NATIONAL DIRECTORY OF CORPORATE GIVING

19TH EDITION

NATIONAL DIRECTORY OF CORPORATE GIVING

Andrew N. Grabois
Editor

CONTRIBUTING STAFF

Vice President, Data Acquisition and Architecture	Jeffrey A. Falkenstein
Director, Foundation Information Management	David G. Jacobs
Regional Product Manager	Margaret Mary Feczko
Director, Grants Information Management	Jeannine Corey
Senior Editorial Associate	Cynthia Y. Manick
Editorial Associate	Emily F. Keller
Corporate Intern	Irina Sverzhanovskaya
Publishing Database Administrator	Kathye Giesler
Programmer	Thomas Provan
System Administrator	Emmy So
Contributing Editors	Claire Charles Linda Calderon
Coordinator, Grants Analysis and Collection	Denise McLeod
Manager, International Data Relations	Yinebon Iniya
Vice President for Marketing and Communications	Anjula Duggal
Production Manager	Christine Innamorato
Graphic Designer/Production Coordinator	Betty Saronson
Catalog/Reference Librarian	Robert Bruno

The editor gratefully acknowledges the many other Foundation Center staff whose support made this volume possible. Thanks also go to the many corporations and foundations whose staffs completed questionnaires or provided information essential to the compilation of this work.

ISBN 978-1-59542-421-1
Printed and bound in the United States of America.

CONTENTS

INTRODUCTION

The 19th Edition of the *National Directory of Corporate Giving* profiles 4,160 companies making contributions to nonprofit organizations. It includes 3,212 foundations and grantmaking public charities identified by the Foundation Center as established and funded primarily by companies and 1,769 direct corporate giving programs. Of these entries, 81 foundations and grantmaking public charities and 64 corporate giving programs are new to this edition.

Companies profiled here range from those with specific interests and structured, formal giving mechanisms to those with broad purposes and informal, unstructured contributions programs. They include 370 *Forbes Global 2000* companies and 578 *Fortune 1000* companies.

We compiled lists of sample grants for foundations when available. In the 19th Edition, there are 8,275 sample grants.

The *Directory* is intended for use by grantseekers in locating potential support, for grantmakers in learning more about other grantmakers, for scholars researching the field, for journalists reporting on the contributions activities of the corporate world, and for anyone generally interested in philanthropy.

The Foundation Center has gathered data on company-sponsored foundations since its creation in 1956 and on direct corporate giving programs since the early 1980s as part of its mission to collect and disseminate information on private, institutionalized giving. The Center makes this data available through its publications, its nationwide network of libraries, and its web site (foundationcenter.org) in the belief that such information exchange enhances the effectiveness and efficiency of the grantmaking process. The Center welcomes comments and suggestions on its data collection and dissemination efforts from both companies and the nonprofit organizations seeking their support.

HOW THE DIRECTORY WAS COMPILED

Entries were prepared using a variety of sources, including materials supplied directly by companies: foundation annual reports, corporate giving reports, informational brochures, and application guidelines. Another primary source of information was the IRS Form 990-PF for the private foundations established by companies and the IRS Form 990 for grantmaking public charities.

Detailed questionnaires for each foundation, grantmaking public charity, and corporate giving program were sent to all of the companies for verification. In all, 585 grantmakers responded to our mailings, providing new and updated information. An additional 131 grantmakers were also reached by telephone.

The Internet is an effective resource used to research companies and their grantmaking activities. Included in this edition are 2,986 grantmaker entries which contain URL and/or e-mail addresses and an additional 3,880 company URL addresses.

Some companies prefer not to divulge information about their charitable activities, or even if they do, often prefer not to give dollar figures. They fear shareholder or employee disapproval of using profits for charitable purposes. Some worry about losing the patronage of portions of the public that might take exception to programs or organizations funded while others worry about unfavorable publicity engendered by grants aimed at controversial issues. Other reasons include the concern over receiving an inordinate amount of requests for support or a company policy that prohibits cooperation with researchers of corporate giving. Additionally, some companies have revealed that they do not track their own giving or that they believe their philanthropic activities to be too informal to be listed.

To ensure accuracy, the *National Directory of Corporate Giving* contains only those entries verified by the companies themselves or compiled from reliable public records. We hope that as corporate giving and community involvement become a greater part of everyday business, more companies will be willing to share information about their charitable endeavors.

HOW TO USE THE NATIONAL DIRECTORY OF CORPORATE GIVING

The *National Directory of Corporate Giving* is a primary tool grantseekers can use to identify corporate grantmakers that might be interested in funding their program or organization. It provides basic descriptions of large and small companies with foundations, grantmaking public charities, and direct corporate giving programs. Indexes help grantseekers quickly identify grantmakers who have expressed an interest in a particular subject field, geographic area, or type of support.

Grantmakers, scholars, journalists, and others interested in the philanthropic field will also find the *Directory* useful in getting a broad overview of corporate giving activities or basic facts about the charitable efforts of specific companies.

When using the *Directory* to identify potential funding sources, be sure to note the limitations statements many grantmakers have provided to determine whether your project falls within the general scope of the company's philanthropic program. Some companies restrict their giving to particular subject or geographic areas; others are not able to provide certain types of support.

ARRANGEMENT

The *Directory* is arranged alphabetically by company name. Each entry is numbered sequentially and references in the indexes are to these entry numbers.

Each company's entry is divided into parts: a general description of the company and its activities and a description of the company's direct corporate giving program, foundation, and/or grantmaking public charity. The "Giving Statement" data element in the company's general description outlines which and how many giving mechanisms the company employs. A company may have a direct corporate giving program, a foundation, a grantmaking public charity, or any combination of all three. A company may also have more than one of any grantmaker type. Each distinct giving entity has a separate description.

WHAT'S IN AN ENTRY?

There are 80 basic data elements that may be included in an entry. The content of entries varies widely due to differences in the size and nature of corporate grantmakers and the availability of information from the companies. The specific data elements that may be included are:

COMPANY

1. The full legal **name of the company.**
2. **"Doing Business As", "Also Known As",** and/or **former company name.**
3. **Street address, city, state, zip code, telephone,** and **fax numbers** of company headquarters.
4. The **URL address** of the company's web site.
5. **Establishment information,** including the year in which the company or its predecessor companies was founded.
6. The **company type,** such as public or private.
7. **Parent company name,** if the company is a subsidiary of another company.
8. **Ultimate parent company name,** if the company is a subsidiary of another company that is not a top-level entity.
9. **Ticker symbol and exchange,** if the company is public.
10. **International Securities Identification Number** (ISIN), that uniquely identifies a security issue independent of where it is traded.
11. A description of the company's principal **business activities;** this listing may not be inclusive of all company activities.
12. **Business type (SIC):** A list of terms, derived from the company's business activities statement, based on the Standard Industrial Classification (SIC) system.
13. A **financial profile** which includes all or some of the following: **number of employees, assets, sales, pre-tax income, expenses, liabilities,** and ***Fortune*** and/or ***Forbes*** **ratings.**
14. The principal **corporate officers.**
15. The company's **board of directors.**

16. Name, city, and state of company **subsidiaries, divisions,** and/or **joint ventures** identified.
17. City and state of **plants** and/or **offices** identified.
18. Countries of **international operations** identified.
19. **Historic mergers:** A list of companies that have merged into the company and the date on which the merger was finalized.
20. A **giving statement** summarizing the methods by which a company gives, such as through a corporate giving program, foundation, or grantmaking public charity.
21. **EIN:** The Employer Identification Number assigned to the company by the Internal Revenue Service.

CORPORATE GIVING PROGRAM

22. **Corporate giving program name.**
23. **Former corporate giving program name.**
24. **Street address, city, state,** and **zip code** of the corporate giving program's principal office.
25. **Telephone number.**
26. Any **additional address** (such as a separate application address) supplied by the company for correspondence or application submission. Additional telephone or fax numbers, as well as e-mail or URL addresses, may also be listed here.
27. **Contact person** name and title.
28. The **year-end date** of the corporate giving program's accounting period for which financial data is supplied.
29. The dollar value and number of **grants paid,** with the largest grant paid **(high)**, smallest grant paid **(low)**, and **average** range of grant payments, if available. Grant figures do not include commitments for future payment. Grant figures may include grants to individuals, employee matching gifts, or in-kind gifts when those figures were not separately available.
30. The dollar value and number of **grants made directly to individuals,** including scholarships, fellowships, awards, or medical payments. When supplied by the company, high, low, and average range are also indicated.
31. The dollar value and number of **employee matching gifts** awarded, excluding employee contributions.
32. The dollar value expended for charitable **programs administered by the company** and the number of company-administered programs. These programs can include museums or other institutions supported exclusively by the company or research programs administered by the company.
33. The dollar value and number of **loans** made to nonprofit organizations by the company. These can include emergency loans to help nonprofits waiting for grants or other income payments. When supplied by the company, high, low, and average range are also indicated.
34. The dollar value and number of **loans to individuals.** When supplied by the company, high, low, and average range are also indicated.
35. The dollar value and number of **in-kind gifts.**
36. The **purpose and activities,** in general terms, of the corporate giving program. This statement may reflect specific funding interests or a general philosophy as expressed by the company.
37. The **fields of interest** reflected by the corporate giving program's charitable activities. The terminology used in this section conforms to the Foundation Center's Grants Classification System (GCS). The terms also provide access to corporate giving program entries through the Subject Index at the back of this volume.
38. The **international giving and interests** of the corporate giving program.
39. The **types of programs** offered by the corporate giving program. Programs are distinctly identified areas of interest which the company supports on a continuing basis or specifically named initiatives created by the company.
40. The **types of support** (such as endowments, seed money, building/renovation, fellowships, etc.) offered by the company. Definitions of the terms used in this section are provided at the beginning of the Types of Support Index at the back of this volume.
41. Any stated **limitations** of the corporate giving program, including geographic preferences and restrictions by type of recipient and type of support.
42. **Publications** or other printed materials distributed by the company that describe its corporate giving program. These can include corporate giving reports, informational brochures, and application guidelines.
43. **Application information,** including the preferred form of application, the number of copies of proposals requested, the preferred method of initial approach, application deadlines, frequency and dates of committee meetings, and the general amount of time the company requires to notify applicants of its decision. A listing of materials that should accompany proposals may also be included. Note: some companies have indicated that applications are not accepted or that funds are currently committed to ongoing projects. Applicants should be aware that the chance of receiving support from these companies is extremely small.
44. The names and titles of corporate giving program **administrators, committee members,** or **officers.**
45. The number of professional and support **staff** employed by the company to handle contributions and an indication of part-time or full-time status of these employees, as reported by the company.

46. A list of **selected grants,** when available. Up to 10 grants reported during a given fiscal year may be provided. Grants to individuals are not included.

FOUNDATION AND GRANTMAKING PUBLIC CHARITY

47. The full legal **name of the grantmaker.**
48. **"Doing Business As", "Also Known As",** or **former grantmaker name.**
49. **Street address, city, state,** and **zip code** of the grantmaker's principal office. The location of the grantmaker may be different from that of the company's headquarters.
50. **Telephone number.**
51. Any **additional address** (such as a separate application address) supplied by the grantmaker for correspondence or application submission. Additional telephone or fax numbers, as well as e-mail or URL addresses, may also be listed here.
52. **Establishment data,** including the legal form (usually a trust or corporation) and the year and state in which the grantmaker was established.
53. A historical record of the **donor(s)** or principal contributor(s) to the grantmaker, including individuals, families, and companies. If a donor is deceased, the symbol ‡ follows the name.
54. **Contact person** name and title.
55. The **year-end date** of the grantmaker's accounting period for which financial data is supplied.
56. **Revenue:** The total amount of contributions and support received by a grantmaking public charity, including investment income, program service revenue, net profits from a sale of assets, etc.
57. **Assets:** the dollar value of the grantmaker's investments at the end of the accounting period. In a few instances, grantmakers that act as "pass-throughs" for annual individual or corporate gifts report zero assets.
58. **Asset type:** generally, assets are reported at market value (M) or ledger value (L).
59. **Gifts received:** the dollar value of new capital received by the grantmaker.
60. **Expenditures:** the dollar value of total disbursements made by the grantmaker, including overhead expenses (salaries, investment, legal, and other professional fees, interest, rent, etc.) and federal excise taxes, as well as the total amount paid for grants, scholarships, and matching gifts.
61. The dollar value of **qualifying distributions** made by the foundation. This figure includes all grants paid, qualifying administrative expenses, loans and program-related investments, set-asides, and amounts paid to acquire assets used directly in carrying out charitable purposes.
62. **Program services expenses:** The total amount of program expenses made by a grantmaking public charity in the year of record. This figure includes all expenses directly involved in carrying out charitable activities, including total grants paid.
63. The dollar value and number of **grants paid,** with the largest grant paid **(high)**, smallest grant paid **(low)**, and **average** range of grant payments, if available. Grant figures generally do not include commitments for future payment or grants to individuals, employee matching gifts, loans, in-kind gifts, or grantmaker-administered programs.
64. The dollar value and number of **grants made directly to or on behalf of individuals,** including scholarships, fellowships, awards, or medical payments. When supplied by the grantmaker, high, low, and average range are also indicated.
65. The dollar value and number of **employee matching gifts** awarded, excluding employee contributions.
66. The dollar value expended for **programs administered by the grantmaker** and the number of grantmaker-administered programs. These programs can include museums or other institutions supported exclusively by the grantmaker or research programs administered by the grantmaker.
67. The dollar value and number of **loans** made to nonprofit organizations by the grantmaker. These can include program-related investments or emergency loans to help nonprofits waiting for grants or other income payments. When supplied by the grantmaker, high, low, and average range are also indicated.
68. The dollar value and number of **loans to individuals.** When supplied by the grantmaker, high, low, and average range are also indicated.
69. The dollar value and number of **in-kind gifts.**
70. The **purpose and activities,** in general terms, of the grantmaker. This statement may reflect specific funding interests or a general philosophy as expressed by the grantmaker or, if no grantmaker statement is available, an analysis of the actual grants awarded by the grantmaker during the most recent two-year period for which public records exist. Many grantmakers leave statements of purpose intentionally broad, indicating only the major program areas within which they fund. More specific areas of interest can often be found in the "Fields of Interest" section of the entry.
71. The **fields of interest** reflected by the grantmaker's giving program. The terminology used in this section conforms to the Foundation Center's Grants Classification System (GCS). The terms also provide access to grantmaker entries through the Subject Index at the back of this volume.
72. The **international giving and interests** of the grantmaker.
73. The **types of programs** offered by the grantmaker. Programs are distinctly identified areas of interest which the grantmaker supports on a continuing basis or specifically named initiatives created by the grantmaker.

74. The **types of support** (such as endowments, seed money, building/renovation, fellowships, etc.) offered by the grantmaker. Definitions of the terms used in this section are provided at the beginning of the Types of Support Index at the back of this volume.
75. Any stated **limitations** of the grantmaker, including geographic preferences and restrictions by type of recipient and type of support.
76. **Publications** or other printed materials distributed by the grantmaker that describe its activities. These can include grantmaker annual reports, informational brochures, and application guidelines.
77. **Application information,** including the preferred form of application, the number of copies of proposals requested, the preferred method of initial approach, application deadlines, frequency and dates of board meetings, and the general amount of time the grantmaker requires to notify applicants of its decision. A listing of materials that should accompany proposals may also be included. Note: some grantmakers have indicated that applications are not accepted or that funds are currently committed to ongoing projects. Applicants should be aware that the chance of receiving support from these grantmakers is extremely small.
78. The names and titles of grantmaker **officers, principal administrators, trustees,** or **directors,** and members of other governing bodies. An asterisk following the individual's name indicates an officer who is also a trustee or director.
79. The number of professional and support **staff** employed by the grantmaker and an indication of part-time or full-time status of these employees, as reported by the grantmaker.
80. **EIN:** the Employer Identification Number assigned to the grantmaker by the Internal Revenue Service for tax purposes. This number can be useful in ordering or looking up copies of the grantmaker's annual IRS Form 990-PF or 990 tax return.
81. A list of **selected grants** when available. Up to ten grants reported during a given fiscal year may be provided. Grants to individuals are not included.

INDEXES

Seven indexes to the descriptive entries are provided at the back of the book.

1. The **Index of Officers, Donors, Trustees, and Administrators** is an alphabetical list of corporate officers, corporate directors, individual and corporate donors, trustees, and administrators whose names appear in *Directory* entries. Many grantseekers find this index helpful in determining if current or prospective members of their own governing boards, alumni of their schools, or current contributors are affiliated with any grantmakers or companies.
2. The **Geographic Index** references companies by the state and city of corporate giving program offices, foundations, corporate headquarters, subsidiaries, divisions, joint ventures, plants, and offices.
3. The **International Giving Index** references companies whose operations, charitable giving, and giving interests extend beyond the United States. A complete alphabetical list of countries, continents, and regions appears at the beginning of the index. Under each country, continent, or region, entry numbers are listed following the abbreviated name of the company. Organizations whose programs benefit people internationally should use this index to identify funders with similar geographic interests.
4. The **Types of Support Index** references companies by the types of support offered by corporate giving programs, foundations, and grantmaking public charities (such as endowments, seed money, building/renovation, fellowships, etc.) A glossary of the types of support listed appears at the beginning of the index. Under each type of support term, entry numbers are listed following the abbreviated name of the company.
5. The **Subject Index** references companies by the fields of interest of corporate giving programs, foundations, and grantmaking public charities. The terminology used in this index conforms to the Foundation Center's Grants Classification System (GCS). A complete alphabetical list of subject headings in the current edition appears at the beginning of the index. Under each subject term, entry numbers are listed following the abbreviated name of the company.
6. The **Types of Business Index** references companies by business activity. The terminology used in this index is based on the phrasing of the Standard Industrial Classification (SIC) system, a standard initiated by the Federal Government's Office of Management and Budget. Under each type of business, entry numbers are listed following the abbreviated name of the company.
7. The **Corporation and Corporate Grantmaker Index** is an alphabetical list of companies, corporate giving programs, foundations, grantmaking public charities, and company subsidiaries that appear in the *Directory*. If a company or grantmaker has changed its name, the former name is also listed.

GUIDELINES FOR GRANTSEEKERS

WHY COMPANIES GIVE

Corporate giving stems from the overlapping of altruism and self-interest. Companies, unlike foundations and other grantmaking organizations, don't exist to give. Their main responsibilities are to their employees, customers, shareholders, and the bottom line.

Companies give to support employee volunteer services, to guarantee a supply of well-trained potential employees, to build community relations, to enhance company image, to return favors, to receive tax deductions, and to influence legislation, policymakers, and other opinion makers. They also give to improve community life, locally and nationwide.

Giving is essential for good corporate business and citizenship. Companies understand the power of publicity and that charitable giving builds a strong community image. Companies also expect concrete rewards for their generosity.

TRENDS

Today companies are reshaping and rethinking their giving programs, narrowing focuses to specific objectives, examining how grants are used, and thinking in terms of possible benefits. They are also developing an increasing number of non-cash giving programs.

Companies often favor causes in the public eye like education, with a focus on math, science, minority education, and school reform. Environmental issues, low-income housing, and preventive health maintenance are also popular areas of giving.

In addition, companies want to maximize the impact of their giving. Direct involvement with students and teachers, in projects like the Adopt-A-School program and other tutoring and mentoring programs, is one approach. Companies often want to plan and manage, foster collaborative donor and nonprofit efforts, and take on long-term projects. They also look to volunteerism in the bid for community standing.

DIRECT CORPORATE GIVING PROGRAMS, COMPANY-SPONSORED FOUNDATIONS, AND GRANTMAKING PUBLIC CHARITIES

Companies provide support to nonprofits through direct corporate giving programs, private foundations, grantmaking public charities, or any combination of all three. Foundations and grantmaking public charities often maintain close ties with their sponsoring company and most giving reflects that company's interests. They generally maintain small endowments and rely on contributions ("gifts received") from the company to support their charitable endeavors. Companies accrue giving funds in fat years that they can tap in lean ones. Foundations must adhere to the appropriate regulations, including filing a yearly IRS Form 990-PF, which details contributions of 5 percent or more of the foundation's market-value assets. Grantmaking public charities must file a yearly IRS Form 990.

Direct corporate giving—all charitable activites outside of a company's foundation or grantmaking public charity—is less regulated. Companies are not required to publicize direct corporate giving programs or sustain prescribed funding levels. For federal tax purposes, they can deduct up to 10 percent of pre-tax income for charitable contributions. They can also make non-cash contributions, sometimes considered operating expenditures, and not necessarily include them in giving statistics. The Conference Board estimates that gifts of non-cash resources (excluding pharmaceutical companies) constitute over 36 percent of corporate giving, the largest share of total contributions.

NON-CASH SUPPORT

Companies are becoming more interested in giving non-cash support with, or in lieu of, monetary grants. Such support includes donated products, donated equipment, use of facilities, and public relations services (including printing and duplicating, event planning, and advertising.) Companies also provide employee expertise in areas such as legal assistance, tax advice, market research, and strategic planning. Many companies encourage and reward employee volunteers and some volunteers are given time off for their efforts. Many companies support organizations where employees volunteer, and in fact, some companies donate to these organizations exclusively. Corporate sponsorship of charitable events, such as dinners, galas, and tournaments, is equally important.

HOW TO FIND CORPORATE FUNDERS

Corporate giving is often found in fields related to corporate activities and in company communities. The grantseeker's search should focus on small local businesses as well as larger national companies.

Corporate giving directories and studies are key resources. This volume includes an extensive "Corporate Funding Bibliography." When referring to a directory, it is important to note grantmaker limitations.

Company-sponsored foundation and grantmaking public charity information returns (IRS Forms 990-PF and 990, respectively) are available through IRS district offices, at a grantmaker's office, through the attorney general for the state in which the grantmaker is chartered, or at the Foundation Center's web site (foundationcenter.org/FindFunders).

Nonprofits should consult public libraries for regional and business indexes. The Chamber of Commerce and Better Business Bureau may also have such guides. Do not overlook the yellow pages and staff community knowledge. In corporate grantseeking, personal contacts are invaluable. Staff, board members, and volunteers may know funders; they should be encouraged to investigate giving policies at these companies.

Additionally, many companies maintain a presence on the Internet, an important, potential source for information about corporate community involvement and grantmaking activities. When available, the *National Directory of Corporate Giving* lists URL addresses for company web sites and corporate grantmaking pages.

THE SUBJECT, GEOGRAPHIC, AND TYPE OF SUPPORT APPROACHES

The *subject* approach leads grantseekers to companies with an interest in funding programs in certain fields related to the company's business activities. The grantseeker should start with the Subject and Types of Business indexes in the *National Directory of Corporate Giving*. Some nonprofit/corporate relationships will be obvious: a sporting goods manufacturer expresses interest in an athletic program for disadvantaged youth; a musical instruments manufacturer supports a music appreciation program; a pharmaceutical company or alcoholic beverage producer funds a drug education program.

The nonprofit should always consider the funder's *motivation*. A corporate giver wants to develop a trained pool of potential employees, support relevant research, improve the respective market, respond to related social issues, and increase sales. Establishing the link with the grantmaker is the grantseeker's key to success. Focus on the company's self-interest rather than benevolence.

The *geographic* approach focuses the nonprofit on the location of corporate headquarters, subsidiaries, divisions, joint ventures, plants, and offices. The grantseeker should refer to the Geographic and International Giving indexes in the *National Directory of Corporate Giving*. A company will support programs that provide direct service to employees and other community residents, that promise public recognition, and that improve customer relations. A company may also want to invest in a community's future.

The *type of support* approach is equally productive. Support includes endowments, seed money, building/renovation, fellowships, etc. It also includes non-cash contributions. The grantseeker should refer to the Types of Support Index in this volume. For example, a clothing manufacturer may have "irregulars" or extra clothing to donate to a homeless shelter. Some connections, however, are less obvious.

DOING YOUR HOMEWORK

Learn about corporate funding before submitting a request. The funder might have an annual report on giving or application guidelines. These will help shape an appeal. Corporate annual reports present company philosophy and often describe company plans for the community, providing vital background information for linking a grant request to company interests. Economic conditions and business news should also be followed. A company laying off employees or running up a deficit may not be the one to ask for a donation.

Follow a corporate giver's guidelines to the letter, especially in regard to submission deadlines. Find out to whom the request should be addressed and the preferred format. At some companies, sponsorships and non-cash support may be handled by the marketing department; employee volunteerism may be coordinated by the human resources department. Different regions may have different application addresses. In the "Additional address" section, the *National Directory of Corporate Giving* indicates when an alternative address exists. Some companies want a preliminary letter of inquiry and a full proposal only after they have expressed an interest; others have formal application forms and some demand multiple copies of proposals. Find this out in advance.

PRESENTING YOUR IDEAS TO A CORPORATE GIVER

A proposal must be honest, clear, concise, and appropriate in tone. Draw up a realistic budget, and be prepared to divulge all sources of income, since corporate grantmakers emphasize the bottom line. Many ask for evidence of fiscally responsible, efficient management. Be explicit. State program or organization goals, include a plan of action, provide a timetable, and indicate a method of evaluation. Be brief but comprehensive.

The company's potential benefits should also be indicated. Consider what a business stands to gain from investing in the program. Involve company volunteers. Highlight an innovative program—a program that tackles a new issue or addresses an unfulfilled need—without undue self-promotion. In addition to requesting cash, nonprofits should also ask for in-kind support and target local businesses for board members and volunteers, likely paths to further contributions. Nonprofit leaders should remember that a good relationship with one company may point the way to others or provide a necessary introduction to funding prospects.

PERSONAL CONTACTS

How important is it to know someone? Personal contacts help, but their impact varies. Corporate grantmakers with specific personnel and explicit guidelines for grantseekers are unlikely to require contacts. Companies with informal contributions programs and guidelines will require a more personal approach.

Nonprofit grantseekers with no personal contacts are not handicapped. Build relationships and establish a local presence. Write an introductory letter to the relevant contact describing your program and expressing interest in a meeting date. Send printed literature and articles about your program. Invite decision makers to see your organization in action and to attend special events. Ask if you should send a preliminary letter of inquiry or a full proposal. Send nothing extraneous. Establishing a rapport with wary grantmakers will be difficult. Remember, cultivation is a long-term effort.

If you receive a grant, send a letter of thanks and submit all agreed-upon reports, following the established timetable. Corporate funders will be very insistent, and will notice a missed deadline. Keep them informed regardless of the agreement. Suggest forms of recognition, such as dinner honors, certificates and plaques, and media coverage. However, grantmaker recognition depends on nonprofit resources, and given the small average donation, such formal recognition is not often required.

Even if you are rejected, continue to nurture the relationship. Thank those in charge for considering your request. Ask why you were not funded if they have not made this clear. Determine whether you will reapply during the next cycle.

Getting corporate support demands creativity, ingenuity, and persistence. Competition will be stiff, but the possibility of support cannot be ignored.

GLOSSARY

The following list includes important terms used by grantmakers and grantseekers. A number of sources have been consulted in compiling this glossary, including *The Handbook on Private Foundations*, 3rd Edition, by David F. Freeman, John A. Edie, Jane C. Nober, and the Council on Foundations (Washington, DC, 2005); *The Law of Tax-Exempt Organizations*, 9th Edition, by Bruce R. Hopkins (Hoboken, NJ: John Wiley & Sons, 2007); and the *AFP Fund-Raising Dictionary*, (2003).

501(c)(3): The section of the Internal Revenue Service code that defines nonprofit, charitable (as broadly defined), tax-exempt organizations. 501(c)(3) organizations are further defined as public charities, private operating foundations, and private non-operating foundations. (See also **Operating Foundation; Private Foundation; Public Charity**)

Annual Report or Corporate Giving Report: A voluntary report issued by a foundation, grantmaking public charity, or company that provides financial data and information on grantmaking activities. Annual reports and corporate giving reports vary in format from simple typewritten documents listing the year's grants to detailed publications that provide substantial information about the grantmaking program.

Assets: The amount of capital or principal—cash, stocks, bonds, real estate, or other resources—controlled by a grantmaker. Generally, assets are invested and the income is used to make grants.

Beneficiary: In philanthropic terms, the donee or grantee receiving funds from a grantmaker is the beneficiary, although society benefits as well. Grantmakers whose legal terms of establishment restrict their giving to one or more named beneficiaries are not included in this publication. Companies making charitable contributions exclusively to "specified beneficiaries" are likewise omitted.

Bricks and Mortar: An informal term given to grants made for construction projects.

Capital Support: Funds provided for endowment purposes, construction, or equipment, and including, for example, grants for "bricks and mortar."

Challenge Grant: A grant that will be paid only if the donee organization is able to raise additional funds from another source(s). Challenge grants are often used to stimulate giving from other donors. (*See also* **Matching Grant**)

Community Foundation: A 501(c)(3) organization that makes grants for charitable purposes in a specific community or region. Funds are usually derived from many donors and held in an endowment independently administered; income earned by the endowment is then used to make grants. Although a few community foundations may be classified by the IRS as private foundations, most are classified as public charities eligible for maximum income tax-deductible contributions from the general public. (*See also* **501(c)(3); Public Charity**)

Community Fund: An organized community program which makes annual appeals to the general public for funds that are usually not retained in an endowment but used for the ongoing operational support of local health and human service agencies. (*See also* **Federated Giving Program**)

Company: A business organized as a legal entity and chartered by a state, with ownership divided into transferable shares of capital stock and the separation of functions of ownership and management. A company has a legal existence apart from that of its owners; it may own property in its own name, pay tax on its earnings, and can sue or be sued in court. In this *Directory*, the words "corporation" and "company" are used interchangeably. "Private company" designates a partnership (owned by two or more persons) or a proprietorship (owned by one person). "Public company" designates a company that has issued shares of ownership to the general public.

Company-Sponsored Foundation (also referred to as **Corporate Foundation**): A private foundation established and primarily funded by a for-profit business organization. The company-sponsored foundation may maintain close ties with the donor company, but it is an independent organization with its own endowment and is subject to the same rules and regulations as other private foundations. (*See also* **Private Foundation**)

Cooperative Venture: A joint effort between or among two or more grantmakers (including foundations, grantmaking public charities, companies, and government agencies). Partners may share in funding responsibilities or contribute information and technical resources.

Corporate Giving Program: A grantmaking program established and administered within a for-profit business organization. Corporate giving programs do not have a separate endowment and their annual grant totals are generally more directly related to current company profits. They are not subject to the same reporting requirements as private foundations or grantmaking public charities. Some companies make charitable contributions through both a corporate giving program and a company-sponsored foundation or grantmaking public charity, or both.

Corporate Report (also referred to as **Annual Report**): As the term is used in this *Directory*, it refers to the annual business report of a company, as distinct from foundation or grantmaking public charity annual reports or corporate giving reports, which concern charitable activities.

Distribution Committee: The board of a grantmaker responsible for making grant decisions. For community foundations, it is intended to be broadly representative of the community served by the foundation.

Donee (also referred to as **Grantee** or **Beneficiary**): The recipient of a grant or contribution.

Donor (also referred to as **Grantor**): The individual or organization that makes a grant or contribution.

Employee Matching Gift: A charitable contribution by a company employee that is matched by a similar contribution from the employer. Many companies have employee matching gift programs for higher education that stimulate employees to give to the college or university of their choice.

Endowment: Funds intended to be kept permanently and invested to provide income for continued support of an organization.

Expenditure Responsibility: In general, when a private foundation makes a grant to an organization that is not classified by the IRS as a "public charity," the foundation is required by law to provide some assurance that the funds will be used for the intended charitable purposes. Special reports on such grants must be filed with the IRS. Most grantee organizations are public charities and many foundations do not make "expenditure responsibility" grants.

Federated Giving Program: A joint fundraising effort usually administered by a nonprofit "umbrella" organization which in turn distributes contributed funds to several nonprofit agencies. The United Way and community chests or funds, the United Jewish Appeal and other religious appeals, the United Negro College Fund, and joint arts councils are examples of federated giving programs. (*See also* **Community Fund**)

Form 990: The annual information return that all tax-exempt organizations, other than private foundations, must submit to the IRS each year and which is also filed with the appropriate state officials. The form requires information on the organization's assets, program services expenses, revenue, contributions and grants, paid staff and salaries, and program funding areas.

Form 990-PF: The annual information return that all private foundations must submit to the IRS each year and which is also filed with appropriate state officials. The form requires information on the foundation's assets, income, operating expenses, contributions and grants, paid staff and salaries, program funding areas, grantmaking guidelines and restrictions, and grant application procedures.

General Purpose Foundation: A private foundation that awards grants in many different fields of interest. (*See also* **Special Purpose Foundation**)

General Purpose Grant: A grant made to further the general purpose or work of an organization, rather than for a specific purpose or project. (*See also* **Operating Support Grant**)

Grantee Financial Report: A report detailing how grant funds were used by an organization. Many companies require this kind of report from grantees. A financial report generally includes a listing of all expenditures from grant funds as well as an overall organizational financial report covering revenue, expenses, assets, and liabilities.

Grassroots Fundraising: Efforts to raise money from individuals or groups of the local community on a broad basis. Usually an organization's own constituents—people who live in the neighborhood served or clients of the agency's services—are the sources of these funds. Grassroots fundraising activities include membership drives, raffles, auctions, benefits, and a range of other activities.

In-Kind Contributions: Contributions of products, equipment, or other property as distinguished from cash grants. Some organizations may also donate meeting space or public relations services as an in-kind contribution.

Letter of Inquiry: A brief letter outlining an organization's activities and its request for funding sent to a grantmaker to determine whether it would be appropriate to submit a full proposal. Many grantmakers prefer to be initially contacted in this way.

Matching Grant: A grant that is made to match funds provided by another donor. (*See also* **Challenge Grant; Employee Matching Gift**)

Operating Foundation: A 501(c)(3) organization classified by the IRS as a private foundation whose primary purpose is to conduct research, social welfare, or other programs determined by its governing body or establishment charter. Some grants may be made, but the sum is generally small relative to the funds used for the foundation's own programs. (*See also* **501(c)(3); Private Foundation**)

Operating Support Grant: A grant to cover the regular personnel, administrative, and other expenses of an existing program or project. (*See also* **General Purpose Grant**)

Payout Requirement: The minimum amount that private foundations are required to expend for charitable purposes (includes grants and, within certain limits, the administrative cost of making grants). In general, a private foundation must meet or exceed an annual payout requirement of 5 percent of the average market value of its assets.

Pre-Tax Income: The income of a company before taxes. Many companies aim to donate at least 2 percent of pre-tax income to charity each year.

Private Foundation: A nongovernmental, nonprofit organization with funds (usually from a single source, such as an individual, family, or company) and programs managed by its own trustees or directors that was established to maintain or aid social, educational, religious, or other charitable activities serving the common welfare, primarily through the awarding of grants. "Private foundation" also means an organization that is tax-exempt under IRS code section 501(c)(3) and is classified by the IRS as a private foundation as defined in the code. The code definition usually, but not always, identifies a foundation with the characteristics first described. (*See also* **501(c)(3); Public Charity**)

Program Amount: Funds that are expended to support a particular charitable program administered internally by an organization.

Program Officer: A staff member of a grantmaker who reviews grant proposals and processes applications for the board of trustees. Only a small percentage of grantmakers have program officers.

Program-Related Investment (PRI): A loan or other investment (as distinguished from a grant) made by a grantmaker to an organization for a project related to the grantmaker's stated charitable purpose and interests. Program-related investments are often made from a revolving fund; the grantmaker generally expects to receive its money back with interest or some other form of return at less than current market rates, and it then becomes available for further program-related investments. When undertaken by a company, PRIs are often called Social Investments.

Proposal: A written application, often with supporting documents, submitted to a grantmaker when requesting a grant. Preferred procedures and formats vary. Consult published guidelines.

Public Charity: In general, an organization that is tax-exempt under IRS code section 501(c)(3) and classified by the IRS as a public charity and not a private foundation. Public charities generally derive their funding or support primarily from the general public in carrying out their social, educational, religious, or other charitable activities serving the common welfare. Some public charities engage in grantmaking activities, although most engage in direct service or other tax-exempt activities. Public charities are eligible for maximum income tax-deductible contributions from the public and are not subject to the same rules and restrictions as private foundations. Some are also referred to as "public foundations" or "publicly supported organizations" and may use the term "foundation" in their names. (*See also* **501(c)(3); Private Foundation**)

Qualifying Distributions: Expenditures of private foundations used to satisfy the annual payout requirement. These can include grants, reasonable administrative expenses, set-asides, loans and program-related investments, and amounts paid to acquire assets used directly in carrying out charitable purposes.

RFP: Request For Proposal. When the government issues a new contract or grant program, it sends out RFPs to agencies that might be qualified to participate. The RFP lists project specifications and application procedures. A few grantmakers occasionally use RFPs in specific fields, but most prefer to consider proposals that are initiated by applicants.

Sales: The price of goods and services that a company renders to its customers. Sales differ from revenue in that revenue includes other sources of income other than sales, such as interest or dividend payments.

Seed Money: A grant or contribution used to start a new project or organization. Seed grants may cover salaries and other operating expenses.

Set-Asides: Funds set aside by a foundation for a specific purpose or project that are counted as qualifying distributions toward the foundation's annual payout requirement. Funding for the project must occur within five years of the first set-aside.

Special Purpose Foundation: A private foundation that focuses its grantmaking activities in one or a few special areas of interest. For example, a foundation may only award grants in the area of cancer research or child development. (*See also* **General Purpose Foundation**)

Technical Assistance: Operational or management assistance given to nonprofit organizations. It can include fundraising assistance, budgeting and financial planning, program planning, legal advice, marketing, and other aids to management. Assistance may be offered directly by a staff member or be offered in the form of a grant to pay for the services of an outside consultant. (*See also* **In-Kind Contributions**)

Trustee (also referred to as **Board Member** or **Director**): A member of a governing board. A grantmaker's board of trustees meets to review grant proposals and make decisions.

ABBREVIATIONS

The following lists contain standard abbreviations frequently used by the Foundation Center's editorial staff. These abbreviations are used most frequently in the addresses of grantmakers and the titles of corporate and grantmaker officers.

STREET ABBREVIATIONS

1st	First*
2nd	Second*
3rd	Third*
Apt.	Apartment
Ave.	Avenue
Bldg.	Building
Blvd.	Boulevard
Cir.	Circle
Ct.	Court
Ctr.	Center
Dept.	Department
Dr.	Drive
E.	East
Expwy.	Expressway
Fl.	Floor
Ft.	Fort
Hwy.	Highway
Ln.	Lane
M.C.	Mail Code
M.S.	Mail Stop
Mt.	Mount
N.	North
N.E.	Northeast
N.W.	Northwest
No.	Number
Pkwy.	Parkway
Pl.	Place
Plz.	Plaza
R.R.	Rural Route
Rd.	Road
Rm.	Room
Rte.	Route
S.	South
S.E.	Southeast
S.W.	Southwest
Sq.	Square
St.	Saint
St.	Street
Sta.	Station
Ste.	Suite
Terr.	Terrace
Tpke.	Turnpike
Univ.	University
W.	West

*Numerics used always

TWO LETTER STATE AND TERRITORY ABBREVIATIONS

AK	Alaska
AL	Alabama
AR	Arkansas
AZ	Arizona
CA	California
CO	Colorado
CT	Connecticut
DC	District of Columbia
DE	Delaware
FL	Florida
GA	Georgia
HI	Hawaii
IA	Iowa
ID	Idaho
IL	Illinois
IN	Indiana
KS	Kansas
KY	Kentucky
LA	Louisiana
MA	Massachusetts
MD	Maryland
ME	Maine
MI	Michigan
MN	Minnesota
MO	Missouri
MS	Mississippi
MT	Montana
NC	North Carolina
ND	North Dakota
NE	Nebraska
NH	New Hampshire
NJ	New Jersey
NM	New Mexico
NV	Nevada
NY	New York
OH	Ohio
OK	Oklahoma
OR	Oregon
PA	Pennsylvania
PR	Puerto Rico
RI	Rhode Island
SC	South Carolina
SD	South Dakota
TN	Tennessee
TX	Texas
UT	Utah
VA	Virginia
VI	Virgin Islands
VT	Vermont
WA	Washington
WI	Wisconsin
WV	West Virginia
WY	Wyoming

ABBREVIATIONS USED FOR OFFICER TITLES

Acctg.	Accounting
ADM.	Admiral
Admin.	Administration
Admin.	Administrative
Admin.	Administrator
Adv.	Advertising
Amb.	Ambassador
Assn.	Association
Assoc(s).	Associate(s)
Asst.	Assistant
Bro.	Brother
C.A.O.	Chief Accounting Officer
C.A.O.	Chief Administration Officer
C.E.O.	Chief Executive Officer
C.F.O.	Chief Financial Officer
C.I.O.	Chief Information Officer
C.I.O.	Chief Investment Officer
C.O.O.	Chief Operating Officer
Capt.	Captain
Chair.	Chairperson
Col.	Colonel
Comm.	Committee
Comms.	Communications
Commo.	Commodore
Compt.	Comptroller
Cont.	Controller
Contrib(s).	Contribution(s)
Coord.	Coordinator
Corp.	Corporate, Corporation
Co(s).	Company(s)
Dep.	Deputy
Devel.	Development
Dir.	Director
Distrib(s).	Distribution(s)
Div.	Division
Exec.	Executive
Ext.	External
Fdn.	Foundation
Fr.	Father
Genl.	General
Gov.	Governor
Govt.	Government
Hon.	Judge
Inf.	Information
Int.	Internal
Intl.	International
Jr.	Junior
Lt.	Lieutenant
Ltd.	Limited
Maj.	Major
Mfg.	Manufacturing
Mgmt.	Management
Mgr.	Manager
Mktg.	Marketing
Msgr.	Monsignor
Mt.	Mount
Natl.	National
Off.	Officer
Opers.	Operations
Org.	Organization
Plan.	Planning
Pres.	President
Prog(s).	Program(s)
RADM.	Rear Admiral
Rels.	Relations
Rep.	Representative
Rev.	Reverend
Rt. Rev.	Right Reverend
Secy.	Secretary
Secy.-Treas.	Secretary-Treasurer
Sen.	Senator
Soc.	Society
Sr.	Senior
Sr.	Sister
Supt.	Superintendent
Supvr.	Supervisor
Svc(s).	Service(s)
Tech.	Technology
Tr.	Trustee
Treas.	Treasurer
Univ.	University
V.P.	Vice President
VADM.	Vice Admiral
Vice-Chair.	Vice Chairperson

ADDITIONAL ABBREVIATIONS

E-mail	Electronic mail
FAX	Facsimile
LOI	Letter of Inquiry
RFP	Request for Proposals
SASE	Self-Addressed Stamped Envelope
TDD, TTY	Telecommunication Device for the Deaf
Tel.	Telephone
URL	Uniform Resource Locator (web site)

Jan.	January
Feb.	February
Mar.	March
Apr.	April
Aug.	August
Sept.	September
Oct.	October
Nov.	November
Dec.	December

CORPORATE PHILANTHROPY BIBLIOGRAPHY

by Rob Bruno, Catalog/Reference Librarian, New York Library, The Foundation Center

This selected bibliography is compiled from the Catalog of Nonprofit Literature, the Foundation Center's bibliographic database with abstracts. Many of the items are available for free reference use in the Center's New York City, Washington, D.C., Cleveland, San Francisco, and Atlanta libraries and in many of its Cooperating Collections throughout the United States. For further references on such topics as corporate philanthropy, fundraising, and proposal development, search the Catalog, which can be accessed at catalog.foundationcenter.org.

2011 Deloitte Volunteer IMPACT Survey. Deloitte, 2011.

Armbruster, Rachel. *Banding Together for a Cause: Proven Strategies for Revenue and Awareness Generation*. Hoboken, NJ: John Wiley & Sons, 2012.

Auerswald, Philip. "Creating Social Value." *Stanford Social Innovation Review*, vol. 7 (Spring 2009): p. 50–5.

Austin, James E.; Seitanidi, Maria May. "Collaborative Value Creation: A Review of Partnering Between Nonprofits and Businesses: Part 1. Value Creation Spectrum and Collaboration Stages." *Nonprofit and Voluntary Sector Quarterly*, vol. 41 (October 2012): p. 726–58.

Austin, James E.; Seitanidi, Maria May. "Collaborative Value Creation: A Review of Partnering Between Nonprofits and Businesses: Part 2. Partnership Processes and Outcomes." *Nonprofit and Voluntary Sector Quarterly, vol. 41* (December 2012): p. 929–68.

Baker, H. Kent; Nofsinger, John R. *Socially Responsible Finance and Investing: Financial Institutions, Corporations, Investors, and Activists*. Hoboken, NJ: Wiley & Sons, 2012.

The BCA Executive Summary: 2010 National Survey of Business Support to the Arts. New York, NY: Business Committee for the Arts, 2010.

Benioff, Marc. *Behind the Cloud*. San Francisco, CA: Jossey-Bass Publishers, 2009.

Bugg-Levine, Antony; Emerson, Jed. *Impact Investing: Transforming How We Make Money While Making a Difference*. Hoboken, NJ: John Wiley & Sons, 2011.

"Cause-Related Marketing: Branding, Buying & Donating." *Wise Giving Guide*, (Spring 2012): p. 2–7.

Cohen, Todd. "Business Value Boosted When Tied to Nonprofit." *NonProfit Times*, vol. 27 (1 April 2013): p. 27–30.

Comunian, Roberta. "Toward a New Conceptual Framework for Business Investments in the Arts: Some Examples from Italy." *Journal of Arts Management, Law and Society*, vol. 39 (Fall 2009): p. 200–20.

Cordes, Joseph J. (ed.); Steuerle, C. Eugene (ed.) *Nonprofits and Business*. Washington, DC: Urban Institute Press, 2009.

Corporate Contributions Report. New York, NY: Conference Board, annual.

"Corporate Giving Strategies." *Essentials*, (Summer 2011): p. 9–12.

Corporate Philanthropy 2008: Data Trends and the Changing Economy. Executive summary. New York, NY: Committee Encouraging Corporate Philanthropy, 2009.

Corporate Philanthropy Report. Wiley Periodicals, monthly.

Damonti, John; Doykos, Patricia; Wanless, R. Sebastian; Kline, Mark. "HIV/AIDS in African Children : the Bristol-Myers Squibb Foundation and Baylor Response." *Health Affairs*, vol. 31 (July 2012): p. 1636–41.

Demacarty, Peter. "Financial Returns of Corporate Social Responsibility, and the Moral Freedom and Responsibility of Business Leaders." *Business and Society Review*, vol. 114 (Fall 2009): p. 393–433.

Donohue, Michele. "Workplace Still Is Productive." *NonProfit Times* (1 November 2011): p. 1, 4.

Edwards, Michael. *Small Change: Why Business Won't Change the World*. San Francisco, CA: Berrett-Koehler Publications, 2010.

Eikenberry, Angela M. "The Hidden Costs of Cause Marketing." *Stanford Social Innovation Review*, vol. 7 (Summer 2009): p. 50–5.

Einstein, Mara. *Compassion, Inc.: How Corporate America Blurs the Line Between What We Buy, Who We Are, and Those We Help*. Berkeley, CA: University of California Press, 2012.

Flandez, Raymund. "Silicon Valley Nonprofits Zero In on Facebook and Its Workers." *Chronicle of Philanthropy*, vol. 24 (31 May 2012): p. 10.

Foster, Mary K.; Meinhard, Agnes G.; Berger, Ida E.; Krpan, Pike. "Corporate Philanthropy in the Canadian Context." *Nonprofit and Voluntary Sector Quarterly*, vol. 38 (June 2009): p. 441–66.

The Foundation and Corporate Response to the Economic Crisis: An Update. New York, NY: Foundation Center, 2009. (Research Advisory).

Frazier, Eric; Lopez-Rivera, Marisa. "Corporate Giving Slow to Recover as Economy Remains Shaky." *Chronicle of Philanthropy* (28 July 2011): p. 1, 23, 26.

Fuller, Stephen S; McClain, John. *Fannie Mae and Freddie Mac: What Does Their Future Mean for the Washington Region's Nonprofit Community?* Center for Regional Analysis, George Mason University, 2011.

Giving in Numbers. New York, NY: Committee to Encourage Corporate Philanthropy, annual.

Giving USA: The Annual Report on Philanthropy. Chicago, IL: Giving USA Foundation, annual.

Gose, Ben. "Nonprofits Worry About California's Effort to Create Social-Business Units." *Chronicle of Philanthropy*, vol. 23 (19 May 2011): p. 9.

Hyatt, Susan A. *Strategy for Good: Business Giving Strategies for the 21st Century*. Denver, CO: GoodWorks, 2011.

IEG Sponsorship Marketplace. Chicago, IL: IEG, LLC., online.

The Index of Global Philanthropy and Remittances 2012. Washington, DC: Hudson Institute, 2012.

"Innovative Financing of Water Projects." *Corporate Philanthropist*, vol. 9 (Spring-Summer 2009): p. 6–7.

Joyce, Maureen, and Motley, Darlene Y. "Boost Your Share of Corporate Sponsorships." *Nonprofit World*, (July–August 2011): p. 10-1.

Key Facts on Corporate Foundations. New York, NY: Foundation Center, annual.

Knowlton, Lisa Wyatt; Phillips, Cynthia C. "Corporate Giving Gets Smarter: ConAgra Foods Foundation Fights Childhood Hunger." *The Foundation Review*, vol. 4 (Issue 2, 2012): p. 72–83.

Kotler, Philip; Hessekiel, David; Lee, Nancy. *Good Works! Marketing and Corporate Initiatives That Build a Better World ... And The Bottom Line*. Hoboken, NJ: John Wiley & Sons, 2012.

Lewis, Nicole; Gipple, Emily. "Target Pledging $1 Billion to Education, But Some Question Its Impact." *Chronicle of Philanthropy*, vol. 25 (6 December 2012): p. 27–8.

Lim, Terence. *Measuring the Value of Corporate Philanthropy: Social Impact, Business Benefits, and Investor Returns*. New York: Committee Encouraging Corporate Philanthropy, 2010.

Liston-Heyes, Catherine; Liu, Gordon. "Cause-Related Marketing in the Retail and Finance Sectors: An Exploratory Study of the Determinants of Cause Selection and Nonprofit Alliances." *Nonprofit and Voluntary Sector Quarterly*, vol. 39 (February 2010): p. 77–101.

Lysakowski, Linda. *Raise More Money from Your Business Community: A Practical Guide to Tapping into Corporate Charitable Giving*. Rancho Santa Margarita, CA: CharityChannel Press, 2012.

Mapping Success in Employee Volunteering: The Drivers of Effectiveness for Employee Volunteering and Giving Programs and Fortune 500 Performance. Chestnut Hill, MA: Boston College. Center for Corporate Citizenship, 2009.

Matching Gift Register. Leesburg, VA: HEP Development Services, annual.

Meijs, Lucas C.P.M.; Tschirhart, Mary; Ten Hoorn, Ester M.; Brudney, Jeffrey L. "Effect of Design Elements for Corporate Volunteer Programs on Volunteerability." *International Journal of Volunteer Administration*, vol. 26 (March 2009): p. 23–32.

Merz, Michael A.; Peloza, John; Chen, Qimei. "Standardization or Localization? Executing Corporate Philanthropy in International Firms." *International Journal of Nonprofit and Voluntary Sector Marketing*, vol. 15 (August 2010): p. 233–52.

Messina, Judith. "Filling Charities' Coffers." *Crain's New York Business*, (12 December 2011): p. 13–4.

Milner, Andrew . "Corporate Philanthropy in Emerging Economies." *Alliance*, vol. 18 (March 2013): p. 50–6.

"Most Big Companies Expect Flat Giving, Despite 2011 Gains." *Chronicle of Philanthropy*, vol. 24 (26 July 2012): p. 1, 7, 10.

Murphy, Richard McGill. "Why Doing Good Is Good for Business." *Fortune*, vol. 161 (8 February 2010): p. 90-5.

National Directory of Corporate Public Affairs. Bethesda, MD: Columbia Books, annual.

Pedrini, Matteo, and Minciullo, Marco. "Italian Corporate Foundations and the Challenge of Multiple Stakeholder Interests." *Nonprofit Management & Leadership*, (Winter 2011): p. 173–197.

Peebles, Laura H. "Mergers and Charitable Giving: Odd Couple or Best Buddies?" *Trusts & Estates*, (June 2011): p. 14–5.

Peebles, Laura H. "Three Good Reasons To Have a Corporate Foundation (And One Not To)." *Trusts & Estates*, vol. 151 (October 2012): p. 16–7.

Pinney, Chris. *Increasing Impact, Enhancing Value: A Practitioner's Guide to Leading Corporate Philanthropy*. Arlington, VA: Council on Foundations, 2012.

Profile of the Practice: Managing Corporate Citizenship as a Business Strategy. Executive summary. Boston, MA: Boston College. Center for Corporate Citizenship, [2010].

"Report: Corporate Philanthropy." *Crain's New York Business*, vol. 26 (13 December 2010): p. 13–5.

Rey-Garcia, Marta; Martin-Cavanna, Javier; Álvarez González, Luis Ignacio. "Assessing and Advancing Foundation Transparency: Corporate Foundations as a Case Study." *The Foundation Review*, vol. 4 (Issue 3, 2012): p. 77–89.

Richey, Lisa Ann; Ponte, Stefano. *Brand Aid: Shopping Well to Save the World*. Minneapolis, MN: University of Minnesota Press, 2011.

Simmons, Maureen. "Corporate Giving Partnerships: The New Paradigm." *AHP Journal*, (Fall 2010): p. 22-3, 25, 27, 29.

Sachar, Emily. "Contests Fund Mission-Driven Firms." *Crain's New York Business*, (5 December 2011): p. 9.

Salopek, Jennifer J. "New Ways to Select Sponsorships." *Associations Now*, vol. 7 (June 2011): p. 42–5.

Souccar, Miriam Kreinin. "Firms Find New Approach." Crain's *New York Business*, vol. 28 (10 December 2012): p. 13-4.

Souccar, Miriam Kreinin. "Surge in Corporate Cash Fills Charities' Coffers." *Crain's New York Business*, vol. 25 (1–17 August 2011): p. 4, 24.

"Stakeholder' Expectation of Business." *Corporate Philanthropist*, vol. 10 (Winter 2010): p. 1–12.

The State of Corporate Citizenship. Chestnut Hill, MA: Boston College Center for Corporate Citizenship, biennial.

Sywulka, Steve T. "How Big Business Can Learn From Tiny Nonprofits (and Vice-Versa)." *Nonprofit World*, vol. 28 (July-August 2010): p. 12-3.

Thompson, Frederick G. "Corporate Partnerships for Nonprofits: A Match Made in Heaven?" *Nonprofit World*, vol. 30 (March–April 2012): p. 6-9.

Thompson, Waddy. "Grant Writers and Corporate Sponsors." *NonProfit Times*, vol. 23 (1 June 2009): p. 16–7.

Urriolagoitia, Lourdes; Vernis, Alfred. "May the Economic Downturn Affect Corporate Philanthropy? Exploring the Contribution Trends in Spanish and U.S. Companies." *Nonprofit and Voluntary Sector Quarterly*, vol. 41 (October 2012): p. 759–85.

Van Huijstee, Mariette; Glasbergen, Pieter. "Business-NGO Interactions in a Multi-Stakeholder Context." *Business and Society Review*, vol. 115 (Fall 2010): p. 249–84.

Veleva, Vesela; Parker, Shoshana. "Measuring the Business Impacts of Community Involvement: The Case of Employee Volunteering at UL." *Business and Society Review*, vol. 117 (Spring 2012): p. 123–42.

Visser, Wayne. *The Age of Responsibility: CSR 2.0 and the New DNA of Business*. Hoboken, NJ: John Wiley & Sons, 2011.

Waddock, Sandra. "Business Unusual: Corporate Responsibility in a 2.0 World." *Business and Society Review*, (Autumn 2011): p. 303–30.

Wallace, Nicole. "Nonprofit Group Devises Credentials for Socially Conscious Business." *Chronicle of Philanthropy*, vol. 23 (7 October 2010): p. 18–9.

Weeden, Curt. *Smart Giving is Good Business: How Corporate Philanthropy Can Benefit Your Company and Society*. San Francisco, CA: Jossey-Bass Publishers, 2011.

Yotsumoto, Yukio. *Americanizing Japanese Firms: The Institutionalization of Corporate Philanthropy and Volunteerism in American Communities*. Lanham, MD: University Press of America, 2010.

Yunus, Muhammad; Weber, Karl. *Building Social Business: The New Kind of Capitalism that Serves Humanity's Most Pressing Needs*. New York, NY: Public Affairs Press, 2010.

RESOURCES OF THE FOUNDATION CENTER

Established in 1956, the Foundation Center is the leading source of information about philanthropy worldwide. Through data, analysis, and training, it connects people who want to change the world to the resources they need to succeed. The Center maintains the most comprehensive database on U.S. and, increasingly, global grantmakers and their grants — a robust, accessible knowledge bank for the sector. It also operates research, education, and training programs designed to advance knowledge of philanthropy at every level. Thousands of people visit the Center's web site each day and are served in its five regional library/learning centers and its network of more than 470 funding information centers located in public libraries, community foundations, and educational institutions nationwide and around the world.

ONLINE DATABASES

FOUNDATION DIRECTORY ONLINE SUBSCRIPTION PLANS

To meet the needs of grantseekers at every level, *Foundation Directory Online* (FDO) offers five plans—each with monthly, annual, and two-year subscription options. With every plan, subscribers can choose from indexed search terms or keyword-search; search for grantmakers geographically by county, metropolitan area, congressional district, and ZIP code, as well as by state and city.

Professional

FDO *Professional* is acclaimed as the best grantseeking tool on the market. Only *Professional* provides immediate access to nine comprehensive databases, updated weekly: grantmakers, companies, grants, and IRS 990s . . . all with indexed search terms and fully keyword-searchable, plus news, jobs, RFPs, IssueLab reports, and nonprofit literature. *Professional* features interactive maps and charts displaying a foundation's giving patterns, and unique funder portfolios with abstracts from *Philanthropy News Digest*, the grantmaker's latest RFPs, job postings, and key staff affiliations.

$179.95: ONE MONTH
$1,295: ONE YEAR

Platinum

The *Platinum* plan includes profiles of all U.S. foundations, corporate funders, and grantmaking public charities in addition to their recently-awarded grants and an index of trustee, officer, and donor names.

$149.95: ONE MONTH
$995: ONE YEAR

Premium

The *Premium* plan features profiles of the nation's top 20,000 funders and an expanded database of recently-awarded grants . . . fully-searchable. With indexed trustee, officer, and donor names, it's a popular starting point for mid-size nonprofits.

$59.95: ONE MONTH
$595: ONE YEAR

Plus

Search two databases: the nation's 10,000 largest foundations and recently-awarded grants. *Plus* includes an index of trustee, officer, and donor names.

$29.95: ONE MONTH
$295: ONE YEAR

Basic

Gain access to profiles of the nation's 10,000 largest foundations. *Basic* includes an index of trustee, officer, and donor names. A great tool for beginning grantseekers.

$19.95: ONE MONTH
$195: ONE YEAR

TO SUBSCRIBE, VISIT foundationcenter.org/fdo

Corporate Giving Online

For nonprofits seeking grants or in-kind donations of equipment, products, professional services, and volunteers from U.S. company-sponsored foundations and giving programs, *Corporate Giving Online* includes three databases, updated weekly: companies, grantmakers, and grants.

$59.95: ONE MONTH
$595: ONE YEAR

TO SUBSCRIBE, VISIT cgonline.foundationcenter.org

Foundation Grants to Individuals Online

Need a scholarship, fellowship or award? Visit the new *Foundation Grants to Individuals Online* built specifically for students, artists, researchers, and individuals like you!

$19.95: ONE MONTH
$36.95: THREE MONTHS
$59.95: SIX MONTHS
$99.95: ONE YEAR

TO SUBSCRIBE, VISIT gtionline.foundationcenter.org

Map of Cross-Border Giving

Who is making a difference outside of the U.S.?

The *Map of Cross-Border Giving* is an online, interactive mapping tool that lets you see over 54,000 grants totaling nearly $15 billion—invaluable for quickly finding U.S. foundations and corporations that support non-U.S. organizations.

$59.95: ONE MONTH
$595: ONE YEAR

TO SUBSCRIBE, VISIT crossborder.foundationcenter.org

TRASI (Tools and Resources for Assessing Social Impact)

Browse or search the TRASI database for proven approaches to social impact assessment, guidelines for creating and conducting an assessment, and ready-to-use tools for measuring social change. TRASI also features a community page where individuals can connect with peers and experts.

FREE

PLEASE VISIT trasi.foundationcenter.org

Philanthropy In/Sight®

A grantmaker's essential planning tool.

Philanthropy In/Sight® is an interactive mapping platform designed for grantmakers, policymakers, researchers, academics—virtually anyone interested in the impact of philanthropy around the world today.

$195: ONE MONTH
$1,495: ONE YEAR

TO SUBSCRIBE, VISIT philanthropyinsight.org

Nonprofit Collaboration Database

This database provides hundreds of real-life examples of how nonprofits are working together.

PLEASE VISIT foundationcenter.org/gainknowledge/collaboration

GRANTMAKER DIRECTORIES

The Foundation Directory, 2013 Edition

Key facts include fields of interest, contact information, financials, names of decision makers, and over 59,000 sample grants. Convenient indexes are provided for all *Foundation Directories*.

MARCH 2013 / ISBN 978-1-59542-417-4 / $215 / PUBLISHED ANNUALLY

The Foundation Directory Part 2, 2013 Edition

Thorough coverage for the next 10,000 largest foundations, with nearly 42,000 sample grants.

MARCH 2013 / ISBN 978-1-59542-422-8 / $185 / PUBLISHED ANNUALLY

The Foundation Directory Supplement, 2013 Edition

This single volume provides updates for thousands of foundations in *The Foundation Directory* and the *Directory Part 2*. Changes in foundation status, contact information, and giving interests are highlighted in new entries.

SEPTEMBER 2013 / ISBN 978-1-59542-430-3 / $125 / PUBLISHED ANNUALLY

Guide to Funding for International & Foreign Programs, 11th Edition

Profiles of more than 2,200 grantmakers that provide international relief, disaster assistance, human rights, civil liberties, community development, and education.

MAY 2012 / ISBN 978-1-59542-408-2 / $125

The Celebrity Foundation Directory 5th Digital Edition

This downloadable directory (PDF) includes detailed descriptions of more than 1,600 foundations started by VIPs in the fields of business, entertainment, politics, and sports.

NOVEMBER 2013 / ISBN 978-1-59542-456-3 / $59.95

National Directory of Corporate Giving, 19th Edition

The *National Directory of Corporate Giving* offers comprehensive profiles of nearly 4,200 companies, more than 3,200 company-sponsored foundations, more than 1,700 corporate giving programs, and over 8,200 sample grants.

AUGUST 2013 / ISBN 978-1-59542-421-1 / $195 / PUBLISHED ANNUALLY

Foundation Grants to Individuals, 22nd Edition

The only publication devoted entirely to foundation grant opportunities for qualified individual applicants, this directory features more than 9,900 entries with current information including foundation name, address, program description, and application guidelines.

JULY 2013 / ISBN 978-1-59542-418-1 / $75 / PUBLISHED ANNUALLY

The PRI Directory, 3rd Edition Charitable Loans and Other Program-Related Investments by Foundations

This *Directory* lists leading funders, recipients, project descriptions, and includes tips on how to secure and manage PRIs. Foundation listings include funder name and state; recipient name, city, and state (or country); and a description of the project funded.

PUBLISHED IN PARTERNSHIP WITH PRI MAKERS NETWORK.

JULY 2010 / ISBN 978-1-59542-214-9 / $95

Grant Guides

Designed for fundraisers who work within specific areas, 25 digital edition *Grant Guides* list actual foundation grants of $10,000 or more. *Guides* include a keyword search tool and indexes to pinpoint grants of interest to you. As a special bonus, each grantmaker entry contains a link to its Foundation Finder profile for even more details, all in a convenient PDF format.

2013 EDITIONS / $39.95 EACH

TO ORDER, VISIT foundationcenter.org/grantguides

FUNDRAISING GUIDES

After the Grant

The Nonprofit's Guide to Good Stewardship

An invaluable and practical resource for anyone seeking funding from foundations, this *Guide* will help you manage your grant to ensure you get the next one.

MARCH 2010 / ISBN 978-1-59542-301-6 / $39.95

Foundation Fundamentals, 8th Edition

Expert advice on fundraising research and proposal development.

A go-to resource in academic programs on the nonprofit sector. *Foundation Fundamentals* describes foundation funding provides advice on research strategies, including how to best use *Foundation Directory Online*.

MARCH 2008 / ISBN 978-1-59542-156-2 / $39.95

The Foundation Center's Guide to Proposal Writing, 6th Edition

Author Jane Geever provides detailed instructions on preparing successful grant proposals, incorporating the results of interviews with 40 U.S. grantmakers.

MAY 2012 / ISBN 978-1-59542-404-4 / $39.95

Guía Para Escribir Propuestas

The Spanish-language translation of *The Foundation Center's Guide to Proposal Writing*, 5th edition.

MARCH 2008 / ISBN 978-1-595423-158-6 / $39.95

The Grantseeker's Guide to Winning Proposals

A collection of 35 actual proposals submitted to international, regional, corporate, and local foundations. Each includes remarks by the program officer who approved the grant.

AUGUST 2008 / ISBN 978-1-59542-195-1 / $39.95

Securing Your Organization's Future

A Complete Guide to Fundraising Strategies, Revised Edition

Author Michael Seltzer explains how to strengthen your nonprofit's capacity to raise funds and achieve long-term financial stability.

FEBRUARY 2001 / ISBN 0-87954-900-9 / $39.95

NONPROFIT MANAGEMENT GUIDES

America's Nonprofit Sector

A Primer

The third edition of this publication, by Lester Salamon, is ideal for people who want a thorough, accessible introduction to the nonprofit sector—as well as the nation's social welfare system.

MARCH 2012 / ISBN 978-1-59542-360-3 / $24.95

The 21St Century Nonprofit

Managing in the Age of Governance

This book details the significant improvements in nonprofit management practice that have taken place in recent years.

SEPTEMBER 2009 / ISBN 978-1-59542-249-1 / $39.95

Foundations and Public Policy

This book presents a valuable framework for foundations as they plan or implement their engagement with public policy.

Published in partnership with The Center on Philanthropy & Public Policy.

MARCH 2009 / ISBN 978-1-59542-218-7 / $34.95

Local Mission-Global Vision

Community Foundations in the 21st Century

This book examines the new role of community foundations, exploring the potential impact of transnational evolution on organized philanthropy.

Published in partnership with Transatlantic Community Foundations Network.

AUGUST 2008 / ISBN 978-1-59542-204-0 / $34.95

Wise Decision-Making in Uncertain Times

Using Nonprofit Resources Effectively

This book highlights the critical challenges of fiscal sustainability for nonprofits, and encourages organizations to take a more expansive approach to funding outreach.

AUGUST 2006 / ISBN 1-59542-099-1 / $34.95

Effective Economic Decision-Making by Nonprofit Organizations

Editor Dennis R. Young offers practical guidelines to help nonprofit managers advance their mission while balancing the interests of trustees, funders, government, and staff.

DECEMBER 2003 / ISBN 1-931923-69-8 / $34.95

The Board Member's Book

Making a Difference in Voluntary Organizations, 3rd Edition

Written by former Independent Sector President Brian O'Connell, this is the perfect guide to the issues, challenges, and possibilities facing a nonprofit organization and its board.

MAY 2003 / ISBN 1-931923-17-5 / $29.95

Philanthropy's Challenge

Building Nonprofit Capacity Through Venture Grantmaking

Author Paul Firstenberg explores the roles of grantmaker and grantee within various models of venture grantmaking. He outlines the characteristics that qualify an organization for a venture grant, and outlines the steps a grantmaker can take to build the grantees' organizational capacity.

FEBRUARY 2003 / SOFTBOUND: ISBN 1-931923-15-9 / $29.95
HARDBOUND: ISBN 1-931923-53-1 / $39.95

Investing in Capacity Building

A Guide to High-Impact Approaches

Author Barbara Blumenthal helps grantmakers and consultants design better methods to help nonprofits, while showing nonprofit managers how to get more effective support.

NOVEMBER 2003 / ISBN 1-931923-65-5 / $34.95

ASSOCIATES PROGRAM

For just $995 a year or $695 for six months, the Associates Program experts will answer all of your questions about foundation giving, corporate philanthropy, and individual donors.

You will receive online access to several lists that are updated monthly, including new grantmakers and grantmaker application deadlines. In addition, you will receive most results within the next business day.

JOIN NOW AT foundationcenter.org/associates

ADDITIONAL ONLINE RESOURCES

foundationcenter.org

- *Philanthropy News Digest* is a daily digest of philanthropy-related articles. Read interviews with leaders, look for RFPs, learn from the experts, and share ideas with others in the field.
- FC Stats provides thousands of tables of national, state, and metropolitan area data on U.S. foundations and their grants, including assets and giving, grant distribution patterns, and top recipients.
- Access research studies to track trends in foundation growth and giving in grantmaker policies and practices.
- To stay current on the latest research trends visit foundationcenter.org/gainknowledge.

grantspace.org

GrantSpace, the Foundation Center's learning community for the social sector, features resources organized under the 13 most common subject areas of funding research — including health, education, and the arts.

- Dig into the GrantSpace knowledge base for answers to more than 150 questions asked about grantseeking and nonprofits.
- Stay up-to-date on classes and events happening in person and online with the GrantSpace training calendar.
- Add your voice and help build a community-driven knowledge base: share your expertise, rate content, ask questions, and add comments.

glasspockets.org

- Learn about the online transparency and accountability practices of the largest foundations, and see who has "glass pockets."
- Transparency Talk, the Glasspockets blog and podcast series, highlights strategies, findings, and best practices related to foundation transparency.
- The Giving Pledge is an effort that encourages the world's wealthiest individuals and families to commit the majority of their assets to philanthropic causes. Eye on the Giving Pledge offers an in-depth picture of Giving Pledge participants, their charitable activities, and the potential impact of the Giving Pledge.
- Learn more about the Reporting Commitment, an initiative aimed at developing more timely, accurate, and precise reporting on the flow of philanthropic dollars.

www.GrantCraft.org

GrantCraft, a former project of the Ford Foundation, operates under the leadership of the Foundation Center in New York and the European Foundation Centre in Brussels. GrantCraft's signature approach has been to tap the "practical wisdom" of a diverse group of experienced grantmakers to improve the practice of philanthropy.

- Find real-life examples and tested solutions for overcoming hurdles faced by funders.
- Learn about grantmaking tools and techniques through guides, case studies, videos, surveys, workshops, and translations.

issuelab.org

IssueLab provides free access to resources that analyze the world's most pressing social, economic, and environmental challenges and their potential solutions. The platform contains more than 12,000 documents and represents one of the largest collections of social sector knowledge.

- Search and browse the database by social issue area, author, publishing organization, or geography.
- Learn how to add resources to the IssueLab collection.

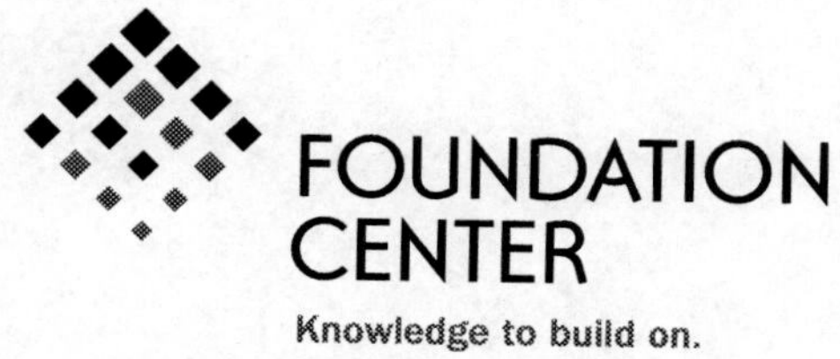

Funding Information Network

In addition to its libraries in Atlanta, Cleveland, New York, San Francisco, and Washington, D.C., the Foundation Center hosts a nationwide network comprised of libraries, community foundations, NGOs, and nonprofit resource centers called the Funding Information Network.

In more than 470 locations, these network partners provide access to the best and most comprehensive information available on foundations and corporate giving, including free access to Foundation Center resources and fundraising research guidance, and other funding-related technical assistance. Additionally, workshops and programs for local nonprofits are offered at many locations.

The Funding Information Network has a presence in all 50 states and in more than a dozen countries globally. Find a location in your area at grantspace.org/Find-Us.

DESCRIPTIVE DIRECTORY

1

The 13th Regional Corporation

1156 Industry Dr.
Seattle, WA 98188-4803 (206) 575-6229

Company URL: http://www.13thregionalcorporation.com
Establishment information: Established in 1975.
Company type: Native corporation
Business activities: Operates native corporation.
Business type (SIC): Nonclassifiable establishments
Corporate officers: Kurt Engelstad, Chair.; Norman L. Ream, Pres.; Peter J. Egan, Secy.; Derek J. Kolar, Treas.
Board of director: Kurt Engelstad, Chair.
Giving statement: Giving through the 13th Regional Heritage Foundation.

The 13th Regional Heritage Foundation

611 12th Ave. S, Ste. 300
Seattle, WA 98144-1911 (425) 443-0763
FAX: (253) 946-1460;
E-mail: the13thheritagefoundation@yahoo.com; Tel. for Elmer Makua: (206) 859-4100; Additional tel.: (253) 221-2621

Establishment information: Established in 1999 in AK.
Donors: The 13th Regional Corp.; 1st Alaskans Foundation; Muckleshoot Indian Tribe.
Contact: Elmer Makua, Exec. Dir.
Financial data (yr. ended 12/31/09): Assets, $46,758 (M); gifts received, $5,000; expenditures, $22,873; qualifying distributions, $0.
Purpose and activities: The foundation awards college scholarships to Alaska Natives who are shareholders or direct descendants or family members of shareholders of the 13th Regional Corp.
Fields of interest: Native Americans/American Indians.
Type of support: Scholarships—to individuals.
Application information: Applications accepted. Application form not required.
Initial approach: Contact foundation for application information
Officers: Tom Harris, Pres.; Chris Kiana, Secy.; George Samuel, Treas.; Elmer Makua, Exec. Dir.
EIN: 912002448

2

1st Source Bank

3600 Portage Ave.
South Bend, IN 46628 (574) 235-2254

Company URL: http://www.1stsource.com
Establishment information: Established in 1863.
Company type: Subsidiary of a public company
Business activities: Operates commercial bank.
Business type (SIC): Banks/commercial
Financial profile for 2010: Number of employees, 8
Corporate officers: Christopher J. Murphy III, Chair., Pres., and C.E.O.; Andrea G. Short, C.F.O. and Treas.; John B. Griffith, Secy. and Genl. Counsel
Board of director: Christopher J. Murphy III, Chair.
Subsidiaries: 1st Source Capital Corp., South Bend, IN; 1st Source Insurance, Inc., South Bend, IN
Giving statement: Giving through the 1st Source Foundation.

1st Source Foundation

c/o 1st Source Bank
P.O. Box 1602
South Bend, IN 46634-1602 (574) 235-2790
URL: https://www.1stsource.com/about-us/community-involvement

Establishment information: Established in 1952 in IN.
Donors: 1st Source Bank; 1st Source Bank Charitable Trust.
Contact: Lee Morton
Financial data (yr. ended 12/31/11): Assets, $18,236,315 (M); gifts received, $500; expenditures, $895,508; qualifying distributions, $816,632; giving activities include $816,632 for grants.
Purpose and activities: The foundation supports organizations involved with arts and culture, education, social welfare and human services, community development, and civic affairs.
Fields of interest: Media, television; Museums (history); Arts; Elementary school/education; Higher education; Education; Hospitals (general); Crime/violence prevention; YM/YWCAs & YM/YWHAs; Human services; Community development, neighborhood development; Community/economic development; Foundations (community); United Ways and Federated Giving Programs; Public affairs.
Type of support: General/operating support.
Geographic limitations: Giving primarily in area of company operations in IN, with emphasis on South Bend.
Publications: Application guidelines; Corporate report.
Application information: Applications accepted. Preference is given to nonprofit, charitable, and community organizations with which 1st Source colleagues play an active role. Application form not required. Applicants should submit the following:
1) detailed description of project and amount of funding requested
2) statement of problem project will address
3) explanation of why grantmaker is considered an appropriate donor for project
4) geographic area to be served
5) results expected from proposed grant
6) how project's results will be evaluated or measured
7) copy of most recent annual report/audited financial statement/990
8) copy of current year's organizational budget and/or project budget
9) listing of additional sources and amount of support
10) listing of board of directors, trustees, officers and other key people and their affiliations

Initial approach: Proposal
Deadline(s): Apr. 25 and Sept. 25
Final notification: 30 days following the board meeting

Directors: Terry Gerber; Wellington D. Jones III; Rex Martin; Christopher J. Murphy III.
Trustee: 1st Source Bank.
EIN: 356034211
Selected grants: The following grants are a representative sample of this grantmaker's funding activity:
$49,479 to United Way of Saint Joseph County, South Bend, IN, 2011.
$17,000 to Community Action of Northeast Indiana, Fort Wayne, IN, 2011.
$15,000 to Boys and Girls Club of Benton Harbor, Benton Harbor, MI, 2011.
$12,000 to Habitat for Humanity, Saint Joseph County, South Bend, IN, 2011.
$11,000 to Bethel College, Mishawaka, IN, 2011.
$10,000 to South Bend Symphony Orchestra, South Bend, IN, 2011.
$10,000 to Urban League of Fort Wayne, Fort Wayne, IN, 2011.
$5,029 to United Way of Porter County, Valparaiso, IN, 2011.
$3,000 to South Bend Heritage Foundation, South Bend, IN, 2011.
$1,000 to Indiana University, South Bend, IN, 2011.

3

3M Company

(formerly Minnesota Mining and Manufacturing Company)
3M Ctr.
St. Paul, MN 55144-1000 (651) 737-6501
FAX: (651) 737-7117

Company URL: http://www.3m.com
Establishment information: Established in 1902.
Company type: Public company
Company ticker symbol and exchange: MMM/NYSE
International Securities Identification Number: US88579Y1010
Business activities: Researches, manufactures, and markets coated and bonded products.
Business type (SIC): Abrasive, asbestos, and nonmetallic mineral products
Financial profile for 2012: Number of employees, 87,677; assets, $33,876,000,000; sales volume, $29,904,000,000; pre-tax net income, $6,351,000,000; expenses, $23,421,000,000; liabilities, $16,301,000,000
Fortune 1000 ranking: 2012—101st in revenues, 42nd in profits, and 166th in assets
Forbes 2000 ranking: 2012—316th in sales, 124th in profits, and 669th in assets
Corporate officers: Inge G. Thulin, Chair., Pres., and C.E.O.; Hak Cheol Shin, Exec. V.P., Opers.; David W. Meline, Sr. V.P. and C.F.O.; Ivan K. Fong, Sr. V.P. and Genl. Counsel; Ian F. Hardgrove, Sr. V.P., Mktg. and Sales; Marlene M. McGrath, Sr. V.P., Human Resources; Scott D. Krohn, V.P. and Treas.
Board of directors: Irene G. Thulin, Chair.; Linda G. Alvarado; Vance D. Coffman; Michael L. Eskew; W. James Farrell; Herbert L. Henkel; Muhtar Kent; Edward M. Liddy; Robert S. Morrison; Aulana L. Peters; Robert J. Ulrich
International operations: Argentina; Australia; Austria; Belgium; Brazil; Canada; China; Denmark; Finland; France; Germany; Hong Kong; India; Italy; Japan; Malaysia; Mexico; Morocco and the Western Sahara; Netherlands; New Zealand; Nigeria; Norway; Pakistan; Panama; Paraguay; Peru; Philippines; Poland; Portugal; Romania; Russia; Saudi Arabia; Singapore; Slovakia; South Africa; South Korea; Spain; Sri Lanka; Sweden; Switzerland; Taiwan; Thailand; Trinidad & Tobago; Turkey; Ukraine; United Arab Emirates; United Kingdom; Uruguay; Venezuela; Vietnam
Giving statement: Giving through the 3M Company Contributions Program and the 3M Foundation.
Company EIN: 410417775

3M Company Contributions Program

3M Ctr.
St. Paul, MN 55144-1000 (888) 364-3577
URL: http://www.3mgiving.com

Purpose and activities: As a complement to its foundation, 3M also makes charitable contributions to nonprofit organizations directly. Support is limited to areas of company operations.

Fields of interest: Arts, cultural/ethnic awareness; Elementary/secondary education; Higher education; Business school/education; Teacher school/education; Engineering school/education; Education, drop-out prevention; Environmental education; Environment; Dental care; Health care; Safety/disasters; Youth development; Human services; Mathematics; Science; Economics Economically disadvantaged.

Program:

3M Ingenuity Grants: 3M provides up to $10,000 each to 47 schools to support new ideas by teaching teams to spark student interest in science, technology, engineering, and math (STEM) classes. Totaling over $400,000, 3M Ingenuity Grants will reach classrooms in 20 states.

Type of support: Curriculum development; Donated products; Employee volunteer services; General/operating support; In-kind gifts; Program development.

Geographic limitations: Giving limited to areas of company operations.

Support limitations: No support for fraternal or social organizations, government agencies, K-12 schools, colleges or universities, religious organizations, animal-related organizations, disease-related organizations, hospitals, clinics, treatment centers, hospice programs, or nursing homes. No grants to individuals, or for advocacy or lobbying efforts to influence legislation, athletic or special events, conferences, seminars, workshops, or symposia, fundraising or testimonial events, film or video production, humanitarian or disaster relief, environmental projects, scholarship funds, travel, or playground or athletic equipment.

Publications: Application guidelines.

Application information: The company utilizes an invitation only Request For Proposal (RFP) process for donations. Unsolicited requests are rarely funded. Unsolicited proposals are not accepted in Minneapolis or St. Paul, MN, or Austin, TX.

Initial approach: Letter of inquiry to nearest company facility addressed to "3M Plant Manager"

Corporate Contributions Committee: A. C. Cirillo, Jr., V.P., Community Affairs; A. H. Janusz, Recording Secy.; Barbara W. Kaufmann, Mgr., Corp. Contribs. and Community Affairs; Cynthia F. Kleven, Mgr., Corp. Contribs.; Thomas A. Boardman; George W. Buckley; J. L. Bushman; M. P. Delkoski; Robert D. MacDonald; R. M. Miller; J. B. Sweeney; S. K. Tokach; S. C. Webster; J. K. Woodworth; J. L. Yeomans.

Number of staff: 4 full-time professional; 1 part-time professional; 2 full-time support.

Selected grants: The following grants are a representative sample of this grantmaker's funding activity:

$50,000 to American Council on Science and Health, New York, NY, 2008.

$37,500 to Society of Hispanic Professional Engineers, City of Industry, CA, 2008.

$25,000 to North Carolina A & T State University, Greensboro, NC, 2008.

$20,000 to HandsOn Twin Cities, Minneapolis, MN, 2008.

$15,000 to University of Minnesota, Minneapolis, MN, 2008.

$10,000 to Friends of the Mississippi River, Saint Paul, MN, 2008.

3M Foundation

(also known as Minnesota Mining and Manufacturing Foundation)
3M Ctr., Bldg., 225-01-S-23
St. Paul, MN 55144-1000 (651) 733-0144
FAX: (651) 737-3061; E-mail: cfkleven@mmm.com;
URL: http://www.3Mgiving.com

Establishment information: Incorporated in 1953 in MN.

Donors: Minnesota Mining and Manufacturing Co.; 3M Co.

Contact: Cynthia F. Kleven, Secy.

Financial data (yr. ended 12/31/11): Assets, $24,605,184 (M); gifts received, $20,000,000; expenditures, $22,259,444; qualifying distributions, $23,907,589; giving activities include $22,154,002 for 2,456 grants (high: $1,000,000; low: $25).

Purpose and activities: The foundation supports organizations involved with arts and culture, education, the environment, health, disaster relief, youth development, human services, science, and economics. Special emphasis is directed toward initiatives with defined and measurable results that target underserved populations.

Fields of interest: Arts, cultural/ethnic awareness; Museums (science/technology); Performing arts, orchestras; Arts; Elementary/secondary education; Education, early childhood education; Higher education; Business school/education; Engineering school/education; Education, services; Education; Environment, climate change/global warming; Environment, natural resources; Environment; Disasters, preparedness/services; Youth development; Human services; United Ways and Federated Giving Programs; Science, formal/general education; Mathematics; Engineering; Science; Economics Children/youth; Minorities; Economically disadvantaged.

Programs:

3M Community Volunteer Award: The foundation annually awards the 3M Community Volunteer Award in recognition of exceptional employee and retiree volunteer contribution. The honor includes a $1,000 grant to a nonprofit organization of the winner's choice.

3M Volunteer Match: The foundation awards $250 grants to nonprofit organizations with which employees and retirees of 3M volunteer at least 20 hours per year.

Arts and Culture: The foundation supports programs designed to enhance the quality of cultural life in communities. Special emphasis is directed toward education and community outreach programs; and artistic and cultural diversity.

Employee Matching Gifts: The foundation matches contributions made by employees, retirees, and directors of 3M to institutions of higher education.

Environment: The foundation supports programs designed to protect the sustainability of Earth's ecosystems. Special emphasis is directed toward programs designed to preserve biodiversity; and mitigate climate change.

Health and Human Services: The foundation supports programs designed to strengthen youth development through prevention; early intervention; school readiness in early childhood; and afterschool initiatives with a learning component. The foundation also provides humanitarian and disaster relief to build and sustain healthy communities.

Higher Education: The foundation supports programs designed to help students prepare for future opportunities in an ever-changing world. Special emphasis is directed toward programs designed to advance excellence in science, engineering, and business; and increase student participation and retention of underserved people in these disciplines.

K-12 Education: The foundation supports programs designed to promote K-12 education. Special emphasis is directed toward initiatives designed to increase student achievement in math, science, and economics; and improve college access and readiness.

Type of support: Capital campaigns; Curriculum development; Employee matching gifts; Employee volunteer services; General/operating support; In-kind gifts; Program development; Scholarship funds.

Geographic limitations: Giving on a national basis in areas of company operations, with emphasis on MN.

Support limitations: No support for religious, fraternal, social, or veterans' organizations, disease-specific organizations, government agencies, hospitals, clinics, or nursing homes, treatment centers or hospices, or individual K-12 schools. No grants to individuals, or for capital endowments, advocacy or lobbying efforts, conferences, seminars, or workshops, publications, film or video production, fundraising, testimonial, athletic or special events, playground or athletic equipment, non-3M equipment, travel, or scholarship funds; no loans or investments.

Publications: Annual report; Application guidelines; Grants list; Program policy statement.

Application information: Applications accepted. Unsolicited requests are rarely funded. The foundation utilizes an invitation only Request For Proposal (RFP) process for organizations located in Minneapolis and St. Paul, MN, and Austin, TX and for humanitarian and disaster relief requests. Application form required.

Initial approach: Complete online eligibility quiz
Copies of proposal: 1
Board meeting date(s): June and Dec.
Deadline(s): None
Final notification: 6 weeks

Officers: Ian F. Hardgrove, Pres.; Kimberly F. Price, V.P.; Cynthia F. Kleven, Secy.; Janet L. Yeomans, Treas.

Number of staff: 6 full-time professional; 3 full-time support.

EIN: 416038262

Selected grants: The following grants are a representative sample of this grantmaker's funding activity:

$2,300,000 to United Way, Greater Twin Cities, Minneapolis, MN, 2011.

$1,000,000 to Nature Conservancy, Arlington, VA, 2011.

$1,000,000 to University of Minnesota, Minneapolis, MN, 2011.

$1,000,000 to University of Minnesota, College of Science and Engineering, Minneapolis, MN, 2011. For Merit Scholarships.

$500,000 to Saint Paul Foundation, Saint Paul, MN, 2011. For Arts Partnership Campaign.

$250,000 to Saint Catherine University, Saint Paul, MN, 2011.

$165,000 to Project Lead the Way, Indianapolis, IN, 2011.

$100,000 to Hope Haven of DeKalb County, DeKalb, IL, 2011.

$100,000 to Minnesota African American Museum and Cultural Center, Minneapolis, MN, 2011.

$75,000 to US FIRST, Manchester, NH, 2011.

$50,000 to Georgia Tech Foundation, Atlanta, GA, 2011.

$50,000 to Zachary Scott Theater Center, Austin, TX, 2011.

$25,000 to Adoption Coalition of Central Texas, Austin, TX, 2011.

$15,000 to Columbia University, New York, NY, 2011. For Nanostructured thin-films for solar photovoltaics beyond the Shockley-Queisser limit and OLED light extraction.
$10,000 to Discovery Science Center of Orange County, Santa Ana, CA, 2011.
$10,000 to River Relief, Columbia, MO, 2011. For Big Muddy Clean Sweep.
$9,000 to BookSpring, Austin, TX, 2011. For RIF Days at Wooten Elementary.
$9,000 to United Way of Douglas and Pope Counties, Alexandria, MN, 2011. For Annual Fundraising Campaign.
$7,000 to VocalEssence, Minneapolis, MN, 2011. For WITNESS 2010-2011.
$5,000 to Clean River Project, Methuen, MA, 2011.

4
7 Day Dental Anaheim
637 N. Euclid St.
2265 W. Lincoln Ave.
Anaheim, CA 92801 (714) 491-8600

Company URL: http://www.7daydentalanaheim.com/
Establishment information: Established in 1990.
Company type: Private company
Business activities: Operates dental practice.
Business type (SIC): Offices and clinics/dentists'
Corporate officer: Chuck Le, Pres. and C.E.O.
Giving statement: Giving through the 7 Day Dental Anaheim Corporate Giving Program.

7 Day Dental Anaheim Corporate Giving Program
2265 W. Lincoln Ave.
Anaheim, CA 92801-6503 (714) 491-8600
E-mail: 7DayDentalAnaheimP@gmail.com;
URL: http://www.7daydentalanaheim.com/

5
7-Eleven, Inc.
(formerly The Southland Corporation)
1 Arts Plz., 1722 Routh St., Ste. 1000
P.O. Box 711
Dallas, TX 75201 (972) 828-7011

Company URL: http://www.7-eleven.com
Establishment information: Established in 1927.
Company type: Subsidiary of a foreign company
Business activities: Operates convenience food stores.
Business type (SIC): Groceries—retail; beverages; miscellaneous prepared foods; soaps, cleaners, and toiletries; chemicals/industrial organic; petroleum refining
Financial profile for 2010: Number of employees, 949; sales volume, $3,980,000,000
Corporate officers: Toshifumi Suzuki, Chair.; Joseph DePinto, Pres. and C.E.O.; Darren Rebelez, Exec. V.P. and C.O.O.; Stanley W. Reynolds, Exec. V.P. and C.F.O.; Wes Hargrove, Sr. V.P. and C.I.O.; Dave Fenton, Sr. V.P., Genl. Counsel, and Secy.; Brad Jenkins, Sr. V.P., Opers.; Krystin Mitchell, Sr. V.P., Human Resources; Cynthia Noren, V.P., Human Resources
Board of directors: Toshifumi Suzuki, Chair.; Joseph M. DePinto
Subsidiary: 7-Eleven Stores, Dallas, TX
Giving statement: Giving through the 7-Eleven, Inc. Corporate Giving Program.

7-Eleven, Inc. Corporate Giving Program
(formerly The Southland Corporation Contributions Program)
c/o Community Rels. Dept.
Loc. 199
P.O. Box 711
Dallas, TX 75221-0711
URL: http://corp.7-eleven.com/InTheCommunity/tabid/471/Default.aspx

Purpose and activities: 7-Eleven makes charitable contributions to nonprofit organizations involved with education, health and wellness, safety, and community revitalization. Special emphasis is directed towards programs designed to focus on youth development. Support is given primarily in areas of company store operations, with emphasis on Dallas, Texas.
Fields of interest: Education; Public health; Crime/law enforcement, police agencies; Safety/disasters; Athletics/sports, amateur leagues; Youth development; Community/economic development.
Program:
Operation Chill: 7-Eleven provides coupons for free 7-Eleven products to enhance relations between police and youth. Law enforcement officers "ticket" kids they observe doing good deeds or exhibiting positive behaviors, such as wearing bicycle helmets, picking up trash, participating in community activities, and deterring crime. The "tickets" are coupons for a free 12-oz Slurpee.
Type of support: Cause-related marketing; Donated products; Employee volunteer services; In-kind gifts; Program development; Sponsorships.
Geographic limitations: Giving primarily in areas of company store operations, particularly in Dallas, TX.
Support limitations: No support for religious, political, or discriminatory organizations. No grants to individuals, or for general operating support, multi-year requests, capital campaigns, or building or endowment campaigns.
Application information: Applications not accepted. Unsolicited requests are not accepted. The Community Relations Department handles giving.

6
A & E Incorporated
5501 21st St.
P.O. Box 1616
Racine, WI 53406-5067 (262) 554-2300

Company URL: http://www.aeincorporated.com
Establishment information: Established in 1932.
Company type: Private company
Business activities: Manufactures hand tools and pressed metal products.
Business type (SIC): Cutlery, hand and edge tools, and hardware; metal forgings and stampings
Corporate officers: John Lang, Chair. and C.E.O.; Alan Biland, Co-Pres.; Andy Eddins, Co-Pres.
Board of director: John Lang, Chair.
Giving statement: Giving through the Lang Family Foundation, Inc.

Lang Family Foundation, Inc.
3836 Aves Island Ct.
Punta Gorda, FL 33950 (507) 931-0430

Establishment information: Established in 1997 in WI.
Donors: Helen Lang†; A&E Inc.
Financial data (yr. ended 12/31/11): Assets, $329,566 (M); gifts received, $4,000; expenditures, $23,472; qualifying distributions, $18,800; giving activities include $18,800 for grants.
Purpose and activities: The foundation supports food banks and organizations involved with arts and culture, education, health, human services, and community development.
Fields of interest: Education; Youth development; Human services.
Type of support: Employee-related scholarships; General/operating support.
Geographic limitations: Giving primarily in MN.
Application information: Applications accepted. Application form required.
Initial approach: Proposal
Deadline(s): Feb. 10
Officers: Sandra P. Lang, Pres.; Gregory A. Ruidl, Secy.; Vickie E. Hein, Recording Secy.; John R. Lang, Treas.
Directors: Amanda B. Knoell; Julie W. Lang; Daniel A. Peterson; Donna Peterson.
EIN: 391884671

7
A.D. Makepeace
158 Tihonet Rd.
Wareham, MA 02571-1104 (508) 295-1000
FAX: (508) 291-7453

Company URL: http://www.admakepeace.com
Establishment information: Established in 1922.
Company type: Private company
Business activities: Operates cranberry farm.
Business type (SIC): Farms/fruit and nut
Corporate officers: Thomas A. Steele, Chair.; Michael P. Hogan, Pres. and C.E.O.; Laurence F. Mulhern, Sr. V.P., Finance and Admin.; Linda M. Burke, V.P., Mktg. and Comms.
Board of directors: Thomas A. Steele, Chair.; Mark B. Bartlett; Thomas Berkley; Joanna Makepeace Bennett; Linda M. Burke; Richard Canning; Samuel Makepeace Coxe; Timothy Crawford; Jeff Crowley; Zelinda Makepeace Douhan; Renee Gonsalves; Michael Hogan; Kim Houdlette; James F. Kane; Robert Karam; Louis Lee Lemmertz; Christopher Makepeace; Laurence F. Mulhern, C.P.A.; Joseph O'Connor; Thomas Otis; George G. Rogers; Steven Sabourin; Joseph Shivell; Robert F. Simmons, Jr.
Giving statement: Giving through the Makepeace Neighborhood Fund.

Makepeace Neighborhood Fund
158 Tihonet Rd.
Wareham, MA 02571-1104 (508) 295-1000
URL: http://www.admakepeace.com/pages/about_adm/adm_neighborhood_fund.asp

Establishment information: Established in 2004 in MA.
Donors: A. D. Makepeace; A.D. Makespeace Company.
Contact: Linda M. Burke, Dir., Mktg. and Comms.
Financial data (yr. ended 12/31/11): Assets, $161,401 (M); gifts received, $160,000; expenditures, $150,674; qualifying distributions, $150,674; giving activities include $149,865 for 29 grants (high: $9,572; low: $1,000).
Purpose and activities: The fund supports organizations involved with historic preservation, education, environmental protection, health care, agriculture, and community housing.
Fields of interest: Historic preservation/historical societies; Education; Environment, natural resources; Environment; Animals/wildlife; Health care; Agriculture/food; Housing/shelter.

Type of support: General/operating support; Program development; Scholarship funds.
Geographic limitations: Giving limited to Carver, Middleborough, Plymouth, Rochester, and Wareham, MA.
Support limitations: No grants to individuals.
Publications: Application guidelines; Grants list.
Application information: Applications accepted. Grants range from $5,000 to $10,000. Application form required. Applicants should submit the following:
1) timetable for implementation and evaluation of project
2) qualifications of key personnel
3) copy of IRS Determination Letter
4) brief history of organization and description of its mission
5) copy of most recent annual report/audited financial statement/990
6) listing of board of directors, trustees, officers and other key people and their affiliations
7) detailed description of project and amount of funding requested
8) listing of additional sources and amount of support

Initial approach: Download application form and mail to foundation
Copies of proposal: 1
Board meeting date(s): Nov.
Deadline(s): Mar. 15
Final notification: May

Trustees: Joanna Bennett; Richard Canning; Michael P. Hogan; Christopher Makepeace; Elizabeth Snow.
EIN: 412163159

8
A.J. Facts Inc.

112 W. 34th St., Ste. 1140
New York, NY 10120-0101 (212) 967-4435

Establishment information: Established in 1993.
Company type: Private company
Business activities: Manufactures girl's apparel.
Business type (SIC): Apparel—girls' and children's outerwear
Corporate officer: Jack Mizarrehi, Owner
Giving statement: Giving through the JVS Charitable Foundation.

JVS Charitable Foundation

c/o A.J. Facts Inc.
112 W. 34th St.
New York, NY 10120-1199 (212) 967-4430

Establishment information: Established in NY.
Donor: A.J. Facts Inc.
Contact: Jack Mizrahi, Tr.
Financial data (yr. ended 12/31/11): Assets, $4,876 (M); gifts received, $86,000; expenditures, $87,604; qualifying distributions, $87,579; giving activities include $87,579 for grants.
Purpose and activities: The foundation supports organizations involved with Judaism.
Fields of interest: Arts; International affairs; Religion.
Type of support: General/operating support.
Geographic limitations: Giving primarily in NY.
Support limitations: No grants to individuals.
Application information: Applications accepted. Application form not required.

Initial approach: Proposal
Deadline(s): None

Trustees: Victor Chouchani; Saul Kredi; Jack Mizrahi.
EIN: 134074980

9
Abacus Wealth Partners, LLC

1818 Market St., Ste. 3740
Philadelphia, PA 19103-3607
(215) 656-4280

Company URL: http://www.abacuswealth.com
Establishment information: Established in 1987.
Company type: Private company
Business activities: Operates wealth management firm.
Business type (SIC): Security and commodity services
Corporate officers: Spencer Sherman, C.E.O.; Jason Cole, Cont.
Offices: Los Angeles, San Francisco, CA
Giving statement: Giving through the Abacus Wealth Partners, LLC Corporate Giving Program.

Abacus Wealth Partners, LLC Corporate Giving Program

1818 Market St.
Philadelphia, PA 19103 (215) 656-4280
E-mail: charity@abacuswealth.com; URL: http://www.abacuswealth.com

Purpose and activities: Abacus Wealth Partners is a certified B Corporation that donates 5 percent of profits to local nonprofit organizations annually.
Fields of interest: Environment; Human services, financial counseling; Microfinance/microlending Economically disadvantaged.
Publications: Application guidelines.
Application information: Applications accepted. There is no formal grant application and applicants are encouraged to be creative in making their case.

Initial approach: E-mail proposal

10
ABARTA, Inc.

1000 Gamma Dr., Ste. 500
Pittsburgh, PA 15238-2927 (412) 963-6226

Company URL: http://www.abarta.com
Establishment information: Established in 1972.
Company type: Private company
Business activities: Operates holding company; produces soft drinks; publishes newspapers and magazines; conducts crude oil and natural gas exploration and development activities.
Business type (SIC): Beverages; extraction/oil and gas; newspaper publishing and/or printing; periodical publishing and/or printing; holding company
Financial profile for 2010: Number of employees, 60
Corporate officers: John F. Bitzer III, Pres. and C.E.O.; Charles R. Hanlon, V.P. and C.F.O.; Frank Nowak, V.P., Human Resources
Giving statement: Giving through the Adams Foundation, Inc. and the Fountainhead Foundation.

Adams Foundation, Inc.

c/o Abarta, Inc.
1000 Gamma Dr., 4th Fl
Pittsburgh, PA 15238-2929 (412) 963-1087

Establishment information: Incorporated in 1955 in PA.
Donors: Rolland L. Adams†; ABARTA Inc.
Contact: Shelley M. Taylor, Pres.
Financial data (yr. ended 12/31/11): Assets, $1,983,168 (M); gifts received, $50,000; expenditures, $276,835; qualifying distributions, $276,500; giving activities include $276,500 for grants.
Purpose and activities: The foundation supports food banks and civic centers and organizations involved with arts and culture, education, mental health, and arthritis.
Fields of interest: Performing arts, ballet; Performing arts, theater; Arts; Higher education; Education; Mental health/crisis services; Arthritis; Food banks; Community development, civic centers.
Type of support: General/operating support.
Geographic limitations: Giving primarily in Ithaca, NY and Pittsburgh, PA.
Support limitations: No grants to individuals.
Application information: Applications accepted. Application form not required. Applicants should submit the following:
1) copy of IRS Determination Letter
2) copy of most recent annual report/audited financial statement/990
3) detailed description of project and amount of funding requested

Initial approach: Proposal
Copies of proposal: 1
Board meeting date(s): Feb. and Aug.
Deadline(s): None

Officers and Directors:* Shelley M. Taylor*, Pres.; Mary R. Hudson*, Secy.; James A. Taylor*, Treas.
EIN: 240866511
Selected grants: The following grants are a representative sample of this grantmaker's funding activity:
$131,000 to Pittsburgh Ballet Theater, Pittsburgh, PA, 2010.
$15,000 to Greater Pittsburgh Community Food Bank, Duquesne, PA, 2010.
$10,000 to Compos Mentis Working Toward Wellness, Ithaca, NY, 2010.
$5,000 to Gabriella Axelrad Education Foundation, Los Angeles, CA, 2010.
$5,000 to Oxfam America, Boston, MA, 2010.
$5,000 to Partners in Health, Boston, MA, 2010.
$1,500 to YMCA of Greater Pittsburgh, Pittsburgh, PA, 2010.
$1,000 to Pittsburgh Foundation, Pittsburgh, PA, 2010.

Fountainhead Foundation

1000 Gamma Dr., Ste. 500
Pittsburgh, PA 15238-2927

Establishment information: Established in 1989 in PA.
Donor: ABARTA Inc.
Contact: Michelle R. Bitzer, Pres.
Financial data (yr. ended 12/31/11): Assets, $662,774 (M); gifts received, $50,000; expenditures, $312,928; qualifying distributions, $309,700; giving activities include $309,700 for grants.
Purpose and activities: The foundation supports organizations involved with education, health, recreation, children, and human services.
Fields of interest: Elementary/secondary education; Higher education; Education; Hospitals (general); Health care; Recreation; Children, services; Human services.
Type of support: General/operating support.
Geographic limitations: Giving on a national basis, with emphasis on PA.
Support limitations: No grants to individuals.

Application information: Applications not accepted.
Officers: Michelle R. Bitzer, Pres.; Astrid S. Bitzer, V.P.; Susan Marie Forsyth, Secy.; John F. Bitzer III, Treas.
EIN: 251605441
Selected grants: The following grants are a representative sample of this grantmaker's funding activity:
$44,900 to Institute for Functional Medicine, Gig Harbor, WA, 2010.
$25,000 to Phillips Exeter Academy, Exeter, NH, 2010.
$11,500 to Childrens Museum of Pittsburgh, Pittsburgh, PA, 2010.
$3,000 to Pittsburgh Public Theater, Pittsburgh, PA, 2010.
$1,750 to Pine Cay Project, Lima, OH, 2010.
$1,500 to Swain School, Allentown, PA, 2010.
$1,250 to Fox Chapel Presbyterian Church, Pittsburgh, PA, 2010.
$1,000 to Pittsburgh Ballet Theater, Pittsburgh, PA, 2010.

11
Abba Technologies, Inc.
1501 San Pedro Dr., N.E.
Albuquerque, NM 87110-6731
(505) 889-3337

Company URL: http://www.abbatech.com
Establishment information: Established in 1993.
Company type: Private company
Business activities: Provides enterprise and scientific application professional services and software and hardware solutions.
Business type (SIC): Computer services
Corporate officers: Andrew L. Baca, Pres. and C.E.O.; Judie Youngman, V.P. and C.O.O.; Pat Koepsell, V.P., Sales
Office: Los Alamos, NM
Giving statement: Giving through the Abba Technologies Foundation, Inc.

Abba Technologies Foundation, Inc.
9390 Research Blvd., Ste. 11-420
Austin, TX 78759-6585
Application address: 12720 Oxen Way, Austin, TX 78732

Establishment information: Established in 2001 in NM.
Donor: Abba Technologies, Inc.
Contact: Bill Boas, Secy.
Financial data (yr. ended 12/31/12): Assets, $81,852 (M); gifts received, $968; expenditures, $5,574; qualifying distributions, $0.
Purpose and activities: The foundation supports organizations involved with opera, nonprofit management, and philanthropy.
Fields of interest: Performing arts, opera; Nonprofit management; Philanthropy/voluntarism.
Type of support: General/operating support.
Geographic limitations: Giving primarily in San Francisco, CA.
Application information: Applications accepted. Application form not required. Applicants should submit the following:
1) detailed description of project and amount of funding requested
2) brief history of organization and description of its mission
3) copy of most recent annual report/audited financial statement/990

Initial approach: Letter of inquiry
Deadline(s): Nov. 1

Officers: Ching-Ching Ganley, Pres.; Bill Boas, Secy.
EIN: 850476590

12
Abbot Machine Company
1500 W. St. Paul Ave.
Milwaukee, WI 53233-2649
(414) 272-6249

Establishment information: Established in 1989.
Company type: Private company
Business activities: Manufactures hydraulic automotive jacks.
Business type (SIC): Machinery/general industry
Financial profile for 2009: Number of employees, 20
Corporate officer: Frederick C. Read, Pres.
Giving statement: Giving through the Abbot Machine Company Charitable Foundation, Inc.

Abbot Machine Company Charitable Foundation, Inc.
519 Elm Spring Ave.
Wauwatosa, WI 53226-4659 (414) 258-3339

Donor: Abbot Machine Co.
Contact: Stuart B. Eiche, Dir.; R.G. Urban, Dir.
Financial data (yr. ended 12/31/11): Assets, $293,086 (M); expenditures, $13,335; qualifying distributions, $13,000; giving activities include $13,000 for grants.
Purpose and activities: The foundation supports organizations involved with education, health, youth development, and Christianity.
Fields of interest: Education; Human services; Religion.
Type of support: General/operating support.
Support limitations: No grants to individuals.
Application information: Applications accepted. Application form not required.

Initial approach: Proposal
Deadline(s): None

Directors: Jocelyn K. Eiche; Stuart B. Eiche; R.G. Urban.
EIN: 396125048

13
Abbott Laboratories
100 Abbott Park Rd.
Abbott Park, IL 60064-3500
(847) 937-6100
FAX: (847) 937-1511

Company URL: http://www.abbott.com
Establishment information: Established in 1888.
Company type: Public company
Company ticker symbol and exchange: ABT/NYSE
International Securities Identification Number: US0028241000
Business activities: Discovers, develops, manufactures, and sells health care products and services.
Business type (SIC): Drugs
Financial profile for 2012: Number of employees, 91,000; assets, $67,234,940,000; sales volume, $21,494,000,000; pre-tax net income, $305,000,000; expenses, $21,142,000,000; liabilities, $40,513,980,000
Fortune 1000 ranking: 2012—70th in revenues, 31st in profits, and 86th in assets
Forbes 2000 ranking: 2012—224th in sales, 88th in profits, and 352nd in assets
Corporate officers: Miles D. White, Chair. and C.E.O.; Thomas C. Freyman, Exec. V.P., Finance and C.F.O.; Stephen R. Fussell, Sr. V.P., Human Resources; Hubert L. Allen, Exec. V.P., Genl. Counsel, and Secy.
Board of directors: Miles D. White, Chair.; Robert J. Alpern, M.D.; Roxanne S. Austin; Sally Blount; W. James Farrell; Edward Liddy; Nancy McKinstry; Phebe Novakovic; William A. Osborn; Samuel C. Scott III; Glenn F. Tilton
Subsidiary: AbbVie Inc., North Chicago, IL
Division: Abbot Nutritional, Columbus, OH
International operations: Argentina; Australia; Austria; Bahamas; Bangladesh; Barbados; Belgium; Bermuda; Brazil; Cambodia; Canada; Chile; China; Colombia; Costa Rica; Croatia; Czech Republic; Denmark; Ecuador; Egypt; El Salvador; Finland; France; Germany; Greece; Grenada; Guatemala; Hong Kong; Hungary; India; Indonesia; Ireland; Italy; Jamaica; Japan; Latvia; Lebanon; Lithuania; Malaysia; Mexico; Mozambique; Netherlands; New Zealand; Norway; Pakistan; Panama; Peru; Philippines; Poland; Portugal; Russia; Singapore; Slovakia; South Africa; South Korea; Spain; Sweden; Switzerland; Tanzania, Zanzibar and Pemba; Thailand; Turkey; United Kingdom; Uruguay; Venezuela
Giving statement: Giving through the Abbott Laboratories Corporate Giving Program, the Abbott Fund, and the Abbott Patient Assistance Foundation.
Company EIN: 360698440

Abbott Laboratories Corporate Giving Program
100 Abbott Park Rd.
Abbott Park, IL 60064-3500
FAX: (847) 935-5051; URL: http://www.abbott.com/citizenship

Financial data (yr. ended 12/31/10): Total giving, $116,177,659, including $116,177,659 for grants.
Purpose and activities: As a complement to its foundation, Abbott also makes charitable contributions to nonprofit organizations directly. Support is given primarily in areas of company operations.
Fields of interest: Education; Environment; Health care; Disasters, preparedness/services; Human services; International development; International relief; Science Children/youth; Youth; Adults; Young adults; Asians/Pacific Islanders; African Americans/Blacks; Hispanics/Latinos; Women; Girls; Men; Boys; AIDS, people with; LGBTQ.
Type of support: Donated products; Employee matching gifts; Employee volunteer services; General/operating support.
Geographic limitations: Giving primarily in areas of company operations.
Application information: Applications not accepted. The Global Citizenship and Policy and Public Affairs Departments handle giving. The company has a staff that only handles contributions.
Number of staff: 12 full-time professional; 2 full-time support.
Selected grants: The following grants are a representative sample of this grantmaker's funding activity:
$1,250,000 to Art Institute of Chicago, Chicago, IL, 2008. For Modern Wing Exhibit.
$1,250,000 to Museum of Science and Industry, Chicago, IL, 2008. For You! The Experience Exhibit.
$375,000 to American Heart Association, Midwest Affiliate, Chicago, IL, 2008. For Go Red Program/Campaign.
$50,000 to Direct Relief International, Santa Barbara, CA, 2008. For monitoring and evaluation.

$25,000 to AmeriCares, Stamford, CT, 2008. For unrestricted support.
$25,000 to CARE, Chicago, IL, 2008. For event.
$25,000 to Sesame Workshop, New York, NY, 2008. For event.
$25,000 to UNICEF of the Greater Chicago Area, Chicago, IL, 2008. For Message of Hope Event.

Abbott Fund

(formerly Abbott Laboratories Fund)
100 Abbott Park Rd., D379/AP6D
Abbott Park, IL 60064-3500 (847) 937-7075
URL: http://www.abbottfund.org

Establishment information: Incorporated in 1951 in IL.
Donor: Abbott Laboratories.
Financial data (yr. ended 12/31/11): Assets, $188,499,579 (M); gifts received, $746,306; expenditures, $39,703,008; qualifying distributions, $39,261,823; giving activities include $24,431,481 for 144 grants (high: $2,500,000; low: $1,000) and $5,114,509 for 2,630 employee matching gifts.
Purpose and activities: The fund supports organizations involved with arts and culture, education, water conservation, health, HIV/AIDS, diabetes, tropical diseases, hunger, nutrition, disaster relief, human services, community development, science, children, minorities, women, and economically disadvantaged people. Special emphasis is directed toward programs designed to promote science and medical innovation; expand access to healthcare; and strengthen communities around the globe.
Fields of interest: Museums; Museums (science/technology); Arts; Elementary/secondary education; Higher education; Libraries (public); Education; Environment, water resources; Medical care, community health systems; Hospitals (general); Health care, clinics/centers; Health care, infants; Health care, rural areas; Reproductive health, OBGYN/Birthing centers; Public health, physical fitness; Health care; AIDS; Diabetes; Tropical diseases; Food services; Food banks; Nutrition; Disasters, preparedness/services; American Red Cross; Family services; Homeless, human services; Human services; Community/economic development; United Ways and Federated Giving Programs; Mathematics; Engineering/technology; Science Children; Minorities; Women; Economically disadvantaged.
Programs:

Abbott Communities: The fund supports programs designed to address unmet needs of the community. The fund supports institutions that serve the public good; health and human service welfare agencies including food banks, homeless shelters, health clinics, museums, libraries, and universities; and humanitarian relief organizations during natural disasters and emergencies.

Access to Health Care: The fund supports programs designed to improve and expand access to health care services for disadvantaged populations through training of medical professionals, building facilities in underserved areas, and engaging in locally appropriate initiatives.

Community Scholarship Program: The fund awards up to 15 $2,000 scholarships to high seniors who plan to pursue a science-related major in college or at a vocational technical school. The program is limited to select high schools in Arizona, California, Illinois, Michigan, Ohio, Puerto Rico, and Virginia. The program is administered by Scholarship America.

Employee Giving Campaign: The fund matches contributions made by employees of Abbot in the United States and Puerto Rico to the United Way and eligible nonprofit organizations.

Employee Matching Grant Plan: The fund matches contributions made by employees of Abbott Laboratories to educational institutions, public broadcasting stations, hospitals, and eligible funds and foundations on a one-for-one bass from $25 to $5,000 per contributor, per year.

Science Education: The fund supports programs designed to promote science education and encourage people to enter science-related fields. Special emphasis is directed toward programs designed to engage and inspire students, families, and teachers to explore science in out-of-school settings; encourage young people to become more proficient in science and attract more scientists to the field; and build strong partnerships that are systemic, replicable, and sustainable for multiple years and locations.
Type of support: Building/renovation; Conferences/seminars; Continuing support; Curriculum development; Employee matching gifts; Faculty/staff development; General/operating support; Management development/capacity building; Program development; Research; Scholarship funds; Sponsorships.
Geographic limitations: Giving on a national and international basis in areas of company operations, with emphasis on AR, CA, CT, Washington, DC, IL, IN, MA, NH, NY, OH, OR, PR, TX, VA, Afghanistan, Africa, Haiti, India, Kenya, and Tanzania; giving also to national and international organizations.
Support limitations: No support for social organizations, political parties or candidates, sectarian religious organizations, or trade or business associations. No grants to individuals, or for scholarships, advertising journals or booklets, capital campaigns, congresses, symposiums, or meetings, medical research that supports Abbott products, political activities, fundraising events, ticket purchases, sporting events, travel, trips, tours, or cultural exchange programs; no employee volunteer services.
Application information: Applications not accepted. The foundation is currently not accepting unsolicited applications. Visit website to view future opportunities for funding.
Officers and Directors:* John B. Thomas*, Pres.; Stephen R. Fussel; Miles D. White.
Number of staff: 1 full-time professional; 1 part-time professional; 1 full-time support; 1 part-time support.
EIN: 366069793
Selected grants: The following grants are a representative sample of this grantmaker's funding activity:
$2,770,000 to Baylor College of Medicine International Pediatric AIDS Initiative, Houston, TX, 2010. For Abbott Fund BIPAI Network Partnership.
$2,500,000 to American Red Cross National Headquarters, Washington, DC, 2011. For Japan Earthquake.
$2,500,000 to Baylor College of Medicine International Pediatric AIDS Initiative, Houston, TX, 2011. For Abbott Fund BIPAI Network Partnership.
$2,484,992 to Partners in Health, Boston, MA, 2011. For the Haiti Nutrition Project.
$2,100,000 to Direct Relief International, Santa Barbara, CA, 2011. For DRI-Abbott PMTCT.
$841,600 to Project HOPE - The People-to-People Health Foundation, Millwood, VA, 2010. For China AFI Nutrition Phase II.
$750,000 to Art Institute of Chicago, Chicago, IL, 2010. For Modern Wing.
$750,000 to Art Institute of Chicago, Chicago, IL, 2011. For Modern Wing.
$600,000 to Kohl Children's Museum of Greater Chicago, Glenview, IL, 2010. For Science Focused Traveling Exhibit.
$550,000 to Operation Smile International, Norfolk, VA, 2011. For Operation Smile programs in Brazil, China, India, Mexico and Russia.
$383,000 to Kohl Children's Museum of Greater Chicago, Glenview, IL, 2011. For Science Focused Traveling Exhibit.
$260,000 to Asian University for Women Support Foundation, Cambridge, MA, 2010. For Investing in Change: Funding Math and Science Teaching at the Asian University for Women.
$260,000 to TOUCH Foundation, New York, NY, 2010. For Laboratory Technician Training at BUCHS, Tanzania.
$240,000 to Feeding America, Chicago, IL, 2011. For Abbott Fund BackPack Grant.
$90,000 to Siempre Unidos, Mill Valley, CA, 2010. For Expanding Medical Care to Hondurans with AIDS.
$50,000 to American Heart Association, Chicago, IL, 2011. For Chicago Go Red for Women: The Faces of Our Community.
$50,000 to Direct Relief International, Santa Barbara, CA, 2010. For Haiti Disaster Relief Efforts.
$50,000 to Project Exploration, Chicago, IL, 2010. For Science Pathways.

Abbott Patient Assistance Foundation

200 Abbott Park Rd., D-031C AP31-3NW
Abbott Park, IL 60064-6214 (800) 222-6885
URL: http://www.abbottpatientassistancefoundation.org/index.asp

Establishment information: Established in 2007 in IL.
Donor: Abbott Laboratories.
Financial data (yr. ended 12/31/11): Assets, $26,269,677 (M); gifts received, $604,125,175; expenditures, $599,264,263; qualifying distributions, $599,264,263; giving activities include $594,182,250 for grants to individuals.
Purpose and activities: The foundation provides Abbott medications, medical nutritionals, and diabetes care products to economically disadvantaged individuals living below the federal poverty line and to individuals lacking prescription drug coverage.
Fields of interest: Health care; Diabetes Economically disadvantaged.
Type of support: Donated products; Grants to individuals.
Geographic limitations: Giving on a national basis, with emphasis on CA, IL, KY, and NJ.
Publications: Application guidelines.
Application information: Applications accepted. Visit website for application addresses. Application form required.
Applications must include copies of all insurance cards (if applicable), proof of income for all household members, including tax returns, Form W2, or pay stubs, a physician's signature, and the patient's signature.

Initial approach: Download application form and mail to application address or contact foundation for application form
Deadline(s): None

Officers and Directors: John Pilotte, Pres.; Thad Smith, V.P.; John Berry, Secy.; Joellen Medley, Treas.; Kevin Dolan; Russell Garich; Kelly Ingold; Dale Johnson; David Ralston; Angela Sekston.
EIN: 261215559

15
AbbyBank
(formerly Abbotsford State Bank)
401 E. Spruce St.
P.O. Box 648
Abbotsford, WI 54405-0648
(715) 223-2345
FAX: (715) 223-6385

Company URL: http://www.abbybank.com
Establishment information: Established in 1968.
Company type: Private company
Business activities: Operates commercial bank.
Business type (SIC): Banks/commercial
Corporate officers: Patrick D. McCrackin, Co-Pres. and C.E.O.; Linda Koch, Co-Pres.; Teri L. Shorer, C.O.O.
Giving statement: Giving through the Abbotsford Story, Inc.

Abbotsford Story, Inc.
401 E. Spruce St.
Abbotsford, WI 54405-9661 (715) 223-2345
E-mail: sretterath@abbybank.com; Application address: P.O. Box 648, Abbotsford, WI 54405, tel.: (800) 288-2229; URL: https://www.abbybank.com/charitablefoundation.shtml

Establishment information: Established in 1985 in WI.
Donors: Abbotsford State Bank; AbbyBank.
Contact: Stacy Retterath
Financial data (yr. ended 12/31/11): Assets, $575,652 (M); gifts received, $48,000; expenditures, $23,722; qualifying distributions, $22,816; giving activities include $22,816 for grants.
Purpose and activities: The foundation supports police agencies and fire departments and organizations involved with music, education, and human services. Special emphasis is directed toward programs designed to serve low-moderate income people.
Fields of interest: Performing arts, music; Middle schools/education; Libraries (public); Education, reading; Education; Crime/law enforcement, police agencies; Disasters, fire prevention/control; Youth development, business; Human services Economically disadvantaged.
Type of support: Building/renovation; Capital campaigns; Equipment; Program development.
Geographic limitations: Giving limited to areas of company operations in Abbotsford, Wausau, and Weston, WI.
Publications: Application guidelines.
Application information: Applications accepted. Application form required. Applicants should submit the following:
1) name, address and phone number of organization
2) copy of IRS Determination Letter
3) detailed description of project and amount of funding requested
4) contact person

Initial approach: Download application form and e-mail or mail to foundation
Board meeting date(s): Semiannually
Deadline(s): Mar. 1 and Sept. 1

Officers: Patrick D. McCrackin, Pres. and Secy.; Dennis Kramer, V.P. and Treas.
Directors: Harold K. Christensen; Curtis Day; Roger Deffner; David Diesen; Donald A. Meyer.
EIN: 391540288

14
Abby's Inc.
(also known as Abby's Legendary Pizza)
1970 River Rd.
Eugene, OR 97404-2502 (541) 461-2229

Company URL: http://www.abbys.com
Establishment information: Established in 1964.
Company type: Private company
Business activities: Operates restaurants.
Business type (SIC): Restaurants and drinking places
Financial profile for 2010: Number of employees, 28
Corporate officers: B. Mills Sinclair, Pres. and C.E.O.; Dave Mahnke, Exec. V.P. and C.O.O.; Rich Olson, C.F.O.
Giving statement: Giving through the Abby's Legendary Pizza Foundation.

The Abby's Legendary Pizza Foundation
1960 River Rd.
Eugene, OR 97404-2502 (541) 689-0019
E-mail: carol@abbys.com; URL: http://www.abbys.com/index.php?option=com_k2&view=item&layout=item&id=10&Itemid=87

Donor: Abby's Inc.
Financial data (yr. ended 12/31/11): Assets, $1,097 (M); gifts received, $24,622; expenditures, $24,440; qualifying distributions, $23,890; giving activities include $23,890 for grants.
Purpose and activities: The foundation supports organizations involved with education, athletics, and youth.
Fields of interest: Elementary/secondary education; Child development, education; Education; Athletics/sports, amateur leagues Youth.
Type of support: General/operating support; Program development; Sponsorships.
Geographic limitations: Giving limited to areas of company operations in OR and WA.
Support limitations: No grants to individuals.
Publications: Application guidelines; Grants list.
Application information: Applications accepted. Application form required. Applicants should submit the following:
1) how project will be sustained once grantmaker support is completed
2) statement of problem project will address
3) principal source of support for project in the past
4) copy of IRS Determination Letter
5) listing of board of directors, trustees, officers and other key people and their affiliations
6) detailed description of project and amount of funding requested
7) listing of additional sources and amount of support

Initial approach: Download application form and mail to foundation
Deadline(s): None

Trustees: Dave Mahnke; Richard Olson; B. Mills Sinclair.
EIN: 931320379

16
ABC Home Furnishings, Inc.
(doing business as A.B.C. Carpet & Home Outlet)
888 Broadway, Fl. 4
New York, NY 10003-1280 (212) 473-3000

Company URL: http://www.abchome.com
Establishment information: Established in 1897.
Company type: Private company
Business activities: Operates specialty home furnishings stores.
Business type (SIC): Furniture and home furnishing stores
Corporate officers: Jerome Weinrib, Co-Pres.; Paulette Cole, Co-Pres. and C.E.O.; Paul Chapman, Exec. V.P., Opers.; David E. Lauber, C.F.O.; Li Kurczewski, V.P., Sales and Mktg.
Giving statement: Giving through the ABC Home and Planet Foundation.

ABC Home and Planet Foundation
888 Broadway E. 19th St.
New York, NY 10003-1258 (646) 602-3581
E-mail: foundation@abchome.com; URL: http://www.abchomeandplanet.org

Financial data (yr. ended 12/31/10): Revenue, $34,232; assets, $46,364 (M); gifts received, $33,172; expenditures, $34,822; program services expenses, $27,658; giving activities include $23,868 for grants.
Purpose and activities: The organization supports the empowerment of disadvantaged people throughout the globe by providing healthcare, literacy, entrepreneurial training, and counseling services.
Officers and Directors:* Paulette Cole*, Pres.; Richard Perl*, V.P. and Treas.; Amy Chender*, Secy.; Amy Llias; Joshua Mailman.
EIN: 300267023

17
Abercrombie & Fitch Co.
6301 Fitch Path
New Albany, OH 43054 (614) 283-6500
FAX: (302) 655-5049

Company URL: http://www.abercrombie.com
Establishment information: Established in 1892.
Company type: Public company
Company ticker symbol and exchange: ANF/NYSE
International Securities Identification Number: US0028962076
Business activities: Operates retail clothing chain.
Business type (SIC): Family apparel and accessory stores
Financial profile for 2013: Number of employees, 98,000; assets, $2,987,400,000; sales volume, $4,510,810,000; pre-tax net income, $366,940,000; expenses, $4,136,570,000; liabilities, $1,169,130,000
Fortune 1000 ranking: 2012—529th in revenues, 538th in profits, and 752nd in assets
Corporate officers: Michael S. Jeffries, Chair. and C.E.O.; Jonathan E. Ramsden, Exec. V.P. and C.F.O.; Ronald A. Robins, Jr., Sr. V.P., Genl Counsel, and Secy.
Board of directors: Michael S. Jeffries, Chair.; James B. Bachmann; Lauren J. Brisky; Michael E. Greenlees; Archie M. Griffin; Kevin S. Huvane; John W. Kessler; Elizabeth M. Lee; Craig R. Stapleton
Giving statement: Giving through the Abercrombie & Fitch Co. Contributions Program.
Company EIN: 311469076

Abercrombie & Fitch Co. Contributions Program

6301 Fitch Path
New Albany, OH 43054-9269 (614) 283-6500
URL: http://www.anfcares.org/philanthropy/

Purpose and activities: Abercrombie & Fitch makes charitable contributions to nonprofit organizations involved with children, healthcare, human services, and on a case by case basis. Support is given primarily in areas of company operations, with emphasis on Columbus, Ohio.
Fields of interest: Elementary/secondary education; Education, reading; Hospitals (general); Hospitals (specialty); Health care; Disasters, preparedness/services; Human services; General charitable giving.
Type of support: Cause-related marketing; Employee volunteer services; General/operating support; In-kind gifts; Program development.
Geographic limitations: Giving primarily in areas of company operations, with emphasis on Columbus, OH; giving also to national organizations.

18
Aberdeen Creek Corporation

1641 Mayacoo Lakes Blvd.
West Palm Beach, FL 33411

Company type: Private company
Business activities: Conducts investment activities; provides business consulting services.
Business type (SIC): Investors/miscellaneous; management and public relations services
Corporate officer: Peter Francis O'Malley, Pres.
Giving statement: Giving through the Good Neighbors Family Trust.

Good Neighbors Family Trust

1641 Mayacoo Lakes Blvd.
West Palm Beach, FL 33411-1851

Establishment information: Established in 2002 in MD.
Donors: Aberdeen Creek Corp.; Peter F. O'Malley; Janice A. O'Malley.
Financial data (yr. ended 12/31/11): Assets, $1,892,093 (M); gifts received, $38,813; expenditures, $86,678; qualifying distributions, $82,475; giving activities include $82,475 for grants.
Purpose and activities: The foundation supports food banks and organizations involved with education, health, eye diseases, homelessness, Christianity, and Catholicism.
Fields of interest: Education; Health care; Religion.
Type of support: Capital campaigns; General/operating support; Program development; Research; Scholarship funds.
Geographic limitations: Giving primarily in FL; giving also to national organizations.
Support limitations: No grants to individuals.
Application information: Applications not accepted. Unsolicited requests for funds not accepted.
Trustees: Mary O. Lunden; Peter J. McKenna; Janice A. O'Malley; Peter F. O'Malley; Susan N. O'Malley.
EIN: 431977430

19
Abita Brewing Company

72011 Holly St.
P.O. Box 1510
Abita Springs, LA 70420 (800) 737-2311

Company URL: http://www.abita.com
Establishment information: Established in 1986.
Company type: Private company
Business activities: Operates brewery.
Business type (SIC): Beverages
Corporate officers: Troy Ashley, Chair. and Secy.; David Blossman, Pres.
Board of director: Troy Ashley, Chair.
Giving statement: Giving through the Abita Brewing Company Contributions Program.

Abita Brewing Company Contributions Program

P.O. Box 1510
Abita Springs, LA 70420-1510
E-mail: friends@abita.com; URL: http://abita.com/learn/giving_back

Purpose and activities: Abita Brewing Company makes charitable in-kind contributions to nonprofit organizations on a case by case basis. Support is given primarily in areas of company operations in Abita Springs, Louisiana.
Fields of interest: Disasters, preparedness/services; Community/economic development.
Type of support: Cause-related marketing; Donated products; In-kind gifts.
Geographic limitations: Giving primarily in areas of company operations in Abita Springs, LA.
Support limitations: No grants to individuals.
Publications: Application guidelines.
Application information: Applications accepted. Application form required.
Initial approach: Complete online application
Deadline(s): None
Final notification: 4 weeks

20
Abt Electronics, Inc.

(formerly Abt Radio)
1200 N. Milwaukee Ave.
Glenview, IL 60025 (847) 967-8830

Company URL: http://www.abtelectronics.com
Establishment information: Established in 1936.
Company type: Private company
Business activities: Operates consumer electronics and appliances store; provides Internet shopping services.
Business type (SIC): Consumer electronics and music stores; appliance stores/household; computer services
Corporate officers: Robert J. Abt, C.E.O.; Jon Abt, Co-Pres.; Michael Abt, Co-Pres.
Giving statement: Giving through the Abt Family Charitable Foundation.

Abt Family Charitable Foundation

1200 Milwaukee Ave.
Glenview, IL 60025-2416

Establishment information: Established in 1987 in IL.
Donor: Abt Electronics, Inc.
Contact: Robert J. Abt, Tr.
Financial data (yr. ended 12/31/11): Assets, $3,198 (M); gifts received, $95,000; expenditures, $103,442; qualifying distributions, $103,440; giving activities include $103,440 for grants.
Purpose and activities: The foundation supports organizations involved with cancer, medical research, karate, human services, and Judaism.
Fields of interest: Cancer; Diabetes research; Medical research; Athletics/sports, amateur leagues; Developmentally disabled, centers & services; Human services; Jewish federated giving programs; Jewish agencies & synagogues.
Type of support: General/operating support; Scholarship funds.
Application information: Applications accepted. Application form not required.
Initial approach: Letter
Deadline(s): None
Trustees: Michael Abt; Richard L. Abt; Robert J. Abt; William P. Abt.
EIN: 363583929

21
Acacia Life Insurance Company

7315 Wisconsin Ave., Ste. 1000 W.
Bethesda, MD 20814-3202 (301) 280-1000
FAX: (301) 280-1161

Establishment information: Established in 1869.
Company type: Subsidiary of a mutual company
Business activities: Sells life insurance.
Business type (SIC): Insurance/life
Corporate officers: Barbara Krumsiek, Chair.; Edward Quinn, Vice-Chair.; Salene Hitchcock-Gear, Pres. and C.E.O.; Robert Barth, C.F.O.; Paul E. Huebner, Sr. V.P. and C.I.O.; Robert-John Hamilton, Secy.; William Wallace Lester, Treas.
Board of directors: Barbara Krumsiek, Chair.; Edward Quinn, Vice-Chair.
Giving statement: Giving through the Acacia Foundation.
Company EIN: 530022880

The Acacia Foundation

(formerly Acacia Charitable Foundation)
7315 Wisconsin Ave.
Bethesda, MD 20814-3202 (301) 280-1223

Establishment information: Established in 2004 in DE.
Donor: Acacia Life Insurance Co.
Contact: Jim Harvey, Treas.
Financial data (yr. ended 12/31/11): Assets, $4,752,039 (M); gifts received, $100,000; expenditures, $375,184; qualifying distributions, $371,367; giving activities include $371,367 for 21 grants (high: $100,000; low: $2,500).
Purpose and activities: The foundation supports organizations involved with education and youth development. Support is given primarily in the Washington, D.C., area.
Fields of interest: Secondary school/education; Education, reading; Education; Boys & girls clubs; Youth development; American Red Cross.
Type of support: Annual campaigns; General/operating support.
Geographic limitations: Giving primarily in the Washington, DC, area.
Support limitations: No support for political organizations or candidates, or social organizations. No grants to individuals.
Publications: Application guidelines.
Application information: Applications accepted. Additional information may be requested at a later date. Application form required. Applicants should submit the following:
1) name, address and phone number of organization

2) copy of IRS Determination Letter
3) brief history of organization and description of its mission
4) copy of most recent annual report/audited financial statement/990
5) listing of board of directors, trustees, officers and other key people and their affiliations
6) detailed description of project and amount of funding requested
7) copy of current year's organizational budget and/or project budget

Initial approach: Proposal
Deadline(s): None

Officers and Directors:* Salene Hitchcock-Gear*, Pres.; Robert-John H. Sands*, V.P.; Shawn Grosser, Corp. Secy.; Jim Harvey, Treas.; Barbara Krumsiek; Patricia McGuire; Edward J. Quinn, Jr.; D. Wayne Silby; Robert M. Willis.
EIN: 201257409
Selected grants: The following grants are a representative sample of this grantmaker's funding activity:
$100,000 to City Year Washington, DC, Washington, DC, 2010. For general purpose.
$10,000 to Alzheimers Association, Fairfax, VA, 2010. For general purpose.
$5,000 to Adoptions Together, Silver Spring, MD, 2010. For general purpose.
$5,000 to Childrens Studio School, Washington, DC, 2010. For general purpose.
$5,000 to Gonzaga College High School, Washington, DC, 2010. For general purpose.
$5,000 to Mentors, Inc., Washington, DC, 2010. For general purpose.
$5,000 to Saint Johns College High School, Washington, DC, 2010. For general purpose.
$5,000 to San Miguel School, Washington, DC, 2010. For general purpose.
$5,000 to Youth Leadership Foundation, Washington, DC, 2010. For general purpose.

22
Accenture, Inc.
1345 Avenue of the Americas
New York, NY 10105 (917) 452-4400

Company URL: http://www.accenture.com
Establishment information: Established in 1989.
Company type: Subsidiary of a foreign company
Business activities: Provides management consulting services.
Business type (SIC): Management and public relations services
Corporate officers: Joe W. Forehand, Chair. and C.E.O.; Jo Deblaere, C.O.O.; Pamela J. Craig, C.F.O.
Board of director: Joe W. Forehand, Chair.
Giving statement: Giving through the Accenture, Inc. Corporate Giving Program and the Accenture Foundation, Inc.

Accenture, Inc. Corporate Giving Program
1345 Avenue of the Americas
New York, NY 10105-0301 (917) 452-4400
FAX: (917) 527-9915; URL: http://www.accenture.com/us-en/company/us-corporate-citizenship/Pages/index.aspx

Purpose and activities: As a complement to its foundation, Accenture also makes charitable contributions to nonprofit organizations directly. Special emphasis is directed towards programs designed to help people build skills that will enable them to find jobs, start businesses, and better their communities. Support is given on a national and international basis in areas of company operations.
Fields of interest: Vocational education; Employment; International development; Community development, small businesses; Engineering/technology.
Type of support: Employee volunteer services; General/operating support; Pro bono services - strategic management; Program development.
Geographic limitations: Giving on a national and international basis in areas of company operations.
Publications: Corporate giving report.

Accenture Foundation, Inc.
161 N. Clark St.
Chicago, IL 60601-3200 (312) 737-0223

Contact: Anne L. Bronson, Exec. Dir.
Financial data (yr. ended 08/31/11): Revenue, $9,671,560; assets, $107,970,033 (M); gifts received, $413,203; expenditures, $5,507,294; giving activities include $413,128 for grants.
Purpose and activities: The foundation supports education, digital opportunities, and enhancement of human life and well-being.
Fields of interest: Education; Safety/disasters.
Type of support: Scholarship funds.
Officers and Directors:* Lisa M. Mascolo*, Pres.; John L. Delsanto*, V.P.; Barrett S. Avigdor*, Secy.; Douglas R. Rees*, Treas.; Anne L. Bronson, Exec. Dir.; Samuel A. Awad; Joel A. Stern; and 6 additional directors.
EIN: 364296414

23
Accupac, Inc.
1501 Industrial Blvd.
P.O. Box 51200
Mainland, PA 19451 (215) 256-7000

Company URL: http://www.accupac.com
Establishment information: Established in 1974.
Company type: Private company
Business activities: Provides manufacturing and packaging services.
Business type (SIC): Soaps, cleaners, and toiletries; drugs; business services/miscellaneous
Corporate officers: Paul Alvater, Pres. and C.E.O.; Malcolm Appelbaum, Co-C.F.O.; Bruce Wright, Co-C.F.O.; Mark Hinkel, V.P., Sales and Mktg.
Giving statement: Giving through the Eileen M. Heck Foundation.

Eileen M. Heck Foundation
c/o Edwin Irwin, C.P.A.
53 Church Rd.
Horsham, PA 19044-3420

Establishment information: Established in 1994 in PA.
Donor: Accupac, Inc.
Financial data (yr. ended 12/31/11): Assets, $223,048 (M); expenditures, $22,268; qualifying distributions, $18,201; giving activities include $18,201 for 8 grants (high: $10,000; low: $25).
Purpose and activities: The foundation supports organizations involved with education.
Fields of interest: Secondary school/education; Higher education; Education.
Type of support: General/operating support.
Geographic limitations: Giving limited to PA.
Support limitations: No grants to individuals.
Application information: Applications not accepted. Unsolicited requests for funds not accepted.
Trustees: Kellyann Cilio; Kimberly Cilio; Eileen Heck Slawek.
EIN: 237788354

24
ACE USA Inc.
436 Walnut St., Ste. 7
P.O. Box 1000
Philadelphia, PA 19106-3703
(215) 640-1000

Company URL: http://www.aceusa.com
Establishment information: Established in 1985.
Company type: Subsidiary of a foreign company
Business activities: Sells property and casualty insurance.
Business type (SIC): Insurance/fire, marine, and casualty
Financial profile for 2009: Number of employees, 2,898
Corporate officers: William Glavin, Chair., Pres. and C.E.O.; David M. Pfeffer, C.F.O.
Board of director: William Glavin, Chair.
Offices: Glendale, San Francisco, CA; Fairfield, CT; Duluth, GA; New Orleans, LA; New York, NY
Giving statement: Giving through the ACE Charitable Foundation.

ACE Charitable Foundation
(formerly ACE INA Foundation)
436 Walnut St., WA 08G
Philadelphia, PA 19106-3786
E-mail: acecharitablefoundation@acegroup.com; URL: http://www.acegroup.com/About-ACE/Philanthropy/Philanthropy.html

Establishment information: Established in 2007 in PA.
Donor: ACE American Insurance Co.
Contact: Eden Kratchman, Exec. Dir.
Financial data (yr. ended 12/31/11): Assets, $2,901,003 (M); gifts received, $1,631,116; expenditures, $2,758,673; qualifying distributions, $2,746,111; giving activities include $2,019,148 for 51 grants (high: $500,000; low: $250) and $726,962 for 1,691 employee matching gifts.
Purpose and activities: The foundation supports organizations involved with education, the environment, health, agriculture and food, relief efforts, and poverty. Special consideration is given to opportunities where ACE employees' time and expertise can be utilized in addition to financial support.
Fields of interest: Higher education; Education; Environment, water resources; Environment, land resources; Environment; Health care; Food services; Food banks; Agriculture/food; Disasters, preparedness/services; American Red Cross; International relief; International migration/refugee issues; Microfinance/microlending; United Ways and Federated Giving Programs Economically disadvantaged.
Type of support: Employee matching gifts; Employee volunteer services; General/operating support; Program development.
Geographic limitations: Giving on a national and international basis in areas of company operations (outside of Bermuda), with some emphasis on Philadelphia, PA.
Application information:

Initial approach: E-mail foundation for application guidelines
Deadline(s): None

Officers and Directors:* Evan Greenberg*, C.E.O.; Brian Dowd*, Exec. V.P.; John Keogh, Exec. V.P.;

Lori Samson*, V.P.; Kathryn Schneider, Secy.; Joseph Jordan, Treas.; Eden M. Kratchman, Exec. Dir.; Robert Hernandez.
EIN: 262456949

25
ACE World Companies

(also known as Ace Trucks Ltd.)
10200 Jacksboro Hwy.
Fort Worth, TX 76135-4706 (817) 237-7700

Company URL: http://www.aceworldcompanies.com
Establishment information: Established in 1987.
Company type: Private company
Business activities: Provides material handling solutions.
Business type (SIC): Machinery/construction, mining, and materials handling
Corporate officers: Ace Ghanemi, C.E.O.; Darwyn Cornwell, Pres.; Camron Ghanemi, C.O.O
Giving statement: Giving through the Ace World Foundation.

Ace World Foundation

10200 Jacksboro Hwy.
Fort Worth, TX 76135-4706

Establishment information: Established in 2000 in TX.
Donor: Ace World Companies, Ltd.
Financial data (yr. ended 12/31/11): Assets, $5,111 (M); expenditures, $5,170; qualifying distributions, $5,000; giving activities include $5,000 for grants.
Fields of interest: Agriculture/food; Human services.
Support limitations: No grants to individuals.
Application information: Applications not accepted. Unsolicited requests for funds not accepted.
Directors: Linda S. Ghanemi; Robert D. Vought.
EIN: 752853030

26
ACF Industries LLC

(also known as ACF Industries, Incorporated)
(formerly ACF Industries, Incorporated)
101 Clark St.
St. Charles, MO 63301 (636) 949-2399

Company URL: http://www.acfindustries.com
Establishment information: Established in 1899.
Company type: Subsidiary of a private company
Business activities: Leases, sells, and manufactures railroad freight and tank cars and parts.
Business type (SIC): Railroad equipment; railroad car rental; industrial machinery and equipment—wholesale
Corporate officers: James E. Bowles, Pres. and C.E.O.; Alan C. Lullman, Sr. V.P., Sales and Mktg.; Mark A. Crinnion, V.P., Treas., and Genl. Counsel; Brenda Schuller, V.P., Mktg.; Harry McKinstry, V.P., Finance and Cont.
Giving statement: Giving through the ACF Foundation, Inc.

ACF Foundation, Inc.

101 Clark St.
St. Charles, MO 63301-2081

Establishment information: Incorporated in 1954 in NY.
Donors: ACF Industries, Inc.; ACF Industries LLC.
Financial data (yr. ended 04/30/12): Assets, $468,116 (M); expenditures, $12,881; qualifying distributions, $12,600; giving activities include $12,600 for 5 grants (high: $4,000; low: $100).
Purpose and activities: The foundation supports organizations involved with higher education, mental health, and youth development.
Fields of interest: Higher education; Mental health/crisis services; Boys & girls clubs; Youth development.
Type of support: Employee matching gifts; General/operating support.
Geographic limitations: Giving limited to areas of company operations, with emphasis on St. Louis and St. Charles, MO.
Support limitations: No grants to individuals.
Application information: Applications accepted. Application form not required.
Initial approach: Proposal
Deadline(s): None
Officers: Carl C. Icahn, Pres.; Umesh Choski, V.P. and Treas.; Alfred D. Kingsley, V.P.; Gail Golden, Secy.
EIN: 136085065

27
ACI Glass Products, LLC

(formerly Vitro America, LLC)
965 Ridge Lake Blvd.
P.O. Box 171173
Memphis, TN 38187 (901) 767-7111

Company URL: http://www.vitroamericacorporate.com
Establishment information: Established in 1872.
Company type: Subsidiary of a private company
Business activities: Manufactures mirrors and multi-purpose glass; provides contract construction services.
Business type (SIC): Glass/flat; contractors/general residential building; contractors/general nonresidential building; glass/pressed or blown; glass products/miscellaneous
Corporate officers: Arturo Carrillo, Pres. and C.E.O.; Ricardo Maiz, V.P. and C.F.O.
Giving statement: Giving through the ACI Glass Products, LLC Corporate Giving Program and the Binswanger Glass Foundation.

ACI Glass Products, LLC Corporate Giving Program

(formerly Vitro America, Inc. Corporate Giving Program)
965 Ridge Lake Blvd.
P.O. Box 171173
Memphis, TN 38187 (901) 767-7111
E-mail: Info@vitroamerica.com; URL: http://www.vitroamericacorporate.com/aboutus_comservice.htm

Purpose and activities: As a complement to its foundation, ACI Glass also makes charitable contributions to nonprofit organizations directly. Support is given primarily in areas of company operations; giving also to national organizations.
Fields of interest: Environment; Health care, research; Medicine/medical care, public education; Housing/shelter, volunteer services; Recreation.
Type of support: Employee volunteer services; General/operating support.
Geographic limitations: Giving primarily in areas of company operations; giving also to national organizations.

Binswanger Glass Foundation

7700 Hill Dr.
Richmond, VA 23225-1929 (804) 272-0551

Donor: Binswanger Glass Co.
Contact: M. I. Binswanger, Pres.
Financial data (yr. ended 12/31/11): Assets, $855,898 (M); expenditures, $35,720; qualifying distributions, $34,400; giving activities include $34,400 for 12 grants (high: $6,850; low: $200).
Purpose and activities: The foundation supports museums and hospitals and organizations involved with K-12 education, cancer research, and human services.
Fields of interest: Museums; Elementary/secondary education; Hospitals (general); Cancer research; Children/youth, services; Developmentally disabled, centers & services; Human services.
Type of support: General/operating support.
Geographic limitations: Giving primarily in Kansas City, MO and Richmond, VA.
Support limitations: No support for private foundations. No grants to individuals.
Application information: Applications accepted. Application form not required. Applicants should submit the following:
1) name, address and phone number of organization
2) copy of IRS Determination Letter
3) detailed description of project and amount of funding requested
Initial approach: Proposal
Deadline(s): None
Officers: Millard I. Binswanger, Pres.; Ellen B. Nolan, V.P.; Betsy W. Binswanger, Secy.-Treas.
Director: Katherine Grubb.
EIN: 546036349

28
Acme Machine Automatics, Inc.

111 Progressive Dr.
Ottoville, OH 45876 (419) 453-0010

Company URL: http://
Establishment information: Established in 1993.
Company type: Private company
Business activities: Manufactures screw machine products.
Business type (SIC): Screw machine products
Corporate officers: David L. Kriegel, C.E.O.; Todd Kriegel, Pres.; Mark Miller, C.F.O.; Randy Mueller, V.P., Opers; Stacy Jent, Secy.
Giving statement: Giving through the Kriegel Family Charitable Trust.

The Kriegel Family Charitable Trust

P.O. Box 752
Van Wert, OH 45891-0752

Establishment information: Established in 1989 in OH.
Donors: Kriegel Holding Co., Inc.; Acme Machine Automatics, Inc.; David L. Kriegel; Kriegel Holdings Inc.
Financial data (yr. ended 12/31/11): Assets, $389,748 (M); gifts received, $110,000; expenditures, $56,106; qualifying distributions, $55,304; giving activities include $55,304 for 19 grants (high: $20,000; low: $25).

Purpose and activities: The foundation supports organizations involved with arts and culture, education, health, and Christianity.
Fields of interest: Arts; Higher education; Education; Health care; United Ways and Federated Giving Programs; Christian agencies & churches.
Geographic limitations: Giving limited to Cincinnati and Lima, OH.
Support limitations: No grants to individuals.
Application information: Applications not accepted. Unsolicited requests for funds not accepted.
Officer: Susan Mosier, C.F.O.
Trustees: David L. Kriegel; Shirley C. Kriegel.
EIN: 346907740

29
Acme-McCrary Corporation

159 North St.
P.O. Box 1287
Asheboro, NC 27204 (336) 625-2161
FAX: (336) 629-2263

Company URL: http://www.acme-mccrary.com
Establishment information: Established in 1909.
Company type: Private company
Business activities: Manufactures women's hosiery.
Business type (SIC): Hosiery and knitted fabrics
Financial profile for 2009: Number of employees, 670
Corporate officers: Larry K. Small, Pres. and Co-C.E.O.; Bill Redding, Co-C.E.O.; Rod Spruill, V.P., Sales
Giving statement: Giving through the Acme-McCrary and Sapona Foundation, Inc.

Acme-McCrary and Sapona Foundation, Inc.

(formerly McCrary-Acme Foundation, Inc.)
159 North St.
Asheboro, NC 27203-5411 (336) 625-2161

Establishment information: Established in 1953.
Donors: Acme-McCrary Corp.; Sapona Manufacturing Co., Inc.
Contact: C.W. McCrary III, Pres.
Financial data (yr. ended 12/31/11): Assets, $1,279,036 (M); expenditures, $61,126; qualifying distributions, $46,900; giving activities include $46,900 for 21 grants (high: $16,000; low: $100).
Purpose and activities: The foundation supports orchestras, hospitals, and zoological societies and organizations involved with education, cancer, baseball, and human services.
Fields of interest: Performing arts, orchestras; Education; Zoos/zoological societies; Hospitals (general); Cancer; Athletics/sports, baseball; Boy scouts; YM/YWCAs & YM/YWHAs; Residential/custodial care, hospices; Human services; United Ways and Federated Giving Programs.
Type of support: General/operating support; Program development; Scholarship funds.
Geographic limitations: Giving primarily in Randolph County, NC.
Support limitations: No grants to individuals.
Application information: Applications accepted. Application form required. Applicants should submit the following:
1) brief history of organization and description of its mission
2) detailed description of project and amount of funding requested

Initial approach: Letter
Board meeting date(s): Dec.
Deadline(s): Early Dec.

Officers: C.W. McCrary, III, Pres.; C. W. McCrary, Jr., V.P.; W. H. Redding, Jr., V.P.; Bruce Patram, Secy.-Treas.
Directors: Mary Ella Pugh; S. Steele Reeding; John O. H. Toledano, Jr.
Number of staff: 1 part-time professional.
EIN: 566047739

30
Activision Blizzard, Inc.

(formerly Activision, Inc.)
3100 Ocean Park Blvd.
Santa Monica, CA 90405 (310) 255-2000
FAX: (302) 636-5454

Company URL: http://www.activisionblizzard.com
Establishment information: Established in 1979.
Company type: Public company
Company ticker symbol and exchange: ATVI/NASDAQ
Business activities: Operates an online, personal computer console and handheld game publishing company.
Business type (SIC): Computer services; consumer electronics and music stores; retail stores/miscellaneous
Financial profile for 2012: Number of employees, 6,700; assets, $14,200,000,000; sales volume, $4,856,000,000; pre-tax net income, $1,458,000,000; expenses, $3,405,000,000; liabilities, $2,883,000,000
Corporate officers: Philippe G.H. Capron, Co-Chair.; Brian G. Kelly, Co-Chair.; Michael J. Griffith, Vice-Chair.; Robert A. Kotick, C.E.O.; Thomas Tippl, C.O.O.; Dennis Durkin, C.F.O.
Board of directors: Philippe G.H. Capron, Co-Chair.; Brian G. Kelly, Co-Chair.; Michael J. Griffith, Vice-Chair.; Jean-Yves Charlier; Robert J. Corti; Frederic Raymond Crepin; Jean-Francois Dubos; Lucian Grainge; Brain G. Kelly; Robert A. Kotick; Robert J. Morgado; Richard Sarnoff; Regis Turrini
Subsidiaries: Activision International, Inc., Mountain View, CA; Infocom, Inc., Cambridge, MA
International operations: Australia; Bermuda; Canada; China; France; Germany; Hong Kong; India; Ireland; Italy; Japan; Luxembourg; Netherlands; Singapore; South Korea; Spain; Sweden; Switzerland; Taiwan; United Kingdom
Giving statement: Giving through the Activision, Inc. Corporate Giving Program, the Continental AG Corporate Giving Program, and the Tony Hawk Foundation.
Company EIN: 954803544

Activision, Inc. Corporate Giving Program

c/o Corp. Citizenship
3100 Ocean Park Blvd.
Santa Monica, CA 90405-3032 (310) 255-2000
URL: http://www.activision.com/index.html?module=locations#about|en_US|type:community

Purpose and activities: Activision makes charitable contributions to nonprofit organizations involved with children, military and veterans, and on a case by case basis. Support is given primarily in areas of company operations, with emphasis on California.
Fields of interest: General charitable giving Children/youth; Military/veterans.
Type of support: Equipment; Sponsorships; Technical assistance.
Geographic limitations: Giving primarily in areas of company operations, with emphasis on CA; giving also to national organizations.

Tony Hawk Foundation

1611-A S. Melrose Dr., Ste. 360
Vista, CA 92081-5471 (760) 477-2479
FAX: (760) 477-2474;
E-mail: kim@tonyhawkfoundation.org; Application e-mail: contact@tonyhawkfoundation.org;
URL: http://www.tonyhawkfoundation.org

Establishment information: Established in 2001 in CA.
Donors: Activision Blizzard, Inc.; Activision, Inc.; Adio Shoes; Richard Barry; Bell Helmets; Birdhouse; Ron Burkle; Cartoon Network; Sean John "Diddy" Combs; Creative Artists Agency, LLC; Janet Crown; Doyle Foundation; DUB; Dynacraft BSC, Inc.; Fuel; Got2b; Adrienne Grant; Brad Greenspan; Anthony "Tony" Hawk; Dennis Hecker; H.J. Heinz Co. Foundation; H.J. Heinz Co.; Infospace; Kathy Ireland; Jeep; Paul Jennings; Jones Soda; Bobby Kotick; LEGO Corp.; Life Changing Lives; Jay Lucarelli; Mattel; Net Jets; Quicksilver Foundations; Quiksilver; Russell Simmons; Six Flags; Tech Deck; T-Mobile; Clair Tunkl; David Tunkl; Ultimate Fighting Champion; Valleycrest Productions, Ltd.; Wasserman Foundation; Dana White, Jr.; Wonka; Zsweet.
Contact: Kim Novick, Devel. Dir.
Financial data (yr. ended 12/31/11): Revenue, $595,577; assets, $2,107,617 (M); gifts received, $581,973; expenditures, $1,077,444; program services expenses, $914,949; giving activities include $572,893 for grants.
Purpose and activities: The primary mission of the foundation is to promote free, high-quality public skateparks in low-income areas throughout the U.S.
Fields of interest: Recreation, parks/playgrounds; Recreation.
Program:
Public Skatepark Grants: The foundation awards grants, ranging from $1,000 to $25,000, to facilitate the construction of new quality skateboard parks, located in low-income communities in the U.S. Grants are based on a one-time, single-year award, although they may be paid over more than one year, if appropriate.
Type of support: Building/renovation; Donated equipment; Donated products; Equipment; Matching/challenge support; Seed money; Technical assistance.
Geographic limitations: Giving on a national basis.
Support limitations: No grants to individuals.
Publications: Annual report; Application guidelines; Grants list.
Application information: Applications accepted. Applications may not be submitted via printed forms, fax, e-mail, or CDs and other computer discs. Application form required. Applicants should submit the following:
1) copy of IRS Determination Letter
2) copy of current year's organizational budget and/or project budget

In addition to the above, applicants should also include documentation (such as newspaper clips or letters from prominent officials) of community support for the skatepark and a copy of the skatepark design. If a professional designer or builder/contractor has been hired, please include a copy of their resume.
Initial approach: Access online application form
Board meeting date(s): Apr. and Dec.
Deadline(s): Mar. 1 and Oct. 1
Final notification: Sixty to ninety days

Officers: Anthony "Tony" Hawk, Pres.; Patricia Hawk, V.P.; Steve Hawk, Secy.-Treas.; Miki Vuckovich, Exec. Dir.
Directors: Gary Arnold; Gerard Cappello; Lenore Hawk Dale; Lhotse Hawk; Bob Kahan; Chris Sacca; Jamie Thomas.
Number of staff: 3 full-time professional; 1 part-time professional.
EIN: 330965889

31
Acuity Management, Inc.
621 N.W. 53rd St., Ste. 240
Boca Raton, FL 33487-8291
(561) 241-3911

Establishment information: Established in 1989.
Company type: Private company
Business activities: Operates holding company.
Business type (SIC): Holding company
Corporate officers: Murray J. Swindell, Pres.; Neil Eisenband, C.F.O.
Giving statement: Giving through the Acuity Foundation, Inc.

Acuity Foundation, Inc.
(formerly The Revere Foundation, Inc.)
621 N.W. 53rd St., Ste. 240
Boca Raton, FL 33487-8285

Establishment information: Established in 1960 in NY.
Donors: Revere Copper and Brass; Peter Cameron; Acuity Management, Inc.; Revere Graphics Worldwide, Inc.
Financial data (yr. ended 12/31/11): Assets, $1,709,829 (M); expenditures, $42,571; qualifying distributions, $41,713; giving activities include $41,713 for grants.
Purpose and activities: The foundation supports museums and organizations involved with education, cancer, brain disorders, senior citizen services, philanthropy, and Christianity.
Fields of interest: Museums; Secondary school/education; Libraries (public); Education; Cancer; Brain disorders; Aging, centers/services; Philanthropy/voluntarism; Christian agencies & churches.
Type of support: Annual campaigns; Capital campaigns; General/operating support; Scholarship funds.
Geographic limitations: Giving primarily in FL, MA, and PA; giving also to national organizations.
Support limitations: No grants to individuals.
Application information: Applications not accepted. Unsolicited requests for funds not accepted.
Officers: Peter Cameron, Pres.; Neil Eisenband, V.P.; Amy Annis, Secy.
EIN: 136098441

32
Acuity Mutual Insurance Company
2800 S. Taylor Dr.
P.O. Box 58
Sheboygan, WI 53081 (920) 458-9131

Company URL: http://www.acuity.com
Establishment information: Established in 1925.
Company type: Mutual company
Business activities: Sells property and casualty insurance.
Business type (SIC): Insurance/accident and health
Corporate officers: James A. Feddersen, Chair.; Benjamin Michael Salzmann, Pres. and C.E.O.; Neal Ruffalo, V.P., Tech. and C.I.O.; Wendy R. Schuler, V.P., Finance and C.F.O.; Wally Waldhart, V.P., Sales and Comms.
Board of directors: James A. Feddersen, Chair.; Michael R. Duckett; Margaret A. Farrow; H. Gaylon Greenhill; Paul J. Hoffman; Rhonda E. Kirkwood; Lisa A. Mauer; Kurt L. Olson; Benjamin M. Salzmann; John F. Schwalbach; Robert T. Willis; Richard G. Zimmermann
Subsidiaries: Acuity Bank, Tomah, WI; Westland Insurance Services Inc., Tomah, WI
Giving statement: Giving through the Acuity Charitable Foundation, Inc.

Acuity Charitable Foundation, Inc.
2800 S. Taylor Dr.
P.O. Box 58
Sheboygan, WI 53082-0058 (920) 458-9131

Establishment information: Established in 2003 in WI.
Donor: Acuity Mutual Insurance Co.
Contact: Lynn Yunger
Financial data (yr. ended 12/31/11): Assets, $5,779,502 (M); expenditures, $591,916; qualifying distributions, $577,812; giving activities include $577,812 for grants.
Purpose and activities: The foundation supports hospices and community foundations and organizations involved with arts and culture, education, cancer, abuse prevention, food distribution, and youth development.
Fields of interest: Media/communications; Performing arts, theater; Arts; Elementary/secondary education; Education; Cancer; Crime/violence prevention, abuse prevention; Food distribution, meals on wheels; Youth development, business; Salvation Army; Residential/custodial care, hospices; Foundations (community); United Ways and Federated Giving Programs.
Type of support: Continuing support; General/operating support; Program development; Sponsorships.
Geographic limitations: Giving primarily in Sheboygan, WI.
Application information: Applications accepted. Proposals should be submitted using organization letterhead. Application form not required.
Initial approach: Proposal
Deadline(s): None
Officers and Directors:* Benjamin M. Salzmann*, C.E.O. and Pres.; Sheri L. Murphy*, V.P.; Laura J. Conklin*, Secy.; Wendy R. Schuler*, Treas.; Edward L. Felchner; Thomas C. Gast; Adam R. Norlander.
EIN: 200354193
Selected grants: The following grants are a representative sample of this grantmaker's funding activity:
$105,000 to United Way, Sheboygan and Plymouth Area, Sheboygan, WI, 2011.
$56,673 to JustGive, San Francisco, CA, 2011.
$25,308 to United Way, Sheboygan and Plymouth Area, Sheboygan, WI, 2011.
$20,000 to Sharon S. Richardson Community Hospice, Sheboygan Falls, WI, 2011.
$7,500 to Mead Public Library Foundation, Sheboygan, WI, 2011.

33
Acumen Solutions, Inc.
1660 International Dr., Ste. 500
McLean, VA 22102 (703) 600-4000

Company URL: http://www.acumensolutions.com/
Establishment information: Established in 1999.
Company type: Private company
Business activities: Operates IT services company.
Business type (SIC): Computer services
Corporate officers: David V. Joubran, Pres. and C.E.O.; Affie Ambrose, Genl. Counsel
Offices: Los Angeles, San Francisco, CA; Boston, MA; New York, NY; Cleveland, OH
International operations: United Kingdom
Giving statement: Giving through the Acumen Solutions, Inc. Contributions Program.

Acumen Solutions, Inc. Contributions Program
1660 International Dr., Ste. 500
Mclean, VA 22102-4854 (703) 600-4055
FAX: (703) 600-4019;
E-mail: mjohnson@acumensolutions.com;
URL: http://www.acumensolutions.com/social-responsibility/

Contact: Margie Johnson, Sr. Dir., Corp. Care
Purpose and activities: Acumen Solutions, Inc. makes charitable contributions to nonprofit organizations directly. Support is given primarily in areas of company operations; giving also to national organizations.
Fields of interest: General charitable giving.
Type of support: Employee matching gifts; Employee volunteer services; Pro bono services.
Geographic limitations: Giving primarily in areas of company operations; giving also to national organizations.

34
Adams & Reese LLP
1 Shell Sq.
701 Poydras St., Ste. 4500
New Orleans, LA 70139-7755
(504) 581-3234

Company URL: http://www.adamsandreese.com
Establishment information: Established in 1988.
Company type: Private company
Business activities: Operates law firm.
Business type (SIC): Legal services
Corporate officers: Powell G. Ogletree, Jr., Chair.; Paul J. Lassalle, C.F.O.; David E. Bender, C.I.O.
Board of director: Powell G. Ogletree, Jr., Chair.
Offices: Birmingham, Mobile, AL; Washington, DC; Saint Petersburg, Sarasota, Tampa, FL; Baton Rouge, New Orleans, LA; Jackson, MS; Chattanooga, Memphis, Nashville, TN; Houston, TX
Giving statement: Giving through the Adams & Reese LLP Corporate Giving Program and the H.U.G.S., Inc.

Adams & Reese LLP Corporate Giving Program
701 Poydras St., Ste. 4500
New Orleans, LA 70139-7755 (504) 581-3234
FAX: (504) 566-0210; Contact for Pro Bono program: Mark Surprenant, Liaison Partner- Pro Bono Svcs., e-mail: Mark.Surprenant@arlaw.com; URL: http://www.adamsandreese.com/community/

Purpose and activities: Adams & Reese makes charitable contributions to nonprofit organizations involved with health, youth development, human services, and on a case by case basis.
Fields of interest: Health organizations; Legal services; Youth development; Human services; General charitable giving.
Type of support: Employee volunteer services; General/operating support; Pro bono services - legal.

H.U.G.S., Inc.

4500 One Shell Sq.
New Orleans, LA 70139-6001
URL: http://www.adamsandreese.com/community/

Establishment information: Established in 1988 in LA.
Donor: Adams and Reese, LLP.
Financial data (yr. ended 12/31/11): Assets, $11,751 (M); gifts received, $104,270; expenditures, $106,042; qualifying distributions, $105,678; giving activities include $105,678 for grants.
Purpose and activities: The foundation supports organizations involved with medical rehabilitation, breast cancer, multiple sclerosis, housing rehabilitation, and human services.
Type of support: Employee volunteer services; General/operating support; Sponsorships.
Geographic limitations: Giving primarily in New Orleans, LA.
Support limitations: No grants to individuals.
Application information: Applications not accepted. Unsolicited requests for funds not accepted.
Officers: Mark C. Surprenant, Pres.; Linda Soileau, Secy.
EIN: 721128842

35
adidas America Inc.

5675 N. Blackstock Rd.
Spartanburg, SC 29303-6329
(864) 587-0700

Company URL: http://www.adidas.com
Establishment information: Established in 1975.
Company type: Subsidiary of a foreign company
Business activities: Manufactures athletic footwear and clothing.
Business type (SIC): Apparel, piece goods, and notions—wholesale; apparel—men's and boys' outerwear
Corporate officers: Patrick Nilsson, Pres.; Mike Turner, C.O.O.
Plants: Los Angeles, CA; New York, NY; Spartanburg, SC
Giving statement: Giving through the adidas America Inc. Corporate Giving Program.

adidas America Inc. Corporate Giving Program

5055 N. Greeley Ave.
Portland, OR 97217-3524
URL: http://www.adidas-group.com/en/sustainability/Community_involvement/default.aspx

Purpose and activities: adidas makes charitable contributions to nonprofit organizations involved with sports within a social context, children, youth, education, preventive health, and disaster relief. Support is given on a national basis primarily in areas of company operations.
Fields of interest: Education; Safety/disasters; General charitable giving Children; Youth.
Program:
Earn Your Stripes Scholarship Program: Through the America Earn Your Stripes Scholarship Program, adidas annually awards 17 financial scholarships to high school seniors from Portland public schools who demonstrate their commitment and achievement in the areas of academics, athletics and community service. In addition to the financial award, each recipient receives a college kit that includes adidas products and school supplies.
Type of support: Donated products; Employee volunteer services; Equipment; General/operating support; Program development; Technical assistance.
Geographic limitations: Giving on a national basis in areas of company operations.
Support limitations: No support for political, discriminatory, or religious organizations. No grants to individuals, or for cultural projects in association with film, music, or theater, advertising, promotion, or research.
Publications: Application guidelines.
Application information: Applications accepted. Proposals should be no longer than 2 pages. The Community Affairs Department handles giving. Application form not required. Applicants should submit the following:
1) copy of IRS Determination Letter
2) brief history of organization and description of its mission
3) copy of most recent annual report/audited financial statement/990
4) listing of board of directors, trustees, officers and other key people and their affiliations
5) detailed description of project and amount of funding requested
6) listing of additional sources and amount of support

Applications should specifically note the nature of the request being made, and include a description of the program's track record.
Initial approach: Proposal to headquarters
Deadline(s): None
Final notification: 4 weeks

36
Adir International Export, Ltd.

(doing business as La Curacao)
1605 W. Olympic Blvd., Ste. 600
Los Angeles, CA 90015-3860
(213) 639-2100

Company URL: http://www.lacuracao.com
Establishment information: Established in 1980.
Company type: Private company
Business activities: Operates consumer electronics stores.
Business type (SIC): Consumer electronics and music stores
Corporate officers: Ron Sahar Azarkman, Pres. and C.E.O.; Jerry Yoram Azarkman, V.P., Mktg.
Giving statement: Giving through the Fundacion La Curacao Para Los Ninos.

Fundacion La Curacao Para Los Ninos

(also known as Curacao Children's Foundation)
c/o Community Rels. Dept.
1605 W. Olympic Blvd., Ste. 600
Los Angeles, CA 90015-3836
E-mail: Foundationinfo@iCuracao.net; URL: http://www.icuracao.net/Community.aspx?p=1#.UNCPeqyrDTM

Establishment information: Established in 2001 in CA.
Donor: Adir International Export, Ltd.
Financial data (yr. ended 12/31/11): Assets, $0 (M); gifts received, $144,552; expenditures, $222,280; qualifying distributions, $126,427; giving activities include $126,427 for 7 grants (high: $81,185; low: $1,309).
Purpose and activities: The foundation improves the quality of life for indigent children and their families through product donations.
Fields of interest: Hospitals (general); Heart & circulatory diseases; American Red Cross; Children, services; Family services; Human services Economically disadvantaged.
Type of support: Donated products; General/operating support; In-kind gifts.
Geographic limitations: Giving primarily in areas of stores operations in CA.
Publications: Application guidelines.
Application information: Applications accepted. Families recommended to the foundation are contacted directly by staff.
Initial approach: Complete online registration to refer a family in need
Deadline(s): None
Officers: Ron Sahar Azarkman, Pres.; Jerry Yoram Azarkman, Secy.-Treas.
EIN: 912168952

37
Admiral Steel, LLC

4152 W. 123rd St.
P.O. Box 2488
Alsip, IL 60803-1869 (708) 388-9600

Company URL: http://www.admiralsteel.com
Establishment information: Established in 1949.
Company type: Private company
Business activities: Operates metals service center.
Business type (SIC): Metals and minerals, except petroleum—wholesale
Corporate officers: Kevin Averill, Co-Pres.; Tolliver J. Mark, Co-Pres.; Terry J. Summers, V.P., Opers.
Giving statement: Giving through the Catherine Tolliver Foundation.

Catherine Tolliver Foundation

c/o George J. Cullen
10 S. Lasalle St., Ste. 1250
Chicago, IL 60603 (312) 332-2545

Donors: Admiral Steel LLC; Harold J. Tolliver.
Financial data (yr. ended 06/30/12): Assets, $844,538 (M); gifts received, $5,026; expenditures, $6,723; qualifying distributions, $5,000; giving activities include $5,000 for 3 grants (high: $2,000; low: $1,000).
Purpose and activities: The foundation supports hospitals and organizations involved with higher education.
Fields of interest: Health care.
Type of support: General/operating support.
Geographic limitations: Giving primarily in IL.

Application information: Applications accepted. Application form not required.

Initial approach: Proposal

Deadline(s): None

Directors: Hugh J. Ahem; Catherine Averill; Mark Tolliver.

EIN: 362941223

38

Adobe Systems Incorporated

345 Park Ave.
San Jose, CA 95110-2704 (408) 536-6000
FAX: (408) 537-6000

Company URL: http://www.adobe.com
Establishment information: Established in 1982.
Company type: Public company
Company ticker symbol and exchange: ADBE/NASDAQ
International Securities Identification Number: US00724F1012
Business activities: Develops, markets, and supports computer software products.
Business type (SIC): Computer services
Financial profile for 2012: Number of employees, 11,144; assets, $9,974,520,000; sales volume, $4,403,680,000; pre-tax net income, $1,118,790,000; expenses, $3,223,490,000; liabilities, $3,309,340,000
Fortune 1000 ranking: 2012—540th in revenues, 232nd in profits, and 390th in assets
Forbes 2000 ranking: 2012—1471st in sales, 832nd in profits, and 1461st in assets
Corporate officers: Charles M. Geschke, Ph.D., Co-Chair.; John E. Warnock, Ph.D., Co-Chair.; Shantanu Narayen, Pres. and C.E.O.; Mark Garrett, Exec. V.P. and C.F.O.; Matthew A. Thompson, Exec. V.P., Opers.; Gerry Martin-Flickinger, Sr. V.P. and C.I.O.; Michael Dillon, Sr. V.P., Genl. Counsel, and Corp. Secy.
Board of directors: Charles M. Geschke, Co-Chair.; John E. Warnock, Co-Chair.; Amy Banse; Edward W. Barnholt; Kelly Barlow; Robert K. Burgess; Frank Calderoni; Michael R. Cannon; James E. Daley; Laura Desmond; Shantanu Narayen; Dan Rosensweig; Robert Sedgewick
Plants: Mountain View, Santa Clara, CA; Seattle, WA
International operations: Belgium; Brazil; Canada; China; Czech Republic; Denmark; France; Germany; Hong Kong; India; Ireland; Israel; Italy; Japan; Netherlands; New Zealand; Norway; Romania; Russia; Singapore; South Africa; Spain; Sweden; Switzerland; Turkey; Ukraine; United Arab Emirates; United Kingdom
Historic mergers: Macromedia, Inc. (December 3, 2005)
Giving statement: Giving through the Adobe Systems Incorporated Corporate Giving Program and the Adobe Foundation.
Company EIN: 770019522

Adobe Systems Incorporated Corporate Giving Program

c/o Community Rels.
345 Park Ave.
San Jose, CA 95110-2704 (408) 536-6000
FAX: (408) 537-6000; URL: http://www.adobe.com/aboutadobe/philanthropy/main.html

Purpose and activities: As a complement to its foundation, Adobe also makes charitable donations to nonprofit organizations directly. For software donations, emphasis is given to schools that focus on digital technology and visual literacy. Support is given nationally and internationally in Australia, Belgium, Canada, China, France, Germany, Hong Kong, India, Ireland, Italy, Japan, the Netherlands, New Zealand, Sweden, and the United Kingdom.
Fields of interest: Arts, cultural/ethnic awareness; Elementary/secondary education; Education, computer literacy/technology training; Environment; Food services; Housing/shelter, homeless; Developmentally disabled, centers & services Economically disadvantaged.
International interests: Australia; Belgium; Canada; China; France; Germany; Hong Kong; India; Ireland; Italy; Japan; Netherlands; New Zealand; Sweden; United Kingdom.

Programs:

Commitment to Community: Adobe supports programs designed to create, promote, and exhibit visual arts, multimedia, and video; reduce hunger and homelessness and provide affordable housing; protect the natural environment and improve public spaces for the enjoyment of the community; and improve access to electronic information for people with disabilities. Grants and scholarships are made through the Adobe Foundation Fund at the Community Foundation Silicon Valley.

International Software Donation Program: Adobe makes charitable contributions of software to K-12 schools and nonprofit organizations involved with K-12 education with programs designed to enable and inspire students to think creatively, communicate effectively, and work collaboratively by focusing on the use of digital technology and visual literacy and programs designed to promote and provide cultural awareness and arts education for the broader community; provide services for low-income families, with emphasis on reducing hunger and homelessness and providing affordable housing; protect the natural environment and improve public spaces for the enjoyment of the community; and improve access to electronic information for people with disabilities. Special emphasis is directed toward programs designed to focus on low-achieving, economically disadvantaged students and/or those who are not succeeding with traditional methods. The program is administered by Gifts in Kind International.

North America Software Donation Program—Education: Adobe makes charitable contributions of software to K-12 public schools with programs designed to enable and inspire students to think creatively, communicate effectively, and work collaboratively by focusing on the use of digital technology and visual literacy. The program is administered by Gifts in Kind International.

North America Software Donation Program—Nonprofit: Adobe makes charitable contributions of software to museums, zoos, libraries, and community centers and programs designed to promote cultural and ethnic awareness, folk arts, visual arts, performing arts, community theater, humanities, art exhibits, and community celebrations; provide arts education and arts service; provide instruction and training in publishing, film production, and broadcasting and conduct nonscientific studies and research and facilitate discussion groups, forums, panels, and lectures in these areas; assist people with disabilities; provide disaster preparedness services; promote inner-city and community benefit activities; serve children in grades K-12 with digital technology training, with an emphasis on low-achieving, economically disadvantaged students and/or those who are not succeeding with traditional methods; promote conservation, environmental protection, and improvement of public spaces for the enjoyment of the community; provide housing services for young people, the elderly, and low- to medium-income individuals; supply money, goods, or services to the poor; and provide job training, counseling, referral services, and employment assistance to individuals. The program is administered by TechSoup.

T3 Program: Through the Train the Teacher (T3) Program, Adobe provides software training to K-12 educators in Silicon Valley and San Francisco, California, and Puget Sound, Washington. These workshops provide teachers with the opportunity to learn how to incorporate digital applications into the classroom across a range of curricular activities, using a variety of Adobe products. Designed around real classroom projects and offered for free or a nominal administrative charge, teachers are given the time and support they need to become proficient at using digital media in their own classrooms.
Type of support: Donated products.
Geographic limitations: Giving nationally and internationally in Australia, Belgium, Canada, China, France, Germany, Hong Kong, India, Ireland, Italy, Japan, the Netherlands, New Zealand, Sweden, and the United Kingdom.
Support limitations: No support for organizations that promote political views, influence legislation, or support candidates for public office, or to churches, houses of worship, religious or sectarian programs not for public benefit, or religious training programs including but not limited to seminaries, theology schools, or yeshivas, private foundations that are themselves grant-making organizations, research or advocacy organizations or think-tanks that do not provide direct services to the end-beneficiary, fraternal or discriminatory organizations. No software donations to international organizations with annual budgets over $10 million. No donations to individuals or for endowments; no software donations for raffles, door prizes, auctions, or other fundraising activities.
Publications: Application guidelines; Corporate giving report.
Application information: Applications accepted. Applications for software donations are processed by Adobe's distribution partners, Good360 and TechSoup. Schools requesting software donations must incorporate digital technology and visual literacy in their curricula, and have an NCES or Canadian Registration number. The software must be used on the organization's premises for its capacity building or educational purposes. Applications are limited to 1 request per organization in any given year. Organizations that request software donations are limited to four individually titled products or one bundled software package per year. Application form required.
Applicants should submit the following:
1) copy of IRS Determination Letter
Completed applications must include supporting documentation to verify an organization's non-discriminatory practices, and the signed anti-piracy contract. International applications must be submitted via fax or airmail with credit card information for processing required fees.

Initial approach: Download and complete online application by region

Final notification: 2 - 3 months for software donation requests

Number of staff: 4 full-time professional.

Adobe Foundation

c/o Foundation Source
501 Silverside Rd., Ste. 123
Wilmington, DE 19809-1377
URL: http://www.adobe.com/corporate-responsibility/community.html

Establishment information: Established in 2007.
Donor: Adobe Systems Incorporated.

Financial data (yr. ended 11/30/11): Assets, $18,349,995 (M); gifts received, $30,000; expenditures, $10,998,587; qualifying distributions, $11,196,032; giving activities include $8,044,669 for 202 grants (high: $515,000; low: $500) and $2,346,120 for 1 foundation-administered program.
Purpose and activities: The foundation supports organizations involved with arts and culture, education, hunger, nutrition, housing, safety, children and youth, and community development. Special emphasis is directed toward programs designed to promote access to underserved communities, giving them the opportunity to develop 21st century skills.
Fields of interest: Visual arts; Visual arts, design; Arts; Education; Food services; Food banks; Nutrition; Housing/shelter, development; Housing/shelter; Safety/disasters; Children/youth, services; Community/economic development.
Programs:
Adobe Youth Voices: Through Adobe Youth Voices (AYV), the foundation empowers youth in underserved communities around the globe with real-world experiences and 21st-century multimedia tools, including audio, video, digital art, web animation, and photography, to communicate their ideas, exhibit their potential, and take action in their communities. The Adobe Youth Voices network includes more than 750 sites in 50 countries. The program includes professional development; strategic partnerships; Adobe Youth Voices Grants that funds youth media organizations and partner with the Adobe Foundation to exhibit youth-produced projects; and the Aspire Awards which recognizes top work by young media artists from around the world. Visit URL http://youthvoices.adobe.com/ for more information.
Community Grants Program - Arts and Creativity Grants: The foundation supports programs designed to empower people to communicate new ideas, tell their stories, and envision solutions. Special emphasis is directed toward programs designed to create or exhibit visual or multimedia art; and programs that use or teach art and design to address social issues and improve lives and communities. The program is by invitation only.
Community Grants Program - Youth Services Grants: The foundation supports programs designed to provide critical services to children and young adults, from birth through age 18, by addressing basic human needs and safety. Special emphasis is directed toward programs designed to provide food and nutrition; provide safe shelter and housing; and promote youth safety in schools, the home environment, and online. The program is by invitation only.
Creativity Scholarship Fund: The foundation awards scholarships to participants in the Adobe Youth Voices program who plan to pursue an academic program or career in a creative field at an accredited college, university, or certification program. Scholarship amounts vary and recipients are chosen based on financial need, academic performance, and potential. The program is designed to empower youth to pursue creative careers or find innovative ways to improve their communities. The scholarship is administered by the Institute of International Education (IIE).
Type of support: Annual campaigns; Continuing support; General/operating support; Program development; Scholarship funds.
Geographic limitations: Giving primarily in areas of company operations, with emphasis on San Francisco and San Jose, CA, Boston, MA, New York, NY, Orem, UT, Seattle, WA, Ottawa, Canada, Beijing, China, London, England, Bangalore and Noida, India, Tokyo, Japan, and Bucharest, Romania.
Publications: Corporate giving report; Grants list.
Application information: Applications not accepted. Contributes only to pre-selected organizations. The foundation utilizes an invitation only process for Community Grants.
Officers and Directors:* Shantanu Narayen*, Pres.; Ann Lewnes, Secy.; Mark Garrett, Treas.; Michelle Crozier Yates, Exec. Dir.; Donna Morris; Kevin Lynch.
EIN: 260233808
Selected grants: The following grants are a representative sample of this grantmaker's funding activity:
$585,000 to Entertainment Industry Foundation, Los Angeles, CA, 2010. For Per Contract Program.
$466,000 to Give2Asia, San Francisco, CA, 2010. For Adobe Foundation Donor Advised Fund.
$350,000 to Education Development Center, Waltham, MA, 2010. For Adobe Youth Voices Project.
$300,000 to PBS Foundation, Arlington, VA, 2010. To engage youth and educators in Adobe Youth Voices through a multifaceted program.
$215,000 to Tech Museum of Innovation, San Jose, CA, 2010. For Infinite Line Exhibit.
$100,000 to Arts Council Silicon Valley, San Jose, CA, 2010. For ACSV Core Grants Programs, Artsopolis.
$50,000 to Friends of the World Food Program, Washington, DC, 2010. For Haiti Disaster Relief Fund.
$49,475 to Free the Children, Mountain View, CA, 2010. To implement Adobe Youth Voices within the Free the Children Network in Toronto and New York.
$30,000 to Childrens Creativity Museum, San Francisco, CA, 2010. For General Operating Support.
$16,000 to Tides Foundation, San Francisco, CA, 2010. For Tides Foundation to be directed to Tides Canada Exchange Fund (No. 1481) for your cross-border.

39
Advance Auto Parts, Inc.

5008 Airport Rd.
Roanoke, VA 24012 (540) 362-4911

Company URL: http://shop.advanceautoparts.com
Establishment information: Established in 1929.
Company type: Public company
Company ticker symbol and exchange: AAP/NYSE
Business activities: Operates auto parts stores.
Business type (SIC): Auto and home supplies—retail
Financial profile for 2012: Number of employees, 55,000; assets, $4,613,810,000; sales volume, $6,205,000,000; pre-tax net income, $624,070,000; expenses, $5,547,690,000; liabilities, $3,403,120,000
Fortune 1000 ranking: 2012—409th in revenues, 410th in profits, and 619th in assets
Forbes 2000 ranking: 2012—1263rd in sales, 1235th in profits, and 1839th in assets
Corporate officers: John C. Brouillard, Chair.; Darren R. Jackson, C.E.O.; George Sherman, Pres.; Michael A. Norona, Exec. V.P. and C.F.O.; Jill A. Livesay, Sr. V.P. and Cont.; Sarah Powell, Sr. V.P., Genl. Counsel, and Corp. Secy.; Mike Pack, Sr. V.P., Opers.; Joe Gonzalez, Sr. V.P., Opers.; Rusty Tweedy, Sr. V.P., Opers.; Tammy Finley, Sr. V.P., Human Resources
Board of directors: John C. Brouillard, Chair.; John F. Bergstrom; Fiona P. Dias; Darren R. Jackson; William S. Oglesby; Paul Raines; Gilbert T. Ray; Carlos A. Saladrigas; Jim Wade
Giving statement: Giving through the Advance Auto Parts, Inc. Corporate Giving Program.
Company EIN: 542049910

Advance Auto Parts, Inc. Corporate Giving Program

5008 Airport Rd.
Roanoke, VA 24012-1601 (540) 362-4911
E-mail: charitable@advance-auto.com; URL: http://corp.advanceautoparts.com/about/public.asp

Purpose and activities: Advance Auto Parts makes charitable contributions to nonprofit organizations involved with health, education, at-risk children and families, and disaster relief. Giving primarily in areas of company operations.
Fields of interest: Education; Health care, blood supply; Health care; Safety/disasters; Human services, fund raising/fund distribution; American Red Cross; Children, services; Family services; United Ways and Federated Giving Programs.
Type of support: Employee volunteer services; General/operating support.
Geographic limitations: Giving primarily in areas of company operations.

40
Advanced Micro Devices, Inc.

(also known as AMD)
1 AMD Pl.
P.O. Box 3453
Sunnyvale, CA 94088 (408) 749-4000
FAX: (408) 982-6164

Company URL: http://www.amd.com
Establishment information: Established in 1969.
Company type: Public company
Company ticker symbol and exchange: AMD/NYSE
International Securities Identification Number: US0079031078
Business activities: Designs and markets digital integrated circuits.
Business type (SIC): Electronic components and accessories
Financial profile for 2012: Number of employees, 10,340; assets, $4,000,000,000; sales volume, $5,422,000,000; pre-tax net income, -$1,217,000,000; expenses, $6,482,000,000; liabilities, $3,462,000,000
Fortune 1000 ranking: 2012—464th in revenues, 985th in profits, and 664th in assets
Corporate officers: Bruce L. Claflin, Chair.; Rory Read, Pres. and C.E.O.; Devinder Kumar, Sr. V.P. and C.F.O.; Harry Wolin, Sr. V.P., Genl. Counsel, and Secy.
Board of directors: Bruce L. Claflin, Chair.; W. Michael Barnes; John E. Caldwell; Henry W. K. Chow; Craig A. Conway; Nicholas M. Donofrio; H. Paulett Eberhart; Martin Edelman; Jack Harding; Ahmed Yahia Al Idrissi; Robert B. Palmer; Rory Read
International operations: Barbados; Belgium; China; France; Germany; Hungary; India; Italy; Japan; Malaysia; Singapore; Sweden; United Kingdom
Giving statement: Giving through the AMD Corporate Giving Program, the NEC Corporation Contributions Program, and the AMD Foundation, Inc.
Company EIN: 941692300

AMD Corporate Giving Program

c/o Community Affairs Dept.
7171 Southwest Pkwy., M.S. 100.3
Austin, TX 78741
FAX: (512) 602-8355;
E-mail: community.affairs@amd.com; URL: http://www.amd.com/corporateresponsibility

Contact: Kristi Fontenot, Community Affairs
Financial data (yr. ended 12/31/11): Total giving, $1,561,711, including $1,561,711 for grants.
Purpose and activities: AMD makes charitable contributions to nonprofit organizations involved with education. Special emphasis is directed toward programs designed to increase student interest and proficiency in science, technology, engineering, and math (STEM skills). Support is given on a national and international basis in areas of company operations.
Fields of interest: Education; Mathematics; Engineering/technology; Science.
Type of support: Continuing support; Employee matching gifts; Employee volunteer services; In-kind gifts; Program development; Use of facilities.
Geographic limitations: Giving on a national and international basis in areas of company operations, with emphasis on Sunnyvale, CA, Fort Collins, CO, Orlando, FL, Boxborough, MA, Austin, TX, and in Beijing and Suzhou, China, Bangalore and Hyderabad, India, Markham, Ontario, Penang, Malaysia, and Singapore.
Support limitations: No support for national organizations without local, financially independent chapters, religious, political, service, or fraternal organizations, arts or cultural organizations, advocacy groups, athletic teams, recreational organizations, individual scouting troops, or discriminatory organizations. No grants to individuals, or for medical research; generally, no grants for capital campaigns.
Application information: Multi-year funding is not automatic. Organizations receiving support are asked to provide periodic progress reports. The Global Community Affairs Department handles giving.
Initial approach: Contact corporate office before submitting application
Number of staff: 4 full-time professional.

AMD Foundation, Inc.

7171 Southwest Pkwy., MS 100.3
Austin, TX 78735-8953
E-mail: amd.foundation@amd.com; URL: http://www.amd.com/foundation

Establishment information: Established in TX.
Donor: Advanced Micro Devices, Inc.
Contact: Kristi Fontenot
Financial data (yr. ended 12/31/11): Assets, $539,060 (M); gifts received, $2,912,507; expenditures, $2,772,348; qualifying distributions, $2,535,738; giving activities include $2,535,738 for grants.
Purpose and activities: The foundation supports programs designed to provide future generations with critical science, technology, engineering, and mathematics (STEM) skills and life skills.
Fields of interest: Higher education; Education; Disasters, preparedness/services; Boys & girls clubs; Youth, services; Human services; Mathematics; Engineering/technology; Science.
Program:
AMD Changing the Game: Through the Changing the Game initiative, the foundation support programs designed to teach youth (9-18) how to create their own digital games on subjects such as energy, environment, health, politics, public policy, and transportation. The program is designed to help students learn science, technology, engineering and math (STEM) skills, problem solving skills, critical thinking, language skills, and teamwork. Special emphasis is directed toward programs that target disadvantaged youth and are based in AMD site communities.
Type of support: Employee matching gifts; Employee volunteer services; General/operating support; Program development.
Geographic limitations: Giving primarily in areas of company operations in San Jose and Silicon Valley, CA, Ft. Collins, CO, Orlando, FL, Boston, MA, Portland, OR, Austin, TX, and Bellevue, WA, and in Beijing, Shanghai, and Suzhou, China, Toronto, Canada, Bangalore and Hyderabad, India, Cyberjaya and Penang, Malaysia, Singapore, and Taipei, Taiwan.
Publications: Application guidelines.
Application information: Applications accepted.
Initial approach: E-mail foundation for AMD Changing the Game
Deadline(s): None for AMD Changing the Game
Officers and Directors:* Alex Brown, Chair.; J. Michael Woollems, Vice-Chair.; Allyson W. Peerman, Pres.; Devinder Kumar, Treas.; Ben Bar-Haim; Robert Feldstein; Annie Flaig; Thomas Seifert; Leslie Sobon; Kathleen Woodhouse.
EIN: 711036553
Selected grants: The following grants are a representative sample of this grantmaker's funding activity:
$251,273 to Boys and Girls Clubs of America, Atlanta, GA, 2011.

41
Advent Software, Inc.

600 Townsend St., 5th Fl.
San Francisco, CA 94103 (415) 543-7696
FAX: (415) 543-5070

Company URL: http://www.advent.com
Establishment information: Established in 1983.
Company type: Public company
Company ticker symbol and exchange: ADVS/NASDAQ
Business activities: Sells enterprise investment management software.
Business type (SIC): Computer services
Financial profile for 2012: Number of employees, 1,222; assets, $658,450,000; sales volume, $358,820,000; pre-tax net income, $47,560,000; expenses, $309,640,000; liabilities, $348,590,000
Corporate officers: John H. Scully, Chair.; David Peter Hess, Jr., Pres. and C.E.O.; James S. Cox, Exec. V.P. and C.F.O.; Doug Yokoyama, Sr. V.P. and C.I.O.; Randall Cook, Sr. V.P., Genl. Counsel. and Corp. Secy.; John P. Brennan, Sr. V.P., Human Resources
Board of directors: John H. Scully, Chair.; Stephanie G. DiMarco; Peter Hess; Asiff S. Hirji; James D. Kirsner; Christine S. Manfredi; Rob Tarkoff; Wendell G. Van Auken
Giving statement: Giving through the Advent Software, Inc. Corporate Giving Program.

Advent Software, Inc. Corporate Giving Program

600 Townsend St.
San Francisco, CA 94103 (415) 543-7696
URL: http://www.advent.com/about/community-involvement

Purpose and activities: Advent Software makes charitable contributions to nonprofit organizations involved with education and low-performing K-12 schools. Support is given primarily in areas of company operations in California, Massachusetts, and New York, and in China, Denmark, India, the Netherlands, Norway, Singapore, Sweden, Switzerland, and the United Kingdom.
Fields of interest: Elementary/secondary education.
International interests: China; Denmark; India; Netherlands; Norway; Singapore; Sweden; Switzerland; United Kingdom.
Type of support: Employee volunteer services; General/operating support.
Geographic limitations: Giving primarily in areas of company operations in CA, MA, and NY, and in China, Denmark, India, the Netherlands, Norway, Singapore, Sweden, Switzerland, and the United Kingdom.

42
AECOM Technology Corporation

555 S. Flower St., Ste. 3700
Los Angeles, CA 90071-2300
(213) 593-8000
FAX: (213) 593-8730

Company URL: http://www.aecom.com
Establishment information: Established in 1990.
Company type: Public company
Company ticker symbol and exchange: ACM/NYSE
Business activities: Provides planning, consulting, architectural and engineering design, and program and construction management services for a broad range of projects, including highways, airports, bridges, mass transit systems, government and commercial buildings, water and wastewater facilities, and power transmission and distribution.
Business type (SIC): Engineering, architectural, and surveying services
Financial profile for 2012: Number of employees, 46,800; assets, $5,664,570,000; sales volume, $8,218,180,000; pre-tax net income, $17,480,000; expenses, $8,164,570,000; liabilities, $3,495,100,000
Fortune 1000 ranking: 2012—320th in revenues, 910th in profits, and 556th in assets
Corporate officers: John M. Dionisio, Chair. and C.E.O.; Daniel R. Tishman, Vice-Chair.; Michael S. Burke, Pres.; Jane Chmielinski, C.O.O.; Stephen M. Kadenancy, Exec. V.P. and C.F.O.; Tom Peck, Sr. V.P. and C.I.O.; Glenn R. Robson, Sr. V.P., Finance; Eric Chen, Sr. V.P., Corp. Finance; Paul J. Gennaro, Sr. V.P., Corp. Comms.; Christina Ching, V.P., Corp. Secy.; Richard G. Newman, Chair. Emeritus
Board of directors: John M. Dionisio, Chair.; Daniel R. Tishman, Vice-Chair.; Francis S. Y. Bong; James H. Fordyce; S. Malcolm Gillis, Ph.D.; Linda M. Griego; David W. Joos; Robert J. Lowe; Richard G. Newman; William G. Ouchi, Ph.D.; Robert J. Routs; William P. Rutledge
Giving statement: Giving through the AECOM Technology Corporation Contributions Program.
Company EIN: 611088522

AECOM Technology Corporation Contributions Program

(also known as AECOM Community Trust)
555 S. Flower St.
Los Angeles, CA 90071-2300 (213) 593-8000

Purpose and activities: AECOM Technology makes charitable contributions to organizations in areas of company operations.
Fields of interest: General charitable giving.
Type of support: Employee volunteer services; General/operating support.
Geographic limitations: Giving primarily in areas of company operations.

43
AEG Houston Soccer Corporation

(doing business as Houston Dynamo)
1001 Avnida De Las Americas 2, Ste. 200
Houston, TX 77002-7360 (713) 276-7500

Establishment information: Established in 2005.
Company type: Private company
Business activities: Operates professional soccer club.
Business type (SIC): Commercial sports
Corporate officers: Oliver Luck, Pres.; Steve Powell, V.P., Sales & Mktg.
Giving statement: Giving through the Houston Dynamo Corporate Giving Program.

Houston Dynamo Corporate Giving Program

c/o Community Rels.
1415 Louisiana, Ste. 3400
Houston, TX 77010-6012 (713) 276-7500
URL: http://www.houstondynamo.com/charities

Purpose and activities: The Houston Dynamo makes charitable contributions of memorabilia to nonprofit organizations involved with helping youths and underserved and at risk children. Support is limited to the greater Houston, Texas, area.
Fields of interest: Youth development; Children/youth, services.
Type of support: Donated products; In-kind gifts.
Geographic limitations: Giving limited to the greater Houston, TX, area.
Publications: Application guidelines.
Application information: Applications accepted. Mailed, faxed, e-mailed, or telephoned applications will not be accepted. Application form required.
Applicants should submit the following:
1) name, address and phone number of organization
2) contact person
Applications should include organization's Tax ID Number, the date, attendance, and location of the event; and the type of fundraiser.
Initial approach: Complete online application form
Deadline(s): 6 weeks prior to need
Final notification: 2 to 4 weeks

44
AEGIS Insurance Services, Inc.

(also known as AEGIS NJ)
1 Meadowlands Plz.
East Rutherford, NJ 07073 (201) 508-2600

Company URL: http://www.aegislink.com
Establishment information: Established in 1975.
Company type: Subsidiary of a foreign company
Business activities: Operates insurance company.
Business type (SIC): Insurance agents, brokers, and services
Financial profile for 2010: Number of employees, 215
Corporate officers: Wesley W. von Schack, Chair.; Alan J. Maguire, Pres. and C.E.O.; Maureen E. Sammon, Sr. V.P. and C.A.O.; Gene Blauvelt, Sr. V.P. and Co-C.I.O.; Rip Reeves, Sr. V.P. and Co-C.I.O.; Michael Johnson, Sr. V.P., Finance; Jay Foley, V.P., Mktg., and Comms.
Board of director: Wesley W. von Schack, Chair.
Giving statement: Giving through the Aegis Foundation Inc.

Aegis Foundation Inc

1 Meadowsland Plz.
East Rutherford, NJ 07073

Establishment information:
Financial data (yr. ended 12/31/11): Assets, $7,500 (M); gifts received, $15,000; expenditures, $11,191; qualifying distributions, $11,191; giving activities include $11,191 for 63 employee matching gifts.
Purpose and activities: The foundation matches contributions made by employees to nonprofit organizations on a one-for-one basis.
Fields of interest: General charitable giving.
Type of support: Employee matching gifts.
Geographic limitations: Giving primarily in CT, NJ, NY, and OK.
Application information: Applications not accepted. Contributes only through employee matching gifts.
Officers: Gilbert Gould, Pres.; Alison Geller, V.P.; Melinda dela Pena, Secy.; Regina Salogiannis, Treas.
EIN: 264187654

45
AEGON USA, Inc.

4333 Edgewood Rd., N.E.
Cedar Rapids, IA 52499-0010
(319) 355-8511

Company URL: http://www.aegonins.com
Establishment information: Established in 1988.
Company type: Subsidiary of a foreign company
Business activities: Sells life and health insurance; provides investment advisory services.
Business type (SIC): Insurance/life; security and commodity services; insurance/accident and health
Corporate officers: Patrick S. Baird, Chair.; Mark William Mullin, Pres. and C.E.O.; Brenda K. Clancy, Exec. V.P. and C.O.O.; Darryl D. Button, Sr. V.P. and C.F.O.; James A. Beardsworth, Sr. V.P. and Treas.; Craig D. Vermie, V.P. and Secy.
Board of director: Patrick S. Baird, Chair.
Subsidiaries: AEGON USA Investment Management, Inc., Cedar Rapids, IA; Diversified Financial Products, Inc., Louisville, KY; Diversified Investment Advisors, Inc., Purchase, NY; Special Markets Group, Inc., Baltimore, MD
Divisions: Equity Group, St. Petersburg, FL; Financial Market Div., Cedar Rapids, IA; Individual Div., Cedar Rapids, IA; Long Term Care Div., Hurst, TX; Monumental Life Div., Baltimore, MD; Worksite Marketing Div., Little Rock, AR
Giving statement: Giving through the AEGON Transamerica Foundation.

AEGON Transamerica Foundation

(formerly AEGON USA Charitable Foundation, Inc.)
c/o Tax Dept.
4333 Edgewood Rd., N.E.
Cedar Rapids, IA 52499-3210
E-mail: shaegontransfound@aegonusa.com; Application contact for organizations in Baltimore, MD: Transamerica Foundation Baltimore, 100 Light St., Fl. 2, Baltimore, MD 21202-2559, Attn: Veronica Mouring, #3237, e-mail: TransamericaFoundationBaltimore@Transamerica.com; URL: http://www.transamerica.com/about_us/aegon_transamerica_foundation.asp

Establishment information: Established around 1994.
Donors: AEGON USA, Inc.; Life Investors Insurance Co. of America; Transmerica Financial Life Insurance Co.
Financial data (yr. ended 12/31/11): Assets, $110,216,791 (M); gifts received, $687,637; expenditures, $5,385,912; qualifying distributions, $5,261,190; giving activities include $4,984,736 for grants and $276,454 for employee matching gifts.
Purpose and activities: The foundation supports programs designed to promote arts and culture; civic and community; education and literacy; and health and welfare.
Fields of interest: Museums; Performing arts; Performing arts, music; Arts; Secondary school/education; Higher education; Education, reading; Education; Health care; Employment; Nutrition; Housing/shelter, homeless; Housing/shelter; Disasters, preparedness/services; Athletics/sports, golf; Children/youth, services; Family services; Human services, financial counseling; Human services; Business/industry; Community/economic development; United Ways and Federated Giving Programs; Leadership development; Public affairs.
Programs:
Arts and Culture: The foundation supports programs designed to foster music and the performing arts, including venues for artistic expression.
Civic and Community: The foundation supports programs designed to promote community development; encourage civic leadership; enhance workforce and business development; and empower people and communities.
Education and Literacy: The foundation supports programs designed to provide knowledge and expand individual's capabilities. Special emphasis is directed toward programs designed to promote financial literacy, financial security, and personal success through financial education and planning for individuals.
Health and Welfare: The foundation supports programs designed to improve the condition of the human body though nutrition, housing for the homeless, disease prevention, and other support services.
Type of support: Building/renovation; Capital campaigns; Employee matching gifts; Employee volunteer services; Equipment; General/operating support; Program development.
Geographic limitations: Giving primarily in areas of company operations, with emphasis on Little Rock, AR, Los Angeles, CA, St. Petersburg, FL, Atlanta, GA, Cedar Rapids, IA, Louisville, KY, Baltimore, MD, Harrison, NY, Exton, PA, and Bedford and Plano, TX.
Support limitations: No support for athletes or athletic organizations, fraternal organizations, political parties or candidates, religious organizations not of direct benefit to the entire community, or social organizations. No grants to individuals, or for conferences, seminars, or trips, courtesy or goodwill advertising, fellowships, K-12 school fundraisers or events, or political campaigns.
Publications: Annual report; Application guidelines.
Application information: Applications accepted. Organizations receiving support are asked to submit a semi-annual report and a final report. Visit website for company facility addresses. Applicants should submit the following:

1) how project will be sustained once grantmaker support is completed
2) qualifications of key personnel
3) statement of problem project will address
4) population served
5) name, address and phone number of organization
6) copy of IRS Determination Letter
7) brief history of organization and description of its mission
8) copy of most recent annual report/audited financial statement/990
9) how project's results will be evaluated or measured
10) listing of board of directors, trustees, officers and other key people and their affiliations
11) detailed description of project and amount of funding requested
12) plans for cooperation with other organizations, if any
13) contact person
14) copy of current year's organizational budget and/or project budget
15) listing of additional sources and amount of support

Applications should include a W-9 statement.
Initial approach: Download application form and mail to nearest company facility; download application form and e-mail to application address for organizations located in Baltimore, MD
Deadline(s): Varies per location

Officers and Directors:* Mark William Mullen*, Chair.; David Blankenship, Pres.; Cynthia Nodorft, V.P.; Lonny Olejniczak, V.P.; David Schulz, V.P.; Greg Tucker, V.P.; Craig D. Vermie, Secy.; Diane Meiners, Treas.
EIN: 421415998
Selected grants: The following grants are a representative sample of this grantmaker's funding activity:
$500,000 to University of Iowa Foundation, Iowa City, IA, 2010. For general support.
$225,213 to United Way of East Central Iowa, Cedar Rapids, IA, 2010. For general support.
$138,828 to Human Services Campus of East Central Iowa, Cedar Rapids, IA, 2010. For general support.
$100,000 to Kennedy Krieger Institute, Baltimore, MD, 2010. For general support.
$100,000 to National Czech and Slovak Museum and Library, Cedar Rapids, IA, 2010. For general support.
$47,044 to United Way of Westchester and Putnam, White Plains, NY, 2010. For general support.
$10,000 to Enoch Pratt Free Library of Baltimore City, Baltimore, MD, 2010. For general support.
$5,000 to Aurora Theater, Lawrenceville, GA, 2010. For general support.
$5,000 to Chase Brexton Health Services, Baltimore, MD, 2010. For general support.
$3,500 to Central City Community Outreach, Los Angeles, CA, 2010. For general support.

46
Aeropostale, Inc.

112 West 34th St., 22nd Fl.
New York, NY 10120 (646) 485-5410
FAX: (302) 636-5454

Company URL: http://www.aeropostale.com
Establishment information: Established in 1995.
Company type: Public company
Company ticker symbol and exchange: ARO/NYSE
Business activities: Mall-based, specialty retailer of casual apparel and accessories.
Business type (SIC): Apparel and accessory stores
Financial profile for 2013: Number of employees, 26,279; assets, $740,840,000; sales volume, $2,386,180,000; pre-tax net income, $59,030,000; expenses, $2,326,670,000; liabilities, $330,480,000
Fortune 1000 ranking: 2012—839th in revenues, 842nd in profits, and 990th in assets
Corporate officers: Karin Hirtler-Garvey, Chair.; Thomas P. Johnson, C.E.O.; Marc D. Miller, Exec. V.P. and C.F.O.; Edward M. Slezak, Sr. V.P., Genl. Counsel, and Secy.; Ann E. Joyce, Sr. V.P. and C.I.O.; Scott K. Birnbaum, Sr. V.P., Mktg.; Kathy E. Gentilozzi, Sr. V.P., Human Resources
Board of directors: Karin Hirtler-Garvey, Chair.; Ronald R. Beegle; Robert B. Chavez; Michael J. Cunningham; Evelyn Dilsaver; Janet E. Grove; John Haugh; John D. Howard; Thomas P. Johnson; Arthur Rubinfeld; David B. Vermylen
Giving statement: Giving through the Aero Gives, Inc. and the Aero Cares, Inc.
Company EIN: 311443880

Aero Gives, Inc.

112 West 34th St., 22nd Fl.
New York, NY 10120 (646) 485-5410
FAX: (464) 304-5267;
E-mail: aerogives@aeropostale.com; URL: http://theaeroway.com/?page_id=403

Contact: Christian Boglivi
Purpose and activities: The foundation supports organizations working to improve the lives of young people.
Fields of interest: Youth development Youth.
Type of support: General/operating support; Program development.
Geographic limitations: Giving primarily in areas of company operations.
Support limitations: No support for political, fraternal, veteran, or religious organizations, or individual K-12 schools, colleges, or universities, or sports teams. No grants to individuals, or for capital campaigns, scholarships, fashion shows, pageants, fundraising, or event sponsorship.
Application information: Applications accepted. Aero Gives will award a grant of up to $5,000 to support operational costs to help an organization continue to work to achieve their overall goals; a grant of up to $10,000 will be awarded to support a specific program, project or initiative. Organizations are eligible to receive funding only one time per calendar year and will be eligible to apply and receive grants for a maximum of two consecutive years. Application form required. Applicants should submit the following:
1) role played by volunteers
2) results expected from proposed grant
3) population served
4) copy of IRS Determination Letter
5) brief history of organization and description of its mission
6) copy of most recent annual report/audited financial statement/990
7) listing of board of directors, trustees, officers and other key people and their affiliations
8) detailed description of project and amount of funding requested
9) contact person
10) copy of current year's organizational budget and/or project budget
11) listing of additional sources and amount of support
Deadline(s): Apr. 1 to May 31
Final notification: Sept. 30

EIN: 275404095

Aero Cares, Inc.

112 West 34th St., 22nd Fl.
New York, NY 10120-2400 (973) 826-1042
URL: http://www.aeropostalecareers.com/community.asp

Establishment information: Established in 2010 in NY.
Financial data (yr. ended 12/31/11): Revenue, $317,399; assets, $515,919 (M); gifts received, $317,299; expenditures, $176,231; giving activities include $147,239 for grants to individuals.
Purpose and activities: The organization provides assistance to Aeropostale employees during times of extreme financial hardship or need resulting from a personal tragedy.
Fields of interest: Disasters, preparedness/services Economically disadvantaged.
Type of support: Donated products; Emergency funds; Grants to individuals; In-kind gifts.
Officers and Directors:* Maro Jo Pile*, Pres.; Kathy Gentilozzi*, V.P.; Edward Slezak*, Secy.; Joseph Pachella*, Treas.; Joyce Donatelli; Robert Hernon; Jennifer Holman; David Parker; Latanya Spellman-Pollard.
EIN: 272040286

47
The AES Corporation

4300 Wilson Blvd., 11th Fl.
Arlington, VA 22203 (703) 522-1315
FAX: (302) 636-5454

Company URL: http://www.aes.com
Establishment information: Established in 1981.
Company type: Public company
Company ticker symbol and exchange: AES/NYSE
International Securities Identification Number: US00130H1059
Business activities: Provides electricity generation and distribution services.
Business type (SIC): Electric services
Financial profile for 2012: Number of employees, 25,000; assets, $41,830,000,000; sales volume, $18,141,000,000; pre-tax net income, $314,000,000; expenses, $17,777,000,000; liabilities, $37,261,000,000
Fortune 1000 ranking: 2012—153rd in revenues, 977th in profits, and 132nd in assets
Corporate officers: Charles O. Rossotti, Chair.; Andres Ricardo Gluski Weilert, Pres. and C.E.O.; Andrew Vesey III, C.O.O.; Thomas O'Flynn, C.F.O.; Elizabeth Hackenson, C.I.O.; Brian A. Miller, Genl. Counsel and Corp. Secy.
Board of directors: Charles O. Rossotti, Chair.; Zhang Guobao; Kristina Johnson; Tarun Khanna; John Koskinen; Philip Lader; Sandra O. Moose; Jay Morse, Jr.; Moises Naim; Sven Sandstrom; Andres Ricardo Gluski Weilert
Subsidiary: IPALCO Enterprises, Inc., Indianapolis, IN
International operations: Argentina; Australia; Austria; Bahamas; Bermuda; Bolivia; Brazil; British Virgin Islands; Bulgaria; Cameroon; Cayman Islands; Chile; China; Colombia; Cyprus; Czech Republic; Dominican Republic; El Salvador; France; Greece; Guernsey; Honduras; Hungary; India; Indonesia; Ireland; Italy; Jordan; Kazakhstan; Luxembourg; Malaysia; Netherlands; Nigeria; Pakistan; Panama; Peru; Philippines; Poland; Qatar; Russia; Singapore; South Africa; Spain; Sri Lanka; Trinidad & Tobago; Turkey; Uganda; Ukraine; United Arab Emirates; United Kingdom; Uruguay; Venezuela
Giving statement: Giving through the AES Corporation Corporate Giving Program.

Company EIN: 541163725

The AES Corporation Corporate Giving Program

4300 Wilson Blvd., 11th Fl.
Arlington, VA 22203-4168 (703) 522-1315
URL: http://www.aes.com/aes/index?page=corporate_responsibility

Purpose and activities: The AES Corporation matches contributions made by its employees to nonprofit organizations. Support is given on a national and international basis primarily in areas of company operations.
Fields of interest: General charitable giving.
Type of support: Employee matching gifts.
Geographic limitations: Giving on a national and international basis primarily in areas of company operations.
Application information: Applications not accepted. Contributes only through employee matching gifts.

48
Aetna Inc.

(formerly Aetna U.S. Healthcare Inc.)
151 Farmington Ave., RE2T
Hartford, CT 06156-0001 (860) 273-0123
FAX: (860) 975-3110

Company URL: http://www.aetna.com
Establishment information: Established in 1850.
Company type: Public company
Company ticker symbol and exchange: AET/NYSE
International Securities Identification Number: US00817Y1082
Business activities: Operates medical service plan; sells dental insurance; sells insurance; provides investment advisory services.
Business type (SIC): Insurance/accident and health; security and commodity services; insurance/title
Financial profile for 2012: Number of employees, 35,000; assets, $41,494,500,000; sales volume, $36,595,000,000; pre-tax net income, $2,545,400,000; expenses, $33,781,700,000; liabilities, $31,088,700,000
Fortune 1000 ranking: 2012—84th in revenues, 125th in profits, and 135th in assets
Forbes 2000 ranking: 2012—264th in sales, 360th in profits, and 558th in assets
Corporate officers: Mark T. Bertolini, Chair., Pres., and C.E.O.; Shawn M. Guertin, Sr. V.P. and C.F.O.; Margaret M. McCarthy, Exec. V.P., Opers.; William J. Casazza, Sr. V.P. and Genl. Counsel; Deanna Fidler, Sr. V.P., Human Resources; Robert M. Mead, V.P., Mktg. and Comms.
Board of directors: Mark T. Bertolini, Chair.; Fernando G. Aguirre; Frank M. Clark; Betsy Z. Cohen; Molly J. Coye, M.D.; Roger N. Farah; Barbara Hackman Franklin; Jeffrey E. Garten; Ellen M. Hancock; Richard J. Harrington; Edward J. Ludwig; Joseph P. Newhouse
Giving statement: Giving through the Aetna Inc. Corporate Giving Program and the Aetna Foundation, Inc.
Company EIN: 232229683

Aetna Inc. Corporate Giving Program

c/o Corp. Contribs.
151 Farmington Ave.
Hartford, CT 06156-3180 (860) 273-6382
URL: http://www.aetna.com/about/aetna/cr/

Financial data (yr. ended 12/31/09): Total giving, $8,772,966, including $8,772,966 for grants.
Purpose and activities: As a complement to its foundation, Aetna also makes charitable contributions to nonprofit organizations directly. Support is given on a national basis in areas of company operations.
Fields of interest: Arts; Nursing school/education; Education; Health care, equal rights; Hospitals (general); Dental care; Public health, obesity; Public health, physical fitness; Health care; End of life care; Palliative care; Mental health, depression; Mental health/crisis services; Diabetes; Nutrition; Housing/shelter, development; Children, services; Residential/custodial care, hospices; Civil/human rights, equal rights; Community/economic development; Public affairs Economically disadvantaged.
Type of support: Conferences/seminars; Continuing support; Employee matching gifts; Employee volunteer services; General/operating support; Program development; Scholarship funds; Sponsorships.
Geographic limitations: Giving on a national basis in areas of company operations.
Publications: Application guidelines; Corporate giving report.

Aetna Foundation, Inc.

(formerly Aetna Life & Casualty Foundation, Inc.)
151 Farmington Ave., RE2R
Hartford, CT 06156-3180
FAX: (860) 273-7764;
E-mail: aetnafoundation@aetna.com; URL: http://www.aetna.com/foundation

Establishment information: Incorporated in 1972 in CT.
Donors: Aetna Inc.; Aetna Life Insurance Company; Aetna Health Inc.
Financial data (yr. ended 12/31/11): Assets, $70,141,641 (M); expenditures, $13,994,163; qualifying distributions, $11,681,417; giving activities include $11,681,417 for 216 grants (high: $2,741,729; low: $100).
Purpose and activities: The foundation supports programs designed to promote wellness, health, and access to high-quality care. Special emphasis is directed toward obesity; racial and ethnic health care equity; and integrated health care.
Fields of interest: Medical school/education; Health care, public policy; Health care, equal rights; Hospitals (general); Health care, clinics/centers; Health care, infants; Medical care, rehabilitation; Public health; Public health, obesity; Public health, physical fitness; Health care, cost containment; Health care, patient services; Health care; Food services; Food banks; Nutrition Children; Minorities; Women; Economically disadvantaged.
Programs:

AcademyHealth/Aetna Foundation Minority Scholars Program: The foundation, in partnership with AcademyHealth, provides professional development, mentoring, and networking opportunities for 15 graduate-level students and postdoctoral fellows to attract men and women from underrepresented groups to the field of racial and ethnic disparities in health outcomes and access to care. The program is administered by AcademyHealth.

Aetna Foundation/National Medical Fellowship Healthcare Leadership Program: The foundation, in partnership with National Medical Fellowships (NMF), provides $5,000 scholarships to second and third-year medical students from underrepresented minority groups. Recipients commit to practice medicine in medically underserved communities. The program as administered by National Medical Fellowships. Visit URL http://www.nmfonline.org/programs/aetna-foundation for more information.

Employee Matching Gifts: The foundation matches contributions made by employees, retirees, directors, selected agents, and the spouses and domestic partners of employees of Aetna for disater relief and to nonprofit organizations from $25 to $5,000 per contributor, per year.

Four Directions Summer Research Program: Through the Four Directions Summer Research Program, American Indian and Alaska Native college students participate in an 8 week basic science or traditional research project at Harvard Medical School and Brigham and Women's Hospital. The program is designed to increase the number of AI/AN representatives in medicine, science, and health care. Students receive career development training, meet faculty from across the hospital and medical school, and participate in a variety of social networking events. Visit URL http://www.fdsrp.org/index.html for more information.

Integrated Health Care: The foundation supports programs designed to advance high-quality health care through care coordination that builds on strong primary care; and promote evidence-based models of care coordination that can lead to high-quality, patient-centered health care services, improve health outcomes, and lower costs.

Obesity: The foundation supports programs designed to address the rising rate of obesity among U.S. adults and children. Special emphasis is directed toward programs designed to address the contributors to obesity among minority populations, and what supports and sustains proper eating and reduces inactivity.

Racial and Ethnic Health Care Equity: The foundation supports programs designed to promote equity in health and health care for common chronic conditions and infant mortality. Special emphasis is directed toward programs designed to improve health and health care among the nation's Medicaid population, particularly in settings with large numbers of minority patients; and address infant mortality.

Volunteer Grants: The foundation awards grants of up to $300 to nonprofit organizations with which employees and retirees of Aetna volunteer at least 20 hours per year.

Type of support: Conferences/seminars; Employee matching gifts; Employee volunteer services; Matching/challenge support; Program development; Research; Scholarship funds; Sponsorships.
Geographic limitations: Giving primarily in areas of company operations in Phoenix, AZ, Los Angeles, Fresno, San Diego, and San Francisco, CA, CT, Washington, DC, Miami and Tampa, FL, Atlanta, GA, Chicago, IL, Baltimore, MD, ME, Charlotte, NC, NJ, New York, NY, Cleveland and Columbus, OH, Philadelphia and Pittsburgh, PA, Austin, Dallas, Houston, and San Antonio, TX, and WA; giving also to national and regional organizations.
Support limitations: No support for religious organizations not of direct benefit to the entire community. No grants to individuals, or for scholarships, endowments, capital campaigns, construction, renovation, or equipment, direct delivery of reimbursable healthcare services, biomedical research, advertising, golf tournaments, advocacy, political causes, or events, or general operating support or deficits.
Publications: Annual report; Application guidelines; Grants list; Newsletter; Program policy statement.
Application information: Applications accepted. Grants range from $50,000 to $150,000 for national grants and from $25,000 to $50,000 for regional grants. Organizations receiving support are asked to show the impact of their work through

measurement and evaluation, communication and dissemination of results, and the sharing of best practices. Support is generally limited to 1 contribution per organization during any given year. Unsolicited requests for national grants are currently not accepted. Sponsorship applications are by invitation only. Applicants should submit the following:
1) timetable for implementation and evaluation of project
2) results expected from proposed grant
3) statement of problem project will address
4) population served
5) brief history of organization and description of its mission
6) geographic area to be served
7) how project's results will be evaluated or measured
8) list of company employees involved with the organization
9) explanation of why grantmaker is considered an appropriate donor for project
10) listing of board of directors, trustees, officers and other key people and their affiliations
11) detailed description of project and amount of funding requested
12) plans for cooperation with other organizations, if any
13) contact person
14) copy of current year's organizational budget and/or project budget

Initial approach: Complete online proposal for regional grants
Board meeting date(s): Apr. and Dec.
Deadline(s): Jan. 1 to Oct. 31 for regional grants
Final notification: 150 days

Officers and Directors:* Mark T. Bertolini*, Chair.; Gilian R. Barclay, D.D.S., DrPH, V.P.; Sharon C. Dalton*, V.P.; Judith Jones, Secy.; Elaine R. Confranceso, Treas.; Sheryl A. Burke; Molly J. Coye, M.D.; Jeffrey E. Garten; Jerald B. Gooden; Steven B. Kelmar; Susan M. Krosman, RN; Andrew J. Lee; Kristi A. Matus; Margaret M. McCarthy; Kay D. Mooney; Joseph P. Newhouse; Sandip Patel; Lonny Reisman, M.D.; Elease E. Wright.
Number of staff: 14 full-time professional.
EIN: 237241940
Selected grants: The following grants are a representative sample of this grantmaker's funding activity:
$200,000 to Project HOPE - The People-to-People Health Foundation, Millwood, VA, 2009. For Health Care Cost Containment Thematic Issue.
$125,000 to American Heart Association, Cleveland, OH, 2009. For Columbus Start and Cleveland Kids at Heart.
$99,620 to Massachusetts General Hospital, Boston, MA, 2009. For Training New Leaders in the Field of Racial and Ethnic Disparities.
$80,000 to Greater Hartford Arts Council, Hartford, CT, 2009. For United Arts Campaign Aetna First Thursdays and Street Banners.
$80,000 to Saint Francis Hospital and Medical Center Foundation, Hartford, CT, 2009. For Building Today for the Miracles of Tomorrow and Honoring Those Who Care.
$75,000 to American Heart Association, Dallas, TX, 2009. For Start Heart Walk Dallas.
$70,000 to Horace Bushnell Memorial Hall, Hartford, CT, 2009. For Lead Sponsor of the Performer newsletter and Bill Cosby show, and Patron Accessibility Sponsor.
$25,000 to Seattle Childrens Hospital Foundation, Seattle, WA, 2009. For Adaptation of Child Obesity Treatment for a Low-Income Setting.
$20,000 to Cathedral Arts Project, Jacksonville, FL, 2009. For Changing Young Lives through the Arts.
$15,000 to Leukemia & Lymphoma Society, Columbus, OH, 2009. For Light the Night.

49
Aexcel Corporation

7373 Production Dr.
Mentor, OH 44060-4858 (440) 974-3800

Company URL: http://www.aexcelcorp.com
Establishment information: Established in 1974.
Company type: Private company
Business activities: Manufactures industrial paints.
Business type (SIC): Paints and allied products
Corporate officer: John S. Milgram, Pres.
Giving statement: Giving through the Paintstone Foundation.

The Paintstone Foundation

7373 Production Dr.
Mentor, OH 44060-4858

Establishment information: Established in 1986 in OH.
Donors: Aexcel Corp.; Joseph B. Milgram, Jr.
Financial data (yr. ended 12/31/11): Assets, $570,757 (M); gifts received, $30,000; expenditures, $73,324; qualifying distributions, $64,000; giving activities include $64,000 for grants.
Purpose and activities: The foundation supports food banks and organizations involved with music, education, health, and international affairs.
Fields of interest: Arts; Agriculture/food; Human services.
Type of support: General/operating support.
Support limitations: No grants.
Application information: Applications not accepted. Unsolicited requests for funds not accepted.
Trustees: Andrew Milgram; John S. Milgram; Joseph B. Milgram, Jr.; Margaretta S.C. Milgram; Thomas Milgram.
EIN: 341538822

50
AFC Enterprises, Inc.

400 Perimeter Ctr. Terr., Ste.1000
Atlanta, GA 30346 (404) 459-4450
FAX: (404) 459-4450

Company URL: http://www.afce.com/
Establishment information: Established in 1992.
Company type: Public company
Company ticker symbol and exchange: AFCE/NASDAQ
Business activities: Develops, operates, and franchises quick-service restaurants, bakeries, and cafes.
Business type (SIC): Restaurants and drinking places
Financial profile for 2012: Number of employees, 1,280; assets, $172,400,000; sales volume, $178,800,000; pre-tax net income, $47,700,000; expenses, $127,500,000; liabilities, $138,200,000
Corporate officers: John M. Cranor III, Chair.; Ralph W. Bower, Pres.; Cheryl A. Bachelder, C.E.O.; Andrew G. Skehan, C.O.O.; H. Melville Hope III, C.F.O.; Harold M. Cohen, Sr. V.P., Genl. Counsel, and Corp. Secy.
Board of directors: John M. Cranor III, Chair.; Krishnan Anand; Victor Arias, Jr.; Cheryl A. Bachelder; Carolyn Hogan Byrd; John F. Hoffner; R. William Ide III; Kelvin J. Pennington
Division: Popeyes Chicken & Biscuits, Atlanta, GA
Giving statement: Giving through the AFC Enterprises, Inc. Corporate Giving Program and the AFC Foundation, Inc.
Company EIN: 582016606

AFC Enterprises, Inc. Corporate Giving Program

c/o Community Affairs
5555 Glenridge Connector NE, Ste. 300
Atlanta, GA 30342 (404) 459-4450
URL: http://popeyes.com/company/corporate-responsibility.php
Additional URL: http://www.popeyes.com/giving.php

Purpose and activities: As a complement to its foundation, AFC also makes charitable contributions to nonprofit organizations directly. Support is given primarily in areas of company operations.
Type of support: Donated products; In-kind gifts.
Geographic limitations: Giving primarily in areas of company operations.
Application information: Applications accepted.
Initial approach: Contact nearest restaurant location in writing

51
Affiliated Managers Group, Inc.

600 Hale St.
Prides Crossing, MA 01965 (617) 747-3300
FAX: (617) 747-3380

Company URL: http://www.amg.com
Establishment information: Established in 1993.
Company type: Public company
Company ticker symbol and exchange: AMG/NYSE
Business activities: Operates global asset management company.
Business type (SIC): Security and commodity services
Financial profile for 2012: Number of employees, 2,230; assets, $6,187,100,000; sales volume, $1,805,500,000; pre-tax net income, $495,200,000; expenses, $1,405,100,000; liabilities, $4,102,900,000
Corporate officers: Sean M. Healey, Chair. and C.E.O.; John Kingston III, Vice-Chair. and Genl. Counsel; Nathaniel Dalton, Pres. and C.O.O.; Jay C. Horgen, Exec. V.P. and C.F.O.
Board of directors: Sean M. Healey, Chair.; Samuel T. Byrne; Dwight D. Churchill; Harold J. Meyerman; William J. Nutt; Tracy P. Palandjian; Rita M. Rodriguez; Patrick T. Ryan; Jide J. Zeitlin
Giving statement: Giving through the Affiliated Managers Group, Inc. and the AMG Charitable Foundation.
Company EIN: 043218510

The AMG Charitable Foundation

600 Hale St.
Prides Crossing, MA 01965

Donor: Affiliated Managers Group, Inc.
Financial data (yr. ended 12/31/11): Assets, $572,757 (M); gifts received, $632,728; expenditures, $47,681; qualifying distributions, $47,681; giving activities include $26,000 for 2 grants (high: $25,000; low: $1,000).
Fields of interest: Human services.
Application information: Applications not accepted. Unsolicited request for funds not accepted.

Officers and Directors:* Sean M. Healey*, Pres.; John Kingston III*, Secy. and Treas.; Jennifer Benson Kelley*, Exec. Dir.
EIN: 364703120

52
Affinity Health Plan
2500 Halsey St.
Bronx, NY 10461-3637 (718) 794-7700

Company URL: http://www.affinityplan.org
Establishment information: Established in 1986.
Company type: Private company
Business activities: Operates medical service plan.
Business type (SIC): Insurance/accident and health
Corporate officers: Bertram Scott, Pres. and C.E.O.; Robert Brown, Exec. V.P. and C.O.O.; Mark T. Corcoran, Exec. V.P. and C.F.O.; Robert Allen, Sr. V.P. and C.I.O.; Ann M. Van Etten, V.P., Human Resources
Giving statement: Giving through the Affinity Health Plan Corporate Giving Program.

Affinity Health Plan Corporate Giving Program
2500 Halsey St.
Bronx, NY 10461-3637 (718) 794-7700
FAX: (718) 794-7815;
E-mail: community@affinityplan.org; URL: https://www.affinityplan.org/Affinity/Who_We_Are/In_the_Community.aspx

Purpose and activities: Affinity makes charitable contributions to nonprofit organizations involved with education, youth development, health care, and housing; giving also to national organizations. Support is given primarily in areas of company operations in Bronx, Kings, New York, Nassau, Orange, Queens, Rockland, Suffolk, and Westchester counties, New York.
Fields of interest: Education; Health care; Housing/shelter; Youth development.
Type of support: Continuing support; General/operating support.
Geographic limitations: Giving primarily in areas of company operations in Bronx, Kings, New York, Nassau, Orange, Queens, Rockland, Suffolk, and Westchester counties, NY.
Application information: Applications accepted.
Initial approach: E-mail proposal to Community Relations

53
AFL Philadelphia, LLC
(doing business as Philadelphia Soul Football Team)
1635 Market St., Ste. 1700
Philadelphia, PA 19103-2208
(215) 636-0421

Establishment information: Established in 2003.
Company type: Private company
Business activities: Operates arena football club.
Business type (SIC): Commercial sports
Corporate officers: Bon Jovi, Chair.; Leo Carlin, Pres.; John Adams, C.O.O.
Board of director: Bon Jovi, Chair.
Giving statement: Giving through the Jon Bon Jovi Soul Foundation.

Jon Bon Jovi Soul Foundation
(formerly Philadelphia Soul Charitable Foundation)
1635 Market St., 17th Fl.
Philadelphia, PA 19103-2208
E-mail: info@jbjsoulfoundation.org; URL: http://www.jonbonjovisoulfoundation.org

Establishment information: Established in 2006 in PA.
Contact: Mimi Box, Exec. Dir.
Financial data (yr. ended 12/31/11): Revenue, $1,527,446; assets, $3,433,426 (M); gifts received, $1,465,000; expenditures, $399,811; giving activities include $31,400 for grants.
Purpose and activities: The foundation seeks to combat issues that force families and individuals into economic despair through the creation of programs and partnerships targeted at breaking the cycle of poverty and homelessness.
Fields of interest: Housing/shelter; Human services Economically disadvantaged.
Application information: Applications not accepted. Unsolicited requests for funds not accepted.
Officers and Board Members:* Jon Bon Jovi*, Chair.; Craig Spencer*, Vice-Chair.; Leo Carlin*, Pres.; Ron Jaworski*, V.P.; Stephen Perna*, V.P.; Sara Peters*, Secy.; Paul Korzilius*, Treas.; Heather Goldfarb*, Asst. Treas.; Mimi Box*, Exec. Dir.; Sr. Mary Scullion.
EIN: 205036346

54
Aflac Incorporated
1932 Wynnton Rd.
Columbus, GA 31999 (706) 323-3431
FAX: (706) 324-6330

Company URL: http://www.aflac.com
Establishment information: Established in 1955.
Company type: Public company
Company ticker symbol and exchange: AFL/NYSE
International Securities Identification Number: US0010551028
Business activities: Operates supplemental health and life insurance company.
Business type (SIC): Insurance/accident and health
Financial profile for 2012: Number of employees, 8,673; assets, $131,094,000,000; sales volume, $25,364,000,000; pre-tax net income, $4,302,000,000; expenses, $21,062,000,000; liabilities, $115,116,000,000
Fortune 1000 ranking: 2012—118th in revenues, 67th in profits, and 48th in assets
Forbes 2000 ranking: 2012—367th in sales, 204th in profits, and 197th in assets
Corporate officers: Daniel P. Amos, Chair. and C.E.O.; Kriss Cloninger III, Pres., C.F.O., and Treas.; Joey M. Loudermilk, Exec. V.P., Genl. Counsel, and Secy.; Laree R. Daniel, Sr. V.P. ,Sales; Eric M. Kirsch, Exec. V.P. and C.I.O.
Board of directors: Daniel P. Amos, Chair.; John Shelby Amos II; Paul S. Amos II; Kriss Cloninger III; Elizabeth J. Hudson; Douglas W. Johnson; Robert B. Johnson; Charles B. Knapp, Ph.D.; E. Stephen Purdom, M.D.; Barbara K. Rimer; Marvin R. Schuster; Melvin T. Stith; David Gary Thompson; Takuro Yoshida
Giving statement: Giving through the Aflac Corporate Giving Program and the Aflac Foundation, Inc.
Company EIN: 581167100

Aflac Corporate Giving Program
1932 Wynnton Rd.
Columbus, GA 31999-0001
URL: http://www.aflac.com/aboutaflac/corporatephilanthropy/communityinvolvement.aspx

Purpose and activities: As a complement to its foundation, Aflac also makes charitable contributions to nonprofit organizations directly. Special emphasis is directed towards programs designed to address pediatric cancer. Support is given primarily in Georgia.
Fields of interest: Arts; Education; Health care; Cancer; Pediatrics; Cancer research; Youth development; Children/youth, services.
Type of support: Employee volunteer services; General/operating support.
Geographic limitations: Giving primarily in GA, with emphasis on Atlanta and the Columbus area; giving on a national basis for pediatric cancer.
Administrators: Francine Medley, Admin., The Aflac Fdn., Inc.; Kathelen Spencer, Chair., Corp. Contribs.
Number of staff: 2 full-time professional; 1 part-time professional.
Selected grants: The following grants are a representative sample of this grantmaker's funding activity:
$50,000 to Carter Center, Atlanta, GA, 2005.
$20,167 to Riley Hospital for Children, Indianapolis, IN, 2005.
$20,000 to Easter Seals North Georgia, Atlanta, GA, 2005.
$16,807 to Saint Jude Childrens Research Hospital, Atlanta, GA, 2005.
$15,000 to Camp Sunshine, Decatur, GA, 2005.
$10,084 to Childrens Hospital of Alabama, Birmingham, AL, 2005.
$10,000 to Prevent Cancer Foundation, Alexandria, VA, 2005.
$5,000 to Columbus Museum, Columbus, GA, 2005.
$5,000 to Juvenile Diabetes Research Foundation International, Atlanta, GA, 2005.
$4,000 to Ronald McDonald House Charities of West Georgia, Columbus, GA, 2005.
$2,000 to Georgia Council for the Hearing Impaired, Decatur, GA, 2005.

The Aflac Foundation, Inc.
1932 Wynnton Rd.
Columbus, GA 31999-0001
FAX: (706) 320-2288; E-mail: fmedley@aflac.com; Additional e-mail: corporatephilanthropy@aflac.com; URL: http://www.aflac.com/us/en/aboutaflac/communityinvolvement.aspx

Establishment information: Established in 1999 in GA.
Donor: American Family Life Assurance Co. of Columbus.
Contact: Francine Medley, Admin.
Financial data (yr. ended 12/31/11): Assets, $3,420,427 (M); gifts received, $4,851,039; expenditures, $5,327,053; qualifying distributions, $5,327,039; giving activities include $5,327,039 for 67 grants (high: $2,000,000; low: $5,000).
Purpose and activities: The foundation supports organizations involved with arts and culture, education, the environment, health, pediatric cancer, cancer research, human services, community development, civic affairs, and minorities.
Fields of interest: Museums; Arts; Education; Environment, water resources; Environment; Cancer; Cancer research; Children/youth, services; Human services; Community/economic development; United Ways and Federated Giving Programs; Public affairs Minorities.

Type of support: Annual campaigns; Capital campaigns; Cause-related marketing; Employee volunteer services; Endowments; Fellowships; General/operating support; Program development; Research; Scholarship funds.
Geographic limitations: Giving primarily in areas of company operations, with emphasis on the greater Atlanta, GA, area.
Support limitations: No support for religious or political organizations or private secondary schools. No grants to individuals.
Publications: Application guidelines.
Application information: Applications accepted. Support is limited to 1 contribution per organization during any given year. Application form not required. Applicants should submit the following:
1) population served
2) copy of IRS Determination Letter
3) geographic area to be served
4) copy of most recent annual report/audited financial statement/990
5) how project's results will be evaluated or measured
6) listing of board of directors, trustees, officers and other key people and their affiliations
7) detailed description of project and amount of funding requested
8) listing of additional sources and amount of support

Initial approach: Download application form and mail to foundation
Copies of proposal: 1
Board meeting date(s): Bi-monthly
Deadline(s): None

Officers: Kathleen V. Amos, Pres.; Audrey Tilman, V.P.; Alfred O. Blackmar, Secy.; Teresa White, Treas.
EIN: 582509396
Selected grants: The following grants are a representative sample of this grantmaker's funding activity:
$2,000,000 to Childrens Healthcare of Atlanta, Atlanta, GA, 2011. For capital campaign.
$600,000 to United Way of the Chattahoochee Valley, Columbus, GA, 2011. For annual campaign.
$543,000 to Community Foundation of the Chattahoochee Valley, Columbus, GA, 2011. For general support.
$285,000 to American Association for Cancer Research, Philadelphia, PA, 2011. For cancer research.
$200,000 to UPtown Columbus, Columbus, GA, 2011. For Chattahoochee River Restoration Project.
$100,000 to National Center for Civil and Human Rights, Atlanta, GA, 2011. For general support.
$100,000 to Saint Anne School, Columbus, GA, 2011. For general support.
$50,000 to Springer Opera House Arts Association, Columbus, GA, 2011. For capital campaign.
$25,000 to Rally Foundation, Sandy Springs, GA, 2011. For general support.
$15,000 to Beads of Courage, Tucson, AZ, 2011. For general support.

55
Ag Processing Inc.

(also known as AGP)
12700 W. Dodge Rd.
P.O. Box 2047
Omaha, NE 68154 (402) 496-7809

Company URL: http://www.agp.com
Establishment information: Established in 1983.
Company type: Cooperative
Business activities: Sells grains and grain products wholesale.
Business type (SIC): Farm-product raw materials—wholesale
Financial profile for 2009: Number of employees, 300; assets, $1,080,000,000; sales volume, $3,380,000,000
Corporate officers: Bradley T. Davis, Chair. and Pres.; Lowell D. Wilson, Vice-Chair.; Keith Spackler, C.E.O.; Mark Craigmile, Sr. V.P., Opers.; Gregory Twist, Sr. V.P., Mktg.; Dean B. Isaacson, Secy.-Treas.
Board of directors: Bradley T. Davis, Chair.; Lowell D. Wilson, Vice-Chair.; Bruce Granquist; Ellis Hein; Dean B. Isaacson; Dave Leiting; Steve Longval; Larry Oltjen; Randy Robeson; Lowell D. Wilson
Giving statement: Giving through the AGP Corporate Giving Program.

AGP Corporate Giving Program

12700 W. Dodge Rd.
Omaha, NE 68154-2154

Contact: Mike Mardnell
Purpose and activities: AGP makes charitable contributions to nonprofit organizations involved with education and agriculture. Support is given primarily in the Midwest.
Fields of interest: Education; Agriculture.
Type of support: Emergency funds; Employee volunteer services; General/operating support; In-kind gifts.
Geographic limitations: Giving primarily in the Midwest.
Application information: Applications not accepted. Contributes only to pre-selected organizations.

56
Agilent Technologies, Inc.

5301 Stevens Creek Blvd.
Santa Clara, CA 95051 (408) 345-8886
FAX: (408) 345-8474

Company URL: http://www.agilent.com
Establishment information: Established in 1983.
Company type: Public company
Company ticker symbol and exchange: A/NYSE
International Securities Identification Number: US00846U1016
Business activities: Designs and manufactures test, measurement, and monitoring instruments, systems, and solutions, semiconductor products, and optical components.
Business type (SIC): Laboratory apparatus; electronic components and accessories
Financial profile for 2012: Number of employees, 20,500; assets, $10,536,000,000; sales volume, $6,858,000,000; pre-tax net income, $1,153,000,000; expenses, $5,739,000,000; liabilities, $5,354,000,000
Fortune 1000 ranking: 2012—371st in revenues, 177th in profits, and 371st in assets
Forbes 2000 ranking: 2012—1192nd in sales, 532nd in profits, and 1422nd in assets
Corporate officers: James G. Cullen, Chair.; William P. Sullivan, C.E.O.; Ron Nersesian, Pres. and C.O.O.; Didier Hirsch, Sr. V.P. and C.F.O.; Marie Oh Huber, Sr. V.P., Genl. Counsel, and Secy.; Jean M. Halloran, Sr. V.P., Human Resources; Neil Dougherty, V.P. and Treas.
Board of directors: James G. Cullen, Chair.; Paul N. Clark; Heidi Fields; Robert J. Herbold; Koh Boon Hwee; David Mckinnon Lawrence, M.D.; A. Barry Rand; Tadataka Yamada, M.D.; William P. Sullivan
International operations: Belgium; Canada; Cayman Islands; China; Germany; Ireland; Italy; Japan; Luxembourg; Malaysia; Netherlands; Singapore; South Korea; Switzerland; Taiwan; United Kingdom
Giving statement: Giving through the Agilent Technologies, Inc. Corporate Giving Program and the Agilent Technologies Foundation.
Company EIN: 770518772

Agilent Technologies, Inc. Corporate Giving Program

5301 Stevens Creek Blvd.
Santa Clara, CA 95051-7201 (408) 345-8886
FAX: (408) 345-8474; URL: http://www.agilent.com/comm_relation/index.html

Purpose and activities: As a complement to its foundation, Agilent Technologies also makes charitable contributions to nonprofit organizations directly. Support is given primarily in areas of company operations, with emphasis on California.
Fields of interest: Education; Science, formal/general education.
Type of support: Continuing support; General/operating support; Program development.
Geographic limitations: Giving primarily in areas of company operations, with emphasis on CA.
Application information: Applications accepted.
Initial approach: Contact nearest public affairs manager for application information

Agilent Technologies Foundation

5301 Stevens Creek Blvd., MS 1B-07
Santa Clara, CA 95051-7201
E-mail: foundation@agilent.com; URL: http://www.agilent.com/contributions/foundation.html

Establishment information: Established in 2001 in CA.
Donor: Agilent Technologies, Inc.
Financial data (yr. ended 10/31/11): Assets, $9,308,199 (M); gifts received, $6,000,000; expenditures, $4,148,096; qualifying distributions, $4,111,433; giving activities include $2,992,391 for 75 grants (high: $310,894; low: $1,000) and $814,251 for employee matching gifts.
Purpose and activities: The foundation supports programs designed to increase student interest and achievement in science education, with an emphasis directed towards populations underrepresented in the technology industry. It also funds university research at the frontiers of measurement in electronics and biosciences.
Fields of interest: Elementary/secondary education; Higher education; Employment, services; Disasters, preparedness/services; Science, formal/general education; Chemistry; Engineering/technology; Biology/life sciences; Science Minorities; Women.
Program:
Pre-University Science Education Grants: The foundation supports programs designed to promote pre-university science education by addressing the future workforce readiness of students for the technology industry and academic research while building general scientific literacy. Special emphasis is directed toward programs that focus on improving science teaching capability, with the intention to create a multiplier effect.
Type of support: Building/renovation; Conferences/seminars; Curriculum development; Employee matching gifts; Employee volunteer services; General/operating support; Program development; Program evaluation; Research; Seed money; Sponsorships.
Geographic limitations: Giving primarily in areas of company operations, with emphasis on CA, CO, DE, Canada, China, Germany, India, Japan, and Taiwan.

Support limitations: No support for home schools, sectarian or denominational organizations, discriminatory organizations, or health or human services organizations. No grants to individuals, or for luncheons, dinners, or auctions, annual campaigns, endowments or capital campaigns, political activities, television or radio productions, or personal websites.
Publications: Corporate giving report; Financial statement.
Application information: Applications not accepted. Unsolicited applications are not accepted.
Board meeting date(s): Apr.
Officers and Directors: William P. Sullivan, Chair. and Pres.; Marie Oh Huber, V.P. and Secy.; Hilliard C. Terry III, V.P. and Treas.; Cynthia D. Johnson, V.P.; Laurie Nichol, Exec. Dir.; Didier Hirsch; Darlene Solomon.
Number of staff: 2 full-time professional; 1 full-time support.
EIN: 770532250

57
AGL Resources Inc.

10 Peachtree Pl., N.E.
P.O. Box 4569
Atlanta, GA 30309 (404) 584-4000
FAX: (404) 584-3945

Company URL: http://www.aglresources.com
Establishment information: Established in 1856.
Company type: Public company
Company ticker symbol and exchange: GAS/NYSE
Business activities: Operates public utility holding company; distributes natural gas.
Business type (SIC): Gas production and distribution; holding company
Financial profile for 2012: Number of employees, 6,121; assets, $14,141,000,000; sales volume, $3,922,000,000; pre-tax net income, $450,000,000; expenses, $3,312,000,000; liabilities, $10,728,000,000
Fortune 1000 ranking: 2012—597th in revenues, 502nd in profits, and 309th in assets
Corporate officers: John W. Somerhalder II, Chair., Pres., and C.E.O.; Andrew W. Evans, Exec. V.P. and C.F.O.; Paul R. Shlanta, Exec. V.P. and Genl. Counsel; Bryan E. Seas, Sr. V.P., and C.A.O.; Joe Surber, Sr. V.P. and C.I.O.; Marshall Lang, Sr. V.P., Mktg.
Board of directors: John W. Somerhalder II, Chair.; Sandra N. Bane; Thomas D. Bell, Jr.; Norman R. Bobins; Charles R. Crisp; Brenda J. Gaines; Arthur E. Johnson; Wyck A. Knox, Jr.; Dennis M. Love; Charles H. McTier; Dean R. O'Hare; Armando J. Olivera; John E. Rau; James A. Rubright; Bettina M. Whyte; Henry C. Wolf
Subsidiaries: Atlanta Gas Light Company, Atlanta, GA; Chattanooga Gas Co., Chattanooga, TN; Georgia Natural Gas Co., Atlanta, GA; Sequent Energy Management, LP, Houston, TX; Virginia Natural Gas , Inc., Norfolk, VA
Historic mergers: NUI Corporation (November 30, 2004); Nicor Inc. (December 9, 2011)
Giving statement: Giving through the AGL Resources Inc. Corporate Giving Program, the AGL Foundation, and the AGL Resources Private Foundation, Inc.
Company EIN: 582210952

AGL Resources Inc. Corporate Giving Program

P.O. Box 4569
Atlanta, GA 30302-4569 (404) 584-4000
URL: http://www.aglresources.com/community/community.aspx

Purpose and activities: As a complement to its foundation, AGL Resources also makes charitable contributions to nonprofit organizations directly. Support is given primarily in areas of company operations in Florida, Georgia, Maryland, New Jersey, Tennessee, and Virginia.
Fields of interest: General charitable giving.
Type of support: Employee volunteer services; General/operating support; In-kind gifts; Sponsorships.
Geographic limitations: Giving primarily in areas of company operations in FL, GA, MD, NJ, TN, and VA.
Number of staff: 2 full-time professional; 2 full-time support.

AGL Foundation

c/o Northen Trust N.A.
P.O. Box 803878
Chicago, IL 60680-3878

Establishment information: Established in 1988 in FL.
Donors: AGL Resources Inc.; Adelyn Luther†.
Financial data (yr. ended 12/31/11): Assets, $9,093,314 (M); gifts received, $9,355,813; expenditures, $250,371; qualifying distributions, $160,784; giving activities include $154,000 for 12 grants (high: $50,000; low: $2,500).
Purpose and activities: The foundation supports clinics and organizations involved with performing arts, education, land conservation, and animal welfare.
Fields of interest: Performing arts; Higher education; Education; Environment, land resources; Animal welfare; Health care, clinics/centers.
Type of support: General/operating support.
Geographic limitations: Giving primarily in MT.
Support limitations: No grants to individuals.
Application information: Applications not accepted. Unsolicited requests for funds not accepted.
Officers: Richard E. Gordon, Pres.; Pattie E. Pastor, V.P.
EIN: 650098771

AGL Resources Private Foundation, Inc.

P.O. Box 4569, M.C. 1080
Atlanta, GA 30302-4569 (404) 584-3791
For organizations in the Nicor Gas service territory contact: amartinez@aglresources.com; URL: http://www.aglresources.com/community/guidelines.aspx

Establishment information: Established in 1998 in GA.
Donors: Georgia Gas Co.; AGL Foundation; AGL Resources Inc.
Contact: Melanie Platt, Pres.
Financial data (yr. ended 12/31/11): Assets, $5,027,141 (M); expenditures, $2,570,839; qualifying distributions, $2,546,043; giving activities include $2,532,135 for 239 grants (high: $500,000; low: $75).
Purpose and activities: The foundation supports organizations involved with arts and culture, K-12 and higher education, literacy, the environment, economic development, business, science, mathematics, leadership development, senior citizens, minorities, women, and economically disadvantaged people.
Fields of interest: Arts; Secondary school/education; Higher education; Education, reading; Environment, air pollution; Environment, natural resources; Environment, energy; Environment, beautification programs; Economic development; Business/industry; United Ways and Federated Giving Programs; Science, formal/general education; Mathematics; Leadership development Aging; Minorities; Women; Economically disadvantaged.
Programs:
Community Enrichment: The foundation supports programs designed to promote energy assistance; minority leadership; women leadership; arts and culture; and programs designed to serve low-income senior citizens.
Education: The foundation supports K-12 public secondary schools, colleges, and universities. Special emphasis is directed toward programs designed to promote literacy, math, and science.
Energy Assistance: The foundation supports programs designed to help low-income households and senior citizens afford natural gas consumption; promote weatherization projects; and provide emergency energy assistance.
Environmental Stewardship: The foundation supports programs designed to promote clean air, conservation, and green space.
Organizational and Supplier Diversity: The foundation supports organizations designed to reflect the diversity of the AGL workplace and provide developmental opportunities and assistance to minority and women-owned businesses.
Type of support: Annual campaigns; Building/renovation; Capital campaigns; Emergency funds; Endowments; Program development; Scholarship funds; Seed money; Sponsorships.
Geographic limitations: Giving primarily in areas of company operations in FL, GA, IL, MD, NJ, TN, TX, and VA.
Support limitations: No support for religious organizations or private K-12 schools. No grants to individuals.
Publications: Application guidelines; Program policy statement.
Application information: Applications accepted. Visit website for application addresses. Application form required. Applicants should submit the following:
1) copy of IRS Determination Letter
2) brief history of organization and description of its mission
3) detailed description of project and amount of funding requested
4) listing of additional sources and amount of support

Initial approach: Download application form and mail application form and proposal to application address
Board meeting date(s): Quarterly
Deadline(s): Education, Environmental Stewardship, and Organizational and Supplier Diversity applications are reviewed in Quarter 1; Community Enrichment Quarter 2; and Energy Assistance in Quarter 3
Officers and Trustees: Melanie M. Platt, Pres.; Beth Reese, V.P.; Myra Bierria, Secy.; Bryan E. Seas, Treas.; Bryan Baston; SunTrust Bank.
EIN: 582399946
Selected grants: The following grants are a representative sample of this grantmaker's funding activity:
$12,500 to Teach for America, New York, NY, 2010. For program support.
$10,000 to American Heart Association, Dallas, TX, 2010. For program support.

$10,000 to Savannah College of Art and Design, Savannah, GA, 2010.
$5,000 to Chesapeake Bay Foundation, Annapolis, MD, 2010.
$5,000 to College of William and Mary, Williamsburg, VA, 2010.
$5,000 to Empty Stocking Fund, Atlanta, GA, 2010.
$5,000 to Southern Methodist University, Dallas, TX, 2010.
$5,000 to Trust for Public Land, San Francisco, CA, 2010. For program support.
$5,000 to United Negro College Fund, Fairfax, VA, 2010. For scholarship program.
$3,000 to Teach for America, New York, NY, 2010.

58
Agora Partnerships

920 U St., N.W.
Washington, DC 20001-4048
(202) 580-8776

Company URL: http://www.agorapartnerships.org
Establishment information: Established in 2004.
Company type: Private company
Business activities: Operates microfinance company.
Business type (SIC): Social services/miscellaneous; business services/miscellaneous
Corporate officers: Ben Powell, C.E.O.; Dorrit Lowsen, C.O.O.
Board of directors: Elizabeth Bibb Binder; Melissa Cheong; Ezra Friedman; Holly Huffman; Sue Igoe; Tabitha Jordan; Ben Powell; Eric Sillman; Sam Sussman
Giving statement: Giving through the Agora Partnerships.

Agora Partnerships

920 U St., NW
Washington, DC 20001-4048 (202) 580-8776
URL: http://www.agorapartnerships.org

Purpose and activities: Agora Partnerships is a certified B Corporation that donates a percentage of profits to charitable organizations. Support is given primarily in Central America, with emphasis on Nicaragua.
Fields of interest: Community development, small businesses Economically disadvantaged.
International interests: Central America.
Type of support: Income development.
Geographic limitations: Giving primarily in Central America, with emphasis on Nicaragua.

59
AgStar Financial Services, ACA

1921 Premier Dr.
P.O. Box 4249
Mankato, MN 56001-5901 (507) 387-4174

Establishment information: Established in 1918.
Company type: Cooperative
Business activities: Provides loans; leases agricultural equipment; sells agricultural, life, and disability insurance; provides financial consulting services; provides accounting services.
Business type (SIC): Non-depository credit institutions; insurance/life; insurance/accident and health; insurance/fire, marine, and casualty; equipment rental and leasing/miscellaneous; accounting, auditing, and bookkeeping services; management and public relations services
Corporate officers: David Kretzschmar, Chair.; Lowell Schafer, Vice-Chair.; Paul A. DeBriyn, Pres. and C.E.O.; Rodney W. Hebrink, Sr. V.P. and C.F.O.; David R. Hoelmer, Sr. V.P. and Genl. Counsel; James G. McKissick, V.P., Comms.
Board of directors: David Kretzschmar, Chair.; Lowell Schafer, Vice-Chair.
Giving statement: Giving through the AgStar Fund for Rural America.

AgStar Fund for Rural America

1921 Premier Dr.
P.O. Box 4249
Mankato, MN 56002-4249 (952) 997-1255
E-mail: Melanie.Olson@Agstar.com; URL: http://www.agstar.com/enhancingamerica/fundforruralamerica/Pages/default.aspx
Additional tel.: (507) 345-5656

Contact: Melanie Olson
Financial data (yr. ended 12/31/09): Total giving, $681,179, including $661,179 for grants and $20,000 for 20 grants to individuals (high: $1,000; low: $1,000).
Purpose and activities: Through the AgStar Fund for Rural America, a direct corporate giving program, AgStar makes charitable contributions to nonprofit organizations involved with agriculture and rural development. Special emphasis is directed toward programs designed to educate young, beginning, or future farmers; maintain or improve the quality of the rural environment; support the advancement and utilization of technology for the benefit of farmers and rural communities; and enhance the quality of life for farmers and rural communities. Support is limited to areas of company operations.
Fields of interest: Libraries (public); Education; Environment; Agriculture; Agriculture, sustainable programs; Agriculture, farmlands; Disasters, preparedness/services; Disasters, fire prevention/control; Recreation, fairs/festivals; Youth development, agriculture; Human services; Rural development; Science.
Programs:

Agriculture Classroom Equipment Grant Program: AgStar awards equipment grants of up to $2,500 to high school agriculture classrooms in rural areas. The program is designed to help alleviate financial constraints for agriculture programs in rural high schools.

AgStar Scholars Program: AgStar, in partnership with the University of Minnesota - St. Paul and the University of Wisconsin - River Valley, supports students in their third year of college who are interested in agricultural financing or agricultural-related careers. The program includes a $2,000 scholarship; an orientation session; guest lectures by AgStar executives; a rural or agriculture-related research project to be completed by the scholar and presented to AgStar and university representatives; and a paid internship with AgStar. Applicants must have a GPA of 3.0 or better.

County Fair Facility Upgrade Grant Program: AgStar awards grants of up to $2,500 to local county fairs to repair livestock buildings, 4-H buildings, and livestock judging areas.

High School Senior Scholarships: AgStar annually awards fifteen $1,000 college scholarships to high school seniors pursuing agriculture-related degrees and five $1,000 scholarships to high school seniors with an agricultural or rural background who plan to continue their education in any field of study. Applicants must live in a AgStar service area and have GPA of 3.0 or higher. Applicants are selected based on academic achievement, leadership characteristics, and community involvement. Preference will be given to children of parents who are client of AgStar Financial Services, ACA.

Rural Feasibility Study Grant Program: AgStar awards grants to nonprofit organizations serving rural areas, educational institutions, and state, county, local, and tribal governments for feasibility studies that result in economic development for rural America.

Type of support: Equipment; General/operating support; Program development; Scholarships—to individuals; Sponsorships; Technical assistance.
Geographic limitations: Giving limited to areas of company operations in MN and northwestern WI.
Support limitations: No support for religious organizations not of direct benefit to the entire community, medical facilities, fraternal or veterans' organizations, arts-related facilities, or discriminatory organizations. No grants for political campaigns, medical research, fundraising activities including benefits, charitable dinners, annual fund drives, or sporting events, sponsorship of sporting teams or activities, construction or maintenance of recreational facilities including ballparks, bleachers, playground equipment, trails, health club memberships, or related transportation, debt reduction, or activities that benefit AgStar employees or directors; no loans.
Publications: Application guidelines; Grants list; Informational brochure.
Application information: Applications accepted. Applications of up to $2,500 will be reviewed by AgStar Fund Staff. Applications of more than $2,500 will be reviewed for approval by the Board of Trustees. Additional information and a site visit may be requested at a later date. Organizations receiving support are asked to provide a final report. Support is limited to $10,000 per organization during any given year. Multi-year funding is not automatic. Application form required.
Requests for scholarships should include letters of recommendation, transcripts, essay, and resume.

Initial approach: Complete online application form; download application form and mail to application address for scholarships and AgStar scholars
Copies of proposal: 1
Deadline(s): Oct. 1 to Nov. 30; Mar. 31 for County Fair Facility Upgrade Grants; May for Agriculture Classroom Equipment Grants; None for Rural Feasibility Study Grants; Jan 1 to Apr. 1 for scholarships; Jan. 14 for AgStar Scholars
Final notification: Mar.

Number of staff: 1 part-time professional.

60
J. F. Ahern Co.

855 Morris St.
P.O. Box 1316
Fond du Lac, WI 54935-5611
(920) 921-9020
FAX: (920) 921-8632

Company URL: http://www.jfahern.com
Establishment information: Established in 1880.
Company type: Private company
Business activities: Provides contract mechanical and fire protection services.
Business type (SIC): Contractors/plumbing, heating, and air-conditioning; contractors/electrical work
Financial profile for 2012: Number of employees, 1,000
Corporate officers: John E. Ahern, Chair.; John E. Ahern III, Pres. and C.E.O.; Ryan J. Bittner, V.P., Finance, and C.F.O.

Board of director: John E. Ahern, Chair.
Divisions: Ahern Fire Protection Div., Fond du Lac, WI; Commercial Contracting Div., Fond du Lac, WI; Industial Contracting Div., Fond du Lac, WI; Pipe Fabrication Div., Fond du Lac, WI
Offices: Itasca, Rockford, IL; Davenport, Des Moines, IA; Grand Rapids, MI; Minneapolis, MN; St. Louis, MO; Omaha, NE; Appleton, Eau Claire, Fond du Lac, Madison, Menomonee Falls, WI
Giving statement: Giving through the J. F. Ahern Company Foundation.

J. F. Ahern Company Foundation

855 Morris St.
Fond du Lac, WI 54935-5611

Establishment information: Established in 1989 in WI.
Donor: J.F. Ahern Co.
Contact: Bob Mathews, Secy. and Dir.
Financial data (yr. ended 06/30/11): Assets, $702,009 (M); gifts received, $50,000; expenditures, $62,649; qualifying distributions, $62,500; giving activities include $62,500 for 15 grants (high: $15,000; low: $1,000).
Purpose and activities: The foundation supports organizations involved with education, health, human services, and civic affairs. Special emphasis is directed toward programs designed to benefit children and youth and economically disadvantaged people.
Fields of interest: Education; Health care; Children/youth, services; Human services.
Type of support: Annual campaigns; Scholarship funds.
Geographic limitations: Giving primarily in western WI.
Support limitations: No grants to individuals.
Application information: Applications accepted. Application form required. Applicants should submit the following:
1) copy of IRS Determination Letter
2) brief history of organization and description of its mission
3) detailed description of project and amount of funding requested

Initial approach: Letter
Copies of proposal: 1
Board meeting date(s): May
Deadline(s): None

Officers and Directors:* John E. Ahern III*, Pres.; Bob Mathews*, Secy.; Alan R. Fox*, Treas.
EIN: 391667434

61
AHS Management Company, Inc.

1 Burton Hills Blvd., Ste. 250
Nashville, TN 37215-6293 (615) 296-3000

Establishment information: Established in 2001.
Company type: Subsidiary of a private company
Business activities: Provides management services.
Business type (SIC): Management and public relations services
Financial profile for 2010: Number of employees, 100
Corporate officers: David T. Vandewater, Pres.; Jamie E. Hopping, V.P. and C.O.O.; R. Dirk Allison, V.P. and C.F.O.; Stephen C. Petrovich, V.P. and Secy.; Ashley M. Crabtree, Treas.
Giving statement: Giving through the Ardent Community Foundation, Inc.

Ardent Community Foundation, Inc.

1 Burton Hills Blvd., Ste. 250
Nashville, TN 37215-6195

Establishment information: Established in 2002 in TN.
Donor: AHS Management Co., Inc.
Financial data (yr. ended 12/31/11): Assets, $12,915 (M); expenditures, $2,832; qualifying distributions, $2,481; giving activities include $2,481 for grants.
Purpose and activities: The foundation supports the United Way of Middle Tennessee.
Type of support: General/operating support.
Support limitations: No grants to individuals.
Application information: Applications not accepted. Unsolicited requests for funds not accepted.
Officers and Directors:* David Vandewater*, Pres.; Clint B. Adams, V.P.; J. Steve Hinkle, V.P.; Steve C. Petrovich*, Secy.; Ashley M. Crabtree, Treas.
EIN: 300122158

62
Air Liquide America L.P.

(formerly Air Liquide America Corp.)
2700 Post Oak Blvd., Ste. 1800
Houston, TX 77056-5797 (713) 624-8000

Company URL: http://www.us.airliquide.com
Establishment information: Established in 1902.
Company type: Subsidiary of a foreign company
Business activities: Manufactures and distributes welding equipment and oil field tools; produces industrial gases.
Business type (SIC): Machinery/metalworking; chemicals/industrial inorganic; machinery/construction, mining, and materials handling; industrial machinery and equipment—wholesale
Corporate officers: Piere Defaur, Pres. and C.E.O.; Fabienne Lecorvaisier, V.P., Finance and Admin.; Francois Abrial, V.P., Human Resources
Subsidiaries: Air Liquide, Houston, TX; Lacona Holdings Inc., Walnut Creek, CA; LAI Properties, Inc., Walnut Creek, CA; Vitalaire Corp., Walnut Creek, CA
Divisions: Alphagaz Div., Walnut Creek, CA; Cardox Div., Walnut Creek, CA; Package Gases Div., Walnut Creek, CA; Tempil Div., South Plainfield, NJ
Giving statement: Giving through the Air Liquide America L.P. Corporate Giving Program and the Air Liquide America Foundation, Inc.

Air Liquide America Foundation, Inc.

(formerly Big Three Industries Foundation, Inc.)
P.O. Box 460149
Houston, TX 77056-8149 (507) 931-1682

Establishment information: Established in 1993 in TX.
Donors: Air Liquide America Corp.; Air Liquide America L.P.; Air Liquid USA, LLC.
Financial data (yr. ended 12/31/11): Assets, $0 (M); gifts received, $90,500; expenditures, $90,500; qualifying distributions, $90,500; giving activities include $80,500 for 1 grant.
Purpose and activities: The foundation awards college scholarships to dependents of employees of Air Liquide America. The scholarship program is administered by Scholarship America, Inc.
Fields of interest: Higher education.
Type of support: Employee-related scholarships.
Application information: Applications accepted. Application form required.

Initial approach: Letter
Deadline(s): Mar. 10

Officers and Directors:* Scott Allen Krapf, Pres.; Kevin M. Feeney, Secy.; James G. Klatt*, Treas.; Art Dubose; Linda W. Krupps; Gary Prezbindowski.
EIN: 760366343

63
Air Products and Chemicals, Inc.

7201 Hamilton Blvd.
Allentown, PA 18195-1501 (610) 481-4911
FAX: (610) 481-5900

Company URL: http://www.airproducts.com
Establishment information: Established in 1940.
Company type: Public company
Company ticker symbol and exchange: APD/NYSE
International Securities Identification Number: US0091581068
Business activities: Manufactures industrial gas and related industrial process equipment; manufactures chemicals.
Business type (SIC): Chemicals/industrial inorganic; chemicals and allied products; laboratory apparatus
Financial profile for 2012: Number of employees, 21,300; assets, $16,941,800,000; sales volume, $9,611,700,000; pre-tax net income, $1,312,500,000; expenses, $8,329,300,000; liabilities, $10,464,600,000
Fortune 1000 ranking: 2012—273rd in revenues, 175th in profits, and 270th in assets
Forbes 2000 ranking: 2012—942nd in sales, 509th in profits, and 1060th in assets
Corporate officers: John E. McGlade, Chair., Pres., and C.E.O.; M. Scott Crocco, Sr. V.P. and C.F.O.; John D. Stanley, Sr. V.P., Genl. Counsel, and C.A.O.; Kevin B. Michaelis, V.P. and C.I.O.; George G. Bitto, V.P. and Treas.; Jennifer L. Grant, V.P., Human Resources; Elizabeth L. Klebe, V.P., Corp. Comms.; Richard Boocock, V.P., Opers.; Mary T. Afflerbach, Corp. Secy.
Board of directors: John E. McGlade, Chair.; Mario L. Baeza; Susan K. Carter; William L. Davis III; Chadwick C. Deaton; Michael J. Donahue; Ursula O. Fairbairn; W. Douglas Ford; Evert Henkes; David H. Y. Ho; Margaret G. McGlynn; Lawrence S. Smith
Subsidiaries: Air Products, L.P., Wilmington, DE; Air Products Manufacturing Corp., Allentown, PA; Prodair Corp., Wilmington, DE
International operations: Argentina; Austria; Bermuda; Brazil; Canada; China; Czech Republic; France; Germany; Indonesia; Ireland; Italy; Japan; Malaysia; Mexico; Netherlands; Norway; Peru; Poland; Portugal; Romania; Russia; Singapore; Slovakia; South Korea; Spain; Switzerland; Taiwan; Thailand; Trinidad & Tobago; United Kingdom
Giving statement: Giving through the Air Products and Chemicals, Inc. Corporate Giving Program and the Air Products Foundation.
Company EIN: 231274455

Air Products and Chemicals, Inc. Corporate Giving Program

c/o Corp. Rels.
7201 Hamilton Blvd.
Allentown, PA 18195-1501
FAX: (610) 706-6088;
E-mail: gostlelj@airproducts.com; URL: http://www.airproducts.com/social_responsibilities

Contact: Laurie Gostley-Hackett, Mgr., Community Rels. and Philanthropy
Purpose and activities: As a complement to its foundation, Air Products and Chemicals also makes

charitable contributions to nonprofit organizations directly. Support is given primarily in areas of company operations.
Fields of interest: Arts; Higher education; Education; Health care; Health organizations; Human services; Community/economic development; United Ways and Federated Giving Programs Economically disadvantaged.
Type of support: Donated equipment; Employee matching gifts; Employee volunteer services; General/operating support; In-kind gifts; Loaned talent; Matching/challenge support; Program development; Scholarship funds; Sponsorships; Use of facilities.
Geographic limitations: Giving primarily in areas of company operations, with emphasis on Allentown, PA.
Publications: Program policy statement.
Application information: Applications accepted. The Corporate Relations Department handles giving. The company has a staff that only handles contributions. Application form not required. Applicants should submit the following:
1) name, address and phone number of organization
2) copy of IRS Determination Letter
3) listing of board of directors, trustees, officers and other key people and their affiliations
4) detailed description of project and amount of funding requested
5) copy of current year's organizational budget and/ or project budget

Initial approach: Proposal to headquarters or nearest company facility
Copies of proposal: 1
Deadline(s): None
Final notification: 3 months

Number of staff: 2 full-time professional; 1 part-time support.

The Air Products Foundation

7201 Hamilton Blvd.
Allentown, PA 18195-1501 (610) 481-7020
E-mail: corprela@airproducts.com; Tel. for Timothy J. Holt: (610) 481-4911; URL: http://www.airproducts.com/company/sustainability/corporate-citizenship/charitable-giving-and-philanthropy.aspx

Establishment information: Incorporated in 1979 in PA.
Donor: Air Products and Chemicals, Inc.
Contact: Timothy J. Holt, Pres.
Financial data (yr. ended 09/30/11): Assets, $66,596,518 (M); expenditures, $5,076,107; qualifying distributions, $4,567,070; giving activities include $4,567,070 for grants.
Purpose and activities: The foundation supports organizations involved with arts and culture, education, the environment, health, safety and sustainability, human services, and community economic development.
Fields of interest: Arts; Higher education; Education; Environment; Health care; Safety/disasters; Human services; Community/economic development; United Ways and Federated Giving Programs.
Program:
Matching Gifts Program: The foundation matches contributions made by employees, retirees, directors, and the spouses of employees of Air Products and Chemicals to institutions of higher education and qualifying arts and cultural organizations on a one-for-one basis from $25 to $5,000 per contributor, per year for education and on a two-for-one basis from $25 to $2,000 per contributor, per year for arts and culture.
Type of support: Annual campaigns; Continuing support; Employee matching gifts; General/operating support.
Geographic limitations: Giving on a national basis in areas of major company operations.
Support limitations: No support for sectarian religious organizations, political or veterans' organizations, labor groups, service clubs, elementary or secondary schools, or United Way-supported organizations. No grants to individuals, or for capital campaigns or general operating support for health organizations or hospitals; no loans.
Publications: Application guidelines.
Application information: Applications accepted. Application form not required. Applicants should submit the following:
1) copy of IRS Determination Letter
2) brief history of organization and description of its mission
3) copy of most recent annual report/audited financial statement/990
4) how project's results will be evaluated or measured
5) list of company employees involved with the organization
6) listing of board of directors, trustees, officers and other key people and their affiliations
7) detailed description of project and amount of funding requested
8) copy of current year's organizational budget and/ or project budget

Initial approach: Proposal
Copies of proposal: 1
Board meeting date(s): Monthly
Deadline(s): May 15

Officers and Trustees:* John D. Stanley*, Chair.; Timothy J. Holt, Pres.; George G. Bitto, V.P. and Treas.; Charles G. Stinner, V.P.; Gregory E. Weigard, V.P.; Benjamin M. Hussa, Secy.; Paul E. Huck; Lynn C. Minella.
EIN: 232130928

65
Airgas, Inc.

259 N. Radnor-Chester Rd., Ste. 100
Radnor, PA 19087-5283 (610) 687-5253
FAX: (610) 225-3271

Company URL: http://www.airgas.com
Establishment information: Established in 1982.
Company type: Public company
Company ticker symbol and exchange: ARG/NYSE
Business activities: Distributes industrial, medical, and specialty gases.
Business type (SIC): Chemicals and allied products —wholesale
Financial profile for 2013: Number of employees, 15,000; assets, $5,618,230,000; sales volume, $4,957,500,000; pre-tax net income, $543,420,000; expenses, $4,361,080,000; liabilities, $4,081,240,000
Fortune 1000 ranking: 2012—509th in revenues, 455th in profits, and 573rd in assets
Forbes 2000 ranking: 2012—1409th in sales, 1462nd in profits, and 1783rd in assets
Corporate officers: Peter McCausland, Chair.; Michael L. Molinini, Pres. and C.E.O.; Robert M. McLaughlin, Sr. V.P. and C.F.O.; Robert A. Dougherty, Sr. V.P. and C.I.O.; Robert H. Young, Jr., Sr. V.P. and Genl. Counsel; Dwight T. Wilson, Sr. V.P., Human Resources
Board of directors: Peter McCausland, Chair.; John P. Clancey; James W. Hovey; Robert L. Lumpkins; Ted B. Miller, Jr.; Michael L. Molinini; Paula A. Sneed; David M. Stout; Lee M. Thomas; John C. van Roden; Ellen C. Wolf
Giving statement: Giving through the Airgas, Inc. Corporate Giving Program.
Company EIN: 560732648

Airgas, Inc. Corporate Giving Program

259 N. Radnor-Chester Rd., Ste. 100
Radnor, PA 19087-5283 (610) 687-5253

Purpose and activities: Airgas makes charitable contributions to organizations in areas of company operations.
Fields of interest: Employment, training; General charitable giving Military/veterans.
Type of support: Employee volunteer services; General/operating support; Technical assistance.
Geographic limitations: Giving primarily in areas of company operations.

64
Air-Rite Heating & Cooling, Inc.

100 Overland Dr.
North Aurora, IL 60542 (630) 264-1150

Company URL: http://www.air-rite.com
Establishment information: Established in 1959.
Company type: Private company
Business activities: Provides contract heating and air-conditioning services.
Business type (SIC): Contractors/plumbing, heating, and air-conditioning
Corporate officers: Lawrence Van Someren, Jr., Pres.; Deborah Evans, Treas.
Giving statement: Giving through the Larry & Dee VanSomeren Foundation.

Larry & Dee VanSomeren Foundation

c/o R. Lloyd & Company Ltd.
15127 S. 73rd Ave.
Orland Park, IL 60462-4398 (708) 429-9500

Establishment information: Established in 1995.
Donors: Air-Rite Heating & Cooling, Inc.; Larry Van Someren, Jr.; Denise Van Someren.
Financial data (yr. ended 03/31/12): Assets, $0 (M); expenditures, $11,108; qualifying distributions, $9,400; giving activities include $9,400 for grants.
Purpose and activities: The foundation supports community centers and organizations involved with youth development, children services, Catholicism, and other areas.
Fields of interest: Human services.
Type of support: General/operating support.
Geographic limitations: Giving limited to Chicago and Naperville, IL.
Support limitations: No grants to individuals.
Application information: Applications not accepted. Unsolicited requests for funds not accepted.
Officers: Larry Van Someren, Jr., Pres.; Denise VanSomeren, Secy.
EIN: 363948903

66

Airtek Construction, Inc.

700 Hudson St.
P.O. Box 388
Troy, AL 36079-8231 (334) 566-7400
FAX: (334) 566-7496

Company URL: http://www.airtek-troy.com
Establishment information: Established in 1988.
Company type: Private company
Business activities: Provides air pollution control equipment including engineering, construction, and maintenance services.
Business type (SIC): Repair shops/miscellaneous
Corporate officers: John Roberts, Pres.; Mark Smith, C.F.O.; Barry Smolcic, V.P., Opers.
Giving statement: Giving through the Burning Bush Foundation, Inc.

Burning Bush Foundation, Inc.

1299 Old Brantley Luverne Rd.
Luverne, AL 36049-4222

Establishment information: Established in 1999 in AL.
Donor: Airtek Construction, Inc.
Financial data (yr. ended 12/31/11): Assets, $34,920 (M); expenditures, $7,646; qualifying distributions, $7,137; giving activities include $4,137 for 4 grants (high: $1,923; low: $496) and $3,000 for 1 grant to an individual.
Purpose and activities: The foundation supports individuals who are poverty stricken in Luverne, Alabama, with emergency food, housing, and clothing; and awards individual grants for day care services and an annual college scholarship award.
Fields of interest: Arts; Education.
Type of support: Grants to individuals.
Application information: Applications not accepted. Unsolicited requests for funds not accepted.
Officers and Directors:* Earl J. Roberts, Jr.*, Pres.; Debarah C. Roberts*, V.P.; Mark A. Smith*, Secy.-Treas.
EIN: 311682310

67

AK Steel Holding Corporation

9227 Centre Pointe Dr.
West Chester, OH 45069 (513) 425-5000
FAX: (302) 636-5454

Company URL: http://www.aksteel.com
Establishment information: Established in 1993.
Company type: Public company
Company ticker symbol and exchange: AKS/NYSE
Business activities: Manufactures flat-rolled steel and blooms.
Business type (SIC): Steel mill products
Financial profile for 2012: Number of employees, 6,400; assets, $3,903,100,000; sales volume, $5,933,700,000; pre-tax net income, -$208,600,000; expenses, $6,061,800,000; liabilities, $4,408,400,000
Fortune 1000 ranking: 2012—430th in revenues, 981st in profits, and 671st in assets
Corporate officers: James L. Wainscott, Chair., Pres., and C.E.O.; David C. Horn, Exec. V.P., Genl. Counsel, and Secy.; Roger K. Newport, Jr., Sr. V.P., Finance and C.F.O.; Keith J. Howell, V.P., Opers.; Gary T. Barlow, V.P., Sales; Stephanie S. Bisselberg, V.P., Human Resources
Board of directors: James L. Wainscott, Chair.; Richard A. Abdoo; John S. Brinzo; Dennis C. Cuneo; William K. Gerber; Bonnie G. Hill; Robert H. Jenkins; Ralph S. Michael III; Shirley D. Peterson; James A. Thomson
International operations: Australia; Belgium; Cayman Islands; France; Italy; Singapore; Spain; United Kingdom; Vanuatu
Giving statement: Giving through the AK Steel Foundation.
Company EIN: 311401455

AK Steel Foundation

9227 Centre Pointe Dr.
West Chester, OH 45069-4822 (513) 425-5038
URL: http://www.aksteel.com/company/corporate-citizenship/
Application address for scholarships: c/o Middletown Community Foundation, 36 Donham Plaza, Middletown, OH 45042, tel.: (513) 424-7369; URL: http://www.mcfoundation.org

Establishment information: Established in 1989 in OH.
Donors: AK Steel Corp.; Kawasaki Steel Investments, Inc.
Financial data (yr. ended 12/31/11): Assets, $12,315,992 (M); expenditures, $1,739,887; qualifying distributions, $1,695,553; giving activities include $1,695,553 for grants.
Purpose and activities: The foundation supports museums and community foundations and organizations involved with health, Down syndrome, cancer, heart disease, diabetes, human services, and international relief and awards college scholarships to the children of employees of AK Steel and to African-American high school seniors attending high schools in Butler and Warren counties, Ohio.
Fields of interest: Museums; Health care, volunteer services; Hospitals (general); Health care, clinics/centers; Health care; Down syndrome; Cancer; Cancer, leukemia; Heart & circulatory diseases; Diabetes; Cancer research; Boy scouts; American Red Cross; YM/YWCAs & YM/YWHAs; Children/youth, services; Aging, centers/services; Developmentally disabled, centers & services; Human services; International relief; Foundations (community); United Ways and Federated Giving Programs African Americans/Blacks.
Programs:
AK Steel Sons and Daughters Scholarships: The foundation awards $5,000 college scholarships annually to the children of AK Steel employees. The scholarship is renewable for a maximum of three years, for a total potential scholarship of $20,000. The program is administered by the Middletown Community Foundation.
Employee Matching Gifts: The foundation matches contributions made by employees of AK Steel Corporation to institutions of higher education and nonprofit organizations.
Louie F. Cox Memorial AK Steel African-American Scholarships: The foundation awards $5,000 college scholarships annually to African-American high school seniors graduating from schools in Butler and Warren counties, OH. The scholarship is renewable for a maximum of three years, for a total potential scholarship of $20,000. The program is administered by the Middletown Community Foundation. Visit URL: http://www.mcfoundation.org/Available_Scholarships.htm#COX for more information.
Steel Magnolia Awards: The foundation awards $1,000 to eight women of all ages who have faced personal adversity and shown strength, courage, compassion, and leadership through their work in support of their communities. The award is given an eligible nonprofit organization selected by each recipient. The program is administered by the Middletown Community Foundation.
Type of support: Annual campaigns; Continuing support; Employee matching gifts; Employee-related scholarships; General/operating support; Scholarships—to individuals.
Geographic limitations: Giving primarily in areas of company operations, with emphasis on OH.
Application information: Applications accepted. The Louis F. Cox Memorial AK Steel African-American Scholarships are administered by the Middletown Community Foundation.
Initial approach: Contact application address for application form for Louis F. Cox Memorial AK Steel African-American Scholarships
Deadline(s): Dec. 31 for Louis F. Cox Memorial AK Steel African-American Scholarships
Officers and Trustees:* James L. Wainscott*, Chair.; Sarah Cunningham, Secy. and Exec. Dir.; Doug Mitterholzer, Treas.; Alan H. McCoy; Albert E. Ferrara, Jr.; David C. Horn; John F. Kaloski.
Number of staff: 1 part-time professional.
EIN: 311284344

68

Akamai Technologies, Inc.

8 Cambridge Ctr.
Cambridge, MA 02142 (617) 444-3000
FAX: (617) 444-3001

Company URL: http://www.akamai.com
Establishment information: Established in 1998.
Company type: Public company
Company ticker symbol and exchange: AKAM/NASDAQ
International Securities Identification Number: US00971T1016
Business activities: Develops Internet computer software.
Business type (SIC): Computer services
Financial profile for 2011: Number of employees, 2,380; assets, $2,600,630,000; sales volume, $1,373,950,000; pre-tax net income, $321,590,000; expenses, $1,059,460,000; liabilities, $254,870,000
Corporate officers: George H. Conrades, Chair.; Tom Leighton, C.E.O.; Jim Benson, Exec. V.P and C.F.O.; Robert Hughes, Exec. V.P., Sales and Mktg.; Kumud Kalia, Sr. V.P. and C.I.O.; Melanie Haratunian, Sr. V.P., Genl. Counsel and Corp. Secy.
Board of directors: George Conrades, Chair.; Martin M. Coyne II; Pamela J. Craig; C. Kim Goodwin; Jill Greenthal; Thomson F. Leighton; Geoffrey A. Moore; Paul Sagan; Frederic V. Salerno; Naomi O. Seligman
International operations: Cayman Islands; China; France; Germany; India; Italy; Japan; Netherlands; Singapore; South Korea; Spain; Sweden; Switzerland; United Kingdom
Giving statement: Giving through the Akamai Foundation, Inc.
Company EIN: 043432319

Akamai Foundation, Inc.

8 Cambridge Ctr.
Cambridge, MA 02142-1413 (617) 444-3920
URL: http://www.akamai.com/html/about/foundation.html

Establishment information: Established in 2000 in MA.
Donors: George Conrades; F. Thomson Leighton; Mrs. F. Thomson Leighton; Paul Sagan; ASU Foundation.
Contact: Mark Heslop

Financial data (yr. ended 12/31/11): Assets, $2,036,884 (M); expenditures, $408,796; qualifying distributions, $389,234; giving activities include $389,234 for grants.
Purpose and activities: The foundation supports programs designed to promote mathematics education in grades K-12.
Fields of interest: Elementary/secondary education; Mathematics.
Type of support: General/operating support.
Geographic limitations: Giving primarily in Washington, DC and MA.
Publications: Application guidelines.
Application information: Applications accepted. Application form not required. Applicants should submit the following:
1) name, address and phone number of organization
2) brief history of organization and description of its mission
3) copy of IRS Determination Letter
4) contact person
5) detailed description of project and amount of funding requested
Initial approach: Proposal
Deadline(s): None
Officers: Wendy Ziner Ravech, Pres. and Secy.; Jonathan Seelig, Treas.
EIN: 043530777
Selected grants: The following grants are a representative sample of this grantmaker's funding activity:
$137,500 to Mathematical Association of America, Washington, DC, 2010.
$72,822 to Mathematical Sciences Research Institute, Berkeley, CA, 2010.
$50,000 to Mass Insight Education and Research Institute, Boston, MA, 2010.
$40,000 to MATCH School Foundation, Boston, MA, 2010.
$25,000 to Center for Excellence in Education, McLean, VA, 2010.

69
Akerman Senterfitt
420 S. Orange Ave., Ste. 1200
Orlando, FL 32801-4904 (407) 423-4000

Company URL: http://www.akerman.com/
Establishment information: Established in 1920.
Company type: Private company
Business activities: Operates law firm.
Business type (SIC): Legal services
Corporate officer: James M. Miller, Chair.
Board of director: James M. Miller, Chair.
Offices: Los Angeles, CA; Denver, CO; Washington, DC; Boca Raton, Fort Lauderdale, Jacksonville, Miami, Naples, Orlando, Palm Beach, Tallahassee, Tampa, FL; Las Vegas, NV; New York, NY; Dallas, TX; Vienna, VA; Madison, WI
Giving statement: Giving through the Akerman Senterfitt Pro Bono Program.

Akerman Senterfitt Pro Bono Program
255 S. Orange Ave., Ste. 1200
Orlando, FL 32801-4904 (305) 374-5600
E-mail: james.miller@akerman.com; Additional tel.: (407) 423-4000; URL: http://www.akerman.com/probono/index.asp

Contact: James M. Miller Esq.
Fields of interest: Legal services.
Type of support: Pro bono services - legal.
Geographic limitations: Giving primarily in areas of company operations in Los Angeles, CA, Denver, CO, Washington, DC, Boca Raton, Fort Lauderdale, Jacksonville, Miami, Naples, Orlando, Palm Beach, Tallahassee, Tampa, and West Palm Beach, FL, Las Vegas, NV, New York, NY, Dallas, TX, Salt Lake City, UT, Vienna, VA, and Madison, WI.
Application information: A Pro Bono Committee manages the pro bono program.

70
Akin Gump Strauss Hauer & Feld LLP
Robert S. Strauss Bldg.
1333 New Hampshire Ave. N.W.
Washington, DC 20036-1564
(202) 887-4000

Company URL: http://www.akingump.com
Establishment information: Established in 1945.
Company type: Private company
Business activities: Operates law firm.
Business type (SIC): Legal services
Corporate officers: R. Bruce McLean, Chair.; Janet L. Mourges, C.F.O.; Lorey A. Hoffman, C.I.O.
Board of director: R. Bruce McLean, Chair.
Offices: Los Angeles, San Francisco, CA; Washington, DC; New York, NY; Philadelphia, PA; Austin, Dallas, Houston, San Antonio, TX
International operations: China; Russia; Sweden; United Arab Emirates; United Kingdom
Giving statement: Giving through the Akin Gump Strauss Hauer & Feld LLP Pro Bono Program.

Akin Gump Strauss Hauer & Feld LLP Pro Bono Program
Robert S. Strauss Bldg.
1333 New Hampshire Ave. N.W.
Washington, DC 20036-1564 (202) 887-4071
FAX: (202) 887-4288;
E-mail: sschulman@akingump.com; Additional tel.: (202) 887-4000; URL: http://www.akingump.com/probono/

Contact: Steven H. Schulman, Partner
Fields of interest: Legal services.
Type of support: Pro bono services - legal.
Geographic limitations: Giving primarily in areas of company operations in Los Angeles, and San Francisco, CA, Washington, DC, Boston, MA, New York, NY, Philadelphia, PA, Austin, Dallas, Houston, and San Antonio, TX, and in China, Russia, Switzerland, United Arab Emirates, and United Kingdom.
Application information: A Pro Bono Committee manages the pro bono program.

71
Alabama Power Company
600 N. 18th St.
P. O. Box 2641
Birmingham, AL 35291-8180
(205) 257-1000

Company URL: http://www.alabamapower.com/
Establishment information: Established in 1906.
Company type: Subsidiary of a public company
Business activities: Generates, transmits, and distributes electricity.
Business type (SIC): Electric services
Financial profile for 2010: Number of employees, 1,300; sales volume, $5,980,000,000
Corporate officers: Charles D. McCrary, Pres. and C.E.O.; Philip C. Raymond, Exec. V.P., C.F.O., and Treas.; Gordon G. Martin, Sr. V.P. and Genl. Counsel.; William E. Zales, Jr., V.P. and Corp. Secy.
Board of directors: Whit Armstrong; Ralph D. Cook; David J. Cooper, Sr.; Thomas A. Fanning; John D. Johns; Patricia M. King; James K. Lowder; Charles D. McCrary; Robert D. Powers; James H. Sanford; John Cox Webb IV
Joint Venture: Southern Electric Generating Co., Birmingham, AL
Giving statement: Giving through the Alabama Power Company Contributions Program and the Alabama Power Foundation, Inc.

Alabama Power Company Contributions Program
c/o Charitable Giving
600 N. 18th St.
P.O. Box 2641
Birmingham, AL 35291 (205) 257-2508
URL: http://www.alabamapower.com/community/home.asp

Purpose and activities: As a complement to its foundation, Alabama Power also makes charitable contributions to nonprofit organizations directly. Support is given primarily in areas of company operations in Alabama.
Fields of interest: Elementary/secondary education; Health care; Housing/shelter, volunteer services; Safety/disasters, fund raising/fund distribution; Recreation, camps; Recreation, parks/playgrounds; Human services; Family resources and services, disability; Human services, gift distribution; Aging, centers/services; Community/economic development Economically disadvantaged.
Programs:
Alabama Wild Power: Alabama Power, in partnership with Tennessee Valley Authority, U.S. Department of Agriculture Natural Resource Conservation Service, and local Soil and Water Conservation Districts, awards grants to property owners with transmission lines crossing their lands for brush removal and plantings that promote, attract, shelter, and feed wildlife in the rights-of-way. The company awards $50 per acre incentive payment capped at $500.
New Teacher Grants: Alabama Power provides $1,000 grants to first-year public school teachers to purchase materials and supplies for their classroom. Winning public school teachers are all graduates of state-approved teacher programs located at Alabama's public four-year colleges and universities.
Project SHARE: Alabama Power, in partnership with American Red Cross, provides assistance to elderly and disabled neighbors who need help with their energy bills. The program is funded by electric utility customers who donate through their monthly electric bill. The program is administered by the American Red Cross.
Renew Our Rivers: Alabama Power supports river-system cleanup in Alabama, Florida, Georgia, and Mississippi with the help of volunteers, homeowner and boat-owner associations, environmental groups, Alabama employees, schools, and civic organizations.
Type of support: Employee volunteer services; Loaned talent; Sponsorships.
Geographic limitations: Giving primarily in areas of company operations in AL.
Support limitations: No support for political organizations. No grants to individuals.
Publications: Application guidelines.
Application information: Applications accepted.
Initial approach: Contact local office for event sponsorship requests

Alabama Power Foundation, Inc.

600 N. 18th St.
P.O. Box 2641
Birmingham, AL 35291-0011
FAX: (205) 257-1860;
E-mail: atsummer@southernco.com; Tel. for Alisa Summerville: (205) 257-4722; Contact for Gateway Grants and Good Roots: Peggy Burnett, Prog. Dir., tel.: (205) 257-2357, e-mail: peburnet@southernco.com; URL: http://alpowercharitablegiving.org/index.php/foundation

Establishment information: Established in 1989 in AL.
Donors: The Charles D. McCrary Family; Alabama Power Co.; Elmer Harris; Glenda Harris; Bruce Hutchins; Priscilla Hutchins.
Contact: Alisa Summerville, Dir. of Charitable Giving
Financial data (yr. ended 12/31/11): Assets, $119,128,828 (M); gifts received, $7,081; expenditures, $8,048,635; qualifying distributions, $6,641,267; giving activities include $6,641,267 for 848 grants (high: $628,586).
Purpose and activities: The foundation supports programs designed to promote education; health and human services; arts and culture; the environment; and programs that promote future growth and neighborhood betterment in underserved communities.
Fields of interest: Arts, cultural/ethnic awareness; Visual arts; Performing arts; Arts; Elementary school/education; Teacher school/education; Education, services; Education; Environment, natural resources; Landscaping; Environment, beautification programs; Environment; Animals/wildlife; Health care; Recreation, parks/playgrounds; Human services; Civil/human rights, equal rights; Community development, neighborhood development; Urban/community development; Community/economic development; United Ways and Federated Giving Programs Minorities; Economically disadvantaged.
Programs:

Alabama Power New Teacher Grant Program: The foundation awards grants to first-year public school teachers for classroom materials and supplies. Candidates are submitted by the state's public teacher colleges and winners are selected by a committee that includes public education school deans. The program is designed to augment the lack of public school funding in communities.

Gateway Grant Program: The foundation awards grants of up to $2,000 to purchase materials for signage to greet visitors to cities, towns, and communities across the state. The program is designed to maintain civic pride in communities; enhance economic development opportunities through signage that is appealing and welcoming; enhance community aesthetics by encouraging physical improvements in the neighborhood; and create a sense of revitalization in areas impacted by natural disasters.

Good Roots: The foundation awards grants of up to $1,000 to local governments, nonprofit organizations, and schools to purchase trees for planting in cities, towns, and communities. The program is designed to maintain an excellent quality of life in the community; improve the quality of the environment in communities across Alabama; and encourage community involvement. Trees must be used in public areas, including parks, in canopies over streets, or in creating shade for a hot parking lot.

Type of support: Capital campaigns; Continuing support; Endowments; General/operating support; Matching/challenge support; Program development; Scholarship funds; Seed money.
Geographic limitations: Giving limited to areas of company operations in central and south AL.
Support limitations: No support for discriminatory organizations, churches or religious organizations not of direct benefit to the entire community, fraternal, athletic, or veterans' organizations, private or secondary private schools, or political organizations. No grants to individuals (except for employee-related scholarships), or for fundraising, general operating support for United Way-supported organizations, athletic tournaments, band trips, research trips, field trips, or other similar events.
Publications: Annual report (including application guidelines); Application guidelines; Informational brochure (including application guidelines).
Application information: Applications accepted. Support is limited to 2 years in length. Video and audio submissions are not accepted. Organizations receiving support are asked to submit a completion report. Application form required. Applicants should submit the following:
1) timetable for implementation and evaluation of project
2) how project will be sustained once grantmaker support is completed
3) signature and title of chief executive officer
4) results expected from proposed grant
5) statement of problem project will address
6) name, address and phone number of organization
7) copy of IRS Determination Letter
8) brief history of organization and description of its mission
9) copy of most recent annual report/audited financial statement/990
10) how project's results will be evaluated or measured
11) listing of board of directors, trustees, officers and other key people and their affiliations
12) detailed description of project and amount of funding requested
13) contact person
14) copy of current year's organizational budget and/or project budget
15) listing of additional sources and amount of support

Initial approach: Complete online application
Board meeting date(s): Mar. 26, June 19, Sept. 18, and Dec. 6
Deadline(s): None for requests under $50,000; Feb. 22, May 24, Aug. 23, and Nov. 15 for requests over $50,000; Apr. 22 for Gateway Grant Program; June 3 for Good Roots
Final notification: 8 weeks; Aug. 6 for Gateway Grant Program; Sept. 10 for Good Roots

Officers and Directors:* Charles D. McCrary*, Chair.; John O. Hudson III, Pres.; William E. Zales, Jr., V.P. and Secy.; Philip C. Raymond*, Treas.; Gregory J. Barker; Mathew W. Bowden; Mark S. Crews; Daniel K. Glover; Bobbie J. Knight; Gordon G. Martin; Donna D. Smith; Zeke W. Smith; Steve R. Spencer.
Number of staff: 4 full-time professional; 1 full-time support.
EIN: 570901832
Selected grants: The following grants are a representative sample of this grantmaker's funding activity:
$628,586 to United Way of Central Alabama, Birmingham, AL, 2011. For general operating support.
$420,382 to Birmingham Urban Revitalization Partnership, Birmingham, AL, 2011. For general operating support.
$250,000 to Birmingham-Southern College, Birmingham, AL, 2011. For general operating support.
$207,650 to University of Alabama, Tuscaloosa, AL, 2011. For general operating support.
$150,000 to National Maritime Museum of the Gulf of Mexico, Mobile, AL, 2011. For general operating support.
$120,500 to United Way of Southwest Alabama, Mobile, AL, 2011. For general operating support.
$9,545 to Hoover City Board of Education, Birmingham, AL, 2011. For general operating support.
$6,600 to United Way of the Chattahoochee Valley, Columbus, GA, 2011. For general operating support.
$5,727 to Alabama Power Service Organization, Eufaula, AL, 2011. For general operating support.
$5,000 to Studio By the Tracks, Irondale, AL, 2011. For general operating support.

72

Alabama Rural Electric Association Of Cooperatives

340 Technacenter Dr.
P.O. Box 244014
Montgomery, AL 36117-6031
(334) 215-2732

Company URL: http://www.areapower.coop/
Establishment information: Established in 1936.
Company type: Cooperative
Business activities: Operates a statewide trade association of electric cooperatives.
Business type (SIC): Business association
Corporate officers: Fred O. Braswell, Pres. and C.E.O.; Karl Rayborn, Sr. V.P. and C.F.O.; Lenore Reese Vickrey, V.P., Comms.; Sean Strickler, V.P., Public Affairs
Board of directors: A. H. Akins; Martin Anderson; Vernon Bagget; Jack Bailey; Leo Bomian; Randy Brannon; Joe Bunch; John Clark; Terry Darby; Max Davis; Steve Foshee; JoAnn Fuller; Leland Fuller; Gary Harrison; David Hembree; Kermit Hill; Lavaughn Holcomb; Patsy Holmes; Bobby Hooper; Max Hyatt; E.A. Jakins; Vince Johnson; Daryl Jones; George Kitchens; Jim McRae; Michael McWaters; Edward Miller; Terry Moseley; Ruby Neeley; O. B. Owens; Waymon Pace; Bruce Purdy; William Rankin; Jimmy Shaver; Ed Short; Mike Simpson; Grady Smith; Heflin Smith; Tom Stackhouse; Jim Stewart; Tommy Thompson; Louie Ward; Van Wardlaw; Irvin Wells; Tommie Werneth; Randal Wilkie; Stan Wilson
Giving statement: Giving through the Electric Cooperative Foundation, Inc.

Electric Cooperative Foundation, Inc.

P.O. Box 244014
Montgomery, AL 36124-4014 (334) 215-2732
URL: http://www.areapower.coop/content.cfm?id=2022

Establishment information: Established in 1998 in AL.
Donors: Tombigbee Electric Cooperative; Alabama Rural Electric Association.
Financial data (yr. ended 12/31/11): Assets, $291,527 (M); gifts received, $155,507; expenditures, $80,489; qualifying distributions, $74,600; giving activities include $74,600 for grants to individuals.
Purpose and activities: The foundation awards college scholarships to children of members of an Alabama electric cooperative that has contributed principal funds to the foundation.
Type of support: Scholarships—to individuals.
Geographic limitations: Giving limited to residents of AL.
Publications: Grants list.

Application information: Applications accepted. Application form required.
Initial approach: Proposal
Deadline(s): None
Officers and Directors:* George Kitchens*, Chair.; Fred O. Braswell, Exec. Dir. and Secy.; Karl G. Rayborn, Treas.; Martin Anderson; Steve Harmon; Ruby Neeley; Grady Smith.
EIN: 631190086

73
Aladdin Industries, LLC

(formerly Aladdin Industries, Inc.)
703 Murfreesboro Rd.
P.O. Box 100255
Nashville, TN 37210-3526 (615) 748-3000

Company URL: http://www.aladdin-pmi.com
Establishment information: Established in 1908.
Company type: Private company
Business activities: Designs and manufactures thermal insulated food and beverageware products.
Business type (SIC): Glass/pressed or blown
Financial profile for 2010: Number of employees, 89
Corporate officers: Frederick R. Meyer, Chair.; Victor S. Johnson III, Vice-Chair.
Board of directors: Frederick R. Meyer, Chair.; Victor S. Johnson III, Vice-Chair.
International operations: Australia; United Kingdom
Giving statement: Giving through the Aladdin Industries Employees Trust and the Aladdin Industries Foundation, Inc.

Aladdin Industries Employees Trust

P.O. Box 100255
Nashville, TN 37224-0255 (615) 748-3000

Donors: Aladdin Industries, Inc.; Aladdin Industries, LLC.
Contact: Lillian B. Jenkins, Secy.
Financial data (yr. ended 12/31/11): Assets, $124,146 (M); expenditures, $5,811; qualifying distributions, $5,486; giving activities include $5,486 for grants.
Purpose and activities: The foundation supports the Nashville Alliance for Public Education in Nashville, Tennessee.
Fields of interest: Education.
Type of support: General/operating support.
Geographic limitations: Giving primarily in Nashville, TN.
Support limitations: No grants to individuals.
Application information: Applications accepted. Application form required. Applicants should submit the following:
1) name, address and phone number of organization
Initial approach: Proposal
Deadline(s): None
Officer: L. B. Jenkins, Secy.
Trustee: V. S. Johnson III.
EIN: 237107691

Aladdin Industries Foundation, Inc.

P.O. Box 100255
Nashville, TN 37224 (615) 748-3000

Establishment information: Incorporated in 1964 in TN.
Donors: Aladdin Industries, Inc.; Aladdin Industries, LLC.
Contact: Lillian B. Jenkins, Secy.-Treas.
Financial data (yr. ended 12/31/11): Assets, $2,468,389 (M); expenditures, $110,551; qualifying distributions, $105,525; giving activities include $105,525 for grants.
Purpose and activities: The foundation supports food banks and organizations involved with arts and culture, health, child welfare, and human services.
Fields of interest: Arts; Agriculture/food; Human services.
Type of support: Annual campaigns; Capital campaigns; Employee-related scholarships; General/operating support; Scholarship funds.
Geographic limitations: Giving primarily in TN.
Application information: Applications accepted. Application form required. Applicants should submit the following:
1) name, address and phone number of organization
2) copy of IRS Determination Letter
3) listing of board of directors, trustees, officers and other key people and their affiliations
4) detailed description of project and amount of funding requested
Initial approach: Proposal
Copies of proposal: 1
Board meeting date(s): Quarterly
Deadline(s): Current calendar year
Officer and Directors:* Lillian B. Jenkins*, Secy.-Treas.; V.S. Johnson III.
EIN: 620701769
Selected grants: The following grants are a representative sample of this grantmaker's funding activity:
$1,000 to Saint Jude Childrens Research Hospital, Memphis, TN, 2010.

74
Alaska Airlines, Inc.

19300 International Blvd.
P.O. Box 68900
Seattle, WA 98168-0900 (206) 392-5040

Company URL: http://www.alaskaair.com
Establishment information: Established in 1932.
Company type: Subsidiary of a public company
Business activities: Provides air transportation services.
Business type (SIC): Transportation/scheduled air
Financial profile for 2010: Number of employees, 300; sales volume, $3,010,000,000
Corporate officers: William S. Ayer, Chair.; Bradley D. Tilden, Pres. and C.E.O.; Ben Minicucci, Exec. V.P., Opers. and C.O.O.; Keith Loveless, Exec. V.P., Genl. Counsel, and Corp. Secy.; Brandon Pedersen, C.F.O.; Keith Loveless, V.P., Finance and Treas.; Joseph Sprague, V.P., Mktg.; Tamara S. Yonng, V.P., Human Resources
Board of directors: William S. Ayer, Chair.; Patricia M. Bedient; Marion C. Blakey; Phyllis J. Campbell; Jessie J. Knight, Jr.; Marc R. Langland; Bryon I. Mallot; Dennis Mandsen; Kenneth J. Thompson; Bradley D. Tilden; Eric K. Yeaman
Giving statement: Giving through the Alaska Airlines, Inc. Corporate Giving Program and the Alaska Airlines Foundation.

Alaska Airlines, Inc. Corporate Giving Program

19300 International Blvd.
Seattle, WA 98188-5304
For requests benefiting the Lower 48/International: c/o Donna Hartman, Mgr., Community Rels., Alaska Airlines, P.O. Box 68900, Seattle, WA 98168, tel.: (206) 392-5383; For requests benefiting the states of Alaska or Hawaii: c/o Susan Bramstedt, Dir., Public Affairs, Alaska Airlines, 4750 Old International Airport Rd., Anchorage, AK 99502, tel.: (907) 266-7230; URL: http://www.alaskaair.com/content/about-us/social-responsibility/corporate-giving.aspx

Purpose and activities: As a complement to its foundation, Alaska Airlines also makes charitable contributions to nonprofit organizations directly. Special emphasis is directed towards programs designed to promote arts and culture, health care, the environment, human services, and community development. Support is given on a national and international basis, with emphasis on Alaska, Oregon, and Washington.
Fields of interest: Arts; Education; Environment; Health care; Human services; Community/economic development.
Programs:
Dollars for Doers: Through the Dollars for Doers Program, Alaska Airlines makes charitable contributions of $10 per hour to nonprofit organizations with which employees volunteer, up to $1,000 per year, per employee.
Employee Matching Gift Program: Alaska Airlines matches employee contributions to nonprofit organizations and educational institutions on a one-for-one basis.
Type of support: Employee matching gifts; Employee volunteer services; In-kind gifts; Sponsorships.
Geographic limitations: Giving on a national and international basis in areas of company operations, with emphasis on AL, OR, and WA.
Support limitations: No support for private businesses, religious organizations not of direct benefit to the entire community, discriminatory organizations, United Way-supported organizations, or educational institutions, (except through the Employee Matching Gift Program). No grants to individuals, or for endowments, pageants, sports teams, United Way campaigns, capital campaigns, or general operating support; no loans.
Publications: Application guidelines.
Application information: Applications accepted. Application form required. Applicants should submit the following:
1) name, address and phone number of organization
2) how company employees can become involved with the organization
3) list of company employees involved with the organization
4) contact person
5) listing of additional sources and amount of support
Applications should include the organization's Tax ID Number and a description of past support by Alaska Airlines with the organization. Ticket donation requests should include the number of tickets requested and intended use of the donation.
Initial approach: Complete online application form
Administrators: Susan Bramstedt, Dir., Public Affairs, AK; Donna R. Hartman, Mgr., Community Rels. and Corp. Giving, Lower 48.
Number of staff: 1 full-time professional.

Alaska Airlines Foundation

4750 International Airport Blvd.
Anchorage, AK 99502 (907) 266-7230

Establishment information: Established in 1998 in AK and WA.
Donor: Alaska Airlines, Inc.
Contact: Tim Thompson, Exec. Dir.
Financial data (yr. ended 12/31/12): Assets, $4,657,005 (M); gifts received, $500,000; expenditures, $101,449; qualifying distributions, $99,500; giving activities include $99,500 for 8 grants (high: $25,000; low: $5,000).
Purpose and activities: The foundation supports organizations involved with education and aviation.

Fields of interest: Museums (specialized); Arts; Education; Space/aviation.
Type of support: Program development.
Geographic limitations: Giving primarily in AK and WA.
Application information: Applications accepted. Focus is on education efforts that address a unique need or value of a community. Application form required.
Initial approach: Letter
Copies of proposal: 1
Deadline(s): Sept. 30
Officers: William S. Ayer, Chair. and Pres.; Keith Loveless, V.P.; Brandon S. Pedersen, V.P.; Marilyn F. Romano, V.P.; Jeanne Gammon, Secy.-Treas.; Timothy Thompson, Exec. Dir.
EIN: 920166198

75
Alaska Communications Systems Group, Inc.

600 Telephone Ave.
Anchorage, AK 99503-6091
(907) 297-3000
FAX: (302) 655-5049

Company URL: http://www.alaskacommunications.com
Establishment information: Established in 1999.
Company type: Public company
Company ticker symbol and exchange: ALSK/NASDAQ
Business activities: Provides local, cellular, long distance, data, and Internet telephone communications services.
Business type (SIC): Telephone communications
Financial profile for 2012: Number of employees, 830; assets, $614,730,000; sales volume, $367,830,000; pre-tax net income, $23,190,000; expenses, $305,110,000; liabilities, $649,410,000
Corporate officers: Edward J. Hayes, Jr., Chair.; Anand Vadapalli, Pres. and C.E.O.; Wayne Graham, C.F.O.; James R. Johnsen, Sr. V.P., Human Resources; Leonard A. Steinberg, V.P., Genl. Counsel, and Corp. Secy.
Board of directors: Edward J. Hayes, Jr., Chair.; David W. Karp; Peter D. Ley; L.Brown Margaret; Brian A. Ross; Anand Vadapalli; John Niles Wanamaker
Historic mergers: Internet Alaska, Inc. (June 16, 2000)
Giving statement: Giving through the Alaska Communications Systems Group, Inc. Corporate Giving Program.
Company EIN: 522126573

Alaska Communications Systems Group, Inc. Corporate Giving Program

600 Telephone Ave.
Anchorage, AK 99503-6010 (907) 297-3000
FAX: (907) 297-3100;
E-mail: letsbetteralaska@acsalaska.com;
URL: http://www.alaskacommunications.com/About-ACS/Our-Work-in-the-Community.aspx

Purpose and activities: Alaska Communications Systems makes charitable contributions to nonprofit organizations involved with education, youth development and access to technology, economic development, and the environment. Support is given primarily in areas of company operations in Alaska.
Fields of interest: Education, computer literacy/technology training; Education; Environment; Boys & girls clubs; Youth development; Economic development; United Ways and Federated Giving Programs.
Programs:
Employee Volunteer Grant Program: Alaska Communications will contribute up to $250 to any eligible nonprofit at which its employees volunteer 20 or more hours per calendar year.
Summer of Heroes: Alaska Communications' Summer of Heroes is a partnership program between Alaska Communications and Boys & Girls Clubs - Alaska to promote awareness and support for youth development programs throughout the state. Running from May through August 2012, the program includes a youth recognition program and a cause-related sales promotion - highlighted by several events. Each year, the program selects five outstanding local heroes based on their nomination forms and essays. The selected heroes receive a $1,500 scholarship and a trip to the 2012 Alaska State Fair where they are recognized in a special ceremony.
Type of support: Employee volunteer services; General/operating support; In-kind gifts.
Geographic limitations: Giving primarily in areas of company operations in AK.
Support limitations: No support for United Way-supported organizations, denominational or sectarian religious organizations, private foundations, political organizations or candidates, or organizations that receive the majority of their funding from State and/or Municipal government. No grants for purposes that may pose a conflict of interest with the company or its values.
Publications: Application guidelines.
Application information: Applications accepted. Organizations requesting support must be existing customers of Alaska Communications Systems. The Alaska Communications Corporate Communications department handles giving. The company may request an expanded proposal or in-person meeting. Application form not required. Applicants should submit the following:
1) timetable for implementation and evaluation of project
2) statement of problem project will address
3) name, address and phone number of organization
4) copy of IRS Determination Letter
5) brief history of organization and description of its mission
6) copy of most recent annual report/audited financial statement/990
7) descriptive literature about organization
8) detailed description of project and amount of funding requested
9) contact person
10) listing of additional sources and amount of support
11) plans for acknowledgement

Requests for event fundraising should include the number of expected attendees.
Initial approach: E-mail proposal
Deadline(s): 2 months prior to need
Number of staff: 1 full-time support.

76
Alaska Railroad Corporation

327 W. Ship Creek Ave.
P.O. Box 107500
Anchorage, AK 99501 (907) 265-2300
FAX: (907) 265-2312

Company URL: http://www.alaskarailroad.com/
Establishment information: Established in 1915.
Company type: Private company
Business activities: Operates railroad.
Business type (SIC): Transportation/railroad
Corporate officers: Linda Leary, Chair.; Bill Sheffield, Vice-Chair.; Christopher Aadnesen, Pres. and C.E.O.; William G. O'Leary, C.O.O.; William R. Hupprich, V.P. and Genl. Counsel
Board of directors: Linda Leary, Chair.; Bill Sheffield, Vice-Chair.; Susan Bell; John Binkley; Jack Burton; John Cook; Pat Kemp; Marc Luiken
Giving statement: Giving through the Alaska Railroad Corporation Contributions Program.

Alaska Railroad Corporation Contributions Program

c/o Corp. Affairs Dept.
P.O. Box 107500
Anchorage, AK 99510-7500 (907) 265-2671
URL: http://www.akrr.com/arrc48.html

Purpose and activities: The Alaska Railroad makes charitable contributions to nonprofit organizations involved with education, community development, and youth development. Support is limited to Alaska, with emphasis on communities located along the railbelt.
Fields of interest: Education; Youth development; Community/economic development.
Type of support: Donated products; In-kind gifts; Program development; Sponsorships.
Geographic limitations: Giving limited to AK, with emphasis on the railbelt.
Support limitations: No support for political, religious, or discriminatory organizations, or sports teams. No grants to individuals, or for endowments, operating budgets, renewal grants, beauty pageants, or travel expenses.
Publications: Application guidelines.
Application information: Applications accepted. A Citizens Advisory Board reviews all requests for cash and some in-kind donations. Application form required. Applicants should submit the following:
1) how project will be sustained once grantmaker support is completed
2) statement of problem project will address
3) copy of IRS Determination Letter
4) list of company employees involved with the organization
5) what distinguishes project from others in its field
6) listing of board of directors, trustees, officers and other key people and their affiliations
7) detailed description of project and amount of funding requested
8) contact person
9) copy of current year's organizational budget and/or project budget
10) listing of additional sources and amount of support
11) plans for acknowledgement

Applications should specifically note the nature of the request being made; and include a description of past support by the Alaska Railroad with the organization.
Initial approach: Download application form and mail to headquarters
Committee meeting date(s): May and Nov.
Deadline(s): Mar. 31 for May consideration and Sept. 30 for Nov. consideration

77
Albany Mutual Telephone Association

131 6th St.
Albany, MN 56307-8322 (320) 845-2101

Company URL: http://www.albanytel.com
Establishment information: Established in 1951.
Company type: Cooperative
Business activities: Operates telephone company.
Business type (SIC): Telephone communications
Corporate officers: Katka Steven, C.E.O.; John Rose, Pres.
Giving statement: Giving through the Albany Mutual Telephone Foundation.

Albany Mutual Telephone Foundation

131 6th St.
P.O. Box 570
Albany, MN 56307-0570 (320) 845-2101

Establishment information: Established in 2007 in MN.
Donor: Central Stearns Comsis, Inc.
Contact: Steve Katka, C.E.O.
Financial data (yr. ended 12/31/11): Assets, $2,808,052 (M); expenditures, $115,906; qualifying distributions, $98,792; giving activities include $98,792 for grants.
Application information: Applications accepted.
Initial approach: Contact foundation for the application form
Deadline(s): None
Officers: Lowell Rushmeyer, Pres.; Roger Wolf, V.P.; Elmer Kohorst, Secy.-Treas.
Directors: Tom Fischer; Joe Hennen; John Klaphake; Norbert Overman; Tony Reber.
EIN: 261561849

78
Albemarle Corporation

451 Florida St.
Baton Rouge, LA 70801 (225) 388-8011
FAX: (225) 388-7686

Company URL: http://www.albemarle.com
Establishment information: Established in 1994.
Company type: Public company
Company ticker symbol and exchange: ALB/NYSE
Business activities: Manufactures polymer products and chemicals.
Business type (SIC): Plastics and synthetics; chemicals and allied products
Financial profile for 2012: Number of employees, 4,304; assets, $3,437,290,000; sales volume, $2,745,420,000; pre-tax net income, $374,590,000; expenses, $2,339,260,000; liabilities, $1,603,690,000
Fortune 1000 ranking: 2012—759th in revenues, 457th in profits, and 709th in assets
Corporate officers: Jim W. Nokes, Chair.; Luther C. Kissam IV, C.E.O.; Scott A. Tozier, Jr., Sr. V.P. and C.F.O.; Karen G. Narwold, Sr. V.P. and Genl. Counsel; Susan M. Kelliher, Sr. V.P., Human Resources; Antony S. Parnell, V.P., Sales
Board of directors: Jim W. Nokes, Chair.; William H. Hernandez; Luther C. Kissam IV; Joseph M. Mahady; James J. O'Brien; Barry W. Perry; John Sherman, Jr.; Harriett Tee Taggart, Ph.D.; Anne Marie Whittemore
Plants: Magnolia, AR; Baton Rouge, LA; Orangeburg, SC; Pasadena, TX
International operations: Belgium; Japan; Netherlands
Giving statement: Giving through the Albemarle Foundation.
Company EIN: 541692118

Albemarle Foundation

451 Florida St.
Baton Rouge, LA 70801-1700 (225) 388-7552
E-mail: AlbemarleFoundation@albemarle.com; E-mail for Sandra Holub: sandra_holub@albemarle.com; URL: http://www.albemarle.com/Sustainability/Albemarle-Foundation-42.html

Establishment information: Established in 2006 in VA.
Donors: M. Rohr; J. Steitz; L. Kissam; Albemarle Corp.
Contact: Sandra Holub, Mgr.
Financial data (yr. ended 12/31/11): Assets, $3,176,747 (M); gifts received, $2,781,787; expenditures, $3,573,662; qualifying distributions, $3,391,237; giving activities include $3,391,237 for grants.
Purpose and activities: The foundation supports programs designed to promote future workforce and education; social and health services; and cultural resources and advocacy.
Fields of interest: Arts education; Arts; Charter schools; Adult/continuing education; Education; Hospitals (general); Health care; Employment, services; Food banks; Housing/shelter, development; Children/youth, services; Family services; Human services; Community/economic development; Engineering/technology.
Programs:
Albemarle Foundation Annual Employee Campaign: Through the Annual Employee Campaign, the foundation supports nonprofit organizations involved with education, health and social services, and cultural initiatives through employee pledges. Pledges are collected by payroll deduction or one-time payment and employees select the year's member agencies.
Cultural Resources and Advocacy: The foundation supports programs designed to provide opportunities for artistic, community education, and specific experiences to the people in Albemarle communities through arts education, jobs, initiatives, and events.
Employee Volunteer Program: The foundation awards $1,000 grants to nonprofit organizations with which employees of Albemarle volunteers.
Foundation Scholarship Program: The foundation awards $2,500 renewable scholarships to children of employees of Albemarle, up to a maximum of $10,000 per eligible student.
Future Workforce and Education: The foundation supports programs designed to strengthen and improve educational opportunities in the areas of technology and science. Special emphasis is directed toward school partnerships and other forums designed to impact technical curriculum; and programs that improve the education system.
Matching Gift Program: The foundation matches contributions made my employees and retirees of Albemarle to nonprofit organizations on a one-for-basis.
Social and Health Services: The foundation supports programs designed to relieve community distress; and help individuals and families overcome barriers to achieving their potential as members of the community. Special emphasis is directed toward building healthy communities; investing in youth; meeting basic needs; strengthening lives; and striding toward independence.
Type of support: Annual campaigns; Building/renovation; Curriculum development; Employee matching gifts; Employee volunteer services; Employee-related scholarships; General/operating support; Program development.
Geographic limitations: Giving limited to communities in which Albemarle Corporation operates in Magnolia, AR, Baton Rouge, LA, South Haven, MI, Twinsburg, OH, Tyrone, PA, Orangeburg, SC, Bayport, Clearlake, and Pasadena, TX, and Richmond, VA.
Support limitations: No support for discriminatory organizations or legislative organizations. No grants for telephone solicitations.
Publications: Application guidelines; Grants list; Informational brochure.
Application information: Applications accepted. Organizations receiving support are asked to submit a final report. Application form required. Applicants should submit the following:
1) timetable for implementation and evaluation of project
2) results expected from proposed grant
3) population served
4) name, address and phone number of organization
5) copy of IRS Determination Letter
6) brief history of organization and description of its mission
7) geographic area to be served
8) how project's results will be evaluated or measured
9) explanation of why grantmaker is considered an appropriate donor for project
10) detailed description of project and amount of funding requested
11) contact person
12) copy of current year's organizational budget and/or project budget
Initial approach: Complete online application
Board meeting date(s): First week of May and Nov.
Deadline(s): Last Tues. of Apr. and Oct.
Final notification: 10 days following board meeting
Officers and Directors: Mark C. Rohr, Pres.; Nicole C. Daniel, Secy.; Richard Fishman, Treas.; Luther C. Kissam IV; John M. Steitz.
EIN: 204798471
Selected grants: The following grants are a representative sample of this grantmaker's funding activity:
$50,000 to City Year, Boston, MA, 2010.
$28,500 to Teach for America, New York, NY, 2010.
$6,300 to Saint Jude Childrens Research Hospital, Memphis, TN, 2010.
$5,500 to University of Tennessee, Knoxville, TN, 2010.
$4,919 to Clemson University, Clemson, SC, 2010.
$3,600 to American Cancer Society, Atlanta, GA, 2010.
$2,500 to Atlanta Legal Aid Society, Atlanta, GA, 2010.
$2,000 to Purdue University, West Lafayette, IN, 2010.
$1,685 to World Vision, Federal Way, WA, 2010.
$1,175 to Multiple Sclerosis Society, National, New York, NY, 2010.

79
Albertsons LLC

(also known as Albertsons Market)
(formerly Albertson's, Inc.)
250 E. Parkcenter Blvd.
Boise, ID 83726-0020 (208) 345-3180

Company URL: http://www.albertsons.com
Establishment information: Established in 1939.
Company type: Subsidiary of a public company
Business activities: Operates supermarkets, drug stores, and warehouse stores.
Business type (SIC): Groceries—retail; general merchandise stores; drug stores and proprietary stores
Financial profile for 2010: Number of employees, 950; sales volume, $5,900,000,000
Corporate officers: Robert G. Miller, C.E.O.; Richard J Navarro, C.F.O.; Mark Bates, C.I.O.; Robert C. Butler, Exec. V.P., Opers.; Paul G. Rowan, Sr. V.P. and Genl. Counsel; Andrew J. Scoggin, Sr. V.P., Human Resources
Subsidiary: American Stores Company, LLC, Salt Lake City, UT
Giving statement: Giving through the Albertsons LLC Corporate Giving Program and the Daimler AG Corporate Giving Program.

Albertsons LLC Corporate Giving Program

(formerly Albertson's, Inc. Corporate Giving Program)
250 E. Parkcenter Blvd.
Boise, ID 83706-3999 (208) 395-6200
E-mail: donations@albertsonsllc.com; URL: http://www.albertsonsmarket.com/our-company/in-the-community/

Purpose and activities: Albertsons makes charitable contributions to nonprofit organizations involved with health, the environment, hunger relief, and nutrition. Support is given primarily in areas of company operations in Arizona, Arkansas, Colorado, Florida, Louisiana, New Mexico, and Texas.
Fields of interest: Education; Environment, recycling; Health care; Agriculture; Food services; Youth development.
Type of support: Donated products; Employee volunteer services; Program development.
Geographic limitations: Giving primarily in areas of company operations in AK, AZ, CO, FL, LA, NM, and TX.
Support limitations: No grants to individuals.
Publications: Application guidelines.
Application information: Applications accepted. Mailed, faxed, or e-mailed applications will not be considered. Videos, DVDs, or similar submissions are not encouraged. Application form required.
Applicants should submit the following:
1) name, address and phone number of organization
2) copy of IRS Determination Letter
3) copy of most recent annual report/audited financial statement/990
4) detailed description of project and amount of funding requested
5) contact person
6) plans for acknowledgement
7) additional materials/documentation
Applications should include the date, website, and expected attendance of the event; and a description of past support by Albertsons with the organization.
Initial approach: Download application form and e-mail to headquarters
Deadline(s): 8 weeks prior to need
Final notification: 6 weeks

80
The Fred W. Albrecht Grocery Company, Inc.

2700 Gilchrist Rd.
Akron, OH 44305-4433 (330) 733-2861

Establishment information: Established in 1891.
Company type: Private company
Business activities: Operates supermarkets, department stores, variety stores, and drug stores.
Business type (SIC): Groceries—retail; drugs, proprietaries, and sundries—wholesale; groceries—wholesale; variety stores; drug stores and proprietary stores
Financial profile for 2012: Number of employees, 5,000; sales volume, $500,000,000
Corporate officers: F. Steven Albrecht, Pres. and C.E.O.; Joseph D. Parsons, V.P. and Secy.; David Hicks, Secy.-Treas.
Board of director: Clark Richards
Subsidiary: Gilcrest Storage, Akron, OH
Giving statement: Giving through the F. W. Albrecht Family Foundation.

F. W. Albrecht Family Foundation

2700 Gilchrist Rd.
Akron, OH 44305-4433 (330) 733-2861

Establishment information: Established in 1990 in OH.
Donors: The Fred W. Albrecht Grocery Co., Inc.; Albrecht Inc.
Contact: Sue Guthier
Financial data (yr. ended 12/31/11): Assets, $1,657,127 (M); gifts received, $204,624; expenditures, $167,395; qualifying distributions, $134,984; giving activities include $134,984 for grants.
Purpose and activities: The foundation supports organizations involved with education, animals and wildlife, and human services.
Fields of interest: Higher education; Education; Animal welfare; Zoos/zoological societies; Animals/wildlife; YM/YWCAs & YM/YWHAs; Human services.
Type of support: General/operating support; Scholarship funds.
Geographic limitations: Giving limited to areas of company operations.
Support limitations: No grants to individuals.
Application information: Applications accepted. Application form required. Applicants should submit the following:
1) copy of IRS Determination Letter
Initial approach: Letter
Deadline(s): None
Directors: F. Steven Albrecht; Douglas A. Flinn; Daniel J. McPeek; James H. Trout.
EIN: 341663626

81
Alcatel Lucent

(formerly Lucent Technologies Inc.)
600-700 Mountain Ave.
Murray Hill, NJ 07974-2008
(908) 582-8200

Company URL: http://www.alcatel-lucent.com/us/
Establishment information: Established in 1954.
Company type: Subsidiary of a foreign company
Business activities: Designs, develops, and manufactures communications systems, software, and products.
Business type (SIC): Telephone communications; communications equipment; computer services
Financial profile for 2006: Number of employees, 29,800; assets, $15,355,000,000; sales volume, $8,796,000,000
Corporate officers: Philippe Camus, Chair.; Bernardus Johannes Maria Verwaayen, C.E.O.; Robert Vrij, Sales and Mktg.
Board of directors: Philippe Camus, Chair.; Bernardus J. Verwaayen
Subsidiaries: AG Communications Systems Corp., Phoenix, AZ; Ortel Corp., Alhambra, CA
Divisions: Business Communications Systems Div., Basking Ridge, NJ; Consumer Products Div., Parsippany, NJ; Microelectronics Div., Berkeley Heights, NJ; Network Systems Div., Morristown, NJ
International operations: Canada; Ireland; Italy; Japan; United Kingdom
Historic mergers: Alcatel USA, Inc. (November 30, 2006)
Giving statement: Giving through the Alcatel-Lucent Corporate Contributions Program and the Alcatel-Lucent Foundation.

Alcatel-Lucent Corporate Contributions Program

(formerly Lucent Technologies Inc. Corporate Giving Program)
600 Mountain Ave.
Murray Hill, NJ 07974-2008
E-mail: foundation@alcatel-lucent.com; URL: http://www.alcatel-lucent.com/csr/htm/en/home.html

Purpose and activities: As a complement to its foundation, Alcatel-Lucent also makes charitable contributions to nonprofit organizations directly. Support is given on a national and international basis primarily in areas of company operations.
Fields of interest: Education; Community/economic development; General charitable giving.
Type of support: Employee volunteer services; General/operating support.
Geographic limitations: Giving on a national and international basis in areas of company operations.

Alcatel-Lucent Foundation

(formerly Lucent Technologies Foundation)
600 Mountain Ave.
Murray Hill, NJ 07974-2008
E-mail: bishalakhi.ghosh@alcatel-lucent.com; URL: http://www2.alcatel-lucent.com/foundation/

Establishment information: Established in 1996.
Donors: Lucent Technologies Inc.; Alcatel-Lucent.
Contact: Bishalakhi Ghosh, Exec. Dir.
Financial data (yr. ended 12/31/11): Assets, $4,228,760 (M); gifts received, $4,000,000; expenditures, $3,588,603; qualifying distributions, $3,576,731; giving activities include $3,368,464 for 14+ grants (high: $2,000,000).
Purpose and activities: The foundation supports programs designed to assist underprivileged youth, with a focus on young women, and to provide youth in underserved communities with access to education and life skills training.
Fields of interest: Elementary/secondary education; Higher education; Education; Employment, training; Disasters, preparedness/services; Youth development, adult & child programs; Big Brothers/Big Sisters; Girl scouts; Youth development, business; Youth development Youth; Young adults, female; Economically disadvantaged.
Type of support: Continuing support; Employee volunteer services; General/operating support; Program development.

Geographic limitations: Giving primarily in areas of company operations, with emphasis on CA, NJ, and NY; giving also to national organizations.
Application information: Applications not accepted. Unsolicited applications are not accepted. Projects must be submitted by employees and supported by senior management.
Board meeting date(s): Bi-annually
Officers and Trustees:* Janet G. Davidson*, Chair.; Barbara Landmann, Vice-Chair.; Yohann Benard, Secy.; Stephanie Vantomme, Treas.; Bishalakhi Ghosh, Exec. Dir.; Frederic Chapelard; Christine Diamente; Marc Kassis; Marco Malfavon; Sandra D. Motley; George (Gee) Rittenhouse; William Reese.
EIN: 223480423

82
Alcoa Inc.

(formerly Aluminum Company of America)
390 Park Ave.
New York, NY 10022-4608 (212) 836-2674
FAX: (212) 298-8436

Company URL: http://www.alcoa.com
Establishment information: Established in 1888.
Company type: Public company
Company ticker symbol and exchange: AA/NYSE
International Securities Identification Number: US0138171014
Business activities: Produces alumina and aluminum; manufactures precision castings, industrial fasteners, vinyl siding, consumer products, food service and flexible packaging products, plastic closures, and car and truck electrical distribution systems.
Business type (SIC): Metal rolling and drawing/nonferrous; paper and paperboard/coated, converted, and laminated; plastic products/miscellaneous; metal refining/primary nonferrous; metal foundries/nonferrous; screw machine products; lighting and wiring equipment/electric
Financial profile for 2012: Number of employees, 61,000; assets, $40,179,000,000; sales volume, $23,700,000,000; pre-tax net income, $324,000,000; expenses, $23,376,000,000; liabilities, $26,980,000,000
Fortune 1000 ranking: 2012—128th in revenues, 592nd in profits, and 140th in assets
Forbes 2000 ranking: 2012—401st in sales, 1602nd in profits, and 577th in assets
Corporate officers: Klaus Kleinfeld, Chair. and C.E.O.; William F. Oplinger, Exec. V.P. and C.F.O.; Audrey Strauss, Exec. V.P. and Corp. Secy.; Peter Hong, V.P. and Treas.; Daniel Cruise, V.P., Public Affairs; Graeme W. Bottger, V.P. and Cont.; Michael T. Barriere, V.P. and Human Resources; Max W. Laun, V.P. and Genl. Counsel.
Board of directors: Klaus Kleinfeld, Chair.; Arthur D. Collins, Jr.; Kathryn S. Fuller; Judith M. Gueron; Michael G. Morris; E. Stanley O'Neal; James W. Owens; Patricia F. Russo; Martin Sorrell; Ratan N. Tata; Ernesto Zedillo
Subsidiaries: Alcoa Brazil Holdings Co., Burlington, VT; Alcoa Composites, Inc., Monrovia, CA; Alcoa Conductor International, Pittsburgh, PA; Alcoa Fujikura, Ltd., Brentwood, TN; Alcoa Generating Corp., Pittsburgh, PA; Alcoa International Holdings Co., Burlington, VT; Alcoa Minerals of Jamaica, Inc., Pittsburgh, PA; Alcoa Properties, Inc., Burlington, VT; Alcoa Recycling Co., Inc., Knoxville, TN; Alcoa Securities Corp., Burlington, VT; Alcoa Services Corp., Pittsburgh, PA; Alumax Inc., Atlanta, GA; ARCTEK Corp., Gettysburg, OH; Bauxite & Northern Railway Co., Pittsburgh, PA; Colockum Transmission Co., Inc., Pittsburgh, PA; H-C Industries, Inc., Crawfordsville, IN; Howmet International Inc., Greenwich, CT; Huck International Inc., Tucson, AZ; Point Comfort & Northern Railway Co., Pittsburgh, PA; Reynolds Metals Company, Richmond, VA; Rockdale Sandow & Southern Railroad, Inc., Pittsburgh, PA; Stolle Corp., Sidney, OH; Suriname Aluminum Co., Inc., Pittsburgh, PA; Tapoco, Inc., Pittsburgh, PA; Yadkin, Inc., Badin, NC
Division: Alcoa Div., Knoxville, TN
Plants: Bauxite, AR; Los Angeles, CA; Lafayette, Newburgh, Richmond, IN; Bettendorf, IA; Massena, NY; Badin, NC; Cleveland, Sidney, OH; Lebanon, New Kensington, PA; Alcoa, TN; Rockdale, TX
International operations: Australia; Bahrain; Brazil; China; France; Germany; Hong Kong; Hungary; Iceland; Italy; Jamaica; Japan; Luxembourg; Mexico; Netherlands; Norway; Russia; Singapore; Spain; Suriname; Switzerland; United Kingdom
Giving statement: Giving through the Alcoa Inc. Contributions Program and the Alcoa Foundation.
Company EIN: 250317820

Alcoa Inc. Contributions Program

390 Park Ave.
New York, NY 10022-4608 (212) 836-2600
URL: http://www.alcoa.com/global/en/community/foundation/info_page/about_community_giving.asp

Financial data (yr. ended 12/31/12): Total giving, $18,000,000, including $18,000,000 for grants.
Purpose and activities: As a complement to its foundation, Alcoa also makes charitable contributions to nonprofit organizations directly. Support is given on a national and international basis in areas of company operations.
Fields of interest: Education; Environment; Disasters, preparedness/services; Community/economic development.
Type of support: General/operating support.
Geographic limitations: Giving on a national and international basis in areas of company operations.

Alcoa Foundation

Alcoa Corporate Ctr.
201 Isabella St.
Pittsburgh, PA 15212-5858 (412) 553-2348
URL: http://www.alcoa.com/global/en/community/foundation.asp

Establishment information: Trust established in 1952 in PA; incorporated in 1964.
Donors: Alcoa Corp.; Aluminum Co. of America; Alcoa Inc.
Financial data (yr. ended 12/31/11): Assets, $442,175,938 (M); gifts received, $500,000; expenditures, $24,327,872; qualifying distributions, $22,839,780; giving activities include $21,096,944 for 1,116 grants (high: $750,000; low: $100).
Purpose and activities: The foundation supports programs designed to engage people to improve the environment, educate tomorrow's leaders, and enhance communities where Alcoa operates around the world. Special emphasis is directed toward programs designed to address the environment, empowerment, education, and sustainable design.
Fields of interest: Higher education; Teacher school/education; Adult/continuing education; Education, services; Education; Environment, public policy; Environment, pollution control; Environment, waste management; Environment, recycling; Environment, climate change/global warming; Environment, natural resources; Environment, water resources; Environment, land resources; Environment, energy; Environment, forests; Environment; Employment, services; Employment, training; Employment; Disasters, preparedness/services; Safety/disasters; Recreation, parks/playgrounds; Girl scouts; Youth development, business; Youth development; American Red Cross; Children/youth, services; Urban/community development; Mathematics; Engineering/technology; Science; Transportation Minorities; Women; Girls.
International interests: Africa; Asia; Australia; Caribbean; Central America; Europe; Mexico; South America.
Programs:
Advancing Sustainability Research Initiative: The foundation, in partnership with NGO's and select universities, supports global sustainability research projects to find answers to environmental issues that impact the quality of life and well-being of communities globally. Special emphasis is directed toward research focusing on energy and environmental economics; materials science and engineering; natural resource management; and sustainable design. Visit URL http://www.iie.org/Programs/Alcoa-Foundation-Advancing-Sustainability-Research for more information.
Alcoa Sons and Daughters Scholarship Program: The foundation awards $7,500 college scholarships to children of U.S. employees of Alcoa. The program is administered by ACT Inc.
Alcoans Coming Together In Our Neighborhoods (ACTION): The foundation awards grants to nonprofit organizations with which teams of Alcoa employees volunteer at least 4 hours on a community service project. Teams of four employees are eligible for $1,500 and teams of eight employees are eligible for $3,000.
Bravo!: The foundation awards $250 grants to nonprofit organizations and non-governmental organizations with which employees of Alcoa volunteer at least 50 hours.
Education: The foundation supports programs designed to promote educational endeavors where Alcoa can offer expertise and make a difference. Special emphasis is directed STEM, including innovative education, training programs, and teaching curriculums in the areas of science, technology, engineering, and math; environment, including environmental awareness and creating environmental community ambassadors among Alcoa employees, students, and community members; safety, including encouraging college students and young professionals to pursue careers in environment, health, and safety (EHS); and workforce development, including education and training opportunities in engineering and manufacturing to promote self-sufficiency.
Employee Matching Gifts: The foundation matches contributions made by full-time employees, directors, and retirees of Alcoa to institutions of higher education on a two-for-one basis from $25 to $5,000 per contributor, per year.
Environment: The foundation supports programs designed to promote systemic improvements in environmental sustainability through research, dialogue, and mobilized action. Special emphasis is directed toward (1) Reduce, Recycle, Replenish - including the use of fewer natural resources, producing less waste, reduced emissions, and mitigated climate change through renewable energy; greater recycling rates and re-used materials; and biodiversity, enhanced parks and land use, reforestation, and water resources conservation; (2) Sustainable Design - including urbanization through the role of architecture and design in building and construction to enable climate change and enhanced environmental and social sustainability of cities; and transportation through improved fuel efficiency and minimized overall environmental

footprint of mass transit; (3) green and blue social enterprises - including environmental-driven innovations and aluminum-enhanced equipment that generates sustainable livelihoods; and (4) Measure and Set Standards - through adoption of standards that measure comprehensive product and industry environmental footprints, including holistic lifecycle analysis.

Make an Impact: The foundation, in partnership with Greening Australia and the Center for Climate and Energy Solutions, promotes reduced carbon footprint through Make an Impact. The environmental stewardship program includes a website with tips, tool, and resources on how to reduce energy bills and live sustainability; a custom built carbon calculator featuring best practice individual carbon "footprint" analysis and personalized action planning; and an outreach program of educational workshops and hands-on activities to support local action and encourage sustainable change. Visit URL http://alcoa.c2es.org/ for more information.

Type of support: Annual campaigns; Building/renovation; Conferences/seminars; Continuing support; Curriculum development; Emergency funds; Employee matching gifts; Employee volunteer services; Employee-related scholarships; Equipment; Management development/capacity building; Matching/challenge support; Program development; Research; Scholarship funds; Sponsorships.

Geographic limitations: Giving on a national and international basis in areas of company operations, with emphasis on New York, NY, Pittsburgh, PA, Africa, Asia, Australia, Brazil, Canada, Caribbean, China, Central America, Europe, Mexico, Russia, and South America.

Support limitations: No support for political or lobbying organizations, sectarian or religious organizations not of direct benefit to the entire community, discriminatory organizations, social clubs or organizations, sports teams, private foundations, or trust funds. No grants to individuals (except for employee-related scholarships), or for endowments, capital campaigns, debt reduction, operating costs or reserves, indirect or overhead costs, fundraising events or sponsorships including walks/runs, golf tournaments, tickets, tables, benefits, raffles, souvenir programs, advertising, or fundraising dinners, trips, conferences, seminars, festivals, one-day events, documentaries, videos, or research projects/programs.

Publications: Application guidelines; Corporate giving report; Grants list; Newsletter; Program policy statement.

Application information: Applications accepted. The minimum grant request is $15,000. Selected applicants will be invited to submit an online application. Organizations receiving support are asked to submit interim reports and a final report. Applicants should submit the following:

1) results expected from proposed grant
2) population served
3) copy of IRS Determination Letter
4) brief history of organization and description of its mission
5) detailed description of project and amount of funding requested
6) contact person
7) copy of current year's organizational budget and/or project budget

Initial approach: Proposal to nearest company facility
Copies of proposal: 1
Board meeting date(s): Monthly
Deadline(s): Contact nearest company facility

Officers and Directors:* Paula Davis*, Pres.; Dean Will, Cont. and Business Mgr.; Nicholas J. Ashooh; Chris L. Ayers; John (Jack) D. Bergen; Alan Cransberg; Franklin L. Feder; Shauna Huang; Lysane Martel; Tim D. Myers; William J. O'Rourke; William F. (Bill) Oplin; Shannon Parks; Rosa Garcia Pineiro; Maxim Smirnov.

Corporate Trustee: The Bank of New York Mellon, N.A.

Number of staff: 6 full-time professional; 1 full-time support.

EIN: 251128857

Selected grants: The following grants are a representative sample of this grantmaker's funding activity:

$1,500,000 to Girl Scouts of the U.S.A., Council of Greater new York, New York, NY, 2011. For Girl Scouts Forever Green program, payable over 2.00 years.
$450,000 to City Year, Boston, MA, 2011. For South Bronx Team Sponsorship Program for Public School 48 and Middle School 424, payable over 2.00 years.
$250,000 to US FIRST, Manchester, NH, 2011. For FIRST Tech Challenge Robotics program, payable over 3.00 years.
$200,000 to Manufacturing Institute, Washington, DC, 2011. For Manufacturing Skills Certification System.
$40,000 to American Enterprise Institute for Public Policy Research, Washington, DC, 2011. For Advancing American Competitiveness: Evaluating U.S. Policy, Ensuring Survival of U.S. Business.
$23,625 to Slavic Village Development, Cleveland, OH, 2011. For Morgana Run Trail Tree Planting and Restoration Project.
$20,000 to California State University at Dominguez Hills Foundation, Carson, CA, 2011. For STEM scholarships.
$19,000 to Boys and Girls Club of Simi Valley, Simi Valley, CA, 2011. For After School Education Program.
$18,000 to Pomona Unified School District, Adult Education, Pomona, CA, 2011. For Machinist CNC Class.

83
Alcon Laboratories, Inc.

6201 S. Fwy.
Fort Worth, TX 76134-2001 (817) 293-0450

Company URL: http://www.alcon.com
Establishment information: Established in 1945.
Company type: Subsidiary of a foreign company
Business activities: Sells eye care products, including surgical, pharmaceutical, and contact lens.
Business type (SIC): Ophthalmic goods; drugs; medical instruments and supplies
Corporate officers: Robert Karsunky, C.F.O.; Elaine E. Whitbeck, Sr. V.P., Genl. Counsel, and Corp. Secy.; Merrick McCracken, Sr. V.P., Human Resources
Giving statement: Giving through the Alcon Cares, Inc. and the Alcon Foundation, Inc.

Alcon Cares, Inc.

6201 S. Freeway
Fort Worth, TX 76134-2001 (817) 293-0450
URL: http://www.alcon.com/en/corporate-responsibility/alcon-foundation.asp

Donor: Alcon Laboratories, Inc.
Contact: Don Doyle, Pres.
Financial data (yr. ended 12/31/11): Assets, $0 (M); gifts received, $226,921; expenditures, $226,921; qualifying distributions, $226,921; giving activities include $226,921 for 19,840 grants (high: $39; low: $1).
Purpose and activities: The foundation provides medications to individuals who cannot afford their medication and to those who lack prescription insurance coverage; and provides access to eye care medication for U.S. medical facilities serving large numbers of Medicare and Medicaid patients.
Fields of interest: Eye diseases; Eye research; Human services Economically disadvantaged.
Type of support: Donated products; Grants to individuals; In-kind gifts.
Geographic limitations: Giving on a national basis and to communities in which Alcon has a facility.
Support limitations: No support for religious, fraternal, labor, political or veteran programs. No support for non 501(c)(3) designated organizations, or for individual or family requests for scholarships, or for fellowship assistance, endowments, or capital and building campaigns outside of community-aligned grants, or for matching gifts, private schools K-12, books, research papers, or articles in professional journals, or for travel expenses.
Publications: Application guidelines.
Application information: Applications accepted. Applications forms must be endorsed and signed by a healthcare pro. Application form required.

Initial approach: Download application form and fax or mail to foundation
Deadline(s): None

Officers and Directors: Don Doyle, Pres.; Sara Woodward, V.P.; Bruce Thorpe, Secy.; Carol Duvall, Treas.; John Reding; Becky Walker.
EIN: 204118713

The Alcon Foundation, Inc.

6201 S. Freeway
Fort Worth, TX 76134-2099 (800) 222-8103
URL: http://www.alcon.com/en/corporate-responsibility/alcon-foundation.asp

Establishment information: Established in 1962 in TX.
Donor: Alcon Laboratories, Inc.
Contact: Matthew Head, Dir., Corp. Giving
Financial data (yr. ended 12/31/11): Assets, $30,000 (M); gifts received, $3,975,157; expenditures, $4,006,097; qualifying distributions, $4,006,094; giving activities include $3,975,157 for 93 grants (high: $943,781; low: $84).
Purpose and activities: The Alcon Foundation supports programs designed to improve the quality of eye care and patient access to eye care; advance eye health education, research, and awareness; and enhance and create sound communities where Alcon has a facility presence.
Fields of interest: Medical school/education; Education; Hospitals (specialty); Optometry/vision screening; Eye diseases; Eye research; Human services; Community/economic development Blind/visually impaired; Economically disadvantaged.
Program:

Community-Aligned Grants: The foundation awards grants to nonprofit organizations located in areas of company operations. Special emphasis is directed toward civic and community programs designed to enhance quality of life; arts and culture programs designed to enrich the cultural environment; and health and human service programs designed to promote patient eye heath education and access to care.

Type of support: Curriculum development; Management development/capacity building; Program development; Research.
Geographic limitations: Giving primarily in areas of company operations in Irvine, CA, Atlanta, GA,

Sinking Spring, PA, Fort Worth and Houston, TX, and Huntington, WV.
Support limitations: No support for fraternal, labor, political, or veterans' organizations, discriminatory organizations, or private K-12 schools. No grants to individuals, or for family requests for scholarships, fellowships, religious activities, endowments, capital or building campaigns, matching gifts, university administrative, management, or indirect fees, golf tournaments, athletic events, league or team sponsorships, school-affiliated orchestras, bands, choirs, student trips or tours, unrestricted grants, books, research papers, articles in professional journals, travel, fundraising activities, or advertising sponsorships.
Publications: Application guidelines; Corporate giving report.
Application information: Applications accepted. Application form required. Applicants should submit the following:
1) copy of IRS Determination Letter
2) brief history of organization and description of its mission
3) copy of most recent annual report/audited financial statement/990
4) listing of board of directors, trustees, officers and other key people and their affiliations
5) detailed description of project and amount of funding requested
6) listing of additional sources and amount of support

Initial approach: Complete online eligibility quiz and application
Board meeting date(s): 4th quarter
Deadline(s): None; Feb. 1 to July 31 for requests of $50,000 or more
Final notification: Final notification for large grant requests is 1st quarter of the following year.

Officers and Directors:* Kevin J. Buehler*, Chair.; Bettina Maunz, Pres.; Christina Ackerman; Robert Kim; Merrick McCracken; Steven Wilson.
EIN: 200166600
Selected grants: The following grants are a representative sample of this grantmaker's funding activity:
$685,195 to United Way of Tarrant County, Fort Worth, TX, 2010.
$600,000 to Johns Hopkins Hospital, Wilmer Institute, Baltimore, MD, 2010.
$565,000 to American Academy of Ophthalmology, Foundation of the, San Francisco, CA, 2010.
$200,000 to Fort Worth Museum of Science and History, Fort Worth, TX, 2010.
$80,000 to American Glaucoma Society, San Francisco, CA, 2010.
$75,219 to United Way of Berks County, Reading, PA, 2010.
$50,000 to Project HOPE - The People-to-People Health Foundation, Millwood, VA, 2010.
$25,000 to International Sister Cities Association of Fort Worth, Fort Worth, TX, 2010.
$14,200 to Casa Manana, Fort Worth, TX, 2010.

84
Aleut Corporation

4000 Old Seward Hwy., Ste. 300
Anchorage, AK 99503-6068
(907) 561-4300

Company URL: http://www.aleutcorp.com
Establishment information: Established in 1972.
Company type: Native corporation
Business activities: Operates native corporation.
Business type (SIC): Nonclassifiable establishments
Corporate officers: Dick Jacobsen, Chair.; Sharon Guenther Lind, Vice-Chair.; David Gillespie, C.E.O.; Thomas Mack, Pres.; Tracy Timothy Woo, C.F.O.; Tara Bourdukofsky, Secy.-Treas.; Robert Hemmen, Cont.
Board of directors: Dick Jacobsen, Chair.; Sharon Guenther Lind, Vice-Chair.; Tara Bourdukofsky; Elary Gromoff, Jr.; Okalena Patricia Lekanoff-Gregory; Jenifer Samuelson-Nelson; Stanley Mack; Carl Moses
Giving statement: Giving through the Aleut Foundation.

The Aleut Foundation

703 W. Tudor Rd., Ste. 102
Anchorage, AK 99503-6650 (907) 646-1929
FAX: (907) 646-1949;
E-mail: taf@thealeutfoundation.org; Additional tel.: (800) 232-4882; URL: http://www.thealeutfoundation.org/

Establishment information: Established in 1987.
Donors: Aleut Corp.; Space Mark Inc.; Aleutian Pribilof Islands Restitution Trust.
Contact: Leatha Merculieff, Exec. Dir.
Financial data (yr. ended 03/31/11): Assets, $387,914 (M); gifts received, $697,381; expenditures, $1,047,088; qualifying distributions, $784,125; giving activities include $784,125 for grants.
Purpose and activities: The foundation awards grants and college scholarships to original enrollees and the descendants of original enrollees of the Aleut Corporation, beneficiaries and the descendants of beneficiaries of the Aleutian Pribilof Islands Restitution Trust, and original enrollees and the descendants of original enrollees of the Isanotski Corporation.
Fields of interest: Native Americans/American Indians.
Programs:

Aleut Foundation Part-Time Scholarships: The foundation awards college scholarships to original enrollees and the descendants of original enrollees of the Aleut Corporation, beneficiaries and the descendants of beneficiaries of the Aleutian Pribilof Islands Restitution Trust, and original enrollees and the descendants of original enrollees of the Isanotski Corporation attending undergraduate, graduate, or master's programs part-time.

Aleut Foundation Scholarships: The foundation awards college scholarships to original enrollees and the descendants of original enrollees of the Aleut Corporation, beneficiaries and the descendants of beneficiaries of the Aleutian Pribilof Islands Restitution Trust, and original enrollees and the descendants of original enrollees of the Isanotski Corporation.

Burial Assistance Grants: The foundation awards $2,000 burial assistance grants to the families of deceased original and the descendents of original enrollees of the Aleut Corporation. Applicant should submit a certified death certificate with the application.

Community Based Education Program: The foundation awards grants to original and descendants of original enrollees of the Aleut Corporation and beneficiaries and descendants of beneficiaries of the Aleutian Pribilof Islands Restitution Trust to attend hazardous medical training and commercial drivers licenses (CDL) off-road driving classes.

Culture Camp Grants: The foundation awards grants to original and the descendants of original enrollees of the Aleut Corporation to attend culture camp.

Lille Hope McGarvey Scholarship: The foundation awards college scholarships to original enrollees and the descendants of original enrollees of the Aleut Corporation, beneficiaries and the descendants of beneficiaries of the Aleutian Pribilof Islands Restitution Trust, and original enrollees and the descendants of original enrollees of the Isanotski Corporation studying in the medical field.

Type of support: Grants to individuals; Internship funds; Scholarships—to individuals.
Geographic limitations: Giving limited to AK.
Publications: Application guidelines; Newsletter; Program policy statement.
Application information: Applications accepted. Application form required.
Requests for scholarships should include a letter of acceptance, a letter of intent, course schedule, official transcripts, two letters of recommendation, and a birth certificate, marriage certificate, or any document linking the applicant's lineage to an original enrollee of the Aleut Corporation and/or a beneficiary of the Aleutian Pribilof Island Restitution Trust. Visit website for detailed application guidelines.

Initial approach: Download application form and mail to foundation
Board meeting date(s): Quarterly
Deadline(s): June 30 and Nov. 28 for scholarships

Officer and Directors:* Kathy Griesbaum*, Chair.; Cynthia H. Lind, Exec. Dir.; Jessica Borenin; Gary Ferguson; Debra Mack; Thomas Mack; Millie McKeown; Boris Merculief.
Number of staff: 2 full-time professional.
EIN: 920124517

85
Alexander & Baldwin, Inc.

822 Bishop St.
P.O. Box 3440
Honolulu, HI 96813 (808) 525-6611
FAX: (808) 525-6652

Company URL: http://www.alexanderbaldwin.com
Establishment information: Established in 1870.
Company type: Public company
Company ticker symbol and exchange: ALEX/NYSE
Business activities: Provides ocean freight transportation services; provides shoreside terminal, stevedoring, and container equipment maintenance services; provides truck brokerage and logistics services; develops and manages real estate; produces sugar cane, coffee, sugar, and molasses; provides trucking services; provides mobile equipment maintenance and repair services; provides self-service storage services; generates electricity.
Business type (SIC): Water transportation; farms, except cash grains/field crop; farms/fruit and nut; sugar, candy, and salted/roasted nut production; miscellaneous prepared foods; trucking and courier services, except by air; warehousing and storage; terminal facilities/motor vehicle maintenance; transportation/deep sea foreign freight; transportation/deep sea domestic freight; transportation services/water; transportation services/freight; electric services; real estate operators and lessors; real estate subdividers and developers
Financial profile for 2012: Number of employees, 946; assets, $1,437,300,000; sales volume, $296,700,000; pre-tax net income, $16,500,000; expenses, $256,300,000; liabilities, $522,900,000
Corporate officers: Stanley M. Kuriyama, Chair. and C.E.O.; Christopher J. Benjamin, Pres. and C.O.O.; Paul K. Ito, Sr. V.P., C.F.O., Treas., and Cont.; Son-Jai Paik, V.P., Human Resources

Board of directors: Stanley M. Kuriyama, Chair.; W. Allen Doane; Walter A. Dods, Jr.; Robert S. Harrison; Charles G. King; Douglas M. Pasquale; Michele K. Saito; Jeffrey N. Watanabe; Eric K. Yeaman
Subsidiaries: A&B Development Co. (California), San Francisco, CA; A&B Properties, Inc., Honolulu, HI; WDCI, Inc., Honolulu, HI
Giving statement: Giving through the Alexander & Baldwin Foundation.
Company EIN: 990032630

Alexander & Baldwin Foundation

P.O. Box 3440
Honolulu, HI 96801-3440 (808) 525-6642
FAX: (808) 525-6677; E-mail: lhowe@abinc.com; Application address for organizations located outside HI and the Pacific: Mathew Cox, Chair. Mainland Contrib. Comm., c/o Matson Navigation Co., Inc., 555 12th St., Oakland, CA 94607; Additional contact for organizations located outside of HI and the Pacific: Paul Merwin, tel.: (707) 421-8121, fax: (707) 421-1835, e-mail: plmifm@aol.com; URL: http://www.alexanderbaldwinfoundation.org

Establishment information: Established in 1991 in HI.
Donors: Alexander & Baldwin, Inc.; A&B Properties, Inc.; East Maui Irrigation Co., Ltd.; Hawaiian Commercial and Sugar Co.; Kahului Trucking and Storage; Kauai Coffee Co.; Kauai Commercial Co., Inc.; Matson Navigation Co., Inc.
Contact: Meredith J. Ching, Pres.
Financial data (yr. ended 12/31/11): Assets, $0 (M); gifts received, $1,002,500; expenditures, $1,646,864; qualifying distributions, $1,620,001; giving activities include $1,620,001 for grants.
Purpose and activities: The foundation supports organizations involved with arts and culture, education, the environment, health, human services, and community development.
Fields of interest: Museums (marine/maritime); Arts; Education, reading; Education; Environment, natural resources; Environment; Health care; Children/youth, services; Human services; Community/economic development; United Ways and Federated Giving Programs.
International interests: Oceania.
Programs:

Employee Matching Gifts Program: The foundation matches contributions made by employees, retirees, and directors of Alexander & Baldwin to educational institutions on a one-for-one basis from $25 to $2,000 per contributor, per year and to organizations involved with arts and culture from $25 to $1,000 per contributor, per year.

Volunteer Matching Gifts Program: The foundation awards $250 grants to nonprofit organizations with which employees of Alexander & Baldwin volunteer at least 25 hours.

Type of support: Annual campaigns; Building/renovation; Capital campaigns; Continuing support; Employee matching gifts; Employee volunteer services; Employee-related scholarships; Equipment; General/operating support; Program development; Seed money.
Geographic limitations: Giving primarily in areas of company operations, with emphasis on AZ, CA, HI, IL, and in the Pacific.
Support limitations: No support for religious organizations or veterans', fraternal, or labor organizations. No grants to individuals, or for travel or endowments, secondary giving, religious activities not of direct benefit to the entire community, advertising, sponsorship of events, or general operating support for United Way agencies; no product or service donations.
Publications: Annual report; Application guidelines; Grants list; Program policy statement.
Application information: Applications accepted. Support is limited to 1 contribution per organization during any given year. Proposals for requests of less than $2,000 should be no longer than 3 pages. Proposals for requests greater than $2,000 should also include an executive summary if proposal exceeds 3 pages. Executive summaries should be no longer than 250 words. Application form required. Applicants should submit the following:
1) results expected from proposed grant
2) statement of problem project will address
3) population served
4) copy of IRS Determination Letter
5) brief history of organization and description of its mission
6) geographic area to be served
7) how project's results will be evaluated or measured
8) list of company employees involved with the organization
9) explanation of why grantmaker is considered an appropriate donor for project
10) listing of board of directors, trustees, officers and other key people and their affiliations
11) detailed description of project and amount of funding requested
12) copy of current year's organizational budget and/or project budget
13) listing of additional sources and amount of support
14) plans for acknowledgement

Initial approach: Download application form and mail proposal and application form to foundation for organizations located in HI and the Pacific; mail to application address for organizations located outside HI and the Pacific
Copies of proposal: 1
Board meeting date(s): Jan., Mar., May, July, Sept., and Nov. for organizations located in HI and the Pacific; monthly for organizations located outside HI and the Pacific
Deadline(s): Feb. 1, Apr. 1, June 1, Aug. 1, Oct. 1, and Dec. 1 for organizations located in HI and the Pacific; first of the month for organizations located outside HI and the Pacific
Final notification: Within 2 weeks of committee meetings

Officers and Directors:* Meredith J. Ching*, Pres.; Christopher J. Benjamin*, V.P. and Treas.; Linda M. Howe, V.P.; Paul K. Ito, V.P.; Alyson J. Nakamura, Secy.; Vic S. Angoco, Jr.; Grant Y.M. Chun; Norbert M. Buelsing; Stanley M. Kuriyama.
Number of staff: 2 part-time professional; 1 part-time support.
EIN: 990291942
Selected grants: The following grants are a representative sample of this grantmaker's funding activity:
$130,000 to United Way, Maui, Wailuku, HI, 2009. For operating support for member agencies.
$100,000 to United Way, Aloha, Honolulu, HI, 2009. For operating support for partner agencies.
$35,000 to Shriners Hospitals for Children, Aloha Chapter, Honolulu, HI, 2009. For capital support for renovation and expansion campaign.
$35,000 to United Way, Aloha, Honolulu, HI, 2009. For operating support for partner agencies.
$25,000 to Child and Family Service, Ewa Beach, HI, 2009. For capital campaign for domestic violence shelter and transitional housing.
$25,000 to University of Hawaii-Maui Community College, Kahului, HI, 2009. For tuition sponsorship/fees for A&B Training Bonus program, which supports Maui small businesses and entrepreneurs.
$20,000 to Alexander and Baldwin Sugar Museum, Puunene, HI, 2009. For general operating support.
$20,000 to United Way of Kauai, Lihue, HI, 2009. For annual support of member agencies.
$15,000 to Helping Hands of Hawaii, Honolulu, HI, 2009. For Ready to Learn program serving Maui schools.
$15,000 to University of Hawaii-Maui Community College, Kahului, HI, 2009. For tuition sponsorship/fees for A&B Training Bonus program, which supports Maui small businesses and entrepreneurs.

86
Alexion Pharmaceuticals, Inc.

352 Knotter Dr.
Cheshire, CT 06410-1138 (203) 272-2596
FAX: (203) 271-8198

Company URL: http://www.alexionpharm.com
Establishment information: Established in 1992.
Company type: Public company
Company ticker symbol and exchange: ALXN/NASDAQ
Business activities: Operates biopharmaceutical company.
Business type (SIC): Drugs
Financial profile for 2012: Number of employees, 1,373; assets, $1,394,750,000; sales volume, $1,134,110,000; pre-tax net income, $397,570,000; expenses, $729,780,000; liabilities, $260,260,000
Forbes 2000 ranking: 2012—1908th in sales, 1450th in profits, and 1957th in assets
Corporate officers: Max Link, Ph.D., Chair.; Leonard Bell, M.D., C.E.O.; Vikas Sinha, Exec V.P. and C.F.O.; John Moriarty, Sr. V.P. Genl. Counsel; James P. Bilotta, V.P. and C.I.O.
Board of directors: Max Link, Ph.D., Chair.; Leonard Bell, M.D.; William Keller; Joseph A. Madri, Ph.D., M.D.; Larry L. Mathis; R. Douglas Norby; Alvin S. Parven; Andreas Rummelt, Ph.D.; Ann M. Veneman
Giving statement: Giving through the Alexion Complement Foundation.
Company EIN: 133648318

Alexion Complement Foundation

352 Knotter Dr.
Cheshire, CT 06410-1138 (888) 765-4747
URL: http://www.alexionpharm.com/SolirisAndPNH/AboutSoliris/Access.aspx

Establishment information: Established in 2007 in CT.
Donor: Alexion Pharmaceuticals, Inc.
Financial data (yr. ended 12/31/10): Assets, $28,098 (M); gifts received, $700,662; expenditures, $703,212; qualifying distributions, $703,212; giving activities include $700,662 for grants to individuals.
Purpose and activities: The foundation provides prescription drug Soliris to uninsured ill patients for treatment of paroxysmal nocturnal hemoglobinura (PNH) and atypical hemolytic uremic syndrome (aHUS).
Fields of interest: Pharmacy/prescriptions; Health care Economically disadvantaged.
Type of support: Donated products; In-kind gifts.
Application information: Applications accepted.

Initial approach: Telephone foundation for application information

Officers: Irving Adler, Pres.; John C. Markow, Secy.; Scott Phillips, Treas.
EIN: 208963321

87

Alfa Mutual Insurance Company

2108 E. South Blvd.
Montgomery, AL 36116-2015
(334) 288-3900

Company URL: https://www.alfains.com/
Establishment information: Established in 1947.
Company type: Mutual company
Business activities: Sells insurance.
Business type (SIC): Insurance carriers
Corporate officers: Jerry A. Newby, Chair., Pres. and C.E.O.; C. Lee Ellis, Exec. V.P., Opers. and Treas.; Ralph C. Forsythe, C.F.O.
Subsidiary: Alfa Corp., Montgomery, AL
Giving statement: Giving through the Alfa Foundation.

Alfa Foundation

P.O. Box 11189
Montgomery, AL 36111-0189 (334) 613-4498

Establishment information: Established in 1996 in AL.
Donors: Alfa Mutual Insurance Co.; Alfa Mutual Fire Insurance Co.
Contact: David R. Proctor
Financial data (yr. ended 10/31/11): Assets, $15,023,540 (M); expenditures, $801,449; qualifying distributions, $765,000; giving activities include $765,000 for grants.
Purpose and activities: The foundation supports organizations involved with secondary, higher, and engineering education, pollution control, health, cancer, equestrianism, and children services.
Fields of interest: Secondary school/education; Higher education; Engineering school/education; Environment, pollution control; Health care; Cancer; Athletics/sports, equestrianism; YM/YWCAs & YM/YWHAs; Children, services; United Ways and Federated Giving Programs.
Type of support: General/operating support.
Geographic limitations: Giving limited to AL.
Support limitations: No grants to individuals.
Application information: Applications accepted. Application form not required.
Initial approach: Proposal
Deadline(s): None
Officers: Jerry A. Newby, Pres.; C. Lee Ellis, Exec. V.P.; H. Al Scott, Secy.; Stephen G. Rutledge, Treas.
EIN: 721373145

88

Alhambra Foundry Company, Ltd.

1147 S. Meridian Ave.
P.O. Box 469
Alhambra, CA 91802-0469 (626) 289-4294

Company URL: http://alhambrafoundry.com/
Establishment information: Established in 1923.
Company type: Private company
Business activities: Manufactures foundry products.
Business type (SIC): Iron and steel foundries; metal products/structural
Corporate officers: Arzhang Baghkhanian, C.E.O.; Mike Bagkhanian, Pres.
Giving statement: Giving through the Alhambra Foundry Company, Ltd. Scholarship Foundation.

Alhambra Foundry Company, Ltd. Scholarship Foundation

1147 Meridian Ave.
Alhambra, CA 91803-1218

Donor: Alhambra Foundry Co., Ltd.
Financial data (yr. ended 12/31/11): Assets, $1 (M); gifts received, $885; expenditures, $1,885; qualifying distributions, $1,000; giving activities include $1,000 for grants.
Purpose and activities: The foundation awards college scholarships to children of employees of Alhambra Foundry. The program is administered by the Foundry Education Foundation.
Type of support: Employee-related scholarships.
Geographic limitations: Giving primarily in areas of company operations.
Application information: Applications not accepted. Unsolicited requests for funds not accepted.
Directors: Arzhang Baghkhanian; Michael Smolski; James Wright.
EIN: 956046932

89

Alice Manufacturing Company, Inc.

208 E. 1st Ave.
Easley, SC 29640-3039 (864) 859-6323

Company URL: http://www.alicemfgco.com
Establishment information: Established in 1923.
Company type: Private company
Business activities: Operates broadwoven cotton fabric mills.
Business type (SIC): Fabrics/broadwoven natural cotton
Financial profile for 2010: Number of employees, 300
Corporate officers: Smyth McKiffick, Chair. and C.E.O.; Bradley S. Wurst, Pres.; Robert Thomas, C.F.O.
Board of director: Smyth McKiffick, Chair.
Giving statement: Giving through the Ellison S. & Noel P. McKissick Foundation.

Ellison S. & Noel P. McKissick Foundation

(formerly Alice Manufacturing Company, Inc. Foundation)
P.O. Box 369
Easley, SC 29641-0369

Establishment information: Established in 1983.
Donors: Alice Manufacturing Co., Inc.; Trust A U/A of Ellison S. Mckissick, Jr.
Financial data (yr. ended 06/30/12): Assets, $16,170,687 (M); expenditures, $848,318; qualifying distributions, $759,054; giving activities include $759,054 for grants.
Purpose and activities: The foundation supports museums and organizations involved with education, land conservation, medical care, children, and Christianity.
Fields of interest: Museums; Elementary/secondary education; Higher education; Business school/education; Education; Environment, land resources; Medical care, rehabilitation; Boys & girls clubs; American Red Cross; Children, services; United Ways and Federated Giving Programs; Christian agencies & churches.
Type of support: General/operating support; Scholarship funds.
Geographic limitations: Giving primarily in NC and SC.
Support limitations: No grants to individuals.
Application information: Applications not accepted. Contributes only to pre-selected organizations.
Officer and Directors: Robert H. Thomas, Treas.; Elizabeth M. Fauntleroy; Ellison Smyth McKissick III; Caroline McKissick Young.
EIN: 570739969
Selected grants: The following grants are a representative sample of this grantmaker's funding activity:
$120,000 to United Way of Pickens County, Easley, SC, 2011.
$120,000 to United Way of Pickens County, Easley, SC, 2011.
$50,000 to Tri-County Technical College, Pendleton, SC, 2011.
$42,162 to Christ Church Episcopal School, Greenville, SC, 2011.
$25,000 to Clemson University, Clemson, SC, 2011.
$25,000 to Clemson University, Clemson, SC, 2011.
$10,000 to Peter-Paul Development Center, Richmond, VA, 2011.
$10,000 to Peter-Paul Development Center, Richmond, VA, 2011.
$5,000 to United Way of Pickens County, Easley, SC, 2011.
$1,500 to Tri-County Technical College, Pendleton, SC, 2011.

90

Alima Cosmetics, Inc.

(doing business as Alima Pure)
18342 S.E. River Rd.
Portland, OR 97267 (503) 786-8224

Company URL: http://www.alimapure.com
Establishment information: Established in 2004.
Company type: Private company
Business activities: Operates cosmetics company.
Business type (SIC): Drugs, proprietaries, and sundries—wholesale
Corporate officer: Kathleen O'Brien, Pres.
Giving statement: Giving through the Alima Cosmetics, Inc. Corporate Giving Program.

Alima Cosmetics, Inc. Corporate Giving Program

18342 SE River Rd.
Portland, OR 97267-6026 (503) 786-8224
URL: http://www.alimapure.com

Purpose and activities: Alima Cosmetics is a certified B Corporation that donates a percentage of net profits to nonprofit organizations. Special emphasis is directed toward organizations involved with the environment. Support is given on a national and international basis, with some emphasis on Portland, Oregon.
Fields of interest: Environment, toxics; Environment; International human rights Women.
Type of support: Continuing support.
Geographic limitations: Giving on a national and international basis, with some emphasis on Portland, OR.

91

Allegheny Technologies Incorporated

(formerly Allegheny Teledyne Incorporated)
1000 6 PPG Pl.
Pittsburgh, PA 15222 (412) 394-2800
FAX: (412) 394-3034

Company URL: http://www.alleghenytechnologies.com
Establishment information: Established in 1996 from the merger of Allegheny Ludlum Corp. with Teledyne, Inc.
Company type: Public company
Company ticker symbol and exchange: ATI/NYSE
Business activities: Manufactures specialty metals, aerospace and electronics products, industrial products, and consumer products.
Business type (SIC): Steel mill products; machinery/metalworking; appliances/household; electronic components and accessories; aircraft and parts
Financial profile for 2012: Number of employees, 11,200; assets, $6,247,800,000; sales volume, $5,031,500,000; pre-tax net income, $244,000,000; expenses, $4,716,100,000; liabilities, $3,768,200,000
Fortune 1000 ranking: 2012—490th in revenues, 640th in profits, and 530th in assets
Corporate officers: Richard J. Harshman, Chair., Pres., and C.E.O.; Dale G. Reid, Exec. V.P., Finance, and C.F.O.; Elliot S. Davis, Sr. V.P., Genl. Counsel, and Corp. Secy.; Danny L. Greenfield, V.P., Corp. Comms.; Mary Beth Moor, V.P., Human Resources; Rose Marie Manley, Treas.; Karl D. Schwartz, Cont. and C.A.O.
Board of directors: Richard J. Harshman, Chair.; Carolyn Corvi; Diane C. Creel; James C. Diggs; J. Brett Harvey; Barbara S. Jeremiah; Michael J. Joyce; John R. Pipski, Jr.; James E. Rohr; Louis J. Thomas; John D. Turner
Subsidiaries: Allegheny Ludlum Corporation, Pittsburgh, PA; ALstrip, Inc., Skokie, IL; ALstrip East, Exton, PA; ALstrip South, Springfield, TN; ALstrip West, Brea, CA
Plants: Wallingford, CT; New Castle, IN; Lockport, NY; Claremore, OK; Brackenridge, Leechburg, Vandergrift, PA
International operations: Australia; Belgium; China; France; Germany; India; Israel; Italy; Japan; Singapore; South Korea; Spain; Taiwan; United Kingdom
Historic mergers: Ladish Co., Inc. (May 6, 2011)
Giving statement: Giving through the Allegheny Technologies Charitable Trust and the Ladish Company Foundation.
Company EIN: 251792394

Allegheny Technologies Charitable Trust

(formerly Allegheny Teledyne Incorporated Charitable Trust)
1000 6 PPG Pl.
Pittsburgh, PA 15222-5479 (412) 394-2800

Establishment information: Established in 1997 in PA.
Donors: Allegheny Teledyne Inc.; Allegheny Technologies Inc.
Contact: Lawrence S. McAndrews, Tr.
Financial data (yr. ended 12/31/11): Assets, $1,360 (M); expenditures, $37,183; qualifying distributions, $37,000; giving activities include $37,000 for 2 grants (high: $20,000; low: $17,000).
Purpose and activities: The trust supports organizations involved with performing arts, secondary and higher education, health, human services, and community development.
Fields of interest: Performing arts; Performing arts, theater; Performing arts, orchestras; Secondary school/education; Higher education; Hospitals (general); Health care; Boy scouts; Human services; Community/economic development; United Ways and Federated Giving Programs.
Geographic limitations: Giving primarily in PA, with emphasis on Pittsburgh.
Support limitations: No support for private foundations. No grants to individuals.
Application information: Applications accepted. Application form not required. Applicants should submit the following:
1) copy of IRS Determination Letter
Initial approach: Proposal
Deadline(s): None
Trustees: Elliot S. Davis; Lauren S. McAndrews.
EIN: 237873055

Ladish Company Foundation

P.O. Box 8902
Cudahy, WI 53110-8902

Establishment information: Established in 1952 in WI.
Donor: Ladish Co., Inc.
Contact: Ronald O. Wiese, Tr.
Financial data (yr. ended 11/30/12): Assets, $29,706,516 (M); expenditures, $1,482,858; qualifying distributions, $1,455,000; giving activities include $1,455,000 for 104 grants (high: $300,000; low: $1,000).
Purpose and activities: The foundation supports organizations involved with arts and culture, education, animal welfare, multiple sclerosis, diabetes, hunger, human services, Christianity, and the visually impaired.
Fields of interest: Museums; Arts; Elementary/secondary education; Higher education; Engineering school/education; Libraries (public); Education; Animal welfare; Multiple sclerosis; Diabetes; Food services; Food banks; YM/YWCAs & YM/YWHAs; Children/youth, services; Human services; United Ways and Federated Giving Programs; Christian agencies & churches Blind/visually impaired.
Type of support: Annual campaigns; Capital campaigns; General/operating support; Program development; Research; Scholarship funds.
Geographic limitations: Giving primarily in WI.
Support limitations: No grants to individuals.
Application information: Applications not accepted. Contributes only to pre-selected organizations.
Board meeting date(s): Oct.
Trustees: Wayne E. Larsen; Gary J. Vroman; Ronald O. Wiese; Kerry L. Woody.
EIN: 396040489
Selected grants: The following grants are a representative sample of this grantmaker's funding activity:
$50,000 to Childrens Hospital of Wisconsin, Milwaukee, WI, 2010.
$50,000 to Saint Marcus Lutheran School, Milwaukee, WI, 2010. For capital campaign.
$50,000 to United Way of Greater Milwaukee, Milwaukee, WI, 2010. For general support.
$40,000 to Zoological Society of Milwaukee County, Milwaukee, WI, 2010.
$34,000 to Hunger Task Force, Milwaukee, WI, 2010.
$30,000 to Badger Association of the Blind and Visually Impaired, Milwaukee, WI, 2010.
$22,000 to Center for Deaf-Blind Persons, Milwaukee, WI, 2010.
$20,000 to Milwaukee Public Museum, Milwaukee, WI, 2010. For general support.
$10,000 to Camp Heartland, Milwaukee, WI, 2010. For general support.
$9,000 to Girl Scouts of the U.S.A., Milwaukee, WI, 2010. For general support.

92

Allegis Group, Inc.

7301 Parkway Dr.
Hanover, MD 21076-1159 (410) 579-4800
FAX: (410) 540-7556

Company URL: http://www.allegisgroup.com
Establishment information: Established in 1983.
Company type: Private company
Business activities: Provides contract employee services; provides consulting services.
Business type (SIC): Personnel supply services; management and public relations services
Financial profile for 2011: Number of employees, 10,000; sales volume, $6,405,960,000
Corporate officers: James C. Davis, Chair.; Michael Salandra, C.E.O.; Paul Bowie, C.F.O.; John Hall, C.A.O.; Michael Varon, V.P., Mktg.; Tracy Johnson, V.P., Human Resources
Board of director: James C. Davis, Chair.
International operations: United Kingdom
Giving statement: Giving through the Allegis Group Foundation, Inc.

Allegis Group Foundation, Inc.

(formerly Team Aerotek Foundation, Inc.)
7301 Parkway Dr.
Hanover, MD 21076-1159 (410) 579-3509

Establishment information: Established in 1998 in MD.
Donors: Aerotek, Inc.; Allegis Group, Inc.
Contact: Hilary Murray
Financial data (yr. ended 12/31/11): Assets, $14,297,573 (M); gifts received, $1,750,000; expenditures, $1,018,901; qualifying distributions, $944,500; giving activities include $944,500 for grants.
Purpose and activities: The foundation supports organizations involved with education, water conservation, cancer, heart disease, recreation, human services, international relief, and Catholicism. Special emphasis is directed toward programs designed to assist underprivileged children.
Fields of interest: Elementary/secondary education; Education; Environment, water resources; Health care, volunteer services; Cancer; Cancer, leukemia; Heart & circulatory diseases; Recreation, parks/playgrounds; Athletics/sports, baseball; Recreation; Boy scouts; American Red Cross; Children, services; Human services; International relief; Catholic agencies & churches Economically disadvantaged.
Program:
Employee Matching Gifts: The foundation matches contributions raised by employees through walks, runs, and bike rides to support their charity.
Type of support: Employee matching gifts; General/operating support; Program development; Scholarship funds.
Geographic limitations: Giving primarily in areas of company operations in Baltimore, MD.
Application information: Applications accepted. Application form not required.
Initial approach: Proposal
Deadline(s): None

Officers and Directors:* James C. Davis*, Pres.; Neil Mann, V.P. and Treas.; Randall D. Sones, Esq., Secy.; Stephen J. Bisciotti.
EIN: 311608900
Selected grants: The following grants are a representative sample of this grantmaker's funding activity:
$50,000 to Parks and People Foundation for Baltimore Recreation and Parks, Baltimore, MD, 2010.
$50,000 to Teach for America, Baltimore, MD, 2010.
$40,000 to Baltimore Jesuit Educational Initiative, Baltimore, MD, 2010.
$40,000 to Living Classrooms Foundation, Baltimore, MD, 2010.
$25,000 to Archdiocese of Baltimore, Baltimore, MD, 2010.
$25,000 to Childrens Scholarship Fund Baltimore, Baltimore, MD, 2010.
$21,373 to American Cancer Society, Baltimore, MD, 2010.
$16,170 to American Heart Association, Baltimore, MD, 2010.
$13,435 to Leukemia & Lymphoma Society, Baltimore, MD, 2010.
$2,500 to Saint Marys Seminary and University, Baltimore, MD, 2010.

93
Allen & Company Incorporated
711 5th Ave., 9th Fl.
New York, NY 10022-3111 (212) 832-8001

Establishment information: Established in 1922.
Company type: Private company
Business activities: Provides investment services.
Business type (SIC): Investors/miscellaneous
Corporate officers: Donald R. Keough, Chair.; Herbert Anthony Allen III, Pres. and C.E.O.
Board of director: Donald R. Keough, Chair.
Giving statement: Giving through the Allen & Company Incorporated Corporate Giving Program.

Allen & Company Incorporated Corporate Giving Program
711 5th Ave.
New York, NY 10022-3111 (212) 832-8000

Contact: Kim M. Wieland, Managing Dir. and C.F.O.
Purpose and activities: Allen makes charitable contributions to nonprofit organizations on a case by case basis. Support is given primarily in areas of company operations.
Fields of interest: General charitable giving.
Type of support: General/operating support; Sponsorships.
Geographic limitations: Giving primarily in areas of company operations.
Support limitations: No grants to individuals.
Application information: Application form not required. Applicants should submit the following:
1) detailed description of project and amount of funding requested
Initial approach: Proposal to headquarters
Copies of proposal: 1
Deadline(s): None
Final notification: 2 to 3 weeks if approved

94
Allen & Overy LLP
1221 Ave. of the Americas
New York, NY 10020-1001 (212) 610-6300

Company URL: http://www.allenovery.com/AOWEB/Home/AllenOveryHome.aspx?prefLangID=410
Establishment information: Established in 1930.
Company type: Private company
Business activities: Operates law firm.
Business type (SIC): Legal services
Corporate officer: Kevin O'Shea, Partner
Office: New York, NY
International operations: Australia; Belgium; Brazil; China; Czech Republic; France; Germany; Greece; Hong Kong; Hungary; India; Indonesia; Italy; Japan; Luxembourg; Netherlands; Poland; Qatar; Romania; Russia; Saudi Arabia; Singapore; Slovakia; Spain; Thailand; United Arab Emirates; United Kingdom
Giving statement: Giving through the Allen & Overy LLP Pro Bono Program.

Allen & Overy LLP Pro Bono Program
1221 Ave. of the Americas
New York, NY 10020-1001 (212) 610-6300
FAX: (212) 610-6399;
E-mail: helen.rogers@allenovery.com; Tel. for Helen Rogers: +44 (0)20 3088 0000; URL: http://www.allenovery.com/corporate-responsibility/probono-community/Pages/default.aspx

Contact: Helen Rogers, Pro Bono and Community Affairs Mgr.
Purpose and activities: Allen & Overy makes charitable contributions to nonprofit organizations involved with improving education and employment, supporting vulnerable people, increasing access to justice, and helping to eradicate poverty.
Fields of interest: Arts; Education; Legal services; Employment; Disasters, preparedness/services; Youth development; Children, services; Homeless, human services; International relief; International human rights; Anti-slavery/human trafficking Economically disadvantaged.
Type of support: Continuing support; Employee volunteer services; General/operating support; Pro bono services - legal; Program development; Scholarships—to individuals.
Application information: A Pro Bono Committee manages the pro bono program.
Initial approach: E-mail letter of inquiry

95
Allen Matkins Leck Gamble Mallory & Natsis LLP
515 S. Figueroa St., 9th Fl.
Los Angeles, CA 90071-3398
(213) 622-5555

Company URL: http://www.allenmatkins.com
Establishment information: Established in 1977.
Company type: Private company
Business activities: Operates law firm.
Business type (SIC): Legal services
Corporate officer: Frederick L. Allen, Partner
Offices: Irvine, Los Angeles, San Diego, San Francisco, Walnut Creek, CA
Giving statement: Giving through the Allen Matkins Leck Gamble Mallory & Natsis LLP Pro Bono Program.

Allen Matkins Leck Gamble Mallory & Natsis LLP Pro Bono Program
515 S. Figueroa St., 9th Fl.
Los Angeles, CA 90071-3398 (213) 955-5584
E-mail: emurray@allenmatkins.com; URL: http://www.allenmatkins.com/en/About-Us/Commitment-to-Community.aspx

Contact: Emily Murray, Partner
Purpose and activities: Allen Matkins makes charitable contributions to nonprofit organizations involved with health, youth development, human services, and on a case by case basis.
Fields of interest: Health care; Legal services; Youth development; Human services; General charitable giving.
Type of support: Employee volunteer services; General/operating support; Pro bono services - legal; Sponsorships.
Application information: A Pro Bono Committee manages the pro bono program.

96
Ivan Allen Workspace, LLC
(formerly Ivan Allen Furniture Co., LLC)
1000 Marietta St. N.W., Ste. 224
Atlanta, GA 30318-5506 (404) 760-8700
FAX: (404) 760-8673

Company URL: http://www.ivanallen.com
Establishment information: Established in 1902.
Company type: Subsidiary of a public company
Business activities: Distributes office furniture and equipment and printing and office supplies; designs and prints office stationery and business forms.
Business type (SIC): Furniture and home furnishings—wholesale; printing/commercial; professional and commercial equipment—wholesale; paper and paper products—wholesale; engineering, architectural, and surveying services
Corporate officers: Inman Allen, Chair. and C.E.O.; John Michael, Pres. and C.O.O.; Laura Wagner, Cont.
Board of director: Inman Allen, Chair.
Giving statement: Giving through the Ivan Allen Workspace, LLC Corporate Giving Program and the Allen Foundation Inc.

Allen Foundation Inc.
P.O. Box 18979
Atlanta, GA 31126 (404) 365-8215

Establishment information: Established in 1956 in GA.
Donors: Ivan Allen Furniture Co., LLC; Ivan Allen Workspace, LLC.
Contact: Marilyn Arkin, Secy.
Financial data (yr. ended 12/31/11): Assets, $22,902 (M); expenditures, $1,375; qualifying distributions, $325; giving activities include $325 for grants.
Purpose and activities: The foundation supports organizations involved with arts and culture, education, and human services.
Fields of interest: Human services.
Type of support: General/operating support.
Geographic limitations: Giving primarily in the South, with emphasis on GA.
Support limitations: No grants to individuals.
Application information: Applications accepted. Application form not required.
Initial approach: Proposal
Copies of proposal: 1
Deadline(s): 4th calendar quarter

Officers: H. Inman Allen, Chair.; Marilyn Arkin, Secy.
Number of staff: None.
EIN: 586037237

97
Allen-Edmonds Shoe Corporation

201 E. Seven Hills Rd.
P.O. Box 998
Port Washington, WI 53074-2504
(262) 235-6000

Company URL: http://www.allenedmonds.com
Establishment information: Established in 1922.
Company type: Private company
Business activities: Manufactures men's shoes.
Business type (SIC): Leather footwear
Corporate officers: Paul D. Grangaard, Pres. and C.E.O.; Jay P. Schauer, C.F.O.; Tim Cronin, Sr. V.P., Sales
Subsidiary: Woodlore Inc., Port Washington, WI
Giving statement: Giving through the Stollenwerk Family Foundation.

Stollenwerk Family Foundation

(formerly Allen-Edmonds Shoe Corporation Charitable Foundation)
10941 N. Range Line Rd.
Mequon, WI 53092-4927

Establishment information: Established in 1998 in WI.
Donors: Allen-Edmonds Shoe Corp.; John & Joellen Stollenwerk.
Financial data (yr. ended 12/31/11): Assets, $358 (M); gifts received, $500; expenditures, $15,564; qualifying distributions, $15,500; giving activities include $15,500 for grants.
Purpose and activities: The foundation supports organizations involved with education, youth, family services, and Catholicism.
Fields of interest: Elementary/secondary education; Higher education; Education; YM/YWCAs & YM/YWHAs; Youth, services; Family services; Catholic agencies & churches.
Type of support: Continuing support; General/operating support.
Geographic limitations: Giving limited to Milwaukee, WI.
Application information: Applications not accepted. Contributes only to pre-selected organizations.
Trustees: S. Pelz; John J. Stollenwerk; J. Stollenwerk, Jr.; P. Stollenwerk.
EIN: 391949021
Selected grants: The following grants are a representative sample of this grantmaker's funding activity:
$100,000 to Northland College, Ashland, WI, 2010.
$26,500 to Skylight Opera Theater, Milwaukee, WI, 2010.
$10,000 to Notre Dame Middle School, Milwaukee, WI, 2010.
$7,848 to UWM Foundation, Milwaukee, WI, 2010.
$5,000 to Boy Scouts of America, Milwaukee, WI, 2010.
$5,000 to Catholic Relief Services, Baltimore, MD, 2010.
$4,000 to Milwaukee Public Library Foundation, Milwaukee, WI, 2010.
$2,500 to Childrens Outing Association, Milwaukee, WI, 2010.
$2,500 to Partners Advancing Values in Education, Milwaukee, WI, 2010.
$2,500 to YMCA of Door County, Sturgeon Bay, WI, 2010.

98
Allens, Inc.

(formerly Allen Canning, Co.)
305 E. Main St.
Siloam Springs, AR 72761-3231
(479) 524-6431

Company URL: http://www.allencanning.com
Establishment information: Established in 1926.
Company type: Private company
Business activities: Produces vegetables.
Business type (SIC): Specialty foods/canned, frozen, and preserved
Corporate officers: Roderick L. Allen, Chair. and C.E.O.; Joshua C. Allen, Exec. V.P., Opers.; Michael D. Hubbard, V.P., Sales and Mktg.; Lori Sherrell, Cont. and Secy.
Board of director: Roderick L. Allen, Chair.
Giving statement: Giving through the Charlotte D. Allen and Delbert E. Allen, Sr. Charitable and Scholarship Trust.

The Charlotte D. Allen and Delbert E. Allen, Sr. Charitable and Scholarship Trust

P.O. Box 7200
Siloam Springs, AR 72761-7200 (479) 238-9811

Establishment information: Established in 1989 in AR.
Donor: Allen Canning Co.
Financial data (yr. ended 12/31/11): Assets, $523,078 (M); expenditures, $27,957; qualifying distributions, $26,860; giving activities include $26,860 for grants.
Purpose and activities: The foundation supports organizations involved with Christianity and awards college scholarships.
Fields of interest: Education; Health care; Religion.
Type of support: Building/renovation; Scholarships—to individuals.
Geographic limitations: Giving primarily in Siloam Springs, AR.
Application information: Applications accepted. Application form required. Applicants should submit the following:
1) copy of most recent annual report/audited financial statement/990
2) detailed description of project and amount of funding requested

Initial approach: Letter
Deadline(s): Jan. 31 through May 31 for scholarships

Trustees: Cheryl Harrison.
EIN: 716138517

99
Allergan, Inc.

2525 Dupont Dr.
Irvine, CA 92612 (714) 246-4500
FAX: (714) 246-6987

Company URL: http://www.allergan.com
Establishment information: Established in 1948.
Company type: Public company
Company ticker symbol and exchange: AGN/NYSE
International Securities Identification Number: US0184901025
Business activities: Manufactures optical wear, eye care, and dermatology products.
Business type (SIC): Ophthalmic goods; drugs
Financial profile for 2012: Number of employees, 10,800; assets, $9,179,300,000; sales volume, $5,646,600,000; pre-tax net income, $1,531,000,000; expenses, $4,035,600,000; liabilities, $3,342,200,000
Fortune 1000 ranking: 2012—440th in revenues, 186th in profits, and 415th in assets
Corporate officers: David E.I. Pyott, Chair., Pres., and C.E.O.; Jeffrey L. Edwards, Exec. V.P., Finance and C.F.O.; Arnold A. Pinkston, Exec. V.P. and Genl. Counsel; Scott D. Sherman, Exec. V.P., Human Resources; James F. Barlow, Sr. V.P. and Corp. Cont.
Board of directors: David E.I. Pyott, Chair.; Deborah L. Dunsire, M.D.; Michael R. Gallagher; Dawn Hudson; Trevor M. Jones, Ph.D.; Louis J. Lavigne, Jr.; Peter J. McDonnell, M.D.; Timothy D. Proctor; Russell T. Ray
International operations: Argentina; Australia; Austria; Belgium; Bermuda; Brazil; Canada; Cayman Islands; Chile; Colombia; Costa Rica; Denmark; France; Germany; Hong Kong; India; Ireland; Italy; Japan; Luxembourg; Malaysia; Mexico; Netherlands; Netherlands Antilles; New Zealand; Norway; Russia; Singapore; South Africa; South Korea; Spain; Sweden; Switzerland; Thailand; United Kingdom; Venezuela
Giving statement: Giving through the Allergan, Inc. Corporate Giving Program and the Allergan Foundation.
Company EIN: 951622442

Allergan, Inc. Corporate Giving Program

c/o Medical Education Dept.
2525 Dupont Dr.
P.O. Box 19534
Irvine, CA 92623-9534 (866) 257-0272
URL: http://www.allergan.com/responsibility/unrestricted_educational_grants.htm

Purpose and activities: As a complement to its foundation, Allergan also supports organizations involved with medical and healthcare education, and post-marketing and clinical medical research. Support is given on a national basis.
Fields of interest: Medical school/education; Health sciences school/education; Health care, association; Health care, research; Health care, patient services; Health care; Health organizations, formal/general education; Medical research, institute.
Type of support: Donated products; Fellowships; Program development.
Geographic limitations: Giving on a national basis.
Support limitations: No grants to individual physicians or group practices, or for travel, promotional exhibits or display booths at conventions/conferences, research, charitable contributions, capital campaigns, building, service contracts, entertainment, general operating expenses, personal or practice development programs, or travel fellowships.
Publications: Application guidelines.
Application information: Applications accepted. Grant Request Letter should be submitted using organization letterhead. The Medical Education Department handles giving. A contributions committee reviews all requests. Application form required. Applicants should submit the following:
1) timetable for implementation and evaluation of project
2) results expected from proposed grant

3) population served
4) name, address and phone number of organization
5) copy of IRS Determination Letter
6) how project's results will be evaluated or measured
7) detailed description of project and amount of funding requested
8) copy of current year's organizational budget and/ or project budget

Initial approach: Complete online application form
Deadline(s): 8 weeks prior to need
Final notification: Following review

The Allergan Foundation

2525 Dupont Dr., T1-4D
P.O. Box 19534
Irvine, CA 92623-9534 (714) 246-5766
E-mail: AllerganFoundation@Allergan.com; Tel. and e-mail for Vanessa Ryan: (714) 246-2077, Ryan_vanessa@allergan.com; URL: http://www.allerganfoundation.org

Establishment information: Established in 1998 in GA.
Donor: Allergan, Inc.
Contact: Vanessa Ryan, Dir., Community Rels.
Financial data (yr. ended 12/31/11): Assets, $47,125,453 (M); expenditures, $5,378,332; qualifying distributions, $5,253,204; giving activities include $4,949,723 for 380 grants (high: $250,000; low: $1,000).
Purpose and activities: The foundation supports programs designed to promote education, research, and awareness of ophthalmologic, dermatologic, neurological, breast, and urologic health, and obesity prevention and intervention; improve the quality of healthcare and patient access to care, with an emphasis on women's health issues and the aging population; and enhance and strengthen the communities where Allergan, Inc. has a facility or employees by supporting the arts, education, and other civic and community causes.
Fields of interest: Arts; Education; Hospitals (general); Public health, obesity; Health care, patient services; Health care; Breast cancer; Eye diseases; Skin disorders; Nerve, muscle & bone diseases; Disasters, preparedness/services; Homeless, human services; Independent living, disability; Human services; Community/economic development; United Ways and Federated Giving Programs; Public affairs Children; Aging; Women.
Programs:

Community Grants: The foundation supports programs designed to promote health and human services, education, civic and community services, and the arts. Special emphasis is directed toward programs serving vulnerable and at-risk populations including children, the elderly, and the infirm.

Focus Grants: The foundation awards grants to patient and health care-focused organizations to improve patient diagnosis, treatment, care, and quality of life, and to promote access to quality healthcare.

We Care Grants: The foundation awards grants to nonprofit organizations with which employees of Allergan take a strong interest through personal donations and time. Grants range from $500 to $1,500.

Type of support: Employee volunteer services; Equipment; Program development; Scholarship funds.
Geographic limitations: Giving primarily in areas of company operations in Orange and Santa Barbara counties, CA, and McLennan County, TX, area; giving also to regional and national organizations.
Support limitations: No support for religious groups not of direct benefit to the entire community, fraternal, labor, political, or veterans' organizations, discriminatory organizations, athletic leagues, school-affiliated orchestras, bands, or choirs, private K-12 schools, pass-through organizations, consumer interest groups, or agencies normally financed by government sources. No grants to individuals, or for family requests for scholarships, fellowship assistance, or other types of support, matching gifts, university administrative, management, or indirect fees, golf tournaments, athletic events, or team sponsorships, student trips or tours, fundraising activities or advertising sponsorships, conferences, workshops, exhibits, surveys, films, or publishing activities, endowments, capital, or building campaigns, general operating support, debt reduction, or contributions in the name of a memorial tribute; no in-kind gifts.
Publications: Annual report (including application guidelines); Application guidelines.
Application information: Applications accepted. Grants range from $2,500 to $10,000. Support is limited to 1 contribution per organization during any given year. The foundation utilizes an invitation only process for Focus Grants. Videos, faxed, or e-mailed applications are not accepted. Application form required. Applicants should submit the following:
1) copy of IRS Determination Letter
2) geographic area to be served
3) copy of most recent annual report/audited financial statement/990
4) descriptive literature about organization
5) listing of board of directors, trustees, officers and other key people and their affiliations
6) detailed description of project and amount of funding requested
7) copy of current year's organizational budget and/ or project budget
8) listing of additional sources and amount of support

Initial approach: Complete online application
Deadline(s): May 1 through July 1
Final notification: Sept.

Officers and Directors:* David E.I. Pyott*, Chair. and C.E.O.; James M. Hindman*, Pres.; Terilea J. Wielenga*, C.F.O.; Matthew J Maletta, Secy. and Genl. Counsel; Daryn A. Martin, Treas.; Gwyn L. Grenrock, Exec. Dir.; Julian S. Gangolli; Gavin S. Herbert; Lynn D. Salo; Scott D. Sherman; Scott M. Whitcup, M.D.
EIN: 330794475

100
ALLETE, Inc.

(formerly Minnesota Power, Inc.)
30 W. Superior St.
Duluth, MN 55802 (218) 279-5000
FAX: " (218) 723-3953"

Company URL: http://www.allete.com
Establishment information: Established in 1906.
Company type: Public company
Company ticker symbol and exchange: ALE/NYSE
Business activities: Generates, transmits, and distributes electricity; transmits and distributes natural gas; mines coal; provides telecommunications services; provides automobile auction services; distributes water.
Business type (SIC): Combination utility services; coal mining; telephone communications; water suppliers; motor vehicles, parts, and supplies—wholesale
Financial profile for 2012: Number of employees, 1,361; assets, $3,253,400,000; sales volume, $961,200,000; pre-tax net income, $135,100,000; expenses, $806,000,000; liabilities, $2,052,400,000
Corporate officers: Alan R. Hodnik, Chair., Pres., and C.E.O.; Mark A. Schober, Sr. V.P. and C.F.O.; Deborah A. Amberg, Sr. V.P., Genl. Counsel, and Secy.; Donald W. Stellmaker, V.P. and Treas.; Steven Q. DeVinck, V.P. and Cont.; Bonnie Keppers, V.P., Human Resources
Board of directors: Alan R. Hodnik, Chair.; Kathleen A. Brekken; Kathryn M. Dindo; Heidi J. Eddins; Sidney W. Emery, Jr.; George Goldfarb; James S. Haines, Jr.; James J. Hoolihan; Madeleine W. Ludlow; Douglas C. Neve; Leonard C. Rodman; Bruce W. Stender
Subsidiaries: ADESA Corp., Indianapolis, IN; BNI Coal, Bismarck, ND; Rain River Energy, Duluth, MN; Superior Water, Light and Power, Superior, WI; Synertec, Duluth, MN
Giving statement: Giving through the ALLETE, Inc. Corporate Giving Program and the Minnesota Power Foundation.
Company EIN: 410418150

Minnesota Power Foundation

30 W. Superior St.
Duluth, MN 55802-2191 (218) 720-2518
E-mail: mhanson@mnpower.com; URL: http://www.mnpowerfoundation.org/
Scholarship Address: c/o Duluth Superior Area Community Foundation, 324 W. Superior St., Ste. 212, Duluth, MN 55802, tel.: (218) 726-0232, e-mail: dhammer@dsacommunityfoundation.com

Establishment information: Established in 2006 in MN.
Donor: ALLETE, Inc.
Contact: Peggy Hanson, Secy. and Fdn. Dir.
Financial data (yr. ended 12/31/11): Assets, $1,494,492 (M); gifts received, $1,000,000; expenditures, $1,098,158; qualifying distributions, $1,069,775; giving activities include $1,069,775 for grants.
Purpose and activities: The foundation supports programs designed to improve the quality of life in communities where Minnesota Power conducts business through education, the environment, community services, youth development, arts and culture, and health and human services. Special emphasis is directed toward programs designed to promote K-12 and post-secondary education; human services; arts and culture; and the preservation of natural resources.
Fields of interest: Arts; Elementary/secondary education; Vocational education; Higher education; Education; Environment, natural resources; Environment; Health care; Food services; Youth development; Human services; Community/ economic development; Foundations (community); United Ways and Federated Giving Programs; Engineering/technology.
Programs:

Community Involvement Scholarship Program: The foundation awards 20 $2,500 scholarships to high school seniors residing in Minnesota Power's service territory. The award is based on student's involvement in the community through volunteer activities, and financial need.

New Generation Scholarships: The foundation awards $1,000 college scholarships to students in the second year of an Associate Degree program and $2,500 scholarships to students in the junior or senior year of a Bachelor Degree program at selected universities. Associate degree students must study electrical or mechanical maintenance, electric technology, environmental water quality, industrial technology, engineering, electrical lineworker technology, electrical construction and maintenance, wind energy, or business, accounting, or finance. Bachelor Degree students must study engineering, economics, teaching including math,

science, or industrial education, accounting, business or finance, information technology, or environmental science. Students must have a GPA of 3.0.
Type of support: Annual campaigns; Building/renovation; Capital campaigns; Equipment; General/operating support; Matching/challenge support; Program development; Scholarship funds; Scholarships—to individuals; Sponsorships.
Geographic limitations: Giving primarily in areas of company operations in MN and ND.
Support limitations: No grants to individuals (except for scholarships) or for travel.
Publications: Application guidelines.
Application information: Applications accepted. Telephone calls and e-mails are discouraged during the application process. Organizations receiving support are asked to provide a final report. Application form required. Applicants should submit the following:
1) name, address and phone number of organization
2) copy of IRS Determination Letter
3) brief history of organization and description of its mission
4) listing of board of directors, trustees, officers and other key people and their affiliations
5) detailed description of project and amount of funding requested
6) contact person
7) copy of current year's organizational budget and/or project budget
8) plans for acknowledgement

Scholarship applications should include official transcripts, letters of recommendation, an essay, and a photograph.
Initial approach: Complete online application; download application form and e-mail for scholarships
Board meeting date(s): Feb., May, Aug., and Nov.
Deadline(s): None; Jan. 14 for Community Involvement Scholarships; Feb. 1 for New Generation Scholarships
Final notification: 90 days; Apr. for scholarships
Officers and Directors: Alan R. Hodnik, Pres.; David J. McMillan, V.P.; Peggy Hanson, Secy. and Fdn. Dir.; Laura Schauer, Treas.; Patrick A. Mullen; Michael A. Perala; Joshua J. Skelton; Todd Simmons; Daniel L. Tonder.
EIN: 562560595
Selected grants: The following grants are a representative sample of this grantmaker's funding activity:
$44,000 to Duluth-Superior Area Community Foundation, Duluth, MN, 2010.
$43,160 to United Way of Greater Duluth, Duluth, MN, 2010.
$31,095 to United Way of 1000 Lakes, Grand Rapids, MN, 2010.
$10,000 to Life House, Duluth, MN, 2010.
$10,000 to Local Initiatives Support Corporation, Duluth, MN, 2010.
$8,464 to University of Minnesota, Duluth, MN, 2010.
$4,458 to University of Minnesota, Duluth, MN, 2010.
$2,200 to Reif Arts Council, Grand Rapids, MN, 2010.
$2,000 to American Red Cross, Duluth, MN, 2010.
$2,000 to Minnesota Ballet, Duluth, MN, 2010.

101
Alliance Data Systems Corporation
7500 Dallas Pkwy.
Plano, TX 75024 (214) 494-3000

Company URL: http://www.alliancedata.com
Establishment information: Established in 1996.
Company type: Public company
Company ticker symbol and exchange: ADS/NYSE
Business activities: Provides data-driven and transaction-based marketing and customer loyalty solutions.
Business type (SIC): Business services/miscellaneous
Financial profile for 2012: Number of employees, 10,700; assets, $12,000,140,000; sales volume, $3,641,390,000; pre-tax net income, $682,900,000; expenses, $2,667,030,000; liabilities, $11,471,650,000
Fortune 1000 ranking: 2012—626th in revenues, 375th in profits, and 348th in assets
Forbes 2000 ranking: 2012—1560th in sales, 1267th in profits, and 1336th in assets
Corporate officers: Robert A. Minicucci, Chair.; Edward J. Heffernan, Pres. and C.E.O.; Charles L. Horn, Exec. V.P. and C.F.O.; Laura Santillan, Sr. V.P. and C.A.O.; Leigh Ann K. Epperson, Sr. V.P., Genl. Counsel, and Secy.
Board of directors: Robert A. Minicucci, Chair.; Bruce K. Anderson; Roger H. Ballou; Lawrence M. Benveniste, Ph.D.; D. Keith Cobb; E. Linn Draper, Jr., Ph.D.; Edward J. Heffernan; Kenneth R. Jensen
Giving statement: Giving through the Alliance Data Systems Corporation Contributions Program.
Company EIN: 311429215

Alliance Data Systems Corporation Contributions Program
17655 Waterview Pkwy.
Dallas, TX 75252 (972) 348-5100
URL: http://www.alliancedata.com/Pages/corporateresponsibility.aspx

Purpose and activities: Alliance Data Systems makes charitable contributions to nonprofit organizations involved with education, literacy, independent living, and children's advocacy. Support is given primarily in areas of company operations.
Fields of interest: Education, early childhood education; Education, special; Higher education, college; Education, reading; Education; Independent housing for people with disabilities; Athletics/sports, Special Olympics; Children, services Children; Minorities; African Americans/Blacks.
Type of support: General/operating support; Scholarship funds.
Geographic limitations: Giving primarily in areas of company operations.

102
AllianceBernstein L.P.
1345 Ave. of the Americas
New York, NY 10105 (212) 969-1000

Company URL: http://www.alliancebernstein.com
Establishment information: Established in 1999.
Company type: Subsidiary of a foreign company
Business activities: Operates global investment management firm.
Business type (SIC): Investment offices
Corporate officers: Peter S. Kraus, Chair. and C.E.O.; David A. Steyn, C.O.O.; John B. Howard, Jr., C.F.O.; Laurence E. Cranch, Genl. Counsel
Board of director: Peter Kraus, Chair.

AllianceBernstein L.P. Corporate Giving Program
1345 Avenue of the Americas
New York, NY 10105

103
Alliant Credit Union
10000 Bessie Coleman Dr.
Chicago, IL 60666 (773) 462-2000

Company URL: http://www.alliantcreditunion.org/
Establishment information: Established in 1935.
Company type: State-chartered credit union
Business activities: Operates a state credit union.
Business type (SIC): Credit unions
Financial profile for 2011: Number of employees, 276,424; assets, $8,235,535,560; liabilities, $8,236
Corporate officers: Marc Krohn, Chair.; Scott Praven, Vice-Chair.; David W. Mooney, Pres., C.E.O., and Treas.; Mona Leung, Sr. V.P., Finance; George Rudolph, Sr. V.P., Opers. and Tech.; Ted Davidson, Secy.
Board of directors: Marc Krohn, Chair.; Scott Praven, Vice-Chair.; Ted Davidson; John Gebo; Irwin I. Gzesh; Shirley Jones; David Leib; Alexandria Marren; David W. Mooney; Anne Pease; Ed Rogowski
Giving statement: Giving through the Alliant Credit Union Foundation.

Alliant Credit Union Foundation
11545 W. Touhy Ave.
Chicago, IL 60666 (773) 462-2000
URL: http://www.alliantcreditunionfoundation.org

Donor: Alliant Credit Union.
Contact: Wayne Rosenwinkel, V.P. and Dir.
Financial data (yr. ended 06/30/11): Assets, $3,693,474 (M); expenditures, $165,185; qualifying distributions, $165,185; giving activities include $160,829 for 61 grants (high: $40,000; low: $20).
Application information: Applications accepted. Application form required.
Initial approach: See website
Deadline(s): None
Officers and Directors: David Mooney, Pres.; Wayne Rosenwinkel, V.P.; Dorothy Skube, Secy.; Michael Gard, Treas.; Robert Russell.
EIN: 711052113
Selected grants: The following grants are a representative sample of this grantmaker's funding activity:
$15,000 to Foster Care to Success, Sterling, VA, 2010. For general operating support.
$3,850 to Breast Cancer Network of Strength, Chicago, IL, 2010. For general operating support.
$2,500 to Great Lakes Adaptive Sports Association, Lake Forest, IL, 2010. For general operating support.
$2,500 to Hadley School for the Blind, Winnetka, IL, 2010. For general operating support.
$2,500 to Little Friends, Naperville, IL, 2010. For general operating support.
$2,500 to Special Olympics Illinois, Normal, IL, 2010. For general operating support.
$1,500 to Chicago Cares, Chicago, IL, 2010. For general operating support.

$1,250 to Boys and Girls Club of West Cook County, Bellwood, IL, 2010. For general operating support.

104
Alliant Energy Corporation

4902 N. Biltmore Ln., Ste. 1000
Madison, WI 53718-2148 (608) 458-3311
FAX: (608) 314-8938

Company URL: http://www.alliantenergy.com
Establishment information: Established in 1981.
Company type: Public company
Company ticker symbol and exchange: LNT/NYSE
Business activities: Generates, transmits, and distributes electricity; transmits and distributes natural gas; produces and distributes steam; distributes water.
Business type (SIC): Combination utility services; water suppliers; steam and air-conditioning supply services
Financial profile for 2012: Number of employees, 4,055; assets, $10,785,500,000; sales volume, $3,094,500,000; pre-tax net income, $430,200,000; expenses, $2,574,800,000; liabilities, $7,445,500,000
Fortune 1000 ranking: 2012—655th in revenues, 448th in profits, and 367th in assets
Forbes 2000 ranking: 2012—1607th in sales, 1442nd in profits, and 1417th in assets
Corporate officers: Patricia Leonard Kampling, Chair., Pres., and C.E.O.; Thomas L. Hanson, Sr. V.P. and C.F.O.; James H. Gallegos, V.P. and Genl. Counsel; John E. Kratchmer, V.P. and Treas.; Wayne A. Reschke, V.P., Human Resources; Robert J. Durian, Cont. and C.A.O.
Board of directors: Patricia Leonard Kampling, Chair.; Patrick E. Allen; Michael L. Bennett; Darryl B. Hazel; Singleton B. McAllister; Ann K. Newhall; Dean C. Oestreich; David A. Perdue; Carol P. Sanders
Subsidiaries: Alliant Energy Resources, Inc., Cedar Rapids, IA; Interstate Power and Light Co., Cedar Rapids, IA; Wisconsin Power and Light Company, Madison, WI
Giving statement: Giving through the Alliant Energy Corporation Contributions Program and the Alliant Energy Foundation, Inc.
Company EIN: 391380265

Alliant Energy Corporation Contributions Program

(formerly Wisconsin Power and Light Company Contributions Program)
c/o Alliant Energy Fdn., Inc.
4902 N. Biltmore Ln.
Ste. 1000
Madison, WI 53718-2148 (800) 255-4268
FAX: (608) 458-0100; URL: http://www.alliantenergy.com/CommunityInvolvement/index.htm

Purpose and activities: As a complement to its foundation, Alliant Energy also makes charitable contributions to local, county, and regional nonprofit organizations directly. Support is given primarily in areas of company operations in Illinois, Iowa, Minnesota, and Wisconsin; giving also to national organizations.
Fields of interest: Environment, energy; Environment; Cancer; Breast cancer; Diabetes; Employment, services; Employment, training; Employment, retraining; Housing/shelter, volunteer services; Human services, fund raising/fund distribution; Economic development; Community/economic development; Financial services.
Type of support: Consulting services; Employee volunteer services; General/operating support; Loaned talent; Program development; Public relations services; Scholarship funds; Sponsorships; Technical assistance.
Geographic limitations: Giving primarily in areas of company operations in IA,IL, MN, and WI; giving also to national organizations.
Publications: Application guidelines; Informational brochure.
Application information: Applications accepted. The Economic and Community Development team reviews applications according to project need, impact, leverage of other funding, innovation, capacity, and sustainability. Projects must be completed in the year that the application was received. Multi-year commitments are not granted under the Partnership Programs. Only one scholarship will be awarded per person annually. Application form required. Applicants should submit the following:

1) timetable for implementation and evaluation of project
2) results expected from proposed grant
3) name, address and phone number of organization
4) copy of IRS Determination Letter
5) listing of board of directors, trustees, officers and other key people and their affiliations
6) detailed description of project and amount of funding requested
7) copy of current year's organizational budget and/ or project budget
8) listing of additional sources and amount of support

An active link to the Alliant Energy Economic and Community Development website must appear on the organization's website. Applications must contain a website address, information about what the funds will be used for specifically, and a follow-up plan.
Initial approach: Complete online application
Copies of proposal: 1
Committee meeting date(s): Monthly
Deadline(s): Jan. 1 to Sept. 30
Number of staff: 3 full-time professional; 1 part-time professional.

Alliant Energy Foundation, Inc.

(formerly Wisconsin Power and Light Foundation, Inc.)
4902 N. Biltmore Ln., Ste. 1000
Madison, WI 53707-1007 (608) 458-4483
FAX: (608) 458-4820;
E-mail: foundation@alliantenergy.com; Additional tel.: (866) 769-3779; contact for Community Service Scholarships: Dawn Lehtinen, Prog. Mgr., tel.: (507) 931-0482, e-mail: dlehtinen@scholarshipamerica.org; URL: http://www.alliantenergy.com/CommunityInvolvement/index.htm

Establishment information: Established in 1984 in WI.
Donors: Wisconsin Power and Light Co.; Alliant Energy Corp.; Interstate Power and Light Co.
Contact: Julie Bauer, Exec. Dir.
Financial data (yr. ended 12/31/10): Assets, $17,141,338 (M); gifts received, $2,000,000; expenditures, $3,555,700; qualifying distributions, $3,489,970; giving activities include $2,357,291 for grants and $866,949 for employee matching gifts.
Purpose and activities: The foundation supports organizations involved with arts and culture, education, the environment, health, employment, housing, safety, human services, community development, civic affairs, and minorities.
Fields of interest: Humanities; Arts; Higher education; Libraries (public); Education; Environment, natural resources; Environmental education; Environment; Health care; Crime/law enforcement, police agencies; Employment, training; Employment; Housing/shelter; Disasters, preparedness/services; Disasters, fire prevention/control; Safety/disasters; Human services; Civil/human rights, equal rights; Economic development; Community/economic development; United Ways and Federated Giving Programs; Leadership development; Public affairs Minorities.
Programs:
Community Grants Program: The foundation supports human needs through the United Way and programs designed to meet local community needs; education programs designed to foster innovation, utilize technology, and develop future leaders; culture and art programs designed to foster knowledge and appreciation of the fine arts and humanities, with an emphasis on broadening access to cultural and art activities; civic programs designed to promote community improvement, economic development, affordable housing, job training, retention, and placement and improved quality of community life; and environmental programs designed to educate, inform, and advance issues that have the potential to impact the community. The foundation also supports safety programs designed to educate and motivate people to live safer and healthier lives; and diversity programs designed to break down barriers, create inclusive environments, and provide opportunities for minorities. Grants range from $500 to $5,000.
Community Service Scholarships: The foundation awards up to twenty-five $1,000 college scholarships to current customers or dependents of current customers of Alliant Energy or its subsidiaries who are first-time college students in recognition of outstanding community leadership. Candidates are selected based on leadership role in the community, volunteer work, academic grade point average, standardized test scores, and an essay. The program is administered by Scholarship America, Inc.
Hometown Challenge Grant Program: The foundation awards matching funds of up to $3,000 to nonprofit organizations and government related agencies to assist local communities in purchasing safety-related equipment that will benefit a large population in the community. Participating organizations must obtain Alliant Energy Foundation approval and commitment prior to fundraising efforts, and organizations must hold at least two fundraising events to quality for the Hometown Challenge program.
Matching Gifts Program: The foundation matches contributions made by employees and retirees of Alliant Energy to nonprofit organizations on a one-for-one basis from $25 to $10,000 per contributor, per year.
Power Team Program: The foundation awards grants of up to $400 to nonprofit organizations when a group of five or more employees of Alliant Energy form a "Power Team" and complete a project for a cause within their community. The "Power Team" chooses one nonprofit organization to receive the grant.
Service Anniversary Grant Program: The foundation awards grants to nonprofit organizations chosen by employees celebrating milestone service anniversaries with Alliant Energy, its predecessors, or subsidiaries. Grants ranging from $25 to $250 are awarded for 10, 15, 25, or 30 years of service.
Volunteer Program: The foundation awards $400 grants to nonprofit organizations with which employees and retirees of Alliant Energy volunteer at least 50 hours per year.

Type of support: Annual campaigns; Building/renovation; Conferences/seminars; Continuing support; Emergency funds; Employee matching gifts; Employee volunteer services; Employee-related scholarships; Equipment; Matching/challenge support; Program development; Research; Scholarship funds; Scholarships—to individuals; Seed money.
Geographic limitations: Giving limited to areas of company operations in IA, MN, and WI.
Support limitations: No support for athletes or teams, fraternal or social clubs, third party funding groups, religious organizations not of direct benefit to the entire community, or discriminatory organizations. No grants to individuals (except for scholarships), or for advertising, door prizes, raffle tickets, dinner tables, golf outings or sponsorships of organized sports teams or activities, sporting events or tournaments, endowments, registration fees or participation fees, books, magazines or professional journal articles, political activities, salaries, facilities costs or general operating expenses, capital campaigns, or "bricks and mortar" projects.
Publications: Annual report (including application guidelines); Application guidelines; Grants list; Informational brochure (including application guidelines); Program policy statement.
Application information: Applications accepted. Additional information may be requested at a later date. Support is limited to 1 contribution per organization during any given year. Organizations receiving support are asked to provide a final report. Application form required. Applicants should submit the following:
1) signature and title of chief executive officer
2) copy of IRS Determination Letter
3) copy of most recent annual report/audited financial statement/990
4) listing of board of directors, trustees, officers and other key people and their affiliations
5) copy of current year's organizational budget and/or project budget

Initial approach: Complete online eligibility quiz and application for Community Grants and Community Service Scholarships; download application form and mail to foundation for Hometown Challenge Grant
Copies of proposal: 1
Board meeting date(s): Quarterly
Deadline(s): Jan. 15, May 15, and Sept. 15 for Community Grants; Feb. 15 for Community Service Scholarships; none for Hometown Challenge Grant
Final notification: Apr. 1, Aug. 2, and Dec. 1 for Community Grants; 15 days for Hometown Challenge Grant

Officers and Directors:* Thomas L. Aller*, Pres.; Patricia L. Kampling*, V.P.; Julie Bauer, Secy. and Exec. Dir.; Colleen Thomas, Treas.; Bob Bartlett; John Larsen.
Number of staff: 3 full-time professional; 3 part-time professional.
EIN: 391444065
Selected grants: The following grants are a representative sample of this grantmaker's funding activity:
$157,982 to JK Group, Plainsboro, NJ, 2010.
$18,500 to Junior Achievement of Wisconsin, Milwaukee, WI, 2010.
$15,000 to Urban League of Greater Madison, Madison, WI, 2010.
$6,025 to Cornshucker Baseball Club, Mount Vernon, IA, 2010.
$6,000 to African American Heritage Foundation, African American Museum of Iowa, Cedar Rapids, IA, 2010.
$6,000 to Dubuque Symphony Orchestra, Dubuque, IA, 2010.
$5,600 to American Players Theater of Wisconsin, Spring Green, WI, 2010.
$5,000 to YM-YWCA of Dubuque, Dubuque, IA, 2010.
$5,000 to YWCA of Madison, Madison, WI, 2010.
$3,900 to YMCA of the Cedar Rapids Metropolitan Area, Cedar Rapids, IA, 2010.
$3,000 to Aldo Leopold Foundation, Baraboo, WI, 2010.
$3,000 to Big Brothers and Big Sisters of Cedar Rapids and East Central Iowa, Cedar Rapids, IA, 2010.
$3,000 to Bluff Elementary, Clinton, IA, 2010.
$2,500 to Oakville, City of, Oakville, IA, 2010.
$1,000 to Habitat for Humanity of Marion County, Knoxville, IA, 2010.

105
Allianz Life Insurance Company of North America

5701 Golden Hills Dr.
P.O. Box 1344
Minneapolis, MN 55416-1297
(800) 950-5872

Company URL: http://www.allianzlife.com
Establishment information: Established in 1896.
Company type: Subsidiary of a foreign company
Business activities: Sells life insurance.
Business type (SIC): Insurance/life
Financial profile for 2009: Number of employees, 2,800
Corporate officers: Gary C. Bhojwani, Chair.; Walter White, Pres. and C.E.O.; Giulio Terzariol, C.F.O.; Cathy Mahone, C.A.O.; Carsten Quitter, C.I.O.; Gretchen Cepek, Genl. Counsel; Suzanne Zeller, Human Resources
Board of director: Gary C. Bhojwani, Chair.
Giving statement: Giving through the Allianz Life Insurance Company of North America Corporate Giving Program.

Allianz Life Insurance Company of North America Corporate Giving Program

P.O. Box 1344
Minneapolis, MN 55416-1297 (800) 950-5872
E-mail: Laura.Juergens@allianzlife.com;
URL: https://www.allianzlife.com/about/community_outreach/community_outreach.aspx

Contact: Laura Juergens
Purpose and activities: Allianz makes charitable contributions to nonprofit organizations involved with financial literacy and the independence and self-sufficiency of senior citizens. Support is given primarily in areas of company operations in the Twin Cities, Minnesota, metropolitan area.
Fields of interest: Health care; Food services; Human services, financial counseling; Human services, gift distribution; Aging, centers/services.
Programs:
Best Prep & Junior Achievement: Allianz has made a three-year commitment to BestPrep and Junior Achievement with the intent of involving employees in their school-based financial literacy efforts. The contribution to each program is $100,000.
Financial Literacy: Alliaz supports programs designed to provide financial literacy education or training and/or educate consumers on retirement planning. Grants typically range from $15,000 to $20,000.
Senior Services: Allianz supports programs that help seniors to be self-sufficient (specifically in relation to food, transportation, adaptive living and basic living needs) and/or enhance the quality of life for seniors through community programming and/or community outreach (specifically social vitality through social activity and interaction). Grants typically range from $15,000 to $20,000.
Type of support: Annual campaigns; Employee volunteer services; General/operating support.
Geographic limitations: Giving primarily in areas of company operations, with emphasis on the Twin Cities, MN, metropolitan area.
Support limitations: No support for fiscal agents. No grants for general operating or capital support.
Publications: Application guidelines.
Application information: Applications accepted. Requests must be submitted in writing via e-mail and mail in a Word document. The narrative portion of the proposal should be no more than 8 pages in length. Application form required. Applicants should submit the following:
1) results expected from proposed grant
2) population served
3) name, address and phone number of organization
4) copy of IRS Determination Letter
5) brief history of organization and description of its mission
6) geographic area to be served
7) copy of most recent annual report/audited financial statement/990
8) how project's results will be evaluated or measured
9) explanation of why grantmaker is considered an appropriate donor for project
10) listing of board of directors, trustees, officers and other key people and their affiliations
11) detailed description of project and amount of funding requested
12) contact person
13) copy of current year's organizational budget and/or project budget
14) plans for acknowledgement

Proposals should include the program or project title, and the name and contact information for the top paid staff member.
Initial approach: Download application form and e-mail and mail completed proposal to headquarters
Deadline(s): Mar. 1 for Financial Literacy; July 1 for Senior Services

106
Allison-Erwin Company

2920 N. Tryon St.
P.O. Box 32308
Charlotte, NC 28206-2761 (704) 334-8621

Establishment information: Established in 1893.
Company type: Private company
Business activities: Sells consumer electronics, furniture, and air conditioners wholesale.
Business type (SIC): Electrical goods—wholesale; furniture and home furnishings—wholesale
Corporate officers: Rhonda Allison, Chair. and Secy.; Gary J. Watkins, Pres.; Bob Allison, C.E.O. and C.F.O.; Brenan Giggey, V.P., Sales and Mktg.
Board of director: Rhonda Allison, Chair.
Giving statement: Giving through the Alwinell Foundation Trust.

Alwinell Foundation Trust

P.O. Box 40200, FL9-100-10-19
Jacksonville, FL 32203-0200 (980) 386-1001
Application address: 150 N. College St., NC1-028-29-01 Charlotte, NC 28255 tel.: (980) 386-1001

Establishment information: Established in 1951 in NC.
Donors: Allison-Erwin Co.; Industrial & Textile Supply Co.
Contact: Marc C. Rock
Financial data (yr. ended 05/31/12): Assets, $1,223,422 (M); expenditures, $52,382; qualifying distributions, $51,800; giving activities include $51,000 for 16 grants (high: $10,000; low: $1,000).
Purpose and activities: The foundation supports organizations involved with educational fundraising, higher education, substance abuse services, employment, housing, and human services.
Fields of interest: Education; Housing/shelter; Human services.
Type of support: General/operating support.
Support limitations: No grants to individuals.
Application information: Applications accepted. Application form required.
Initial approach: Proposal
Deadline(s): None
Officers: James R. Allison, Chair.; Henry J. Allison, Jr., Secy.
Board Member: Carol A. Marlee.
Trustee: Bank of America, N.A.
EIN: 566039491

107
Allstate Insurance Company

2775 Sanders Rd., Ste. F7
Northbrook, IL 60062-6127 (847) 402-5000

Company URL: http://www.allstate.com
Establishment information: Established in 1931.
Company type: Subsidiary of a public company
International Securities Identification Number: US0200021014
Business activities: Sells property and casualty insurance.
Business type (SIC): Insurance/fire, marine, and casualty
Corporate officers: Thomas J. Wilson, Chair., Pres., and C.E.O.; Danny L. Hale, Sr. V.P. and C.F.O.; Michael Escobar, Asst. V.P. and Chief Diversity Off.
Board of directors: Thomas J. Wilson, Chair.; F. Duane Ackerman; Robert D. Beyer; Kermit R. Crawford; W. James Farrell; Jack M. Greenberg; Herbert L. Henkel; Ronald T. LeMay; Andrea Redmond; H. John Riley, Jr.; John W. Rowe; Joshua I. Smith; Judith A. Sprieser; Mary Alice Taylor
Giving statement: Giving through the Allstate Insurance Company Contributions Program and the Allstate Foundation.
Company EIN: 360719665

Allstate Insurance Company Contributions Program

2775 Sanders Rd.
Northbrook, IL 60062-6110 (847) 402-5175
E-mail: SocialResponsibilityFeedback@allstate.com ; URL: http://www.allstate.com/social-responsibility.aspx

Financial data (yr. ended 12/31/11): Total giving, $3,800,000, including $3,800,000 for 120 grants.
Purpose and activities: As a complement to its foundation, Allstate also makes charitable contributions to nonprofit organizations directly. Support is given primarily in areas of company operations.
Fields of interest: Arts, cultural/ethnic awareness; Museums; Hospitals (general); Safety, automotive safety; Safety/disasters; Human services, financial counseling; Civil/human rights, equal rights; Community/economic development.
Type of support: Advocacy; Employee volunteer services; General/operating support; Sponsorships.
Geographic limitations: Giving primarily in areas of company operations.
Publications: Corporate giving report.
Application information: Application form required.
Copies of proposal: 1

The Allstate Foundation

2775 Sanders Rd., Ste. F4
Northbrook, IL 60062-6127 (847) 402-7849
FAX: (847) 402-7568; E-mail: Grants@Allstate.com; Additional e-mails: Jan Epstein - jepstein@allstate.com; Sue Duchak - sue.duchak@allstate.com; Jennifer McGrath - jennifermcgrath@allstate.com; Chindaly Griffith - chindaly.griffith@allstate.com; e-mail for High School Award: KeeptheDrive@allstate.com; URL: http://www.allstatefoundation.org/
E-mail for High School Award: KeeptheDrive@allstate.com

Establishment information: Incorporated in 1952 in IL.
Donors: The Allstate Corp.; Allstate Insurance Co.; Allstate New Jersey Insurance Co.
Contact: Patricia Lara Garza, Dir., Strategic Philanthropy
Financial data (yr. ended 12/31/12): Assets, $65,952,209 (M); gifts received, $36,275,138; expenditures, $19,764,214; qualifying distributions, $19,764,214; giving activities include $17,065,547 for 3,165 grants (high: $825,515; low: $25), $203,580 for employee matching gifts and $17,065,547 for 6 foundation-administered programs.
Purpose and activities: The foundation supports programs designed to address teen safe driving and domestic violence. Additionally, the Foundation also supports programs designed to promote safe and vital communities; economic empowerment; and tolerance, inclusion, and diversity.
Fields of interest: Crime/violence prevention, youth; Employment, services; Employment, training; Employment; Disasters, preparedness/services; Safety, automotive safety; Safety/disasters; Youth, services; Family services, domestic violence; Human services, financial counseling; Civil/human rights, equal rights; Civil rights, race/intergroup relations; Community development, neighborhood development; Economic development Children/youth; Disabilities, people with; Minorities; Asians/Pacific Islanders; African Americans/Blacks; Hispanics/Latinos; Native Americans/American Indians; Economically disadvantaged; LGBTQ; Gay men; Bisexual.

Programs:

Act Out Loud: The foundation, in partnership with National Youth Traffic Safety Month, sponsors a teen-led and school-based activism competition to promote safe driving and to encourage youth to make a difference in their community. Teams of high school students participate in three different activities that focus on stronger teen driver safety laws. Points are awarded based on school participation and project quality. Activities include a SAFE-TEE shirt design contest, creative sign contest, and a Facebook yearbook application. A $10,000 grand prize is awarded. Visit URL: http://www.actoutloud.org/ for more information.

Agency Hands in the Community Grants: The foundation awards $1,000 grants to support the local volunteer efforts of full-time agency owners and personal financial representatives of Allstate. Grants are awarded to nonprofit organizations that seek to improve the quality of life in local communities.

Domestic Violence Program: Moving Ahead Economic Empowerment Grants: The foundation awards grants to state domestic violence coalitions and local programs to enhance projects that help survivors overcome economic challenges and achieve financial independence. Special emphasis is directed toward financial education through the use of Allstate's Moving Ahead Through Money Management Curriculum; matched saving programs including Individual Development Accounts; job readiness and job training; and microloans and microenterprise.

Domestic Violence Program: Moving Ahead Through Financial Empowerment Curriculum: The foundation, in partnership with the National Network to End Domestic Violence, produces the Moving Ahead Through Financial Management Curriculum which packages tools and information designed to empower survivors to understand and manage their finances. The curriculum is distributed through partnerships with state domestic violence coalitions and is used to educate and train advocates and Allstate volunteers to help domestic violence survivors achieve financial security.

Economic Empowerment: The foundation supports programs designed to empower people with economic resources and knowledge to make informed financial decisions about their future. Special emphasis is directed toward financial and economic literacy; and helping domestic violence survivors live and stay free through financial security.

Helping Hands Grant Program: The foundation awards $500 grants to charitable, social, or humanitarian organizations with which employees of Allstate volunteer 25 hours or more or teams of employees who volunteer 20 hours or more.

Keep the Drive High School Journalism Awards: The foundation annually awards grants to high school teens who address through print or broadcast journalism the importance of stronger driver laws at the state or national level. Applicants for the print journalism category and must submit published newspaper articles and applications for the broadcast journalism category must upload broadcast video segments on YouTube. Grand prize winners receive $2,000, second place winners receive $1,000, and a third place winner receives $750. See Web site for additional information, http://www.keepthedrive.com/.

Matching Grant Program for Higher Education: The foundation matches contributions made by full-time employees of Allstate to institutions of higher education on a one-for-one basis from $25 to $1,000 per employee, per year.

Regional Domestic Violence Grant Program: The foundation provides grants and local resources to national, statewide, local domestic violence organizations to empower survivors of domestic violence. Special emphasis is directed toward programs designed to help domestic violence survivors build their financial independence through financial education; job readiness and job training; matched savings initiatives; and microenterprise.

Safe and Vital Communities: The foundation supports programs designed to foster communities that are economically solvent, crime-free, and that give residents a sense of belonging and commitment. Special emphasis is directed toward rebuilding lives after a natural disaster through catastrophe response; nurturing safe, strong, and healthy communities through neighborhood revitalization; and encouraging safe driving attitudes and behaviors through teen safe driving programs.

Teen Safe Driving Program: Through the Teen Safe Driving initiative, the foundation encourages teens to develop safe driving attitudes and behaviors to reduce the risk of teen driving-related accidents. The program includes Keep the Drive, a teen-led smart driving movement that educates teens about the issues and empowers them to become smart driving activists in their schools and communities; community outreach, to surround teens with smart driving messages from key teen influencers, including parents; leadership and advocacy education, to advance public understanding of teen safe driving and inform public policy decision-makers; and public awareness, to elevate teen driving as a chronic public health issue through social marketing and public relations campaigns.

Tolerance, Inclusion, and Diversity: The foundation supports programs designed to foster tolerance, inclusion, and values for people of all backgrounds. Special emphasis is directed toward programs designed to teach tolerance to youth to foster a generation free of bias; and encourage communities to be free of prejudice to alleviate discrimination.

Type of support: Cause-related marketing; Conferences/seminars; Curriculum development; Emergency funds; Employee matching gifts; Employee volunteer services; Film/video/radio; General/operating support; Grants to individuals; Loaned talent; Management development/capacity building; Pro bono services; Pro bono services - communications/public relations; Pro bono services - financial management; Pro bono services - human resources; Pro bono services - interactive/website technology; Pro bono services - legal; Pro bono services - marketing/branding; Pro bono services - strategic management; Pro bono services - technology infrastructure; Program development; Research; Technical assistance.

Geographic limitations: Giving in on a national basis in areas of company operations, in AK, AL, AR, AZ, CA, CO, CT, DC, DE, FL, GA, HI, IA, ID, IL, IN, KS, KY, LA, MA, MD, ME, MI, MN, MO, MS, MT, NC, ND, NE, NH, NJ, NM, NV, NY, OH, OK, OR, PA, RI, SC, TN, TX, UT, VA, VT, WA, WI, WV, and WY; giving also to regional and national organizations.

Support limitations: No support for religious organizations not of direct benefit to the entire community. Also, ONLY 501(c)3 tax status organizations are eligible. No grants to individuals (except for Keep the Drive High School Journalism Awards), or for fundraising events or sponsorships, equipment not part of a community outreach program, athletic events, memorials, travel, or audio, film, or video production.

Publications: Application guidelines; Program policy statement.

Application information: Application form required. Applicants should submit the following:

1) role played by volunteers
2) timetable for implementation and evaluation of project
3) qualifications of key personnel
4) name, address and phone number of organization
5) copy of IRS Determination Letter
6) how company employees can become involved with the organization
7) brief history of organization and description of its mission
8) geographic area to be served
9) copy of most recent annual report/audited financial statement/990
10) how project's results will be evaluated or measured
11) list of company employees involved with the organization
12) explanation of why grantmaker is considered an appropriate donor for project
13) listing of board of directors, trustees, officers and other key people and their affiliations
14) detailed description of project and amount of funding requested
15) contact person
16) copy of current year's organizational budget and/or project budget
17) listing of additional sources and amount of support
18) plans for acknowledgement

Visit Website for detailed application deadlines.

Initial approach: Complete online eligibility quiz and application; For Teen Safe Driving programs complete online application for Keep the Drive High School Journalism Awards and Act Out Loud

Board meeting date(s): Aug. and Nov.

Deadline(s): Varies for Teen Safe Driving, Domestic Violence, Safe and Vital Communities, Economic Empowerment, and Tolerance, Inclusion, and Diversity; None; Oct. 1 to Mar. 1 for Keep the Drive High School Journalism Awards; Oct. 14 to Jan. 31 for Act Out Loud registration

Final notification: Varies

Officers and Trustees:* Thomas J. Wilson*, Chair. and Pres.; Joan H. Walker, Exec. V.P. and Secy.; Judith P. Greffin*, Exec. V.P. and C.I.O; Susie Lees, Exec. Dir. and Genl. Counsel; Mario Rizzo, Sr. V.P. and Treas.; D. Scott Harper, Sr. V.P.; Don Civgin; Michele C. Mayes; Mathew E. Winter.

EIN: 366116535

Selected grants: The following grants are a representative sample of this grantmaker's funding activity:

$825,515 to National Safety Council, Itasca, IL, 2012. For Drive it Home Multi-City Launch.

$500,000 to United Way of Metropolitan Chicago, Chicago, IL, 2012. For Promoting Financial Stability for Domestic Violence Survivors.

$425,000 to Facing History and Ourselves National Foundation, Brookline, MA, 2012. For Community Conversations.

$400,000 to Junior Achievement, National, Colorado Springs, CO, 2012. For Title Sponsorship Renewal JA Economics for Success, $ave USA and Teens and Personal Finance Survey, and technology/operating support.

$400,000 to National Network to End Domestic Violence, Washington, DC, 2012. For NNEDV/TAF Economic Empowerment Project.

$35,000 to White Plains Library Foundation, White Plains, NY, 2012. For Allstate Readiness Series.

$1,000 to Boys and Girls Club of the Columbia Basin, Moses Lake, WA, 2012. For Agency Owner Volunteerism.

$1,000 to Mississippi Childrens Museum, Jackson, MS, 2012. For Agency Owner Volunteerism.

$1,000 to YMCA, Shenango Valley, Hermitage, PA, 2012. For Agency Owner Volunteerism.

108
AllStyle Coil Company, L.P.

7037 Brittmoore Dr.
P.O. Box 40696
Houston, TX 77041 (713) 466-6333

Company URL: http://www.allstyle.com
Establishment information: Established in 1990.
Company type: Private company
Business activities: Manufactures direct expansion indoor heating and cooling coils.
Business type (SIC): Machinery/refrigeration and service industry
Corporate officer: Lendell Martin, Partner
Giving statement: Giving through the Martin Foundation, Inc.

Martin Foundation, Inc.

7037 Brittmoore Rd.
Houston, TX 77041-3210

Establishment information: Established in 2001 in TX.
Donors: AllStyle Coil Co., L.P.; Lawanna S. Martin; Lendell Martin.
Financial data (yr. ended 12/31/11): Assets, $953,203 (M); gifts received, $5,841; expenditures, $77,929; qualifying distributions, $39,955; giving activities include $650 for 3 grants (high: $500; low: $50).
Purpose and activities: The foundation supports organizations involved with Christianity.
Fields of interest: Christian agencies & churches.
Type of support: General/operating support.
Geographic limitations: Giving limited to TX.
Support limitations: No grants to individuals.
Application information: Applications not accepted. Unsolicited requests for funds not accepted.
Officers: Lendell Martin, Pres.; Roger D. Martin, V.P.; Lawanna S. Martin, Secy.-Treas.
EIN: 760671303

109
Allyis, Inc.

10210 N.E. Points Dr., Ste. 200
Kirkland, WA 98033-7872 (425) 691-3000

Company URL: http://www.allyis.com
Establishment information: Established in 1996.
Company type: Private company
Business activities: Operates information management company.
Business type (SIC): Computer services
Corporate officers: Ethan Yarbrough, Vice-Chair.; Jason Herman, C.E.O.; Suzette McClintock, C.O.O.
Board of director: Ethan Yarbrough, Vice-Chair.
Giving statement: Giving through the Allyis, Inc. Corporate Giving Program.

Allyis, Inc. Corporate Giving Program

Plz. at Yarrow Bay
10210 NE Points Dr., Ste. 200
Kirkland, WA 98033-7872 (425) 691-3000
FAX: (425) 691-3001; E-mail: klaw@allyis.com;
URL: http://www.allyis.com/about/Pages/CorporateCitizenship.aspx

Contact: Kristy Law, Dir., Corp. Citizenship
Purpose and activities: Allyis makes charitable contributions to nonprofit organizations that support families, community health and welfare, and the environment. Support is given primarily in areas of company operations.
Fields of interest: Environment; Family services; Community/economic development.
Type of support: Employee matching gifts; Employee volunteer services; General/operating support.
Geographic limitations: Giving primarily in areas of company operations.

110
Almar Sales Company Inc.

320 5th Ave., 3rd Fl.
New York, NY 10001 (212) 594-6920
FAX: (212) 564-1097

Company URL: http://www.almarsales.com
Establishment information: Established in 1965.
Company type: Private company
Business activities: Sells hair accessories, health and beauty aids, jewelry, toys, cosmetics, and party goods wholesale.
Business type (SIC): Non-durable goods—wholesale; durable goods—wholesale; paper and paper products—wholesale; drugs, proprietaries, and sundries—wholesale
Corporate officer: Jackie Ash, V.P., Sales
Giving statement: Giving through the Jack H. Ashkenazie Foundation, Inc.

Jack H. Ashkenazie Foundation, Inc.

c/o Almar Sales Co., Inc.
320 Fifth Ave., 3rd Fl.
New York, NY 10001-3115
URL: http://www.almarsales.com/about.asp

Establishment information: Established in 2001 in NY.
Donor: Almar Sales Co. Inc.
Financial data (yr. ended 12/31/11): Assets, $421 (M); gifts received, $531,734; expenditures, $532,067; qualifying distributions, $531,853; giving activities include $531,853 for grants.
Purpose and activities: The foundation supports hospitals and organizations involved with education, hunger, human services, and Judaism.
Fields of interest: Education; Hospitals (general); Food services; Children, services; Human services, gift distribution; Homeless, human services; Human services; Jewish federated giving programs; Jewish agencies & synagogues.
Type of support: General/operating support.
Geographic limitations: Giving primarily in NY.
Support limitations: No grants to individuals.
Application information: Applications not accepted. Contributes only to pre-selected organizations.
Officer and Directors: Jack R. Ashkenazie, Treas.; Harry J. Ashkenazie; Raymond J. Ashkenazie.
EIN: 134161819

111
Alpenrose Dairy

(doing business as Alpenrose Velodrome)
6149 S.W. Shattuck Rd.
Portland, OR 97221-1044 (503) 244-1133

Company URL: http://alpenrose.com
Establishment information: Established in 1916.
Company type: Private company
Business activities: Operates dairy farm.
Business type (SIC): Dairy products
Corporate officers: Carl Cadanau III, Pres.; John Pedersen, Cont.
Board of directors: Roderick C. Birkland; Wendall R. Birkland
Giving statement: Giving through the VC Fund.

VC Fund

6149 S.W. Shattuck Rd.
Portland, OR 97221-1044 (503) 244-1133

Establishment information: Established in 1994 in OR.
Donors: Alpenrose Dairy, Inc.; VC Trust IRA; Carl H. Cadonau, Jr.
Contact: Carl H. Cadonau, Tr.
Financial data (yr. ended 12/31/11): Assets, $2,889,406 (M); expenditures, $165,961; qualifying distributions, $96,550; giving activities include $94,500 for 2 grants (high: $89,500; low: $5,000).
Purpose and activities: The foundation supports organizations involved with youth, homelessness, and Christianity.
Fields of interest: Youth, services; Homeless, human services; Christian agencies & churches.
Type of support: Program development.
Geographic limitations: Giving primarily in OR.
Support limitations: No grants to individuals.
Application information: Applications accepted. Application form required. Applicants should submit the following:
1) copy of IRS Determination Letter
Initial approach: Letter
Deadline(s): None
Trustees: Anita J. Cadonau; Carl H. Cadonau, Jr.; Randall E. Cadonau; Barbara Samsel-Deeming.
EIN: 943189006
Selected grants: The following grants are a representative sample of this grantmaker's funding activity:
$25,000 to Birch Community Services, Portland, OR, 2010.
$20,000 to Portland Rescue Mission, Portland, OR, 2010.

112
Alpha Natural Resources, Inc.

1 Alpha Pl.
P.O. Box 16429
Bristol, VA 24209 (276) 619-4410
FAX: (302) 636-5454

Company URL: http://www.alphanr.com
Establishment information: Established in 2002.
Company type: Public company
Company ticker symbol and exchange: ANR/NYSE
Business activities: Operates coal producing company.
Business type (SIC): Mining/coal and lignite surface
Financial profile for 2012: Assets, $13,100,000,000; sales volume, $7,000,000,000
Fortune 1000 ranking: 2012—365th in revenues, 994th in profits, and 325th in assets
Forbes 2000 ranking: 2012—1182nd in sales, 1963rd in profits, and 1274th in assets
Corporate officers: Kevin S. Crutchfield, Chair. and C.E.O.; Paul H. Vining, Pres.; Frank J. Wood, Exec. V.P. and C.F.O.; Vaughn R. Groves, Exec. V.P., Genl. Counsel, and Secy.
Board of directors: Kevin S. Crutchfield, Chair.; Angelo C. Brisimitzakis, kis; William J. Crowley, Jr.; E. Linn Draper, Jr.; Glenn A. Eisenberg; Deborah M. Fretz; P. Michael Giftos; L. Patrick Hassey; Joel Richards III; James F. Roberts; Ted G. Wood
Giving statement: Giving through the Alpha Natural Resources, Inc. Corporate Giving Program.
Company EIN: 421638663

Alpha Natural Resources, Inc. Corporate Giving Program

c/o Community Involvement Committee
1 Alpha Pl.
P.O. Box 16429
Bristol, VA 24209 (276) 619-4410
URL: http://www.alphanr.com/community/Pages/default.aspx

Purpose and activities: Alpha Natural Resources makes contributions to nonprofit organizations involved with children and families, education, arts and culture, and social services helping those in need of health care and emergency fuel. Giving is limited to areas of company operations in Kentucky, Pennsylvania, Virigina, West Virginia, and Wyoming.
Fields of interest: Arts; Higher education, college; Higher education, university; Education; Environment, energy; Environment; Health care; Substance abuse, prevention; Food services; Housing/shelter, services; Youth development; Children, services; Family services; Human services, emergency aid; Aging, centers/services; Human services.
Type of support: Annual campaigns; Donated products; Employee volunteer services; Employee-related scholarships; General/operating support; In-kind gifts; Scholarship funds.
Geographic limitations: Giving is limited to areas of company operations in KY, PA, VA, WV, and WY.
Publications: Annual report (including application guidelines); Application guidelines.
Application information: Applications accepted. The company is no longer processing grant requests for 2012. An employee-led Community Involvement Committee handles giving. Application form required. Applicants should submit the following:
1) role played by volunteers
2) name, address and phone number of organization
3) copy of IRS Determination Letter
4) brief history of organization and description of its mission
5) geographic area to be served
6) detailed description of project and amount of funding requested
7) contact person
8) plans for acknowledgement
Applications should note the nearest Alpha Operation, and an explanation of the organization's current programs, activities, and objectives.
Initial approach: Complete online application for requests of $10,000 or more; Letter to headquarters or e-mail for smaller requests
Committee meeting date(s): Annually
Deadline(s): 90 days prior to need

113
Alro Steel Corporation

3100 E. High St.
P.O. Box 927
Jackson, MI 49204-0927 (517) 787-5500
FAX: (517) 787-6390

Company URL: http://www.alro.com
Establishment information: Established in 1948.
Company type: Private company
Business activities: Sells steel wholesale.
Business type (SIC): Metals and minerals, except petroleum—wholesale
Corporate officers: Alvin L. Glick, Chair. and C.E.O.; Barry J. Glick, Vice-Chair.; Mark Alyea, Pres. and C.O.O.; Carl Glick, V.P. and Secy.; Randy Glick, V.P., Opers.; Marlin Hanstad, V.P., Sales; David Zontek, V.P. Human Resources; Keith Wood, V.P., Inf. Systems; James Norman, Cont.

Board of directors: Alvin L. Glick, Chair.; Barry J. Glick, Vice-Chair
Plants: Boca Raton, Clearwater, Orlando, FL; Melrose Park, IL; Kalamazoo, Redford, MI; Tonawanda, NY; Charlotte, NC; Perrysburg, OH; Menomonee Falls, WI
Giving statement: Giving through the Alro Steel Foundation.

The Alro Steel Foundation

3100 E. High St.
Jackson, MI 49203-3467

Establishment information: Established in 2004 in MI.
Donors: Li-Cor of Lincoln LLC; Alro Steel Corp.
Financial data (yr. ended 12/31/11): Assets, $6,914,918 (M); gifts received, $2,400,000; expenditures, $1,587,722; qualifying distributions, $1,587,702; giving activities include $1,587,702 for grants.
Purpose and activities: The foundation supports organizations involved with education, health, diabetes research, children and youth, and business.
Fields of interest: Higher education; Education; Hospitals (general); Health care, clinics/centers; Health care; Diabetes research; American Red Cross; Children/youth, services; Business/industry; United Ways and Federated Giving Programs.
Type of support: Building/renovation; General/operating support; Program development; Scholarship funds.
Geographic limitations: Giving primarily in MI, with emphasis on Jackson.
Support limitations: No grants to individuals.
Application information: Applications not accepted. Contributes only to pre-selected organizations.
Officers: Alvin L. Glick, Pres.; Barry J. Glick, V.P.; Carlton L. Glick, Secy.; Randal L. Glick, Treas.
EIN: 300254220
Selected grants: The following grants are a representative sample of this grantmaker's funding activity:
$1,000,000 to University of Michigan, Ann Arbor, MI, 2010.
$15,000 to United Way of Jackson County, Jackson, MI, 2010. For general support.
$10,000 to Center for Family Health, Jackson, MI, 2010. For general support.
$5,000 to Central Michigan University, Mount Pleasant, MI, 2010.
$3,000 to Junior Achievement of the Michigan Edge, Jackson, MI, 2010. For general support.
$2,750 to United Way of Central Indiana, Indianapolis, IN, 2010. For general support.
$1,000 to First United Methodist Church of Warren, Warren, MI, 2010. For general support.

114
Alsan Realty LP

18 Central Blvd.
South Hackensack, NJ 07606-1802
(201) 641-1642

Establishment information: Established in 2007.
Company type: Private company
Business activities: Operate real estate agency.
Business type (SIC): Real estate agents and managers
Corporate officers: Robert D. Duncan, Chair.; Stephen R. Quazzo, C.E.O.
Board of director: Robert D. Duncan, Chair.
Giving statement: Giving through the Alfred N. Sanzari Family Foundation, Inc.

Alfred N. Sanzari Family Foundation, Inc.

P.O. Box 2187
South Hackensack, NJ 07606-2187 (201) 342-2777

Establishment information: Established in 2006 in NJ.
Donors: Alsan Realty Co.; Mary A. Sanzari.
Contact: David Sanzari, Tr.
Financial data (yr. ended 12/31/11): Assets, $2,095,337 (M); expenditures, $4,560; qualifying distributions, $2,560.
Purpose and activities: The foundation supports organizations involved with education, conservation, and Catholicism.
Fields of interest: Education; Health care.
Type of support: General/operating support.
Geographic limitations: Giving primarily in NJ and PA.
Application information: Applications accepted. Application form required. Applicants should submit the following:
1) detailed description of project and amount of funding requested
Initial approach: Proposal
Deadline(s): None
Trustees: Frank Huttle III; Ben F. Sanzari; Joni Sanzari; David Sanzari; Mary A. Sanzari.
EIN: 204215473
Selected grants: The following grants are a representative sample of this grantmaker's funding activity:
$100,000 to Villanova University, Villanova, PA, 2009. For general support.
$5,500 to Archdiocese of Newark, Newark, NJ, 2009. For general support.

115
Alsco, Inc.

(formerly Steiner Corporation)
175 S. West Temple St., Ste. 510
Salt Lake City, UT 84101-1463
(801) 328-8831

Company URL: http://www.alsco.com
Establishment information: Established in 1889.
Company type: Private company
Business activities: Supplies linen and towels; processes food; leases equipment.
Business type (SIC): Laundry, cleaning, and garment services; specialty foods/canned, frozen, and preserved
Corporate officers: Kevin K. Steiner, Co-Pres. and Co-C.E.O.; Robert C. Steiner, Co-Pres. and Co-C.E.O.; James Kearns, C.F.O.
Subsidiaries: American Fine Food, Inc., Payette, ID; American Fine Food Nyssa, Nyssa, OR; American Uniform Co., Cleveland, TN; Change-O-Matic/Wesco, Aurora, IL; Farm Store No. 1, Boise, ID; Reclamizer, Philadelphia, PA; Steiner Co., Inc., Chicago, IL
Divisions: Steiner Foreign Linen Div., Salt Lake City, UT; Steiner U.S. Linen Div., Salt Lake City, UT
Giving statement: Giving through the Steiner Foundation, Inc.

Steiner Foundation, Inc.

505 E. South Temple St.
Salt Lake City, UT 84102-1004 (801) 328-8831

Establishment information: Established in 1959 in UT.
Donors: Steiner Corp.; Alsco Inc.; Richard R. Steiner†.
Contact: Kevin K. Steiner, Pres.
Financial data (yr. ended 06/30/11): Assets, $5,049,066 (M); gifts received, $500,000; expenditures, $6,706,128; qualifying distributions, $6,689,950; giving activities include $6,689,950 for grants.
Purpose and activities: The foundation supports organizations involved with theater, education, family planning, substance abuse services, human services, and economically disadvantaged people.
Fields of interest: Performing arts, theater; Elementary/secondary education; Higher education; Education, services; Education; Reproductive health, family planning; Substance abuse, services; Boy scouts; Homeless, human services; Human services Economically disadvantaged.
Type of support: General/operating support; Scholarship funds.
Geographic limitations: Giving primarily in UT.
Application information: Applications accepted. Application form not required. Applicants should submit the following:
1) name, address and phone number of organization
2) copy of most recent annual report/audited financial statement/990
3) detailed description of project and amount of funding requested
Initial approach: Proposal
Deadline(s): None
Officers: Kevin K. Steiner, Pres.; Timothy L. Weiler, Secy.
EIN: 876119190
Selected grants: The following grants are a representative sample of this grantmaker's funding activity:
$100,000 to Boy Scouts of America, Salt Lake City, UT, 2010.
$100,000 to Boy Scouts of America, Salt Lake City, UT, 2010.
$30,000 to buildOn, Stamford, CT, 2010.
$20,000 to Odyssey House, Salt Lake City, UT, 2010.
$20,000 to Pioneer Theater Company, Salt Lake City, UT, 2010.
$20,000 to Road Home, Salt Lake City, UT, 2010.
$20,000 to Rowland Hall-Saint Marks School, Salt Lake City, UT, 2010.
$5,500 to University of Utah, Salt Lake City, UT, 2010. For scholarship.
$3,000 to Literacy Action Center, Salt Lake City, UT, 2010.
$2,000 to Springville Museum of Art, Springville, UT, 2010.

116
Alston & Bird LLP

1 Atlantic Ctr.
1201 W. Peachtree St.
Atlanta, GA 30309-3424 (404) 881-7000

Company URL: http:///www.alston.com
Establishment information: Established in 1982.
Company type: Private company
Business activities: Operates law firm.
Business type (SIC): Legal services
Corporate officers: Richard G. Levinson, C.F.O.; Robert Marburger, C.I.O.
Offices: Los Angeles, Menlo Park, Westlake Village, CA; Washington, DC; Atlanta, GA; New York, NY; Charlotte, Durham, NC; Dallas, TX
International operations: Belgium
Giving statement: Giving through the Alston & Bird LLP Pro Bono Program.

Alston & Bird LLP Pro Bono Program
1 Atlantic Ctr.
1201 W. Peachtree St.
Atlanta, GA 30309-3424 (404) 881-7255
E-mail: mary.benton@alston.com; Additional tel.: (404) 881-7000; URL: http://www.alston.com/firm/community/probono/

Contact: Mary Benton, Pro Bono Partner
Fields of interest: Legal services.
Type of support: Pro bono services - legal.
Geographic limitations: Giving primarily in areas of company operations in Los Angeles, Menlo Park, and Westlake Village, CA, Washington, DC, Atlanta, GA, Charlotte, and Durham, NC, Dallas, TX, and in Belgium.
Application information: A Pro Bono Committee manages the pro bono program.

117
Altair Learning Management, Inc.
305 W. Nationalwide Blvd.
P.O. Box 2886
Columbus, OH 43215-2309
(614) 222-0882

Establishment information: Established in 2003.
Company type: Private company
Business activities: Operates educational software and web-based course delivery company.
Business type (SIC): Educational services/ miscellaneous
Corporate officer: William L. Lager, C.E.O.
Giving statement: Giving through the Michael John Lager Foundation.

Michael John Lager Foundation
P.O. Box 2886
Columbus, OH 43216-2886 (614) 738-0028
E-mail: mjlfoundation@columbus.rr.com

Establishment information: Established in 2004 in OH.
Donors: Altair Learning Management I, Inc.; William J. Lager.
Financial data (yr. ended 12/31/11): Assets, $14,135 (M); gifts received, $20,156; expenditures, $28,114; qualifying distributions, $5,900; giving activities include $1,100 for 2 grants (high: $600; low: $500) and $4,800 for 10 grants to individuals (high: $1,000; low: $125).
Purpose and activities: Giving primarily for group homes and direct assistance to individuals.
Fields of interest: Human services.
Type of support: Grants to individuals; Scholarships —to individuals.
Geographic limitations: Giving limited to OH.
Application information: Applications accepted. Application form required.
Initial approach: Proposal
Deadline(s): None
Officer: Zita Hunt, Treas.
Directors: Nathan Case; Jerry McMannamy; Melissa Vasil.
EIN: 200985519

118
Altec Industries, Inc.
210 Inverness Center Dr.
Birmingham, AL 35242-4834
(205) 991-7733
FAX: (205) 408-8601

Company URL: http://www.altec.com
Establishment information: Established in 1929.
Company type: Private company
Business activities: Operates electric utility and telecommunications equipment and services company.
Business type (SIC): Machinery/construction, mining, and materials handling
Corporate officers: Lee J. Styslinger, Jr., Chair.; Lee J. Styslinger III, Pres. and C.E.O.; J.D. Williams, Sr. V.P., Secy., and C.F.O.; Robert D. Hunter, Secy.; Jerry Moore, Treas. and Cont.
Board of director: Lee J. Styslinger, Jr., Chair.
Giving statement: Giving through the Altec Industries, Inc. Contributions Program and the Altec/Styslinger Foundation.

Altec Industries, Inc. Contributions Program
210 Inverness Center Dr.
Birmingham, AL 35242-4834 (205) 991-7733
URL: http://www.altec.com

Purpose and activities: As a complement to its foundation, Altec Industries also makes charitable contributions to nonprofit organizations directly.

Altec/Styslinger Foundation
210 Inverness Center Dr.
Birmingham, AL 35242-4834

Establishment information: Established in 1997 in AL.
Donors: Lee J. Styslinger, Jr.; Altec Industries, Inc.; Global Rental Co.
Financial data (yr. ended 12/31/11): Assets, $12,247,120 (M); gifts received, $3,050,000; expenditures, $997,748; qualifying distributions, $917,750; giving activities include $917,750 for grants.
Purpose and activities: Giving primarily for arts and culture, education, health associations, human services, children and youth services, the United Way, and religion.
Fields of interest: Performing arts; Arts; Elementary/secondary education; Higher education; Education; Zoos/zoological societies; Animals/wildlife; Health organizations, association; Youth development, centers/clubs; Human services; Children/youth, services; United Ways and Federated Giving Programs; Christian agencies & churches.
Geographic limitations: Giving primarily in AL.
Support limitations: No grants to individuals.
Application information: Applications not accepted. Contributes only to pre-selected organizations.
Officers and Directors:* Lee J. Styslinger, Jr.*, Chair.; Lee J. Styslinger III*, C.E.O. and Pres.; Allen W. Ritchie, Secy.
EIN: 721372302
Selected grants: The following grants are a representative sample of this grantmaker's funding activity:
$20,000 to University of Alabama, Birmingham, AL, 2010. For general operating budget.
$10,000 to Birmingham Zoo, Birmingham, AL, 2010. For general operating budget.
$10,000 to Innovation Depot, Birmingham, AL, 2010. For general operating budget.
$5,000 to Black Warrior Riverkeeper, Birmingham, AL, 2010. For general operating budget.
$5,000 to Boy Scouts of America, Birmingham, AL, 2010. For general operating budget.
$5,000 to Linly Heflin Unit, Birmingham, AL, 2010. For general operating budget.
$5,000 to Red Mountain Theater Company, Birmingham, AL, 2010. For general operating budget.
$2,500 to Campus Crusade for Christ, Birmingham, AL, 2010. For general operating budget.
$2,500 to Crippled Childrens Foundation, Birmingham, AL, 2010. For general operating budget.
$2,000 to Exceptional Foundation, Birmingham, AL, 2010. For general operating budget.

119
The Altman Company
1251 Fairwood Ave.
Columbus, OH 43206-3313
(614) 253-8611

Company URL: http://www.altmangc.com/
Establishment information: Established in 1931.
Company type: Private company
Business activities: Provides general contract construction services.
Business type (SIC): Building construction general contractors and operative builders
Corporate officers: Jonathan S. Altman, Pres.; Norm J. Altman, Secy. and Treas.
Giving statement: Giving through the Altman Family Foundation.

Altman Family Foundation
(formerly Norman & Nettie Altman Foundation)
1251 Fairwood Ave.
Columbus, OH 43206-3313

Donor: The Altman Co.
Financial data (yr. ended 12/31/11): Assets, $2,330 (M); gifts received, $13,000; expenditures, $12,520; qualifying distributions, $12,520; giving activities include $12,520 for grants.
Purpose and activities: The foundation supports fire departments and organizations involved with higher and theological education and Catholicism.
Fields of interest: Education; Housing/shelter.
Type of support: General/operating support.
Geographic limitations: Giving primarily in Columbus, OH.
Support limitations: No grants to individuals.
Application information: Applications not accepted. Contributes only to pre-selected organizations.
Trustees: James P. Altman; Jon Altman; Norman J. Altman III; Judith Briley.
EIN: 311052997

120
Altria Group, Inc.
(doing business as Philip Morris)
(formerly Philip Morris Companies Inc.)
6601 W. Broad St.
Richmond, VA 23230 (804) 274-2200

Company URL: http://www.altria.com
Establishment information: Established in 1902.
Company type: Public company
Company ticker symbol and exchange: MO/NYSE
International Securities Identification Number: US02209S1033

Business activities: Operates tobacco products company.
Business type (SIC): Tobacco products—cigarettes; food and kindred products; beverages
Financial profile for 2012: Number of employees, 9,100; assets, $35,329,000,000; sales volume, $24,618,000,000; pre-tax net income, $6,477,000,000; expenses, $18,239,000,000; liabilities, $32,161,000,000
Fortune 1000 ranking: 2012—159th in revenues, 45th in profits, and 160th in assets
Forbes 2000 ranking: 2012—535th in sales, 133rd in profits, and 639th in assets
Corporate officers: Martin J. Barrington, Chair. and C.E.O.; David R. Beran, Pres. and C.O.O.; Howard A. Willard III, Exec. V.P. and C.F.O.; Denise F. Keane, Exec. V.P. and Genl. Counsel; Charles N. Whitaker, Sr. V.P., Human Resources
Board of directors: Martin J. Barrington, Chair.; Elizabeth E. Bailey; Gerald L. Baliles; John T. Casteen III; Dinyar S. Devitre; Thomas F. Farrell II; Thomas W. Jones; W. Leo Kiely III; Kathryn McQuade; George Munoz; Nabil Y. Sakkab
Subsidiaries: Philip Morris Capital Corp., Stamford, CT; Philip Morris USA, Inc., Richmond, VA; Philip Morris USA Inc., Richmond, VA; U.S. Smokeless Tobacco Company LLC, Greenwich, CT
International operations: Brazil; Canada
Giving statement: Giving through the Altria Group, Inc. Corporate Giving Program and the Altria Companies Employee Community Fund.
Company EIN: 133260245

Altria Group, Inc. Corporate Giving Program

(formerly Philip Morris Companies Inc. Corporate Giving Program)
c/o Corp. Contribs. Dept.
6601 West Broad St.
Richmond, VA 23230-1723 (804) 274-2200
URL: http://www.altria.com/Pages/default.aspx

Purpose and activities: Altria makes charitable contributions to nonprofit organizations involved with arts and culture, education, the environment, and positive youth development. Support is given on a national basis, with emphasis on the greater Richmond, Virginia, area, including Washington, DC.
Fields of interest: Arts education; Visual arts; Museums; Performing arts; Arts; Education, public education; Elementary/secondary education; Vocational education; Higher education; Scholarships/financial aid; Environment, natural resources; Environment, water resources; Environment, land resources; Environment, beautification programs; Substance abuse, prevention; Agriculture; Food banks; Youth development; Leadership development.
Programs:

Arts: Altria supports programs designed to promote visual and performing arts. Special emphasis is directed toward programs designed to develop new audiences and increase access to the arts; sponsorships that bring world-class cultural experiences to the community; and arts education programs designed to enhance the overall performance and development of middle school students, primarily in greater Richmond, Virginia public schools.

Dollars for Doers: Altria awards grants to nonprofit organizations with which Altria employees volunteer a minimum of 25 hours per calendar year.

Education: Altria supports programs designed to improve educational outcomes for underserved youth and address the demand for a diverse, highly skilled workforce. Special emphasis is directed toward middle and high-school enrichment programs for urban public schools that contribute to everyday student success, math and science excellence, and access to and preparation for higher education; technical education at community colleges and universities, including agricultural studies programs at select land-grant institutions; strengthening management skills among school leaders; and higher education and scholarship support.

Environment: Altria support supports programs designed to reduce environmental impact and promote sustainability of natural resources. Special emphasis is directed toward sustainable agriculture and land conservation; watershed stewardship; and trash cleanup and litter prevention.

Matching Gifts Program: Altria matches contributions made by its employees to nonprofit organizations one a one-for-one basis up to $30,000 per employee, per year.

Positive Youth Development: Altria, through Philip Morris USA, supports youth programs designed to help kids develop the confidence and skills they to need to avoid risky behaviors, including underage tobacco use. Special emphasis is directed toward programs designed to provide evidence-based initiatives for kids including mentoring, life skills education, and substance abuse prevention; assist national youth-serving organizations reach more kids, improve program quality, and better measure their impact; help community leaders align youth programs and policies; and conduct research on effective PYD programs.
Type of support: Building/renovation; Emergency funds; Employee matching gifts; Employee volunteer services; General/operating support; In-kind gifts; Program development; Sponsorships.
Geographic limitations: Giving on a national basis in areas of company operations, with emphasis on the greater Richmond, VA area, including Washington, DC.
Support limitations: No support for political, lobbying organizations, religious, fraternal, veterans' or discriminatory organizations. No grants to individuals, or for capital campaigns, endowments, building fund drives, television, film, or video production, or athletic or sports-related activities.
Publications: Grants list.
Application information: Applications not accepted. Unsolicited applications are generally not accepted. The company utilizes an invitation only process for giving.
Number of staff: 15 full-time professional; 3 part-time professional; 8 full-time support; 1 part-time support.

Altria Companies Employee Community Fund

(formerly Philip Morris Employee Community Fund)
6603 W. Broad St.
Richmond, VA 23230-1723 (804) 484-8631
URL: http://www.pmusa.com/en/cms/Responsibility/Investing_in_Our_Communities/default.aspx

Establishment information: Established in 2000 in VA.
Donor: Philip Morris USA Inc.
Financial data (yr. ended 12/31/11): Revenue, $2,645,085; assets, $1,781,550 (M); gifts received, $2,644,805; expenditures, $2,575,000; giving activities include $2,575,000 for grants.
Purpose and activities: The fund enables employees of subsidiaries of Altria Group and other interested donors to make contributions that can be combined for distribution to existing nonprofit organizations in their communities, with a focus on hunger relief, services to seniors, youth development, emergency services, homelessness, and domestic violence.
Fields of interest: Food services; Housing/shelter, homeless; Youth, services; Family services, domestic violence; Human services, emergency aid; Aging, centers/services.
Geographic limitations: Giving primarily in Cabarrus County, NC and central VA.
Support limitations: No grants for general operating deficits, research projects, endowments, or building or capital campaigns.
Application information: Applications not accepted. Unsolicited requests for funds not accepted.
Officers and Directors:* Jennifer L. Hunter*, Chair.; Joseph S. Amado*, Secy.; Henry P. Long*, Treas.; James E. Dillard; Sheila G. Mitchell; Patrick L. Neal; Gary R. Ruth; Craig G. Schwartz; James W. Wareen.
EIN: 311733311

121
Alyeska Pipeline Service Company

900 E. Benson St.
Anchorage, AK 99519 (907) 787-8700

Company URL: http://www.alyeska-pipe.com
Establishment information: Established in 1970.
Company type: Joint venture
Business activities: Operates crude oil pipeline system.
Business type (SIC): Pipelines (except natural gas/operation of)
Corporate officers: Thomas Barrett, Pres.; Ed Hendrickson, Sr. V.P. and C.F.O.; Mike Joynor, Sr. V.P., Opers.; Susan Parks, V.P. and Genl. Counsel
Giving statement: Giving through the Alyeska Pipeline Service Company Contributions Program.

Alyeska Pipeline Service Company Contributions Program

P.O. Box 196660
Anchorage, AK 99519-6660 (907) 787-8700
E-mail: alyeskamail@alyeska-pipeline.com; Corporate donation addresses: Anchorage Corp. Comms. - Donations, Alyeska Pipeline Service Company, P.O. Box 196660, MS 542, Anchorage, AK 99519-6660, email: AnchComm@alyeska-pipeline.com, tel.: (907) 787-8870, fax: (907) 787-8240; Fairbanks Corp. Comms.- Donations, Alyeska Pipeline Service Company, 615 Bidwill Ave., MS 815, Fairbanks, AK, 99701, e-mail: FBKSComm@alyeska-pipeline.com, tel.: (907) 450-5857; Valdez Corp. Comms. - Donations, Alyeska Pipeline Service Company, P.O. Box 300, MS 701, Valdez, AK, 99686, e-mail: VLDZComm@alyeska-pipeline.com, tel.: (907) 834-7303, fax: (907) 834-7585; Gift/Volunteer Matching: Plan Administrator, Matching Gift/Volunteer Matching Plan, Alyeska Pipeline Service Company, P.O. Box 19660, MS 542, Anchorage, AK, 99519-6660, e-mail: donationmatching@alyeska-pipeline.com, tel.: (907) 787-8243, fax: (907) 787-8240; URL: http://www.alyeska-pipe.com/AboutUs/InTheCommunity

Purpose and activities: Alyeska makes charitable contributions to nonprofit organizations involved with education, employment, volunteerism, community safety, diversity, and the environment. Giving limited to Alaska, primarily in areas of company operations in Anchorage, Fairbanks, Prince William Sound, and Valdez, Alaska, and along the pipeline corridor. Emphasis is given to organizations with employee involvement.

Fields of interest: Arts, cultural/ethnic awareness; Elementary/secondary education; Adult/continuing education; Environment; Employment, volunteer services; Employment; Safety/disasters; Civil/human rights, equal rights; Community/economic development.
Type of support: Employee volunteer services; General/operating support.
Geographic limitations: Giving limited to AK, primarily in areas of company operations in Anchorage, Fairbanks, Prince William Sound, and Valdez, AK, and along the pipeline corridor.
Support limitations: No support for No support religious organizations not of direct public benefit, political organizations, or campaigns, discriminatory organizations. No grants to individuals or for the benefit of one person, or for travel expenses, programs that duplicate existing services, or for endowments.
Publications: Application guidelines; Informational brochure.
Application information: Applications accepted. Form letters are not accepted. Phone calls are discouraged. Application form not required. Applicants should submit the following:
1) listing of additional sources and amount of support
2) copy of current year's organizational budget and/or project budget
3) contact person
4) plans for cooperation with other organizations, if any
5) detailed description of project and amount of funding requested
6) list of company employees involved with the organization
7) how project's results will be evaluated or measured
8) geographic area to be served
9) copy of IRS Determination Letter
10) name, address and phone number of organization
11) population served
12) results expected from proposed grant
13) how project will be sustained once grantmaker support is completed

Initial approach: Mail completed proposal to regional application address listed on website
Copies of proposal: 1

122
Amazon.com, Inc.
410 Terry Ave., N.
Seattle, WA 98109-5210 (206) 266-1000
FAX: (302) 636-5454

Company URL: http://www.amazon.com
Establishment information: Established in 1994.
Company type: Public company
Company ticker symbol and exchange: AMZN/NASDAQ
Business activities: Operates online retail store and marketplace.
Business type (SIC): Nonstore retailers
Financial profile for 2012: Number of employees, 88,400; assets, $32,555,000,000; sales volume, $61,093,000,000; pre-tax net income, $544,000,000; expenses, $60,417,000,000; liabilities, $24,363,000,000
Fortune 1000 ranking: 2012—49th in revenues, 902nd in profits, and 173rd in assets
Forbes 2000 ranking: 2012—131st in sales, 1781st in profits, and 688th in assets
Corporate officers: Jeffrey P. Bezos, Chair., Pres., and C.E.O.; Thomas J. Szkutak, Sr. V.P. and C.F.O.; David A. Zapolsky, V.P., Genl. Counsel, and Secy.; Shelley L. Reynolds, V.P. and Cont.
Board of directors: Jeffrey P. Bezos, Chair.; Tom A. Alberg; John Seely Brown; Jamie S. Gorelick; William B. Gordon; Alain Monie; Jonathan Rubinstein; Thomas O. Ryder; Patricia Q. Stonesifer
Subsidiaries: A9, Palo Alto, CA; Alexa, San Francisco, CA; Audible, Newark, NJ; BookSurge, Charleston, SC; Brilliance Audio, Grand Haven, MI; IMDb, Seattle, WA; Lab126, Cupertino, CA; shopbop, Madison, WI; SmallParts, Miami Lakes, FL; Zappos.com, Inc., Henderson, NV
International operations: Luxembourg
Giving statement: Giving through the Amazon.com, Inc. Corporate Giving Program.
Company EIN: 911646860

Amazon.com, Inc. Corporate Giving Program
1200 12th Ave. South, Ste. 1200
Seattle, WA 98144-2734 (206) 266-1000
URL: http://www.amazon.com/b/ref=gw_m_b_ourcomm?ie=UTF8&node=13786411

Purpose and activities: Amazon.com makes charitable contributions to nonprofit organizations involved with literary education for youth, publishing, theater, art, and disaster relief. Support is given primarily to national organizations; giving also to local organizations in areas of company operations.
Fields of interest: Arts, public education; Media, print publishing; Performing arts, theater; Performing arts, theater (playwriting); Literature; Arts; Secondary school/education; Safety/disasters, fund raising/fund distribution.
Type of support: Computer technology; Donated products; Employee volunteer services; General/operating support; In-kind gifts; Public relations services; Publication; Sponsorships; Technical assistance.
Geographic limitations: Giving primarily to national organizations; giving also to local organizations in areas of company operations.
Publications: Application guidelines.
Application information: Applications accepted. Application form required. Applicants should submit the following:
1) contact person
2) copy of IRS Determination Letter

Proposals should include a link to the organization's website, and a brief description of how the organization helps to foster the creation, discussion, publication, and dissemination of books to a wide audience.
Initial approach: Complete online application

123
Ambac Financial Group, Inc.
1 State St. Plz.
New York, NY 10004-1505 (212) 658-7470
FAX: (212) 509-9190

Company URL: http://www.ambac.com
Establishment information: Established in 1971.
Company type: Public company
Company ticker symbol and exchange: ABK/Pink Sheets
Business activities: Operates holding company; sells surety insurance; provides investment advisory services.
Business type (SIC): Insurance/surety
Financial profile for 2012: Number of employees, 226; assets, $27,007,160,000; sales volume, $685,690,000; pre-tax net income, -$256,500,000; expenses, $942,190,000; liabilities, $30,914,690,000
Forbes 2000 ranking: 2012—1950th in sales, 1876th in profits, and 801st in assets
Corporate officers: Victor Mandel, Chair.; Diana N. Adams, Pres. and C.E.O.; David Trick, Treas. and C.F.O.; Michael Reilly, C.I.O. and Co-C.A.O.; Robert B. Eisman, Co-C.A.O.; Stephen M. Ksenak, Genl. Counsel and Corp. Secy.
Board of directors: Victor Mandel, Chair.; Diana N. Adams; Diane B. Glossman; Thomas P. Gybel; Gary Stern; Jeffrey S. Stein; Nader Tavakoli
Subsidiary: Ambac Capital Corp., New York, NY
Giving statement: Giving through the Ambac Financial Group, Inc. Corporate Giving Program.
Company EIN: 133621676

Ambac Financial Group, Inc. Corporate Giving Program
One State Street Plz.
New York, NY 10004 (212) 668-0340
FAX: (212) 509-9190; URL: http://www.ambac.com/aboutus.asp

Program:
Matching Gifts Program: Ambac matches contributions made by its employees to nonprofit organizations on a one-for-one basis from $100 to $20,000 per employee, per year.
Corporate Contributions Committee: Susan Oehrig, Chair.; Jessie Adams; Gregg Bienstock; Don Farrell; Louise Minford.

124
Amboy National Bank
3590 U.S. Hwy. 9, S.
Old Bridge, NJ 08857 (732) 591-8700

Company URL: http://www.amboybank.com
Establishment information: Established in 1888.
Company type: Subsidiary of a private company
Business activities: Operates commercial bank.
Business type (SIC): Banks/commercial
Corporate officer: Stanley J. Koreyva, C.O.O.
Offices: Hillsborough, Hopewell, Howell, Laurence Harbor, Manalapan, Millstone Township, Monroe, New Brunswick, Oakhurst, Old Bridge, Port Monmouth, Red Bank, Rocky Hill, Sayreville, South Amboy, Woodbridge, NJ
Giving statement: Giving through the Amboy Foundation, Inc.

The Amboy Foundation, Inc.
c/o Amboy Bank
3590 U.S. Hwy. 9
Old Bridge, NJ 08857-2837
URL: http://www.amboybank.com/home/about/amboy

Establishment information: Established in 1996 in NJ.
Donor: Amboy National Bank.
Contact: Karen Casey
Financial data (yr. ended 12/31/11): Assets, $2,319,402 (M); expenditures, $170,229; qualifying distributions, $170,000; giving activities include $170,000 for 38 grants (high: $10,000; low: $1,000).
Purpose and activities: The foundation supports organizations involved with education, civic affairs, health, human services, social services, and culture. Special emphasis is directed toward programs designed to promote community development and social welfare, including local

shelters and health and welfare clinics; benefit low to moderate income populations; provide educational initiatives to meet the housing needs of low to moderate income populations; and promote higher education, with a focus on business programs.
Fields of interest: Arts; Higher education; Business school/education; Education; Hospitals (general); Health care; Housing/shelter, development; Housing/shelter; Children/youth, services; Family services; Human services; Community/economic development; Public affairs Economically disadvantaged.
Type of support: General/operating support; Program development; Sponsorships.
Geographic limitations: Giving primarily in central NJ.
Support limitations: No support for private clubs or fraternal organizations, labor groups, or pass-through organizations. No grants to individuals or for political causes.
Publications: Application guidelines.
Application information: Applications accepted. Grants range from $1,000 to $10,000. Proposals should be no longer than 2 pages. Support is limited to 1 contribution per organization during any given year. Application form not required. Applicants should submit the following:
1) timetable for implementation and evaluation of project
2) how project will be sustained once grantmaker support is completed
3) staff salaries
4) qualifications of key personnel
5) statement of problem project will address
6) name, address and phone number of organization
7) copy of IRS Determination Letter
8) brief history of organization and description of its mission
9) copy of most recent annual report/audited financial statement/990
10) list of company employees involved with the organization
11) descriptive literature about organization
12) listing of board of directors, trustees, officers and other key people and their affiliations
13) detailed description of project and amount of funding requested
14) contact person
15) copy of current year's organizational budget and/or project budget
16) listing of additional sources and amount of support

Proposals should include a description of past involvement by the foundation with the organization.
Initial approach: Proposal
Copies of proposal: 1
Board meeting date(s): Quarterly
Deadline(s): None
Final notification: 30 days following board meetings

Officers and Trustees:* Mary Kay Riccardi, V.P.; Patricia M. Keys*, Secy.; George G. Brennan*, Treas.; Marguerite DiSepio; George E. Scharpf.
EIN: 223484075

125
AMC Entertainment Inc.

(doing business as AMC)
920 Main St.
Kansas City, MO 64105 (816) 221-4000

Company URL: http://www.amctheaters.com
Establishment information: Established in 1920.
Company type: Subsidiary of a foreign company
Business activities: Operates holding company; operates movie theaters.
Business type (SIC): Motion picture theaters
Financial profile for 2011: Number of employees, 8,800; assets, $3,653,200,000; sales volume, $2,417,700,000
Fortune 1000 ranking: 2012—787th in revenues, 921st in profits, and 691st in assets
Corporate officers: Aaron J. Stone, Chair.; Gerardo I. Lopez, Pres. and C.E.O.; Craig R. Ramsey, Exec. V.P. and C.F.O.; Michael Czinege, C.I.O.; Keith Weidenkeller, Sr. V.P., Human Resources; Terry W. Crawford, V.P. and Treas.; Michael W. Zwonitzer, V.P., Finance
Board of directors: Aaron J. Stone, Chair.; Gerardo I. Lopez; Craig R. Ramsey
Giving statement: Giving through the AMC Entertainment Inc. Corporate Giving Program.
Company EIN: 431304369

AMC Entertainment Inc. Corporate Giving Program

920 Main St.
Kansas City, MO 64105-2017
URL: http://www.amctheatres.com/corporate/in-the-community

Purpose and activities: AMC Entertainment makes charitable contributions to nonprofit organizations involved with autism, lung research, children services, and community development. Support is given primarily in areas of company operations, with emphasis on Kansas City, Missouri.
Fields of interest: Autism; Lung research; Children, services; Community/economic development.
Program:
Education: AMC thanks and rewards teachers who dedicate their time to educating kindergarten through 12th grade students. Several times a year teachers throughout the U.S. and Canada are invited to escape from everyday life and view select movies free of charge. AMC partners with select film distributors to provide the free movie passes.
Type of support: Donated products; Employee volunteer services; General/operating support; Program development; Sponsorships; Use of facilities.
Geographic limitations: Giving primarily in areas of company operations, with emphasis Kansas City, MO; giving also to national organizations.
Application information: Applications not accepted. Contributes only to pre-selected organizations.

126
AMC Networks Inc.

(formerly Rainbow Media Holdings, Inc.)
11 Penn Plz.
New York, NY 10001 (212) 324-8500

Company URL: http://www.amcnetworks.com
Establishment information: Established in 1980.
Company type: Subsidiary of a public company
Business activities: Provides cable television services; operates sports arena; operates professional basketball club; operates professional ice hockey club; provides advertising services.
Business type (SIC): Cable and other pay television services; advertising; commercial sports
Corporate officers: Charles Doran, Chair.; Josh Sapan, Pres. and C.E.O.; Ed Carroll, C.O.O.; Sean S. Sullivan, Exec. V.P. and C.F.O.; Jamie Gallagher, Exec. V.P. and Genl. Counsel; John P. Giraldo, C.A.O.; John Huffman, Exec. V.P., Finance; Ellen Kroner, Exec. V.P., Comms. and Mktg.; Rob Doodian, Exec. V.P., Human Resources
Board of director: Charles Doran, Chair.
Giving statement: Giving through the Rainbow Media Holdings LLC Corporate Giving Program.

Rainbow Media Holdings LLC Corporate Giving Program

(formerly Rainbow Media Holdings, Inc. Corporate Giving Program)
200 Jericho Quadrangle
Jericho, NY 11753-2701
FAX: (516) 803-5143

Contact: Matthew Frankel, Dir., Media Rels. and Public Affairs
Purpose and activities: Rainbow Media makes charitable contributions to nonprofit organizations involved with arts and culture and education. Support is given primarily in the New York, New York, tri-state area.
Fields of interest: Media/communications; Arts; Education.
Type of support: Annual campaigns; Conferences/seminars; General/operating support; In-kind gifts; Scholarship funds; Sponsorships.
Geographic limitations: Giving primarily in the New York, NY, tri-state area.
Application information: The Corporate Communications Department handles giving. Application form not required. Applicants should submit the following:
1) detailed description of project and amount of funding requested

Initial approach: Proposal to headquarters
Copies of proposal: 1
Deadline(s): None
Final notification: 1 month

Administrators: Matthew Frankel, Dir., Media Rels. and Public Affairs; Christine Levesque, Sr. V.P., Comms. and Mktg.

127
AMCOL International Corporation

2870 Forbs Ave.
Hoffman Estates, IL 60192 (847) 851-1500
FAX: (847) 851-1699

Company URL: http://www.amcol.com
Establishment information: Established in 1927.
Company type: Public company
Company ticker symbol and exchange: ACO/NYSE
Business activities: Mines, processes, and distributes clays; provides trucking services; provides freight brokerage services.
Business type (SIC): Mining and quarrying of nonmetallic minerals (except fuels); mining/clay, ceramic, and refractory mineral; trucking and courier services, except by air; transportation services/freight
Financial profile for 2012: Number of employees, 2,824; assets, $910,600,000; sales volume, $985,600,000; pre-tax net income, $84,300,000; expenses, $887,500,000; liabilities, $449,200,000
Corporate officers: John Hughes, Chair.; Ryan F. McKendrick, Pres. and C.E.O.; Donald W. Pearson, Sr. V.P. and C.F.O.
Board of directors: John Hughes, Chair.; Arthur Brown; Daniel P. Casey; Donald J. Gallagher; Ryan McKendrick; Frederick J. Palensky, Ph.D.; Jay D. Proops; Clarence O. Redman; William H. Schumann; Dale E. Stahl; Audrey L. Weaver; Paul C. Weaver

Subsidiaries: Ameri-Co Carriers, Inc., Scottsbluff, NE; American Colloid Co., Arlington Heights, IL; Colloid Environmental Technologies Co., Arlington Heights, IL; Nanocor, Inc., Arlington Heights, IL
International operations: Australia; United Kingdom
Giving statement: Giving through the Paul Bechtner Education Foundation.
Company EIN: 360724340

Paul Bechtner Education Foundation

(formerly American Colloid Company Foundation)
2870 Forbs Ave.
Hoffman Estates, IL 60192-3702

Establishment information: Established in 1994 in IL.
Donors: AMCOL International Corp.; Everett P. Weaver; Paul Bechner Foundation.
Contact: Amiel Naiman
Financial data (yr. ended 12/31/11): Assets, $31,520 (M); gifts received, $50,800; expenditures, $33,000; qualifying distributions, $33,000; giving activities include $33,000 for 22 grants (high: $1,500; low: $1,500).
Purpose and activities: The foundation awards college scholarships to children of employees of AMCOL International Corp.
Fields of interest: Education.
Type of support: Employee-related scholarships.
Application information: Applications accepted. Application form required.
Initial approach: Proposal
Deadline(s): Apr. 20
Officers: Ryan F. McKendrick, Pres.; James W. Ashley, Secy.; Donald W. Pearson, Treas.
EIN: 363892273

128
Ameren Corporation

1901 Chouteau Ave.
St. Louis, MO 63103 (314) 621-3222
FAX: (314) 621-2888

Company URL: http://www.ameren.com/
Establishment information: Established in 1902.
Company type: Public company
Company ticker symbol and exchange: AEE/NYSE
International Securities Identification Number: US0236081024
Business activities: Operates holding company; generates, transmits, and distributes electricity; transmits and distributes natural gas.
Business type (SIC): Combination utility services; holding company
Financial profile for 2012: Number of employees, 9,097; assets, $21,835,000,000; sales volume, $6,828,000,000; pre-tax net income, -$1,654,000,000; expenses, $8,068,000,000; liabilities, $15,219,000,000
Fortune 1000 ranking: 2012—373rd in revenues, 979th in profits, and 228th in assets
Corporate officers: Thomas R. Voss, Chair., Pres., and C.E.O.; Martin J. Lyons, Exec. V.P. and C.F.O.; Gregory L. Nelson, Sr. V.P., Genl. Counsel, and Secy.; Bruce A. Steinke, Sr. V.P., Finance, and C.A.O.; S. Mark Brawley, V.P., Internal Audit
Board of directors: Thomas R. Voss, Chair.; Catherine S. Brune; Ellen M. Fitzsimmons; Walter J. Galvin; Gayle P.W. Jackson, Ph.D.; James C. Johnson; Steven H. Lipstein; Patrick T. Stokes; Stephen R. Wilson; Jack D. Woodard
Subsidiaries: Ameren Development Co., St. Louis, MO; Ameren Energy, Inc., St. Louis, MO; Ameren Energy Resources Co., St. Louis, MO; Ameren Illinois Company, Peoria, IL; Ameren Services Co., St. Louis, MO; Central Illinois Light Company, Peoria, IL; Central Illinois Public Service Company, Springfield, IL; CIPSCO Investment Co., Springfield, IL; Union Electric Company, St. Louis, MO
Giving statement: Giving through the Ameren Corporation Contributions Program and the Ameren Corporation Charitable Trust.
Company EIN: 431723446

Ameren Corporation Contributions Program

(formerly Union Electric Company Contributions Program)
1901 Chouteau Ave.
St. Louis, MO 63103-3003 (800) 552-7583
Application address for Illinois: Corp. Contribs., Ameren Illinois, 300 Liberty St., Peoria, IL 61602; for Missouri: Corp. Contribs., Ameren Missouri, P.O. Box 66149, MC 100, St. Louis, MO 63166-6149. E-mail for Illinois: CommunityRelationsIL@ameren.com; e-mail for Missouri: CommunityRelations@ameren.com.; URL: http://www.ameren.com/CommunityMembers/Pages/default.aspx

Contact: Brian Leonard, Mgr., Business and Community Affairs
Purpose and activities: As a complement to its foundation, Ameren also makes charitable contributions to nonprofit organizations directly. Emphasis is given to civic, environmental, and cultural organizations, educational institutions and programs, senior citizens' organizations, social services, and youth activities. Support is given primarily in areas of company operations.
Fields of interest: Arts; Education; Environment, energy; Environment; Health care; Food banks; Youth development; Human services; United Ways and Federated Giving Programs Aging.
Program:
Ameren VIP/TEAMS Grant Program: Through the Ameren VIP/TEAMS Grant Program, Ameren makes charitable contributions to nonprofit organizations with which company employees volunteer. VIP grants are made to organizations for projects in which at least one Ameren employee is involved. TEAMS grants are made to organizations for projects in which at least three Ameren employees are involved. Grants range from $50 to $500.
Type of support: Annual campaigns; Building/renovation; Capital campaigns; Cause-related marketing; Curriculum development; Donated equipment; Emergency funds; Employee volunteer services; Equipment; General/operating support; In-kind gifts; Matching/challenge support; Program development; Seed money; Sponsorships.
Geographic limitations: Giving primarily in areas of company operations in IL and MO.
Support limitations: No support for political organizations or candidates, or religious, fraternal, veterans', social, or similar organizations. No grants to individuals; no electric or natural gas service donations.
Publications: Application guidelines.
Application information: Applications accepted. Application guidelines are available here: http://www.ameren.com/sites/aiu/Community/Pages/HowtoapplyGrant.aspx. Application form required. Applicants should submit the following:
1) timetable for implementation and evaluation of project
2) population served
3) name, address and phone number of organization
4) copy of IRS Determination Letter
5) brief history of organization and description of its mission
6) copy of most recent annual report/audited financial statement/990
7) list of company employees involved with the organization
8) listing of board of directors, trustees, officers and other key people and their affiliations
9) detailed description of project and amount of funding requested
10) contact person
11) copy of current year's organizational budget and/or project budget
12) listing of additional sources and amount of support
13) plans for acknowledgement

Application should include the number of people served by the organization annually, the percentage of the total budget that is spent on administration and fundraising costs, and whether the organization has received funding from Ameren in the past five years.
Initial approach: Download online application form and mail completed form to application address in Illinois or Missouri
Copies of proposal: 1
Deadline(s): None
Administrators: Susan M. Bell, Sr. Supvr., Business and Community Affairs (MO); Brian Leonard, Mgr., Business and Community Affairs (MO); Sean Vanslyke, Mgr., Community and Public Rels. (IL).
Number of staff: 3 full-time professional; 2 full-time support.

Ameren Corporation Charitable Trust

(formerly Union Electric Company Charitable Trust)
c/o Corp. Contribs., Ameren
P.O. Box 66149, M.C. 100
St. Louis, MO 63166-6149
FAX: (314) 554-2888;
E-mail: bleonard@ameren.com; Application address for organizations located in IL: Corp. Contribs., Ameren, 300 Liberty St., Peoria, IL 61602-1404, tel.: (877) 426-3736, ext. 75001; tel.: (314) 554-6441; e-mail: CommunityRelations@ameren.com; URL: http://www.ameren.com/CommunityMembers/CharitableTrust/Pages/Corporationcharitabletrust.aspx

Establishment information: Trust established in 1944 in MO.
Donors: Union Electric Co.; Ameren Corp.
Contact: Brian K. Leonard, Dir., Business and Community Affairs
Financial data (yr. ended 12/31/12): Assets, $6,353,738 (M); expenditures, $4,837,773; qualifying distributions, $4,822,739; giving activities include $4,811,382 for 180 grants (high: $1,304,100; low: $25).
Purpose and activities: The trust supports organizations involved with arts and culture, human services, and civic affairs. Special emphasis is directed toward organizations involved with education, the environment, youth, and senior citizens.
Fields of interest: Arts; Higher education; Education; Environment, energy; Hospitals (general); Youth development, business; Salvation Army; Youth, services; Human services; United Ways and Federated Giving Programs; Public affairs Aging.
Type of support: Annual campaigns; Building/renovation; Capital campaigns; Continuing support; Donated equipment; Donated land; Emergency funds; Employee matching gifts; Equipment; General/operating support; In-kind gifts; Matching/challenge support; Program development; Scholarship funds; Sponsorships.

Geographic limitations: Giving limited to areas of company operations in IL and MO.
Support limitations: No support for political organizations or candidates or religious, fraternal, veterans', social, or similar organizations. No grants to individuals; no electric or natural gas service donations.
Publications: Annual report; Application guidelines; Corporate giving report (including application guidelines).
Application information: Applications accepted. Application requests under $5,000 require a cover letter and IRS determination letter; requests over $5,000 require additional information. Application form required. Applicants should submit the following:
1) results expected from proposed grant
2) qualifications of key personnel
3) population served
4) copy of IRS Determination Letter
5) brief history of organization and description of its mission
6) geographic area to be served
7) copy of most recent annual report/audited financial statement/990
8) listing of board of directors, trustees, officers and other key people and their affiliations
9) detailed description of project and amount of funding requested
10) copy of current year's organizational budget and/or project budget

Initial approach: Download application form and mail to foundation for organizations located in MO; download application form and mail to application address for organizations located in IL
Copies of proposal: 1
Board meeting date(s): 2 or 3 times per month
Deadline(s): None
Final notification: 4 to 6 weeks

Trustee: Bank of America, N.A.
Number of staff: 2 full-time professional; 1 full-time support.
EIN: 436022693
Selected grants: The following grants are a representative sample of this grantmaker's funding activity:
$1,304,100 to United Way of Greater Saint Louis, Saint Louis, MO, 2012. For operating support.
$270,000 to Energy Assistance Foundation, Decatur, IL, 2012. For Warm Neighbors Program.
$100,000 to BioSTL, Saint Louis, MO, 2012. For operating support.
$100,000 to University of Missouri, College of Business Administration, Saint Louis, MO, 2012. For capital campaign.
$80,000 to Arts and Education Council, Saint Louis, MO, 2012. For annual campaign.
$50,000 to Ronald McDonald House Charities of Metro Saint Louis, Saint Louis, MO, 2012. For capital campaign.
$50,000 to Urban League of Metropolitan Saint Louis, Saint Louis, MO, 2012. For outreach center.
$30,000 to World Bird Sanctuary, Valley Park, MO, 2012. For Summer Education Program.
$15,000 to American Red Cross, Saint Louis Chapter, Saint Louis, MO, 2012. For Harrisburg, IL Relief.
$10,000 to Opera Theater of Saint Louis, Saint Louis, MO, 2012. For season support.

129
Ameren Illinois Company

(formerly Illinois Power Company)
300 Liberty St.
Peoria, IL 61602 (309) 677-5271

Company URL: http://www.ameren.com
Establishment information: Established in 1902.
Company type: Subsidiary of a public company
Business activities: Operates gas and electric services company.
Business type (SIC): Combination utility services
Corporate officers: Richard J. Mark, Chair., Pres., and C.E.O.; Martin J. Lyons, Jr., C.F.O.; Bruce Steinke, Sr. V.P., Finance and C.A.O.; Gregory L. Nelson, Sr. V.P., Genl. Counsel and Secy.; Ronald D. Pate, V.P., Opers.
Board of director: Richard J. Mark, Chair.
Giving statement: Giving through the Ameren Illinois Corporate Giving Program and the Energy Assistance Foundation.

Ameren Illinois Corporate Giving Program

(formerly Illinois Power Company Contributions Program)
c/o Corp. Contribs.
300 Liberty St.
Peoria, IL 61602-1404
E-mail: communityrelationsil@ameren.com; URL: http://www.ameren.com/sites/aiu/Community/Pages/default.aspx
Scholarship address: Wanda Cruz, Ameren Illinois, 370 South Main St., E-05, Decatur, IL 62523, e-mail: wcruz@ameren.com

Purpose and activities: Ameren Illinois makes charitable contributions to nonprofit organizations on a case by case basis. Support is limited to areas of company operations in Illinois.
Fields of interest: Higher education; Scholarships/financial aid; Environment, energy; Environmental education; Engineering; Utilities; General charitable giving Minorities.
Program:
Ameren Illinois Minority Scholarship: Through the Ameren Illinois Minority Scholarship program, Ameren Illinois awards one, annually renewable, $2,500 scholarship every year to a minority graduating, high school senior accepted to an accredited two year or four year college or university in the United States. Scholarship recipients must earn a 2.6 GPA on a 4.0 scale or its equivalent, major in an engineering discipline, and are invited to work at Ameren each summer as a summer intern. Applicant must be a permanent resident with the Ameren Illinois distribution service area at the time the scholarship is first awarded.
Type of support: Conferences/seminars; Employee volunteer services; General/operating support; Program development; Publication; Scholarships—to individuals.
Geographic limitations: Giving limited to areas of company operations in IL.
Support limitations: No support for political or religious organizations, or fraternal, veterans', social, or similar organizations. No grants to individuals (except for Ameren Illinois Minority Scholarship) or for political campaigns.
Publications: Application guidelines.
Application information: Applications accepted. Application form required. Applicants should submit the following:
1) timetable for implementation and evaluation of project
2) statement of problem project will address
3) population served
4) copy of IRS Determination Letter
5) brief history of organization and description of its mission
6) copy of most recent annual report/audited financial statement/990
7) list of company employees involved with the organization
8) explanation of why grantmaker is considered an appropriate donor for project
9) descriptive literature about organization
10) listing of board of directors, trustees, officers and other key people and their affiliations
11) detailed description of project and amount of funding requested
12) copy of current year's organizational budget and/or project budget
13) plans for acknowledgement
14) additional materials/documentation

Scholarship applications should include an essay and official transcripts.
Initial approach: Download application form and mail to headquarters; download application form and mail to application address for Ameren Illinois Minority Scholarship
Deadline(s): Apr. 8 for Ameren Illinois Minority Scholarship

Energy Assistance Foundation

P.O. Box 1758
Decatur, IL 62525-1758
FAX: (217) 424-6515; E-mail: ssams@ameren.com

Establishment information: Established in 1982 in IL.
Donor: Illinois Power Co.
Contact: Susan Sams, Exec. Dir.
Financial data (yr. ended 12/31/11): Revenue, $1,580,458; assets, $1,472,958 (M); gifts received, $1,572,347; expenditures, $928,482; giving activities include $841,997 for grants to individuals.
Purpose and activities: The foundation assists with energy payment and conservation for the elderly and handicapped who do not qualify for other programs.
Fields of interest: Environment, energy Aging; Disabilities, people with.
Programs:
Non-Residential Hardship Program: Monetary assistance is provided to businesses and nonprofit organizations with increased power bills.
Warm Neighbors Bill Payment Program: Applicants must be in danger of losing their primary source of heating, and, if eligible, have already applied for federal and/or state fuel assistance. Applicants must also have a household income at or below 200 percent of the poverty level or demonstrate personal or family crisis. This program runs from Dec. 1 through May 31.
Weatherization Program: Provides home weatherization to the elderly and disabled who do not qualify for other programs. Thirteen volunteer agencies help to approve grantees for this purpose.
Type of support: Grants to individuals.
Officers and Directors:* Carol Brandt*, Pres.; Larry Altenbaumer*, V.P.; Dave Carr*, V.P.; Mike Mowen*, Secy.-Treas.; Susan Sams, Exec. Dir.; Stan Ogden.
Number of staff: 1
EIN: 363216406

131
American Advertising Federation

(formerly Tulsa Advertising Federation, Inc.)
7720 S. Erie Ave.
P.O. Box 4452
Tulsa, OK 74159 (918) 806-2552

Company URL: http://www.tulsaadfed.com/
Establishment information: Established in 1937.
Company type: Private company
Business activities: Provides advertising services.
Business type (SIC): Advertising
Corporate officer: Susan Bramsch, Pres.
Board of directors: Leslie Blanchet; Susan Bramsch; Hunter Cates; Alyssa Guempel; Bill Hinkle; Rosie Hinkle; Justin Johnson; Chelsea McGuire; Kyra McNamara; Jessica Medina; Solange O'Brein; Danni Powell; Jared Rencher; Sarah Smith; Taylor Smith
Giving statement: Giving through the Tulsa Advertising Foundation.

Tulsa Advertising Foundation

P.O. Box 4452
Tulsa, OK 74159-0452 (918) 806-2550
E-mail: rosiehinkle@cox.net

Establishment information: Established in 1986 in OK as a company-sponsored operating foundation.
Donor: Tulsa Advertising Federation, Inc.
Contact: Rosemarie Hinkle, Treas.
Financial data (yr. ended 12/31/11): Assets, $39,797 (M); gifts received, $2,500; expenditures, $3,263; qualifying distributions, $2,500; giving activities include $2,500 for 3 grants to individuals (high: $1,000; low: $750).
Purpose and activities: The foundation awards college scholarships to students located in the Tulsa, Oklahoma, area interested in advertising.
Type of support: Scholarships—to individuals.
Geographic limitations: Giving primarily in the Tulsa, OK, area.
Application information: Applications accepted. Application form required.
Proposals should include a resume and a narrative on the applicant's interest in marketing and advertising.
Initial approach: Proposal
Deadline(s): None
Directors: Wes Alexander; Lesile Blanchet; Rita Moschovidis Burke; Hunter Cates; Amanda Clinton; Jessica Fossard; Maria Gaw; Amber Hinkle; Bill Hinkle; Tom Holiday; Paige Laughlin; Chelsea McGuire; Leigh Anne Self; Taylor Smith.
Officers: Susan Bramsch, Pres.; Sarah Smith, V.P. and Secy.; Rosie Hinkle, Treas.
EIN: 731253534

132
American Appraisal Associates, Inc.

411 E. Wisconsin Ave., Ste. 1900
Milwaukee, WI 53202-4409
(414) 271-7240

Company URL: http://www.american-appraisal.com
Establishment information: Established in 1896.
Company type: Private company
Business activities: Provides valuation consulting services.
Business type (SIC): Management and public relations services
Corporate officers: Joseph P. Zvesper, Chair. and C.E.O.; Kimberly L. Russo, Exec. V.P. and C.F.O.; Dale Egan, Sr. V.P. and Genl. Counsel; Lee Hackett, Exec. V.P., Opers.
Board of director: Joseph P. Zvesper, Chair.
Subsidiaries: American Appraisal Asia, Inc., Milwaukee, WI; American Appraisal Capital Services, Inc., Milwaukee, WI; American Appraisal China, Inc., Milwaukee, WI; The American Appraisal Co., Milwaukee, WI
Division: Real Estate Advisory Group, Atlanta, GA
Office: New York, NY
International operations: Austria; Canada; Czech Republic; Germany; Greece; Hong Kong; Hungary; Italy; Japan; Mexico; Morocco and the Western Sahara; Portugal; Russia; Spain; Thailand; United Kingdom
Giving statement: Giving through the American Appraisal Trust.

American Appraisal Trust

411 E. Wisconsin Ave., Ste. 1900
Milwaukee, WI 53202-4466

Establishment information: Established in 1952 in WI.
Donor: American Appraisal Associates, Inc.
Financial data (yr. ended 06/30/12): Assets, $0 (M); gifts received, $28,200; expenditures, $28,200; qualifying distributions, $28,200; giving activities include $28,200 for grants.
Purpose and activities: The foundation supports art museums and hospitals and organizations involved with education and human services.
Fields of interest: Museums (art); Higher education; Engineering school/education; Education; Hospitals (general); Children/youth, services; Family services; Human services; United Ways and Federated Giving Programs.
Type of support: Program development.
Geographic limitations: Giving primarily in Milwaukee, WI.
Support limitations: No grants to individuals.
Application information: Applications not accepted. Unsolicited requests for funds not accepted.
Officers: Joseph P. Zvesper, Chair.; Amanda Ripley, Secy.
EIN: 386048265

133
American Biltrite, Inc.

57 River St.
Wellesley Hills, MA 02481-2097
(781) 237-6655
FAX: (781) 237-6880

Company URL: http://www.ambilt.com
Establishment information: Established in 1908.
Company type: Public company
Company ticker symbol and exchange: ABLT/Pink Sheets
Business activities: Manufactures industrial rubber and plastic products.
Business type (SIC): Rubber products/fabricated; plastic products/miscellaneous
Financial profile for 2011: Number of employees, 600; assets, $120,400,000; sales volume, $208,730,000; pre-tax net income, -$1,470,000; expenses, $209,860,000; liabilities, $77,440,000
Corporate officers: Roger S. Marcus, Chair. and C.E.O.; Richard G. Marcus, Pres. and C.O.O.; William M. Marcus, Exec. V.P. and Treas.; Howard N. Feist III, V.P., Finance, and C.F.O.; Henry W. Winkleman, V.P. and Secy.; Diane Lew, Cont.
Board of directors: Roger S. Marcus, Chair.; Leo R. Breitman; John C. Garrels III; Mark N. Kaplan, Esq.; James S. Marcus; Richard G. Marcus; William M. Marcus; Mark S. Newman; Kenneth I. Watchmaker
Subsidiaries: Congoleum Corp., Trenton, NJ; Ideal Tape Co., Lowell, MA; K&M Assocs., Providence, RI
Division: Tape Products Div., Moorestown, NJ
International operations: Canada; Hong Kong
Giving statement: Giving through the American Biltrite Charitable Trust.
Company EIN: 041701350

American Biltrite Charitable Trust

57 River St., Ste. 302
Wellesley Hills, MA 02481-2058

Donor: American Biltrite, Inc.
Financial data (yr. ended 09/30/11): Assets, $6,864 (M); gifts received, $10,000; expenditures, $7,069; qualifying distributions, $7,096; giving activities include $6,475 for 9 grants (high: $1,500; low: $150).
Purpose and activities: The trust supports community centers and organizations involved with education and religion.
Fields of interest: Education; Human services; Religion.
Type of support: General/operating support.
Support limitations: No grants to individuals.
Application information: Applications not accepted. Unsolicited requests for funds not accepted.
Trustees: Richard G. Marcus; Roger S. Marcus; William M. Marcus.
EIN: 042775257

134
American Building Supply, Inc.

8360 Elder Creek Rd.
Sacramento, CA 95828-1705
(916) 503-4100

Company URL: http://www.abs-hardware.com
Establishment information: Established in 1985.
Company type: Private company
Business activities: Sells doors wholesale.
Business type (SIC): Lumber and construction materials—wholesale
Corporate officers: Mark Ballantyne, Pres.; Linda Roberts, Cont.
Giving statement: Giving through the ABS Foundation, Inc.

ABS Foundation, Inc.

P.O. Box 276227
Sacramento, CA 95827-6227

Establishment information: Established in 2003 in CA.
Donors: American Building Supply, Inc.; JBL Hawaii, Ltd.
Financial data (yr. ended 12/31/11): Assets, $1,210,560 (M); expenditures, $91,036; qualifying distributions, $91,000; giving activities include $91,000 for grants.
Purpose and activities: The foundation supports organizations involved with arts and culture, education, youth development, and human services.
Fields of interest: Arts; Education; Youth development; Human services.
Type of support: Capital campaigns; Endowments; General/operating support.

Geographic limitations: Giving primarily in areas of company operations, with emphasis on CA, CO, GA, and HI.
Support limitations: No grants for religious programs or programs not of direct benefit to the entire community.
Publications: Application guidelines.
Application information: Applications accepted. Application form required.
Initial approach: Contact foundation for application form
Officers: Mark Ballantyne, Pres.; Dave Baker, V.P.; Sharee Ballantyne, Secy.; Sharon Van Osdol, C.F.O.
EIN: 260024575

135
American Buildings Company

(formerly Steel Builders, Inc.)
1150 State Docks Rd.
Eufaula, AL 36027 (334) 687-2032
FAX: (334) 688-2261

Company URL: http://www.americanbuildings.com
Establishment information: Established in 1947.
Company type: Subsidiary of a public company
Business activities: Manufactures and markets metal building systems.
Business type (SIC): Metal products/structural
Financial profile for 2009: Number of employees, 950
Corporate officers: Robert T. Ammerman, C.E.O.; Ray S. Napolitan, Pres.; R. Charles Blackmon, Exec. V.P. and C.F.O.; William R. Buchholz, V.P., Opers.; Wes Brooker, V.P., Mktg.; Byron Brumfield, V.P., Human Resources; Anne Savage, Cont.
Plants: Modesto, CA; El Paso, IL; Columbus, MS; Carson City, NV; Rocky Mount, NC; Jamestown, OH; La Crosse, VA
Giving statement: Giving through the No Other Foundation.

No Other Foundation

c/o John C. Stutes, II
1843 Foreman Dr.
Cookeville, TN 38501-4192

Establishment information: Established in 1999 in TN.
Donors: American Buildings Co.; J&S Construction Co., Inc; John D. Stites II; XI Properties.
Financial data (yr. ended 03/31/12): Assets, $75,841 (M); expenditures, $3,074; qualifying distributions, $0.
Purpose and activities: The foundation supports organizations involved with higher education, youth development, and Christianity.
Fields of interest: Higher education; Boy scouts; Christian agencies & churches.
Type of support: General/operating support.
Application information: Applications not accepted. Unsolicited requests for funds not accepted.
Officers: John D. Stites II, Pres.; James R. Stites, V.P.; Rosemary T. Stites, Secy.
Trustees: Donnie Davidson; Sarah Davidson; Mary Stites.
EIN: 621790241
Selected grants: The following grants are a representative sample of this grantmaker's funding activity:
$50,000 to Timothy Hill Childrens Ranch, Riverhead, NY, 2009.

136
American Campus Communities, Inc.

12700 Hill Country Blvd., Ste. T-200
Austin, TX 78738 (512) 732-1000
FAX: (512) 732-2450

Company URL: http://www.americancampus.com/
Establishment information: Established in 1996.
Company type: Public company
Company ticker symbol and exchange: ACC/NYSE
Business activities: Operates student housing real estate investment trust (REIT).
Business type (SIC): Investors/miscellaneous
Financial profile for 2012: Number of employees, 2,913; assets, $5,118,960,000; sales volume, $491,290,000; pre-tax net income, $57,470,000; expenses, $375,770,000; liabilities, $2,470,580,000
Corporate officers: R.D. Burck, Chair.; William C. Bayless, Jr., Pres. and C.E.O.; Greg A. Dowell, Sr. Exec. V.P. and C.O.O.; Jonathan A. Graf, Exec. V.P., C.F.O., and Treas.; Kim K. Voss, Sr. V.P. and Cont.; Ronald A. Weaver, Sr. V.P., Human Resources
Board of directors: R.D. Burck, Chair.; William C. Bayless, Jr.; G. Steven Dawson; Cydney Donnell; Edward Lowenthal; Oliver Luck; Winston Walker
Giving statement: Giving through the American Campus Charities Foundation.
Company EIN: 760753089

American Campus Charities Foundation

12700 Hill Country Blvd., Ste. T-2400
Austin, TX 78738

Establishment information: Established in 2006 in TX.
Donors: Locke, Liddell & Sapp, LLP; Glast, Phillips & Murray; Merrill Lynch; GPS Construction Services, LLC; KeyBank Capital Markets; Apex Construction; Davis Brothers Construction; American Campus Communities Services, Inc.; Morley Group, Inc.; Hardison Downey Kitchell; Hardman Signs; University Loft Co.; Community Bank of Texas; Faver Gray; RBC Capital Markets; Hunter Roberts Construction; Ryan Reid.
Financial data (yr. ended 12/31/11): Assets, $547,730 (M); gifts received, $279,699; expenditures, $213,701; qualifying distributions, $69,181; giving activities include $69,181 for grants.
Fields of interest: Education; Health organizations; Youth development.
Geographic limitations: Giving primarily in Washington, DC, and Austin, TX.
Support limitations: No grants to individuals.
Application information: Applications not accepted. Unsolicited requests for funds not accepted.
Officers: William Bayless, Pres.; Greg Dowell, V.P.; Jonathan Graf, Secy.
EIN: 743061377

137
American Century Companies, Inc.

4500 Main St.
P.O. Box 419200
Kansas City, MO 64111-1816
(816) 531-5575
FAX: (816) 340-7692

Company URL: http://www.americancentury.com
Establishment information: Established in 1958.
Company type: Private company
Business activities: Provides investment advisory services.
Business type (SIC): Security and commodity services
Financial profile for 2011: Number of employees, 1,300
Corporate officers: James E. Stowers, Jr., Chair.; Jonathan Stuart Thomas, Pres. and C.E.O.; Barry Fink, Exec. V.P and C.O.O.; Enrique Chang, Exec. V.P. and C.I.O.; Patrick Bannigan, Exec. V.P. and C.O.O.
Board of director: James E. Stowers, Jr., Chair.
Giving statement: Giving through the American Century Investments Foundation.

American Century Investments Foundation

(formerly American Century Companies Foundation)
4500 Main St.
P.O. Box 418210
Kansas City, MO 64141-0210 (816) 340-7046
E-mail: grants@gkccf.org; Additional tel.: (816) 627-3468; URL: https://www.americancentury.com/about_us/community_investments.jsp

Establishment information: Established in 2000 in MO.
Donor: American Century Cos., Inc.
Contact: Scott Oberkrom, Exec. Dir.
Financial data (yr. ended 12/31/11): Assets, $3,968,114 (M); gifts received, $2,600,000; expenditures, $1,450,000; qualifying distributions, $1,450,000; giving activities include $1,450,000 for 1 grant.
Purpose and activities: The foundation supports programs designed to provide innovative opportunities that are sustainable and inspire growth in communities. Special emphasis is directed toward health and human service organizations designed to provide direct services to individuals.
Fields of interest: Hospitals (general); Health care, patient services; Health care; Children/youth, services; Family services, domestic violence; Human services; Community/economic development; Foundations (community); United Ways and Federated Giving Programs Economically disadvantaged.
Program:
Dollars for Donors: The foundation awards grants to nonprofit organizations with which employees of American Century contribute their time or money.
Type of support: Employee matching gifts; Employee volunteer services; General/operating support; Program development.
Geographic limitations: Giving primarily in areas of company operations in Mountain View, CA, Kansas City, MO, and New York, NY.
Support limitations: No support for religious organizations not of direct benefit to the entire community, social, labor, veterans', alumni, or fraternal organizations, athletic teams, or political

candidates. No grants to individuals, or for special events, capital campaigns, recreational sporting events, political causes or legislative lobbying efforts, debt reduction, travel, or conferences.
Publications: Application guidelines.
Application information: Applications accepted. The application process is managed by the Greater Kansas City Community Foundation. Preference will be given to organizations in which American Century Investments employees are involved as board members, volunteers, and/or donors. Grants range from $5,000 to $25,000. Application form required.
Applicants should submit the following:
1) population served
2) copy of IRS Determination Letter
3) brief history of organization and description of its mission
4) copy of most recent annual report/audited financial statement/990
5) list of company employees involved with the organization
6) listing of board of directors, trustees, officers and other key people and their affiliations
7) copy of current year's organizational budget and/or project budget
Initial approach: Complete online application
Board meeting date(s): Semi-annually
Deadline(s): Apr. 7 and Oct. 7
Final notification: 8 weeks
Officers and Directors:* Mark Gilstrap*, Pres.; Jon W. Zindel*, Sr. V.P. and Treas.; Lisa H. Lattan*, V.P. and Secy.; Scott Oberkrom, Exec. Dir.
EIN: 431881225
Selected grants: The following grants are a representative sample of this grantmaker's funding activity:
$1,441,000 to Greater Kansas City Community Foundation, Kansas City, MO, 2010. For operating expenses.

138
American Direct Mail Marketing, Inc.

8136 Old Keene Mill Rd., Ste. A-312
Springfield, VA 22152-1850
(703) 569-8600

Company URL: http://www.admm.com/
Establishment information: Established in 1984.
Company type: Private company
Business activities: Provides mail advertising services.
Business type (SIC): Mailing, reproduction, commercial art, photography, and stenographic service
Corporate officer: Margo Friedmann, Pres.
Giving statement: Giving through the IHFR Foundation.

IHFR Foundation

8136 Old Keene Mill Rd., A-312
Springfield, VA 22152-1843 (703) 569-8600
URL: http://www.inhopefreedomrings.org

Establishment information: Established in 2005 in VA.
Donors: American Direct Mail Marketing, Inc.; CouponsToGo.com; F.W. Harris, Inc.; MSS, Inc.; Papa John's; Prince William Home Improvement; Springfield Lorton Dental Group; Burke Centre Automotive, Inc.; Cropp-Metcalfe; Hadeed Carpet Cleaning, Inc.
Financial data (yr. ended 12/31/11): Assets, $18,542 (M); gifts received, $21,229; expenditures, $22,744; qualifying distributions, $22,744; giving activities include $20,000 for 2 grants to individuals (high: $10,000; low: $10,000).
Purpose and activities: The foundation awards college scholarships to high school seniors in Fairfax County, Virginia.
Fields of interest: Higher education.
Program:
In Hope Freedom Rings Foundation Scholarship: The foundation awards $10,000 scholarships to high school seniors who plan to pursue higher education at a two or four-year college or university. Recipients are selected based on academic excellence, financial need, extracurricular activities, and community service. This program is limited to high schools in Fairfax County, Virginia.
Type of support: Scholarships—to individuals.
Geographic limitations: Giving primarily in Fairfax County, VA.
Publications: Application guidelines.
Application information: Applications accepted. Application form required.
Applications should include a signed copy of pages 1 and 2 of form 1040 of the applicant's parent's or guardian's Federal Tax Return; transcripts; resume; a teacher or counselor recommendation; and an essay.
Initial approach: Proposla
Deadline(s): Mid Nov.
Officers: Margo Friedman, Pres. and Treas.; David Shapiro, V.P. and Secy.
EIN: 203849277

139
American Dredging Company

1060 First Ave., Ste. 400
King of Prussia, PA 19406 (610) 768-8020

Company type: Private company
Business activities: Provides dredging services.
Business type (SIC): Construction/miscellaneous heavy; contractors/miscellaneous special trade
Giving statement: Giving through the ADCO Foundation.

ADCO Foundation

1060 1st Ave., Ste. 400
King of Prussia, PA 19406-1337

Donor: American Dredging Co.
Contact: James J. Clarke, Jr., Tr.
Financial data (yr. ended 12/31/11): Assets, $863,900 (M); expenditures, $46,466; qualifying distributions, $40,000; giving activities include $40,000 for grants.
Purpose and activities: The foundation supports organizations involved with media, Alzheimer's disease, and Judaism.
Fields of interest: Media/communications; Alzheimer's disease; Jewish federated giving programs; Jewish agencies & synagogues.
Type of support: General/operating support; Scholarship funds.
Geographic limitations: Giving primarily in New York, NY.
Application information: Applications accepted. Application form required.
Initial approach: Letter
Deadline(s): None
Trustees: Bruce A. Beal; James J. Clarke, Jr.
EIN: 236278135

140
American Eagle Outfitters, Inc.

77 Hot Metal St.
Pittsburgh, PA 15203-2329 (412) 432-3300
FAX: (302) 655-5049

Company URL: http://www.ae.com
Establishment information: Established in 1977.
Company type: Public company
Company ticker symbol and exchange: AEO/NYSE
Business activities: Operates apparel stores; provides Internet shopping services.
Business type (SIC): Family apparel and accessory stores; computer services
Financial profile for 2013: Number of employees, 44,000; assets, $1,756,050,000; sales volume, $3,475,800,000; pre-tax net income, $402,040,000; expenses, $3,081,200,000; liabilities, $534,870,000
Fortune 1000 ranking: 2012—642nd in revenues, 544th in profits, and 883rd in assets
Corporate officers: Jay L. Schottenstein, Chair.; Roger S. Markfield, Vice-Chair.; Robert L. Hanson, C.E.O.; Mary M. Boland, Exec. V.P., C.F.O., and C.A.O.; Michael Rempell, Exec. V.P. and C.O.O.
Board of directors: Jay L. Schottenstein, Chair.; Roger S. Markfield, Vice-Chair.; Robert L. Hanson; Michael G. Jesselson; Thomas R. Ketteler; Cary D. McMillan; Janice E. Page; David M. Sable; Noel J. Spiegel
International operations: Canada; Hong Kong
Giving statement: Giving through the American Eagle Outfitters, Inc. Corporate Giving Program and the American Eagle Outfitters Foundation.
Company EIN: 132721761

American Eagle Outfitters, Inc. Corporate Giving Program

c/o Gift Card Donations
77 Hot Metal St.
Pittsburgh, PA 15203-2382
URL: http://www.aebetterworld.org/

Purpose and activities: As a complement to its foundation, American Eagle also makes charitable contributions of gift cards to high schools and colleges. Support is given primarily in areas of company operations.
Fields of interest: Secondary school/education; Higher education; Substance abuse, prevention.
Type of support: Donated products; Sponsorships.
Geographic limitations: Giving primarily in areas of company operations.
Application information: Applications accepted. Proposals should be submitted using organization letterhead. Application form not required. Applicants should submit the following:
1) copy of IRS Determination Letter
2) brief history of organization and description of its mission
3) plans for acknowledgement
Applications should include the organization's Tax ID Number and a brief description of the event.
Initial approach: Proposal to headquarters
Copies of proposal: 1
Deadline(s): 6 weeks prior to need
Final notification: 6 weeks

American Eagle Outfitters Foundation

77 Hot Metal St.
Pittsburgh, PA 15203-2382 (412) 432-4552
E-mail: AEBetterWorld@ae.com; URL: http://www.ae.com/web/corpResp/community/index.jsp

Establishment information: Established in 1999 in PA.

Donor: American Eagle Outfitters, Inc.
Contact: Marcie Eberhart, Dir.
Financial data (yr. ended 01/31/12): Assets, $3,249,639 (M); gifts received, $159,370; expenditures, $525,556; qualifying distributions, $485,484; giving activities include $485,484 for grants.
Purpose and activities: The foundation supports programs designed to promote conservation and youth development.
Fields of interest: Environment, natural resources; Environment; Youth development, adult & child programs; Big Brothers/Big Sisters; Youth development.
Program:
Gift Card Donations: The foundation donates $25 gift cards to college and high school sponsored drug-free volunteer events that strive to keep teens and college students safe.
Type of support: Donated products; Employee volunteer services; General/operating support; Program development; Scholarship funds.
Geographic limitations: Giving primarily in Ottawa, KS, New York, NY, and Pittsburgh, PA.
Support limitations: No support for organizations budgeting over 30 percent of funds for fundraising purposes, discriminatory organizations, individual religious organizations, political organizations or candidates, lobbying groups, or veterans' or fraternal organizations. No grants to individuals, or for fashion shows, political campaigns, medical or health-related causes, goodwill advertising, or capital campaigns.
Publications: Application guidelines.
Application information: Applications accepted. Grants range from $1,000 to $10,000. Proposals should be no longer than 3 to 4 pages. Letters of inquiry should be submitted using organization letterhead. Organizations receiving support are asked to provide a final report. Application form not required. Applicants should submit the following:
1) timetable for implementation and evaluation of project
2) results expected from proposed grant
3) statement of problem project will address
4) population served
5) copy of IRS Determination Letter
6) brief history of organization and description of its mission
7) copy of most recent annual report/audited financial statement/990
8) how project's results will be evaluated or measured
9) list of company employees involved with the organization
10) explanation of why grantmaker is considered an appropriate donor for project
11) listing of board of directors, trustees, officers and other key people and their affiliations
12) detailed description of project and amount of funding requested
13) plans for cooperation with other organizations, if any
14) contact person
15) copy of current year's organizational budget and/or project budget
16) listing of additional sources and amount of support
17) plans for acknowledgement

Initial approach: Proposal; letter of inquiry for gift card donations
Copies of proposal: 1
Board meeting date(s): Twice per year
Deadline(s): None; 6 weeks prior to need for gift card donations
Final notification: 2 weeks following board meetings; 6 weeks for gift card donations

Officers and Directors: Fred Grover, Pres.; Steve Lyman, V.P.; Michael Jennings, Secy.; Scott Griffith, Treas.; Kristin Boyle; Tom DiDonato; Marcie Eberhart; Monica Gorman; Roz Johnson; Rick Milazzo.
EIN: 251827476
Selected grants: The following grants are a representative sample of this grantmaker's funding activity:
$10,000 to Pittsburgh Symphony, Pittsburgh, PA, 2010.
$10,000 to United Way of Allegheny County, Pittsburgh, PA, 2010.
$7,500 to Educational Network of Artists in Creative Theater, New York, NY, 2010.
$7,500 to Figure Skating in Harlem, New York, NY, 2010.
$7,000 to Allegheny County Library Association, Pittsburgh, PA, 2010.
$6,000 to East Central Kansas Area Agency on Aging, Ottawa, KS, 2010.
$5,000 to Carnegie Science Center, Pittsburgh, PA, 2010.
$5,000 to Ottawa University, Ottawa, KS, 2010.

141
American Electric Power Company, Inc.

(also known as AEP)
1 Riverside Plz.
Columbus, OH 43215-2372
(614) 716-1000
FAX: (614) 223-1823

Company URL: http://www.aep.com
Establishment information: Established in 1906.
Company type: Public company
Company ticker symbol and exchange: AEP/NYSE
International Securities Identification Number: US0255371017
Business activities: Operates public utility holding company; generates, transmits, and distributes electricity.
Business type (SIC): Holding company; electric services
Financial profile for 2012: Number of employees, 18,513; assets, $54,367,000,000; sales volume, $14,945,000,000; pre-tax net income, $1,822,000,000; expenses, $12,289,000,000; liabilities, $39,130,000,000
Fortune 1000 ranking: 2012—185th in revenues, 161st in profits, and 101st in assets
Forbes 2000 ranking: 2012—638th in sales, 478th in profits, and 426th in assets
Corporate officers: Michael G. Morris, Chair.; Nicholas K. Akins, Pres. and C.E.O.; Robert P. Powers, Exec. V.P. and C.O.O.; Brian X. Tierney, Exec. V.P. and C.F.O.; Dennis Welch, Exec. V.P. and C.A.O.; David M. Feinberg, Sr. V.P., Genl. Counsel, and Secy.
Board of directors: Michael G. Morris, Chair.; Nick Akins; David J. Anderson; James F. Cordes; Ralph D. Crosby, Jr.; Linda A. Goodspeed; Thomas E. Hoaglin; Sandra Beach Lin; Richard C. Notebaert; Lionel L. Nowell III; Steve Rasmussen; Richard L. Sandor; Sara Martinez Tucker; John F. Turner
Subsidiaries: American Electric Power Service Corp., Columbus, OH; Appalachian Power Co., Roanoke, VA; Central and South West Corp., Dallas, TX; Columbus Southern Power Company, Columbus, OH; Franklin Real Estate Co., Philadelphia, PA; Indiana Michigan Power Co., Fort Wayne, IN; Kentucky Power Co., Ashland, KY; Kingsport Power Co., Kingsport, TN; Ohio Power Co., Canton, OH; Wheeling Power Co., Wheeling, WV
Plant: Cheshire, OH
Giving statement: Giving through the AEP Corporate Giving Program, the American Electric Power Foundation, and the American Electric Power System Educational Trust Fund.
Company EIN: 134922640

AEP Corporate Giving Program

1 Riverside Plz.
Columbus, OH 43215-2355
E-mail: blschumann@aep.com; Additional contact: Jennah Nelson, Community Rels. Representative, e-mail: jlnelson@aep.com; URL: http://www.aep.com/community/CorporateGivingGuidelines/

Contact: Barry Schumann, Community Rels. Coord.
Purpose and activities: AEP makes charitable contributions to nonprofit organizations involved with K-12 education. Support is given primarily in areas of company operations.
Fields of interest: Elementary/secondary education.
Type of support: Employee matching gifts; General/operating support; Sponsorships.
Geographic limitations: Giving primarily in areas of company operations in AR, IN, KY, LA, MI, OH, OK, TN, TX, VA, and WV.
Application information: Application form not required.
Initial approach: Proposal to headquarters
Deadline(s): None
Final notification: Varies

American Electric Power Foundation

1 Riverside Plz.
Columbus, OH 43216-2355 (614) 716-1000
URL: http://www.aep.com/community/AEPFoundation/

Establishment information: Established in 2005 in OH.
Donor: American Electric Power Service Corp.
Financial data (yr. ended 12/31/11): Assets, $62,129,297 (M); expenditures, $22,378,302; qualifying distributions, $22,279,232; giving activities include $22,279,232 for 42+ grants (high: $1,500,000).
Purpose and activities: The foundation supports programs designed to improve lives through education from early childhood through higher education; protect the environment; provide basic human services in the areas of hunger, housing, health, and safety; and enrich the quality of life of communities through art, music, and cultural heritage.
Fields of interest: Arts, cultural/ethnic awareness; Museums (art); Performing arts, music; Arts; Elementary/secondary education; Education, early childhood education; Higher education; Education; Environment, natural resources; Environmental education; Environment; Hospitals (general); Health care; Food services; Food banks; Housing/shelter, development; Housing/shelter; Safety/disasters; Boys & girls clubs; Big Brothers/Big Sisters; Human services; Community/economic development.
Type of support: Building/renovation; Capital campaigns; Continuing support; Endowments; General/operating support; Program development; Scholarship funds.
Geographic limitations: Giving primarily in areas of company operations in AR, IN, KY, LA, MI, OH, OK, TN, TX, VA, and WV.
Support limitations: No support for religious, fraternal, athletic or veterans' organizations. No grants to individuals.

Publications: Annual report; Application guidelines; IRS Form 990 or 990-PF printed copy available upon request.
Application information: Applications accepted. Proposals should be submitted using organization letterhead. Proposals for multi-state or national projects should be limited to a one-page synopsis and submitted in Microsoft Word format to Educate@AEP.com. Visit website for local AEP regional utility addresses. Application form not required. Applicants should submit the following:
1) copy of IRS Determination Letter
2) brief history of organization and description of its mission
3) copy of most recent annual report/audited financial statement/990
4) how project's results will be evaluated or measured
5) detailed description of project and amount of funding requested
6) copy of current year's organizational budget and/or project budget
7) plans for acknowledgement
Proposals should include an executed IRS Form W-9.
Initial approach: E-mail or mail proposal to nearest company regional utility for local projects; e-mail one-page proposal for multi-state or national projects
Copies of proposal: 1
Deadline(s): None
Trustees: Nicholas K. Akins; Carl L. English; Teresa L. McWain; Michael G. Morris; Robert M. Powers; Brian X. Tierney; Susan Tomasky; Dennis E. Welch.
EIN: 203886453
Selected grants: The following grants are a representative sample of this grantmaker's funding activity:
$1,500,000 to Eastern Michigan University Foundation, Ypsilanti, MI, 2011. For general support.
$1,350,000 to Ohio State University Foundation, Columbus, OH, 2011. For general support.
$1,250,000 to COSI Columbus, Columbus, OH, 2011. For general support.
$1,000,000 to Columbus Downtown Development Corporation, Columbus, OH, 2011. For general support.
$845,000 to Jane Goodall Institute for Wildlife Research, Education and Conservation, Arlington, VA, 2011. For general support.
$500,000 to Columbus Museum of Art, Columbus, OH, 2010. For general support.
$500,000 to Columbus Museum of Art, Columbus, OH, 2011. For general support.
$500,000 to COSI Columbus, Columbus, OH, 2010. For general support.
$500,000 to Jane Goodall Institute for Wildlife Research, Education and Conservation, Arlington, VA, 2010. For Roots and Shoots Program, international environmental and humanitarian program for children and youth where they can learn about problems and issues in their local communities and then discover ways to make the world a better place. Projects are focused on improving the lives of people, animals and the environment. Kids who belong to Roots & Shoots groups have the opportunity to network with R&S members from around the world to learn about other cultures and gain a deeper understanding of the global impact of their actions.
$500,000 to West Virginia Community Action Partnerships, Charleston, WV, 2011. For general support.
$385,000 to Jane Goodall Institute for Wildlife Research, Education and Conservation, Arlington, VA, 2010. For work on reduced emissions initiatives.
$250,000 to Columbus Housing Partnership, Columbus, OH, 2011. For general support of Homeport.
$250,000 to Dubuque County Historical Society, National Mississippi River Museum and Aquarium, Dubuque, IA, 2010. For general support.
$250,000 to Northeast Texas Community College Foundation, Mount Pleasant, TX, 2011. For general support.
$250,000 to Ohio State University Foundation, Columbus, OH, 2010. For general support.
$200,000 to Ronald McDonald House Charities of the Tri-State, Huntington, WV, 2010. For general support.
$200,000 to Virginia Tech Foundation, Blacksburg, VA, 2010. For general support.
$166,667 to Science Central, Fort Wayne, IN, 2011. For general support.
$150,000 to Habitat for Humanity, Greater Columbus, Columbus, OH, 2010. For Green Building program.
$150,000 to Habitat for Humanity, Greater Columbus, Columbus, OH, 2010. For Green Practices Program.

The American Electric Power System Educational Trust Fund

c/o Tax Dept.
P.O. Box 16428
Columbus, OH 43216-0428 (614) 223-1000
Scholarship address: AEP, Human Resources, 1 Riverside Plaza, Columbus, OH 43215

Donors: American Electric Power Co., Inc.; Columbus Southern Power Co.; Ohio Power Co.; CSW Foundation.
Financial data (yr. ended 02/28/12): Assets, $5,084,414 (M); expenditures, $299,942; qualifying distributions, $291,500; giving activities include $291,500 for grants to individuals.
Purpose and activities: The foundation awards college scholarships to children of AEP employees.
Fields of interest: Higher education.
Type of support: Employee-related scholarships.
Geographic limitations: Giving primarily in areas of company operations, including IN, OH, and VA.
Publications: Program policy statement.
Application information: Applications not accepted. Contributes only through employee-related scholarships.
Trustees: Carl L. English; Venita McCellon-Allen; Robert P. Powers; Susan Tomasky.
EIN: 237418083

142
American Equity Mortgage, Inc.

11993 Westline Industrial Dr.
St. Louis, MO 63146-3203 (314) 878-9999

Company URL: http://www.americanequity.com
Establishment information: Established in 1992.
Company type: Private company
Business activities: Mortgage and home loan lender.
Business type (SIC): Brokers and bankers/mortgage
Corporate officer: Deanna Daughhetee, Pres. and C.E.O.
Giving statement: Giving through the American Equity Mortgage Charitable Foundation.

American Equity Mortgage Charitable Foundation

11933 Westline Industrial Dr.
St. Louis, MO 63146-3203

Establishment information: Established in 2005 in MO.
Donors: American Equity Mortgage; Validata Lender Services, LLC; Premium Settlements of MD, LLC.
Financial data (yr. ended 12/31/11): Assets, $77,299 (M); gifts received, $135,316; expenditures, $143,125; qualifying distributions, $142,160; giving activities include $141,186 for 45 grants (high: $25,000; low: $7,500).
Purpose and activities: The foundation supports food banks and organizations involved with patient services, breast cancer, children services, and programs designed to assist victims of abuse.
Fields of interest: Health care, patient services; Breast cancer; Food banks; Children, services; Women, centers/services Women; Crime/abuse victims.
Type of support: General/operating support; Sponsorships.
Geographic limitations: Giving primarily in MD, St. Louis, MO, and OH; giving also to national organizations.
Support limitations: No grants to individuals.
Application information: Applications not accepted. Contributes only to pre-selected organizations.
Officers: Deanna Daughhetee, Pres.; Robert Bower, Secy.
Director: Jeannine Beck.
EIN: 203985928

143
American Express Company

World Financial Ctr.
200 Vesey St.
New York, NY 10285 (212) 640-2000
FAX: (212) 640-0404

Company URL: http://www.americanexpress.com
Establishment information: Established in 1850.
Company type: Public company
Company ticker symbol and exchange: AXP/NYSE
International Securities Identification Number: US0258161092
Business activities: Provides consumer and business loans; provides travel services.
Business type (SIC): Credit institutions/personal; credit institutions/business
Financial profile for 2012: Number of employees, 63,500; assets, $153,140,000,000; sales volume, $33,808,000,000; pre-tax net income, $6,451,000,000; expenses, $27,357,000,000; liabilities, $134,254,000,000
Fortune 1000 ranking: 2012—90th in revenues, 41st in profits, and 42nd in assets
Forbes 2000 ranking: 2012—281st in sales, 122nd in profits, and 177th in assets
Corporate officers: Kenneth I. Chenault, Chair. and C.E.O.; Edward P. Gilligan, Pres.; Daniel T. Henry, Exec. V.P. and C.F.O.; Marc C. Gordon, Exec. V.P. and C.I.O.; Louise M. Parent, Exec. V.P. and Genl. Counsel
Board of directors: Kenneth I. Chenault, Chair.; Charlene Barshefsky; Ursula M. Burns; Samuel J. Palmisano; Peter Chernin; Anne Lauvergeon; Theodore J. Leonsis; Richard C. Levin; Richard A. McGinn; Steven S. Reinemund; Daniel L. Vasella; Robert D. Walter; Ronald A. Williams
Subsidiary: American Express Travel Related Services Co., Inc., New York, NY

Offices: Phoenix, AZ; Fort Lauderdale, Miami, FL; Minneapolis, MN; Greensboro, NC; Salt Lake City, UT
International operations: Austria; Canada; Netherlands; Russia; United Kingdom
Giving statement: Giving through the American Express Company Contributions Program, the American Express Charitable Fund, and the American Express Foundation.
Company EIN: 134922250

American Express Company Contributions Program

c/o Philanthropic Prog.
3 World Financial Ctr., M.C. 01-48-04
New York, NY 10285-4805 (212) 640-5661
URL: http://about.americanexpress.com/csr/?inav=CorporateResponsibility

Purpose and activities: As a complement to its foundation, American Express also makes charitable contributions to nonprofit organizations directly. Support is given on a national and international basis.
Fields of interest: Arts, cultural/ethnic awareness; Historic preservation/historical societies; Arts; Environment; Animals/wildlife; Health care; Disasters, preparedness/services; Recreation, fairs/festivals; American Red Cross; Human services; Community/economic development; Leadership development; General charitable giving.
Program:
Members Project: The company, in partnership with TakePart, supports an innovative online initiative in the areas of arts and culture, community development, environment and wildlife, education, and health and wellness. American Express card members and the general public are invited to vote online for the charity they think deserves funding from American Express. Five selected charities will receive a total of $1,000,000.
Type of support: Annual campaigns; Continuing support; Emergency funds; Employee volunteer services; General/operating support; Program development; Sponsorships.
Geographic limitations: Giving on a national and international basis in areas of company operations, with emphasis on NY.
Support limitations: No support for religious organizations not of direct benefit to the entire community or political candidates or organizations. No grants to individuals, or for fundraising, goodwill advertising, souvenir journals, or dinners, travel, political causes or campaigns, books, magazines, or articles in professional journals, endowments, or capital campaigns, traveling exhibitions, or sports sponsorships.
Publications: Application guidelines; Grants list.
Application information: Applications accepted. Letters of inquiry should be no longer than 1 to 2 pages. The Community Affairs Department handles giving. The company has a staff that only handles contributions. A contributions committee at each company location reviews all requests originating from that particular area. Application form not required. Applicants should submit the following:
1) timetable for implementation and evaluation of project
2) brief history of organization and description of its mission
3) how project's results will be evaluated or measured
4) explanation of why grantmaker is considered an appropriate donor for project
5) copy of current year's organizational budget and/or project budget
6) listing of additional sources and amount of support

Initial approach: Letter of inquiry to nearest company facility; vote online for Members Project
Copies of proposal: 1
Committee meeting date(s): Varies
Deadline(s): Varies per facility; weekly for Members Project

Number of staff: 9 full-time professional; 4 full-time support.

American Express Charitable Fund

200 Vesey St., 48th Fl.
New York, NY 10285-1000
Application address for organizations located outside of Phoenix, AZ, south FL, and Salt Lake City, UT: 3 World Financial Ctr., M.C. 01-48-04, New York, NY 10285-4804; E-mail for Phoenix, AZ: American Express Co., c/o Community Affairs, PhoenixLOIs@aexp.com; E-mail for south Florida: American Express Co., c/o Community Affairs, FtLauderdaleLOIs@aexp.com; E-mail for Salt Lake City, UT: American Express Co., c/o Community Affairs, SaltLakeCityLOIs@aexp.com; URL: http://about.americanexpress.com/csr/e-driven.aspx

Establishment information: Established in 2007 in NY.
Donor: American Express.
Financial data (yr. ended 12/31/11): Assets, $18,368,593 (M); expenditures, $9,344,587; qualifying distributions, $9,344,587; giving activities include $2,865,750 for 341 grants (high: $250,000; low: $500) and $6,439,748 for 15,408 employee matching gifts.
Purpose and activities: The fund supports programs designed to promote historic preservation; leadership; and community service.
Fields of interest: Arts, cultural/ethnic awareness; Museums; Performing arts; Historic preservation/historical societies; Arts; Higher education; Education; Food services; Disasters, preparedness/services; American Red Cross; YM/YWCAs & YM/YWHAs; Human services; Community/economic development; Foundations (community); United Ways and Federated Giving Programs; Leadership development; Public affairs.
Programs:
Employee Matching Gifts Program: The fund matches contributions made by employees of American Express to nonprofit organizations on a one-for-one basis from $25 to $8,000 per employee, per year.
Employee Scholarships: The fund awards four-year college scholarships of up to $4,000 to children of employees of American Express and its subsidiaries based on merit and financial need. Applicants who demonstrate no financial need are considered for a one-time honorarium of $750. The program is administered by Scholarship America, Inc.
Serve2Gether Grants: The fund awards grants to nonprofit organizations with which American Express employees or teams of employees volunteer their time and expertise and submit a proposal for support.
Type of support: Annual campaigns; Building/renovation; Employee matching gifts; Employee volunteer services; Employee-related scholarships; General/operating support; Program development; Sponsorships.
Geographic limitations: Giving primarily on a national basis in areas of company operations, with emphasis on Phoenix, AZ, Los Angeles and San Francisco, CA, Washington, DC, southern FL, Atlanta, GA, Chicago, IL, Boston, MA, New York, NY, Philadelphia, PA, Dallas and Houston, TX, and Salt Lake City, UT.
Support limitations: No support for discriminatory organizations, religious organizations not of direct benefit to the entire community, or political organizations. No grants to individuals (except for employee-related scholarships), or for fundraising, goodwill advertising, souvenir journals, or dinner programs, travel, books, magazines, or articles in professional journals, endowments or capital campaigns, traveling exhibitions, or sports sponsorships.
Publications: Application guidelines; Grants list; Program policy statement.
Application information: Applications accepted. Letters of inquiry should be no longer than 1 to 3 pages. Historic preservation applications for archival projects are discouraged. Leadership applications for youth leadership programs are discouraged. Organizations receiving support of at least $7,500 are asked to provide a final report. Application form not required. Applicants should submit the following:
1) timetable for implementation and evaluation of project
2) name, address and phone number of organization
3) copy of IRS Determination Letter
4) brief history of organization and description of its mission
5) geographic area to be served
6) copy of most recent annual report/audited financial statement/990
7) how project's results will be evaluated or measured
8) listing of board of directors, trustees, officers and other key people and their affiliations
9) detailed description of project and amount of funding requested
10) contact person
11) copy of current year's organizational budget and/or project budget
12) listing of additional sources and amount of support

Initial approach: Letter of inquiry to application address; e-mail letter of inquiry to organizations located in Phoenix, AZ, southern FL, and Salt Lake City, UT
Deadline(s): None; Feb. 1 and July 1 for Phoenix, AZ, southern FL, and Salt Lake City, UT
Final notification: 3 to 4 months

Officers and Trustees:* Timothy J. McClimon*, Pres.; Mary Ellen Craig, Secy.; David L . Yowan, Treas.; Tammy D. Fried, Counsel; Vernon E. Jordan, Jr.; Frank P. Popoff.
EIN: 261607898
Selected grants: The following grants are a representative sample of this grantmaker's funding activity:
$376,000 to Scholarship America, Saint Peter, MN, 2010. For Employee Scholarship.
$76,087 to Charities Aid Foundation UK, West Malling, England, 2010. For Global Volunteer Action Fund.
$50,000 to City Year, Boston, MA, 2010.
$49,000 to Florida Sterling Council, Tallahassee, FL, 2010.
$40,000 to Florence Crittenton Services of Arizona, Phoenix, AZ, 2010.
$25,000 to Ballet Arizona, Phoenix, AZ, 2010.
$16,500 to Young at Art Childrens Museum, Davie, FL, 2010.
$10,000 to Boys and Girls Clubs of Metropolitan Phoenix, Phoenix, AZ, 2010.
$10,000 to Duet: Partners in Health and Aging, Phoenix, AZ, 2010.
$10,000 to Reading Connections, Greensboro, NC, 2010.

American Express Foundation

World Financial Ctr.
200 Vesey St., 48th Fl.
New York, NY 10285-4804
Application address for organizations located outside of Phoenix, AZ, south FL, and Salt Lake City, UT: 3 World Financial Center, M.C. 01-48-04, New York, NY 10285-4804; E-mail for Phoenix, AZ: American Express Co., c/o Community Affairs, PhoenixLOIs@aexp.com; E-mail for south Florida: American Express Co., c/o Community Affairs, FtLauderdaleLOIs@aexp.com; E-mail for Salt Lake City, UT: American Express Co., c/o Community Affairs, SaltLakeCityLOIs@aexp.com; URL: http://about.americanexpress.com/csr/?inav=about_CorpResponsibility

Establishment information: Incorporated in 1954 in NY.
Donor: American Express Co.
Financial data (yr. ended 12/31/11): Assets, $10,957,285 (M); expenditures, $8,710,640; qualifying distributions, $8,703,807; giving activities include $8,591,500 for 155 grants (high: $1,000,000; low: $330).
Purpose and activities: The foundation supports programs designed to promote historic preservation; leadership; and community service.
Fields of interest: Visual arts; Museums; Performing arts; Historic preservation/historical societies; Arts; Higher education; Education; Hospitals (general); Food services; Food banks; Food distribution, meals on wheels; Disasters, preparedness/services; American Red Cross; Children/youth, services; Human services; Economic development; Nonprofit management; Community/economic development; Foundations (community); Voluntarism promotion; Leadership development; Public affairs.
Programs:
Community Service: The foundation supports programs designed to cultivate meaningful opportunities for civic engagement and encourage community service. Special emphasis is directed toward capacity building of nonprofits through community engagement, including volunteers, audience members, and donors; encouraging citizens to play an active role in civic processes; and the engagement of community members and American Express employees in philanthropy, volunteerism, or participation in local civic organizations. The foundation also supports disaster relief and preparedness programs that allow relief agencies to be better equipped in responding to emergencies as they occur.
Historic Preservation: The foundation supports programs and projects designed to preserve, restore, or sustain historic places, landmarks, and public spaces; and preserve sites that represent diverse cultures. Special emphasis is directed toward projects designed to restore historic places to ensure ongoing public access and interaction with the sites; preserve historic places for future or innovative use; and sustain historic places by creating systems to manage increased visitor activities and environmental impact.
Leadership: The foundation supports programs designed to provide current and future nonprofit leaders with practical opportunities to learn and build leadership skills. Special emphasis is directed toward programs designed to address the leadership deficit in the nonprofit sector by enabling new executive directors or supporting the training and development of emerging leaders; diversify the current landscape of nonprofit leaders; and transform organizations through best-in-class management and leadership practices through board leadership, implementing management principles, or expanding an organization's capacity to attract, develop and retain leadership talent.
Type of support: Annual campaigns; Conferences/seminars; Continuing support; Emergency funds; General/operating support; Management development/capacity building; Program development.
Geographic limitations: Giving on a national and international basis in areas of company operations with emphasis on greater Phoenix, AZ, Los Angeles and San Francisco, CA, Washington, DC, south FL, Atlanta, GA, Chicago, IL, Boston, MA, New York, NY, Philadelphia, PA, Puerto Rico, Houston, TX, Salt Lake City, UT, Argentina, Austria, Canada, China, France, Germany, Hong Kong, Italy, Japan, Mexico, Netherlands, Singapore, Spain, Taiwan, and the United Kingdom.
Support limitations: No support for discriminatory organizations, religious organizations not of direct benefit to the entire community, or political organizations. No grants to individuals, or for fundraising, goodwill advertising, souvenir journals, or dinner programs, travel, books, magazines, or articles in professional journals, endowments or capital campaigns, traveling exhibitions, or sports sponsorships.
Publications: Application guidelines; Grants list; Program policy statement.
Application information: Applications accepted. Letter of inquiry should be no longer than 1 to 3 pages. Historic preservation applications for archival projects are discouraged. Leadership applications for youth leadership programs are discouraged. Organizations receiving support of at least $7,500 are asked to provide a final report. Application form not required. Applicants should submit the following:
1) timetable for implementation and evaluation of project
2) statement of problem project will address
3) copy of IRS Determination Letter
4) brief history of organization and description of its mission
5) explanation of why grantmaker is considered an appropriate donor for project
6) detailed description of project and amount of funding requested
7) copy of current year's organizational budget and/or project budget
8) listing of additional sources and amount of support

Initial approach: Letter of inquiry to application address; e-mail letter of inquiry to organizations located in Phoenix, AZ, southern FL, and Salt Lake City, UT
Board meeting date(s): Biannually
Deadline(s): None; Feb. 1 and July 1 for Phoenix, AZ, southern FL, and Salt Lake City, UT
Final notification: 3 to 4 months

Officers and Trustees:* Thomas Schick*, Chair.; Timothy J. McClimon, Pres.; Judy Tenzer, Secy.; Mary Ellen Craig, Compt.; Kenneth I. Chenault; Edward P. Gilligan; Daniel T. Henry; Stephen J. Squeri.
EIN: 136123529
Selected grants: The following grants are a representative sample of this grantmaker's funding activity:
$2,000,000 to World Trade Center Memorial Foundation, New York, NY, 2010. For Special Projects.
$1,000,000 to My Good Deed, Newport Beach, CA, 2011. For special projects.
$1,000,000 to Smithsonian Institution, Washington, DC, 2011. For special projects.
$500,000 to National Academy Foundation, New York, NY, 2010.
$400,000 to National Academy Foundation, New York, NY, 2011. For leadership.
$200,000 to Feeding America, Chicago, IL, 2010.
$150,000 to Independent Sector, Washington, DC, 2010.
$130,000 to Entrepreneurial Training for Innovative Community, Tokyo, Japan, 2010.
$122,000 to Common Purpose International, London, England, 2011. For international work.
$100,000 to Common Purpose International, London, England, 2010.
$100,000 to Taproot Foundation, San Francisco, CA, 2011.
$67,000 to Dom Romer GmbH, Frankfurt, Germany, 2010.
$50,000 to Asociacion Amigos del Museo Nacional de Bellas Artes, Buenos Aires, Argentina, 2010.
$50,000 to Mobilize.org, Washington, DC, 2011. For leadership.
$50,000 to Points of Light Institute, Atlanta, GA, 2011.
$47,000 to Fundacion Cimientos, Buenos Aires, Argentina, 2010.
$35,000 to National Trust for Historic Preservation, Washington, DC, 2011. For leadership.
$25,000 to Craigslist Foundation, San Francisco, CA, 2011. For leadership.
$25,000 to Wave Hill, Bronx, NY, 2011. For historic preservation.

144
American Family Mutual Insurance Company

(also known as American Family Insurance Group)
6000 American Pkwy.
Madison, WI 53783 (608) 249-2111

Company URL: http://www.amfam.com
Establishment information: Established in 1927.
Company type: Mutual company
Business activities: Sells fire, casualty, business, health, property, and life insurance.
Business type (SIC): Insurance/fire, marine, and casualty; security and commodity services; insurance/life; insurance/accident and health; holding company
Financial profile for 2011: Number of employees, 7,893; assets, $17,302,037,000; sales volume, $6,491,800,000; liabilities, $11,590,886
Corporate officers: Jack C. Salzwedel, Chair. and C.E.O.; Daniel R. Schultz, Pres. and C.O.O.; Daniel J. Kelly, C.F.O. and Treas.; Richard A. Fetherston, Sr. V.P., Comms.; Kristin R. Kirkconnell, C.I.O.; Peter C. Gunder, C.I.O.; Annette S. Knapstein, V.P., Mktg.; Kari E. Grasee, V.P. and Cont.; David C. Holman, Secy.
Board of directors: Jack C. Salzwedel, Chair.; David R. Anderson; Rakesh Khurana; Daniel R. Schultz; Michael M. Knetter; Paul S. Shain; Londa J. Dewey; R. Scott Malmgren; Thomas J. Zimbrick; Leslie Ann Howard; Walter M. Oliver; Ted D. Kellner; Eliot G. Protsch
Subsidiaries: American Family Brokerage, Inc., Madison, WI; American Family Financial Services, Inc., Madison, WI; American Family Life Insurance Co., Madison, WI; American Family Mutual Insurance Co., Madison, WI; American Standard Insurance Co. of Wisconsin, Madison, WI
Giving statement: Giving through the American Family Insurance Group Corporate Giving Program.

American Family Insurance Group Corporate Giving Program

c/o Community Rels.
6000 American Pkwy.
Madison, WI 53783-0001
E-mail: Community-Relations@amfam.com;
URL: http://www.amfam.com/company/values_contributions.asp

Purpose and activities: American Family Insurance makes charitable contributions to nonprofit organizations involved with arts and culture, education, health, human services, and youth. Support is limited to areas of company operations in Arizona, Colorado, Georgia, Illinois, Indiana, Iowa, Kansas, Minnesota, Missouri, Nebraska, Nevada, North Dakota, Ohio, Oregon, South Dakota, Utah, Washington, and Wisconsin.
Fields of interest: Arts; Education; Health care; Food services; Housing/shelter; Youth development; Human services.
Type of support: Employee volunteer services; Equipment; General/operating support; Program development; Scholarship funds; Sponsorships.
Geographic limitations: Giving limited to areas of company operations in AZ, CO, GA, IA, ID, IL, IN, KS, MN, MO, ND, NE, NV, OH, OR, SD, UT, WA, and WI.
Support limitations: No support for teams. No grants to individuals.
Application information: Applications accepted. The Community Relations Department handles giving. Application form required.
Initial approach: Complete online application form
Deadline(s): None
Final notification: Following review

145
American Fidelity Assurance Company

(also known as American Fidelity Group)
2000 N. Classen Blvd., Ste. 10E
P.O. Box 25523
Oklahoma City, OK 73106-6013
(405) 523-2000

Company URL: http://www.afadvantage.com
Establishment information: Established in 1960.
Company type: Subsidiary of a private company
Business activities: Sells accident, health, and life insurance.
Business type (SIC): Insurance/accident and health; insurance/life
Corporate officers: William M. Cameron, Co-Chair. and C.E.O.; William E. Durrett, Co-Chair.; David R. Carpenter, Vice-Chair., Pres., and C.O.O.; Robert D. Brearton, C.F.O.; Gary E. Tredway, Sr. V.P. and Secy.; Stephen P. Garrett, Sr. V.P. and Cont.
Board of directors: William M. Cameron, Co-Chair.; William E. Durrett, Co-Chair.; David R. Carpenter, Vice-Chair.; Gregory S. Allen; John M. Bendheim; Lynda L. Cameron; Charles R. Eitel; Theodore M. Elam; Theodore M. Elam; Paula Marshall; Tommie J. McDaniel; Stephen M. Prescott, M.D.
Giving statement: Giving through the American Fidelity Group Corporate Giving Program and the American Fidelity Foundation.

American Fidelity Group Corporate Giving Program

2000 N. Classen Blvd.
Oklahoma City, OK 73106-6007 (405) 523-2000
URL: http://www.afadvantage.com/about-afa/serving-our-community.aspx

Purpose and activities: As a complement to its foundation, American Fidelity Group also makes charitable contributions to nonprofit organizations directly. Support is given primarily in Oklahoma City, Oklahoma.
Fields of interest: Elementary school/education; Education, reading; Education; Health care, blood supply; Food services; Safety/disasters.
Type of support: Employee volunteer services; Sponsorships.
Geographic limitations: Giving primarily in Oklahoma City, OK.
Application information: Application form not required.

American Fidelity Foundation

(formerly American Fidelity Corporation Founders Fund, Inc.)
2000 N. Classen., Ste. 7N
Oklahoma City, OK 73106-6023
FAX: (405) 523-5421;
E-mail: JoElla.Ramsey@af-group.com; Additional contact: Tom McDaniel, Pres., e-mail: Tom.McDaniel@af-group.com; URL: http://www.americanfidelityfoundation.org

Establishment information: Established in 1984 in OK.
Donor: American Fidelity Assurance Co.
Contact: Jo Ella Ramsey, Admin.; David R. Lopez, Pres.
Financial data (yr. ended 12/31/11): Assets, $12,099,306 (M); gifts received, $2,000,000; expenditures, $826,282; qualifying distributions, $786,793; giving activities include $786,793 for grants.
Purpose and activities: The foundation supports organizations involved with arts and culture, education, heath, human services, community economic development, and civic affairs.
Fields of interest: Museums; Arts; Education, early childhood education; Higher education; Education; Health care; Children/youth, services; Family services; Human services; Community/economic development; United Ways and Federated Giving Programs; Public affairs.
Type of support: Annual campaigns; Employee matching gifts; Employee volunteer services; General/operating support; Program development; Program evaluation; Research; Seed money; Sponsorships.
Geographic limitations: Giving primarily in areas of company operations in OK.
Support limitations: No support for private clubs, religious, fraternal, or sectarian organizations, or for organizations that seek to influence or initiate legislation, political candidates, political parties, or political campaigns. No grants to individuals, or for capital campaigns, endowments (except to fund scholarships or for other specific education projects), or for travel expenses.
Publications: Application guidelines; Grants list; Quarterly report.
Application information: Applications accepted. Grants range from $500 to $5,000. A formal application may be requested at a later date. Support is limited to one contribution per organization during any given year. Application form not required. Applicants should submit the following:
1) name, address and phone number of organization
2) detailed description of project and amount of funding requested
3) contact person
4) copy of current year's organizational budget and/or project budget

Initial approach: E-mail or mail letter of interest
Copies of proposal: 1
Board meeting date(s): Quarterly
Deadline(s): None
Final notification: 2 weeks

Officers and Directors:* William M. Cameron*, Chair.; Tom McDaniel*, Pres.; Robert D. Brearton*, Exec. V.P. and Treas.; Stephen P. Garrett*, Secy.; Jo Carol Cameron; David R. Carpenter; William E. Durrett.
EIN: 731236059

146
American Future Systems, Inc.

(also known as Progressive Business Publications)
370 Technology Dr.
Malvern, PA 19355 (610) 695-8600

Company URL: http://www.pbp.com
Establishment information: Established in 1959.
Company type: Private company
Business activities: Publishes newsletters.
Business type (SIC): Publishing/miscellaneous
Corporate officers: Edward M. Satell, Pres.; Dana Dovberg, Corp. Cont.
Giving statement: Giving through the Progressive Business Publications Charitable Trust and the Progressive Business Publications Foundation.

Progressive Business Publications Charitable Trust

c/o Edward M. Satell
376 Technology Dr.
Malvern, PA 19355-1315

Establishment information: Established in 1996 in PA.
Donors: American Future Systems, Inc.; Edward M. Satell.
Financial data (yr. ended 12/31/11): Assets, $816,081 (M); gifts received, $200,000; expenditures, $244,507; qualifying distributions, $145,020; giving activities include $145,020 for grants.
Purpose and activities: The foundation supports organizations involved with arts and culture, food services, business youth development, and international affairs.
Fields of interest: Museums (history); Performing arts, theater; Arts; Food services; Youth development, business; International affairs; United Ways and Federated Giving Programs.
Type of support: General/operating support.
Geographic limitations: Giving primarily in Philadelphia, PA.
Support limitations: No grants to individuals.
Application information: Applications not accepted. Contributes only to pre-selected organizations.
Trustee: Edward M. Satell.
EIN: 237835073
Selected grants: The following grants are a representative sample of this grantmaker's funding activity:
$39,500 to Walnut Street Theater, Philadelphia, PA, 2010.
$15,000 to International House, New York, NY, 2010.

$12,050 to Junior Achievement of Delaware Valley, Chester, PA, 2010.
$10,000 to National Constitution Center, Philadelphia, PA, 2010.
$1,180 to American Red Cross, Philadelphia, PA, 2010.
$1,000 to Center for Advancement in Cancer Education, Wynnewood, PA, 2010.

Progressive Business Publications Foundation

370 Technology Dr.
Malvern, PA 19355-0719 (610) 695-8600

Establishment information: Established in 2000 in PA.
Donor: American Future Systems, Inc.
Financial data (yr. ended 12/31/11): Assets, $0 (M); gifts received, $25,644; expenditures, $25,644; qualifying distributions, $25,644; giving activities include $25,644 for 11 grants to individuals (high: $2,500; low: $644).
Purpose and activities: The foundation awards college scholarships to children of employees of American Future Systems.
Fields of interest: Higher education.
Type of support: Employee-related scholarships.
Geographic limitations: Giving primarily in Malvern, PA.
Application information: Applications accepted.
Initial approach: Proposal
Deadline(s): Sep. 30
Trustees: Marc S. Maser; Edward J. Satell.
EIN: 256665358

147
American General Corporation

2929 Allen Pkwy., Ste. 3800
Houston, TX 77019-7104 (713) 522-1111

Company URL: http://www.americangeneral.com
Establishment information: Established in 1926.
Company type: Subsidiary of a public company
Business activities: Provides investment advisory services; sells life insurance; provides consumer loans.
Business type (SIC): Insurance/life; credit institutions/personal; security and commodity services
Corporate officers: Maurice Geenbeg, Chair.; Rodney O. Martin, Jr., C.E.O.
Board of directors: Maurice Geenbeg, Chair.; Bob Herbert
Subsidiaries: AGC Life Insurance Co., Nashville, TN; American General Finance, Inc., Evansville, IN; American General Investment Management Corp., New York, NY; USLIFE Corp., New York, NY
Division: Retirement Services Div., Houston, TX
Offices: Springfield, IL; Milwaukee, WI
Historic mergers: Home Beneficial Corporation (April 16, 1997)
Giving statement: Giving through the AIG American General Corporate Giving Program.

AIG American General Corporate Giving Program

(formerly American General Corporation Contributions Program)
c/o Community Rels.
2929 Allen Pkwy., AT-40
Houston, TX 77019-2155
E-mail: Jennifer.Waldner@aglife.com; Additional Community Relations Contacts: For Chicago, Illinois: Eileen Hampton, Human Resources Consultant, 1000 East Woodfield Rd., Schaumburg, IL,60173, e-mail: Eileen.Hampton@aglife.com; For Springfield, Illinois: Jay Lohman, Financial Compliance, 3051 Hollis Dr., Springfield, IL 62704, e-mail: jay.v.lohman@aglife.com; For Neptune, New Jersey: Eileen Hampton, Human Resources Consultant, 3600 Rte. 66, Neptune, NJ 07754, e-mail: Eileen.Hampton@aglife.com; For Nashville, Tennessee: Linda Hughes, Human Resources, American General Ctr., Brentwood, TN 37027, e-mail: linda.f.hughes@aglife.com; For Dallas, Texas: Sandy Kelley, Human Resources, 6363 Forest Park Rd., Dallas, TX 75235, e-mail:Sandy.Kelley@aglife.com; For Milwaukee, Wisconsin: Chris Briskie, Dir., Human Resources, 750 West Virginia St. Milwaukee, WI 53204, e-mail: Chris.Briskie@aglife.com; URL: http://www.aigag.com/life/life.nsf/contents/aboutus_community

Contact: Jennifer Waldner
Purpose and activities: AIG American General makes charitable contributions to nonprofit organizations involved with helping at-risk children, and on a case by case basis. Support is given primarily in areas of company operations in Schaumburg and Springfield, Illinois, Neptune, New Jersey, Brentwood, Tennessee, and Dallas and Houston, Texas.
Fields of interest: Education; Community/economic development; General charitable giving Children.
Program:
Community Spirit Awards: Through the Community Spirit Awards program, AIG American General annually awards grants of $5,000 to a select group of employees in recognition of their outstanding volunteer efforts, to be donated to a charity of their choice.
Type of support: Employee matching gifts; Employee volunteer services; General/operating support; Seed money.
Geographic limitations: Giving primarily in areas of company operations, with emphasis on Schaumburg and Springfield, IL, Neptune, NJ, Brentwood, TN, Dallas and Houston, TX, and Milwaukee, WI.
Application information: Applications not accepted. Unsolicited applications are currently not accepted.

148
American Golf Corporation

2951 28th St., Ste. 300
Santa Monica, CA 90405-2961
(310) 664-4000

Company URL: http://www.americangolf.com
Establishment information: Established in 1969.
Company type: Subsidiary of a public company
Business activities: Operates golf courses.
Business type (SIC): Amusement and recreation services/miscellaneous
Corporate officers: Paul Major, Pres. and C.E.O.; Keith Brown, Sr. V.P. and C.O.O.; Joe Stegman, V.P., Human Resources
Giving statement: Giving through the American Golf Foundation.

American Golf Foundation

2951 28th St.
Santa Monica, CA 90405-2961 (480) 838-1546
URL: http://www.americangolffoundation.org

Establishment information: Established in 1995 in CA.
Financial data (yr. ended 12/31/11): Revenue, $624,049; assets, $275,059 (M); gifts received, $575,652; expenditures, $590,803; giving activities include $493,848 for grants and $11,643 for grants to individuals.
Purpose and activities: The foundation promotes the game of golf and its ideals through charity, education, and community service.
Fields of interest: Athletics/sports, golf.
Geographic limitations: Giving on a national basis.
Officers and Board Members:* Joe Stegman*, Pres.; Darryl Cluster*, Secy.; Keith Brown, C.F.O.; John Flaschner*; Pete McDaniel; Kathy Whitworth.
EIN: 954539145

149
American Greetings Corporation

1 American Rd.
Cleveland, OH 44144 (216) 252-7300
FAX: (216) 252.6778

Company URL: http://www.corporate.americangreetings.com
Establishment information: Established in 1906.
Company type: Public company
Company ticker symbol and exchange: AM/NYSE
Business activities: Prints greeting cards; manufactures gift wrapping paper and related products and picture frames and haircare products.
Business type (SIC): Greeting cards; wood products/miscellaneous; manufacturing/miscellaneous
Financial profile for 2013: Number of employees, 25,400; assets, $1,583,460,000; sales volume, $1,868,740,000; pre-tax net income, $85,910,000; expenses, $1,774,570,000; liabilities, $901,590,000
Corporate officers: Morry Weiss, Chair.; Zev Weiss, C.E.O.; Jeffrey Weiss, Pres. and C.O.O.; Robert D. Tyler, C.A.O. and Corp. Cont.; Stephen J. Smith, Sr. V.P. and C.F.O.; Douglas W. Rommel, Sr. V.P. and C.I.O.; Catherine M. Kilbane, Sr. V.P., Genl. Counsel, and Secy.; Brian T. McGrath, Sr. V.P., Human Resources; Christopher W. Haffke, V.P. and Genl. Counsel
Board of directors: Morry Weiss, Chair.; Scott S. Cowen; Jeffrey D. Dunn; William E. MacDonald III; Michael J. Merriman, Jr.; Charles A. Ratner; Jerry Sue Thornton, Ph.D.; Jeffrey Weiss; Zev Weiss
Subsidiaries: A.G. Industries, Inc., Forest City, NC; Acme Frame Products, Inc., Chicago, IL; Plus Mark, Inc., Afton, TN; Those Characters From Cleveland, Inc., Independence, OH; Wilhold, Sunbury, PA
International operations: Canada; United Kingdom
Giving statement: Giving through the American Greetings Corporation Contributions Program.
Company EIN: 340065325

American Greetings Corporation Contributions Program

1 American Rd.
Cleveland, OH 44144-2398 (216) 252-7300
FAX: (216) 252-6778; URL: http://www.corporate.americangreetings.com/aboutus/sustainability.html

Purpose and activities: American Greetings makes charitable contributions to nonprofit organizations on a case by case basis. Support is given primarily in Cleveland, Ohio.
Fields of interest: United Ways and Federated Giving Programs; General charitable giving.

Type of support: Employee volunteer services; General/operating support; Sponsorships.
Geographic limitations: Giving primarily in Cleveland, OH.

150
American Honda Motor Co., Inc.

1919 Torrance Blvd.
P.O. Box 100-1W-5A
Torrance, CA 90501-2746 (310) 783-2000

Company URL: http://corporate.honda.com/
Establishment information: Established in 1959.
Company type: Subsidiary of a foreign company
Business activities: Imports, distributes, and manufactures automobiles; manufactures motorcycles, power equipment, and allied parts.
Business type (SIC): Motor vehicles and equipment; motorcycles, bicycles, and parts; motor vehicles, parts, and supplies—wholesale; motorcycles—retail
Financial profile for 2010: Number of employees, 2,375
Corporate officers: Tetsuo Iwamura, Pres. and C.E.O.; Hiroyuki Suganuma, C.F.O.; John W. Mendel, Exec. V.P., Sales; Gary Kessler, Sr. V.P., Human Resources and Admin.
Board of director: Gary Kessler
Subsidiaries: American Honda Finance Corp., Torrance, CA; Honda of South Carolina Mfg., Inc., Timmonsville, SC; Honda Power Equipment Mfg., Inc., Swepsonville, NC; Honda Trading America Corp., Torrance, CA
Giving statement: Giving through the American Honda Motor Co., Inc. Corporate Giving Program, the Mitsubishi Electric Corporation Contributions Program, and the American Honda Foundation.

American Honda Motor Co., Inc. Corporate Giving Program

1919 Torrance Blvd.
Torrance, CA 90501-2722 (310) 783-2000
URL: http://corporate.honda.com/america/philanthropy.aspx?id=philanthropy_overview

Purpose and activities: As a complement to its foundation, American Honda also makes charitable contributions to nonprofit organizations directly. Emphasis is given to organizations involved with youth and education, and science and technology. Support is given on a national basis.
Fields of interest: Arts, cultural/ethnic awareness; Arts; Elementary/secondary education; Education; Environment; Aquariums; Public health; Medical research; Athletics/sports, professional leagues; Youth development; Human services; Civil/human rights, equal rights; Community/economic development; Engineering/technology; Science; Public affairs Economically disadvantaged.
Type of support: Employee volunteer services; General/operating support; In-kind gifts; Sponsorships.
Geographic limitations: Giving on a national basis.
Support limitations: No support for religious or political organizations. No grants to individuals.
Publications: Application guidelines.
Application information: Applications accepted. The Community Relations department handles giving. Application form required.
Initial approach: Complete online application form
Final notification: 6-8 weeks

American Honda Foundation

1919 Torrance Blvd., M.S. 100-1W-5A
Torrance, CA 90501-2746 (310) 781-4090
FAX: (310) 781-4270; E-mail: ahf@ahm.honda.com; URL: http://corporate.honda.com/america/philanthropy.aspx?id=ahf

Establishment information: Established in 1984 in CA.
Donor: American Honda Motor Co., Inc.
Financial data (yr. ended 03/31/12): Assets, $30,712,688 (M); gifts received, $168,175; expenditures, $2,359,654; qualifying distributions, $1,666,410; giving activities include $1,666,410 for grants.
Purpose and activities: The foundation supports programs designed to promote youth education. Special emphasis is directed toward science, technology, engineering, mathematics, the environment, job training, and literacy.
Fields of interest: Elementary/secondary education; Vocational education; Higher education; Education, reading; Education; Environment; Employment, training; Science, formal/general education; Physical/earth sciences; Mathematics; Engineering/technology; Science Youth; Minorities.
Type of support: Continuing support; Curriculum development; General/operating support; Matching/challenge support; Program development; Scholarship funds; Seed money.
Geographic limitations: Giving on a national basis with some emphasis on CA.
Support limitations: No support for private foundations, for-profit organizations, churches, religious groups, or sectarian organizations, arts and culture organizations, health and welfare, disaster relief, legislative organizations, political organizations or candidates, advocacy, veterans' or fraternal organizations, or labor groups. No grants to individuals, or for scholarships, operating funds for hospitals, medical or educational research, research papers, fundraising, dinners, parties, receptions, auction charity balls, or 5k walks or runs, sponsorships, advertising, building funds or capital campaigns, endowments, corporate memberships, conferences or seminars, service club activities, youth recreational activities or playground equipment, student foreign exchange programs, trips or tours, or beauty or talent contests; no vehicle or product donations; no loans for small businesses.
Publications: Application guidelines; Grants list; Informational brochure (including application guidelines).
Application information: Applications accepted. Grants range from $20,000 to $75,000. No faxed applications are accepted. Support is limited to 1 contribution per organization during any given year. A site visit may be requested. Application form required. Applicants should submit the following:
1) copy of IRS Determination Letter
2) brief history of organization and description of its mission
3) copy of most recent annual report/audited financial statement/990
4) descriptive literature about organization
5) listing of board of directors, trustees, officers and other key people and their affiliations
6) detailed description of project and amount of funding requested
7) copy of current year's organizational budget and/or project budget
8) listing of additional sources and amount of support
9) additional materials/documentation

Organizations with a gross revenue of $500,000 or more must have two years of audited financial statements examined by an independent CPA for the purpose of expressing an opinion. Organizations with a gross revenue of less than $500,000 that do not have audits, are welcome to submit two years of financial statements accompanied by an independent CPA's review report instead.
Initial approach: Complete online eligibility quiz and application form
Board meeting date(s): Jan., Apr., July, and Oct.
Deadline(s): Feb. 1, May 1, Aug. 1, and Nov. 1
Final notification: May 1, Aug. 1., Nov. 1. and Feb. 1

Officers and Directors:* Gary Kessler*, Pres.; Naoji Ono, V.P.; Steve Center*, Secy.-Treas.; Oraetta Minor; DeWayne Odom; Michael Rickey; Gail Rodkin; Cicely Salatino; Urvi Sutariya.
Number of staff: 4 full-time professional.
EIN: 953924667
Selected grants: The following grants are a representative sample of this grantmaker's funding activity:
$60,000 to Classroom Central, Charlotte, NC, 2012. For Classroom Central STEM Initiative, which enables low-income students to succeed academically. Classroom Central allows teachers to shop for free school supplies twice a month throughout the school year. Low-income students receive basic Science, Technology, Engineering and Mathematics (STEM) supplies and books necessary to enhance their ability to excel in math and science-related disciplines. These supplies include compasses, protractors, science books and quarterly science magazines, graphing paper and science calculators.
$60,000 to Community Foundation of Northeast Iowa, Waterloo, IA, 2012. For Leader Valley - Leader in Me Program, school-wide transformational model using 7 Habits of Highly Effective People as a common language and integrating the Habits directly into the curriculum, traditions and culture of schools. This result in instilling important leadership principles, improving academic achievement, decreasing discipline issues and raising accountability and engagement among teachers, students and parents.
$60,000 to DC Children and Youth Investment Trust Corporation, Washington, DC, 2012. For DC Inquiry-Based Learning (DCIBL), designed to turn up the volume on Science, Technology, Engineering and Mathematics (STEM) education by providing training to youth workers from selected community-based organizations in hands-on STEM curriculum. Serving as co-explorers, these nontraditional teachers deliver engaging STEM activities to students who typically have little to no exposure to STEM. Students then use what they have learned to address a specific issue occurring in their communities - giving them a real world application of STEM. At the culminating fair, students showcase their findings before peers, family members and community leaders.
$60,000 to Delaware Foundation for Science and Mathematics Education, Wilmington, DE, 2012. For NBC Learn News Archives on Demand, providing middle schools in Delaware with access to NBC Learn Archives on Demand, media tool aligned to state standards in curriculu. The tool is a collection of NBC News videos, primary source documents, photos and images, graphs and charts; designed for use in school classrooms. Teachers and their students can access and download material covering subjects such as science, mathematics, language arts and social studies, from any internet-connected computer.
$60,000 to Freedom School Partners, Charlotte, NC, 2012. For Summer Literacy Program, which targets Title-1 schools serving students in grades K-8. Six-week literacy-based camps are offered free of charge and are led by trained college interns who

serve as role models. Daily activities, books and other materials are selected to incorporate culturally relevant themes in effort to make the content engaging and relatable to students. At the end of each week, the children are given a book to take home to ensure that reading continues at home.
$60,000 to Living Arts, Detroit, MI, 2012. For El Arte STEAM/READ (Science, Technology, Engineering, Arts, Math and Literacy Initiative), program which enlists local artists in arts residencies, serving students in grades Pre-Kindergarten through eight Teaching artists partner with classroom teachers in Southwest Detroit to provide innovative arts-based curricula, aligned with academic standards to improve students' science, math, technology and literacy skills. This unique approach integrates the arts into day-to-day education resulting in significant improvement in student performance.
$60,000 to Rainier Scholars, Seattle, WA, 2012. For Academic Enrichment Program, which puts 6th graders on the path to college preparatory success through a 14-month intensive academic boot camp. Students attend rigorous courses focused on science, mathematics, literature and writing, and history. Academic and support services lead to placement into top independent and public schools and continues until the Scholars' final day of college.
$60,000 to San Mateo County Superintendent of Schools, Redwood City, CA, 2012. For Integrated Outdoor Education and the New California Education Environment Initiative State Adopted Curriculum (EEI). 5th and 6th grade teachers receive professional development training and strategies to effectively integrate California's newly adopted EEI curriculum with hands-on outdoor education curriculum taught at week-long residential outdoor science schools. EEI includes 85 instructional units, integrating California science and social studies/ history standards.
$50,000 to Young Women's Leadership Charter School of Chicago, Chicago, IL, 2012. For Real Women Do Real Science, program for girls in grades 7-12. They gain a deep understanding of the scientific method through inquiry and experimentation. In addition to year-long science courses, students engage in unique research-based projects and career exploration via extra-curricular activities, internships and Saturday Academies offered through local partnerships. A key component of the curriculum is its annual Science Fair in which all projects are based on the Chicago River, with students analyzing the river based on their grade level's science focus.
$30,400 to Boys and Girls Clubs of Greater Dallas, Dallas, TX, 2012. For CSI-Project Learn which pairs youth ages 13-18 with seasoned detectives within the Dallas Police Department who will work closely teaching them about the necessary skills and levels of education required to pursue careers in Law Enforcement, Forensic Science, as a Medical Examiner and more. Participants will go beyond the yellow tape and work a mock crime scene from investigation to a mock trial. Students will receive real-world experience and hands-on activities focused on toxicology, chemistry, DNA testing, fingerprinting and courtroom testimony.

151
American Hospice, Inc.

6421 Camp Bowie Blvd., Ste. 200
Fort Worth, TX 76116-5401 (817) 551-0945

Company URL: http://www.americanhospice.com/
Establishment information: Established in 1992.
Company type: Private company
Business activities: Operates hospice management company.
Business type (SIC): Home healthcare services
Giving statement: Giving through the American Hospice of Texas Foundation.

American Hospice of Texas Foundation

6421 Camp Bowie Blvd., Ste. 200
Fort Worth, TX 76116-5401 (817) 551-0945

Establishment information: Established in 2003 in TX.
Donors: American Hospice, Inc.; Kemmie Adair.
Contact: Sharon Horn, Secy.
Financial data (yr. ended 12/31/10): Assets, $0 (M); expenditures, $1,846; qualifying distributions, $1,846; giving activities include $941 for 1 grant.
Purpose and activities: Giving for education about hospice care, and occasionally to subsidize care for needy individuals.
Fields of interest: Health care.
Type of support: Grants to individuals; Program development.
Geographic limitations: Giving primarily in Austin and Fort Worth, TX.
Application information: Applications accepted. Application form required.
Initial approach: Letter or telephone
Deadline(s): None
Officers: Jay Koeper, Pres.; Sharon Horn, Secy.; Mike Miller, Treas.
EIN: 043768638

152
American Hospitality Group, Inc.

(formerly American Health Care Centers, Inc.)
200 Smokerise Dr., Ste. 300
Wadsworth, OH 44281-9460
(330) 336-6684

Company URL: http://www.americanhg.com
Establishment information: Established in 1972.
Company type: Private company
Business activities: Operates restaurant; operates hotels; operates retirement and assisted living facilities; operates nursing homes; provides home health care services.
Business type (SIC): Restaurants and drinking places; hotels and motels; nursing and personal care facilities; home healthcare services; residential care
Corporate officers: Robert Leatherman, Sr., Chair. and Pres.; Phyllis Leatherman, Secy.-Treas.; Laura Groves, Cont.
Board of director: Robert Leatherman, Sr., Chair.
Giving statement: Giving through the Leatherman Family Foundation.

Leatherman Family Foundation

200 Smokerise Dr., Ste. 300
Wadsworth, OH 44281-9460

Establishment information: Established in 1992 in OH.
Donors: Robert Leatherman; American Health Care Centers, Inc.; Premier Island Group, LLC; Phyllis Leatherman.
Financial data (yr. ended 12/31/11): Assets, $1,962 (M); gifts received, $7,800; expenditures, $8,195; qualifying distributions, $6,770; giving activities include $6,770 for 2 grants (high: $5,770; low: $1,000).
Purpose and activities: The foundation supports hospices and organizations involved with historic preservation, substance abuse treatment, cancer, and Christianity.
Fields of interest: Historic preservation/historical societies; Substance abuse, treatment; Cancer; Cancer, leukemia; Residential/custodial care, hospices; Christian agencies & churches.
Type of support: General/operating support; Publication.
Geographic limitations: Giving primarily in NY and OH.
Support limitations: No grants to individuals.
Application information: Applications not accepted. Unsolicited requests for funds not accepted.
Officers and Trustees:* Robert Leatherman*, Pres. and Treas.; Phyllis Leatherman*, V.P. and Secy.; Karen Friedt; Robert J. Leatherman, Jr.; Sean Leatherman; Robin Wenger.
EIN: 346981592

153
American Income Life Insurance Company

1200 Wooded Acres Dr.
Waco, TX 76710-4436 (254) 761-6400

Company URL: https://www.ailife.com
Establishment information: Established in 1954.
Company type: Subsidiary of a public company
Business activities: Sells life and health insurance.
Business type (SIC): Insurance/life; insurance/ accident and health
Corporate officers: Scott Alan Smith, Pres.; Roger C. Smith, C.E.O.
Giving statement: Giving through the American Income Life Insurance Company Contributions Program.

American Income Life Insurance Company Contributions Program

c/o Corp. Contribs.
1200 Wooded Acres Dr.
Waco, TX 76710-4436 (254) 761-6400
URL: http://www.american-income-life-giving.com/

Purpose and activities: American Income Life makes charitable contributions to nonprofit organizations involved with fair trade, good jobs, healthcare reform, environmental sustainability, and electing fair-minded candidates. Support is given on a national basis.
Fields of interest: Education; Environment; Health care; Employment; Food banks; Family services; International economics/trade policy; Labor rights; Public policy, research; Public affairs, political organizations.
Type of support: Employee volunteer services; General/operating support; In-kind gifts; Scholarship funds.
Geographic limitations: Giving on a national basis in areas of company operations, with emphasis on central Texas.

154
American Industrial Center
830 S. Reagan Blvd., Ste. 162
Longwood, FL 32750 (407) 331-8666

Establishment information: Established in 1994.
Company type: Private company
Business activities: Operates nonresidential buildings.
Business type (SIC): Real estate operators and lessors
Corporate officer: Daniel J. Woods, Mgr.
Giving statement: Giving through the Sapphire Foundation, Inc.

Sapphire Foundation, Inc.
474 Glenshore Dr.
Cullowhee, NC 28723
E-mail: info@sapphirefound.org; URL: http://sapphirefound.org/

Establishment information: Established in 2004 in FL.
Donors: American Industrial Center; Daniel J. Woods; Mary Jane Woods.
Financial data (yr. ended 12/31/10): Assets, $602,565 (M); gifts received, $15,000; expenditures, $28,531; qualifying distributions, $28,245; giving activities include $28,245 for 6 grants (high: $25,000; low: $80).
Fields of interest: Arts; Education; Youth development.
Type of support: General/operating support.
Geographic limitations: Giving primarily in IL.
Support limitations: No grants to individuals.
Application information: Applications not accepted. Unsolicited requests for funds not accepted.
Directors: Kathy S. Adkins-Shawgo; Daniel J. Woods; Laurel R. Woods.
EIN: 202005288

155
American Industries, Inc.
(doing business as American Steel, Inc.)
1750 N.W. Naito Pkwy., Ste. 106
Portland, OR 97209-2530 (503) 222-0060

Establishment information: Established in 1944.
Company type: Private company
Business activities: Operates holding company.
Business type (SIC): Holding company
Corporate officers: Howard H. Hedinger, Chair. and Pres.; John Dempsey, V.P and C.F.O.
Board of director: Howard H. Hedinger, Chair.
Giving statement: Giving through the Hedinger Family Foundation.

Hedinger Family Foundation
1750 N.W. Front Ave., Ste. 106
Portland, OR 97209-2532
FAX: (503) 222-0070

Establishment information: Established in 1998 in OR.
Donor: American Industries, Inc.
Contact: Stacey Graves, Grants Officer
Financial data (yr. ended 12/31/11): Assets, $1,175,272 (M); gifts received, $747,399; expenditures, $1,342,816; qualifying distributions, $1,325,399; giving activities include $1,325,399 for grants.
Purpose and activities: The foundation supports science museums and organizations involved with education, animals and wildlife, health, cancer, youth development, and human services.
Fields of interest: Museums (science/technology); Elementary/secondary education; Secondary school/education; Higher education; Education; Animal welfare; Veterinary medicine, hospital; Animals/wildlife, training; Animals/wildlife; Hospitals (general); Health care; Cancer; Youth development, centers/clubs; Youth development; Children/youth, services; Residential/custodial care; Human services.
Type of support: Building/renovation; General/operating support; Program development; Scholarship funds.
Geographic limitations: Giving primarily in the greater Portland, OR, area.
Support limitations: No grants to individuals.
Application information: Applications not accepted. Contributes only to pre-selected organizations.
Directors: Hillary Hedinger Guelfi; Blake H. Hedinger; Howard H. Hedinger.
EIN: 931255431
Selected grants: The following grants are a representative sample of this grantmaker's funding activity:
$205,000 to Self Enhancement, Inc., Portland, OR, 2010.
$118,800 to Guide Dogs for the Blind, Boring, OR, 2010.
$105,000 to DoveLewis Emergency Animal Hospital, Portland, OR, 2010.
$100,000 to Oregon Museum of Science and Industry, Portland, OR, 2010.
$50,000 to Doernbecher Childrens Hospital, Portland, OR, 2010.
$50,000 to Medical Teams International, Tigard, OR, 2010.
$50,000 to Saint Marys Home for Boys, Beaverton, OR, 2010.
$48,005 to Candlelighters for Children with Cancer, Portland, OR, 2010.
$46,000 to Okizu Foundation, Novato, CA, 2010.
$28,900 to Central Catholic High School, Portland, OR, 2010.

156
American International Group, Inc.
(also known as AIG)
70 Pine St.
180 Maiden Ln.
New York, NY 10038 (212) 770-7000
FAX: (212) 943-1125

Company URL: http://www.aigcorporate.com/index.html
Establishment information: Established in 1919.
Company type: Public company
Company ticker symbol and exchange: AIG/NYSE
International Securities Identification Number: US0268747849
Business activities: Operates holding company; sells general and life insurance.
Business type (SIC): Holding company; insurance/life; insurance/fire, marine, and casualty
Financial profile for 2012: Number of employees, 63,000; assets, $548,633,000,000; sales volume, $65,656,000,000; pre-tax net income, $9,322,000,000; expenses, $56,334,000,000; liabilities, $450,631,000,000
Fortune 1000 ranking: 2012—38th in revenues, 55th in profits, and 12th in assets
Forbes 2000 ranking: 2012—122nd in sales, 167th in profits, and 52nd in assets
Corporate officers: Robert S. Miller, Chair.; Robert H. Benmosche, Pres. and C.E.O.; David L. Herzog, Exec. V.P. and C.F.O.; Thomas A. Russo, Exec. V.P. and Genl. Counsel; Michael R. Cowan, Exec. V.P. and C.A.O.; Brian T. Schreiber, Exec. V.P. and Treas.; Jeffrey Hurd, Sr. V.P., Human Resources and Comms.; Christina Pretto, Sr. V.P., Corp. Comms.
Board of directors: Robert S. Miller, Jr., Chair.; Robert H. Benmosche; W. Don Cornwell; John H. Fitzpatrick; Christopher S. Lynch; Arthur C. Martinez; George L. Miles, Jr.; Henry S. Miller; Suzanne Nora Johnson; Morris W. Offit; Ronald A. Rittenmeyer; Douglas M. Steenland
Subsidiaries: American General Corporation, Houston, TX; The Hartford Steam Boiler Inspection and Insurance, Co., Hartford, CT; Springleaf Finance Corporation, Evansville, IN
International operations: Bermuda; Canada; China; France; Israel; Kazakhstan; Liechtenstein; Luxembourg; Philippines; Russia; Switzerland; Taiwan
Giving statement: Giving through the AIG Corporate Giving Program, the AIG Disaster Relief Fund-New York, and the AIG Foundation, Inc.
Company EIN: 132592361

AIG Corporate Giving Program
180 Maiden Ln.
New York, NY 10038 (212) 770-7000
E-mail: corporate.responsibility@aig.com;
URL: http://www.aig.com/citizenship_3171_437858.html

Purpose and activities: As a complement to its foundation, AIG also makes charitable donations to nonprofit organizations directly. Support is given primarily in areas of company operations.
Fields of interest: Education; Health care; Safety/disasters; Self-advocacy services, disability; Homeless, human services; Economic development; Social entrepreneurship; Public affairs.
Program:
Employee Matching Gifts: AIG matches contributions made by its employees to nonprofit organizations on a one-for-one basis, up to $3,000 per employee per year.
Type of support: Employee matching gifts; General/operating support; Scholarship funds.
Geographic limitations: Giving primarily in areas of company operations.
Support limitations: No support for fraternal organizations, or organizations that advocate, support, or practice activities inconsistent with AIG's non-discrimination policies. No grants to individuals, or for sectarian activities, or political purposes.
Application information: Unsolicited proposals are not accepted. Letters of inquiry may be e-mailed in PDF or MS Word format to corporate.giving@aig.com.
Initial approach: E-mail letter of inquiry
Deadline(s): None

AIG Disaster Relief Fund-New York
180 Maiden Ln.
New York, NY 10038
URL: http://www.aig.com/citizenship_3171_437858.html

Establishment information: Established in 2003 in NY.
Donors: Starr Foundation; American International Group, Inc.
Financial data (yr. ended 12/31/11): Assets, $486 (M); gifts received, $3,019,041; expenditures, $3,099,328; qualifying distributions, $3,096,159;

giving activities include $3,058,992 for 4 grants (high: $2,505,000; low: $80,000).
Purpose and activities: The foundation supports programs designed to assist victims of natural and manmade disasters around the world.
Fields of interest: Disasters, preparedness/services; American Red Cross; Human services.
Type of support: Emergency funds.
Geographic limitations: Giving on a national basis, with emphasis on Washington, DC and Tokyo, Japan.
Support limitations: No grants to individuals.
Application information: Applications not accepted. Contributes only to pre-selected organizations.
Officers and Directors:* Jeffrey J. Hurd*, Pres.; Tal S. Kaissar*, V.P.; Christina L. Pretto*, V.P.; Kathleen E. Shannon*, Secy.; Brian T. Schreiber*, Treas.
EIN: 743085338

AIG Foundation, Inc.

c/o Linda Sabo
180 Maiden Lane, 22nd Fl.
New York, NY 10038-4925

Establishment information: Established in 2005 in NY.
Donor: American International Group, Inc.
Financial data (yr. ended 12/31/11): Assets, $3,390 (M); gifts received, $3,257,249; expenditures, $3,257,249; qualifying distributions, $3,257,249; giving activities include $2,881,652 for 580 grants to individuals (high: $14,000; low: $95).
Purpose and activities: The foundation awards college scholarships to dependents of employees of American International Group, Inc.
Fields of interest: Higher education.
Type of support: Employee-related scholarships.
Geographic limitations: Giving on a national and international basis in areas of company operations.
Publications: Corporate giving report.
Application information: Applications not accepted. Contributes only through employee-related scholarships.
Officers: David Herzog, Chair.; Kathleen Shannon, V.P. and Secy.; Robert Gender, V.P. and Treas.
EIN: 203713472

157
American Manufacturing Corporation

(doing business as Wind River Holdings)
(also known as Wind River Holdings)
Croton Rd. Corp. Ctr.
555 Croton Rd., Ste. 200
King of Prussia, PA 19406-3171
(610) 962-3770

Company URL: http://www.windriverholdings.com/default.asp
Establishment information: Established in 1982.
Company type: Private company
Business activities: Operates holding company; manufactures power transmission equipment.
Business type (SIC): Machinery/general industry
Financial profile for 2010: Number of employees, 17
Corporate officers: Robert Strouse, C.O.O.; John F. Yaglenski, C.F.O.
Subsidiary: Philadelphia Gear Corp., King of Prussia, PA
Giving statement: Giving through the Ball Family Foundation.

The Ball Family Foundation

(formerly Russell C. Ball Foundation)
555 Croton Rd., Ste. 200
King of Prussia, PA 19406-3176

Donors: Philadelphia Gear Corp.; American Manufacturing Corp.; Lehigh Consumer Products Corp.; Goddard Systems, Inc.; Wind River Holdings, LP.
Financial data (yr. ended 12/31/11): Assets, $17,566 (M); gifts received, $705,000; expenditures, $693,360; qualifying distributions, $691,950; giving activities include $691,950 for grants.
Purpose and activities: The foundation supports hospitals and organizations involved with arts and culture and education.
Fields of interest: Arts education; Museums (art); Historic preservation/historical societies; Arts; Secondary school/education; Higher education; Education; Hospitals (general).
Type of support: Annual campaigns; Capital campaigns; General/operating support; Program development.
Geographic limitations: Giving limited to PA.
Application information: Applications not accepted. Contributes only to pre-selected organizations.
Officers and Directors:* Russell C. Ball III*, Pres. and Treas.; Andrew L. Ball*, V.P.; Robert H. Strouse, V.P.; Paul F. Brennan, Secy.
EIN: 516017780
Selected grants: The following grants are a representative sample of this grantmaker's funding activity:
$250,000 to Harvard University, Cambridge, MA, 2010.
$130,000 to Baldwin School, Bryn Mawr, PA, 2010.
$50,000 to Bryn Mawr Hospital, Bryn Mawr, PA, 2010.
$25,000 to Olana Partnership, Hudson, NY, 2010. For general fund.
$10,000 to Baldwin School, Bryn Mawr, PA, 2010.
$9,910 to Pennsylvania Academy of the Fine Arts, Philadelphia, PA, 2010.
$9,515 to Whitney Museum of American Art, New York, NY, 2010.
$7,600 to Baker Industries, Malvern, PA, 2010. For general fund.
$4,520 to Philadelphia Live Arts Festival and Philly Fringe, Philadelphia, PA, 2010.
$2,430 to American Cancer Society, Philadelphia, PA, 2010.

158
American Medical Systems Holdings, Inc.

10700 Bren Rd. W.
Minnetonka, MN 55343-9679
(952) 930-6000

Company URL: http://www.americanmedicalsystems.com
Establishment information: Established in 1972.
Company type: Subsidiary of a public company
Business activities: Operates medical technology company that provides solutions to physicians treating men's and women's pelvic health conditions.
Business type (SIC): Medical instruments and supplies
Financial profile for 2011: Number of employees, 1,255; assets, $1,053,430,000; sales volume, $542,320,000; pre-tax net income, $135,880,000; expenses, $387,580,000; liabilities, $384,870,000
Corporate officers: Anthony P. Bihl III, C.E.O.; Camille Farhat, Pres.
Giving statement: Giving through the American Medical Systems Holdings, Inc. Corporate Giving Program.
Company EIN: 411978822

American Medical Systems Holdings, Inc. Corporate Giving Program

c/o Charitable Grant Application
10700 Bren Rd. W.
Minnetonka, MN 55343-9679 (952) 930-6000
FAX: (952) 930-6373;
E-mail: GrantRequest@ammd.com; URL: http://www.amsgiving.org

Purpose and activities: American Medical Systems supports organizations and programs involved with improving healthcare delivery and access to high quality healthcare around the world. Special emphasis is directed toward programs that promote patient education and/or awareness related to male and female pelvic health conditions, symptoms, and treatment options; patient access and indigent care related to male and female pelvic health conditions; and global disaster relief. Support is given on an international basis, primarily in areas of company operations.
Fields of interest: Mental health/crisis services, formal/general education; Medical research, public education; Medical specialties research; Medical research; Disasters, preparedness/services; Patients' rights Economically disadvantaged.
Type of support: Conferences/seminars; Curriculum development; Donated products; Fellowships; General/operating support; In-kind gifts; Research.
Geographic limitations: Giving primarily in areas of company operations, and internationally.
Publications: Application guidelines.
Application information: Applications accepted. Organizations are limited to one application per year. Application form required. Applicants should submit the following:
1) name, address and phone number of organization
2) copy of IRS Determination Letter
3) brief history of organization and description of its mission
4) detailed description of project and amount of funding requested
5) contact person

Initial approach: Download application form and e-mail completed form (preferred) or mail to headquarters
Committee meeting date(s): Quarterly
Deadline(s): None

159
American Optical Corporation

14 Mechanic St.
Southbridge, MA 01550-2570
(508) 765-7085

Establishment information: Established in 1850.
Company type: Private company
Business activities: Manufactures ophthalmic lenses, frames and cases, sunglasses, safety products, and precision molded and coated plastics.
Business type (SIC): Ophthalmic goods; textile goods/miscellaneous; plastic products/miscellaneous; abrasive, asbestos, and nonmetallic mineral products; professional and commercial equipment—wholesale

Corporate officers: Maurice J. Cunniffe, Chair.; William D. Cotter, V.P. and Secy.; Steven J. Beckett, V.P. and Co-Treas.; Gary Bridgman, Co-Treas.
Board of directors: Maurice J. Cunniffe, Chair.; John W. Van Dyke
Giving statement: Giving through the American Optical Foundation.

American Optical Foundation
100 Mechanic St., Bldg. 80
Southbridge, MA 01550-2570 (508) 765-7085

Establishment information: Established in 1968.
Donors: American Optical Corp.; Jane Cunniffe; Maurice Cunniffe.
Financial data (yr. ended 12/31/11): Assets, $1,125,990 (M); expenditures, $89,490; qualifying distributions, $75,555; giving activities include $75,555 for grants.
Purpose and activities: The foundation supports museums, police agencies, fire departments, and service clubs and organizations involved with historical activities and education.
Fields of interest: Museums; Historical activities; Education; Crime/law enforcement, police agencies; Disasters, fire prevention/control; Community development, service clubs; United Ways and Federated Giving Programs.
Type of support: Employee matching gifts; Employee-related scholarships; General/operating support.
Geographic limitations: Giving primarily in MA.
Trustees: Gary Bridgman; Allen Skott; John Van Dyke; American Optical Corp.
EIN: 046028058

160
American Paper & Twine Company
7400 Cockrill Bend Blvd.
Nashville, TN 37209 (615) 350-9000

Company URL: http://www.aptcommerce.com
Establishment information: Established in 1926.
Company type: Private company
Business activities: Manufactures industrial paper and office, maintenance, and restaurant supplies.
Business type (SIC): Paper and paper products—wholesale
Corporate officers: Robert S. Doochin, Pres. and C.E.O.; William David Morris, Exec. V.P. and C.F.O.; Mark Wright, V.P., Sales; Van Tomlinson, Secy.
Giving statement: Giving through the American Paper & Twine Charitable Trust.

American Paper & Twine Charitable Trust
7400 Cockrill Bend Blvd.
Nashville, TN 37209-1047

Donor: American Paper & Twine Co.
Contact: Robert S. Doochin, Tr.
Financial data (yr. ended 12/31/11): Assets, $1,679 (M); gifts received, $44,000; expenditures, $44,200; qualifying distributions, $44,200; giving activities include $44,200 for grants.
Purpose and activities: The trust supports museums and organizations involved with orchestras, historic preservation, K-12 and higher education, and animal welfare.
Fields of interest: Arts; Education; Religion.
Type of support: General/operating support.
Geographic limitations: Giving primarily in Nashville, TN.
Support limitations: No grants to individuals.
Application information: Applications not accepted. Unsolicited requests for funds not accepted.
Trustees: Julie Doochin; Robert S. Doochin; William David Morris; Jason Ritchason; Karen Shaffer.
EIN: 626046717

161
American Power Conversion Corporation
132 Fairgrounds Rd.
West Kingston, RI 02892 (401) 789-5735

Company URL: http://www.apcc.com
Establishment information: Established in 1981.
Company type: Subsidiary of a foreign company
Business activities: Designs, develops, manufactures, and markets computer and electronic application power protection and management solutions.
Business type (SIC): Electrical industrial apparatus
Corporate officers: Laurent Vernerey, Pres. and C.E.O.; Karen Miranda, C.F.O.; Chris Hanley, Sr. V.P., Sales and Mktg; Kevin Roche, Sr. V.P., Human Resources
International operations: France; Germany; Italy; Netherlands; Poland; Russia; Singapore; Spain; Sweden
Giving statement: Giving through the American Power Conversion Corporation Contributions Program.

American Power Conversion Corporation Contributions Program
c/o Contribs. Comm.
132 Fairgrounds Rd.
West Kingston, RI 02892-1511
FAX: (401) 788-2739;
E-mail: CommunityImpACT@apc.com; URL: http://www.apcc.com/corporate/community/

Purpose and activities: American Power Conversion makes charitable contributions to nonprofit organizations involved with K-12 and higher education. Support is given primarily in areas of company operations.
Fields of interest: Elementary/secondary education; Higher education; Disasters, preparedness/services.
Type of support: Donated products; Employee matching gifts; Employee volunteer services; General/operating support; Scholarship funds; Sponsorships.
Geographic limitations: Giving primarily in areas of company operations in RI.
Application information: Applications not accepted. Contributes only to pre-selected organizations.

162
American Product Distributors Inc.
8350 Arrowbridge Blvd.
Charlotte, NC 28273-5755 (704) 522-9411

Company URL: http://www.americanproduct.com/
Establishment information: Established in 1992.
Company type: Private company
Business activities: Sells and distributes office supplies.
Business type (SIC): Paper and paper products—wholesale
Corporate officers: C. Ray Kennedy, C.E.O.; Cy Kennedy, Pres.; Eva Dinion, Sr. V.P., Opers.; Ronard F. Dixon, Cont.
Board of director: Michael Jones
Giving statement: Giving through the C. Ray & Cynthia M. Kennedy Foundation, Inc.

C. Ray & Cynthia M. Kennedy Foundation, Inc.
8350 Arrowridge Blvd.
Charlotte, NC 28273-5755 (704) 549-4029

Establishment information: Established in NC.
Donor: American Product Distributors, Inc.
Contact: C. Ray Kennedy, Dr.
Financial data (yr. ended 12/31/10): Assets, $17,753 (M); gifts received, $234,594; expenditures, $222,601; qualifying distributions, $221,303; giving activities include $12,555 for 6 grants to individuals (high: $8,743; low: $100).
Purpose and activities: The foundation supports organizations involved with legal aid, housing, sports, youth development, and human services.
Type of support: General/operating support; Sponsorships.
Geographic limitations: Giving primarily in NC.
Application information: Applications accepted. Application form required.
Attach a Copy of Contact Information and Purpose of Organization.
Initial approach: Proposal
Deadline(s): None
Directors: C. Ray Kennedy; Cynthia M. Kennedy.
EIN: 020661874

163
American Retail Group, Inc.
1114 Ave. of the Americas, Ste. 2801
New York, NY 10036-7773 (212) 704-5300

Establishment information: Established in 1999.
Company type: Subsidiary of a foreign company
Business activities: Operates clothing stores.
Business type (SIC): Apparel and accessory stores
Corporate officers: Hans Brenninkmeyer, Chair. and Pres.; Soledad Bayazit, C.E.O. and C.F.O.
Board of directors: Hans Brenninkmeyer, Chair.; Soledad Bayazit
Giving statement: Giving through the Christina Foundation.

The Christina Foundation
277 Park Ave., 29th Fl.
New York, NY 10172-0003 (212) 704-2306

Establishment information: Established in 1968.
Donors: American Retail Group, Inc.; American Retail Properties, Inc.; Argidius Foundation; Stiftung Auxilium.
Contact: Carlos De La Rosa, Treas.
Financial data (yr. ended 12/31/11): Assets, $264 (M); expenditures, $399; qualifying distributions, $0.
Purpose and activities: The foundation supports organizations involved with Christianity.
Application information: Applications accepted. Application form not required.
Initial approach: Proposal
Deadline(s): None
Officers: David Verzeis, Pres. and V.P.; Maria Regina Garvey, Secy.; Carlos De La Rosa, Treas.
EIN: 136277184

164
American Schlafhorst Company

8801 South Blvd.
Charlotte, NC 28273-6931 (704) 643-8049

Company type: Private company
Business activities: Manufactures textile machinery and equipment.
Business type (SIC): Industrial machinery and equipment—wholesale
Giving statement: Giving through the American Schlafhorst Foundation, Inc.

American Schlafhorst Foundation, Inc.

P.O. Box 240828
Charlotte, NC 28224-0828 (704) 554-0800

Establishment information: Established in 1987 in NC.
Donor: American Schlafhorst Co.
Contact: Dan W. Loftis, Exec. Dir.
Financial data (yr. ended 12/31/11): Assets, $1,696,239 (M); expenditures, $172,558; qualifying distributions, $90,000; giving activities include $90,000 for 9 grants (high: $10,000; low: $10,000).
Purpose and activities: The foundation supports museums, botanical gardens, and hospitals and organizations involved with higher education, employment, housing, and youth services.
Fields of interest: Museums; Higher education; Higher education, college (community/junior); Botanical gardens; Hospitals (general); Employment; Housing/shelter; Youth, services.
Type of support: General/operating support; Scholarship funds.
Geographic limitations: Giving primarily in Charlotte, NC.
Support limitations: No grants to individuals.
Application information: Applications accepted. Application form not required.
Initial approach: Proposal
Deadline(s): None
Officers: Tracy E. Tindal, Pres.; Ernest Reigel, Secy.; Dan W. Loftis*, Exec. Dir.
Director: Charles B. Park III.
EIN: 561590110

165
American Snuff Company, LLC

(formerly Conwood Company)
813 Ridge Lake Blvd., Ste. 100
P.O. Box 217
Memphis, TN 38120-9470 (901) 761-2050

Company URL: http://www.americansnuff.com/
Establishment information: Established in 1900.
Company type: Subsidiary of a public company
Business activities: Manufactures smokeless tobacco products.
Business type (SIC): Tobacco products—chewing, smoking, and snuff
Corporate officers: Michael D. Flaherty, V.P. and C.F.O.; Kevan A. Ostrander, V.P. and C.I.O.
Subsidiaries: Scott Tobacco, Bowling Green, KY; Taylor Bros., Winston-Salem, NC
Giving statement: Giving through the American Snuff Charitable Trust.

American Snuff Charitable Trust

(formerly Conwood Charitable Trust)
c/o Trust Dept., Regions Bank
1100 Ridgeway Loop, Ste. 100
Memphis, TN 38120-4053
Additional address: c/o Ed Roberson, American Snuff Co., 813 Ridge Lake Blvd., Memphis, TN 38119, tel.: (901) 761-2050; URL: http://www.reynoldsamerican.com/community-support.cfm?plank=communitySupport5

Establishment information: Established in 1952 in TN.
Donors: American Snuff Co.; Conwood Co.
Financial data (yr. ended 12/31/11): Assets, $4,527,777 (M); expenditures, $525,726; qualifying distributions, $487,247; giving activities include $466,600 for 69 grants (high: $30,000; low: $1,000).
Purpose and activities: The trust supports food banks and organizations involved with education, health, housing development, human services, and religion.
Fields of interest: Higher education; Education; Health care, clinics/centers; Health care; Food banks; Housing/shelter, development; Children/youth, services; Family services; Residential/custodial care, hospices; Aging, centers/services; Developmentally disabled, centers & services; Human services; Christian agencies & churches; Religion.
Type of support: Building/renovation; Capital campaigns; General/operating support; Scholarship funds; Sponsorships.
Geographic limitations: Giving primarily in areas of company operations in Memphis, TN; limited giving in NC.
Support limitations: No grants to individuals.
Application information: Applications accepted. Application form not required. Applicants should submit the following:
1) detailed description of project and amount of funding requested
Initial approach: Proposal
Deadline(s): None
Officer and Trustees: Wally Philips, Chair.; Ed Roberson; Regions Bank.
EIN: 626036034
Selected grants: The following grants are a representative sample of this grantmaker's funding activity:
$28,000 to Rhodes College, Memphis, TN, 2010.
$15,000 to Mid-South Food Bank, Memphis, TN, 2010.
$15,000 to Shrine School, Memphis, TN, 2010.
$12,500 to Brinkley Heights Urban Academy, Memphis, TN, 2010.
$12,500 to Kings Daughters and Sons Home, Bartlett, TN, 2010.
$12,500 to Shelby Residential and Vocational Services, Memphis, TN, 2010.
$9,000 to Memphis Child Advocacy Center, Memphis, TN, 2010.
$5,000 to Memphis Athletic Ministries, Memphis, TN, 2010.
$3,500 to Boy Scouts of America, Memphis, TN, 2010.
$1,500 to Les Passees, Memphis, TN, 2010.

166
American State Bank

1401 Ave. Q
Lubbock, TX 79408-3819 (806) 767-7000

Company URL: http://www.asbonline.com
Establishment information: Established in 1948.
Company type: Subsidiary of a private company
Business activities: Operates commercial bank.
Business type (SIC): Banks/commercial
Corporate officers: Scott Collier, Chair. and Pres.; Michael F. Epps, C.F.O.
Board of directors: Scott Collier, Chair.; W.R. Collier; Michael F. Epps; Gary R. Galbraith; Don Hufstedler; Harold E. Humphries; Greg C. Jones; Mark Kirkpatrick; Clay Leaverton; Michael Marshall; Van May; Susie Moore; Don Pickering; R.H. Pickering; C. Richard Sivalls; Tony Whitehead; Harry Zimmerman
Giving statement: Giving through the American State Bank Endowed Scholarship Fund for Nursing (LCU) and the American State Bank Endowed Scholarship Fund for Nursing Charitable Trust.

American State Bank Endowed Scholarship Fund for Nursing (LCU)

1401 Ave. Q
Lubbock, TX 79401 (806) 720-7676

Establishment information: Established in 1993 in TX.
Donor: American State Bank.
Financial data (yr. ended 12/31/11): Assets, $18,649 (M); expenditures, $984; qualifying distributions, $500; giving activities include $500 for grants.
Purpose and activities: The fund awards college scholarships to juniors and seniors enrolled in the School of Nursing at Lubbock Christian University in Lubbock, Texas.
Type of support: Scholarships—to individuals.
Application information: Applications accepted. Contact Lubbock Christian University for Applications and Application Deadline. Application form required.
Requests should include transcripts and letters of reference.
Initial approach: Proposal
Deadline(s): None
Trustee: American State Bank.
EIN: 752474107

167
American Tower Corporation

116 Huntington Ave., 11th Fl.
Boston, MA 02116 (617) 375-7500
FAX: (617) 375-7575

Company URL: http://www.americantower.com
Establishment information: Established in 1995.
Company type: Public company
Company ticker symbol and exchange: AMT/NYSE
Business activities: Operates broadcast and wireless communications towers company.
Business type (SIC): Communications services/miscellaneous
Financial profile for 2012: Number of employees, 2,432; assets, $14,089,130,000; sales volume, $2,875,960,000; pre-tax net income, $701,290,000; expenses, $1,756,640,000; liabilities, $10,516,030,000
Fortune 1000 ranking: 2012—734th in revenues, 278th in profits, and 312th in assets

Forbes 2000 ranking: 2012—1629th in sales, 876th in profits, and 1223rd in assets
Corporate officers: James D. Taiclet, Jr., Chair., Pres., and C.E.O.; Tom Bartlett, Exec. V.P. and C.F.O.; Edmund DiSanto, Exec. V.P., C.A.O., and Genl. Counsel; Hal Hess, Exec. V.P., Opers.
Board of directors: James D. Taiclet, Jr., Chair.; Raymond P. Dolan; Ronald M. Dykes; Carolyn F. Katz; Gustavo Lara Cantu; JoAnn A. Reed; Pamela D.A. Reeve; David E. Sharbutt; Samme L. Thompson
Giving statement: Giving through the American Tower Corporation Contributions Program.
Company EIN: 650723837

American Tower Corporation Contributions Program

116 Huntington Ave., 11th Fl.
Boston, MA 02116 (617) 375-7500
URL: http://www.americantower.com/atcweb/AboutUs/SocialResponsibility.htm

Purpose and activities: American Tower makes charitable contributions to nonprofit organizations on a case by case basis. Support is given primarily in areas of company operations in Arizona, California, Colorado, Georgia, Illinois, Massachusetts, Nebraska, South Carolina, and Texas, and in Brazil, Chile, Colombia, Ghana, India, Mexico, Peru, South Africa and the United Kingdom.
Fields of interest: General charitable giving.
International interests: Brazil; Chile; Colombia; Ghana; India; Mexico; Peru; South Africa; United Kingdom.
Type of support: Employee volunteer services; General/operating support.
Geographic limitations: Giving primarily in areas of company operations in AZ, CA, CO, GA, IL, MA, NE, SC, and TX, and in Brazil, Chile, Colombia, Ghana, India, Mexico, Peru, South Africa and the United Kingdom.

168
American Trading and Production Corporation

10 E. Baltimore St., Ste. 1600
Baltimore, MD 21202-1630
(410) 347-7150

Company URL: http://www.atapco.com
Establishment information: Established in 1931.
Company type: Private company
Business activities: Develops real estate.
Business type (SIC): Real estate subdividers and developers
Corporate officer: Daniel B. Hirschhorn, Chair., Pres., and C.E.O.
Board of director: Daniel B. Hirschhorn, Chair.
Giving statement: Giving through the American Trading and Production Corporation Contributions Program.

American Trading and Production Corporation Contributions Program

10 E. Baltimore St., Ste. 1111
Baltimore, MD 21202-1630 (410) 347-7201
FAX: (410) 347-7210

Contact: Betsy F. Ringel, Exec. Dir.; Daniel B. Hirschhorn, C.E.O.
Financial data (yr. ended 12/31/08): Total giving, $355,137, including $340,142 for 80 grants (high: $66,142; low: $50) and $14,995 for 38 employee matching gifts.
Purpose and activities: American Trading and Production makes charitable contributions to nonprofit organizations involved with employment training, community development, and on a case by case basis. Support is given primarily in the greater Baltimore, Maryland, metropolitan area.
Fields of interest: Arts; Education; Employment, training.
Type of support: Employee matching gifts; General/operating support.
Geographic limitations: Giving primarily in the greater Baltimore, MD, metropolitan area.
Support limitations: No support for religious organizations. No grants to individuals.
Application information: Applications accepted. Proposals should be submitted using organization letterhead. The company has a staff that only handles contributions. Association of Baltimore Area Grantmakers Common Grant Application Form accepted. Application form not required. Applicants should submit the following:
1) detailed description of project and amount of funding requested
Initial approach: Proposal to headquarters
Copies of proposal: 1
Deadline(s): None
Final notification: 2 months
Administrators: Lara A. Hall, Prog. Off.; Betsy F. Ringel, Exec. Dir.
Number of staff: 2 part-time professional.

169
American United Life Insurance Company

(also known as OneAmerica Financial Partners, Inc.)
1 American Sq.
P.O. Box 6010
Indianapolis, IN 46206-0368
(317) 285-1877

Company URL: http://www.oneamerica.com
Establishment information: Established in 1936.
Company type: Subsidiary of a mutual company
Business activities: Sells life insurance, and retirement plan products and services.
Business type (SIC): Security and commodity services; insurance carriers
Corporate officers: Dayton H. Molendorp, Chair., Co-Pres. and C.E.O.; J. Scott Davison, Co-Pres.; Constance E. Lund, Sr. V.P., Corp. Finance and Treas.; Mark C. Roller, Sr. V.P., Human Resources; Emet C. Talley, V.P. and C.I.O.; Thomas M. Zurek, Genl. Counsel and Secy.
Board of director: Dayton H. Molendorp, Chair.
Giving statement: Giving through the OneAmerica Financial Partners Corporate Giving Program and the OneAmerica Foundation, Inc.

OneAmerica Foundation, Inc.

(formerly AUL Foundation, Inc.)
P.O. Box 368
Indianapolis, IN 46206-4257
FAX: (317) 285-1979

Establishment information: Established in 1985 in IN.
Donor: American United Life Insurance Co.
Contact: Jim Freeman
Financial data (yr. ended 12/31/11): Assets, $8,798,862 (M); expenditures, $623,101; qualifying distributions, $615,708; giving activities include $615,708 for grants.
Purpose and activities: The foundation supports museums and zoological societies and organizations involved with orchestras, education, human services, and leadership development.
Fields of interest: Museums; Performing arts, orchestras; Higher education; Education; Zoos/zoological societies; American Red Cross; Children, services; Human services; Leadership development.
Type of support: General/operating support.
Geographic limitations: Giving limited to the Indianapolis, IN, area.
Support limitations: No grants to individuals.
Application information: Applications accepted. Application form not required. Applicants should submit the following:
1) detailed description of project and amount of funding requested
2) copy of IRS Determination Letter
Initial approach: Letter of inquiry
Deadline(s): Sept. 30
Officers and Directors:* Dayton H. Molendorp*, Chair. and Pres.; James W. Freeman, V.P.; Kaye A. Palmer, Secy.; Daniel Schluge, Treas.; David W. Goodrich; William P. Johnson; James T. Morris.
EIN: 311146437
Selected grants: The following grants are a representative sample of this grantmaker's funding activity:
$125,000 to Marian University, Indianapolis, IN, 2010.
$63,000 to United Way of Central Indiana, Indianapolis, IN, 2010.
$63,000 to United Way of Central Indiana, Indianapolis, IN, 2010.
$63,000 to United Way of Central Indiana, Indianapolis, IN, 2010.
$63,000 to United Way of Central Indiana, Indianapolis, IN, 2010.
$25,000 to Indiana University Foundation, Indianapolis, IN, 2010.
$20,000 to Center for Leadership Development, Indianapolis, IN, 2010.
$17,829 to United Way of Central Indiana, Indianapolis, IN, 2010.
$12,500 to Gleaners Food Bank of Indiana, Indianapolis, IN, 2010.
$10,000 to Indianapolis Museum of Art, Indianapolis, IN, 2010.

170
American Woodmark Corporation

3102 Shawnee Dr.
Winchester, VA 22601-4208
(540) 665-9100
FAX: (540) 665-9176

Company URL: http://www.americanwoodmark.com
Establishment information: Established in 1980.
Company type: Public company
Company ticker symbol and exchange: AMWD/NASDAQ
Business activities: Manufactures and sells kitchen cabinets and vanities.
Business type (SIC): Wood millwork
Financial profile for 2012: Number of employees, 3,791; assets, $265,120,000; sales volume, $515,810,000; pre-tax net income, -$33,290,000; expenses, $549,260,000; liabilities, $135,100,000
Corporate officers: Kent B. Guichard, Chair., Pres., and C.E.O.; S. Cary Dunston, Exec. V.P., Opers.; Jonathan H. Wolk, Sr. V.P., C.F.O., and Corp. Secy.

Board of directors: Kent B. Guichard, Chair.; William F. Brandt, Jr.; Andrew B. Cogan; Martha M. Dally; James G. Davis, Jr.; Daniel T. Hendrix; Kent J. Hussey; Carol B. Moerdyk; Vance W. Tang
Giving statement: Giving through the American Woodmark Foundation, Inc.
Company EIN: 541138147

American Woodmark Foundation, Inc.

3102 Shawnee Dr.
Winchester, VA 22601-4282 (540) 665-9129
E-mail: awfoundation@woodmark.com; URL: http://www.americanwoodmark.com/about.asp?iAreaID=1&iSectionID=7

Establishment information: Established in 1995 in VA.
Donor: American Woodmark Corp.
Contact: Brenda K. Dupont, Chair.
Financial data (yr. ended 04/30/12): Assets, $457,551 (M); gifts received, $200,000; expenditures, $261,619; qualifying distributions, $261,064; giving activities include $260,634 for 150 grants (high: $27,500; low: $234).
Purpose and activities: The foundation supports organizations involved with education, domestic violence, housing, and public safety. Support is limited to areas of company operations.
Fields of interest: Education; Crime/violence prevention, domestic violence; Housing/shelter; Disasters, preparedness/services.
Type of support: Annual campaigns; Building/renovation; Capital campaigns; Continuing support; Curriculum development; Equipment; General/operating support.
Geographic limitations: Giving limited to areas of company operations in Kingman, AZ, Jackson and Toccoa, GA, Grant County, IN, Monticello and Hazard, KY, Cumberland, MD, Tahlequah, OK, Humboldt, TN, Winchester-Frederick County, Clarke County and Orange, VA, and Moorefield, WV.
Support limitations: No support for private foundations, political organizations, or religious organizations not of direct benefit to the entire community. No grants to individuals.
Application information: Applications accepted. Application form not required. Applicants should submit the following:
1) signature and title of chief executive officer
2) copy of IRS Determination Letter
3) detailed description of project and amount of funding requested
4) contact person

Initial approach: Letter of inquiry signed by official with organization applying
Copies of proposal: 1
Board meeting date(s): Jan., Apr., July, and Oct.
Deadline(s): None
Final notification: Within 3 months

Officers and Directors:* Brenda K. Dupont*, Chair.; Wendy W. Armel, Secy.; Douglas Boucher*, Treas.
EIN: 541759773
Selected grants: The following grants are a representative sample of this grantmaker's funding activity:
$11,000 to Free Medical Clinic of the Northern Shenandoah Valley, Winchester, VA, 2011.
$6,500 to Barns of Rose Hill, Berryville, VA, 2011.
$5,000 to Barns of Rose Hill, Berryville, VA, 2011.
$5,000 to Blue Ridge Area Food Bank, Winchester, VA, 2011.
$5,000 to Kingman Aid to Abused People, Kingman, AZ, 2011.
$2,500 to Saint Jude Childrens Research Hospital, Memphis, TN, 2011. For operating expenses.
$2,000 to Boy Scouts of America, Jackson, TN, 2011. For operating expenses.
$2,000 to Warm the Children, Higganum, CT, 2011. For operating expenses.
$1,500 to American Cancer Society, Somerset, KY, 2011. For operating expenses.
$1,000 to Lord Fairfax Community College Educational Foundation, Middletown, VA, 2011. For scholarships.

130
America's Incredible Pizza Company, LLC

1835 E. Republic Rd., Ste. 102
Springfield, MO 65804 (417) 886-7925

Company URL: http://www.incrediblepizza.com/
Establishment information: Established in 1999.
Company type: Private company
Business activities: Operates family entertainment centers.
Business type (SIC): Restaurants and drinking places
Corporate officers: Richard A. Barsness, Chair.; Larry Abbe, Pres. and C.E.O.; George R. Ward II, C.F.O.
Board of director: Richard A. Barsness, Chair.
Giving statement: Giving through the Incredible Pizza Charitable Foundation.

Incredible Pizza Charitable Foundation

2522 S. Campbell Ave.
Springfield, MO 65807

Establishment information: Established in 2007 in MO.
Donors: Incredible Pizza Franchise Group, LLC; Richard A. Barsness; Cheryl Barsness.
Financial data (yr. ended 12/31/11): Assets, $255 (M); gifts received, $30,550; expenditures, $30,717; qualifying distributions, $29,624; giving activities include $29,624 for 8 grants (high: $11,560; low: $230).
Fields of interest: Education; Health care; Human services.
Geographic limitations: Giving primarily in MO.
Application information: Applications not accepted. Unsolicited requests for funds not accepted.
Officer: Amber Mattingly, Fdn. Mgr.
Trustees: Cheryl Barsness; Richard A. Barsness.
EIN: 766226663

171
AMERIGROUP Corporation

4425 Corporation Ln.
Virginia Beach, VA 23462 (757) 490-6900

Company URL: http://www.amerigroupcorp.com
Establishment information: Established in 1994.
Company type: Public company
Parent company: WellPoint, Inc.
Company ticker symbol and exchange: AGP/NYSE
Business activities: Operates medical service plan. At press time, the company is in the process of merging with WellPoint, Inc.
Business type (SIC): Insurance/accident and health
Financial profile for 2011: Number of employees, 5,100; assets, $2,801,350,000; sales volume, $6,318,390,000; pre-tax net income, $309,850,000; expenses, $6,008,550,000; liabilities, $1,516,830,000
Corporate officers: James G. Carlson, Chair., Pres., and C.E.O.; Richard C. Zoretic, Exec. V.P. and C.O.O.; James W. Truess, Exec. V.P. and C.F.O.; Margaret M. Roomsburg, Sr. V.P. and C.A.O.; Timothy Skeen, Sr. V.P. and C.I.O.
Board of directors: James G. Carlson, Chair.; Thomas E. Capps; Jeffrey B. Child; Emerson U. Fullwood; Kay Coles James; William J. McBride; Hala Moddelmog; Adm. Joseph W. Prueher; Uwe E. Reinhardt, Ph.D.; Richard D. Shirk; John W. Snow
Giving statement: Giving through the AMERIGROUP Foundation.
Company EIN: 541739323

AMERIGROUP Foundation

P.O. Box 62509
Virginia Beach, VA 23466-2509 (757) 490-6900
FAX: (757) 222-2360;
E-mail: AmerigroupFoundation@amerigroup.com; URL: http://www.amerigroup.com/about-amerigroup/amerigroup-foundation

Donor: AMERIGROUP Corp.
Financial data (yr. ended 12/31/11): Assets, $4,780,113 (M); gifts received, $2,107,242; expenditures, $2,092,093; qualifying distributions, $2,090,269; giving activities include $1,685,955 for 299 grants (high: $175,000; low: $115) and $172,091 for employee matching gifts.
Purpose and activities: The foundation supports programs designed to foster access to healthcare; encourage safe and healthy children and families; and promote community improvement and healthy neighborhoods. Special emphasis is directed toward programs designed to serve the financially disadvantaged, seniors, and people with disabilities.
Fields of interest: Higher education; Health sciences school/education; Education; Health care, research; Reproductive health; Reproductive health, prenatal care; Public health; Health care, insurance; Health care; Genetic diseases and disorders; Kidney diseases; YM/YWCAs & YM/YWHAs; Children/youth, services; Children, services; Family services; Aging, centers/services; Developmentally disabled, centers & services; Independent living, disability; Community/economic development; United Ways and Federated Giving Programs Aging; Disabilities, people with; Economically disadvantaged.
Type of support: Building/renovation; Continuing support; Employee matching gifts; General/operating support; Program development; Research; Sponsorships.
Geographic limitations: Giving primarily in Washington, DC, FL, GA, KS, LA, MD, NJ, NV, NY, and TX, with emphasis on VA.
Support limitations: No support for private foundations, fraternal, social, athletic, labor, or veterans' organizations, political parties or candidates, for profit-entities including start-up businesses, or for organizations not of direct benefit to the entire community. No grants to individuals, or for tickets, tables, benefits, raffles, souvenir programs, fundraising dinners, golf outings, trips, tours, or similar events.
Publications: Application guidelines.
Application information: Applications accepted. Application form required. Applicants should submit the following:
1) name, address and phone number of organization
2) how project's results will be evaluated or measured
3) detailed description of project and amount of funding requested
4) contact person
5) population served
6) plans for acknowledgement

Initial approach: Complete online application

Deadline(s): Feb. 15, May 17, and Aug. 16
Final notification: Mar. 29, June 28, and Sept. 27
Officers and Directors:* John E. Littel*, Chair. and Pres.; Nicholas J. Pace, V.P. and Secy.; Scott W. Anglin, V.P. and Treas.; James G. Carlson*, V.P.; Richard C. Zoretic*, V.P.
EIN: 542014061
Selected grants: The following grants are a representative sample of this grantmaker's funding activity:
$50,000 to Saint Marys Home for Disabled Children, Norfolk, VA, 2010. For general use.
$25,000 to American Association of People with Disabilities, Washington, DC, 2010. For general use.
$25,000 to League for People with Disabilities, Baltimore, MD, 2010. For general use.
$25,000 to Morningside College, Sioux City, IA, 2010. For general use.
$15,000 to Virginia Gentlemen Foundation, Virginia Beach, VA, 2010. For general use.
$10,000 to Business Consortium for Arts Support, Norfolk, VA, 2010. For general use.
$10,000 to Families of Autistic Children of Tidewater, Virginia Beach, VA, 2010. For general use.
$10,000 to FC Harlem, New York, NY, 2010. For general use.
$10,000 to FORKids, Norfolk, VA, 2010. For general use.
$5,000 to Food and Friends, Washington, DC, 2010. For general use.

172
AmeriPlan Corporation
5700 Democracy Dr.
Plano, TX 75024-7124 (469) 229-4500
FAX: (469) 229-4589

Company URL: http://www.ameriplanusa.com
Establishment information: Established in 1992.
Company type: Private company
Business activities: Provides supplemental health care benefit services.
Business type (SIC): Insurance/accident and health
Financial profile for 2009: Number of employees, 250
Corporate officers: Dennis Bloom, Chair. and C.E.O.; Daniel Bloom, Pres. and C.O.O.; Hattie McCutcheon, V.P., and C.I.O.; Mark Dixon, V.P., Comms.
Board of director: Dennis Bloom, Chair.
Giving statement: Giving through the AmeriPlan Foundation.

AmeriPlan Foundation
5700 Democracy Dr., Ste. 1000
Plano, TX 75024-7126

Establishment information: Established in 2001 in TX.
Donor: AmeriPlan Corp.
Financial data (yr. ended 12/31/11): Assets, $20 (M); gifts received, $4,174; expenditures, $4,233; qualifying distributions, $4,148; giving activities include $4,148 for grants.
Purpose and activities: The foundation supports the Sportmen's Legacy Foundation in McKinney, Texas.
Type of support: General/operating support; Grants to individuals; Scholarship funds.
Geographic limitations: Giving primarily in Dallas, TX.
Application information: Applications not accepted. Unsolicited requests for funds not accepted.
Officers: Dennis Bloom, Pres.; Daniel Bloom, Secy.
Director: Cecil Mathis.
EIN: 752793733

173
AmeriPride Services Inc.
10801 Wayzata Blvd.
Minnetonka, MN 55305-5510
(952) 738-4200

Company URL: http://www.ameripride.com
Establishment information: Established in 1889.
Company type: Private company
Business activities: Manufactures linen products; provides garment services.
Business type (SIC): Textile goods/miscellaneous; laundry, cleaning, and garment services
Corporate officers: Bill Evans, Pres. and C.E.O.; Maria Snyder, C.I.O.; Dan Lagermeier, Sr. V.P., and C.F.O.; Lance Westfall, V.P., Sales and Mktg.
Giving statement: Giving through the AmeriPride Services Inc. Corporate Giving Program.

AmeriPride Services Inc. Corporate Giving Program
10801 Wayzata Blvd.
Minnetonka, MN 55305 (952) 738-4200
FAX: (952) 738-4252; URL: http://www.ameripride.com/US_Info/AboutAmeriPride/CommitmenttoCommunity.jsp?bmUID=1237990444223

Purpose and activities: AmeriPride makes charitable contributions to nonprofit organizations on a case-by-case basis. Support is given in areas of company operations.
Fields of interest: Education; Breast cancer; Multiple sclerosis; Recreation; Youth development; Children, services; Human services, gift distribution.
Type of support: Cause-related marketing; Employee volunteer services; General/operating support.
Geographic limitations: Giving primarily in areas of company operations.

174
Ameriprise Financial, Inc.
(formerly American Express Financial Corporation)
55 Ameriprise Financial Ctr.
Minneapolis, MN 55474 (612) 671-3131
FAX: (302) 655-5049

Company URL: http://www.ameriprise.com
Establishment information: Established in 1894.
Company type: Public company
Company ticker symbol and exchange: AMP/NYSE
Business activities: Provides investment advisory services.
Business type (SIC): Security and commodity services
Financial profile for 2012: Number of employees, 12,235; assets, $134,729,000,000; sales volume, $10,259,000,000; pre-tax net income, $1,238,000,000; expenses, $9,021,000,000; liabilities, $125,637,000,000
Fortune 1000 ranking: 2012—263rd in revenues, 194th in profits, and 44th in assets
Forbes 2000 ranking: 2012—909th in sales, 616th in profits, and 188th in assets
Corporate officers: James M. Cracchiolo, Chair. and C.E.O.; Walter S. Berman, Exec. V.P. and C.F.O.; Randy Kupper, Exec. V.P. and C.I.O.; John C. Junek, Exec. V.P. and Genl. Counsel; Deirdre N. Davey, Exec. V.P., Corp. Comms.; Kelli A. Hunter, Exec. V.P., Human Resources
Board of directors: James M. Cracchiolo, Chair.; Lon R. Greenberg; Warren D. Knowlton; W. Walker Lewis; Siri S. Marshall; Jeffrey Noddle; H. Jay Sarles; Robert F. Sharpe, Jr.; William H. Turner
International operations: India; Luxembourg
Giving statement: Giving through the Ameriprise Financial, Inc. Corporate Giving Program.
Company EIN: 133180631

Ameriprise Financial, Inc. Corporate Giving Program
(formerly American Express Financial Corporation Contributions Program)
c/o Community Rels.
1099 Ameriprise Financial Ctr.
Minneapolis, MN 55474-0010
E-mail: community.relations@ampf.com;
URL: http://www.ameriprise.com/about-ameriprise-financial/company-information/ameriprise-community-relations.asp

Purpose and activities: Ameriprise makes charitable contributions to nonprofit organizations with which its employees are involved. Special emphasis is directed towards programs designed to meet basic human needs and support community vitality. Support is limited to areas of company operations in Phoenix, Arizona, Boston, Massachusetts, Minneapolis, Minnesota, Las Vegas, Nevada, and DePere, Wisconsin,.
Fields of interest: Arts; Environment; Employment; Food services; Housing/shelter; Disasters, preparedness/services; Human services, financial counseling; Community/economic development; Public affairs.
Programs:
Ameriprise Financial Advisor Gift Matching Program: Ameriprise awards $2,000 grants to nonprofit organizations with which its advisors volunteer at least 50 hours per year.
Ameriprise Financial Employee Gift Matching Program: Ameriprise matches contributions made by its employees to nonprofit organizations up to $2,000 per employee, per year.
Employee- and Advisor-Driven Causes: Ameriprise makes charitable contributions to nonprofit organizations with which its employees and advisors volunteer.
Type of support: Employee matching gifts; Employee volunteer services; General/operating support; Program development; Sponsorships.
Geographic limitations: Giving limited to areas of company operations in Phoenix, AZ, Boston, MA, Twin Cities, MN, Las Vegas, NV, and DePere, WI.
Support limitations: No support for discriminatory organizations, political or religious organizations, hospitals or clinics, or fraternal, social, labor, trade, athletics, veterans, or other membership organizations. No grants to individuals, or for capital campaigns, endowments, medical programs, advertising or marketing initiatives, benefits or charitable dinners, fundraising events, galas, performance sponsorships, sporting tournaments and events (i.e., golf, tennis tournaments) or advertising or tickets to these events, research, travel, programs solely focused on youth mentoring, Individual Development Accounts (IDAs), sports-related activities, or multi-year support.
Publications: Application guidelines.
Application information: Applications accepted. The Community Relations Department handles giving.

Requests should not be made more than 6 weeks before deadlines. Application form required.
Applicants should submit the following:
1) population served
2) how project's results will be evaluated or measured
3) explanation of why grantmaker is considered an appropriate donor for project
4) what distinguishes project from others in its field
5) detailed description of project and amount of funding requested
Proposals should include a track record of successful programs and projects.
Initial approach: Complete online application form
Deadline(s): Feb. 1 and May 15
Final notification: By the end of Apr. and Aug.

175
AmerisourceBergen Corporation
1300 Morris Dr., Ste. 100
Chesterbrook, PA 19087-5559
(610) 727-7000
FAX: (610) 647-0141

Company URL: http://www.amerisourcebergen.com
Establishment information: Established in 2001 from the merger of AmeriSource Health Corp. with Bergen Brunswig Corp.
Company type: Public company
Company ticker symbol and exchange: ABC/NYSE
Business activities: Sells pharmaceutical products wholesale.
Business type (SIC): Drugs, proprietaries, and sundries—wholesale
Financial profile for 2012: Number of employees, 14,500; assets, $15,500,000,000; sales volume, $80,600,000,000; pre-tax net income, $1,163,130,000; expenses, $78,236,870,000; liabilities, $12,987,410,000
Fortune 1000 ranking: 2012—32nd in revenues, 261st in profits, and 293rd in assets
Forbes 2000 ranking: 2012—85th in sales, 775th in profits, and 1154th in assets
Corporate officers: Richard C. Gozon, Chair.; Steven H. Collis, Pres. and C.E.O.; John G. Chou, Exec. V.P. and Genl. Counsel; Tim G. Guttman, Sr. V.P. and C.F.O.; Dale Danilewitz, Sr. V.P. and C.I.O.; June Barry, Sr. V.P., Human Resources; J.F. Quinn, V.P. and Corp. Treas.; Lazarus Krikorian, V.P. and Corp. Cont.
Board of directors: Richard C. Gozon, Chair.; Steven H. Collis; Douglas R. Conant; Richard W. Gochnauer; Edward E. Hagenlocker; Jane E. Henney, M.D.; Kathleen W. Hyle; Michael J. Long; Henry W. McGee
Subsidiary: C.D. Smith Healthcare, Inc., St. Joseph, MO
Giving statement: Giving through the AmerisourceBergen Corporation Contributions Program.
Company EIN: 233079390

AmerisourceBergen Corporation Contributions Program
(formerly AmeriSource Health Corporation Contributions Program)
1300 Morris Dr.
Chesterbrook, PA 19087-5559 (610) 727-7000
URL: http://www.amerisourcebergen.com/abc/Charitable_Giving/index.jsp

Purpose and activities: AmerisourceBergen makes charitable contributions to nonprofit organizations involved with improving the mental, social, and physical well-being of the elderly. Support is given primarily in North Carolina, Pennsylvania, Texas, and in Canada.
Fields of interest: Public health; Health care; United Ways and Federated Giving Programs Aging.
International interests: Canada.
Type of support: Employee volunteer services; General/operating support.
Geographic limitations: Giving primarily in areas of company operations in NC, PA, and TX, and in Canada.
Application information: Applications not accepted. Unsolicited requests are currently not accepted.

176
Ameristar Casinos, Inc.
3773 Howard Hughes Pkwy., Ste. 490 S.
Las Vegas, NV 89169 (702) 567-7000
FAX: (702) 755-2737

Company URL: http://www.ameristar.com
Establishment information: Established in 1993.
Company type: Public company
Company ticker symbol and exchange: ASCA/NASDAQ
Business activities: Operates casino hotels.
Business type (SIC): Hotels and motels
Financial profile for 2012: Number of employees, 7,210; assets, $2,074,270,000; sales volume, $1,195,220,000; pre-tax net income, $104,300,000; expenses, $977,060,000; liabilities, $2,096,530,000
Corporate officers: Luther P. Cochrane, Chair.; Gordon R. Kanofsky, C.E.O.; Larry A. Hodges, Pres. and C.O.O.; Thomas M. Steinbauer, Sr. V.P., Finance, C.F.O., Secy., and Treas.; Peter C. Walsh, Sr. V.P., Genl. Counsel, and C.A.O.
Board of directors: Luther P. Cochrane, Chair.; Carl Brooks; Larry A. Hodges; Gordon R. Kanofsky; Leslie Nathanson Juris, Ph.D.; J. William Richardson; Thomas M. Steinbauer; Peter C. Walsh
Giving statement: Giving through the Foundations of East Chicago, Inc.
Company EIN: 880304799

The Foundations of East Chicago, Inc.
100 West Chicago Ave.
East Chicago, IN 46312-3260 (219) 392-4225
FAX: (219) 392-4245; Contact for RFPs: Rosie Pena, rpena@foundationsec.org; URL: http://www.foundationsec.org

Donor: Ameristar East Chicago.
Contact: Russel G. Taylor, Exec. Dir.
Financial data (yr. ended 12/31/11): Assets, $29,796,517 (M); gifts received, $21,859,294; expenditures, $5,214,534; qualifying distributions, $2,813,667; giving activities include $2,268,032 for 185 grants (high: $241,242; low: $125).
Purpose and activities: The foundation supports programs designed to promote education; public safety; youth development; family support; health; financial independence and community economic development; and awards college scholarships.
Fields of interest: Arts; Elementary/secondary education; Vocational education; Education, drop-out prevention; Education, reading; Education; Public health; Health care; Crime/violence prevention; Employment, services; Employment, training; Food services; Food banks; Safety/disasters; Youth development; Children/youth, services; Family services; Human services, financial counseling; Human services; Community development, neighborhood development; Community/economic development.
Programs:
Collaboration Grants: The foundation awards collaboration grants to nonprofit organizations that collaborate with at least two additional organizations to address education, public safety, youth development, health, family support, or financial independence and community development.
Continuing Education Scholarships: The foundation awards college scholarships of up to $1,000 to adults undertaking continuing education.
Financial Independence and Community Development: The foundation supports programs designed to assist East Chicagoans become financially independent through job training, job creation, and money management skills; and programs designed to improve East Chicago and its neighborhoods.
General Support Grants: The foundation awards general support grants to help nonprofit organizations cover expenditures associated with its general operation. Special emphasis is directed toward administration expenses, rent, office supplies, capital expenditures, and staff education and training.
High School Scholarships: The foundation annually awards 38 college scholarships to East Chicago Central High School students. Scholarships are renewable and range from $1,500 to $6,000.
Public Safety: The foundation supports programs designed to improve public safety. Special emphasis is directed toward enforcement and other preventive efforts on specific 'at risk' or 'offender' populations; building neighborhood networks so that residents can feel safer, enforce community norms, and reclaim public spaces; strengthening families through improved parental capacity and skills; building a continuum of care, including case management through early interventions with high risk families where young children are present, or will soon be present.
RFP: The foundation currently issued a Request for Proposals in areas of public relations and marketing; website and social media; nonprofit capacity building; and program measurement and reporting. Visit URL http://foundationsofeastchicago.org/04-29-2013-notice-of-requests-for-proposal-in-four-service-areas for RFP announcement. All responses are due in May.
Type of support: Building/renovation; Capital campaigns; General/operating support; Management development/capacity building; Scholarship funds; Scholarships—to individuals.
Geographic limitations: Giving limited to East Chicago, IN.
Publications: Application guidelines; Financial statement; Grants list; Newsletter (including application guidelines); Program policy statement.
Application information: Applications accepted. Additional information may be requested at a later date. An interview may be requested for scholarships. Organizations receiving support are asked to submit an interim report and a final report. Requests for scholarships should include transcripts, 3 letters of recommendation, and a 300-word essay.
Initial approach: Complete online application form; inquire in person for Continuing Education Scholarships; download application form and mail to foundation for High School Scholarships; e-mail proposals for RFPs
Copies of proposal: 1

Deadline(s): Oct. 4 for General Support Grants; Sept. for Collaboration Grants; Varies for High School Scholarships; May 17 for RFPs
Final notification: Mid-Nov. for General Support and Collaboration Grants
Officers and Directors:* Nadyne Kokot*, Pres.; George Weems*, V.P.; Peter Smith*, Secy.; James Rajchel*, Treas.; Russel G. Taylor, Exec. Dir.; Sylvia Morrisroe; Mario Palacios.
EIN: 208445003
Selected grants: The following grants are a representative sample of this grantmaker's funding activity:
$15,000 to Community Reinvestment Project of East Chicago, East Chicago, IN, 2010.
$15,000 to Community Reinvestment Project of East Chicago, East Chicago, IN, 2010. For general operations.
$10,050 to East Chicago Education Foundation, East Chicago, IN, 2010.
$10,000 to Greater First Baptist Church, East Chicago, IN, 2010.
$9,283 to East Chicago Education Foundation, East Chicago, IN, 2010.
$7,000 to East Chicago Public Library, East Chicago, IN, 2010.
$4,970 to East Chicago Education Foundation, East Chicago, IN, 2010.
$2,000 to East Chicago Education Foundation, East Chicago, IN, 2010.

177
Amerisure Mutual Insurance Company

(formerly Michigan Mutual Insurance Company)
26777 Halsted Rd., Ste. 200
Farmington Hills, MI 48331-3586
(248) 615-9000

Company URL: http://www.amerisure.com
Establishment information: Established in 1912.
Company type: Mutual company
Business activities: Sells property and casualty insurance.
Business type (SIC): Insurance/fire, marine, and casualty
Financial profile for 2010: Number of employees, 400; sales volume, $2,229,313,000
Corporate officers: James B. Nicholson, Chair.; Richard F. Russell, Pres. and C.E.O.; Thomas E. Hoeg, Exec. V.P. and C.O.O.; Matthew J. Simon, V.P., C.F.O., and Treas.; Gregory J. Crabb, V.P. and C.A.O.; Susan Gailey Vincent, V.P., Genl. Counsel, and Secy.; Angela M. McBride, V.P., Human Resources; Gerald K. Chiddick, V.P., Mktg.
Board of directors: James B. Nicholson, Chair.; Karen Batchelor; Robert K. Burgess; Dennis R. Herrick; Phillip E. Love; Richard F. Russell; Thomas A. Player, Esq.; Bettina M. Whyte; William P. Vititoe
Giving statement: Giving through the Amerisure Mutual Insurance Company Contributions Program and the Amerisure Charitable Foundation, Inc.

Amerisure Mutual Insurance Company Contributions Program

c/o Corp. Contribs.
26777 Halsted Rd.
Farmington Hills, MI 48331-3586 (800) 257-1900
URL: http://www.amerisure.com/Community_Service.asp

Purpose and activities: As a complement to its foundation, Amerisure also makes charitable contributions to organizations directly. Special emphasis is directed toward programs designed to promote children and youth development. Support is given primarily in areas of company operations in Arizona, Florida, Georgia, Illinois, Indiana, Minnesota, Missouri, North Carolina, Tennessee, and Texas, with emphasis on Michigan.
Fields of interest: Arts; Education, association; Education, reform; Education; Health care, patient services; Health care; Genetic diseases and disorders; Heart & circulatory diseases; Neuroscience; Breast cancer research; Athletics/sports, Special Olympics; Boys & girls clubs; Youth development, business; Salvation Army; Children/youth, services; Economics.
Type of support: Employee matching gifts; Employee volunteer services; General/operating support; Sponsorships.
Geographic limitations: Giving primarily in areas of company operations in AZ, FL, GA, IL, IN, MN, MO, NC, TN, and TX, with emphasis on MI; giving also to national organizations.
Application information:
Number of staff: 5 full-time professional.

Amerisure Charitable Foundation, Inc.

26777 Halsted Rd.
Farmington Hills, MI 48331-3577
URL: http://www.amerisure.com/Community_Service.asp

Establishment information: Established in 2005 in MI.
Donor: Amerisure Mutual Insurance Co.
Financial data (yr. ended 12/31/11): Assets, $1,484,279 (M); gifts received, $428,306; expenditures, $445,360; qualifying distributions, $437,500; giving activities include $437,500 for grants.
Purpose and activities: The foundation supports organizations involved with arts and culture, education, health, mental health, housing development, athletics, human services, the insurance industry, and economics.
Fields of interest: Arts; Higher education; Education; Health care, patient services; Health care; Mental health/crisis services; Housing/shelter, development; Athletics/sports, Special Olympics; Boys & girls clubs; Youth development, business; Children/youth, services; Residential/custodial care, hospices; Human services; Business/industry; United Ways and Federated Giving Programs; Economics.
Type of support: General/operating support; Program development.
Geographic limitations: Giving primarily in areas of company operations in MI.
Support limitations: No grants to individuals.
Application information: Applications not accepted. Contributes only to pre-selected organizations.
Officers and Directors:* Richard F. Russell*, C.E.O. and Pres.; Thomas E. Hoeg*, C.O.O. and Exec. V.P.; Matthew J. Simon*, Exec. V.P. and Treas.; Susan Gailey Vincent*, V.P., Secy., and Genl. Counsel; Derick W. Adams*, V.P.; Gregory J. Crabb*, V.P.; Michael M. Dieterle*, V.P.; Edward H. Wagner*, V.P.
EIN: 300289445
Selected grants: The following grants are a representative sample of this grantmaker's funding activity:
$15,000 to Michigan Colleges Foundation, Southfield, MI, 2010. For general support.
$12,500 to Detroit Institute of Arts, Detroit, MI, 2010. For general support.
$10,000 to Michigan Council on Economic Education, Novi, MI, 2010. For general support.
$10,000 to Shepherd Center Foundation, Atlanta, GA, 2010. For general support.
$7,000 to Illinois State University Foundation, Normal, IL, 2010. For general support.
$5,000 to Cornerstone Schools Association, Detroit, MI, 2010. For general support.
$5,000 to Detroit Symphony Orchestra, Detroit, MI, 2010. For general support.
$5,000 to Habitat for Humanity of Pinellas, Saint Petersburg, FL, 2010. For general support.
$5,000 to Starfish Initiative, Indianapolis, IN, 2010. For general support.

178
Ameritas Life Insurance Corp.

(formerly Bankers Life Insurance Company of Nebraska)
5900 O St.
P.O. Box 81889
Lincoln, NE 68501-1889 (402) 467-1122

Company URL: http://www.ameritas.com
Establishment information: Established in 1887.
Company type: Subsidiary of a mutual company
Business activities: Sells life insurance; provides investment advisory services; sells dental and vision insurance.
Business type (SIC): Insurance/life; security and commodity services; insurance/accident and health
Financial profile for 2011: Assets, $17,746,174; liabilities, $15,310,376
Corporate officer: JoAnn M. Martin, Chair., Pres., and C.E.O.
Board of directors: JoAnn M. Martin, Chair.; James P. Abel; James M. Anderson; Michael S. Cambron; James R. Krieger; Patricia A. McGuire; Tonn M. Ostergard; Edward J. Quinn, Jr.; Kim M. Robak; Paul C. Schorr IV; Wayne D. Silby; Robert M. Willis
Giving statement: Giving through the Ameritas Charitable Foundation.

Ameritas Charitable Foundation

(formerly BLN Charitable Foundation)
5900 O St.
Lincoln, NE 68510-2234

Establishment information: Established in 1985 in NE.
Donor: Ameritas Life Insurance Corp.
Contact: JoAnn M. Martin, Dir.; Sue Wilkinson, Secy.
Financial data (yr. ended 12/31/11): Assets, $9,289,023 (M); expenditures, $1,147,325; qualifying distributions, $1,143,440; giving activities include $1,143,440 for grants.
Purpose and activities: The foundation has primary interest in education programs, but will consider civic, cultural, and health and welfare requests.
Fields of interest: Museums (children's); Arts; Secondary school/education; Higher education; Education; Animal welfare; Hospitals (general); Health care; Crime/violence prevention, child abuse; Boy scouts; YM/YWCAs & YM/YWHAs; Children, services; Family services; Human services.
Type of support: Annual campaigns; Capital campaigns; Continuing support; Equipment; General/operating support; Program development; Scholarship funds; Sponsorships.
Geographic limitations: Giving primarily in Lincoln, NE.
Support limitations: No support for organizations that utilize a major portion of their budget for administration and solicitation. No grants to individuals.
Publications: Application guidelines.

Application information: Applications accepted. Additional information may be requested at a later date. Application form required. Applicants should submit the following:
1) name, address and phone number of organization
2) copy of IRS Determination Letter
3) brief history of organization and description of its mission
4) copy of most recent annual report/audited financial statement/990
5) listing of board of directors, trustees, officers and other key people and their affiliations
6) detailed description of project and amount of funding requested
7) copy of current year's organizational budget and/ or project budget

Initial approach: Proposal
Board meeting date(s): May and Dec.
Deadline(s): Apr. 1 and Nov. 1

Officers and Directors:* James P. Abel*, Pres.; Sue Wilkinson, Secy. and Cont.; William W. Lester*, Treas.; JoAnn M. Martin*.
Number of staff: None.
EIN: 363428705
Selected grants: The following grants are a representative sample of this grantmaker's funding activity:
$10,000 to Boy Scouts of America, Cornhusker Council, Walton, NE, 2011.
$10,000 to BryanLGH Medical Center Foundation, Lincoln, NE, 2011.
$10,000 to Humane Society of Capital, Lincoln, NE, 2011.
$10,000 to Leadership Lincoln, Lincoln, NE, 2011.
$10,000 to Lincoln-Lancaster County Child Advocacy Center, Lincoln, NE, 2011.
$10,000 to Madonna Foundation, Lincoln, NE, 2011.
$10,000 to Nebraska Community Foundation, Lincoln, NE, 2011.
$8,000 to Lincoln Childrens Museum, Lincoln, NE, 2011.
$5,000 to Omaha Botanical Center, Omaha, NE, 2011. For Japanese Garden Project.
$5,000 to Wayne State College Foundation, Wayne, NE, 2011.

179
Ameritec Corporation

760 Arrow Grand Cir.
Covina, CA 91722-2147 (626) 915-5441
FAX: (626) 915-7181

Company URL: http://www.ameritec.com
Establishment information: Established in 1980.
Company type: Private company
Business activities: Manufactures telephone and telegraph equipment.
Business type (SIC): Communications equipment
Corporate officers: William Speight, Pres.; Brett Isley, V.P., Sales
Giving statement: Giving through the Ameritec Foundation.

Ameritec Foundation

760 Arrow Grand Cir.
Covina, CA 91722-2147 (626) 915-5441
URL: http://www.ameritec.com/ameritecfoundation/

Establishment information: Established in 1987 in CA.
Donor: Ameritec Corp.
Contact: John Watson, Pres. and Dir.
Financial data (yr. ended 12/31/11): Assets, $1,392,472 (M); expenditures, $32,948; qualifying distributions, $32,948; giving activities include $30,000 for 3 grants (high: $10,000; low: $10,000).
Purpose and activities: The foundation supports organizations involved with education, human services, and economically disadvantaged people and awards grants to individuals conducting spinal cord injury medical research.
Fields of interest: Higher education; Education; Spine disorders research; YM/YWCAs & YM/YWHAs; Children/youth, services; Human services, gift distribution; Human services Economically disadvantaged.
Type of support: Emergency funds; Equipment; Matching/challenge support; Program development.
Geographic limitations: Giving primarily in the east Covina, CA area.
Support limitations: No support for religious or political organizations. No grants to individuals.
Application information: Applications accepted. Application form required. Applicants should submit the following:
1) detailed description of project and amount of funding requested

Initial approach: Proposal
Deadline(s): None

Officers and Directors:* John Watson, Pres.; Tom Hollfelder, C.F.O.; Michael P. Newman*, Secy.; Miguel Garcia; Van Windham.
Number of staff: None.
EIN: 954147156

180
AmeriVision Communications, Inc.

(doing business as Affinity4)
999 Waterside Dr., Ste. 1910
Norfolk, VA 23510 (800) 684-4880

Company URL: http://www.affinity4.com
Establishment information: Established in 1991.
Company type: Private company
Business activities: Provides cellular telephone communications services; provides long distance telephone communications services; provides Internet access services.
Business type (SIC): Telephone communications
Corporate officers: Stephen D. Halliday, Chair., Pres., and C.E.O.; David Bingham, C.O.O.; Loni Lyle Woodley, V.P. and C.F.O. Treas.
Board of director: Stephen D. Halliday, Chair.
Giving statement: Giving through the Affinity4 Give Back Program.

Affinity4 Give Back Program

(formerly LifeLine Communications Give Back Program)
c/o Give Back Prog.
999 Waterside Dr., Ste. 1910
Norfolk, VA 23510-3319 (866) 591-0702
URL: http://www.affinity4.com/giveBack/

Contact: Katie King
Purpose and activities: Through its cause-related marketing business plan, Affinity4 makes charitable contributions to churches and nonprofit organizations that support families and children, constitutional and religious freedoms, and traditional Christian values. Support is given on a national and international basis.
Fields of interest: Family services; United Ways and Federated Giving Programs; Christian agencies & churches.
Type of support: Cause-related marketing.
Geographic limitations: Giving on a national and international basis.
Application information: Applications accepted. Applicants should submit the following:
1) name, address and phone number of organization
2) contact person

Applications should indicate the organization's donor base.
Initial approach: Complete online application form

181
AMETEK, Inc.

1100 Cassatt Rd.
P.O. Box 1764
Berwyn, PA 19312 (610) 647-2121
FAX: (215) 323-9337

Company URL: http://www.ametek.com
Establishment information: Established in 1930.
Company type: Public company
Company ticker symbol and exchange: AME/NYSE
Business activities: Manufactures electronic instruments and electric motors.
Business type (SIC): Electrical industrial apparatus; electronic and other electrical equipment and components
Financial profile for 2012: Number of employees, 13,700; assets, $5,190,060,000; sales volume, $3,334,210,000; pre-tax net income, $662,480,000; expenses, $2,588,340,000; liabilities, $2,654,910,000
Fortune 1000 ranking: 2012—662nd in revenues, 355th in profits, and 582nd in assets
Forbes 2000 ranking: 2012—1586th in sales, 1055th in profits, and 1801st in assets
Corporate officers: Frank S. Hermance, Chair. and C.E.O.; David A. Zapico, Exec. V.P. and C.O.O.; Robert R. Mandos, Jr., Exec. V.P. and C.F.O.
Board of directors: Frank S. Hermance, Chair.; Anthony Conti; Charles D. Klein; Steven W. Kohlhagen; James R. Malone; Elizabeth R. Varet; Dennis K. Williams
Subsidiaries: AMETEK Motors Holding, Inc., Chambersburg, PA; EDAX Inc., Mahwah, NJ; Rotron Inc., Woodstock, NY
International operations: Bermuda; Canada; Denmark; England; Germany; Hong Kong; Italy; Japan; Mexico; Singapore; United Kingdom
Giving statement: Giving through the AMETEK, Inc. Corporate Giving Program and the AMETEK Foundation, Inc.
Company EIN: 141682544

AMETEK Foundation, Inc.

1100 Cassatt Rd.
Berwyn, PA 19312-1177

Establishment information: Incorporated in 1960 in NY.
Donor: AMETEK, Inc.
Contact: Kathryn E. Sena, Secy.-Treas.
Financial data (yr. ended 12/31/11): Assets, $4,050,559 (M); gifts received, $500,000; expenditures, $1,261,000; qualifying distributions, $1,241,780; giving activities include $1,241,780 for grants.
Purpose and activities: The foundation supports hospitals and organizations involved with arts and culture, education, the environment, cancer, diabetes, human services, international affairs, and community economic development.

Fields of interest: Museums; Arts; Elementary school/education; Higher education; Scholarships/ financial aid; Education; Environment, natural resources; Environment; Hospitals (general); Cancer; Diabetes; American Red Cross; Youth, services; Human services; International affairs; Business/industry; Community/economic development; United Ways and Federated Giving Programs.
Type of support: Annual campaigns; Building/ renovation; Endowments; Equipment; Exchange programs; General/operating support; Matching/ challenge support; Program development; Research; Scholarship funds; Technical assistance.
Geographic limitations: Giving primarily in areas of company operations, with emphasis on PA.
Support limitations: No support for organizations lacking significant employee interest or involvement. No grants to individuals; no loans.
Application information: Applications accepted. Application form not required.

Initial approach: Proposal
Copies of proposal: 1
Board meeting date(s): Apr. and Oct.
Deadline(s): None

Officers and Directors:* Frank S. Hermance*, Chair. and Pres.; Elizabeth R. Varet*, V.P.; Kathryn E. Sena, Secy.-Treas.; Dennis K. Williams.
EIN: 136095939
Selected grants: The following grants are a representative sample of this grantmaker's funding activity:
$2,000 to American Cancer Society, Atlanta, GA, 2010.

182
Amgen Inc.

1 Amgen Center Dr.
Thousand Oaks, CA 91320-1799
(805) 447-1000
FAX: (805) 447-1010

Company URL: http://www.amgen.com
Establishment information: Established in 1980.
Company type: Public company
Company ticker symbol and exchange: AMGN/ NASDAQ
International Securities Identification Number: US0311621009
Business activities: Discovers, develops, manufactures, and markets human therapeutics.
Business type (SIC): Drugs
Financial profile for 2012: Number of employees, 18,100; assets, $54,298,000,000; sales volume, $17,265,000,000; pre-tax net income, $5,009,000,000; expenses, $11,688,000,000; liabilities, $35,238,000,000
Fortune 1000 ranking: 2012—162nd in revenues, 43rd in profits, and 102nd in assets
Forbes 2000 ranking: 2012—541st in sales, 127th in profits, and 427th in assets
Corporate officers: Robert A. Bradway, Chair., Pres. and C.E.O.; Jonathan M. Peacock, Exec. V.P. and C.F.O.; Fabrizio Bonanni, Exec. V.P., Opers.; Diana McKenzie, Sr. V.P. and C.I.O.; David J. Scott, Sr. V.P., Genl. Counsel, and Secy.; Brian M. McNamee, Sr. V.P., Human Resources
Board of directors: Robert A. Bradway, Chair.; David Baltimore; Frank J. Biondi, Jr.; Vance D. Coffman; Francois De Carbonnel; Robert A. Eckert; Rebecca M. Henderson, Ph.D.; Frank C. Herringer; Tyler Jacks; Gilbert S. Omenn, M.D., Ph.D; Judith C. Pelham; J. Paul Reason; Leonard D. Schaeffer; Ronald D. Sugar
Subsidiary: Amgen Puerto Rico, Inc., Juncos, PR
Plants: Boulder, Longmont, CO
International operations: Bermuda
Historic mergers: Immunex Corporation (July 15, 2002)
Giving statement: Giving through the Amgen Inc. Corporate Giving Program and the Amgen Foundation, Inc.
Company EIN: 953540776

Amgen Inc. Corporate Giving Program

1 Amgen Ctr. Dr., M/S 27-3-A
Thousand Oaks, CA 91320-1799 (866) 442-6436
E-mail for Healthcare Donation requests: HCCDonations@amgen.com; for Independent Medical Education requests: HCCIME@amgen.com; URL: http://www.amgen.com/citizenship/ overview.html

Purpose and activities: As a complement to its foundation, Amgen Inc. also makes charitable contributions to nonprofit organizations directly.
Fields of interest: Medical school/education; Health care; Science Economically disadvantaged.
Type of support: Donated products; Equipment; General/operating support; In-kind gifts.
Publications: Application guidelines.
Application information: Applications accepted. Application form required.

Initial approach: Complete online applications for Independent Medical Education grants and equipment donations; letter of inquiry for Healthcare Donations;
Deadline(s): None
Final notification: 60 days

Amgen Foundation, Inc.

c/o Jewel Smith, Mgr.
1 Amgen Center Dr., M.S. 28-1-B
Thousand Oaks, CA 91320-1799 (805) 447-4056
FAX: (805) 376-1258;
E-mail: amgenfoundation@amgen.com; Additional e-mail for Eduardo Cetlin: ecetlin@amgen.com; additional e-mail for Jewel Smith: jewels@amgen.com; URL: http://www.amgen.com/ citizenship/foundation.html

Establishment information: Established in 1991 in CA.
Donor: Amgen Inc.
Contact: Eduardo Cetlin, Sr. Mgr., Corp. Contribs.
Financial data (yr. ended 12/31/11): Assets, $88,812,847 (M); gifts received, $13,935,001; expenditures, $20,075,829; qualifying distributions, $19,715,955; giving activities include $14,415,120 for 201 grants (high: $1,500,000; low: $5,000) and $4,150,603 for employee matching gifts.
Purpose and activities: The foundation supports programs designed to advance science education; improve quality of care and access for patients; and create sound communities where Amgen staff members live and work.
Fields of interest: Arts; Higher education; Teacher school/education; Education; Health care, reform; Health care, equal rights; Health care, information services; Health care, patient services; Health care; Food banks; Disasters, preparedness/services; Human services; Community/economic development; United Ways and Federated Giving Programs; Science, formal/general education; Mathematics; Engineering/technology; Science.
Programs:

Amgen Award for Science Teaching Excellence (AASTE): The foundation annually awards grants to K-12 educators who elevate the level of science literacy in the classroom. Recipients are selected based on creativity and effectiveness of teaching methods; the plan for the use of grant money to improve science education resources in their schools; and an innovative science lesson plan showcasing innovative methods in the classroom. The selected winners receive $5,000 and the winner's school receive a restricted grant of $5,000 for expansion or enhancement of a school science program, for science resources, or for the professional development of the school's science teachers. The program is limited to California, Colorado, Kentucky, Massachusetts, Rhode Island, Washington, Puerto Rico, and Canada.

Amgen Fellows: The foundation, in partnership with Teach For America, supports math and science graduates who wish to teach in low-income communities. The foundation sponsors recruitment, training and development for 50 fellows a year; a annual mathematics and science summit, and a $2,000 signing bonus for each fellow. The program is administered by Teach For America.

Amgen Scholars: The foundation, in partnership with select universities, invites undergraduates students interested in pursing a graduate degree and a career in science or engineering to engage in hands-on-research during the summer. The program includes seminars, workshops, networking events and a three-day symposium led by scientists from the industry and academia. The program is open to students in the U.S and in Europe and is administered by the host universities. Visit URL: http://www.amgenscholars.com/ for more information.

Amgen Staff Volunteer Program (ASVP): The foundation awards $500 grants to nonprofit organizations with which employees of Amgen volunteer at least 15 hours. Each hour of service after the initial 15 hours earns $25 per hour for that same organization, up to an annual maximum of $2,000 per full-time staff member and $1,000 per part-time staff member. The foundation also recognizes outstanding volunteer efforts of staff in the U.S. and Puerto Rico through the Amgen Excellence in Volunteering Awards. Honorees receive $5,000 to be donated to the nonprofit organization of their choice.

Community Life: The foundation supports programs designed to strengthen and enrich the community, thereby making it a more desirable place to live and work; and help make the richness of the arts, the excitement of the sciences, the promise of education, and the provision of essential health and social services more accessible to all members of the community.

Excellence in Volunteering Awards: The foundation honors Amgen employees who make a difference to local communities through volunteerism. The award includes a $5,000 donation to the nonprofit organization of the winner's choice.

Matching Gift Program: The foundation matches contributions made by employees of Amgen to nonprofit organizations on a one-for-one basis from $50 to $20,000 per employee, per year.

Patients | Choices | Empowerment Competition: The foundation, in partnership with Ashoka's Changemakers, sponsors a competition to promote patients' empowerment and improve health outcomes. The contest is open to current and past patients, healthcare practitioners and advocates, and anyone in the general public who has a patient empowerment solution to elevate patients' voices. Ideas are posted online at the Changemaker website where finalists are open to the public for online voting. Three winners receive a $10,000 grant and selected entries are invited to submit proposals to the foundation for future funding. Visit

URL: http://www.changemakers.com/empower-patient for more information.

Quality of Care and Access for Patients: The foundation supports programs designed to provide patients, caregivers, and healthcare practitioners with information, education, and access. Special emphasis is directed toward patient empowerment programs that enable patients to become active partners in their healthcare, make informed decisions, and contribute to a wider perspective in the healthcare system; and healthcare disparities/health inequalities programs designed to close gaps and address population-specific differences in the presence of disease, health outcomes, or access to healthcare.

Science Education: The foundation supports programs designed to raise the value of science literacy in the community; provide hands-on-science experiences for students; promote teacher quality; and provide professional development. Special emphasis is directed toward programs designed to enhance the quality of math and science teachers entering the classroom; promote development opportunities that have a positive impact on student achievement; and provide students and teachers with hands-on inquiry-based learning experiences that impact students' excitement about science and scientific careers.

Type of support: Capital campaigns; Continuing support; Employee matching gifts; Employee volunteer services; Endowments; Equipment; General/operating support; Grants to individuals; Matching/challenge support; Program development; Program evaluation; Research.

Geographic limitations: Giving on a national and international basis in areas of company operations, with emphasis on Los Angeles, San Francisco, and Ventura, CA, CO, KY, Greater Boston, Middlesex, and Suffolk counties, MA, Juncos, PR, RI, King and South Snohomish counties, WA, and Europe; giving also to regional and national organizations.

Support limitations: No support for religious organizations not of direct benefit to the entire community, political organizations, labor unions or fraternal, service, or veterans' organizations, international organizations, private foundations, or discriminatory organizations. No grants to individuals (except for AASTE), or for fundraising or sports-related events, corporate sponsorships, or lobbying activities.

Publications: Annual report; Application guidelines; Grants list; Program policy statement.

Application information: Applications accepted. A full proposal may be requested at a later date. Support is limited to 1 contribution per organization during any given year. Application form required. Applicants should submit the following:

1) role played by volunteers
2) timetable for implementation and evaluation of project
3) how project will be sustained once grantmaker support is completed
4) results expected from proposed grant
5) qualifications of key personnel
6) statement of problem project will address
7) population served
8) name, address and phone number of organization
9) copy of IRS Determination Letter
10) brief history of organization and description of its mission
11) geographic area to be served
12) copy of most recent annual report/audited financial statement/990
13) how project's results will be evaluated or measured
14) explanation of why grantmaker is considered an appropriate donor for project
15) listing of board of directors, trustees, officers and other key people and their affiliations
16) detailed description of project and amount of funding requested
17) contact person
18) copy of current year's organizational budget and/or project budget
19) listing of additional sources and amount of support

Initial approach: Complete online letter of inquiry; complete online application for AASTE
Board meeting date(s): Quarterly
Deadline(s): None; Feb. for AASTE
Final notification: June for AASTE

Officers and Directors:* Jean Lim Terra, Pres.; Richard T. Benson, Secy.; Laurie Stelzer, Treas.; Stephen Canepa, C.F.O.; David Beier; Fabrizio Bonanni; Laura Hamill; Brian M. McNamee; Joseph P. Miletich; Jonathan M. Peacock; David J. Scott.

EIN: 770252898

Selected grants: The following grants are a representative sample of this grantmaker's funding activity:

$500,000 to Massachusetts General Hospital, Schwartz Center for Compassionate Healthcare, Boston, MA, 2011. For Schwartz Center Rounds brings together clinical caregivers to discuss social and emotional challenges of patient care. National Consensus Project ensures that compassionate care becomes a top priority in healthcare.
$480,000 to European Schoolnet, Brussels, Belgium, 2011. For European Amgen Teacher Programme.
$373,707 to European Schoolnet, Brussels, Belgium, 2012. For European Amgen Teacher Programme.
$356,200 to Cancer Support Community, Washington, DC, 2011. For Open To Options: Dissemination of Treatment Decision Support for People with Cancer.
$337,805 to University of Puerto Rico, Mayaguez, PR, 2011. For Amgen Biotechnology Training and Learning Enhancement for Students (Amgen BioTalents).
$300,000 to FOOD Share, Oxnard, CA, 2011. To support Ventura County's regional food bank.
$300,000 to Health Leads Boston, Boston, MA, 2012. For Advancing Health Leads Through Operational Excellence, Evaluation Preparation, and Alumni Engagement.
$250,000 to United Network for Organ Sharing, Richmond, VA, 2012. For Automation of the Kidney Paired Donation Program of the Organ Procurement and Transplantation Network/United Network for Organ Sharing.
$229,878 to Education Development Center, Waltham, MA, 2012. For Curriculum Update for the Amgen-Bruce Wallace Biotechnology Lab Program.
$119,062 to University of California, Berkeley, CA, 2012. For San Francisco Bay Area Site: Amgen-Bruce Wallace Biotechnology Laboratory Program.
$75,000 to Alianza para un Puerto Rico Sin Drogas, San Juan, PR, 2011. For Prevention Stage: a community based program for high-risk youth.
$54,000 to Youth Connection of Ventura County, Casa Pacifica Centers for Children and Families, Camarillo, CA, 2012. For Programs for Abused, Neglected, and At-Risk Children.
$50,000 to Home and Hospice Care of Rhode Island, Providence, RI, 2012. To Continue to Expand and Develop Palliative Care Education, Collaboration and Outreach Program Year Two.
$40,000 to College Crusade of Rhode Island, Providence, RI, 2011. For RI GEAR UP: Proven College Access Programming and Services for Disadvantaged Youth.
$30,000 to Biotech Partners, Berkeley, CA, 2011. For Biotech Partners' High School Biotech Academies and Community College Bioscience Career Institute.
$30,000 to Free Clinic of Simi Valley, Simi Valley, CA, 2011. To provide services to meet the growing health care needs of the economically disadvantaged members of Simi Valley.
$25,000 to National Math and Science Initiative, Dallas, TX, 2012. For Military Families Program Expansion.
$25,000 to Rhode Island Free Clinic, Providence, RI, 2012. For Healthy Lifestyles for Today and Tomorrow.
$20,000 to Meals on Wheels of San Francisco, San Francisco, CA, 2011. For Home Delivered Meals Program for San Francisco Seniors.
$20,000 to Senior Resource Services, Greeley, CO, 2012. For assisting the elderly population to remain independent at home as long as possible.

183
Amica Mutual Insurance Company

100 Amica Way
Lincoln, RI 02865 (800) 652-6422

Company URL: http://www.amica.com
Establishment information: Established in 1907.
Company type: Mutual company
Business activities: Sells insurance.
Business type (SIC): Insurance carriers
Financial profile for 2011: Number of employees, 3,012; assets, $4,126,651,274; sales volume, $1,492,306,568; expenses, $1,563,306,647; liabilities, $1,866,231,994
Fortune 1000 ranking: 2012—977th in revenues, 780th in profits, and 574th in assets
Corporate officers: Robert A. DiMuccio, Chair., Pres., and C.E.O.; James P. Loring, Sr. V.P., C.F.O., and Treas.; Robert K. Benson, Sr. V.P. and C.I.O.; Suzanne E. Casey, Sr. V.P. and Secy.; Robert P. Suglia, Sr. V.P. and Genl. Counsel; Mary Q. Williamson, V.P. and Cont.
Board of directors: Jeffrey P. Aiken; Patricia W. Chadwick; Edward F. DeGraan; Andrew M. Erickson; Robert A. DiMuccio; Barry G. Hittner; Michael D. Jeans; Ronald K. Machtley; Richard A. Plotkin; Donald J. Reaves; Cheryl W. Snead; Thomas A. Taylor
Subsidiaries: Amica Life Insurance Company, Lincoln, RI; Amica Lloyd's of Texas, Inc., Sugar Land, TX; Amica Property and Casualty Insurance Company, Lincoln, RI
Giving statement: Giving through the Amica Companies Foundation.
Company EIN: 050348344

Amica Companies Foundation

100 Amica Way
Lincoln, RI 02865-1156
E-mail: amicacofoundations@amica.com; URL: http://www.amica.com/about_us/in_your_community/events.html

Establishment information: Established in 1997 in RI.
Donor: Amica Mutual Insurance Co.
Contact: Paul S. Bruno, Cash Mgr.
Financial data (yr. ended 12/31/11): Assets, $21,275,208 (M); gifts received, $500,000; expenditures, $1,451,453; qualifying distributions, $1,438,771; giving activities include $642,477 for

152 grants and $796,294 for 878 employee matching gifts.
Purpose and activities: The foundation supports organizations involved with arts and culture, education, the environment, health, youth development, human services, and civic and community development.
Fields of interest: Humanities; Arts; Education; Environment; Health care; Youth development; Human services; Community/economic development; United Ways and Federated Giving Programs.
Programs:
Citizenship Grant Program: The foundation annually awards grants to qualified nonprofit organizations with which Amica employees are actively involved. Grants are awarded by committee to selected nonprofit organizations in the name of the employee submitting the application.
Matching Gift Program: The foundation matches contributions made by employees, pensioners, and directors of Amica to schools or other nonprofit organizations at a rate fluctuating from 1:1 to 1.5:1. The 2011 matching rate was 1.5:1, for a match limit of $19,800 per person.
Type of support: Annual campaigns; Building/renovation; Capital campaigns; Continuing support; Employee matching gifts; Employee volunteer services; Endowments; General/operating support; Matching/challenge support; Research; Scholarship funds.
Geographic limitations: Giving primarily in RI.
Support limitations: No support for political, lobbying, or religious organizations, or discriminatory organizations. No grants to individuals.
Publications: Application guidelines; Financial statement.
Application information: Applications accepted. Application form not required. Applicants should submit the following:
1) copy of IRS Determination Letter
2) brief history of organization and description of its mission
3) descriptive literature about organization
4) listing of board of directors, trustees, officers and other key people and their affiliations
5) detailed description of project and amount of funding requested

Initial approach: E-mail or mail proposal to foundation
Copies of proposal: 1
Board meeting date(s): Bimonthly
Deadline(s): None
Final notification: Up to 8 weeks

Officers and Directors:* Robert A. DiMuccio*, Pres.; Robert K. MacKenzie, Secy.; Robert P. Suglia, Genl. Counsel; James P. Loring, Treas.; Robert K. Benson, C.I.O.; Jeffrey P. Aiken; Patricia W. Chadwick; Edward F. DeGraan; Andrew M. Erickson; Barry G. Hittner; Michael D. Jeans; Ronald K. Machtley; Richard A. Plotkin; Donald J. Reaves; Cheryl W. Snead; Thomas A. Taylor.
Number of staff: None.
EIN: 050493445
Selected grants: The following grants are a representative sample of this grantmaker's funding activity:
$45,600 to Community Preparatory School, Providence, RI, 2011.
$20,325 to Bryant University, Smithfield, RI, 2011.
$15,075 to Downtown Chapel, Portland, OR, 2011.
$11,025 to McAuley Ministries, Providence, RI, 2011.
$10,000 to Dana-Farber Cancer Institute, Boston, MA, 2011.
$10,000 to Rhode Island for Community and Justice, Providence, RI, 2011.
$7,500 to Greenwich Music Festival Company, Greenwich, CT, 2011.
$6,349 to Providence Rescue Mission, Providence, RI, 2011.
$6,050 to Miriam Hospital, Providence, RI, 2011.
$2,500 to Meals on Wheels, Lexington, NC, 2011.

184
AMN Healthcare Services, Inc

12400 High Bluff Dr., Ste. 100
San Diego, CA 92130 (866) 871-8519
FAX: (800) 282-1211

Company URL: http://www.amnhealthcare.com/
Establishment information: Established in 1985.
Company type: Public company
Company ticker symbol and exchange: AHS/NYSE
Business activities: Provides temporary healthcare staffing.
Business type (SIC): Personnel supply services
Financial profile for 2012: Number of employees, 1,700; assets, $517,390,000; sales volume, $953,950,000; pre-tax net income, $27,320,000; expenses, $910,420,000; liabilities, $335,270,000
Corporate officers: Douglas D. Wheat, Chair.; Susan R. Salka, Pres. and C.E.O.; Denise L. Jackson, Sr. V.P., Genl. Counsel, and Secy.; Marcia R. Faller, Sr. V.P., Opers.; Wendy Newman, Sr. V.P., Mktg.; Julie Fletcher, Sr. V.P., Human Resources; Brain M. Scott, C.F.O., C.A.O., and Treas.
Board of directors: Douglas D. Wheat, Chair.; R. Jeffrey Harris; Michael M.E. Johns III, M.D.; Martha H. Marsh; Susan R. Salka; Mark G. Foletta; Andrew M. Stern; Paul E. Weaver
Giving statement: Giving through the AMN Healthcare Services, Inc. Corporate Giving Program.
Company EIN: 061500476

AMN Healthcare Services, Inc. Corporate Giving Program

c/o Community Rels.
12400 High Bluff Dr.
San Diego, CA 92130 (877) 282-0369
E-mail: steve.wehn@amnhealthcare.com;
URL: http://amnhealthcare.mediaroom.com/index.php?s=25713

Contact: Steve Wehn, V.P. of Govt. and Community Rels.
Purpose and activities: AMN Healthcare Services, Inc. makes charitable contributions to nonprofit organizations involved with health care, medical education, breast cancer, social services, and public health awareness. Support is given primarily in areas of company operations.
Fields of interest: Nursing school/education; Health care, formal/general education; Public health; Health care; Breast cancer; Medical research, fund raising/fund distribution; Human services; Biology/life sciences.
Type of support: Employee volunteer services; Scholarships—to individuals; Sponsorships.
Geographic limitations: Giving primarily in areas of company operations.

185
Amnews Corporation

(also known as New York Amsterdam News)
2340 8th Ave.
New York, NY 10027 (212) 932-7400

Company URL: http://www.amsterdamnews.org
Establishment information: Established in 1909.
Company type: Private company
Business activities: Publishes newspapers.
Business type (SIC): Newspaper publishing and/or printing
Corporate officer: Wilbert Tatum, Chair.
Board of director: Wilbert Tatum, Chair.
Giving statement: Giving through the Amsterdam News Educational Foundation, Inc.

Amsterdam News Educational Foundation, Inc.

2340 Frederick Douglass Blvd.
New York, NY 10027 (212) 674-8391
Application address: 41 2nd Ave., New York, NY 10003

Donors: Amnews Corp.; Moet Hennessy; CocaCola.
Contact: Elinor Tatum
Financial data (yr. ended 12/31/10): Assets, $761,554 (M); gifts received, $20,970; expenditures, $59,892; qualifying distributions, $59,275; giving activities include $33,435 for 8 grants (high: $10,185; low: $250).
Purpose and activities: The foundation supports organizations involved with education and journalism.
Fields of interest: Arts; Education; Human services.
Type of support: General/operating support.
Application information: Applications accepted. Application form required.
Initial approach: Letter
Deadline(s): None
Officers and Directors: Susan Tatum*, Pres.; Elinor Tatum*, V.P.; Frank Graziadei*, Secy.; Curtis Simmons; Phyllis Harrison Ross, M.D.
EIN: 133634817

186
AMPCO-Pittsburgh Corporation

600 Grant St., Ste. 4600
P. O. Box 358015
Pittsburgh, PA 15219-2700 (412) 456-4400
FAX: (412) 456-4404

Company URL: http://www.ampcopittsburgh.com/
Establishment information: Established in 1929.
Company type: Public company
Company ticker symbol and exchange: AP/NYSE
Business activities: Manufactures steel products and specialty metal products.
Business type (SIC): Machinery/metalworking; steel mill products; machinery/special industry; machinery/general industry; machinery/refrigeration and service industry
Financial profile for 2012: Number of employees, 1,178; assets, $533,180,000; sales volume, $292,900,000; pre-tax net income, $15,170,000; expenses, $276,610,000; liabilities, $341,090,000
Corporate officers: Robert A. Paul, Chair. and C.E.O.; Rose Hoover, Exec. V.P., C.A.O., and Corp. Secy.; Dee Ann Johnson, V.P., Cont., and Treas.
Board of directors: Robert A. Paul, Chair.; Robert J. Appel; Leonard M. Carroll; Paul A. Gould; William K.

Lieberman; Laurence E. Paul; Stephen E. Paul; Carl H. Pforzheimer III; Ernest G. Siddons
Subsidiaries: Aerofin Corp., Lynchburg, VA; Buffalo Forge Company, Buffalo, NY; Buffalo Pumps, Inc., North Tonawanda, NY; NewCastle Industries, Inc., New Castle, PA; Pittsburgh Forgings Company, Pittsburgh, PA; Union Electric Steel Corp., Carnegie, PA
Plant: Valparaiso, IN
International operations: Belgium; United Kingdom
Giving statement: Giving through the Fair Oaks Foundation, Inc.
Company EIN: 251117717

Fair Oaks Foundation, Inc.

(formerly AMPCO-Pittsburgh Foundation II, Inc.)
600 Grant St., Ste. 4600
Pittsburgh, PA 15219-2903 (412) 456-4418

Establishment information: Established in 1988 in PA.
Donors: Pittsburgh Forgings Foundation; AMPCO-Pittsburgh Foundation.
Contact: Rose Hoover, V.P.
Financial data (yr. ended 12/31/11): Assets, $5,240,793 (M); expenditures, $446,907; qualifying distributions, $439,500; giving activities include $439,500 for grants.
Purpose and activities: The foundation supports botanical gardens, zoos, food banks, and community centers and organizations involved with orchestras, higher education, animal welfare, and human services.
Fields of interest: Performing arts, orchestras; Higher education; Botanical gardens; Animal welfare; Zoos/zoological societies; Food banks; American Red Cross; Salvation Army; Women, centers/services; Human services; Community development, civic centers; United Ways and Federated Giving Programs; Jewish federated giving programs.
Type of support: Program development.
Geographic limitations: Giving primarily in PA and VA.
Application information: Applications accepted. Application form not required.
Initial approach: Proposal
Deadline(s): Oct. 31
Officers and Trustees:* Robert A. Paul*, Chair.; Ernest G. Siddons*, Pres.; Rose Hoover*, V.P.
EIN: 251576560
Selected grants: The following grants are a representative sample of this grantmaker's funding activity:
$100,000 to Cornell University, Ithaca, NY, 2010.
$25,000 to University of Pittsburgh, Pittsburgh, PA, 2010.
$20,000 to United Way of Allegheny County, Pittsburgh, PA, 2010.
$10,000 to Pittsburgh Zoo and PPG Aquarium, Pittsburgh, PA, 2010.
$5,000 to Cooper-Siegel Community Library, Pittsburgh, PA, 2010.
$5,000 to Pittsburgh Promise Foundation, Pittsburgh, PA, 2010.
$2,500 to Light of Life Rescue Mission, Pittsburgh, PA, 2010.
$2,500 to Pittsburgh Trust for Cultural Resources, Pittsburgh, PA, 2010.
$2,000 to Pittsburgh Ballet Theater, Pittsburgh, PA, 2010.
$1,500 to Little Sisters of the Poor, Pittsburgh, PA, 2010.

187
AMR Corp.

4333 Amon Carter Blvd.
Fort Worth, TX 76155-2605 (817) 963-1234

Company URL: http://www.aa.com
Establishment information: Established in 1934.
Company type: Public company
Company ticker symbol and exchange: AAMRQ/Pink Sheets
Business activities: Operates holding company; provides air transportation services.
Business type (SIC): Transportation/scheduled air
Financial profile for 2012: Number of employees, 77,750; assets, $23,510,000,000; sales volume, $24,855,000,000; pre-tax net income, -$2,445,000,000; expenses, $26,956,000,000; liabilities, $31,497,000,000
Fortune 1000 ranking: 2012—121st in revenues, 993rd in profits, and 215th in assets
Forbes 2000 ranking: 2012—373rd in sales, 1956th in profits, and 887th in assets
Corporate officers: Thomas W. Horton, Chair., Pres., and C.E.O.; Isabella D. Goren, Sr. V.P. and C.F.O.; Gary F. Kennedy, Sr. V.P. and Genl. Counsel; Kenneth W. Wimberly, Corp. Secy.
Board of directors: Thomas W. Horton, Chair.; John W. Bachmann; Stephen M. Bennett; Armando M. Codina; Alberto Ibarguen; Ann McLaughlin Korologos; Michael A. Miles; Philip J. Purcell; Ray M. Robinson; Judith Rodin; Matthew K. Rose; Roger T. Staubach
Subsidiary: American Airlines, Inc., Fort Worth, TX
International operations: Bermuda
Giving statement: Giving through the AMR Corporation Contributions Program and the AMR/American Airlines Foundation.
Company EIN: 751825172

AMR/American Airlines Foundation

P.O. Box 619616, M.D. 5656
Dallas, TX 75261-9616

Establishment information: Established in 1985 in TX.
Donors: AMR Corp.; Flagship Charities; Chicago Charities.
Contact: Timothy J. Doke, Secy.
Financial data (yr. ended 12/31/11): Assets, $675,914 (M); gifts received, $405,275; expenditures, $396,235; qualifying distributions, $260,000.
Purpose and activities: The foundation supports organizations involved with health, pediatrics, human services, and children.
Fields of interest: Health care, clinics/centers; Health care, patient services; Health care; Pediatrics; Family services; Aging, centers/services Children; Economically disadvantaged.
Type of support: General/operating support.
Geographic limitations: Giving primarily in areas of company operations, with emphasis on CA and Fort Worth, TX; giving also to regional and national organizations.
Support limitations: No support for discriminatory organizations, religious, fraternal, social, or veterans' organizations, political or partisan organizations or candidates, or lobbying organizations. No grants to individuals, or for endowments, annual campaigns, basic academic or scientific research, athletic events or sponsorships, or social functions or advertising; generally, no multi-year grants.
Application information: Applications not accepted. Contributes only to pre-selected organizations.
Officers and Directors:* Thomas W. Horton*, Pres.; Andrew M. Backover*, V.P.; Kenneth W. Wimberly*, Secy.; Beverly K. Goulet, Treas.
EIN: 762086656
Selected grants: The following grants are a representative sample of this grantmaker's funding activity:
$62,000 to Pediatric and Family Medical Center, Los Angeles, CA, 2009.
$62,000 to Volunteer League of the San Fernando Valley, Van Nuys, CA, 2009.

188
Amsted Industries Incorporated

2 Prudential Plz.
180 N. Stetson St., Ste. 1800
Chicago, IL 60601 (312) 645-1700

Company URL: http://www.amsted.com
Establishment information: Established in 1902.
Company type: Private company
Business activities: Manufactures diversified industrial parts and equipment.
Business type (SIC): Steel mill products; iron and steel foundries; metal products/fabricated; engines and turbines; machinery/general industry; machinery/refrigeration and service industry; machinery/industrial and commercial
Corporate officers: W. Robert Reum, Chair., Pres., and C.E.O.; Thomas E. Bergmann, V.P., Finance and C.F.O.; Stephen R. Smith, V.P., Genl. Counsel, and Secy.; Glenn Chamberlin, V.P. and Treas.; Steven E. Obendorf, Cont.
Board of director: Robert W. Reum, Chair.
Subsidiaries: Amsted Rail, Chicago, IL; ASF-Keystone, Granite City, IL; Baltimore Aircoil Co., Jessup, MD; Brenco, Petersburg, VA; Burgess-Norton Mfg. Co., Geneva, IL; Consolidated Metco, Portland, OR; Diamond Chain Co., Indianapolis, IN; Griffin Pipe Products Co., Downers Grove, IL; Griffin Wheel Co., Chicago, IL; Means Industries, Saginaw, MI
International operations: Canada
Giving statement: Giving through the Amsted Industries Foundation.

Amsted Industries Foundation

2 Prudential Plz.
180 N. Stetson St., Ste. 1800
Chicago, IL 60601-6808 (312) 645-1700

Establishment information: Established in 1953 in IL.
Donor: Amsted Industries Inc.
Contact: Shirley Whitesell, Tr.
Financial data (yr. ended 09/30/11): Assets, $958 (M); expenditures, $380,764; qualifying distributions, $378,170; giving activities include $378,170 for grants.
Purpose and activities: The foundation supports organizations involved with arts and culture, education, health, and human services.
Fields of interest: Arts; Education; Health care; Health organizations, association; Human services; United Ways and Federated Giving Programs; Government/public administration.
Type of support: Building/renovation; Continuing support; Employee matching gifts; General/operating support.
Geographic limitations: Giving limited to areas of company operations, with some emphasis on Chicago, IL.
Support limitations: No support for religious organizations or veterans' organizations. No grants

to individuals, or for endowments, scholarships, fellowships, or advertising; no loans.
Application information: Applications not accepted.
Trustees: Matthew J. Hower; W. Robert Reum; Shirley J. Whitesell.
Number of staff: 1 part-time professional; 1 part-time support.
EIN: 366050609
Selected grants: The following grants are a representative sample of this grantmaker's funding activity:
$10,000 to United Way of Metropolitan Chicago, Chicago, IL, 2010.
$5,000 to Boy Scouts of America, Dallas, TX, 2010.
$5,000 to Chicago Horticultural Society, Glencoe, IL, 2010.
$5,000 to Colgate University, Hamilton, NY, 2010.
$5,000 to Hubbard Street Dance Chicago, Chicago, IL, 2010.
$5,000 to Morton Arboretum, Lisle, IL, 2010.
$3,000 to United Way of Saginaw County, Saginaw, MI, 2010.
$2,011 to Big Brothers Big Sisters of Central Iowa, Clive, IA, 2010.
$2,000 to Central Catholic High School, Portland, OR, 2010.
$1,000 to Museum of Science and Industry, Chicago, IL, 2010.

189
Amway Corporation

(formerly Quixtar)
7575 Fulton St. E.
Ada, MI 49355-0001 (616) 787-7550

Company URL: http://www.amway.com
Establishment information: Established in 1959.
Company type: Subsidiary of a private company
Business activities: Manufactures and produces vitamins and food supplements, skin care products and cosmetics, therapeutic magnets, and laundry products.
Business type (SIC): Drugs; soaps, cleaners, and toiletries; metal products/fabricated
Financial profile for 2011: Number of employees, 14,000; sales volume, $9,200,000,000
Corporate officers: Steve Van Andel, Chair.; Doug DeVos, Pres.; Al Koop, C.O.O.; Michael Cazer, Exec. V.P. and C.F.O.
Board of director: Steve Van Andel, Chair.
International operations: Argentina; Australia; Austria; Brazil; Canada; Chile; China; Colombia; Costa Rica; Czech Republic; France; Germany; Greece; Guatemala; Hungary; Indonesia; Italy; Japan; Malaysia; Mexico; Netherlands; New Zealand; Panama; Philippines; Poland; Portugal; Slovakia; Slovenia; South Africa; South Korea; Spain; Switzerland; Taiwan; Thailand; Turkey; United Kingdom; Uruguay
Giving statement: Giving through the Amway Corporation Contributions Program.

Amway Corporation Contributions Program

5101 Spaulding Plz. S.E.
Ada, MI 49355-0001
E-mail: contributions@amway.com; URL: http://www.amwayonebyone.com

Purpose and activities: Amway makes charitable contributions to nonprofit organizations involved with at-risk children. Support is given primarily in areas of company operations in Buena Park, California, Lakeview, California, Norcross, Georgia, Honolulu, Hawaii, Arlington, Texas, and Kent, Washington, with emphasis on the greater Grand Rapids, Michigan, area, and in Africa, Asia, Australia, Europe, and Latin America.
Fields of interest: Arts; Health care; Nutrition; Disasters, preparedness/services; Boys & girls clubs; Children, services; Developmentally disabled, centers & services Children.
International interests: Africa; Asia; Australia; Europe; Latin America.
Type of support: Employee volunteer services; General/operating support; In-kind gifts.
Geographic limitations: Giving primarily in areas of company operations in Buena Park and Lakeview, CA, Norcross, GA, Honolulu, HI, Arlington, TX, and Kent, WA, with emphasis on the greater Grand Rapids, MI, area, and in Africa, Asia, Australia, Europe, and Latin America.
Support limitations: No support for fraternal organizations or school athletic teams, bands, or choirs, political, legislative, or lobbying organizations. No grants to individuals, or for travel, scholarships, religious projects, sports or fundraising events, movie, film, or television documentaries, general awareness campaigns, marketing sponsorships, cause-related marketing, or advertising projects; no in-kind gifts for conferences or conventions, personal use, distribution at an expo, fair, or event, family reunions, or sports fundraising events.
Publications: Application guidelines.
Application information: Applications accepted. Videos, reports, publications, and other unsolicited materials are not encouraged. In-kind donation values do not exceed $250. Application form required.
Initial approach: Complete online application form
Deadline(s): None
Final notification: 2 months

190
Anadarko Petroleum Corporation

1201 Lake Robbins Dr.
The Woodlands, TX 77380-1046
(832) 636-1000
FAX: (302) 655-5049

Company URL: http://www.anadarko.com
Establishment information: Established in 1959.
Company type: Public company
Company ticker symbol and exchange: APC/NYSE
International Securities Identification Number: US0325111070
Business activities: Conducts crude oil, natural gas, and natural gas liquids exploration, production, and marketing activities.
Business type (SIC): Extraction/oil and gas
Financial profile for 2012: Number of employees, 5,200; assets, $52,589,000,000; sales volume, $13,411,000,000; pre-tax net income, $3,565,000,000; expenses, $9,684,000,000; liabilities, $31,960,000,000
Fortune 1000 ranking: 2012—207th in revenues, 84th in profits, and 106th in assets
Forbes 2000 ranking: 2012—720th in sales, 243rd in profits, and 438th in assets
Corporate officers: R.A. Walker, Chair., Pres., and C.E.O.; Robert G. Gwin, Sr. V.P., Finance. and C.F.O.; Robert K. Reeves, Sr. V.P., Genl. Counsel, and C.A.O.
Board of directors: R.A. Walker, Chair.; Kevin P. Chilton; Luke R. Corbett; H. Paulett Eberhart; Peter J. Fluor; Richard L. George; Preston M. Geren III; Charles W. Goodyear; John R. Gordon; Eric D. Mullins; Paula Rosput Reynolds
Subsidiaries: Kerr-McGee Corporation, Oklahoma City, OK; Western Gas Resources, Inc., Denver, CO
International operations: Bahamas; Netherlands
Historic mergers: Kerr-McGee Corporation (August 10, 2006)
Giving statement: Giving through the Anadarko Petroleum Corporation Contributions Program.
Company EIN: 760146568

Anadarko Petroleum Corporation Contributions Program

c/o Anadarko Community Affairs
P.O. Box 1330
Houston, TX 77251-1330 (800) 800-1101
URL: http://www.anadarko.com/Responsibility/Pages/CommunityInvolvement.aspx

Purpose and activities: Anadarko makes charitable contributions to nonprofit organizations involved with arts and culture, education, health, and human services. Support is limited to areas of company operations.
Fields of interest: Arts, cultural/ethnic awareness; Education; Health care; Food services, commodity distribution; Housing/shelter, volunteer services; Safety/disasters; Human services, financial counseling; Human services; United Ways and Federated Giving Programs; Engineering; Science.
Program:
Anadarko in Action: Anadarko awards grants to nonprofit organizations in which its employees volunteer.
Type of support: Employee matching gifts; Employee volunteer services; General/operating support; Scholarship funds.
Geographic limitations: Giving is limited to areas of company operations.
Support limitations: No support for sports organizations or individual United Way agencies. No grants to individuals, or for sporting events, or film or video projects.
Publications: Application guidelines.
Application information: Applications accepted. Application form not required. Applicants should submit the following:
1) statement of problem project will address
2) population served
3) copy of IRS Determination Letter
4) brief history of organization and description of its mission
5) detailed description of project and amount of funding requested
6) copy of current year's organizational budget and/or project budget
7) listing of additional sources and amount of support

Initial approach: Mail proposal to headquarters
Copies of proposal: 1

191
Anaheim Ducks Hockey Club, LLC

(also known as ADHC)
(formerly The Mighty Ducks of Anaheim)
2695 E. Katella Ave.
Anaheim, CA 92806-5904 (714) 704-2700

Company URL: http://ducks.nhl.com
Establishment information: Established in 1993.
Company type: Private company
Business activities: Operates professional ice hockey club.
Business type (SIC): Commercial sports

Corporate officers: Michael Schulman, C.E.O.; Tim Ryan, Exec. V.P. and C.O.O.; Douglas Heller, V.P., Finance and C.F.O.; Steve Obert, V.P., Sales and Mktg.; Jay Scott, V.P., Human Resources; Melody Martin, Cont.; Bernard Schneider, Genl. Counsel
Giving statement: Giving through the Anaheim Ducks Corporate Giving Program.

Anaheim Ducks Corporate Giving Program

(formerly The Mighty Ducks of Anaheim Corporate Giving Program)
c/o Honda Center
2695 E. Katella Ave.
Anaheim, CA 92806-5904
URL: http://ducks.nhl.com/club/page.htm?id=60697

Purpose and activities: The Anaheim Ducks and Honda Center makes charitable contributions to nonprofit organizations involved with children and families, education, broadening access to hockey, and health and wellness. Support is limited to organizations in southern California.
Fields of interest: Education; Health care; Athletics/sports, amateur leagues; Children, services; Family services.
Type of support: Donated products; In-kind gifts.
Geographic limitations: Giving primarily in Support is limited to organizations in southern CA.
Publications: Application guidelines.
Application information: Applications accepted. Requests via phone, fax, writing, or e-mail are not accepted. Donation address must not include a P.O. box. Applications are limited to 1 request per organization for any given event. Donations are limited to 1 contribution per organization in any given year. Donation items are typically sent in the month prior to the event date. The organization does not facilitate personal items to be autographed by players or coaches. Application form required.
Applicants should submit the following:
1) name, address and phone number of organization
2) copy of IRS Determination Letter
3) contact person
Applications should include event details, including date, description, what the donation will be used for, and number of attendees expected.
Initial approach: Complete online application
Copies of proposal: 1
Deadline(s): 8 weeks prior to event

192
Anchor Fabricators, Inc.

386 Talmadge Rd.
P.O. Box 99
Clayton, OH 45315-9621 (937) 836-5117
FAX: (937) 836-2644

Company URL: http://www.anchorfab.com
Establishment information: Established in 1949.
Company type: Private company
Business activities: Manufactures metal products.
Business type (SIC): Fabricated metal products (except machinery and transportation equipment)
Corporate officers: Thomas S. Saldoff, Pres.; Marshall Ruchman, Secy.
Giving statement: Giving through the Saldoff-Semmelman Family Foundation, Inc.

Saldoff-Semmelman Family Foundation, Inc.

386 Talmadge Rd.
P.O. Box 99
Clayton, OH 45315-9621

Establishment information: Established in 1996 as a company-sponsored operating foundation.
Donors: Anchor Fabricators, Inc.; Ruth D. Saldoff Family; Thomas S. Saldoff; Ruth D. Saldoff Charitable Trust.
Financial data (yr. ended 07/31/09): Assets, $224,189 (M); expenditures, $11,391; qualifying distributions, $11,391; giving activities include $11,205 for 8 grants (high: $8,160; low: $120).
Purpose and activities: The foundation supports organizations involved with arts and culture, education, the environment, animal welfare, cancer, human services, and Judaism.
Fields of interest: Education; Human services; Religion.
Type of support: General/operating support.
Geographic limitations: Giving primarily in FL and OH.
Support limitations: No grants to individuals.
Application information: Applications not accepted. Unsolicited requests for funds not accepted.
Directors: Marshall Ruchman; Ruth D. Saldoff; Thomas S. Saldoff.
EIN: 311478276

193
AnchorBank, fsb

1516 W. Main St.
Sun Prairie, WI 53590-1824
(608) 837-5181

Company URL: http://www.anchorbank.com
Establishment information: Established in 1919.
Company type: Subsidiary of a public company
Business activities: Operates savings bank.
Business type (SIC): Savings institutions
Corporate officers: David L. Omachinski, Chair.; Chris Michael Bauer, C.E.O.; Mark D. Timmerman, Pres. and C.O.O.; Dale C. Ringgenberg, Sr. V.P., Treas. and C.F.O.
Board of director: David L. Omachinski, Chair.
Giving statement: Giving through the Anchor Foundation, Inc.

Anchor Foundation, Inc.

c/o Mark Timmerman
1509 Red Tail Dr.
Verona, WI 53593-7969

Establishment information: Established in 2003 in WI.
Donor: AnchorBank, FSB.
Financial data (yr. ended 12/31/11): Assets, $1,545,049 (M); expenditures, $107,785; qualifying distributions, $28,700; giving activities include $28,700 for grants.
Purpose and activities: The foundation supports museums and medical centers and organizations involved with higher education, cancer, youth development, and Christianity.
Fields of interest: Museums (marine/maritime); Higher education; Health care, clinics/centers; Cancer; Boy scouts; Youth development, business; Christian agencies & churches.
Type of support: Building/renovation; Program development.
Geographic limitations: Giving primarily in Madison, Osceola, Oshkosh, and Platteville, WI.
Application information: Applications not accepted. Contributes only to pre-selected organizations.
Officers: Mark D. Timmerman, Pres. and Secy.; Douglas J. Timmerman, V.P. and Treas.
EIN: 710929809

194
Andersen Corporation

100 4th Ave. N.
Bayport, MN 55003-1096 (651) 264-5150
FAX: (651) 264-5107

Company URL: http://
http:www.andersenwindows.com
Establishment information: Established in 1903.
Company type: Private company
Business activities: Manufactures wood windows, patio doors, and related accessories.
Business type (SIC): Wood millwork
Financial profile for 2011: Number of employees, 9,000; sales volume, $2,160,000,000
Corporate officers: James E. Humphrey, Chair.; Jay Lund, Pres. and C.E.O.; Philip E. Donaldson, Exec. V.P. and C.F.O.; Mary D. Carter, Sr. V.P. and C.A.O.
Board of director: James E. Humphrey, Chair.
Subsidiary: Andersen Windows, Inc., Bayport, MN
Giving statement: Giving through the Andersen Corporation Contributions Program and the Andersen Corporate Foundation.

Andersen Corporation Contributions Program

c/o Corp. Comms.
100 4th Ave. N.
Bayport, MN 55003-1058 (651) 264-5150

Contact: Susan Roeder
Financial data (yr. ended 12/31/08): Total giving, $1,395,000, including $1,395,000 for grants.
Purpose and activities: As a complement to its foundation, Andersen also makes charitable contributions to nonprofit organizations directly. Support is given primarily in areas of company operations.
Fields of interest: Visual arts, architecture; Housing/shelter; Business/industry; Community/economic development.
Type of support: Building/renovation; General/operating support; In-kind gifts; Sponsorships.
Geographic limitations: Giving primarily in areas of company operations.
Support limitations: No grants to individuals.
Publications: Application guidelines.
Application information: Applications accepted. Application form required.
Initial approach: Contact headquarters for application form
Final notification: 1 month

Andersen Corporate Foundation

(formerly The Bayport Foundation of Andersen Corporation)
White Pine Bldg.
342 5th Ave. N., Ste. 200
Bayport, MN 55003-1201 (651) 275-4450
FAX: (651) 439-9480;
E-mail: andersencorpfdn@srinc.biz; Additional tel.: (651) 439-1557; URL: http://www.srinc.biz/bp/index.html

Establishment information: Incorporated in 1941 in MN.
Donor: Andersen Corp.
Contact: Chloette Haley, Prog. Off.

Financial data (yr. ended 11/30/12): Assets, $43,349,719 (M); expenditures, $2,230,196; qualifying distributions, $2,085,255; giving activities include $1,914,400 for 139 grants (high: $100,000; low: $1,500).
Purpose and activities: The foundation supports programs designed to provide community, social, and support services to better people's lives and strengthen communities. Special emphasis is directed toward programs designed to promote affordable housing; health and safety; education and youth development; human services; and civic support.
Fields of interest: Media/communications; Visual arts; Museums; Performing arts; Performing arts, music; Arts; Elementary/secondary education; Education, services; Education; Environment, natural resources; Hospitals (general); Public health; Health care; Substance abuse, prevention; Mental health/crisis services; Employment, services; Housing/shelter, temporary shelter; Housing/shelter, owner/renter issues; Housing/shelter; Disasters, preparedness/services; Safety/disasters; Recreation; Aging, centers/services; Minorities/immigrants, centers/services; Independent living, disability; Human services; Mathematics; Engineering/technology; Science Children/youth; Aging; Disabilities, people with; Economically disadvantaged.
International interests: Canada.
Programs:

Affordable Housing: The foundation supports programs designed to provide affordable housing to low-income families. Special emphasis is directed towards sustainable housing that does not convert to market-rate housing; owner-occupied rental homes, apartments, and assisted living; and support services for emergency shelter and short term transitional housing.

Civic Support: The foundation supports programs designed to build, promote, and preserve communities. Special emphasis is directed toward organizations that provide a public service, such as public radio, public television, and museums; and cultural organizations including performing arts, visual arts, and music designed to make a significant contribution to the life of the community.

Education and Youth Development: The foundation supports organizations that offer intellectual and social opportunities for K-12 young people. Special emphasis is directed toward programs for public and private schools that are not funded in the general operating budget, and a responsible, independent group oversees allocation of the funds; programs that focus on science, technology, engineering, and mathematics; preservation of environmental quality; and after school programs, drug prevention, and career planning.

Health and Safety: The foundation supports programs designed to promote safe and healthy environments, and improve health through prevention and education for young people, senior citizens, and people in vulnerable situations. Special emphasis is directed toward prevention and outreach programs; programs and services that promote mental health, wellness, and safety; facilities and equipment; emergency preparedness; and recreational programs for people with special needs.

Human Services: The foundation supports programs designed to enhance self-sufficiency for people living in poverty, senior citizens, and the disabled. Special emphasis is directed toward basic needs of daily life, including food and transportation; new immigrant services; and national organizations providing emergency recovery services for communities suffering from natural disasters.

Type of support: Annual campaigns; Building/renovation; Capital campaigns; Emergency funds; General/operating support; Program development.
Geographic limitations: Giving primarily in areas of company operations in Des Moines and Dubuque, IA, East Metro, MN, North Brunswick, NJ, Luray and Page County, VA, Dunn County, Menomonie, and St. Croix Valley, WI, and to national organizations; some giving also in Huron, London, Middlesex, and Perth, Ontario Province, Canada.
Support limitations: No support for national research organizations. No grants to individuals, or for endowments, or the purchase of Andersen products.
Publications: Application guidelines; IRS Form 990 or 990-PF printed copy available upon request.
Application information: Applications accepted. Call foundation before sending request. Visit foundation Web site for application address and guidelines. Application form required. Applicants should submit the following:
1) timetable for implementation and evaluation of project
2) how project will be sustained once grantmaker support is completed
3) signature and title of chief executive officer
4) copy of IRS Determination Letter
5) brief history of organization and description of its mission
6) copy of most recent annual report/audited financial statement/990
7) list of company employees involved with the organization
8) descriptive literature about organization
9) listing of board of directors, trustees, officers and other key people and their affiliations
10) detailed description of project and amount of funding requested
11) copy of current year's organizational budget and/or project budget
12) listing of additional sources and amount of support

Proposals should include a description of past support by the foundation.

Initial approach: Download application form and mail proposal and application form to nearest application address
Copies of proposal: 1
Board meeting date(s): Jan., Apr., July, and Nov.
Deadline(s): Apr. 15, July 15, Oct. 15, and Dec. 15
Final notification: 10 working days

Officers and Directors: Keith D. Olson, Pres.; Susan Roeder, V.P., Grants Admin. and Secy.; Phil Donaldson, Treas.; Laurie Bauer; Jay Lund; Jerry Redmond.
Number of staff: 1 full-time professional; 1 full-time support.
EIN: 416020912
Selected grants: The following grants are a representative sample of this grantmaker's funding activity:
$50,000 to Regions Hospital, Saint Paul, MN, 2012. For campaign to transform mental health.
$40,000 to Partnership Plan for Stillwater Area Schools, Stillwater, MN, 2012. For Math and Science Partnership Plan Programs.
$30,000 to Habitat for Humanity, Saint Croix Valley, River Falls, WI, 2012. For Eco Village project.
$20,000 to Canvas Health, Oakdale, MN, 2012. For Integrative Health Initiative.
$10,000 to Junior Achievement of the Upper Midwest, Maplewood, MN, 2012. For JA BizTown and STEM program.
$8,000 to Operation Help, Hudson, WI, 2012. For general operating support.
$2,500 to Bridge to Hope, Menomonie, WI, 2012. For general operating support.

195
Anderson Packaging, Inc.

4545 Assembly Dr.
Rockford, IL 61109-3081 (815) 484-8900
FAX: (815) 484-8904

Company URL: http://www.andersonpackaging.com
Establishment information: Established in 1967.
Company type: Subsidiary of a public company
Business activities: Manufactures pharmaceutical and personal care packaging products.
Business type (SIC): Paper and paperboard/coated, converted, and laminated
Financial profile for 2009: Number of employees, 1,000
Corporate officers: Shawn Reilley, C.E.O.; Jerry Boxleitner, Pres.; Peter Belden, V.P., Sales and Mktg.; Rosalyn Wesley, V.P., Human Resources
Giving statement: Giving through the Anderson Family Charitable Fund.

Anderson Family Charitable Fund

330 Spring Creek Rd.
Rockford, IL 61107-1035

Establishment information: Established in 2000 in IL.
Donors: Anderson Packaging, Inc.; John R. Anderson.
Financial data (yr. ended 12/31/11): Assets, $16,013 (M); expenditures, $1,187; qualifying distributions, $1,000; giving activities include $1,000 for 1 grant.
Purpose and activities: The fund supports art museums and organizations involved with performing arts, higher education, land conservation, sports, and community development.
Fields of interest: Museums (art); Performing arts; Higher education; Environment, land resources; Athletics/sports, amateur leagues; Community/economic development.
Type of support: General/operating support.
Geographic limitations: Giving primarily in Rockford, IL.
Support limitations: No grants to individuals.
Application information: Applications not accepted. Unsolicited requests for funds not accepted.
Officers and Directors:* John R. Anderson*, Pres.; Linda Anderson*, V.P.; David J. Anderson*, Secy.; Duane R. Bach, Treas.; Jeffrey R. Anderson; Tracy E. Fitzgerald; Kristin L. Pecora.
EIN: 364332912

196
Hanna Andersson Corporation

1010 N.W. Flanders
Portland, OR 97209-3119 (503) 242-0920

Company URL: http://www.hannaandersson.com
Establishment information: Established in 1983.
Company type: Subsidiary of a private company
Business activities: Provides catalog shopping services; operates clothing stores.
Business type (SIC): Nonstore retailers; apparel and accessory stores
Corporate officers: Adam Stone, Pres. and C.E.O.; Rod Rice, C.F.O.; Randy Rieder, V.P., Opers.; Alison Hiatt, V.P., Mktg.; Gretchen A. Peterson, V.P., Human Resources; Steve Dunn, V.P., Inf. Systems
Giving statement: Giving through the Hanna Helps.

Hanna Helps
1010 N.W. Flanders
Portland, OR 97209-3119 (503) 242-0920
URL: http://www.hannaandersson.com/aboutHanna.asp?pg=166

Purpose and activities: Hanna Andersson makes charitable contributions to nonprofit organizations involved with improving the lives of young children. Special emphasis is directed toward programs designed to address early childhood education and literacy, poverty and neglect, domestic violence, homelessness, and mental healthcare. Support is given on a national basis in areas of company operations, with emphasis on Louisville, Kentucky, and Portland, Oregon.
Fields of interest: Elementary/secondary education; Education, reading; Mental health, treatment; Children, services; Family services, domestic violence; Homeless, human services Economically disadvantaged.
Program:
Employee Matching Gift Program: Hanna Andersson matches contributions made by employees to nonprofit organizations on a one-for-one basis up to $500 per employee, per year.
Type of support: Donated products; Employee matching gifts; Employee volunteer services; General/operating support.
Geographic limitations: Giving on a national basis in areas of company operations, with emphasis on Louisville, KY, and Portland, OR; giving also to regional and national organizations.
Support limitations: No support for discriminatory organizations. No grants to individuals, or for auctions, capital campaigns or buildings, scholarships, or religious activities.
Application information: Applications not accepted. Unsolicited requests for grants are not accepted.

197
Andretti International, Inc.
(also known as Michael Andretti Foundation)
630 Selvaggio Dr., Ste. 340
Nazareth, PA 18064-9234 (610) 365-0500

Company URL: http://www.andretti.com
Establishment information: Established in 1985.
Company type: Private company
Business activities: Races cars; produces wine; operates car dealerships; operates motorcycle accessories stores; operates racing school; operates indoor entertainment facility; operates carwashes; distributes fuel.
Business type (SIC): Commercial sports; beverages; motor vehicles—retail; motorcycles—retail; fuel dealers—retail; motor vehicle services, except repair; amusement and recreation services/miscellaneous; educational services/miscellaneous
Corporate officer: J.F. Thormann, Exec. V.P. and C.O.O.
Giving statement: Giving through the Michael Andretti Foundation.

The Michael Andretti Foundation
7615 Zionsville Rd.
Indianapolis, IN 46268-2174 (317) 872-2700
E-mail: foundation@andretti.com; URL: http://andrettiautosport.com/home.php?cid=team-profile-mafoundation

Establishment information: Established in 2003.
Financial data (yr. ended 12/31/11): Revenue, $284,816; assets, $41,268 (M); gifts received, $158,120; expenditures, $342,881; giving activities include $317,385 for grants.
Purpose and activities: The foundation seeks to focus national resources on people who have shown need and help promote programs for better health, education, and welfare of all of America's children and citizens.
Fields of interest: Education; Health care Children/youth.
Geographic limitations: Giving on a national basis.
Support limitations: No grants to individuals.
Officers: Michael Andretti, Pres.; J.F. Thormann, V.P.; Michael Morrisey, Treas.; Ryann Rigsby, Exec. Dir.
Director: John Caponigro.
EIN: 571163960

198
Andrews Kurth LLP
600 Travis, Ste. 4200
Houston, TX 77002-2910 (713) 220-4200

Company URL: http://www.andrewskurth.com
Establishment information: Established in 1902.
Company type: Private company
Business activities: Operates law firm.
Business type (SIC): Legal services
Corporate officers: Thomas J. Perich, Chair.; Charles L. "Lynn" McGuire, C.I.O.
Offices: Washington, DC; New York, NY; Austin, Dallas, Houston, The Woodlands, TX
International operations: China; United Kingdom
Giving statement: Giving through the Andrews Kurth LLP Corporate Giving Program.

Andrews Kurth LLP Corporate Giving Program
600 Travis, Ste. 4200
Houston, TX 77002-2910 (713) 220-4200
FAX: (713) 220-4285; URL: http://www.andrewskurth.com/about-service.html

Purpose and activities: Andrew Kurth makes charitable contributions to nonprofit organizations involved with education, food services, human services, and on a case by case basis.
Fields of interest: Education; Legal services; Food services; Human services; General charitable giving.
Type of support: Employee volunteer services; General/operating support; Pro bono services - legal.

199
Androscoggin Bank
30 Lisbon St.
Lewiston, ME 04240-7116 (207) 784-9164
FAX: (207) 783-5211

Company URL: http://www.androscogginbank.com
Establishment information: Established in 1870.
Company type: Private company
Business activities: Operates savings bank.
Business type (SIC): Savings institutions
Corporate officer: Paul H. Andersen, Pres. and C.E.O.
Giving statement: Giving through the Mainstreet Foundation Investment Management Account.

Mainstreet Foundation Investment Management Account
(also known as MainStreet Foundation)
(formerly Androscoggin Savings Bank Foundation)
c/o Androscoggin Bank
P.O. Box 1407
Lewiston, ME 04243-1407 (207) 376-2545
E-mail: bankoncommunity@androscogginbank.com; Additional tel.: (207) 777-6651; URL: http://www.androscogginbank.com/mainstreet-foundation.aspx

Establishment information: Established in 1997 in ME.
Donor: Androscoggin Bank.
Contact: Melissa Rock
Financial data (yr. ended 12/31/11): Assets, $903,832 (M); expenditures, $50,831; qualifying distributions, $43,014; giving activities include $42,330 for 13 grants (high: $5,000; low: $1,500).
Purpose and activities: The foundation supports programs designed to foster the development and welfare of at-risk youth. Special emphasis is directed towards programs designed to promote after-school and mentoring initiatives; leadership development experiences of all types; literacy and a love of learning; coping with homelessness and family dynamics; mental health and developing effective change and coping mechanisms; learning life-management skills such as learning about earning, saving, budgeting money, and spending money; and general welfare of youth.
Fields of interest: Education, services; Education, reading; Mental health/crisis services; Youth development, adult & child programs; Youth development; Youth, services; Family services; Human services, financial counseling; Homeless, human services; Human services; Leadership development Youth.
Type of support: Program development; Seed money.
Geographic limitations: Giving primarily in areas of company operations in ME.
Support limitations: No grants for general operating support, annual campaigns, endowments, conferences or seminars, training of trainers or teachers, or facilities renovation or improvements; no multi-year support or capital campaigns.
Publications: Application guidelines; Grants list.
Application information: Applications accepted. The foundation awards impact grants and seed grants. Additional information may be requested at a later date. Support is limited to 1 contribution per organization during any given year. Organizations receiving support are asked to submit a final report. Application form required. Applicants should submit the following:
1) detailed description of project and amount of funding requested
2) geographic area to be served
3) copy of current year's organizational budget and/or project budget
4) timetable for implementation and evaluation of project
5) explanation of why grantmaker is considered an appropriate donor for project
6) how project's results will be evaluated or measured
7) brief history of organization and description of its mission
8) listing of additional sources and amount of support

Initial approach: Download application form and mail to foundation
Board meeting date(s): Feb., May, and Nov.
Deadline(s): Jan. 15, Apr. 15, and Oct. 15

Officer: Gwendolyn B. Moore, Chair.

Directors: Ronald Aseltine, Esq.; Normand Bilodeau; Steven A. Closson; Christine Conrad; Lindy Fogg; Debra Griffin; Kate Landry; David Pease.
EIN: 311573495

200
Angels Baseball, LP

(also known as Los Angeles Angels of Anaheim)
2000 E. Gene Autry Way
Anaheim, CA 92806-6143 (714) 940-2000

Company URL: http://losangeles.angels.mlb.com
Establishment information: Established in 1960.
Company type: Private company
Business activities: Operates professional baseball club.
Business type (SIC): Commercial sports
Corporate officers: Dennis Kuhl, Chair.; John Carpino, Pres.; Bill Beverage, C.F.O.; Molly Taylor Jolly, Sr. V.P., Finance and Admin.; Robert Alvarado, V.P., Mktg.; Tim Mead, V.P., Comms.; Cris Lacoste, Cont.
Board of director: Dennis Kuhl, Chair.
Giving statement: Giving through the Los Angeles Angels of Anaheim Corporate Giving Program and the Angels Baseball Foundation.

Los Angeles Angels of Anaheim Corporate Giving Program

c/o Community Rels.
2000 Gene Autry Way
Anaheim, CA 92806-6143 (888) 796-4256
Application address for speaker requests: Angels BaseballSpeakers Bureau, 2000 Gene Autry Way, Anaheim, CA 92806; Application address for donation requests: Angels Baseball, Community Rels., 2000 Gene Autry Way, Anaheim, CA 92806; URL: http://losangeles.angels.mlb.com/NASApp/mlb/ana/community/index.jsp

Purpose and activities: As a complement to its foundation, the Los Angeles Angels of Anaheim also makes charitable contributions of memorabilia to nonprofit organizations directly. Support is given primarily in southern California.
Fields of interest: Education, reading; Education; Health care, blood supply; Health care; Cancer, leukemia; Breast cancer; Food banks; Recreation.
Type of support: Employee volunteer services; In-kind gifts.
Geographic limitations: Giving primarily in southern CA.
Publications: Application guidelines.
Application information: Applications accepted. Proposals should be submitted using organization letterhead. Proposals are not accepted via fax or e-mail. Application form not required. Applicants should submit the following:
1) population served
2) name, address and phone number of organization
3) copy of IRS Determination Letter
4) detailed description of project and amount of funding requested
5) contact person
Proposals should indicate the date and location of the event.
Initial approach: Proposal to headquarters
Copies of proposal: 1
Deadline(s): 1 month prior to event for speaker requests; 6 weeks prior to need for donation requests

Angels Baseball Foundation

2000 E. Gene Autry Way
Anaheim, CA 92806-6100 (714) 940-2174
FAX: (714) 940-2244; URL: http://losangeles.angels.mlb.com/ana/community/baseball_foundation.jsp

Establishment information: Established in 2004 in CA.
Financial data (yr. ended 12/31/10): Revenue, $1,689,254; assets, $2,127,102 (M); gifts received, $1,693,064; expenditures, $1,598,766; giving activities include $1,524,815 for grants and $40,000 for grants to individuals.
Purpose and activities: The foundation focuses on initiatives aimed to create and improve education, health care, arts and sciences, and community related youth programs, in addition to providing children the opportunity to experience the game of baseball.
Fields of interest: Arts; Education; Health care; Cancer; Cancer research; Athletics/sports, baseball; Boys & girls clubs; Youth development; American Red Cross; Children, services; Community/economic development; Science.
Geographic limitations: Giving limited to the greater Los Angeles, CA area.
Officers and Directors:* Mark Merhab*, Chair.; Bill Beverage*, Secy.-Treas.; Ed Arnold; Bobby Grich; Dennis Kuhl; Tim Mead; Arte Moreno; Carole Moreno; Anne Scioscia.
EIN: 200713975

201
ANH Refractories Company

400 Fairway Dr.
Moon Township, PA 15108-3190
(412) 375-6600

Company URL: http://www.anhrefractories.com
Establishment information: Established in 2000.
Company type: Private company
Business activities: Manufactures and sells refractory products.
Business type (SIC): Clay structural products
Corporate officers: Guenter D. Karhut, Chair. and C.E.O.; Jon A. Allegretti, Pres.; Viktor Fischer, Exec. V.P., Sales and Mktg.; Gabriel Faimann, C.F.O.
Board of director: Guenter Karhut, Chair.
Giving statement: Giving through the ANH Refractories Company Foundation.

ANH Refractories Company Foundation

(formerly Global Industrial Technologies Foundation)
400 Fairway Dr.
Moon Township, PA 15108-3190 (412) 375-6755

Establishment information: Established in 1996 in TX.
Donor: Global Industrial Technologies, Inc.
Contact: Gabriel Faimann, C.F.O. and Treas.
Financial data (yr. ended 10/31/11): Assets, $1,067,527 (M); gifts received, $2,787; expenditures, $58,490; qualifying distributions, $48,656; giving activities include $48,656 for 17 grants (high: $16,217; low: $484).
Purpose and activities: The foundation supports orchestras and organizations involved with health, diabetes, and human services.
Fields of interest: Performing arts, orchestras; Hospitals (general); Health care, patient services; Palliative care; Health care; Diabetes; Big Brothers/Big Sisters; Salvation Army; Children, services; Residential/custodial care, hospices; Human services.
Type of support: General/operating support.
Geographic limitations: Giving primarily in PA.
Application information: Applications accepted. Application form required. Applicants should submit the following:
1) copy of IRS Determination Letter
2) detailed description of project and amount of funding requested
Initial approach: Proposal
Deadline(s): None
Officers and Directors:* Jon A. Allegretti*, Pres. and Secy.; Guenter D. Karhut*, C.O.O.; Gabriel Faimann*, C.F.O. and Treas.
EIN: 752699251

202
Anheuser-Busch Companies, Inc.

1 Busch Pl.
St. Louis, MO 63118-1852 (314) 577-2000

Company URL: http://www.anheuser-busch.com
Establishment information: Established in 1852.
Company type: Subsidiary of a foreign company
Business activities: Operates holding company; produces beer; manufactures metal cans and lids; recycles aluminum containers; manufactures pressure sensitive, metalized, plastic, and paper labels; operates theme parks.
Business type (SIC): Beverages; paper and paperboard/coated, converted, and laminated; metal containers; holding company; amusement and recreation services/miscellaneous
Financial profile for 2010: Number of employees, 30,236; assets, $113,800,000,000; sales volume, $36,800,000,000
Corporate officers: Luiz Fernando Edmond, Pres.; Gary L. Rutledge, V.P. and Genl. Counsel; Joao Guerra, V.P., Finance; David Almeida, V.P., Sales; Paul Chibe, V.P., Mktg.; James Villeneuve, V.P., Corp. Affairs, and Comms.
Subsidiaries: Anheuser-Busch, Inc., St. Louis, MO; Anheuser-Busch Recycling Corp., Marion, OH; Busch Media Group, Inc., St. Louis, MO; Busch Properties, Inc., Columbus, OH; Metal Container Corp., Oklahoma City, OK; Precision Printing and Packaging, Inc., Clarksville, TN; SeaWorld of Florida, Inc., Orlando, FL; SeaWorld of Texas, Inc., San Antonio, TX; SeaWorld Parks & Entertainment, Orlando, FL
International operations: Bermuda; Brazil; British Virgin Islands; Cayman Islands; Chile; China; Hong Kong; Mexico; Spain; United Kingdom
Giving statement: Giving through the Anheuser-Busch Companies, Inc. Corporate Giving Program and the Anheuser-Busch Foundation.

Anheuser-Busch Companies, Inc. Corporate Giving Program

1 Busch Pl.
St. Louis, MO 63118-1849
URL: http://anheuser-busch.com/index.php/our-responsibility/

Purpose and activities: As a complement to its foundation, Anheuser-Busch also makes charitable contributions to nonprofit organizations directly. Support is given primarily in areas of company operations in California, Colorado, Florida, Georgia, Hawaii, Kentucky, Massachusetts, Missouri, New

Hampshire, New Jersey, New York, Ohio, Oklahoma, and Virginia.
Fields of interest: Education; Environment; Disasters, preparedness/services; Economic development Minorities; Military/veterans.
Type of support: Donated products; General/operating support; Sponsorships.
Geographic limitations: Giving primarily in areas of company operations in CA, CO, FL, GA, HI, KY, MA, MO, NH, NJ, NY, OH, OK, TX, and VA.
Support limitations: No support for political candidates or organizations, religious organizations, fraternal, social, or similar organizations, or athletic organizations. No grants to individuals, or for general operating support for hospitals, capital campaigns for secondary schools, or general operating support for United Way member organizations.
Publications: Application guidelines.
Application information: Applications accepted. Video submissions are not encouraged. Application form not required. Applicants should submit the following:
1) name, address and phone number of organization
2) copy of IRS Determination Letter
3) brief history of organization and description of its mission
4) copy of most recent annual report/audited financial statement/990
5) listing of board of directors, trustees, officers and other key people and their affiliations
6) detailed description of project and amount of funding requested
7) copy of current year's organizational budget and/or project budget
8) listing of additional sources and amount of support

Proposals should include a description of past support by Anheuser-Busch with the organization; indicate whether the organization is a United Way member agency; and indicate whether the organization has a permanent liquor license.
Initial approach: Proposal to headquarters
Copies of proposal: 1
Administrators: Cynthia Garrone, Mgr., Charitable Contribs.; Judy Vonder Haar, Asst. Mgr., Charitable Contribs.
Number of staff: 1 full-time professional; 1 part-time professional.

Anheuser-Busch Foundation

c/o Anheuser-Busch Cos., Inc.
1 Busch Pl.
St. Louis, MO 63118-1849 (314) 577-2000
URL: http://anheuser-busch.com/index.php/our-responsibility/

Establishment information: Established in 1975 in MO.
Donor: Anheuser-Busch Cos., Inc.
Financial data (yr. ended 12/31/11): Assets, $69,112,586 (M); expenditures, $12,098,229; qualifying distributions, $11,567,015; giving activities include $10,536,299 for 162 grants (high: $2,000,000; low: $1,000) and $821,173 for 1,176 employee matching gifts.
Purpose and activities: The foundation supports programs designed to promote disaster relief and preparedness; increase access to and completion of higher education; raise consciousness and action for water conservation and recycling; and increase the quality of life through homeownership and entrepreneurship.
Fields of interest: Higher education; Scholarships/financial aid; Education; Environment, recycling; Environment, natural resources; Environment, water resources; Environmental education; Housing/shelter, development; Housing/shelter; Disasters, preparedness/services; American Red Cross; Human services; Economic development; Community/economic development; United Ways and Federated Giving Programs; Military/veterans' organizations Minorities; African Americans/Blacks; Hispanics/Latinos; Economically disadvantaged.
Programs:
Employee Matching Gifts: The foundation matches contributions made by employees, directors, and retirees of Anheuser-Busch to educational institutions on a one-for-one basis from $25 to $5,000 per contributor, per year.
Employee Volunteer Grants: The foundation awards grants to nonprofit organizations with which employees of Anheuser-Busch volunteer.
Type of support: Building/renovation; Continuing support; Employee matching gifts; Employee volunteer services; General/operating support; Matching/challenge support; Program development; Scholarship funds.
Geographic limitations: Giving primarily in areas of company operations, with emphasis on Fairfield, Los Angeles, and San Diego, CA, Fort Collins, CO, Jacksonville, Orlando, and Tampa, FL, Cartersville, GA, St. Louis, MO, Merrimack, NH, Newark, NJ, Baldwinsville, NY, Columbus, OH, Houston and San Antonio, TX, and Williamsburg, VA.
Support limitations: No support for discriminatory, political, fraternal, social, or religious organizations, legislators, athletic organizations or teams, charter schools, pre-schools, elementary, middle, or high schools, or hospitals or healthcare-related organizations. No grants to individuals, or for political campaigns, annual or capital campaigns, conferences or seminars, travel or organized field trips, family reunions, general operating support for United Way agencies, or endowments; no multi-year commitments.
Application information: Applications not accepted. Contributes only to pre-selected organizations.
Board meeting date(s): Approximately every 3 months
Trustees: Gary L. Rutledge; James Villeneuve; U.S. Bank, N.A.
EIN: 510168084
Selected grants: The following grants are a representative sample of this grantmaker's funding activity:
$2,000,000 to United Way of Greater Saint Louis, Saint Louis, MO, 2010.
$2,000,000 to United Way of Greater Saint Louis, Saint Louis, MO, 2011.
$1,699,550 to ABMRF/The Foundation for Alcohol Research, Baltimore, MD, 2010.
$800,000 to American Red Cross, Saint Louis, MO, 2010.
$785,129 to ABMRF/The Foundation for Alcohol Research, Baltimore, MD, 2011.
$600,000 to Saint Louis University, Saint Louis, MO, 2010.
$600,000 to Saint Louis University, Saint Louis, MO, 2011.
$500,000 to University of Missouri, Saint Louis, MO, 2010.
$500,000 to University of Missouri, Saint Louis, MO, 2011.
$276,512 to University of Virginia, Charlottesville, VA, 2011.
$275,000 to American Red Cross, Saint Louis, MO, 2011.
$222,000 to Old Spanish Missions, San Antonio, TX, 2010.
$200,000 to YMCA of Greater Saint Louis, Saint Louis, MO, 2011.
$138,400 to Washington University, Saint Louis, MO, 2010.
$80,000 to United Way of Essex and West Hudson, Newark, NJ, 2010.
$50,000 to Smithsonian Center for Latino Initiatives, Washington, DC, 2010.
$46,383 to United Way of Larimer County, Fort Collins, CO, 2011.
$35,000 to Clay Scholarship, Saint Louis, MO, 2011.
$25,000 to American Red Cross, Saint Louis, MO, 2011.
$25,000 to Boys Hope Girls Hope of Saint Louis, Saint Louis, MO, 2010.

203
Ann's Trading Co., Inc.

4461 Santa Fe Ave.
Los Angeles, CA 90058 (323) 277-7930
FAX: (323) 277-7938

Company URL: http://www.annstrading.com
Establishment information: Established in 1981.
Company type: Private company
Business activities: Sells handbags, accessories, and home accessories wholesale.
Business type (SIC): Apparel, piece goods, and notions—wholesale; furniture and home furnishings—wholesale
Corporate officer: Hyung D. Kim, Pres. and C.E.O.
Giving statement: Giving through the Elim Ministry Foundation.

Elim Ministry Foundation

4461 S. Santa Fe Ave.
Los Angeles, CA 90058-2101 (323) 277-7930

Establishment information: Established in 2004 in CA.
Donor: Ann's Trading Co., Inc.
Contact: Mi Hye Kim, Pres.
Financial data (yr. ended 12/31/11): Assets, $68,864 (M); gifts received, $12,000; expenditures, $9,905; qualifying distributions, $8,980; giving activities include $8,980 for 6 grants (high: $3,600; low: $300).
Purpose and activities: The foundation supports organizations involved with Christianity and awards scholarships to individuals.
Fields of interest: Christian agencies & churches.
Type of support: General/operating support; Grants to individuals; Scholarships—to individuals.
Geographic limitations: Giving primarily in CA; giving also in Korea.
Application information: Applications accepted. Application form required.
Scholarship application should include a transcript, essay, and reference.
Deadline(s): None
Officers: Mi Hye Kim, Pres.; Hyung Don Kim, Secy.
Director: John Lee.
EIN: 030535740

204
Anocoil Corporation

60 E. Main St.
P.O. Box 1318
Rockville, CT 06066-3245 (860) 871-1200

Company URL: http://www.anocoil.com
Establishment information: Established in 1958.
Company type: Private company
Business activities: Manufactures lithographic plates.
Business type (SIC): Printing trade services

Corporate officers: Howard A. Fromson, C.E.O.; David M. Bujese, Pres.; Michael Fromson, V.P., Opers.
Giving statement: Giving through the Howard A. Fromson Foundation, Inc.
Company EIN: 018800458

Howard A. Fromson Foundation, Inc.

(formerly Fromson Foundation, Inc.)
c/o Anocoil Corp.
P.O. Box 1318
Rockville, CT 06066 (860) 871-1200

Establishment information: Established in 1982 in CT.
Donors: Howard A. Fromson; Anocoil Corp.
Financial data (yr. ended 11/30/11): Assets, $900,305 (M); expenditures, $74,124; qualifying distributions, $73,206; giving activities include $41,350 for 5 grants (high: $25,000; low: $350) and $17,910 for 30 grants to individuals (high: $1,410; low: $250).
Purpose and activities: The foundation supports programs designed to promote education and health.
Fields of interest: Arts; Education; Health care.
Type of support: General/operating support; Scholarships—to individuals.
Geographic limitations: Giving primarily in the northeastern U.S., with emphasis on CT.
Application information: Applications accepted. Application form not required.
Initial approach: Letter
Deadline(s): None
Officer: Howard A. Fromson, Pres.
EIN: 061074374

205
Anschutz New York Soccer Inc.

(also known as Red Bull New York)
1 Harmon Plz., 3rd Fl.
Secaucus, NJ 07094-2800 (201) 583-7000

Establishment information: Established in 1994.
Company type: Subsidiary of a private company
Ultimate parent company: The Anschutz Corporation
Business activities: Operates professional soccer club.
Business type (SIC): Commercial sports
Corporate officer: Greg Domico, V.P., Finance
Giving statement: Giving through the New York Red Bulls Corporate Giving Program.

New York Red Bulls Corporate Giving Program

(formerly New York/New Jersey MetroStars Corporate Giving Program)
c/o Community Rels.
600 Cape May St.
Harrison, NJ 07029-2400
E-mail: christinagiunta@newyorkredbulls.com;
URL: http://www.newyorkredbulls.com/community

Contact: Christina Guinta, Community Rels. Mgr.
Purpose and activities: The New York Red Bulls make charitable contributions of memorabilia to nonprofit organizations on a case by case basis. Support is limited to the tri-state Connecticut, New Jersey, and New York area.
Fields of interest: General charitable giving.
Type of support: In-kind gifts; Loaned talent.
Geographic limitations: Giving limited to the tri-state CT, NJ, and NY area.
Application information: Applications accepted. Proposals should be submitted using organization letterhead. Telephone calls during the application process are not encouraged. Application form not required.
Initial approach: Proposal to headquarters
Copies of proposal: 1
Final notification: 1 month prior to need

206
Anthony Timberland Inc.

(formerly Bearden Lumber Company, Inc.)
111 S. Plum St.
P.O. Box 137
Bearden, AR 71720 (870) 687-3611
FAX: (870) 687-2283

Company URL: http://www.anthonytimberlands.com
Establishment information: Established in 1907.
Company type: Private company
Business activities: Manufactures lumber and hardwood lumber products.
Business type (SIC): Lumber and wood products
Corporate officers: John E. Anthony, Chair.; Steven M. Anthony, Pres.; James R. Green, Exec. V.P. and C.F.O.; Rick Green, V.P., Finance
Board of director: John E. Anthony, Chair.
Giving statement: Giving through the Bearden Lumber Company Scholarship Foundation, Inc.

Bearden Lumber Company Scholarship Foundation, Inc.

P.O. Box 137
Bearden, AR 71720-0137 (870) 687-2246

Donors: Bearden Lumber Co., Inc.; Anthony Timberlands, Inc.
Financial data (yr. ended 12/31/11): Assets, $1 (M); gifts received, $25,000; expenditures, $25,000; qualifying distributions, $25,000; giving activities include $25,000 for grants.
Purpose and activities: The foundation awards college scholarships to graduates of Bearden High School in Bearden, Arkansas.
Type of support: Scholarships—to individuals.
Geographic limitations: Giving limited to Bearden, AR.
Application information: Applications accepted. Application form required.
Initial approach: Contact foundation for application form
Deadline(s): Mar. 15
Directors: Steven M. Anthony; Rick Green; Ken Riley.
EIN: 710510772

207
The Antioch Company, LLC

(doing business as Creative Memories)
(also known as Creative Memories)
3001 Clearwater Rd.
P.O. Box 1839
St. Cloud, MN 56302-1839 (800) 468-9335

Company URL: http://www.creativememories.com/
Establishment information: Established in 1987.
Company type: Private company
Business activities: Sells albums, scrapbooking materials, digital photobooks, and photo organization software.
Business type (SIC): Printing/commercial; blankbooks, bookbinding, and looseleaf binders
Corporate officers: Chris Veit, Pres. and C.E.O.; Karen Felix, C.F.O.
Subsidiary: Our Own Image, Yellow Springs, OH
Divisions: Antioch Publishing Div., Yellow Springs, OH; Creative Memories Div., St. Cloud, MN
Plants: Sparks, NV; Colonial Heights, VA
Giving statement: Giving through the Antioch Company Contributions Program.

The Antioch Company Contributions Program

3001 Clearwater Rd.
St. Cloud, MN 56302-1839
FAX: (320) 529-5863;
E-mail: rhorgen@creativememories.com

Contact: Becy Horgen, Exec. Asst.
Purpose and activities: As a complement to its foundation, Antioch also makes charitable contributions to nonprofit organizations on a case by case basis. Special emphasis is directed toward programs designed to help at-risk populations. Support is given primarily in the St. Cloud, Minnesota, and Yellow Springs, Ohio, areas.
Fields of interest: Children, services; Family services, domestic violence; Human services; Civil/human rights Children; Aging; Economically disadvantaged.
Type of support: General/operating support.
Geographic limitations: Giving primarily in the St. Cloud, MN, and Yellow Springs, OH, areas.
Support limitations: No support for religious or political organizations.
Application information: Applications not accepted. The Office of the President handles giving.
Committee meeting date(s): Ongoing

208
ANZA, Incorporated

312 9th Ave. S.E., Ste. B
Watertown, SD 57201 (605) 886-3889

Company URL: http://www.anza.com
Establishment information: Established in 1992.
Company type: Subsidiary of a private company
Business activities: Manufactures telecommunications transformers; manufactures machine tools; manufactures signs.
Business type (SIC): Communications equipment; machinery/metalworking; manufacturing/miscellaneous
Corporate officers: Dennis D. Holien, Pres. and C.E.O.; Greg Kulesa, C.F.O.; Dave Peterson, V.P., Sales
Giving statement: Giving through the ANZA Foundation.

ANZA Foundation

312 9th Ave. S.E., Ste. B
P.O. Box 1445
Watertown, SD 57201-5602

Establishment information: Established in 1995 in SD.
Donor: ANZA, Inc.
Contact: Michele Holien, Mgr.
Financial data (yr. ended 12/31/11): Assets, $25,983 (M); expenditures, $3,510; qualifying distributions, $3,510; giving activities include $3,500 for 1 grant.
Purpose and activities: The foundation supports organizations involved with education and religion.

Fields of interest: Education; United Ways and Federated Giving Programs; Religion.
Type of support: General/operating support.
Geographic limitations: Giving limited to areas of company operations in SD.
Application information: Applications accepted. Application form required. Applicants should submit the following:
1) copy of IRS Determination Letter
2) copy of most recent annual report/audited financial statement/990
Initial approach: Proposal
Deadline(s): None
Directors: Dennis D. Holien; Greg Kulesa.
EIN: 460438174

209
AOL Inc.

(also known as AOL)
(formerly AOL LLC)
770 Broadway
New York, NY 10003 (212) 654-6400
FAX: (302) 636-5454

Company URL: http://http:/corp.aol.com
Establishment information: Established in 1985.
Company type: Public company
Company ticker symbol and exchange: AOL/NYSE
Business activities: Provides interactive online services; develops Web brands; provides Internet technology solutions; provides electronic commerce services.
Business type (SIC): Computer services
Financial profile for 2012: Number of employees, 5,660; assets, $2,797,300,000; sales volume, $2,191,700,000; pre-tax net income, $1,210,100,000; expenses, $989,800,000; liabilities, $6,592,000,000
Fortune 1000 ranking: 2012—880th in revenues, 191st in profits, and 773rd in assets
Forbes 2000 ranking: 2012—1744th in sales, 595th in profits, and 1948th in assets
Corporate officers: Tim Armstrong, Chair. and C.E.O.; Karen Dykstra, Exec. V.P. and C.F.O.; Julie Jacobs, Exec. V.P. and Genl. Counsel; Peter Land, Sr. V.P., Comms.
Board of directors: Tim Armstrong, Chair.; Richard L. Dalzell; Alberto Ibarguen; Hugh F. Johnston; Dawn G. Lepore; Susan M. Lyne; Patricia E. Mitchell; Fredric G. Reynolds; James R. Stengel
Subsidiaries: AOL International LLC, Dulles, VA; CompuServe Interactive Services, Inc., Columbus, OH; Digital City, Inc., Vienna, VA; The ImagiNation Network, Inc., Burlingame, CA; MovieFone, Inc., New York, NY; Netscape Communications Corp., Mountain View, CA
International operations: Canada
Giving statement: Giving through the AOL Inc. Corporate Giving Program.
Company EIN: 204268793

AOL Inc. Corporate Giving Program

(formerly AOL LLC Corporate Giving Program)
c/o Community Rels.
770 Broadway
New York, NY 10003 (212) 206-4466
URL: http://corp.aol.com/category/community-relations/

Contact: Rachel Gross, Community Rels.
Purpose and activities: AOL makes charitable contributions to nonprofit organizations involved with children's safety and health. Special emphasis is directed toward citizen philanthropy and public service advertising. Support is given on a national basis.
Fields of interest: Children, services; Children's rights; Philanthropy/voluntarism, information services; Voluntarism promotion.
Programs:
AOL Aspires: Through the AOL Aspires program, AOL supports programs designed to help disadvantaged youth reach their potential, envision positive futures, open doors of opportunity to educational and career opportunities, and nurture creative talent relating to media and technology.
Cultural and Ethnic Awareness: AOL supports programs designed to promote peace, tolerance, and an appreciation for diverse cultures and perspectives.
Employee Volunteerism: AOL makes charitable contributions to nonprofit organizations with which employees volunteer.
Technology: AOL seeks to increase digital opportunity and 21st century technology literacy by helping nonprofit organizations, schools, and individuals in disadvantaged communities use online resources and other technologies more effectively to further their goals.
Type of support: Cause-related marketing; Employee volunteer services; General/operating support; Technical assistance.
Support limitations: No support for religious organizations not of direct benefit to the entire community, discriminatory organizations, political, labor, or fraternal organizations, or sports teams. No grants to individuals (except for scholarships), or for general operating support or sports events.
Application information: Unsolicited requests are accepted but not encouraged. A contributions committee reviews all requests. Application form required. Applicants should submit the following:
1) copy of IRS Determination Letter
2) brief history of organization and description of its mission
3) how project's results will be evaluated or measured
4) explanation of why grantmaker is considered an appropriate donor for project
5) descriptive literature about organization
6) detailed description of project and amount of funding requested
7) copy of current year's organizational budget and/or project budget
8) listing of additional sources and amount of support
Initial approach: Download application form and mail letter of inquiry and application form to headquarters
Copies of proposal: 1
Committee meeting date(s): Quarterly
Deadline(s): None

210
Aon Corporation

200 E. Randolph St.
Chicago, IL 60601 (312) 381-1000

Company URL: http://www.aon.com
Establishment information: Established in 1979.
Company type: Public company
Company ticker symbol and exchange: AON/NYSE
International Securities Identification Number: GB00B5BT0K07
Business activities: Operates risk management services and management consulting company; also insurance and reinsurance brokerage.
Business type (SIC): Insurance/life; insurance/accident and health; insurance agents, brokers, and services; holding company
Financial profile for 2012: Assets, $30,500,000,000; sales volume, $11,500,000,000
Forbes 2000 ranking: 2012—842nd in sales, 611th in profits, and 731st in assets
Corporate officers: Lester B. Knight, Chair.; Gregory C. Case, Pres. and C.E.O.; Christa Davies, Exec. V.P. and C.F.O.; Peter Lieb, Exec. V.P. and Genl. Counsel; Laurel Meissner, Sr. V.P. and Cont.
Board of directors: Lester B. Knight, Chair.; Gregory C. Case; Fulvio Conti; Cheryl A. Francis; Edgar D. Jannotta; J. Michael Losh; Robert S. Morrison; Richard B. Myers; Richard C. Notebaert; Gloria Santona; Carolyn Y. Woo
Giving statement: Giving through the Aon Foundation and the Aon Memorial Education Fund.
Company EIN: 363051915

Aon Foundation

(formerly Combined International Foundation)
200 East Randolph
Chicago, IL 60601-6419 (312) 381-3555
FAX: (312) 381-6166;
E-mail: aon_foundation@aon.com

Establishment information: Established in 1984 in IL.
Donor: Aon Corp.
Contact: Carolyn Barry Frost, Pres. and Treas.
Financial data (yr. ended 12/31/11): Assets, $50,014 (M); gifts received, $10,109,436; expenditures, $10,647,115; qualifying distributions, $10,647,115; giving activities include $10,647,090 for 3,322 grants (high: $500,000; low: $25).
Purpose and activities: The Aon Foundation is the principal vehicle for Aon's philanthropic programs in the U.S. and focuses on empowering people and working with communities at risk. Aon invests in educational programs that make a marked difference in the academic achievement of young people, as well as in organizations that help develop the future workforce.
Fields of interest: Arts; Education; Environment; Disasters, preparedness/services; Youth development; American Red Cross; Human services; Community/economic development Youth; Disabilities, people with; Minorities; Economically disadvantaged.
Type of support: Employee matching gifts; Employee volunteer services; General/operating support; Program development.
Geographic limitations: Giving on a national basis in areas of company operations, with emphasis on Chicago, IL.
Support limitations: No support for fraternal, labor, political, religious, or discriminatory organizations. No grants to individuals.
Publications: Corporate giving report.
Application information: Applications not accepted. Contributes only to pre-selected organizations. The foundation utilizes an invitation only process for giving.
Board meeting date(s): 3 times per year
Officers and Directors: Carolyn Barry Frost, Pres. and Treas.; Ram Padmanabhan, Secy.; Gregory J. Besio; Gregory C. Case; Christa Davies.
Number of staff: 4
EIN: 363337340
Selected grants: The following grants are a representative sample of this grantmaker's funding activity:
$500,000 to American Red Cross, Greater Chicago Chapter, Chicago, IL, 2011. For disaster preparedness and response programs.

$399,775 to Find a Better Way, Manchester, England, 2011.
$358,926 to INSEAD Management Education Foundation, New York, NY, 2011.
$250,000 to United Way of Metropolitan Chicago, Chicago, IL, 2011.
$145,000 to World Trade Center Memorial Foundation, New York, NY, 2011.
$100,000 to Childrens Memorial Foundation, Chicago, IL, 2011.
$25,000 to Hull House Association, Chicago, IL, 2011.
$25,000 to Institute for Business and Home Safety, Tampa, FL, 2011.
$10,000 to Chicago Film Critics Association, Arlington Heights, IL, 2011.
$2,500 to Park University, Parkville, MO, 2011. For undergraduate and advanced degree programs.

Aon Memorial Education Fund

200 E. Randolph St., 8th Fl.
Chicago, IL 60601-6419 (312) 381-3551
E-mail: beth.gallagher@aon.com; URL: http://www.aon.com/usa/about-aon/aon-memorial-education-fund.jsp

Contact: Beth Gallagher, V.P.
Financial data (yr. ended 12/31/11): Assets, $6,458,781 (M); gifts received, $163,438; expenditures, $362,047; qualifying distributions, $398,451; giving activities include $267,362 for grants to individuals.
Purpose and activities: The fund provides scholarships to children of Aon employees lost on September 11th. Scholarships are awarded to individuals for post-secondary education, as well as funding for education at various levels for individuals with special needs.
Fields of interest: Higher education; Education; Disasters, 9/11/01 Disabilities, people with.
Program:
Post-Secondary Education Scholarships: Scholarships in the amount of $20,000 are awarded annually to each individual for tuition and related expenses such as books, supplies and equipment required for courses. Applicant must maintain a "C" GPA or its equivalent for undergraduate studies, and a "B" GPA for graduate studies. An individual will continue to qualify for annual awards as long as he/she is enrolled for study at an approved educational institution and maintains a minimum GPA as stated, and will not qualify for more than six years of annual awards without making a special application to the Fund. The award does not cover room and board costs.
Type of support: Employee-related scholarships; Scholarships—to individuals.
Application information: Applications not accepted.
Officers and Directors:* Ram Padmanabhan, V.P. and Secy.; Justin Dygert, V.P.; Beth Gallagher, V.P.; Paul A. Hagy*, V.P.; Robert E. Lee, V.P.; Katie Rooney, V.P.; Jeremy G.O. Farmer; Harvey N. Medvin.
EIN: 364468038

211
Apache Corporation

2000 Post Oak Blvd., Ste. 100
Houston, TX 77056-4400 (713) 296-6000
FAX: (302) 655-5049

Company URL: http://www.apachecorp.com
Establishment information: Established in 1954.
Company type: Public company
Company ticker symbol and exchange: APA/NYSE
International Securities Identification Number: US0374111054
Business activities: Conducts oil and natural gas exploration and production activities.
Business type (SIC): Extraction/oil and gas
Financial profile for 2012: Number of employees, 5,976; assets, $60,737,000,000; sales volume, $17,078,000,000; pre-tax net income, $4,877,000,000; expenses, $12,201,000,000; liabilities, $29,406,000,000
Fortune 1000 ranking: 2012—167th in revenues, 100th in profits, and 93rd in assets
Forbes 2000 ranking: 2012—545th in sales, 308th in profits, and 388th in assets
Corporate officers: G. Steven Farris, Chair. and C.E.O.; Rodney J. Eichler, Co-Pres. and C.O.O.; Roger B. Plank, Co-Pres.; Thomas P. Chambers, Exec. V.P. and C.F.O.; P. Anthony Lannie, Exec. V.P. and Genl. Counsel; Margery M. Harris, Exec. V.P., Human Resources; Matthew W. Dundrea, Sr. V.P., Treas., and Admin.; Robert J. Dye, Sr. V.P., Comms.; Rebecca A. Hoyt, V.P., C.A.O., and Cont.; Cheri L. Peper, Corp. Secy.
Board of directors: G. Steven Farris, Chair.; Randolph M. Ferlic, M.D.; Eugene C. Fiedorek; A.D. Frazier, Jr.; Patricia Albjerg Graham; Chansoo Joung; John A. Kocur; George D. Lawrence; William C. Montgomery; Rodman D. Patton; Charles J. Pitman
Subsidiaries: Apache Crude Oil Marketing, Inc., Houston, TX; Apache Delaware Investment, L.L.C., Wilmington, DE; Apache Foundation, Houston, TX; Apache Gathering Co., Houston, TX; Apache International, L.L.C., Houston, TX; Apache Louisiana Minerals, Inc., Cameron, LA; Apache Marketing, Inc., Houston, TX; Apache North America, Inc., Houston, TX; Apache Shady Lane Ranch, Inc., Houston, TX; Apache Transmission Corporation-Texas, Houston, TX; Clear Creek Hunting Preserve, Inc., Clearmont, WY; Cottonwood Aviation, Inc., Houston, TX; Dek Energy Co., Houston, TX; Gom Shelf, L.L.C., Houston, TX; Phoenix Exploration Resources, Ltd., Oklahoma City, OK
International operations: Australia; Cayman Islands; England; United Kingdom; Wales
Giving statement: Giving through the Apache Corporation Contributions Program, the Apache Foundation, and the Apache Employee Relief Fund.
Company EIN: 410747868

Apache Corporation Contributions Program

2000 Post Oak Blvd., Ste. 100
Houston, TX 77056-4497 (713) 296-6000
URL: http://www.apachecorp.com/Resources/Upload/Sustainability/community/index.html

Contact: Debbie Carter, Corp. Outreach Coord.
Purpose and activities: As a complement to its foundation, Apache also makes charitable contributions to nonprofit organizations directly. Support is given primarily in areas of company operations on a national and international basis.
Fields of interest: Arts; Education; Environment, natural resources; Environment; Health care; Independent living, disability; Human services; Community/economic development; Public affairs.
Program:
Apache Matching Gift Program: The program matches donations to charitable organizations in social welfare, education, conservation and ecology, health and human services, arts and culture, and civic improvements. Apache matches employee contributions on a dollar-for-dollar basis up to $10,000 per employee per year.
Type of support: Annual campaigns; Donated products; Employee matching gifts; Employee volunteer services; General/operating support; In-kind gifts; Scholarship funds; Sponsorships.
Geographic limitations: Giving on a national and international basis in areas of company operations, with emphasis on Denver, CO, Tulsa, OK, and Houston and Midland, TX, and in Australia, Argentina, Canada, Egypt, Kenya, and the United Kingdom.
Support limitations: No grants to individuals, or for annual tithes, building campaigns, or religious activities.
Publications: Application guidelines; Corporate giving report (including application guidelines).
Application information: Applications accepted. The Investor Relations Department handles giving. Proposals should be limited to 2 pages. Application form not required. Applicants should submit the following:
1) results expected from proposed grant
2) population served
3) name, address and phone number of organization
4) brief history of organization and description of its mission
5) how project's results will be evaluated or measured
6) detailed description of project and amount of funding requested
7) contact person
8) listing of additional sources and amount of support
9) copy of most recent annual report/audited financial statement/990
10) copy of current year's organizational budget and/or project budget
11) copy of IRS Determination Letter
12) listing of board of directors, trustees, officers and other key people and their affiliations

Proposals should include the purpose, goals, objectives, and action plan for the project, and the plan for continuing the activity beyond Apache's support, if appropriate.
Initial approach: Proposal to headquarters
Copies of proposal: 1
Deadline(s): Jan. 1 to Dec. 1
Final notification: 45 days
Number of staff: 1 full-time professional.

Apache Employee Relief Fund

2000 Post Oak Blvd., Ste. 100
Houston, TX 77056-4400 (713) 296-6000

Establishment information: Established in 2001 in TX.
Financial data (yr. ended 12/31/09): Assets, $60,402 (M).
Purpose and activities: The fund provides disaster relief for employees of Apache.
Fields of interest: Human services, emergency aid.
Type of support: Grants to individuals.
Officers and Directors:* Karen C. Kovach-Webb*, Chair. and Pres.; William A. Mintz*, V.P.; Cheri L. Peper*, Corp. Secy.; Peter J. Czerniakowski*, Treas.; Margery M. Harris; Robert R. Rayphole.
EIN: 760686831

212
Apex Aridyne Corporation

168 Doughty Blvd.
P.O. Box 960670
Inwood, NY 11096-2010 (516) 239-4400

Company URL: http://www.apexmills.com/aboutus.php
Establishment information: Established in 1943.
Company type: Subsidiary of a private company

Business activities: Manufactures textile products.
Business type (SIC): Textile mill products
Corporate officer: Edward Schlussel, Pres.
Giving statement: Giving through the Kurz-Kneiger Foundation, Inc.

Kurz-Kneiger Foundation, Inc.

168 Doughty Blvd.
Inwood, NY 11096-2010

Establishment information: Established in 1984 in NY.
Donors: Apex Aridyne Corp.; Milton Kurz.
Financial data (yr. ended 12/31/11): Assets, $778,774 (M); gifts received, $500; expenditures, $42,740; qualifying distributions, $37,860; giving activities include $37,860 for grants.
Purpose and activities: The foundation supports art museums and organizations involved with theological education, health, and Judaism.
Fields of interest: Health care; Health organizations; Religion.
Type of support: General/operating support.
Application information: Applications not accepted. Unsolicited requests for funds not accepted.
Officers: Milton Kurz, Pres.; Edward Schlussel, V.P.; Jonathan Kurz, Secy.; David Kurz, Treas.
EIN: 112680139

213
Apex CoVantage, LLC

(formerly Apex Data Services, Inc.)
198 Van Buren St.
200 Presidents Plz.
Herndon, VA 20170-5338 (703) 709-3000
FAX: (703) 709-0333

Company URL: http://www.apexcovantage.com
Establishment information: Established in 1988.
Company type: Private company
Business activities: Provides electronic publishing services; provides engineering services.
Business type (SIC): Computer services; engineering, architectural, and surveying services
Financial profile for 2010: Number of employees, 2,500
Corporate officers: James O. Edwards, Chair.; Shashikant Gupta, Pres.; Margaret Boryczka, C.O.O.; Tandy Harris, V.P., Human Resources; Jack J. Mueller, Exec. Dir.
Board of director: James O. Edwards, Chair.
Giving statement: Giving through the Apex Foundation.

The Apex Foundation

198 Van Buren St., Ste. 120
Herndon, VA 20170-5338 (703) 709-3000
E-mail: info@apexcovantage.com; Application address: 615 S. Hancock St., Philadelphia, PA 19147, tel.: (703) 753-0580; URL: http://www.apexfoundation.org

Establishment information: Established in 2002 in VA.
Donors: Apex Data Services, Inc.; Apex CoVantage, LLC; Radhika Murari; Aravind Natarajan.
Contact: Karen Kuranz
Financial data (yr. ended 12/31/11): Assets, $6,182 (M); gifts received, $80,775; expenditures, $84,611; qualifying distributions, $80,000; giving activities include $80,000 for grants.
Purpose and activities: The foundation supports programs designed to provide social assistance to people challenged by poverty, disability, or discrimination and inspire them to achieve self-sufficiency.
Fields of interest: Food services; Disasters, preparedness/services; Children/youth, services; Developmentally disabled, centers & services; Women, centers/services; Homeless, human services; Human services Disabilities, people with; Minorities; Economically disadvantaged.
Type of support: General/operating support; Program development.
Geographic limitations: Giving primarily in VA, Cambodia, and India.
Support limitations: No support for sectarian organizations.
Application information: Applications accepted. Unsolicited applications are currently not accepted.
Copies of proposal: 1
Officers and Directors:* Shashikant Gupta*, Pres.; Kristin Abbott, Secy.; John Kuranz, Exec. Dir.; Margaret Boryczka; Karen Kuranz; Srini Vasan.
EIN: 542048512
Selected grants: The following grants are a representative sample of this grantmaker's funding activity:
$14,000 to Miriams Kitchen, Washington, DC, 2010.
$5,000 to Herndon-Reston FISH, Herndon, VA, 2010.
$3,000 to Arlington Food Assistance Center, Arlington, VA, 2010.

214
Apex Oil Company, Inc.

8235 Forsyth Blvd., Ste. 400
St. Louis, MO 63105 (314) 889-9600
FAX: (314) 854-8539

Company URL: http://www.apexoil.com
Establishment information: Established in 1932.
Company type: Private company
Business activities: Sells petroleum products wholesale.
Business type (SIC): Petroleum and petroleum products—wholesale
Financial profile for 2011: Number of employees, 700; sales volume, $4,260,000,000
Corporate officers: Paul Anthony Novelly, C.E.O.; Edwin L. Wahl, Pres.; Douglas D. Hommert, Exec. V.P. and Genl. Counsel; John L. Hank, Jr., V.P., C.F.O., and Treas.; Jeffrey D. Baltz, Cont.
Subsidiaries: Clark Oil Trading Co., St. Louis, MO; Edgington Oil Co., Long Beach, CA
Giving statement: Giving through the Apex Oil Company Charitable Foundation.

Apex Oil Company Charitable Foundation

8235 Forsyth Blvd., Ste. 400
Clayton, MO 63105-1621

Establishment information: Established in 2002 in MO.
Donors: Apex Oil Co., Inc.; Edgington Oil Co.
Contact: Chandra N. Niemann, Treas.
Financial data (yr. ended 12/31/11): Assets, $7,732,327 (M); gifts received, $2,120,000; expenditures, $3,066,095; qualifying distributions, $3,050,600; giving activities include $3,050,600 for 18 grants (high: $1,225,000; low: $500).
Purpose and activities: The foundation supports organizations involved with orchestras, education, health, and human services.
Fields of interest: Performing arts, orchestras; Secondary school/education; Higher education; Scholarships/financial aid; Education; Hospitals (general); Health care, clinics/centers; Health care; Residential/custodial care, hospices; Human services.
Type of support: Building/renovation; Capital campaigns; General/operating support; Program development; Scholarship funds.
Geographic limitations: Giving primarily in Washington, DC, New York, NY, St. Louis, MO, and New Zealand.
Application information: Applications accepted. Application form not required. Applicants should submit the following:
1) name, address and phone number of organization
2) copy of IRS Determination Letter
3) detailed description of project and amount of funding requested
Initial approach: Proposal
Deadline(s): None
Officers and Directors:* Paul A. Novelly*, Pres.; Karon M. Burns, Secy.; Chandra N. Nieman*, Treas.; Paul A. Novelly II.
EIN: 710914470
Selected grants: The following grants are a representative sample of this grantmaker's funding activity:
$1,492,000 to Horatio Alger Association of Distinguished Americans, Alexandria, VA, 2010. To provide scholarships.
$360,000 to Fulton School at Saint Albans, Saint Albans, MO, 2010. To maintain facility and provide tuition assistance.
$200,000 to Beth Israel Medical Center, New York, NY, 2010. For Parkinson's research.
$100,000 to Barnes-Jewish Hospital Foundation, Saint Louis, MO, 2010. For sclerosis research.
$100,000 to Saint Anthonys Charitable Foundation, Saint Louis, MO, 2010. To provide health care to the needy.
$15,000 to John F. Kennedy Center for the Performing Arts, Washington, DC, 2010. For arts education.
$10,000 to Villa Duchesne, Saint Louis, MO, 2010.
$10,000 to Visitation Academy of Saint Louis, Saint Louis, MO, 2010.
$3,000 to Saint Louis ARC, Saint Louis, MO, 2010. To provide services to the disabled.
$1,500 to Winter Opera, Saint Louis, MO, 2010. For opera theater in Saint Louis.

215
Apogee Enterprises, Inc.

4400 W. 78th St., Ste. 520
Minneapolis, MN 55435 (952) 835-1874
FAX: (952) 835-1874

Company URL: http://www.apog.com
Establishment information: Established in 1949.
Company type: Public company
Company ticker symbol and exchange: APOG/NASDAQ
Business activities: Designs, develops, and manufactures glass products, services, and systems.
Business type (SIC): Glass products/miscellaneous
Financial profile for 2013: Number of employees, 3,871; assets, $520,140,000; sales volume, $700,220,000; pre-tax net income, $26,570,000; expenses, $672,800,000; liabilities, $186,820,000
Corporate officers: Bernard P. Aldrich, Chair.; Joseph F. Puishys, Pres. and C.E.O.; James S. Porter, C.F.O.; John A. Klein, Sr. V.P., Opers.; Gary

R. Johnson, V.P. and Treas.; Patricia A. Beithon, Genl. Counsel and Secy.
Board of directors: Bernard P. Aldrich, Chair.; Jerome L. Davis; Sara L. Hays; Robert J. Marzec; Stephen C. Mitchell; J. Terry Manning; Joseph F. Puishys; Richard V. Reynolds; David E. Weiss
Subsidiaries: Harmon Contract, Inc., Minneapolis, MN; Harmon Glass Co., Minneapolis, MN; Viracon, Inc., Owatonna, MN; Viracon/Curvlite, Inc., Owatonna, MN
Giving statement: Giving through the Apogee Enterprises, Inc. Corporate Giving Program.
Company EIN: 410919654

Apogee Enterprises, Inc. Corporate Giving Program
440 W. 78th St., Ste. 520
Minneapolis, MN 55435-5446 (952) 835-1874
URL: http://www.apog.com/Culture/community.html

Purpose and activities: Apogee makes charitable contributions to nonprofit organizations involved with education, cancer, food services, and athletics. Support is given primarily in areas of company operations.
Fields of interest: Cancer; Cancer research; Cancer, leukemia research; Food services; Athletics/sports, Special Olympics; United Ways and Federated Giving Programs.
Type of support: Employee volunteer services; General/operating support.
Geographic limitations: Giving on a national basis in areas of company operations.

216
Apollo Group, Inc.
(doing business as University Of Phoenix)
4025 S. Riverpoint Pkwy.
Phoenix, AZ 85040 (480) 966-5394
FAX: (480) 379-3503

Company URL: http://www.apollogrp.edu/
Establishment information: Established in 1973.
Company type: Public company
Company ticker symbol and exchange: APOL/NASDAQ
Business activities: Provider of higher education programs for working adults.
Business type (SIC): Colleges, universities, and professional schools
Financial profile for 2012: Number of employees, 49,992; assets, $2,868,320,000; sales volume, $4,253,340,000; pre-tax net income, $666,250,000; expenses, $3,577,000,000; liabilities, $1,939,940,000
Fortune 1000 ranking: 2012—554th in revenues, 374th in profits, and 764th in assets
Corporate officers: Peter V. Sperling, Chair.; Terri C. Bishop, Vice-Chair.; Gregory W. Cappelli, C.E.O.; Curt Uehlein, C.O.O.; Brian Swartz, Sr. V.P. and C.F.O.; Jeff Langenbach, Sr. V.P. and C.A.O.; Sean B.W. Martin, Sr. V.P., Genl. Counsel, and Secy.; Mark Brenner, Sr. V.P., Corp. Comms.
Board of directors: Peter V. Sperling, Chair.; Terri C. Bishop, Vice-Chair.; Gregory W. Cappelli; Matthew Carter, Jr.; Richard H. Dozer; Roy A. Herberger, Jr.; Ann Kirschner; Robert S. Murley; Manuel F. Rivelo; Darby E. Shupp; Margaret Spellings; John G. Sperling; Allen Weiss
Giving statement: Giving through the University of Phoenix Foundation.
Company EIN: 860419443

University of Phoenix Foundation
4025 S. Riverpoint Pkwy., Stop CF-K815
Phoenix, AZ 85040-0723
E-mail: upxfoundation@phoenix.edu; URL: http://www.upxfoundation.org

Establishment information: Established in 2006 in AZ.
Donors: Apollo Group, Inc.; Liberty Mutual; Inmart Group; Herff Jones, Inc.
Financial data (yr. ended 08/31/11): Assets, $1,157,993 (M); gifts received, $1,700,000; expenditures, $2,004,615; qualifying distributions, $2,003,642; giving activities include $2,003,642 for grants.
Purpose and activities: The foundation supports programs designed to increase access to education, with emphasis on underrepresented and low-income students.
Fields of interest: Education, research; Higher education; Education, services; Education; Youth, services Economically disadvantaged.
Type of support: General/operating support; Program development; Research; Scholarship funds; Sponsorships.
Geographic limitations: Giving primarily in AZ, CA, and Washington, DC.
Application information: The foundation is in the process of revising its application guidelines. Please visit website for updated information.
Officers and Director:* Nina Munson*, Chair.; Nancy Hennigan, Secy.; Mathew Beckler, Treas.; Pat Gottfried, Exec. Dir.; Charlotte Saylors.
EIN: 205964568
Selected grants: The following grants are a representative sample of this grantmaker's funding activity:
$150,000 to WestEd, San Francisco, CA, 2010. For general support.
$100,000 to California Tomorrow, Oakland, CA, 2010. For general support.
$100,000 to Center for American Progress, Washington, DC, 2010. For general support.
$100,000 to College Track, Oakland, CA, 2010. For general support.
$50,000 to Childrens Museum of Phoenix, Phoenix, AZ, 2010. For general support.
$50,000 to East Bay Zoological Society, Oakland, CA, 2010. For general support.
$50,000 to MIND Research Institute, Santa Ana, CA, 2010. For general support.
$50,000 to Robert Toigo Foundation, Oakland, CA, 2010. For general support.
$50,000 to Save San Francisco Bay Association, Oakland, CA, 2010. For general support.
$46,800 to Junior Achievement Worldwide, Colorado Springs, CO, 2010. For general support.

217
Apple, Inc.
(formerly Apple Computer, Inc.)
1 Infinite Loop
Cupertino, CA 95014 (408) 996-1010
FAX: (408) 996-0275

Company URL: http://www.apple.com
Establishment information: Established in 1976.
Company type: Public company
Company ticker symbol and exchange: AAPL/NASDAQ
Business activities: Designs, manufactures and markets personal computers, mobile communication and media devices, and portable digital music players.
Business type (SIC): Computer and office equipment
Financial profile for 2012: Number of employees, 72,800; assets, $176,064,000,000; sales volume, $156,508,000,000; pre-tax net income, $55,763,000,000; expenses, $101,267,000,000; liabilities, $57,854,000,000
Fortune 1000 ranking: 2012—6th in revenues, 2nd in profits, and 37th in assets
Forbes 2000 ranking: 2012—15th in sales, 2nd in profits, and 141st in assets
Corporate officers: Arthur D. Levinson, Ph.D., Chair.; Timothy Cook, C.E.O.; Peter Oppenheimer, Sr. V.P. and C.F.O.; D. Bruce Sewell, Sr. V.P. and Genl. Counsel; Jeff Williams, Sr. V.P., Opers.; Phillip W. Schiller, Sr.V.P., Marketing
Board of directors: Arthur D. Levinson, Ph.D., Chair.; William V. Campbell; Timothy Cook; Millard S. Drexler; Albert A. Gore, Jr.; Robert A. Iger; Andrea Jung; Ronald D. Sugar, Ph.D.
Subsidiary: FileMaker, Inc., Santa Clara, CA
Giving statement: Giving through the Apple Inc. Contributions Program and the Farris, Vaughan, Wills & Murphy LLP Pro Bono Program.
Company EIN: 942404110

Apple Inc. Contributions Program
1 Infinite Loop
Cupertino, CA 95014 (408) 996-1010

Purpose and activities: Apple Inc. matches contributions made by its employees to nonprofit organizations.
Fields of interest: General charitable giving.
Type of support: Employee matching gifts.
Application information: Applications not accepted. Contributes only through employee matching gifts.

218
Apple Bank for Savings
122 E. 42nd St., 9th Fl.
New York, NY 10168 (212) 224-6400
FAX: (212) 224-6580

Company URL: http://www.theapplebank.com
Establishment information: Established in 1863.
Company type: Private company
Business activities: Operates savings bank.
Business type (SIC): Banks/commercial; savings institutions
Financial profile for 2011: Assets, $7,582,245,000; liabilities, $7,582,245,000
Corporate officers: Alan Shamoon, Chair., Pres., and C.E.O.; Steven C. Bush, Exec. V.P. and C.A.O.; Douglas L. Van Horne, Sr. V.P. and C.I.O.; Bruce Herman, Sr. V.P., Genl. Counsel, and Secy.; Louis Rawden, Sr. V.P. and Cont.
Board of director: Alan Shamoon, Chair.
Giving statement: Giving through the Apple Bank for Savings Corporate Giving Program.

Apple Bank for Savings Corporate Giving Program
1075 Central Park Ave.
Scarsdale, NY 10583 (914) 721-2155

Contact: Richard O' Brien, V.P.
Purpose and activities: Apple makes charitable contributions to nonprofit organizations involved with substance abuse, law enforcement, employment, housing, community development, and senior citizens. Support is given primarily in areas of company operations.

Fields of interest: Substance abuse, services; Crime/law enforcement; Housing/shelter; Community/economic development Aging.
Type of support: Building/renovation; In-kind gifts; Program development; Sponsorships.
Geographic limitations: Giving primarily in areas of company operations, with emphasis on NY.
Application information: Application form not required.
Initial approach: Proposal to headquarters
Deadline(s): None

219
Applied Industrial Technologies, Inc.

(formerly Bearings, Inc.)
1 Applied Plz.
Cleveland, OH 44115-2511 (216) 426-4000
FAX: (216) 426-4845

Company URL: http://web.applied.com
Establishment information: Established in 1923.
Company type: Public company
Company ticker symbol and exchange: AIT/NYSE
Business activities: Sells industrial and fluid power products and systems wholesale; provides fluid power, mechanical, electrical, and rubber shop services.
Business type (SIC): Industrial machinery and equipment—wholesale; machinery/industrial and commercial
Financial profile for 2012: Number of employees, 4,664; assets, $962,180,000; sales volume, $2,375,450,000; pre-tax net income, $166,830,000; expenses, $2,207,050,000; liabilities, $290,050,000
Fortune 1000 ranking: 2012—843rd in revenues, 721st in profits, and 972nd in assets
Corporate officers: John F. Meier, Chair.; Neil A. Schrimsher, C.E.O.; Benjamin J. Mondics, Pres. and C.O.O.; Mark O. Eisele, V.P., C.F.O., and Treas.; Fred D. Bauer, V.P., Genl. Counsel, and Secy.; Thomas E. Armold, V.P., Mktg.; Daniel T. Brezovec, Corp. Cont.
Board of directors: John F. Meier, Chair.; William G. Bares; Thomas A. Commes; Peter A. Dorsman; L. Thomas Hiltz; Edith Kelly-Green; Dan P. Komnenovich; Michael J. Moore; Vincent K. Petrella; Neil A. Schrimsher; Jerry Sue Thornton, Ph.D.; Peter C. Wallace
Subsidiary: Applied Industrial Technologies-Mainline, Inc., Appleton, WI
International operations: Barbados; Canada
Giving statement: Giving through the Applied Industrial Technologies, Inc. Corporate Giving Program.
Company EIN: 340117420

Applied Industrial Technologies, Inc. Corporate Giving Program

(formerly Bearings, Inc. Corporate Giving Program)
1 Applied Plz.
Cleveland, OH 44115-2511 (216) 426-4000
URL: http://web.applied.com/base.cfm?page_id=1545

Purpose and activities: Applied Industrial Technologies makes charitable contributions to nonprofit organizations involved with tutoring and education, community and economic development, infant health, and food banks. Giving also to national organizations.
Fields of interest: Elementary school/education; Health care, infants; Food banks; Housing/shelter, volunteer services; Boys & girls clubs; Salvation Army; Pregnancy centers; Community/economic development, fund raising/fund distribution; Community/economic development; United Ways and Federated Giving Programs.
Type of support: Employee volunteer services; Sponsorships.
Geographic limitations: Giving on a local and national basis.
Publications: Annual report.
Application information:
Copies of proposal: 1

220
Applied Materials, Inc.

3050 Bowers Ave.
P.O. Box 58039
Santa Clara, CA 95054-3299
(408) 727-5555

Company URL: http://www.appliedmaterials.com
Establishment information: Established in 1967.
Company type: Public company
Company ticker symbol and exchange: AMAT/NASDAQ
International Securities Identification Number: US0382221051
Business activities: Researches, develops, and manufactures semiconductor production equipment.
Business type (SIC): Machinery/special industry; electronic components and accessories
Financial profile for 2012: Assets, $11,700,000,000; sales volume, $8,100,000,000
Fortune 1000 ranking: 2012—302nd in revenues, 719th in profits, and 345th in assets
Forbes 2000 ranking: 2012—1090th in sales, 1781st in profits, and 1363rd in assets
Corporate officers: Michael R. Splinter, Chair. and C.E.O.; Gary E. Dickerson, Pres.; George S. Davis, Exec. V.P. and C.F.O.; Joseph J. Sweeney, Sr. V.P., Genl. Counsel, and Corp. Secy.; Joseph Flanagan, Sr. V.P., Opers.; Mary Humiston, Sr. V.P., Human Resources
Board of directors: Michael R. Splinter, Chair.; Aart J. De Geus; Stephen R. Forrest, Ph.D.; Thomas J. Iannotti; Susan M. James; Alexander A. Karsner; James C. Morgan; Gerhard H. Parker; Dennis D. Powell; Willem P. Roelandts; James E. Rogers; Robert H. Swan
Plant: Austin, TX
Offices: Chandler, Phoenix, AZ; Santa Clara, CA; Boise, ID; Gloucester, MA; Kalispell, MT; Rio Rancho, NM; Hopewell Junction, NY; Hillsboro, OR; Richardson, TX; Manassas, VA
Giving statement: Giving through the Applied Materials, Inc. Corporate Giving Program and the Applied Materials Foundation.
Company EIN: 941655526

Applied Materials, Inc. Corporate Giving Program

3050 Bowers Ave.
P.O. Box 58039
Santa Clara, CA 95054-3299 (408) 727-5555
E-mail: community_affairs@appliedmaterials.com;
URL: http://www.appliedmaterials.com/about/cr

Purpose and activities: As a complement to its foundation, Applied Materials also makes charitable contributions to K-12 educational institutions and nonprofit organizations directly. Support is limited to areas of company operations in California, Massachusetts, Montana, Texas, and Utah, with emphasis on Silicon Valley, California, and in Canada, China, France, Germany, India, Israel, Japan, Malaysia, the Philippines, Singapore, South Korea, Switzerland, and Taiwan.
Fields of interest: Arts; Elementary/secondary education; Environment, energy; Environmental education; Human services; Community/economic development.
International interests: Canada; China; France; Germany; India; Israel; Japan; Malaysia; Philippines; Singapore; South Korea; Switzerland; Taiwan.
Type of support: Continuing support; Curriculum development; Faculty/staff development; Program development.
Geographic limitations: Giving limited to areas of company operations in CA, MA, MT, TX, and UT, with emphasis on Silicon Valley, CA, and in Canada, China, France, Germany, India, Israel, Japan, Malaysia, the Philippines, Singapore, South Korea, Switzerland, and Taiwan.
Support limitations: No support for fraternal, religious, or political organizations, or missing children's organizations. No grants to individuals, or for general operating support, research, commencements, PTAs, alumni groups, health-related programs or sponsorships, fundraisers such as walk-a-thons, runs, teams in training, sporting events for school or civic teams, capital campaigns, brick and morta projects, equipment, home building, or physical structures.
Application information: Applications accepted. Application form required.
Initial approach: Complete online application form; e-mail letter of inquiry for organizations located outside of the U.S.
Committee meeting date(s): Semi-annually
Deadline(s): Jan. 15 and June 15

The Applied Materials Foundation

3050 Bowers Ave., MS 0106
Santa Clara, CA 95054-3201
E-mail: applied_materials_foundation@amat.com; E-mail contact for organizations located outside of the U.S.: community_affairs@amat.com;
URL: http://www.appliedmaterials.com/about/cr

Establishment information: Established in 1994.
Donor: Applied Materials, Inc.
Contact: Claudia Schwiefert, Grant Mgr.
Financial data (yr. ended 10/31/11): Assets, $29,390,741 (M); gifts received, $19,966,513; expenditures, $6,486,733; qualifying distributions, $6,393,756; giving activities include $6,321,408 for 165 grants (high: $338,505; low: $20).
Purpose and activities: The foundation supports programs designed to promote arts and culture; education; environmental awareness and sustainability; and civic engagement.
Fields of interest: Performing arts, theater; Arts; Elementary/secondary education; Higher education; Adult/continuing education; Education, reading; Education; Environmental education; Environment; Food services; Food banks; Housing/shelter; Disasters, preparedness/services; Youth development, adult & child programs; Youth, services; Homeless, human services; Human services; International relief; Mathematics; Science; Leadership development Economically disadvantaged.
Programs:
Arts and Culture Grants: The foundation supports arts and culture programs designed to have broad community appeal; initiatives that take arts and culture outside traditional settings to reach young people of diverse backgrounds, particularly in economically disadvantaged neighborhoods; bring the arts to educational programs and organizations; offer opportunities for employee engagement; and

serves the North America communities in which Applied Materials does business.

Civic Engagement Grants: The foundation supports programs designed to meet basic needs such as food, water, and housing; support the infrastructure of the nonprofit sector and its leadership; provide initiatives that can be replicated to reach multiple communities; offer opportunities for employee engagement; and address community needs in North American sites where Applied Materials does business.

Education Grants: The foundation supports programs designed to serve students in grades K-12; promote traditional skills such as reading, writing, math, science and technology, and other subjects that prepare young people for entering the workforce; address critical education needs through innovative approaches to learning; expand existing efforts in order to reach more students or a wider geographic area; partner with other nonprofit groups to create, implement or evaluate shared programs; provide adult education and training in communities where unemployment or underemployment are particular challenges; offer opportunities for employee engagement; and address community needs in North America sites where Applied Materials does business.

Employee Matching Gifts: The foundation matches contributions made by its employees to K-12 schools and nonprofit organizations on a one-for-one basis up to $2,000 per employee, per year.

Environmental Grants: The foundation support programs designed to demonstrate the benefits of solar energy; promote environmental education for young people, especially in underserved communities; encourage hands on opportunities for employee volunteers and their families; provide innovative initiatives that can be replicated to reach more communities; and address community needs in sites where Applied Materials does business.

Type of support: Annual campaigns; Continuing support; Curriculum development; Program development; Sponsorships.

Geographic limitations: Giving primarily in areas of company operations, with emphasis on San Jose, CA, Gloucester, MA, Kalispell, MT and Austin, TX; giving also to organizations outside of the United States.

Support limitations: No support for missing children organizations, fraternities, religious or political organizations, commencements, PTAs, or alumni groups. No grants to individuals, or for general operating support, capital campaigns, research, sporting events for schools or civic teams, health-related programs or sponsorships, fundraisers such as walk-a-thons, runs, team in training, etc., or bricks/mortar, equipment, home building, or physical structures.

Publications: Application guidelines; Corporate giving report.

Application information: Applications accepted. Applicants should submit the following:

1) name, address and phone number of organization
2) detailed description of project and amount of funding requested
3) contact person

Initial approach: Complete online application; e-mail community affairs for organizations located outside of the United States

Board meeting date(s): Semi-annually

Deadline(s): Jan. 15 and June 15

Final notification: Mar. 15 to 31 and Aug. 15 to 31

Officers and Directors:* Michael R. Splinter*, Pres.; Charmaine F. Mesina, Secy.; Robert M. Friess, C.F.O.; Siobhan Kenney, Exec. Dir.; George S. Davis; James C. Morgan.

EIN: 770386898

Selected grants: The following grants are a representative sample of this grantmaker's funding activity:

$250,000 to San Jose Unified School District, San Jose, CA, 2011. For Closing the Achievement Gap.

$200,000 to Capital Area Food Bank of Texas, Austin, TX, 2011. For The Comprehensive Campaign.

$200,000 to Santa Clara University, Santa Clara, CA, 2011. For CSTS Collaborative, 5 Year Commitment.

$200,000 to Second Harvest Food Bank of Santa Clara and San Mateo Counties, San Jose, CA, 2011. For Freedom from Hunger Campaign.

$162,934 to Global Impact, Alexandria, VA, 2011. For Japan Earthquake/Tsunami Disaster Relief Matching.

$130,000 to Arts Council Silicon Valley, San Jose, CA, 2011. For Excellence in the Arts.

$30,000 to Teach for America, Phoenix, AZ, 2011. To sponsor a School.

$15,000 to American Red Cross, Central Texas, Austin, TX, 2011. For Donation for Victims of Central Texas Fires.

$15,000 to Meals on Wheels and More, Austin, TX, 2011. For Adopt-A-Route.

$15,000 to TheaterWorks, Palo Alto, CA, 2011. For Theatreworks for Schools.

221
AptarGroup, Inc.

475 W. Terra Cotta Ste. E
Crystal Lake, IL 60014-9695
(815) 477-0424
FAX: (815) 477-0481

Company URL: http://www.aptargroup.com/

Establishment information: Established in 1992.

Company type: Public company

Company ticker symbol and exchange: ATR/NYSE

Business activities: Manufactures pumps, molding, and aerosol valves.

Business type (SIC): Machinery/general industry; plastic products/miscellaneous

Financial profile for 2012: Number of employees, 12,000; assets, $2,324,410,000; sales volume, $2,331,040,000; pre-tax net income, $241,370,000; expenses, $2,072,120,000; liabilities, $944,520,000

Fortune 1000 ranking: 2012—852nd in revenues, 631st in profits, and 819th in assets

Corporate officers: King W. Harris, Chair.; Stephen J. Hagge, Pres. and C.E.O.; Robert W. Kuhn, Exec. V.P., C.F.O., and Secy.; Ursula Saint-Leger, V.P., Human Resources

Board of directors: King W. Harris, Chair.; Alain Chevassus; Leslie A. Desjardins; George L. Fotiades; Leo Guthart; Stephen J. Hagge; Giovanna Kampouri-Monnas; Peter H. Pfeiffer; Joanne Smith; Ralf K. Wunderlich

International operations: India; Mexico

Giving statement: Giving through the AptarGroup Charitable Foundation.

Company EIN: 363853103

AptarGroup Charitable Foundation

475 W. Terra Cotta Ste. E
Crystal Lake, IL 60014-3407 (815) 477-0424

Establishment information: Established in 1994 in IL.

Donor: AptarGroup, Inc.

Contact: Lawrence Lowrimore, Secy.

Financial data (yr. ended 12/31/11): Assets, $145,836 (M); gifts received, $183,300; expenditures, $272,504; qualifying distributions, $272,504; giving activities include $236,254 for grants and $36,250 for grants to individuals.

Purpose and activities: The foundation supports organizations involved with arts and culture, education, health, and human services.

Fields of interest: Performing arts; Arts; Higher education; Education; Health care; Family services; Family services, domestic violence; Human services; United Ways and Federated Giving Programs.

Program:

Employee Matching Gift Program: The foundation matches contributions made by employees of AptarGroup to nonprofit organizations on a one-for-one basis, up to $6,000 per employee per year.

Type of support: Employee matching gifts; General/operating support; Scholarships—to individuals.

Geographic limitations: Giving primarily in areas of company operations in CT, IL, MA, and WI.

Support limitations: No support for nursing homes, animal welfare groups, national or international relief organizations, primary, secondary, or theological schools, or religious, civic, fraternal, veterans', social, or political organizations. No grants to individuals (except for scholarships), or for testimonial dinners, fundraising events, courtesy advertising, or trips or tours.

Publications: Application guidelines.

Application information: Applications accepted. Application form required. Applicants should submit the following:

1) copy of IRS Determination Letter
2) brief history of organization and description of its mission
3) geographic area to be served
4) copy of most recent annual report/audited financial statement/990
5) listing of board of directors, trustees, officers and other key people and their affiliations
6) detailed description of project and amount of funding requested
7) copy of current year's organizational budget and/or project budget
8) listing of additional sources and amount of support

Initial approach: Contact foundation for application form

Board meeting date(s): June and Dec.

Deadline(s): Mar. 15 and Oct. 15

Officers and Directors:* Stephen J. Hagge*, Chair., Pres., and Treas.; Patrick Doherty*, V.P.; Phil Miller*, V.P.; Eric S. Ruskoski*, V.P.; Lawrence Lowrimore*, Secy.

EIN: 363927834

Selected grants: The following grants are a representative sample of this grantmaker's funding activity:

$16,500 to United Way of McHenry County, McHenry, IL, 2010.

$6,840 to American Cancer Society, Waukesha, WI, 2010.

$6,000 to Woodstock Mozart Festival, Woodstock, IL, 2010.

$5,000 to McHenry County College Foundation, Crystal Lake, IL, 2010.

$5,000 to Sterling House Community Center, Stratford, CT, 2010.

$4,100 to American Cancer Society, Batavia, IL, 2010.

$4,100 to Raue Center for the Arts, Crystal Lake, IL, 2010.

$4,000 to Bradley University, Peoria, IL, 2010.

$2,100 to Illinois State University Foundation, Normal, IL, 2010.
$2,000 to Family Service of Waukesha, Waukesha, WI, 2010.

222
Aqua America, Inc.

762 W. Lancaster Ave.
Bryn Mawr, PA 19010-3489
(610) 527-8000
FAX: (610) 645-1061

Company URL: https://www.aquaamerica.com
Establishment information: Established in 1886.
Company type: Public company
Company ticker symbol and exchange: WTR/NYSE
Business activities: Operates water and wastewater services utility holding company.
Business type (SIC): Water suppliers
Financial profile for 2012: Number of employees, 1,619; assets, $4,858,520,000; sales volume, $757,760,000; pre-tax net income, $250,970,000; expenses, $436,240,000; liabilities, $3,472,810,000
Corporate officers: Nicholas DeBenedictis, Chair., Pres., and C.E.O.; David P. Smeltzer, Exec. V.P. and C.F.O.; Robert A. Rubin, Sr. V.P., C.A.O., and Cont.; Christopher H. Franklin, Sr. V.P., Genl. Counsel and Secy.
Board of directors: Nicholas DeBenedictis, Chair.; Mary C. Carroll; Richard Glanton; Lon R. Greenberg; William P. Hankowsky; Wendell F. Holland, Esq.; Mario Mele; Ellen T. Ruff; Andrew J. Sordoni III
Giving statement: Giving through the Aqua America, Inc. Corporate Giving Program.
Company EIN: 231702594

Aqua America, Inc. Corporate Giving Program

c/o Dir., Corp. Giving, Corp. & Public Affairs
762 W. Lancaster Ave.
Bryn Mawr, PA 19010-3402 (877) 987-2782
URL: https://www.aquaamerica.com/about-aqua/corporate-giving.aspx

Purpose and activities: As a complement to its foundation, Aqua America, Inc. makes charitable donations to nonprofit organizations involved with the environment and environmental advocacy. Support is given primarily in areas of company operations.
Fields of interest: Environment.
Type of support: Advocacy; General/operating support.
Geographic limitations: Giving primarily in areas of company operations in FL, IL, IN, NC, NJ, NY, OH, PA, TX, and VA.
Application information: Applications accepted.
Initial approach: Letter of inquiry to headquarters
Trustee: Batholomew P. Baron.

223
ARAMARK Corporation

ARAMARK Tower
1101 Market St.
Philadelphia, PA 19107 (215) 238-3000

Company URL: http://www.aramark.com
Establishment information: Established in 1959.
Company type: Subsidiary of a private company
Business activities: Provides food and facility services; rents and markets uniform and career apparel.
Business type (SIC): Restaurants and drinking places; personal services/miscellaneous
Financial profile for 2011: Number of employees, 208,000; assets, $10,221,900,000; sales volume, $12,571,700,000
Corporate officers: Joseph Neubauer, Chair.; Eric J. Foss, Pres. and C.E.O.; L. Frederick Sutherland, Exec. V.P. and C.F.O.; Lynn B. McKee, Exec. V.P., Human Resources; Christopher S. Holland, Sr. V.P. and Treas.
Board of directors: Joseph Neubauer, Chair.; Eric J. Foss; Christopher S. Holland; L. Frederick Sutherland
Subsidiary: ARAMARK Uniform & Career Apparel Group, Inc., Burbank, CA
International operations: Argentina; Belgium; British Virgin Islands; Canada; Chile; China; Colombia; Czech Republic; Germany; Greece; Hong Kong; Ireland; Japan; Luxembourg; Mexico; Netherlands; Peru; Singapore; South Korea; Spain; United Kingdom
Giving statement: Giving through the ARAMARK Corporation Contributions Program.
Company EIN: 952051630

ARAMARK Corporation Contributions Program

ARAMARK Tower
1101 Market St.
Philadelphia, PA 19107-2934
URL: http://www.aramark.com/SocialResponsibility/CommunityInvolvement/

Contact: Donna Irvin, Exec. Dir., Corp. Contribs.
Purpose and activities: ARAMARK makes charitable contributions to nonprofit organizations involved with community development. Support is given primarily in areas of company operations; giving also to national organizations.
Fields of interest: Disasters, preparedness/services; Family services; Community/economic development.
Type of support: Annual campaigns; Capital campaigns; Employee matching gifts; Employee-related scholarships; In-kind gifts.
Geographic limitations: Giving primarily in areas of company operations.

224
Aramco Services Company

9009 W. Loop S.
Houston, TX 77096-1719 (713) 432-4000

Company URL: http://www.aramcoservices.com
Establishment information: Established in 1991.
Company type: Subsidiary of a foreign company
Business activities: Produces crude oil; conducts mining activities.
Business type (SIC): Extraction/oil and gas
Corporate officers: Mohammed Y. Al-Qahtani, Pres. and C.E.O.; Richard Hall, V.P., Finance
Giving statement: Giving through the Aramco Services Company Contributions Program.

Aramco Services Company Contributions Program

9009 W. Loop S.
Houston, TX 77096-1799 (713) 432-4000
URL: http://www.aramcoservices.com/community/

Purpose and activities: Aramco makes charitable contributions to nonprofit organizations involved with education, safe neighborhoods, health care, and the environment. Support is given primarily in areas of company operations in Houston, Texas.
Fields of interest: Media, television; Education, public education; Environment, natural resources; Environment; Health care; Neuroscience research; Housing/shelter, volunteer services; Safety/disasters; Human services, fund raising/fund distribution; Social sciences, fund raising/fund distribution.
Type of support: Continuing support; Employee volunteer services; Sponsorships.
Geographic limitations: Giving primarily in areas of company operations in Houston, TX.
Support limitations: No support for political or religious organizations.

225
Arbeit & Co.

601 2nd Ave. S., Ste. 4950
Minneapolis, MN 55402-4608
(612) 333-7660

Establishment information: Established in 1995.
Company type: Private company
Business activities: Provides investment services; holding company.
Business type (SIC): Investment offices; holding company
Corporate officers: Gerald Rauenhorst, Principal; Henriette Rauenhorst, Principal
Giving statement: Giving through the Better Way Foundation, Inc.

Better Way Foundation, Inc.

(formerly Alpha Omega Foundation, Inc.)
10350 Bren Rd. West
Minnetonka, MN 55343-9014 (952) 656-4597
E-mail: info@betterwayfoundation.org; URL: http://betterwayfoundation.org/

Establishment information: Established around 1994 in FL.
Donors: North Star Ventures; Arbeit Investment, LP; Arbeit & Co.; Opus Corp.
Financial data (yr. ended 12/31/11): Assets, $31,626,422 (M); expenditures, $1,538,467; qualifying distributions, $1,159,943; giving activities include $1,159,943 for grants.
Purpose and activities: The foundation supports programs designed to provide holistic and cost-effective development opportunities to young children and families. Special emphasis is directed toward programs designed to improve early childhood outcomes.
Fields of interest: Education, early childhood education; Higher education; Health care; Nutrition; Family services; Human services; United Ways and Federated Giving Programs; Catholic agencies & churches Children; Economically disadvantaged.
Type of support: Capital campaigns; Continuing support; General/operating support; Program development; Research; Scholarship funds.
Geographic limitations: Giving primarily in CA, IN, MN, WA, and Tanzania.
Support limitations: No grants to individuals.
Publications: Application guidelines.
Application information: Applications accepted. Unsolicited full proposals are not accepted. Organizations interested in presenting an idea for funding must submit a brief letter of inquiry. Application form not required. Applicants should submit the following:

1) name, address and phone number of organization
2) detailed description of project and amount of funding requested
3) contact person

Initial approach: Complete online letter of inquiry
Deadline(s): None

Officers and Directors:* Matthew G. Rauenhorst*, Chair. and Pres.; Amy R. Goldman*, V.P.; Sophie Kelley, V.P.; Mary Pickard, V.P.; Fr. Kevin McDonough*, Secy.; Judy Mahoney*, Treas.; Kristin Grubb, Tax Off.; Anne Mahony; Louise Myers; Gia Rauenhorst; Steve Cashin.
EIN: 411795984

226
Arbella, Inc.

(doing business as Arbella Mutual Insurance Co.)
1100 Crown Colony Dr.
Quincy, MA 02169 (617) 328-2800
FAX: (617) 328-2970

Company URL: https://www.arbella.com
Establishment information: Established in 1988.
Company type: Subsidiary of a private company
Business activities: Sells fire and casualty insurance.
Business type (SIC): Insurance/fire, marine, and casualty
Corporate officers: John F. Donohue, Chair., Pres. and Co-C.E.O.; Douglas R. Jones, Co-C.E.O.; Robert P. Medwid, Exec. V.P., Treas., and C.F.O.
Board of director: John F. Donohue, Chair.
Giving statement: Giving through the Arbella Insurance Group Charitable Foundation, Inc.

Arbella Insurance Group Charitable Foundation, Inc.

(formerly Arabella Charitable Foundation, Inc.)
101 Arch St., Ste. 1860
Boston, MA 02110-1118 (617) 769-3040
E-mail: charitable.foundation@arbella.com;
URL: https://www.arbella.com/arbella-insurance/why-arbella/arbella-insurance-foundation

Establishment information: Established in 2004 in MA.
Donor: Arbella, Inc.
Financial data (yr. ended 12/31/10): Assets, $29,465,858 (M); gifts received, $15,000,000; expenditures, $2,273,994; qualifying distributions, $1,010,701; giving activities include $1,010,701 for 446 grants (high: $125,000; low: $18) and $939,066 for 1 foundation-administered program.
Purpose and activities: The foundation supports hospitals and organizations involved with orchestras, education, genetic diseases, cancer, medical research, legal aid, hunger, automotive safety, human services, immigration, and community development.
Fields of interest: Performing arts, orchestras; Law school/education; Education; Hospitals (general); Genetic diseases and disorders; Cancer; Cancer research; Medical research; Legal services; Food services; Safety, automotive safety; Athletics/sports, Special Olympics; Children/youth, services; Children, services; Family services; Homeless, human services; Human services; Civil/human rights, immigrants; Community/economic development; United Ways and Federated Giving Programs.
Type of support: Employee volunteer services; General/operating support; Program development; Scholarship funds.
Geographic limitations: Giving primarily in areas of company operations, with emphasis on CT and MA.
Support limitations: No grants to individuals.
Application information: Applications not accepted. Contributes only to pre-selected organizations.
Officers and Directors:* John F. Donohue*, Chair. and Pres.; Frances X. Bellotti*, Vice-Chair.; Gail Eagan, Sr. V.P. and Genl. Counsel; Beverly Tangvik, Secy. and Dir. of Charitable Giving; Christoper E. Hall, Treas.; Patricia B. Bailey; Thomas S. Carpenter; Anne DeFrancesco; Edmund J. Doherty; J. Robert Dowling; William H. DuMouchel; Andrea Gargiulo; David W. Hattman; Thomas R. Kiley; Jeannette M. Orsino.
EIN: 050613355
Selected grants: The following grants are a representative sample of this grantmaker's funding activity:
$125,000 to Boston Symphony Orchestra, Boston, MA, 2010.
$48,535 to Dana-Farber Cancer Institute, Boston, MA, 2010.
$29,344 to Father Bills and MainSpring, Quincy, MA, 2010.
$28,725 to Irish International Immigrant Center, Boston, MA, 2010.
$25,000 to Greater Boston Legal Services, Boston, MA, 2010.
$22,000 to United Way of Massachusetts Bay, Boston, MA, 2010.
$11,150 to Boston Celtics Shamrock Foundation, Boston, MA, 2010.
$10,720 to American Cancer Society, Framingham, MA, 2010.
$10,000 to Boston Educational Development Foundation, Boston, MA, 2010.
$5,000 to South Shore Mental Health Center, Quincy, MA, 2010.

227
Arbitron Inc.

(formerly Ceridian Corporation)
9705 Patuxent Woods Dr.
Columbia, MD 21046 (410) 312-8000
FAX: (302) 655-5049

Company URL: http://www.arbitron.com
Establishment information: Established in 1912.
Company type: Public company
Company ticker symbol and exchange: ARB/NYSE
Business activities: Provides radio audience measurement information services; develops computer software; provides consumer, shopping, and media usage information services.
Business type (SIC): Research, development, and testing services; computer services
Financial profile for 2012: Number of employees, 1,720; assets, $269,090,000; sales volume, $449,860,000; pre-tax net income, $94,950,000; expenses, $361,630,000; liabilities, $115,680,000
Corporate officers: Philip Guarascio, Chair.; Sean R. Creamer, Pres. and C.E.O.; Debra Delman, Exec. V.P., Finance and C.F.O.; Marilou Legge, Exec. V.P., Comms.
Board of directors: Philip Guarascio, Chair.; Shellye Archambeau; Sean R. Creamer; David W. Devonshire; John A. Dimling; Erica Farber; Ronald G. Garriques; Larry E. Kittelberger; Larry E. Kittelberger; William T. Kerr; Luis G. Nogales; Richard A. Post
Subsidiaries: The Arbitron Co., New York, NY; Ceridian Human Resources Group, Minneapolis, MN; Comdata Corp., Brentwood, TN; Computing Devices International, Bloomington, MN
International operations: India
Giving statement: Giving through the Arbitron Inc. Corporate Giving Program.
Company EIN: 520278528

Arbitron Inc. Corporate Giving Program

(formerly Ceridian Corporation Contributions Program)
9705 Patuxent Woods Dr.
Columbia, MD 21046-1565 (410) 312-8000

Contact: Wendy Mellon
Purpose and activities: Arbitron makes charitable contributions to nonprofit organizations involved with literacy and to libraries and on a case by case basis. Support is given primarily in areas of company operations.
Fields of interest: Libraries/library science; Education, reading; General charitable giving.
Type of support: Donated equipment; Employee volunteer services; General/operating support.
Geographic limitations: Giving primarily in areas of company operations.
Application information: Applications accepted. Contributions are currently very limited.
Initial approach: Contact headquarters for application information
Deadline(s): None

228
Arby's Restaurant Group, Inc.

1155 Perimeter Ctr. W., 12th Fl.
Atlanta, GA 30338 (678) 514-4100
FAX: (678) 514-5346

Company URL: http://www.arbys.com
Establishment information: Established in 1964.
Company type: Private company
Business activities: Franchises restaurants.
Business type (SIC): Restaurants and drinking places
Corporate officers: Hala G. Moddelmog, Pres. and C.E.O.; George M. Condos, C.O.O.; John Dasis, C.F.O.; Warren Chang, C.I.O.; Melissa Strait, Sr. V.P., Human Resources
Giving statement: Giving through the Arby's Foundation, Inc.

Arby's Foundation, Inc.

1155 Perimeter Ctr. W., Ste. 1200
Atlanta, GA 30338-5464 (678) 514-5158
FAX: (678) 514-5334;
E-mail: info@arbysfoundation.org; URL: http://www.arbysfoundation.org

Establishment information: Established in 1986.
Donor: Arby's Restaurant Group.
Financial data (yr. ended 12/31/11): Revenue, $4,197,388; assets, $13,226,495 (M); gifts received, $3,571,043; expenditures, $3,959,076; giving activities include $1,736,643 for grants.
Purpose and activities: The foundation seeks to make a difference in the communities Arby's serves by supporting leadership, education, and mentoring initiatives.
Fields of interest: Education; Big Brothers/Big Sisters; Youth development, services; Youth development.
Program:
Partner Grants: The foundation provides grant money to the selected organizations that already benefit from partnering with Arby's locally with their golf tournaments.

Type of support: Endowments; Management development/capacity building; Scholarship funds.
Application information: Applications not accepted.
Officers and Trustees: Hala Moddelmog*, Chair.; Jo Ann Herold, Vice-Chair.; John L. Gray, Secy.; Danton Nolan, Treas.; Susan Adzick; David Cox; Chuck Sliker; and 13 additional trustees.
Number of staff: 16 full-time professional.
EIN: 581692997

229
Arcelormittal USA, Inc.

1 S. Dearborn St., 18th Fl.
Chicago, IL 60603-9888 (312) 899-3440

Company URL: http://www.arcelormittal.com/
Establishment information: Established in 2002.
Company type: Subsidiary of a foreign company
Business activities: Operates steel company.
Business type (SIC): Steel mill products
Financial profile for 2010: Number of employees, 20,500
Corporate officers: Lakshmi Niwas Mittal, Chair.; Michael G. Rippey, Pres. and C.E.O.; Aditya Mittal, C.F.O.; Andy Harshaw, Exec. V.P., Opers.; Daniel Mull, Exec. V.P., Sales and Mktg.; Brian Kurtz, V.P. and Treas.; John Brett, Cont.; Carlos Hernandez, Genl. Counsel
Board of director: Lakshmi Niwas Mittal, Chair.
Giving statement: Giving through the ArcelorMittal USA Inc. Corporate Giving Program and the ArcelorMittal USA Foundation, Inc.

ArcelorMittal USA Inc. Corporate Giving Program

1 S. Dearborn St.
Chicago, IL 60603 (312) 899-3440
URL: http://www.arcelormittal.com/corp/corporate-responsibility

Purpose and activities: As a complement to its foundation, ArcelorMittal USA supports nonprofit organizations involved with the environment, education, road projects, healthcare, and safety. Support is given primarily in areas of company operations on an international basis.
Fields of interest: Elementary/secondary education; Education, computer literacy/technology training; Environment, energy; Environment; Health care; Employment, training; Housing/shelter; Transportation.
Type of support: Employee volunteer services; General/operating support; In-kind gifts.
Geographic limitations: Giving primarily in areas of company operations on an international basis.

ArcelorMittal USA Foundation, Inc.

(formerly Mittal Steel USA Foundation, Inc.)
1 S. Dearborn St., 19th Fl.
Chicago, IL 60603-2302

Establishment information: Established in 2000 in IN.
Donors: Mittal Steel USA Inc.; ArcelorMittal USA, Inc.
Contact: William C. Steers, Pres.
Financial data (yr. ended 12/31/11): Assets, $623,415 (M); gifts received, $2,000,477; expenditures, $2,220,641; qualifying distributions, $2,220,411; giving activities include $2,220,411 for 16 grants (high: $700,000; low: $1,500).
Purpose and activities: The foundation supports organizations involved with education, animal welfare, disaster relief, and to the United Way.
Fields of interest: Education; Animal welfare; Disasters, preparedness/services; United Ways and Federated Giving Programs.
Type of support: General/operating support; Program development; Scholarship funds.
Geographic limitations: Giving in the U.S., with emphasis on IN and MN.
Application information: Applications accepted. Application form not required. Applicants should submit the following:
1) name, address and phone number of organization
2) detailed description of project and amount of funding requested

Initial approach: Letter
Deadline(s): None

Officers and Directors:* William C. Steers, Pres.; Paul Liebenson, Secy.; Martha Gonzelez*, Treas.; Joseph Heil; Gary Lefko; Heather Loebner; Cordell Petz.
EIN: 352121803
Selected grants: The following grants are a representative sample of this grantmaker's funding activity:
$700,000 to National Fish and Wildlife Foundation, Fort Snelling, MN, 2010.
$460,881 to Legacy Foundation, Merrillville, IN, 2010.
$300,000 to United Way, Lake Area, Griffith, IN, 2010.
$195,000 to United Way of Greater Cleveland, Cleveland, OH, 2010.
$175,000 to United Way of Porter County, Valparaiso, IN, 2010.
$47,000 to United Way of Chester County, West Chester, PA, 2010.
$30,000 to United Way of Metropolitan Chicago, Chicago, IL, 2010.
$23,000 to United Way of the Capital Region, Enola, PA, 2010.
$20,000 to United Way of Weirton, Weirton, WV, 2010.
$11,000 to United Way of Saint Joseph County, South Bend, IN, 2010.

230
Arch Chemicals, Inc.

501 Merritt 7
P.O. Box 5204
Norwalk, CT 06856-5204 (203) 229-2900

Company URL: http://www.archchemicals.com
Establishment information: Established in 1984.
Company type: Subsidiary of a foreign company
Business activities: Manufactures specialty chemicals.
Business type (SIC): Chemicals and allied products
Financial profile for 2010: Number of employees, 2,504; assets, $1,238,000,000; sales volume, $1,377,400,000; pre-tax net income, $94,500,000; expenses, $1,283,500,000; liabilities, $795,000,000
Corporate officer: Rolf Soiron, Chair.
Board of director: Rolf Soiron, Chair.
Subsidiary: Arch Wood Products, Inc., Smyrna, GA
Plant: Mesa, AZ
International operations: Belgium; France; Germany; Hong Kong; Ireland; Italy; Japan; Mexico; South Africa; United Kingdom; Venezuela
Giving statement: Giving through the Arch Chemicals, Inc. Corporate Giving Program.
Company EIN: 061526315

Arch Chemicals, Inc. Corporate Giving Program

501 Merritt 7, P.O. Box 5204
Norwalk, CT 06856-5204 (203) 229-2900
URL: http://www.archchemicals.com/Fed/Corporate/About/community.htm

Purpose and activities: Arch makes charitable contributions to nonprofit organizations involved with education, the environment, public safety, health, diversity, water resources, science, and technology. Support is given on a national and international basis, with emphasis on areas of company operations, including in Bangladesh, Guatemala, Haiti, Honduras, Ireland, Mali, and South Africa.
Fields of interest: Elementary/secondary education; Education; Environment, water resources; Environment; Public health, communicable diseases; Medical research, public education; Safety/disasters, volunteer services; Recreation, camps; Civil/human rights, equal rights; Science, public education; Chemistry; Engineering/technology; Public utilities, water Economically disadvantaged.
International interests: Bangladesh; Guatemala; Haiti; Honduras; Ireland; Mali; Southern Africa.
Program:
Arch Chemicals, Inc. Scholarship Program: Through the Arch Chemicals, Inc. Scholarship Program, the company encourages and provides support to the children of employees for higher education achievements and recognize the employee parents who have guided their children to high accomplishments.
Type of support: Employee matching gifts; Employee volunteer services; Employee-related scholarships; Film/video/radio; In-kind gifts; Sponsorships.
Geographic limitations: Giving on a national and international basis, with emphasis on areas of company operations, including in Bangladesh, Guatemala, Haiti, Honduras, Ireland, Mali, and South Africa.
Publications: Program policy statement.
Application information: Applications not accepted. Contributes only to pre-selected organizations.

231
Arch Coal, Inc.

1 City Place Dr., Ste. 300
St. Louis, MO 63141 (314) 994-2700

Company URL: http://www.archcoal.com
Establishment information: Established in 1969.
Company type: Public company
Company ticker symbol and exchange: ACI/NYSE
Business activities: Mines, refines, and distributes coal.
Business type (SIC): Mining/coal and lignite surface
Financial profile for 2012: Number of employees, 6,424; assets, $10,006,780,000; sales volume, $4,159,040,000; pre-tax net income, -$1,017,400,000; expenses, $4,864,290,000; liabilities, $7,152,210,000
Fortune 1000 ranking: 2012—564th in revenues, 966th in profits, and 389th in assets
Corporate officers: Steven F. Leer, Chair.; John W. Eaves, Pres. and C.E.O.; Paul A. Lang, Exec. V.P. and C.O.O.; John T. Drexler, Sr. V.P. and C.F.O.; Robert G. Jones, Sr. V.P., Genl. Counsel, and Secy.; Deck S. Slone, Sr. V.P., Public Affairs; Kenneth D. Cochran, Sr. V.P., Opers.; John W. Lorson, V.P. and C.A.O.; David E. Hartley, V.P. and C.I.O.; John

Ziegler, Jr., V. P., Human Resources; James E. Florczak, Treas.
Board of directors: Steven F. Leer, Chair.; John W. Eaves; David D. Freudenthal; Patricia Fry Godley; Paul T. Hanrahan; Douglas H. Hunt; J. Thomas Jones; George C. Morris III; A. Michael Perry; Theodore D. Sands; Wesley M. Taylor; Peter I. Wold
Giving statement: Giving through the Arch Coal Foundation.
Company EIN: 430921172

Arch Coal Foundation

1 Cityplace Dr., Ste. 300
St. Louis, MO 63141-7066
Contact for Teacher Achievement Awards: archteacherawards@gmail.com; URL: http://www.archcoal.com/community/foundation.aspx

Establishment information: Established in 2006 in MO.
Contact: Deck S. Sloane, Pres.
Financial data (yr. ended 12/31/11): Assets, $4,077,487 (M); expenditures, $1,527,893; qualifying distributions, $1,508,733; giving activities include $1,275,387 for grants.
Purpose and activities: The foundation supports organizations involved with arts and culture, education, and the environment; awards grants to K-12 classroom teachers in recognition of outstanding achievement; and awards grants to K-12 classroom teachers to invent and test innovative teaching ideas in the classroom.
Fields of interest: Museums (art); Performing arts, theater; Arts; Elementary/secondary education; Higher education; Environment, natural resources; Environment.
Programs:

Innovative Teaching Grants Program: The foundation awards grants of up to $10,000 to K-12 teachers in Delta County's schools to invent and test innovative teaching ideas in their classrooms. The program is designed to encourage other teachers to replicate the best ideas; and individual classroom awards will be limited to $500 each.

Teacher Achievement Awards: The foundation annually honors K-12 teachers for outstanding achievement in West Virginia, Wyoming, and four counties in Utah, including Carbon, Emery, Sanpete, and Sevier. Gants of up to $3,500 are awarded and teachers also receive a commemorative plaque and statuette.

Type of support: Capital campaigns; Continuing support; Employee-related scholarships; General/operating support; Grants to individuals; Sponsorships.
Geographic limitations: Giving primarily in areas of company operations in CO, IL, KY, MO, UT, WV, and WY.
Publications: Application guidelines; Grants list.
Application information: Applications accepted. Unsolicited requests for grants are not accepted.
Initial approach: Complete online nomination form for Teacher Achievement Awards; download application form and mail to foundation for Innovative Teaching Grants Program
Deadline(s): None for Teacher Achievement Awards; varies for Innovative Teaching Grants Program
Officers and Directors:* Deck S. Sloane*, Pres.; James E. Florczak, V.P., Finance; Joe Ploetz*, Secy.; John W. Lorson; R. Gregory Schaefer; John D. Snider.
EIN: 203980901
Selected grants: The following grants are a representative sample of this grantmaker's funding activity:
$300,000 to University of Wyoming Foundation, Laramie, WY, 2011.
$50,000 to University of Utah, Salt Lake City, UT, 2011.
$25,000 to State of Saint Louis Foundation, Saint Louis, MO, 2011. For general fund.
$19,500 to Wyoming Community Foundation, Laramie, WY, 2011.
$15,000 to American Red Cross, Saint Louis, MO, 2011.
$10,000 to Boy Scouts of America, Saint Louis, MO, 2011. For general fund.
$10,000 to Fords Theater Society, Washington, DC, 2011. For general fund.
$10,000 to Gunnison, City of, Gunnison, CO, 2011.
$5,000 to Blanchette Rockefeller Neurosciences Institute, Morgantown, WV, 2011.
$2,500 to Safe Connections, Saint Louis, MO, 2011. For general fund.

232
Archer & Greiner, P.C.

1 Centennial Sq.
33 E. Euclid Ave.
Haddonfield, NJ 08033-0968
(856) 795-2121

Company URL: http://www.archerlaw.com/
Establishment information: Established in 1928.
Company type: Private company
Business activities: Operates law firm.
Business type (SIC): Legal services
Corporate officers: Robert Lehman, C.E.O.; Christopher R. Gibson, Pres.; John Tait, C.F.O.; Kathleen Laimkuhler, C.A.O.
Offices: Georgetown, Wilmington, DE; Flemington, Hackensack, Haddonfield, Princeton, NJ; New York, NY; Philadelphia, PA
Giving statement: Giving through the Archer & Greiner, P.C. Corporate Giving Program.

Archer & Greiner, P.C. Corporate Giving Program

1 Centennial Sq.
P.O. Box 3000
Haddonfield, NJ 08033-0968 (856) 795-2121
FAX: (856) 795-0574; URL: http://www.archerlaw.com/firm.php?category=Firm+Overview&headline=Community+Service

Purpose and activities: Archer & Greiner makes charitable contributions to religious agencies and nonprofit organizations involved with arts and culture, human services, and on a case by case basis.
Fields of interest: Arts; Law school/education; Legal services; Human services; Christian agencies & churches; Jewish agencies & synagogues; General charitable giving.
Type of support: Conferences/seminars; Employee volunteer services; Pro bono services - legal; Scholarship funds.

233
Archer-Daniels-Midland Company

(also known as ADM)
4666 Faries Pkwy.
P.O. Box 1470
Decatur, IL 62525 (217) 424-5200

Company URL: http://www.admworld.com
Establishment information: Established in 1902.
Company type: Public company
Company ticker symbol and exchange: ADM/NYSE
Business activities: Produces oilseed products; produces corn products; sells agricultural commodities wholesale.
Business type (SIC): Agricultural services—crop; grain mill products, including pet food; fats and oils; farm-product raw materials—wholesale
Financial profile for 2012: Number of employees, 30,000; assets, $45,136,000,000; sales volume, $46,729,000,000; pre-tax net income, $997,000,000; expenses, $45,732,000,000; liabilities, $26,216,000,000
Fortune 1000 ranking: 2012—27th in revenues, 165th in profits, and 134th in assets
Forbes 2000 ranking: 2012—74th in sales, 441st in profits, and 511th in assets
Corporate officers: Patricia A. Woertz, Chair., Pres., and C.E.O.; Juan R. Luciano, Exec. V.P. and C.O.O.; Ray G. Young, Sr. V.P. and C.F.O.; Marshall I Smith, Sr. V.P., Secy., and Genl. Counsel; Michael D'Ambrose, Sr. V.P., Human Resources; Douglas R. Ostermann, V.P. and Treas.; John P. Stott, V.P. and Cont.; Vikram Luthar, V.P., Finance
Board of directors: Patricia A. Woertz, Chair.; Alan Boeckmann; George W. Buckley; Mollie Hale Carter; Terrell K. Crews; Pierre Dufour; Donald E. Felsinger; Antonio Maciel Neto; Patrick J. Moore; Thomas F. O'Neill; Daniel T. Shih; Kelvin R. Westbrook
Subsidiaries: ADM Investor Services, Inc., Chicago, IL; ADM Milling Co., Shawnee Mission, KS; American River Transportation Co., Decatur, IL; Hickory Point Bank & Trust Co., Decatur, IL; Moorman Manufacturing Company, Quincy, IL; Tabor Grain Co., Decatur, IL
International operations: Canada
Giving statement: Giving through the Archer Daniels Midland Company Contributions Program.
Company EIN: 208529150

Archer Daniels Midland Company Contributions Program

4666 Faries Pkwy.
Decatur, IL 62526-5678 (217) 424-5200
E-mail: responsibility@adm.com; URL: http://origin.adm.com/en-US/responsibility/2010CR/Pages/default.aspx

Purpose and activities: Archer Daniels Midland makes charitable contributions to nonprofit organizations involved with agricultural development and education. Special emphasis is directed towards educational programs for children and young adults. Support is given on a national and international basis in areas of company operations, with some emphasis on central Illinois.
Fields of interest: Education; Environment; Employment; Agriculture/food, formal/general education; Agriculture, sustainable programs; Food services; Disasters, preparedness/services; International development; United Ways and Federated Giving Programs Children; Young adults.
Type of support: Employee matching gifts; Employee volunteer services; General/operating support; Program development.

Geographic limitations: Giving on a national and international basis in areas of company operations, with some emphasis on central IL.

234
Arctic Slope Regional Corporation

(also known as ASRC)
3900 C St., Ste. 801
P.O. Box 129
Anchorage, AK 99503-5963
(907) 339-6000

Company URL: http://www.asrc.com
Establishment information: Established in 1972.
Company type: Native corporation
Business activities: Operates native corporation.
Business type (SIC): Nonclassifiable establishments
Financial profile for 2011: Number of employees, 11,000; sales volume, $2,330,000,000
Corporate officers: Crawford Patkotak, Chair.; George Sielak, Vice-Chair.; Rex Allen Rock, Sr., Pres. and C.E.O.; Butch Lincoln, Exec. V.P. and C.O.O.; Charlie Kozak, Exec. V.P. and C.F.O.; Denali Kemppel, Exec. V.P. and Genl. Counsel; Cheryl Stine, Sr. V.P. and C.A.O.; Flossie Chrestman, V.P., Admin.; Forrest D. Olemaun, V.P., Opers.; Mary Ellen Ahmaogak, Corp. Secy.
Board of directors: Crawford Patkotak, Chair.; George Sielak, Vice-Chair.; Patsy Aamodt; Jacob Adams, Sr.; Mary Ellen Ahmaogak; Eddie Ahyakak; Paul Bodfish, Sr.; C. Eugene Brower; Richard Savik Glenn; George T. Kaleak, Sr.; Thomas Nukapigak; Ida Olemaun; Raymond Paneak; Rex Allen Rock, Sr.; Sandra Stuermer
Subsidiaries: Alaska Lube and Fuel, Anchorage, AK; ASCG, Inc., Anchorage, AK; ASCG Inspection Svcs., Anchorage, AK; ASRC Contacting Co., Inc., Sacramento, CA; ASRC Parsons Engineering, LLC, Anchorage, AK; Barrow Cable TV, Barrow, AK; Eskimos, Inc., Barrow, AK; FSEC, Inc., Pasadena, CA; Leedshill-Herkenhoff, Inc., Albuquerque, NM; Natchiq, Inc., Anchorage, AK; Petro Star Inc., Anchorage, AK; Piquniq Management Corp., Anchorage, AK; Puget Plastics Corp., Tualatin, OR; SKW/Eskimos Inc., Anchorage, AK; Sourdough Fuel, Inc., Fairbanks, AK; Top of the World Hotel, Barrow, AK; Tundra Mesa Constructors, Scottsdale, AZ; Tundra Tours, Inc., Barrow, AK; Western Arctic Coal, Anchorage, AK
Giving statement: Giving through the Arctic Education Foundation.

Arctic Education Foundation

P.O. Box 129
Barrow, AK 99723-0129 (907) 852-9456
FAX: (907) 852-2774; E-mail: arcticed@asrc.com; Tel. and e-mail for Carolyn M. Edwards: (907) 852-8633, cmedwards@asrc@com; Additional tel.: (800) 770-2772; URL: http://www.arcticed.com

Establishment information: Established in 1978 in AK.
Donors: Arctic Slope Regional Corp.; Chevron U.S.A., Inc.; BP Alaska; Shell Oil Co.; Amoco Corp.; Piqunik Management Corp.; UIC Construction LLC.
Contact: Carolyn M. Edwards, Mgr.
Financial data (yr. ended 12/31/11): Assets, $25,732,280 (M); gifts received, $652,978; expenditures, $1,422,140; qualifying distributions, $1,284,598; giving activities include $1,284,598 for grants to individuals.
Purpose and activities: The foundation awards scholarships for training and higher education to Northern Alaska Inupiat Natives currently residing in the Artic Slope Region, original 1971 shareholders of the Artic Slope Regional Corporation, and lineal descendants of original 1971 shareholders of the Arctic Slope Regional Corporation.
Fields of interest: Vocational education; Higher education; Education Native Americans/American Indians.
Program:
Anagi Leadership Award: The foundation awards one scholarship to an original ASRC shareholder or direct lineal descendant of an original ASRC shareholder. The scholarship covers tuition, fees, books, and room and board, and is awarded to acknowledge the leadership of retired Arctic Slope Regional Corporation President, Jacob Anagi Adams.
Type of support: Scholarships—to individuals.
Geographic limitations: Giving limited to AK.
Publications: Application guidelines.
Application information: Applications accepted. For college students pursuing a four-year degree and for graduate students the maximum is $6,000 per year, and for training students the limit is $2,500 per training term. Application form required.
Requests should include a determination of eligibility form, a letter of acceptance or certificate of admission from an educational institution or vocational training program, a budget forecast, high school or college transcripts, 3 letters of recommendation, and a letter detailing future plans after education or vocational training.
Initial approach: Complete online application or download application form and mail to foundation
Board meeting date(s): Jan. and Aug.
Deadline(s): Mar. 1, May 1, Aug. 1, and Dec. 1; Apr. 15 for Anagi Leadership Award
Officers and Directors:* George Sielak*, Chair.; Lucinda Stackhouse, Secy.; Eugene Brower; Elizabeth Hollingsworth; Raymond Paneak; Crawford Patkotak; Sandra Stuermer.
Number of staff: 1 full-time professional.
EIN: 920068447

235
Arent Fox LLP

1050 Connecticut Ave., NW, Ste. 600
Washington, DC 20036-5339
(202) 857-6000

Company URL: http://www.arentfox.com
Establishment information: Established in 1942.
Company type: Private company
Business activities: Operates law firm.
Business type (SIC): Legal services
Corporate officers: Mark M. Katz, Chair.; Matthew J. Clark, Managing Partner
Offices: Los Angeles, CA; Washington, DC; New York, NY
Giving statement: Giving through the Arent Fox LLP Corporate Giving Program.

Arent Fox LLP Corporate Giving Program

1050 Connecticut Ave., NW, Ste. 600
Washington, DC 20036-5339 (202) 857-6000
FAX: (202) 857-6395; Contact for Pro Bono program: Deanne Ottaviano, Partner & Pro Bono Comm. Chair., tel.: (202) 775-5781, e-mail: ottaviano.deanne@arentfox.com; URL: http://www.arentfox.com/firm/probono/index.cfm?fa=community

Purpose and activities: Arent Fox makes charitable contributions to K-12 educational institutions and nonprofit organizations involved with arts and culture, family services, historical preservation, and community development.
Fields of interest: Historic preservation/historical societies; Arts; Elementary/secondary education; Legal services; Neighborhood centers; Family services; Community/economic development.
Type of support: Employee volunteer services; General/operating support; Pro bono services - legal.
Application information: A Pro Bono Committee manages the Pro Bono Program.

236
AREVA NC, Inc.

(formerly COGEMA, Inc.)
1 Bethesda Ctr.
4800 Hampden Ln., Ste. 1100
Bethesda, MD 20814-2969 (301) 841-1600

Company URL: http://www.areva.com/
Establishment information: Established in 1982.
Company type: Subsidiary of a foreign company
Business activities: Mines uranium.
Business type (SIC): Mining/uranium, radium, vanadium, and other miscellaneous metal
Financial profile for 2011: Number of employees, 4,000
Corporate officers: Michael W. Rencheck, Pres. and C.E.O.; Jean-Claude Hunel, V.P. and C.F.O.; Thomas Pennington, V.P. and Secy.
Giving statement: Giving through the AREVA NC, Inc. Corporate Giving Program.

AREVA NC, Inc. Corporate Giving Program

(formerly COGEMA, Inc. Corporate Giving Program)
4800 Hampden Ln., Ste. 1100
Bethesda, MD 20814-2969 (301) 986-8585
URL: http://www.areva.com/EN/group-869/other-patronage-programsnbsp-local-development-energy-access-culture-and-emergency-aid.html

Purpose and activities: AREVA makes charitable contributions to nonprofit organizations involved with the environment, human services, and economic development. Support is given primarily in areas of company operations.
Fields of interest: Environment; Human services; Community/economic development.
Type of support: General/operating support; Sponsorships.
Geographic limitations: Giving primarily in areas of company operations.

237
Ariel Corporation

35 Blackjack Rd. Ext.
Mount Vernon, OH 43050 (740) 397-0311

Company URL: http://www.arielcorp.com
Establishment information: Established in 1966.
Company type: Private company
Business activities: Manufactures gas compression equipment.
Business type (SIC): Machinery/general industry
Corporate officers: Karen Buchwald Wright, Chair.; Kenneth Reynolds, C.F.O.

Giving statement: Giving through the Ariel Foundation.

Ariel Foundation

101 E. Gambier St.
Mount Vernon, OH 43050-3509 (740) 392-0364
FAX: (740) 392-0370;
E-mail: jreynolds@ariel-foundation.org; URL: http://www.ariel-foundation.org/

Establishment information: Established in 2009 in OH.
Donors: Karen Buchwald Wright; Ariel Corporation.
Contact: Jan Reynolds, Secy.-Treas.
Financial data (yr. ended 12/31/11): Assets, $13,834,959 (M); gifts received, $5,153,042; expenditures, $1,102,366; qualifying distributions, $954,100; giving activities include $954,100 for grants.
Purpose and activities: The foundation supports programs designed to improve quality of life. Special emphasis is directed toward arts and culture, education, parks, and the pursuit of happiness.
Fields of interest: Arts; Higher education; Engineering school/education; Libraries (public); Education; Recreation, parks/playgrounds; YM/YWCAs & YM/YWHAs; Human services; Community/economic development; United Ways and Federated Giving Programs; Engineering; Science.
Program:
James P. Buschwald & Tom Rastin Engineering Scholarships: The foundation annually awards $5,000 to students of sophomore status or above who are enrolled at a four-year engineering college in the fields of chemical, electrical, or mechanical engineering. Applicant must be a graduate of Mount Vernon High School, of Mount Vernon, OH, or a resident of Mount Vernon, OH at the time of high school graduation. Applicants are selected based on academic achievement, recommendation from instructors, personal qualities, and financial need.
Type of support: Building/renovation; Capital campaigns; Equipment; General/operating support; Scholarship funds; Scholarships—to individuals.
Geographic limitations: Giving primarily in the Mount Vernon, OH area.
Support limitations: No support for non-501(c)(3) organizations, or for religious organizations not of direct benefit to the entire community, or fraternal and veterans' organizations. No grants for athletic events or political campaigns.
Publications: Application guidelines; Grants list.
Application information: Applications accepted. Letters of inquiry should be short and concise. Full grant applications may be requested at a later date. Applicants should submit the following:
1) population served
2) name, address and phone number of organization
3) detailed description of project and amount of funding requested
4) contact person
Scholarship applications should include transcripts, 2 letters of recommendation, and wallet size photo.
Initial approach: E-mail, fax, or mail letter of inquiry; download application form and mail to foundation for scholarships
Board meeting date(s): Quarterly
Deadline(s): None; July 7 for scholarships
Officers and Directors:* Karen Buchald Wright*, Chair. and Pres.; Thomas Rastin*, Vice-Chair. and V.P.; Janet L. Reynolds*, Secy.-Treas.
EIN: 270226408

238
Ariens Company

655 W. Ryan St.
P.O. Box 157
Brillion, WI 54110 (920) 756-2141
FAX: (920) 756-2407

Company URL: http://www.arienscorp.com
Establishment information: Established in 1933.
Company type: Private company
Business activities: Manufactures power garden equipment.
Business type (SIC): Machinery/farm and garden
Financial profile for 2009: Number of employees, 700
Corporate officers: Michael Ariens, Chair.; Daniel T. Ariens, Pres. and C.E.O.; Stewart Witkov, Exec. V.P. and C.F.O.; Bob Bradford, Sr. V.P., Opers.; Regina Kramer, V.P., Admin.; John Horn, V.P., Sales; Steve Demsien, V.P., Mktg.
Board of director: Michael Ariens, Chair.
Giving statement: Giving through the Ariens Foundation, Ltd.

Ariens Foundation, Ltd.

655 W. Ryan St.
Brillion, WI 54110-1072

Establishment information: Established in 1967 in WI.
Donors: Ariens Corp.; Francis Ariens Memorial; Ariens Co.
Contact: Mary M. Ariens, Pres.
Financial data (yr. ended 06/30/12): Assets, $442,151 (M); gifts received, $160,975; expenditures, $153,495; qualifying distributions, $153,539; giving activities include $141,684 for 23 + grants and $11,325 for 1 grant to an individual.
Purpose and activities: The foundation supports community foundations and organizations involved with secondary and higher education, the environment, homeless shelters, athletics, civil liberties, and human services and awards scholarships to individuals.
Fields of interest: Secondary school/education; Higher education; Environmental education; Environment; Housing/shelter, homeless; Athletics/sports, amateur leagues; Youth development, business; Human services; Civil liberties, right to life.
Type of support: Building/renovation; General/operating support; Scholarship funds; Scholarships—to individuals.
Geographic limitations: Giving primarily in northeastern WI, with emphasis on Brillion.
Application information: Applications accepted. Application form required.
Scholarship applicants should submit a brief resume of qualifications.
Initial approach: Proposal
Deadline(s): None
Officers: Mary M. Ariens, Pres.; H. James Jensen, Treas.
EIN: 396102058

239
Arizona Public Service Company

(also known as APS)
400 N. 5th St.
Phoenix, AZ 85004 (602) 250-1000

Company URL: http://www.aps.com
Establishment information: Established in 1920.
Company type: Subsidiary of a public company
Business activities: Generates, transmits, and distributes electricity.
Business type (SIC): Combination utility services; electric services
Financial profile for 2010: Number of employees, 600; sales volume, $3,180,000,000
Corporate officers: Donald E. Brandt, Chair. and C.E.O.; Donald G. Robinson, Pres. and C.O.O.; David P. Falck, Exec. V.P., Genl. Counsel, and Secy.; James R. Hatfield, Sr. V.P. and C.F.O.; Cindy Berger, V.P. and C.I.O.; Denise R. Danner, V.P., Cont., and C.A.O.; Lee R. Nickloy, V.P. and Treas.
Board of director: Donald E. Brandt, Chair.
Subsidiaries: Bixco, Inc., Phoenix, AZ; Stagg Systems, Inc., Houston, TX
Giving statement: Giving through the APS Corporate Giving Program and the APS Foundation, Inc.
Company EIN: 860011170

APS Corporate Giving Program

400 N. 5th St.
Phoenix, AZ 85004-3992
For scholarships: Louise Moskowitz, tel.: (602) 250-2291, e-mail: Louise.Moskowitz@aps.com; URL: http://www.aps.com/en/communityandenvironment/charitablegiving/ourgivingprograms/Pages/community.aspx

Purpose and activities: As a complement to its foundation, APS also makes charitable contributions to nonprofit organizations directly. Support is given primarily in areas of company operations in Arizona and northwestern New Mexico.
Fields of interest: Arts; Education; Environment; Human services; Community/economic development.
Program:
Employee Matching Gifts: APS matches contributions made by its employees and retirees to nonprofit organizations on a one-for-two basis.
Type of support: Employee matching gifts; Employee volunteer services; Employee-related scholarships; General/operating support; In-kind gifts; Research; Scholarships—to individuals.
Geographic limitations: Giving primarily in areas of company operations in AZ and northwestern NM.

APS Foundation, Inc.

P.O. Box 53999, M.S. 8657
Phoenix, AZ 85072
E-mail: joanna.deshay@aps.com

Establishment information: Established in 1981 in AZ.
Donor: Arizona Public Service Co.
Contact: Joanna de'Shay
Financial data (yr. ended 12/31/11): Assets, $25,792,301 (M); expenditures, $1,575,550; qualifying distributions, $1,575,550; giving activities include $1,575,550 for 20 grants (high: $243,000; low: $5,000).
Purpose and activities: The foundation supports organizations involved with arts and culture, education, the environment, health, human services, and community development.

Fields of interest: Arts; Education; Environment; Hospitals (general); Health care; Children/youth, services; Human services; Community/economic development.
Type of support: Capital campaigns; General/operating support; Matching/challenge support.
Geographic limitations: Giving primarily in AZ.
Support limitations: No support for charter or private schools, religious, political, fraternal, legislative, or lobbying organizations, or private or family foundations. No grants to individuals, or for travel-related or hotel expenses, salaries, or debt reduction.
Application information: Applications accepted. Organizations receiving support are asked to provide a final report. Application form not required. Applicants should submit the following:
1) results expected from proposed grant
2) statement of problem project will address
3) copy of IRS Determination Letter
4) brief history of organization and description of its mission
5) how project's results will be evaluated or measured
6) listing of board of directors, trustees, officers and other key people and their affiliations
7) detailed description of project and amount of funding requested
8) copy of current year's organizational budget and/or project budget
9) listing of additional sources and amount of support

Proposals should include a description of past involvement by the foundation with the organization and the organization's website and e-mail address, if available.
Initial approach: E-mail proposal to nearest local representative
Copies of proposal: 1
Final notification: 30 to 60 days
Officers and Directors:* Donald E. Brandt*, Chair. and Pres.; Donald P. Falck*, V.P. and Secy.; Tommy D. McLeod*, V.P. and Treas.; Donald G. Robinson*, V.P.; Mark A. Schiavoni*, V.P.
Number of staff: 2 full-time professional; 1 part-time support.
EIN: 953735903

240
Arkansas Blue Cross and Blue Shield

601 S. Gaines St.
Little Rock, AR 72201 (501) 378-2000

Company URL: http://www.arkansasbluecross.com
Establishment information: Established in 1948.
Company type: Mutual company
Business activities: Operates medical service plan.
Business type (SIC): Insurance/accident and health
Financial profile for 2011: Assets, $1,221,696,000; pre-tax net income, $62,434,000; expenses, $1,213,669,000; liabilities, $640,038,000
Corporate officers: Robert L. Shoptaw, Chair.; George K. Mitchell, M.D., Vice-Chair.; P. Mark White, Pres. and C.E.O.; Mike Brown, Exec. V.P. and C.O.O.; Gary Dillard, Sr. V.P. and C.F.O.; Joseph Smith, Sr. V.P. and C.I.O.; Karen Raley, V.P., Comms.
Board of directors: Robert L. Shoptaw, Chair.; Carolyn Blakely, Ph.D.; Susan Brittain; Robert V. Brothers; Mark Greenway; Bradley D. Jesson; James V. Kelley; Mahlon O. Maris, M.D.; J. Thomas May; George K. Mitchell, M.D.; Dan Nabholz; Marla Johnson Norris; Ben Owens; Patty Smith; Sherman Tate; Mark White; Leslie Wyatt, Ph.D.
Giving statement: Giving through the Blue & You Foundation for a Healthier Arkansas.

Blue & You Foundation for a Healthier Arkansas

(formerly ABC Foundation)
USAble Corporate Ctr.
320 W. Capitol, Ste. 200
Little Rock, AR 72201-3506 (501) 378-3300
FAX: (501) 378-2051;
E-mail: posullivan@arkbluecross.com; Tel. for Patrick O'Sullivan: (501) 378-2221; Additional contact: Suzanne Baldwin, Admin. Asst., tel. (501) 378-2223, e-mail: lsbaldwin@arkbluecross.com; URL: http://www.blueandyoufoundationarkansas.org

Establishment information: Established in 2001 in AR.
Donor: Arkansas Blue Cross and Blue Shield.
Contact: Patrick O'Sullivan, Exec. Dir.; Suzanne Baldwin, Admin. Asst.
Financial data (yr. ended 12/31/12): Assets, $52,866,832 (M); expenditures, $2,635,855; qualifying distributions, $2,272,910; giving activities include $2,272,910 for 68 grants (high: $159,000; low: $1,000).
Purpose and activities: The foundation supports programs designed to improve health in Arkansas. Special emphasis is directed towards programs designed to affect health care delivery, health care policy, and health care economics in Arkansas.
Fields of interest: Health care, public policy; Health care, reform; Hospitals (general); Health care, clinics/centers; Health care, infants; Dental care; Health care, patient services; Health care; Diabetes; Children/youth, services; Family services.
Type of support: General/operating support; Program development; Program evaluation; Research.
Geographic limitations: Giving limited to AR.
Support limitations: No support for private foundations, organizations with a contractual relationship with Arkansas Blue Cross and Blue Shield, political or lobbying organizations, fraternal, athletic, or social organizations, or religious organizations not of direct benefit to the entire community. No grants to individuals, or for fundraising events or celebrations, capital campaigns or endowments, facilities or equipment, conferences, indirect costs, or tobacco-related programs.
Publications: Application guidelines; Grants list.
Application information: Applications accepted. Mini-Grants are for requests of $1,000. Regular grants are for requests of $5,000 to $150,000. Regular grant recipients file 6-month and 12-month reports and receive a site visit. Mini-Grant recipients file a one-page report within six months. Application form required. Applicants should submit the following:
1) timetable for implementation and evaluation of project
2) how project will be sustained once grantmaker support is completed
3) results expected from proposed grant
4) qualifications of key personnel
5) statement of problem project will address
6) population served
7) copy of IRS Determination Letter
8) brief history of organization and description of its mission
9) geographic area to be served
10) copy of most recent annual report/audited financial statement/990
11) how project's results will be evaluated or measured
12) listing of board of directors, trustees, officers and other key people and their affiliations
13) detailed description of project and amount of funding requested
14) plans for cooperation with other organizations, if any
15) copy of current year's organizational budget and/or project budget
16) listing of additional sources and amount of support

Applications should include the resume of the Project Manager or Director.
Initial approach: Complete online application
Deadline(s): Mar., Apr., and May for Mini-Grants; July 15 for Regular Grants
Final notification: 30 days for Mini-Grants; mid-Nov. for Regular Grants
Officers and Directors:* Robert D. Cabe*, Chair.; Lee Douglass, Secy.; Gray Dillard, Treas.; Steve Short, Treas.; Patrick O'Sullivan, Exec. Dir.; Carolyn Blakely, Ph.D.; Sybil Jordan Hampton; Mahlon Maris, M.D.; George K. Mitchell, M.D.; Marla Johnson Norris; P. Mark White.
Number of staff: 2 full-time professional.
EIN: 710862108

241
Arkansas Steel Associates, LLC

2803 Van Dyke Rd.
Newport, AR 72112-9755 (870) 523-3693

Company URL: http://www.arkansassteel.com
Establishment information: Established in 1989.
Company type: Subsidiary of a foreign company
Business activities: Manufactures steel plates.
Business type (SIC): Steel mill products
Corporate officers: Toshinori Nakanishi, Pres. and C.E.O.; Jerry Park, C.F.O.
Giving statement: Giving through the Arkansas Steel Associates Charitable Trust.

Arkansas Steel Associates Charitable Trust

2803 Van Dyke Rd.
Newport, AR 72112-9755 (870) 523-3693

Establishment information: Established in 1999 in AR.
Donor: Arkansas Steel Assocs.
Contact: Barry Hulett
Financial data (yr. ended 12/31/11): Assets, $407,658 (M); expenditures, $20,433; qualifying distributions, $20,050; giving activities include $20,050 for grants.
Purpose and activities: The foundation supports organizations involved with music and education.
Fields of interest: Performing arts, music; Higher education; Education.
Type of support: Employee-related scholarships; General/operating support; Sponsorships.
Geographic limitations: Giving primarily in areas of company operations in Newport, AR.
Support limitations: No grants to individuals (except for employee-related scholarships).
Application information: Applications accepted.
Initial approach: Proposal
Deadline(s): None
Officer and Trustees: Ted Nakanishi, Pres.; Edward Boyce; Jim Gowen, Sr.; Mike Turner; Larry Williams.
EIN: 716178691

242
Arkema Inc.
(formerly Atofina Chemicals, Inc.)
900 First Ave.
King Of Prussia, PA 19406 (215) 419-7000

Company URL: http://www.arkema-inc.com/index.cfm
Establishment information: Established in 2000.
Company type: Subsidiary of a foreign company
Business activities: Manufactures chemicals.
Business type (SIC): Chemicals and allied products
Financial profile for 2010: Number of employees, 2,369; sales volume, $1,680,000,000
Corporate officers: Bernard Roche, Pres. and C.E.O.; Patricia McCarthy, Sr. V.P. and C.F.O.; Mike Keough, C.I.O.; William Hamel, Sr. V.P. and Genl. Counsel; Chris Giangrasso, V.P., Human Resources and Comms.
International operations: Brazil; Canada; Germany; Mexico
Giving statement: Giving through the Arkema Inc. Foundation.

Arkema Inc. Foundation
(formerly Atofina Chemicals, Inc. Foundation)
900 First Ave.
King of Prussia, PA 19406-1308 (215) 419-7735
E-mail: diane.milici@arkema.com; URL: http://www.arkema-inc.com/index.cfm?pag=590

Establishment information: Trust established in 1957 in PA.
Donors: Elf Atochem North America, Inc.; Atofina Chemicals, Inc.; Arkema Inc.
Contact: Diane Milici, Admin.
Financial data (yr. ended 12/31/11): Assets, $369,133 (M); gifts received, $300,000; expenditures, $201,561; qualifying distributions, $200,570; giving activities include $170,892 for 71 grants (high: $20,000; low: $250) and $25,000 for 50 grants to individuals.
Purpose and activities: The foundation supports organizations involved with arts and culture, education, and civic affairs. Special emphasis is directed toward programs designed to advance elementary school science education.
Fields of interest: Media/communications; Museums; Arts; Elementary school/education; Higher education; Education; United Ways and Federated Giving Programs; Science; Public affairs.
Program:
Science Teacher Program: The foundation supports an intensive week long session for elementary and secondary school teachers to promote science education. Teachers work with Arkema chemical engineers and research scientists and receive science experiment kits to explore topics including life, earth and physical science, and technology. The program is designed to teach new ways to illustrate scientific concepts. Participating teachers also receive a donation to purchase additional science experiment supplies for their classrooms and the mentoring guidance of Arkema research scientists throughout the school year.
Type of support: Annual campaigns; Building/renovation; Continuing support; Emergency funds; Employee matching gifts; Employee-related scholarships; Equipment; General/operating support; Matching/challenge support.
Geographic limitations: Giving primarily in areas of company operations, with some emphasis on the Philadelphia, PA, area; giving in Axis, AL, Calvert City, Carrollton, and Louisville, KY, Blooming Prairie, MN, Geneseo, NY, Birdsboro, PA, Memphis, TN, and Beaumont, Crosby, and Houston, TX for the Science Teacher Program.
Support limitations: No support for veterans', fraternal, labor, or sectarian religious organizations, or sports teams. No grants to individuals (except for employee-related scholarships), or for endowments, special projects, research, publications, conferences, courtesy advertising, entertainment promotions, event sponsorships, public education, athletic competitions, or political causes or campaigns; no loans.
Publications: Application guidelines.
Application information: Applications accepted. Letters of inquiry should be no longer than 2 pages. Application form not required. Applicants should submit the following:
1) copy of IRS Determination Letter
2) detailed description of project and amount of funding requested

Initial approach: Letter of inquiry; download application form and mail to nearest participating company facility for Science Teacher Program
Copies of proposal: 1
Board meeting date(s): Mar., June, Sept., and Dec.
Deadline(s): None
Final notification: 1 to 3 months

Trustees: Ryan Dirkx; Chris Giangrasso; Bernard Roche.
Number of staff: 1 part-time professional.
EIN: 236256818
Selected grants: The following grants are a representative sample of this grantmaker's funding activity:
$15,000 to Pennsylvania State University, University Park, PA, 2010.
$10,000 to Chemical Heritage Foundation, Philadelphia, PA, 2010.
$5,967 to Franklin Institute Science Museum, Philadelphia, PA, 2010.
$4,700 to Arts and Business Council of Greater Philadelphia, Philadelphia, PA, 2010.
$4,000 to Cornell University, Ithaca, NY, 2010.
$4,000 to Drexel University, Philadelphia, PA, 2010.
$4,000 to George Washington University, Washington, DC, 2010.
$4,000 to Harding University, Searcy, AR, 2010.
$4,000 to Princeton University, Princeton, NJ, 2010.
$4,000 to United States Military Academy, West Point, NY, 2010.

243
Armbrust International Ltd.
(formerly Armbrust Chain Company)
735 Allens Ave.
Providence, RI 02905-5412 (401) 781-3300

Company URL: http://www.armbrustintl.com
Establishment information: Established in 1920.
Company type: Private company
Business activities: Manufactures jewelry chains.
Business type (SIC): Metal products/fabricated
Corporate officers: Erwin Pearl, Chair.; Thomas J. Baker, C.E.O.; Donald Armbrust, Pres.; Karen Kase, C.F.O. and Compt.; Steven Armbust, Treas.
Board of director: Erwin Pearl, Chair.
Giving statement: Giving through the Armbrust Foundation.

Armbrust Foundation
7710 Ashley Cir.
University Park, FL 34201-2090

Establishment information: Established about 1951 in RI.
Donors: Donald G. Armbrust; Armbrust Chain Co.; Howard Armbrust.
Financial data (yr. ended 12/31/11): Assets, $1,249,348 (M); expenditures, $90,025; qualifying distributions, $73,450; giving activities include $63,900 for 31 grants (high: $10,000; low: $100).
Purpose and activities: The foundation supports hospitals and organizations involved with arts and culture, education, conservation, children, and religion.
Fields of interest: Arts; Education; Religion.
Type of support: General/operating support.
Geographic limitations: Giving primarily in RI.
Support limitations: No grants to individuals.
Application information: Applications not accepted. Unsolicited requests for funds not accepted.
Trustee: Howard W. Armbrust.
EIN: 056088332

244
Armor Healthcare, LLC
1031 2nd St.
Hudson, WI 54016-1208 (715) 381-9868

Company URL: http://www.armorhealthcare.com
Establishment information: Established in 2007.
Company type: Private company
Business type (SIC): Chemicals/industrial inorganic
Corporate officers: Robert J. Simmons, Jr., C.E.O.; Brian K. Martin, Pres.
Giving statement: Giving through the Armor Healthcare, LLC Contributions Program.

Armor Healthcare, LLC Contributions Program
1031 2nd St.
Hudson, WI 54016-1208 (715) 381-9868
E-mail: info@armorhealthcare.com; URL: http://www.armorhealthcare.com

245
Armstrong Utilities, Inc.
1 Armstrong Pl.
Butler, PA 16001 (724) 283-0925

Company URL: http://www.agoc.com/index.htm
Establishment information: Established in 1946.
Company type: Subsidiary of a private company
Business activities: Provides cable television and telephone services.
Business type (SIC): Cable and other pay television services
Corporate officers: Jay L. Sedwick, Chair.; Kirby J. Campbell, Vice-Chair.; Dru A. Sedwick, Pres.; Bryan Cipoletti, C.F.O; Eric Aulbach, C.I.O; Christopher King, Exec. V.P., Finance
Board of directors: Jay L. Sedwick, Chair.; Kirby J. Campbell, Vice-Chair.
Giving statement: Giving through the Sedwick Foundation.

Sedwick Foundation
c/o Kirby J. Campbell, Tr.
1 Armstrong Pl.
Butler, PA 16001-1951 (724) 283-0925

Establishment information: Established in 1986 in PA.

Donors: Armstrong Utilities, Inc.; Jay L. Sedwick; Linda Sedwick; Armstrong Communications, Inc.; Armstrong Telephone Co. of West Virginia; Armstrong Telephone Co. of Maryland; Guardian Protection Services, Inc.
Financial data (yr. ended 06/30/12): Assets, $32,915,205 (M); expenditures, $2,163,760; qualifying distributions, $1,854,500; giving activities include $1,854,500 for 39 grants (high: $500,000; low: $2,000).
Purpose and activities: The foundation supports camps and medical centers and organizations involved with higher education, human services, public policy, and Christianity.
Fields of interest: Higher education; Health care, clinics/centers; Recreation, camps; YM/YWCAs & YM/YWHAs; Human services; Public policy, research; Christian agencies & churches.
Type of support: General/operating support.
Geographic limitations: Giving primarily in Butler, PA.
Support limitations: No grants to individuals.
Application information: Applications not accepted. Contributes only to pre-selected organizations.
Trustees: Kirby J. Campbell; Dru A. Sedwick; Jay L. Sedwick; William C. Stewart.
EIN: 256284774
Selected grants: The following grants are a representative sample of this grantmaker's funding activity:
$500,000 to Grove City College, Grove City, PA, 2011.
$100,000 to Christian and Missionary Alliance, Colorado Springs, CO, 2011.
$100,000 to Leadership Institute, Arlington, VA, 2011.
$100,000 to Renaissance Charitable Foundation, Indianapolis, IN, 2011.
$60,000 to Pine Valley Bible Conference, Ellwood City, PA, 2011.
$50,000 to Dallas Theological Seminary, Dallas, TX, 2011.
$40,000 to Judicial Watch, Washington, DC, 2011.
$30,000 to Food for the Hungry, Phoenix, AZ, 2011.
$30,000 to Mission Aviation Fellowship, Nampa, ID, 2011.
$9,500 to Community Alliance Church, Butler, PA, 2011.

246
Armstrong World Industries, Inc.

2500 Columbia Ave.
P.O. Box 3001
Lancaster, PA 17604 (717) 397-0611
FAX: (717) 396-6133

Company URL: http://www.armstrong.com
Establishment information: Established in 1891.
Company type: Public company
Company ticker symbol and exchange: AWI/NYSE
Business activities: Designs and manufactures floors, ceilings and cabinets.
Business type (SIC): Furniture/household; paper mills; clay structural products; abrasive, asbestos, and nonmetallic mineral products; lighting and wiring equipment/electric; furniture and home furnishings—wholesale
Financial profile for 2012: Number of employees, 8,500; assets, $2,854,300,000; sales volume, $2,618,900,000; pre-tax net income, $220,500,000; expenses, $2,347,700,000; liabilities, $2,135,200,000
Fortune 1000 ranking: 2012—762nd in revenues, 681st in profits, and 766th in assets
Corporate officers: Matthew J. Espe, C.E.O.; Thomas B. Mangas, Sr. V.P. and C.F.O.; Mark Hershey, Sr. V.P., Genl. Counsel, and Corp. Secy.; Donald R. Maier, Sr. V.P., Opers.; Tom Kane, Sr. V.P., Human Resources; Stephen F. McNamara, V.P. and Cont.
Board of directors: Stan A. Askren; Kevin R. Burns; Matthew J. Espe; James J. Gaffney; Tao Huang; Michael F. Johnston; Larry S. McWilliams; Jeffrey Liaw; James Clinton Melville; James J. O'Connor; John J. Roberts; Richard E. Wenz
Subsidiaries: American Olean Tile Co., Lansdale, PA; Armstar, Lenoir City, TN; Armstrong Cork Finance Corp., Wilmington, DE; Armstrong Realty Group, Inc., Lancaster, PA; Armstrong World Industries Delaware, Inc., Wilmington, DE; BEGA/FS, Inc., Carpinteria, CA; The W.W. Henry Co., Huntington Park, CA; IWF, Inc., Reno, NV
Plants: Mobile, AL; Warren, AR; South Gate, CA; Pensacola, FL; Macon, GA; Kankakee, IL; Somerset, KY; Braintree, MA; Jackson, Vicksburg, MS; West Plains, MO; Auburn, NE; Fulton, NY; Statesville, NC; Hilliard, OH; Stillwater, OK; St. Helens, OR; Beaver Falls, Beech Creek, Lancaster, Marietta, Thompsontown, Titusville, PA; Jackson, TN; Center, TX
International operations: Australia; Austria; Canada; Germany; Netherlands; Spain; Sweden; Switzerland; United Kingdom
Giving statement: Giving through the Armstrong Foundation.
Company EIN: 230366390

Armstrong Foundation

2500 Columbia Ave.
Lancaster, PA 17603-4117
FAX: (717) 396-6055;
E-mail: Foundation@armstrongfoundation.com; Additional address: P.O. Box 3001, Lancaster, PA 17604-3001; URL: http://www.armstrongfoundation.com/

Establishment information: Established in 1985 in PA.
Donor: Armstrong World Industries, Inc.
Contact: Janice E. Biagio, Coord.
Financial data (yr. ended 12/31/11): Assets, $2,912,369 (M); expenditures, $1,480,116; qualifying distributions, $1,461,119; giving activities include $1,442,332 for 237 grants (high: $525,000; low: $50) and $18,787 for 4 grants to individuals (high: $11,990; low: $1,500).
Purpose and activities: The foundation supports organizations involved with education, health, substance abuse, hunger, housing development, human services, and community development.
Fields of interest: Higher education; Education; Hospitals (general); Health care; Substance abuse, services; Substance abuse, treatment; Food services; Food banks; Food distribution, meals on wheels; Housing/shelter, development; Boys & girls clubs; Boy scouts; Youth development, business; American Red Cross; Children/youth, services; Family services; Human services; Community/economic development.
Programs:
Armstrong Scholarship Program: The foundation awards four-year $2,500 college scholarships to high school juniors who are children of employees of Armstrong. The program is administered by National Merit Scholarship Corporation.
Employee Choice Gift Matching - Volunteer Time: The foundation awards $500 grants to nonprofit organizations with which employees of Armstrong volunteer at least 36 hours per year.
Employee Choice Gift Matching - Monetary: The foundation matches contributions made by employees of Armstrong to nonprofit organizations on a one-for-one basis from $50 to $500 per employee, per year.
Employee Hardship Program: The foundation awards grants to economically disadvantaged employees experiencing financial hardship, and who are victims of natural disasters or catastrophic illness.
Higher Education Gift Matching: The foundation matches contributions made by employees and directors of Armstrong to institutions of higher education on a one-for-one basis from $50 to 10,000 per employee, per year.
U.S. Plant Discretionary: The foundation awards grants of $1,000 and up to nonprofit organizations recommended by Armstrong U.S. plant managers.
Type of support: Annual campaigns; Building/renovation; Employee matching gifts; Employee volunteer services; Employee-related scholarships; General/operating support; Grants to individuals; Scholarship funds.
Geographic limitations: Giving primarily in areas of company operations.
Support limitations: No grants to individuals (except for employee-related scholarships and hardship grants), or for legislative or political activities.
Publications: Application guidelines; Program policy statement.
Application information: Applications accepted. Application form required.
Initial approach: Complete online application form
Deadline(s): July 1
Officers and Directors:* William C. Rodruan*, Pres.; Thomas J. Waters, V.P. and Treas.; Mary J. Huwaldt, Secy.; Michele M. Nicholas, Secy.; David S. Cookson; Linda Toth; Ellen R. Romano.
EIN: 232387950

247
Arnall Golden Gregory LLP

171 17th St., N.W., Ste. 2100
Atlanta, GA 30363-1031 (404) 873-8500

Company URL: http://www.agg.com
Establishment information: Established in 1949.
Company type: Private company
Business activities: Operates law firm.
Business type (SIC): Legal services
Corporate officers: Jonathan Golden, Partner; Glenn P. Hendrix, Partner
Offices: Washington, DC; Atlanta, GA
Giving statement: Giving through the Arnall Golden Gregory LLP Pro Bono Program.

Arnall Golden Gregory LLP Pro Bono Program

171 17th St., N.W., Ste. 2100
Atlanta, GA 30363-1031 (404) 873-8500
FAX: (404) 873-8501; E-mail: robert.dow@agg.com; URL: http://www.agg.com/Contents/ProBonoActivities.aspx

Contact: Robert Dow, Partner
Purpose and activities: Arnall Golden Gregory makes charitable contributions to nonprofit organizations involved with helping victims of domestic violence and low-income individuals, and on a case by case basis.
Fields of interest: Legal services; Family services, domestic violence; Homeless, human services; General charitable giving Economically disadvantaged.
Type of support: Employee volunteer services; General/operating support; Pro bono services - legal.

Application information: A Pro Bono Committee manages the Pro Bono Program.

Officer: Abe Krash, Pres.
Director: Stuart Land.
EIN: 521656501

Application information: Applications accepted. Application form required.
Initial approach: Complete online application form

248
Arnold & Porter LLP

555 12th St., N.W.
Washington, DC 20004-1206
(202) 942-5000

Company URL: http://www.arnoldporter.com/home.cfm
Establishment information: Established in 1946.
Company type: Private company
Business activities: Operates law firm.
Business type (SIC): Legal services
Corporate officer: Richard M. Alexander, Managing Partner
Offices: Los Angeles, Palo Alto, San Francisco, CA; Denver, CO; Washington, DC; New York, NY; McLean, VA
International operations: Belgium; United Kingdom
Giving statement: Giving through the Arnold & Porter LLP Corporate Giving Program and the Arnold & Porter Foundation.

Arnold & Porter LLP Corporate Giving Program

555 12th St., N.W.
Washington, DC 20004-1206 (202) 942-5000
FAX: (202) 942-5999; Contact for Pro Bono program: Marsha Tucker, Social Worker, tel.: (202) 942-5313, e-mail: marsha.tucker@aporter.com; URL: http://www.arnoldporter.com/about_the_firm_diversity_community_involvement.cfm

Contact: Marsha Tucker, Social Worker
Purpose and activities: Arnold & Porter makes charitable contributions to nonprofit organizations involved with promoting diversity.
Fields of interest: Legal services; Civil/human rights, equal rights Minorities; Women; LGBTQ.
Type of support: General/operating support; Pro bono services - legal.
Geographic limitations: Giving primarily in areas of company operations in Los Angeles, Palo Alto, and San Francisco, CA, Denver, CO, Washington, DC, New York, NY, McLean, VA, and in Belgium, United Kingdom.

Arnold & Porter Foundation

555 12th St. N.W.
Washington, DC 20004-1200

Establishment information: Established in 1989 in DC.
Donors: Arnold & Porter; Washington Lawyer's Committee; American Civil Liberties Union.
Financial data (yr. ended 12/31/11): Assets, $1,365,344 (M); gifts received, $15,561; expenditures, $97,812; qualifying distributions, $97,500; giving activities include $90,000 for 1 grant.
Purpose and activities: The foundation supports the LSUHSC Foundation in New Orleans, Louisiana.
Fields of interest: Medical school/education; Health care.
Type of support: Fellowships; General/operating support.
Geographic limitations: Giving primarily in New Orleans, LA.
Support limitations: No grants to individuals.
Application information: Applications not accepted. Unsolicited requests for funds not accepted.

249
Arrow Electronics, Inc.

50 Marcus Dr.
Melville, NY 11747-4210 (631) 847-5449
FAX: (631) 847-5458

Company URL: http://www.arrow.com/
Establishment information: Established in 1946.
Company type: Public company
Company ticker symbol and exchange: ARW/NYSE
Business activities: Provider of products, services, and solutions to industrial and commercial users of electronic components and enterprise computing solutions.
Business type (SIC): Electrical goods—wholesale
Financial profile for 2012: Number of employees, 16,500; assets, $10,785,690,000; sales volume, $20,405,130,000; pre-tax net income, $710,360,000; expenses, $19,601,010,000; liabilities, $6,802,470,000
Fortune 1000 ranking: 2012—141st in revenues, 331st in profits, and 366th in assets
Forbes 2000 ranking: 2012—461st in sales, 1056th in profits, and 1417th in assets
Corporate officers: Michael J. Long, Chair., Pres., and C.E.O.; John C. Waddell, Vice-Chair.; Paul J. Reilly, Exec. V.P., Opers. and Finance and C.F.O.; Peter S. Brown, Sr. V.P., Genl. Counsel, and Secy.; Gretchen Zech, Sr. V.P., Human Resources; Vincent P. Melvin, V.P. and C.I.O.
Board of directors: Michael J. Long, Chair.; John C. Waddell, Vice-Chair.; Philip K. Asherman; Gail E. Hamilton; John N. Hanson; Richard S. Hill; Martha Frances Keeth; Andrew C. Kerin; Stephen C. Patrick; Barry W. Perry
International operations: Argentina; Belgium; Brazil; Canada; Cayman Islands; Hong Kong; Japan; Mexico; South Africa; Taiwan
Giving statement: Giving through the Arrow Electronics, Inc. Corporate Giving Program.
Company EIN: 111806155

Arrow Electronics, Inc. Corporate Giving Program

50 Marcus Dr.
Melville, NY 11747-4210 (631) 947-2000
E-mail: jcuniglio@arrow.com; URL: http://www.arrow.com/community/

Contact: James Cuniglio
Purpose and activities: Arrow Electronics makes charitable contributions to nonprofit organizations involved with education, the environment, and technology. Support is given on a national basis in areas of company operations.
Fields of interest: Arts; Education; Environment; Health care; Human services; Engineering/technology.
Type of support: Employee volunteer services; General/operating support; Program development.
Geographic limitations: Giving on a national basis in areas of company operations.
Support limitations: No support for political or religious organizations, government agencies, pass-through organizations, organizations that pose a conflict of interest to Arrow Electronics, discriminatory organizations, or membership organizations. No grants to individuals, or for athletic teams or events, or capital campaigns.
Publications: Application guidelines.

250
Arrowhead Properties, L.P.

500 Steed Rd.
P.O. Box 6100
Ridgeland, MS 39158 (601) 853-7300

Establishment information: Established in 1977.
Company type: Private company
Business activities: Conducts investment activities.
Business type (SIC): Investors/miscellaneous
Giving statement: Giving through the Arrowhead Foundation.

Arrowhead Foundation

P.O. Box 6100
Ridgeland, MS 39158-6100 (601) 853-7300

Establishment information: Established in 1997 in MS.
Donors: Arrowhead Properties, L.P.; Hap Hederman.
Contact: H. Doug Hederman, Tr.
Financial data (yr. ended 12/31/11): Assets, $164,688 (M); gifts received, $224,461; expenditures, $112,749; qualifying distributions, $110,700; giving activities include $110,700 for grants.
Purpose and activities: The foundation supports hospitals and organizations involved with higher education, theological education, and automotive safety.
Fields of interest: Education; Health care; Religion.
Type of support: General/operating support; Scholarship funds.
Application information: Applications accepted. Application form not required.
Initial approach: Proposal
Deadline(s): None
Trustees: H. Doug Hederman; Richard W. Hussey, Jr.; Thomas H. Hussey; Mollie Hederman Young.
EIN: 646213378

251
Arrowpoint Capital Corp.

(formerly Royal & Sun Alliance USA, Inc.)
Whitehall Corp. Ctr., Ste. 3
3600 Arco Corporate Dr.
Charlotte, NC 28273-8135 (704) 522-2000

Company URL: http://www.arrowpointcap.com
Establishment information: Established in 1851.
Company type: Private company
Business activities: Operates insurance company.
Business type (SIC): Insurance/fire, marine, and casualty; holding company
Corporate officers: John Tighe, Pres. and C.E.O.; Dennis Cahill, C.O.O.; Sean Beatty, C.F.O.; Dave Shumway, C.I.O.; Dave Davenport, Cont.; Jim Meehan, Genl. Counsel
Subsidiary: Royal Group Inc., Charlotte, NC
Giving statement: Giving through the Arrowpoint Insurance Foundation, Inc.

Arrowpoint Insurance Foundation, Inc.

(formerly The Royal & Sun Alliance Insurance Foundation Inc.)
3600 Arco Corporate Dr.
Charlotte, NC 28273-8100
URL: http://www.arrowpointcap.com/arrowpoint/index.aspx

Establishment information: Established in 1989 in NC.
Donor: Royal Group Inc.
Contact: Linda Y. Pettigrew, Secy.
Financial data (yr. ended 12/31/11): Assets, $424,496 (M); expenditures, $39,559; qualifying distributions, $39,168; giving activities include $39,168 for 15 grants (high: $10,000; low: $225).
Purpose and activities: The foundation supports hospitals, food banks, and charter schools and organizations involved with higher education and family services.
Fields of interest: Charter schools; Higher education; Hospitals (general); Food banks; Family services; United Ways and Federated Giving Programs.
Type of support: Annual campaigns; General/operating support; Program development; Sponsorships.
Geographic limitations: Giving primarily in Charlotte, NC, Princeton, NJ, and Rock Hill, SC.
Support limitations: No support for religious, veterans', or fraternal organizations or civic or social clubs. No grants to individuals, or for medical research, endowments (except for occasional scholarships and fellowships for insurance-related university programs), or telethons or televised appeals; generally, no grants for capital campaigns.
Publications: Informational brochure (including application guidelines).
Application information: Applications accepted. Application form required. Applicants should submit the following:
1) population served
2) name, address and phone number of organization
3) copy of IRS Determination Letter
4) brief history of organization and description of its mission
5) copy of most recent annual report/audited financial statement/990
6) explanation of why grantmaker is considered an appropriate donor for project
7) descriptive literature about organization
8) listing of board of directors, trustees, officers and other key people and their affiliations
9) detailed description of project and amount of funding requested

Initial approach: Letter
Board meeting date(s): Quarterly
Deadline(s): None

Officers and Directors:* Catherine A. Carlino*, Chair. and Pres.; David M. Davenport*, V.P. and Treas.; Linda Y. Pettigrew, Secy.; John Szczepek.
EIN: 561658178

252
Arroyo Paloma Inc.

(doing business as Villa Royal Apartments)
5800 Dashwood Dr.
Houston, TX 77081-5109 (713) 664-3335
FAX: (713) 664-3370

Company type: Private company
Business activities: Operates apartment buildings.
Business type (SIC): Real estate operators and lessors
Corporate officers: Robert M. Wilford, Pres.; J.F. Wilford, Secy.
Giving statement: Giving through the Gente Ayudando Gente S.A.

Gente Ayudando Gente S.A.

14107 Swiss Hill Dr.
Houston, TX 77077-1027

Establishment information: Established in 2001 in TX.
Donors: Robert M. Wilford; Arroyo Paloma, Inc.; RJW Properties, LP.
Financial data (yr. ended 12/31/11): Assets, $8,094 (M); gifts received, $850; expenditures, $810; qualifying distributions, $0.
Purpose and activities: The foundation supports organizations that assist the residents of the Republic of Panama to improve quality of life through improved housing and increased education.
Type of support: General/operating support.
Support limitations: No grants to individuals.
Application information: Applications not accepted. Contributes only to pre-selected organizations.
Officer: Robert M. Wilford, Pres.
EIN: 760685272

253
Arthur's Enterprises, Inc.

2010 2nd Ave.
Huntington, WV 25703-1108
(304) 523-7491

Establishment information: Established in 1986.
Company type: Private company
Business activities: Sells electrical equipment wholesale.
Business type (SIC): Electrical goods—wholesale
Corporate officers: Clarence Martin, C.E.O.; Arthur Weisberg, Pres.; James Roma, C.I.O.
Subsidiaries: Ligon Electric Supply Co. Inc. of NC, Huntington, WV; State Electric Supply Co., Huntington, WV
Giving statement: Giving through the Arthur's Enterprises, Inc. Scholarship Foundation.

Arthur's Enterprises, Inc. Scholarship Foundation

P.O. Box 5654
Huntington, WV 25703-0654
Application address: P.O. Box 5346, Huntington, WV 25703

Establishment information: Established in 1991 in WV.
Donor: Arthur's Enterprises, Inc.
Contact: Joan Weisberg, Secy. and Dir.
Financial data (yr. ended 06/30/12): Assets, $1,891 (M); gifts received, $26,000; expenditures, $26,602; qualifying distributions, $26,500; giving activities include $26,500 for grants to individuals.
Purpose and activities: The foundation awards college scholarships to children of employees of Arthur's Enterprises, Inc. and its subsidiaries.
Fields of interest: Higher education.
Type of support: Employee-related scholarships.
Geographic limitations: Giving limited to areas of company operations in WV.
Application information: Applications accepted. Application form required.
Have One Parent who has been a full-time employee of .

Initial approach: Proposal
Deadline(s): Mar. 1

Officers and Directors:* Arthur Weisberg, Pres.; Clarence Martin, V.P. and Treas.; Joan Weisberg, Secy.; John Spoor.
EIN: 550709058

254
Artichoke Joe's, Inc.

659 Huntington Ave.
San Bruno, CA 94066-3608
(650) 589-8812

Company URL: http://www.artichokejoes.com
Establishment information: Established in 1916.
Company type: Private company
Business activities: Operates gaming parlor.
Business type (SIC): Amusement and recreation services/miscellaneous
Corporate officers: Dennis J. Sammut, Pres. and Treas.; Melanie Maraffio, Cont.
Giving statement: Giving through the Sammut Family Foundation.

Sammut Family Foundation

659 Huntington Ave.
San Bruno, CA 94066-3608

Establishment information: Established in 1990 in CA.
Donor: Artichoke Joe's, Inc.
Financial data (yr. ended 11/30/11): Assets, $239,018 (M); gifts received, $300,000; expenditures, $112,761; qualifying distributions, $110,901; giving activities include $104,850 for 18 grants (high: $31,600; low: $200).
Purpose and activities: The foundation supports organizations involved with education, human services, and community development.
Fields of interest: Libraries (public); Education; Human services; Community development, service clubs; Community/economic development.
Type of support: General/operating support; Program development; Scholarship funds.
Geographic limitations: Giving limited to San Mateo County, CA, with emphasis on San Bruno.
Support limitations: No grants to individuals.
Application information: Applications not accepted. Unsolicited requests for funds not accepted.
Officers: Dennis J. Sammut, Pres.; Helen Sammut, C.F.O.; Sally S. Johnson, V.P.
EIN: 943113076

255
Ascena Retail Group Inc.

(formerly The Dress Barn, Inc.)
30 Dunnigan Dr.
Suffern, NY 10901 (845) 369-4602

Company URL: http://www.ascenaretail.com/
Establishment information: Established in 1962.
Company type: Public company
Company ticker symbol and exchange: ASNA/NASDAQ
Business activities: Operates women's clothing stores.
Business type (SIC): Women's apparel stores
Financial profile for 2012: Number of employees, 46,000; assets, $2,807,100,000; sales volume, $3,353,300,000; pre-tax net income, $279,000,000; expenses, $3,074,700,000; liabilities, $1,466,200,000
Fortune 1000 ranking: 2012—659th in revenues, 632nd in profits, and 769th in assets

Corporate officers: Elliot S. Jaffe, Chair.; David R. Jaffe, Pres. and C.E.O.; John J. Sullivan, Exec. V.P. and C.O.O.; Dirk A. Montgomery, Exec. V.P. and C.F.O.; Jay Levine, Sr. V.P., C.A.O., and Corp. Cont.; David Johns, Sr. V.P., C.I.O; Gene L. Wexler, Esq., Sr. V.P. and Genl. Counsel
Board of directors: Elliot S. Jaffe, Chair.; Kate Buggeln; Klaus Eppler; David R. Jaffe; Roslyn S. Jaffe; Randy L. Pearce; Michael W. Rayden; John Usdan
Giving statement: Giving through the Ascena Foundation.
Company EIN: 492312960

Ascena Foundation

(formerly The Dress Barn Fund)
30 Dunnigan Dr.
Suffern, NY 10901-4101

Establishment information: Established in 1985 in CT.
Donors: The Dress Barn, Inc.; Maurices, Inc.
Financial data (yr. ended 12/31/11): Assets, $42,653 (M); gifts received, $295,000; expenditures, $318,772; qualifying distributions, $318,772; giving activities include $318,712 for 42 + grants (high: $100,896; low: $20).
Purpose and activities: The foundation supports organizations involved with higher education, health, employment services, human services, international relief and conflict resolution, business and industry, and women.
Fields of interest: Higher education; Health care, volunteer services; Hospitals (general); Health care; Employment, services; American Red Cross; Children/youth, services; Human services, gift distribution; Human services; International relief; International conflict resolution; Business/industry Women.
Type of support: Employee matching gifts; General/operating support; Scholarship funds.
Geographic limitations: Giving primarily in NY; giving also to national organizations.
Application information: Applications not accepted. Contributes only to pre-selected organizations.
Officer: Elliot S. Jaffe, Pres.
Trustee: Roslyn E. Jaffe.
EIN: 222731305
Selected grants: The following grants are a representative sample of this grantmaker's funding activity:
$7,500 to Seeds of Peace, New York, NY, 2010.
$5,000 to American Heart Association, Dallas, TX, 2010.
$5,000 to University of Michigan, Ann Arbor, MI, 2010. For scholarship.
$5,000 to University of Pittsburgh, Pittsburgh, PA, 2010. For scholarship.
$5,000 to University of Wisconsin, Madison, WI, 2010. For scholarship.
$5,000 to West Virginia University, Morgantown, WV, 2010. For scholarship.
$2,500 to Autism Speaks, New York, NY, 2010.
$1,595 to American Cancer Society, Atlanta, GA, 2010.

256
Ash Grove Cement Company

11011 Cody St.
Overland Park, KS 66210 (913) 451-8900
FAX: (913) 451-8324

Company URL: http://www.ashgrove.com
Establishment information: Established in 1882.
Company type: Private company
Business activities: Manufactures cement; produces lime.
Business type (SIC): Cement/hydraulic; concrete, gypsum, and plaster products
Corporate officers: Charles T. Sunderland, Chair. and C.E.O.; Kenton W. Sunderland, Vice-Chair. and Secy.; J. Randall Vance, Sr. V.P., Admin.; Stephen D. Ryan, V.P. and Genl. Counsel; David W. Ezell, V.P., Human Resources
Board of directors: Charles T. Sunderland, Chair.; Kent W. Sunderland, Vice-Chair.; Eileen Flink; Patrick J. Gorup; Michael J. Hrizuk; Charles W. Larson; F. Lynn Markel; J. Randall Vance; John W. Webster; George M. Wells
Subsidiaries: Ash Grove Materials Corp., Shawnee Mission, KS; Cedar Creek Properties, Inc., Olathe, KS
Giving statement: Giving through the Ash Grove Charitable Foundation.

Ash Grove Charitable Foundation

P.O. Box 25900
Overland Park, KS 66225-5900

Establishment information: Established in 1997 in KS.
Donor: Ash Grove Cement Co.
Contact: Kenton W. Sunderland, Pres.
Financial data (yr. ended 12/31/11): Assets, $9,202,065 (M); expenditures, $524,699; qualifying distributions, $430,461; giving activities include $430,461 for grants.
Purpose and activities: The foundation supports community foundations and organizations involved with education, conservation, cancer, crime and violence prevention, human services, and community development.
Fields of interest: Higher education; Libraries (public); Education; Environment, natural resources; Cancer; Crime/violence prevention; Housing/shelter, development; Boy scouts; Homeless, human services; Human services; Community/economic development; Foundations (community).
Type of support: Annual campaigns; Building/renovation; Capital campaigns; Employee matching gifts; Equipment; General/operating support.
Geographic limitations: Giving primarily in areas of company operations in AR, ID, KS, MO, MT, NE, OR, and WA.
Support limitations: No support for secondary schools.
Publications: Grants list.
Application information: Applications accepted. Application form not required.
Initial approach: Proposal
Copies of proposal: 1
Board meeting date(s): As needed
Final notification: 3 months
Officers: Kenton W. Sunderland, Pres.; Charles T. Sunderland, V.P.; Eileen Flink, Secy.
Number of staff: 1 part-time professional.
EIN: 431765963
Selected grants: The following grants are a representative sample of this grantmaker's funding activity:
$100,000 to Foreman Public Schools, Foreman, AR, 2010.
$20,000 to Greater Kansas City Community Foundation, Kansas City, MO, 2010.
$20,000 to Iowa Natural Heritage Foundation, Des Moines, IA, 2010.
$17,500 to Boy Scouts of America, Heart of America Council, Kansas City, MO, 2010.
$10,000 to American Cancer Society, Dallas, TX, 2010.
$10,000 to Library Foundation, Portland, OR, 2010.
$10,000 to Restart, Kansas City, MO, 2010.
$5,000 to Catholic Community Services Foundation, Keizer, OR, 2010.
$2,500 to Saint Joseph Institute for the Deaf, Lenexa, KS, 2010.
$2,000 to Girl Scouts of the U.S.A., Wichita, KS, 2010.

257
Ashby & Geddes, P.A.

500 Delaware Ave.
P.O. Box 1150
Wilmington, DE 19899 (302) 654-1888

Company URL: http://www.ashby-geddes.com
Establishment information: Established in 1980.
Company type: Private company
Business activities: Operates law firm.
Business type (SIC): Legal services
Corporate officer: Lawrence C. Ashby, Partner
Giving statement: Giving through the Ashby & Geddes, P.A. Pro Bono Program.

Ashby & Geddes, P.A. Pro Bono Program

500 Delaware Ave., 8th Fl.
Wilmington, DE 19801 (302) 654-1888
E-mail: ptrainer@ashby-geddes.com; URL: http://www.ashby-geddes.com/about-service.html

Contact: Philip Trainer
Fields of interest: Legal services.
Type of support: Pro bono services - legal.

258
Ashland Inc.

(formerly Ashland Oil, Inc.)
50 E. RiverCenter Blvd.
P.O. Box 391
Covington, KY 41012-0391 (859) 815-3333
FAX: (859) 815-5188

Company URL: http://www.ashland.com
Establishment information: Established in 1936.
Company type: Public company
Company ticker symbol and exchange: ASH/NYSE
Business activities: Provides general contract asphalt and concrete construction services; manufactures and produces asphaltic and ready-mix concrete, crushed stone, and aggregate; sells chemicals, plastics, and resins wholesale; manufactures specialty chemicals; manufactures and markets motor oil and automotive chemicals; operates automotive oil change outlets; refines petroleum.
Business type (SIC): Chemicals and allied products—wholesale; mining/crushed and broken stone; construction/highway and street (except elevated); chemicals and allied products; petroleum refining; asphalt and roofing materials; concrete, gypsum, and plaster products; motor vehicle services, except repair
Financial profile for 2012: Number of employees, 15,000; assets, $12,400,000,000; sales volume, $8,100,000,000; pre-tax net income, -$14,000,000; expenses, $7,904,000,000; liabilities, $8,495,000,000
Fortune 1000 ranking: 2012—321st in revenues, 859th in profits, and 340th in assets
Forbes 2000 ranking: 2012—1080th in sales, 1741st in profits, and 1317th in assets

Corporate officers: James J. O'Brien, Chair. and C.E.O.; J. Kevin Willis, Sr. V.P. and C.F.O.; Peter Ganz, Sr. V.P., Genl. Counsel, and Secy.; Eric N. Boni, V.P. and Treas.; J. William Heitman, V.P. and Cont.; Steven E. Post, V.P., Opers.
Board of directors: James J. O'Brien, Chair.; Brendan Cummins; Roger W. Hale; Kathleen Ligocki; Vada O. Manager; Barry W. Perry; Mark C. Rohr; George A. Schaefer, Jr.; Janice J. Teal, Ph.D.; John F. Turner; Michael J. Ward
International operations: Australia; Brazil; Canada; China; Finland; France; Germany; Italy; Japan; Mauritius; Netherlands; Singapore; Spain; United Kingdom
Historic mergers: Hercules Incorporated (November 13, 2008)
Giving statement: Giving through the Ashland Inc. Corporate Giving Program.
Company EIN: 200865835

Ashland Inc. Corporate Giving Program

(formerly Ashland Inc. Foundation)
50 E. River Center Blvd.
Covington, KY 41011-1850 (859) 815-3409
FAX: (859) 815-3693;
E-mail: dsgeorge@ashland.com; URL: http://www.ashland.com/commitments

Contact: Deborah S. George, Mgr., Contribs. Prog.
Purpose and activities: Ashland makes charitable contributions to nonprofit organizations involved with education, mentoring, and the environment. Support is given primarily in areas of company operations.
Fields of interest: Education; Environment.
Type of support: Annual campaigns; Employee matching gifts; General/operating support; Program development; Program-related investments/loans; Scholarship funds.
Geographic limitations: Giving primarily in areas of company operations.
Support limitations: No support for fraternal, veterans', labor, athletic, or sectarian organizations or organizations not of direct benefit to the entire community. No grants to individuals, or for travel or audio, video, or film production.
Publications: Corporate report.
Application information: Applications accepted. Unsolicited requests are accepted but not encouraged. The Human Resources and Communications Department handles giving. The company has a staff that only handles contributions. A contributions committee reviews all requests. Application form not required.
Initial approach: Proposal to headquarters
Copies of proposal: 1
Committee meeting date(s): Varies
Deadline(s): Jun. or Jul. for the next year's funding
Final notification: 4 months
Administrators: Susan B. Esler, V.P., Human Resources and Comms.; Deborah S. George, Mgr., Contribs. Prog.
Number of staff: 2 part-time professional.

259
Ashley Furniture Industries, Inc.

1 Ashley Way
Arcadia, WI 54612-1218 (608) 323-3377
FAX: (608) 323-6008

Company URL: http://www.ashleyfurniture.com/
Establishment information: Established in 1945.
Company type: Private company
Business activities: Manufactures and imports upholstered, leather, and hardwood furniture.
Business type (SIC): Furniture/household
Financial profile for 2011: Number of employees, 13,650; sales volume, $2,900,000,000
Corporate officers: Ronald G. Wanek, Chair.; Charles Vogel, Vice-Chair.; Todd Wanek, Pres. and C.E.O.; Robert White, Exec. V.P. and C.I.O.; Dale Barneson, C.F.O.
Board of directors: Ronald G. Wanek, Chair.; Charles Vogel, Vice-Chair.
Giving statement: Giving through the Wanek-Vogel Foundation, Ltd.

The Wanek-Vogel Foundation, Ltd.

c/o Ashley Furniture Industries, Inc.
1 Ashley Way
Arcadia, WI 54612-1218 (608) 323-6249

Establishment information: Established in WI.
Donor: Ashley Furniture Industries.
Contact: Paulette Rippley
Financial data (yr. ended 12/31/11): Assets, $16,890,476 (M); gifts received, $5,000,000; expenditures, $2,663,229; qualifying distributions, $2,606,979; giving activities include $2,606,979 for 35 grants (high: $2,114,171; low: $50).
Purpose and activities: Giving primarily to local government for community development; Some giving for medical research and human services.
Fields of interest: Historic preservation/historical societies; Cystic fibrosis research; Agriculture/food; Recreation, community; Human services; Community/economic development.
Type of support: General/operating support.
Geographic limitations: Giving primarily in WI.
Support limitations: No grants to individuals.
Application information: Applications accepted. Applicants should submit the following:
1) signature and title of chief executive officer
2) name, address and phone number of organization
3) copy of IRS Determination Letter
4) descriptive literature about organization
5) detailed description of project and amount of funding requested
Initial approach: 1-page typewritten letter, with margin of 1 inch on all sides, and type not smaller than 10 point
Deadline(s): None
Final notification: 12 weeks
Directors: Benjamin Charles Vogel; Charles H.E. Vogel; Ronald G. Wanek; Todd R. Wanek.
EIN: 391948289
Selected grants: The following grants are a representative sample of this grantmaker's funding activity:
$109,036 to Arcadia, City of, Arcadia, WI, 2011. For general support.
$48,000 to City of Hope, Los Angeles, CA, 2011. For general support.

260
Aspen Skiing Company

117 ABC
Aspen, CO 81611 (970) 925-1220

Company URL: http://www.aspensnowmass.com
Establishment information: Established in 1947.
Company type: Private company
Business activities: Operates ski resorts.
Business type (SIC): Hotels and motels
Corporate officers: Mike Kaplan, Pres. and C.E.O.; Matt Jones, V.P. and C.F.O.; John Rigney, V.P., Sales; Christian Knapp, V.P., Mktg.
Giving statement: Giving through the Environment Foundation.

Environment Foundation

(formerly Aspen Skiing Company Environment Foundation)
P.O. Box 1248
Aspen, CO 81612-1248 (970) 300-7153
FAX: (970) 300-7154;
E-mail: mhamilton@aspensnowmass.com; Email for Matthew Hamilton: mamilton@aspensnowmass.com; fax for Matthew Hamilton: (970) 300-7154

Contact: Matthew Hamilton, Exec. Dir.
Financial data (yr. ended 12/31/11): Revenue, $203,481; assets, $77,631 (M); gifts received, $203,398; expenditures, $176,836; giving activities include $162,904 for grants.
Purpose and activities: The foundation is dedicated to the enhancement and protection of the environmental quality of the Roaring Fork Valley region, and supports projects that promote environmental education and research.
Fields of interest: Environment, alliance/advocacy; Environment, management/technical assistance; Environment, association; Environment, administration/regulation; Environment, research; Environment, public policy; Environment, reform; Environment, ethics; Environment, fund raising/fund distribution; Environment, legal rights; Environment, information services; Environment, public education; Environment, volunteer services; Environment, government agencies; Environment, formal/general education; Environment, pollution control; Environment, air pollution; Environment, water pollution; Environment, noise pollution; Environment, radiation control; Environment, toxics; Environment, waste management; Environment, recycling; Environment, climate change/global warming; Environment, natural resources; Environment, water resources; Environment, land resources; Environment, energy; Environment, forests; Environment, plant conservation; Environment, beautification programs; Environmental education; Environment; Animals/wildlife, management/technical assistance; Animal welfare.
Program:
Grants: Applications are accepted for projects that work to improve or protect the Roaring Fork Valley environment. Potential projects include ecological research, vegetation improvement programs, resource conservation programs, conservation of lands, riparian or wildlife habitats, transportation issues, air quality initiatives, open space preservation, recreational improvements, environmental education, and trail restoration. Eligible recipients may be private or nonprofit organizations, government agencies, or individuals; typical grant requests range from $2,000 to $10,000, though grant requests for less that $8,000 will be given priority.
Type of support: Consulting services; Continuing support; Curriculum development; Emergency funds; Equipment; Land acquisition; Management development/capacity building; Program development; Program evaluation; Research; Seed money; Technical assistance.
Geographic limitations: Giving primarily in the Roaring Fork Valley, CO.
Publications: Application guidelines; Grants list.
Application information: Applications must be received by 4:30 PM EST; potential applicants must contact mhamilton@aspensnowmass.com to request an application and discuss proposal in general.

Initial approach: Telephone or email for application
Deadline(s): Mar. 1 for Grants
Officers: Mark Cornish, Chair.; Georgie Bremner, Vice-Chair.; Matthew Hamilton, Exec. Dir.
Number of staff: 1 full-time professional.
EIN: 841428863

261
Associated Banc-Corp
1200 Hansen Rd.
Green Bay, WI 54304-5448 (920) 491-7000
FAX: (920) 433-3261

Company URL: http://www.assocbank.com
Establishment information: Established in 1970.
Company type: Public company
Company ticker symbol and exchange: ASBC/ NASDAQ
Business activities: Operates bank holding company; operates commercial bank.
Business type (SIC): Banks/commercial; holding company
Financial profile for 2012: Number of employees, 4,900; assets, $23,487,740,000; pre-tax net income, $254,460,000; liabilities, $20,551,340,000
Corporate officers: William R. Hutchinson, Chair.; Philip B. Flynn, Pres. and C.E.O.; James Yee, Exec. V.P., C.O.O., and C.I.O.; Christopher J. Del Moral-Niles, Exec. V.P. and C.F.O.; Randall J. Erickson, Exec. V.P., Genl. Counsel, and Corp. Secy.
Board of directors: William R. Hutchinson, Chair.; John F. Bergstrom; Ruth M. Crowley; Philip B. Flynn; Ronald Richard Harder; Robert A. Jeffe; Eileen A. Kamerick; Richard T. Lommen; J. Douglas Quick; Karen T. Van Lith; John Brian Williams
Subsidiaries: Appraisal Services, Inc., Milwaukee, WI; Associated Banc-Corp Services, Inc., Green Bay, WI; Associated Bank, N.A., Neenah, WI; Associated Bank Chicago, Chicago, IL; Associated Bank Green Bay, N.A., Green Bay, WI; Associated Bank Illinois, N.A., Rockford, IL; Associated Bank Lakeshore, N.A., Manitowoc, WI; Associated Bank Milwaukee, Milwaukee, WI; Associated Bank Minnesota, Minneapolis, MN; Associated Bank North, Wausau, WI; Associated Bank South Central, Madison, WI; Associated Card Services Bank, N.A., Stevens Point, WI; Associated Commercial Finance, Inc., St. Cloud, MN; Associated Commercial Mortgage, Inc., Milwaukee, WI; Associated Investment Management, LLC, Green Bay, WI; Associated Investment Services, Inc., Green Bay, WI; Associated Leasing, Inc., Menomonee Falls, WI; Associated Mortgage, Inc., De Pere, WI; Associated Trust Co., N.A., Milwaukee, WI; Banc Life Insurance Corp., Phoenix, AZ; Citizens Financial Services, Inc., Quincy, IL; Wisconsin Finance Corp., Shawano, WI
Office: Marshfield, WI
Giving statement: Giving through the Associated Banc-Corp Foundation Charitable Trust and the Associated Banc-Corp Founders Scholarship, Inc.
Company EIN: 391098068

Associated Banc-Corp Foundation Charitable Trust
(formerly First Financial Foundation, Inc.)
P.O. Box 12800
Green Bay, WI 54307-2800
E-mail: jon.drayna@associatedbank.com; Application address: c/o Associated Banc-Corp, P.O. Box 13307, 112 N. Adams St., Green Bay, WI 54307-3307

Establishment information: Established in 1977 in WI.
Donors: First Financial Bank; Associated Banc-Corp.
Contact: Jonathan Drayna, Dir.
Financial data (yr. ended 12/31/11): Assets, $1,789 (M); expenditures, $866,278; qualifying distributions, $863,341; giving activities include $863,341 for grants.
Purpose and activities: The trust supports hospitals and organizations involved with television, cancer, youth development, and community development.
Fields of interest: Media, television; Hospitals (general); Cancer; Youth development, business; Community/economic development.
Type of support: Program development.
Geographic limitations: Giving limited to areas of company operations in IL and WI; giving also to national organizations.
Support limitations: No support for political, labor, or veterans' organizations or religious organizations. No grants to individuals.
Application information: Applications accepted. Application form required.
Initial approach: Contact foundation for application form
Deadline(s): Sept. 1
Officer and Directors:* Brian R. Bodager*, Pres.; Joanne P. Radeske.
Trustee: Associated Banc-Corp.
Number of staff: 1 part-time professional.
EIN: 391277461

Associated Banc-Corp Founders Scholarship, Inc.
P.O. Box 12800
Green Bay, WI 54307-2800 (920) 491-7102
Application address: 112 N. Adams St., P.O. Box 13307, Green Bay, WI 54307-3307, tel.: 920-491-7102

Establishment information: Established in 1984 in WI.
Donors: Associated Banc-Corp; Associated Trust Co.
Contact: Jonathan Drayna, Secy.
Financial data (yr. ended 12/31/11): Assets, $249,200 (M); expenditures, $68,385; qualifying distributions, $68,322; giving activities include $64,000 for 45 grants to individuals (high: $1,500; low: $250).
Purpose and activities: The foundation awards college scholarships to children of employees of Associated Banc-Corp and its affiliates.
Fields of interest: Higher education.
Type of support: Employee-related scholarships.
Geographic limitations: Giving primarily in areas of company operations in WI.
Application information: Applications not accepted. Contributes only through employee-related scholarships.
Officers: Tom Graham, Pres.; Jon Drayna, Secy.
Trustee: Associated Trust Co.
Directors: Lori Flanagan; Mark Melum; James Noffke; Joe Selner.
EIN: 391482448

262
Associated Food Stores, Inc.
(also known as W-H Food Products)
1800 Rockaway Ave., Ste. 200
Hewlett, NY 11557-1668 (516) 256-3100

Company URL: http:// www.associatedsupermarkets.com
Establishment information: Established in 1940.
Company type: Private company
Business activities: Produces food, produce, frozen foods, meat, bakery goods, and non-food products.
Business type (SIC): Groceries—wholesale
Financial profile for 2009: Number of employees, 32
Corporate officer: Harry Laufer, Pres.
Giving statement: Giving through the Hordo & Bennett Pro Bono Program and the Associated Food Stores Charitable Foundation, Inc.

Associated Food Stores Charitable Foundation, Inc.
1800 Rockaway Ave.
Hewlett, NY 11557-1668

Establishment information: Established in 1987 in NY.
Donor: Associated Food Stores, Inc.
Financial data (yr. ended 12/31/11): Assets, $23,666 (M); expenditures, $48,183; qualifying distributions, $48,033; giving activities include $48,033 for grants.
Purpose and activities: The foundation supports organizations involved with education, cancer, and Judaism.
Fields of interest: Education; Cancer; Jewish agencies & synagogues; Religion.
Type of support: General/operating support.
Geographic limitations: Giving primarily in NY.
Support limitations: No grants to individuals.
Application information: Applications not accepted. Unsolicited requests for funds not accepted.
Directors: Ira Gober; Harry Laufer.
EIN: 112866371

263
Associated Oregon Loggers, Inc.
(doing business as AOL, Inc.)
1127 25th St., S.E.
P.O. Box 12339
Salem, OR 97301-5026 (503) 364-1330

Company URL: http://www.oregonloggers.org
Establishment information: Established in 1969.
Company type: Business league
Business activities: Operates trade association providing business services to contract logging firms and related businesses.
Business type (SIC): Business association; logging
Corporate officer: Tracy Brostrom, Pres.
Giving statement: Giving through the Friends of Paul Bunyan Foundation.

The Friends of Paul Bunyan Foundation
P.O. Box 12339
Salem, OR 97309-0339

Establishment information: Established in 1997 in OR.
Donors: Associated Oregon Loggers, Inc.; AOL Services, Inc.
Financial data (yr. ended 06/30/12): Assets, $452,648 (M); expenditures, $49,623; qualifying distributions, $29,250; giving activities include $29,250 for grants.
Purpose and activities: The foundation promotes scientific and educational projects related to forestry and resource education.
Fields of interest: Arts; Environment; Youth development.

Type of support: Annual campaigns; Building/renovation; Curriculum development; Research.
Geographic limitations: Giving limited to areas of company operations in OR.
Support limitations: No support for political candidates or parties. No grants to individuals, or for political activism projects or propaganda.
Publications: Application guidelines.
Application information: Applications accepted. Application form required.
Initial approach: Proposal
Copies of proposal: 1
Deadline(s): None
Officers and Board Members:* Hap Huffman*, Pres.; Bob Mahon*, V.P.; Doug Littlejohn*, Treas.; Mike Miller, Exec. Dir.; Gary Betts; Gary Jensen; Bob Luoto; Dick Powell; Robert Van Natta; Steve Woodward.
Number of staff: 1 full-time professional; 1 part-time professional.
EIN: 911830032

264
Associated Printers, Inc.

(also known as Pegasus InterPrint, Inc.)
7111 Hayvenhurst Ave.
Van Nuys, CA 91406 (818) 989-3600

Company URL: http://www.interprintusa.com
Establishment information: Established in 1983.
Company type: Private company
Business activities: Provides commercial printing services.
Business type (SIC): Printing/commercial
Corporate officer: Robert D. Pollard, Pres.
Board of director: Robert D. Pollard
Giving statement: Giving through the Vartanian & Topalian Foundation.

Vartanian & Topalian Foundation

P.O. Box 571191
Tarzana, CA 91357-1191

Establishment information: Established in 2001 in CA.
Donor: Associated Printers, Inc.
Financial data (yr. ended 12/31/11): Assets, $325,435 (M); expenditures, $135,000; qualifying distributions, $133,800; giving activities include $133,800 for 9 grants (high: $115,000; low: $800).
Purpose and activities: The foundation supports organizations involved with arts and culture, education, international relief, Catholicism, and Armenian culture.
Fields of interest: Arts, cultural/ethnic awareness; Museums; Arts; Education, early childhood education; Education; International relief; Catholic agencies & churches.
Type of support: General/operating support; Program development.
Geographic limitations: Giving primarily in CA.
Support limitations: No grants to individuals.
Application information: Applications not accepted. Contributes only to pre-selected organizations.
Officers: Vahe Vartanian, Pres.; Shake Vartanian, C.F.O.; Krikor Gary Topalian, Secy.
Number of staff: None.
EIN: 300005828

265
Association for Unmanned Vehicle Systems International

(doing business as AUVSI)
2700 S. Quincy St., Ste. 400
Arlington, VA 22206-2226 (703) 845-9671

Company URL: http://www.auvsi.org
Establishment information: Established in 1972.
Company type: Business league
Business activities: Operates a business association dedicated to promoting unmanned vehicle systems and related technologies.
Business type (SIC): Business association
Corporate officers: Peter Bale, Chair.; Ralph Alderson, Co-Vice-Chair.; John Lademan, Co-Vice-Chair.; Michael Toscano, Pres. and C.E.O.; Bob Thomson, Sr. V.P., Opers.; Brett Davis, V.P., Comms.; Joe Brannan, Treas.
Board of directors: Peter Bale, Chair.; Ralph Alderson, Co-Vice-Chair.; John Lademan, Co-Vice-Chair.
Giving statement: Giving through the Association for Unmanned Vehicle Systems Foundation, Inc.

Association for Unmanned Vehicle Systems Foundation, Inc.

2700 S. Quincy St., Ste. 400
Arlington, VA 22206-2226
FAX: (703) 845-9679;
E-mail: davidson@auvsifoundation.org; URL: http://www.auvsi.org/FOUNDATION

Establishment information: Established in 1992 in DC;.
Donors: AUVSI Capital Chapter; Association for Unmanned Vehicle Systems Intl.
Contact: Daryl Davidson, Exec. Dir.
Financial data (yr. ended 12/31/11): Revenue, $1,496,299; assets, $535,640 (M); gifts received, $1,240,067; expenditures, $1,242,225; giving activities include $120,085 for grants.
Purpose and activities: The foundation supports activities designed to increase public awareness of unmanned systems technology; promotes public education in the field of unmanned systems technology through discussion groups, forums, panels, and other programs; and provides grants to aid in the formal training and education of individuals in unmanned systems technology.
Fields of interest: Education; Science, research; Engineering/technology.
Type of support: General/operating support.
Geographic limitations: Giving primarily in VA.
Support limitations: No grants to individuals.
Officers: David Anderson, Pres.; Robert D. Brown, Treas.; Daryl Davidson, Exec. Dir.
Trustees: Joe Brannan; Larry Felder.
EIN: 521797483

266
Assurant, Inc.

1 Chase Manhattan Plz., 41st Fl.
New York, NY 10005 (212) 859-7000
FAX: (302) 655-5049

Company URL: http://www.assurant.com
Establishment information: Established in 1892.
Company type: Public company
Company ticker symbol and exchange: AIZ/NYSE
Business activities: Sells property, credit, health, dental, disability, life, and funeral insurance.
Business type (SIC): Insurance/accident and health; insurance/life; insurance/fire, marine, and casualty; insurance/surety
Financial profile for 2012: Number of employees, 14,600; assets, $28,946,610,000; sales volume, $8,508,270,000; pre-tax net income, $757,750,000; expenses, $7,750,520,000; liabilities, $23,761,240,000
Fortune 1000 ranking: 2012—309th in revenues, 343rd in profits, and 191st in assets
Forbes 2000 ranking: 2012—1047th in sales, 1076th in profits, and 756th in assets
Corporate officers: Elaine D. Rosen, Ph.D., Chair.; Robert B. Pollock, Pres. and C.E.O.; Michael J. Peninger, Exec. V.P. and C.F.O.; Bart R. Schwartz, Exec. V.P. and Secy.; Christopher J. Pagano, Exec. V.P. and Treas.; Alan B. Colberg, Exec. V.P. and Mktg.; Sylvia R. Wagner, Exec. V.P., Human Resources
Board of directors: Elaine D. Rosen, Chair.; Howard L. Carver; Juan N. Cento; Elyse B. Douglas; Lawrence V. Jackson; David B. Kelso; Charles John Koch; Jean-Paul L. Montupet; Robert B. Pollock; Paul J. Reilly; Robert W. Stein
Subsidiaries: Assurant Health, Milwaukee, WI; Assurant Solutions, Miami, FL; Fortis Benefits Insurance Company, Kansas City, MO; United Family Life Insurance Company, Atlanta, GA
International operations: Argentina; Bermuda; Brazil; Canada; Cayman Islands; Chile; China; Denmark; Dominican Republic; England; Germany; Ireland; Italy; Mexico; Spain; United Kingdom
Giving statement: Giving through the Assurant, Inc. Corporate Giving Program and the Assurant Foundation.
Company EIN: 391126612

Assurant, Inc. Corporate Giving Program

One Chase Manhattan Plz.
New York, NY 10005 (212) 859-7000
E-mail: Debbie.Burbridge@assurant.com;
URL: http://www.assurant.com/inc/assurant/community/index.html

Purpose and activities: As a complement to its foundation, Assurant also makes charitable contributions to nonprofit organizations directly. Support is given primarily in areas of company operations.
Fields of interest: Education; Health care; Food services; Housing/shelter, homeless; Housing/shelter, expense aid; Human services; Children/youth, services; Human services.
Type of support: Employee volunteer services; General/operating support; Sponsorships.
Geographic limitations: Giving primarily in areas of company operations.
Support limitations: No support for political parties or candidates or religious organizations.

Assurant Foundation

(formerly Fortis Foundation)
1 Chase Manhattan Plz., 41st Fl.
New York, NY 10005-1420 (212) 859-7026
E-mail: Taryn.Moskowitz@assurant.com;
URL: http://www.assurant.com/inc/assurant/community/new-york.html

Establishment information: Established in 1982 in NY.
Donors: Time Insurance Co.; Fortis Insurance Co.; Fortis, Inc.; Fortis Benefits Insurance Co.
Contact: Taryn Moskowitz, Corp. Comms. Consultant
Financial data (yr. ended 12/31/11): Assets, $9,592,959 (M); gifts received, $5,000,000;

expenditures, $471,339; qualifying distributions, $435,931; giving activities include $435,931 for grants.
Purpose and activities: The foundation supports organizations involved with education, health, nutrition, housing, human services, and community development. Special emphasis is directed toward health and wellness; homes and property; and hometown help.
Fields of interest: Museums (art); Education; Health care; Nutrition; Housing/shelter; Family services; Human services; Community/economic development.
Type of support: Employee matching gifts; General/operating support; Program development.
Geographic limitations: Giving primarily in areas of company operations in the New York, NY, metropolitan area.
Support limitations: No support for religious or political organizations. No grants to individuals or for lobbying or fundraising.
Publications: Application guidelines.
Application information: Applications accepted. Application form required. Applicants should submit the following:
1) principal source of support for project in the past
2) copy of IRS Determination Letter
3) copy of most recent annual report/audited financial statement/990
4) listing of board of directors, trustees, officers and other key people and their affiliations
5) detailed description of project and amount of funding requested
6) copy of current year's organizational budget and/or project budget

Initial approach: Download application form and mail to foundation
Copies of proposal: 1
Deadline(s): Feb. 16, May 16, Aug. 16, and Nov. 16

Trustees: Robert B. Pollock; Lesley Silvester.
EIN: 133156497
Selected grants: The following grants are a representative sample of this grantmaker's funding activity:
$7,223 to Share Our Strength, Washington, DC, 2009. For matching funds.
$3,000 to Learning Ally, Princeton, NJ, 2009.
$2,500 to Big Brothers Big Sisters of New York City, New York, NY, 2009.
$2,500 to Duke University, Durham, NC, 2009.
$2,000 to Fresh Air Fund, New York, NY, 2009.

267
Assurant Health

(formerly Fortis Insurance Company)
501 W. Michigan St.
P.O. Box 624
Milwaukee, WI 53201-3050
(414) 271-3011

Company URL: http://www.assuranthealth.com
Establishment information: Established in 1892.
Company type: Subsidiary of a public company
Business activities: Sells health insurance; operates medical service plan.
Business type (SIC): Insurance/accident and health
Corporate officers: Adam Lamnin, Pres. and C.E.O.; Donald Hamm, C.O.O.; Chris Dowler, Sr. V.P. and C.I.O.
Giving statement: Giving through the Assurant Health Foundation.

Assurant Health Foundation

(formerly Fortis Health Foundation, Inc.)
501 W. Michigan St.
Milwaukee, WI 53203-2706 (414) 299-1358
FAX: (414) 299-6749;
E-mail: MaryGrace.Curatola@assurant.com;
URL: http://www.assurant.com/inc/assurant/community/health.html

Establishment information: Established in 1973 in WI.
Donors: Time Insurance Co.; Fortis Insurance Co.
Contact: MaryGrace Curatola, V.P.
Financial data (yr. ended 12/31/11): Assets, $1,278,756 (M); expenditures, $328,502; qualifying distributions, $327,902; giving activities include $327,902 for grants.
Purpose and activities: The foundation supports organizations involved with arts and culture, education, healthcare access and affordability, health promotion, disease prevention, and public policy.
Fields of interest: Performing arts, theater; Performing arts, music; Arts; Education; Medical care, community health systems; Health care, clinics/centers; Public health; Health care, cost containment; Health care, patient services; Health care; United Ways and Federated Giving Programs; Public policy, research.
Programs:

Arts and Culture: The foundation supports arts and cultural groups; employee involvement in the arts and culture arena; opportunities to increase exposure to the arts; and groups serving diverse communities and artistic forms.

Employee Matching Grant Program: The foundation matches contributions made my employees of Assurant Health to cultural organizations, educational institutions, and social service organizations on a one-for-one basis from $20 to $7,500 per employee, per year.

Expanding Access to Care: The foundation supports programs designed to expand access to healthcare, including health clinics and centers and other human service organizations.

REAP Program: Through Reaching Excellence in Academic Performance (REAP) program, the foundation provides funding to five Milwaukee Public Schools to address performance gaps in the Milwaukee Public School (MPS) system. The program is designed to raise the level of student academic performance, school attendance, parental involvement, and the learning environment.

Type of support: Continuing support; Employee matching gifts; Employee volunteer services; General/operating support; Matching/challenge support; Program development.
Geographic limitations: Giving primarily in areas of company operations in Milwaukee and southeastern WI; giving also to national public policy initiatives.
Support limitations: No support for labor, political, fraternal, municipal, or religious organizations. No grants to individuals.
Application information: Applications not accepted. The foundation utilizes an invitation only Request For Proposal (RFP) process. Unsolicited requests are not accepted.

Board meeting date(s): Quarterly

Officers: Rob Guilbert, Pres.; MaryGrace Curatola, V.P.; Jennifer Kopps-Wagner, Secy.; Howard Miller, Treas.
Director: Laurel Call.
Trustee: Mary Hinderliter.
EIN: 237346436
Selected grants: The following grants are a representative sample of this grantmaker's funding activity:
$30,000 to United Way of Greater Milwaukee, Milwaukee, WI, 2011.
$25,000 to Milwaukee Public Museum, Milwaukee, WI, 2011.
$5,000 to Big Brothers Big Sisters of Metropolitan Milwaukee, Milwaukee, WI, 2011.
$5,000 to Milwaukee Rescue Mission, Milwaukee, WI, 2011.
$2,350 to Big Brothers Big Sisters of Metropolitan Milwaukee, Milwaukee, WI, 2011.
$1,500 to Milwaukee Rescue Mission, Milwaukee, WI, 2011.
$1,450 to Milwaukee Rescue Mission, Milwaukee, WI, 2011.
$1,050 to Milwaukee Rescue Mission, Milwaukee, WI, 2011.

268
Assurant Solutions

11222 Quail Roost Dr.
Miami, FL 33157-6543 (305) 253-2244

Company URL: http://www.assurantsolutions.com
Establishment information: Established in 1980.
Company type: Subsidiary of a public company
Business activities: Develop, underwrite and market specialty insurance, extended service contracts and other risk management solutions.
Business type (SIC): Insurance/life; holding company
Financial profile for 2009: Number of employees, 80
Corporate officers: S. Craig Lemasters, Pres. and C.E.O.; Carey L. Bongard, Exec. V.P., Human Resources; Ivan C. Lopez Morales, Sr. V.P. and C.F.O.
Board of directors: Manuel Becerra; Joseph E. Erdeman
Subsidiaries: American Bankers Insurance Co. of Florida, Miami, FL; American Bankers Life Assurance Co. of Florida, Miami, FL
Giving statement: Giving through the Assurant Corporate Giving Program.

Assurant Corporate Giving Program

c/o Charitable Giving Prog. Office
11222 Quail Roost Dr.
Miami, FL 33157-6596
E-mail: debbie.burbridge@assurant.com;
URL: http://www.assurantsolutions.com/inCommunity.html
Additional URL: http://www.assurant.com/inc/assurant/community/solutions.html

Contact: Debbie Burbridge
Financial data (yr. ended 12/31/10): Total giving, $1,584,369, including $832,098 for grants and $752,271 for employee matching gifts.
Purpose and activities: As a complement to its foundation, Assurant also makes charitable contributions to nonprofit organizations directly. Special emphasis is directed towards programs designed to address arts and culture, education, health care, and human services. Support is given primarily in areas of company operations, with emphasis on southern Florida, Atlanta, Georgia, and Lawton, Oklahoma, and in Argentina, Brazil, Canada, Chile, China, Germany, Ireland, Italy, Mexico, Puerto Rico, Spain, and the United Kingdom.
Fields of interest: Arts; Education; Health care; Food services; Housing/shelter; Disasters, preparedness/services; United Ways and Federated Giving Programs Children/youth.

International interests: Argentina; Brazil; Canada; Chile; China; Germany; Ireland; Italy; Mexico; Spain; United Kingdom.

Program:

United Way Gift Matching Program: Assurant matches charitable contributions made by its employees to United Way member agencies on a one-for-one basis, up to $1,000, per employee.

Type of support: Continuing support; Employee matching gifts; Employee volunteer services; General/operating support; Program development; Scholarship funds; Sponsorships.

Geographic limitations: Giving primarily in areas of company operations, with emphasis on southern FL, Atlanta, GA, and Lawton OK, and in Argentina, Brazil, Canada, Chile, China, Germany, Ireland, Italy, Mexico, Puerto Rico, Spain, and the United Kingdom.

Support limitations: No support for government agencies, social, or political organizations, religious organizations not of direct benefit to the entire community, trade, industry, or professional associations, or fraternal, labor, or veterans' organizations. No grants to individuals, or for sports events or sponsorships or fundraising, advertising or tickets, travel, or discretionary social functions.

Publications: Application guidelines; Corporate giving report; Informational brochure; Program policy statement (including application guidelines).

Application information: Applications accepted. Proposals should be submitted using organization letterhead. Multi-year funding is not automatic. The Corporate Communications Department handles giving. The company has a staff that only handles contributions. Application form not required.

Applicants should submit the following:

1) timetable for implementation and evaluation of project
2) site description
3) results expected from proposed grant
4) name, address and phone number of organization
5) copy of IRS Determination Letter
6) brief history of organization and description of its mission
7) copy of most recent annual report/audited financial statement/990
8) listing of board of directors, trustees, officers and other key people and their affiliations
9) detailed description of project and amount of funding requested
10) copy of current year's organizational budget and/or project budget
11) listing of additional sources and amount of support

Requests for continuing support should include a description of the benefit realized or received from the previous contribution.

Initial approach: Proposal to headquarters
Copies of proposal: 1
Committee meeting date(s): Quarterly
Deadline(s): None
Final notification: 6 to 8 weeks

Number of staff: 1 full-time professional.

269
Assurity Life Insurance Company

1526 K St.
P.O. Box 82533
Lincoln, NE 68501-2533 (402) 476-6500

Company URL: http://www.assurity.com
Establishment information: Established in 1890.
Company type: Subsidiary of a private company
Business activities: Sells life insurance.
Business type (SIC): Insurance/life
Financial profile for 2010: Number of employees, 350
Corporate officers: Thomas E. Henning, Chair., Pres., and C.E.O.; Susan L. Keisler-Munro, Sr. V.P. and C.O.O.; Marvin P. Ehly, V.P., C.F.O., and Treas.; William R. Schmeeckie, V.P. and C.I.O.
Board of director: Thomas E. Henning, Chair.
Giving statement: Giving through the Assurity Life Foundation.

Assurity Life Foundation

(formerly Security Financial Life Foundation)
2000 Q St.
Lincoln, NE 68503-3609 (402) 437-9504

Establishment information: Established in 1993 in NE.
Donors: Security Mutual Life Insurance Co.; Security Financial Life Insurance Co.; Assurity Life Insurance Co.
Contact: Tammy Halvorsen
Financial data (yr. ended 12/31/11): Assets, $3,524,398 (M); gifts received, $2,000,000; expenditures, $60,715; qualifying distributions, $60,000; giving activities include $60,000 for 1 grant.
Purpose and activities: The foundation supports organizations involved with performing arts, higher education, land conservation, health, heart disease, human services, and economic development.
Fields of interest: Performing arts; Performing arts, theater; Performing arts, orchestras; Higher education; Environment, land resources; Health care, insurance; Health care; Heart & circulatory diseases; YM/YWCAs & YM/YWHAs; Human services; Economic development; United Ways and Federated Giving Programs.
Type of support: General/operating support.
Geographic limitations: Giving primarily in Lincoln, NE.
Support limitations: No grants to individuals.
Application information: Applications accepted. Application form not required.

Initial approach: Proposal
Board meeting date(s): Quarterly
Deadline(s): None

Officers and Directors:* Thomas E. Henning*, C.E.O. and Pres.; William R. Schmeeckle, V.P.; Carol S. Watson, Secy.; Marvin P. Enly*, Treas.; William R. Cintani; Frank H. Hilsabeck; Angela L. Muhleisen; David T. Wallman; Lyn W. Ziegenbein.
Number of staff: None.
EIN: 470775374

270
Astoria Energy, LLC

17-10 Steinway St.
Astoria, NY 11375 (718) 274-7700
FAX: (718) 274-7892

Company URL: http://www.astoriaenergy.com
Establishment information: Established in 1999.
Company type: Private company
Business activities: Generates, transmits, and distributes electric power.
Business type (SIC): Electric services
Corporate officers: Charles McCall, C.E.O.; Louis M. St. Maurice, C.F.O.
Giving statement: Giving through the SCS Astoria Energy Foundation, Inc.

SCS Astoria Energy Foundation, Inc.

1990 Post Oak Blvd., Ste. 1900
Houston, TX 77056-3831

Establishment information: Established in 2005 in NY.
Donor: Astoria Energy, LLC.
Financial data (yr. ended 12/31/11): Assets, $29,857 (M); expenditures, $58; qualifying distributions, $0.
Purpose and activities: The foundation supports hospitals and organizations involved with education, tennis, human services, community economic development, and civic affairs.
Fields of interest: Elementary/secondary education; Higher education; Education; Hospitals (general); Athletics/sports, racquet sports; Children/youth, services; Human services; Business/industry; Community/economic development; Public affairs.
Type of support: Program development; Scholarship funds.
Geographic limitations: Giving primarily in NY.
Support limitations: No grants to individuals.
Application information: Applications not accepted. Unsolicited requests for funds not accepted.
Officers: Charles McCall, Pres.; Stephan Secru, V.P. and Secy.; Philippe Habib, Treas.
EIN: 202197026

271
Astoria Federal Savings and Loan Association

1 Astoria Federal Plz.
Lake Success, NY 11042-1085
(516) 327-3000

Company URL: http://www.astoriafederal.com
Establishment information: Established in 1888.
Company type: Subsidiary of a public company
Business activities: Operates savings and loan institutions.
Business type (SIC): Savings institutions
Corporate officers: Ralph F. Palleschi, Chair.; Gerard C. Keegan, Vice-Chair., Sr. Exec. V.P., and C.O.O.; John J. Conefry, Jr., Vice-Chair.; Monte N. Redman, Pres. and C.E.O.; Frank E. Fusco, Sr. Exec. V.P., Treas., and C.F.O.; Alan P. Eggleston, Sr. Exec. V.P. and Secy.; Robert J. DeStefano, Exec. V.P. and C.I.O.
Board of directors: Ralph F. Palleschi, Chair.; John J. Conefry, Jr., Vice-Chair.; Gerard Keegan, Vice-Chair.; John R. Chrin; Peter C. Haeffner, Jr.; Gerard C. Keegan; Brian M. Leeney; Monte N. Redman
Giving statement: Giving through the Astoria Federal Savings and Loan Association Corporate Giving Program.
Company EIN: 113170868

Astoria Federal Savings and Loan Association Corporate Giving Program

1 Astoria Federal Plz.
Lake Success, NY 11042-1085 (516) 327-3000
URL: https://www.astoriafederal.com/about-us-2/community-connections/

272
AstraZeneca Pharmaceuticals LP

(formerly Zeneca Inc.)
1800 Concord Pike
Wilmington, DE 19850-5437
(302) 886-3000

Company URL: http://www.astrazeneca-us.com
Establishment information: Established in 1999.
Company type: Subsidiary of a foreign company
Business activities: Discovers, develops, manufactures, and provides health care products and solutions.
Business type (SIC): Drugs
Financial profile for 2010: Number of employees, 20,800; sales volume, $14,800,000,000
Corporate officers: Richard Fante, Pres.; Marion McCourt, C.O.O.; Maria Brito Perez, V.P., Human Resources
Giving statement: Giving through the AstraZeneca Pharmaceuticals LP Corporate Giving Program, the AstraZeneca HealthCare Foundation, and the AstraZeneca Patient Assistance Organization.

AstraZeneca HealthCare Foundation

(formerly Zeneca HealthCare Foundation)
1800 Concord Pike
P.O. Box 15437
Wilmington, DE 19850-5437 (302) 886-3000
E-mail: ConnectionsforCardiovascularHealth@astrazeneca.com; Additional tel.: (800) 236-9933; URL: http://www.astrazeneca-us.com/foundation/

Establishment information: Established as a company-sponsored operating foundation in 1993 in DE.
Donors: Zeneca Inc.; AstraZeneca Pharmaceuticals LP.
Financial data (yr. ended 12/31/11): Assets, $18,909,789 (M); gifts received, $20,601; expenditures, $3,922,800; qualifying distributions, $3,922,800; giving activities include $3,682,942 for 20 grants (high: $295,000; low: $153,600).
Purpose and activities: The foundation promotes public awareness of healthcare issues and provides public education of medical knowledge.
Fields of interest: Education; Health care; Cancer; Heart & circulatory diseases; Health organizations; Disasters, preparedness/services.
Program:
Connections for Cardiovascular Health: Through the Connections for Cardiovascular Health program, the AstraZeneca HealthCare Foundation will award annual grants of $150,000 and greater to US-based nonprofit organizations involved with improving cardiovascular health within the United States.
Type of support: Annual campaigns; Continuing support; General/operating support; Program development.
Support limitations: No support for religious or faith-based programs not of direct benefit to the entire community, for-profit organizations, or discriminatory organizations. No grants to individuals, or for capital investments, unsolicited capital campaigns, enhancements of existing hospital services or hospital software systems, professional education, training for healthcare professionals, research or clinical trials, healthcare providers or cardiologist salaries, endowments, journals, or advertising.
Publications: Application guidelines.
Application information: Applications accepted. Grants range from $150,000 to $250,000. Multi-year funding is not automatic. Application form required. Applicants should submit the following:
1) results expected from proposed grant
2) population served
3) name, address and phone number of organization
4) copy of IRS Determination Letter
5) brief history of organization and description of its mission
6) copy of most recent annual report/audited financial statement/990
7) detailed description of project and amount of funding requested
8) plans for cooperation with other organizations, if any
9) contact person
10) copy of current year's organizational budget and/or project budget

Initial approach: Complete online application for Connections for Cardiovascular Health
Deadline(s): Feb. 1 to Feb. 28 for Connections for Cardiovascular Health grants

Officers and Directors:* James Blasetto*, Chair.; David P. Nicoli*, Pres.; Ann V. Booth-Barbarin*, Secy.; David White, Treas.; Joyce Jacobson, Exec. Dir.; John Buse; Timothy J. Gardner; Howard G. Hutchinson; Jennifer H. Mieres; Michael Miller; Robert W. Perkins.
EIN: 510349682

AstraZeneca Patient Assistance Organization

1800 Concord Pike
P.O. Box 15437
Wilmington, DE 19850-5437
URL: http://www.astrazeneca-us.com/help-affording-your-medicines/prescription-saving-program/
Mailing address: AZ&Me Prescription Savings Prog., P.O. Box 898, Somerville, NJ 08876, fax: (800) 961-8323

Establishment information: Established in 2006 in DE.
Financial data (yr. ended 12/31/11): Revenue, $629,187,333; gifts received, $629,187,333; expenditures, $629,187,333; program services expenses, $629,187,333; giving activities include $629,187,333 for 344,206 grants to individuals.
Purpose and activities: The organization works to provide pharmaceutical drugs to the sick, poor, and needy.
Fields of interest: Pharmacy/prescriptions; Health care.
Type of support: In-kind gifts.
Application information: Applications not accepted. Unsolicited requests for funds not considered or acknowledged.
Officers and Trustees :* David P. Nicoli*, Chair. and Pres.; Ann V. Booth-Barbarin*, Secy.; David E. White, Treas.; Robert L. Busch; Robert N. Jenkins; Carolyn H. Miclucci; Robert Perkins.
EIN: 562591004

273
AT&T Inc.

(formerly SBC Communications Inc.)
208 S. Akard St.
Dallas, TX 75202-2233 (210) 821-4105

Company URL: http://www.att.com
Establishment information: Established in 1876.
Company type: Public company
Company ticker symbol and exchange: T/NYSE
International Securities Identification Number: US00206R1023
Business activities: Operates holding company; provides IP-based business communications services; local, wireless, and long distance telephone communications services; wireless Internet access and voice services; publishes telephone directories; provides satellite television services.
Business type (SIC): Telephone communications; publishing/miscellaneous; cable and other pay television services; holding company
Financial profile for 2012: Number of employees, 242,000; assets, $272,315,000,000; sales volume, $127,434,000,000; pre-tax net income, $10,439,000,000; expenses, $114,494,000,000; liabilities, $179,953,000,000
Fortune 1000 ranking: 2012—11th in revenues, 25th in profits, and 21st in assets
Forbes 2000 ranking: 2012—33rd in sales, 62nd in profits, and 109th in assets
Corporate officers: Randall L. Stephenson, Chair., Pres., and C.E.O.; John Stephens, Sr. Exec. V.P. and C.F.O.; Wayne Watts, Sr. Exec. V.P. and Genl. Counsel; Ronald E. Spears, Sr. Exec. V.P., Opers.; William A. Blase, Jr., Sr. Exec. V.P., Human Resources; Ann E. Meuleman, Sr. V.P. and Secy.
Board of directors: Randall L. Stephenson, Chair.; Gilbert F. Amelio, Ph.D.; Reuben V. Anderson; James H. Blanchard; Scott T. Ford; James P. Kelly; Jon C. Madonna; Michael B. McCallister; John B. McCoy; Jaime Chico Pardo; Joyce M. Roche; Matthew K. Rose; Laura D'Andrea Tyson
Subsidiaries: AT&T Alascom, Anchorage, AK; AT&T Corp., Bedminster, NJ; AT&T International Inc., San Antonio, TX; AT&T Mobility, Atlanta, GA; AT&T Teleholdings, Inc., Chicago, IL; BellSouth Corporation, Atlanta, GA; BellSouth Telecommunications, Inc., Atlanta, GA; Southwestern Bell Telephone Company, Dallas, TX; Southwestern Bell Yellow Pages, Inc., St. Louis, MO; Sterling Commerce, Dublin, OH
Office: San Antonio, TX
Historic mergers: AT&T Wireless Services, Inc. (October 25, 2004); BellSouth Corporation (December 29, 2006); Centennial Communications Corp. (November 6, 2009)
Giving statement: Giving through the AT&T Inc. Corporate Giving Program and the AT&T Foundation.
Company EIN: 431301883

AT&T Inc. Corporate Giving Program

(formerly AT&T Corp. Contributions Program)
130 E. Travis, Rm. 350
San Antonio, TX 78205 (800) 591-9663
E-mail: sustainability@attnews.us; URL: http://www.att.com/gen/landing-pages?pid=7735

Financial data (yr. ended 12/31/10): Total giving, $129,632,968, including $129,632,968 for grants.
Purpose and activities: As a complement to its foundation, AT&T also makes charitable contributions to nonprofit organizations directly. Support is given on a national basis in areas of company operations.
Fields of interest: Arts; Higher education; Education; Health care; Housing/shelter, development; Disasters, preparedness/services; Youth development, business; Human services; Civil/human rights, equal rights; Community/economic development; Engineering/technology; Military/veterans' organizations Minorities; Military/veterans; Economically disadvantaged.
Type of support: Donated products; Employee volunteer services; General/operating support; Program development; Scholarship funds; Sponsorships; Technical assistance.
Geographic limitations: Giving on a national basis in areas of company operations; giving also to national organizations.

AT&T Foundation

(formerly SBC Foundation)
208 S. Akard, Ste. 100
Dallas, TX 75202-4206
FAX: (210) 351-2599; Application address: 130 E. Travis, Ste. 350, San Antonio, TX 78205; Additional tel.: (800) 591-9663; URL: http://www.att.com/gen/landing-pages?pid=7735

Establishment information: Established in 1984 in MO.
Donors: Southwestern Bell Corp.; SBC Communications Inc.; AT&T Inc.
Financial data (yr. ended 12/31/11): Assets, $18,655,778 (M); expenditures, $16,272,288; qualifying distributions, $15,514,402; giving activities include $12,580,064 for grants and $2,934,338 for 2,985 employee matching gifts.
Purpose and activities: The foundation supports programs designed to advance education. Special emphasis is directed toward programs designed to create learning opportunities, promote academic and economic achievement, and address community needs. The foundation also supports organizations involved with arts and culture, health, human services, community development, and civic affairs.
Fields of interest: Arts; Secondary school/education; Higher education; Scholarships/financial aid; Education, drop-out prevention; Education; Health care; Employment, training; Employment; Disasters, preparedness/services; Human services; Community development, neighborhood development; Community development, small businesses; Community/economic development; Mathematics; Engineering/technology; Science; Leadership development; Public affairs Minorities; Economically disadvantaged.

Programs:

AT&T Aspire Initiative: AT&T and the foundation support programs designed to help students graduate from high school ready for college and careers to become better prepared to meet global competition. Special emphasis is directed toward technology; people; and local communities. Technology is addressed through AT&T Foundry innovation centers to discover new approaches to educational obstacles; collaborations with organizations to develop interactive learning tools to better engage students; the use of gamification, the Internet, video, and social media in educational programs; internships in areas related to 21st century skills; and collaborations with GameDesk to transform traditional instruction and equalize education. People are served through the involvement of AT&T employees and the Aspire Mentoring Academy; expansion of the Job Shadow Initiative with Junior Achievement; skill-based mentoring where students and employees are paired based on shared interests; and the engagement of AT&T customers, companies, and stakeholders to address the education crisis. Communities through local education-focused groups; partnerships with groups that embrace social innovation, 21st century skills, and science, technology, engineering, and mathematics (STEM) disciplines in underserved communities; contributions to organizations that specialize in students and improved quality of education; and through Aspire Local Impact Request for Proposals (RFPs).

AT&T Aspire Local High School Impact Initiative: The foundation, under the AT&T Aspire initiative, awards grants to schools and nonprofit organizations that have evidence-based practices and data-driven outcomes that improve high school graduation rates in their communities. Special emphasis is directed toward programs that incorporate social innovation; integrate the disciplines of science, technology, engineering, and math (STEM); and increase the number of minority and underrepresented students in STEM fields. Grants range from $100,000 to $300,000 for 24 months.

AT&T Foundation Employee Disaster Relief Fund: The foundation provides grants, short-term financial assistance, and long-term financial assistance for food, clothing, physical and mental health care, housing, transportation, education, and childcare to employees and retirees of AT&T affected by a disaster.

Higher Education and Cultural Matching Gifts: The foundation matches contributions made by directors, employees, and retirees of AT&T to institutions of higher education and organizations involved with arts and culture on a one-for-one basis from $25 to $3,000 per retiree, per year, and from $25 to $15,000 per employee and director, per year.

Type of support: Curriculum development; Employee matching gifts; Employee volunteer services; Equipment; Matching/challenge support; Program development; Scholarship funds.
Geographic limitations: Giving on a national basis in areas of company operations, with emphasis on TX.
Support limitations: No support for religious organizations not of direct benefit to the entire community, or for political, discriminatory, or disease-specific organizations, or medical clinics or research. No grants to individuals (except for employee-related disaster grants) or for capital campaigns, endowment funds, goodwill ads, ticket or dinner purchases, sports programs or events, or cause-related marketing; no product donations.
Publications: Corporate giving report; Program policy statement.
Application information: Applications accepted. Company facility addresses can be found on the 990. Multi-year funding is not automatic. AT&T Aspire applications are accepted on an invitation-only basis. Visit website for RFP announcements. Applicants should submit the following:
1) timetable for implementation and evaluation of project
2) how project will be sustained once grantmaker support is completed
3) statement of problem project will address
4) copy of IRS Determination Letter
5) copy of most recent annual report/audited financial statement/990
6) explanation of why grantmaker is considered an appropriate donor for project
7) listing of board of directors, trustees, officers and other key people and their affiliations
8) detailed description of project and amount of funding requested
9) copy of current year's organizational budget and/or project budget
10) listing of additional sources and amount of support

Initial approach: Contact nearest statewide facility for general funding; proposal to application address for general national funding
Board meeting date(s): Twice per year
Deadline(s): None for general funding

Officers and Directors:* James W. Cicconi*, Chair.; Beth Shiroishi, Pres.; Thomas R. Giltner, V.P. and Secy.; Jonathan P. Klug, V.P. and Treas.; Charlene Lake, V.P.; William A. Blase, Jr.; Catherine Coughlin; Ralph De La Vega; Wayne Watts; John Stephens.
Number of staff: 11 full-time professional; 1 full-time support.
EIN: 431353948
Selected grants: The following grants are a representative sample of this grantmaker's funding activity:
$1,634,693 to Scholarship America, Saint Peter, MN, 2011. For first half of total amount for the 2011-2012 AT&T Foundation Scholarship Program, and 2011 AT&T Foundation Scholarship Program Management Fee.
$1,634,693 to Scholarship America, Saint Peter, MN, 2011. For second half of total amount for the 2011-2012 AT&T Foundation Scholarship Program.
$1,000,000 to Bexar County Performing Arts Center Foundation, San Antonio, TX, 2011. For the Bexar County Performing Arts Center Foundation in the creation of a world-class performance facility that will serve as a permanent home for the major performing and cultural arts organizations of San Antonio and Bexar County.
$1,000,000 to George W. Bush Foundation, Dallas, TX, 2011. For the George W. Bush Institute's administration, leadership, program services, and evaluation components of the Alliance to Reform Education Leadership (AREL) program.
$500,000 to United Way of San Antonio and Bexar County, San Antonio, TX, 2011. For United Way Corporate Contribution Request.
$456,352 to United Way of Metropolitan Atlanta, Atlanta, GA, 2011. For United Way Corporate Contribution Request.
$260,000 to Symphony Society of San Antonio, San Antonio, TX, 2011. For the San Antonio Symphony's Music Scholars program at three low-income San Antonio high schools. The program aims to keep the youth connected through training and accomplishment in music.
$75,000 to Associated Colleges of Illinois, Chicago, IL, 2011. For the Associated Colleges of Illinois (ACI's) College Readiness Program created for at-risk students to successfully graduate from high school. The program offers year-round academic enrichment, personal growth, and leadership development activities at member College and University campuses.
$50,000 to Texas Governors Mansion Restoration Fund, Austin, TX, 2011. For restoration of the historic Texas Governor's Mansion that was badly fire damaged by arsonist attack.
$1,100 to United Fund of Walker County, Huntsville, TX, 2011. For United Way Corporate Contribution Request.

274
AT&T Mobility, LLC

(formerly Cingular Wireless LLC)
Glenridge Highlands 2
5565 Glenridge Connector Ste. 1664D
Atlanta, GA 30342 (404) 236-6000

Company URL: http://www.wireless.att.com/
Establishment information: Established in 1987.
Company type: Subsidiary of a public company
Business activities: Provides cellular telephone communications services.
Business type (SIC): Telephone communications
Financial profile for 2009: Number of employees, 43,100; sales volume, $53,600,000,000
Corporate officers: Randall L. Stephenson, Chair.; Ralph De La Vega, Pres. and C.E.O.; Peter A. Ritcher, C.F.O.; F. Thaddeus Arroyo, C.I.O.
Board of director: Randall L. Stephenson, Chair.
Offices: Birmingham, AL; Pleasanton, Tustin, CA; Lake Mary, FL; Hoffman Estates, IL; Indianapolis, IN; Greenbelt, MD; Westwood, MA; St. Louis, MO; Roseland, NJ; King of Prussia, PA; Dallas, TX

Giving statement: Giving through the Cingular Wireless LLC Corporate Giving Program.

Cingular Wireless LLC Corporate Giving Program

c/o Charitable Contribs. and Sponsorships
5565 Glenridge Connector, Ste. 2070-B
Atlanta, GA 30342-4756
E-mail: charitable.contributions@cingular.com; URL: http://www.wireless.att.com/about/community-support/index.jsp

Purpose and activities: Cingular Wireless makes charitable contributions to nonprofit organizations involved with arts and culture, education, disaster relief, domestic violence, and human services. Special emphasis is directed toward programs designed to focus specifically on teaching/developing modes of expression. Support is given primarily in areas of company operations.
Fields of interest: Arts; Education; Disasters, preparedness/services; Family services, domestic violence; Human services Disabilities, people with.
Type of support: Employee volunteer services; Program development.
Geographic limitations: Giving primarily in areas of company operations; giving also to national organizations.
Publications: Application guidelines.
Application information: Applications accepted. Application form not required. Applicants should submit the following:
1) copy of current year's organizational budget and/or project budget
2) copy of most recent annual report/audited financial statement/990
3) listing of additional sources and amount of support
4) copy of IRS Determination Letter

Proposals should include a copy of the organization's non-discrimination policy.
Initial approach: Proposal to headquarters

275
Atayne, LLC

96 Maine St., Ste. 131
Brunswick, ME 04011 (888) 456-0470

Company URL: http://www.atayne.com
Establishment information: Established in 2007.
Company type: Private company
Business activities: Manufactures recycled outdoor clothing and performance apparel.
Business type (SIC): Apparel and other finished products made from fabrics and similar materials
Corporate officers: Jeremy Litchfield, Pres.; Kathleen Lendway, V.P., Opers.
Giving statement: Giving through the Atayne Corporate Giving Program.

Atayne Corporate Giving Program

96 Maine St., Ste. 131
Brunswick, ME 04011-2013 (888) 456-0470
URL: http://www.atayne.com

Purpose and activities: Atayne is a certified B Corporation that donates a percentage of net profits to nonprofit organizations. Special emphasis is directed toward organizations involved with the environment.
Fields of interest: Environment.

276
Athletics Investment Group, LLC

(also known as Oakland Athletics)
7000 Coliseum Way
Oakland, CA 94621 (510) 638-4900

Company URL: http://oakland.athletics.mlb.com
Establishment information: Established in 1901.
Company type: Private company
Business activities: Operates professional baseball club.
Business type (SIC): Commercial sports
Financial profile for 2009: Number of employees, 2,000
Corporate officers: Michael Crowley, Pres.; Paul Wong, V.P., Finance; Kendall R. Pries, V.P., Comms.; Jim Leahey, V.P., Sales and Mktg.; Neil Kraetsch, Genl. Counsel
Giving statement: Giving through the Oakland Athletics Community Fund.

The Oakland Athletics Community Fund

(also known as The Oakland A's Community Fund)
McAfee Coliseum
7000 Coliseum Way
Oakland, CA 94621-1917
FAX: (510) 562-1633;
E-mail: community@oaklandathletics.com.; Additional contact: Detra G. Paige, tel.: (510) 563-2241, e-mail: dpaige@oaklandathletics.com; Tel. for A's Amigos, Little A's, and Senior Days: (510) 563-2329; URL: http://oakland.athletics.mlb.com/NASApp/mlb/oak/community/index.jsp

Establishment information: Established in 1981 in CA.
Donors: Athletics Investment Group, LLC; Hofmann Foundation; Citation Homes Central; Teammates for Kids Foundation; The Gifford Foundation; Ross Stores, Inc.
Contact: Kendall R. Pries, Dir.
Financial data (yr. ended 12/31/11): Assets, $685,845 (M); gifts received, $1,442,351; expenditures, $1,376,150; qualifying distributions, $1,375,879; giving activities include $873,314 for 132 grants (high: $178,300; low: $50) and $10,000 for 4 grants to individuals (high: $3,000; low: $2,000).
Purpose and activities: The foundation supports programs designed to improve education; aid the underprivileged; promote crime and drug prevention; promote health awareness; and champion children and senior welfare.
Fields of interest: Media, radio; Media, journalism; Secondary school/education; Education; Hospitals (general); Public health, physical fitness; Health care; Substance abuse, prevention; Cancer; Breast cancer; Diabetes research; Crime/violence prevention; Athletics/sports, amateur leagues; Athletics/sports, baseball Children; Aging; Disabilities, people with; Economically disadvantaged.
Programs:
A's Amigos: Through the foundations A's Amigos program, Oakland A's bilingual speaking players interact with local Hispanic children. Children learn about the value of sportsmanship and hard work from their role models. The program includes a game ticket and an A's cap.
Bay Area All-Star Scholarship Team: The foundation awards $3,000 scholarships to successful high seniors residing within the Bay Area's nine counties. Candidates must have a grade point average of 3.0, display leadership qualities and/or inspirational qualities on the athletic field, and demonstrate the value of education, good work ethic, and community outreach.
Bill Kings College Scholarship: The foundation awards one $3,000 scholarship to an undergraduate student majoring in journalism or broadcasting. Applicants must prove financial need, have a grade point average of 3.0, and show a strong interest in pursuing a career in broadcasting or journalism. The recipient will also receive the opportunity to intern with the A's Broadcasting Department.
Little A's: The foundation invites Bay Area non-profit organizations to bring low to moderate income children to enjoy an Oakland A's game. Groups receive game tickets and souvenirs.
Mathletics: The foundation distributes "Mathletics" workbooks to Bay Area youths to promote the importance of math. The workbook utilizes formulas for calculating statistics of A's players. Students who complete the workbooks correctly and submits the answers will receive two ticket vouchers from the A's. One school that demonstrates outstanding participation in the program will receive a visit from an A's player.
Science of the Game: The foundation, in partnership with Chevron, promote science education through educational workbooks. Students in grades 1-8 will earn two free ticket vouchers to an A's game by learning about baseball and the role science plays.
Senior Days: The foundation hosts Bay Area seniors throughout the regular baseball season. Free tickets are available for senior groups, centers and facilities, and those senior enjoy the game from their own section of the ballpark.
Type of support: Donated products; Equipment; General/operating support; In-kind gifts; Matching/challenge support; Program development; Scholarships—to individuals; Sponsorships.
Geographic limitations: Giving limited to northern CA, with emphasis on the Bay Area counties.
Publications: Application guidelines.
Application information: Applications accepted. Proposals should be submitted using organization letterhead. Requests via fax, e-mail, or phone are not accepted. Telephone calls during the application process are not encouraged. Support is limited to 1 contribution per organization within a baseball season. Applicants should submit the following:
1) population served
2) name, address and phone number of organization
3) copy of IRS Determination Letter
4) detailed description of project and amount of funding requested
5) contact person

Applications for the Bill King Scholarship should include a 2-3 page essay, 2 letters of recommendation, and official transcripts from each college attended.
Initial approach: Proposal; contact participating high schools for Bay Area All-Star Scholarship Team; complete online application for Bill King College Scholarship, Mathletics, and Science of the Game; e-mail foundation for A's Amigos, Little A's, and Senior Days
Deadline(s): 6 to 8 weeks prior to need; Feb. 13 for Bay Area All-Star Scholarship Team; May 31 for the Bill King Scholarship
Officers and Directors: Michael Crowley, Pres.; Detra G. Paige; Kendall R. Pries; Lisa H. Seeno; Jane Spray; Kari Wolff.
EIN: 942826655

277
Atlanta Falcons Football Club, LLC

4400 Falcon Pkwy.
Flowery Branch, GA 30542-3176
(770) 965-3115
FAX: (770) 965-2766

Company URL: http://www.atlantafalcons.com
Establishment information: Established in 1965.
Company type: Private company
Business activities: Operates professional football club.
Business type (SIC): Commercial sports
Financial profile for 2010: Number of employees, 130
Corporate officers: Arthur M. Blank, Chair.; Richard McKay, Pres. and C.E.O.; Gregory Beadles, Exec. V.P., Admin. and C.F.O.; Jim Smith, Sr. V.P., Sales and Mktg.; Robert Geoffrey, Cont.
Board of director: Arthur M. Blank, Chair.
Giving statement: Giving through the Atlanta Falcons Football Club, LLC Corporate Giving Program.

Atlanta Falcons Football Club, LLC Corporate Giving Program

c/o Community Rels., Donation Requests
4400 Falcon Pkwy.
Flowery Branch, GA 30542-3176
URL: http://www.atlantafalcons.com/Community/Donation-Requests/

Purpose and activities: The Atlanta Falcons make charitable contributions of memorabilia to nonprofit organizations involved with youth sports, recreation, and fitness. Support is given primarily in Georgia.
Fields of interest: Recreation Youth.
Type of support: In-kind gifts.
Geographic limitations: Giving is limited to GA.
Support limitations: No support for churches, synagogues, or other places of worship. No grants for fundraising for the benefit of individuals or families.
Application information: Applications accepted. Proposals should be submitted using organization letterhead. Support is limited to 1 contribution per organization during any given year. The Community Relations Department handles giving. Application form not required. Applicants should submit the following:
1) population served
2) name, address and phone number of organization
3) copy of IRS Determination Letter
4) contact person

Proposals should indicate the date of the event, the type of fundraiser, and the expected number of attendees.
Initial approach: Mail proposal to headquarters
Copies of proposal: 1
Deadline(s): 6 weeks prior to event

278
Atlanta Hawks, L.P.

Centennial Tower
101 Marietta St., N.W., Ste. 1900
Atlanta, GA 30303-2720 (404) 827-3800

Company URL: http://www.nba.com/hawks
Establishment information: Established in 1946.
Company type: Private company
Business activities: Operates professional basketball club.
Business type (SIC): Commercial sports
Corporate officers: Bob Williams, Pres.; Phil Ebinger, Exec. V.P. and C.F.O.; Peter Sorckoff, V.P., Mktg.
Giving statement: Giving through the Atlanta Hawks, L.P. Corporate Giving Program and the Atlanta Hawks Foundation, Inc.

Atlanta Hawks, L.P. Corporate Giving Program

c/o Community Affairs Donation Request
Centennial Tower
101 Marietta St. N.W., Ste. 1900
Atlanta, GA 30303-2771
FAX: (404) 827-3042; URL: http://www.nba.com/hawks/community

Purpose and activities: The Atlanta Hawks make charitable contributions of game tickets and memorabilia to nonprofit organizations involved with children. Support is given primarily within a 50-mile radius of Atlanta, Georgia.
Fields of interest: Education; Children, services.
Type of support: Donated products; In-kind gifts.
Geographic limitations: Giving primarily within a 50-mile radius of Atlanta, GA.
Application information: Applications accepted. Proposals should be submitted using organization letterhead. Support is limited to 1 contribution per organization during any given year. Application form not required. Applicants should submit the following:
1) population served
2) brief history of organization and description of its mission
3) detailed description of project and amount of funding requested

Proposals should specifically note the nature of the request being made; and indicate the date, time, and location of the event and the type of fundraiser.
Initial approach: Mail or fax proposal to headquarters
Copies of proposal: 1
Deadline(s): 1 month prior to need

Atlanta Hawks Foundation, Inc.

101 Marietta St., 19th Fl.
Atlanta, GA 30303-2720 (404) 878-3500
E-mail: andrea.carter@atlantaspirit.com;
URL: http://www.nba.com/hawks/community/Atlanta_Hawks_Foundation-79913-33.html

Establishment information: Established in 1989 in GA.
Contact: Tracy White, Pres.
Financial data (yr. ended 06/30/12): Revenue, $56,131; assets, $661,416 (M); gifts received, $79,613; expenditures, $100,284; giving activities include $41,953 for grants.
Purpose and activities: The foundation is dedicated to improving quality of life for Georgia's youth by inspiring them to develop a passion for learning and a commitment to physical fitness and recreation.
Fields of interest: Public health, physical fitness; Recreation; Youth development.
Geographic limitations: Giving limited to GA.
Application information: Applications not accepted. Unsolicited requests for funds not accepted.
Officers: Tracy White*, Pres.; Ailey Penningroth*, V.P.; Caren Cook*, Secy.; Phill Ebinger*, Treas.
Directors: Andrea Carter; Phil Ebinger; Bernie Mullin; David Payne.
EIN: 581762732

279
Atlanta Hockey Club, LLC

(also known as Atlanta Thrashers)
Centennial Tower
101 Marietta St. N.W., Ste. 1900
Atlanta, GA 30303-2771 (404) 878-3800

Company URL: http://thrashers.nhl.com
Establishment information: Established in 1997.
Company type: Subsidiary of a private company
Business activities: Operates professional ice hockey club.
Business type (SIC): Commercial sports
Financial profile for 2009: Number of employees, 40
Corporate officers: Bernard J. Mullin, Pres. and C.E.O.; Bill Duffy, Exec. V.P. and C.F.O.; Greg Hughes, Sr. V.P., Public Rels.; Phil Ebinger, V.P., Finance; Jim Pfeifer, V.P., Mktg.; Ginni Siler, V.P., Human Resources; David Kane, Cont.
Giving statement: Giving through the Atlanta Thrashers Foundation.

Atlanta Thrashers Foundation

101 Marietta St., Ste. 1900
Atlanta, GA 30303-2720 (404) 878-3500
E-mail: andrea.carter@atlantaspirit.com;
URL: http://thrashers.nhl.com/team/app/?service=page&page=NHLPage&id=13898

Establishment information: Established in 1999 in GA.
Financial data (yr. ended 06/30/11): Revenue, $168,699; assets, $274,763 (M); gifts received, $222,416; expenditures, $234,758; giving activities include $174,651 for grants.
Purpose and activities: The foundation supports nonprofit education and health organizations and key amateur hockey groups dedicated to improving the quality of life of Georgia's children.
Fields of interest: Education; Health care; Athletics/sports, amateur leagues; Athletics/sports, winter sports Children.
Geographic limitations: Giving limited to GA.
Support limitations: No support for religious purposes. No grants to individuals, or for endowments, endowed faculty chairs, indirect costs, overhead, general support, fundraising events, sponsorships, capital or endowment campaigns, or multi-year pledge requests.
Publications: Application guidelines; Grants list.
Application information: Applications accepted. Applicants should submit the following:
1) copy of IRS Determination Letter
2) listing of board of directors, trustees, officers and other key people and their affiliations
3) copy of current year's organizational budget and/or project budget

Initial approach: Download application
Deadline(s): Mar. 31
Final notification: Apr. 30
Officers: Don Waddell, Pres.; Ailey Penningroth, V.P.; Caren Cook, Secy.; Phil Ebinger, Treas.
Directors: Andrea Carter; David Payne; Scott Wilkinson; Tracy White.
EIN: 582485233

280
Atlanta National League Baseball Club, Inc.

(also known as Atlanta Braves)
755 Hank Aaron Dr., S.W.
P.O. Box 4064
Atlanta, GA 30315-1120 (404) 522-7630

Company URL: http://atlanta.braves.mlb.com
Establishment information: Established in 1912.
Company type: Subsidiary of a public company
Ultimate parent company: Time Warner Inc.
Business activities: Operates professional baseball club.
Business type (SIC): Commercial sports
Corporate officers: Terence F. McGuirk, Chair. and C.E.O.; John Schuerholz, Pres.; Mike Plant, Exec. V.P., Opers.; Derek Schiller, Exec. V.P., Sales and Mktg.; Chip Moore, C.F.O.; Greg Heller, Sr. V.P. and Genl. Counsel; William C. Bartholomay, Chair. Emeritus
Board of director: Terence F. McGuirk, Chair.
Giving statement: Giving through the Atlanta Braves Corporate Giving Program and the Atlanta Braves Foundation.

Atlanta Braves Corporate Giving Program

c/o Donation Requests
755 Hank Aaron Dr., SW
Atlanta, GA 30315-1120 (404) 494-1020
URL: http://atlanta.braves.mlb.com/atl/community/atl_fundraisers.jsp

Purpose and activities: As a complement to its foundation, the Atlanta Braves also make charitable contributions of autographed memorabilia to nonprofit organizations directly. Support is limited to Georgia.
Fields of interest: General charitable giving.
Type of support: In-kind gifts.
Geographic limitations: Giving limited to GA.
Publications: Application guidelines.
Application information: Applications accepted. Proposals should be submitted using organization letterhead. Application form not required. Proposals should include the date and a description of the event, and an explanation of how the proceeds will be used.
Initial approach: Proposal to headquarters
Deadline(s): 5 weeks prior to the event

Atlanta Braves Foundation

755 Hank Aaron Dr.
Atlanta, GA 30315-1120 (404) 614-1330
URL: http://atlanta.braves.mlb.com/atl/community/atl_foundation.jsp

Establishment information: Established in 1992 in GA.
Financial data (yr. ended 12/31/11): Revenue, $714,186; assets, $1,612,860 (M); gifts received, $378,560; expenditures, $722,395; giving activities include $290,476 for grants.
Purpose and activities: The foundation contributes to youth organizations and educational programs that provide young people (ages 12 and younger) with the alternatives and the support needed to become knowledgeable and productive citizens.
Fields of interest: Athletics/sports, baseball; Youth development.
Programs:
Community Coach Award: Grants of $1,000 are awarded to youth baseball and softball coaches who provide superior levels of leadership both on and off the field, for equipment, uniforms or field improvements.
Grants: The foundation grants funds to youth-serving organizations that focus on health, education, and recreation. Grants of between $500 and $10,000 each will be awarded in support of afterschool programs, health and wellness efforts, anti-bullying campaigns, educational projects, and athletic programs. To be eligible, organizations must be tax exempt under Section 501(c)(3) of the Internal Revenue Code and serve youth within the Atlanta metro area.
High School Scholarship Program: The foundation offers scholarships to graduating high school seniors throughout Georgia. Six $2,000 scholarships are awarded to students who have demonstrated strong community involvement as well as solid academic performance throughout their high school careers.
Pinch Hitter Fund: The fund has been established to alleviate unforeseen expenses and help organizations in dire need by providing relief for lost or stolen equipment, damaged facilities or for uniform and equipment shortages. Support may be provided in the form of financial or in-kind assistance. Applications will be reviewed on a quarterly basis throughout the calendar year.
Type of support: Equipment; In-kind gifts; Scholarship funds.
Geographic limitations: Giving primarily in GA.
Publications: Application guidelines.
Application information: Applications accepted. Application form required.
Initial approach: Complete online nomination form for Community Coach Award; Download application form for Grants and Pinch Hitter Fund
Deadline(s): Apr. 15 for High School Scholarship Program; May 31 for Community Coach Award; July 31 for Grants
Officers and Directors:* Terry McGuirk*, Pres.; Mike Plant*, V.P.; Chip Moore*, Treas.; Gus Eurton; Rubye Lucas; Ericka Newsome; Derek Schiller; John Schuerholz.
EIN: 582071299

281
Atlantic City Coin And Slot Service Company, Inc.

201 W. Decatur Ave.
Pleasantville, NJ 08232-3151
(609) 641-7811
FAX: (609) 272-0279

Company URL: http://www.ac-coin.com
Establishment information: Established in 1978.
Company type: Private company
Business activities: Manufactures slot machines and other products for the gaming industry.
Business type (SIC): Manufacturing/miscellaneous
Corporate officers: Mac R. Seelig, Pres.; Jason Seelig, Exec. V.P., Sales and Mktg.; Thomas McCormick, Exec. V.P. and Genl. Counsel; Jeffrey Seelig, C.F.O.
Giving statement: Giving through the Seelig Family Foundation, Inc.

Seelig Family Foundation, Inc.

111 E. Parkway Dr.
Egg Harbor Township, NJ 08234-5112 (609) 641-9525

Establishment information: Established in 1993 in NJ.
Donors: AC Coin & Slot, Inc.; Globe Vending Corp.
Contact: Debby Johnson
Financial data (yr. ended 12/31/11): Assets, $5,258 (M); gifts received, $5,000; expenditures, $3,950; qualifying distributions, $3,875; giving activities include $3,875 for grants.
Fields of interest: Education; Human services; Religion.
Type of support: General/operating support.
Geographic limitations: Giving primarily in NJ.
Support limitations: No grants to individuals.
Application information: Applications accepted. Application form not required.
Initial approach: Letter
Deadline(s): None
Directors: Kay Seelig; Mac Seelig.
EIN: 521833325

282
Atlantic Services Group, Inc.

1002 Trident St.
Hanahan, SC 29410 (843) 740-9200

Establishment information: Established in 1979.
Company type: Private company
Business activities: Provides administrative management, storage, and financial services; rents furniture; leases steamships.
Business type (SIC): Management and public relations services; fertilizers and agricultural chemicals; warehousing and storage; transportation services/water; equipment rental and leasing/miscellaneous
Giving statement: Giving through the Atlantic Services of Charleston Charitable Trust.

The Atlantic Services of Charleston Charitable Trust

P.O. Box 62948
Charleston, SC 29419-2948 (843) 740-9200

Establishment information: Established in 1982.
Donors: Atlantic Services Group, Inc.; David Maybank, Jr.; Louise J. Maybank.
Contact: David Maybank, Jr., Tr.
Financial data (yr. ended 06/30/11): Assets, $383,483 (M); gifts received, $8,000; expenditures, $26,980; qualifying distributions, $26,500; giving activities include $26,500 for 10 grants (high: $10,000; low: $500).
Purpose and activities: The trust supports museums and organizations involved with historic preservation, education, environmental law, conservation, health, and Christianity.
Fields of interest: Education; Health care; Religion.
Type of support: General/operating support.
Geographic limitations: Giving primarily in Charleston, SC.
Support limitations: No grants to individuals.
Application information: Applications accepted. Application form not required. Applicants should submit the following:
1) qualifications of key personnel
2) brief history of organization and description of its mission
3) detailed description of project and amount of funding requested
Initial approach: Letter
Deadline(s): None
Trustees: David Maybank, Jr.; Louise J. Maybank.
EIN: 570741318

283
Atlantic Stewardship Bank, Inc.
630 Godwin Ave.
Midland Park, NJ 07432-1405
(201) 444-7100

Company URL: https://www.asbnow.com
Establishment information: Established in 1985.
Company type: Subsidiary of a public company
Business activities: Operates state commercial bank.
Business type (SIC): Banks/commercial
Corporate officers: William C. Hanse, Esq., Chair.; Abraham Van Wingerden, Vice-Chair.; Paul Van Ostenbridge, Pres. and C.E.O.; Claire M. Chadwick, Sr. V.P. and C.F.O.
Board of directors: William C. Hanse, Chair.; Abraham Van Wingerden, Vice-Chair.; Richard W. Culp; Harold Dyer; Margo Lane; Arie Leegwater; John L. Steen; Robert J. Turner; William J. Vander Eems; Paul Van Ostenbridge; Michael A. Westra; Howard R. Yeaton
Giving statement: Giving through the Atlantic Stewardship Foundation.

Atlantic Stewardship Foundation
630 Godwin Ave.
Midland Park, NJ 07432-1405 (201) 444-7100

Establishment information: Established in 2007 in NJ.
Donor: Atlantic Stewardship Bank.
Contact: Claire Chadwick
Financial data (yr. ended 12/31/11): Assets, $40,937 (M); gifts received, $28,750; expenditures, $32,180; qualifying distributions, $30,950; giving activities include $30,950 for grants.
Purpose and activities: The foundation supports nonprofit organizations involved with religious education and health care. Support is given primarily in areas of company operations in New Jersey.
Fields of interest: Health care; Christian agencies & churches; Religion.
Type of support: General/operating support.
Geographic limitations: Giving primarily in areas of company operations in NJ.
Support limitations: No grants to individuals.
Application information: Applications accepted. Application form not required. Applicants should submit the following:
1) detailed description of project and amount of funding requested

Initial approach: Proposal
Deadline(s): None
Final notification: 3 months

Trustees: Richard Culp; Harold Dyer; William Hanse; Margo Lane; Arie Leegwater; John Steen; Robert Turner; William Vander Eems; Paul Van Ostenbridge; Michael Westra; Howard Yeaton.
EIN: 266392972

284
Atlas Foundry Company, Inc.
601 N. Henderson Ave.
Marion, IN 46952-3348 (765) 662-2525

Company URL: http://www.atlasfdry.com/about.htm
Establishment information: Established in 1893.
Company type: Private company
Business activities: Manufactures gray iron castings.
Business type (SIC): Iron and steel foundries
Corporate officers: James M. Gartland, Jr., Pres.; Bill Gartland, C.F.O.; Chuck Rice, V.P., Opers.; Joseph C. Gartland, V.P., Sales
Giving statement: Giving through the Atlas Foundry Foundation, Inc.

Atlas Foundry Foundation, Inc.
Factory and Henderson St.
Marion, IN 46953

Donor: Atlas Foundry Co.
Financial data (yr. ended 12/31/11): Assets, $804,357 (M); gifts received, $51,478; expenditures, $81,257; qualifying distributions, $79,935; giving activities include $79,025 for 37 grants (high: $28,300; low: $50).
Purpose and activities: The foundation supports organizations involved with education, children and youth, civic affairs, and religion.
Fields of interest: Education; Human services; Religion.
Type of support: General/operating support.
Support limitations: No grants to individuals.
Application information: Applications not accepted. Unsolicited requests for funds not accepted.
Directors: Greg Gartland; James M. Gartland, Jr.
EIN: 356041739

285
Atmos Energy Corporation
3 Lincoln Centre, Ste. 1800, 5430 LBJ Fwy.
P.O. Box 650205
Dallas, TX 75240 (972) 934-9227
FAX: (972) 855-3040

Company URL: http://www.atmosenergy.com
Establishment information: Established in 1906.
Company type: Public company
Company ticker symbol and exchange: ATO/NYSE
Business activities: Distributes natural gas.
Business type (SIC): Gas production and distribution
Financial profile for 2012: Number of employees, 4,759; assets, $7,495,680,000; sales volume, $3,438,480,000; pre-tax net income, $290,420,000; expenses, $2,992,240,000; liabilities, $5,136,430,000
Fortune 1000 ranking: 2012—634th in revenues, 554th in profits, and 467th in assets
Corporate officers: Robert W. Best, Chair.; Kim R. Cocklin, Pres. and C.E.O.; Bret Eckert, Sr. V.P. and C.F.O.; Louis P. Gregory, Sr. V.P., Genl. Counsel, and Corp. Secy.; Michael E. Haefner, Sr. V.P., Human Resources; Richard J. Gius, V.P. and C.I.O.; Daniel M. Meziere, V.P. and Treas.; Christopher T. Forsythe, V.P. and Cont.; Verlon R. Aston, Jr., V.P., Public Affairs
Board of directors: Robert W. Best, Chair.; Kim Cocklin; Richard W. Douglas; Ruben E. Esquivel; Richard K. Gordon; Robert C. Grable; Thomas C. Meredith; Nancy K. Quinn; Richard A. Sampson; Lee E. Schlessman; Stephen R. Springer; Charles K. Vaughan; Richard Ware II
Subsidiary: Atmos Energy Holdings, Inc., Dallas, TX
International operations: Bermuda
Giving statement: Giving through the Atmos Energy Corporation Contributions Program and the Arthur K. and Sylvia S. Lee Scholarship Foundation.
Company EIN: 751743247

Arthur K. and Sylvia S. Lee Scholarship Foundation
P.O. Box 681943
Franklin, TN 37068-1943 (615) 771-8300
Application address: 810 Crescent Centre Dr., Ste. 600, Franklin, TN 37067

Establishment information: Established in 1962 in IL.
Donors: M. Mervyn K. Wrench; Chapman and Cutler; United Cities Gas Co.; Atmos Energy Corp.
Contact: James B. Ford, Secy.-Treas.
Financial data (yr. ended 12/31/11): Assets, $1,072,941 (M); gifts received, $10,000; expenditures, $110,616; qualifying distributions, $84,567; giving activities include $84,567 for grants.
Purpose and activities: The foundation awards college scholarships to students. Special emphasis is directed toward children and dependents of employees of Atmos Energy.
Fields of interest: Education.
Type of support: Employee-related scholarships; Scholarships—to individuals.
Application information: Applications accepted. Priority given to children or dependents of employees. Application form required.

Initial approach: Contact foundation for application form
Deadline(s): June 1

Officer and Trustees:* James B. Ford, Secy.-Treas.; Adrienne Brandon; Bradford Gioia; Glenn R. King; Malcolm Liles; Mack S. Linebaugh, Jr.; Ogden Stokes.
EIN: 366069067

286
Audubon State Bank
315 Broadway St.
Audubon, IA 50025-1101 (712) 563-2644

Company URL: http://www.audubonstatebank.com
Establishment information: Established in 1876.
Company type: Private company
Business activities: Operates holding company; operates commercial bank.
Business type (SIC): Banks/commercial; holding company
Corporate officers: Elizabeth Garst, Chair.; Brett Irlmeier, Pres. and C.E.O.; Linda Koenig, Co.-Secy.; Kelley Christensen, Co.-Secy.
Board of directors: Elizabeth Garst, Chair.; Sarah Christensen; Jennifer Garst; Lyle Hansen, Jr.; Brett Irlmeier; Doug McDermott; Daryl Olsen
Giving statement: Giving through the Audubon State Bank Charitable Foundation.

Audubon State Bank Charitable Foundation
P.O. Box 149
Audubon, IA 50025-1101 (712) 563-2644

Establishment information: Established in 1990 in IA.
Donor: The Audubon State Bank.
Contact: Brett Irlmeier, Pres.
Financial data (yr. ended 12/31/11): Assets, $39,994 (M); gifts received, $28,550; expenditures, $12,695; qualifying distributions, $12,395; giving activities include $12,395 for grants.
Purpose and activities: The foundation supports hospitals and community foundations and organizations involved with education, cancer,

community development, civic affairs, and Protestantism.
Fields of interest: Health care; Human services; Religion.
Type of support: General/operating support.
Geographic limitations: Giving primarily in areas of company operations in Audubon, IA, area.
Support limitations: No grants to individuals.
Application information: Applications accepted. Application form required. Applicants should submit the following:
1) detailed description of project and amount of funding requested
Initial approach: Letter
Copies of proposal: 1
Board meeting date(s): Monthly
Deadline(s): None
Officers and Directors:* Brett Irlmeier*, Pres.; Steven Shaffer, Secy.-Treas.; Sarah Christensen; Elizabeth Garst; Jennifer Garst; Lyle Hanson, Jr.; Doug McDermott; Daryl Olsen; John C. Parrott, Jr.
EIN: 421366431

287
Auntie Anne's, Inc.

(doing business as Auntie Anne's)
48-50 W. Chestnut St., Ste. 200
Lancaster, PA 17603 (717) 435-1435

Company URL: http://www.auntieannes.com/
Establishment information: Established in 1988.
Company type: Private company
Business activities: Franchises soft pretzel stores.
Business type (SIC): Restaurants and drinking places
Corporate officers: Samuel R. Beiler, Chair. and C.E.O.; William P. Dunn, Jr., Pres. and C.O.O.; Mitch Blocher, C.F.O.; Beth Monaghan, C.A.O.; Douglas Martin, V.P., Opers.
Board of director: Samuel R. Beiler, Chair.
Giving statement: Giving through the C.A.R.E.S. Committee.

C.A.R.E.S. Committee

48-50 W. Chestnut St., No. 200
Lancaster, PA 17603

Establishment information: Established in 2000 in PA.
Donors: Auntie Anne's, Inc.; Nestle Waters North America.
Financial data (yr. ended 12/31/11): Assets, $3,439 (M); gifts received, $78,238; expenditures, $103,046; qualifying distributions, $59,460; giving activities include $59,460 for grants.
Fields of interest: Youth development; Human services.
Support limitations: No grants to individuals.
Application information: Applications not accepted. Unsolicited requests for funds not accepted.
Officers: Stefanie Stamatopoulos, Chair.; Tracy Barley, Secy.; Tom Perella, Treas.
EIN: 233026106

288
Austin Industries, Inc.

3535 Travis St., Ste. 300
P.O. Box 1590
Dallas, TX 75204-1466 (214) 443-5500
FAX: (214) 443-5581

Company URL: http://www.austin-ind.com
Establishment information: Established in 1918.
Company type: Private company
Business activities: Provides nonresidential general contract construction services.
Business type (SIC): Contractors/general nonresidential building
Financial profile for 2010: Number of employees, 6,000; sales volume, $2,000,000,000
Corporate officers: Ronald J. Gafford, Chair., Pres., and C.E.O.; J.T. Fisher, C.F.O.; Stan Smith, C.I.O.; John Foley, V.P., Human Resources
Board of director: Ronald J. Gafford, Chair.
Subsidiaries: Austin Bridge & Road, Inc., Irving, TX; Austin Commercial, Inc., Dallas, TX; Austin Industrial, Inc., Houston, TX
Giving statement: Giving through the Austin Industries, Inc. Corporate Giving Program.

Austin Industries, Inc. Corporate Giving Program

3535 Travis St., Ste. 300
Dallas, TX 75204-1466 (214) 443-5500
URL: http://www.austin-ind.com/industries/community

Purpose and activities: Austin Industries makes charitable contributions to nonprofit organizations involved with youth, arts and culture, education, and health care. Support is given primarily in areas of company operations in Texas.
Fields of interest: Arts; Education; Environment; Health care Youth; Minorities.
Type of support: General/operating support; In-kind gifts.
Geographic limitations: Giving primarily in areas of company operations in TX.

289
Autodesk, Inc.

111 McInnis Pkwy.
San Rafael, CA 94903-2773
(415) 507-5000
FAX: (415) 507-5100

Company URL: http://usa.autodesk.com
Establishment information: Established in 1982.
Company type: Public company
Company ticker symbol and exchange: ADSK/NASDAQ
International Securities Identification Number: US0527691069
Business activities: Designs computer software and multimedia tools.
Business type (SIC): Computer services
Financial profile for 2013: Number of employees, 7,300; assets, $4,308,400,000; sales volume, $2,312,200,000; pre-tax net income, $310,000,000; expenses, $2,006,300,000; liabilities, $2,265,200,000
Fortune 1000 ranking: 2012—853rd in revenues, 526th in profits, and 635th in assets
Corporate officers: Crawford W. Beveridge, Chair.; Carl Bass, Pres. and C.E.O.; Mark J. Hawkins, Exec. V.P. and C.F.O.; Pascal W. DiFronzo, Sr. V.P., Genl. Counsel, and Secy.; Steve Blum, Sr. V.P., Sales; Jan Becker, Sr. V.P., Human Resources
Board of directors: Crawford W. Beveridge, Chair.; Carl Bass; J. Hallam Dawson; Thomas Georgens; Per-Kristian Halvorsen, Ph.D.; Mary T. McDowell; Lorrie McNorrington; Charles J. Robel; Stacy J. Smith; Steven M. West
Offices: Petaluma, San Francisco, CA; Greenwood Village, CO; Washington, DC; Chicago, Itasca, IL; Novi, MI; Manchester, NH; Ithaca, NY; Lake Oswego, OR; Plano, TX; McLean, VA
International operations: Australia; Austria; Brazil; Canada; China; Czech Republic; France; Germany; Hungary; India; Ireland; Italy; Japan; Mexico; Netherlands; Poland; Portugal; Russia; Singapore; South Korea; Spain; Sweden; Switzerland; Taiwan; Turkey; United Kingdom; Venezuela
Giving statement: Giving through the Autodesk, Inc. Corporate Giving Program.
Company EIN: 942819853

Autodesk, Inc. Corporate Giving Program

c/o Community Rels. Dept.
111 McInnis Pkwy.
San Rafael, CA 94903-2773 (415) 507-6603
E-mail: julie.wilder@autodesk.com; Application address for product donations: Good360, 1330 Bradock Pl. Alexandria, VA 22314; URL: http://usa.autodesk.com/community-relations/

Contact: Julie Wilder, Mgr., Employee Impact Progs.
Financial data (yr. ended 01/31/13): Total giving, $2,150,000, including $2,150,000 for grants.
Purpose and activities: Autodesk makes charitable contributions to nonprofit organizations involved with arts and culture, education, the environment, health and human services, and community development. Support is given on a national and international basis.
Fields of interest: Arts; Education; Environment; Health care; Human services; Community/economic development; Engineering/technology; Science Infants/toddlers; Children/youth; Children; Youth; Adults; Aging; Young adults; Disabilities, people with; Physically disabled; Blind/visually impaired; Deaf/hearing impaired; Mentally disabled; Minorities; Asians/Pacific Islanders; African Americans/Blacks; Hispanics/Latinos; Native Americans/American Indians; Indigenous peoples; Women; Infants/toddlers, female; Girls; Adults, women; Young adults, female; Men; Infants/toddlers, male; Boys; Adults, men; Young adults, male; Military/veterans; Substance abusers; AIDS, people with; Single parents; Crime/abuse victims; Terminal illness, people with; Immigrants/refugees; Economically disadvantaged; Homeless; Migrant workers; LGBTQ; Lesbians; Gay men; Bisexual; Transgender and gender nonconforming.
International interests: Asia; Canada; Central America; Europe; South America.
Type of support: Annual campaigns; Building/renovation; Capital campaigns; Continuing support; Curriculum development; Donated products; Emergency funds; Employee matching gifts; Employee volunteer services; Equipment; General/operating support; In-kind gifts; Matching/challenge support; Program development; Scholarship funds; Sponsorships; Use of facilities.
Geographic limitations: Giving on a national and international basis primarily in areas of company operations, including in Canada, Asia, and Europe; also giving in Latin America via employee matching.
Support limitations: No support for athletic teams, religious organizations, political organizations, or discriminatory organizations. No grants for sporting events or advertising through Community Relations.

Application information: Applications not accepted. The Autodesk Impact Design Foundation will replace Community Relations Program and relaunch sometime in 2013 with a new focus and funding approach.
Administrator: Julie Wilder, Mgr., Worldwide Community Rels.
Number of staff: 2 full-time professional.
Selected grants: The following grants are a representative sample of this grantmaker's funding activity:
$20,000 to Intel Computer Clubhouse/BACR, San Rafael, CA, 2012. For after-school education program support.
$5,000 to Habitat for Humanity East Bay/Silicon Valley, Oakland, CA, 2012.
$4,000 to WildCare: Terwilliger Nature Education and Wildlife Rehabilitation, San Rafael, CA, 2012. For annual gala.
$3,000 to Farallones Marine Sanctuary Association, San Francisco, CA, 2012. For environmental program.
$1,500 to Special Olympics New Hampshire, Manchester, NH, 2012.
$500 to HAVEN, Pontiac, MI, 2012.

290
Autoliv ASP, Inc.

(also known as Autoliv, Inc.)
3350 Airport Rd.
Ogden, UT 84405-1563 (801) 625-4800

Company URL: http://www.autoliv.com
Establishment information: Established in 1996.
Company type: Subsidiary of a foreign company
Business activities: Designs, develops, and manufactures airbag inflators, modules, and cushions, seat belts, and steering wheels.
Business type (SIC): Motor vehicles and equipment; fabricated textile products/ miscellaneous
Financial profile for 2009: Number of employees, 7,250
Corporate officers: Lars Westerberg, Co-Pres. and C.E.O.; Michael Ward, Co-Pres.; Scott Olson, C.I.O.; Ryan Woolf, Treas.
Giving statement: Giving through the US Autoliv ASP, Inc. Corporate Giving Program.

US Autoliv ASP, Inc. Corporate Giving Program

3350 Airport Rd.
Ogden, UT 84405-1563

Purpose and activities: US Autoliv ASP makes charitable contributions to nonprofit organizations on a case by case basis. Support is given primarily in areas of company operations, with emphasis on Ogden, Utah.
Fields of interest: General charitable giving.
Type of support: Employee matching gifts; General/ operating support; In-kind gifts.
Geographic limitations: Giving primarily in areas of company operations, with emphasis on Ogden, UT.
Application information: Applications not accepted. Contributes only to pre-selected organizations.

291
Automatic Data Processing, Inc.

(also known as ADP)
1 ADP Blvd., Bldg. 433
Roseland, NJ 07068-1786 (973) 974-5000

Company URL: http://www.adp.com
Establishment information: Established in 1949.
Company type: Public company
Company ticker symbol and exchange: ADP/ NASDAQ
International Securities Identification Number: US0530151036
Business activities: Provides computing services.
Business type (SIC): Computer services
Financial profile for 2012: Number of employees, 57,000; assets, $30,815,500,000; sales volume, $10,665,200,000; pre-tax net income, $2,122,100,000; expenses, $8,543,100,000; liabilities, $24,701,500,000
Fortune 1000 ranking: 2012—255th in revenues, 147th in profits, and 182nd in assets
Forbes 2000 ranking: 2012—876th in sales, 433rd in profits, and 680th in assets
Corporate officers: Leslie A. Brun, Chair.; Carlos A. Rodriguez, Pres. and C.E.O.; Edward B. Flynn III, Exec. V.P., Sales and Mktg.; Jan Siegmund, V.P. and C.F.O.; Michael L. Capone, V.P. and C.I.O.; Michael A. Bonarti, V.P., Genl. Counsel, and Secy.
Board of directors: Leslie A. Brun, Chair.; Ellen R. Alemany; Gregory D. Brenneman; Richard T. Clark; Eric C. Fast; Linda R. Gooden; Robert Glenn Hubbard; John P. Jones III; Carlos Rodriguez; Enrique T. Salem; Gregory L. Summe
Subsidiary: ProBusiness Services, Inc., Pleasanton, CA
International operations: Australia; Belgium; Brazil; Canada; China; Denmark; France; Germany; Italy; Netherlands; Spain; United Kingdom
Giving statement: Giving through the ADP Foundation.
Company EIN: 221467904

ADP Foundation

1 ADP Blvd., MS 433
Roseland, NJ 07068-1728

Establishment information: Established in 1978 in NJ.
Financial data (yr. ended 12/31/10): Revenue, $1,009,342; assets, $18,378,746 (M); gifts received, $992,027; expenditures, $4,972,487; giving activities include $4,856,323 for grants.
Purpose and activities: The foundation provides scholarships to children of ADP associates and matching grants to nonprofit organizations.
Fields of interest: Education.
Type of support: Employee matching gifts; Employee-related scholarships.
Publications: Annual report.
Directors: James Benson; Gary C. Butler; Michael Capone; Regina Lee; Henry Taub; Arthur F. Weinbach.
EIN: 222222589

292
AutoNation, Inc.

(formerly Republic Industries, Inc.)
110 S.E. 6th St.
Fort Lauderdale, FL 33301-5000
(954) 769-6000

Company URL: http://www.autonation.com
Establishment information: Established in 1991.
Company type: Public company
Company ticker symbol and exchange: AN/NYSE
Business activities: Operates car dealerships.
Business type (SIC): Motor vehicles—retail
Financial profile for 2012: Assets, $6,600,000,000; sales volume, $15,700,000,000
Fortune 1000 ranking: 2012—177th in revenues, 450th in profits, and 483rd in assets
Forbes 2000 ranking: 2012—598th in sales, 1492nd in profits, and 1706th in assets
Corporate officers: Michael J. Jackson, Chair. and C.E.O.; Michael E. Maroone, Pres. and C.O.O.; Michael J. Short, Exec. V.P. and C.F.O.; Jonathan P. Ferrando, Exec. V.P., Genl. Counsel, and Secy.; Kevin P. Westfall, Sr. V.P., Sales; Marc Cannon, Sr. V.P., Corp. Comm.
Board of directors: Michael J. Jackson, Chair.; Robert J. Brown; Rick L. Burdick; William C. Crowley; David B. Edelson; Robert R. Grusky; Michael J. Maroone; Carlos A. Migoya
International operations: Cayman Islands
Giving statement: Giving through the AutoNation, Inc. Corporate Giving Program.
Company EIN: 731105145

AutoNation, Inc. Corporate Giving Program

(formerly Republic Industries, Inc. Corporate Giving Program)
110 S.E. 6th St.
Fort Lauderdale, FL 33301-5005 (954) 769-7209
FAX: (954) 769-6494;
E-mail: butlerg@autonation.com

Contact: Gale M. Butler, V.P., Corp. Affairs
Financial data (yr. ended 12/31/07): Total giving, $2,200,000, including $2,175,000 for 200 grants, $5,000 for 4,025 employee matching gifts and $20,000 for 50 in-kind gifts.
Purpose and activities: AutoNation makes charitable contributions to nonprofit organizations involved with arts and culture, education, the environment, children and youth safety, families, and civic affairs. Support is given on a national basis in areas of company operations.
Fields of interest: Arts; Education; Environment; Safety/disasters; Family services; Public affairs Children; Youth.
Type of support: Cause-related marketing; Continuing support; Donated equipment; Donated products; Employee matching gifts; Employee volunteer services; General/operating support; In-kind gifts; Loaned talent; Public relations services; Scholarship funds; Scholarships—to individuals; Sponsorships; Use of facilities.
Geographic limitations: Giving on a national basis in areas of company operations, with some emphasis on southern FL.
Support limitations: No support for religious or fraternal organizations not of direct benefit to the entire community, political organizations, or international organizations. No grants to individuals (except for scholarships), or for travel or political campaigns; no new or used vehicle donations.
Publications: Application guidelines.

Application information: Applications accepted. Proposals should be no longer than 1 to 2 pages. Support is limited to 1 contribution per organization during any given year. Multi-year funding is not automatic. The Corporate Affairs Department handles giving. The company has a staff that only handles contributions. A contributions committee reviews all requests. Application form not required. Applicants should submit the following:

1) timetable for implementation and evaluation of project
2) signature and title of chief executive officer
3) results expected from proposed grant
4) statement of problem project will address
5) copy of IRS Determination Letter
6) brief history of organization and description of its mission
7) how project's results will be evaluated or measured
8) descriptive literature about organization
9) listing of board of directors, trustees, officers and other key people and their affiliations
10) detailed description of project and amount of funding requested
11) copy of current year's organizational budget and/or project budget
12) listing of additional sources and amount of support

Proposals should include a prioritized menu of the organization's annual events and a description of past involvement by AutoNation with the organization.

Initial approach: Mail or E-mail proposal to headquarters
Copies of proposal: 1
Committee meeting date(s): Fall
Deadline(s): Early fall
Final notification: Following review

Number of staff: 1 full-time professional; 1 part-time support.

293
Autonomie Project, Inc.

119 Braintree Street, Ste. 510
Boston, MA 02134 (877) 218-9131

Company URL: http://www.autonomieproject.com
Establishment information: Established in 2007.
Company type: Private company
Business activities: Manufactures footwear, clothing and accessories.
Business type (SIC): Apparel and other finished products made from fabrics and similar materials
Corporate officers: Gina Williams, Co-Owner; Anne O'Loughlin, Co-Owner
Giving statement: Giving through the Autonomie Project, Inc. Corporate Giving Program.

Autonomie Project, Inc. Corporate Giving Program

119 Braintree St., Ste. 510
Boston, MA 02134-1640 (877) 218-9131
URL: http://www.autonomieproject.com

Purpose and activities: Autonomie Project is a certified B Corporation that donates a percentage of net profits to nonprofit organizations. Special emphasis is directed toward organizations that promote fair trade and environmentally friendly practices.
Fields of interest: Environment; Employment; Business/industry.
Type of support: General/operating support.

294
AutoZone, Inc.

123 S. Front St.
Memphis, TN 38103-3607 (901) 495-6500
FAX: (901) 495-8300

Company URL: http://www.autozone.com
Establishment information: Established in 1979.
Company type: Public company
Company ticker symbol and exchange: AZO/NYSE
Business activities: Operates automotive parts and accessories stores.
Business type (SIC): Auto and home supplies—retail
Financial profile for 2012: Number of employees, 70,000; assets, $6,265,640,000; sales volume, $8,603,860,000; pre-tax net income, $1,452,990,000; expenses, $6,974,970,000; liabilities, $7,813,660,000
Fortune 1000 ranking: 2012—306th in revenues, 213th in profits, and 529th in assets
Forbes 2000 ranking: 2012—1027th in sales, 573rd in profits, and 1700th in assets
Corporate officers: William C. Rhodes III, Chair., Pres., and C.E.O.; William T. Giles, Exec. V.P., Finance, and C.F.O.; Harry L. Goldsmith, Exec. V.P., Genl. Counsel, and Secy.; Ronald B. Griffin, Sr. V.P. and C.I.O.; Charlie Pleas III, Sr. V.P. and Cont.; Albert Saltiel, Sr. V.P., Mktg.
Board of directors: William C. Rhodes III, Chair.; Sue E. Gove; Earl G. Graves, Jr.; Enderson Guimaraes; J.R. Hyde III; George R. Mrkonic, Jr.; Luis P. Nieto
International operations: Mexico
Giving statement: Giving through the AutoZone, Inc. Corporate Giving Program.
Company EIN: 621482048

AutoZone, Inc. Corporate Giving Program

123 S. Front St.
Memphis, TN 38103-3607 (901) 495-6500
E-mail: community.relations@autozone.com; Application address for matching gifts: AutoZone Matching Gift Prog., P.O. Box 2198, Dept. 8014, Memphis, TN 38101.; URL: http://www.autozoneinc.com/about_us/community_relations/index.html

Purpose and activities: AutoZone makes charitable contributions to museums and food banks and nonprofit organizations involved with education, women's empowerment, children's services, baseball and softball programs, and theater; and participates in blood drives. Support is limited to areas of company operations, with emphasis on Memphis, Tennessee.
Fields of interest: Museums; Performing arts, theater; Arts; Secondary school/education; Hospitals (specialty); Health care, blood supply; Food banks; Athletics/sports, baseball; Salvation Army; Children, services; Women, centers/services; United Ways and Federated Giving Programs Economically disadvantaged.
Programs:

AutoZone Scholarships: AutoZone annually awards fifteen $3,000 college scholarships to the children or dependents of AutoZone associates. Eligible recipients must have at least one year of service and have demonstrated academic achievement, leadership, school activity, and community service.

Matching Gifts Program: AutoZone matches employees' contributions to eligible nonprofit organizations. AutoZone will match eligible contributions dollar for dollar. A minimum of $25 up to a maximum of $500 per employee, per fiscal year may be matched when all program requirements are met.

Type of support: Annual campaigns; Donated equipment; Donated products; Employee matching gifts; Employee volunteer services; Employee-related scholarships; General/operating support; In-kind gifts; Sponsorships.
Geographic limitations: Giving is limited to areas of company operations, with emphasis on Memphis, TN.
Support limitations: No support for political organizations, athletic organizations or teams, or churches or religious organizations. No grants to individuals (except employee-related scholarships), or for school advertising (e.g., calendars, posters, yearbooks), general advertising, family reunions, or beauty contests.
Publications: Application guidelines.
Application information: Applications accepted. The Community Relations Department handles giving. AutoZone does not respond to requests by phone or fax. Application form required. Applicants should submit the following:

1) name, address and phone number of organization
2) copy of IRS Determination Letter
3) brief history of organization and description of its mission
4) copy of most recent annual report/audited financial statement/990
5) list of company employees involved with the organization
6) listing of board of directors, trustees, officers and other key people and their affiliations
7) detailed description of project and amount of funding requested
8) contact person
9) listing of additional sources and amount of support

Proposals should include an explanation of the organization's achievements and goals within the past year.

Initial approach: Download application form and e-mail completed proposal
Deadline(s): Feb. 28 for grants; none for United Way and in-kind requests
Final notification: Sept. 1 for grants; a minimum of 4 to 6 weeks for United Way and in-kind requests

295
Aveda Corporation

4000 Pheasant Ridge Dr.
Blaine, MN 55449 (763) 783-4250

Company URL: http://www.aveda.com
Establishment information: Established in 1978.
Company type: Private company
Business activities: Manufactures personal care and lifestyle products.
Business type (SIC): Soaps, cleaners, and toiletries
Corporate officers: Dominique Consell, Pres.; Christopher J. Werle, V.P., Comms.; Tom Petrillo, Sr. V.P., Sales; Darrin Johnson, Cont.
Giving statement: Giving through the Aveda Corporation Contributions Program.

Aveda Corporation Contributions Program

4000 Pheasant Ridge Dr. N.E.
Blaine, MN 55449-7101
URL: http://www.aveda.com/aboutaveda/giving.tmpl

Purpose and activities: Aveda Corporation makes charitable contributions to nonprofit organizations committed to social and environmental improvement. Support is given primarily in areas of company operations; giving also to national and international organizations.
Fields of interest: Environment; Breast cancer research; Community/economic development.
Type of support: General/operating support.
Geographic limitations: Giving primarily in areas of company operations; giving also to national and international organizations.

296
The Avelina Companies, Inc.

3 Belcher St.
Plainville, MA 02762-1303 (508) 695-3252
FAX: (508) 695-1130

Establishment information: Established in 1998.
Company type: Private company
Business activities: Sells sand and gravel wholesale.
Business type (SIC): Lumber and construction materials—wholesale
Corporate officers: Gerard C. Lorusso, Pres.; Henry G. Grilli, Cont.
Giving statement: Giving through the Avelina Charitable Foundation, Inc.

Avelina Charitable Foundation, Inc.

3 Belcher St.
Plainville, MA 02762-1303 (508) 695-3252

Establishment information: Established in 2001 in MA.
Donors: The Avelina Cos., Inc.; Joseph J. Lorusso.
Financial data (yr. ended 12/31/11): Assets, $2,961 (M); gifts received, $22,500; expenditures, $24,552; qualifying distributions, $24,500; giving activities include $24,500 for grants.
Purpose and activities: The foundation supports hospitals and organizations involved with education.
Fields of interest: Education; Health care; Human services.
Type of support: General/operating support; Program development; Scholarship funds.
Application information: Applications accepted. Application form required.
Initial approach: Letter
Deadline(s): None
Officers and Trustees:* Gerard C. Lorusso*, Pres. and Treas.; Henry G. Grilli, Clerk; Joseph J. Lorusso.
EIN: 010563707

297
Avery Dennison Corporation

(formerly Avery International Corporation)
150 N. Orange Grove Blvd.
Pasadena, CA 91103-3596 (626) 304-2000
FAX: (626) 792-7312

Company URL: http://www.averydennison.com
Establishment information: Established in 1935.
Company type: Public company
Company ticker symbol and exchange: AVY/NYSE
International Securities Identification Number: US0536111091
Business activities: Manufactures labeling equipment and products, self-adhesive products, tapes, office products, and specialty chemicals.
Business type (SIC): Paper and paperboard/coated, converted, and laminated; chemical preparations/miscellaneous; machinery/general industry
Financial profile for 2012: Number of employees, 29,800; assets, $5,105,300,000; sales volume, $6,035,600,000; pre-tax net income, $255,500,000; expenses, $5,780,100,000; liabilities, $3,524,400,000
Fortune 1000 ranking: 2012—375th in revenues, 556th in profits, and 588th in assets
Corporate officers: Dean A. Scarborough, Chair., Pres., and C.E.O.; Susan C. Miller, Sr. V.P., Genl. Counsel, and Secy.; Mitchell R. Butier, Sr. V.P. and C.F.O.; Richard W. Hoffman, Sr. V.P. and C.I.O.; Lori J. Bondar, V.P., Cont., and C.A.O.; Karyn E. Rodriguez, V.P. and Treas.
Board of directors: Dean A. Scarborough, Chair.; Brad A. Alford; Anthony K. Anderson; Peter K. Barker; Rolf L. Borjesson; John T. Cardis; Ken C. Hicks; Charles H. Noski; David E. I. Pyott; Patrick Thomas Siewert; Julia A. Stewart; Martha N. Sullivan
Subsidiaries: Avery, Inc., New York, NY; Avery Corporation, Pasadena, CA; Avery Dennison Foundation, Pasadena, CA; Avery Dennison Overseas Corp., Framingham, MA; Avery Graphic Systems, Inc., Schererville, IN; Dennison Manufacturing Co., Framingham, MA; DM Label, Inc., Covina, CA; Monarch Industries, Inc., Warren, RI; Paxar Corp., White Plains, NY; RF Identics, Inc., Grand Rapids, MI; Rvl Packaging, Inc., Westlake Village, CA; RVL Printed Labels, L.L.C., Statesville, NC; Security Printing Division, Inc., Clinton, SC
International operations: Argentina; Australia; Austria; Bangladesh; Belgium; Brazil; British Virgin Islands; Bulgaria; Canada; Chile; China; Colombia; Czech Republic; Denmark; Dominican Republic; El Salvador; Finland; France; Germany; Gibraltar; Guatemala; Honduras; Hong Kong; Hungary; India; Indonesia; Ireland; Italy; Japan; Luxembourg; Malaysia; Malta; Mauritius; Morocco and the Western Sahara; Netherlands; New Zealand; Nicaragua; Norway; Pakistan; Peru; Philippines; Poland; Romania; Russia; Singapore; South Africa; South Korea; Sri Lanka; Sweden; Switzerland; Taiwan; Thailand; Turkey; United Arab Emirates; United Kingdom; Venezuela; Vietnam
Giving statement: Giving through the Avery Dennison Foundation.
Company EIN: 951492269

Avery Dennison Foundation

(formerly Avery International Foundation)
150 N. Orange Grove Blvd.
Pasadena, CA 91103-3534 (626) 304-2000
E-mail: AveryDennison.Foundation@averydennison.com; URL: http://www.averydennison.com/avy/en_us/Sustainability/Community

Establishment information: Established in 1977.
Donor: Avery Dennison Corp.
Contact: Alicia Procello Maddox, Pres. and Exec. Dir.
Financial data (yr. ended 12/31/11): Assets, $15,245,641 (M); expenditures, $931,158; qualifying distributions, $808,567; giving activities include $808,567 for grants.
Purpose and activities: The foundation supports programs designed to promote education and environmental sustainability.
Fields of interest: Visual arts; Visual arts, design; Elementary/secondary education; Vocational education; Higher education; Environment, waste management; Environment, recycling; Environment, natural resources; Environment, water resources; Environment, energy; Environment, forests; Environment; Youth, services; Business/industry; Community/economic development; United Ways and Federated Giving Programs; Mathematics; Engineering/technology; Science Economically disadvantaged.
Programs:
Avery Dennison Granting Wishes: The foundation awards $1,000 to nonprofit and non-governmental organizations (NGOs) identified by employees in each facility in the United States and Europe. The program is designed to encourage employee engagement.
Education: The foundation supports programs designed to provide direct services to traditionally underserved populations based on gender, socioeconomic status, geography, or community need; provide educational improvements in elementary, secondary, post-secondary, or vocational schools; and promote science, math, technology, and the graphic and visual arts.
Environment: The foundation supports programs designed to improve the physical environment; promote community-based implementation with resident and youth engagement; and promote responsible care of the environment and knowledge of environmental issues relevant to the manufacturing industry, including energy, water conservation, waste reduction, recycling, responsible forestry, sustainable packaging, product safety, and resource conservation.
Global Grantmaking Initiative: The foundation, in collaboration with local Avery Dennison business units, awards grants to nonprofit, non-governmental organizations (NGOs), and educational institutions. Organizations must provide services to benefit the public where Avery Dennison has facilities and a significant workforce. Organizations must also incorporate Avery Dennison employees into the community programs offered.
H. Russell Smith Volunteer Award: The foundation recognizes five employees for their exemplary volunteer community service. The award includes a $5,000 grant to the nonprofit, nongovernmental organization (NGO), or school selected by the recipients.
Matching Gifts: The foundation matches contributions made by employees of Avery Dennison to educational institutions on a one-for-one basis up to $3,000 per employee, per year.
Type of support: Continuing support; Curriculum development; Employee matching gifts; Employee volunteer services; General/operating support; Program development; Scholarship funds.
Geographic limitations: Giving primarily in areas of company operations, with emphasis on CA, Brazil, China, and India.
Support limitations: No support for discriminatory organizations, for-profit organizations or ventures, government agencies, service clubs or veterans' or fraternal organizations, churches or religious organizations, private foundations, political organizations or candidates, or United Way-supported organizations (over 30 percent of budget). No grants to individuals, or for conferences, fundraisers, or special events, sponsorships, institutional endowments, beauty or talent contests, political activities, or general operating support for hospitals.
Publications: Application guidelines; Grants list; Occasional report.
Application information: Applications accepted. Support is limited to 1 contribution per organization during any given year. Multi-year funding is not automatic. Application form required. Applicants should submit the following:
1) timetable for implementation and evaluation of project
2) results expected from proposed grant
3) copy of IRS Determination Letter

4) brief history of organization and description of its mission
5) copy of most recent annual report/audited financial statement/990
6) how project's results will be evaluated or measured
7) listing of board of directors, trustees, officers and other key people and their affiliations
8) detailed description of project and amount of funding requested
9) copy of current year's organizational budget and/or project budget
10) listing of additional sources and amount of support

Initial approach: Complete online application
Deadline(s): None
Final notification: 3 to 6 months

Officers: Alicia Procello Maddox, Pres. and Exec. Dir.; Kim Caldwell, V.P.; Judy Abelman, V.P.; David N. Edwards, V.P.; Anne Hill, V.P.; Kim Macaulay, V.P.; Karyn E. Rodriguez, V.P.; Raj Srinivasan, V.P.; Judith K. Gain, Treas.
Number of staff: 1 full-time professional.
EIN: 953251844
Selected grants: The following grants are a representative sample of this grantmaker's funding activity:
$170,000 to United Way of Greater Los Angeles, Los Angeles, CA, 2009.
$88,191 to Institute of International Education, New York, NY, 2009.
$80,000 to Pasadena Educational Foundation, Pasadena, CA, 2009.
$50,000 to City of Hope, Duarte, CA, 2009.
$45,000 to Art Center College of Design, Pasadena, CA, 2009.
$40,000 to Institute of International Education, New York, NY, 2009.
$27,800 to Institute of International Education, New York, NY, 2009.
$2,314 to Southern California Grantmakers, Los Angeles, CA, 2009.

298
Avidia Bank

42 Main St.
Hudson, MA 01749-2123 (978) 562-6944

Company URL: http://www.avidiabank.com
Establishment information: Established in 1869.
Company type: Private company
Business activities: Operates savings institution.
Business type (SIC): Savings institutions
Corporate officers: David Lamson, Chair.; Mark Connell, Pres.; Paul Sheehan, Sr. V.P. and C.O.O.; John Casagrande, Sr. V.P. and C.F.O.
Board of directors: David Lamson, Chair.; Brian Parker
Giving statement: Giving through the Avidia Charitable Foundation, Inc.

Avidia Charitable Foundation, Inc.

(formerly Hudson Savings Charitable Foundation)
42 Main St.
Hudson, MA 01749-2123 (978) 567-3541

Establishment information: Established in 1997 in MA.
Donor: The Hudson Savings Bank.
Contact: Margaret B. Melo Sullivan, Treas.
Financial data (yr. ended 12/31/11): Assets, $530,465 (M); expenditures, $76,309; qualifying distributions, $76,139; giving activities include $73,667 for 17 grants (high: $20,000; low: $1,000).
Purpose and activities: The foundation supports hospitals and organizations involved with education, legal aid, baseball, and human services.
Fields of interest: Adult/continuing education; Education; Hospitals (general); Legal services; Athletics/sports, baseball; Boys & girls clubs; YM/YWCAs & YM/YWHAs; Children/youth, services; Family services; Aging, centers/services; Human services.
Type of support: Capital campaigns; Continuing support; General/operating support; Program development.
Geographic limitations: Giving primarily in MA.
Support limitations: No grants to individuals.
Application information: Applications accepted. Application form required.

Initial approach: Contact foundation for application form
Deadline(s): See application

Officers: Mark R. O'Connell, Pres.; Carol Parker, Clerk; Margaret B. Sullivan, Treas.
Directors: Paul Blazar; M. Neil Flanagan; David F. Lamson; Joseph MacDonough; James Tashjian; Fred Williams; Nicholas Zayka.
EIN: 043371516

299
Avis Budget Group, Inc.

6 Sylvan Way
Parsippany, NJ 07054 (973) 496-4700
FAX: (302) 636-5454

Company URL: http://www.avisbudgetgroup.com
Establishment information: Established in 1946.
Company type: Public company
Company ticker symbol and exchange: CAR/NYSE
Business activities: Operates vehicle rental company.
Business type (SIC): Motor vehicle rentals and leasing
Financial profile for 2012: Number of employees, 28,000; assets, $15,218,000,000; sales volume, $7,357,000,000; pre-tax net income, $300,000,000; expenses, $7,057,000,000; liabilities, $14,461,000,000
Fortune 1000 ranking: 2012—350th in revenues, 483rd in profits, and 296th in assets
Forbes 2000 ranking: 2012—1143rd in sales, 1387th in profits, and 1170th in assets
Corporate officers: Ronald L. Nelson, Chair. and C.E.O.; David B. Wyshner, Sr. Exec. V.P. and C.F.O.; Michael K. Tucker, Exec. V.P. and Genl. Counsel; Gerard Insall, Sr. V.P. and C.I.O.
Board of directors: Ronald L. Nelson, Chair.; Alun Cathcart; Mary C. Choksi; Leonard S. Coleman; John D. Hardy, Jr.; Lynn Krominga; Eduardo G. Mestre; F. Robert Salerno; Stender E. Sweeney
Subsidiaries: Avis Rent A Car System, LLC, Parsippany, NJ; Budget Rent A Car System, Inc., Parsippany, NJ
Giving statement: Giving through the Avis Budget Charitable Foundation.
Company EIN: 060918165

The Avis Budget Charitable Foundation

(formerly The Cendant Charitable Foundation)
6 Sylvan Way
Parsippany, NJ 07054-4407 (973) 496-2579

Establishment information: Established in 2001 in DE.
Donors: Cendant Corp.; First American Real Estate Tax Svcs.
Contact: Jean Sera, V.P. and Secy.
Financial data (yr. ended 12/31/11): Assets, $675,721 (M); expenditures, $128,195; qualifying distributions, $128,195; giving activities include $128,195 for 31 grants (high: $18,500; low: $250).
Purpose and activities: The foundation supports organizations involved with arts and culture, education, health, cancer, human services, community development, youth, and minorities.
Fields of interest: Museums; Performing arts, dance; Arts; Education; Hospitals (general); Health care; Cancer; American Red Cross; Human services; Business/industry; Community/economic development; United Ways and Federated Giving Programs Youth; Minorities.
Type of support: General/operating support; Scholarship funds.
Geographic limitations: Giving primarily in CA, NJ, and NY.
Application information: Applications accepted. Application form required. Applicants should submit the following:
1) copy of IRS Determination Letter
2) detailed description of project and amount of funding requested
3) contact person
4) copy of current year's organizational budget and/or project budget

Initial approach: Proposal
Deadline(s): None

Officers and Directors:* Henry Silverman, Chair. and Pres.; Jean Sera, V.P. and Secy.; Mark Servodidio, V.P.; David Wyshner, Treas. and C.F.O.; Michael Tucker.
EIN: 223758292
Selected grants: The following grants are a representative sample of this grantmaker's funding activity:
$15,650 to American Cancer Society, Atlanta, GA, 2010.
$6,000 to Teach for America, New York, NY, 2010.
$1,500 to Multiple Sclerosis Society, National, New York, NY, 2010.
$1,500 to Phoenix House, New York, NY, 2010.
$1,400 to Loyola High School of Los Angeles, Los Angeles, CA, 2010.
$1,000 to Childrens Defense Fund, Washington, DC, 2010.
$1,000 to Childrens Tumor Foundation, New York, NY, 2010.
$1,000 to Stanford University, Stanford, CA, 2010.

300
Avis Rent A Car System, LLC

6 Sylvan Way
Parsippany, NJ 07054 (973) 496-3500

Company URL: http://www.avis.com
Establishment information: Established in 1946.
Company type: Subsidiary of a public company
Business activities: Operates car rental company.
Business type (SIC): Motor vehicle rentals and leasing
Corporate officers: Ronald L. Nelson, Chair. and C.E.O.; David B. Wyshner, Sr. Exec. V.P. and C.F.O.; Mark J. Servodidio, Exec. V.P. and C.A.O.; Michael K. Tucker, Exec. V.P. and Genl. Counsel.; Gerard Insall, Sr. V.P. and C.I.O.
Board of director: Ronald L. Nelson, Chair.
Giving statement: Giving through the Avis Rent A Car System, LLC Corporate Giving Program.

Avis Rent A Car System, LLC Corporate Giving Program

(formerly Cendant Corporation Contributions Program)
6 Sylvan Way
Parsippany, NJ 07054 (973) 496-3500
URL: http://www.avis.com/car-rental/content/display.ac?navId=T6M21S06

Purpose and activities: Avis Rent A Car System makes charitable contributions to national organizations involved with minority education, economic development, cancer research, support for seriously ill patients, passenger safety and related safety initiatives, and transportation as a component of social services. Support is given primarily in areas of company operations.
Fields of interest: Education; Health care, support services; Health care, patient services; Parkinson's disease; Cancer research; Food distribution, meals on wheels; Safety, automotive safety; Youth development, equal rights; Children, services; Women, centers/services; Human services; Civil/human rights, LGBTQ; Economic development; Community development, business promotion; Community/economic development; Military/veterans' organizations; Transportation Minorities.
Program:
Upromise: Through the Upromise program, Avis contributes five percent of Upromise members' time-and-mileage charges into their college savings account for a child, grandchild, or any other future college student they choose to support.
Type of support: Donated products; General/operating support; In-kind gifts.
Geographic limitations: Giving primarily in areas of company operations.
Publications: Application guidelines.
Application information: Applications accepted. Unsolicited requests (particularly cash requests) are unlikely to be funded. Application form required. Applicants should submit the following:
1) name, address and phone number of organization
2) brief history of organization and description of its mission
3) detailed description of project and amount of funding requested
4) contact person

Applications should include e-mail address and website address.
Initial approach: Complete online application
Deadline(s): 3 weeks prior to need for vehicle donations; 60 days for cash donations

301
Avista Corporation

(formerly The Washington Water Power Company)
1411 E. Mission Ave.
P.O. Box 3727
Spokane, WA 99220-3727 (509) 489-0500
FAX: (509) 777-5075

Company URL: http://www.avistacorp.com
Establishment information: Established in 1889.
Company type: Public company
Company ticker symbol and exchange: AVA/NYSE
Business activities: Generates, transmits, and distributes electricity; distributes natural gas.
Business type (SIC): Combination utility services
Financial profile for 2012: Number of employees, 1,682; assets, $4,313,180,000; sales volume, $1,547,000,000; pre-tax net income, $120,060,000; expenses, $1,356,930,000; liabilities, $3,053,700,000
Corporate officers: Scott L. Morris, Chair., Pres., and C.E.O.; Mark T. Thies, Sr. V.P. and C.F.O.; Marian M. Durkin, Sr. V.P. and Genl. Counsel; Karen S. Feltes, Sr. V.P., Human Resources and Corp. Secy.; James M. Kensok, V.P. and C.I.O.; Christy M. Burmeister-Smith, V.P. and Cont.
Board of directors: Scott L. Morris, Chair.; Erik J. Anderson; Kristianne Blake; Donald Burke; Rick R. Holley; John F. Kelly; Rebecca A. Klein; Michael L. Noel; Marc F. Racicot; Heidi B. Stanley; R. John Taylor
Subsidiaries: Avista Advantage, Inc., Spokane, WA; Avista Energy, Inc., Spokane, WA; Pentzer Corp., Spokane, WA
Plants: Coeur d'Alene, Lewiston, ID; Medford, OR; Pullman, WA
Giving statement: Giving through the Avista Corporation Contributions Program and the Avista Foundation.
Company EIN: 910462470

Avista Corporation Contributions Program

(formerly The Washington Water Power Company Contributions Program)
P.O. Box 3727
Spokane, WA 99220-3727 (509) 495-8031
E-mail: debbie.simock@avistacorp.com;
URL: http://www.avistautilities.com/community/Pages/default.aspx

Contact: Debbie Simock, Community Rels. Strategist
Financial data (yr. ended 12/31/10): Total giving, $1,796,796, including $1,796,796 for grants.
Purpose and activities: As a complement to its foundation, Avista also makes charitable contributions to nonprofit organizations directly. Support is given primarily in areas of company operations.
Fields of interest: Museums; Arts; Elementary/secondary education; Higher education; Education; Youth, services; Economic development; Community/economic development Minorities.
Type of support: Capital campaigns; Continuing support; Curriculum development; Donated equipment; Emergency funds; Employee volunteer services; General/operating support; In-kind gifts; Internship funds; Land acquisition; Program development; Seed money; Sponsorships; Technical assistance; Use of facilities.
Geographic limitations: Giving primarily in areas of company operations, with emphasis on northern ID, southern OR, and eastern WA.
Support limitations: No grants for endowments.
Publications: Application guidelines.
Application information: The Public Affairs Department handles giving. Application form required.
Initial approach: Visit website for application information
Copies of proposal: 1
Deadline(s): None
Final notification: 1 month
Number of staff: 1 part-time professional; 1 part-time support.

The Avista Foundation

MSC-68
P.O. Box 3727
Spokane, WA 99220-3727 (509) 495-8156
FAX: (509) 494-4144;
E-mail: contributions@avistacorp.com; URL: http://www.avistafoundation.org

Establishment information: Established in 2002 in WA.
Donors: Avista Corp.; Avista Capital, Inc.
Contact: Anne-Marie Axworthy, Chair. and Pres.
Financial data (yr. ended 12/31/11): Assets, $3,678,513 (M); expenditures, $427,226; qualifying distributions, $417,949; giving activities include $417,949 for 202 grants (high: $95,000; low: $25).
Purpose and activities: The foundation supports organizations involved with education, energy conservation, community economic development, science, senior citizens, and economically disadvantaged people.
Fields of interest: Elementary/secondary education; Higher education; Education; Environment, energy; Community/economic development; Physical/earth sciences; Engineering/technology; Science Aging; Economically disadvantaged.
Programs:
Economic and Cultural Vitality: The foundation supports programs designed to help communities and citizens grow and prosper.
Education: The foundation supports programs designed to promote K-12 science, math, and technology education and higher education.
Matching Gift Program: The foundation matches contributions made by employees of Avista Utilities to nonprofit organizations.
Vulnerable and Limited Income Populations: The foundation supports programs designed to provide assistance to those with limited incomes; and develop initiatives to reduce poverty.
Type of support: Capital campaigns; Employee matching gifts; Equipment; General/operating support; Program development; Scholarship funds; Seed money.
Geographic limitations: Giving primarily in areas of company operations in northern ID, Sanders County, MT, southern OR, and eastern WA.
Support limitations: No support for religious, veterans', or fraternal organizations, discriminatory organizations, or national health organizations (or their local affiliates) or research/disease advocacy organizations. No grants to individuals, or for teams or extra-curricular school events, fundraising events, trips or tours, the development or production of books, films, videos, or television campaigns, or memorial campaigns.
Publications: Application guidelines; Informational brochure (including application guidelines); IRS Form 990 or 990-PF printed copy available upon request.
Application information: Applications accepted. Application form required. Applicants should submit the following:
1) statement of problem project will address
2) population served
3) copy of IRS Determination Letter
4) brief history of organization and description of its mission
5) copy of most recent annual report/audited financial statement/990
6) how project's results will be evaluated or measured
7) listing of board of directors, trustees, officers and other key people and their affiliations

Initial approach: Complete online application or download application and fax or mail to foundation
Copies of proposal: 1
Board meeting date(s): Feb., May, Aug., and Nov.
Deadline(s): None
Final notification: 90 days
Officers and Directors:* Anne Marie Axworthy*, Chair. and Pres.; Robert Beitz*, V.P.; Mike Thomason*, Secy.; Christy Burmeister-Smith*,

Treas.; Kristine Meyer, Exec. Dir.; Patrick Lynch; David J. Meyer; Dennis Vermillion.
EIN: 753003371
Selected grants: The following grants are a representative sample of this grantmaker's funding activity:
$95,000 to United Way of Spokane County, Spokane, WA, 2010. For general program support.
$20,000 to Gonzaga University, Spokane, WA, 2010.
$10,500 to Gonzaga University, Spokane, WA, 2010.
$10,500 to University of Idaho Foundation, Moscow, ID, 2010.
$10,500 to Washington State University Foundation, Pullman, WA, 2010.
$10,000 to ARC of Spokane, Spokane, WA, 2010.
$8,000 to United Way of Jackson County, Medford, OR, 2010. For general program support.
$5,000 to Oregon Tech Development Foundation, Klamath Falls, OR, 2010.
$3,500 to American Red Cross, Spokane, WA, 2010.
$2,250 to United Way of Moscow/Latah County, Moscow, ID, 2010. For general program support.

302
Aviva USA Corporation

(formerly AmerUs Group Co.)
7700 Mills Civic Pkwy.
West Des Moines, IA 50266
(515) 362-3600

Company URL: http://www.avivausa.com
Establishment information: Established in 1896.
Company type: Subsidiary of a foreign company
Business activities: Operates holding company; sells life insurance.
Business type (SIC): Insurance/life; holding company
Corporate officers: Thomas C. Godlasky, Chair.; Chrisopher Littlefield, Pres. and C.E.O.; Brenda Jean Cushing, Exec. V.P. and C.F.O.; Michael H. Miller, Exec. V.P., Sales
Board of director: Thomas C. Godlasky, Chair.
Subsidiary: Indianapolis Life Insurance Company, Indianapolis, IN
Giving statement: Giving through the Aviva Charitable Foundation.

Aviva Charitable Foundation

(formerly AmerUs Group Charitable Foundation)
699 Walnut St., Ste. 2000
Des Moines, IA 50309-3929 (515) 557-3916
E-mail: AvivaFoundation@avivausa.com; E-mail for Karen Lynn: karen.lynn@avivausa.com; URL: http://www.avivausa.com/wps/portal/avivausa/about/corporate-responsibility

Establishment information: Established in 1994 in IA.
Donors: American Mutual Life Insurance Co.; AmerUs Group Co.
Contact: Karen Lynn, V.P.
Financial data (yr. ended 12/31/11): Assets, $1,539,091 (M); gifts received, $1,000,000; expenditures, $1,156,234; qualifying distributions, $1,156,059; giving activities include $1,156,059 for grants.
Purpose and activities: The foundation supports organizations involved with arts and culture, education, community development, and civic affairs.
Fields of interest: Media, television; Visual arts; Museums; Performing arts; Arts; Higher education; Education; Health care, association; Community/economic development; United Ways and Federated Giving Programs; Economics; Public affairs.
Type of support: Continuing support; Employee matching gifts; Employee volunteer services; General/operating support; Scholarship funds.
Geographic limitations: Giving primarily in areas of company operations in Des Moines, IA, Indianapolis, IN, Topeka, KS, Quincy, MA, and Woodbury, NY.
Support limitations: No support for athletes or athletic organizations, fraternal organizations, hospitals or health care facilities, K-8 schools, military or veterans' groups, pass-through organizations, political parties, candidates, or organizations, private foundations, sectarian, religious or denominational organizations, social organizations, trade, industry, or professional associations, or United Way organizations seeking funds for operating expenses of United Way-funded programs. No grants to individuals, or for conference or seminar attendance, courtesy or goodwill advertising, endowments, fellowships, festival participation, or political campaigns.
Publications: Application guidelines.
Application information: Applications accepted. Support is limited to 1 contribution per organization during any given year. Multi-year funding is not automatic. Organizations receiving support are asked to provide a final report. Application form required. Applicants should submit the following:
1) copy of IRS Determination Letter
2) brief history of organization and description of its mission
3) geographic area to be served
4) copy of most recent annual report/audited financial statement/990
5) how project's results will be evaluated or measured
6) list of company employees involved with the organization
7) listing of board of directors, trustees, officers and other key people and their affiliations
8) detailed description of project and amount of funding requested
9) plans for cooperation with other organizations, if any
10) copy of current year's organizational budget and/or project budget
11) role played by volunteers

Initial approach: Download application form and mail to foundation
Copies of proposal: 1
Board meeting date(s): Three times per year
Deadline(s): June 1
Final notification: 8 weeks

Officers and Director:* Christopher J. Littlefield, Pres.; Karen Lynn, V.P.; Michael H. Miller, Secy.; Brenda J. Cushing, Treas.; Mark V. Heitz.
Number of staff: 2 part-time professional.
EIN: 421431745
Selected grants: The following grants are a representative sample of this grantmaker's funding activity:
$647,721 to United Way of Central Iowa, Des Moines, IA, 2011.
$50,000 to Central Iowa Shelter and Services, Des Moines, IA, 2011.
$39,486 to United Way of Greater Topeka, Topeka, KS, 2011.
$30,075 to Civic Center of Greater Des Moines, Des Moines, IA, 2011.
$25,000 to Des Moines Arts Festival, Des Moines, IA, 2011.
$15,400 to Des Moines Art Center, Des Moines, IA, 2011.
$12,000 to Des Moines Symphony, Des Moines, IA, 2011.
$10,000 to Bravo Greater Des Moines, Des Moines, IA, 2011.
$10,000 to Simpson College, Indianola, IA, 2011.
$7,500 to Hospice of Central Iowa, West Des Moines, IA, 2011.

303
Avlon Industries, Inc.

1999 N. 15th Ave.
Melrose Park, IL 60160 (708) 563-0363

Company URL: http://www.avlon.com
Establishment information: Established in 1984.
Company type: Private company
Business activities: Develops, manufactures, and markets personal care products.
Business type (SIC): Soaps, cleaners, and toiletries
Corporate officers: Ali N. Syed, Pres.; William Stewart, Exec. V.P. and C.F.O.; Dure S. Syed, Corp. Secy.
Giving statement: Giving through the Hasnia Foundation.

Hasnia Foundation

1999 N. 15th Ave.
Melrose Park, IL 60160-1402 (708) 325-1322

Establishment information: Established in 2000 in IL.
Donors: Avlon Industries, Inc.; Ali Syed; Islamic Mission and Mosque, Inc.
Financial data (yr. ended 12/31/11): Assets, $153,608 (M); gifts received, $90,000; expenditures, $25,126; qualifying distributions, $17,015; giving activities include $9,356 for 3 grants (high: $5,701; low: $1,655) and $7,659 for grants to individuals.
Purpose and activities: The foundation supports organizations involved with education, youth, and Islam and awards college scholarships to students in Pakistan.
Fields of interest: Education; Human services; Religion.
International interests: Pakistan.
Type of support: General/operating support; Scholarships—to individuals.
Geographic limitations: Giving limited to IL and Pakistan.
Application information: Applications accepted. Application form required.
Scholarship applicants must have a GPA of at least 3.0.

Initial approach: Contact foundation for application information; contact foundation for application form for scholarships
Deadline(s): May for scholarships

Officer: Ijlal Hussain Zaidi, Pres.
Directors: Tehseen Naqvi; Ali N. Syed; Dure S. Syed.
EIN: 364415277

304
Avnet, Inc.

2211 S. 47th St.
Phoenix, AZ 85034-6403 (480) 643-2000
FAX: (480) 643-7370

Company URL: http://www.avnet.com
Establishment information: Established in 1955.
Company type: Public company
Company ticker symbol and exchange: AVT/NYSE
Business activities: Manufactures and distributes electronic components and computer, electrical,

electroautomotive, and video communications products.
Business type (SIC): Electronic components and accessories; metal foundries/nonferrous; communications equipment; motor vehicles, parts, and supplies—wholesale; electrical goods—wholesale
Financial profile for 2012: Number of employees, 19,100; assets, $10,167,870,000; sales volume, $25,707,520,000; pre-tax net income, $790,780,000; expenses, $24,820,440,000; liabilities, $6,262,130,000
Fortune 1000 ranking: 2012—117th in revenues, 306th in profits, and 384th in assets
Corporate officers: William H. Schumann III, Chair.; Richard P. Hamada, C.E.O.; Ray Sadowski, C.A.O.; Kevin Moriarty, Sr. V.P., C.F.O. and Cont.; Stephen R. Phillips, Sr. V.P. and C.I.O.; Erin Lewin, Sr. V.P. and Genl. Counsel; MaryAnn Miller, Sr. V.P., Human Resources and Comms.
Board of directors: William H. Schumann III, Chair.; J. Veronica Biggins; Michael A. Bradley; R. Kerry Clark; Richard Hamada; James A. Lawrence; Frank R. Noonan; Ray M. Robinson; William P. Sullivan
Subsidiaries: Avnet Development Labs, Inc., Durham, NC; Brownell Electro, Inc., New York, NY; Channel Master, Smithfield, NC; I.W. Rice, New York, NY; Valley Forge Die Casting, Inc., Chicago, IL; Valley Forge Products Co., Inwood, NY
International operations: Australia; Austria; Belgium; Brazil; Canada; China; Czech Republic; England; Estonia; France; Germany; Greece; Hong Kong; Hungary; India; Ireland; Israel; Italy; Malaysia; Mexico; New Zealand; Philippines; Poland; Romania; Singapore; Slovakia; South Africa; South Korea; Spain; Sweden; Switzerland; Thailand; Ukraine; United Kingdom; Wales
Giving statement: Giving through the Avnet, Inc. Corporate Giving Program.
Company EIN: 111890605

Avnet, Inc. Corporate Giving Program

c/o Avnet Contribs. Council
2211 S. 47th St.
Phoenix, AZ 85034-6403 (480) 643-4811
E-mail: Jessie.Ferris@avnet.com; URL: http://www.avnet.com/

Contact: Jessie Ferris
Purpose and activities: Avnet makes charitable contributions to nonprofit organizations involved with education, children's issues, community, and technology. Support is given primarily in areas of company operations.
Fields of interest: Education, reading; Education, computer literacy/technology training; Education; Children, services; Community/economic development; Philanthropy/voluntarism, volunteer services; Engineering/technology.

Program:

Dollars for Doers Program: The Avnet Cares Governing Board has expanded its Dollars for Doers pilot program across the Americas, pledging to donate cash grants to qualified nonprofit organizations based on the level of employee involvement. Employees volunteering 20 hours before Sept. 30 may apply for organizations to receive $200, and organizations where employees volunteer 40 hours before Sept. 30 may receive $400.

Type of support: Annual campaigns; Employee volunteer services; General/operating support; Sponsorships.
Geographic limitations: Giving primarily in areas of company operations.
Publications: Application guidelines.
Application information: Applications accepted. The Avnet Contributions Council handles giving. Application form required. Applicants should submit the following:
1) results expected from proposed grant
2) copy of IRS Determination Letter
3) copy of most recent annual report/audited financial statement/990
4) how project's results will be evaluated or measured
5) listing of board of directors, trustees, officers and other key people and their affiliations
6) copy of current year's organizational budget and/or project budget
7) listing of additional sources and amount of support
8) contact person
9) brief history of organization and description of its mission
10) name, address and phone number of organization
11) population served

Applications should include the amount requested, a statement of need, and a description of beneficiaries.
Initial approach: Download application and mail completed proposal to Avnet Contributions Council
Copies of proposal: 1

305
Avon Products, Inc.

777 3rd Ave.
New York, NY 10017 (212) 282-7000

Company URL: http://www.avon.com
Establishment information: Established in 1886.
Company type: Public company
Company ticker symbol and exchange: AVP/NYSE
International Securities Identification Number: US0543031027
Business activities: Manufactures and markets beauty products.
Business type (SIC): Soaps, cleaners, and toiletries; drugs, proprietaries, and sundries—wholesale
Financial profile for 2012: Number of employees, 39,100; assets, $7,382,500,000; sales volume, $10,717,100,000; pre-tax net income, $218,600,000; expenses, $10,402,300,000; liabilities, $6,165,400,000
Fortune 1000 ranking: 2012—252nd in revenues, 906th in profits, and 474th in assets
Forbes 2000 ranking: 2012—889th in sales, 1781st in profits, and 1641st in assets
Corporate officers: Doglas R. Conant, Chair.; Sheri S. McCoy, C.E.O.; Kimberly A. Ross, Exec. V.P. and C.F.O.; Donagh Herlihy, Sr. V.P. and C.I.O.; Jeff Benjamin, Sr. V.P. and Genl. Counsel; Scott Crum, Sr. V.P., Human Resources
Board of directors: Douglas R. Conant, Chair.; W. Don Cornwell; V. Ann Hailey; Maria Elena Lagomasino; Ann S. Moore; Sheri S. McCoy; Charles H. Noski; Gary M. Rodkin; Kimberly A. Ross; Paula Stern, Ph.D.
Offices: Pasadena, CA; Newark, DE; Atlanta, GA; Morton Grove, IL; New York, Rye, Suffern, NY; Springdale, OH; Caguas, PR
International operations: Albania; Argentina; Australia; Austria; Bermuda; Bolivia; Bosnia-Herzegovina; Brazil; Brunei; Bulgaria; Canada; Cayman Islands; Chile; China; Colombia; Croatia; Czech Republic; Dominican Republic; Ecuador; Egypt; El Salvador; England; Estonia; Finland; France; Germany; Greece; Guatemala; Honduras; Hong Kong; Hungary; India; Indonesia; Ireland; Israel; Italy; Japan; Kazakhstan; Kyrgyzstan; Latvia; Lithuania; Luxembourg; Macedonia; Malaysia; Mauritius; Mexico; Moldova; Montenegro; Morocco and the Western Sahara; Netherlands; New Zealand; Nicaragua; Panama; Peru; Philippines; Poland; Portugal; Romania; Russia; Saudi Arabia; Serbia; Singapore; Slovenia; South Africa; South Korea; Spain; Switzerland; Taiwan; Thailand; Turkey; Ukraine; Uruguay; Venezuela; Vietnam; Wales
Giving statement: Giving through the Avon Foundation for Women.
Company EIN: 130544597

Avon Foundation for Women

(also known as Avon Products Foundation, Inc.)
(formerly Avon Foundation)
777 Third Ave., 2nd Fl.
New York, NY 10017-1401 (212) 282-5000
E-mail: info@avonfoundation.org; URL: http://www.avonfoundation.org

Establishment information: Incorporated in 1955 in NY.
Donor: Avon Products, Inc.
Contact: Carol Kurzig, Pres.
Financial data (yr. ended 12/31/12): Revenue, $55,075,531; assets, $35,104,686 (M); gifts received, $55,151,124; expenditures, $59,596,256; program services expenses, $46,315,204; giving activities include $33,154,275 for grants.
Purpose and activities: The foundation's mission is to improve the lives of women and their families.
Fields of interest: Breast cancer; Crime/violence prevention, domestic violence Adults, women; Young adults, female.

Programs:

Avon Breast Cancer Research Program: Proposals for up to $150,000 per year for up to two years are accepted from organizations that seek to advance understanding of causes of breast cancer and prevention.

Avon Foundation Breast Health Outreach Program: This program supports community-based organizations to provide outreach and breast health education, and to connect women and men to screening services and follow-up care in partnership with local medical providers. Funding is awarded to programs that successfully implement breast cancer early detection programs that include breast health education, regular mamography screening, clinical breast examination, and breast self-examination for at-risk, medically underserved women 40 years-old and older.

Avon Safety Net Program: The program supports institutions and organizations that have traditionally cared for uninsured, at-risk, low-income, and minority patients to enable medically underserved women and men to access post-screening diagnostics and care. Applicants may request up to $125,000 per year for two years for support for patient navigation programs, equipment, other personnel and infrastructure needs that will enhance breast cancer care services to the medically underserved.

Domestic and Sexual Assault Training Programs: This program funds the development of, and offer assistance in launching, a comprehensive series of targeted prevention and intervention training tools to help bystanders recognize, respond to, and make appropriate referrals in situations when partner abuse, dating abuse, or sexual assault are suspected or observed. Up to four grants of up to $125,000 each will be awarded - one for each of the following categories, including Children - how to recognize and respond, prevent, or assist when family violence affects children; Teens and Young Adults - how to recognize, respond to or prevent dating abuse or sexual assault, or to assist victims;

Female and Male Victims - how to recognize, respond to or prevent incidents of domestic violence, or to assist victims ; Female and Male Victims - how to recognize, respond to or prevent incidents of sexual assault, or to assist victims.

Domestic Violence Survivor Empowerment Program: This program funds full-time economic empowerment coordinator positions in domestic violence victim service agencies across the United States with the goal to provide domestic violence survivors with the resources and economic empowerment tools necessary to develop self-sufficiency. Since its inception, the program has awarded $4 million to nearly seventy-five coordinators. Examples of successful programs include those that have increased the numbers of clients who receive comprehensive case management support, have developed and sustained community support linkages to enhance client outcomes, and have incorporated effective client mentoring programs in addition to core services already provided. Up to twenty grants of up to $65,000 each will be awarded in December 2013. The funding period will be from January 1 to December 31, 2014.

Employee Matching Gifts: The foundation matches contributions made by employees and directors of Avon to nonprofit organizations on a two-for-one basis up to $500, and on a one-for-one basis thereafter up to $15,000 per year.

Healthy Relationship College Program: This program, open to nonprofit college and university organizations in the United States, funds programs that deal with dating abuse, sexual assault, and stalking prevention and awareness, including campus-wide outreach events, trainings, and/or workshops; peer education programs to increase the number of student ambassadors; awareness materials, including resource guides, Web site pages, posters, cards, and buttons; and video or print PSAs or short films. The program should emphasize awareness and prevention through education. Twenty-five grants of up to $5,000 will be awarded.

James E. Preston Community Service Scholarship: The foundation annually awards one four-year $5,000 college scholarship to a dependent child of a full-time employee of Avon who demonstrates outstanding community service experience that is deemed most exemplary.

m.powerment by mark: The program is dedicated to breaking the cycle of dating abuse and partner violence. All funds raised are awarded as grants to programs and organizations that are making strides in breaking this cycle. Since 2008 when m.powerment by mark was launched, more than $725,000 has been raised. Focus is targeted primarily to young women, ages 16-34, with a special prevention and education "Healthy Relationship Peer Educator" model program at colleges nationwide.

President's Recognition Program Scholarship for Children and Grandchildren: The foundation awards $2,000 college scholarships to children and grandchildren of members of the Avon President's Recognition Program Scholarship Program for Representatives.

Scholarship Program for Children of Associates: One scholarship of $12,000, paid in installments of $3,000 over a four-year period, is available to dependent children of a current, regular, full-time U.S. or Puerto Rico associate.

Scholarship Program for Representatives: The foundation awards full-time and part-time college scholarships, ranging from $1,500 to $2,500, to representatives of Avon.

Speak Out Against Domestic Violence Program: The program supports domestic violence awareness, education, direct services and prevention initiatives. Specifically, the Avon Foundation funds model pilot programs and new approaches in the following areas: economic self-sufficiency for DV survivors, dating abuse and prevention programs implemented on college and university campuses, and programs that are targeted to help children affected by domestic violence. Grants range from $1,000 to $100,000 depending on the scope, size, and impact of the program proposed. Grants are non-renewable; however an organization may submit a new proposal the following year for continued funding.

Type of support: Continuing support; Employee matching gifts; Employee-related scholarships; Equipment; General/operating support; Program development; Research.

Geographic limitations: Giving on a national basis, with limited international giving for special foundation initiatives.

Support limitations: No support for political, religious, veterans', or fraternal organizations. No grants to individuals (except for employee-related scholarships), or for endowments, fundraising events, telethons, marathons, races, benefits, courtesy advertising, or films; no loans.

Publications: Annual report; Application guidelines; Financial statement; Grants list; Informational brochure; Newsletter.

Application information: Applications accepted. See web site for specific regional application guidelines and deadlines. Application form required. Applicants should submit the following:

1) results expected from proposed grant
2) population served
3) name, address and phone number of organization
4) copy of IRS Determination Letter
5) detailed description of project and amount of funding requested
6) contact person
7) copy of current year's organizational budget and/or project budget
8) additional materials/documentation

Initial approach: Online application only
Copies of proposal: 1
Board meeting date(s): Five times per year
Deadline(s): Varies
Final notification: Varies

Officers: Robert J. Corti, Chair.; Carol Kurzig, Pres.; Kim Azzarelli, V.P.; John P. Higson, V.P.; Meg Lerner, V.P.; Patricia Perez-Ayala, V.P.; Michael Schwartz, V.P.; Cheryl Heinonen, Secy.; Shalabh Gupta, Treas.

EIN: 136128447

306
AVX Corporation

1 AVX Blvd.
Fountain Inn, SC 29644-9039
(843) 448-9411
FAX: (302) 655-5049

Company URL: http://www.avx.com/
Establishment information: Established in 1972.
Company type: Public company
Company ticker symbol and exchange: AVX/NYSE
Business activities: Operates passive electronic components and related products company.
Business type (SIC): Electronic components and accessories
Financial profile for 2013: Number of employees, 10,700; assets, $2,601,990,000; sales volume, $1,414,400,000; pre-tax net income, -$113,320,000; expenses, $1,534,240,000; liabilities, $629,070,000

Corporate officers: John S. Gilbertson, Chair. and C.E.O.; John Lawing, Pres.; Kurt P. Cummings, V.P., C.F.O., and Secy.-Treas.; Peter Venuto, V.P., Sales; Kathleen M. Kelly, V.P., Human Resources
Board of directors: John S. Gilbertson, Chair.; Shoichi Aoki; Donald B. Christiansen; David A. Decenzo; Kazuo Inamori; Makoto Kawamura; Tetsuo Kuba; Tatsumi Maeda; Joseph Stach
Giving statement: Giving through the AVX/Kyocera Foundation.
Company EIN: 330379007

AVX/Kyocera Foundation

1 AVX Blvd.
Fountain Inn, SC 29644-9039

Establishment information: Established in 1996 in SC.
Donor: AVX Corp.
Financial data (yr. ended 03/31/12): Assets, $9,902,196 (M); gifts received, $2,500; expenditures, $574,857; qualifying distributions, $481,959; giving activities include $467,460 for 57 grants (high: $110,000; low: $500) and $14,499 for 13 grants to individuals (high: $3,000; low: $250).
Purpose and activities: The foundation supports museums and organizations involved orchestras, education, health, and heart disease and awards undergraduate scholarships to individuals.
Fields of interest: Museums; Museums (art); Performing arts, orchestras; Secondary school/education; Higher education; Education; Hospitals (general); Health care, clinics/centers; Health care; Heart & circulatory diseases; International relief.
Type of support: General/operating support; Scholarships—to individuals; Sponsorships.
Geographic limitations: Giving primarily in the U.S., with emphasis on SC; giving also in Czech Republic, El Salvador, and Malaysia.
Application information: Applications not accepted. Unsolicited requests for funds not accepted.
Officers: John S. Gilbertson, Pres.; C. Marshall Jackson, V.P.; Kathleen M. Kelly, V.P.; Kurt P. Cummings, Treas.
EIN: 571057142
Selected grants: The following grants are a representative sample of this grantmaker's funding activity:
$55,000 to Brookgreen Gardens, Murrells Inlet, SC, 2011.
$50,000 to Alfred University, Alfred, NY, 2011.
$30,000 to Webber Hospital Association, Biddeford, ME, 2011.
$25,000 to Coastal Carolina University, Conway, SC, 2011.
$25,000 to Greenville County Museum of Art, Greenville, SC, 2011.
$25,000 to Greenville Technical College, Greenville, SC, 2011.
$25,000 to Olean General Hospital, Olean, NY, 2011.
$9,000 to Clemson University, Clemson, SC, 2011.
$4,000 to College of Charleston, Charleston, SC, 2011.
$1,500 to Florida State College, Jacksonville, FL, 2011.

307
AXA Equitable

(formerly The Equitable Companies Incorporated)
1290 Ave. of the Americas
New York, NY 10104-0101 (212) 554-1234

Company URL: http://www.axa-equitable.com
Establishment information: Established in 1859.
Company type: Subsidiary of a foreign company
Business activities: Operates financial services company.
Business type (SIC): Insurance/life; security and commodity services; holding company
Financial profile for 2012: Number of employees, 8,800
Corporate officers: Mark Pearson, Chair. and C.E.O.; Andrew McMahon, Pres.
Board of director: Mark Pearson, Chair.
Giving statement: Giving through the AXA Foundation, Inc.

AXA Foundation, Inc.

(formerly The Equitable Foundation, Inc.)
1290 Ave. of the Americas, 12th Fl.
New York, NY 10104-0101 (212) 314-3662
FAX: (212) 314-4480; E-mail for AXA Achievement Community Scholarships: axacommunity@scholarshipamerica.org; URL: http://www.axa-foundation.com

Establishment information: Established in 1986 in NY.
Donors: The Equitable Cos. Inc.; The Equitable Life Assurance Society of the U.S.; AXA Financial, Inc.; The MONY Group, Inc.
Contact: Faith Frank, Chair., C.E.O., and Pres.
Financial data (yr. ended 12/31/11): Assets, $30,322,240 (M); expenditures, $4,713,851; qualifying distributions, $4,528,412; giving activities include $1,904,064 for 62 grants (high: $335,000; low: $500) and $1,655,883 for 5,455 employee matching gifts.
Purpose and activities: The foundation supports programs designed to improve the quality of life in communities where AXA Financial has a presence. The foundation operates and awards college scholarships through AXA Achievement, a program which provides youth with advice and access to succeed in college.
Fields of interest: Higher education Youth; Minorities.
Programs:

AXA Achievement Community Scholarship Program: The foundation annually awards up to twelve $2,000 college scholarships to high school seniors in each AXA Advisors branch office area. The program is administered by Scholarship America, Inc.

AXA Achievement Scholarship: The foundation, in association with U.S. News & World Report, annually awards 52 $10,000 college scholarships to high school seniors, one in each state, the District of Columbia, and Puerto Rico. Ten top winners receive an additional $15,000. The program is administered by Scholarship America, Inc.

AXA Family Scholarship: The foundation annually awards up to 50 $2,000 college scholarships to high school seniors who are children of AXA Equitable employees or financial professionals. The program is administered by Scholarship America, Inc.

AXA Matching Gifts Program: The foundation matches contributions made by AXA Equitable employees and financial professionals to nonprofit organizations on a one-for-one basis.

Type of support: Employee matching gifts; Employee-related scholarships; General/operating support; Scholarship funds; Scholarships—to individuals.
Geographic limitations: Giving on a national basis with some emphasis in Washington, DC, St. Peter, MN, and New York, NY.
Support limitations: No support for private foundations or religious or international organizations. No grants to individuals (except for scholarships), or for capital campaigns, or media-related projects.
Publications: Application guidelines.
Application information: Unsolicited requests for non-AXA Achievement scholarships are not accepted. Application form required.

Initial approach: Complete online application for AXA Achievement Scholarships and AXA Achievement Community Scholarships
Board meeting date(s): As needed
Deadline(s): Dec. 1 for AXA Achievement Scholarships; Feb. 1 for AXA Achievement Community Scholarships
Final notification: Mid-Mar. for AXA Achievement Scholarships

Officers and Directors:* Faith Frank*, Chair., Pres., and C.E.O.; Jan Goldstein, Secy.; John C. Taroni, Treas.; Mark Pearson; Amy Radin.
Number of staff: 3 full-time professional.
EIN: 131340512
Selected grants: The following grants are a representative sample of this grantmaker's funding activity:
$670,000 to Scholarship America, Saint Peter, MN, 2012. For AXA Achievement U.S. News Scholarship awards.
$602,000 to Scholarship America, Saint Peter, MN, 2012. For AXA Achievement Community Scholarship awards.
$200,005 to American Red Cross National Headquarters, Washington, DC, 2013. For Disaster Responder Program.
$200,000 to National PTA-National Congress of Parents and Teachers, Chicago, IL, 2012. For general support.
$100,000 to National Association for College Admission Counseling, Arlington, VA, 2012. For National College Fairs.

308
Axinn, Veltrop & Harkrider LLP

114 West 47th St.
New York, NY 10036-1508 (212) 728-2200

Company URL: http://www.avhlaw.com
Establishment information: Established in 1997.
Company type: Private company
Business activities: Operates law firm.
Business type (SIC): Legal services
Corporate officer: Lauren S. Albert, Partner
Giving statement: Giving through the Axinn, Veltrop & Harkrider LLP Pro Bono Program.

Axinn, Veltrop & Harkrider LLP Pro Bono Program

114 W. 47th St., Fl. 22
New York, NY 10036-1508 (212) 728-2200
E-mail: LSA@avhlaw.com; URL: http://www.avhlaw.com

Contact: Lauren Albert, Partner
Fields of interest: Legal services.
Type of support: Pro bono services - legal.
Geographic limitations: Giving primarily in areas of company operations in Hartford, CT, Washington, DC, and New York, NY.
Application information: An attorney coordinates pro bono projects.

309
Azavea, Inc.

340 N. 12th St., Ste. 402
Philadelphia, PA 19107-1102
(215) 925-2600
FAX: (215) 925-2663

Company URL: http://www.azavea.com/about-us/
Establishment information: Established in 2000.
Company type: Private company
Business type (SIC): Business services/ miscellaneous
Corporate officer: Robert Cheetham, Pres. and C.E.O
Giving statement: Giving through the Azavea Inc. Contributions Program.

Azavea Inc. Contributions Program

340 N. 12th St., Ste. 402
Philadelphia, PA 19107 (215) 925-2600
E-mail: info@azavea.com; URL: http://www.azavea.com

Purpose and activities: Azavea is a certified B Corporation that donates a percentage of profits to charitable organizations. Support is given primarily in Philadelphia, Pennsylvania.
Fields of interest: Arts; Environment; Human services; International development; Community/ economic development; Computer science.
Type of support: Pro bono services - interactive/ website technology.
Geographic limitations: Giving primarily in Philadelphia, PA; giving also to national and international organizations.

310
AZPB L.P.

(also known as Arizona Diamondbacks)
Chase Field
401 E. Jefferson St.
Phoenix, AZ 85004-2438 (602) 462-6500

Company URL: http://arizona.diamondbacks.mlb.com
Establishment information: Established in 1995.
Company type: Private company
Business activities: Operates professional baseball club.
Business type (SIC): Commercial sports
Corporate officers: Derrick M. Hall, Pres. and C.E.O.; Thomas Harris, Exec. V.P. and C.F.O.; Cullen Maxey, Exec. V.P., Opers.; Nona Lee, Sr. V.P. and Genl. Counsel; Marian Rhodes, Sr. V.P., Human Resources; Josh Rawitch, Sr. V.P., Comms.; Bob Zweig, V.P. and C.I.O.; Craig Bradley, V.P., Finance; Karina Bohn, V.P., Mktg.
Giving statement: Giving through the Arizona Diamondbacks Corporate Giving Program and the Arizona Diamondbacks Foundation.

Arizona Diamondbacks Corporate Giving Program

c/o Community Affairs
P.O. Box 2095
Phoenix, AZ 85001-2095 (602) 462-6500
E-mail: backsfoundation@dbacks.com; Application address for in-kind donation requests: Arizona Diamondbacks, Attn: Community Affairs, 401 E. Jefferson St., Phoenix, AZ 85004; URL: http://arizona.diamondbacks.mlb.com/NASApp/mlb/ari/community/index.jsp

Purpose and activities: As a complement to its foundation, the Arizona Diamondbacks also make charitable contributions of memorabilia and game tickets to nonprofit organizations directly. Support is given primarily in Arizona.
Fields of interest: Education, reading; Hospitals (specialty); Athletics/sports, training; Boys & girls clubs; Children/youth, services; Human services, gift distribution.
Type of support: Donated products; Employee volunteer services; In-kind gifts.
Geographic limitations: Giving primarily in AZ.
Publications: Application guidelines.
Application information: Applications accepted. The Community Affairs department handles giving. Application form required. Applicants should submit the following:
1) name, address and phone number of organization
2) copy of IRS Determination Letter
3) brief history of organization and description of its mission
4) contact person
Proposals should include the number of tickets requested, three game dates (weekdays preferred) for ticket requests, event location and date, and estimated number of attendees for player appearance requests.
Initial approach: Proposal to headquarters
Final notification: 30 days for in-kind donation requests

Arizona Diamondbacks Foundation

(formerly Arizona Diamondbacks Charities, Inc.)
401 E. Jefferson St.
Phoenix, AZ 85004-2438 (602) 462-6500
FAX: (602) 462-6599; E-mail: mroyer@dbacks.com; URL: http://arizona.diamondbacks.mlb.com/ari/community/foundation.jsp

Establishment information: Established in 1997 in AZ.
Contact: Dianne Aguilar, Exec. Dir.
Financial data (yr. ended 12/31/10): Revenue, $1,980,129; assets, $1,020,852 (M); gifts received, $2,118,400; expenditures, $1,949,806; program services expenses, $1,949,806; giving activities include $1,685,935 for grants and $14,244 for grants to individuals.
Purpose and activities: The foundation focuses its efforts on three main areas of need: homelessness, indigent healthcare and children's programs of all types, including education and youth baseball field development.
Fields of interest: Education; Health care; Housing/shelter, homeless; Athletics/sports, baseball; Youth development Children.
Programs:
Diamonds Back Field Building Program: Through this program, the foundation builds and refurbishes baseball fields. Fields are dedicated in Diamondbacks players' names and generally feature new lights, an electronic scoreboard, new fencing and backstops, new irrigation and new dirtwork and/or grass.
Grand Slam Award: The award was established to make a larger impact on community organizations by providing a grant in the amount of $100,000 or more.
Pinch Hitter Fund: The fund provides relief to Arizona youth leagues and organizations for lost or stolen equipment, damaged facilities or for uniform/equipment shortage.
Play Ball Scholarship Fund: The fund provides support to Arizona youth baseball and softball leagues that have players requiring scholarship funding. Funds are awarded for up to $5,000. Organizations cannot receive more than one award per year.
Program Grants: The foundation supports community programs statewide through program grants. These grants are awarded in amounts of between $1,000 and $5,000. All 501(c)(3) nonprofit organizations in Arizona are welcome to apply for funding; however, priority is given to organizations who fall under the Diamondbacks foundation's focus areas (homelessness, indigent healthcare, and children's programs of all types, including education and youth baseball field development).
Type of support: In-kind gifts; Program development; Scholarship funds.
Geographic limitations: Giving limited to AZ.
Support limitations: No support for religious organizations which are purely denominational or sectarian in purpose. No grants for debt reduction.
Publications: Application guidelines.
Application information: Applications accepted. Application form required.
Initial approach: Download application form for Diamonds Back Field Building Program; e-mail to request application for Grand Slam Award and Program Grants; complete online application for Pinch Hitter Fund and Play Ball Scholarship Fund
Board meeting date(s): Biannually
Deadline(s): Dec. 31 for Diamonds Back Field Building Program
Officers and Directors:* Ken Kendrick, Chair.; Michael Kennedy*, Pres.; Derrick M. Hall*, V.P.; Dianne Aguilar, Exec. Dir.; Annette Auxier; Roy Hendrickson, Jr.; Brad Nelsen; Hope H. Ozer; William Perry; Isaac Serna; Michael Yates.
EIN: 860901615

311
Azulay, Horn, & Seiden, LLC

(formerly Azulay & Azulay, P.C.)
205 N. Michigan Ave., 40th Fl.
Chicago, IL 60601-5914 (312) 861-0860

Establishment information: Established in 1982.
Company type: Private company
Business activities: Provides legal services.
Business type (SIC): Legal services
Corporate officer: Ira Azulay, C.E.O.
Giving statement: Giving through the Azulay Family Foundation.

Azulay Family Foundation

203 N. Lasalle St., Ste. 1550
Chicago, IL 60601

Establishment information: Established around 1993.
Donors: Azulay & Azulay, P.C.; Azulay, Horn, Khalaf & Yoo; Y. Judd Azulay.
Contact: Y. Judd Azulay, Pres.
Financial data (yr. ended 12/31/11): Assets, $242,803 (M); gifts received, $53,731; expenditures, $63,863; qualifying distributions, $60,633; giving activities include $60,633 for 35 grants (high: $18,500; low: $27).
Purpose and activities: The foundation supports Jewish agencies and temples.
Fields of interest: Education; Religion.
Type of support: Annual campaigns; Continuing support; General/operating support; Program development; Seed money; Sponsorships.
Support limitations: No grants to individuals.
Application information: Applications accepted. Application form not required.
Initial approach: Proposal
Deadline(s): None
Officers: Y. Judd Azulay, Pres.; Gladys Azulay, V.P.; Ira Azulay, V.P.
EIN: 363740650

312
B & B Holdings, Inc.

(doing business as Arizona Cardinals)
8701 S. Hardy Dr.
Tempe, AZ 85284-2800 (602) 379-0101

Company URL: http://www.azcardinals.com
Establishment information: Established in 1898.
Company type: Private company
Business activities: Operates professional football club.
Business type (SIC): Commercial sports
Corporate officers: William V. Bidwell, Sr., Chair.; Michael J. Bidwell, Pres.; Ron Minegar, Exec. V.P. and C.O.O.; Greg Lee, C.F.O.; Lisa Manning, V.P., Mktg.; David Koeninger, Genl. Counsel; Steve Ryan, V.P., Business Devel.
Board of director: William V. Bidwill, Chair.
Giving statement: Giving through the Arizona Cardinals Corporate Giving Program and the Cardinal Charities, Inc.

Arizona Cardinals Corporate Giving Program

c/o Community Rels. Dept.
8701 S. Hardy Dr.
Tempe, AZ 85284-2800
FAX: (480) 785-7327; Application address: P.O. Box 888, Phoenix, AZ 85001-0888; URL: http://www.azcardinals.com/community

Contact: Lisa Mardeusz
Purpose and activities: The Arizona Cardinals make charitable contributions of memorabilia to nonprofit organizations on a case by case basis. Support is given primarily in Arizona.
Fields of interest: Children, services; Women, centers/services; Minorities/immigrants, centers/services; General charitable giving.
Type of support: General/operating support; In-kind gifts.
Geographic limitations: Giving primarily in AZ.
Application information: Applications accepted. Proposals should be submitted using organization letterhead. Support is limited to 1 contribution per organization during any given year. Application form not required. Applicants should submit the following:
1) name, address and phone number of organization
2) copy of IRS Determination Letter
3) descriptive literature about organization
4) detailed description of project and amount of funding requested
5) contact person
Proposals should indicate the date of the event and the type of fundraiser.
Initial approach: Mail proposal to headquarters

Copies of proposal: 1
Deadline(s): 45 days prior to event

Cardinal Charities, Inc.

P.O. Box 888
Phoenix, AZ 85001-0888
FAX: (480) 785-7327; URL: http://www.azcardinals.com/community/charities.html

Establishment information: Established in 1990 in AZ.
Contact: Michael J. Bidwill, Pres.
Financial data (yr. ended 01/31/12): Revenue, $948,731; assets, $891,258 (M); gifts received, $475,925; expenditures, $761,678; giving activities include $728,527 for grants.
Purpose and activities: The organization seeks to support programs designed to improve the quality of life and enhance opportunities for children, women, and minorities throughout Arizona.
Fields of interest: Children; Minorities; Women.
Geographic limitations: Giving primarily in AZ.
Support limitations: No grants to individuals.
Publications: Application guidelines; Grants list.
Application information: Applications accepted. Application form required.
Initial approach: Request application by fax or mail
Deadline(s): Aug. 1
Officers: William V. Bidwill, Chair.; Michael J. Bidwill, Pres.; William V. Bidwill, Jr., V.P.; Greg Lee, C.F.O.
EIN: 860653587

313
Badger Meter, Inc.

4545 W. Brown Deer Rd.
P.O. Box 245036
Milwaukee, WI 53223 (414) 355-0400
FAX: (414) 355-7499

Company URL: http://www.badgermeter.com/
Establishment information: Established in 1905.
Company type: Public company
Company ticker symbol and exchange: BMI/NYSE
Business activities: Manufactures and markets precision valves, natural gas instrumentation, and mechanical, electro-mechanical, and ultrasonic flow measurement devices.
Business type (SIC): Laboratory apparatus
Financial profile for 2012: Number of employees, 1,366; assets, $290,450,000; sales volume, $319,660,000; pre-tax net income, $43,470,000; expenses, $275,190,000; liabilities, $119,210,000
Corporate officers: Richard A. Meeusen, Chair., Pres., and C.E.O.; Richard E. Johnson, Sr. V.P., Finance, C.F.O., and Treas.; William R. Bergum, V.P., Genl. Counsel, and Secy.; Beverly L.P. Smiley, V.P. and Cont.; Kimberly K. Stoll, V.P., Sales and Mktg.; Horst E. Gras, V.P., Opers
Board of directors: Richard A. Meeusen, Chair.; Ronald H. Dix; Thomas J. Fischer; Gale E. Klappa; Gail A. Lione; Andrew J. Policano; Steven J. Smith; Todd Teske
Subsidiary: Badger Meter, PMI, Tulsa, OK
Divisions: Badger Meter Industrial Div., Milwaukee, WI; Badger Meter Utility Div., Milwaukee, WI
Plants: Rio Rico, AZ; Tulsa, OK
International operations: Canada; Czech Republic; France; Germany; Mexico; Slovakia
Giving statement: Giving through the Badger Meter Foundation, Inc.
Company EIN: 390143280

Badger Meter Foundation, Inc.

P.O. Box 245036
Milwaukee, WI 53224-9536 (414) 371-5704
Application address: 4545 W. Brown Deer Rd., Milwaukee, WI 53223, tel.: (414) 371-5704

Establishment information: Incorporated in 1952 in WI.
Donor: Badger Meter, Inc.
Contact: Ronald H. Dix, Pres. and Dir.
Financial data (yr. ended 12/31/11): Assets, $1,795,377 (M); expenditures, $139,203; qualifying distributions, $129,855; giving activities include $129,845 for 53 grants (high: $25,000; low: $25).
Purpose and activities: The foundation supports organizations involved with arts and culture, education, health, and human services.
Fields of interest: Museums; Performing arts; Arts; Elementary/secondary education; Higher education; Medical school/education; Education; Health care, blood supply; Health care; YM/YWCAs & YM/YWHAs; Human services.
Type of support: Continuing support; Employee matching gifts; General/operating support; Program development; Scholarship funds.
Geographic limitations: Giving limited to WI, with emphasis on the greater Milwaukee area.
Support limitations: No grants to individuals, or for scholarships, fellowships, publications, or conferences; no loans.
Application information: Applications accepted. Application form required. Applicants should submit the following:
1) copy of IRS Determination Letter
2) detailed description of project and amount of funding requested
Initial approach: Letter
Copies of proposal: 1
Board meeting date(s): Apr., and Oct.
Deadline(s): Apr. and Oct.
Officers and Directors:* Ronald H. Dix, Pres.; Richard E. Johnson, V.P.; Kristie Zahn, Secy.; John P. Biever, Treas.; Peter W. Bruce; Richard S. Gallagher; Barbara M. Wiley.
Number of staff: 1 part-time professional.
EIN: 396043635

314
Badger Mining Corporation

409 S. Church St.
P.O. Box 328
Berlin, WI 54923 (920) 361-2388

Company URL: http://www.badgerminingcorp.com
Establishment information: Established in 1979.
Company type: Private company
Business activities: Provides sand and silica mining services.
Business type (SIC): Mining/sand and gravel
Corporate officers: Michael D. Hess, C.E.O.; Timothy J. Wuest, Pres.; Beth J. Nighbor, V.P., Human Resources; Robert L. Brooks, Secy.-Treas.
Giving statement: Giving through the Badger Mining Corporate Associate Scholarship Trust and the Badger Mining Scholarship Trust.

Badger Mining Corporate Associate Scholarship Trust

(formerly BMC Associate Scholarship Trust)
P.O. Box 270
Markesan, WI 53946-0270 (920) 398-2358

Donor: Badger Mining Corp.
Financial data (yr. ended 12/31/11): Assets, $17,089 (M); gifts received, $28,000; expenditures, $34,905; qualifying distributions, $34,500; giving activities include $34,500 for grants.
Purpose and activities: The trust awards college scholarships to employees and the children and spouses of employees of Badger Mining.
Fields of interest: Higher education.
Type of support: Employee-related scholarships.
Geographic limitations: Giving limited to WI.
Application information: Applications accepted. Application form required.
Initial approach: Proposal
Deadline(s): Feb. 1
Trustee: Markesan State Bank.
EIN: 396642667

Badger Mining Scholarship Trust

P.O. Box 270
Markesan, WI 53946-0270 (920) 398-2358

Donor: Badger Mining Corporation.
Financial data (yr. ended 12/31/11): Assets, $40,008 (M); gifts received, $43,000; expenditures, $34,405; qualifying distributions, $34,000; giving activities include $34,000 for grants.
Purpose and activities: The trust awards college scholarships to students attending high schools in Berlin, Markesan, and Taylor, Wisconsin, interested in pursuing studies in mining engineering, engineering curriculum, or environmental science.
Type of support: Scholarships—to individuals.
Geographic limitations: Giving limited to WI.
Application information: Applications accepted. Application form required.
Initial approach: Proposal
Deadline(s): None
Trustee: Markesan State Bank.
EIN: 396433973

315
Bailey Nurseries, Inc.

1325 Bailey Rd.
Newport, MN 55055-1502 (651) 459-9744

Company URL: http://www.baileynursery.com
Establishment information: Established in 1905.
Company type: Private company
Business activities: Sells nursery stock wholesale.
Business type (SIC): Non-durable goods—wholesale
Financial profile for 2010: Number of employees, 500
Corporate officers: Gordon Bailey, Jr., Chair.; Rodney P. Bailey, Co-Pres.; Terri McEnery, Co-Pres.; John Brailey, C.F.O.
Board of director: Gordon Bailey, Jr., Chair.
Plants: Yamhill, OR; Sunnyside, WA
Giving statement: Giving through the Bailey Nursery Foundation.

Bailey Nursery Foundation

c/o John Bailey
1325 Bailey Rd.
Newport, MN 55055-1502

Establishment information: Established in 1997 in MN.
Donor: Bailey Nurseries, Inc.
Financial data (yr. ended 12/31/11): Assets, $547,495 (M); expenditures, $70,703; qualifying

distributions, $66,889; giving activities include $66,889 for grants.
Purpose and activities: The foundation supports organizations involved with arts and culture, education, conservation, and horticulture.
Fields of interest: Museums; Museums (science/technology); Arts; Higher education; Education; Horticulture/garden clubs; Landscaping; Environment.
Type of support: General/operating support.
Geographic limitations: Giving primarily in MN.
Support limitations: No grants to individuals.
Application information: Applications not accepted. Unsolicited requests for funds not accepted.
Officers: Gordon Bailey, Chair.; Rodney P. Bailey, Pres.; John P. Bailey, Secy.; Theresa McEnaney, Treas.
EIN: 411890034

316
Baird & Warner Holding Company

120 S. LaSalle St., 20th Fl.
Chicago, IL 60603 (312) 368-1855
FAX: (312) 368-1490

Company URL: http://www.bairdwarner.com
Establishment information: Established in 1855.
Company type: Private company
Business activities: Operates real estate agency.
Business type (SIC): Real estate agents and managers
Financial profile for 2010: Number of employees, 400
Corporate officers: John W. Baird, Chair.; Stephen W. Baird, Pres. and C.E.O.; Warren Habib, Exec. V.P. and C.F.O.; Charlie Melidosian, V.P. and C.I.O.; Vicki Clavins, V.P. and Cont.; Peter Papakyriacou, V.P., Mktg. and Comms.; Jeanine McShea, V.P., Sales; Wendy A. Dahm, V.P., Human Resources
Board of director: John W. Baird, Chair.
Giving statement: Giving through the Baird Foundation.

Baird Foundation

120 S. LaSalle St., Ste. 2000
Chicago, IL 60603-3594

Establishment information: Established in 1996 in IL.
Donors: Baird & Warner, Inc.; Neil McKay; Olive B. McKay; John Baird.
Financial data (yr. ended 02/28/12): Assets, $1,736,639 (M); gifts received, $270,098; expenditures, $191,954; qualifying distributions, $180,500; giving activities include $180,500 for 26 grants (high: $100,000; low: $100).
Purpose and activities: The foundation supports arboretums and organizations involved with arts and culture, education, land conservation, crime and law enforcement, civic affairs, and Christianity.
Fields of interest: Historic preservation/historical societies; Arts; Higher education; Education; Environment, land resources; Botanical gardens; Crime/law enforcement; Human services; United Ways and Federated Giving Programs; Public affairs; Christian agencies & churches.
Type of support: General/operating support.
Geographic limitations: Giving primarily in Chicago, IL.
Support limitations: No grants to individuals.
Application information: Applications not accepted. Contributes only to pre-selected organizations.
Officers: Olive B. McKay, Pres.; John W. Baird, Secy.-Treas.
EIN: 366042924
Selected grants: The following grants are a representative sample of this grantmaker's funding activity:
$37,500 to Trust for Public Land, San Francisco, CA, 2010.

317
Robert W. Baird and Company

777 E. Wisconsin Ave.
P.O. Box 0672
Milwaukee, WI 53201-0672
(800) 792-2473

Company URL: http://www.rwbaird.com/
Establishment information: Established in 1919.
Company type: Private company
Business activities: Provides investment banking services.
Business type (SIC): Brokers and dealers/security
Corporate officers: Paul Purcell, Chair., Pres., and C.E.O.; C.H. Randolph Lyon, Co-Vice-Chair.; Richard Waid, Co-Vice-Chair.; Dominick P. Zarcone, C.F.O.; Russell P. Schwei, C.P.A., C.O.O.; Mary Ellen Stanek, C.I.O.; Glen F. Hackmann, Genl. Counsel and Secy.
Board of directors: Paul Purcell, Chair.; C.H. Randolph Lyon, Co-Vice-Chair.; Richard Waid, Co-Vice-Chair.
Giving statement: Giving through the Baird Foundation, Inc.

Baird Foundation, Inc.

(formerly Robert W. Baird and Company Foundation, Inc.)
777 E. Wisconsin Ave.
Milwaukee, WI 53202-5302 (414) 298-5199
E-mail: bairdfoundation@rwbaird.com; E-mail for Deanna Singh: dsingh@rwbaird.com; URL: http://www.rwbaird.com/about-baird/culture/baird-foundation.aspx

Establishment information: Established in 1967 in WI.
Donor: Robert W. Baird and Co.
Contact: Deanna Singh, Prog. Off.
Financial data (yr. ended 12/31/11): Assets, $16,447,495 (M); gifts received, $3,964,400; expenditures, $2,753,705; qualifying distributions, $2,736,905; giving activities include $2,736,905 for grants.
Purpose and activities: The foundation supports programs designed to promote education; health and human services; the arts; and diversity and organizations with which Baird associates are actively engaged in order to maximize the impact on those organizations and communities.
Fields of interest: Museums (art); Performing arts; Performing arts, ballet; Performing arts, opera; Arts; Secondary school/education; Higher education; Education; Hospitals (general); Health care; Mental health, grief/bereavement counseling; Cystic fibrosis; Boys & girls clubs; Boy scouts; American Red Cross; YM/YWCAs & YM/YWHAs; Children/youth, services; Human services; Civil/human rights, equal rights; Community/economic development; United Ways and Federated Giving Programs.
Type of support: Annual campaigns; Capital campaigns; Employee matching gifts; Employee volunteer services; General/operating support; Program development.
Geographic limitations: Giving on a national basis, with emphasis on WI; giving also to national and international organizations.
Support limitations: No grants to individuals.
Publications: Annual report.
Application information: Applications not accepted. Contributes only to pre-selected organizations.
Officers: James D. Bell, Jr.*, Chair.; Paul E. Purcell, Pres.; Leslie H. Dixon, V.P.; Peter S. Kies, V.P.; C.H. Randolph Lyon, V.P.; Mary Ellen Stanek, V.P.; Glen F. Hackmann, Secy.; Leonard M. Rush, Treas.
EIN: 396107937
Selected grants: The following grants are a representative sample of this grantmaker's funding activity:
$75,000 to United Way of Greater Milwaukee, Milwaukee, WI, 2010.
$50,000 to United Performing Arts Fund, Milwaukee, WI, 2010.
$30,000 to University of Chicago, Chicago, IL, 2010.
$15,000 to Childrens Health System, Milwaukee, WI, 2010.
$7,500 to Childrens Outing Association, Milwaukee, WI, 2010.
$3,750 to Saint Ann Center for Intergenerational Care, Milwaukee, WI, 2010.
$3,000 to Milwaukee Repertory Theater, Milwaukee, WI, 2010.
$2,500 to Cristo Rey Network, Chicago, IL, 2010.
$2,500 to Social Development Foundation, Milwaukee, WI, 2010.
$1,250 to Tampa Jewish Community Center/Federation, Tampa, FL, 2010.

318
Baker & Baker Real Estate Developers, LLC

1400 Pickens St., 5th Fl.
Columbia, SC 29201-3424 (803) 254-8987

Company URL: http://www.bakerred.com
Establishment information: Established in 1950.
Company type: Private company
Business activities: Operates nonresidential buildings.
Business type (SIC): Real estate operators and lessors
Corporate officer: Vickie Schermbeck, Cont.
Giving statement: Giving through the Baker and Baker Foundation, Inc.

Baker and Baker Foundation, Inc.

P.O. Box 12397
Columbia, SC 29211-2397

Establishment information: Established in 1982 in SC.
Donors: Baker and Baker Real Estate Developer, LLC; Patricia M. Baker.
Financial data (yr. ended 12/31/11): Assets, $106,557 (M); gifts received, $172,500; expenditures, $167,115; qualifying distributions, $165,525; giving activities include $165,525 for 17 grants (high: $103,000; low: $100).
Purpose and activities: The foundation supports community foundations and museums and organizations involved with birth defects, family services, and Judaism.
Fields of interest: Museums; Genetic diseases and disorders; Family services; Foundations (community); United Ways and Federated Giving Programs; Jewish federated giving programs; Jewish agencies & synagogues.

Type of support: General/operating support.
Publications: Annual report.
Application information: Applications not accepted. Unsolicited requests for funds not accepted.
Officers: John Baker, Pres.; Steven M. Anastasion, V.P.
EIN: 570752311
Selected grants: The following grants are a representative sample of this grantmaker's funding activity:
$13,750 to United Way of the Midlands, Columbia, SC, 2010.
$10,000 to Columbia Museum of Art, Columbia, SC, 2010.
$3,500 to American Heart Association, Glen Allen, VA, 2010.
$1,000 to Historic Columbia Foundation, Columbia, SC, 2010.
$1,000 to Keep the Midlands Beautiful, Columbia, SC, 2010.
$1,000 to Sistercare, Columbia, SC, 2010.
$1,000 to Tree of Life Congregation, Columbia, SC, 2010.

319
Baker & Hostetler LLP

PNC Ctr.
1900 E. 9th St., Ste. 3200
Cleveland, OH 44114-3482 (216) 621-0200

Company URL: http://www.bakerlaw.com
Establishment information: Established in 1916.
Company type: Private company
Business activities: Operates law firm.
Business type (SIC): Legal services
Corporate officer: Kevin L. Cash, C.F.O.
Offices: Costa Mesa, Los Angeles, CA; Denver, CO; Washington, DC; Orlando, FL; Chicago, IL; New York, NY; Cincinnati, Cleveland, Columbus, OH; Houston, TX
International operations: Brazil; Mexico
Giving statement: Giving through the Baker & Hostetler LLP Pro Bono Program and the Baker Hostetler Foundation.

Baker & Hostetler LLP Pro Bono Program

PNC Ctr.
1900 E. 9th St., Ste. 3200
Cleveland, OH 44114-3482 (513) 929-3400
FAX: (216) 696-0740;
E-mail: knickolas@bakerlaw.com; URL: http://www.bakerlaw.com/aboutus/probono/

Contact: Kimberlee Nickolas, Recruiting Coord.
Fields of interest: Legal services.
Type of support: Pro bono services - legal.
Geographic limitations: Giving primarily in areas of company operations in Costa Mesa, and Los Angeles, CA, Denver, CO, Washington, DC, Orlando, FL, Chicago, IL, New York, NY, Cincinnati, Cleveland, and Columbus, OH, and Houston, TX, and in Brazil, and Mexico.
Application information: A Pro Bono Committee manages the pro bono program.

The Baker Hostetler Foundation

(formerly Baker & Hostetler Founders Trust)
c/o William J. Culbertson, Esq.
PNC Center
1900 E. 9th St., Rm. 3200
Cleveland, OH 44114-3485

Establishment information: Established in 1965.
Donors: Baker & Hostetler LLP; John D. Drinko†; Hazel P. Hostetler†.
Financial data (yr. ended 12/31/11): Assets, $331,246 (M); gifts received, $150,750; expenditures, $44,332; qualifying distributions, $41,717; giving activities include $40,000 for 5 grants (high: $20,000; low: $5,000).
Purpose and activities: The foundation supports organizations involved with orchestras and law school.
Fields of interest: Performing arts, orchestras; Law school/education.
Type of support: Annual campaigns; General/operating support.
Geographic limitations: Giving primarily in OH.
Support limitations: No grants to individuals or for fellowships; no loans.
Application information: Applications not accepted. Contributes only to pre-selected organizations.
Officers and Directors:* R. Steven Kestner*, Pres.; G. Thomas Ball*, V.P.; Hewitt B. Shaw*, Secy.-Treas.
EIN: 263495996

320
Baker & McKenzie, LLP

1 Prudential Plz.
130 E. Randolph Dr., Ste. 2500
Chicago, IL 60601-6317 (312) 861-8000

Company URL: http://www.bakermckenzie.com
Establishment information: Established in 1949.
Company type: Private company
Business activities: Operates law firm.
Business type (SIC): Legal services
Corporate officers: Eduardo C. Leite, Chair.; Greg C. Walters, Global C.O.O.; Robert (Bob) S. Spencer, Global C.F.O.
International operations: Argentina; Australia; Austria; Azerbaijan; Bahrain; Belgium; Brazil; Canada; Chile; China; Colombia; Czech Republic; Egypt; France; Germany; Hungary; Indonesia; Italy; Japan; Kazakhstan; Luxembourg; Malaysia; Mexico; Netherlands; Philippines; Poland; Qatar; Russia; Saudi Arabia; Singapore; Spain; Sweden; Switzerland; Taiwan; Thailand; Ukraine; United Arab Emirates; United Kingdom; Venezuela; Vietnam
Giving statement: Giving through the Baker & McKenzie, LLP Pro Bono Program.

Baker & McKenzie, LLP Pro Bono Program

1 Prudential Plz.
130 E. Randolph Dr., Ste. 2500
Chicago, IL 60601-6317 (305) 789-8904
FAX: (305) 789-8953;
E-mail: angela.vigil@bakermckenzie.com;
URL: http://www.bakermckenzie.com/globalprobonocommunity/

Contact: Angela Vigil, Partner/ N. American Pro Bono Dir.
Fields of interest: Legal services.
Type of support: Pro bono services - legal.
Geographic limitations: Giving primarily in areas of company operations in Palo Alto, San Diego, and San Francisco, CA, Washington, DC, Miami, FL, Chicago, IL, Dallas, and Houston, TX, and in Argentina, Australia, Austria, Azerbaijan, Bahrain, Belgium, Brazil, Canada, Chile, China, Colombia, Czech Republic, Egypt, France, Germany, Hungary, Indonesia, Italy, Japan, Kazakhstan, Luxembourg, Malaysia, Mexico, Netherlands, Philippines, Poland, Qatar, Russia, Saudi Arabia, Singapore, Spain, Sweden, Switzerland, Taiwan, Thailand, Ukraine, United Arab Emirates, United Kingdom, Venezuela, and Vietnam.
Application information: A Pro Bono Committee manages the pro bono program.

321
Baker Botts L.L.P.

1 Shell Plz.
910 Louisiana St.
Houston, TX 77002-4995 (713) 229-1234

Company URL: http://www.bakerbotts.com
Establishment information: Established in 1840.
Company type: Private company
Business activities: Operates law firm.
Business type (SIC): Legal services
Corporate officers: Lydia Companion, C.F.O.; Mark White, C.A.O.; Charles Szalkowski, Genl. Counsel
Offices: Palo Alto, CA; Washington, DC; New York, NY; Austin, Dallas, Houston, TX
International operations: China; Hong Kong; Russia; Saudi Arabia; United Arab Emirates; United Kingdom
Giving statement: Giving through the Baker Botts L.L.P. Corporate Giving Program.

Baker Botts L.L.P. Corporate Giving Program

1 Shell Plz.
910 Louisiana St.
Houston, TX 77002-4995 (713) 229-1234
FAX: (713) 229-1522; Contact for Pro Bono program: Rob Fowler, Partner; URL: http://www.bakerbotts.com/about/community/

Purpose and activities: Baker Botts makes charitable contributions to nonprofit organizations involved with arts and culture, K-12 education, children and family services, civil rights, and community development.
Fields of interest: Arts; Elementary/secondary education; Legal services; Children/youth, services; Family services; Homeless, human services; Human services; Civil/human rights; Community/economic development; General charitable giving.
Type of support: Employee volunteer services; General/operating support; Pro bono services - legal.
Application information: A Pro Bono Committee manages the Pro Bono Program.

322
Baker Coarsey Enterprises, Inc.

(also known as Coarsey Groves Gift Shop)
6703 N. Armenia Ave.
Tampa, FL 33604-5715

Company type: Private company
Business activities: Operates fruit and vegetable store; produces fruits and vegetables.
Business type (SIC): Farms/vegetable and melon; farms/fruit and nut
Corporate officers: Stephen L. Baker, Pres.; Mary C. Baker, Secy.
Board of directors: Mary C. Baker; Stephen L. Baker; John A. Grant
Giving statement: Giving through the Warren L. Baker Foundation Inc.

Warren L. Baker Foundation Inc.
10025 Orange Grove Dr.
Tampa, FL 33618-4011

Establishment information: Established in 1992 in FL.
Donors: Baker Coarsey Enterprises, Inc.; Mary G. Baker.
Financial data (yr. ended 10/31/11): Assets, $76,762 (M); expenditures, $185,585; qualifying distributions, $68,300; giving activities include $68,300 for 14 grants (high: $10,650; low: $500).
Purpose and activities: The foundation supports organizations involved with financial aid and other areas.
Fields of interest: Scholarships/financial aid; General charitable giving.
Type of support: Scholarship funds.
Geographic limitations: Giving primarily in Tampa, FL.
Support limitations: No grants to individuals.
Application information: Applications not accepted. Unsolicited requests for funds not accepted.
Officer: Stephen L. Baker, Pres.
EIN: 593158655

323
Michael Baker Corporation
Airside Business Park
100 Airside Dr.
Moon Township, PA 15108 (412) 269-6300
FAX: (412) 375-3980

Company URL: http://www.mbakercorp.com
Establishment information: Established in 1940.
Company type: Public company
Company ticker symbol and exchange: BKR/AMEX
Business activities: Provides engineering services; provides consulting services.
Business type (SIC): Engineering, architectural, and surveying services; management and public relations services
Financial profile for 2012: Number of employees, 3,109; assets, $373,410,000; sales volume, $593,400,000; pre-tax net income, $6,740,000; expenses, $589,450,000; liabilities, $148,810,000
Corporate officers: Robert N. Bontempo, Ph.D., Chair.; Michael J. Zugay, C.P.A., Exec. V.P. and C.F.O.; Jeremy Gill, V.P. and C.I.O; David G. Higie, V.P., Corp. Comms.
Board of directors: Robert N. Bontempo, Ph.D., Chair.; Nicholas P. Constantakis; David L. DeNinno; Robert H. Foglesong; Mark E. Kaplan; Pamela S. Pierce; David N. Wormley, Ph.D.
Subsidiaries: Baker Engineering, Inc., Chicago, IL; Baker Engineering NY, Inc., Elmsford, NY; Baker Environmental, Inc., Coraopolis, PA; Michael Baker Jr., Inc., Beaver, PA; Baker Mellon Stuart Construction, Inc., Pittsburgh, PA; Baker Support Services, Inc., Dallas, TX; Baker/MO Services, Inc., Houston, TX
International operations: United Kingdom
Giving statement: Giving through the Michael Baker Corporation Contributions Program and the Michael Baker Corporation Foundation.
Company EIN: 250927646

Michael Baker Corporation Foundation
100 Airside Dr.
Moon Township, PA 15108-2783

Establishment information: Established in 2006 in PA.
Donor: Michael Baker Corporation.
Financial data (yr. ended 12/31/11): Assets, $289,724 (M); gifts received, $258,731; expenditures, $452,112; qualifying distributions, $433,639; giving activities include $433,639 for grants.
Purpose and activities: The foundation supports hospitals and organizations involved with education, children services, community economic development, and engineering.
Fields of interest: Higher education; Education; Hospitals (general); Children, services; Community/economic development; United Ways and Federated Giving Programs; Engineering/technology.
Type of support: Continuing support; Employee matching gifts; General/operating support; Program development; Scholarship funds; Sponsorships.
Geographic limitations: Giving primarily in areas of company operations in PA.
Support limitations: No grants to individuals.
Application information: Applications not accepted. Contributes only to pre-selected organizations.
Officers and Directors:* Bradley L. Mallory, Pres.; H. James McKnight*, Secy.; James M. Kempton*, Treas.; David G. Higie*, Exec. Dir.
EIN: 830448116
Selected grants: The following grants are a representative sample of this grantmaker's funding activity:
$60,000 to United Way of Beaver County, Monaca, PA, 2010.
$36,751 to American Red Cross, Des Moines, IA, 2010. For operating support.
$30,000 to Childrens Hospital of Pittsburgh Foundation, Pittsburgh, PA, 2010.
$25,000 to Geneva College, Beaver Falls, PA, 2010.
$25,000 to Pittsburgh Foundation, Pittsburgh, PA, 2010. For operating support.
$9,895 to American Cancer Society, Oklahoma City, OK, 2010. For operating support.
$8,000 to Allegheny Conference on Community Development, Pittsburgh, PA, 2010.
$5,000 to Carnegie Institute, Pittsburgh, PA, 2010. For program support.
$2,000 to Reach Out and Care Wheels, Bozeman, MT, 2010. For program support.
$2,000 to University of Alaska Anchorage, Anchorage, AK, 2010.

324
Baker Hughes Incorporated
2929 Allen Pkwy., Ste. 2100
Houston, TX 77019-2118 (713) 439-8600
FAX: 302) 655-5049

Company URL: http://www.bakerhughes.com
Establishment information: Established in 1987.
Company type: Public company
Company ticker symbol and exchange: BHI/NYSE
International Securities Identification Number: US0572241075
Business activities: Provides oilfield downhole tool technologies, products, and services; sells integrated chemical technology solutions; designs and manufactures water treatment systems; provides solid/liquid separation equipment and systems; manufactures centrifuges and specialty filters.
Business type (SIC): Machinery/construction, mining, and materials handling; chemicals/industrial inorganic; machinery/general industry; machinery/refrigeration and service industry
Financial profile for 2012: Assets, $26,700,000,000; sales volume, $21,400,000,000
Fortune 1000 ranking: 2012—135th in revenues, 155th in profits, and 203rd in assets
Forbes 2000 ranking: 2012—440th in sales, 466th in profits, and 808th in assets
Corporate officers: Martin S. Craighead, Chair. and C.E.O.; Peter A. Ragauss, Sr. V.P. and C.F.O.; Alan R. Crain, Sr. V.P. and Genl. Counsel; Didier Charreton, V.P., Human Resources
Board of directors: Martin Craighead, Chair.; Larry D. Brady; Clarence P. Cazalot, Jr.; Lynn Elsenhans; Anthony G. Fernandes; Claire W. Gargalli; Pierre H. Jungels, Ph.D.; James A. Lash; J. Larry Nichols; James W. Stewart; Charles L. Watson
Subsidiary: Western Atlas Inc., Houston, TX
International operations: Argentina; Australia; Austria; Brazil; Canada; China; Germany; Malaysia; Mexico; Netherlands; Singapore; United Kingdom; Venezuela
Historic mergers: Petrolite Corporation (July 2, 1997)
Giving statement: Giving through the Baker Hughes Foundation.
Company EIN: 760207995

Baker Hughes Foundation
P.O. Box 3045
Houston, TX 77253-3045

Establishment information: Established in 1994 in TX.
Donor: Baker Hughes Inc.
Contact: Isaac C. Kerridge, Exec. Dir.
Financial data (yr. ended 12/31/11): Assets, $4,293,834 (M); gifts received, $2,588,558; expenditures, $1,690,009; qualifying distributions, $1,688,769; giving activities include $1,685,820 for grants.
Purpose and activities: The foundation supports nonprofit organizations on a case by case basis in areas of company operations.
Fields of interest: Arts; Higher education; Education; Health care; Food services; Boys & girls clubs; American Red Cross; YM/YWCAs & YM/YWHAs; Children/youth, services; Human services; United Ways and Federated Giving Programs.
Program:
Matching Gifts Program: The foundation matches contributions made by employees of Baker Hughes to nonprofit organizations and academic institutions on a one-for-one basis.
Type of support: Employee matching gifts; Scholarship funds.
Geographic limitations: Giving in areas of company operations in the greater Tulsa, OK, and Houston, TX, areas; and on an international basis in Angola.
Support limitations: No support for religious or political organizations or secondary schools.
Application information: Applications accepted. Application form not required. Applicants should submit the following:
1) detailed description of project and amount of funding requested
2) copy of IRS Determination Letter
Initial approach: Proposal
Copies of proposal: 1
Deadline(s): None
Officers and Trustees:* Chad C. Deaton, Chair. and Pres.; Didier Charreton, V.P.; Alan R. Crain, Jr.*, V.P.; Peter A. Ragauss*, V.P.; Sandra E. Alford, Secy.-Treas.; Isaac C. Kerridge*, Exec. Dir.
Number of staff: 1 full-time professional.
EIN: 760441292
Selected grants: The following grants are a representative sample of this grantmaker's funding activity:

$393,291 to Institute of International Education, New York, NY, 2011. For general support.
$160,000 to Pennsylvania State University, University Park, PA, 2011. For general support.
$62,250 to Alley Theater, Houston, TX, 2011. For general support.
$47,501 to Susan G. Komen for the Cure, Houston, TX, 2011. For general support.
$29,501 to Junior Achievement of Southeast Texas, Houston, TX, 2011. For general support.
$15,000 to Holocaust Museum Houston, Houston, TX, 2011. For general support.
$10,000 to Asia Society Texas Center, Houston, TX, 2011. For general support.
$10,000 to Interfaith Ministries for Greater Houston, Houston, TX, 2011. For general support.
$10,000 to Memorial Hermann Foundation, Houston, TX, 2011. For general support.
$2,600 to Sam Houston State University, Huntsville, TX, 2011. For general support.

325
Baker, Donelson, Bearman, Caldwell & Berkowitz, PC

1st Tennessee Bldg.
165 Madison Ave., Ste. 2000
Memphis, TN 38103-2723 (901) 526-2000

Company URL: http://www.bakerdonelson.com
Establishment information: Established in 1888.
Company type: Private company
Business activities: Operates law firm.
Business type (SIC): Legal services
Corporate officers: Ben C. Adams, Chair. and C.E.O.; Jerry Stauffer, Pres. and C.O.O.; John D. Green, C.I.O.; Joyce Rhodes, Admin.
Board of director: Ben C. Adams, Chair.
Offices: Birmingham, Montgomery, AL; Washington, DC; Atlanta, Macon, GA; Baton Rouge, Mandeville, New Orleans, LA; Jackson, MS; Chattanooga, Huntsville, Johnson City, Knoxville, Memphis, Nashville, TN
International operations: United Kingdom
Giving statement: Giving through the Baker, Donelson, Bearman, Caldwell & Berkowitz, PC Corporate Giving Program.

Baker, Donelson, Bearman, Caldwell & Berkowitz, PC Corporate Giving Program

1st Tennessee Bldg., Ste. 2000
165 Madison Ave.
Memphis, TN 38103-2723 (205) 328-0480
Contact for Pro Bono program: Lisa Borden, Pro Bono Shareholder, tel.: (205) 244-3803, fax: (205) 488-3803, e-mail: lborden@bakerdonelson.com; URL: http://www.bakerdonelson.com/civic-involvement-ourfirm-practices/

Purpose and activities: Baker, Donelson, Bearman, Caldwell & Berkowitz makes charitable contributions to nonprofit organizations involved with the arts, health, youth development, and human services.
Fields of interest: Arts; Health care; Health organizations; Legal services; Youth development; Human services.
Type of support: Employee volunteer services; General/operating support; Pro bono services - legal.
Application information: A Pro Bono Committee manages the Pro Bono Program.

326
Bakewell Corp.

7800 Forsyth Blvd., 8th Fl.
St. Louis, MO 63105-3311 (314) 862-5555

Establishment information: Established in 1950.
Company type: Private company
Business activities: Provides non-residential building management and real estate brokerage services.
Business type (SIC): Real estate operators and lessors; real estate agents and managers
Financial profile for 2009: Number of employees, 19
Corporate officer: Edward L. Bakewell Lii, Mgr.
Giving statement: Giving through the Bakewell Foundation.

The Bakewell Foundation

(formerly The Edward L. Bakewell, Jr. Family Foundation)
7800 Forsyth Blvd., 8th Fl.
St. Louis, MO 63105-3311 (314) 862-5555

Establishment information: Established in 1987 in MO.
Donors: Bakewell Corp.; Edward L. Bakewell, Jr.; Edward L. Bakewell III.
Contact: Richard W. Meier, Secy.
Financial data (yr. ended 12/31/11): Assets, $6,484,831 (M); gifts received, $300,000; expenditures, $344,548; qualifying distributions, $318,000; giving activities include $318,000 for grants.
Purpose and activities: The foundation supports museums, hospitals, and health clinics and organizations involved with higher education and sustainability research.
Fields of interest: Museums; Higher education; Environment, research; Environment, natural resources; Environment, water resources; Hospitals (general); Health care, clinics/centers.
Type of support: General/operating support.
Geographic limitations: Giving primarily in CA, CO, FL, MO, and WY.
Application information: Applications accepted. Application form not required. Applicants should submit the following:
1) detailed description of project and amount of funding requested
Initial approach: Proposal
Deadline(s): None
Officers and Directors:* Edward L. Bakewell III*, Pres.; Richard W. Meier*, Secy.
EIN: 431434313
Selected grants: The following grants are a representative sample of this grantmaker's funding activity:
$125,000 to University of Southern California, Los Angeles, CA, 2010.
$2,500 to Neighborhood Health Clinic, Naples, FL, 2010. For general operating funds.
$1,500 to Rocky Mountain Institute, Snowmass, CO, 2010. For general operating funds.

327
Balch & Bingham LLP

1901 6th Ave. N., Ste. 1500
Birmingham, AL 35203-4642
(205) 251-8100

Company URL: http://www.balch.com
Establishment information: Established in 1922.
Company type: Private company
Business activities: Operates law firm.
Business type (SIC): Legal services
Corporate officer: Alan T. Rogers, Partner
Offices: Birmingham, Montgomery, AL; Washington, DC; Atlanta, GA; Gulfport, Jackson, MS
Giving statement: Giving through the Balch & Bingham LLP Corporate Giving Program.

Balch & Bingham LLP Corporate Giving Program

1901 6th Ave. N., Ste. 1500
Birmingham, AL 35203-4642 (205) 251-8100
FAX: (205) 488-5713; URL: http://www.balch.com/about/community/

Purpose and activities: Balch & Bingham make charitable contributions to K-12 educational institutions and nonprofit organizations involved with youth development.
Fields of interest: Elementary/secondary education; Legal services; Youth development.
Type of support: Employee volunteer services; Pro bono services - legal; Sponsorships.

328
Ball Corporation

10 Longs Peak Dr.
P.O.Box 5000
Broomfield, CO 80021-2510
(303) 469-3131
FAX: (303) 460-2315

Company URL: http://www.ball.com
Establishment information: Established in 1880.
Company type: Public company
Company ticker symbol and exchange: BLL/NYSE
International Securities Identification Number: US0584981064
Business activities: Manufactures metal and plastic packaging; manufactures and provides aerospace and other technologies and services.
Business type (SIC): Metal containers; plastic products/miscellaneous; aircraft and parts
Financial profile for 2012: Number of employees, 15,000; assets, $7,507,100,000; sales volume, $8,735,700,000; pre-tax net income, $595,600,000; expenses, $7,945,200,000; liabilities, $6,329,500,000
Fortune 1000 ranking: 2012—301st in revenues, 392nd in profits, and 466th in assets
Corporate officers: John A. Hayes, Chair., Pres. and C.E.O.; Scott C. Morrison, Sr. V.P. and C.F.O.; Lisa A. Pauley, Sr. V.P., Human Resources, and Admin.; Jeff A. Knobel, V.P. and Treas.; Shawn M. Barker, V.P. and Cont.; Charles E. Baker, V.P., Genl. Counsel, and Corp. Secy.; James N. Peterson, V.P., Mktg.
Board of directors: John A. Hayes, Chair.; Robert W. Alspaugh; Hanno C. Fiedler; R. David Hoover; John F. Lehman; Pedro Henrique Mariani; Georgia R. Nelson; Jan Nicholson; George M. Smart; Theodore M. Solso; Stuart A. Taylor II
Subsidiary: Ball Aerospace & Technologies Corp., Broomfield, CO
International operations: Canada
Giving statement: Giving through the Ball Corporation Contributions Program.
Company EIN: 350160610

Ball Corporation Contributions Program

P.O. Box 5000
Broomfield, CO 80038-5000 (303) 460-2126
FAX: (303) 460-2127

Contact: Harold L. Sohn, Sr. V.P., Corp. Rels.
Financial data (yr. ended 12/31/09): Total giving, $2,249,014, including $1,873,891 for grants and $375,123 for employee matching gifts.
Purpose and activities: Ball makes charitable contributions to nonprofit organizations on a case by case basis. Support is given primarily in areas of company operations.
Fields of interest: General charitable giving.
Type of support: Employee matching gifts; General/operating support.
Geographic limitations: Giving primarily in areas of company operations, with emphasis on Broomfield, CO.
Support limitations: No grants to individuals.
Publications: Newsletter.
Application information: Applications accepted. The Corporate Relations Department handles giving. Application form not required. Applicants should submit the following:
1) detailed description of project and amount of funding requested
Initial approach: Mail proposal to headquarters
Copies of proposal: 1
Deadline(s): None
Final notification: 2 weeks if approved
Number of staff: 2 full-time professional.

329
Ballard Spahr LLP

1735 Market St., 51st Fl.
Philadelphia, PA 19103-7599
(215) 665-8500

Company URL: http://www.ballardspahr.com
Establishment information: Established in 1885.
Company type: Private company
Business activities: Operates law firm.
Business type (SIC): Legal services
Offices: Phoenix, AZ; Los Angeles, San Diego, CA; Denver, CO; Wilmington, DE; Washington, DC; Atlanta, GA; Baltimore, Bethesda, MD; Las Vegas, NV; Cherry Hill, NJ; Philadelphia, PA; Salt Lake City, UT
Giving statement: Giving through the Ballard Spahr LLP Pro Bono Program.

Ballard Spahr LLP Pro Bono Program

1735 Market St., 51st Fl.
Philadelphia, PA 19103-7599 (215) 864-8912
FAX: (215) 864-8999;
E-mail: scanlonm@ballardspahr.com; URL: http://www.ballardspahr.com/en/Pro_Bono.aspx

Contact: Mary Gay Scanlon, Pro Bono Counsel
Fields of interest: Legal services.
Type of support: Pro bono services - legal.
Geographic limitations: Giving primarily in areas of company operations in Phoenix, AZ, Los Angeles, and San Diego, CA, Denver, CO, Washington, DC, Wilmington, DE, Atlanta, GA, Baltimore, and Bethesda, MD, Cherry Hill, NJ, Las Vegas, NV, Philadelphia, PA, and Salt Lake City, UT.
Application information: A Pro Bono Committee manages the pro bono program.

330
Bally Total Fitness Holding Corporation

8700 W. Bryn Mawr Ave., 2nd Fl.
Chicago, IL 60631-3512 (773) 380-3000
FAX: (773) 380-7679

Company URL: http://www.ballyfitness.com
Establishment information: Established in 1983.
Company type: Private company
Business activities: Operates fitness centers.
Business type (SIC): Amusement and recreation services/miscellaneous
Financial profile for 2010: Number of employees, 19,200
Corporate officers: Don R. Kornstein, Chair.; Michael Sheehan, C.E.O.; Steven D. Barnhart, Sr. V.P. and C.F.O.
Board of directors: Don R. Kornstein, Chair.; Michael Sheehan
Subsidiary: Bally Total Fitness Corp., Chicago, IL
Giving statement: Giving through the Bally Total Fitness Holding Corporation Contributions Program.
Company EIN: 363228107

Bally Total Fitness Holding Corporation Contributions Program

c/o Public Rels. Dept.
8700 W. Bryn Mawr Ave.
Chicago, IL 60631-3512 (773) 380-3000
FAX: (773) 399-0476; URL: http://www.ballyfitness.com/bfit-communities.aspx

Contact: Karyn Petkus
Purpose and activities: Bally Total Fitness makes charitable contributions to nonprofit organizations on a case by case basis. Support is given primarily in areas of company operations.
Fields of interest: General charitable giving.
Program:
BFIT Communities Program: Bally Total Fitness supports programs designed to help communities get physically fit. The company donates used equipment to charitable organizations.
Type of support: Cause-related marketing; Donated equipment; Sponsorships.
Geographic limitations: Giving primarily in areas of company operations.
Application information: Applications accepted. Application form required.
Initial approach: Download application form and fax to headquarters for equipment donations

331
Baltimore County Savings Bank, M.H.C.

4111 E. Joppa Rd., Ste. 300
Baltimore, MD 21236-2289
(410) 256-5000

Company URL: http://www.baltcosavings.com
Establishment information: Established in 1955.
Company type: Subsidiary of a public company
Business activities: Operates federal savings institution.
Business type (SIC): Savings institutions
Corporate officer: Joseph J. Bouffard, Pres. and C.E.O.
Giving statement: Giving through the Baltimore County Savings Bank Foundation.

Baltimore County Savings Bank Foundation

(also known as The BCSB Foundation)
4111 E. Joppa Rd., Ste. 300
Baltimore, MD 21236-2289
URL: http://www.baltcosavings.com/about_bcsb/charitable_foundation.asp

Establishment information: Established in 2003 in MD.
Financial data (yr. ended 09/30/12): Assets, $258,760 (M); expenditures, $4,962; qualifying distributions, $4,060; giving activities include $4,060 for grants.
Fields of interest: Education; Human services.
Support limitations: No grants to individuals.
Application information: Applications not accepted. Unsolicited requests for funds not accepted.
Officers: David M. Meadows, Secy.; Bonnie M. Klein, Treas.
Directors: H. Adrian Cox; Frank W. Dunton; Henry V. Kahl; William J. Kappauf, Jr.; Elmer Klein; Michael C. Klein; Vincent Pecora; George Wilbanks.
EIN: 522108339

332
The Baltimore Equitable Society

1 Charles Ctr.
100 N. Charles St., Ste. 640
Baltimore, MD 21201-3808
(410) 727-1794

Company URL: http://www.1794insurance.com/index.html
Establishment information: Established in 1794.
Company type: Private company
Business activities: Sells insurance.
Business type (SIC): Insurance agents, brokers, and services
Financial profile for 2011: Assets, $123,204,000; liabilities, $52,805,000
Corporate officers: Sharon V. Woodward, Pres. and Treas.; Alice P. Jones, Secy.
Board of directors: Richard O. Berndt; George L. Bunting, Jr.; Juliet A. Eurich; Freeman A. Hrabowski III; Hugh W. Mohler; Philip J. Raub; Arnold I. Richman; James S. Riepe; Marjorie Rodgers Cheshire
Giving statement: Giving through the Baltimore Equitable Insurance Foundation.

Baltimore Equitable Insurance Foundation

100 N. Charles St., Ste. 640
Baltimore, MD 21201-1794 (410) 727-1794
FAX: (410) 539-1073

Establishment information: Established in 1990 in MD.
Donor: The Baltimore Equitable Society.
Contact: Timothy J. Swartz, Pres. and Treas.
Financial data (yr. ended 12/31/11): Assets, $4,782,736 (M); expenditures, $271,715; qualifying distributions, $261,100; giving activities include $261,100 for grants.
Purpose and activities: The foundation supports organizations involved with elementary education, health, human services, and community development.
Fields of interest: Elementary school/education; Health care; Housing/shelter; Human services;

Community/economic development; United Ways and Federated Giving Programs.
Type of support: General/operating support; Program development.
Geographic limitations: Giving limited to the Baltimore, MD, area.
Support limitations: No grants to individuals.
Application information: Applications accepted. Application form required.
Initial approach: Contact foundation for application form
Board meeting date(s): Quarterly
Deadline(s): Jan. 1, Apr. 1, July 1, and Oct. 1
Officers and Directors:* Richard O. Berndt*, Chair.; Sharon V. Woodward*, Pres. and Treas.; Juliet A. Eurich*, Secy.; George L. Hunting, Jr.; Betsy Nelson.
EIN: 521645633

333
The Baltimore Life Insurance Company

(also known as The Baltimore Life Companies)
10075 Red Run Blvd.
Owings Mills, MD 21117-4871
(410) 581-6600

Company URL: http://www.baltlife.com
Establishment information: Established in 1882.
Company type: Private company
Business activities: Sells life insurance.
Business type (SIC): Insurance/life
Corporate officers: Gerard E. Holthaus, C.P.A., Chair.; David K. Ficca, Pres. and C.E.O.; John J. Patterson, Exec. V.P. and C.O.O.; Richard A. Spencer III, Sr. V.P. and C.F.O.; Harold B. Rojas, Esq., Sr. V.P., Genl. Counsel, and Secy.; Tiffany T. King, C.P.A., V.P. and Cont.; James P. Seeberger, Jr., V.P., Admin.; Garry H. Voith, V.P., Mktg. and Comms.; Thomas R. Cranston, Treas.
Board of directors: Gerard E. Holthaus, C.P.A., Chair.; Stephen C. Achuff, M.D.; Nancy S. Brodie; Paul J. Chew; Robert W. Crandall; David K. Ficca; John F. Gaburick, C.P.A.; Benjamin H. Griswold IV; Robert J. Lawless; John A. MacColl; Walter D. Pinkard, Jr.; Stephanie L. Reel
Subsidiaries: Baltimore Financial Brokerage, Owings Mills, MD; Life of Maryland Inc., Owings Mills, MD
Giving statement: Giving through the Baltimore Life Companies Contributions Program.

The Baltimore Life Companies Contributions Program

10075 Red Run Blvd.
Owings Mills, MD 21117-4865
URL: http://www.baltlife.com/aboutcorp_citizenship.aspx

Purpose and activities: Baltimore Life makes charitable contributions to nonprofit organizations involved with family, safety, and community enhancement. Support is given primarily in Delaware, Maryland, and Pennsylvania.
Fields of interest: Safety/disasters; Family services; Community/economic development.
Program:
Community Grants Program: Baltimore Life awards $500 grants to programs designed to enhance family, safety, and community. Special emphasis is directed toward programs designed to assist distressed families; enhance public safety and the community; and combat community deterioration. The program is open to certified nonprofit organizations and organizations under the direction of government agencies such as public libraries, senior centers, homeless shelters, and similar organizations.
Type of support: Employee volunteer services; General/operating support.
Geographic limitations: Giving primarily in DE, MD, and PA.
Officer: L. John Pearson, Chair., Pres., and C.E.O.

334
Baltimore Orioles L.P.

333 W. Camden St.
Baltimore, MD 21201 (410) 685-9800
FAX: (410) 547-6277

Company URL: http://baltimore.orioles.mlb.com
Establishment information: Established in 1901.
Company type: Private company
Business activities: Operates professional baseball club.
Business type (SIC): Commercial sports; amusement and recreation services/miscellaneous
Financial profile for 2010: Number of employees, 135
Corporate officers: Peter G. Angelos, Chair. and C.E.O.; Thomas L. Clancy, Jr., Vice-Chair.; Doug Duennes, Exec. V.P., Opers.; Robert A. Ames, C.P.A., V.P. and C.F.O.; Gregory E. Bader, V.P., Mktg. and Comms.; Michael D. Hoppes, C.P.A., V.P., Finance; H. Russell Smouse, Genl. Counsel
Board of director: Peter G. Angelos, Chair.
Giving statement: Giving through the Baltimore Orioles Corporate Giving Program and the Baltimore Orioles Foundation, Inc.

Baltimore Orioles Corporate Giving Program

c/o Community Outreach/Donations
333 W. Camden St.
Baltimore, MD 21201-2496 (410) 685-9800
URL: http://baltimore.orioles.mlb.com/bal/community/fundraising.jsp

Purpose and activities: As a complement to its foundation, the Baltimore Orioles also make charitable contributions of memorabilia to nonprofit organizations directly. Support is limited to Washington, DC, Delaware, Maryland, southern Pennsylvania, and Virginia.
Fields of interest: Education; Athletics/sports, amateur leagues; Youth development; General charitable giving.
Type of support: In-kind gifts.
Geographic limitations: Giving limited to Washington, DC, DE, MD, southern PA, and VA.
Support limitations: No grants to individuals.
Publications: Application guidelines.
Application information: Applications accepted. Proposals should be submitted using organization letterhead. Donation requests are not accepted via e-mail. The Community Outreach Department handles giving. Application form not required. Applicants should submit the following:
1) name, address and phone number of organization
2) copy of IRS Determination Letter
3) contact person
Proposals should indicate the date of the event and how the proceeds will be used.
Initial approach: Mail proposal to headquarters
Deadline(s): 6 weeks prior to event

The Baltimore Orioles Foundation, Inc.

333 W. Camden St.
Baltimore, MD 21201-2435
URL: http://baltimore.orioles.mlb.com/bal/community/giving.jsp

Establishment information: Established around 1965 in MD.
Donors: Orioles Reach; Baltimore Orioles L.P.; ARAMARK Corp.; Touch Em All Foundation; Teammates for Kids; Azek Trim Boards; Kris Benson; Jeremy Fefel; Melvin Mora; Miguel Tejada; Brian Roberts.
Financial data (yr. ended 10/31/11): Assets, $759,700 (M); gifts received, $615,782; expenditures, $548,734; qualifying distributions, $357,900; giving activities include $357,900 for grants.
Purpose and activities: The foundation supports sports museums and community foundations and organizations involved with orchestras, higher education, health, baseball, youth development, and human services.
Fields of interest: Museums (sports/hobby); Performing arts, orchestras; Higher education; Health care; Athletics/sports, baseball; Youth development; Human services; Foundations (community).
Type of support: General/operating support.
Geographic limitations: Giving primarily in the Baltimore, MD area.
Support limitations: No grants to individuals.
Application information: Applications accepted. Application form not required.
Initial approach: Proposal
Deadline(s): None
Directors: Georgia K. Angelos; John Peter Angelos; Louis Francis Angelos; Peter G. Angelos; Joseph E. Foss.
EIN: 526058645
Selected grants: The following grants are a representative sample of this grantmaker's funding activity:
$75,000 to Baltimore Symphony Orchestra, Baltimore, MD, 2010.
$30,000 to Baltimore Community Foundation, Baltimore, MD, 2010.
$25,000 to Jackie Robinson Foundation, New York, NY, 2010.
$5,000 to Kennedy Krieger Institute, Baltimore, MD, 2010.
$1,690 to University of Maryland Medical System, Baltimore, MD, 2010.

335
Baltimore Ravens L.P.

1 Winning Dr.
Owings Mills, MD 21117-4776
(410) 701-4000
FAX: (410) 701-4140

Company URL: http://www.baltimoreravens.com
Establishment information: Established in 1946.
Company type: Private company
Business activities: Operates professional football club.
Business type (SIC): Commercial sports
Financial profile for 2010: Number of employees, 125
Corporate officers: Richard W. Cass, Pres.; Jeffrey Goering, V.P. and C.F.O.; Bob Eller, V.P., Opers.; Gabrielle Dow, V.P., Mktg.; Jim Coller, Cont.
Giving statement: Giving through the Baltimore Ravens Corporate Giving Program and the Ravens All-Community Team Foundation, Inc.

Baltimore Ravens Corporate Giving Program

c/o Community Rels.
1 Winning Dr.
Owings Mills, MD 21117-4776
Tel. for Ravens Champions Athlete of the Week: (410) 701-4117.; URL: http://www.baltimoreravens.com/News/Community/Contact_Community_Relations.aspx

Purpose and activities: As a complement to its foundation, the Baltimore Ravens also makes charitable contributions of team memorabilia to nonprofit organizations directly, and provides player, staff, and coach appearances. Support is given primarily in areas of company operations in Maryland.
Fields of interest: Elementary/secondary education; Athletics/sports, training; Athletics/sports, school programs; Youth, services; Community/economic development; United Ways and Federated Giving Programs.
Programs:
NFL Community Quarterback: The Community Quarterback Award program - funded by NFL Charities - salutes Maryland volunteers who exhibit exceptional leadership, dedication and commitment to bettering their local communities. Each Community Quarterback for 2011 received tickets for themselves and a guest, as well as Ravens memorabilia and merchandise, a trophy and a $2,500 grant to their respective nonprofit organization. The three recipients were also recognized on the field prior to kickoff.
Ravens Champions Athlete of the Week: The Baltimore Ravens are promoting academic, athletic, and community excellence through the Ravens Champions Athlete of the Week, a program that recognizes the athletic achievements of Baltimore area youth and promotes local high school athletics. Eight times during the NFL regular season (corresponding with Ravens home games), two student athletes (a male and a female athlete) are awarded the honor of Ravens Champions Athlete of the Week, presented by Toyota. Potential candidates include all Baltimore area high school athletes. Benefits awarded to Ravens Champions Athletes of the Week include tickets to that week's home game, official media recognition, and a $500 donation to the recipients' athletic programs.
Ravens High School Coach of the Week: Presented by Toyota, the Ravens High School Coach of the Week program honors a Baltimore-area high school football coach who makes a significant impact on his or her athletes. Weekly recipients receive a $2,000 donation to the school's football program, an award certificate signed by Ravens head coach John Harbaugh, and a specially designed hat.
Type of support: Donated products; Employee volunteer services; In-kind gifts; Loaned talent.
Geographic limitations: Giving primarily in areas of company operations in MD.
Publications: Application guidelines.
Application information: Applications accepted. Letters should be submitted using organization letterhead. Requests are not accepted via phone, fax, or e-mail. Applications are limited to 1 request per organization during any given year. Donations are in the form of team memorabilia. The Community Relations Department handles giving. Application form not required. Applicants should submit the following:
1) copy of IRS Determination Letter
2) brief history of organization and description of its mission
3) descriptive literature about organization
Letters should include the date of the event.
Initial approach: Mail proposal to headquarters
Deadline(s): 6 weeks prior to event

Ravens All-Community Team Foundation, Inc.

(formerly Ravens Foundation for Families, Inc.)
1 Winning Dr.
Owings Mills, MD 21117-4776 (410) 701-4166

Establishment information: Established in 1996 in MD.
Financial data (yr. ended 12/31/11): Revenue, $925,746; assets, $1,056,702 (M); gifts received, $915,471; expenditures, $1,107,399; giving activities include $888,928 for grants and $50,000 for grants to individuals.
Purpose and activities: The foundation seeks to change fundamental ills with which Baltimore, MD area families must deal in the pursuit of healthy and productive lives for themselves and their community.
Fields of interest: Family services.
Program:
Baltimore Ravens Scholarship Program: Five $5,000 scholarship enable local youth to continue their education on a collegiate level. Applicants must be U.S. citizens or permanent residents. This scholarship is renewable.
Geographic limitations: Giving primarily in the Baltimore, MD area.
Application information: Applications accepted. Application form required.
Initial approach: Contact foundation for application form
Deadline(s): None
Officers: Richard Cass, Chair.; Kevin Byrne, Vice-Chair.; Rebecca Koppelman, Treas.; Melanie Legrande, Exec. Dir.
Board Members: Ed Burchell; Marques Charbonnet; Donald Diraddo; Kim Ferguson; Jeff Goering; Erin Howland; Elizabeth Jackson; Jerry Rosburg.
EIN: 521987065

336
BancorpSouth Bank

1 Mississippi Plz.
201 S. Spring St.
Tupelo, MS 38804-4826 (662) 680-2000

Company URL: http://www.bancorpsouth.com
Establishment information: Established in 1876.
Company type: Subsidiary of a public company
Business activities: Operates commercial bank.
Business type (SIC): Banks/commercial
Corporate officers: Aubrey B. Patterson, Jr., Chair. and C.E.O.; Gordon R. Lewis, Vice-Chair.; James Virgil Kelly, Pres. and C.O.O.; Cathy S. Freeman, Exec. V.P. and Corp. Secy.
Board of directors: Aubrey B. Patterson, Jr., Chair.; Gordon Lewis, Vice-Chair.
Giving statement: Giving through the BancorpSouth Bank Corporate Giving Program and the BancorpSouth Foundation.

BancorpSouth Foundation

P.O. Box 789
Tupelo, MS 38802-0789 (662) 680-2000

Establishment information: Established in 1999 in MS.
Donor: BancorpSouth, Inc.
Contact: Gary Bonds
Financial data (yr. ended 12/31/11): Assets, $2,991,394 (M); expenditures, $158,907; qualifying distributions, $136,900; giving activities include $136,900 for 18 grants (high: $25,000; low: $500).
Purpose and activities: The foundation supports organizations involved with orchestras, secondary and higher education, legal aid, housing, youth development, and human services.
Fields of interest: Youth development; Human services.
Type of support: General/operating support.
Application information: Applications accepted. Application form required. Applicants should submit the following:
1) detailed description of project and amount of funding requested
Initial approach: Letter
Deadline(s): None
Trustee: BancorpSouth, Inc.
EIN: 646217237

337
BancTrust Financial Group, Inc.

(formerly First National Bank of Brewton, Alabama)
100 St. Joseph St.
P.O. Box 3067
Mobile, AL 36602-3615 (251) 431-7800
FAX: (251) 431-7851

Company URL: http://www.banctrustfinancialgroupinc.com
Establishment information: Established in 1986.
Company type: Public company
Company ticker symbol and exchange: BTFG/NASDAQ
Business activities: Operates commercial bank.
Business type (SIC): Banks/commercial
Financial profile for 2011: Number of employees, 540; assets, $2,031,880,000; pre-tax net income, -$40,480,000; liabilities, $1,917,600,000
Corporate officers: W. Bibb Lamar, Jr., Chair., Pres., and C.E.O.; F. Michael Johnson, Exec. V.P., C.F.O., and Secy.; J. Dianne Hollingsworth, Sr. V.P., Human Resources; Mark Thompson, V.P., Finance; Rebecca S. Minto, V.P., Mktg.
Board of directors: W. Bibb Lamar, Jr., Chair.; Tracy T. Conerly; Stephen G. Crawford; David C. De Laney; Robert M. Dixon, Jr.; Broox G. Garrett, Jr.; Carol F. Gordy; Barry E. Gritter; James M. Harrison, Jr.; Clifton C. Inge, Jr.; Kenneth S. Johnson; John H. Lewis, Jr.; Harris V. Morrissette; Paul D. Owens, Jr.; Mary Ann Morthland Patterson; Peter C. Sherman; Dennis A. Wallace
Giving statement: Giving through the First National Bank Charitable Foundation.
Company EIN: 630909434

First National Bank Charitable Foundation

P.O. Box 469
Brewton, AL 36427-0469 (251) 867-3231

Donor: First National Bank of Brewton, Alabama.
Contact: Raymond Lynn
Financial data (yr. ended 12/31/11): Assets, $1,108,403 (M); expenditures, $59,562; qualifying distributions, $55,683; giving activities include $54,821 for 41 grants (high: $3,000; low: $100).
Purpose and activities: The foundation supports community foundations and organizations involved with education, the environment, cancer, hunger, school athletics, and human services.
Fields of interest: Elementary/secondary education; Higher education; Libraries (public);

Education; Environment, beautification programs; Environment; Cancer; Food distribution, meals on wheels; Athletics/sports, school programs; Human services; Foundations (community).
Type of support: Building/renovation; Equipment; General/operating support; Scholarship funds; Sponsorships.
Geographic limitations: Giving primarily in Escambia County, AL.
Application information: Applications accepted. Application form required. Applicants should submit the following:
1) detailed description of project and amount of funding requested
Initial approach: Letter
Deadline(s): None
Directors: John Barnett; Broox G. Garrett, Jr.; Mark Manning; Thomas E. McMillan, Jr.; J. Stephen Nelson.
EIN: 630935188

338
Bangor Savings Bank

99 Franklin St.
P.O. Box 930
Bangor, ME 04401 (207) 942-5211

Company URL: http://www.bangor.com
Establishment information: Established in 1852.
Company type: Private company
Business activities: Operates savings bank.
Business type (SIC): Banks/commercial
Financial profile for 2012: Assets, $2,585,586,000; liabilities, $2,585,586,000
Corporate officers: James H. Goff, Chair.; Robert A. Strong, Vice-Chair.; James J. Conlon, Pres. and C.E.O.; Bruce G. Nickerson, Exec. V.P., Treas., and C.F.O.; Robert S. Montgomey-Rice, Exec. V.P. and C.O.O.; Yellow Light Breen, Exec. V.P. and Clerk
Board of directors: James H. Goff, Chair.; Robert A. Strong, Vice-Chair.; Kathryn L. Barber; Gena R. Canning; James J. Conlon; George F. Eaton II, Esq.; Charles E. Hewett, Ph.D.; Richard J. McGoldrick; Martha G. Newman; Scott Oxley; William D. Purington; Vincent P. Veroneu
Giving statement: Giving through the Bangor Savings Bank Corporate Giving Program and the Bangor Savings Bank Foundation.

Bangor Savings Bank Corporate Giving Program

c/o Corp. Giving
P.O. Box 930
Bangor, ME 04402-0930 (877) 226-4671
E-mail: customercare@bangor.com; URL: http://www.bangor.com/Why-Bangor-Savings/Supporting-Our-Communities.aspx

Purpose and activities: As a complement to its foundation, Bangor Savings Bank also makes charitable contributions to nonprofit organizations directly. Support is given primarily in Maine.
Fields of interest: Arts; Education; Health care; Human services; United Ways and Federated Giving Programs.
Type of support: Employee volunteer services; General/operating support; Program development.
Geographic limitations: Giving primarily in areas of company operations in ME.
Publications: Application guidelines.
Application information: Applications accepted. Application form not required. Applicants should submit the following:
1) detailed description of project and amount of funding requested
Initial approach: E-mail or mail proposal to headquarters
Deadline(s): None

Bangor Savings Bank Foundation

99 Franklin St.
P.O. Box 930
Bangor, ME 04402-0930 (877) 226-4671
E-mail: foundation@bangor.com; Additional tel.: (207) 942-5211; E-mail for Stacy Haskell: stacey.haskell@bangor.com; URL: http://www.bangor.com/Why-Bangor-Savings/Supporting-Our-Communities.aspx

Establishment information: Established in 1996 in ME.
Donor: Bangor Savings Bank.
Contact: Stacy Haskell, Asst. V.P., Community Rels.
Financial data (yr. ended 03/31/12): Assets, $4,221,773 (M); gifts received, $477,000; expenditures, $693,932; qualifying distributions, $667,607; giving activities include $667,607 for grants.
Purpose and activities: The foundation supports programs designed to promote culture and arts; education; health and wellness; and social and civic services. Special emphasis is directed toward initiatives designed to increase workforce education levels and address out-migration of youth; increase regional income levels and economic activity in rural communities; and support Maine entrepreneurs and micro-enterprise businesses whose needs are not met by existing programs.
Fields of interest: Arts; Higher education; Business school/education; Education, services; Education; Public health, physical fitness; Health care; Mental health/crisis services; Employment, services; Employment; Youth, services; Economic development; Rural development; Business/industry; Social entrepreneurship; Community development, small businesses; United Ways and Federated Giving Programs; Economics; Public affairs.
Programs:
Community Matters More: Through the Community Matters More Program, the foundation will award a total of $100,000 to 68 local nonprofit organizations. The organizations awarded will be selected through an online public voting process. The top organizations in each region will receive $5,000 each, and the remaining 60 organizations will receive $1,000 each.
Culture and Arts: The foundation supports creative arts programs designed to educate and entertain while providing a forum for local talent; and activities designed to enhance the role of art organizations as economic enterprises.
Education: The foundation supports programs designed to raise student aspirations at the primary, secondary, and post-secondary levels; transfer knowledge in specific skill sets such as public speaking and economics; and initiatives designed to support education through dissemination of information.
Health and Wellness: The foundation supports unduplicated programs essential to the underlying medical care of a community; and initiatives focused on physical and mental wellness for people of all ages.
Social and Civic Services: The foundation supports programs designed to improve quality of life in communities served by Bangor Savings.
Type of support: Annual campaigns; Building/renovation; Capital campaigns; Equipment; Matching/challenge support; Program development.
Geographic limitations: Giving limited to areas of company operations in ME.
Support limitations: No support for political organizations or candidates, or religious organizations. No grants to individuals, or for annual operating budgets of United Way agencies, conferences or seminars, or endowments.
Publications: Application guidelines; Grants list; Program policy statement.
Application information: Applications accepted. Grants range from $2,000 to $50,000. Support is limited to 1 contribution per organization during any given year. Application form required. Applicants should submit the following:
1) statement of problem project will address
2) population served
3) copy of IRS Determination Letter
4) brief history of organization and description of its mission
5) geographic area to be served
6) copy of most recent annual report/audited financial statement/990
7) how project's results will be evaluated or measured
8) listing of board of directors, trustees, officers and other key people and their affiliations
9) detailed description of project and amount of funding requested
10) listing of additional sources and amount of support
Initial approach: Download application form and mail to foundation; complete online voting form for Community Matters More
Copies of proposal: 1
Board meeting date(s): Quarterly
Deadline(s): Jan. 1, Apr. 1, July 1, and Oct. 1; Mar. 7 for Community Matters More
Final notification: 60 to 90 days
Officers and Directors:* Gary W. Smith*, Chair.; James J. Conlon*, Pres.; Yellow Light Breen, V.P., Secy., and Clerk; Bruce G. Nickerson, Treas.; Kathryn L. Barber; Gena R. Canning; George F. Eaton II, Esq.; James H. Goff; Charles E. Hewett, Ph.D.; Richard J. McGoldrick; Martha G. Newman; William D. Purington; Robert A. Strong, CFA.
EIN: 043353896
Selected grants: The following grants are a representative sample of this grantmaker's funding activity:
$56,000 to Good Shepherd Food-Bank, Auburn, ME, 2010.
$50,000 to Maine Community College System, Augusta, ME, 2010.
$25,000 to Boy Scouts of America, Bangor, ME, 2010.
$25,000 to Childrens Museum and Theater of Maine, Portland, ME, 2010.
$15,000 to Our Town Belfast, Belfast, ME, 2010.
$10,000 to Alpha One, South Portland, ME, 2010.
$10,000 to Maine Food Producers Alliance, Augusta, ME, 2010.
$2,500 to Aroostook County Action Program, Presque Isle, ME, 2010.
$2,500 to Cobscook Community Learning Center, Lubec, ME, 2010.
$2,000 to Northeast Historic Film, Bucksport, ME, 2010.

339
Bank of America, N.A.

(formerly Bank of America National Trust and Savings Association)
100 N. Tryon St., Ste. 1000
Charlotte, NC 28280-0010 (704) 386-5681

Company URL: http://www.bankofamerica.com
Establishment information: Established in 1921.
Company type: Subsidiary of a public company
Business activities: Operates commercial bank.
Financial profile for 2010: Number of employees, 8,000; sales volume, $71,610,000,000; pre-tax net income, $9,080,000,000
Giving statement: Giving through the Clorinda Giannini Memorial Benefit Fund.

Clorinda Giannini Memorial Benefit Fund

c/o Bank of America, N.A.
P.O. Box 831041
Dallas, TX 75283-1041 (877) 444-1012

Establishment information: Established in 1942 in CA.
Donors: Bank of America National Trust and Savings Assn.; Bank of America, N.A.
Financial data (yr. ended 04/30/12): Assets, $585,891 (M); expenditures, $86,584; qualifying distributions, $86,032; giving activities include $84,872 for 34 grants to individuals (high: $9,495; low: $79).
Purpose and activities: The foundation awards grants to employees, dependents of employees, and retirees of Bank of America for relief of distress caused by illness, accident, disability, surgery, medical and nursing care, hospitalization, financial difficulties, loss of income, or other emergencies.
Fields of interest: Economically disadvantaged.
Type of support: Grants to individuals.
Geographic limitations: Giving limited to CA.
Application information: Applications not accepted. Unsolicited requests for funds not accepted.
Trustee: Bank of America, N.A.
EIN: 946073513

340
Bank of America Corporation

(formerly BankAmerica Corporation)
Bank of America Corp. Ctr.
100 N. Tryon St.
Charlotte, NC 28255-0001 (704) 386-5681
FAX: (302) 655-5049

Company URL: http://www.bankofamerica.com
Establishment information: Established in 1874.
Company type: Public company
Company ticker symbol and exchange: BAC/NYSE
International Securities Identification Number: US0605051046
Business activities: Operates bank holding company; operates commercial bank.
Business type (SIC): Banks/commercial; holding company
Financial profile for 2012: Number of employees, 267,000; assets, $2,209,974,000,000; pre-tax net income, $3,072,000,000; liabilities, $1,973,018,000,000
Fortune 1000 ranking: 2012—21st in revenues, 44th in profits, and 3rd in assets
Forbes 2000 ranking: 2012—63rd in sales, 132nd in profits, and 11th in assets
Corporate officers: Charles O. Holliday, Jr., Chair.; Brian T. Moynihan, Pres. and C.E.O.; David C. Darnell, Co-C.O.O.; Thomas K. Montag, Co-C.O.O.; Bruce R. Thompson, C.F.O.; Gary G. Lynch, Genl. Counsel
Board of directors: Charles O. Holliday, Jr., Chair.; Mukesh Dhirubhai Ambani; Susan S. Bies; Frank P. Bramble, Sr.; Virgis W. Colbert; Charles K. Gifford; Monica C. Lozano; Thomas J. May; Brian T. Moynihan; Donald E. Powell; Charles O. Rossotti; Robert W. Scully
Subsidiaries: BancBoston Investments Inc., Boston, MA; Bank of America, N.A., Charlotte, NC; Bank of America, N.A., Charlotte, NC; Bank of America Texas, N.A., Dallas, TX; Fleet National Bank, Providence, RI; Merrill Lynch & Co., Inc., New York, NY
International operations: Argentina; Australia; Bahamas; Bermuda; Brazil; British Virgin Islands; Canada; Cayman Islands; Chile; China; Colombia; England; France; Germany; Gibraltar; Guernsey; Hong Kong; India; Indonesia; Ireland; Isle of Man; Japan; Lebanon; Luxembourg; Malaysia; Mauritius; Mexico; Netherlands; Peru; Philippines; Poland; Romania; Saudi Arabia; Scotland; Singapore; Slovakia; South Africa; South Korea; Spain; Sweden; Switzerland; Taiwan; Thailand; Turkey; United Kingdom; Uruguay
Historic mergers: Bank South Corporation (January 9, 1996); Boatmen's Bancshares, Inc. (January 7, 1997); Barnett Banks, Inc. (January 9, 1998); BankAmerica Corporation (September 30, 1998); FleetBoston Financial Corporation (April 1, 2004); MBNA America Bank, N.A. (January 1, 2006); U.S. Trust Corporation (July 1, 2007); LaSalle Bank Midwest N.A. (October 1, 2007); LaSalle Bank N.A. (October 1, 2007); Countrywide Home Loans, Inc. (July 1, 2008)
Giving statement: Giving through the Bank of America Corporation Contributions Program, the Bank of America Charitable Foundation, Inc., the A. P. Giannini Foundation for Employees, and the Bank of America Charitable Gift Fund.
Company EIN: 560906609

Bank of America Corporation Contributions Program

(formerly BankAmerica Corporation Contributions Program)
100 N. Tryon St., #170
Charlotte, NC 28202 (980) 335-3561
URL: http://www.bankofamerica.com/foundation/

Purpose and activities: As a complement to its foundation, Bank of America also makes charitable contributions to nonprofit organizations directly. Support is given on a national and international basis in areas of company operations.
Fields of interest: Arts; Education; Health care; Human services; Community/economic development.
Type of support: Building/renovation; Employee matching gifts; Employee volunteer services; General/operating support; Program development; Sponsorships.
Geographic limitations: Giving on a national and international basis in areas of company operations, including Canada and the United Kingdom.
Support limitations: No support for athletic organizations or political organizations. No grants to individuals, or for political activities, tuition, or debt reduction.

The Bank of America Charitable Foundation, Inc.

401 N. Tryon St., NC1-021-02-20
Charlotte, NC 28255-0001 (800) 218-9946
URL: http://www.bankofamerica.com/foundation/index.cfm

Establishment information: Established in 1958; reincorporated in 2004.
Donors: Bank of America Corp.; Bank of America, N.A.; FleetBoston Financial Foundation; The Holden Trust; Merrill Lynch & Co., Inc.
Financial data (yr. ended 12/31/11): Assets, $86,383,791 (M); gifts received, $276,374,979; expenditures, $198,332,854; qualifying distributions, $198,213,418; giving activities include $198,213,345 for 26,004 grants (high: $3,378,856; low: $8).
Purpose and activities: The Bank of America Charitable Foundation provides philanthropic support to address specific needs vital to the health of local communities by focusing on community and economic development initiatives, addressing critical human needs such as hunger, and educating the workforce for 21st century jobs. Special emphasis is directed toward programs supporting low and moderate income communities. Support is given primarily in areas of company operations.
Fields of interest: Arts; Secondary school/education; Higher education; Education; Environment; Hospitals (general); Employment, services; Employment, training; Employment; Food services; Food banks; Nutrition; Housing/shelter, home owners; Housing/shelter; Youth development; Family services; Human services, financial counseling; Homeless, human services; Human services; Community development, neighborhood development; Community development, small businesses; Community/economic development; United Ways and Federated Giving Programs; Leadership development.
Programs:

Community Development: The foundation supports programs designed to address housing foreclosure counseling and mitigation, real estate owned disposition, and affordable housing. The foundation also supports financial education and coaching and financial empowerment initiatives. Special emphasis is directed toward preserving neighborhoods and community revitalization.

Critical Needs: The foundation supports programs designed help individuals in need through food access, shelter, and addressing financial wellness and stability issues facing low-income communities. Special emphasis is directed toward hunger relief and food access; emergency shelter and supportive housing; and benefits access and referrals.

Local Heroes: The foundation annually awards five $5,000 grants to nonprofit organizations chosen by outstanding community leaders in each of the 44 Bank of America markets. Chosen heroes are recognized at a public awards ceremony in their local community.

Matching Gifts: The foundation matches contributions made by employees and directors of Bank of America to nonprofit organizations on a one-for-one basis from $25 to $5,000 per contributor, per year.

Neighborhood Builders: Through the Neighborhood Builders program, the foundation provides funding to outstanding nonprofit organizations who are meeting pressing community issues in community development, education and workforce development, and critical needs, and also provide leadership development for their staff. The program is by invitation only.

Student Leaders: The Student Leaders program recognizes community-minded students with a paid non-profit internship and participation in a Student Leadership Summit in Washington, D.C. It is one of the ways the foundation is helping youth gain valuable work experience and skills to help put them on a path for future success.

Workforce Development and Education: The foundation supports programs designed to provide workforce development and educational opportunities to the unemployed and underserved. Special emphasis is directed toward high school graduation and post-secondary access; post-secondary completion; job readiness for unemployed and underemployed; and small business support.

Type of support: Conferences/seminars; Continuing support; Employee matching gifts; Employee volunteer services; Employee-related scholarships; General/operating support; Internship funds; Management development/capacity building; Program development.

Geographic limitations: Giving on a national and international basis in areas of company operations.

Support limitations: No support for discriminatory organizations, political, labor, or fraternal organizations, civic clubs, religious organizations not of direct benefit to the entire community, or public or private pre-K-12 schools. No grants to individuals or for fellowships, sports, athletic events or programs, travel-related events, student trips or tours, development or production of books, films, videos, or televisions programs, or memorial campaigns.

Application information: Applications accepted. Support is limited to 1 contribution per organization during any given year. Application form required.

Initial approach: Complete online eligibility quiz and application

Deadline(s): Jan. 22 to Feb. 13 for Workforce Development and Education; Apr. 15 to May 10 for Community Development; and July 8 to Aug 2 for Critical Needs

Officers and Directors:* Anne M. Finucane*, Chair.; Kerry H. Sullivan, Pres.; Suzette Finger, Sr. V.P. and Treas.; Thomas M. Brantley, Sr. V.P., Tax; Dannielle C. Campos, Sr. V.P.; Anna Cowenhoven, Sr. V.P.; Rena M. DeSisto, Sr. V.P.; Stephen B. Fitzgerald, Sr. V.P.; Robert E. Gallery, Sr. V.P.; Angie Garcia-Lathrop, Sr. V.P.; Abigail Goward, Sr. V.P.; Charles R. Henderson, Jr., Sr. V.P.; Teresa M. Ingwall, Sr. V.P.; Daniel Letendre, Sr. V.P.; Alexandra C. Liftman, Sr. V.P.; Jennifer Locane, Sr. V.P.; Susan Portugal, Sr. V.P.; Tish Secrest, Sr. V.P.; Michael F. Shriver, Sr. V.P.; Brenda L. Suits, Sr. V.P.; Kristen L. Teskey, Sr. V.P.; Colleen O. Johnson, Secy.; Keith T. Banks; Catherine P. Bessant; Amy Woods Brinkley; Helen B. Eggers; Walter B. Elcock; Claire A. Huang; Janet W. Lamkin; Andrew D. Plepler; Martin Richards; Purna R. Saggurti.

EIN: 200721133

Selected grants: The following grants are a representative sample of this grantmaker's funding activity:

$4,000,050 to Georgia State University, Atlanta, GA, 2011. For program and operating support.
$3,378,856 to Center for Leadership Innovation, Ellicott City, MD, 2011. For program and operating support.
$2,451,700 to Enterprise Community Partners, Columbia, MD, 2011. For program and operating support.
$2,172,791 to American Red Cross National Headquarters, Washington, DC, 2011. For program and operating support.
$1,339,577 to United Way of Central Carolinas, Charlotte, NC, 2011. For program and operating support.
$1,004,710 to Museum of Fine Arts, Boston, MA, 2011. For program and operating support.
$555,000 to City Year, Boston, MA, 2011. For program and operating support.
$5,075 to Discovery Science Place, Tyler, TX, 2011. For program and operating support.
$5,000 to Urban League of Rochester, Rochester, NY, 2011. For program and operating support.
$3,600 to College of Wooster, Wooster, OH, 2011. For program and operating support.

A. P. Giannini Foundation for Employees

c/o Bank of America, N.A.
P.O. Box 831041
Dallas, TX 75283-1041 (877) 444-1012

Establishment information: Established in 1927 in CA.

Donor: Bank of America Corp.

Financial data (yr. ended 12/31/11): Assets, $1,766,177 (M); expenditures, $86,673; qualifying distributions, $85,101; giving activities include $85,101 for 35 grants to individuals (high: $6,992; low: $543).

Purpose and activities: The foundation awards grants and loans to employees and family members of employees of Bank of America and its subsidiaries for medical bills or other emergencies.

Type of support: Grants to individuals; Loans—to individuals.

Application information: Applications accepted. Application form required.

Initial approach: Proposal

Deadline(s): None

Trustee: Bank of America, N.A.

EIN: 946089550

Bank of America Charitable Gift Fund

(formerly Fleet Charitable Gift Fund)
c/o Bank of America, N.A. Philanthropic Solutions
P.O. Box 1802
Providence, RI 02901-1802
URL: http://www.bankofamerica.com/grantmaking

Establishment information: Established in 1955 in MA by declaration of trust.

Financial data (yr. ended 12/31/11): Revenue, $115,812,292; assets, $335,024,478 (M); gifts received, $78,184,283; expenditures, $76,955,412; giving activities include $74,912,376 for grants.

Purpose and activities: The fund administers a donor-advised fund that considers support in the areas of human services, urban programs, youth and family services, health care programs, and education.

Geographic limitations: Giving primarily in MA.

Support limitations: No support for national organizations. No grants to individuals, or for conferences, film production, travel, projects requiring a multi-year commitment, endowment funds, research not under the aegis of recognized charitable organizations, publications, or matching gifts; no loans.

Application information: Applications not accepted. Contributes only to pre-selected organizations.

Trustee: Bank of America, N.A.

EIN: 046010342

Selected grants: The following grants are a representative sample of this grantmaker's funding activity:

$35,000 to Pine Street Inn, Boston, MA, 2010. For general operations of the organization to support the emergency shelter services we provide to Boston's homeless population.
$25,000 to Boston Building Materials Cooperative Charitable and Educational Fund, Boston, MA, 2010. For general operations of the organization. These funds will make it possible for us to continue our daily work of providing high quality affordable materials and valuable advice to low- and moderate-income homeowners in Greater Boston.
$25,000 to On the Rise, Cambridge, MA, 2010. For general operating support to continue to offer our core programs (the Safe Haven Program for homeless women and our new Keep The Keys/ housing stabilization services).
$20,000 to Homestart, Boston, MA, 2010. For general operating funds to help to support the housing services.
$10,000 to Merrimack Valley Food Bank, Lowell, MA, 2010. For Food Distribution Program.
$10,000 to United Way of Greater Plymouth County, Brockton, MA, 2010. For South Shore Network to End Homelessness. This request will help fund the South Shore Network's regional coordinator who is based at United Way.
$5,000 to Boston Youth Symphony Orchestras, Boston, MA, 2010. For Intensive Community Program (ICP), a rigorous stringed-instrument training program serving students from Boston's inner city.

341
The Bank of Greene County

425 Main St.
P.O. Box 470
Catskill, NY 12414-1300 (518) 943-3700

Company URL: http://www.thebankofgreenecounty.com

Establishment information: Established in 1889.

Company type: Subsidiary of a public company

Business activities: Operates savings bank.

Business type (SIC): Savings institutions

Corporate officers: Martin C. Smith, Chair.; Donald E. Gibson, Pres. and C.E.O.; Michelle M. Plummer, C.P.A., Exec. V.P., C.O.O., and C.F.O.; Gregory W. Spampinato, C.I.O.; Rebecca R. Main, Sr. V.P. and Human Resources; John Olivett, V.P., Opers.; Betsy Darrow, Cont.

Board of directors: Martin C. Smith, Chair.; Donald E. Gibson; David H. Jenkins; Dennis R. O'Grady; Arthur Place; Charles Schaefer; Paul Slutzky; J. Bruce Whittaker

Giving statement: Giving through the Bank of Greene County Charitable Foundation.

Bank of Greene County Charitable Foundation

P.O. Box 470
302 Main St.
Catskill, NY 12414-1300
URL: https://www.thebankofgreenecounty.com/index.php?p=14

Establishment information: Established in 1999 in DE and NY.

Donor: The Bank of Greene County.

Financial data (yr. ended 06/30/12): Assets, $1,506,283 (M); expenditures, $75,780; qualifying distributions, $72,700; giving activities include $72,700 for 89 grants (high: $10,000; low: $250).

Purpose and activities: The foundation supports organizations involved with arts and culture, health and wellness, housing, human services, civic affairs, and economically disadvantaged people.

Fields of interest: Arts; Higher education; Hospitals (general); Health care; Housing/shelter; YM/YWCAs & YM/YWHAs; Residential/custodial care, hospices; Human services; Public affairs Economically disadvantaged.

Type of support: Annual campaigns; Building/renovation; Equipment; General/operating support; Program development.
Geographic limitations: Giving primarily in areas of company operations in NY.
Support limitations: No support for political candidates or religious organizations. No grants to individuals, or for activities for sectarian purposes, seminars, conferences, or endowments.
Publications: Application guidelines.
Application information: Applications accepted. Proposals should be submitted using organization letterhead. Support is limited to 1 contribution per organization during any given year. Application form required. Applicants should submit the following:
1) name, address and phone number of organization
2) copy of IRS Determination Letter
3) brief history of organization and description of its mission
4) listing of board of directors, trustees, officers and other key people and their affiliations
5) detailed description of project and amount of funding requested
6) contact person
7) copy of current year's organizational budget and/or project budget
8) listing of additional sources and amount of support

Initial approach: Letter
Copies of proposal: 1
Deadline(s): Dec. 1 to Jan. 15
Final notification: 90 days

Officers and Directors:* Martin C. Smith*, Chair.; Donald E. Gibson, C.E.O. and Pres.; Michelle M. Plummer, Exec. V.P., C.O.O., and C.F.O.; Rebecca R. Main, Sr. V.P. and Secy.; Stephen Nelson, Sr. V.P.; Cynthia Dupilka, V.P.; David H. Jenkins; Dennis R. O'Grady; Arthur Place; Charles H. Schaefer, Esq.; Paul Slutzky; J. Bruce Whittaker.
EIN: 141810419

342
Bank of Hawaii

130 Merchant St., 20th Fl.
Honolulu, HI 96813-4450 (808) 694-8389

Company URL: https://www.boh.com
Establishment information: Established in 1897.
Company type: Subsidiary of a public company
Business activities: Operates commercial bank.
Business type (SIC): Banks/commercial
Financial profile for 2011: Number of employees, 2,400; assets, $13,846,390,000; pre-tax net income, $226,980,000; liabilities, $12,843,720,000
Corporate officers: Peter S. Ho, Chair., Pres., and C.E.O.; Kent T. Lucien, Vice-Chair. and C.F.O.; Mark A. Rossi, Vice-Chair., C.A.O., Genl. Counsel, and Secy.; Peter M. Biggs, Vice-Chair.; Wayne Y. Hamano, Vice-Chair.; Alton T. Kuioka, Vice-Chair.; Mary E. Sellers, Vice-Chair.; Donna A. Tanoue, Vice-Chair.; Shelley B. Thompson, Vice-Chair.; Derek A. Baughman, Sr. Exec. V.P. and C.I.O.; Dean Y. Shigemura, Sr. Exec.V.P. and Treas.; Derek J. Norris, Sr. Exec. V.P. and Cont.
Board of directors: Peter S. Ho, Chair.; Peter M. Biggs, Vice-Chair.; Wayne Y. Hamano, Vice-Chair.; Alton T. Kuiko, Vice-Chair.; Kent T. Lucien, Vice-Chair.; Mark A. Rossi, Vice-Chair.; Mary E. Sellers, Vice-Chair.; Donna A. Tanoue, Vice-Chair.
Giving statement: Giving through the Bank of Hawaii Corporate Giving Program and the Bank of Hawaii Foundation.

Bank of Hawaii Corporate Giving Program

130 Merchant St. #1910
Honolulu, HI 96813 (808) 694-8196
URL: https://www.boh.com/community/385.asp

Purpose and activities: As a complement to its foundation, Bank of Hawaii makes charitable contributions to nonprofit organizations on a case by case basis. Support is limited to areas of company operations in American Samoa, Guam, Hawaii, Palau, and Saipan.
Fields of interest: Arts; Environment; Food services; Food banks; YM/YWCAs & YM/YWHAs; Children/youth, services; Children, foster care; Human services, financial counseling; Aging, centers/services.
Type of support: Annual campaigns; Employee volunteer services; General/operating support; In-kind gifts; Sponsorships.
Geographic limitations: Giving is limited to areas of company operations in AS, CM, GU, HI, and in Palau; giving also to national organizations.

Bank of Hawaii Foundation

(formerly Bancorp Hawaii Charitable Foundation)
Foundation Admin. No. 758
P.O. Box 3170
Honolulu, HI 96802-3170 (808) 538-4944
FAX: (808) 538-4006; E-mail: emoniz@boh.com; Additional contacts: Flora Williams, Asst. V.P., tel.: (808) 694-4393, e-mail: flora.williams@boh.com; Paula Boyce, Grants Admin., tel.: (808) 538-4945, e-mail: pboyce@boh.com; URL: https://www.boh.com/customer-service/689.asp

Establishment information: Established in 1981 in HI.
Donors: Bank of Hawaii; Allan R. Landon.
Contact: Elaine Moniz, Trust Specialist
Financial data (yr. ended 12/31/11): Assets, $7,478,149 (M); gifts received, $2,362,326; expenditures, $2,221,719; qualifying distributions, $1,875,278; giving activities include $1,875,278 for grants.
Purpose and activities: The foundation supports organizations involved with arts and culture, education, health, hunger, housing, human services, and community development. Special emphasis is directed toward programs designed serve children and youth, indigenous peoples, and economically disadvantaged people; and strengthen low- to moderate-income communities.
Fields of interest: Arts education; Arts; Higher education; Education; Health care; Food services; Housing/shelter; Salvation Army; Human services, financial counseling; Human services; Economic development; Community/economic development Children/youth; Indigenous peoples; Economically disadvantaged.
Type of support: Annual campaigns; Building/renovation; Capital campaigns; Continuing support; Emergency funds; Endowments; Equipment; General/operating support; Matching/challenge support; Program development; Scholarship funds; Technical assistance.
Geographic limitations: Giving primarily in areas of company operations in American Samoa, Guam, HI, and Saipan.
Support limitations: No support for pass-through organizations. No grants to individuals, or for deficit budgets, general fundraising campaigns, religious purposes, or trips or tours.
Publications: Application guidelines; Informational brochure.
Application information: Applications accepted. Grants range from $1,000 to $25,000. Letters of inquiry are strongly encouraged for unsolicited ideas or projects. Executive summaries should be no longer than 1 page and include a summary of the proposal and a brief overview of the organization. A full formal proposal may be requested at a later date. Support is limited to 1 contribution per organization during any given year. Application form required. Applicants should submit the following:
1) copy of IRS Determination Letter
2) brief history of organization and description of its mission
3) listing of board of directors, trustees, officers and other key people and their affiliations

Initial approach: Download letter of inquiry cover sheet and mail cover sheet and executive summary to foundation
Copies of proposal: 1
Board meeting date(s): Biannually
Deadline(s): Postmarked by Jan. 15 or July 15
Final notification: 60 days

Officers and Directors:* Donna A. Tanoue*, Pres.; Stafford J. Kiguchi, V.P.; Peter S. Ho*, V.P.; Cynthia G. Wyrick, Secy.; Kent Lucien*, Treas.; S. Haunani Apoliona; Mary G.F. Bitterman; Mark A. Burak; Michael J. Chun, Ph.D.; Clinton R. Churchill; David A. Heenan; Robert A. Huret; Alton T. Kuioka; Martin A. Stein; Donald M. Takaki; Barbara J. Tanabe; Robert W. Wo, Jr.
Trustee: Bank of Hawaii.
EIN: 990210467
Selected grants: The following grants are a representative sample of this grantmaker's funding activity:
$125,000 to United Way, Aloha, Honolulu, HI, 2009. For campaign.
$62,500 to United Way, Aloha, Honolulu, HI, 2009. For campaign.
$62,500 to United Way, Aloha, Honolulu, HI, 2009. For campaign.
$35,000 to American Red Cross, Hawaii State Chapter, Honolulu, HI, 2009. For Charity Walk.
$35,000 to Family Promise of Hawaii, Kailua, HI, 2009. For Charity Walk.
$25,000 to Bishop Museum, Honolulu, HI, 2009. For Hawaiian Hall Restoration Project.
$25,000 to Child and Family Service, Ewa Beach, HI, 2009. For anniversary campaign to rebuild domestic abuse shelter facility.
$25,000 to Le Jardin Academy, Kailua, HI, 2009. For construction of classrooms and gymnasium.
$23,500 to United Way, Maui, Wailuku, HI, 2009. For campaign.
$15,000 to Iolani School, Honolulu, HI, 2009. For Stone Scholarship to cover tuition for high school students.

343
The Bank of Maine

(formerly Savings Bank of Maine)
190 Water St.
P.O. Box 190
Gardiner, ME 04345-0190 (207) 582-5550

Company URL: https://www.thebankofmaine.com
Establishment information: Established in 1834.
Company type: Private company
Business activities: Operates savings bank.
Business type (SIC): Banks/commercial
Corporate officers: John W. Everets, Chair. and C.E.O.; Willard B. Soper, Pres. and C.O.O.; Anita M. Nored, Treas.
Board of directors: John W. Everets, Chair.; Willard B. Soper

Giving statement: Giving through the Bank of Maine Charitable Foundation and the Savings Bank of Maine Scholarship Foundation.

The Bank of Maine Charitable Foundation

(formerly Savings Bank of Maine, FSB Charitable Foundation)
190 Water St.
Gardiner, ME 04345-2109 (207) 582-5550

Establishment information: Established in 1988 in ME.
Donors: Gardiner Savings Institution, F.S.B.; Savings Bank of Maine.
Contact: Dennis A. Carolin
Financial data (yr. ended 12/31/11): Assets, $1,496,322 (M); expenditures, $315,006; qualifying distributions, $295,858; giving activities include $295,858 for grants.
Purpose and activities: The foundation supports fire departments and festivals and organizations involved with arts and culture, education, the environment, health, human services, and community development.
Fields of interest: Performing arts; Historic preservation/historical societies; Arts; Higher education, college (community/junior); Libraries (public); Education; Botanical gardens; Environment; Hospitals (general); Health care; Disasters, fire prevention/control; Recreation, fairs/festivals; Boys & girls clubs; YM/YWCAs & YM/YWHAs; Human services; Community/economic development; United Ways and Federated Giving Programs.
Type of support: General/operating support.
Geographic limitations: Giving primarily in Gardiner, ME.
Application information: Applications accepted. Application form not required.
Initial approach: Proposal
Deadline(s): None
Officers and Directors:* Richard L. Goodwin*, Chair.; Everett L. Ayer, Vice-Chair.; Arthur C. Markos*, Pres.; Al C. Graceffa; Daniel L. Hollingdale; Robert P. Lacasse; John G. Rizzo.
EIN: 010446023
Selected grants: The following grants are a representative sample of this grantmaker's funding activity:
$346,179 to Gardiner, City of, Gardiner, ME, 2010.
$50,000 to YMCA, Kennebec Valley, Augusta, ME, 2010.
$21,000 to Johnson Hall, Gardiner, ME, 2010.
$5,000 to Maine State Music Theater, Brunswick, ME, 2010.
$1,000 to Calumet Club, Le Club Calumet Franco-American Festival, Augusta, ME, 2010.
$500 to Readfield Historical Society, Readfield, ME, 2010.
$500 to Riverview Foundation, Topsham, ME, 2010.
$500 to YMCA, Kennebec Valley, Augusta, ME, 2010.
$300 to Heartwood Regional Theater Company, Damariscotta, ME, 2010.
$250 to Readfield Union Meeting House, Readfield, ME, 2010.

Savings Bank of Maine Scholarship Foundation

(formerly Gardiner Savings Institution FSB Scholarship Foundation Savings Bank of Maine Scholarship Foundation)
P.O. Box 190
Gardiner, ME 04345 (207) 582-5550

Establishment information: Established in 1985 in ME.
Donor: Gardiner Savings Institution, F.S.B.
Contact: Dennis Carolin, Treas.
Financial data (yr. ended 03/31/12): Assets, $348,146 (M); expenditures, $28,690; qualifying distributions, $26,000; giving activities include $26,000 for grants to individuals.
Purpose and activities: The foundation awards college scholarships to high school seniors located in areas of Gardiner Savings Institution operations.
Type of support: Scholarships—to individuals.
Geographic limitations: Giving primarily in Augusta, Gardiner, Hallowell, Manchester, Richmond, and Wiscasset, ME.
Support limitations: No employee-related scholarships.
Application information: Applications accepted. Application form not required.
Initial approach: Proposal
Deadline(s): None
Officers: Willard Soper, Pres.; Dennis Caroln, Treas.
Board Members: John Everets; Sheryl Milliard; Anita Nored; Dennis Townley.
EIN: 222853667

344
The Bank of New York Mellon Corporation

(formerly The Bank of New York Company, Inc.)
1 Wall St.
New York, NY 10286 (212) 495-1784
FAX: (302) 655-5049

Company URL: http://www.bnymellon.com
Establishment information: Established in 1784.
Company type: Public company
Company ticker symbol and exchange: BK/NYSE
Business activities: Operates bank holding company.
Business type (SIC): Holding company; banks/commercial
Financial profile for 2012: Number of employees, 49,500; assets, $358,990,000,000; pre-tax net income, $3,302,000,000; liabilities, $322,559,000,000
Fortune 1000 ranking: 2012—180th in revenues, 81st in profits, and 15th in assets
Corporate officers: Gerald L. Hassell, Co-Chair. and C.E.O.; Stephen D. Lackey, Co-Chair.; Thomas P. Gibbons, Vice-Chair. and C.F.O.; Curtis Y. Arledge, Vice-Chair.; Timothy F. Keaney, Vice-Chair.; James P. Palermo, Vice-Chair.; Brian G. Rogan, Vice-Chair.; Karen B. Peetz, Pres.; Suresh Kumar, Sr. Exec. V.P. and C.I.O.; Jane Sherburne, Genl. Counsel and Corp. Secy
Board of directors: Gerald L. Hassell, Co-Chair.; Stephen D. Lackey, Co-Chair.; Curtis Y. Arledge, Vice-Chair.; Thomas P. Gibbons, Vice-Chair.; Timothy F. Keaney, Vice-Chair.; James P. Palermo, Vice-Chair.; Brian G. Rogan, Vice-Chair.; Ruth E. Bruch; Nicholas M. Donofrio; Edmund F. Kelly; Richard J. Kogan; Michael J. Kowalski; John A. Luke, Jr.; Mark A. Nordenberg; Karen B. Peetz; Catherine A. Rein; William C. Richardson; Samuel C. Scott III; Wesley W. Von Schack
Subsidiary: The Bank of New York, New York, NY
International operations: Bermuda; Brazil; Canada; Chile; England; Ireland; Japan; Luxembourg; Netherlands; Scotland; Singapore; United Kingdom
Historic mergers: Mellon Financial Corporation (July 2, 2007)
Giving statement: Giving through the Bank of New York Mellon Corporate Giving Program, the BNY Mellon Foundation, Inc., and the BNY Mellon Foundation of Southwestern PA.
Company EIN: 132614959

The Bank of New York Mellon Corporate Giving Program

(formerly The Bank of New York Corporate Giving Program)
1 Wall St.
New York, NY 10005-2501 (212) 495-1784
E-mail: powering.potential@bnymellon.com;
URL: http://www.bnymellon.com/about/communitycommitment.html

Purpose and activities: As a complement to its foundation, BNY Mellon also makes charitable contributions to nonprofit organizations directly. Special emphasis is directed towards programs designed to promote workforce development and basic needs provision. Support is given primarily in areas of company operations, with emphasis on Connecticut, Massachusetts, New Jersey, New York, and Pennsylvania.
Fields of interest: Humanities; Arts; Education; Health care; Employment; Human services; Community/economic development.
Program:
Global Workforce Development Initiative: Through the Global Workforce Development Initiative, the company partners with nonprofit organizations to enhance education, job training, and career development for youth at-risk for chronic unemployment, poverty, and homelessness.
Type of support: Employee matching gifts; Employee volunteer services; General/operating support; Program development; Sponsorships.
Geographic limitations: Giving primarily in areas of company operations, with emphasis on CT, MA, NJ, NY, and PA.
Publications: Application guidelines.
Application information: Applications accepted. Letters of inquiry should be no longer than 2 to 3 pages. Subject line of e-mail should include the organization's name, Tax ID Number, and geographic location. Application form not required. Applicants should submit the following:
1) population served
2) name, address and phone number of organization
3) brief history of organization and description of its mission
4) geographic area to be served
5) detailed description of project and amount of funding requested
Initial approach: E-mail letter of inquiry
Deadline(s): None

BNY Mellon Foundation, Inc.

(formerly The Bank of New York Mellon Corporation Foundation)
P.O. Box 185
Pittsburgh, PA 15230-9897 (412) 234-8679
E-mail: powering.potential@bnymellon.com;
URL: http://www.bnymellon.com/about/communitycommitment.html

Establishment information: Established in 1997 in NY.
Donors: The Bank of New York; BNY Capital Corp.; Bank of New York Mellon Corp. Foundation.
Financial data (yr. ended 12/31/11): Assets, $30,874,639 (M); expenditures, $1,777,094; qualifying distributions, $1,698,750; giving activities include $1,698,750 for grants.
Purpose and activities: The foundation supports programs designed to address workforce development and basic needs provision.

Fields of interest: Employment, services; Employment, training; Employment; Human services, financial counseling; Human services; Economic development.
Type of support: Employee matching gifts; General/operating support.
Geographic limitations: Giving on a national basis through throughout the U.S., except for southwestern PA.
Support limitations: No grants to individuals.
Publications: Application guidelines.
Application information: Applications accepted. Letters of inquiry should be no longer than 2 to 3 pages. A full application may be requested at a later date. Applicants should submit the following:
1) name, address and phone number of organization
2) copy of IRS Determination Letter
3) brief history of organization and description of its mission
4) geographic area to be served
5) detailed description of project and amount of funding requested
6) statement of problem project will address

Initial approach: E-mail letter of inquiry
Deadline(s): None

Officers and Directors:* R. Jeep Byant*, Chair.; Daisy Holmes, Pres.; Lisa Concepcion, Secy.; Michael McFadden, Treas.; Raymond Dorado; Gerald L. Hassell; Joanne Jaxtimer; David F. Lamere; James P. McDonald; Karen Peetz; Patricia Sampson; Kurt Woetzel.
EIN: 311605320

BNY Mellon Foundation of Southwestern PA

(formerly The BNY Mellon Charitable Foundation)
BNY Mellon Ctr. Ste. 1830
500 Grant St.
Pittsburgh, PA 15258-0001
E-mail: powering.potential@bnymellon.com;
URL: http://www.bnymellon.com/about/charitablegiving-howto.html

Establishment information: Established in 1974 in PA.
Donors: Mellon Bank; Mellon Financial Corp.
Contact: James P. McDonald, Pres.
Financial data (yr. ended 12/31/11): Assets, $67,998,521 (M); expenditures, $3,916,018; qualifying distributions, $3,737,000; giving activities include $3,737,000 for 70 grants (high: $200,000; low: $1,000).
Purpose and activities: The foundation supports organizations involved with economic development, education, and human services. Special emphasis is directed toward programs designed to promote basic needs and workforce development.
Fields of interest: Higher education; Education; Employment, services; Employment, training; Food banks; Housing/shelter; Human services, financial counseling; Human services; Community/economic development; Jewish federated giving programs.
Type of support: Program development.
Geographic limitations: Giving limited to southwestern PA.
Support limitations: No support for fraternal or religious organizations, United Way agencies, or national organizations. No grants to individuals, or for emergency needs, debt reduction, endowments, equipment, land acquisition, scholarships, fellowships, research, publications, travel, conferences, continuing support, or specialized health campaigns or other highly specialized projects with little or no positive impact on communities; no loans.
Application information: Applications accepted. Letters of inquiry should be no longer than 3 pages. Grantmakers of Western Pennsylvania's Common Grant Application Format accepted. Application form not required. Applicants should submit the following:
1) population served
2) copy of IRS Determination Letter
3) copy of most recent annual report/audited financial statement/990
4) how project's results will be evaluated or measured
5) descriptive literature about organization
6) listing of board of directors, trustees, officers and other key people and their affiliations
7) detailed description of project and amount of funding requested
8) copy of current year's organizational budget and/or project budget
9) listing of additional sources and amount of support

Initial approach: Letter of inquiry
Copies of proposal: 1
Board meeting date(s): Quarterly
Deadline(s): None
Final notification: 2 months

Officers and Directors:* Steven G. Elliott*, Chair.; James P. McDonald*, Pres.; Barry Athol, Treas.; R. Jeep Bryant; Jared L. Cohon; Frank M. Hammond; Donald J. Heberle; Mark A. Nordenberg; Lisa B. Peters; Vincent V. Sands; David S. Shapira; William E. Strickland, Jr.
Number of staff: None.
EIN: 237423500

345
Bank of Stockton

301 E. Minor Ave.
Stockton, CA 95202-2501 (209) 929-1336
FAX: (209) 948-5475

Company URL: http://www.bankofstockton.com
Establishment information: Established in 1867.
Company type: Subsidiary of a private company
Business activities: Operates commercial bank.
Business type (SIC): Banks/commercial
Corporate officers: Douglass M. Eberhardt, Chair., Pres., and C.E.O.; Thomas H. Shaffer, Exec. V.P. and C.O.O.
Board of directors: Douglass M. Eberhardt, Chair.; Philip C. Berolzheimer; Bernard L. Caldwe ll; Bill L. Dozier; Douglass M. Eberhardt II; Mary D. Eberhardt; Mary Elizabeth Eberhardt-Sandstrom; Timothy J. Hachman; Robert A. McHugh III; Thomas H. Shaffer
Giving statement: Giving through the Bank of Stockton Corporate Giving Program and the Bank of Stockton Educational Foundation.

Bank of Stockton Corporate Giving Program

c/o Mktg. Dept.: Donations & Sponsorships
P.O. Box 1110
Stockton, CA 95201-3003 (209) 929-1246
FAX: (209) 929-1434; URL: http://www.bankofstockton.com/Main.aspx?TabID=20&PageID=71

Purpose and activities: As a complement to its foundation, Bank of Stockton also makes charitable contributions to nonprofit organizations directly. Support is given primarily in areas of company operations of California.
Fields of interest: General charitable giving.
Type of support: Employee volunteer services; General/operating support; Sponsorships.
Geographic limitations: Giving primarily in areas of company operations in CA.
Publications: Application guidelines.
Application information: Applications accepted. Proposals should be submitted using organization letterhead. Application form not required. Applicants should submit the following:
1) population served
2) copy of IRS Determination Letter
3) copy of most recent annual report/audited financial statement/990
4) contact person
5) copy of current year's organizational budget and/or project budget
6) plans for acknowledgement
7) list of company employees involved with the organization

Proposals should indicate the date and location of the event, if applicable; and any applicable deadlines.

Initial approach: Mail or fax proposal to headquarters or local branch
Deadline(s): 1 month prior to event

Bank of Stockton Educational Foundation

P.O. Box 1110
Stockton, CA 95201-1110

Establishment information: Established in 2000 in CA.
Donor: Bank of Stockton.
Financial data (yr. ended 06/30/12): Assets, $444,711 (M); expenditures, $10; qualifying distributions, $0.
Purpose and activities: The foundation awards student loans to individuals.
Type of support: Student loans—to individuals.
Application information: Applications not accepted. Unsolicited requests for funds not accepted.
Officers and Directors:* Douglass M. Eberhardt*, C.E.O.; Thomas H. Shaffer*, V.P.; Douglass M. Eberhardt II*, Secy.; W. Henry Claussen, Dir.
EIN: 311801280

346
Bank of the West

(formerly United California Bank)
180 Montgomery St., 4th Fl.
San Francisco, CA 94104 (323) 727-3777

Company URL: http://www.bankofthewest.com
Establishment information: Established in 1874.
Company type: Subsidiary of a foreign company
Business activities: Operates commercial bank.
Business type (SIC): Banks/commercial
Financial profile for 2010: Number of employees, 1,000; assets, $57,650,000,000; sales volume, $2,690,000,000
Corporate officers: J. Michael Shepherd, Chair. and C.E.O.; Thibault Fulconis, Vice-Chair.; Maura Markus, Pres. and C.O.O.; Duke Dayal, C.F.O.; Michael Bracco, Sr. Exec. V.P. and C.A.O.; Vanessa L. Washington, Sr. Exec. V.P., Genl. Counsel, and Secy.
Board of directors: J. Michael Shepherd, Chair.; Thibault Fulconis, Vice-Chair.; Frank Bonetto; Bernard Brasseur; Francois Dambrine; Gerard Denot; Walter A. Dods, Jr.; Stuart A. Hall; Guido Van Hauwermeiren; Conrad W. Hewitt; Vivien Levy-Garboua; A. Ewan MacDonald; Yves Martrenchar; Isao Matsuuara; Don J. McGrath; Rodney R. Peck; Frank Roncey; Robert L. Toney; Jacqes H. Wahl
Giving statement: Giving through the Bank of the West Corporate Giving Program and the Bank of the West Charitable Foundation.
Company EIN: 940475440

Bank of the West Corporate Giving Program

(formerly United California Bank Corporate Giving Program)
c/o Corp. Compliance Dept.
180 Montgomery St.
San Francisco, CA 94104 (415) 765-4800
URL: http://www.bankofthewest.com/BOW/main.jsp?ChId=fdb75f9c6072ff00VgnVCM10000087c35c92____

Purpose and activities: Bank of the West makes charitable contributions to nonprofit organizations involved with education, job training, healthcare, human services, community and economic development, and civic affairs.
Fields of interest: Arts; Environment; Health care; Employment, training; Housing/shelter; Human services; Community/economic development; Public affairs.
Programs:
Community and Civic: Bank of the West supports organizations involved with youth development, community development, and civic affairs.
Community Development: Bank of the West supports programs designed to promote affordable housing and lending; provide credit, homeownership, and home maintenance education; promote economic development; and provide financial services education.
Cultural: Bank of the West supports programs designed to provide well-managed cultural activities.
Education and Job Training: Bank of the West supports programs designed to provide basic skills education, including reading, writing, and mathematics; provide business and economic system education; provide scholarships to students who require financial assistance in obtaining an education in business, financial accounting, and economic disciplines; provide scholarships to students who require financial assistance in obtaining vocational and technical training in other fields; provide after-school tutoring and mentoring; promote literacy and provide library programs for youth and adults; provide education in arts and sciences; provide school-to-work and welfare-to-work transition services; provide job training; and promote self-sufficiency.
Health and Human Care: Bank of the West supports hospitals and clinics, specific care centers in hospitals and clinics, and other health agencies; mental health counseling centers, including those for the elderly and the disabled; alcohol and drug recovery centers; homeless and crisis shelters and battered women shelters; homeless organizations, including those that provide services to adults and adults with children; and soup kitchens.
Type of support: Employee volunteer services; General/operating support; Program development; Sponsorships.
Geographic limitations: Giving primarily in areas of company operations.
Support limitations: No support for No support. No grants.

Bank of the West Charitable Foundation

(formerly Commercial Federal Charitable Foundation)
P.O. Box 5155
San Ramon, CA 94583-5155 (415) 399-7285
E-mail: rebeca.rangel@bankofwest.com; Application address: Community Affairs Dept., 180 Montgomery St., 14th Fl., San Francisco, CA 94104; URL: http://www.bankofthewest.com/about-us/community-support.html

Establishment information: Established in 2001 in NE.
Donor: Commercial Federal Bank, FSB.
Contact: Rebeca Rangel, Tr.
Financial data (yr. ended 12/31/11): Assets, $2,792,196 (M); expenditures, $184,979; qualifying distributions, $155,000; giving activities include $150,000 for 14 grants (high: $15,000; low: $5,000).
Purpose and activities: The foundation supports programs designed to promote education and job training; and community and economic development. Special emphasis is directed toward programs designed to serve low-to-moderate income individuals.
Fields of interest: Higher education; Education, reading; Education; Employment, training; Employment; Housing/shelter, home owners; Housing/shelter; Human services, financial counseling; Homeless, human services; Human services; Business/industry; Community development, business promotion; Community development, small businesses; Microfinance/microlending; Community/economic development Economically disadvantaged.
Type of support: Annual campaigns; Building/renovation; Capital campaigns; General/operating support; Program development; Scholarship funds.
Geographic limitations: Giving in areas of company operations in AZ, CA, CO, IA, ID, KS, MN, MO, ND, NE, NM, NV, OK, OR, SD, UT, WA, WI and WY.
Support limitations: No support for fraternal or alumni organizations, political action committees, political candidates, or lobbying organizations. No grants to individuals, or for capital campaigns, trips or tours, or talent or beauty contests.
Publications: Application guidelines.
Application information: Applications accepted. A full on-line application may be requested at a later date. Support is limited to 1 contribution per organization during any given year. Application form required. Applicants should submit the following:
1) copy of IRS Determination Letter
2) copy of most recent annual report/audited financial statement/990
3) listing of board of directors, trustees, officers and other key people and their affiliations
4) detailed description of project and amount of funding requested

Applications should include a W-9 Form.
Initial approach: Complete online letter of inquiry
Deadline(s): None
Trustees: Michael Bracco; Rebeca Rangel; Vanessa L. Washington.
EIN: 396765096

347
The Bank of Tokyo-Mitsubishi UFJ, Ltd.

1251 Ave. of the Americas
New York, NY 10020-1104 (212) 782-4000
FAX: (212) 782-6448

Company URL: http://www.bk.mufg.jp/english/network/americas.html
Establishment information: Established in 1955.
Company type: Subsidiary of a foreign company
Business activities: Operates commercial bank.
Business type (SIC): Banks/commercial
Corporate officers: Minoru Shimada, Pres. and C.E.O.; Johannes H. Worsoe, C.A.O.; Robert E. Hand, Sr. V.P. and Secy.
Giving statement: Giving through the BTMU Foundation, Inc.

The BTMU Foundation, Inc.

(formerly The BTM Foundation, Inc.)
c/o Bank of Tokyo-Mitsubishi UFJ, Ltd.
1251 Ave. of the Americas, 15th Fl.
New York, NY 10020-1168 (212) 782-4926
E-mail: ynakamura@us.mufg.jp

Establishment information: Established in 1997 in NY.
Donors: Bank of Tokyo-Mitsubishi Trust Co.; Bank of Tokyo-Mitsubishi UFJ Trust Co.
Contact: Yuka Nakamura
Financial data (yr. ended 12/31/11): Assets, $5,223,727 (M); gifts received, $858,529; expenditures, $937,130; qualifying distributions, $930,514; giving activities include $930,514 for grants.
Purpose and activities: The foundation supports nonprofit organizations involved with education, community development, and human services. Special emphasis is directed toward programs serving low and moderate income people and neighborhoods.
Fields of interest: Arts education; Education, reading; Health care; Food services; Housing/shelter, development; Aging, centers/services; Urban/community development; Community/economic development Physically disabled; Mentally disabled; Economically disadvantaged.
Type of support: General/operating support; Program development.
Geographic limitations: Giving primarily in New York, NY.
Support limitations: No support for political, religious, sectarian, fraternal, veterans, labor, or lobbying organizations. No grants to individuals, or for advertising, fundraising, capital campaigns, tickets or memberships, or debt reduction.
Publications: Application guidelines; Grants list.
Application information: Applications accepted. Application form required. Applicants should submit the following:
1) staff salaries
2) qualifications of key personnel
3) population served
4) principal source of support for project in the past
5) copy of IRS Determination Letter
6) geographic area to be served
7) copy of most recent annual report/audited financial statement/990
8) listing of board of directors, trustees, officers and other key people and their affiliations
9) detailed description of project and amount of funding requested
10) contact person
11) copy of current year's organizational budget and/or project budget
12) listing of additional sources and amount of support

Initial approach: Contact foundation for application form
Copies of proposal: 1
Board meeting date(s): 4th quarter
Deadline(s): Mid-June to late July
Final notification: Dec.
Officers and Directors:* Masa Tanaka*, Chair.; Yukiyasu Nishio*, Pres.; Johannes Worsoe*, Exec. V.P.; Liz Lyman, Sr. V.P.; Beth Gilroy, V.P.; Andrew Rasanen, V.P.; Thomas Pennington, Secy.; Thomas Greene, Treas.; Noriaki Goto; Isaac Shapiro.
EIN: 133916201
Selected grants: The following grants are a representative sample of this grantmaker's funding activity:
$40,000 to Enterprise Community Partners, New York, NY, 2010.
$20,000 to Local Initiatives Support Corporation, New York, NY, 2010.

$20,000 to Neighborhood Housing Services of New York City, New York, NY, 2010.
$15,000 to ACCION USA, New York, NY, 2010.
$15,000 to Corporation for Supportive Housing, New York, NY, 2010.
$15,000 to Low Income Investment Fund, New York, NY, 2010.
$10,000 to Housing Partnership Development Corporation, New York, NY, 2010.
$10,000 to New York City Financial Network Action Consortium, Brooklyn, NY, 2010.
$10,000 to Nonprofit Finance Fund, New York, NY, 2010.
$10,000 to Primary Care Development Corporation, New York, NY, 2010.

348
Bank of Utica

222 Genesee St.
Utica, NY 13502 (315) 797-2700

Company URL: http://www.bankofutica.com
Establishment information: Established in 1927.
Company type: Private company
Business activities: Operates commercial bank.
Business type (SIC): Banks/commercial
Corporate officers: Tom E. Sinnott, Pres. and C.E.O.; Marie L. Bord, V.P., Human Resources and Cont.; David A. Lashure, V.P., Inf. Systems
Giving statement: Giving through the Bank of Utica Foundation, Inc.

Bank of Utica Foundation, Inc.

c/o M&H
P.O. Box 477
Utica, NY 13503-0477

Establishment information: Established in 1992 in NY.
Donor: Bank of Utica.
Financial data (yr. ended 12/31/11): Assets, $1,944,950 (M); expenditures, $126,294; qualifying distributions, $124,894; giving activities include $124,894 for grants.
Purpose and activities: The foundation supports health centers and organizations involved with arts and culture, education, housing, golf, human services, and community economic development.
Fields of interest: Arts councils; Performing arts; Arts; Higher education; Libraries (public); Scholarships/financial aid; Education; Health care, clinics/centers; Housing/shelter; Athletics/sports, golf; Community/economic development; United Ways and Federated Giving Programs.
Type of support: General/operating support; Program development.
Geographic limitations: Giving limited to Utica, NY.
Support limitations: No grants to individuals.
Officers: Tom E. Sinnott, Chair.; Joan M. Sinnott, Pres.; Barry J. Sinnott, V.P.
EIN: 161423958
Selected grants: The following grants are a representative sample of this grantmaker's funding activity:
$20,000 to Saint Elizabeth Medical Center Foundation, Utica, NY, 2010.
$8,500 to Munson Williams Proctor Institute, Utica, NY, 2010.
$5,000 to Economic Development Growth Enterprises Corporation, Rome, NY, 2010.
$5,000 to Hope House, Utica, NY, 2010.
$5,000 to Utica Public Library, Utica, NY, 2010.
$2,500 to Sculpture Space, Utica, NY, 2010.
$2,000 to Oneida County Historical Society, Utica, NY, 2010.
$2,000 to Utica Zoological Society, Utica, NY, 2010.
$1,250 to For The Good, Utica, NY, 2010.

349
Bank Rhode Island

(also known as BankRI)
1 Turks Head Pl.
P.O. Box 9488
Providence, RI 02903 (401) 456-5000

Company URL: http://www.bankri.com
Establishment information: Established in 1996.
Company type: Subsidiary of a public company
Business activities: Operates a state commercial bank.
Business type (SIC): Banks/commercial
Corporate officers: John A. Yena, Chair.; Meredith A. Curren, Vice-Chair.; Mark J. Meiklejohn, Co-Pres. and Co-C.E.O.; Merrill W. Sherman, Co-Pres. and Co-C.E.O.; Linda H. Simmons, C.F.O. and Treas.; Robert H. Wischnowsky, C.I.O.; Alan P. Melidossian, V.P., Mktg. and Comms.
Board of directors: John A. Yena, Chair.; Meredith A. Curren, Vice-Chair.; Anthony F. Andrade; John R. Berger; Richard L. Bready; Ernest J. Chornyei, Jr.; Edward J. Mack II; Mark Meiklejohn; Paul Perrault; Pablo Rodriguez, M.D.; Cheryl W. Snead
Giving statement: Giving through the Bank Rhode Island Corporate Giving Program.
Company EIN: 050509802

Bank Rhode Island Corporate Giving Program

c/o Corp. & Community Rels.
P.O. Box 9488
Providence, RI 02940-9488
URL: https://www.bankri.com/AboutBankRI/IntheCommunity/tabid/229/Default.aspx

Contact: Patricia O. Saracino, V.P., Corp. and Community Rels.
Purpose and activities: Bank Rhode Island makes charitable contributions to nonprofit organizations involved with neighborhood preservation and revitalization, critical services, education, and diversity. Support is given primarily in areas of company operations in Kent, Providence, and Washington counties, Rhode Island.
Fields of interest: Arts, cultural/ethnic awareness; Education; Employment, training; Youth development; Family services; Human services; Civil/human rights, equal rights; Community/economic development Minorities.
Type of support: Employee volunteer services; General/operating support; In-kind gifts; Technical assistance; Use of facilities.
Geographic limitations: Giving primarily in areas of company operations in Kent, Providence, and Washington counties, RI.
Support limitations: No support for religious or sectarian organizations, fraternal or political organizations, colleges or universities (non-capital campaigns), or local chapters of national health organizations related to a single disease. No grants to individuals, or for endowments, trips, tours or conferences.
Publications: Application guidelines.
Application information: Applications accepted. Bank Rhode Island's contributions range in size, with an average contribution less than $2,000. Smaller requests ($100 or less) may be made at a branch. Bank Rhode Island will review only one proposal per organization within a 12-month period. Applicants should submit the following:
1) copy of IRS Determination Letter
Initial approach: Proposal
Copies of proposal: 1
Deadline(s): None

350
BankSouth

(formerly Citizens Union Bank)
200 N. East St.
P.O. Box 89
Greensboro, GA 30642 (706) 453-2236
FAX: (706) 453-0155

Company URL: http://www.banksouth.biz
Establishment information: Established in 1977.
Company type: Private company
Business activities: Operates commercial bank.
Business type (SIC): Banks/commercial
Corporate officers: Harold Reynolds, Chair. and C.E.O.; Mike Sleeth, C.F.O.; David S. Cowles, Exec. V.P. and C.O.O.
Board of directors: Harold Reynolds, Chair.; Lewis Duvall; Richard H. Maddux; Marguerite R. McInteer; Carolyn Reynolds Parker; James M. Reynolds III; Frances R. Strickland; Jerry Shaifer; Bobby L. Voyles
Office: Savannah, GA
Giving statement: Giving through the BankSouth Foundation, Ltd.

BankSouth Foundation, Ltd.

(formerly Citizens Union Bank Foundation, Ltd.)
P.O. Box 89
Greensboro, GA 30642-0089
Application address: 200 N. East St., Greensboro, GA 30642, tel.: (706) 453-2236

Donors: Citizens Union Bank; BankSouth.
Contact: Bobby L. Voyles, Chair.
Financial data (yr. ended 12/31/11): Assets, $436,389 (M); expenditures, $25,095; qualifying distributions, $24,500; giving activities include $24,500 for grants.
Purpose and activities: The foundation supports organizations involved with education and awards college scholarships to individuals nominated by their high schools in Green County, Georgia.
Fields of interest: Education; Human services; Religion.
Type of support: General/operating support; Scholarships—to individuals.
Geographic limitations: Giving limited to Greene County, GA.
Application information: Applications accepted. Application form required.
Initial approach: Proposal
Deadline(s): None
Officers and Directors:* Bobby L. Voyles*, Chair.; Dean B. Rizner*, Secy.-Treas.; Neal Dolvin; Richard Schmidt; Frances Strickland.
EIN: 581541701

351
Banner & Witcoff, Ltd.

10 S. Wacker Dr., Ste. 3000
Chicago, IL 60606-7407 (312) 463-5000

Company URL: http://www.bannerwitcoff.com
Establishment information: Established in 1920.
Company type: Private company
Business activities: Operates law firm.
Business type (SIC): Legal services
Corporate officer: Charles L. Miller, Pres.

Giving statement: Giving through the Banner & Witcoff, Ltd. Pro Bono Program.

Banner & Witcoff, Ltd. Pro Bono Program

10 S. Wacker Dr., Ste. 3000
Chicago, IL 60606-7407 (202) 824-3000
E-mail: info@bannerwitcoff.com; URL: http://www.bannerwitcoff.com/

Contact: Darrell Mottley, Attorney
Fields of interest: Legal services.
Type of support: Pro bono services - legal.
Geographic limitations: Giving primarily in areas of company operations in Washington, DC, Chicago, IL, Boston, MA, and Portland, OR.
Application information: A Pro Bono Committee manages the pro bono program.

352
Banner Seventeen, LLC

(doing business as Boston Celtics)
226 Causeway St., 4th Fl.
Boston, MA 02114-2155 (617) 854-8000

Company URL: http://www.nba.com/celtics
Establishment information: Established in 1946.
Company type: Subsidiary of a private company
Business activities: Operates professional basketball club.
Business type (SIC): Commercial sports
Corporate officers: Wyc Grousbeck, C.E.O.; Rich Gotham, Pres.; Bill Reissfelder, Sr. V.P. and C.F.O.; Tim Rath, V.P. and Cont.
Giving statement: Giving through the Boston Celtics Shamrock Foundation, Inc.

Boston Celtics Shamrock Foundation, Inc.

(formerly Boston Celtics Charitable Foundation, Inc.)
226 Causeway St., 4th Fl.
Boston, MA 02114-2155 (617) 854-8000
FAX: (617) 367-4286; URL: http://www.nba.com/celtics/community/shamrock/index.html

Establishment information: Established in 1993 in MA.
Contact: William J. Reissfelder, Treas.
Financial data (yr. ended 12/31/10): Revenue, $1,434,029; assets, $2,997,557 (M); gifts received, $1,528,913; expenditures, $1,201,097; giving activities include $869,002 for 18 grants (high: $100,000; low: $5,000).
Purpose and activities: As the philanthropic arm of the Boston Celtics, the foundation seeks to benefit children through programs that provide education and support, and partners with community-based organizations that provide health care, shelter, and vital services for children in need.
Fields of interest: Health care; Health care, home services; Housing/shelter.
Geographic limitations: Giving primarily in MA.
Officers and Directors:* Stephen Pagliuca*, Pres.; William J. Reissfelder*, Treas.; Leigh Trimmier*, Exec. Dir.; Robert Epstein; H. Irving Grousbeck; Wycliffe Grousbeck; Glenn Hutchins; James Pallotta.
EIN: 043174933

353
Barack Ferrazzano Kirschbaum & Nagelberg LLP

200 W. Madison St., Ste. 3900
Chicago, IL 60606-3459 (312) 984-3100

Company URL: http://www.bfkn.com
Establishment information: Established in 1984.
Company type: Private company
Business activities: Operates law firm.
Business type (SIC): Legal services
Corporate officer: Douglas W. Anderson, Partner
Giving statement: Giving through the Barack Ferrazzano Kirschbaum & Nagelberg LLP Pro Bono Program and the BFKN Foundation, Inc.

Barack Ferrazzano Kirschbaum & Nagelberg LLP Pro Bono Program

200 W. Madison St., Ste. 3900
Chicago, IL 60606-3459 (312) 984-3100
E-mail: randall.oyler@bfkn.com; URL: http://www.bfkn.com/about-probono.html

Contact: Randall Oyler, Partner
Fields of interest: Legal services.
Type of support: Pro bono services - legal.
Geographic limitations: Giving primarily in areas of company operations in Chicago, IL.
Application information: A Pro Bono Committee manages the pro bono program.

BFKN Foundation, Inc.

200 W. Madison St., Ste. 3900
Chicago, IL 60606-3465 (312) 984-3100
URL: http://www.bfkn.com/about-community.html

Establishment information: Established in 2005.
Financial data (yr. ended 12/31/09): Revenue, $23,047; assets, $9,971 (M); gifts received, $23,039; expenditures, $19,897; program services expenses, $19,882.
Purpose and activities: The foundation supports the creation and furtherance of peer review and instruction programs relating to conflict management among primary and secondary education school students. Special emphasis is directed toward programs designed to assist and encourage economically disadvantaged students. Support is given primarily in areas of company operations in the greater Chicago, Illinois area.
Geographic limitations: Giving primarily in areas of company operations in the greater Chicago, IL area.
Officers and Directors:* Rachel M. Trummel, Pres.; Roger H. Stetson, Secy.; Mark S. Bernstein, Treas.; Sarah M. Bernstein; Ray G. Rezner.
EIN: 203116348

354
Barbara Oil Company

21 S. Clark St., Ste. 3990
Chicago, IL 60603-2008 (312) 726-5555

Establishment information: Established in 1916.
Company type: Private company
Business activities: Operates security brokerage.
Business type (SIC): Brokers and dealers/security
Corporate officers: Kimball T. Brooker, Co-Pres.; Thomas K. Brooker, Co-Pres.; Anita D. Mik, Secy.
Giving statement: Giving through the Brooker Family Foundation.

Brooker Family Foundation

21 S. Clark St., Ste. 3990
Chicago, IL 60603-2008

Establishment information: Established in 2004 in IL.
Donors: T. Kimball Brooker; Barbara Oil Co.
Financial data (yr. ended 10/31/11): Assets, $476,898 (M); expenditures, $32,275; qualifying distributions, $30,000; giving activities include $30,000 for 4 grants (high: $10,000; low: $5,000).
Fields of interest: Education; Religion.
Support limitations: No grants to individuals.
Application information: Applications not accepted. Unsolicited requests for funds not accepted.
Officer: T. Kimball Brooker, Pres. and Treas.
EIN: 202004088

355
Barber Gale Group, Inc.

172 N. Hanover St.
Pottstown, PA 19464-5434 (610) 705-3606
FAX: (610) 705-3565

Company URL: http://www.barbergale.com
Establishment information: Established in 1993.
Company type: Private company
Business type (SIC): Business services/miscellaneous
Corporate officer: Cynthia Barber Gale, C.E.O.
Giving statement: Giving through the Barber Gale Group, Inc. Corporate Giving Program.

Barber Gale Group, Inc. Corporate Giving Program

172 N Hanover St.
Pottstown, PA 19464-5434 (610) 705-3606
URL: http://www.barbergale.com

356
Barber, Fred Lee Co., Inc.

515 Madison Ave., Ste. 3300
New York, NY 10022-5414 (212) 888-0373

Establishment information: Established in 1974.
Company type: Private company
Business activities: Provides business consulting services.
Business type (SIC): Management and public relations services
Corporate officer: Fred Lee Barber, Chair. and C.E.O.
Board of director: Fred L. Barber, Chair.
Giving statement: Giving through the Blue Hill Road Foundation, Inc.

Blue Hill Road Foundation, Inc.

c/o Leshkowitz & Co.
270 Madison Ave.
New York, NY 10016-0602 (212) 532-5550
Application address: 8 E. 96th St., New York, NY 10028-0706

Establishment information: Established in 1994 in NY.
Donors: Fred Lee Barber Co., Inc.; Fred Lee Barber; David Barber.
Contact: Fred Lee Barber, Pres.
Financial data (yr. ended 12/31/11): Assets, $2,347,350 (M); gifts received, $80,000; expenditures, $122,292; qualifying distributions,

$121,500; giving activities include $121,500 for grants.
Purpose and activities: Giving primarily for education and hospitals.
Geographic limitations: Giving primarily in NY.
Support limitations: No grants to individuals.
Application information: Applications accepted. Application form required. Applicants should submit the following:
1) descriptive literature about organization
2) detailed description of project and amount of funding requested
Initial approach: Letter
Deadline(s): None
Officers: Fred Lee Barber, Pres.; David Barber, Secy.; Daniel Barber, Treas.
EIN: 133799422

357
Barclays PLC (USA)
745 Seventh Ave.
New York, NY 10019 (212) 526-7000

Company URL: http://group.barclays.com/about-barclays/about-us/usa#Community
Establishment information: Established in 1690.
Company type: Subsidiary of a foreign company
Business activities: Operates financial services company.
Business type (SIC): Banks/commercial
Corporate officer: Antony P. Jenkins, C.E.O.
Giving statement: Giving through the Barclays PLC (USA) Corporate Giving Program.

Barclays PLC (USA) Corporate Giving Program
745 Seventh Ave.
New York, NY 10019 (212) 526-7000
E-mail: philanthropyamericas@barclays.com; Additional e-mail: Communityrelations@barclaycardus.com; URL: http://group.barclays.com/about-barclays/about-us/usa#Community

358
C.R. Bard, Inc.
730 Central Ave.
Murray Hill, NJ 07974-1139
(908) 277-8000
FAX: (908) 277-8412

Company URL: http://www.crbard.com/
Establishment information: Established in 1907.
Company type: Public company
Company ticker symbol and exchange: BCR/NYSE
Business activities: Designs, manufactures, packages, distributes, and sells medical, surgical, diagnostic, and patient care devices.
Business type (SIC): Medical instruments and supplies
Financial profile for 2012: Number of employees, 12,200; assets, $4,151,300,000; sales volume, $2,958,100,000; pre-tax net income, $732,400,000; expenses, $2,225,700,000; liabilities, $2,225,600,000
Fortune 1000 ranking: 2012—721st in revenues, 320th in profits, and 651st in assets
Forbes 2000 ranking: 2012—1617th in sales, 1127th in profits, and 1866th in assets
Corporate officers: Timothy M. Ring, Chair. and C.E.O.; John H. Weiland, Pres. and C.O.O.; Christopher S. Holland, Sr. V.P. and C.F.O.; Jean Holloway, V.P., Genl. Counsel, and Secy.; Scott T. Lowry, V.P. and Treas.; Frank Lupisella, Jr., V.P. and Cont.; Bronwen K. Kelly, V.P., Human Resources
Board of directors: Timothy M. Ring, Chair.; David M. Barrett, M.D.; Marc C. Breslawsky; Herbert L. Henkel; John C. Kelly; Gail K. Naughton, Ph.D.; Tommy G. Thompson; Tony L. White; John H. Weiland; Anthony Welters
Subsidiaries: Bard Access Systems, Inc., Salt Lake City, UT; Bard International, Inc., Murray Hill, NJ; Dymax Corp., Pittsburgh, PA
Divisions: Bard Electrophysiology Div., Lowell, MA; Bard Medical Div., Covington, GA; Bard Peripheral Vascular Div., Tempe, AZ; Corporate Healthcare Services Div., Murray Hill, NJ; Davol, Inc., Warwick, RI
Plants: Glens Falls, NY; Las Piedras, PR; Moncks Corner, SC
International operations: Canada; England; France; Ireland
Giving statement: Giving through the C. R. Bard, Inc. Corporate Giving Program and the C. R. Bard Foundation, Inc.
Company EIN: 221454160

C. R. Bard, Inc. Corporate Giving Program
730 Central Ave.
New Providence, NJ 07974-1139
FAX: (908) 277-8098

Contact: Linda A. Hrevnack, Mgr., Community Affairs and Contribs.
Financial data (yr. ended 12/31/10): Total giving, $1,374,608, including $1,006,869 for 114 grants and $367,739 for employee matching gifts.
Purpose and activities: As a complement to its foundation, C.R. Bard also makes charitable contributions to nonprofit organizations directly. Support is given primarily in areas of company operations.
Fields of interest: Education; Health care; Human services.
Type of support: Donated products; General/operating support.
Geographic limitations: Giving primarily in areas of company operations.
Support limitations: No support for private foundations, political parties, fraternal, religious, or sectarian groups, or veterans' organizations. No grants to individuals.
Application information: Applications not accepted. Contributes only to pre-selected organizations. The Community Affairs Department handles giving. A contributions committee reviews all requests.
Committee meeting date(s): Quarterly
Corporate Contributions Committee: Linda Hrevnack, Mgr., Community Affairs and Contribs.
Number of staff: 1 full-time professional.

C. R. Bard Foundation, Inc.
730 Central Ave.
Murray Hill, NJ 07974-1139
FAX: (908) 277-8098; URL: http://www.crbard.com/Community_Outreach/C_R__Bard_Foundation,_Inc_.html

Establishment information: Established in 1987 in NY.
Donor: C.R. Bard, Inc.
Contact: Linda Hrevnack
Financial data (yr. ended 12/31/11): Assets, $749,521 (M); gifts received, $2,154,000; expenditures, $2,391,616; qualifying distributions, $2,391,616; giving activities include $1,799,499 for 176 grants (high: $89,969; low: $52) and $575,193 for 1,270 employee matching gifts.
Purpose and activities: The foundation supports organizations involved with education, health, and human services. Special emphasis is directed toward programs designed to promote urology, oncology, vascular, and surgical medicine.
Fields of interest: Education; Health care; Medical specialties; Human services; United Ways and Federated Giving Programs.
Programs:
Community Commitment: The foundation supports programs designed to improve quality of life in Bard communities in the U.S. and Puerto Rico. Special emphasis is directed towards programs designed to promote arts and culture, education, health care, and social welfare. Projects are selected by division locations and special emphasis is geared toward organizations with employee volunteerism.
Health Care Commitment: The foundation supports programs designed to improve quality of life through health care. Special emphasis is directed toward programs designed to promote urology, oncology, vascular, and surgical medicine.
Matching Gifts Program: The foundation matches contributions made by employees and directors of C.R. Bard to the United Way and nonprofit organizations involved with education, health, social welfare, and arts and culture.
Type of support: Employee matching gifts; General/operating support; Program development; Scholarship funds; Sponsorships.
Geographic limitations: Giving primarily in areas of company operations.
Support limitations: No support for private foundations, political parties, fraternal, religious, or sectarian groups, or veterans' organizations. No grants to individuals, or for events that provide a non-charitable benefit to C.R. Bard, or capital campaigns.
Publications: Application guidelines.
Application information: Applications accepted. Application form not required. Applicants should submit the following:
1) statement of problem project will address
2) name, address and phone number of organization
3) copy of IRS Determination Letter
4) brief history of organization and description of its mission
5) copy of most recent annual report/audited financial statement/990
6) listing of board of directors, trustees, officers and other key people and their affiliations
7) detailed description of project and amount of funding requested
8) copy of current year's organizational budget and/or project budget
Initial approach: Proposal
Copies of proposal: 2
Board meeting date(s): Quarterly
Deadline(s): None
Officers: Timothy M. Ring, Pres.; Scott T. Lowry, V.P. and Treas.; John H. Weiland, V.P.; Bronwen Kelly, Secy.
EIN: 222840708
Selected grants: The following grants are a representative sample of this grantmaker's funding activity:
$100,000 to Institute for Health Technology Studies, Washington, DC, 2010.
$83,261 to United Way of Greater Union County, Elizabeth, NJ, 2010.
$79,184 to Johns Hopkins University, Baltimore, MD, 2010.
$73,055 to United Way, Valley of the Sun, Phoenix, AZ, 2010.

$67,158 to Cleveland Clinic Foundation, Cleveland, OH, 2010.
$58,422 to Community Health Charities of New Jersey, Monroe Township, NJ, 2010.
$50,000 to Siena College, Loudonville, NY, 2010.
$50,000 to Vascular Disease Foundation, Lakewood, CO, 2010.
$33,000 to John F. Kennedy Center for the Performing Arts, Washington, DC, 2010.

359
Bardes Corporation
4730 Madison Rd.
Cincinnati, OH 45227-1426 (513) 533-6200

Company URL: https://www.ilsco.com//Default.aspx?ght=bMkOFOntbLmb8V6JsfOkpg%3d%3d
Establishment information: Established in 1996.
Company type: Subsidiary of a private company
Business activities: Operates holding company; manufactures industrial machinery and wiring devices; provides construction and financial services.
Business type (SIC): Holding company; operative builders; machinery/industrial and commercial; lighting and wiring equipment/electric
Corporate officers: Merrilyne Bardes, Chair.; David J. Fitzgibbon, Pres. and C.E.O.
Board of director: Merrilyne Bardes, Chair.
Subsidiary: FTZ Industries, Inc., Simpsonville, SC
Giving statement: Giving through the Bardes Fund.

Bardes Fund
4730 Madison Rd.
Cincinnati, OH 45227-1426

Establishment information: Established in 1955 in OH.
Donors: Bardes Corp.; Brittain B. Cudlip.
Financial data (yr. ended 12/31/11): Assets, $1,537,835 (M); gifts received, $50,000; expenditures, $84,146; qualifying distributions, $74,950; giving activities include $74,950 for 10 grants (high: $20,000; low: $2,000).
Purpose and activities: The foundation supports organizations involved with arts and culture and human services.
Fields of interest: Performing arts, orchestras; Arts; Human services; United Ways and Federated Giving Programs.
Type of support: Annual campaigns; Capital campaigns; General/operating support; Program development.
Geographic limitations: Giving primarily in FL and OH.
Application information: Applications not accepted. Unsolicited requests for funds not accepted.
Officers: Merrilyn Bardes, Pres.; Thomas Quinn, Secy.; Rebecca Barron, Treas.
EIN: 316036206

360
Barnes & Noble, Inc.
122 5th Ave.
New York, NY 10011-5605 (212) 633-3300

Company URL: http://www.barnesandnobleinc.com
Establishment information: Established in 1986.
Company type: Public company
Company ticker symbol and exchange: BKS/NYSE
Business activities: Operates book stores; operates video game and entertainment software stores; provides Internet shopping services.
Business type (SIC): Shopping goods stores/miscellaneous; consumer electronics and music stores; computer services
Financial profile for 2012: Number of employees, 35,000; assets, $3,765,250,000; sales volume, $7,129,200,000; pre-tax net income, -$96,610,000; expenses, $7,190,500,000; liabilities, $2,825,320,000
Fortune 1000 ranking: 2012—360th in revenues, 915th in profits, and 682nd in assets
Corporate officers: Leonard Riggio, Chair.; Stephen Riggio, Vice-Chair.; Mitchell S. Klipper, Co-C.E.O.; William J. Lynch, Jr., Co-C.E.O.; Michael P. Huseby, C.F.O.; Christopher Grady-Troia, C.I.O.; Mary Ellen Keating, Sr. V.P., Corp. Comms., and Public Affairs; Allen W. Lindstrom, V.P. and Corp. Cont.; Gene DeFelice, V.P., Genl. Counsel, and Corp. Secy.; Michelle Smith, V.P., Human Resources
Board of directors: Leonard Riggio, Chair.; Stephen Riggio, Vice-Chair.; George Campbell, Jr.; Mark D. Carleton; William T. Dillard II; David G. Golden; Patricia L. Higgins; William J. Lynch, Jr.; Gregory B. Maffei; David A. Wilson
Subsidiary: B. Dalton Bookseller, Inc., New York, NY
International operations: Bermuda
Giving statement: Giving through the Barnes & Noble, Inc. Corporate Giving Program.
Company EIN: 061196501

Barnes & Noble, Inc. Corporate Giving Program
122 5th Ave.
New York, NY 10011 (800) 962-6177
FAX: (201) 559-6910;
E-mail: contributions@bn.com; URL: http://www.barnesandnobleinc.com/our_company/community/community.html

Purpose and activities: Barnes & Noble makes charitable contributions to nonprofit organizations involved with arts and culture, literacy, and education. Support is given on a national basis in areas of company operations.
Fields of interest: Arts; Elementary/secondary education; Higher education; Education, reading; Education; Human services, gift distribution.
Program:
My Favorite Teacher Program: The Barnes & Noble My Favorite Teacher program provides middle and high school students the opportunity to tell their communities how much they appreciate their teachers. Teachers from grades 1 through 12 are eligible for nomination, and awards include cash prizes for the teachers and schools, NOOKs and more. The winning teacher from each store is entered into the regional contest, where regional winners receive a NOOK and a $500 Barnes & Noble gift card. From the pool of regional winners, Barnes & Noble names one teacher the Barnes & Noble National Teacher of the Year. The winning teacher receives $5,000 and the title of "Barnes & Noble My Favorite Teacher of the Year." The winner is recognized at a special community celebration at their local Barnes & Noble store, and the winning teacher's school receives $5,000.
Type of support: Donated products; Employee volunteer services; Sponsorships.
Geographic limitations: Giving on a national basis in areas of company operations.
Publications: Application guidelines.
Application information: Applications accepted. Application form not required.
Initial approach: Proposal to local store manager or community relations manager for local requests; e-mail proposal for corporate sponsorship and donation requests
Copies of proposal: 1

361
Barnes & Thornburg LLP
11 S. Meridian St.
Indianapolis, IN 46204-3535
(317) 236-1313

Company URL: http://www.btlaw.com
Establishment information: Established in 1940.
Company type: Private company
Business activities: Operates law firm.
Business type (SIC): Legal services
Corporate officers: Larry R. Lambert, C.F.O.; Kenneth Kobe, C.A.O.
Giving statement: Giving through the Barnes & Thornburg LLP Pro Bono Program.

Barnes & Thornburg LLP Pro Bono Program
11 S. Meridian St.
Indianapolis, IN 46204-3535 (317) 231-7464
FAX: (317) 231-7433;
E-mail: john.maley@btlaw.com; URL: http://www.btlaw.com/aboutus/xpqGC.aspx?xpST=AboutUsGC&key=f98890c8-372c-4c30-aa40-6f05fe10e339&activeEntry=d0ba4e3a-c7e9-4932-b4ca-e67d54e0a69d

Contact: John Maley, Partner
Fields of interest: Legal services.
Type of support: Pro bono services - legal.
Geographic limitations: Giving primarily in areas of company operations in Los Angeles, CA, Washington, DC, Wilmington, DE, Atlanta, GA, Chicago, IL, Elkhart, Fort Wayne, Indianapolis, and South Bend, IN, Grand Rapids, MI, Minneapolis, MN, Columbus, OH.
Application information: A Pro Bono Committee manages the pro bono program.

362
Barnes Group Inc.
123 Main St.
Bristol, CT 06011 (860) 583-7070
FAX: (302) 674-5266

Company URL: http://www.bginc.com
Establishment information: Established in 1857.
Company type: Public company
Company ticker symbol and exchange: B/NYSE
Business activities: Manufactures mechanical and nitrogen gas springs and manifold systems; manufactures aerospace components and assemblies; provides jet engine component repair services; sells maintenance, repair, and operating supplies and engineered metal components wholesale.
Business type (SIC): Metal products/fabricated; aircraft and parts; industrial machinery and equipment—wholesale; repair shops/miscellaneous
Financial profile for 2012: Number of employees, 5,100; assets, $1,868,600,000; sales volume, $1,229,960,000; pre-tax net income, $121,650,000; expenses, $1,093,400,000; liabilities, $1,068,480,000
Corporate officers: Thomas O. Barnes, Chair.; Patrick J. Dempsey, Pres. and C.E.O.; Christopher J.

Stephens, Jr., Sr. V.P., Finance and C.F.O.; Claudia S. Toussaint, Sr. V.P., Genl. Counsel, and Secy.; Dawn N. Edwards, Sr. V.P., Human Resources; Kenneth Hopson, V.P. and Treas.; Marian Acker, Jr., V.P. and Cont.
Board of directors: Thomas O. Barnes, Chair.; Thomas J. Albani; John W. Alden; Gary G. Benanav; William S. Bristow, Jr.; George T. Carpenter; Patrick J. Dempsey; Mylle H. Mangum; Hassell H. McClellan; Gregory F. Milzcik; William J. Morgan
Divisions: Associated Spring Div., Bristol, CT; Barnes Aerospace Div., Windsor, CT
Plants: Bakersfield, CA; Windsor, CT; Norcross, GA; Rockford, IL; Elizabethtown, KY; Saline, Ypsilanti, MI; Edison, NJ; Syracuse, NY; Arden, NC; Maumee, OH; Corry, PA; Arlington, Dallas, TX; Auburn, WA; Milwaukee, New Berlin, WI
International operations: Canada; France; Mexico; Singapore; United Kingdom
Giving statement: Giving through the Barnes Group Foundation Inc.
Company EIN: 060247846

Barnes Group Foundation Inc.

123 Main St.
Bristol, CT 06010-0489
URL: http://www.barnesgroupinc.com/about_foundation.php
Scholarship application address: Citizens Scholarship Foundation of America, Inc., 1505 Riverview Rd., P.O. Box 297, St. Peter, MN 56082

Establishment information: Incorporated in 1973 in CT.
Donor: Barnes Group Inc.
Financial data (yr. ended 12/31/11): Assets, $825,206 (M); gifts received, $1,850,000; expenditures, $1,024,867; qualifying distributions, $1,012,503; giving activities include $1,012,503 for grants.
Purpose and activities: The foundation supports organizations involved with arts and culture, education, the environment, health, cancer, youth services, and civic affairs.
Fields of interest: Arts; Higher education; Education; Environment, natural resources; Environment, land resources; Environment; Health care; Cancer; American Red Cross; Youth, services; United Ways and Federated Giving Programs; Public affairs.
Programs:
Matching Gift Program: The foundation matches contributions made by employees and directors of Barnes Group to organizations involved with arts and culture, education, and health care.
Scholarship Program: The foundation awards college scholarships to children of employees Barnes Group. The program is administered by Citizens Scholarship Foundation of America, Inc.
Type of support: Annual campaigns; Building/renovation; Employee matching gifts; Employee volunteer services; Employee-related scholarships; General/operating support.
Geographic limitations: Giving primarily in areas of company operations, with emphasis on CT.
Support limitations: No grants to individuals (except for employee-related scholarships).
Officers and Directors:* Gregory F. Milzcik*, Pres.; Thomas O. Barnes*, Secy.; Dawn N. Edwards; Christopher J. Stephens, Jr.; Claudia S. Toussaint.
EIN: 237339727

363
Barrasso Usdin Kupperman Freeman & Sarver LLC

909 Poydras St., 24th Fl.
New Orleans, LA 70112-4053
(504) 589-9700

Company URL: http://www.barrassousdin.com
Establishment information: Established in 2003.
Company type: Private company
Business activities: Operates law firm.
Business type (SIC): Legal services
Corporate officer: Meredith A. Cunningham, Partner
Office: Lake Charles, LA
Giving statement: Giving through the Barrasso Usdin Kupperman Freeman & Sarver LLC Corporate Giving Program.

Barrasso Usdin Kupperman Freeman & Sarver LLC Corporate Giving Program

909 Poydras St., 24th Fl.
New Orleans, LA 70112-4053 (504) 589-9700
FAX: (504) 589-9701;
E-mail: kbeckman@barrassousdin.com; Contact for Pro Bono program: Meredith Cunningham, Member, Hiring Attorney, tel.: (504) 589-9734, e-mail: mcunningham@barrassousdin.com; URL: http://www.barrassousdin.com/community.php

Contact: Kristin Beckman, Pro Bono Partner
Purpose and activities: Barrasso Usdin Kupperman Freeman & Sarver makes charitable contributions to educational institutions and nonprofit organizations involved with arts and culture, health care, and youth development.
Fields of interest: Arts; Education; Health care; Legal services; Youth development.
Type of support: Employee volunteer services; General/operating support; Pro bono services - legal; Program development; Scholarship funds.

364
Barron's Educational Series, Inc.

250 Wireless Blvd.
Hauppauge, NY 11788 (631) 434-3311
FAX: (631) 434-3217

Company URL: http://www.barronseduc.com
Establishment information: Established in 1941.
Company type: Private company
Business activities: Publishes test preparation manuals; publishes directories; publishes books; produces electronic learning materials.
Business type (SIC): Publishing/miscellaneous; book publishing and/or printing
Corporate officers: Manuel H. Barron, Pres.; Alex Holtz, Sr. V.P., Sales and Mktg.; Michael Rozansky, Cont.
Giving statement: Giving through the Gloria M. Barron Foundation.

Gloria M. Barron Foundation

927 Ripley Ln.
Oyster Bay, NY 11771-4605

Donors: Barron's Educational Series, Inc.; Manuel H. Barron.
Financial data (yr. ended 12/31/11): Assets, $94,486 (M); expenditures, $53,639; qualifying distributions, $53,219; giving activities include $53,000 for 5 grants (high: $45,000; low: $1,000).
Purpose and activities: The foundation supports art museums and libraries and organizations involved with secondary education, children services, and disability services.
Fields of interest: Museums (art); Secondary school/education; Libraries (public); Boys & girls clubs; Children, services; Developmentally disabled, centers & services.
Type of support: General/operating support; Program development; Scholarship funds.
Geographic limitations: Giving primarily in the New York, NY, area.
Support limitations: No grants to individuals.
Application information: Applications not accepted. Unsolicited requests for funds not accepted.
Trustee: Manuel H. Barron.
EIN: 237038551

365
Bartlett and Company

4800 Main St., Ste. 1200
Kansas City, MO 64112-2509
(816) 753-6300

Company URL: http://www.bartlettandco.com
Establishment information: Established in 1907.
Company type: Private company
Business activities: Provides grain merchandising and storage services; produces cattle; conducts milling activities.
Business type (SIC): Farm-product raw materials—wholesale; farms/livestock; grain mill products, including pet food; non-durable goods—wholesale
Corporate officers: Paul D. Bartlett, Jr., Chair.; James B. Hebenstreit, Pres. and C.E.O.; Jack Moran, Sr. V.P. and C.I.O.; Tom Steele, C.F.O.; Arnold F. Wheeler, V.P. and Secy.-Treas.; Simon B. Buckner IV, Genl. Counsel
Board of directors: Paul D. Bartlett, Jr., Chair.; Bruce R. Bartlett
Giving statement: Giving through the Bartlett and Company Contributions Program and the Bartlett and Company Grain Charitable Foundation.

Bartlett and Company Grain Charitable Foundation

4900 Main St., Ste. 1200
Kansas City, MO 64112-2683

Establishment information: Established in 1986 in MO.
Donor: Bartlett and Co.
Financial data (yr. ended 04/30/12): Assets, $2,876,238 (M); expenditures, $132,670; qualifying distributions, $130,180; giving activities include $130,180 for 50 grants (high: $30,000; low: $30).
Purpose and activities: The foundation supports organizations involved with arts and culture, education, trichotillomania disorder, legal aid, children services, and public policy.
Fields of interest: Health care; Agriculture/food; Human services.
Type of support: General/operating support.
Geographic limitations: Giving primarily in Washington, DC, Kansas City, MO, and VA.
Support limitations: No grants to individuals.
Application information: Applications accepted. Application form required.
Initial approach: Proposal
Deadline(s): None

Trustees: Paul D. Bartlett, Jr.; James B. Hebenstreit.
EIN: 436323269

366
Barton-Malow Enterprises, Inc.

26500 American Dr.
Southfield, MI 48034 (248) 436-5000

Company URL: http://www.bartonmalow.com/default.htm
Establishment information: Established in 1924.
Company type: Private company
Business activities: Provides general contract construction services.
Business type (SIC): Engineering, architectural, and surveying services; contractors/general nonresidential building; management and public relations services
Corporate officers: Benjamin C. Maibach III, Chair. and C.E.O.; Ryan Maibach, Pres.; Phil Go, C.I.O.; Michael Dishaw, Sr. V.P. and C.F.O.
Board of director: Benjamin C. Maibach III, Chair.
Subsidiaries: The ARGOS Group, Southfield, MI; Barton-Malow Co., Southfield, MI; Barton-Malow Rigging Co., Oak Park, MI
Giving statement: Giving through the Barton-Malow Company Foundation.

Barton-Malow Company Foundation

c/o Mike Dish
26500 American Dr.
Southfield, MI 48034-2252 (248) 436-5000

Establishment information: Established in 1954 in MI.
Donors: Barton-Malow Enterprises, Inc.; Cloverdale Equipment Co.; Barton Malow Company.
Financial data (yr. ended 03/31/12): Assets, $174,195 (M); gifts received, $200,000; expenditures, $194,106; qualifying distributions, $194,106; giving activities include $194,045 for 25 grants (high: $70,000; low: $100).
Purpose and activities: The foundation supports community foundations and organizations involved with education, health, heart disease, housing development, and children services.
Fields of interest: Higher education; Education; Hospitals (general); Health care; Heart & circulatory diseases; Housing/shelter, development; American Red Cross; Children, services; Foundations (community); United Ways and Federated Giving Programs.
Type of support: General/operating support; Scholarship funds.
Geographic limitations: Giving primarily in FL, MD, MI, and VA.
Support limitations: No grants to individuals.
Application information: Applications accepted. Application form required.
Initial approach: Letter
Deadline(s): None
Trustee: Douglas Maibach.
EIN: 386088176
Selected grants: The following grants are a representative sample of this grantmaker's funding activity:
$20,000 to American Heart Association, Southfield, MI, 2010.
$7,500 to American Red Cross, Detroit, MI, 2010.
$7,500 to Learning Ally, Charlottesville, VA, 2010.
$5,000 to American Red Cross, Detroit, MI, 2010.
$2,500 to Mosaic Youth Theater of Detroit, Detroit, MI, 2010.
$1,000 to Engineering Society of Detroit, Southfield, MI, 2010.
$1,000 to University of Detroit Mercy, Detroit, MI, 2010.
$1,000 to Valencia Foundation, Orlando, FL, 2010.
$1,000 to YMCA of Metropolitan Detroit, Detroit, MI, 2010.

367
The Baseball Club of Seattle, L.P.

(also known as Seattle Mariners)
1250 1st Ave. S.
P.O. Box 4100
Seattle, WA 98134 (206) 346-4001

Company URL: http://seattle.mariners.mlb.com
Establishment information: Established in 1977.
Company type: Subsidiary of a foreign company
Business activities: Operates professional baseball club.
Business type (SIC): Commercial sports
Corporate officers: Howard A. Lincoln, Chair. and C.E.O.; Chuck Armstrong, Pres. and C.O.O.; Bob Aylward, Exec. V.P., Opers.; Kevin Mather, Exec. V.P., Finance; Randy Adamack, Sr. V.P., Comms.; Marianne Short, Sr. V.P., Human Resources; Tim Kornegay, V.P., Finance; Frances Traisman, V.P., Sales; Kevin Martinez, V.P., Mktg.; Greg Massey, Cont.; John Ellis, Chair. Emeritus
Board of directors: Howard A. Lincoln, Chair.; Minoru Arakawa; John Ellis; Rob Glaser; Chris Larson; Wayne Perry; Frank Shrontz
Giving statement: Giving through the Seattle Mariners Corporate Giving Program and the Mariners Care.

Seattle Mariners Corporate Giving Program

c/o Charitable Donations
P.O. Box 4100
Seattle, WA 98194-0100 (206) 346-4000
URL: http://seattle.mariners.mlb.com/sea/community/mariners_care_donations.jsp

Purpose and activities: As a complement to its foundation, the Seattle Mariners also make charitable contributions of memorabilia and game tickets to nonprofit organizations directly. Support is limited to Alaska, Hawaii, Idaho, Montana, Oregon, Washington, and British Columbia.
Fields of interest: General charitable giving.
International interests: Canada.
Type of support: Donated products; In-kind gifts.
Geographic limitations: Giving limited to AK, HI, ID, MT, OR, WA, and British Columbia.
Support limitations: No grants to individuals.
Publications: Application guidelines.
Application information: Proposals should be submitted using organization letterhead. Faxed or e-mailed proposals are not accepted. Personal items or fan merchandise to be autographed are not accepted. Support is limited to 1 contribution per organization during any given year. The Community Relations Department handles giving. Applicants should submit the following:
1) name, address and phone number of organization
2) contact person
Applications should include the Tax ID Number of the organization, and the date and a description of the event.
Initial approach: Mail proposal to headquarters
Deadline(s): 6 weeks prior to event

Mariners Care

1250 1st Ave. S.
Seattle, WA 98134-1216 (206) 346-4026
E-mail: mariners@mariners.org; URL: http://seattle.mariners.mlb.com/sea/community/index.jsp

Establishment information: Established in 1991 in WA.
Contact: Charles G. Armstrong, Pres.
Financial data (yr. ended 12/31/11): Revenue, $228,147; assets, $852,080 (M); gifts received, $53,225; expenditures, $330,182; giving activities include $324,590 for grants.
Purpose and activities: The foundation is dedicated to serving the community, especially young people, by providing grants for youth-oriented community service programs and other worthy projects in the Pacific Northwest.
Fields of interest: Recreation, community; Athletics/sports, baseball; Youth, services; Economic development.
Geographic limitations: Giving limited to the northwestern U.S.
Officers: Charles G. Armstrong, Pres.; Joseph Chard, V.P.; Gina Hanson, Secy.; Tim Kornegay, Treas.
EIN: 943138515

368
BASF Corporation

100 Campus Dr.
Florham Park, NJ 07932 (973) 245-6000

Company URL: http://www.basf.com/corporate/index.html
Establishment information: Established in 1986.
Company type: Subsidiary of a foreign company
Business activities: Manufactures chemicals, agricultural products, and pharmaceuticals.
Business type (SIC): Chemicals and allied products; drugs; fertilizers and agricultural chemicals
Financial profile for 2011: Number of employees, 16,167
Corporate officers: Hans Engel, Chair. and C.E.O.; Fried-Walter Munstermann, Exec. V.P. and C.F.O.; David Stryker, Sr. V.P. and Genl. Counsel
Board of director: Hans Engel, Chair.
Plants: Wyandotte, MI; Charlotte, NC
Historic mergers: Cognis Corporation (December 10, 2010)
Giving statement: Giving through the BASF Corporation Contributions Program and the BASF Foundation USA.

BASF Corporation Contributions Program

c/o Community Rels.
100 Campus Dr.
Florham Park, NJ 07932-1089 (973) 245-6000
URL: http://www.basf.com/group/corporate/us/en/about-basf/worldwide/north-america/USA/community/index

Purpose and activities: BASF makes charitable contributions to nonprofit organizations involved with education, health and human services, youth development, science, and civic affairs. Support is given primarily in areas of company operations in Alabama, Arizona, Colorado, Connecticut, Delaware, Florida, Georgia, Kentucky, Louisiana, Michigan, Minnesota, Missouri, New Jersey, New York, North Carolina, Ohio, Pennsylvania, Puerto Rico, South Carolina, Tennessee, Texas, and Virginia.

Fields of interest: Education; Environment; Health care; Youth development; Human services; Science; Public affairs.
Type of support: Donated products; Employee volunteer services; General/operating support; In-kind gifts.
Geographic limitations: Giving primarily in areas of company operations in AL, AZ, CO, CT, DE, FL, GA, KY, LA, MI, MN, MO, NC, NJ, NY, OH, PA, PR, SC, TN, TX, and VA.
Support limitations: No support for political, sectarian, fraternal, or veterans' organizations. No grants for telephone solicitation.
Application information: Applications accepted.
Initial approach: Contact headquarters for application information

The BASF Foundation USA

(formerly Cognis Foundation)
23700 Chagrin Blvd.
Beachwood, OH 44122
Application address: 100 Park Ave., Florham Park, NJ 07932

Establishment information: Established in 2003 in OH.
Donor: Cognis Corp.
Contact: Maureen Paukert, Secy.
Financial data (yr. ended 12/31/11): Assets, $0 (M); gifts received, $104,778; expenditures, $157,890; qualifying distributions, $157,890; giving activities include $157,890 for 20 grants (high: $87,550; low: $500).
Purpose and activities: The foundation supports services clubs and organizations involved with arts and culture, education, cancer, and chemistry.
Fields of interest: Arts; Elementary/secondary education; Higher education; Higher education, college (community/junior); Scholarships/financial aid; Education; Cancer; Community development, service clubs; United Ways and Federated Giving Programs; Chemistry.
Type of support: General/operating support; Scholarship funds.
Geographic limitations: Giving primarily in IL, OH, PA, and SC.
Support limitations: No support for religious or political organizations. No grants for capital campaigns or brick or mortar projects.
Application information: Applications accepted. Application form required. Applicants should submit the following:
1) detailed description of project and amount of funding requested
Initial approach: Letter
Copies of proposal: 1
Deadline(s): None
Final notification: Within 3 months
Officers: Frank Bozich, Pres.; Maureen Paukert, Secy.; Robert Malone, Treas.
EIN: 562312894

369
Bashas', Inc

22402 S. Basha Rd.
P.O. Box 488
Chandler, AZ 85248 (480) 895-9350

Company URL: http://www.bashas.com
Establishment information: Established in 1932.
Company type: Private company
Business activities: Operates grocery stores.
Business type (SIC): Groceries—retail
Corporate officers: Edward N. Basha, Jr., Chair. and C.E.O.; Johnny Basha, Vice-Chair.; James Buhr, Sr. V.P., Finance and C.F.O.; Christie Frazier-Coleman, Sr. V.P., Sales
Board of directors: Edward N. Basha, Jr., Chair.; Johnny Basha, Vice-Chair.
Giving statement: Giving through the Bashas' Inc. Corporate Giving Program.

Bashas' Inc. Corporate Giving Program

c/o Corp. Contribs.
P.O. Box 488
Chandler, AZ 85244-0488

Purpose and activities: Bashas' makes charitable contributions to nonprofit organizations on a case by case basis. Support is given primarily in areas of company operations in Arizona.
Fields of interest: General charitable giving.
Type of support: Donated products; Employee-related scholarships; General/operating support; In-kind gifts.
Geographic limitations: Giving primarily in areas of company operations in AZ.
Support limitations: No grants for out-of-state travel, beauty pageants, capital campaigns, individual competitions, or contact sports.
Publications: Application guidelines.
Application information: A contributions committee reviews all requests. Application form not required. Applicants should submit the following:
1) copy of IRS Determination Letter
2) timetable for implementation and evaluation of project
3) population served
4) detailed description of project and amount of funding requested
Initial approach: Proposal to headquarters
Copies of proposal: 1
Committee meeting date(s): Varies
Deadline(s): 4 to 6 weeks prior to need
Final notification: Following review

370
The Basketball Club of Seattle, LLC

(also known as Seattle Supersonics)
351 Elliott Ave. W., Ste. 500
Seattle, WA 98119-4153 (206) 281-5800

Company URL: http://www.nba.com/sonics
Establishment information: Established in 1967.
Company type: Private company
Business activities: Operates professional basketball club.
Business type (SIC): Commercial sports
Corporate officers: Howard Schultz, Chair.; Wally Walker, Pres. and C.E.O.; Danny Barth, Exec. V.P. and C.A.O.; Brian M. Byrnes, Sr. V.P., Sales and Mktg.; Dan Mahoney, V.P., Comms.; Katy Semtner, V.P., Human Resources
Board of director: Howard Schultz, Chair.
Giving statement: Giving through the Seattle Sonics and Storm Foundation.

The Seattle Sonics and Storm Foundation

(formerly Sonics & Storm T.E.A.M. Foundation)
3421 Thorndyke Ave. W.
Seattle, WA 98119-1606 (206) 272-2696
FAX: (206) 272-2697

Establishment information: Established in 1967 in WA.
Contact: Wyjuana Montgomery, Community Progs. Mgr.
Financial data (yr. ended 12/31/10): Revenue, $39,909; assets, $180,202 (M); gifts received, $13,000; expenditures, $32,765; program services expenses, $27,525; giving activities include $23,252 for grants and $4,273 for grants to individuals.
Purpose and activities: The foundation supports community programs that 'teach, encourage and motivate' children, young adults, and families in Washington, and also that supports educational and athletic initiatives.
Fields of interest: Education; Athletics/sports, basketball; Youth development, community service clubs.
Program:
Inspirational Prep Athlete of the Year Scholarship Program: Awarded in conjunction with King County Journal Newspapers, the scholarship is designed to honor student-athletes that have overcome severe circumstances to achieve their goals. Four student-athletes are selected: one male and one female athlete from eastern King County and one male and one female athlete from southern King County. The scholarship recipients are honored at the annual King County Journal Newspapers prep sports banquet. Each scholarship recipient receives a $2,500 cash award to apply toward his or her college education.
Type of support: In-kind gifts; Scholarships—to individuals.
Geographic limitations: Giving limited to WA.
Support limitations: No support for organizations lacking 501(c)(3) status or political, religious, labor, or fraternal organizations. No grants to individuals (except for scholarships), or for capital campaigns, advertising, fundraising drives, salaries, stipends, travel expenses, general or administrative costs, or endowments.
Officers: Dawn Trudeau, Pres.; Lisa Brummel, V.P.; Ginny Gilder, V.P.; Anne Levinson, Secy.; Karen Bryant, Treas.
EIN: 912130853

371
Bass, Berry & Sims PLC

150 3rd Ave. S., Ste. 2800
Nashville, TN 37201-2017 (615) 742-6200

Company URL: http://www.bassberry.com
Establishment information: Established in 1922.
Company type: Private company
Business activities: Operates law firm.
Business type (SIC): Legal services
Corporate officer: Keith B. Simmons, Managing Partner
Offices: Knoxville, Memphis, Nashville, TN
Giving statement: Giving through the Bass, Berry & Sims PLC Pro Bono Program.

Bass, Berry & Sims PLC Pro Bono Program

150 3rd Ave. S., Ste. 2800
Nashville, TN 37201-2017 (615) 742-7285
E-mail: desquivel@bassberry.com; URL: http://www.bassberry.com/aboutus/communityinvolvement/#Pro_Bono

Contact: David Esquivel, Pro Bono Comm. Chair
Fields of interest: Legal services.
Type of support: Pro bono services - legal.

Geographic limitations: Giving primarily in areas of company operations in Knoxville, Memphis, and Nashville, TN.
Application information: A Pro Bono Committee manages the pro bono program.

372
Bassett Furniture Industries, Inc.

3525 Fairystone Park Hwy.
P.O. Box 626
Bassett, VA 24055 (276) 629-6000
FAX: (276) 629-6346

Company URL: http://www.bassettfurniture.com
Establishment information: Established in 1902.
Company type: Public company
Company ticker symbol and exchange: BSET/NASDAQ
Business activities: Manufactures furniture.
Business type (SIC): Furniture/household
Financial profile for 2012: Number of employees, 1,412; assets, $227,180,000; sales volume, $269,670,000; pre-tax net income, $12,010,000; expenses, $265,400,000; liabilities, $69,900,000
Corporate officers: Paul Fulton, Chair.; Robert H. Spilman, Jr., Pres. and C.E.O.; J. Michael Daniel, Sr. V.P. and C.F.O.; Bruce R. Cohenour, Sr. V.P., Sales; Jay R. Hervey, Esq., V.P., Genl. Counsel, and Secy.; Edward H. White, V.P., Human Resources
Board of directors: Paul Fulton, Chair.; Peter W. Brown; Kristina K. Cashman; Howard H. Haworth; George W. Henderson III; J. Walter McDowell; Dale C. Pond; Robert H. Spilman, Jr.; William C. Wampler, Jr.; William C. Warden, Jr.
Plants: Phoenix, AZ; Dumas, AR; Los Angeles, Stockton, CA; Lake Wales, West Palm Beach, FL; Dublin, Macon, Newnan, GA; Booneville, Saltillo, MS; Tipton, MO; Amherst, NH; Hickory, High Point, Mount Airy, Newton, Statesville, Taylorsville, NC; Columbus, OH; Pottstown, PA; Austin, TX; Burkeville, Christiansburg, Fredericksburg, Martinsville, VA; Chehalis, WA; Walworth, WI
Joint Venture: Triwood, Inc., Ridgeway, VA
Giving statement: Giving through the Bassett Furniture Industries Foundation, Inc.
Company EIN: 540135270

Bassett Furniture Industries Foundation, Inc.

P.O. Box 626
Bassett, VA 24055-0626

Establishment information: Established in 1992 in VA.
Donor: Bassett Furniture Industries, Inc.
Financial data (yr. ended 11/30/11): Assets, $1,646,071 (M); expenditures, $108,218; qualifying distributions, $108,218; giving activities include $92,000 for 10 grants (high: $25,000; low: $1,000).
Purpose and activities: The foundation supports organizations involved with arts and culture, higher education, athletics, children's services, and Christianity.
Fields of interest: Museums (natural history); Arts; Higher education; Athletics/sports, amateur leagues; Boy scouts; Children, services.
Type of support: General/operating support; Program development.
Geographic limitations: Giving primarily in VA.
Support limitations: No grants to individuals.
Application information: Applications not accepted. Unsolicited requests for funds not accepted.
Officers and Director:* Robert H. Spilman, Jr., Pres.; Jay R. Hervey, Secy.
EIN: 541652381

373
Batson-Cook, Co.

817 4th Ave.
P.O. Box 151
West Point, GA 31833 (706) 643-2500

Company URL: http://www.batson-cook.com
Establishment information: Established in 1915.
Company type: Subsidiary of a private company
Business activities: Provides general contract construction services.
Business type (SIC): Building construction general contractors and operative builders
Corporate officers: R. Randall Hall, Pres. and C.E.O.; Jeffery H. Turner, C.F.O. and Treas.; J. Littleton Glover, Jr., V.P. and Genl. Counsel; Alesia Wessinger, Corp. Secy.
Giving statement: Giving through the Batson-Cook Foundation, Inc.

Batson-Cook Foundation, Inc.

P.O. Box 151
West Point, GA 31833-0151

Establishment information: Established in 1987 in GA.
Donor: Batson-Cook Co.
Financial data (yr. ended 12/31/10): Assets, $209,327 (M); expenditures, $0; qualifying distributions, $0.
Purpose and activities: The foundation supports organizations involved with performing arts, health, housing, youth development, leadership development, and Christianity.
Fields of interest: Performing arts; Performing arts, orchestras; Elementary/secondary education; Higher education; Education; Health care; Housing/shelter; Boy scouts; Leadership development; Christian agencies & churches.
Type of support: Annual campaigns; Endowments; General/operating support; Program development.
Geographic limitations: Giving primarily in areas of company operations in GA.
Support limitations: No grants to individuals.
Application information: Applications not accepted. Unsolicited requests for funds not accepted.
Officers: Edmund C. Glover, Chair.; Cecil G. Hood, Treas.
Trustees: J. Littleton Glover, Jr.; Raymond L. Moody.
EIN: 581762604

374
The Batts Group, Ltd.

3855 Sparks Dr. S.E., Ste. 222
Grand Rapids, MI 49546-2427
(616) 956-3053

Establishment information: Established in 1998.
Company type: Private company
Business activities: Operates holding company; develops real estate.
Business type (SIC): Real estate subdividers and developers; holding company
Corporate officer: John H. Batts, Chair. and Pres.
Board of director: John H. Batts, Chair.
Subsidiary: Belfry Development Corp., Grand Rapids, MI
Giving statement: Giving through the Batts Foundation.

The Batts Foundation

3855 Sparks Dr. S.E., Ste. 222
Grand Rapids, MI 49546-2427 (616) 956-3053
E-mail: jsand@battsgroup.com

Establishment information: Established in 1988 in MI.
Donor: The Batts Group, Ltd.
Financial data (yr. ended 12/31/11): Assets, $1,829,310 (M); expenditures, $103,899; qualifying distributions, $100,000; giving activities include $100,000 for grants.
Purpose and activities: The foundation supports organizations involved with arts and culture, K-12 and higher education, disease, and human services.
Fields of interest: Education; Health care; Human services.
Type of support: Annual campaigns; Building/renovation; Capital campaigns; Continuing support; Endowments; General/operating support; Matching/challenge support; Program development; Scholarship funds.
Support limitations: No grants to individuals.
Application information: Applications accepted. Application form not required.
Initial approach: Proposal
Copies of proposal: 1
Deadline(s): None
Officer and Directors:* John H. Batts*, Pres.; James L. Batts; John T. Batts; Michael A. Batts; Robert H. Batts.
Number of staff: 1 part-time support.
EIN: 382782168

375
Otto Baum Company, Inc.

866 N. Main St.
Morton, IL 61550-1602 (309) 266-7114

Company URL: http://www.ottobaum.com
Establishment information: Established in 1937.
Company type: Private company
Business activities: Provides general contract construction services.
Business type (SIC): Building construction general contractors and operative builders
Corporate officers: Kenneth D. Baum, Co.-Pres. and C.E.O.; Terry L. Baum, Co.-Pres. and Treas.; Kurt L. Baum, V.P., Opers.; Glen Sullivan, Secy.; Scott Wallace, Cont.
Office: Decatur, IL
Giving statement: Giving through the Otto Baum Company, Inc. Foundation.

Otto Baum Company, Inc. Foundation

866 N. Main St.
Morton, IL 61550-1602

Establishment information: Established in 1998 in IL.
Donor: Otto Baum Co., Inc.
Financial data (yr. ended 12/31/11): Assets, $33,543 (M); gifts received, $25,000; expenditures, $35,050; qualifying distributions, $35,050; giving activities include $35,025 for 27 grants (high: $8,525; low: $100).
Purpose and activities: The foundation supports camps and organizations involved with arts and culture, vocational rehabilitation, and human services.

Fields of interest: Museums; Arts; Employment, vocational rehabilitation; Recreation, camps; Boy scouts; American Red Cross; Residential/custodial care; Developmentally disabled, centers & services; Human services; United Ways and Federated Giving Programs.
Type of support: General/operating support.
Geographic limitations: Giving primarily in Peoria, IL.
Support limitations: No grants to individuals.
Application information: Applications not accepted. Contributes only to pre-selected organizations.
Officers and Directors:* Wayne E. Baum*, Pres.; Kenneth D. Baum*, V.P.; Craig R. Baum*, Secy.; Terry L. Baum*, Treas.
EIN: 371376985

376
Bausch & Lomb, Inc
1 Bausch & Lomb Pl.
Rochester, NY 14604-2701 (585) 338-6000

Company URL: http://www.bausch.com
Establishment information: Established in 1853.
Company type: Private company
Business activities: Manufactures contact lenses, lens care products, sunglasses, and ophthalmic pharmaceutical products.
Business type (SIC): Ophthalmic goods
Financial profile for 2011: Number of employees, 10,000; sales volume, $2,600,000,000
Corporate officers: Fred Hassan, Chair.; Brent L. Saunders, Pres. and C.E.O.; Brian J. Harris, Exec. V.P. and C.F.O.; Alan H. Farnsworth, Exec. V.P. and C.I.O.; A. Robert D. Bailey, Exec. V.P. and Genl. Counsel
Board of directors: Fred Hassan, Chair.; Sean D. Carney; R. Kerry Clark; Joseph P. Landy; D. Scott Mackesy; Robert J. Palmisano; Brent L. Saunders; Richard F. Wallman; Elizabeth H. Weatherman
Subsidiaries: B&L Pharmaceuticals, Inc., Tampa, FL; Bausch & Lomb Insurance Co., Rochester, NY; Bausch & Lomb Opticare, Inc., Rochester, NY; Bausch & Lomb Puerto Rico, Inc., San Juan, PR; Outlook Eyewear Co., Broomfield, CO; Polymer Technology Corp., Wilmington, MA; Revo, Inc., Mountain View, CA
Divisions: Bausch & Lomb Contact Lens Div.-FL, Sarasota, FL; Bausch & Lomb Eyewear Div.-TX, San Antonio, TX; Bausch & Lomb Hearing Systems Div., Golden Valley, MN; Bausch & Lomb International Div., Rochester, NY; Bausch & Lomb Personal Products Div.-NY, Rochester, NY; Bausch & Lomb Personal Products Div.-SC, Greenville, SC; Bausch & Lomb Pharmaceutical Div., Tampa, FL; Contact Lens Div., Rochester, NY; Eyewear Div., Rochester, NY; Thin Film Technology Div., Rochester, NY
Plants: San Dimas, CA; Miami, Sarasota, Summerland Key, Tampa, FL; Tucker, GA; Westbrook, ME; Portage, MI; Eden Prairie, MN; O'Fallon, MO; Omaha, NE; Pittsfield, NH; Newfield, NJ; Hauppauge, Stone Ridge, NY; Raleigh, NC; San Juan, PR; Cranston, RI; Greenville, SC; Houston, San Antonio, TX; Oregon, WI
International operations: Australia; Brazil; Canada; China; India; Japan; Malaysia; Mexico; New Zealand; Philippines; Russia; Singapore; South Korea; Taiwan; United Kingdom; Venezuela
Giving statement: Giving through the Bausch & Lomb Foundation, Inc.
Company EIN: 160345235

Bausch & Lomb Foundation, Inc.
c/o Bausch & Lomb Inc.
1 Bausch & Lomb Pl.
Rochester, NY 14604-2701 (585) 338-5000

Establishment information: Incorporated in 1927 in NY.
Donor: Bausch & Lomb Inc.
Contact: Adam Grossberg, V.P.
Financial data (yr. ended 12/31/11): Assets, $136,737 (M); expenditures, $302; qualifying distributions, $0.
Purpose and activities: The foundation supports museums and organizations involved with education, optometry, diabetes, and the visually impaired.
Fields of interest: Museums; Higher education; Medical school/education; Optometry/vision screening; Diabetes Blind/visually impaired.
Type of support: Continuing support; General/operating support; Program development.
Geographic limitations: Giving primarily in areas of company operations in Rochester, NY.
Support limitations: No grants to individuals.
Application information: Applications accepted. Application form not required. Applicants should submit the following:
1) copy of IRS Determination Letter
2) listing of board of directors, trustees, officers and other key people and their affiliations
3) detailed description of project and amount of funding requested
4) copy of current year's organizational budget and/or project budget

Initial approach: Proposal
Copies of proposal: 1
Deadline(s): None

Officers and Directors:* Rick A. Heinick*, Pres.; Brian J. Harris*, V.P. and Treas.; Adam Grossberg*, V.P.; A. Robert D. Bailey*, Secy.
Number of staff: 1 full-time professional.
EIN: 166039442
Selected grants: The following grants are a representative sample of this grantmaker's funding activity:
$10,000 to American Diabetes Association, Alexandria, VA, 2010.

377
Baxter International Inc.
1 Baxter Pkwy.
Deerfield, IL 60015-4625 (224) 948-1812
FAX: (224) 948-1813

Company URL: http://www.baxter.com
Establishment information: Established in 1931.
Company type: Public company
Company ticker symbol and exchange: BAX/NYSE
International Securities Identification Number: US0718131099
Business activities: Develops, manufactures, and distributes health care products, systems, and services.
Business type (SIC): Medical instruments and supplies
Financial profile for 2012: Number of employees, 51,000; assets, $20,390,000,000; sales volume, $14,190,000,000; pre-tax net income, $2,889,000,000; expenses, $11,301,000,000; liabilities, $13,452,000,000
Fortune 1000 ranking: 2012—193rd in revenues, 88th in profits, and 236th in assets
Forbes 2000 ranking: 2012—674th in sales, 248th in profits, and 963rd in assets
Corporate officers: Robert L. Parkinson, Jr., Chair. and C.E.O.; Robert J. Hombach, Corp. V.P. and C.F.O.; Paul E. Martin, Corp. V.P. and C.I.O.; Stephanie A. Shinn, Corp. V.P. and Corp. Secy.; James K. Saccaro, Corp. V.P. and Treas.; Sebastian J. Bufalino, Corp. V.P. and Cont.; David P. Scharf, Corp. V.P. and Genl. Counsel; Jeanne K. Mason, Corp. V.P., Human Resources
Board of directors: Robert L. Parkinson, Jr., Chair.; Blake E. Devitt; John D. Forsyth; Gail D. Fosler; James R. Gavin III, M.D., Ph.D.; Peter S. Hellman; Wayne T. Hockmeyer, Ph.D.; Carole J. Shapazian; Thomas T. Stallkamp; Kornelis J. Storm; Albert P.L. Stroucken
Giving statement: Giving through the Baxter International Inc. Corporate Giving Program and the Baxter International Foundation.
Company EIN: 360781620

Baxter International Inc. Corporate Giving Program
1 Baxter Pkwy.
Deerfield, IL 60015-4625 (224) 948-2000
URL: http://sustainability.baxter.com/community_support/index.html

Financial data (yr. ended 12/31/10): Total giving, $75,300,000, including $27,200,000 for grants and $48,100,000 for in-kind gifts.
Purpose and activities: As a complement to its foundation, Baxter also makes charitable contributions to nonprofit organizations directly. Support is given primarily in areas of company operations.
Fields of interest: Elementary/secondary education; Teacher school/education; Education; Environment; Health care, equal rights; Health care; Hemophilia; Kidney diseases; Health organizations; Immunology; Employment, services; Disasters, preparedness/services; Youth, services; Patients' rights; Mathematics; Science Economically disadvantaged.
Type of support: Conferences/seminars; Curriculum development; Donated products; Employee volunteer services; General/operating support; In-kind gifts; Sponsorships.
Geographic limitations: Giving primarily in areas of company operations.
Publications: Corporate report.
Application information: The Global Community Relations Department handles giving.
Number of staff: 2 part-time professional; 2 part-time support.

The Baxter International Foundation
(formerly The Baxter Allegiance Foundation)
1 Baxter Pkwy.
Deerfield, IL 60015-4633 (847) 948-4605
FAX: (847) 948-4559; E-mail: fdninfo@baxter.com; Additional tel.: (847) 948-2000; URL: http://www.baxter.com/about_baxter/sustainability/international_foundation/index.html

Establishment information: Established in 1982 in IL.
Donors: Baxter International Inc.; American Hospital Supply Corp.; Allegiance Corp.
Contact: Donna Namath, Secy. and Exec. Dir.
Financial data (yr. ended 12/31/11): Assets, $33,035,912 (M); expenditures, $4,112,720; qualifying distributions, $4,004,341; giving activities include $2,814,324 for 131 grants (high: $210,000; low: $200) and $777,691 for employee matching gifts.
Purpose and activities: The foundation supports programs designed to improve access, quality, and cost-effectiveness of direct healthcare. Special

emphasis is directed toward programs designed to expand access to direct healthcare services to disadvantaged or underserved populations in communities where a significant number of Baxter employees live and work.
Fields of interest: Dental care; Health care, insurance; Health care, cost containment; Health care; Substance abuse, services; Mental health/crisis services; Crime/violence prevention, domestic violence; Crime/violence prevention, child abuse; Crime/violence prevention, sexual abuse Aging; Disabilities, people with; Military/veterans; Economically disadvantaged.
Programs:
Employee Dollars for Doers: The foundation awards grants to nonprofit organizations with which employees of Baxter volunteer.
Employee Matching Gifts: The foundation matches contributions made by employees of Baxter to nonprofit organizations involved with arts and culture, education, and health on a one-for-one basis from $25 to $5,000 per employee, per year.
Episteme Award: The foundation, in partnership with the Honor Society of Nursing, awards a $15,000 grant to a nurse who has contributed significantly to nursing knowledge development, application, or discovery that results in a sizable benefit to the public. The program is administered by Sigma Theta Tau International (STTI).
Foster G. McGraw Prize: Through the Foster G. McGraw Prize program, the foundation honors health delivery organizations such as hospitals, health systems, integrated networks, or self-defined community partnerships that have demonstrated exceptional commitment to community service. The honoree is awarded a grant of $100,000 and up to three finalists are awarded a grant of $10,000. The program is administered by the American Hospital Association.
Scholarship Program for Children of Employees: The foundation awards $1,000 college scholarships to children of employees of Baxter.
William B. Graham Prize: The foundation, in partnership with the Association of University Programs in Health Administration, awards grants to recognize worldwide contributions to improving the health of the public through research. The prize consists of $25,000 for an individual and $25,000 to the nonprofit institution designated by the recipient to support his or her work. The program is administered by the Association of University Programs in Health Administration.
Type of support: Continuing support; Employee matching gifts; Employee volunteer services; Employee-related scholarships; Program development.
Geographic limitations: Giving on a national and international basis in areas of company operations, including CA, Cook, Lake, and McHenry County, IL, IN, Austria, Brazil, China, Costa Rica, France, Ireland, Portugal, and Mexico.
Support limitations: No support for disease or condition-specific organizations, hospitals, lobbying or political organizations, or organizations with a limited constituency, such as fraternal, veterans', or religious organizations. No grant to individuals (except for employee-related scholarships) or for capital or endowment campaigns, non-healthcare activities at educational institutions, general operating support or maintenance of effort, magazines, professional journals, documentaries, film, video, radio, or website productions, medical missions, advertising, tickets to dinners, benefits, social or fund-raising events, sponsorships or promotional materials, or research.
Publications: Application guidelines; Grants list; IRS Form 990 or 990-PF printed copy available upon request.
Application information: Applications accepted. Multi-year funding is not automatic. The majority of grants are awarded based on recommendations from Baxter facilities' staff and employees. Organizations receiving support are asked to provide an interim report and a final report. Application form not required. Applicants should submit the following:
1) how project will be sustained once grantmaker support is completed
2) staff salaries
3) name, address and phone number of organization
4) copy of IRS Determination Letter
5) brief history of organization and description of its mission
6) copy of most recent annual report/audited financial statement/990
7) how project's results will be evaluated or measured
8) listing of board of directors, trustees, officers and other key people and their affiliations
9) detailed description of project and amount of funding requested
10) contact person
11) copy of current year's organizational budget and/or project budget
12) listing of additional sources and amount of support

Applications should include a description of the organization's past involvement with a local Baxter facility or employee, if available.
Initial approach: Complete online application
Copies of proposal: 1
Board meeting date(s): Three times a year
Deadline(s): Feb. 15, June 14, and Oct. 11
Final notification: Following board meetings
Officers and Directors: Robert J. Hombach, Pres.; Donna Namath, Secy. and Exec. Dir.; Charles W. Thurman, Treas.; Katherine Azuara; Alice J. Campbell; Robert M. Davis; Shaun Newlon; Peter Nicklin; John S. Park.
Number of staff: 1 full-time professional; 1 full-time support.
EIN: 363159396

378
Bay Alarm Company
60 Berry Dr.
Pacheco, CA 94553-5601 (925) 935-1100

Establishment information: Established in 1946.
Company type: Private company
Business activities: Provides security systems services.
Business type (SIC): Business services/miscellaneous
Corporate officers: Roger L. Westphal, C.E.O.; Matthew Westphal, Co-Pres; Graham Westphal, Co-Pres; Mark Jones, C.F.O.
Giving statement: Giving through the Bay Alarm Company Contributions Program and the Westphal Family Foundation.

Bay Alarm Company Contributions Program
60 Berry Dr.
Pacheco, CA 94553
E-mail: sponsorships@bayalarm.com; URL: http://www.bayalarm.com/about/community/

Purpose and activities: As a complement to its foundation, Bay Alarm Company also makes charitable contributions to nonprofit organizations directly.
Fields of interest: Crime/law enforcement; Athletics/sports, amateur leagues; Community/economic development Children/youth.
Type of support: General/operating support; Sponsorships.
Geographic limitations: Giving primarily in Oakland, CA area; giving also to national organizations.

The Westphal Family Foundation
60 Berry Dr.
Pacheco, CA 94553-5601

Establishment information: Established in 1999 in CA.
Donors: Bay Alarm Co.; Balco Holdings, Inc.
Financial data (yr. ended 12/31/11): Assets, $105,331 (M); gifts received, $134,000; expenditures, $38,060; qualifying distributions, $38,000; giving activities include $38,000 for 17 grants (high: $4,000; low: $1,000).
Purpose and activities: The foundation supports organizations involved with education, health, ALS, child welfare, and children and youth.
Fields of interest: Elementary school/education; Higher education; Education; Hospitals (general); Health care; ALS; Crime/violence prevention, child abuse; Girls clubs; Children/youth, services.
Type of support: Annual campaigns; Employee-related scholarships; General/operating support; Program development.
Geographic limitations: Giving limited to CA.
Support limitations: No grants to individuals (except for employee-related scholarships).
Application information: Applications not accepted. Contributes only through employee-related scholarships and pre-selected organizations.
Trustees: Bruce A. Westphal; Patricia A. Westphal; Penny L. Westphal; Roger L. Westphal.
EIN: 916491365

379
Bay Chevrolet Inc.
2900 Government Blvd.
Mobile, AL 36606-2609 (251) 476-8080
FAX: (251) 476-5289

Company URL: http://www.baychevrolet.net
Establishment information: Established in 1943.
Company type: Private company
Business activities: Operates used car dealership.
Business type (SIC): Motor vehicles—retail
Corporate officer: John S. Moses, Pres.
Giving statement: Giving through the Moses Foundation.

The Moses Foundation
2900 Government Blvd.
Mobile, AL 36606-2609 (251) 476-8080

Establishment information: Established in 1993 in AL.
Donor: Bay Chevrolet.
Contact: John S. Moses, Treas.
Financial data (yr. ended 08/31/11): Assets, $557,119 (M); expenditures, $33,842; qualifying distributions, $26,220; giving activities include $23,764 for 31 grants (high: $7,564; low: $50).
Fields of interest: Arts; Education; Human services; Protestant agencies & churches.
Type of support: General/operating support.
Geographic limitations: Giving primarily in the greater Mobile, AL, area.
Support limitations: No grants to individuals.

Application information: Applications accepted. Application form not required.
Initial approach: Letter
Deadline(s): None
Officers: Marilyn N. Moses, Pres.; Jennifer F. Moses, 1st V.P.; E. Linhart Moses, 2nd V.P.; John S. Moses, Treas.
EIN: 631107871

380
Bay State Savings Bank

28 Franklin St.
Worcester, MA 01608 (508) 890-9000

Company URL: http://www.baystatesavingsbank.com
Establishment information: Established in 1895.
Company type: Private company
Business activities: Operates savings bank.
Business type (SIC): Savings institutions
Financial profile for 2011: Assets, $266,449,523; liabilities, $266,449,523
Corporate officers: George F. Sullivan, Jr., Chair.; Peter B. Alden, Pres., Treas., and C.E.O.; Paul D. Gildody, Exec. V.P. and C.O.O.; Robert B. Duquette, Sr. V.P., C.F.O., and Treas.; Diane M. Giampa, Sr. V.P., Mktg. and Human Resources; Lisa A. Duquette, V.P., Opers.; Andrew A. Brown, Clerk
Board of directors: George F. Sullivan, Jr., Chair.; Peter B. Alden; F. Stephen Harvey, Jr.; Patricia L. Jones; John H. McCabe; Andrew C.J. Meagher; Joni Milluzzo; John J. Monahan; William J. Mulford; Gerald J. Power; Robert P. Powers
Offices: Ausurn, Holden, MA
Giving statement: Giving through the Bay State Savings Bank Corporate Giving Program and the Bay State Savings Charitable Foundation, Inc.

Bay State Savings Bank Corporate Giving Program

28 Franklin St.
Worcester, MA 01608 (508) 890-9000
FAX: (508) 792-5217; URL: http://www.baystatesavingsbank.com

Contact: Sarah Day
Purpose and activities: As a complement to its foundation, Bay State Savings Bank also makes charitable contributions to nonprofit organizations directly through its Champions for Children program. Special emphasis is directed toward programs or individuals that provide education, mentoring, training, life skills development, or recreational opportunities to the youth of the community. Support is given in areas of company operations in central Massachusetts.
Fields of interest: Elementary/secondary education; Youth development; Children/youth, services.
Type of support: Cause-related marketing; Employee volunteer services; General/operating support; Grants to individuals; Public relations services.
Geographic limitations: Giving primarily in areas of company operations in central MA.
Publications: Application guidelines.
Application information: Applications accepted. Application form required. Applicants should submit the following:
1) name, address and phone number of organization
2) copy of IRS Determination Letter
3) brief history of organization and description of its mission
4) contact person
Initial approach: Download nomination form and mail or fax to headquarters
Deadline(s): None

Bay State Savings Charitable Foundation, Inc.

(formerly Bay State Charitable Foundation, Inc.)
28 Franklin St.
Worcester, MA 01608-1904 (508) 890-9000
Additional tel.: (800) 244-8161, (508) 890-9011;
URL: https://www.baystatesavingsbank.com/index.php/about-us/community-involvement/

Establishment information: Established in 2002 in MA.
Donor: Bay State Savings Bank.
Contact: Diane Giampa, Clerk
Financial data (yr. ended 12/31/11): Assets, $151,261 (M); expenditures, $27,377; qualifying distributions, $27,350; giving activities include $27,300 for 11 grants (high: $4,500; low: $1,500).
Purpose and activities: The foundation supports organizations involved with education, health, housing, human services, and community development.
Fields of interest: Education; Health care; Housing/shelter; Human services; Community/economic development.
Type of support: Capital campaigns; General/operating support; Program development; Scholarship funds.
Geographic limitations: Giving limited to areas of company operations in Auburn, Barre, Berlin, Boylston, Charlton, Clinton, Douglas, Dudley, Grafton, Holden, Hubbardston, Jefferson, Lancaster, Leicester, Leominster, Millbury, Northborough, Northbridge, Oxford, Paxton, Princeton, Rutland, Shrewsbury, Spencer, Sterling, Sutton, Upton, Webster, West Boylston, Westminster, Whitinsville, and Worcester, MA.
Support limitations: No support for political organizations or candidates, religious institutions, fraternal organizations, employment unions, or fully tax-supported entities such as schools or libraries. No grants to individuals.
Publications: Application guidelines.
Application information: Applications accepted. Grants range from $1,000 to $3,000. Proposals should be limited to 4 pages. Application form required. Applicants should submit the following:
1) timetable for implementation and evaluation of project
2) how project will be sustained once grantmaker support is completed
3) statement of problem project will address
4) population served
5) name, address and phone number of organization
6) copy of IRS Determination Letter
7) brief history of organization and description of its mission
8) copy of most recent annual report/audited financial statement/990
9) how project's results will be evaluated or measured
10) listing of board of directors, trustees, officers and other key people and their affiliations
11) detailed description of project and amount of funding requested
12) plans for cooperation with other organizations, if any
13) contact person
14) copy of current year's organizational budget and/or project budget
Initial approach: Download application form and mail completed proposal and form to foundation
Copies of proposal: 9
Board meeting date(s): Mar. and Oct.
Deadline(s): Feb. 15 and Sept. 15
Final notification: 30 days following board meeting
Officers and Directors:* Peter B. Alden*, Pres. and Treas.; Diane M. Giampa, Clerk; Jay Z. Aframe; John Graham; Lisa Piehler; George F. Sullivan.
EIN: 800038576

381
Bayer Corporation

(formerly Miles Inc.)
100 Bayer Rd., Bldg. 4
Pittsburgh, PA 15205-9741 (412) 777-2000

Company URL: http://www.bayerus.com
Establishment information: Established in 1884.
Company type: Subsidiary of a foreign company
Business activities: Manufactures chemicals, health care products, pharmaceuticals, and imaging technologies.
Business type (SIC): Chemicals/industrial inorganic; drugs; soaps, cleaners, and toiletries; chemicals/industrial organic; fertilizers and agricultural chemicals; medical instruments and supplies
Financial profile for 2009: Number of employees, 17,000
Corporate officers: Gregory S. Babe, Pres. and C.E.O.; Willy Scherf, C.F.O.; Jens Lohmann, C.A.O.; Tracy E. Spagnol, V.P. and Treas.
Subsidiary: Bayer Healthcare Pharmaceuticals Inc., Wayne, NJ
Giving statement: Giving through the Bayer Corporation Contributions Program, the Bayer USA Foundation, and the Institute for Healthcare Communication.

Bayer Corporation Contributions Program

100 Bayer Rd.
Pittsburgh, PA 15205-9741 (412) 777-2000
Making Science Make Sense tel.: (800) 422-9374;
C.A.U.S.E. Challenge Hotline: (412) 237-1552;
SciTech Days: Geri Baker, School Prog. Mgr., tel.: (412) 237-1552,
e-mail: BakerG@carnegiesciencecenter.org.;
URL: http://www.bayerus.com/csr_sustainability.aspx

Purpose and activities: As a complement to its foundation, Bayer also makes charitable contributions to nonprofit organizations directly. Support is given in areas of company operations.
Fields of interest: Education, reading; Education; Environment; Children/youth, services; Science, formal/general education; Mathematics; Engineering/technology; Science.
Programs:
C.A.U.S.E. Challenge High School Film Festival: Bayer, in partnership with Carnegie Science Center's Regional SciTech initiative and Pittsburgh Filmmakers, invites 9th to 12th-grade students and student teams to write, produce, and edit videos or films on the theme "Mutual Impact: The Environment and You." The grand prize winner receives $1,000, a digital video camera and case, a Pittsburgh Filmmakers class, director's chair, Carnegie Science Center passes, and three Rivers Film Festival tickets. Other film awards include an Abstract/Art/Experimental Film Award, Narrative Film Award, Documentary Film Award, and Communicating Science Award, each with a $300 value. Each school that produces a prize-winning film

will also receive $1,500 to support their media and science programs.

Making Science Make Sense: Through the company-wide initiative Making Science Make Sense, Bayer supports science literacy and advancement through hands-on, inquiry-based science learning, employee volunteerism, and public education.

Partners for Youth and the Environment: Bayer is the first company in the world to enter a long-term partnership with the United Nations Environment Programme (UNEP) in the area of youth and environment. The cooperation focuses on children and young people from all over the world who are interested in environmental issues and committed to protecting the world around them. The partnership projects cover a range of events and creative competitions for children and young people. These include international conferences, study trips, science forums and painting and photo competitions. Another initiative is the publication of the TUNZA magazine - the environmental magazine for young people.

World Environment Day/International Children's Painting Competition: Bayer, in partnership with the United Nations Environment Programme Regional Office for North America, invites elementary and middle school students ages 6 to 14 to learn more about the environment and reflect that knowledge creatively through art. The program is designed to link science literacy and the environment and reinforce the notion that everyone has a responsibility when it comes to environmental and climate protection.

Type of support: Curriculum development; Employee volunteer services; General/operating support; In-kind gifts.

Geographic limitations: Giving in areas of company operations, with emphasis on Berkeley, CA, Elkhart and Mishawaka, IN, Shawnee, KS, Kansas City, MO, Research Triangle Park, NC, Morristown, NJ, Tarrytown, NY, Pittsburgh, PA, Baytown, TX, and Institute, New Martinsville, and South Charleston, WV; and in Columbia, France, Italy, Japan, Taiwan, and United Kingdom.

Application information:

Initial approach: Visit website for C.A.U.S.E. Challenge High School Film Festival registration information

Deadline(s): Registration starts Jan. 2 for C.A.U.S.E. Challenge High School Film Festival

Bayer USA Foundation

(formerly Bayer Foundation)
100 Bayer Rd.
Pittsburgh, PA 15205-9741 (412) 777-2000
URL: http://www.bayerus.com/Foundation/Foundation_Home.aspx

Establishment information: Established in 1985 in PA.

Donor: Bayer Corp.

Contact: Sarah Toulouse, Exec. Dir.

Financial data (yr. ended 12/31/11): Assets, $35,533,065 (M); gifts received, $7,714,862; expenditures, $9,654,227; qualifying distributions, $9,592,869; giving activities include $9,310,307 for 143 grants (high: $3,000,000; low: $75).

Purpose and activities: The foundation supports programs designed to promote education and workforce development; and environment and sustainability.

Fields of interest: Museums; Museums (science/technology); Arts; Higher education; Engineering school/education; Education; Environment, energy; Environmental education; Environment; Cancer; Diabetes; Employment, services; Food banks; Housing/shelter; American Red Cross; Youth, services; Human services; Economic development; Community/economic development; Mathematics; Engineering/technology; Science Youth; Minorities; Women.

Programs:

Arts and Culture: The foundation provides limited supports to organizations involved with arts, culture, and social services. Special emphasis is directed toward education or advocacy initiatives aimed at youth or underserved populations.

Education and Workforce Development: The foundation supports programs designed to promote hands-on inquiry-based science, technology, engineering, and math (STEM) education; and initiatives designed to provide innovative solutions to encourage more female and minority students to pursue a career in STEM.

Environment and Sustainability: The foundation supports programs designed to provide environmental education opportunities for youth; promote green building and energy-efficiency; and support issue-related work around sustainability.

Type of support: Capital campaigns; Conferences/seminars; Continuing support; Curriculum development; Equipment; Program development; Scholarship funds.

Geographic limitations: Giving primarily in areas of company operations in Berkeley and northern CA, Shawnee, KS, Kansas City, MO, Raleigh-Durham, NC, northern NJ, Newark, OH, Allegheny county and Pittsburgh, PA, and Baytown and Houston, TX; giving also to national organizations.

Support limitations: No support for discriminatory, political, or religious organizations, primary or secondary schools, or organizations outside of the U.S. No grants to individuals, or for general operating support for United Way affiliated organizations, endowments, debt reduction or operating reserves, charitable dinners, events, sponsorships, conferences, or seminars, community or event advertising, research projects, student trips or exchange programs, athletic sponsorships or scholarships, or telephone solicitations.

Publications: Application guidelines; Program policy statement.

Application information: Applications accepted. A full proposal may be requested at a later date. The Bayer USA Foundation application follows the Common Grant application process. Collateral materials including books, binders, videos, CDs, DVDs, programs, brochures, etc. will not be accepted unless specifically requested by the foundation. Application form not required.

Applicants should submit the following:

1) timetable for implementation and evaluation of project
2) name, address and phone number of organization
3) copy of IRS Determination Letter
4) brief history of organization and description of its mission
5) geographic area to be served
6) detailed description of project and amount of funding requested
7) contact person
8) copy of current year's organizational budget and/or project budget
9) listing of additional sources and amount of support

Applications should include a W-9 Form.

Initial approach: Complete online application
Copies of proposal: 1
Board meeting date(s): Feb. and Oct.
Deadline(s): None
Final notification: Following board meetings

Officers and Directors:* Richard K. Heller, V.P., Tax; Robert J. Koch, Secy.; James Martin, Treas.; Sarah Toulouse, Exec. Dir.; Claudio Abreu; Lars Benecke; Jack Boyne; Andrew J. Diana; Micheal J. McDonald; Elizabeth Roden.

EIN: 251508079

382
Bayer Healthcare Pharmaceuticals Inc.

(formerly Bayer Healthcare LLC)
6 W. Belt Plz.
Wayne, NJ 07470-6806 (973) 694-4100

Company URL: http://pharma.bayer.com

Establishment information: Established in 1979.

Company type: Subsidiary of a foreign company

Business activities: Manufactures pharmaceuticals, consumer health care products, diagnostic products, biological products, and animal health products.

Business type (SIC): Drugs

Corporate officers: Marijn Dekkers, Chair.; Reinhart Franzen, Pres. and C.E.O.; Jane Kramer, V.P., Public Affairs

Board of director: Marijn Dekkers, Chair.

Divisions: Bayer Agriculture Div., Shawnee Mission, KS; Bayer Biological Products Div., Research Triangle Park, NC; Bayer Consumer Care Div., Morristown, NJ; Bayer Diagnostics Div., Tarrytown, NY; Bayer Pharmaceutical Div., West Haven, CT

Historic mergers: Berlex Inc. (September 14, 2007)

Giving statement: Giving through the Bayer Hemophilia Awards Program and the ARCH Foundation.

The Bayer Hemophilia Awards Program

c/o Charitable Contribs.
2 T.W. Alexander Dr.
Research Triangle Park, NC 27709-0144
E-mail: programadministrator@bayer-hemophilia-awards.com; URL: http://www.bayer-hemophilia-awards.com

Purpose and activities: Bayer Biological Products awards grants to researchers, physicians in training, and caregivers and allied health professionals for research, the development of clinical expertise, and educational activities in the hemophilia field. Support is given on a national and international basis.

Fields of interest: Hemophilia; Hemophilia research.

Programs:

Caregiver Award: Bayer Biological Products annually awards six grants of up to $25,000 for educational activities in the field of hemophilia for caregivers and allied health professionals who work with hemophilia patients. The award can be used for educational seminars/symposia, mentored experiences, or training workshops.

Clinical Training Award: Bayer Biological Products annually awards four $100,000 two-year grants to mentored physicians in training for the development of specific clinical expertise in the field of hemophilia and, if desired, research projects in the field of hemostasis.

Early Career Investigator Award: Bayer Biological Products annually awards five $100,000 two-year grants to junior faculty members for mentored basic and/or clinical research projects in the bleeding disorders field. Special emphasis is directed toward clinical studies; properties and delivery of clotter factor proteins; assays and models; genetic and epidemiology; and molecular aspects and mechanisms of clotting factor inhibitor formation.

Special Project Award: Bayer Biological Products annually awards five grants of up to $200,000 for research projects conducted by individuals affiliated with facilities that provide care to hemophilia patients. Special emphasis is directed toward clinical research; basic research; assessment and intervention in psychosocial issues facing patients and their families; and assessment of quality of life and other health economic outcomes in patients with bleeding disorders and the effect of treatment modalities on such outcomes.
Type of support: Conferences/seminars; Equipment; Grants to individuals; Publication; Research; Seed money.
Geographic limitations: Giving on a national and international basis in the U.S. and in Australia, Canada, China, Europe, India, and Japan.
Support limitations: No grants for research focused on products or technologies licensed or patented by competitors of Bayer, cancer diagnosis or therapy, non-hemophilia-related AIDS diagnosis or hepatitis therapy, cardiovascular disease diagnosis or therapy, or purely thrombotic disorders.
Publications: Application guidelines.
Application information: Applications accepted. Letter of intent should be 500 words or less. A full proposal may be requested at a later date. Individuals receiving support are asked to provide periodic progress reports and a final report. A Grants Review and Awards Committee reviews all letters of intent and full proposals. Application form required.
Initial approach: Download letter of intent and e-mail to administrator
Copies of proposal: 1
Deadline(s): None for letter of intent; Mar. for those invited to submit full proposals
Final notification: May
Grants Review and Awards Committee: Gil White, M.D., Chair.; Erik Berntorp, M.D.; Paul Giangrande, M.D.; Barbara Konkle, M.D.; David Lillicrap, M.D.; Pier Mannucci, M.D.; Claude Negrier, M.D.; Brenda Riske; Alok Srivastava, M.D.

ARCH Foundation

6 W. Belt
Wayne, NJ 07470-6806 (973) 305-5022
Additional application addresses: P.O. Box 220908, Charlotte, NC 29222-0908, tel.: (877) 393-9071, Fax: (877) 229-1421; URL: http://www.archfoundation.com/

Establishment information: Established in 2001 in NJ; status changed to company-sponsored operating foundation in 2005.
Donors: Berlex Laboratories, Inc.; Berlex Inc.; Bayer Healthcare Pharmaceuticals Inc.; Bauer USA Foundation.
Contact: Donald Nerz, Treas.
Financial data (yr. ended 12/31/11): Assets, $172,540 (M); gifts received, $10,643,600; expenditures, $10,974,448; qualifying distributions, $10,973,817; giving activities include $10,143,600 for grants to individuals.
Purpose and activities: The foundation provides the birth control medication Mirena to economically disadvantaged women who live below the federal poverty level and have no insurance coverage.
Fields of interest: Health care Women; Economically disadvantaged.
Type of support: Donated products; Grants to individuals.
Geographic limitations: Giving on a national basis.
Publications: Application guidelines.
Application information: Applications accepted. Applications must be completed in part by a healthcare provider. Application form required. Applicants should submit the following:
1) copy of most recent annual report/audited financial statement/990
Initial approach: Download application form and fax or mail to application address
Deadline(s): None
Officers and Trustees:* Leo Plouffe*, Chair.; Paul Bedard, Pres.; Peter Currie, Secy.; Donald Nerz, Treas.; David Grimes, M.D.; Anita Nelson, M.D.; Ruth Merkatz; Sandy Oliver; Mary Pendergast; Jim Sailer.
EIN: 221231236

383
Bays Lung Rose & Holma

1099 Alakea St., Ste. 1600
Honolulu, HI 96813-4500 (808) 523-9000

Company URL: http://www.legalhawaii.com
Establishment information: Established in 1986.
Company type: Private company
Business activities: Operates law firm.
Business type (SIC): Legal services
Corporate officer: A. Bernard Bays, Partner
Giving statement: Giving through the Bays Lung Rose & Holma Pro Bono Program.

Bays Lung Rose & Holma Pro Bono Program

1099 Alakea St., 16th Fl.
Honolulu, HI 96813-4500 (808) 523-9000
URL: http://www.legalhawaii.com

Fields of interest: Legal services.
Type of support: Pro bono services - legal.
Geographic limitations: Giving primarily in areas of company operations in Honolulu, HI.
Application information: Pro bono cases handled by individual attorneys.

384
Bayview Financial Holdings, L.P.

4425 Ponce De Leon Blvd., 5th Fl.
Coral Gables, FL 33146 (877) 764-3238

Company URL: http://www.bayviewfinancial.com
Establishment information: Established in 1998.
Company type: Private company
Business activities: Provides consulting services; purchases mortgages and commercial real estate loans; provides commercial real estate loans.
Business type (SIC): Management and public relations services; credit institutions/business; investors/miscellaneous
Financial profile for 2011: Number of employees, 1,000
Corporate officers: John H. Fischer, Chair., Secy., and C.F.O.; David Quint, Pres.; Richard O'Brien, C.O.O.
Board of directors: John H. Fischer, Chair.; David Quint
Subsidiary: BayView Portfolio Services, Inc., Miami, FL
Giving statement: Giving through the Bayview Foundation, Inc.

Bayview Foundation, Inc.

4425 Ponce De Leon Blvd., 5th Fl.
Coral Gables, FL 33146-1837 (305) 646-6505
FAX: (305) 817-5206

Establishment information: Established in 1999 in FL.
Donor: BayView Financial Trading Group, L.P.
Contact: Sonya Hamilton, Coord.
Financial data (yr. ended 12/31/11): Assets, $1,069,364 (M); gifts received, $407,786; expenditures, $452,698; qualifying distributions, $171,908; giving activities include $171,908 for grants.
Purpose and activities: The foundation supports programs designed to enrich the lives of children through educational outreach and tutoring services.
Fields of interest: Education, services; Education Children.
Type of support: Equipment; General/operating support; Program development; Sponsorships.
Geographic limitations: Giving limited to FL.
Support limitations: No grants to individuals.
Application information: Applications not accepted. Contributes only to pre-selected organizations.
Officers and Directors:* David Ertel*, Pres.; Brian E. Bomstein, V.P. and Secy.; Robert A. Wegner, V.P. and Treas.; Eve Lominac, V.P.; John H. Fischer, V.P.; David Quint*, V.P.; Marvin Williams, V.P.; Beth Ertel.
EIN: 650890514
Selected grants: The following grants are a representative sample of this grantmaker's funding activity:
$50,000 to City Year Miami, Miami, FL, 2010.

385
BB&T Corporation

(formerly Southern National Corporation)
200 W. 2nd St.
Winston-Salem, NC 27101-4019
(336) 733-2000
FAX: (336) 721-3499

Company URL: http://www.bbt.com/
Establishment information: Established in 1897.
Company type: Public company
Company ticker symbol and exchange: BBT/NYSE
Business activities: Operates bank holding company; operates commercial bank; sells insurance.
Business type (SIC): Banks/commercial; insurance carriers
Financial profile for 2012: Number of employees, 34,000; assets, $183,872,000,000; pre-tax net income, $2,792,000,000; liabilities, $162,714,000,000
Fortune 1000 ranking: 2012—251st in revenues, 102nd in profits, and 34th in assets
Corporate officers: Kelly S. King, Chair. and C.E.O.; Christopher L. Henson, C.O.O.; Daryl N. Bible, Sr. Exec. V.P. and C.F.O.
Board of directors: Kelly S. King, Chair.; John A. Allison IV; Jennifer S. Banner; K. David Boyer, Jr.; Anna R. Cablik; Ronald E. Deal; J. Littleton Glover, Jr.; Jane P. Helm; Valeria Lynch Lee; John P. Howe III, M.D.; Nido R. Qubein; Thomas E. Skains; Thomas N. Thompson; Edwin Welch; Stephen T. Williams
Subsidiaries: Branch Banking and Trust Company, Winston-Salem, NC; Regional Acceptance Corp., Greenville, NC; Scott & Stringfellow, Inc., Richmond, VA
International operations: Bermuda
Historic mergers: BB&T Financial Corporation (February 28, 1995); Virginia Capital Bancshares, Inc. (June 27, 2001); First Virginia Banks, Inc. (July 1, 2003); BankAtlantic (July 31, 2012)
Giving statement: Giving through the BB&T Corporation Contributions Program, the BankAtlantic Foundation, Inc., the BB&T Charitable Foundation, the BB&T Foundation of Robeson

County, the BB&T Foundation of Wilson County, the BB&T West Virginia Foundation, Inc., the Citizens Savings Bank, SSB Foundation, and the Fredericksburg Savings Charitable Foundation.
Company EIN: 560939887

BB&T Corporation Contributions Program

(formerly Southern National Corporation Contributions Program)
P.O. Box 1290, M.C. 001-05-04-30
Winston-Salem, NC 27102-1290
FAX: (336) 733-0118;
E-mail: esimpson@bbandt.com

Contact: Ed Simpson, Sr. V.P., Financial Projects
Purpose and activities: As a complement to its foundation, BB&T also makes charitable contributions to nonprofit organizations directly. Support is given primarily in the Mid-Atlantic and Southeast.
Fields of interest: Arts; Education; Health care; Human services; Economic development; Community/economic development.
Type of support: Annual campaigns; Building/renovation; Capital campaigns; Curriculum development; Emergency funds; Endowments; General/operating support; In-kind gifts; Matching/challenge support; Professorships; Program development; Publication; Scholarship funds; Sponsorships.
Geographic limitations: Giving primarily in the Mid-Atlantic and Southeast.
Support limitations: No grants to individuals.
Application information: Applications not accepted. Contributes only to pre-selected organizations. The Financial Management Department handles giving. The company has a staff that only handles contributions. A contributions committee reviews all requests.
Committee meeting date(s): Bi-Monthly
Number of staff: 1 full-time professional; 1 full-time support.

BankAtlantic Foundation, Inc.

2100 W. Cypress Creek Rd.
Fort Lauderdale, FL 33309-1823 (954) 940-5058
FAX: (954) 940-5030;
E-mail: mbarrysmith@bankatlantic.com; Additional fax: (954) 940-6350; URL: http://www.bankatlantic.com/bafoundation

Establishment information: Established in 1994 in FL.
Donors: BankAtlantic, F.S.B.; The Annenberg Foundation; BankAtlantic; BankAtlantic Bancorp, Inc.
Contact: Marcia Barry-Smith, Secy. and Exec. Dir.
Financial data (yr. ended 12/31/11): Assets, $2,243,790 (M); gifts received, $50,150; expenditures, $223,593; qualifying distributions, $200,265; giving activities include $200,265 for grants.
Purpose and activities: The foundation supports organizations involved with arts and culture, education, human services, and community development.
Fields of interest: Museums (art); Performing arts; Arts; Elementary school/education; Education; Children/youth, services; Children, foster care; Homeless, human services; Human services; Economic development; Community/economic development.
Type of support: Continuing support; General/operating support; Program development.
Geographic limitations: Giving limited to areas of company operations in FL.
Support limitations: No support for hospitals, K-12 schools, national health-related organizations, political or lobbying organizations, religious, veteran, or fraternal organizations, school athletic teams, cheerleading squads, bands, or choirs. No grants to individuals, or for capital or building campaigns, courtesy or goodwill advertising to benefit publications, endowments, fundraising events, ticket purchases , travel, medical research, social functions, or sporting events.
Publications: Application guidelines.
Application information: Applications accepted. Grants range from $1,000 to $3,000. Faxed applications are not accepted. Support is limited to 1 contribution per organization during any given year for three years in length. Multi-year funding is not automatic. Additional information may be requested at a later date. A site visit may be requested. Application form not required. Applicants should submit the following:
1) signature and title of chief executive officer
2) statement of problem project will address
3) name, address and phone number of organization
4) copy of IRS Determination Letter
5) brief history of organization and description of its mission
6) listing of board of directors, trustees, officers and other key people and their affiliations
7) detailed description of project and amount of funding requested
8) contact person
9) copy of current year's organizational budget and/or project budget
10) listing of additional sources and amount of support

Proposals should include a copy of the organization's Charitable Solicitation License.
Initial approach: Proposal
Copies of proposal: 1
Deadline(s): Mar. 30 to Oct. 31
Final notification: 90 days
Officers and Trustees:* Alan B. Levan*, Pres.; Jarett Levan, V.P.; Marcia Barry-Smith*, Secy. and Exec. Dir.; Lewis F. Sarrica*, Treas.
Number of staff: None.
EIN: 650499150
Selected grants: The following grants are a representative sample of this grantmaker's funding activity:
$25,000 to Broward County School District, Fort Lauderdale, FL, 2008.
$20,000 to Broward Public Library Foundation, Fort Lauderdale, FL, 2008.
$20,000 to Dade Public Education Fund, Miami, FL, 2008.
$15,000 to Hispanic Unity of Florida, Hollywood, FL, 2008.
$15,000 to Museum of Science and Industry, Tampa, FL, 2008.
$10,000 to Broward Partnership for the Homeless, Fort Lauderdale, FL, 2008.
$10,000 to Donors Forum of South Florida, Miami, FL, 2008.
$10,000 to Leadership Broward Foundation, Fort Lauderdale, FL, 2008.
$10,000 to Urban League of Broward County, Fort Lauderdale, FL, 2008.
$8,500 to Fort Lauderdale Childrens Theater, Fort Lauderdale, FL, 2008.
$5,000 to American Association of Caregiving Youth, Boca Raton, FL, 2008.

BB&T Charitable Foundation

P.O. Box 1547, M.C. 001-05-04-30
Winston-Salem, NC 27102-1547
FAX: (336) 733-0118;
E-mail: esimpson@bbandt.com

Establishment information: Established in 1998 in NC.
Donors: BB&T Corp.; First Virginia Bank.
Contact: Ed Simpson, Exec. Dir.
Financial data (yr. ended 12/31/11): Assets, $3,457,723 (M); expenditures, $4,575,480; qualifying distributions, $4,547,925; giving activities include $4,546,925 for 188 grants (high: $750,000; low: $250).
Purpose and activities: The foundation supports organizations involved with arts and culture, education, the environment, health, human services, and community development.
Fields of interest: Arts; Education; Environment; Health care; Human services; Economic development; Community/economic development.
Type of support: Annual campaigns; Building/renovation; Capital campaigns; Curriculum development; Emergency funds; Endowments; General/operating support; Matching/challenge support; Professorships; Program development; Publication; Scholarship funds.
Geographic limitations: Giving primarily in areas of company operations in the mid-Atlantic and southeastern U.S.
Support limitations: No grants to individuals.
Application information: Applications not accepted. Contributes only to pre-selected organizations.
Board meeting date(s): Bi-monthly
Officer: Ed Simpson, Exec. Dir.
Trustee: BB&T Corp.
Number of staff: None.
EIN: 562093089
Selected grants: The following grants are a representative sample of this grantmaker's funding activity:
$500,000 to YWCA of Winston-Salem and Forsyth County, Winston-Salem, NC, 2010.
$200,000 to University of North Carolina at Greensboro Excellence Foundation, Greensboro, NC, 2010.
$175,000 to WilMed Healthcare Foundation, Wilson, NC, 2010.
$125,000 to United Way of Wilson County, Wilson, NC, 2010.
$50,000 to North Carolina Museum of Natural Sciences, Friends of the, Raleigh, NC, 2010.
$30,000 to Moses H. Cone Memorial Hospital Operating Corporation, Greensboro, NC, 2010.
$25,000 to Hill Center, Durham, NC, 2010.
$20,000 to Historic Preservation Foundation of North Carolina, Raleigh, NC, 2010.
$20,000 to Hospice and Palliative CareCenter, Winston-Salem, NC, 2010.
$20,000 to North Carolina Community Foundation, Raleigh, NC, 2010.

BB&T Foundation of Robeson County

c/o Branch Banking & Trust Co.
434 Fayetteville St., 14th Fl.
Raleigh, NC 27601-1701

Establishment information: Established in 1996 in NC.
Donor: BB&T Corp.
Financial data (yr. ended 12/31/11): Assets, $42,365 (M); expenditures, $1,000; qualifying distributions, $1,000.
Purpose and activities: The foundation supports the Robeson County Partnership for Children.
Fields of interest: Children, services.
Support limitations: No grants to individuals.

Application information: Applications not accepted. Unsolicited requests for funds not accepted.
Trustee: Branch Banking & Trust Co.
EIN: 566474893

BB&T Foundation of Wilson County

c/o Branch Banking & Trust Co.
434 Fayetteville St., 14th Fl.
Raleigh, NC 27601-1701

Donor: BB&T Corp.
Financial data (yr. ended 12/31/11): Assets, $146,382 (M); expenditures, $34,000; qualifying distributions, $33,000; giving activities include $33,000 for grants.
Purpose and activities: The foundation supports science museums and organizations involved with children's services, and disability services.
Fields of interest: Arts; Religion.
Type of support: General/operating support.
Support limitations: No grants to individuals.
Application information: Applications not accepted. Unsolicited requests for funds not accepted.
Trustee: Branch Banking & Trust Co.
EIN: 566474894

BB&T West Virginia Foundation, Inc.

(formerly One Valley Bank Foundation, Inc.)
434 Fayetteville St., 14th Fl.
Raleigh, NC 27601

Establishment information: Established in 1954 in WV.
Donors: One Valley Bank, N.A.; BB&T Corp.; OVB Charitable Trust.
Contact: John M. Barry
Financial data (yr. ended 12/31/11): Assets, $9,947,548 (M); gifts received, $100,250; expenditures, $571,737; qualifying distributions, $553,421; giving activities include $553,421 for grants.
Purpose and activities: The foundation supports community foundations and organizations involved with arts and culture, education, health, human services, and community economic development.
Fields of interest: Performing arts, orchestras; Arts; Higher education; Libraries (public); Education; Hospitals (general); Health care, clinics/centers; Health care; YM/YWCAs & YM/YWHAs; Human services; Foundations (community); United Ways and Federated Giving Programs.
Type of support: General/operating support.
Geographic limitations: Giving limited to WV.
Support limitations: No grants to individuals.
Application information: Applications accepted. Application form required.
Initial approach: Proposal
Copies of proposal: 1
Board meeting date(s): As needed
Deadline(s): None
Officers and Trustees: John M. Barry, Exec. Dir.; Phyllis H. Arnold; Calvin E. Barker; Nelle Ratrie Chilton; C. Edward Gaunch; J. Holmes Morrison; Steven M. Rubin; K. Richard C. Sinclair; Edwin H. Welch.
EIN: 556017269
Selected grants: The following grants are a representative sample of this grantmaker's funding activity:
$53,000 to West Virginia Independent Colleges and Universities, Charleston, WV, 2009.
$37,450 to United Way of Central West Virginia, Charleston, WV, 2009.
$23,900 to Capital Area Development Corporation, Charleston, WV, 2009.
$20,000 to West Virginia University Foundation, Morgantown, WV, 2009.
$17,000 to YWCA of Charleston, Charleston, WV, 2009. For Sojourners Program.
$15,000 to Cabell Huntington Hospital Foundation, Huntington, WV, 2009.
$15,000 to Clay Center for the Arts and Sciences of West Virginia, Charleston, WV, 2009.
$10,588 to Charleston Area Medical Center Foundation, Charleston, WV, 2009.
$10,000 to Fairmont State Foundation, Fairmont, WV, 2009.
$10,000 to Shepherd University Foundation, Shepherdstown, WV, 2009.

Citizens Savings Bank, SSB Foundation

c/o Branch Banking & Trust Co.
434 Fayetteville St., 14th Fl.
Raleigh, NC 27601-1701

Establishment information: Established in 1994.
Donor: Citizens Savings Bank, SSB.
Financial data (yr. ended 12/31/11): Assets, $69,479 (M); expenditures, $6,009; qualifying distributions, $5,000; giving activities include $5,000 for grants.
Purpose and activities: The foundation supports Presbyterian College in Clinton, South Carolina.
Fields of interest: Education.
Type of support: General/operating support.
Support limitations: No grants to individuals.
Application information: Applications not accepted. Unsolicited requests for funds not accepted.
Trustee: Branch Banking & Trust Co.
EIN: 566436047

Fredericksburg Savings Charitable Foundation

P.O. Box 783
400 George St.
Fredericksburg, VA 22404-0783 (540) 371-9617

Establishment information: Established in 1998 in DE and VA.
Donor: Virginia Capital Bancshares, Inc.
Contact: Samuel C. Harding, Jr., Dir.
Financial data (yr. ended 12/31/11): Assets, $8,397,492 (M); expenditures, $575,997; qualifying distributions, $554,000; giving activities include $554,000 for grants.
Purpose and activities: The foundation supports programs designed to expand home ownership opportunities; and contribute to the quality of life in communities where Fredericksburg Savings Bank operates.
Fields of interest: Hospitals (general); Health care, clinics/centers; Food banks; Housing/shelter; Boys & girls clubs; American Red Cross; Salvation Army; YM/YWCAs & YM/YWHAs; Children/youth, services; Homeless, human services; Human services; Community/economic development.
Type of support: General/operating support.
Geographic limitations: Giving primarily in areas of company operations in Caroline, King George, Orange, Spotsylvania, and Stafford counties, VA, and Fredericksburg, VA.
Support limitations: No grants to individuals.
Application information: Applications accepted. Application form required.
Initial approach: Contact foundation for application form
Directors: O'Conner G. Ashby; Ernest N. Donahoe; Samuel C. Harding, Jr.; William B. Young.
EIN: 541913172
Selected grants: The following grants are a representative sample of this grantmaker's funding activity:
$2,500 to American Cancer Society, Atlanta, GA, 2010.
$2,500 to Special Olympics, Washington, DC, 2010.

386
BBCN Bank

(formerly Nara Bank)
3731 Wilshire Blvd., Ste. 1000
Los Angeles, CA 90010-2830
(213) 639-1700

Company URL: http://www.bbcnbank.com
Establishment information: Established in 1989.
Company type: Subsidiary of a foreign company
Business activities: Operates commercial bank.
Business type (SIC): Banks/commercial
Corporate officers: Alvin D. Kang, Pres. and C.E.O.; Bonita I. Lee, Exec. V.P. and C.O.O.; Philip E. Guldeman, C.P.A., Exec. V.P. and C.F.O.; Brian E. Van Dyk, Exec. V.P. and C.I.O.
Giving statement: Giving through the BBCN Bank Scholarship Foundation.

BBCN Bank Scholarship Foundation

(formerly The Nara Bank Scholarship Foundation)
3731 Wilshre Blvd., Ste. 1000
Los Angeles, CA 90010-2830 (213) 639-1700
URL: http://www.bbcnbank.com/community_support.asp

Establishment information: Established in 2001 in CA.
Donor: Nara Bank.
Contact: Paul Choi, Secy.
Financial data (yr. ended 12/31/10): Assets, $0; gifts received, $75,659; expenditures, $94,659; qualifying distributions, $94,659; giving activities include $90,000 for 45 grants to individuals (high: $2,000; low: $2,000).
Purpose and activities: The foundation awards college scholarships to high school seniors located in Alameda, Los Angeles, Orange, and Santa Clara counties, California, Bergen County, New Jersey, and New York, Bronx, Kings, and Queens counties, New York.
Fields of interest: Higher education.
Program:
Scholarships: The foundation awards $2,000 college scholarships to underserved high school graduates located in select counties of California, New Jersey, and New York. Applicants must plan to attend an accredited junior college or four-year college and have an overall GPA of 3.3 or higher. Recipients are selected based on financial need, academic excellence, and leadership in the community.
Type of support: Scholarships—to individuals.
Geographic limitations: Giving limited to areas of company operations in Alameda, Los Angeles, Orange, and Santa Clara counties, CA, Bergen County, NJ, and New York, Bronx, Kings, and Queens counties, NY.
Publications: Application guidelines; Grants list.
Application information: Applications accepted. Application form required.
Applications should include an official high school transcripts, a one-page essay, and a copy of a signed family tax return.
Initial approach: Contact foundation for application form or download application form when available
Copies of proposal: 1
Deadline(s): Feb. 28

Officers and Directors:* John Hampton, C.E.O.; Christine Oh*, C.F.O.; Paul Choi, Secy.; Alvin D. Kang; Min Kim.
EIN: 912156704

387
BC International Group, Inc.

(formerly Birger Christensen (USA) Inc.)
922 Riverview Dr.
Totowa, NJ 07512-1127 (973) 826-1140

Company URL: http://www.birgerusa.com
Establishment information: Established in 1993.
Company type: Private company
Business activities: Operates women's clothing and accessories stores.
Business type (SIC): Women's specialty and accessory stores
Corporate officers: Chris Spiropoulos, Pres. and C.E.O.; Galatia Asprou, C.F.O.
Giving statement: Giving through the Iordanis Spyropoulos Foundation.

Iordanis Spyropoulos Foundation

922 Riverview Dr.
Totowa, NJ 07512-1127

Establishment information: Established in 2005 in NJ.
Donor: BC International Group, Inc.
Financial data (yr. ended 12/31/11): Assets, $1,707,677 (M); gifts received, $85,000; expenditures, $104,008; qualifying distributions, $98,440; giving activities include $98,440 for grants.
Purpose and activities: The foundation supports organizations involved with senior citizen services and Christianity.
Fields of interest: Religion.
Type of support: General/operating support.
Geographic limitations: Giving primarily in Hicksville, Whitestone, and Yonkers, NY.
Support limitations: No grants to individuals.
Application information: Applications not accepted. Unsolicited requests for funds not accepted.
Officers: Christos Spyropoulos, Pres. and C.E.O.; Galatia Asprou, C.F.O.; Stella Spyropoulos, V.P.
EIN: 510534361

388
BDP International, Inc.

510 Walnut St.
Philadelphia, PA 19106 (215) 629-8940

Company URL: http://www.bdpinternational.com
Establishment information: Established in 1966.
Company type: Private company
Business activities: Provides customized global transportation and logistics services.
Business type (SIC): Transportation services/ freight
Corporate officers: Richard J. Bolte, Jr., Pres. and C.E.O.; Frank P. Osusky, C.F.O. and Treas.; John M. Bolte, C.O.O.; Albert Fenaroli, Chair. Emeritus
Board of director: Albert J. Fenaroli
Giving statement: Giving through the Bolte Family Foundation.

The Bolte Family Foundation

c/o BDP International
510 Walnut St., Fl. 14
Philadelphia, PA 19106-3619

Establishment information: Established in 2007 in PA.
Donor: BDP International, Inc.
Financial data (yr. ended 12/31/11): Assets, $30,407 (M); gifts received, $901,000; expenditures, $909,326; qualifying distributions, $909,326; giving activities include $908,750 for 12 grants (high: $800,000; low: $250).
Purpose and activities: The foundation supports children's hospitals and organizations involved with higher education, patient services, breast cancer, and chemistry.
Fields of interest: Higher education; Hospitals (general); Health care, patient services; Breast cancer; Salvation Army; Children, services; Chemistry.
Type of support: General/operating support.
Geographic limitations: Giving primarily in PA.
Support limitations: No grants to individuals.
Application information: Applications not accepted. Contributes only to pre-selected organizations.
Officers: William Connors, Pres.; Thomas Kramer, V.P.; Midge Clark, Treas.
EIN: 412237563

389
Beall's, Inc.

1806 38th Ave., E.
Bradenton, FL 34208 (941) 747-2355
FAX: (941) 746-1171

Company URL: http://www.beallsinc.com
Establishment information: Established in 1915.
Company type: Private company
Business activities: Operates department stores; operates discount stores.
Business type (SIC): Department stores; variety stores
Corporate officers: Dan Love, Pres.; Michael Maddaloni, Treas.; Stephen M. Knopik, C.E.O.; Richard Judd, C.O.O.; Alison Smith, V.P., Finance
Board of director: Dan Love, Chair.
Subsidiaries: Beall's Department Stores, Inc., Bradenton, FL; Beall's Outlet Stores, Inc., Bradenton, FL
Giving statement: Giving through the R. M. Beall, Sr. Charitable Foundation.

R. M. Beall, Sr. Charitable Foundation

1806 38th Ave. E.
Bradenton, FL 34208-4708

Establishment information: Established in 1987 in FL.
Donors: Beall's Department Stores, Inc.; Beall's, Inc.
Contact: Patricia Johnson
Financial data (yr. ended 12/31/11): Assets, $3,758,824 (M); gifts received, $6,460; expenditures, $272,826; qualifying distributions, $242,010; giving activities include $126,417 for 62 grants to individuals (high: $8,335; low: $250).
Purpose and activities: The foundation supports organizations involved with education and youth development and awards college scholarships to student members of the Palmetto Youth Center in Palmetto, Florida.
Fields of interest: Higher education; Students, sororities/fraternities; Education, reading; Education; Girls clubs; Youth development.
Program:
Palmetto Youth Center Scholarship Program: The foundation awards college scholarships of up to $5,000 to student members of the Palmetto Youth Center in Palmetto, Florida. Recipients are chosen based on the extent of involvement with the Palmetto Youth Center, academic achievement, extracurricular activities, and financial need.
Type of support: Employee-related scholarships; General/operating support; Scholarships—to individuals.
Geographic limitations: Giving primarily in Bradenton, FL.
Application information: Applications accepted. Application form required.
Applications for scholarships should include transcripts and letters of recommendation.
Initial approach: Proposal
Deadline(s): None
Board Members: Beverly Beall; Robert M. Beall II; Betty B. Szymanski; Clifford L. Walters.
EIN: 592851924

390
Beam Inc.

(formerly Beam Global Spirits & Wine, Inc.)
510 Lake Cook Rd., Ste. 200
Deerfield, IL 60015-4964 (847) 948-8888
FAX: (847) 948-8610

Company URL: http://www.beamglobal.com
Establishment information: Established in 1995.
Company type: Public company
Company ticker symbol and exchange: BEAM/ NYSE
Business activities: Produces spirits and wine.
Business type (SIC): Beverages
Financial profile for 2012: Number of employees, 3,400; assets, $8,636,900,000; sales volume, $2,465,900,000; pre-tax net income, $502,000,000; expenses, $1,890,000,000; liabilities, $4,024,800,000
Fortune 1000 ranking: 2012—822nd in revenues, 415th in profits, and 436th in assets
Corporate officers: David Mackay, Chair.; Matthew J. Shattock, Pres. and C.E.O.; Robert Probst, Sr. V.P. and C.F.O.; Kenton R. Rose, Sr. V.P., Genl. Counsel, C.A.O., and Secy.; Clarkson Hine, Sr. V.P., Corp. Comms., and Public Affairs; Mindy Mackenzie, Sr. V.P., Human Resources
Board of directors: David Mackay, Chair.; Richard A. Goldstein; Stephen W. Golsby; Ann Fritz Hackett; Gretchen W. Price; Matt Shattock; Robert A. Steele; Peter Wilson
International operations: Canada
Giving statement: Giving through the Beam Inc. Corporate Giving Program.
Company EIN: 133295276

Beam Inc. Corporate Giving Program

(formerly Beam Global Spirts & Wine Angels' Share Program)
510 Lake Cook Rd.
Deerfield, IL 60015-4971
URL: http://beamglobal.com/responsibility/ philanthropy

Purpose and activities: Beam Global Spirits & Wine makes charitable contributions to nonprofit organizations involved with health and human services, and on a case by case basis. Support is given primarily in areas of company operations.
Fields of interest: Public health; Health care; Human services; General charitable giving Military/ veterans.

Type of support: Donated products; Employee matching gifts; Employee volunteer services; General/operating support; Sponsorships.
Geographic limitations: Giving primarily in areas of company operations.
Application information: Applications accepted. Contact form should include the date, location, expected attendance, and a brief description of the event.
Initial approach: Complete contact form on website
Deadline(s): 90 days prior to need

391
D. D. Bean & Sons Co., Inc.
207 Peterborough St.
P.O. Box 348
Jaffrey, NH 03452 (603) 532-8311

Company URL: http://www.ddbean.com
Establishment information: Established in 1938.
Company type: Private company
Business activities: Manufactures match books.
Business type (SIC): Manufacturing/miscellaneous
Corporate officers: Vernon Bean, Chair.; Delcie Bean, Pres. and C.E.O.; Stephen H. Krause, Secy.
Board of director: Vernon Bean, Chair.
Subsidiaries: Jaffrey Fire Protection Co., Jaffrey, NH; W.W. Cross, Inc., Jaffrey, NH
Giving statement: Giving through the Bean Foundation.

The Bean Foundation
P.O. Box 348
Jaffrey, NH 03452-0348 (603) 532-8311

Establishment information: Established in 1954 in NH.
Donor: D.D. Bean & Sons Co., Inc.
Financial data (yr. ended 12/31/11): Assets, $923,008 (M); expenditures, $104,217; qualifying distributions, $101,050; giving activities include $101,050 for grants.
Purpose and activities: The foundation supports Christian agencies and churches and organizations involved with arts and culture, education, human services, and civic affairs and awards college scholarships and health insurance grants to indigent individuals.
Fields of interest: Arts; Housing/shelter; Human services.
Type of support: General/operating support; Grants to individuals; Scholarships—to individuals.
Application information: Applications accepted. Application form not required.
Initial approach: Proposal
Deadline(s): None
Officer: Susan E. Leach, Pres.; Charles H. Krause, V.P. and Treas.; Christopher V. Bean, Secy.
Directors: Delcie D. Bean; Mark C. Bean; Bonnie B. Bennett; Caroline K. Hollister; Laura Redmond.
EIN: 026005330

392
L. L. Bean, Inc.
3 Campus Dr.
Freeport, ME 04033-0001 (207) 552-3028
FAX: (207) 552-4080

Company URL: http://www.llbean.com
Establishment information: Established in 1912.
Company type: Private company
Business activities: Operates apparel stores; provides Internet shopping services; provides catalog shopping services.
Business type (SIC): Apparel and accessory stores; nonstore retailers; computer services
Financial profile for 2010: Number of employees, 4,600; sales volume, $1,440,000,000
Corporate officers: Leon A. Gorman, Chair.; Christopher J. McCormick, Pres. and C.E.O.; Mark Fasold, C.F.O.; Robert Peixotto, C.O.O.; John Oliver, V.P., Public Affairs; Martha Cyr, V.P., Human Resources
Board of director: Leon A. Gorman, Chair.
Giving statement: Giving through the L. L. Bean, Inc. Corporate Giving Program.

L. L. Bean, Inc. Corporate Giving Program
c/o Community Rels.
15 Casco St.
Freeport, ME 04033-0001
E-mail: donationrequest@llbean.com; URL: http://www.llbean.com/customerService/aboutLLBean/charitable_giving.html

Purpose and activities: L. L. Bean makes charitable contributions to nonprofit organizations involved with arts and culture, education, the environment, health, and human services. Special emphasis is directed towards programs designed to promote outdoor recreation and conservation. Support is given primarily in Maine.
Fields of interest: Arts; Education; Environment; Health care; Recreation; Human services.
Type of support: Donated products; General/operating support; Program development.
Geographic limitations: Giving limited to Bangor, Brunswick, Freeport, Lewiston, and Portland, ME for arts and culture; giving limited to ME for education, health, and human services; giving to regional and national organizations for outdoor recreation and conservation.
Support limitations: No support for political, sectarian, fraternal, or religious organizations, animal welfare groups, or national health organizations and their local affiliates, individual schools, or teacher or parent organizations. No grants to individuals, or for conferences, pageants or fashion shows, treks, sporting events or athletic teams, travel, advertising, film or television productions, individual youth clubs or scout troops, classrooms, or teams.
Publications: Application guidelines.
Application information: Applications accepted. Proposals should be no longer than 3 pages. The Community Relations Department handles giving. The company has a staff that only handles contributions. Application form not required. Applicants should submit the following:
1) copy of current year's organizational budget and/or project budget
2) detailed description of project and amount of funding requested
3) how project's results will be evaluated or measured
4) brief history of organization and description of its mission
5) copy of IRS Determination Letter
6) population served
7) timetable for implementation and evaluation of project

Initial approach: E-mail or mail proposal to headquarters
Copies of proposal: 1
Deadline(s): 4 weeks prior to need
Final notification: 4 weeks
Number of staff: 1 full-time professional; 2 full-time support.

393
The Lewis Bear Company
6120 Enterprise Dr.
Pensacola, FL 32505-1858 (850) 432-9368

Company URL: http://www.floridasgreatnorthwest.com
Establishment information: Established in 1876.
Company type: Private company
Business activities: Sells beer wholesale.
Business type (SIC): Beer, wine, and distilled beverages—wholesale
Corporate officers: John L. Hutchinso, Chair.; Ed Gardner, Jr., Vice-Chair.; Lewis Bear, Jr., Pres. and C.E.O.; Roger Weir, C.O.O.; Edward L. Koontz, V.P., Sales and Mktg.; Belle Y. Bear, Secy.
Board of directors: John L. Hutchinson, Chair.; Ed Gardner, Vice-Chair.
Giving statement: Giving through the Bear Family Foundation, Inc.

The Bear Family Foundation, Inc.
6120 Enterprise Dr.
Pensacola, FL 32505-1858

Establishment information: Established in 2002 in FL.
Donors: The Lewis Bear Co.; Lewis Bear, Jr.
Financial data (yr. ended 12/31/11): Assets, $2,259,544 (M); gifts received, $1,000,000; expenditures, $69,195; qualifying distributions, $57,714; giving activities include $57,714 for grants.
Purpose and activities: The foundation supports art councils, zoos, hospitals, and organizations involved with elementary education, heart disease, and human services.
Fields of interest: Education; Health care; Human services.
Type of support: General/operating support; Program development.
Geographic limitations: Giving limited to Pensacola, FL.
Support limitations: No grants to individuals.
Application information: Applications not accepted. Unsolicited requests for funds not accepted.
Officers: Lewis Bear, Jr., Chair.; Belle Y. Bear, Vice-Chair.; Cindi Bear Bonner, Secy.; Lewis Bear III, Treas.
EIN: 753064392

394
Beaver Street Fisheries, Inc.
1741 W. Beaver St.
P.O. Box 41430
Jacksonville, FL 32203-1430
(904) 493-4954
FAX: (904) 633-7271

Company URL: http://www.beaverfish.com
Establishment information: Established in 1950.
Company type: Private company
Business activities: Sells seafood wholesale.
Business type (SIC): Groceries—wholesale
Corporate officers: Harry Frisch, Chair.; Benjamin P. Frisch, Pres.; Jeff Edwards, C.F.O.; Scott Lane, C.I.O.
Board of director: Harry Frisch, Chair.
Giving statement: Giving through the Beaver Street Foundation, Inc.

Beaver Street Foundation, Inc.

P.O. Box 41430
Jacksonville, FL 32203-1430

Establishment information: Established in 1986 in FL.
Donor: Beaver Street Fisheries, Inc.
Financial data (yr. ended 12/31/11): Assets, $12,639,211 (M); gifts received, $503,955; expenditures, $542,204; qualifying distributions, $535,268; giving activities include $535,268 for grants.
Purpose and activities: The foundation supports organizations involved with higher education, animal welfare, health, cancer, human services, and Judaism.
Fields of interest: Higher education; Animal welfare; Hospitals (general); Health care, clinics/centers; Health care; Cancer; Cancer, leukemia; Youth development, business; Children, services; Human services; United Ways and Federated Giving Programs; Jewish federated giving programs; Jewish agencies & synagogues.
Type of support: Annual campaigns; Continuing support; General/operating support; Sponsorships.
Geographic limitations: Giving primarily in Jacksonville, FL.
Support limitations: No grants to individuals.
Application information: Applications not accepted. Contributes only to pre-selected organizations.
Directors: Adam Frisch; Benjamin P. Frisch; Hans Frisch; Mark Frisch.
EIN: 592714980
Selected grants: The following grants are a representative sample of this grantmaker's funding activity:
$20,000 to University of North Florida Foundation, Jacksonville, FL, 2010.
$12,000 to United Way of Northeast Florida, Jacksonville, FL, 2010.
$10,000 to Congregation Ahavath Chesed, Jacksonville, FL, 2010.
$10,000 to Jacksonville University, Jacksonville, FL, 2010.
$7,000 to Jacksonville Wolfson Childrens Hospital, Jacksonville, FL, 2010.
$5,000 to HandsOn Jacksonville, Jacksonville, FL, 2010.
$5,000 to Junior Achievement of North Florida, Jacksonville, FL, 2010.
$3,000 to Jewish Family and Community Services, Jacksonville, FL, 2010.
$2,000 to OneJax, Jacksonville, FL, 2010.
$1,000 to American Red Cross, Jacksonville, FL, 2010.

395
Bechtel Group, Inc.

50 Beale St.
San Francisco, CA 94105 (415) 768-1234

Company URL: http://www.bechtel.com
Establishment information: Established in 1898.
Company type: Private company
Business activities: Provides engineering services; provides nonresidential general contract construction services.
Business type (SIC): Engineering, architectural, and surveying services; contractors/general nonresidential building
Financial profile for 2011: Number of employees, 52,700; sales volume, $27,900,000,000
Corporate officers: Riley P. Bechtel, Chair. and C.E.O.; Adrian Zaccaria, Vice-Chair.; Bill Dudley, Pres. and C.O.O.; Peter A. Dawson, C.F.O.; Michael C. Bailey, Genl. Counsel
Board of directors: Riley Bechtel, Chair.; Adrian Zaccaria, Vice-Chair.; Mike Adams; Michael Bailey; Steve Bechtel, Jr.; Leigh Clifford; Peter Dawson; Alan Dachs; Bill Dudley; Jack Futcher; Andy Greig; Bob Joss; David O'Reilly; John MacDonald; Nick Moore; Dan Warmenhoven
Subsidiaries: Bechtel Corp., San Francisco, CA; Bechtel Enterprises, Inc., San Francisco, CA; Becon Construction Co., Inc., Houston, TX
Plant: Frederick, MD
International operations: Canada; Egypt; United Kingdom
Giving statement: Giving through the Bechtel Group, Inc. Corporate Giving Program and the Bechtel Group Foundation.
Company EIN: 942681915

Bechtel Group Foundation

(formerly Bechtel Foundation)
50 Beale St.
San Francisco, CA 94105-1813 (415) 768-1842
E-mail: becfoun@bechtel.com; Application address: P.O. Box 193965, San Francisco, CA 94119-3965; URL: http://www.bechtel.com/foundation.html

Establishment information: Incorporated in 1953 in CA.
Donors: Bechtel Group, Inc.; Bechtel Power Corp.; Bechtel Systems of Infrastructure, Inc.; Bechtel Corp.
Contact: Marthe Patterson, Comms. and Grants Off.
Financial data (yr. ended 12/31/11): Assets, $20,023,311 (M); gifts received, $3,000,000; expenditures, $2,753,996; qualifying distributions, $2,603,828; giving activities include $2,603,828 for grants.
Purpose and activities: The foundation supports organizations involved with arts and culture, education, human services, science, and civic affairs.
Fields of interest: Arts; Higher education; Business school/education; Engineering school/education; Education; Human services; United Ways and Federated Giving Programs; Mathematics; Engineering; Science; Public affairs.
Programs:
Bechtel Global Scholar Grants: The foundation awards $3,000 college scholarships to children of employees of Bechtel. The program is administered through Scholarship America.
Building Positive Relationships Grants: The foundation awards grant of up to $5,000 to educational, civic, cultural, and social service programs located in communities that host major Bechtel offices and projects.
Improving the Pipeline of Engineering and Construction Talent Grants: The foundation supports university-level education through scholarship funds and supports business, technical, and engineering programs at universities.
Matching Gift Grants: The foundation matches contributions made by employees and retirees of Bechtel to institutions of higher education on a one-for-one basis from $100 to $1,000 per contributor, per year.
Type of support: Employee matching gifts; Employee volunteer services; Employee-related scholarships; General/operating support; Program development; Scholarship funds.
Geographic limitations: Giving on a national and international basis in areas of company operations, with emphasis on CA, Washington, DC, MD, MN, PA, and VA.
Support limitations: No support for religious organizations. No grants to individuals (except for employee-related scholarships), or for endowments or special projects.
Application information: Applications accepted. Application form not required. Applicants should submit the following:
1) copy of IRS Determination Letter
2) descriptive literature about organization
Initial approach: Proposal
Board meeting date(s): Annually
Deadline(s): None
Final notification: Varies
Officers and Directors:* Riley P. Bechtel*, Chair.; Adrian Zaccaria*, Pres.; Michael C. Bailey*, Sr. V.P.; Peter A. Dawson*, Sr. V.P.; M. W. Quazzo, V.P. and Secy.; Annette M. Sparks, V.P. and Cont.; J.K. Deshong, V.P.; Charlene A. Wellness*, V.P.; K. C. Leader, Treas.; William N. Dudley, Jr.
Number of staff: 1 full-time professional; 1 part-time professional; 1 full-time support; 1 part-time support.
EIN: 946078120

396
The Beck Group

(also known as HCBeck, Ltd.)
1807 Ross Ave., Ste. 500
Dallas, TX 75201-8006 (214) 303-6200
FAX: (214) 303-6300

Company URL: http://www.beckgroup.com/
Establishment information: Established in 1912.
Company type: Private company
Business activities: Operates full-service, general contracting company specializing in commercial projects; also provides real estate development services.
Business type (SIC): Contractors/general nonresidential building
Financial profile for 2010: Number of employees, 500
Corporate officers: Henry C. Beck III, Co-C.E.O.; C. Samuel Ellison, Co-C.E.O.; Mark Collins, C.F.O.; Tonya Johannsen, Genl. Counsel
Board of director: Lawrence A. Wilson
Giving statement: Giving through the Beck Community Development Foundation.

Beck Community Development Foundation

1807 Ross Ave., Ste. 500
Dallas, TX 75201-8006 (214) 303-6456
URL: http://www.beckgroup.com/#/beck-community-involvement

Establishment information: Established in 2007 in TX.
Donors: The Beck Company; Henry C. Beck Charitable Lead Trust; HC Beck, Ltd.; HCB Jr. Lead Trust.
Contact: James A. Gettman, Pres.
Financial data (yr. ended 12/31/11): Assets, $178,395 (M); gifts received, $128,420; expenditures, $184,566; qualifying distributions, $54,398; giving activities include $54,398 for grants.
Purpose and activities: The foundation supports programs designed to break the cycle of poverty, undereducation, poor hygiene, and sickness. Special emphasis is directed toward programs designed to promote water; shelter; education; and microfinance.
Fields of interest: Higher education; Education; Environment, water resources; Public health,

hygiene; Housing/shelter; Microfinance/microlending; Community/economic development.
International interests: Mexico.
Type of support: Building/renovation; General/operating support; Scholarship funds.
Geographic limitations: Giving primarily in TX for the benefit of Mexico.
Application information: Applications accepted. Application form required.
Initial approach: Proposal
Deadline(s): None
Officers: James A. Gettman, Pres.; Gillett Berger, V.P. and Secy.
Directors: Henry C. Beck III; Gregg Powell.
EIN: 743237285

397
Beckman Coulter, Inc.

(formerly Beckman Instruments, Inc.)
250 S. Kraemer Blvd.
Brea, CA 92821-6232 (714) 993-5321

Company URL: http://www.beckmancoulter.com
Establishment information: Established in 1935.
Company type: Subsidiary of a public company
Business activities: Designs, manufactures, and markets laboratory systems.
Business type (SIC): Laboratory apparatus
Financial profile for 2010: Number of employees, 11,900; assets, $4,882,800,000; sales volume, $3,663,400,000; pre-tax net income, $308,900,000; expenses, $3,263,900,000; liabilities, $2,751,300,000
Corporate officers: Tom Joyce, Pres., Diagnostics Div.; Chuck McLaughlin, Sr. V.P. and C.F.O.; Jeff Linton, Sr. V.P. and Genl. Counsel; Allison Blackwell, Sr. V.P., Human Resources
Subsidiary: Coulter Corporation, Miami, FL
International operations: Panama
Giving statement: Giving through the Beckman Coulter, Inc. Corporate Giving Program and the Beckman Coulter Foundation.
Company EIN: 951040600

Beckman Coulter, Inc. Corporate Giving Program

(formerly Beckman Instruments, Inc. Corporate Giving Program)
c/o Community Rels.
250 S. Kraemer Blvd.
Brea, CA 92821-6232 (714) 961-4002
E-mail: communityrelations@beckman.com;
URL: https://www.beckmancoulter.com/wsrportal/wsr/company/about-us/community-relations/index.htm

Purpose and activities: As a complement to its foundation, Beckman Coulter also makes charitable contributions to nonprofit organizations directly. Support is given primarily in areas of company operations.
Fields of interest: Health care, research; Medical research.
Programs:
Beckman Coulter Founders Scholarship Program: The company awards 13 $5,000 college scholarships to children of employees of Beckman Coulter.
Research-Related Health Care: The company supports hospitals, research laboratories, nonprofit organizations, medical foundations, and medical symposia to help health organizations in their battle against disease.
Science: The company supports organizations and institutions designed to further the outreach and enhancement of science and technology in our everyday lives.
Science Education: The company supports educational organizations, universities, and schools. Special emphasis is directed toward programs designed to encourage students to pursue higher education, especially in the areas of science, math, and technology.
Type of support: Employee matching gifts; Employee volunteer services; Employee-related scholarships; Sponsorships.
Geographic limitations: Giving primarily in areas of company operations.
Number of staff: 2 full-time professional.

Beckman Coulter Foundation

250 S. Kraemer Blvd., M363
Brea, CA 92821-6229
URL: http://www.beckmancoulterfoundation.org/

Establishment information: Established in 2007 in CA.
Donor: Beckman Coulter, Inc.
Contact: Catherine Dougherty, Grant Dir.
Financial data (yr. ended 12/31/11): Assets, $5,048,421 (M); expenditures, $1,073,146; qualifying distributions, $1,027,507; giving activities include $1,027,507 for grants.
Purpose and activities: The foundations supports programs designed to promote science; science education; and healthcare-related research that improves patient health and quality of life.
Fields of interest: Higher education; Education; Health care; Medical research; American Red Cross; Science, formal/general education; Mathematics; Engineering/technology; Science.
Programs:
Employee Matching Gifts: The foundation matches contributions made by employees of Beckman Coulter to primary and secondary educational institutions, colleges, and universities on a one-for-one basis up to $10,000 per employee, per year.
Volunteer Matching: The foundation matches fundraising commitments made by volunteer teams of Beckman Coulter employees up to $100 per event.
Type of support: Employee matching gifts; Employee volunteer services; General/operating support; Program development; Sponsorships.
Geographic limitations: Giving primarily in areas of company operations in CA.
Support limitations: No support for fraternal, labor, or veterans' organizations, for-profit organizations, discriminatory organizations, private foundations, political organizations, or religious organizations or groups. No grants for advertising, beauty or talent contests, capital or building campaigns (including new construction or renovations), fundraisers, galas or dinners, golf tournaments, media productions including radio, TV., film, web-casts, or publications, meetings, conferences, symposia, or workshops unrelated to Beckman Coulter, political campaigns or activities, or sports affiliated activities.
Application information: Applications not accepted. The foundation is not currently accepting any new requests for support.
Officers and Directors:* G. Russell Bell*, Pres.; Jeffrey Linton*, Secy.; Roger B. Plotkin*, C.F.O.; Sibil Lin, Treas.; Peter Heseltine; James C. Osborne.
EIN: 261126986
Selected grants: The following grants are a representative sample of this grantmaker's funding activity:
$63,244 to Women and Infants Hospital of Rhode Island, Providence, RI, 2010.
$60,000 to Emory University, Atlanta, GA, 2010.
$45,000 to Harvey Mudd College, Claremont, CA, 2010.
$20,000 to Rose-Hulman Institute of Technology, Terre Haute, IN, 2010.
$20,000 to University of Washington Foundation, Seattle, WA, 2010.
$10,000 to Harvey Mudd College, Claremont, CA, 2010.
$10,000 to National Organization for Renal Disease, Studio City, CA, 2010.
$5,000 to Leukemia & Lymphoma Society, Indianapolis, IN, 2010.
$2,500 to City of Hope, Los Angeles, CA, 2010.
$1,168 to Leukemia & Lymphoma Society, Indianapolis, IN, 2010.

398
Becton, Dickinson and Company

(also known as BD)
1 Becton Dr.
Franklin Lakes, NJ 07417-1880
(201) 847-6800
FAX: (201) 847-6475

Company URL: http://www.bd.com
Establishment information: Established in 1897.
Company type: Public company
Company ticker symbol and exchange: BDX/NYSE
International Securities Identification Number: US0758871091
Business activities: Manufactures and sells medical supplies and devices, laboratory equipment, and diagnostic products.
Business type (SIC): Medical instruments and supplies; drugs
Financial profile for 2012: Number of employees, 29,555; assets, $11,360,910,000; sales volume, $7,708,380,000; pre-tax net income, $1,472,410,000; expenses, $6,150,500,000; liabilities, $7,225,020,000
Fortune 1000 ranking: 2012—332nd in revenues, 174th in profits, and 358th in assets
Forbes 2000 ranking: 2012—1114th in sales, 420th in profits, and 1373rd in assets
Corporate officers: Vincent A. Forlenza, Chair., Pres., and C.E.O.; Jeffrey S. Sherman, Sr. V.P. and Genl. Counsel; Donna M. Boles, Sr. V.P., Human Resources; Suketu Upadhyay, Sr. V.P. and Cont.; Gary M. DeFazio, V.P. and Corp. Secy.; John E. Gallagher, V.P. and Treas.
Board of directors: Vincent A. Forlenza, Chair.; Basil L. Anderson; Henry P. Becton, Jr.; Catherine M. Burzik; Edward F. DeGraan; Claire M. Fraser-Liggett; Christopher Jones; Marshall O. Larsen; Adel A.F. Mahmoud; Gary A. Mecklenburg; James F. Orr; Willard J. Overlock, Jr.; Rebecca W. Rimel; Bertram L. Scott; Alfred Sommer
International operations: Argentina; Australia; Austria; Barbados; Belgium; Bermuda; Brazil; British Virgin Islands; Canada; Cayman Islands; China; Colombia; Czech Republic; Denmark; Finland; France; Ghana; Greece; Guatemala; Hong Kong; Hungary; India; Ireland; Japan; Kenya; Mauritius; Mexico; Netherlands; New Zealand; Norway; Pakistan; Philippines; Poland; Singapore; Slovakia; South Africa; South Korea; Spain; Sweden; Switzerland; Thailand; Turkey; United Kingdom; Uruguay; Venezuela
Giving statement: Giving through the BD Corporate Giving Program.
Company EIN: 220760120

BD Corporate Giving Program

1 Becton Dr.
Franklin Lakes, NJ 07417-1815
E-mail: BD_Sustainability_Office@bd.com;
URL: http://www.bd.com/responsibility

Contact: Jennifer Farrington, Mgr., Community Partnerships
Financial data (yr. ended 12/31/11): Total giving, $14,500,000, including $5,100,000 for grants, $1,000,000 for employee matching gifts and $8,400,000 for in-kind gifts.
Purpose and activities: BD makes charitable contributions to nonprofit organizations involved with health and human services and community development. Support is given on a national and international basis.
Fields of interest: Public health; Health care; Human services; Community/economic development.
International interests: Africa; Asia; Europe; Latin America; Middle East.
Programs:
BD Global Healthcare Fund: Through the BD Global Healthcare Fund, BD supports programs designed to address unmet health care needs and help all people live healthy lives.
BD Local Initiatives Fund: Through the BD Local Initiatives Fund, BD makes charitable contributions to nonprofit organizations involved with health and human services and community development.
BD Matching Gifts Program: BD matches contributions made by its employees and retirees to nonprofit organizations involved with arts and culture, education, the environment, and health and human services.
Type of support: Donated equipment; Donated products; Employee matching gifts; Employee volunteer services; General/operating support; In-kind gifts; Program development.
Geographic limitations: Giving on a national and international basis, with emphasis on areas of company operations.
Support limitations: No grants to individuals, or for fundraising, workshops, sporting events, dinners, or event-driven activities.
Application information: Applications not accepted. Contributes only to pre-selected organizations. The Community Relations Department handles giving. A contributions committee reviews all requests.
Committee meeting date(s): Semi-annual
Number of staff: 1 full-time professional; 2 part-time support.

399
Bed Bath & Beyond Inc.

650 Liberty Ave.
Union, NJ 07083 (908) 688-0888
FAX: (908) 688-6483

Company URL: http://www.bedbathandbeyond.com
Establishment information: Established in 1971.
Company type: Public company
Company ticker symbol and exchange: BBBY/ NASDAQ
Business activities: Operates chain of domestic merchandise retail stores.
Business type (SIC): Furniture and home furnishings—wholesale
Financial profile for 2013: Number of employees, 57,000; assets, $6,279,950,000; sales volume, $10,914,580,000; pre-tax net income, $1,634,060,000; expenses, $9,276,370,000; liabilities, $2,200,220,000
Fortune 1000 ranking: 2012—285th in revenues, 200th in profits, and 552nd in assets
Forbes 2000 ranking: 2012—919th in sales, 580th in profits, and 1723rd in assets
Corporate officers: Warren Eisenberg, Co-Chair.; Leonard Feinstein, Co-Chair.; Steven H. Temares, C.E.O.; Arthur Stark, Pres.; Eugene A. Castagna, C.F.O. and Treas.; Allan N. Rauch, V.P. and Genl. Counsel; Richard C. McMahon, V.P., Opers.
Board of directors: Warren Eisenberg, Co-Chair.; Leonard Feinstein, Co-Chair.; Dean S. Adler; Stanley F. Barshay; Klaus Eppler; Patrick R. Gaston; Jordan Heller; Victoria A. Morrison; Steven H. Temares
Giving statement: Giving through the Bed Bath & Beyond Inc. Contributions Program.
Company EIN: 112250488

Bed Bath & Beyond Inc. Contributions Program

650 Liberty Ave.
Union, NJ 07083 (908) 688-0888
E-mail: corporateresponsibility@bedbath.com;
URL: http://www.bedbathandbeyond.com/corpResponsibility.asp?

Purpose and activities: Bed Bath & Beyond makes charitable contributions to nonprofit organizations in areas of company operations.
Fields of interest: Environment, water pollution; Brain disorders Women.
Type of support: Donated products; In-kind gifts.
Geographic limitations: Giving primarily in areas of company operations.

400
Beech-Nut Nutrition Corp.

100 Hero Dr.
Amsterdam, NY 12010 (518) 595-6600
FAX: (518) 595-6601

Company URL: http://www.beechnut.com
Establishment information: Established in 1931.
Company type: Private company
Business activities: Operates baby food company.
Business type (SIC): Specialty foods/canned, frozen, and preserved
Financial profile for 2012: Number of employees, 4,000
Corporate officers: Christoph Rudolf, Pres. and C.E.O.; Tim Kennedy, C.F.O.; Gary Stenzel, V.P., Opers.; Matthew Smith, V.P. and Mktg.
Giving statement: Giving through the Beech-Nut Nutrition Corporation Contributions Program.

Beech-Nut Nutrition Corporation Contributions Program

100 Hero Dr.
Amsterdam, NY 12010-8348 (518) 595-6600
URL: http://www.beechnut.com/

401
Bekins Investments

201 Pierce St., Ste. 205
Sioux City, IA 51101-1479 (712) 233-1882

Company URL: http://bekinsinvestments.com/
Establishment information: Established in 2005.
Company type: Private company
Business activities: Operates investment company.
Business type (SIC): Security and commodity services
Corporate officers: Greg Deman, Owner; Dave Furlong, Mgr.
Giving statement: Giving through the VMP Nutrition Foundation.

VMP Nutrition Foundation

(formerly CCS Foundation)
8650 Freeport Pkwy., Ste. 250
Irving, TX 75063

Establishment information: Established in 2002.
Donors: Bekins Distribution Center Co.; Greg Deman; Bekins Investments.
Financial data (yr. ended 12/31/11): Assets, $427,717 (M); expenditures, $728,463; qualifying distributions, $700,374; giving activities include $700,374 for grants.
Purpose and activities: The foundation supports organizations involved with education, health, youth development, and Catholicism.
Fields of interest: Arts; Education; Religion.
Type of support: General/operating support.
Geographic limitations: Giving primarily in Sioux City, IA.
Support limitations: No grants to individuals.
Application information: Applications not accepted. Contributes only to pre-selected organizations.
Director: Dale C. Tigges.
EIN: 421517830
Selected grants: The following grants are a representative sample of this grantmaker's funding activity:
$60,000 to Bishop Heelan Catholic Schools, Sioux City, IA, 2009.
$25,000 to Pontifical North American College, Washington, DC, 2009.
$1,500 to Saturday in the Park, Sioux City, IA, 2009.

402
The Belden Brick Company

700 W. Tuscarawas St.
Canton, OH 44702 (330) 456-0031

Company URL: http://www.beldenbrick.com
Establishment information: Established in 1885.
Company type: Private company
Business activities: Manufactures face, floor, and acid-proof bricks and tiles.
Business type (SIC): Clay structural products
Corporate officers: William H. Belden, Jr., Chair.; Robert F. Belden, Pres. and C.E.O.; Jeff Adams, C.I.O.; Robert T. Belden, V.P., Opers.; John Belden, V.P., Sales and Mktg.; Jim Leahy, Treas.
Board of director: William H. Belden, Jr., Chair.
Giving statement: Giving through the Belden Brick Company Charitable Trust.

The Belden Brick Company Charitable Trust

P.O. Box 20910
Canton, OH 44701-0910 (330) 456-0031
E-mail: bill.belden@beldenbrick.com; Application address: 700 W. Tuscarawas St., Canton, OH 44702, tel.: (330) 456-0031

Donors: Belden Brick Co.; Belden Holding & Acquisition Co.
Contact: William H. Belden, Jr., Tr.
Financial data (yr. ended 12/31/11): Assets, $1,940,786 (M); expenditures, $90,422; qualifying distributions, $90,422; giving activities include $89,450 for 50 grants (high: $12,000; low: $200).
Purpose and activities: The foundation supports organizations involved with arts and culture,

education, health, football, youth development, and human services.
Fields of interest: Arts; Education; Human services.
Type of support: Annual campaigns; Capital campaigns; General/operating support.
Geographic limitations: Giving primarily in areas of company operations in OH.
Support limitations: No grants to individuals.
Application information: Applications accepted. Application form required. Applicants should submit the following:
1) name, address and phone number of organization
2) copy of IRS Determination Letter
3) detailed description of project and amount of funding requested

Initial approach: Proposal
Deadline(s): None
Final notification: Within 2 months

Trustees: Robert F. Belden; William H. Belden, Jr.; David L. Hartung.
EIN: 346565519

403
Belk, Inc.
2801 W. Tyvola Rd.
Charlotte, NC 28217-4500 (704) 357-1000

Company URL: http://www.belk.com
Establishment information: Established in 1888.
Company type: Private company
Business activities: Operates department stores.
Business type (SIC): Department stores
Financial profile for 2011: Number of employees, 24,000; assets, $2,389,631,000; sales volume, $3,513,280,000
Fortune 1000 ranking: 2012—592nd in revenues, 597th in profits, and 789th in assets
Corporate officers: Thomas M. Belk, Jr., Chair. and C.E.O.; H.W. McKay Belk, Vice-Chair.; John R. Belk, Co-Pres. and C.O.O.; Kathryn Bufano, Co-Pres.; Brian T. Marley, Exec. V.P. and C.F.O.; Ralph A. Pitts, Exec. V.P., Genl. Counsel, and Secy.
Board of directors: Thomas M. Belk, Jr., Chair.; H.W. McKay Belk, Vice-Chair.; John R. Belk; Jerri L. DeVard; Sarah Belk Gambrell; J. Kirk Glenn, Jr.; Elizabeth Valk Long; Thomas C. Nelson; John R. Thompson; John L. Townsend III
Subsidiary: Belk-Simpson Company, Charlotte, NC
Giving statement: Giving through the Belk, Inc. Contributions Program and the Belk Foundation.
Company EIN: 562058574

Belk, Inc. Contributions Program
2801 W. Tyvola Rd.
Charlotte, NC 28217-4500 (704) 357-1000
URL: http://www.belk.com/AST/Misc/Belk_Stores/About_Us/Community.jsp

Purpose and activities: As a complement to its foundation, Belk, Inc. makes charitable contributions to nonprofit organizations directly. Support is given primarily in areas of company operations.
Fields of interest: Education; Breast cancer research; Community/economic development.
Type of support: Cause-related marketing; Employee volunteer services; General/operating support.
Geographic limitations: Giving primarily in areas of company operations in AL, AR, FL, GA, KY, LA, MD, MO, MS, NC, OK, SC, TN, TX, VA and WV.

The Belk Foundation
2801 W. Tyvola Rd.
Charlotte, NC 28217-4500 (704) 426-8396
E-mail: info@belkfoundation.org; E-mail for Susan Blount: susan_blount@belk.com; URL: http://belkfoundation.org

Establishment information: Trust established in 1928 in NC.
Donors: The Belk Department Stores; Matthews Belk; Belk Enterprises; Belk, Inc.
Contact: Susan Blount, Admin.
Financial data (yr. ended 05/31/12): Assets, $46,699,572 (M); gifts received, $750,000; expenditures, $2,899,983; qualifying distributions, $2,545,090; giving activities include $2,404,915 for 57 grants (high: $440,000; low: $695).
Purpose and activities: The foundation supports programs designed to ensure all students graduate from high school and continue on an intentional path toward college, a career, and quality of life.
Fields of interest: Arts; Secondary school/education; Higher education; Education, services; Education; Hospitals (general); Health care; Breast cancer; Boys & girls clubs; Boy scouts; YM/YWCAs & YM/YWHAs; Children/youth, services; Human services; United Ways and Federated Giving Programs.
Type of support: Annual campaigns; Building/renovation; Capital campaigns; Continuing support; Emergency funds; Endowments; General/operating support; Matching/challenge support; Program development; Scholarship funds; Sponsorships.
Geographic limitations: Giving primarily in areas of company operations, with emphasis on Birmingham, AL, Atlanta, GA, and Charlotte, NC.
Support limitations: No support for private elementary or secondary schools or international organizations. No grants to individuals or for fundraising.
Publications: Application guidelines; Grants list; IRS Form 990 or 990-PF printed copy available upon request.
Application information: Applications accepted. Final applications are by invitation only and are issued mid-Feb. and mid-Aug. The foundation awards the majority of its grants to organizations identified by Belk Foundation staff and board. Application form not required. Applicants should submit the following:
1) name, address and phone number of organization
2) geographic area to be served
3) detailed description of project and amount of funding requested
4) contact person

Initial approach: Complete online eligibility quiz and letter of inquiry form
Deadline(s): None; Apr. 1 and Oct. 1 for applications
Final notification: May and Nov. for applications

Officers and Directors:* Katherine B. Morris*, Chair.; John R. Belk, Vice-Chair. and Treas.; Mary Claudia Belk Pilon*, Secy.; Johanna Edens Anderson, Exec. Dir.; Thomas M. Belk, Jr.; Ophelia Garmon-Brown; Peter Gorman; Louise Martin.
EIN: 270237197

404
Belk-Simpson Company
2801 W. Tyvola Rd.
Charlotte, NC 28217 (704) 357-1000

Company URL: http://www.belk.com
Establishment information: Established in 1891.
Company type: Subsidiary of a private company
Business activities: Operates department stores.
Business type (SIC): Department stores
Corporate officer: Thomas M. Belk, Jr., Chair. and C.E.O.
Board of director: Thomas M. Belk, Jr., Chair.
Giving statement: Giving through the Harvest Charities.

Harvest Charities
(formerly Belk-Simpson Foundation)
c/o Wachovia Bank, N.A.
1525 West Wt. Harris Blvd. D1114-044
Charlotte, NC 28288-1161

Establishment information: Trust established in 1944 in SC.
Donors: Belk-Simpson Co.; J. A. Kuhn.
Contact: Todd Ripley
Financial data (yr. ended 12/31/11): Assets, $9,274,840 (M); expenditures, $585,297; qualifying distributions, $494,500; giving activities include $494,500 for grants.
Purpose and activities: The foundation supports museums and organizations involved with education, health, human services, and religion.
Fields of interest: Museums; Secondary school/education; Higher education; Education; Hospitals (general); Health care, clinics/centers; Health care; Human services; United Ways and Federated Giving Programs; Protestant agencies & churches; Religion.
Type of support: Capital campaigns; General/operating support; Program development; Scholarship funds.
Geographic limitations: Giving primarily in SC.
Support limitations: No grants to individuals.
Application information: Applications not accepted. Contributes only to pre-selected organizations.

Board meeting date(s): May 1 and Nov. 1

Trustee: Wachovia Bank, N.A.
Board of Advisors: Claire Efird; John A. Kuhn; Lucy S. Kuhn; William D.S. Kuhne; Nell M. Rice; Caroline Schmitt; Katherine Sullivan.
EIN: 576020261
Selected grants: The following grants are a representative sample of this grantmaker's funding activity:
$5,000 to First Presbyterian Church, Winston-Salem, NC, 2010. For general support.

405
Belleville Shoe Manufacturing Co.
100 Premier Dr.
Belleville, IL 62220 (618) 233-5600

Company URL: http://www.bellevilleshoe.com/about.php
Establishment information: Established in 1904.
Company type: Private company
Business activities: Manufactures military boots.
Business type (SIC): Footwear/rubber and plastic; apparel—men's and boys' coats and suits
Corporate officer: Mark Ferguson, Pres.
Giving statement: Giving through the Walter E. Weidmann Charitable Foundation.

Walter E. Weidmann Charitable Foundation

c/o Regions Morgan Keegan Trust
1 S. Church St.
Belleville, IL 62220-2237 (231) 334-7588
Application address: 8996 S. Dunns Farm Rd., Maple City, MI 49664, tel.: (231) 334-7588

Donor: Belleville Shoe Manufacturing Company.
Contact: David Herr
Financial data (yr. ended 11/30/11): Assets, $257,822 (M); expenditures, $28,550; qualifying distributions, $21,500; giving activities include $21,500 for 6 grants (high: $5,000; low: $500).
Purpose and activities: The foundation supports organizations involved with bereavement counseling, children and youth, and family services.
Fields of interest: Mental health, grief/bereavement counseling; YM/YWCAs & YM/YWHAs; Children/youth, services; Family services; United Ways and Federated Giving Programs.
Type of support: General/operating support.
Geographic limitations: Giving primarily in IL and St. Louis, MO.
Support limitations: No grants to individuals.
Application information: Applications accepted. Application form not required.
Initial approach: Proposal
Deadline(s): None
Trustee: Regions Morgan Keegan Trust.
EIN: 376211937

406
Belo Corp.

(formerly A.H. Belo Corporation)
400 S. Record St.
P.O. Box 655237
Dallas, TX 75202-4841 (214) 977-6606
FAX: (214) 977-6603

Company URL: http://www.belo.com
Establishment information: Established in 1842.
Company type: Public company
Company ticker symbol and exchange: BLC/NYSE
Business activities: Broadcasts television; publishes newspapers; provides Internet information services; provides cable television services.
Business type (SIC): Newspaper publishing and/or printing; radio and television broadcasting; cable and other pay television services; computer services
Financial profile for 2012: Number of employees, 2,696; assets, $1,499,590,000; sales volume, $714,720,000; pre-tax net income, $156,660,000; expenses, $485,640,000; liabilities, $1,199,430,000
Corporate officers: Robert W. Decherd, Chair.; Dunia A. Shive, Pres. and C.E.O.; Carey P. Hendrickson, Sr. V.P., C.F.O., and Treas.; Russell F. Coleman, Sr. V.P. and Genl. Counsel; Sandra J. Martin, V.P. and Cont.; William L. Hamersly, V.P., Human Resources
Board of directors: Robert W. Decherd, Chair.; Peter A. Altabef; Henry P. Becton, Jr., M.D.; Judith L. Craven, M.D.; Dealey D. Herndon; James M. Moroney, III; Wayne R. Sanders; Dunia A. Shive; M. Anne Szostak; McHenry T. Tichenor, Jr.; Lloyd D. Ward
Subsidiaries: KASW-TV, Phoenix, AZ; KENS-TV, San Antonio, TX; KGW-TV, Portland, OR; KHOU-TV, L.P., Houston, TX; KING-TV, Seattle, WA; KMOV-TV, St. Louis, MO; KMOV-TV, Inc., St. Louis, MO; KMSB-TV, Tucson, AZ; KONG-TV, Seattle, WA; KREM-TV, Spokane, WA; KSKM-TV, Spokane, WA; KTTU-TV, Tucson, AZ; KTVB-TV, Boise, ID; KTVK-TV, Phoenix, AZ; KVUE-TV, Austin, TX; Press-Enterprise Co., Riverside, CA; WCNC-TV, Charlotte, NC; WFAA-TV, L.P., Dallas, TX; WHAS-TV, Louisville, KY; WUPL-TV, New Orleans, LA; WVEC TV, Hampton, VA; WWL-TV, New Orleans, LA; WWL-TV, Inc., New Orleans, LA
Giving statement: Giving through the Belo Foundation.
Company EIN: 750135890

The Belo Foundation

(formerly A. H. Belo Corporation Foundation)
400 South Record St.
Dallas, TX 75202-4841 (214) 977-6661
FAX: (214) 977-6620;
E-mail: ameadows@belo.com; Application address: P.O. Box 655237, Dallas, TX 75265-5237;
URL: http://www.belo.com/about/foundation

Establishment information: Established in 1995 in TX as successor to the Dallas Morning News-WFAA Foundation, established in 1952.
Donors: A.H. Belo Corp.; Belo Corp.
Contact: Amy M. Meadows, V.P., Secy., and Exec. Dir.
Financial data (yr. ended 12/31/11): Assets, $35,413,328 (M); expenditures, $2,637,183; qualifying distributions, $2,065,000; giving activities include $2,065,000 for grants.
Purpose and activities: The foundation supports college-level journalism education and the development of urban public parks and green space.
Fields of interest: Media, print publishing; Higher education; Recreation, parks/playgrounds.
Type of support: Building/renovation; Capital campaigns; Continuing support; Curriculum development; Endowments; General/operating support; Program development; Scholarship funds.
Geographic limitations: Giving primarily in areas of company operations, with emphasis on Phoenix and Tucson, AZ, Riverside, CA, Boise, ID, Louisville, KY, New Orleans, LA, St. Louis, MO, Charlotte, NC, Portland, OR, Providence, RI, Austin, Dallas, Fort Worth, Houston, and San Antonio, TX, Hampton and Norfolk, VA, and Seattle, Spokane, and Tacoma, WA.
Support limitations: No grants to individuals or for sponsorships.
Publications: Application guidelines.
Application information: Applications accepted. Grants generally range from $5,000 to $50,000. Additional information may be requested at a later date. Visit website for e-mail addresses for general managers. Application form not required. Applicants should submit the following:
1) how project will be sustained once grantmaker support is completed
2) copy of IRS Determination Letter
3) brief history of organization and description of its mission
4) explanation of why grantmaker is considered an appropriate donor for project
5) listing of board of directors, trustees, officers and other key people and their affiliations
6) detailed description of project and amount of funding requested
7) listing of additional sources and amount of support

Initial approach: E-mail letter of inquiry to nearest television general manager or contact foundation to discuss request for funding
Copies of proposal: 1
Board meeting date(s): Twice annually
Deadline(s): None
Final notification: Varies
Officers and Trustees:* Robert W. Decherd*, Chair.; Marian Spitzberg*, Pres.; Amy M. Meadows, V.P., Secy., and Exec. Dir.; Guy H. Kerr; Dunia A. Shive.
Number of staff: 1 part-time professional; 1 part-time support.
EIN: 752564365
Selected grants: The following grants are a representative sample of this grantmaker's funding activity:
$1,750,000 to University of Texas, Austin, TX, 2010. To construct Belo Center for New Media.
$25,000 to Dallas Foundation, Dallas, TX, 2010. For International Federation for Artificial Organs Burl Osborne Award.
$20,000 to National Association of Broadcasters Education Foundation, Washington, DC, 2010. For general operating support.
$15,000 to American Press Institute, Reston, VA, 2010. For general operating support.
$10,000 to American Society of Newspaper Editors Foundation, Columbia, MO, 2010. For general operating support.
$10,000 to Dallas County Heritage Society, Dallas, TX, 2010. For publication of Legacies Magazine.
$10,000 to Media Institute, Arlington, VA, 2010. For general operating support.
$10,000 to Southern Methodist University, Dallas, TX, 2010. For Belo Archives housed at SMU DeGolyer Library.

407
Bemis Company, Inc.

1 Neenah Ctr., 4th Fl.
P.O. Box 669
Neenah, WI 54956-0669 (920) 727-4100

Company URL: http://www.bemis.com
Establishment information: Established in 1858.
Company type: Public company
Company ticker symbol and exchange: BMS/NYSE
International Securities Identification Number: US0814371052
Business activities: Manufactures flexible packaging products and pressure sensitive materials.
Business type (SIC): Paper and paperboard/coated, converted, and laminated
Financial profile for 2012: Number of employees, 19,600; assets, $4,185,700,000; sales volume, $5,139,200,000; pre-tax net income, $278,600,000; expenses, $4,793,700,000; liabilities, $2,544,800,000
Fortune 1000 ranking: 2012—479th in revenues, 613th in profits, and 647th in assets
Corporate officers: William J. Bolton, Chair.; Henry J. Theisen, Pres. and C.E.O.; Scott B. Ullem, V.P. and C.F.O.; Sheri H. Edison, V.P., Genl. Counsel, and Secy.; Melanie E.R. Miller, V.P. and Treas.; Jerry Krempa, V.P. and Cont.; Timothy S. Fliss, Jr., V.P., Human Resources
Board of directors: William J. Bolton, Chair.; Ronald J. Floto; David S. Haffner; Barbara L. Johnson; Timothy M. Manganello; William L. Mansfield; Roger D. O'Shaughnessy; Paul S. Peercy; Edward N. Perry; David T. Szczupak; Henry J. Theisen; Holly A. Van Deursen; Philip G. Weaver
Subsidiaries: Bemis Clysar, Inc., Clinton, IA; Curwood, Inc., Oshkosh, WI; MacKay, Inc., Florence, KY; Milprint, Inc., Oshkosh, WI
Plants: Crossett, AR; Terre Haute, IN; Centerville, IA; Monkato, MN; Omaha, NE; Flemington, NJ; Fremont, OH; Pauls Valley, OK; Hazleton, Lebanon, Philadelphia, PA; Shelbyville, TN; Longview, TX; Vancouver, WA; Appleton, New London, Oskosh, WI
International operations: Belgium; Brazil; China; Czech Republic; Denmark; Finland; France; Germany; Hungary; Mexico; Sweden; United Kingdom

Giving statement: Giving through the Bemis Company Foundation.
Company EIN: 430178130

Bemis Company Foundation

One Neenah Ctr., 4th Fl.
P.O. Box 669
Neenah, WI 54957-0669 (920) 527-5300
E-mail: slebel@bemis.com; Application contact and address: Kim Wetzel, Fdn. Consultant, tel.: (920) 734-2707, e-mail: kwetzel@bemis.com;
URL: http://www.bemis.com/citizenship/

Establishment information: Trust established in 1959 in MO.
Donor: Bemis Co., Inc.
Contact: Sandra L. Ebel, Fdn. Admin.
Financial data (yr. ended 12/31/11): Assets, $23,582 (M); gifts received, $3,100,000; expenditures, $2,808,412; qualifying distributions, $2,808,411; giving activities include $2,742,749 for 984 grants (high: $593,951; low: $25).
Purpose and activities: The foundation supports programs designed to encourage through basic needs and emergency assistance; empower though basic education and health and fitness; and elevate through higher education and arts and culture.
Fields of interest: Performing arts; Arts; Higher education; Education; Public health, physical fitness; Health care; Food services; Food banks; Youth development; Salvation Army; Human services; United Ways and Federated Giving Programs; Public affairs.
Programs:
Cultural & Civic Programs: The foundation supports cultural and civic programs, with emphasis on the communities in which Bemis operates and its employees live.
Educational Gift Matching: The foundation matches contributions made by employees of Bemis to educational institutions on a two-for-one basis up to $2,000 per employee, per year.
Educational Programs: The foundation supports programs designed to help individuals become knowledgeable and productive citizens; and provides support to help individuals and organizations realize their educational goals.
Foodshare Program: Through the Foodshare Program, the foundation matches contributions made by employees of Bemis to local food banks and food shelves on a two-for-one basis.
Nonprofit Gift Matching: The foundation matches contributions made by employees of Bemis to nonprofit organizations on a one-for-one basis from $25 to $500 per employee, per year.
Scholarship Program: The foundation awards college scholarships to children of current and former employees of Bemis. The program is administered by Scholarship America, Inc.
Social Welfare & Health Programs: The foundation supports programs designed to help those in need build and improve their lives, including basic needs for food, shelter, and healthcare, intervention, and support programs for facilitating change.
Type of support: Annual campaigns; Building/renovation; Capital campaigns; Continuing support; Employee matching gifts; Employee-related scholarships; General/operating support.
Geographic limitations: Giving limited to areas of company operations in Crossett and Russellville, AR, Centerville, Clinton, and Des Moines, IA, Batavia and Bellwood, IL, Columbus and Terre Haute, IN, Shelbyville, KY, West Monroe, LA, Mankato and Minneapolis, MN, Joplin, MO, Omaha, NE, Edgewood, NY, Akron, Fremont, and Stow, OH, Pauls Valley, OK, Lebanon, Philadelphia, Scranton, and West Hazleton, PA, Shelbyville, TN, Vancouver, WA, and Appleton, Boscobel, Lancaster, Menasha, Neenah, New London, and Oshkosh, WI.
Support limitations: No support for religious, lobbying, or political organizations, hospitals, or other foundations. No grants to individuals (except for employee-related scholarships), or for endowments, research, educational capital campaigns, or trips or tours; no loans.
Publications: Application guidelines.
Application information: Applications accepted. Grants are limited to 3 years in length. Telephone calls during the application process are not encouraged. Application form required. Applicants should submit the following:
1) principal source of support for project in the past
2) name, address and phone number of organization
3) copy of IRS Determination Letter
4) brief history of organization and description of its mission
5) geographic area to be served
6) copy of most recent annual report/audited financial statement/990
7) how project's results will be evaluated or measured
8) listing of board of directors, trustees, officers and other key people and their affiliations
9) detailed description of project and amount of funding requested
10) copy of current year's organizational budget and/or project budget
11) listing of additional sources and amount of support

Initial approach: Download application form and e-mail or mail to application address
Copies of proposal: 1
Board meeting date(s): Mar. 15, June 15, Sept. 15, and Dec. 15
Deadline(s): None

Trustees: Timothy S. Fliss, Jr.; Jerry Krempa; Stanley A. Jaffy; Scott B. Ullem.
Number of staff: 2 part-time professional.
EIN: 416038616

408
Bemis Manufacturing Company

300 Mill St.
P.O. Box 901
Sheboygan Falls, WI 53085-0901
(800) 558-7651

Company URL: http://www.bemismfg.com
Establishment information: Established in 1901.
Company type: Private company
Business activities: Manufactures wood, plastic, medical, and household products.
Business type (SIC): Wood products/miscellaneous; plastic products/miscellaneous; appliances/household
Corporate officer: Peter Bemis, Pres.
Giving statement: Giving through the F. K. Bemis Family Foundation, Inc.

F. K. Bemis Family Foundation, Inc.

300 Mill St.
Sheboygan Falls, WI 53085-1807 (920) 467-4621

Establishment information: Established about 1953 in WI.
Donor: Bemis Manufacturing Co.
Contact: Karen Hoefler, Secy.
Financial data (yr. ended 12/31/11): Assets, $527,479 (M); gifts received, $340,001; expenditures, $325,070; qualifying distributions, $325,070; giving activities include $325,070 for grants.
Purpose and activities: The foundation supports gardens and hospices and organizations involved with arts and culture, education, children and youth, and community development.
Fields of interest: Performing arts; Historic preservation/historical societies; Arts; Higher education; Education; Botanical gardens; Boys & girls clubs; Salvation Army; YM/YWCAs & YM/YWHAs; Children/youth, services; Residential/custodial care, hospices; Community/economic development.
Type of support: Building/renovation; Capital campaigns; General/operating support; Scholarship funds; Scholarships—to individuals.
Geographic limitations: Giving primarily in Sheboygan County, WI.
Application information: Applications accepted. Application form not required. Applicants should submit the following:
1) copy of IRS Determination Letter
2) detailed description of project and amount of funding requested

Initial approach: Proposal
Deadline(s): Dec. 1

Officers: Peter F. Bemis, Pres.; Erin Bemis, V.P.; Karen E. Hoefler, Secy.
EIN: 396067930

409
Ben & Jerry's Homemade, Inc.

30 Community Dr.
South Burlington, VT 05403-6828
(802) 846-1543

Company URL: http://www.benjerry.com
Establishment information: Established in 1978.
Company type: Subsidiary of a foreign company
Business activities: Produces and sells ice cream, frozen yogurt, sorbet, and novelty products; franchises ice cream parlors.
Business type (SIC): Dairy products; restaurants and drinking places; investors/miscellaneous
Financial profile for 2010: Number of employees, 200
Corporate officers: Jostein Solheim, C.E.O.; Michael Graning, C.F.O.; Barbara Jackson, V.P., Mktg.
Board of directors: Jostein Solheim; Jeff Furman; Pierre Ferrari; Jennifier Henderson; Helen Jones; Terry Mollner; Anuradha Mittal; Kees Van der Graaf
International operations: United Kingdom
Giving statement: Giving through the Ben & Jerry's Homemade Inc. Corporate Giving Program and the Ben & Jerry's Foundation, Inc.

Ben & Jerry's Homemade Inc. Corporate Giving Program

30 Community Dr.
South Burlington, VT 05403-6828 (802) 846-1500
E-mail: BJ.Donations@benjerry.com; Sponsorship and donation tel.: 802-846-1543, ext. 7986;
URL: http://www.benjerry.com/activism/

Purpose and activities: As a complement to its foundation, Ben & Jerry's also makes charitable contributions to nonprofit organizations, schools, and municipal organizations. Support is given on a national basis, with emphasis on Vermont.
Fields of interest: Environment; Agriculture, sustainable programs; Agriculture, farmlands; Children/youth, services; Family services.

Type of support: Donated products; In-kind gifts; Sponsorships.
Geographic limitations: Giving on a national basis, with emphasis on VT.
Support limitations: No support for religious organizations. No grants to individuals, or for scholarships; no product donations for sale or fundraising purposes (coupons may be used for fundraising).
Publications: Application guidelines.
Application information: Applications accepted. Support is limited to 1 contribution per organization for product donations, and 50 free pint coupons per event during any given year. Organizations that receive product donations are prohibited from using the company name in distribution (except for coupons). Donations are provided solely for events. Phone calls are discouraged. Application form required. Applicants should submit the following:
1) name, address and phone number of organization
2) detailed description of project and amount of funding requested
3) contact person
4) copy of IRS Determination Letter

Proposals for product donations should include the title, date, and location of the event, and the number of bulk containers requested.
Initial approach: Complete online application for product donations in VT, and sponsorships; contact nearest company facility for product donations to organizations outside of VT
Deadline(s): 6 weeks prior to event
Number of staff: None.

Ben & Jerry's Foundation, Inc.

30 Community Dr.
South Burlington, VT 05403-6828 (802) 846-1500
E-mail: info@benandjerrysfoundation.org;
URL: http://www.benandjerrysfoundation.org

Establishment information: Established in 1985 in NY.
Donors: Ben & Jerry's Homemade, Inc.; Ben & Jerry's Corp.; Bennett Cohen.
Contact: Lisa Pendolino, Managing Dir.
Financial data (yr. ended 12/31/11): Assets, $5,126,856 (M); gifts received, $2,226,660; expenditures, $2,293,629; qualifying distributions, $2,028,591; giving activities include $2,028,591 for grants.
Purpose and activities: The foundation promotes progressive social change by supporting grassroots organizations that utilize community organizing strategies to advance social justice, environmental justice, and food justice.
Fields of interest: Environment; Agriculture, community food systems; Civil/human rights, immigrants; Civil rights, race/intergroup relations; Labor rights; Civil/human rights; Community/economic development; Public affairs, citizen participation Economically disadvantaged.
Programs:
Employee Matching Gift Program: The foundation matches contributions made by employees of Ben & Jerry's to nonprofit organizations on a one-for-one basis up to $2,000 per employee, per year.
Grassroots Organizing for Social Change Program: The Grassroots Organizing for Social Change Program supports non-profit grassroots, constituent-led organizations across the country that are using direct action, grassroots community-organizing strategies to accomplish their goals. The foundation considers proposals that are aligned with the its broad interests in social justice, environmental justice and socially just food systems.
National Movement Building Grant Program: The foundation supports national progressive movement-building organizations and coalitions designed to advance social justice, environmental protection, and sustainable food systems. Special emphasis is directed toward programs that work across sectors and implementing approaches and knowledge and models that build the movement and lead to positive change. The foundation's current building movement is immigrant and low-income workers rights. Grants range from $25,000 to $50,000. This program is invitation only.
Vermont Capacity Building Grant Program: The foundation supports Vermont statewide nonprofit organizations working toward broad systemic change designed to promote social justice, environmental protection, and family farms and local food systems. Grants can be used for consultation, technology, organizational developmental work, infrastructure development, staff development, or staff needs. Grants of up to $25,000 are awarded.
Vermont Community Action Teams Program (CATs): The foundation awards grants of up to $2,000 to local community organizations providing services, activities, and events with emphasis on social services, cultural, recreational, arts programs, and underserved populations including seniors, at-risk youth, and low-income communities. The program is administered by Vermont Community Action Teams comprised of non-management employees of Ben & Jerry's.
Type of support: Employee matching gifts; General/operating support; Management development/capacity building; Program development.
Geographic limitations: Giving on a national basis, with emphasis on St. Albans, South Burlington, and Waterbury, VT.
Support limitations: No support for schools, colleges or universities, state agencies, businesses or business associations, other foundations or regranting organizations, organizations and programs that are focused or based outside of the United States, or organizations with annual budgets over $500,000. No grants to individuals, or for scholarship programs, advocacy programs, discretionary or emergency funds, research projects, capital campaigns, religious programs, international or foreign-based programs, government sponsored programs, social service programs, or arts and media programs.
Publications: Annual report; Application guidelines; Grants list; IRS Form 990 or 990-PF printed copy available upon request; Program policy statement.
Application information: Applications accepted. A full proposal may be requested at a later date for the Grassroots Organizing for Social Change Program. Additional information and a site visit may be requested for Vermont Capacity Building Grant Program. Application form required. Applicants should submit the following:
1) timetable for implementation and evaluation of project
2) staff salaries
3) results expected from proposed grant
4) qualifications of key personnel
5) statement of problem project will address
6) population served
7) name, address and phone number of organization
8) copy of IRS Determination Letter
9) brief history of organization and description of its mission
10) copy of most recent annual report/audited financial statement/990
11) detailed description of project and amount of funding requested
12) contact person
13) copy of current year's organizational budget and/or project budget
14) listing of additional sources and amount of support

Initial approach: Complete online letter of interest for Grassroots Organizing for Social Change Program; complete online proposals for Vermont Capacity Building Grant Program, Vermont Economic Justice Grant Program and Vermont Community Action Teams Grant Program
Board meeting date(s): Monthly
Deadline(s): Mar. 15th and Sept. 15th for Grassroots Organizing for Social Change Program; June 15th for Vermont Capacity Building Grant Program; June 15th for Vermont Economic Justice Grant Program; None for Vermont Community Action Teams
Final notification: 30 days for letters of interest; Nov. for Vermont Capacity Building Grant Program
Officers and Trustees:* Jerry Greenfield*, Pres.; Elizabeth Bankowski*, Secy.; Jeffrey Furman*, Treas.; Anuradha Mittal.
Number of staff: 2 part-time professional; 1 full-time support.
EIN: 030300865
Selected grants: The following grants are a representative sample of this grantmaker's funding activity:
$50,000 to Jobs with Justice, Montpelier, VT, 2011. For U-Fund grant for Excluded Workers Congress.
$25,000 to Highfields Institute, Hardwick, VT, 2011. For capacity building.
$25,000 to Jobs with Justice, Montpelier, VT, 2011. For U-Fund grant for Caring Across Generations National Campaign.
$15,000 to Centro por la Justicia, San Antonio, TX, 2011. For Southwest Workers' Union.
$15,000 to Clean Air Coalition of Western New York, Buffalo, NY, 2011. For Project TAPP.
$15,000 to Faith Action for Community Equity, Honolulu, HI, 2011. For Maui Immigrant Rights Project.
$15,000 to Lakeview Action Coalition, Chicago, IL, 2011. For community organizing general support.
$15,000 to Pleasant Street Neighborhood Network Center, Worcester, MA, 2011. For Worcester Homeless Action Committee.
$15,000 to Teachers Unite, New York, NY, 2011. For general support.
$12,000 to Occidental Arts and Ecology Center, Occidental, CA, 2011. For California Climate and Agriculture Network.

410
Benedict-Miller, LLC

123 N. 8th St.
Kenilworth, NJ 07033-1108 (908) 497-1477

Company URL: http://www.benedict-miller.com
Establishment information: Established in 1940.
Company type: Subsidiary of a private company
Business activities: Operates metals service company.
Business type (SIC): Metals and minerals, except petroleum—wholesale
Corporate officers: John P. Benedict, Pres.; Gail Snyder, Cont.
Giving statement: Giving through the Benedict-Miller Foundation.

The Benedict-Miller Foundation

178 Main St.
P.O. Box 174
New Britain, CT 06050-2229 (201) 438-3000
Application address: c/o Frederick C. Remmeli, P.O. Box 912, Lyndhurst, NJ, 07071

Establishment information: Established in NJ.
Contact: John Benedict, Jr., Chair.
Financial data (yr. ended 06/30/11): Assets, $576,018 (M); expenditures, $36,063; qualifying distributions, $31,955; giving activities include $30,000 for 45 grants (high: $4,500; low: $50).
Purpose and activities: The foundation supports music festivals and food banks and organizations involved with media, education, land conservation, health, human services, and Christianity.
Fields of interest: Arts; Education; Human services.
Type of support: General/operating support.
Geographic limitations: Giving primarily in CO, NJ, NY, and VA.
Support limitations: No grants to individuals.
Application information: Applications accepted. Application form not required.
Initial approach: Letter
Deadline(s): Prior to last week in May
Trustee: TD Bank, N.A.
EIN: 226022176

411
Beneficial Company, LLC

(formerly Beneficial Corporation)
2700 Sanders Rd.
Prospect Heights, IL 60070-2701
(847) 564-5000

Company URL: http://www.beneficial.com
Establishment information: Established in 1923.
Company type: Subsidiary of a public company
Business activities: Operates bank holding company; provides consumer loans; sells insurance.
Business type (SIC): Holding company; banks/commercial; savings institutions; credit institutions/personal; brokers and bankers/mortgage; insurance/surety; real estate subdividers and developers
Corporate officers: Patti Prairie, C.I.O.; Jonathan Macey, Sr. V.P., C.A.O., and Cont.; Scott A. Siebels, Sr. V.P. and Secy.
Subsidiaries: Bencharge Credit Service of America, Wilmington, DE; Beneficial Data Processing Corp., Wilmington, DE; Beneficial Management Corporation of America, Wilmington, DE; Beneficial National Bank, Wilmington, DE; Beneficial Savings Bank, FSB, Tampa, FL; Harbour Island, Inc., Tampa, FL
Plants: Hanford, CA; New Haven, CT; Shenandoah, PA
Giving statement: Giving through the CTW Foundation, Inc.

CTW Foundation, Inc.

(formerly Beneficial Foundation, Inc.)
P.O. Box 911
Wilmington, DE 19899-0911 (302) 429-9427
Application address: c/o Hodson Svcs., LLC, 300 Bellevue Pkwy., Ste. 100, Wilmington, DE 19809

Establishment information: Incorporated in 1951 in DE.
Donors: Beneficial Corp.; Beneficial New Jersey.
Contact: Robert A. Tucker, Pres.
Financial data (yr. ended 12/31/10): Assets, $1,293,011 (M); expenditures, $475,541; qualifying distributions, $410,000; giving activities include $410,000 for grants.
Purpose and activities: The foundation supports hospices and hospitals and organizations involved with arts and culture, secondary, higher, and law education, conservation, and nursing.
Fields of interest: Museums; Performing arts, theater; Arts; Secondary school/education; Higher education; Law school/education; Environment, natural resources; Hospitals (general); Nursing care; Medical research; Residential/custodial care, hospices.
Type of support: Annual campaigns; Continuing support; Employee-related scholarships; General/operating support; Program development; Research.
Geographic limitations: Giving primarily in MA, NJ, NY, and RI.
Support limitations: No grants for endowments; no loans.
Application information: Applications accepted. Application form not required.
Initial approach: Proposal
Board meeting date(s): Usually in May and Dec.
Deadline(s): Oct. 1; Apr. 15 for scholarships
Officers and Directors:* Robert A. Tucker*, Pres.; Eileen D. Dickey, Secy.; Charles W. Bower*, Treas.; Finn M.W. Caspersen; Finn M.W. Caspersen, Jr.
Number of staff: 2 part-time support.
EIN: 516011637
Selected grants: The following grants are a representative sample of this grantmaker's funding activity:
$250,000 to Hospital for Special Surgery, New York, NY, 2009.
$25,000 to Brown University, Providence, RI, 2009.
$20,000 to Shakespeare Theater of New Jersey, Madison, NJ, 2009.
$15,000 to Wesleyan University, Middletown, CT, 2009.
$13,500 to Visiting Nurse Association of Somerset Hills, Basking Ridge, NJ, 2009.
$10,000 to Harness Racing Museum and Hall of Fame, Goshen, NY, 2009.
$10,000 to New Jersey Conservation Foundation, Far Hills, NJ, 2009.
$8,500 to Cardigan Mountain School, Canaan, NH, 2009.
$5,000 to Shakespeare Theater of New Jersey, Madison, NJ, 2009.

412
Beneficial Mutual Bancorp, Inc.

510 Walnut St., 19th Fl.
Philadelphia, PA 19106 (215) 864-6000

Company URL: https://www.thebeneficial.com/
Establishment information: Established in 1853.
Company type: Public company
Company ticker symbol and exchange: BNCL/NASDAQ
Business activities: Operates savings bank.
Business type (SIC): Savings institutions
Financial profile for 2012: Number of employees, 874; assets, $5,006,400,000; pre-tax net income, $15,940,000; liabilities, $4,372,530,000
Corporate officers: Frank Farnesi, Chair.; Gerard P. Cuddy, Pres. and C.E.O.; Thomas D. Cestare, Exec. V.P. and C.F.O.
Board of directors: Frank Farnesi, Chair.; Gerard P. Cuddy; Edward G. Boehne; Karen Dougherty Buchholz; Donald F. Gayhardt, Jr.; Elizabeth H. Gemmill; Thomas J. Lewis; Joseph J. McLaughlin; Michael J. Morris; George W. Nise; Marcy C. Panzer; Roy D. Yates
Giving statement: Giving through the Beneficial Foundation.
Company EIN: 562480744

The Beneficial Foundation

530 Walnut St.
Philadelphia, PA 19106-3603
FAX: (215) 864-6177;
E-mail: rjuliano@thebeneficial.com; Additional tel.: (267) 519-5749; URL: https://www.thebeneficial.com/foundation-mission.asp

Establishment information: Established in 2007 in PA.
Donor: Beneficial Mutual Bancorp, Inc.
Contact: Robert Juliano, V.P., Community Dev.
Financial data (yr. ended 12/31/11): Assets, $6,321,296 (M); expenditures, $487,090; qualifying distributions, $482,325; giving activities include $482,325 for grants.
Purpose and activities: The foundation supports programs designed to address children in crisis; youth and education; and human service programs designed to improve the needs of low- and moderate income communities.
Fields of interest: Education; Human services; Community/economic development Children/youth; Children; Youth; Adults; Aging; Young adults; Disabilities, people with; Physically disabled; Blind/visually impaired; Mentally disabled; Minorities; Asians/Pacific Islanders; African Americans/Blacks; Hispanics/Latinos; Women; Infants/toddlers, female; Girls; Adults, women; Young adults, female; Men; Infants/toddlers, male; Boys; Adults, men; Young adults, male; Military/veterans; Substance abusers; AIDS, people with; Single parents; Crime/abuse victims; Immigrants/refugees; Economically disadvantaged; Homeless.
Type of support: Annual campaigns; Building/renovation; Capital campaigns; Emergency funds; Equipment; Program development; Scholarship funds; Technical assistance.
Geographic limitations: Giving primarily in areas of company operations in NJ and PA.
Support limitations: No support for political or fraternal organizations. No grants to individuals.
Publications: Annual report; Application guidelines; Program policy statement (including application guidelines); Quarterly report.
Application information: Applications accepted. Proposal should be submitted using organization letterhead. A site visit may be requested. Application form required. Applicants should submit the following:
1) results expected from proposed grant
2) population served
3) principal source of support for project in the past
4) copy of IRS Determination Letter
5) brief history of organization and description of its mission
6) geographic area to be served
7) copy of most recent annual report/audited financial statement/990
8) listing of board of directors, trustees, officers and other key people and their affiliations
9) detailed description of project and amount of funding requested
10) listing of additional sources and amount of support
Initial approach: Proposal
Copies of proposal: 1
Board meeting date(s): Quarterly
Deadline(s): None
Final notification: 2-3 weeks
Officers and Directors:* Gerard P. Cuddy*, Pres.; Wiliam Kline, Secy.; Cheryl Giles*, Secy.; Loretta T. Ross*, Treas.; James T. Connor; Elizabeth H.

Gemmill; Robert Juliano; Rev. Nicholas Rashford, S.J.
Number of staff: 3 full-time professional; 3 full-time support.
EIN: 260542636
Selected grants: The following grants are a representative sample of this grantmaker's funding activity:
$15,000 to Philadelphia Orchestra Association, Philadelphia, PA, 2011.
$5,000 to Neighborhood Housing Services of Philadelphia, Philadelphia, PA, 2011.
$3,000 to Mercy Neighborhood Ministries of Philadelphia, Philadelphia, PA, 2011.
$3,000 to Philadelphia Chinatown Development Corporation, Philadelphia, PA, 2011.
$2,500 to Archdiocese of Philadelphia, Philadelphia, PA, 2011.
$2,500 to Free Library of Philadelphia, Philadelphia, PA, 2011.
$2,500 to Network for Teaching Entrepreneurship, New York, NY, 2011.
$2,500 to Philadelphia Reads, Philadelphia, PA, 2011.
$2,500 to Philadelphia VIP, Philadelphia, PA, 2011.
$1,500 to Greensgrow Philadelphia Project, Philadelphia, PA, 2011.

413
Benesch, Friedlander, Coplan & Aronoff LLP

200 Public Sq., Ste. 2300
Cleveland, OH 44114-2309 (216) 363-4500

Company URL: http://www.beneschlaw.com
Establishment information: Established in 1938.
Company type: Private company
Business activities: Operates law firm.
Business type (SIC): Legal services
Corporate officers: James M. Hill, Chair.; John H. Banks, C.O.O. and C.F.O.
Board of director: James M. Hill, Chair.
Offices: Wilmington, DE; Indianapolis, IN; White Plains, NY; Cleveland, Columbus, OH; Philadelphia, PA
International operations: China
Giving statement: Giving through the Benesch, Friedlander, Coplan & Aronoff LLP Pro Bono Program.

Benesch, Friedlander, Coplan & Aronoff LLP Pro Bono Program

200 Public Sq., Ste. 2300
Cleveland, OH 44114-2309 (216) 363-4500
FAX: (216) 363-4588;
E-mail: dmellott@beneschlaw.com; URL: http://www.beneschlaw.com/aboutus/xprGeneralContent2.aspx?xpST=AboutUsGeneral&key=ddd41bab-1cbd-4c25-8a0f-c6d6a16f18f0

Contact: Dave Mellott, Practice Group Leader
Fields of interest: Legal services.
Type of support: Pro bono services - legal.
Geographic limitations: Giving primarily in areas of company operations in Wilmington, DE, Indianapolis, IN, White Plains, NY, Cleveland, and Columbus, OH, and Philadelphia, PA.
Application information: A Pro Bono Manager coordinates the program.

414
Benevento & Mayo Partners

46 Public Sq.
Wilkes Barre, PA 18701-2609
(570) 824-7895

Company type: Private company
Business activities: Provides investment advisory services.
Business type (SIC): Security and commodity services
Giving statement: Giving through the Benevento and Mayo Foundation.

Benevento and Mayo Foundation

46 Public Sq., Ste. 500
Wilkes-Barre, PA 18701-2600

Establishment information: Established in 1997 in PA.
Donors: Benevento & Mayo Partners; Marlco Investment Corp.
Financial data (yr. ended 12/31/11): Assets, $939,086 (M); gifts received, $4,750; expenditures, $40,645; qualifying distributions, $39,139; giving activities include $38,334 for 6 grants (high: $20,000; low: $1,000).
Purpose and activities: The foundation supports organizations involved with education, human services, and Catholicism.
Fields of interest: Education; Human services; Religion.
Type of support: General/operating support; Scholarship funds.
Geographic limitations: Giving limited to PA.
Application information: Applications not accepted. Unsolicited requests for funds not accepted.
Trustees: Brian J. Parente; Charles E. Parente; Charles E. Parente, Jr.; John Parente; Mary M. Parente; Marla Parente Sgarlat.
EIN: 237880441

415
Bennett Thrasher PC

1 Overton Park
3625 Cumberland Blvd., Ste. 1000
Atlanta, GA 30339-3361 (770) 396-2200

Company URL: http://www.btcpa.net
Establishment information: Established in 1980.
Company type: Private company
Business activities: Operates certified public accounting and consulting firm.
Business type (SIC): Accounting, auditing, and bookkeeping services
Corporate officers: Kenneth L. Thrasher, Chair.; Gregory Kosinski, C.O.O.; Robert Koney, C.F.O.; Chris Benner, V.P., Finance; William Eckerson, V.P., Human Resources
Board of director: Kenneth L. Thrasher, Chair.
Giving statement: Giving through the Bennett Thrasher Foundation, Inc.

Bennett Thrasher Foundation, Inc.

(formerly BT Foundation, Inc.)
3625 Cumberland Blvd., No. 1000
Atlanta, GA 30339 (770) 396-2200
E-mail: btfoundation@btcpa.net; URL: http://www.btcpa.net/Foundation/About/tabid/111/Default.aspx

Establishment information: Established in 2004 in GA.
Donor: Bennett Thrasher.
Contact: Chris Gilligan, Pres.
Financial data (yr. ended 12/31/11): Assets, $4,111 (M); gifts received, $100,103; expenditures, $98,936; qualifying distributions, $95,958; giving activities include $95,958 for grants.
Purpose and activities: The foundation supports organizations that foster the long-term development and success of individuals in the greater Atlanta, Georgia, metropolitan area.
Fields of interest: Youth development; Community/economic development; Religion.
Type of support: General/operating support.
Geographic limitations: Giving limited to the greater Atlanta, GA, metropolitan area.
Application information: Applications accepted. Application form required.
Initial approach: Letter
Deadline(s): None
Officers: Chris Gilligan, Pres.; David Thompson, V.P.; Paul Dobsky, Secy.; William Howell, Treas.
Board Members: Stephanie Crawford; Cary Rodin; Tiffany Scales; Ken Thrasher; Justin Walker.
EIN: 743111939

416
Bentley Manufacturing Company

520 Park Industrial Dr.
La Habra, CA 90631 (562) 501-2955

Company URL: http://www.gasketsonline.com
Establishment information: Established in 1955.
Company type: Private company
Business activities: Manufactures washers and cork gaskets.
Business type (SIC): Plastic products/miscellaneous; gaskets, packing and sealing devices, and rubber hose and belting
Corporate officers: Kevin Crampton, Pres. and C.E.O.; Deena Campana, V.P., Opers.
Giving statement: Giving through the Kevin P. Crampton Foundation.

The Kevin P. Crampton Foundation

110 Leola Way
Anaheim, CA 92807-3514 (714) 279-0060
URL: http://crampton.org/

Establishment information: Established in 1998 in CA.
Donor: Bentley Manufacturing Co., Inc.
Financial data (yr. ended 05/31/11): Assets, $509,582 (M); expenditures, $28,795; qualifying distributions, $22,312; giving activities include $22,312 for grants.
Purpose and activities: The foundation supports organizations involved with health.
Fields of interest: Education; Health care; Human services.
Type of support: General/operating support.
Support limitations: No grants to individuals.
Application information: Applications accepted. Application form not required.
Initial approach: Proposal
Deadline(s): None
Officers: Kevin P. Crampton, Pres.; Kristine M. Crampton, Secy.
EIN: 330811215

417
Benton Homebuilders

1000 Executive Pkwy., Ste. 106
Creve Coeur, MO 63141 (314) 336-5555

Company URL: http://www.bentonhomebuilders.com
Establishment information: Established in 1970.
Company type: Private company
Business activities: Operates new home construction and development company.
Business type (SIC): Real estate subdividers and developers; contractors/general residential building
Corporate officer: William Levinson, Pres.
Giving statement: Giving through the Community Partnership At Benton Homebuilders.

Community Partnership At Benton Homebuilders

(formerly Community Partnership At Taylor-Morley Homes)
1000 Executive Pkwy., Ste. 106
St. Louis, MO 63141-6369 (314) 336-5555

Establishment information: Established in 2002 in MO.
Donor: Taylor-Morley, Inc.
Financial data (yr. ended 12/31/11): Assets, $64,427 (M); expenditures, $17,386; qualifying distributions, $16,250; giving activities include $16,250 for grants.
Purpose and activities: The foundation supports organizations involved with cancer, abuse services, and children and youth. Special emphasis is directed toward programs designed to restore the quality of life of children and families in the greater St. Louis, Missouri, area.
Fields of interest: Health organizations; Youth development; Religion.
Type of support: General/operating support.
Geographic limitations: Giving primarily in the greater St. Louis, MO, area.
Application information: Applications accepted. Application form required.
Initial approach: Proposal
Deadline(s): None
Officers and Directors:* John E. Bennett*, Pres.; Courtney Adams*, Secy.; William A. Levinson*, Treas.
EIN: 300018491

418
Berghammer Construction Corporation

4750 N. 132nd St.
Butler, WI 53007-1629 (262) 790-4750
FAX: (262) 790-4755

Company URL: http://www.berghammer.com
Establishment information: Established in 1929.
Company type: Private company
Business activities: Provides residential and nonresidential general contract construction services.
Business type (SIC): Contractors/general nonresidential building; contractors/general residential building
Corporate officers: Leif A. Nesheim, Pres.; Cheryl Hebel, V.P., Finance
Giving statement: Giving through the Nesheim Family Foundation, Inc.

Nesheim Family Foundation, Inc.

4750 N. 132nd St.
Butler, WI 53007-1629

Establishment information: Established in 2002 in WI.
Donor: Berghammer Construction Corp.
Financial data (yr. ended 12/31/11): Assets, $174,644 (M); expenditures, $3,467; qualifying distributions, $2,150; giving activities include $2,150 for grants.
Purpose and activities: The foundation supports organizations involved with literacy and community development.
Fields of interest: Housing/shelter; Human services; Community/economic development.
Type of support: General/operating support.
Geographic limitations: Giving limited to Milwaukee, WI.
Support limitations: No grants to individuals.
Application information: Applications not accepted. Unsolicited requests for funds not accepted.
Officer and Directors:* Leif Nesheim*, Pres.; Andrew Nesheim; Patricia Nesheim.
Number of staff: None.
EIN: 020560726

419
Berglund Chevrolet Buick Pontiac

1824 Williamson Rd.
Roanoke, VA 24012-5228 (540) 344-1461

Company URL: http://www.berglundcars.com
Establishment information: Established in 1970.
Company type: Private company
Business activities: Operates auto dealership.
Business type (SIC): Motor vehicles—retail
Corporate officers: Bruce M. Farrell, Pres.; Anne Feazelle, Secy.
Giving statement: Giving through the Farrell Foundation.

Farrell Foundation

(formerly Berglund Foundation)
1824 Williamson Rd.
Roanoke, VA 24012-5298 (540) 344-1461

Establishment information: Established in 1988 in VA.
Donors: Berglund Chevrolet; Shane Farrell.
Contact: Anne Feazelle, Secy.
Financial data (yr. ended 04/30/12): Assets, $1,707,681 (M); gifts received, $101,826; expenditures, $137,206; qualifying distributions, $136,410; giving activities include $136,410 for 17 grants (high: $65,000; low: $200).
Purpose and activities: The foundation supports festivals and organizations involved with higher education, cancer, human services, economic development, and Catholicism.
Fields of interest: Arts; Housing/shelter; Human services.
Type of support: General/operating support.
Geographic limitations: Giving primarily in Roanoke, VA.
Application information: Applications accepted. Application form required. Applicants should submit the following:
1) descriptive literature about organization
Initial approach: Letter
Deadline(s): None
Officers: Bruce M. Farrell, Pres.; Anne Feazelle, Secy.
EIN: 541475736

420
The Bergquist Company

18930 W. 78th St.
Chanhassen, MN 55317-9347
(952) 835-2322
FAX: (952) 835-0430

Company URL: http://www.bergquistcompany.com
Establishment information: Established in 1964.
Company type: Private company
Business activities: Manufactures, markets, and sells electronic thermal materials, electronic thermal substrates, electronic components, membrane switches, and touch screens.
Business type (SIC): Electronic and other electrical equipment and components; electronic components and accessories
Corporate officers: Carl R. Bergquist, Jr., Chair., Pres., and Co-C.E.O.; Carl R. Bergquist, Sr., Co-C.E.O.; James G. Plewacki, Sr. V.P. and C.F.O.; Tim Schaefer, C.I.O.; John Camp, V.P., Human Resources; Madeline Foss, Cont.
Board of director: Carl R. Bergquist, Jr., Chair.
Plants: Wareham, MA; Big Fork, Cannon Falls, MN; Prescott, WI
International operations: Germany; Hong Kong; Ireland; Netherlands; South Korea; United Kingdom
Giving statement: Giving through the People in Business Care, Inc.

People in Business Care, Inc.

P.O. Box 977
Chanhassen, MN 55317-0977

Establishment information: Established in 1983 in MN.
Donor: The Berquist Co.
Financial data (yr. ended 07/31/09): Assets, $2,941,724 (M); gifts received, $890,581; expenditures, $660,261; qualifying distributions, $660,261; giving activities include $525,945 for 556 grants (high: $7,200; low: $47) and $128,430 for 117 grants to individuals (high: $3,000; low: $42).
Purpose and activities: The foundation supports organizations involved with health, hunger, human services, community development, and Christianity and awards medical assistance and emergency aid grants to residents of CA and MN.
Fields of interest: Health care, clinics/centers; Dental care; Health care; Food services; Food banks; Children, services; Family services; Residential/custodial care, hospices; Human services; Community/economic development; Christian agencies & churches.
Type of support: Equipment; General/operating support; Grants to individuals; Program development; Scholarship funds; Sponsorships.
Geographic limitations: Giving primarily in MN.
Application information: Applications accepted. Application form not required. Applicants should submit the following:
1) detailed description of project and amount of funding requested
Initial approach: Letter of inquiry
Copies of proposal: 1
Board meeting date(s): Monthly
Deadline(s): None
Officers: James Plewacki, Chair.; John Camp, Secy.; Don Conroy, Treas.
EIN: 363261419

Selected grants: The following grants are a representative sample of this grantmaker's funding activity:
$4,250 to Hope Academy, Minneapolis, MN, 2009.
$3,000 to Friends of Hospice, Litchfield, CT, 2009.
$2,800 to Camp Victory, Zumbro Falls, MN, 2009.
$2,000 to Minnesota Assistance Council for Veterans, Saint Paul, MN, 2009.
$2,000 to Special Olympics Minnesota, Minneapolis, MN, 2009.
$1,600 to Banyan Foundation, Minneapolis, MN, 2009.
$1,600 to Banyan Foundation, Minneapolis, MN, 2009.
$1,500 to YMCA of Greater Saint Paul, Minneapolis, MN, 2009.
$1,300 to Campus Crusade for Christ International, Orlando, FL, 2009.
$1,300 to Campus Crusade for Christ International, Orlando, FL, 2009.

421
Bergstrom, Inc.

(doing business as Bergstrom Climate Systems)
(formerly Bergstrom Manufacturing Company, Inc.)
2390 Blackhawk Rd.
P.O. Box 6007
Rockford, IL 61125 (815) 874-7821
FAX: (815) 874-2144

Company URL: http://www.bergstrominc.com
Establishment information: Established in 1949.
Company type: Private company
Business activities: Manufactures vehicle heaters, air conditioners, and ventilators.
Business type (SIC): Motor vehicles and equipment
Financial profile for 2010: Number of employees, 1,385
Corporate officers: David R. Rydell, Chair. and C.E.O.; Jack Shaffer, Pres. and C.O.O.; Steven Boyle, C.F.O.; Jim Elliott, V.P., Opers.
Board of director: David R. Rydell, Chair.
Giving statement: Giving through the Bergstrom Inc. Charitable Foundation.

Bergstrom Inc. Charitable Foundation

c/o JP Morgan Chase Bank
10 S. Dearborn, 21st Fl.
Chicago, IL 60603
Application address: Bergstrom Inc., 2390 Blackhawk Rd., Rockford, IL 61109, tel.: (815) 394-4655

Establishment information: Established in 1979.
Donors: Bergstrom Manufacturing Co., Inc.; Bergstrom Climate Systems, Inc.; Bergstrom Inc.
Contact: David R. Rydell, Tr.
Financial data (yr. ended 04/30/12): Assets, $934,822 (M); gifts received, $1,130,000; expenditures, $445,903; qualifying distributions, $443,480; giving activities include $443,480 for grants.
Purpose and activities: The foundation supports history museums, parks, and community foundations and organizations involved with education, health, golf, and human services.
Fields of interest: Education; Health care; Human services.
Type of support: Program development.
Geographic limitations: Giving primarily in Rockford, IL.
Support limitations: No grants to individuals.
Application information: Applications accepted. Application form required. Applicants should submit the following:
1) detailed description of project and amount of funding requested
Initial approach: Proposal
Deadline(s): None
Trustees: David R. Rydell; JPMorgan Chase Bank, N.A.
EIN: 366692339
Selected grants: The following grants are a representative sample of this grantmaker's funding activity:
$50,000 to Lutheran Social Services of Illinois, Des Plaines, IL, 2009.
$50,000 to United Way of Rock River Valley, Rockford, IL, 2009.
$25,000 to Midway Village and Museum Center, Rockford, IL, 2009.
$20,000 to Rockford Park District, Rockford, IL, 2009.
$11,000 to Community Foundation of Northern Illinois, Rockford, IL, 2009.
$10,000 to Rockford College, Rockford, IL, 2009.
$9,834 to Friends of the Coronado, Rockford, IL, 2009.
$8,334 to Janet Wattles Foundation, Rockford, IL, 2009.
$5,000 to Augustana College, Rock Island, IL, 2009.
$2,500 to Northern Illinois Hospice Association, Rockford, IL, 2009.

422
Bering Straits Native Corporation

(also known as BSNC)
110 Front St., Ste. 300
P.O. Box 1008
Nome, AK 99762 (907) 443-5252

Company URL: http://www.beringstraits.com
Establishment information: Established in 1972.
Company type: Native corporation
Business activities: Operates native corporation.
Business type (SIC): Nonclassifiable establishments
Corporate officers: Henry Ivanoff, Chair.; Eugene Asicksik, Vice-Chair.; Gail Schubert, Pres. and C.E.O.; Peggy Hoogendorn, V.P., Admin.; Roy Ashenfelter, Secy.; Clara Langton, Treas.
Board of directors: Henry Ivanoff, Chair.; Eugene Asicksik, Vice-Chair.; Martha Aarons; Roy Ashenfelter; Jason Evans; Neal W. Foster; Louis Green, Jr.; Homer E. Hoogendorn; Stephen Ivanoff; Clara Langton; Percy Nayokpuk; Fred Sagoonick; Gail R. Schubert; Tim Towarak; Tony Weyiouanna, Sr.
Subsidiaries: Eagle Electric, LLC, Anchorage, AK; Inuit Services Inc., Nome, AK; Knik Construction Inc., Nome, AK
Giving statement: Giving through the Bering Straits Foundation.

Bering Straits Foundation

P.O. Box 1008
Nome, AK 99762-1008 (907) 443-4305
FAX: (907) 443-2985;
E-mail: foundation@beringstraits.com; Toll-free tel.: (800) 478-5079; URL: http://www.beringstraits.com/

Establishment information: Established in 1991.
Contact: Carolyn Crowder, Pres.
Financial data (yr. ended 12/31/10): Revenue, $185,971; assets, $270,159 (M); gifts received, $139,064; expenditures, $314,487; giving activities include $189,454 for grants to individuals.
Purpose and activities: The foundation is dedicated to enhancing educational and cultural preservation opportunities for Bering Straits Native Corporation shareholders, their descendants, and the people of the Bering Straits region.
Fields of interest: Higher education Native Americans/American Indians.

Programs:

Fellowships: The foundation offers cultural and heritage fellowships to individuals who plan to attend non-credit workshops, conferences, or seminars that perpetuate the understanding of Bering Straits Native culture and heritage. Sixteen fellowships of $250 each will be awarded to individuals who plan to attend the Kawerak Regional Conference; twenty fellowships of $500 each will also be available to individuals who plan to attend national/international events that meet the stated guidelines.

Scholarships: The foundation awards scholarships to full- or part-time students enrolled in an accredited college or vocational school. Eligible applicants must be a shareholder, or lineal descendent of a shareholder of, the Bering Straits Native Corporation, and must have maintained a 3.0 GPA for his/her high school career.

Type of support: Fellowships; Public relations services; Scholarships—to individuals; Student loans—to individuals.
Publications: Application guidelines; Newsletter; Occasional report; Program policy statement; Quarterly report.
Application information: Applications accepted. Application form required.
Initial approach: Download application
Board meeting date(s): 2nd Tuesday of each month
Deadline(s): June 30 (fall) and Dec. 31 (spring) for applications
Final notification: Biannually
Officers and Directors:* Carolyn Crowder*, Pres.; Moriah Sallaffie*, Exec. V.P.; Clara Langton*, Secy.-Treas.; Arthur Martin; Tabetha Toloff.
Number of staff: 1 full-time professional.
EIN: 920138528

424
Berkel & Co. Contractors, Inc.

2649 S. 142nd St.
P.O. Box 335
Bonner Springs, KS 66012 (913) 422-5125

Company URL: http://www.berkelandcompany.com/
Establishment information: Established in 1959.
Company type: Private company
Business activities: Constructs specialized building foundations.
Business type (SIC): Contractors/miscellaneous special trade; contractors/concrete work
Corporate officers: Charles J. Berkel, Chair.; Alan R. Roach, Pres.; Grant D. White, C.F.O.; Edith M. Cantrell, Secy.; Susan E. Martley, Treas.
Board of director: Charles J. Berkel, Chair.
Giving statement: Giving through the C. D. Terry Scholarship Foundation.

C. D. Terry Scholarship Foundation
c/o Brotherhood Bank & Trust
756 Minnesoto Ave.
Kansas City, KS 66101-2704 (913) 667-8022

Establishment information: Established in 1992 in KS.
Donor: Berkel & Company Contractors, Inc.
Financial data (yr. ended 12/31/11): Assets, $7,135 (M); expenditures, $33,832; qualifying distributions, $33,832; giving activities include $33,732 for 42 grants to individuals (high: $1,500; low: $500).
Purpose and activities: The foundation awards college scholarships to children, spouses, and grandchildren of full-time employees and children of directors of Berkel & Co. Contractors, Inc.
Type of support: Employee-related scholarships.
Geographic limitations: Giving limited to areas of company operations, with emphasis on Bonner Springs, KS.
Application information: Applications accepted. Application form required.
Initial approach: Letter
Deadline(s): Varies
Advisory Board: James G. Butler, Jr.; Paul A. Hustad; Gerald L. Miller, Ph.D; Robert J. Reintjes, Sr.
EIN: 486316064

425
H. A. Berkheimer, Inc.
50 N. 7th St.
P.O. Box 900
Bangor, PA 18013-1731 (610) 588-0965
FAX: (610) 588-5765

Company URL: http://www.hab-inc.com
Establishment information: Established in 1946.
Company type: Private company
Business activities: Provides tax administration services.
Business type (SIC): Business services/ miscellaneous
Financial profile for 2009: Number of employees, 184
Corporate officer: John Berkheimer, Chair. and C.E.O.
Board of director: John Berkheimer, Chair.
Giving statement: Giving through the Berkheimer Foundation.
Company EIN: 231669661

Berkheimer Foundation
1883 Jury Rd.
Pen Argyl, PA 18072-9652

Establishment information: Established in 1989 in PA.
Donors: H.A. Berkheimer, Inc.; Berkheimer Oursourcing, Inc.
Financial data (yr. ended 12/31/11): Assets, $319,286 (M); gifts received, $5,000; expenditures, $2,543; qualifying distributions, $1,250.
Purpose and activities: The foundation supports the Girl Scouts - Great Valley Council and other organizations on a case by case basis.
Fields of interest: Girl scouts; General charitable giving.
Type of support: Annual campaigns; Building/ renovation; Capital campaigns.
Geographic limitations: Giving primarily in PA.
Support limitations: No grants to individuals.
Application information: Applications not accepted. Unsolicited requests for funds not accepted.
Board meeting date(s): Quarterly
Officers: John D. Berkheimer, Pres.; Henry U. Sandt, Secy.-Treas.
Directors: William Carson; Dennis J. Harris; Robert Pharo; William Sykes.
Number of staff: None.
EIN: 232582881

426
W.R. Berkley Corporation
475 Steamboat Rd.
Greenwich, CT 06830 (203) 629-3000
FAX: (203) 629-3073

Company URL: http://www.wrberkley.com/
Establishment information: Established in 1967.
Company type: Public company
Company ticker symbol and exchange: WRB/NYSE
Business activities: Operates holding company; sells property and casualty insurance.
Business type (SIC): Insurance/fire, marine, and casualty; holding company
Financial profile for 2012: Number of employees, 6,642; assets, $20,155,900,000; sales volume, $5,823,550,000; pre-tax net income, $701,930,000; expenses, $5,121,630,000; liabilities, $15,849,680,000
Fortune 1000 ranking: 2012—438th in revenues, 330th in profits, and 239th in assets
Corporate officers: William R. Berkley, Chair. and C.E.O.; W. Robert Berkley, Jr., Pres. and C.O.O.; Eugene G. Ballard, Sr. V.P. and C.F.O.; Ira S. Lederman, Sr. V.P., Genl. Counsel, and Corp. Secy.; Carol J. LaPunzina, Sr. V.P., Human Resources
Board of directors: William R. Berkley, Chair.; Christopher L. Augostini; W. Robert Berkley; Ronald E. Blaylock; Mark E. Brockbank; George G. Daly, Ph.D.; Mary C. Farrell; Jack H. Nusbaum; Mark L. Shapiro
Subsidiaries: Berkley International, LLC, Greenwich, CT; Carolina Casualty Insurance Co., Jacksonville, FL; Key Risk Management Services, Inc., Greensboro, NC; Monitor Liability Managers, Inc., Rolling Meadows, IL; Monitor Surety Managers, Inc., Chatham, NJ; Signet Star Holdings, Inc., Greenwich, CT
Giving statement: Giving through the W. R. Berkley Corporation Charitable Foundation.
Company EIN: 221867895

W. R. Berkley Corporation Charitable Foundation
c/o Foundation Source
501 Silverside Rd., Ste. 123
Wilmington, DE 19809-1377

Establishment information: Established in 2002 in DE.
Donors: W.R. Berkley Corp.; Acadia Insurance Company; Berkley Aviation LLC; Berkley Risk Administrators Company, LLC; Carolina Casualty Insurance Company; Continental Western Insurance Company; Monitor Liability Managers, Inc.; Nautilus Insurance Company; Union Insurance Company.
Financial data (yr. ended 12/31/11): Assets, $310,788 (M); gifts received, $397,199; expenditures, $368,619; qualifying distributions, $365,473; giving activities include $365,473 for grants.
Purpose and activities: The foundation supports food banks and organizations involved with arts and culture, education, diabetes, legal aid, human services, and public policy.
Fields of interest: Performing arts; Performing arts, orchestras; Arts; Higher education; Education; Diabetes; Legal services; Food banks; Boys & girls clubs; Children/youth, services; Human services; Public policy, research.
Type of support: General/operating support; Program development.
Geographic limitations: Giving primarily in CT, Washington, DC, IA, MA, ME, NY, and PA.
Support limitations: No grants to individuals.
Application information: Applications not accepted. Contributes only to pre-selected organizations.
Officers and Directors:* William R. Berkley*, Pres.; Josephine A. Ralmondi*, V.P. and Secy.; William R. Berkley, Jr.*, V.P. and Treas.
Trustee: W.R. Berkley Corp.
EIN: 364516560
Selected grants: The following grants are a representative sample of this grantmaker's funding activity:
$50,000 to New York University, New York, NY, 2010.
$10,000 to Civic Builders, New York, NY, 2010.
$10,000 to Washington Legal Foundation, Washington, DC, 2010.
$6,000 to Des Moines Area Religious Council, Des Moines, IA, 2010.
$5,500 to Children and Families of Iowa, Des Moines, IA, 2010.
$5,000 to Central Park Conservancy, New York, NY, 2010.
$4,500 to Penobscot Theater Company, Bangor, ME, 2010.
$3,000 to Friendship Home of Lincoln, Lincoln, NE, 2010.
$2,000 to Computers for Kids, Boise, ID, 2010.
$2,000 to New Horizons for New Hampshire, Manchester, NH, 2010.

427
J. E. Berkowitz, L.P.
1 Gateway Blvd.
P.O. Box 427
Pedricktown, NJ 08067 (856) 456-7800

Company URL: http://www.jeberkowitz.com
Establishment information: Established in 1920.
Company type: Private company
Business activities: Manufactures and sells insulating, tempered, and spandrel glass and store front metals.
Business type (SIC): Glass/flat; metal products/ structural
Corporate officers: Edwin J. Berkowitz, Chair.; Arthur M. Berkowitz, Pres.
Board of directors: Edwin J. Berkowitz, Chair.; Thomas J. Lynch
Giving statement: Giving through the Edwin J. Berkowitz Scholarship Foundation Inc.

Edwin J. Berkowitz Scholarship Foundation Inc.
c/o J.E. Berkowitz, L.P.
P.O. Box 427
Pedricktown, NJ 08067

Establishment information: Established in 1995 in NJ.
Donor: J.E. Berkowitz, L.P.
Financial data (yr. ended 09/30/11): Assets, $24,956 (M); gifts received, $5,000; expenditures, $10,000; qualifying distributions, $10,000; giving

activities include $10,000 for 4 grants to individuals (high: $2,500; low: $2,500).
Purpose and activities: The foundation awards college scholarships to employees and the children of employees of J.E. Berkowitz.
Fields of interest: Higher education.
Type of support: Employee-related scholarships.
Geographic limitations: Giving limited to areas of company operations in NJ.
Application information: Applications not accepted. Contributes only through employee-related scholarships.
Trustees: Arthur M. Berkowitz; Joseph A. Durcanin; Joe Rotondo.
EIN: 223402191

428
Berkshire Bank

(formerly Berkshire County Savings Bank)
24 North St.
P.O. Box 1308
Pittsfield, MA 01202-1308 (800) 773-5601

Company URL: http://www.berkshirebank.com
Establishment information: Established in 1846.
Company type: Subsidiary of a public company
Business activities: Operates commercial bank.
Business type (SIC): Banks/commercial
Financial profile for 2011: Assets, $3,484,000,000; liabilities, $3,007,800,000
Corporate officers: Michael P. Daly, Pres. and C.E.O.; Kevin P. Riley, Exec. V.P., C.F.O., and Treas.; Linda A. Johnston, Exec. V.P., Human Resources; Gordon Prescott, Corp. Secy. and Genl. Counsel
Board of directors: Lawrence A. Bossidy, Chair.; Robert M. Curley; John Davis; James Williar Dunlaevy; Michael P. Daly; Rodney C. Dimock; Susan M. Hill; Cornelius D. Mahoney; Catherine B. Miller; David E. Phelps; Barton D. Raser; Jeffrey D. Templeton
Historic mergers: Rome Bancorp, Inc. (May 31, 2011); Legacy Banks (July 21, 2011); The Connecticut Bank and Trust Company (April 20, 2012)
Giving statement: Giving through the Berkshire Bank Foundation, Inc., the Berkshire Bank Foundation -Legacy Region, and the C.B.T. Charitable Foundation, Inc.

Berkshire Bank Foundation, Inc.

(formerly Greater Berkshire Charitable Foundation)
P.O. Box 1308
Pittsfield, MA 01202-1308 (413) 447-1724
E-mail: foundation@berkshirebank.com; E-mail for Peter J. Lafayette: plafayette@berkshirebank.com; Contact for Recycle, Renew, and Reuse Program: Gary R. Levante, tel.: (413) 447-1737, e-mail: glevante@berkshirebank.com; URL: http://www.berkshirebank.com/about-us/in_the_community/berkshire-bank-foundation
E-mail for scholarships: scholarshipinfo@berkshirebank.com

Establishment information: Established in 1996 in MA.
Donor: Berkshire Bank.
Contact: Peter J. Lafayette, Exec. Dir.
Financial data (yr. ended 12/31/11): Assets, $15,463,123 (M); expenditures, $1,423,971; qualifying distributions, $867,762; giving activities include $867,762 for grants.
Purpose and activities: The foundation supports organizations involved with arts and culture, environmental education, employment, housing, mentoring, human services, immigrant advocacy, military and veterans, and economically disadvantaged people. Special emphasis is directed toward programs designed to promote education and community economic development.
Fields of interest: Museums; Arts; Education, early childhood education; Higher education; Adult education—literacy, basic skills & GED; Libraries (public); Education; Environmental education; Employment, services; Housing/shelter, temporary shelter; Housing/shelter, homeless; Housing/shelter, home owners; Housing/shelter; Youth development, adult & child programs; Human services, financial counseling; Human services; Civil/human rights, immigrants; Urban/community development; Community/economic development Military/veterans; Economically disadvantaged.
Programs:
Berkshire Bank Foundation Scholarship Awards Program: The foundation awards $2,000 college scholarships to high school seniors in a town or city in MA, NY, and VT served by Berkshire Bank. Applicants must have a record of volunteerism in the community in non-school sponsored activities and participation in extracurricular activities, a minimum 3.0 GPA, a family income under $75,000, and a plan to attend a two or four year college or technical school.
Employee Volunteer Program: The foundation awards employees of Berkshire Bank 8 hours of paid leave to participate in volunteer projects put on by the bank during business hours. The foundation also selects employee volunteers of the year, where employees who have made outstanding contributions to their communities through volunteerism is given a $500 donation to the nonprofit organization of their choice.
Recycle, Renew, and Reuse Program: Berkshire Bank donates surplus computers, telephones, and other technology equipment to nonprofit organizations that can not afford new purchases due to reduced income and funding cutbacks. Technology equipment includes monitors, keyboards, servers, printers, storage devices, and routers. The program is limited to Berkshire County, Massachusetts and is administered by the Berkshire Bank Foundation.
Type of support: Annual campaigns; Capital campaigns; Continuing support; Donated equipment; Employee volunteer services; General/operating support; Program development; Publication; Scholarship funds; Scholarships—to individuals; Sponsorships.
Geographic limitations: Giving primarily in areas of company operations in Berkshire County and Pioneer Valley, MA, NY, and southern VT.
Support limitations: No support for religious organizations, fraternal, labor, or political organizations, including fraternal orders of police and firefighters, lobbying groups, private foundations, pass-through organizations, or national health organizations. No grants to individuals (except for scholarships), or for golf tournaments, fundraising dinners, annual memberships or annual appeals, endowments, or conferences or seminars.
Publications: Application guidelines.
Application information: Applications accepted. Requests of less than $1,500 should include a 1 page project letter describing the proposed project, description, purpose, timetable, goals, cost, and impact. Small Project Requests between $1,500 and $4,999 should include a 2 to 3 page narrative. Large Project Requests for $5,000 or more should include a 2 to 3 page narrative and are processed on a quarterly basis. Support is limited to 1 contribution per organization during any given year for three years in length. Application form required. Applicants should submit the following:
1) timetable for implementation and evaluation of project
2) population served
3) copy of IRS Determination Letter
4) copy of most recent annual report/audited financial statement/990
5) how project's results will be evaluated or measured
6) listing of board of directors, trustees, officers and other key people and their affiliations
7) detailed description of project and amount of funding requested
8) copy of current year's organizational budget and/or project budget
9) listing of additional sources and amount of support

Scholarship applications should include an essay, resume, and school transcripts.
Initial approach: Complete online application form; download application and mail for scholarships; e-mail request letter for Recycle, Renew, and Reuse Program
Copies of proposal: 1
Board meeting date(s): Mar., June, Sept. and Dec.
Deadline(s): None for requests of up to $5,000; Mar. 1, June. 1, Sept. 1, and Dec. 1 for requests of $5,000 or more; Mar. 28 for scholarships; none for Recycle, Renew, and Reuse Program
Final notification: May for scholarships; several months for Recycle, Renew, and Reuse Program
Officers and Directors:* Michael J. Ferry*, Chair. and Pres.; Catherine B. Miller, Vice-Chair.; Michael P. Daly, V.P.; Michael Oleksak, V.P.; Peter J. Lafayette, Secy. and Exec. Dir.; Kevin P. Riley, Treas.; Thomas R. Creed; Robert M. Curley; Sean Gray; D. Jeffrey Templeton; Corydon L. Thurston.
EIN: 043365869
Selected grants: The following grants are a representative sample of this grantmaker's funding activity:
$2,000 to Johnson and Wales University, Providence, RI, 2009.
$2,000 to Northeastern University, Boston, MA, 2009.
$2,000 to University of Vermont, Burlington, VT, 2009.
$1,000 to American Cancer Society, Atlanta, GA, 2009.

Berkshire Bank Foundation -Legacy Region

(formerly The Legacy Banks Foundation)
P.O. Box 1308
Pittsfield, MA 01201-5114 (413) 447-1724
E-mail: plafayette@berkshirebank.com; Application address: Lori Gazzillo, V.P., Community Rels., P.O. Box 1148, Pittsfield, MA 01202-1148; URL: http://www.berkshirebank.com/about-us/in_the_community/berkshire-bank-foundation

Establishment information: Established in 2005 in DE and MA.
Donor: Legacy Banks.
Contact: Richard M. Sullivan, Pres.
Financial data (yr. ended 12/31/11): Assets, $9,992,099 (M); expenditures, $521,689; qualifying distributions, $401,353; giving activities include $401,353 for grants.
Purpose and activities: The foundation supports education and community and economic development projects that enhance opportunities for children and adults in Berkshire County, Massachusetts. Special emphasis is directed toward programs that target disadvantaged communities or populations.

Fields of interest: Education, early childhood education; Education; Community/economic development Children; Adults; Economically disadvantaged.
Type of support: General/operating support; Program development.
Geographic limitations: Giving limited to areas of company operations in Berkshire County, MA.
Support limitations: No support for religious, political, fraternal, lobbying, national health, or discriminatory organizations, or intermediary organizations that raise and distribute funds in their own name, or private foundations. No grants to individuals, or for golf tournaments, fundraising dinners, annual memberships and appeals, or endowments, or underwriting support for conferences or seminars.
Publications: Application guidelines.
Application information: Applications accepted. Support is limited to 1 contribution per organization during any given year. Multi-year funding is not automatic. Application form required. Applicants should submit the following:
1) population served
2) copy of IRS Determination Letter
3) how project's results will be evaluated or measured
4) listing of board of directors, trustees, officers and other key people and their affiliations
5) detailed description of project and amount of funding requested
6) copy of current year's organizational budget and/ or project budget
7) listing of additional sources and amount of support
8) plans for acknowledgement
Initial approach: Complete online application
Board meeting date(s): Quarterly
Deadline(s): Mar. 1, June 1, Sept. 1, and Dec. 1 for requests $5,000 and over
Officers and Directors:* J. Williar Dunlaevy*, Chair. and C.E.O.; Patrick J. Sullivan*, Vice-Chair.; Richard M. Sullivan*, Pres.; Lori Gazzillo, V.P.; Daniel Kinney, V.P.; Heather A. King, Secy.; Dianne M. Supranowicz, Treas.; Lawrence J. Lane; Susan Lombard; Anne W. Pasko; Bruce H. Person; Mary Jo Piretti-Miller.
EIN: 203661535
Selected grants: The following grants are a representative sample of this grantmaker's funding activity:
$40,000 to Berkshire Museum, Pittsfield, MA, 2010. For capital campaign.
$29,884 to United Way, Berkshire, Pittsfield, MA, 2010.
$20,000 to Barrington Stage Company, Pittsfield, MA, 2010. For capital campaign.
$10,000 to Berkshire Community College Foundation, Pittsfield, MA, 2010.
$6,500 to Barrington Stage Company, Pittsfield, MA, 2010.
$5,000 to Berkshire Community Action Council, Pittsfield, MA, 2010.
$5,000 to Elizabeth Freeman Center, Pittsfield, MA, 2010.
$5,000 to Hancock Shaker Village, Pittsfield, MA, 2010. For capital campaign.
$5,000 to Massachusetts Museum of Contemporary Art, North Adams, MA, 2010.
$1,000 to Lenox Library Association, Lenox, MA, 2010.

C.B.T. Charitable Foundation, Inc.
58 State House Sq.
Hartford, CT 06103-3902

Establishment information: Established in 2004 in CT.
Donor: The Connecticut Bank and Trust Co.
Contact: Anson C. Hall, Exec. Dir.
Financial data (yr. ended 12/31/11): Assets, $195,116 (M); gifts received, $291; expenditures, $73,598; qualifying distributions, $72,884; giving activities include $72,884 for grants.
Purpose and activities: The foundation supports House of Bread in Hartford, Connecticut.
Fields of interest: Arts; Human services; Science.
Type of support: General/operating support.
Geographic limitations: Giving limited to areas of company operations in CT.
Application information: Applications accepted. Application form required.
Initial approach: Letter
Deadline(s): None
Officers and Directors:* David A. Lentini*, Chair.; Virginia B. Springer, Secy.; Anson C. Hall*, Exec. Dir.
Number of staff: None.
EIN: 161703567

429
Berkshire Hathaway Inc.
3555 Farnam St., Ste. 1440
Omaha, NE 68131 (402) 346-1400
FAX: (212) 783-3833

Company URL: http://www.berkshirehathaway.com
Establishment information: Established in 1889.
Company type: Public company
Company ticker symbol and exchange: BRK.A/ NYSE
Business activities: Operates holding company; sells insurance and reinsurance.
Business type (SIC): Insurance carriers; holding company
Financial profile for 2012: Number of employees, 288,500; assets, $427,452,000,000; sales volume, $162,463,000,000; pre-tax net income, $22,236,000,000; expenses, $140,227,000,000; liabilities, $239,805,000,000
Fortune 1000 ranking: 2012—5th in revenues
Forbes 2000 ranking: 2012—17th in sales, 20th in profits, and 70th in assets
Corporate officers: Warren E. Buffett, Chair. and C.E.O.; Charles T. Munger, Vice-Chair.; Marc D. Hamburg, Sr. V.P. and C.F.O.; Daniel J. Jaksich, V.P. and Cont.; Forrest N. Krutter, Secy.; Kerby S. Ham, Treas.
Board of directors: Warren E. Buffett, Chair.; Charles T. Munger, Vice-Chair.; Howard G. Buffett; Stephen B. Burke; Susan L. Decker; William H. Gates III; Charlotte Guyman; Donald R. Keough; Thomas S. Murphy; Ronald L. Olson; Walter Scott, Jr.
Subsidiaries: Associated Retail Stores, Inc., Long Island City, NY; Blue Chip Stamps, Los Angeles, CA; H.H. Brown Shoe Co., Greenwich, CT; Buffalo News, Buffalo, NY; Burlington Northern Santa Fe, LLC, Fort Worth, TX; Clayton Homes, Inc., Maryville, TN; Edina Realty, Inc., Minneapolis, MN; Fechheimer Bros. Co., Cincinnati, OH; The Scott Fetzer Company, Westlake, OH; Fruit of the Loom, Inc., Bowling Green, KY; GEICO Corporation, Chevy Chase, MD; General Reinsurance Corporation, Stamford, CT; Government Employees Insurance Company, Washington, DC; H.J. Heinz Company, Pittsburgh, PA; Johns Manville Corporation, Denver, CO; Justin Industries Inc., Fort Worth, TX; K & W Products Div., Santa Fe Springs, CA; The Lubrizol Corporation, Wickliffe, OH; MidAmerican Energy Company, Des Moines, IA; MidAmerican Energy Holdings Company, Des Moines, IA; Benjamin Moore & Co., Montvale, NJ; Nebraska Furniture Mart, Omaha, NE; PacifiCorp, Portland, OR; The Pampered Chef, Ltd., Addison, IL; Russell Corporation, Atlanta, GA; See's Candies, San Francisco, CA; Shaw Industries Group, Inc., Dalton, GA; World Book, Chicago, IL; XTRA Corporation, St. Louis, MO
International operations: Australia; Canada; South Africa; United Kingdom
Giving statement: Giving through the Berkshire Hathaway Inc. Corporate Giving Program and the Buffett Foundation, Inc.
Company EIN: 470813844

Berkshire Hathaway Inc. Corporate Giving Program
3555 Farnam St., Ste.1440
Omaha, NE 68131-3302
URL: http://www.berkshirehathaway.com/sholdqa.html

Purpose and activities: Berkshire Hathaway makes charitable contributions to nonprofit organizations as designated by the company's shareholders. Support is given on a national basis.
Fields of interest: General charitable giving.
Type of support: General/operating support.
Geographic limitations: Giving on a national basis.
Application information: Applications not accepted. Contributes only to pre-selected organizations designated by the company's shareholders.

Buffett Foundation, Inc.
8212 Harwood Ave. N.E.
Albuquerque, NM 87110-1518

Establishment information: Established in 1988 in NM.
Donors: Berkshire Hathaway Inc.; United Way of Central NM; B&H Company, Inc.; George Buffett; Jeanett Buffett.
Financial data (yr. ended 12/31/11): Assets, $4,027 (M); expenditures, $1,390; qualifying distributions, $0.
Purpose and activities: The foundation supports organizations involved with higher education and family planning.
Fields of interest: Higher education; Reproductive health, family planning.
Type of support: General/operating support.
Geographic limitations: Giving primarily in Hillsdale, MI and Albuquerque, NM.
Application information: Applications not accepted. Unsolicited requests for funds not accepted.
Officers: George Buffett, Pres.; Jeannette Buffett, V.P.; Patricia M. Buffett, Secy.; George Buffett II, Treas.
Director: John Buffett.
EIN: 850360365

430
Berkshire Life Insurance Company of America
(formerly Berkshire Life Insurance Company)
700 South St.
Pittsfield, MA 01201-8212 (413) 499-4321
FAX: (413) 499-4831

Company URL: http://www.guardianlife.com/AboutGuardian/CompanyOverview/Guardian%20Subsidiaries/index.htm
Establishment information: Established in 2001.
Company type: Subsidiary of a private company
Business activities: Sells disability insurance.
Business type (SIC): Insurance/accident and health

Corporate officer: Gordon G. Dinsmore, Pres.
Giving statement: Giving through the Berkshire Life Insurance Company of America Corporate Giving Program.

Berkshire Life Insurance Company of America Corporate Giving Program

700 South St.
Pittsfield, MA 01201-8212 (413) 395-4467
FAX: (413) 395-5986;
E-mail: wendy_coakley@berkshirelife.com

Contact: Wendy Webster Coakley, Chair., Corp. Contribs.; Lorraine Allessio
Purpose and activities: As a complement to its foundation, Berkshire also makes charitable contributions to nonprofit organizations directly. Support is limited to Berkshire County, Massachusetts.
Fields of interest: Arts education; Environmental education; Environment; Government/public administration.
Type of support: General/operating support.
Geographic limitations: Giving limited to Berkshire County, MA.

423
Berk-Tek, Inc.

(doing business as Nexans USA Inc.)
132 White Oak Rd.
New Holland, PA 17557-8303
(717) 354-6200

Company URL: http://www.nexans.us/
Establishment information: Established in 2000.
Company type: Subsidiary of a foreign company
Business activities: Manufactures wire and cable.
Business type (SIC): Metal products/fabricated
Corporate officers: Paul Trunk, Pres.; Yves Trezieres, C.I.O; Kevin Cyr, Sr. V.P., Sales and Mktg.
Board of directors: Frederic Vincent, Chair.; Robert Brunck; Guillermo Luksic Craig; Gianpaolo Caccini; Georges Chodron de Courcel; Francois Polge de Combret; Cyrille Duval; Jerome Gallot; Veronique Guillot-Pelpel; Colette Lewiner; Francisco Perez Mackenna; Hubert Porte; Mouna Sepehri; Nicolas de Tavernost; Lena Wujek
Giving statement: Giving through the Boscov-Berk-Tek, Inc., Scholarship Fund.

Boscov-Berk-Tek, Inc., Scholarship Fund

c/o Kevin St., Cyr., Nexans Inc.
132 White Oak Rd.
New Holland, PA 17557-8300 (717) 354-6200

Establishment information: Established in 1994 in PA.
Donor: Berk-Tek, Inc.
Contact: Kevin St. Cyr, Tr.
Financial data (yr. ended 12/31/11): Assets, $254,779 (M); expenditures, $11,117; qualifying distributions, $10,000; giving activities include $10,000 for grants.
Purpose and activities: The foundation awards college scholarships to children, descendants, and spouses of employees of Berk-Tek, Inc.
Type of support: Employee-related scholarships.
Geographic limitations: Giving limited to PA.
Application information: Applications accepted. Application form required.
Initial approach: Contact foundation for application form
Deadline(s): None
Trustee: Kevin St. Cyr.
EIN: 237763668

431
Bernecker's Nursery, Inc.

16900 S.W. 216 St.
Goulds, FL 33170 (305) 247-8577

Company URL: http://www.berneckers.com
Establishment information: Established in 1961.
Company type: Private company
Business activities: Raises and distributes indoor tropical plants.
Business type (SIC): Horticultural specialties
Corporate officer: Robert Bernecker, C.E.O.
Giving statement: Giving through the Bernecker Charitable Foundation, Inc.

Bernecker Charitable Foundation, Inc.

P.O. Box 913
Waxahachie, TX 75168

Establishment information: Established in 1993 in FL.
Donors: Bernecker's Nursery, Inc.; Robert Bernecker.
Financial data (yr. ended 12/31/10): Assets, $1,233,298 (M); gifts received, $46,000; expenditures, $194,175; qualifying distributions, $194,000; giving activities include $194,000 for grants.
Fields of interest: Christian agencies & churches.
Support limitations: No grants to individuals.
Application information: Applications not accepted. Contributes only to pre-selected organizations.
Officer and Directors:* Robert Bernecker*, Pres. and Secy.-Treas.; Luke Benson; Donald Bernecker.
EIN: 650416459

432
Bernhardt Furniture Company

1839 Morganton Blvd.
P.O. Box 740
Lenoir, NC 28645-0740 (828) 758-9811
FAX: (828) 759-6259

Company URL: http://www.bernhardt.com
Establishment information: Established in 1889.
Company type: Private company
Business activities: Manufactures upscale casegoods and upholstered furniture.
Business type (SIC): Furniture/household
Financial profile for 2010: Number of employees, 2,100
Corporate officers: G. Alexander Bernhardt, Sr., Chair. and C.E.O.; Anne Bernhardt, Vice-Chair.; Lewis G. Norman, Vice-Chair.; Alex Bernhardt, Jr., Pres. and C.E.O.
Board of directors: G. Alexander Bernhardt, Sr., Chair.; Anne Bernhardt, Vice-Chair.; Lewis Norman, Vice-Chair.
Giving statement: Giving through the Bernhardt Furniture Foundation.

Bernhardt Furniture Foundation

(formerly Lenoir Community Foundation, Inc.)
P.O. Box 740
Lenoir, NC 28645-0740 (828) 759-6288

Establishment information: Established in NC.
Donors: Bernhardt Furniture Company; John C. Bernhardt, Jr.; Alex Bernhardt, Sr.; Alex Bernhardt, Jr.; Mary Bernhardt Busko; Lillian Bernhardt Sutcliffe.
Contact: William F. Howard III, Treas.
Financial data (yr. ended 10/31/12): Assets, $1,580,994 (M); gifts received, $187,500; expenditures, $122,347; qualifying distributions, $114,706; giving activities include $95,600 for 16 grants (high: $15,000; low: $1,000).
Purpose and activities: The foundation supports health clinics and organizations involved with arts and culture, education, cancer, hunger, human services, and Christianity.
Fields of interest: Education; Health care; Community/economic development.
Type of support: General/operating support.
Geographic limitations: Giving limited to Caldwell County, NC.
Support limitations: No grants to individuals.
Application information: Applications accepted. Application form required.
Initial approach: Contact foundation for application form
Board meeting date(s): Jan. or Feb.
Deadline(s): May 30
Officers: G. Alex Bernhardt, Sr., Pres.; James R. Collett, Jr., V.P.; G. Alex. Bernhardt, Jr., V.P.; Jason M. Hensley, Secy.; William F. Howard III, Treas.
EIN: 510202755

433
Bernstein Shur Sawyer & Nelson

100 Middle St., Fl. 6, West Twr.
P.O. Box 9729
Portland, ME 04101-5029 (207) 774-1200

Company URL: http://www.bernsteinshur.com/
Establishment information: Established in 1915.
Company type: Private company
Business activities: Operates law firm.
Business type (SIC): Legal services
Corporate officers: Charles E. Miller, C.E.O.; Julie W. Gerard, C.O.O.
Offices: Augusta, Portland, ME; Manchester, NH
Giving statement: Giving through the Bernstein Shur Sawyer & Nelson Pro Bono Program.

Bernstein Shur Sawyer & Nelson Pro Bono Program

100 Middle St., Fl. 6
P.O. Box 9729
Portland, ME 04101-4100 (207) 774-1200
FAX: (207) 774-1127;
E-mail: jkeenan@bernsteinshur.com; URL: http://www.bernsteinshur.com/

Contact: Rachel Strong, Pro Bono Counsel
Fields of interest: Legal services.
Type of support: Pro bono services - legal.
Geographic limitations: Giving primarily in Augusta, and Portland, ME, and Manchester, NH.
Application information: A Pro Bono Committee manages the program.

434
L. M. Berry and Company

(doing business as The Berry, Co.)
3100 Kettering Blvd.
Dayton, OH 45439-1975 (937) 296-2121

Company URL: http://www.lmberry.com
Establishment information: Established in 1910.
Company type: Subsidiary of a public company
Business activities: Provides advertising sales services.
Business type (SIC): Advertising
Financial profile for 2010: Number of employees, 650
Corporate officers: Scott A. Pomeroy, Pres. and C.E.O.; Linda Martin, Exec. V.P. and C.O.O.; Dan Graham, Exec. V.P. and C.A.O.; Scott A. Berman, C.F.O.; Daphne Young, V.P., Opers.; Michele Hutchison, V.P., Opers. and Sales; Mark Williams, V.P., Comms.; John Fischer, Genl. Counsel
Giving statement: Giving through the L. M. Berry and Company Contributions Program.

L. M. Berry and Company Contributions Program

3170 Kettering Blvd.
Dayton, OH 45439-1924 (937) 296-2121

Contact: Pam White
Purpose and activities: L.M. Berry makes charitable contributions to nonprofit organizations involved with arts and culture, health, human services, and economic development. Support is given primarily in areas of company operations.
Fields of interest: Visual arts; Performing arts; Arts; Education; Hospitals (general); Health care; Children/youth, services; Economic development.
Type of support: Employee volunteer services; General/operating support; Program development.
Geographic limitations: Giving primarily in areas of company operations, with emphasis on Dayton, OH.
Application information: The company is in the process of reviewing its charitable giving guidelines.

435
Berry Companies Inc.

3223 N. Hydraulic St.
Wichita, KS 67219 (316) 832-0171
FAX: (316) 832-1055

Company URL: http://www.berrycompaniesinc.com/
Establishment information: Established in 1957.
Company type: Private company
Business activities: Sells and leases heavy construction equipment.
Business type (SIC): Industrial machinery and equipment—wholesale
Corporate officers: Fred F. Berry, Jr., Chair.; Walter T. Berry, Pres.; Rod Opliger, C.F.O. and Cont.; Judy Worrell, V.P. and Secy.-Treas.
Board of director: Fred F. Berry, Jr., Chair.
Plant: Denver, CO
Giving statement: Giving through the Berry Foundation Inc.

Berry Foundation Inc.

3223 N. Hydraulic
P.O. Box 829
Wichita, KS 67201-0829

Establishment information: Established in 2006 in KS.
Donor: Berry Company.
Contact: Judy Worrell, Secy.-Treas. and Dir.
Financial data (yr. ended 12/31/11): Assets, $316,035 (M); gifts received, $173,071; expenditures, $134,568; qualifying distributions, $134,398; giving activities include $132,623 for 88 grants (high: $15,000; low: $100).
Fields of interest: Arts; Education, early childhood education; Secondary school/education; Education; Zoos/zoological societies; Boys & girls clubs; Children, services; Developmentally disabled, centers & services; Human services; Business/industry; United Ways and Federated Giving Programs; Christian agencies & churches.
Type of support: Annual campaigns; Building/renovation; Endowments; General/operating support; Scholarship funds.
Geographic limitations: Giving primarily in KS.
Support limitations: No grants to individuals.
Application information: Applications accepted. Application form not required.
Initial approach: Proposal
Deadline(s): None
Officers and Directors:* Fred F. Berry, Jr., Pres.; Judy Worrell, Secy.-Treas.; Walter T. Berry; Daniel J. Scheer.
EIN: 203942107

436
Berry Investment Company

(also known as Michigan Metals And Manufacturing, Inc.)
29100 Northwestern Hwy.
Southfield, MI 48034-1046 (248) 358-5220

Establishment information: Established in 1974.
Company type: Private company
Business activities: Conducts investment activities.
Business type (SIC): Investors/miscellaneous
Corporate officers: Isaac Lakritz, Pres.; Larry A. Berry, V.P., Finance
Giving statement: Giving through the Berry Foundation.

The Berry Foundation

29100 Northwestern Hwy., Ste. 290
Southfield, MI 48034-1069

Donors: Berry Investment Co.; Louis Berry†; Harold Berry; Lawrence Berry; Louis Berry Marital Trust; Berry Ventures; Vivian Berry; Barbara Berry; Selma B. Schwartz; Peter Seagle; Elliott B. Berry; Miriam Seagle; Betsy Heuer; Peter Seagle.
Financial data (yr. ended 12/31/11): Assets, $125 (M); gifts received, $32,075; expenditures, $50,880; qualifying distributions, $50,235; giving activities include $49,615 for 174 grants (high: $12,000; low: $20).
Purpose and activities: The foundation supports organizations involved with education, health, cancer, children and youth services, and Judaism.
Fields of interest: Education; Health care; Health organizations.
Type of support: General/operating support; Program development.
Geographic limitations: Giving primarily in Washington, DC, FL, MI, and New York, NY.
Support limitations: No grants to individuals.
Application information: Applications not accepted. Unsolicited requests for funds not accepted.
Officers: Harold Berry, Pres. and Treas.; Lawrence Berry, V.P.; Peter C. Seagle, Secy.
Trustees: Barbara Berry; Elliott B. Berry; Betsy Heuer; Selma B. Schwartz; Miriam Seagle.
EIN: 386064574

437
Berry Petroleum Company

1999 Broadway, Ste. 3700
Denver, CO 80202 (303) 999-4400
FAX: (302) 655-5049

Company URL: http://www.bry.com
Establishment information: Established in 1909.
Company type: Public company
Company ticker symbol and exchange: BRY/NYSE
Business activities: Conducts crude oil and natural gas exploration, development, acquisition, exploitation, and production activities.
Business type (SIC): Extraction/oil and gas
Financial profile for 2012: Number of employees, 374; assets, $3,325,400,000; sales volume, $978,600,000; pre-tax net income, $259,660,000; expenses, $718,940,000; liabilities, $2,310,610,000
Corporate officers: Martin H. Young, Jr., Chair.; Robert F. Heinemann, Pres. and C.E.O.; Michael Duginski, Exec. V.P. and C.O.O.; David D. Wolf, Exec. V.P. and C.F.O.; Davis O. O'Connor, V.P., Genl. Counsel, and Secy.; Shawn M. Canaday, V.P., Finance and Treas.; Walter B. Ayers, V.P., Human Resources; Jamie L. Wheat, Cont.
Board of directors: Martin H. Young, Jr., Chair.; Ralph B. Busch III; William E. Bush, Jr.; Stephen L. Cropper; J. Herbert Gaul, Jr.; Robert F. Heinemann; Stephen J. Hadden; Thomas J. Jamieson; J. Frank Keller; Michael S. Reddin
Plant: Oxnard, CA
Giving statement: Giving through the Berry Petroleum Company Contributions Program.
Company EIN: 770079387

Berry Petroleum Company Contributions Program

1999 Broadway, Suite 3700
Denver, CO 80202-5703 (303) 999-4400
URL: http://www.bry.com/pages/community2.html

Purpose and activities: Berry Petroleum makes charitable contributions to museums, hospitals, and nonprofit organizations involved with education, cancer, and hunger, and awards college scholarships to graduating seniors. Support is given primarily in areas of company operations, and to national organizations.
Fields of interest: Museums; Higher education, college; Higher education, university; Education; Environment, energy; Hospitals (general); Cancer; Food banks; Recreation, camps; Boy scouts; Girl scouts; American Red Cross; Family resources and services, disability; Human services, gift distribution; United Ways and Federated Giving Programs.
Program:
Berry Petroleum Company Scholarship: Berry Petroleum annually awards college scholarships (generally $1,500) to graduating seniors residing in areas of company operations who plan to pursue a two-year associate degree or four-year academic degree at an accredited college or university.
Type of support: Employee matching gifts; Employee volunteer services; General/operating support; In-kind gifts; Scholarships—to individuals.
Geographic limitations: Giving primarily in areas of company operations, and to national organizations.

438
Berry Plastics Corporation
101 Oakley St.
P.O. Box 959
Evansville, IN 47710 (812) 424-2904

Company URL: http://www.berryplastics.com
Establishment information: Established in 1967.
Company type: Subsidiary of a private company
Parent company: BPC Holding Corporation
Business activities: Manufactures injection molded packaging.
Business type (SIC): Plastic products/ miscellaneous
Financial profile for 2011: Number of employees, 16,000; assets, $5,630,000,000; sales volume, $4,257,000,000
Fortune 1000 ranking: 2012—503rd in revenues, 878th in profits, and 587th in assets
Corporate officers: Ira G. Boots, Co-Chair and Co-C.E.O.; Jonathan Rich, Co-Chair and Co-C.E.O.; Ralph B. Beeler, Pres. and C.O.O.; Jim Kratochvil, C.F.O.; Mark Miles, Exec. V.P., Treas., and Cont.
Board of directors: Ian G. Boots, Co-Chair.; Jonathan Rich, Co-Chair.
Subsidiaries: Kerr Group, Inc., Lancaster, PA; Landis Plastics, Inc., Chicago, IL; Setco, LLC, Monroe Township, NJ; Tubed Products, LLC, Easthampton, MA
Plants: Sarasota, FL; Baltimore, MD
International operations: Belgium; Canada; India; Mexico
Giving statement: Giving through the Berry Plastics Corporation Contributions Program.
Company EIN: 351813706

Berry Plastics Corporation Contributions Program
P.O. Box 959
Evansville, IN 47706-0959 (812) 424-2904
URL: http://www.berryplastics.com/catalog/content/corporate/community

Purpose and activities: Berry Plastics makes charitable contributions to nonprofit organizations involved with economically disadvantaged people. Support is given primarily in Evansville, Indiana.
Fields of interest: Environment, recycling; Housing/shelter; Salvation Army Economically disadvantaged.
Type of support: Employee volunteer services; In-kind gifts.
Geographic limitations: Giving primarily in Evansville, IN.

439
Bertelsmann, Inc.
1540 Broadway, Fl. 24
New York, NY 10036-4039 (212) 782-1000

Company URL: http://www.bertelsmann.com
Establishment information: Established in 1975.
Company type: Subsidiary of a foreign company
Business activities: Publishes books.
Business type (SIC): Book publishing and/or printing
Corporate officers: Hans-Marti Sorge, Chair.; Gerd Schulte-Hillen, Vice-Chair.; Wayne D. Taylor, Pres.; Greg Brown, V.P., Human Resources; Gordon Taylor, V.P., Finance; Mark Rosson, V.P., Sales
Board of directors: Hans-Marti Sorge, Chair.; Gerd Schulte-Hillen, Vice-Chair.
Subsidiaries: Bertelsmann Printing & Manufacturing Corp., Berryville, VA; Doubleday Book Club, Garden City, NY; Doubleday Direct, Garden City, NY; Military Book Club, Garden City, NY; Mystery Guild, Garden City, NY; Penguin Random House, New York, NY; Science Fiction Book Club, Garden City, NY
Giving statement: Giving through the Bertelsmann, Inc. Corporate Giving Program and the Bertelsmann Foundation U.S., Inc.

Bertelsmann Foundation U.S., Inc.
1745 Broadway
New York, NY 10019-4305

Establishment information: Established in 1996 in NY.
Donors: Bertelsmann, Inc.; Bertelsmann Stiftung; The Chase Manhattan Bank; BMG Music; Random House, Inc.
Contact: Melanie Fallon-Houska
Financial data (yr. ended 12/31/11): Assets, $16,015 (M); gifts received, $200,000; expenditures, $207,536; qualifying distributions, $195,995; giving activities include $105,000 for 59 grants (high: $10,000; low: $500).
Purpose and activities: The foundation supports organizations involved with higher education and awards college scholarships to New York City public high school students.
Fields of interest: Higher education.
Type of support: Employee-related scholarships; General/operating support; Scholarships—to individuals.
Geographic limitations: Giving limited to New York, NY.
Application information: Applications accepted. Unsolicited requests from organizations are not accepted. Application form required.
Initial approach: Letter
Deadline(s): Mar. 1 for scholarships
Officers and Directors:* Robert J. Sorrentino*, Pres.; Jacqueline Chasey*, V.P. and Secy.; Evelyn Pena, Treas.; Wolfgang Keochstadt.
EIN: 133777740

440
Bessemer Trust Company, N.A.
630 Fifth Ave.
New York, NY 10111 (212) 708-9100

Company URL: http://www.bessemertrust.com
Establishment information: Established in 1907.
Company type: Subsidiary of a private company
Business activities: Operates wealth management firm.
Business type (SIC): Security and commodity services
Corporate officers: John Allen Hilton, Jr., Co-Pres. and C.E.O.; George H. Wilcox, Co-Pres.
Offices: Los Angeles, San Francisco, CA; Wilmington, DE; Washington, DC; Miami, Naples, Palm Beach, FL; Chicago, IL; Boston, MA; Woodbridge, NJ; Dallas, TX
Giving statement: Giving through the Bessemer National Gift Fund.

The Bessemer National Gift Fund
c/o Bessemer Trust Co., N.A.
100 Woodbridge Center Dr.
Woodbridge, NJ 07095-1162 (732) 855-0800

Establishment information: Established in 1997 in NJ.
Financial data (yr. ended 12/31/11): Revenue, $9,302,045; assets, $36,854,619 (M); gifts received, $8,430,892; expenditures, $10,641,077; program services expenses, $10,318,347; giving activities include $10,318,347 for 131 grants (high: $1,505,000; low: $5,780).
Fields of interest: Higher education.
Application information: Applications not accepted. Contributes only to pre-selected organizations.
Trustees: J. Dinsmore Adams, Jr.; Molly Parkinson; Bessemer Trust Co., N.A.
EIN: 137111099

441
Best Best & Krieger LLP
3750 University Ave., Ste. 400
P.O. Box 1028
Riverside, CA 92501-3369 (951) 686-1450

Company URL: http://bbklaw.com/
Establishment information: Established in 1891.
Company type: Private company
Business activities: Operates law firm.
Business type (SIC): Legal services
Corporate officer: Eric L. Garner, Managing Partner
Offices: Indian Wells, Irvine, Los Angeles, Ontario, Riverside, Sacramento, San Diego, Walnut Creek, CA; Washington, DC
Giving statement: Giving through the Best Best & Krieger LLP Pro Bono Program.

Best Best & Krieger LLP Pro Bono Program
3750 University Ave., Ste. 400
P.O. Box 1028
Riverside, CA 92501-3369 (619) 525-1300
FAX: (619) 233-6118;
E-mail: jamie.zamoff@bbklaw.com; Additional: tel.: (951) 686-1450, fax: (951) 686-3083; URL: http://bbklaw.com/

Contact: Jamie Zamoff, C.O.O.
Fields of interest: Legal services.
Type of support: Pro bono services - legal.
Geographic limitations: Giving primarily in areas of company operations in Indian Wells, Irvine, Los Angeles, Riverside, Sacramento, San Diego, Ontario, and Walnut Creek, CA, and Washington, DC.
Application information: A Pro Bono Committee manages the program.

442
Best Buy Co., Inc.
7601 Penn Ave. S.
Richfield, MN 55423 (612) 291-1000
FAX: (612) 292-4001

Company URL: http://www.bby.com
Establishment information: Established in 1966.
Company type: Public company
Company ticker symbol and exchange: BBY/NYSE
International Securities Identification Number: US0865161014
Business activities: Operates consumer electronics, home office equipment, entertainment software, and appliance stores; provides Internet shopping services.
Business type (SIC): Consumer electronics and music stores; appliance stores/household; computer services

Financial profile for 2012: Number of employees, 165,000; assets, $16,787,000,000; sales volume, $45,085,000,000; pre-tax net income, -$186,000,000; expenses, $45,210,000,000; liabilities, $13,726,000,000
Fortune 1000 ranking: 2012—61st in revenues, 958th in profits, and 271st in assets
Forbes 2000 ranking: 2012—178th in sales, 1873rd in profits, and 1083rd in assets
Corporate officers: Hatim A. Tyabji, Chair.; Hubert Joly, Pres. and C.E.O.; Sharon L. McCollam, Exec. V.P., C.A.O., and C.F.O.; Keith J. Nelsen, Exec. V.P., Genl. Counsel, and Secy.; Susan S. Grafton, Sr. V.P., Cont., and C.A.O.; Christopher K.K. Gould, V.P. and Treas.
Board of directors: Hatim A. Tyabji, Chair.; Bradbury H. Anderson; Lisa M. Caputo; Russ Fradin; Ronald James; Hubert Joly; Sanjay Khosla; Allen U. Lenzmeier; Kathy J. Higgins Victor; Gerard Vittecoq
Subsidiary: Magnolia Hi-Fi, Inc., Kent, WA
International operations: Mauritius; United Kingdom
Giving statement: Giving through the Best Buy Co., Inc. Corporate Giving Program and the Best Buy Children's Foundation.
Company EIN: 410907483

Best Buy Co., Inc. Corporate Giving Program

7601 Penn Ave.
Minneapolis, MN 55423
URL: http://www.bestbuy-communityrelations.com/

Purpose and activities: As a complement to its foundation, Best Buy Co. also makes charitable contributions to nonprofit organizations directly. Support is given on a national basis in areas of company operations.
Fields of interest: Elementary/secondary education; Libraries (public); Youth development Youth.
Type of support: Donated products.
Geographic limitations: Giving on a national basis in areas of company operations.
Support limitations: No support for religious organizations not of direct benefit to the entire community. No grants to individuals, or for endowments, national ceremonies, memorials, conferences, testimonials or other similar events.
Publications: Application guidelines.
Application information: Applications accepted.
Initial approach: Contact local Best Buy facility for store donations
Final notification: 6 to 8 weeks for store donations

Best Buy Children's Foundation

7601 Penn Ave. S.
Richfield, MN 55423-3645
FAX: (612) 292-4001;
E-mail: bestbuygrants@easymatch.com; E-mail for Best Buy Scholarships: bestbuy@scholarshipamerica.org; URL: https://pr2-887076246.us-east-1.elb.amazonaws.com/community-relations/overview/

Establishment information: Established in 1994 in MN.
Donor: Best Buy Co., Inc.
Financial data (yr. ended 03/03/12): Assets, $617,468 (M); gifts received, $9,704,568; expenditures, $9,756,041; qualifying distributions, $7,868,790; giving activities include $7,528,432 for 440 grants (high: $1,200,000; low: $1,000).
Purpose and activities: The foundation supports programs designed to provide access to opportunities for youth through technology. Special emphasis is directed toward programs designed to empower teens to excel in school and develop 21st century skills.
Fields of interest: Elementary/secondary education; Education; Disasters, preparedness/services; Boys & girls clubs; Human services; United Ways and Federated Giving Programs; Engineering/technology; Leadership development Youth; Economically disadvantaged.
Programs:
@15: Through @15, Best Buy and the foundation supports teen empowerment through scholarships, contests, grants, and a website that promotes youth engagement.
Best Buy Scholarships: The foundation awards $1,000 scholarships to high school students in grades 9-12 who volunteer time to their communities, excel in academics, and participate in extracurricular activities. The program is administered by Scholarship America, Inc.
Best Buy Tech Centers: Through Best Buy Tech Centers, Best Buy and the Foundation create afterschool centers where teens explore the world of technology, including graphic design software, video cameras, digital music mixing tools, and online tutorials. Tech centers will open in partnership with the Intel Computer Clubhouse Networks in Chicago, Miami, San Antonio, and Minneapolis/St. Paul.
Community Grants Program: The foundation awards grants to nonprofit organizations located within 50 miles of a Best Buy store designed to empower teens to excel in school and develop 21st century skills through access to technology. Grants amounts will average $4,000 to $6,000 and will not exceed $10,000.
National Program: The foundation supports programs designed to serve a national audience; programs that have a national distribution plan and national partnerships in place; and programs designed to encourage teens to learn and play with the latest technologies so that youth will become fluent and develop skills and experiences to help them succeed in their careers, contribute to their communities, and lead outstanding lives.
Twin Cities Fund: The foundation supports programs designed to serve the Twin Cities audience; provide access to opportunities for teens through technology; and promote the vibrancy of the Twin Cities area. The program is open to nonprofit organizations in the Twin Cities, Minnesota area.
Type of support: Capital campaigns; Continuing support; Curriculum development; General/operating support; Program development; Scholarship funds.
Geographic limitations: Giving limited to areas of company operations, with emphasis on the Twin Cities, MN area.
Support limitations: No support for fraternal organizations or social clubs, units of government or quasi-governmental agencies, labor or lobbying organizations, for-profit organizations, religious organizations not of direct benefit to the entire community, or athletic teams. No grants to individuals or for political campaigns, general operating support, endowments, travel, national ceremonies, memorials, fundraising dinners, testimonials, conferences, or similar events, health, medical, therapeutic programs, or living subsidies, athletic events, or multi-year requests; no product donations.
Publications: Application guidelines; Grants list; Program policy statement.
Application information: Applications accepted. Capital requests are limited to the Twin Cities, MN, area organizations that have previously received funding from the foundation. Support is limited to 1 contribution per organization during any given year. Organizations receiving support are asked to provide a final report. Multi-year funding is not automatic. Application form required. Applicants should submit the following:
1) role played by volunteers
2) timetable for implementation and evaluation of project
3) how project will be sustained once grantmaker support is completed
4) principal source of support for project in the past
5) copy of IRS Determination Letter
6) geographic area to be served
7) copy of most recent annual report/audited financial statement/990
8) how project's results will be evaluated or measured
9) list of company employees involved with the organization
10) listing of board of directors, trustees, officers and other key people and their affiliations
11) detailed description of project and amount of funding requested
12) copy of current year's organizational budget and/or project budget
13) listing of additional sources and amount of support

Initial approach: Complete online eligibility quiz and application form
Copies of proposal: 1
Board meeting date(s): Annually
Deadline(s): June 1 to July 1 for Community Grants; Feb. 1, May 1, Aug. 1, and Nov. 1 for National Program and Twin Cities Fund; Feb. 15 for Best Buy Scholarships
Final notification: Sept. 15 for Community Grants; Mar. for scholarships
Officers and Trustees:* Susan S. Hoff*, Chair.; Shawn Score, Pres.; Todd Hartman, Secy.; Marc D. Gordon*, Treas.; Matt Furman; Stephen Gillett; Bill Hoffman; Patricia Mcphee; Raymond Slivia.
Number of staff: 1 full-time professional.
EIN: 411784382
Selected grants: The following grants are a representative sample of this grantmaker's funding activity:
$1,300,000 to Scholarship America, Saint Peter, MN, 2011. For National Partnership Grant.
$957,153 to Washington DC Martin Luther King, Jr. National Memorial Project Foundation, Washington, DC, 2011. For National Partnership Grant.
$400,000 to Mercy Corps, Portland, OR, 2011. For National Partnership Grant.
$365,000 to Youth Venture, Minneapolis, MN, 2011. For National Partnership Grant.
$250,000 to Boys and Girls Clubs of America, National Headquarters, Atlanta, GA, 2011. For National Partnership Grant.
$225,000 to Urban League, National, New York, NY, 2011. For National Partnership Grant.
$15,000 to MacPhail Center for Music, Minneapolis, MN, 2011. For Twin City Metro Hometown Grant.
$15,000 to Telavision.org, Lake Elmo, MN, 2011. For Twin City Metro Hometown Grant.
$10,000 to Big Brothers Big Sisters of Ventura County, Camarillo, CA, 2011. For Community Partnership Grant.
$8,000 to YMCA of Greater Grand Rapids, Grand Rapids, MI, 2011. For Community Partnership Grant.

443
Best Chairs, Inc.
1 Best Dr.
Ferdinand, IN 47532-9537 (812) 367-1761

Company URL: http://www.besthf.com
Establishment information: Established in 1962.
Company type: Private company
Business activities: Manufactures chairs.
Business type (SIC): Furniture/household
Financial profile for 2011: Number of employees, 1,000
Corporate officers: Clement M. Lange, Jr., Chair.; Glenn A. Lange, C.E.O.; Brian Lange, Pres.; Ron Swick, C.I.O.; Sheila M. Wendholt, V.P., Public Rels.
Board of director: Clement M. Lange, Jr., Chair.
Giving statement: Giving through the Best Chairs Foundation, Inc.

Best Chairs Foundation, Inc.
P.O. Box 158
Ferdinand, IN 47532-0158

Establishment information: Established in 2002 in IN.
Donor: Best Chairs, Inc.
Financial data (yr. ended 12/31/11): Assets, $616 (M); gifts received, $18,000; expenditures, $18,000; qualifying distributions, $18,000; giving activities include $18,000 for grants.
Purpose and activities: The foundation awards college scholarships to individuals.
Type of support: Scholarships—to individuals.
Application information: Applications not accepted. Unsolicited requests for funds not accepted.
Officers: Glenn A. Lange, Pres.; Joseph L. Lange, V.P.; Sheila M. Wendholt, Secy.; Steven M. Wahl, Treas.
EIN: 743061519

444
Bestway, Inc.
(also known as Bestway Rental, Inc.)
12400 Coit Rd, Ste. 950
Dallas, TX 75251 (214) 630-6655

Company URL: http://www.bestwayrto.com
Establishment information: Established in 1972.
Company type: Private company
Business activities: Owns and operates household good, electronic, appliance, and jewelry rental stores.
Business type (SIC): Equipment rental and leasing/ miscellaneous
Corporate officers: R. Brooks Reed, Chair.; David A. Kraemer, Pres. and C.E.O.; Beth A. Durrett, Secy. and C.F.O.
Board of director: R. Brooks Reed, Chair.
Giving statement: Giving through the Bestway Rentals Edwin Anderson Scholarship Foundation, Inc.
Company EIN: 810332743

Bestway Rentals Edwin Anderson Scholarship Foundation, Inc.
12400 Coit Rd., Ste. 950
Dallas, TX 75251

Establishment information: Established in 2001 in TX.
Donors: Bestway, Inc.; Bestway Rentals, Inc.
Financial data (yr. ended 12/31/10): Assets, $157 (M); gifts received, $3,000; expenditures, $3,000; qualifying distributions, $2,750; giving activities include $2,500 for 1 grant to an individual.
Purpose and activities: The foundation awards college scholarships to children of employees of Bestway.
Type of support: Employee-related scholarships.
Application information: Applications not accepted. Unsolicited requests for funds not accepted.
Officers and Directors:* David A. Kraemer*, Pres.; Beth A. Durrett*, Secy.
EIN: 752901174

445
Bethel Industries, Inc.
3423 John F. Kennedy Blvd.
Jersey City, NJ 07307-4107
(201) 656-8222

Establishment information: Established in 1992.
Company type: Private company
Business activities: Manufactures men's and boy's clothing.
Business type (SIC): Apparel—men's and boys' outerwear
Corporate officer: Sun Kim, Pres.
Giving statement: Giving through the CSK Charitable Foundation.

CSK Charitable Foundation
70 Anderson Ave.
Englewood Cliffs, NJ 07632-1502

Establishment information: Established in 2006 in NJ.
Donors: Young Kil Kim; Sun Chong Kim; Bethel Industries, Inc.
Financial data (yr. ended 12/31/11): Assets, $1,481,739 (M); expenditures, $87,572; qualifying distributions, $74,550; giving activities include $74,550 for grants.
Fields of interest: Human services; Religion.
Support limitations: No grants to individuals.
Application information: Applications not accepted. Unsolicited requests for funds not accepted.
Trustees: Sun Chong Kim; Young Kil Kim.
EIN: 205738876

446
Bethpage Federal Credit Union Inc.
899 S. Oyster Bay Rd.
Bethpage, NY 11714-1031 (516) 349-6700

Company URL: https://www.bethpagefcu.com
Establishment information: Established in 1941.
Company type: Private company
Business activities: Operates federal credit union.
Business type (SIC): Credit unions
Financial profile for 2012: Assets, $5,000,000,000
Corporate officers: Robert F. Kelly, Chair.; Don Balducci, Vice-Chair.; Kirk Kordeleski, Pres. and C.E.O.; Wayne N. Grosse, C.O.O.; Brian Clarke, Sr. V.P. and C.F.O.; Doug O'Neill, Sr. V.P., Human Resources
Board of directors: Robert F. Kelly, Chair.; Don Balducci, Vice-Chair.; John C. Komst; Jorge Martinez; Sam Piazzola; Richard B. Turan
Giving statement: Giving through the Bethpage Federal Credit Union Inc. Contributions Program.

Bethpage Federal Credit Union Inc. Contributions Program
899 S. Oyster Bay Rd.
Bethpage, NY 11714-1031 (516) 349-6700
E-mail: charitablegiving@bethpagefcu.com;
URL: https://www.bethpagefcu.com/community/heart-of-bethpage.aspx

447
Better Brands, Inc.
908 Jackson St.
Myrtle Beach, SC 29577 (843) 626-9402
FAX: (843) 839-6474

Company URL: http://www.budbeach.com
Establishment information: Established in 1959.
Company type: Private company
Business activities: Sells beer wholesale.
Business type (SIC): Beer, wine, and distilled beverages—wholesale
Corporate officers: Brenda Zilonka III, Pres.; Tony Hagerud, C.F.O. and Cont.
Giving statement: Giving through the Spadoni Foundation.

The Spadoni Foundation
1101 Norwalk st.
Greensboro, NC 27407-2022

Establishment information: Established in 1997 in SC.
Donor: Better Brands, Inc.
Contact: Brenda L. Spadoni-Urquhart, Dir.
Financial data (yr. ended 12/31/11): Assets, $2,044 (M); expenditures, $168; qualifying distributions, $0.
Purpose and activities: The foundation supports community foundations and organizations involved with higher education and other areas.
Fields of interest: Higher education; Foundations (community); General charitable giving.
Type of support: General/operating support.
Geographic limitations: Giving primarily in SC.
Support limitations: No grants to individuals.
Application information: Applications accepted. Application form required.
Initial approach: Proposal
Deadline(s): None
Directors: Julia S. Spadoni; Brenda L. Spadoni-Urquhart.
EIN: 562063503

448
Better World Books
11560 Great Oaks Way, Ste. 100
Alpharetta, GA 30022 (678) 527-1580

Company URL: http://www.betterworldbooks.com
Establishment information: Established in 2002.
Company type: Private company
Business activities: Operates online bookstore.
Business type (SIC): Shopping goods stores/ miscellaneous; nonstore retailers
Corporate officers: Andy Perlmutter, Pres. and C.E.O.; Doug Smith, Sr. V.P. and C.I.O.; Mike Miller, Sr. V.P., Opers.; John Ujda, V.P., Mktg.; Paul Sansone, V.P., Finance, Admin. and C.F.O.
Giving statement: Giving through the Better World Books Corporate Giving Program.

Better World Books Corporate Giving Program

1105 Lakewood Pkwy.
Alpharetta, GA 30009-7624 (678) 405-3855
URL: http://www.betterworldbooks.com/info.aspx?f=facts

Purpose and activities: Better World Books is a certified B Corporation that donates products and a percentage of profits to nonprofit organizations. Special emphasis is directed toward organizations involved with worldwide literacy initiatives.
Fields of interest: Education, reading.
Program:
Literacy and Education in Action Program (LEAP) Grants: The Literacy and Education in Action Program (LEAP) funds literacy and educational nonprofits and libraries for specific projects - putting the program on the front lines of the fight to reduce global poverty through education. Nonprofit groups or libraries write up what they will do with their grant (down to the dollar), and then Better World Books funds the projects expected to have the greatest impact.
Type of support: Donated products; General/operating support; Program development.

449
BetterWorld Telecom, LLC

11951 Freedom Dr., 13th Fl.
Reston, VA 20190 (703) 797-1750

Company URL: http://www.betterworldtelecom.com
Establishment information: Established in 2002.
Company type: Private company
Business activities: Operates voice and data telecommunications carrier.
Business type (SIC): Telephone communications
Corporate officers: James F. Kenefick, Chair.; Matt Bauer, Pres.
Board of director: James K. Kenefick, Chair.
Offices: Sacramento, San Diego, San Francisco, CA; McLean, VA; Seattle, WA
Giving statement: Giving through the BetterWorld Telecom, LLC Corporate Giving Program.

BetterWorld Telecom, LLC Corporate Giving Program

11951 Freedom Dr., 13th Fl.
Reston, VA 20190-5686 (866) 567-2273
URL: http://www.betterworldtelecom.com/donations/

Purpose and activities: BetterWorld Telecom is a certified B Corporation that donates 3 percent of revenues to nonprofit organizations. Special emphasis is directed toward organizations involved with children, education, fair trade, and the environment.
Fields of interest: Education; Environment; International economics/trade policy; Labor rights Children.
Type of support: Employee volunteer services; General/operating support.

450
Betts Cadillac, Inc.

(also known as Willis Cadillac, Inc.)
2121 N.W. 100th St.
Des Moines, IA 50325-5348
(515) 253-9600

Company URL: http://www.willisautocampus.com/
Establishment information: Established in 1947.
Company type: Private company
Business activities: Operates car dealership.
Business type (SIC): Motor vehicles—retail
Corporate officers: Richard M. Willis, Pres.; Ann M. Jeffries, Cont.
Giving statement: Giving through the Betts Foundation.

Betts Foundation

2121 N.W. 100th St.
Des Moines, IA 50325-5348

Establishment information: Established in 1964.
Donors: Betts Cadillac, Inc.; Betts Lexus.
Financial data (yr. ended 12/31/11): Assets, $346,412 (M); expenditures, $29,246; qualifying distributions, $26,150; giving activities include $26,150 for grants.
Purpose and activities: The foundation supports civic centers and organizations involved with secondary and higher education, cancer, and Protestantism.
Fields of interest: Education; Human services; Religion.
Type of support: General/operating support.
Geographic limitations: Giving primarily in Des Moines, IA.
Support limitations: No grants to individuals.
Application information: Applications not accepted. Unsolicited requests for funds not accepted.
Trustee: Charles H. Betts, Jr.
EIN: 426059607

451
Betts Industries, Inc.

1800 Pennsylvania Ave., W.
Warren, PA 16365-1932 (814) 723-1250

Company URL: http://www.bettsindustries.com
Establishment information: Established in 1901.
Company type: Private company
Business activities: Manufactures utility covers, dome covers, valves, and transportation tank safety lamps.
Business type (SIC): Metal products/fabricated; iron and steel foundries; lighting and wiring equipment/electric
Corporate officers: Richard T. Betts, Chair.; Thomas E. Mooney, V.P., Sales.
Board of director: Richard T. Betts, Chair.
Giving statement: Giving through the Betts Foundation.

Betts Foundation

1800 Pennsylvania Ave. W.
Warren, PA 16365-1932 (814) 723-1250

Establishment information: Established in 1957 in PA.
Donor: Betts Industries, Inc.
Financial data (yr. ended 12/31/11): Assets, $4,033,945 (M); gifts received, $200,000; expenditures, $252,867; qualifying distributions, $213,242; giving activities include $213,242 for grants.
Purpose and activities: The foundation supports organizations involved with theater, higher education, animal welfare, legal aid, human services, and community development.
Fields of interest: Performing arts, theater; Higher education; Animal welfare; Legal services; Boy scouts; YM/YWCAs & YM/YWHAs; Children/youth, services; Human services; Community/economic development.
Type of support: Building/renovation; Capital campaigns; Equipment; General/operating support; Scholarship funds.
Geographic limitations: Giving primarily in Warren County, PA.
Application information: Applications accepted. Application form not required.
Initial approach: Letter or telephone call
Deadline(s): None
Trustees: C.R. Betts; R.E. Betts; Richard T. Betts; T.E. Betts; M.D. Hedges.
EIN: 256035169

452
Beverage Distributors, Inc.

3800 King Ave.
Cleveland, OH 44114-3703 (216) 431-1600
FAX: (216) 472-1628

Company URL: http://www.beveragedist.com/
Establishment information: Established in 1933.
Company type: Private company
Business activities: Sells beer wholesale.
Business type (SIC): Beer, wine, and distilled beverages—wholesale
Corporate officers: James V. Conway, Chair. and C.E.O.; Mike Conway, Pres.; Michelle F. Bates, Cont.
Board of director: James V. Conway, Chair.
Giving statement: Giving through the Conway Family Foundation.

The Conway Family Foundation

(formerly The Beverage Distributors Inc. Foundation)
3800 King Ave.
Cleveland, OH 44114-3703

Establishment information: Established in 2001 in OH.
Donor: Beverage Distributors, Inc.
Financial data (yr. ended 12/31/11): Assets, $209,176 (M); gifts received, $7,318; expenditures, $103,212; qualifying distributions, $100,465; giving activities include $100,465 for grants.
Purpose and activities: The foundation supports health clinics and organizations involved with arts and culture, breast cancer, hunger, youth development, human services, Catholicism, and philanthropy.
Fields of interest: Arts; Health care, clinics/centers; Breast cancer; Food services; Youth development; Human services; United Ways and Federated Giving Programs; Philanthropy/voluntarism; Catholic agencies & churches.
Type of support: General/operating support.
Application information: Applications not accepted. Unsolicited requests for funds not accepted.
Officers and Trustees:* James V. Conway*, Pres.; Patrick M. Flanagan*, Secy.; Michelle Brown*, Treas.
EIN: 341964921
Selected grants: The following grants are a representative sample of this grantmaker's funding activity:

$5,000 to Georgetown University, Washington, DC, 2010.

453
Beverage Distributors, Inc.

200 Ferry St.
Clarksburg, WV 26301-2831
(304) 624-4261

Company URL: http://beveragewv.com/index.html
Establishment information: Established in 1950.
Company type: Private company
Business activities: Sells beer, wine, and distilled beverages on a wholesale basis.
Business type (SIC): Beer, wine, and distilled beverages—wholesale
Corporate officer: Vincent D'Annunzio, Pres.
Giving statement: Giving through the D'Annunzio Foundation, Inc.

D'Annunzio Foundation, Inc.

P.O. Box 866
Clarksburg, WV 26302-0866 (304) 624-9720
Application address: 200 Ferry St., Clarksburg, WV 26301, tel.: (304) 624-9720

Establishment information: Established in 1979 in WV.
Donors: Beverage Distributors, Inc.; Vincent D'Annunzio; David D'Annunzio; Michael D'Annunzio.
Contact: Vincent F. D'Annunzio, Dir.
Financial data (yr. ended 12/31/11): Assets, $299,782 (M); gifts received, $81,200; expenditures, $119,115; qualifying distributions, $119,115; giving activities include $114,000 for 29 grants (high: $21,000; low: $500).
Fields of interest: Education; Health care; Human services.
Application information: Applications accepted. Application form not required.
Initial approach: Proposal
Deadline(s): None
Directors: David D'Annunzio; Michael D'Annunzio; Vincent F. D'Annunzio.
EIN: 550589828

454
Beyer Crushed Rock Co. Inc.

4600 State Rte. Y
Cleveland, MO 64734-8216
(816) 618-7625

Establishment information: Established in 1989.
Company type: Subsidiary of a private company
Business activities: Produces aggregate.
Business type (SIC): Mining/crushed and broken stone
Corporate officer: Joseph T. Fahey, Pres.
Giving statement: Giving through the Joseph M. Fahey and Mary Elizabeth Rogers Fahey Foundation, Inc.

The Joseph M. Fahey and Mary Elizabeth Rogers Fahey Foundation, Inc.

408 High Grove Dr.
Grandview, MO 64030-2338

Establishment information: Established in 1986 in MO.
Donors: J.M. Fahey Construction Co.; Beyer Crushed Rock Co.
Financial data (yr. ended 12/31/11): Assets, $868,323 (M); gifts received, $155,000; expenditures, $87,876; qualifying distributions, $82,600; giving activities include $82,600 for grants.
Purpose and activities: The foundation supports organizations involved with education, human services, and the disabled.
Fields of interest: Education; Human services; Religion.
Type of support: General/operating support.
Geographic limitations: Giving limited to Kansas City, MO.
Support limitations: No grants to individuals.
Application information: Applications not accepted. Contributes only to pre-selected organizations.
Officers: Joseph T. Fahey, Pres. and Treas.; Kevin F. Fahey, Secy.
Directors: Bridget K. Fahey; Mark C. Owens; Mary E. Stone.
EIN: 431418114

455
BHP Billiton Petroleum (Americas), Inc

(formerly BHP Petroleum (Americas) Inc.)
1360 Post Oak Blvd., Ste. 150
Houston, TX 77056-3030 (713) 961-8500

Company URL: http://www.bhpbilliton.com/bb/aboutUs/companyOverview.jsp
Establishment information: Established in 1963.
Company type: Subsidiary of a foreign company
Business activities: Conducts crude petroleum exploration activities.
Business type (SIC): Extraction/oil and gas
Corporate officers: Jacques Nasser, Chair.; J. Michael Yeager, C.E.O.; Ivan Arriagada, Pres.; David D. Powell, C.F.O.; Jeffrey L. Sahlberg, V.P. and Treas; David J. Nelson, V.P., Human Resources; Jamie Dykes, Genl. Counsel
Board of directors: Jacques Nasser, Chair.; Malcolm Broomhead; John Buchanan; Carlos Cordeiro; David Crawford; Pat Davies; Carolyn Hewson; Marius Kloppers; Lindsay Maxsted; Wayne Murdy; Keith Rumble; John Schubert; Baroness Shriti Vadera
Giving statement: Giving through the BHP Billiton Petroleum (Americas) Inc. Corporate Giving Program.

BHP Billiton Petroleum (Americas) Inc. Corporate Giving Program

(formerly BHP Petroleum (Americas) Inc. Corporate Giving Program)
BHP Tower
1360 Post Oak Blvd., Ste. 500
Houston, TX 77056-3020
FAX: (713) 961-8680

Purpose and activities: BHP Billiton Petroleum makes charitable contributions to nonprofit organizations involved with arts and culture, education, the environment, health, and youth development. Support is given primarily in areas of company operations.
Fields of interest: Arts; Education; Environment; Health care; Youth development.
Type of support: Employee volunteer services; General/operating support.
Geographic limitations: Giving primarily in areas of company operations.
Application information: Application form not required.
Initial approach: Proposal to headquarters

457
Bickel & Brewer

1717 Main St., Ste. 4800
Dallas, TX 75201 (214) 653-4000

Company URL: http://www.bickelbrewer.com
Establishment information: Established in 1984.
Company type: Private company
Business activities: Provides complex litigation and dispute resolution services.
Business type (SIC): Legal services
Corporate officers: John W. Bickel II, Partner; William A. Brewer III, Partner
Office: New York, NY
Giving statement: Giving through the Bickel & Brewer Foundation.

Bickel & Brewer Foundation

(formerly Bickel & Brewer Legal Foundation)
4800 Comerica Bank Tower
1717 Main Street
Dallas, TX 75201 (214) 653-4026
E-mail: aburnett@bickelbrewer.com; URL: http://www.bickelbrewer.com/#/thefoundation

Establishment information: Established in 1995 in TX.
Donor: Bickel & Brewer.
Contact: Andrea Burnett, Mgr. of Media & Community Rels.
Financial data (yr. ended 12/31/11): Assets, $3,878 (M); gifts received, $2,118,340; expenditures, $2,333,303; qualifying distributions, $878,250; giving activities include $878,250 for grants.
Purpose and activities: The foundation supports organizations involved with arts and culture, health, community reinvestment, and civic affairs. Special emphasis is directed toward programs designed to promote law and education.
Fields of interest: Performing arts; Arts; Elementary/secondary education; Higher education; Education; Health care; Legal services; Children/youth, services; Human services; Civil/human rights; Community/economic development; Public policy, research; Public affairs.
Programs:
Future Leaders Program: Through the Future Leaders Program, the foundation provides enhanced academic resources to 5th - 12th grade students from economically disadvantaged communities, particularly greater South and West Dallas, to encourage students to graduate from high school, college, and take their place as leaders in the community. The program focuses on academic enrichment, cultural awareness, and leadership and personal development, and includes enriched curriculum, student trips, and guest speakers.
Latino Institute for Human Rights: Through the Latino Institute for Human Rights, Bickel & Becker and the NYU School of Law recruits and trains lawyers committed to advancing the interests of Latino communities and promoting human rights. The Institute offers students a scholarship, NYU legal education, vocational training, and the opportunity to participate in a wide variety of community forums, workshops, and conferences. Participants who graduate from law school or complete a judicial clerkship work two years at an organization that serves the social and legal needs of the Latino community.

National Public Policy Forum: The foundation in partnership with Bickel & Brewer and New York University sponsors an international contest that gives teams of high school students the opportunity to participate in written and oral debates on issues of public policy. The top 32 teams receives a cash award and the grand champion receives $5,000 for the school, $5,000 for the participating team, and the Bickel & Brewer Cup.
Type of support: Annual campaigns; General/operating support; Program development.
Geographic limitations: Giving primarily in New York, NY, and TX, with some emphasis on the Dallas area.
Support limitations: No grants to individuals.
Publications: Application guidelines.
Application information: Applications accepted. Application form required. Applicants should submit the following:
1) detailed description of project and amount of funding requested
2) brief history of organization and description of its mission
3) geographic area to be served
4) population served
5) copy of current year's organizational budget and/or project budget
6) listing of additional sources and amount of support

Initial approach: Download application form and mail to foundation
Copies of proposal: 1
Deadline(s): None
Officers: William A. Brewer III, Chair.; John W. Bickel II, Pres.; James S. Renard, Secy.-Treas.; Kat Sewers, Exec. Dir.
EIN: 752625364
Selected grants: The following grants are a representative sample of this grantmaker's funding activity:
$25,000 to Dallas Symphony Orchestra, Dallas, TX, 2009.
$10,000 to Dallas Theater Center, Dallas, TX, 2009.
$5,000 to Episcopal School of Dallas, Dallas, TX, 2009.
$1,000 to American Jewish Committee, New York, NY, 2009.

458
Bicon, Inc.

501 Arborway
Boston, MA 02130-3663 (617) 524-4443
FAX: (6170 524-0096

Company URL: http://www.bicon.com
Establishment information: Established in 1985.
Company type: Private company
Business activities: Manufactures dental implants.
Business type (SIC): Medical instruments and supplies
Corporate officers: Vincent J. Morgan, Pres.; Craig Morgan, C.F.O.
Board of director: Vincent J. Morgan
Giving statement: Giving through the Southanson Trust.

Southanson Trust

501 Arborway
Jamaica Plain, MA 02130

Establishment information: Established in 2006 in MA.
Donors: Vincent J. Morgan; Bicon, LLC.
Contact: Craig A. Morgan, Tr.
Financial data (yr. ended 11/30/11): Assets, $135,366 (M); expenditures, $11,516; qualifying distributions, $10,000; giving activities include $10,000 for 1 grant.
Fields of interest: Education.
Geographic limitations: Giving primarily in MA.
Application information: Applications accepted. Application form required. Applicants should submit the following:
1) detailed description of project and amount of funding requested

Initial approach: Proposal
Deadline(s): None
Trustees: Christina E. Morgan; Craig A. Morgan; Vincent J. Morgan; Vincent J. Morgan, Jr.; Jennifer M. Peterson.
EIN: 776256995

459
Bierlein Companies, Inc.

2000 Bay City Rd.
Midland, MI 48642-6932 (989) 496-0066
FAX: (989) 496-0144

Company URL: http://www.bierlein.com
Establishment information: Established in 1957.
Company type: Private company
Business activities: Provides demolition, rigging and dismantling, asbestos abatement, and environmental services.
Business type (SIC): Contractors/miscellaneous special trade; oil and gas field services; sanitary services
Financial profile for 2011: Number of employees, 300
Corporate officers: Michael D. Bierlein, Pres. and C.E.O.; Patrick A. Wurtzel, V.P., Opers.; D.J. DiBlasi, V.P., Sales and Mktg.; John W. Fleming, C.P.A., Cont.
Giving statement: Giving through the Bierlein Companies Foundation.
Company EIN: 381940783

Bierlein Companies Foundation

2000 Bay City Rd.
Midland, MI 48642-6932

Establishment information: Established in 1985 in MI.
Donors: Bierlein Demolition Contractors, Inc.; Bierlein Environmental Services, Inc.; Bierlein Cos., Inc.; Bierlein Services, Inc.
Contact: Michael D. Bierlein, Pres.; Ken LeCureux, Secy.
Financial data (yr. ended 12/31/11): Assets, $886,776 (M); gifts received, $350,000; expenditures, $123,080; qualifying distributions, $123,080; giving activities include $123,080 for grants.
Purpose and activities: The foundation supports organizations involved with arts and culture, education, health, children and youth, human services, community development, and Christianity.
Fields of interest: Arts; Higher education; Education; Health care; Children/youth, services; Human services; Community/economic development; United Ways and Federated Giving Programs; Christian agencies & churches.
Type of support: Annual campaigns; Capital campaigns; General/operating support.
Geographic limitations: Giving primarily in the Saginaw Valley, MI.
Support limitations: No support for political organizations. No grants to individuals.
Application information: Applications not accepted. Contributes only to pre-selected organizations.
Officers and Directors:* Michael D. Bierlein*, Pres.; Thomas L. Bierlein*, V.P.; Kenneth W. LeCureux*, Secy.-Treas.
EIN: 382615341

460
Big Lots, Inc.

300 Phillipi Rd.
P.O. Box 28512
Columbus, OH 43228-5311
(614) 278-6800
FAX: (614) 278-6676

Company URL: http://www.biglots.com
Establishment information: Established in 1967.
Company type: Public company
Company ticker symbol and exchange: BIG/NYSE
International Securities Identification Number: US0893021032
Business activities: Operates broadline closeout retail company.
Business type (SIC): Variety stores
Financial profile for 2013: Number of employees, 37,400; assets, $1,753,630,000; sales volume, $5,400,120,000; pre-tax net income, $294,310,000; expenses, $5,101,660,000; liabilities, $995,480,000
Fortune 1000 ranking: 2012—466th in revenues, 612th in profits, and 884th in assets
Corporate officers: Philip E. Mallott, Chair.; David J. Campisi, Pres. and C.E.O.; Lisa Bachmann, Exec. V.P., C.O.O., and C.I.O.; Charles W. Haubiel, Exec. V.P., C.A.O., Genl. Counsel, and Corp. Secy.; Timothy A. Johnson, Sr. V.P. and C.F.O.; Robert Claxton, Sr. V.P., Mktg.; Michael A. Schlonsky, Sr. V.P., Human Resources; Paul Schroeder, V.P. and Cont.
Board of directors: Philip E. Mallott, Chair.; Jeffrey P. Berger; David J. Campisi; James R. Chambers; Peter J. Hayes; Brenda J. Lauderback; Russell Solt; James R. Tener; Dennis B. Tishkoff
Giving statement: Giving through the Big Lots, Inc. Contributions Program.
Company EIN: 061119097

Big Lots, Inc. Contributions Program

300 Phillipi Rd.
Columbus, OH 43228-5311 (614) 278-6800
URL: http://www.biglots.com/corporate/community-relations

Purpose and activities: Big Lots makes charitable contributions to nonprofit organizations involved with K-12 education, family services, and children. Support is given primarily in areas of company operations.
Fields of interest: Elementary/secondary education; Food services; Children, services; Family services; Human services; General charitable giving.
Type of support: Cause-related marketing; Employee volunteer services; General/operating support; In-kind gifts.
Geographic limitations: Giving primarily in areas of company operations; giving also to national organizations.

461
Big Y Foods, Inc.
2145 Roosevelt Ave.
P.O. Box 7840
Springfield, MA 01102-7840
(413) 784-0600
FAX: (413) 731-0087

Company URL: http://www.bigy.com
Establishment information: Established in 1936.
Company type: Private company
Business activities: Operates supermarkets.
Business type (SIC): Groceries—retail
Corporate officers: Donald H. D'Amour, Chair. and C.E.O.; Charles L. D'Amour, Pres. and C.O.O.; William D. White, Co-C.F.O.; Herb Dotterer, Sr. V.P. and C.F.O.; Michael S. Gold, V.P. and Genl. Counsel; Kevin Regan, V.P., Finance; Michael D'Amour, V.P., Sales; Claire D'Amour-Daley, V.P., Corp. Comms.; Libby Pidgeon, V.P., Human Resources
Board of director: Donald H. D'Amour, Chair.
Giving statement: Giving through the Big Y Foods, Inc. Corporate Giving Program, the Big Y 50th Anniversary Employee Commemorative Scholarship Foundation, the Paul H. D'Amour Fellowship Foundation, and the Gerald and Paul D'Amour Founders Scholarship for Academic Excellence.

Big Y Foods, Inc. Corporate Giving Program
c/o Mrs. Boggis
2145 Roosevelt Ave.
Springfield, MA 01104-1650 (413) 504-4000
URL: http://www.bigy.com/Community#.T2o3mxHy8kR

Purpose and activities: As a complement to its foundations, Big Y Foods also makes charitable donations to nonprofit organizations directly. Support is given primarily in areas of company operations in Connecticut and Massachusetts.
Fields of interest: Education; Health organizations, fund raising/fund distribution; Breast cancer; Food services.
Type of support: Donated products; Employee volunteer services; In-kind gifts; Scholarships—to individuals.
Geographic limitations: Giving primarily in areas of company operations in CT and MA.

Big Y 50th Anniversary Employee Commemorative Scholarship Foundation
2145 Roosevelt Ave.
Springfield, MA 01104-1650 (413) 504-4218

Establishment information: Established in 1987 in MA.
Donors: Big Y Foods, Inc.; Cooley, Shrair, Labovitz.
Financial data (yr. ended 06/30/11): Assets, $73,810 (M); gifts received, $6,050; expenditures, $6,053; qualifying distributions, $6,050; giving activities include $6,050 for 2 grants (high: $6,000; low: $50).
Purpose and activities: The foundation awards college scholarships to employees and the children of employees of Big Y Foods, Inc.
Fields of interest: Higher education.
Type of support: Employee-related scholarships.
Geographic limitations: Giving limited to areas of company operations in CT and MA.
Application information: Applications accepted. Application form required.
Initial approach: Letter
Deadline(s): Feb. 1
Trustees: Charles L. D'Amour; Donald H. D'Amour.
EIN: 042909526

The Paul H. D'Amour Fellowship Foundation
2145 Roosevelt Ave.
Springfield, MA 01104-1650 (413) 504-4218

Donor: Big Y Foods, Inc.
Financial data (yr. ended 07/01/12): Assets, $146,159 (M); gifts received, $10,070; expenditures, $10,071; qualifying distributions, $10,000; giving activities include $10,000 for 5 grants to individuals (high: $2,000; low: $2,000).
Purpose and activities: The foundation awards college scholarships to children of employees of Big Y Foods.
Type of support: Employee-related scholarships.
Geographic limitations: Giving limited to CT and central and western MA.
Support limitations: No grants to individuals (except for employee-related scholarships).
Application information: Applications accepted. Application form required.
Submit transcripts of students' grades, college board scores, and 3 letters of recommendation.
Initial approach: Letter
Deadline(s): Feb. 1st
Trustees: Charles L. D'Amour; Donald H. D'Amour.
EIN: 222626366

The Gerald and Paul D'Amour Founders Scholarship for Academic Excellence
P.O. Box 7840
2145 Roosevelt Ave.
Springfield, MA 01102-7840 (413) 504-4218
URL: http://www.bigy.com/Community/Scholarships
Application address: Scholarship Comm., Big Y Foods Inc., P.O. Box 7840, Springfield, MA 01102-7840

Establishment information: Established in 1994 in MA.
Donor: Big Y Foods, Inc.
Financial data (yr. ended 06/26/11): Assets, $1,563,566 (M); gifts received, $237,123; expenditures, $209,244; qualifying distributions, $208,500; giving activities include $208,500 for 289 grants to individuals (high: $1,000; low: $500).
Purpose and activities: The foundation awards college scholarships to students residing in Big Y Foods, Inc. marketing areas.
Fields of interest: Higher education.
Type of support: Employee-related scholarships; Scholarships—to individuals.
Geographic limitations: Giving limited to areas of company operations in CT and central and western MA.
Publications: Application guidelines; Grants list.
Application information: Applications accepted. Scholarships are based on academic achievement. Application form required.
Requests for scholarships should include transcripts, college board scores, and 3 letters of recommendation.
Initial approach: Download application and mail to application address
Deadline(s): Feb. 1
Trustees: Charles L. D'Amour; Donald H. D'Amour.
EIN: 223305742

462
R. C. Bigelow Inc.
201 Black Rock Tpke.
Fairfield, CT 06825-5504 (203) 334-1212
FAX: (203) 334-5114

Company URL: http://www.bigelowtea.com
Establishment information: Established in 1945.
Company type: Private company
Business activities: Produces specialty teas.
Business type (SIC): Miscellaneous prepared foods
Financial profile for 2010: Number of employees, 350
Corporate officers: David C. Bigelow, Jr., Co-Chair. and Co-C.E.O.; Eunice J. Bigelow, Co-Chair. and Co-C.E.O.; Robert M. Crawford, Co-C.E.O.; Cynthia R. Bigelow, Pres.; Donald Janezic, C.F.O.
Board of directors: David C. Bigelow, Jr., Co-Chair.; Eunice Bigelow, Co-Chair.
Giving statement: Giving through the R. C. Bigelow Inc. Corporate Giving Program.

R. C. Bigelow Inc. Corporate Giving Program
201 Black Rock Tpke.
Fairfield, CT 06825-5504 (888) 244-3569
URL: http://www.bigelowtea.com/our-story/mission-statement.aspx

Purpose and activities: Bigelow makes charitable contributions to nonprofit organizations involved with community fundraising, volunteer home building, school mentoring programs, book drives, and business lecture programs for public schools. Support is given primarily in areas of company operations in Fairfield, Connecticut, and to national organizations.
Fields of interest: Education, reading; Education; Housing/shelter, volunteer services; Housing/shelter, repairs; Youth development, volunteer services; Human services, fund raising/fund distribution; Human services, public education Economically disadvantaged.
Type of support: Annual campaigns; Building/renovation; Continuing support; Employee volunteer services.
Geographic limitations: Giving primarily in areas of company operations in Fairfield, CT, and to national organizations.

456
BI-LO, LLC
(formerly BI-LO, Inc.)
208 BI-LO Blvd.
P.O. Box 99
Greenville, SC 29607 (864) 213-2500
FAX: (864) 297-5870

Company URL: http://www.bi-lo.com
Establishment information: Established in 1961.
Company type: Subsidiary of a private company
Business activities: Operates grocery stores.
Business type (SIC): Groceries—retail
Financial profile for 2010: Number of employees, 15,000
Corporate officers: R. Randall Onstead, Jr., Chair.; Michael D. Byars, Pres. and C.E.O.; Brian P. Carney, Exec. V.P. and C.F.O.
Board of director: R. Randall Onstead, Jr., Chair.
Giving statement: Giving through the BI-LO, LLC Corporate Giving Program and the BI-LO Charities, Inc.

BI-LO Charities, Inc.
P.O. Box 5000
Mauldin, SC 29662-5000 (864) 234-1780

Establishment information: Established in 1998 in SC.
Financial data (yr. ended 12/31/11): Revenue, $3,297,640; assets, $1,257,378 (M); gifts received, $3,931,688; expenditures, $3,468,637; giving activities include $3,231,527 for grants.
Purpose and activities: The organization raises funds for donation to recognized charities based in communities where BI-LO grocery stores are located.
Fields of interest: Human services.
Geographic limitations: Giving limited to SC.
Officers and Directors:* Brian Hotarek*, Pres.; Jim Smits*, V.P.; Dwane Bryant*, Secy.; Phil Barker*, Treas.; Lynn Faust; Joyce Smart; and 2 additional directors.
EIN: 571063898

463
Bingham McCutchen LLP
1 Federal St.
Boston, MA 02110-1726 (617) 951-8000

Company URL: http://www.bingham.com
Company type: Private company
Business activities: Operates law firm.
Business type (SIC): Legal services
Corporate officers: William A. Bachman, C.O.O.; Carol Sabochick, C.F.O.; Robert Meadows, C.I.O.
Offices: Costa Mesa, East Palo Alto, Los Angeles, San Francisco, Santa Monica, CA; Hartford, CT; Washington, DC; Portland, ME; Boston, MA; New York, NY
International operations: Germany; Hong Kong; Japan; United Kingdom
Giving statement: Giving through the Bingham McCutchen LLP Pro Bono Program.

Bingham McCutchen LLP Pro Bono Program
1 Federal St.
Boston, MA 02110-1726 (202) 373-6743
E-mail: rachel.strong@bingham.com; URL: http://www.bingham.com/Explore-Bingham

Contact: Rachel Strong, Pro Bono Counsel
Fields of interest: Legal services.
Type of support: Pro bono services - legal.
Geographic limitations: Giving primarily in areas of company operations in Costa Mesa, East Palo Alto, Los Angeles, San Francisco, and Santa Monica, CA, Hartford, CT, Washington, DC, Boston, MA, Portland, ME, New York, NY, and in Germany, Hong Kong, Japan, United Kingdom.
Application information: A Pro Bono Committee manages the program.

464
Binswanger Corporation
(also known as Binswanger Management Corporation)
2 Logan Sq., Ste. 400
Philadelphia, PA 19103 (215) 448-6000
FAX: (215) 448-6238

Company URL: http://www.binswanger.com/
Establishment information: Established in 1931.
Company type: Private company
Business activities: Operates commercial real estate agency.
Business type (SIC): Real estate agents and managers
Corporate officers: Frank G. Binswanger, Jr., Co-Chair.; John K. Binswanger, Co-Chair.; Clive G. Mendelow, Vice-Chair. and Co-C.O.O.; John J. Dues, Vice-Chair.; David R. Binswanger, Pres. and C.E.O.; Johnny Brooks, Co-C.O.O.; Beth Ganss, C.F.O.; Daniel F. Cullen, V.P. and Genl. Counsel
Board of directors: Frank G. Binswanger, Jr., Co-Chair.; John K. Binswanger, Co-Chair.; John J. Dues, Vice-Chair.; Clive Mendelow, Vice-Chair.
Plants: Englewood, CO; Chicago, IL; Charlotte, NC
Giving statement: Giving through the Binswanger Foundation.

Binswanger Foundation
2 Logan Sq., 4th Fl.
Philadelphia, PA 19103-2759 (215) 448-6000

Establishment information: Established in 1942.
Donors: John K. Binswanger; Elizabeth Binswanger; Binswanger Corp.; Frank G. Binswanger, Jr.
Contact: John K. Binswanger, Pres.
Financial data (yr. ended 12/31/11): Assets, $4,553 (M); expenditures, $7,000; qualifying distributions, $7,000; giving activities include $7,000 for grants.
Purpose and activities: The foundation supports hospitals and organizations involved with higher education and parks and playgrounds.
Fields of interest: Arts; Youth development.
Geographic limitations: Giving primarily in Philadelphia, PA.
Support limitations: No grants to individuals.
Application information: Applications accepted. Application form not required. Applicants should submit the following:
1) detailed description of project and amount of funding requested
Initial approach: Proposal
Deadline(s): None
Officers: Frank G. Binswanger, Jr., Chair.; Robert B. Binswanger, Vice-Chair.; John K. Binswanger, Pres.; Frank G. Binswanger III, Secy.; David R. Binswanger, Treas.
EIN: 236296506

465
Biogen Idec Inc.
(formerly IDEC Pharmaceuticals Corporation)
133 Boston Post Rd.
Weston, MA 02493 (781) 464-2000
FAX: (617) 679-2617

Company URL: http://www.biogenidec.com
Establishment information: Established in 1978.
Company type: Public company
Company ticker symbol and exchange: BIIB/NASDAQ
International Securities Identification Number: US09062X1037
Business activities: Develops, manufactures, and markets human health care therapies.
Business type (SIC): Drugs
Financial profile for 2012: Number of employees, 5,950; assets, $10,130,120,000; sales volume, $5,516,460,000; pre-tax net income, $1,855,110,000; expenses, $3,666,110,000; liabilities, $3,168,590,000
Fortune 1000 ranking: 2012—454th in revenues, 149th in profits, and 387th in assets
Forbes 2000 ranking: 2012—1337th in sales, 436th in profits, and 1470th in assets
Corporate officers: William D. Young, Chair.; George A. Scangos, Ph.D, C.E.O.; Paul J. Clancy, Exec. V.P., Finance and C.F.O.; Susan H. Alexander, Esq., Exec. V.P., Genl. Counsel, and Corp. Secy.; Kenneth DiPietro, Exec. V.P., Human Resources; Ray Pawlicki, Sr. V.P. and C.I.O.
Board of directors: William D. Young, Chair.; Alexander J. Denner, Ph.D.; Caroline D. Dorsa; Nancy L. Leaming; Richard C. Mulligan, Ph.D.; Robert W. Pangia; Stelios Papadopoulos, Ph.D.; Brian S. Posner; Eric K. Rowinsky, M.D.; George A. Scangos, Ph.D.; Lynn Schenk; Stephen A. Sherwin, M.D.
International operations: Argentina; Australia; Austria; Belgium; Brazil; Czech Republic; Finland; France; Germany; India; Ireland; Italy; Japan; Mexico; Netherlands; New Zealand; Norway; Portugal; Slovakia; Slovenia; Spain; Sweden; Switzerland; United Kingdom
Historic mergers: Biogen, Inc. (November 12, 2003)
Giving statement: Giving through the Biogen Idec Inc. Corporate Giving Program and the Biogen Idec Foundation Inc.
Company EIN: 330112644

Biogen Idec Inc. Corporate Giving Program
(formerly Biogen, Inc. Corporate Giving Program)
14 Cambridge Ctr.
Cambridge, MA 02142-1453 (617) 679-2000
Additional tel.: (617) 679-2851; URL: http://www.biogenidec.com/community.aspx?ID=11586

Contact: Kathryn R. Bloom
Purpose and activities: As a complement to its foundation, Biogen Idec also makes charitable contributions to nonprofit organizations directly. Support is given primarily in areas of company operations.
Fields of interest: Education; Community/economic development.
Program:
Science Education: Biogen Idec supports programs designed to encourage young people to pursue careers in science and engineering.
Type of support: Employee volunteer services; General/operating support.
Geographic limitations: Giving primarily in Oceanside and San Diego, CA, Cambridge and the greater Boston, MA, area, and Durham and Raleigh, NC.
Support limitations: No support for religious or political organizations. No grants to individuals.
Application information: Applications accepted. The Public Affairs Department handles giving. Proposals should be no longer than 3 pages. Telephone calls are not encouraged. Application form not required. Proposals should include a description of past involvement by Biogen Idec with the organization.
Initial approach: Proposal to headquarters
Copies of proposal: 2
Deadline(s): None
Final notification: Following review
Number of staff: 1 full-time professional.

Biogen Idec Foundation Inc.
(formerly Biogen Foundation, Inc.)
c/o Biogen Idec Inc.
133 Boston Post Rd.
Weston, MA 02493-2525
FAX: (617) 679-3223;
E-mail: foundation@biogenidec.com; URL: http://www.biogenidec.com/biogen_idec_foundation.aspx?ID=9515

Establishment information: Established in 2002 in MA.
Donor: Biogen, Inc.
Financial data (yr. ended 12/31/10): Assets, $24,013,859 (M); expenditures, $1,649,779; qualifying distributions, $1,550,158; giving activities include $1,426,939 for 243 grants (high: $200,000; low: $15).
Purpose and activities: The foundation supports programs designed to improve quality of life for communities in which Biogen operates. Special emphasis is directed toward programs designed to promote science literacy and encourage young people to consider careers in science.
Fields of interest: Museums (science/technology); Arts; Middle schools/education; Secondary school/education; Higher education; Education; Disasters, preparedness/services; Human services; Community/economic development; Science Youth.
Programs:
Academic Matching Gift Program: The foundation matches contributions made by employees and directors of Biogen to institutions of higher education on a one-for-one basis from $15 to $5,000 per employee, per institution, per year.
Enhancing Community-Based Science: The foundation awards micro-grants to schools and nonprofits to extend their work in science education and provide the extra support needed to make science engaging. Grants range from $250 to $2,500.
Transformational Grants: The foundation supports science programs designed to serve middle and high school students, with an emphasis on those from diverse and underserved backgrounds.
Type of support: Annual campaigns; Continuing support; Employee matching gifts; General/operating support; Program development; Sponsorships.
Geographic limitations: Giving primarily in areas of company operations in San Diego, CA, Cambridge and greater Boston, MA, and Durham and Raleigh, NC.
Support limitations: No support for discriminatory, religious, or political organizations, or government agencies. No grants to individuals, or for political candidates, special events, fundraising, or capital campaigns.
Publications: Application guidelines.
Application information: Applications accepted. Application form not required. Applicants should submit the following:
1) copy of IRS Determination Letter
2) detailed description of project and amount of funding requested
Initial approach: Complete online eligibility quiz and application
Board meeting date(s): Quarterly
Deadline(s): None
Officers and Directors:* Tony Kingsley*, Chair.; Susan Alexander, Secy.; Mike Dambach, Treas.; Kara DiGiacomo, Exec. Dir.; Paul Clancy; Jo Ann Taormina; Jo Viney.
Number of staff: 1 full-time professional.
EIN: 161636254
Selected grants: The following grants are a representative sample of this grantmaker's funding activity:
$33,333 to American Cancer Society, Atlanta, GA, 2009.
$20,000 to Greater Boston Food Bank, Boston, MA, 2009.
$20,000 to Indiana University, Bloomington, IN, 2009.
$5,000 to Boston Medical Center, Boston, MA, 2009.
$5,000 to Operation Homefront, San Antonio, TX, 2009.
$2,500 to Boston Symphony Orchestra, Boston, MA, 2009.
$1,500 to University of Arkansas, Fayetteville, AR, 2009.
$1,000 to University of California, Berkeley, CA, 2009.

466
Biomet, Inc.
56 E. Bell Dr.
P.O. Box 587
Warsaw, IN 46581-0587 (574) 267-6639

Company URL: http://www.biomet.com
Establishment information: Established in 1977.
Company type: Subsidiary of a private company
Business activities: Designs, manufactures, and markets musculoskeletal medical products.
Business type (SIC): Medical instruments and supplies
Financial profile for 2011: Number of employees, 7,469; assets, $11,969,000,000; sales volume, $2,698,000,000
Corporate officers: Jeffrey R. Binder, Pres. and C.E.O.; Renaat Vermeulen, Sr. V.P.; Daniel P. Florin, Sr. V.P. and C.F.O.; Bradley J. Tandy, Sr. V.P., Genl. Counsel, and Secy.; Robin T. Barney, Sr. V.P., Opers.; Peggy Taylor, Sr. V.P., Human Resources
Board of directors: Jeffrey R. Binder; Jonathan J. Coslet; Michael Dal Bello; Adrian Jones; Max C. Lin; David McVeigh; Michael Michelson; Dane A. Miller, Ph.D.; Andrew Y. Rhee; Todd Sisitsky
Subsidiaries: Arthrotek, Inc., Ontario, CA; Biomet Fair Lawn, L.P., Fair Lawn, NJ; EBI, L.P., Parsippany, NJ; EBI Medical Systems, Inc., Parsippany, NJ; Electro-Biology, Inc., Guaynabo, PR; Implant Innovations, Inc., Palm Beach Gardens, FL; Kirschner Medical Corp., Hunt Valley, MD; Walter Lorenz Surgical, Inc., Jacksonville, FL
International operations: Australia; Austria; Belgium; Bermuda; Brazil; Canada; Chile; China; Czech Republic; Denmark; Finland; France; Germany; Gibraltar; Greece; Hong Kong; Hungary; Italy; Japan; Luxembourg; Mexico; Netherlands; New Zealand; Norway; Poland; Portugal; South Africa; South Korea; Spain; Sweden; Switzerland; Turkey; United Kingdom
Giving statement: Giving through the Biomet, Inc. Corporate Giving Program and the Dr. Dane & Mary Louise Miller Foundation, Inc.
Company EIN: 351418342

Biomet, Inc. Corporate Giving Program
56 East Bell Dr.
PO Box 587
Warsaw, IN 46581-0587 (574) 267-6639

Purpose and activities: Biomet makes charitable contributions to nonprofit organizations involved with community development, medical missions, and disaster relief. Support is given primarily in areas of company operations; giving also to national and international organizations.
Fields of interest: Disasters, preparedness/services; Community/economic development.
Type of support: Donated products; General/operating support; In-kind gifts.
Geographic limitations: Giving primarily in areas of company operations; giving also to national and international organizations.

Dr. Dane & Mary Louise Miller Foundation, Inc.
(formerly The Biomet Foundation, Inc.)
700 Park Ave., Ste. G
Winona Lake, IN 46590-1066 (573) 267-2535

Establishment information: Established in 1990 in IN.
Donors: Biomet, Inc.; Dane A. Miller; Mrs. Dane A. Miller; Jerry L. Ferguson; Mrs. Jerry L. Ferguson.
Contact: Cindy Helper, Secy.
Financial data (yr. ended 12/31/11): Assets, $15,256,036 (M); expenditures, $811,707; qualifying distributions, $770,925; giving activities include $595,425 for 77 grants (high: $125,000; low: $100) and $175,500 for 61 grants to individuals (high: $3,000; low: -$3,000).
Purpose and activities: The foundation supports organizations involved with arts and culture, education, breast cancer research, recreation, human services, and Christianity.
Fields of interest: Media, television; Arts; Secondary school/education; Higher education; Education; Breast cancer research; Recreation, fairs/festivals; Recreation; Children/youth, services; Family services, adolescent parents; Pregnancy centers; Developmentally disabled, centers & services; Human services; United Ways and Federated Giving Programs.
Type of support: Annual campaigns; Employee-related scholarships; General/operating support; Matching/challenge support; Program development; Scholarship funds; Sponsorships.
Geographic limitations: Giving primarily in Kosciusko County, IN.
Support limitations: No support for political or religious organizations.
Publications: Informational brochure.
Application information: Applications accepted. Additional information may be requested at a later date. Application form not required. Applicants should submit the following:
1) copy of most recent annual report/audited financial statement/990
2) detailed description of project and amount of funding requested
Initial approach: Proposal
Copies of proposal: 1
Board meeting date(s): Quarterly
Deadline(s): None
Final notification: Up to 3 months
Officers and Directors:* Mrs. Dane A. Miller*, Pres.; Mary Louise Miller*, V.P.; Cindy Hepler*, Secy.; Daniel P. Hann; Stephanie Mullen; Kimberly Vanssessen; Darlene K. Whaley.
EIN: 351806314
Selected grants: The following grants are a representative sample of this grantmaker's funding activity:
$5,000 to Leukemia & Lymphoma Society, White Plains, NY, 2010. For general contribution.
$3,200 to Muscular Dystrophy Association, Tucson, AZ, 2010.

467
The Bionetics Corporation
11833 Canon Blvd., Ste. 100
Newport News, VA 23606-2589
(757) 873-0900

Company URL: http://www.bionetics.com
Establishment information: Established in 1969.
Company type: Private company
Business activities: Operates engineering and applied science company.

Business type (SIC): Research, development, and testing services; management and public relations services
Corporate officer: Charles J. Stern, C.E.O.
Offices: Jefferson, AR; Kennedy Space Center, FL; Fort Benning, GA; Tallulah, LA; Omaha, NE; Heath, OH; Oklahoma City, OK; Oak Ridge, TN; Hill AFB, UT; Alexandria, Dahlgren, VA
Giving statement: Giving through the Bionetics Corporation Charitable Trust.

Bionetics Corporation Charitable Trust

11833 Canon Blvd., Ste. 100
Newport News, VA 23606-2589

Donor: The Bionetics Corp.
Financial data (yr. ended 12/31/09): Assets, $28,312 (M); gifts received, $38,994; expenditures, $48,432; qualifying distributions, $48,432; giving activities include $48,432 for 31 grants (high: $12,750; low: $50).
Fields of interest: Education; Health care; Human services.
Support limitations: No grants to individuals.
Application information: Applications not accepted. Unsolicited requests for funds not accepted.
Officer: Charles J. Stern, Pres.
EIN: 546263704

468
Bird-in-Hand Corporation

2715 Old Philadelphia Pike, Rte. 340
P.O. Box 402
Bird in Hand, PA 17505-9707
(717) 768-1501

Company URL: http://www.bird-in-hand.com
Establishment information: Established in 1911.
Company type: Private company
Business activities: Operates motels; operates restaurants; operates bakery; operates deli; operates campground.
Business type (SIC): Hotels and motels; bakeries; restaurants and drinking places; camps/recreational
Corporate officers: John E. Smucker, Jr., Chair. and C.E.O.; Vickie Unruh, C.F.O.
Board of director: John E. Smucker, Jr., Chair.
Giving statement: Giving through the Paul M. Smucker Family Foundation.

Paul M. Smucker Family Foundation

2727 Old Philadelphia Pike
Bird in Hand, PA 17505-9707

Donor: Bird-in-Hand Corp.
Financial data (yr. ended 08/31/12): Assets, $768 (M); gifts received, $800; expenditures, $834; qualifying distributions, $0.
Purpose and activities: The foundation supports the Anabaptist Heritage Center of Lancaster County in Lancaster, PA.
Fields of interest: Religion.
Type of support: General/operating support.
Support limitations: No grants to individuals.
Application information: Applications not accepted. Unsolicited requests for funds not accepted.
Trustees: Connie Rivera; James Smucker; John E. Smucker II.
EIN: 232267540

469
Birds Eye Foods, LLC

(formerly Agrilink Foods, Inc.)
90 Linden Oaks
P.O. Box 20670
Rochester, NY 14625 (585) 383-1850

Company URL: http://www.birdseyefoods.com
Establishment information: Established in 1961.
Company type: Subsidiary of a private company
Business activities: Operates canned and frozen food products company.
Business type (SIC): Specialty foods/canned, frozen, and preserved
Corporate officers: Christopher Puma, Pres. and C.O.O.; Neil Harrison, C.E.O.; Christopher Puma, C.F.O.; Linda K. Nelson, Exec. V.P., C.F.O., and Secy.; Lois Warlick-Jarvie, Sr. V.P., Admin.
Plants: Montezuma, GA; Ridgeway, IL; Benton Harbor, Fennville, Sodus, MI; Vineland, NJ; Alton, Barker, Bergen, Brockport, Oakfield, Red Creek, NY; Alamo, TX; Enumclaw, Tacoma, WA
Giving statement: Giving through the New York Vegetable Research Association Inc.
Company EIN: 160845824

New York Vegetable Research Association Inc.

c/o William Harris
10018 Asbury Rd.
Leroy, NY 14482

Establishment information: Established in NY.
Donors: Birdseye Foods; Agrilink Foods, Inc.
Financial data (yr. ended 12/31/10): Assets, $122,405 (M); gifts received, $96,944; expenditures, $80,318; qualifying distributions, $79,222; giving activities include $79,222 for 1 grant.
Fields of interest: Education.
Support limitations: No grants to individuals.
Application information: Applications not accepted. Unsolicited requests for funds not accepted.
Officer: William Harris, Pres.
Board Members: Larry Christiansen; Michael Gardinier; Ronald B. Glazier; Tom Porter.
EIN: 161575593

470
Birdsong Corporation

612 Madison Ave.
Suffolk, VA 23434-4028 (757) 539-3456
FAX: (757) 539-7360

Company URL: http://www.birdsong-peanuts.com
Establishment information: Established in 1911.
Company type: Private company
Business activities: Markets nuts and nut by-products; provides food refrigeration and storage services.
Business type (SIC): Farm-product raw materials—wholesale; warehousing and storage
Financial profile for 2010: Number of employees, 700
Corporate officers: Thomas H. Birdsong Lii, Chair.; George Y. Birdsong, C.E.O.; Jeffrey B. Johnson, Pres.; Stephen L. Huber, C.F.O.
Board of director: Thomas H. Birdsong Lii, Chair.
Giving statement: Giving through the Birdsong Charitable Foundation and the Birdsong Trust Fund.

Birdsong Charitable Foundation

P.O. Box 1400
Suffolk, VA 23439-1400

Establishment information: Established in 1991 in VA.
Donor: Birdsong Corp.
Contact: Stephen L. Huber, Dir.
Financial data (yr. ended 12/31/11): Assets, $4,525,059 (M); gifts received, $1,250,000; expenditures, $765,828; qualifying distributions, $732,825; giving activities include $732,825 for grants.
Purpose and activities: The foundation supports organizations involved with arts and culture, education, science, and religion.
Fields of interest: Historic preservation/historical societies; Arts; Elementary/secondary education; Higher education; Education; Food services; Nutrition; Athletics/sports, amateur leagues; Salvation Army; Youth, services; Homeless, human services; Philanthropy/voluntarism.
Type of support: General/operating support.
Geographic limitations: Giving primarily in VA.
Support limitations: No grants to individuals.
Application information: Applications not accepted. Contributes only to pre-selected organizations.
Board meeting date(s): Varies
Officers and Directors:* W. J. Spain, Jr.*, Pres.; Stephen L. Huber*, Secy.; George Y. Birdsong, Treas.; Thomas H. Birdsong III.
EIN: 541607210
Selected grants: The following grants are a representative sample of this grantmaker's funding activity:
$300,000 to Randolph-Macon College, Ashland, VA, 2011.
$156,000 to Virginia Wesleyan College, Norfolk, VA, 2011.
$3,500 to Chesapeake Bay Foundation, Norfolk, VA, 2011.
$1,125 to Future Farmers of America Foundation, National, Indianapolis, IN, 2011.

Birdsong Trust Fund

c/o William L. Chorey, Sr.
P.O. Box 916
Suffolk, VA 23439-1876

Donor: Birdsong Corp.
Financial data (yr. ended 12/31/11): Assets, $1,258,357 (M); gifts received, $20,000; expenditures, $78,945; qualifying distributions, $66,000; giving activities include $66,000 for 7 grants (high: $25,000; low: $5,000).
Purpose and activities: The foundation supports health centers and organizations involved with historic preservation and human services.
Fields of interest: Historic preservation/historical societies; Health care, clinics/centers; American Red Cross; Family services, domestic violence; Human services.
Type of support: Capital campaigns; General/operating support; Program development; Sponsorships.
Geographic limitations: Giving limited to the Suffolk, VA, area.
Support limitations: No grants to individuals, or for scholarships.
Application information: Applications accepted. Application form required. Applicants should submit the following:
1) detailed description of project and amount of funding requested
Initial approach: Letter
Deadline(s): None
Officers: John C. Harrell, Pres.; William L. Chorey, Secy.-Treas.

Trustees: R. Leroy Howell; W.R. Savage III; Kent Spain.
EIN: 546039845

471
Birmingham Hide & Tallow Company, Inc.

700 Maple St., Ste. A
P.O. Box 1596
Birmingham, AL 35210 (205) 252-1197
FAX: (205) 251-1522

Company URL: http://www.bhtonline.com
Establishment information: Established in 1900.
Company type: Private company
Business activities: Operates waste management company.
Business type (SIC): Farm-product raw materials—wholesale
Corporate officers: Bill Vickers, Chair.; Cleve McDaniel, C.E.O.; T. Owen Vickers, Pres.; Michael S. Glenn, V.P. and C.F.O.; Harry G. Vickers, Secy.
Board of director: Bill Vickers, Chair.
Giving statement: Giving through the Birmingham Hide and Tallow Charitable Foundation Inc.

Birmingham Hide and Tallow Charitable Foundation Inc.

P.O. Box 1596
Birmingham, AL 35201-1596
URL: http://www.bhtonline.com/charities.html

Establishment information: Established in 2005 in AL.
Donor: Birmingham Hide & Tallow, Inc.
Financial data (yr. ended 12/31/11): Assets, $149,969 (M); gifts received, $170,000; expenditures, $29,800; qualifying distributions, $29,800; giving activities include $29,800 for 8 grants (high: $10,000; low: $300).
Purpose and activities: The foundation supports camps and organizations involved with education, health, cancer, human services, and Christianity.
Fields of interest: Higher education; Education; Hospitals (general); Health care, patient services; Health care; Cancer; Recreation, camps; Children/youth, services; Residential/custodial care; Residential/custodial care, group home; Developmentally disabled, centers & services; Human services; Christian agencies & churches.
Type of support: General/operating support; Program development.
Geographic limitations: Giving primarily in Birmingham, AL.
Support limitations: No grants to individuals.
Application information: Applications not accepted. Unsolicited requests for funds not accepted.
Officers: Marsha Vickers, Pres.; Julia V. Wright, V.P.; Michael S. Glenn, Secy.-Treas.
EIN: 202077546
Selected grants: The following grants are a representative sample of this grantmaker's funding activity:
$40,000 to University of Alabama, Tuscaloosa, AL, 2010.
$20,000 to Church of the Highlands, Birmingham, AL, 2010.
$11,000 to Society for the Blind, Sacramento, CA, 2010.
$10,000 to Humane Society of Greater Birmingham, Birmingham, AL, 2010.
$5,000 to Mitchells Place, Birmingham, AL, 2010.
$3,000 to Camp Smile-A-Mile, Birmingham, AL, 2010.
$3,000 to Ducks Unlimited, Memphis, TN, 2010.
$3,000 to Glenwood, Inc., Birmingham, AL, 2010.
$2,000 to Alabama Symphonic Association, Birmingham, AL, 2010.
$2,000 to American Heart Association, Dallas, TX, 2010.

472
The Birmingham News

2201 4th Ave. N.
Birmingham, AL 35203-3863
(205) 325-3425
FAX: (205) 325-3205

Company URL: http://www.bhamnews.com
Establishment information: Established in 1888.
Company type: Private company
Business activities: Publishes newspaper.
Business type (SIC): Newspaper publishing and/or printing
Corporate officers: Victor H. Hanson, Pres.; Steve Irvine, C.O.O.; John W. Schmid, Cont.
Giving statement: Giving through the Birmingham News Corporate Giving Program.

The Birmingham News Corporate Giving Program

2200 4th Ave. N.
Birmingham, AL 35203-3802
URL: http://www.bhamnews.com/indexmain.html

Purpose and activities: The Birmingham News makes charitable contributions to nonprofit organizations involved with education. Support is limited to areas of company operations in Birmingham, Alabama.
Fields of interest: Elementary/secondary education; Education.
Program:
Newspaper in Education Program (NIE): Birmingham News provides educators with materials to assist in teaching all curriculum. The company provides classroom copies of The Birmingham News; teacher programs, workshops, and demonstration classes; materials that schools lack which are aligned with Alabama Course of Study Objectives as set by the Alabama Department of Education; and academic contests throughout the year.
Type of support: Curriculum development; Donated products; In-kind gifts.
Geographic limitations: Giving limited to areas of company operations in Birmingham, AL.

473
BJ's Wholesale Club, Inc.

25 Research Dr.
Westborough, MA 01581 (508) 651-7400
FAX: (508) 651-6114

Company URL: http://www.bjs.com
Establishment information: Established in 1984.
Company type: Private company
Business activities: Operates warehouse club stores.
Business type (SIC): Variety stores
Corporate officers: Laura J. Sen, Pres. and C.E.O.; Robert W. Eddy, Exec. V.P. and C.F.O.; Peter Amalfi, Exec. V.P. and C.I.O.
Board of director: Laura J. Sen
Giving statement: Giving through the BJ's Charitable Foundation.
Company EIN: 043360747

BJ's Charitable Foundation

(formerly BJ's Charitable Foundation, Inc.)
25 Research Dr.
Westborough, MA 01581-0001
E-mail for Adopt -A-School: school@bjs.com;
URL: http://www.bjs.com/charity

Financial data (yr. ended 09/29/09): Total giving, $842,081, including $842,081 for 14 grants (high: $290,000; low: $10,000).
Purpose and activities: BJ's Charitable Foundation supports programs designed to promote the safety, security, and well-being of children and families; support education and health; provide community service opportunities; and aid in hunger, homelessness, and disaster relief. Special emphasis is directed toward programs that provide basic needs services to those in need. Support is limited to areas of company operations in Connecticut, Delaware, Florida, Georgia, Maine, Maryland, Massachusetts, New Hampshire, New Jersey, New York, North Carolina, Ohio, Pennsylvania, Rhode Island, and Virginia.
Fields of interest: Education; Health care; Food services; Disasters, preparedness/services; Safety, education; Children, services; Family services; Homeless, human services; Voluntarism promotion.
Program:
Adopt-A-School Program: Through the Adopt-A-School Program, BJ's gives "adopted" schools support they can use to enhance existing programs and curriculum objectives while providing students with opportunities that will help them grow into active citizens in their communities. BJ's makes a one-time donation to use toward discretionary programs, such as field trips and special events, reading enhancement programs or other educational needs.
Type of support: Building/renovation; Equipment; General/operating support; Program development.
Geographic limitations: Giving limited to areas of company operations in CT, DE, FL, GA, MA, ME, MD, NH, NJ, NY, NC, OH, PA, RI, and VA.
Support limitations: No support for discriminatory organizations, political organizations, fraternal groups, or social clubs engaging in political activity, religious organizations not of direct benefit to the entire community, or private foundations that have been in place for less than 1 year. No grants to individuals, or for scholarships, programs established less than one year ago, capital campaigns, music, film, or art festival sponsorships, business expositions or conferences, journal or program advertisements, or fees for participating in competitive programs.
Publications: Application guidelines; Grants list.
Application information: Applications accepted. BJ's Charitable Foundation is a donor-advised fund at a national public charity. All contributions to BJ's Charitable Foundation go directly to the public charity that sponsors the donor-advised fund and all grants from the donor-advised fund are made at the recommendation of BJ's Charitable Foundation and its delegates and at the discretion of the sponsoring charity. Applicants should submit the following:
1) population served
2) name, address and phone number of organization
3) copy of IRS Determination Letter
4) brief history of organization and description of its mission
5) copy of most recent annual report/audited financial statement/990

6) how project's results will be evaluated or measured
7) listing of board of directors, trustees, officers and other key people and their affiliations
8) detailed description of project and amount of funding requested
9) contact person
10) copy of current year's organizational budget and/or project budget
11) listing of additional sources and amount of support

Cover letters should be no longer than 1 page. Proposals should include the organization's fax number and the contact person's E-mail address, if available; a description of the historic success rate of project/program participants and the method used to track or measure their success; the cost per client served per month; and the percentage of funds budgeted for administrative costs and programs for the program and the organization.

Initial approach: Complete online application
Copies of proposal: 1
Deadline(s): Jan. 6, Apr. 6, and July 6
Final notification: July, Sept, and Nov.

Officers and Directors:* Herbert J. Zarkin*, Chair.; Paul M. Bass*, Pres.; Lon F. Povich*, Exec. V.P. and Secy.; Frank D. Forward*, Exec. V.P. and Treas.; Michael P. Atkinson; Laura Sen.

474
Black Hills Corporation

625 9th St.
P.O. Box 1400
Rapid City, SD 57701-2428
(605) 721-1700
FAX: (605) 348-4748

Company URL: http://www.blackhillscorp.com
Establishment information: Established in 1941.
Company type: Public company
Company ticker symbol and exchange: BKH/NYSE
Business activities: Generates, transmits, and distributes electricity; mines coal; produces crude oil and natural gas.
Business type (SIC): Electric services
Financial profile for 2012: Number of employees, 1,925; assets, $3,729,470,000; sales volume, $1,173,880,000; pre-tax net income, $136,910,000; expenses, $930,170,000; liabilities, $2,496,960,000
Corporate officers: David R. Emery, Chair., Pres., and C.E.O.; Anthony S. Cleberg, Exec. V.P. and C.F.O.; Scott A. Buchholz, C.I.O.; Steven J. Helmers, Sr. V.P. and Genl. Counsel
Board of directors: David R. Emery, Chair.; Jack W. Eugster; Michael H. Madison; Steven R. Mills; Stephen D. Newlin; Gary L. Pechota; Rebecca B. Roberts; Warren L. Robinson; John B. Vering; Thomas J. Zeller
Subsidiaries: Universal Transportation, Rapid City, SD; Western Production Co., Newcastle, WY; Wyodak Resources Development Corp., Gillette, WY
Giving statement: Giving through the Black Hills Corporation Contributions Program and the Black Hills Corporation Foundation.
Company EIN: 460458824

Black Hills Corporation Contributions Program

625 9th St.
Rapid City, SD 57701-2674 (605) 721-1700
URL: http://www.blackhillscorp.com/social.htm

Purpose and activities: As a complement to its foundation, Black Hills also makes charitable contributions to nonprofit organizations directly. Support is given primarily in areas of company operations in Colorado, Iowa, Kansas, Montana, Nebraska, South Dakota, and Wyoming.
Fields of interest: Environment; Recreation, community; Family services; Community/economic development; Utilities; General charitable giving.
Type of support: Building/renovation; Employee volunteer services; Employee-related scholarships; General/operating support; In-kind gifts.
Geographic limitations: Giving primarily in areas of company operations in CO, IA, KS, MT, NE, SD, and WY.

Black Hills Corporation Foundation

625 9th St.
P.O. Box 1400
Rapid City, SD 57709-1400 (605) 721-2384
E-mail: hillary.dobbs@blackhillscorp.com.;
URL: http://www.blackhillscorp.com/social.htm

Establishment information: Established in 2001 in SD.
Donor: Black Hills Corp.
Contact: Hilary Dobbs
Financial data (yr. ended 12/31/11): Assets, $3,925,876 (M); expenditures, $334,267; qualifying distributions, $334,082; giving activities include $334,082 for grants.
Purpose and activities: The foundation supports organizations involved with arts and culture, education, the environment, youth development, human services, community development, and civic affairs.
Fields of interest: Arts; Higher education; Education; Environment; Youth development; Human services; Community/economic development; United Ways and Federated Giving Programs; Public affairs.
Type of support: Capital campaigns; General/operating support.
Geographic limitations: Giving primarily in areas of company operations in CO, SD and WY.
Support limitations: No support for political organizations, religious organizations not of direct benefit to the entire community, or discriminatory organizations. No grants to individuals, or for endowments, conferences, seminars, or festivals, tours, trips, or pageants, endowments, debt reduction, or athletic sponsorships.
Publications: Application guidelines.
Application information: Applications accepted. Application form required. Applicants should submit the following:

1) timetable for implementation and evaluation of project
2) results expected from proposed grant
3) copy of IRS Determination Letter
4) brief history of organization and description of its mission
5) copy of most recent annual report/audited financial statement/990
6) how project's results will be evaluated or measured
7) listing of board of directors, trustees, officers and other key people and their affiliations
8) detailed description of project and amount of funding requested
9) copy of current year's organizational budget and/or project budget

Initial approach: Download application form and mail proposal and application form to nearest External Affairs Manager
Board meeting date(s): Mar. 11, June 17, Sept. 16, and Dec. 16
Deadline(s): 2 weeks prior to board meeting

Officers: Jason Ketchum, Pres.; Linda R. Evans, V.P.; Mark Lux, Secy.; Perry Krush, Treas.
Directors: Susan Bailey; David R. Emery; Jafar Karim; Steve Pella; Penny Schild; Stuart Wevik.
EIN: 752986866
Selected grants: The following grants are a representative sample of this grantmaker's funding activity:
$90,000 to South Dakota School of Mines and Technology Foundation, Rapid City, SD, 2009.
$26,250 to United Way of the Black Hills, Rapid City, SD, 2009.
$25,000 to Black Hills State University, Spearfish, SD, 2009.
$15,000 to Honor Flight South Dakota, Sioux Falls, SD, 2009.
$15,000 to Wildlife Experiences, Rapid City, SD, 2009.
$13,334 to Dubuque County Historical Society, National Mississippi River Museum and Aquarium, Dubuque, IA, 2009.
$12,500 to South Dakota Parks and Wildlife Foundation, Pierre, SD, 2009.
$10,000 to Allied Arts Fund Drive, Rapid City, SD, 2009.
$10,000 to Central States Fair, Rapid City, SD, 2009.
$10,000 to Church Response, Rapid City, SD, 2009.

475
Black River Management Company

60 Cuttermill Rd., Ste. 214
Great Neck, NY 11021-3104
(516) 684-4800

Company type: Private company
Business activities: Provides investment banking services.
Business type (SIC): Management and public relations services
Financial profile for 2009: Number of employees, 1,946
Corporate officer: Gilbert Butler, Chair. and C.E.O.
Subsidiary: Beckley-Cardy, Inc., Duluth, MN
Giving statement: Giving through the Butler Conservation Fund, Inc. and the Gilbert and Ildiko Butler Family Foundation, Inc.

Butler Conservation Fund, Inc.

(formerly Gilbert & Ildiko Butler Foundation, Inc.)
60 Cutter Mill Rd., Ste. 214
Great Neck, NY 11021-3104
URL: http://butlerconservationfund.org/

Establishment information: Established in 1988 in MA.
Donors: Gilbert Butler; Butler Capital Corp.
Financial data (yr. ended 12/31/11): Assets, $137,168,426 (M); gifts received, $63,780; expenditures, $7,215,171; qualifying distributions, $4,682,757; giving activities include $4,237,606 for 50 grants (high: $1,073,382; low: $250).
Purpose and activities: The foundation supports parks and organizations involved with the environment and animals and wildlife.
Fields of interest: Historic preservation/historical societies; Environment, natural resources; Environment, water resources; Environment, land resources; Botanical gardens; Environmental education; Environment; Animal welfare; Animals/wildlife; Recreation, parks/playgrounds.

Type of support: Capital campaigns; General/operating support; Program development; Research.
Geographic limitations: Giving primarily in MA, ME, NY, SC, and VA; giving also to national organizations.
Application information: Applications not accepted. Unsolicited applications are not accepted.
Officers and Directors:* Gilbert Butler*, Chair. and Pres.; Anthony P. Grassi*, Vice-Chair.; Christopher J. Elliman*, V.P.; Tomer Inbar, Secy.; Dhruvika Patel Amin, Cont.; Dana Beach; Peter Lehner; Kristine Tompkins.
EIN: 043032409
Selected grants: The following grants are a representative sample of this grantmaker's funding activity:
$1,507,889 to Butler Fund for the Environment, New York, NY, 2007.
$685,101 to Conservacion Patagonica, Sausalito, CA, 2007.
$333,333 to Nature Conservancy, Arlington, VA, 2007. For Great Bear Rainforest program in British Columbia, Canada.
$250,000 to Appalachian Mountain Club, Boston, MA, 2007.
$250,000 to Central Park Conservancy, New York, NY, 2007.
$166,666 to Downeast Lakes Land Trust, Grand Lake Stream, ME, 2007.
$155,000 to South Carolina Coastal Conservation League, Charleston, SC, 2007.
$110,000 to Friends of Acadia, Bar Harbor, ME, 2007.
$60,000 to Blaine County Recreation District, Hailey, ID, 2007.
$50,000 to Nature Conservancy, Maine Field Office, Brunswick, ME, 2007.

The Gilbert and Ildiko Butler Family Foundation, Inc.

60 Cutter Mill Rd.
Great Neck, NY 11021-3104

Establishment information: Established in 2006 in MA.
Donors: Gilbert Butler; Ildiko Butler.
Financial data (yr. ended 12/31/10): Assets, $8,813,410 (M); expenditures, $483,407; qualifying distributions, $321,910; giving activities include $311,617 for 43 grants (high: $112,527; low: $135).
Fields of interest: Performing arts, music; Performing arts, education; Arts; Education; Human services; Children/youth, services.
Type of support: General/operating support.
Geographic limitations: Giving primarily in NY.
Support limitations: No grants to individuals.
Application information: Applications not accepted. Contributes only to pre-selected organizations.
Officer: Gilbert Butler, Pres. and Treas.
Directors: Fred Butler; Ildiko Butler; Emily Rafferty; Winthrop Rutherfurd, Jr.
EIN: 270141384
Selected grants: The following grants are a representative sample of this grantmaker's funding activity:
$25,000 to Irish Georgian Society, New York, NY, 2009.
$20,000 to Metropolitan Museum of Art, New York, NY, 2009.
$10,150 to Project Sunshine, New York, NY, 2009.
$10,000 to Visiting Nurse Service of New York, New York, NY, 2009.
$5,000 to American Friends of Aphrodisias, New York, NY, 2009.
$5,000 to Hospital for Special Surgery, New York, NY, 2009.
$5,000 to Save Venice, New York, NY, 2009.
$2,500 to New York City Ballet, New York, NY, 2009.
$2,000 to New York Public Library, New York, NY, 2009.
$1,000 to Central Park Conservancy, New York, NY, 2009.

476
V.H. Blackinton and Co., Inc.

221 John L. Dietsch Blvd.
P.O. Box 1300
Attleboro Falls, MA 02763-1031
(508) 699-4436

Company URL: http://www.blackinton.com
Establishment information: Established in 1852.
Company type: Private company
Business activities: Manufactures badges and uniform insignias for law enforcement departments and public service agencies.
Business type (SIC): Fabricated textile products/miscellaneous
Corporate officers: Peter A. Roque, Pres. and C.E.O.; David T. Long, C.O.O.; Rick Isacco, V.P., Human Resources; Jeff Boutin, Cont.
Board of director: Tim Convery
Giving statement: Giving through the North Attleboro Scholarship Foundation.

North Attleboro Scholarship Foundation

P.O. Box 926
North Attleboro, MA 02760

Establishment information: Established in 1992 in MA.
Donors: Louise Farrands; Mary L. McKenna; Estate of Emma Irvine†; Constance Rezza.
Financial data (yr. ended 06/30/12): Assets, $2,294,321 (M); gifts received, $82,903; expenditures, $78,824; qualifying distributions, $62,970; giving activities include $62,970 for grants to individuals.
Purpose and activities: The foundation awards scholarships to graduates of North Attleboro High School in Massachusetts.
Type of support: Scholarships—to individuals.
Geographic limitations: Giving limited to North Attleboro, MA.
Application information: Applications not accepted. Unsolicited requests for funds not accepted.
Officers: Donald McHoul, V.P.
Directors: Steve Doucette; Louise Farrands; Laura Gaulin; Linda Gay; James K. Hale; Kristen Kraskouskas; Matthew Lacasse; Wendy McCrae; Mary McKenna; Catherine E. Shuman; Maura Sullivan; Michael Vigonto.
EIN: 046056778

477
The Blackstone Group LP

345 Park Ave., 31st Fl.
New York, NY 10154 (212) 583-5000
FAX: (212) 583-5749

Company URL: http://www.blackstone.com
Establishment information: Established in 1985.
Company type: Public company
Company ticker symbol and exchange: BX/NYSE
Business activities: Operates private equity firm.
Business type (SIC): Investors/miscellaneous
Financial profile for 2012: Number of employees, 1,780; assets, $28,931,550,000; sales volume, $4,019,440,000; pre-tax net income, $1,014,900,000; expenses, $3,260,680,000; liabilities, $23,464,710,000
Fortune 1000 ranking: 2012—585th in revenues, 552nd in profits, and 192nd in assets
Corporate officers: Stephen A. Schwarzman, Chair. and C.E.O.; J. Tomilson Hill, Vice-Chair.; Hamilton E. James, Pres. and C.O.O.; Laurence A. Tosi, C.F.O.
Board of directors: Stephen A. Schwarzman, Chair.; J. Tomilson Hill, Vice-Chair.; Jonathan D. Gray; Hamilton E. James; Richard Hampton Jenrette; Jay O. Light; Brian Mulroney; William G. Parrett
Giving statement: Giving through the Blackstone Charitable Foundation.
Company EIN: 208875684

The Blackstone Charitable Foundation

345 Park Ave.
New York, NY 10154-0004 (212) 583-5465
E-mail: foundation@blackstone.com; URL: http://www.blackstone.com/citizenship/the-blackstone-charitable-foundation

Establishment information: Established in 2007 in DE.
Financial data (yr. ended 06/30/11): Revenue, $5,830,375; assets, $79,508,327 (M); gifts received, $3,981,703; expenditures, $7,238,926; giving activities include $6,119,664 for grants.
Purpose and activities: The organization aims to invest in initiatives that encourage and support economic growth, with a primary focus on promoting entrepreneurship.
Fields of interest: Economic development; Urban/community development; Community development, business promotion; Community development, small businesses.
Application information: Applications accepted.
Officers: Robert L. Friedman, Chair.; Slyvia F. Moss, Pres.; John Mccormick, Secy.; Sean Klimczak, Treas.
Directors: Peter Rose; Mary Frances Metrick.
EIN: 260462996

478
William Blair & Company, L.L.C.

222 W. Adams St.
Chicago, IL 60606-5312 (312) 236-1600

Company URL: http://www.williamblair.com
Establishment information: Established in 1935.
Company type: Private company
Business activities: Operates investment bank; provides investment advisory services; provides securities brokerage services.
Business type (SIC): Brokers and dealers/security; security and commodity services
Corporate officers: Edgar D. Jannotta, Chair.; E. David Coolidge III, Vice-Chair.; John R. Ettelson, Pres. and C.E.O.; Timothy L. Burke, C.F.O.; Arthur J. Simon, Genl. Counsel
Board of directors: Edgar Jannotta, Chair.; E. David Coolidge, Vice-Chair.
Giving statement: Giving through the William Blair & Company Foundation.

William Blair & Company Foundation

222 W. Adams St., 28th Fl.
Chicago, IL 60606-5307

Establishment information: Established in 1980 in IL.
Donor: William Blair & Co., L.L.C.
Contact: E. David Coolidge III, V.P.
Financial data (yr. ended 12/31/12): Assets, $7,069,255 (M); gifts received, $1,520,000; expenditures, $1,487,211; qualifying distributions, $1,482,784; giving activities include $1,482,784 for 355 grants (high: $75,000; low: $250).
Purpose and activities: The foundation supports organizations involved with arts and culture, higher education, health, cancer, human services, civic affairs, Christianity, and Judaism.
Fields of interest: Arts; Higher education; Hospitals (general); Health care; Cancer; Cancer research; Children/youth, services; Human services; Government/public administration; Public affairs; Catholic agencies & churches; Jewish agencies & synagogues.
Type of support: Annual campaigns; Building/renovation; Capital campaigns; Continuing support; Endowments; Fellowships; General/operating support; Internship funds; Scholarship funds.
Geographic limitations: Giving primarily in the metropolitan Chicago, IL, area.
Support limitations: No grants to individuals.
Application information: Applications accepted. Application form not required.
Initial approach: Proposal
Copies of proposal: 1
Deadline(s): None
Officers: Edgar D. Jannotta, Pres.; E. David Coolidge III, V.P.; Michelle S. Seitz, V.P.; Thomas W. Pace, Secy.; John R. Ettelson, Treas.
EIN: 363092291
Selected grants: The following grants are a representative sample of this grantmaker's funding activity:
$75,000 to Greater Chicago Food Depository, Chicago, IL, 2011. For general purposes.
$15,000 to Chicago Council on Global Affairs, Chicago, IL, 2011. For general purposes.
$15,000 to Chicago Summer Business Institute, Chicago, IL, 2011. For general purposes.
$15,000 to Chicago Symphony Orchestra, Chicago, IL, 2011. For general purposes.
$10,000 to American Jewish Committee, New York, NY, 2011. For general purposes.
$10,000 to Chicago Public Library Foundation, Chicago, IL, 2011. For general purposes.
$7,000 to Cystic Fibrosis Foundation, Bethesda, MD, 2011. For general purposes.
$5,000 to Catholic Charities of the Archdiocese of Chicago, Chicago, IL, 2011. For general purposes.
$5,000 to Infant Welfare Society of Chicago, Chicago, IL, 2011. For general purposes.
$2,500 to Chicago Community Trust, Chicago, IL, 2011. For general purposes.

479
Blair Construction, Inc.
23020 U.S. Hwy. 29
Gretna, VA 24557 (434) 656-6243

Company URL: http://www.blair-construction.com/
Establishment information: Established in 1911.
Company type: Private company
Business activities: Provides nonresidential general contract construction services.
Business type (SIC): Contractors/general nonresidential building
Corporate officers: Fred A. Blair, Pres.; Timothy J. Clark, V.P., Opers.; Greg Nichols, Treas.; Matt Doss, Cont.
Giving statement: Giving through the Blair Construction Scholarship Foundation.

Blair Construction Scholarship Foundation
P.O. Box 612
Gretna, VA 24557-0612 (434) 656-6243

Establishment information: Established in 1999 in VA.
Donor: Blair Construction, Inc.
Contact: J. Matthew Doss, Treas.
Financial data (yr. ended 12/31/11): Assets, $4,627 (M); gifts received, $6,800; expenditures, $6,125; qualifying distributions, $6,100; giving activities include $6,100 for grants.
Purpose and activities: Scholarship awards to graduates from the Gretna, Virginia, area.
Fields of interest: Higher education.
Type of support: Scholarships—to individuals.
Geographic limitations: Giving limited to residents of the Gretna, VA, area.
Application information: Applications accepted. Application form required.
Initial approach: Proposal
Deadline(s): Feb. 28
Officers: Fred A. Blair, Pres.; Brenda M. Blair, V.P.; Timothy J. Clark, Secy.; J. Matthew Doss, Treas.
EIN: 541915821

480
Blakely Sokoloff Taylor Zafman LLP
1279 Oakmead Pkwy.
Sunnyvale, CA 94085-4040 (408) 720-8300

Company URL: http://www.bstz.com
Establishment information: Established in 1975.
Company type: Private company
Business activities: Operates law firm.
Business type (SIC): Legal services
Corporate officer: Thomas C. Webster, Partner
Offices: Costa Mesa, Los Angeles, Sunnyvale, CA; Denver, CO; Beaverton, OR; Seattle, WA
Giving statement: Giving through the Blakely Sokoloff Taylor Zafman LLP Corporate Giving Program.

Blakely Sokoloff Taylor Zafman LLP Corporate Giving Program
1279 Oakmead Pkwy.
Sunnyvale, CA 94085-4040 (408) 720-8300
FAX: (408) 720-8383; URL: http://www.bstz.com/

Fields of interest: Legal services.
Type of support: General/operating support; Pro bono services - legal.
Geographic limitations: Giving primarily in areas of company operations in Costa Mesa, Los Angeles, and Sunnyvale, CA, Denver, CO, Beaverton, OR, and Seattle, WA.

481
Block Communications, Inc.
(formerly Blade Communications, Inc.)
405 Madison Ave., Ste 2100
Toledo, OH 43604 (419) 724-6212

Company URL: http://www.blockcommunications.com
Establishment information: Established in 1900.
Company type: Private company
Business activities: Publishes newspapers.
Business type (SIC): Newspaper publishing and/or printing; cable and other pay television services
Financial profile for 2010: Number of employees, 14
Corporate officers: Gary J. Blair, Pres.; Jodi L. Miehls, C.F.O.
Board of directors: Gary J. Blair; Cyrus Block
Giving statement: Giving through the Blade Foundation.

Blade Foundation
405 Madison Ave.
Toledo, OH 43604

Establishment information: Established in 1969 in OH.
Donors: Blade Communications, Inc.; Block Communications, Inc.
Contact: Jodi Miehls, Treas.
Financial data (yr. ended 12/31/11): Assets, $4,895 (M); gifts received, $87,200; expenditures, $92,732; qualifying distributions, $92,500; giving activities include $92,500 for grants.
Purpose and activities: The foundation supports organizations involved with arts and culture, education, health, human services, community development, Christianity, and Judaism.
Fields of interest: Arts; Education; Health care.
Type of support: Employee-related scholarships; General/operating support.
Application information: Applications accepted. Application form not required. Applicants should submit the following:
1) name, address and phone number of organization
2) detailed description of project and amount of funding requested
Initial approach: Letter
Copies of proposal: 1
Deadline(s): None for grants; Mar. 1 for scholarships
Officers: Allan Block, V.P.; John R. Block, V.P.; Sandra J. Chavez, Secy.; Jodi Miehls, Treas.
EIN: 346559843

482
Block Electric Co., Inc.
7107 N. Milwaukee Ave.
Niles, IL 60714 (847) 647-4030

Company URL: http://www.blockelectric.com
Establishment information: Established in 1920.
Company type: Private company
Business activities: Provides general contract electrical services.
Business type (SIC): Contractors/electrical work
Corporate officers: Jack G. Block, Pres.; Jeffrey S. Underwood, V.P. and C.F.O.
Giving statement: Giving through the Block Family Foundation.

Block Family Foundation

(formerly Block Electric Company, Inc. Foundation)
7107 N. Milwaukee Ave.
Niles, IL 60714-4424 (847) 647-4030

Establishment information: Established in 1991 in IL.
Donors: Block Electric Co., Inc.; John G. Block.
Financial data (yr. ended 12/31/11): Assets, $1,350,178 (M); gifts received, $299,988; expenditures, $193,297; qualifying distributions, $185,408; giving activities include $185,408 for 32 grants (high: $50,000; low: $100).
Purpose and activities: The foundation supports organizations involved with higher education, medical education, health, cancer, and human services.
Fields of interest: Higher education; Medical school/education; Hospitals (general); Health care; Cancer; Human services.
Type of support: General/operating support.
Geographic limitations: Giving limited to IL.
Support limitations: No grants to individuals.
Application information: Applications not accepted. Contributes only to pre-selected organizations.
Directors: John G. Block; Michael J. Deger; Jeffrey Underwood.
EIN: 363811476
Selected grants: The following grants are a representative sample of this grantmaker's funding activity:
$50,000 to University of Portland, Portland, OR, 2011. For unrestricted contribution.
$32,000 to Silver Cross Hospital and Medical Centers, Joliet, IL, 2011. For unrestricted contribution.
$13,860 to Silver Cross Foundation, Joliet, IL, 2011. For unrestricted contribution.
$7,500 to Leukemia & Lymphoma Society, Pittsfield, MA, 2011. For unrestricted contribution.
$5,180 to City of Hope, Chicago, IL, 2011. For unrestricted contribution.
$4,500 to Rush University Medical Center, Chicago, IL, 2011. For unrestricted contribution.
$2,500 to Boy Scouts of America, Chicago Area Council, Chicago, IL, 2011. For unrestricted contribution.
$2,300 to Childrens Medical Research Foundation, Western Springs, IL, 2011. For unrestricted contribution.
$1,600 to Ingalls Development Foundation, Harvey, IL, 2011. For unrestricted contribution.
$1,500 to Saint Vincent de Paul Center, Chicago, IL, 2011. For unrestricted contribution.

483
Blockbuster L.L.C.

(formerly Blockbuster, Inc.)
1201 Elm St.
Dallas, TX 75270-2102 (214) 854-3000

Company URL: http://www.blockbuster.com
Establishment information: Established in 1982.
Company type: Subsidiary of a public company
Business activities: Operates home videocassette, DVD, and video game rental stores.
Business type (SIC): Video tape rental
Financial profile for 2010: Number of employees, 27,000; assets, $1,538,300,000; sales volume, $4,062,400,000; pre-tax net income, -$505,800,000; expenses, $4,447,500,000; liabilities, $1,852,600,000
Corporate officers: Michael Kelly, Pres. and Co-C.E.O.; James W. Keyes, Co-C.E.O.; Dennis McGill, Exec. V.P. and C.F.O.; Rod J. McDonald, V.P., Secy., and Genl. Counsel; Kevin Lewis, Sr. V.P., Mktg.
Board of directors: Edward Bleier; Gary J. Fernandes; Joseph J. Fitzsimmons; Jules Haimovitz; Gregory S. Meyer; Strauss Zelnick
International operations: Argentina; Canada; Ireland; Italy; Mexico; New Zealand; Spain; United Kingdom; Uruguay
Giving statement: Giving through the Blockbuster Inc. Corporate Giving Program.
Company EIN: 521655102

Blockbuster Inc. Corporate Giving Program

c/o Corp. Contribs.
3000 Redbud Blvd.
McKinney, TX 75069-8228
URL: http://www.blockbuster.com/corporate/communityRelations

Purpose and activities: Blockbuster makes charitable contributions to nonprofit organizations involved with impacting children and families, with a film/video industry focus. Support is given to national organizations.
Fields of interest: Media, film/video; Employment; Children, services; Family services; Civil/human rights, equal rights.
Type of support: Employee volunteer services; In-kind gifts; Program development.
Geographic limitations: Giving to national organizations.
Support limitations: No support for political, religious, or fraternal organizations. No grants to individuals, or for capital campaigns, endowments, scholarships, independent film and video productions, or sporting events.
Publications: Application guidelines.
Application information: Applications accepted. Application form not required.
Initial approach: Proposal to headquarters

484
Blommer Chocolate Company

600 W. Kinzie St.
Chicago, IL 60654-5585 (312) 226-7700
FAX: (312) 226-4141

Company URL: http://www.blommer.com
Establishment information: Established in 1939.
Company type: Private company
Business activities: Produces chocolate coating, cocoa powder, cocoa butter, and chocolate bars.
Business type (SIC): Sugar, candy, and salted/roasted nut production
Financial profile for 2009: Number of employees, 358
Corporate officers: Henry J. Blommer, Jr., Chair. and C.E.O.; Jack S. Larsen, C.F.O.; Steve Blommer, V.P., Opers.; Peter Drake, V.P., Sales and Mktg.; Linda Melampy, Corp. Cont.
Board of director: Henry J. Blommer, Jr., Chair.
Giving statement: Giving through the Blommer Chocolate Foundation.

Blommer Chocolate Foundation

600 W. Kinzie St.
Chicago, IL 60610-3977

Establishment information: Established in 1957 in IL.
Donor: Blommer Chocolate Co., Inc.
Contact: Joseph Blommer, Secy.
Financial data (yr. ended 05/31/11): Assets, $252,963 (M); gifts received, $100,000; expenditures, $85,081; qualifying distributions, $85,000; giving activities include $85,000 for 3 grants (high: $50,000; low: $10,000).
Purpose and activities: The foundation supports organizations involved with education and cancer.
Fields of interest: Education.
Type of support: General/operating support.
Geographic limitations: Giving primarily in Washington, DC, Worcester, MA, and New York, NY.
Support limitations: No grants to individuals.
Application information: Applications not accepted. Unsolicited requests for funds not accepted.
Officers: Henry J. Blommer, Jr., Pres.; Joseph Blommer, Secy.
Director: Peter Blommer.
EIN: 366075919

485
The Blood-Horse Inc.

3101 Beaumont Centre Cir., Ste. 100
Lexington, KY 40513-1961 (859) 278-2361

Company URL: http://www.bloodhorse.com
Establishment information: Established in 1916.
Company type: Subsidiary of a private company
Business activities: Publishes magazines and newsletters about thoroughbred racing and breeding.
Business type (SIC): Periodical publishing and/or printing
Corporate officers: G. Watts Humphrey, Chair.; Stacy V. Bearse, Pres. and C.E.O.; Mike Gallenstein, C.I.O.
Board of director: G. Watts Humphrey, Chair.
Giving statement: Giving through the Blood-Horse Charitable Foundation, Inc.

The Blood-Horse Charitable Foundation, Inc.

3101 Beaumont Centre Cir., Ste. 100
Lexington, KY 40513-1959 (859) 278-2361
Application address: P.O. Box 919003, Lexington, KY 40591-9003

Establishment information: Established in 1988 in KY.
Donor: The Blood-Horse, Inc.
Contact: Stacy V. Bearse, Secy.
Financial data (yr. ended 05/31/11): Assets, $0 (M); expenditures, $1,965; qualifying distributions, $1,720; giving activities include $1,550 for grants.
Purpose and activities: The foundation supports museums and organizations involved with equestrianism and human services.
Type of support: General/operating support.
Geographic limitations: Giving primarily in KY.
Support limitations: No grants to individuals.
Application information: Applications accepted. Application form required. Applicants should submit the following:
1) copy of IRS Determination Letter
2) detailed description of project and amount of funding requested
Initial approach: Letter
Board meeting date(s): Apr.
Deadline(s): Before Apr.
Officers: Stuart S. Janney, III, Pres.; G. Watts Humphrey, Jr., V.P.; Stacy V. Bearse, Secy.; Ellen A. Kiser, Treas.
EIN: 611142154

486
Bloomberg L.P.
731 Lexington Ave.
New York, NY 10022 (212) 318-2000

Company URL: http://www.bloomberg.com
Establishment information: Established in 1982.
Company type: Private company
Business activities: Financial information services, news, and media company.
Business type (SIC): Security and commodity services; periodical publishing and/or printing; radio and television broadcasting; cable and other pay television services; computer services; business services/miscellaneous
Financial profile for 2012: Number of employees, 15,000
Corporate officers: Peter T. Grauer, Chair.; Daniel L. Doctoroff, Pres. and C.F.O.
Board of directors: Peter T. Grauer, Chair.; Thomas F. Secunda
Giving statement: Giving through the Bloomberg L.P. Corporate Giving Program.

Bloomberg L.P. Corporate Giving Program
731 Lexington Ave.
New York, NY 10022-1331
E-mail: philanthropy@bloomberg.net; URL: http://www.bloomberg.com/about/philanthropy/

Contact: Erana Stennett
Purpose and activities: Bloomberg makes charitable contributions to nonprofit organizations involved with arts and culture, education, the environment, health, medical research, human services, and science. Support is given on a national and international basis in areas of company operations.
Fields of interest: Humanities; Arts; Education, reading; Education; Environment; Health care; Medical research; Recreation, parks/playgrounds; Human services; Science.
Programs:
Dollars for Your Hours: Through the Dollars for Your Hours program, Bloomberg L.P. enables employees to convert volunteer hours at charities into dollars.
Employee Matching Program: Through the Employee Matching Program, Bloomberg will review one employee matching contribution to a list of approved charities outside of disaster relief matches.
Type of support: Emergency funds; Employee matching gifts; Employee volunteer services; Endowments; Fellowships; General/operating support; In-kind gifts; Matching/challenge support; Research; Scholarship funds; Sponsorships.
Geographic limitations: Giving on a national and international basis in areas of company operations, with emphasis on the New York, NY, area.
Support limitations: No support for religious or political organizations, or individual schools, colleges, or universities.
Publications: Newsletter.
Application information: Applications accepted. The Philanthropy Department handles giving. The company has a staff that only handles contributions. A contributions committee reviews all requests. Application form not required. Applicants should submit the following:
1) population served
2) copy of IRS Determination Letter
3) geographic area to be served
4) detailed description of project and amount of funding requested
5) copy of current year's organizational budget and/or project budget
6) listing of additional sources and amount of support

The company prefers U.S. proposals to be submitted in English; outside the U.S. proposals can be submitted in the language of the requesting nonprofit.
Initial approach: Proposal to headquarters
Copies of proposal: 1
Committee meeting date(s): Bi-weekly
Deadline(s): None
Final notification: 6 to 8 weeks
Number of staff: 6 full-time professional.

487
Bloomin Brands, Inc.
(formerly OSI Restaurant Partners, LLC)
2202 N. West Shore Blvd., 5th Fl., Ste. 500
Tampa, FL 33607 (813) 282-1225

Company URL: http://www.osirestaurantpartners.com
Establishment information: Established in 1988.
Company type: Private company
Business activities: Operates casual-dining restaurants.
Business type (SIC): Restaurants and drinking places
Financial profile for 2011: Number of employees, 96,000; assets, $2,480,000,000; sales volume, $3,630,000,000
Corporate officers: Elizabeth A. Smith, Chair. and C.E.O.; David Deno, Exec. V.P. and C.F.O.; Charles Weston, Sr. V.P. and C.I.O.
Board of directors: Elizabeth A. Smith, Chair.; Andrew B. Balson; Robert D. Basham; J. Michael Chu; Mindy Grossman; David Humphrey; John J. Mahoney; Mark E. Nunnelly; Chris T. Sullivan
Giving statement: Giving through the OSI Restaurant Partners, LLC Corporate Giving Program and the Tampa Bay Bowl Association, Inc.

OSI Restaurant Partners, LLC Corporate Giving Program
2202 N. West Shore Blvd.
Tampa, FL 33607 (813) 282-1225

Purpose and activities: OSI Restaurant Partners makes charitable contributions to nonprofit organizations directly.
Fields of interest: Disasters, preparedness/services Military/veterans.
Type of support: General/operating support; Sponsorships.

Tampa Bay Bowl Association, Inc.
(doing business as Outback Bowl)
4211 W. Boy Scout Blvd., Ste. 560
Tampa, FL 33607-5724 (813) 874-2695
FAX: (813) 873-1959; URL: http://www.outbackbowl.com

Establishment information: Established in 1985 in FL.
Financial data (yr. ended 01/31/11): Revenue, $10,638,639; assets, $10,208,185 (M); expenditures, $10,325,455; program services expenses, $9,709,529; giving activities include $6,800,000 for 2 grants (high: $3,400,000).
Purpose and activities: The association sponsors a post-season college bowl football game. The proceeds of the game benefit the playing teams' colleges.
Fields of interest: Higher education, college; Higher education, university.
Application information: Applications not accepted. Contributes only to pre-selected organizations.
Officers and Directors:* Mitch Shribert*, Chair.; Dale Dignum*, Vice-Chair.; Jim McVay, Pres. and C.E.O.; Ken Hoverman, Secy.; William Cammarata, Treas.; Bob Basham; Terry Bien; Anthony Borrell, Jr.; Dick Christian; and 27 additional directors.
EIN: 592643123

488
Bloomingdale's, Inc.
1000 3rd Ave.
New York, NY 10022-1231 (212) 705-2000

Company URL: http://www.bloomingdales.com
Establishment information: Established in 1872.
Company type: Subsidiary of a public company
Business activities: Operates department stores.
Business type (SIC): Department stores
Corporate officers: Michael Gould, Chair. and C.E.O.; Tony Spring, Pres. and C.O.O.; Bruce Berman, C.F.O.; Frank Berman, Sr. V.P., Mktg.
Board of director: Michael Gould, Chair.
Giving statement: Giving through the Bloomingdale's, Inc. Corporate Giving Program.

Bloomingdale's, Inc. Corporate Giving Program
1000 3rd Ave.
New York, NY 10022-1230 (212) 705-2000
URL: http://www.bloomingdalesjobs.com/bloomingdales/about/community.asp

Purpose and activities: Bloomingdale's makes charitable contributions to nonprofit organizations involved with arts and culture, HIV/AIDS, health, hunger, and women. Support is given primarily in areas of company operations in California, Florida, Georgia, Illinois, Maryland, Massachusetts, Minnesota, Nevada, New Jersey, New York, Pennsylvania, and Virginia.
Fields of interest: Arts; Animal welfare; Cancer; AIDS; Diabetes; Health organizations; Food services; Homeless, human services; United Ways and Federated Giving Programs; General charitable giving Children/youth; Women.
Type of support: Employee volunteer services; General/operating support; Sponsorships.
Geographic limitations: Giving primarily in areas of company operations in CA, FL, GA, IL, MA, MD, MN, NJ, NV, NY, PA, and VA; giving also to national organizations.

489
Blue Chip Casino, Inc.
777 Blue Chip Dr.
Michigan City, IN 46360-2422
(219) 879-7711

Company URL: http://www.bluechipcasino.com
Establishment information: Established in 1999.
Company type: Private company
Business activities: Operates hotel and casino.
Business type (SIC): Hotels and motels
Corporate officers: William Boyd, Chair. and C.E.O.; Keith Smith, Pres. and C.O.O.
Board of director: William Boyd, Chair.
Giving statement: Giving through the Michigan City Community Enrichment Corporation.

Michigan City Community Enrichment Corporation

100 E. Michigan Blvd.
Michigan City, IN 46360-3265

Establishment information: Established in 1998 in IN.
Donor: Blue Chip Casino, Inc.
Financial data (yr. ended 12/31/11): Assets, $448,349 (M); gifts received, $733,966; expenditures, $757,626; qualifying distributions, $747,534; giving activities include $740,462 for grants.
Purpose and activities: The foundation supports the Michigan City Zoo and programs designed to benefit children.
Fields of interest: Zoos/zoological societies Children.
Type of support: Building/renovation; Equipment; Program development.
Geographic limitations: Giving primarily in Michigan City, IN.
Support limitations: No support for churches or sectarian religious organizations. No grants to individuals, or for endowments, debt reduction, general operating support, or basic municipal or educational functions or services.
Application information: Applications accepted. Support is limited to 1 contribution per organization during any given year. Application form required. Applicants should submit the following:
1) statement of problem project will address
2) population served
3) copy of IRS Determination Letter
4) geographic area to be served
5) copy of most recent annual report/audited financial statement/990
6) how project's results will be evaluated or measured
7) descriptive literature about organization
8) listing of board of directors, trustees, officers and other key people and their affiliations
9) detailed description of project and amount of funding requested
10) contact person
11) copy of current year's organizational budget and/or project budget
12) listing of additional sources and amount of support

Initial approach: Contact foundation for application form
Copies of proposal: 9
Deadline(s): Varies

Officers and Directors: Jim Kintzele, Pres.; Bob Worek, V.P.; Stephanie Adams, Treas.; Hassan Dabagia; Robert Lee; Peggy Thomas; Brenda Tillison-Dusenburg; Freddi Valdez.
EIN: 352036426

490
Blue Cross & Blue Shield of Mississippi

3545 Lakeland Dr.
P.O. Box 1043
Jackson, MS 39215-1043 (601) 932-3704

Company URL: http://www.bcbsms.com
Establishment information: Established in 1947.
Company type: Mutual company
Business activities: Operates medical service plan.
Business type (SIC): Insurance/accident and health
Financial profile for 2011: Assets, $778,731,898; liabilities, $217,655,051
Corporate officers: Richard J. Hale, Pres. and C.E.O.; Carol Berry Pigott, C.O.O.; Jeffrey T. Leber, C.F.O.
Subsidiaries: Advanced Health Systems, Inc., Jackson, MS; Bluebonnet Life Insurance Co., Flowood, MS; Capstone Corp., Jackson, MS; United Healthcorp Inc., Jackson, MS
Giving statement: Giving through the Blue Cross & Blue Shield of Mississippi Foundation.

Blue Cross & Blue Shield of Mississippi Foundation

3545 Lakeland Dr.
Flowood, MS 39232-8839 (601) 664-4281
FAX: (601) 952-8344;
E-mail: foundation@bcbms.com; Additional tel.: (601) 664-4525; Application address: P.O. Box 1043, Jackson, MS 39215-1043; E-mail for Healthy Hometown Award: healthyhometown@bcbsms.com; URL: http://www.healthiermississippi.org

Donor: Blue Cross and Blue Shield of Mississippi.
Contact: Sheila Grogan, Exec. Dir.
Financial data (yr. ended 12/31/11): Assets, $62,504,342 (M); gifts received, $10,000,000; expenditures, $2,958,582; qualifying distributions, $2,845,502; giving activities include $2,574,049 for 58 grants (high: $315,219; low: $1,000).
Purpose and activities: The foundation supports programs designed to improve the health and wellness of Mississippians; and promote preventive health as a solution for the heath care crisis. Special emphasis is directed toward programs designed to promote children's health and wellness; community health initiatives; and healthy lifestyles and choices.
Fields of interest: Public health; Public health, obesity; Public health, physical fitness; Health care; Nutrition; Recreation Children.
Program:
Healthy Hometown Award: The foundation awards $25,000 grants to municipalities to promote community health and wellness. Three categories will receive awards: large town with 15,000 or more residents; medium town with 5,001 to 14,999 residents; and small town with fewer than 5,000 residents. One town will be selected as The Healthiest Town in Mississippi and receive a $50,000 grant. In addition to the monetary reward, recipients receive a congratulatory ad in the local newspaper and statewide publications; a wall plaque for City Hall and/or a promotional road sign at the town's entrance; and promotion of the winning towns on the foundation and corporate websites.
Type of support: Building/renovation; Continuing support; Curriculum development; Equipment; General/operating support; Program development; Sponsorships.
Geographic limitations: Giving limited to areas of company operations in MS.
Support limitations: No support for discriminatory organizations, denominational or religious organizations, political caucuses or candidates, hospitals, college alumni associations, or high school or college sports teams. No support for individuals, or for political campaigns, special occasion or commemorative advertising, journals, or dinner programs (unless part of overall sponsorship effort), hospital building funds, or high school or college sports events.
Publications: Annual report; Application guidelines; Financial statement; Grants list.
Application information: Applications accepted. Letter of inquiry should not exceed 3 pages. Additional information may be requested at a later date. A site visit may be requested for Healthy Hometown Award. Organizations receiving support are asked to provide a final report. Application form required. Applicants should submit the following:
1) qualifications of key personnel
2) population served
3) name, address and phone number of organization
4) how project's results will be evaluated or measured
5) detailed description of project and amount of funding requested
6) contact person
7) copy of current year's organizational budget and/or project budget

Initial approach: Complete online letter of inquiry or mail letter of inquiry to foundation; download application form and mail to foundation for Healthy Hometown Award
Copies of proposal: 1
Deadline(s): None; Apr. 1 for Healthy Hometown Award
Final notification: Within 6 weeks

Officers and Directors:* John L. Sewell*, Chair.; Thomas C. Fenter, M.D.*, Vice-Chair.; Jeffery T. Leber*, Pres.; Scott T. Williamson*, Secy.; Douglas R. Garrett*, Treas.; Sheila Grogan, Exec. Dir.; J. Edward Hill; Harry M. Walker.
EIN: 200471034
Selected grants: The following grants are a representative sample of this grantmaker's funding activity:
$286,270 to Pearl River Community College, Poplarville, MS, 2011.
$250,000 to Health Care Foundation of North Mississippi, Tupelo, MS, 2011.
$101,217 to Regional Rehabilitation Center, Tupelo, MS, 2011.
$24,967 to Lawhon Elementary School, Tupelo, MS, 2011.
$24,967 to North Bay Elementary School, Bay Saint Louis, MS, 2011.
$24,967 to Pecan Park Elementary School, Ocean Springs, MS, 2011.
$24,967 to Pierce Street Elementary School, Tupelo, MS, 2011.
$24,967 to Pillow Academy, Greenwood, MS, 2011.
$10,000 to Project Fit America, Boyes Hot Springs, CA, 2011.

491
Blue Cross & Blue Shield of Rhode Island

500 Exchange St.
Providence, RI 02903 (401) 459-1000

Company URL: https://www.bcbsri.com
Establishment information: Established in 1939.
Company type: Private company
Business activities: Operates medical service plan.
Business type (SIC): Insurance/accident and health
Corporate officers: Chuck LoCurto, Chair.; Carol A. Mumford, Vice-Chair.; Peter Andruszkiewicz, Pres. and C.E.O.; William K. Wray, C.O.O.; Michael Hudson, Exec. V.P. and C.F.O.; Michele B. Lederberg, Exec. V.P., Genl. Counsel, and C.A.O.; Paul Hanlon, V.P. and C.I.O.; Brian O'Malley, V.P., Finance; Eric Gasbarro, V.P., Human Resources
Board of directors: Chuck LoCurto, Chair.; Carol A. Mumford, Vice-Chair.; Denise A. Barge; Fredric V. Christian, M.D.; Fredric V. Christian, M.D.; Meredith Curren; Michael V. D'Ambra; Scott Duhamel; James Harrington; Samuel H. Havens; Peter C. Hayes; Juana I. Horton; Elizabeth B. Lange, M.D.; Warren E. Licht, M.D.; John P. Maguire; Robert G. Norton; Anne E. Powers; Merrill Sherman; Randy A. Wyrofsky, C.P.A.

Giving statement: Giving through the Blue Cross & Blue Shield of Rhode Island Corporate Giving Program.

Blue Cross & Blue Shield of Rhode Island Corporate Giving Program

c/o Community Rels. Dept.
500 Exchange St.
Providence, RI 02903 (401) 459-1000
E-mail for volunteer program: blueangel_news@bcbsri.org.; URL: https://www.bcbsri.com/about-us/community

Purpose and activities: Blue Cross & Blue Shield of Rhode Island makes charitable contributions to nonprofit and social welfare organizations directly. Special emphasis is directed toward programs that increase access to healthcare for the uninsured. Support is limited to Rhode Island.
Fields of interest: Health care, insurance; Health care Economically disadvantaged.
Programs:
BlueAngel Community Champion Grant: Employees who have volunteered at least 25 hours in the current or most recent calendar year at one nonprofit organization can apply for this grant. The organization and the community benefit twice - from the employee's time and talent and from a $500 BlueAngel Community Champion Grant.
Time to Give: Every full-time employee receives eight hours of paid time off annually to volunteer at Rhode Island nonprofit organizations during regular business hours.
Type of support: Employee volunteer services; General/operating support; In-kind gifts; Sponsorships.
Geographic limitations: Giving limited to RI.
Support limitations: No support for religious organizations not of direct benefit to the entire community, or political, fundraising, or discriminatory organizations, or individual Rhode Island elementary or secondary schools (unless the request is for a new and innovative program specifically designed to address health and wellness), or sports teams. No grants to individuals, or for capital campaigns.
Publications: Application guidelines.
Application information: Applications accepted. The Community Relations Department handles giving. Application form not required. Applicants should submit the following:
1) name, address and phone number of organization
2) brief history of organization and description of its mission
3) listing of board of directors, trustees, officers and other key people and their affiliations
4) detailed description of project and amount of funding requested
5) contact person
6) listing of additional sources and amount of support
Initial approach: Letter of inquiry
Copies of proposal: 1
Deadline(s): None
Final notification: 6 weeks

492
Blue Cross and Blue Shield of Alabama, Inc.

450 Riverchase Pkwy. E.
Birmingham, AL 35244 (205) 220-2100

Company URL: http://www.bcbsal.com
Establishment information: Established in 1936.
Company type: Mutual company
Business activities: Operates medical service plan.
Business type (SIC): Insurance/accident and health
Financial profile for 2012: Number of employees, 3,700
Corporate officers: M. Eugene Moor, Jr., Chair.; Terry D. Kellogg, Pres. and C.E.O.; Cynthia Mizell, Sr. V.P. and C.F.O.; Scott McGlaun, Sr. V.P. and C.I.O.
Board of director: M. Eugene Moor, Chair.
Giving statement: Giving through the Caring Foundation.

The Caring Foundation

450 Riverchase Pkwy. E.
Birmingham, AL 35244-2858

Establishment information: Established in 1990 in AL.
Donor: Blue Cross and Blue Shield of Alabama, Inc.
Contact: Barbara A. Hutchinson
Financial data (yr. ended 12/31/11): Assets, $43,917,895 (M); gifts received, $10,146,696; expenditures, $3,837,750; qualifying distributions, $3,729,335; giving activities include $3,729,335 for 269 grants (high: $255,000; low: $100).
Purpose and activities: The foundation supports organizations involved with education, health, safety, and children and youth.
Fields of interest: Education; Hospitals (general); Health care; Safety, education; Children/youth, services; United Ways and Federated Giving Programs.
Type of support: General/operating support; Program development.
Geographic limitations: Giving primarily in AL.
Support limitations: No grants to individuals, or for capital campaigns.
Application information: Applications accepted. Application form not required. Applicants should submit the following:
1) name, address and phone number of organization
2) brief history of organization and description of its mission
3) detailed description of project and amount of funding requested
Initial approach: Proposal
Copies of proposal: 1
Board meeting date(s): 4th Wed. in Apr.
Deadline(s): None
Final notification: 1 to 2 months
Officers and Directors:* M. Eugene Moor, Jr.*, Chair.; Terry D. Kellogg, Pres.; Timothy L. Kirkpatrick, V.P.; Carol D. Mackin, Secy.; Cynthia M. Vice, Treas.; James M. Aycock; L. Keith Granger; Kenneth E. Hubbard; Fred D. Hunker, M.D.; Helen Shores Lee; William J. Stevens.
EIN: 631035261
Selected grants: The following grants are a representative sample of this grantmaker's funding activity:
$870,647 to Alabama Child Caring Foundation, Birmingham, AL, 2009.
$367,210 to United Way of Central Alabama, Birmingham, AL, 2009.
$200,000 to Explore Center, Mobile, AL, 2009.
$168,000 to University of Alabama, Tuscaloosa, AL, 2009.
$100,500 to Salvation Army of Birmingham, Birmingham, AL, 2009.
$100,000 to Community Foundation of Greater Birmingham, Birmingham, AL, 2009.
$40,000 to Multiple Sclerosis Society, National, Birmingham, AL, 2009.
$35,000 to HEAL, Birmingham, AL, 2009.
$30,000 to Troy University, Troy, AL, 2009.
$12,500 to Birmingham History Center, Birmingham, AL, 2009.

493
Blue Cross and Blue Shield of Florida, Inc.

4800 Deerwood Campus Pkwy.
Jacksonville, FL 32246-6498
(904) 791-6111

Company URL: http://www.bcbsfl.com
Establishment information: Established in 1945.
Company type: Mutual company
Business activities: Operates medical service plan.
Business type (SIC): Insurance/accident and health
Financial profile for 2010: Number of employees, 5,000; sales volume, $8,530,000,000
Corporate officers: Robert I. Lufrano, Chair. and C.E.O.; Arnold Livermore, Exec. V.P. and C.O.O.; R. Chris Doerr, Exec. V.P. and C.F.O.; Bob Well, Sr. V.P., Human Resources
Board of directors: Robert I. Lufrano, Chair.; John B. Ramil
Giving statement: Giving through the Blue Cross and Blue Shield of Florida, Inc. Corporate Giving Program and the Blue Cross Blue Shield of Florida Foundation, Inc.

Blue Cross and Blue Shield of Florida, Inc. Corporate Giving Program

c/o Community Rels.
4800 Deerwood Campus Pkwy., DC3-4
Jacksonville, FL 32246-8273
E-mail: communityrelations@bcbsfl.com; URL: http://www.bcbsfl.com/index.cfm?section=visitors&fuseaction=Community.home

Purpose and activities: As a complement to its foundation, Blue Cross and Blue Shield of Florida also makes charitable contributions to nonprofit organizations involved with culture, education, health, and human services. Support is limited to Florida.
Fields of interest: Arts; Education; Health care; Human services; Community/economic development.
Type of support: Consulting services; Donated equipment; General/operating support; In-kind gifts; Loaned talent; Program development; Public relations services; Sponsorships; Technical assistance.
Geographic limitations: Giving limited to FL.
Support limitations: No support for organizations in communities where Blue Cross and Blue Shield of Florida already supports a similar organization, religious organizations not of direct benefit to the entire community, political organizations or candidates, organizations posing a conflict of interest with Blue Cross and Blue Shield of Florida, discriminatory organizations, or parent-teacher organizations. No grants to individuals, or for general operating support for civic or fraternal organizations.
Publications: Application guidelines.
Application information: Applications accepted. The Community Relations Department handles giving. Application form required. Applicants should submit the following:
1) results expected from proposed grant
2) statement of problem project will address
3) population served
4) name, address and phone number of organization
5) geographic area to be served
6) copy of most recent annual report/audited financial statement/990
7) listing of board of directors, trustees, officers and other key people and their affiliations

8) detailed description of project and amount of funding requested
9) contact person
10) copy of current year's organizational budget and/or project budget
11) listing of additional sources and amount of support
12) additional materials/documentation

Applications should include the organization's Tax ID Number, an annual report, the levels of sponsorship and benefits of each; and indicate how the program/event would help control heath care costs.

Initial approach: Download application form and mail to headquarters
Deadline(s): 15th of each month
Final notification: 60 days

Number of staff: 1 full-time professional; 1 part-time support.

Blue Cross Blue Shield of Florida Foundation, Inc.

(formerly The Blue Foundation for a Healthy Florida, Inc.)
4800 Deerwood Campus Pkwy., DC 3-4
Jacksonville, FL 32246-6498
FAX: (904) 357-8367;
E-mail: thebluefoundationfl@bcbsfl.com; E-mail for Susan B. Towler: susan.towler@bcbsfl.com; E-mail for Sapphire Award: TheSapphireAward@bcbsfl.com; E-mail for Embrace a Healthy Florida: embrace@bcbsfl.com; E-mail for Improve Quality of Life Grants: communityrelations@floridablue.com; URL: http://www3.bcbsfl.com/wps/portal/bcbsfl/bluefoundation

Establishment information: Established in 2001 in FL.
Donors: Blue Cross and Blue Shield of Florida, Inc.; Health Options, Inc.; Tracy Leinbach.
Contact: Susan B. Towler, V.P.; Susan F. Wildes, Sr. Prog. Mgr.
Financial data (yr. ended 12/31/11): Assets, $114,028,784 (M); gifts received, $30,682,888; expenditures, $7,463,530; qualifying distributions, $6,960,855; giving activities include $5,348,556 for 157 grants (high: $1,600,001; low: $1,000) and $313,179 for 2 foundation-administered programs.
Purpose and activities: The foundation supports programs designed to improve the health of Floridians and their communities. Special emphasis is directed toward programs designed to improve access to health care; consumer health; the quality and safety of patient care; quality of life; and the healthcare system.
Fields of interest: Arts; Elementary/secondary education; Higher education; Nursing school/education; Education, reading; Education; Health care, alliance/advocacy; Health care, public policy; Health care, equal rights; Health care, clinics/centers; Dental care; Optometry/vision screening; Public health; Public health, obesity; Public health, physical fitness; Health care, financing; Health care, patient services; Health care; Mental health, counseling/support groups; Mental health/crisis services; Nutrition; Disasters, preparedness/services; Family services; Human services; Civil/human rights, equal rights; Community/economic development; Leadership development Children; Minorities; Economically disadvantaged.
Programs:
Embrace a Healthy Florida - Addressing Childhood Obesity: The foundation supports programs designed address the causes of childhood obesity that goes beyond traditional nutrition and fitness. The foundation provides grants to nonprofit organizations, fund research, and foster community collaboration and engagement. The program is limited to Jacksonville, Miami, Orlando, Tallahassee, and Tampa, Florida. Visit URL http://embraceahealthyfl.org/ for more information.
Improve Access to Health Care Grants Program: Through IMPACT grants, the foundation supports programs designed to increase access to quality health-related services for Floridians, especially the uninsured and underserved. Special emphasis is directed toward initiatives designed to incorporate new innovative and evidence-based approaches; build program and/or organizational capacity; address health care disparities in a culturally-competent manner; promote collaboration; leverage financial, human and other resources to maximize measurable impact; and programs that are forward-focused and cognizant of a changing health care system. Health-related services include primary care; dental care; vision care; specialty care; mental health services and counseling; case management and health care navigation; outreach, awareness, and education; and advocacy and public policy. Grants range from $10,000 to $100,000.
Improve Quality and Safety of Patient Care: The foundation, in partnership with The Robert Wood Johnson Foundation, the Florida Action Coalition, and the Florida Center for Nursing, supports programs designed to increase educational capacity, workforce diversity, continuing education, and professional development of nurses.
Improve Quality of Life: The foundation supports programs designed to address critical issues in local communities. Special emphasis is directed toward arts and culture; education and literacy; human and social services; disaster relief and preparedness; and diversity and community development.
Sapphire Award: The foundation annually recognizes community heath organizations that have demonstrated excellence in improving access to health-related services and health-related outcomes for Florida's at-risk populations and communities. The award is divided into three categories: organization, programs, and services and its designed to promote support for improved services and systems that can be sustained over time.
Type of support: Capital campaigns; Continuing support; Equipment; General/operating support; Management development/capacity building; Program development; Scholarship funds; Technical assistance.
Geographic limitations: Giving limited to areas of company operations in FL.
Support limitations: No support for political or lobbying organizations, fraternal, athletic, or social organizations, or religious organizations not of direct benefit to the entire community, private foundations, or Type III supporting organizations. No grants to individuals (except for the Sapphire Award) or for fundraising.
Publications: Application guidelines; Corporate giving report; Grants list.
Application information: Applications accepted. A site visit may be requested for IMPACT Health Care Grants. Organizations may apply for support only once during a 12-moth period. Unsolicited applications for Embrace a Healthy Florida are not accepted. An interview may be requested for the Sapphire Award. Organizations receiving support are asked to submit a final report. Application form required. Applicants should submit the following:
1) qualifications of key personnel
2) population served
3) copy of IRS Determination Letter
4) geographic area to be served
5) copy of most recent annual report/audited financial statement/990
6) how project's results will be evaluated or measured
7) listing of board of directors, trustees, officers and other key people and their affiliations
8) detailed description of project and amount of funding requested
9) copy of current year's organizational budget and/or project budget
10) listing of additional sources and amount of support

Nominations for the Sapphire Award must include 3 letters of support from people familiar with the nominated organization or individual.

Initial approach: Complete online letter of inquiry and application for IMPACT Health Care Grants; complete online nomination form for Sapphire Award; complete online application for Improve Quality of Life Grants
Board meeting date(s): Feb., Apr., June, Aug., Oct., and Dec.
Deadline(s): Mar. 28th for letter of inquiry for IMPACT Health Care Grants; June 29 for full application for IMPACT Health Care Grants; Aug. 31 for Sapphire Award; None for Improve Quality of Life Grants
Final notification: Oct. for IMPACT Health Care Grants; Feb. for Sapphire Award

Officers and Directors:* Cyrus M. "Russ" Jollivette*, Chair.; Charles S. Joseph*, Vice-Chair; Susan B. Towler, V.P.; Mark S. McGowan*, Secy.; Cheryl O. Mose*, Treas.; Michael Cascone, Jr.; Gary M. Healy; V. Sheffield Kenyon; Joyce A. Kramer; Penelope S. Shaffer; Darnell Smith.
Number of staff: 4 full-time professional.
EIN: 593707820
Selected grants: The following grants are a representative sample of this grantmaker's funding activity:
$1,600,001 to University of Florida Foundation, Gainesville, FL, 2011. To sponsor Chair in Health Disparities and Health Disparities Support.
$250,000 to Florida Association of Food Banks, Fort Myers, FL, 2011. For food for the entire State of Florida.
$150,000 to University of Central Florida, Orlando, FL, 2011. For Center for Nursing and Nursing Education.
$125,000 to Americas Health Insurance Plans Foundation, Washington, DC, 2011. For ChildObesity180 Initiative.
$122,500 to Susan B. Anthony Center, Pembroke Pines, FL, 2011. For medical care for homeless and recovering women by offering substance abuse treatment services and quality physical and mental health care programs.
$104,000 to War on Poverty - Florida, Jacksonville, FL, 2011. For coordination of local efforts, Lead Agency for Opa-Locka Embrace Initiative.
$76,500 to Hebni Nutrition Consultants, Orlando, FL, 2011. For programs providing nutrition education and intervention strategies to prevent diet-related diseases.
$49,242 to Institute for Child and Family Health, Miami, FL, 2011. For Pediatric Capacity.
$18,000 to Good Samaritan Health Centers, Saint Augustine, FL, 2011. For Wildflower Clinic Dental Program Manager.
$9,000 to Hialeah Public Libraries, Hialeah, FL, 2011. For Healthy Lifestyle at your Library.

494
Blue Cross and Blue Shield of Illinois, Inc.
300 E. Randolph St.
Chicago, IL 60601-5099 (312) 653-6000

Company URL: http://www.bcbsil.com
Establishment information: Established in 1936.
Company type: Subsidiary of a private company
Business activities: Operates medical service plan.
Business type (SIC): Insurance/accident and health
Corporate officers: Raymond Mc Caskey, C.E.O.; Karen M. Atwood, Pres.
Giving statement: Giving through the Blue Cross and Blue Shield of Illinois, Inc. Corporate Giving Program.

Blue Cross and Blue Shield of Illinois, Inc. Corporate Giving Program
300 E. Randolph St.
Chicago, IL 60601-5099
E-mail: regina_m_high@bcbsil.com; Additional contact: Clarita Santos, Dir. of Community Health Initiatives, e-mail: clarita_santos@bcbsil.com; URL: http://www.bcbsil.com/company_info/community/index.html

Contact: Regina High, Community Investments Mgr.
Purpose and activities: Blue Cross and Blue Shield of Illinois makes charitable contributions to nonprofit organizations involved with arts and culture, education, health, human services, diversity, and civic affairs. Special emphasis is directed towards programs designed to promote health and proper nutrition among children. Support is given primarily in Illinois.
Fields of interest: Arts; Education; Public health; Public health, physical fitness; Health care; Employment; Nutrition; Recreation, parks/playgrounds; Human services; Civil/human rights, equal rights; Community/economic development Children; Economically disadvantaged.
Type of support: General/operating support; In-kind gifts; Sponsorships.
Geographic limitations: Giving primarily in IL.
Support limitations: No support for hospitals, or individual schools or universities. No grants for political campaigns or religious activities.
Application information: Applications accepted. Application form required.
Initial approach: Complete online application form
Deadline(s): Mar. 31; 3 months prior to need for sponsorships
Final notification: June

495
Blue Cross and Blue Shield of Kansas, Inc.
1133 S.W. Topeka Blvd.
Topeka, KS 66629-0001 (785) 291-4180

Company URL: http://www.bcbsks.com/AboutUs/
Establishment information: Established in 1942.
Company type: Mutual company
Business activities: Operates medical service plan.
Business type (SIC): Insurance/accident and health
Corporate officers: Steven D. Marsh, C.P.A., Chair.; Gary Shorman, Vice-Chair.; Andrew C. Corbin, Pres. and C.E.O.; Matthew D. All, V.P. and Genl. Counsel; Shelley Pittman, V.P., Opers.; Beryl Lowery-Born, V.P., Finance; Mark G. Dolsky, V.P., Sales and Mktg.
Board of directors: Steven D. Marsh, Chair.; Gary D. Shorman, Vice-Chair.; James M. Alley III; Leon J. Boor; Anderw C. Corbin; Robin R. LacKamp; Diane L. Lee; Steven D. Marsh; Edward J. Miller; Louis E. Mosiman; Robert L. Mullen; Thomas C. Simpson; Steve W. Sloan; Susan M. Smith; Cathy Mith Taylor; Kenneth W. Winter
Giving statement: Giving through the Blue Cross and Blue Shield of Kansas Foundation, Inc.

Blue Cross and Blue Shield of Kansas Foundation, Inc.
1133 S.W. Topeka Blvd.
Topeka, KS 66629-0001 (785) 291-7246
FAX: (785) 291-7664;
E-mail: marlou.wegener@bcbsks.com; URL: http://www.bcbsks.com/AboutUs/Foundation/index.htm

Establishment information: Established in 2005 in KS.
Donor: Blue Cross and Blue Shield of Kansas, Inc.
Contact: Marlou Wegener, C.O.O.
Financial data (yr. ended 12/31/11): Assets, $11,399,491 (M); gifts received, $2,000,000; expenditures, $599,044; qualifying distributions, $543,333; giving activities include $543,333 for grants.
Purpose and activities: The foundation supports programs designed to address health improvement; healthcare access; health education; healthy behaviors and prevention; and direct health services for the uninsured.
Fields of interest: Health care, clinics/centers; Public health; Public health, obesity; Public health, physical fitness; Health care, insurance; Health care, patient services; Health care.
Program:
Healthy Habits for Life: The foundation awards grants of up to $1,000 to assist schools in promoting healthy lifestyle choices for their students and to address childhood obesity. Special emphasis is directed toward programs designed to help youth reduce cardiovascular risk; increase physical activity; and learn healthy eating habits.
Type of support: Curriculum development; General/operating support; Program development.
Geographic limitations: Giving in areas of company operations in KS.
Support limitations: No support for religious organizations or parent-teacher organizations. No grants to individuals, or for sponsorships of sports or athletic teams, capital campaigns, or political campaigns, events, or activities.
Publications: Application guidelines.
Application information: Applications accepted. Application form required. Applicants should submit the following:
1) results expected from proposed grant
2) brief history of organization and description of its mission
3) how project's results will be evaluated or measured
4) explanation of why grantmaker is considered an appropriate donor for project
5) detailed description of project and amount of funding requested
6) copy of current year's organizational budget and/or project budget
7) plans for acknowledgement

Initial approach: Download application form and fax or mail for requests of $1,000 or less; telephone or e-mail foundation for requests over $1,000; download application and mail for Healthy Habits for Life
Deadline(s): None; Oct. 14 for Healthy Habits for Life
Final notification: Dec. 1 for Healthy Habits for Life
Officers and Directors:* Andrew C. Corbin*, Pres.; S. Graham Bailey*, C.O.O.; Scott H. Raymond, Secy.; Beryl Lowery-Born*, Treas.; Robin R. LacKamp; Louis E. Mosiman.
EIN: 203085640
Selected grants: The following grants are a representative sample of this grantmaker's funding activity:
$50,000 to Kansas Childrens Discovery Center, Topeka, KS, 2010.
$35,000 to United Way of Greater Topeka, Topeka, KS, 2010. For general support.
$5,000 to Douglas County Dental Clinic, Lawrence, KS, 2010.
$5,000 to Guadalupe Clinic, Wichita, KS, 2010.
$5,000 to Health Care Access, Lawrence, KS, 2010.
$5,000 to Mother Mary Anne Clinic, Wichita, KS, 2010.
$5,000 to Oral Health Kansas, Topeka, KS, 2010.
$5,000 to United Way of the Plains, Wichita, KS, 2010. For general support.
$4,210 to Caritas Clinics, Leavenworth, KS, 2010.
$1,000 to Manhattan Community Foundation, Manhattan, KS, 2010.

496
Blue Cross and Blue Shield of Minnesota
3535 Blue Cross Rd.
Saint Paul, MN 55122-1154
(651) 662-8000

Company URL: http://www.bluecrossmn.com
Establishment information: Established in 1933.
Company type: Mutual company
Business activities: Operates medical service plan.
Business type (SIC): Insurance/accident and health
Corporate officers: Pamela A. Wheelock, Chair.; Peter H. McNerney, Vice-Chair.; Michael Guyette, Pres. and C.E.O.; James Eppel, Jr., Sr. V.P. and C.O.O.; Jamison Rice, Sr. V.P. and C.F.O.; James Egan, Sr. V.P. and C.I.O.; Jackie Jennifer, Sr. V.P., Opers.; Kathleen Mock, Sr. V.P., Public Affairs; Colleen Connors, Sr. V.P., Human Resources and Comms.
Board of directors: Pamela A. Wheelock, Chair.; Peter H. McNerney, Vice-Chair.; Kathleen A. Blatz; Walter T. Chesley; Judi H. Dutcher; William F. Farley; Benjamin R. Field III; Patrick Geraghty; Kevin R. Green; Rita J. Heise; Jan K. Malcolm; Vance K. Opperman, Esq.; James T. Porter; Hugh C. Smith, M.D.
Giving statement: Giving through the Blue Cross and Blue Shield of Minnesota Foundation, Inc.

Blue Cross and Blue Shield of Minnesota Foundation, Inc.
1750 Yankee Doodle Rd., N159
Eagan, MN 55122-1613 (651) 662-3950
FAX: (651) 662-4266;
E-mail: foundation@bluecrossmn.com; Additional address: P.O. Box 64560, St. Paul, MN 55164-0560; Additional tel.: (866) 812-1593; Contact for Growing Up Healthy: Jocelyn Ancheta, Prog. Off., tel.: (651) 662-2894, e-mail: Jocelyn_L_Ancheta@bluecrossmn.com; Contact for Public Libraries for Health and Building Health Equity Together: Stacey Millett, Sr. Prog. Off, tel.: (651) 662-1019, e-mail:

Stacey_D_Millett@bluecrossmn.com; URL: http://www.bcbsmnfoundation.org

Establishment information: Established in 1986 in MN.
Donors: Blue Cross and Blue Shield of Minnesota; American Healthways; HMO Minnesota.
Financial data (yr. ended 12/31/11): Assets, $65,755,717 (M); gifts received, $10,000,404; expenditures, $3,879,493; qualifying distributions, $3,590,664; giving activities include $2,198,855 for 63 grants (high: $310,830; low: $2,500) and $415,586 for 4 foundation-administered programs.
Purpose and activities: The foundation supports programs designed to improve community conditions that have an impact on the health of children and families. Special emphasis is directed toward health and early childhood development; health and housing; health and social connectedness; health and the environment; and healthier Minnesota communities.
Fields of interest: Child development, education; Libraries (public); Education; Environment, toxics; Environment; Health care, equal rights; Health care, clinics/centers; Public health; Public health, environmental health; Health care; Mental health/crisis services; Employment; Nutrition; Housing/shelter; Safety/disasters; Family services; Human services; Community/economic development Children; Minorities; African Americans/Blacks; Native Americans/American Indians; Immigrants/refugees; Economically disadvantaged.

Programs:

Building Health Equity Together: The foundation awards grants of up to $75,000 to partnerships between Minnesota local governments and local nonprofit organizations with programs designed to create conditions that allow all community members to reach their full health potential. Partnerships must address one or more factors that influence health outcomes including education, employment, income, family and social support, and community. Special emphasis is directed toward political subdivisions or tribal governments with a significant percentage of low-income households.

Connect for Health Challenge: The foundation awards grants of up to $500,000 to nonprofits, schools, and local units of government with programs designed to strengthen social connections in low-income communities. Applicants are selected and voted on by the public and are judged on alignment with the challenge topic, collaboration, effectiveness and impact, organizational capacity, and sustainability. Visit URL http://challenges.incommons.org/connectforhealth for more information.

Growing Up Healthy: Kids and Communities: The foundation supports programs designed to improve children's health through the intersection of two or more of the following health determinants: early childhood development; stable, affordable housing; and the physical environment. Special emphasis is directed toward projects designed to address the needs of children of color and children living in poverty; and originate from and work with Native American communities where significant socioeconomic and health disparities exist. The foundation awards planning grants of up to $25,000 and three-year implementation grants of up to $150,000.

Health Equity: The foundation supports programs designed to build positive community relationships at the organizational and individual level. The foundation builds on current work in early childhood development, social connectedness, and links between neighborhood and life expectancy to improve community conditions that affect health equity and to promote practices that reduce inequities.

Health Impact Assessments: The foundation, in partnership with the Robert Wood Johnson Foundation and The Pew Charitable Trusts, supports health impact assessments (HIA) through grants and technical assistance. Special emphasis is directed toward HIA initiatives designed to demonstrate projects that inform a specific decision and help build the case for the value of HIA; and initiatives that enable organizations with previous HIA experience to conduct HIAs and develop sustainable, self-supporting HIA programs at the local, state, or tribal level. The program is administered by The Pew Charitable Trusts. Visit URL http://www.healthimpactproject.org/ for more information.

Healthy Children: The foundation supports programs designed to improve the quality of housing; reduce children's exposure to harmful chemicals; increase readiness for kindergarten; and increase children's access to healthy foods and safe places to play.

Healthy Neighborhoods: The foundation supports programs designed to build strong bonds between neighbors in communities across the state through improving or extending the reach of gathering places that build connections in low-income communities.

Public Libraries for Health: Through Public Libraries for Health, the foundation partners with up to four public libraries to improve health for low-income communities and communities of color and to advance health equity. Projects must address education, employment, income, family and social support, or community safety. Grants of up to $50,000 are awarded and may be used for an existing project or new opportunity.

Resilient Organizations Fund: Through the Resilient Organization Fund, the foundation awards grants to current Blue Cross Foundation grantees to strengthen long-term sustainability and organizational capacity.

Type of support: Continuing support; Management development/capacity building; Program development; Technical assistance.
Geographic limitations: Giving limited to MN; giving also to statewide and regional organizations.
Support limitations: No support for athletic organizations or groups. No grants to individuals, or for lobbying, political, or fraternal activities, legal services, sports events, religious activities, clinical quality improvement activities, biomedical research, capital campaigns, endowments or travel, fundraising events, or development campaigns, debt reduction, the payment of services or benefits reimbursable from other sources, the supplanting of funds already secured for budgeted staff and/or services, or long-term support; no loans.
Publications: Annual report; Application guidelines; Corporate giving report; Grants list; Informational brochure; Newsletter; Occasional report.
Application information: Applications accepted. Support is limited to 1 contribution per organization during any given year. Site visits may be requested for Building Health Equity Together. Application form not required. Applicants should submit the following:
1) copy of IRS Determination Letter
2) geographic area to be served
3) how project's results will be evaluated or measured
4) detailed description of project and amount of funding requested

Initial approach: Telephone foundation; mail letter of inquiry to foundation; proposal for Public Libraries for Health; complete online application for Building Health Equity Together
Board meeting date(s): Feb., May, Aug., and Nov.
Deadline(s): Visit website for deadlines; July 20 for Public Libraries for Health; Aug. 27 to Sept. 28 for Building Health Equity Together
Final notification: Sept. for Public Libraries for Health; Mid-Dec. for Building Health Equity Together

Officers and Directors: Pamela A. Wheelock*, Chair.; Kathy Gaalswyk*, Vice-Chair.; Marsha Shotley*, Pres.; Denise Bergevin, V.P.; John Orner, V.P.; Nancy Nelson*, Secy.-Treas.; Carolyn Link, Exec. Dir.; Colleen Connors; Frank Fernandez; Shirley Hughes; Jan K. Malcolm; Deborah Meehan.
Number of staff: 6 full-time professional.
EIN: 363525653
Selected grants: The following grants are a representative sample of this grantmaker's funding activity:
$500,000 to Minnesota Community Action Association Resource Fund, Saint Paul, MN, 2012. For distribution to eight Community Action Partnership agencies serving the ten counties with the highest rates of poverty and the surrounding service areas.
$333,000 to Pew Charitable Trusts, Philadelphia, PA, 2012. For up to three Minnesota health impact assessments, training, mentoring and technical assistance and reasonable staff support.
$312,127 to United e-Way, Alexandria, VA, 2013. For 2012 Community Giving Campaign.
$310,830 to Pew Charitable Trusts, Philadelphia, PA, 2011. For two health impact assessment demonstration projects and training and technical assistance for grantees.
$272,244 to United Ways of the Greater New York, New Jersey and Connecticut Tri-State Area, New York, NY, 2011. For Community Giving Campaign.
$150,000 to American Cancer Society, Mendota Heights, MN, 2011. To advance Minnesota CHW field-building work and establish a sustainable organizational infrastructure for its future.
$100,000 to Second Harvest Heartland, Saint Paul, MN, 2011. For Hunger-Free Minnesota initiative.
$75,000 to Anoka-Hennepin School District No. 11, Coon Rapids, MN, 2012. For College Possible Expansion to Champlin Park High School.
$60,000 to Peta Wakan Tipi, Saint Paul, MN, 2012. For indigenous food network that will encompass from farm to fork nutrition within the American Indian community in a cultural context.
$60,000 to United Way, Greater Mankato Area, Mankato, MN, 2011. For First Steps Collaborative Coordinator position to deliver a coordinated and integrated approach to address social determinants of health issues in four counties.
$50,000 to Austin Public Library, Austin, MN, 2012. For Healthy Cooking on a Budget program.
$50,000 to Heartland Community Action Agency, Willmar, MN, 2012. For second year funding for the Healthy Foundations project.
$50,000 to Local Initiatives Support Corporation, Twin Cities, Saint Paul, MN, 2012. For second year funding for advancing comprehensive community development strategies in two targeted communities - Aurora St. Anthony and Frogtown.
$50,000 to Minnewaska Area Schools, Glenwood, MN, 2012. For second year funding for Pope County Growing Up Healthy project.
$50,000 to Open Cities Health Center, Saint Paul, MN, 2012. For second year funding for health navigator to provide health outreach and education as part of the Frogtown-Summit University Expanded Community Resource Hub.
$25,000 to First Childrens Finance, Minneapolis, MN, 2011. For Minnesota Based Childcare Business Improvement Programs.
$25,000 to GiveMN.org, Saint Paul, MN, 2011. For sponsorship of small nonprofit leaderboard grant prizes during the Give to the Max Day event.

$25,000 to Greater Minneapolis Council of Churches, Foodshare, Minneapolis, MN, 2011. For Minnesota Foodshare Drive.
$25,000 to ISAIAH, Saint Paul, MN, 2011. For Healthy Heartlands-California Endowment Event: Power to Thrive/Organizing for Public Health.
$20,000 to Community Design Center of Minnesota, Saint Paul, MN, 2012. For Growing Healthy Youth and Communities.
$5,570 to Council on Foundations, Arlington, VA, 2011. For Funding Partner.

497
Blue Cross and Blue Shield of North Carolina, Inc.

P.O. Box 2291
Durham, NC 27702 (919) 765-4102

Company URL: http://www.bcbsnc.com
Establishment information: Established in 1968.
Company type: Mutual company
Business activities: Operates medical service plan; sells life, dental, long-term care, and disability insurance.
Business type (SIC): Insurance/accident and health; insurance/life
Corporate officers: J. Bradley Wilson, Pres. and C.E.O.; Ian K. Gordon, Sr. V.P. and C.O.O.; Gerald Petkau, Sr. V.P. and C.F.O.; Alan Hughes, Sr. V.P. and C.I.O.; N. King Prather, Sr. V.P., Genl. Counsel, and Corp. Secy.
Giving statement: Giving through the Blue Cross and Blue Shield of North Carolina, Inc. Corporate Giving Program and the Blue Cross and Blue Shield of North Carolina Foundation.

Blue Cross and Blue Shield of North Carolina, Inc. Corporate Giving Program

c/o Community Rels.
P.O. Box 2291
Durham, NC 27702-2291 (919) 765-4600
E-mail: jasmine.smith@bcbsnc.com; Additional e-mail: Kristy Kent, Community Leadership and Volunteerism: kristy.kent@bcbsnc.com;
URL: http://www.bcbsnc.com/content/corporate/community.htm

Contact: Jasmine Smith, Community Sponsorships
Purpose and activities: As a complement to its foundation, Blue Cross and Blue Shield of North Carolina also makes charitable contributions to nonprofit organizations directly. Support is given primarily in areas of company operations in North Carolina, and to national organizations.
Fields of interest: Education, fund raising/fund distribution; Health care, blood supply; Health care; Health organizations, fund raising/fund distribution; Heart & circulatory diseases; Cancer research; Agriculture, sustainable programs; Food services; Independent living, disability; United Ways and Federated Giving Programs Economically disadvantaged.
Type of support: Donated products; Employee volunteer services; General/operating support.
Geographic limitations: Giving primarily in areas of company operations in NC, and to national organizations.
Application information: The Community Relations Department handles giving.
Initial approach: Contact Community Relations department for application information
Administrators: JoAnn Holder, Admin. Asst.; Kristy Kent, Community Leadership and Volunteerism; Jasmine Smith, Community Sponsorships.

Blue Cross and Blue Shield of North Carolina Foundation

c/o Grant Review Comm.
P.O. Box 2291
5901 Old Chapel Hill Rd.
Durham, NC 27702-2291 (919) 765-7347
FAX: (919) 765-7288;
E-mail: info@bcbsncfoundation.org; E-mail for Jill Mallatratt: jill.mallatratt@bcbsncfoundation.org; Contact for Health of Vulnerable Populations: Katie Eyes, Prog. Mgr., tel.: (919) 765-4024, e-mail: katie.eyes@bcbsncfoundation.org; Contact for Healthy Active Communities: Jennifer MacDougall, Prog. Mgr., tel.: (919) 765-2128, e-mail: jennifer.macDougall@bcbsncfoundation.org; Contact for Community Impact through Nonprofit Excellence: Valerie Stewart, Prog. Mgr., tel.: (919) 765-4514, e-mail: valerie.stewart@bcbsncfoundation.org; Additional contact: Michael Gay, Opers. Mgr., tel. (919) 765-2826, e-mail: michael.gay@bcbsncfoundation.org; URL: http://www.bcbsnc.com/foundation

Establishment information: Established in 2000 in NC.
Donors: Blue Cross and Blue Shield of North Carolina, Inc.; Golden Leaf Foundation.
Contact: Jill Mallatratt, Assoc. Project Mgr.
Financial data (yr. ended 06/30/11): Assets, $114,282,807 (M); gifts received, $10,000,000; expenditures, $12,217,042; qualifying distributions, $11,100,075; giving activities include $10,762,781 for 132 grants (high: $2,000,000; low: $2,050) and $284,728 for 4 foundation-administered programs.
Purpose and activities: The foundation supports programs designed to improve the health and well-being of North Carolinians. Special emphasis is directed toward programs designed to attain measurable results and sustained community impact.
Fields of interest: Medical care, community health systems; Health care, clinics/centers; Dental care; Public health; Public health, obesity; Public health, physical fitness; Health care, patient services; Health care; Cancer; Breast cancer; Heart & circulatory diseases; Diabetes; Food services; Nutrition; Athletics/sports, school programs; Children/youth, services; Family services, parent education; Rural development; Leadership development Aging; Disabilities, people with; Economically disadvantaged.
Programs:
Be Active Kids: Through Be Active Kids, the foundation and Be Active North Carolina, educates preschool children about the importance of eating healthy and staying alive through an interactive nutrition and physical program. The program includes a curriculum-based Be Active Kids kit with lesson plans, recipes, and activity ideas, storyboards, classroom posters, and a parent newsletter. Kits are free of charge to child-care providers in North Carolina when they attend a free Be Active Kids training. Visit URL http://beactivekids.org/bak/Front/Default.aspx for more information.
Community Impact through Nonprofit Excellence: The foundation supports programs designed to strengthen the organizational capacity of nonprofit organizations in North Carolina by addressing program delivery and impact; fundraising and long-term financial stability; board leadership and contributions to the organization; operational efficiencies and infrastructure; and collaborations and partnerships with other organizations to better serve stakeholders. The initiative also includes the Healthy Community Institute, a two-day board and staff training program designed to build organizational capacity; 5 Good Ideas, a half-day interactive training for nonprofit leaders focusing on management skills and leadership development; and Community TIEs, and grant program honoring achievement in Technology, Innovation, and Evaluation.
Health of Vulnerable Populations: The foundation supports programs designed to improve health outcomes for North Carolinians served by health care safety-net organizations. Special emphasis is directed toward programs designed to increase quality, supply, and access to medical and dental care through coordination and continuity of care; increased number of providers serving vulnerable populations; increased provider use of evidence-based protocol and quality improvement measures; and enhanced operations and infrastructure of health care safety-net organizations. The foundation also supports programs designed to improve individual health, with a focus on diabetes, cardiovascular, and oral health; self-care and preventative behavior; reduced number of visits to emergency departments for non-urgent care; blood pressure control; A1C less than or equal to 7; and increased rate of completion of phase 1 dental treatment plan.
Healthy Active Communities: The foundation supports programs designed to increase physical activity and access to healthy food through the use of the physical environment to create space, and places for physical activity and healthy food options; organizational and institutional policies that support increased activity and healthy eating; initiatives that increase physical activity and knowledge of healthy foods both during and upon completion of the program; and plans that address the built and policy environment for physical activity and healthy eating in local communities.
Healthy Active Communities - Equipment: The foundation awards grants of up to $5,000 for tools or accessories designed to enhance the capability of an agency to increase levels of physical activity or access to healthy food for rural communities or vulnerable populations in urban communities. Equipment requests may include pedometers, heart rate monitors, exercise balls, yoga mats, dyna bands, weights, age-appropriate play equipment, and garden tools and supplies.
Robert K. Greczyn, Jr. Community Health Center Leadership Award: The foundation, in partnership with the North Carolina Community Health Center, annually honors a community health center professional who excels in service to his or her fellow North Carolinians in the field of public health and primary care. Recipients receive $25,000 to advance the work of his or her community health center and a commissioned handcrafted vase.
Type of support: Capital campaigns; Conferences/seminars; Consulting services; Continuing support; Curriculum development; Equipment; General/operating support; Management development/capacity building; Matching/challenge support; Program development; Program evaluation; Technical assistance.
Geographic limitations: Giving primarily in areas of company operations in NC.
Support limitations: No support for religious organizations, individual sports teams, or organizations with the sole purpose of receiving goods and entitlements from other charitable organizations. No grants to individuals, or for bricks and mortar, annual campaigns, political campaigns,

religious purposes, endowments, advertising, or direct service or program-related costs including salaries, benefits, materials, or supplies.
Publications: Annual report; Application guidelines; Financial statement; Grants list; IRS Form 990 or 990-PF printed copy available upon request; Program policy statement.
Application information: Applications accepted. A full proposal may be requested at a later date for Health of Vulnerable Populations and Healthy Active Communities. Support is limited to 1 contribution per organization during any given year. Application form required. Applicants should submit the following:
1) copy of IRS Determination Letter
2) copy of most recent annual report/audited financial statement/990
3) listing of board of directors, trustees, officers and other key people and their affiliations
4) copy of current year's organizational budget and/or project budget
5) listing of additional sources and amount of support

Financial documentation required is based on the organization's size and type.
Initial approach: Complete online application
Deadline(s): Varies - visit website for deadline announcements
Final notification: Varies
Officers and Directors:* J. Bradley Wilson*, Chair.; Kathy Higgins, Pres.; Danielle Breslin, V.P., Opers.; Stran Summers, V.P., Finance; N. King Prather, Secy.; Steve Cherrier, Treas.; Daniel E. Glaser; Robert J. Greczyn, Jr.; Jeffrey L. Houpt, M.D.; Maureen O'Connor; Gerald Petkau; John T. Roos.
EIN: 562226009
Selected grants: The following grants are a representative sample of this grantmaker's funding activity:
$2,000,000 to North Carolina Association of Free Clinics, Winston-Salem, NC, 2011. To support existing NCAFC member free clinics and pharmacies and the creation of new free clinics in underserved counties. The focus is on the stability and sustainability of all member clinics.
$1,000,000 to North Carolina Partnership for Children, Raleigh, NC, 2011. To improve the health of young children, ages 0-5, and child care workers through a statewide strategy of comprehensive coordinated early childhood obesity prevention, outreach, and technical assistance that will address change at the individual, programmatic, built environment and policy levels.
$1,000,000 to University of North Carolina at Asheville Foundation, Asheville, NC, 2011. To continue partnership that seeks to discover the best practices about health and wellness and to broadly communicate those to the public, through undergraduate research, internships, and equipment support for the North Carolina Center for Health and Wellness.
$805,000 to North Carolina State University Foundation, Raleigh, NC, 2011. To improve health policy decision making through the development of interactive, data-driven tools and forums that develop consensus and enhance collaboration.
$350,000 to Rensselaerville Institute, Rensselaerville, NY, 2011. To identify and equip NC community sparkplugs with the direction, planning, support, and resources they need to succeed in bringing more healthy lifestyles and opportunities to residents within their communities.
$250,000 to North Carolina Institute of Medicine, Morrisville, NC, 2011. To identify workable solutions to important health problems facing the state by bringing together stakeholder groups to study and make recommendations about health issues.
$250,000 to North Carolina Public Health Foundation, Raleigh, NC, 2011. For collaboration between leaders in public health and health care to build the expertise and capacity for proven quality improvement methodologies statewide.
$211,580 to East Carolina University, Greenville, NC, 2011. To decrease the prevalence of obesity in ten rural eastern North Carolina middle schools through the MATCH (Motivating Adolescents with Technology to Choose Health) program, and to refine and package the program so that it can be easily replicated in any area of the state by the end of the three-year investment.
$198,000 to Wake County Medical Society Community Health Foundation, Raleigh, NC, 2011. To increase access to medical care for uninsured and underinsured adults in Wake County through implementation of a web-based coordination of care tool in hospitals and community clinics.
$95,226 to Office of Rural Health and Community Care, Raleigh, NC, 2011. To increase access to preventative and primary health services for 1,650 farmworkers and their families in the Piedmont/Triad Region by implementing a farmworker health outreach program and increasing the accessibility of local health care providers.

498
Blue Cross and Blue Shield of South Carolina

2501 Faraway Dr.
Columbia, SC 29223 (803) 788-0222

Company URL: http://www.southcarolinablues.com
Establishment information: Established in 1946.
Company type: Mutual company
Business activities: Operates medical service plan.
Business type (SIC): Insurance/accident and health
Corporate officers: M. Edward Sellers, Chair.; David S. Pankau, Pres. and C.E.O.; Robert Leichtle, C.F.O.; Mike Mizeur, Exec. V.P. and C.F.O.
Board of director: M. Edward Sellers, Chair.
Subsidiaries: Alpine Agency Inc., Columbia, SC; Alpine Agency of the Midlands, Camden, SC; CCM Advisors Corp., Columbia, SC; Companion Benefit Alternatives Inc., Columbia, SC; Companion Commercial Insurance Co., Columbia, SC; Companion Healthcare Corp., Columbia, SC; Companion Life Insurance Co., Columbia, SC; Companion Property & Casualty Insurance Co., Inc., Columbia, SC; Companion Technologies Corp., Columbia, SC; Companion Technologies Corp. of Tennessee, Knoxville, TN; Companion Technologies of North Carolina, Morrisville, NC; Megawest Systems Inc., Midvale, UT; Palmetto Government Benefit Administrators Inc., Columbia, SC; Planned Administrators Inc., Columbia, SC; Preferred Health Systems Inc., Columbia, SC
Giving statement: Giving through the Blue Cross and Blue Shield of South Carolina Foundation.

Blue Cross and Blue Shield of South Carolina Foundation

I-20 at Alpine Rd., MC AX-G22
Columbia, SC 29219-0001
E-mail: info.foundation@bcbssc.com; URL: http://www.bcbsscfoundation.org

Donors: Bluechoice Health Plan of SC, Inc.; Blue Cross and Blue Shield of South Carolina; Companion Healthcare Corp.
Contact: Harvey L. Galloway, Exec. Dir.
Financial data (yr. ended 12/31/11): Assets, $95,651,319 (M); gifts received, $7,000,000; expenditures, $2,904,111; qualifying distributions, $2,666,795; giving activities include $2,666,795 for 37 grants (high: $926,314; low: $500).
Purpose and activities: The foundation supports programs designed to the promote good health of South Carolinians and to increase access to healthcare for the economically disadvantaged. Special emphasis is directed toward programs designed to assist the uninsured and underinsured, children, and adolescents.
Fields of interest: Health care, clinics/centers; Public health; Public health, obesity; Health care, insurance; Health care, patient services; Nursing care; Health care; Mental health/crisis services; Health organizations; Children/youth, services Children; Youth; Economically disadvantaged.
Programs:
Childhood/Adolescent Health: The foundation supports programs designed to increase access to healthcare and services; improve individuals' well-being; promote health status; and identify solutions to issues that affect children's and adolescents' health.
Community Health: The foundation supports programs designed to increase early identification of diseases; and improve individuals' ability to manage their diseases.
Giving Back Grant Program: The foundation awards $500 grants to nonprofit organizations in South Carolina with which employees and retirees of Blue Cross and Blue Shield volunteer at least 40 hours in a service year.
Health Care and Free Medical Clinics: The foundation supports programs designed to increase the number of uninsured and underinsured individuals who receive needed medical care.
Mental Health: The foundation supports programs designed to increase the number of uninsured and underinsured individuals who have access to mental health services.
Nursing Issues: The foundation supports programs designed to increase the number of credentialed nurses who are practicing in South Carolina.
Prevention of Obesity: The foundation supports programs designed to decrease obesity rates, especially in children and adolescents.
Type of support: Employee volunteer services; Equipment; General/operating support; Program development; Research.
Geographic limitations: Giving limited to areas of company operations in SC.
Support limitations: No support for political, lobbying, or religious organizations. No grants to individuals, or for annual campaigns, capital campaigns, sports tournaments, raffles, or auctions, fundraising events, or membership drives.
Publications: Application guidelines; Grants list; Program policy statement.
Application information: Applications accepted. Letter of intent should be no longer than 2 pages. A full proposal may be requested at a later date. Support is limited to 1 contribution per organization during any given year. Application form not required. Applicants should submit the following:
1) timetable for implementation and evaluation of project
2) statement of problem project will address
3) population served
4) name, address and phone number of organization
5) brief history of organization and description of its mission
6) how project's results will be evaluated or measured
7) detailed description of project and amount of funding requested

8) contact person
9) listing of additional sources and amount of support

Initial approach: Complete online letter of intent or download letter of intent and e-mail or mail to foundation
Board meeting date(s): Spring and Fall
Deadline(s): Spring (Feb. 20) and Fall (Aug. 21)

Officers and Directors:* M. Edward Sellers*, Chair.; Judith M. Davis*, Secy.; Mike Mizeur, Treas.; Harvey L. Galloway, Exec. Dir.; Bill L. Amick; Minor M. Shaw; Joseph F. Sullivan.
EIN: 223847938
Selected grants: The following grants are a representative sample of this grantmaker's funding activity:
$1,253,216 to South Carolina Office of Rural Health, Lexington, SC, 2010. For community health.
$809,675 to Childrens Trust Fund of South Carolina, Columbia, SC, 2010. For childhood health.
$500,000 to South Carolina Nurses Foundation, Columbia, SC, 2010. For nursing issues.
$266,022 to South Carolina Coalition for Promoting Physical Activity, Irmo, SC, 2010. For obesity prevention.
$173,536 to South Carolina Campaign to Prevent Teen Pregnancy, Columbia, SC, 2010. For childhood health.
$77,000 to Children in Crisis in Dorchester County, Summerville, SC, 2010. For childhood health.
$50,000 to Dee Norton Lowcountry Childrens Center, Charleston, SC, 2010. For childhood health.
$50,000 to Orangeburg Calhoun Free Medical Clinic, Orangeburg, SC, 2010. For free medical clinic.
$50,000 to Sistercare, Columbia, SC, 2010. For mental health.
$27,685 to Colleton County School District, Walterboro, SC, 2010. For school-based mental health program.

499
Blue Cross and Blue Shield of Vermont

445 Industrial Ln.
Berlin, VT 05602-4415 (802) 223-6131

Company URL: http://www.bcbsvt.com
Establishment information: Established in 1944.
Company type: Private company
Business activities: Operates health insurance company.
Business type (SIC): Insurance/accident and health
Corporate officers: Don George, Pres. and C.E.O.; John Trifone, V.P., Treas., C.F.O., and C.I.O.; Christopher R. Gannon, V.P., Genl. Counsel, and C.A.O.
Board of directors: Karen Nystrom-Meyer, Chair.; John Collins, Vice-Chair.; Guy Boyer; Jo Bradley; John Bramley; Peter Crosby; Nancy Eldridge; John Ewing; Don C. George; Deborah Granquist; Thomas Huebner; Charlie Kireker; Mary G. Powell; Charles Smith; Donald Webster
Giving statement: Giving through the Blue Cross and Blue Shield of Vermont Corporate Giving Program.

Blue Cross and Blue Shield of Vermont Corporate Giving Program

P.O. Box 186
Montpelier, VT 05602-4415 (802) 223-6131
URL: http://www.bcbsvt.com/visitor/CommunityInvolvement/

Contact: Kathy Parry, Ext. Affairs Coord.
Purpose and activities: The foundation supports nonprofit organizations involved with health-related causes.
Fields of interest: Health care.
Type of support: General/operating support; In-kind gifts; Sponsorships.
Geographic limitations: Giving limited to VT.
Support limitations: No support for religious organizations or for youth and school sports programs. No grants to individuals.
Publications: Application guidelines.
Application information: Applications accepted. Application form not required.

Initial approach: Proposal
Copies of proposal: 1
Deadline(s): None

500
Blue Cross Blue Shield of Arizona

2444 W. Las Palmaritas Dr.
Phoenix, AZ 85021 (602) 864-4400

Company URL: http://www.azblue.com
Establishment information: Established in 1939.
Company type: Private company
Business activities: Operates medical service plan.
Business type (SIC): Insurance/accident and health
Corporate officers: Barbara J. Ralston, Chair.; Harry A. Papp, Vice-Chair.; Richard L. Boals, Pres. and C.E.O.; Karen Abraham, Sr. V.P. and C.F.O.; Elizabeth A. Messina, Sr. V.P. and C.I.O.; Deanna Salazar, Sr. V.P. and Genl. Counsel; Jeff Stelnik, Sr. V.P., Sales and Mktg.; Alton J. Washington, Secy.
Board of directors: Barbara J. Ralston, Chair.; Harry A. Papp, Vice-Chair.; Richard L. Boals; Robert B. Bulla; Rebecca L. Burnham; Dan C. Coleman; Lattie F. Coor, Ph.D.; Richard H. Dozer; Kathleen H. Goeppinger, Ph.D.; Larry Landry; Kay J. McKay; James S. Pignatelli; William J. Post; Thomas C. Rothe, M.D.; Gary L. Trujillo; Alton J. Washington
Giving statement: Giving through the Blue Cross Blue Shield of Arizona Corporate Giving Program.

Blue Cross Blue Shield of Arizona Corporate Giving Program

c/o Community Rels.
P.O. Box 13466
Phoenix, AZ 85002-3466 (602) 864-4100
E-mail: MBarrios@azblue.com; Within Maricopa County, tel. for Sue Glawe: (602) 864-4602; Outside Maricopa County, tel. for Maribel Barrios: (602) 864-5107; URL: http://www.azblue.com/about-us/Community.aspx

Contact: Maribel Barrios, Community Rels.
Purpose and activities: Blue Cross Blue Shield of Arizona makes charitable contributions to nonprofit organizations involved with arts and culture, economic development and civic initiatives, youth and education, health, wellness, and human services. Support is limited to Arizona.
Fields of interest: Arts; Education; Health care; Human services; Community/economic development Youth.
Type of support: Employee volunteer services; General/operating support; Sponsorships.
Geographic limitations: Giving limited to AZ.
Publications: Application guidelines.
Application information: Applications accepted. Application form required. Applicants should submit the following:

1) name, address and phone number of organization
2) copy of IRS Determination Letter
3) brief history of organization and description of its mission
4) listing of board of directors, trustees, officers and other key people and their affiliations
5) contact person
6) listing of additional sources and amount of support
7) plans for acknowledgement

Applications should specify what percentage of the funds will remain in Arizona; and event date, time, and location.

Initial approach: Complete online application
Deadline(s): 60 days prior to event

501
Blue Cross Blue Shield of Massachusetts, Inc.

401 Park Dr., Landmark Ctr.
Boston, MA 02215-3326 (617) 246-5000

Company URL: http://www.bluecrossma.com
Establishment information: Established in 1937.
Company type: Private company
Business activities: Operates medical service plan.
Business type (SIC): Insurance/accident and health
Financial profile for 2012: Number of employees, 3,500
Corporate officers: Andrew Dreyfus, Pres. and C.E.O.; Bruce M. Bullen, C.O.O.; Allen P. Maltz, Exec. V.P. and C.F.O.; William Fandrich, Sr. V.P. and C.I.O.; Stephanie Lovell, Sr. V.P. and Genl. Counsel; Timothy O'Brien, Sr. V.P., Sales; Jay McQuaide, Sr. V.P., Corp. Comms.; Jason Robart, Sr. V.P., Human Resources
Board of directors: George R. Alcott III; Brian M. Barefoot; Andrew C. Dreyfus; Helen G. Drinan; Richard C. Garrison; Paul Guzzi; Bruce Hamory; Philip W. Johnston; Gloria C. Larson; James H. Lunt; Ralph C. Martin II, Esq.; Robert F. Meenan, M.D.; Paul Toner; Dorothy E. Puhy; Timothy Sweeney; William C. Van Faasen; Benaree P. Wiley; Phyllis R. Yale
Giving statement: Giving through the Blue Cross Blue Shield of Massachusetts, Inc. Corporate Giving Program and the Blue Cross Blue Shield of Massachusetts Foundation, Inc. for Expanding Healthcare Access.
Company EIN: 041045815

Blue Cross Blue Shield of Massachusetts, Inc. Corporate Giving Program

Landmark Ctr.
401 Park Dr.
Boston, MA 02215-3326 (617) 246-4339
FAX: (617) 246-2259;
E-mail: jeffrey.bellows@bcbsma.com; URL: http://www.bluecrossma.com/visitor/community-leadership/good-business/index.html

Contact: Jeff Bellows, Sr. Dir., Community Rels.
Financial data (yr. ended 12/31/10): Total giving, $4,890,000, including $4,890,000 for grants.
Purpose and activities: As a complement to its foundation, Blue Cross and Blue Shield of Massachusetts makes charitable contributions to nonprofit organizations directly. Special emphasis is directed toward programs that promote healthy child development, education enrichment, healthy environments/family nutrition, and sustainable

health care. Support is limited to those living and working in Massachusetts.
Fields of interest: Education; Environment, pollution control; Environment, beautification programs; Environment; Health care, research; Health care, public policy; Health care; Agriculture, sustainable programs; Food services; Nutrition; Youth development, adult & child programs; Youth development; Child development, services; Human services; Patients' rights; Financial services Infants/toddlers; Children; Youth; Economically disadvantaged.
Type of support: Employee volunteer services; General/operating support; Program development; Program-related investments/loans; Sponsorships.
Geographic limitations: Giving limited to MA.
Support limitations: No support for religious organizations not of direct benefit to the entire community, or college alumni, or school associations. No grants to individuals or organizations, or for fellowships, travel, capital campaigns, new construction, renovation, equipment, endowments, cash reserves, publications, or sports promotions or events; no educational loans; no non-501c3 entities.
Publications: Annual report; Corporate giving report.
Application information: Applications accepted. The Community Relations Department handles giving. The company has a staff that only handles contributions. A contributions committee reviews all requests. Application form not required. Applicants should submit the following:
1) copy of IRS Determination Letter
Initial approach: Letter of inquiry
Copies of proposal: 1
Committee meeting date(s): Bi-weekly
Deadline(s): Rolling
Final notification: 3 to 4 weeks
Administrators: Jeff Bellows, Sr. Dir., Community Rels.; Lucy Darragh, Mgr. , Community Rels.; Yvonne Tang, Mgr. , Community Rels.
Number of staff: 7 full-time professional.

Blue Cross Blue Shield of Massachusetts Foundation, Inc. for Expanding Healthcare Access

(formerly Wellchild, the Foundation of Health for Life)
Landmark Ctr.
401 Park Dr.
Boston, MA 02215-3325 (617) 246-3744
FAX: (617) 246-3992;
E-mail: info@bluecrossmafoundation.org; Tel. and e-mail for Celeste Reid Lee: (617) 246-8406, celeste.lee@bcbsma.com; Additional contact: Jennifer Lee, Grantmaking Prog. Mgr., Jennifer.Lee@bcbsma.com; E-mail for Massachusetts Institute for Community Health Leadership: mmccorma@hsph.harvard.edu; URL: http://www.bcbsmafoundation.org
Contacts for fellowships: Larry Tye, 26 Grant St., Lexington, MA 02420, e-mail: larrytye@aol.com; Anna Gosline, e-mail: Anna.Gosline@bcbsma.com

Establishment information: Established in 2001 in MA; status changed to a private foundation in 2006.
Donors: Blue Cross and Blue Shield of Massachusetts, Inc.; Robert Wood Johnson Foundation; CT Health Foundation; Bingham Betterment Fund; Ottauquechee Health Foundation; Cox Charitable Lead Trust; Tufts.
Contact: Celeste Reid Lee, Interim Pres.
Financial data (yr. ended 12/31/11): Assets, $91,601,500 (M); gifts received, $6,162,810; expenditures, $6,870,289; qualifying distributions, $6,813,177; giving activities include $3,203,154 for 86 grants (high: $125,000; low: $1,494).
Purpose and activities: The foundation seeks to expand access to health care by working with public and private organizations to broaden health coverage and reduce barriers to care.
Fields of interest: Health care, research; Health care, public policy; Health care, equal rights; Hospitals (general); Health care, clinics/centers; Public health; Public health, environmental health; Health care, insurance; Health care; Leadership development.
Programs:
Catalyst Fund: The foundation awards grants to support one-time capacity-building expenses for organizations that serve the health care needs of uninsured and low-income people. The program is designed to strengthen an organization's ability to expand access to health care. Grants range from $1,000 to $5,000.
Connecting Consumers with Care: The foundation awards two-year grants of up to $40,000 to community-based organizations, community health centers, and hospital-based programs designed to help consumers enroll in and maintain access to coverage; address system-level barriers through collaboration; and educate and equip consumers to utilize the healthcare system more effectively.
Cost and Affordability Policy and Research Grants: The foundation supports programs designed to promote research, policy analysis, and evaluation of health care costs and spending. Special emphasis is directed toward the creation of information that guides policy makers; and guide delivery systems based programs designed to reduce or slow the growth in health care spending. Grants range from $30,000 to $150,000.
Health Coverage Fellowship: Through the Health Coverage Fellowship, the foundation trains members of the media to cover critical healthcare issues. The program focuses on issues ranging from insuring the uninsured to mental illness, backups in emergency rooms, ethnic and economic disparities in the delivery of care, and environmental health. The fellowship is housed at Babson College's Center for Executive Education in Wellesley, and brings journalists together with leading health officials, policy makers, and researchers. The fellows also learn first-hand how the system works, from joining mental health case workers patrolling the streets at night to riding a Medflight helicopter. The foundation selects ten journalists each year from across the country for an intensive nine days and nights of training.
Making Health Care Affordable: Preserving Access and Improving Value: The foundation awards up to three years of funding to programs designed to demonstrate substantive cost containment while maintaining access and quality of care. This program is closed until Summer 2014.
Massachusetts Institute for Community Health Leadership: Through the Massachusetts Institute of Community Health Leadership initiative, the foundation builds leadership capacity among healthcare organizations in the Commonwealth that serve the needs of low-income and uninsured residents. The 18-day educational program is designed to help those with leadership potential increase their own personal impact, strengthen their effectiveness in their organization, and enhance the organization's influence in the healthcare system.
Strengthening the Voice for Access: The foundation awards two-year grants of up to $70,000 to initiatives designed to promote the interests of the uninsured, underinsured, and underserved through strategic advocacy. The program is designed to strengthen community-based policy activities, increase citizen participation in public policy development, and promote collaboration among state policy and advocacy organizations on healthcare coverage for vulnerable populations, and healthcare affordability.
Type of support: Continuing support; Fellowships; Management development/capacity building; Program development; Sponsorships.
Geographic limitations: Giving primarily in areas of company operations in MA.
Support limitations: No grants for events or sponsorships.
Publications: Application guidelines; Grants list; IRS Form 990 or 990-PF printed copy available upon request; Program policy statement.
Application information: Applications accepted. Applicants for the Catalyst Fund and the Massachusetts Institute for Community Health Leadership should submit 5 copies of the application. Letters of inquiry should be no longer than 2 pages. Organizations receiving support are asked to submit an interim report and a final report. Applicants should submit the following:
1) copy of IRS Determination Letter
2) listing of board of directors, trustees, officers and other key people and their affiliations
3) detailed description of project and amount of funding requested
4) copy of current year's organizational budget and/or project budget
Initial approach: Download application and mail for Catalyst Fund and Massachusetts Institute for Community Health Leadership; download application and mail to application address for Health Coverage Fellowship; download letter of inquiry form and mail for Connecting Consumers with Care, Cost and Affordability Grants, and Strengthening the Voice for Access
Deadline(s): Varies for Catalyst Fund, Massachusetts Institute for Community Health Leadership, Connecting Consumers with Care, Strengthening the Voice for Access, and Health Coverage Fellowship; Sept. 7 for Cost and Affordability Grants
Final notification: 6 to 7 weeks for Catalyst Fund
Officers and Directors:* Philip W. Johnston*, Chair.; Robert Meenan, M.D.*, Vice-Chair.; Audrey Shelto, Pres.; Helen Caulton-Harris; Andrew Dreyfus; Barbara Ferrer, Ph.D., MPH; Matt Fishman; Milton Glass; James W. Hunt, Jr.; Rachel Kaprielian; Nick Littlefield; Richard C. Lord; Robert Restuccia; Charlotte S. Yeh, M.D., FACEP.
EIN: 043148824

502
Blue Cross Blue Shield of Michigan

600 E. Lafayette Blvd.
Detroit, MI 48226-2998 (313) 225-9000

Company URL: http://www.bcbsm.com
Establishment information: Established in 1939.
Company type: Mutual company
Business activities: Operates medical service plan.
Business type (SIC): Insurance/accident and health
Financial profile for 2012: Assets, $12,851,300,000; liabilities, $9,381,000,000
Corporate officers: Gregory A. Sudderth, Chair.; Spencer Johnson, M.D., Vice-Chair.; Daniel J. Loepp, Pres. and C.E.O.; Mark R. Barlett, Exec. V.P. and C.F.O.; Darrell E. Middleton, Exec. V.P., Opers.; Tricia A. Keith, Sr. V.P. and Corp. Secy.; Lynda M. Rossi, Sr. V.P., Public Affairs; Carolynn Walton, V.P. and Treas.
Board of directors: Gregory A. Sudderth, Chair.; Spencer C. Johnson, Vice-Chair.; James G. Agee; Jon E. Barfield; William H. Black; Terry Burns; Brian

M. Connolly; Patrick J. Devlin; Mark T. Gaffney; Thomas J. Hadrych; John M. Hamilton; Melvin L. Larsen; Daniel J. Loepp; Gary J. McInerney; Livio Mezza; John Vander Molen; Robert A. Patzer; Calvin T. Rapson; James W. Richards; Iris K. Salters; James U. Settles, Jr.; Gregory A. Sudderth; S. Martin Taylor; Gary H. Torgow
Giving statement: Giving through the Blue Cross Blue Shield of Michigan Corporate Giving Program and the Blue Cross Blue Shield of Michigan Foundation.

Blue Cross Blue Shield of Michigan Corporate Giving Program

c/o Corp. Contribs.
600 E. Lafayette Blvd., M.C. 1808
Detroit, MI 48226-2927 (313) 225-0539
FAX: (313) 225-9693;
E-mail: volunteer@bcbsm.com; URL: http://www.bcbsm.com/home/diversity/community.shtml

Purpose and activities: As a complement to its foundation, Blue Cross Blue Shield of Michigan also makes charitable contributions to nonprofit organizations directly. Support is limited to Michigan.
Fields of interest: Public health; Public health, physical fitness; Health care; Nutrition Youth; Aging.
Type of support: Employee volunteer services; General/operating support.
Geographic limitations: Giving limited to areas of company operations in MI.
Support limitations: No support for political organizations or candidates or alumni associations. No grants to individuals, or for political campaigns, extracurricular school activities, endowments, scholarships, research, multi-year pledges, general operating expenses, group travel, or capital campaigns.
Publications: Application guidelines.
Application information: Applications accepted. Application form required. Applicants should submit the following:
1) results expected from proposed grant
2) population served
3) name, address and phone number of organization
4) copy of IRS Determination Letter
5) brief history of organization and description of its mission
6) listing of board of directors, trustees, officers and other key people and their affiliations
7) detailed description of project and amount of funding requested
8) contact person
9) additional materials/documentation

Applications should include an annual report, all sponsorship levels and benefits of each, and additional sources being solicited for funding; and indicate any previous support received from Blue Cross Blue Shield in the past 3 years.
Initial approach: Download application form and mail with proposal to headquarters
Deadline(s): None
Final notification: 15 days
Number of staff: 2 part-time professional; 2 part-time support.

Blue Cross Blue Shield of Michigan Foundation

(formerly Michigan Health Care Education and Research Foundation/MHCERF)
600 Lafayette E., Ste. X520
Detroit, MI 48226-2998 (313) 225-8706
FAX: (313) 225-7730;
E-mail: foundation@bcbsm.com; Additional tel.: (313) 225-7560; URL: http://www.bcbsm.com/foundation/

Establishment information: Established in 1980 in MI.
Donor: Blue Cross and Blue Shield of Michigan.
Contact: Ira Strumwasser Ph.D., C.E.O. and Exec. Dir.
Financial data (yr. ended 12/31/10): Revenue, $1,650,586; assets, $51,661,290 (M); expenditures, $2,624,732; giving activities include $1,416,255 for grants and $60,750 for grants to individuals.
Purpose and activities: The foundation is dedicated to improving the health of Michigan residents through the support of research and innovative programs.
Fields of interest: Health care; Medical research, institute.
Programs:
Community Health Matching Grants Program: The program focuses on community efforts to increase access to health care, address critical public health issues, improve the quality of care and enhance efficiency. The program's purpose is to encourage nonprofit community based organizations to develop, implement and evaluate new approaches to address community health problems. Up to $25,000 per year for two years is available. Matching funds are required based on the size of the applicant organization's budget as well as the percent of Medicaid and uninsured patients served.
Excellence in Research Awards for Students: This program identifies and acknowledges Michigan's university students who have made significant contributions to health and health care through applied research in health policy or medical care. Awards are presented to doctoral or medical students for published papers that represent a contribution to health policy or clinical care. Three awards will be given: the first place winner receives $1,000, the second place winner receives $750, and the third place winner receives $500.
Frank J. McDevitt, D.O. Excellence in Research Awards for Health Services, Policy & Clinical Care: This program provides four awards of $10,000 each for research projects in progress or planned by the recipient in the fields of health policy, health services, and clinical care. Proposals should focus on such topics as public health, the financing and organization of health services, population health, reimbursement, or resource allocation. Eligible applicants include Michigan-based researchers with terminal research degrees (e.g. Ph.D. or Dr.PH) and Michigan-based physicians (M.D. or D.O.); separate awards will be offered to physician- and doctoral-level researchers. The financial award will be made to the recipient's 501(c)(3) nonprofit or educational organization, and is unrestricted.
Investigator-Initiated Research Program: This program encourages Michigan-based applied research projects designed to improve health care in the state of Michigan. It does not support basic science or biomedical research, including drug studies or studies using animals. Projects that focus on the quality and cost of health care and appropriate access are considered priority and include: the organization and delivery of health care services; evaluation of new methods or approaches to containing health care costs and providing access to high quality health care; assessment and assurance of quality care; and identification and validation of clinical protocols and evidence-based practice guidelines. Grants are typically in the $50,000 to $75,000 per year range; exceptional projects will be considered for multiyear funding or funding requests in excess of $75,000.
Patient Safety Grants: The purpose of this program is to encourage the development and expanded use of checklists in medicine and surgery to enhance patient safety. We are particularly interested in evidence based projects that will seamlessly integrate checklists into providers' work flow so that they will be readily adopted and utilized. The Foundation expects to provide up to ten (10) $50,000 grants to develop, implement and evaluate the effectiveness of using checklists to prevent medical and surgical errors in acute care hospital settings.
Physician-Investigator Research Award Program: This program is for physicians who have an interest in health and medical care research. The purpose is to provide seed money to physicians to explore the merits of a potential research idea. The proposed project might be in the form of a pilot study, feasibility study, or a small research study. Grants of $10,000 are available for research related to the quality of care, cost, and appropriate access to health and medical care. The program does not support basic science, biomedical research (including drug studies) or studies using animals.
Proposal Development Award Program: The award is intended to help Michigan-based nonprofit community organizations develop grant proposals for new health care initiatives. This award of up to $3,500 is available to help nonprofits obtain grant writing resources so they may secure the funding they need to bring creative community-based health care programs to life.
RFP Program: The foundation may periodically offer special requests for proposals from Michigan-based nonprofits or qualified individuals that focus on specific aims concerning its mission. Currently, up to ten grants of $50,000 each are available to implement and evaluate patient safety checklists in medicine and surgery.
Student Awards Program: The program provides a $3,000 one-year stipend to students for applied research addressing health, health services, or policy. The intent is to support the next generation of applied researchers in health and health care policy and delivery by supporting doctoral and medical student research.
Type of support: Fellowships; Grants to individuals; Income development; Matching/challenge support; Program development; Research; Seed money; Technical assistance.
Geographic limitations: Giving primarily in MI.
Publications: Annual report (including application guidelines); Application guidelines; Informational brochure (including application guidelines).
Application information: Applications accepted. See web site for current requests for proposals and application guidelines/deadlines. Application form required.
Board meeting date(s): May, Aug., and Nov.
Deadline(s): Jan. 1 for Excellence in Research Awards and Excellence in Research Awards for Students; Apr. 3 for Research Award for Improving Patient Safety and Research Award for Identification and Treatment of Depression; and Apr. 30 for Student Awards Program
Final notification: Aug. for Student Awards Program; quarterly for Matching Grants Program
Officers and Directors:* Shauna Ryder Diggs, M.D.*, Chair.; Joel I. Ferguson*, Vice-Chair.; Ira Strumwasser, Ph.D., C.E.O. and Exec. Dir.; Kevin L. Seitz*, Pres.; Marla Larkin, Secy.; Peter B. Ajluni, D.O.*, Treas.; Haifa Fakhouri, Ph.D.; Joel I. Ferguson; John M. MacKeigan, M.D.; Willard S. Stawski, M.D.
Number of staff: 3 full-time professional; 2 full-time support.
EIN: 382338506

503
Blue Cross Blue Shield of Wyoming
4000 House Ave.
Cheyenne, WY 82001 (307) 634-1393
FAX: (307) 634-5742

Company URL: http://www.bcbswy.com
Establishment information: Established in 1945.
Company type: Mutual company
Business activities: Operates medical service plan.
Business type (SIC): Insurance/accident and health
Financial profile for 2009: Number of employees, 250
Corporate officers: Cliff Kirk, Chair.; Thomas Lockhart, Vice-Chair.; Tim J. Crilly, Pres., Secy., and C.E.O.; Diane Gore, C.F.O.; Karen Dobson, V.P., Opers.; Richard (Rick) Schum, V.P., Mktg.
Board of directors: Cliff Kirk, Chair.; Tom Lockhart, Vice-Chair.; Rex Arney
Giving statement: Giving through the Caring Foundation of Wyoming.

Caring Foundation of Wyoming
P.O. Box 2266
Cheyenne, WY 82003-2266
URL: https://www.bcbswy.com/company_info/community/

Donors: Blue Cross and Blue Shield of Wyoming; Wyoming Affiliate Of Susan G. Komen.
Financial data (yr. ended 12/31/11): Assets, $4,709,767 (M); gifts received, $276,863; expenditures, $453,437; qualifying distributions, $5,350; giving activities include $5,350 for grants.
Purpose and activities: The foundation provides health expenditures for the benefit of economically disadvantaged Wyoming residents.
Fields of interest: Education.
Type of support: Grants to individuals.
Geographic limitations: Giving limited to WY.
Application information: Applications not accepted. Unsolicited requests for funds not accepted.
Officers: Dan Sullivan, Chair.; Michael Healy, Vice-Chair.; Rick Schum, Treas.
EIN: 830292601

504
Blue Cross of Idaho Health Service, Inc.
3000 E. Pine Ave.
Meridian, ID 83642 (208) 345-4550

Company URL: http://www.bcidaho.com
Establishment information: Established in 1945.
Company type: Mutual company
Business activities: Operates medical service plan.
Business type (SIC): Insurance/accident and health
Corporate officers: Michael J. Shirley, Chair.; Jo Anne Stringfield, Vice-Chair.; Zelda Geyer-Sylvia, Pres. and C.E.O.; Jack A. Myers, Exec. V.P. and C.F.O.; Steve Tobiason, Sr. V.P. and Genl. Counsel; David Jeppesen, Sr. V.P., Mktg. and Comms.; Debra M. Henry, Sr. V.P., Human Resources; Lance Hatfield, V.P. and C.I.O.
Board of directors: Michael J. Shirley, Chair.; Jo Anne Stringfield, Vice-Chair.; Zelda Geyer-Sylvia; Jack W. Gustavel; N. Charles Hedemark; Kenlon P. Johnson; Thomas F. Kealey; Ward Parkinson
Subsidiary: Idaho Benefits Administration, Inc., Boise, ID
Giving statement: Giving through the Blue Cross of Idaho Foundation for Health, Inc.
Company EIN: 820344294

Blue Cross of Idaho Foundation for Health, Inc.
3000 E. Pine Ave.
Meridian, ID 83642-5995 (208) 387-6817
FAX: (208) 331-7321;
E-mail: info@bcidahofoundation.org; E-mail for Childhood Obesity Prevention Grants: grants@bcidahofoundation.org; Additional address: P.O. Box 8419, Boise, ID 83707-2419; Additional tel.: (866) 482-2252; Contact for Color Me Healthy, Touch to Quit, and Good Health Club: Kendra Witt, PhD, MPH, tel.: (208) 286-3461, e-mail: kwitt@bcidaho.com; URL: http://www.bcidahofoundation.org/

Establishment information: Established in 2001 in ID.
Donors: Blue Cross of Idaho Health Service, Inc.; American Legacy Foundation.
Financial data (yr. ended 12/31/11): Assets, $12,172,294 (M); gifts received, $83,406; expenditures, $670,509; qualifying distributions, $513,266; giving activities include $513,266 for grants.
Purpose and activities: The foundation supports programs and organizations that work to improve the health and wellness of all Idahoans.
Fields of interest: Nursing school/education; Education; Hospitals (general); Public health; Public health, obesity; Public health, physical fitness; Health care; Mental health, smoking; Health organizations; Food services; Nutrition; Children, day care Children; Economically disadvantaged.
Programs:
Childhood Obesity Prevention Grants: The foundation awards grants of up to $20,000 to address childhood obesity in Idaho. Special emphasis is directed toward programs designed to promote healthy food and beverage options for children; increase the intensity and frequency of physical activity among children; and promote research exploring the obesity epidemic in Idaho.
Color Me Healthy (CMH): Through the Color Me Healthy program, the foundation provides Color Me Healthy curriculums to childcare centers throughout Idaho to encourage healthy eating and nutrition. The program includes interactive lessons that teach preschool age children about eating fruits and vegetables of different colors and physical activity, a teacher's guide, picture cards, classroom posters, music CD, hand stamp, and a reproducible parent newsletter.
Good Health Club: The foundation provides Good Health Club Toolkits to physician offices to fight childhood obesity; and to encourage the "5-2-1-0" approach to living, portion control, and actionable advice for parents and kids to increase healthy behaviors.
Touch to Quit: Through the Touch to Quit program, the foundation promotes tobacco cessation for hospital patients. The program includes a touch screen monitor that offers tailored videos consisting of messages from a medical doctor and former tobacco users, strategies for dealing with smoking addiction, and information about free quitting resources in Idaho.
Type of support: Annual campaigns; Continuing support; Curriculum development; Donated equipment; Matching/challenge support; Program development; Program evaluation; Research; Sponsorships.
Geographic limitations: Giving limited to ID.
Support limitations: No grants to individuals.
Publications: Application guidelines.
Application information: Applications accepted. Proposals for Childhood Obesity Prevention Grants should be no longer than 2 pages. A full proposal may be requested at a later date. The foundation accepts funding requests for specific initiatives. Please visit website for announcements regarding funding. Applicants should submit the following:
1) how project will be sustained once grantmaker support is completed
2) statement of problem project will address
3) population served
4) detailed description of project and amount of funding requested
5) copy of current year's organizational budget and/or project budget

Initial approach: E-mail proposal for Childhood Obesity Prevention Grants
Board meeting date(s): Quarterly
Deadline(s): Oct. 14 for Childhood Obesity Prevention Grants
Final notification: 2 weeks for Childhood Obesity Prevention Grants

Officers: Raymond R. Flachbart*, Chair. and Pres.; Zelda Geyer-Sylvia*, Vice-Chair. and V.P.; Bruce Croffy, Secy.-Treas.
Number of staff: 1 full-time professional.
EIN: 260024334

505
Blue Cross of Northeastern Pennsylvania
(also known as Hospital Service Association of Northeastern Pennsylvania)
19 N. Main St.
Wilkes Barre, PA 18711-0302
(570) 200-4300

Company URL: http://www.bcnepa.com
Establishment information: Established in 1938.
Company type: Mutual company
Business activities: Operates medical service plan.
Business type (SIC): Insurance/accident and health
Corporate officers: John P. Moses, Esq., Chair.; Denise S. Cesare, Pres. and C.E.O.; William J. Farrell, C.F.O.
Board of directors: John P. Moses, Esq., Chair.; Frank E. Apostolico; Paul J. Canevari; Denise S. Cesare; Peter J. Danchak; Louis A. DeNaples; Bart E. Ecker, Esq.; John H. Graham; Alan S. Hollander, Esq.; Gary F. Lamont; Richard K. Mangan; John D. McCarthy, Jr; John J. Menapace; Paul H. Rooney, Jr.; Rhea P. Simms; David J. Williams
Giving statement: Giving through the Blue Ribbon Foundation of Blue Cross of Northeastern Pennsylvania.

The Blue Ribbon Foundation of Blue Cross of Northeastern Pennsylvania
(formerly Hospital Service Association of Northeastern Pennsylvania Foundation)
19 N. Main St.
Wilkes-Barre, PA 18711-0300 (570) 200-6305
FAX: (570) 200-6699;
E-mail: Cynthia.Yevich@bcnepa.com; Additional contact: Jennifer R. Deemer, Grants Specialist, Jennifer.Deemer@@bcenpa.com; URL: https://www.bcnepa.com/Community/BlueRibbon.aspx

Establishment information: Established in 2001 in PA.
Donors: Blue Cross of Northeastern Pennsylvania; Hospital Service Assn. of N.E. PA.

Contact: Cynthia A. Yevich, Exec. Dir.
Financial data (yr. ended 12/31/11): Assets, $90,683 (M); gifts received, $280,000; expenditures, $285,520; qualifying distributions, $209,729; giving activities include $209,729 for 27 grants (high: $34,142; low: $1,000).
Purpose and activities: The foundation supports programs designed improve the heath and wellness of residents in Pennsylvania communities. Special emphasis is directed toward programs designed to address critical health issues through creative, community-based, programmatic initiatives; produce measurable health and wellness results; foster collaboration and partnership among community organizations; and address the root causes of specific diseases and conditions to help moderate escalating healthcare costs.
Fields of interest: Child development, education; Medical school/education; Education, reading; Health care, equal rights; Medicine/medical care, public education; Health care, clinics/centers; Dental care; Pharmacy/prescriptions; Public health; Public health, obesity; Public health, physical fitness; Health care, insurance; Health care; Mental health/crisis services, public education; Substance abuse, services; Substance abuse, prevention; Substance abuse, treatment; Mental health, treatment; Health organizations, public education; Cancer; Heart & circulatory diseases; Diabetes; Nutrition; Family services; Human services, financial counseling; Human services; United Ways and Federated Giving Programs Children; Aging; Disabilities, people with; Women; Crime/abuse victims.
Programs:

Access to Health Care for the Uninsured and Underinsured Initiative: The foundation supports programs designed to provide health care services to the uninsured and underinsured in northeastern and north central Pennsylvania. Special emphasis is directed toward unfunded pharmaceutical needs, medical supplies, medical personnel, diagnostic testing, translation services, and dental services. Grants of up to $20,000 will be awarded to individual organizations, and grants of up to $75,000 will be awarded to collaborative projects.

Health and Wellness Impact Grants - Behavioral Health Awareness: The foundation supports programs designed to promote awareness and education on the diagnosis and treatment of behavioral disorders. Special emphasis is directed toward programs designed to improve community awareness and acceptance of behavioral disorders, or provide clinicians, patients, and families with information and organizational support to identify, diagnose, treat, and manage these disorders.

Health and Wellness Impact Grants - Cancer Awareness: The foundation supports programs designed to improve community awareness of routine cancer screenings, including when and how they are done; stress the importance of early detection and the impact it has on cancer survival; promote increased awareness and education among health care professionals; improve health status for cancer patients; and foster future prevention needs for cancer survivors.

Health and Wellness Impact Grants - Cardiovascular Disease Awareness: The foundation supports programs designed to promote awareness and prevention of cardiovascular diseases such as coronary heart disease, stroke, high blood pressure, and heart failure and their risk factors. Special emphasis is directed toward programs designed to incorporate proven risk factor interventions, including nutrition, exercise or lifestyle change, and education for health care professionals or for patients with cardiovascular disease and their families.

Health and Wellness Impact Grants - Diabetes Awareness: The foundation supports programs designed to improve awareness and education about pre-diabetes, Type 1 and Type 2 diabetes, and related risk factors. Special emphasis is directed toward programs designed to provide clinicians, patients, and families with information and support to identify, treat, and manage diabetes; and incorporate proven interventions such as nutrition and lifestyle change.

Health and Wellness Impact Grants - Drug, Alcohol, or Tobacco Awareness: The foundation supports programs designed to educate the community on the prevention and/or treatment of drug, alcohol, and tobacco abuse, incorporating the behavioral aspects of resisting drug, alcohol, or tobacco usage; and include interventions that are age specific and targeted to promote a positive attitude for resisting peer pressure in the use of drugs, alcohol, or tobacco.

Health and Wellness Impact Grants - Overweight and Obesity Awareness: The foundation supports programs designed integrate nutritional, physical, behavioral and/or medical interventions to promote healthy behaviors, eating habits, and increased physical activity; improve community awareness of the complications caused by being overweight or obese; and promote healthy lifestyles education.

Health and Wellness Mini-Grants - Health Education and Prevention: The foundation supports programs designed to improve awareness of health and wellness issues in the community; address health, reading, and financial literacy; and increase medical education for the provider community. Grants range from $2,500 to $10,000.

Health and Wellness Mini-Grants - Healthy Children and Families: The foundation supports programs designed to improve early childhood intervention; assist abused, special needs, and at-risk children; provide preventive services for families; and promote special dental initiatives. Grants range from $2,500 to $10,000.

Health and Wellness Mini-Grants - Human Services: The foundation supports programs designed to address women and children's health issues; increase independence for the elderly and disabled; and provide crisis intervention support. Grants range from $2,500 to $10,000.
Type of support: Program development.
Geographic limitations: Giving limited to areas of company operations in Bradford, Carbon, Clinton, Lackawanna, Luzerne, Lycoming, Monroe, Pike, Sullivan, Susquehanna, Tioga, Wayne, and Wyoming counties, PA.
Support limitations: No support for schools, parent/teacher organizations, camps, organizations not of direct benefit to the entire community, camps of any kind, emergency response organizations, or political candidates or organizations. No grants to individuals, or for equipment or fixed assets, tours, trips, or conferences, capital campaigns or building, annual campaigns, general operating support, scholarships, endowments, debt reduction, or fundraising.
Publications: Annual report; Application guidelines; Grants list; Informational brochure; Program policy statement.
Application information: Applications accepted. Grant requests should not exceed $15,000. Potential applicants are encouraged to contact the foundation to discuss proposals and/or projects. Support is limited to 1 contribution per organization during any given year. Organizations receiving support are asked to provide an interim report and a final report. Application form required. Applicants should submit the following:
1) timetable for implementation and evaluation of project
2) how project will be sustained once grantmaker support is completed
3) copy of IRS Determination Letter
4) brief history of organization and description of its mission
5) copy of most recent annual report/audited financial statement/990
6) how project's results will be evaluated or measured
7) listing of board of directors, trustees, officers and other key people and their affiliations
8) detailed description of project and amount of funding requested
9) copy of current year's organizational budget and/or project budget
10) listing of additional sources and amount of support

Initial approach: Download application form and mail proposal and application form to foundation
Board meeting date(s): Apr. 16, July 11, and Nov. 12
Deadline(s): Mar. 8, June 7, and Oct. 4

Officers and Directors:* Denise S. Cesare*, Pres.; William J. Farrell, C.F.O. and Treas.; Gertude McGowan, Secy.; Cynthia A. Yevich, Exec. Dir.; Judith O. Graziano; Alan S. Hollander, Esq.; Sir. M. Martin de Porres Mc-Hale; John J. Menapace; John P. Moses, Esq.; Paul H. Rooney, Jr.
EIN: 233101673
Selected grants: The following grants are a representative sample of this grantmaker's funding activity:
$25,100 to North Penn Comprehensive Health Services, Wellsboro, PA, 2009. For Project Reach.
$20,000 to Rural Health Corporation of Northeastern Pennsylvania, Wilkes Barre, PA, 2009. For dental services for the uninsured.
$16,000 to Trehab Center, Montrose, PA, 2009. For workshops on medical consequences of substance abuse.
$10,000 to MetroAction, Inc., Scranton, PA, 2009. For Kindergarten Readiness Nutrition Education Program.
$9,300 to Pocono Healthy Communities Alliance, Stroudsburg, PA, 2009. For Healthy Start Screening Program.
$7,680 to Pennsylvania Environmental Council, Harrisburg, PA, 2009. For Community Garden Nutrition Workshops.
$7,000 to Serento Gardens, Hazleton, PA, 2009. For MED-ED Workshops for Seniors.
$6,525 to North Penn Legal Services, Scranton, PA, 2009. For Living Will Outreach Project.

506
Blue Diamond Growers

1802 C St.
P.O. Box 1768
Sacramento, CA 95811 (916) 446-8500

Company URL: http://www.bluediamond.com
Establishment information: Established in 1910.
Company type: Cooperative
Business activities: Sells almonds wholesale.
Business type (SIC): Farm-product raw materials—wholesale
Financial profile for 2012: Assets, $310,300,000; liabilities, $215,425,000
Corporate officers: Clinton Shick, Chair.; Dale Van Groningen, Vice-Chair.; Mark D. Jansen, Pres. and C.E.O.; Dean LaVallee, Corp. Secy. and C.F.O.
Board of directors: Clinton Shick, Chair.; Dale Van Groningen, Vice-Chair.; Charles Crivelli III; Dan Cummings; Kevin Fondse; George Goshgarian;

Elaine Rominger; Steve Van Duyn; Robert J. Weimer; Donald Yee
Giving statement: Giving through the Blue Diamond Growers Corporate Giving Program.

Blue Diamond Growers Corporate Giving Program

c/o Community Rels. Dept.
P.O. Box 1768
Sacramento, CA 95812-1768
URL: http://www.bluediamond.com/index.cfm?navid=88

Purpose and activities: Blue Diamond makes charitable contributions to nonprofit organizations involved with youth development. Support is given primarily in midtown Sacramento, California.
Fields of interest: Youth development.
Type of support: Program development.
Geographic limitations: Giving primarily in midtown Sacramento, CA, with emphasis on the company's immediate neighborhood.
Support limitations: No product donations.
Publications: Application guidelines.
Application information: Applications accepted. Application form required. Applicants should submit the following:
1) timetable for implementation and evaluation of project
2) name, address and phone number of organization
3) copy of IRS Determination Letter
4) brief history of organization and description of its mission
5) geographic area to be served
6) copy of most recent annual report/audited financial statement/990
7) how project's results will be evaluated or measured
8) detailed description of project and amount of funding requested
9) contact person
10) copy of current year's organizational budget and/or project budget
11) listing of additional sources and amount of support
12) plans for acknowledgement
Initial approach: Download application form and mail to headquarters
Committee meeting date(s): July
Deadline(s): Apr.1 to July 1

507
BlueCross BlueShield of Tennessee, Inc.

1 Cameron Hill Cir.
Chattanooga, TN 37402-9815
(423) 535-5600
FAX: (423) 535-6255

Company URL: http://www.bcbst.com/
Establishment information: Established in 1945.
Company type: Private company
Business activities: Operates not-for-profit, locally governed health plan company.
Business type (SIC): Insurance/accident and health
Financial profile for 2010: Number of employees, 5,373; assets, $2,910,242,000; sales volume, $5,240,790,000; liabilities, $1,319,242,000
Corporate officers: Lamar J. Partridge, Chair.; Betty W. DeVinney, Vice-Chair.; Vicky B. Gregg, C.E.O.; William M. Gracey, Pres. and C.O.O.; John Giblin, Exec. V.P. and C.F.O.; Bill Young, Sr., V.P. and Genl. Counsel; Ron Harr, Sr. V.P., Human Resources and Public Affairs
Board of directors: Lamar J. Partridge, Chair.; Betty W. DeVinney, Vice-Chair.; Hulet M. Chaney; Gus B. Denton; DeWitt Ezell; Vicky B. Gregg; Herbert H. Hilliard; James M. Phillips; Gloria S. Ray; Emily J. Reynolds; Paul E. Stanton, Jr., M.D.; Scott Wallace
Giving statement: Giving through the Tennessee Health Foundation, Inc.

Tennessee Health Foundation, Inc.

1 Cameron Hill Cir.
Chattanooga, TN 37402-9815 (423) 535-7163
FAX: (423) 535-7173;
E-mail: Kathy_Bingham@bcbst.com; Additional address: 801 Pine St., Chattanooga, TN 37402-2555; URL: http://www.bcbst.com/about/community/TN-health-foundation/

Establishment information: Established in 2003 in TN.
Donor: Blue Cross and Blue Shield of Tennessee.
Contact: Kathy Bingham, Mgr.
Financial data (yr. ended 12/31/11): Assets, $128,947,850 (M); gifts received, $18,000,000; expenditures, $5,636,460; qualifying distributions, $5,430,235; giving activities include $5,406,618 for grants.
Purpose and activities: The foundation supports programs designed to improve health, public education, and economic development for Tennesseans. Special emphasis is directed towards programs designed to address health disparities and at-risk populations; infant mortality and childhood obesity; and patient safety and quality.
Fields of interest: Higher education; Medical school/education; Hospitals (general); Health care, clinics/centers; Health care, infants; Public health; Public health, obesity; Health care, insurance; Health care, patient services; Health care; Disasters, preparedness/services; Human services; Economic development Children; Economically disadvantaged.
Type of support: General/operating support; Program development.
Geographic limitations: Giving primarily in areas of company operations in TN.
Support limitations: No support for private clubs, private schools, organizations not eligible for tax deductible support, religious organizations, political candidates or organizations, hospitals or hospital building funds, or sports facilities or sports teams. No grants to individuals, or for political causes or campaigns, or special occasion or commemorative advertising.
Publications: Application guidelines; Informational brochure.
Application information: Applications accepted. Letter of inquiry must be submitted using organization letterhead and should be no longer than 2 pages. A full proposal may be requested at a later date. Applicants should submit the following:
1) how project will be sustained once grantmaker support is completed
2) signature and title of chief executive officer
3) statement of problem project will address
4) population served
5) name, address and phone number of organization
6) brief history of organization and description of its mission
7) how project's results will be evaluated or measured
8) explanation of why grantmaker is considered an appropriate donor for project
9) detailed description of project and amount of funding requested
10) plans for cooperation with other organizations, if any
11) contact person
Initial approach: Download letter of inquiry cover sheet and mail letter of inquiry and cover sheet to foundation
Deadline(s): Last day of Jan., May 1, and Sept. 1
Officers and Directors:* Lamar J. Partridge*, Chair.; Betty De Vinney*, Vice-Chair.; Vicky Gregg*, C.E.O.; Sheila Clemons, Secy.; John Giblin, C.F.O.; Danny Timblin, Treas.; Calvin Anderson*, Exec. Dir.; DeWitt Ezell, Jr.; Hulet Chaney; Gus B. Denton; John F. Germ; William M. Gracey; Herbert H. Hilliard; James M. Phillips; Gloria S. Ray; Emily J. Reynolds; Paul E. Stanton; Scott E. Wallace.
EIN: 200298456
Selected grants: The following grants are a representative sample of this grantmaker's funding activity:
$991,935 to Tennessee Hospital Education and Research Foundation, Nashville, TN, 2010. For Tennessee Patient Safety Program.
$980,000 to Tennessee Hospital Education and Research Foundation, Nashville, TN, 2010. For Tennessee Surgical Quality Improvement Project.
$500,000 to American Red Cross, Nashville, TN, 2010. For disaster relief.
$422,000 to University of Tennessee Health Science Center, Memphis, TN, 2010. For Phase III of Blues Project, infant mortality initiative.
$422,000 to University of Tennessee Health Science Center, Memphis, TN, 2010. For Phase III of Blues Project, infant mortality initiative.
$300,000 to Governors Books from Birth Foundation, Nashville, TN, 2010. For general support.
$200,000 to Tennessee State Collaborative on Reforming Education, SCORE, Nashville, TN, 2010. For general support.
$168,000 to Mountain States Foundation, Johnson City, TN, 2010. For Growing Healthy Program.
$100,000 to Knoxville Academy of Medicine Foundation, Knoxville, TN, 2010. For Project Access Emergency Department Utilization Initiative.
$90,000 to Church Health Center of Memphis, Memphis, TN, 2010. For program to encourage weight loss for obese diabetic patients.

508
BMC Software, Inc.

2101 CityWest Blvd.
Houston, TX 77042-2827 (713) 918-1371
FAX: (713) 918-8000

Company URL: http://www.bmc.com
Establishment information: Established in 1980.
Company type: Public company
Company ticker symbol and exchange: BMC/NASDAQ
Business activities: Develops computer software.
Business type (SIC): Computer services
Financial profile for 2013: Number of employees, 6,700; assets, $4,720,300,000; sales volume, $2,201,400,000; pre-tax net income, $427,900,000; expenses, $1,736,000,000; liabilities, $3,901,800,000
Fortune 1000 ranking: 2012—890th in revenues, 396th in profits, and 603rd in assets
Corporate officers: Robert E. Beauchamp, Chair., Pres., and C.E.O.; William D. Miller, C.O.O.; Stephen B. Solcher, Sr. V.P. and C.F.O.; Patrick K. Tagtow, Sr. V.P., Genl. Counsel, and Secy.; Brian Bergdoll, Sr. V.P., Sales; Hollie S. Castro, Sr. V.P., Admin.; T. Cory Bleuer, V.P., Cont., and C.A.O.
Board of directors: Robert E. Beauchamp, Chair.; Jon E. Barfield; Gary L. Bloom; John M. Dillon; Meldon K. Gafner; Mark J. Hawkins; Stephan A.

James; P. Thomas Jenkins; Louis J. Lavigne, Jr.; Kathleen A. O'Neil; Alex Pinchev; Carl James "Jim" Schaper; Tom C. Tinsley
Offices: Costa Mesa, Sacramento, San Jose, CA; Waltham, MA; New York, NY; West Conshohocken, PA; McLean, VA; Bellevue, WA
International operations: Argentina; Australia; Austria; Belgium; Brazil; Canada; China; Denmark; Finland; France; Germany; Hong Kong; Ireland; Israel; Italy; Japan; Malaysia; Netherlands; Norway; Singapore; South Korea; Spain; Sweden; Switzerland; United Kingdom
Giving statement: Giving through the BMC Software, Inc. Corporate Giving Program.
Company EIN: 742126120

BMC Software, Inc. Corporate Giving Program

2101 CityWest Blvd.
Houston, TX 77042-2828 (713) 918-8800
E-mail: dan_darmond@bmc.com; URL: http://www.bmc.com/corporate/corporate-commitment

Contact: Dan D'Armond, Dir., Community and Govt. Rels.
Purpose and activities: BMC Software makes charitable contributions to nonprofit organizations involved with social services, and health and wellness. Support is given primarily in areas of company operations, with emphasis on San Jose, California, Boston, Massachusetts, and Houston and Austin, Texas, and in India, Israel, the Netherlands, and Singapore.
Fields of interest: Public health; Human services.
International interests: India; Israel; Netherlands; Singapore.
Type of support: Employee volunteer services; General/operating support; Program development.
Geographic limitations: Giving on a national and international basis in areas of company operations, with emphasis on San Jose, CA, Boston, MA, Houston and Austin, TX, and in India, Israel, the Netherlands, and Singapore.
Application information:
Initial approach: E-mail headquarters for application information
Administrator: Dan D'Armond, Dir., Comms. and Govt. Rels.

509
BMW of North America, LLC

(formerly BMW of North America, Inc.)
300 Chestnut Ridge Rd.
Woodcliff Lake, NJ 07677-7731
(201) 307-4000

Company URL: http://www.bmwusa.com
Establishment information: Established in 1975.
Company type: Subsidiary of a foreign company
Business activities: Operates holding company; markets automobiles, motorcycles, parts and accessories, and marine engines wholesale.
Business type (SIC): Holding company; motor vehicles, parts, and supplies—wholesale; industrial machinery and equipment—wholesale
Corporate officers: Norbert Reithofer, Chair.; Ludwig Willisch, Pres.; Peter Miles, Exec. V.P., Opers.; Stefan Sengewald, Exec. V.P., Finance and C.F.O.; Tom Kowaleski, V.P., Corp. Comms.
Board of director: Norbert Reithofer, Chair.
Giving statement: Giving through the BMW of North America, LLC Corporate Giving Program.

BMW of North America, LLC Corporate Giving Program

(formerly BMW of North America, Inc. Corporate Giving Program)
P.O. Box 1227
Westwood, NJ 07675-1227
URL: http://www.bmwusa.com/Standard/Content/Uniquely/BMWInTheCommunity/Philanthropy.aspx

Purpose and activities: BMW makes charitable contributions to nonprofit organizations involved with education, road safety, and the environment. Support is given primarily in areas of company operations.
Fields of interest: Arts; Education; Environment; Safety, automotive safety; Community/economic development.
Type of support: General/operating support; Program development.
Geographic limitations: Giving primarily in areas of company operations.
Support limitations: No support for religious organizations not of direct benefit to the entire community, political, lobbying, fraternal, labor, or veterans' organizations, or disease-specific organizations. No grants to individuals (except for scholarships), or for general operating support, sponsorships, advertising, group or individual travel, team sponsorships, athletic scholarships, national conferences, sports events, or short-term events.
Publications: Application guidelines.
Application information: Applications accepted. Unsolicited requests for general operating support are generally not accepted. Multi-year funding is not automatic. Application form required. Applicants should submit the following:
1) timetable for implementation and evaluation of project
2) qualifications of key personnel
3) statement of problem project will address
4) name, address and phone number of organization
5) brief history of organization and description of its mission
6) copy of most recent annual report/audited financial statement/990
7) how project's results will be evaluated or measured
8) listing of board of directors, trustees, officers and other key people and their affiliations
9) detailed description of project and amount of funding requested
10) contact person
11) copy of current year's organizational budget and/or project budget
12) plans for acknowledgement

Initial approach: Proposal to headquarters
Final notification: 6 to 8 weeks

510
Boart Longyear Company

10808 South River Front Pkwy, Ste. 600
South Jordan, UT 84095 (801) 972-6430

Company URL: http://www.boartlongyear.com
Establishment information: Established in 1974.
Company type: Subsidiary of a foreign company
Business activities: Manufactures drilling products; provides contract drilling services.
Business type (SIC): Machinery/construction, mining, and materials handling; mining services/metal; mining services/coal; mining services/nonmetallic mineral (except fuels)
Corporate officers: David McLemore, Chair.; Joe Ragan, C.F.O.; Fabrizio Rasetti, Sr. V.P., Genl. Counsel, and Secy.; Brad Baker, Sr. V.P., Human Resources
Board of directors: David McLemore, Chair.; Bruce Brook; Roger Brown; Roy Franklin; Tanya Fratto; Barbara Jeremiah; Peter St. George
Giving statement: Giving through the Boart Longyear Company Contributions Program.

Boart Longyear Company Contributions Program

2640 W. 1700 S.
Salt Lake City, UT 84104-4269 (801) 972-6430
FAX: (801) 977-3374

Contact: Nancy Allen, Exec. Asst.
Purpose and activities: Boart Longyear makes charitable contributions to hospitals and nonprofit organizations involved with arts and culture and civic affairs. Support is given primarily in Utah.
Fields of interest: Arts; Medical care, in-patient care; Public affairs.
Type of support: Annual campaigns; Donated equipment; Emergency funds; Employee-related scholarships; General/operating support; Sponsorships.
Geographic limitations: Giving primarily in UT.
Support limitations: No support for religious organizations.
Application information: Applications accepted. The Human Resources Department handles giving. A contributions committee reviews all requests. Application form not required. Applicants should submit the following:
1) detailed description of project and amount of funding requested

Initial approach: Proposal to nearest company facility
Copies of proposal: 1
Committee meeting date(s): Quarterly
Deadline(s): None
Final notification: Varies
Number of staff: 2 full-time professional; 3 full-time support.

512
Bobcats Basketball Holdings, LLC

(also known as Charlotte Bobcats)
333 E. Trade St.
Charlotte, NC 28202 (704) 688-8600

Company URL: http://www.nba.com/bobcats
Establishment information: Established in 2003.
Company type: Private company
Business activities: Operates professional basketball club.
Business type (SIC): Commercial sports
Corporate officers: Michael Jordan, Chair.; Curtis J. Polk, Vice-Chair.; Fred A. Whitfield, Pres. and C.O.O.; Bill Duffy, Exec. V.P., C.F.O., and C.A.O.; Colleen Millsap, Exec. V.P., Admin.; Kay Lowery, V.P., Human Resources; Andy Feffer, V.P., Mktg.; Sheryl Willie, Cont.
Board of directors: Michael Jordan, Chair.; Curtis J. Polk, Vice-Chair.
Giving statement: Giving through the Charlotte Bobcats Corporate Giving Program and the Bobcats Youth Foundation, Inc.

Charlotte Bobcats Corporate Giving Program

c/o Community Rels. Dept.
129 W. Trade St., Ste. 700
Charlotte, NC 28202-5301 (704) 688-8791
FAX: (704) 688-8733; URL: http://www.nba.com/bobcats/community_relations.html

Contact: Kimberly Beal
Purpose and activities: The Charlotte Bobcats makes charitable contributions of game tickets and memorabilia to nonprofit organizations involved with youth development and on a case by case basis. Support is given primarily in North Carolina and South Carolina.
Fields of interest: Youth development; General charitable giving.
Type of support: Donated products; In-kind gifts.
Geographic limitations: Giving primarily in NC and SC.
Application information: Applications accepted. Support is limited to 1 contribution per organization during any given year. Proposals should be submitted using organization letterhead. Support is limited to 50 tickets per organization for game ticket donations. Applicants should submit the following:
1) population served
2) name, address and phone number of organization
3) copy of IRS Determination Letter
4) descriptive literature about organization
5) detailed description of project and amount of funding requested
6) contact person

Proposals should indicate the date, time, and location of the event, the expected number of attendees, and the type of fundraiser; the nature of the request being made; and the applicant's e-mail address, if available.
Initial approach: Mail or fax proposal to headquarters for memorabilia donations; complete online application form for game ticket donations
Deadline(s): 1 month prior to need
Final notification: 2 weeks for memorabilia donations; 2 weeks prior to game for game ticket donations

Bobcats Youth Foundation, Inc.

(formerly Bobcats Charitable Foundation, Inc.)
333 E. Trade St.
Charlotte, NC 28202-2425 (704) 688-8790
E-mail: lbarber@bobcatsse.com; URL: http://www.nba.com/bobcats/charitable_foundation.html

Establishment information: Established in 2004 in NC.
Contact: Larita L. Barber, Pres.
Financial data (yr. ended 09/30/11): Revenue, $381,020; assets, $353,044 (M); gifts received, $494,802; expenditures, $228,937; program services expenses, $222,209; giving activities include $222,209 for grants.
Purpose and activities: As the philanthropic arm of the Charlotte Bobcats, the foundation supports organizations involved with arts and culture, literacy, education, health, and fitness; special emphasis is directed toward programs designed to offer enrichment to children and youth.
Fields of interest: Arts; Education, reading; Education; Health care; Recreation Children/youth.
Program:
Grants Program: The foundation provides grants in the areas of literacy, fitness, and wellness to organizations, to support programs that offer enrichment to the children and youth of the Charlotte, NC region. Funding priorities include excellence in education (supporting organizations whose work impacts literacy and the educational advancement of underserved and underperforming children and youth) and health and fitness (supporting organization whose work impacts healthy and positive by youth in recreational sports, especially basketball, and organizations who promote the development of healthy lifestyles for young people through proper nutrition, exercise, and positive life choices). Eligible organizations must have had 501(c)(3) status for at least twelve months prior to application submission and have at least a two-to-three year operating history.
Type of support: Program development; Seed money.
Geographic limitations: Giving limited to the Charlotte, NC, area.
Support limitations: No support for government agencies or government-supported organizations (over 40 percent of budget), organizations with a fiscal agent relationship, religious organizations not of direct benefit to the entire community, or discriminatory organizations. No grants to individuals (except for scholarships), or for general operating support, building/renovation, endowments, conferences, research, salaries, stipends, or travel.
Publications: Application guidelines.
Application information: Applications accepted. Application form required.
Initial approach: Contact foundation for application
Board meeting date(s): Annually
Officers: William T. Duffy*, Chair.-Pres.; Andre Walters*, Secry.; James Dunlevy*, Treas.
EIN: 200946449

511
Bob's Discount Furniture, LLC

428 Tolland Tpke.
Manchester, CT 06040-1715
(860) 645-3208
FAX: (860) 645-4056

Company URL: http://www.mybobs.com
Establishment information: Established in 1991.
Company type: Private company
Business activities: Operates furniture stores.
Business type (SIC): Furniture and home furnishing stores
Financial profile for 2010: Number of employees, 1,800
Corporate officers: Gene Rosenberg, Chair.; Edmond J. English, C.E.O.; Robert Kaufman, Pres.; Steven Caprario, C.O.O.; Bill Ballou, Sr. V.P. and C.F.O.; Bob Dawley, V.P., Human Resources; Jason Olivieri, Cont.
Board of director: Gene Rosenberg, Chair.
Giving statement: Giving through the Bob's Discount Furniture, LLC Corporate Giving Program and the Bob's Discount Furniture Charitable Foundation, Inc.

Bob's Discount Furniture, LLC Corporate Giving Program

(also known as Bob's Outreach)
428 Tolland Tpke.
Manchester, CT 06040-1765 (860) 645-3208
E-mail: outreachvan@mybobs.com; URL: http://www.mybobs.com/outreach/

Purpose and activities: As a complement to its foundation, Bob's Discount Furniture makes charitable contributions to nonprofit organizations directly through its Random Acts of Kindness program; and awards scholarship funds to eligible high schools through its High School Heroes Scholarship Program. Support is given primarily in areas of company operations in Connecticut, Massachusetts, Maine, New Hampshire, New Jersey, New York, and Rhode Island.
Fields of interest: Vocational education; Higher education; General charitable giving.
Program:
High School Heroes Scholarship Program: The Bob's Discount Furniture $100,000 High School Heroes Scholarship Program offers high school students the opportunity to help save lives while earning scholarship money. Winners can receive a scholarship for up to $8,000.
Type of support: General/operating support; Scholarship funds.
Geographic limitations: Giving primarily in areas of company operation in CT, MA, ME, NH, NJ, NY, and RI.
Application information:
Deadline(s): June 1 to May 15 for High School Heroes Scholarship Program

Bob's Discount Furniture Charitable Foundation, Inc.

428 Tolland Tpke.
Manchester, CT 06042-1765
E-mail: info@bobscares.com; Additional tel.: (860) 233-6200; URL: http://bobscares.org/

Establishment information: Established in 1997 in CT.
Donors: Stan Adelstein; John Espinosa; Julieus Feinblum; Joseph Goodman; Lee Goodman; Rick Guyan; Roy Hester; Michael Hoffman; Burt Homonoff; Randy Jaffee; Robert Kaufman; Alan Parvizian; Gene Rosenberg; W.R. Allen Company; BH Associates; Bob's Discount Furniture of Mass., LLC; Bob's Discount Furniture, Inc.; Bob's Discount Furniture, LLC; Furniture Auctions of America; Gene Rosenberg Associates; Great American Group; Powell Company.
Contact: Kathryn Pianta, Charity Coord.
Financial data (yr. ended 12/31/11): Assets, $321,714 (M); gifts received, $605,541; expenditures, $533,142; qualifying distributions, $480,714; giving activities include $480,714 for grants.
Purpose and activities: The foundation supports organizations involved with education, health, cancer, human services, and children.
Fields of interest: Elementary/secondary education; Education; Health care, clinics/centers; Health care, patient services; Health care; Cancer; Big Brothers/Big Sisters; American Red Cross; Children/youth, services; Family services; Human services Children.
Type of support: General/operating support; Sponsorships.
Geographic limitations: Giving primarily in areas of company operations.
Support limitations: No grants to individuals.
Publications: Application guidelines.
Application information: Applications accepted. Letter of inquiry should be submitted on organization letterhead. Application form not required. Applicants should submit the following:
1) copy of IRS Determination Letter
2) detailed description of project and amount of funding requested
3) name, address and phone number of organization
4) contact person

Initial approach: Letter of inquiry
Deadline(s): 60 days prior to need

Officers and Directors:* Robert Kaufman*, Pres.; Ilene Kaufman*, Secy.; Eugene Rosenberg.
EIN: 061475682
Selected grants: The following grants are a representative sample of this grantmaker's funding activity:
$2,000 to Arthritis Foundation, Atlanta, GA, 2010.
$1,500 to Boston Public Schools, Boston, MA, 2010.
$1,050 to National Kidney Foundation, New York, NY, 2010.

513
Bodine Aluminum, Inc.

2100 Walton Rd.
St. Louis, MO 63114-5808 (314) 423-8200

Company URL: http://www.bodinealuminum.com
Establishment information: Established in 1912.
Company type: Subsidiary of a foreign company
Business activities: Manufactures aluminum sand and permanent mold castings.
Business type (SIC): Metal foundries/nonferrous
Corporate officer: Robert W. Lloyd, Pres. and C.E.O.
Giving statement: Giving through the Bodine Aluminum, Inc. Corporate Giving Program.

Bodine Aluminum, Inc. Corporate Giving Program

c/o Corp. Affairs
100 Cherry Blossom Way
Troy, MO 63379-2516
URL: http://www.trybodinealuminum.com/

Purpose and activities: Bodine makes charitable contributions to nonprofit organizations involved with education, the environment, and youth development. Support is given primarily in Missouri.
Fields of interest: Education; Environment; Youth development.
Type of support: General/operating support.
Geographic limitations: Giving primarily in MO, with emphasis on Lincoln County and the St. Charles area.
Application information: Applications accepted. Application form not required. Applicants should submit the following:
1) statement of problem project will address
2) name, address and phone number of organization
3) descriptive literature about organization
4) detailed description of project and amount of funding requested
5) contact person
6) additional materials/documentation
Initial approach: Proposal to headquarters
Copies of proposal: 1
Deadline(s): None

514
Bodman PLC

1901 St. Antoine St., 6th Fl. at Ford Field
Detroit, MI 48226-2310 (313) 259-7777

Company URL: http://www.bodmanlaw.com
Establishment information: Established in 1929.
Company type: Private company
Business activities: Operates law firm.
Business type (SIC): Legal services
Corporate officer: Michael E. Starrs, C.O.O.
Offices: Ann Arbor, Cheboygan, Detroit, Troy, MI; Dallas, TX
Giving statement: Giving through the Bodman PLC Pro Bono Program.

Bodman PLC Pro Bono Program

1901 Saint Antoine St.
6th Fl. at Ford Field
Detroit, MI 48226-2310 (313) 259-7777
E-mail: skornfield@bodmanlaw.com; URL: http://www.bodmanlaw.com/givingback.php

Contact: Susan M. Kornfield, Member
Fields of interest: Legal services.
Type of support: Pro bono services - legal.
Geographic limitations: Giving primarily in areas of company operations in Ann Arbor, Cheboygan, Detroit, and Troy, MI, Dallas, TX.
Application information: A Pro Bono Committee manages the program.

515
Boehringer Ingelheim, Corp.

900 Ridgebury Rd.
P.O. Box 368
Ridgefield, CT 06877-1058 (203) 798-9988

Company URL: http://us.boehringer-ingelheim.com
Establishment information: Established in 1971.
Company type: Subsidiary of a foreign company
Business activities: Discovers, develops, manufactures, and markets human and animal health care products.
Business type (SIC): Drugs
Financial profile for 2009: Number of employees, 6,000
Corporate officers: J. Martin Carroll, Pres. and C.E.O.; Marla Persky, Sr. V.P., Genl. Counsel., and Corp. Secy.; Paul R. Fonteyne, Sr. V.P., Mktg.
Subsidiaries: Boehringer Ingelheim Chemicals, Inc., Petersburg, VA; Boehringer Ingelheim Pharmaceuticals, Inc., Ridgefield, CT; Boehringer Ingelheim Roxane, Inc., Columbus, OH; Boehringer Ingelheim Vetmedica, Inc., St. Joseph, MO; Roxane Laboratories, Inc., Columbus, OH; Ben Venue Laboratories, Inc., Cleveland, OH
Giving statement: Giving through the Boehringer Ingelheim Cares Foundation, Inc.

Boehringer Ingelheim Cares Foundation, Inc.

900 Ridgebury Rd.
P.O. Box 368
Ridgefield, CT 06877-0358
E-mail: bicaresfoundation.rdg@boehringer-ingelheim.com; Contact for Patient Assistance Program: c/o Express Scripts SDS, Inc., P.O. Box 66555, St. Louis, MO 63166-6555, tel.: (800) 556-8317, fax: (866) 851-2827; For Patient Assistance Program for Medicare Beneficiaries: P.O. Box 66745, St. Louis, MO 63166-6745, tel.: (800) 556-8317, fax: (866) 727-5891; URL: http://us.boehringer-ingelheim.com/our_responsibility/grants-and-funding/charitable_donations.html

Establishment information: Established as a company-sponsored operating foundation in 2001 in CT.
Donors: Boehringer Ingelheim Pharmaceuticals, Inc.; Boehringer Ingelheim USA Corp.; Roxane Laboratories, Inc.
Contact: Frank A. Pomer Esq., V.P. and Treas.
Financial data (yr. ended 12/31/11): Assets, $25,384,492 (M); gifts received, $148,612,637; expenditures, $143,029,528; qualifying distributions, $142,976,721; giving activities include $3,189,752 for 47 grants (high: $2,380,252; low: $25) and $136,571,705 for grants to individuals.
Purpose and activities: The foundation supports programs designed to improve access to healthcare for underserved patients, and enhance math and science education for teachers and students in underserved communities; and provides Boehringer Ingelheim pharmaceuticals to uninsured patients in need.
Fields of interest: Higher education; Education; Health care, equal rights; Health care, clinics/centers; Health care; Disasters, preparedness/services; Youth, services; Human services; United Ways and Federated Giving Programs; Science, formal/general education; Mathematics; Science Economically disadvantaged.
Programs:
Charitable Donations Program: The foundation supports programs designed to provide access to medical care for those in need; promote math and science education; and enhance the communities in which Boehringer Ingelheim operates.
Patient Assistance Program: The foundation provides Boehringer Ingelheim pharmaceuticals to patients who are without pharmaceutical insurance and who meet household income levels. Special emphasis is directed toward those who are most in need, including senior citizens and families on limited incomes. For additional information see web site: URL http://us.boehringer-ingelheim.com/our_responsibilty/patients_families.html.
Product Donation Program: The foundation provides Boehringer Ingelheim pharmaceuticals to qualified nonprofit, health, and government organizations including AmeriCares, Direct Relief International, and MAP International. Patients in need who are served by those organizations may access medications that are critically important to their health and well-being free of charge.
Type of support: Donated products; Employee volunteer services; Equipment; General/operating support; Grants to individuals; In-kind gifts; Program development; Research.
Geographic limitations: Giving primarily in northern Fairfield County, CT; giving also to national organizations for Patient Assistance and Product Donation Program.
Support limitations: No support for political or religious organizations. No grants for event sponsorships.
Publications: Application guidelines; Program policy statement.
Application information: Applications accepted. Application form required. Applicants should submit the following:
1) qualifications of key personnel
2) population served
3) name, address and phone number of organization
4) copy of IRS Determination Letter
5) brief history of organization and description of its mission
6) geographic area to be served
7) copy of most recent annual report/audited financial statement/990
8) how project's results will be evaluated or measured
9) listing of board of directors, trustees, officers and other key people and their affiliations
10) detailed description of project and amount of funding requested
11) contact person
12) copy of current year's organizational budget and/or project budget
13) listing of additional sources and amount of support

Applications for the Patient Assistance Program must be filled out by a doctor and should include proof of the applicant's income.

Initial approach: Complete online eligibility quiz and application; download application form and fax or mail completed application for Patient Assistance Program
Board meeting date(s): Semi-annually
Deadline(s): None

Officers and Directors:* Paul Fonteyne*, Chair.; Lilly Ackley, Pres.; Frank A. Pomer, Esq., V.P. and Treas.; Tina Clark Beamon, Esq., Secy.; Amy Fry; Stefan Rinn.
EIN: 311810072
Selected grants: The following grants are a representative sample of this grantmaker's funding activity:
$350,000 to Connecticut United for Research Excellence, New Haven, CT, 2010. For Science Quest.
$200,000 to AmeriCares Free Clinics, Stamford, CT, 2010. For clinic.
$133,081 to United Way of Western Connecticut, Danbury, CT, 2010.
$100,000 to Pharmaceutical Research and Manufacturers of America Foundation, Washington, DC, 2010. For corporate contribution.
$50,000 to AmeriCares, Stamford, CT, 2010. For program support.
$50,000 to Catholic Medical Mission Board, New York, NY, 2010. For annual support.
$50,000 to MAP International, Brunswick, GA, 2010. For annual support for programs.
$34,200 to Anns Place, The Home of I CAN, Danbury, CT, 2010. For Family Day/Family Program Services.
$25,000 to Direct Relief International, Santa Barbara, CA, 2010. For annual support.
$23,400 to Womens Center of Greater Danbury, Danbury, CT, 2010. For volunteer coordinator.
$22,500 to Science Horizons, Danbury, CT, 2010. For Science Fair.
$18,000 to Ridgefield Symphony Orchestra, Ridgefield, CT, 2010. For concerts.
$10,000 to American Cancer Society, Wilton, CT, 2010. For Bethel Danbury and Reading Relay for Life.
$10,000 to Gwynedd-Mercy College, Gwynedd Valley, PA, 2010. For Adult Health Center.
$10,000 to Junior Achievement of Western Connecticut, Bridgeport, CT, 2010. For education programs.

516
The Boeing Company

100 N. Riverside Plz.
Chicago, IL 60606-1596 (312) 544-2000
FAX: (312) 544-2140

Company URL: http://www.boeing.com
Establishment information: Established in 1916.
Company type: Public company
Company ticker symbol and exchange: BA/NYSE
Business activities: Manufactures commercial airplanes, military aircraft and missile systems, and space and communications products.
Business type (SIC): Aircraft and parts; guided missiles and space vehicles; search and navigation equipment
Financial profile for 2012: Number of employees, 174,400; assets, $88,896,000,000; sales volume, $81,698,000,000; pre-tax net income, $5,910,000,000; expenses, $75,387,000,000; liabilities, $83,029,000,000
Fortune 1000 ranking: 2012—30th in revenues, 50th in profits, and 70th in assets
Forbes 2000 ranking: 2012—84th in sales, 141st in profits, and 278th in assets
Corporate officers: W. James McNerney, Jr., Chair., Pres., and C.E.O.; Gregory Smith, Exec. V.P. and C.F.O.; J. Michael Luttig, Exec. V.P. and Genl. Counsel; Kim Hammonds, C.I.O.; John J. Tracy, Sr. V.P., Opers.; Tony Parasida, Sr. V.P., Human Resources and Admin.; Thomas J. Downey, Sr. V.P., Comms.
Board of directors: W. James McNerney, Jr., Chair.; David L. Calhoun; Arthur D. Collins, Jr.; Linda Z. Cook; Kenneth M. Duberstein; Adm. Edmund P. Giambastiani, Jr.; Lawrence W. Kellner; Edward M. Liddy; Amb. Susan C. Schwab; Ronald A. Williams; Mike S. Zafirovski
Subsidiaries: Aviall Inc., Dallas, TX; Boeing Aerospace Operations, Inc., Cocoa Beach, FL; Boeing Realty Corp., Long Beach, CA; Jeppesen Sanderson, Inc., Englewood, CO; McDonnell Douglas Corporation, St. Louis, MO
Divisions: Commercial Airplanes Div., Renton, WA; Shared Services Group, Seattle, WA
Joint Venture: United Space Alliance, LLC, Houston, TX
International operations: Argentina; Australia; Barbados; Bermuda; Brazil; Canada; Cayman Islands; China; Cyprus; Czech Republic; Germany; Gibraltar; Greece; Hong Kong; India; Ireland; Italy; Japan; Malaysia; Mexico; Netherlands; Netherlands Antilles; New Zealand; Norway; Poland; Russia; Saudi Arabia; Singapore; South Africa; South Korea; Spain; Sweden; United Kingdom
Giving statement: Giving through the Boeing Company Global Corporate Citizenship, the Boeing Company Charitable Trust, the Employees Community Fund of Boeing, and the Employees Community Fund of Boeing-St. Louis.
Company EIN: 910425694

The Boeing Company Global Corporate Citizenship

100 N. Riverside
Chicago, IL 60606 (312) 544-2000
Additional tel.: (312) 544-3958; URL: http://www.boeing.com/companyoffices/aboutus/community/

Contact: Nora Moreno Cargie, Dir., Global Corp. Citizenship; Mark Schulze, Office Admin.
Purpose and activities: As a complement to its foundation, Boeing also makes charitable contributions to nonprofit organizations directly. Support is given to organizations involved with arts and culture, civic engagement, early learning and primary/secondary education, the environment, and health and human services. Support is given on a national and international basis.
Fields of interest: Arts; Elementary/secondary education; Education, early childhood education; Education; Environment; Health care; Family services, domestic violence; Human services; Public affairs.
Type of support: Building/renovation; Capital campaigns; Conferences/seminars; Consulting services; Continuing support; Donated equipment; Emergency funds; Employee matching gifts; Employee volunteer services; Equipment; Fellowships; In-kind gifts; Loaned talent; Matching/challenge support; Professorships; Program development; Public relations services; Research; Scholarship funds; Seed money; Sponsorships; Technical assistance; Use of facilities.
Geographic limitations: Giving on a national and international basis in areas of company operations, including AL, AZ, CA, CO, FL, GA, HI, IL, KS, MD, MO, NV, NM, OH, OK, OR, PA, SC, TX, UT, DC, WA, and in Australia, Canada, including Richmond, British Columbia and Winnipeg, Manitoba, and in Africa, and Europe including France, Germany, Great Britain, Spain, Italy, Russia and Commonwealth of Independent States, and Central, Eastern and Northern Europe, and The Middle East and Persian Gulf, including Saudi Arabia, Israel, Turkey, and Latin America including Brazil, and Mexico.
Support limitations: No support for political candidates, committees, or organizations, religious organizations, hospital or medical research organizations, or athletic organizations. No grants to individuals, or for travel, agency-sponsored walks, runs, or golf tournaments, auction booklet printing, tickets, or one-time events.
Application information: Applications accepted. Application form required.

Initial approach: Visit website for guidelines in each eligible state and country
Copies of proposal: 1

The Boeing Company Charitable Trust

c/o Bank of America, N.A.
P.O. Box 831041
Dallas, TX 75283-1041
Application contact: Bridget Sweeney-Renzulli, Community and Education Rels., MC-5002-8450, 100 N. Riverside Plaza, Chicago, IL 60606, tel.: (312) 544-2071; URL: http://www.boeing.com/companyoffices/aboutus/community/index.html

Establishment information: Trust established in 1964 in WA as successor to the Boeing Airplane Company Charitable Trust, established in 1952.
Donor: The Boeing Co.
Financial data (yr. ended 12/31/11): Assets, $57,843,114 (M); expenditures, $240,364; qualifying distributions, $96,061.
Purpose and activities: The foundation supports organizations involved with arts and culture, education, the environment, health, employment, human services, community development, science, civic affairs, and economically disadvantaged people.
Fields of interest: Visual arts; Performing arts; Arts; Elementary/secondary education; Education, early childhood education; Education, services; Education, reading; Education; Environment, pollution control; Environment, recycling; Environment, climate change/global warming; Environment, natural resources; Environment; Health care; Employment, training; Employment; Family services, parent education; Human services, financial counseling; Human services; Civil/human rights, equal rights; Economic development; Business/industry; Community/economic development; Science, formal/general education; Mathematics; Government/public administration; Public affairs Economically disadvantaged.

Programs:

Arts and Culture: The foundation supports programs designed to promote participation in arts and cultural activities and experiences. Special emphasis is directed toward performances and exhibitions that introduce new voices and perspectives to the community; collaborative efforts developed to create a more sustainable arts and cultural environment; and programs designed to engage people to become lifelong arts and cultural participants, patrons, and practitioners.

Civic: The foundation supports programs designed to increase public understanding of and engagement in the processes and issues that affect the community. Special emphasis is directed toward programs designed to address globalization; conservation and sustainability; community building; economic development; workforce development; scientific literacy and uses of technology; cultural, ethnic, and religious diversity; and strengthening the democratic process.

Education - Early Learning: The foundation supports programs designed to promote the development of social, emotional, and cognitive skills in children from birth to age five that are needed to succeed in school and in life. Special emphasis is directed toward programs designed to support parents as a child's first and most important teachers; provide access to an adequate level of information and support to parents; develop formal and informal caregivers; and promote public awareness.

Education - Primary and Secondary: The foundation supports programs designed to promote the development of quality learning environments in the areas of math, science, and literacy for future success in the workforce and in life. Special emphasis is directed toward programs designed to promote teachers' professional development and improve school leadership; improve outcomes for the largest number of students possible, including targeted investments for underserved populations; and encourage school systems to adopt a standard, aligned curriculum.

Environment: The foundation supports programs designed to address climate change and pollution. Special emphasis is directed toward programs designed to inspire environmental citizenship and educate citizens to minimize their impact on the environment; reduce greenhouse gas emissions and increase recycling and energy efficiency; and protect and restore critical natural assets and habitats.

Health and Human Services: The foundation supports programs designed to promote the economic well-being and health of the communities' most vulnerable residents. Special emphasis is directed toward programs designed to foster job training; promote social enterprises; provide new business to low-income communities; promote collaborations that coordinate healthcare services and economic self-sufficiency; address disparities in healthcare; and support projects that improve the efficiency of health and human services systems, including food, housing, and healthcare.

Type of support: Building/renovation; Curriculum development; Emergency funds; Equipment; In-kind gifts; Matching/challenge support; Program development; Research; Seed money; Sponsorships.

Geographic limitations: Giving on a national and international basis in areas of company operations, with emphasis on WA.

Support limitations: No support for political candidates or organizations, religious organizations not of direct benefit to the entire community, athletic groups, hospitals, school-affiliated orchestras, bands, choirs, or drama groups. No grants to individuals, or for adoption services, memorials, endowments, travel, walk-a-thons, athletic events (except for Special Olympics), door prizes or raffles, medical research, school-affiliated trips, yearbooks, or class parties, general operating support, fundraising events or activities, advertising, t-shirts, giveaways or promotional items, documentary films or books, debt reduction, dissertations or student research projects, loans, scholarships, fellowships, gifts, honoraria, gratuities, or capital campaigns for rental properties.

Publications: Annual report (including application guidelines); Application guidelines; Corporate giving report; Program policy statement.

Application information: Applications accepted. Additional information may be requested at a later date. A site visit may be requested. Organizations receiving support are asked to submit an interim report and a final report. Application form required.

Initial approach: Complete online application form

Deadline(s): Varies; visit website for local deadlines

Trustee: Bank of America, N.A.

EIN: 916056738

Employees Community Fund of Boeing-St. Louis

c/o UMB Bank
P.O. Box 415044
Kansas City, MO 64141-6692 (816) 860-7749
URL: http://www.boeing.com/companyoffices/aboutus/community/ecf_apply_stl.html

Establishment information: Established in 1997 in MO.

Contact: Angela Most, Mgr., Charitable Giving

Financial data (yr. ended 12/31/11): Revenue, $16,789,061; assets, $9,560,530 (M); gifts received, $16,692,186; expenditures, $17,324,751; program services expenses, $17,315,896; giving activities include $17,315,896 for 16 grants (high: $13,404,803; low: $10,000).

Purpose and activities: The fund is administered under the Boeing Company and supports the communities where St. Louis-based employees live and work.

Fields of interest: Arts; Elementary/secondary education; Environment; Health care; Human services; Public affairs.

Program:

Grants: The foundation considers grant applications from nonprofit organizations with 501 (c)(3) status in its service area, in the areas of health and human services, education (primarily K-12), arts and culture, and civics and environment.

Type of support: Building/renovation; Continuing support; Curriculum development; Emergency funds; Equipment; General/operating support; Internship funds; Program development; Program evaluation; Publication; Scholarship funds.

Geographic limitations: Giving primarily in St. Louis City and Franklin, Jefferson, Lincoln, St. Charles, St. Clair, St. Louis, and Warren counties, MO; consideration also given in Calhoun, Clinton, Greene, Macoupin, Madison, Monroe, and Randolph counties, IL.

Support limitations: No support for political organizations or programs, private foundations, or sectarian, fraternal, social, religious, or similar organizations. No grants to individuals, or for conferences or seminars.

Publications: Annual report (including application guidelines); Application guidelines; Grants list; Informational brochure.

Application information: Applications accepted. Applicant must be a 501(c)(3) nonprofit agency. Application form required. Applicants should submit the following:

1) contact person
2) listing of board of directors, trustees, officers and other key people and their affiliations
3) copy of current year's organizational budget and/or project budget
4) copy of most recent annual report/audited financial statement/990

Initial approach: Download application online

Copies of proposal: 1

Board meeting date(s): Monthly

Deadline(s): Jan. 31

Final notification: Sept. 1

Officers and Directors:* Laura Coughlin*, Pres.; Kim Jones*, V.P.; Angela Most*, Secy.-Treas.; Nani Bond; Kim Brestal; Mike Carosone; Bryan Chatmon; Mary Cisiewski; Kristin Favre; William Locke; Mandy Mills.

Trustee: UMB Bank, N.A.

Number of staff: 1 full-time professional; 1 part-time support.

EIN: 436023034

517
Boh Bros. Construction Co., LLC

730 S. Tonti St.
P.O. Drawer 53266
New Orleans, LA 70119 (800) 284-3377

Company URL: http://www.bohbros.com

Establishment information: Established in 1909.

Company type: Private company

Business activities: Provides construction services.

Business type (SIC): Construction/miscellaneous heavy; construction/highway and street (except elevated)

Financial profile for 2010: Number of employees, 100

Corporate officers: Robert H. Boh, Chair.; Robert S. Boh, Pres. and C.E.O.; G. Arthur Seaver III, Sr. V.P., Opers.

Board of director: Robert H. Boh, Chair.

Offices: Mobile, AL; Baton Rouge, Westlake, LA; Houston, TX

Giving statement: Giving through the Boh Foundation.

Boh Foundation

730 S. Tonti St.
New Orleans, LA 70119-7551
URL: http://www.nola.com

Establishment information: Established in 1975 in LA.

Donor: Boh Bros. Construction Co., L.L.C.

Financial data (yr. ended 01/31/12): Assets, $931,895 (M); expenditures, $84,879; qualifying distributions, $84,500; giving activities include $84,500 for 15 grants (high: $20,000; low: $1,000).

Purpose and activities: The foundation supports organizations involved with arts and culture, education, youth development, children and youth, and Catholicism.

Fields of interest: Museums; Arts; Secondary school/education; Higher education; Education; Youth development; Children/youth, services; Catholic agencies & churches.

Type of support: Building/renovation.

Geographic limitations: Giving primarily in New Orleans, LA.

Support limitations: No grants to individuals.

Application information: Applications not accepted. Unsolicited requests for funds not accepted.

Officer and Trustees:* Robert H. Boh*, Chair.; Robert S. Boh; John F. Lipani.

EIN: 510167756

518
Boies, Schiller & Flexner LLP

575 Lexington Ave., 7th Fl.
New York, NY 10022-6138 (212) 446-2300

Company URL: http://www.bsfllp

Establishment information: Established in 1997.

Company type: Private company

Business activities: Operates law firm.
Business type (SIC): Legal services
Corporate officer: David A. Barrett, Partner
Offices: Hollywood, Oakland, Santa Monica, CA; Washington, DC; Fort Lauderdale, Miami, Orlando, FL; Las Vegas, NV; Hanover, NH; Albany, Armonk, New York, NY
Giving statement: Giving through the Boies, Schiller & Flexner LLP Pro Bono Program.

Boies, Schiller & Flexner LLP Pro Bono Program

575 Lexington Ave., Fl. 7
New York, NY 10022-6138 (212) 446-2300
FAX: (212) 446-2350; URL: http://www.bsfllp.com/practices/180

Contact: Jonathan Schiller, Managing Partner
Fields of interest: Legal services.
Type of support: Pro bono services - legal.
Geographic limitations: Giving primarily in areas of company operations in Oakland, and Santa Monica, CA, Washington, DC, Fort Lauderdale, Hollywood, Miami, and Orlando, FL, Hanover, NH, Las Vegas, NV, Albany, Armonk, and New York, NY.
Application information: A Pro Bono Committee manages the program.

519
Boiron-Bornema, Inc.

6 Campus Blvd.
Newtown Square, PA 19073-3267
(610) 325-7464

Company URL: http://www.boironusa.com
Establishment information: Established in 1932.
Company type: Subsidiary of a foreign company
Business activities: Manufactures and distributes homeopathic medicines.
Business type (SIC): Drugs
Financial profile for 2010: Number of employees, 42
Corporate officers: Christian Boiron, Chair.; Janick Boudazin, Pres. and C.E.O.; Barbara Burger, C.I.O.
Board of director: Christian Boiron, Chair.
Giving statement: Giving through the Boiron Research Foundation.

Boiron Research Foundation

6 Campus Blvd., Bldg. A
Newtown Square, PA 19073-3200

Establishment information: Established in 1987 in MD.
Donors: Boiron-Borneman Co.; International Foundation for Clinical Homeopathy.
Contact: Thierry Boiron, Pres.
Financial data (yr. ended 12/31/11): Assets, $144,533 (M); expenditures, $322; qualifying distributions, $0.
Purpose and activities: The foundation awards grants to individuals for homeopathic medical research.
Type of support: Grants to individuals.
Application information: Applications accepted. Application form required. Applicants should submit the following:
1) copy of current year's organizational budget and/or project budget
Initial approach: Proposal
Deadline(s): Sept. 30
Officers: Thierry Boiron, Pres.; Ludovic Rassat, V.P.; Gilles Chaufferin, Secy.; Philippe Belon; Bruno Joet.
EIN: 521268329

520
The Boler Company, Inc.

500 Park Blvd., Ste. 1010
Itasca, IL 60143-2608 (630) 773-9111

Establishment information: Established in 1977.
Company type: Private company
Business activities: Manufactures automotive parts and chassis.
Business type (SIC): Motor vehicles and equipment; plastic products/miscellaneous; metal products/fabricated; industrial machinery and equipment—wholesale
Corporate officers: John M. Boler, Chair.; Matthew J. Boler, Pres. and C.E.O.; John M. Gaynor, C.F.O.; James Colley, V.P. and Treas.; Nancy B. Coons, V.P., Admin.
Board of director: John M. Boler, Chair.
International operations: Mexico
Giving statement: Giving through the Boler Family Foundation.

The Boler Family Foundation

(formerly The Boler Company Foundation)
500 Park Blvd., Ste. 1010
Itasca, IL 60143-1285

Establishment information: Established in 1987 in IL.
Donors: The Boler Co., Inc.; John M. Boler; James W. Boler; Matthew J. Boler; Michael J. Boler; Judith B. McCormack; Jill B. McCormack.
Financial data (yr. ended 12/31/11): Assets, $23,624,399 (M); gifts received, $9,088,455; expenditures, $1,723,426; qualifying distributions, $1,662,436; giving activities include $1,659,653 for 8 grants (high: $500,000; low: $50,000).
Purpose and activities: The foundation supports organizations involved with education, health, autism, and children with special needs.
Fields of interest: Elementary/secondary education; Higher education; Education; Health care, clinics/centers; Speech/hearing centers; Health care; Autism Children; Disabilities, people with.
Type of support: General/operating support; Program development.
Geographic limitations: Giving limited to IL.
Support limitations: No grants to individuals.
Application information: Applications not accepted. Contributes only to pre-selected organizations.
Trustees: John M. Boler; Jill B. McCormack; Judith B. McCormack.
EIN: 366854134
Selected grants: The following grants are a representative sample of this grantmaker's funding activity:
$250,000 to University of Chicago, Chicago, IL, 2010. For general fund.
$100,000 to Heights Foundation, Fort Myers, FL, 2010. For general fund.
$75,000 to Yampa Valley Autism Program, Steamboat Springs, CO, 2010. For general fund.
$25,000 to Julie Billiart School, Lyndhurst, OH, 2010. For general fund.
$10,000 to Center for Speech and Language Disorders, Elmhurst, IL, 2010. For general fund.
$10,000 to Notre Dame-Cathedral Latin School, Chardon, OH, 2010. For general fund.

522
Bond, Schoeneck & King, PLLC

1 Lincoln Ctr.
110 W. Fayette St.
Syracuse, NY 13202-1355 (315) 218-8000

Company URL: http:///www.bsk.com
Establishment information: Established in 1897.
Company type: Private company
Business activities: Operates law firm.
Business type (SIC): Legal services
Corporate officer: James E. Mackin, Partner
Offices: Naples, FL; Overland Park, KS; Albany, Buffalo, Garden City, Ithaca, New York, Oswego, Rochester, Syracuse, Utica, NY
Giving statement: Giving through the Bond, Schoeneck & King, PLLC Pro Bono Program.

Bond, Schoeneck & King, PLLC Pro Bono Program

1 Lincon Ctr.
Syracuse, NY 13202-1355 (315) 218-8000
FAX: (315) 218-8100; URL: http://www.bsk.com/bond/pro-bono

Contact: Thomas Myers, Member
Fields of interest: Legal services.
Type of support: Pro bono services - legal.
Geographic limitations: Giving primarily in areas of company operations in Naples, FL, Overland Park, KS, Albany, Buffalo, Garden City, Ithaca, New York, Oswego, Rochester, Syracuse, and Utica, NY.

523
Boneal Inc.

6962 US Hwy. 460
P.O. Box 49
Means, KY 40346-8909 (606) 768-3620

Company URL: http://www.boneal.com
Establishment information: Established in 1980.
Company type: Private company
Business activities: Provides manufacturing outsourcing solutions.
Business type (SIC): Fabricated metal products (except machinery and transportation equipment); plastic products/miscellaneous
Corporate officers: Keith Gannon, C.E.O.; David B. Ledford, Pres.; Georgetta Hollon Gannon, C.F.O.
Board of director: Jeffrey B. Compton
Subsidiary: The Lonmore Co., Lexington, KY
Plants: Buckner, KY; Ann Arbor, MI
Giving statement: Giving through the Boneal Charitable Foundation, Inc.

Boneal Charitable Foundation, Inc.

611 Winchester Rd.
P.O. Box 640
Mount Sterling, KY 40353
Application address: P.O. Box 49, Means, KY 40346

Establishment information: Established in 1999 in KY.
Donor: Boneal Inc.
Contact: Georgetta H. Gannon, Dir.
Financial data (yr. ended 12/31/11): Assets, $127,085 (M); gifts received, $12,000; expenditures, $4,381; qualifying distributions, $4,000; giving activities include $4,000 for grants.
Purpose and activities: The fund supports organizations involved with arts and culture and higher education and awards college scholarships to students in Menifee County, Kentucky.

Fields of interest: Youth development.
Type of support: Program development; Scholarships—to individuals.
Application information: Applications accepted. Application form required.
Initial approach: Letter or Telephone
Deadline(s): None
Directors: Georgetta H. Gannon; O. Keith Gannon; David Ledford.
EIN: 611358724

524
Bonitz, Inc.
645 Rosewood Dr.
P.O. Box 82
Columbia, SC 29202-4603 (803) 799-0181
FAX: (803) 748-9223

Company URL: http://www.bonitz.us/
Establishment information: Established in 1954.
Company type: Private company
Business activities: Provides general contract construction services.
Business type (SIC): Building construction general contractors and operative builders
Corporate officers: George W. Rogers, Chair.; Tom Edens, Pres.; Laurence Newton, V.P., Finance; Richard Ames, V.P., Mktg.
Board of director: George W. Rogers, Chair.
Subsidiaries: Bonitz Contracting Co., Inc., Columbia, SC; Bonitz Flooring Group, Inc., Columbia, SC; Bonitz Insulation Co., Inc., Columbia, SC; Merovan Business Pank Corp., Greenville, SC; Sam Wood Associates, Inc., Raleigh, NC
Giving statement: Giving through the Bill Rogers Bonitz Scholarship Fund.

Bill Rogers Bonitz Scholarship Fund
1525 W. WT. Harris Blvd.
Charlotte, NC 28288-5709 (336) 747-8182
E-mail: sallyking@bellsouth.net; URL: https://www.csascholars.org/bntz/index.php

Establishment information: Established in 1999 in SC.
Donor: Bonitz of South Carolina, Inc.
Financial data (yr. ended 06/30/12): Assets, $149,361 (M); expenditures, $6,546; qualifying distributions, $4,000; giving activities include $4,000 for grants.
Purpose and activities: The foundation awards college scholarships to children of full-time employees of Bonitz of South Carolina for technical or trade school.
Fields of interest: Education.
Type of support: Employee-related scholarships.
Geographic limitations: Giving limited to SC.
Application information: Applications not accepted. Contributes only through employee-related scholarships.
Trustee: Wells Fargo Bank, N.A.
EIN: 566549889

521
The Bon-Ton Stores, Inc.
2801 E. Market St.
York, PA 17402-2406 (717) 757-7660
FAX: (717) 751-3196

Company URL: http://www.bonton.com
Establishment information: Established in 1898.
Company type: Public company
Company ticker symbol and exchange: BONT/NASDAQ
Business activities: Operates department stores.
Business type (SIC): Department stores
Financial profile for 2013: Number of employees, 27,100; assets, $1,634,210,000; sales volume, $2,978,840,000; pre-tax net income, -$21,320,000; expenses, $2,917,320,000; liabilities, $1,523,600,000
Fortune 1000 ranking: 2012—719th in revenues, 896th in profits, and 906th in assets
Corporate officers: Byron L. Bergren, Chair.; Brendan L. Hoffman, Pres. and C.E.O.; Keith E. Plowman, Exec. V.P. and C.F.O.; Dennis R. Clouser, Exec. V.P., Human Resources; Thomas M. Grumbacher, Chair. Emeritus
Board of directors: Byron L. Bergren, Chair.; Lucinda M. Baier; Philip M. Browne; Marsha M. Everton; Michael L. Gleim; Thomas M. Grumbacher; Brendan L. Hoffman; Todd McCarty; Jeffrey B. Sherman
Giving statement: Giving through the Bon-Ton Foundation.
Company EIN: 232835229

The Bon-Ton Foundation
(also known as The Bon-Ton Stores Foundation)
2801 E. Market St.
York, PA 17402-2420

Establishment information: Established in 1991 in PA.
Donor: The Bon-Ton Stores, Inc.
Financial data (yr. ended 01/31/12): Assets, $294,595 (M); gifts received, $211,690; expenditures, $200,296; qualifying distributions, $195,576; giving activities include $114,582 for 39 + grants (high: $20,307), $41,800 for 24 grants to individuals (high: $2,000; low: $600) and $35,624 for employee matching gifts.
Purpose and activities: The foundation supports organizations involved with arts and culture, education, water conservation, health, cancer, human services, and Judaism.
Fields of interest: Performing arts; Arts; Medical school/education; Education; Environment, water resources; Health care, clinics/centers; Health care; Genetic diseases and disorders; Cancer; Cancer research; Breast cancer research; YM/YWCAs & YM/YWHAs; Children/youth, services; Human services; Community/economic development; Jewish agencies & synagogues.
Type of support: Employee matching gifts; Employee volunteer services; General/operating support; Grants to individuals; Program development; Scholarship funds; Sponsorships.
Geographic limitations: Giving primarily in areas of store operations in PA.
Support limitations: No grants to individuals (except for disaster grants).
Application information: Applications not accepted. Contributes only to pre-selected organizations and through disaster grants.
Board meeting date(s): Quarterly
Officers and Directors:* Mary Kerr*, Pres.; Gregory Yawman*, Secy.; Michael Webb*, Treas.; Kimberly Krummerich; Christine Hojnacki; Cindy Hupf; Colleen Mayer; Pamela Pratt; Kathleen Weber.
EIN: 232656774
Selected grants: The following grants are a representative sample of this grantmaker's funding activity:
$2,000 to Milwaukee Art Museum, Milwaukee, WI, 2009.

525
Booz-Allen & Hamilton Inc.
8283 Greensboro Dr.
McLean, VA 22102-4904 (703) 902-5000

Company URL: http://www.bah.com
Establishment information: Established in 1914.
Company type: Private company
Business activities: Provides management and technology consulting services.
Business type (SIC): Management and public relations services
Financial profile for 2010: Number of employees, 23,315; sales volume, $5,122,600,000
Corporate officers: Ralph W. Shrader, Chair., Pres., and C.E.O.; Samuel R. Strickland, Exec. V.P., C.F.O., and C.A.O.; Frank S. Smith III, Sr. V.P. and C.I.O.
Board of directors: Ralph W. Shrader, Chair.; Daniel F. Akerson; Peter Clare; Ian Fujiyama; Charles O. Rossotti; Philip A. Odeen; Samuel R. Strickland
Giving statement: Giving through the Booz-Allen & Hamilton Inc. Corporate Giving Program.

Booz-Allen & Hamilton Inc. Corporate Giving Program
8283 Greensboro Dr.
McLean, VA 22102-4904 (703) 902-5000
URL: http://www.boozallen.com/about/community

Purpose and activities: Booz-Allen & Hamilton makes charitable contributions to nonprofit organizations involved with arts and culture, youth, education, the environment, health, and human services. Support is given on a national, with emphasis on the District of Columbia, Maryland, and Virginia. Support is also given on an international basis, including in Honduras.
Fields of interest: Museums (art); Performing arts; Arts; Education, volunteer services; Education; Environment, pollution control; Environment, water pollution; Environment, climate change/global warming; Environment; Health care, research; Hospitals (general); Public health; ALS; Food services; Housing/shelter, rehabilitation; Athletics/sports, Special Olympics; Youth development, public education; Girl scouts; Human services; Children, services; Homeless, human services; Engineering/technology.
International interests: Honduras.
Type of support: Conferences/seminars; Employee volunteer services; General/operating support; Pro bono services; Program development; Sponsorships; Technical assistance.
Geographic limitations: Giving in areas of company operations, with emphasis on DC, MD, and VA, and on a national and international basis, including in Honduras.
Application information: Applications not accepted. Contributes only to pre-selected organizations.

526
Borcherding Enterprises, Inc.
9737 Kings Auto Mall Rd.
Cincinnati, OH 45249-8243 (513) 677-9200

Company URL: http://www.borcherdingbpg.com
Establishment information: Established in 1983.
Company type: Private company
Business activities: Operates automobile dealership.
Business type (SIC): Motor vehicles—retail
Corporate officers: Kim Borcherding, Co-Pres.; John Borcherding, Co-Pres.

Giving statement: Giving through the Borcherding Foundation, Inc.

Borcherding Foundation, Inc.

9737 Kings Auto Mall Rd.
Cincinnati, OH 45249-8243

Establishment information: Established in 2003 in OH.
Donor: Borcherding Enterprises, Inc.
Financial data (yr. ended 12/31/11): Assets, $1,500 (M); expenditures, $0; qualifying distributions, $0.
Purpose and activities: The foundation supports organizations involved with K-12 education, patient services, cancer, and children and youth.
Type of support: General/operating support.
Geographic limitations: Giving primarily in Cincinnati, OH; giving also in Phoenix, AZ.
Support limitations: No grants to individuals.
Application information: Applications not accepted. Unsolicited requests for funds not accepted.
Director: Kim Borcherding.
EIN: 200349836

527
Borden Manufacturing Company

1506 E. Ash St.
Goldsboro, NC 27530-5204
(919) 734-4301

Company type: Private company
Business activities: Produces cotton and synthetic yarns.
Business type (SIC): Yarn and thread mills
Corporate officer: Ralph Borden, Pres.
Giving statement: Giving through the Borden Fund, Inc.

The Borden Fund, Inc.

(formerly Borden Manufacturing Company Fund, Inc.)
P.O. Drawer P
Goldsboro, NC 27533-9715

Establishment information: Established in 1952 in NC.
Donor: Borden Manufacturing Co.
Financial data (yr. ended 12/31/11): Assets, $1,817,321 (M); expenditures, $109,885; qualifying distributions, $66,039; giving activities include $66,039 for grants.
Purpose and activities: The foundation supports hospices and organizations involved with performing arts, higher education, and youth development.
Fields of interest: Health care; Human services; Religion.
Type of support: General/operating support.
Geographic limitations: Giving primarily in areas of company operations, with emphasis on Goldsboro, NC.
Support limitations: No grants to individuals.
Application information: Applications not accepted. Unsolicited requests for funds not accepted.
Officers: W. Lee Borden, Pres. and Treas.; Robert H. Borden, V.P.; Edwin B. Borden III, Secy.
EIN: 566045689

528
BorgWarner, Inc.

3850 Hamlin Rd.
Auburn Hills, MI 48326 (248) 754-9200
FAX: (302) 655-5049

Company URL: http://www.borgwarner.com
Establishment information: Established in 1928.
Company type: Public company
Company ticker symbol and exchange: BWA/NYSE
Business activities: Manufactures vehicle powertrain application systems and components.
Business type (SIC): Motor vehicles and equipment
Financial profile for 2012: Number of employees, 19,100; assets, $6,400,800,000; sales volume, $7,183,200,000; pre-tax net income, $761,000,000; expenses, $6,430,300,000; liabilities, $3,318,200,000
Fortune 1000 ranking: 2012—358th in revenues, 335th in profits, and 516th in assets
Forbes 2000 ranking: 2012—1162nd in sales, 1141st in profits, and 1723rd in assets
Corporate officers: Timothy M. Manganello, Chair. and C.E.O.; Robin J. Adams, Vice-Chair., Exec. V.P., and C.A.O.; James R. Verrier, Pres. and C.O.O.; Ronald T. Hundzinski, V.P. and C.F.O.; Jamal M. Farhat, V.P. and C.I.O.; Thomas J. McGill, V.P. and Treas.; Steven G. Carlson, V.P. and Cont.; John J. Gasparovic, V.P., Genl. Counsel, and Secy.; Scott D. Gallett, V.P., Mktg., Public Rels., and Comms.; Janice K. McAdams, V.P., Human Resources
Board of directors: Timothy M. Manganello, Chair.; Robin J. Adams, Vice-Chair.; Phyllis O. Bonanno; David T. Brown; Jan Carlson; Dennis C. Cuneo; Jere A. Drummond; John R. McKernan, Jr.; Alexis P. Michas; Ernest J. Novak, Jr.; Richard O. Schaum; Thomas T. Stallkamp
Subsidiary: BorgWarner Cooling Systems Inc., Marshall, MI
International operations: Brazil; Canada; China; France; Hong Kong; Hungary; India; Japan; Mexico; Monaco; Poland; South Korea; Taiwan; Thailand
Giving statement: Giving through the BorgWarner Inc. Corporate Giving Program and the BorgWarner Foundation.
Company EIN: 133404508

BorgWarner Inc. Corporate Giving Program

3850 Hamlin Rd.
Auburn Hills, MI 48326-2872 (248) 754-9200
URL: http://www.borgwarner.com/en/Company/SocialResponsibility/default.aspx

Purpose and activities: Borg Warner makes charitable contributions to nonprofit organizations involved with children, education, and the environment. Support is given primarily in areas of company operations in Illinois, Michigan, Mississippi, New York, North Carolina, South Carolina, and Texas, and in Brazil, China, France, Germany, Hungary, India, Ireland, Italy, Japan, Mexico, Monaco, Poland, Portugal, South Korea, Spain, and the United Kingdom.
Fields of interest: Education; Environment, energy; Environment; Health care, patient services; Health care; Disasters, preparedness/services; Children, services; Science; Engineering/technology; General charitable giving Children.
International interests: Brazil; China; France; Germany; Hungary; India; Ireland; Italy; Japan; Mexico; Monaco; Poland; Portugal; South Korea; Spain; United Kingdom.
Type of support: Employee matching gifts; Employee volunteer services; General/operating support.
Geographic limitations: Giving primarily in areas of company operations in IL, MI, MS, NC, NY, SC, and TX, and in Brazil, China, France, Germany, Hungary, India, Ireland, Italy, Japan, Mexico, Monaco, Poland, Portugal, South Korea, Spain, and the United Kingdom.

BorgWarner Foundation

3850 Hamlin Rd.
Auburn Hills, MI 48326-2872

Establishment information: Established in 2001 in IL.
Donor: BorgWarner Inc.
Financial data (yr. ended 12/31/11): Assets, $0 (M); gifts received, $326,592; expenditures, $326,592; qualifying distributions, $326,592; giving activities include $326,592 for grants.
Purpose and activities: The foundation supports organizations involved with education, health, and human services.
Fields of interest: Higher education; Engineering school/education; Education; Health care; Food services; American Red Cross; Human services.
Type of support: Endowments; General/operating support; Scholarship funds.
Geographic limitations: Giving primarily in MI.
Support limitations: No grants to individuals.
Application information: Applications not accepted. Unsolicited requests for funds not accepted.
Officers: Laurene H. Horiszny, Pres.; Jan Bertsch, Treas.
Directors: Phyllis Bonanno; Jere Drummond.
EIN: 311776016

529
Robert Bosch, LLC

(formerly Robert Bosch Corporation)
38000 Hills Tech Dr.
Farmington Hills, MI 48331 (248) 876-1000

Company URL: http://www.bosch.us
Establishment information: Established in 1906.
Company type: Subsidiary of a foreign company
Business activities: Develops and manufactures automotive parts, power tools, and home appliances.
Business type (SIC): Motor vehicles and equipment; machinery/metalworking; appliances/household
Financial profile for 2010: Number of employees, 500; sales volume, $8,800,000,000
Corporate officers: Peter J. Marks, Chair., Pres., and C.E.O.; Luke Baer, Sr. V.P., Genl. Counsel, and Secy.
Board of director: Peter J. Marks, Chair.
Division: Video Equipment Div., Salt Lake City, UT
Giving statement: Giving through the Robert Bosch Corporation Contributions Program and the Robert Bosch Fair Share Fund.

Robert Bosch Fair Share Fund

8101 Dorchester Rd.
Charleston, SC 29418-2906 (843) 760-7000

Establishment information: Established in 1976 in SC; supporting organization of Berkeley Citizens, Berkeley Seniors, Caregivers, Carolina Youth Development Center, Coastal Carolina Council, Crisis Ministries, Dorchester Outreach Ministry, Florence Crittenden Home, Good News Christian School, Helping Hands of Goose Creek, Lowcounty Children's Center, Lowcounty Crisis Pregnancy Center, Meals on Wheels - East Cooper, MUSC

Foundation, My Sister's House, Salvation Army, Tricounty Family Ministries, Trident Literacy Association, Trident United Way.
Contact: Vickey Middleton, Recording Secy.
Financial data (yr. ended 12/31/11): Revenue, $85,204; assets, $14,978 (M); gifts received, $66,924; expenditures, $122,875; giving activities include $122,875 for grants.
Purpose and activities: The fund supports various charitable organizations, with a focus on youth and human services.
Fields of interest: Human services; Youth, services.
Type of support: In-kind gifts.
Geographic limitations: Giving limited to Berkeley, Charleston, and Dorchester counties, SC.
Officers: Thomas Piness, Pres.; Eric Kuker, Treas.
Directors: Hank Bennett; David Brown; Steven Kremser; Rubysteen Major; Stephanie Myers; Vanessa White.
EIN: 570620740

530
BOSE Corporation

The Mountain
P.O. Box 9168
Framingham, MA 01701-9168
(508) 879-7330
FAX: (508) 820-3465

Company URL: http://www.bose.com
Establishment information: Established in 1964.
Company type: Private company
Business activities: Produces loudspeakers and electronic equipment.
Business type (SIC): Audio and video equipment/ household
Financial profile for 2011: Number of employees, 9,300; sales volume, $2,280,000,000
Corporate officers: Amar G. Bose, C.E.O.; Bob Maresca, Pres.; Rob Ramrath, C.I.O.; Daniel A. Grady, V.P., Finance and C.F.O; Drew Geiger, V.P., Mktg.
International operations: Australia; Brazil; Canada; Denmark; France; Germany; Italy; Japan; Mexico; Netherlands; United Kingdom
Giving statement: Giving through the BOSE Foundation, Inc.

BOSE Foundation, Inc.

c/o BOSE Corp.
The Mountain, Ste. MS6B1
Framingham, MA 01701-9168 (508) 879-7330

Establishment information: Established in 1987 in MA.
Donor: BOSE Corp.
Financial data (yr. ended 03/31/11): Assets, $1,784,130 (M); expenditures, $361,471; qualifying distributions, $361,221; giving activities include $361,221 for grants.
Purpose and activities: The foundation supports organizations involved with music, higher education, health, and housing development and awards research grants to academic institutions in the areas of electric engineering, business, and computer science.
Fields of interest: Performing arts, music; Higher education; Engineering school/education; Health care; Housing/shelter, development; American Red Cross; Business/industry; United Ways and Federated Giving Programs; Engineering/ technology.
Type of support: General/operating support; Research.
Geographic limitations: Giving limited to MD and MA; giving also to national organizations.
Application information: Applications not accepted. Contributes only to pre-selected organizations.
Officers and Directors:* Robert Maresca*, Pres.; Mark E. Sullivan, Clerk; Herbert W. Batchelder, Treas.
EIN: 042967717
Selected grants: The following grants are a representative sample of this grantmaker's funding activity:
$6,620 to American Cancer Society, Atlanta, GA, 2011.
$1,762 to Multiple Sclerosis Society, National, New York, NY, 2011.
$1,000 to American Diabetes Association, Alexandria, VA, 2011.
$1,000 to Autism Speaks, New York, NY, 2011.
$1,000 to Cystic Fibrosis Foundation, Bethesda, MD, 2011.

531
Bose McKinney & Evans LLP

111 Monument Cir., Ste. 2700
Indianapolis, IN 46204-5120
(317) 684-5000

Company URL: http://www.boselaw.com
Establishment information: Established in 1955.
Company type: Private company
Business activities: Operates law firm.
Business type (SIC): Legal services
Corporate officer: Vicki Bruce Hansen, C.O.O.
Offices: Washington, DC; Fort Wayne, Indianapolis, West Lafayette, IN
Giving statement: Giving through the Bose McKinney & Evans LLP Pro Bono Program.

Bose McKinney & Evans LLP Pro Bono Program

111 Monument Cir., Ste. 2700
Indianapolis, IN 46204-5120 (317) 684-5000
FAX: (317) 684-5173; URL: http:// www.boselaw.com

Contact: Sam Laurin, Partner
Fields of interest: Legal services.
Type of support: Pro bono services - legal.
Geographic limitations: Giving primarily in areas of company operations in Indianapolis, IN.

532
Bossong Hosiery Mills, Inc.

840 W. Salisbury St.
P.O. Box 789
Asheboro, NC 27203-4327 (336) 625-2175

Establishment information: Established in 1927.
Company type: Private company
Business activities: Manufactures women's hosiery.
Business type (SIC): Hosiery and knitted fabrics
Financial profile for 2012: Number of employees, 275
Corporate officer: F.Huntley Bossong, Pres.
Giving statement: Giving through the Bossong Foundation.

Bossong Foundation

(formerly SA Bossong Trust Fund)
1525 W. W.T. Harris Blvd., D1114-044
Charlotte, NC 28288-5709
Application address: Joseph C. Bossong, V.P., c/o Bossong Hosiery Mills, Inc., P.O. Box 789, Asheboro, NC 27023

Establishment information: Established around 1977 in NC.
Donor: Bossong Hosiery Mills, Inc.
Financial data (yr. ended 11/30/11): Assets, $155,466 (M); expenditures, $13,400; qualifying distributions, $11,150; giving activities include $10,000 for 8 grants (high: $3,000; low: $250).
Purpose and activities: The foundation supports organizations involved with higher education, youth services, and Christianity.
Fields of interest: Education; Human services; Public affairs.
Type of support: General/operating support.
Geographic limitations: Giving limited to NC.
Support limitations: No grants to individuals.
Application information: Applications not accepted. Unsolicited requests for funds not accepted.
Officer: Joseph C. Bossong, V.P.
Trustee: Wells Fargo Bank, N.A.
EIN: 136028097

533
The Boston Beer Company , Inc.

1 Design Ctr., Ste. 850
Boston, MA 02110 (617) 368-5000
FAX: (617) 368-5500

Company URL: http://www.bostonbeer.com
Establishment information: Established in 1984.
Company type: Public company
Company ticker symbol and exchange: SAM/NYSE
Business activities: Operates microbrewing company.
Business type (SIC): Beverages
Financial profile for 2012: Number of employees, 950; assets, $359,480,000; sales volume, $580,220,000; pre-tax net income, $95,520,000; expenses, $484,640,000; liabilities, $114,390,000
Corporate officers: C. James Koch, Chair.; Martin F. Roper, Pres. and C.E.O.; William F. Urich, C.F.O. and Treas.; Kathleen H. Wade, V.P. and Corp. Secy.; Thomas W. Lance, V.P., Opers.; John C. Geist, V.P., Sales; Ai-Li Lim, V.P., Human Resources; Al-Li Lim, V.P., Human Resources
Board of directors: C. James Koch, Chair.; David A. Burwick; Pearson C. Cummin III; Cynthia A. Fisher; Jay Margolis; Martin F. Roper; Gregg A. Tanner; Jean-Michel Valette
Giving statement: Giving through the Boston Beer Company, Inc. Contributions Program.
Company EIN: 043284048

The Boston Beer Company, Inc. Contributions Program

1 Design Ctr., Ste. 850
Boston, MA 02110-2300 (617) 368-5000
URL: http://www.samueladams.com/company/ community-involvement.aspx

Purpose and activities: The Boston Beer Co. makes charitable contributions to nonprofit organizations directly. Support is given primarily in areas of company operations in Massachusetts.
Fields of interest: Cancer; Business/industry; Voluntarism promotion Children.

Type of support: Donated products; General/operating support; In-kind gifts; Mission-related investments/loans.
Geographic limitations: Giving primarily in areas of company operations in MA.

534
Boston Capital Holdings, LP

1 Boston Pl., Ste. 2100
Boston, MA 02108-4405 (617) 624-8900

Company URL: http://www.bostoncapital.com
Establishment information: Established in 1974.
Company type: Subsidiary of a private company
Business activities: Operates holding company.
Business type (SIC): Holding company
Corporate officers: Jack Manning, Chair., Pres., and C.E.O.; Jeff Goldstein, C.O.O.; Marc N. Teal, Sr. V.P. and C.F.O.; Karen A. Germano, Sr. V.P. and Cont.; Nestor M. Nicholas, Genl. Counsel
Board of director: Jack Manning, Chair.
Giving statement: Giving through the Boston Capital Foundation.

The Boston Capital Foundation

1 Boston Pl., 21st Fl.
Boston, MA 02108-4406

Establishment information: Established in 1995 in MA.
Donors: A Celebrity Salute to Boston Garden; Boston Capital Holdings, LP.
Financial data (yr. ended 12/31/11): Assets, $5,868 (M); gifts received, $90,326; expenditures, $95,768; qualifying distributions, $95,698; giving activities include $95,698 for grants.
Purpose and activities: The foundation supports libraries and organizations involved with arts and culture, disease, housing, human services, international affairs, and economic development.
Fields of interest: Arts; Education; Community/economic development.
Type of support: General/operating support.
Application information: Applications not accepted. Unsolicited requests for funds not accepted.
Trustees: Kevin Costello; Jeffrey Goldstein; John P. Manning.
EIN: 043257822

535
The Boston Consulting Group

Exchange Pl., 31st Fl.
Boston, MA 02109 (617) 973-1200

Company URL: http://www.bcg.com
Establishment information: Established in 1963.
Company type: Private company
Business activities: Operates management consulting firm.
Business type (SIC): Management and public relations services
Financial profile for 2011: Number of employees, 5,600; sales volume, $3,550,000,000
Corporate officers: Rich Lesser, Pres. and C.E.O.; Debbie Simpson, C.F.O.; Jeremy Barton, Genl. Counsel
Giving statement: Giving through the Boston Consulting Group Corporate Giving Program.

The Boston Consulting Group Corporate Giving Program

Exchange Pl., 31st Fl.
Boston, MA 02109 (617) 973-1200
URL: http://www.bcg.com/about_bcg/social_impact/default.aspx

Purpose and activities: The Boston Consulting Group makes charitable contributions to nonprofit organizations on a case-by-case basis.
Fields of interest: General charitable giving.
Type of support: Employee volunteer services; General/operating support; In-kind gifts.

536
Boston Market Corp.

14103 Denver W. Pkwy., Ste. 100
Golden, CO 80401-3124 (303) 278-9500

Company URL: http://www.bostonmarket.com
Establishment information: Established in 1985.
Company type: Subsidiary of a public company
Business activities: Operates restaurants.
Business type (SIC): Restaurants and drinking places
Corporate officers: George Michel, C.E.O.; Gregory S. Uhing, Sr. V.P. and C.F.O.; J. Randal Miller, C.A.O. and Genl. Counsel; Phyllis Hammond, Sr. V.P., Corp. Comms.; Gretchen Paules, V.P., Mktg.; Joe Dennen, V.P., Finance
Giving statement: Giving through the Boston Market Corporation Contributions Program.

Boston Market Corporation Contributions Program

14103 Denver West Pkwy.
Golden, CO 80401-3124
URL: http://www.bostonmarket.com/fundraisers/index.jsp

Purpose and activities: Boston Market makes charitable contributions to nonprofit organizations involved with food services, children, and military and veterans. Support is given to national organizations.
Fields of interest: Food services; Children, services; Military/veterans' organizations.
Type of support: Cause-related marketing; Donated products; In-kind gifts; Sponsorships.
Geographic limitations: Giving to national organizations.

537
Boston Professional Hockey Association, Inc.

(also known as Boston Bruins)
TD Banknorth Garden
100 Legends Way
Boston, MA 02114-1390 (617) 624-1900

Company URL: http://www.bostonbruins.com
Establishment information: Established in 1924.
Company type: Subsidiary of a private company
Business activities: Operates professional ice hockey club.
Business type (SIC): Commercial sports
Corporate officers: Jeremy M. Jacobs, Sr., Chair. and C.E.O.; Cam Neely, Pres.; Amy Latimer, Sr. V.P., Sales and Mktg.; James K. Bednarek, V.P., Finance; Jen Compton, V.P., Mktg.
Board of director: Jeremy M. Jacobs, Sr., Chair.
Giving statement: Giving through the Boston Bruins Corporate Giving Program and the Boston Bruins Foundation, Inc.

Boston Bruins Corporate Giving Program

TD Garden
100 Legends Way
Boston, MA 02114-1300 (617) 624-1900
URL: http://bruins.nhl.com/club/page.htm?id=38784

Purpose and activities: As a complement to its foundation, the Boston Bruins also make charitable contributions of memorabilia to nonprofit organizations directly. Support is limited to New England.
Fields of interest: General charitable giving.
Type of support: In-kind gifts.
Geographic limitations: Giving limited to New England.
Support limitations: No grants to individuals.
Application information: Applications accepted. Requests for monetary donations are not accepted. Application form required. Applicants should submit the following:
1) contact person
2) name, address and phone number of organization
Applications should include the organization's Tax ID number, and the name, date, and a description of the event.
Initial approach: Complete online application form
Deadline(s): 6 weeks prior to event

Boston Bruins Foundation, Inc.

(formerly Boston Bruins Charitable Foundation, Inc.)
c/o TD Banknorth Garden
100 Legends Way
Boston, MA 02114-1300 (617) 624-1924
E-mail: bsweeney@bostonbruins.com; Grant process contact inf.: tel.: (617) 624-1928, E-mail: jsouthwood@bostonbruins.com; URL: http://bruins.nhl.com/club/microhome.htm?location=/foundation

Establishment information: Established in 2003 in MA.
Contact: Bob Sweeney, Dir., Devel.
Financial data (yr. ended 06/30/11): Revenue, $1,489,246; assets, $1,008,907 (M); gifts received, $986,957; expenditures, $1,478,786; giving activities include $1,359,676 for grants.
Purpose and activities: The mission of the foundation is to assist charitable organizations that demonstrate a strong commitment to enhancing the quality of life for children in the community.
Fields of interest: Children, services Children.
Geographic limitations: Giving primarily in New England, with emphasis on MA.
Support limitations: No support for organizations lacking 501(c)(3) status, fraternal, veterans', labor, religious, or governmental agencies, or start-up organizations seeking first-time cash grant support. No grants to individuals.
Application information: Applications accepted. Requests submitted by fax or e-mail not considered. See foundation Web site for additional application information. Application form required. Applicants should submit the following:
1) copy of IRS Determination Letter
2) copy of most recent annual report/audited financial statement/990
3) listing of board of directors, trustees, officers and other key people and their affiliations
4) copy of current year's organizational budget and/or project budget

5) listing of additional sources and amount of support
Initial approach: Download application form
Officers: Charlie Jacobs, Chair.; Jessica Rahuba, C.F.O.
EIN: 200172439

538
Boston Red Sox Baseball Club L.P.

4 Yawkey Way
Boston, MA 02215 (617) 267-9440

Company URL: http://boston.redsox.mlb.com
Establishment information: Established in 1901.
Company type: Subsidiary of a private company
Business activities: Operates professional baseball club.
Business type (SIC): Commercial sports
Corporate officers: Thomas C. Werner, Chair.; David Ginsberg, Co.-Vice-Chair.; Phillip H. Morse, Co.-Vice-Chair.; Larry Lucchino, Pres. and C.E.O.; Sam Kennedy, Exec. V.P. and C.O.O.; Steve Fitch, Sr. V.P. and C.F.O.; Mark Solitro, V.P. and Cont.; Amy Waryas, V.P., Human Resources
Board of directors: Thomas Werner, Chair.; David Ginsberg, Co.-Vice-Chair.; Phillip Morse, Co.-Vice-Chair.
Giving statement: Giving through the Boston Red Sox Corporate Giving Program and the Red Sox Foundation, Inc.

Boston Red Sox Corporate Giving Program

c/o Community Rels.
4 Yawkey Way
Boston, MA 02215-3409 (617) 226-6717
URL: http://boston.redsox.mlb.com/bos/community/in_kind_donations.jsp

Purpose and activities: As a complement to its foundation, the Boston Red Sox also make charitable contributions to nonprofit organizations directly. Support is limited to Connecticut, Maine, Massachusetts, New Hampshire, Rhode Island, and Vermont.
Fields of interest: General charitable giving.
Type of support: In-kind gifts.
Geographic limitations: Giving limited to CT, MA, ME, NH, RI, and VT.
Support limitations: No grants to individuals; no ticket donations.
Publications: Application guidelines.
Application information: Applications accepted. Support is limited to 1 contribution during any given year. Personal items or fan merchandise to be autographed are not accepted. The Community Relations Department handles giving. Application form required. Applicants should submit the following:
1) name, address and phone number of organization
2) detailed description of project and amount of funding requested
3) contact person
Applications should include the organization's Tax ID Number; the name, date, location, description, and expected attendance of the event; the type of fundraiser; and the event sponsor/underwriter.
Initial approach: Complete online application form
Deadline(s): 8 weeks prior to need

The Red Sox Foundation, Inc.

4 Yawkey Way
Boston, MA 02215-3409 (617) 226-6614
E-mail: redsoxfoundation@redsox.com; URL: http://www.redsoxfoundation.org

Establishment information: Established in 2002 in MA.
Contact: Meg Vaillancourt, Exec. Dir.
Financial data (yr. ended 12/31/10): Revenue, $6,609,862; assets, $8,629,641 (M); gifts received, $2,929,270; expenditures, $8,004,362; program services expenses, $7,609,104; giving activities include $6,210,304 for 60 grants (high: $4,076,809; low: $6,000) and $236,597 for grants to individuals.
Purpose and activities: The foundation aims to improve the health, educational, and recreational opportunities for children in New England as well as addressing social issues that affect the quality of life in urban neighborhoods.
Fields of interest: Education; Health care; Recreation Children.
Program:
Red Sox Scholars: Each year, the foundation provides tutoring, mentoring, enrichment opportunities to economically disadvantaged 6th and 7th graders in Boston public schools with college scholarships of $10,000 each pending graduation from high school. The scholarships, which are held in their name and will be paid directly to the college of their choice, are conditional upon the students maintaining their academic standing and good citizenship.
Type of support: Scholarship funds.
Geographic limitations: Giving limited to the New England area, with emphasis on MA.
Officer: Meg Vaillancourt, Exec. Dir.; Tom Werner*, Chair.; Lawrence Lucchino*, Pres. and C.E.O.
Board Members: Michael Egan; Chad Gifford; Mike Gordon; Sean McGrail; Tom Werner; Linda Henry.
EIN: 331007984

539
Boston Sand & Gravel Company

100 N. Washington St.
P.O. Box 9187
Boston, MA 02114 (617) 227-9000

Company URL: http://www.bostonsand.com
Establishment information: Established in 1914.
Company type: Private company
Business activities: Manufactures ready-mix concrete; processes gravel, sand, and stone.
Business type (SIC): Mining/sand and gravel; mining/crushed and broken stone; aircraft and parts
Corporate officers: Dean M. Boylan, Sr., C.E.O.; Dean M. Boylan, Jr., Pres.; Jeanne-Marie Boylan, Exec. V.P., C.F.O., and Treas.
Giving statement: Giving through the Boston Sand & Gravel Company Charitable Foundation, Inc.

Boston Sand & Gravel Company Charitable Foundation, Inc.

100 N. Washington St., 2nd Fl.
Boston, MA 02114-2128

Establishment information: Established in 1993 in MA.
Donor: Boston Sand & Gravel Co.
Financial data (yr. ended 12/31/11): Assets, $118,400 (M); expenditures, $70,583; qualifying distributions, $68,500; giving activities include $68,500 for grants.
Purpose and activities: The foundation supports organizations involved with education, health, recreation, and human services.
Fields of interest: Education; Health care; Human services.
Application information: Applications not accepted. Unsolicited requests for funds not accepted.
Officers and Directors:* Dean M. Boylan*, Pres.; Jeanne-Marie Boylan*, Treas.
EIN: 043174009

540
Boston Scientific Corporation

1 Boston Scientific Pl.
Natick, MA 01760-1537 (508) 650-8000
FAX: (508) 650-8923

Company URL: http://www.bostonscientific.com
Establishment information: Established in 1979.
Company type: Public company
Company ticker symbol and exchange: BSX/NYSE
International Securities Identification Number: US1011371077
Business activities: Develops, manufactures, and markets medical devices.
Business type (SIC): Medical instruments and supplies
Financial profile for 2012: Number of employees, 24,000; assets, $17,154,000,000; sales volume, $7,249,000,000; pre-tax net income, -$4,107,000,000; expenses, $11,117,000,000; liabilities, $10,284,000,000
Fortune 1000 ranking: 2012—357th in revenues, 997th in profits, and 266th in assets
Forbes 2000 ranking: 2012—1165th in sales, 1981st in profits, and 1069th in assets
Corporate officers: Peter M. Nicholas, Chair.; Michael F. Mahoney, Pres. and C.E.O.; Timothy A. Pratt, Exec. V.P., Genl. Counsel, Secy., and C.A.O.; Jeffrey D. Capello, Exec. V.P. and C.F.O.; Kenneth J. Pucel, Exec. V.P., Opers.; Wendy Carruthers, Sr. V.P., Human Resources
Board of directors: Peter M. Nicholas, Chair.; Katharine T. Bartlett; Bruce L. Byrnes; Nelda J. Connors; Kristina M. Johnson, Ph.D.; Michael F. Mahoney; Ernest Mario, Ph.D.; N.J. Nicholas, Jr.; Uwe E. Reinhardt, Ph.D.; John E. Sununu
Subsidiaries: Boston Scientific Scimed, Inc., Maple Grove, MN; Cardiac Pathways Corp., Sunnyvale, CA; EP Technologies, Inc., San Jose, CA; Scimed Life Systems, Inc., Maple Grove, MN
Plants: Valencia, CA; Miami, FL; Spencer, IN; Plymouth, MN; Redmond, WA
International operations: Argentina; Australia; Belgium; Bermuda; Bulgaria; Canada; Colombia; Czech Republic; Denmark; England; Finland; France; Germany; Greece; Hong Kong; Hungary; India; Ireland; Israel; Italy; Japan; Lebanon; Luxembourg; Malaysia; Mexico; Netherlands; New Zealand; Panama; Philippines; Poland; Portugal; Singapore; South Africa; South Korea; Spain; Switzerland; Thailand; Turkey; Uruguay; Venezuela
Historic mergers: Guidant Corporation (April 21, 2006)
Giving statement: Giving through the Boston Scientific Corporation Contributions Program, the Boston Scientific Foundation, Inc., and the Sally Smith Taylor Charitable Trust.
Company EIN: 042695240

Boston Scientific Corporation Contributions Program

c/o Charitable Donations Admin.
1 Boston Scientific Pl.
Natick, MA 01760-1537 (508) 650-8000
E-mail: charitableadmin@bsci.com; URL: http://www.bostonscientific.com/CorporateResponsibility.bsci/,,/navRelId/1004.1071/seo.serve

Purpose and activities: As a complement to its foundation, Boston Scientific also makes charitable contributions to individuals and nonprofit organizations directly. Support is given to organizations that support global, national, and local initiatives that expand access to quality healthcare and provide educational opportunities for the underserved. Emphasis is given to programs that encourage students to pursue career paths in the fields of health, science, and technology. The Boston Scientific HCP and National Associations Charitable Donations program is limited to charitable fundraisers, public health education awareness, general community health research, charitable sponsorships, and indigent care. Giving primarily in areas of company operations.
Fields of interest: Secondary school/education; Higher education, college; Health sciences school/education; Education, reading; Education; Health care, association; Medical care, community health systems; Health care, patient services; Health care; Heart & circulatory diseases; Diabetes; Food banks; Human services, fund raising/fund distribution; Children, services; Family services; Human services, gift distribution; Developmentally disabled, centers & services; United Ways and Federated Giving Programs; Science, public education; Mathematics; Engineering/technology; Biology/life sciences; Military/veterans' organizations Economically disadvantaged.

Program:
The Community Energy Project: The Community Energy Project offers free home weatherization services for low-income senior citizens and people with disabilities who live in Portland, Oregon. PacifiCorp employee volunteers and others install energy-saving materials.
Type of support: Annual campaigns; Conferences/seminars; Donated products; Employee volunteer services; Equipment; General/operating support; Grants to individuals; In-kind gifts; Program development; Sponsorships.
Geographic limitations: Giving primarily in areas of company operations.
Support limitations: No support for organizations that are not national associations, clubs, fraternal groups, or lobbying groups, religious organizations not of direct benefit to the entire community, MA-licensed HCPs that are not recognized by the Internal Revenue Service as 501(c)(3) entities or Vermont-licensed HCPs, individuals or entities that are debarred/excluded from participation in federal health care programs, for Boston Scientific HCP and National Associations Charitable Donations. No grants for political campaigns, physical plant improvements (e.g., "bricks and mortar"), purchase of equipment used in patient care, recreation or entertainment (e.g., golf tournaments), or to supplement Medicare or Medicaid coverage gaps, and no product donations, for Boston Scientific HCP and National Associations Charitable Donations.
Publications: Application guidelines.
Application information: Applications accepted. Applications for educational grants should be submitted on organization letterhead. Application form required. Applicants should submit the following:
1) timetable for implementation and evaluation of project
2) population served
3) name, address and phone number of organization
4) brief history of organization and description of its mission
5) list of company employees involved with the organization
6) listing of board of directors, trustees, officers and other key people and their affiliations
7) detailed description of project and amount of funding requested
8) contact person
9) copy of current year's organizational budget and/or project budget
10) listing of additional sources and amount of support
11) additional materials/documentation
Applications for medical fellowship grants should include Federal Tax I.D., Form W-9, list of key faculty, medical affiliations, fellowship details, and information on practice and research work as well as past grants. Applications for educational grants should include conference title, date, location, speakers, and brochure, accreditation information, Form W-9, and number of attendees. Applications for product donations should include procedure to be performed, number of patients to be treated, and product name, size, and quantity. Applications for Boston Scientific HCP and National Associations Charitable Donations should include a Form W-9, a list of available sponsorship levels, and a copy of the event brochure or invitation, event details, and past funding.
Initial approach: Download application and mail completed form and additional materials to headquarters for medical fellowship grants and educational grants; E-mail request for Boston Scientific HCP and National Associations Charitable Donations; Scan and fax or e-mail form for product donations.
Copies of proposal: 1
Deadline(s): 4 weeks prior to event for Boston Scientific HCP and National Associations Charitable Donations

Boston Scientific Foundation, Inc.

1 Boston Scientific Pl., MS B2
Natick, MA 01760-1537 (508) 650-8554
FAX: (508) 650-8579;
E-mail: bscifoundation@bsci.com; URL: http://www.bostonscientific.com/CorporateResponsibility.bsci/,,/method/lvl1/navRelId/1071.1077/seo.serve

Establishment information: Established in 2001 in MA.
Donors: Boston Scientific Corp.; John Abele; G. David Jang.
Contact: Jacqueline Boas, Fdn Admin.
Financial data (yr. ended 12/31/11): Assets, $18,309,798 (M); gifts received, $4,253,395; expenditures, $5,700,260; qualifying distributions, $5,675,258; giving activities include $5,362,785 for 347 grants (high: $400,000; low: $1,600).
Purpose and activities: The foundation supports programs designed to improve the lives of the economically disadvantaged in the areas of health and education.
Fields of interest: Elementary/secondary education; Higher education; Medical school/education; Education; Hospitals (general); Health care, clinics/centers; Health care; Cancer; Breast cancer; Boys & girls clubs; Youth development; YM/YWCAs & YM/YWHAs; Children/youth, services; Human services; Mathematics; Science Economically disadvantaged; Homeless.

Programs:
Education: The foundation supports programs designed to promote educational opportunities and skill development for the economically disadvantaged or those at risk. Special emphasis is directed toward improved educational outcomes, skill development, and long-term economic self-sufficiency.
Employee-related Scholarships: The foundation awards college scholarships to children of active, full-time employees of Boston Scientific.
Fellowship Grants: The foundation awards post-graduate medical fellowships in fields of study that are of interest to Boston Scientific. Fields of study include Cardiac Rhythm Management & Electrophysiology, Endoscopy, Interventional Cardiology & Peripheral Interventions, Neurovascular, Neuromodulation, and Urology & Women's Health. The program is designed to inspire the next generation of leaders, innovators, and caregivers. The program is administered by Boston Scientific's CRM Grant Committee.
Health: The foundation supports programs designed to improve health through enhanced access and quality of care; and promote disease prevention and awareness efforts.
Type of support: Curriculum development; Employee volunteer services; Employee-related scholarships; Fellowships; Program development.
Geographic limitations: Giving primarily in areas of company operations in Fremont, San Jose, and Valencia, CA, Spencer, IN, Greater Boston, Marlborough, Natick, and Quincy, MA, and Twin Cities, MN.
Support limitations: No support for political or religious organizations or discriminatory organizations. No grants to individuals (except for fellowships and employee-related scholarships), or for general operating support, capital campaigns, event-based fundraising or corporate sponsorships.
Publications: Annual report; Application guidelines.
Application information: Applications accepted. Visit website for application address. Support is limited to 1 contribution per organization during any given year. Application form required. Applicants should submit the following:
1) timetable for implementation and evaluation of project
2) copy of IRS Determination Letter
3) brief history of organization and description of its mission
4) copy of most recent annual report/audited financial statement/990
5) how project's results will be evaluated or measured
6) listing of board of directors, trustees, officers and other key people and their affiliations
7) detailed description of project and amount of funding requested
8) contact person
9) copy of current year's organizational budget and/or project budget
10) additional materials/documentation
Fellowship applications should include a copy of the institution's Form W9, a comprehensive fellowship description, and a letter of request on the institution's letterhead signed by the director of the fellowship program.
Initial approach: Complete online application; download application form and mail to application address for Fellowships
Copies of proposal: 1
Board meeting date(s): Quarterly
Deadline(s): None; Mar. 15 for fellowships
Final notification: 3 to 6 months
Officers and Directors:* Otha T. "Ski"p Spriggs III*, Pres.; Jean Lance*, V.P.; Timothy Pratt*, Clerk;

Robert Castagna*, Treas.; Marilee Grant; Alison J. Osattin; Doug Teany.
Number of staff: 1 full-time professional.
EIN: 043556844
Selected grants: The following grants are a representative sample of this grantmaker's funding activity:
$36,137 to Family Van, Roxbury, MA, 2011. To demonstrate how preventive interventions reduce barriers to health and health services across the United States.
$35,000 to Citizen Schools, Boston, MA, 2011. To create more experiences in the STEM fields that can intrigue and inspire students, helping them advance their learning and explore new opportunities, using core program element, apprenticeships, to engage students and scientists together in hands-on projects at five sites in San Mateo and Santa Clara counties, operating exclusively in school districts in low-income, disadvantaged communities.
$30,000 to Breakthrough Cambridge, Cambridge, MA, 2011. For Breakthrough Cambridge (BTC), the only year-round, tuition-free academic program in Cambridge, MA that serves at-risk and under-resourced middle and high school student.
$25,000 to School Health Clinics of Santa Clara County, San Jose, CA, 2011. For immunizations to low income children in Santa Clara.
$25,000 to ServeMinnesota, Minneapolis, MN, 2011. For Minnesota Math Corps, AmeriCorps program that deploys members to use research-based math intervention to teach students required math skills, which has expanded to serve more than 750 participants in 31 sites in St. Cloud, St. Paul, and the St. Croix River Education District in East Central Minnesota.
$22,000 to Sabathani Community Center, Minneapolis, MN, 2011. For health and wellness initiatives to address pervasive problem of health disparities affecting residents of color in South Minneapolis, including creation of solutions to address problems of affordability and access to fitness activities, health care for the senior population and lack of culturally competent nutrition education for children and youth.
$20,000 to Boston Partners in Education, Boston, MA, 2011. For Math Rules!, weekly math mentoring program serving students in grades 1-5 across Boston in Ralph W. Emerson Elementary School, the Nathan Hale Elementary School, and the Mission Hill K-8 School in Roxbury; the John Marshall Elementary School in Dorchester; the William Blackstone Elementary School in the South End; the John Eliot K-8 School in the North End; and the Josiah Quincy Elementary School in Chinatown.
$15,000 to A Little Easier Recovery, North Andover, MA, 2011. For A Little Easier Recovery Initiative, to address a clear unmet need for advanced breast cancer patients facing the worst case scenario beginning with extensive surgery typically followed by chemotherapy and radiation.
$15,000 to Hmong American Partnership, Saint Paul, MN, 2011. For HAP's Academic and Career Mentorship Program (ACMP) to provide academic support and mentorship to high-risk Hmong girls and young women (ages 13-18) in Saint Paul, Minnesota, provided through ACMP help participants improve their academic performance in math and science and broaden their knowledge of educational and professional opportunities with: after-school and summer math and science enrichment programs; one-on-one tutoring in math and science; career mentorship; college preparation; and mother/daughter support groups.
$12,000 to Urban Ventures Leadership Foundation, Minneapolis, MN, 2011. For Learning Lab to provide enhancement in math, reading and science for urban youth in year-round, out-of school time, using state-of-the art computers, smart boards and have access to technology for projects and research.

Sally Smith Taylor Charitable Trust

One Post Office Sq., 33rd Fl.
Boston, MA 02109-2106 (617) 261-1000

Establishment information: Established in 2006 in NC.
Donor: Boston Scientific Corp.
Contact: John O'keefe
Financial data (yr. ended 12/31/11): Assets, $67,893 (M); expenditures, $4,004; qualifying distributions, $4,004; giving activities include $3,500 for 3 grants to individuals (high: $2,500; low: $500).
Purpose and activities: Scholarship awards to North Carolina residents studying science, math, or engineering in an educational institution in North Carolina.
Fields of interest: Higher education.
Type of support: Scholarships—to individuals.
Geographic limitations: Giving limited to NC.
Application information: Applications accepted. Application form required.
Initial approach: Letter
Deadline(s): None
Trustee: James H. Taylor, Jr.
EIN: 203827822

541
Bound To Stay Bound Books, Inc.

1880 W. Morton Ave.
Jacksonville, IL 62650-2619
(217) 245-5191

Company URL: http://www.btsb.com
Establishment information: Established in 1920.
Company type: Private company
Business activities: Manufactures prebound children's library books.
Business type (SIC): Blankbooks, bookbinding, and looseleaf binders
Corporate officers: Robert L. Sibert, Chair.; Bob Sibert, Pres.; Joe Agner, C.I.O.; Steven R. Flynn, Treas.
Board of director: Robert L. Sibert, Chair.
Giving statement: Giving through the Bound To Stay Bound Books Foundation.

Bound To Stay Bound Books Foundation

1211 W. Morton Ave.
Jacksonville, IL 62650-2770
URL: http://www.btsb.com/aboutus/index.php

Establishment information: Established in 1984 in IL.
Donor: Bound To Stay Bound Books, Inc.
Financial data (yr. ended 12/31/11): Assets, $3,971,352 (M); gifts received, $134; expenditures, $192,056; qualifying distributions, $170,500; giving activities include $170,500 for 42 grants (high: $17,000; low: $250).
Purpose and activities: The foundation supports historical societies and organizations involved with education, conservation, and human services and awards scholarships to students pursuing graduate library degrees.
Fields of interest: Historic preservation/historical societies; Elementary/secondary education; Higher education; Libraries/library science; Education, reading; Education; Environment, natural resources; YM/YWCAs & YM/YWHAs; Human services; United Ways and Federated Giving Programs.
Programs:
ALSC Bound to Stay Bound Books Scholarship: The foundation annually awards four $7,000 scholarships to individuals pursuing a master's or advanced degree in children's librarianship. Recipients are selected based on academic excellence, leadership qualities, and the desire to work with children up to and including the age of 14 in any type of library. The program is administered by the American Library Association.
The Robert F. Sibert Award: The foundation annually recognizes the author of the most distinguished informational book for children published during the preceding year. The award is named in honor of Robert F. Sibert, the President of Bound to Stay Bound Books, who established standards for book binding through the American Library Association. The award is administered by the Association for Library Service to Children.
Type of support: Annual campaigns; Conferences/seminars; Endowments; General/operating support; Program development; Scholarship funds; Scholarships—to individuals; Sponsorships.
Geographic limitations: Giving primarily in IL.
Application information: Applications not accepted. Unsolicited requests for funds not accepted.
Trustee: Jacksonville Savings Bank, N.A.
EIN: 376227827

542
Bourns, Inc.

1200 Columbia Ave.
Riverside, CA 92507-2114 (951) 781-5690

Company URL: http://www.bourns.com
Establishment information: Established in 1952.
Company type: Private company
Business activities: Manufactures electronic products.
Business type (SIC): Electronic and other electrical equipment and components
Financial profile for 2010: Number of employees, 300
Corporate officers: Gordon L. Bourns, Chair. and C.E.O.; John J. Halenda, Pres. and C.O.O.; William P. McKenna, C.F.O. and Treas.; L. L. White, Secy.
Board of directors: Gordon L. Bourns, Chair.; John J. Halenda; William P. McKenna
Subsidiary: Recon/Optical, Inc., Barrington, IL
Divisions: Bourns Sensors/Controls Div., Riverside, CA; Pacific Optical Div., Riverside, CA
Plant: Logan, UT
International operations: China; Germany; Hungary; Ireland; Mexico; Switzerland; Taiwan; United Kingdom
Giving statement: Giving through the Bourns Foundation.

The Bourns Foundation

1200 Columbia Ave.
Riverside, CA 92507-2129 (951) 781-5025

Establishment information: Established in 1956.
Donor: Bourns, Inc.
Contact: Karen J. Smarr, Secy.-Treas.
Financial data (yr. ended 11/30/11): Assets, $8,819 (M); expenditures, $50,033; qualifying distributions, $50,000; giving activities include $50,000 for 12 grants (high: $16,000; low: $1,000).

Purpose and activities: The foundation supports programs designed to promote education, science, and technology.
Fields of interest: Education; Science; Religion.
Type of support: General/operating support; Program development.
Geographic limitations: Giving primarily in southern CA.
Support limitations: No grants to individuals.
Publications: Application guidelines.
Application information: Applications accepted. Application form required.
Initial approach: Contact foundation for application form
Copies of proposal: 1
Board meeting date(s): Quarterly
Deadline(s): None
Officers and Directors:* Gordon L. Bourns*, Pres.; Linda A. Hill*, V.P.; Karen J. Smarr*, Secy.-Treas.; Gordon L. Bourns II; Anita L. Macbeth; Denise L. Moyles; Gerald T. Young.
EIN: 956044472

543
Bowater, Inc.

55 E. Camperdown Way
Greenville, SC 29601 (864) 282-9473

Company URL: http://www.bowater.com
Establishment information: Established in 1881.
Company type: Subsidiary of a public company
Business activities: Manufactures, produces, distributes, and sells newsprint, uncoated specialty paper, coated groundwood paper, market pulp, lumber, and timber.
Business type (SIC): Paper mills; logging; lumber and wood products; pulp mills; paperboard mills
Financial profile for 2011: Sales volume, $44,940,000
Corporate officers: Richard B. Evans, Chair.; Richard Garneau, C.E.O. and Pres.; Jo-Ann Longworth, Sr. V.P. and C.F.O.; Pierre Laberge, Sr. V.P., Human Resources
Board of directors: Richard B. Evans, Chair.; Richard D. Falconer; Richard Garneau; Jeffrey A. Hearn; Bradley P. Martin; Alain Rheaume; Micheal S. Rousseau; David H. Wilkins
Divisions: Coated and Specialty Papers Div., Greenville, SC; Coated and Specialty Papers Div., Greenville, SC
International operations: Canada
Giving statement: Giving through the Bowater Incorporated Corporate Giving Program.
Company EIN: 620721803

Bowater Incorporated Corporate Giving Program

55 E. Camperdown Way
P.O. Box 1028
Greenville, SC 29601-3511

Contact: Gordon R. Manuel, Dir., Govt. Affairs
Purpose and activities: Bowater makes charitable contributions to nonprofit organizations involved with arts and culture, education, health and human services, civic affairs, and on a case by case basis. Support is given primarily in areas of company operations.
Fields of interest: Arts; Education; Health care; Human services; Public affairs; General charitable giving.
Type of support: Annual campaigns; Capital campaigns; Continuing support; Employee matching gifts; Employee volunteer services; General/operating support; Sponsorships.
Geographic limitations: Giving primarily in areas of company operations.
Application information: Applications accepted. A contributions committee reviews all requests. Application form not required. Applicants should submit the following:
1) detailed description of project and amount of funding requested
Initial approach: Proposal to nearest company facility
Copies of proposal: 1
Final notification: Following review
Number of staff: 1 full-time professional.

544
Bowles Rice McDavid Graff & Love, PLLC

600 Quarrier St.
Charleston, WV 25301-2121
(304) 347-1100

Company URL: http://www.bowlesrice.com
Establishment information: Established in 1920.
Company type: Private company
Business activities: Provides legal services.
Business type (SIC): Legal services
Corporate officers: Scott Ball, C.I.O; Robert Dinsmore, Treas.
Board of director: Mark Nelson
Giving statement: Giving through the Bowles Rice Foundation.

Bowles Rice Foundation

600 Quarrier St.
P.O. Box 1386
Charleston, WV 25325-1386

Establishment information: Established in 2005 in WV.
Donors: Billy Atkins; Carolyn Atkins; Bowles, Rice, McDavid, Graff & Love, LLP.
Financial data (yr. ended 12/31/11): Assets, $1,146,397 (M); gifts received, $102,500; expenditures, $84,655; qualifying distributions, $60,924; giving activities include $60,167 for 8 grants (high: $25,000; low: $1,667).
Fields of interest: Secondary school/education; Higher education; Crime/law enforcement, fund raising/fund distribution; Legal services; Foundations (community).
Support limitations: No grants to individuals.
Application information: Applications not accepted. Unsolicited requests for funds not accepted.
Officers: Thomas A. Heywood, Pres.; Leslie Russo, Secy.; Robert S. Kiss, Treas.
Directors: Greg Bailey; Robert L. Bays; Andy Fusco; Stan Lee; Mike Lorensen; Ellen Maxwell-Hoffman; Stuart McMillan; Chazz Printz; Howard Seufer; Tim Wills; John Woods.
EIN: 202077682

545
Boyd Coffee Company

19730 N.E. Sandy Blvd.
Portland, OR 97230-7310 (503) 666-4545

Company URL: http://www.boyds.com
Establishment information: Established in 1900.
Company type: Private company
Business activities: Produces and sells coffee wholesale.
Business type (SIC): Groceries—wholesale
Corporate officers: David D. Boyd, Co-Chair.; Richard D. Boyd, Co-Chair.; Jeffrey Newman, C.E.O.; Steve Weeks, C.F.O. and Treas.
Board of directors: David D. Boyd, Co-Chair.; Richard D. Boyd, Co-Chair.
Giving statement: Giving through the Boyd Family Foundation.

Boyd Family Foundation

P.O. Box 28372
Portland, OR 97228-8372

Establishment information: Established in 2000 in OR.
Donors: Boyd Coffee Co.; Richard Boyd; David Boyd.
Financial data (yr. ended 12/31/11): Assets, $317,792 (M); expenditures, $18,957; qualifying distributions, $16,800; giving activities include $16,800 for grants.
Purpose and activities: The foundation supports organizations involved with animal welfare, grief counseling, and human services.
Fields of interest: Animals/wildlife; Youth development; Human services.
Type of support: General/operating support; Program development.
Geographic limitations: Giving primarily in Portland, OR.
Support limitations: No support for political organizations. No grants to individuals.
Application information: Applications not accepted. Unsolicited requests for funds not accepted.
Board meeting date(s): Quarterly
Officers: Sean Kiffe, Pres.; John Dutt, V.P.; Maryellen Kiffe, Secy.; Michael Boyd, Treas.
Directors: Brenda Boyd; Christopher Boyd; David Boyd; Jody Boyd; Judy Boyd; Karri Boyd; Kelsey Boyd; Richard Boyd; Stephen Boyd; Katy Dutt.
EIN: 931294466

546
Boyd Gaming Corporation

3883 Howard Hughes Pkwy., 9th Fl.
Las Vegas, NV 89169 (702) 792-7200
FAX: (702) 792-7313

Company URL: http://www.boydgaming.com
Establishment information: Established in 1941.
Company type: Public company
Company ticker symbol and exchange: BYD/NYSE
Business activities: Operates casinos.
Business type (SIC): Amusement and recreation services/miscellaneous
Financial profile for 2012: Number of employees, 25,247; assets, $6,332,190,000; sales volume, $2,487,430,000; pre-tax net income, -$1,143,850,000; expenses, $3,342,300,000; liabilities, $6,028,400,000
Fortune 1000 ranking: 2012—814th in revenues, 976th in profits, and 526th in assets
Corporate officers: William S. Boyd, Chair.; Marianne Boyd Johnson, Vice-Chair.; Keith E. Smith, Pres. and C.E.O.; Paul J. Chakmak, Exec. V.P. and C.O.O.; Brian A. Larson, Exec. V.P., Genl. Counsel, and Secy.; Josh Hirsberg, Sr. V.P., C.F.O., and Treas.
Board of directors: William S. Boyd, Chair.; Marianne Boyd Johnson, Vice-Chair.; Robert L. Boughner; William R. Boyd; Richard E. Flaherty; Thomas V. Girardi; Billy G. McCoy; Frederick J. Schwab; Keith E. Smith; Christine J. Spadafor; Peter M. Thomas; Veronica J. Wilson
Subsidiary: Coast Hotels and Casinos, Inc., Las Vegas, NV

Giving statement: Giving through the Boyd Gaming Corporation Contributions Program.
Company EIN: 880242733

Boyd Gaming Corporation Contributions Program

3883 Howard Hughes Pkwy., 9th Fl.
Las Vegas, NV 89169-0928 (702) 792-7200
URL: http://www.boydgaming.com/community

Financial data (yr. ended 12/31/10): Total giving, $2,000,000, including $2,000,000 for 1,000 grants.
Purpose and activities: Boyd Gaming makes charitable contributions to nonprofit organizations on a case by case basis. Support is limited to areas of company operations in Illinois, Indiana, Louisiana, Mississippi, Nevada, and New Jersey.
Fields of interest: Boys & girls clubs; United Ways and Federated Giving Programs; General charitable giving.
Type of support: Employee volunteer services; General/operating support; In-kind gifts.
Geographic limitations: Giving limited to areas of company operations in IL, IN, LA, MS, NJ, and NV.
Support limitations: No support for discriminatory organizations, or for teams. No grants to individuals, or for school-sponsored endeavors.
Application information: Applications accepted. Application form required. Applicants should submit the following:
1) detailed description of project and amount of funding requested
2) contact person
3) name, address and phone number of organization
Applications should indicate the date of the event, if applicable.
Initial approach: Complete online application form

547
BP America

(formerly BP Amoco Corporation)
501 Westlake Park Blvd.
Houston, TX 77079-2604 (281) 366-2000

Company URL: http://www.bp.com
Establishment information: Established in 1899.
Company type: Subsidiary of a foreign company
Business activities: Operates energy company; explores, extracts, refines and processes oil and natural gas.
Business type (SIC): Petroleum refining; extraction/oil and gas; extraction/natural gas liquids; chemicals and allied products; pipelines (except natural gas/operation of); gas production and distribution
Financial profile for 2009: Number of employees, 23,000; assets, $47,000,000,000
Corporate officers: Lamar McKay, Chair. and Co-Pres.; William G. Lowrie, Co-Pres.
Board of director: Lamar McKay, Chair.
Plants: Denver, CO; Atlanta, Augusta, GA; Joliet, Naperville, Oakbrook Terrace, IL; Whiting, IN; Des Moines, IA; New Orleans, LA; Mandan, ND; Marietta, OH; Tulsa, OK; Cooper River, Rock Hill, SC; Alvin, Cedar Bayou, Chocolate Bayou, Houston, Texas City, TX; Salt Lake City, UT; Yorktown, VA; Chippewa Falls, WI
Offices: Anchorage, AK; La Palma, CA; Chicago, Warrenville, IL
Giving statement: Giving through the BP America Corporate Giving Program and the BP Foundation, Inc.

BP America Corporate Giving Program

(formerly BP Amoco Corporation Contributions Program)
501 Westlake Park Blvd.
Houston, TX 77079-2604 (281) 366-2000
For environmental hotline & community info: (866) 448-5816; for wildlife distress hotline: (866) 557-1401; for claims: (800) 440-0858;
URL: http://www.bp.com/en/global/corporate/sustainability.html

Purpose and activities: BP America makes charitable contributions to nonprofit organizations selected by their employees; giving also for disaster relief. Support is given primarily in areas of company operations.
Fields of interest: Environment, research; Environment, pollution control; Environment, water pollution; Disasters, preparedness/services; Safety/disasters.
Programs:
Fabric of America Fund: BP has agreed to contribute funds to an escrow account to be used to pay claims submitted to the GCCF. The GCCF is administered by Kenneth R. Feinberg (the "Claims Administrator"), a neutral fund administrator responsible for all decisions relating to the administration and processing of claims by the GCCF.
Gulf Coast Claims Facility: BP has agreed to contribute funds to an escrow account to be used to pay claims submitted to the Gulf Coast Claims Facility (GCCF). The GCCF is administered by Kenneth R. Feinberg (the "Claims Administrator"), a neutral fund administrator responsible for all decisions relating to the administration and processing of claims by the GCCF.
Gulf Research Initiative: Through the Gulf of Mexico Research Initiative (GRI), three research institutions in the Gulf region will receive a total of $25 million in fast-track funding for high-priority studies of the distribution, composition and ecological interactions of oil and dispersant.
Rig Worker Assistance Fund: Through the Rig Worker Assistance Fund, BP will provide support to unemployed rig workers experiencing economic hardship as a result of the moratorium on deepwater drilling imposed by the United States federal government. The Fund will be administered through the Gulf Coast Restoration and Protection Foundation, a supporting organization of The Baton Rouge Area Foundation (BRAF).
Type of support: Emergency funds; Employee volunteer services; General/operating support.
Geographic limitations: Giving primarily in areas of company operations.
Application information: Applications not accepted. Contributes only to pre-selected organizations.

BP Foundation, Inc.

(formerly BP Amoco Foundation, Inc.)
501 Westlake Park Blvd., 25th Fl
Houston, TX 77079-2604
URL: http://www.bp.com/en/global/corporate/sustainability/society/host-communities-and-societies/community-investment.html

Establishment information: Incorporated in 1952 in IN.
Donors: Amoco Corp.; BP Amoco Corp.; BP Corp. North America Inc.; BP America Inc.; Amoco Production Co.; Atlantic Richfield Co.; BP Products North America, Inc.
Financial data (yr. ended 12/31/11): Assets, $62,303,190 (M); gifts received, $3,491,282; expenditures, $21,325,904; qualifying distributions, $21,032,886; giving activities include $20,179,496 for 68 grants (high: $4,486,132; low: $67).
Purpose and activities: The foundation supports organizations involved with arts and culture, education, the environment, animals and wildlife, disaster relief, human services, international relief, and community development.
Fields of interest: Museums; Museums (art); Arts; Higher education; Libraries (public); Scholarships/financial aid; Education; Environment, air pollution; Environment, climate change/global warming; Environment, natural resources; Environment, energy; Environment; Animals/wildlife; Disasters, preparedness/services; American Red Cross; Human services; International relief; Community/economic development Economically disadvantaged.
Program:
BP Employee Matching Fund: The foundation matches personal donations, volunteer time, and fundraising made by employees of BP to charitable organizations, up to $5,000 per employee per year.
Type of support: Emergency funds; Employee matching gifts; Employee volunteer services; General/operating support; Program development; Research; Scholarship funds; Sponsorships.
Geographic limitations: Giving primarily in AK, AL, CA, Washington, DC, GA, Chicago, IL, IN, NY, and OH; giving also in Australia, Brazil, China, Germany, Indonesia, Italy, Japan, Spain, and the United Kingdom.
Support limitations: No support for religious, fraternal, political, social, or athletic organizations; generally, no support for organizations already receiving general operating support through the United Way. No grants to individuals, or for endowments, medical research, publications, or conferences.
Application information: Applications not accepted. Contributes only to pre-selected organizations.
Board meeting date(s): Apr., July, and Nov.
Officers and Directors:* Andy P. Hopwood*, Chair.; Ray C. Dempsey*, Pres.; Steven L. Bray, Secy.; Don Eldred*, C.F.O.; Mark E. Thompson, Treas.; Benjamin E. Cannon, Exec. Dir.; Sherry Strasner, Assoc. Dir.; Claire Bebbington; Iris M. Cross.
Number of staff: 4 full-time professional; 1 full-time support.
EIN: 366046879
Selected grants: The following grants are a representative sample of this grantmaker's funding activity:
$4,486,132 to JK Group, Plainsboro, NJ, 2011. For unrestricted support.
$2,460,000 to Los Angeles County Museum of Art, Los Angeles, CA, 2011. For unrestricted support.
$2,000,000 to Art Institute of Chicago, Chicago, IL, 2011. For unrestricted support.
$1,500,000 to Stanford University, Stanford, CA, 2011. For unrestricted support.
$700,576 to BirdLife International, Cambridge, England, 2011. For unrestricted support.
$284,965 to Wildlife Conservation Society, Bronx, NY, 2011. For unrestricted support.
$100,000 to University of Alaska Foundation, Fairbanks, AK, 2011. For unrestricted support.
$85,792 to American Red Cross National Headquarters, Washington, DC, 2011. For unrestricted support.
$75,000 to Arctic Education Foundation, Anchorage, AK, 2011. For unrestricted support.

548
BPI Technology, Inc.

(also known as Beef Products, Inc.)
891 Two Rivers Dr.
Dakota Dunes, SD 57049-5156
(605) 217-8000

Company URL: http://www.beefproducts.com
Establishment information: Established in 1976.
Company type: Private company
Business activities: Produces boneless lean beef.
Business type (SIC): Meat packing plants and prepared meats and poultry
Financial profile for 2010: Number of employees, 80
Corporate officer: Eldon N. Roth, C.E.O.
Giving statement: Giving through the Food Safety Research & Education Foundation, Inc.

Food Safety Research & Education Foundation, Inc.

891 Two Rivers Dr.
Dakota Dunes, SD 57049-5156
URL: http://www.beefproducts.com/

Establishment information: Established in 2002 in SD.
Donors: BPI Technology, Inc.; Cooperating for food safety, Inc.
Financial data (yr. ended 03/31/11): Assets, $10,153 (M); gifts received, $9,942; expenditures, $49; qualifying distributions, $49.
Purpose and activities: The foundation supports Cooperating for Food Safety in Washington, DC.
Fields of interest: Agriculture/food.
Type of support: General/operating support.
Geographic limitations: Giving limited to Washington, DC.
Support limitations: No grants to individuals.
Application information: Applications not accepted. Unsolicited requests for funds not accepted.
Officers and Directors:* Eldon Roth*, Pres.; Ronald Yockey*, V.P.; Regina Roth*, Secy.-Treas.
EIN: 200152625

549
Bracewell & Giuliani LLP

711 Louisiana, Ste. 2300
S. Tower Pennzoil Pl.
Houston, TX 77002-2770 (713) 223-2300

Company URL: http://www.bracewellgiuliani.com
Establishment information: Established in 1945.
Company type: Private company
Business activities: Operates law firm.
Business type (SIC): Legal services
Corporate officers: Patrick Oxford, Chair.; Mark C. Evans, Managing Partner; Brenda Cook Cialone, C.O.O.; Keith Marlow, C.F.O.
Offices: Hartford, CT; Washington, DC; New York, NY; Austin, Dallas, Houston, San Antonio, TX; Seattle, WA
International operations: United Arab Emirates; United Kingdom
Giving statement: Giving through the Bracewell & Giuliani LLP Pro Bono Program.

Bracewell & Giuliani LLP Pro Bono Program

711 Louisiana, Ste. 2300
S. Tower Pennzoil Pl.
Houston, TX 77002-2770
URL: http://www.bracewellgiuliani.com/about/community-involvement

Purpose and activities: Bracewell & Giuliani makes charitable contributions to educational institutions and nonprofit organizations involved with arts and culture, health care, youth development, homeless people, and law.
Fields of interest: Arts; Law school/education; Health care; Legal services; Youth development; Homeless, human services; Law/international law Minorities.
Type of support: Conferences/seminars; Employee volunteer services; General/operating support; Pro bono services - legal.
Application information: A Pro Bono Committee manages the pro bono program.

550
Bradley Arant Boult Cummings LLP

1 Federal Pl.
1819 5th Ave. N.
Birmingham, AL 35203-2119
(205) 521-8000

Company URL: http://www.babc.com
Establishment information: Established in 1871.
Company type: Private company
Business activities: Operates law firm.
Business type (SIC): Legal services
Corporate officer: Scott E. Adams, Partner
Offices: Birmingham, Huntsville, Montgomery, AL; Washington, DC; Jackson, MS; Charlotte, NC; Nashville, TN
Giving statement: Giving through the Bradley Arant Boult Cummings LLP Pro Bono Program.

Bradley Arant Boult Cummings LLP Pro Bono Program

1 Federal Pl.
1819 5th Ave. N.
Birmingham, AL 35203-2104 (205) 521-8387
E-mail: jchristie@babc.com; Additional tel.: (205) 521-8000; URL: http://www.babc.com/pro-bono/

Contact: Chris Christie, Chair, Pro Bono Comm.
Fields of interest: Legal services.
Type of support: Pro bono services - legal.
Geographic limitations: Giving primarily in areas of company operations in Birmingham, Huntsville, and Montgomery, AL, Washington, DC, Jackson, MS, Charlotte, NC, Nashville, TN.
Application information: A Pro Bono Committee manages the pro-bono program.

551
Vera Bradley Designs, Inc.

2208 Production Rd.
Fort Wayne, IN 46808 (260) 482-4673

Company URL: http://www.verabradley.com
Establishment information: Established in 1982.
Company type: Public company
Company ticker symbol and exchange: VRA/NASDAQ
Business activities: Manufactures quilted cotton luggage, handbags, and accessories.
Business type (SIC): Leather luggage; leather goods/personal
Financial profile for 2012: Number of employees, 2,078
Corporate officers: Robert J. Hall, Chair.; Michael C. Ray, C.E.O; Matthew C. Wojewuczki, Exec. V.P., Opers.; Kevin J. Sierks, V.P., C.F.O., and Corp. Cont.; David O. Thompson, V.P., Sales
Board of directors: Robert J. Hall, Chair.; Barbara Bradley Baekgaard; Richard Baum; Karen Kaplan; John E. Kyees; Matthew McEvoy; P. Michael Miller; Patricia R. Miller; Frances P. Philip; Michael C. Ray; Edward M. Schmults
Giving statement: Giving through the Vera Bradley Foundation for Breast Cancer, Inc.

Vera Bradley Foundation for Breast Cancer, Inc.

P.O. Box 80201
Fort Wayne, IN 46898-0201 (260) 207-5153
E-mail: foundation@verabradley.com; URL: http://www.verabradley.org

Establishment information: Established in 1998.
Contact: Catherine H. Hill, Dir.
Financial data (yr. ended 10/31/11): Revenue, $2,496,077; assets, $3,431,597 (M); gifts received, $2,591,416; expenditures, $2,808,256; giving activities include $2,700,000 for grants.
Purpose and activities: The foundation promotes, sponsors, and supports breast cancer research, education, and services.
Fields of interest: Breast cancer; Breast cancer research.
Type of support: Research.
Geographic limitations: Giving limited to IN.
Publications: Informational brochure; Newsletter.
Application information: Applications not accepted. Contributes to pre-selected organizations.
Officers and Board Members:* Richard Doermer*, Pres.; Barbara Baekgaard; Michael Miller; Patricia Miller; Jill Nichols; Kathleen Randolph.
Number of staff: 2 full-time professional; 1 full-time support.
EIN: 352058177

552
Brady Corporation

6555 W. Good Hope Rd.
P.O. Box 571
Milwaukee, WI 53201-0571
(800) 541-1686
FAX: (800) 292-2289

Company URL: http://www.bradycorp.com
Establishment information: Established in 1914.
Company type: Public company
Company ticker symbol and exchange: BRC/NYSE
Business activities: Manufactures and markets identification solutions and specialty products that identify and protect premises, products and people.
Business type (SIC): Manufacturing/miscellaneous
Financial profile for 2012: Number of employees, 6,900; assets, $1,607,720,000; sales volume, $1,324,270,000; pre-tax net income, $22,750,000; expenses, $1,284,510,000; liabilities, $598,370,000
Corporate officers: Frank M. Jaehnert, Pres. and C.E.O.; Bentley N. Curran, C.I.O.; Thomas J. Felmer, Sr. V.P. and C.F.O.; Allan J. Klotsche, Sr. V.P., Human Resources; Kathy Johnson, V.P., Finance and C.A.O.; Paul Meyer, Treas.

Board of directors: Patrick W. Allender; Gary S. Balkema; Conrad G. Goodkind; Frank W. Harris; Frank M. Jaehnert; Paul Meyer; Elizabeth P. Pungello; Bradley C. Richardson
Giving statement: Giving through the Brady Corporation Foundation, Inc.
Company EIN: 390178960

Brady Corporation Foundation, Inc.

6555 W. Good Hope Rd.
Milwaukee, WI 53223-4634
E-mail: foundation@bradycorp.com; URL: http://www.foundation.bradycorp.org

Establishment information: Established in 2005 in WI.
Donor: Brady Corporation.
Financial data (yr. ended 07/31/11): Assets, $3,979,904 (M); gifts received, $1,426,629; expenditures, $269,036; qualifying distributions, $269,036; giving activities include $147,070 for grants and $121,966 for in-kind gifts.
Purpose and activities: The foundation supports programs designed to promote formative development; skills development; and leadership development. Special emphasis is directed toward programs focusing on education.
Fields of interest: Elementary/secondary education; Education, early childhood education; Child development, education; Elementary school/education; Education; Youth development, association; Leadership development.
Type of support: Continuing support; Donated products; In-kind gifts; Program development.
Geographic limitations: Giving primarily in areas of company operations in WI.
Publications: Application guidelines.
Application information: Applications accepted. Generally, unsolicited requests for funds not accepted. The foundation utilizes a RFP process for giving. Organizations wishing to provide unsolicited general information may send a letter of intent via email only. Applicants should submit the following:
1) copy of IRS Determination Letter
2) copy of most recent annual report/audited financial statement/990
3) detailed description of project and amount of funding requested
4) contact person

Initial approach: E-mail letter of intent
Board meeting date(s): June
Deadline(s): Feb. 15
Final notification: May 15

Officers: Frank M. Jaehnert, Pres.; Allan Klotsche, C.O.O.; Elizabeth Pungello, Secy.; Barbara Bolens, Treas.
Directors: Bentley Curran; Dave Hawke; Thomas J. Felmer.
EIN: 203304824
Selected grants: The following grants are a representative sample of this grantmaker's funding activity:
$19,000 to Milwaukee School of Engineering, Milwaukee, WI, 2009.
$10,000 to United Way of Greater Milwaukee, Milwaukee, WI, 2009.
$4,000 to Milwaukee Rescue Mission, Milwaukee, WI, 2009.
$4,000 to Ohio State University, Columbus, OH, 2009.

553
Brady Homes

2203 Eastland Dr., Ste. 8
Bloomington, IL 61704 (309) 663-5301

Company URL: http://bradyhomes.com/
Establishment information: Established in 1964.
Company type: Private company
Business activities: Operates residential construction company.
Business type (SIC): Contractors/general residential building
Corporate officer: Ed Brady, Pres.
Giving statement: Giving through the Brady Foundation.

The Brady Foundation

2201 Eastland Dr., Ste. 1
Bloomington, IL 61704-2201 (309) 828-8571

Establishment information: Established in 2000 in IL.
Donors: Pinehurst Development, Inc.; APEX Properties, Inc.; W.E.B. Construction Co., Inc.
Contact: Nancy K. Brady
Financial data (yr. ended 06/30/11): Assets, $19,851 (M); gifts received, $1,059; expenditures, $1,978; qualifying distributions, $1,950; giving activities include $1,950 for 5 grants (high: $1,000; low: $50).
Purpose and activities: The foundation supports organizations involved with K12 education and human services.
Fields of interest: Human services.
Type of support: General/operating support.
Support limitations: No grants to individuals.
Application information: Applications accepted. Application form required.

Initial approach: Letter
Deadline(s): None

EIN: 371401149

554
Bragg Live Food Products, Inc.

P.O. Box 7
Santa Barbara, CA 93102 (805) 968-1020

Company URL: http://www.bragg.com
Establishment information: Established in 1912.
Company type: Private company
Business activities: Produces organic apple cider vinegar, organic olive oil, and soybean protein concentrate; publishes books.
Business type (SIC): Miscellaneous prepared foods; fats and oils
Corporate officers: Patricia Bragg, Pres. and C.E.O.; Jeannie Shin, Cont.
Giving statement: Giving through the Bragg Health Foundation.

Bragg Health Foundation

(formerly Bragg Health Crusades)
Box 7
Santa Barbara, CA 93102-0007

Establishment information: Established in 2001 in CA.
Donors: Live Food Products, Inc.; Patricia Bragg; Bragg Live Food Products, Inc.
Financial data (yr. ended 12/31/11): Assets, $1,431,387 (M); gifts received, $25,000; expenditures, $12,866; qualifying distributions, $5,374; giving activities include $3,480 for 7 grants (high: $500; low: $480).
Purpose and activities: The foundation supports organizations involved with oceans, animal welfare, cancer, human services, and Christianity.
Fields of interest: Environment, water resources; Animal welfare; Animals/wildlife, preservation/protection; Cancer; Family services; Human services; Christian agencies & churches.
Type of support: General/operating support.
Geographic limitations: Giving primarily in CA; some giving in CO, HI, and TX.
Support limitations: No grants to individuals.
Application information: Applications not accepted. Contributes only to pre-selected organizations.
Officers: Patricia Bragg, Pres.; Cindy A. Duerrner, Secy.
Director: John Westerdahl.
EIN: 300033989

555
Bramco, LLC

1801 Watterson Trail
P.O. Box 32230
Louisville, KY 40232-2230 (502) 493-4300

Company URL: http://www.bramco.com/
Establishment information: Established in 1908.
Company type: Private company
Business activities: Sell, rents, and services construction, mining, and industrial equipment.
Business type (SIC): Industrial machinery and equipment—wholesale
Corporate officers: Joseph A. Paradis III, Chair. and C.E.O.; Charles H. Leis, Pres. and C.O.O.; Michael Brennan, Exec. V.P. and C.F.O.; J.J. Lancaster, Cont.
Board of director: Joseph A. Paradis III, Chair.
Giving statement: Giving through the Paradis Foundation, Inc.

Paradis Foundation, Inc.

1801 Watterson Tr.
P.O. Box 32230
Louisville, KY 40232-2230

Establishment information: Established in 1978 in KY.
Donor: Bramco, Inc.
Contact: Pat Riddle, Secy.
Financial data (yr. ended 03/31/12): Assets, $1,982,536 (M); gifts received, $50,000; expenditures, $99,047; qualifying distributions, $86,145; giving activities include $86,145 for 16 grants (high: $12,000; low: $1,000).
Purpose and activities: The foundation supports art museums and hospitals and organizations involved with education and human services.
Fields of interest: Arts; Education; Human services.
Type of support: Endowments; General/operating support.
Geographic limitations: Giving primarily in Louisville, KY.
Support limitations: No grants to individuals.
Application information: Applications accepted. Application form required. Applicants should submit the following:
1) copy of IRS Determination Letter

Initial approach: Proposal
Deadline(s): None

Officers and Directors:* Joseph A. Paradis*, Pres.; Joseph A. Paradis III*, V.P.; Pat Riddle, Secy.; Charles H. Leis*, Treas.; Steven J. Paradis.
EIN: 310908284

556
Peter Brasseler Holdings LP
1 Brasseler Blvd.
Savannah, GA 31419-9576 (912) 925-8525

Establishment information: Established in 1989.
Company type: Private company
Business activities: Operates medical products company.
Business type (SIC): Professional and commercial equipment—wholesale
Corporate officers: Don Waters, Pres. and C.E.O.; Bill Miller, V.P., Admin.
Giving statement: Giving through the Peter & Inge Brasseler Foundation, Inc.

The Peter & Inge Brasseler Foundation, Inc.
(formerly The Brasseler USA Foundation, Inc.)
1 Brasseler Blvd.
Savannah, GA 31419-9576 (912) 925-8525

Establishment information: Established in 1999 in GA.
Donor: Brasseler USA Dental, LLC.
Contact: Don L. Waters, Pres.
Financial data (yr. ended 12/31/11): Assets, $1,902 (M); gifts received, $100,000; expenditures, $100,750; qualifying distributions, $100,000; giving activities include $100,000 for grants.
Purpose and activities: The foundation supports New York University College of Dentistry.
Fields of interest: Education.
Type of support: General/operating support.
Application information: Applications accepted. Application form required.
Initial approach: Proposal
Deadline(s): Dec. 1
Officers: Don L. Waters, Pres.; Roland Minnis, Secy.
EIN: 582443012

557
Bressler, Amery & Ross, P.C.
325 Columbia Tpke., Ste. 301
Florham Park, NJ 07932-1212
(973) 514-1200

Company URL: http://www.bressler.com
Establishment information: Established in 1960.
Company type: Private company
Business activities: Operates law firm.
Business type (SIC): Legal services
Corporate officer: Brian F. Amery, Managing Partner
Offices: Miramar, FL; Florham Park, NJ; New York, NY
Giving statement: Giving through the Bressler, Amery & Ross, P.C. Corporate Giving Program.

Bressler, Amery & Ross, P.C. Corporate Giving Program
325 Columbia Tpke., Ste. 301
Florham Park, NJ 07932-1212 (973) 514-1200
FAX: (973) 514-1660; Contact for Pro Bono program: Diana Manning, Esq., Member, e-mail: dmanning@bressler.com; URL: http://www.bressler.com/diversity.asp

Contact: Samuel J. Thomas, Member
Purpose and activities: Bressler, Amery & Ross make charitable contributions to nonprofit organizations involved with human services, civil rights, minorities, and women, and law.
Fields of interest: Education; Legal services; Civil/human rights; Law/international law Minorities; Women.
Type of support: Employee volunteer services; General/operating support; Pro bono services - legal; Sponsorships.

558
Brewer Foods Inc.
1021 Noell Ln.
P.O. Box 1908
Rocky Mount, NC 27804-1761
(252) 937-2000
FAX: (252) 927-2816

Establishment information: Established in 1972.
Company type: Private company
Business activities: Operates restaurants.
Business type (SIC): Restaurants and drinking places
Financial profile for 2009: Number of employees, 340
Corporate officers: Joe B. Brewer, Jr., Pres.; Douglas E. Anderson, Secy.; Lucy B. Wheeless, Treas.
Giving statement: Giving through the Brewer Foundation, Inc.

Brewer Foundation, Inc.
P.O. Box 7906
Rocky Mount, NC 27804-0906 (252) 443-1333

Establishment information: Established in 1969 in NC.
Donors: Joseph B. Brewer, Jr.; Lucy Ann Brewer†; Brewer Foods Inc.; Lucy Brewer Trust.
Contact: Joseph B. Brewer, Jr., Pres. and Dir.
Financial data (yr. ended 08/31/12): Assets, $1,211,923 (M); gifts received, $20,000; expenditures, $77,149; qualifying distributions, $58,527; giving activities include $58,527 for grants.
Purpose and activities: The foundation supports organizations involved with education, human services, and Christianity, and awards college scholarships.
Fields of interest: Education; Human services; Christian agencies & churches.
Type of support: General/operating support; Scholarships—to individuals.
Geographic limitations: Giving limited to NC.
Application information: Applications accepted. Application form required. Applicants should submit the following:
1) detailed description of project and amount of funding requested
Initial approach: Letter
Deadline(s): None
Officer and Directors:* Joseph B. Brewer, Jr., Pres.; Joseph B. Brewer III; Virginia H. Brewer.
EIN: 560941242

559
Bricker & Eckler LLP
100 S. 3rd St.
Columbus, OH 43215-4291
(614) 227-2300

Company URL: http://www.bricker.com
Establishment information: Established in 1945.
Company type: Private company
Business activities: Operates law firm.
Business type (SIC): Legal services
Corporate officers: Richard A. King, C.O.O.; Steven P. Odum, C.F.O.; Ahmad Sinno, C.I.O.
Offices: Cleveland, Columbus, West Chester, OH
Giving statement: Giving through the Bricker & Eckler LLP Corporate Giving Program.

Bricker & Eckler LLP Corporate Giving Program
100 S. 3rd St.
Columbus, OH 43215-4236 (614) 227-2300
FAX: (614) 227-2390; Contact for Pro Bono: Kimberly Brown, Coord., Chair., e-mail: kbrown@bricker.com; URL: http://www.bricker.com/about-us/community.aspx

Contact: Sally Bloomfield, Coord. and Chair
Purpose and activities: Bricker & Eckler makes charitable contributions to nonprofit organizations involved with arts and culture, education, the environment, health care, human services, and civic affairs.
Fields of interest: Arts; Law school/education; Education; Environment; Health care; Legal services; Human services; Public affairs.
Type of support: Employee volunteer services; General/operating support; Pro bono services - legal; Program development.

560
Bridgestone Americas, Inc.
(formerly Bridgestone/Firestone Americas Holding, Inc.)
535 Marriot Dr.
Nashville, TN 37214 (615) 937-1000

Company URL: http://www.bridgestone-americas.com
Establishment information: Established in 1994.
Company type: Subsidiary of a foreign company
Business activities: Manufactures tires; manufactures air springs, building materials, synthetic and natural rubber products, and industrial fibers and textiles; operates tire stores.
Business type (SIC): Tires and inner tubes; rubber products/fabricated; motor vehicles and equipment; auto and home supplies—retail
Financial profile for 2010: Number of employees, 250; sales volume, $4,690,000,000
Corporate officers: Mark A. Emkes, Chair., Pres., and C.E.O.; Eduardo Minardi, C.O.O.
Board of director: Mark A. Emkes, Chair.
Giving statement: Giving through the Bridgestone Americas, Inc. Corporate Giving Program and the Bridgestone Americas Trust Fund.
Company EIN: 880335067

Bridgestone Americas, Inc. Corporate Giving Program
535 Marriott Dr.
Nashville, TN 37214-5092
FAX: (615) 937-3621; URL: http://www.bridgestone-americas.com/community/csr/index.html

Purpose and activities: As a complement to its fund, Bridgestone Americas Holding makes charitable contributions to nonprofit organizations directly. Support is given on a local, national, and international basis, with emphasis on areas of company operations.

Fields of interest: Media, television; Media, radio; Museums; Adult education—literacy, basic skills & GED; Libraries/library science; Environment, water pollution; Environment, natural resources; Environmental education; Animals/wildlife, preservation/protection; Medical care, rehabilitation; Health care; Substance abuse, services; Housing/shelter, volunteer services; Housing/shelter, aging; Independent housing for people with disabilities; Housing/shelter, home owners; Housing/shelter, repairs; Safety/disasters, volunteer services; Disasters, preparedness/services; Boy scouts; Girl scouts; Civil/human rights, alliance/advocacy; United Ways and Federated Giving Programs.
Type of support: Building/renovation; Donated land; Donated products; Employee volunteer services; General/operating support; Program development; Scholarship funds; Sponsorships.
Geographic limitations: Giving on a local, national, and international basis, with emphasis on areas of company operations.

The Bridgestone Americas Trust Fund

(formerly The Bridgestone/Firestone Trust Fund)
535 Marriott Dr.
Nashville, TN 37214-5092 (615) 937-1415
FAX: (615) 937-1414;
E-mail: bfstrustfund@bfusa.com; URL: http://www.bridgestone-firestone.com/community/trustfund/index.html

Establishment information: Trust established in 1952 in OH.
Donors: The Firestone Tire and Rubber Co.; Bridgestone/Firestone, Inc.; Bridgestone Americas Holding, Inc.; Bridgestone Americas, Inc.
Contact: Bernice Csaszar, Admin.
Financial data (yr. ended 12/31/11): Assets, $14,410,064 (M); expenditures, $2,620,009; qualifying distributions, $2,521,248; giving activities include $2,439,278 for 788 grants (high: $195,050; low: $50).
Purpose and activities: The foundation supports organizations involved with arts and culture, agriculture, housing development, disaster relief, automotive safety, human services, and the automotive industry. Special emphasis is directed towards programs designed to address education; the environment and conservation; and children.
Fields of interest: Media, television; Media, radio; Performing arts, orchestras; Performing arts, opera; Arts; Higher education; Scholarships/financial aid; Education; Environment, natural resources; Environment; Agriculture; Housing/shelter, development; Disasters, preparedness/services; Safety, automotive safety; YM/YWCAs & YM/YWHAs; Children, services; Human services; Business/industry; United Ways and Federated Giving Programs Children.
Program:
Employee Matching Gifts: The foundation matches contributions made by full-time employees and retirees of Bridgestone Americas to institutions of higher education on a one-for-one basis from $50 to $5,000 per contributor, per year.
Type of support: Annual campaigns; Building/renovation; Capital campaigns; Continuing support; Emergency funds; Employee matching gifts; Employee-related scholarships; Endowments; General/operating support; Matching/challenge support; Program development; Research; Scholarship funds; Sponsorships.
Geographic limitations: Giving on a national basis, with emphasis on areas of company operations in AR, IN, OH, and TN; giving also to regional and national organizations.
Support limitations: No support for partisan political organizations, discriminatory organizations, or religious organizations not of direct benefit to the entire community. No grants to individuals (except for employee-related scholarships), or for debt reduction, equipment, land acquisition, or publications; no loans.
Publications: Application guidelines; Grants list.
Application information: Applications accepted. Proposals should be no longer than 2 pages. Application form not required. Applicants should submit the following:
1) population served
2) copy of IRS Determination Letter
3) brief history of organization and description of its mission
4) copy of most recent annual report/audited financial statement/990
5) how project's results will be evaluated or measured
6) listing of board of directors, trustees, officers and other key people and their affiliations
7) detailed description of project and amount of funding requested
8) copy of current year's organizational budget and/or project budget
9) listing of additional sources and amount of support

Proposals should indicate the percentage of funding requested of the foundation by the organization; and, if benefits are involved, include a breakdown of deductible versus non-deductible portions.
Initial approach: Proposal to nearest company facility; proposal to foundation for national organizations
Copies of proposal: 1
Board meeting date(s): As required
Deadline(s): None
Officer and Committee Members:* Christine Karbowiak*, Chair.; David Dumas; Truman Hyde; Eugene Stephens.
Trustee: KeyBank N.A.
Number of staff: 1 full-time support.
EIN: 346505181

561
The Bridgewater Candle Company, LLC

951 S. Pine St., Ste. 120
Spartanburg, SC 29302-3370
(864) 542-8062

Company URL: http://www.bridgewatercandles.com
Establishment information: Established in 1998.
Company type: Private company
Business activities: Manufactures candles.
Business type (SIC): Manufacturing/miscellaneous
Corporate officer: Robert Caldwell, Sr., Pres.
Giving statement: Giving through the Bridgewater Foundation.

Bridgewater Foundation

951 S. Pine St.
Spartanburg, SC 29302-3370 (864) 542-8062

Donor: The Bridgewater Candle Co., LLC.
Contact: Mark E. Johnson, Chair.
Financial data (yr. ended 12/31/11): Assets, $674,303 (M); expenditures, $26,204; qualifying distributions, $10,000; giving activities include $10,000 for 1 grant.
Purpose and activities: The foundation supports Christian community foundations.
Fields of interest: Foundations (community); Christian agencies & churches.
Type of support: General/operating support.
Geographic limitations: Giving primarily in Spartanburg, SC.
Support limitations: No grants to individuals.
Application information: Applications accepted. Application form required. Applicants should submit the following:
1) copy of IRS Determination Letter
Initial approach: Letter
Deadline(s): None
Officers: Mark E. Johnson, Chair.; T. Dodd Caldwell, Vice-Chair.; Sarah R. Caldwell, Secy.; Kathleen C. Johnson, Treas.
Directors: Hugh H. Brantley; Robert E. Caldwell, Jr.; Robert E. Caldwell, Sr.; Sylvia R. Caldwell.
EIN: 582421520

562
Bridgewater Savings Bank

756 Orchard St.
Raynham, MA 02767-1028 (508) 697-6908

Company URL: http://www.bridgewatersavings.com
Establishment information: Established in 1872.
Company type: Mutual company
Business activities: Operates savings bank.
Business type (SIC): Savings institutions
Financial profile for 2011: Assets, $485,037,000; pre-tax net income, $2,210,000; liabilities, $441,385
Corporate officers: Robert L. Todd, Sr., Chair.; James C. Lively, C.E.O and Pres.; Richard Burgess, V.P. and C.F.O; Stephen F. Banks, Sr. V.P. and C.I.O; Matthew Burke, Cont.
Board of director: Robert L. Todd, Sr., Chair.
Giving statement: Giving through the Bridgewater Savings Charitable Foundation, Inc.

Bridgewater Savings Charitable Foundation, Inc.

756 Orchard St.
Raynham, MA 02767-1028 (508) 884-3311
URL: http://www.bridgewatersavings.com/AbouttheBank/CharitableFoundation.aspx

Establishment information: Established in 2002 in MA.
Donors: Bridgewater Savings Bank; All-Players Golf Tournament.
Financial data (yr. ended 09/30/11): Assets, $196,471 (M); expenditures, $45,603; qualifying distributions, $25,417; giving activities include $22,915 for 16 grants (high: $5,500; low: $500).
Purpose and activities: The foundation supports programs designed to assist children of low- to moderate-income families.
Fields of interest: Education; Health care; Human services.
Type of support: Annual campaigns; Building/renovation; Capital campaigns; Continuing support; General/operating support; Program development.
Geographic limitations: Giving primarily in areas of company operations in Barnstable, Bristol, and Plymouth counties, MA.
Support limitations: No support for political organizations. No grants to individuals.
Publications: Application guidelines.
Application information: Applications accepted. Application form required. Applicants should submit the following:

1) timetable for implementation and evaluation of project
2) signature and title of chief executive officer
3) population served
4) copy of IRS Determination Letter
5) geographic area to be served
6) detailed description of project and amount of funding requested
7) copy of current year's organizational budget and/ or project budget
8) listing of additional sources and amount of support

Initial approach: Download application form and mail cover letter and application form to foundation
Board meeting date(s): Monthly
Deadline(s): None

Officers and Directors:* James C. Lively*, Pres.; Suzanne M. Blom*, Clerk; Richard Burgess, Jr.*, Treas.; Joseph W. Mitchell; Peter Dello Russo; Edward F. Sousa.
EIN: 113689271

563
Bridgeway Capital Management, Inc.

20 Greenway Plz., Ste. 450
Houston, TX 77046 (713) 661-3500

Company URL: http://www.bridgewayfund.com
Establishment information: Established in 1993.
Company type: Subsidiary of a private company
Business activities: Provides investment advisory services.
Business type (SIC): Security and commodity services
Corporate officers: Miles Douglas Harper III, Chair.; Michael Mulcahy, Pres.; Debbie Hanna, Secy.; Linda Giuffre, Treas.
Board of directors: Miles Douglas Harper III, Chair.; Kirbyjon Caldwell; Karen Gerstner; Linda Giuffre; Debbie Hanna; Evan Harrel; John Montgomery; Michael Mulcahy
Giving statement: Giving through the Bridgeway Charitable Foundation.

Bridgeway Charitable Foundation

20 Greenway Plz. ste. 450
Houston, TX 77046-2009 (832) 204-8170
FAX: (713) 807-8071;
E-mail: info@bridgewayfoundation.org.; URL: http://www.bridgewayfoundation.org/

Establishment information: Established in 2000 in TX.
Donor: Bridgeway Capital Management, Inc.
Financial data (yr. ended 12/31/11): Assets, $3,875 (M); gifts received, $297,358; expenditures, $646,924; qualifying distributions, $635,489; giving activities include $635,489 for grants.
Purpose and activities: The foundation supports programs designed to eliminate genocide; promote peace and reconciliation; and promote human rights.
Fields of interest: Higher education; Education; Health care; Disasters, preparedness/services; Children/youth, services; Human services; International relief; International peace/security; International conflict resolution; Civil/human rights; Christian agencies & churches Economically disadvantaged.
Programs:
Eliminating Genocide: The foundation partners with organizations that demand equality and safety for everyone regardless of family, tribe, religion, location, or skin color; and with organizations that promote a world without genocide.
Human Rights: The foundation supports programs designed to protect and care for human life; and initiatives centered around working globally toward justice and equality.
Peacemaking and Reconciliation: The foundation support programs designed to create and encourage sustainable peace; and rebuild the lives of people afflicted by racial, political, and economic discrimination.
Type of support: Capital campaigns; Emergency funds; General/operating support; Matching/ challenge support; Program development; Scholarship funds.
Geographic limitations: Giving primarily in TX and the United Kingdom.
Support limitations: No grants to individuals, or for scholarships, fellowships, sponsorship of golf tournaments, galas, award dinners, or other fundraising events, debt reduction, endowments, or religious activities not of direct benefit to the entire community.
Application information: Applications not accepted. Unsolicited applications are currently not accepted.
Board meeting date(s): Quarterly
Officers and Directors:* John Montgomery*, Pres.; Ann M. Montgomery*, V.P.; Bill Baumeyer*, V.P.; Ashley Rodriguez*, Secy.; Von Celestine, Treas.
Officer & Director: Shannon Sedgwick Davis; Rebecca Hove.
EIN: 760666069
Selected grants: The following grants are a representative sample of this grantmaker's funding activity:
$333,333 to Better World Fund, Washington, DC, 2010.
$66,000 to Chinquapin School, Highlands, TX, 2010.
$50,000 to Furman University, Greenville, SC, 2010.
$30,365 to Reconciliation Ministries, Medina, WA, 2010.
$25,000 to Casa de Esperanza de los Ninos, Houston, TX, 2010.
$20,000 to Mona Foundation, Kirkland, WA, 2010.
$15,000 to ArtBridge, Houston, TX, 2010. For operating fund.

564
Briggs & Morgan, P.A.

2200 IDS Ctr.
80 S. 8th St.
Minneapolis, MN 55402-2100
(612) 977-8400

Company URL: http:///www.briggs.com
Establishment information: Established in 1960.
Company type: Private company
Business activities: Operates law firm.
Business type (SIC): Legal services
Corporate officers: Brian D. Wenger, Chair.; Alan H. Maclin, Pres.; Philip R. Schenkenberg, Secy.; Elizabeth M. Brama, Treas.
Board of directors: Brian D. Wenger, Chair.; Thomas L. Bray; Darlene M. Cobian; James E. Duffy; Alan H. Maclin; Michael T. Miller; Philip R. Schenkenberg; Frank A. Taylor; Timothy R. Thornton
Offices: Minneapolis, Saint Paul, MN
Giving statement: Giving through the Briggs & Morgan, P.A. Pro Bono Program and the Briggs and Morgan Foundation.

Briggs & Morgan, P.A. Pro Bono Program

2200 IDS Ctr.
80 S. 8th St.
Minneapolis, MN 55402-2100 (612) 977-8582
E-mail: jlong@briggs.com; URL: http://www.briggs.com/about/probono/

Contact: Jim Long, Pro-Bono Comm. Chair.
Fields of interest: Legal services.
Type of support: Pro bono services - legal.
Geographic limitations: Giving primarily in areas of company operations in Minneapolis, and St. Paul, MN.
Application information: A Pro Bono Chair. coordinates the pro bono program.

Briggs and Morgan Foundation

(formerly Chancery Lane Foundation)
80 S. 8th St., Ste. 2200
Minneapolis, MN 55402
URL: http://www.briggs.com/about/community/

Establishment information: Established in 1960 in MN.
Financial data (yr. ended 12/31/11): Assets, $138,093 (M); gifts received, $316,237; expenditures, $350,652; qualifying distributions, $350,369; giving activities include $350,369 for grants.
Fields of interest: Performing arts; Arts; Higher education; Legal services; Disasters, Hurricane Katrina; United Ways and Federated Giving Programs.
Type of support: Annual campaigns; Capital campaigns; Continuing support; Program development.
Geographic limitations: Giving primarily in the Minneapolis and St. Paul, MN, area.
Support limitations: No grants to individuals.
Application information: Applications not accepted. Contributes only to pre-selected organizations.
Officers and Directors:* Alan Maclin*, Pres.; Brian Wenger*, V.P.; Charles Rogers*, Treas.
EIN: 416009924

565
Briggs & Stratton Corporation

12301 W. Wirth St.
Wauwatosa, WI 53222-2110
(414) 259-5333
FAX: (414) 259-5338

Company URL: http://www.briggsandstratton.com
Establishment information: Established in 1909.
Company type: Public company
Company ticker symbol and exchange: BGG/NYSE
Business activities: Manufactures air-cooled gasoline engines.
Business type (SIC): Engines and turbines; motor vehicles and equipment
Financial profile for 2012: Number of employees, 6,321; assets, $1,608,230,000; sales volume, $2,066,530,000; pre-tax net income, $29,870,000; expenses, $2,025,300,000; liabilities, $976,260,000
Fortune 1000 ranking: 2012—926th in revenues, 854th in profits, and 909th in assets
Corporate officers: Todd J. Teske, Chair., Pres., and C.E.O.; David J. Rodgers, Sr. V.P. and C.F.O.; Robert

F. Heath, V.P., Genl. Counsel, and Secy.; Randall R. Carpenter, V.P., Mktg.; Andrea L. Golvach, V.P. and Treas.
Board of directors: Todd J. Teske, Chair.; William F. Achtmeyer; James E. Humphrey; Patricia L. Kampling; Keith R. McLoughlin; Robert J. O'Toole; Henrik C. Slipsager; Charles I. Story; Brian C. Walker
Plants: Auburn, AL; Statesboro, GA; Murray, KY; Poplar Bluff, MO; Jefferson, Menomonee Falls, WI
International operations: Australia; Austria; Brazil; Canada; China; Czech Republic; France; Germany; Italy; Japan; Mexico; Netherlands; New Zealand; South Africa; Spain; Sweden; United Kingdom
Giving statement: Giving through the Briggs & Stratton Corporation Contributions Program and the Briggs & Stratton Corporation Foundation, Inc.
Company EIN: 390182330

Briggs & Stratton Corporation Contributions Program

12301 W. Wirth St.
Wauwatosa, WI 53222-2110 (414) 259-5333
URL: http://www.briggsandstratton.com/corp/about_us/community.aspx

Purpose and activities: As a complement to its foundation, Briggs & Stratton also makes charitable contributions to nonprofit organizations directly. Support is given primarily in areas of company operations, with emphasis on Wisconsin.
Fields of interest: Arts; Education; Environment; Health care; Disasters, preparedness/services; Human services; Public affairs.
Type of support: Employee volunteer services; General/operating support; Program development; Scholarships—to individuals; Sponsorships.
Geographic limitations: Giving primarily in areas of company operations, with emphasis on WI.

Briggs & Stratton Corporation Foundation, Inc.

12301 W. Wirth St.
Wauwatosa, WI 53222-2110 (414) 259-5496
Application address for grants to public charities: c/o Robert F. Heath, P.O. Box 702, Milwaukee, WI 53201; URL: http://www.basco.com/Sustainability/Community%20Involvement/

Establishment information: Incorporated in 1953 in WI.
Donor: Briggs & Stratton Corp.
Contact: Robert F. Heath, Secy.-Treas.
Financial data (yr. ended 11/30/11): Assets, $10,369,611 (M); gifts received, $1,000,000; expenditures, $1,255,610; qualifying distributions, $1,249,750; giving activities include $1,249,750 for 109 grants (high: $205,000; low: $500).
Purpose and activities: The foundation supports organizations involved with arts and culture and education.
Fields of interest: Performing arts; Arts; Education; Boys & girls clubs; YM/YWCAs & YM/YWHAs; United Ways and Federated Giving Programs.
Type of support: Annual campaigns; Building/renovation; Capital campaigns; Employee-related scholarships; General/operating support; Program development.
Geographic limitations: Giving primarily in areas of company operations in Auburn, AL, Statesboro, GA, Murray, KY, Poplar Bluff, MO, and Milwaukee, WI.
Support limitations: No support for religious organizations. No grants to individuals (except for employee-related scholarships).
Application information: Applications accepted. Application form not required. Applicants should submit the following:
1) detailed description of project and amount of funding requested
2) copy of current year's organizational budget and/or project budget
Initial approach: Proposal
Copies of proposal: 1
Board meeting date(s): June and Nov.
Deadline(s): None

Officers and Directors:* Frederick P. Stratton, Jr.*, Pres.; John S. Shiely*, V.P.; Robert F. Heath, Secy.-Treas.; Michael D. Hamilton; Todd J. Teske.
EIN: 396040377
Selected grants: The following grants are a representative sample of this grantmaker's funding activity:
$205,000 to United Way of Greater Milwaukee, Milwaukee, WI, 2010.
$105,000 to United Performing Arts Fund, Milwaukee, WI, 2010.
$100,000 to Childrens Hospital of Wisconsin, Milwaukee, WI, 2010. For operating support.
$35,000 to Future Farmers of America Foundation, National, Indianapolis, IN, 2010. For program support.
$35,000 to Milwaukee Development Corporation, Milwaukee, WI, 2010.
$31,000 to Acton Institute for the Study of Religion and Liberty, Grand Rapids, MI, 2010. For operating support.
$30,000 to Hoover Institution on War, Revolution and Peace, Stanford, CA, 2010.
$25,000 to Students in Free Enterprise, Springfield, MO, 2010. For operating support.
$10,000 to Milwaukee Art Museum, Milwaukee, WI, 2010. For operating support.
$5,000 to United Community Center, Milwaukee, WI, 2010. For operating support.

566

Bright Horizons Family Solutions, Inc.

200 Talcott Ave. S.
Watertown, MA 02472 (617) 673-8000

Company URL: http://www.brighthorizons.com
Establishment information: Established in 1986.
Company type: Private company
Business activities: Provides early child care and education services; provides strategic work/life consulting services.
Business type (SIC): Day care services/child; management and public relations services
Financial profile for 2009: Number of employees, 18,484
Corporate officers: Linda A. Mason, Chair.; Roger H. Brown, Vice-Chair.; David H. Lissy, C.E.O.; Mary Ann Tocio, Pres. and C.O.O.; Elizabeth J. Boland, C.F.O.; Stephen I. Dreier, C.A.O.; Jackie Legg, Sr. V.P., Opers.; Gary O'Neill, Sr. V.P., Mktg.
Board of directors: Linda A. Mason, Chair.; Roger H. Brown, Vice-Chair.; Joshua Bekenstein; JoAnne Brandes; E.Townes Ducan; Fred K. Foulkes; David Gergen; Gabrielle Greene; Sara lawrence-Lightfoot; Marguerite W. Kondracke; David H. Lissy; Ian M. Rolland; Mary Ann Tocio
Giving statement: Giving through the Bright Horizons Foundation for Children.
Company EIN: 621742957

Bright Horizons Foundation for Children

105 Westwood Pl., Ste. 125
Brentwood, TN 37027-5039 (615) 256-9915
FAX: (615) 254-3766;
E-mail: bhfoundation@brighthorizons.com;
URL: http://www.brighthorizons.com/foundation/

Establishment information: Established in 1999 in TN.
Contact: Karin Weaver, Exec. Dir.
Financial data (yr. ended 12/31/11): Revenue, $848,264; assets, $918,543 (M); gifts received, $860,911; expenditures, $780,175; giving activities include $388,375 for grants.
Purpose and activities: The foundation supports nonprofit organizations in the areas of children, child and youth education, and child care.
Fields of interest: Education; Children/youth, services.

Programs:
Founders Grants: Provides general operating grants of up to $5,000 to nonprofit organizations that serve at-risk children aged 12 years and under, with an emphasis on the early education years of those ages zero to six. Priority will be given to nonprofit organizations located in communities where Bright Horizons employees live and work.
Gleason Grants: Provides grants of $250 each to qualified nonprofit organizations receiving 40 hours of employee volunteer service.
Type of support: General/operating support.
Geographic limitations: Giving on a national basis.
Support limitations: No support for colleges, universities, or religious organizations. No grants to individuals, or for advertising, multi-year commitments, fundraising, or athletic teams or events.
Publications: Application guidelines.
Application information: Applications accepted. Application form not required. Applicants should submit the following:
1) how project will be sustained once grantmaker support is completed
2) copy of IRS Determination Letter
3) brief history of organization and description of its mission
4) copy of most recent annual report/audited financial statement/990
5) listing of board of directors, trustees, officers and other key people and their affiliations
6) contact person
7) copy of current year's organizational budget and/or project budget
8) additional materials/documentation
Initial approach: Mail or fax proposal to foundation
Board meeting date(s): Apr., July, Oct., and Jan.
Deadline(s): Feb. 26, May 28, Aug. 27, and Nov. 26

Officers and Directors:* Gary O'Neil*, Chair.; Dave Gleason*, Pres.; Elizabeth Boland*, Secy.-Treas.; Becky Bowman, Exec. Dir.; Dave Lissy.
EIN: 621782263

567

Brightpoint, Inc.

7635 Interactive Way, Ste. 200
Indianapolis, IN 46278 (317) 707-2355

Company URL: http://www.brightpoint.com
Establishment information: Established in 1989.
Company type: Public company
Company ticker symbol and exchange: CELL/NASDAQ

Business activities: Distributes wireless devices and accessories and provides customized logistic services to the wireless industry.
Business type (SIC): Electrical goods—wholesale
Financial profile for 2011: Number of employees, 6,176; assets, $1,506,910,000; sales volume, $5,244,380,000; pre-tax net income, $57,180,000; expenses, $5,171,690,000; liabilities, $1,215,750,000
Corporate officers: Robert J. Laikin, Chair. and C.E.O.; Vincent Donargo, Exec. V.P., C.F.O., and Treas.; John Alexander Du Plessis Currie, Exec. V.P. and C.I.O.; Craig M. Carpenter, Exec. V.P., Genl. Counsel, and Secy.; Robert L. Colin, Sr. V.P., C.A.O., and Cont.; Annette Cyr, Sr. V.P., Human Resources
Board of directors: Robert J. Laikin, Chair.; Eliza Hermann; John F. Levy; Cynthia L. Lucchese; Thomas J. Ridge; Richard W. Roedel; Jerry L. Stead; Michael L. Smith; Jerre L. Stead; Kari-Pekka Wilska
International operations: Australia; Austria; Belgium; British Virgin Islands; Colombia; Denmark; Finland; France; Germany; Guatemala; India; Italy; Luxembourg; Mexico; Netherlands; New Zealand; Norway; Philippines; Poland; Portugal; Russia; Singapore; Slovakia; South Africa; Spain; Sweden; Switzerland; United Arab Emirates; Venezuela
Giving statement: Giving through the Brightpoint, Inc. Corporate Giving Program.
Company EIN: 351778566

Brightpoint, Inc. Corporate Giving Program

c/o Charitable Contribution Request
501 Airtech Pkwy.
Plainfield, IN 46168-7408 (800) 952-2355
FAX: (317) 707-2329; URL: http://www.brightpoint.com/Brightpoint/PageServlet?locationid=26&languageid=73&pageid=13480

Purpose and activities: Brightpoint makes charitable contributions to nonprofit organizations involved with the arts and culture, humanities, education, health, and sports. Support is given primarily in areas of company operations, with emphasis on Indiana.
Fields of interest: Humanities; Arts; Education; Health care; Athletics/sports, amateur leagues; General charitable giving.
Type of support: Employee volunteer services; General/operating support; Sponsorships.
Geographic limitations: Giving primarily in areas of company operations, with emphasis on IN.
Publications: Application guidelines.
Application information: Applications accepted. Additional information may be requested at a later date. A contributions committee reviews all requests.
Initial approach: Mail proposal to headquarters
Copies of proposal: 1
Deadline(s): 3rd quarter for following calendar year
Final notification: 4th quarter

568
Brilliant Earth, Inc.

26 O'Farrell St., 10th Fl.
San Francisco, CA 94108-5832
(415) 354-4623

Company URL: http://www.brilliantearth.com
Establishment information: Established in 2005.
Company type: Private company
Business activities: Operates ethically produced jewelry boutique and online store.
Business type (SIC): Shopping goods stores/ miscellaneous
Corporate officers: Beth Gerstein, Co.-C.E.O.; Eric Grossberg, Co.-C.E.O.
Giving statement: Giving through the Brilliant Earth, Inc. Corporate Giving Program.

Brilliant Earth, Inc. Corporate Giving Program

12 Geary St., Ste. 605
San Francisco, CA 94108-5716 (415) 354-4623
URL: http://www.brilliantearth.com/giving-back/

Purpose and activities: Brilliant Earth makes charitable donations to nonprofit organizations involved with helping communities in gemstone regions recover from abuses in the past and develop the skills needed to manage their natural resources effectively.
Fields of interest: Environment; International human rights; Children's rights; Business/industry Children.
Type of support: General/operating support.
Geographic limitations: Giving primarily in gemstone producing regions in Africa.

569
Brillion Iron Works, Inc.

200 Park Ave.
Brillion, WI 54110-1145 (920) 756-2121

Company URL: http://www.brillionironworks.com
Establishment information: Established in 1900.
Company type: Subsidiary of a public company
Business activities: Manufactures gray and ductile iron castings; designs, manufactures, and markets farm equipment.
Business type (SIC): Iron and steel foundries; machinery/farm and garden
Corporate officers: David G. Adams, Pres.; Bill Jones, V.P., Finance
Giving statement: Giving through the Brillion Foundation Inc.

Brillion Foundation Inc.

200 Park Ave.
P.O. Box 127
Brillion, WI 54110 (920) 756-2121

Establishment information: Established in 1953 in WI.
Donor: Brillion Iron Works, Inc.
Contact: Julie Malliett, Secy.
Financial data (yr. ended 06/30/11): Assets, $142,052 (M); expenditures, $7,038; qualifying distributions, $7,038; giving activities include $1,750 for 2 grants (high: $1,000; low: $750) and $5,000 for 4 grants to individuals (high: $1,250; low: $1,250).
Purpose and activities: The foundation supports organizations involved with education, health, youth, community development, government and public administration, and Christianity, and awards college scholarships.
Fields of interest: Education; Health care; Youth, services; Community/economic development; Government/public administration; Christian agencies & churches.
Type of support: Capital campaigns; General/ operating support; Scholarship funds; Scholarships —to individuals.
Application information: Applications not accepted. Unsolicited requests for funds not accepted.
Officers: Randy Brull, Pres.; Michael A. Miller, V.P.; Julie Malliett, Secy.; Michael Julien, Treas.
Directors: Mary Larson; Kenneth E. Wagner.
EIN: 396043916

570
Brinckerhoff & Neuville, Inc.

1134 Main St.
P.O. Box 424
Fishkill, NY 12524-3665 (845) 896-4700

Company URL: http://www.bninsurancegroup.com
Establishment information: Established in 1961.
Company type: Private company
Business activities: Sells insurance.
Business type (SIC): Insurance carriers
Corporate officers: Philip Cosentino, Co.-Pres.; Sterling Gaston, Co.-Pres.; Mary Brinckerhoff, Exec. V.P. and Secy.; Ben R. Adams, Treas.
Giving statement: Giving through the Brinckerhoff Foundation.

The Brinckerhoff Foundation

68 Main St.
Fishkill, NY 12524-1329

Establishment information: Established in 1998 in DE.
Donor: Brinckerhoff & Neuville, Inc.
Financial data (yr. ended 10/31/11): Assets, $0 (M); expenditures, $60,656; qualifying distributions, $59,250; giving activities include $59,250 for 11 grants (high: $25,000; low: $350).
Purpose and activities: The foundation supports hospitals and organizations involved with arts and culture and higher education.
Fields of interest: Arts; Education.
Type of support: General/operating support.
Geographic limitations: Giving primarily in NY.
Support limitations: No grants to individuals.
Application information: Applications not accepted. Unsolicited requests for funds not accepted.
Officers: Barbara B. Tead, Pres.; Beverly B. Brinckerhoff, V.P.; Mary E. Brinckerhoff, Secy.; Margaret Brinckerhoff Gentsch, Treas.
EIN: 141805812

572
Brinker International, Inc.

6820 LBJ Fwy.
Dallas, TX 75240 (972) 980-9917
FAX: (972) 770-9593

Company URL: http://www.brinker.com/
Establishment information: Established in 1975.
Company type: Public company
Company ticker symbol and exchange: EAT/NYSE
Business activities: Operates and franchises restaurants.
Business type (SIC): Restaurants and drinking places
Financial profile for 2012: Number of employees, 100,400; assets, $1,436,070,000; sales volume, $2,820,720,000; pre-tax net income, $208,810,000; expenses, $2,588,890,000; liabilities, $1,126,200,000
Fortune 1000 ranking: 2012—744th in revenues, 648th in profits, and 927th in assets
Corporate officers: Douglas H. Brooks, Chair., Pres., and C.E.O.; Wyman T. Roberts, Pres. and C.E.O; Guy Constant, Exec. V.P. and C.F.O.; Roger F.

Thomson, Exec. V.P., C.A.O., Genl. Counsel, and Secy.; Dora Cortinas, C.I.O
Board of directors: Douglas H. Brooks, Chair.; Joseph M. DePinto; Harriet Edelman; Mike George; William T. Giles; Gerardo I. Lopez; Jon L. Luther; John W. Mims; George R. Mrkonic; Rosendo G. Parra; Wyman T. Roberts
Giving statement: Giving through the Brinker International, Inc. Corporate Giving Program.
Company EIN: 751914582

Brinker International, Inc. Corporate Giving Program

c/o Charitable Comm.
6820 LBJ Fwy.
Dallas, TX 75240-6511
FAX: (972) 770-5977; URL: http://www.brinker.com/company/givingback.asp#res

Purpose and activities: Brinker International makes charitable contributions to nonprofit organizations involved with arts and culture, health, and human services. Support is given primarily in areas of company operations.
Fields of interest: Arts; Health care; Human services.
Type of support: Employee volunteer services; General/operating support.
Geographic limitations: Giving primarily in areas of company operations.
Support limitations: No support for religious or political organizations, or organizations that receive United Way funding. No grants to individuals, or for conferences or seminars, reunions, capital campaigns, travel, or research.
Publications: Application guidelines.
Application information: Applications accepted. Proposals should be submitted using organization letterhead and should be no longer than 2 pages. Telephone calls are not accepted. A contributions committee reviews all requests. Application form not required. Applicants should submit the following:
1) statement of problem project will address
2) copy of IRS Determination Letter
3) brief history of organization and description of its mission
4) list of company employees involved with the organization
5) listing of additional sources and amount of support

Initial approach: Mail or fax proposal to headquarters
Copies of proposal: 1
Deadline(s): None
Final notification: 4 to 6 weeks

571
The Brink's Company

(formerly The Pittston Company)
1801 Bayberry Ct.
P.O. Box 18100
Richmond, VA 23226-8100 (804) 289-9600
FAX: (804) 289-9770

Company URL: http://www.brinkscompany.com
Establishment information: Established in 1859.
Company type: Public company
Company ticker symbol and exchange: BCO/NYSE
Business activities: Provides armored car transportation services; provides monitored security services; provides freight transportation services.
Business type (SIC): Business services/miscellaneous; transportation/scheduled air
Financial profile for 2012: Number of employees, 70,000; assets, $2,553,900,000; sales volume, $3,842,100,000; pre-tax net income, $154,500,000; expenses, $3,670,900,000; liabilities, $2,052,100,000
Fortune 1000 ranking: 2012—594th in revenues, 761st in profits, and 797th in assets
Corporate officers: Thomas C. Schievelbein, Chair., Pres., and C.E.O.; Joseph W. Dziedzic, V.P. and C.F.O.; McAlister C. Marshall II, V.P., Genl. Counsel and Secy.; Jonathan Andrew Leon, Treas.; Matthew A.P. Schumacher, Cont.
Board of directors: Thomas C. Schievelbein, Chair.; Betty C. Alewine; Paul G. Boynton; Marc C. Breslawsky; Reginald D. Hedgebeth; Michael J. Herling; Murray D. Martin; Ronald L. Turner
Subsidiary: BAX Global Inc., Irvine, CA
Giving statement: Giving through the Brink's Company Contributions Program and the Brink's Foundation.
Company EIN: 541317776

The Brink's Foundation

(formerly The Pittston Foundation)
1801 Bayberry Ct.
P.O. Box 18100
Richmond, VA 23226-8100

Establishment information: Established in 1997 in VA.
Donors: The Pittston Co.; The Brink's Co.
Financial data (yr. ended 12/31/11): Assets, $318,532 (M); gifts received, $33,026; expenditures, $63,026; qualifying distributions, $60,000; giving activities include $60,000 for 2 grants (high: $50,000; low: $10,000).
Purpose and activities: The foundation supports children's hospitals and organizations involved with education.
Fields of interest: Health care.
Type of support: General/operating support; Scholarship funds.
Geographic limitations: Giving primarily in VA.
Support limitations: No grants to individuals.
Application information: Applications not accepted. Unsolicited requests for funds not accepted.
Officers and Directors:* Frank T. Lennon*, Pres.; McAlister C. Marschall II, V.P. and Secy.; Joseph W. Dzledzic, V.P.; Jonathan Andrew Leon, Treas.
EIN: 541815655

573
Brinks Hofer Gilson & Lione

NBC Tower, Ste. 3600
455 N. Cityfront Plz. Dr.
Chicago, IL 60611-5599 (312) 321-4200

Company URL: http://www.brinkshofer.com/firm_info
Establishment information: Established in 1917.
Company type: Private company
Business activities: Operates law firm.
Business type (SIC): Legal services
Corporate officer: Lee Rendino, C.F.O.
Offices: Washington, DC; Chicago, IL; Indianapolis, IN; Ann Arbor, MI; Research Triangle Park, NC; Salt Lake City, UT
Giving statement: Giving through the Brinks Hofer Gilson & Lione Pro Bono Program.

Brinks Hofer Gilson & Lione Pro Bono Program

NBC Tower, Ste. 3600
455 N. Cityfront Plz. Drive
Chicago, IL 60611-5599 (312) 321-4200
E-mail: vgnoffo@brinkshofer.com; URL: http://www.brinkshofer.com/firm_info/community-involvement

Contact: Vincent J. Gnoffo, Pro Bono Comm. Chair
Purpose and activities: Brinks Hofer Gilson & Lione Corporate Giving Program makes charitable contributions to elementary and secondary schools and nonprofit organizations involved with youth development.
Fields of interest: Elementary/secondary education; Legal services; Employment, training; Youth development.
Type of support: Internship funds; Pro bono services - legal; Program development.
Application information: A Pro Bono Committee manages the pro bono program.

574
Brinkster Communications Corporation

2600 N. Central Ave., Ste. 310
Phoenix, AZ 85004 (480) 388-3777

Company URL: http://www.brinkster.com
Establishment information: Established in 1999.
Company type: Private company
Business activities: Operates a web hosting company.
Business type (SIC): Business services/miscellaneous
Corporate officers: Jared P. Stauffer, Chair., Pres., and C.E.O.; Clint Poole, C.O.O.; Nathaniel Kemberling, C.F.O.
Board of director: Jared P. Stauffer, Chair.
Giving statement: Giving through the Eugene W. Kemberling Foundation.

Eugene W. Kemberling Foundation

2600 N. Central Ave., Ste. 310
Phoenix, AZ 85004-3003

Establishment information: Established in 2005 in VA.
Donors: Brinkster Communications, Inc.; Nathaniel Kemberling; Mary Lou Kemberling; Brinkster.
Financial data (yr. ended 01/31/12): Assets, $5,496 (M); gifts received, $34,790; expenditures, $373; qualifying distributions, $0.
Fields of interest: Christian agencies & churches.
Type of support: General/operating support.
Application information: Applications not accepted. Unsolicited requests for funds not accepted.
Officer: Mary Lou Kemberling, Pres.
EIN: 371458317

575
Bristlecone Advisors, LLC

1000 2nd Ave., Ste. 3110
Seattle, WA 98104-1046 (206) 664-2500
FAX: (206) 664-2523

Company URL: http://www.bristleconeadvisors.com
Establishment information: Established in 1999.
Company type: Private company

Business type (SIC): Security and commodity services; business services/miscellaneous
Corporate officer: Keith R. Vernon, Partner
Giving statement: Giving through the Bristlecone Advisors, LLC Contributions Program.

Bristlecone Advisors, LLC Contributions Program

1000 Second Ave., Ste. 3110
Seattle, WA 98104-1046 (206) 664-2500
E-mail: info@bristleconeadvisors.com; URL: http://www.bristleconeadvisors.com

Purpose and activities: Bristlecone Advisors is a certified B Corporation that donates a percentage of profits to charitable organizations. Support is given primarily in areas of company operations in Washington.
Fields of interest: Environment; Children, adoption; Children, foster care; Child development, services; Family services, domestic violence; Homeless, human services; Venture philanthropy.
Type of support: General/operating support.
Geographic limitations: Giving primarily in areas of company operations in WA.

576
Bristol Bay Native Corporation

111 W. 16th Ave., Ste. 400
Anchorage, AK 99501-6206
(907) 278-3602

Company URL: http://www.bbnc.net
Establishment information: Established in 1971.
Company type: Native corporation
Business activities: Operates native corporation.
Business type (SIC): Nonclassifiable establishments; holding company
Corporate officers: Joseph L. Chythlook, Chair.; Jason Metrokin, Pres. and C.E.O.; Scott Torrison, V.P. and C.O.O.; Jeffrey Sinz, V.P. and C.F.O.; April Ferguson, V.P. and Genl. Counsel; Greg French, Treas.
Board of directors: Joseph L. Chythlook, Chair.; Peter Andrew, Jr.; Shawn Aspelund; Melvin C. Brown; Robert J. Clark; Moses Kritz; Dorothy M. Larson; Russell S. Nelson; Hjalmar E. Olson; Marie Paul; H. Robin Samuelsen, Jr.; Daniel Seybert
Giving statement: Giving through the Bristol Bay Native Corporation Contributions Program and the Bristol Bay Native Corp. Education Foundation.

Bristol Bay Native Corp. Education Foundation

111 W. 16th Ave., Ste. 400
Anchorage, AK 99501-6299 (907) 278-3602
FAX: (907) 276-3924; E-mail: pelagiol@bbnc.net; Additional tel.: (800) 426-3602; URL: http://www.bbnc.net/index.php?option=com_content&view=category&layout=blog&id=19&Itemid=40

Establishment information: Established in 1992 in AK.
Donor: Bristol Bay Native Corp.
Contact: Luanne Pelagio, Exec. Dir.
Financial data (yr. ended 12/31/11): Assets, $4,862,238 (M); gifts received, $214,652; expenditures, $291,476; qualifying distributions, $252,012; giving activities include $252,012 for grants to individuals.
Purpose and activities: The foundation awards college and vocational scholarships to Alaska Native shareholders of Bristol Bay Native Corporation.
Fields of interest: Vocational education; Higher education Native Americans/American Indians.
Programs:
H. Noble Dick Scholarship: Through the H. Noble Dick Scholarship program, the foundation awards one college scholarship of up to $1,000 to a college junior or senior who is an Alaska Native shareholder of Bristol Bay Native Corporation and is majoring in accounting or business management.
Higher Education Scholarships: Through the Higher Education Scholarship program, the foundation awards college scholarships of up to $3,500 to high school seniors who are Alaska Native shareholders of Bristol Bay Native Corporation. The award is based on academic standing, leadership, financial need, and life experiences.
Pedro Bay Scholarship: Through the Pedro Bay Scholarship program, the foundation awards college scholarships of up to $3,000 to high school juniors, seniors, or advanced degree candidates enrolled at a 4 year college who are shareholders of Pedro Bay Corporation.
Short-Term Vocational/Technical Education Program Scholarship: Through the Short-Term Vocational/Technical Education Program, the foundation awards scholarships of up to $600 to Alaska Native shareholders of Bristol Bay Native Corporation to attend short term trainings to enhance their work and career opportunities.
Vocational Education Scholarships: Through the Vocational Education Scholarship program, the foundation awards $500 college scholarships to high school seniors who are Alaska Native shareholders of Bristol Bay Native Corporation. The award is given to encourage educational and career advancement.
Wells Fargo - BBNC Scholarship: Through the Wells Fargo - BBNC Scholarship program, the foundation, in partnership with Wells Fargo, awards one college scholarship of up to $5,000 to a college junior or senior who is an Alaska Native shareholder of Bristol Bay Native Corporation. The scholarship is awarded to further advance the education of Alaska Natives and to encourage interest in the banking profession.
Type of support: Scholarships—to individuals.
Geographic limitations: Giving primarily in AK.
Publications: Application guidelines; Newsletter (including application guidelines).
Application information: Applications accepted. Applicants for Short-Term Vocational Education Program Scholarships must also submit a letter of request that includes employment goals, how the training will relate to your employment goals, and employment opportunities after completion of the training. Application form required.
Requests should include an essay describing interest in the field of study, financial and academic performance, and level of desire to work in the region or for the Bristol Bay Native Corporation or its subsidiaries; proof of application or acceptance to a vocational institute or institution of higher education; 2 letters of recommendation; a resume; and a wallet size photo.
Initial approach: Download application form and mail to foundation
Board meeting date(s): Quarterly
Deadline(s): Apr. 1 for Higher Education and Vocational Education Scholarships; None for Short-Term Vocational Education Program Scholarships
Officers and Directors: Marie Paul, Pres.; Richard Y. Lopez, V.P.; April Ferguson, Secy.; Cynthia Tisher, Treas.; Luanne Pelagio, Exec. Dir.; Jerry Liboff; Evelyn Mujica-Larson; Patrick Patterson III.
Number of staff: 1 full-time professional.
EIN: 920141709

577
Bristol County Savings Bank

35 Broadway
P.O. Box 4002
Taunton, MA 02780-3120 (508) 828-5300
FAX: (508) 824-6626

Company URL: http://www.bristolcountysavings.com
Establishment information: Established in 1846.
Company type: Private company
Business activities: Operates savings bank.
Business type (SIC): Savings institutions
Financial profile for 2011: Assets, $1,346,246; liabilities, $1,158,739
Corporate officers: Robert Hallock, Chair.; Patrick J. Murray, Jr., Pres. and C.E.O.; Julie D. S. Chapman, Exec. V.P. and C.O.O.; Dennis F. Leahy, Exec. V.P., C.F.O., and Treas.; Robert J. DeMoura, Exec. V.P. and C.I.O.; Kevin M. McCarthy, Sr. V.P., Opers.
Board of director: Robert Hallock, Chair.
Giving statement: Giving through the Bristol County Savings Charitable Foundation, Inc.

Bristol County Savings Charitable Foundation, Inc.

35 Broadway, 2nd FL
Taunton, MA 02780-3120
FAX: (508) 828-5455;
E-mail: community.involvement@bcsbmail.com; Application address: 29 Broadway, 2nd Fl., Taunton, MA 02780, tel.: (508) 462-3106; URL: http://www.bristolcountysavings.com/community-foundation.htm

Establishment information: Established in 1996 in MA.
Donor: Bristol County Savings Bank.
Contact: Michele L. Roberts, Clerk
Financial data (yr. ended 10/31/11): Assets, $7,307,634 (M); gifts received, $615,896; expenditures, $1,049,139; qualifying distributions, $995,727; giving activities include $995,727 for grants.
Purpose and activities: The foundation supports historical and zoological societies and organizations involved with education, water resources, health, human services, and community economic development.
Fields of interest: Historic preservation/historical societies; Elementary/secondary education; Higher education; Education; Environment, water resources; Zoos/zoological societies; Hospitals (general); Health care; Boys & girls clubs; Boy scouts; YM/YWCAs & YM/YWHAs; Human services; Community/economic development; United Ways and Federated Giving Programs.
Type of support: Building/renovation; Equipment; Matching/challenge support; Program development; Scholarship funds; Seed money.
Geographic limitations: Giving limited to the greater Attleboro, Berkley, Dartmouth, Dighton, Fall River, Franklin, New Bedford, North Attleborough, Norton, Plainville, Raynham, Rehoboth, Seekonk, Taunton, Westport, and Wrentham, MA, and Pawtucket, RI.
Support limitations: No support for religious organizations. No grants for general operating support.
Publications: Application guidelines.
Application information: Applications accepted. Organizations receiving support are asked to submit a final report. Application form required. Applicants should submit the following:
1) copy of IRS Determination Letter
2) listing of board of directors, trustees, officers and other key people and their affiliations

3) detailed description of project and amount of funding requested
   Initial approach: Contact foundation for a letter of interest
   Board meeting date(s): May and Nov. for Massachusetts; Jan., May, and Aug. for Pawtucket, Rhode Island
   Deadline(s): Mar. 11 and Sept. 16 for Massachusetts; Apr. 1, Aug. 5, and Dec. 3 for Pawtucket, Rhode Island

Officers and Trustees:* E. Dennis Kelley, Jr., Chair.; Patrick J. Murray, Jr., Pres.; Michele L. Roberts, Clerk; Dennis F. Leahy, Treas.; J. Jerome Coogan; Marjorie L. Largey; Russel F. Martorana; Edward P. Pariseau; Louis M. Ricciardi; Koreen A. Santos; Frank Teixeira; Suzanne Withers.
EIN: 043332966
Selected grants: The following grants are a representative sample of this grantmaker's funding activity:
$50,000 to Bridgewater State College, Bridgewater, MA, 2011.
$35,000 to Community Care Services, Taunton, MA, 2011.
$27,000 to Pawtucket Foundation, Pawtucket, RI, 2011.
$25,000 to YMCA of Attleboro, Attleboro, MA, 2011.
$20,000 to Southcoast Hospitals Group, New Bedford, MA, 2011.
$18,000 to Boy Scouts of America, Annawon Council, Norton, MA, 2011.
$13,500 to Old Dartmouth Historical Society, New Bedford, MA, 2011.
$10,000 to Highlander Dunn Institute, Providence, RI, 2011.
$7,500 to Attleboro Area Council of Churches, Attleboro, MA, 2011.
$6,600 to Preparatory Rehabilitation for Individual Development and Employment, Taunton, MA, 2011.

578
Bristol-Myers Squibb Company

345 Park Ave.
New York, NY 10154-0004 (212) 546-4000
FAX: (302) 655-5049

Company URL: http://www.bms.com
Establishment information: Established in 1858.
Company type: Public company
Company ticker symbol and exchange: BMY/NYSE
International Securities Identification Number: US1101221083
Business activities: Manufactures and sells pharmaceuticals.
Business type (SIC): Drugs
Financial profile for 2012: Number of employees, 28,000; assets, $35,897,000,000; sales volume, $17,621,000,000; pre-tax net income, $2,340,000,000; expenses, $15,281,000,000; liabilities, $22,274,000,000
Fortune 1000 ranking: 2012—158th in revenues, 105th in profits, and 157th in assets
Forbes 2000 ranking: 2012—528th in sales, 309th in profits, and 627th in assets
Corporate officers: James M. Cornelius, Chair.; Lamberto Andreotti, C.E.O.; Charles Bancroft, Exec. V.P. and C.F.O.; Paul von Autenried, Sr. V.P. and C.I.O.; Sandra Leung, Genl. Counsel and Corp. Secy.; John Elicker, Sr. V.P., Public Affairs; Ann Powell Judge, Sr. V.P., Human Resources
Board of directors: James M. Cornelius, Chair.; Lamberto Andreotti; Lewis B. Campbell; Laurie H. Glimcher, M.D.; Michael Grobstein; Alan J. Lacy; Vicki L. Sato, Ph.D.; Elliott Sigal, M.D., Ph.D.; Gerlad L. Storch; Togo Dennis West, Jr.
Subsidiaries: E. R. Squibb & Sons, L.L.C., Princeton, NJ; Westwood-Squibb Pharmaceuticals, Inc., Buffalo, NY
Plants: Wallingford, CT; Evansville, IN; Zeeland, MI; Hopewell, NJ
Offices: Nassau Park, New Brunswick, Plainsboro, NJ
International operations: Austria; Belgium; Brazil; Canada; China; Colombia; Germany; Greece; Italy; Malaysia; Mexico; Netherlands; Panama; Peru; Spain; Sweden; Switzerland; Taiwan; United Kingdom; Venezuela
Historic mergers: Amylin Pharmaceuticals, Inc. (August 8, 2012)
Giving statement: Giving through the Bristol-Myers Squibb Company Contributions Program, the Bristol-Myers Squibb Foundation, Inc., and the Bristol-Myers Squibb Patient Assistance Foundation, Inc.
Company EIN: 220790350

Bristol-Myers Squibb Company Contributions Program

345 Park Ave.
New York, NY 10154-0037 (212) 546-4000
Contact for Community Grants Program: Frederick Egenolf, Dir., Community Affairs, tel.: (609) 252-4983; E-mail for Independent Medical Education: medicalgrants.administration@bms.com ; URL: http://www.bms.com/responsibility/grantsandgiving/Pages/default.aspx

Contact: John L. Damonti, V.P., Corp. Philanthropy
Purpose and activities: As a complement to its foundation, Bristol-Myers Squibb also makes charitable contributions to nonprofit organizations directly. Support is given primarily in areas of company operations.
Fields of interest: Higher education; Medical school/education; Education; Health care, equal rights; Hospitals (general); Health care, clinics/centers; Pharmacy/prescriptions; Health care, patient services; Health care; Mental health/crisis services; Cancer; Neuroscience; Health organizations; Children/youth, services; Aging, centers/services; Homeless, human services; Human services; Community/economic development; Science, formal/general education; Chemistry; Mathematics; Engineering/technology; Biology/life sciences; Science; Public affairs Economically disadvantaged.
Programs:
Community Grants: Bristol-Myers supports programs designed to improve health and well-being in communities where Bristol-Myers has facilities and where its people live and work. Special emphasis is directed toward programs designed to address unmet medical needs; reduce health disparities; eliminate barriers to treatment, especially for patients with chronic diseases; improve the quality of science, technology, and mathematics education in local schools; and provide essential services to people in need through civic and community initiatives.
Corporate Memberships: Bristol-Myers supports national and regional disease-related organizations and medical societies that permit corporate members.
Fellowships, Scholarships, & Awards: Bristol-Myers awards grants to hospitals, health care facilities, academic medical centers at universities, educational institutions for graduate or post-graduate programs in healthcare-related fields, and professional societies in support of fellowships, scholarships, and awards. Special emphasis is directed toward fellowships, scholarships, and visiting professorships; scholarships for healthcare professionals to attend national medical meetings; and awards to recognize academic contributions in science, medicine, or patient care.
Independent Medical Education (IME): Through IME, Bristol-Myers supports programs designed to address recognized gaps in healthcare delivery to improve patient care; and enhance the professional skills and knowledge of healthcare professionals. Special emphasis is directed toward the following disease areas: cardiovascular, immunoscience, metabolics, neuroscience, oncology, and virology.
Independent-Sponsored Research Grants: Bristol-Myers supports programs designed to help patients prevail over serious diseases through investigator-sponsored research. The company supports clinical research, non-interventional research, and non-clinical research. Special emphasis is directed toward clinical research trials that support cardiovascular/metabolics, neuroscience, cancer, immunology, and virology.
Scientific Organizations: Bristol-Myers supports organizations involved with science. Special emphasis is directed toward conferences and events in biology, chemistry, pharmaceutical development, regulatory sciences, and enabling technologies.
Sponsorships: Bristol-Myers provides sponsorships to healthcare organizations and institutions, independent medical or professional societies, and patient advocacy-related organizations. Special emphasis is directed toward patient education; community healthcare activities; disease awareness initiatives; and activities related to improving patient access to healthcare and medications.
Type of support: Conferences/seminars; Continuing support; Employee-related scholarships; Fellowships; General/operating support; In-kind gifts; Program development; Research; Scholarship funds; Sponsorships.
Geographic limitations: Giving on a national and international basis in areas of company operations in Wallingford, CT, Mount Vernon, IN, Devens, MA, Hopewell, New Brunswick, Plainsboro, Princeton, and West Windsor, NJ, New York and Syracuse, NY, and PA.
Support limitations: No support for political, fraternal, social, or veterans' organizations, religious or sectarian organizations not of direct benefit to the entire community, or discriminatory organizations. No grants to individuals (except for employee-related scholarships), or for endowments, capital campaigns, or general operational deficits; no loans.
Publications: Application guidelines.
Application information: Applications accepted. The company has a staff that only handles contributions. A contributions committee reviews all requests. Application form required. Applicants should submit the following:
1) copy of IRS Determination Letter
2) copy of most recent annual report/audited financial statement/990
3) listing of board of directors, trustees, officers and other key people and their affiliations
4) detailed description of project and amount of funding requested
5) copy of current year's organizational budget and/or project budget
   Initial approach: Complete online application
   Copies of proposal: 1
   Deadline(s): 8 weeks prior to need; 6 weeks prior to need for scientific organizations grants; 12 weeks prior to need for Community Grants; None for Independent Medical Education grants under $10,000; July 5 to Sept. 30 and Jan. 2 to Mar. 30 for IME grants over $10,000;

June 30 for Investigator-Sponsored Research Grants
Final notification: 8 weeks; 6 weeks for scientific organizations grants and Community Grants; 8 weeks for Independent Medical Education grants; Aug. 15 for Investigator-Sponsored Research Grants

Number of staff: 6 full-time professional; 4 full-time support.

The Bristol-Myers Squibb Foundation, Inc.

(formerly The Bristol-Myers Fund, Inc.)
345 Park Ave., 3rd Fl.
New York, NY 10154-0004 (212) 546-4000
E-mail: bms.foundation@bms.com; E-mail for Together on Diabetes in the U.S: Patricia Doykos, patricia.doykos@bms.com or togetherondiabetes@bms.com; E-mail for Together on Diabetes in China and India: Phangisile Mtshali, phangisile.mtshali@bms.com; Contact for Mental Health & Well-Being: Catharine Grimes, e-mail: Catharine.Grimes@bms.com; Contact for Secure the Future - Technical Assistance and Skills Transfer Program: Secure the Future, P.O. Box 1408, Bedfordview, 2008, South Africa, tel.: +21 11 456 6400, fax: +27 11 456 6589, e-mail: archie.smuts@bms.com or beryl.mohr@bms.com; URL: http://www.bms.com/foundation/Pages/home.aspx

Establishment information: Incorporated in 1982 in FL as successor to a foundation established in 1953.

Donor: Bristol-Myers Squibb Co.

Contact: John L. Damonti, Pres.

Financial data (yr. ended 12/31/11): Assets, $151,701,668 (M); gifts received, $35,850,207; expenditures, $31,790,817; qualifying distributions, $28,850,815; giving activities include $25,581,391 for 196+ grants (high: $1,761,552) and $3,269,424 for employee matching gifts.

Purpose and activities: The foundation supports programs designed to reduce health disparities around the world. Special emphasis is directed toward programs designed to improve the health outcomes of populations disproportionately affected by HIV/AIDS in Africa; hepatitis in Asia; type 2 diabetes; mental health and well-being in the United States; and cancer in Europe.

Fields of interest: Higher education; Medical school/education; Education; Health care, public policy; Health care, equal rights; Medical care, community health systems; Hospitals (general); Health care, clinics/centers; Pharmacy/prescriptions; Public health; Public health, STDs; Public health, communicable diseases; Palliative care; Nursing care; Health care; Mental health, treatment; Mental health/crisis services; Cancer; AIDS; Diabetes; Health organizations; Cancer research; AIDS research; American Red Cross; Residential/custodial care, hospices; Human services Children; Aging; African Americans/Blacks; Women; Military/veterans; Economically disadvantaged.

International interests: Africa; China; Europe; India; Japan; Sub-Saharan Africa.

Programs:

Cancer in Europe - Bridging Cancer Care Initiative: The foundation supports programs designed to narrow the difference in care and outcomes experienced by countries in central and eastern Europe. Special emphasis is directed toward programs designed to improve cancer nursing skills and knowledge among oncology and general practice nurses; and community education and support services that remove barriers to care and support patients as they manage their disease at home and in the community.

Employee Giving Program: The foundation matches contributions made by employees of Bristol-Myers Squibb to the United Way, educational institutions, nonprofit organizations, and organizations involved with combating specific global health disparities.

Employee Volunteer Award Program: The foundation awards grants to nonprofit organizations with which employees of Bristol-Myers Squibb volunteer.

Hepatitis in Asia - Delivering Hope: The foundation supports programs designed to raise awareness and promote prevention and care related to hepatitis B and C in China, Japan, India, and Taiwan. Special emphasis is directed toward capacity building for healthcare professionals and lay health workers; disease education and awareness; and best practices in the prevention and management of hepatitis B and C to inform public health policy.

HIV/AIDS in Africa - Secure the Future: The foundation supports programs designed to develop and replicate innovative and sustainable solutions for vulnerable populations, including women and children who are infected and affected by HIV/AIDS in sub-Saharan Africa. The foundation also operates the Technical Assistance and Skills Transfer Program (TAP) designed to empower communities to harness resources and capacity to improve the effectiveness and sustainability of community-based HIV/AIDS programs. Special emphasis is directed toward expanding Secure the Future technical assistance and skills transfer into Africa; improving diagnosis, support, education, and treatment for people co-infected with HIV and tuberculosis; and pharmacist-based HIV/AIDS services. Visit URL: http://www.securethefuture.com/ for more information.

Mental Health & Well-Being in the U.S.: The foundation supports programs designed to reduce mental health disparities through healthcare capacity building and support services for patients at the community level. Special emphasis is directed toward programs designed to address the mental health and re-integration needs of service members, veterans, and military families; and of people with mental illness involved in the criminal justice system.

Together on Diabetes: The foundation supports programs designed to improve health outcomes of people living with type 2 diabetes in China, India, and the United States. Special emphasis is directed toward programs designed to help adults living with type 2 diabetes self-manage the disease and navigate care; build and coordinate medical, non-medical, and policy efforts at the community level and empower the individuals and organizations involved with bringing education, reach, and influence to the fight against type 2 diabetes; and promote new ideas about diabetes control efforts given the current and future scale of the epidemic and the duration of the disease experience. The foundation awards grants to non-governmental organizations and academic institutions working at the community level and partnerships are encouraged. The foundation also announces a themed request for proposals (RFP) every November during National Diabetes Month. Visit: http://www.bms.com/togetherondiabetes/pages/home.aspx for more information.

Type of support: Continuing support; Curriculum development; Employee matching gifts; Employee volunteer services; Employee-related scholarships; General/operating support; In-kind gifts; Management development/capacity building; Program development; Program evaluation; Research; Seed money; Technical assistance.

Geographic limitations: Giving primarily in areas of company operations in Wallingford, CT, Washington, DC, Mount Vernon, IN, Devens, MA, Hopewell, New Brunswick, Plainsboro, Princeton, and West Windsor, NJ, New York and Syracuse, NY, PA, TX, Africa (especially Sub-Saharan Africa), China, Europe, India, Japan, Taiwan, and Thailand.

Support limitations: No support for political, fraternal, social, or veterans' organizations, religious or sectarian organizations not of direct benefit to the entire community, or federated campaign-supported organizations. No grants to individuals (except for employee-related scholarships), or for endowments, capital campaigns, debt reduction, conferences, sponsorships, or independent medical research, or specific public broadcasting or films; no loans.

Publications: Application guidelines; Grants list; Informational brochure; Program policy statement.

Application information: Applications accepted. Organizations receiving support are asked to submit biannual reports and a final report. Application form required. Applicants should submit the following:

1) timetable for implementation and evaluation of project
2) how project will be sustained once grantmaker support is completed
3) results expected from proposed grant
4) statement of problem project will address
5) population served
6) copy of IRS Determination Letter
7) geographic area to be served
8) copy of most recent annual report/audited financial statement/990
9) how project's results will be evaluated or measured
10) listing of board of directors, trustees, officers and other key people and their affiliations
11) detailed description of project and amount of funding requested
12) plans for cooperation with other organizations, if any
13) contact person
14) copy of current year's organizational budget and/or project budget
15) listing of additional sources and amount of support

Initial approach: Complete online application; e-mail for Together on Diabetes; complete online application for Secure the Future - Technical Assistance and Skills Transfer Program
Board meeting date(s): Dec. and as needed
Deadline(s): None
Final notification: 6 to 8 weeks

Officers and Directors:* Lamberto Andreotti, Chair.; John L. Damonti*, Pres.; Mary Vanhatten, Secy.; Jeffrey Galik, Treas.; Beatrice Cazala; Giovanni Caforio, M.D.; John E. Celentano; Brian Daniels, M.D.; Sandra Leung.

Number of staff: 6 full-time professional; 4 full-time support.

EIN: 133127947

Selected grants: The following grants are a representative sample of this grantmaker's funding activity:

$1,761,552 to American Academy of Family Physicians Foundation, Leawood, KS, 2011.
$1,497,348 to American Pharmacists Association Foundation, Washington, DC, 2011.
$1,338,323 to Duke University, Durham, NC, 2011.
$1,073,722 to Johns Hopkins University, Baltimore, MD, 2011.
$373,577 to Research Foundation for Mental Hygiene, Menands, NY, 2011.
$219,689 to Liver Foundation West Bengal, Kolkata, India, 2011.

$84,600 to International Society of Nurses in Cancer Care, Vancouver, Canada, 2011.
$60,000 to University of Lubumbashi, Lubumbashi, Democratic Republic of the Congo, 2011.
$50,000 to Polish Amazons Social Movement, Warsaw, Poland, 2011.

The Bristol-Myers Squibb Patient Assistance Foundation, Inc.

345 Park Ave.
New York, NY 10154-0004 (800) 736-0003
FAX: (866) 736-1611; Application address: P.O. Box 220769, Charlotte, NC 28222-0769; URL: http://www.bmspaf.org/index.html

Establishment information: Established in 1999 in NJ as a company-sponsored operating foundation.
Donors: E.R. Squibb & Sons, Inc.; E.R. Squibb & Sons, L.L.C.; Bristol-Myers Squibb Co.; Otsuka American Pharmaceutical, Inc.; BMS/Sanofi Pharmaceuticals Partnership.
Financial data (yr. ended 12/30/11): Assets, $1,667,529 (M); gifts received, $482,597,734; expenditures, $482,597,734; qualifying distributions, $482,597,734; giving activities include $472,208,171 for grants to individuals.
Purpose and activities: The foundation provides prescription medicines to patients with financial hardships who have no private prescription drug insurance and are not eligible for prescription drug coverage through Medicaid or other government programs.
Fields of interest: Economically disadvantaged.
Type of support: Donated products; Grants to individuals.
Geographic limitations: Giving on a national basis.
Publications: Application guidelines; Informational brochure.
Application information: Applications accepted. Applications must be completed by the patient and a healthcare provider. Application form required. Applicants must attach a photocopy of the annual household income, including Federal tax form (1040), social security income (SSA 1099), pension, interest, retirement, or child support, if applicable.
Initial approach: Download application form and fax or mail to foundation
Deadline(s): 1 month prior to need
Officers and Trustees:* John L. Damonti*, Chair.; Sandra Leung, Esq., Secy.; David J. Marlow, Treas.; Alicia Coghlan; Ronald C. Miller.
EIN: 223622487

579
Broadcom Corporation

5300 California Ave., Bldg. 1-8
Irvine, CA 92617-3038 (949) 926-5000
FAX: (949) 926-5203

Company URL: http://www.broadcom.com
Establishment information: Established in 1991.
Company type: Public company
Company ticker symbol and exchange: BRCM/NASDAQ
International Securities Identification Number: US1113201073
Business activities: Manufactures semiconductors for wired and wireless communications.
Business type (SIC): Electronic components and accessories
Financial profile for 2012: Number of employees, 11,300; assets, $11,208,000,000; sales volume, $8,006,000,000; pre-tax net income, $656,000,000; expenses, $7,330,000,000; liabilities, $3,369,000,000
Fortune 1000 ranking: 2012—327th in revenues, 261st in profits, and 359th in assets
Forbes 2000 ranking: 2012—1094th in sales, 838th in profits, and 1391st in assets
Corporate officers: Henry Samueli, Ph.D., Chair.; Scott A. McGregor, Pres. and C.E.O.; Eric K. Brandt, Exec. V.P. and C.F.O.; Arthur Chong, Exec. V.P., Genl. Counsel, and Corp. Secy.; Neil Y. Kim, Exec. V.P., Opers.; Terri Timberman, Exec. V.P., Human Resources; Robert L. Tirva, Sr. V.P. and Corp. Cont.
Board of directors: Henry Samueli, Ph.D., Chair.; Robert J. Finocchio, Jr.; Nancy H. Handel; Eddy W. Hartenstein; Maria M. Klawe, Ph.D.; John E. Major; Scott A. McGregor; William T. Morrow; Robert E. Switz
Giving statement: Giving through the Broadcom Corporation Contributions Program and the Broadcom Foundation.
Company EIN: 330480482

Broadcom Corporation Contributions Program

5300 California Ave.
Irvine, CA 92617-3038 (949) 946-5000
URL: http://www.broadcom.com/global_citizenship/

Purpose and activities: As a complement to its foundation, Broadcom also makes charitable contributions directly to nonprofit organizations involved with education, healthcare, disaster relief, fundraising, children and youth, math and science, and housing. Support is given primarily in areas of company operations.
Fields of interest: Education; Health care; Breast cancer; Housing/shelter, volunteer services; Safety/disasters; Human services, fund raising/fund distribution; Children/youth, services; Mathematics; Science.
Type of support: Employee volunteer services; General/operating support.
Geographic limitations: Giving primarily in areas of company operations.

Broadcom Foundation

5300 California Ave., Ste. 14067
Irvine, CA 92617-3038 (949) 926-9500
FAX: (949) 926-9244;
E-mail: feedback@broadcomfoundation.org;
URL: http://www.broadcomfoundation.org/

Establishment information: Established in 2009 in CA.
Donor: Broadcom Corp.
Financial data (yr. ended 12/31/11): Assets, $73,650,517 (M); gifts received, $25,000,000; expenditures, $2,931,899; qualifying distributions, $2,709,535; giving activities include $2,525,167 for 70 grants (high: $1,000,000; low: $2,500).
Purpose and activities: The foundation supports programs designed to advance STEM education; inspire youth to pursue careers in engineering; reduce economic disparity; close the STEM education gap among women, ethnic, and minority populations; improve quality of life in Broadcom communities; create opportunities for volunteerism and civic engagement among Broadcom employees; and strengthen Broadcom Corporation social responsibility and global citizenship.
Fields of interest: Elementary/secondary education; Higher education; Education; Health care; Human services; Economic development; Mathematics; Engineering/technology; Science Youth; Minorities; Women.
Programs:
Community Engagement: The foundation supports organizations involved with K-12 STEM education, health, and human services in communities where Broadcom Corporation employees live and work. Special emphasis is directed toward programs with volunteer opportunities for Broadcom employees, including competition judges, mentors, or educators.
Global Community Heroes: The foundation recognizes volunteerism and civic engagement by honoring 10 employees throughout Broadcom's global offices for service to their community. The award includes $500 in honor of a winner to a qualifying charity of his or her choice.
STEM Education & Research: The foundation supports programs designed to promote a greater understanding of science, technology, engineering, and mathematics and their practical applications. Special emphasis is directed toward graduate and post-graduate STEM research, scholarship and education initiatives; undergraduate STEM education; The National Broadcom MASTERS Competition for Middle Schoolers; and opportunities to close the K-12 STEM education gap among women and diverse populations in Broadcom Communities.
Type of support: Continuing support; Employee volunteer services; Program development; Research; Sponsorships.
Geographic limitations: Giving primarily in areas of company operations in Tempe, AZ, Irvine, Petaluma, San Diego, San Jose, Santa Clara, and Sunnyvale, CA, Colorado Springs, Fort Collins, and Longmont, CO, Duluth, GA, Andover, Burlington, and Marlborough, MA, Germantown, MD, Edina, MN, Morrisville, NC, Matawan, NJ, Yardley, PA, Austin and Houston, TX, and Federal Way, WA; giving also internationally in select cities in Australia, Belgium, China, Denmark, France, Greece, India, Israel, Japan, Korea, Netherlands, Singapore, Spain, Taiwan, and United Kingdom.
Support limitations: No support for fraternal, labor, political, or social organizations, political candidates, sectarian religious organizations, private K-12 schools, trade or business associations, discriminatory organizations, third party organizations, or agencies normally financed by government sources. No grants to individuals, or for equipment, capital campaigns, advertising journals or booklets, congresses, symposiums, or meetings, scholarships, fellowships, lobbying, technical research in support of Broadcom products, sporting events, tickets, or sponsorships, travel, trips, tours, or cultural exchange programs, university administrative, management, or indirect fees, endowments, ongoing general operating support, debt reduction, memorial tributes, special fundraising event table or ticket purchase, or matching gifts.
Publications: Annual report; Application guidelines; IRS Form 990 or 990-PF printed copy available upon request.
Application information: Applications accepted. Most of the foundation funding is by invitation only; however qualified organizations may apply during the open proposal period. Application form required.
Initial approach: Complete online application
Deadline(s): Apr. 30 to June 30
Final notification: 3 months
Officers and Directors:* Scott McGregor*, Pres.; Lauri D. Fischer, Secy.; Gregg S. Morrison, C.F.O.; Maria Wronski, Treas.; Paula Golden, Exec. Dir.; Eric K. Brandt; Arthur Chong; Henry Samueli, Ph.D.; Terri L. Timberman.
EIN: 264754581

580
Brocchini Farms, Inc.

(doing business as Mid-Cal Produce)
(also known as Albert Brocchini Farms)
27011 S. Austin Rd.
Ripon, CA 95366-9625 (209) 599-4229

Establishment information: Established in 1948.
Company type: Private company
Business activities: Operates grape vineyards.
Business type (SIC): Farms/fruit and nut
Corporate officers: Robert Brocchini, Pres.; Ingrid Treadway, Cont.; Dolores Sanchez, Human Resources
Board of director: Dolores Sanchez
Giving statement: Giving through the Albert & Rina Brocchini Family Foundation.

Albert & Rina Brocchini Family Foundation

27011 S. Austin Rd.
Ripon, CA 95366-9625 (209) 599-4229

Establishment information: Established in 2004 in CA.
Donors: Brocchini Farms, Inc.; A&R Enterprises.
Contact: Robert Brocchini, Pres.
Financial data (yr. ended 08/31/12): Assets, $1,695,185 (M); expenditures, $257,660; qualifying distributions, $245,025; giving activities include $245,025 for 29 grants (high: $105,100; low: $250).
Purpose and activities: The foundation supports organizations involved with arts and culture, education, nerve disorders, athletics, and human services.
Fields of interest: Arts; Secondary school/ education; Education; Nerve, muscle & bone diseases; Athletics/sports, amateur leagues; Children, services; Aging, centers/services; Human services.
Type of support: General/operating support; Scholarship funds.
Geographic limitations: Giving primarily in CA.
Support limitations: No grants to individuals.
Application information: Applications accepted. Application form required.
Initial approach: Contact foundation for application form
Deadline(s): None
Officers: Robert Brocchini, Pres.; Stephen Brocchini, V.P.; Kristine Brocchini, Secy.-Treas.
EIN: 270106523

581
Brochsteins, Inc.

(also known as Fashion Square Merchants Association Inc.)
11530 Main St.
Houston, TX 77025-5988 (713) 666-2881

Company URL: http://www.brochsteins.com
Establishment information: Established in 1935.
Company type: Private company
Business activities: Manufactures wood office furniture.
Business type (SIC): Furniture/office
Corporate officers: Raymond. D. Brochstein, Chair.; Deborah Brochstein, Pres. and C.E.O.; Melissa P. Burgess, V.P. and Secy.
Board of directors: Raymond D. Brochstein, Chair.; Deborah Brochstein; Steven Hecht
Giving statement: Giving through the Lynn and Joel Brochstein Foundation, Inc.

Lynn and Joel Brochstein Foundation, Inc.

(formerly Brochstein Foundation)
3350 McCue, Ste. 2002
Houston, TX 77056

Establishment information: Established in 1975 in TX.
Donors: Brochsteins, Inc.; Architectural Woodwork Corp.; Joel Brochstein; Lynn Brochstein.
Financial data (yr. ended 10/31/12): Assets, $827,489 (M); expenditures, $58,911; qualifying distributions, $44,446; giving activities include $44,446 for 9 grants (high: $19,386; low: $50).
Purpose and activities: The foundation supports organizations involved with arts and culture, education, health, cancer, human services, and senior citizens.
Fields of interest: Education; Health organizations; Religion.
Type of support: General/operating support.
Support limitations: No grants to individuals.
Application information: Applications not accepted. Unsolicited requests for funds not accepted.
Trustees: Joel Brochstein; Lynn Brochstein.
EIN: 746039346

582
Bromelkamp Company, LLC

106 E. 24th St.
Minneapolis, MN 55404-3522
(612) 870-9087

Company URL: http://bromelkamp.com
Establishment information: Established in 1978.
Company type: Private company
Business activities: Provides an integrated software solution for managing grants and contacts.
Business type (SIC): Computer services
Corporate officer: Henry A. Bromelkamp, Pres.
Giving statement: Giving through the Bromelkamp Company Foundation.

Bromelkamp Company Foundation

106 East 24th St.
Minneapolis, MN 55404-3522 (612) 870-9087
FAX: (612) 767-6709; URL: http://bromelkamp.com/Home/OurFoundation/tabid/57/Default.aspx

Purpose and activities: The foundation supports nonprofit organizations on a case by case basis. Support is given in areas of company operations in Jackson, Berkley, and Midland, Michigan; Minneapolis, Minnetonka, Maple Grove, and New Hope, Minnesota; Omaha, Nebraska; and Jarvisburg, North Carolina.
Fields of interest: Education, reading; Employment, training; Food banks; Housing/shelter, homeless; Computer science; Accessibility/universal design.
Program:
Group Volunteer Event: Bromelkamp Foundation offers a group volunteer event grant. The grant consists of a single event in which the staff of 14 will volunteer a block of time (2-3 hours) to assist an organization. Examples of projects the company has worked on in the past are: organizing and shelving donations given to a food shelf, and singing Christmas carols at a nursing home.
Type of support: Employee matching gifts; Employee volunteer services; General/operating support; Technical assistance.
Geographic limitations: Giving primarily in areas of company operations in Jackson, Berkley, and Midland, MI, Minneapolis, Minnetonka, Maple Grove, and New Hope, MN, Jarvisburg, NC, and Omaha, NE.
Publications: Application guidelines; Grants list.
Application information: Applications accepted. The maximum grant amount is $2,000. The company's grant making priority for 2013 is homelessness. Applicants for Technical Assistance grants are strongly encourage to call and discuss their project prior to making a request. Application form required. Applicants should submit the following:
1) copy of IRS Determination Letter
Initial approach: Create an eGrant.net account and complete online application for grants; call to discuss project for technical assistance
Committee meeting date(s): Annually
Deadline(s): Mar. 30, 2013
Final notification: Apr. 25, 2013

583
Brookline Bancorp, MHC

160 Washington St.
Brookline, MA 02447-0469 (617) 730-3520

Company URL: http://www.brooklinesavings.com
Establishment information: Established in 1871.
Company type: Subsidiary of a public company
Business activities: Operates bank holding company; operates savings bank.
Business type (SIC): Savings institutions; holding company
Financial profile for 2008: Number of employees, 219; assets, $2,613,010,000
Corporate officer: Richard P. Chapman, Jr., Pres. and C.E.O.
Subsidiary: Brookline Bancorp, Inc., Brookline, MA
Giving statement: Giving through the Brookline Savings Bank Charitable Foundation.
Company EIN: 043402944

Brookline Savings Bank Charitable Foundation

P.O. Box 470469
Brookline, MA 02447 (617) 927-7974
Application address: P. O. Box 179179, Boston, MA 02117, tel.: (617) 927-7974

Establishment information: Established in 1999 in MA.
Donor: Brookline Bancorp, MHC.
Contact: Wesley K. Blair III
Financial data (yr. ended 12/31/11): Assets, $0 (M); gifts received, $697; expenditures, $72,245; qualifying distributions, $72,075; giving activities include $72,075 for 34 grants (high: $10,000; low: $100).
Purpose and activities: The foundation supports the United Way in Boston, Massachusetts.
Fields of interest: United Ways and Federated Giving Programs.
Type of support: General/operating support.
Geographic limitations: Giving primarily in MA.
Support limitations: No grants to individuals.
Application information: Applications accepted. Application form required.
Initial approach: Proposal
Deadline(s): None
Officers: Paul A. Perrault, Pres.; Jane M. Wolchonok, Sr. V.P.

Directors: David C. Chapin; John J. Doyle, Jr.; John A. Hackett; John L. Hall II; Thomas I. Hollister; Charles H. Peck; Hollis W. Plimpton, Jr.; Joseph J. Slotnik; Rosamond B. Value; Peter O. Wilde.
EIN: 043498480

584
Brooklyn Nets

(formerly New Jersey Basketball LLC)
Barclays Ctr.
15 Metrotech Ctr., 11th Fl.
Brooklyn, NY 11201 (718) 933-3000

Company URL: http://www.nba.com/nets
Establishment information: Established in 1967.
Company type: Subsidiary of a foreign company
Business activities: Operates professional basketball club.
Business type (SIC): Commercial sports
Corporate officers: Christophe Charlier, Chair.; Irina Pavlova, Pres.; Brett Yormark, C.E.O.; Charlie Mierswa, Exec. V.P., Business Opers., and C.F.O.
Giving statement: Giving through the Brooklyn Nets Corporate Giving Program and the Nets Foundation, Inc.

Brooklyn Nets Corporate Giving Program

(formerly New Jersey Nets Corporate Giving Program)
c/o Community Rels. Dept.
15 MetroTech Center, 11th Fl.
Brooklyn, NY 11201
FAX: (718) 522-3544;
E-mail: donations@brooklynnets.com; Contact for Student Rewards Program: Mike Wisniewski, tel.: (201) 635-3145; URL: http://www.nba.com/nets/community/donation-requests

Purpose and activities: The Brooklyn Nets make charitable contributions to nonprofit organizations on a case by case basis. Support is given primarily in New York and New Jersey.
Fields of interest: Education, reading; Education; Public health, physical fitness; Nutrition; Athletics/sports, basketball; Boys & girls clubs; Youth, services; Human services, gift distribution; General charitable giving.
Programs:

Get Net Fit: The Nets, in partnership with the American Dairy Association, teaches kids the importance of nutrition and fitness. The program includes clinics, court refurbishments, and a nutrition challenge during the school year.

Hometown Hero: The Nets, in partnership with TD Bank, honors individuals who have made a significant contributions and performed selfless acts in their communities. The honorees receive game tickets, and an on-court ceremony during a home game.

Nets Athlete Assist Program: Through the Nets Athlete Assist Program, Nets players purchase and donate blocks of tickets to Nets home games to youth groups and nonprofit organizations. Ticket recipients are recognized during the game and participates in some of the in-game entertainment activities.

Newspapers in Education: The Nets, in partnership with Newark Star Ledger, provides newspapers and lessons plans for teachers to use in class to enhance students critical thinking. Selected students are chosen by their students to interview a Nets player after a Nets practice and have their article published in the Star Ledger.

Read to Achieve: The Nets, in partnership with Western Union, visit schools and libraries to emphasize the importance of reading and receiving an education. The program also includes reading time-outs and book donations.

Student Reward Program: The Nets, in partnership with the U.S. Army, annually rewards students who excel academically and athletically in their community with tickets to Nets games.
Type of support: Donated products; In-kind gifts; Income development; Loaned talent.
Geographic limitations: Giving primarily in areas of company operations in NJ and NY.
Support limitations: No monetary donations or sponsorships.
Publications: Application guidelines.
Application information: Applications accepted. Proposals should be submitted using organization letterhead. Support is limited to 1 contribution per organization during any given year. Player, dancer, or mascot appearances are only available from Oct. to Mar. The Community Relations Department handles giving. Application form not required. Applicants should submit the following:
1) population served
2) brief history of organization and description of its mission
3) descriptive literature about organization
4) detailed description of project and amount of funding requested

Proposals should specifically note the nature of the request being made; and indicate the date, time, and location of the event and the type of fundraiser.
Initial approach: Mail or fax proposal to headquarters for memorabilia, tickets, player, dancer, and mascot appearances, and the Nets Athlete Assist Program; telephone headquarters for Student Rewards Program
Copies of proposal: 1
Deadline(s): 6 weeks prior to need for memorabilia, tickets, and player, dancer, or mascot appearances; None for the Nets Athlete Assist Program
Final notification: 6 weeks

The Nets Foundation, Inc.

c/o Brooklyn Nets
15 Metrotech Ctr., 11th Fl.
Brooklyn, NY 11201

Establishment information: Established in 2007 in NJ.
Donors: Barclays Capital; Forest City Ratner Companies; Forest City Ratner Companies Foundation; New Jersey Basketball, LLC.
Financial data (yr. ended 06/30/11): Assets, $767,666 (M); gifts received, $1,067,632; expenditures, $928,155; qualifying distributions, $901,405; giving activities include $901,405 for 34 grants (high: $100,000; low: $2,000).
Purpose and activities: The foundation supports programs designed to promote youth; foster education; and strengthen communities.
Fields of interest: Historic preservation/historical societies; Arts; Higher education; Education; Recreation, parks/playgrounds; Athletics/sports, amateur leagues; Athletics/sports, basketball; Boys & girls clubs; Big Brothers/Big Sisters; Human services; Children/youth, services; Community/economic development Youth.
Type of support: General/operating support; Program development.
Geographic limitations: Giving primarily in NJ and NY.
Application information: Applications not accepted. Contributes only to pre-selected organizations.
Officers and Directors:* Brett Yormark*, Pres.; Leo Ehrline*, V.P. and Secy.; Charlie Mierswa*, V.P. and Treas.; Bruce Ratner.
EIN: 205370246
Selected grants: The following grants are a representative sample of this grantmaker's funding activity:
$175,000 to Out2Play, New York, NY, 2010. For general support.
$110,000 to Brooklyn Childrens Museum, Brooklyn, NY, 2010. For general support.
$100,000 to Brooklyn Historical Society, Brooklyn, NY, 2010.
$100,000 to New York Police and Fire Widows and Childrens Benefit Fund, New York, NY, 2010. For general support.
$75,000 to Police Athletic League, New York, NY, 2010. For general support.
$70,000 to Camp Sunshine at Sebago Lake, Casco, ME, 2010. For general support.
$50,000 to Brooklyn Conservatory of Music, Brooklyn, NY, 2010.
$50,000 to Lutheran Medical Center, Brooklyn, NY, 2010.
$25,000 to Saint Johns University, Jamaica, NY, 2010. For general support.
$10,000 to Neighbors Helping Neighbors, Brooklyn, NY, 2010.

585
Brooks Resources Corporation

409 N.W. Franklin Ave.
Bend, OR 97701 (541) 382-1662

Company URL: http://www.brooks-resources.com/
Establishment information: Established in 1969.
Company type: Private company
Business activities: Provides real estate brokerage services.
Business type (SIC): Real estate subdividers and developers
Corporate officers: Michael P. Hollern, Pres. and C.E.O.; Jade Mayer, C.F.O.; Romy Mortensen, V.P., Sales and Mktg.
Subsidiaries: Awbrey Glen Golf Club, Inc., Bend, OR; Mount Bachelor Village Corp., Bend, OR
Giving statement: Giving through the Bend Foundation.

Bend Foundation

730 2nd Ave. S., Ste. 1300
Minneapolis, MN 55402-2475 (612) 752-1770
E-mail: barb@brooksresources.com; Additional tel.: (541) 382-1662; URL: http://brooks-resources.com/about-us/community-contributions/

Establishment information: Established in 1947 in IL.
Donors: Brooks Resources Corp.; Brooks-Scanlon, Inc.
Contact: Michael P. Hollern, Tr.
Financial data (yr. ended 12/31/11): Assets, $4,389,397 (M); expenditures, $266,053; qualifying distributions, $230,420; giving activities include $230,420 for grants.
Purpose and activities: The foundation supports health clinics and organizations involved with arts and culture, education, land conservation, hunger, and human services.
Fields of interest: Media, film/video; Museums; Performing arts, theater; Arts; Higher education; Education; Environment, land resources; Health care, clinics/centers; Food services; Boys & girls

clubs; Children, services; Family services; Family services, domestic violence; Human services.
Type of support: Annual campaigns; Building/renovation; Equipment; Program development; Seed money.
Geographic limitations: Giving limited to central OR, with emphasis on Deschutes County.
Support limitations: No grants for general operating support, debt reduction, endowments, special projects, research, publications, or conferences; no loans.
Application information: Applications accepted. Application form not required. Applicants should submit the following:
1) copy of IRS Determination Letter
2) how project's results will be evaluated or measured
3) detailed description of project and amount of funding requested
4) copy of current year's organizational budget and/or project budget
Initial approach: Proposal
Copies of proposal: 1
Board meeting date(s): Feb. or Mar.
Deadline(s): None
Final notification: A few months
Trustees: Conley Brooks; Conley Brooks, Jr.; Michael P. Hollern; William L. Smith.
EIN: 416019901
Selected grants: The following grants are a representative sample of this grantmaker's funding activity:
$20,000 to BendFilm, Bend, OR, 2009. For general support.
$20,000 to Crook County Foundation, Prineville, OR, 2009. For general support.
$20,000 to Kids Intervention and Diagnostic Service Center, Bend, OR, 2009. For general support.
$15,750 to Saving Grace, Bend, OR, 2009. For general support.
$11,000 to High Desert Museum, Bend, OR, 2009. For general support.
$10,000 to Deschutes Land Trust, Bend, OR, 2009. For general support.
$10,000 to Tower Theater Foundation, Bend, OR, 2009. For general support.
$7,000 to Saint Charles Medical Center Foundation, Bend, OR, 2009. For general support.

586
Brookstone, Inc.

1 Innovation Way
Merrimack, NH 03054 (603) 880-9500

Company URL: http://www.brookstone.com
Establishment information: Established in 1965.
Company type: Subsidiary of a private company
Business activities: Operates specialty retailing company.
Business type (SIC): Shopping goods stores/miscellaneous
Corporate officers: Jackson P. Tai, Chair.; Stephen Bebis, Pres. and C.E.O.; James M. Speltz, V.P. and C.O.O.; Thomas F. Moynihan, V.P. and C.F.O.; William E. Wood, V.P. and C.I.O.; Stephen A. Gould, V.P. and Genl. Counsel; Deirdre A. Zimmermann, V.P., Mktg.; Robert M. Chessen, V.P., Human Resources
Board of director: Jackson P. Tai, Chair.
Giving statement: Giving through the Brookstone, Inc. Corporate Giving Program.
Company EIN: 061182895

Brookstone, Inc. Corporate Giving Program

1 Innovation Way
Merrimack, NH 03054-4873 (603) 577-8005
URL: http://www.brookstone.com/brookstone-donate-to-tsunami-relief.html?bkiid=hmpg|hdr|banner|donate

Purpose and activities: Brookstone, Inc. makes charitable contributions to nonprofit organizations on a case by case basis.
Fields of interest: Disasters, preparedness/services; Disasters, floods; International relief.
Type of support: General/operating support.

587
Brother International Corporation

100 Somerset Corporate Blvd.
Bridgewater, NJ 08807-0911
(908) 704-1700

Company URL: http://www.brother-usa.com
Establishment information: Established in 1954.
Company type: Subsidiary of a foreign company
Business activities: Markets industrial products, home appliances, and business products.
Business type (SIC): Professional and commercial equipment—wholesale
Financial profile for 2010: Number of employees, 2,000; sales volume, $1,560,000,000
Corporate officers: Tadashi Ishiguro, Pres.; Anthony Melfi, V.P. and C.F.O.; Dennis Upton, C.I.O.
Subsidiary: Brother Industries (USA), Inc., Bartlett, TN
Giving statement: Giving through the Brother International Corporation Contributions Program.

Brother International Corporation Contributions Program

100 Somerset Corporate Blvd.
Bridgewater, NJ 08807-0911 (908) 704-1700
FAX: (908) 704-8235; URL: http://www.brother.com/en/csr/index.htm

Purpose and activities: Brother makes charitable contributions to nonprofit organizations involved with employment training and business promotion. Support is given on a national and international basis in areas of company operations.
Fields of interest: Environmental education; Employment, training; Disasters, preparedness/services; Community development, business promotion; General charitable giving.
Type of support: Donated products; Employee volunteer services; General/operating support.
Geographic limitations: Giving on a national and international basis in areas of company operations.

588
Brotherhood Mutual Insurance Company

6400 Brotherhood Way
P.O. Box 2227
Fort Wayne, IN 46825 (260) 482-8668

Company URL: http://www.brotherhoodmutual.com/
Establishment information: Established in 1917.
Company type: Mutual company
Business activities: Provides property, casualty, liability, and foreign liability insurance, for Christian churches and related ministries.
Business type (SIC): Insurance/fire, marine, and casualty
Financial profile for 2010: Number of employees, 250; sales volume, $2,583,451,000
Corporate officers: Mark A. Robison, C.P.A., Chair. and Pres.; Michael J. Allison, V.P. and Secy.; Matthew G. Hirschy, C.P.A., V.P. and Treas.; Kathleen J. Turpin, V.P., Human Resources; Daryl G. Pannabecker, V.P., Inf. Systems; Mitzi Thomas, Asst. V.P., Mktg. and Comms.
Board of directors: Mark A. Robison, Chair.; Michael J. Allison; James A. Blum; David Boyer; Kathy B. Bruns; John L. Cooley; Garrett W. Cooper; Phillip A. Dabill; Chris L. Goeglein; Ronald J. Habegger; Matthew G. Hirschy; Allen H. Leatherman; Sammy T. Mah; Pamela J. Moret
Giving statement: Giving through the Brotherhood Mutual Foundation, Inc.

Brotherhood Mutual Foundation, Inc.

6400 Brotherhood Way
Fort Wayne, IN 46825-4235

Establishment information: Established in 2005 in IN.
Donor: Brotherhood Mutual Insurance Co.
Financial data (yr. ended 12/31/11): Assets, $84,811 (M); gifts received, $344,449; expenditures, $354,138; qualifying distributions, $353,960; giving activities include $353,960 for grants.
Purpose and activities: The foundation supports health clinics and organizations involved with education, reproductive health, human services, international relief, civic affairs, and Christianity.
Fields of interest: Higher education; Education; Health care, clinics/centers; Reproductive health; Youth, services; Homeless, human services; Human services; International relief; Public affairs, citizen participation; Christian agencies & churches.
Type of support: Annual campaigns; Building/renovation; Capital campaigns; General/operating support; Program development; Sponsorships.
Geographic limitations: Giving primarily in IN.
Support limitations: No grants to individuals.
Application information: Applications not accepted. Contributes only to pre-selected organizations.
Officers: James A. Blum, Chair.; Mark A. Robison, Pres.; Hugh W. White, V.P.; Michael J. Allison, Secy.; Matthew G. Hirschy, Treas.
EIN: 203618117
Selected grants: The following grants are a representative sample of this grantmaker's funding activity:
$35,153 to World Relief, Baltimore, MD, 2010.
$30,000 to Taylor University, Fort Wayne, IN, 2010.
$25,000 to Youth for Christ, Fort Wayne, IN, 2010.
$10,000 to Advance America, Indianapolis, IN, 2010.
$7,200 to Samaritans Purse, Boone, NC, 2010.
$5,000 to Keystone Schools, Fort Wayne, IN, 2010. For general support.
$3,500 to Griffith Foundation for Insurance Education, Worthington, OH, 2010.
$2,800 to World Relief, Baltimore, MD, 2010.
$2,080 to Youth for Christ, Fort Wayne, IN, 2010.
$2,000 to Boy Scouts of America, Fort Wayne, IN, 2010.

589
Brown Brothers Harriman & Co.
(also known as BBH)
140 Broadway
New York, NY 10005-1101 (212) 483-1818

Company URL: http://www.bbh.com
Establishment information: Established in 1818.
Company type: Private company
Business activities: Operates commercial bank.
Business type (SIC): Banks/commercial
Corporate officers: Charles H. Schreiber, Sr. V.P., C.F.O., C.A.O., and Treas.; Jonathan D. Oestreich, Sr. V.P., Finance
Subsidiaries: Brown Brothers Harriman Trust Co. of New York, New York, NY; Brown Brothers Harriman Trust Co. of Texas, Dallas, TX
Offices: Palm Beach, FL; Chicago, IL; Boston, MA; Charlotte, NC; Philadelphia, PA
International operations: China; Hong Kong; Ireland; Japan; Luxembourg; Switzerland; United Kingdom
Giving statement: Giving through the Brown Brothers Harriman & Co. Undergraduate Fund.

The Brown Brothers Harriman & Co. Undergraduate Fund
140 Broadway
New York, NY 10005-1108

Establishment information: Established in 1964.
Donor: Brown Brothers Harriman & Co.
Financial data (yr. ended 07/31/11): Assets, $1,375,445 (M); expenditures, $62,895; qualifying distributions, $54,600; giving activities include $54,600 for grants.
Purpose and activities: The foundation awards college scholarships to children of employees of Brown Brothers Harriman & Co. The program is administered by Scholarship America, Inc.
Type of support: Employee-related scholarships.
Geographic limitations: Giving limited to areas of company operations.
Application information: Applications accepted. Application form required.
Initial approach: Proposal
Deadline(s): May 1
Officers and Trustees:* William Carter Sullivan III*, Chair.; Marla Barr, Secy.; Scott Clemons; Andrew Hofer; Maroa Velez; John Walsh.
EIN: 136169140

590
Brown Rudnick LLP
1 Financial Ctr.
Boston, MA 02111 (212) 209-4800

Company URL: http://www.brownrudnick.com
Establishment information: Established in 1948.
Company type: Private company
Business activities: Operates law firm.
Business type (SIC): Legal services
Financial profile for 2008: Number of employees, 350
Corporate officers: Joseph F. Ryan, C.E.O.; Elizabeth M. Hurley, C.A.O.
Offices: Hartford, CT; Washington, DC; Boston, MA; New York, NY; Providence, RI
International operations: Ireland; United Kingdom
Giving statement: Giving through the Brown Rudnick LLP Corporate Giving Program and the Brown Rudnick Charitable Foundation Corporation.

Brown Rudnick LLP Corporate Giving Program
1 Financial Ctr.
Boston, MA 02111-2600 (617) 856-8200
FAX: (617) 856-8201;
E-mail: awallis@brownrudnick.com; Contact for Pro Bono program: Albert Wallis, Exec. Dir., Ctr. for Public Interest, tel.: (617) 856-8119, fax: (617) 856-8201, e-mail: awallis@brownrudnick.com; URL: http://www.brownrudnickcenter.com/involvement

Contact: Albert Wallis, Exec. Dir., Brown Rudnick Center for the Public Interest
Purpose and activities: As a complement to its foundation, Brown Rudnick also makes charitable contributions to nonprofit organizations directly.
Fields of interest: Legal services; General charitable giving.
Type of support: Employee volunteer services; General/operating support; Pro bono services - legal.

Brown Rudnick Charitable Foundation Corporation
1 Financial Ctr.
Boston, MA 02111-2621 (617) 856-8200
FAX: (617) 856-8201;
E-mail: awallis@brownrudnick.com; URL: http://www.brownrudnickcenter.com/foundation/

Establishment information: Established in 2000 in MA.
Contact: Albert W. Wallis, Exec. Dir.
Financial data (yr. ended 12/31/11): Revenue, $159,740; assets, $1,582,246 (M); gifts received, $116,154; expenditures, $258,200; giving activities include $222,740 for grants.
Purpose and activities: The foundation's mission is to improve inner-city education in the communities in which the law firm of Brown Rudnick has its offices.
Fields of interest: Education Economically disadvantaged.
Programs:
Community Grants: These are small grants, capped at $2,000, designed to address a one-time, tangible, immediate need. The purposes of the program are to simultaneously encourage those involved broadly with the Brown Rudnick Center for the Public Interest to actively think about the educational needs in the communities the served by the foundation; recognize, encourage and collaborate with front-line workers within the educational system who often do not have a voice in funding decisions; and provide funding to assist with small, concrete projects or needs which will make an improvement in inner city education in communities served by the foundation.
Relationship Grants: The program seeks to improve inner-city education by developing a relationship with a nonprofit organization that includes providing financial support, pro bono legal representation, and volunteer time. Grants are awarded annually to organizations for the purpose of addressing the educational needs of less-enfranchised individuals and groups within the geographic boundaries of Boston, MA; Hartford, CT; New York City; Washington, DC; and/or Providence, RI. Proposals may be in any amount between $5,000 and $50,000 each (a project encompassing more than one city may exceed this amount up to a total of $75,000).
Type of support: Building/renovation; Curriculum development; Equipment; Film/video/radio; General/operating support; In-kind gifts; Internship funds; Management development/capacity building; Program development; Program evaluation; Publication.
Geographic limitations: Giving limited to Hartford, CT; Washington, DC; Boston, MA; New York, NY; and Providence, RI.
Support limitations: No grants for sponsorship of a fundraising or table event.
Publications: Application guidelines; Grants list; Informational brochure; Newsletter.
Application information: Applications accepted. Application form required.
Initial approach: Complete proposal form for Relationship Grants; complete online application for Community Grants
Board meeting date(s): Monthly
Deadline(s): Varies for Relationship Grants; applications considered on a monthly basis for Community Grants
Officers and Directors:* Joseph Ryan*, Chair.; Jeffery Jonas, Pres.; Catherine Gardner, V.P.; Henry W. Men, III, V.P.; Michael J. Camilleri, Treas.; Douglas A. Cohen, Clerk; Albert W. Wallis, Exec. Dir.; Daniel Brown; Mary D. Bucci; Wayne Dennison; and 8 additional directors.
EIN: 043527056

591
Brown Shoe Company, Inc.
(formerly Brown Group, Inc.)
8300 Maryland Ave.
P.O. Box 29
St. Louis, MO 63105-3693 (314) 854-4000
FAX: (314) 854-4274

Company URL: http://www.brownshoe.com
Establishment information: Established in 1878.
Company type: Public company
Company ticker symbol and exchange: BWS/NYSE
Business activities: Operates shoe stores; sells footwear wholesale.
Business type (SIC): Shoe stores; leather footwear; apparel, piece goods, and notions—wholesale
Financial profile for 2013: Number of employees, 14,100; assets, $1,171,260,000; sales volume, $2,598,070,000; pre-tax net income, $38,550,000; expenses, $2,536,460,000; liabilities, $746,130,000
Fortune 1000 ranking: 2012—788th in revenues, 856th in profits, and 952nd in assets
Corporate officers: Ronald A. Fromm, Chair.; Diane M. Sullivan, Pres. and C.E.O.; Mark Schmitt, C.I.O.; Russ Hammer, Sr. V.P. and C.F.O.; Michael I. Oberlander, Sr. V.P., Genl. Counsel, and Secy.
Board of directors: Ronald A. Fromm, Chair.; Mario L. Baeza; Mahendra Gupta; Carla Hendra; Ward M. Klein; Steven W. Korn; Patricia G. McGinnis; W. Patrick McGinnis; Michael F. Neidorff; Diane M. Sullivan; Hal J. Upbin; Harold B. Wright
Subsidiaries: Brown Group Retail, Inc., Madison, WI; Pagoda Trading North America, Inc., St. Louis, MO
International operations: Brazil; British Virgin Islands; Canada; Cayman Islands; Hong Kong; Ireland; Italy; Macau
Giving statement: Giving through the Brown Shoe Company, Inc. Charitable Trust.
Company EIN: 430197190

Brown Shoe Company, Inc. Charitable Trust
(formerly Brown Group, Inc. Charitable Trust)
8300 Maryland Ave.
St. Louis, MO 63105-3693
FAX: (314) 854-4205; URL: http://www.brownshoe.com/contact/charitable.asp

Establishment information: Trust established in 1951 in MO.
Donors: Brown Group, Inc.; Brown Shoe Co., Inc.
Financial data (yr. ended 12/31/11): Assets, $2,493,756 (M); expenditures, $1,288,169; qualifying distributions, $1,267,272; giving activities include $1,254,512 for 101 grants (high: $303,500; low: $100).
Purpose and activities: The foundation supports organizations involved with arts and culture, education, health, human services, and civic affairs.
Fields of interest: Arts councils; Media, television; Museums (art); Performing arts, theater; Performing arts, orchestras; Arts; Elementary/secondary education; Higher education; Education; Hospitals (general); Health care, clinics/centers; Health care; Cancer; Boy scouts; Youth development, business; YM/YWCAs & YM/YWHAs; Human services; United Ways and Federated Giving Programs; Jewish federated giving programs; Public affairs.
Program:
Employee Matching Gifts: The foundation matches contributions made by full-time employees and directors of Brown Shoe Company to institutions of higher education, art museums, performing art groups, historical societies, science museums, libraries, art groups, and public radio and television stations on a two-for-one basis from $50 to $2,500 per contributor, per year.
Type of support: Annual campaigns; Capital campaigns; Continuing support; General/operating support; Program development.
Geographic limitations: Giving limited to areas of major company operations, with emphasis on St. Louis, MO.
Support limitations: No support for private foundations, organizations primarily funded by state or federal taxes, fraternal organizations, political or advocacy groups, organizations located outside of the U.S. operating primarily in the U.S., international charities, religious organizations not of direct benefit to the entire community, pass-through organizations, or United Way-supported organizations. No grants to individuals, or for endowments, special projects, research, publications, or conferences; no loans.
Publications: Application guidelines.
Application information: Applications accepted. Application form not required. Applicants should submit the following:
1) copy of IRS Determination Letter
2) brief history of organization and description of its mission
3) listing of board of directors, trustees, officers and other key people and their affiliations
4) detailed description of project and amount of funding requested
5) copy of current year's organizational budget and/or project budget

Initial approach: Proposal
Copies of proposal: 1
Board meeting date(s): Every 2 months
Deadline(s): None
Final notification: 1 to 3 months

Officer and Directors: Ronald A. Fromm, Chair.; Bill Berberich; Ann Joos; Michael Oberlander.
Trustee: SunTrust Bank.
EIN: 237443082
Selected grants: The following grants are a representative sample of this grantmaker's funding activity:
$16,500 to American Heart Association, Dallas, TX, 2011. For general charitable purpose.
$2,500 to American Liver Foundation, New York, NY, 2011. For general charitable purpose.
$2,500 to Boys Hope Girls Hope, Bridgeton, MO, 2011. For general charitable purpose.
$2,500 to University of Chicago, Chicago, IL, 2011. For general charitable purpose.

592
Brown-Forman Corporation

850 Dixie Hwy.
Louisville, KY 40210-1038 (502) 585-1100
FAX: (502) 774-6633

Company URL: http://www.brown-forman.com
Establishment information: Established in 1870.
Company type: Public company
Company ticker symbol and exchange: BF.B/NYSE
International Securities Identification Number: US1156372096
Business activities: Operates holding company; manufactures and markets consumer products.
Business type (SIC): Holding company
Financial profile for 2012: Number of employees, 4,000; assets, $3,500,000,000; sales volume, $2,400,000,000; pre-tax net income, $760,000,000; expenses, $1,935,000,000; liabilities, $1,408,000,000
Fortune 1000 ranking: 2012—767th in revenues, 329th in profits, and 704th in assets
Forbes 2000 ranking: 2012—1707th in sales, 1244th in profits, and 1906th in assets
Corporate officers: Garvin Brown, IV, Co-Chair.; Paul C. Varga, Co-Chair. and C.E.O.; James S. Welch, Jr., Vice-Chair.; Mark McCallum, Exec. V.P. and C.O.O.; Donald C. Berg, Exec. V.P. and C.F.O.; Matthew E. Hamel, Exec. V.P., Genl. Counsel, and Secy.; Lisa Steiner, Sr. V.P., Human Resources
Board of directors: George Garvin Brown IV, Co-Chair.; Paul C. Varga, Co-Chair.; James S. Welch, Jr., Vice-Chair.; Joan Amble; Patrick Bousquet-Chavanne; Martin S. Brown, Jr.; Bruce L. Byrnes; John D. Cook; Sandra A. Frazier; William E. Mitchell; Dace Brown Stubbs
Subsidiaries: Brown-Forman Beverage Worldwide, Louisville, KY; Brown-Forman Enterprises, Louisville, KY; Brown-Forman International Ltd., Louisville, KY; Dansk, Gorham, and Kirk Stieff, Mount Kisco, NY; Hartmann Luggage and Leather Goods Group, Lawrenceville, NJ; Lenox, Inc., Lawrenceville, NJ; Lenox China and Crystal, Lawrenceville, NJ; Lenox Collections, Langhorne, PA; Lenox Manufacturing, Lawrenceville, NJ; Lenox Merchandising, Lawrenceville, NJ; Lenox Tabletop Group, Lawrenceville, NJ
Giving statement: Giving through the Brown-Forman Corporation Contributions Program.
Company EIN: 610143150

Brown-Forman Corporation Contributions Program

850 Dixie Hwy.
Louisville, KY 40210-1038 (502) 585-1100
FAX: (502) 774-7189

Contact: Lois Mateus
Purpose and activities: Brown-Forman makes charitable contributions to nonprofit organizations involved with arts and culture, education, the environment, housing, and civic affairs. Support is given primarily in areas of company operations.
Fields of interest: Arts; Education; Environment; Housing/shelter; Public affairs.
Type of support: Employee matching gifts; General/operating support; In-kind gifts.
Geographic limitations: Giving primarily in areas of company operations, with emphasis on Louisville, KY.
Application information: Proposals should be submitted using organization letterhead. Application form not required. Applicants should submit the following:
1) copy of IRS Determination Letter

Initial approach: Proposal to headquarters
Committee meeting date(s): Bi-monthly
Deadline(s): 4-6 months prior to need

593
Brownstein Hyatt Farber Schreck, LLP

410 17th St., Ste. 2200
Denver, CO 80202-4432 (303) 223-1100

Company URL: http://www.bhfs.com
Establishment information: Established in 1968.
Company type: Private company
Business activities: Operates law firm.
Business type (SIC): Legal services
Corporate officers: Norman Brownstein, Chair.; Blane R. Prescot, C.E.O.; Steven W. Farber, Pres.; Dean A. Nakayama, C.O.O.
Board of director: Norman Brownstein, Chair.
Offices: Phoenix, AZ; Los Angeles, Sacramento, San Clemente, San Diego, Santa Barbara, CA; Denver, CO; Washington, DC; Las Vegas, Reno, NV; Albuquerque, Santa Fe, NM
Giving statement: Giving through the Brownstein Hyatt Farber Schreck, LLP Pro Bono Program.

Brownstein Hyatt Farber Schreck, LLP Pro Bono Program

410 17th St., Ste. 2200
Denver, CO 80202-4432 (303) 223-1100
FAX: (303) 223-1111; E-mail: hfarbes@bhfs.com; URL: http://www.bhfs.com/Careers/Associates/ProBono

Contact: Lauren Schmidt Farber Jr, Pro Bono Partner
Fields of interest: Legal services.
Type of support: Pro bono services - legal.
Geographic limitations: Giving primarily in areas of company operations in Phoenix, AZ, Sacramento, San Clemente, San Diego, and Santa Barbara, CA, Denver, CO, Washington, DC, Albuquerque, and Santa Fe, NM, Las Vegas, and Reno, NV.
Application information: A Pro Bono Committee manages the pro-bono program.

594
G.L. Bruno Associates Inc.

(also known as Bruno Enterprises, Inc.)
855 M St., Ste. 1010
Fresno, CA 93721-2753 (559) 454-7744

Company URL: http://www.glbruno.com/
Establishment information: Established in 1978.
Company type: Private company
Business activities: Operates real estate development company.
Business type (SIC): Real estate subdividers and developers
Corporate officers: Gary L. Bruno, Pres. and C.E.O.; Cynthia B. Wynkoop, C.O.O.; Stacy Saenz, C.F.O.; Helen Martinez, Cont.
Giving statement: Giving through the G. L. Bruno Foundation.

G. L. Bruno Foundation
855 M St., 10th Fl.
Fresno, CA 93721-2753
URL: http://www.glbrunofamily.org

Establishment information: Established in 1995 in CA.
Donor: G.L. Bruno Assocs., Inc.
Financial data (yr. ended 12/31/11): Assets, $7,492 (M); gifts received, $3,400; expenditures, $74,726; qualifying distributions, $48,300; giving activities include $48,300 for grants.
Fields of interest: Health care; Health organizations.
Support limitations: No grants to individuals.
Application information: Applications not accepted. Unsolicited requests for funds not accepted.
Officer: Gary L. Bruno, Pres.
EIN: 770419307

595
Brunswick Corporation
1 N. Field Ct.
Lake Forest, IL 60045-4811
(847) 735-4700
FAX: (847) 735-4765

Company URL: http://www.brunswick.com
Establishment information: Established in 1845.
Company type: Public company
Company ticker symbol and exchange: BC/NYSE
Business activities: Manufactures motor vehicle parts and engines, industrial machinery, recreational equipment, and defense and aerospace products.
Business type (SIC): Engines and turbines; aircraft and parts; ship and boat building and repair; guided missiles and space vehicles; games, toys, and sporting and athletic goods
Financial profile for 2012: Number of employees, 16,177; assets, $2,424,200,000; sales volume, $3,717,600,000; pre-tax net income, $181,000,000; expenses, $3,469,800,000; liabilities, $2,346,500,000
Fortune 1000 ranking: 2012—615th in revenues, 823rd in profits, and 810th in assets
Corporate officers: Dustan E. McCoy, Chair. and C.E.O.; William L. Metzger, Sr. V.P and C.F.O.; Alan L. Lowe, V.P. and Cont.; Kristin M. Coleman, V.P., Genl. Counsel, and Corp. Secy.; Randall S. Altman, V.P. and Treas.
Board of directors: Dustan E. McCoy, Chair.; Nolan D. Archibald; Anne E. Belec; Jeffrey L. Bleustein; Cambria W. Dunaway; David C. Everitt; Manuel A. Fernandez; Graham H. Phillips; Ralph C. Stayer; J. Steven Whisler; Roger J. Wood; Lawrence A. Zimmerman
Subsidiary: Igloo Holdings Inc., Houston, TX
Plant: Brookfield, WI
International operations: Belgium; Bermuda; Brazil; Canada; China; England; Finland; France; Germany; Hong Kong; Hungary; Italy; Mexico; Netherlands; Norway; Poland; Singapore; Wales
Giving statement: Giving through the Brunswick Foundation, Inc.
Company EIN: 360848180

The Brunswick Foundation, Inc.
1 N. Field Ct.
Lake Forest, IL 60045-4811 (847) 735-4344
FAX: (847) 735-4765; URL: http://www.brunswick.com/company/community/brunswickfoundation.php

Establishment information: Incorporated in 1957 in IL.
Donors: Brunswick Corp.; Peter N. Larson.
Contact: Judith P. Zelisko, Pres.
Financial data (yr. ended 12/31/11): Assets, $2,315,539 (M); gifts received, $120,000; expenditures, $337,127; qualifying distributions, $329,664; giving activities include $329,664 for 172 grants (high: $5,000; low: $500).
Purpose and activities: The foundation supports organizations involved with arts and culture, education, health, and welfare; and programs that promote boating, indoor recreation, fitness and related industry interests.
Fields of interest: Arts; Higher education; Education; Public health, physical fitness; Health care; Athletics/sports, water sports; Recreation; Boy scouts; Human services.
Programs:
Dollars for Doers Program: The foundation awards grants to nonprofit organizations for which an individual employee or group of employees has completed volunteer work. Individuals grants range from $50 to $150 and group volunteer grants range up to $1,000.
Sons & Daughters Scholarship Program: The foundation awards single-year scholarships of up to $2,500 to high school seniors and college freshman, sophomores, and juniors who are children of Brunswick employees to attend a college, university, or vocational school. Scholarships are awarded based on academic record, achievement test scores, and leadership abilities as demonstrated by extracurricular activities, and work record.
The Dealer Sons & Daughters Scholarship Program: The foundation awards single-year college scholarships of up to $2,000 to high school seniors and college freshman, sophomores, and juniors who are children of Brunswick Dealers attend a college, university, or vocational school. Brunswick Deals must have achieved "Gold" or "Platinum" level status as determined by Brunswick Dealer Advantage.
Type of support: Building/renovation; Capital campaigns; Continuing support; Employee matching gifts; Employee volunteer services; Employee-related scholarships; General/operating support; Program development; Scholarship funds.
Geographic limitations: Giving primarily in areas of company operations.
Support limitations: No support for religious organizations, preschools, primary or secondary schools, fraternal orders, or veterans' or labor organizations. No grants to individuals (except for employee-related scholarships), or for endowments or capital campaigns, trips, tours, tickets, or advertising; no in-kind product or equipment donations.
Publications: Application guidelines.
Application information: Applications accepted. Common application forms are also accepted. Application form required. Applicants should submit the following:
1) how project will be sustained once grantmaker support is completed
2) population served
3) copy of IRS Determination Letter
4) brief history of organization and description of its mission
5) geographic area to be served
6) listing of board of directors, trustees, officers and other key people and their affiliations

Initial approach: Contact foundation for application form
Board meeting date(s): Quarterly
Deadline(s): None

Officers and Directors:* Judith P. Zelisko*, Pres.; B. Russell Lockridge*, V.P.; Marsha T. Vaughn, Secy.; William L. Metzger*, Treas.
Number of staff: 1 full-time professional.
EIN: 366033576
Selected grants: The following grants are a representative sample of this grantmaker's funding activity:
$5,000 to Southern Utah University, Cedar City, UT, 2009.
$5,000 to Syracuse University, Syracuse, NY, 2009.
$2,500 to Appalachian State University, Boone, NC, 2009.
$2,500 to Arizona State University, Tempe, AZ, 2009.
$2,500 to Bethel University, Saint Paul, MN, 2009.
$2,500 to Birmingham-Southern College, Birmingham, AL, 2009.
$2,500 to Bradley University, Peoria, IL, 2009.
$2,500 to Carson-Newman College, Jefferson City, TN, 2009.
$2,500 to Carson-Newman College, Jefferson City, TN, 2009.
$2,500 to Marquette University, Milwaukee, WI, 2009.

596
Bryan Cave LLP
1 Metropolitan Sq.
211 N. Broadway, Ste. 3600
Saint Louis, MO 63102-2750
(314) 259-2000

Company URL: http:///www.bryancave.com
Establishment information: Established in 1873.
Company type: Private company
Business activities: Operates law firm.
Business type (SIC): Legal services
Offices: Phoenix, AZ; Irvine, Los Angeles, San Francisco, CA; Washington, DC; Atlanta, GA; Chicago, Edwardsville, IL; Kansas City, Overland Park, KS; Jefferson City, Saint Louis, MO; New York, NY; Charlotte, NC; Dallas, TX
International operations: China; France; Germany; Hong Kong; Indonesia; Japan; Malaysia; Philippines; Singapore; Thailand; United Kingdom
Giving statement: Giving through the Bryan Cave LLP Pro Bono Program.

Bryan Cave LLP Pro Bono Program
1 Metropolitan Sq.
211 N. Broadway, Ste. 3600
Saint Louis, MO 63102-2750 (202) 508-6025
E-mail: dcschwartz@bryancave.com; URL: http://www.bryancave.com/bryancave/probono/

Contact: Daniel C. Schwartz, Partner
Fields of interest: Legal services.
Type of support: Pro bono services - legal.
Geographic limitations: Giving primarily in areas of company operations in Phoenix, AZ, Irvine, Los Angeles, and San Francisco, CA, Washington, DC, Atlanta, GA, Chicago, and Edwardsville, IL, Overland Park, KS, Jefferson City, Kansas City, and St. Louis, MO, Charlotte, NC, New York, NY, and Dallas, TX, and in China, France, Germany, Hong Kong, Indonesia, Japan, Malaysia, Philippines, Singapore, Thailand, and United Kingdom.
Application information: A Pro Bono Committee manages the pro-bono program.

597
BSA LifeStructures, Inc.

(formerly BSA Design, Inc.)
9365 Counselors Row
Indianapolis, IN 46240-6422
(317) 819-7878

Company URL: http://www.bsalifestructures.com
Establishment information: Established in 1975.
Company type: Private company
Business activities: Provides architectural and engineering services.
Business type (SIC): Engineering, architectural, and surveying services
Corporate officers: Samuel Reed, Chair.; Keith Smith, Pres.
Board of director: Samuel Reed, Chair.
Giving statement: Giving through the BSA LifeStructures Foundation Inc.

BSA LifeStructures Foundation Inc.

9365 Counselors Row, Ste. 120
Indianapolis, IN 46240-3809 (317) 819-7878
E-mail: kminx@bsals.com

Establishment information: Established in 2001 in IN.
Donors: BSA Design, Inc.; BSA LifeStructures, Inc.
Contact: Donald B. Altemeyer, Dir.
Financial data (yr. ended 12/31/11): Assets, $31,753 (M); expenditures, $82,021; qualifying distributions, $80,000; giving activities include $80,000 for 3 grants (high: $50,000; low: $10,000).
Purpose and activities: The foundation supports organizations involved with arts and culture, higher education, medical education, and health.
Fields of interest: Arts; Higher education; Medical school/education; Hospitals (general); Health care.
Type of support: Capital campaigns; General/operating support; Scholarship funds.
Geographic limitations: Giving primarily in Indianapolis, IN.
Application information: Applications accepted. Application form required. Applicants should submit the following:
1) detailed description of project and amount of funding requested
Initial approach: Proposal
Board meeting date(s): Nov.
Deadline(s): Dec. 1
Directors: Donald B. Altemeyer; Monte L. Hoover; Shawn P. Mulholland.
EIN: 300007233

598
Steve Bubalo Construction Company, Inc.

128 Live Oak Ave.
Monrovia, CA 91016-5050 (626) 574-7570

Establishment information: Established in 1960.
Company type: Private company
Business activities: Provides general contract underground utility construction services.
Business type (SIC): Construction/miscellaneous heavy
Corporate officers: Steve Bubalo, C.E.O.; John C. Schiller, Pres.; Louise Esther Bubalo, Secy.-Treas.
Giving statement: Giving through the Bubalo Family Foundation.

Bubalo Family Foundation

P.O. Box 1048
Monrovia, CA 91017-1048 (626) 574-7570

Establishment information: Established in 1992 in CA.
Donors: Steve Bubalo Construction Co., Inc.; S.L.S. & N., Inc.; Steve Bubalo; Louise Bubalo.
Contact: Louise Bubalo, V.P. and Treas.
Financial data (yr. ended 12/31/11): Assets, $92,649 (M); expenditures, $7,405; qualifying distributions, $6,100; giving activities include $6,100 for grants.
Purpose and activities: The foundation supports organizations involved with education, health, international relief, and Catholicism.
Fields of interest: Education; Health care; Human services.
International interests: Croatia.
Type of support: General/operating support; Scholarship funds.
Application information: Applications accepted. Proposals or brochure should list applicant's tax exempt number. Application form required. Applicants should submit the following:
1) copy of IRS Determination Letter
Initial approach: Proposal or brochure
Deadline(s): None
Officers: Steve Bubalo, Pres.; Louise Bubalo, V.P. and Treas.
EIN: 954353411

599
Buccaneer L.P.

(also known as Tampa Bay Buccaneers)
1 Buccaneer Pl.
Tampa, FL 33607 (813) 870-2700

Company URL: http://www.buccaneers.com
Establishment information: Established in 1974.
Company type: Private company
Business activities: Operates professional football club.
Business type (SIC): Commercial sports
Corporate officers: Bryan Glazer, Co-Chair.; Edward Glazer, Co-Chair.; Joel Glazer, Co-Chair.; Malcolm Glazer, Pres.; Brian Ford, C.O.O.; Joe Fada, C.F.O.
Board of directors: Bryan Glazer, Co-Chair.; Edward Glazer, Co-Chair.; Joel Glazer, Co-Chair.
Giving statement: Giving through the Tampa Bay Buccaneers Corporate Giving Program, the Glazer Family Foundation, Inc., and the Tampa Bay Buccaneers Charities, Inc.

Tampa Bay Buccaneers Corporate Giving Program

c/o Community Rels.
Donation Requests
One Buccaneer Pl.
Tampa, FL 33607
URL: http://web2.buccaneers.com/community/donation-requests

Purpose and activities: As a complement to its foundation, the Tampa Bay Buccaneers also make charitable donations of memorabilia to nonprofit organizations directly, for use in charitable fundraising events. Giving limited to Charlotte, Citrus, De Soto, Hardee, Hernando, Highlands, Hillsborough, Lake, Manatee, Marion, Orange, Osceola, Pasco, Pinellas, Polk, Sarasota, Seminole, and Sumter counties, Florida.
Fields of interest: General charitable giving.
Type of support: Donated products; In-kind gifts.
Geographic limitations: Giving limited to Charlotte, Citrus, De Soto, Hardee, Hernando, Highlands, Hillsborough, Lake, Manatee, Marion, Orange, Osceola, Pasco, Pinellas, Polk, Sarasota, Seminole, and Sumter counties, FL.
Support limitations: Generally no donations for fundraisers to benefit individuals or families.
Publications: Application guidelines.
Application information: Applications accepted. Memorabilia requests submitted via form letter, fax, or e-mail are not accepted. Proposals must be submitted by mail using organization letterhead. Fan merchandise for the purpose of autographing is not accepted and will be returned. Support is limited to 1 contribution per organization during any given year. Requests for player appearances must be submitted separately. The Community Relations Department handles giving. Applicants should submit the following:
1) name, address and phone number of organization
2) copy of IRS Determination Letter
3) contact person
Giving limited to charitable organizations that provide direct service to clients, are located in the specified counties or have an affiliate there that retains all generated funds, and hold a Florida Consumer Certificate of Exemption. Proposals must contain the date of the event, the type of fundraiser, and where the proceeds go.
Initial approach: Mail proposal to headquarters for memorabilia requests; Complete online application form for player, coach, or representative appearance requests
Deadline(s): 8 to 10 weeks prior to event for memorabilia; 6 weeks prior to event for appearances
Final notification: Up to one week prior to event for appearance requests that will be fulfilled

Glazer Family Foundation, Inc.

c/o Coord.
1 Buccaneer Pl.
Tampa, FL 33607-5701 (813) 870-2700
E-mail: GlazerFamilyFoundation@buccaneers.nfl.com; URL: http://www.glazerfamilyfoundation.com/

Establishment information: Established in 1999 in FL.
Donors: Buccaneer L.P.; Florida Sports Foundation.
Financial data (yr. ended 12/31/11): Assets, $11,522 (M); gifts received, $2,993,285; expenditures, $2,995,080; qualifying distributions, $2,923,423; giving activities include $2,923,423 for grants.
Purpose and activities: The foundation supports programs designed to serve disadvantaged youth and families; and supports positive social and economic development within the community.
Fields of interest: Museums; Libraries (public); Education, reading; Education; Hospitals (general); Health care, clinics/centers; Optometry/vision screening; Health care, patient services; Health care; Food services; Safety/disasters; Athletics/sports, amateur leagues; Athletics/sports, football; Recreation; Children/youth, services; Human services; Community/economic development Youth; Economically disadvantaged.

Programs:

Buc-Packs for Back-To-School: The foundation provides backpacks filled with school supplies and Buccaneers merchandise to youth organizations located in Marion, Citrus, Lake, Sumter, Hernando, Orange, Seminole, Pasco, Polk, Osceola, Hillsborough, Pinellas, Manatee, Hardee, Highlands, De Soto, Sarasota and Charlotte counties, Florida.

Cheering You On: The foundation provides pediatric patients admitted to eight hospitals located in Hillsborough, Orange, and Pinellas Counties with a Tampa Bay Buccaneers stuffed teddy bear and activity book.

Gameday for Kids: Through Gameday for Kids, the foundation hosts children who attend nonprofit programs in Central Florida area at Tampa Bay Buccaneers home games. Selected children are rewarded for academic achievement and positive behavior. The program includes reserved seating, food vouchers, and Buccaneers battle flags to cheer on the team.

Grant Program: The foundation biannually awards grants of up to $5,000 to programs designed to address the welfare of disadvantaged children and their families. Special emphasis is directed toward programs designed to promote health; safety; recreation; and education.

Holiday Shopping Spree: The foundation annually sponsors a holiday shopping spree for disadvantaged children at Target store in Tampa, Florida. The program is administered in partnership with local nonprofit organizations like the Tampa Boys and Girls Club and Directions for Mental Health, where children from these programs are invited to Target before the store is open to the public. The event is also attended by Buccaneers staff, Captain Fear, cheerleaders, and the Buccaneers Women's Organization.

Make Reading Your Goal: The foundation provides area libraries with Buccaneer bookmarks to encourage reading among youth. Children receive a free bookmark when they check out a book from their local public library.

Vision Mobile: The foundation supports "Vision Mobile," a mobile unit that travels throughout Florida where certified doctors provide vision exams and prescription glasses to children from Title 1 schools at no charge. The program is limited to Hillsborough, Manatee, Pinellas, Pasco, Polk, Orange, Osceola, and Sarasota counties.

Type of support: Donated products; Equipment; In-kind gifts; Program development.

Geographic limitations: Giving primarily in Tampa Bay and central FL, with emphasis on Charlotte, Citrus, De Soto, Hardee, Hernando, Highlands, Hillsborough, Lake, Manatee, Marion, Orange, Osceola, Pasco, Pinellas, Polk, Sarasota, Seminole, Sumter counties.

Support limitations: No support for political organizations. No grants to individuals, or for fundraising, celebrations, administrative/training costs, capital campaigns, sponsorships, scholarships, basic research/conferences, or political campaigns.

Publications: Application guidelines; Program policy statement.

Application information: Applications accepted. Support is limited to 1 contribution per organization during any given year. Organizations receiving support are asked to provide a final report. Application form required. Applicants should submit the following:

1) statement of problem project will address
2) population served
3) copy of IRS Determination Letter
4) copy of most recent annual report/audited financial statement/990
5) how project's results will be evaluated or measured
6) explanation of why grantmaker is considered an appropriate donor for project
7) descriptive literature about organization
8) listing of board of directors, trustees, officers and other key people and their affiliations
9) detailed description of project and amount of funding requested

Initial approach: Complete online application form

Deadline(s): Sept. 1 to Nov. 1; May 4 to July 1 for Buc-Packs for Back-to-School and Gameday for Kids

Final notification: Within 1 month following deadlines; Aug. 1 for Buc-Packs for Back-to-School and Gameday for Kids

Officers and Directors: Darcie Glazer Kassewitz, Co-Pres.; Edward Glazer, Co-Pres.; Bryan Glazer; Joel Glazer.

EIN: 593578188

Selected grants: The following grants are a representative sample of this grantmaker's funding activity:

$1,000,000 to Cleveland Clinic, Cleveland, OH, 2010.
$6,093 to Childrens Home, Tampa, FL, 2010.
$4,675 to YMCA, Central Florida, Orlando, FL, 2010.
$4,573 to Pinellas Village, Largo, FL, 2010.
$3,049 to Spring of Tampa Bay, Tampa, FL, 2010.

600
Buchalter, Nemer, Fields, & Younger

1000 Wilshire Blvd., Ste. 1500
Los Angeles, CA 90017-2457
(213) 891-0700

Company URL: http://www.buchalter.com
Establishment information: Established in 1948.
Company type: Private company
Business activities: Provides legal services.
Business type (SIC): Legal services
Corporate officers: Stewart Buchalter, Chair.; Holly J. Fujie, Pres.
Board of directors: Stewart Buchalter, Chair.; Shawn M. Christianson
Offices: Newport Beach, San Francisco, CA
Giving statement: Giving through the Buchalter, Nemer, Fields, & Younger Charitable Foundation.

Buchalter, Nemer, Fields, & Younger Charitable Foundation

1000 Wilshire Blvd., Ste. 1500
Los Angeles, CA 90017-2457 (213) 891-0700

Establishment information: Trust established in 1965 in CA.
Donors: Buchalter, Nemer, Fields, & Younger; Irwin R. Buchalter; Murray M. Fields.
Contact: Urusla Bower
Financial data (yr. ended 12/31/11): Assets, $22,200 (M); expenditures, $10; qualifying distributions, $0.
Purpose and activities: The foundation supports organizations involved with television, human services, and women.
Fields of interest: Arts; Public affairs.
Type of support: General/operating support.
Support limitations: No grants to individuals, or for endowments, research, scholarships, or fellowships; no loans.
Application information: Applications accepted. Application form not required.

Initial approach: Proposal
Deadline(s): None

Trustees: Bernard Bollinger; Arthur Chinski; Shawn M. Christianson; Philip J. Wolman.
EIN: 956112980

601
Buckeye Diamond Logistics, Inc.

15 Sprague Rd.
P.O. Box E
South Charleston, OH 45368-9644
(937) 462-8361

Company URL: http://www.buckeyediamond.com/
Establishment information: Established in 1968.
Company type: Private company
Business activities: Manufactures wood pallets, plastic pallets, and packaging products.
Business type (SIC): Wood containers
Financial profile for 2010: Number of employees, 120
Corporate officers: Sam J. McAdow, Sr., Chair.; Samuel J. McAdow, Jr., C.E.O.; Ken Lachey, Pres.; Marianne Hinson, C.F.O.
Board of director: Sam J. McAdow, Sr., Chair.
Giving statement: Giving through the Sam and Carol McAdow Family Foundation.

Sam and Carol McAdow Family Foundation

15 Sprague Rd.
South Charleston, OH 45368-9644
Application address: c/o Beth Sullivan, 4802 Macallan Ct. E., Dublin, OH 43017-8288, tel.: (614) 792-6216

Establishment information: Established in 2001 in OH.
Donors: Sam McAdow; Carol McAdow; McAdow Investment Group; Buckeye Diamond Logistics, Inc.
Financial data (yr. ended 12/31/11): Assets, $272,381 (M); expenditures, $21,164; qualifying distributions, $14,575; giving activities include $14,575 for grants.
Purpose and activities: The foundation supports organizations involved with cancer, Alzheimer's disease, cleft lip and palate, human services, and Christianity.
Fields of interest: Education; Health care; Human services.
Type of support: General/operating support.
Geographic limitations: Giving primarily in OH.
Support limitations: No grants to individuals, or to organizations lacking 501 (c)(3) status.
Application information: Applications accepted. Application form required. Applicants should submit the following:

1) detailed description of project and amount of funding requested
2) descriptive literature about organization
3) listing of additional sources and amount of support

Initial approach: Proposal
Deadline(s): None

Officers: Carol B. McAdow, Pres.; John M. McAdow, V.P.; Michael R. McAdow, V.P.; Samuel J. McAdow, V.P.; Elizabeth M. Sullivan, Secy.; Samuel James McAdow, Treas.
EIN: 311779858

602
Buckley Associates, Inc.

385 King St.
Hanover, MA 02339-2447 (781) 878-5000

Company URL: http://www.buckleyonline.com/
Establishment information: Established in 1970.
Company type: Private company

Business activities: Manufactures and distributes, heating, ventilation, and air conditioning products.
Business type (SIC): Hardware, plumbing, and heating equipment—wholesale
Corporate officers: Robert L. Buckley II, Co-Pres.; Al Madison, Co-Pres.; Kevin Reynolds, C.I.O.; Susan J. Mielbye, Secy.
Giving statement: Giving through the Buckley Charitable Trust.

Buckley Charitable Trust

385 King St.
P.O. Box 1411
Hanover, MA 02339-1010 (781) 878-5000

Establishment information: Established in 1985 in MA.
Donor: Buckley Associates, Inc.
Contact: Susan J. Mielbye, Tr.
Financial data (yr. ended 11/30/12): Assets, $21,225 (M); gifts received, $5,000; expenditures, $4,257; qualifying distributions, $3,000; giving activities include $3,000 for 4 grants (high: $1,000; low: $500).
Fields of interest: Education.
Type of support: Scholarship funds.
Geographic limitations: Giving primarily in MA.
Support limitations: No grants to individuals.
Application information: Applications accepted. Application form required.
Initial approach: Proposal
Deadline(s): None
Trustees: Robert L. Buckley II; Susan J. Mielbye.
EIN: 046553587

603
Buckleysandler LLP

1250 24th St. N.W., Ste. 700
Washington, DC 20037-1222
(202) 349-8000

Company URL: http://www.buckleysandler.com
Establishment information: Established in 2003.
Company type: Private company
Business activities: Operates law firm.
Business type (SIC): Legal services
Financial profile for 2012: Number of employees, 150
Corporate officers: Emily Barry, C.F.O.; James Dillon, C.I.O.
Giving statement: Giving through the BuckleySandler LLP Pro Bono Program.

BuckleySandler LLP Pro Bono Program

1250 24th St., N.W., Ste. 700
Washington, DC 20037-1222 (202) 349-8000
E-mail: sschlatter@buckleysandler.com;
URL: http://www.buckleysandler.com/the-firm/probono

Contact: Stephanie Schlatter, Pro Bono Coord.
Fields of interest: Legal services.
Type of support: Pro bono services - legal.

604
Budget Rent A Car System, Inc.

6 Sylvan Way, Ste. 1
Parsippany, NJ 07054-3826
(973) 496-3500

Company URL: https://www.budget.com
Establishment information: Established in 1958.
Company type: Subsidiary of a public company
Business activities: Operates car rental company.
Business type (SIC): Motor vehicle rentals and leasing
Corporate officers: Ronald L. Nelson, Chair. and C.E.O.; David B. Wyshner, Sr. Exec. V.P. and C.F.O.; Mark J. Servodidio, Exec. V.P. and C.A.O.; Michael K. Tucker, Exec. V.P. and Genl. Counsel; Gerard Insall, Sr. V.P. and C.I.O.
Board of director: Ronald L. Nelson, Chair.
Giving statement: Giving through the Budget Rent A Car System, Inc. Corporate Giving Program.

Budget Rent A Car System, Inc. Corporate Giving Program

6 Sylvan Way
Parsippany, NJ 07054 (973) 496-3500
URL: https://www.budget.com/budgetWeb/html/en/aboutus/companyinfo/responsibility.html

Purpose and activities: Budget Rent A Car makes charitable contributions to national organizations in areas of company operations.
Fields of interest: Community/economic development; General charitable giving.
Type of support: Donated products; General/operating support; In-kind gifts.
Geographic limitations: Giving primarily in areas of company operations.
Publications: Application guidelines.
Application information: Applications accepted. Application form required. Applicants should submit the following:
1) population served
2) name, address and phone number of organization
3) copy of IRS Determination Letter
4) brief history of organization and description of its mission
5) geographic area to be served
6) copy of most recent annual report/audited financial statement/990
7) list of company employees involved with the organization
8) explanation of why grantmaker is considered an appropriate donor for project
9) detailed description of project and amount of funding requested
10) contact person
11) copy of current year's organizational budget and/or project budget
12) listing of additional sources and amount of support
13) plans for acknowledgement

Applications should include the number of full-time staff members at the organization, the percent of the project cost that is being requested, past support from Budget or Avis and the organization's use of its services, if applicable, the type of vehicle requested and dates needed, the number of people served by the project, and the address of the nearest Budget location.
Initial approach: Complete online application

605
Budweiser of Columbia, Inc.

(also known as K W Associates, LLC)
825 Bluff Rd.
Columbia, SC 29201-4709 (803) 799-5490

Company URL: http://www.budweiser.com
Establishment information: Established in 1876.
Company type: Private company
Business activities: Sells beer wholesale.
Business type (SIC): Beer, wine, and distilled beverages—wholesale
Financial profile for 2010: Number of employees, 215
Corporate officer: Gene E. Williams, Pres. and C.E.O.
Giving statement: Giving through the Budweiser of Columbia and Greenville Foundation, Inc.

Budweiser of Columbia and Greenville Foundation, Inc.

(formerly Budweiser of Columbia, Anderson and Greenville Foundation, Inc.)
825 Bluff Rd.
Columbia, SC 29202-0684 (803) 799-5490
Application address: P.O. Box 684, Columbia, SC 29202-0684, tel.: 803-799-5490

Establishment information: Established in 1981.
Donors: Budweiser of Columbia, Inc.; Budweiser of Anderson, Inc.; Budweiser of Greenville, Inc.
Contact: James F. Kirkham, C.F.O. and Secy.-Treas.
Financial data (yr. ended 12/31/11): Assets, $1,144,434 (M); expenditures, $117,394; qualifying distributions, $105,286; giving activities include $105,286 for 27 grants (high: $17,000; low: $250).
Purpose and activities: The foundation supports arts councils and organizations involved with higher education and recreation.
Fields of interest: Arts; Education; Animals/wildlife.
Type of support: General/operating support.
Application information: Applications accepted. Application form required. Applicants should submit the following:
1) brief history of organization and description of its mission
Initial approach: Letter
Deadline(s): None
Officers: Gene E. Williams, Chair.; Rodney G. Williams, C.E.O.; James F. Kirkham, C.F.O. and Secy.-Treas.; Kelly English, Cont. and Exec. Dir.
EIN: 570734278

606
Buffalo Bills, Inc.

1 Bills Dr.
Orchard Park, NY 14127-2237
(716) 648-1800

Company URL: http://www.buffalobills.com
Establishment information: Established in 1960.
Company type: Private company
Business activities: Operates professional football club.
Business type (SIC): Commercial sports
Corporate officers: Russ Brandon, Pres. and C.E.O.; Marc Honan, Sr. V.P., Mktg.; Jeffrey C. Littmann, C.F.O.; Scott Berchtold, V.P., Comms.; P.J. Wright, Secy.; Frank Wojnicki, Cont.
Giving statement: Giving through the Buffalo Bills Inc. Corporate Giving Program and the Buffalo Bills Youth Foundation, Inc.

Buffalo Bills Inc. Corporate Giving Program

c/o Community Rels. Dept.
1 Bills Dr.
Orchard Park, NY 14127-2237
URL: http://www.buffalobills.com/community

Purpose and activities: As a complement to its foundation, the Buffalo Bills also make charitable contributions of memorabilia to nonprofit organizations directly. Support is given primarily in New York.
Fields of interest: General charitable giving.
Type of support: In-kind gifts; Loaned talent.
Geographic limitations: Giving primarily in NY, with emphasis on western NY.
Application information: Applications accepted. Application form not required. Applicants should submit the following:
1) name, address and phone number of organization
2) contact person
Proposals should indicate the date, time, length, and location of the event.
Initial approach: Proposal to headquarters
Copies of proposal: 1
Deadline(s): 4 to 6 weeks prior to need

Buffalo Bills Youth Foundation, Inc.

63 Kercheval Ave., Ste. 200
Grosse Pointe Farms, MI 48236-3652
Application address: 1 Bills Dr., Orchard Pk., NY 14127; URL: http://www.buffalobills.com/community/youth-foundation.html

Establishment information: Established in 1987 in NY.
Donors: Buffalo Bills Inc.; The Boston Beer Co.; Teammates for Kids Foundation; Jason Peters; NFL Charities; NFL Youth Football Fund; Marcel Dareus.
Contact: Gretchen Geitter
Financial data (yr. ended 12/31/11): Assets, $359,586 (M); gifts received, $150,070; expenditures, $272,188; qualifying distributions, $272,188; giving activities include $266,245 for 75 grants (high: $30,000; low: $500).
Purpose and activities: The foundation supports programs designed to promote education, health and fitness, and youth football. Special emphasis is directed toward programs designed to improve the lives of youth and young adults.
Fields of interest: Education; Public health, physical fitness; Athletics/sports, football Youth.
Type of support: Equipment; General/operating support; Program development; Research.
Geographic limitations: Giving primarily in western NY.
Support limitations: No grants to individuals, or for fund drives, or political campaigns.
Publications: Application guidelines.
Application information: Applications accepted. Proposals should be no longer than 3 pages. Application form required. Applicants should submit the following:
1) population served
2) copy of IRS Determination Letter
3) copy of most recent annual report/audited financial statement/990
4) listing of board of directors, trustees, officers and other key people and their affiliations
5) detailed description of project and amount of funding requested
6) copy of current year's organizational budget and/or project budget
7) listing of additional sources and amount of support
Initial approach: Download application form and mail proposal and application form to foundation
Copies of proposal: 1
Deadline(s): Mar. 31
Final notification: Within 3 months
Officers and Directors:* Ralph C. Wilson, Jr.*, Chair.; Mary M. Owen*, Pres. and Secy.; Jeffrey C. Littmann*, V.P. and Treas.
EIN: 161291395
Selected grants: The following grants are a representative sample of this grantmaker's funding activity:
$30,000 to American Heart Association, Amherst, NY, 2010.
$25,000 to United Way of Buffalo and Erie County, Buffalo, NY, 2010.
$16,400 to United Way of Buffalo and Erie County, Buffalo, NY, 2010.
$15,000 to Encompass Resources for Learning, Rochester, NY, 2010.
$15,000 to Gateway-Longview, Buffalo, NY, 2010.
$5,000 to Catholic Charities of Buffalo, Buffalo, NY, 2010.
$2,500 to Sheas OConnell Preservation Guild, Buffalo, NY, 2010.
$2,000 to Research Center for Stroke and Heart Disease, Buffalo, NY, 2010.
$1,500 to Erie County Society for the Prevention of Cruelty to Animals, Tonawanda, NY, 2010.
$1,500 to Lothlorien Therapeutic Riding Center, East Aurora, NY, 2010.

607
Bufftree Building Company, Inc.

193-R. Pope's Island
New Bedford, MA 02740-7252
(508) 997-5357

Company type: Private company
Business activities: Provides nonresidential general contract construction services.
Business type (SIC): Contractors/general nonresidential building
Corporate officer: Andrew Tillet, Pres.
Giving statement: Giving through the Bufftree Foundation.

The Bufftree Foundation

193-R Popes Island
New Bedford, MA 02740-7252

Establishment information: Established in 2002 in MA.
Donor: Bufftree Building Co., Inc.
Financial data (yr. ended 12/31/11): Assets, $5,360 (M); expenditures, $893; qualifying distributions, $0.
Purpose and activities: The foundation supports organizations involved with children and youth services.
Fields of interest: Human services.
Type of support: General/operating support.
Application information: Applications not accepted. Unsolicited requests for funds not accepted.
Officers: Andrew B. Tillet, Pres. and Clerk; Scott W. Costa, Treas.
Directors: Robert Baarsvik; Matthew J. Downey.
EIN: 043611908

608
Build-A-Bear Workshop, Inc.

1954 Innerbelt Business Center Dr.
St. Louis, MO 63114 (314) 423-8000
FAX: (302) 636-5454

Company URL: http://www.buildabear.com
Establishment information: Established in 1997.
Company type: Public company
Company ticker symbol and exchange: BBW/NYSE
Business activities: Operates teddy bear-themed retail stores.
Business type (SIC): Shopping goods stores/miscellaneous
Financial profile for 2011: Number of employees, 4,800; assets, $241,570,000; sales volume, $394,380,000; pre-tax net income, -$2,650,000; expenses, $397,030,000; liabilities, $112,330,000
Corporate officers: Mary Lou Fiala, Chair.; Maxine Clark, C.E.O.; Tina Klocke, C.O.O., C.F.O., Treas., and Secy.; Dave Finnegan, C.I.O.; Eric R. Fencl, Genl. Counsel
Board of directors: Mary Lou Fiala, Chair.; Maxine Clark; Barney A. Ebsworth; Mary Lou Fiala; James M. Gould; Virginia H. Kent; Louis M. Mucci; Coleman Peterson; Thomas Pinnau
Giving statement: Giving through the Build-A-Bear Workshop, Inc. Corporate Giving Program, the Build-A-Bear Workshop Bear Hugs Foundation, and the Build-A-Bear Workshop Foundation, Inc.
Company EIN: 431883836

Build-A-Bear Workshop, Inc. Corporate Giving Program

1954 Innerbelt Business Center Dr.
St. Louis, MO 63114
URL: http://www.buildabear.com/shopping/contents/content.jsp?catId=400002&id=700016&sc_hpan=footer&sc_hpdr=footer_veryright

Purpose and activities: Build-A-Bear Workshop makes charitable contributions of teddy bears and gift cards to schools and nonprofit organizations involved with animals, children, and families.
Fields of interest: Education; Animal welfare; Children, services; Family services.
Program:
Stuffed with Hugs: Since Stuffed with Hugs began in 2001, more than 325,000 donations have been made to community organizations around the world including children's hospitals, firefighters and police officers, the USO, UNICEF, Ronald McDonald House Charities, American Red Cross, children in foster and adoptive care organizations, children's health and wellness initiatives, children's literacy organizations, and humane education programs. Build-A-Bear Workshop also conducts Stuffed with Hugs events in response to natural disaster situations such as hurricanes and floods to bring children in need of a hug some special comfort.
Type of support: Donated products.
Geographic limitations: Giving on a national basis.
Support limitations: No grants for advertising or monetary donations.
Publications: Application guidelines.
Application information: Applications accepted. Application form required.
Initial approach: Complete online application

Build-A-Bear Workshop Bear Hugs Foundation

1954 Innerbelt Business Center Dr.
St. Louis, MO 63114-5760 (314) 423-8000
E-mail: giving@buildabear.com; URL: http://www.buildabear.com/shopping/contents/content.jsp?catId=400002&id=700013

Establishment information: Established in 2006 in MO.
Donors: Build-A-Bear Workshop, Inc.; Build-A-Bear Workshop Canada Ltd.
Financial data (yr. ended 12/31/11): Assets, $828,448 (M); gifts received, $543,174; expenditures, $165,143; qualifying distributions, $128,081; giving activities include $128,081 for 65 grants (high: $10,000; low: $400).
Purpose and activities: The foundation supports programs designed to promote health and wellness of children and families; care and welfare of animals; and literacy and education.
Fields of interest: Education, early childhood education; Education, special; Education, reading; Education; Animals/wildlife, public education; Animal welfare; Animals/wildlife, special services; Animals/wildlife; Health care; Pediatrics research; Medical research; Safety, education; Children, services Children.
International interests: Canada.
Programs:
Children's Health and Wellness: The foundation supports programs designed to make the world a healthier and happier place for kids. Special emphasis is directed toward childhood disease research, child safety, and children with special needs. The program is sponsored by the sale of Champ - A Champion Fur Kids, where one dollar from each sale is donated through the foundation to children health and wellness. Grants typically range from $1,000 to $10,000.
Domestic Pets: The foundation supports programs designed to support domestic animals including animal welfare, pet rescue and rehabilitation, and therapeutic and humane education pet initiatives. The program is sponsored by the sale of Bearemy's Kennel Pals where one dollar from each sale is donated through the foundation for domestic pets. Grants range from $1,000 to $10,000.
Literacy and Education: The foundation supports programs designed to promote children literacy and education. Special emphasis is directed toward summer reading programs, early childhood education, and literacy programs for children with special needs. The program is sponsored by the sale of Turner the Owl where $0.50 of each sale is donated through the foundation to literacy. Grants range from $1,000 to $10,000.
Type of support: General/operating support; Matching/challenge support; Program development; Research.
Geographic limitations: Giving on a national basis primarily in areas of company operations in CA, CO, KY, MN, MO, NJ, PA, and WI, and in Canada.
Support limitations: No support for private foundations, or for religious organizations not of direct benefit to the entire community, or political organizations. No grants for salaries for administrators, therapists, or medial personnel, professional development for staff, advertising, fuel for mobile clinics, research projects or experimental testing, capital campaigns, construction or "new facility" expense, fundraising or special events, or political activities; generally, no grants to individuals.
Publications: Application guidelines; Grants list; IRS Form 990 or 990-PF printed copy available upon request.
Application information: Applications accepted. Additional information may be requested at a later date. Support is limited to 1contribution per organization during any given year. Organizations receiving support may be asked to provide a final report. Application form required. Applicants should submit the following:
1) copy of IRS Determination Letter
2) copy of most recent annual report/audited financial statement/990
3) listing of board of directors, trustees, officers and other key people and their affiliations
4) copy of current year's organizational budget and/or project budget
Initial approach: Complete online application
Copies of proposal: 1
Deadline(s): Feb. 1 to Oct. 31; requests received after Sept. 1 will not be awarded until after Jan. 1
Final notification: 4 to 6 months
Officers and Directors:* Dorrie Krueger*, Pres.; Jill Saunders, V.P.; Teresa Kroll*, Secy.; Jeff Fullmer*, Treas.; Heather Barksdale; Bob Buer; Mike Early; Jennifer Guinn; Michael Segura.
EIN: 204961009
Selected grants: The following grants are a representative sample of this grantmaker's funding activity:
$5,000 to Arkansas Rice Depot, Little Rock, AR, 2010.
$5,000 to Cerebral Palsy Association of Chester County, Exton, PA, 2010.
$5,000 to Youth in Need, Saint Charles, MO, 2010.
$3,000 to Education Clinic, Inc., New York, NY, 2010.
$2,500 to Miracle Flights for Kids, Henderson, NV, 2010.
$2,000 to Colettes Childrens Home, Huntington Beach, CA, 2010.
$1,600 to Center for Mental Health, Great Falls, MT, 2010.
$1,500 to Humane Society, Ark-Valley, Buena Vista, CO, 2010.
$1,000 to Florence Crittenton Agency, Knoxville, TN, 2010.
$1,000 to Southern California Bulldog Rescue, Santa Ana, CA, 2010.

Build-A-Bear Workshop Foundation, Inc.

1954 Innerbelt Business Center Dr.
Saint Louis, MO 63114-5760 (314) 423-8000
E-mail: giving@buildabear.com; URL: http://www.buildabear.com/shopping/contents/content.jsp?catid=400002&id=700012

Establishment information: Established in 2003 in MO.
Donor: Build-A-Bear Workshop, Inc.
Contact: Maxine Clark, Pres.
Financial data (yr. ended 12/31/11): Revenue, $1,896,370; assets, $1,273,986 (M); gifts received, $1,893,344; expenditures, $1,215,075; giving activities include $1,165,383 for grants.
Purpose and activities: The foundation is committed to improving communities and impacting lives through meaningful philanthropic programs that support causes for children and families, including children's cancer research and treatment programs; promote literacy; preserve endangered animals and their habitats; and support local animal shelters.
Fields of interest: Animal welfare; Animals/wildlife, preservation/protection; Hospitals (specialty); Cancer research; Disasters, preparedness/services; Children, services; Family services Children.
Programs:
Bearemy's Kennel Pals Grants: These grants provide direct support for domestic pet programs, including animal welfare organizations, pet rescue and rehabilitation organizations, and therapeutic and humane education pet programs.
Champ-A Champion Fur Kids Grants: These grants provide direct support for children in the areas of health and wellness. Potential grantees include childhood disease research foundation, child safety organizations, and organizations that serve children with special needs.
Grants: Funding, ranging from $1,000 to $10,000, is available to support organizations that help children and families, animals, and the environment directly.
Huggable Heroes: A 'Huggable Hero' is a young person 18 years of age or under seeking to make a difference in their neighborhood, school, or community. Each year Build-A-Bear Workshop honors twelve 'Huggable Heroes' chosen from the U.S. and Canada for their outstanding community service.
Literacy and Education Grants: These grants provide support for children in literacy and education programs, such as summer reading programs, early childhood education programs, and literacy programs for children with special needs.
Geographic limitations: Giving on a national basis.
Publications: Application guidelines.
Application information: Applications accepted.
Initial approach: Submit application
Deadline(s): Feb., May, Aug., and Nov. for Literacy and Education Grants; Mar., June, Sept., and Dec. for Bearemy's Kennel Pals Grants; Apr., July, and Oct. for Champ-A Champion Fur Kids Grants; rolling basis for Grants
Officers: Maxine Clark, Pres.; Barry Erdos, V.P.; Tina Klocke, Secy.-Treas.
EIN: 331007188

609
Builders Incorporated

1081 S. Glendale
P.O. Box 20050
Wichita, KS 67208 (316) 684-1400

Company URL: http://www.buildersinc.com/
Establishment information: Established in 1941.
Company type: Private company
Business activities: Operates residential, commercial, and industrial real estate development company.
Business type (SIC): Real estate agents and managers
Corporate officer: Mike Garvey, Pres.
Giving statement: Giving through the Garvey Family Charitable Trust.

Garvey Family Charitable Trust

c/o Heritage Group LC
7309 E. 21st St., Ste. 120
Wichita, KS 67206-1178

Establishment information: Established in 1987 in KS.
Donor: Builders, Inc.
Financial data (yr. ended 12/31/11): Assets, $1,274,352 (M); gifts received, $72,000; expenditures, $106,868; qualifying distributions, $103,500; giving activities include $103,500 for grants.
Fields of interest: Recreation; Youth development; Human services.

Geographic limitations: Giving primarily in Wichita, KS.
Support limitations: No grants to individuals.
Application information: Applications not accepted. Unsolicited requests for funds not accepted.
Trustee: James W. Garvey.
EIN: 486283076

610
Building 19, Inc.

319 Lincoln St.
Hingham, MA 02043-1729 (781) 749-6900

Company URL: http://www.building19.com
Establishment information: Established in 1964.
Company type: Private company
Business activities: Operates general merchandise stores.
Business type (SIC): Merchandise stores/general
Corporate officers: Gerald Elovitz, Chair.; William Elovitz, Pres.; Wendy Linehan, V.P., Opers.; Donna J. Sweeney, V.P., Human Resources; Norman Greenberg, Secy.
Board of director: Gerald Elovitz, Chair.
Giving statement: Giving through the Building 19 Foundation.

Building 19 Foundation

319 Lincoln St.
Hingham, MA 02043-1729 (781) 749-6900
E-mail: Foundation@Building19.com; URL: http://www.building19.com/building19foundation/donations.htm

Establishment information: Established in 1989 in MA.
Donor: Building 19, Inc.
Contact: Judi Greenberg
Financial data (yr. ended 12/31/11): Assets, $788,886 (M); expenditures, $30,016; qualifying distributions, $3,946; giving activities include $3,946 for 6 grants (high: $2,571; low: $100).
Purpose and activities: The foundation supports organizations involved with education, health, diabetes, cancer, human services, community development, Judaism, and other areas.
Fields of interest: Secondary school/education; Education; Hospitals (general); Health care; Diabetes; Salvation Army; Children/youth, services; Human services; Community/economic development; Jewish agencies & synagogues; General charitable giving.
Type of support: Annual campaigns; General/operating support; Scholarship funds; Sponsorships.
Geographic limitations: Giving primarily in areas of company operations in MA.
Support limitations: No grants to individuals.
Publications: Application guidelines.
Application information: Applications accepted. Proposals should be submitted using organization letterhead. Application form required. Applicants should submit the following:
1) statement of problem project will address
2) copy of IRS Determination Letter
3) detailed description of project and amount of funding requested
Initial approach: Proposal
Board meeting date(s): Nov.
Deadline(s): None
Final notification: 30 days
Directors: Debra Elovitz; Elaine Elovitz; Gerald Elovitz.
EIN: 043064072

611
Buist Electric, Inc.

8650 Byron Center Ave. S.W.
Byron Center, MI 49315 (616) 878-3315

Company URL: http://www.buistelectric.com
Establishment information: Established in 1964.
Company type: Private company
Business activities: Provides general contract electrical services.
Business type (SIC): Contractors/electrical work
Corporate officers: Larry Buist, Pres. and C.E.O.; Cheryl Van Solkema, C.F.O.; Pete Westerhoff, Cont.
Giving statement: Giving through the Buist Foundation.

Buist Foundation

8650 Byron Center Ave. S.W.
Byron Center, MI 49315-9201 (616) 878-3315
URL: http://www.buistelectric.com/company_info/community/buist_foundation.php

Establishment information: Established as a company-sponsored operating foundation in 1998.
Donor: Buist Electric, Inc.
Contact: Brent Brinks, Pres.
Financial data (yr. ended 12/31/10): Assets, $128,297 (M); gifts received, $363,647; expenditures, $310,772; qualifying distributions, $304,554; giving activities include $99,606 for 31 grants (high: $28,000) and $204,948 for grants to individuals.
Purpose and activities: The foundation supports organizations involved with secondary education, health, housing, human services, and Christianity and awards grants to needy families.
Fields of interest: Secondary school/education; Education; Health care; Housing/shelter; Pregnancy centers; Human services; Christian agencies & churches.
Type of support: Continuing support; General/operating support; Grants to individuals; Scholarship funds.
Geographic limitations: Giving primarily in Grand Rapids, MI.
Publications: Application guidelines.
Application information: Applications accepted. Application form not required.
Initial approach: Proposal
Board meeting date(s): Monthly
Deadline(s): None
Officers and Directors: Brent Brinks, Pres.; Andy Vermunen, Secy.; Kathy Burgess; Aaron Cooper; Matt DeVries; Jim Etzinga; Dave Houseman; Cindy Meengs.
EIN: 383314509
Selected grants: The following grants are a representative sample of this grantmaker's funding activity:
$5,000 to South Christian High School, Grand Rapids, MI, 2010. For scholarship.
$3,000 to Lakeshore Pregnancy Center, Holland, MI, 2010. For ongoing support.
$2,252 to Alpha Womens Center, Grand Rapids, MI, 2010.
$2,100 to Pregnancy Resource Center, Grand Rapids, MI, 2010.
$2,000 to Health Intervention Services, Grand Rapids, MI, 2010.
$2,000 to Kalamazoo Gospel Mission, Kalamazoo, MI, 2010.
$2,000 to Other Way Ministries, Grand Rapids, MI, 2010.
$2,000 to Safe Haven Ministries, Grand Rapids, MI, 2010.
$1,000 to Kids Food Basket, Grand Rapids, MI, 2010.
$1,000 to Theological Book Network, Grand Rapids, MI, 2010.

612
Bunge North America, Inc.

11720 Borman Dr.
St. Louis, MO 63146-4129 (314) 292-2000

Company URL: http://www.bungenorthamerica.com
Establishment information: Established in 1818.
Company type: Subsidiary of a public company
Business activities: Imports and exports grain, castor oil, corn, processed fruits, and flavors; processes soybeans; sells food products wholesale.
Business type (SIC): Farm-product raw materials—wholesale; fats and oils; warehousing and storage
Financial profile for 2009: Number of employees, 4,749
Corporate officers: Soren W. Schroder, Pres. and C.E.O.; Todd A. Bastean, V.P. and C.F.O.; Chris Brunk, V.P. and C.I.O.; Geralyn F. Hayes, V.P., Human Resources
Subsidiaries: Bunge Edible Oil Corp., Bradley, IL; Lauhoff Grain Co., Danville, IN
Giving statement: Giving through the Bunge North America Foundation.

Bunge North America Foundation

(formerly Bunge Corporation Foundation)
11720 Borman Dr.
St. Louis, MO 63146-4129 (314) 292-2300

Establishment information: Established in 1993 in MO.
Donor: Bunge North America, Inc.
Contact: Geralyn F. Hayes
Financial data (yr. ended 12/31/11): Assets, $20,108 (M); gifts received, $850,000; expenditures, $801,063; qualifying distributions, $801,063; giving activities include $801,063 for grants.
Purpose and activities: The foundation supports organizations involved with arts and culture, education, the environment, and community development.
Fields of interest: Museums (art); Arts; Higher education; Education; Botanical gardens; Environment; Agriculture; Community/economic development; United Ways and Federated Giving Programs.
Program:
Employee-Matching Grants Program: The foundation matches contributions made by employees of Bunge North America to educational, cultural, and civic institutions on a one-for-one basis.
Type of support: Employee matching gifts; General/operating support; Program development; Sponsorships.
Geographic limitations: Giving primarily in areas of company operations, with emphasis on KS, MA, MO, and NY.
Support limitations: No grants to individuals.
Application information: Applications accepted. Application form not required. Applicants should submit the following:
1) copy of most recent annual report/audited financial statement/990
2) detailed description of project and amount of funding requested
Initial approach: Proposal
Deadline(s): None

Officers: Carl L. Hausmann, Pres.; Michael M. Scharf, Sr. V.P.; Philip W. Staggs, V.P.; David G. Kabbes, Secy.; John P. Gilsinn, Treas.; John E. Sabourin, Cont.
EIN: 431617648
Selected grants: The following grants are a representative sample of this grantmaker's funding activity:
$55,000 to Harvard University, Cambridge, MA, 2011.
$10,000 to Saint Louis Art Museum, Saint Louis, MO, 2011.
$5,000 to Saint Louis Symphony Orchestra, Saint Louis, MO, 2011.
$5,000 to Saint Louis Zoo, Saint Louis, MO, 2011.
$3,365 to Texas A & M University, College Station, TX, 2011.
$2,800 to YMCA of Greater Saint Louis, Saint Louis, MO, 2011.
$1,000 to Massachusetts Institute of Technology, Cambridge, MA, 2011.
$1,000 to Shakespeare Festival Saint Louis, Saint Louis, MO, 2011.

613
Burger King Holdings, Inc.

(formerly Burger King Corporation)
5505 Blue Lagoon Dr.
Miami, FL 33126-2029 (305) 378-3000

Company URL: http://www.burgerking.com
Establishment information: Established in 1954.
Company type: Subsidiary of a private company
Business activities: Operates fast-food restaurants.
Business type (SIC): Restaurants and drinking places; holding company
Financial profile for 2011: Number of employees, 35,020; assets, $5,770,000,000; sales volume, $2,330,000,000
Corporate officers: Alexandre Behring, Co-Chair.; John W. Chidsey, Co-Chair.; Bernardo Hees, C.E.O.; Daniel S. Schwartz, Exec. V.P. and C.F.O.
Board of directors: Alexandre Behring, Co-Chair.; John W. Chidsey, Co-Chair.
Giving statement: Giving through the Burger King Holdings, Inc. Contributions Program, the Burger King Scholars, Inc., and the Have it Your Way Foundation.
Company EIN: 753095469

Burger King Holdings, Inc. Contributions Program

(formerly Burger King Corporation Contributions Program)
5505 Blue Lagoon Dr.
Miami, FL 33126-2029 (305) 378-3000
URL: http://www.bk.com/en/us/company-info/corporate-responsibility/index.html

Purpose and activities: As a complement to its foundation, Burger King also makes charitable contributions to nonprofit organizations directly. Support is given primarily in areas of company operations, with emphasis on southern Florida.
Fields of interest: Elementary/secondary education; Big Brothers/Big Sisters; Youth development; Children, services.
Type of support: Employee volunteer services; General/operating support; In-kind gifts; Program development; Sponsorships.
Geographic limitations: Giving primarily in areas of company operations, with emphasis on southern FL.

Burger King Scholars, Inc.

910 Triangle St.
Blacksburg, VA 24060-7716
E-mail: burgerkingscholars@scholarshipamerica.org ; URL: http://www.haveityourwayfoundation.org/burger_king_scholars_program.html

Establishment information: Established in 2007 in VA.
Contact: Darlene Hodges
Financial data (yr. ended 06/30/12): Assets, $10,195 (M); expenditures, $700; qualifying distributions, $0; giving activities include $0 for grants to individuals.
Purpose and activities: The foundation awards scholarships to graduating high school seniors and Burger King restaurant employees in the U.S., Puerto Rico, and in Canada who are planning to pursue higher education.
International interests: Canada.
Type of support: Employee-related scholarships; Scholarships—to individuals.
Geographic limitations: Giving on a national and international basis primarily in areas of company operations in the U.S., Puerto Rico, and in Canada.
Publications: Application guidelines; Grants list.
Application information: Applications accepted. Application form required.
Applications should include a list of work experiences and involvement in school and community activities; a current transcript of grades; and employment information if your application is affiliated with a Burger King employee.
Initial approach: Proposal
Deadline(s): Dec. 15
Final notification: May
Officers: John Newcomb, Pres.; Peggy M. Meade, V.P.
EIN: 205136286

Have it Your Way Foundation

5505 Blue Lagoon Dr.
Miami, FL 33126-2029 (305) 378-3186
FAX: (305) 378-7017;
E-mail: BK_HIYWFoundation@whopper.com; E-Mail for Andrea M. Tejada : atejada@whopper.com; Tel. for Andrea M. Tejada : (305)-378-3183; Fax for Andrea M. Tejada : (305)-378-7017; URL: http://haveityourwayfoundation.org

Establishment information: Established in 2005 in FL.
Contact: Andrea M. Tejada, Exec. Dir.
Financial data (yr. ended 12/31/11): Revenue, $5,092,161; assets, $13,703,775 (M); gifts received, $3,099,778; expenditures, $2,275,922; giving activities include $1,264,422 for grants and $109,998 for grants to individuals.
Purpose and activities: The foundation supports organizations that alleviate hunger, prevent diseases and support youth programs. It also focuses on improving education and offering scholastic opportunity by providing grants to service organizations that have a mission of honoring students scholastic achievements and community efforts.
Fields of interest: Education; Youth development; Human services.
Program:
Burger King Scholars Program: Every year, this program helps graduating high school seniors build brighter futures. The awards ($1,000 each) are sponsored annually by the fundraising efforts of Burger King Corporation, Burger King franchisees, and restaurant guests in the United States, Canada, and Puerto Rico. Awards must be used for educational expenses, such as tuition or required fees and books, and must be used during the first year of college or post-secondary vocational/technical school.
Type of support: Grants to individuals.
Publications: Annual report; Newsletter.
Application information:
Initial approach: Online application
Officers: Jonathan Fitzpatrick, Co-Chair.; Steve Lewis, Co-Chair.; Jill Granat, Pres.; Lisa Giles-Klein, Secy.; Jackie Friesner, Treas.; Andrea M. Tejada, Exec. Dir.
Directors: Jerry Comstock; Ken Donahue; Glen Helton; James Joy; Steve Pattison; Robes St. Juste.
EIN: 061765327

614
Burger's Ozark Country Cured Hams Inc.

32819 Hwy. 87
California, MO 65018-3227 (573) 796-3134
FAX: (573) 796-3137

Company URL: http://www.smokehouse.com
Establishment information: Established in 1952.
Company type: Private company
Business activities: Produces prepared and specialty meats.
Business type (SIC): Meat packing plants and prepared meats and poultry
Corporate officers: Steven F. Burger, Pres.; Rodney J. Anderson, V.P., Sales
Giving statement: Giving through the E. M. Burger Memorial Foundation.

E. M. Burger Memorial Foundation

32819 Hwy. 87
California, MO 65018-9803
Application address: 205 Kelly, California, MO 65108

Establishment information: Established in 1974 in MO.
Donor: Burger Ozark Country Cured Hams.
Contact: Mary Keil, V.P.
Financial data (yr. ended 12/31/11): Assets, $1,290,378 (M); gifts received, $1,000; expenditures, $70,657; qualifying distributions, $68,199; giving activities include $68,199 for 38 grants (high: $24,241; low: $50).
Fields of interest: Arts; Education; Human services.
Geographic limitations: Giving primarily in MO.
Support limitations: No grants to individuals.
Application information: Applications accepted. Application form not required.
Initial approach: Proposal
Deadline(s): None
Officers: Robert E. Keil, Pres.; Mary K. Keil, V.P. and Treas.; Sara Rohrbach, Secy.
EIN: 237416312

615
Burke-Divide Electric Cooperative, Inc.

(also known as BDEC)
9549 Hwy. 5 W.
Columbus, ND 58727 (701) 939-6671

Company URL: http://www.bdec.coop
Establishment information: Established in 1945.
Company type: Cooperative
Business activities: Distributes electricity.

Business type (SIC): Electric services
Corporate officers: David Sigloh, Pres.; Lynn Jacobson, Secy.-Treas.
Board of directors: Jeff Dahlin; Kent Haugland; Lynn Jacobson; Kurt Koppelsloen; Steven Overlee; David Sigloh; Lane Titus
Plant: Kenmare, ND
Giving statement: Giving through the Burke-Divide Memorial Foundation.

Burke-Divide Memorial Foundation

P.O. Box 6
Columbus, ND 58727-0006 (701) 939-6671

Establishment information: Established in 2001.
Contact: Jason Brothen, Exec.Tr.
Financial data (yr. ended 12/31/10): Assets, $9,952 (M); gifts received, $130; expenditures, $112; qualifying distributions, $111; giving activities include $110 for 1 grant to an individual.
Purpose and activities: The foundation awards college scholarships to children of members of Burke-Divide Electric Cooperative.
Type of support: Scholarships—to individuals.
Geographic limitations: Giving primarily in ND.
Application information: Applications accepted. Application form required.
Submit a resume and statement of purpose.
Initial approach: Letter
Deadline(s): None
Trustees: Jason Brothen; Erin Fagerbakke; Iola Rosenquist; David Sigloh.
EIN: 456014666

616
Burlington Capital Group LLC

(formerly America First Companies)
1 Burlington Pl.
1004 Farnam St., Ste. 400
Omaha, NE 68102 (402) 444-1630

Company URL: http://www.burlingtoncg.com
Establishment information: Established in 1984.
Company type: Private company
Business activities: Operates investment bank.
Business type (SIC): Brokers and dealers/security
Corporate officers: Lisa Yanney Roskens, Chair., Pres., and C.E.O.; Mark A. Hiatt, C.O.O.; Timothy Francis, C.F.O.; Michael B. Yanney, Chair. Emeritus
Board of directors: Lisa Y. Roskens, Chair.; Mariann Byerwalter; William Carter; Patrick J. Jung; George H. Krauss; Martin A. Massengale; Gail Walling Yanney; Michael B. Yanney; Clayton K. Yeutter
Giving statement: Giving through the America First Foundation.

America First Foundation

1004 Farnam St., Ste. 400
Omaha, NE 68102-1885 (402) 444-1630
URL: http://www.am1stfoundation.org/index.html

Establishment information: Established in 2002 in NE.
Donors: America First Cos. L.L.C.; The Burlington Capital Group LLC.
Contact: Lisa Y. Roskens, Pres.
Financial data (yr. ended 12/31/11): Assets, $1,455,214 (M); expenditures, $327,326; qualifying distributions, $308,775; giving activities include $308,775 for 26 grants (high: $70,000; low: $1,000).
Purpose and activities: The foundation supports programs designed to promote arts and culture, education, senior care, and programs designed to promote strong family values.
Fields of interest: Arts; Higher education; Education; Animals/wildlife; Athletics/sports, amateur leagues; Recreation; Family services; Aging, centers/services.
Type of support: General/operating support.
Geographic limitations: Giving primarily in IA and NE; some giving to national organizations.
Support limitations: No support for national or religious organizations (unless their programs address specific local community needs), elementary or secondary schools (except to provide special initiatives or programs not covered by regular school budgets), political action or advocacy groups, organizations whose primary purpose is to support other non-profit organizations, fraternal groups, athletic teams, bands, veteran's organizations, volunteer firefighters, or similar groups. No grants to individuals, or for religious doctrines or tenets, endowments, golf events or fundraisers, or tables at fundraisers.
Publications: Application guidelines.
Application information: Applications accepted. Application form required. Applicants should submit the following:
1) name, address and phone number of organization
2) copy of IRS Determination Letter
3) brief history of organization and description of its mission
4) detailed description of project and amount of funding requested

Initial approach: Download application form and mail to foundation
Board meeting date(s): Third Thurs. of Mar., June, Sept. and Dec.
Deadline(s): 1 week before scheduled board meetings
Officers: Lisa Y. Roskens, Pres.; Michael J. Draper, Secy.-Treas.
Directors: Mark A. Hiatt; Michael B. Yanney.
EIN: 010658759

617
Burlington Coat Factory Warehouse Corporation

1830 Rte. 130 N.
Burlington, NJ 08016 (609) 387-7800

Company URL: http://
www.burlingtoncoatfactory.com
Establishment information: Established in 1924.
Company type: Subsidiary of a private company
Business activities: Operates off-price apparel and home product company.
Business type (SIC): Family apparel and accessory stores
Financial profile for 2012: Number of employees, 28,729; assets, $2,680,000,000; sales volume, $4,081,500,000
Fortune 1000 ranking: 2012—577th in revenues, 868th in profits, and 787th in assets
Corporate officers: Thomas Kingsbury, Pres. and C.E.O.; Todd Weyhrich, Exec. V.P. and C.F.O.
Giving statement: Giving through the Burlington Coat Factory Warehouse Corporation Contributions Program.

Burlington Coat Factory Warehouse Corporation Contributions Program

1830 Rte. 130 N.
Burlington, NJ 08016 (609) 387-7800
URL: http://www.burlingtoncoatfactory.com/AboutUs/CommunityRelations.aspx

618
Burlington Northern Santa Fe, LLC

(doing business as BNSF Railroad)
(formerly Burlington Northern Santa Fe Corporation)
2650 Lou Menk Dr., 2nd Fl.
P.O. Box 961039
Fort Worth, TX 76131-2830 (817) 352-1000

Company URL: http://www.bnsf.com
Establishment information: Established in 1995 from the merger of Burlington Northern Inc. with Santa Fe Pacific Corp.
Company type: Subsidiary of a public company
Business activities: Operates railroad.
Business type (SIC): Transportation/railroad; mining/coal and lignite surface; holding company
Financial profile for 2011: Number of employees, 40,000; sales volume, $39,000,000,000
Corporate officers: Matthew K. Rose, Chair. and C.E.O.; Carl R. Ice, Pres. and C.O.O.; Thomas N. Hund, Exec. V.P. and C.F.O.; Roger Nober, Exec. V.P. and Secy.; Gregory C. Fox, Exec. V.P., Opers.; Jo-ann M. Olsovsky, V.P. and C.I.O.; Julie A. Piggott, V.P. and Cont.; Charles W. Shewmake, V.P. and Genl. Counsel; C. Alec Vincent, Asst. V.P., Finance, and Treas.; Riz Chand, Asst. V.P., Human Resources
Board of director: Matthew K. Rose, Chair.
International operations: Bermuda; Canada
Giving statement: Giving through the BNSF Railway Foundation.
Company EIN: 411804964

BNSF Railway Foundation

(formerly BNSF Foundation)
2650 Lou Menk Dr.
Fort Worth, TX 76131-2830 (817) 867-6458
FAX: (817) 352-7925;
E-mail: BNSFFoundation@bnsf.com; URL: http://www.bnsffoundation.org/giving.html
Contact for Diversity Scholarship Program: Teresa Beman, E-mail: teresa.beman@bnsf.com

Donors: BNSF Railway; Burlington Northern Santa Fe Corp.
Contact: Deanna Dugas, Mgr., BNSF Railway Fdn.
Financial data (yr. ended 12/31/11): Assets, $286,549 (M); gifts received, $8,200,000; expenditures, $8,656,098; qualifying distributions, $8,656,098; giving activities include $7,560,934 for 894 grants (high: $330,000; low: $200) and $1,056,261 for 1,172 employee matching gifts.
Purpose and activities: The foundation supports organizations involved with arts and culture, higher education, the environment, health, substance abuse services, crime and violence prevention, recreation, human services, diversity, community development, children and youth, minorities, women, and economically disadvantaged people, and awards college scholarships to high school seniors, college sophomores, and Native Americans.
Fields of interest: Visual arts; Museums; Performing arts; Arts; Vocational education; Higher education; Education; Environment; Hospitals (general); Health care; Substance abuse, services; Crime/violence prevention, domestic violence; Crime/violence prevention, child abuse; Recreation, parks/playgrounds; Recreation; Boys & girls clubs; Boy scouts; Camp Fire; Youth development, business; American Red Cross; YM/YWCAs & YM/YWHAs; Residential/custodial care; Human services; Civil/human rights, equal rights; Business/industry; Community/economic development; United Ways and Federated Giving Programs Children/youth;

Minorities; Hispanics/Latinos; Native Americans/American Indians; Women; Economically disadvantaged.

Programs:

BNSF College Scholarship Program: The foundation annually awards up to 40 college scholarships to high school seniors who are children of employees of BNSF. Renewable scholarships of $2,500 per year are awarded to BNSF Scholarship winners and renewable scholarships of $5,000 are awarded to students who are selected as National Merit Scholars. The program is administered by International Scholarship and Tuition Services (ISTS).

Civic: The foundation support programs designed to promote the environment; crime prevention; parks and recreation; diversity; and community development.

Cultural: The foundation supports programs designed to promote performing, visual, and fine arts; museums; and programs designed to offer opportunities for underserved children to experience cultural learning events.

Educational: The foundation supports public and private educational institutions, primarily at the college level, and vocational and non-college schools. Special emphasis is directed toward programs designed to improve the quality of education.

Employee Matching Gifts Program: The foundation matches contributions made by employees and directors of BNSF to nonprofit organizations on a one-for-one basis.

Future Farmers of America Scholarships: The foundation annually awards ten $5,000 college scholarships to high school seniors who are members of Future Farmers of America (FFA) in California, Illinois, Iowa, Kansas, Minnesota, Montana, Nebraska, North Dakota, South Dakota, and Texas planning to major in areas related to agriculture, including business management, economics, finance, or sales and marketing. The program is administered by the National Future Farmers of America office.

Health and Human Services: The foundation supports YMCA/YWCA's, hospitals, medical programs, and programs designed to address chemical dependency treatment and prevention; spouse and child abuse; and women's and children's aid, and transitional shelters.

Native American Scholarships: The foundation annually awards five 4-year annual college scholarships to outstanding Native American high school seniors in Arizona, California, Colorado, Kansas, Minnesota, Montana, New Mexico, North Dakota, Oklahoma, Oregon, South Dakota, and Washington. Special emphasis is directed toward students planning to study medicine, engineering, natural and physical sciences, business, education, and health administration. The program is administered by the American Indian Science and Engineering Society (AISES).

Youth: The foundation supports programs designed to serve youth, including Boys & Girls Clubs, Camp Fire, Scouts, Junior Achievement, and similar groups.

Type of support: Annual campaigns; Building/renovation; Employee matching gifts; Employee-related scholarships; Management development/capacity building; Matching/challenge support; Program development; Scholarship funds; Scholarships—to individuals.
Geographic limitations: Giving limited to communities located on main BNSF Railway operating lines.
Support limitations: No support for religious organizations, veterans' or fraternal organizations, national health organizations, corporate memberships, taxpayer associations or other bodies whose activities are expected to directly benefit the corporation, or political organizations or candidates. No grants to individuals (except for scholarships), or for general operating support, endowments, national health programs, loans, travel, corporate memberships, political campaigns, computers or computer-related projects, benefit tickets or courtesy advertising, tables and/or tickets to gala fundraisers, salaries, wages, or administrative expenses, or capital campaigns.
Publications: Application guidelines.
Application information: Applications accepted. Support is limited to 1 contribution per organization during any given year. Telephone calls during the application process are not encouraged. Priority is given to organizations that have an established relationship with the BNSF Foundation. Grants range between $1,000 and $10,000. Application form required. Applicants should submit the following:
1) results expected from proposed grant
2) statement of problem project will address
3) population served
4) copy of IRS Determination Letter
5) brief history of organization and description of its mission
6) how project's results will be evaluated or measured
7) list of company employees involved with the organization
8) explanation of why grantmaker is considered an appropriate donor for project
9) detailed description of project and amount of funding requested
10) contact person
11) listing of additional sources and amount of support

Initial approach: Complete online application
Board meeting date(s): Monthly
Deadline(s): None
Final notification: 3 to 6 months

Officers and Directors:* John O. Ambler, Pres.; Michael R. Annis, V.P.; C. Alec Vincent, Treas.; Amy Hawkins; Carl R. Ice; Andrew Johnsen; Roger Nober; Matthew K. Rose.
EIN: 261635887
Selected grants: The following grants are a representative sample of this grantmaker's funding activity:
$330,000 to International Scholarship and Tuition Services, Nashville, TN, 2011.
$307,239 to United Way of Tarrant County, Fort Worth, TX, 2011.
$143,750 to Horatio Alger Association of Distinguished Americans, Alexandria, VA, 2011.
$100,000 to Amon Carter Museum of Western Art, Fort Worth, TX, 2011.
$100,000 to Cornerstone Assistance Network, Fort Worth, TX, 2011.
$51,250 to Future Farmers of America Foundation, National, Indianapolis, IN, 2011.
$10,000 to Minnesota Private College Fund, Saint Paul, MN, 2011.
$5,000 to Salt Creek Ballet Company, Westmont, IL, 2011.
$5,000 to YMCA, Beatrice Mary Family, Beatrice, NE, 2011.
$4,000 to United Way of Central Texas, Temple, TX, 2011.

619
Leo Burnett Company, Inc.

35 W. Wacker Dr.
Chicago, IL 60601 (312) 220-5959
FAX: (312) 220-3299

Company URL: http://www.leoburnett.com
Establishment information: Established in 1935.
Company type: Subsidiary of a foreign company
Business activities: Operates advertising agency.
Business type (SIC): Advertising
Corporate officers: Thomas Bernardin, Chair. and C.E.O.; Jaun Carlos Ortiz, Pres.; Paul Eichelman, C.F.O.
Board of director: Thomas Bernardin, Chair.
Giving statement: Giving through the Leo Burnett Company Charitable Foundation.

Leo Burnett Company Charitable Foundation

35 W. Wacker Dr., 4th Fl
Chicago, IL 60601-1608 (312) 220-5781
tel.: (312) 220-5781

Establishment information: Established in 1985 in IL.
Donors: Leo Burnett Co., Inc.; Leo Burnett USA, Inc.
Contact: Alice O'Hara
Financial data (yr. ended 12/31/11): Assets, $786,666 (M); gifts received, $257,894; expenditures, $298,831; qualifying distributions, $298,831; giving activities include $297,820 for 1 + grant.
Purpose and activities: The foundation supports organizations involved with advertising and education.
Fields of interest: Media, print publishing; Higher education; Business school/education; Education.

Program:

Matching Gifts Plan: The foundation matches contributions made by employees of Leo Burnett Company to nonprofit organizations on a one-for-one basis from $25 to $5,000 per employee, per year.

Type of support: Employee matching gifts; General/operating support.
Geographic limitations: Giving primarily in CO, GA, KS, and Richmond, VA.
Support limitations: No grants to individuals.
Application information: Applications accepted. Application form required.

Initial approach: Proposal
Board meeting date(s): Biannually
Deadline(s): None

Officers: Thomas Bernardin, Pres.; Richard Stoddart, Exec. V.P.; Richard Meehan, V.P.; Sondra J. Thorson, V.P.; Robert S. Westphal, V.P.; Carla Michelotti, Secy.; Paul Eichelman, Treas.
Number of staff: 1 full-time professional; 1 part-time professional; 1 full-time support.
EIN: 363379336
Selected grants: The following grants are a representative sample of this grantmaker's funding activity:
$6,000 to Columbia College, Chicago, IL, 2009.
$5,000 to Dartmouth College, Hanover, NH, 2009.
$3,340 to Leukemia & Lymphoma Society, White Plains, NY, 2009.
$3,231 to Prostate Cancer Foundation, Santa Monica, CA, 2009.
$3,000 to University of Colorado, Boulder, CO, 2009.
$2,750 to Rush University Medical Center, Chicago, IL, 2009.
$2,500 to Lyric Opera of Chicago, Chicago, IL, 2009.

$2,321 to Greater Chicago Food Depository, Chicago, IL, 2009.
$1,750 to University of Notre Dame, Notre Dame, IN, 2009.
$1,500 to Chicago Symphony Orchestra, Chicago, IL, 2009.

620
Burns & McDonnell, Inc.

9400 Ward Pkwy.
Kansas City, MO 64114 (816) 333-9400
FAX: (816) 822-3028

Company URL: http://www.burnsmcd.com
Establishment information: Established in 1898.
Company type: Private company
Business activities: Provides engineering and architectural design services; provides hazardous waste and air pollution management services.
Business type (SIC): Engineering, architectural, and surveying services; sanitary services; administration/environmental quality program
Financial profile for 2010: Number of employees, 2,000
Corporate officers: Gregory M. Graves, Chair., Pres. and C.E.O.; Mark H. Taylor, V.P., Treas., and C.F.O.; Dennis W. Scott, V.P. and C.A.O.
Board of director: Gregory M. Graves, Chair.
Giving statement: Giving through the Burns & McDonnell Foundation.

Burns & McDonnell Foundation

9400 Ward Pkwy.
Kansas City, MO 64114-3319 (816) 333-9400
FAX: (816) 822-3516;
E-mail: mlavin@burnsmcd.com; Tel. for Melissa Lavin-Hickey: (816) 822-3024; URL: http://www.burnsmcd.com/Company/Community-Involvement-co

Establishment information: Established in 1987 in MO.
Donor: Burns & McDonnell, Inc.
Contact: Melissa Lavin-Hickey, Community Rels. Dir.
Financial data (yr. ended 12/31/11): Assets, $15,740,283 (M); gifts received, $2,000,000; expenditures, $681,054; qualifying distributions, $676,550; giving activities include $676,550 for grants.
Purpose and activities: The foundation supports organizations involved with arts and culture, environmental practices, and human services. Special emphasis is directed toward science, technology, engineering, and math education.
Fields of interest: Museums (science/technology); Performing arts; Performing arts, theater; Historic preservation/historical societies; Arts; Elementary/secondary education; Higher education; Engineering school/education; Education; Environment; Children/youth, services; Human services; Foundations (community); United Ways and Federated Giving Programs; Mathematics; Engineering/technology; Science.
Program:
Burns & McDonnell Battle of the Brains: Through Battle of the Brains, the foundation invites small groups of students to design the next great exhibit for Science City. The contest has an elementary division for K-6 grades and a secondary division for 7-12 grades. Projects are judged on creativity and inspiration; interactive exhibit engagement; student involvement; constructability; and presentation. Projects are judged by experts from Science City and Burns & McDonnell and in the third round judging is determined by public vote. Groups are eligible to win up to $50,000 for STEM education at their school. Visit URL http://battleofthebrainskc.com/ for more information.
Type of support: Annual campaigns; Endowments; General/operating support; Program development.
Geographic limitations: Giving primarily in areas of company operations in Kansas City, MO.
Support limitations: No support for religious or political organizations.
Application information: Applications accepted. Application form not required.
Initial approach: Proposal
Deadline(s): None
Officers and Directors:* Gregory M. Graves*, Chair. and Pres.; Dennis W. Scott, V.P; G. William Quatman, Secy.; Mark H. Taylor*, Treas.; Donald F. Greenwood; Raymond J. Kowalik; John E. Nobles; Walter C. Womack; David G. Yeamans.
EIN: 431448871
Selected grants: The following grants are a representative sample of this grantmaker's funding activity:
$21,100 to University of Missouri, Columbia, MO, 2010.
$11,740 to Leukemia & Lymphoma Society, White Plains, NY, 2010.
$9,000 to University of Missouri, Columbia, MO, 2010.
$8,000 to Multiple Sclerosis Society, National, New York, NY, 2010.
$6,000 to Alzheimers Association, Chicago, IL, 2010.
$5,500 to Kansas State University, Manhattan, KS, 2010.
$5,050 to American Lung Association, New York, NY, 2010.
$4,800 to American Cancer Society, Atlanta, GA, 2010.
$4,240 to American Heart Association, Dallas, TX, 2010.
$4,000 to University of Kansas, Lawrence, KS, 2010.

621
Burr & Forman LLP

420 N. 20th St., Ste. 3400
Birmingham, AL 35203-5210
(205) 251-3000

Company URL: http:///www.burr.com
Establishment information: Established in 1905.
Company type: Private company
Business activities: Operates law firm.
Business type (SIC): Legal services
Corporate officers: James W. Lowery, Jr., C.O.O.; David S. Michel, C.I.O.
Offices: Birmingham, Mobile, Montgomery, AL; Orlando, Winter Park, FL; Atlanta, GA; Jackson, MS; Nashville, TN
Giving statement: Giving through the Burr & Forman LLP Corporate Giving Program.

Burr & Forman LLP Corporate Giving Program

420 N. 20th St., Ste. 3400
Birmingham, AL 35203-5210 (205) 251-3000
FAX: (205) 458-5100; URL: http://www.burr.com/About%20Burr/In%20the%20Community.aspx#.UHR7ea6Xf_w

Purpose and activities: Burr & Forman make charitable contributions to nonprofit organizations involved with children, health, youth development, human services, and on a case by case basis.
Fields of interest: Health organizations; Legal services; Youth development; Children, services; Human services; General charitable giving.
Type of support: Employee volunteer services; General/operating support; Pro bono services - legal.

622
Burrtec Waste Industries, Inc.

9890 Cherry Ave.
Fontana, CA 92335 (909) 429-4200

Company URL: http://www.burrtec.com/
Establishment information: Established in 1955.
Company type: Private company
Business activities: Operates solid waste company.
Business type (SIC): Sanitary services
Corporate officer: Cole Burr, Pres. and C.E.O.
Giving statement: Giving through the Burrtec Waste Industries, Inc. Contributions Program.

Burrtec Waste Industries, Inc. Contributions Program

9890 Cherry Ave.
Fontana, CA 92335 (909) 429-4200
URL: http://www.burrtec.com/our-community

Purpose and activities: Burrtec Waste Industries makes charitable contributions to nonprofit organizations in areas of company operations. Emphasis is given to organizations involved with fairs, festivals, and fundraisers.
Fields of interest: Environment, waste management; Environment, recycling; Recreation, fairs/festivals; Community/economic development, fund raising/fund distribution; General charitable giving.
Type of support: Donated products; Employee volunteer services; General/operating support; In-kind gifts.
Geographic limitations: Giving primarily in areas of company operations in CA.

624
The Burton Corporation

(doing business as Burton Snowboards)
80 Industrial Pkwy.
Burlington, VT 05401-5434 (802) 862-4500

Company URL: http://www.burton.com
Establishment information: Established in 1977.
Company type: Private company
Business activities: Manufactures snowboards.
Business type (SIC): Games, toys, and sporting and athletic goods
Corporate officers: Jake Burton, Chair. and C.E.O.; Mike Rees, C.O.O.
Board of director: Jake Burton, Chair.
Subsidiaries: Gravis Footwear Inc., Burlington, VT; Red Corp., Burlington, VT
Giving statement: Giving through the CHILL Foundation.

The CHILL Foundation

(formerly The Burton Foundation)
80 Industrial Pkwy.
Burlington, VT 05401-5434
URL: http://chill.org/

Establishment information: Established as a company-sponsored operating foundation in 1997.

Donors: Burton Snowboards; Islands Fund; Jeffrey Jones; JP Morgan Chase; Responsys; Tom Kartsotis; Harmon Foundation; Mountain Creek; Pepsico Inc.; Turner Construction Co.
Financial data (yr. ended 04/30/12): Assets, $222,168 (M); gifts received, $930,165; expenditures, $1,085,750; qualifying distributions, $999,478; giving activities include $80,218 for 1 grant.
Purpose and activities: The foundation operates a learn to snowboard intervention program for disadvantaged inner-city youth.
Application information: Applications not accepted. Unsolicited requests for funds not accepted.
Officers: Jake Burton Carpenter, Co-Chair.; Donna Carpenter, Co-Chair.; Scott Barrett, Secy.; Andrew McConnell, Treas.; June D. Heston, Exec. Dir.
Board Members: Jeff Boliba; Barry Saunders; Abby Young.
EIN: 030353892

623
Burt's Bees, Inc.

633 Davis Dr., Ste. 600
Morrisville, NC 27560 (919) 998-5200

Company URL: http://www.burtsbees.com
Establishment information: Established in 1984.
Company type: Subsidiary of a public company
Business activities: Manufactures natural personal care products.
Business type (SIC): Soaps, cleaners, and toiletries
Corporate officer: Nick Vlahos, C.E.O.
Giving statement: Giving through the Burt's Bees Greater Good Foundation.

The Burt's Bees Greater Good Foundation

c/o Foundation Source
501 Silverside Rd., Ste. 123
Wilmington, DE 19809-1377
E-mail: ycarlough@burtsbees.com; Application address: c/o Burt's Bees, 210 W. Pettigrew St., Durham, NC 27701, tel (919) 433-4580

Establishment information: Established in 2007 in DE.
Donor: Burt's Bees.
Contact: Yola Carlough
Financial data (yr. ended 12/31/11): Assets, $98,505 (M); gifts received, $270,308; expenditures, $267,557; qualifying distributions, $243,750; giving activities include $243,750 for grants.
Support limitations: No grants to individuals.
Application information: Applications accepted. Application form required. Applicants should submit the following:
1) detailed description of project and amount of funding requested
2) name, address and phone number of organization
Initial approach: Letter or email.
Deadline(s): None
Officer and Director:* John B. Replogle*, Pres. and Secy.
EIN: 260143643
Selected grants: The following grants are a representative sample of this grantmaker's funding activity:
$30,000 to Teach for America, New York, NY, 2010.
$25,000 to Triangle Land Conservancy, Raleigh, NC, 2010.
$15,000 to Doc Arts, Durham, NC, 2010. For charitable event.
$15,000 to North Carolina Conservation Network, Raleigh, NC, 2010.
$10,000 to North Carolina Agricultural Foundation, Raleigh, NC, 2010. For charitable event.
$5,000 to Durham Chamber Legacy Foundation, Durham, NC, 2010.
$5,000 to North Carolina Conservation Network, Raleigh, NC, 2010. For charitable event.
$5,000 to Triangle Community Foundation, Durham, NC, 2010. For charitable event.
$3,000 to North Carolina Sustainability Center, Raleigh, NC, 2010.
$2,500 to Leadership Triangle, Durham, NC, 2010. For charitable event.

625
Business Impact Group, LLC

(also known as BIG)
2411 Galpin Ct., Ste. 120
Chanhassen, MN 55317-4634
(952) 278-7800

Company URL: http://www.impactgroup.us
Establishment information: Established in 2003.
Company type: Private company
Business activities: Manufactures and markets children's, men's, and women's apparel.
Business type (SIC): Apparel, piece goods, and notions—wholesale
Corporate officers: Paul Taunton, Pres. and C.E.O.; Peter Vos, C.F.O.; Tracey Walke, Human Resources
Giving statement: Giving through the STAR Foundation.

The STAR Foundation

9980 Deerbrook Dr.
Chanhassen, MN 55317-8551

Establishment information: Established in 2006 in MN.
Donors: Paul Taunton; Cyndee Taunton; Business Impact Group, LLC.
Financial data (yr. ended 12/31/11): Assets, $50,162 (M); gifts received, $50,000; expenditures, $4,405; qualifying distributions, $4,405.
Geographic limitations: Giving primarily in areas of company operations in MN.
Support limitations: No grants to individuals.
Application information: Applications not accepted. Unsolicited requests for funds not accepted.
Director: Paul Taunton.
EIN: 205330274

626
Butler Manufacturing Company

1540 Genessee St.
P.O. Box 419917
Kansas City, MO 64102 (816) 968-3000

Company URL: http://www.butlermfg.com
Establishment information: Established in 1901.
Company type: Subsidiary of a foreign company
Business activities: Designs, manufactures, and markets nonresidential structure building systems and components; provides construction management services; develops real estate.
Business type (SIC): Metal products/structural; real estate subdividers and developers; management and public relations services
Corporate officers: John J. Holland, Chair. and C.E.O.; Ronald E. Rutledge, Pres. and C.O.O.; Larry C. Miller, V.P., Finance and C.F.O.
Board of director: John J. Holland, Chair.
Subsidiaries: BUCON, Inc., Kansas City, MO; Butler Real Estate, Inc., Kansas City, MO
Division: Vistawall Group, Terrell, TX
Plants: Birmingham, AL; Modesto, Visalia, CA; Tucker, GA; Galesburg, IL; Laurinburg, NC; Annville, PA; Warwick, RI; Greeneville, TN; San Marcos, TX; Wausau, WI
International operations: China; New Zealand; Saudi Arabia
Giving statement: Giving through the Butler Manufacturing Company Contributions Program and the Butler Manufacturing Company Foundation.

Butler Manufacturing Company Foundation

1540 Genessee St.
P.O. Box 419917
Kansas City, MO 64141-0917 (816) 968-3208
FAX: (816) 627-8946;
E-mail: jcharmon@butlermfg.com

Establishment information: Incorporated in 1952 in MO.
Donor: Butler Manufacturing Co.
Contact: Jill C. Harmon, Admin.
Financial data (yr. ended 06/30/12): Assets, $5,852,698 (M); gifts received, $98,073; expenditures, $405,450; qualifying distributions, $327,306; giving activities include $327,306 for grants.
Purpose and activities: The foundation supports organizations involved with arts and culture, education, health, employment, housing, youth development, community development, disabled people, minorities, women, and economically disadvantaged people.
Fields of interest: Arts; Elementary/secondary education; Higher education; Education; Hospitals (general); Health care; Employment, training; Employment; Housing/shelter; Youth development; Community development, neighborhood development; Community/economic development; United Ways and Federated Giving Programs Disabilities, people with; Minorities; Women; Economically disadvantaged.
Programs:

Butler Manufacturing Employee Program: The foundation awards grants to employees of Butler Manufacturing Co. and its wholly-owned subsidiaries who are in financial distress because of serious illness, accidents, or loss or damage to property from weather or fire.

Community Needs: The foundation supports the United Way; minority assistance programs designed to provide jobs or job training for the disadvantaged, and foster the movement of minorities into the mainstream of economic life; youth programs designed to promote education and social development of youth; hospitals that provide unique services or serve the medically indigent; and neighborhood and housing programs designed to encourage revitalization and the preservation of neighborhoods.

Culture: The foundation supports professional minority arts organizations and programs designed to have a cultural impact on a broad segment of those communities where employees of Butler Manufacturing reside; and bring cultural opportunity to the economically disadvantaged.

Education: The foundation supports programs designed to supply a significant number of employees to Butler Manufacturing and/or provide opportunities for continuing education to Butler

Manufacturing employees in plant cities; provide education to residents of Butler Manufacturing plant cities; contribute to a community's ability to provide quality educational opportunities for its citizens; help disadvantaged students who demonstrate ability and desire to prepare for and remain in college; provide educational opportunities that advance minorities, women, and people with disabilities; and develop marketable career skills in young people.

Matching Gifts - Culture: The foundation matches contributions made by full-time employees and retirees of Butler Manufacturing and its wholly-owned subsidiaries to nonprofit organizations involved with arts and culture on a one-for-one basis from $25 up to $2,000 per contributor, per year.

Matching Gifts - Education: The foundation matches contributions made by full-time employees and retirees of Butler Manufacturing and its wholly-owned subsidiaries to institutions of higher education on a one-for-one basis from $25 up to $2,000 per contributor, per year.

Scholarship Program: The foundation annually awards eight four-year $2,500 college scholarships to children of full-time employees of Butler Manufacturing and its wholly-owned subsidiaries. Awards are based on academic achievement, financial need, personal characteristics, and future promise.

Type of support: Annual campaigns; Capital campaigns; Continuing support; Employee matching gifts; Employee volunteer services; Employee-related scholarships; General/operating support; Grants to individuals; Seed money.
Geographic limitations: Giving primarily in areas of company operations, with emphasis on the greater Kansas City, MO, area.
Support limitations: No support for political organizations, religious organizations not of direct benefit to the entire community, pre-K-12 educational institutions, fraternal or veterans' organizations, national health organizations, local or regional chapters of national health organizations, or grantmaking foundations. No grants to individuals (except for employee-related hardship grants and employee-related scholarships), or for tours, conferences, seminars, workshops, or similar events, fundraising, or endowments.
Publications: Application guidelines; Informational brochure (including application guidelines).
Application information: Applications accepted. Application form not required. Applicants should submit the following:
1) statement of problem project will address
2) copy of IRS Determination Letter
3) brief history of organization and description of its mission
4) copy of most recent annual report/audited financial statement/990
5) descriptive literature about organization
6) listing of board of directors, trustees, officers and other key people and their affiliations
7) detailed description of project and amount of funding requested
8) copy of current year's organizational budget and/or project budget
9) listing of additional sources and amount of support

Proposals should indicate the total funds needed to complete a project, if applicable.

Initial approach: Proposal to nearest company facility; proposal to foundation for organizations located in the greater Kansas City, MO, area
Copies of proposal: 1
Board meeting date(s): Mar., June, Sept., and Dec.
Deadline(s): 2 months prior to board meetings
Final notification: Following board meetings

Officers and Trustees: Patrick Finan, Pres.; Harry Yeatman, V.P. and Secy.; Justin Powell, Treas.; Gary Coder; Tanya Bennett; Alec Hignam.
Number of staff: 1 part-time support.
EIN: 440663648
Selected grants: The following grants are a representative sample of this grantmaker's funding activity:
$59,000 to United Way of Greater Kansas City, Kansas City, MO, 2010.
$6,000 to Kansas State University, Manhattan, KS, 2010.
$6,000 to Missouri State University, Springfield, MO, 2010.
$5,500 to University of Missouri, Kansas City, MO, 2010.
$5,000 to United Way of Lebanon County, Lebanon, PA, 2010.
$4,500 to Family Conservancy, Kansas City, KS, 2010.
$4,500 to United Way of Hays County, San Marcos, TX, 2010.
$3,000 to Gillis Center, Kansas City, MO, 2010.
$3,000 to Purdue University, West Lafayette, IN, 2010.
$2,000 to Cross-Lines Community Outreach, Kansas City, KS, 2010.

627
Butler Rubin Saltarelli & Boyd LLP

70 W. Madison St., Ste. 1800
Chicago, IL 60602-4257 (312) 444-9660

Company URL: http://www.butlerrubin.com
Establishment information: Established in 1980.
Company type: Private company
Business activities: Operates law firm.
Business type (SIC): Legal services
Corporate officer: Michael P. Motyka, C.O.O.
Giving statement: Giving through the Butler Rubin Saltarelli & Boyd LLP Corporate Giving Program.

Butler Rubin Saltarelli & Boyd LLP Corporate Giving Program

70 W. Madison St., Ste. 1800
Chicago, IL 60602-4257 (312) 444-9660
FAX: (312) 444-9287; Contact for Pro Bono program: James A. Morsch, Partner, tel.: (312) 696-4457, fax: (312) 444-9702, e-mail: jmorsch@butlerrubin.com; For Butler Rubin in the community: Andrea Gordon, Dir., Mktg. and Client Svcs., tel.: (312) 696-4466, e-mail: agordon@butlerrubin.com; URL: http://www.butlerrubin.com/our-commitment/community-service/

Purpose and activities: Butler Rubin makes charitable contributions to nonprofit organizations involved with helping underprivileged youths and families.
Fields of interest: Arts; Health organizations; Legal services; Youth development; Minorities/immigrants, centers/services; Homeless, human services; Civil/human rights; United Ways and Federated Giving Programs; Public affairs Economically disadvantaged.
Type of support: Employee volunteer services; General/operating support; Pro bono services - legal.

628
H. E. Butt Grocery Company

646 S. Main Ave.
San Antonio, TX 78204-1210
(210) 938-8000

Company URL: http://www.heb.com
Establishment information: Established in 1905.
Company type: Private company
Business activities: Operates grocery stores.
Business type (SIC): Groceries—retail
Financial profile for 2011: Number of employees, 76,000; sales volume, $15,600,000,000
Corporate officers: Charles C. Butt, Chair. and C.E.O.; Craig Boyan, Pres. and C.O.O.; Martin Otto, C.F.O.; Robert D. Loeffler, C.A.O; Gavin L. Gallagher, C.I.O.; Caryn Conrad, V.P., Mktg.; Mike Pardoe, Human Resources
Board of directors: Charles C. Butt, Chair.; Salman Manzur
Giving statement: Giving through the H. E. Butt Grocery Company Contributions Program and the H. E. Butt Foundation.

H. E. Butt Grocery Company Contributions Program

646 S. Main Ave.
San Antonio, TX 78204-1210 (210) 938-8592
E-mail: campos.dya@heb.com; Additional application addresses: Austin and central TX: Leslie Sweet, Dir., Public Affairs, 6929 Airport, Ste. 176, Austin, TX 78752, tel.: (512) 421-1017; Houston, TX: Cyndy Garza-Roberts, Dir., Public Affairs, 4301 Windfern, Houston, TX 77041, tel.: (713) 329-3920; Gulf Coast, TX, area: Shelley Parks, Dir., Public Affairs, 4428 Kostoryz, Corpus Christi, TX 78415, tel.: (361) 857-1708; Border Region: Virginia Perez, Public Affairs Specialist, 2502 Cornerstone Blvd., Edinburg, TX 78752, tel.: (956) 225-3659; URL: http://www.heb.com/sectionpage/about-us/community/community-involvement/sd80002
Excellence in Education Awards: Jill Reynolds, 6929 Airport Blvd., Ste. 176, Austin, TX 78752, e-mail: reynolds.jill@heb.com

Contact: Dya Campos, Dir., Public Affairs
Purpose and activities: H.E. Butt makes charitable contributions to nonprofit organizations involved with arts and culture, education, hunger, recreation, economic development, and to food banks and awards grants to K-12 teachers. Support is given primarily in areas of company operations.
Fields of interest: Arts; Elementary/secondary education; Education; Health care; Food services; Food banks; Nutrition; Recreation; Economic development.
International interests: Mexico.
Programs:

Excellence in Education Awards: H.E. Butt annually awards grants to K-12 and special area public school educators whose leadership and dedication inspire a love of learning in students of all backgrounds and abilities. The teacher award is divided into three categories: the rising star award, the leadership award, and the lifetime achievement award. Three elementary school and three secondary school teachers and their schools receive $5,000, $10,000, and $25,000, respectively, based on years of service. Thirty regional finalists will also receive $1,000 each plus $1,000 for their schools. Excellence awards also include principal award categories to elementary and secondary school principals and district award categories for large, small, and regional districts. The program is limited to Texas.

Excellence in Education Healthy Campus Grant: H.E. Butt annually awards $15,000 grants to area schools to increase health and nutrition education for students. The program is designed to develop, implement, and promote the three pillars of H-E-B's statewide health improvement effort: Food, Body, and Life.
Type of support: Consulting services; Donated equipment; Donated products; General/operating support; Grants to individuals; Loaned talent; Program development; Research.
Geographic limitations: Giving primarily in areas of company operations in TX and in Mexico; giving also to national organizations.
Publications: Application guidelines; Grants list.
Application information: Applications accepted. Proposals should be submitted using organization letterhead. Organizations located in the Dallas, TX, area should use headquarters application address. Application form required. Applicants should submit the following:
1) copy of IRS Determination Letter
2) descriptive literature about organization
Applications for Excellence in Education Awards should include, a resume, essay, and letters of support.
Initial approach: Download application form and mail proposal and application form to nearest application address; complete online application for Excellence in Education Awards and Healthy Campus Grant
Deadline(s): 60 days prior to need; Jan. 6 for Excellence in Education Awards; Nov. 11 for Healthy Campus Grant
Final notification: 30 days

H. E. Butt Foundation
P.O. Box 290670
Kerrville, TX 78029-0670
FAX: (830) 257-3137; Tel. for Jennifer Hargrave: (830) 792-1246; URL: http://www.laityrenewal.org/aboutFoundation.php

Establishment information: Incorporated as a company-sponsored operating foundation in 1933 in TX.
Donors: Howard E. Butt, Sr.†; Howard E. Butt, Jr.; H.E. Butt Grocery Co.
Contact: Jennifer D. Hargrave, Cont.
Financial data (yr. ended 12/31/11): Assets, $204,344,964 (M); gifts received, $106,589,287; expenditures, $8,396,148; qualifying distributions, $12,014,603; giving activities include $777,754 for 18 grants (high: $256,290; low: $100) and $8,194,996 for 4 foundation-administered programs.
Purpose and activities: The foundation supports camps in Texas used by qualifying organizations related to church renewal, summer Christian youth camps, and organizations involved with lay theological education and mental health.
Fields of interest: Theological school/education; Mental health/crisis services; Recreation, camps; Christian agencies & churches Children/youth; Youth; Adults.
Type of support: General/operating support.
Geographic limitations: Giving limited to TX.
Support limitations: No grants to individuals, or for building or endowments.
Publications: Newsletter.
Application information: Applications not accepted. Contributes only to pre-selected organizations. The foundation's giving is limited to its own giving programs, including a Christian adult retreat center, a youth camp, a family camp, and camping facilities administered through Foundations for Laity Renewal.
Board meeting date(s): Dec.
Officers and Directors:* Howard E. Butt, Jr.*, Pres.; David M. Rogers*, Exec. V.P. and C.O.O.; F. Dwight Lacy*, Sr. V.P.; Barbara Dan Butt*, V.P. and Secy.-Treas.; Deborah Butt Rogers*, V.P.; Jennifer D. Hargrave, Cont.
Number of staff: 25 full-time professional; 20 full-time support; 1 part-time support.
EIN: 741239819
Selected grants: The following grants are a representative sample of this grantmaker's funding activity:
$229,954 to Laity Lodge Foundation, Kerrville, TX, 2009.
$123,862 to Laity Renewal Foundation, Kerrville, TX, 2009.
$5,000 to First Baptist Church, Leakey, TX, 2009.
$3,000 to Leakey Volunteer Fire Dapartment, Leakey, TX, 2009.
$2,500 to Frio Canyon EMS, Leakey, TX, 2009.
$1,500 to Friends of the Library Association, Leakey, TX, 2009.
$1,000 to Divide Volunteer Fire Department, Divide, TX, 2009.
$1,000 to Real County Junior Livestock, 2009.
$500 to Canyon Performing Arts, Leakey, TX, 2009.

629
Butzel Long, PC
150 W. Jefferson Ave., Ste. 100
Detroit, MI 48226-4430 (313) 225-7000

Company URL: http://www.butzel.com
Establishment information: Established in 1854.
Company type: Private company
Business activities: Operates law firm.
Business type (SIC): Legal services
Corporate officer: Justin G. Klimko, Pres.
Board of directors: Richard B. Brosnick; Carey A. DeWitt; W. Patrick Dreisig; Justin G. Klimko; Louis Theros; James E. Wynne
Offices: Washington, DC; Ann Arbor, Bloomfield Hills, Detroit, Lansing, MI; New York, NY
Giving statement: Giving through the Butzel Long, PC Pro Bono Program and the Butzel Long Charitable Trust.

Butzel Long, PC Pro Bono Program
150 W. Jefferson, Ste. 100
Detroit, MI 48266-4430 (313) 225-7000
URL: http://www.butzel.com/about-pro-bono/

Contact: Jennifer Consiglio, Shareholder
Fields of interest: Legal services.
Type of support: Pro bono services - legal.
Geographic limitations: Giving primarily in areas of company operations in Washington, DC, Ann Arbor, Bloomfield Hills, Detroit, and Lansing, MI, New York, NY.
Application information: A Pro Bono Committee manages the pro-bono program.

Butzel Long Charitable Trust
(formerly The Butzel Long Gust & Van Zile Charitable Trust)
150 W. Jefferson Ave., Ste. 100
Detroit, MI 48226-4450

Establishment information: Established in 1983 in MI.
Donor: Butzel Long.
Contact: Joseph J. Melnick, Tr.
Financial data (yr. ended 12/31/11): Assets, $3,184 (M); gifts received, $2,850; expenditures, $4,935; qualifying distributions, $4,935; giving activities include $4,700 for 8 grants (high: $1,500; low: $100).
Purpose and activities: The foundation supports organizations involved with education, hunger, and human services. Special emphasis is directed toward legal institutions and Bar related activities.
Fields of interest: Education; Legal services; Food services; YM/YWCAs & YM/YWHAs; Children/youth, services; Human services Economically disadvantaged.
Type of support: Annual campaigns; General/operating support; Scholarship funds; Sponsorships.
Geographic limitations: Giving primarily in MI.
Application information: Applications accepted. Application form not required. Applicants should submit the following:
1) copy of IRS Determination Letter
2) detailed description of project and amount of funding requested
Initial approach: Proposal
Deadline(s): Dec. 31
Trustees: Joseph J. Melnick; Richard E. Rassel.
EIN: 382510263

630
Byers Choice Ltd.
4355 County Line Rd.
P.O. Box 158
Chalfont, PA 18914-1825 (215) 822-6700
FAX: (215) 822-3847

Company URL: http://www.byerschoice.com
Company type: Private company
Business activities: Manufactures specialty gifts and ornaments.
Business type (SIC): Glass products/miscellaneous; metal products/fabricated
Corporate officers: Robert L. Byers, Jr., Pres. and C.E.O.; Joe Giedgowd, C.F.O.
Giving statement: Giving through the Byers Foundation.

The Byers Foundation
P.O. Box 158
Chalfont, PA 18914-0158 (215) 822-6700

Establishment information: Established in 1986 in PA.
Donor: Byers Choice, Ltd.
Contact: Joyce F. Byers, Secy.-Treas.
Financial data (yr. ended 12/31/11): Assets, $2,182,652 (M); gifts received, $125,000; expenditures, $46,163; qualifying distributions, $35,000; giving activities include $35,000 for 2 grants (high: $25,000; low: $10,000).
Purpose and activities: The foundation supports historical societies and organizations involved with health, cancer, human services, and Christianity.
Fields of interest: Historic preservation/historical societies; Health care; Cancer; Salvation Army; Christian agencies & churches.
Type of support: General/operating support; Program development.
Geographic limitations: Giving primarily in southeastern PA, with emphasis on the Doylestown and Philadelphia areas.
Application information: Applications accepted. Application form required.
Initial approach: Proposal
Copies of proposal: 1
Board meeting date(s): Annually
Deadline(s): None

Officers: Robert L. Byers, Pres.; Jeffrey D. Byers, V.P.; Robert L. Byers, Jr., V.P.; Joyce F. Byers, Secy.-Treas.
EIN: 232406657
Selected grants: The following grants are a representative sample of this grantmaker's funding activity:
$50,000 to Bucks County Historical Society, Doylestown, PA, 2010.

631
Byrd Cookie Company
6700 Waters Ave.
P.O. Box 13086
Savannah, GA 31406-2718 (912) 355-1716

Company URL: http://www.byrdcookiecompany.com
Establishment information: Established in 1924.
Company type: Private company
Business activities: Produces cookies, cheese biscuits, and condiments.
Business type (SIC): Bakery products; specialty foods/canned, frozen, and preserved
Corporate officers: Geoff Repella, Pres.; Kay Curl, Secy.-Treas.
Giving statement: Giving through the Curl Family Foundation, Inc.

The Curl Family Foundation, Inc.
704 View Point Dr.
Savannah, GA 31406

Establishment information: Established in 1998 in GA.
Donors: Byrd Cookie Co.; Benny Curl.
Financial data (yr. ended 12/31/11): Assets, $14,173 (M); gifts received, $5,792; expenditures, $5,042; qualifying distributions, $16,624; giving activities include $5,033 for 3 grants (high: $3,993; low: $300).
Purpose and activities: The foundation supports organizations involved with education, the environment, human services, and religion.
Fields of interest: Education.
Type of support: General/operating support.
Application information: Applications not accepted. Unsolicited requests for funds not accepted.
Director: Benny Curl.
EIN: 582422772

632
C & C Ford Sales, Inc.
1100 Easton Rd.
Horsham, PA 19044-1405 (215) 674-3600

Company URL: http://www.candcford.com
Establishment information: Established in 1991.
Company type: Private company
Business activities: Operates new and used car dealership.
Business type (SIC): Motor vehicles—retail
Corporate officer: Michael D. Chapman, Vice-Chair.
Board of director: Michael D. Chapman, Vice-Chair.
Giving statement: Giving through the Commonwealth National Foundation.

Commonwealth National Foundation
c/o Brett Rhode
250 Babylon Rd.
Horsham, PA 19044-1319

Establishment information: Established in 1999 in PA.
Donors: Bank of America, N.A.; C & C Ford; Chapman Auto Group; David Urbach; Alan Gubernick; Chapman Auto Group; Matthew Newman.
Financial data (yr. ended 12/31/11): Assets, $40,514 (M); gifts received, $51,213; expenditures, $119,725; qualifying distributions, $77,102; giving activities include $76,000 for 7 grants (high: $20,000; low: $1,000).
Fields of interest: Health care; Human services; Civil/human rights.
Geographic limitations: Giving primarily in PA.
Support limitations: No grants to individuals.
Application information: Applications not accepted. Unsolicited requests for funds not accepted.
Officers: Brett J. Rhode, Pres. and Treas.; Terrance Turnolo, V.P. and Secy.
Directors: Barbara Augustine; Alan Gubernick; Jonathan Marks; Noreen Moskalski; David Urbach.
EIN: 233015337

633
C & C Metal Products Corporation
456 Nordhoff Pl.
Englewood, NJ 07631-4808
(201) 569-7300

Company URL: http://www.ccmetal.com
Establishment information: Established in 1914.
Company type: Private company
Business activities: Manufactures fashion and home furnishing metal products.
Business type (SIC): Jewelry and notions/costume
Corporate officers: Gerald Nathel, Chair. and C.E.O.; Mitchell Chalfin, V.P. and Secy.; Matheew Nathel, V.P. and Treas.; Jack Slominsky, Cont.
Board of director: Gerald Nathel, Chair.
Offices: Los Angeles, CA; New York, NY
Giving statement: Giving through the Harry Chalfin Foundation, Inc.

Harry Chalfin Foundation, Inc.
456 Nordhoff Pl.
Englewood, NJ 07631-4808

Establishment information: Established in 1945 in NY.
Donors: Gannett Outdoor; C&C Metal Products Corp.
Financial data (yr. ended 12/31/11): Assets, $190 (M); expenditures, $10; qualifying distributions, $0.
Purpose and activities: The foundation supports organizations involved with theater and Judaism.
Type of support: General/operating support.
Support limitations: No grants to individuals.
Application information: Applications not accepted. Unsolicited requests for funds not accepted.
Trustee: Mitchell Chalfin.
EIN: 136162748

634
C & S Wholesale Grocers, Inc.
7 Corporate Dr.
Keene, NH 03431-5042 (603) 354-7000

Company URL: http://www.cswg.com
Establishment information: Established in 1918.
Company type: Private company
Business activities: Sells groceries wholesale.
Business type (SIC): Groceries—wholesale
Financial profile for 2011: Number of employees, 16,681; sales volume, $20,400,000,000
Corporate officers: Rick Cohen, Chair. and C.E.O.; Michael F. Newbold, C.A.O; Joe Caracappa, C.I.O.; Scott Charlton, Exec. V.P., Opers.; Richard L. Wyckoff, Exec. V.P., Sales and Mktg.; Bruce Johnson, Exec. V.P. and Human Resources
Board of directors: Richard B. Cohen, Chair.; Nat Silverman
Giving statement: Giving through the C & S Wholesale Grocers, Inc. Corporate Giving Program.

C & S Wholesale Grocers, Inc. Corporate Giving Program
7 Corporate Dr.
Keene, NH 03431-5042
URL: http://community.cswg.com

Contact: Gina Goff, Dir., Community Involvement
Purpose and activities: C&S Wholesale Grocers supports initiatives designed to stop hunger; and promote the health and enrichment of communities in which its employees and facilities have homes. Support is limited to areas within 20 miles of company operations.
Fields of interest: Education, reading; Medical care, in-patient care; Health care; Crime/violence prevention, child abuse; Food services; Food banks; Disasters, preparedness/services; Children, services; United Ways and Federated Giving Programs; Leadership development.
Programs:
C&S Team Up & Make Strides: Through the C&S Team Up & Make Strides program, C&S Wholesale Grocers makes charitable contributions of up to $140 to nonprofit organizations with which teams of at least four full-time and part-time employees are involved in a fundraising event.
Dollars for Doers: Through the Dollars for Doers program, C&S Wholesale Grocers makes charitable contributions of $1 per hour to nonprofit organizations with which full-time and part-time employees volunteer at least 15 hours per year.
Type of support: Donated products; Employee volunteer services; General/operating support; Public relations services; Sponsorships.
Geographic limitations: Giving limited to areas of company operations in Birmingham, AL, Fresno, Sacramento, and Stockton, CA, Suffield and Windsor Locks, CT, Kapolei and Honolulu, HI, Aberdeen, North East, and Upper Marlboro, MD, North Hatfield, South Hatfield, and Westfield, MA, Keene, NH, Avenel, Dayton, New Brunswick, North Brunswick, and Woodbridge, NJ, greater Buffalo, Chester, Montgomery, and Newburgh, NY, Bethlehem, DuBois, Dunmore, and Harrisburg, PA, Mauldin, SC, and Brattleboro, VT, areas; giving also to statewide and regional food banks near the company's distribution centers.
Support limitations: No support for national health organizations or statewide or regional branches of national health organizations, religious organizations, fraternal, veterans', or political organizations, discriminatory organizations, organizations established less than two years ago, or sports teams. No grants to individuals, or for capital campaigns, multi-year support, endowments, scholarships, mass mailings, travel, general operating support for non-hunger United Way member agencies, or golf tournaments.
Publications: Application guidelines; Corporate giving report.
Application information: Applications accepted. Major grant requests by invitation only. Support is limited to 1 contribution per organization during any given year for 1 year in length. Telephone calls are

not encouraged. Mini-Grants are grants less than $1,000, product donations less than $100 in value, and sponsorships less than $500; sponsorships generally do not exceed $5,000. The Community Involvement Department handles giving. The company has a staff that only handles contributions. A contributions committee reviews all requests. Application form required.

Initial approach: Complete online application form for Mini-Grants
Copies of proposal: 1
Deadline(s): The first of each month for Mini-Grants; Feb. 1, June 1, and Oct. 1 for sponsorships
Final notification: 2 weeks following deadlines for Mini-Grants

Administrators: Gina Goff, Dir., Community Involvement.
Number of staff: 3 full-time professional.

635
C L D Investments Ltd.

101 N.E. 16th Ave.
Ocala, FL 34470-6904 (352) 732-4464

Establishment information: Established in 2000.
Company type: Private company
Business activities: Operates real estate investment company.
Business type (SIC): Investors/miscellaneous
Giving statement: Giving through the Dinkins Family Foundation, Inc.

Dinkins Family Foundation, Inc.

101 N.E. 16th Ave.
Ocala, FL 34470-6904

Establishment information: Established in 2006 in FL.
Donors: CLD Investments, Ltd.; C.L. Dinkins Trust.
Financial data (yr. ended 12/31/11): Assets, $385,004 (M); expenditures, $21,431; qualifying distributions, $18,450; giving activities include $18,450 for grants.
Fields of interest: Education; Human services; Religion.
Geographic limitations: Giving primarily in FL; some giving in AZ, CA, CO, DC, GA, KY, NE, OK, PA, and TN.
Application information: Applications not accepted. Unsolicited requests for funds not accepted.
Directors: Brad Dinkins; Michael Dinkins; Tracy Rains.
EIN: 208068017

636
C Spire Wireless

(formerly Cellular South, Inc.)
1018 Highland Colony Pkwy., Ste. 300
Ridgeland, MS 39157-2060
(601) 974-7757

Company URL: http://www.cspire.com/
Establishment information: Established in 1988.
Company type: Private company
Business activities: Provides wireless services and products.
Business type (SIC): Telephone communications
Financial profile for 2010: Number of employees, 268
Corporate officers: Hu Meena, Pres. and C.E.O.; Kevin Hankins, C.O.O.; Suzy Hays, Sr. V.P., Mktg.
Giving statement: Giving through the C Spire Wireless Foundation.

C Spire Wireless Foundation

(formerly The Cellular South Charitable Foundation)
1018 Highland Colony Pkwy., Ste. 360
Ridgeland, MS 39157-2060 (601) 355-1522
URL: http://www.cspire.com/company_info/about/programs/foundation.jsp

Establishment information: Established in 2005 in MS.
Donors: James H. Creekmore, Sr.; Wade Creekmore; Brightpoint North America, LP; Meredith Creekmore; V. Hugo Meena, Jr.; Beth Byrd; Sidney Crews; Cellular South, Inc.
Contact: Beth C. Byrd, Exec. Dir.
Financial data (yr. ended 12/31/11): Assets, $21,354 (M); gifts received, $534,000; expenditures, $533,926; qualifying distributions, $534,411; giving activities include $488,900 for 57 grants (high: $100,000; low: $400).
Purpose and activities: The foundation supports programs designed to improve quality of life in markets where C Spire Wireless operates and organizations involved with academics, athletics, heath, wellness, safety, and civic affairs. Special emphasis is directed toward programs designed to improve opportunities for education in Mississippi.
Fields of interest: Museums; Secondary school/education; Higher education; Education; Health care; Disasters, preparedness/services; Safety/disasters; Athletics/sports, amateur leagues; Human services; Public affairs; Christian agencies & churches.
Type of support: Annual campaigns; Endowments; General/operating support; Program development; Scholarship funds; Sponsorships.
Geographic limitations: Giving primarily in areas of company operations in AL, FL, MS, and TN.
Support limitations: No support for political candidates or groups, amateur sports teams, or religious organizations. No grants to individuals, or for administrative expenses, capital campaigns, or purchase of uniforms or trips for school-related organizations; no loans.
Publications: Application guidelines.
Application information: Applications accepted. Support is limited to 1 contribution per organization during any given year. Organizations receiving support are asked to submit a final report. Application form required. Applicants should submit the following:
1) statement of problem project will address
2) population served
3) brief history of organization and description of its mission
4) how project's results will be evaluated or measured
5) detailed description of project and amount of funding requested
6) copy of current year's organizational budget and/or project budget

Initial approach: Complete online application
Deadline(s): 150 days prior to need
Final notification: 90 days

Officers and Directors: Hu Meena, Pres.; Wesley Goings, V.P.; Meredith Creekmore, Secy.-Treas.; Beth C. Byrd, Exec. Dir.; Jim Richmond.
EIN: 203426826

637
C.M. Capital Corporation

525 University Ave., Ste. 200
Palo Alto, CA 94301-1903 (650) 326-6480

Company URL: http://www.ccapital.com
Establishment information: Established in 1949.
Company type: Subsidiary of a foreign company
Business activities: Operates holding company; provides investment advisory services.
Business type (SIC): Holding company; security and commodity services
Financial profile for 2009: Number of employees, 30
Corporate officers: Johnson M.D. Cha, Chair.; John C. Couch, Vice-Chair.; Bruce W. Madding, C.P.A., Pres., C.E.O., and C.I.O.; Fernando R. Sucre, Sr. V.P. and C.F.O.; Mary Theresa Muniz, V.P., Admin. and Human Resources; Peter G. Morrissey, Genl. Counsel
Board of directors: Johnson M.D. Cha, Chair.; John C. Couch, Vice-Chair.; James H. Boettcher; Robert K. Jaedicke; Robert L. Joss; F. Van Kasper; Lawrence J. Lau; Stephan F. Newhouse; Teh Kok Peng; William F. Sharpe; Tony Sun
Giving statement: Giving through the C.M. Capital Foundation.

C.M. Capital Foundation

525 University Ave., Ste. 1400
Palo Alto, CA 94301-1910 (650) 326-6480
FAX: (650) 325-4762;
E-mail: ehammack@ccapital.com

Donors: Alphamill Trust; C.M. Capital Corp.
Contact: Elizabeth M. Hammack, V.P. and Secy.
Financial data (yr. ended 12/31/11): Assets, $1,090,282 (M); expenditures, $62,970; qualifying distributions, $57,650; giving activities include $57,650 for grants.
Purpose and activities: The foundation supports hospitals and organizations involved with arts and culture, education, cancer, children and youth, and community development. Support is given primarily in Santa Clara county, California.
Fields of interest: Education; Health organizations; Human services.
Type of support: Employee matching gifts; General/operating support.
Geographic limitations: Giving primarily in CA, with emphasis on Santa Clara County.
Support limitations: No support for political, religious, or for-profit organizations. No grants to individuals, or for fundraisers or conferences.
Application information: Applications accepted. Application form required.

Initial approach: Letter
Deadline(s): Jan. 15, Apr. 15, July 15, and Oct. 15

Officers and Directors:* John C. Couch*, Chair.; Lucia Cha*, Pres.; Jenchyn Luh, Sr. V.P. and Treas.; Elizabeth M. Hammack, V.P., Secy., and Exec. Dir.; Selina Cha; Priscilla Chou; Richard Eigner.
EIN: 770583870

638
CA, Inc.

(doing business as CA Technologies)
(formerly Computer Associates International, Inc.)
1 CA Plz.
Islandia, NY 11749 (800) 225-5224
FAX: (631) 342-6800

Company URL: http://www.ca.com
Establishment information: Established in 1976.
Company type: Public company
Company ticker symbol and exchange: CA/NASDAQ
Business activities: Designs, develops, and markets computer software.
Business type (SIC): Computer services
Financial profile for 2013: Number of employees, 13,600; assets, $11,811,000,000; sales volume, $4,643,000,000; pre-tax net income, $1,318,000,000; expenses, $3,281,000,000; liabilities, $6,361,000,000
Fortune 1000 ranking: 2012—499th in revenues, 207th in profits, and 349th in assets
Forbes 2000 ranking: 2012—1421st in sales, 665th in profits, and 1373rd in assets
Corporate officers: Arthur F. Weinbach, Chair.; Russell M. Artzt, Vice Chair.; Michael P. Gregoire, C.E.O.; Richard Beckert, Exec. V.P. and C.F.O.; Amy Fliegelman Olli, Exec. V.P. and Genl. Counsel; Paul Pronsati, Sr. V.P., Comms.
Board of directors: Arthur F. Weinbach, Chair.; Jens Adler; Raymond J. Bromark; Gary J. Fernandes; Michael P. Gregoire; Rohit Kapoor; Kay Koplovitz; Christopher B. Lofgren; Richard Sulpizio; Laura S. Unger; Ron Zambonini
Subsidiary: Sterling Software, Inc., Dallas, TX
Plants: Birmingham, AL; Phoenix, AZ; Huntington Beach, CA; Aurora, CO; East Windsor, CT; Maitland, FL; Marietta, GA; Honolulu, HI; Lisle, IL; Indianapolis, IN; Calverton, MD; Metairie, Westwood, MA; Dearborn, MI; Bloomington, MN; St. Louis, MO; Omaha, NE; Princeton, NJ; Fairport, NY; Durham, NC; Beavercreek, OH; Portland, OR; West Conshohocken, PA; Austin, TX; Midvale, UT; Reston, VA; Bellevue, WA; Milwaukee, WI
International operations: Argentina; Australia; Austria; Bahrain; Belgium; Canada; Cayman Islands; Chile; China; Colombia; Cyprus; Czech Republic; Denmark; Finland; France; Germany; Greece; Hong Kong; India; Indonesia; Israel; Italy; Japan; Luxembourg; Malaysia; Mexico; Netherlands; New Zealand; Norway; Peru; Philippines; Poland; Saudi Arabia; Singapore; South Africa; South Korea; Spain; Sweden; Switzerland; Taiwan; Thailand; Turkey; United Kingdom; Venezuela
Giving statement: Giving through the CA, Inc. Corporate Giving Program.
Company EIN: 132857434

CA, Inc. Corporate Giving Program

(formerly Computer Associates International, Inc. Corporate Giving Program)
c/o Community Affairs
1 CA Plz., Ste. 100
Islandia, NY 11749-5303 (800) 225-5224
FAX: (631) 342-6800; URL: http://www.ca.com/us/community-affairs.aspx

Purpose and activities: CA makes charitable contributions to nonprofit organizations involved with education, technology, health care, human services, and the advancement of women in IT. Support is given on a national and international basis in areas of company operations.
Fields of interest: Education; Health care; Human services; Engineering/technology Adults, women.
Program:
Matching Gifts Program: CA Technologies matches contributions made by its employees to nonprofit organizations on a one-for-one basis up to $5,000 per employee, per year.
Type of support: Building/renovation; Continuing support; Donated equipment; Donated products; Employee matching gifts; Employee volunteer services; General/operating support; In-kind gifts.
Geographic limitations: Giving on a national and international basis in areas of company operations.

639
Cable News Network, Inc.

(also known as CNN)
1 CNN Ctr.
Atlanta, GA 30303 (404) 827-1600
FAX: (404) 878-0011

Company URL: http://www.cnn.com
Establishment information: Established in 1980.
Company type: Subsidiary of a public company
Business activities: Operate cable news network.
Business type (SIC): Cable and other pay television services
Corporate officer: Ann Moore, Chair. and C.E.O.
Board of director: Ann Moore, Chair.

CNN Heroes

1 Time Warner Ctr.
New York, NY 10019-6038
URL: http://www.cnnheroes.com

Purpose and activities: CNN Heroes: An All-Star Tribute is an annual television special that recognizes 10 individuals who have made meaningful contributions to humanity. The program marks the end of a year-long CNN Heroes campaign, in which viewers are invited to nominate candidates they would like to be honored. Each Top 10 CNN Hero is awarded $50,000 to aid them in their projects, with the CNN Hero of the Year receiving an additional $250,000 grant. Categories for recognition include: Championing Children: Commitment to the welfare of young people; Community Crusader: Creating solutions to a local problem or social issue; Defending the Planet: Innovative efforts to preserve and protect the environment; Medical Marvel: Dedication to the enhancement of human health; Protecting the Powerless: Advancing the cause of human or equal rights; and Young Wonder: Outstanding achievement by a person 25 or under.
Fields of interest: Environment; Health care; Civil/human rights; Community/economic development Children.
Program:
CNN Heroes Awards Program: Awards to individuals in the U.S. and abroad who are making a difference in their communities and beyond, who are at least thirteen years of age or older as of Nov. 25, 2010, and some portion of the nominee's activities must have taken place on Nov. 25, 2010 or be ongoing. Each finalist will receive $50,000 and the winner will receive $250,000. Nominees cannot have previously been selected as a CNN Hero Finalist or Winner.
Type of support: Grants to individuals.
Geographic limitations: Giving on a national basis.
Publications: Application guidelines; Grants list.
Application information: Applications accepted. Nominations are only accepted online through the CNN Heroes website. Mailed in submissions or other information will not be accepted. Application form required.
Initial approach: Complete online application
Deadline(s): Aug. 31 for 2011; Aug. 1 for 2012

640
Cablevision of Michigan, Inc.

21170 Allen Rd.
Trenton, MI 48183-1602 (313) 382-1500

Company URL: http://www.cablevision.com/about/index.jsp
Company type: Private company
Business activities: Provides cable television services.
Business type (SIC): Cable and other pay television services
Giving statement: Giving through the Dearborn Cable Communications Fund.

Dearborn Cable Communications Fund

22211 W. Warren St.
Dearborn Heights, MI 48127-2597 (313) 277-5800
Application address: 908 New York St., Dearborn, MI 48128, tel.: (313) 277-5800

Establishment information: Established in 1984 in MI.
Donors: Group W Cable, Inc.; Cablevision of Michigan, Inc.
Contact: Michael F. Katona, Pres.
Financial data (yr. ended 12/31/11): Assets, $730,668 (M); expenditures, $73,864; qualifying distributions, $46,411; giving activities include $46,411 for 7 grants (high: $15,943; low: $1,200).
Purpose and activities: The foundation supports programs designed to provide cable television programming of interest to the general community.
Fields of interest: Media/communications.
Type of support: Conferences/seminars; Equipment; General/operating support; Technical assistance.
Geographic limitations: Giving primarily in the Dearborn, MI, area.
Application information: Applications accepted. Application form required.
Initial approach: Letter
Board meeting date(s): Bimonthly
Deadline(s): None
Final notification: 60 Days
Officers: Michael Katona, Pres.; Andy Fradkin, V.P.; Barbara Parker, Secy.; Mark Campbell, Treas.
Directors: Joe Caruso; Nancy Daher; Said Deep; Kurt Doelle; Russ Gibb.
EIN: 382571195

641
Cablevision Systems Corporation

1111 Stewart Ave.
Bethpage, NY 11714 (516) 803-2300
FAX: (516) 364-4913

Company URL: http://www.cablevision.com
Establishment information: Established in 1973.
Company type: Public company
Company ticker symbol and exchange: CVC/NYSE

Business activities: Operates holding company; provides cable television services; operates motion picture theaters.
Business type (SIC): Cable and other pay television services; holding company; motion picture theaters
Financial profile for 2012: Number of employees, 18,889; assets, $7,246,220,000; sales volume, $6,705,460,000; pre-tax net income, $57,180,000; expenses, $6,012,160,000; liabilities, $12,885,390,000
Fortune 1000 ranking: 2012—382nd in revenues, 542nd in profits, and 481st in assets
Corporate officers: Charles F. Dolan, Chair.; Gregg G. Seibert, Vice-Chair. and C.F.O.; James L. Dolan, Pres. and C.E.O.; David Ellen, Exec. V.P. and Genl. Counsel; Victoria D. Salhus, Sr. V.P. and Secy.; Kevin Watson, Sr. V.P. and Treas.; Victoria Mink, Sr. V.P. and Cont.
Board of directors: Charles F. Dolan, Chair.; Gregg G. Seibert, Vice-Chair.; Rand V. Araskog; Edward C. Atwood; Frank J. Biondi, Jr.; Zachary W. Carter; James L. Dolan; Kathleen M. Dolan; Kristin A. Dolan; Patrick F. Dolan; Deborah Dolan-Sweeney; Thomas C. Dolan; Thomas V. Reifenheiser; John R. Ryan; Brian G. Sweeney; Vincent Tese; Leonard Tow; Marianne Dolan Weber
Subsidiaries: AMC Networks Inc., New York, NY; Madison Square Garden Company, New York, NY
International operations: Israel
Giving statement: Giving through the Cablevision Systems Corporation Contributions Program and the Marc Lustgarten Pancreatic Cancer Foundation.
Company EIN: 113415180

Cablevision Systems Corporation Contributions Program

1111 Stewart Ave.
Bethpage, NY 11714-3533 (877) 766-4633
E-mail: edinfo@cablevision.com; URL: http://www.cablevision.com/comm_ed/index.jsp

Purpose and activities: As a complement to its foundation, Cablevision makes charitable contributions of internet access technology to K-12 schools and school libraries. Support is given primarily in areas of company operations in Colorado, Connecticut, Montana, New Jersey, Utah, and Wyoming with emphasis on the New York, New York metropolitan area.
Fields of interest: Elementary/secondary education; Libraries (school).
Type of support: Donated products; Employee volunteer services.
Geographic limitations: Giving primarily in areas of company operations in CO, CT, MT, NJ, UT, and WY, with emphasis on the New York, NY, metropolitan area.
Application information:
Initial approach: Telephone or e-mail headquarters for application information

Marc Lustgarten Pancreatic Cancer Foundation

1111 Stewart Ave.
Bethpage, NY 11714-3533 (516) 803-2304
FAX: (516) 803-2303; Toll-free tel.: (866) 789-1000; URL: http://www.lustgartenfoundation.org/

Establishment information: Established in 1998 in NY.
Contact: Kerri Kaplan, Exec. Dir.
Financial data (yr. ended 12/31/11): Revenue, $13,085,372; assets, $33,576,010 (M); gifts received, $8,854,801; expenditures, $8,102,402; program services expenses, $7,148,037; giving activities include $6,001,054 for 30 grants (high: $1,046,934; low: $22,000).
Purpose and activities: The foundation supports efforts to advance the scientific and medical research related to the diagnosis, treatment, cure, and prevention of pancreatic cancer.
Fields of interest: Cancer research.
Programs:
Correlative Studies Award Program: Awarded in conjunction with the National Cancer Institute's Cancer Therapy Evaluation Program (CTEP), this program will fund selected correlative research applications directly linked to a CTEP-sponsored clinical trial of novel therapeutics for pancreatic cancer. Proposals must be focused on pancreatic ductal adenocarcinoma studies, and must be based on strong and testable hypotheses. Eligible projects for funding include, but are not limited to: phenotypic or genotypic alterations that correlate with response to therapy; phenotypic or genotypic alterations that explain the development of therapy resistance; phenotypic or genotypic alterations related to prognosis; studies that determine if test agents reach their cellular targets; studies that define the mechanisms of action of test agents in target tissues; early surrogate markers of later clinical responses; phenotypic or genotypic alterations that may be used for risk assessment, early detection, or prognosis; characterization of immune response with association to new immunotherapies for prevention or treatment; defining and targeting specific signal transduction pathways and populations of cells for therapy; or evaluation of accessible sites for monitoring changes occurring in less accessible sites (for example, the oral cavity as a surrogate site for cells in the pancreas).
Innovator Awards Program: This program provides a one-year, $100,000 award to fund novel, 'out-of-the-box' concepts in both translational and basic research. Applicants must hold an M.D. or Ph.D. and an independent, faculty-level position with or without tenure at the time of review; proposed investigations must be conducted at a university, hospital, or research institution possessing non-profit status.
Type of support: Research.
Geographic limitations: Giving on a national basis.
Publications: Annual report; Application guidelines; Newsletter.
Application information: Applications accepted.
Initial approach: Visit web site for current requests for proposals and/or request for applications
Deadline(s): Sept. 12 (concept proposals) and Oct. 31 (full proposals) for Innovator Awards; Oct. 15, Jan. 31, and May 31 for Correlative Studies Awards Program
Officers and Directors:* Charles F. Dolan*, Chair.; Robert F. Vizza, Ph.D.*, Pres.; William J. Bell*, Treas.; Kerri Kaplan, Exec. Dir.; James L. Dolan; Andrew Lustgarten; Marcia Lustgarten; Shelia A. Mahony; Matthew Modine; Charles R. Schueler; Alan D. Schwartz; Adam Silver.
EIN: 311611837

642
Cabot Corporation

2 Seaport Ln., Ste. 1300
Boston, MA 02210-2019 (617) 345-0100
FAX: (617) 342-6103

Company URL: http://www.cabot-corp.com
Establishment information: Established in 1882.
Company type: Public company
Company ticker symbol and exchange: CBT/NYSE
Business activities: Manufactures specialty chemicals and performance materials.
Business type (SIC): Chemical preparations/miscellaneous
Financial profile for 2012: Number of employees, 4,826; assets, $4,399,000,000; sales volume, $3,300,000,000; pre-tax net income, $245,000,000; expenses, $3,010,000,000; liabilities, $2,586,000,000
Fortune 1000 ranking: 2012—660th in revenues, 409th in profits, and 630th in assets
Corporate officers: John F. O'Brien, Chair.; Patrick M. Prevost, Pres. and C.E.O.; Eduardo E. Cordeiro, Exec. V.P. and C.F.O.; Brian A. Berube, Sr. V.P. and Genl. Counsel; Robby D. Sisco, Sr. V.P., Human Resources
Board of directors: John F. O'Brien, Chair.; John S. Clarkeson; Juan Enriquez-Cabot; Gautam S. Kaji; Henry McCance; John K. McGillicuddy; Roderick C.G MacLeod; Patrick Prevost; Sue Rataj; Ronaldo H. Schmitz; Lydia W. Thomas; Mark S. Wrighton
Plants: Atlanta, GA; Tuscola, IL; Franklin, Ville Platte, LA; Billerica, Everett, MA; Boyertown, PA; Pampa, TX
International operations: Argentina; Australia; Belgium; Brazil; British Virgin Islands; Canada; China; Colombia; Czech Republic; England; France; Germany; India; Indonesia; Italy; Japan; Luxembourg; Malaysia; Netherlands; Scotland; Singapore; South Korea; Spain; Switzerland; United Kingdom; Venezuela
Giving statement: Giving through the Cabot Corporation Contributions Program and the Cabot Corporation Foundation, Inc.
Company EIN: 042271897

Cabot Corporation Foundation, Inc.

2 Seaport Ln., Ste. 1300
Boston, MA 02210-2058 (617) 345-0100
E-mail: jane_bell@cabot-corp.com; Additional Contact: Cynthia L. Gullotii, e-mail: Cynthia_Gullotti@cabot-corp.com; URL: http://www.cabot-corp.com/About-Cabot/Corporate-Giving

Establishment information: Incorporated in 1953 in MA.
Donor: Cabot Corp.
Contact: Jane A. Bell, V.P. and Exec. Dir.
Financial data (yr. ended 09/30/11): Assets, $751,132 (M); gifts received, $1,000,000; expenditures, $1,290,570; qualifying distributions, $1,290,300; giving activities include $1,290,300 for grants.
Purpose and activities: The foundation supports organizations involved with education, health, human services, community development, science and technology, and civic affairs.
Fields of interest: Elementary/secondary education; Education, early childhood education; Higher education; Education, reading; Education; Health care; Residential/custodial care, hospices; Human services; Community/economic development; United Ways and Federated Giving Programs; Chemistry; Mathematics; Engineering/technology; Computer science; Biology/life sciences; Science.
Type of support: Building/renovation; Capital campaigns; Continuing support; Equipment; General/operating support; Program development; Publication; Scholarship funds.
Geographic limitations: Giving primarily in Support is given primarily in areas of company operations in Alpharetta, GA, Tuscola, Il, Franklin, and Ville Platte, LA, Billerica, Boston, and Haverhill, MA, Midland, MI, Boyertown, PA, Pampa, and The Woodlands, TX, and in Argentina, Belgium, Brazil, Canada, China, Columbia, Czech Republic, Dubai, France, Germany, India, Indonesia, Italy, Japan, Malaysia, Mexico,

Netherlands, Norway, Spain, Switzerland, Venezuela, and Wales.
Support limitations: No support for religious organizations not of direct benefit to the entire community, or political or fraternal organizations. No grants to individuals, or for capital campaigns or endowments, tickets or tables at fundraising events, or advertising.
Publications: Annual report; Application guidelines.
Application information: Applications accepted. Organizations receiving support are asked to submit periodic progress reports. Application form required. Applicants should submit the following:
1) timetable for implementation and evaluation of project
2) how project will be sustained once grantmaker support is completed
3) results expected from proposed grant
4) qualifications of key personnel
5) copy of IRS Determination Letter
6) brief history of organization and description of its mission
7) copy of most recent annual report/audited financial statement/990
8) explanation of why grantmaker is considered an appropriate donor for project
9) listing of board of directors, trustees, officers and other key people and their affiliations
10) detailed description of project and amount of funding requested
11) listing of additional sources and amount of support

Initial approach: Download application form and e-mail proposal and application form to foundation
Copies of proposal: 1
Board meeting date(s): Jan., Apr., July, and Oct.
Deadline(s): 30 days prior to board meetings
Final notification: 3 months

Officers and Directors:* Patrick M. Prevost*, Pres.; Jane A. Bell*, V.P. and Exec. Dir.; Karen Abrams, Clerk; John J. Lawler*, Treas.; Christina Bramante; Andrew O'Donovan; Janet Ryan; Robby D. Sisco.
EIN: 046035227
Selected grants: The following grants are a representative sample of this grantmaker's funding activity:
$60,000 to Washington University, Saint Louis, MO, 2009.
$54,000 to Scholarship America, Saint Peter, MN, 2009.
$2,100 to Atlanta Day Shelter for Women and Children, Atlanta, GA, 2009.

643
Samuel Cabot Incorporated

100 Hale St.
Newburyport, MA 01950-3504
(978) 465-1900

Company URL: http://www.cabotstain.com
Establishment information: Established in 1877.
Company type: Subsidiary of a public company
Business activities: Develops, manufactures, and distributes exterior wood stains and surface finishing products.
Business type (SIC): Paints and allied products
Corporate officers: Samuel Cabot III, Chair.; John E. Schutz, Pres. and C.E.O.
Board of director: Samuel Cabot III, Chair.
Plants: Hayward, Union City, CA
Giving statement: Giving through the Samuel Cabot Inc. Corporate Giving Program.

Samuel Cabot Inc. Corporate Giving Program

100 Hale St.
Newburyport, MA 01950-3504 (978) 465-1900
FAX: (978) 462-0511

Contact: Wendy Machaud
Purpose and activities: Samuel Cabot makes charitable contributions to nonprofit organizations involved with education. Support is given primarily in Newburyport, Massachusetts.
Fields of interest: Elementary/secondary education.
Type of support: Donated products; General/operating support.
Geographic limitations: Giving primarily in Newburyport, MA.
Application information: Applications accepted. A contributions committee reviews all requests. Application form not required.
Initial approach: Proposal to headquarters

644
Cacique, Inc.

(doing business as Cacique USA Food)
14923 Proctor Ave.
P.O. Box 91270
La Puente, CA 91746 (626) 961-3399

Company URL: http://www.caciqueusa.com
Establishment information: Established in 1973.
Company type: Private company
Business activities: Manufactures Hispanic-style dairy products.
Business type (SIC): Dairy products
Financial profile for 2009: Number of employees, 242
Corporate officers: Gilbert de Cardenas, Sr., C.E.O.; Gilbert L. de Cardenas, Jr., Pres.; Lio Mograbi, V.P., Opers.; Bob Hubberard, V.P., Finance; Abel Cordero, V.P., Sales; Will Parker, V.P., Mktg.; Carl Lau, Cont.
Giving statement: Giving through the Cacique Foundation.

Cacique Foundation

14940 Proctor Ave.
City of Industry, CA 91744 (626) 961-3399

Establishment information: Established in 1996 in CA.
Donors: Cacique, Inc.; Cacique Distributors, U.S.
Contact: Ana de Cardenas-Raptis, Pres.
Financial data (yr. ended 12/31/11): Assets, $10,580 (M); gifts received, $175,000; expenditures, $175,427; qualifying distributions, $175,367; giving activities include $175,367 for 21 grants (high: $50,000; low: $10).
Purpose and activities: The foundation supports hospitals and organizations involved with arts and culture, education, athletics and sports, human services, and civil and human rights.
Fields of interest: Arts; Secondary school/education; Higher education; Education; Hospitals (general); Athletics/sports, amateur leagues; Children/youth, services; Human services; Civil/human rights.
Program:
Scholarship Program: The foundation provides scholarship funds for individuals to study at Mt. San Antonio College. The funds are awarded to students sponsored by the Buenanueva Foundation, Cacique employees, and Mt. SAC students who are single parents. The program is administered by Mt. SAC Foundation.
Type of support: General/operating support; Scholarship funds.
Geographic limitations: Giving primarily in CA and FL.
Application information: Applications accepted. Scholarship information is available at the office of the Mount San Antonio College Foundation on the campus of Mount San Antonio College.
Initial approach: Contact foundation for grant application information; contact Mt. SAC Foundation for scholarships
Officers: Gilbert L. De Cardenas, Chair.; Ana de Cardenas-Raptis, Pres.
EIN: 954518246
Selected grants: The following grants are a representative sample of this grantmaker's funding activity:
$20,000 to Pasadena Hospital Association, Pasadena, CA, 2009.
$5,000 to Misioneros del Camino, Miami, FL, 2009.
$1,000 to Cal Poly Pomona Foundation, Pomona, CA, 2009.

645
Caddell Construction Co., Inc.

2700 Lagoon Park Dr.
P.O. Box 210099
Montgomery, AL 36109-1110
(334) 272-7723
FAX: (334) 272-8844

Company URL: http://www.caddell.com
Establishment information: Established in 1983.
Company type: Private company
Business activities: Provides general contract construction services.
Business type (SIC): Building construction general contractors and operative builders
Corporate officers: John A. Caddell, Chair.; J. Kirby Caddell, Vice-Chair.; B.E. Stewart, Pres. and C.O.O.; Earl Jones, V.P. and C.A.O.
Board of directors: John A. Caddell, Chair.; J. Kirby Caddell, Vice-Chair.
Giving statement: Giving through the Caddell Foundation.

The Caddell Foundation

2700 Lagoon Park Dr.
Montgomery, AL 36109-1110

Donor: Caddell Construction Co., Inc.
Contact: Earl Jones
Financial data (yr. ended 12/31/11): Assets, $6,131,540 (M); gifts received, $900,000; expenditures, $234,407; qualifying distributions, $233,200; giving activities include $233,200 for grants.
Purpose and activities: The foundation supports fairs and festivals and organizations involved with performing arts, higher education, and cancer.
Fields of interest: Performing arts; Performing arts, theater; Performing arts, music; Performing arts, orchestras; Higher education; Cancer; Recreation, fairs/festivals; United Ways and Federated Giving Programs.
Type of support: General/operating support.
Geographic limitations: Giving primarily in Montgomery, AL.
Support limitations: No grants to individuals.
Application information: Applications accepted. Application form not required. Applicants should submit the following:

1) brief history of organization and description of its mission
Initial approach: Proposal
Deadline(s): None

Officers and Directors:* John A. Caddell*, Pres.; Joyce K. Caddell*, Secy.-Treas.; Cathy L. Caddell; Christopher P. Caddell; Jeffrey P. Caddell; John K. Caddell; Michael A. Caddell.
EIN: 631133304
Selected grants: The following grants are a representative sample of this grantmaker's funding activity:
$25,000 to Alabama Shakespeare Festival, Montgomery, AL, 2010.
$18,089 to Georgia Tech Foundation, Atlanta, GA, 2010.
$7,500 to American Cancer Society, Montgomery, AL, 2010.
$7,500 to Cloverdale Playhouse, Montgomery, AL, 2010.
$7,500 to Huntingdon College, Montgomery, AL, 2010.
$7,500 to Samford University, Birmingham, AL, 2010.

646
Cadence Design Systems, Inc.

2655 Seely Ave., Bldg. 5
San Jose, CA 95134 (408) 943-1234
FAX: (408) 428-5001

Company URL: http://www.cadence.com
Establishment information: Established in 1988.
Company type: Public company
Company ticker symbol and exchange: CDNS/NASDAQ
Business activities: Develops computer software; manufactures computer technology.
Business type (SIC): Computer services; computer and office equipment
Financial profile for 2012: Number of employees, 5,200; assets, $2,287,000,000; sales volume, $1,326,420,000; pre-tax net income, $188,270,000; expenses, $1,115,860,000; liabilities, $1,371,830,000
Corporate officers: John B. Shoven, Ph.D., Chair.; Lip-Bu Tan, Pres. and C.E.O.; Geoffrey G. Ribar, Sr. V.P. and C.F.O.; James J. Cowie, Sr., V.P., Genl. Counsel, and Secy.; Tina Jones, Sr., Sr. V.P., Human Resources; Pankaj Mayor, V.P., Mktg.
Board of directors: John B. Shoven, Ph.D., Chair.; Susan L. Bostrom; James D. Plummer; Alberto Sangiovanni-Vincentelli, Ph.D.; George M. Scalise; Roger S. Siboni; Young K. Sohn; Lip-Bu Tan
Subsidiary: Cooper & Chyan Technology Inc., Cupertino, CA
International operations: Bermuda; Canada; Cayman Islands; China; Cyprus; France; Germany; Hong Kong; Hungary; India; Ireland; Israel; Italy; Japan; Netherlands; Russia; Singapore; Sweden; Taiwan; United Kingdom
Giving statement: Giving through the Cadence Design Systems, Inc. Corporate Giving Program.
Company EIN: 770148231

Cadence Design Systems, Inc. Corporate Giving Program

c/o Community Involvement
2655 Seely Ave.
San Jose, CA 95134-1931 (408) 943-1234
E-mail: kwheeler@cadence.com; URL: http://www.cadence.com/community/

Contact: Kathy Wheeler, Mgr., Community Rels.
Purpose and activities: Cadence makes charitable contributions to nonprofit organizations involved with education, the military, homeless women, children, and youth, and technology. Support is given primarily in areas of company operations in Arizona, Florida, Maryland, Massachusetts, Minnesota, New Jersey, New York, North Carolina, Oregon, Pennsylvania, Texas, Utah, and Washington, with emphasis on California, and in India, Japan, and the United Kingdom.
Fields of interest: Museums (science/technology); Elementary/secondary education; Vocational education; Children/youth, services; Women, centers/services; Homeless, human services; Engineering/technology; General charitable giving Military/veterans.
International interests: India; Japan; United Kingdom.
Program:
Matching Gift Program: Cadence matches contributions made by its part-time and full-time employees in Canada and the US to nonprofit organizations on a one-for-one basis.
Type of support: Donated equipment; Employee matching gifts; Employee volunteer services; General/operating support; In-kind gifts; Sponsorships.
Geographic limitations: Giving primarily in areas of company operations in AZ, FL, MA, MD, MN, NC, NJ, NY, OR, PA, TX, UT, and WA, with emphasis on CA, and in India, Japan, and the United Kingdom.
Application information: Unsolicited requests for general operating support and sponsorships are not accepted.
Initial approach: Letter of inquiry for equipment donations

647
Cades Schutte LLP

1000 Bishop St., Ste. 1200
Honolulu, HI 96813-4298 (808) 521-9200

Company URL: http://cades.com
Establishment information: Established in 1922.
Company type: Private company
Business activities: Operates law firm.
Business type (SIC): Legal services
Giving statement: Giving through the Cades Schutte LLP Corporate Giving Program.

Cades Schutte LLP Corporate Giving Program

Cades Schutte Bldg.
1000 Bishop St., 10th Fl.
Honolulu, HI 96813-4298 (808) 521-9200
FAX: (808) 521-9210; URL: http://cades.com/FirmBio/dsp_FirmProfile.cfm

Contact: Patricia J. McHenry, Attorney
Purpose and activities: Cades Schutte makes charitable contributions to nonprofit organizations involved with arts and culture, education, and human services.
Fields of interest: Arts; Law school/education; Education; Legal services; Human services; United Ways and Federated Giving Programs; General charitable giving.
Type of support: General/operating support; Pro bono services - legal; Scholarship funds.

648
Cadillac Products Inc.

5800 Crooks Rd.
Troy, MI 48098-2830 (248) 879-5000

Company URL: http://www.cadprod.com
Establishment information: Established in 1942.
Company type: Private company
Business activities: Manufactures interior automotive trim, packaging materials, and specialty papers.
Business type (SIC): Motor vehicles and equipment; paper and paperboard/coated, converted, and laminated; plastic products/miscellaneous
Financial profile for 2010: Number of employees, 50
Corporate officers: Robert J. Williams, Sr., Chair.; Robert J. Williams, Jr., Pres. and C.E.O.; Debra Osborn, C.F.O.; Roger Williams, Treas.; Jim Krizan, Cont.
Board of director: Robert J. Williams, Sr., Chair.
Giving statement: Giving through the Cadillac Products Inc. Foundation.

Cadillac Products Inc. Foundation

5800 Crooks Rd.
Troy, MI 48098-2830 (248) 879-5000

Establishment information: Established in 1985 in MI.
Donors: Cadillac Products Inc.; Robert J. Williams, Sr.
Contact: Roger K. Williams, Treas.
Financial data (yr. ended 07/31/11): Assets, $809,655 (M); expenditures, $10,363; qualifying distributions, $10,000; giving activities include $10,000 for 1 grant.
Purpose and activities: The foundation supports organizations involved with higher education and youth development.
Fields of interest: Higher education; Boys & girls clubs.
Type of support: General/operating support.
Geographic limitations: Giving primarily in Phoenix, AZ, and IN.
Application information: Applications accepted. Application form required. Applicants should submit the following:
1) detailed description of project and amount of funding requested
Initial approach: Letter
Deadline(s): None

Officers: Robert J. Williams, Sr., Pres.; Michael P. Williams II, V.P.; Robert J. Williams, Jr., Secy.; Roger K. Williams, Treas.
EIN: 382636705

649
Cadwalader, Wickersham & Taft LLP

1 World Financial Ctr.
New York, NY 10281-1003 (212) 504-6000

Company URL: http://www.cadwalader.com
Establishment information: Established in 1792.
Company type: Private company
Business activities: Operates law firm.
Business type (SIC): Legal services
Offices: Washington, DC; New York, NY; Charlotte, NC; Houston, TX
International operations: Belgium; China; Hong Kong; United Kingdom

Giving statement: Giving through the Cadwalader, Wickersham & Taft LLP Pro Bono Program.

Cadwalader, Wickersham & Taft LLP Pro Bono Program

1 World Financial Ctr.
New York, NY 10281-1003 (212) 504-6665
E-mail: annie.mohan@cwt.com; Additional tel.: (212) 504-6000; URL: http://www.cadwalader.com/About_Cadwalader/Public_Service/Pro_Bono_Reports/32

Contact: Annie Mohan, Mgr. of Pro Bono
Fields of interest: Legal services.
Type of support: Pro bono services - legal.
Geographic limitations: Giving primarily in areas of company operations in Washington, DC, Charlotte, NC, New York, NY, Houston, TX, and in Belgium, China, Hong Kong, and United Kingdom.
Application information: The Pro Bono Committee manages the pro-bono program.

650
Caesars Entertainment Corporation

(formerly Harrah's Entertainment, Inc.)
1 Caesars Palace Dr.
Las Vegas, NV 89109 (702) 407-6000

Company URL: http://www.caesars.com
Establishment information: Established in 1937.
Company type: Private company
Business activities: Operates hotel casinos and related facilities.
Business type (SIC): Amusement and recreation services/miscellaneous; hotels and motels
Financial profile for 2012: Assets, $28,000,000,000; sales volume, $8,600,000,000
Forbes 2000 ranking: 2012—1037th in sales, 1947th in profits, and 778th in assets
Corporate officers: Gary W. Loveman, Chair., Pres., and C.E.O.; Jonathan S. Halkyard, Sr. V.P. and C.F.O.; Tim Donovan, Sr. V.P. and Genl. Counsel; Jan Jones, Sr. V.P., Comms.
Board of director: Gary W. Loveman, Chair.
Subsidiaries: Caesars World, Inc., Las Vegas, NV; Harrah's Operating Company, Inc., Las Vegas, NV
Divisions: Harrah's Ak-Chin, Phoenix, AZ; Harrah's Atlantic City, Atlantic City, NJ; Harrah's Casino Cruises, Joliet, IL; Harrah's Casino Hotel, Laughlin, NV; Harrah's Casino Vicksburg, Vicksburg, MS; Harrah's Las Vegas, Las Vegas, NV; Harrah's North Kansas City, North Kansas City, NV; Harrah's Prairie Band, Topeka, KS; Harrah's Reno, Reno, NV; Harrah's Shreveport, Shreveport, LA; Harrah's Skagit Valley, Skagit Valley, WA; Harrah's St. Louis-Riverport Casino & Hotel, Maryland Heights, MO; Harrah's Tahoe, Lake Tahoe, NV; Harrah's Tunica Mardi Gras Casino, Tunica, MS
International operations: Bermuda
Historic mergers: Caesars Entertainment, Inc. (June 13, 2005)
Giving statement: Giving through the Caesars Entertainment Corporation Contributions Program and the Caesars Foundation.
Company EIN: 621411755

Caesars Entertainment Corporation Contributions Program

(formerly Harrah's Entertainment, Inc. Corporate Giving Program)
1 Caesars Palace Dr.
Las Vegas, NV 89109-8969
URL: http://www.caesars.com/corporate/about-us-charitable-giving.html

Purpose and activities: As a complement to its foundation, Caesars Entertainment Corporation also makes charitable contributions to nonprofit organizations directly. Special emphasis is directed towards programs that serve senior citizens, health-related causes, and diverse populations. Support is given primarily in areas of company operations.
Fields of interest: Health care; Human services; Aging, centers/services.
Type of support: Employee volunteer services; General/operating support; In-kind gifts.
Geographic limitations: Giving primarily in areas of company operations.
Support limitations: No support for religious organizations not of direct benefit to the entire community, or for political organizations, discriminatory organizations, athletic teams, or treatment centers. No grants to individuals.
Publications: Application guidelines.
Application information: Applications accepted. Applicants should submit the following:
1) name, address and phone number of organization
2) copy of IRS Determination Letter
3) brief history of organization and description of its mission
4) copy of most recent annual report/audited financial statement/990
5) listing of board of directors, trustees, officers and other key people and their affiliations
6) detailed description of project and amount of funding requested
7) copy of current year's organizational budget and/or project budget
8) listing of additional sources and amount of support

Applications should include an annual report and statement of diversity; and indicate accrediting agencies, if applicable. Cultural organizations should submit their most recent 12-month audience statistics.
Initial approach: Complete online application form
Deadline(s): 60 days prior to need

Caesars Foundation

(formerly The Harrah's Foundation)
1 Caesars Palace Dr.
Las Vegas, NV 89109-8969 (702) 880-4728
FAX: (702) 407-6520;
E-mail: caesarsfoundation@caesars.com; Additional address: P.O. Box 2332, Princeton, NJ 08543-2332, tel.: (855) 645-6328; URL: http://www.caesarsfoundation.com/

Establishment information: Established in 2002 in NV.
Donors: Caesars Entertainment Operating Company, Inc.; Harrah's Operating Co., Inc.
Contact: Judi Brown, Admin.
Financial data (yr. ended 12/31/11): Assets, $1,793,347 (M); gifts received, $7,868,749; expenditures, $7,779,618; qualifying distributions, $7,596,517; giving activities include $7,129,322 for 99 grants (high: $1,000,000; low: $5,000).
Purpose and activities: The foundation supports programs designed to help older individuals live longer, healthier, and more fulfilling lives; promote a safe and clean environment; and improve the quality of life in communities where Caesars operates.
Fields of interest: Higher education; Environment, land resources; Environment, energy; Environment; Hospitals (general); Health care, clinics/centers; Health care, patient services; Health care; Mental health/crisis services; Alzheimer's disease; Food services; Food distribution, meals on wheels; Nutrition; Disasters, preparedness/services; American Red Cross; Youth, services; Human services, mind/body enrichment; Aging, centers/services; Developmentally disabled, centers & services; Human services; Public affairs Aging.
Type of support: Building/renovation; Capital campaigns; Continuing support; Employee volunteer services; General/operating support; Program development; Research; Scholarship funds; Sponsorships.
Geographic limitations: Giving primarily in areas of company operations in AZ, CA, IA, IL, IN, LA, MO, MS, NC, NJ, Las Vegas and Reno, NV, and PA.
Support limitations: No grants to individuals; no in-kind gifts.
Publications: Application guidelines; Informational brochure.
Application information: Applications accepted. The foundation generally funds programs and projects of $10,000 or more. Application form required. Applicants should submit the following:
1) copy of IRS Determination Letter
2) brief history of organization and description of its mission
3) copy of most recent annual report/audited financial statement/990
4) listing of board of directors, trustees, officers and other key people and their affiliations
5) detailed description of project and amount of funding requested
6) copy of current year's organizational budget and/or project budget
7) listing of additional sources and amount of support
8) plans for acknowledgement

Applications must also include a diversity statement that reflects the applicants policy toward non-discrimination.
Initial approach: Complete online application
Board meeting date(s): Quarterly
Deadline(s): None
Officers and Trustees:* Janet Beronio*, Chair.; Jan Jones Blackhurst*, Vice-Chair.; Scott Weigand*, Secy.; Torben Cohrs, Treas.; Thom Reilly, Exec. Dir.; Thomas M. Jenkin; Fred Keeton; Dan Nita; John Payne; Diane Wilfong.
EIN: 743050638
Selected grants: The following grants are a representative sample of this grantmaker's funding activity:
$1,100,000 to AARP Foundation, Las Vegas, NV, 2010. For program support.
$1,000,000 to University of Nevada at Las Vegas Foundation, Las Vegas, NV, 2010. For Innovation Village.
$500,000 to American Cancer Society, Memphis and Shelby County Unit, Memphis, TN, 2010. For program support.
$500,000 to Meals on Wheels Association of America, Alexandria, VA, 2010. For March for Meals campaigns, delivery vehicles and program.
$250,000 to Opportunity Village, Las Vegas, NV, 2010. For program endowment of Seniors with Disabilities.
$250,000 to Second Wind Dreams, Alpharetta, GA, 2010. For event sponsorship.
$200,000 to AtlantiCare Regional Medical Center, Atlantic City, NJ, 2010. For new trauma center facility.

$182,200 to Nevada Public Radio Corporation, Las Vegas, NV, 2010. For program support.
$60,000 to Calumet College of Saint Joseph, Whiting, IN, 2010. For Capital Campaign for New Student Center Building.
$25,000 to National Association of Area Agencies on Aging, Washington, DC, 2010. For event sponsorship.

651
Cahill Gordon & Reindel LLP

80 Pine St.
New York, NY 10005-1702 (212) 701-3000

Company URL: http:///www.cahill.com
Establishment information: Established in 1919.
Company type: Private company
Business activities: Operates law firm.
Business type (SIC): Legal services
Corporate officer: Floyd Abrams, Partner
Offices: Washington, DC; New York, NY
International operations: United Kingdom
Giving statement: Giving through the Cahill Gordon & Reindel LLP Pro Bono Program.

Cahill Gordon & Reindel LLP Pro Bono Program

80 Pine St.
New York, NY 10005-1702 (212) 701-3000
E-mail: djanuszewski@cahill.com; URL: http://www.cahill.com/firm/080

Contact: David Januszewski, Pro Bono Partner
Fields of interest: Legal services.
Type of support: Pro bono services - legal.
Geographic limitations: Giving primarily in areas of company operations in Washington, DC, New York, NY, and in United Kingdom.
Application information: The Pro Bono Committee manages the pro-bono program.

652
Cajun Industries, LLC

15635 Airline Hwy.
P.O. Box 104
Baton Rouge, LA 70817 (225) 753-5857
FAX: (225) 751-9777

Company URL: http://www.cajunusa.com/
Establishment information: Established in 1973.
Company type: Private company
Business activities: Builds oil refineries, power plants, and other industrial and infrastructure projects.
Business type (SIC): Construction/miscellaneous heavy
Corporate officers: Lane Grigsby, Chair.; Kenneth Jacob, Pres. and C.E.O.; Shane Recile, C.F.O.; John English, V.P., Mktg.; Dawn Grigsby, V.P., Sales
Board of director: Lane Grigsby, Chair.
Giving statement: Giving through the Merice "Boo" Johnson Grigsby Foundation.

The Merice "Boo" Johnson Grigsby Foundation

15635 Airline Hwy.
Baton Rouge, LA 70817-7318
E-mail: info@boogrigsbyfoundation.org; Additional address: 12540 W. Lake Estates, Baton Rouge, LA 70810; URL: http://www.boogrigsbyfoundation.com

Establishment information: Established in 2006 in LA.
Donor: Cajun Constructors, Inc.
Financial data (yr. ended 12/31/10): Assets, $1,678,661 (M); gifts received, $280,000; expenditures, $240,369; qualifying distributions, $220,500; giving activities include $220,500 for grants.
Purpose and activities: The foundation supports organizations involved with arts and culture, education, the environment, health, human services, and community development.
Fields of interest: Arts education; Visual arts; Performing arts; Humanities; Arts; Higher education; Education; Environment, natural resources; Environmental education; Environment; Health care; Family services; Human services; Community/economic development.
Type of support: Continuing support; General/operating support; Program development; Scholarship funds.
Geographic limitations: Giving primarily in Baton Rouge, LA; giving also to national organizations.
Application information: Applications not accepted. Unsolicited requests for funds not accepted.
Directors: L. Lane Grigsby; Todd William Grigsby; Tami Grigsby Moran; Tricia Grigsby Sanchez.
EIN: 208091007

653
California Bank & Trust

11752 El Camino Real
San Diego, CA 92130-2049
(858) 720-9300
FAX: (858) 720-9330

Company URL: http://ttp://www.calbanktrust.com
Establishment information: Established in 1952.
Company type: Subsidiary of a public company
Business activities: Operates commercial bank.
Business type (SIC): Banks/commercial
Corporate officer: David Blackford, Chair., Pres., and C.E.O.
Board of director: David Blackford, Chair.
Giving statement: Giving through the California Bank & Trust Corporate Giving Program.

California Bank & Trust Corporate Giving Program

c/o Community Reinvestment Dept.
16041 Goldenwest St., 2nd Fl.
Huntington Beach, CA 92647-3405
URL: http://www.calbanktrust.com/about/community-grant.html#more_grant

Purpose and activities: California Bank & Trust makes charitable contributions to nonprofit organizations involved with affordable housing, small business and micro-enterprise development, and community economic development. Support is given primarily in areas of company operations.
Fields of interest: Housing/shelter; Business/industry; Community/economic development.
Geographic limitations: Giving primarily in areas of company operations in CA.
Publications: Application guidelines.
Application information: Applications accepted. Applicants should submit the following:
1) population served
2) listing of board of directors, trustees, officers and other key people and their affiliations
3) listing of additional sources and amount of support
4) copy of IRS Determination Letter
5) copy of current year's organizational budget and/or project budget
6) contact person
7) brief history of organization and description of its mission

Initial approach: Proposal
Deadline(s): None

654
California Casualty Group

1900 Alameda de las Pulgas
San Mateo, CA 94403 (650) 574-4000

Company URL: http://www.calcas.com
Establishment information: Established in 1914.
Company type: Private company
Business activities: Sells automobile and property insurance.
Business type (SIC): Insurance/fire, marine, and casualty
Corporate officers: Carl Beau Brown, Chair. and C.E.O.; Michael Ray, Sr. V.P., C.F.O., and Treas.; Vasu Kadambi, Sr. V.P. and C.I.O; James R. Englese, Sr. V.P., Corp. Secy., and Genl. Counsel.; James F. Grady, Ph.D., Sr. V.P., Admin.
Board of directors: Carl Beau Brown, Chair.; Jon H. Hamm; Thomas H. Tongue, Esq.
Giving statement: Giving through the California Casualty Group Corporate Giving Program.

California Casualty Group Corporate Giving Program

P.O. Box M, M.C. CD-1
San Mateo, CA 94402-0080 (650) 572-4408
FAX: (650) 572-4491; E-mail: pgrandov@calcas.com

Contact: Patti Grandov, Coord., Contribs. Comm.
Financial data (yr. ended 12/31/10): Total giving, $33,000, including $33,000 for 8 grants.
Purpose and activities: California Casualty Group makes charitable contributions to nonprofit organizations supported/sponsored by affinity groups participating in California Casualty insurance programs and organizations involved with education and youth development. Support is given primarily in areas of company operations.
Fields of interest: Elementary/secondary education; Higher education; Education; Youth development Children/youth; Children.
Type of support: Continuing support; General/operating support.
Geographic limitations: Giving primarily in areas of company operations.
Support limitations: No support for widely known or "household name" organizations, fundraising organizations, sports teams or leagues. No grants for luncheons, dinners, or banquets, research not incidental to an organization's main purpose, equipment, or construction projects.
Publications: Application guidelines.
Application information: Applications accepted. Support is limited to 3 years in length. The Corporate Development handles giving. A contributions committee reviews all requests. Application form required.

Initial approach: Contact headquarters for application form
Copies of proposal: 1
Committee meeting date(s): Contact headquarters for dates
Deadline(s): Contact headquarters for deadline
Final notification: Contact headquarters for dates

Number of staff: 1 part-time support.

655
California Physicians' Service Agency Inc.

(doing business as Blue Shield of California)
50 Beale St.
San Francisco, CA 94105-1808
(415) 229-5000

Company URL: http://www.blueshieldca.com
Establishment information: Established in 1939.
Company type: Mutual company
Business activities: Operates medical service plan.
Business type (SIC): Insurance/accident and health
Financial profile for 2011: Number of employees, 4,800; sales volume, $9,700,000,000
Corporate officers: Robert Lee, Chair.; Paul Markovich, Pres. and C.E.O.; Ed Cymerys, Exec. V.P., Chief Actuary, and C.F.O.; Seth A. Jacobs, Sr. V.P., Genl. Counsel, and Corp. Secy.; Rob Geyer, Sr. V.P., Customer Quality; Marcus Thygeson, M.D., Sr. V.P., Chief Health Off.; Marianne Jackson, Sr. V.P., Human Resources; Christopher Gorecki, V.P. and Corp. Cont.
Board of directors: Robert Lee, Chair.; Doug Busch; Vanessa Chang; Evelyn Dilsaver; Hector Flores, M.D.; Alan Fohrer; Hector Flores; William Hauck; Sandra Hernandez, M.D.; Paul Markovich; Mohammad Qayoumi, Ph.D.
Subsidiaries: California Physicians Insurance Corp., San Francisco, CA; HIH America, Irvine, CA
Offices: Costa Mesa, El Dorado Hills, El Segundo, Fresno, Gold River, Lodi, Ontario, Redding, Sacramento, San Diego, San Francisco, San Jose, Ventura, Walnut Creek, Woodland Hills, CA
Giving statement: Giving through the Blue Shield of California Corporate Giving Program and the California Physicians' Service Foundation.

Blue Shield of California Corporate Giving Program

50 Beale St.
San Francisco, CA 94105-1808 (415) 229-5000
URL: https://www.blueshieldca.com/bsca/about-blue-shield/social-responsibility/home.sp

Purpose and activities: As a complement to its foundation, Blue Shield of California also makes charitable contributions to nonprofit organizations directly. Emphasis is given to organizations that are involved with improving health and quality of life. Support is limited to community events, programs, and organizations in California with which Blue Shield of California employees are involved.
Fields of interest: Health care, support services; Health care; Health organizations, single organization support; Cancer; AIDS; Alzheimer's disease; Cancer, leukemia research; Heart & circulatory research; Crime/violence prevention; Food services; Housing/shelter, homeless; Boys clubs; Girls clubs; Children/youth, services; Human services; Military/veterans' organizations.
Program:
Matching Gifts Program: Blue Shield matches employee donations to healthcare organizations 2-to-1 and donations to human services organizations 1-to-1, up to $1,000. In 2011, employee and matching gifts totaled nearly $400,000.
Type of support: Employee matching gifts; Employee volunteer services; General/operating support.
Geographic limitations: Giving limited to CA.

California Physicians' Service Foundation

(doing business as Blue Shield of California Foundation)
50 Beale St., 14th Fl.
San Francisco, CA 94105-1819
FAX: (415) 229-6268;
E-mail: bscf@blueshieldcafoundation.org; E-mail for Gwyneth Tripp:
gwyneth.tripp@blueshieldcafoundation.org;
URL: http://www.blueshieldcafoundation.org/

Establishment information: Established in 1981 as a grantmaking public charity; status changed to company-sponsored foundation in 2004.
Donor: California Physicians' Service Agency Inc.
Contact: Gwyneth Tripp, Grant Admin.
Financial data (yr. ended 12/31/11): Assets, $61,993,650 (M); gifts received, $38,195,000; expenditures, $29,134,222; qualifying distributions, $29,056,418; giving activities include $24,522,346 for 343 grants (high: $1,049,722; low: $5,000; average: $15,000–$500,000).
Purpose and activities: The foundation supports programs designed to improve the lives of Californians, particularly underserved populations, by making health care accessible, effective, and affordable for all Californians, and by ending domestic violence.
Fields of interest: Health care, public policy; Health care, reform; Health care, clinics/centers; Health care, insurance; Health care, cost containment; Health care, financing; Health care; Health organizations, reform; Crime/violence prevention, domestic violence; Family services, domestic violence; Leadership development Economically disadvantaged.
Programs:
Blue Shield Against Violence: The foundation supports programs designed to end domestic violence and strengthen California's domestic violence safety net through grantmaking and operating programs. Special emphasis is directed toward programs designed to build a stronger shield through a coordinated network of services and domestic violence organizations, and increased efficiency across that network; spur innovation through new solutions to reach high-need populations; and advance and influence domestic violence policy.
Clinic Leadership Institute: The foundation operates an 18-month professional development training program for 25 leaders of California clinics and health centers. The program includes a personal learning plan, seminars, inter-sessions, peer networking, community clinic leadership projects, professional coaching, and leadership network and alumni activities. The program is designed to build the next generation of safety net providers and leaders and is administered by the Center for the Health Professions at the University of California, San Francisco.
Health Care and Coverage: The foundation provides technical assistance to state and local policymakers to successfully implement national health reform and supports safety net institutions that are the essential health providers in their communities. Special emphasis is directed toward programs designed to strengthen community clinics and other safety net providers through innovation; encourage innovative approaches to expand access to care for the uninsured through advocacy, convenings, and other efforts; promote policy efforts around Medi-Cal enrollment modernization; develop policy solutions, financing, and access models for underserved populations; and foster solutions to bend the healthcare cost curve and help Californians get better value for their healthcare spending.
Strong Field Project: The Strong Field Project is a four-year, $7 million effort by Blue Shield of California Foundation's Blue Shield Against Violence program. Started in 2010, the Project focuses on building a stronger, more coordinated network of DV service providers in California. In collaboration with the California Partnership to End Domestic Violence, CompassPoint Nonprofit Services, Jemmott Rollins Group, and Women's Foundation of California, the Project will develop individual leadership skills, stronger organizations, and networking and expanded knowledge-sharing opportunities across California's domestic violence field.
Type of support: Conferences/seminars; Continuing support; Employee-related scholarships; General/operating support; Management development/capacity building; Program development; Program evaluation; Research; Scholarship funds; Technical assistance.
Geographic limitations: Giving limited to CA.
Support limitations: No support for religious organizations not of direct benefit to the entire community or political candidates or organizations. No grants to individuals (except for employee-related scholarships), or for stand-alone sponsorships, award dinners, athletic events, competitions, special events, or tournaments, conferences or seminars, capital construction, television, film, or media production, political causes or campaigns, direct medical, specialty, or social services, subsidies to individuals for insurance coverage, outreach and enrollment activities for public health insurance programs, or case management.
Publications: Annual report; Application guidelines; Financial statement; Grants list; Newsletter; Occasional report; Program policy statement (including application guidelines).
Application information: Applications accepted. Unsolicited requests for general operating support grants are not accepted. Organizations may be asked to submit a full proposal. Additional information may be requested at a later date. Organizations receiving support are asked to submit final reports, and, potentially, interim reports. Application form required.
Initial approach: Complete online eligibility quiz and letter of inquiry form
Board meeting date(s): Quarterly
Deadline(s): Feb. 8, May 17, and July 19 for online letter of inquiry form
Final notification: 90 days
Officer and Trustees:* David J. Kears*, Chair.; Peter Long, Ph.D.*, Pres. and C.E.O.; Scott Travasos, C.F.O. and Dir., Finance & Opers.; Vivian Clecak; Thomas W. Epstein; Franklin D. Gilliam, Jr.; William Hauck; Antonia Hernandez; Sandra Hernandez, M.D.; Marianne Jackson.
Number of staff: 13 full-time professional; 4 full-time support; 1 part-time support.
EIN: 942822302
Selected grants: The following grants are a representative sample of this grantmaker's funding activity:
$675,000 to Insure the Uninsured Project, Santa Monica, CA, 2011. To implement health reform in California.
$500,000 to Health Plan of San Joaquin, French Camp, CA, 2011. For Safety Net Health Information Exchange.
$495,650 to California Regional Extension Center, Oakland, CA, 2011. For data analytics platform pilot project.
$300,000 to California School Health Centers Association, Oakland, CA, 2011. For strengthening school-based health centers as part of health care safety net.

$300,000 to Nonprofit Finance Fund, New York, NY, 2011. To build financial knowledge and capacity among California domestic violence organizations.
$300,000 to TechSoup Global, San Francisco, CA, 2011. For technology capacity-building for domestic violence field.
$120,000 to Alliance for Rural Community Health, Ukiah, CA, 2011. For Clinic Consortia Data Capacity.
$102,146 to Deaf Hope, Oakland, CA, 2011. To strength cultural competency in California ¿'s domestic violence field for high need, underserved populations.
$100,000 to Arrowhead Regional Medical Center Foundation, Colton, CA, 2011. For low-income health program implementation.
$20,000 to Watts Healthcare Corporation, Los Angeles, CA, 2011. For community clinic and core support.

656
California Pizza Kitchen, Inc.

6053 W. Century Blvd., 11th Fl.
Los Angeles, CA 90045-6438
(310) 342-5000

Company URL: http://www.cpk.com
Establishment information: Established in 1985.
Company type: Subsidiary of a private company
Business activities: Operates, licenses, and franchises pizza restaurants.
Business type (SIC): Restaurants and drinking places
Financial profile for 2011: Number of employees, 14,000; assets, $330,940,000; sales volume, $642,230,000; pre-tax net income, -$6,250,000; expenses, $648,460,000; liabilities, $136,530,000
Corporate officers: Gerard J. Hart, Chair., Pres., and C.E.O.; H. G. Carrington, Jr., C.F.O.
Board of director: Gerard J. Hart, Chair.
Giving statement: Giving through the California Pizza Kitchen, Inc. Corporate Giving Program and the California Pizza Kitchen Foundation.

California Pizza Kitchen, Inc. Corporate Giving Program

6053 W. Century Blvd., Ste. 1100
Los Angeles, CA 90045-6442 (310) 342-5000
FAX: (310) 342-4640; URL: http://www.cpk.com/about/community-relations/

Purpose and activities: As a complement to its foundation, California Pizza Kitchen also makes charitable contributions to nonprofit organizations directly. Special emphasis is directed towards programs designed to focus on children, education, and youth sports. Support is given primarily in areas of company restaurant operations.
Fields of interest: Education; Athletics/sports, amateur leagues; Youth, services Children.
Type of support: Donated products; Use of facilities.
Geographic limitations: Giving primarily in areas of company restaurant operations.
Application information:
Initial approach: Telephone nearest company restaurant

California Pizza Kitchen Foundation

6053 W. Century Blvd., 11th Fl.
Los Angeles, CA 90045-6430 (310) 342-5000
URL: http://www.cpk.com/company/community-relations/

Establishment information: Established in 2000 in CA.
Donor: California Pizza Kitchen, Inc.
Contact: Sarah Goldsmith Grover, Pres.
Financial data (yr. ended 12/31/11): Assets, $4,363 (M); gifts received, $39,818; expenditures, $261,980; qualifying distributions, $253,000; giving activities include $253,000 for grants.
Purpose and activities: The foundation supports organizations involved with K-12 education, health, cancer, HIV/AIDS, employment, recreation, human services, and children.
Fields of interest: Elementary/secondary education; Health care; Cancer; AIDS; Employment; Recreation; Human services Children.
Geographic limitations: Giving on a national basis, with emphasis on areas of company operations; giving also to national organizations.
Support limitations: No grants to individuals.
Application information: Applications accepted. Application form not required.
Initial approach: Letter of inquiry
Trustee: Sarah Goldsmith Grover, Pres.
EIN: 954790812
Selected grants: The following grants are a representative sample of this grantmaker's funding activity:
$266,939 to Starlight Childrens Foundation, Los Angeles, CA, 2010. For unrestricted contribution.
$6,936 to Global Impact, Alexandria, VA, 2010.
$5,000 to John Wayne Cancer Institute, Santa Monica, CA, 2010. For unrestricted contribution.

657
Calista Corporation

301 Calista Ct., Ste. A
Anchorage, AK 99518-3000
(907) 279-5516

Company URL: http://www.calistacorp.com
Establishment information: Established in 1972.
Company type: Native corporation
Business activities: Operates native corporation.
Business type (SIC): Nonclassifiable establishments
Corporate officers: Arthur S. Heckman, Chair.; Willie Kasayulie, Vice-Chair.; Andrew J. Guy, Pres. and C.E.O.; Christine Klein, C.O.O.; Sharon Weddleton, C.F.O.; Otis Armstrong, C.I.O.; Marcia Davis, Genl. Counsel
Board of directors: Arthur S. Heckman, Chair.; Willie Kasayulie, Vice-Chair.; Mike Akerelrea; John P. Angaiak; Robert L. Beans; George Guy; Art Heckman; Robert Hoffman; William Igkurak; Margaret P. Pohjola; Marcie Sherer; JoAnn Werning
Giving statement: Giving through the Calista Scholarship Fund.

Calista Scholarship Fund

(formerly David K. Nicolai Memorial Scholarship Fund)
301 Calista Ct., Ste. A
Anchorage, AK 99518-3028 (907) 279-5516
FAX: (907) 644-6376;
E-mail: scholarships@calistacorp.com; Toll-free tel.: (800) 277-5516; URL: http://www.calistacorp.com/shareholders/scholarshipscalista-heritage-foundation

Establishment information: Established in 1994 in AK.
Donors: Alyeska Pipeline Co.; Barrick Gold Corporation; Calista Corporation; Donlin Creek, LLC; Keybank N.A.
Contact: June McAtee, Pres.
Financial data (yr. ended 12/31/11): Revenue, $504,315; assets, $2,358,845 (M); gifts received, $528,380; expenditures, $683,257; giving activities include $318,714 for grants to individuals.
Purpose and activities: The fund provides financial assistance to Alaska Natives to enable recipients to participate in continuing educational activities, formal programs of study, and programs to improve their stature.
Fields of interest: Education Asians/Pacific Islanders; Native Americans/American Indians; Indigenous peoples.
Program:
Scholarships: Awards scholarships, ranging from $500 to $1,000 per semester for up to two semesters, to Alaska Native shareholders of Calista Corporation or lineal descendants of an Alaska Native shareholder. Applicants must have earned a G.E.D. and be in good academic standing and have at least a 2.0 GPA.
Type of support: Scholarships—to individuals.
Geographic limitations: Giving limited to AK.
Publications: Application guidelines; Informational brochure.
Application information: Applications accepted. Application form required.
Initial approach: Download application form
Deadline(s): June 30
Officers and Directors:* Margaret P. Pohjola*, Chair.; Joann Werning*, Vice-Chair.; June McAtee*, Pres.; Mary Martinez*, V.P.; Arthur S. Heckman, Secy.-Treas.; John Angaiack.
EIN: 920088631

658
Calkain Companies, Inc.

11150 Sunset Hills Rd., Ste. 300
Reston, VA 20190 (703) 787-4714

Company URL: http://www.calkain.com/
Company type: Private company
Business activities: Operates commercial real estate company.
Corporate officers: Jonathan Hipp, Pres. and C.E.O.; Geoffrey Bobsin, C.F.O.
Giving statement: Giving through the Hipp Family Foundation.

The Hipp Family Foundation

11150 Sunset Hills Rd., Ste. 300
Reston, VA 20190-5335
E-mail: info@hippfamilyfoundation.com;
URL: http://www.hippfamilyfoundation.com/

Establishment information: Established in 2005 in VA.
Donors: Calkain Realty, Inc.; Jonathan W. Hipp.
Financial data (yr. ended 12/31/11): Assets, $870 (M); expenditures, $0; qualifying distributions, $0.
Fields of interest: Human services.
Geographic limitations: Giving primarily in FL.
Support limitations: No grants to individuals.
Application information: Applications not accepted. Unsolicited requests for funds not accepted.
Officer and Director:* Jonathan W. Hipp*, Pres.
EIN: 202210887

659
Callanan Industries, Inc.
1245 Kings Rd.
P.O. Box 15097
Albany, NY 12212-5097 (518) 374-2222

Company URL: http://www.callanan.com
Establishment information: Established in 1883.
Company type: Subsidiary of a foreign company
Business activities: Manufactures aggregates, asphalt paving, and ready-mixed concrete.
Business type (SIC): Concrete, gypsum, and plaster products; asphalt and roofing materials
Corporate officers: Ciaran Brennan, Pres.; David Rayno, C.F.O.
Giving statement: Giving through the Callanan Industries, Inc. Corporate Giving Program.

Callanan Industries, Inc. Corporate Giving Program
P.O. Box 15097
Albany, NY 12212-5097 (518) 374-2222

Purpose and activities: Callanan makes charitable contributions to nonprofit organizations on a case by case basis. Support is given primarily in the Albany, New York, area.
Fields of interest: General charitable giving.
Type of support: Building/renovation; Sponsorships.
Geographic limitations: Giving primarily in the Albany, NY, area.

660
Callaway Golf Company
2180 Rutherford Rd.
Carlsbad, CA 92008-7328 (760) 931-1771
FAX: (760) 931-8013

Company URL: http://www.callawaygolf.com
Establishment information: Established in 1982.
Company type: Public company
Company ticker symbol and exchange: ELY/NYSE
Business activities: Manufactures and distributes golf clubs.
Business type (SIC): Games, toys, and sporting and athletic goods; durable goods—wholesale
Financial profile for 2012: Number of employees, 1,500; assets, $637,640,000; sales volume, $834,070,000; pre-tax net income, -$118,050,000; expenses, $950,300,000; liabilities, $318,650,000
Corporate officers: Ronald S. Beard, Chair.; Bradley J. Holiday, Sr. Exec. V.P. and C.F.O.; Brian P. Lynch, Sr. V.P., Genl. Counsel, and Corp. Secy.; Mark Leposky, Sr. V.P., Opers.
Board of directors: Ronald S. Beard, Chair.; Samuel H. Armacost; John C. Cushman III; Yotaro Kobayashi; John F. Lundgren; Adebayo O. Ogunlesi; Richard L. Rosenfield; Anthony S. Thornley
International operations: Australia; Canada; Japan; South Korea; United Kingdom
Giving statement: Giving through the Callaway Golf Company Contributions Program and the Callaway Golf Company Foundation.
Company EIN: 953797580

Callaway Golf Company Contributions Program
(also known as Callaway Golf Community Giving Program)
2180 Rutherford Rd.
Carlsbad, CA 92008-7328
URL: http://www.callawaygolf.com/global/en-us/corporate/commitment-to-community.html

Purpose and activities: As a complement to its foundation, Callaway Golf Company also makes charitable contributions to nonprofit organizations directly. Donations are limited to organizations focused on at-risk youth and essential health services for under-insured individuals and families. Giving primarily to San Diego County chapters of national organizations; giving also in Chicopee, MA and Austin, TX, and to deployed military units in Afghanistan and Iraq.
Fields of interest: Medical care, rehabilitation; Health care, insurance; Health care; Athletics/sports, golf; Youth development Youth; Military/veterans; Economically disadvantaged.
Type of support: Donated products; Employee volunteer services; In-kind gifts.
Geographic limitations: Giving primarily in areas of company operations in San Diego County, CA; giving also in Chicopee, MA and Austin, TX, and to deployed military units in Afghanistan and Iraq.
Support limitations: No support for schools, PTAs, hospitals, or sports league associations.
Application information: Applications accepted. Proposals for the Equipment for Growth Program should include a letter from the principal on school letterhead stating that the school is receiving Title 1 funding.
Initial approach: Complete online application form; letter to headquarters for the Equipment Growth Program

Callaway Golf Company Foundation
2180 Rutherford Rd.
Carlsbad, CA 92008-7328 (760) 930-8686
FAX: (760) 930-5021;
E-mail: cgcfoundation@callawaygolf.com;
URL: http://www.callawaygolf.com/Global/en-US/Corporate/CallawayGolfFoundation.html

Establishment information: Established in 1993 in CA.
Donors: Callaway Golf Co.; Ely R. Callaway, Jr.†; Cindy Callaway.
Financial data (yr. ended 12/31/11): Assets, $4,485,596 (M); gifts received, $20; expenditures, $241,711; qualifying distributions, $214,451; giving activities include $130,400 for 3 grants (high: $99,000; low: $11,400) and $74,464 for employee matching gifts.
Purpose and activities: The foundation supports organizations involved with education, health, athletics, and youth development.
Fields of interest: Education; Health care; Athletics/sports, amateur leagues; Athletics/sports, golf; Boys & girls clubs; Youth development; American Red Cross.
Programs:
Dollars for Doers: The foundation awards grants to nonprofit organizations with which employees of Callaway volunteer at least 25 hours during a given year.
Employee Matching Gifts: The foundation matches contributions made by employees and directors of Callaway Golf to nonprofit organizations on a one-for-one basis up to $5,000 per contributor, per year.
Scholarship Program: The foundation awards scholarships to children of employees of Callaway Golf. The program is administered by Scholarship Management Services.
Type of support: Employee matching gifts; Employee-related scholarships; General/operating support; In-kind gifts; Matching/challenge support; Program development.
Geographic limitations: Giving primarily in northern San Diego County, CA.
Support limitations: No support for political or religious organizations or arts and culture, environmental, or animal welfare organizations. No grants to individuals (except for employee-related scholarships), or for fundraising; no product donations.
Publications: IRS Form 990 or 990-PF printed copy available upon request.
Application information: Applications not accepted. Contributes only to pre-selected organizations.
Board meeting date(s): Feb., May, Aug., and Nov.
Officers and Directors:* Bradley J. Holiday*, Chair.; Marty Hochman, Secy.; Jennifer Thomas, C.F.O.; Timothy Buckman; Christopher O. Carroll; Steven C. McCracken; Michele M. Szynal.
Number of staff: 2 full-time professional; 1 full-time support; 1 part-time support.
EIN: 330590291
Selected grants: The following grants are a representative sample of this grantmaker's funding activity:
$99,000 to Scholarship America, Saint Peter, MN, 2011.
$5,000 to Valparaiso University, Valparaiso, IN, 2011.
$1,300 to Childrens Tumor Foundation, New York, NY, 2011.
$1,000 to Academy at Charlemont, Charlemont, MA, 2011.
$1,000 to Academy at Charlemont, Charlemont, MA, 2011.

661
Calpine Corporation
717 Texas Ave., Ste. 1000
Houston, TX 77002 (713) 830-2000
FAX: (713) 830-2001

Company URL: http://www.calpine.com
Establishment information: Established in 1984.
Company type: Public company
Company ticker symbol and exchange: CPN/NYSE
Business activities: Generates, transmits, and distributes electricity; produces natural gas.
Business type (SIC): Electric services; extraction/oil and gas
Financial profile for 2012: Number of employees, 2,151; assets, $16,549,000,000; sales volume, $5,478,000,000; pre-tax net income, $218,000,000; expenses, $4,534,000,000; liabilities, $12,555,000,000
Fortune 1000 ranking: 2012—459th in revenues, 577th in profits, and 276th in assets
Corporate officers: J. Stuart Ryan, Chair.; Jack A. Fusco, Pres. and C.E.O.; Thad Hill, Exec. V.P. and C.O.O.; Zamir Rauf, Exec. V.P. and C.F.O.; W. Thaddeus Miller, Exec. V.P. and Secy.; Jim D. Deidiker, Sr. V.P. and C.A.O.; Dennis Fishback, Sr. V.P. and C.I.O.; Hether Benjamin-Brown, Sr. V.P., Human Resources
Board of directors: J. Stuart Ryan, Chair.; Frank Cassidy; Jack A. Fusco; Robert C. Hinckley; David C. Merritt; W. Benjamin Moreland; Robert A. Mosbacher, Jr.; William E. Oberndorf; Denise M. O'Leary
International operations: Canada

Giving statement: Giving through the Calpine Corporation Contributions Program and the Calpine Foundation.
Company EIN: 770212977

Calpine Foundation

717 Texas Ave., Ste. 1000
Houston, TX 77002-2761 (713) 830-8883
E-mail: foundation@calpine.com

Establishment information: Established in 2002 in CA.
Donors: Calpine Corp.; Paramount Pictures; Gas Turbine Efficiency; TRS Services; Calpine Corporation.
Contact: Norma Dunn, Pres. and Dir.
Financial data (yr. ended 12/31/11): Assets, $447,902 (M); gifts received, $126,553; expenditures, $123,055; qualifying distributions, $123,055; giving activities include $89,000 for 10 grants (high: $30,000; low: $1,000).
Purpose and activities: The foundation supports organizations involved with arts and culture, education, lung disease, housing, human services, and community development.
Fields of interest: Museums; Historic preservation/historical societies; Arts; Education; Lung diseases; Housing/shelter, development; Housing/shelter; American Red Cross; Children/youth, services; Developmentally disabled, centers & services; Homeless, human services; Human services; Community/economic development.
Type of support: Employee matching gifts; Employee volunteer services; General/operating support.
Geographic limitations: Giving primarily in TX; giving also to national organizations.
Support limitations: No support for religious or political organizations.
Publications: Application guidelines.
Application information: Applications accepted. Application form required.
Initial approach: E-mail
Copies of proposal: 1
Deadline(s): None
Officers and Directors:* Jack A. Fusco*, Chair. and C.E.O.; Norma Dunn*, Pres.; Michael Rogers*, V.P.; Thaddeus W. Miller*, Secy.; Zamir Rauf*, Treas.
EIN: 260025038
Selected grants: The following grants are a representative sample of this grantmaker's funding activity:
$1,000 to Alzheimers Association, Chicago, IL, 2011.

662
Calumet Enterprises, Inc.

24 Meadow Ln.
Smoketown, PA 17576-9703
(717) 392-7123

Establishment information: Established in 2000.
Company type: Private company
Business activities: Leases restaurant equipment; leases automobiles.
Business type (SIC): Equipment rental and leasing/miscellaneous; motor vehicle rentals and leasing
Corporate officer: M. Clark, Owner
Giving statement: Giving through the Clark Associates Charitable Foundation.

Clark Associates Charitable Foundation

c/o Fred E. Clark
2205 Old Philadelphia Pike
Lancaster, PA 17602-3416
URL: http://www.clarkassociatesinc.biz/charitablefoundation.html

Establishment information: Established in 2001 in PA.
Donors: Fred E. Clark; Calumet Enterprises Inc.; Commercial Stainless, Inc.; Hawk Industries, Inc.; Clark Associates, Inc.; The Webstaurant Store Inc.; Noble Chemical Inc.
Financial data (yr. ended 12/31/11): Assets, $920,351 (M); gifts received, $798,804; expenditures, $157,040; qualifying distributions, $155,385; giving activities include $155,385 for 81 grants (high: $43,940; low: $50).
Purpose and activities: The foundation supports fire departments and organizations involved with arts and culture, education, health, human services, and Christianity.
Fields of interest: Performing arts, orchestras; Arts; Higher education; Education; Health care; Disasters, fire prevention/control; American Red Cross; Homeless, human services; Human services; Christian agencies & churches.
Type of support: General/operating support.
Geographic limitations: Giving primarily in Lancaster, PA.
Application information: Applications not accepted. Contributes only to pre-selected organizations.
Trustees: Elizabeth A. Clark; Fred E. Clark.
EIN: 256773373

663
Calvert Group, Ltd.

4550 Montgomery Ave., Ste. 1125N
Bethesda, MD 20814 (301) 951-4800

Company URL: http://www.calvert.com
Establishment information: Established in 1976.
Company type: Subsidiary of a mutual company
Business activities: Provides investment advisory services.
Business type (SIC): Security and commodity services
Corporate officers: Barbara Janet Krumsiek, Chair., Pres., and C.E.O.; Lynne Ford, Exec. V.P., Sales and Mktg.; Ronald M. Wolfsheimer, Sr. V.P., C.F.O., and C.A.O.; William M. Tartikoff, Sr. V.P., Secy., and Genl. Counsel
Board of directors: Barbara J. Krumsiek, Chair.; Richard L. Baird, Jr.; Rebecca L. Adamson; John G. Guffey, Jr.
Giving statement: Giving through the TEAM Foundation and the Calvert Social Investment Foundation.

TEAM Foundation

105 Park Ave. N.W.
Bagley, MN 56621-9558 (218) 694-3550
URL: http://www.team-foundation.org/

Establishment information: Established in 2003 in MN.
Donors: TEAM Industries, Inc.; Okuma America Corporation; Toyoda Machinety USA; Ch Robinson Company; Interdyn BMI.
Contact: Tricia Young, Treas.
Financial data (yr. ended 12/31/11): Assets, $281,434 (M); gifts received, $415,540; expenditures, $220,629; qualifying distributions, $192,833; giving activities include $190,251 for 13 grants (high: $39,114; low: $1,000).
Purpose and activities: The foundation supports programs designed to promote education; health; and community.
Fields of interest: Elementary/secondary education; Education, early childhood education; Education, reading; Education; Hospitals (general); Health care; Food services; Nutrition; Children, services; Residential/custodial care, hospices; Aging, centers/services; Human services; Community/economic development; Mathematics; Engineering/technology Youth; Aging.
Programs:
Community: The foundation supports community and human service programs designed to feed the hungry; care for the elderly; nurture the young; and strengthen the community. Special emphasis is directed toward food shelves; youth programs; senior centers; senior nutrition; and crisis centers.
Education: The foundation supports programs designed to promote education starting at the pre-K level. Special emphasis is directed toward early childhood learning; accelerated reading and math programs; and elementary, middle, and high school technology.
Health Care: The foundation supports programs designed to ensure quality healthcare for rural Minnesotans. Special emphasis is directed toward hospices, regional children hospitals, and programs designed to promote advanced medical technology.
Type of support: Building/renovation; Continuing support; Endowments; Equipment; General/operating support; Program development; Sponsorships.
Geographic limitations: Giving primarily in areas of company operations in MN.
Publications: Application guidelines; Program policy statement.
Application information: Applications accepted. Application form required. Applicants should submit the following:
1) statement of problem project will address
2) population served
3) name, address and phone number of organization
4) copy of IRS Determination Letter
5) brief history of organization and description of its mission
6) geographic area to be served
7) copy of most recent annual report/audited financial statement/990
8) detailed description of project and amount of funding requested
9) copy of current year's organizational budget and/or project budget
10) listing of additional sources and amount of support
Initial approach: Download application form and mail to foundation
Deadline(s): None
Officers: Debra Matthews, Pres.; Steve Kast, V.P.; Sara Gordon, Secy.; Tricia Young, Treas.
Director: Beatrice Ricke.
EIN: 061696861

Calvert Social Investment Foundation

(also known as Calvert Foundation)
7315 Wisconsin Ave., Ste. 1100W
Bethesda, MD 20814-3238 (800) 248-0337
E-mail: info@calvertfoundation.org; Toll-free tel.: (800) 248-0337; Additional address: 7 Elizabeth St., San Francisco, CA 94110-3014, tel.: (415) 824-2948, fax: (415) 255-9687; URL: http://www.calvertfoundation.org

Establishment information: Established in 1988 in MD.

Contact: Liz Sessler, Mktg. and Sales Assoc.; Justin Conway, Rels. Off.
Financial data (yr. ended 12/31/11): Revenue, $19,563,480; assets, $251,374,053 (M); gifts received, $10,268,467; expenditures, $16,429,261; program services expenses, $15,575,422; giving activities include $3,462,025 for 133 grants (high: $128,963; low: $5,225).
Purpose and activities: The foundation invests in community development through financial organizations working in urban and rural communities by making loans to those groups that will re-lend the money to individuals or fund projects in their respective communities; supported programs include low-income housing funds, community development funds, community development banks and credit unions, international intermediaries working in developing countries, and microenterprise funds.
Fields of interest: Housing/shelter, development; Urban/community development; Rural development; Community/economic development.
Program:
Loans: Loans, ranging from $50,000 to $2.5 million (or ten percent of the applicant's total assets, whichever is less), are available to community organizations that serve as financial intermediaries for their communities (including loan funds, microfinance institutions, affordable housing developers, and social enterprises) and are in need of flexible, affordable capital. Eligible organizations must have at least three years of operating experience, a solid base of net assets or net worth, evidence of good operating performance, and a track record of raising and repaying debt capital. Loans can be for one to five years; loans are often recommended for renewal at maturity if borrowers have demonstrated good credit risk.
Type of support: Program-related investments/ loans.
Geographic limitations: Giving primarily on a national basis; some lending on an international basis.
Support limitations: No support for soliciting organizations. No loans to individuals.
Publications: Annual report; Financial statement; Informational brochure; Newsletter.
Application information: Applications accepted.
Initial approach: Letter of request
Board meeting date(s): Quarterly
Officers and Directors:* John G. Guffey, Jr.*, Co-Chair.; D. Wayne Silby*, Co-Chair.; Lisa Hall*, Pres. and C.E.O.; Margaret Clark; Mary Houghton; Barbara J. Krumsiek; Ira Lieberman; Terrence J. Mollner; Katherine Stearns.
Number of staff: 22 full-time professional; 1 part-time professional.
EIN: 521591398

664
Calvi Electric Company
14 S. California Ave., Ste. 1
Atlantic City, NJ 08401-6491
(609) 345-0151

Company URL: http://www.calvielectric.com/ index.html
Establishment information: Established in 1909.
Company type: Private company
Business activities: Provides general contract electrical services.
Business type (SIC): Contractors/electrical work
Corporate officers: George Brestle, Pres.; Deborah McAuliffe, Secy.-Treas.
Giving statement: Giving through the Francis L. Calvi Memorial Foundation.

Francis L. Calvi Memorial Foundation
14 S. California Ave.
Atlantic City, NJ 08401-6413 (609) 345-0151

Establishment information: Established in 1986 in NJ.
Donor: Calvi Electric Co.
Contact: George Brestle, Tr.
Financial data (yr. ended 12/31/12): Assets, $162,221 (M); gifts received, $213; expenditures, $12,199; qualifying distributions, $12,000; giving activities include $12,000 for 7 grants to individuals (high: $2,500; low: $1,000).
Purpose and activities: The foundation awards college scholarships to employees and children of employees of Calvi Electric Co.
Type of support: Employee-related scholarships.
Geographic limitations: Giving limited to NJ.
Application information: Applications not accepted. Contributes only through employee-related scholarships.
Trustees: Charles Bauernhuber; George Brestle; Alan Staller.
EIN: 222769316

665
Cambia Health Solutions
(formerly The Regence Group)
100 S.W. Market St., Ste. 1500
P.O. Box 1071
Portland, OR 97201 (503) 225-5221

Company URL: http://www.regence.com/
Establishment information: Established in 1996.
Company type: Private company
Business activities: Operates managed care companies.
Business type (SIC): Insurance/accident and health
Financial profile for 2010: Number of employees, 6,543
Corporate officers: Mark B. Ganz, Pres. and C.E.O.; Vince Price, Exec. V.P. and C.F.O.; John Cimral, Sr. V.P. and C.I.O.
Giving statement: Giving through the Cambia Health Foundation.

Cambia Health Foundation
(formerly The Regence Foundation)
P.O. Box 1271, M.S. E12C
Portland, OR 97207-1271 (503) 276-1965
FAX: (503) 276-1996;
E-mail: RegenceFoundation@regence.com;
URL: http://www.regencefoundation.org/index.html

Establishment information: Established in 2007 in OR.
Donor: The Regence Group.
Contact: Monique Barton, Exec. Dir.
Financial data (yr. ended 12/31/11): Assets, $58,180,462 (M); gifts received, $8,000,000; expenditures, $2,440,441; qualifying distributions, $1,781,074; giving activities include $1,781,074 for grants.
Purpose and activities: The foundation supports programs designed to increase access to medical care for those who cannot afford it; and promote innovating methods that improve outcomes and address disparities in care.
Fields of interest: Medical care, in-patient care; Medical care, community health systems; Hospitals (general); Health care, clinics/centers; Public health; Health care; Health care, insurance; Health care, patient services; End of life care; Palliative care.
Programs:
Building Healthier Communities - Access to Healthcare: The foundation supports programs designed to promote access to healthcare. Special emphasis is directed toward expanding the healthcare safety net; decreasing inefficiencies and gaps in local healthcare systems; engaging people in their own healthcare; improving health outcomes; addressing healthcare disparities; and matching eligible individuals with existing insurance options. Grants range from $20,000 to $90,000.
Building Healthier Communities - Healthcare Connections: The foundation supports emerging partnerships between organizations that are striving to improve healthcare access and a community healthcare system as a whole. Special emphasis is directed toward community needs assessments; data analysis; community meetings; training and technical assistance; and organizations infrastructure and capacity building. Grants range from $20,000 to $35,000.
Building Healthier Communities - Transforming Healthcare: The foundation supports healthcare systems that gives people information and tools they need to be healthy; address the origins of rising healthcare costs; and improve health outcomes via better communication between patients and providers. Special emphasis is directed programs designed to address healthcare transparency and factors that affect long-term behavioral changes; increase the public's access and usage of information about healthcare quality and cost; develop and implement tools that allow people to make healthy decisions; encourage people to be their own advocates with their physicians and healthcare team; and engage provides in quality assessment and improvement. Grants range from $20,000 to $75,000.
Sojourn Award: The foundation awards a $50,000 grant to inspirational leaders in the field of palliative and end-of-life care.
Sojourns Pathway: The foundation awards grants to programs designed to ensure that palliative care is available to all patients with advanced illness. Special emphasis is directed toward programs designed to improve patients' and family members' satisfaction with overall care; integrate palliative care with local healthcare systems through partnerships between hospitals and their communities; reduce patients' pain and suffering; and promote sustainable business models for hospital-based palliative care. The foundation awards planning grants for up to $25,000 for up to six months; implementation grants ranging from $50,000 to $115,000 for one or two years; and innovation grants ranging from $30,000 to $100,00 for up to two years.
Type of support: Management development/ capacity building; Program development; Research; Technical assistance.
Geographic limitations: Giving limited to ID, OR, UT, and WA.
Support limitations: No support for political organizations, or for religious organizations not of direct benefit to the entire community. No grants to individuals (except for Sojourns Awards), or capital construction, award dinners, athletic events, competitions, special events, or tournaments, or conferences or seminars.
Publications: Application guidelines; Program policy statement.
Application information: Applications accepted. Unsolicited applications for Sojourns Pathway planning grants are not accepted. Organizations

receiving support are asked to submit a final report. Application form required.

Initial approach: Complete online eligibility quiz and letter of inquiry for Building Healthier Communities; complete online application for Sojourns Pathways; complete online nomination form for Sojourns Award

Board meeting date(s): Quarterly

Deadline(s): None for Building Healthier Communities; Jan. 8 to Aug. 6 for Sojourns Pathways implementation grants; None for Sojourns Pathways innovation grants; Dec. 3 for Sojourns Awards

Final notification: 60 days for Building Healthier Communities; 45 days for Sojourns Pathways; Mar. for Sojourns Award

Officers and Directors: Michael C. Alexander*, Chair.; Kieren Porter, Pres.; Kerry Barnett, Secy.; Lynn Harden, Exec. Dir.; Jennifer Cannaday; Vivian Chi; Mark Ganz; Scott Kreiling; John Stellmon.

Number of staff: 3 full-time professional.

EIN: 320200578

Selected grants: The following grants are a representative sample of this grantmaker's funding activity:

$250,000 to Salem Hospital Foundation, Salem, OR, 2010. To implement Palliative Care plan, payable over 2.00 years.

$246,981 to IHC Health Services, McKay-Dee Hospital, Salt Lake City, UT, 2010. To implement Palliative Care plan at Dixie Regional Medical Center, payable over 2.00 years.

$238,354 to Asante Health System, Medford, OR, 2010. To implement Palliative Care plan, payable over 2.00 years.

$237,800 to Saint John Medical Center Foundation, Longview, WA, 2010. To implement Palliative Care plan, payable over 2.00 years.

$165,745 to Providence Health Care Foundation, Centralia, WA, 2010. To implement Palliative Care plan, payable over 2.00 years.

$150,000 to Overlake Hospital Foundation, Bellevue, WA, 2010. To implement Palliative Care plan, payable over 1.50 years.

$123,686 to Saint Joseph Regional Medical Center, Lewiston, ID, 2010. To implement Palliative Care plan, payable over 2.00 years.

$100,000 to Evergreen Healthcare Foundation, Kirkland, WA, 2010. To build community partnerships through Evergreen Palliative Care Program.

$100,000 to University of Washington Foundation, Seattle, WA, 2010. For Primary Palliative Care Program at Harborview Medical Center: Innovation and Partnership in the Care of Terminally Ill Patients, payable over 2.00 years.

$50,000 to Idaho End-of-Life Coalition, Boise, ID, 2010. For Sojourns Award, initiative to recognize inspirational leaders in the field of palliative and end-of-life care within Idaho, Oregon, Utah and Washington.

666
Cambridge Savings Bank

1374 Massachusetts Ave.
Cambridge, MA 02138-3822
(617) 441-4155

Company URL: http://www.cambridgesavings.com
Establishment information: Established in 1834.
Company type: Subsidiary of a private company
Business activities: Operates savings bank.
Business type (SIC): Savings institutions
Corporate officers: Wayne Patenaude, Pres. and C.E.O.; Dana S. Philbrook, Sr. V.P. and Cont.; Diane M. Ryan, V.P., Human Resources
Offices: Acton, Arlington, Bedford, Belmont, Burlington, Lexington, Newton, MA
Giving statement: Giving through the Cambridge Savings Charitable Foundation, Inc.

Cambridge Savings Charitable Foundation, Inc.

1374 Massachusetts Ave.
Cambridge, MA 02138-3822 (617) 441-4313
E-mail: jfoutter@cambridgesavings.com;
URL: https://www.cambridgesavings.com/pg_View.aspx?PageID=745

Establishment information: Established in 2003 in MA.
Donor: 1834 Realty Inc.
Contact: Jeff Foutter, Community Rels. & CRA
Financial data (yr. ended 12/31/11): Assets, $1,621,503 (M); gifts received, $500,000; expenditures, $453,010; qualifying distributions, $452,760; giving activities include $445,060 for 74 grants (high: $25,000; low: $1,000).
Purpose and activities: The foundation supports organizations involved with the arts and culture, education, health, housing, recreation, human services, and youth and awards college scholarships to graduating high school seniors from Acton-Boxborough, Arlington, Bedford, Belmont, Burlington, Cambridge, Concord-Carlisle, Lexington, Minuteman Regional High School, Newton, Somerville, and Watertown.
Fields of interest: Arts; Education; Health care; Housing/shelter; Recreation; Human services Youth.
Program:

Kevin J. Fitzgerald Scholarship Program: The foundation awards college scholarships to graduating high school seniors attending schools in Acton-Boxborough, Arlington, Bedford, Belmont, Burlington, Cambridge, Concord-Carlisle, Lexington, Newton, Somerville, and Watertown. Two scholarships will be awarded to seniors from each high school, one $2,500 scholarship to a senior attending a four-year college, and the second to a senior attending a vocational school, community college, or other two-year college program.

Type of support: Annual campaigns; General/operating support; Scholarships—to individuals.
Geographic limitations: Giving primarily in areas of company operations in Acton, Arlington, Bedford, Belmont, Brookline, Burlington, Cambridge, Concord, Lexington, Lincoln, Medford, Newton, Somerville, Waltham, Watertown, Winchester, and Woburn, MA.
Publications: Application guidelines.
Application information: Applications accepted. Support is limited to 1 contribution per organization during any given year. Application form required. Applicants should submit the following:

1) timetable for implementation and evaluation of project
2) signature and title of chief executive officer
3) population served
4) copy of IRS Determination Letter
5) brief history of organization and description of its mission
6) copy of most recent annual report/audited financial statement/990
7) how project's results will be evaluated or measured
8) listing of board of directors, trustees, officers and other key people and their affiliations
9) detailed description of project and amount of funding requested
10) copy of current year's organizational budget and/or project budget

Initial approach: Download application form and mail or e-mail proposal and application form to foundation; contact participating school's guidance office for application form for scholarships

Copies of proposal: 1

Board meeting date(s): Jan. 31, Mar. 31, June 30, and Sept. 30

Deadline(s): None

Officers: Robert M. Wilson*, C.E.O. and Pres.; Stephen J. Coukos, Exec. V.P., Genl. Counsel, and Clerk; Susan Lapierre, Sr. V.P.; Wayne Patenaude, Treas.
Directors: Anne Adams Cushman; Charlie Lyons; Robert J. Ramsey; Robert P. Reardon.
EIN: 481307731
Selected grants: The following grants are a representative sample of this grantmaker's funding activity:

$7,500 to University of Massachusetts, Amherst, MA, 2011.
$3,600 to Cooperative Elder Services, Lexington, MA, 2011.
$2,500 to Boston University, Boston, MA, 2011.
$2,500 to University of Miami, Coral Gables, FL, 2011.
$2,500 to University of New Hampshire, Durham, NH, 2011.
$2,500 to University of Rhode Island, Kingston, RI, 2011.

667
Cameron International Corporation

(also known as Cameron)
1333 W. Loop S., Ste. 1700
Houston, TX 77027 (713) 513-3300
FAX: (713) 513-3456

Company URL: http://www.c-a-m.com/
Establishment information: Established in 1920.
Company type: Public company
Company ticker symbol and exchange: CAM/NYSE
Business activities: Manufactures oil and gas pressure control equipment; manufactures gas turbines, centrifugal gas and air compressors, integral and separable reciprocating engines, compressors, and turbochargers.
Business type (SIC): Machinery/general industry; engines and turbines; machinery/construction, mining, and materials handling
Financial profile for 2012: Number of employees, 27,000; assets, $11,158,200,000; sales volume, $8,502,100,000; pre-tax net income, $938,000,000; expenses, $7,579,800,000; liabilities, $5,592,100,000
Fortune 1000 ranking: 2012—310th in revenues, 255th in profits, and 362nd in assets
Forbes 2000 ranking: 2012—1046th in sales, 741st in profits, and 1391st in assets
Corporate officers: Jack B. Moore, Chair.; Charles M. Sledge, Sr. V.P. and C.F.O.; William C. Lemmer, Sr. V.P. and Genl. Counsel; Christopher Krummel, V.P., C.A.O., and Cont.; Grace B. Holmes, V.P. and Corp. Secy.; H. Keith Jennings, V.P. and Treas.; Edward E. Will, V.P., Mktg.; Roslyn Larkey, V.P., Human Resources
Board of directors: Jack B. Moore, Chair.; C. Baker Cunningham; Sheldon R. Erikson; Peter J. Fluor; Douglas L. Foshee; James T. Hackett; Rodolfo Landim; Michael E. Patrick; Jon Erik Reinhardsen; David A. Ross III; Bruce W. Wilkinson

Historic mergers: LeTourneau Technologies, Inc. (October 24, 2011)
Giving statement: Giving through the Cooper Cameron Corporation Contributions Program and the LeTourneau, Inc. Community Actions Council.
Company EIN: 760451843

LeTourneau, Inc. Community Actions Council

2400 S. MacArthur Blvd.
Longview, TX 75602-5300
Application address: P.O. Box 2307, Longview TX 75606-2307

Establishment information: Established in 2006 in TX.
Donor: LeTourneau, Inc.
Contact: Daniel Flourney, Pres.
Financial data (yr. ended 12/31/09): Assets, $9,437 (M); expenditures, $28,430; qualifying distributions, $27,770; giving activities include $27,770 for 15 grants (high: $5,575; low: $250).
Purpose and activities: The foundation supports health centers and organizations involved with literacy, cancer, heart disease, housing development, youth development, and gift distribution.
Fields of interest: Education; Health care; Health organizations.
Type of support: General/operating support.
Geographic limitations: Giving primarily in TX.
Application information: Applications accepted. Application form not required.
Initial approach: Proposal
Deadline(s): None
Officers: Daniel W. Flourney, Pres.; Glenn Randolph, Secy.
Directors: David Blazek.
EIN: 752792907

668
James Campbell Company, LLC

James Campbell Bldg., Ste. 200
1001 Kamokila Blvd.
Kapolei, HI 96707-2014 (808) 674-6674

Company URL: http://www.jamescampbell.com
Establishment information: Established in 1900.
Company type: Private company
Business activities: Operates diversified real estate company.
Business type (SIC): Real estate operators and lessors; real estate subdividers and developers
Corporate officers: Richard J. Dahl, Chair., Pres., and C.E.O.; Landon H. W. Chun, Exec. V.P. and C.F.O.
Board of directors: Richard J. Dahl, Chair.; Linda Assante; W. David P. Carey III; Stephen H. MacMillan; T. Michael May; Kristin F. Gannon
Office: San Francisco, CA
Giving statement: Giving through the James Campbell Corporation Community Fund.

James Campbell Corporation Community Fund

1001 Kamokila Blvd.
Kapolei, HI 96707-2005

Contact: D. Keola Lloyd
Purpose and activities: James Campbell makes charitable contributions to nonprofit organizations involved with K-12 education, youth development, community development, and on a case by case basis. Support is given primarily in areas of company operations in Hawaii.
Fields of interest: Elementary/secondary education; Youth development; Community/economic development; General charitable giving.
Programs:
Community Building: James Campbell makes charitable contributions to nonprofit organizations involved with community development.
Community Partnerships: James Campbell makes charitable contributions to nonprofit organizations with historic ties to the Estate of James Campbell or the Campbell name.
Education: James Campbell makes charitable contributions to K-12 public schools and early childhood education. Special emphasis is directed toward programs designed to promote parent involvement and provide teacher training workshops.
Employee Involvement: James Campbell makes charitable contributions to nonprofit organizations with which employees are involved.
Youth: James Campbell supports programs designed to address the needs of at-risk young people by providing them with positive, alternative activities.
Type of support: Capital campaigns; Employee volunteer services; Equipment; General/operating support.
Geographic limitations: Giving primarily in Ewa, Ewa Beach, Kapolei/Makakilo, and Waianae Coast, HI.
Support limitations: No support for sectarian or religious organizations. No grants to individuals, or for political activities or highly technical research projects; no loans.
Publications: Corporate giving report.
Application information: Applications accepted. Support is limited to 1 contribution per organization during any given year for 1 year in length. Proposals should be no longer than 2 to 3 pages. Organizations receiving support are asked to formally acknowledge the contribution and provide a final report. A contributions committee reviews all requests. Application form not required. Applicants should submit the following:
1) statement of problem project will address
2) population served
3) detailed description of project and amount of funding requested
4) brief history of organization and description of its mission
Initial approach: Proposal to headquarters
Copies of proposal: 1
Committee meeting date(s): Monthly
Deadline(s): 1st of the month
Final notification: 2 months

669
Campbell Soup Company

1 Campbell Pl.
Camden, NJ 08103-1701 (856) 342-4800
FAX: (856) 342-3878

Company URL: http://www.campbellsoup.com
Establishment information: Established in 1869.
Company type: Public company
Company ticker symbol and exchange: CPB/NYSE
International Securities Identification Number: US1344291091
Business activities: Produces and markets convenience food products.
Business type (SIC): Food and kindred products
Financial profile for 2012: Number of employees, 17,700; assets, $6,530,000,000; sales volume, $7,707,000,000; pre-tax net income, $1,106,000,000; expenses, $6,495,000,000; liabilities, $5,632,000,000
Fortune 1000 ranking: 2012—338th in revenues, 248th in profits, and 510th in assets
Forbes 2000 ranking: 2012—1091st in sales, 807th in profits, and 1573rd in assets
Corporate officers: Paul R. Charron, Chair.; Denise Morrison, Pres. and C.E.O.; B. Craig Owens, Sr. V.P., C.F.O., and C.A.O.; Joseph C. Spagnoletti, Sr. V.P. and C.I.O.; Anthony P. DiSilvestro, Sr. V.P., Finance; Ellen Oran Kaden, Sr. V.P., Public Affairs; Andy Ridler, V.P., Finance.
Board of directors: Paul R. Charron, Chair.; Edmund M. Carpenter; Bennett Dorrance; Lawrence C. Karlson; Randall W. Larrimore; Mary Alice D. Malone; Sara S. Mathew; Denise M. Morrison; Charles R. Perrin; A. Barry Rand; Nick Shreiber; Tracey T. Travis; Archbold D. van Beuren, Jr.; Les C. Vinney; Charlotte C. Weber
Subsidiaries: Campbell Finance Corp., Wilmington, DE; CSC Advertising, Inc., Camden, NJ
Plants: Fayetteville, AR; City of Industry, CA; Clinton, CT; Millsboro, DE; Miami, FL; Atlanta, GA; Thornton, IL; Howe, IN; Bridgeport, MI; Worthington, MN; Omaha, Tecumseh, NE; South Plainfield, NJ; Maxton, NC; Jackson, OH; Blandon, PA; Barceloneta, PR; Aiken, SC; Hillsboro, TX; Richmond, VA; Bonduel, WI
International operations: Australia; Belgium; Canada; China; France; Germany; Hong Kong; Indonesia; Ireland; Japan; Malaysia; Mexico; Netherlands; New Zealand; Russia; Singapore; Sweden; United Kingdom
Giving statement: Giving through the Campbell Soup Company Contributions Program and the Campbell Soup Foundation.
Company EIN: 210419870

Campbell Soup Company Contributions Program

1 Campbell Pl.
Camden, NJ 08103-1701 (856) 342-4800
FAX: (856) 342-3878; URL: http://www.campbellsoupcompany.com/csr/default.aspx

Purpose and activities: As a complement to its foundation, Campbell Soup also makes charitable contributions to nonprofit organizations directly. Support is given primarily in areas of company operations, with emphasis on Camden, New Jersey.
Fields of interest: Public health, obesity; Health care; Food services; Agriculture/food; Youth development; Children, services; Human services; Civil/human rights, equal rights; Community/economic development; United Ways and Federated Giving Programs.
Programs:
Labels for America: Campbell soup awards up to 2,000 bonus Labels for Education points to participating K-12 schools that complete a volunteer project, fitness activity, or educational program that promotes learning, caring, and sharing within the community.
Labels for Education: Campbell Soup awards educational equipment including computers, software, sports equipment, musical instruments, library books, and vehicles to K-12 schools in exchange for proofs of purchase from Campbell products brought in by customers participating in the program.
Stamp Out Hunger: Campbell Soup, in partnership with the National Association of Letter Carriers, operates a large single day food drive. Customers and the general public donate a grocery bag containing non-perishable foods like canned soup, canned vegetables, pasta, rice, or cereal. The grocery back is placed next to their mailbox and is

collected by letter carriers and delivered to local food banks.
Type of support: Cause-related marketing; Donated products; Employee volunteer services; Equipment; General/operating support; In-kind gifts; Program development.
Geographic limitations: Giving primarily in areas of company operations, with emphasis on Camden, NJ.

Campbell Soup Foundation

(formerly Campbell Soup Fund)
1 Campbell Pl.
Camden, NJ 08103-1799 (856) 342-4800
E-mail: community_relations@campbellsoup.com;
URL: http://www.campbellsoupcompany.com/community_center.asp

Establishment information: Incorporated in 1953 in NJ.
Donor: Campbell Soup Co.
Contact: Jerry S. Buckley, Chair.
Financial data (yr. ended 06/30/12): Assets, $20,145,632 (M); gifts received, $2,000,000; expenditures, $1,660,713; qualifying distributions, $1,515,075; giving activities include $1,393,558 for grants and $121,517 for employee matching gifts.
Purpose and activities: The foundation supports programs designed to promote hunger relief; wellness; education; and community revitalization.
Fields of interest: Performing arts; Higher education; Education; Health care; Food services; Nutrition; Recreation, camps; Recreation; Children/youth, services; Human services; Economic development; Community/economic development; United Ways and Federated Giving Programs.
Programs:
Camden Beacons: The foundation supports programs designed to promote positive change and improve the quality of life for the Camden, New Jersey community.
Dollars for Doers: The foundation awards grants to nonprofit organizations with which employees of Campbell Soup volunteer.
Matching Gifts: The foundation matches contributions made by employees of Campbell Soup to educational institutions on a one-for-one basis from $100 to $5,000 per employee, per year.
Plant Communities: The foundation supports programs designed to provide tangible results for local residents in U.S. communities where Campbell Soup has facilities.
Type of support: Building/renovation; Employee matching gifts; Employee volunteer services; Employee-related scholarships; Equipment; General/operating support; Matching/challenge support; Program development.
Geographic limitations: Giving primarily in areas of company operations in Davis, Sacramento, and Stockton, CA, Bloomfield and Norwalk, CT, Lakeland, FL, Downers Grove, IL, Marshall, MI, Maxton, NC, South Plainfield, NJ, Napoleon, Wauseon, and Willard, OH, Denver and Downingtown, PA, Aiken, SC, Paris, TX, Richmond, UT, Everett, WA, and Milwaukee, WI, with emphasis on Camden, NJ.
Support limitations: No support for religious organizations not of direct benefit to the entire community, political organizations, or units of government. No grants to individuals (except for employee-related scholarships), or for events or sponsorships.
Publications: Application guidelines.
Application information: Applications accepted. Support is limited to 1 contribution per organization during any given year. Application form not required. Applicants should submit the following:
1) results expected from proposed grant
2) statement of problem project will address
3) name, address and phone number of organization
4) copy of IRS Determination Letter
5) explanation of why grantmaker is considered an appropriate donor for project
6) detailed description of project and amount of funding requested
7) contact person
8) copy of current year's organizational budget and/or project budget
9) listing of additional sources and amount of support

Initial approach: E-mail proposal to foundation
Copies of proposal: 1
Board meeting date(s): As required
Deadline(s): None
Final notification: Up to 3 months

Officers and Trustees:* Jerry S. Buckley*, Chair.; Carlos M. Del Sol*, Vice-Chair.; Wendy A. Milanese, Secy.; Ashok Madhaven, Treas.; Anthony P. DiSilvestro, Cont.; Michael Dunn; Karen J. Lewis; Maureen Linder; Steve White.
Number of staff: 1 part-time professional; 1 part-time support.
EIN: 216019196

670
Candlesticks, Inc.

112 W. 34th St., Ste. 901
New York, NY 10120-0999 (212) 947-8900

Establishment information: Established in 1968.
Company type: Private company
Business activities: Sells women's and children's undergarments and swimwear wholesale.
Business type (SIC): Apparel—women's, girls', and children's undergarments; apparel—girls' and children's outerwear
Corporate officer: Leonard S. Bernstein, Pres. and C.E.O.
Giving statement: Giving through the Lawrence Foundation.

The Lawrence Foundation

112 W. 34th St.
New York, NY 10120-0101

Donors: Candlesticks, Inc.; Lancaster Industries, Inc.; Jay S. Bernstein; Leonard S. Bernstein.
Financial data (yr. ended 09/30/12): Assets, $1,129,528 (M); expenditures, $61,028; qualifying distributions, $59,006; giving activities include $58,600 for 18 grants (high: $10,000; low: $250).
Purpose and activities: The foundation supports organizations involved with education, air pollution, crime, human services, international human rights, civil rights, Judaism, and homeless people and awards college scholarships to students attending Donegal High School in Mount Joy, Pennsylvania.
Fields of interest: Environment; Housing/shelter; Human services.
Type of support: General/operating support; Scholarships—to individuals.
Geographic limitations: Giving limited to Mount Joy, PA, for scholarships.
Application information: Applications not accepted. Unsolicited requests for funds not accepted.
Trustees: Jay S. Bernstein; Lawrence Bernstein; Leonard S. Bernstein.
EIN: 132880731

671
Cannon Valley Telecom, Inc.

202 S. 1st St.
Bricelyn, MN 56014-2006 (507) 653-4444

Establishment information: Established in 1983.
Company type: Private company
Business activities: Operates telephone telecommunications company.
Business type (SIC): Telephone communications
Financial profile for 2010: Number of employees, 18
Corporate officers: Scott W. Johnson, Pres.; Loretta Johnson, Secy.-Treas.
Giving statement: Giving through the Cannon Valley Communications Foundation.

Cannon Valley Communications Foundation

51285 Lakeland Ln.
P.O. Box 213
Elysian, MN 56028

Donors: Miriam Johnson; Cannon Valley Telecom, Inc.; Cannon Valley Cellular, Inc.; Scott W. Johnson; Loretta A. Johnson; Aaron M. Johnson; Matthew J. Johnson; Jesse R. Johnson.
Financial data (yr. ended 12/31/11): Assets, $1,556,165 (M); expenditures, $95,633; qualifying distributions, $80,350; giving activities include $78,100 for 16 grants (high: $14,700; low: $500).
Purpose and activities: The foundation supports organizations involved with education, youth services, and community development.
Fields of interest: Elementary/secondary education; Youth, services; Community/economic development.
Type of support: Employee matching gifts; General/operating support; Grants to individuals.
Geographic limitations: Giving primarily in MN.
Application information: Applications not accepted. Unsolicited requests for funds not accepted.
Officers and Directors: Scott W. Johnson*, Pres.; Aaron M. Johnson*, V.P.; Loretta A. Johnson*, Secy.-Treas.; Jesse R. Johnson; Matthew J. Johnson.
EIN: 204474578

672
Canon U.S.A., Inc.

1 Canon Plz.
Lake Success, NY 11042-1198
(516) 328-5000

Company URL: http://www.usa.canon.com
Establishment information: Established in 1965.
Company type: Subsidiary of a foreign company
Business activities: Manufactures professional and consumer imaging equipment and information systems.
Business type (SIC): Photographic equipment and supplies; computer and office equipment; communications equipment
Financial profile for 2011: Number of employees, 700; sales volume, $3,557,000,000
Corporate officers: Joe Adachi, Pres. and C.E.O.; Seymour Liebman, Exec. V.P., C.A.O., and Genl. Counsel; Kunihiko Tedo, Sr. V.P., C.F.O., Treas., and Finance; Joseph G. Warren, Sr. V.P. and Corp. Human Resources
Subsidiaries: Canon Business Solutions-Central, Inc., Schaumburg, IL; Canon Business Solutions-East, Inc., New York, NY; Canon Business

Solutions-West, Inc., Gardena, CA; Canon Financial Services, Inc., Burlington, NJ; Canon Latin America, Inc., Miami, FL; Canon Research Center America, Inc., Palo Alto, CA; Canon Virginia, Inc., Newport News, VA
Division: Broadcasting Equipment Div., Englewood Cliffs, NJ
Offices: Irvine, Santa Clara, CA; Norcross, GA; Honolulu, HI; Itasca, IL; Jamesburg, NJ; Irving, TX; Arlington, VA
Giving statement: Giving through the Canon U.S.A., Inc. Corporate Giving Program and the Canon Envirothon.

Canon U.S.A., Inc. Corporate Giving Program

1 Canon Plz.
Lake Success, NY 11042-1198
URL: http://www.usa.canon.com/templatedata/AboutCanon/ciwccresp.html

Contact: Michael R. Virgintino, Sr. Mgr., Corp. Social Responsibility
Purpose and activities: Canon makes charitable contributions to nonprofit organizations involved with natural resources conservation and protection, youth development, and on a case by case basis. Support is given on a national basis and in Canada, Central America, and South America.
Fields of interest: Environment, natural resources; Youth development; General charitable giving.
International interests: Canada; Central America; South America.
Type of support: Donated equipment; Donated products; Employee volunteer services; General/operating support; Scholarship funds; Scholarships—to individuals.
Geographic limitations: Giving in areas of company operations in CA, Washington, DC, GA, HI, IL, NJ, NY, TX, and UT; giving also to national organizations.
Support limitations: No support for religious, political, or labor organizations. No grants to individuals (except for scholarships).
Publications: Corporate giving report.
Application information: Applications accepted. The Corporate Social Responsibility Department handles giving. A contributions committee reviews all requests. Application form not required.
Initial approach: Proposal to headquarters
Copies of proposal: 1
Deadline(s): None
Final notification: 1 to 3 months
Number of staff: 2 full-time professional; 1 part-time professional.

Canon Envirothon

P.O. Box 855
League City, TX 77574-0855
FAX: (281) 332-5259; Additional tel.: (800) 825-5547; URL: http://www.envirothon.org/

Establishment information: Established in 2007 in TX.
Donors: Canon-USA, Inc.; US Forest Service.
Financial data (yr. ended 12/31/11): Assets, $285,293 (M); gifts received, $373,454; expenditures, $771,653; qualifying distributions, $770,198; giving activities include $288,638 for 121 grants (high: $59,080; low: $100).
Purpose and activities: The foundation supports environmental education, awareness, and science through scholarships and through sponsorship of the annual Canon Envirothon Competition for high school students.
Fields of interest: Secondary school/education; Higher education; Environment, natural resources; Environment, water resources; Environment, land resources; Environment, forests; Environment; Science.
Programs:
Canon Envirothon Competition: The foundation annual sponsors a competition to expose teams of high school students to environmental issues, ecosystems, and topography. The problem solving competition takes place at the local level at participating states and in Canada. The foundation awards mini-grants to those states to help run the competition. State winners with the highest scores advance to the national competition where they compete for scholarships by demonstrating their knowledge of environmental science and natural resource management at five training/testing stations including soils/land use, aquatic ecology, forestry, wildlife, and current environmental issues.
Canon Scholarships: The foundation awards scholarships of up to $5,000 to students who place in the top 10 at the Canon Envirothon Competition. Scholarships are to be used toward a four year university, two year college, or trade school and students will have up to two years after graduation from high school to use the Canon scholarship money.
Diversity Grant Program: The foundation, in partnership with U.S. Forest Services, awards grants to state and provincial Envirothon programs to increase the diversity of participants. The program welcomes Native Americans and First Nations population, French speaking Canadian students, urban and inner-city youth, and those separate by geographic and/or economic barriers.
Envirothon Extra Mile Award: The foundation, in partnership with the National Association of Conservation Districts Auxiliary, awards a $100 cash prize and a plaque or trophy to the team demonstrating the most sprit, cooperation, leadership, and friendship during the Canon Envirothon Competition.
Mini-Grants: The foundation awards grants of up to $1,250 to states and provinces to help publicize and grow local programs and support Canon Envirothon awareness.
Rookie Team Award: The foundation, in partnership with the National Association of Conservation Districts Auxiliary, awards a $100 cash prize and a plaque or trophy to the highest scoring team representing a state/province that has not previously participated at the Canon Envirothon Competition. Teams that have participated as a "demonstration team" will also be eligible to compete for the award.
Type of support: General/operating support; Program development; Scholarships—to individuals.
Geographic limitations: Giving on a national basis and in Canada.
Application information: Applications not accepted. Unsolicited requests for funds not accepted.
Officers and Directors:* Craig Zinter*, Chair.; Sandy Huey*, Vice-Chair.; Kristen Moore*, Secy.; Peggy Lemons, Treas.; Clay Burns, Exec. Dir.; Valerie Archibald; Sid Lowrance; Terry Seehorn.
EIN: 300367267
Selected grants: The following grants are a representative sample of this grantmaker's funding activity:
$9,500 to Duke University, Durham, NC, 2010. For scholarship awards.
$8,000 to Duke University, Durham, NC, 2010. For scholarship awards.
$7,000 to Swarthmore College, Swarthmore, PA, 2010. For scholarship awards.
$6,000 to University of Delaware, Newark, DE, 2010. For scholarship awards.
$5,000 to Duke University, Durham, NC, 2010. For scholarship awards.
$5,000 to Occidental College, Los Angeles, CA, 2010. For scholarship awards.
$5,000 to Ohio State University, Columbus, OH, 2010. For scholarship awards.
$5,000 to Yale University, New Haven, CT, 2010. For scholarship awards.
$3,500 to Cornell University, Ithaca, NY, 2010. For scholarship awards.
$1,250 to Pennsylvania Envirothon, Bedford, PA, 2010.

673
Caparo Steel Co.

(formerly Sharon Steel Corporation)
15 Roemer Blvd.
Farrell, PA 16121 (724) 983-1919

Company URL: http://
Establishment information: Established in 1994.
Company type: Subsidiary of a private company
Business activities: Produces steel.
Business type (SIC): Steel mill products
Corporate officer: Chuck Emmenegger, Pres.
Subsidiaries: Alaska Gold Co., Nome, AK; Carpentertown Coal and Coke Co., Templeton, PA; Mueller Brass Co., Port Huron, MI; U.S.S. Lead Refinery, Inc., East Chicago, IN; Union Steel Corp., Union, NJ; United States Fuel Co., Yorklyn, DE; Utah Railroad Co., Yorklyn, DE
Plants: Dearborn, MI; Farrell, PA
Giving statement: Giving through the Sharon Steel Foundation.

Sharon Steel Foundation

c/o Arthur Y. Fox
126 E. 56th St., 12th Fl.
New York, NY 10022-3613
Application address: c/o Hume R. Steyer, Seward & Kissel, 1 Battery Park Plz., New York, NY 10004

Establishment information: Established in 1953 in PA.
Donor: Sharon Steel Corp.
Financial data (yr. ended 12/31/11): Assets, $3,330,940 (M); expenditures, $312,555; qualifying distributions, $302,880; giving activities include $302,880 for grants.
Purpose and activities: The foundation supports organizations involved with education and human services.
Fields of interest: Secondary school/education; Higher education; Education; Children/youth, services; Children, foster care; Human services; United Ways and Federated Giving Programs.
Type of support: General/operating support; Program development; Scholarship funds.
Geographic limitations: Giving primarily in CT, NH, NY, OH, PA, and RI.
Support limitations: No grants to individuals.
Application information: Applications accepted. Application form not required. Applicants should submit the following:
1) copy of IRS Determination Letter
2) copy of most recent annual report/audited financial statement/990
3) detailed description of project and amount of funding requested
4) brief history of organization and description of its mission
Initial approach: Proposal
Deadline(s): None
Trustees: Christian L. Oberbeck; Malvin G. Sandler; Hume R. Steyer.
EIN: 256063133

Selected grants: The following grants are a representative sample of this grantmaker's funding activity:
$20,000 to Brown University, Providence, RI, 2010.

674
Cape Cod Five Cents Savings Bank

19 West Rd.
P.O. Box 10
Orleans, MA 02653-3204 (508) 240-0555
FAX: (508) 240-1895

Company URL: http://www.capecodfive.com
Establishment information: Established in 1855.
Company type: Private company
Business activities: Operates savings bank; provides mortgages.
Business type (SIC): Banks/commercial; brokers and bankers/mortgage
Financial profile for 2011: Assets, $2,104,458,000; liabilities, $2,104,458,000
Corporate officers: Dorothy A. Savarese, Pres. and C.E.O.; Robert A. Talerman, Exec. V.P. and C.O.O.; Phillip W. Wong, Exec. V.P., C.F.O., and Treas.; Anthony P. Massaro, Sr. V.P. and C.I.O.; Michael S. Kiceluk, V.P. and C.I.O.; John J. McNamara, V.P. and Compt.
Offices: Brewster, Centerville, Chatham, East Harwich, Harwichport, Hyannis, Mashpee, South Yarmouth, Wellfleet, MA
Giving statement: Giving through the Cape Cod Five Cents Savings Bank Charitable Trust.

Cape Cod Five Cents Savings Bank Charitable Trust

P.O. Box 10
Orleans, MA 02653-0010
E-mail: jpollock@capecodfive.com; Additional Tel.: (508) 240-0555; URL: https://www.capecodfive.com/home/fou/abt

Establishment information: Established in 1998 in MA.
Donor: Cape Cod Five Cents Savings Bank.
Financial data (yr. ended 12/31/11): Assets, $10,617,718 (M); gifts received, $60,000; expenditures, $609,742; qualifying distributions, $546,249; giving activities include $546,249 for grants.
Purpose and activities: The foundation supports programs designed to address health and elder services; culture and art including historic heritage; human services including economic development; youth education; conservation and the environment.
Fields of interest: Historic preservation/historical societies; Arts; Elementary/secondary education; Education; Environment, natural resources; Environment; Hospitals (general); Health care; Food banks; Children/youth, services; Residential/custodial care, hospices; Aging, centers/services; Human services; Economic development.
Type of support: Building/renovation; Capital campaigns; Continuing support; Equipment; Program development; Sponsorships.
Geographic limitations: Giving limited to areas of company operations in MA, with emphasis on Cape Cod and the islands.
Support limitations: No support for religious organizations. No grants to individuals, or for travel, social functions, athletic events or activities, annual memberships, or appeals.
Publications: Annual report; Application guidelines.
Application information: Applications accepted. Application form required. Applicants should submit the following:
1) principal source of support for project in the past
2) copy of IRS Determination Letter
3) brief history of organization and description of its mission
4) copy of most recent annual report/audited financial statement/990
5) detailed description of project and amount of funding requested
6) copy of current year's organizational budget and/or project budget

Initial approach: Download application form and e-mail or mail to foundation
Copies of proposal: 1
Board meeting date(s): Quarterly
Deadline(s): Feb. 17, May 11, July 13, and Sept. 28

Officers: Dorothy A. Savarese, Chair.; David B. Williard, Secy.; Phillip W. Wong, Treas.; Elliott Carr, Exec. Mgr.
EIN: 043423249
Selected grants: The following grants are a representative sample of this grantmaker's funding activity:
$20,000 to Cape Symphony Orchestra, Yarmouth Port, MA, 2010.
$15,000 to Falmouth Service Center, Falmouth, MA, 2010.
$15,000 to Housing Assistance Corporation, Hyannis, MA, 2010.
$10,000 to Brewster Conservation Trust, Brewster, MA, 2010.
$8,500 to Community Health Center of Cape Cod, Mashpee, MA, 2010.
$5,000 to Cape Cod Commercial Hook Fishermens Association, North Chatham, MA, 2010.
$5,000 to Compassionate Care ALS, West Falmouth, MA, 2010.
$5,000 to United Way, Cape and Islands, Hyannis, MA, 2010.
$3,000 to radKIDS, South Dennis, MA, 2010.
$2,500 to Big Brothers Big Sisters of Cape Cod and the Islands, Centerville, MA, 2010.

675
Capezio/Ballet Makers, Inc

1 Campus Rd.
Totowa, NJ 07512 (917) 595-9000

Company URL: http://www.capeziodance.com
Establishment information: Established in 1887.
Company type: Private company
Business activities: Manufactures dance shoes, bodywear, and miscellaneous accessories.
Business type (SIC): Leather footwear; apparel—women's outerwear
Corporate officers: Michael Terlizzi, Pres. and C.E.O.; Marc Terlizzi, C.O.O.; Ruth Swanson, C.I.O.; Harry Krawitz, V.P., Finance; Ben Pignataro, V.P., Sales
Giving statement: Giving through the Capezio/Ballet Makers Dance Foundation, Inc.

Capezio/Ballet Makers Dance Foundation, Inc.

1 Campus Rd.
Totowa, NJ 07512-1201
E-mail: dfiorenzi@balletmakers.com; URL: http://www.capezio.com/all-access/dance-foundation/

Establishment information: Incorporated in 1953 in NY.
Donor: Capezio/Ballet Makers Inc.
Contact: Jane Remer, Exec. Dir.
Financial data (yr. ended 12/31/11): Assets, $635 (M); gifts received, $70,000; expenditures, $70,000; qualifying distributions, $70,000; giving activities include $60,000 for 45 grants (high: $6,000; low: $750) and $10,000 for 1 grant to an individual.
Purpose and activities: The foundation supports programs designed to provide services to the dance field and promote the public awareness of dance as a diverse art form.
Fields of interest: Performing arts, dance; Performing arts, theater; Recreation, fairs/festivals.
Program:
Capezio Dance Award: Through the Capezio Dance Award, the foundation annually awards $10,000 to an individual, company, or organization that has made a significant contribution to American dance. Candidates must be nominated from a group indentified by the trustees and the award is presented at a ceremony honoring the awarded.
Type of support: Conferences/seminars; Continuing support; General/operating support; Grants to individuals; Program development.
Geographic limitations: Giving primarily in CA, Washington, DC, MA, MD, NC, and NY; giving also to statewide and regional organizations; giving on a national basis for Capezio Dance Award.
Support limitations: No support for dance schools or colleges or universities. No grants to individuals (except for the Capezio Dance Award), or for endowments, cash reserves, or capital fund drives; no in-kind, technical, or consulting assistance.
Publications: Application guidelines; Grants list.
Application information: Applications accepted. Proposals should be no longer than 2 pages and submitted using organization letterhead. Telephone calls during the application process are not encouraged. Unsolicited requests for the Capezio Dance Award are not accepted. Application form required. Applicants should submit the following:
1) signature and title of chief executive officer
2) brief history of organization and description of its mission
3) listing of board of directors, trustees, officers and other key people and their affiliations
4) detailed description of project and amount of funding requested
5) copy of current year's organizational budget and/or project budget
6) listing of additional sources and amount of support
7) additional materials/documentation

Initial approach: Download application form and mail proposal and application form to foundation
Copies of proposal: 1
Board meeting date(s): Bi-annually
Deadline(s): Apr. 1
Final notification: June 30

Officers and Trustees:* Anthony Giacoio, Sr.*, Pres.; Donald Terlizzi*, Treas.; Jane Remer, Exec. Dir.; Lawrence Freedman*; Nicholas P. Terlizzi, Jr.*; Michael Terlizzi*.
Number of staff: 1 part-time professional.
EIN: 136161198

676
Capital City Bank
217 N. Monroe St.
P.O. Box 900
Tallahassee, FL 32301-7619
(850) 402-7700

Company URL: http://www.ccbg.com
Establishment information: Established in 1895.
Company type: Subsidiary of a public company
Business activities: Operates commercial bank.
Business type (SIC): Banks/commercial
Corporate officers: William G. Smith, Jr., Chair., Co-Pres., and C.E.O.; Tom Barron, Co-Pres.; J. Kimbrough Davis, Exec. V.P. and C.F.O.
Board of director: William G. Smith, Jr., Chair.
Giving statement: Giving through the Capital City Bank Group Foundation, Inc.

Capital City Bank Group Foundation, Inc.
217 N. Monroe St.
Tallahassee, FL 32301-7619 (850) 402-8521
Additional address: P.O. Box 11248, Tallahassee, FL 32302; URL: https://www.ccbg.com/our-communities.htm

Establishment information: Established in 1983.
Donors: Capital City First National Bank; Capital City Bank.
Financial data (yr. ended 12/31/11): Assets, $2,363,382 (M); gifts received, $126,993; expenditures, $250,308; qualifying distributions, $249,047; giving activities include $249,047 for 216 grants (high: $21,700; low: $25).
Purpose and activities: The foundation supports organizations involved with arts and culture, education, health, heart disease, Alzheimer's, housing development, school athletics, human services, and community development.
Fields of interest: Performing arts, theater; Arts; Higher education; Education; Hospitals (general); Health care; Heart & circulatory diseases; Alzheimer's disease; Housing/shelter; Athletics/sports, school programs; Boys & girls clubs; American Red Cross; Children/youth, services; Residential/custodial care, hospices; Developmentally disabled, centers & services; Human services; Community/economic development; United Ways and Federated Giving Programs.
Program:
Tipping Points Grants: The foundation will award a one-time gift to jump-start an organization to get its feet off the ground, or propel an organization to close the gap on what may seem to be an unattainable goal. The foundation will award a $50,000 grant to one organization, or two $25,000 grants to two different organizations.
Type of support: General/operating support; Scholarship funds.
Geographic limitations: Giving primarily in areas of company operations in FL.
Support limitations: No support for athletic teams. No grants for advertising, association memberships, athletic or fundraising event sponsorships, professional telephone sale solicitations, tickets to attend community functions or fundraisers, or activities with religious or political affiliation.
Publications: Application guidelines; Grants list.
Application information: Applications accepted. Application form required. Applicants should submit the following:
1) timetable for implementation and evaluation of project
2) statement of problem project will address
3) copy of IRS Determination Letter
4) brief history of organization and description of its mission
5) explanation of why grantmaker is considered an appropriate donor for project
6) detailed description of project and amount of funding requested
7) copy of current year's organizational budget and/or project budget

Initial approach: Contact nearest bank facility for an application form
Copies of proposal: 3
Board meeting date(s): Annually
Deadline(s): Apr. 1 and Oct. 1
Final notification: 30 days

Officers: William G. Smith, Jr., Chair.; Robert H. Smith, Pres.; Brooke Hallock, Secy.; Ray A Johnson, Treas.
EIN: 592276367
Selected grants: The following grants are a representative sample of this grantmaker's funding activity:
$2,000 to Ducks Unlimited, Memphis, TN, 2009.
$2,000 to Tallahassee Lenders Consortium, Tallahassee, FL, 2009.

677
The Capital Group Companies, Inc.
333 S. Hope St., 53rd Fl.
Los Angeles, CA 90071-1406
(213) 486-9200
FAX: (213) 486-9217

Company URL: http://www.capgroup.com
Establishment information: Established in 1931.
Company type: Private company
Business activities: Provides investment advisory services.
Business type (SIC): Security and commodity services
Financial profile for 2011: Number of employees, 7,000; sales volume, $7,530,000,000
Corporate officers: Philip de Toledo, Pres.; James M. Brown, Sr. V.P. and Treas.
Subsidiaries: The Capital Group Intl., Los Angeles, CA; The Capital Research and Management Co., Los Angeles, CA
Giving statement: Giving through the Capital Group Companies Charitable Foundation and the Capital Group Foundation.

The Capital Group Companies Charitable Foundation
333 S. Hope St.
Los Angeles, CA 90071-1406
URL: http://thecapitalgroup.com/our-company/company-culture.html

Establishment information: Established in 1997 in CA.
Donors: Capital Management Services, Inc.; Capital Bank & Trust Co.; The Capital Group Cos., Inc.; Capital Research & Management Co.; Capital International, Inc.
Financial data (yr. ended 06/30/12): Assets, $268,529,833 (M); gifts received, $38,373,131; expenditures, $19,155,368; qualifying distributions, $18,369,264; giving activities include $18,332,473 for 5,289 grants.
Purpose and activities: The foundation supports community foundations and organizations involved with arts and culture, education, the environment, health, youth development, human services, international relief, and leadership development.
Fields of interest: Media, television; Media, radio; Museums; Museums (art); Performing arts; Performing arts, theater; Performing arts, opera; Arts; Middle schools/education; Secondary school/education; Higher education; Libraries (public); Education, reading; Education; Environment; Hospitals (general); Health care; Youth development; Children, services; Family services; Family services, domestic violence; Human services; International relief; Foundations (community); Leadership development.
Programs:
Anniversary Gift Program: The foundation awards grants to nonprofit organizations chosen by an employee who is celebrating an anniversary with Capital Group. An employee is eligible for this program every five years, beginning with his or her fifth anniversary.
Associate Matching Gift Program: The foundation matches contributions made by associates of Capital Group to nonprofit organizations on a two-for-one basis, up to $5,000 per employee, per year.
Dollars for Doers: The foundation awards grants to nonprofit organizations with which employees of Capital Group volunteer, $100 for every 10 hours of service, up to $500 per fiscal year.
Grant Making Program: Through the Grant Making Program, the foundation awards grants on behalf of Capital Group employees who volunteer or serve on the board of a nonprofit organization.
Type of support: Employee matching gifts; Employee volunteer services; General/operating support.
Geographic limitations: Giving on a national and international basis, with emphasis on CA, CT, Washington, DC, NY, and TX.
Support limitations: No support for religious, political, fraternal, or professional organizations. No grants to individuals.
Application information: Applications not accepted. Contributes only to pre-selected organizations.
Officers and Directors:* Thomas J. Condon*, Chair.; Naomi H. Kobayashi, Secy.; Edith H.L. Van Huss, C.F.O.; James B. Lovelace; Bruce E. Meikle; Theodore R. Samuels.
EIN: 954658856
Selected grants: The following grants are a representative sample of this grantmaker's funding activity:
$278,100 to K C E T Community Television of Southern California, Burbank, CA, 2011.
$243,500 to Rim of the World High School, Regional Occupational Program, Lake Arrowhead, CA, 2011.
$175,200 to Salzburg Global Seminar, Washington, DC, 2011.
$63,300 to Childrens Hospital Los Angeles, Los Angeles, CA, 2011.
$46,100 to Advocates for Survivors of Domestic Violence and Sexual Assault, Hailey, ID, 2011.
$5,000 to California Science Center Foundation, Los Angeles, CA, 2011.
$4,000 to UMMA Community Clinic, Los Angeles, CA, 2011.
$3,800 to HELPS International, Addison, TX, 2011.
$3,750 to Westside Neighborhood School, Los Angeles, CA, 2011.
$3,500 to Pacific Asian Counseling Services, Los Angeles, CA, 2011.

678
Capital Investments & Ventures Corp.

(also known as PADI)
30151 Tomas St.
Rancho Santa Margarita, CA 92688-2125
(949) 858-0647

Company URL: http://www.padi.com
Establishment information: Established in 1975.
Company type: Private company
Business activities: Operates holding company; provides scuba diving and snorkeling instructional services.
Business type (SIC): Amusement and recreation services/miscellaneous
Corporate officers: Brian Cronin, Chair. and C.E.O.; Drew Richardson, Pres. and C.O.O.; Gary Prenovost, C.F.O.; Sheryl Beck, Cont.
Board of director: Brian Cronin, Chair.
Subsidiary: PADI, Inc., Rancho Santa Margarita, CA
Giving statement: Giving through the PADI Foundation and the Project AWARE Foundation.

PADI Foundation

(also known as Professional Association of Diving Instructors Foundation)
9150 Wilshire Blvd., Ste. 300
Beverly Hills, CA 90212-3430 (310) 281-3200
FAX: (310) 859-1430;
E-mail: grants@padifoundation.org; URL: http://www.padifoundation.org

Establishment information: Established as a company-sponsored operating foundation in 1991 in CA.
Donors: Department of Justice, State of California; Capital Investments & Ventures Corp.
Contact: Charles P. Rettig, Pres.
Financial data (yr. ended 05/31/12): Assets, $3,514,211 (M); gifts received, $100,000; expenditures, $267,394; qualifying distributions, $245,084; giving activities include $222,775 for 25 grants to individuals (high: $9,073; low: $1,500).
Purpose and activities: The foundation supports organizations involved with underwater science, the underwater environment, education, and sports diving and awards grants to individuals undertaking projects in underwater science.
Fields of interest: Education; Environment, water pollution; Environment, natural resources; Environment, water resources; Environment; Athletics/sports, water sports; Marine science.
International interests: Asia; Australia; Brazil; Europe; South Africa.
Type of support: Grants to individuals; Research.
Geographic limitations: Giving on a national and international basis.
Support limitations: No grants for diving equipment, standard photographic equipment, personal computers, overhead costs, or indirect expenses.
Publications: Application guidelines; Financial statement; Grants list.
Application information: Applications accepted. The foundation utilizes the Common Grant Application, a web-based management program to receive and administer grant proposals. Application form not required. Applicants should submit the following:
1) timetable for implementation and evaluation of project
2) statement of problem project will address
3) name, address and phone number of organization
4) detailed description of project and amount of funding requested
5) copy of current year's organizational budget and/or project budget

Initial approach: Complete online application
Copies of proposal: 1
Board meeting date(s): Apr.
Deadline(s): Nov. 1 to Feb. 1
Final notification: May 3

Officer and Directors:* Charles P. Rettig*, Pres.; Paul K. Dayton, Ph.D.; Daniel M. Hanes, Ph.D.; Jeff Nadler; Andrew Saxon, M.D.
EIN: 954326850

Project AWARE Foundation

30151 Tomas St., Ste. 200
Rancho Santa Margarita, CA 92688-2125 (949) 858-7657
FAX: (949) 858-7521;
E-mail: grants@projectaware.org; Toll-free tel. (U.S. and Canada): (866) 80AWARE; URL: http://www.projectaware.org

Establishment information: Established in 1992 in CA.
Contact: Jenny Miller Garmendia, Exec. Dir.
Financial data (yr. ended 12/31/11): Revenue, $635,139; assets, $510,074 (M); gifts received, $537,087; expenditures, $695,920; giving activities include $5,000 for grants to individuals.
Purpose and activities: The foundation encourages awareness of the fragile nature of the aquatic world through education, and assists in its protection.
Fields of interest: Environment, water pollution; Environment.

Program:

Grants Program: Provides grants to a variety of nonprofit organizations, institutions and individuals involved in activities directly related to the conservation of underwater environments. Funding requests will be accepted up to a maximum of $10,000 depending on the location of the project. The average grant awarded ranges between $1,500 and $3,000.

Geographic limitations: Giving on a national and international basis.
Support limitations: No grants for equipment, political campaigns, overhead expenses, travel or living expenses, or product design for resale.
Publications: Application guidelines.
Application information: Applications accepted. Faxed or mailed proposals will not be accepted. Application form required. Applicants should submit the following:
1) timetable for implementation and evaluation of project
2) copy of current year's organizational budget and/or project budget

Initial approach: Download application form
Copies of proposal: 1
Board meeting date(s): Jan., Apr., July, and Oct.
Deadline(s): Mar. 15, June 15, Sept. 15, and Dec. 15
Final notification: Within two weeks

Officers and Directors:* Drew Richardson, Ed.D.*, Chair.; Kristin Valette*, Secy.-Treas.; Jenny Miller Garmendia, Exec. Dir.; Deborah Brosnan, Ph.D.; Roger McManus.
EIN: 330540475

679
Capital One Financial Corporation

1680 Capital One Dr., Ste. 1400
McLean, VA 22102-3407 (703) 720-1000
FAX: (302) 636-5454

Company URL: http://www.capitalone.com
Establishment information: Established in 1988.
Company type: Public company
Company ticker symbol and exchange: COF/NYSE
International Securities Identification Number: US14040H1059
Business activities: Operates holding company; provides consumer loans; operates savings bank.
Business type (SIC): Credit institutions/personal; banks/commercial; savings institutions; holding company
Financial profile for 2012: Number of employees, 39,593; assets, $312,918,000,000; pre-tax net income, $5,035,000,000; liabilities, $272,419,000,000
Fortune 1000 ranking: 2012—127th in revenues, 53rd in profits, and 18th in assets
Forbes 2000 ranking: 2012—396th in sales, 161st in profits, and 94th in assets
Corporate officers: Richard D. Fairbank, Chair., Pres., and C.E.O.; Gary L. Perlin, C.F.O.; Robert M. Alexander, C.I.O.; John G. Finnerman, Jr., Genl. Counsel and Corp. Secy.
Board of directors: Richard D. Fairbank, Chair.; W. Ronald Dietz; Patrick W. Gross; Ann Fritz Hackett; Lewis Hay III; Pierre E. Leroy; Peter E. Raskind; Mayo A. Shattuck III; Bradford H. Warner
Subsidiary: ING Bank, fsb, Wilmington, DE
Historic mergers: Hibernia Corporation (November 30, 2005); North Fork Bancorporation, Inc. (December 1, 2006); Chevy Chase Bank, F.S.B. (February 27, 2009)
Giving statement: Giving through the Capital One Financial Corporation Contributions Program and the Capital One Foundation.
Company EIN: 541719854

Capital One Financial Corporation Contributions Program

1680 Capital One Dr.
McLean, VA 22102-3491 (703) 720-1000
URL: http://www.capitalone.com/about/?linkid=WWW_1009_Z_A0B2084C0D22A0E8F33F8CB2G1F85H5AF4I7CC8_GBLFO_F1_01_T_ABT

Purpose and activities: As a complement to its foundation, Capital One Bank also makes charitable contributions to nonprofit organizations directly. Support is limited to areas of company operations in Louisiana, New Jersey, New York, Texas, Virginia, and Washington.
Fields of interest: Education, early childhood education; Secondary school/education; Higher education, college; Adult/continuing education; Adult education—literacy, basic skills & GED; Education, services; Employment; Housing/shelter, rehabilitation; Housing/shelter, homeless; Housing/shelter, expense aid; Youth development, public education; Youth development, services; Human services, financial counseling; Community development, business promotion; Community development, small businesses Economically disadvantaged.

Programs:

Matching Gifts Program: Capital One matches contributions made by its employees to institutions of higher education on a one-for-one basis.

Scholarships: Capital One awards $5,000 and $10,000 college scholarships to graduating high school seniors.

Volunteer One Program: Through the Volunteer One Program, Capital One makes charitable contributions of up to $500 to nonprofit organizations with which employees volunteer.

Type of support: Consulting services; Employee volunteer services; General/operating support; Loaned talent; Pro bono services; Sponsorships.
Geographic limitations: Giving on a national basis in areas of company operations in DC, LA, NJ, NY, TX, and VA.
Support limitations: Generally no support for political, labor, fraternal, religious, athletic, health, or civic organizations, or for sports programs. Generally no grants to individuals, or for fundraising, fellowships, advertising, marketing, sporting or athletic events, travel, student trips or tours, memorial campaigns, capital campaign projects, or development or production of books, films, videos, or television programs.
Publications: Application guidelines.
Application information: Applications accepted.
Initial approach: Complete online eligibility quiz. Contact nearest branch or corporate office to request an application form

Capital One Foundation

(formerly North Fork Foundation)
1680 Capital One Dr.
McLean, VA 22102-3407 (804) 284-2118
E-mail: communityaffairs@capitalone.com;
URL: http://www.capitalone.com/about/corporate-citizenship/partnerships/

Establishment information: Established in 1994 in NY.
Donor: GreenPoint Bank.
Contact: Mary Johnson Fain, Sr. Mgr., Opers.
Financial data (yr. ended 09/30/11): Assets, $39,615,504 (M); gifts received, $4,615,000; expenditures, $3,423,458; qualifying distributions, $3,216,171; giving activities include $3,216,171 for 64 grants (high: $599,000; low: $4,000).
Purpose and activities: The foundation supports education-centered community development programs that expand economic opportunity among low-to-moderate-income families. Special emphasis is directed toward neighborhood approaches that address the education and well-being of children and youth.
Fields of interest: Elementary/secondary education; Education, early childhood education; Education, services; Education, reading; Education; Employment, services; Employment, training; Housing/shelter; Youth development; Children, day care; Human services, financial counseling; Community development, small businesses; Community/economic development.
Type of support: Continuing support; Employee matching gifts; General/operating support; Program development.
Geographic limitations: Giving primarily in Washington, DC, greater New Orleans, LA, MD, northern and central NJ, New York City and Long Island, NY, the greater Dallas and Houston, TX, areas, and Fairfax County, VA; giving also to national organizations.
Support limitations: No support for political, labor, fraternal organizations, or civic clubs, religious organizations not of direct benefit of the entire community, or health-related organizations. No grants to individuals, or for fundraising or fellowships, advertising or marketing activities, sports, athletic events, or athletic programs, travel-related events including student trips or tours, development or production of books, films, videos, or television programs, or memorial campaigns.
Publications: Application guidelines; Corporate giving report.
Application information: Applications accepted. Applicants should submit the following:
1) detailed description of project and amount of funding requested
2) geographic area to be served
3) contact person
4) name, address and phone number of organization

Initial approach: Complete online letter of inquiry form
Deadline(s): None

Officers and Directors:* Carolyn S. Berkowitz*, Pres.; Amy D. Cook, Secy.; Andrew D. Labenne, Treas.; Guenet M. Beshah; Dorothy Broadman; Lynn A. Carter; Heather M. Cox; John G. Finneran, Jr.; Nicole Moran; Richard A. Woods*.
EIN: 113276603

680
Capitol Federal Financial, Inc.

700 Kansas Ave.
P.O. Box 3505
Topeka, KS 66603-3505 (785) 235-1341

Company URL: http://www.capfed.com
Establishment information: Established in 1999.
Company type: Public company
Company ticker symbol and exchange: CFFN/NASDAQ
Business activities: Operates bank holding company; operates savings bank.
Business type (SIC): Savings institutions; holding company
Financial profile for 2012: Number of employees, 677; assets, $9,378,300,000; pre-tax net income, $116,000,000; liabilities, $7,571,850,000
Corporate officers: John B. Dicus, Chair., Pres., and C.E.O.; Kent G. Townsend, Exec. V.P., C.F.O., and Treas.; Natalie G. Haag, Exec. V.P. and Genl. Counsel.
Board of directors: John B. Dicus, Chair.; Morris Jack Huey II; Jeffrey M. Johnson; James G. Morris; Michael T. McCoy, M.D.; Reginald L. Robinson; Jeffrey R. Thompson; Marilyn S. Ward
Subsidiary: Capitol Federal Savings Bank, Topeka, KS
Giving statement: Giving through the Capitol Federal Financial Corporate Giving Program and the Capitol Federal Foundation.
Company EIN: 481212142

Capitol Federal Financial Corporate Giving Program

700 Kansas Ave.
Topeka, KS 66603-3829 (785) 235-1341
URL: http://www.capfed.com/content/site/en/home/community.html

Purpose and activities: Capitol Federal makes charitable contributions to nonprofit organizations involved with arts and culture, higher education, housing, and community development. Support is given primarily in areas of company operations in Kansas.
Fields of interest: Arts; Higher education; Housing/shelter; Community development, neighborhood development.
Type of support: Pro bono services.
Geographic limitations: Giving primarily in areas of company operations in KS.

Capitol Federal Foundation

700 S. Kansas Ave., Ste. 517
Topeka, KS 66603-3809 (785) 270-6040
FAX: (785) 270-6046; Additional tel.: (785) 270-6041; URL: http://www.capfed.com/site/en/home/community.html

Establishment information: Established in 1999 in KS.
Donor: Capitol Federal Financial.
Contact: Tammy Dishman, Pres.
Financial data (yr. ended 12/31/11): Assets, $91,228,140 (M); expenditures, $3,576,831; qualifying distributions, $2,985,742; giving activities include $2,881,894 for 343 grants (high: $400,000; low: $34).
Purpose and activities: The foundation supports performing art centers and organizations involved with education, health, affordable housing, human services, and community development.
Fields of interest: Performing arts centers; Higher education; Education; Health care; Housing/shelter; Boys & girls clubs; Big Brothers/Big Sisters; Youth, services; Human services; Community/economic development; Foundations (community); United Ways and Federated Giving Programs.
Type of support: Annual campaigns; Building/renovation; Capital campaigns; Conferences/seminars; Continuing support; Emergency funds; Employee matching gifts; Employee volunteer services; Equipment; Fellowships; General/operating support; Income development; Internship funds; Management development/capacity building; Matching/challenge support; Professorships; Program development; Scholarship funds; Seed money; Technical assistance.
Geographic limitations: Giving limited to areas of company operations in central and northeastern KS.
Support limitations: No support for religious or political organizations.
Application information: Applications accepted. Application form not required. Applicants should submit the following:
1) copy of IRS Determination Letter
2) listing of board of directors, trustees, officers and other key people and their affiliations
3) copy of current year's organizational budget and/or project budget
4) listing of additional sources and amount of support

Initial approach: Letter or telephone
Copies of proposal: 1
Board meeting date(s): Quarterly
Deadline(s): None
Final notification: 90 to 120 days

Officers: John B. Dicus, Chair.; Tammy Dishman, Pres.; John B. Dicus, Secy.-Treas.
Number of staff: 1 full-time professional.
EIN: 481214952
Selected grants: The following grants are a representative sample of this grantmaker's funding activity:
$400,000 to Washburn University Foundation, Topeka, KS, 2011.
$200,000 to Kansas Masonic Foundation, Topeka, KS, 2011.
$132,988 to United Way of Greater Topeka, Topeka, KS, 2011.
$100,000 to Johnson County Community College Foundation, Overland Park, KS, 2011.
$100,000 to Lawrence Community Theater, Lawrence, KS, 2011.
$62,400 to United Way of Douglas County, Lawrence, KS, 2011.
$33,000 to Topeka Symphony Society, Topeka, KS, 2011.
$20,000 to Ronald McDonald House of Northeast Kansas, Topeka, KS, 2011.

$20,000 to Washburn University Foundation, Topeka, KS, 2011.
$15,615 to Topeka Community Foundation, Topeka, KS, 2011.

681
Caplin & Drysdale, Chartered

1 Thomas Cir., N.W., Ste. 1100
Washington, DC 20005-5802
(202) 862-5000

Company URL: http://www.caplindrysdale.com
Establishment information: Established in 1964.
Company type: Private company
Business activities: Operates law firm.
Business type (SIC): Legal services
Corporate officer: Scott D. Michel, Pres.
Offices: Washington, DC; New York, NY
Giving statement: Giving through the Caplin & Drysdale, Chartered Corporate Giving Program.

Caplin & Drysdale, Chartered Corporate Giving Program

1 Thomas Cir., N.W., Ste. 1100
Washington, DC 20005-5802 (202) 862-5000
FAX: (202) 429-3301; Contact for Pro Bono program: Elihu Inselbuch, Member, tel.: (212) 319-7125, (212) 644-6755, e-mail:ei@capdale.com; URL: http://www.caplindrysdale.com/233

Purpose and activities: Caplin & Drysdale makes charitable contributions to nonprofit organizations involved with human services.
Fields of interest: Legal services; Housing/shelter; Salvation Army; Human services; Women, centers/services; Homeless, human services.
Type of support: Continuing support; Employee volunteer services; General/operating support; Pro bono services - legal.

682
Capri, Inc.

6867 N. Oracle Rd., Ste. 101
Tucson, AZ 85704-4264 (520) 219-1856

Establishment information: Established in 1972.
Company type: Private company
Business activities: Operates and manages hotel/motel radio broadcast station.
Business type (SIC): Management and public relations services
Financial profile for 2010: Number of employees, 5
Corporate officers: Jim O'Connell, Pres. and C.E.O.; Mary Graham, Secy.
Giving statement: Giving through the Eddy Foundation.

Eddy Foundation

6867 N. Oracle Rd., Ste. 101
Tucson, AZ 85704-4265

Establishment information: Established in 2000 in MT.
Donor: Capri, Inc.
Contact: Jim O'Connell, Pres.
Financial data (yr. ended 12/31/11): Assets, $225,293 (M); expenditures, $10,882; qualifying distributions, $10,443; giving activities include $10,443 for grants.
Fields of interest: Health care; Agriculture/food; Human services.
Support limitations: No grants to individuals.
Application information: Applications accepted. Application form required. Applicants should submit the following:
1) descriptive literature about organization
Initial approach: Letter
Deadline(s): None
Officers: Jim O'Connell, Pres.; Brad Bruno, Treas.
Director: Kelly Kuntz.
EIN: 810537109

683
The Caprock Group, Inc.

805 W. Idaho St., Ste. 200
Boise, ID 83702-8916 (208) 368-9600
FAX: (208) 368-9602

Company URL: http://www.thecaprockgroup.com
Establishment information: Established in 2005.
Company type: Private company
Business type (SIC): Business services/miscellaneous
Corporate officer: Gregory A. Brown, Owner
Giving statement: Giving through the Caprock Group, Inc.

The Caprock Group, Inc.

805 West Idaho St., Ste. 200
Boise, ID 83702-8916 (208) 368-9600
E-mail: Contact@thecaprockgroup.com; URL: http://www.thecaprockgroup.com

Purpose and activities: The Caprock Group is a certified B Corporation that donates a percentage of net profits to charitable organizations.

684
Capstone Publishers, Inc.

151 Good Counsel Dr.
P.O. Box 669
Mankato, MN 56002-0069 (507) 388-6650

Company URL: http://www.capstonepub.com
Establishment information: Established in 1990.
Company type: Subsidiary of a private company
Business activities: Operates book publishing company.
Business type (SIC): Book publishing and/or printing
Corporate officers: G. Thomas Ahern, C.E.O.; Todd R. Brekhus, Pres.; William R. Rouse, C.O.O and C.F.O; Eric S. Fitzgerald, V.P., Sales
Board of directors: G. Thomas Ahern; James P. Coughlan; Robert J. Coughlan; William L. Kozitza; Dennis E. Miller; Paul J. Schleich
Offices: Bloomington, North Mankato, MN
Giving statement: Giving through the Capstone Publishers, Inc. Corporate Giving Program.

Capstone Publishers, Inc. Corporate Giving Program

5050 Lincoln Drive, Ste. 200
Edina, MN 55436 (507) 388-6650
E-mail: community.giving@coughlancompanies.com ; URL: http://www.capstonepub.com/content/ABOUTUS_COMMUNITYOUTREACH

Purpose and activities: Capstone Publishers makes charitable contributions to nonprofit organizations involved with literacy, education, and the environment. Support is given primarily in areas of company operations in Minnesota; giving also to national and international organizations.
Fields of interest: Elementary school/education; Adult education—literacy, basic skills & GED; Education, reading; Education; Environmental education; Environment.
Type of support: Donated products; Employee volunteer services; General/operating support; In-kind gifts.
Geographic limitations: Giving primarily in areas of company operations in MN; giving also to national and international organizations.
Support limitations: No support for political organizations or where direct competitors of Coughlan Companies are also involved as sponsors. No grants for activities in which there is no charitable partner or beneficiary.
Publications: Application guidelines.
Application information: Applications accepted. Phone calls are not encouraged. Proposals should be limited to 5 pages (not including budget) using a font size no smaller than 10 pt. Application form required. Applicants should submit the following:
1) copy of IRS Determination Letter
2) copy of current year's organizational budget and/or project budget
3) plans for acknowledgement
4) name, address and phone number of organization
5) contact person
Initial approach: E-mail completed grant proposal application
Committee meeting date(s): Quarterly
Deadline(s): Feb. 8, May 10, Aug. 9, and Nov. 8 for grant proposals

685
Cardinal Health, Inc.

7000 Cardinal Pl.
Dublin, OH 43017-1091 (614) 757-5000
FAX: (614) 757-6000

Company URL: http://www.cardinal.com
Establishment information: Established in 1971.
Company type: Public company
Company ticker symbol and exchange: CAH/NYSE
International Securities Identification Number: US14149Y1082
Business activities: Sells pharmaceutical products wholesale; provides pharmaceutical management services; sells and provides medical and surgical products and services wholesale; manufactures and provides pharmaceutical technologies and services; provides pharmaceutical automation and information services.
Business type (SIC): Drugs, proprietaries, and sundries—wholesale; machinery/special industry; professional and commercial equipment—wholesale; computer services; management and public relations services
Financial profile for 2012: Number of employees, 23,300; assets, $24,260,000,000; sales volume, $107,552,000,000; pre-tax net income, $1,698,000,000; expenses, $105,760,000,000; liabilities, $18,016,000,000
Fortune 1000 ranking: 2012—19th in revenues, 189th in profits, and 213th in assets
Forbes 2000 ranking: 2012—54th in sales, 540th in profits, and 862nd in assets
Corporate officers: George S. Barrett, Chair. and C.E.O.; Steve Falk, Exec. V.P., Genl. Counsel, and Corp. Secy.; Patricia Morrison, Exec. V.P. and C.I.O.; Shelley Bird, Exec. V.P., Public Affairs; Jeffrey W. Henderson, C.F.O.

Board of directors: George S. Barrett, Chair.; Colleen F. Arnold; Glenn A. Britt; Carrie S. Cox; Calvin Darden; Bruce L. Downey; John F. Finn; Clayton M. Jones; Gregory B. Kenny; David P. King; Richard C. Notebaert; Jean G. Spaulding, M.D.
Subsidiaries: Allegiance Corp., McGaw Park, IL; Automatic Liquid Packaging, Inc., Woodstock, IL; Bindley Western Industries, Inc., Indianapolis, IN; Comprehensive Reimbursement Consultants, Inc., Minneapolis, MN; CORD Logistics, Inc., La Vergne, TN; Medicine Shoppe International, Inc., St. Louis, MO; National Pharmpak Services, Inc., Zanesville, OH; National Specialty Services, Inc., Nashville, TN; Owen Healthcare, Inc., Houston, TX; PCI Services, Inc., Philadelphia, PA; Pyxis Corp., San Diego, CA
Giving statement: Giving through the Cardinal Health, Inc. Corporate Giving Program and the Cardinal Health Foundation.
Company EIN: 310958666

Cardinal Health, Inc. Corporate Giving Program

c/o Community Rels.
7000 Cardinal Pl.
Dublin, OH 43017-1091 (614) 757-7481
FAX: (614) 652-9601;
E-mail: communityrelations@cardinalhealth.com;
URL: http://www.cardinal.com/us/en/community/index.asp

Contact: Dianne Radigan, Dir., Community Rels.
Financial data (yr. ended 06/30/12): Total giving, $3,274,473, including $3,274,473 for grants.
Purpose and activities: As a complement to its foundation, Cardinal Health also makes charitable contributions to nonprofit organizations directly. Support is given to healthcare programs designed to improve efficiency, enhance quality, and enable cost-effectiveness; to increase awareness of prescription drug abuse, and to build healthy communities. Giving primarily in areas of company operations.
Fields of interest: Medical care, community health systems; Health care; Health care; Substance abuse, services; Community/economic development.
Type of support: Donated products; General/operating support; In-kind gifts.
Geographic limitations: Giving primarily in areas of company operations, with emphasis on Little Rock, AR, northern Chicago, Lake, and McHenry County, IL, Radcliff, KY, Albuquerque, NM, central OH, PR, LaVergne, TN, El Paso, TX, and Kenosha County, WI; giving also to national organizations and internationally in China, Dominican Republic and Mexico.
Support limitations: No support for fraternal, athletic, or social clubs, member-based organizations, including chambers of commerce, rotary clubs, or IRS 501(c)(4) legions or associations, municipalities, including fire departments or police departments, organizations classified as IRS 509(a)(3), discriminatory organizations, organizations with divisive or litigious public agendas, religious organizations not of direct benefit to the entire community, sports teams, veterans', labor, or political organizations, private foundations or deferred giving trusts, marching bands, or youth clubs. No grants to individuals (except for employee-related scholarships), or for advertising, capital campaigns outside of central Ohio, endowments, event sponsorships, general operating support, debt reduction, political campaigns, athletic competitions, memberships, subscriptions, club dues, or travel; no loans.
Application information: Applications accepted. Organizations requesting product or financial donations in response to a national or international disaster should contact one of the company's international disaster relief partners directly. Application form not required.
Initial approach: Submit letter of inquiry online

Cardinal Health Foundation

c/o Community Rels.
7000 Cardinal Pl.
Dublin, OH 43017-1091 (614) 757-7481
E-mail: communityrelations@cardinalhealth.com; E-mail for Dianne Radigan: Dianne.Radigan@cardinalhealth.com; URL: http://www.cardinal.com/

Establishment information: Established in 2000 in OH.
Donors: The Baxter Allegiance Foundation; Cardinal Health, Inc.; World Reach.
Contact: Dianne Radigan, Dir., Community Rels.
Financial data (yr. ended 06/30/12): Assets, $54,801,555 (M); expenditures, $7,766,859; qualifying distributions, $7,766,959; giving activities include $7,766,859 for grants.
Purpose and activities: The foundation supports healthcare programs designed to improve efficiency, enhance quality, and enable cost-effectiveness; increase awareness of prescription drug abuse; and build healthy communities.
Fields of interest: Education; Medical care, community health systems; Hospitals (general); Health care, clinics/centers; Pharmacy/prescriptions; Public health; Public health, physical fitness; Health care, patient services; Health care; Disasters, preparedness/services; Safety/disasters Children; Youth; Aging.
Programs:
E3 Grants - Effectiveness, Efficiency, and Excellence in Healthcare: The foundation awards grants to health systems, hospitals, and clinics designed to promote healthcare efficiency, quality, and cost of care. Special emphasis is directed toward programs designed to develop medication safety across transitions of care from the acute setting to the community and/or home; and implement WHO checklists in the operating room. Grants range from $15,000 to $35,000.
Employee Matching Gifts: The foundation matches contributions made by employees of Cardinal Health to nonprofit organizations from $25 to $1,000 per employee, per year. Donations to health-related, school, and scholarship programs are matched 100%, and donations to other nonprofits organizations are matched 50%.
Employee-Related Scholarships: The foundation awards $2,000 college scholarships to children and dependents of employees of Cardinal Health. The program is administered by Scholarship America.
Essential to Wellness Grants: The foundation supports programs designed to improve health and wellness in communities served by Cardinal Health. Special emphasis is directed toward programs designed to promote active, healthy lifestyles for children, families, and the elderly; and encourage healthy literacy, patient education, and engagement.
Preventing the Abuse and Misuse of Prescription Drugs Grant Program: The foundation supports programs designed to reduce the abuse and misuse of prescription drugs in youth and adults. Special emphasis is directed toward programs designed to increase awareness of prescription drug abuse; increase knowledge of how to reduce access to prescription drugs and/or proper disposal and the dangers of misusing prescription drugs; and increase willingness to openly discuss the prescription drug abuse problem. Grants range from $5,000 to $15,000.
Team Building Grants: The foundation awards grants of up to $5,000 to nonprofit organizations with which teams of three or more employees of Cardinal Health volunteer their time for a hands-on service project.
Team Fundraising Grants: The foundation awards grants of up to $2,500 to recognize teams of three or more employees of Cardinal Health who join together to raise funds for a local nonprofit organization.
Volunteer Leadership Grants: The foundation awards grants of up to $3,500 to nonprofit organizations with which employees of Cardinal Health serve as volunteer board members, committee chairs, or fundraising chairs.
Type of support: Conferences/seminars; Continuing support; Donated products; Employee matching gifts; Employee volunteer services; Employee-related scholarships; In-kind gifts; Matching/challenge support; Program development; Research; Scholarship funds.
Geographic limitations: Giving primarily in areas of company operations, with emphasis on Little Rock, AR, northern Chicago, Lake, and McHenry County, IL, Radcliff, KY, Albuquerque, NM, central OH, LaVergne, TN, El Paso, TX, PR, Kenosha County, WI; giving also to national organizations and internationally in China, Dominican Republic, and Mexico.
Support limitations: No support for fraternal, athletic, or social clubs, member-based organizations, including chambers of commerce, rotary clubs, or IRS 501(c)(4) legions or associations, municipalities, including fire departments or police departments, organizations classified as IRS 509(a)(3), discriminatory organizations, organizations with divisive or litigious public agendas, religious organizations not of direct benefit to the entire community, sport teams, veterans', labor, or political organizations, private foundations or deferred giving trusts, marching bands, or youth clubs. No grants to individuals (except for employee-related scholarships), or for advertising, capital campaigns outside of Ohio, endowments, general operating support, debt reduction, political campaigns, athletic competitions, memberships, subscriptions, club dues, or travel; no loans.
Publications: Application guidelines; IRS Form 990 or 990-PF printed copy available upon request; Program policy statement.
Application information: Applications accepted. Organizations receiving E3 Grants are asked to submit a mid-year progress report and a final report. Organizations receiving Preventing the Abuse and Misuse of Prescription Medications Grant Program support are asked to participate in webinars or conference calls, submit a program/project evaluation, and submit a year-end summary report. Application form not required. Applicants should submit the following:
1) results expected from proposed grant
2) statement of problem project will address
3) copy of IRS Determination Letter
4) how project's results will be evaluated or measured
5) detailed description of project and amount of funding requested
6) copy of current year's organizational budget and/or project budget

Initial approach: Complete online proposal for E3 Grants, Preventing the Abuse and Misuse of Prescription Medications Grant Program, and Essential to Wellness Grants
Deadline(s): Dec. 7 for E3 Grants; May 11 for Preventing the Abuse and Misuse of

Prescription Medications Grant Program; Jan. 18 for Essential to Wellness Grants
Final notification: May for Preventing the Abuse and Misuse of Prescription Medications Grant Program; Apr. for Essential to Wellness Grants
Officers and Directors:* Shirley Bird*, Chair.; Tony Caprio*, Vice-Chair.; Stephen Falk*, Secy.; Jorge Gomez*, Treas.; Lisa Ashby; Jon Giacomin; Carole Watkins; Connie Woodburn.
EIN: 311746458
Selected grants: The following grants are a representative sample of this grantmaker's funding activity:
$450,000 to Ohio Childrens Hospital Association Foundation, Columbus, OH, 2011. For Solutions for Patient safety.
$250,000 to Columbus Museum of Art, Columbus, OH, 2011. For capital campaign.
$250,000 to Institute for Healthcare Improvement, Cambridge, MA, 2011. For Thought Leadership.
$183,500 to Scholarship America, Saint Peter, MN, 2011. For EE Scholarship.
$180,300 to Boston University, School of Management, Boston, MA, 2011. For Professional development.
$66,667 to Action for Children Council of Franklin County, Kids Come First, Columbus, OH, 2011. For capital campaign.
$27,846 to OhioHealth, Columbus, OH, 2011. For E3 - Effectiveness, Efficiency, Excellence.
$5,000 to National Dance Institute New Mexico, Santa Fe, NM, 2011. For community focused.
$3,500 to Saint Stephens Community House, Columbus, OH, 2011. For volunteer leadership grant.
$3,500 to University of Illinois Foundation, Urbana, IL, 2011. For volunteer leadership grant.

686
Care2.com, Inc.

275 Shoreline Dr., Ste. 300
Redwood City, CA 94065-1490
(650) 622-0860
FAX: 650-622-0870

Company URL: http://www.Care2.com
Establishment information: Established in 1998.
Company type: Private company
Business type (SIC): Business services/ miscellaneous
Corporate officers: Randy Paynter, Pres. and C.E.O.; Marlin Miller, C.O.O.; Randy Ferrell, V.P., Sales
Giving statement: Giving through the Care2.com, Inc. Contributions Program.

Care2.com, Inc. Contributions Program

275 Shoreline Dr., Ste. 300
Redwood City, CA 94065-1490 (650) 622-0860
URL: http://www.Care2.com

Purpose and activities: Care2.com is a certified B Corporation that donates a percentage of net profits to charitable organizations.

687
CareFirst of Maryland, Inc.

(doing business as CareFirst BlueCross BlueShield)
10455 and 104853 Mill Run Cir.
Owings Mills, MD 21117 (410) 581-3000

Company URL: http://www.carefirst.com
Establishment information: Established in 1937.
Company type: Subsidiary of a private company
Business activities: Operates medical service plan.
Business type (SIC): Insurance/accident and health
Financial profile for 2012: Number of employees, 5,200
Corporate officers: Joseph G. Hall, Co-Chair.; Michael J. Kelly, Co-Chair.; Chet Burrell, Pres. and C.E.O.; G. Mark Chaney, Exec. V.P. and C.F.O.; John A. Picciotto, Esq., Exec. V.P. and Genl Counsel; Michael Filber, Sr. V.P., Sales
Board of directors: Joseph G. Hall, Co-Chair.; Micheal J. Kelly, Co-Chair.; Andrea M. Amprey; Barbara Blount Armstrong; Gregory V. Billups; James A. D'Orta; James G. Hall; Richard N. Kramer; John F. Reim; Margaret Scott Schiff; Loretta L. Schmitzer, Esq.; Kevin G. Quinn
Giving statement: Giving through the CareFirst BlueCross BlueShield Corporate Giving Program.

CareFirst BlueCross BlueShield Corporate Giving Program

c/o Community Affairs
10455 Mill Run Cir.
Owings Mills, MD 21117-5559
E-mail: community.affairs@carefirst.com; URL: http://www.carefirstcommitment.com/html/index.html

Purpose and activities: CareFirst makes charitable contributions to nonprofit organizations involved with improving access to health care, addressing health disparities, improving health care quality and safety, and supporting health and wellness initiatives. Support is limited to areas of company operations in Washington, DC, Maryland, and northern Virginia.
Fields of interest: Public health; Health care.
Type of support: Employee matching gifts; Employee volunteer services; General/operating support; Sponsorships.
Geographic limitations: Giving limited to areas of company operations in Washington, DC, and MD, and northern VA.
Support limitations: No support for religious or political organizations, national organizations with local chapters, organizations posing a conflict of interest to CareFirst or a subsidiary company, discriminatory organizations, service clubs, or parent-teacher organizations. No grants to individuals, or for political candidates.
Publications: Application guidelines.
Application information: Applications accepted. The Office of Public Policy and Community Affairs handles giving. Application form required. Applicants should submit the following:
1) timetable for implementation and evaluation of project
2) statement of problem project will address
3) population served
4) copy of IRS Determination Letter
5) brief history of organization and description of its mission
6) geographic area to be served
7) copy of most recent annual report/audited financial statement/990
8) how project's results will be evaluated or measured
9) explanation of why grantmaker is considered an appropriate donor for project
10) what distinguishes project from others in its field
11) detailed description of project and amount of funding requested
12) copy of current year's organizational budget and/or project budget

Applications should include a description of the program's track record and indicate any affiliations with federated funds or public agencies.
Initial approach: Complete online application form
Deadline(s): None
Final notification: 4 to 8 weeks; 12 weeks for requests over $100,000

688
CareFusion Corporation

3750 Torrey View Ct.
San Diego, CA 92130 (858) 617-2000
FAX: (302) 655-5049

Company URL: http://www.carefusion.com
Establishment information: Established in 2009.
Company type: Public company
Company ticker symbol and exchange: CFN/NYSE
Business activities: Operates global medical technology company.
Business type (SIC): Medical instruments and supplies
Financial profile for 2012: Number of employees, 15,000; assets, $8,488,000,000; sales volume, $3,598,000,000; pre-tax net income, $487,000,000; expenses, $3,024,000,000; liabilities, $3,257,000,000
Fortune 1000 ranking: 2012—622nd in revenues, 479th in profits, and 442nd in assets
Forbes 2000 ranking: 2012—1551st in sales, 1412th in profits, and 1590th in assets
Corporate officers: Kieran T. Gallahue, Chair. and C.E.O.; James F. Hinrichs, C.F.O.; Michael Zill, Exec. V.P. and C.I.O.; Joan B. Stafslien, Exec. V.P., Genl. Counsel, and Secy.; Roger Marchetti, Exec. V.P., Human Resources; Ron Frisbie, Exec. V.P., Opers.; James Mazzola, Sr. V.P., Mktg. and Comms.
Board of directors: Kieran T. Gallahue, Chair.; Philip L. Francis; Robert F. Friel; Jacqueline B. Kosecoff; J. Michael Losh; Gregory T. Lucier; Edward D. Miller; Michael D. O'Halleran; Robert P. Wayman
Giving statement: Giving through the CareFusion Foundation.
Company EIN: 264123274

CareFusion Foundation

3750 Torrey View Ct.
San Diego, CA 92130-2622
E-mail: carefustion@sdfoundation.org; URL: http://www.carefusion.com/company/citizenship/giving/

Establishment information: Established in 2009 in CA.
Donor: CareFusion 303, Inc.
Financial data (yr. ended 12/31/12): Assets, $3,600,831 (M); gifts received, $1,150; expenditures, $408,664; qualifying distributions, $382,796; giving activities include $382,796 for 5 grants (high: $250,000; low: $1,150).
Purpose and activities: The foundation supports programs designed to improve patient care and enhance community health and wellness.
Fields of interest: Hospitals (general); Health care, clinics/centers; Health care, patient services; Health care.

Programs:

Clinical Excellence Grants: The foundation supports programs designed to achieve clinical excellence and establish best practices in health care safety and efficiency. Grants of up to $50,000 are currently awarded to improve infection prevention. Special emphasis is directed toward organizations designed to implement measurable clinical initiatives to improve infection prevention; and hospital-led patient education or outreach related to infection prevention within the local community. Grants are approved and administered by The San Diego Foundation.

Community Leadership Grants: The foundation awards community leadership grants to organizations on behalf of individual employees who demonstrate commitment to improving community health and wellness.

Community Wellness Grants: The foundation supports programs designed to improve the wellness of communities where CareFusion employees live and work. Grants are awarded based on employee recommendations.

Type of support: Employee volunteer services; Program development.
Geographic limitations: Giving primarily in areas of company operations in CA.
Support limitations: No support for religious organizations, veterans', labor, or political organizations, fraternal, athletic, or social membership groups, member-based organizations including chambers of commerce, rotary clubs, or IRS 501(c)(4) legions or associations, municipalities including fire or police departments, IRS 509(a)(3) supporting organizations, litigious organizations, or sports teams. No grants to individuals, or for advertising or event sponsorships, capital campaigns for health systems, hospitals, or clinics, endowments, general operating support or emergency operating funds, tickets for fundraising events or raffles, athletic competitions, golf outings, or debt retirements; no loans.
Publications: Application guidelines.
Application information: Organizations receiving support are asked to submit a final report. Applicants should submit the following:
1) timetable for implementation and evaluation of project
2) results expected from proposed grant
3) copy of IRS Determination Letter
4) how project's results will be evaluated or measured
5) detailed description of project and amount of funding requested
6) copy of current year's organizational budget and/or project budget

Initial approach: Visit website for application information
Deadline(s): Varies

Officers and Directors:* James Mazzola*, Pres.; Joan B. Stafslien*, Secy.; Jean Maschal, C.F.O.
EIN: 272071842

689
Caremore Medical Enterprises

12900 Park Plaza Dr., Ste. 150
Cerritos, CA 90703 (855) 242-9607

Company URL: http://www.caremore.com
Company type: Subsidiary of a public company
Business activities: Operates healthcare management company.
Business type (SIC): Health services
Giving statement: Giving through the CareMore Foundation.

CareMore Foundation

120 Monument Cir.
Indianapolis, IN 46204

Donor: Caremore Medical Enterprises.
Financial data (yr. ended 12/31/11): Assets, $173,000 (M); gifts received, $250,000; expenditures, $77,000; qualifying distributions, $77,000; giving activities include $77,000 for 23 grants (high: $5,000; low: $2,500).
Fields of interest: Environment; Health care; Human services.
Application information: Applications not accepted. Unsolicited requests for funds not accepted.
Officers: Leeba Lessin, C.E.O.; Michael Foster, Secy.; Brendan Baker, Treas.
Directors: Alan Hoops; John Kao.
EIN: 800623537

690
CareSource Management Group

230 N. Main St.
Dayton, OH 45402 (937) 224-3300
FAX: (937) 224-2272

Company URL: http://www.caresource.com/en/Pages/default.aspx
Establishment information: Established in 1989.
Company type: Private company
Business activities: Operates public-sector managed care company.
Business type (SIC): Insurance/accident and health
Financial profile for 2010: Number of employees, 1,015; sales volume, $2,457,000,000
Corporate officers: Pamela B. Morris, Pres. and C.E.O.; Bobby Jones, C.O.O.; L. Tarlton Thomas III, C.F.O.; Dan McCabe, C.A.O.; Paul Stoddard, C.I.O.; Mark Chilson, Exec. V.P. and Genl. Counsel
Board of directors: Kevin Brown; Michael E. Ervin; Jocelyn Guyer; Ellen S. Leffak; J. Thomas Maultsby; John P. Monahan; Pamela Morris; Terry Rapoch
Giving statement: Giving through the CareSource Foundation.

The CareSource Foundation

c/o CareSource Management Group
230 N. Main St.
Dayton, OH 45402-1263 (937) 531-2808
Mailing address: P.O. Box 8738, Dayton, OH 45401-8738; URL: http://www.caresourcefoundation.com

Establishment information: Established in 2006 in OH; supporting organization of Caresource and Caresource Michigan.
Donor: CareSource Management Group.
Contact: Cathy Ponitz, Exec. Dir.
Financial data (yr. ended 12/31/11): Revenue, $2,214,402; assets, $1,238,540 (M); gifts received, $2,214,402; expenditures, $1,601,167; giving activities include $1,515,750 for grants.
Purpose and activities: The foundation provides opportunities to advance innovative solutions and address healthcare needs of the underserved through grants, outreach, medical expertise, strategic community partnerships and volunteerism, with focus in the following areas: issues of the uninsured, community health issues, and critical health trends.
Fields of interest: Medical care, community health systems; Pharmacy/prescriptions; Public health; Health care, insurance.
Geographic limitations: Giving primarily in geographical areas in which CareSource has the highest concentration of members, with emphasis on the greater Dayton, OH, area.
Support limitations: No support for organizations lacking 501(c)(3) status, individual primary or secondary schools, sectarian organizations having a predominantly religious purpose, fraternal or veteran organizations, tax-supported colleges and universities for operating purposes, or for organizations who cannot provide adequate accounting records or procedures. No grants to individuals, or for majority capital campaigns, scholarships or educational fees, fundraising, or debt retirement.
Officers and Trustees: J. Thomas Maultsby*, Chair.; William Marsteller, D.C.*, Vice-Chair.; Pamela Morris*, Pres. and C.E.O.; RoNita Hawes-Saunders*, Secy.-Treas.; Cathy Ponitz*, Exec. Dir.; Thomas Breitenbach; Morris L. Brown, M.D.; Lisa Grigsby; Ken Herr.
EIN: 562582561

691
Cargill, Incorporated

P.O. Box 9300
Minneapolis, MN 55440-9300
(952) 742-7575

Company URL: http://www.cargill.com
Establishment information: Established in 1865.
Company type: Private company
Business activities: Manufactures and produces food and agricultural products; provides risk management services.
Business type (SIC): Food and kindred products; fertilizers and agricultural chemicals; management and public relations services
Financial profile for 2011: Number of employees, 126,800; sales volume, $109,560,000,000
Corporate officers: Gregory R. Page, Chair. and C.E.O.; Paul D. Conway, Vice-Chair.; David W. MacLennan, Pres., C.O.O., and C.F.O.; John E. Geisler, Corp. V.P. and C.I.O.; Jayme D. Olson, Corp. V.P. and Treas.; Kimberly A. Lattu, Corp. V.P. and Cont.; Laura Witte, Corp. V.P., Genl. Counsel, and Corp. Secy.; Thomas M. Hayes, Corp. V.P., Opers.; Peter Vrijsen, Corp. V.P., Human Resources
Board of directors: Gregory R. Page, Chair.; Paul D. Conway, Vice-Chair.; Richard H. Anderson; Arthur D. Collins, Jr.; Linda Zarda Cook; Curtis Johnson; Richard M. Kovacevich; Bernard Poussot
Subsidiaries: The Mosaic Company, Plymouth, MN; Mosaic Global Holdings Inc., Lake Forest, IL
International operations: Belgium; Canada
Giving statement: Giving through the Cargill, Incorporated Corporate Giving Program and the Cargill Foundation.
Company EIN: 410177680

Cargill, Incorporated Corporate Giving Program

c/o Corp. Affairs
P.O. Box 5650
Minneapolis, MN 55440-5650 (952) 742-2931
E-mail: stacey_smida@cargill.com; Additional contact: Stacey Smida, Grants Mgr.: tel.: (952) 742-4311, e-mail: stacey_smida@cargill.com; URL: http://www.cargill.com/corporate-responsibility/community-engagement/charitable-giving/index.jsp

Contact: Michelle Grogg, Sr. Dir., Corp. Contribs.
Purpose and activities: As a complement to its foundation, Cargill also makes charitable

contributions to nonprofit organizations directly. Special emphasis is directed towards programs designed to address nutrition and health, education, and environmental stewardship. Giving primarily in areas of company operations; giving also to regional, national, and international organizations.
Fields of interest: Education; Environment, natural resources; Environment, water resources; Environment; Health care; Agriculture/food, formal/general education; Agriculture, sustainable programs; Food services; Nutrition; Human services; International development; Rural development; Community/economic development; Science, formal/general education; Engineering/technology; Public affairs.
Programs:
Demonstrating Responsible Stewardship of Natural Resources: Cargill supports programs designed to protect and improve accessibility to water resources; educate children about conservation and preservation; and promote agricultural management practices that reduce impact and promote sustainability.
Ensuring A Safe, Nutritious, Accessible Global Food Supply: Cargill supports programs designed to provide long-term solutions to alleviate hunger; improve food safety; educate consumers about healthy and nutritious food; and promote a global, open food supply chain.
Promoting Innovation in Education: Cargill supports programs designed to help develop logic and thinking skills; promote leadership development; and increase access to education for socio-economically disadvantaged youth.
Type of support: Employee matching gifts; Employee volunteer services; Program development; Scholarship funds; Scholarships—to individuals.
Geographic limitations: Giving primarily in areas of company operations; giving also to regional, national, and international organizations.
Support limitations: No support for lobbying, political, or fraternal organizations. No grants to individuals (except for employee-related scholarships), or for athletic scholarships, advertising, or event sponsorships, religious purposes, public service, or political campaigns, benefit dinners or tickets to dinners, fundraising, walk-a-thons, promotions to eradicate or control specific diseases, publications, audio-visual productions, special broadcasts, endowments, ambulances, defibrillators, or other medical equipment. Generally, no grants for general operating expenses or capital campaigns.
Publications: Application guidelines.
Application information: Applications accepted. A contributions committee reviews all requests. Letters of inquiry should be no longer than 2 to 3 pages. Additional information or a site visit may be requested at a later date. Application form required. Applicants should submit the following:
1) explanation of why grantmaker is considered an appropriate donor for project
2) detailed description of project and amount of funding requested
3) name, address and phone number of organization
Initial approach: Mail or e-mail letter of inquiry
Deadline(s): None
Final notification: 90 days
Number of staff: 4 full-time professional.

The Cargill Foundation

P.O. Box 5626
Minneapolis, MN 55440-5626 (952) 742-4311
FAX: (952) 742-7224;
E-mail: stacy_smida@cargill.com; Application address: c/o Mark Murphy, P.O. Box 5650, Minneapolis, MN 55440-5632, tel.: (952) 742-4311; URL: http://www.cargill.com/corporate-responsibility/community-engagement/charitable-giving/headquarters-giving/index.jsp

Establishment information: Incorporated in 1952 in MN.
Donors: Agualia Foundation; Cargill, Inc.; Cargill Charitable Trust.
Contact: Stacy Smida, Grants Mgr.
Financial data (yr. ended 12/31/11): Assets, $121,635,585 (M); gifts received, $1,393,160; expenditures, $10,165,715; qualifying distributions, $9,484,668; giving activities include $9,484,668 for 68 grants (high: $1,200,000; low: $1,000).
Purpose and activities: The foundation supports programs designed to educate socio-economically disadvantaged children and eliminate barriers to their educational success.
Fields of interest: Museums (science/technology); Performing arts, orchestras; Arts; Elementary/secondary education; Education, early childhood education; Higher education; Education, services; Education; Learning disorders; YM/YWCAs & YM/YWHAs; Developmentally disabled, centers & services; United Ways and Federated Giving Programs Children; Youth; Economically disadvantaged.
Programs:
Education: The foundation supports programs and services that take place during the day, typically within the classroom with teacher instruction. Special emphasis is directed toward programs and services that are curriculum-driven and embedded in other areas of learning.
Eliminating Barriers to Educational Success: The foundation supports programs and services that occur before or after school, which are typically provided by paid program staff or volunteers. Students are recommended to the programs by the school staff; or the programs recruit students or parents directly.
Type of support: Capital campaigns; Continuing support; Curriculum development; General/operating support; Program development.
Geographic limitations: Giving primarily in Minneapolis and its northern and western suburbs with emphasis on Brooklyn Center, Brooklyn Park, Crystal, Eden Prairie, Edina, Golden Valley, Hopkins, Minnetonka, New Hope, Plymouth, Robbinsdale, and St. Louis Park, MN.
Support limitations: No support for religious organizations not of direct benefit to the entire community, or for individual schools, or organizations that serve mental or dental needs of children. No grants to individuals, or for athletic scholarships, memberships in civic organizations or trade associations, fundraising events, tickets or campaigns, endowments, recognition or testimonial events, public service or political campaigns, lobbying activities, conferences, travel, programs serving adults (including domestic violence), youth employment, summer, or juvenile justice programs, or programs that serve children whose parents are incarcerated or have serious medical problems.
Publications: Application guidelines; Program policy statement.
Application information: Applications accepted. Organizations requesting Education support are asked to contact Cargill Foundation staff for more information. Education program support is given primarily by invitation rather than through applications. A full proposal may be requested at a later date for Eliminating Barriers. Video and audio submissions are not encouraged. Application form required. Applicants should submit the following:
1) statement of problem project will address
2) population served
3) name, address and phone number of organization
4) copy of IRS Determination Letter
5) brief history of organization and description of its mission
6) geographic area to be served
7) detailed description of project and amount of funding requested
Initial approach: Complete online letter of intent for Eliminating Barriers
Copies of proposal: 1
Board meeting date(s): Mar., June, Sept., and Dec.
Deadline(s): None for Education; Varies for Eliminating Barriers
Final notification: Within 4 weeks
Officers: Robbin S. Johnson, Pres.; Terri D. Barreiro, V.P.; Marsha MacMilan, V.P.; Marianne Short, V.P.; Scott Portnoy, Secy.; Mark Murphy, Exec. Dir.
Number of staff: 2 full-time professional; 1 full-time support.
EIN: 416020221

692
Caribou Coffee Company, Inc.

3900 Lakebreeze Ave., N. Brooklyn Ctr.
Minneapolis, MN 55429 (763) 592-2200
FAX: (763) 592-2300

Company URL: http://www.cariboucoffee.com
Establishment information: Established in 1992.
Company type: Public company
Company ticker symbol and exchange: CBOU/NASDAQ
Business activities: Operates coffee shops.
Business type (SIC): Restaurants and drinking places
Financial profile for 2012: Number of employees, 6,086; assets, $143,360,000; sales volume, $326,500,000; pre-tax net income, $14,930,000; expenses, $311,310,000; liabilities, $42,230,000
Corporate officers: Gary A. Graves, Chair.; Michael J. Tattersfield, Pres. and C.E.O.; Timothy J. Hennessy, C.F.O.; Alfredo V. Martel, Sr. V.P., Mktg.; Daniel E. Lee, V.P., Genl. Counsel, and Secy.; Karen E. McBride-Raffel, V.P., Human Resources
Board of directors: Gary A. Graves, Chair.; Kip R. Caffey; Sarah Palisi Chapin; Wallace B. Doolin; Charles H. Ogburn; Philip H. Sanford; Michael J. Tattersfield
Giving statement: Giving through the Caribou Coffee Charitable Foundation.
Company EIN: 411731219

Caribou Coffee Charitable Foundation

(formerly Caribou Coffee Charitable Trust)
3900 Lakebreeze Ave. N.
Minneapolis, MN 55429-3839

Establishment information: Established in 2002 in MN.
Donors: Caribou Coffee Co.; LA Expo, LLC.
Financial data (yr. ended 12/31/11): Assets, $94,770 (M); gifts received, $75,000; expenditures, $29,850; qualifying distributions, $28,850; giving activities include $28,850 for 9 grants (high: $10,000; low: $100).
Purpose and activities: The foundation supports organizations involved with cancer, coffee-farming, and human services.
Fields of interest: Health organizations; Youth development; Human services.
Type of support: General/operating support.
Geographic limitations: Giving in areas of company operations on a local and national level.
Support limitations: No grants to individuals.

Application information: Applications not accepted. Unsolicited requests for funds not accepted.
Officers: Michael Tattersfield, Pres.; Nate Hjelseth, Treas.
Director: Karen McBride.
EIN: 753047181

693
Carlson Companies, Inc.

701 Carlson Pkwy.
Minnetonka, MN 55305-8212
(763) 212-5000

Company URL: http://www.carlson.com
Establishment information: Established in 1938.
Company type: Private company
Business activities: Provides marketing services; provides business travel management services; operates restaurants; operates hotels; operates cruise line; operates travel agency.
Business type (SIC): Restaurants and drinking places; transportation/water passenger; travel and tour arrangers; hotels and motels; management and public relations services
Financial profile for 2011: Number of employees, 52,500; sales volume, $4,130,000,000
Corporate officers: Marilyn Carlson Nelson, Chair.; Trudy Rautio, Pres. and C.E.O.; William A. Van Brunt, Exec. V.P. and Genl. Counsel; James Porter, Exec. V.P., Human Resources, and Comms.
Board of directors: Marilyn Carlson Nelson, Chair.; Brad Anderson; Lee A. Chaden; Edwin C. Gage; Geoffrey Gage; Scott C. Gage; Diana L. Nelson; Wendy Nelson; Gregory R. Page; Lawrence Perlman; Trudy Rautio
Subsidiaries: Carlson Hospitality Group, Inc., Minneapolis, MN; Carlson Leasing, Inc., Minneapolis, MN; Carlson Marketing Group, Inc., Minneapolis, MN; Carlson Properties, Inc., Minneapolis, MN; Carlson Showrooms, Inc., Minneapolis, MN; Country Kitchen International, Inc., Minneapolis, MN; Curtis Homes, Inc., Minneapolis, MN; Radisson Group, Inc., Minneapolis, MN; TGI Friday's, Inc., Addison, TX
International operations: Australia; Canada; Japan; United Kingdom
Giving statement: Giving through the Carlson Companies, Inc. Corporate Giving Program and the Curtis L. Carlson Family Foundation.

Carlson Companies, Inc. Corporate Giving Program

701 Carlson Pkwy.
Hopkins, MN 55305-5240
E-mail: CarlsonPublicRelations@carlson.com; URL: http://www.carlson.com/responsible-business/stakeholders.php

Purpose and activities: Carlson makes charitable contributions to nonprofit organizations involved with children, military, and HIV/AIDS. Support is given primarily areas of company operations, with some emphasis on Minnesota.
Fields of interest: AIDS; Tropical diseases; Crime/violence prevention, child abuse; Crime/violence prevention, sexual abuse; Big Brothers/Big Sisters; Children/youth, services; Children, adoption Military/veterans.
Type of support: Employee volunteer services; General/operating support; Sponsorships.
Geographic limitations: Giving primarily in areas of company operations, with some emphasis on MN.

The Curtis L. Carlson Family Foundation

550 Tonkawa Rd.
Long Lake, MN 55356-9724 (952) 404-5605
FAX: (952) 404-5051; Contact for C. David Nelson: tel.: (952) 404-5636, fax: (952) 358-2405, e-mail: david.nelson@carlson.com; Additional contact: Joanie Weis, Grants Mgr., tel.: (952) 404-5605, fax: (952) 358-2405, e-mail: jweis@carlson.com; URL: http://www.clcfamilyfoundation.com

Establishment information: Incorporated in 1959 in MN, originally as The Curtis L. Carlson Foundation.
Donors: Curtis L. Carlson†; Arleen M. Carlson†; Glen D. Nelson; Marilyn C. Nelson; Arleen M. Carlson 2000 BCG Charitable Annuity Trust; Arleen M. Carlson 2000 MCN Charitable Annuity Trust; Carlson Companies, Inc.
Contact: C. David Nelson, Exec. Dir.
Financial data (yr. ended 12/31/11): Assets, $191,877,496 (M); gifts received, $95,267,695; expenditures, $7,247,767; qualifying distributions, $6,319,921; giving activities include $5,706,256 for 277 grants (high: $400,000; low: $35).
Purpose and activities: The foundation supports organizations involved with education, at-risk children and youth, and youth mentoring.
Fields of interest: Secondary school/education; Higher education; Education; Youth development, adult & child programs; Big Brothers/Big Sisters; American Red Cross; Children/youth, services; Human services Children/youth.
Type of support: Annual campaigns; General/operating support; Management development/capacity building; Matching/challenge support; Program development.
Geographic limitations: Giving primarily in the Twin Cities, MN metropolitan area.
Support limitations: No support for political activities or causes. No grants to individuals, (including scholarships), or for endowment funds, dinners, benefits, conferences, travel, athletic events, or endowments.
Publications: Application guidelines; Grants list.
Application information: Applications accepted. A site visit and additional information may be requested. Applicants for youth mentoring grants are required to complete the Mentoring Partnership of Minnesota's Quality Mentoring Assessment Path (QMAP) before an application can be submitted. Organizations receiving support are asked to submit a Minnesota Common Grant Report Form. Application form required. Applicants should submit the following:

1) how project will be sustained once grantmaker support is completed
2) name, address and phone number of organization
3) copy of IRS Determination Letter
4) brief history of organization and description of its mission
5) copy of most recent annual report/audited financial statement/990
6) how project's results will be evaluated or measured
7) listing of board of directors, trustees, officers and other key people and their affiliations
8) detailed description of project and amount of funding requested
9) plans for cooperation with other organizations, if any
10) copy of current year's organizational budget and/or project budget
11) listing of additional sources and amount of support

Initial approach: Complete online application
Board meeting date(s): Apr., July, and Oct.
Deadline(s): Jan. 1, Apr. 1, and July 1
Final notification: Following a board meeting

Officers and Trustees:* Barbara Carlson Gage*, Chair. and Pres.; Marilyn Carlson Nelson*, Vice-Chair.; Diana L. Nelson, V.P.; Rick Carlson Gage, Treas.; C. David Nelson, Exec. Dir.; Geoffrey Carlson Gage; Scott Carlson Gage*; Wendy M. Nelson.
EIN: 416028973

694
CarMax Business Services, LLC.

(doing business as CarMax Auto Finance)
225 Chastain Meadows Ct.
Kennesaw, GA 30144 (770) 792-4750

Company URL: http://www.carmax.com
Establishment information: Established in 1993.
Company type: Subsidiary of a public company
Business activities: Provides on-site auto financing services.
Business type (SIC): Credit institutions/business
Corporate officers: Tom Folliard, Pres. and C.E.O.; Tom Reedy, Exec. V.P. and C.F.O.
Giving statement: Giving through the CarMax Foundation.

The CarMax Foundation

12800 Tuckahoe Creek Pkwy.
Richmond, VA 23238-1115 (804) 747-0422
FAX: (804) 935-4516;
E-mail: kmxfoundation@carmax.com; URL: http://www.carmaxcares.com

Establishment information: Established in 2003 in VA.
Donors: CarMax Auto Superstores, Inc.; CarMax Business Services, LLC.
Contact: Sharon R. Handley, Mgr.
Financial data (yr. ended 02/28/12): Assets, $9,062,232 (M); gifts received, $6,000,400; expenditures, $2,657,665; qualifying distributions, $2,482,892; giving activities include $2,482,892 for grants.
Purpose and activities: The foundation supports programs designed to promote education, youth leadership, and wellness in the communities where CarMax associates live and work.
Fields of interest: Elementary/secondary education; Vocational education; Education; Youth development; Family services; Human services; Leadership development Children/youth; Economically disadvantaged.
Programs:

Board Service Donations: The foundation awards grants to nonprofit organizations with which associates serve on governing or advisory board.

CarMax Cares Award: The foundation honors one associate from each of the eight national regions, the Home Office, and CarMax Auto Finance for their personal volunteer efforts and leadership in CarMax community giving. Recipients are recognized at a company event and their selected nonprofits receive $5,000 on their behalf.

Matching Dollars Program: The foundation matches contributions made by associates of CarMax to nonprofit organizations on a one-for-one basis from $25 to $10,000 per associate, per year.

Matching Hours Program: The foundation awards grants of $10 per hour to nonprofit organizations with which associates of CarMax volunteer at least ten hours up to $10,000 per associate, per year.

Regional Giving Program: The foundation supports programs designed to improve educational opportunities for children and families; promote youth leadership; and promote wellness. Grant requests are accepted by invitation only. Nonprofits are nominated by CarMax employees.

Richmond Funding Program: The foundation supports programs designed to promote educational opportunities for children and families; youth leadership; and wellness. Support is given primarily in the greater Richmond, Virginia, area.

Volunteer Team-Builders: The foundation awards $500 grants to nonprofit organizations with which associates participate in volunteer team-builder events. Events with more than 50 volunteers are eligible for a $1,000 volunteer grant.

Type of support: Employee matching gifts; Employee volunteer services; Program development.

Geographic limitations: Giving primarily in areas of company operations, with emphasis on the greater Richmond, VA, area; giving also to national organizations.

Support limitations: No support for discriminatory organizations, organizations posing a conflict of interest with CarMax's mission, goals, programs, or products, fraternal, athletic, social, labor, or political organizations. No grants for debt reduction, political campaigns, or capital campaigns, endowments, event sponsorships, or scholarships; no vehicle donations.

Publications: Annual report; Application guidelines; IRS Form 990 or 990-PF printed copy available upon request.

Application information: Applications accepted. Letters of inquiry should include a statement describing the project; and indicate the approximate date when an application will be submitted. Application form required.

Initial approach: Mail letter of inquiry and complete online application
Copies of proposal: 1
Board meeting date(s): Quarterly
Deadline(s): Feb. 15 for Richmond Giving Program
Final notification: Mar. 31 for Richmond Giving Program

Officers and Directors:* Lynn Mussatt*, Pres.; Dan Bickett*, V.P.; Dodie Fix*, V.P.; Jong Han*, V.P.; Alice Heinz*, V.P.; Eric Tam*, V.P.; Dugald Yska*, V.P.; Christine Collins, Secy.; Michelle M. Halasz, Secy.; John M. Stuckey, Secy.; Veronica Hinckle*, Treas.

Number of staff: 1 full-time professional; 1 part-time professional.

EIN: 383681796

Selected grants: The following grants are a representative sample of this grantmaker's funding activity:

$25,000 to Reach Out and Read Virginia, Richmond, VA, 2011.
$15,000 to Big Brothers Big Sisters of Tampa Bay, Tampa, FL, 2011.
$15,000 to Chicago Cares, Chicago, IL, 2011.
$15,000 to Kids in Distress, Wilton Manors, FL, 2011.
$10,000 to Childrens Health Education Center, Milwaukee, WI, 2011.
$10,000 to DC Youth Orchestra Program, Washington, DC, 2011.
$10,000 to FeedMore, Richmond, VA, 2011.
$10,000 to FORKids, Norfolk, VA, 2011.
$6,000 to Epilepsy Foundation of Georgia, Atlanta, GA, 2011.
$5,586 to Virginia Athletics Foundation, Charlottesville, VA, 2011.

695
Carmody & Torrance LLP

50 Leavenworth St.
Waterbury, CT 06721-1110 (203) 573-1200

Company URL: http:///www.carmodylaw.com
Establishment information: Established in 1902.
Company type: Private company
Business activities: Operates law firm.
Business type (SIC): Legal services
Corporate officers: Ann H. Rubin, Managing Partner; Timothy R. Carmody, Partner
Offices: New Haven, Southbury, Waterbury, CT
Giving statement: Giving through the Carmody & Torrance LLP Corporate Giving Program.

Carmody & Torrance LLP Corporate Giving Program

50 Leavenworth St.
Waterbury, CT 06702-2112 (203) 573-1200
FAX: (203) 575-2600; URL: http://www.carmodylaw.com/aboutus/xprGeneralContent2.aspx?xpST=AboutUsCommunity

Purpose and activities: Carmody & Torrance makes charitable contributions to nonprofit organizations involved with arts and culture, education, the environment, public health, and human services.

Fields of interest: Arts; Education; Environment; Public health; Substance abuse, treatment; Legal services; Food services; Athletics/sports, school programs; Family services; Human services.

Type of support: Employee volunteer services; General/operating support; Pro bono services - legal.

696
Carnival Corporation & plc

3655 N.W. 87th Ave.
Miami, FL 33178-2428 (305) 599-2600
FAX: (305) 471-4700

Company URL: http://www.carnivalcorp.com
Establishment information: Established in 1972.
Company type: Public company
Company ticker symbol and exchange: CCL/NYSE
International Securities Identification Number: GB0031215220
Business activities: Operates passenger cruise ship and travel company.
Business type (SIC): Transportation/water passenger
Financial profile for 2012: Number of employees, 13,700; assets, $39,161,000,000; sales volume, $15,382,000,000; pre-tax net income, $1,302,000,000; expenses, $13,740,000,000; liabilities, $15,232,000,000
Forbes 2000 ranking: 2012—617th in sales, 403rd in profits, and 590th in assets
Corporate officers: Micky Arison, Chair. and C.E.O.; Howard S. Frank, Vice-Chair. and C.O.O.; David Bernstein, Sr. V.P. and C.F.O.; Arnaldo Perez, Sr. V.P., Genl. Counsel, and Secy.; Larry Freedman, V.P., Cont., and C.A.O.
Board of directors: Micky Arison, Chair.; Howard S. Frank, Vice-Chair.; Jonathon Band; Arnold W. Donald; Pier Luigi Foschi; Richard J. Glasier; Debra Kelly-Ennis; John Parker; Stuart Subotnick; Laura Weil; Randall J. Weisenburger
Subsidiary: Holland America Line Inc., Seattle, WA
Giving statement: Giving through the Carnival Corporation & plc Corporate Giving Program.
Company EIN: 591562976

Carnival Corporation & plc Corporate Giving Program

3655 N.W. 87th Ave.
Miami, FL 33178-2418 (305) 599-2600
URL: http://phx.corporate-ir.net/phoenix.zhtml?c=200767&p=irol-community

Purpose and activities: Carnival Corporation makes charitable contributions to nonprofit organizations in areas of company operations in south Florida; giving also to national and international organizations. Emphasis is given to organizations involved with disaster relief and the arts.

Fields of interest: Arts; Environment; Safety/disasters, volunteer services; Children, services; General charitable giving.

Type of support: Donated products; Employee volunteer services; General/operating support; In-kind gifts.

Geographic limitations: Giving primarily in areas of company operations and on a national and international basis, with emphasis on south Florida, the Caribbean, and Haiti.

697
Carolina Containers Company

909 Prospect St.
High Point, NC 27260-8273
(336) 883-7146

Company URL: http://www.carolinacontainer.com
Establishment information: Established in 1928.
Company type: Private company
Business activities: Manufactures corrugated boxes.
Business type (SIC): Paperboard containers
Corporate officers: Paul Ingle, Pres.; Ken H. Hanner, C.F.O.
Giving statement: Giving through the Carolina Containers Company Foundation.

Carolina Containers Company Foundation

P.O. Box 2166
High Point, NC 27261-2166

Establishment information: Established in 2003 in NC.
Donor: Carolina Containers Co.
Financial data (yr. ended 12/31/11): Assets, $27,930 (M); expenditures, $100; qualifying distributions, $100; giving activities include $100 for grants.
Purpose and activities: The foundation supports camps and organizations involved with education, housing, and human services.
Fields of interest: Education; Human services.
Type of support: General/operating support.
Application information: Applications not accepted. Unsolicited requests for funds not accepted.
Officers and Directors:* Robert T. Amos III*, Pres.; William B. Millis*, Secy.-Treas.; Pat Foy Brady; Edward H. Covington; Henry G. Foy.
EIN: 470921299

698
Carolina Hurricanes Hockey Club

(also known as Carolina Hurricanes)
(formerly Hurricanes Hockey L.P.)
1400 Edwards Mill Rd.
Raleigh, NC 27607-3624 (919) 467-7825

Company URL: http://www.carolinahurricanes.com
Establishment information: Established in 1971.
Company type: Private company
Business activities: Operates professional ice hockey club.
Business type (SIC): Commercial sports
Corporate officers: Peter Karmanos, Jr., Chair. and C.E.O.; Jim Rutherford, Pres.; Michael Amendola, Exec. V.P. and C.F.O.
Board of director: Peter Karmanos, Jr., Chair.
Giving statement: Giving through the Carolina Hurricanes Corporate Giving Program and the Carolina Hurricanes Foundation, Inc.

Carolina Hurricanes Corporate Giving Program

1400 Edwards Mill Rd.
Raleigh, NC 27607-3624
URL: http://hurricanes.nhl.com/club/page.htm?id=46111

Purpose and activities: The Carolina Hurricanes make charitable contributions of game tickets and memorabilia to nonprofit organizations on a case by case basis. Support is given primarily in North Carolina.
Fields of interest: General charitable giving.
Type of support: Donated products; In-kind gifts.
Geographic limitations: Giving primarily in NC.
Application information: Applications accepted. Support is limited to 1 contribution per organization during any given year. Proposals should be submitted using organization letterhead. Application form not required. Applicants should submit the following:
1) population served
2) detailed description of project and amount of funding requested

Proposals should indicate the expected number of attendees and the type of fundraiser.
Initial approach: Proposal to headquarters
Copies of proposal: 1
Deadline(s): 6 weeks prior to need

Carolina Hurricanes Foundation, Inc.

(also known as Kids N Community Foundation)
1400 Edwards Mill Rd.
Raleigh, NC 27607-3624 (919) 861-5467
URL: http://hurricanes.nhl.com/club/page.htm?id=46202

Establishment information: Established in 1986 in NC.
Financial data (yr. ended 07/31/11): Revenue, $727,023; assets, $477,025 (M); gifts received, $520,599; expenditures, $599,052; program services expenses, $527,771; giving activities include $527,771 for 44 grants (high: $40,000; low: $5,000).
Purpose and activities: As the philanthropic arm of the Carolina Hurricanes, the foundation makes contributions to various organizations, primarily charitable in nature, in order to support local causes and general goodwill.
Fields of interest: Human services.
Geographic limitations: Giving limited to NC.
Support limitations: No support for religious or political organizations. No grants for capital campaigns, conferences, debt retirement, operating deficits, endowments, sponsorships, or grants to individuals.
Application information: Applications accepted.
Initial approach: Download application
Directors: Doris Barksdale; Blake Coules; Jim Davis; George Habel; Kathy Higgins; Robert Ingram; Orage Quarles III; Billie Redmond; Harvey Schmitt; Doug Warf.
EIN: 222652765

699
Carolina Ice Inc.

2466 Old Poole Rd.
Kinston, NC 28504-9234 (252) 527-3178

Company URL: http://www.carolinaice.com
Establishment information: Established in 1983.
Company type: Private company
Business activities: Manufactures ice.
Business type (SIC): Miscellaneous prepared foods
Corporate officers: Thomas L. Edwards, Pres.; James Bradshaw, C.F.O.
Giving statement: Giving through the E. Merle & Ollie W. Edwards Foundation, Inc.

The E. Merle & Ollie W. Edwards Foundation, Inc.

2466 Old Poole Rd.
Kinston, NC 28504-9061

Establishment information: Established in 2000 in NC.
Donors: Edwards Investment Group, LLC; Carolina Ice Co., Inc.; Coastal Wholesale, Inc.; E. Merle Edwards; Ollie W. Edwards.
Financial data (yr. ended 12/31/11): Assets, $1,141,840 (M); expenditures, $69,857; qualifying distributions, $67,250; giving activities include $67,250 for grants.
Fields of interest: Education; Youth development; Human services.
Geographic limitations: Giving primarily in Kinston, NC.
Support limitations: No grants to individuals.
Application information: Applications not accepted. Unsolicited requests for funds not accepted.
Officers: Thomas L. Edwards, Pres.; Merle W. Edwards, V.P.; David C. Edwards, Secy.-Treas.
Directors: Edwin M. Edwards; Stuart M. Edwards; Thomas L. Edwards, Jr.
EIN: 562166688

700
Carpenter Technology Corporation

2 Meridian Blvd.
Wyomissing, PA 19610-1339
(302) 658-7581

Company URL: http://www.cartech.com
Establishment information: Established in 1889.
Company type: Public company
Company ticker symbol and exchange: CRS/NYSE
Business activities: Manufactures, fabricates, and distributes specialty metals and engineered products.
Business type (SIC): Steel mill products
Financial profile for 2012: Number of employees, 4,800; assets, $2,627,800,000; sales volume, $2,028,700,000; pre-tax net income, $188,600,000; expenses, $1,818,600,000; liabilities, $1,524,000,000
Fortune 1000 ranking: 2012—941st in revenues, 701st in profits, and 791st in assets
Corporate officers: Gregory A. Pratt, Chair.; William A. Wulfsohn, Pres. and C.E.O.; James A. Johnson III, C.I.O.; Tony R. Thene, Sr. V.P. and C.F.O.; David L. Strobel, Sr. V.P., Opers.; James D. Dee, V.P., Genl. Counsel, and Secy.; John L. Rice, V.P., Human Resources
Board of directors: Gregory A. Pratt, Chair.; Carl G. Anderson, Jr.; Philip M. Anderson, Ph.D.; Thomas Hicks; I. Martin Inglis; Steven Karol; Robert R. McMaster; Peter N. Stephans; Kathryn C. Turner; Jeffrey Wadsworth; Stephen M. Ward, Jr.; William A. Wulfsohn
Subsidiary: Dynamet Inc., Washington, PA
Plants: Auburn, El Cajon, CA; Clearwater, FL; Wood Ridge, NJ; Elyria, Twinsburg, OH; Bridgeville, Orwigsburg, Reading, Washington, Wilkes Barre, PA; Hartsville, Orangeburg, SC
Giving statement: Giving through the Carpenter Technology Corporation Contributions Program.
Company EIN: 230458500

Carpenter Technology Corporation Contributions Program

2 Meridian Blvd.
Wyomissing, PA 19610-1339
URL: http://www.cartech.com/about.aspx?id=134

Purpose and activities: Carpenter Technology makes charitable contributions to nonprofit organizations involved with arts and culture, science and math education in public schools, and human services. Support is given primarily in areas of company operations in Pennsylvania.
Fields of interest: Arts; Education, public education; Elementary/secondary education; Housing/shelter; Boys & girls clubs; Youth development; Human services; United Ways and Federated Giving Programs; Science; Mathematics; Engineering/technology; General charitable giving.
Type of support: Annual campaigns; Capital campaigns; Employee volunteer services; General/operating support; Scholarship funds.
Geographic limitations: Giving primarily in areas of company operations.
Number of staff: 1 full-time support.

701
Carrington Coleman Sloman & Bluementhal L.L.P

901 Main St., Ste. 5500
Dallas, TX 75202-3767 (214) 855-3000

Company URL: http://www.carringtoncoleman.com
Company type: Private company
Business activities: Operates law firm.
Business type (SIC): Legal services
Corporate officer: Timothy F. Gavin, Managing Partner
Giving statement: Giving through the Carrington Coleman Sloman & Bluementhal L.L.P. Corporate Giving Program.

Carrington Coleman Sloman & Bluementhal L.L.P. Corporate Giving Program

901 Main St., Ste. 5500
Dallas, TX 75202-3767 (214) 855-3566
FAX: (214) 758-3762; E-mail: caltman@ccsb.com; Additional tel.: (214) 855-3000; Contact for Pro Bono program: Cathy Altman, Partner, tel.: (214) 855-3083, fax: (214) 758-3783, e-mail: caltman@ccsb.com; URL: http://www.carringtoncoleman.com/community.html

Contact: Cathy Altman, Partner
Purpose and activities: Carrington Coleman makes charitable contributions to nonprofit organizations involved with arts and culture, education, and human services.
Fields of interest: Arts; Education; Legal services; Human services.
Type of support: Employee volunteer services; General/operating support; Pro bono services - legal.

702
Carris Financial Corp.

49 Main St.
Proctor, VT 05765-1178

Company URL: http://www.carris.com
Establishment information: Established in 1951.
Company type: Private company
Business activities: Manufactures reels as packaging for wire and cable.
Business type (SIC): Metal products/fabricated; wood millwork; wood containers; wood products/miscellaneous; furniture/household; plastic products/miscellaneous
Corporate officer: William H. Carris, Pres.
Giving statement: Giving through the Carris Corporate Foundation, Inc.

Carris Corporate Foundation, Inc.

(formerly The Carris Reels Fund)
49 Main St.
Proctor, VT 05765-1178

Establishment information: Established in 1990.
Donors: Carris Reels, Inc.; Bridge Manufacturing, Inc.; Vermont Tubbs, Inc.; Carris Financial Corp.; Carris Reels of Connecticut, Inc.; Carris Reels of California, Inc.
Financial data (yr. ended 12/31/11): Assets, $54,450 (M); gifts received, $139,102; expenditures, $179,587; qualifying distributions, $179,530; giving activities include $173,550 for 106 grants (high: $46,000; low: $150).
Purpose and activities: The foundation makes charitable contributions to nonprofit organizations recommended by Carris employees and approved by local giving committees.
Fields of interest: United Ways and Federated Giving Programs; General charitable giving.
Type of support: General/operating support.
Geographic limitations: Giving primarily in areas of company operations in VT.
Support limitations: No grants to individuals.
Application information: Applications not accepted. Contributes only to pre-selected organizations.
Officers: Michael Curran, Pres.; David Fitz-Gerald, V.P. and Treas.; David Ferraro*, Secy.
EIN: 030326934
Selected grants: The following grants are a representative sample of this grantmaker's funding activity:
$40,000 to Chaffee Arts Center, Rutland, VT, 2009.
$38,000 to Center for Scholarship Administration, Taylors, SC, 2009.
$20,000 to Chaffee Arts Center, Rutland, VT, 2009.
$20,000 to Mariposa Arts Foundation, Bayside, TX, 2009.
$10,000 to College of Mount Saint Joseph, Cincinnati, OH, 2009.
$10,000 to College of Saint Joseph, Rutland, VT, 2009.
$10,000 to United Way of Rutland County, Rutland, VT, 2009.

703
Carroll Enterprises, Inc.

554 Main St.
P.O. Box 15014
Worcester, MA 01615-0014
(508) 756-3513

Company URL: http://www.subconnector.com/
Establishment information: Established in 1967.
Company type: Private company
Business activities: Provides small business consulting services.
Business type (SIC): Management and public relations services
Corporate officers: Francis R. Carroll, Chair.; Brian K. Carroll, Pres. and C.E.O.; Kevin A. Cullinan, V.P., Finance; David Briggs, V.P., Mktg.; Katherine Hessel, V.P., Human Resources; Mark Petter, V.P., Inf. Systems
Board of director: Francis R. Carroll, Chair.
Subsidiary: Small Business Service Bureau, Inc., Worcester, MA
Giving statement: Giving through the Carroll Charitable Foundation.

Carroll Charitable Foundation

(formerly Small Business Service Bureau, Inc. Charitable Foundation)
554 Main St.
P.O. Box 15014
Worcester, MA 01615-0014 (508) 756-3513

Donors: Small Business Service Bureau, Inc.; Carroll Enterprises, Inc.
Contact: Francis Carroll, Tr.
Financial data (yr. ended 06/30/11): Assets, $508,295 (M); gifts received, $250,548; expenditures, $43,811; qualifying distributions, $41,455; giving activities include $41,455 for grants.
Purpose and activities: The foundation supports war memorials and organizations involved with health sciences education and other areas and awards college scholarships to children of employees of the Small Business Service Bureau and college students conducting research on small businesses.
Fields of interest: Arts; Education; Religion.
Type of support: Employee-related scholarships; General/operating support; Scholarships—to individuals.
Geographic limitations: Giving primarily in areas of company operations in Worcester, MA.
Support limitations: No grants to individuals (except for scholarships).
Application information: Applications accepted. Application form required. Applicants should submit the following:
1) descriptive literature about organization
Initial approach: Letter
Deadline(s): None
Trustees: Francis Carroll; Lisa Carroll; Mary M. Carroll; Patricia A. Greenlaw.
EIN: 222546670

704
Carrols Corporation

968 James St.
P.O. Box 6969
Syracuse, NY 13203-2596 (315) 424-0513

Company URL: http://www.carrols.com
Establishment information: Established in 1960.
Company type: Subsidiary of a public company
Business activities: Owns and operates fast food restaurants; distributes food.
Business type (SIC): Restaurants and drinking places; business services/miscellaneous
Corporate officers: Alan Vituli, Chair. and Co-C.E.O.; Daniel T. Accordino, Pres., C.O.O., and Co-C.E.O.; Paul R. Flanders, V.P., C.F.O., and Treas.; Jeffery Kent, C.I.O.; Timothy J. LaLonde, V.P. and Cont.; William E. Myers, Esq., V.P., Genl. Counsel, and Secy.; Jerry DiGenova, V.P., Human Resources
Board of directors: Alan Vituli, Chair.; Daniel T. Accordino
Subsidiary: Quanta Advertising Corp., Syracuse, NY
Giving statement: Giving through the Carrols Corporation Contributions Program.

Carrols Corporation Contributions Program

968 James St.
Syracuse, NY 13203-2503 (315) 424-0513
Tel. for Dollars for Doers: (800) 348-1074 ext. 2219; URL: http://www.carrols.com/community/

Purpose and activities: Carrols makes charitable contributions to nonprofit organizations on a case by case basis. Support is given primarily in areas of company operations.
Fields of interest: General charitable giving.
Program:
Dollars for Doers: Carrols Corporation awards $250 grants to nonprofit organizations where employees volunteers for a minimum of 48 hours during a six-month period. Giving is limited to two grants per person per year.
Type of support: Continuing support; Employee volunteer services; General/operating support; In-kind gifts.
Geographic limitations: Giving primarily in areas of company operations.

705
Kit Carson Electric Cooperative, Inc.

118 Cruz Alta Rd.
P.O. Box 578
Taos, NM 87571-6490 (575) 758-2258

Company URL: http://www.kitcarson.com
Establishment information: Established in 1944.
Company type: Cooperative
Business activities: Distributes electricity.
Business type (SIC): Electric services
Corporate officers: Luis Reyes, C.E.O.; Bobby Ortega, Pres.; Alex C. Romero, C.O.O.; Chris Duran, Secy.; Bruce Jassman, Treas.
Board of directors: Francis Cordova; Toby Martinez; Manuel Medina; Luisa Valerio-Mylet

Giving statement: Giving through the Kit Carson Electric Education Foundation.

Kit Carson Electric Education Foundation

P.O. Box 578
Taos, NM 87571-0587 (575) 758-2258
URL: http://www.kitcarson.com/index.php?option=com_content&view=article&id=76&Itemid=161

Establishment information: Established in 1997 in NM.
Donor: Kit Carson Electric Cooperative, Inc.
Contact: David Arguello, Pres.
Financial data (yr. ended 12/31/11): Assets, $53,009 (M); gifts received, $23,453; expenditures, $40,914; qualifying distributions, $39,568; giving activities include $38,000 for 38 grants to individuals (high: $1,000; low: $1,000).
Purpose and activities: The foundation supports organizations involved with education and athletics and awards college scholarships to members and children of members of Kit Carson Electric Cooperative.
Fields of interest: Elementary/secondary education; Higher education; Education, services; Education; Athletics/sports, school programs; Athletics/sports, amateur leagues; Athletics/sports, baseball.
Program:
Kit Carson Electric Education Foundation Scholarship: The foundation annually awards one-time scholarships to high school seniors who are children of members of the Kit Carson Electric Cooperative service area. Applicants are selected based on character, academic achievement, demonstration of a degree plan, and willingness to pursue higher education.
Type of support: General/operating support; Program development; Scholarships—to individuals.
Geographic limitations: Giving limited to areas of company operations in NM.
Publications: Application guidelines; Grants list.
Application information: Applications accepted. Application form required.
Scholarship applications should include official transcripts and a letter of recommendation. Applicants must also provide an original class schedule from the college or school they will be attending before funds can be released.
Initial approach: Letter
Deadline(s): Apr. 15 for scholarships
Final notification: 30 days
Officers: Rudy Martinez, Pres.; David Arguello, V.P.; Steve Archuleta, Secy.-Treas.
Directors: Catherine Garduno; Diane Steinman.
EIN: 311578049

706
Carter Law Group, P.C.

849 N. 3rd Ave.
Phoenix, AZ 85003-1408 (602) 456-0071
FAX: 602-296-0415

Company URL: http://carternonprofitlaw.com/
Establishment information: Established in 2001.
Company type: Private company
Business type (SIC): Business services/miscellaneous
Corporate officer: Ellis McGehee Carter, Founder
Giving statement: Giving through the Carter Law Group, P.C. Contributions Program.

Carter Law Group, P.C. Contributions Program

849 N. 3rd Ave.
Phoenix, AZ 85003-1408 (602) 456-0071
URL: http://carternonprofitlaw.com

Purpose and activities: Carter Law Group is a certified B Corporation that commits a percentage of billable hours to pro bono work.
Type of support: Pro bono services - legal.

707
Carter Ledyard & Milburn LLP

2 Wall St.
New York, NY 10005-2001 (212) 732-3200

Company URL: http://www.clm.com
Establishment information: Established in 1854.
Company type: Private company
Business activities: Operates law firm.
Business type (SIC): Legal services
Corporate officer: Rose Auslander, Partner
Offices: Washington, DC; New York, NY
Giving statement: Giving through the Carter Ledyard & Milburn LLP Pro Bono Program.

Carter Ledyard & Milburn LLP Pro Bono Program

2 Wall St.
New York, NY 10005-2001 (212) 238-8603
E-mail: lockhart@clm.com; Additional tel.: (212) 732- 3200; URL: http://www.clm.com/content.cfm/ID/1061

Contact: Judith A. Lockhart, Managing Partner
Fields of interest: Legal services.
Type of support: Pro bono services - legal.
Geographic limitations: Giving primarily in areas of company operations in Washington, DC, New York, NY.
Application information: The Pro Bono Committee manages the pro-bono program.

708
Carter's, Inc.

1170 Peachtree St. N.E., Ste. 900
Atlanta, GA 30309-7649 (404) 745-2700
FAX: (404) 892-0968

Company URL: http://www.carters.com
Establishment information: Established in 1865.
Company type: Public company
Company ticker symbol and exchange: CRI/NYSE
Business activities: Manufactures children's apparel; operates children's apparel stores.
Business type (SIC): Apparel—girls' and children's outerwear; children's apparel and accessory stores
Financial profile for 2012: Number of employees, 11,786; assets, $1,630,110,000; sales volume, $2,381,730,000; pre-tax net income, $255,390,000; expenses, $2,119,750,000; liabilities, $644,630,000
Fortune 1000 ranking: 2012—841st in revenues, 633rd in profits, and 908th in assets
Corporate officers: Michael D. Casey, Chair. and C.E.O.; Brian J. Lynch, Pres.; Richard F. Westenberger, Exec. V.P. and C.F.O.; William Greg Foglesong, Sr. V.P., Mktg.; Jill A. Wilson, Sr. V.P., Human Resources
Board of directors: Michael D. Casey, Chair.; Amy Woods Brinkley; Vanessa J. Castagna; A. Bruce Cleverly; Jevin S. Eagle; Paul Fulton; William J. Montgoris; David Pulver; John R. Welch; Thomas E. Whiddon
Giving statement: Giving through the Carter's, Inc. Contributions Program.
Company EIN: 133912933

Carter's, Inc. Contributions Program

1170 Peachtree St. N.E., Ste. 900
Atlanta, GA 30309-7706 (404) 745-2700
URL: http://www.carters.com/about/community.aspx

Purpose and activities: Carter's, Inc. makes charitable contributions to nonprofit organizations designed to serve children through arts and culture, education, and health, safety, and human services. Support is given primarily in areas of company operations on a national and international basis.
Fields of interest: Arts; Elementary school/education; Health care; Cancer, leukemia; Safety/disasters; Children/youth, services; Human services, gift distribution; Homeless, human services; Human services.
Type of support: Annual campaigns; Donated products; Employee volunteer services; General/operating support; In-kind gifts; Sponsorships.
Geographic limitations: Giving in areas of company operations on a national and international basis.

709
Caruso Kitchen Designs Inc.

10050 W. 41st Ave.
Wheat Ridge, CO 80033-4157
(303) 432-9131

Company URL: http://www.carusokitchens.com/
Establishment information: Established in 1998.
Company type: Private company
Business activities: Sells lumber and building materials.
Business type (SIC): Lumber and other building materials—retail
Corporate officers: Jerry Caruso, Pres.; Jared Caruso, V.P., Opers.
Giving statement: Giving through the Caruso Family Charities.

Caruso Family Charities

10050 W. 41st Ave.
Wheat Ridge, CO 80033-4701 (303) 421-4475
URL: http://www.carusofamilycharities.net

Establishment information: Established in 2006 in CO.
Donors: Caruso Kitchen Designs; Decor Cabinets; Richard K. Brown.
Contact: Gerard Caruso, Pres.
Financial data (yr. ended 12/31/11): Assets, $0 (M); gifts received, $32,521; expenditures, $117,137; qualifying distributions, $38,939; giving activities include $24,355 for 2 grants (high: $23,855; low: $500) and $14,584 for 5 grants to individuals (high: $5,500; low: $1,500).
Fields of interest: Health care; Health organizations.
Geographic limitations: Giving primarily in CO.
Support limitations: No grants to individuals.
Application information: Applications accepted. Application form required.
Initial approach: Proposal
Deadline(s): Dec. 31
Officers: Gerard Caruso, Pres.; Andrea Caruso, V.P.; Karen Caruso, Secy.

Directors: Richard King Brown; Jared A. Caruso; John A. Caruso.
EIN: 205904999

710
The Carvel Corporation

200 Glenridge Point Pkwy., Ste. 200
Atlanta, GA 30342 (404) 255-3250

Company URL: http://www.carvel.com
Establishment information: Established in 1934.
Company type: Subsidiary of a private company
Business activities: Operates franchised ice cream outlets.
Business type (SIC): Restaurants and drinking places
Corporate officer: Scott Colwell, Pres.
Giving statement: Giving through the Carvel Corporation Contributions Program.

The Carvel Corporation Contributions Program

200 Glenridge Point Pkwy., Ste. 200
Atlanta, GA 30342 (404) 255-3250
URL: http://www.carvel.com

711
Carver Federal Savings Bank

75 W. 125th St.
New York, NY 10027-4512 (718) 230-2900

Company URL: http://www.carverbank.com
Establishment information: Established in 1948.
Company type: Subsidiary of a public company
Business activities: Operates savings bank.
Business type (SIC): Savings institutions
Corporate officers: Deborah C. Wright, Chair., Pres., and C.E.O.; Chris A. McFadden, Exec. V.P. and C.F.O.; Mark A. Ricca, Exec. V.P. and Genl. Counsel
Board of director: Deborah C. Wright, Chair.
Giving statement: Giving through the Carver Federal Savings Bank Corporate Giving Program and the Carver Scholarship Fund, Inc.

Carver Federal Savings Bank Corporate Giving Program

c/o Carver Community Development Corporation
75 West 125th St.
New York, NY 10027-4512 (718) 230-2900
E-mail: ccdc@carverbank.com; URL: http://www.carverbank.com/home/about/community/contributions

Purpose and activities: As a complement to its foundation, Carver Federal Savings Bank also makes charitable contributions to nonprofit organizations directly. Support is limited to Carver Federal customers in areas of company operations in New York City.
Fields of interest: Economic development; Community/economic development.
Type of support: Program development.
Geographic limitations: Giving limited to organizations that are Carver customers in areas of company operations in New York City.
Support limitations: No grants to individuals.
Publications: Application guidelines.
Application information: Applications accepted. Carver's contributions budget has been expended for the current fiscal year. Proposals should be from organizations that are current customers of Carver Federal Savings Bank and for programs that promote wealth and economic development. Support is limited to 1 contribution per organization during any given year.

Carver Scholarship Fund, Inc.

75 W. 125th St.
New York, NY 10027-4512 (212) 876-4747

Donor: Carver Federal Savings Bank.
Contact: Richard T. Greene, Chair.
Financial data (yr. ended 12/31/10): Assets, $278,225 (M); expenditures, $24,900; qualifying distributions, $15,000; giving activities include $15,000 for grants.
Purpose and activities: The foundation awards college scholarships to students in New York, New York.
Fields of interest: Education.
Type of support: Scholarships—to individuals.
Geographic limitations: Giving primarily in New York, NY.
Publications: Informational brochure.
Application information:
Initial approach: Contact foundation for application information
Officers and Directors:* Deborah Wright, Chair.; Richard T. Greene, Jr.*, Vice-Chair.; Earl Andrews; Marcelia Maxwell.
EIN: 133277661

712
Cary Oil Company, Inc.

110 MacKenan Dr.
P.O. Box 5189
Cary, NC 27511 (919) 462-1100
FAX: (919) 481-6862

Company URL: http://www.caryoil.com
Establishment information: Established in 1959.
Company type: Private company
Business activities: Operates gasoline service stations; sells petroleum products wholesale.
Business type (SIC): Gasoline service stations; petroleum and petroleum products—wholesale
Corporate officers: Don Stephenson, Pres.; Craig Stephenson, V.P., Sales and Mktg.; Betty Phillips, V.P., Finance and Admin.
Giving statement: Giving through the Cary Oil Foundation, Inc.

Cary Oil Foundation, Inc.

P.O. Box 5189
Cary, NC 27519-5189

Establishment information: Established in 1996 in NC.
Donors: Cary Oil Co., Inc.; Stanly Lorren.
Contact: Anthony Craig Stephenson, Secy.-Treas.
Financial data (yr. ended 12/31/11): Assets, $3,423,435 (M); gifts received, $175,000; expenditures, $393,189; qualifying distributions, $165,210; giving activities include $165,210 for grants.
Purpose and activities: The foundation supports organizations involved with education, health, hunger, human services, international relief, and Christianity.
Fields of interest: Education; Hospitals (general); Health care; Food services; Human services, volunteer services; Salvation Army; YM/YWCAs & YM/YWHAs; Children/youth, services; Family services, home/homemaker aid; Human services; International relief; Christian agencies & churches.
Type of support: General/operating support.
Geographic limitations: Giving primarily in NC.
Support limitations: No grants to individuals.
Application information: Applications not accepted. Contributes only to pre-selected organizations.
Officers and Directors:* Harry D. Stephenson*, Pres.; Thomas C. Stephenson*, V.P.; Anthony Craig Stephenson*, Secy.-Treas.
EIN: 561950150

713
Cascade Natural Gas Corporation

222 Fairview Ave. N.
Seattle, WA 98109-5312 (206) 624-3900

Company URL: http://www.cngc.com
Establishment information: Established in 1953.
Company type: Subsidiary of a private company
Business activities: Distributes natural gas.
Business type (SIC): Gas production and distribution
Corporate officers: David L. Goodin, Pres. and C.E.O.; Scott Madison, C.A.O.; Eric Martuscelli, V.P., Opers.
Subsidiaries: Cascade Land Leasing Co., Seattle, WA; CGC Energy, Inc., Seattle, WA; CGC Properties, Inc., Seattle, WA; CGC Resources, Inc., Seattle, WA
Offices: Baker City, Bend, Hermiston, Ontario, Pendleton, OR; Aberdeen, Anacortes, Bellingham, Bremerton, Kennewick, Longview, Moses Lake, Mount Vernon, Sunnyside, Walla Walla, Wenatchee, Yakima, WA
Giving statement: Giving through the Cascade Natural Gas Corporation Contributions Program.
Company EIN: 910599090

Cascade Natural Gas Corporation Contributions Program

c/o Customer Svc. Dept.
222 Fairview Ave. N.
Seattle, WA 98109-5312 (206) 624-3900
FAX: (206) 624-7215; E-mail: jmarshall@cngc.com; Additional fax: (206) 654-4069; Additional contact: Debbie Banry, Mgr., Customer Svc., e-mail: dbanry@cngc.com; URL: http://www.cngc.com/in-your-community

Contact: Julie Marshall, V.P., Customer Svc.
Purpose and activities: Cascade makes charitable contributions to nonprofit organizations involved with arts and culture, the environment, health and human services, community development, and civic affairs. Support is given primarily in areas of company operations.
Fields of interest: Arts; Environment, natural resources; Environment; Health care; Human services; Community/economic development; Public affairs.
Programs:
Arts and Culture: Cascade supports programs designed to enrich the communities they serve.
Civic and Community: Cascade supports programs designed to protect and improve economic health.
Environment and Conservation: Cascade supports programs designed to promote environment and conservation.
Health and Human Services: Cascade supports programs designed to promote basic health and welfare needs.

Type of support: Annual campaigns; Curriculum development; Donated equipment; Emergency funds; Employee matching gifts; Employee volunteer services; General/operating support; In-kind gifts; Matching/challenge support; Program development; Use of facilities.
Geographic limitations: Giving primarily in areas of company operations in OR and WA.
Support limitations: No support for national organizations, political organizations, lobbying organizations, sectarian religious organizations, or fraternal or labor organizations. No grants for fundraising or travel.
Publications: Application guidelines; Program policy statement (including application guidelines).
Application information: Applications accepted. The Customer Service Department handles giving. A contributions committee reviews all requests of over $1000. Application form required.
Initial approach: Download application form
Copies of proposal: 1
Committee meeting date(s): As needed
Deadline(s): None
Final notification: Following review
Administrators: Debbie Banry, Mgr., Customer Svc.; Julie Marshall, V.P., Customer Svc.
Number of staff: 2 part-time professional.

714
Casino Queen, Inc.

200 S. Front St.
East Saint Louis, IL 62201-1222
(618) 874-5000

Company URL: http://www.casinoqueen.com
Establishment information: Established in 1991.
Company type: Private company
Business activities: Operates casino hotel.
Business type (SIC): Hotels and motels
Corporate officers: Charles W. Bidwill III, Co-Pres.; James Koman, Co-Pres.; Robert Barrows, C.F.O.
Giving statement: Giving through the Casino Queen Community Development Foundation.

Casino Queen Community Development Foundation

c/o Casino Queen, Inc.
200 S. Front St.
East St. Louis, IL 62201-1222 (618) 874-5000

Establishment information: Established in 1993 in IL.
Donor: Casino Queen, Inc.
Financial data (yr. ended 04/30/12): Revenue, $6,500; assets, $2,025 (M); gifts received, $6,500; expenditures, $6,500.
Fields of interest: Community/economic development.
Geographic limitations: Giving limited to the East St. Louis, IL area.
Application information: Applications not accepted. Contributes only to a pre-selected organization.
Directors: Charles W. Bidwill III; Timothy J. Rand.
EIN: 363902704

715
Cassidy Turley

(formerly Cassidy & Pinkard, Inc.)
2101 L St., N.W., Ste. 700
Washington, DC 20037 (202) 463-2100

Company URL: http://www.cassidyturley.com/
Company type: Private company
Business activities: Provides real estate brokerage services.
Business type (SIC): Real estate agents and managers
Financial profile for 2011: Number of employees, 3,600
Corporate officers: Walter D. Pinkard, Jr., Chair.; William M. Collins, Vice-Chair.; Joseph Stettinius, Jr., C.E.O.; John J. Fleury, C.O.O.; Maureen C. Wheeler, Sr. V.P., Comms.
Board of directors: Walter D. Pinkard, Jr., Chair.; William M. Collins, Vice-Chair.
Offices: Rockville, MD; Vienna, VA
Giving statement: Giving through the Cassidy & Pinkard Foundation.

The Cassidy & Pinkard Foundation

2900 K St NW., Ste. 401
Washington, DC 20037-1556

Establishment information: Established in 1988 in DC.
Donors: Cassidy & Pinkard, Inc.; Blane Dodson; John M. Benziger; Peter J. Farrell; Robert M. Pinkard.
Financial data (yr. ended 11/30/11): Assets, $134,871 (M); expenditures, $7,863; qualifying distributions, $7,815; giving activities include $6,000 for 1 grant.
Purpose and activities: The foundation supports organizations involved with education.
Fields of interest: Education.
Type of support: General/operating support; Scholarship funds.
Support limitations: No grants to individuals.
Application information: Applications not accepted. Unsolicited requests for funds not accepted.
Officers: Robert M. Pinkard, Pres.; Mary Petersen, V.P.; John M. Benziger, Secy.; Peter Farrell, Treas.
Board Members: Brendan Cassidy; Zeke Dodson.
EIN: 521609921

716
A.M. Castle & Co.

1420 Kensington Rd., Ste. 220
Oak Brook, IL 60523 (847) 455-7111
FAX: (847) 455-0587

Company URL: http://www.amcastle.com
Establishment information: Established in 1890.
Company type: Public company
Company ticker symbol and exchange: CAS/NYSE
Business activities: Sells metals wholesale.
Business type (SIC): Metals and minerals, except petroleum—wholesale
Financial profile for 2012: Number of employees, 1,701; assets, $788,810,000; sales volume, $1,270,370,000; pre-tax net income, -$1,554,000,000; expenses, $1,229,220,000; liabilities, $451,470,000
Corporate officers: Brian P. Anderson, Chair.; Scott Dolan, Pres. and C.E.O.; Scott F. Stephens, C.F.O. and Treas.; Kevin H. Glynn, V.P. and C.I.O.; Robert J. Perna, V.P., Genl. Counsel, and Secy.; Anne D. Scharm, V.P., Human Resources
Board of directors: Brian P. Anderson, Chair.; Scott Dolan; Reuben Simpson Donnelley; Ann M. Drake; Patrick J. Herbert III; Terrence J. Keating; James D. Kelly; Pamela Forbes Lieberman, C.P.A.; Gary A. Masse; John McCartney
Plants: Phoenix, AZ; Paramount, San Diego, Stockton, CA; Marietta, GA; Chicago, IL; Wichita, KS; Worcester, MA; Kansas City, MO; Charlotte, NC; Bedford Heights, Cincinnati, OH; Tulsa, OK; Fairless Hills, PA; Grand Prairie, Houston, TX
International operations: Canada; China; Mexico; Spain; United Kingdom
Giving statement: Giving through the Castle Foundation Inc.
Company EIN: 360879160

Castle Foundation Inc.

1420 Kensington Rd., Ste. 220
Oak Brook, IL 60523-2143

Establishment information: Established in 1952.
Donor: A.M. Castle & Co.
Contact: Karen A. Vanderveen, Secy.-Treas. and Dir.
Financial data (yr. ended 12/31/11): Assets, $196,012 (M); expenditures, $125,254; qualifying distributions, $125,224; giving activities include $125,224 for grants.
Purpose and activities: The foundation supports organizations involved with education and human services.
Fields of interest: Elementary/secondary education; Higher education; Education; Human services; United Ways and Federated Giving Programs.
Type of support: Employee matching gifts; General/operating support; Program development.
Geographic limitations: Giving primarily in IL.
Support limitations: No grants to individuals (except for employee-related scholarships).
Application information: Applications accepted. Application form not required.
Initial approach: Proposal
Board meeting date(s): Apr.
Deadline(s): None
Officers and Directors:* Michael H. Goldberg, Pres.; Scott F. Stephens, V.P.; Karen A. Vanderveen, Secy.-Treas.; Patrick J. Herbert.
EIN: 366109305
Selected grants: The following grants are a representative sample of this grantmaker's funding activity:
$60,000 to Communities in Schools of Chicago, Chicago, IL, 2010.
$6,000 to University of Michigan, Ann Arbor, MI, 2010.
$6,000 to University of Wisconsin, Madison, WI, 2010.
$3,500 to California State University, Long Beach, CA, 2010.
$3,500 to Kent State University, Kent, OH, 2010.
$3,000 to Michigan State University, East Lansing, MI, 2010.
$1,200 to University of Chicago, Chicago, IL, 2010.
$1,200 to University of Utah, Salt Lake City, UT, 2010.
$1,000 to University of Notre Dame, Notre Dame, IN, 2010.

717
Castle & Cooke, Inc.

10900 Wilshire Blvd., Ste. 1600
Los Angeles, CA 90024 (310) 208-3636

Company URL: http://www.castlecooke.net
Establishment information: Established in 1851.
Company type: Subsidiary of a private company

Business activities: Develops real estate; owns real estate; leases transportation equipment; provides trucking services; manufactures brick and building materials; operates resorts.
Business type (SIC): Real estate subdividers and developers; clay structural products; trucking and courier services, except by air; real estate operators and lessors; hotels and motels; motor vehicle rentals and leasing
Corporate officers: David H. Murdock, Chair., Pres., and C.E.O.; Edward C. Roohan, Pres. and C.O.O; Scott A. Griswold, Co-Exec. V.P., Opers.; Roberta Wieman, Co-Exec. V.P., Opers.; Gary Wong, V.P. and C.F.O.; Christine Dzwonczyk, V.P. and Treas.; Jason Burnett, V.P. and Genl. Counsel; Philip M. Young, V.P., Human Resources
Board of director: David H. Murdock, Chair.
Subsidiaries: Castle & Cooke California, Inc., Bakersfield, CA; Castle & Cooke Homes Hawaii, Inc., Mililani, HI; Lanai Co., Inc., Lanai City, HI
Giving statement: Giving through the David H. Murdock Institute for Business and Culture.
Company EIN: 770412800

David H. Murdock Institute for Business and Culture

(formerly Castle & Cooke Institute for Business and Culture)
10900 Wilshire Blvd., Ste. 1600
Los Angeles, CA 90024-6500

Establishment information: Established in 1988 in HI.
Donors: David H. Murdock; Dole Food Co., Inc.; Castle & Cooke, Inc.
Contact: Bill Leigh, Acct. Mgr.
Financial data (yr. ended 12/31/11): Assets, $1,902 (M); gifts received, $2,001,500; expenditures, $2,002,450; qualifying distributions, $2,002,450; giving activities include $2,001,000 for 2 grants (high: $2,000,000; low: $1,000).
Purpose and activities: The foundation supports Duke University and organizations involved with civic affairs.
Fields of interest: Higher education; Public affairs.
Type of support: General/operating support; Research.
Geographic limitations: Giving limited to CA and NC.
Support limitations: No support for religious organizations. No grants to individuals.
Application information: Applications not accepted. Contributes only to pre-selected organizations.
Officers and Directors:* David H. Murdock*, C.E.O.; Roberta Wieman*, Exec. V.P., Admin., and Corp. Secy.; Scott A. Griswold, Exec. V.P., Finance; Phil Young, V.P., Human Resources.
EIN: 954195213
Selected grants: The following grants are a representative sample of this grantmaker's funding activity:
$5,000,000 to Duke University, Durham, NC, 2010. For general support.
$920,000 to David H. Murdock Research Institute, Kannapolis, NC, 2010. For general support.
$50,000 to New York City Opera, New York, NY, 2010. For general support.
$24,000 to Pacific Aviation Museum Pearl Harbor, Honolulu, HI, 2010. For general support.

718
Castle & Cooke California, Inc.

10000 Stockdale Hwy., Ste. 300
Bakersfield, CA 93311 (661) 664-6500
FAX: (661) 664-6042

Company URL: http://www.castlecooke.com/who-we-are.html
Establishment information: Established in 1851.
Company type: Subsidiary of a private company
Business activities: Develops real estate.
Business type (SIC): Real estate subdividers and developers
Corporate officers: David H. Murdock, Chair. and C.E.O.; Bruce Freeman, Pres.; David A. Lari, V.P. and Cont.
Board of director: David H. Murdock, Chair.
Giving statement: Giving through the Castle & Cooke California, Inc. Corporate Giving Program.

Castle & Cooke California, Inc. Corporate Giving Program

10900 Wilshire Blvd., Ste. 1600
Los Angeles, CA 90024-6538

Purpose and activities: Castle & Cooke California makes charitable contributions to nonprofit organizations on a case by case basis. Support is given primarily in Sierra Vista, Arizona, Bakersfield, California, and Keene's Pointe, Florida.
Fields of interest: General charitable giving.
Type of support: General/operating support.
Geographic limitations: Giving primarily in Sierra Vista, AZ, Bakersfield, CA, and Keene's Pointe, FL.

719
Catalina Marketing Corporation

200 Carillon Pkwy.
St. Petersburg, FL 33716-1242
(727) 579-5000
FAX: (727) 556-2700

Company URL: http://www.catalinamarketing.com
Establishment information: Established in 1983.
Company type: Private company
Business activities: Provides electronic marketing services.
Business type (SIC): Advertising
Financial profile for 2010: Number of employees, 1,200
Corporate officers: Jamie Egasti, C.E.O.; Michael Barna, Exec. V.P. and C.F.O.; Claire DeMatteis, Exec. V.P., Genl. Counsel, and Corp. Secy.
Giving statement: Giving through the Catalina Marketing Charitable Foundation.

Catalina Marketing Charitable Foundation

200 Carillon Pkwy.
St. Petersburg, FL 33716-1242 (727) 579-5000

Establishment information: Established in 1991 in CA.
Donor: Catalina Marketing Corp.
Contact: Bill Protz, Pres.
Financial data (yr. ended 07/31/11): Assets, $2,917,684 (M); gifts received, $252,267; expenditures, $311,786; qualifying distributions, $284,951; giving activities include $284,951 for grants.
Purpose and activities: The foundation supports organizations involved with education, water conservation, health, hunger, housing development, athletics, youth business development, and children services.
Fields of interest: Higher education; Scholarships/financial aid; Education; Environment, water resources; Hospitals (general); Health care, clinics/centers; Health care; Food services; Housing/shelter, development; Athletics/sports, amateur leagues; Youth development, business; Children, services; United Ways and Federated Giving Programs.
Type of support: Annual campaigns; Continuing support; General/operating support; Program development; Scholarship funds.
Geographic limitations: Giving primarily in FL.
Application information: Applications accepted. Application form not required.
Initial approach: Proposal
Deadline(s): None
Officers and Directors:* Debbie Booth, Chair.; Bill Protz*, Pres.; Justin Summer*, Secy.; Rick Frier*, Treas.; Simon Banfield; Edward Kuehlne; Eric N. Williams.
EIN: 330489905
Selected grants: The following grants are a representative sample of this grantmaker's funding activity:
$30,000 to Pinellas County Education Foundation, Largo, FL, 2010. For general support.
$10,000 to Police Athletic League, Saint Petersburg, FL, 2010. For general support.
$10,000 to Tampa Baywatch, Tierra Verde, FL, 2010. For general support.
$5,000 to All Childrens Hospital, Saint Petersburg, FL, 2010. For general support.
$5,000 to Eckerd College, Saint Petersburg, FL, 2010. For general support.
$5,000 to United Way of Tampa Bay, Tampa, FL, 2010. For general support.
$3,500 to Southeastern Guide Dogs, Palmetto, FL, 2010. For general support.
$2,000 to Big Brothers Big Sisters of Pinellas County, Largo, FL, 2010. For general support.
$1,200 to Tampa Baywatch, Tierra Verde, FL, 2010. For general support.
$1,000 to YMCA of Greater Saint Petersburg, Saint Petersburg, FL, 2010. For general support.

720
Catawissa Wood and Components, Inc.

(formerly Catawissa Lumber & Specialty Company, Inc.)
1015 W. Valley Ave.
P.O. Box 176
Elysburg, PA 17824-7259 (570) 644-1928

Company URL: http://www.catawissalumber.com
Establishment information: Established in 1957.
Company type: Subsidiary of a foreign company
Business activities: Manufactures hardwood dimension lumber and allied products.
Business type (SIC): Lumber and wood products
Financial profile for 2009: Number of employees, 413
Corporate officer: James E. Smith, C.F.O.
Giving statement: Giving through the Catawissa Lumber & Specialty Co., Inc. Trust.

Catawissa Lumber & Specialty Co., Inc. Trust

c/o First Columbia Bank & Trust Co.
1199 Lightstreet Rd.
Bloomsburg, PA 17815-1702
Application address: 11 W. Main St., Bloomsburg, PA 17815

Donor: Catawissa Lumber & Specialty Co., Inc.
Contact: Janice Dreese
Financial data (yr. ended 12/31/11): Assets, $119,383 (M); expenditures, $7,195; qualifying distributions, $5,000; giving activities include $5,000 for grants.
Purpose and activities: The foundation awards college scholarships and student loans to graduates of Shamokin Area Senior High School, Mount Carmel Area High School, Southern Columbia Area High School, Bloomsburg Area High School, Central Columbia High School, Danville Area High School, and Columbia-Montour Area Vocational Technical High School in Pennsylvania.
Fields of interest: Education.
Type of support: Scholarships—to individuals.
Geographic limitations: Giving limited to the Catawissa, PA, area.
Application information: Applications accepted. Application form required. Applicants should submit the following:
1) copy of most recent annual report/audited financial statement/990
Initial approach: Contact foundation for application form
Deadline(s): Apr. 16
Trustee: First Columbia Bank & Trust Co.
EIN: 237676581

721
Catchafire, Inc.

31 E. 32nd St., 10 Fl., Ste. 610
New York, NY 10016-5509 (212) 213-8014

Company URL: http://www.catchafire.org
Establishment information: Established in 2009.
Company type: Private company
Business type (SIC): Business services/miscellaneous
Corporate officer: Rachael Chong, C.E.O.
Giving statement: Giving through the Catchafire Incorporated Contributions Program.

Catchafire Incorporated Contributions Program

118 E. 28th St., Ste.1012
New York, NY 10016-8451 (212) 213-8014
E-mail: catchus@catchafire.org; URL: http://www.bcorporation.net/catchafire

Purpose and activities: Catchafire is a certified B Corporation that donates a percentage of profits to charitable organizations.

722
Caterpillar Inc.

100 N.E. Adams St.
Peoria, IL 61629-0001 (309) 675-1000
FAX: (309) 675-6620

Company URL: http://www.cat.com
Establishment information: Established in 1925.
Company type: Public company
Company ticker symbol and exchange: CAT/NYSE
Business activities: Designs, manufactures, markets, and sells construction, mining, and forestry machinery; designs, manufactures, markets, and sells engines; provides loans; sells insurance; conducts investment activities.
Business type (SIC): Machinery/construction, mining, and materials handling; engines and turbines; non-depository credit institutions; insurance carriers; investors/miscellaneous
Financial profile for 2012: Number of employees, 125,341; assets, $89,356,000,000; sales volume, $65,875,000,000; pre-tax net income, $8,236,000,000; expenses, $57,304,000,000; liabilities, $71,824,000,000
Fortune 1000 ranking: 2012—42nd in revenues, 33rd in profits, and 68th in assets
Forbes 2000 ranking: 2012—121st in sales, 93rd in profits, and 273rd in assets
Corporate officers: Douglas R. Oberhelman, Chair. and C.E.O.; Bradley M. Halverson, C.F.O; Jananne A. Copeland, C.A.O.; Christopher M. Reitz, Corp. Secy.; Edward J. Scott, Treas.; Michael DeWalt, Corp. Cont.
Board of directors: Douglas R. Oberhelman, Chair.; David L. Calhoun; Daniel M. Dickinson; Juan Gallardo; David R. Goode; Jesse J. Greene, Jr.; Jon M. Huntsman, Jr.; Peter A. Magowan; Dennis A. Muilenburg; William A. Osborn; Charles D. Powell; Edward B. Rust, Jr.; Susan C. Schwab, Ph.D.; Joshua I. Smith; Miles D. White
Subsidiaries: Anchor Coupling Inc., Menominee, MI; Carter Machinery Company, Inc., Salem, VA; Caterpillar AccessAccount Corp., Nashville, TN; Caterpillar Americas Co., Peoria, IL; Caterpillar Americas Services Co., Miami, FL; Caterpillar Commercial, L.L.C., Peoria, IL; Caterpillar Elkader, L.L.C., Elkader, IA; Caterpillar Engine Systems Inc., Peoria, IL; Caterpillar Forest Products Inc., Zebulon, NC; Caterpillar GB, L.L.C., Peoria, IL; Caterpillar Global Services, L.L.C., Peoria, IL; Caterpillar Insurance Co., Nashville, TN; Caterpillar Insurance Services Corp., Nashville, TN; Caterpillar Life Insurance Co., Nashville, TN; Caterpillar Logistics Services, Inc., Morton, IL; Caterpillar Logistics Services, Inc., Peoria, IL; Caterpillar of Delaware, Inc., Atlanta, GA; Caterpillar Paving Products, Inc., Minneapolis, MN; Caterpillar Paving Products Inc., Minneapolis, MN; Caterpillar Power Systems Inc., Peoria, IL; Caterpillar Product Services Corp., Nashville, TN; Caterpillar Reman Powertrain Indiana, L.L.C., Franklin, IN; Caterpillar Reman Powertrain Services, Inc., Summerville, SC; Caterpillar Remanufacturing Drivetrain, L.L.C., West Fargo, ND; Caterpillar Services Limited, Peoria, IL; Caterpillar Work Tools, Inc., Wamego, KS; Caterpillar World Trading Corp., Peoria, IL; Chemetron-Railway Products, Inc., Albertville, AL; F.G. Wilson (USA), L.L.C., Newberry, SC; Federal Financial Services, L.L.C., Clinton, MD; Ironmart, L.L.C., Lexington, SC; Kentuckiana Railcar Repair & Storage Facility, L.L.C., Charlestown, IN; Magnum Power Products, L.L.C., Indianapolis, IN; MaK Americas Inc., Miramar, FL; Perkins Engines, Inc., Mossville, IL; Perkins Shibaura Engines, L.L.C., Griffin, GA; Perkins Technology Inc., Troy, MI; Pioneer Distribution, Inc., Compton, CA; Pioneer Machinery, L.L.C., West Columbia, SC; PMHC, L.L.C., West Columbia, SC; Progress Metal Reclamation Co., Ashland, KY; Solar Turbines, Inc., San Diego, CA
Plants: Aurora, Decatur, Joliet, Mapleton, Morton, Mossville, Pontiac, IL; Lafayette, IN
International operations: Argentina; Australia; Barbados; Belgium; Bermuda; Brazil; Canada; Chile; China; Costa Rica; Czech Republic; Egypt; England; France; Germany; Guernsey; Hong Kong; Hungary; India; Ireland; Italy; Japan; Luxembourg; Malaysia; Mexico; Netherlands; New Zealand; Nicaragua; Nigeria; Northern Ireland; Norway; Pakistan; Panama; Peru; Philippines; Poland; Russia; Singapore; South Africa; Spain; Sri Lanka; Sweden; Switzerland; Thailand; Trinidad & Tobago; Tunisia; Turkey; Ukraine; United Arab Emirates; Uruguay; Venezuela; Wales
Giving statement: Giving through the Caterpillar Inc. Corporate Giving Program, the Caterpillar Foundation, and the Illinois High School Activities Foundation.
Company EIN: 370602744

Caterpillar Inc. Corporate Giving Program

100 N.E. Adams St.
Peoria, IL 61629-1480

Contact: Leith Robotham, Social Responsibility
Purpose and activities: As a complement to its foundation, Caterpillar also makes charitable contributions to nonprofit organizations directly. Support is given primarily in areas of company operations.
Fields of interest: Education; Environment; Human services Children/youth; Adults; Young adults; Minorities; Economically disadvantaged.
Type of support: Employee matching gifts; General/operating support; Program development; Scholarship funds.
Geographic limitations: Giving primarily in areas of company operations; giving also to national organizations.
Support limitations: No support for fraternal organizations, political organizations, sectarian religious organizations, or United Way-supported organizations. No grants to individuals, or for tickets or advertising.
Application information: Applications not accepted. Contributes only to pre-selected organizations. The Social Responsibility Department handles giving. The company has a staff that only handles contributions.
Administrator: Jennifer Zammuto, V.P.
Number of staff: 3 part-time professional; 1 part-time support.

Caterpillar Foundation

100 N.E. Adams St.
Peoria, IL 61629-1480 (309) 675-5941
E-mail: Foundation@cat.com; Additional tel.: (309) 675-4464; URL: http://www.cat.com/foundation

Establishment information: Established in 1952 in IL.
Donor: Caterpillar Inc.
Contact: Jennifer Zammuto, V.P.
Financial data (yr. ended 12/31/11): Assets, $33,035,371 (M); gifts received, $49,885,000; expenditures, $49,959,370; qualifying distributions, $49,789,926; giving activities include $49,789,926 for 1,140 grants (high: $4,000,000; low: $50).
Purpose and activities: The foundation supports programs designed to advance knowledge and education; protect the environment and conservation of resources; and promote access to basic human services.
Fields of interest: Media/communications; Media, television; Museums; Arts; Higher education; Education; Environment, natural resources; Environment, water resources; Environment, land resources; Environment, forests; Environment; Zoos/zoological societies; Hospitals (general); Health care; Breast cancer; Youth development, business; Human services; Microfinance/microlending; Community/economic development; United Ways and Federated Giving Programs; Mathematics; Engineering/technology; Public

policy, research; Public affairs Economically disadvantaged.
Programs:
Community Service Awards: The foundation honors employees who have shown an outstanding volunteer commitment to their communities. The award includes a $25,000 donation to the nonprofit of the recipient's choice.
Employee Matching Gifts: The foundation matches contributions made by employees, retirees, and directors of Caterpillar to institutions of higher education and organizations involved with arts and culture, the environment, and public policy on a one-for-one basis from $50 to $2,000 per contributor, per year.
Type of support: Annual campaigns; Building/renovation; Capital campaigns; Curriculum development; Employee matching gifts; Employee volunteer services; Equipment; General/operating support; Matching/challenge support; Program development; Scholarship funds; Sponsorships.
Geographic limitations: Giving primarily in areas of company operations in North Little Rock, AR, Tucson, AZ, San Diego, CA, Griffin, LaGrange, and Spalding, GA, Aurora, Decatur, Joliet, and Pontiac, IL, Franklin and Lafayette, IN, Wamego, KS, Danville, KY, Minneapolis, MN, Boonville and West Plains, MO, Boonville, Corinth, and Prentiss, MS, Cary, Clayton, Morgantown, Sanford, and Winston-Salem, NC, Fargo, ND, Sumter, SC, Victoria, TX, and Milwaukee, WI, with emphasis on Peoria, IL.
Support limitations: No support for fraternal organizations or exclusive membership societies, hospitals, political action committees or candidates, private foundations, religious organizations not of direct benefit to the entire community, or discriminatory organizations. No grants to individuals, or for graduate student scholarships or fellowships, capital campaigns, building construction, debt reduction, development or production of books, videos, films, or television programs, research papers or articles in professional journals, endowments, general operating or agency programs funded by the United Way, political causes, research, sponsorships, tickets, or advertising for fund-raising, or travel; no product or service donations; no loans.
Publications: Application guidelines; Corporate giving report (including application guidelines); Program policy statement.
Application information: Applications accepted. Application form required. Applicants should submit the following:
1) timetable for implementation and evaluation of project
2) qualifications of key personnel
3) statement of problem project will address
4) population served
5) name, address and phone number of organization
6) copy of IRS Determination Letter
7) brief history of organization and description of its mission
8) copy of most recent annual report/audited financial statement/990
9) how project's results will be evaluated or measured
10) list of company employees involved with the organization
11) explanation of why grantmaker is considered an appropriate donor for project
12) listing of board of directors, trustees, officers and other key people and their affiliations
13) detailed description of project and amount of funding requested
14) contact person
15) copy of current year's organizational budget and/or project budget
16) listing of additional sources and amount of support
17) additional materials/documentation

Initial approach: Complete online application for organizations located in Peoria, IL; download application and e-mail to nearest facility for organizations located outside of Peoria, IL
Board meeting date(s): Dec. 1
Deadline(s): None
Final notification: 2 months

Officers and Directors:* Douglas R. Oberhelman*, Pres.; E. J. Rapp*, Exec. V.P.; J. A. Baumgartner*, V.P.; M. H. Collier, V.P.; K. S. Hauer, V.P.; M. L. Sullivan, V.P.; Jennifer L. Zammuto, V.P.; M. C. Marshall, Secy.; Robin D. Beran, Treas.
EIN: 376022314
Selected grants: The following grants are a representative sample of this grantmaker's funding activity:
$4,000,000 to United Way, Heart of Illinois, Peoria, IL, 2011.
$3,711,857 to International Youth Foundation, Baltimore, MD, 2011.
$1,696,979 to Bradley University, Peoria, IL, 2011.
$1,500,000 to Lakeview Museum of Arts and Sciences, Peoria, IL, 2011.
$78,000 to Engineers Without Borders USA, Boulder, CO, 2011.
$50,000 to Living Lands and Waters Restoration Organization, East Moline, IL, 2011.
$4,000 to Judson University, Elgin, IL, 2011.

Illinois High School Activities Foundation

2715 McGraw Dr.
Bloomington, IL 61704-2715
URL: http://www.ihsa.org/

Establishment information: Established around 1994 in IL.
Donors: Catapillar, Inc.; The Quaker Oats Company.
Financial data (yr. ended 12/31/11): Assets, $117,933 (M); gifts received, $56,627; expenditures, $45,035; qualifying distributions, $45,035; giving activities include $26,000 for 26 grants to individuals (high: $1,000; low: $1,000).
Purpose and activities: The foundation awards scholarships to members of the Illinois High School Association's All-State Academic Team.
Fields of interest: Higher education.
Type of support: Scholarships—to individuals.
Geographic limitations: Giving limited to residents of IL.
Application information: Applications accepted. Scholarships are limited to members of the Illinois High School Association's All-State Academic Team. Application form required.

Initial approach: Contact participating high schools for All-State Academic Team information and application
Deadline(s): None

Officers and Directors:* Jim Woodward*, Pres.; Marty Hickman, Treas.; Allan Chapman; Ron McGraw.
EIN: 371322645

723
Cathay Bank

777 N. Broadway St.
Los Angeles, CA 90012 (213) 625-4700

Company URL: http://www.cathaybank.com/
Establishment information: Established in 1962.
Company type: Subsidiary of a public company
Business activities: Operates a state commercial bank.
Business type (SIC): Banks/commercial
Corporate officers: Dunson K. Cheng, Ph.D., Chair., Pres., and C.E.O.; Peter Wu, Ph.D., Vice-Chair. and C.O.O.; Heng W. Chen, Exec. V.P. and C.F.O.; Perry P. Oei, Sr. V.P., Secy., and Genl. Counsel; Dennis Kwok, Sr. V.P. and Treas.
Board of directors: Dunson K. Cheng, Chair.; Peter Wu, Vice-Chair.
Giving statement: Giving through the Cathay Bank Foundation.

Cathay Bank Foundation

777 N. Broadway
Los Angeles, CA 90012-2819 (213) 625-4899
E-mail: foundation@cathaybank.com; URL: http://www.cathaybank.org

Donors: Ted Stein; Mrs. Ted Stein; Cathay Bank; Diamond Ridge Development, LLC; PrimeVest; Shilo Inn; Highland Capital; Alpha Industries; Pacific BMW; Transcontinental Realty Investors, Inc.; 3 A Holdings, LLC.
Contact: Thomas Wilson
Financial data (yr. ended 12/31/11): Assets, $108,776 (M); gifts received, $1,461,348; expenditures, $1,395,432; qualifying distributions, $1,395,432; giving activities include $1,227,000 for 95 grants (high: $60,000; low: $1,500).
Purpose and activities: The foundation supports nonprofit organizations involved with community and economic development, education, health and welfare, and arts and culture. Special emphasis is directed toward programs that target low and moderate-income communities. Support is given primarily in areas of company operations.
Fields of interest: Arts education; Arts; Education; Employment, training; Food services; Housing/shelter; Human services; Family services; Family services, domestic violence; Community/economic development.
Type of support: General/operating support.
Geographic limitations: Giving primarily in areas of company operations, with emphasis on CA, IL, MA, NJ, NY, TX, and WA.
Support limitations: No support for political, religious, fraternal, labor, veterans, or military organizations, or private foundations, or organizations that channel grant funds to third parties. No grants to individuals, or for operating funds for hospitals or other patient care facilities, or travel.
Publications: Application guidelines.
Application information: Applications accepted. A full grant application may be requested at a later date. Support is limited to 1 contribution per organization during any given year. Grant awards generally range from $1,000 to $10,000. Application form required. Applicants should submit the following:
1) name, address and phone number of organization
2) contact person
3) detailed description of project and amount of funding requested
4) geographic area to be served
5) population served

Initial approach: Letter of intent
Copies of proposal: 3
Board meeting date(s): Quarterly
Deadline(s): None

Officers and Directors:* Peter Wu, Chair., C.E.O., and Pres.; Irwin Wong*, V.P., C.F.O., and Treas.; David Nakagaki, V.P. and Secy.; Alex Lee*, V.P.; Dominic Lee*, V.P.; Pin Tai*, V.P.; Wilson Tang*, V.P.; Deborah Ching; Patrick Lee.
EIN: 743052411

Selected grants: The following grants are a representative sample of this grantmaker's funding activity:
$60,000 to Food Bank for New York City, New York, NY, 2011.
$13,000 to International Institute of Los Angeles, Los Angeles, CA, 2011.
$10,000 to Boston Chinatown Neighborhood Center, Boston, MA, 2011.
$10,000 to City Year Los Angeles, Los Angeles, CA, 2011.
$10,000 to Los Angeles Regional Food Bank, Los Angeles, CA, 2011.
$10,000 to Neighborhood Housing Services of Chicago, Chicago, IL, 2011.
$5,000 to Network for Teaching Entrepreneurship, New York, NY, 2011.
$2,500 to Coalition for Humane Immigrant Rights of Los Angeles, Los Angeles, CA, 2011.

724
Cavaliers Holdings, LLC

(also known as Cleveland Cavaliers)
1 Center Ct.
Cleveland, OH 44115-4001 (216) 420-2000

Company URL: http://www.nba.com/cavaliers
Establishment information: Established in 1947.
Company type: Subsidiary of a private company
Business activities: Operates professional basketball club.
Business type (SIC): Commercial sports
Corporate officers: Daniel R. Gilbert, Chair.; Jeffrey Cohen, Vice-Chair.; Len Komoroski, C.E.O.; Mozelle Jackson, C.F.O.; David Griffin, V.P., Opers.
Board of directors: Daniel R. Gilbert, Chair.; Jeffrey Cohen, Vice-Chair.
Giving statement: Giving through the Cleveland Cavaliers Corporate Giving Program.

Cleveland Cavaliers Corporate Giving Program

1 Center Ct.
Cleveland, OH 44115-4001
FAX: (215) 420-2010; E-mail: cavscare@cavs.com; URL: http://www.nba.com/cavaliers/community/index.html

Contact: Holly Yank
Purpose and activities: The Cleveland Cavaliers make charitable contributions to nonprofit organizations involved with education, physical fitness, nutrition, recreation, youth, and life skills. Support is given primarily in areas of company operations in Ohio.
Fields of interest: Elementary school/education; Secondary school/education; Education, reading; Education; Public health, physical fitness; Nutrition; Recreation; Youth, services; Human services, gift distribution; Human services; Mathematics; General charitable giving.
Programs:

All-Star Kids: Through All-Star Kids, the Cavaliers honors one middle school student each month who is setting a positive example for their peers. The student is visited at his or her school by Cavaliers Mascot Moondog and Cavaliers "Hype Man" Ahmaad Crump and receives a super-sized ticket to a Cavaliers game.

Cavaliers/FirstMerit Scholarship Program: The Cavaliers, in partnership with FirsMerit Bank, awards 10 $2,000 college scholarships to graduating high school seniors from Northeast Ohio.

Cavaliers/Majestic Steel Scholarship Program: The Cavaliers, in partnership with Majestic Steel USA, awards six $2,000 scholarships to graduating high school seniors or college students already enrolled in a manufacturing program at Cuyahoga Community College, Lakeland Community College, or Lorain Community College.

Fit As A Pro: The Cavaliers, in partnership with Medical Mutual, encourage exercise and well-balanced eating among elementary and middle school students in Cuyahoga, Geauga, Lake, Lorain, Medina, Portage, and Summit counties. Classrooms receive a nutrition poster for display and students receive Fit As A Pro fitness cards to track the among of physical activity each day with a goal of 30-60 minutes.

Full Court Press: The Cavaliers, in partnership with Chancellor University, selects 15 high schools in Northeast Ohio to learn about the world of journalism and sports. Students attend "Media Day" to tour the Quicken Loans Arena, participate in media availability following the Cavaliers on game day, attend a roundtable discussion with media members and public relation staff, and receives 2 tickets to attend the Cavaliers vs. Detroit Piston game. Students are encourage to write about the experience for his/her newspaper and the winning submission will be featured on the Cavaliers website.

Head of the Class: Through Head of the Class, the Cavaliers honors one teacher each month in Cuyahoga County who is making a difference in their students lives both inside and outside of the classroom. The teacher is visited at his or her school by Cavaliers Mascot Moondog and Cavaliers "Hype Man" Ahmaad Crump and receives a super-sized ticket to a Cavaliers game.

Kindness In Action: Through the Kindness In Action program, the Cavaliers initiates random acts of generosity targeted toward those in need in economically depressed areas of the community.

Read to Achieve: The Cavaliers encourage elementary school students in Cuyahoga, Geauga, Lake, Lorain, Medina, Portage, and Summit counties to develop a love for reading and to encourage adults to read regularly with children. Classrooms receive progress cards for each student who must read outside of the classroom daily and track the number of minutes they read each day for a month.

Reading & Learning Centers: The Cavaliers create reading and learning centers in community-based organizations and schools to provide children with regular access to books and technology. The program is designed to improve conditions of current facilities and to improve quality of literacy and educational programming.

Straight "A" All Stars: The Cavaliers rewards students in grades K-8 in Ashtabula, Cuyahoga, Geauga, Lorain, Medina, Portage, and Summit counties who receive straight A's. Students are entered into a contest to win 2 tickets to a Cavaliers game and a t-shirt. All applicants receive an official Straight "A" All-Stars certificate and a book cover.

Type of support: Curriculum development; Donated products; General/operating support; In-kind gifts; Income development; Loaned talent; Program development; Scholarships—to individuals.
Geographic limitations: Giving primarily in areas of company operations in Cuyahoga, Geauga, Lake, Lorain, Medina, Portage, and Summit counties, OH.
Publications: Application guidelines.
Application information: Applications accepted. Proposals should be submitted using organization letterhead. Support is limited to 1 contribution per organization during any given year. Application form not required. Applicants should submit the following:
1) detailed description of project and amount of funding requested
2) geographic area to be served
3) population served
4) brief history of organization and description of its mission

Proposals should indicate the type of fundraiser, and the number of tickets needed if applicable. Cavaliers/Majestic Steel applications should include high school transcripts and a current FAFSA form. Cavaliers/FirstMerit Scholarship applications should include high school transcripts, ACT or SAT scores, one letter of recommendation, and a 500 word essay.

Initial approach: Proposal to headquarters for autographs, player appearances, and ticket donations; download application form and mail to headquarters for scholarships and Reading & Learning Centers; submit writing samples for Full Court Press; complete online nomination form for All-Star Kids and Head of the Class
Copies of proposal: 1
Deadline(s): 6 weeks prior to need; Feb. 15 for Cavaliers/FirstMerit Scholarships; Mar. 5 for Cavaliers/Majestic Steel Scholarships; Mar. 1 for Full Court Press; None for All-Star Kids, Head of the Class, and Reading & Learning Centers

725
CB Richard Ellis Group, Inc.

11150 Santa Monica Blvd., Ste. 1600
Los Angeles, CA 90025 (310) 405-8900
FAX: (302) 655-5049

Company URL: http://www.cbre.com
Establishment information: Established in 1906.
Company type: Public company
Company ticker symbol and exchange: CBG/NYSE
International Securities Identification Number: US12504L1098
Business activities: Operates commercial real estate agency.
Business type (SIC): Real estate; real estate agents and managers
Financial profile for 2012: Number of employees, 37,000; assets, $7,809,540,000; sales volume, $6,514,100,000; pre-tax net income, $489,480,000; expenses, $5,929,020,000; liabilities, $6,270,330,000
Fortune 1000 ranking: 2012—387th in revenues, 452nd in profits, and 457th in assets
Corporate officers: Richard C. Blum, Chair.; Robert E. Sulentic, Pres. and C.E.O; Gil Borok, C.F.O.; Laurence H. Midler, Exec. V.P. and Genl. Counsel; Arlin E. Gaffner, Co-C.A.O.; Chris Kirk, Co-C.A.O.; Jim Groch, C.I.O.
Board of directors: Richard C. Blum, Chair.; Brandon B. Boze; Curtis F. Feeny; Bradford M. Freeman; Michael Kantor; Frederic V. Malek; Bob Sulentic; Jane J. Su; Laura D'Andrea Tyson; Gary L. Wilson; Ray Wirta
Subsidiaries: CB Richard Ellis, Inc., Los Angeles, CA; CB Richard Ellis Services, Inc., Chicago, IL; CBRE Melody & Co., Houston, TX
Joint Venture: CB Commercial/Whittier Partners, L.P., Boston, MA
International operations: Netherlands; United Kingdom
Giving statement: Giving through the CB Richard Ellis—Kenny/Farley Foundation, Inc.
Company EIN: 943391143

CB Richard Ellis—Kenny/Farley Foundation, Inc.

c/o Eastern Bank
605 Broadway, LF 42
Saugus, MA 01906-3200

Establishment information: Established in 1999 in MA.
Donors: CB Richard Ellis Services, Inc.; CB Richard Ellis Group, Inc.
Financial data (yr. ended 10/31/11): Assets, $412,410 (M); gifts received, $5,700; expenditures, $10,072; qualifying distributions, $6,175; giving activities include $5,000 for 1 grant.
Purpose and activities: The foundation supports the Kenneth B. Schwartz Center in Saugas, Massachusetts.
Fields of interest: Health care, clinics/centers.
Type of support: General/operating support.
Geographic limitations: Giving limited to MA.
Support limitations: No grants to individuals.
Application information: Applications not accepted. Unsolicited requests for funds not accepted.
Officers: Kevin M. Doyle, Pres.; Jennifer E. Fox, Clerk.
Directors: Robert J. Daglio; Charles T. Francis; Mark F. Tassinari; Benjamin C. Terry.
EIN: 043489211

726
CBI Polymers LLC

1946 Young St., Ste. 480
Honolulu, HI 96826 (808) 949-2208

Company URL: http://www.decongel.com
Company type: Private company
Business activities: Operates sustainable polymer products company.
Business type (SIC): Chemicals/industrial inorganic
Corporate officers: Hank C. Wuh, Co-Pres. and C.E.O.; Larry J. Stack, Co-Pres. and C.O.O.; Douglas M. Tonokawa, C.F.O.
Giving statement: Giving through the CBI Polymers LLC Contributions Program.

CBI Polymers LLC Contributions Program

1946 Young St., Ste. 288
Honolulu, HI 96826-2150
URL: http://www.skaiventures.com/technology/decongel/

727
CBS Corporation

(formerly Viacom Inc.)
51 W. 52nd St.
New York, NY 10019-6188 (212) 975-4321

Company URL: http://www.cbscorporation.com
Establishment information: Established in 1928.
Company type: Public company
Company ticker symbol and exchange: CBS/NYSE
International Securities Identification Number: US1248572026
Business activities: Broadcasts television; produces television programming; provides cable television services; broadcasts radio; provides outdoor advertising services; publishes books; operates theme parks.
Business type (SIC): Radio and television broadcasting; book publishing and/or printing; cable and other pay television services; advertising; amusement and recreation services/miscellaneous
Financial profile for 2012: Number of employees, 20,930; assets, $26,466,000,000; sales volume, $14,089,000,000; pre-tax net income, $2,561,000,000; expenses, $11,138,000,000; liabilities, $16,253,000,000
Fortune 1000 ranking: 2012—186th in revenues, 134th in profits, and 206th in assets
Forbes 2000 ranking: 2012—680th in sales, 398th in profits, and 813th in assets
Corporate officers: Sumner M. Redstone, Chair.; Shari E. Redstone, Vice-Chair.; Leslie Moonves, Pres. and C.E.O.; Joseph R. Ianniello, Exec. V.P. and C.F.O.; Louis J. Briskman, Exec. V.P. and Genl. Counsel; Anthony G. Ambrosio, Exec. V.P., Human Resources and Admin.; Lawrence Liding, Jr., Sr. V.P., Cont., and C.A.O.; Angeline C. Straka, Sr. V.P. and Secy.
Board of directors: Sumner M. Redstone, Chair.; Shari E. Redstone, Vice-Chair.; David R. Andelman; Joseph A. Califano, Jr.; William S. Cohen; Gary L. Countryman; Charles K. Gifford; Leonard Goldberg; Bruce S. Gordon; Linda M. Griego; Arnold Kopelson; Leslie Moonves; Douglas Morris; Frederic V. Salerno
Subsidiaries: Showtime Networks Inc., New York, NY; Simon & Schuster, Inc., New York, NY; Viacom Pictures Inc., Universal City, CA; Viacom Productions LLC, Universal City, CA
International operations: Australia; Brazil; Canada; France; Japan; Switzerland
Giving statement: Giving through the CBS Foundation Inc.
Company EIN: 042949533

CBS Foundation Inc.

(formerly Viacom Foundation Inc.)
51 W. 52 St.
New York, NY 10019-6119 (212) 975-5245

Establishment information: Incorporated in 1953 in NY.
Donors: CBS Inc.; Westinghouse Electric Corp.; CBS Corp.; Westinghouse Foundation; Viacom Inc.
Contact: Martin D. Franks, Pres. and Dir.
Financial data (yr. ended 12/31/11): Assets, $15,591 (M); expenditures, $0; qualifying distributions, $0.
Purpose and activities: The foundation supports programs designed to promote arts and culture, education, and community revitalization. Support is given primarily in areas of company operations.
Fields of interest: Arts; Education; Community/economic development.
Type of support: General/operating support; Sponsorships.
Geographic limitations: Giving primarily in areas of company operations.
Support limitations: No support for labor or discriminatory organizations. No grants to individuals, or for building or endowments; no matching gifts; no loans.
Application information: Applications accepted. Application form required. Applicants should submit the following:
1) copy of IRS Determination Letter
2) brief history of organization and description of its mission
3) copy of most recent annual report/audited financial statement/990
4) listing of board of directors, trustees, officers and other key people and their affiliations
5) detailed description of project and amount of funding requested

Initial approach: Proposal
Copies of proposal: 1
Board meeting date(s): Quarterly
Deadline(s): None
Officers and Directors:* Martin D. Franks, Pres.; John S. Orlando, V.P. and Treas.; Lisa M. Tanzi.
Number of staff: 1 full-time professional; 1 full-time support.
EIN: 136099759

728
CC Partners

(doing business as Golden State Warriors)
1011 Broadway
Oakland, CA 94607-4019 (510) 986-2200

Company URL: http://www.nba.com/warriors
Establishment information: Established in 1946.
Company type: Private company
Business activities: Operates professional basketball club.
Business type (SIC): Commercial sports
Corporate officers: Joe Lacob, Co-Chair. and C.E.O.; Peter Guber, Co-Chair.; Vivek Ranadive, Vice-Chair.; Rick Welts, Pres. and C.O.O.; Marty Glick, C.F.O.; David Kelly, V.P., Genl. Counsel; Kellie Vugrincic, V.P., Human Resources
Board of directors: Joe Lacob, Co-Chair. and C.E.O.; Peter Guber, Co-Chair.; Vivek Ranadive, Vice-Chair.; Fred Harman; Bruce Karsh; Chamath Palihapitiya; Bob Piccinini; Jerry West
Giving statement: Giving through the Golden State Warriors Corporate Giving Program and the Golden State Warriors Foundation.

Golden State Warriors Corporate Giving Program

c/o Community Rels.
1011 Broadway
Oakland, CA 94607-4019 (510) 986-2215
Contact for Read to Achieve: Erika Smith, tel.: (510) 986-2217; URL: http://www.nba.com/warriors/community/home.html

Purpose and activities: The Golden State Warriors make charitable contributions to nonprofit organizations on a case by case basis. Support is given primarily in the greater San Francisco Bay Area, California.
Fields of interest: Elementary school/education; Education, reading; Education; Public health, physical fitness; Crime/violence prevention, child abuse; Nutrition; Athletics/sports, amateur leagues; Athletics/sports, basketball; Youth development; Youth, services; Family services; General charitable giving.
Programs:
Get Fit: The Golden State Warriors, in partnership with Kaiser Permanente, educates Bay Area youth on the importance of healthy eating and active living. The program includes visits by Warrior players to local schools and clinics and nutrition and health-themed performances by actors from Kaiser Permanente's Educational Theatre Program.
Read to Achieve: Through Read to Achieve, the Golden State Warriors encourage literacy to Bay Area children through monthly Reading Time, Reading & Learning Centers, and other literary activities. The program is conducted in partnership with elementary and middle schools, public library systems, and local youth agencies.
Type of support: Donated products; General/operating support; In-kind gifts; Loaned talent.
Geographic limitations: Giving primarily in areas of company operations in the greater San Francisco Bay Area, CA.

Publications: Application guidelines.
Application information: Applications accepted. Proposals should be submitted using organization letterhead. Support is limited to 1 contribution per organization during any given year. Telephone calls during the application process are not encouraged. The Community Relations Department handles giving. Application form not required. Applicants should submit the following:
1) population served
2) copy of IRS Determination Letter
3) detailed description of project and amount of funding requested
Proposals should indicate the date and location of the event.
Initial approach: Proposal to headquarters for grants, memorabilia, promotional items, or player appearances; download application form and mail to headquarters for ticket donations
Copies of proposal: 1
Deadline(s): 6 to 8 weeks prior to need
Final notification: 2 to 3 weeks

Golden State Warriors Foundation
1011 Broadway
Oakland, CA 94607-4019 (510) 986-2200
URL: http://www.nba.com/warriors/community_index.html

Establishment information: Established in 1998 in CA.
Contact: Angela Cohan, Pres.
Financial data (yr. ended 06/30/11): Revenue, $217,806; assets, $310,507 (M); gifts received, $168,264; expenditures, $188,930; giving activities include $152,210 for grants and $3,500 for grants to individuals.
Purpose and activities: The foundation provides financial assistance and opportunities to other nonprofit civic and community organizations that benefit and enrich the lives of children, youth, and those in need.
Fields of interest: Youth; Aging; Economically disadvantaged.
Type of support: In-kind gifts.
Geographic limitations: Giving primarily in northern CA.
Officers and Directors:* Angela Cohan*, Pres.; Robert Rowell*, V.P.; Neda Kia*, Secy.; Dwayne Redmon*, Treas.; Alvin Attles; Rod Higgins.
EIN: 943253780

729
CDW Corporation
Business Technology Ctr.
200 N. Milwaukee Ave.
Vernon Hills, IL 60061 (847) 465-6000
FAX: (847) 465-6800

Company URL: http://www.cdw.com
Establishment information: Established in 1984.
Company type: Private company
Business activities: Operates a technology products company.
Business type (SIC): Consumer electronics and music stores
Financial profile for 2010: Number of employees, 6,200; sales volume, $8,800,000,000
Fortune 1000 ranking: 2012—267th in revenues, 703rd in profits, and 554th in assets
Corporate officers: Thomas E. Richards, Chair., Pres., and C.E.O.; Ann E. Ziegler, Sr. V.P. and C.F.O.; Jonathan J. Stevens, Sr. V.P., Opers. and C.I.O.; Christine A. Leahy, Sr. V.P., Genl. Counsel, and Corp. Secy.
Board of directors: Thomas E. Richards, Chair.; Steven W. Alesio; Barry K. Allen; Benjamin D. Chereskin; Glenn M. Creamer; Michael J. Dominguez; Paul J. Finnegan; Robin P. Selati; Donna F. Zarcone
Offices: Chandler, AZ; Shelton, CT; Chicago, Mettawa, IL; North Las Vegas, NV; Eatontown, Voorhees, NJ; Herndon, VA; Madison, WI
International operations: Canada
Giving statement: Giving through the CDW Corporation Contributions Program.

CDW Corporation Contributions Program
Business Technology Ctr.
200 N. Milwaukee Ave.
Vernon Hills, IL 60061-1577 (847) 465-6000
E-mail for product and in-kind donation requests: donations@cdw.com; URL: http://www.cdw.com/content/about/community-involvement.asp

Purpose and activities: CDW Corporation makes charitable contributions to nonprofit organizations involved with technology, education, and children. Support is given primarily in areas of company operations in Chandler, Arizona, Shelton Connecticut, Chicago, Mettawa, and Vernon Hills, Illinois, Eatontown and Voorhees, New Jersey, North Las Vegas, Nevada, Herndon, Virginia, and Madison Wisconsin.
Fields of interest: Education, computer literacy/technology training; Education Children.
Type of support: Donated products; Employee matching gifts; Employee volunteer services; General/operating support; In-kind gifts.
Geographic limitations: Giving primarily in Chandler, AZ, Shelton CT, Chicago, Mettawa, and Vernon Hills, IL, Eatontown and Voorhees, NJ, North Las Vegas, NV, Herndon, VA, and Madison WI.
Support limitations: No support for political or religious organizations, or for local organizations that raise funds to send overseas. No grants to individuals, or for capital campaigns.
Publications: Application guidelines.
Application information: Applications accepted. Application form required.
Initial approach: Complete online application
Deadline(s): None
Final notification: 4 weeks for product donation requests

730
Celanese Americas Corporation
(formerly Hoechst Corporation)
550 U.S. Hwy. 202/206
Bedminster, NJ 07921-1537
(908) 901-4500

Company URL: http://www.celanese.com/index/about_home.html
Establishment information: Established in 2004.
Company type: Subsidiary of a public company
Business activities: Provides business services.
Business type (SIC): Business services/miscellaneous
Corporate officer: David N. Weidman, Chair., Pres., and C.E.O.
Board of director: David N. Weidman, Chair.
Giving statement: Giving through the Celanese Americas Foundation Inc.

Celanese Americas Foundation Inc
(formerly Hoechst Corporation Foundation)
1601 W. LBJ Fwy.
Dallas, TX 75234

Establishment information: Established in 1984 in NJ.
Donors: Hoechst Corp.; Celanese Americas Corp.
Financial data (yr. ended 12/31/11): Assets, $0 (M); expenditures, $0; qualifying distributions, $0.
Purpose and activities: The foundation supports organizations involved with education, sports, human services, and Judaism.
Type of support: Employee matching gifts.
Support limitations: No support for religious or fraternal organizations. No grants to individuals, or for general operating support for United Way-supported organizations; special projects of hospitals have low priority.
Application information: Applicants should submit the following:
1) copy of IRS Determination Letter
2) copy of most recent annual report/audited financial statement/990
Initial approach: None
Deadline(s): None
Officers and Trustees:* Chirstopher W. Jensen, Pres. and Treas.; John W. Howard*, V. P.; Dougles M. Madden*, V. P.; Gjon N. Nivica, Jr.*, Secy.
Number of staff: 1 full-time professional; 1 part-time professional.
EIN: 222577170

731
Celebrity International Inc.
100 W. 33rd St., Ste. 800
New York, NY 10001-2909 (212) 279-1616

Company URL: http://www.vitaminsbaby.com
Establishment information: Established in 1965.
Company type: Private company
Business activities: Manufactures baby apparel for newborns and infants.
Business type (SIC): Apparel, piece goods, and notions—wholesale
Financial profile for 2010: Number of employees, 35
Corporate officer: Eli Matalon, Pres. and C.E.O.
Giving statement: Giving through the Celebrity Foundation, Inc.

The Celebrity Foundation, Inc.
19667 Turnberry Way, Ste. 26D
Aventura, FL 33180-2514

Establishment information: Established in 2002 in FL.
Donors: Celebrity International, Inc.; Vitamins Playwear, Ltd.; Amar Industries, Inc.; Morris D. Matalon; Samuel Matalon; Eli Matalon; Michael Matalon; Luna Investments, Inc.
Financial data (yr. ended 09/30/12): Assets, $1,797,166 (M); gifts received, $70,000; expenditures, $194,253; qualifying distributions, $186,904; giving activities include $186,904 for 37 grants (high: $87,800; low: $36).
Fields of interest: Cancer; Jewish agencies & synagogues.
Geographic limitations: Giving primarily in NY.
Support limitations: No grants to individuals.
Application information: Applications not accepted. Unsolicited requests for funds not accepted.
Officer and Directors:* Morris D. Matalon*, Chair.; Eli Matalon; Michael Matalon; Samuel Matalon.
EIN: 810587000

732
Celgene Corporation
86 Morris Ave.
Summit, NJ 07901 (908) 673-9000
FAX: (908) 673-9001

Company URL: http://www.celgene.com/
Establishment information: Established in 1986.
Company type: Public company
Company ticker symbol and exchange: CELG/NASDAQ
International Securities Identification Number: US1510201049
Business activities: Operates biopharmaceutical company.
Business type (SIC): Drugs
Financial profile for 2012: Number of employees, 4,700; assets, $11,734,310,000; sales volume, $5,506,710,000; pre-tax net income, $1,681,490,000; expenses, $3,760,270,000; liabilities, $6,039,840,000
Fortune 1000 ranking: 2012—456th in revenues, 142nd in profits, and 354th in assets
Corporate officers: Robert J. Hugin, Chair., Pres., and C.E.O.; Perry A. Karsen, Exec. V.P. and C.O.O.; Jacqualyn A. Fouse, Ph.D., Exec. V.P. and C.F.O.
Board of directors: Robert J. Hugin, Chair.; Richard Barker, D.Phill.; Michael D. Casey; Carrie S. Cox; Rodman L. Drake; Michael A. Friedman, M.D.; Gilla Kaplan, Ph.D.; James Loughlin; Ernest Mario, Ph.D.
Giving statement: Giving through the Celgene Corporation Patient Assistance Program.
Company EIN: 222711928

Celgene Corporation Patient Assistance Program
86 Morris Ave.
Summit, NJ 07901-3915 (908) 673-9000
URL: http://www.celgenepatientsupport.com/financial_resources.aspx

Purpose and activities: Celgene offers free or low cost drugs to individuals who are unable to pay for their medication. Support is given on a national basis.
Fields of interest: Pharmacy/prescriptions.
Type of support: Donated products; Grants to individuals; In-kind gifts.
Geographic limitations: Giving on a national basis.
Application information: Applications accepted. Application form required.
Initial approach: Visit RxAssist website for application information

733
Cellco Partnership
(doing business as Verizon Wireless)
1 Verizon Way
Basking Ridge, NJ 07920 (908) 306-7000

Company URL: http://www.verizonwireless.com
Establishment information: Established in 1995.
Company type: Joint venture
Business activities: Provides wireless communications services.
Business type (SIC): Telephone communications
Financial profile for 2010: Number of employees, 4,300; sales volume, $63,400,000,000
Corporate officers: Lowell C. McAdam, Chair.; Daniel S. Mead, Pres. and C.E.O.; John G. Stratton, Exec. V.P. and C.O.O.; Ajay Waghray, C.I.O.; Andrew Davies, V.P. and C.F.O.; Marquett Smith, V.P., Corp. Comms.; M. Alan Gardner, V.P., Human Resources; Martha Delehanty, V.P., Human Resources
Board of director: Lowell C. McAdam, Chair.
Giving statement: Giving through the Verizon Wireless Corporate Giving Program.
Company EIN: 223372889

Verizon Wireless Corporate Giving Program
(formerly AirTouch Connections)
180 Washington Valley Rd.
Bedminster, NJ 07921-2120
URL: http://aboutus.verizonwireless.com/communityservice/hopeLine.html

Contact: Debra Lewis, Mgr., Public Affairs
Purpose and activities: Verizon Wireless makes charitable contributions to nonprofit organizations involved with domestic violence and on a case by case basis. Support is given in areas of company operations.
Fields of interest: Crime/violence prevention, domestic violence; Family services, domestic violence; General charitable giving.
Program:
HopeLine: Through the HopeLine program, Verizon Wireless supports programs designed to help prevent domestic violence and assist in the life rebuilding process for victims of domestic violence. In addition to making monetary donations, the company also distributes previously owned wireless handsets for the benefit of domestic violence victims and nonprofit advocacy organizations.
Type of support: Donated equipment; Donated products; General/operating support; Sponsorships.
Geographic limitations: Giving in areas of company operations.
Support limitations: No support for private foundations, religious organizations, fraternal, social, trade, veterans', or labor organizations, or regional or statewide organizations not of benefit to Verizon Wireless customers or employees. No grants to individuals, or for continuing support, contests, mass mailings, trips or tours, endowments, capital campaigns, memorials, books, magazines, or articles in professional journals, advertising, film or video production, or political campaigns or issues.

734
CEMEX, Inc.
920 Memorial City Way, Ste. 100
Houston, TX 77024 (713) 650-6200

Company URL: http://www.cemexusa.com
Establishment information: Established in 1930.
Company type: Subsidiary of a foreign company
Business activities: Manufactures cement and ready-mixed concrete.
Business type (SIC): Cement/hydraulic; concrete, gypsum, and plaster products
Financial profile for 2010: Number of employees, 500
Corporate officers: Karl Watson, Jr., Pres.; Leslie S. White, Exec. V.P. and Genl. Counsel; Richard G. Shapiro, Exec. V.P., Public Affairs and Mktg.
Giving statement: Giving through the CEMEX Foundation.

CEMEX Foundation
(formerly Southdown Foundation)
P.O. Box 1500
Houston, TX 77251-1500 (713) 650-6200
Application address: c/o Human Resources, CEMEX Inc., 92 Memorial City Way, Ste. 100, Houston, TX 77024

Establishment information: Established in 1993.
Donors: Medusa Corp.; CEMEX Corp.
Financial data (yr. ended 12/31/11): Assets, $6,132,538 (M); expenditures, $619,949; qualifying distributions, $607,790; giving activities include $607,790 for grants.
Purpose and activities: The foundation supports organizations involved with education, birth defects, human services, and the masonry trade.
Fields of interest: Higher education; Education; Genetic diseases and disorders; Women, centers/services; Human services; Business/industry.
Type of support: General/operating support.
Geographic limitations: Giving primarily on FL, NY, and OH.
Support limitations: No grants to individuals.
Application information: Applications accepted. Application form not required. Applicants should submit the following:
1) copy of IRS Determination Letter
2) detailed description of project and amount of funding requested
3) brief history of organization and description of its mission

Initial approach: Proposal
Deadline(s): None
Officers and Trustees:* Gilberto Perez*, Chair. and Pres.; Leslie S. White*, Secy.-Treas.; R. Frank Craddock, Jr.; Andrew M. Miller.
EIN: 346505254
Selected grants: The following grants are a representative sample of this grantmaker's funding activity:
$124,001 to University of Florida Foundation, Gainesville, FL, 2010.
$70,000 to Chico State CIM Patrons, Forest Ranch, CA, 2010.
$25,678 to Saint Agnes Academy, Houston, TX, 2010.
$18,403 to Wright State University Foundation, Dayton, OH, 2010.
$15,000 to American Heart Association, Houston, TX, 2010.
$6,564 to Stanford University, Stanford, CA, 2010.

735
Centene Corporation
Centene Plz.
7700 Forsyth Blvd.
St. Louis, MO 63105 (314) 725-4477
FAX: (212) 759-1260

Company URL: http://www.centene.com
Establishment information: Established in 1984.
Company type: Public company
Company ticker symbol and exchange: CNC/NYSE
Business activities: Operates medical service plan.
Business type (SIC): Insurance/accident and health
Financial profile for 2012: Number of employees, 6,800; assets, $2,741,680,000; sales volume, $8,667,610,000; pre-tax net income, -$11,620,000; expenses, $8,694,730,000; liabilities, $1,788,630,000
Fortune 1000 ranking: 2012—303rd in revenues, 881st in profits, and 783rd in assets

Corporate officers: Michael F. Neidorff, Chair., Pres., and C.E.O.; William N. Scheffel, Exec. V.P., C.F.O., and Treas.; Carol E. Goldman, Exec. V.P. and C.A.O.; Donald G. Imholz, Exec. V.P. and C.I.O.; Keith H. Williamson, Exec. V.P., Corp. Secy., and Genl. Counsel.; Jeffrey A. Schwaneke, Sr. V.P., C.A.O., and Cont.; Edmund E. Kroll, Sr. V.P., Finance
Board of directors: Michael F. Neidorff, Chair.; Orlando Ayala; Robert K. Ditmore; Frederick H. Eppinger, Jr.; Richard A. Gephardt; Pamela A. Joseph; John R. Roberts; David L. Steward; Tommy G. Thompson
Giving statement: Giving through the Centene Charitable Foundation and the Centene Foundation for Quality Health Care.
Company EIN: 421406317

The Centene Charitable Foundation

7700 Forsyth Blvd., Ste. 800
St. Louis, MO 63105-1837
E-mail: CenteneCharitableFoundation@centene.com ; URL: http://www.centene.com/about-us/responsible-enterprise/charitablefoundation/

Establishment information: Established in 2005 in MO.
Donor: Centene Management Company, LLC.
Financial data (yr. ended 05/31/12): Assets, $1,986,662 (M); gifts received, $3,500,000; expenditures, $4,596,608; qualifying distributions, $4,595,294; giving activities include $4,594,548 for 251 grants (high: $291,528; low: $100).
Purpose and activities: The foundation supports fairs and festivals and organizations involved with arts and culture, education, health, birth defects, sports, human services, community development, and minorities.
Fields of interest: Museums; Performing arts; Performing arts centers; Performing arts, dance; Performing arts, opera; Arts; Secondary school/education; Higher education; Education; Hospitals (general); Health care; Genetic diseases and disorders; Recreation, fairs/festivals; Athletics/sports, amateur leagues; Boys & girls clubs; Children, services; Developmentally disabled, centers & services; Human services; Community/economic development; United Ways and Federated Giving Programs Minorities.
Type of support: Annual campaigns; Building/renovation; Continuing support; General/operating support; Program development; Scholarship funds; Sponsorships.
Geographic limitations: Giving primarily in areas of company operations, with emphasis on St. Louis, MO.
Publications: Application guidelines.
Application information: Applications accepted. Application form required. Applicants should submit the following:
1) detailed description of project and amount of funding requested
2) copy of IRS Determination Letter
Initial approach: Complete online application
Deadline(s): 6 months prior to need
Final notification: 1 month
Officers: Michael F. Neidorff, Pres.; Keith H. Williamson, Secy.; William N. Scheffel, Treas.
EIN: 201298192
Selected grants: The following grants are a representative sample of this grantmaker's funding activity:
$497,180 to John F. Kennedy Center for the Performing Arts, Washington, DC, 2011.
$100,000 to State of Saint Louis Foundation, Saint Louis, MO, 2011. For general fund.
$100,000 to Urban League, National, New York, NY, 2011.
$86,468 to Boys and Girls Club, Mathews-Dickey, Saint Louis, MO, 2011.
$50,000 to Provident, Inc., Saint Louis, MO, 2011. For general fund.
$48,500 to Manhattan School of Music, New York, NY, 2011.
$48,000 to National Marfan Foundation, Port Washington, NY, 2011.
$40,000 to Wisconsin Womens Health Foundation, Madison, WI, 2011. For general fund.
$26,975 to American Liver Foundation, Saint Louis, MO, 2011.
$25,000 to Saint Louis Sports Foundation, Saint Louis, MO, 2011. For general fund.

The Centene Foundation for Quality Health Care

Centene Pl.
7700 Forsyth Blvd., Ste. 800
St. Louis, MO 63105
URL: http://www.centene.com/about-us/responsible-enterprise/centene-foundation-for-quality-healthcare/

Establishment information: Established in 2004 in MO.
Donors: The Centene Charitable Foundation; Centene Managment Co., LLC.
Financial data (yr. ended 05/31/11): Assets, $561,503 (M); gifts received, $528,042; expenditures, $42,418; qualifying distributions, $37,459; giving activities include $32,500 for 2 grants (high: $17,500; low: $15,000).
Purpose and activities: The foundation supports programs designed to improve the quality, access, effectiveness, and value of healthcare for low-income families and individuals. Special emphasis is directed toward indigent care and prevention; cultural diversity; collaborative initiatives; and public policy.
Fields of interest: Health care.
Programs:

Collaborations: The foundation supports collaborations that seek to implement innovative approaches to healthy communities. Special emphasis is directed toward collaborations that are inclusive of the target populations, health care professionals, faith-based and community-based organizations, and local governments; and programs that encourage philanthropy in the area of health.

Cultural Diversity: The foundation supports programs designed to increase diversity in the health field in the areas of recruitment, retention, and recognition. Special emphasis is directed toward cultural diversity in the health field; the availability of trained and certified medical interpreters; effective life skills to live in a multi-cultural society; and programs that increase cultural competency from awareness to proficiency in the health field.

Increasing Access to Quality Healthcare: The foundation supports programs designed to increase access to primary care and prevention. Special emphasis is directed toward health literacy; initiatives that improve the quality of medical interpreters; direct access to primary healthcare for women and children; and increasing physical activity, improving nutritional habits, and decreasing adverse behaviors including smoking and drinking among youth.

Public Policy: The foundation supports programs designed to educate local, state, and federal policy makers to identify innovative approaches that increase the availability of care, enhance the quality of care, and manage the cost of care.

Type of support: General/operating support; Matching/challenge support; Program development; Seed money.
Application information: Applications not accepted. Unsolicited requests for funds not accepted.
Officers and Board Members:* Cary D. Hobbs*, Chair.; Kathy Bradley-Wells, Pres.; Daniel J. Godar*, Secy.; William N. Scheffel*, Treas.; Mary Eggert; Edward Fischer; Gloria Wilder; Shelly Steward.
EIN: 201516497

736
The Center for Business Intelligence

600 Unicorn Park Dr.
Woburn, MA 01801 (339) 298-2100

Company URL: http://ttp://www.cbinet.com
Establishment information: Established in 1995.
Company type: Subsidiary of a private company
Business activities: Operates biotechnology, pharmaceutical and healthcare conferences company.
Business type (SIC): Business services/miscellaneous
Corporate officer: Kelly Rose, Mgr.
Giving statement: Giving through the Center for Business Intelligence Corporate Giving Program.

The Center for Business Intelligence Corporate Giving Program

600 Unicorn Park Dr.
Woburn, MA 01801 (339) 298-2100
URL: http://www.cbinet.com

737
Center Ice, LLC

(doing business as Tampa Bay Lightning)
401 Channelside Dr.
Tampa Bay Times Forum
Tampa, FL 33602-5400 (813) 301-6500

Company URL: http://www.tampabaylightning.com
Establishment information: Established in 1992.
Company type: Subsidiary of a private company
Business activities: Operates professional ice hockey club.
Business type (SIC): Commercial sports
Corporate officers: Jeff Vinik, Chair.; Thomas S. Wilson, C.E.O.; Ronald J. Campbell, Pres.; Harry Hutt, Exec. V.P., Corp. Sales and Mktg.; Bill Wickett, Exec. V.P., Comms.
Board of director: Jeff Vinik, Chair.
Giving statement: Giving through the Tampa Bay Lightning Corporate Giving Program and the Lightning Foundation, Inc.

Tampa Bay Lightning Corporate Giving Program

c/o Community Rels.
401 Channelside Dr.
Tampa, FL 33602-5400 (813) 301-6607
FAX: (813) 301-1494; URL: http://lightning.nhl.com/club/page.htm?id=50496

Purpose and activities: The Tampa Bay Lightning makes charitable contributions of memorabilia to nonprofit organizations on a case by case basis. Support is given primarily in the Tampa Bay, Florida, area.

Fields of interest: Education; Athletics/sports, winter sports; General charitable giving Youth.
Type of support: Donated products; In-kind gifts; Income development.
Geographic limitations: Giving primarily in areas of company operations in the Tampa Bay, FL, area.
Publications: Application guidelines.
Application information: Applications accepted. Proposals should be submitted using organization letterhead. Support is limited to 1 contribution per organization during any given year. The Community Relations Department handles giving. Application form not required. Applicants should submit the following:
1) name, address and phone number of organization
2) detailed description of project and amount of funding requested
3) contact person
Proposals should indicate the type of fundraiser and the date, time, and location of the event.
Initial approach: Mail or fax proposal to headquarters for memorabilia donations
Copies of proposal: 1
Deadline(s): 6 weeks prior to need for memorabilia donations

Lightning Foundation, Inc.

401 Channelside Dr.
Tampa, FL 33602-5400 (813) 301-6500
URL: http://lightning.nhl.com/club/page.htm?id=50496

Establishment information: Established in FL.
Contact: Nancy Crane, Exec. Dir.
Financial data (yr. ended 12/31/11): Revenue, $2,712,630; assets, $4,021,292 (M); gifts received, $2,206,338; expenditures, $1,497,412; program services expenses, $1,281,307; giving activities include $1,043,112 for 25 grants (high: $90,221; low: $5,300).
Purpose and activities: The foundation is dedicated to the support of local organizations that enrich the lives of those living throughout the Tampa Bay community through focusing its resources on advancing amateur hockey and educational enrichment opportunities for children, along with medical research and treatment for those in need.
Fields of interest: Education; Cancer; Medical research; Athletics/sports, amateur leagues; Athletics/sports, winter sports; Boys & girls clubs; Boy scouts; Girl scouts; YM/YWCAs & YM/YWHAs.
Program:
Grants: The foundation awards grants, ranging from $2,500 to $10,000, to programs focusing on amateur hockey, educational enrichment opportunities for children and families, and medical research and treatment.
Geographic limitations: Giving primarily in the Tampa Bay, FL area.
Publications: Application guidelines.
Application information: Applications accepted. Requests must be typed on official organization letterhead. Donations will only be granted to charitable or nonprofit organizations, or events, hosted in the Tampa Bay area and surrounding local communities.
Initial approach: Download application form
Deadline(s): Six weeks prior to the event date
Officer: Nancy Crane, Exec. Dir.
Directors: Ronald J. Campell; Sean Henry; Bill Wickett.
EIN: 593542305

738
CenterPoint Energy, Inc.

1111 Louisiana St.
Houston, TX 77002 (713) 207-1111
FAX: (713) 207-3169

Company URL: http://www.centerpointenergy.com
Establishment information: Established in 1882.
Company type: Public company
Company ticker symbol and exchange: CNP/NYSE
Business activities: Operates public utility holding company; generates, transmits, and distributes electricity.
Business type (SIC): Electric services; holding company
Financial profile for 2012: Assets, $22,900,000,000; sales volume, $7,500,000,000
Fortune 1000 ranking: 2012—344th in revenues, 383rd in profits, and 220th in assets
Forbes 2000 ranking: 2012—1140th in sales, 1341st in profits, and 900th in assets
Corporate officers: Milton Carroll, Chair.; David M. McClanahan, Pres. and C.E.O.; Scott M. Prochazka, Exec. V.P. and C.O.O.; Gary L. Whitlock, Exec. V.P. and C.F.O.; Scott E. Rozzell, Exec. V.P., Genl. Counsel, and Corp. Secy.
Board of directors: Milton Carroll, Chair.; Michael P. Johnson; Janiece M. Longoria; David M. McClanahan; Susan O. Rheney; R. A. Walker; Peter S. Wareing
Subsidiaries: CenterPoint Energy Houston Electric, LLC, Houston, TX; CenterPoint Energy Resources Corp., Minneapolis, MN
Giving statement: Giving through the CenterPoint Energy, Inc. Corporate Giving Program.
Company EIN: 740694415

CenterPoint Energy, Inc. Corporate Giving Program

(formerly Reliant Energy, Incorporated Corporate Giving Program)
P.O. Box 4567
Houston, TX 77210-4567 (713) 207-1111
E-mail: Diane.Hasell@CenterPointEnergy.com; Grants application addresses: TX/Corporate, CenterPoint Energy, Diane Hasell, P.O. Box 1700, Houston, TX 77251, e-mail: Diane.Hasell@CenterPointEnergy.com; for Arkansas, Louisiana, Mississippi, and Oklahoma: CenterPoint Energy, Rose McQuillon, P.O. Box 1700, Houston, TX 77251, e-mail: Rose.McQuillon@CenterPointEnergy.com; for Minnesota: CenterPoint Energy, Jean Krause, 800 LaSalle Avenue S., Minneapolis, MN 55402, e-mail: Jean.Krause@CenterPointEnergy.com; sponsorships contact: Alicia Dixon, Corp. Comms., tel.: (713) 207-5885, e-mail: Alicia.Dixon@CenterPointEnergy.com; URL: http://www.centerpointenergy.com/community/AR/

Contact: Diane Hasell
Purpose and activities: CenterPoint Energy makes charitable contributions to nonprofit organizations involved with education, community development, the environment, civic issues, and health and human services. Support is given primarily in areas of company operations.
Fields of interest: Elementary/secondary education; Higher education; Education; Environment; Health care, infants; Health care, blood supply; Health care; Cancer; Employment; Food services; Disasters, preparedness/services; Human services; Community/economic development; Military/veterans' organizations; Public affairs.
Type of support: Annual campaigns; Emergency funds; Employee volunteer services; General/operating support; In-kind gifts; Sponsorships.
Geographic limitations: Giving primarily in areas of company operations in AR, LA, MN, MS, OK, and TX.
Support limitations: No support for political, or religious organizations, or sports or athletic programs. No grants to national organizations. No grants to individuals, or for capital campaigns, endowments, start-ups, fundraising, conferences, travel, or multi-year funding.
Publications: Application guidelines; Corporate giving report.
Application information: Applications accepted. Proposals should be limited to 4 or 5 pages, excluding attachments. Application form not required. Applicants should submit the following:
1) timetable for implementation and evaluation of project
2) results expected from proposed grant
3) statement of problem project will address
4) copy of IRS Determination Letter
5) brief history of organization and description of its mission
6) copy of most recent annual report/audited financial statement/990
7) how project's results will be evaluated or measured
8) list of company employees involved with the organization
9) what distinguishes project from others in its field
10) listing of board of directors, trustees, officers and other key people and their affiliations
11) detailed description of project and amount of funding requested
12) plans for cooperation with other organizations, if any
13) copy of current year's organizational budget and/or project budget
14) listing of additional sources and amount of support
Proposals should include a Form W-9, and a statement regarding whether the program being proposed has a broad base of support.
Initial approach: Proposal to headquarters
Copies of proposal: 1
Deadline(s): June 1 to July 31

739
CenterPoint Energy Resources Corp.

800 LaSalle Ave.
P.O. Box 59038
Minneapolis, MN 55459-0038
(612) 321-5099

Company URL: http://www.centerpointenergy.com/about/companyoverview
Company type: Subsidiary of a public company
Ultimate parent company: CenterPoint Energy, Inc.
International Securities Identification Number: US15189T1079
Business activities: Transmits and distributes natural gas.
Business type (SIC): Gas production and distribution
Financial profile for 2009: Number of employees, 20
Corporate officers: Milton Carroll, Chair.; David M. McClanahan, Pres. and C.E.O.; Gary L. Whitlock, Exec. V.P. and C.F.O.; Scott M. Prochazka, Exec. V.P. and C.O.O.; Scott E. Rozzell, Exec. V.P., Genl. Counsel, and Corp. Secy.
Board of director: Milton Carroll, Chair.
Division: Minnesota Gas, Minneapolis, MN

Giving statement: Giving through the Minnesota Gas Corporate Giving Program.

Minnesota Gas Corporate Giving Program

(formerly CenterPoint Energy Minnegasco Corporate Giving Program)
800 LaSalle Ave., HQ14
Minneapolis, MN 55402-2006
E-mail: jeankrause@centerpointenergy.com;
URL: http://www.centerpointenergy.com/community/inthecommunity/MN/

Contact: Suzanne Pierazek, Mgr., Community Rels.; Jean Krause, Dir., Community and Public Rels.
Purpose and activities: Minnesota Gas makes charitable contributions to nonprofit organizations involved with the environment and housing. Support is given primarily in areas of company operations.
Fields of interest: Environment; Housing/shelter.
Type of support: Employee volunteer services; General/operating support; Sponsorships.
Geographic limitations: Giving primarily in areas of company operations in MN.
Support limitations: No support for United Way-supported organizations or religious or political organizations. No grants to individuals, or for travel, conferences, fundraising, capital campaigns, endowments, contingencies, reserve purposes, debt reduction, national fund drives, continuing support, or athletic activities.
Publications: Application guidelines.
Application information: Applications accepted. The Community Relations Department handles giving. Application form required.
Initial approach: Download application form and mail to headquarters
Copies of proposal: 1
Deadline(s): July 1
Final notification: Following review
Administrators: Jean Krause, Dir., Community Rels.; Suzanne Pierazek, Mgr., Community Rels.
Number of staff: None.

740
CentiMark Corporation

12 Grandview Cir.
Canonsburg, PA 15317-8533
(724) 743-7777

Company URL: http://www.centimark.com/
Establishment information: Established in 1967.
Company type: Private company
Business activities: Operates a commercial and industrial roofing contracting company.
Business type (SIC): Contractors/roofing, siding, and sheet metal work
Corporate officers: Edward B. Dunlap, Chair. and C.E.O.; Timothy M. Dunlap, Pres. and C.O.O.; John L. Heisey, Exec. V.P. and C.F.O.; Thor DiCesare, Sr. V.P. and Genl. Counsel; Greg Wilson, V.P. and C.I.O.; Landon Connolly, V.P., Human Resources
Board of director: Edward B. Dunlap, Chair.
Giving statement: Giving through the CentiMark Foundation.

CentiMark Foundation

12 Grandview Cir.
Canonsburg, PA 15317-8533 (724) 514-8572
E-mail: Kathy.Slencak@CentiMark.Com

Establishment information: Established in 2007 in PA.
Donors: Timothy M. Dunlap; CentiMark Corp.
Contact: Kathy Slencak, Mgr., Community Rels.
Financial data (yr. ended 12/31/11): Assets, $219,588 (M); gifts received, $2,000,000; expenditures, $1,847,993; qualifying distributions, $1,844,105; giving activities include $1,844,105 for grants.
Purpose and activities: The foundation supports organizations involved with education, health, hunger, housing, human services, and Catholicism.
Fields of interest: Elementary/secondary education; Higher education; Education; Hospitals (general); Health care; Food services; Food banks; Food distribution, meals on wheels; Housing/shelter; Salvation Army; Children/youth, services; Family services; Pregnancy centers; Developmentally disabled, centers & services; Homeless, human services; Human services; Catholic agencies & churches.
Type of support: Capital campaigns; General/operating support; Program development.
Geographic limitations: Giving primarily in PA.
Application information: Applications not accepted. Contributes only to pre-selected organizations.
Officers and Trustees:* Edward B. Dunlap, Jr.*, Pres.; Timothy M. Dunlap*, V.P.; Thor D. DiCesare, Secy.; John A. Rudzik*, Treas. and Exec. Dir.; John L. Heisey.
EIN: 208911858
Selected grants: The following grants are a representative sample of this grantmaker's funding activity:
$95,000 to Washington City Mission, Washington, PA, 2011.
$64,000 to Blessings in a Backpack, Louisville, KY, 2011.
$54,355 to Washington City Mission, Washington, PA, 2011.
$25,000 to North Hills Affordable Housing Task Force, Pittsburgh, PA, 2011. For operating expenses.
$15,000 to Allegheny Valley School, Coraopolis, PA, 2011.
$15,000 to Sisters Place, Clairton, PA, 2011. For operating expenses.
$10,000 to Holy Family Foundation, Pittsburgh, PA, 2011. For operating expenses.
$5,000 to Cancer League of Colorado, Englewood, CO, 2011. For operating expenses.
$5,000 to Dialysis Clinic, Nashville, TN, 2011. For operating expenses.
$5,000 to Early Learning Institute, Pittsburgh, PA, 2011. For operating expenses.

741
Central Maine Power Company

(also known as CMP)
83 Edison Dr.
Augusta, ME 04336 (207) 623-3521

Company URL: http://www.cmpco.com
Establishment information: Established in 1899.
Company type: Subsidiary of a public company
Business activities: Generates, transmits, and distributes electricity.
Business type (SIC): Electric services
Corporate officers: Sara J. Burns, Pres. and C.E.O.; Eric N. Stinneford, V.P., Cont., and Treas.
Board of directors: Sara J. Burns; Robert D. Kump; F. Michael McClain; Wesley Von Schack
Subsidiary: Maine Electric Power Co., Inc., Augusta, ME
Giving statement: Giving through the Central Maine Power Company Contributions Program.

Central Maine Power Company Contributions Program

c/o Public Affairs Dept.
83 Edison Dr.
Augusta, ME 04336-0002 (800) 565-0121
URL: http://www.cmpco.com/GivingBack/inthecommunity/corpspon.html

Purpose and activities: Central Maine Power contributes primarily to schools or educational enrichment programs that raise math, science, and technology achievement or that support aspirations for educational and career achievement. Support is given primarily in areas of company operations in Maine.
Fields of interest: Education; Science; Mathematics; Engineering/technology.
Type of support: Donated equipment; Employee volunteer services; General/operating support; Sponsorships.
Geographic limitations: Giving primarily in areas of company operations in ME.
Support limitations: No support for United Way-supported organizations. No grants to individuals.
Publications: Application guidelines.
Application information: Applications accepted. A contributions committee reviews all requests. Application form not required. Applicants should submit the following:
1) name, address and phone number of organization
2) brief history of organization and description of its mission
3) detailed description of project and amount of funding requested
4) copy of current year's organizational budget and/or project budget
Initial approach: Proposal to headquarters
Copies of proposal: 1
Final notification: Following review
Number of staff: 1 part-time professional; 1 part-time support.

742
The Central National Bank

802 N. Washington St.
P.O. Box 700
Junction City, KS 66441-2447
(785) 238-4114
FAX: (785) 761-2953

Company URL: http://www.centralnational.com
Establishment information: Established in 1884.
Company type: Subsidiary of a private company
Business activities: Operates bank holding company; operates commercial bank.
Business type (SIC): Banks/commercial; holding company
Corporate officers: William C. McAdams, C.E.O.; Ed C. Rolfs, Pres.
Giving statement: Giving through the Central Charities Foundation Inc.

Central Charities Foundation Inc.

P.O. Box 700
Junction City, KS 66441-0700

Establishment information: Established in 1997 in KS.
Donors: Central National Bank; Edward C. Rolfs; Edward J. Rolfs; Mary Beerhalter.
Financial data (yr. ended 12/31/11): Assets, $2,769,355 (M); gifts received, $24,556; expenditures, $203,908; qualifying distributions,

$184,196; giving activities include $182,196 for 8 grants (high: $12,387; low: $68).
Purpose and activities: The foundation supports organizations involved with education, youth development, children and youth, senior citizen services, and Christianity.
Fields of interest: Higher education; Education; Boy scouts; Girl scouts; American Red Cross; Salvation Army; YM/YWCAs & YM/YWHAs; Children/youth, services; Aging, centers/services; United Ways and Federated Giving Programs; Christian agencies & churches.
Type of support: General/operating support.
Geographic limitations: Giving limited to Junction City and Geary County, KS.
Application information: Applications accepted. Application form required.
Initial approach: Proposal
Deadline(s): None
Directors: Sara Girard; Christine A. Munson; Edward J. Rolfs; Betty Waters.
EIN: 486143983

743
Central National-Gottesman, Inc.

3 Manhattanville Rd.
Purchase, NY 10577-2110 (914) 696-9000
FAX: (914) 696-1066

Company URL: http://www.cng-inc.com/
Establishment information: Established in 1886.
Company type: Private company
Business activities: Sells and distributes pulp and paper.
Business type (SIC): Paper and paper products—wholesale; durable goods—wholesale
Financial profile for 2012: Number of employees, 1,000; sales volume, $3,000,000,000
Corporate officers: Kenneth L. Wallach, Chair. and C.E.O.; Jim Panos, C.I.O.; Louise Caputo, V.P., Human Resources; Edward J. Rapa, V.P., Opers.; David Jones, V.P., Finance; Steven Eigen, Treas.
Board of director: Kenneth L. Wallach, Chair.
International operations: Spain
Giving statement: Giving through the Central National-Gottesman Foundation.

The Central National-Gottesman Foundation

3 Manhattanville Rd.
Purchase, NY 10577-2110

Establishment information: Established in 1981 in NY.
Donor: Central National-Gottesman, Inc.
Contact: Steven Eigen, Treas.
Financial data (yr. ended 12/31/11): Assets, $19,261,546 (M); expenditures, $1,311,276; qualifying distributions, $1,181,057; giving activities include $402,500 for 65 grants (high: $125,000; low: $100) and $601,552 for 27 grants to individuals (high: $40,000; low: $5,020).
Purpose and activities: The foundation supports hospitals and organizations involved with higher education, pulp and paper industry, and the visually impaired.
Fields of interest: Higher education; Hospitals (general); Business/industry; United Ways and Federated Giving Programs; Jewish federated giving programs Blind/visually impaired.
Program:
Employee Scholarship Program: The foundation awards college scholarships to the children of full-time employees of Central National-Gottesman and its Lindenmeyer divisions.
Type of support: Employee-related scholarships; General/operating support.
Geographic limitations: Giving primarily in NY.
Support limitations: No grants to individuals (except for employee-related scholarships).
Application information: Applications not accepted. Contributes only through employee-related scholarships and to pre-selected organizations.
Officers and Director: Kenneth L. Wallach, Pres.; Peter Sigefried, Secy.; Steven Eigen, Treas.; Andrew Wallach.
EIN: 133047546
Selected grants: The following grants are a representative sample of this grantmaker's funding activity:
$76,400 to New York Public Library, New York, NY, 2009.
$57,500 to UJA-Federation of New York, New York, NY, 2009.
$55,000 to Bates College, Lewiston, ME, 2009.
$50,000 to City Harvest, New York, NY, 2009.
$50,000 to National Book Foundation, New York, NY, 2009.
$40,000 to Harvard University, Cambridge, MA, 2009.
$25,000 to Council on Foreign Relations, New York, NY, 2009.
$25,000 to White Plains Hospital Center, White Plains, NY, 2009.
$18,350 to Poets and Writers, New York, NY, 2009.
$12,416 to Amherst College, Amherst, MA, 2009.

744
Central New Mexico Electric Cooperative

810 1st St.
P.O. Box 669
Moriarty, NM 87035 (505) 832-4483

Company URL: http://www.cnmec.org
Establishment information: Established in 1939.
Company type: Cooperative
Business activities: Generates, transmits, and distributes electricity.
Business type (SIC): Electric services
Corporate officers: Jerry Britton, Pres.; Alena Brandenberger, C.F.O.; J. T. Turner, Secy.; Wayne Connell, Treas.
Board of directors: Leandro Abeyta; Jerry Britton; Wayne Connell; Duane Frost; Kenneth Shaw; J.T. Turner; Mike Valdez; Phil Wallin
Giving statement: Giving through the Central New Mexico Electric Education Foundation.

Central New Mexico Electric Education Foundation

P.O. Box 157
Mountainair, NM 87036-0157 (505) 832-4483
Application address: P.O. Box 669, Moriarty, NM 87035, tel.: (505) 832-4483; URL: http://www.cnmec.org/

Establishment information: Established in 1990 in NM.
Donor: Central New Mexico Electric Cooperative.
Contact: Dolores Jones
Financial data (yr. ended 12/31/11): Assets, $88,161 (M); gifts received, $3,187; expenditures, $6,316; qualifying distributions, $4,750; giving activities include $4,750 for 15 grants to individuals (high: $500; low: $250).
Purpose and activities: The foundation awards college scholarships to members and the children of members of Central New Mexico Electric Cooperative.
Fields of interest: Higher education.
Type of support: Scholarships—to individuals.
Geographic limitations: Giving limited to areas of company operations in NM.
Publications: Application guidelines; Grants list.
Application information: Applications accepted. Application form required.
Applications must include 3 letters of recommendation and official transcripts.
Initial approach: Download application form and mail to foundation
Deadline(s): Feb. 1
Officers: Jerry Britton, Pres.; Duane Frost, V.P.; J. T. Turner, Secy.; Wayne Connell, Treas.
Trustees: Leandro Abeyta; Mike Valdez; Phil Wallin.
EIN: 850366030

745
Central State Bank

301 Iowa Ave.
P.O. Box 146
Muscatine, IA 52761-3850 (563) 263-3131

Company URL: http://www.centralstate.com
Establishment information: Established in 1933.
Company type: Subsidiary of a private company
Business activities: Operates commercial bank.
Business type (SIC): Banks/commercial
Corporate officers: Gregory J. Kistler, Chair.; John B. Rigler, Vice-Chair.; Robert J. Howard, Pres. and C.E.O.; Roger Kline, C.F.O.
Board of directors: Gregory J. Kistler, Chair.; John B. Rigler, Vice-Chair.
Giving statement: Giving through the Central Bancshares Charitable Foundation.

The Central Bancshares Charitable Foundation

c/o Jeff Pattison
301 Iowa Ave.
Muscatine, IA 52761-3837
Application address: 21 E. Main St., Galesburg, IL 61401; 1060 W. Monroe St., Washington, IA 52353; 140 Holiday Rd., Coralville, IA 52241

Establishment information: Established in 2004 in IA.
Donors: Central State Bank; The Farmers & Mechanics Bank; West Chester Savings Bank.
Contact: Greg Kistler, Dir.; Douglas Sanders, Dir.; Steven Olson, Dir.; Daniel Uphoff, Dir.
Financial data (yr. ended 12/31/11): Assets, $193,834 (M); gifts received, $82,625; expenditures, $82,515; qualifying distributions, $82,515; giving activities include $82,515 for 171 grants (high: $14,250; low: $25).
Purpose and activities: The foundation supports community foundations and organizations involved with arts and culture, education, and human services.
Fields of interest: Historical activities; Arts; Secondary school/education; Higher education; Libraries (public); Education; American Red Cross; YM/YWCAs & YM/YWHAs; Human services; Foundations (community); United Ways and Federated Giving Programs.
Type of support: Annual campaigns; Continuing support; General/operating support; Program development; Scholarship funds; Sponsorships.

Geographic limitations: Giving primarily in Muscatine, IA.
Application information: Applications accepted. Application form not required.
Initial approach: Proposal
Deadline(s): None
Directors: Gregory J. Kistler; Steven C. Olson; Jeff Pattison; Doug Sanders; Dan Uphoff.
EIN: 200510383

746
Central Storage & Warehouse Company

4309 Cottage Grove Rd.
Madison, WI 53716-1201 (608) 221-7600

Company URL: http://www.csw-wi.com
Establishment information: Established in 1947.
Company type: Private company
Business activities: Provides trucking and storage services.
Business type (SIC): Trucking and courier services, except by air
Corporate officers: Kenneth R. Williams, Chair.; John Winegarden, C.E.O.; Jeannie Plautz, Pres.; Jack Williams, V.P., Opers; Steve Sharratt, V.P., Sales and Mktg.
Board of director: Kenneth R. Williams, Chair.
Giving statement: Giving through the C. J. Williams Central Storage Foundation, Inc.

C. J. Williams Central Storage Foundation, Inc.

4309 Cottage Grove Rd.
P.O. Box 7034
Madison, WI 53707-7034 (608) 221-7600

Establishment information: Established in 1984 in WI.
Donors: Central Storage & Warehouse Co.; Kenneth R. Williams.
Contact: Kenneth R. Williams, Pres. and Treas.
Financial data (yr. ended 12/31/11): Assets, $1,021 (M); gifts received, $30,000; expenditures, $30,000; qualifying distributions, $30,000; giving activities include $30,000 for grants.
Purpose and activities: The foundation supports organizations involved with arts and culture.
Fields of interest: Arts.
Type of support: Annual campaigns; General/operating support.
Geographic limitations: Giving primarily in FL and WI.
Support limitations: No grants to individuals.
Application information: Applications accepted. Application form not required.
Initial approach: Letter
Deadline(s): None
Officers: Kenneth R. Williams, Pres. and Treas.; Leslie Jean Plautz, V.P. and Secy.
EIN: 391524830

747
Central Valley Electric Cooperative, Inc.

1505 N. 13th St.
P.O. Box 230
Artesia, NM 88210-3404 (575) 746-3571

Company URL: http://www.cvecoop.org/
Establishment information: Incorporated in June 23, 1937.
Company type: Cooperative
Business activities: Generates, transmits, and distributes electricity.
Business type (SIC): Electric services
Financial profile for 2012: Number of employees, 80; assets, $125,370,716; liabilities, $125,370,716
Corporate officers: Darrell W. Atkins, Pres.; Wesley Pilley, Secy.-Treas.
Board of directors: Darrell Atkins; Michael Bennett; Larry Benedict; Jack Case; Jason Ciempa; Wesley Pilley; Chuck Wagner
Giving statement: Giving through the Central Valley Electric Education Foundation.

Central Valley Electric Education Foundation

P.O. Box 230
Artesia, NM 88211-0230 (505) 746-3571
URL: http://www.cvecoop.org/content/scholarships

Donor: Central Valley Electric Cooperative, Inc.
Contact: Mike Anderson
Financial data (yr. ended 12/31/11): Assets, $1,243,537 (M); gifts received, $136,675; expenditures, $132,463; qualifying distributions, $132,000; giving activities include $132,000 for grants.
Purpose and activities: The foundation awards college scholarships to members and the children of members of Central Valley Electric Cooperative attending a college or university in New Mexico.
Fields of interest: Higher education.
Type of support: Scholarships—to individuals.
Geographic limitations: Giving limited to NM.
Publications: Application guidelines.
Application information: Applications accepted. Scholarships of up to $2,000 are awarded. Applicants must maintain a 2.5 GPA on a 4.0 scale. Multi-year funding is not automatic. Application form required.
Applications should include official transcripts and 3 letters of recommendation.
Initial approach: Download application form and mail to foundation
Deadline(s): Apr. 15
Final notification: 60 days
Trustees: Darrell Atkins; Wesley Pilley; Chuck Wagner.
EIN: 850323120

748
Century 21 Department Stores, Inc.

22 Cortlandt St., Fl. 33
New York, NY 10007-3140 (212) 227-9092
FAX: (212) 528-0758

Company URL: http://www.c21stores.com
Establishment information: Established in 1961.
Company type: Private company
Business activities: Operates department stores.
Business type (SIC): Department stores
Financial profile for 2009: Number of employees, 2,105
Corporate officers: Raymond Giroi, Chair.; Abraham Gindi, C.E.O.; J. Jindi, Pres.; Gerald Shotts, C.O.O.; Ezra Sultan, C.F.O.
Board of director: Raymond Gindi, Chair.
Giving statement: Giving through the Century 21 Associates Foundation, Inc.

Century 21 Associates Foundation, Inc.

(formerly Gindi Associates Foundation, Inc.)
22 Cortlandt St.
New York, NY 10007-3107

Establishment information: Established in 1982 in NJ.
Donors: Century 21, Inc.; ASG Equities LLC.
Financial data (yr. ended 05/31/12): Assets, $5,809,396 (M); gifts received, $4,000,000; expenditures, $6,501,415; qualifying distributions, $6,501,411; giving activities include $6,450,686 for 1,163 grants (high: $1,000,000; low: $18).
Purpose and activities: The foundation supports organizations involved with education, human services, and Judaism.
Fields of interest: Higher education; Theological school/education; Education; Human services; Jewish federated giving programs; Jewish agencies & synagogues.
Type of support: Continuing support; General/operating support; Sponsorships.
Geographic limitations: Giving primarily in NJ and Brooklyn and New York, NY.
Support limitations: No grants to individuals.
Application information: Applications not accepted. Contributes only to pre-selected organizations.
Trustees: Abraham Gindi; Raymond Gindi.
EIN: 222412138

749
Century Construction Company, Inc.

7416 Forest Hill Ave.
Richmond, VA 23225 (804) 330-4400

Company URL: http://www.centuryconstruction.com
Establishment information: Established in 1963.
Company type: Private company
Business activities: Provides nonresidential general contract construction services.
Business type (SIC): Contractors/general nonresidential building
Corporate officers: Stuart K. Morgan, Chair.; Mark G. Meland, Pres.; Neil A. Palmer, V.P., Sales
Board of director: Stuart K. Morgan, Chair.
Giving statement: Giving through the Century Foundation.

The Century Foundation

7416 Forest Hill Ave.
Richmond, VA 23225-1528 (804) 330-4400
URL: http://www.centuryconstruction.com

Establishment information: Established in 1986 in VA.
Donors: Century Construction Co., Inc.; Construction Assocs.
Contact: William G. Hollowell, Dir.

Financial data (yr. ended 12/31/11): Assets, $77,109 (M); expenditures, $4,735; qualifying distributions, $4,000; giving activities include $4,000 for 4 grants (high: $1,000; low: $1,000).
Purpose and activities: The foundation awards college scholarships to individuals for research and training in the construction industry.
Fields of interest: Education.
Type of support: Scholarships—to individuals.
Geographic limitations: Giving primarily in VA.
Application information: Applications accepted. Application form required.
Initial approach: Proposal
Deadline(s): May 21st
Directors: William G. Hollowell; Stuart K. Morgan.
EIN: 541384796

750
Century Life Assurance Company

101 N. Broadway Ave., Ste. 950
Oklahoma City, OK 73102-8403
(405) 270-1086

Company URL: http://
Establishment information: Established in 1988.
Company type: Subsidiary of a public company
Business activities: Sells credit life insurance, credit accident and health insurance, and life insurance.
Business type (SIC): Insurance/surety; insurance/life; insurance/accident and health
Corporate officer: Dee White, Pres.
Giving statement: Giving through the BancFirst Charitable Foundation.

BancFirst Charitable Foundation

P.O. Box 26788
Oklahoma City, OK 73126-0788

Establishment information: Established as a company-sponsored operating foundation in 1989 in OK.
Donors: American Trend Life Insurance Co.; Century Life Assurance Co.; BancFirst.
Financial data (yr. ended 12/31/11): Assets, $1,143,034 (M); expenditures, $73,458; qualifying distributions, $69,681; giving activities include $67,500 for 3 grants (high: $50,000; low: $7,500).
Purpose and activities: The foundation supports organizations involved with arts and culture and children services.
Fields of interest: Museums (history); Performing arts, theater; Arts; Children, services.
Type of support: General/operating support; Sponsorships.
Geographic limitations: Giving limited to OK.
Application information: Applications not accepted. Unsolicited requests for funds not accepted.
Officers and Directors:* H. E. Rainbolt*, Pres.; David E. Rainbolt*, V.P.; Debbie Hodde, Secy.-Treas.
EIN: 731343258

751
CenturyLink, Inc.

(doing business as CenturyLink)
(formerly CenturyTel, Inc.)
100 CenturyTel Dr.
Monroe, LA 71203 (318) 388-9000
FAX: (318) 388-9562

Company URL: http://www.centurylink.com/
Establishment information: Established in 1930.
Company type: Public company
Company ticker symbol and exchange: CTL/NYSE
International Securities Identification Number: US1567001060
Business activities: Provides local and wireless telephone communications services.
Business type (SIC): Telephone communications
Financial profile for 2012: Number of employees, 47,000; assets, $54,020,000,000; sales volume, $18,376,000,000; pre-tax net income, $1,250,000,000; expenses, $15,842,000,000; liabilities, $34,731,000,000
Fortune 1000 ranking: 2012—150th in revenues, 245th in profits, and 103rd in assets
Forbes 2000 ranking: 2012—500th in sales, 717th in profits, and 428th in assets
Corporate officers: William Arthur Owens, Chair.; Harvey P. Perry, Vice-Chair.; Glen F. Post III, Pres. and C.E.O.; Karen A. Puckett, Exec. V.P. and C.O.O.; R. Stewart Ewing, Jr., Exec. V.P. and C.F.O.; Stacey W. Goff, Exec. V.P., Genl. Counsel, and Secy.
Board of directors: William A. Owens, Chair.; Harvey P. Perry, Vice-Chair.; Virginia Boulet; Peter C. Brown; Richard A. Gephardt; W. Bruce Hanks; Gregory J. McCray; C.G. Melville, Jr.; Fred R. Nichols; Glen F. Post III; Michael J. Roberts; Laurie A. Siegel; Joseph R. Zimmel
Subsidiaries: CenturyTel of Adamsville, Inc., Adamsville, TN; CenturyTel of Arkansas, Inc., Hardy, AR; CenturyTel of Central Louisiana, LLC, Jena, LA; CenturyTel of Claiborne, Inc., New Tazewell, TN; CenturyTel of Evangeline, LLC, Welsh, LA; CenturyTel of Idaho, Inc., Salmon, ID; CenturyTel of Lake Dallas, Inc., Lake Dallas, TX; CenturyTel of Michigan, Inc., Pinconning, MI; CenturyTel of Mountain Home, Inc., Mountain Home, AR; CenturyTel of North Louisiana, LLC, Plain Dealing, LA; CenturyTel of Wisconsin, Inc., La Crosse, WI; CenturyTel/Area Long Lines, Inc., La Crosse, WI
Offices: Alexandria, LA; Vancouver, WA
Historic mergers: Embarq Corporation (July 1, 2009); Qwest Communications International Inc. (April 1, 2011)
Giving statement: Giving through the CenturyLink-Clarke M. Williams Foundation.
Company EIN: 720651161

CenturyLink-Clarke M. Williams Foundation

(formerly Qwest Foundation)
100 Centurylink Dr.
Monroe, LA 71203-2041
E-mail: qwest.foundation@qwest.com

Establishment information: Established in 1985 in CO.
Donors: U S WEST, Inc.; Qwest Communications International Inc.
Contact: David Bromberg, Mgr.
Financial data (yr. ended 12/31/11): Assets, $17,010,578 (M); expenditures, $2,080,442; qualifying distributions, $1,926,669; giving activities include $1,902,597 for 628 grants (high: $150,000; low: $500).
Purpose and activities: The foundation supports programs designed to enrich the lives of children in pre-kindergarten through 12th grade education. Special emphasis is directed toward programs designed to effectively use technology to improve pre-k through 12 public school instruction; promote innovative models to strengthen pre-k through 12 public school education; improve the skills and leadership of educators and parents; promote innovative early childhood education; and promote diversity awareness and cultural competency.
Fields of interest: Arts, cultural/ethnic awareness; Elementary/secondary education; Education, early childhood education; United Ways and Federated Giving Programs; Engineering/technology; Assistive technology Children.
Programs:
Employee Volunteer Grant Program: The foundation awards $500 grants to nonprofit organizations with which employees of Qwest volunteer at least 40 hours per six-month period.
Quest Teacher and Technology Grants: The foundation awards grants to teachers and schools to improve K-12 education and support enhanced student learning through teacher innovation in the classroom. The foundation partners with selected organizations in states located in Qwest service territories. Grants are advertised and reviewed statewide and then awarded to teachers who use technology in the classroom.
Type of support: Continuing support; Employee volunteer services; General/operating support; Grants to individuals; Program development.
Geographic limitations: Giving on a national basis in areas of company operations in AR, IA, ID, CO, MN, MO, ND, NE, NM, OR, SD, UT, WA, and WY.
Support limitations: No support for political organizations, private foundations, pass-through organizations, or organizations that receive 3 percent or more funding from the United Way. No grants to individuals (except for Qwest Teacher Grants), or for scholarships, sectarian religious activities, capital campaigns, chairs, endowments, general operating support for single-disease health groups, or goodwill advertising.
Publications: Application guidelines.
Application information: Applications accepted. The foundation is in the process of transitioning to a new management process. Applications for general funding are currently not accepted. Qwest Teacher and Technology Grants are administered through partner agencies located in Qwest service territories.
Officers and Directors:* Stacey Goff*, Pres.; Christine Searls, Secy.; Jon Robinson, Treas.; Steven Davis; Tony Davis; Odell Riley.
Number of staff: 2 full-time professional.
EIN: 840978668
Selected grants: The following grants are a representative sample of this grantmaker's funding activity:
$663,452 to United Way, Mile High, Denver, CO, 2010. For Qwest Corporate Match.
$200,000 to Public Education and Business Coalition, Denver, CO, 2010. For Colorado Teachers and Technology.
$189,245 to United Way, Greater Twin Cities, Minneapolis, MN, 2010. For Qwest Corporate Match.
$100,000 to Arizona Technology in Education Association, Tempe, AZ, 2010. For AzTEA/Qwest Foundation for Education Grants.
$78,055 to Junior Achievement Rocky Mountain, Denver, CO, 2010. For JA in a Day and JA Hispanic Initiative Parent Outreach.
$50,000 to Denver Museum of Nature and Science, Denver, CO, 2010. For Professional Development.
$6,000 to Hennepin County Library, Friends of the, Minneapolis, MN, 2010. For Homework Hub.

$5,000 to Big Brothers Big Sisters Columbia Northwest, Portland, OR, 2010. For School-Based Mentoring Program.
$5,000 to Foundations for a Better Oregon, Portland, OR, 2010. For CLASS Project (Creative Leadership Achieves Student Success).
$5,000 to Omaha Childrens Museum, Omaha, NE, 2010. For Where Our Reading Meets Science (WORMS).

752
Cephalon, Inc.
41 Moores Rd.
P.O. Box 4011
Frazer, PA 19355 (610) 344-0200

Company URL: http://www.cephalon.com
Establishment information: Established in 1987.
Company type: Subsidiary of a foreign company
Business activities: Discovers, develops, and markets pharmaceutical products.
Business type (SIC): Drugs
Financial profile for 2010: Number of employees, 3,726; assets, $4,891,830,000; sales volume, $2,811,060,000; pre-tax net income, $618,800,000; expenses, $2,093,500,000; liabilities, $2,258,400,000
Corporate officers: J. Kevin Buchi, C.E.O.; Wilco Groenhuysen, Exec. V.P. and C.F.O.; Carl A. Savini, Exec. V.P. and C.A.O.; Gerald J. Pappert, Esq., Exec. V.P., Genl. Counsel, and Secy.
Board of directors: J. Kevin Buchi; William P. Egan; Martyn D. Greenacre; Charles J. Homcy, M.D.; Vaughn M. Kailian; Kevin E. Moley; Charles A. Sanders; Gail R. Wilensky, Ph.D.; Dennis L. Winger
Office: Salt Lake City, UT
International operations: Bermuda; Denmark; France; Germany; Ireland; Italy; Luxembourg; Netherlands; Poland; Spain; Switzerland; United Kingdom
Giving statement: Giving through the Cephalon, Inc. Corporate Giving Program and the Cephalon Cares Foundation.
Company EIN: 232484489

Cephalon, Inc. Corporate Giving Program
c/o Mgr., Corp. Contribs.
41 Moores Rd.
P.O. Box 4011
Frazer, PA 19355-1113
URL: http://www.cephalon.com/our-responsibility.html

Purpose and activities: As a complement to its foundation, Cephalon also makes charitable contributions to nonprofit organizations directly. Support is given primarily in Minneapolis, Minnesota, the greater Philadelphia, Pennsylvania area, and Salt Lake City, Utah, and in Australia, France, Germany, and Switzerland.
Fields of interest: Cancer, leukemia; Disasters, preparedness/services; Residential/custodial care, hospices; General charitable giving Disabilities, people with.
International interests: Australia; France; Germany; Switzerland.
Type of support: Employee volunteer services; General/operating support.
Geographic limitations: Giving primarily in Minneapolis, MN, the greater Philadelphia, PA area, and Salt Lake City, UT, and in Australia, France, Germany, and Switzerland.
Application information: Applications not accepted. Unsolicited requests for funds are not accepted.

Cephalon Cares Foundation
41 Moores Rd.
Frazer, PA 19355-113 (877) 237-4881
Application address: 6900 College Blvd., Ste. 1000, Overland Park, KS 66211, tel.: (877) 237-4881; URL: http://www.cephalon.com/cephaloncares-foundation.html

Establishment information: Established in 2009.
Financial data (yr. ended 12/31/11): Assets, $14,715,274 (M); gifts received, $37,355,224; expenditures, $29,938,224; qualifying distributions, $29,938,224; giving activities include $29,117,310 for grants to individuals.
Purpose and activities: The foundation provides prescription medication to economically disadvantaged individuals who lack prescription drug coverage and who meet certain income criteria.
Fields of interest: Economically disadvantaged.
Type of support: Donated products; In-kind gifts.
Publications: Application guidelines.
Application information: Applications accepted. Applications are accepted for Fentora, Nuvigil, Treanda, Gabitril, Tev-Tropin, and Trisenox. Application form required.
Applications must be signed by a physician and should also include proof of income.
Initial approach: Telephone foundation for application form or download application form and fax or mail to application address
Deadline(s): None
Officers and Directors:* Denise Bradley*, Chair.; Randy Bradway, Vice-Chair.; Laurie Thibodeau*, Pres.; Kristen Bauer*, Secy.; Felicia Ladin, Treas.; Rick Gulino*, Secy.
EIN: 263977456

753
Ceridian Corporation
3311 E. Old Shakopee Rd.
Minneapolis, MN 55425-1361
(952) 853-8100

Company URL: http://www.ceridian.com
Establishment information: Established in 1957.
Company type: Joint venture
Business activities: Provides human resource managed business solutions.
Business type (SIC): Management and public relations services
Financial profile for 2009: Number of employees, 9,579; sales volume, $1,490,000,000
Corporate officers: Stuart C. Harvey, Jr., Chair., Pres., and C.E.O.; Lois M. Martin, Exec. V.P. and C.F.O.; Kairus K. Tarapore, Exec. V.P., Human Resources; Ann C. Shaw, Sr. V.P., Genl. Counsel, and Secy.
Board of directors: L. White Matthews III; Ronald T. LeMay; George R. Lewis; William L. Trubeck; Alan F. White
Subsidiary: Comdata Network, Inc., Brentwood, TN
International operations: Canada; United Kingdom
Giving statement: Giving through the Ceridian Corporation Contributions Program.

Ceridian Corporation Contributions Program
3311 E. Old Shakopee Rd.
Minneapolis, MN 55425-1361
URL: http://www.ceridian.com/about_us_nav/1,6267,15599,00.html

Purpose and activities: Ceridian makes charitable contributions to nonprofit organizations on a case by case basis. Support is given on a national and international basis in areas of company operations.
Fields of interest: Education; United Ways and Federated Giving Programs; General charitable giving.
Program:
Community Action Field Program: Through the Community Action Field Program, Ceridian makes grants of up to $500 to nonprofit organizations with which employees volunteer.
Type of support: Employee volunteer services; General/operating support; Scholarships—to individuals.
Geographic limitations: Giving on a national and international basis in areas of company operations; giving also to national organizations.

754
Cerner Corporation
2800 Rockcreek Pkwy.
North Kansas City, MO 64117
(816) 221-1024

Company URL: http://www.cerner.com
Establishment information: Established in 1979.
Company type: Public company
Company ticker symbol and exchange: CERN/NASDAQ
Business activities: Develops health care information technology solutions.
Business type (SIC): Computer services
Financial profile for 2012: Number of employees, 11,900; assets, $3,704,470,000; sales volume, $2,665,440,000; pre-tax net income, $587,710,000; expenses, $2,093,770,000; liabilities, $870,820,000
Fortune 1000 ranking: 2012—774th in revenues, 400th in profits, and 686th in assets
Forbes 2000 ranking: 2012—1651st in sales, 1177th in profits, and 1894th in assets
Corporate officers: Neal L. Patterson, Chair., Pres., and C.E.O.; Clifford W. Illig, Vice-Chair.; Mike Nill, Exec. V.P. and C.O.O.; Marc G. Naughton, Exec. V.P. and C.F.O.
Board of directors: Neal L. Patterson, Chair.; Clifford W. Illig, Vice-Chair.; Gerald E. Bisbee, Jr., Ph.D.; Denis A. Cortese; John C. Danforth; Linda M. Dillman; William B. Neaves, Ph.D.; William D. Zollars
Offices: Irvine, CA; Atlanta, GA; Burlington, MA; Southfield, MI; Dallas, TX; Herndon, VA; Bellevue, WA
Giving statement: Giving through the First Hand Foundation.
Company EIN: 431196944

First Hand Foundation
2800 Rockcreek Pkwy.
Kansas City, MO 64117-2521 (816) 201-1569
FAX: (816) 571-1569;
E-mail: firsthandfoundation@cerner.com; E-mail for Mary Nelson: nelson@cerner.com; Additional e-mail: firstha@firsthandfoundation.org; Contact for Love Bag Program: Tammy Ankey, tel.: (816) 201-5984, e-mail: tammy.ankney@cerner.com; URL: http://www.firsthandfoundation.org/

Establishment information:
Donor: Cerner Corp.
Contact: Mary Nelson
Financial data (yr. ended 12/31/11): Revenue, $4,328,591; assets, $10,670,470 (M); gifts received, $4,037,597; expenditures, $4,726,522; program services expenses, $4,083,160; giving activities include $1,620,704 for grants and $1,339,459 for grants to individuals.

Purpose and activities: The foundation supports programs designed to directly impact the health status of young life. Special emphasis is directed toward programs designed to help children with health-related needs when insurance and other financial resources have been exhausted.
Fields of interest: Health care; Children/youth, services.
Programs:
Healthe Kids: Through Healthe Kids, the foundation provides community-based health screening for school-age children. The program is designed to identify possible health issues for children regardless of insurance circumstances and without requiring an out-of-pocket expense.
Individual Care Grants: The foundation awards grants to provide assistance to children with health-related needs. Special emphasis is directed toward treatment including clinical procedures, medicine, therapy, and prosthesis; equipment including wheelchairs, assistive technology, care devices, and hearing aids; displacement, associated with families of seriously ill children who must travel away from their home during treatment, including lodging, food, gas, parking, and transportation; and vehicle modification, including lifts, ramps, and transfer boards.
Love Bag Program: Through the Love Bag program, the foundation and community organizations create and distribute bags filled with personal items including blankets, pajamas, and books to children in need. The program is designed to comfort children as they transition into foster care. Bags are distributed by local social service agencies.
Type of support: Equipment; General/operating support; Program development.
Geographic limitations: Giving on a national and international basis with some emphasis on KS, LA, and MO.
Support limitations: No support for discriminatory organizations, or political or lobbying activities. No grants for home modification projects, alternative or experimental drugs, treatment or the therapy where there is significant controversy in the medical community, wheelchair-accessible van purchases, research, debt reduction, capital campaigns, multi-year projects, or overhead costs.
Publications: Application guidelines; Financial statement; Newsletter.
Application information: Applications accepted. Additional information may be requested at a later date.
Applications for Individual Care Gants should include a letter from a doctor explaining the child's diagnosis, history of illness, specific request for funding, and other relevant information; a letter from a provider on letterhead showing the original cost and estimated discount on procedure or equipment requested; letter from therapist on letterhead if applying for therapy or therapy equipment; letter from social worker on letterhead if requesting displacement assistance; evidence of the family's financial situation; and a letter of denial from insurance company.
Initial approach: Download application and mail to foundation for Individual Care Grants
Board meeting date(s): First Wed. the month
Deadline(s): Before last Wed. of the month for Individual Care Grants
Final notification: 7 to 10 days following review for Individual Care Grants
Officers and Directors:* Jeanne Lillig-Patterson*, Chair.; Neal L. Patterson*, Pres.; Melissa Frerking, V.P. and Exec. Dir.; Randy D. Sims, Secy.; Marc G. Naughton*, Treas.; Clifford W. Illig; Brian Irwin; Lisa Kiene; Francie McNair-Stoner; Dan Schipfer; Brian Streich; Julie Wilson.
EIN: 431725294
Selected grants: The following grants are a representative sample of this grantmaker's funding activity:
$56,000 to American Royal Association, Kansas City, MO, 2009. For general support.
$38,608 to Project Explore, Overland Park, KS, 2009. For general support.
$32,077 to EMDR Humanitarian Assistance Programs, Hamden, CT, 2009. For general support.
$24,000 to Ellis Foundation, Fort Scott, KS, 2009. For general support.
$10,000 to Operation Breakthrough, Kansas City, MO, 2009.
$8,400 to Good Shepherd Catholic Church, Shawnee, KS, 2009. For general support.
$7,500 to Church of the Nativity, Leawood, KS, 2009. For general support.
$5,000 to Morningside Presbyterian Church, Atlanta, GA, 2009. For general support.

755
CF Industries, Inc.
4 Pkwy., N., Ste. 400
Deerfield, IL 60015-2590 (847) 405-2400

Company URL: http://www.cfindustries.com
Establishment information: Established in 1946.
Company type: Subsidiary of a public company
Business activities: Manufacturers and distributes nitrogen and phosphate fertilizer products.
Business type (SIC): Fertilizers and agricultural chemicals
Financial profile for 2010: Number of employees, 210
Corporate officers: Stephen R. Wilson, Chair.; Brad Gordon, Pres.; Dennis Kelleher, Sr. V.P. and C.F.O.; Bert Frost, V.P., Sales
Board of director: Stephen R. Wilson
Giving statement: Giving through the CF Industries, Inc. Corporate Giving Program.

CF Industries, Inc. Corporate Giving Program
c/o Community Rels.
4 Pkwy. N., Ste. 400
Deerfield, IL 60015-2590
URL: http://www.cfindustries.com/community_relations.html

Purpose and activities: CF Industries makes charitable contributions to nonprofit organizations involved with K-12 education, the environment, youth development, and human services. Support is given primarily in areas of company operations in Florida, Iowa, Illinois, Mississippi, and Oklahoma, and in Canada.
Fields of interest: Elementary/secondary education; Environment; Youth development; Human services; General charitable giving.
International interests: Canada.
Program:
Classroom Minigrant Program: Through the Classroom Minigrant Program, CF Industries awards grants to educators who find innovative ways to incorporate agriculture or the environment into a classroom project.
Type of support: General/operating support; Grants to individuals; Program development.
Geographic limitations: Giving primarily in areas of company operations in FL, IA, IL, MS, and OK, and in Canada.
Application information:
Initial approach: Contact nearest plant distribution facility for Classroom Minigrant Program

756
CFS Bancorp, Inc.
707 Ridge Rd.
Munster, IN 46321-1612 (219) 836-2960

Company URL: http://www.cfsbancorp.com
Establishment information: Established in 1998.
Company type: Public company
Company ticker symbol and exchange: CITZ/NASDAQ
Business activities: Operates bank holding company; operates savings bank.
Business type (SIC): Savings institutions; holding company
Financial profile for 2012: Number of employees, 261; assets, $1,138,110,000; pre-tax net income, $6,360,000; liabilities, $1,026,290,000
Corporate officers: Robert R. Ross, Chair.; Darryl D. Pomranke, Pres. and C.E.O.; Jerry A. Weberling, Exec. V.P. and C.F.O.
Board of directors: Robert R. Ross, Chair.; Gregory W. Blaine; Gene Diamond; John William Palmer; Daryl D. Pomranke; Joyce M. Simon
Giving statement: Giving through the Citizens Savings Foundation.
Company EIN: 332042093

The Citizens Savings Foundation
707 Ridge Rd.
Munster, IN 46321-1611 (219) 836-2960
URL: http://www.mybankcitizens.com/aboutcitizens/citizens_savings_foundation/

Establishment information: Established in 1998 in IN.
Donors: CFS Bancorp, Inc.; Citizens Helping Citizens Fund; Citizens Financial Bank.
Contact: Monica F. Sullivan, V.P. and Secy.
Financial data (yr. ended 06/30/12): Assets, $816,653 (M); gifts received, $20,340; expenditures, $37,033; qualifying distributions, $37,033; giving activities include $30,799 for 10 grants (high: $3,625; low: $1,600).
Purpose and activities: The foundation supports organizations involved with education and human services. Special emphasis is directed toward programs designed to expand home ownership opportunities and provide access to affordable housing; youth development programs designed to improve life options through education and work skills; and community organizations designed to contribute to quality of life.
Fields of interest: Secondary school/education; Higher education; Education; Housing/shelter, development; Housing/shelter; Boys & girls clubs; Youth development; American Red Cross; YM/YWCAs & YM/YWHAs; Residential/custodial care, hospices; Residential/custodial care, senior continuing care; Human services; Community/economic development.
Program:
Employee Matching Grants: The foundation matches contributions made by employees of CFS to institutions of higher education on a one-for-one basis.
Type of support: Building/renovation; Employee matching gifts; Equipment; General/operating support; Program development; Scholarship funds; Sponsorships.

Geographic limitations: Giving primarily in areas of company operations in Southern Cook County, IL, and Porter counties, IN.
Support limitations: No grants to individuals.
Publications: Application guidelines; Grants list.
Application information: Applications accepted. Application form required. Applicants should submit the following:
1) copy of IRS Determination Letter
2) copy of most recent annual report/audited financial statement/990
3) listing of board of directors, trustees, officers and other key people and their affiliations
4) copy of current year's organizational budget and/or project budget
5) listing of additional sources and amount of support
6) population served

Initial approach: Contact foundation for application form
Deadline(s): None

Officers and Directors: Thomas F. Prisby, Chair. and C.E.O.; Monica F. Sullivan, V.P. and Secy.; Jerry A. Weberling, Treas.; Peter J. Doherty; Bruce E. Huey; Timothy D. Johnson; Rocharda Moore-Morris; Jerome J. Reppa.
EIN: 352056076

757
CH Energy Group, Inc.

284 S. Ave.
Poughkeepsie, NY 12601-4879
(845) 452-2000
FAX: (914) 486-5415

Company URL: http://www.chenergygroup.com
Establishment information: Established in 1982.
Company type: Public company
Company ticker symbol and exchange: CHG/NYSE
Business activities: Operates holding company; generates, transmits, and distributes electricity; transmits and distributes natural gas.
Business type (SIC): Combination utility services; holding company
Financial profile for 2012: Number of employees, 869; assets, $1,784,950,000; sales volume, $924,720,000; pre-tax net income, $66,750,000; expenses, $833,400,000; liabilities, $1,266,630,000
Corporate officers: Steven V. Lant, Chair., Pres., and C.E.O.; Christopher M. Capone, Exec. V.P. and C.F.O.; John E. Gould, Exec. V.P. and Genl. Counsel.; Denise Doring VanBuren, V.P., Public Rels. and Corp. Secy.; Kimberly J. Wright, V.P. and Cont.; Stacey A. Renner, Treas.
Board of directors: Steven V. Lant, Chair.; Margarita K. Dilley; Steven M. Fetter; Stanley J. Grubel; Manuel J. Iraola; E. Michel Kruse; Edward T. Tokar; Jeffrey D. Tranen; Ernest R. Verebelyi
Subsidiaries: Central Hudson Energy Services, Inc., Poughkeepsie, NY; Central Hudson Gas & Electric Corp., Poughkeepsie, NY
Giving statement: Giving through the CH Energy Group, Inc. Corporate Giving Program.
Company EIN: 141804460

CH Energy Group, Inc. Corporate Giving Program

284 South Ave.
Poughkeepsie, NY 12601-4838 (845) 452-2000
E-mail: dvanburen@cenhud.com; URL: http://www.cenhud.com/about_us/employee_matching.html

Contact: Denise D. VanBuren, V.P., Corp. Comms.
Purpose and activities: CH Energy matches contributions made by its employees to nonprofit organizations. Support is given primarily in areas of company operations in New York.
Fields of interest: General charitable giving.
Program:
Employee Matching Gift Program: CH Energy matches contributions made by its part-time and full-time employees to nonprofit organizations on a one-for-one basis from $50 to $500 per employee, per year.
Type of support: Employee matching gifts.
Geographic limitations: Giving primarily in areas of company operations in NY.
Application information: Applications not accepted. Contributes only through employee-matching gifts.

758
CH2M HILL Companies, Ltd.

9191 S. Jamaica St.
Englewood, CO 80112-5946
(303) 771-0900

Company URL: http://www.ch2m.com
Establishment information: Established in 1946.
Company type: Private company
Business activities: Provides full-service engineering, consulting, construction, and operations services.
Business type (SIC): Engineering, architectural, and surveying services
Financial profile for 2011: Number of employees, 23,000; assets, $1,967,100,000; sales volume, $5,422,800,000
Corporate officers: Lee A. McIntire, Chair. and C.E.O.; Michael Lucki, C.P.A., C.F.O.; Margaret B. McLean, Sr. V.P. and Corp. Secy.
Board of directors: Lee A. McIntire, Chair.; Nancy R. Tuor; Bob Bailey; Robert G. Card; William T. Dehn; Jerry D. Geist; Garry M. Higdem; Chad Holliday; Mike McKelvy; Georgia Nelson; David B. Price, Jr.; Jacque Rast; Nancy Tuor; Barry L. Williams
Giving statement: Giving through the CH2M HILL Companies Contributions Program and the CH2M Hill Foundation.

CH2M HILL Companies Contributions Program

9191 S. Jamaica St.
Englewood, CO 80112-5946 (303) 771-0900
URL: http://www.ch2m.com/corporate/about_us/corporate_responsibility/default.asp

Purpose and activities: As a complement to its foundation, CH2M Hill also makes charitable contributions to nonprofit organizations directly. Support is given primarily in areas of company operations.
Fields of interest: Education, fund raising/fund distribution; Elementary/secondary education; Higher education, university; Engineering school/education; Environment, climate change/global warming; Environment, natural resources; Environment, water resources; Environment, energy; Environment; Public health, clean water supply; Disasters, preparedness/services; Recreation, parks/playgrounds; Recreation, fairs/festivals; Children/youth, services; Independent living, disability; Science, fund raising/fund distribution; Science, formal/general education; Mathematics; Engineering/technology Economically disadvantaged.
Type of support: Annual campaigns; Curriculum development; Employee volunteer services; General/operating support; In-kind gifts; Program development; Sponsorships.
Geographic limitations: Giving primarily in areas of company operations.
Application information: Applications not accepted. Contributes only to pre-selected organizations.

CH2M Hill Foundation

P.O. Box 803878
Chicago, IL 60680-3878

Establishment information: Established in 1992.
Donors: James W. Poirot; CH2M Hill.
Financial data (yr. ended 12/31/11): Assets, $639,692 (M); expenditures, $1,006,420; qualifying distributions, $991,118; giving activities include $991,118 for grants.
Purpose and activities: The foundation supports undergraduate and graduate engineering and science programs, and technology initiatives designed to promote sustainable communities, clean water, a healthy environment, safe transportation systems, renewable energy, and efficient industry.
Fields of interest: Higher education; Engineering.
Type of support: Capital campaigns; General/operating support; Scholarship funds.
Geographic limitations: Giving primarily in CA, CO, Washington, DC, OR, and WA.
Support limitations: No grants to individuals.
Application information: Applications not accepted. Contributes only to pre-selected organizations.
Board meeting date(s): Varies
Officers and Directors: William Dehn, V.P.; Patrick O'Keefe, V.P.; Margaret B. McClean, Secy.; Lee McIntire; Catherine M. Santee.
EIN: 841227384
Selected grants: The following grants are a representative sample of this grantmaker's funding activity:
$157,371 to American Red Cross, Denver, CO, 2010. For general support.
$40,000 to American Red Cross, Denver, CO, 2010. For general support.
$40,000 to Engineers Without Borders USA, Boulder, CO, 2010. For general support.
$40,000 to National Engineers Week Foundation, Alexandria, VA, 2010. For general support.
$20,000 to Womens Foundation of Colorado, Denver, CO, 2010. For general support.
$18,500 to Engineers Without Borders USA, Boulder, CO, 2010. For general support.
$15,000 to Project CURE, Centennial, CO, 2010. For general support.
$10,000 to Thunderbird, The Garvin School of International Management, Glendale, AZ, 2010. For general support.
$3,500 to Thorne Ecological Institute, Boulder, CO, 2010. For general support.
$1,500 to Childrens Museum of Oak Ridge, Oak Ridge, TN, 2010. For general support.

759
Chadbourne & Parke LLP

30 Rockefeller Plz.
New York, NY 10112 (212) 408-5338

Company URL: http://www.chadbourne.com
Establishment information: Established in 1902.
Company type: Private company
Business activities: Operates law firm.
Business type (SIC): Legal services

Corporate officers: Hal M. Stewart, C.O.O.; Lisa Palestine, C.F.O.; Curt Cunningham, C.I.O.
Offices: Los Angeles, CA; Washington, DC
Giving statement: Giving through the Chadbourne & Parke LLP Pro Bono Program and the Chadbourne & Parke LLP Foundation.

Chadbourne & Parke LLP Pro Bono Program

30 Rockefeller Plz.
New York, NY 10112-0015 (212) 408-5365
E-mail: co'neill@chadbourne.com; Additional tel.: (212) 408-5338; URL: http://www.chadbourne.com/probono/

Contact: Charles K. O'Neill, Chair, Pro Bono Committee
Purpose and activities: Chadbourne & Parke makes charitable contributions to nonprofit organizations on a case by case basis.
Fields of interest: Legal services; General charitable giving.
Type of support: Advocacy; Pro bono services - legal.
Application information: A Pro Bono Committee manages the pro-bono program.

Chadbourne & Parke LLP Foundation

30 Rockefeller Plz.
New York, NY 10112-0002
URL: http://www.chadbourne.com/foundation/

Establishment information: Established in 2001 in DE.
Donor: Chadbourne & Parke LLP.
Financial data (yr. ended 12/31/11): Assets, $53,618 (M); expenditures, $2; qualifying distributions, $0.
Purpose and activities: The foundation supports programs designed to provide financial assistance to families and individuals affected by a disaster.
Fields of interest: Disasters, preparedness/services; Disasters, 9/11/01.
Type of support: General/operating support.
Geographic limitations: Giving primarily in Washington, DC, FL, MA, and NY.
Support limitations: No grants to individuals.
Application information: Applications not accepted. Contributes only to pre-selected organizations.
Officers: Andrew A. Giaccia*, Pres.; Lauren D. Kelly, V.P. and Secy.; Hal M. Stewart*, V.P. and Treas.
EIN: 134197648

760
Chandler-Frates & Reitz, Inc.

(also known as CFR)
5314 S. Yale Ave., Ste. 900
Tulsa, OK 74135-2198 (918) 747-8631

Company URL: http://www.cfr-ins.com
Establishment information: Established in 1994.
Company type: Private company
Business activities: Sells insurance.
Business type (SIC): Insurance carriers
Corporate officers: Jack Allen, Jr., Chair.; Robert Gardner, C.E.O.; Trey Biggs, Pres.; Michelle Rakes, V.P., Opers.
Board of director: Jack Allen, Jr., Chair.
Giving statement: Giving through the CFR Education Foundation, Inc.

CFR Education Foundation, Inc.

4501 E. 31st St.
Tulsa, OK 74135-2132

Establishment information: Established in 2002 in OK.
Donor: Chandler-Frates & Reitz, Inc.
Contact: Jack Allen, Pres.
Financial data (yr. ended 12/31/09): Assets, $0; expenditures, $270,150; qualifying distributions, $269,972; giving activities include $269,972 for 2 grants (high: $269,341; low: $631).
Purpose and activities: The foundation supports the Tulsa Community Foundation.
Fields of interest: Foundations (community).
Type of support: General/operating support; Program development.
Geographic limitations: Giving primarily in OK.
Support limitations: No grants to individuals.
Application information: Applications accepted. Application form not required. Applicants should submit the following:
1) detailed description of project and amount of funding requested

Initial approach: Proposal
Deadline(s): None

Officers and Directors:* Jack Allen*, Pres.; Robert Atherton, Secy.; Andrew Allen; Jack B. Allen.
EIN: 731645339

761
Chaney Enterprises, L.P.

12480 Mattawoman Dr., Fl. 3
P.O. Box 548
Waldorf, MD 20604-1548 (301) 932-5000

Company URL: http://www.chaney-ent.com
Establishment information: Established in 1962.
Company type: Private company
Business activities: Sells concrete, concrete block, and sand and gravel wholesale.
Business type (SIC): Lumber and construction materials—wholesale
Corporate officers: Francis H. Chaney II, Chair.; Donna Chaney Bunn, Vice-Chair.; William F. Child IV, Pres. and C.E.O.; Thomas W. Flynn, C.F.O.; Christopher R. Bunn, V.P. and C.I.O.
Board of directors: Francis H. Chaney II, Chair.; Donna Chaney Bunn, Vice-Chair.; William F. Childs IV
Giving statement: Giving through the Chaney Foundation, Ltd.

Chaney Foundation, Ltd.

(formerly Eugene Chaney Foundation, Ltd.)
12480 Mattawoman Dr.
P.O. Box 548
Waldorf, MD 20604-0548 (301) 932-5000
FAX: (301) 870-8086;
E-mail: ssantana@ChaneyEnterprises.com; Additional tel.: (301) 932-5665; Additional contact: Blair Selby, e-mail: bselby@chaneyenterprises.com; URL: http://www.chaney-ent.com/chaney_foundation/index.htm

Establishment information: Established in 1987 in MD.
Donors: Chaney Enterprises, L.P.; B.P.O.E.; Southstar, LP.
Contact: Sherry Santana, Community Rels. Specialist
Financial data (yr. ended 12/31/10): Assets, $780,150 (M); gifts received, $3,514; expenditures, $370,707; qualifying distributions, $370,729; giving activities include $349,664 for 86 grants (high: $20,000; low: $300).
Purpose and activities: The foundation supports programs designed to promote children advocacy and services; cultural arts; education; the environment; health care and health education; and historical education and preservation.
Fields of interest: Historic preservation/historical societies; Arts; Higher education; Business school/education; Education; Environment, water resources; Environment, beautification programs; Environmental education; Environment; Health care, clinics/centers; Public health; Health care; Mental health/crisis services; Cancer; American Red Cross; Children/youth, services; Human services; Foundations (community); United Ways and Federated Giving Programs; Engineering.
Programs:
Beautification Grants: The foundation awards grants to community organizations, schools, and nonprofit organizations to establish aesthetic and environmental improvement projects that benefit residents of Charles, Calvert, St. Mary's, Anne Arundel, or Caroline County, MD. Preference is given to projects that use native plant species and/or incorporate other "green" gardening practices like water conservation measures, organic fertilizers, mulch, compost, and compost teas. Grants of up to $1,000 are awarded and must be matched by applicants organization in cash, services, labor, or a combination.
Chaney Foundation Scholarship: The foundation awards $1,000 college scholarships to high school seniors or graduates residing in Charles, Calvert, St. Mary's, and Caroline Counties, MD. Preference is given to students majoring in building trades, drafting, design, construction or concrete management, environmental science, architecture, or business.
Type of support: Annual campaigns; Building/renovation; Capital campaigns; Equipment; General/operating support; Matching/challenge support; Program development; Scholarship funds; Scholarships—to individuals.
Geographic limitations: Giving primarily in Waldorf, MD, with emphasis on Anne Arundel, Calvert, Caroline, Charles, and St. Mary's County.
Support limitations: No support for religious organizations. No grants for endowments.
Publications: Application guidelines.
Application information: Applications accepted. The foundation is in the process of evaluating its grant cycle for general grants. Visit website for updated deadlines for general funding. Applicants for Beautification Grants must agree to submit before and after photos of their projects if selected to receive a grant. Application form required. Applicants should submit the following:
1) brief history of organization and description of its mission
2) listing of board of directors, trustees, officers and other key people and their affiliations
3) detailed description of project and amount of funding requested
4) copy of current year's organizational budget and/or project budget

Applications for scholarships should include a 300-word essay, 2 letters of recommendation, a copy of photo identification, letter(s) of acceptance if not currently attending college, and high school or college transcripts.

Initial approach: Complete online eligibility quiz and application; download application form and mail to foundation for Beautification Grants and scholarships
Deadline(s): Varies for general grants; Apr. 30 for Beautification Grants and scholarships
Final notification: End of May for Beatification Grants

Officers and Directors:* Francis H. Chaney II*, Pres.; William F. Childs IV*, V.P.; Carol M. Jackson*,

Secy.; Robert D. Agee; Rebekah Lare; Barbara Lawson; Michael L. Middleton.
EIN: 521525001
Selected grants: The following grants are a representative sample of this grantmaker's funding activity:
$20,000 to Summit School, Edgewater, MD, 2009.
$10,000 to Bay Area Community Church, Annapolis, MD, 2009.
$5,000 to American Red Cross, La Plata, MD, 2009.
$5,000 to Calverton School, Huntingtown, MD, 2009.
$5,000 to Enterprise Community Partners, Columbia, MD, 2009.
$5,000 to Key School, Annapolis, MD, 2009.
$5,000 to Sotterley Foundation, Hollywood, MD, 2009.
$4,000 to Maryland Hall for the Creative Arts, Annapolis, MD, 2009.
$3,000 to Calverton School, Huntingtown, MD, 2009.
$1,500 to Hospice of the Chesapeake, Annapolis, MD, 2009.

762
Chapman and Cutler LLP
111 W. Monroe St., Ste. 1700
Chicago, IL 60603-4080 (312) 845-3000

Company URL: http://www.chapman.com
Establishment information: Established in 1913.
Company type: Private company
Business activities: Operates law firm.
Business type (SIC): Legal services
Giving statement: Giving through the Chapman and Cutler LLP Pro Bono Program.

Chapman and Cutler LLP Pro Bono Program
111 W. Monroe St., Ste. 1700
Chicago, IL 60603-4080 (312) 845-3428
E-mail: lombardo@chapman.com; Additional tel.: (312) 845-3000; URL: http://www.chapman.com/about.php?&id=51

Contact: Joseph Lombardo, Pro Bono Partner
Fields of interest: Legal services.
Type of support: Pro bono services - legal.
Geographic limitations: Giving primarily in areas of company operations in San Francisco, CA, Chicago, IL, New York, NY, and Salt Lake City, UT.
Application information: A Pro Bono Coordinator manages the pro-bono program.

763
Chapman Insurance
(also known as G.S. Chapman & Associates Insurance Brokers, Inc.)
(formerly Chapman & Associates, Inc.)
265 N. San Gabriel Blvd.
P.O. Box 72
Pasadena, CA 91107-3423 (626) 405-8031

Company URL: http://www.chapmanins.com
Establishment information: Established in 1973.
Company type: Subsidiary of a public company
Business activities: Provides insurance brokerage services.
Business type (SIC): Insurance agents, brokers, and services
Corporate officers: Gregory Chapman, Pres. and C.E.O.; Valli Bowman, Co-C.O.O.; Melissa Cerny, Co-C.O.O.
Giving statement: Giving through the Chapman & Associates Foundation.

Chapman & Associates Foundation
265 N. San Gabriel Blvd.
Pasadena, CA 91107-3423
E-mail: mperez@chapmanins.com; URL: http://www.chapmanins.com/about/foundation

Establishment information: Established in 2001 in CA.
Donors: Chapman & Associates; Gil Younger; Philadelphia Insurance Company.
Contact: Mari Perez
Financial data (yr. ended 12/31/11): Assets, $1,370,227 (M); gifts received, $913,000; expenditures, $451,224; qualifying distributions, $447,778; giving activities include $447,778 for grants.
Purpose and activities: The foundation supports organizations involved with education, forest conservation, health, human services, and religion.
Fields of interest: Education; Environment, forests; Hospitals (general); Health care, clinics/centers; Health care; Children/youth, services; Children, foster care; Human services; Christian agencies & churches; Religion.
Type of support: General/operating support.
Geographic limitations: Giving primarily in CA.
Support limitations: No grants to individuals.
Publications: Application guidelines.
Application information: Applications accepted. Letters of inquiry should be no longer than 1 page. Additional information may be requested at a later date. The foundation utilizes a Recommendation Committee to select potential grantees. Application form not required.
Initial approach: E-mail or mail letter of inquiry
Board meeting date(s): Quarterly
Deadline(s): None
Officers and Directors: James Hull, Pres.; Harold Parker, Jr., V.P.; Ryan Dietz, Secy.; Gerald S. Chapman; Gregory S. Chapman.
EIN: 954835227
Selected grants: The following grants are a representative sample of this grantmaker's funding activity:
$25,000 to Pacific Clinics, Arcadia, CA, 2009.
$20,000 to Pasadena Hospital Association, Pasadena, CA, 2009.
$11,843 to Life Steps Foundation, Culver City, CA, 2009.
$11,500 to City CarShare, San Francisco, CA, 2009.
$7,500 to Foothill Family Service, Pasadena, CA, 2009.
$6,000 to Five Acres, Altadena, CA, 2009.
$5,000 to Conservation Corps of Long Beach, Long Beach, CA, 2009.
$5,000 to Ettie Lee Youth and Family Services, Baldwin Park, CA, 2009.
$5,000 to Intercommunity Child Guidance Center, Whittier, CA, 2009.
$5,000 to John Tracy Clinic, Los Angeles, CA, 2009.

764
Charles River Laboratories, Inc.
251 Ballardvale St.
Wilmington, MA 01887-1000
(781) 222-6000

Company URL: http://www.criver.com
Establishment information: Established in 1951.
Company type: Subsidiary of a public company
Business activities: Breeds scientific and medical research animals.
Business type (SIC): Farms/animal and livestock specialty; animal services, except veterinary
Financial profile for 2011: Number of employees, 7,100
Corporate officers: James C. Foster, Chair., Pres., and C.E.O.; Thomas F. Ackerman, Corp. Exec. V.P. and C.F.O.
Board of directors: James C. Foster, Chair.; Robert J. Bertolini; Stephen D. Chubb; George E. Massaro; Deborah Kochevar; George M. Milne, Jr.; C. Richard Reese; Samuel O. Thier; Richard F. Wallman; William H. Waltrip
Plants: Westbrook, ME; Portage, MI; Pittsfield, NH; Newfield, NJ; Port Washington, Stone Ridge, NY; Raleigh, NC
International operations: Canada; France; Germany; Italy; Japan; United Kingdom
Giving statement: Giving through the Charles River Laboratories Foundation, Inc.
Company EIN: 760509980

Charles River Laboratories Foundation, Inc.
(formerly Charles River Foundation)
251 Ballardvale St.
Wilmington, MA 01887-1096
FAX: (802) 785-2900

Donor: Charles River Laboratories, Inc.
Financial data (yr. ended 10/31/12): Assets, $4,654 (M); expenditures, $138; qualifying distributions, $138.
Purpose and activities: The foundation supports programs designed to educate the public about biomedical research; enhance education furthering the humane care of laboratory animals; and advance the three R's of animal welfare: reduction, refinement, and replacement.
Type of support: General/operating support; Grants to individuals; Program development; Research; Sponsorships.
Geographic limitations: Giving primarily in MA.
Application information: Applications not accepted. Unsolicited requests for funds not accepted.
Officers: James C. Foster, Pres.; Marilyn Brown, V.P.; David Johst, Clerk; Thomas F. Ackerman, Treas.
EIN: 510188208
Selected grants: The following grants are a representative sample of this grantmaker's funding activity:
$20,000 to States United for Biomedical Research, Raleigh, NC, 2009.
$5,400 to Foundation for Biomedical Research, Cherie Proctor, Director of Membership and Development, Washington, DC, 2009.
$1,000 to California Society for Biomedical Research, Sacramento, CA, 2009.
$1,000 to North Carolina Association for Biomedical Research, Raleigh, NC, 2009.
$1,000 to Pennsylvania Society for Biomedical Research, Camp Hill, PA, 2009.

765
Charter Communications, Inc.

12405 Powerscourt Dr., Ste. 100
St. Louis, MO 63131-3660 (314) 965-0555
FAX: (302) 636-5454

Company URL: http://www.charter.com
Establishment information: Established in 1993.
Company type: Public company
Company ticker symbol and exchange: CHTR/NASDAQ
Business activities: Provides cable television services. The company filed for Chapter 11 bankruptcy in 2009 to restructure its debt.
Business type (SIC): Cable and other pay television services
Financial profile for 2012: Number of employees, 17,800; assets, $15,599,000,000; sales volume, $7,504,000,000; pre-tax net income, -$47,000,000; expenses, $6,643,000,000; liabilities, $15,450,000,000
Fortune 1000 ranking: 2012—340th in revenues, 949th in profits, and 290th in assets
Forbes 2000 ranking: 2012—1137th in sales, 1874th in profits, and 1149th in assets
Corporate officers: Eric L. Zinterhofer, Chair.; Thomas M. Rutledge, Pres. and C.E.O.; John Bickahm, C.O.O.; Christopher L. Winfrey, Exec. V.P. and C.F.O.; Robert Quicksilver, Exec. V.P. and C.A.O.; Kevin D. Howard, Sr. V.P., C.A.O., and Cont.; Richard R. Dykhouse, Sr. V.P., Genl. Counsel, and Corp. Secy.
Board of directors: Eric L. Zinterhofer, Chair.; W. Lance Conn; Michael Huseby; Craig A. Jacobson; Gregory Maffei; Jeffrey A. Marcus; John D. Markley, Jr.; John Malone; David C. Merritt; Balan Nair; Thomas M. Rutledge
Offices: Birmingham, AL; Beatrice, Scottsbluff, NE
Giving statement: Giving through the Charter Communications, Inc. Corporate Giving Program.
Company EIN: 431857213

Charter Communications, Inc. Corporate Giving Program

12405 Powerscourt Dr., Ste. 100
St. Louis, MO 63131-3673

Contact: Anita Lamont
Purpose and activities: Charter Communications makes charitable contributions to nonprofit organizations involved with education and human services. Support is given on a national basis in areas of company operations.
Fields of interest: Education; Children, services; Human services.
Type of support: Donated products; Employee volunteer services; General/operating support; Scholarships—to individuals; Sponsorships.
Geographic limitations: Giving on a national basis in areas of company operations.
Application information: Applications accepted. Application form not required. Applicants should submit the following:
1) detailed description of project and amount of funding requested

Initial approach: Proposal to headquarters
Final notification: Following review

766
Charter Manufacturing Company, Inc.

1212 W. Glen Oaks Ln.
P.O. Box 217
Mequon, WI 53092-0217 (262) 243-4700

Company URL: http://www.chartermfg.com
Establishment information: Established in 1936.
Company type: Private company
Business activities: Manufactures steel billets, cold-finished steel shapes, miscellaneous steel and wire products, and miscellaneous fabricated metal products.
Business type (SIC): Steel mill products; metal products/fabricated
Corporate officers: Charles A. Mellowes, Chair. and C.E.O.; Thomas Glaister, Pres. and C.O.O.; John M. Couper, C.F.O.; Marc Crankshaw, C.I.O; John A. Mellowes, Chair. Emeritus
Board of director: Charles A. Mellowes, Chair.
Plant: Milwaukee, WI
Giving statement: Giving through the Charter Manufacturing Company Foundation, Inc.

Charter Manufacturing Company Foundation, Inc.

411 E. Wisconsin Ave., Ste. 2040
Milwaukee, WI 53202-4497

Establishment information: Established in 1984 in WI.
Donor: Charter Manufacturing Co., Inc.
Financial data (yr. ended 12/31/11): Assets, $5,551,123 (M); gifts received, $2,000,000; expenditures, $1,133,557; qualifying distributions, $1,131,534; giving activities include $1,131,534 for grants.
Purpose and activities: The foundation supports organizations involved with performing arts, higher, medical, and engineering education, conservation, health, housing development, and youth development.
Fields of interest: Performing arts; Higher education; Medical school/education; Engineering school/education; Environment, natural resources; Hospitals (general); Health care; Housing/shelter, development; Youth development, business; United Ways and Federated Giving Programs.
Type of support: Annual campaigns; Capital campaigns; General/operating support.
Geographic limitations: Giving primarily in Milwaukee, WI.
Support limitations: No grants to individuals.
Application information: Applications not accepted. Contributes only to pre-selected organizations.
Officers and Directors:* Linda T. Mellowes*, Pres.; John A. Mellowes*, V.P. and Treas.; Patrick J. Goebel, Secy.; Charles A. Mellowes; John W. Mellowes.
EIN: 391486363
Selected grants: The following grants are a representative sample of this grantmaker's funding activity:
$408,250 to Medical College of Wisconsin, Milwaukee, WI, 2010. For general support.
$401,250 to University School of Milwaukee, Milwaukee, WI, 2010. For general support.
$125,635 to United Way of Greater Milwaukee, Milwaukee, WI, 2010. For general support.
$120,000 to Milwaukee School of Engineering, Milwaukee, WI, 2010. For general support.
$67,060 to United Performing Arts Fund, Milwaukee, WI, 2010. For general support.
$60,000 to Junior Achievement of Wisconsin, Milwaukee, WI, 2010. For general support.
$50,000 to Cornell University, Ithaca, NY, 2010. For general support.
$20,000 to City Year, Boston, MA, 2010. For general support.
$10,000 to Milwaukee Public Museum, Milwaukee, WI, 2010. For general support.
$5,000 to Milwaukee Art Museum, Milwaukee, WI, 2010. For general support.

767
Charter One Financial Inc.

(formerly Charter One Bank, N.A.)
1215 Superior Ave., Ste. 245
Cleveland, OH 44114-3257 (216) 566-5300

Company URL: http://www.charterone.com
Company type: Subsidiary of a private company
Business activities: Operates commercial bank.
Business type (SIC): Banks/commercial
Corporate officer: Kenneth Marblestone, Pres.
Giving statement: Giving through the Charter One Foundation.

Charter One Foundation

(formerly Charter One Bank Bank Foundation)
1215 Superior Ave.
Cleveland, OH 44114
Additional addresses: Illinois: 71 S. Wacker, Ste. 2900, Chicago, IL 60606, Michigan: 27777 Franklin Rd., Southfield, MI 48034; URL: http://www.charterone.com/community/

Purpose and activities: Charter One makes charitable contributions to nonprofit organizations that promote affordable housing, encourage the development of innovative responses to basic human needs, encourage community-based services targeted to low- and moderate-income families and individuals, support community development initiatives that are catalysts for economically distressed areas, and promote new ways to address issues of economic self-sufficiency. Support is given primarily in areas of company operations.
Fields of interest: Housing/shelter; Human services, financial counseling; Human services; Community/economic development Economically disadvantaged.
Type of support: Annual campaigns; Capital campaigns; Donated products; Employee matching gifts; Employee volunteer services; Program development; Sponsorships; Use of facilities.
Geographic limitations: Giving primarily in areas of company operations in IL, MI, and OH.
Support limitations: No support for religious, political, labor, fraternal, veterans, governmental, quasi-governmental, research, or discriminatory organizations, foundations, or public or private educational institutions. No grants to individuals, or for annual appeals, single disease/issue information, annual operating support, endowments, conferences and seminars, trips and tours, historic preservation, or payment on bank loans (including loans from Charter One).
Publications: Application guidelines.
Application information: Applications accepted. Application form required.

Initial approach: Complete online application
Deadline(s): None
Final notification: Up to 8 weeks

768
The Chartis Group, LLC
60 State St., Ste. 700
Boston, MA 02109-1894 (617) 878-2178

Company URL: http://www.chartisgroup.com
Establishment information: Established in 2001.
Company type: Private company
Business activities: Provides management consulting services.
Business type (SIC): Management and public relations services
Corporate officer: Thomas Kiesau, Principal
Board of directors: Steve Levin; Greg Maddrey; Mellisa D. McCain; Michelle Moratti; George Sauter; Raphe Schwartz
Giving statement: Giving through the Chartis Foundation.

The Chartis Foundation
20 Bow St.
Cohasset, MA 02025-1330

Establishment information: Established in 2005 in IL.
Donor: Chartis Group, LLC.
Financial data (yr. ended 12/31/11): Assets, $413,036 (M); gifts received, $145,000; expenditures, $206,895; qualifying distributions, $205,000; giving activities include $205,000 for grants.
Purpose and activities: The foundation supports organizations involved with higher education and health.
Fields of interest: Higher education, university; Health care, infants; Health care.
Type of support: General/operating support.
Geographic limitations: Giving primarily in CT, LA, and SD.
Support limitations: No grants to individuals.
Application information: Applications not accepted. Contributes only to pre-selected organizations.
Directors: Ethan Arnold; Ken Graboys; Chris Regan.
EIN: 203996418
Selected grants: The following grants are a representative sample of this grantmaker's funding activity:
$80,000 to Tulane University, New Orleans, LA, 2010.
$25,000 to Partners in Health, Boston, MA, 2010.

769
Lynn Chase Designs, Inc.
45 E. End Ave., Ste. 12J
New York, NY 10026 (212) 288-1990

Company URL: http://www.lynnchasedesigns.com
Establishment information: Established in 1988.
Company type: Private company
Business activities: Designs and markets dinnerware, giftware, and accessories.
Business type (SIC): Pottery
Corporate officer: Lynn Chase, C.E.O.
Giving statement: Giving through the Chase Wildlife Foundation.

Chase Wildlife Foundation
c/o Lynn Chase
45 E. End Ave., Ste. 5C
New York, NY 10028-7980
E-mail: tina@lynnchasedesigns.com; URL: http://www.lynnchase.com/wildlife-foundation.html

Establishment information: Established in 1988 in DE.
Contact: Hifza Nosheen, Admin.
Financial data (yr. ended 12/31/10): Revenue, $9,866; assets, $58,706 (M); gifts received, $5,905; expenditures, $29,667.
Purpose and activities: The foundation promotes the preservation of wildlife and the environment on a global scale. It operates with two goals: first, to stop the destruction of animal habitats by human growth and expansion; and second, to focus on the survival and re-establishment of key species in that environment. To these ends, the foundation provides individual grants and joins cooperative efforts with other preservation and conservation organizations worldwide.
Fields of interest: Environment, climate change/global warming; Environment; Animals/wildlife, preservation/protection.
Type of support: Equipment; Grants to individuals; Program development; Research; Seed money.
Geographic limitations: Giving on a national basis.
Publications: Financial statement; Newsletter.
Application information:
Board meeting date(s): 3 times per year
Officers and Directors:* Marianna Baker*, Pres.; Dani Luyten*, Secy.; Richard A. Flintoft*, Treas.; William T. Baker; Lynn Chase; Michael Kraus; Renee Landegger.
EIN: 222968708

770
Chase Oil Corporation
11352 Lovington Hwy.
Artesia, NM 88210-9634 (575) 746-9853
FAX: (575) 746-9539

Establishment information: Established in 1992.
Company type: Private company
Business activities: Provides oil and gas field management services.
Business type (SIC): Oil and gas field services
Corporate officers: Robert C. Chase, Pres.; Rebecca Ericson, Secy.-Treas.
Giving statement: Giving through the Chase Foundation.

Chase Foundation
510 Texas Ave.
Artesia, NM 88210-2041 (575) 746-4610
E-mail: richardprice@chasefoundation.com; Additional e-mail: info@chasefoundation.com; Additional Contact: Ginny Bush, Assoc. Dir., e-mail: GinnyBush@chasefoundation.com; URL: http://www.chasefoundation.com

Establishment information: Established in 2006 in NM.
Donors: Gerene Furguson; Mack C. Chase; Marilyn Y. Chase; Chase Oil Co.
Contact: Richard Price, Exec. Dir.
Financial data (yr. ended 12/31/11): Assets, $42,127,508 (M); gifts received, $41,451; expenditures, $2,025,503; qualifying distributions, $1,360,100; giving activities include $1,360,100 for grants.
Purpose and activities: The foundation supports organizations involved with pre-school through 12th grade education, higher education, substance abuse, domestic violence, community development, charity infrastructure, youth development, and emergency and critical human services.
Fields of interest: Elementary/secondary education; Higher education; Substance abuse, services; Crime/violence prevention, domestic violence; Youth development; Human services; Community/economic development; Philanthropy/voluntarism.
Program:
Chase Foundation Scholarship: The foundation, in partnership with the New Mexico Community Foundation, awards renewable college scholarships to graduating seniors from Artesia High School and to children of employees of Mack Energy Corporation, Chase Farms, Deerhorn Aviation employed outside Artesia, NM. Scholarships range from $500 up to $5,000 for New Mexico college and universities, and up to $2,500 for out of state colleges and universities. Recipients are selected based on GPA, ACT or SAT scores, and participation in honor or advanced classes.
Type of support: Building/renovation; Employee-related scholarships; General/operating support; Program development; Scholarship funds; Scholarships—to individuals.
Geographic limitations: Giving primarily in southeastern NM; some giving also in west TX.
Support limitations: No support for political or lobbying organizations or international organizations,. No grants to individuals (except for scholarships), or for general operating expenses of established programs, interests or programs detrimental to the oil and gas industry, ticketed events, or projects that do not have sustainability for a 5 year period; no loans.
Publications: Annual report; Application guidelines; Grants list.
Application information: Applications accepted. Application form required. Applicants should submit the following:
1) qualifications of key personnel
2) statement of problem project will address
3) population served
4) name, address and phone number of organization
5) copy of IRS Determination Letter
6) brief history of organization and description of its mission
7) geographic area to be served
8) copy of most recent annual report/audited financial statement/990
9) listing of board of directors, trustees, officers and other key people and their affiliations
10) plans for cooperation with other organizations, if any
11) contact person
12) listing of additional sources and amount of support

Scholarships applications should include high school transcripts; an acceptance letter from the educational institution to which the scholarship will be paid; and a financial aid award letter from the educational institution.
Initial approach: Compete online application
Board meeting date(s): 2nd Tues. of Mar., June, Sept., and Dec.
Deadline(s): 4 weeks prior to quarterly board meeting; May 2 for scholarships
Officer and Directors: Richard Price*, Exec. Dir.; Deb Chase; Karla Chase; Mack C. Chase; Marilyn Y. Chase; Richard Chase; Robert Chase; Gerene Dianne Chase Ferguson; Johnny Knorr.
Advisor: Brad Bartek.
Trustee: JPMorgan Chase Bank, N.A.
EIN: 367466258
Selected grants: The following grants are a representative sample of this grantmaker's funding activity:
$1,770,932 to New Mexico Community Foundation, Santa Fe, NM, 2010. For Chase Foundation Scholarship Fund.
$200,000 to Lubbock Christian School, Lubbock, TX, 2010. For building fund.

$125,000 to George W. Bush Foundation, Dallas, TX, 2010. For program support.
$50,000 to Valley Christian Academy, Roswell, NM, 2010. For Building a Future Campaign.
$25,000 to Sidney Gutierez Middle School, Roswell, NM, 2010. For program support.
$25,000 to Wayland Baptist University, Plainview, TX, 2010. For program support.
$10,000 to University of New Mexico Foundation, Albuquerque, NM, 2010. For program support.

771
Chehalis Industrial Commission

1611 N. National Ave.
Chehalis, WA 98532 (360) 748-7661

Establishment information: Established in 1957.
Company type: Private company
Business activities: Provides business consulting services.
Business type (SIC): Management and public relations services
Corporate officer: Charles Hubbert, Pres.
Giving statement: Giving through the Community Partners.

Community Partners

P.O. Box 1501
Chehalis, WA 98532-0409 (360) 748-7661

Establishment information: Established in 1999 in WA.
Donor: The Industrial Commission, Inc.
Contact: C.A. "Buck" Hubbert, Pres.
Financial data (yr. ended 03/31/11): Assets, $8,779,085 (M); gifts received, $610; expenditures, $837,262; qualifying distributions, $624,532; giving activities include $624,532 for grants.
Purpose and activities: The foundation supports programs designed to promote economic development; encourage job creation; promote social welfare; and educate the public.
Fields of interest: Education; Employment; Children, services; Human services; Community/economic development.
Type of support: General/operating support.
Geographic limitations: Giving primarily in Chehalis, Centralia, and Lewis County, WA.
Support limitations: No grants to individuals.
Application information: Applications accepted. Applicants should submit the following:
1) detailed description of project and amount of funding requested
Initial approach: Proposal
Deadline(s): None

Officers: C.A. "Buck" Hubert, Pres.; Frank Devaul, V.P.; Norman Forsyth, Secy.-Treas.
Board Members: Alex Goehard; Bill Lotto; Bruce Roberts; Gail Shaw; Larry Tornow.
EIN: 911985089
Selected grants: The following grants are a representative sample of this grantmaker's funding activity:
$7,500 to Lewis County Work Opportunities Services, Chehalis, WA, 2009.

772
Chelsea Groton Savings Bank

1 Franklin Sq.
Norwich, CT 06360 (860) 823-4913

Company URL: http://www.chelseagroton.com
Establishment information: Established in 1854.
Company type: Private company
Business activities: Operates savings bank.
Business type (SIC): Savings institutions
Financial profile for 2011: Assets, $835,796,000
Corporate officers: B. Michael Rauh, Jr., Pres. and C.E.O.; Richard J. Morelli, Sr. V.P., C.F.O., and Treas.; Patricia A. Magao, Corp. Secy.; Jessica L. Todd, Compt.
Board of directors: D. Ben Benoit; Dennis J. Cambria; Mary Ellen Jukoski; P. Michael Lahan; Wilhelm W. Meya; B. Michael Rauh, Jr.; George W. Strouse; Thomas R. Switz
Offices: Groton, Mystic, Niantic, North Stonington, Pawcatuck, Salem, Sprague, Waterford, CT
Giving statement: Giving through the Chelsea Groton Foundation, Inc.

Chelsea Groton Foundation, Inc.

1 Franklin Sq.
Norwich, CT 06360-5825 (860) 823-4800
URL: http://www.chelseagroton.com/foundation.php

Establishment information: Established in 1998 in CT.
Donor: Chelsea Groton Savings Bank.
Financial data (yr. ended 12/31/11): Assets, $2,366,311 (M); expenditures, $131,147; qualifying distributions, $126,090; giving activities include $124,440 for 46 grants (high: $6,000; low: $965).
Purpose and activities: The foundation supports organizations involved with arts and culture, education, health, and human services.
Fields of interest: Arts; Higher education; Education, reading; Education; Hospitals (general); Health care; Children/youth, services; Human services; United Ways and Federated Giving Programs.
Type of support: Building/renovation; Continuing support; Equipment; General/operating support; Program development; Scholarship funds.
Geographic limitations: Giving primarily in areas of company operations in southeastern CT.
Support limitations: No support for municipal, public, political, or religious entities. No grants to individuals.
Application information: Applications accepted. Application form required. Applicants should submit the following:
1) copy of IRS Determination Letter
2) copy of most recent annual report/audited financial statement/990
3) copy of current year's organizational budget and/or project budget
Initial approach: Letter
Deadline(s): Apr. 30 for the awards May 31; Aug. 31 for the awards Oct. 31

Trustees: Mary Ellen Jukoski; Harry Colonis; Jeffrey Godley; Eric Janney; Michael Rauh; Robert Niderno; Zuzanna Olszewski; Lori-Ellen Wesolowski; Anne Wilkinson.
EIN: 061520330

773
Chemed Corporation

(formerly Roto-Rooter, Inc.)
2600 Chemed Ctr., 255 E. 5th St.
Cincinnati, OH 45202-4726 (513) 762-6900
FAX: (302) 655-5049

Company URL: http://www.chemed.com
Establishment information: Established in 1970.
Company type: Public company
Company ticker symbol and exchange: CHE/NYSE
Business activities: Operates hospices; provides plumbing and drain cleaning services.
Business type (SIC): Miscellaneous repair services; nursing and personal care facilities
Financial profile for 2012: Number of employees, 14,096; assets, $859,630,000; sales volume, $1,430,040,000; pre-tax net income, $145,820,000; expenses, $1,273,620,000; liabilities, $406,330,000
Corporate officers: George J. Walsh III, Chair.; Kevin J. McNamara, Pres. and C.E.O.; David P. Williams, Exec. V.P. and C.F.O.; Lisa A. Reinhard, V.P. and C.A.O.; Naomi C. Dallob, V.P. and Secy.; Arthur V. Tucker, Jr., V.P. and Cont.
Board of directors: George J. Walsh III, Chair.; Joel F. Gemunder; Patrick P. Grace; Thomas C. Hutton; Walter L. Krebs; Andrea R. Lindell; Kevin J. McNamara; Thomas P. Rice; Donald E. Saunders; Frank E. Wood
Subsidiaries: Roto-Rooter Group, Inc., Cincinnati, OH; Vitas, Miami, FL
Giving statement: Giving through the Chemed Foundation.
Company EIN: 310791746

Chemed Foundation

255 E. 5th St., Ste. 2600
Cincinnati, OH 45202-4726
FAX: (513) 762-6919;
E-mail: sandra.laney@chemed.com

Establishment information: Established in 1991 in OH.
Donors: Chemed Corp.; Roto-Rooter, Inc.
Contact: Sandra E. Laney, Pres.
Financial data (yr. ended 12/31/11): Assets, $6,124,233 (M); expenditures, $334,845; qualifying distributions, $329,860; giving activities include $296,575 for 84 grants (high: $40,000; low: $145).
Purpose and activities: The foundation supports organizations involved with arts and culture, education, housing, and human services.
Fields of interest: Arts; Elementary/secondary education; Higher education; Education; Housing/shelter; Human services; United Ways and Federated Giving Programs.
Type of support: Annual campaigns; Capital campaigns; General/operating support; Scholarship funds.
Geographic limitations: Giving primarily in OH.
Support limitations: No grants to individuals.
Publications: Annual report.
Application information: Applications accepted. Application form not required. Applicants should submit the following:
1) detailed description of project and amount of funding requested
Initial approach: Proposal
Copies of proposal: 1
Board meeting date(s): Mar., June, Sept., and Dec.
Deadline(s): None

Officers and Directors:* Sandra E. Laney*, Pres.; Kevin J. McNamara*, Secy.; David J. Lohbeck, Treas.; Thomas C. Hutton.
EIN: 311326421

774
Chemical Financial Corporation

(doing business as Chemical Bank)
235 E. Main St.
P.O. Box 2049
Midland, MI 48641-2049 (989) 839-5350
FAX: (517) 839-5337

Company URL: http://www.chemicalbankmi.com
Establishment information: Established in 1973.
Company type: Public company
Company ticker symbol and exchange: CHFC/NASDAQ
Business activities: Operates bank holding company; operates commercial bank.
Business type (SIC): Banks/commercial; holding company
Financial profile for 2012: Number of employees, 1,859; assets, $5,917,250,000; pre-tax net income, $71,810,000; liabilities, $5,320,910,000
Corporate officers: David B. Ramaker, Chair., Pres., and C.E.O.; Lori A. Gwizdala, Exec. V.P., Treas., and C.F.O.; William C. Collins, Exec. V.P., Genl. Counsel, and Secy.
Board of directors: David B. Ramaker, Chair.; Gary E. Anderson; J. Daniel Bernson; Nancy Bowman; James R. Fitterling; Thomas T. Huff; Michael T. Laethem; James B. Meyer; Terence F. Moore; Grace O. Shearer; Larry D. Stauffer; Franklin C. Wheatlake
Subsidiaries: CFC Data Corp., Midland, MI; Chemical Bank and Trust Company, Midland, MI; Chemical Bank Shoreline, Benton Harbor, MI; Chemical Bank West, Grand Rapids, MI
Historic mergers: Bank West Financial Corporation (September 14, 2001)
Giving statement: Giving through the Chemical Financial Corporation Contributions Program.
Company EIN: 382022454

Chemical Financial Corporation Contributions Program

333 E. Main St.
P.O. Box 569
Midland, MI 48640-6511 (800) 567-9757
URL: http://www.chemicalbankmi.com/cb/About_Chemical.htm

Purpose and activities: Chemical Financial Corporation makes charitable contributions to nonprofit organizations involved with cancer research, housing, youth development, and community development. Support is given primarily in areas of company operations in Michigan.
Fields of interest: Cancer research; Housing/shelter; Youth development, business; Youth development; Community/economic development; United Ways and Federated Giving Programs.
Type of support: Employee volunteer services; General/operating support.
Geographic limitations: Giving primarily in areas of company operations in MI.

775
Chemtura Corporation

(formerly Crompton Corporation)
1818 Market St., Ste. 3700
Philadelphia, PA 19103 (203) 573-2000
FAX: (302) 636-5454

Company URL: http://www.chemtura.com
Establishment information: Established in 1900.
Company type: Public company
Company ticker symbol and exchange: CHMT/NYSE
Business activities: Manufactures and sells specialty chemicals and polymer processing equipment. The company's US operations filed for Chapter 11 bankruptcy protection on Mar. 18, 2009.
Business type (SIC): Chemicals/industrial organic; plastics and synthetics; industrial and commercial machinery and computer equipment
Financial profile for 2012: Number of employees, 4,600; assets, $3,030,000,000; sales volume, $2,629,000,000; pre-tax net income, $162,000,000; expenses, $2,424,000,000; liabilities, $1,969,000,000
Fortune 1000 ranking: 2012—710th in revenues, 738th in profits, and 747th in assets
Corporate officers: Craig A. Rogerson, Chair., Pres., and C.E.O.; Stephen C. Forsyth, Exec. V.P. and C.F.O.; Billie S. Flaherty, Sr. V.P., Genl. Counsel, and Corp. Secy.; Alan M. Swiech, Sr. V.P., Human Resources; Laurence Orton, V.P. and Corp. Cont.
Board of directors: Craig A. Rogerson, Chair.; Jeffrey D. Benjamin; Timothy J. Bernlohr; Anna C. Catalano; Alan S. Cooper; James W. Crownover; Robert A. Dover; Jonathan F. Foster; John K. Wulff
Subsidiaries: Great Lakes Chemical Corporation, Indianapolis, IN; Uniroyal Chemical Co., Inc., Middlebury, CT
International operations: Argentina; Australia; Belgium; Brazil; Canada; Chile; China; Denmark; Ecuador; France; Germany; Hong Kong; Hungary; Ireland; Italy; Japan; Kazakhstan; Mexico; Netherlands; New Zealand; Singapore; Slovenia; South Africa; South Korea; Spain; Switzerland; Taiwan; Thailand; United Kingdom
Giving statement: Giving through the Chemtura Corporation Contributions Program.
Company EIN: 522183153

Chemtura Corporation Contributions Program

(formerly Crompton Corporation Contributions Program)
1818 Market St., Ste. 3700
Philadelphia, PA 19103-3640 (215) 446-3911
URL: http://www.chemtura.com

Purpose and activities: Chemtura makes charitable contributions to nonprofit organizations involved with education, health care, human services, economic development. Special emphasis is directed towards programs designed to provide educational and economic opportunities for disadvantaged people. Support is given in areas of company operations in California, Connecticut, Georgia, Illinois, Indiana, and Pennsylvania, and on an international basis in areas of company operations.
Fields of interest: Education; Health care; Human services; Community/economic development Economically disadvantaged.
Type of support: Building/renovation; Employee volunteer services; General/operating support; In-kind gifts.
Geographic limitations: Giving in areas of company operations in CA, CT, GA, IL, IN, and PA, and on an international basis in areas of company operations.

776
Chenega Corporation

3000 C St., Ste. 301
Anchorage, AK 99503 (907) 277-5706

Company URL: http://www.chenega.com/
Establishment information: Established in 1974.
Company type: Native corporation
Business activities: Operates native corporation.
Business type (SIC): Nonclassifiable establishments
Corporate officers: Charles W. Totemoff, Pres. and C.E.O.; Paul T. Selanoff, Treas.
Giving statement: Giving through the Chenega Future, Inc.

Chenega Future, Inc.

3000 C St., Ste. 200 S. Wing
Anchorage, AK 99503-3975 (907) 751-6901
FAX: (907) 569-6939;
E-mail: pandrews@chenegacorp.com.; Additional contact: Molly Merrit-Duren, tel.: (907) 677-4987, e-mail: shareholderdevelopment@chenega.com; Additional tel.: (888) 442-5388; URL: http://www.chenegafuture.com/
Application address: Chenega Future Inc., Shareholder Development Manager, P.O. Box 240988, Anchorage, AK 99524

Establishment information: Classified as a company-sponsored operating foundation in 1990.
Donor: Chenega Corp.
Contact: Patti Andrews, Secy.
Financial data (yr. ended 12/31/11): Assets, $36,412 (M); gifts received, $1,810,081; expenditures, $1,790,001; qualifying distributions, $360,483; giving activities include $360,483 for 104 grants to individuals (high: $9,000; low: $25).
Purpose and activities: The foundation awards scholarships for education and training to shareholders and their spouses and descendants of shareholders of Chenega Corp.
Fields of interest: Vocational education; Higher education Native Americans/American Indians.
Type of support: Internship funds; Scholarships—to individuals.
Geographic limitations: Giving limited to AK.
Publications: Application guidelines.
Application information: Applications accepted. Application form required.
Applications should include high school transcripts, a letter of acceptance, financial statements, progress reports indicating grade at the end of each semester, three letters of recommendation, a letter concerning goals, and an educational plan.
Initial approach: Download application form and mail to foundation
Deadline(s): May 1 for summer semester, Dec. 1 for spring semester, Aug. 1 for fall semester, 10 days prior to need for short-term vocational or technical training, and Sept. 30 for Chugach School District
Officers and Directors: Patrick C. Selanof, Pres.; Phyllis Pipkin, V.P.; Patricia Totemoff Andrews, Secy.; Joyce L. Kompkoff, Treas.; Lloyd Kompkoff, Exec. Dir.; LaVon Johnson.
EIN: 943111730
Selected grants: The following grants are a representative sample of this grantmaker's funding activity:

$100,000 to Alaska Vocational Technical Center, Seward, AK, 2009. For education endowment.
$100,000 to Chugach School District, Anchorage, AK, 2009. For education endowment.
$21,024 to Saint Innocent of Irkutsk Orthodox Church, Anchorage, AK, 2009. For Native Culture and Heritage.
$10,000 to Saint Michael the Archangel Orthodox Church, Cordova, AK, 2009. For Native Culture and Heritage.

777
Chesapeake Energy Corporation

6100 N. Western Ave.
Oklahoma City, OK 73118 (405) 935-3500

Company URL: http://www.chk.com/
Establishment information: Established in 1989.
Company type: Public company
Company ticker symbol and exchange: CHK/NYSE
Business activities: Producer of natural gas.
Business type (SIC): Extraction/oil and gas
Financial profile for 2012: Number of employees, 12,000; assets, $41,611,000,000; sales volume, $12,316,000,000; pre-tax net income, -$974,000,000; expenses, $14,210,000,000; liabilities, $26,042,000,000
Fortune 1000 ranking: 2012—223rd in revenues, 974th in profits, and 133rd in assets
Forbes 2000 ranking: 2012—779th in sales, 1916th in profits, and 556th in assets
Corporate officers: Archie W. Dunham, Chair.; Aubrey K. McClendon, C.E.O.; Steven C. Dixon, C.O.O.; Domenic J. Dell'Osso, Jr., Exec. V.P. and C.F.O.; Michael A. Johnson, Sr. V.P., C.A.O., and Cont.; Cathlyn L. Tompkins, Sr. V.P. and C.I.O.; Jennifer M. Grigsby, Sr. V.P., Treas., and Corp. Secy.; James R. Webb, Sr. V.P. and Genl. Counsel; James C. Johnson, Sr. V.P., Mktg.; Martha A. Burger, Sr. V.P., Human Resources
Board of directors: Archie W. Dunham, Chair.; Bob G. Alexander; Vincent J. Intrieri; R. Brad Martin; Merrill A. Miller, Jr.; Frederic M. Poses; Louis A. Raspino; Thomas L. Ryan
Giving statement: Giving through the Chesapeake Energy Corporation Contributions Program.
Company EIN: 731395733

Chesapeake Energy Corporation Contributions Program

c/o Community Rels. Dept.
P.O. Box 18496
Oklahoma City, OK 73154-0496 (405) 935-8000
E-mail: contributions@chk.com; URL: http://www.chk.com/Corporate-Responsibility/Community/Pages/Information.aspx

Purpose and activities: Chesapeake Energy makes charitable contributions to nonprofit organizations involved with education, health, social services, and community development. Support is given primarily in areas of company operations in Colorado, Kentucky, New Mexico, New Mexico, New York, North Dakota, Northwest Louisiana, Oklahoma, Ohio, Pennsylvania, Texas, West Virginia, and Wyoming.
Fields of interest: Education; Environment; Health care; Health organizations; Human services; Community/economic development.
Type of support: Donated equipment; Employee volunteer services; General/operating support; In-kind gifts; Scholarship funds; Sponsorships.
Geographic limitations: Giving primarily in areas of company operations in CO, KY, Northwest LA, ND, NM, NY, OH, OK, PA, TX, WVA, and WY.
Support limitations: No support for political organizations or religious organizations not of direct benefit to the entire community. No grants to individuals, or for travel expenses, nonprofit and school-sponsored walk-a-thons, athletic events and athletic group sponsorships other than Special Olympics, door prizes or raffles, school-affiliated orchestras, bands, choirs, trips, drama groups, yearbooks and class parties, or fraternity/sorority-related events or fund-raisers.
Publications: Application guidelines.
Application information: Applications accepted. Application form required.
Initial approach: Complete online application form

778
Chesapeake Pharmaceutical Packaging Company, Inc.

(formerly Chesapeake Corporation)
325 Duffy Ave., Ste. 1
Hicksville, NY 11801-3644 (516) 277-8600

Company URL: http://www.chesapeakecorp.com
Establishment information: Established in 2009.
Company type: Subsidiary of a foreign company
Business activities: Develops, manufactures, and sells specialty packaging products.
Business type (SIC): Paperboard mills
Corporate officers: Robin Henfling, Pres.; Christopher J. Cassidy, V.P., Sales and Mktg.
Subsidiaries: Chesapeake Display and Packaging Co., Winston-Salem, NC; Chesapeake Forest Products Co. LLC, West Point, VA; Chesapeake Printing and Packaging Company, Lexington, NC; Delmarva Properties, Inc., Richmond, VA; Stonehouse Inc., Williamsburg, VA
International operations: United Kingdom
Giving statement: Giving through the Chesapeake Corporation Contributions Program.
Company EIN: 540166880

Chesapeake Corporation Contributions Program

1021 E. Cary St.
Richmond, VA 23219-4058
FAX: (804) 697-1199; Application address: P.O. Box 2350, Richmond, VA 23218-2350

Contact: Joseph C. Vagi, Mgr., Corp. Comms.
Purpose and activities: As a complement to its foundation, Chesapeake also makes charitable contributions to nonprofit organizations directly. Support is given primarily in the Richmond, Virginia, area.
Fields of interest: Education; Environmental education.
Type of support: Annual campaigns; General/operating support.
Geographic limitations: Giving primarily in the Richmond, VA, area.
Support limitations: No support for religious or political organizations. No grants to individuals.
Application information: Applications accepted. The Corporate Communications Department handles giving. A contributions committee reviews all requests. Application form not required. Applicants should submit the following:
1) copy of IRS Determination Letter
2) geographic area to be served
3) detailed description of project and amount of funding requested
Initial approach: Proposal to headquarters
Copies of proposal: 1
Committee meeting date(s): Quarterly
Deadline(s): Prior to committee meetings
Final notification: 1 week following committee meetings
Number of staff: 1 part-time support.

779
Cheviot Savings Bank

3723 Glenmore Ave.
Cheviot, OH 45211-4744 (513) 661-0457
FAX: (513) 389-4634

Company URL: http://www.cheviotsavings.com
Establishment information: Established in 1911.
Company type: Subsidiary of a mutual company
Business activities: Operates savings bank.
Business type (SIC): Savings institutions
Corporate officers: Thomas J. Linneman, Pres.; Scott T. Smith, C.F.O.; Jeffrey J. Lenzer, V.P., Opers.; Kimberly Siener, C.A.O.; Tricia Walter, Cont.
Offices: Cincinnati, Harrison, West Chester, OH
Giving statement: Giving through the Cheviot Savings Bank Charitable Foundation.

Cheviot Savings Bank Charitable Foundation

3723 Glenmore Ave.
Cincinnati, OH 45211-4720

Establishment information: Established in 2004 in OH.
Donor: Cheviot Savings Bank.
Financial data (yr. ended 12/31/11): Assets, $847,251 (M); expenditures, $87,636; qualifying distributions, $84,700; giving activities include $84,700 for grants.
Purpose and activities: The foundation supports fire departments and parks and playgrounds and organizations involved with secondary education, cystic fibrosis, Parkinson's disease, housing, and youth development.
Fields of interest: Education; Health care; Human services.
Type of support: Building/renovation; Equipment; General/operating support; Scholarship funds.
Support limitations: No grants to individuals.
Application information: Applications not accepted. Unsolicited requests for funds not accepted.
Officers: Thomas J. Linneman, C.E.O. and Pres.; James Williamson, Secy.; Scott T. Smith, Treas.
Directors: Kevin Kappa; Jeffrey J. Lenzer; William Westerhaus.
EIN: 300228735

780
Chevron Corporation

(formerly ChevronTexaco Corporation)
6001 Bollinger Canyon Rd.
San Ramon, CA 94583-2324
(925) 842-1000
FAX: (415) 894-6817

Company URL: http://www.chevron.com
Establishment information: Established in 1879.
Company type: Public company
Company ticker symbol and exchange: CVX/NYSE
International Securities Identification Number: US1667641005

Business activities: Conducts crude oil and natural gas exploration activities; develops and produces crude oil and natural gas; refines crude oil; markets crude oil, natural gas, and petroleum products; transports crude oil, natural gas, and petroleum products; manufactures and markets industrial chemicals; mines coal.
Business type (SIC): Extraction/oil and gas; mining/coal and lignite surface; chemicals/ industrial inorganic; petroleum refining; pipelines (except natural gas/operation of); gas production and distribution; petroleum and petroleum products —wholesale
Financial profile for 2012: Number of employees, 62,000; assets, $233,000,000,000; sales volume, $222,600,000,000; pre-tax net income, $46,332,000,000; expenses, $195,577,000,000; liabilities, $96,458,000,000
Fortune 1000 ranking: 2012—3rd in revenues, 3rd in profits, and 22nd in assets
Forbes 2000 ranking: 2012—10th in sales, 8th in profits, and 116th in assets
Corporate officers: John S. Watson, Chair. and C.E.O.; George L. Kirkland, Vice-Chair.; Patricia E. Yarrington, V.P. and C.F.O.; Paul Bennett, V.P. and Treas.; Matthew J. Foehr, V.P. and Compt.; R. Hewitt Pate, V.P. and Genl. Counsel; Stephen W. Green, V.P., Public Affairs; Joe W. Laymon, V.P., Human Resources; Lydia I. Beebe, Corp. Secy.
Board of directors: John S. Watson, Chair.; George L. Kirkland, Vice-Chair.; Linnet F. Deily; Robert E. Denham; Charles T. Hagel; Enrique Hernandez, Jr.; Charles W. Moorman; Kevin W. Sharer; John G. Stumpf; Ronald D. Sugar; Carl Ware
Subsidiaries: Chevron Chemical Co., San Ramon, CA; Chevron U.S.A. Inc., San Francisco, CA; The Pittsburg & Midway Coal Mining Co., Englewood, CO; Union Oil Company of California, San Ramon, CA; Unocal Corporation, El Segundo, CA
Plants: Bakersfield, El Segundo, La Habra, Los Angeles, Morro Bay, Richmond, Sacramento, Walnut Creek, CA; Washington, DC; Atlanta, GA; Honolulu, HI; New Orleans, LA; Jackson, Pascagoula, MS; New York, NY; Marietta, OH; Austin, Baytown, Cedar Bayou, El Paso, Houston, Port Arthur, TX; Salt Lake City, UT
International operations: Argentina; Australia; Bahamas; Bermuda; Brazil; Canada; England; France; Indonesia; Nigeria; Philippines; Singapore; Wales
Giving statement: Giving through the Chevron Corporation Contributions Program, the Nissan Motor Co., Ltd. Contributions Program, the Chevron Community Foundation, and the Chevron Global Fund.
Company EIN: 940890210

Chevron Corporation Contributions Program

(formerly ChevronTexaco Corporation Contributions Program)
6001 Bollinger Canyon Rd.
San Ramon, CA 94583-2324 (925) 842-1000
URL: http://www.chevron.com/globalissues/economiccommunitydevelopment/

Purpose and activities: As a complement to its foundation, Chevron also makes charitable contributions to nonprofit organizations directly. Special emphasis is directed towards programs designed to promote education, health, and economic development. Support is given on a national and international basis in areas of company operations.
Fields of interest: Vocational education; Education; Health care; Heart & circulatory diseases; Lung diseases; AIDS; Tropical diseases; Employment; Economic development; Community development, small businesses; Science, formal/general education; Mathematics; Engineering/technology Women.
Type of support: Employee matching gifts; Employee volunteer services; General/operating support; Loans—to individuals; Program development; Scholarships—to individuals.
Geographic limitations: Giving on a national and international basis in areas of company operations.
Number of staff: 7 full-time professional; 3 full-time support.

Chevron Community Foundation

(formerly ChevronTexaco Foundation)
6001 Bollinger Canyon Rd., Rm. A2328
San Ramon, CA 94583-2324
FAX: (925) 842-3617

Establishment information: Incorporated in 1979 in DE.
Donors: Texaco Inc.; ChevronTexaco Corp.; Chevron Corp.
Financial data (yr. ended 12/31/10): Assets, $3,800,680 (M); expenditures, $62,014; qualifying distributions, $0.
Purpose and activities: The foundation supports programs designed to enhance quality of life through music education and scientific discovery for children.
Fields of interest: Performing arts, music; Arts; Education; Children, services; Science.
Type of support: Curriculum development; Employee-related scholarships; Program development; Research; Scholarship funds.
Geographic limitations: Giving primarily in areas of company operations; giving also to national organizations.
Support limitations: No support for religious organizations, private foundations, or fraternal, social, or veterans' organizations. No grants for general operating support, non-hospital capital campaigns, endowments, films, videos, or television projects, courtesy advertising, social functions, commemorative journals, meetings, or political activities; no loans.
Application information: Applications not accepted. Unsolicited requests for funds not accepted.
Directors: John E. Bethancourt; John Fitzpatrick; Franklyn G. Jenifer; David Krattebol; J.W. Rhodes; Patricia Yarrington.
Number of staff: 3
EIN: 133007516

Chevron Global Fund

(formerly ChevronTexaco Global Fund)
c/o Chevron Corp., Public and Govt. Affairs
6001 Bollinger Canyon Rd.
San Ramon, CA 94583-2324 (925) 842-1000

Establishment information: Established in 1999 in NY.
Donor: Texaco Inc.
Financial data (yr. ended 12/31/11): Assets, $1,921,360 (M); expenditures, $68,737; qualifying distributions, $47,358; giving activities include $44,788 for 1 grant.
Purpose and activities: The foundation supports organizations involved with disaster relief.
Fields of interest: Disasters, preparedness/ services; American Red Cross.
International interests: Global programs.
Type of support: General/operating support.
Geographic limitations: Giving to international organizations located in Silver Spring, MD and Portland, OR.
Support limitations: No grants to individuals.
Application information: Applications not accepted. Contributes only to pre-selected organizations.
Officers and Directors:* Matthew Lonner*, Pres.; Rhonda Zygocki.
EIN: 311634478

781
The Chicago Bears Football Club, Inc.

1000 Football Dr.
Lake Forest, IL 60045-4829
(847) 295-6600

Company URL: http://www.chicagobears.com
Establishment information: Established in 1920.
Company type: Private company
Business activities: Operates professional football club.
Business type (SIC): Commercial sports
Corporate officers: George J. McCaskey, Chair.; Ted Phillips, Pres. and C.E.O.; Virginia McCaskey, Secy.
Board of directors: George McCaskey, Chair.; Andrew McKenna; Brian J. McCaskey; Ed McCaskey, Jr.; Michael McCaskey; Patrick McCaskey; Virginia McCaskey; Ted Phillips; Pat Ryan
Giving statement: Giving through the Chicago Bears Football Club, Inc. Corporate Giving Program.

Chicago Bears Football Club, Inc. Corporate Giving Program

Halas Hall
1000 Football Dr.
Lake Forest, IL 60045-4829
URL: http://www.chicagobears.com/community

Purpose and activities: The Chicago Bears make charitable contributions of memorabilia to nonprofit organizations on a case by case basis. Support is given primarily in Illinois and the Chicagoland, Illinois, area.
Fields of interest: Education; Public health, physical fitness; Athletics/sports, football; General charitable giving.
Type of support: Donated products; In-kind gifts.
Geographic limitations: Giving primarily in IL and the Chicagoland, IL, area.
Support limitations: No game ticket donations.
Publications: Application guidelines.
Application information: Applications accepted. Support is limited to 1 contribution per organization during any given year. Telephone calls are not encouraged. Application form required.
Initial approach: Complete online application form
Copies of proposal: 1
Deadline(s): 6 weeks prior to need

782
Chicago Blackhawks Hockey Team, Inc.

1901 W. Madison St.
United Ctr.
Chicago, IL 60612-2459 (312) 455-7000

Company URL: http://www.chicagoblackhawks.com
Establishment information: Established in 1926.
Company type: Subsidiary of a private company
Business activities: Operates professional ice hockey club.

Business type (SIC): Commercial sports
Corporate officers: William Rockwell Wirtz, Chair.; John F. McDonough, Pres. and C.E.O.
Board of director: William Rockwell Wirtz, Chair.
Giving statement: Giving through the Chicago Blackhawks Hockey Team, Inc. Corporate Giving Program.

Chicago Blackhawks Hockey Team, Inc. Corporate Giving Program

1901 W. Madison St.
Chicago, IL 60612-2459
URL: http://blackhawks.nhl.com/club/microhome.htm?location=/charities

Purpose and activities: The Chicago Blackhawks makes charitable contributions to nonprofit organizations involved with education, children, homelessness, human services, people with disabilities, and the prevention of crime, abuse, and drug use. Support is limited to Illinois and northwest Indiana.
Fields of interest: Education, reading; Education; Hospitals (specialty); Cancer; Crime/violence prevention, abuse prevention; Housing/shelter, homeless; Human services, fund raising/fund distribution; Family resources and services, disability; Human services, gift distribution; Homeless, human services.
Type of support: Donated products; General/operating support; In-kind gifts.
Geographic limitations: Giving limited to IL and northwest IN.
Publications: Application guidelines.
Application information: Applications accepted. Application form required. Applicants should submit the following:
1) name, address and phone number of organization
2) brief history of organization and description of its mission
Requests must include the date, time, location, expected number of attendees, and a description of the event. Request should be addressed to the name of the player requested.
Initial approach: Complete online application for speaker requests
Copies of proposal: 1

783
Chicago Fire Soccer, LLC

(also known as Chicago Fire)
7000 S. Harlem Ave.
Bridgeview, IL 60455-1160 (708) 594-7200

Company URL: http://www.chicago-fire.com
Establishment information: Established in 1997.
Company type: Private company
Ultimate parent company: The Anschutz Corporation
Business activities: Operates professional soccer club.
Business type (SIC): Commercial sports
Corporate officers: Julian Posada, Pres.; Mike Humes, C.O.O.; Guillermo Petrei, V.P., Opers.
Giving statement: Giving through the Chicago Fire Corporate Giving Program and the Chicago Fire Foundation Toyota Park.

Chicago Fire Corporate Giving Program

Toyota Park
7000 S. Harlem Ave.
Bridgeview, IL 60455-1160 (708) 594-7200
FAX: (708) 496-6050; URL: http://www.chicago-fire.com/community

Purpose and activities: The Chicago Fire makes charitable contributions of team memorabilia and merchandise to nonprofit organizations for fundraising events. Support is given primarily in the greater Chicago, Illinois, area.
Fields of interest: General charitable giving.
Type of support: Donated products; In-kind gifts.
Geographic limitations: Giving primarily in the greater Chicago, IL, area.
Support limitations: No grants for general operating support, or sponsorships.
Publications: Application guidelines.
Application information: Applications accepted. Applications submitted by e-mail, fax, or mail are not accepted. Telephone calls are discouraged. Items sent for autograph will not be accepted and may not be returned. Organizations must be based in Illinois. Requests are limited to 1 application in any given year. Application form required. Applicants should submit the following:
1) name, address and phone number of organization
2) contact person
3) copy of IRS Determination Letter
Requests should include event name and date, as well as how many years the event has been held, the expected number of attendees, the amount raised in the prior year, and what the donated items will be used for.
Initial approach: Complete online application form
Deadline(s): 6 weeks prior to need
Final notification: 4 weeks from submission date

Chicago Fire Foundation Toyota Park

(formerly Fireworks for Kids Foundation)
7000 S. Harlem Ave.
Bridgeview, IL 60455-1160 (708) 496-6740
FAX: (312) 705-7393;
E-mail: jyavitz@chicago-fire.com; URL: http://www.chicago-fire.com/sites/chicago/files/grant_guidelines.pdf

Establishment information: Established in 1998 in IL.
Contact: Jessica Yavitz, Exec. Dir.
Financial data (yr. ended 12/31/11): Revenue, $186,501; assets, $314,221 (M); gifts received, $186,072; expenditures, $292,961; giving activities include $190,526 for grants.
Purpose and activities: As the philanthropic arm of the Chicago Fire, the foundation supports organizations whose programs provide educational and recreational opportunities for economically or otherwise challenged children.
Fields of interest: Education; Recreation, community Economically disadvantaged.
Program:
Grants: The foundation makes grants to programs in the metropolitan Chicago area that focus on health and wellness, education, and the environment, particularly with youth. Eligible organizations must be based in Cook, Lake, DuPage, McHenry, Kane, Kankakee, or Will counties, Illinois; or Lake County, Indiana.
Geographic limitations: Giving limited to the metropolitan Chicago area, IL and IN.
Publications: Annual report; Application guidelines; Newsletter.
Application information: Applications accepted. Applicants should submit the following:
1) statement of problem project will address
2) qualifications of key personnel
3) population served
4) detailed description of project and amount of funding requested
5) copy of IRS Determination Letter
6) listing of board of directors, trustees, officers and other key people and their affiliations
7) copy of most recent annual report/audited financial statement/990
8) contact person
9) listing of additional sources and amount of support
10) additional materials/documentation
Initial approach: Submit letter of inquiry
Deadline(s): Oct. 1
Officers and Directors:* Andrew Hauptman, Hon. Chair.; Tony Lopez, V.P. and Treas.; Frank Klopas*, Pres.; Jessica Yavitz, Exec. Dir.; Dean Magdalin; Jill Matesic; Sheila Moore; and 9 additional directors.
EIN: 911931487

784
Chicago National League Ball Club, Inc.

(also known as Chicago Cubs)
1060 W. Addison St.
Chicago, IL 60613-4397 (773) 404-2827

Company URL: http://www.cubs.com
Establishment information: Established in 1876.
Company type: Subsidiary of a private company
Business activities: Operates professional baseball club.
Business type (SIC): Commercial sports
Corporate officers: Tom Ricketts, Chair.; Crane H. Kenney, Pres.; Michael Lufrano, Exec. V.P. and Genl. Counsel; Mark McGuire, Exec. V.P., Opers.; Julian Green, V.P., Comms.
Board of directors: Tom Ricketts, Chair.; Laura Ricketts; Pete Ricketts; Todd Ricketts
Giving statement: Giving through the Chicago Cubs Charities.

Chicago Cubs Charities

c/o Community Affairs
1060 W. Addison St.
Chicago, IL 60613-4566 (773) 404-4073
URL: http://www.cubs.com/donations

Purpose and activities: The Chicago Cubs makes charitable contributions of memorabilia and game tickets to nonprofit organizations for fundraising auctions and raffles.
Fields of interest: General charitable giving.
Type of support: Donated products; In-kind gifts.
Publications: Application guidelines.
Application information: Applications accepted. Mail and phone requests are not accepted. Requests are limited to 1 application per organization in any given year. Items for autograph are not accepted. Organizations that receive an item must complete an online reply form after the event, including the amount the item raised for the event, to be considered for future requests. Applications for group tickets must be submitted separately. Groups are limited to 50 people. The Community Affairs Department handles giving. Application form required.
Requests must include the event name, date, location, number of guests, sponsor or underwriter, and what the donation will be used for.
Initial approach: Complete online application
Deadline(s): 6 weeks prior to need

Administrator: Jennifer Dedes Nowak, Mgr., Community Outreach, Grants and Donations.
Number of staff: 4 full-time professional; 2 full-time support.

785
Chicago Professional Sports L.P.

(also known as Chicago Bulls)
1901 W. Madison St., United Ctr.
Chicago, IL 60612-2459 (312) 455-4000

Company URL: http://www.nba.com/bulls
Establishment information: Established in 1966.
Company type: Private company
Business activities: Operates professional basketball club.
Business type (SIC): Commercial sports
Corporate officers: Jerry M. Reinsdorf, Chair.; Michael Reinsdorf, Pres. and C.O.O.; Steve Schanwald, Exec. V.P., Opers.; Irwin B. Mandel, Sr. V.P., Finance; John Viola, V.P., Corp. Sales; Susan Goodenow, V.P., Comms.; Stuart Bookman, Cont.
Board of director: Jerry M. Reinsdorf, Chair.
Giving statement: Giving through the CharitaBulls.

CharitaBulls

c/o Chicago Professional Sports L.P.
1901 W. Madison St.
Chicago, IL 60612-2459 (312) 455-4000
URL: http://www.nba.com/bulls/community/charitabulls.html

Establishment information: Established in 1987 in IL.
Contact: Stuart Bookman
Financial data (yr. ended 06/30/11): Revenue, $1,684,331; assets, $4,423,447 (M); gifts received, $968,507; expenditures, $1,365,766; giving activities include $561,704 for grants.
Purpose and activities: The foundation raises and contributes funds to projects benefiting worthy causes in the Chicago, Illinois, area, such as basketball court renovation programs, midnight basketball, Special Olympics, and an upgrading equipment project of the Chicago Public Library.
Fields of interest: Elementary/secondary education; Libraries (public); Recreation, parks/playgrounds; Athletics/sports, basketball; Athletics/sports, Special Olympics; Youth development, community service clubs.
Program:
Bulls Scholars: Bulls Scholars offers seventh and eighth grade students in the Chicago Public Schools system the option to enroll in an additional English and/or algebra course during after-school hours. Students successfully completing the program earn high school credit and learn valuable skills that will assist them with the transition into higher education.
Type of support: Building/renovation; Equipment; Program development; Scholarships—to individuals.
Geographic limitations: Giving primarily in Chicago, IL.
Application information: Applications accepted. Application form required.
Initial approach: Contact local high school for scholarship application
Officers and Directors:* Steven M. Schanwald*, Pres.; Irwin B. Mandel*, V.P.; David Kurland, Secy.; Stuart Bookman, Treas.; Robert A. Judelson; Jerry Reinsdorf.
EIN: 363544506

786
Chicago Sun-Times, Inc.

350 N. Orleans St., 10th Fl.
Chicago, IL 60654 (312) 321-3000

Company URL: http://www.suntimes.com
Establishment information: Established in 1948.
Company type: Subsidiary of a foreign company
Business activities: Publishes newspapers. The company has filed for Chapter 11 protection.
Business type (SIC): Newspaper publishing and/or printing
Corporate officers: Timothy P. Knight, C.E.O.; Matthew A. Saleski, V.P., Mktg.; Ted Rilea, V.P., Human Resources
Subsidiaries: Daily Southtown, Chicago, IL; Star Publications, Chicago Heights, IL
Giving statement: Giving through the Chicago Sun-Times Charity Trust.

Chicago Sun-Times Charity Trust

350 N. Orleans St., 10th Fl.
Chicago, IL 60654-1700 (312) 321-3000
E-mail: charitytrust@suntimes.com; Tel. for Patricia L. Dudek: (312) 321-2213, e-mail: pdudek@suntimes.com; URL: http://www.suntimes.com/charitytrust

Establishment information: Trust established in 1936 in IL as the Times Charity Fund.
Donors: Season of Sharing; Chicago Sun-Times, Inc.; Frederick F. Burgmann†.
Contact: Patricia L. Dudek, Pres.
Financial data (yr. ended 09/30/11): Assets, $879,750 (M); gifts received, $56,708; expenditures, $319,207; qualifying distributions, $305,000; giving activities include $305,000 for grants.
Purpose and activities: The foundation supports programs designed to serve youth. Special emphasis is directed toward programs designed to promote education and literacy; arts and culture; and social services and civic affairs.
Fields of interest: Performing arts, music; Arts; Education, services; Education, reading; Education; Food banks; Boys & girls clubs; Youth, services; Human services; Public affairs Youth.
Program:
Sun Shine Project: Through the Sun Shine Project, the foundation awards grants to charities involved with youth in education, art, and civic engagement. The public is invited to nominate deserving charities on the Sun Shine Project website and charities with the most votes and comments will be considered for funding. The program is limited to charities located in the Chicago region. Visit URL http://www.chicagosunshineproject.com/ for more information.
Type of support: Capital campaigns; General/operating support; Program development.
Geographic limitations: Giving limited to areas of company operations in the metropolitan Chicago, IL, area.
Support limitations: No support for religious organizations not of direct benefit to the entire community or primary or secondary schools. No grants to individuals, or for medical research, fellowships, national health agency drives, scholarships, benefit dinners, advertisements, commemorative journals, or sponsorships at fundraising events.
Publications: Application guidelines.
Application information: Applications accepted. Applicants should submit the following:
1) how project will be sustained once grantmaker support is completed
2) statement of problem project will address
3) copy of IRS Determination Letter
4) brief history of organization and description of its mission
5) copy of most recent annual report/audited financial statement/990
6) how project's results will be evaluated or measured
7) listing of board of directors, trustees, officers and other key people and their affiliations
8) detailed description of project and amount of funding requested
9) copy of current year's organizational budget and/or project budget

Initial approach: Proposal; complete online nomination form for the Sun Shine Project
Copies of proposal: 1
Board meeting date(s): Mar. and Oct.
Deadline(s): None; Oct. 9 for the Sun Shine Project
Final notification: Dec. for the Sun Shine Project
Officers and Trustees:* James D. McDonough*, Chair.; Patricia L. Dudek*, Pres.; John Barron; Jeremy Halbreich; Dan Knight; Mary Mitchell; Theodore Rilea; Mark Roth; Mathew Saleski.
EIN: 366059459
Selected grants: The following grants are a representative sample of this grantmaker's funding activity:
$50,000 to Greater Chicago Food Depository, Chicago, IL, 2010.
$20,000 to Gildas Club Chicago, Chicago, IL, 2010.
$15,000 to Boys and Girls Clubs of Chicago, Chicago, IL, 2010.
$10,000 to Chicago Academy of Sciences, Chicago, IL, 2010.

787
Chicago Title and Trust Company

171 N. Clark St., 4th Fl.
Chicago, IL 60601-3309 (312) 223-2000

Company URL: https://www.ctic.com/default.asp
Establishment information: Established in 1891.
Company type: Subsidiary of a public company
Business activities: Sells title insurance.
Business type (SIC): Insurance/title
Corporate officers: John E. Rau, Pres. and C.E.O.; Peter G. Leemputte, Exec. V.P. and C.A.O.
Subsidiary: Chicago Title Insurance Co., Los Angeles, CA
Giving statement: Giving through the Chicago Title and Trust Company Foundation.

Chicago Title and Trust Company Foundation

c/o John Rau Miami Corp.
410 N. Michigan Ave., Ste. 590
Chicago, IL 60611-4220 (312) 644-6720

Establishment information: Established in 1951 in IL.
Donor: Chicago Title and Trust Co.
Contact: Eileen Hughes, Treas.
Financial data (yr. ended 12/31/11): Assets, $1,174,832 (M); expenditures, $224,940; qualifying distributions, $201,758; giving activities include $189,250 for 33 grants (high: $10,000; low: $250).
Purpose and activities: The foundation supports libraries, hospitals, aquariums, and festivals and organizations involved with arts and culture, higher

education, youth development business, human services, and community development.
Fields of interest: Performing arts; Performing arts, theater; Performing arts, opera; Arts; Higher education; Libraries (public); Aquariums; Hospitals (general); Recreation, fairs/festivals; Youth development, business; Community/economic development.
Type of support: Annual campaigns; Building/renovation; General/operating support; Program development.
Geographic limitations: Giving primarily in Chicago, IL.
Support limitations: No support for religious organizations. No grants to individuals, or for debt reduction.
Application information: Applications accepted. Application form not required.
Initial approach: Proposal
Copies of proposal: 1
Board meeting date(s): Apr. and Oct.
Deadline(s): None
Officers and Trustees:* John Rau*, Chair.; Eileen Hughes, Treas.; Norman R. Bobins; Robert Stucker.
Number of staff: 1 part-time support.
EIN: 366036809
Selected grants: The following grants are a representative sample of this grantmaker's funding activity:
$10,000 to Chicago Public Library Foundation, Chicago, IL, 2010. For general fund.
$10,000 to Chicago Shakespeare Theater, Chicago, IL, 2010. For general fund.
$10,000 to Chicago Shakespeare Theater, Chicago, IL, 2010. For general fund.
$10,000 to Lyric Opera of Chicago, Chicago, IL, 2010. For general fund.
$5,000 to Chamber of Commerce Foundation, Chicagoland, Chicago, IL, 2010. For general fund.
$5,000 to Chicago Public Library Foundation, Chicago, IL, 2010. For general fund.
$5,000 to Junior Achievement of Chicago, Chicago, IL, 2010. For general fund.
$2,500 to Chicago Humanities Festival, Chicago, IL, 2010. For general fund.
$1,000 to Indiana University Foundation, Bloomington, IN, 2010. For general fund.

788
Chicago Tribune Company
435 N. Michigan Ave., Ste. 1400
Chicago, IL 60611-4066 (312) 222-3232

Company URL: http://www.chicagotribune.com
Establishment information: Established in 1847.
Company type: Subsidiary of a private company
Business activities: Publishes newspapers.
Business type (SIC): Newspaper publishing and/or printing
Financial profile for 2009: Number of employees, 3,070
Corporate officer: Sam Zell, Chair. and Co-C.E.O.
Giving statement: Giving through the Chicago Tribune Company Community Giving Program and the Chicago Tribune Foundation.

Chicago Tribune Foundation
c/o Community Giving
435 N. Michigan Ave., 2nd Fl.
Chicago, IL 60611-4041 (312) 222-3928
FAX: (312) 222-3882;
E-mail: jwoelffer@tribune.com; URL: http://www.chicagotribune.com/communitygiving

Establishment information: Incorporated in 1958 in IL.
Donor: Chicago Tribune Co.
Contact: Jan Ellen Woelffer, Grant and Charitable Prog. Specialist
Financial data (yr. ended 12/31/11): Assets, $1,027,119 (M); expenditures, $267,582; qualifying distributions, $264,776; giving activities include $264,776 for grants.
Purpose and activities: The foundation supports organizations involved with journalism, arts and culture, and civic affairs. Special emphasis is directed toward programs that foster education for under-served populations.
Fields of interest: Media, print publishing; Arts; Civil liberties, first amendment; Public affairs Youth; Adults; Minorities.

Programs:
Civic: The foundation supports programs designed to help low-income youth through education engage in the Chicago area. Grants range from $2,500 to $5,000. By invitation only.
Culture: The foundation supports programs designed to provide educational support in the arts for youth from low-income communities. Arts education programs can be in-school or after-school support. Grants range from $2,500 to $5,000. Priority is given to community-based arts organizations with budgets under $2 million.
Employee Matching Gifts: The foundation matches contributions made by employees of Chicago Tribune to nonprofit organizations on a two-for-one basis up to $1,000 per employee, per year.
Journalism: The Chicago Tribune Foundation strives for journalistic excellence by building a diverse pool of journalists to serve readers in Chicago and encouraging youths to have a voice. While there are many worthy approaches and organizations, the foundation seeks to focus its resources on local programs that will help train journalists who might otherwise not enter the field, and help them thrive in newsrooms. Support is considered for five categories of journalism programs that promote the development of a journalistic workforce that better reflects the makeup of the communities served by newspapers, including minorities and individuals from economically disadvantaged backgrounds. The journalism grant range is $5,000 to $7,500. Support is not provided to individual college or high school newspapers. Proposals are due August 1 for a board meeting in November. The funding areas are: 1) Internships offered by local journalism organizations or Chicago-area colleges and universities that foster entry-level journalism reporting, photography and editing experiences for diverse candidates in metropolitan Chicago. 2) Training and education programs offered by local or national journalism nonprofit organizations for diverse professional journalists. 3) Hands-on journalism production or media literacy programs offered by local nonprofit organizations that reach low-income youth and diverse students in metropolitan Chicago. 4) Local reading services of media news and information that are broadcast and serve metropolitan Chicago.
Type of support: Employee matching gifts; General/operating support; Program development.
Geographic limitations: Giving primarily in the metropolitan Chicago, IL, area; giving also to national organizations for Journalism.
Support limitations: No support for high school or college newspapers or international organizations. No grants to individuals, or for capital campaigns.
Publications: Application guidelines; Corporate giving report; Grants list.
Application information: Applications accepted. Proposals are by invitation only; contact staff before submitting. Proposals may be submitted using the Chicago Area Grant Application Form or as a Letter of Inquiry plus grant information. Proposals should be no longer than 2 to 5 pages. Support is limited to 1 contribution per organization during any given year for three years. Application form not required. Applicants should submit the following:
1) copy of IRS Determination Letter
2) copy of most recent annual report/audited financial statement/990
3) descriptive literature about organization
4) listing of board of directors, trustees, officers and other key people and their affiliations
5) copy of current year's organizational budget and/or project budget
6) listing of additional sources and amount of support
7) additional materials/documentation
Proposals should include information requested on the Chicago Area Grant Application Form.
Initial approach: Letter, e-mail, or telephone
Copies of proposal: 1
Board meeting date(s): June for Culture; Nov. for Journalism
Deadline(s): Feb. 1 for Culture; Aug. 1 for Journalism
Final notification: Following board meetings
Officers and Directors:* Tony Hunter, Chair.; Sheila Solomon, Secy.; Janice Jacobs.
EIN: 366050792
Selected grants: The following grants are a representative sample of this grantmaker's funding activity:
$5,000 to Albany Park Theater Project, Chicago, IL, 2012. For after-school theater programs in writing, acting and production for teens.
$5,000 to Chicago Lighthouse for People Who Are Blind or Visually Impaired, Chicago, IL, 2012. For radio reading services for CRIS (Chicagoland Radio Information Service), radio reading service of news and ads for people with visual impairment or disabilities.
$5,000 to Chicago Sinfonietta, Chicago, IL, 2012. For music education programs in schools for low-income youth. To allow parent outreach for families to receive tickets to attend concerts.
$2,500 to Asian American Journalists Association, San Francisco, CA, 2012. For print or Internet internship for entry-level journalism opportunities in the Chicago area.

789
Chicago White Metal Casting Company, Inc.
649 N. Rte. 83
Bensenville, IL 60106-1340
(630) 595-4424
FAX: (630) 595-4474

Company URL: http://www.cwmdiecast.com
Establishment information: Established in 1937.
Company type: Private company
Business activities: Manufactures metal die-castings.
Business type (SIC): Metal foundries/nonferrous
Corporate officers: Walter G. Treiber, Chair. and Treas.; Eric Treiber, Pres. and C.E.O.; Anthony R. LoCoco, Exec. V.P. and C.F.O.; Jonathan Miller, V.P., Sales and Mktg.
Board of director: Walter G. Treiber, Chair.
Giving statement: Giving through the Chicago White Metal Charitable Foundation.

Chicago White Metal Charitable Foundation

649 N., Rte. 83
Bensenville, IL 60106 (630) 595-4424

Establishment information: Established in 1995 in IL.
Donors: Chicago White Metal Casting Co., Inc.; Walter G. Treiber, Jr.
Financial data (yr. ended 10/31/11): Assets, $51,354 (M); gifts received, $17,500; expenditures, $20,961; qualifying distributions, $20,708; giving activities include $20,708 for 13 grants (high: $7,500; low: $100).
Purpose and activities: The foundation supports organizations involved with opera, higher education, recreation, youth development, human services, community development, and government and public administration.
Fields of interest: Performing arts, opera; Higher education; Recreation; Youth development; Human services; Community/economic development; Government/public administration.
Type of support: Employee-related scholarships; General/operating support.
Geographic limitations: Giving primarily in the Chicago, IL, area.
Application information: Applications accepted. Application form required.
Initial approach: Letter
Deadline(s): None
Officers: Walter Treiber, Pres.; Eric Treiber, Secy.-Treas. and Mgr.
EIN: 366069669

790
Chicago White Sox, Ltd.

333 W. 35th St.
Chicago, IL 60616-3651 (312) 674-1000
FAX: (312) 674-5119

Company URL: http://chicago.whitesox.mlb.com
Establishment information: Established in 1901.
Company type: Private company
Business activities: Operates professional baseball club.
Business type (SIC): Commercial sports
Corporate officers: Jerry M. Reinsdorf, Chair.; Edward M. Einhorn, Vice-Chair.; Tim Buzard, Sr. V.P. and Admin.; Brooks Boyer, Sr. V.P., Sales and Mktg.; Scott Reifert, Sr. V.P., Comms.; John Corvino, Genl. Counsel
Board of directors: Jerry M. Reinsdorf, Chair.; Edward M. Einhorn, Vice-Chair.; Robert Judelson; Judd Malkin; Robert Mazer; Allan Muchin; Jay Pinsky; Lee Stern; Burton Ury; Charles Walsh
Giving statement: Giving through the Chicago White Sox, Ltd. Corporate Giving Program and the Chicago White Sox Charities, Inc.

Chicago White Sox, Ltd. Corporate Giving Program

c/o Community Rels.
333 W. 35th St.
Chicago, IL 60616-3651
FAX: (312) 674-5119; URL: http://chicago.whitesox.mlb.com/NASApp/mlb/cws/community/index.jsp

Purpose and activities: The Chicago White Sox provides financial support to organizations involved with education, cancer, recreation, and children and families in crisis; and provides memorabilia and game tickets on a case by case basis. Support is given primarily in Illinois and the greater Chicagoland, Illinois and northwestern Indiana, area.
Fields of interest: Education; Cancer; Youth development, centers/clubs; Youth development; Children/youth, services; Family services; Human services; General charitable giving.
Type of support: Donated products; General/operating support; In-kind gifts.
Geographic limitations: Giving primarily in IL and the greater Chicagoland, IL and northwestern IN, area.
Application information: Applications accepted. Proposals should be submitted using organization letterhead. Support is limited to 1 contribution per organization during any given year. Application form not required. Applicants should submit the following:
1) name, address and phone number of organization
2) detailed description of project and amount of funding requested
3) contact person

Proposals should indicate the date and location of the event, if applicable.
Initial approach: Mail or fax proposal to headquarters
Copies of proposal: 1
Deadline(s): 4 to 6 weeks prior to need

Chicago White Sox Charities, Inc.

333 W. 35th St.
Chicago, IL 60616-3621 (312) 674-5387
FAX: (312) 674-5119; E-mail: coreilly@chisox.com; URL: http://chicago.whitesox.mlb.com/NASApp/mlb/cws/community/index.jsp?program=charities

Establishment information: Established in 1990 in IL.
Contact: Christine O'Reilly, Exec. Dir.
Financial data (yr. ended 12/31/10): Revenue, $1,152,576; assets, $4,680,739 (M); gifts received, $568,260; expenditures, $1,639,547; giving activities include $1,333,871 for grants.
Purpose and activities: The charity provides financial and emotional support to hundreds of Chicago-based organizations, including those leading the fight against cancer, dedicated to improving the lives of youth through recreation and education, and offering support to children and families in crisis.
Fields of interest: Education; Cancer research; Recreation; Youth development, formal/general education; Youth development; Family services.
Program:
Grants: Grants are available to organizations in the greater Chicago metropolitan region that work in youth education programs, health and wellness programs, child abuse prevention and treatment programs, and cancer research and treatment programs.
Type of support: Building/renovation; Continuing support; Equipment; Fellowships; Management development/capacity building; Program development; Publication; Research; Scholarship funds.
Geographic limitations: Giving primarily in the greater metropolitan Chicago, IL, area.
Publications: Annual report; Grants list; Newsletter.
Application information: Applications accepted. Letter of interest should be limited to 2 pages and submitted on organization letterhead. Application form required. Applicants should submit the following:
1) population served
2) detailed description of project and amount of funding requested
3) descriptive literature about organization
4) results expected from proposed grant
5) how project's results will be evaluated or measured
6) copy of most recent annual report/audited financial statement/990
7) copy of IRS Determination Letter
8) listing of board of directors, trustees, officers and other key people and their affiliations

Initial approach: Letter of interest to headquarters
Copies of proposal: 1
Board meeting date(s): Dec.
Deadline(s): Varies
Officers: Scott Reifert, Pres.; Howard Pizer, Secy.; Timothy Buzard, Treas.
Directors: Brooks Boyer; Jerry M. Reinsdorf; Terry Savarise; Ken Williams.
EIN: 363719918

791
Chick-fil-A, Inc.

5200 Buffington Rd.
Atlanta, GA 30349-2945 (404) 765-8000
FAX: (800) 232-2677

Company URL: http://www.chick-fil-a.com
Establishment information: Established in 1946.
Company type: Private company
Business activities: Operates restaurants.
Business type (SIC): Restaurants and drinking places
Financial profile for 2009: Number of employees, 6,152; sales volume, $3,217,000,000
Corporate officers: S. Truett Cathy, Chair. and C.E.O.; Dan T. Cathy, Pres. and C.O.O.; James Buck McCabe, Sr. V.P., Finance, and C.F.O.; Timothy Tassopoulos, Sr. V.P., Opers.; Michael F. Erbrick, V.P. and C.I.O.; Philip A. Barrett, V.P. and Cont.; Barry V. White, V.P., Comms.
Board of director: S. Truett Cathy, Chair.
Giving statement: Giving through the Chick-fil-A, Inc. Corporate Giving Program, the Chick-Fil-A Foundation, and the WinShape Foundation, Inc.

Chick-fil-A, Inc. Corporate Giving Program

5200 Buffington Rd.
Atlanta, GA 30349-2945 (404) 765-8000
URL: http://www.chick-fil-a.com/#ourcommitment

Purpose and activities: As a complement to its foundation, Chick-fil-A also makes charitable contributions to schools and nonprofit organizations directly. Support is given in areas of company operations.
Fields of interest: Education, fund raising/fund distribution; Elementary school/education; Athletics/sports, football; Recreation; Children, services; Family services.
Programs:
Chick-fil-A Leadership Scholarship Program: Chick-fil-A offers $1,000 college scholarships to certain qualified franchised Operator Restaurant employees, a Chick-fil-A tradition that has awarded over $30 million in scholarships.
S. Truett Cathy Scholar Awards: Chick-fil-A awards additional $1,000 college scholarships to high school students who demonstrate excellence in academics, leadership, and community service.
Type of support: Donated products; Employee volunteer services; Employee-related scholarships; General/operating support; In-kind gifts; Program development; Scholarship funds; Sponsorships.
Geographic limitations: Giving on a national basis in areas of company operations.
Publications: Application guidelines.

Application information: Applications accepted. Franchised Restaurant Operators handle giving at individual locations. Application form not required.
Initial approach: Contact nearest franchise for product donations, local events, and sponsorships
Deadline(s): None

WinShape Foundation, Inc.

(formerly WinShape Centre, Inc.)
5200 Buffington Rd.
Atlanta, GA 30349-2998
FAX: (706) 238-7742;
E-mail: rskelton@winshape.org; Additional tel.: (877) 977-3873, e-mail: info@winshape.org; URL: http://www.winshape.org
Scholarship application address: c/o Berry College, P.O. Box 490159, Mt. Berry, GA 30149-0009, tel.: (706) 236-2215, e-mail: admissions@berry.edu, collegeprogram@winshape.org

Establishment information: Established as a company-sponsored operating foundation in 1984 in GA.
Donors: Chick-fil-A, Inc.; S. Truett Cathy; CFA Properties, Inc.
Financial data (yr. ended 12/31/11): Assets, $67,828,167 (M); gifts received, $25,459,075; expenditures, $27,748,074; qualifying distributions, $24,875,190; giving activities include $5,919,311 for 24 grants (high: $2,896,438; low: $100) and $22,118,960 for 4 foundation-administered programs.
Purpose and activities: The foundation supports programs involved with education, children and youth, families, marriage enrichment, and religion; also awards college scholarships to undergraduate students attending Berry College.
Fields of interest: Child development, education; Secondary school/education; Education; Youth development; Children/youth, services; Child development, services; Family services; Christian agencies & churches; Religion Children/youth; Children.
Program:
WinShape College Scholarship Program: The foundation awards college scholarships of up to $32,000 to undergraduate students attending Berry College who agree to pre-determined standards of living including christ-followership, integrity, servanthood, and unity.
Type of support: Continuing support; Scholarships —to individuals.
Geographic limitations: Giving primarily in GA.
Publications: Application guidelines; Informational brochure (including application guidelines).
Application information: Applications accepted. Unsolicited requests accepted only for scholarship program. An interview may be required for scholarships. Scholarship applicants must apply to the WinShape College Program and to Berry College. Application form required.
Scholarship applications should include 3 references, a resume, and an essay.
Initial approach: Complete online application form or contact foundation for application form for scholarships
Board meeting date(s): Varies
Deadline(s): Feb. 1 for scholarships
Final notification: Apr. 15 for scholarships
Officers: S. Truett Cathy, Pres.; Donald M. Cathy, V.P.; James B. McCabe, Secy.-Treas.; Robert M. Skelton, Exec. Dir.
Number of staff: 62 full-time professional.
EIN: 581595471

792
Chicopee Bancorp, Inc.

70 Center St.
P.O. Box 300
Chicopee, MA 01014-0300 (413) 594-6692
FAX: (413) 594-8197

Company URL: http://www.chicopeesavings.com/
Establishment information: Established in 1854.
Company type: Public company
Company ticker symbol and exchange: CBNK/ NASDAQ
Business activities: Operates savings bank.
Business type (SIC): Savings institutions
Financial profile for 2012: Number of employees, 38; assets, $599,980,000; pre-tax net income, $3,050,000; liabilities, $510,010,000
Corporate officers: William J. Wagner, Chair., Pres., and C.E.O.; Guida R. Sajdak, Sr. V.P. and C.F.O.; Maria J.C. Aigner, Sr. V.P., Human Resources; Theresa C. Szlosek, Corp. Secy.
Board of directors: William J. Wagner, Chair.; Thomas J. Bardon; James H. Bugbee; Douglas K. Engebretson; Gary G. Fitzgerald; William J. Giokas; James P. Lynch; William D. Masse; Gregg F. Orlen; Paul C. Picknelly; Judith T. Tremble
Giving statement: Giving through the Chicopee Savings Bank Charitable Foundation.
Company EIN: 204840562

Chicopee Savings Bank Charitable Foundation

70 Center St.
P.O. Box 300
Chicopee, MA 01014-0300 (413) 598-3107
E-mail: foundation@chicopeesavings.com; URL: http://www.chicopeesavings.com/default.asp?LINKNAME=COMMUNITY

Establishment information: Established in 2006 in DE and MA.
Donor: Chicopee Bancorp, Inc.
Contact: Berdie Thompson, Coord.
Financial data (yr. ended 12/31/11): Assets, $6,021,725 (M); expenditures, $406,725; qualifying distributions, $398,240; giving activities include $381,278 for 160 grants (high: $50,000; low: $25).
Purpose and activities: The foundation supports programs designed to preserve and enhance quality of life within local neighborhoods and communities. Special emphasis is directed toward community development; preservation of affordable housing; human service programs that serve low- and moderate-income individuals; art programs that serve the disadvantaged; and education.
Fields of interest: Arts; Higher education; Education; Housing/shelter, development; Housing/shelter; Boys & girls clubs; Human services; Community/economic development Economically disadvantaged.
Type of support: Annual campaigns; Continuing support; General/operating support; In-kind gifts; Program development; Scholarship funds; Sponsorships.
Geographic limitations: Giving primarily in areas of company operations in Chicopee, Ludlow, South Hadley, Ware, and West Springfield, MA.
Support limitations: No support for political or fraternal organizations. No grants to individuals.
Publications: Application guidelines.
Application information: Applications accepted. The foundation is currently accepting requests for general operating support from organizations that provide vital community services. Proposals should be no longer than 1 to 2 pages in length. A site visit may be requested. Multi-year funding is not automatic. Organizations receiving support are asked to submit periodic reports. Application form not required. Applicants should submit the following:
1) results expected from proposed grant
2) statement of problem project will address
3) population served
4) copy of IRS Determination Letter
5) geographic area to be served
6) copy of most recent annual report/audited financial statement/990
7) listing of board of directors, trustees, officers and other key people and their affiliations
8) detailed description of project and amount of funding requested
9) copy of current year's organizational budget and/or project budget
10) listing of additional sources and amount of support
Initial approach: Proposal
Deadline(s): None; 90 days prior to need for sponsorships, events, or in-kind requests
Officers and Directors:* William J. Wagner*, Pres.; Theresa C. Szlosek, Secy.; Guida R. Sajdak, Treas.; Thomas J. Bardon; James H. Bugbee; Douglas Engebretson; William J. Gikoas; Russell J. Omer; Gregg F. Orlen; Michael Sobon.
EIN: 223940271
Selected grants: The following grants are a representative sample of this grantmaker's funding activity:
$3,000 to Boston College, Chestnut Hill, MA, 2011.
$1,500 to American Heart Association, Dallas, TX, 2011.
$1,000 to Muscular Dystrophy Association, Tucson, AZ, 2011.

793
Chief Industries, Inc.

3942 W. Old Hwy. 30
P.O. Box 2078
Grand Island, NE 68802-2078
(308) 389-7200

Company URL: http://www.chiefind.com
Establishment information: Established in 1954.
Company type: Private company
Business activities: Manufactures electronic display systems, grain bins, steel buildings, mobile and modular housing, recreational vehicles, security windows and doors, sewage treatment systems, and ethanol fuel; operates golf course.
Business type (SIC): Electronic components and accessories; chemicals/industrial organic; metal refining/secondary nonferrous; machinery/special industry; machinery/refrigeration and service industry; transportation equipment/miscellaneous
Corporate officers: Robert G. Eihusen, Chair., Pres., and C.E.O.; Dave Ostdiek, V.P., Treas., and C.F.O.; Donald L. Dunn, Secy.; Susan Albers, Corp. Cont.
Board of director: Robert G. Eihusen, Chair.
Giving statement: Giving through the Chief Foundation, Inc. and the Virgil Eihusen Foundation, Inc.

The Chief Foundation, Inc.

P.O. Box 2078
Grand Island, NE 68802-2078 (308) 389-7200

Establishment information: Established in 2006 in NE.
Donor: Chief Industries, Inc.
Contact: Barbara Saladen, Secy.-Treas.

Financial data (yr. ended 12/31/11): Assets, $749,377 (M); expenditures, $57,297; qualifying distributions, $57,000; giving activities include $57,000 for 6 grants (high: $20,000; low: $5,000).
Purpose and activities: The foundation supports organizations involved with theater, education, and human services.
Fields of interest: Performing arts, theater; Education; Girl scouts; YM/YWCAs & YM/YWHAs; Children/youth, services; Homeless, human services; Human services.
Type of support: Capital campaigns.
Geographic limitations: Giving primarily in Grand Island, NE.
Application information: Applications accepted. Application form required.
Initial approach: Letter
Deadline(s): None
Officers: D. J. Eihusen, Pres.; Barbara Saladen, Secy.-Treas.
Director: Susan Albers.
EIN: 204896971

Virgil Eihusen Foundation, Inc.

(formerly Eihusen-Chief Foundation, Inc.)
4100 W. Husker Hwy.
Grand Island, NE 68803-6539 (308) 383-1425

Establishment information: Established in 1988 in NE.
Donors: Chief Industries, Inc.; Virgil Eihusen Estate.
Contact: Jack Henry, V.P.
Financial data (yr. ended 06/30/12): Assets, $2,674,645 (M); expenditures, $59,500; qualifying distributions, $47,525; giving activities include $47,525 for grants.
Purpose and activities: The foundation supports health centers and organizations involved with agriculture, recreation, and youth mentoring.
Fields of interest: Arts; Health care; Human services.
Type of support: Building/renovation; Capital campaigns; Scholarship funds.
Geographic limitations: Giving primarily in Grand Island, NE.
Support limitations: No grants to individuals.
Application information: Applications accepted. Application form required.
Initial approach: Letter
Deadline(s): None
Officers and Directors:* Marilyn Eihusen*, Pres.; Jack Henry*, V.P.; Jill Fargo*, Secy.
EIN: 363661287

794
Chinese Healing Institute

12381 Wilshire Blvd., Ste. 104
West Los Angeles, CA 90025-1063
(310) 826-1314
FAX: (310) 571-3168

Company URL: http://chinesehealinginstitute.com
Establishment information: Established in 1995.
Company type: Private company
Business activities: Provides health services.
Business type (SIC): Medical offices and clinics/ miscellaneous
Corporate officers: Yi Pan, Owner; Xiao Ming Xu, Owner
Giving statement: Giving through the Weiner Family Foundation.

Weiner Family Foundation

12401 Wilshire Blvd., 2nd Fl.
Los Angeles, CA 90025-1086

Establishment information: Established in 2002 in CA.
Donors: Chinese Healing Institute; Beryl Weiner.
Financial data (yr. ended 12/31/11): Assets, $263,348 (M); gifts received, $50,000; expenditures, $16,563; qualifying distributions, $15,500; giving activities include $15,500 for grants.
Purpose and activities: The foundation supports the Los Angeles Philharmonic Association.
Fields of interest: Arts.
Type of support: General/operating support.
Support limitations: No grants to individuals.
Application information: Applications not accepted. Unsolicited requests for funds not accepted.
Officer and Director:* Beryl Weiner*, Pres.
EIN: 010674806

795
Chiquita Brands International, Inc.

(formerly United Brands Company)
550 S Caldwell St.
Charlotte, NC 28202 (980) 636-5000

Company URL: http://www.chiquita.com
Establishment information: Established in 1899.
Company type: Public company
Company ticker symbol and exchange: CQB/NYSE
Business activities: Produces, markets, and distributes fruits, vegetables, and processed foods.
Business type (SIC): Agricultural production crops; farms/vegetable and melon; farms/fruit and nut; specialty foods/canned, frozen, and preserved
Financial profile for 2012: Number of employees, 20,000; assets, $1,697,760,000; sales volume, $3,078,340,000; pre-tax net income, -$297,800,000; expenses, $3,332,170,000; liabilities, $1,327,360,000
Fortune 1000 ranking: 2012—700th in revenues, 955th in profits, and 894th in assets
Corporate officers: Kerrii B. Anderson, Chair.; Edward F. Lonergan, Pres. and C.E.O.; Brian W. Kocher, Sr. V.P. and C.O.O.; Rick P. Kocher, Sr. V.P. and C.F.O.; James E. Thompson, Sr. V.P., Genl. Counsel, and Secy.; Joseph B. Johnson, V.P., Cont., and C.A.O.
Board of directors: Kerrii B. Anderson, Chair.; Howard W. Barker, Jr.; William H. Camp; Clare M. Hasler-Lewis, Ph.D.; Edward F. Lonergan; Jaime Serra; Jeffrey N. Simmons; Steven P. Stanbrook; Ronald V. Waters III
Giving statement: Giving through the Chiquita Brands International Foundation.
Company EIN: 041923360

Chiquita Brands International Foundation

(formerly United Brands Foundation)
250 E. 5th St.
Cincinnati, OH 45202-4119

Establishment information: Incorporated in 1954 in IL.
Donor: Chiquita Brands International, Inc.
Contact: Heather Higdon
Financial data (yr. ended 12/31/11): Assets, $1 (M); expenditures, $0; qualifying distributions, $0.
Purpose and activities: The foundation supports organizations involved with natural resources, agriculture, and nutrition.
Fields of interest: Environment, natural resources; Agriculture; Nutrition.
Type of support: In-kind gifts; Program development.
Application information: Applications accepted. Application form not required.
Initial approach: Proposal
Copies of proposal: 1
Deadline(s): None
Officers: Joseph W. Bradley, Pres.; Lori Ritchey, V.P.; Michael Sims, V.P.; James E. Thompson, Secy.
EIN: 366051081

796
Choate, Hall & Stewart LLP

2 International Pl.
Boston, MA 02110-4104 (617) 248-5000

Company URL: http://www.choate.com
Company type: Private company
Business activities: Operates law firm.
Business type (SIC): Legal services
Corporate officers: Bill Gelnaw, Managing Partner; John Nadas, Managing Partner
Giving statement: Giving through the Choate, Hall & Stewart LLP Pro Bono Program.

Choate, Hall & Stewart LLP Pro Bono Program

2 International Pl.
Boston, MA 02110-4104 (617) 248-5000
E-mail: jbaraniak@choate.com; Additional tel.: (617) 248-5000; URL: http://www.choate.com/firm.php?FirmID=5

Contact: John R. Baraniak, Partner
Fields of interest: Legal services.
Type of support: Pro bono services - legal.
Geographic limitations: Giving primarily in areas of company operations in Boston, MA.
Application information: An attorney coordinates pro bono projects.

797
Choggiung Limited

104 Main St. Ste. 201
P.O. Box 330
Dillingham, AK 99576-0330
(907) 842-5218

Company URL: http://www.choggiung.com
Establishment information: Established in 1973.
Company type: Native corporation
Business activities: Operates native corporation.
Business type (SIC): Nonclassifiable establishments
Corporate officers: Lance Nunn, C.E.O; Bryce Edgmon, Pres.; Olga Kropoff, Secy.; John A. Heyano, Treas.
Board of directors: Bryce Edgmon; Ida M. Backford; LouAnn Backford; John A. Heyano; Olga Kropoff; Cameron Poindexter; Jack A. Savo, Jr.; Thomas Tilden; Frank G. Woods III
Subsidiaries: Nuna Contractors, Anchorage, AK; Quvaq, Dillingham, AK
Giving statement: Giving through the Choggiung Education Endowment Foundation.

Choggiung Education Endowment Foundation

P.O. Box 330
Dillingham, AK 99576-0330 (907) 842-5218

Establishment information: Established in 1995 in AK.
Donors: Choggiung Ltd.; Nuna Contractors; Dylan Hopper.
Financial data (yr. ended 09/30/12): Assets, $289,597 (M); expenditures, $14,210; qualifying distributions, $13,505; giving activities include $13,505 for 17 grants (high: $2,000; low: $23).
Purpose and activities: The foundation awards college scholarships and work enhancement scholarships to shareholders and children of shareholders of Choggiung Limited.
Fields of interest: Education.
Type of support: Scholarships—to individuals.
Geographic limitations: Giving primarily in Dillingham, AK.
Publications: Application guidelines; Program policy statement.
Application information: Applications accepted. Application form required.
Applications for college scholarships should include a letter of interest that includes applicant's intentions, expected field of study, goals, and expectations; recent transcripts; 2 letters of reference; and a letter of acceptance from the institution that the applicant plans to attend.
Initial approach: Letter
Board meeting date(s): June 30
Deadline(s): April 30
Officers: John A. Heyano, Pres.; Louann Backford, V.P.; Jack A. Savo, Jr., Secy.-Treas.
Trustee: Darlene Olson.
EIN: 920155519

798
Choice Hotels International, Inc.

10750 Columbia Pike
Silver Spring, MD 20901 (301) 592-5000
FAX: (301) 592-6157

Company URL: http://www.choicehotels.com
Establishment information: Established in 1939.
Company type: Public company
Company ticker symbol and exchange: CHH/NYSE
Business activities: Franchises hotels.
Business type (SIC): Hotels and motels; investors/miscellaneous
Financial profile for 2012: Number of employees, 1,431; assets, $510,770,000; sales volume, $691,510,000; pre-tax net income, $169,170,000; expenses, $498,890,000; liabilities, $1,059,680,000
Corporate officers: Stewart W. Bainum, Jr., Chair.; Stephen P. Joyce, Pres. and C.E.O.; Patrick Pacious, Exec. V.P., Opers.; David L. White, C.F.O.; Simone Wu, Sr. V.P., Genl. Counsel, and Corp. Secy.; Scott Oaksmith, Cont.
Board of directors: Stewart Bainum, Jr., Chair.; Barbara T. Alexander; William L. Jews; Stephen P. Joyce; Scott A. Renschler; John T. Schwieters; Ervin R. Shames; Gordon A. Smith; John P. Tague
Giving statement: Giving through the Choice Hotels International Foundation.
Company EIN: 521209792

Choice Hotels International Foundation

10750 Columbia Pike
Silver Spring, MD 20901-4427 (301) 592-5000
FAX: (301) 592-6274;
E-mail: choice_foundation@choicehotels.com;
URL: http://www.choicehotels.com/en/responsibility/roomtogive?sid=xBzpH.WEwNOgSY3.10
Scholarship application address: 4225 E. Windrose Dr., Phoenix, AZ 85032; Tel. for Women's Business Alliance Scholarship Program: (602) 953-4478

Establishment information: Established in 1999 in MD.
Donor: Choice Hotels International, Inc.
Contact: Kelly Kane, Exec. Dir.
Financial data (yr. ended 12/31/11): Assets, $431,778 (M); gifts received, $854,838; expenditures, $776,562; qualifying distributions, $728,853; giving activities include $728,853 for grants.
Purpose and activities: The foundation supports programs designed to provide shelter and food to those in need; enhance educational efforts of schools, workforce entry organizations, and the hospitality industry; and promote the growth and development of tourism.
Fields of interest: Education; Employment; Food services; Housing/shelter; Human services; Economic development, visitors/convention bureau/tourism promotion; Community/economic development Adults, women.
Programs:
Matching Contributions Program: The foundation matches contributions made by employees of Choice Hotels to nonprofit organizations on a one-for-one basis up to $3,000 per employee, per organization, per year.
Scholarship Program for Dependent Children: The foundation awards $2,000 college scholarships to the dependents of associates of Choice Hotels.
Volunteer Matching Program: The foundation awards grants to nonprofit organizations with which Choice Hotels employees volunteer, $500 for every 100 volunteer hours, up to $1,000 per organization.
Women's Business Alliance Scholarship Program: The foundation annually awards a $2,000 college scholarship to a deserving female with an interest in or link to the hospitality industry. This award is open to undergraduate and post-graduate students. Visit URL: http://www.choicehotels.com/en/about-choice/wba for more information.
Type of support: Employee matching gifts; Employee volunteer services; Employee-related scholarships; General/operating support; Program development; Research; Scholarship funds; Scholarships—to individuals.
Geographic limitations: Giving primarily in areas of company operations in Phoenix, AZ, Grand Junction, CO, Silver Spring, MD, and Minot, ND; giving also to national organizations.
Support limitations: No support for religious organizations not of direct benefit to the entire community, lobbying, political, or fraternal organizations, for-profit ventures, or medical- or health-related organizations. No grants to individuals (except for scholarships), or for capital campaigns, endowments, or memorials, golf tournaments, dinners, or events where Choice Hotels International Foundation receives a tangible benefit.
Publications: Annual report; Application guidelines.
Application information: Applications accepted. Unsolicited applications for general funding are currently not accepted. Application form required. Scholarship requests should include high school or college transcripts, letters of recommendation, and a 500-word essay.
Initial approach: Download application form and mail to foundation for Women's Business Alliance Scholarship Program
Copies of proposal: 1
Board meeting date(s): Rolling
Deadline(s): Feb. 2 for Women's Business Alliance Scholarship Program
Final notification: May 14 for scholarships
Officer and Trustees: Kelly Kane, Exec. Dir.; Phyllis Burkhard; Patrick Cimerola; Maria D'Ambrosio; Brett Limage; Anne Madison; Thomas Mirgon; David L. White.
EIN: 522184905

799
The Chotin Group Corp.

6400 S. Fiddlers Green Cir.. Ste. 1200
Greenwood Village, CO 80111-4950
(303) 741-0100

Company URL: http://www.chotin.com
Establishment information: Established in 1984.
Company type: Private company
Business activities: Provides financial consulting and management services.
Business type (SIC): Management and public relations services
Corporate officers: Steven B. Chotin, Chair.; Helen M. Dickens, Pres. and C.O.O.; David D. Frederick, C.F.O.; Paul Isherwood, C.I.O.; Jennifer M. Land, V.P., Human Resources
Board of director: Steven B. Chotin, Chair.
Giving statement: Giving through the Chotin Foundation.

The Chotin Foundation

Plz. Tower One
6400 S. Fiddlers Green Cir., Ste. 1200
Englewood, CO 80111-4958
FAX: (303) 741-6944; E-mail: jland@chotin.com; Additional tel.: (800) 943-008; URL: http://www.chotinfoundation.org/

Establishment information: Established in 2004 in CO.
Donors: Steven B. Chotin; The Chotin Group Corp.; Cayrac Corp.
Contact: Jennifer M. Land, Exec. Dir.
Financial data (yr. ended 12/31/11): Assets, $9,489 (M); gifts received, $212,360; expenditures, $208,255; qualifying distributions, $201,131; giving activities include $201,131 for grants.
Purpose and activities: The foundation supports organizations involved with arts and culture, education, health, human services, and leadership development. Special emphasis is directed toward Judaism and economically disadvantaged people.
Fields of interest: Arts; Education, early childhood education; Education; Hospitals (general); Public health; Health care; Children/youth, services; Family services; Aging, centers/services; Human services; Foundations (community); Leadership development; Jewish agencies & synagogues Economically disadvantaged.
Programs:
Arts and Culture: The foundation supports programs designed to expand access to arts and culture; and create cultural experiences for underprivileged children and youth.
Education: The foundation supports programs designed to promote early childhood education;

motivate students to gain skills that will help them academically and in a career; and foster leadership development.

Health and Wellness: The foundation supports programs designed to improve the health and well being of underprivileged children, youth, families, and seniors through health education and research.

Jewish Community: The foundation supports programs designed to serve underprivileged children and youth through education and cultural experiences; and help Jewish children, families, and seniors thrive through human services.

Type of support: General/operating support; Program development; Research.
Geographic limitations: Giving primarily in Denver, CO.
Support limitations: No grants to individuals.
Application information: Applications not accepted. Contributes only to pre-selected organizations.
Officers and Directors:* Helen M. Dickens*, Pres.; Jack Keane, Exec. V.P.; Jennifer M. Land*, Secy. and Exec. Dir.; David D. Frederick*, Treas.; Steven B. Chotin; Robin Chotin.
EIN: 710950446
Selected grants: The following grants are a representative sample of this grantmaker's funding activity:
$50,200 to Allied Jewish Federation of Colorado, Denver, CO, 2009.
$12,500 to Allied Jewish Federation of Colorado, Denver, CO, 2009.
$10,350 to Allied Jewish Federation of Colorado, Denver, CO, 2009.
$10,200 to Allied Jewish Federation of Colorado, Denver, CO, 2009.
$10,000 to Allied Jewish Federation of Colorado, Denver, CO, 2009.
$5,180 to Allied Jewish Federation of Colorado, Denver, CO, 2009.
$5,120 to Allied Jewish Federation of Colorado, Denver, CO, 2009.
$4,850 to Allied Jewish Federation of Colorado, Denver, CO, 2009.
$2,980 to Allied Jewish Federation of Colorado, Denver, CO, 2009.
$2,336 to Jewish Community Foundation of Colorado, Denver, CO, 2009.

800
Christie, Parker & Hale, LLP
350 W. Colorado Blvd., Ste. 500
P.O. Box 7068
Pasadena, CA 91105-1821 (626) 795-9900

Company URL: http://www.cph.com
Establishment information: Established in 1954.
Company type: Private company
Business activities: Operates law firm.
Business type (SIC): Legal services
Corporate officer: Gregory S. Lampert, Partner
Giving statement: Giving through the Christie, Parker & Hale, LLP Pro Bono Program.

Christie, Parker & Hale, LLP Pro Bono Program
350 W. Colorado Blvd., Ste. 500
Pasadena, CA 91105-1821 (626) 683-4599
E-mail: byron.hibdon@cph.com; URL: http://www.cph.com

Contact: Byron Hibdon, Exec. Dir.
Fields of interest: Legal services.
Type of support: Pro bono services - legal.
Geographic limitations: Giving primarily in areas of company operations in Irvine, and Pasadena, CA.
Application information: The Management Committee coordinates the pro-bono program.

801
Chrysler Group LLC
(formerly Chrysler LLC)
1000 Chrysler Dr.
Auburn Hills, MI 48326-2766
(248) 576-5741

Company URL: http://www.chrysler.com
Establishment information: Established in 1925.
Company type: Private company
Business activities: Manufactures and provides automotive and transportation products and services.
Business type (SIC): Motor vehicles and equipment
Financial profile for 2010: Number of employees, 51,623; assets, $35,449,000,000; sales volume, $41,946,000,000
Corporate officers: Sergio Marchionne, Chair. and C.E.O.; Richard Palmer, C.F.O.; Holly E. Leese, Sr. V.P., Genl. Counsel, and Secy.; Gualberto Ranieri, Sr. V.P., Comms.; Nancy A. Rae, Sr. V.P., Human Resources; Scott A. Sandschafer, V.P. and C.I.O.
Board of directors: Sergio Marchionne, Chair.; Alfredo Altavilla; Leo W. Houle; John B. Lanaway; Erickson N. Perkins; Ruth J. Simmons; Douglas M. Steenland; Ronald L. Thompson; Stephen M. Wolf
Subsidiaries: Chrysler International Corporation, Auburn Hills, MI; Global Electric Motor Cars, Inc., Fargo, ND
Division: Toledo Precision Machining Div., Perrysburg, OH
Plants: Yucca, AZ; Belvidere, IL; Indianapolis, Kokomo, IN; Chelsea, Detroit, Sterling Heights, Trenton, Warren, MI; Toledo, Twinsburg, OH
International operations: Canada
Giving statement: Giving through the Chrysler Group LLC Contributions Program and the Chrysler Foundation.

Chrysler Group LLC Contributions Program
1000 Chrysler Dr.
Auburn Hills, MI 48326-2766 (248) 576-5741
URL: http://www.chryslergroupllc.com/company/AboutUs/Pages/AboutUs.aspx

The Chrysler Foundation
(formerly DaimlerChrysler Corporation Fund)
1000 Chrysler Dr.
CIMS: 485-13-35
Auburn Hills, MI 48326-2766
FAX: (248) 512-2503; URL: http://www.media.chrysler.com/newsroom.do?id=137&mid=202

Establishment information: Incorporated in 1953 in MI.
Donors: Chrysler Corp.; DaimlerChrysler Corp.; Chrysler Group LLC.
Contact: Brian G. Glowiak, V.P. and Secy.
Financial data (yr. ended 12/31/11): Assets, $1,536,508 (M); expenditures, $1,169,012; qualifying distributions, $1,168,108; giving activities include $922,809 for 97 grants (high: $290,000; low: $250).
Purpose and activities: The foundation supports organizations involved with arts and culture, education, workforce development, disaster relief, youth development, human services, diversity, community development, science and technology, and public policy and marketplace issues. Special emphasis is directed toward programs designed to enrich the physical, educational, and cultural needs of local Chrysler Group communities.
Fields of interest: Arts, cultural/ethnic awareness; Arts; Vocational education; Higher education; Business school/education; Engineering school/education; Education; Employment, training; Employment; Disasters, preparedness/services; Safety, automotive safety; Youth development; American Red Cross; Human services; Civil/human rights, equal rights; Economic development; Business/industry; Community/economic development; Engineering/technology; Science; Public policy, research Infants/toddlers; Children/youth; Children; Youth; Adults; Aging; Young adults; Disabilities, people with; Physically disabled; Blind/visually impaired; Minorities; Asians/Pacific Islanders; African Americans/Blacks; Hispanics/Latinos; Native Americans/American Indians; Indigenous peoples; Women; Infants/toddlers, female; Girls; Young adults, female; Men; Infants/toddlers, male; Boys; Young adults, male; Military/veterans; Single parents; Terminal illness, people with; Economically disadvantaged; Homeless; LGBTQ.
Type of support: Annual campaigns; Building/renovation; Cause-related marketing; Continuing support; Curriculum development; Emergency funds; Employee matching gifts; Employee volunteer services; Employee-related scholarships; General/operating support; Program development; Scholarship funds; Sponsorships.
Geographic limitations: Giving primarily in areas of company operations in Yucca, AZ, Irvine, CA, Englewood, CO, Washington, DC, Orlando, FL, Belvidere and Lisle, IL, Indianapolis and Kokomo, IN, Elkridge, MD, Detroit, MI, Syracuse and Tappan, NY, Perrysburg, Toledo, and Twinsburg, OH, Addison, TX, and Kenosha, WI; giving also to regional and national organizations.
Support limitations: No support for discriminatory organizations or private or corporate foundations. No grants to individuals (except for employee-related scholarships), or for endowments, general operating support for local United Way agencies, direct health care delivery programs, additions or renovations to real estate, fundraising activities related to individual sponsorship, debt reduction, religious or sectarian programs, or athletic programs involving individual teams; no loans; no vehicle donations; no multi-year pledges.
Application information: Applications not accepted. The foundation utilizes an invitation only Request For Proposal (RFP) process. Unsolicited requests are not accepted.

Board meeting date(s): As required, usually quarterly

Officers and Trustees:* Joseph "Jody" Trapasso, Pres.; Brian G. Glowiak, V.P. and Secy.; Walter P. Bodden, Jr., V.P. and Treas.; R. J. Elder, Cont.; Fred Diaz; Scott R. Garberding; Scott Kunselman; Nancy A. Rae; Gialberto Ranier.
Number of staff: 2 full-time professional; 1 full-time support.
EIN: 386087371
Selected grants: The following grants are a representative sample of this grantmaker's funding activity:
$195,000 to Howard University, Washington, DC, 2012.
$100,000 to California Latino Legislative Caucus Institute for Public Policy, Los Angeles, CA, 2012.
$100,000 to National Italian American Foundation, Washington, DC, 2012.
$85,000 to Hispanic Scholarship Fund, San Francisco, CA, 2012.
$60,000 to Gleaners Community Food Bank, Detroit, MI, 2012.

$50,000 to Michigan Science Center, Detroit, MI, 2012.
$40,000 to Think Detroit PAL, Detroit, MI, 2012.
$37,000 to Inforum Center for Leadership, Detroit, MI, 2012.
$26,000 to Forgotten Harvest, Oak Park, MI, 2012.
$2,250 to Missouri University of Science and Technology, Rolla, MO, 2012.

802
CHS Inc.

(formerly Cenex Harvest States Cooperatives)
5500 Cenex Dr.
Inver Grove Heights, MN 55077-1733
(651) 355-6000

Company URL: http://www.chsinc.com
Establishment information: Established in 1929.
Company type: Cooperative
Company ticker symbol and exchange: CHSCP/NASDAQ
Business activities: Diversified energy grains and food company.
Business type (SIC): Farm-product raw materials—wholesale; non-durable goods—wholesale
Financial profile for 2012: Number of employees, 10,216; assets, $13,423,150,000; sales volume, $40,599,290,000; pre-tax net income, $1,416,570,000; expenses, $39,086,380,000; liabilities, $8,967,810,000
Corporate officers: David Bielenberg, Chair.; Dennis Carlson, Vice-Chair.; Steven Fritel, Vice-Chair.; Carl M. Casale, Pres. and C.E.O.; David A. Kastelic, Exec. V.P. and C.F.O.; Lisa A. Zell, Exec. V.P. and Genl. Counsel; Daniel Schurr, Secy.-Treas.
Board of directors: David Bielenberg, Chair.; Dennis Carlson, Vice-Chair.; Steven Fritel, Vice-Chair.; Donald Anthony; Robert Bass; Clinton J. Blew; Curt Eischens; Jon Erickson; David Johnsrud; David Kayser; Randy Knecht; Greg Kruger; Edward Malesich; Steve Riegel
Subsidiary: National Cooperative Refinery Association, McPherson, KS
Joint Ventures: Agriliance, LLC, Inver Grove Heights, MN; Cofina Financial, LLC, Inver Grove Heights, MN; Provista Renewable Fuels Marketing, LLC, Inver Grove Heights, MN
International operations: Brazil; Canada; China; Hong Kong; Netherlands; Russia; Switzerland; Ukraine
Giving statement: Giving through the CHS Inc. Corporate Giving Program and the CHS Foundation.

CHS Inc. Corporate Giving Program

(formerly CHS Cooperatives Corporate Giving Program)
5500 Cenex Dr.
Inver Grove Heights, MN 55077-1721 (651) 355-5129
FAX: (651) 355-5073;
E-mail: info@chsfoundation.org; URL: http://www.chsfoundation.org/stewardship.html

Purpose and activities: As a complement to its foundation, CHS also makes charitable contributions to nonprofit organizations directly. Support is given primarily in areas of company operations.
Fields of interest: Education; Agriculture; Rural development; United Ways and Federated Giving Programs.
Type of support: Annual campaigns; Conferences/seminars; Employee volunteer services; General/operating support.
Geographic limitations: Giving primarily in areas of company operations.
Publications: Application guidelines.
Application information: Applications accepted.
Initial approach: Complete online application
Copies of proposal: 1
Deadline(s): None
Administrators: Vanessa Magnus, Intern; William J. Nelson, Pres.; Jennifer Thatcher, Mgr.
Number of staff: 1 part-time professional; 1 part-time support.

CHS Foundation

5500 Cenex Dr.
Inver Grove Heights, MN 55077-1733 (800) 814-0506
FAX: (651) 355-5073;
E-mail: info@chsfoundation.org; URL: http://www.chsfoundation.org
Contact for scholarships: Jennifer Thatcher, Mgr., tel.: (800) 814-0506 ext. 3

Establishment information: Trust established in 1947 in MN.
Donors: Farmers Union Central Exchange, Inc.; CENEX, Inc.; Cenex Harvest States Cooperatives; CHS Inc.
Contact: William J. Nelson, Pres.
Financial data (yr. ended 12/31/11): Assets, $28,677,312 (M); gifts received, $3,078,610; expenditures, $2,692,664; qualifying distributions, $2,650,348; giving activities include $2,213,107 for grants.
Purpose and activities: The foundation supports organizations involved with education, agriculture, safety, youth development, rural development, and leadership development. Special emphasis is directed toward programs that invest in the future of rural America, agriculture, and cooperative business.
Fields of interest: Higher education; Education, community/cooperative; Education; Agriculture; Disasters, preparedness/services; Youth development, agriculture; Youth development; American Red Cross; Rural development; Leadership development Children/youth; Youth; Adults; Young adults.
Programs:
Cooperative Education Grants Program: The foundation supports programs on a national basis designed to provide quality education opportunities that foster cooperative understanding and growth.
Farm and Agriculture Safety: The foundation supports programs designed to keep farm families, children, and agribusiness professionals safe.
High School Scholarship Program: The foundation awards 50 $1,000 scholarships to graduating high school students entering into an agricultural field of study at a two or four-year college. Applicant must U.S. citizen or permanent resident.
Mini-Grants: The foundation awards grants of up to $1,000 to academic and leadership programs designed to strengthen student learning and enhance professional development. Applicants must be a campus-sanctioned club or organization; agricultural-related; and an advisor must be listed as a contact.
Returning Value to Rural Communities: The foundation supports programs designed to build vibrant communities in rural America through education and leadership development. Special emphasis is directed toward building leadership capacity through adult education and leadership initiatives; and innovative and collaborative approaches to address emerging issues and opportunities in rural communities.
Rural Youth and Leadership Development: The foundation supports programs designed to foster leaders of tomorrow, and promote youth development. Special emphasis is directed toward programs designed to emphasize leadership development through education.
Two-Year Scholarship Program: The foundation annually awards 25 $1,000 college scholarships to first-year college students at two-year institutions studying an agricultural-related major. Student must be a U.S. citizen or permanent resident.
University Scholarship Program: The foundation annually awards 150 $1,000 college scholarships to students pursing agricultural-related majors. The program is administered by participating universities.
Type of support: Annual campaigns; Conferences/seminars; Curriculum development; General/operating support; Program development; Program evaluation; Research; Scholarship funds; Scholarships—to individuals; Seed money; Sponsorships; Use of facilities.
Geographic limitations: Giving on a national basis, primarily in areas of company operations in CO, IA, ID, IL, IN, KS, MI, MN, MO, MT, NE, ND, OH, OK, OR, SD, TX, UT, WA, WI, and WY.
Support limitations: No support for religious or political organizations. No grants for building projects, debt reduction, community development, or program related loans.
Publications: Application guidelines; Informational brochure; Program policy statement.
Application information: Applications accepted. Application form required. Applicants should submit the following:
1) copy of IRS Determination Letter
2) copy of current year's organizational budget and/or project budget
Initial approach: Complete online application form
Board meeting date(s): Monthly
Deadline(s): None; Apr. 1 for High School Scholarships and Two-Year Scholarships; Sept. 30 for Cooperative Education Grants Program
Final notification: 30 to 90 days; Dec. for Cooperative Education Grants Program
Officer and Trustees:* Michael Toelle*, Chair.; Robert Bass*, Vice-Chair.; William J. Nelson, Pres.; Jerry Hasnedl*, Secy.-Treas.; Bruce Anderson*; Donald Anthony; Dave Bielenberg; C.J. Blew; Dennis Carlson; Curt Eischens; Steve Fritel; David Kayser; Randy Knecht; Greg Kruger; Michael Mulcahey; Richard Owen; Steve Riegel; Dan Schurr.
Number of staff: 1 part-time professional; 2 part-time support.
EIN: 416025858

803
Chuao Chocolatier

2345 Camino Vida Roble
Carlsbad, CA 92011 (760) 476-1668
FAX: (760) 476-1355

Company URL: http://www.chuaochocolatier.com
Establishment information: Established in 2002.
Company type: Private company
Business activities: Manufactures candy and confectionary products.
Business type (SIC): Sugar, candy, and salted/roasted nut production
Financial profile for 2010: Number of employees, 30
Corporate officers: Richard Antonorsi, Chair.; Sergio Alvarez, C.E.O.; Michael Antonorsi, Pres.; Kim Rhode, C.F.O.
Board of director: Richard Antonorsi, Chair.

Giving statement: Giving through the Chuao Chocolatier Corporate Giving Program.

Chuao Chocolatier Corporate Giving Program

2345 Camino Vida Roble
Carlsbad, CA 92011-1505 (760) 476-1668
E-mail: info@chuaochocolatier.com; URL: http://www.chuaochocolatier.com

804
The Chubb Corporation

15 Mountain View Rd.
Warren, NJ 07059 (908) 903-2000
FAX: (908) 903-2027

Company URL: http://www.chubb.com
Establishment information: Established in 1967.
Company type: Public company
Company ticker symbol and exchange: CB/NYSE
International Securities Identification Number: US1712321017
Business activities: Operates holding company; sells property and casualty insurance.
Business type (SIC): Insurance/fire, marine, and casualty; holding company
Financial profile for 2012: Number of employees, 10,200; assets, $52,184,000,000; sales volume, $13,595,000,000; pre-tax net income, $1,996,000,000; expenses, $11,599,000,000; liabilities, $36,357,000,000
Fortune 1000 ranking: 2012—202nd in revenues, 137th in profits, and 108th in assets
Forbes 2000 ranking: 2012—708th in sales, 404th in profits, and 443rd in assets
Corporate officers: John D. Finnegan, Chair., Pres., and C.E.O.; Richard G. Spiro, Exec. V.P. and C.F.O.; Ned I. Gerstman, Exec. V.P. and Co-C.I.O.; Robert M. Witkoff, Exec. V.P. and Co-C.I.O.; Maureen A. Brundage, Exec. V.P. and Genl. Counsel; John Kennedy, Sr. V.P. and C.A.O.
Board of directors: John D. Finnegan, Chair.; Zoe Baird; Sheila P. Burke; James I. Cash, Jr.; Lawrence W. Kellner; Martin G. McGuinn; Lawrence M. Small; Jess Soderberg; Daniel E. Somers; William C. Weldon; James M. Zimmerman; Alfred W. Zollar
Subsidiaries: Associated Aviation, Inc., Short Hills, NJ; Associated Aviation Underwriters, Chicago, IL; Chubb & Son, Inc., Warren, NJ; The Chubb Institute, Parsippany, NJ; DHC, Warren, NJ; Federal Insurance Co., Warren, NJ; Sovereign Life Insurance Co., Santa Barbara, CA; Touchette Corp., East Syracuse, NY; Vigilant Insurance Co., New York, NY
International operations: Bermuda
Giving statement: Giving through the Chubb Corporation Contributions Program.
Company EIN: 132595722

The Chubb Corporation Contributions Program

15 Mountain View Rd.
P.O. Box 1615
Warren, NJ 07059-6711 (908) 903-2000
FAX: (908) 903-2027; URL: http://www.chubb.com/corporate/chubb12285.html

Purpose and activities: Chubb makes charitable contributions to nonprofit organizations involved with arts and culture, education, health care, employment, and youth development. Support is given primarily in areas of company operations.
Fields of interest: Arts; Education; Health care; Employment; Youth development.
Type of support: Employee matching gifts; Employee volunteer services; General/operating support; Program development.
Geographic limitations: Giving on a national and international basis in areas of company operations.

805
Chugach Alaska Corporation

3800 Centerpoint Dr., Ste. 700
Anchorage, AK 99503-4161
(907) 563-8866

Company URL: http://www.chugach-ak.com
Establishment information: Established in 1972.
Company type: Native corporation
Business activities: Operates native corporation.
Business type (SIC): Nonclassifiable establishments
Corporate officers: Sherri D. Bueretta, Chair.; Donna J. Platt, Vice-Chair.; Mike Anderson, Pres.; Ed Herndon, C.E.O.; Connie Baehr, C.F.O.; Mel Lynch, V.P., Opers.; David J. Totemoff, Sr., Corp. Secy.; Matthew P. McDaniel, Corp. Treas.
Board of directors: Sheri D. Buretta, Chair.; Donna J. Platt, Vice-Chair.; Julie E. Kitka; Gabriel D. Kompkoff; James Kvasnikoff; Michael McCanna; David J. Totemoff, Sr.; Violet F. Yeaton
Subsidiaries: Chugach Development Corp., Anchorage, AK; Chugach Management Services Inc., Anchorage, AK; Chugach Telecommunications & Computers Inc., Anchorage, AK
Giving statement: Giving through the Chugach Heritage Foundation.

Chugach Heritage Foundation

3800 Centerpoint Dr., Ste. 601
Anchorage, AK 99503-4196 (907) 563-8866
FAX: (907) 550-4147;
E-mail: stephen.grantier@chugach-ak.com; Additional tel.: (800) 858-2768; E-mail for scholarships: scholarships@chugach-ak.com; URL: http://www.chugachheritagefoundation.org/

Establishment information: Established in 1994 in AK.
Donors: Chugach Alaska Regional Corp.; Chugach Alaska Corp.
Contact: Stephen Grantier, Prog. Mgr.
Financial data (yr. ended 12/31/11): Assets, $39,550 (M); gifts received, $975,594; expenditures, $969,385; qualifying distributions, $970,481; giving activities include $885,092 for 232 grants (high: $12,000; low: -$8,956).
Purpose and activities: The foundation awards college scholarships, vocational certificates, and job training to shareholders and the descendants of shareholders of Chugach Alaska Corporation.
Fields of interest: Vocational education; Higher education; Employment, training Native Americans/American Indians.
Type of support: Scholarships—to individuals.
Geographic limitations: Giving primarily in AK and WA.
Publications: Application guidelines.
Application information: Applications accepted. The foundation awards associate level scholarships of up to $4,800 annually, junior and senior level undergraduate scholarships of up to $6,000 annually, graduate level scholarships of up to $12,000 annually, and vocational training scholarships of up to $4,000 per academic year. Checks are issued to the educational institution on behalf of the student. Application form required. Requests should include official transcripts, a college acceptance letter, class schedule, and proof of relationship to a Chugach Alaska Corporation shareholder.
Initial approach: Download application form and e-mail, fax, hand deliver, or mail to foundation
Deadline(s): None; Aug. 15 for repeat applicants
Officers and Trustees:* Michael McCanna*, Chair. and Pres.; Sherri D. Buretta; Marchell Espe; Gabriel Kompkoff.
EIN: 920116128

806
Church Mutual Insurance Company

3000 Schuster Ln.
P.O. Box 357
Merrill, WI 54452-0357 (715) 536-5577
FAX: (715) 539-4650

Company URL: http://www.churchmutual.com
Establishment information: Established in 1897.
Company type: Private company
Business activities: Operates insurance company.
Business type (SIC): Insurance/fire, marine, and casualty
Financial profile for 2012: Number of employees, 922; assets, $1,229,671,441; liabilities, $814,391,979
Corporate officers: Allen L. Leverett, Chair.; Michael E. Ravn, Pres. and C.E.O.; Richard V. Poirier, C.O.O.; John F. Cleary, V.P., Secy., and Genl. Counsel; Herman W. Vandenberg, V.P., Treas., and Corp. Cont.; Kevin D. Root, C.P.A., V.P. and C.F.O.; Christopher A. Graham, V.P. and C.I.O.; Craig D. Wessman, V.P., Sales; Patrick M. Moreland, V.P., Mktg.; Richard A. Huseby, V.P., Human Resources
Board of directors: Allen L. Leverett, Chair.; Michael W. Grebe; Marsha A. Lindsay; James J. McIntyre; Michael E. Ravn; Michael J. Riley; Lori A. Weyers; Walter H. White, Jr.; John B. Williams
Giving statement: Giving through the Church Mutual Insurance Company Contributions Program.

Church Mutual Insurance Company Contributions Program

3000 Schuster Ln.
P.O. Box 357
Merrill, WI 54452-0357 (715) 536-5577
URL: http://www.churchmutual.com

807
Churchill Downs Incorporated

700 Central Ave.
Louisville, KY 40208-1212 (502) 636-4400
FAX: (502) 636-4430

Company URL: http://www.churchilldownsincorporated.com
Establishment information: Established in 1928.
Company type: Public company
Company ticker symbol and exchange: CHDN/NASDAQ
Business activities: Operates horse race track.
Business type (SIC): Commercial sports
Financial profile for 2012: Number of employees, 2,300; assets, $1,114,340,000; sales volume, $732,380,000; pre-tax net income, $91,430,000; expenses, $635,630,000; liabilities, $470,040,000
Corporate officers: Robert L. Evans, Chair. and C.E.O.; William C. Carstanjen, Pres. and C.O.O.; William E. Mudd, Exec. V.P. and C.F.O.; Alan K. Tse,

Exec. V.P. and Genl. Counsel; Chuck Kenyon, Sr. V.P., Human Resources
Board of directors: Robert L. Evans, Chair.; Ulysses Lee Bridgeman; Leonard S. Coleman, Jr.; Craig J. Duchossois; Richard L. Duchossois; Robert L. Fealy; Daniel P. Harrington; G. Watts Humphrey, Jr.; James F. McDonald; R. Alex Rankin; Darrell R. Wells
Subsidiaries: Churchill Downs Management Co., Louisville, KY; Hoosier Park, L.P., Anderson, IN
Giving statement: Giving through the Churchill Downs Incorporated Contributions Program and the Churchill Downs Incorporated Foundation.
Company EIN: 610156015

Churchill Downs Incorporated Contributions Program

600 N. Hurstbourne Pkwy., Ste. 400
Louisville, KY 40222 (502) 636-4400
E-mail: dana.johnson@kyderby.com; URL: http://www.churchilldownsincorporated.com/about-cdi/community-involvement

Purpose and activities: As a complement to its foundation, Churchill Downs also makes charitable contributions to nonprofit organizations directly. Support is given primarily in areas of company operations in Florida, Illinois, Kentucky, and Louisiana.
Fields of interest: Arts; Education; Public health; Mental health, gambling addiction; Housing/shelter, volunteer services; Athletics/sports, equestrianism; Youth development; Salvation Army; Homeless, human services.
Type of support: Employee volunteer services; General/operating support; In-kind gifts; Public relations services.
Geographic limitations: Giving primarily in areas of company operations in FL, IL, KY, and LA.
Application information: The Community Relations department handles giving.
Initial approach: Contact a member of the Community Relations team via phone or mail

Churchill Downs Incorporated Foundation

(formerly Churchill Downs Foundation, Inc.)
600 N. Hurstbourne Pkwy., Ste. 400
Louisville, KY 40222-5385 (502) 636-4400
FAX: (502) 535-4577;
E-mail: Foundation@kyderby.com; E-mail for Dana Johnson: Dana.Johnson@kyderby.com; Application address: P.O. Box 3704, Midway, KY 40347; URL: http://www.churchilldownsincorporated.com/about-cdi/community-involvement

Establishment information: Established in 2000 in KY.
Donors: Churchill Downs Inc.; Yum Brands, Inc.
Contact: Dana Johnson, Sr. Dir. of Corp. Responsibility and Community Affairs
Financial data (yr. ended 12/31/11): Assets, $517,543 (M); gifts received, $99,953; expenditures, $1,189,085; qualifying distributions, $1,185,533; giving activities include $1,182,500 for 20 grants (high: $1,000,000; low: $2,000).
Purpose and activities: The foundation supports organizations involved with arts and culture, education, horse racing industry, and public welfare.
Fields of interest: Museums; Arts; Education; Food services; Food banks; Athletics/sports, equestrianism; Recreation; Youth, services; Family services; Human services.
Type of support: Equipment; General/operating support; Program development; Scholarship funds; Sponsorships.
Geographic limitations: Giving primarily in Louisville, KY and New Orleans, LA.
Support limitations: No support for national or regional organizations unless their programs address specific local community needs, religious organizations, social, labor, political, veterans', or fraternal organizations, or political action committees. No grants to individuals, or for staff, or administrative payroll, seed money, lobbying efforts, legislative purposes, or travel.
Publications: Application guidelines; Corporate giving report.
Application information: Applications accepted. Application form required. Applicants should submit the following:
1) copy of IRS Determination Letter
2) geographic area to be served
3) detailed description of project and amount of funding requested
4) listing of additional sources and amount of support

Initial approach: Download application form and mail to foundation
Board meeting date(s): June, Sept., and Nov.
Deadline(s): Postmarked by June 1
Final notification: Sept.

Officers and Directors: Brett Hale, Pres.; Ekumene Lysonge, V.P.; William C. Carstanjen, Pres.; Rebecca C. Reed, Secy.; Michael W. Anderson, Treas.; John Asher; Julia Carstanjen; Kristine M. Stabler.
EIN: 611380215

808
Cianbro Corporation

1 Cianbro Square
Pittsfield, ME 04967 (207) 487-3311
FAX: (207) 487-3861

Company URL: http://www.cianbro.com
Establishment information: Established in 1949.
Company type: Private company
Business activities: Provides nonresidential general contract construction services; provides metal coating services; provides integrated computer system design services.
Business type (SIC): Contractors/general nonresidential building; metal coating and plating; computer services
Financial profile for 2011: Number of employees, 4,000
Corporate officers: Peter G. Vigue, Chair. and C.E.O.; Peter A. Virgue, Pres. and C.O.O.; Aldo Servello, Treas. and C.F.O.
Board of director: Petre G. Vigue, Chair.
Giving statement: Giving through the Cianbro Charitable Foundation.

Cianbro Charitable Foundation

P.O. Box 1000
Pittsfield, ME 04967-1000 (207) 487-3311
Application address: 1 Hunnewell Sq., Pittsfield, ME 04967

Establishment information: Established in 1989 in ME.
Donor: Cianbro Corp.
Contact: H. Bonnie Brown
Financial data (yr. ended 12/31/11): Assets, $1,365,292 (M); gifts received, $501,780; expenditures, $349,515; qualifying distributions, $340,521; giving activities include $340,521 for grants.
Purpose and activities: The foundation supports organizations involved with arts and culture, education, forest conservation, the construction industry, and community development.
Fields of interest: Museums; Historic preservation/historical societies; Arts; Secondary school/education; Higher education; Education; Environment, forests; Cancer; Boy scouts; YM/YWCAs & YM/YWHAs; Business/industry; Community/economic development.
Type of support: Capital campaigns; Employee-related scholarships; Program development; Scholarship funds.
Geographic limitations: Giving limited to ME.
Support limitations: No grants to individuals (except for employee-related scholarships).
Application information: Applications accepted. Application form not required. Applicants should submit the following:
1) copy of IRS Determination Letter
2) detailed description of project and amount of funding requested

Initial approach: Proposal
Board meeting date(s): Quarterly
Deadline(s): None

Trustees: Alan Burton; Peter G. Vigue.
EIN: 223020020
Selected grants: The following grants are a representative sample of this grantmaker's funding activity:
$10,000 to Boy Scouts of America, Pine Tree Council, Portland, ME, 2010.
$10,000 to Maine Maritime Academy, Castine, ME, 2010.
$6,250 to Boy Scouts of America, Bangor, ME, 2010.
$6,000 to Forest Society of Maine, Bangor, ME, 2010.
$5,000 to Maine Discovery Museum, Bangor, ME, 2010.
$5,000 to Maine Maritime Museum, Bath, ME, 2010.
$5,000 to University of Maine, Orono, ME, 2010.
$5,000 to University of New England, Portland, ME, 2010.
$5,000 to YMCA, Kennebec Valley, Augusta, ME, 2010.
$1,000 to Alzheimers Association, Falmouth, ME, 2010.

809
CIBA Insurance Services, Inc.

655 N. Central Ave., Ste. 2100
Glendale, CA 91203 (818) 638-8525

Company URL: http://www.cibaservices.com
Establishment information: Established in 1993.
Company type: Private company
Business activities: Operates commercial insurance company.
Business type (SIC): Insurance agents, brokers, and services
Corporate officers: Michael Marino, Pres. and C.E.O.; Geri Relich, C.F.O.
Offices: Chicago, IL; Las Vegas, NV; Dallas, TX
Giving statement: Giving through the CIBA Foundation.

CIBA Foundation

655 N. Central Ave., Ste. 2100
Glendale, CA 91203-1443
URL: http://www.cibafoundation.com

Establishment information: Established in 2005 in CA.
Donor: Ciba Insurance Services, Inc.
Financial data (yr. ended 12/31/11): Assets, $70,424 (M); gifts received, $13,914; expenditures, $43,905; qualifying distributions,

$28,535; giving activities include $28,500 for 3 grants (high: $15,000; low: $5,000).
Purpose and activities: The foundation supports nonprofit organizations involved with disadvantaged and disabled children and others in need.
Fields of interest: Health care; Human services.
Type of support: Employee matching gifts; Program development.
Application information: Applications not accepted. Unsolicited requests for funds not accepted.
Officers: Michael Marino, Chair.; Dwain Bender, Pres.; Geri Relich, C.F.O.; Robert Baker, Secy.
Director: Charles Bates.
EIN: 203380617

810
CIBA Vision Corporation
11460 Johns Creek Pkwy.
Duluth, GA 30097-1556 (678) 415-3937

Company URL: http://www.cibavision.com
Establishment information: Established in 1980.
Company type: Subsidiary of a foreign company
Business activities: Manufactures medical eyecare products.
Business type (SIC): Drugs
Corporate officers: Andrea Saia, Pres.; John McKenna, C.F.O.; Scott Chyatte, Genl. Counsel
Giving statement: Giving through the CIBA Vision Corporation Contributions Program.

CIBA Vision Corporation Contributions Program
11460 Johns Creek Pkwy.
Duluth, GA 30097-1518 (678) 415-3937
E-mail: communityrelations@cibavision.com

Purpose and activities: CIBA makes charitable contributions to nonprofit organizations involved with education, vision, and community development. Support is given primarily in areas of company operations.
Fields of interest: Education; Optometry/vision screening; Eye diseases; Eye research; Community/economic development.
Type of support: Donated products; General/operating support; In-kind gifts.
Geographic limitations: Giving primarily in the Atlanta, GA, metro area.
Support limitations: No support for political organizations. No grants to individuals, or for capital campaigns, fundraising, general operating support, athletic activities, or trips.
Application information: A contributions committee reviews all requests. Applicants should submit the following:
1) name, address and phone number of organization
2) copy of IRS Determination Letter
3) brief history of organization and description of its mission
4) how project's results will be evaluated or measured
5) detailed description of project and amount of funding requested
6) listing of additional sources and amount of support

Committee meeting date(s): Monthly

811
Cic Mortgage Credit Inc.
(formerly Credit Bureau of Nashville, Inc.)
2206 21st Ave. S., Ste. 303
Nashville, TN 37212-4922 (615) 386-2282

Company URL: http://www.ciccredit.com
Establishment information: Established in 1992.
Company type: Private company
Business activities: Provides credit reporting services.
Business type (SIC): Credit reporting and collection agencies
Corporate officer: Trish Pendleton, C.O.O.
Giving statement: Giving through the CIC Foundation, Inc.

CIC Foundation, Inc.
2206 21st Ave. S., Ste. 301
Nashville, TN 37212-4922 (615) 386-2296

Establishment information: Established in 2003 in TN.
Donor: Credit Bureau of Nashville, Inc.
Contact: Donna Tilley, Treas.
Financial data (yr. ended 12/31/11): Assets, $5,700,001 (M); expenditures, $2,408,398; qualifying distributions, $1,878,108; giving activities include $1,227,049 for grants and $644,453 for employee matching gifts.
Purpose and activities: The foundation supports organizations involved with health, substance abuse, human services, and Christianity and awards college scholarships to students located in Kentucky and Tennessee.
Fields of interest: Hospitals (general); Health care, patient services; Health care; Substance abuse, services; Children/youth, services; Family services; Residential/custodial care, hospices; Human services; Christian agencies & churches.
Type of support: Building/renovation; General/operating support; Program development; Scholarship funds; Scholarships—to individuals.
Geographic limitations: Giving primarily in KY and TN.
Application information: Applications accepted. Application form required.
Initial approach: Contact foundation for scholarship application
Deadline(s): Apr. 1 for scholarships
Officers and Directors:* William D. Maxfield, Chair.; Gary V. Forsythe, Pres.; Charles C. Martin, Secy.; Donna Tilley, Treas.; Leslie B. Enoch II; W. Dale Maxfield, Sr.; J. Terry Olive; M. Terry Turner.
EIN: 562348880
Selected grants: The following grants are a representative sample of this grantmaker's funding activity:
$150,000 to Monroe Carell Jr. Childrens Hospital at Vanderbilt, Nashville, TN, 2011.
$50,000 to Alzheimers Association, Nashville, TN, 2011.
$35,000 to Tennesseans for Alternatives to the Death Penalty, Nashville, TN, 2011.
$22,500 to Sexual Assault Center, Nashville, TN, 2011.
$21,000 to Nashville Rescue Mission, Nashville, TN, 2011.
$21,000 to Our Kids, Nashville, TN, 2011.
$20,000 to Hospital Hospitality House, Nashville, TN, 2011.
$15,000 to Association for Guidance, Aid, Placement and Empathy, Nashville, TN, 2011.
$15,000 to Salvus Center, Gallatin, TN, 2011.
$10,217 to Hendersonville Samaritan Association, Hendersonville, TN, 2011.

812
CIGNA Corporation
2 Liberty Pl.
1601 Chestnut St.
Philadelphia, PA 19192-1550
(215) 761-1000

Company URL: http://www.cigna.com
Establishment information: Established in 1792.
Company type: Public company
Company ticker symbol and exchange: CI/NYSE
International Securities Identification Number: US1255091092
Business activities: Sells health, life, and accident insurance; provides investment advisory services.
Business type (SIC): Insurance/accident and health; security and commodity services; insurance/life
Financial profile for 2012: Number of employees, 35,800; assets, $53,734,000,000; sales volume, $29,119,000,000; pre-tax net income, $2,477,000,000; expenses, $26,642,000,000; liabilities, $43,965,000,000
Fortune 1000 ranking: 2012—103rd in revenues, 128th in profits, and 104th in assets
Forbes 2000 ranking: 2012—324th in sales, 390th in profits, and 431st in assets
Corporate officers: Isaiah Harris, Jr., Chair.; David M. Cordani, Pres. and C.E.O.; Matt Manders, Pres., Opers.; Ralph Nicoletti, C.F.O.; Mark L. Boxer, Exec. V.P. and C.I.O.; Nicole S. Jones, Exec. V.P. and Genl. Counsel; John M. Murabito, Exec. V.P., Human Resources
Board of directors: Isaiah Harris, Jr., Chair.; David M. Cordani; Eric J. Foss; Jane E. Henney, M.D.; Roman Martinez IV; John M. Partridge; James E. Rogers; Joseph P. Sullivan; Eric C. Wiseman; Donna F. Zarcone; William D. Zollars
Subsidiary: Healthsource Inc., Hooksett, NH
Giving statement: Giving through the CIGNA Corporation Contributions Program and the CIGNA Foundation.
Company EIN: 061059331

CIGNA Corporation Contributions Program
c/o Civic Affairs
900 Cottage Grove Rd.
Bloomfield, CT 06002-2920
E-mail: FoundationGrants@cigna.com; URL: http://www.cigna.com/about_us/community/index.html

Purpose and activities: As a complement to its foundation, Cigna also supports events and activities designed to promote health and wellness, leadership development, provide opportunities to underprivileged people, and help communities address social and environmental challenges. Support is given primarily in Bloomfield/Hartford, Connecticut and Philadelphia, Pennsylvania.
Fields of interest: Environment; Public health; Health care; Human services; Community/economic development, equal rights; Community development, neighborhood development; Leadership development.
Type of support: Employee volunteer services; Program development; Sponsorships.
Geographic limitations: Giving primarily in areas of company operations in Bloomfield/Hartford, CT and Philadelphia, PA.
Support limitations: No support for fraternal, social, religious, or political organizations, or discriminatory organizations. No grants to individuals or families, or for capital campaigns.

Application information: Applications accepted. The Civic Affairs Department handles giving. Application form required.

Initial approach: Complete online application form
Deadline(s): 3 months prior to need
Final notification: 4 weeks

CIGNA Foundation

1601 Chestnut St., TL15C
Philadelphia, PA 19192-1540 (215) 761-4328
E-mail: communityrelations@cigna.com; Application address: CIGNA Grant Program, P.O. Box 2332, Princeton, NJ 08543-2332, tel.: 866) 865-5277; URL: http://www.cigna.com/about_us/community/index.html

Establishment information: Incorporated in 1962 in PA.
Donor: CIGNA Corp.
Contact: Gianna S. Jackson, Exec. Dir.
Financial data (yr. ended 12/31/10): Assets, $5,352,890 (M); gifts received, $5,917,955; expenditures, $1,958,885; qualifying distributions, $1,888,993; giving activities include $1,888,993 for grants.
Purpose and activities: The foundation supports programs designed to promote wellness; develop leaders; expand opportunities; and embrace communities.
Fields of interest: Arts; Elementary school/education; Higher education; Education; Environment; Health care, equal rights; Public health; Health care, patient services; Health care; Genetic diseases and disorders; Breast cancer; Recreation, parks/playgrounds; American Red Cross; YM/YWCAs & YM/YWHAs; Children/youth, services; Developmentally disabled, centers & services; Human services; Civil/human rights, equal rights; Civil/human rights, advocacy; Community/economic development; Foundations (public); Public policy, research; Leadership development.
Programs:

Community Caring Awards: Through the Community Caring Awards program, the foundation awards grants to nonprofit organizations with which employees, retirees, and directors of CIGNA volunteer through Grants for Givers; honors volunteers whose work is particularly creative or beneficial through Volunteer of the Month; recognizes exceptional volunteer service through the Volunteer of the Year award chosen by the Points of Light Foundation; and supports projects with which three or more CIGNA employees participate through Team Volunteer Awards.

Developing Leaders: The foundation supports community service that encourages talented individuals to become future leaders.

Embracing Communities: The foundation supports programs designed to connect neighbors to create networks that will address complex social and environmental challenges.

Employee Matching Gifts: The foundation matches contributions made by employees of CIGNA to institutions of higher education, special-education schools, and organizations involved with arts and culture on a one-for-one basis.

Expanding Opportunities: The foundation supports programs designed to reach across barriers including gender, ethnicity, or physical condition to tap the talents of every person.

Promoting Wellness: The foundation supports programs designed to build awareness; help people manage their health challenges; and make health services available and affordable for all.

Type of support: Annual campaigns; Conferences/seminars; Employee matching gifts; Employee volunteer services; General/operating support; Program development; Scholarship funds.
Geographic limitations: Giving primarily in Hartford, CT, Washington, DC, and Philadelphia, PA; giving also to national organizations.
Support limitations: No support for fraternal organizations, social or political organizations, faith-based organizations not of direct of the entire community, or discriminatory groups. No grants to individuals, or for capital campaigns, or discriminatory projects.
Publications: Annual report; Application guidelines; Corporate giving report (including application guidelines).
Application information: Applications accepted. Support is limited to 1 contribution per organization during any given year. Application form required.

Initial approach: Complete online application form
Board meeting date(s): Biannually
Deadline(s): None, but Oct. 15 is encouraged
Final notification: All funds distributed on an annual basis by Nov. 30

Officers and Directors:* John M. Murabito*, Chair.; Michael Anthony Fernandez, Co-Pres.; Anthony Perez, Co-Pres.; Thomas A. McCarthy, V.P.; Lindsay K. Blackwood, Secy.; Gianna S. Jackon, Exec. Dir.; David M. Cordani; H. Edward Hanway; Carol Ann Petren; Karen S. Rohan.
EIN: 236261726

813
Cincinnati Bengals, Inc.

1 Paul Brown Stadium
Cincinnati, OH 45202-3418 (513) 621-3550
FAX: (513) 621-3570

Company URL: http://www.bengals.com
Establishment information: Established in 1937.
Company type: Private company
Business activities: Operates professional football club.
Business type (SIC): Commercial sports
Financial profile for 2010: Number of employees, 50
Corporate officers: Michael Brown, Pres.; Bill Scanlon, C.F.O.; Johanna Kappner, Cont.
Giving statement: Giving through the Cincinnati Bengals, Inc. Corporate Giving Program.

Cincinnati Bengals, Inc. Corporate Giving Program

1 Paul Brown Stadium
Cincinnati, OH 45202-3418
URL: http://www.bengals.com/community

Purpose and activities: The Cincinnati Bengals make charitable contributions of memorabilia to nonprofit organizations on a case by case basis. Support is given primarily in the Cincinnati, Ohio, area.
Fields of interest: General charitable giving Economically disadvantaged.
Type of support: Donated products; In-kind gifts.
Geographic limitations: Giving primarily in the Cincinnati, OH, area.
Application information: Applications accepted. Proposals should be submitted using organization letterhead. Support is limited to 1 contribution per organization during any given year. Applicants should submit the following:
1) name, address and phone number of organization
2) descriptive literature about organization
3) detailed description of project and amount of funding requested
4) contact person

Initial approach: Contact headquarters for application information
Copies of proposal: 1
Deadline(s): 4 to 6 weeks prior to need for memorabilia donations and game ticket donations for fundraising

814
The Cincinnati Reds LLC

100 Main St.
Cincinnati, OH 45202-4109 (513) 765-7000

Company URL: http://cincinnati.reds.mlb.com
Establishment information: Established in 1866.
Company type: Private company
Business activities: Operates professional baseball club.
Business type (SIC): Commercial sports
Corporate officers: W. Joseph Williams, Jr., Chair.; Thomas L. Williams, Vice-Chair. and Treas.; Robert H. Castellini, Pres. and C.E.O.; Phillip J. Castellini, C.O.O.; Doug Healy, V.P., Finance and C.F.O.; James A. Marx, Esq., V.P. and Genl. Counsel; Bill Reinberger, V.P., Corp. Sales; Ralph Mitchell, V.P., Comms. and Mktg.; Christopher L. Fisher, Secy.; Bentley Viator, Cont.
Board of directors: W. Joseph Williams, Jr., Chair.; Thomas Williams, Vice-Chair.
Giving statement: Giving through the Cincinnati Reds LLC Corporate Giving Program and the Cincinnati Reds Community Fund.

The Cincinnati Reds LLC Corporate Giving Program

c/o Donation Request
Great American Ball Park
100 Joe Nuxhall Way
Cincinnati, OH 45202-4109
Application address for non-fundraising game ticket donations: c/o Community Rels., Special Reds, 100 Main St., Cincinnati, OH 45202, fax: (513) 765-7153; URL: http://cincinnati.reds.mlb.com/NASApp/mlb/cin/community/index.jsp

Purpose and activities: The Cincinnati Reds make charitable contributions of memorabilia and game tickets for fundraising to nonprofit organizations on a case by case basis and non-fundraising game tickets to nonprofit organizations involved with less fortunate people. Support is given primarily in Indiana, Kentucky, and Ohio.
Fields of interest: Education; Athletics/sports, baseball; Human services; General charitable giving.
Type of support: Donated products; In-kind gifts.
Geographic limitations: Giving primarily in IN, KY, and OH, with emphasis on the greater Cincinnati area.
Support limitations: No grants for general operating support, advertising, or sponsorships.
Application information: Applications accepted. Proposals should be submitted using organization letterhead. Support is limited to 1 contribution per organization during any given year. Non-fundraising game ticket donations are limited to 1 game per organization during any given year. Application form not required. Applicants should submit the following:
1) name, address and phone number of organization
2) descriptive literature about organization
3) detailed description of project and amount of funding requested
4) contact person
Proposals for memorabilia donations or game ticket donations for fundraising should indicate the date of the event. Proposals for non-fundraising game ticket

donations should indicate how attending a game would benefit the organization's clients, whether any special seating is needed, the number of tickets needed, and the first and second choice of game dates.

Initial approach: Mail proposal to headquarters for memorabilia donations and game ticket donations for fundraising; mail or fax proposal to application address for non-fundraising game ticket donations
Copies of proposal: 1
Deadline(s): 4 to 6 weeks prior to need for memorabilia donations and game ticket donations for fundraising; 3 weeks prior to need for non-fundraising game ticket donations

The Cincinnati Reds Community Fund

100 Joe Nuxhall Way
Cincinnati, OH 45202-4109 (513) 765-7000
E-mail: info@redsyouthbaseball.org; Tel. for Charles Frank: (513)-765-7231; E-Mail for Charles Frank: cfrank@reds.com; URL: http://redsyouthbaseball.org/

Establishment information: Established in 2001 in OH.
Contact: Charles Frank, Exec. Dir.
Financial data (yr. ended 10/31/11): Revenue, $1,732,693; assets, $645,735 (M); gifts received, $966,797; expenditures, $1,524,361; giving activities include $78,762 for grants.
Purpose and activities: As the philanthropic arm of the Cincinnati Reds, the fund is dedicated to improving the lives of youth by leveraging the tradition of the Cincinnati Reds and the game of baseball.
Fields of interest: Education; Animal welfare; Health care; Athletics/sports, baseball; Youth development.
Geographic limitations: Giving limited to the greater Cincinnati, OH, area.
Officers: Owen Wrassman, Pres.; Kitty Strauss, V.P.; Lorrie Platt, Secy.; Doug Healy, Treas.; Charley Frank, Exec. Dir.
Board Members: Amin Akbar; John L. Allen; Brad Blettner; Bob Castellini; Phil Castellini; Darrick Dansby; Ozie Davis III; Jenny Gardner; Victor Gray; Jennifer Green; Tamara Harkavy; Mike Hartmann; Joe Hoffecker; Jerry Karalson; Dr. Tim Kremchek; and 13 additional board members.
EIN: 311790195

815
Cinemark USA, Inc.

3900 Dallas Pkwy., Ste. 500
Plano, TX 75093-7865 (972) 665-1000

Company URL: http://www.cinemark.com
Establishment information: Established in 1984.
Company type: Subsidiary of a public company
Business activities: Operates movie theaters.
Business type (SIC): Motion picture theaters
Financial profile for 2010: Number of employees, 22,000; assets, $3,420,000,000; sales volume, $2,140,000,000
Corporate officers: Lee Roy Mitchell, Chair.; Timothy Warner, Pres. and C.E.O.; Robert D. Copple, Exec. V.P., C.F.O., and Treas.; Michael D. Cavalier, Sr. V.P., Genl. Counsel, and Secy.
Board of director: Lee Roy Mitchell, Chair.
Giving statement: Giving through the Cinemark USA, Inc. Corporate Giving Program.

Cinemark USA, Inc. Corporate Giving Program

c/o Donations
3900 Dallas Pkwy., Ste. 500
Plano, TX 75093-7871
FAX: (972) 665-1004;
E-mail: mzrnol@cinemark.com

Contact: Michele Zrno, Exec. Asst. to V.P., Mktg.
Purpose and activities: Cinemark makes charitable contributions of movie tickets to nonprofit organizations on a case by case basis. Support is given primarily in areas of company theater operations.
Fields of interest: General charitable giving.
Type of support: Donated products; In-kind gifts.
Geographic limitations: Giving primarily in areas of company theater operations.
Publications: Application guidelines.
Application information: Applications accepted. Proposals should be submitted using organization letterhead. Telephone calls and faxes are not encouraged. Organizations receiving support are asked to publicly acknowledge the donation. The Marketing Department handles giving. Application form not required. Applicants should submit the following:
1) copy of IRS Determination Letter
2) brief history of organization and description of its mission
3) detailed description of project and amount of funding requested
4) contact person

Proposals should indicate how, when, and where movie tickets will be used.
Initial approach: Proposal to headquarters
Copies of proposal: 1
Deadline(s): At least 5 weeks prior to need
Final notification: Following review
Number of staff: 1

816
Cintas Corporation

6800 Cintas Blvd.
P.O. Box 625737
Cincinnati, OH 45262-5737 (513) 459-1200
FAX: (513) 573-4030

Company URL: http://www.cintas.com
Establishment information: Established in 1929.
Company type: Public company
Company ticker symbol and exchange: CTAS/NASDAQ
Business activities: Provides uniform rental services; manufactures and sells uniforms.
Business type (SIC): Apparel—men's and boys' outerwear; laundry, cleaning, and garment services
Financial profile for 2012: Number of employees, 30,000; assets, $4,160,910,000; sales volume, $4,102,000,000; pre-tax net income, $470,940,000; expenses, $356,237,000,000; liabilities, $2,021,770,000
Fortune 1000 ranking: 2012—574th in revenues, 474th in profits, and 650th in assets
Corporate officers: Robert J. Kohlhepp, Chair.; Scott D. Farmer, C.E.O.; J. Phillip Holloman, Pres. and C.O.O.; William C. Gale, Sr. V.P. and C.F.O.; Thomas Frooman, V.P., Secy., and Genl. Counsel; J. Michael Hansen, V.P. and Treas.; Richard T. Farmer, Chair. Emeritus
Board of directors: Robert J. Kohlhepp, Chair.; Gerald S. Adolph; John F. Barrett; Melanie W. Barstad; Scott D. Farmer; Richard T. Farmer; James J. Johnson; Joseph M. Scaminace; Ronald W. Tysoe
Subsidiary: Unitog Company, Mason, OH
International operations: Canada; China; Honduras; Hong Kong; Mexico; Netherlands
Giving statement: Giving through the Cintas Cares.
Company EIN: 311188630

Cintas Cares

(formerly Cintas Corporation Contributions Program)
6800 Cintas Blvd.
P.O. Box 625737
Cincinnati, OH 45262-5737
URL: http://www.cintas.com/company/

Purpose and activities: Cintas makes charitable contributions to nonprofit organizations involved with the military, human services, international relief, and on a case by case basis. Support is given primarily in areas of company operations.
Fields of interest: Disasters, preparedness/services; Human services; International relief; General charitable giving Military/veterans.
Type of support: Donated products; Employee volunteer services; General/operating support; In-kind gifts.
Geographic limitations: Giving primarily in areas of company operations; giving also to national and international organizations.

817
Circle K Stores, Inc.

(formerly The Circle K Corporation)
1130 W. Warner Rd., Bldg. B
P.O. Box 52085
Tempe, AZ 85284-1213 (602) 728-8000

Company URL: http://www.circlek.com
Establishment information: Established in 1957.
Company type: Subsidiary of a foreign company
Business activities: Operates convenience stores.
Business type (SIC): Groceries—retail
Financial profile for 2010: Number of employees, 500; sales volume, $1,773,900,000
Corporate officer: Geoffrey C. Haxel, Pres.
Giving statement: Giving through the Circle K Corporation Contributions Program.

The Circle K Corporation Contributions Program

c/o Donations Comms. Dept.
P.O. Box 52085
Phoenix, AZ 85072-2085
Application addresses: AZ, NV: P.O. Box 52085, Phoenix, AZ 85072; FL (except Panhandle area): 12911 N. Telecom Pkwy., Temple Terrace, FL 33637; AL, AR, Panhandle, FL, LA, MS, and TN: 25 W. Cedar St., Ste. 100, Pensacola, FL 32502; GA, NC, and SC: 2440 Whitehall Park Dr., Ste. 800, Charlotte, NC 28273; CA, OR, and WA: 495 E. Rincon Ste. 150, Corona, CA 91709; CO, NM, OK, and TX: 3001 Gateway Dr. Ste. 130, Irving, TX 75063; IA, IL, IN, and KY: P.O. Box 347, Columbus, IN 47201; and MI, OH, and PA: 935 E. Talmadge Ave., Akron, OH 44310; URL: http://www.circlek.com/CircleK/AboutUs/CommunityService.htm

Purpose and activities: Circle K makes charitable contributions to nonprofit organizations involved with education, cerebral palsy, hunger, community development, and at-risk youth. Giving primarily in areas of company operations in Alabama, Arizona, Arkansas, California, Colorado, Florida, Georgia, Illinois, Iowa, Indiana, Kentucky, Los Angeles, Michigan, Mississippi, Nevada, New Mexico, North Carolina, Ohio, Oklahoma, Oregon, Pennsylvania,

South Carolina, Tennessee, Texas, and Washington. Giving also to national organizations.
Fields of interest: Education; Cerebral palsy; Food services; Housing/shelter, volunteer services; Boys clubs; Girls clubs; Youth development; Community/economic development Economically disadvantaged.
Type of support: Employee volunteer services; General/operating support; In-kind gifts; Sponsorships.
Geographic limitations: Giving primarily in areas of company operations in AL, AR, AZ, CA, CO, FL, GA, IA, IL, IN, KY, LA, MI, MS, NC, NM, NV, OH, OK, OR, PA, SC, TN, TX, and WA. Giving also to national organizations.
Publications: Application guidelines.
Application information: Applications accepted. Requests for financial contributions are reviewed in Jan. and Feb. for funding the next fiscal year. The Communications Department handles giving. Application form not required.
Proposals should be sent to: Circle K Stores, Inc., c/o Comms. Dept., Attention: Donations, at regional application address.
Initial approach: Proposal to nearest regional application address
Deadline(s): None
Final notification: 4 to 6 weeks

818
Cisco Systems, Inc.
170 W. Tasman Dr.
San Jose, CA 95134-1706 (408) 526-4000

Company URL: http://www.cisco.com
Establishment information: Established in 1984.
Company type: Public company
Company ticker symbol and exchange: CSCO/NASDAQ
International Securities Identification Number: US17275R1023
Business activities: Manufactures and provides Internet network hardware and software equipment and solutions.
Business type (SIC): Computer and office equipment
Financial profile for 2012: Number of employees, 66,639; assets, $91,759,000,000; sales volume, $46,061,000,000; pre-tax net income, $10,159,000,000; expenses, $35,996,000,000; liabilities, $40,473,000,000
Fortune 1000 ranking: 2012—60th in revenues, 22nd in profits, and 66th in assets
Forbes 2000 ranking: 2012—186th in sales, 48th in profits, and 261st in assets
Corporate officers: John T. Chambers, Chair. and C.E.O.; Gary B. Moore, Co-Pres. and C.O.O.; Robert W. Lloyd, Co-Pres., Sales; Frank A. Calderoni, Exec. V.P. and C.F.O.; Randy Pond, Exec. V.P., Opers.; Mark Chandler, Sr. V.P., Genl. Counsel, and Secy.; Kelly A. Kramer, Sr. V.P., Corp. Finance
Board of directors: John T. Chambers, Chair.; Carol A. Bartz; Marc Benioff; Greg Brown; M. Michele Burns; Michael D. Capellas; Larry R. Carter; Brian L. Halla; John L. Hennessy, Ph.D.; Kristina M. Johnson, Ph.D.; Richard M. Kovacevich; Roderick C. McGeary; Arun Sarin; Steven M. West
Subsidiary: Scientific-Atlanta, Inc., Lawrenceville, GA
International operations: Albania; Algeria; Argentina; Asia; Australia; Austria; Bahrain; Belgium; Bermuda; Bosnia-Herzegovina; Brazil; Bulgaria; Cameroon; Canada; Chile; China; Colombia; Costa Rica; Croatia; Cyprus; Czech Republic; Denmark; Dominican Republic; Ecuador; Egypt; El Salvador; Estonia; Ethiopia; Finland; France; Germany; Greece; Hong Kong; Hungary; Iceland; India; Indonesia; Ireland; Israel; Italy; Japan; Jordan; Latvia; Luxembourg; Macedonia; Malaysia; Mauritius; Mexico; Netherlands; New Zealand; Nigeria; Norway; Pakistan; Panama; Peru; Poland; Portugal; Qatar; Romania; Senegal; Serbia; Singapore; Slovakia; South Africa; South Korea; Spain; Sweden; Switzerland; Taiwan; Thailand; Trinidad & Tobago; Tunisia; United Kingdom; Venezuela; Vietnam
Historic mergers: Scientific-Atlanta, Inc. (February 27, 2006)
Giving statement: Giving through the Cisco Systems, Inc. Corporate Giving Program and the Cisco Systems Foundation.
Company EIN: 770059951

Cisco Systems, Inc. Corporate Giving Program
170 W. Tasman Dr.
San Jose, CA 95134-1706 (408) 526-4000
URL: http://csr.cisco.com/

Purpose and activities: As a complement to its foundation, Cisco also makes charitable contributions to nonprofit organizations directly. Emphasis is given to organizations involved with education, healthcare, economic empowerment, and critical human needs. Support is given in areas of company operations and on a national and international basis.
Fields of interest: Education, computer literacy/technology training; Education; Food services; Housing/shelter; Safety/disasters, management/technical assistance; Children, services; Human services, financial counseling; Human services; International affairs, management/technical assistance; Microfinance/microlending; Community/economic development; Engineering/technology; Military/veterans' organizations Economically disadvantaged.
Type of support: Donated products; Equipment; General/operating support; Program development.
Geographic limitations: Giving in areas of company operations and on a national and international basis.
Application information: Applications accepted. Applications are not accepted via postal mail or e-mail attachments. Cisco considers maximum requests of $75,000 (USD) for first-time applicants for the Global Impact Cash Grant program. Application form required.
Initial approach: Complete online eligibility quiz and Initial Information Form

Cisco Systems Foundation
170 W. Tasman Dr.
San Jose, CA 95134-1706 (408) 527-3040
URL: http://www.cisco.com/go/foundation

Establishment information: Established in 1997 in CA.
Donors: Cisco Systems, Inc.; Scientific-Atlanta Fdn. Inc.
Contact: Peter Tavernise, Exec. Dir.
Financial data (yr. ended 07/31/11): Assets, $133,016,137 (M); gifts received, $2,851; expenditures, $13,420,193; qualifying distributions, $12,510,292; giving activities include $6,616,192 for 115 grants (high: $880,000; low: $15,000) and $5,657,284 for employee matching gifts.
Purpose and activities: The foundation supports programs designed to improve access to basic human needs, education, and economic opportunity. Special emphasis is directed toward programs designed to address underserved communities; and provide solutions that utilizes the power of the internet and communications technology.
Fields of interest: Elementary/secondary education; Vocational education; Health sciences school/education; Adult/continuing education; Education, reading; Education; Public health, obesity; Public health, clean water supply; Health care; Crime/violence prevention; Employment, training; Employment, retraining; Food services; Housing/shelter, development; Housing/shelter; Disasters, preparedness/services; Children, services; Human services, financial counseling; Human services; Economic development; Social entrepreneurship; Community development, small businesses; Microfinance/microlending; Mathematics; Engineering/technology; Science Children/youth; Minorities; Women; Girls; Economically disadvantaged; Homeless.
Programs:
Community Impact Cash Grants - Silicon Valley: The foundation awards grants of up to $15,000 to local organizations for programs designed to address the unmet needs of underserved communities in areas of education and critical human needs. Special emphasis is directed toward health programs, including disease prevention, positive healthy habits, and obesity and violence prevention; and K-8 education programs designed to make it possible for every child to attain quality education.
Employee Volunteer Program: The foundation awards grants to nonprofit organizations with which employees of Cisco Systems volunteer.
Global Impact Cash Grants: The foundation awards grants to organizations with a national or multi-national scope of operations. Special emphasis is directed toward programs designed to promote education including STEM, curriculum development, student-centricity, teacher development, and parental participation; economic empowerment, including underserved populations transitioning from education to workforce, microfinance institutions, and access to knowledge and skills to upgrade individuals and entrepreneurs; and critical human needs, including basic needs of underserved communities, web-based tools to increase access to products and services, natural disasters, and humanitarian crises. Grants of up to $75,000 are awarded.
Type of support: Continuing support; Curriculum development; Employee matching gifts; Employee volunteer services; General/operating support; Program development.
Geographic limitations: Giving primarily within a 50 mile radius of company operations in Lawrenceville, GA, Boxborough, MA, Research Triangle Park, NC, Richardson, TX, Toronto, Canada, Beijing and Shanghai, China, and Bangalore, India, with emphasis on San Jose, CA.
Support limitations: No support for discriminatory organizations, religious, political, or sectarian organizations not of direct benefit to the entire community, public schools or school systems, charter schools, school foundations, booster clubs, colleges or universities, pass-through organizations, or grantmaking foundations. No grants to individuals, or for research, start-up needs, scholarships, stipends, loans, athletic events, competitions, tournaments, conferences, seminars, festival or similar one-day events, field trips, fundraising events, sponsorships, capital campaigns, or challenge or matching grants; generally, no equipment funding.
Publications: Application guidelines; Grants list; IRS Form 990 or 990-PF printed copy available upon request.

Application information: Applications accepted. A full proposal may be requested at a later date for Global Impact Grants. Organizations receiving Community Impact Cash Grants - Silicon Valley are asked to provide periodic progress reports. Application form required.

Initial approach: Complete online eligibility quiz and application form
Board meeting date(s): Fall and spring
Deadline(s): None for Global Impact Grants; Jan. 28 to Feb. 15 for Community Impact Cash Grants - Silicon Valley
Final notification: June for Community Impact Cash Grants - Silicon Valley

Officer and Trustees:* John P. Morgridge*, Chair.; John T. Chambers, Pres.; Larry R. Carter*, Secy.-Treas.; Peter Tavernise, Exec. Dir.; Carlos Dominguez; Patrick Finn; Karen McFadzen; Randy Pond; Michael Quinn; Michael Vessey; Tae Yoo.
Number of staff: 1 part-time support.
EIN: 770443347
Selected grants: The following grants are a representative sample of this grantmaker's funding activity:
$880,000 to National Center for Learning Disabilities, New York, NY, 2011. For RTI Action Network-Leadership Network.
$600,000 to Community Voice Mail National Office, Seattle, WA, 2011. For Next Generation of ICT Phase II.
$480,000 to City Year, Boston, MA, 2011. For Cisco's continued investment in learning and development initiatives to enhance collaboration and enhance corps member and student outcomes.
$250,000 to American Red Cross National Headquarters, Washington, DC, 2011. For Japan Earthquake and Tsunami Relief.
$250,000 to Citizen Schools, Boston, MA, 2011. For expanding opportunity and supporting educational achievement for middle school students.
$250,000 to ImagineNations Group, Pasadena, MD, 2011. For ImagineNations Network.
$250,000 to MIND Research Institute, Santa Ana, CA, 2011. For Arizona Pilot of ST Math Project.
$200,000 to Blue Planet Run Foundation, Redwood City, CA, 2011. For AnalytiX 2.0.
$15,000 to YMCA of San Francisco, Urban Services, San Francisco, CA, 2011. For Starr King and Malcolm X After School Program(s) Cyber Tutoring through EPGY (Education Program for Gifted Youth).

819
CIT Group Inc.

(formerly Tyco Capital Corporation)
11 W. 42 St.
New York, NY 10036 (212) 461-5200

Company URL: http://www.cit.com
Establishment information: Established in 1908.
Company type: Public company
Company ticker symbol and exchange: CIT/NYSE
Business activities: Provides commercial and consumer loans.
Business type (SIC): Credit institutions/business; credit institutions/personal
Financial profile for 2012: Number of employees, 3,560; assets, $44,012,000,000; pre-tax net income, -$454,800,000; liabilities, $35,677,200,000
Fortune 1000 ranking: 2012—589th in revenues, 963rd in profits, and 125th in assets
Forbes 2000 ranking: 2012—1511th in sales, 1899th in profits, and 523rd in assets
Corporate officers: John A. Thain, Chair. and C.E.O.; Nelson J. Chai, Pres.; Robert J. Ingato, Exec. V.P., Genl. Counsel, and Secy.; Andrew Brandman, Exec. V.P. and C.A.O.; Scott T. Parker, C.F.O.
Board of directors: John A. Thain, Chair.; Michael J. Embler; William M. Freeman; David M. Moffett; R. Brad Oates; Marianne Miller Parrs; Gerald Rosenfeld; John R. Ryan; Seymour Sternberg; Peter J. Tobin; Laura S. Unger
Subsidiaries: The CIT Group/Business Credit, Inc., New York, NY; The CIT Group/Capital Finance, Inc., New York, NY; The CIT Group/Commercial Services, Inc., New York, NY; The CIT Group/Consumer Finance, Inc., Livingston, NJ; The CIT Group/Equipment Financing, Inc., Livingston, NJ; The CIT Group/Equity Investments, Inc., Livingston, NJ; The CIT Group/Sales Financing, Inc., Livingston, NJ; Education Lending Group, Inc., San Diego, CA
International operations: Aruba; Australia; Austria; Barbados; Belgium; Bermuda; Brazil; Canada; Cayman Islands; Chile; China; Colombia; France; Germany; Hong Kong; Hungary; Ireland; Italy; Japan; Luxembourg; Malaysia; Mexico; Netherlands; New Zealand; Poland; Portugal; Russia; Singapore; South Korea; Spain; Sweden; United Kingdom
Giving statement: Giving through the CIT Group Inc. Corporate Giving Program.
Company EIN: 651051192

CIT Group Inc. Corporate Giving Program

11 W 42 St.
New York, NY 10036
E-mail: stacy.papas@cit.com; URL: http://www.cit.com/about-cit/corporate-citizenship/corporate-giving/index.htm

Contact: Stacy Papas, V.P., Corp. Giving and Community and Employee Affairs
Purpose and activities: CIT makes charitable contributions to nonprofit organizations on a case by case basis. Support is given on a national and international basis in areas of company operations.
Fields of interest: General charitable giving.
International interests: Canada.
Type of support: Continuing support; Employee volunteer services; General/operating support; Program development.
Geographic limitations: Giving on a national and international basis in areas of company operations.
Support limitations: No support for religious, political, legislative, veteran, fraternal, conference, or sports organizations, or for political candidates. No grants to individuals.
Publications: Application guidelines.
Application information: Grantmaking is currently suspended. The Corporate Giving Department handles giving. Multi-year funding is not automatic. Application form not required. Applicants should submit the following:
1) copy of IRS Determination Letter
2) brief history of organization and description of its mission
3) listing of board of directors, trustees, officers and other key people and their affiliations
4) detailed description of project and amount of funding requested

Applications should include a description of past support by CIT Group with the organization.

Initial approach: Proposal to headquarters
Committee meeting date(s): Annually
Deadline(s): None

820
CITGO Petroleum Corporation

1293 Eldridge Pkwy.
P.O. Box 4689
Houston, TX 77210-4689 (800) 992-4846

Company URL: http://www.citgo.com
Establishment information: Established in 1910.
Company type: Subsidiary of a foreign company
Business activities: Refines, markets, and transports petroleum products.
Business type (SIC): Petroleum refining
Corporate officers: Alejandro Granado, Chair., Pres., and C.E.O.; Maritza Villanueva, V.P., Finance and Treas.; Gustavo Velasquez, V.P., Mktg.; Daniel Cortez, V.P., Public Affairs; John Butts, Corp. Cont.; Dean M. Hasseman, Genl. Counsel
Board of directors: Alejandro Granado, Chair.; Victor Aular; Asdrubal Chavez; Eulogio Del Pino
Giving statement: Giving through the CITGO Petroleum Corp. Contributions Program and the Simon Bolivar Foundation, Inc.

CITGO Petroleum Corp. Contributions Program

P.O. Box 4689
Houston, TX 77210-4689
URL: http://www.citgo.com/SocialResponsibility.jsp

Purpose and activities: CITGO makes charitable contributions to nonprofit organizations involved with reading, education, energy, the environment, animal welfare, public health, muscular dystrophy, women centers, and human services. Support is given primarily in areas of company operations.
Fields of interest: Education, reading; Education; Environment, energy; Environment; Animal welfare; Public health; Muscular dystrophy; Women, centers/services; Human services; United Ways and Federated Giving Programs; General charitable giving.
Program:
CITGO-Venezuela Heating Oil Program: CITGO, in partnership with Bolivarian Republic of Venezuela and the Citizens Energy Corporation, provides discounted heating oil to low-income households and social service providers in areas of the country most affected by cold winters. The program is available to families in need, those who receive fuel assistance from the federal government, homeless shelters, multi-unit buildings, and Native American tribes.
Type of support: In-kind gifts; Sponsorships.
Geographic limitations: Giving on a national basis in areas of company operations.

Simon Bolivar Foundation, Inc.

c/o Dr. Dario Merchan
P.O. Box 4689
Houston, TX 77210-4689
E-mail: sbf@citgo.com; URL: http://www.simonbolivarfoundation.org/

Establishment information: Established in 2007 in TX.
Donor: CITGO Petroleum Corporation.
Contact: Brenda Estrada-Torres
Financial data (yr. ended 12/31/11): Assets, $12,678,183 (M); gifts received, $11,163,134; expenditures, $11,065,137; qualifying distributions, $10,449,934; giving activities include $3,654,817 for 39 grants (high: $2,000,000; low: $601) and $6,667,721 for 2 foundation-administered programs.

Purpose and activities: The foundation supports programs designed to expand access to healthcare to underprivileged individuals who are affected by critical illness and poverty.
Fields of interest: Environment; Hospitals (general); Health care, clinics/centers; Speech/hearing centers; Health care, support services; Health care, organ/tissue banks; Health care, patient services; Health care; Disasters, preparedness/services; Human services Economically disadvantaged.
International interests: Venezuela.
Programs:
Bone Marrow Transplant: The foundation provides financial assistance for pre- and post-medical treatment for underprivileged children and young adults in need of bone marrow transplants. The program is administered in partnership with Fundacion para el Trasplante de Medula Osea in Maracaibo, Venezuela and a network of hospitals throughout Italy.
Bronx Social Programs: The foundation awards grants to South Bronx nonprofit organizations that are critical in the process of the region's social development and environmental restoration.
Critical Care: The foundation supports critically ill patients who can not afford necessary medical treatment and patients who live in countries where specialized treatments are not available. The foundation provides access to specialized medical treatment and financial assistance to help with excessive medical costs for patient and their families.
Hearing Solutions: The foundation, in partnership with Petroleos de Venezuela and Fundacion Venezolana de Otologia, provides financial assistance to people who are severely deaf and require hearing aids or cochlear implants.
Liver Transplant: The foundation provides financial assistance to underprivileged children in need of liver transplants and related medical treatment. Qualified patients typically receive transplants and assistance through the Hospital Italiano in Buenos Aires, Argentina.
Type of support: Building/renovation; Equipment; Program development.
Geographic limitations: Giving primarily in Washington, DC, New York, NY, Argentina, Italy, and Venezuela.
Publications: Application guidelines; Program policy statement.
Application information: Applications accepted. Application form required.
Initial approach: Complete online application for medical assistance and Bronx Social Programs
Deadline(s): None for medical assistance; Dec. 21 for Bronx Social Programs
Officers and Directors:* Maritza Rojas de Villanueva*, Chair.; Dario Merchan, Pres.; Patricia Milano, V.P.; Arnaldo Arcay, Secy.; Fatima Romero, Treas.; Daniel Cortez; Brian O'Kelly.
EIN: 205787382

821
Citigroup Inc.

399 Park Ave.
New York, NY 10022 (212) 559-1000

Company URL: http://www.citigroup.com
Establishment information: Established in 1988.
Company type: Public company
Company ticker symbol and exchange: C/NYSE
International Securities Identification Number: US1729674242
Business activities: Operates financial services holding company; operates commercial bank.
Business type (SIC): Banks/commercial; holding company
Financial profile for 2012: Number of employees, 259,000; assets, $1,864,660,000,000; pre-tax net income, $7,936,000,000; liabilities, $1,675,611,000,000
Fortune 1000 ranking: 2012—26th in revenues, 23rd in profits, and 5th in assets
Forbes 2000 ranking: 2012—73rd in sales, 60th in profits, and 17th in assets
Corporate officers: Michael E. O'Neill, Chair.; Michael S. Helfer, Vice-Chair.; Michael L. Corbat, C.E.O.; John C. Gerspach, C.F.O.; Rohan Seneka Weerasinghe, Genl. Counsel and Corp. Secy.
Board of directors: Michael E. O'Neill, Chair.; Michael Helfer, Vice-Chair.; Michael L. Corbat; Franz B. Humer; Robert L. Joss, Ph.D.; Judith Rodin; Robert L. Ryan; Anthony M. Santomero; Joan E. Spero, Ph.D.; Diana L. Taylor; William S. Thompson, Jr.; Ernesto Zedillo
Subsidiaries: CitiFinancial Auto Corp., Dallas, TX; CitiFinancial Co., Baltimore, MD; Citigroup Global Markets, Inc., New York, NY; CitiMortgage, Inc., St. Louis, MO
International operations: Argentina; Aruba; Australia; Bahamas; Bahrain; Belgium; Bermuda; Brazil; British Virgin Islands; Canada; Cayman Islands; Chile; China; Colombia; Congo; Costa Rica; Czech Republic; Dominican Republic; Ecuador; Egypt; El Salvador; Finland; France; Germany; Greece; Guatemala; Guernsey; Haiti; Honduras; Hong Kong; Hungary; India; Indonesia; Ireland; Italy; Ivory Coast; Jamaica; Japan; Jersey; Kazakhstan; Kenya; Luxembourg; Macau; Malaysia; Mauritius; Mexico; Morocco and the Western Sahara; Netherlands; New Zealand; Nigeria; Panama; Peru; Philippines; Poland; Portugal; Romania; Russia; Saint Kitts-Nevis; Singapore; Slovakia; South Africa; South Korea; Spain; Switzerland; Taiwan; Tanzania, Zanzibar and Pemba; Thailand; Trinidad & Tobago; Turkey; Uganda; Ukraine; United Kingdom; Uruguay; Venezuela; Zambia
Historic mergers: European American Bank (July 17, 2001)
Giving statement: Giving through the Citigroup Inc. Corporate Giving Program and the Citi Foundation.
Company EIN: 521568099

Citigroup Inc. Corporate Giving Program

(formerly Travelers Group Inc. Corporate Giving Program)
425 Park Ave., 2nd. Fl.
New York, NY 10022-3527
URL: http://www.citigroup.com/citi/about/global_citizenship.html

Purpose and activities: As a complement to its foundation, Citigroup also makes charitable contributions to nonprofit organizations directly.
Fields of interest: Environment; Human services, financial counseling; Civil/human rights, equal rights; Civil/human rights; Community/economic development; Public affairs Economically disadvantaged.
Type of support: Employee volunteer services; General/operating support.
Geographic limitations: Giving in areas of company operations.
Publications: Corporate report; Informational brochure.

Citi Foundation

(formerly Citigroup Foundation)
1 Court Sq., Fl. 43
Long Island City, NY 11120
E-mail: citifoundation@citi.com; URL: http://www.citifoundation.com

Establishment information: Established in 1994 in NY.
Donors: Citicorp; Citibank, N.A.; Citigroup Inc.; Citigroup Venture Capital Ltd.; Charles Prince.
Contact: Lia Cartagena, Grants Assoc.
Financial data (yr. ended 12/31/11): Assets, $62,791,324 (M); gifts received, $78,002,273; expenditures, $78,616,970; qualifying distributions, $78,616,000; giving activities include $78,614,500 for 492 grants (high: $2,000,000; low: $10,000).
Purpose and activities: The foundation supports organizations and programs designed to enhance economic opportunities for individuals and families, particularly those in need, in areas of company operations. The foundation provides grant support for programs that are aligned with it's economic empowerment mission, promote collaboration and effective use of philanthropic resources, engage it's employees, and demonstrate impact and positive outcomes. Special emphasis is directed toward programs designed to promote financial capability and asset building; microfinance; enterprise development; college success; youth education and livelihoods; neighborhood revitalization; and disaster response. The foundation also strives to partner with organizations that demonstrate a commitment to the environment and environmental innovations in each of the core priority areas.
Fields of interest: Higher education; Education, reading; Disasters, preparedness/services; Youth development, business; Human services, financial counseling; Community/economic development, management/technical assistance; Community development, neighborhood development; Economic development; Business/industry; Community development, small businesses; Microfinance/microlending; Community/economic development; Financial services Youth; Minorities; Women; Economically disadvantaged.
Programs:
College Success: The foundation supports programs designed to increase the number of low- to moderate-income secondary school students who are meeting the academic, financial, and social milestones to pursue higher education. This program is limited to the U.S.
Disaster Response: The foundation supports programs designed to promote preparedness, immediate response, and rebuilding efforts that lead to long-term recovery of communities.
Enterprise Development: The foundation supports programs designed to increase the number of micro or small enterprises that provide new income generation and/or employment opportunities for low- to moderate-income individuals.
Financial Capability and Asset Building: The foundation supports programs designed to increase the number of low-to moderate-income adults and/or youth who adopt positive financial behaviors and accumulate financial assets.
Microfinance: The foundation supports programs designed to increase the supply and use of financial products, supplied by microfinance institutions, that improve financial inclusion of low-to moderate-income individuals.
Neighborhood Revitalization: The foundation supports programs designed to promote small businesses, affordable housing units, or community facilities that contribute to the economic and/or environmental sustainability of low-to

moderate-income communities. This program is limited to the U.S.

Youth Education and Livelihoods: The foundation supports programs designed to increase the number of low-to moderate-income youth, ages 13-25, who become employed, start their own-income-generating business, or obtain postsecondary education or training. This program is limited to organizations located outside of the U.S.

Type of support: Continuing support; Management development/capacity building; Program development.

Geographic limitations: Giving on a national and international basis in Algeria, Argentina, Australia, Bahamas, Bahrain, Bangladesh, Belgium, Brazil, Brunei, Bulgaria, Cameroon, Canada, China, Colombia, Costa Rica, Cote d'Ivoire, Czech Republic, Democratic Rep. of Congo, Denmark, Dominican Republic, Ecuador, Egypt, El Salvador, Finland, France, Germany, Ghana, Greece, Guam, Guatemala, Honduras, Hong Kong, Hungary, India, Indonesia, Ireland, Israel, Italy, Jamaica, Japan, Jordan, Kazakhstan, Kenya, Korea (South), Kuwait, Lebanon, Luxembourg, Malaysia, Morocco, Netherlands, New Zealand, Nicaragua, Nigeria, Norway, Pakistan, Panama, Paraguay, Peru, Philippines, Poland, Portugal, Qatar, Romania, Russia, Senegal, Singapore, Slovakia, South Africa, Spain, Sri Lanka, Sweden, Switzerland, Taiwan, Tanzania, Thailand, Trinidad & Tobago, Tunisia, Turkey, Uganda, Ukraine, United Arab Emirates, United Kingdom, Uruguay, Venezuela, Vietnam, and Zambia.

Support limitations: No support for political candidates or religious, veterans', or fraternal organizations not of direct benefit to the entire community. No grants to individuals, or for political causes, fundraising events, telethons, marathons, races, or benefits, advertising, sponsorships, dinners or luncheons, or membership fees.

Publications: Corporate giving report; Grants list; Informational brochure.

Application information: Applications not accepted. The foundation utilizes an invitation only process; unsolicited proposals are not accepted.

Board meeting date(s): 4-5 times yearly

Officers and Directors:* Lewis B. Kaden*, Chair.; Pamela P. Flaherty, Pres.; Brandee McHale, C.O.O.; Bob Annibale; Shirish Apte; Jim Cowles; Raymond J. McGuire; Paul McKinnon; William J. Mills; Edward Skyler; Francesco Vanni d'Archirafi; Alberto Verme.

Number of staff: 22 full-time professional; 2 full-time support; 3 part-time support.

EIN: 133781879

Selected grants: The following grants are a representative sample of this grantmaker's funding activity:

$5,000,000 to Financial Innovations Center, Chicago, IL, 2012. For Financial Capability Innovation Fund.

$200,000 to Neighborhood Reinvestment Corporation, Washington, DC, 2012. For Counselor Training and Technology and Capacity Program.

$160,000 to Junior Achievement Worldwide, Colorado Springs, CO, 2012. For youth financial capability and entrepreneur program in LATAM region.

$40,000 to Local Initiatives Support Corporation, New York, NY, 2012. For Technical Assistance Program.

822
Citizen Watch Company of America, Inc.

1200 Wall St. W.
Lyndhurst, NJ 07071 (800) 321-1023
FAX: (310) 225-4926

Company URL: http://www.citizenwatch.com
Establishment information: Established in 1924.
Company type: Subsidiary of a foreign company
Business activities: Operates watch and timepiece company.
Business type (SIC): Watches, clocks, and parts
Financial profile for 2010: Number of employees, 300
Corporate officers: Laurence R. Grunstein, Pres.; Ronald F. Luino, V.P., Opers. and Admin.
Giving statement: Giving through the Citizen Watch Company of America, Inc. Contributions Program.

Citizen Watch Company of America, Inc. Contributions Program

1200 Wall St. W.
Lyndhurst, NJ 07071 (800) 321-1023
E-mail: press@citizenwatch.com; URL: http://www.citizenwatch.com/COA/English/home.asp

823
Citizens Building and Loan Association

229 Trade St.
P.O. Box 388
Greer, SC 29651 (864) 877-2054

Company URL: http://www.cblgreer.com/
Establishment information: Established in 1907.
Company type: Private company
Business activities: Operates savings and loan bank.
Business type (SIC): Savings institutions
Corporate officers: Benjamin B. Waters III, Chair.; J. Thomas Johnson, Pres. and C.E.O.; Rhonda P. Turner, V.P., Opers.
Board of directors: Benjamin B. Waters III, Chair.; W. Terry Dobson; Hayne P. Griffin, Jr.; Laurens I. James; Ralph W. Johnson; Paul J. Rogers
Giving statement: Giving through the Citizens Building & Loan Charitable Foundation.

Citizens Building & Loan Charitable Foundation

229 Trade St.
Greer, SC 29651-3427 (864) 877-2054
URL: http://www.cblgreer.com/cbl-in-the-community.php

Establishment information: Established in 1999 in SC.
Financial data (yr. ended 12/31/11): Assets, $598,050 (M); gifts received, $1,000; expenditures, $75,000; qualifying distributions, $75,000; giving activities include $75,000 for 9 grants (high: $30,000; low: $2,000).
Fields of interest: Human services; Religion.
Geographic limitations: Giving primarily in SC, with some giving in NY.
Support limitations: No grants to individuals.
Application information: Applications accepted. Application form required. Applicants should submit the following:
1) additional materials/documentation

Initial approach: Letter
Deadline(s): Jan. 1, Apr. 1, Sept. 1, and Dec. 1
Directors: Terry Dobson; Hayne Griffin; Laurens I. James, Jr.; Ralph Johnson; Tommy Johnson; Paul Rogers; Benjamin Waters.
EIN: 562158345

824
Citizens Business Bank

701 N. Haven Ave.
Ontario, CA 91764-4920 (909) 980-4030

Company URL: https://www.cbbank.com
Establishment information: Established in 1974.
Company type: Subsidiary of a public company
Business activities: Operates commercial bank.
Business type (SIC): Banks/commercial
Corporate officer: Christopher D. Myers, Pres. and C.E.O.

Citizens Business Bank Corporate Giving Program

701 N Haven Ave.
Ontario, CA 91764-4920 (609) 980-4030

Purpose and activities: Support is given to nonprofit organizations involved with civic and community issues.
Fields of interest: Hospitals (general); Hospitals (specialty); Health care; Boys clubs; Girls clubs; YM/YWCAs & YM/YWHAs; Children, services; Community/economic development; United Ways and Federated Giving Programs; Public affairs.
Type of support: Annual campaigns; Employee volunteer services; General/operating support; Loaned talent.
Geographic limitations: Giving primarily in areas of company operations.

825
The Citizens First National Bank

E. 5th & Lake Ave.
P.O. Box 1227
Storm Lake, IA 50588 (712) 732-5440

Company URL: http://www.citizensfnb.com
Establishment information: Established in 1902.
Company type: Private company
Business activities: Operates commercial bank.
Business type (SIC): Banks/commercial
Corporate officer: Harry P. Schaller, Pres.
Giving statement: Giving through the Citizens First National Bank Foundation.

Citizens First National Bank Foundation

P.O. Box 1227
Storm Lake, IA 50588-1227 (712) 732-5440

Donor: Citizens First National Bank Foundation.
Contact: Harry P. Schaller, Tr.
Financial data (yr. ended 12/31/11): Assets, $421,778 (M); expenditures, $22,254; qualifying distributions, $21,130; giving activities include $21,130 for grants.
Purpose and activities: The foundation supports organizations involved with higher education, Christianity, and other areas.
Fields of interest: Education; Religion.

Geographic limitations: Giving primarily in the Early and Storm Lake, IA, areas.
Support limitations: No grants to individuals.
Application information: Applications accepted. Application form required.
Initial approach: Letter
Deadline(s): Nov. 1
Trustees: George H. Schaller; Harry P. Schaller.
EIN: 426073539

826
Citizens National Bank Inc.

44 Public Sq.
Somerset, KY 42501-1414 (606) 679-6341

Company URL: http://www.cnbsomerset.com
Establishment information: Established in 1920.
Company type: Subsidiary of a private company
Business activities: Operates commercial bank.
Business type (SIC): Banks/commercial
Corporate officers: Harris Rakestraw III, Chair.; Cy Waddle, Vice-Chair.; Donald E. Bloomer, Pres. and C.E.O.; Lisa Compton, Exec. V.P., Opers.
Board of directors: Harris Rakestraw III, Chair.; Cy Waddle, Vice-Chair.; Ron Absher; Donald E. Bloomer; Clay Parker Davis; Robert S. Harris; Charles R. Hembree; Steve Merrick; Harold D. Rogers; Larry VanHook; William J. Wilson
Giving statement: Giving through the Citizens Community Foundation, Inc.

Citizens Community Foundation, Inc.

145 Woodland Dr.
Somerset, KY 42502-1351

Establishment information: Established in 2005 in KY.
Donor: Citizens National Bank.
Financial data (yr. ended 12/31/11): Assets, $320,450 (M); expenditures, $25,520; qualifying distributions, $25,000; giving activities include $25,000 for grants.
Fields of interest: Higher education.
Type of support: Scholarship funds.
Geographic limitations: Giving primarily in KY.
Support limitations: No grants to individuals.
Application information: Applications not accepted. Unsolicited requests for funds not accepted.
Directors: Clay Parker Davis; Harris Rakestraw III; Cy Waddle.
EIN: 203537437

827
Citizens Republic Bancorp, Inc.

(formerly Citizens Banking Corporation)
328 S. Saginaw St.
Flint, MI 48502-2401 (810) 766-7500
FAX: (810) 257-2570

Company URL: http://www.citizensbanking.com
Establishment information: Established in 1871.
Company type: Public company
Company ticker symbol and exchange: CRBC/NASDAQ
Business activities: Operates bank holding company; operates commercial bank.
Business type (SIC): Banks/commercial; holding company
Financial profile for 2012: Number of employees, 1,973; assets, $9,586,680,000; pre-tax net income, $99,270,000; liabilities, $8,216,180,000
Corporate officers: James L. Wolohan, Chair.; Cathleen H. Nash, Pres. and C.E.O.; Lisa T. McNeely, Exec. V.P. and C.F.O.; Gerald D. Bettens, Exec. V.P. and C.I.O.; Thomas W. Gallagher, Exec. V.P., Genl. Counsel, and Secy.; Susan P. Brockett, Exec. V.P., Human Resources; Joseph C. Czopek, Sr. V.P. and Corp. Cont.; Brian D.J. Boike, Sr. V.P. and Treas.
Board of directors: James L. Wolohan, Chair.; Lizabeth A. Ardisana; George J. Butvilas; Madeleine L. Champion; Robert S. Cubbin; William M. Fenimore, Jr.; Gary J. Hurand; Benjamin W. Laird; Stephen J. Lazaroff; Cathleen H. Nash; Kendall B. Williams
Giving statement: Giving through the Citizens Banking Corporation Contributions Program and the Citizens Banking Corporation Charitable Foundation.
Company EIN: 382378932

Citizens Banking Corporation Charitable Foundation

328 S. Saginaw St., M/C 001065
Flint, MI 48502-1923

Establishment information: Established in 1999 in MI.
Donor: Citizens Banking Co.
Financial data (yr. ended 12/31/11): Assets, $162,702 (M); expenditures, $8,324; qualifying distributions, $5,330; giving activities include $5,000 for 1 grant.
Purpose and activities: The foundation supports food banks and organizations involved with arts and culture, education, housing, sports, human services, and community economic development.
Fields of interest: Performing arts, music; Arts; Education; Food banks; Housing/shelter; Athletics/sports, amateur leagues; Athletics/sports, winter sports; Human services; Community/economic development; United Ways and Federated Giving Programs.
Type of support: General/operating support.
Geographic limitations: Giving primarily in IA, MI, and WI.
Support limitations: No grants to individuals.
Application information: Applications not accepted. Unsolicited requests for funds not accepted.
Trustee: Citizens Bank, N.A.
EIN: 386742630

828
Citizens State Bank

114 W. Main St.
P.O. Box 198
Wyoming, IA 52362-7748 (563) 488-2211

Company URL: http://www.csbwyoming.com
Establishment information: Established in 1913.
Company type: Private company
Business activities: Operates commercial bank.
Business type (SIC): Banks/commercial
Corporate officers: Leo Ahrendsen, Chair.; David C. Butterworth, Pres. and C.E.O.; Theresa Westhoff, Secy.
Board of director: Leo Ahrendsen, Chair.
Giving statement: Giving through the Citizens State Foundation.

Citizens State Foundation

200 N. Main St.
P.O. Box 159
Pocahontas, IA 50574-0159 (712) 335-3222

Establishment information: Established in 1988 in IA.
Donor: Citizens State Bank.
Contact: Stephen R. Baade, Pres.
Financial data (yr. ended 12/31/11): Assets, $50,404 (M); gifts received, $24,000; expenditures, $19,030; qualifying distributions, $19,030; giving activities include $19,030 for grants.
Purpose and activities: The foundation supports hospices and organizations involved with education, health, heart disease, crime and law enforcement, disability services, and community development.
Fields of interest: Higher education; Education; Health care; Heart & circulatory diseases; Crime/law enforcement; Residential/custodial care, hospices; Developmentally disabled, centers & services; Community/economic development.
Type of support: Annual campaigns; Building/renovation; General/operating support; Program development; Research; Scholarship funds.
Geographic limitations: Giving primarily in IA.
Support limitations: No grants to individuals.
Application information: Applications accepted. Application form required. Applicants should submit the following:
1) copy of IRS Determination Letter
2) detailed description of project and amount of funding requested
Initial approach: Contact foundation for application form
Deadline(s): None
Officers: Stephen R. Baade, Pres.; Donald D. Schnell, V.P.; Denise Nielson, Secy.-Treas.
EIN: 421303083

829
City Carton Company, Inc.

(also known as City Carton Recycling)
3 E. Benton St.
Iowa City, IA 52240-1509 (319) 351-2848

Company URL: http://www.citycarton.com
Establishment information: Established in 1967.
Company type: Private company
Business activities: Recycles paper.
Business type (SIC): Durable goods—wholesale
Corporate officers: Andy Ockenfels, Pres. and C.E.O.; Thomas P. Rowland, C.F.O.; Daryl Russ, V.P., Opers.
Giving statement: Giving through the Ockenfels Family Foundation.

Ockenfels Family Foundation

3 E. Benton St.
Iowa City, IA 52240

Establishment information: Established in 2000 in IA.
Donor: City Carton Co. Inc.
Financial data (yr. ended 12/31/11): Assets, $89,352 (M); gifts received, $122,563; expenditures, $39,884; qualifying distributions, $0.
Purpose and activities: The foundation supports organizations involved with cancer.
Type of support: General/operating support.
Support limitations: No grants to individuals.
Application information: Applications not accepted. Unsolicited requests for funds not accepted.
Officers and Trustees: Andrew Ockenfels, Pres.; Timothy A. Ockenfels, V.P.; Christopher J. Ockenfels, Secy.-Treas.; Deb Ockenfels; John L. Ockenfels; Mark Ockenfels.
EIN: 421510256

830
City National Bank

City National Plz.
555 S. Flowers St., 9th Fl.
Los Angeles, CA 90071-2303
(213) 673-7700
FAX: (310) 858-3334

Company URL: http://www.cnb.com
Establishment information: Established in 1954.
Company type: Subsidiary of a public company
Business activities: Operates commercial bank.
Business type (SIC): Banks/commercial
Corporate officers: Russell D. Goldsmith, Chair. and C.E.O.; Christopher J. Warmuth, Pres.; Christopher J. Carey, Exec. V.P. and C.F.O.; John J. Beale, Exec. V.P. and C.I.O.; Michael B. Cahill, Exec. V.P., Genl. Counsel, and Corp. Secy.; Marianne Lamutt, Exec. V.P., Human Resources; Thomas R. Miller, Exec. V.P., Mktg.
Board of director: Russell D. Goldsmith, Chair.
Giving statement: Giving through the City National Bank Corporate Giving Program.

City National Bank Corporate Giving Program

(formerly City National Corporation Contributions Program)
555 S. Flower St., 9th Fl.
Los Angeles, CA 90071 (213) 673-7603
FAX: (213) 673-7646;
E-mail: jennifer.nickerson@cnb.com; URL: http://cnb.com/aboutus/community/

Contact: Jennifer Nickerson, V.P. and Community Rels. Mgr.
Financial data (yr. ended 12/31/10): Total giving, $3,597,247, including $3,429,523 for 1,743 grants, $50,000 for 10 grants to individuals and $117,724 for 105 in-kind gifts.
Purpose and activities: City National Bank makes charitable contributions to nonprofit organizations on a case by case basis. Support is given primarily in California, Nevada, and New York.
Fields of interest: General charitable giving.
Type of support: Cause-related marketing; Conferences/seminars; Consulting services; Curriculum development; Donated equipment; Donated products; Emergency funds; Employee volunteer services; General/operating support; In-kind gifts; Loaned talent; Program development; Program evaluation; Public relations services; Scholarship funds; Sponsorships; Technical assistance; Use of facilities.
Geographic limitations: Giving primarily in CA, Las Vegas and Reno, NV, and New York, NY.
Support limitations: No support for political organizations.
Publications: Corporate report.
Application information: Applications accepted. The Marketing Dept. handles giving. The company has a staff that only handles contributions. Application form not required.
Initial approach: Letter of inquiry
Copies of proposal: 1
Deadline(s): None
Officer: Jennifer Nickerson, V.P. and Community Rels. Mgr.
Number of staff: 1 full-time professional; 1 full-time support.

831
Cityside Management Corp.

186 Granite St., Ste. 301
Manchester, NH 03101 (603) 423-0313
FAX: (603) 420-1122

Company URL: http://www.citysidecorp.com/
Establishment information: Established in 1997.
Company type: Private company
Business activities: Operates real estate asset management company serving U.S. Department of Housing and Urban Development (HUD).
Business type (SIC): Business services/miscellaneous
Corporate officers: Christopher Dolloff, Pres. and C.E.O.; Lionel Hotard, C.O.O.; Sue Murtagh, C.F.O.; Jim Stikeman, C.A.O.; Dan Hanson, V.P., Opers.; Peter Chaloner, Cont.
Giving statement: Giving through the Cityside Management Corporation Contributions Program.

Cityside Management Corporation Contributions Program

22 Greeley Street, Ste. #5
Merrimack, NH 03054-4434
URL: http://www.citysidecorp.com

832
CLARCOR Inc.

840 Crescent Centre Dr., Ste. 600
Franklin, TN 37067 (615) 771-3100
FAX: (615) 771-5616

Company URL: http://www.clarcor.com
Establishment information: Established in 1904.
Company type: Public company
Company ticker symbol and exchange: CLC/NYSE
Business activities: Manufactures engine and mobile filtration products; manufactures industrial and environmental filtration products; manufactures packaging products.
Business type (SIC): Motor vehicles and equipment; paperboard containers; machinery/general industry
Financial profile for 2012: Number of employees, 5,417; assets, $1,205,500,000; sales volume, $1,121,770,000; pre-tax net income, $183,000,000; expenses, $939,050,000; liabilities, $304,660,000
Corporate officers: Chris Conway, Chair. and C.E.O.; David Fallon, V.P., Finance and C.F.O.; David J. Lindsay, V.P., Admin. and C.A.O.; Richard M. Wolfson, V.P., Genl. Counsel, and Corp. Secy.
Board of directors: Christopher L. Conway, Chair; Robert Burgstahler; Paul Donovan; Mark A. Emkes; Robert H. Jenkins; Philip R. Lochner, Jr.; James L. Packard
Subsidiaries: Baldwin Filters, Inc., Kearney, NE; CLARCOR Air Filtration Products, Inc., Jeffersonville, IN; J.L. Clark, Inc., Rockford, IL; Clark Filter, Inc., Lancaster, PA; Keddeg Company, Lenexa, KS; Martin Kurz & Company, Inc., New York, NY; Perry Equipment Corporation, Mineral Wells, TX; Purolator EFP, LLC, Houston, TX; Purolator Facet, Inc., Greensboro, NC; Purolator Liquid Process, Sacramento, CA; Total Filtration Services, Inc., Rochester Hills, MI; United Air Specialists, Inc., Cincinnati, OH
International operations: Australia; Canada; China; France; Germany; Italy; Malaysia; Mexico; Netherlands; Singapore; South Africa; Spain; United Kingdom
Giving statement: Giving through the CLARCOR Foundation.
Company EIN: 360922490

CLARCOR Foundation

840 Crescent Centre Dr., Ste. 600
Franklin, TN 37067-4687

Establishment information: Established in 1954 in IL.
Donor: CLARCOR Inc.
Contact: Kim Orr, Chair.
Financial data (yr. ended 12/31/11): Assets, $7,234,471 (M); expenditures, $253,222; qualifying distributions, $220,577; giving activities include $220,577 for grants.
Purpose and activities: The foundation supports organizations involved with arts and culture, education, hunger, and human services. Support is limited to areas of company operations.
Fields of interest: Museums; Performing arts, orchestras; Arts; Education; Food services; Athletics/sports, golf; American Red Cross; YM/YWCAs & YM/YWHAs; Children/youth, services; Human services; United Ways and Federated Giving Programs.
Type of support: Annual campaigns; Capital campaigns; General/operating support.
Geographic limitations: Giving limited to areas of company operations in IL, IN, KY, NC, NE, OH, OK, PA, TN, and TX.
Support limitations: No support for foundations or political or religious organizations. No grants to individuals, or for endowments, research, scholarships, or fellowships; no loans.
Publications: Application guidelines; Program policy statement.
Application information: Applications accepted. Application form required. Applicants should submit the following:
1) copy of most recent annual report/audited financial statement/990
Initial approach: Contact nearest company facility for application form
Copies of proposal: 1
Board meeting date(s): Feb., May, Aug., and Nov.
Deadline(s): None
Officers and Trustees:* Kim Orr*, Chair.; Bonnie Tucker, Secy.; Marybeth Averill; Norman E. Johnson; Brian Keith; Bruce A. Klein; David J. Lindsay.
Number of staff: None.
EIN: 366032573
Selected grants: The following grants are a representative sample of this grantmaker's funding activity:
$25,000 to Vanderbilt University, Nashville, TN, 2009.
$20,000 to Nashville Symphony, Nashville, TN, 2009.
$20,000 to Rockford Park District, Rockford, IL, 2009.
$10,000 to American Red Cross, Murfreesboro, TN, 2009.
$10,000 to Lifesong for Orphans, Gridley, IL, 2009.
$8,794 to United Way of Greater Greensboro, Greensboro, NC, 2009.
$6,571 to United Way of Williamson County, Franklin, TN, 2009.
$5,000 to Boy Scouts of America, Middle Tennessee Council, Nashville, TN, 2009.
$5,000 to YMCA of Southern Indiana, Jeffersonville, IN, 2009.
$2,500 to Literacy Council, Rockford, IL, 2009.

833
Claremont Savings Bank
145 Broad St.
Claremont, NH 03743-3610
(603) 542-7711

Company URL: http://www.claremontsavings.com
Establishment information: Established in 1907.
Company type: Mutual company
Business activities: Operates savings bank.
Business type (SIC): Savings institutions
Corporate officers: Mark S. Thompson, Chair.; Thomas P. Connair, Vice-Chair.; Sherwood C. Moody, Pres., C.E.O., and Treas.; Jolene D. Tenney, Sr. V.P., Opers.; Lynn H. Smith, V.P. and Cont.
Board of directors: Mark S. Thompson, Chair.; Thomas P. Connair, Vice Chair.; Joseph J. Gorman, Jr.; H. Clay Hawkins IV; Wayne C. McCutcheon; Sherwood C. Moody; Robert H. Porter; Frank E. Reed
Giving statement: Giving through the Claremont Savings Bank Foundation.

Claremont Savings Bank Foundation
P.O. Box 1600
Claremont, NH 03743-1600
URL: https://www.claremontsavings.com/About-CSB/Foundation

Establishment information: Established in 2002 in NH.
Donor: Claremont Savings Bank.
Contact: Candace T. Crawford, Tr.
Financial data (yr. ended 06/30/12): Assets, $601,903 (M); expenditures, $1,078,110; qualifying distributions, $1,074,890; giving activities include $1,074,890 for grants.
Purpose and activities: The foundation supports organizations involved with arts and culture, education, health, affordable housing, human services, and civic affairs.
Fields of interest: Arts; Education; Health care; Housing/shelter; Human services; Public affairs.
Type of support: Capital campaigns; Continuing support; General/operating support; Program development.
Geographic limitations: Giving primarily in Claremont, Charlestown, and Cornish, NH; some giving in surrounding communities in NH and VT.
Support limitations: No support for religious organizations or municipalities. No grants to individuals.
Publications: Application guidelines.
Application information: Applications accepted. Applications should include a 1 to 3 page memo describing the applicant organization and the program for which it seeks funding. Grants range from $1,000 to $5,000. Application form required.
Applicants should submit the following:
1) name, address and phone number of organization
2) copy of IRS Determination Letter
3) brief history of organization and description of its mission
4) geographic area to be served
5) copy of most recent annual report/audited financial statement/990
6) descriptive literature about organization
7) detailed description of project and amount of funding requested
8) contact person
9) copy of current year's organizational budget and/or project budget
10) listing of additional sources and amount of support

Initial approach: Download application form and mail to foundation
Deadline(s): June 8
Final notification: June 29

Trustees: Thomas Connair; Candace T. Crawford; Jill M. Edson; H. Clay Hawkins IV; Sherwood C. Moody.
EIN: 331014741

834
The Clarity Project
2784 Homestead Rd.
Santa Clara, CA 95051-5353
(408) 921-1990

Company URL: http://www.the-clarity-project.com
Establishment information: Established in 2009.
Company type: Private company
Business type (SIC): Business services/miscellaneous
Corporate officers: Jesse Finfrock, Co-Founder; Rachel Lichte, Co-Founder; Shane Rogers, Co-Founder
Giving statement: Giving through the Clarity Project Contributions Program.

The Clarity Project Contributions Program
2784 Homestead Rd.
Santa Clara, CA 95051-5353 (408) 921-1990
E-mail: info@clarityproject.com; URL: http://www.the-clarity-project.com

Purpose and activities: The Clarity Project donates 100 percent of profits to charitable organizations. Support is given primarily in Sierra Leone.
Fields of interest: Elementary/secondary education; Education, reading; Employment, training; International development; Rural development.
International interests: Sierra Leone.
Type of support: General/operating support; Program development.
Geographic limitations: Giving primarily in Sierra Leone.

835
Clark Electric Cooperative
124 N. Main St.
P.O. Box 190
Greenwood, WI 54437 (715) 267-6188

Company URL: http://www.cecoop.com
Establishment information: Established in 1937.
Company type: Cooperative
Business activities: Generates, transmits, and distributes electricity.
Business type (SIC): Electric services
Corporate officers: Tim Stewart, C.E.O.; Tony Jarocki, Pres.; Clarence Hoesly, Secy.
Board of directors: Chuck Bena; Jeremy Baxter; Wilmer Griepentrog; Clarence Hoesly; Tony Jarocki; Ron Schmidt; Howard Schultz
Giving statement: Giving through the Adler-Clark Electric Community Commitment Foundation Trust.

Adler-Clark Electric Community Commitment Foundation Trust
P.O. Box 190
Greenwood, WI 54437-9419 (715) 267-6188
Application address: 124 N Main St., Greenwood, WI 54437

Establishment information: Established in 2004 in WI.
Donor: Clark Electric Appliance & Satellite.
Contact: Timothy E. Stewart, Tr.
Financial data (yr. ended 12/31/11): Assets, $758,362 (M); expenditures, $26,946; qualifying distributions, $24,325; giving activities include $24,325 for grants.
Purpose and activities: The foundation supports organizations involved with education, hunger, fire and ambulance services, and recreation.
Fields of interest: Libraries (public); Education; Health care, EMS; Food services; Food banks; Disasters, fire prevention/control; Athletics/sports, amateur leagues; Recreation; Human services.
Type of support: Equipment; General/operating support; Program development.
Geographic limitations: Giving primarily in Clark County, WI and surrounding communities.
Application information: Applications accepted. Application form required. Applicants should submit the following:
1) copy of IRS Determination Letter
2) copy of most recent annual report/audited financial statement/990

Initial approach: Contact foundation for application form
Deadline(s): Dec. 1

Trustees: Wilmer Gripentrog; Patricia Lindner; Timothy E. Stewart.
EIN: 202040648

836
Clark Hill PLC
500 Woodward Ave., Ste. 3500
Detroit, MI 48226-3435 (313) 965-8300

Company URL: http://www.clarkhill.com
Establishment information: Established in 1890.
Company type: Private company
Business activities: Operates law firm.
Business type (SIC): Legal services
Corporate officer: John J. Hern, Jr., C.E.O.
Offices: Los Angeles, CA; Washington, DC; New York, NY
International operations: Brazil; China; Kazakhstan; Mexico; Poland; Russia; Ukraine; United Arab Emirates; United Kingdom
Giving statement: Giving through the Clark Hill PLC Corporate Giving Program.

Clark Hill PLC Corporate Giving Program
500 Woodward Ave., Ste. 3500
Detroit, MI 48226-3435 (313) 965-8300
FAX: (313) 965-8252; Contact for Pro Bono program: Paul Scheidemantel, Attorney, tel.: (313) 965-8310, e-mail: pscheidemantel.clarkhill.com; URL: http://www.clarkhill.com/community.aspx

Purpose and activities: Clark Hill makes charitable contributions to nonprofit organizations on a case by case basis.
Fields of interest: Legal services; General charitable giving.
Type of support: Employee volunteer services; General/operating support; Pro bono services - legal.

837

Clarke Environmental Mosquito Management, Inc.

110 E. Irving Park Rd., 4th Fl.
Roselle, IL 60172-1734 (630) 894-2000

Company URL: http://www.clarkemosquito.com/whoisclarke.cfm
Establishment information: Established in 1946.
Company type: Private company
Business activities: Operates pest control company.
Business type (SIC): Sanitary services
Financial profile for 2010: Number of employees, 30
Corporate officers: J. Lyell Clarke III, Pres. and C.E.O.; Joseph Drago, C.F.O.; Julie Reiter, V.P., Human Resources
Giving statement: Giving through the John and Mary Kemp Clarke Foundation.

John and Mary Kemp Clarke Foundation

c/o Andrew P. Tecson
30 S. Wacker Dr., Ste. 2600
Chicago, IL 60606-7413

Establishment information: Established in 2007 in IL.
Donor: Clarke Environmental Mosquito Management, Inc.
Financial data (yr. ended 12/31/11): Assets, $103,184 (M); expenditures, $7,290; qualifying distributions, $6,115; giving activities include $5,000 for 1 grant.
Fields of interest: Human services.
Support limitations: No grants to individuals.
Application information: Applications not accepted. Unsolicited requests for funds not accepted.
Officers and Directors:* Mary Kemp Clarke*, Pres.; John L. Clarke III*, V.P.; Mary Rob Clarke*, V.P.; Andrew P. Tecson, Secy.
EIN: 208925077

838

Clarks Companies, N.A.

620 S. Union St.
Kennett Square, PA 19348-3534
(610) 444-6550

Company URL: http://clarks.zappos.com/aboutus.zhtml
Establishment information: Established in 1899.
Company type: Subsidiary of a foreign company
Business activities: Manufactures shoes.
Business type (SIC): Leather footwear; apparel, piece goods, and notions—wholesale
Corporate officers: Robert Infantino, Pres.; H. Richard Scheerer, C.I.O.; Margaret Newville, V.P., Mktg.
Giving statement: Giving through the Clarks Companies Foundation.

The Clarks Companies Foundation

c/o Sharon Schuler
156 Oak St.
Newton Upper Falls, MA 02464-1440

Establishment information: Established in 2006 in MA.
Donors: The Clarks Companies, N.A.; Stella International Holdings Ltd.; Headlines International Ltd.; Gao Yao Chung Jye Shoes Mfg.; Win Profile Factory; Robert Infantino; Jim Salzano; Earth, Inc.; Pangea Leather Services Ltd; Prime International India Pvt Ltd; Shang Hai Kotoni Shoe Co. Ltd; Stella International Holdings Ltd; T. Abdul Wahid And Co.; Enk International/wsa; Mound Printing; Zappos.com.
Financial data (yr. ended 12/31/11): Assets, $969,056 (M); gifts received, $224,792; expenditures, $158,175; qualifying distributions, $66,407; giving activities include $66,407 for grants to individuals.
Type of support: Scholarships—to individuals.
Geographic limitations: Giving limited to residents of Bridgewater, MA.
Application information: Applications accepted. Only graduating seniors of Bridgewater, MA High School are eligible. Application form required. Submit the copy of high school transcript.
Initial approach: Proposal
Deadline(s): None
Officers and Directors: Robert Infantino, Pres.; James Salzano, V.P.; Margie Glazer, Secy.; Sharon Schuler, Treas.; Jason Isaarel; Karla Jarvis; Steve Katsirubus; Steve Lawrence; Steve Mahoney.
EIN: 204511300

839

Clarkson Eyecare, Inc.

217 Clarkson Rd.
Ellisville, MO 63011-2219 (636) 227-2600

Company URL: http://www.clarksoneyecare.com/
Establishment information: Established in 1979.
Company type: Private company
Business activities: Provides medical eye care services.
Business type (SIC): Medical offices and clinics/miscellaneous
Corporate officers: Lawrence J. Jehling, Co-Chair.; Gerald R. Jehling, Co-Chair. and Pres.; Amanda J. Ditch, C.O.O.; Anthony G. Nunn, C.F.O.; Cynthia M. Muessig, V.P., Finance; Kerri L. Beers, V.P., Opers.
Board of directors: Lawrence J. Jehling, Co-Chair.; Gerald R. Jehling, Co-Chair.
Giving statement: Giving through the Clarkson Eyecare Foundation.

Clarkson Eyecare Foundation

217 Clarkson Rd.
Ellisville, MO 63011-2219 (636) 227-2600
FAX: (636) 200-4020;
E-mail: tpeel@clarksoneyecare.com; URL: http://www.theclarksoneyecarefoundation.org

Establishment information: Established in 2004 in MO.
Donor: Entergy Arkansas, Inc.
Financial data (yr. ended 12/31/11): Revenue, $140,489; assets, $233,600 (M); gifts received, $108,725; expenditures, $131,826; giving activities include $540 for grants.
Purpose and activities: The foundation is dedicated to enhancing quality of life by providing vision improvement and access to a brighter future, including funding Lasik surgery for individuals who are physically challenged and have difficulty wearing eyeglasses and/or contacts.
Fields of interest: Blind/visually impaired.
International interests: Dominican Republic; Vietnam.
Type of support: Annual campaigns; Equipment.
Geographic limitations: Giving primarily in MO.
Publications: Application guidelines; Occasional report.
Application information: Applications accepted. Application form required.
Initial approach: Letter
Copies of proposal: 1
Board meeting date(s): Quarterly
Deadline(s): None
Final notification: 1 week
Officers and Directors:* Eric Messmer*, Pres.; Tesha Peel, Exec. Dir.; Henry Allhoff; Kathleen Doan; Craig Doiron; Matt Iovaldi; William Jehling; Michael Klein; Jim Landry; Stephen Menzel; Dan Rosen; Dr. James Wachter.
Number of staff: 1 part-time professional.
EIN: 200265693

840

Classic Leather, Inc.

(formerly Classic Upholstery, Inc.)
203 Simpson St. S.W., Ste. 220
P.O. Box 2404
Conover, NC 28613-8207 (828) 328-2046

Company URL: http://www.classic-leather.com
Establishment information: Established in 1966.
Company type: Private company
Business activities: Manufactures upholstered home and office furniture.
Business type (SIC): Furniture/household; furniture/office
Corporate officers: Thomas H. Shores, Jr., Pres. and C.E.O.; Charles D. Dixon, Secy.
Giving statement: Giving through the Classic Foundation, Inc.

Classic Foundation, Inc.

P.O. Box 2404
Hickory, NC 28603-2404

Establishment information: Established in 1976 in NC.
Donor: Classic Leather, Inc.
Financial data (yr. ended 10/31/11): Assets, $23,218 (M); expenditures, $75; qualifying distributions, $75.
Purpose and activities: The foundation supports organizations involved with education and Christianity.
Fields of interest: Education; YM/YWCAs & YM/YWHAs; Christian agencies & churches.
Type of support: General/operating support.
Geographic limitations: Giving limited to Hickory, NC.
Support limitations: No grants to individuals.
Application information: Applications not accepted. Unsolicited requests for funds not accepted.
Officers: Thomas H. Shores, Jr., Pres.; Kim Long, Secy.
EIN: 581351062

841

Clayton Homes, Inc.

500 Alcoa Trail
Maryville, TN 37804-5550 (865) 380-3000

Company URL: http://www.claytonhomes.com/
Establishment information: Established in 1934.
Company type: Subsidiary of a public company
Business activities: Manufactures, sells, finances, and insures homes; develops, owns, and manages housing communities.
Business type (SIC): Wood buildings and mobile homes; operative builders; insurance/fire, marine,

and casualty; real estate subdividers and developers
Corporate officers: Kevin T. Clayton, Pres. and C.E.O.; John J. Kalec, Exec. V.P. and C.F.O.; Ralph Warchol, V.P. and C.I.O.; Jerry Creel, Sr. V.P., Human Resources
Subsidiaries: CMH Homes, Inc., Knoxville, TN; CMH Manufacturing, Inc., Knoxville, TN; CMH Parks, Inc., Knoxville, TN; Vanderbilt Mortgage & Finance, Inc., Knoxville, TN
Giving statement: Giving through the Clayton Homes, Inc. Corporate Giving Program.

Clayton Homes, Inc. Corporate Giving Program

5000 Clayton Rd.
Maryville, TN 37804-5550
URL: http://www.claytonhomes.com/giving_back.cfm

Purpose and activities: Clayton Homes makes charitable contributions to nonprofit organizations involved with education and housing. Support is given primarily in areas of company operations.
Fields of interest: Education; Housing/shelter; United Ways and Federated Giving Programs.
Type of support: Employee matching gifts; Employee volunteer services; Program development; Seed money.
Geographic limitations: Giving primarily in areas of company operations; giving also to national organizations.

842
Clear Channel Communications, Inc.

200 E. Basse Rd.
San Antonio, TX 78209-8328
(210) 822-2828

Company URL: http://www.clearchannel.com
Establishment information: Established in 1972.
Company type: Subsidiary of a public company
Business activities: Broadcasts radio; broadcasts television; provides outdoor advertising services.
Business type (SIC): Advertising; radio and television broadcasting
Corporate officers: Robert W. Pittman, C.E.O.; Thomas W. Casey, Exec. V.P. and C.F.O.; Robert H. Walls, Jr., Exec. V.P. and Genl. Counsel
Subsidiary: Eller Media Corp., Phoenix, AZ
Historic mergers: The Ackerley Group, Inc. (June 14, 2002)
Giving statement: Giving through the Clear Channel Communications Foundation.

Clear Channel Communications Foundation

200 E. Basse Rd.
San Antonio, TX 78209-8328

Establishment information: Established in 1999 in TX.
Donors: Clear Channel Communications, Inc.; J. Walter Thompson USA, Inc.
Financial data (yr. ended 12/31/11): Assets, $1,953,718 (M); expenditures, $394,891; qualifying distributions, $380,475; giving activities include $380,475 for grants.
Purpose and activities: The foundation supports parks and playgrounds and organizations involved with arts and culture, education, health, disaster relief, human services, and minority civil rights.
Fields of interest: Media/communications; Arts; Education, management/technical assistance; Elementary/secondary education; Secondary school/education; Education; Health care; Disasters, preparedness/services; Recreation, parks/playgrounds; Boy scouts; Children, services; Family services; Homeless, human services; Human services; Civil/human rights, minorities.
Type of support: Building/renovation; Conferences/seminars; General/operating support.
Geographic limitations: Giving limited to San Antonio, TX.
Support limitations: No grants to individuals.
Application information: Applications not accepted. Contributes only to pre-selected organizations.
Officers and Directors:* L. Lowry Mays*, Pres.; Mark P. Mays*, V.P. and Secy.; Randall T. Mays*, V.P. and Treas.
EIN: 742908486
Selected grants: The following grants are a representative sample of this grantmaker's funding activity:
$35,000 to Teach for America, New York, NY, 2010. For general support.
$25,000 to Old Spanish Missions, San Antonio, TX, 2010. For general support.
$20,000 to League of United Latin American Citizens, Washington, DC, 2010. For general support.
$11,000 to Family Service Association of San Antonio, San Antonio, TX, 2010. For general support.
$5,000 to Child Guidance Center of San Antonio, San Antonio, TX, 2010. For general support.
$2,500 to Catholic Television of San Antonio, San Antonio, TX, 2010. For general support.
$2,500 to Cibolo Nature Center, Boerne, TX, 2010. For general support.
$2,500 to Girl Scouts of the U.S.A., San Antonio, TX, 2010. For general support.
$2,500 to San Antonio Bar Foundation, San Antonio, TX, 2010. For general support.
$2,500 to San Antonio, City of, San Antonio, TX, 2010. For general support.

843
Cleary Gottlieb Steen & Hamilton LLF

1 Liberty Plz.
New York, NY 10006-1404 (212) 225-2000

Company URL: http://www.cgsh.com
Establishment information: Established in 1946.
Company type: Private company
Business activities: Operates law firm.
Business type (SIC): Legal services
Corporate officer: Michael Lechner, C.I.O.
Offices: Washington, DC; New York, NY
International operations: Argentina; Belgium; China; France; Germany; Hong Kong; Italy; Russia; United Kingdom
Giving statement: Giving through the Cleary Gottlieb Steen & Hamilton LLP Pro Bono Program.

Cleary Gottlieb Steen & Hamilton LLP Pro Bono Program

1 Liberty Plz.
New York, NY 10006-1404 (212) 225-2348
E-mail: jkroman@cgsh.com; Additional tel.: (212) 225-2000; URL: http://www.cgsh.com/about/pro_bono_and_community_service/

Contact: Jennifer Kroman, Director of Pro Bono Practice
Purpose and activities: Cleary Gottlieb Steen & Hamilton makes charitable contributions to nonprofit organizations involved with immigration law, affordable housing, family services, and criminal defense.
Fields of interest: Elementary/secondary education; Legal services; Legal services, guardianship; Housing/shelter, homeless; Housing/shelter; Disasters, preparedness/services; Family services, domestic violence; Minorities/immigrants, centers/services; International human rights Disabilities, people with; Offenders/ex-offenders.
Type of support: General/operating support; Matching/challenge support; Pro bono services - legal.
Application information: The Pro Bono Committee manages the pro-bono program.

844
Clemens Markets, Inc.

1555 Bustard Rd.
Kulpsville, PA 19443 (215) 361-9000

Establishment information: Established in 1939.
Company type: Subsidiary of a private company
Business activities: Operates supermarkets.
Business type (SIC): Groceries—retail; real estate operators and lessors
Corporate officer: Jack S. Clemens, Pres. and C.E.O.
Giving statement: Giving through the Clemens Foundation.

Clemens Foundation

P.O. Box 1555
Kulpsville, PA 19443

Establishment information: Established in 1966 in PA.
Donors: Clemens Markets, Inc.; Abram S. Clemens†; James C. Clemens†; Lillian H. Clemens.
Financial data (yr. ended 09/30/11): Assets, $985,507 (M); expenditures, $8,253; qualifying distributions, $0.
Purpose and activities: The foundation supports hospitals and organizations involved with education, hunger, human services, and Christianity.
Fields of interest: Education; Health care; Religion.
Type of support: Building/renovation; Equipment; General/operating support; Program development; Scholarship funds.
Geographic limitations: Giving primarily in PA.
Application information: Applications accepted. Application form required.
Initial approach: Contact foundation for application form
Copies of proposal: 1
Board meeting date(s): Oct. or Nov.
Deadline(s): Sept. 30
Officers: Jack S. Clemens, Pres.; Douglas C. Moyer, C.F.O.; Mark Clemens, V.P.; Cheryl Mehl, V.P.; Jill Clemens, Secy.; Marilyn Clemens Rohrbach, Treas.
EIN: 231675035

845
Clements Foods Co.
6601 N. Harvey Pl.
P.O. Box 14538
Oklahoma City, OK 73118 (405) 842-3308
FAX: (405) 843-6894

Company URL: http://www.clementsfoods.com/index.html
Establishment information: Established in 1953.
Company type: Private company
Business activities: Produces food condiments.
Business type (SIC): Specialty foods/canned, frozen, and preserved; miscellaneous prepared foods
Corporate officers: Richard Clements, Chair.; Edward B. Clements, Pres. and C.E.O.
Board of director: Richard Clements, Chair.
Subsidiaries: American Nut Co., Lewisville, TX; Clements Nut Co., Lewisville, TX; Clements Vinegar Co., Oklahoma City, OK
Giving statement: Giving through the Clements Food Foundation.

Clements Food Foundation
P.O. Box 14538
Oklahoma City, OK 73113-0538 (405) 842-3308
Application address: 6601 N. Harvey Pl., Oklahoma City, OK 73113, tel.: (405) 842-3308

Establishment information: Established in 1986 in OK.
Donor: Clements Foods Co.
Contact: Robert H. Clements, Secy.
Financial data (yr. ended 02/28/12): Assets, $2,404,515 (M); expenditures, $106,088; qualifying distributions, $103,550; giving activities include $103,550 for grants.
Purpose and activities: The foundation supports food banks and organizations involved with arts and culture, K-12 and higher education, vision health, and Christianity.
Fields of interest: Arts; Education; Community/economic development.
Type of support: General/operating support; Program development.
Geographic limitations: Giving primarily in Oklahoma City, OK.
Application information: Applications accepted. Application form required.
Initial approach: Letter
Deadline(s): None
Officers: Richard H. Clements, Pres.; Robert H. Clements, Secy.; Richard L. Clements, Treas.
EIN: 731304657

846
Cleveland Browns, LLC
76 Lou Groza Blvd.
Berea, OH 44017 (440) 891-5000

Company URL: http://www.clevelandbrowns.com
Establishment information: Established in 1946.
Company type: Private company
Business activities: Operates professional football club.
Business type (SIC): Commercial sports
Corporate officers: Mike Holmgren, Pres.; Bryan Wiedmeier, Exec. V.P., Opers.; David A. Jenkins, Sr. V.P., Finance and Admin.; Brett Reynolds, V.P., Mktg.; Laurie Rice, Cont.; Frederick R. Nance, Genl. Counsel
Giving statement: Giving through the Cleveland Browns Corporate Giving Program and the Cleveland Browns Foundation.

Cleveland Browns Corporate Giving Program
c/o Community Outreach Dept.
76 Lou Groza Blvd.
Berea, OH 44017-1238
FAX: (440) 891-7529; URL: http://www.clevelandbrowns.com/community/in-kind-support.html

Purpose and activities: As a complement to its foundation, the Cleveland Browns also make charitable contributions and in-kind donations to nonprofit organizations directly. Support is given primarily in the greater Cleveland area and Northeast Ohio region.
Fields of interest: General charitable giving.
Type of support: Donated products; In-kind gifts; Sponsorships.
Geographic limitations: Giving primarily in OH, with emphasis on the greater Cleveland area and northeast OH region.
Publications: Application guidelines.
Application information: Applications accepted. Sponsorship requests should be submitted using organization letterhead. In-kind support is limited to 1 contribution per organization during any given year. Personal items to be autographed are not accepted. Applicants should submit the following:
1) name, address and phone number of organization
2) contact person
Applications for in-kind donations should include Tax ID Number of the organization; the name, date, and a description of the event; and the type of fundraiser. Sponsorship requests should include the Tax ID Number of the organization; the type of event or program; the date, time, length, and location of the event; and the sponsorship levels available.
Initial approach: Complete online application form for in-kind donations and player appearances; mail or fax proposal to headquarters for sponsorships
Deadline(s): 4 weeks in advance of event for in-kind donations and player appearances; 6 weeks in advance of event for sponsorships

Cleveland Browns Foundation
76 Lou Groza Blvd.
Berea, OH 44017-1238 (440) 891-5000
FAX: (440) 891-7529; URL: http://www.clevelandbrowns.com/community/foundation.html

Establishment information: Established in 1999 in OH.
Contact: George W. White, Pres.
Financial data (yr. ended 12/31/11): Revenue, $392,005; assets, $908,284 (M); gifts received, $496,834; expenditures, $576,592; giving activities include $376,103 for grants and $100,000 for grants to individuals.
Purpose and activities: As the philanthropic arm of the Cleveland Browns, the foundation helps meet the needs of disadvantaged and inner-city youth in the northeast Ohio area from childhood through teenage years.
Fields of interest: Arts; Education; Health care; Employment, services; Disasters, preparedness/services.
Program:
Marion Motley Scholarship: Two scholarships are awarded to students for four years to attend college. Recipients must demonstrate a commitment to and a continued involvement in their community. To recognize and honor Marion Motley, each applicant will be asked to research his life and career and provide insight on how he impacted the Cleveland Browns and the NFL.
Type of support: Curriculum development; Program development.
Geographic limitations: Giving limited to the northeast OH area.
Support limitations: No support for religious organizations for sectarian religious purposes. No grants for general or annual operation expenses, capital or building funds, fundraising, sponsorship events, or donation requests.
Publications: Application guidelines; Biennial report (including application guidelines).
Application information: Applications accepted. Applications submitted via fax or e-mail not accepted. See Web site for further application information. Application form required. Applicants should submit the following:
1) timetable for implementation and evaluation of project
2) signature and title of chief executive officer
3) results expected from proposed grant
4) copy of IRS Determination Letter
5) copy of most recent annual report/audited financial statement/990
6) how project's results will be evaluated or measured
7) explanation of why grantmaker is considered an appropriate donor for project
8) listing of board of directors, trustees, officers and other key people and their affiliations
9) copy of current year's organizational budget and/or project budget
Copies of proposal: 3
Deadline(s): Nov. 6 for the Marion Motley Scholarship Fund
Officers and Trustee:* George W. White*, Pres.; Randolph Lerner*, V.P.; James H. Berick*, Secy.; Douglas C. Jacobs*, Treas.; Lorne Novick.
Number of staff: 1 full-time professional.
EIN: 341885593

847
Cleveland Indians Baseball Company, Inc.
Progressive Field
2401 Ontario St.
Cleveland, OH 44115 (216) 420-4200

Company URL: http://cleveland.indians.mlb.com
Establishment information: Established in 1901.
Company type: Private company
Business activities: Operates professional baseball club; operates baseball field.
Business type (SIC): Commercial sports
Corporate officers: Paul J. Dolan, Chair. and C.E.O.; Mark S. Shapiro, Pres.; Kenneth E. Stefanov, Sr. V.P., Finance and C.F.O.; Neil Weiss, Sr. V.P. and C.I.O.; Victor Gregorits, Sr. V.P., Sales; Bob DiBiasio, Sr. V.P., Public Affairs; Joe Znidarsic, V.P., Genl. Counsel; Sara Lehrke, V.P., Human Resources; Sarah Taylor, Cont.
Board of director: Paul J. Dolan, Chair.
Giving statement: Giving through the Cleveland Indians Baseball Company, Inc. Corporate Giving Program and the Cleveland Indians Charities, Inc.

Cleveland Indians Baseball Company, Inc. Corporate Giving Program

c/o Community Rels., Donated Item Request
2401 Ontario St.
Cleveland, OH 44115-4003

Purpose and activities: The Cleveland Indians make charitable contributions of memorabilia to nonprofit organizations on a case by case basis. Support is given primarily in areas of company operations.
Fields of interest: General charitable giving.
Type of support: In-kind gifts.
Geographic limitations: Giving primarily in areas of company operations, with emphasis on OH and Erie, PA.
Application information: Applications accepted. Proposals should be submitted using organization letterhead. Application form not required. Applicants should submit the following:
1) name, address and phone number of organization
2) descriptive literature about organization
3) detailed description of project and amount of funding requested
4) contact person
Proposals should indicate the date of the event, if applicable.
Initial approach: Proposal to headquarters
Copies of proposal: 1
Deadline(s): 1 month prior to need

Cleveland Indians Charities, Inc.

c/o Progressive Field
2401 Ontario St.
Cleveland, OH 44115-4003 (216) 420-4400
E-mail: cic@indians.com; Additional tel.: (216) 420-HITS; URL: http://cleveland.indians.mlb.com/NASApp/mlb/cle/community/cic.jsp

Establishment information: Established in 1989 in OH.
Donors: Huntington Bancshares Inc.; McDonald Investments, Inc.; Cleveland Indians Baseball Co., Inc.; Jim Thome; Ellis Burks; CC Sabathia; Medical Mutual of Ohio; Travis Hafner.
Financial data (yr. ended 12/31/11): Assets, $2,021,402 (M); gifts received, $941,898; expenditures, $1,095,804; qualifying distributions, $452,599; giving activities include $452,599 for grants.
Purpose and activities: The foundation support programs designed to promote youth education and recreation.
Fields of interest: Education; Athletics/sports, baseball; Recreation; Boys & girls clubs Youth.
Type of support: General/operating support; In-kind gifts; Scholarship funds.
Geographic limitations: Giving limited to Cleveland, OH.
Support limitations: No grants to individuals.
Application information: Applications not accepted. Contributes only to pre-selected organizations.
Officers and Trustees:* Paul J. Dolan*, Chair.; Robert A. DiBiasio*, Pres.; Sarah Taylor, Treas.; Chris Antonetti; Rick Manning.
Number of staff: 2 full-time professional; 12 part-time support.
EIN: 341618536
Selected grants: The following grants are a representative sample of this grantmaker's funding activity:
$5,000 to Major League Baseball Players Alumni Association, Colorado Springs, CO, 2010. For general operating support.

848
Clif Bar, Inc.

1451 66th St.
Emeryville, CA 94608-1004 (510) 558-7855

Company URL: http://www.clifbar.com
Establishment information: Established in 1986.
Company type: Private company
Business activities: Makes natural energy, nutrition, and snack bars.
Business type (SIC): Bakery products
Corporate officers: Gary J. Erickson, C.E.O.; Kevin Cleary, Pres. and C.O.O.; Richard Boragno, C.F.O.; Rick Collins, Sr. V.P., Sales; Karen Jobb, V.P., Sales; Bruce Lymburn, Genl. Counsel
Giving statement: Giving through the Clif Bar Family Foundation.

Clif Bar Family Foundation

1451 66th St.
Emeryville, CA 94608-1004 (510) 596-6383
E-mail: familyfoundation@clifbar.com; E-mail for Seed Matters Program: seedmatters@clifbarfamilyfoundation.org; URL: http://www.clifbarfamilyfoundation.org

Establishment information: Established in 2006 in CA.
Donor: Clif Bar & Co.
Financial data (yr. ended 12/31/11): Assets, $104,631 (M); gifts received, $2,164,725; expenditures, $2,316,807; qualifying distributions, $2,049,721; giving activities include $2,049,721 for grants.
Purpose and activities: The foundation supports programs designed to strengthen the food system and community; enhance public health; and safeguard the environment and natural resources. Special emphasis is directed toward grassroots organizations that have the ability to engage local groups.
Fields of interest: Arts; Education; Environment, pollution control; Environment, air pollution; Environment, waste management; Environment, climate change/global warming; Environment, natural resources; Environment, land resources; Environment, energy; Environment; Employment; Agriculture, community food systems; Agriculture, sustainable programs; Agriculture, farmlands; Food services; Agriculture/food; Housing/shelter; Youth, services; Human services; Community development, small businesses.
Programs:
Building Stronger Communities: The foundation supports programs designed to promote innovation in education; create safe and healthy housing; generate green jobs and small business; and increase youth access to arts and culture.
Creating A Robust Healthy Food System: The foundation supports programs designed to expand organic food and farming; reconnect farms to families; safeguard the seeds farmers depend on; and address hunger and malnutrition.
Increasing Opportunities for Outdoor Activity: The foundation supports programs designed to conserve open spaces; develop pedestrian and bike-friendly towns and cities; and enable more Americans to enjoy nature.
Protecting Earth's Beauty & Bounty: The foundation supports programs designed to preserve wild places and backcountry; reduce waste and advance renewable energy; and keep climate action in the forefront.
Reduce Environmental Health Hazards: The foundation supports programs designed to improve air quality; clean-up water supplies; and reduce exposures to toxic materials.
Seed Matters: The foundation, in partnership with Organic Farming Research Foundation, Organic Seed Alliance, and the Center for Food Safety, supports the development of organic seed systems. The foundation provides organic farmers with new varieties of seed adapted to organic systems and fellowships to Ph.D. students to study organic plant breeding at public land grant universities. The initiative is designed to conserve crop genetic diversity; promote farmers' role and rights as seed innovators and stewards; and reinvigorate public seed research and education. Visit URL: http://www.seedmatters.org/index.html for more information.
Type of support: Annual campaigns; Consulting services; Donated products; Fellowships; General/operating support; Management development/capacity building; Program development.
Geographic limitations: Giving primarily in CA.
Support limitations: No support for religious groups or state agencies. No grants to individuals, or for seminar, media, or fundraising events that are not an integral part of a broader program, capital construction, endowments, or debt reduction.
Publications: Application guidelines; Grants list.
Application information: Applications accepted. The average award for Small Grants is $8,000. Capacity-Building Grants, Long-Term Partnerships, and Consulting Grants are by invitation only. Application form required.
Initial approach: Complete online questionnaire and application for Small Grants
Board meeting date(s): Quarterly
Deadline(s): Feb. 15, May 15, Aug. 15, and Nov. 15 for Small Grants
Officers: Kathleen F. Crawford, Pres.; Gary J. Erickson, Secy.-Treas.
EIN: 204345935
Selected grants: The following grants are a representative sample of this grantmaker's funding activity:
$95,000 to Breast Cancer Fund, San Francisco, CA, 2010. For general support.
$50,000 to Organic Farming Research Foundation, Santa Cruz, CA, 2010. For general support.
$25,000 to Childrens Health Environmental Coalition, Los Angeles, CA, 2010. For general support.
$20,000 to Womens Earth Alliance, Berkeley, CA, 2010. For general support.
$10,000 to Engage Network, Oakland, CA, 2010. For general support.
$10,000 to Luna Kids Dance, Berkeley, CA, 2010. For general support.
$10,000 to Red Feather Development Group, Bozeman, MT, 2010. For general support.
$10,000 to Vipani, Inc., Mountain View, CA, 2010. For general support.
$7,500 to Childrens Village of Sonoma County, Santa Rosa, CA, 2010. For general support.
$5,000 to Neighborhood Parks Council, San Francisco, CA, 2010. For general support.

849
Clifford Chance US LLP

31 W. 52nd St.
New York, NY 10019-6131 (212) 878-8000

Company URL: http://www.cliffordchance.com
Establishment information: Established in 1987.
Company type: Private company
Business activities: Operates law firm.
Business type (SIC): Legal services

Corporate officers: David Childs, Managing Partner; Amanda Burton, C.O.O.; Stephen Purse, C.F.O.
International operations: Australia; Belgium; Brazil; China; Czech Republic; France; Germany; Hungary; India; Italy; Japan; Luxembourg; Netherlands; Poland; Qatar; Romania; Russia; Saudi Arabia; Singapore; Spain; Thailand; Turkey; Ukraine; United Arab Emirates; United Kingdom
Giving statement: Giving through the Clifford Chance US LLP Pro Bono Program and the Clifford Chance Foundation, Inc.

The Clifford Chance Foundation, Inc.

c/o Clifford Chance, LLP
31 W. 52nd St., 3rd Fl.
New York, NY 10019-6131
URL: http://www.cliffordchance.com/about_us/corporate_responsibility/community_pro_bono/clifford_chance_foundation.html

Establishment information: Established in 2007 in DE and NY.
Donors: Brian Hoffmann; John Carroll; Craig Medwick; Clifford Chance US LLP.
Financial data (yr. ended 12/31/11): Assets, $176,800 (M); gifts received, $156,324; expenditures, $173,089; qualifying distributions, $168,052; giving activities include $168,052 for grants.
Fields of interest: Education.
Support limitations: No grants to individuals.
Application information: Applications not accepted. Unsolicited requests for funds not accepted.
Officers: Craig Medwick, Pres.; Diana Koshel, V.P.; Jason Young, Secy.; David Moldenhauer, Treas.; Rita Stephanz, Genl. Counsel.
Board Members: Laurence Cranch; Anthony Essaye; Richard McDermott; Margaret Blair Soyster; and 5 additional board members.
EIN: 743203078

850
Cliffs Natural Resources Inc.

(formerly Cleveland-Cliffs Inc)
200 Public Sq., Ste. 3300
Cleveland, OH 44114-2544 (216) 694-5700

Company URL: http://www.cleveland-cliffs.com
Establishment information: Established in 1847.
Company type: Public company
Company ticker symbol and exchange: CLF/NYSE
International Securities Identification Number: US18683K1016
Business activities: Mines iron ore.
Business type (SIC): Metal mining
Financial profile for 2012: Number of employees, 7,589; assets, $13,574,900,000; sales volume, $5,872,700,000; pre-tax net income, -$501,800,000; expenses, $6,181,500,000; liabilities, $8,942,200,000
Fortune 1000 ranking: 2012—424th in revenues, 975th in profits, and 316th in assets
Forbes 2000 ranking: 2012—1291st in sales, 1921st in profits, and 1248th in assets
Corporate officers: Joseph A. Carrabba, Chair., Pres., and C.E.O.; Laurie Brlas, Exec. V.P., Opers.; Terrance M. Paradie, Sr. V.P. and C.F.O.; James Michaud, Sr. V.P., Human Resources
Board of directors: Joseph A. Carrabba, Chair.; Susan M. Cunningham; Barry J. Eldridge; Andres Ricardo Gluski Weilert; Susan M. Green; Janice K. Henry; James F. Kirsch; Francis R. McAllister; Richard K. Riederer; Richard A. Ross
Plants: Hueytown, AL; Ishpeming, MI; Eveleth, Hibbing, Silver Bay, MN; Pineville, WV
International operations: Australia; Brazil; Canada; Luxembourg; Netherlands; Peru
Giving statement: Giving through the Cliffs Foundation.
Company EIN: 341464672

The Cliffs Foundation

(formerly The Cleveland-Cliffs Foundation)
1100 Superior Ave., Ste. 1500
Cleveland, OH 44114-2544
URL: http://www.cliffsnaturalresources.com/EN/Sustainability/WordsinAction/Pages/CliffsFoundation.aspx

Establishment information: Established in 1962 in OH.
Donors: Cleveland-Cliffs Inc.; Tilden Mining Co.; Empire Iron Mining Partnership; Hibbing Taconite Co.; Northshore Mining Co.; Cliffs Natural Resources.
Contact: Dana W. Byrne, V.P. and Asst. Treas.
Financial data (yr. ended 12/31/11): Assets, $3,857,659 (M); gifts received, $2,000,000; expenditures, $2,420,112; qualifying distributions, $2,420,112; giving activities include $2,377,894 for grants and $42,018 for 37 employee matching gifts.
Purpose and activities: The foundation supports organizations involved with arts and culture, health, human services, and civic affairs. Special emphasis is directed toward education.
Fields of interest: Museums; Performing arts, theater; Performing arts, orchestras; Arts; Higher education; Education; Hospitals (general); Health care; Children/youth, services; Human services; United Ways and Federated Giving Programs; Public affairs.
Program:
Matching Gifts: The foundation matches contributions made by employees of Cleveland-Cliffs to private secondary schools and institutions of higher education on a one-for-one basis from $25 to $4,000 per employee, per year.
Type of support: Annual campaigns; Building/renovation; Capital campaigns; Employee matching gifts; General/operating support; Scholarship funds.
Geographic limitations: Giving primarily in areas of company operations, with emphasis on northwest AL, the upper MI peninsula, northeastern MN, Cleveland, OH, and southern WV.
Support limitations: No grants to individuals; no loans.
Publications: Application guidelines.
Application information: Applications accepted. Support is limited to 1 contribution per organization during any given year. Application form not required.
Initial approach: Proposal
Copies of proposal: 1
Deadline(s): None
Officers and Trustees:* Joseph A. Carrabba*, Pres.; Donald J. Gallagher*, V.P. and Treas.; Dana W. Byrne, V.P.; George W. Hawk, Jr., Secy.; Laurie Brlas; William R. Calfee.
EIN: 346525124
Selected grants: The following grants are a representative sample of this grantmaker's funding activity:
$400,000 to Bell Memorial Hospital, Ishpeming, MI, 2011.
$100,000 to American Red Cross, Birmingham, AL, 2011.
$100,000 to Great Lakes Museum of Science, Environment and Technology, Cleveland, OH, 2011.
$20,000 to University of Minnesota, Minneapolis, MN, 2011.
$17,500 to Colorado School of Mines, Golden, CO, 2011.
$10,000 to Boys and Girls Club of Central Alabama, Birmingham, AL, 2011.
$5,500 to Pennsylvania State University, University Park, PA, 2011.
$5,000 to Cleveland Foodbank, Cleveland, OH, 2011.
$5,000 to Friendship Ventures, Annandale, MN, 2011.
$5,000 to United States Hockey Hall of Fame, Eveleth, MN, 2011.

851
Clinton Savings Bank

200 Church St.
Clinton, MA 01510-2502 (978) 365-4591
FAX: (978) 365-3719

Company URL: http://www.clintonsavings.com
Establishment information: Established in 1851.
Company type: Private company
Business activities: Operates savings bank.
Business type (SIC): Savings institutions
Financial profile for 2010: Assets, $492,025; liabilities, $451,242
Corporate officers: William E. O'Neil, Jr., Chair.; Robert M. Farragher, Vice-Chair.; Robert J. Paulhus, Jr., Pres. and C.E.O.; Richard R. Hayward, Jr., Sr. V.P., Treas., and C.F.O.; Michael D. Tenaglia, Sr. V.P., Opers. and C.I.O.; Sheila A. Azorandia, V.P. and Compt.; Holly A. Connors, V.P., Opers.
Board of directors: William E. O'Neil, Jr., Chair.; Robert M. Farragher, Vice-Chair.; Paul B. Cherubini; John F. Hogan; John F. Kilcoyne; Barbara E. King; Maureen K. Quill; Robert J. Paulhus, Jr.; David E. Ross; John A. Schmidt
Offices: Berlin, Bolton, Sterling, West Boylston, MA
Giving statement: Giving through the Clinton Savings Charitable Foundation, Inc.

Clinton Savings Charitable Foundation, Inc.

200 Church St.
Clinton, MA 01510-0770 (978) 365-3700

Establishment information: Established in 2000 in MA.
Donor: Clinton Savings Bank.
Contact: Robert Paulhus, Pres. and C.E.O.
Financial data (yr. ended 12/31/11): Assets, $191,011 (M); gifts received, $20,000; expenditures, $23,575; qualifying distributions, $22,980; giving activities include $22,980 for grants.
Purpose and activities: The foundation supports organizations involved with education.
Fields of interest: Education; Health care; Human services.
Type of support: General/operating support; Scholarship funds.
Geographic limitations: Giving primarily in MA.
Support limitations: No grants to individuals.
Application information: Applications accepted. Application form required.
Initial approach: Contact foundation
Deadline(s): Contact foundation
Officers and Directors: David E. Ross*, Chair.; Robert M. Farragher*, Vice-Chair.; Robert Paulhus, Pres.; Paul B. Cherubini; John M. Davis; John F. Hogan; John F. Kilcoyne; Barbara E. King; William E. O'Neil, Jr.; Maureen K. Quill; John A. Schmidt; Timothy H. Wheeler.
EIN: 043538396

852
The Clorox Company
1221 Broadway
Oakland, CA 94612-1888 (510) 271-7000

Company URL: http://www.thecloroxcompany.com
Establishment information: Established in 1913.
Company type: Public company
Company ticker symbol and exchange: CLX/NYSE
Business activities: Produces and markets non-durable consumer products.
Business type (SIC): Soaps, cleaners, and toiletries
Financial profile for 2012: Number of employees, 8,400; assets, $4,500,000,000; sales volume, $5,600,000,000; pre-tax net income, $791,000,000; expenses, $4,677,000,000; liabilities, $4,490,000,000
Fortune 1000 ranking: 2012—461st in revenues, 318th in profits, and 632nd in assets
Forbes 2000 ranking: 2012—1328th in sales, 893rd in profits, and 1849th in assets
Corporate officers: Donald R. Knauss, Chair. and C.E.O.; Stephen M. Robb, Sr. V.P. and C.F.O.; Wayne L. Delker, Ph.D., Sr. V.P. and C.I.O.; Laura Stein, Sr. V.P. and Genl. Counsel; Jacqueline P. Kane, Sr. V.P., Human Resources
Board of directors: Donald R. Knauss, Chair.; Daniel Boggan, Jr.; Richard H. Carmona, M.D.; Tully M. Friedman; George Harad; Robert W. Matschullat; Edward A. Mueller; Jeffrey Noddle; Rogelio Rebolledo; Pamela Thomas-Graham; Carolyn M. Ticknor
Subsidiaries: Burt's Bees, Inc., Morrisville, NC; First Brands Corporation, Danbury, CT; The Kingsford Products Co., Oakland, CA
Plants: Rogers, AR; Los Angeles, Pleasanton, CA; Tampa, FL; Alpharetta, Cartersville, Forest Park, Kennesaw, GA; Chicago, Wheeling, IL; Spring Hill, KS; Burnside, Summershade, KY; Aberdeen, MD; Pearl, MI; Belle, MO; Reno, NV; Paulsboro, NJ; Cleveland, Painesville, OH; Springfield, OR; Caguas, PR; Houston, TX; Amherst, VA; Beryl, Parsons, WV
International operations: Argentina; Australia; Barbados; Bermuda; Brazil; British Virgin Islands; Canada; Cayman Islands; Chile; China; Colombia; Dominican Republic; Ecuador; Egypt; Germany; Hong Kong; Hungary; Japan; Luxembourg; Malaysia; Mexico; Netherlands; New Zealand; Panama; Peru; Philippines; Russia; Saudi Arabia; South Africa; South Korea; Switzerland; United Kingdom; Uruguay; Venezuela; Yemen
Giving statement: Giving through the Clorox Company Contributions Program and the Clorox Company Foundation.
Company EIN: 310595760

The Clorox Company Contributions Program
1221 Broadway
Oakland, CA 94612 (510) 271-2199
Application address: The Clorox Co. Fdn., P.O. Box 24305, Oakland, CA 94623-1305; Additional tel.: (510) 271-7751; URL: http://www.cloroxcsr.com/

Contact: Carmella J. Johnson, Mgr., Contribs.
Purpose and activities: As a complement to its foundation, Clorox also makes product donations to nonprofit organizations on a case by case basis. Support is given on an national and international basis.
Fields of interest: Disasters, preparedness/services.
Type of support: Donated products; Employee volunteer services; Sponsorships.
Geographic limitations: Giving on an international basis in areas of company operations, particularly Fairfield, Los Angeles, Oakland, and Pleasanton, CA, Tampa, FL, Atlanta, GA, Bedford Park, Chicago, and Wheeling, IL, Rosedale, KS, Burnside and Louisville, KY, Aberdeen, MD, Jackson, MS, Belle and Kansas City, MO, Reno, NV, Springfield, OR, Caguas, PR, Houston, TX, Beryl and Parsons, WV, Moose Jaw, Canada, and Tlalnepantla, Mexico.
Support limitations: No support for religious organizations, athletic leagues, or veterans' or political organizations. No grants to individuals, or for travel, television production, national conventions, benefit advertising, or dinners.
Application information: Unsolicited proposals for product donations are not accepted. The Community Affairs Department handles giving. Application form required.
Initial approach: Contact headquarters for application form
Copies of proposal: 1
Deadline(s): 2 months prior to event
Final notification: Following review

The Clorox Company Foundation
1221 Broadway
Oakland, CA 94612-1888 (510) 836-3223
E-mail: cloroxfndt@eastbaycf.org; Mailing address: c/o East Bay Community Foundation, De Domenico Bldg., 200 Frank Ogawa Plz., Oakland, CA 94612; URL: http://www.thecloroxcompany.com/corporate-responsibility/purpose/clorox-company-foundation/

Establishment information: Incorporated in 1980 in CA.
Donor: The Clorox Co.
Financial data (yr. ended 06/30/12): Assets, $2,370,796 (M); gifts received, $5,664,991; expenditures, $5,387,617; qualifying distributions, $5,417,617; giving activities include $5,182,502 for grants.
Purpose and activities: The foundation supports organizations involved with arts and culture, K-12 education, disaster relief, and youth development. Grants are administered by the East Bay Community Foundation.
Fields of interest: Visual arts; Performing arts; Arts; Elementary/secondary education; Disasters, preparedness/services; Youth development; Voluntarism promotion Children/youth; Children; Youth; Girls; Boys; Economically disadvantaged.
Programs:
Arts Mini-Grants Initiative: The foundation annually awards 25 $1,000 grants to nonprofit organizations involved with visual and performing arts.
Commitment Awards: The foundation awards $300 grants to nonprofit organizations with which employees of Clorox have volunteered at least 24 hours.
Culture/Civic Programs: The foundation supports programs designed to advance civic and cultural initiatives; and increase awareness of, participation in, and appreciation of arts and culture.
Education and Youth Development: The foundation supports programs designed to prepare young people to participate successfully in an increasingly global society and to contribute back to the communities in which they live. Special emphasis is directed toward programs designed to improve the academic performance of children, especially through strategies that foster reform within the public schools; prepare young people for the world of work and for community leadership; and promote positive relationships among young people from diverse cultural and ethnic groups.
Employee Matching Gifts: The foundation matches contributions made by full-time employees of Clorox to nonprofit organizations from $10 to $2,500 per employee, per year and to institutions of higher education on a one-for-one basis from $10 to $5,000 per employee, per year.
Type of support: Donated products; Employee matching gifts; Employee volunteer services; Employee-related scholarships; General/operating support; Program development; Scholarship funds.
Geographic limitations: Giving primarily in areas of company operations, with emphasis on the Oakland, CA, area; giving on a national and international basis for disaster relief.
Support limitations: No support for national organizations, religious organizations not of direct benefit to the entire community, political parties, candidates, or organizations, or exclusive membership organizations. No grants for fundraising, athletic events or league sponsorships, travel, advertising or promotional sponsorships, tickets, conferences, conventions, meetings, or similar events, media production, political activities, dues, debt reduction, capital campaigns, or individual school projects.
Publications: Annual report (including application guidelines); Application guidelines.
Application information: Applications accepted. Unsolicited requests for scholarship funds are not accepted. Application form required. Applicants should submit the following:
1) detailed description of project and amount of funding requested
2) brief history of organization and description of its mission
3) population served
4) geographic area to be served
5) results expected from proposed grant
6) how project's results will be evaluated or measured
7) copy of IRS Determination Letter
8) listing of board of directors, trustees, officers and other key people and their affiliations
9) copy of current year's organizational budget and/or project budget
10) listing of additional sources and amount of support
11) copy of most recent annual report/audited financial statement/990

Initial approach: Complete online application form
Board meeting date(s): Mar. and Sept.
Deadline(s): Jan. 1, Apr. 1, July 1, and Oct. 1
Final notification: 2 months following deadlines

Officers and Trustees:* Donald R. Knauss*, Chair.; Jacqueline P. Kane*, Pres.; Victoria Jones, V.P. and Secy.; Charles R. Conradi, V.P. and Treas.; Jeffrey R. Brubaker; Benno Dorer; Paola Gonzalez.
EIN: 942674980
Selected grants: The following grants are a representative sample of this grantmaker's funding activity:
$1,676,278 to JK Group, Plainsboro, NJ, 2011. For Gift Campaign Employee Contributions.
$389,441 to JK Group, Plainsboro, NJ, 2011.
$234,050 to JK Group, Plainsboro, NJ, 2011. For Corporate Match.
$133,000 to East Bay Community Foundation, Oakland, CA, 2011. For education/youth program.
$117,211 to JK Group, Plainsboro, NJ, 2011. For One Time Payroll Deduction Match.
$111,500 to East Bay Community Foundation, Oakland, CA, 2011. For cultural/civic program.
$107,000 to East Bay Community Foundation, Oakland, CA, 2011. For culture/civic program.
$98,390 to Scholarship America, Saint Peter, MN, 2011. For scholarship program.
$63,379 to JK Group, Plainsboro, NJ, 2011. For Higher Education Match.
$50,000 to East Bay Community Foundation, Oakland, CA, 2011. For civic/cultural program.

$12,500 to Brothers on the Rise, Oakland, CA, 2012.
$12,500 to Dimensions Dance Theater, Oakland, CA, 2012.
$10,000 to Super Stars Literacy, Oakland, CA, 2012.
$7,500 to Oakland Kids First, Oakland, CA, 2012.
$7,500 to Oakland LEAF Foundation, Oakland, CA, 2012.
$6,300 to Friends of Sausal Creek, Oakland, CA, 2012.
$5,000 to AXIS Dance Company, Oakland, CA, 2012.
$5,000 to Youth Movement Records, Oakland, CA, 2012.

853
CME Group Inc.

(formerly Chicago Mercantile Exchange Holdings Inc.)
20 S. Wacker
Chicago, IL 60606-7413 (312) 930-1000
FAX: (302) 655-5049

Company URL: http://www.cmegroup.com/
Establishment information: Established in 1898.
Company type: Public company
Company ticker symbol and exchange: CME/ NASDAQ
Business activities: Operates futures exchange.
Business type (SIC): Security and commodity brokers, dealers, exchanges, and services; security and commodity exchange
Financial profile for 2012: Number of employees, 2,600; assets, $38,863,200,000; sales volume, $2,914,600,000; pre-tax net income, $1,693,400,000; expenses, $122,260; liabilities, $17,444,100,000
Fortune 1000 ranking: 2012—726th in revenues, 218th in profits, and 143rd in assets
Forbes 2000 ranking: 2012—1631st in sales, 675th in profits, and 588th in assets
Corporate officers: Terrence A. Duffy, Chair. and Pres.; Charles P. Carey, Vice-Chair.; Phupinder S. Gill, C.E.O.; Bryan T. Durkin, C.O.O.; James E. Parisi, C.F.O., Finance.; Kevin Kometer, C.I.O.; Kathleen M. Cronin, Genl. Counsel and Corp. Secy.
Board of directors: Terrence A. Duffy, Chair.; Charles P. Carey, Vice-Chair.; Jeffrey M. Bernacchi; Timothy S. Bitsberger; Mark E. Cermak; Dennis H. Chookaszian; Jackie Clegg; James A. Donaldson; Martin J. Gepsman; Larry G. Gerdes; Daniel R. Glickman; J. Dennis Hastert; Bruce F. Johnson; Gary M. Katler; Leo Melamed; William P. Miller II; James E. Newsome; Joseph Niciforo; C.C. Odom II; James E. Oliff; John L. Pietrzak; Alex J. Pollock; John F. Sandner; Terry L. Savage; William R. Shepard; Howard J. Siegel; Christopher Stewart; Dennis A. Suskind; David J. Wescott
International operations: Brazil; Singapore; United Kingdom
Historic mergers: Board of Trade of the City of Chicago, Inc. (July 12, 2007); New York Mercantile Exchange, Inc. (August 22, 2008)
Giving statement: Giving through the Chicago Board of Trade Foundation and the CME Group Community Foundation.
Company EIN: 364459170

Chicago Board of Trade Foundation

141 W. Jackson Blvd., Ste. 1801
Chicago, IL 60604-2929 (312) 435-3609
E-mail: krogers@henningcarey.com; URL: http://www.cmegroup.com/company/foundations/cbot-foundation.html

Establishment information: Established in 1984 in IL.
Donors: Board of Trade of the City of Chicago, Inc.; Trader's Foundation Endowment Fund; Chicago Board of Trade.
Contact: Katie Rogers, Admin.
Financial data (yr. ended 12/31/11): Assets, $3,506,005 (M); expenditures, $262,049; qualifying distributions, $232,678; giving activities include $212,500 for 53 grants (high: $20,000; low: $1,000).
Purpose and activities: The foundation supports organizations involved with education, animals and wildlife, social and human services, seniors, and children in need.
Fields of interest: Secondary school/education; Education; Zoos/zoological societies; Animals/wildlife; Hospitals (general); Health care, patient services; Health care; Children/youth, services; Developmentally disabled, centers & services; Human services Children; Aging.
Type of support: Continuing support; General/operating support; Scholarship funds.
Geographic limitations: Giving primarily in areas of company operations in the Chicago, IL area.
Support limitations: No support for discriminatory or ancillary organizations, exclusionary organizations, private foundations, political candidates or lobbying organizations, religious, fraternal, social, or other membership organizations providing services to their own constituencies, or athletic teams. No grants to individuals, or for operating or capital expenses, memorials, endowments, multi-year pledges, fundraising, special events including conferences, symposia, or sports tournaments, or video or film production.
Publications: Application guidelines.
Application information: Applications accepted. Applications should include a cover letter on company letterhead. Application form required. Applicants should submit the following:
1) timetable for implementation and evaluation of project
2) results expected from proposed grant
3) population served
4) copy of IRS Determination Letter
5) brief history of organization and description of its mission
6) copy of most recent annual report/audited financial statement/990
7) how project's results will be evaluated or measured
8) listing of board of directors, trustees, officers and other key people and their affiliations
9) detailed description of project and amount of funding requested
10) listing of additional sources and amount of support

Initial approach: Download application form and mail to foundation
Copies of proposal: 1
Board meeting date(s): 1st quarter annually
Deadline(s): Check CME Group website for deadlines

Officers and Directors:* Charles P. Carey*, Chair.; Robert Corvino*, Vice-Chair.; Jill A. Harley, Treas.; David Brennan; Michael J. Daley.
EIN: 363348469
Selected grants: The following grants are a representative sample of this grantmaker's funding activity:
$20,000 to INFANT, Inc., Winnetka, IL, 2011.
$10,000 to San Miguel Schools Chicago, Chicago, IL, 2011.
$5,000 to Make-A-Wish Foundation of Illinois, Chicago, IL, 2011.
$2,500 to Evans Scholars Foundation, Golf, IL, 2011.

CME Group Community Foundation

(formerly New York Mercantile Exchange Charitable Foundation)
20 South Wacker Dr.
Chicago, IL 60606-7499 (312) 559-4966
URL: http://www.cmegroup.com/company/corporate-citizenship/index.html

Establishment information: Established in 1989 in NY.
Donors: New York Mercantile Exchange, Inc.; Steven Berkson; Chicago Mercantile Exchange, Inc.; Madison Tyler LLC; MF Global.
Contact: Nancy Choi, Mgr., Community Rels.
Financial data (yr. ended 12/31/11): Assets, $1,062,843 (M); gifts received, $649,411; expenditures, $658,896; qualifying distributions, $637,150; giving activities include $637,150 for grants.
Purpose and activities: The foundation supports organizations involved with children in need, education, and health and human services.
Fields of interest: Education; Health care; Disasters, preparedness/services; Children/youth, services; Human services.
Program:
Matching Gift Program: The foundation matches contributions made by members and employees of CME, COBT, NYMEX, and COMEX to nonprofit organizations on a one-for-one basis from $25 to $1,000 per individual, per calendar year.
Type of support: Annual campaigns; Building/renovation; Emergency funds; Employee matching gifts; Equipment; General/operating support; Program development; Research; Scholarship funds; Seed money; Sponsorships.
Geographic limitations: Giving primarily in areas of company operations, with emphasis on Chicago, IL and New York, NY.
Support limitations: No support for exclusionary organizations, private foundations, political candidates or lobbying organizations, religious, fraternal, social, or other membership organizations providing services to their own constituencies, or athletic teams. No grants to individuals, or for general operating costs, capital expenses, memorials, endowments, multi-year pledges, fundraising, special events including conferences, symposia, or sports tournaments, or video/film production.
Publications: Application guidelines.
Application information: Applications accepted. Application form required. Applicants should submit the following:
1) timetable for implementation and evaluation of project
2) results expected from proposed grant
3) population served
4) copy of IRS Determination Letter
5) brief history of organization and description of its mission
6) geographic area to be served
7) copy of most recent annual report/audited financial statement/990
8) how project's results will be evaluated or measured
9) listing of board of directors, trustees, officers and other key people and their affiliations
10) listing of additional sources and amount of support

11) plans for acknowledgement
Proposals should include a completed W-9 and an explanation of any deficits or changes in funding, if applicable.
Initial approach: Download application form and mail proposal and application form to foundation
Deadline(s): Rolling basis through Oct. 1
Final notification: 10 to 12 weeks after receipt
Officers and Directors:* Terrance A. Duffy, Pres.; Meg Wright, Secy.; Jill A. Harley*, Treas.; Neil Citrone; Bryan T. Durkin; Phupinder S. Gill; Hilda Harris Piell; Kristin K. Wood.
EIN: 133586378
Selected grants: The following grants are a representative sample of this grantmaker's funding activity:
$25,000 to Summer Camp Opportunities Provide An Edge, New York, NY, 2009.
$12,500 to Cystic Fibrosis Foundation, New York, NY, 2009.
$10,000 to Big Apple Circus, Brooklyn, NY, 2009.
$10,000 to Camp AmeriKids, Stamford, CT, 2009.
$10,000 to City Harvest, New York, NY, 2009.
$10,000 to Jewish Community Council of Greater Coney Island, Brooklyn, NY, 2009.
$7,500 to Atlantic Theater Company, New York, NY, 2009.
$5,000 to Hispanic AIDS Forum, New York, NY, 2009.
$5,000 to New York Junior Tennis League, Woodside, NY, 2009.
$5,000 to Shelter Our Sisters, Hackensack, NJ, 2009.

854
CMS Energy Corporation
1 Energy Plz.
Jackson, MI 49201 (517) 788-0550

Company URL: http://www.cmsenergy.com
Establishment information: Established in 1886.
Company type: Public company
Company ticker symbol and exchange: CMS/NYSE
International Securities Identification Number: US1258961002
Business activities: Operates holding company; generates, transmits, and distributes electricity; transmits and distributes natural gas.
Business type (SIC): Holding company; combination utility services
Financial profile for 2012: Number of employees, 7,514; assets, $17,131,000,000; sales volume, $6,253,000,000; pre-tax net income, $622,000,000; expenses, $5,250,000,000; liabilities, $13,937,000,000
Fortune 1000 ranking: 2012—406th in revenues, 416th in profits, and 267th in assets
Forbes 2000 ranking: 2012—1242nd in sales, 1293rd in profits, and 1071st in assets
Corporate officers: David W. Joos, Chair.; John G. Russell, Pres. and C.E.O.; Thomas J. Webb, Exec. V.P. and C.F.O.; James E. Brunner, Sr. V.P. and Genl. Counsel; Glenn P. Barba, V.P., C.A.O., and Cont.; Mamatha Chamarthi, V.P. and C.I.O.; Catherine M. Reynolds, V.P. and Corp. Secy.; Venkat Dhenuvakonda Rao, V.P. and Treas.
Board of directors: David W. Joos, Chair.; Merribel S. Ayres; Jon E. Barfield, Jr.; Stephen E. Ewing; Richard M. Gabrys; William D. Harvey; Philip R. Lochner, Jr.; Michael T. Monahan; John G. Russell; Kenneth L. Way; Laura H. Wright; John B. Yasinsky
Subsidiaries: CMS Enterprises, Inc., Jackson, MI; Consumers Energy Company, Jackson, MI
Giving statement: Giving through the CMS Energy Foundation.
Company EIN: 382726431

CMS Energy Foundation
1 Energy Plz., EP 8-210
Jackson, MI 49201-2276 (517) 788-0432

Establishment information: Established in 2001 in MI.
Donor: CMS Energy Corp.
Contact: Carolyn A. Bloodworth, Secy.-Treas.
Financial data (yr. ended 12/31/11): Assets, $40,720 (M); expenditures, $43,350; qualifying distributions, $43,350; giving activities include $43,330 for 3 grants (high: $25,000; low: $1,000).
Purpose and activities: The foundation supports organizations involved with arts and culture, higher education, the environment, human services, community economic development, and civic affairs. Special emphasis is directed toward programs that reach underserved populations and communities.
Fields of interest: Arts; Secondary school/education; Higher education; Environment; Children/youth, services; Family services; Human services; Economic development; Community/economic development; United Ways and Federated Giving Programs Economically disadvantaged.
Type of support: Building/renovation; Capital campaigns; Employee volunteer services; Equipment; General/operating support; Program development.
Geographic limitations: Giving primarily in areas of company operations in NC, LA, MI, and PA.
Support limitations: No support for discriminatory organizations, United Way-supported organizations, political organizations, religious organizations not of direct benefit to the entire community, or labor, veterans', fraternal, or social organizations. No grants to individuals, or for fundraising, debt reduction, endowments, sports tournaments, talent or beauty contests, or political campaigns; no loans for small business.
Publications: Application guidelines.
Application information: Applications accepted. Application form required. Applicants should submit the following:
1) copy of IRS Determination Letter
Initial approach: 2 page letter
Deadline(s): None
Officers and Directors:* John G. Russell*, Chair.; David G. Mengebier*, Pres.; Carolyn A. Bloodworth*, Secy.-Treas.; James E. Brunner; John M. Butler; Timothy L. Mehl; Philip G. Polyak; Thomas J. Webb.
EIN: 383575175

855
CNA Financial Corporation
333 S. Wabash
Chicago, IL 60604 (312) 822-5000
FAX: (312) 755-7215

Company URL: http://www.cna.com
Establishment information: Established in 1897.
Company type: Public company
Company ticker symbol and exchange: CNA/NYSE
Business activities: Sells insurance.
Business type (SIC): Insurance/accident and health; insurance/life; insurance/fire, marine, and casualty; pension, health, and welfare funds
Financial profile for 2012: Number of employees, 7,500; assets, $58,522,000,000; sales volume, $9,547,000,000; pre-tax net income, $872,000,000; expenses, $8,675,000,000; liabilities, $46,208,000,000
Corporate officers: Thomas F. Motamed, Chair. and C.E.O.; D. Craig Mense, Exec. V.P. and C.F.O.; Thomas Pontarelli, Exec. V.P. and C.A.O.; Jonathan D. Kantor, Exec. V.P., Genl. Counsel, and Secy.; Ray Oral, Sr. V.P. and C.I.O.; Sarah Pang, Sr. V.P., Corp. Comms.; Debbie Nutley, Sr. V.P., Human Resources
Board of directors: Thomas F. Motamed, Chair.; Paul J. Liska; Jose O. Montemayor; Don M. Randel; Joseph W. Rosenberg; Andrew H. Tisch; James S. Tisch; Marvin Zonis
Subsidiary: Continental Assurance Company, Chicago, IL
International operations: United Kingdom
Giving statement: Giving through the CNA Financial Corporation Contributions Program and the CNA Foundation.
Company EIN: 366169860

CNA Financial Corporation Contributions Program
333 S. Wabash Ave.
Chicago, IL 60604-4107 (312) 822-5000
URL: http://www.cna.com/portal/site/cna/about/

Purpose and activities: As a complement to its foundation, CNA also makes charitable contributions to nonprofit organizations directly. Support is given primarily in areas of company operations.
Fields of interest: General charitable giving.
Type of support: Employee volunteer services; General/operating support; In-kind gifts.
Geographic limitations: Giving primarily in areas of company operations.

CNA Foundation
(formerly CNA Insurance Companies Foundation)
333 S. Wabash Ave., 44th Fl.
Chicago, IL 60604-4107 (312) 822-5000
E-mail: rita.wilmes@cna.com; Tel. for Rita Wilmes: (312) 822-2606; Additional contact: Marlene Rotstein, Dir., tel.: (312) 822-7065, e-mail: marlene.rotstein@cna.com; Additional e-mail: cna_foundation@cna.com; URL: http://www.cna.com/portal/site/cna/about/

Establishment information: Established in 1995.
Donor: CNA Financial Corp.
Contact: Rita Wilmes, Prog. Coord.
Financial data (yr. ended 12/31/11): Assets, $761,689 (M); gifts received, $2,000,000; expenditures, $2,526,304; qualifying distributions, $2,526,304; giving activities include $2,526,304 for grants.
Purpose and activities: The CNA Foundation helps to limit risks by helping to build healthy, vibrant communities, by funding a variety of programs and organizations that support current and prospective employees; ensure field involvement; and build industry relationships. Special emphasis is directed toward programs designed to meet the educational needs of children; assist and support children, youth, and adults in developing vocational and education skills; and support economically disadvantaged children and families.
Fields of interest: Elementary/secondary education; Vocational education; Education; Health care; Employment, training; Employment; Human services; Community/economic development; Public affairs Children; Economically disadvantaged.
Programs:
Community Involvement Grants: Through Community Involvement Grants (CIG Award), the foundation awards grants to nonprofit organizations involved with arts and culture, education, health,

workforce development, human services, community development, and civic affairs in the six regions where CNA does business. This program is administered by the Public Affairs Department.

Education: The foundation supports programs designed to strengthen schools through the advancement of basic curriculum, enhanced learning opportunities, and faculty development.

Matching Gift Program: The foundation matches contributions made by employees of CNA to nonprofit organizations on a one-for-one basis up to $5,000 per employee, per year.

Support for the Economically Disadvantaged: The foundation supports programs designed to enhance quality of life for the economically disadvantaged; and help children and families through difficult times.

Work Force Development: The foundation supports programs designed to enhance the competitiveness of U.S. workers in the global economy; and encourage and prepare children, youth, and adults for entry into and success in the workplace.

Type of support: Continuing support; Curriculum development; Employee matching gifts; Employee-related scholarships; Grants to individuals; Program development; Scholarship funds.

Geographic limitations: Giving primarily in Chicago, IL.

Support limitations: No support for political organizations, professional associations, labor, alumni, or fraternal organizations or social clubs, religious organizations not of direct benefit to the entire community, discriminatory organizations, or grantmaking foundations. No grants to individuals (except for employee-related emergency disaster relief grants), or for political, legislative, lobbying, or advocacy efforts, endowed chairs or professorships, endowments, advertising or raffles, tickets for testimonial events or similar benefit events from which only a portion of the revenue reaches the sponsor, or dinners or golf tournaments.

Publications: Application guidelines.

Application information: Applications accepted. Limited discretionary funds available. Additional information may be requested at a later date. Multi-year funding is not automatic. Requests for Community Involvement Grants are accepted from employees only. Application form required.

Applicants should submit the following:

1) copy of IRS Determination Letter
2) brief history of organization and description of its mission
3) copy of most recent annual report/audited financial statement/990
4) how project's results will be evaluated or measured
5) listing of board of directors, trustees, officers and other key people and their affiliations
6) detailed description of project and amount of funding requested
7) copy of current year's organizational budget and/ or project budget
8) listing of additional sources and amount of support

Initial approach: Download application form and mail proposal and application form to foundation

Copies of proposal: 1

Deadline(s): None

Final notification: 6 months

Officers and Directors:* Thomas F. Motamed, Chair.; Thomas Pontarelli*, Pres.; Stathy Darcy, V.P. and Secy.; Stephen Westman, V.P.; James Doyle, Treas.; Sarah Pang, Exec. Dir.; Craig D. Mense; Deborah Nutley; Timothy Szerlong.

Number of staff: 2 part-time professional.

EIN: 364029026

856
CNH America LLC

6900 Veterans Blvd.
Burr Ridge, IL 60527-5640 (630) 887-2233

Company URL: http://www.cnh.com/Pages/home.aspx

Establishment information: Established in 1999.

Company type: Subsidiary of a foreign company

Business activities: Manufactures farm and construction equipment.

Business type (SIC): Machinery/farm and garden

Financial profile for 2010: Number of employees, 208

Corporate officer: Sergio Marchionne, Chair.

Board of directors: Sergio Marchionne, Chair.; Harold D. Boyanovsky; Thomas J. Colligan; Edward A. Hiler; Leo W. Houle; Rolf M. Jeker; Peter Kalantzis; John Lanaway; Kenneth Lipper; Paolo Monferino; Jacques Theurillat; Richard Tobin

Giving statement: Giving through the CNH America LLC.

CNH America LLC

6900 Veterans Blvd.
Burr Ridge, IL 60527-5640
E-mail: lisa.moran@cnh.com; URL: http://cnh.com/Company/Pages/ethicalCommunityCommitment.aspx

Contact: Lisa Moran

Purpose and activities: CNH America makes charitable contributions to organizations located in areas of company operations.

Fields of interest: General charitable giving.

Type of support: Annual campaigns; Building/renovation; Capital campaigns; Donated equipment; In-kind gifts; Research; Scholarship funds; Sponsorships.

Geographic limitations: Giving is limited to areas of company operations.

Support limitations: No support for religious organizations or for sports teams. No grants to individuals.

Publications: Corporate report; Informational brochure.

Application information: Applications accepted. All required documentation listed on application must be submitted or request will not be considered. The Human Resources Department handles giving. A contributions committee reviews all requests. Application form required.

Initial approach: Letter and application to headquarters

Copies of proposal: 1

Committee meeting date(s): Quarterly

Deadline(s): Mar. 1, June 1, Sept. 1, and Dec. 1

Final notification: 30 days

Number of staff: 1 full-time professional.

857
CNO Financial Group, Inc.

(formerly Conseco, Inc.)
11825 N. Pennsylvania St.
Carmel, IN 46032 (317) 817-6100
FAX: (302) 636-5454

Company URL: http://www.cnoinc.com

Establishment information: Established in 1979.

Company type: Public company

Company ticker symbol and exchange: CNO/NYSE

Business activities: Operates holding company involved with life and health insurance.

Business type (SIC): Insurance/accident and health; insurance/life

Financial profile for 2012: Number of employees, 4,200; assets, $34,131,400,000; sales volume, $4,342,700,000; pre-tax net income, $155,700,000; expenses, $4,187,000,000; liabilities, $29,082,100,000

Fortune 1000 ranking: 2012—548th in revenues, 549th in profits, and 165th in assets

Forbes 2000 ranking: 2012—1477th in sales, 1582nd in profits, and 667th in assets

Corporate officers: Neal Schneider, Chair.; Edward J. Bonach, C.E.O.; Bruce Baude, Exec. V.P. and C.O.O.; Frederick J. Crawford, Exec. V.P. and C.F.O.; Matthew J. Zimpfer, Exec. V.P. and Genl. Counsel; Susan L. Menzel, Exec. V.P., Human Resources; John R. Kline, Sr. V.P. and C.A.O.

Board of directors: Neal C. Schneider, Chair.; Edward J. Bonach; Ellyn L. Brown; Robert C. Greving; Mary R. Henderson; R. Keith Long; Frederick J. Sievert; Michael T. Tokarz; John G. Turner

Subsidiaries: American Travellers Corp., Bensalem, PA; Association Management Corp., Rockford, IL; Bankers Life Holding Co., Chicago, IL; Bankers National Life Insurance Co., Carmel, IN; Beneficial Standard Life Insurance Co., Carmel, IN; Business Information Group, Rockford, IL; Capital American Finance, Cleveland, OH; CHIC, Carmel, IN; Conseco Capital Management, Inc., Carmel, IN; Conseco Capital Partners II, L.P., New York, NY; Conseco Risk Management, Inc., Carmel, IN; Great American Reserve Insurance Co., Carmel, IN; Lincoln American Life Insurance Co., Carmel, IN; National Fidelity Life Insurance Co., Carmel, IN; National Group Life Insurance Co., Rockford, IL; National Group Marketing Corp., Irving, TX; National Health Services, Inc., Milwaukee, WI; Network Air Medical Systems, Inc., Rockford, IL; Pioneer Direct Corp., Rockford, IL; Pioneer Life Insurance Co. of Illinois, Rockford, IL; Union Benefit Life Insurance Co., Rockford, IL

International operations: Canada

Giving statement: Giving through the CNO Financial Group, Inc. Corporate Giving Program.

Company EIN: 753108137

CNO Financial Group, Inc. Corporate Giving Program

(formerly Conseco, Inc. Corporate Giving Program)
11825 N. Pennsylvania St.
Carmel, IN 46032-4555 (317) 817-3768
Additional contact: Barbara Ciesemier, tel.: (312) 396-7461; URL: http://www.cnoinc.com/about-cno/in-the-community

Contact: Media Oakes

Purpose and activities: Conseco makes charitable contributions to nonprofit organizations involved with education, cancer, arthritis, Alzheimer's disease, housing development, basketball, human services, and senior citizens. Support is given primarily in Indiana.

Fields of interest: Education; Cancer; Arthritis; Alzheimer's disease; Food distribution, meals on wheels; Housing/shelter, development; Athletics/sports, basketball; American Red Cross; Aging, centers/services; Human services; United Ways and Federated Giving Programs Aging.

Type of support: Employee volunteer services; General/operating support; Program development; Sponsorships.

Geographic limitations: Giving primarily in IN; giving also to national organizations.

858
Coach, Inc.

516 W. 34th St.
New York, NY 10001-1394 (212) 594-1850
FAX: (212) 594-1682

Company URL: http://www.coach.com
Establishment information: Established in 1941.
Company type: Public company
Company ticker symbol and exchange: COH/NYSE
Business activities: Designs and manufactures high-end leather goods and accessories.
Business type (SIC): Leather goods/personal
Financial profile for 2012: Number of employees, 18,000; assets, $3,104,320,000; sales volume, $4,763,180,000; pre-tax net income, $1,505,660,000; expenses, $3,251,190,000; liabilities, $1,111,390,000
Fortune 1000 ranking: 2012—504th in revenues, 192nd in profits, and 743rd in assets
Forbes 2000 ranking: 2012—1403rd in sales, 548th in profits, and 1920th in assets
Corporate officers: Lew Frankfort, Chair. and C.E.O.; Jerry Stritzke, Co-Pres. and C.O.O.; Reed Krakoff, Co-Pres.; Jane Nielsen, Exec. V.P., C.A.O., and C.F.O.; Todd Kahn, Exec. V.P., Genl. Counsel, and Secy.; Sarah Dunn, Exec. V.P., Human Resources
Board of directors: Lew Frankfort, Chair.; Susan J. Kropf; Gary W. Loveman; Ivan Menezes; Irene R. Miller; Michael Murphy; Stephaine Tilenius; Jide J. Zeitlin
Giving statement: Giving through the Coach, Inc. Corporate Giving Program and the Coach Foundation, Inc.
Company EIN: 522242751

Coach, Inc. Corporate Giving Program

516 W. 34th St.
New York, NY 10001-1394 (212) 594-1850

Purpose and activities: As a complement to its foundation, Coach also makes charitable product donations to nonprofit organizations directly.
Fields of interest: Health care; Medical research; Housing/shelter, homeless; Homeless, human services Homeless.
Type of support: Donated products.

Coach Foundation, Inc.

c/o Coach, Inc.
516 W. 34th St.
New York, NY 10001-1311
E-mail: coachfoundation@coach.com; URL: http://www.coach.com/online/handbags/genWCM-10551-10051-en-/Coach_US/CompanyInformation/CoachFoundation/

Establishment information: Established in 2008 in NY.
Donor: Coach, Inc.
Financial data (yr. ended 06/30/12): Assets, $75,463,364 (M); expenditures, $3,409,471; qualifying distributions, $3,242,525; giving activities include $3,242,525 for 66 grants (high: $523,525; low: $5,000).
Purpose and activities: The foundation supports programs designed to empower, educate, and support women and children around the world.
Fields of interest: Secondary school/education; Higher education; Education; Environment; Hospitals (general); Breast cancer; Dispute resolution; Disasters, preparedness/services; American Red Cross; Children, services; Family services; Family services, domestic violence; Women, centers/services; Business/industry Women.
Programs:
The Coach Education Initiative: The foundation supports programs designed to improve educational opportunities for the underserved, enabling them to learn, grow, and contribute to society.
The Coach Women's Initiative: The foundation supports programs designed to help women realize their full potential through personal and economic empowerment.
Type of support: Continuing support; Employee matching gifts; Employee volunteer services; General/operating support; Program development; Scholarship funds.
Geographic limitations: Giving primarily in areas of company operations, with some emphasis in New York City; giving also to national organizations.
Application information: Applications not accepted. The foundation primarily funds projects recommended by its employees and board members.
Officers and Directors:* Lew Frankfort*, Chair., Pres., and C.E.O.; Jerry Stritzke*, C.O.O.; Todd Kahn*, V.P. and Secy.; Nancy H. Walsh, Treas.; Jane Nielson, C.F.O.; Felice Schulaner, Exec. Dir.; Sarah Dunn; Susan J. Kropf; Jason Weisenfeld.
EIN: 262939018
Selected grants: The following grants are a representative sample of this grantmaker's funding activity:
$100,000 to Childrens Defense Fund, Washington, DC, 2011.
$25,000 to Teach for America, New York, NY, 2011.
$15,000 to Autism Speaks, New York, NY, 2011.

859
Coastal Electric Cooperative

1265 S. Coastal Hwy.
Midway, GA 31320-5230 (912) 884-3311

Company URL: http://www.coastalelectriccooperative.com
Establishment information: Established in 1940.
Company type: Cooperative
Business activities: Operates a member-owned electric cooperative providing electric service.
Business type (SIC): Electric services
Corporate officers: Stephen Mullice, Pres.; F. Whit Hollowell, Jr., Exec. V.P. and C.E.O.; J. Mark Bolton, V.P., Mktg and Comms.; Chris Fettes, V.P., Opers.; Rebecca Tharpe, V.P., Human Resources; Barbara Davis, Secy.-Treas.
Board of directors: Billy Bland; Barbara Davis; Eric Hartley; Johnny Kearns; Ken Luke; Laura McGee; Stephen Mullice; Jack Waters; John Woods III
Giving statement: Giving through the Coastal EMC Foundation.

Coastal EMC Foundation

P.O. Box 109
Midway, GA 31320-0109 (912) 884-3311
FAX: (912) 884-2789; URL: http://www.coastalemc.com/foundation.aspx?section=c
Scholarship e-mail: scholarship@coastalemc.com

Financial data (yr. ended 12/31/11): Revenue, $134,863; assets, $149,230 (M); gifts received, $134,047; expenditures, $68,877; giving activities include $68,877 for grants.
Purpose and activities: The foundation's mission is to assist with the food, health, safety, education and shelter needs of citizens in counties served by Coastal Electric Cooperative.
Fields of interest: Education; Health care; Food services; Housing/shelter; Human services.
Programs:
Bright Ideas: This program awards grants of up to $2,000 to certified school teachers instructing students in grades K-12 in south Bryan, Liberty, and McIntosh counties, GA. The program encourages teachers to develop creative, innovative programs that might not otherwise be funded through the school system. The competition is open to public and private schools accredited by the Southern Association of Colleges and Schools.
Coastal Electric Cooperative Foundation Scholarships: Scholarships of $1,000 each are available to residents of south Bryan, Liberty, and McIntosh counties who are graduating seniors, college students, or adult students returning to school. Applications are evaluated on the basis of commitment to community, integrity, accountability, innovation, and financial need.
Walter Harrison Scholarship: Each year, the foundation selects three nominees to compete in a state-wide competition for scholarships of $1,000 each. Eligible applicants must be members of the Coastal Electric Cooperative, or dependent children who are graduating seniors or college students. Applications are judged on the basis of academic achievement and financial need.
Type of support: Grants to individuals; Scholarships—to individuals.
Geographic limitations: Giving primarily in GA.
Publications: Application guidelines.
Application information: Applications accepted. Application form required.
Initial approach: Submit application
Deadline(s): Feb. 13 for Walter Harrison Scholarship; Mar. 30 for Coastal Electric Cooperative Foundation Scholarships; Apr. 31 for Bright Ideas
Board Members: Ronald Burns; Robert Carpenter; Kimberly Carter; Runette Parker; Roger Sapp; Barbara Smith; William B. Smith; Lynne Stevens; Thomas Wallace.
EIN: 582076664

860
Coats American, Inc.

3430 Toringdon Way, Ste. 301
Charlotte, NC 28277-2446 (704) 329-5800

Company URL: http://www.coatsandclark.com
Establishment information: Established in 1898.
Company type: Subsidiary of a foreign company
Business activities: Manufactures cotton, synthetic, and blended thread and yarns; dyes and finishes fabrics.
Business type (SIC): Yarn and thread mills; farm-product raw materials—wholesale
Corporate officers: Steven Baune, C.E.O.; James Lamon, Pres.
Subsidiaries: Calico Printers Assn., Marion, NC; Coats & Clark, Charlotte, NC; Coats Trim Resources, Matthews, NC
Giving statement: Giving through the Coats North American Educational Foundation.

Coats North American Educational Foundation

(formerly American Thread Educational Foundation, Inc.)
3430 Toringdon Way, Ste. 301
Charlotte, NC 28277-2576 (704) 329-5800

Donors: Coats American Inc.; Thread Mill Athletic Assn.
Contact: Peggy Sullivan, Secy. and Co-Treas.
Financial data (yr. ended 12/31/11): Assets, $740,299 (M); expenditures, $64,084; qualifying distributions, $63,927; giving activities include $59,000 for 18 grants to individuals (high: $6,000; low: $1,000).
Purpose and activities: The foundation awards college scholarships to children of employees of Coats American Inc. and Coats & Clark earning below a stated salary level.
Type of support: Employee-related scholarships; Program-related investments/loans.
Geographic limitations: Giving primarily in areas of company operations.
Application information: Applications not accepted. Contributes only through employee-related scholarships.
Board meeting date(s): May 1
Officers: Bill Graham, Pres.; Peggy Sullivan, Secy. and Co-Treas.; Scott Willis, Co-Treas.
Director: Kim Robinson.
EIN: 566093510

861
Coca-Cola Bottling Co. Consolidated

4100 Coca-Cola Plz.
P.O. Box 31487
Charlotte, NC 28211 (704) 557-4000

Company URL: http://www.cokeconsolidated.com
Establishment information: Established in 1902.
Company type: Public company
Company ticker symbol and exchange: COKE/NASDAQ
Business activities: Produces, markets, and distributes carbonated and noncarbonated beverages.
Business type (SIC): Beverages
Financial profile for 2012: Number of employees, 5,000; assets, $1,283,470,000; sales volume, $1,614,430,000; pre-tax net income, $53,350,000; expenses, $1,525,750,000; liabilities, $1,148,210,000
Corporate officers: J. Frank Harrison III, Chair. and C.E.O.; William B. Elmore, Vice-Chair.; Henry W. Flint, Pres. and C.O.O.; James E. Harris, Sr. V.P. and C.F.O.; Umesh M. Kasbekar, Sr. V.P., Admin.; David L. Hopkins, Sr. V.P., Opers.; Robert G. Chambless, Sr. V.P., Sales and Mktg.; Michael A. Strong, Sr. V.P., Human Resources; William J. Billiard, V.P. and C.A.O.; Clifford M. Deal III, V.P. and Treas.
Board of directors: J. Frank Harrison III, Chair.; William B. Elmore, Vice-Chair.; H.W. McKay Belk; Alexander Benedict Cummings, Jr.; Sharon A. Decker; Morgan H. Everett; Deborah H. Everhart; Henry W. Flint; William H. Jones; James H. Morgan; John W. Murrey III; Dennis A. Wicker
International operations: Netherlands
Giving statement: Giving through the Coca-Cola Bottling Co. Consolidated Corporate Giving Program.
Company EIN: 560950585

Coca-Cola Bottling Co. Consolidated Corporate Giving Program

4100 Coca-Cola Plz.
Charlotte, NC 28211-3481 (704) 557-4400
URL: http://www.cokeconsolidated.com/stewardship.html

Purpose and activities: Coca-Cola Bottling makes charitable contributions to nonprofit organizations involved with education, recreation, children and youth, and families. Support is given primarily in areas of company operations.
Fields of interest: Education; Athletics/sports, school programs; Recreation; YM/YWCAs & YM/YWHAs; Children/youth, services; Family services.
Type of support: Donated products; Employee volunteer services; General/operating support; In-kind gifts; Program development; Sponsorships.
Geographic limitations: Giving primarily in areas of company operations in AL, FL, GA, MS, NC, SC, TN, VA, and WV.
Support limitations: No grants for national events or programs.
Publications: Application guidelines.
Application information: Applications accepted. Application form not required.
Initial approach: Proposal to nearest company facility for product donations and sponsorships
Copies of proposal: 1
Deadline(s): None
Final notification: Following review

862
The Coca-Cola Company

1 Coca-Cola Plz.
P.O. Box 1734
Atlanta, GA 30313-2420 (404) 676-2121
FAX: (404) 676-6792

Company URL: http://www.coca-cola.com
Establishment information: Established in 1892.
Company type: Public company
Company ticker symbol and exchange: KO/NYSE
International Securities Identification Number: US1912161007
Business activities: Produces, markets, and distributes beverage concentrates and syrups.
Business type (SIC): Beverages
Financial profile for 2012: Number of employees, 150,900; assets, $86,174,000,000; sales volume, $48,017,000,000; pre-tax net income, $11,809,000,000; expenses, $37,238,000,000; liabilities, $53,384,000,000
Fortune 1000 ranking: 2012—57th in revenues, 19th in profits, and 71st in assets
Forbes 2000 ranking: 2012—182nd in sales, 49th in profits, and 284th in assets
Corporate officers: Muhtar Kent, Chair. and C.E.O.; Gary P. Fayard, Exec. V.P. and C.F.O.; Alexander B. Cummings, Exec. V.P. and C.A.O.; Bernhard Goepelt, Sr. V.P. and Genl. Counsel
Board of directors: Muhtar Kent, Chair.; Herbert A. Allen; Ronald W. Allen; Howard G. Buffett; Richard M. Daley; Barry Diller; Helene D. Gayle; Evan G. Greenberg; Alexis M. Herman; Robert A. Kotick; Maria Elena Lagomasino; Donald F. McHenry; Samuel Nunn; James D. Robinson III; Peter V. Ueberroth; Jacob Wallenberg
Plants: Tempe, AZ; Los Angeles, San Diego, San Francisco, CA; Denver, CO; Daytona Beach, FL; Lenexa, KS; New Orleans, LA; Columbia, MD; Needham Heights, MA; Detroit, Lansing, MI; Akron, OH; Wilsonville, OR; Dallas, TX; Bellevue, WA
International operations: Angola; Argentina; Australia; Belgium; Brazil; Canada; Cayman Islands; Chile; China; Costa Rica; Egypt; France; Germany; India; Ireland; Japan; Mexico; Netherlands; Norway; Peru; Philippines; South Africa; Spain; Sweden; United Kingdom; Venezuela
Giving statement: Giving through the Coca-Cola Company Contributions Program, the Coca-Cola Chile Foundation, the Coca-Cola China Foundation Ltd., the Coca-Cola Educational & Environmental Foundation, the Coca-Cola Foundation, Inc., the Coca-Cola Foundation of Bolivia, the Coca-Cola Foundation of Ecuador, the Coca-Cola Foundation of Mexico, the Coca-Cola Foundation Philippines, the Coca-Cola Foundation Thailand, the Coca-Cola Great Britain, the Coca-Cola India Foundation, the Coca-Cola Korea Youth Foundation, the Coca-Cola Spain Foundation, the Inca Kola Foundation, the SAS & Coca-Cola Environmental Foundation, and the Coca-Cola Scholars Foundation, Inc.
Company EIN: 580628465

The Coca-Cola Company Contributions Program

1 Coca-Cola Plz.
Atlanta, GA 30313-2420 (404) 676-2121
URL: http://www.thecoca-colacompany.com/citizenship/our_communities.html

Purpose and activities: As a complement to its foundation, Coca-Cola also makes charitable contributions to nonprofit organizations directly. Special emphasis is directed toward programs designed to address healthy active lifestyles, education, and youth development. Support is given on a national and international basis in areas of company operations.
Fields of interest: Scholarships/financial aid; Education, drop-out prevention; Education; Environment, recycling; Environment, water resources; Public health, physical fitness; AIDS; Tropical diseases; Nutrition; Youth development; Civil/human rights, equal rights.
Type of support: Donated products; Employee matching gifts; Employee volunteer services; General/operating support; In-kind gifts; Program development; Scholarship funds; Sponsorships.
Geographic limitations: Giving on a national and international basis in areas of company operations.
Support limitations: No support for discriminatory organizations, religious, political, legislative, lobbying, or fraternal organizations, or for U.S.-based schools. No grants to individuals, or for movie, film, or television documentaries, advertising or marketing sponsorships, web site development, beauty contests, fashion shows, or hair shows, local sports or athletic teams, or travel.
Publications: Application guidelines.
Application information: Applications accepted. Application form required.
Initial approach: Complete online application eligibility quiz and application form

The Coca-Cola Foundation, Inc.

1 Coca-Cola Plaza, N.W.
Atlanta, GA 30313-2420 (404) 676-2568
FAX: (404) 676-8804;
E-mail: cocacolacommunityrequest@na.ko.com; Additional tel.: (404) 676-3525; URL: http://www.thecoca-colacompany.com/citizenship/foundation_coke.html

Establishment information: Incorporated in 1984 in GA.
Donor: The Coca-Cola Co.
Contact: Helen Smith Price, Exec. Dir.
Financial data (yr. ended 12/31/11): Assets, $244,016,915 (M); gifts received, $77,000; expenditures, $76,738,040; qualifying distributions, $76,230,474; giving activities include $71,248,566 for 273 grants (high: $12,095,000; low: $9,500) and $4,981,743 for employee matching gifts.
Purpose and activities: The foundation supports programs designed to promote water stewardship; healthy and active lifestyles; community recycling, and education.

Fields of interest: Higher education; Scholarships/financial aid; Education, services; Education, drop-out prevention; Education; Environment, water pollution; Environment, recycling; Environment, water resources; Hospitals (general); Public health, obesity; Public health, physical fitness; Public health, clean water supply; Public health, sanitation; AIDS; Nutrition; Disasters, preparedness/services; Big Brothers/Big Sisters; Girl scouts; Youth development; Public affairs.
International interests: Africa; Europe; Latin America.

Programs:

Coca-Cola First Generation Scholarship: The foundation supports students who are the first in their immediate family to attend college or university through scholarships. The program is administered by participating schools.

Community Recycling: The foundation supports programs designed to increase litter abatement efforts; advance recovery and reuse; increase community recycling awareness; and support research and innovation.

Education: The foundation awards scholarships and supports programs designed to promote school drop-out prevention; access to education; and other educational initiatives per local business unit priorities.

Healthy and Active Lifestyles: The foundation supports programs designed to promote access to exercise, physical activity, and nutritional education; motivate behavior modification; and programs designed to encourage lifestyle/behavioral changes.

Matching Gift Program: The foundation matches contributions made by employees of Coca-Cola to nonprofit organizations on a two-for-one basis.

Water Stewardship: The foundation supports programs designed to promote access to clean water and sanitation; watershed protection in water-stressed regions; utilization of water for production and/or multiple use systems that do more than provide clean water; and education and awareness programs designed to promote water conservation within communities and industry.

Type of support: Continuing support; Emergency funds; Employee matching gifts; Fellowships; General/operating support; Program development; Scholarship funds; Sponsorships.
Geographic limitations: Giving on a national and international basis in areas of company operations, with emphasis on CA, Washington, DC, Atlanta, GA, New York, NY, TX, VA, Africa, Australia, Chile, China, Colombia, Europe, Italy, Japan, Latin America, Philippines, and Russia.
Support limitations: No support for discriminatory organizations, political, legislative, or lobbying organizations, fraternal organizations, athletic teams, or U.S. based local schools, including charter schools, pre-schools, elementary schools, middle schools, or high schools. No grants to individuals (except for the Coca-Cola First Generation Scholarship), or for movie, film, or television documentaries, website development, concerts or other entertainment events, beauty contests, fashion shows, or hair shows, local sports, travel or organized field trips, family reunions, marketing sponsorships, cause marketing, or advertising projects, land, building, or equipment, or construction or renovation projects.
Publications: Application guidelines; Grants list; Program policy statement.
Application information: Applications accepted. Faxed or e-mailed applications are not accepted. Application form required. Applicants should submit the following:
1) timetable for implementation and evaluation of project
2) staff salaries
3) results expected from proposed grant
4) qualifications of key personnel
5) copy of IRS Determination Letter
6) brief history of organization and description of its mission
7) explanation of why grantmaker is considered an appropriate donor for project
8) listing of board of directors, trustees, officers and other key people and their affiliations
9) detailed description of project and amount of funding requested
10) copy of current year's organizational budget and/or project budget
11) additional materials/documentation

Initial approach: Complete online application form; contact participating universities for Coca-Cola First Generation Scholarship
Copies of proposal: 1
Board meeting date(s): Quarterly
Deadline(s): None
Final notification: 60 days

Officers and Directors:* Ingrid Saunders Jones*, Chair.; Alexander B. Cummings, Secy.; Gary P. Fayard*, Treas.; Lawton Hawkins, Genl. Legal Counsel; William Hawkins*, Genl. Tax Counsel; Helen Smith Price*, Exec. Dir.; Ahmet C. Bozer; Beatriz Perez; Sonya Soutus; Dominique Reiniche; Clyde C. Tuggle.
Number of staff: 6 full-time professional; 5 full-time support.
EIN: 581574705
Selected grants: The following grants are a representative sample of this grantmaker's funding activity:
$12,095,000 to Coca-Cola Africa Foundation, Manzini, Swaziland, 2011.
$11,130,770 to Coca-Cola Africa Foundation, Manzini, Swaziland, 2010. For various community programs.
$6,000,000 to China Youth Development Foundation, Beijing, China, 2010. For Disaster Relief for the Sichuan Earthquake.
$6,000,000 to Coca-Cola Africa Foundation, Manzini, Swaziland, 2011. To provide support for strategic community partnership programs via Safe Water for Africa, launched by The Coca-Cola Africa Foundation, in partnership with Diageo plc, the International Finance Corporation and WaterHealth International. SWA will work with communities to drive the expansion of WHI's innovative water service delivery model across the continent. The grant provides seed funding to deliver sustainable safe water access for communities across Ghana, Nigeria, and Liberia in 2011, with new country programs expected in 2012 and beyond.
$3,000,000 to China Youth Development Foundation, Beijing, China, 2011. For Disaster Relief for the Sichuan Earthquake - China.
$3,000,000 to Global Environment and Technology Foundation, Arlington, VA, 2011. For the Replenish Africa Initiative (RAIN) by working with local stakeholders to develop community-based water projects in select African countries.
$2,000,000 to Better World Fund, Washington, DC, 2010. For Inclusive Community Based Water Management Program, with United Nations Foundation.
$1,720,000 to Coca-Cola Environmental Educational Foundation, Tokyo, Japan, 2010. For Foundation Programs.
$1,000,000 to Atlanta International School, Atlanta, GA, 2010. For See Beyond: The Campaign for Atlanta International School.
$1,000,000 to Community Foundation for Greater Atlanta, Atlanta, GA, 2011. For Centers of Hope Initiative.
$640,000 to AVINA Americas, Washington, DC, 2010. For Regional Recycling Initiative for Latin America.
$250,000 to Pakistan Red Crescent Society, Lahore, Pakistan, 2010. For Disaster Relief.
$125,000 to World Wildlife Fund Canada, Toronto, Canada, 2011. For the establishment of new water flow management plans and start restoration work along the St. Lawrence River in Canada.
$116,000 to China Youth Development Foundation, Beijing, China, 2010. For Project Hope Teacher Training Program and Coca-Cola Hope Star Scholarship Program.
$100,000 to American Red Cross National Headquarters, Washington, DC, 2011. For Joplin Missouri Tornado Relief.
$100,000 to National Park Foundation, Washington, DC, 2010. For Active Trails.
$100,000 to Recycling Congress of Ontario, Toronto, Canada, 2010. For Zero Waste Event Certification Program.
$100,000 to Sugar Industry Foundation, Makati City, Philippines, 2011. For construction of School Buildings at Quezon National High School -Annex situated at Brgy Butong, Municipality of Butong, province of Bukindnon.
$75,000 to Vive en Forma, Lake Villa, IL, 2011. For Vive en Forma.

Coca-Cola Scholars Foundation, Inc.

P.O. Box 442
Atlanta, GA 30301-0442 (404) 733-5420
FAX: (404) 733-5439;
E-mail: questions@coca-colascholars.org; Toll-free tel.: (800) 306-2653; address for Coca-Cola Two-Year College Scholarship: P.O. Box 1615, Atlanta, GA 30301-1615, tel.: (800) 306-2653;
URL: http://www.coca-colascholars.org

Establishment information: Established in 1986 in GA.
Contact: Patricia A. Ross, V.P. and Secy.
Financial data (yr. ended 12/31/10): Revenue, $4,723,718; assets, $34,953,260 (M); gifts received, $2,430,985; expenditures, $6,304,552; program services expenses, $5,412,997; giving activities include $400,000 for 2 grants (high: $350,000; low: $50,000), $3,492,361 for 1,132 grants to individuals and $1,495,636 for foundation-administered programs.
Purpose and activities: The foundation presents awards to well-rounded, college-bound high school students with highly developed ethics and goals.
Fields of interest: Youth.

Programs:

Coca-Cola Scholars Program: Seniors at secondary schools throughout the United States who meet eligibility requirements may apply for one of 250 four-year merit-based scholarships. Fifty of these are four-year $20,000 scholarships ($5,000 per year for four years), while 200 are designated as four-year $10,000 scholarships ($2,500 per year for four years). Scholarships can be used at any accredited U.S. college or university. Eligible applicants must: be current high school (or home-schooled) seniors attending schools in the U.S. (or select Department of Defense schools); be U.S. citizens, nationals, permanent residents, temporary residents, refugees, asylees, Cuban-Haitian emigrants, or humanitarian parolees; anticipate completion of a high-school diploma at the time of application; plan to pursue a degree at an accredited U.S. post-secondary institution; and carry a minimum 3.0 GPA at the end of their junior year of high school.

Educator of Distinction: Two hundred and fifty educators are designated annually by 250

Coca-Cola Scholars in recognition of excellence in teaching and mentoring.

GRADS (Get Ready and Do Something): The mission of this program is to be a quality community service endeavor that prepares teens for the challenges of life beyond high school by promoting education and encouraging self-reliance through an engaging, interactive method.

Type of support: Scholarships—to individuals.
Geographic limitations: Giving on a national basis.
Support limitations: No scholarships to Coca-Cola employees or employees' dependents.
Publications: Annual report; Application guidelines; Informational brochure (including application guidelines).
Application information: Applications accepted. Application form required.
Initial approach: Complete online application form; write to or telephone foundation for application information for Coca-Cola Two-Year College Scholarship
Copies of proposal: 1
Board meeting date(s): Quarterly
Deadline(s): May 31 for Coca-Cola Two-Year College Scholarships; Oct. 31 for Coca-Cola Scholars
Final notification: Mid-Dec.
Officers and Directors:* Claude B. Nielsen*, Chair.; J. Mark Davis, Pres.; Jane H. Hopkins, V.P., Finance; Patricia A. Ross, V.P. and Secy.; J.A.M. Douglas, Jr.; William Douglas III; Ingrid Saunders Jones; Vicki R. Palmer; Jack Pelo; Hagar Rand; Edwin C. "Cookie" Rice; H.L. Williams, Jr.; Brian Wynne.
Number of staff: 7 full-time professional.
EIN: 581686023

863
Coca-Cola Enterprises Inc.

2500 Windy Ridge Pkwy.
Atlanta, GA 30339 (678) 260-3000
FAX: (302) 655-5049

Company URL: http://www.cokecce.com
Establishment information: Established in 1944.
Company type: Public company
Company ticker symbol and exchange: CCE/NYSE
International Securities Identification Number: US19122T1097
Business activities: Produces, markets, sells, and distributes nonalcoholic beverages.
Business type (SIC): Beverages
Financial profile for 2012: Number of employees, 13,000; assets, $9,510,000,000; sales volume, $8,062,000,000; pre-tax net income, $837,000,000; expenses, $7,134,000,000; liabilities, $6,817,000,000
Fortune 1000 ranking: 2012—339th in revenues, 271st in profits, and 403rd in assets
Forbes 2000 ranking: 2012—1083rd in sales, 842nd in profits, and 1509th in assets
Corporate officers: John F. Brock, Chair. and C.E.O.; William W. Douglas III, Exec. V.P. and C.F.O.; Esat Sezer, Sr. V.P. and C.I.O.; John R. Parker, Jr., Sr. V.P. and Genl. Counsel; Laura Brightwell, Sr. V.P., Public Affairs and Comms.; Pamela O. Kimmet, Sr. V.P., Human Resources; William T. Plybon III, V.P. and Secy.; Joyce King-Lavinder, V.P. and Treas.; Suzanne D. Patterson, V.P., Cont., and C.A.O.; Jacques Purnode, V.P., Finance; Nigel Miller, V.P., Human Resources
Board of directors: John F. Brock, Chair.; Jan Bennink; Calvin Darden; L. Phillip Humann; Orrin H. Ingram II; Thomas H. Johnson; Suzanne B. Labarge; Veronique Morali; Andrea L. Saia; Garry Watts; Curtis R. Welling; Phoebe A. Wood
Subsidiaries: BCI Coca-Cola Bottling Co. of Los Angeles, Los Angeles, CA; The Laredo Coca-Cola Bottling Co., Inc., Laredo, TX
International operations: Canada; France; Luxembourg; United Kingdom
Giving statement: Giving through the Coca-Cola Enterprises Inc. Corporate Giving Program and the Coca-Cola Enterprises Charitable Foundation.
Company EIN: 580503352

Coca-Cola Enterprises Inc. Corporate Giving Program

2500 Windy Ridge Pkwy.
Atlanta, GA 30339-5677 (678) 260-3000
URL: http://www.cokecce.com/corporate-responsibility-sustainability

Purpose and activities: Coca-Cola Enterprises makes charitable contributions to nonprofit organizations involved with water conservation, recycling, healthy active living, youth development, and diversity. Support is given primarily in areas of company operations in Belgium, Great Britain, France, Luxembourg, Monaco, and the Netherlands.
Fields of interest: Environment, recycling; Environment, water resources; Public health, physical fitness; Nutrition; Youth development; Civil/human rights, equal rights; General charitable giving.
International interests: Belgium; England; France; Luxembourg; Monaco; Netherlands; Scotland; Wales.
Type of support: Employee volunteer services; General/operating support; In-kind gifts; Program development.
Geographic limitations: Giving primarily in areas of company operations in Belgium, Great Britain, France, Luxembourg, Monaco, and the Netherlands.

The Coca-Cola Enterprises Charitable Foundation

2500 Windy Ridge Pkwy., Ste. 1500
Atlanta, GA 30339-5676
Application address: c/o Coca-Cola Scholars Foundation, P.O. Box 1615, Atlanta, GA 30301-1615

Establishment information: Established in 2002.
Donor: Coca-Cola Enterprises Inc.
Financial data (yr. ended 12/31/10): Assets, $1,556,418 (M); expenditures, $650,938; qualifying distributions, $650,000; giving activities include $650,000 for grants to individuals.
Purpose and activities: The foundation awards college scholarships to children of employees of Coca-Cola Enterprises and its subsidiaries.
Fields of interest: Vocational education; Higher education.
Program:

CCE Johnston Legacy Scholarship: The foundation annually awards one-time $5,000 scholarships to high school seniors who are children of current or part-time employees of Coca-Cola Enterprises or its subsidiaries who plan to pursue a degree at an accredited college or university. Applicants with a 3.0 GPA are also eligible for one of ten four-year scholarships of up to $20,000.

Type of support: Employee-related scholarships.
Geographic limitations: Giving primarily in areas of company operations.
Application information: Applications not accepted. Contributes only through employee-related scholarships.
Officer and Directors:* John H. Downs*, Chair.; Laura Brightwell; Bill Douglas; Pam Kimmet; Bill Plybon; Greg Whitson.
EIN: 582660344

864
Coghlin Companies, Inc.

17 Briden St.
Worcester, MA 01605-2639
(508) 753-2354

Company URL: http://www.columbiatech.com/home/page.asp?pn=financial
Establishment information: Established in 1885.
Company type: Private company
Business activities: Manufactures electronic equipment.
Business type (SIC): Electronic and other electrical equipment and components
Corporate officers: James W. Coghlin, Pres. and C.E.O.; Christopher Palermo, C.F.O.
Giving statement: Giving through the Coghlin Family Foundation.

The Coghlin Family Foundation

17 Briden St.
Worcester, MA 01605-2639 (508) 713-4714

Establishment information: Established in 2000 in MA.
Donor: Coghlin Cos., Inc.
Contact: James W. Coghlin, Sr., Pres.
Financial data (yr. ended 12/31/11): Assets, $160,844 (M); gifts received, $100,000; expenditures, $32,522; qualifying distributions, $30,356; giving activities include $30,356 for grants.
Purpose and activities: The foundation supports hospitals and organizations involved with higher education and human services.
Fields of interest: Education; Recreation; Youth development.
Type of support: General/operating support; Scholarship funds.
Support limitations: No grants to individuals.
Application information: Applications accepted. Application form required.
Initial approach: Letter
Deadline(s): None
Officer and Trustees:* James W. Coghlin, Sr.*, Pres.; Christopher Coghlin; James W. Coghlin, Jr.
EIN: 043519886

865
Coghlin Construction Services, Inc.

100 Prescott St.
Worcester, MA 01605-1713
(508) 793-0300

Company URL: http://www.coghlin.com
Establishment information: Established in 1885.
Company type: Private company
Business activities: Provides electrical, telecommunications, and computer networking contract construction services.
Business type (SIC): Contractors/electrical work
Corporate officers: Susan M. Mailman, C.E.O.; Steve Wentzell, C.F.O.; Rita Brantl, C.I.O.; Cathleen E. Coonan, Cont.

Subsidiaries: Coghlin Electrical Contractors, Inc., Worcester, MA; Coghlin Network Svcs., Worcester, MA
Giving statement: Giving through the Coghlin Services Fund.

Coghlin Services Fund

100 Prescott St.
Worcester, MA 01605-1713 (508) 793-0373

Establishment information: Established in 2000 in MA as successor to the Coghlin Fund.
Donors: Coghlin Construction Services, Inc.; Coghlin Electrical Contractors Inc.
Contact: Susan M. Mailman, Tr.
Financial data (yr. ended 12/31/11): Assets, $740,796 (M); gifts received, $25,031; expenditures, $174,876; qualifying distributions, $160,888; giving activities include $160,888 for 53 grants (high: $53,250; low: $100).
Purpose and activities: The fund supports organizations involved with human services and religion.
Fields of interest: Human services; United Ways and Federated Giving Programs; Religion.
Type of support: General/operating support.
Support limitations: No grants to individuals.
Application information: Applications accepted. Application form required. Applicants should submit the following:
1) detailed description of project and amount of funding requested
Initial approach: Letter
Deadline(s): None
Trustees: Edwin B. Coghlin, Jr.; Susan M. Mailman; Stephen F. Wentzell.
EIN: 043517737
Selected grants: The following grants are a representative sample of this grantmaker's funding activity:
$50,000 to Anna Maria College, Paxton, MA, 2010.
$5,195 to Chamber of Commerce of Worcester, Worcester, MA, 2010.
$4,500 to Fallon Clinic Foundation, Worcester, MA, 2010.
$3,500 to Youth Opportunities Upheld, Worcester, MA, 2010.
$1,300 to Childrens Friend, Worcester, MA, 2010.
$1,200 to Boy Scouts of America, Worcester, MA, 2010.

866
J.H. Cohn LLP

(formerly J.H. Cohn & Company)
4 Becker Farm Rd.
Roseland, NJ 07068-1600 (973) 228-3500

Company URL: http://www.jhcohn.com/About.aspx
Establishment information: Established in 1919.
Company type: Private company
Business activities: Provides accounting services.
Business type (SIC): Accounting, auditing, and bookkeeping services
Corporate officers: Thomas J. Marino, C.E.O.; Domenick Esposito, C.O.O.; Edward Betzler, Cont.
Giving statement: Giving through the J. H. Cohn & Company Foundation.

J. H. Cohn & Company Foundation

c/o Peter H. Alpert, Inc.
601 South Figueroa St., Ste. 2330
Los Angeles, CA 90017-5704 (213) 687-1510

Establishment information: Established in 1954.
Donors: J.H. Cohn & Co.; Benjamin Alpert†.
Contact: Peter H. Alpert, Mgr.
Financial data (yr. ended 03/31/11): Assets, $27,649 (M); expenditures, $2,590; qualifying distributions, $2,275; giving activities include $2,000 for 1 grant.
Purpose and activities: The foundation supports organizations involved with Judaism.
Fields of interest: Jewish federated giving programs; Jewish agencies & synagogues.
Type of support: General/operating support.
Geographic limitations: Giving primarily in CA.
Support limitations: No support for private foundations. No grants to individuals.
Application information: Applications accepted. Application form required. Applicants should submit the following:
1) brief history of organization and description of its mission
2) detailed description of project and amount of funding requested
Initial approach: Letter
Deadline(s): None
Officer: Peter H. Alpert, Mgr.
Trustee: Richard Alpert.
EIN: 226059842

867
Cole Haan Holdings, Inc.

1 Cole Haan Dr.
Yarmouth, ME 04096-6709 (207) 846-2500

Company URL: http://www.colehaan.com
Establishment information: Established in 1928.
Company type: Subsidiary of a public company
Business activities: Manufactures dress and casual footwear and accessories.
Business type (SIC): Leather footwear
Corporate officers: Dave McTague, Co-C.E.O.; James Seuss, Pres. and Co-C.E.O.; Chad Furlong, C.I.O.
Giving statement: Giving through the Mark Goodwin Memorial Trust.

Mark Goodwin Memorial Trust

c/o KeyBank
4900 Tiedeman Rd., OH-01-49-0150
Brooklyn, OH 44144-2302 (518) 257-9661

Establishment information: Established in 1991 in ME.
Donors: Cole Haan Holdings, Inc.; Yarmouth Redemption Center.
Contact: Christine Moughton
Financial data (yr. ended 08/31/12): Assets, $176,272 (M); expenditures, $22,282; qualifying distributions, $20,072; giving activities include $18,797 for 23 grants to individuals (high: $2,000; low: $120).
Purpose and activities: The foundation awards college scholarships to employees and children of employees of Cole Haan Holdings.
Fields of interest: Education.
Type of support: Employee-related scholarships.
Geographic limitations: Giving limited to areas of company operations.
Application information: Applications not accepted. Contributes only through employee-related scholarships.
Trustee: KeyBank N.A.
EIN: 223226157

868
Cole, Schotz, Meisel, Forman & Leonard, P.A.

Court Plz. N.
25 Main St.
Hackensack, NJ 07601-7015
(201) 489-3000

Company URL: http://www.coleschotz.com
Establishment information: Established in 1928.
Company type: Private company
Business activities: Operates law firm.
Business type (SIC): Legal services
Corporate officer: Larry Rabinowitz, Partner
Offices: Wilmington, DE; Baltimore, MD; Hackensack, NJ; New York, NY; Fort Worth, TX
Giving statement: Giving through the Cole, Schotz, Meisel, Forman & Leonard, P.A. Pro Bono Program.

Cole, Schotz, Meisel, Forman & Leonard, P.A. Pro Bono Program

Court Plz. N.
25 Main St.
Hackensack, NJ 07601-7015 (201) 525-6267
E-mail: dkohane@coleshotz.com; Additional tel.: (201) 489-3000, fax:(201) 489-1536; URL: http://www.coleschotz.com/about-initiative.html

Contact: David M. Kohane, Member
Purpose and activities: Cole Schotz makes charitable contributions to nonprofit organizations involved with child development and education, and on a case by case basis.
Fields of interest: Education, early childhood education; Child development, education; Legal services; Food services; Children, services; Child development, services; Family services; General charitable giving.
Type of support: Employee volunteer services; Pro bono services - legal; Sponsorships.
Application information: The Pro Bono Committee manages the pro-bono program.

869
Colgate-Palmolive Company

300 Park Ave.
New York, NY 10022-7402 (212) 310-2000

Company URL: http://www.colgate.com
Establishment information: Established in 1806.
Company type: Public company
Company ticker symbol and exchange: CL/NYSE
International Securities Identification Number: US1941621039
Business activities: Manufactures consumer products.
Business type (SIC): Soaps, cleaners, and toiletries
Financial profile for 2012: Number of employees, 37,700; assets, $13,394,000,000; sales volume, $17,085,000,000; pre-tax net income, $3,874,000,000; expenses, $13,196,000,000; liabilities, $11,205,000,000
Fortune 1000 ranking: 2012—165th in revenues, 79th in profits, and 321st in assets
Forbes 2000 ranking: 2012—547th in sales, 232nd in profits, and 1258th in assets
Corporate officers: Ian M. Cook, Chair.; Franck J. Moison, C.O.O.; Dennis Hickey, C.F.O.; Tom Greene, C.I.O.; Daniel Marsili, Sr. V.P., Human Resources; Elaine Paik, V.P. and Corp. Treas.; Victoria Dolan, V.P. and Corp. Cont.; Jan Guifarro, V.P., Corp. Comms.; Andrew D. Hendry, Secy.

Board of directors: Ian M. Cook, Chair.; Nikesh Arora; John T. Cahill; Helene D. Gayle; Ellen M. Hancock; Joseph Jimenez; Richard J. Kogan; Delano E. Lewis; J. Pedro Reinhard; Stephen I. Sadove
Subsidiaries: Colgate-Hoyt Laboratories, Canton, MA; Colgate-Palmolive International Div., New York, NY; CPL Industries Inc., Tenafly, NJ; Hill's Pet Products, Inc., Topeka, KS; Mennen, Morristown, NJ; Softsoap, Chaska, MN; Technology Center, Piscataway, NJ; Tom's of Maine, Inc., Kennebunk, ME
Plants: Jeffersonville, IN; Kansas City, KS; Bowling Green, KY; Morristown, NJ; Cambridge, OH
International operations: Argentina; Australia; Belgium; Brazil; British Virgin Islands; Canada; China; Czech Republic; Denmark; Dominican Republic; Ecuador; France; Germany; Greece; Guatemala; India; Ireland; Italy; Japan; Malaysia; Mexico; Morocco and the Western Sahara; Netherlands; New Zealand; Peru; Philippines; Portugal; Senegal; Singapore; South Africa; Spain; Sweden; Switzerland; Thailand; United Kingdom; Uruguay; Vietnam
Giving statement: Giving through the Colgate-Palmolive Company Contributions Program.
Company EIN: 131815595

Colgate-Palmolive Company Contributions Program

c/o Contribs. Dept.
300 Park Ave.
New York, NY 10022-7402
URL: http://www.colgate.com/app/Colgate/US/Corp/CommunityPrograms/HomePage.cvsp
Additional URL: http://HealthyColgate

Financial data (yr. ended 12/31/10): Total giving, $17,809,000, including $17,809,000 for grants.
Purpose and activities: Colgate-Palmolive makes charitable contributions to nonprofit organizations involved with education and youth. Support is given on a national and international basis, primarily in areas of company operations.
Fields of interest: Higher education; Education; Dental care; Health care, rural areas; Public health; Health care, patient services; Children/youth, services Children; Youth; Minorities; Young adults, female; Economically disadvantaged.
Programs:

Bright Smiles, Bright Futures Global Program: Through the Bright Smiles, Bright Futures Global Program, Colgate supports programs designed to promote oral health through education and prevention by providing educational materials and dental screenings.

Colgate Women's Games: Colgate Women's Games gives girls and young women the opportunity to participate in athletic competitions, with the aim of promoting self-esteem, teamwork, and the importance of education. Finalists compete for trophies and educational grants-in-aid.

Give Kids a Smile: Colgate, in collaboration with the American Dental Association, provides education, along with preventative and restorative care, to low-income children who do not have access to dental care.

Type of support: Donated products; Employee matching gifts; General/operating support.
Geographic limitations: Giving on a national and international basis, primarily in areas of company operations.
Application information: Applications accepted. Proposals should be no longer than 2 pages. Application form not required. Applicants should submit the following:
1) copy of IRS Determination Letter
2) brief history of organization and description of its mission
3) detailed description of project and amount of funding requested

Initial approach: Proposal to headquarters
Deadline(s): None
Final notification: Following review

870
COLHOC L.P.

(also known as Columbus Blue Jackets)
Nationwide Arena
200 W. Nationwide Blvd., 3rd Fl.
Columbus, OH 43215 (614) 246-4625

Company URL: http://www.bluejackets.com
Establishment information: Established in 1997.
Company type: Private company
Business activities: Operates professional ice hockey club.
Business type (SIC): Commercial sports
Corporate officers: John P. McConnell, Chair.; Michael A. Priest, Pres.; Larry Hoepfner, Exec. V.P., Opers.; T.J. LaMendola, C.F.O.; Gregory Kirstein, Sr. V.P. and Genl. Counsel; J.D. Kershaw, V.P., Mktg.; Todd Sharrock, V.P., Comms.; Wendy Rohaly, Cont.
Board of director: John P. McConnell, Chair.
Giving statement: Giving through the Columbus Blue Jackets Foundation.

Columbus Blue Jackets Foundation

200 W. Nationwide Blvd.
Columbus, OH 43215-2563 (614) 246-3707
FAX: (614) 246-3738;
E-mail: cbjfoundation@bluejackets.com;
URL: http://www.bluejacketsfoundation.org/

Establishment information: Established in 2000 in OH.
Contact: Jen Bowden, Exec. Dir.
Financial data (yr. ended 12/31/11): Revenue, $478,652; assets, $1,265,139 (M); gifts received, $33,102; expenditures, $613,916; giving activities include $460,676 for grants and $20,000 for grants to individuals.
Purpose and activities: The foundation donates time, resources and financial support to organizations committed to meeting the educational, cultural, health, and wellness needs of people throughout central Ohio.
Fields of interest: Education; Public health; Health care; Cancer; Pediatrics.
Program:

Scholarships: Scholarships are available to high school seniors planning to attend a two- or four-year accredited college or university in the U.S. as a full-time student, no later than the fall after the applicant graduates high school. Applicants must have a 3.0 GPA or better, and have demonstrated leadership, positive attitude, and credible character toward both their schools and their hockey teams. Applicants must be a member of the Thomas Worthington, Worthington Kilbourne, Dublin Scioto, Dublin Coffman, Upper Arlington, St. Charles, Hilliard, Olentangy, Westerville, Gahanna, Northeast Storm, Pickerington/Reynoldsburg, Newark, or Athens high school hockey team.

Type of support: Building/renovation; Cause-related marketing; Donated equipment; Equipment; Matching/challenge support; Program development; Research; Scholarship funds; Scholarships—to individuals; Sponsorships.
Geographic limitations: Giving limited to OH, with a focus on central OH.
Support limitations: No support for religious or political organizations.
Publications: Annual report; Application guidelines; Grants list.
Application information: Applications accepted. Application form required. Applicants should submit the following:
1) how project will be sustained once grantmaker support is completed
2) name, address and phone number of organization
3) copy of IRS Determination Letter
4) brief history of organization and description of its mission
5) how project's results will be evaluated or measured
6) contact person
7) copy of current year's organizational budget and/or project budget
8) listing of additional sources and amount of support

Initial approach: Download application
Copies of proposal: 1
Board meeting date(s): Quarterly
Deadline(s): Mar. 1
Final notification: End of every hockey season

Officers and Directors:* John P. McConnell*, Pres.; Cathy M. Lyttle*, V.P.; Greg Kirstein*, Secy.; Thomas J. LaMendola*, Treas.; Jen Bowden, Exec. Dir.; Antoinette Mongillo.
EIN: 311688700

871
Collective Brands, Inc.

(formerly Payless ShoeSource, Inc.)
3231 S.E. 6th Ave.
P.O. Box 1189
Topeka, KS 66607-2207 (785) 233-5171

Company URL: http://www.collectivebrands.com/
Establishment information: Established in 1956.
Company type: Public company
Company ticker symbol and exchange: PSS/NYSE
Business activities: Operates shoe stores.
Business type (SIC): Shoe stores
Financial profile for 2012: Number of employees, 14,100; assets, $2,047,200,000; sales volume, $3,461,700,000; pre-tax net income, -$65,800,000; expenses, $3,489,000,000; liabilities, $1,402,400,000
Corporate officers: D. Scott Olivet, Chair.; W. Paul Jones, Co-C.E.O.; Michael J. Massey, Pres., Genl. Counsel, Secy., and Co-C.E.O.; Douglas J. Treff, Exec. V.P. and C.A.O.; Douglas G. Boessen, Sr. V.P., C.F.O., and Treas.; Jeff Lauro, Sr. V.P. and C.I.O.; Betty J. Click, Sr. V.P., Human Resources
Board of directors: D. Scott Olivet, Chair.; Daniel Boggan, Jr.; Myldred H. Mangum; Richard L. Markee; John F. McGovern; Robert F. Moran; Matthew A. Ouimet; Michael A. Weiss; Robert C. Wheeler
Subsidiary: The Stride Rite Corporation, Lexington, MA
International operations: Australia; Bermuda; British Virgin Islands; Canada; Cayman Islands; China; Colombia; Dominican Republic; Ecuador; El Salvador; Germany; Guatemala; Honduras; Hong Kong; Ireland; Netherlands; Nicaragua; Panama; Spain; Trinidad & Tobago; United Kingdom; Uruguay
Giving statement: Giving through the Collective Brands Foundation.
Company EIN: 431813160

Collective Brands Foundation

(formerly Payless ShoeSource Foundation)
3231 S.E. 6th Ave.
Topeka, KS 66607-2260 (877) 902-4437
E-mail: grants@greaterhorizons.org; URL: http://www.collectivebrands.com/foundation

Establishment information: Established in 1998 in KS and MO.
Donor: Payless ShoeSource, Inc.
Contact: Shirley A. Steele
Financial data (yr. ended 01/31/11): Assets, $562,143 (M); gifts received, $275,000; expenditures, $316,885; qualifying distributions, $316,760; giving activities include $316,760 for grants.
Purpose and activities: The foundation supports programs designed to address women's preventative health; promote children's physical activity and fitness; improve the lives of children and youth in need; preserve the environment; and support the footwear industry.
Fields of interest: Arts; Education; Environment; Public health, physical fitness; Health care; Children/youth, services; Human services; Business/industry; United Ways and Federated Giving Programs Children; Women.
Type of support: Annual campaigns; Building/renovation; Capital campaigns; Continuing support; In-kind gifts; Program development; Scholarship funds; Sponsorships.
Geographic limitations: Giving primarily in areas of company operations, with emphasis on Redlands, CA, Denver, CO, Topeka, the Kansas City metropolitan area, and Lawrence, KS, greater Boston and Lexington, MA, New York, NY, and Brookville, OH.
Support limitations: No support for private charities or foundations, private schools, or religious or political organizations. No grants to individuals, or for capital campaigns, debt reduction, travel, or conferences.
Publications: Application guidelines.
Application information: Applications accepted. Application form required. Applicants should submit the following:
1) name, address and phone number of organization
2) copy of IRS Determination Letter
3) brief history of organization and description of its mission
4) copy of most recent annual report/audited financial statement/990
5) detailed description of project and amount of funding requested
6) contact person
7) explanation of why grantmaker is considered an appropriate donor for project
8) results expected from proposed grant
9) copy of current year's organizational budget and/or project budget

Initial approach: Complete online application for grants and sponsorship requests
Board meeting date(s): Quarterly
Deadline(s): Aug. 15
Final notification: 10 weeks

Officers and Directors:* Betty J. Click*, Pres.; Curtis Sneden*, V.P. and Secy.; Gary C. Madsen*, V.P. and Treas.; Rob Hallam, V.P.
EIN: 481196508
Selected grants: The following grants are a representative sample of this grantmaker's funding activity:
$90,000 to United Way of Greater Topeka, Topeka, KS, 2011.
$41,500 to Greater Horizons, Kansas City, MO, 2011. To support programs.
$25,000 to Kansas Childrens Discovery Center, Topeka, KS, 2011. For general support.
$15,000 to Community Foundation of Middle Tennessee, Nashville, TN, 2011.
$7,500 to New School, New York, NY, 2011.
$5,000 to Germantown Community Theater, Germantown, TN, 2011. To support programs.
$5,000 to Kansas Childrens Service League, Topeka, KS, 2011.
$5,000 to Special Olympics Kansas, Mission, KS, 2011. To support programs.
$3,000 to Topeka Youth Project, Topeka, KS, 2011.
$2,500 to Rose Brooks Center, Kansas City, MO, 2011.

872
Collette Travel Service, Inc.

162 Middle St.
Pawtucket, RI 02860-1057 (800) 340-5158

Company URL: http://www.collettevacations.com
Establishment information: Established in 1918.
Company type: Private company
Business activities: Tour operator.
Business type (SIC): Travel and tour arrangers
Corporate officers: Daniel J. Sullivan, Jr., Pres. and C.E.O.; John Galvin, C.F.O.
Giving statement: Giving through the Collette Foundation and the Alice I. Sullivan Charitable Foundation.

Collette Foundation

162 Middle St.
Pawtucket, RI 02860-1013 (401) 642-4576
E-mail: info@collettefoundation.org; URL: http://www.collettefoundation.org/

Establishment information: Established in 2007 in RI.
Donors: Jack Carley; Collette Travel Service, Inc.
Contact: Allison Villasenor, Prog. Mgr.
Financial data (yr. ended 12/31/11): Assets, $823,689 (M); gifts received, $219,315; expenditures, $299,707; qualifying distributions, $294,180; giving activities include $294,180 for grants.
Purpose and activities: The foundation supports programs designed to improve and extend the quality of life of children in worldwide destinations with which Collette explores.
Fields of interest: Education; Human services; International relief Children; Economically disadvantaged.
Type of support: Annual campaigns; Building/renovation; Continuing support; Employee volunteer services; Equipment; General/operating support; Matching/challenge support; Program development; Sponsorships.
Geographic limitations: Giving primarily in areas of company operations in Brazil, Cambodia, China, Costa Rica, Kenya, Mexico, Peru, and South Africa.
Support limitations: No grants to individuals.
Application information: Applications not accepted. Contributes only to pre-selected organizations.
Directors: John Galvin; Michael Horan.
Trustee: Daniel J. Sullivan, Jr.
EIN: 208256603

The Alice I. Sullivan Charitable Foundation

162 Middle St.
Pawtucket, RI 02860-1013 (401) 642-4655
E-mail: lkelly@collettevacations.com; Additional Address: Collette Vacations, Community Rels. Dept., 180 Middle St., Pawtucket, RI 02860, Kathy Sullivan, tel.: (401) 727-9000 x3222, e-mail: ksullivan@collettevacations.com

Establishment information: Established in 2007 in RI.
Donors: Collette Travel Service, Inc.; Tides Foundation.
Contact: Lynne Kelly, Mgr., Community Rels.
Financial data (yr. ended 12/31/11): Assets, $312,310 (M); gifts received, $452,930; expenditures, $494,619; qualifying distributions, $491,084; giving activities include $491,084 for 117 grants (high: $50,000; low: $50).
Purpose and activities: The foundation supports organizations involved with arts and culture, education, health, hunger, athletics, human services, and community development.
Fields of interest: Performing arts, theater; Arts; Secondary school/education; Higher education; Education; Hospitals (general); Health care; Food services; Athletics/sports, amateur leagues; Boys & girls clubs; Children/youth, services; Family services; Homeless, human services; Human services; Urban/community development; Community/economic development.
Type of support: Annual campaigns; Capital campaigns; Employee volunteer services; Program development; Scholarship funds; Sponsorships.
Geographic limitations: Giving primarily in RI.
Support limitations: No grants to individuals.
Application information: Applications not accepted. Contributes only to pre-selected organizations.
Directors: John Galvin; Michael Horan.
Trustee: Daniel J. Sullivan, Jr.
EIN: 208256471
Selected grants: The following grants are a representative sample of this grantmaker's funding activity:
$2,000 to American Heart Association, Dallas, TX, 2010.
$2,000 to Indiana University, Bloomington, IN, 2010. For scholarships.
$1,000 to Brown University, Providence, RI, 2010. For scholarships.

873
Collins Development Corporation

11750 Sorrento Valley Rd., Ste. 2
San Diego, CA 92121-1025
(858) 481-7767

Establishment information: Established in 1962.
Company type: Private company
Business activities: Develops commercial real estate.
Business type (SIC): Real estate subdividers and developers
Corporate officer: Harry A. Collins, Pres.
Giving statement: Giving through the Collins Companies Foundation.

The Collins Companies Foundation

11750 Sorrento Valley Rd., Ste. 209
San Diego, CA 92121-1085

Establishment information: Established in 1990 in CA.
Donor: Collins Development Corp.
Financial data (yr. ended 12/31/11): Assets, $81,629 (M); gifts received, $100,000; expenditures, $19,049; qualifying distributions, $17,400; giving activities include $17,400 for 2 grants (high: $12,000; low: $5,400).

Purpose and activities: The foundation supports organizations involved with secondary and higher education.
Fields of interest: Secondary school/education; Higher education; American Red Cross.
Type of support: General/operating support; Scholarship funds.
Geographic limitations: Giving limited to San Diego, CA.
Support limitations: No grants to individuals.
Application information: Applications not accepted. Unsolicited requests for funds not accepted.
Officers: E. Tyler Miller, Jr., Pres.; William A. Tribolet, Secy.; Robert E. Petersen, Treas.
EIN: 330389001

874
Colonial Life & Accident Insurance Company

(also known as Colonial Supplemental Insurance)
1200 Colonial Life Blvd. W.
P.O. Box 1365
Columbia, SC 29202-1365 (803) 798-7000

Company URL: http://www.coloniallife.com
Establishment information: Established in 1939.
Company type: Subsidiary of a public company
Business activities: Sells personal, accident, and life insurance.
Business type (SIC): Insurance/life; insurance/accident and health
Financial profile for 2009: Number of employees, 950; sales volume, $1,130,000,000
Corporate officers: Randall C. Horn, Pres. and C.E.O.; Tim Arnold, Sr. V.P., Sales and Mktg.
Giving statement: Giving through the Colonial Supplemental Insurance Corporate Giving Program.

Colonial Supplemental Insurance Corporate Giving Program

1200 Colonial Life Blvd.
Columbia, SC 29210-7670
E-mail: ammcgehee@coloniallife.com; URL: http://www.coloniallife.com/About/CorporateSocialResponsibility.aspx

Contact: Marie McGehee, Mgr., Community Rels.
Financial data (yr. ended 12/31/10): Total giving, $705,000, including $705,000 for grants.
Purpose and activities: Colonial Supplemental Insurance makes charitable contributions to nonprofit organizations involved with arts and culture, education, healthcare, and community and economic development. Support is given primarily in Columbia, South Carolina.
Fields of interest: Arts; Education; Health care; Community/economic development.
Type of support: Employee matching gifts; Employee volunteer services; General/operating support; In-kind gifts; Loaned talent; Sponsorships; Use of facilities.
Geographic limitations: Giving primarily in Columbia, SC.
Publications: Corporate giving report.
Administrator: Marie McGehee, Community and Customer Rels. Consultant.
Number of staff: 2 full-time professional.

875
Colonial Oil Industries, Inc.

101 N. Lathrop Ave.
Savannah, GA 31415 (912) 236-1331

Company URL: http://www.colonialgroupinc.com
Establishment information: Established in 1921.
Company type: Subsidiary of a private company
Business activities: Sells petroleum wholesale.
Business type (SIC): Petroleum and petroleum products—wholesale
Financial profile for 2011: Number of employees, 900; sales volume, $5,200,000,000
Corporate officers: Robert H. Demere, Jr., Pres. and C.E.O.; Francis A. Brown, C.F.O.; Bob May, C.I.O.; William A. Baker, V.P., Opers.; Charles H. Hodges, Treas.
Subsidiaries: Chatham Towing Co., Savannah, GA; Colonial Drilling & Exploration Corp., Savannah, GA; Colonial Marine Industries, Inc., Savannah, GA; Colonial Terminals, Inc., Savannah, GA; Emark Stations, Inc., Savannah, GA; Interstate Stations, Inc., Savannah, GA
Giving statement: Giving through the Colonial Foundation, Inc.

Colonial Foundation, Inc.

P.O. Box 576
Savannah, GA 31402-0576 (912) 236-1331
Application address: 1010 N. Lathrop Ave., Savannah, GA 31415

Establishment information: Established in 1986 in GA.
Donor: Colonial Oil Industries, Inc.
Contact: Frances A. Brown, V.P., Finance and Treas.
Financial data (yr. ended 12/31/11): Assets, $6,985,922 (M); gifts received, $800,267; expenditures, $1,333,120; qualifying distributions, $1,295,161; giving activities include $1,289,051 for 74 grants (high: $100,000; low: $200) and $6,110 for 19 employee matching gifts.
Purpose and activities: The foundation supports organizations involved with arts and culture, education, health, cancer, hunger, human services, and business promotion.
Fields of interest: Museums; Historic preservation/historical societies; Arts; Elementary/secondary education; Higher education; Engineering school/education; Education; Health care; Cancer; Food services; Youth development, business; YM/YWCAs & YM/YWHAs; Human services; Community development, business promotion; United Ways and Federated Giving Programs.
Type of support: Annual campaigns; Employee matching gifts; General/operating support; Scholarship funds; Sponsorships.
Geographic limitations: Giving primarily in Savannah, GA.
Support limitations: No grants to individuals.
Application information: Applications accepted. Applicants should submit the following:
1) copy of IRS Determination Letter
Initial approach: Proposal
Deadline(s): None
Officers: Robert H. Demere, Jr., Pres. and Secy.; Frances A. Brown, V.P., Finance and Treas.; William A. Baker, Jr., V.P.
EIN: 581693323
Selected grants: The following grants are a representative sample of this grantmaker's funding activity:
$35,000 to Nature Conservancy, Arlington, VA, 2011.
$5,000 to Leukemia & Lymphoma Society, White Plains, NY, 2011.
$2,500 to Nature Conservancy, Arlington, VA, 2011. For membership.

876
Colonial Pipeline Company

1185 Sanctuary Pkwy., Ste. 100
P.O. Box 1624
Alpharetta, GA 30009-4738
(678) 762-2200

Company URL: http://www.colpipe.com
Establishment information: Established in 1962.
Company type: Private company
Business activities: Operates petroleum product pipelines.
Business type (SIC): Pipelines (except natural gas/operation of)
Corporate officers: Tim Felt, Pres. and C.E.O.; Michael Pubois, C.I.O.; Doug Belden, V.P., Opers.; Trey Almond, Treas.
Giving statement: Giving through the Colonial Pipeline Company Contributions Program.

Colonial Pipeline Company Contributions Program

P.O. Box 1624
Alpharetta, GA 30009-9934 (678) 762-2200
Tel. for Corporate and Public Affairs office: (678) 762-2289; URL: http://www.colpipe.com/ab_com.asp

Purpose and activities: Colonial Pipeline makes charitable contributions to emergency response organizations, fire departments, and nonprofit organizations involved with education, the environment, and community development. Support is given primarily in areas of company operations.
Fields of interest: Elementary/secondary education; Education; Environmental education; Environment; Health care, EMS; Disasters, fire prevention/control; Safety/disasters; Recreation; Community/economic development.
Type of support: Employee volunteer services; Equipment; General/operating support; Sponsorships.
Geographic limitations: Giving primarily in areas of company operations in AL, GA, LA, MD, MS, NY, SC, TN, VA, and TX.
Application information: The Corporate and Public Affairs Department handles giving.

877
Colorado Avalanche, LLC

Pepsi Ctr.
1000 Chopper Cir.
Denver, CO 80204 (303) 405-1100
FAX: (303) 575-1920

Company URL: http://www.coloradoavalanche.com
Establishment information: Established in 1979.
Company type: Subsidiary of a private company
Business activities: Operates professional ice hockey club.
Business type (SIC): Commercial sports
Corporate officers: Pierre Lacroix, Pres.; Jean Martineau, Sr. V.P., Comms.
Giving statement: Giving through the Colorado Avalanche, LLC Corporate Giving Program.

Colorado Avalanche, LLC Corporate Giving Program

c/o Community Rels.
Pepsi Ctr.
1000 Chopper Cir.
Denver, CO 80204-5805
E-mail: llinscott@pepsiecenter.com; URL: http://avalanche.nhl.com/club/page.htm?id=32582

Contact: Lesley Linscott, Sr. Dir., Community Rels.
Purpose and activities: The Colorado Avalanche makes charitable contributions of game tickets and memorabilia to nonprofit organizations involved with children and on a case by case basis. Support is limited to Colorado.
Fields of interest: Children, services; General charitable giving.
Type of support: In-kind gifts.
Geographic limitations: Giving limited to CO.
Publications: Application guidelines; Corporate giving report.
Application information: Applications accepted. Support is limited to 1 contribution per organization during any given year. Telephone calls are not encouraged. Application form required. Applicants should submit the following:
1) population served
2) name, address and phone number of organization
3) brief history of organization and description of its mission
4) contact person
Requests for memorabilia donations should include the name, date, location, and a description of the event. Requests for ticket donations should indicate whether the group requires handicap accessible seating, and the intended use of the ticket donation.
Initial approach: Complete online application form
Deadline(s): 6 weeks prior to need for memorabilia donations; Sept. 1 for ticket donations

878
Colorado Dental Service, Inc.

(also known as Delta Dental of Colorado)
4582 S. Ulser St., Ste. 800
Denver, CO 80237-2567 (303) 741-9300

Company URL: http://www.deltadentalco.com
Establishment information: Established in 1958.
Company type: Private company
Business activities: Sells dental insurance.
Business type (SIC): Insurance/accident and health
Financial profile for 2011: Assets, $104,746,000; sales volume, $269,873,000; liabilities, $23,703,000
Corporate officers: Cynthia A. Evans, Chair.; Kathryn A. Paul, Pres. and C.E.O.; David Beal, V.P. and C.F.O.; Linda M. Arneson, V.P. and C.O.O.; Barbara B. Springer, V.P., Genl. Counsel, and Admin.; Jean Lawhead, V.P., Mktg. and Sales
Board of directors: Cynthia A. Evans, Chair.; Douglas Berkey; John P. Hopkins; Denise Kassebaum; Victor Lazzaro, Jr.; Mary Noonan; B. LaRae Orullian; Kathryn Paul; Donald Safer; Gail Schoettler, Ph.D.; Thomas Swain; Marilyn Taylor; Walt Vogl; Mark Wehrle
Giving statement: Giving through the Delta Dental Plan of Colorado Foundation, Inc.

Delta Dental Plan of Colorado Foundation, Inc.

4582 S. Ulster St., Ste. 800
Denver, CO 80237-2567 (303) 741-9300
FAX: (303) 741-4233;
E-mail: bspringer@ddpco.com; URL: http://www.deltadentalco.com/deltadentalfoundation.aspx

Establishment information: Established in 1997 in CO; supporting organization of Colorado Dental Service, Inc. (doing business as Delta Dental of Colorado).
Donor: Delta Dental of Colorado.
Contact: Kathryn Paul, Pres. and C.E.O.
Financial data (yr. ended 12/31/11): Revenue, $4,789,411; assets, $15,278,998 (M); gifts received, $3,644,239; expenditures, $2,904,171; giving activities include $1,742,500 for grants and $416,309 for grants to individuals.
Purpose and activities: The foundation supports projects that promote the prevention of oral diseases and the advancement of the science and practice of dentistry. The foundation currently provides funding for projects focused on: 1) promoting awareness of pregnant women and new mothers of the importance of oral health; 2) promoting education of medical and dental students on the oral/systemic connection; 3) placing hygienists in pediatric offices; and 4) providing sealants to low-income children.
Fields of interest: Dental care.
Geographic limitations: Giving limited to CO.
Support limitations: No support for religious or political organizations.
Publications: Annual report.
Application information: Applications not accepted. Unsolicited requests for funds not accepted.
Officers and Trustees:* Kathryn Paul*, Pres. and C.E.O.; Linda Arneson*, V.P. and C.O.O.; David Beal, V.P. and C.F.O.; Jean Lawhead, V.P., Sales and Mktg.; Barbara Springer, J.D., V.P., Admin. and Gen. Counsel; Jonathon Anderson, D.D.S.; Douglas Berkey, D.M.D.; Cynthia Evans; John P. Hopkins; and 10 additional directors.
Number of staff: 2 part-time professional.
EIN: 841389431

879
Colorado Rockies Baseball Club, Ltd.

Coors Field
2001 Blake St.
Denver, CO 80205-2000 (303) 292-0200

Company URL: http://colorado.rockies.mlb.com
Establishment information: Established in 1993.
Company type: Private company
Business activities: Operates professional baseball club.
Business type (SIC): Amusement and recreation services/miscellaneous
Corporate officers: Richard L. Monfort, Chair. and C.E.O.; Gregory D. Feasel, Exec. V.P. and C.O.O.; Harold R. Roth, Exec. V.P., C.F.O., and Genl. Counsel; Sue Ann McClaren, V.P., Opers.; Michael J. Kent, V.P., Finance; Marcy E. Glasser, V.P., Corp. Sales; Jay E. Alves, V.P., Comms.; Elizabeth E. Stecklein, V.P., Human Resources
Board of director: Richard L. Monfort, Chair.
Giving statement: Giving through the Colorado Rockies Baseball Club, Ltd. Corporate Giving Program and the Colorado Rockies Baseball Club Foundation.

Colorado Rockies Baseball Club, Ltd. Corporate Giving Program

c/o Community Donations
Coors Field
2001 Blake St.
Denver, CO 80205-2000
URL: http://colorado.rockies.mlb.com/NASApp/mlb/col/community/index.jsp

Purpose and activities: The Colorado Rockies make charitable contributions to nonprofit organizations involved with literacy, education, drug and alcohol abuse prevention, and youth baseball and softball. Support is given primarily in the Rocky Mountain region.
Fields of interest: Elementary/secondary education; Education, reading; Education; Substance abuse, prevention; Athletics/sports, baseball; Youth development; Children/youth, services.
Programs:
Care & Share Program: The Rockies in partnership with The Children's Hospital, Make A Wish Foundation, and the Starlight Foundation, gives seriously ill children the opportunity to watch batting practice while standing on Coors Field and get autographs from their favorite Rockies players and coaches.
Colorado Rockies Educational Packet: The Rockies supports education for K-12 classrooms through an educational packet that meets the educational standards set by the Department of Education. The packet is designed to demonstrate the way learning can be tied to the game of baseball and focuses on art, English, geography, health and nutrition, history, math, music, science, speech, and drama. The packet is available at the Rockies website.
Community Ticket Program: The Rockies provides game tickets to nonprofit organizations for individuals who would otherwise not have the opportunity to attend a Rockies baseball game.
Hispanic Adult Leadership Award: The Rockies awards season tickets to individuals who have demonstrated a commitment to the Hispanic community. Winners are selected based on leadership, promotion of family values, community involvement, and personal achievements, and their name will appear on a plaque displayed inside the home plate entrance at Coors Field.
Make an Impact School Program: Through the Make an Impact Program, the Rockies hold "Rockies School Rallies" for grades K-8 at local schools during an assembly. The program is designed to show students how to make an impact in their lives and communities through staying in school, refusing drugs, getting involved, and showing respect. The program includes a 45 interactive program, a visit from Rockies mascot Dinger, and prizes.
Type of support: Curriculum development; Donated products; In-kind gifts; Publication.
Geographic limitations: Giving primarily in areas of company operations in the Rocky Mountain region, CO.
Publications: Application guidelines.
Application information: Applications accepted. Proposals and letters of inquiries should be submitted using organization letterhead. The Community Relations Department handles giving. Applicants should submit the following:
1) copy of IRS Determination Letter
2) descriptive literature about organization
3) detailed description of project and amount of funding requested
Initial approach: Proposal to headquarters; mail letter of inquiry to headquarters for Community Ticket Program
Deadline(s): 4 to 6 weeks prior to need

Colorado Rockies Baseball Club Foundation

c/o Colorado Rockies Baseball Club, Ltd.
2001 Blake St.
Denver, CO 80205-2000 (303) 292-0200
URL: http://colorado.rockies.mlb.com/col/community/index.jsp

Establishment information: Established in 1991 in CO.
Contact: Keli S. McGregor, Pres.
Financial data (yr. ended 12/31/11): Revenue, $137,054; assets, $281,496 (M); gifts received, $136,846; expenditures, $93,764; giving activities include $93,764 for grants.
Purpose and activities: The foundation targets underprivileged and at-risk youth through programs for youth baseball, drug and alcohol abuse awareness and prevention, and education and literacy.
Fields of interest: Education, reading; Education; Substance abuse, prevention; Athletics/sports, baseball.
Type of support: Program development.
Geographic limitations: Giving limited to the Rocky Mountain, CO region.
Publications: Annual report.
Application information:
Board meeting date(s): Varies
Officers: Charles K. Monfort, Chair.; Richard L. Monfort, Vice-Chair.; Keli S. McGregor, Pres.; Gregory D. Feasel, Sr. V.P.; Jim Kellogg, V.P.; Harold R. Roth, Treas.
Number of staff: 1 part-time professional.
EIN: 841178557

880
Colorado State Bank and Trust

1600 Broadway, 3rd Fl.
Denver, CO 80202-4927 (303) 863-4478

Company URL: http://www.csbt.com
Establishment information: Established in 1908.
Company type: Subsidiary of a public company
Business activities: Operates commercial bank.
Business type (SIC): Banks/commercial
Corporate officers: Greg Symons, Chair.; Stanley A. Lybarger, Pres. and C.E.O.; Steven E. Nell, Exec. V.P. and C.F.O.; Don Parker, Exec. V.P. and C.I.O.
Board of directors: Greg Symons, Chair.; Stanley A. Lybarger
Giving statement: Giving through the Colorado State Bank Foundation.

Colorado State Bank Foundation

P.O. Box 1620
Tulsa, OK 74101-1620 (303) 863-4478
FAX: (303) 863-4459; E-mail: mjhanson@csbt.com; Application address: 1600 Broadway, Denver, CO 80202; URL: https://www.csbt.com/en/Other/Community_Commitment.page

Establishment information: Established in 1955.
Donor: Colorado State Bank and Trust.
Contact: Margie Hanson, Secy.
Financial data (yr. ended 06/30/12): Assets, $360,370 (M); expenditures, $24,035; qualifying distributions, $19,150; giving activities include $19,150 for grants.
Purpose and activities: The foundation supports organizations involved with human services, youth and aging, and community development.
Fields of interest: Human services; Community/economic development Youth; Aging.
Type of support: Building/renovation; Capital campaigns; Equipment; General/operating support; Program development.
Geographic limitations: Giving limited to areas of company operations in the Denver, CO metropolitan area.
Support limitations: No support for religious organizations, schools, or hospitals. No grants to individuals, or for endowments, cover deficits, debt reduction, or sponsorships of special events, tournaments, or tables.
Publications: Application guidelines; IRS Form 990 or 990-PF printed copy available upon request.
Application information: Applications accepted. Grants range from $250 to $1,000. Support is limited to 1 contribution per organization during any given year. Organizations receiving support are asked to submit a final report. Application form required. Applicants should submit the following:
1) name, address and phone number of organization
2) copy of IRS Determination Letter
3) brief history of organization and description of its mission
4) contact person
5) results expected from proposed grant
6) copy of current year's organizational budget and/or project budget
7) listing of board of directors, trustees, officers and other key people and their affiliations
Initial approach: Proposal
Board meeting date(s): Quarterly
Deadline(s): Jan. 1, Apr. 1, July 1, and Oct. 1
Final notification: 2 to 3 months
Officers: Bill Sullivan, Pres.; Mike Burns, V.P.; Margie Hanson, Secy.; Mike Nation, Treas.
EIN: 846020256

881
Colt Investments, Inc.

7400 State Line Rd., Ste. 208
Prairie Village, KS 66208-3448
(913) 385-5010

Establishment information: Established in 1964.
Company type: Private company
Business activities: Provides insurance brokerage services; operates commercial bank.
Business type (SIC): Insurance agents, brokers, and services; banks/commercial
Corporate officer: Mack V. Colt, Pres. and C.E.O.
Giving statement: Giving through the Colt Family Charitable Trust.

The Colt Family Charitable Trust

7400 State Line Rd., Ste. 208
Prairie Village, KS 66208-4100 (913) 385-5010

Establishment information: Established in 2001.
Donors: Colt Investments, Inc.; Mack V. Colt.
Contact: Mack V. Colt, Tr.
Financial data (yr. ended 12/31/11): Assets, $5,956 (M); expenditures, $44,934; qualifying distributions, $44,500; giving activities include $44,500 for 6 grants (high: $17,000; low: $500).
Purpose and activities: The foundation supports organizations involved with education, prisoner rehabilitation, youth development, human services, and Christianity.
Fields of interest: Education; Offenders/ex-offenders, rehabilitation; Youth development, centers/clubs; Youth development; Human services; United Ways and Federated Giving Programs; Christian agencies & churches.
Type of support: General/operating support.
Geographic limitations: Giving primarily in KS, Kansas City, MO, and VA.
Support limitations: No grants to individuals.
Application information: Applications accepted. Application form not required.
Initial approach: Proposal
Deadline(s): None
Trustees: Mack V. Colt; Sara C. Colt; Elizabeth C. Deckert.
EIN: 266005858
Selected grants: The following grants are a representative sample of this grantmaker's funding activity:
$20,000 to Christ Community Church, Leawood, KS, 2010.
$15,000 to Hope Center, Kansas City, MO, 2010.
$5,000 to International Foundation, Washington, DC, 2010.
$2,500 to Gracious Promise Foundation, Kansas City, KS, 2010.
$2,000 to Desire Street Ministries, Decatur, GA, 2010.
$2,000 to Integrity Resource Center, Olathe, KS, 2010.
$1,000 to Prison Fellowship Ministries, Lansdowne, VA, 2010.

882
Columbia Financial Inc.

19-01 Rte. 208 N.
Fair Lawn, NJ 07410 (201) 796-2194

Company URL: http://www.columbiabankonline.com
Company type: Subsidiary of a private company
Business activities: Operates bank holding company; operates commercial bank.
Business type (SIC): Banks/commercial; holding company
Corporate officer: Thomas J. Kemly, Pres. and C.E.O.
Subsidiary: Columbia Bank, Fair Lawn, NJ
Giving statement: Giving through the Columbia Bank Foundation.

Columbia Bank Foundation

19-01 Rte. 208
Fair Lawn, NJ 07410-2832
FAX: (201) 794-5612;
E-mail: dwoods@columbiabankonline.com;
URL: http://www.columbiabankonline.com/home/about/foundation/

Establishment information: Established in 2004 in NJ and incorporated in DE.
Donor: Columbia Financial Inc.
Contact: Dorothy Woods, Dir.
Financial data (yr. ended 12/31/11): Assets, $30,204 (M); gifts received, $274,000; expenditures, $248,335; qualifying distributions, $245,100; giving activities include $245,100 for grants.
Purpose and activities: The foundation supports organizations involved with health, affordable housing, human services, financial literacy, and community development. Special emphasis is directed toward organizations serving low- and moderate-income individuals and communities.
Fields of interest: Education, early childhood education; Education, special; Education; Health care; Employment; Housing/shelter, development; Housing/shelter, home owners; Housing/shelter, services; Housing/shelter; Human services, financial counseling; Human services; Community/

economic development Economically disadvantaged.

Programs:

Affordable Housing: The foundation supports initiatives designed to promote affordable housing for low- and moderate-income individuals and communities.

Community Investment and Economic Development: The foundation supports initiatives designed to improve the quality of life, sustain economic development, and support job skills for low- and moderate-income individuals and communities; and promote community development.

Financial Literacy and Education: The foundation supports initiatives designed to enrich a child's educational opportunities, promote early childhood development, and provide special education programs, with preferences given to those programs targeting low- and moderate-income persons; provide homeownership counseling, home maintenance, and other financial services education.

Health and Human Services: The foundation supports initiatives designed to revitalize or stabilize low- and moderate-income areas and/or target low- and moderate-income persons; and sustain access to quality health care for individuals.

Type of support: Building/renovation; Capital campaigns; Equipment; Program development.
Geographic limitations: Giving primarily in areas of company operations in NJ.
Support limitations: No support for national health organizations, research/disease advocacy organizations, religious, political, labor, or fraternal organizations, or civic clubs. No grants to individuals, or for scholarships, general operating support, sports, athletic events or athletic programs, or travel-related events.
Publications: Application guidelines; Program policy statement.
Application information: Applications accepted. Cover letters should be submitted using organization letterhead. Support is limited to 1 contribution per organization during any given year. Multi-year funding is not automatic. Application form required. Applicants should submit the following:
1) role played by volunteers
2) name, address and phone number of organization
3) copy of IRS Determination Letter
4) brief history of organization and description of its mission
5) copy of most recent annual report/audited financial statement/990
6) list of company employees involved with the organization
7) descriptive literature about organization
8) listing of board of directors, trustees, officers and other key people and their affiliations
9) detailed description of project and amount of funding requested
10) contact person
11) listing of additional sources and amount of support

Proposals should indicate the organization's date of incorporation.

Initial approach: Download application form and mail proposal and application form to foundation
Copies of proposal: 1
Board meeting date(s): Quarterly
Deadline(s): Last business day of the month preceding board meeting
Final notification: 3 months

Officers and Directors:* Raymond G. Hallock*, Pres.; Diane L. Weiss, Secy.; E. Thomas Allen*, Treas.; Eugene M. Schwartz, Genl. Counsel; Noel R. Holland; Thomas J. Kemly; Henry Kuiken; Elizabeth Randall; Dorothy M. Woods.
EIN: 201115566
Selected grants: The following grants are a representative sample of this grantmaker's funding activity:
$10,000 to Covenant House, New York, NY, 2010.

883
Columbia Gas of Ohio, Inc.

200 Civic Center Dr.
Columbus, OH 43215 (614) 460-6000

Company URL: http://www.columbiagasohio.com
Establishment information: Established in 1951.
Company type: Subsidiary of a public company
Business activities: Transmits and distributes natural gas.
Business type (SIC): Gas production and distribution
Corporate officers: John W. Partridge, Jr., Pres.; Stephen P. Smith, C.F.O.
Giving statement: Giving through the Columbia Gas of Ohio, Inc. Corporate Giving Program.

Columbia Gas of Ohio, Inc. Corporate Giving Program

200 Civic Center Dr.
Columbus, OH 43215-4138 (614) 460-4629
FAX: (614) 460-5502; Additional tel.: (800) 952-3037.; URL: http://www.columbiagasohio.com/en/doing-more-for-you/community-service/community-programs.aspx

Purpose and activities: Columbia Gas of Ohio makes charitable contributions to nonprofit organizations involved with education, energy assistance, and human services. Special emphasis is directed towards programs that provide assistance to low-income families. Support is given primarily in areas of company operations in Ohio.
Fields of interest: Education; Environment, energy; Human services; American Red Cross; Human services, emergency aid; United Ways and Federated Giving Programs; Utilities Economically disadvantaged.
Type of support: Employee volunteer services.
Geographic limitations: Giving primarily in areas of company operations in OH.

884
Columbia Gas of Pennsylvania, Inc.

(also known as Columbia Gas of Maryland, Inc.)
501 Technology Dr.
Canonsburg, PA 15317 (724) 416-6300

Company URL: http://www.columbiagaspamd.com
Establishment information: Established in 1885.
Company type: Subsidiary of a public company
Business activities: Transmits and distributes natural gas.
Business type (SIC): Gas production and distribution
Corporate officers: M. Carol Fox, Co-Pres.; Mark R. Kempic, Co-Pres.; Edward Santry, V.P., Human Resources
Giving statement: Giving through the Columbia Gas of Pennsylvania, Inc./Columbia Gas of Maryland, Inc. Corporate Giving Program.

Columbia Gas of Pennsylvania, Inc./ Columbia Gas of Maryland, Inc. Corporate Giving Program

501 Technology Dr.
Canonsburg, PA 15317-9585
FAX: (724) 416-6383;
E-mail: mmarcus@nisource.com; URL: http://www.columbiagaspa.com/en/community-outreach.aspx

Contact: Mike Marcus, Mgr., Comms. and Community Rels.
Purpose and activities: Columbia Gas of Pennsylvania/Maryland makes charitable contributions to nonprofit organizations involved with environmental preservation, education, natural resources, public safety, human services, community development, senior citizens, minorities, women, and first responders. Support is given primarily in Maryland and Pennsylvania.
Fields of interest: Historic preservation/historical societies; Education; Environment, natural resources; Disasters, preparedness/services; Safety/disasters; Youth, services; Human services; Economic development; Community/economic development Children; Aging; Minorities; Women.
Type of support: Cause-related marketing; Donated equipment; Employee volunteer services; In-kind gifts; Program development; Sponsorships.
Geographic limitations: Giving primarily in MD and PA.
Support limitations: No support for fraternal, political, municipal, veterans', or athletic organizations or United Way-supported organizations. No grants to individuals.
Publications: Corporate giving report (including application guidelines); Informational brochure (including application guidelines).
Application information: Applications accepted. Faxes are not encouraged. The Communications and Community Relations Department handles giving. A contributions committee reviews all requests. Application form required. Applicants should submit the following:
1) population served
2) copy of IRS Determination Letter
3) geographic area to be served
4) copy of most recent annual report/audited financial statement/990
5) how project's results will be evaluated or measured
6) listing of board of directors, trustees, officers and other key people and their affiliations
7) detailed description of project and amount of funding requested
8) listing of additional sources and amount of support

Initial approach: Mail proposal and application form to headquarters
Copies of proposal: 1
Committee meeting date(s): Monthly
Deadline(s): None
Final notification: Varies

885
Columbus Electric Cooperative, Inc.

900 N. Gold Ave.
P.O. Box 631
Deming, NM 88030-3127 (575) 546-8838

Company URL: http://www.columbusco-op.org/index.cfm
Establishment information: Established in 1946.

Company type: Cooperative
Business activities: Generates, transmits, and distributes electricity.
Business type (SIC): Electric services
Corporate officers: Edward Elbrock, Co-Pres.; Hal B. Keeler, Co-Pres.; William C. Miller, Jr., Secy.-Treas.
Board of directors: Nancy Clopton; William J. Cloudt; Eddie Diaz; Edward Elbrock; Joe Johnson; Hal B. Keeler; Randy L. Massey; William C. Miller, Jr.; Jay Peterson
Giving statement: Giving through the Columbus Electric Scholarship, Inc.

Columbus Electric Scholarship, Inc.

P.O. Box 631
Deming, NM 88031-0631 (575) 546-8838
URL: http://www.columbusco-op.org/Education/scholarship.cfm

Establishment information: Established in 1991 in NM.
Donor: Columbus Electric Cooperative, Inc.
Financial data (yr. ended 12/31/11): Assets, $7,776 (M); gifts received, $3,509; expenditures, $7,253; qualifying distributions, $7,250; giving activities include $7,250 for grants.
Purpose and activities: The foundation awards college scholarships to members and the children of members of Columbus Electric Cooperative attending college in Arizona or New Mexico.
Fields of interest: Education.
Type of support: Scholarships—to individuals.
Application information: Applications accepted. Application form required.
Requests should include three letters of reference.
Initial approach: Contact foundation for application form
Deadline(s): June 30 for fall semester; Dec. 31 for spring semester
Final notification: Within 60 days
Officers: Edward Elbrock, Pres.; Randy L. Massey, V.P.; William C. Miller, Jr., Secy.-Treas.
Board Members: Nancy Clopton; William Cloudt; Joe Johnson; Hal B. Keeler; Jay Peterson.
EIN: 850373471

886
Columbus Team Soccer, LLC

(also known as Columbus Crew)
Columbus Crew Stadium
1 Black and Gold Blvd.
Columbus, OH 43211-2091
(614) 447-2739

Company URL: http://www.thecrew.com
Establishment information: Established in 1995.
Company type: Private company
Business activities: Operates professional soccer club.
Business type (SIC): Commercial sports
Corporate officers: Mark McCullers, Co-Pres.; James Smith, Co-Pres.; Mike Malo, Sr. V.P., Sales and Mktg.; Tom Patton, V.P., Finance and Admin.; Scott DeBolt, V.P., Opers.
Giving statement: Giving through the Columbus Crew Corporate Giving Program and the Crew Soccer Foundation.

Columbus Crew Corporate Giving Program

c/o Community Outreach Dept.
1 Black & Gold Blvd.
Columbus, OH 43211-2091
FAX: (614) 447-4109; URL: http://www.thecrew.com/content/donation-requests

Purpose and activities: The Columbus Crew makes charitable contributions of game tickets and memorabilia to nonprofit organizations involved with education, youth soccer, community development, and on a case by case basis. Support is given primarily in Ohio.
Fields of interest: Education; Athletics/sports, soccer; Youth development; Community/economic development; General charitable giving.
Type of support: In-kind gifts.
Geographic limitations: Giving primarily in OH, with emphasis on central OH.
Support limitations: No grants for general operating support or sponsorships.
Application information: Applications accepted. Proposals should be submitted using organization letterhead. Support is limited to 1 contribution per organization during any given year. Telephone calls during the application process are not encouraged. Application form not required. Applicants should submit the following:
1) name, address and phone number of organization
2) copy of IRS Determination Letter
3) detailed description of project and amount of funding requested
4) contact person
Proposals should indicate the type of fundraiser and the date, time, and location of the event.
Initial approach: Mail or fax proposal to headquarters
Copies of proposal: 1
Deadline(s): 6 weeks prior to need
Final notification: 2 weeks prior to need

Crew Soccer Foundation

1 Black and Gold Blvd.
Columbus, OH 43211-2091 (614) 447-4170
URL: http://www.crewsoccerfoundation.org

Financial data (yr. ended 12/31/11): Revenue, $188,091; assets, $355,876 (M); gifts received, $187,982; expenditures, $94,493; giving activities include $60,579 for grants.
Purpose and activities: The foundation is the charitable arm of Major League Soccer's Columbus Crew and is dedicated to serving as a catalyst for community investment and development; the foundation also works to advance the sport at all levels and enrich the overall quality of life in central Ohio and beyond, with an emphasis on developing the potential of the area's young people.
Fields of interest: Athletics/sports, soccer; Youth development.
Officers and Directors:* Mark McCullers*, Pres.; Scott DeBolt*, Secy.; Brad Eldridge*, C.F.O.; Dave Stephany, Exec. Dir.; Lisa Wu Fate; Tod Friedman; C. Todd Jones; Juan Jose Perez; Jamie Ryan; Matt Starkey.
EIN: 710913027

887
Comcast Corporation

(formerly AT&T Comcast Corp.)
1 Comcast Ctr.
1500 Market St.
Philadelphia, PA 19103-2838
(215) 286-1700
FAX: (215) 981-7790

Company URL: http://www.comcast.com
Establishment information: Established in 1963.
Company type: Public company
Company ticker symbol and exchange: CMCSA/NASDAQ
Business activities: Provides broadband communications services; provides television shopping services; produces television programming.
Business type (SIC): Cable and other pay television services; nonstore retailers; motion pictures/production and services allied to
Financial profile for 2012: Number of employees, 129,000; assets, $164,971,000,000; sales volume, $62,570,000,000; pre-tax net income, $11,609,000,000; expenses, $50,415,000,000; liabilities, $115,615,000,000
Fortune 1000 ranking: 2012—46th in revenues, 26th in profits, and 39th in assets
Forbes 2000 ranking: 2012—129th in sales, 79th in profits, and 165th in assets
Corporate officers: Brian L. Roberts, Chair., Pres., and C.E.O.; Michael J. Angelakis, Vice-Chair. and C.F.O.; Lawrence J. Salva, Sr. V.P., C.A.O., and Cont.; William E. Dordelman, Sr. V.P. and Treas.; Arthur R. Block, Esq., Sr. V.P., Genl. Counsel, and Secy.; Karen Dougherty Buchholz, V.P., Admin.; Jennifer Khoury Newcomb, V.P., Corp. Comms.; Ralph J. Roberts, Chair. Emeritus
Board of directors: Brian L. Roberts, Chair.; Michael J. Angelakis, Vice-Chair.; Kenneth J. Bacon; Sheldon M. Bonovitz; Joseph J. Collins; J. Michael Cook; Gerald L. Hassell; Jeffrey A. Honickman; Eduardo G. Mestre; Ralph J. Roberts; Jonathan A. Rodgers; Judith Rodin
Subsidiaries: Comcast Business Communications, Inc., Plymouth Meeting, PA; Comcast Cable Communications, Inc., Philadelphia, PA; Comcast Holdings Corporation, Philadelphia, PA; Comcast MO Group, Inc., Englewood, CO; Comcast of Brockton, Inc., Brockton, MA; Comcast Spectacor, L.P., Philadelphia, PA; Comcast Telephony Communications, LLC, Philadelphia, PA; Diamonique Corp., Horsham, PA; Jones Cable Holdings, Inc., Philadelphia, PA; M H Lightnet Inc., Union, NJ; NBC Universal, Inc., New York, NY; Philadelphia 76ers, L.P., Philadelphia, PA; Philadelphia Flyers, L.P., Philadelphia, PA; QVC, Inc., West Chester, PA; QVC Chesapeake, Inc., Chesapeake, VA; QVC San Antonio, Inc., San Antonio, TX; TGC, Inc., Orlando, FL
International operations: Australia; Belgium; Brazil; Canada; Denmark; France; Germany; Greece; Hong Kong; Hungary; India; Italy; Netherlands; Netherlands Antilles; Singapore; Switzerland; United Kingdom
Giving statement: Giving through the Comcast Corporation Contributions Program and the Comcast Foundation.
Company EIN: 270000798

Comcast Corporation Contributions Program

1 Comcast Ctr.
Philadelphia, PA 19130-2838 (215) 286-7058
E-mail: bill_black@comcast.com; URL: http://www.comcast.com/Corporate/About/InTheCommunity/Literacy/digital-literacy.html

Contact: Bill Black, Sr. Dir., Community Investment
Purpose and activities: As a complement to its foundation, Comcast also makes charitable contributions to nonprofit organizations directly. Support is given primarily in areas of company operations.
Fields of interest: Education, reading; Youth development; Voluntarism promotion; Leadership development.
Type of support: Program development.
Geographic limitations: Giving primarily in areas of company operations.
Application information: Applications not accepted. Contributes only to pre-selected organizations.

The Comcast Foundation

1 Comcast Ctr., 48th Fl.
Philadelphia, PA 19103-2838 (215) 286-1700
E-mail for Leaders and Achievers Scholarships: comcast@applyists.com; URL: http://www.comcast.com/corporate/about/inthecommunity/foundation/comcastfoundation.html

Establishment information: Established in 1999 in DE.
Donors: Comcast CICG, LP; Comcast QVC, Inc.; MOC Holdco II, Inc.
Contact: William D. Black, V.P. and Exec. Dir.
Financial data (yr. ended 12/31/11): Assets, $19,812,943 (M); expenditures, $15,528,734; qualifying distributions, $15,460,060; giving activities include $13,519,060 for 1,053 grants (high: $500,000; low: $250) and $1,941,000 for 1,789 grants to individuals (high: $10,000; low: $1,000).
Purpose and activities: The foundation supports programs designed to expand digital literacy; promote community service; and build tomorrow's leaders; and awards college scholarships to high school seniors.
Fields of interest: Education, reading; Education, computer literacy/technology training; Education, e-learning; Education; Employment, training; Boys & girls clubs; Big Brothers/Big Sisters; Youth development, services; YM/YWCAs & YM/YWHAs; Children/youth, services; Voluntarism promotion; United Ways and Federated Giving Programs; Computer science; Military/veterans' organizations; Leadership development Economically disadvantaged.
Programs:
Comcast Leaders and Achievers Scholarship Program: The foundation awards $1,000 college scholarships to high school seniors who demonstrate strong commitment to community service and displays leadership ability in school activities or through work experience. Applicants must have a GPA of 2.8 or higher and must be nominated by a school principal or guidance counselor. The program is administered by International Scholarship and Tuition Services.
Gustave G. Amsterdam Leadership Award: The foundation annually awards $5,000 scholarships to two Philadelphia public high school graduates planning to attend a Philadelphia college or university. The recipients are chosen among Philadelphia area finalists in the Comcast Leaders and Achievers Scholarship Program.
Type of support: Conferences/seminars; Continuing support; Employee volunteer services; General/operating support; Program development; Publication; Scholarship funds; Scholarships—to individuals; Sponsorships.
Geographic limitations: Giving on a national basis in areas of company operations, with emphasis on CA, MA, and PA.
Support limitations: No support for discriminatory organizations, donor-advised funds, private foundations, political candidates or organizations, or Type III Non-Supporting organizations as defined by the IRS. No grants to individuals (except for scholarships), or for marketing sponsorships, sporting events, trips or tours, capital campaigns, endowments, research studies, or lobbying campaigns.
Publications: Application guidelines.
Application information: Applications accepted. Contributes only to individuals nominated by high school principals for scholarships. Unsolicited applications for grants or sponsorships are not accepted. Local Comcast systems and employees identify non-profit organizations as potential grant recipients. Application form required.
Initial approach: Principals should e-mail foundation to verify school eligibility status and request nomination form for scholarships
Deadline(s): Dec. 7 for Comcast Leaders and Achievers Scholarship Program
Officers and Directors:* David L. Cohen*, Co-Chair.; Ralph J. Roberts*, Co-Chair.; Charisse Lillie, Pres.; Kristine A. Dankenbrink*, Sr. V.P. and Secy.; Jospeh F. Ditrolio*, Sr. V.P. and Treas.; Tracy J. Baumgartner, Sr. V.P.; William E. Dordelman, Sr. V.P.; William D. Black, V.P. and Exec Dir.; Dave R. Breidinger; Julian A. Brodsky; Kevin M. Casey; William Connors; Thomas J. Donnelly; A. Melissa Maxfield; Adam L. Miller; David A. Scott; Steven A. White.
EIN: 510390132
Selected grants: The following grants are a representative sample of this grantmaker's funding activity:
$1,200,000 to City Year, Boston, MA, 2010. For leadership development and training, team sponsorships, and events sponsorship.
$350,000 to United Way of Greater Philadelphia and Southern New Jersey, Philadelphia, PA, 2010. For Employee Campaign.
$270,000 to Big Brothers Big Sisters of America, Philadelphia, PA, 2010. For Beyond School Walls program. This payment includes the second year of support for the four Beyond School Walls programs begun last year and the addition of five new sites. This grant will support a total of 225 Big/Little matches.
$260,000 to One Economy Corporation, Washington, DC, 2010. For ongoing support of the Comcast Digital Connectors program, including the salary of the program director who was hired because of the rapid expansion of the Comcast partnership.
$200,000 to One Economy Corporation, Washington, DC, 2010. For additional funding for the unanticipated rapid expansion of Digital Connectors, which is now expected to grow to 14 sites (instead of the planned 4 sites), including the hire of a program director needed to oversee the program's rapid expansion.
$25,000 to American Red Cross, Southeastern Pennsylvania Chapter, Philadelphia, PA, 2010. For the relief efforts for the victims of the earthquake in Haiti.
$15,000 to Boys and Girls Clubs of Sarasota County, Sarasota, FL, 2010. For Club Tech.
$10,000 to Big Brothers Big Sisters of Bucks County, Jamison, PA, 2010. For general mentoring support, but to continue the program which focuses on establishing matches for Littles who have family members who have been incarcerated.
$4,900 to United Way, Pikes Peak, Colorado Springs, CO, 2010. For Employee Campaign.

888
Comcast Spectacor, L.P.

Wachovia Ctr. Complex
3601 S. Broad St.
Philadelphia, PA 19148 (215) 336-3600

Company URL: http://www.comcast-spectacor.com
Establishment information: Established in 1996.
Company type: Subsidiary of a public company
Business activities: Operates professional ice hockey clubs; operates professional basketball club; operates ice skating rinks; operates professional baseball clubs; operates arenas; provides cable television services.
Business type (SIC): Commercial sports; cable and other pay television services; amusement and recreation services/miscellaneous
Corporate officers: Edward M. Snider, Chair.; Fred A. Shabel, Vice-Chair.; Peter A. Luukko, Pres. and C.O.O.; Russ Chaldler, Exec. V.P. and C.F.O.; Phil Weinberg, Exec. V.P. and Genl. Counsel; Sanford Lipstein, Chair. Emeritus
Board of directors: Edward M. Snider, Chair.; Fred A. Shabel, Vice-Chair.
Subsidiaries: Philadelphia 76ers, L.P., Philadelphia, PA; Philadelphia Flyers, L.P., Philadelphia, PA
Giving statement: Giving through the Sports Complex Special Services District and the Comcast-Spectacor Foundation.

Sports Complex Special Services District

(formerly South Village Community Development Corp.)
3300 S. 7th St.
Philadelphia, PA 19148-5319
FAX: (215) 271-1702;
E-mail: sjalosinski@scssd.org; URL: http://www.scssd.org

Establishment information: Established in PA.
Donors: Philadelphia Eagles; Philadelphia Phillies; Comcast-Spectator.
Financial data (yr. ended 12/31/11): Assets, $2,299,698 (M); gifts received, $1,206,227; expenditures, $1,264,102; qualifying distributions, $60,937; giving activities include $60,937 for grants.
Fields of interest: Education; Youth development; Religion.
Geographic limitations: Giving primarily in Philadelphia, PA.
Support limitations: No grants to individuals.
Application information: Applications not accepted. Unsolicited requests for funds not accepted.
Officers and Directors:* John Page*, Pres.; Barbara A. Capozzi*, V.P.; Don Smolenski*, Secy.; John Sfrisi*, Treas.; Shawn Jalosinski, Exec. Dir.; Judy Cerrone; Theodore Scairato; Michael R. Stiles.
EIN: 232822048

Comcast-Spectacor Foundation

(also known as Flyers Wives Charities, Inc.)
c/o Wachovia Bank, N.A.
3601 S. Broad St.
Philadelphia, PA 19148-5250 (215) 389-9426
FAX: (215) 389-9507;
E-mail: csfoundation@comcast-spectacor.com;

E-mail for Mary Ann Saleski: msaleski@comcast-spectacor.com; URL: http://www.comcastspectacorfoundation.org/

Establishment information: Established in 1988 in PA.
Financial data (yr. ended 06/30/11): Revenue, $1,252,713; assets, $1,941,697 (M); gifts received, $100,128; expenditures, $1,085,804; giving activities include $603,332 for grants.
Purpose and activities: The foundation seeks to improve the quality of life and to be an active and positive force in the community in the greater Philadelphia region.
Fields of interest: Hospitals (general); Youth development; Community/economic development.
Geographic limitations: Giving primarily in greater Philadelphia, PA region.
Officers: Fred Shabel, Vice-Chair.; Peter Luko, Pres.-C.O.O.; Russ Chandler*, Exec. V.P. and C.F.O.; Philip Weinberg*, Exec. V.P. and Genl. Counsel; Mary Ann Saleski, Sr. V.P.; Shawn Tilger, Sr. V.P.
EIN: 232513233

889
Comerica Incorporated

Comerica Bank Tower
1717 Main St., MC 6404
Dallas, TX 75201 (214) 462-4000
FAX: (214) 462-4010

Company URL: http://www.comerica.com
Establishment information: Established in 1849.
Company type: Public company
Company ticker symbol and exchange: CMA/NYSE
International Securities Identification Number: US2003401070
Business activities: Operates bank holding company; operates commercial bank.
Business type (SIC): Banks/commercial; holding company
Financial profile for 2012: Number of employees, 9,306; assets, $65,359,000,000; pre-tax net income, $710,000,000; liabilities, $58,417,000,000
Fortune 1000 ranking: 2012—772nd in revenues, 327th in profits, and 88th in assets
Forbes 2000 ranking: 2012—1667th in sales, 1108th in profits, and 362nd in assets
Corporate officers: Ralph W. Babb, Jr., Chair., Pres., and C.E.O.; Karen L. Parkhill, Vice-Chair. and C.F.O.; Paul R. Obermeyer, Exec. V.P. and C.I.O.
Board of directors: Ralph W. Babb, Jr., Chair.; Karen L. Parkhill, Vice-Chair.; Roger A. Cregg; T. Kevin DeNicola; Jacqueline P. Kane; Richard G. Lindner; Alfred A. Piergallini; Robert S. Taubman; Reginald M. Turner, Jr.; Nina G. Vaca
Subsidiaries: Comerica Bank, Detroit, MI; Comerica Bank & Trust, N.A., Ann Arbor, MI; Comerica Insurance Services, Inc., Southfield, MI; Comerica Leasing Corp., Southfield, MI; Comerica Securities, Inc., Detroit, MI; Comerica West Inc., Las Vegas, NV; Imperial Management, Inc., City of Industry, CA; Munder Capital Management, Birmingham, MI; Professional Life Underwriters Services, Inc., Southfield, MI; Wilson, Kemp & Associates, Inc., Detroit, MI
International operations: Bermuda; Brazil; British Virgin Islands; Cayman Islands; Hong Kong; Luxembourg
Historic mergers: Imperial Bancorp (January 29, 2001)
Giving statement: Giving through the Comerica Incorporated Corporate Giving Program and the Comerica Charitable Foundation.
Company EIN: 381998421

Comerica Incorporated Corporate Giving Program

c/o Corp. Contribs. Mgr.
MC 3390, P.O. Box 75000
Detroit, MI 48275-3390
Florida application address: MC 5172, 1675 N. Military Trail, Ste. 600, Boca Raton, FL 33486; Michigan application address: MC 3390, P.O. Box 75000, Detroit, MI 48275; Texas application address: MC 6503, P.O. Box 650282, Dallas, TX 75265; Western application address: MC 4805, 333 West Santa Clara St., San Jose, CA 95113; URL: http://www.comerica.com/vgn-ext-templating/v/index.jsp?vgnextoid=25fa788635bd2010VgnVCM1000004302a8c0RCRD

Purpose and activities: As a complement to its foundation, Comerica also makes charitable contributions to nonprofit organizations directly. Support is limited to Arizona, California, Florida, Michigan, and Texas.
Fields of interest: Education; Business/industry; Community development, small businesses; Community/economic development; Economics; Public affairs, finance Minorities; Adults, women.
Type of support: Employee volunteer services; Equipment; General/operating support; Sponsorships.
Geographic limitations: Giving limited to AZ, CA, FL, MI, and TX.
Support limitations: No grants for capital funding or program development.
Publications: Application guidelines.
Application information: Applications accepted. Application form not required. Applicants should submit the following:
1) how project will be sustained once grantmaker support is completed
2) results expected from proposed grant
3) statement of problem project will address
4) population served
5) name, address and phone number of organization
6) brief history of organization and description of its mission
7) copy of most recent annual report/audited financial statement/990
8) how project's results will be evaluated or measured
9) explanation of why grantmaker is considered an appropriate donor for project
10) what distinguishes project from others in its field
11) listing of board of directors, trustees, officers and other key people and their affiliations
12) detailed description of project and amount of funding requested
13) listing of additional sources and amount of support

Proposals should include any applicable deadlines and indicate whether the organization has received prior funding from Comerica or the Comerica Charitable Foundation.
Initial approach: Mail proposal to nearest application address

Comerica Charitable Foundation

c/o Corp. Contribs.
P.O. Box 75000, M.C. 3390
Detroit, MI 48275-3390
FAX: (313) 222-5555; Application addresses: Florida: Corp. Contribs. Mgr., M.C. 5172, 1675 N. Military Trail, Ste. 600, Boca Raton, FL 33486, Michigan: Corp. Contribs. Mgr., M.C. 3390, P.O. Box 75000, Detroit, MI 48275-3390, Texas: Corp. Contribs. Mgr., M.C. 6503, P.O. Box 650282, Dallas, TX 75265-0282, Western Market: Corp. Contribs. Mgr., M.C. 4805, 333 W. Santa Clara St., San Jose, CA 95113; Tel. for Caroline E. Chambers: (313) 222-3571; URL: http://www.comerica.com/about-us/community-involvement/pages/charitable-giving.aspx

Establishment information: Established in 1997 in MI.
Donors: Comerica Bank; Comerica Inc.
Contact: Janice E. Tessier, Pres.
Financial data (yr. ended 12/31/11): Assets, $138,403 (M); gifts received, $4,020,488; expenditures, $4,048,182; qualifying distributions, $4,048,182; giving activities include $4,048,182 for 513 grants (high: $504,500; low: $150).
Purpose and activities: The foundation supports organizations involved with education, health, employment, housing, financial literacy, community development, and economically disadvantaged people, and programs designed to promote diversity and inclusion.
Fields of interest: Elementary/secondary education; Business school/education; Adult/continuing education; Education; Health care; Employment, training; Employment; Housing/shelter; Human services, financial counseling; Civil/human rights, equal rights; Business/industry; Community development, small businesses; Community/economic development Economically disadvantaged.
Programs:
Access to Health Care: The foundation support programs designed to provide preventive care for the uninsured and underinsured.
Economic Self-Sufficiency: The foundation supports programs designed to promote economic self-sufficiency for low and moderate income individuals and families through financial literacy, job readiness, job creation and retention, small business training and development, and transitional and supportive housing.
Education: The foundation supports programs designed to promote financial literacy in K-12 and adult students; and provide scholarships for students with income needs for studies in business, finance, and growth industries.
Neighborhood Revitalization: The foundation supports programs designed to promote affordable housing and neighborhood business development.
Type of support: Capital campaigns; General/operating support; Program development; Scholarship funds.
Geographic limitations: Giving primarily in areas of company operations in AZ, CA, FL, MI, and TX.
Publications: Application guidelines; Program policy statement.
Application information: Applications accepted. Application form not required. Applicants should submit the following:
1) how project will be sustained once grantmaker support is completed
2) copy of IRS Determination Letter
3) brief history of organization and description of its mission
4) copy of most recent annual report/audited financial statement/990
5) listing of board of directors, trustees, officers and other key people and their affiliations
6) copy of current year's organizational budget and/or project budget
7) listing of additional sources and amount of support

Initial approach: Proposal to application address
Deadline(s): Mar. 15, June 15, Sept 15, and Nov. 15
Final notification: Apr. 15, July 15, Oct. 15, and Dec. 15
Officers and Directors:* Linda D. Forte*, Chair.; Janice M. Tessier*, Pres.; Jon W. Bilstrom*, V.P.;

Nicole V. Gersch, Secy.; Michael H. Michalak, Treas..; Caroline E. Chambers.
EIN: 383373052
Selected grants: The following grants are a representative sample of this grantmaker's funding activity:
$600,000 to United Way for Southeastern Michigan, Detroit, MI, 2010. For general fund.
$150,000 to National Council for Community Development, New York, NY, 2010. For general fund.
$100,000 to Detroit Institute of Arts, Detroit, MI, 2010. For general fund.
$50,000 to Mabuhay Alliance, San Diego, CA, 2010. For general fund.
$34,000 to Michigan State University, East Lansing, MI, 2010. For general fund.
$10,000 to Jewish Federation of Metropolitan Detroit, Bloomfield Hills, MI, 2010. For general fund.
$6,500 to Michigan Neighborhood Partnership, Detroit, MI, 2010. For general fund.
$5,000 to San Jose Conservation Corps and Charter School, San Jose, CA, 2010. For general fund.
$3,000 to Alliance for Multicultural Community Services, Houston, TX, 2010. For general fund.
$3,000 to Sphinx Organization, Detroit, MI, 2010. For general fund.

890
Commerce Bancshares, Inc.

1000 Walnut
P.O. Box 13686
Kansas City, MO 64106 (816) 234-2000
FAX: (800) 892-7100

Company URL: http://www.commercebank.com
Establishment information: Established in 1966.
Company type: Public company
Company ticker symbol and exchange: CBSH/NASDAQ
Business activities: Operates bank holding company; operates commercial bank.
Business type (SIC): Banks/commercial; holding company
Financial profile for 2012: Number of employees, 4,878; assets, $22,159,590,000; pre-tax net income, $398,610,000; liabilities, $19,992,460,000
Forbes 2000 ranking: 2012—1899th in sales, 1409th in profits, and 915th in assets
Corporate officers: David W. Kemper, Chair. and C.E.O.; Jonathan M. Kemper, Co-Vice-Chair.; Seth M. Leadbeater, Co-Vice-Chair.; John W. Kemper, Pres. and C.O.O.; Charles G. Kim, C.F.O.
Board of directors: David W. Kemper, Chair.; Jonathan M. Kemper, Co-Vice-Chair.; Seth M. Leadbeater, Co-Vice-Chair.; Terry Bassham; John R. Capps; Earl H. Devanny III; W. Thomas Grant II; James B. Hebenstreit; Terry O. Meek; Benjamin F. Rassieur III; Todd R. Schnuck; Andrew C. Taylor; Kimberly G. Walker
Subsidiaries: Capital for Business, Inc., Kansas City, MO; CBI Insurance Co., Kansas City, MO; CBI-Illinois, Inc., Kansas City, MO; CBI-Kansas, Inc., Kansas City, MO; CFB Partners II, LLC, Kansas City, MO; CFB Venture Fund I, Inc., Clayton, MO; CFB Venture Fund II, L.P., Kansas City, MO; Commerce Bank, N.A., Omaha, NE; Commerce Mortgage Corp., Kansas City, MO; Mid-America Financial Corp., Kansas City, MO; UBI Financial Services, Inc., Wichita, KS
Giving statement: Giving through the Commerce Bancshares Foundation.
Company EIN: 430889454

The Commerce Bancshares Foundation

(formerly The Commerce Foundation)
922 Walnut, Ste. 200
Kansas City, MO 64106-1809
URL: http://www.commercebank.com/about/social-responsibility/involvement.asp

Establishment information: Incorporated in 1952 in MO.
Donor: Commerce Bancshares, Inc.
Contact: Elizabeth Radtke, V.P.
Financial data (yr. ended 12/31/11): Assets, $1,089,180 (M); gifts received, $1,877,895; expenditures, $2,500,926; qualifying distributions, $1,486,788; giving activities include $1,475,204 for 814 grants (high: $242,978; low: $64).
Purpose and activities: The foundation supports organizations involved with arts and culture, education, health, human services, and civic affairs.
Fields of interest: Arts; Higher education; Education; Health care; American Red Cross; YM/YWCAs & YM/YWHAs; Human services; United Ways and Federated Giving Programs; Public affairs.
Programs:
Commerce Commendations: The foundation honors employees who have demonstrated exceptional commitment to the community. Employees are nominated by other Commerce employees and winners select a charity to receive a contribution in their honor.
Community Recognition Awards: The foundation, in partnership with the William T. Kemper Foundation, recognizes individuals who have contributed time and talent to help those in need. The honor includes a luncheon and a contribution in their name to the charity of their choice. Nominees are selected by Commerce's advisory boards.
Type of support: Annual campaigns; Building/renovation; Capital campaigns; Conferences/seminars; Continuing support; Curriculum development; Emergency funds; Employee volunteer services; Equipment; General/operating support; Professorships; Program development; Scholarship funds; Seed money.
Geographic limitations: Giving primarily in areas of company operations in Kansas City and St. Louis, MO.
Support limitations: No support for private foundations or non-501(c)(3) organizations. No grants to individuals, or for loans or matching gifts.
Application information: Applications not accepted. Contributes only to organizations recommended by Commerce Bank groups and executives. Unsolicited applications and proposals are not accepted.
Board meeting date(s): As required
Officers and Directors:* Jonathan M. Kemper, Pres.; Edward J. Reardon II, V.P. and Treas.; Elizabeth Radtke*, V.P.; James L. Swarts, Secy.; Kevin G. Barth; David W. Kemper.
EIN: 446012453

891
Commercial Bank

208 E. Main St.
Grayson, KY 41143-1304 (606) 474-7811

Company URL: http://www.cbgrayson.com/2023/mirror/
Establishment information: Established in 1891.
Company type: Subsidiary of a private company
Business activities: Operates commercial bank.
Business type (SIC): Banks/commercial
Corporate officer: Jack W. Strother, Jr., Chair.
Board of directors: Jack W. Strother, Jr., Chair.; Fred Buck; Phyllis Davis; John Jordan; Mary Blanche Jungers; Von Loy Kiser; Willie D. Patton; Sam Perry; Jack W. Strother, Sr.; Mark Strother
Giving statement: Giving through the Commercial Bank Foundation.

Commercial Bank Foundation

208 E. Main St.
Grayson, KY 41143-1304 (606) 474-7811

Donors: Commercial Bank; The Commercial Bank of Grayson.
Contact: Jack W. Strother, Jr., Tr.; Mark Strother, Tr.
Financial data (yr. ended 12/31/11): Assets, $581,178 (M); gifts received, $25,000; expenditures, $28,902; qualifying distributions, $28,500; giving activities include $28,500 for grants.
Purpose and activities: The foundation supports community foundations and organizations involved with higher education and awards college scholarships to students attending high school in Carter County, Kentucky.
Fields of interest: Education.
Type of support: General/operating support; Scholarship funds; Scholarships—to individuals.
Geographic limitations: Giving limited to Carter County, KY.
Application information: Applications accepted. An application form is required for scholarships. Application form required.
Scholarship applicants must have a GPA. of 3.50 or better. Scholarship applications should include a 1,000 word essay.
Initial approach: Proposal; contact foundation for application form for scholarships
Deadline(s): Apr. 15 for scholarships
Trustees: Jack W. Strother, Jr.; Mark Strother.
EIN: 611087988

892
Commercial Brick Corporation

Old Hwy. 270 W.
P.O. Box 1382
Wewoka, OK 74884 (405) 257-6613
FAX: (405) 257-6440

Company URL: http://www.commercialbrick.com
Establishment information: Established in 1973.
Company type: Private company
Business activities: Manufactures clay bricks and tiles.
Business type (SIC): Clay structural products
Corporate officers: Dick Liddell, Chair.; Robert Hartsock, Pres.
Board of director: Dick Liddell, Chair.
Giving statement: Giving through the Robert Clay Liddell Foundation.

Robert Clay Liddell Foundation

3000 Berry Rd., Ste. 120
Norman, OK 73072-7472 (405) 310-3103

Establishment information: Established in 2004 in OK.
Donors: Richard D. Liddell; Kelly Rose; Suzanne Rose; Commercial Brick Corp.
Financial data (yr. ended 12/31/11): Assets, $0 (M); gifts received, $528,728; expenditures, $528,554; qualifying distributions, $292,306; giving activities include $292,306 for grants.

Fields of interest: Mental health, addictions; Residential/custodial care; Christian agencies & churches.
Application information: Applications accepted. Applicants should submit the following:
1) detailed description of project and amount of funding requested
Initial approach: Letter
Deadline(s): None
Director: Lloyd R. Trenary.
EIN: 200420550
Selected grants: The following grants are a representative sample of this grantmaker's funding activity:
$23,800 to FaithWorks of the Inner City, Edmond, OK, 2010.
$12,000 to Work Activity Center, Moore, OK, 2010. For general assistance.
$9,250 to Ellis Foundation, Fort Scott, KS, 2010.
$9,000 to Jim Riley Outreach, Edmond, OK, 2010. For general assistance.

893
Commercial Metals Company
6565 N. MacArthur Blvd., Ste. 800
Irving, TX 75039 (214) 689-4300
FAX: (214) 689-5886

Company URL: http://www.cmc.com
Establishment information: Established in 1915.
Company type: Public company
Company ticker symbol and exchange: CMC/NYSE
Business activities: Manufactures, recycles, markets, and distributes steel and metal products and related materials.
Business type (SIC): Steel mill products
Financial profile for 2012: Number of employees, 9,860; assets, $3,441,250,000; sales volume, $7,828,440,000; pre-tax net income, $162,790,000; expenses, $7,665,650,000; liabilities, $2,194,880,000
Fortune 1000 ranking: 2012—335th in revenues, 568th in profits, and 708th in assets
Corporate officers: Joseph Alvarado, Chair., Pres., and C.E.O.; Barbara R. Smith, Sr. V.P. and C.F.O.; Ann J. Bruder, Sr. V.P., Genl. Counsel, and Secy.; Tracy Nolan, V.P. and C.I.O.; Paul Kirkpatrick, V.P. and Corp. Secy.; Carey Dubois, V.P. and Treas.; Adam Hickey, V.P. and Cont.
Board of directors: Joseph Alvarado, Chair.; Harold L. Adams; Rhys J. Best; Robert L. Guido; Richard B. Kelson; Anthony A. Massaro; Rick J. Mills; Sarah E. Raiss; J. David Smith; Joseph C. Winkler
Subsidiaries: CMC Steel Fabricators, Inc., Seguin, TX; Commercial Metals Railroad Salvage Co., Dallas, TX; Commercial Metals-Austin Inc., Austin, TX; Howell Metal Co., New Market, VA; SMI Steel Inc., Birmingham, AL; SMI-Owen Steel Co., Inc., Columbia, SC; Structural Metals, Inc., Seguin, TX
Plants: Arcadia, CA; Jacksonville, Tampa, FL; Chattanooga, TN; Clute, Corpus Christi, Fort Worth, Galveston, Houston, Victoria, Vinton, TX
International operations: Australia; China; Croatia; England; Germany; Hong Kong; Mexico; Poland; Singapore; Switzerland; United Kingdom
Giving statement: Giving through the Commercial Metals Company Contributions Program.
Company EIN: 750725338

Commercial Metals Company Contributions Program
6565 N. MacArthur Blvd., Ste. 800
Irving, TX 75039-6283 (214) 689-4300
FAX: (214) 689-5886; URL: http://www.cmc.com/en/americas/ourcompany/Pages/communityinvolvement.aspx

Purpose and activities: Commercial Metals makes charitable contributions to nonprofit organizations involved with arts and culture, education, and health and social issues dealing with the family. Support is given primarily in the Dallas-Fort Worth, Texas, area.
Fields of interest: Arts; Education; Health care; Employment, training; Human services Mentally disabled.
Type of support: Employee volunteer services; General/operating support; In-kind gifts; Program development.
Geographic limitations: Giving primarily in the Dallas-Fort Worth, TX, area.

894
Commonwealth Bank & Trust Company
4912 US Hwy. 42., Ste. 202
Louisville, KY 40222-6358 (502) 259-2330

Company URL: http://www.cbandt.com
Establishment information: Established in 1991.
Company type: Private company
Business activities: Operates commercial bank.
Business type (SIC): Banks/commercial
Financial profile for 2011: Assets, $713,700,000,000; sales volume, $49,500,000,000
Corporate officers: Ann Cowley Wells, Chair. and C.E.O.; John W. Key, Pres.; Michael E. Miller, C.O.O
Board of directors: Ann Cowley Wells, Chair.; Diane Cornwell; Garrett W. Dering; Robert C. Gatewood; Bobby Hudson; Betty Baird Kregor; James E. Mason; John A. Stough, Jr.; Carl M. Thomas; Darrell Wells; Wayne Wells
Offices: Anchorage, Shelbyville, Simpsonville, KY
Giving statement: Giving through the Commonwealth Bank & Trust Company Charitable Foundation.

Commonwealth Bank & Trust Company Charitable Foundation
(formerly Shelby County Trust Bank Charitable Foundation, Inc.)
4350 Brownsboro Rd., Ste. 310
Louisville, KY 40207

Establishment information: Established in 1985 in KY.
Donor: Shelby County Trust Bank.
Financial data (yr. ended 06/30/11): Assets, $253,517 (M); expenditures, $14,624; qualifying distributions, $14,610; giving activities include $14,610 for 1 grant.
Purpose and activities: The foundation supports libraries and organizations involved with the theater, parks and playgrounds, and human services.
Fields of interest: Human services.
Type of support: Equipment; General/operating support.
Geographic limitations: Giving is limited to Jefferson and Shelby counties, KY.
Application information: Applications not accepted. Unsolicited requests for funds not accepted.
Director: Margaret Ann Wells.
EIN: 311147866

895
Commonwealth Edison Company
(also known as ComEd)
440 S. Lasalle St.
Chicago, IL 60605-1028 (312) 394-2231

Company URL: https://www.comed.com
Establishment information: Established in 1887.
Company type: Subsidiary of a public company
Parent company: Exelon Corporation
Business activities: Operates electric power company.
Business type (SIC): Electric services
Financial profile for 2009: Number of employees, 5,819; sales volume, $5,770,000,000
Corporate officers: Anne R. Pramaggiore, C.E.O.; Terence Donnelly, Exec. V.P., Opers.; Joseph Trpik, Jr., Sr. V.P., C.F.O., and Treas.
Giving statement: Giving through the Commonwealth Edison Company Contributions Program.
Company EIN: 360938600

Commonwealth Edison Company Contributions Program
440 S. Lasalle St.
Chicago, IL 60605-1028 (312) 394-4321
E-mail: exeloncorporatecontributions@exeloncorp.com; URL: https://www.comed.com/about-us/community-involvement/Pages/default.aspx

Purpose and activities: Commonwealth Edison makes charitable contributions to nonprofit organizations involved with arts and culture, community economic development, math and science education, and the environment. Support is limited to service area in northern Illinois.
Fields of interest: Arts; Environment; Community/economic development; United Ways and Federated Giving Programs; Science, public education; Mathematics.
Type of support: Employee volunteer services; General/operating support; Sponsorships.
Geographic limitations: Giving limited to areas of company operations in northern IL.
Support limitations: No support for discriminatory organizations. No grants to individuals.
Publications: Application guidelines.
Application information: Applications accepted.
Initial approach: Complete online application
Deadline(s): None

896
Communications Products, Inc.
(also known as CPI)
7301 E. 90th St., Ste. 111
Indianapolis, IN 46256-1282
(317) 576-0332

Company URL: http://www.commprod.com
Establishment information: Established in 1983.
Company type: Private company
Business activities: Operates technology integration company that provides voice, data and cabling services.
Business type (SIC): Telephone communications
Corporate officers: Cliff Arellano, Pres.; Robert Peterson, V.P., Opers.; Carla Kraus, V.P.,Sales
Giving statement: Giving through the CIACO, Inc.

CIACO, Inc.
4563 W. 200 N.
Anderson, IN 46011-8788 (317) 637-2050

Establishment information: Established in IN.
Donors: Communication Products Inc.; Clifford I. Arellano; Nancy M. Arellano; James Currier; Barbara Currier; Sandra Clabaugh; Isabelle Moore.
Contact: Nancy M. Arellano, Dir.
Financial data (yr. ended 12/31/11): Assets, $636 (M); gifts received, $32,000; expenditures, $35,267; qualifying distributions, $35,266; giving activities include $34,317 for 15 grants (high: $7,500; low: $50).
Purpose and activities: The foundation supports organizations involved with education, community development, and Christianity; awards scholarships to students graduating from Anderson High School; and provides financial aid grants to the indigent.
Fields of interest: Education; Community/economic development; Christian agencies & churches Economically disadvantaged.
Type of support: General/operating support; Grants to individuals; Scholarships—to individuals.
Geographic limitations: Giving primarily in Anderson, IN.
Application information: Applications accepted. Application form required.
Initial approach: Proposal
Deadline(s): None
Directors: Clifford I. Arellano; Nancy M. Arellano; Christy Poturkovic.
EIN: 351756007

897
Community Bancshares of Mississippi, Inc.
1225 W. Government St.
Brandon, MS 39042-3048 (601) 469-1611

Company URL: http://www.communitybank.net/
Establishment information: Established in 1978.
Company type: Private company
Business activities: Operates bank holding company; operates commercial bank.
Business type (SIC): Banks/commercial; holding company
Corporate officers: Thomas W. Colbert, Chair.; Charles W. Nicholson, Jr., Vice-Chair. and C.O.O.; Freddie J. Bagley, Pres. and C.E.O.; William C. Lehr, Sr. V.P. and C.I.O.
Board of directors: Thomas W. Colbert, Chair.; Charles W. Nicholson, Jr., Vice-Chair.
Subsidiary: Community Bank, Blountsville, AL
Giving statement: Giving through the CB Foundation, Inc.
Company EIN: 630868361

CB Foundation, Inc.
P.O. BOX 1869
Brandon, MS 39043 (601) 825-4323
Application address: 1255 W. Government St., Brandon, MS 39042

Establishment information: Established in 2002 in MS.
Donors: Bankers Capital Corp.; Community Bancshares of Mississippi, Inc.
Contact: William C. Lehr, Secy.-Treas.
Financial data (yr. ended 12/31/11): Assets, $209,604 (M); expenditures, $1,048; qualifying distributions, $0.
Purpose and activities: The foundation supports organizations involved with theater, theological education, and public policy research.
Fields of interest: Performing arts, theater; Theological school/education; Public policy, research.
Type of support: General/operating support.
Geographic limitations: Giving primarily in Jackson, MS.
Application information: Applications accepted. Application form not required.
Initial approach: Proposal
Deadline(s): None
Officers: Thomas W. Colbert, Chair.; Freddie J. Bagley, Pres.; William C. Lehr, Secy.-Treas.
EIN: 753052579

898
Community Bank
(formerly Huntington Park Bank)
790 E. Colorado Blvd.
Pasadena, CA 91101 (800) 788-9999

Company URL: https://www.cbank.com/default.aspx
Establishment information: Established in 1945.
Company type: Private company
Business activities: Operates commercial bank.
Business type (SIC): Banks/commercial
Financial profile for 2012: Assets, $3,060,641,000; pre-tax net income, $42,094,000; liabilities, $2,803,806,000
Corporate officers: David P. Malone, Chair. and C.E.O.; Charles L. Rosen, C.O.O.; Nancy L. Karlson, C.F.O.; Deborah K. Hart, C.A.O.; Tom Baker, C.I.O.
Board of directors: David P. Malone, Chair.; Charles E. Cook; Harold Harrigian; Kyle R. Jones; Charles D. McCluer; Douglas J. McEachern; DuWayne J. Peterson; Craig H. Stewart; Kristen Stovesand
Giving statement: Giving through the Community Bank Foundation.

Community Bank Foundation
790 E. Colorado Blvd., Ste. MS-205
Pasadena, CA 91101-2113 (626) 568-2140

Establishment information: Established in 1990 in CA.
Donors: Community Bank, N.A.; Charles and Dorothy Cook Living Trust; Charles and Dorothy Cook Residuary Trust.
Contact: Wendy Welch-Keller, Secy.
Financial data (yr. ended 12/31/11): Assets, $3,907 (M); expenditures, $10; qualifying distributions, $0.
Purpose and activities: The foundation supports organizations involved with arts and culture, education, animal welfare, human services, community development, children, women, and economically disadvantaged people.
Programs:
Community Service: The foundation supports programs designed to enrich the lives of low income families, especially woman and children.
Education: The foundation supports programs designed to promote education. Special emphasis is directed toward programs designed to benefit disadvantaged students.
Human Services: The foundation supports programs designed to promote the well-being of low-and moderate income households, and promote community and economic development in lower income areas.
Type of support: General/operating support; Program development; Scholarship funds.
Geographic limitations: Giving primarily in Los Angeles, Orange, Riverside, and San Bernardino counties, CA.
Support limitations: No grants to individuals.
Application information: Applications accepted. Application form not required. Applicants should submit the following:
1) population served
2) name, address and phone number of organization
3) copy of IRS Determination Letter
4) brief history of organization and description of its mission
5) copy of most recent annual report/audited financial statement/990
6) listing of board of directors, trustees, officers and other key people and their affiliations
7) detailed description of project and amount of funding requested
8) contact person
9) copy of current year's organizational budget and/or project budget
10) listing of additional sources and amount of support
11) additional materials/documentation
Initial approach: Proposal
Copies of proposal: 1
Deadline(s): None
Officers and Director:* David P. Malone*, Pres.; Nancy Karlson Parker, C.F.O.; Wendy Welch-Keller, Secy.
EIN: 954262497

899
Community Coffee Company, LLC
P.O. Box 2311
Baton Rouge, LA 70821 (225) 368-3900

Company URL: http://www.communitycoffee.com
Establishment information: Established in 1919.
Company type: Private company
Business activities: Produces coffee.
Business type (SIC): Miscellaneous prepared foods
Corporate officers: Matthew Saurage, Chair., Pres., and C.E.O.; David Belanger, C.O.O.; Annette L. Vaccaro, Sr. V.P., C.F.O., and Treas.; Danny Hebert, V.P., Human Resources
Board of directors: Matthew C. Saurage, Chair.; C. Thomas Bromley III; Donald E. Brunson; David E. Hogberg; Ralph J. Nicoletti; H. N. Saurage IV
Giving statement: Giving through the Community Coffee Company LLC Corporate Giving Program.

Community Coffee Company LLC Corporate Giving Program
c/o Donation Requests
P.O. Box 2311
Baton Rouge, LA 70821-2311
FAX: (225) 368-4584;
E-mail: donations@communitycoffee.com;
URL: http://www.communitycoffee.com/AboutUs/Donations.aspx

Purpose and activities: Community Coffee makes charitable contributions of coffee to local pre-K-12 schools and to nonprofit organizations on a case by case basis. Support is given on a national basis in areas of company operations, with some emphasis on Louisiana.
Fields of interest: Elementary/secondary education; General charitable giving Military/veterans.
Type of support: Donated products; Sponsorships.

Geographic limitations: Giving on a national basis in areas of company operations; support for pre-K-12 educational systems is limited to LA.
Application information: Applications accepted. Application form required. Applicants should submit the following:
1) brief history of organization and description of its mission
2) contact person
Applications should indicate the organization's Tax ID Number and the intended use of donation; and the name, date, location, and expected attendance of the event, if applicable.
Initial approach: Download application form and e-mail or fax to headquarters for product donation
Deadline(s): 1 month prior to need
Final notification: 2 weeks

900
Community Health Systems, Inc.

4000 Meridian Blvd.
Franklin, TN 37067 (615) 465-7000

Company URL: http://www.chs.net
Establishment information: Established in 1986.
Company type: Public company
Company ticker symbol and exchange: CYH/NYSE
Business activities: Operates hospitals and surgery centers.
Business type (SIC): Hospitals
Financial profile for 2012: Number of employees, 96,000; assets, $16,606,330,000; sales volume, $13,028,990,000; pre-tax net income, $503,770,000; expenses, $11,944,310,000; liabilities, $13,875,130,000
Fortune 1000 ranking: 2012—184th in revenues, 507th in profits, and 274th in assets
Forbes 2000 ranking: 2012—657th in sales, 1505th in profits, and 1093rd in assets
Corporate officers: Wayne T. Smith, Chair., Pres., and C.E.O.; W. Larry Cash, Exec. V.P. and C.F.O.; Rachel A. Seifert, Exec. V.P., Genl. Counsel, and Secy.; J. Gary Seay, Sr. V.P. and C.I.O.; Martin G. Schweinhart, Sr. V.P., Opers.; Kevin J. Hammons, V.P., Corp. Cont., and C.A.O.; James W. Doucette, V.P. and Treas.; Tomi Galin, V.P., Corp. Comms.; Robert A. Horrar, V.P., Admin. and Human Resources
Board of directors: Wayne T. Smith, Chair.; W. Larry Cash; John A. Clerico; James S. Ely III; John A. Fry; William Norris Jennings, M.D.; Julia B. North; H. Mitchell Watson, Jr.
Giving statement: Giving through the Community Health Systems Foundation.
Company EIN: 133893191

Community Health Systems Foundation

4000 Meridian Blvd.
Franklin, TN 37067-6325

Establishment information: Established in 2005 in TN.
Donor: Community Health Systems.
Financial data (yr. ended 12/31/11): Assets, $7,849,293 (M); expenditures, $245,779; qualifying distributions, $245,679; giving activities include $245,679 for grants.
Purpose and activities: The foundation supports organizations involved with education, health, human services, and international development.
Fields of interest: Elementary/secondary education; Higher education; Medical school/education; Nursing school/education; Hospitals (general); Health care; Youth development, services; American Red Cross; Children/youth, services; Human services; International development; International relief; United Ways and Federated Giving Programs.
Type of support: Employee matching gifts; General/operating support; Program development; Scholarship funds.
Geographic limitations: Giving primarily in KY, MA, NY, PA, and TN.
Support limitations: No grants to individuals.
Application information: Applications not accepted. Contributes only to pre-selected organizations.
Officers and Directors:* Wayne T. Smith*, Chair. and Pres.; W. Larry Cash*, Exec. V.P.; Rachel A. Seifert*, Sr. V.P. and Secy.; Martin G. Schweinhart*, Sr. V.P.; James W. Doucette, V.P. and Treas.; T. Mark Buford, V.P.; Linda K. Parsons, V.P.
EIN: 203323391

901
Compass Bank

15 S. 20th St., Ste. 801
Birmingham, AL 35233-2000
(205) 297-6785

Company URL: http://www.bbvacompass.com/
Establishment information: Established in 1964.
Company type: Subsidiary of a public company
Business activities: Operates commercial bank.
Business type (SIC): Banks/commercial
Corporate officers: Jose Maria Garcia Meyer, Chair.; Manuel Sanchez, Co-Pres. and C.E.O.; Angel Cano, Co-Pres. and C.F.O.
Board of director: Jose Maria Garcia Meyer, Chair.
Giving statement: Giving through the BBVA Compass Foundation.

BBVA Compass Foundation

(formerly Compass Bank Foundation)
P.O. Box 10566, M.C. AL/BI/CH/ACT
Birmingham, AL 35296-0002 (205) 297-3464
E-mail: corporateresponsibility@bbvacompass.com; Additional contact: Joye Hehn, Mgr., Corp. Responsibility and Reputation; Application address: 2001 Kirby Dr., Ste. C110, Houston, TX 77019, tel.: (713) 831-5705; URL: http://www.bbvacompass.com/compass/responsibility/foundations.cfm

Establishment information: Established in 1981 in AL.
Donor: Compass Bank.
Contact: Reymundo Ocanas, V.P. and Exec. Dir.
Financial data (yr. ended 12/31/11): Assets, $636,069 (M); gifts received, $3,800,000; expenditures, $4,731,450; qualifying distributions, $4,731,350; giving activities include $4,731,350 for 660 grants (high: $500,000; low: $25).
Purpose and activities: The foundation supports organizations involved with arts and culture, education, the environment, health, housing, human services, diversity and inclusion, community development, minorities, and economically disadvantaged people.
Fields of interest: Museums; Arts; Elementary/secondary education; Higher education; Teacher school/education; Education; Environment, natural resources; Environment, energy; Environmental education; Environment; Health care, equal rights; Public health; Health care; Housing/shelter; Children/youth, services; Human services, financial counseling; Human services; Civil rights, race/intergroup relations; Community development, neighborhood development; Business/industry; Community/economic development; United Ways and Federated Giving Programs; Leadership development Minorities; Economically disadvantaged.
Programs:
Arts and Culture: The foundation supports programs designed to facilitate access to and participation in cultural experiences for persons with low- to moderate-income levels; and ensure the availability of artistic opportunities and venues that reflect the diversity of the community.
Community Development: The foundation supports programs designed to create and sustain affordable housing; provide alternative financial services and products to low- to moderate-income communities; revitalize low- to moderate-income neighborhoods and facilitate job creation; deliver financial education and financial literacy to children, adolescents, and adults; and promote entrepreneurship and economic development for minority and underserved groups and/or low- to moderate-income areas.
Diversity and Inclusion: The foundation provides capacity building to organizations serving minority segments with emphasis on low-income populations; and supports programs designed to provide leadership development of underrepresented groups; and promote tolerance and understanding among mainstream and minority populations.
Education: The foundation supports programs designed to address needs in PreK-12 education through public school-sponsored or facilitated curriculum-based initiatives; advance PreK-12 student performance through professional development and retention of teachers; facilitate merit-based access to higher education for underrepresented groups; and promote research and special initiatives at higher education institutions.
Environment and Natural Resources: The foundation supports programs designed to enable and sustain access to green technology and sustainable sources of energy to low- to moderate-income communities; promote projects with significant impact on the protection of the environment and sustainable practices; and promote public education about the environment and sustainability.
Health and Human Services: The foundation supports programs designed to enable and sustain independence for individuals and families; promote access to health education; and ensure access to quality healthcare.
Type of support: Annual campaigns; Curriculum development; Employee-related scholarships; General/operating support; Management development/capacity building; Matching/challenge support; Program development; Research; Scholarship funds; Sponsorships.
Geographic limitations: Giving primarily in areas of company operations in AL, AZ, CO, FL, NM, NY, PR, and TX.
Support limitations: No support for political committees or candidates, veterans' or fraternal organizations, alumni organizations, religious organizations not of direct benefit to the entire community, discriminatory organizations, individual pre-college schools including private, parochial, charter, or home schools, or individual schools in public school systems. No grants for sponsorships, golf tournaments, tables at events, fundraising activities that includes tickets, meals, or other benefits, general operating support for

organizations supported by the United Way, or political causes.
Publications: Application guidelines; Program policy statement.
Application information: Applications accepted. All applicants are invited to attend the semi-monthly Charitable Contributions Process conference calls and webinar presentations. Application form required.
Initial approach: Complete online eligibility quiz and application
Deadline(s): Jan. 3 to Sept. 30
Officers and Trustees:* Manolo Sanchez*, Chair.; Tiffany Dunne, Pres.; Reymundo Ocanas, V.P. and Exec. Dir.; Joseph B. Cartee, Secy.; Kirk Pressley, Treas.; Shelaghmichael Brown; Rafael Bustillo; B. Shane Clanton; Isabel Goiri; Bill Helms; James G. Heslop; Krister Holm.
EIN: 630823545
Selected grants: The following grants are a representative sample of this grantmaker's funding activity:
$200,000 to Texas A & M International University, Outreach Office of Institutional Advancement, Laredo, TX, 2010.
$100,000 to American Red Cross, Chicago, IL, 2010.
$90,000 to Houston Symphony Orchestra, Houston, TX, 2010.
$50,000 to United Way of Central Alabama, Birmingham, AL, 2010.
$40,000 to Habitat for Humanity, Dallas Area, Dallas, TX, 2010.
$40,000 to PeopleFund, Austin, TX, 2010.
$35,000 to George Gervin Youth Center, San Antonio, TX, 2010.
$5,775 to Childrens Museum of Houston, Houston, TX, 2010.
$5,000 to Denver Public Library Friends Foundation, Denver, CO, 2010.
$5,000 to United Way, Pikes Peak, Colorado Springs, CO, 2010.

902
Compuware Corporation

1 Campus Martius
Detroit, MI 48266-5099 (313) 227-7300
FAX: (313) 227-7555

Company URL: http://www.compuware.com
Establishment information: Established in 1973.
Company type: Public company
Company ticker symbol and exchange: CPWR/NASDAQ
International Securities Identification Number: US2056381096
Business activities: Operates software company.
Business type (SIC): Computer services
Financial profile for 2013: Number of employees, 4,491; assets, $1,973,280,000; sales volume, $944,550,000; pre-tax net income, $1,040,000; expenses, $942,340,000; liabilities, $975,060,000
Corporate officers: Gurminder S. Bedi, Chair.; Bob Paul, C.E.O.; Joseph Angileri, Pres. and C.O.O.; Laura Fournier, Exec. V.P., C.F.O., and Treas.; Denise Starr, Exec. V.P., Admin. and C.A.O.; Daniel S. Follis, Jr., Sr. V.P., Genl. Counsel, and Secy.; Lisa Elkin, Sr. V.P., Mktg. and Comms.
Board of directors: Gurminder S. Bedi, Chair.; Dennis W. Archer; William O. Grabe; Frederick A. Henderson; Faye Alexander Nelson; Robert C. Paul; Glenda D. Price, Ph.D.; W. James Prowse; G. Scott Romney; Ralph J. Szygenda
Giving statement: Giving through the Compuware Corporation Contributions Program.
Company EIN: 382007430

Compuware Corporation Contributions Program

1 Campus Martius
Detroit, MI 48266-5099 (313) 227-7300
URL: http://www.compuware.com/about/community-involvement.html

Purpose and activities: Compuware makes charitable contributions to nonprofit organizations involved with arts and culture, health care, youth development, technology education, and diversity. Support is given primarily in areas of company operations.
Fields of interest: Arts; Education; Health care; Cancer research; Youth development; Children/youth, services; Civil/human rights, equal rights; Engineering/technology; Public affairs Minorities; Women.
Type of support: Capital campaigns; Continuing support; Employee volunteer services; In-kind gifts; Program development; Sponsorships.
Geographic limitations: Giving primarily in areas of company operations.
Support limitations: No support for labor, fraternal, or social organizations, organizations with overhead expenses exceeding 25 percent of the total operating budget, or political organizations. No grants to individuals, or for political candidates or committees, general operating support, or projects or programs that could result in personal benefit to a Compuware director or employee.
Publications: Application guidelines.
Application information: Applications accepted. A contributions committee reviews all requests. Organizations receiving support are asked to provide periodic progress reports. Application form required. Applicants should submit the following:
1) contact person
2) detailed description of project and amount of funding requested
3) copy of IRS Determination Letter
4) name, address and phone number of organization
Applications should include a description of past support by Compuware with the organization.
Initial approach: Complete online letter of inquiry form
Committee meeting date(s): Monthly
Deadline(s): None
Final notification: 30 to 60 days

904
ConAgra Foods, Inc.

(formerly ConAgra, Inc.)
1 ConAgra Dr.
Omaha, NE 68102-5001 (402) 240-4000

Company URL: http://www.conagrafoods.com
Establishment information: Established in 1999.
Company type: Public company
Company ticker symbol and exchange: CAG/NYSE
International Securities Identification Number: US2058871029
Business activities: Produces branded and value-added packaged foods.
Business type (SIC): Meat packing plants and prepared meats and poultry; food and kindred products
Financial profile for 2012: Number of employees, 26,100; assets, $11,441,900,000; sales volume, $13,262,600,000; pre-tax net income, $625,200,000; expenses, $12,637,400,000; liabilities, $7,002,400,000
Fortune 1000 ranking: 2012—209th in revenues, 348th in profits, and 357th in assets
Forbes 2000 ranking: 2012—701st in sales, 787th in profits, and 1310th in assets
Corporate officers: Steven Goldstone, Chair.; Gary M. Rodkin, Pres. and C.E.O.; John F. Gehring, Exec. V.P. and C.F.O.; Brian Keck, Exec. V.P. and C.A.O.; Colleen Batcheler, Exec. V.P., Genl. Counsel, and Corp. Secy.; Nicole Theophilus, Sr. V.P., Human Resources; Robert Wise, V.P. and Cont.
Board of directors: Steven F. Goldstone, Chair.; Mogens C. Bay; Stephen G. Butler; Joie A. Gregor; Rajive Johri; William G. Jurgensen; Richard H. Lenny; Ruth Ann Marshall; Gary M. Rodkin; Andrew J. Schindler; Kenneth E. Stinson
Giving statement: Giving through the ConAgra Foods Feeding Children Better Foundation and the ConAgra Foods Foundation.
Company EIN: 710248710

ConAgra Foods Feeding Children Better Foundation

1 ConAgra Dr.
Omaha, NE 68102-5001
FAX: (402) 595-4595;
E-mail: foundation@conagrafoods.com; URL: http://www.nourishkidstoday.org

Establishment information: Established in 1999 in NE.
Donors: ConAgra, Inc.; ConAgra Foods, Inc.
Contact: Candy Becker, Fdn. Coord.
Financial data (yr. ended 05/31/12): Assets, $8,828,026 (M); expenditures, $4,929,712; qualifying distributions, $4,929,712; giving activities include $4,888,019 for 16 grants (high: $2,261,460; low: $2,500).
Purpose and activities: The foundation, under the umbrella of Nourish Today, Flourish Tomorrow, supports programs designed to provide solutions for child hunger and nutrition education. Special emphasis is directed toward programs designed to help children in need.
Fields of interest: Health organizations, research; Health organizations, public education; Agriculture/food, public policy; Agriculture/food, public education; Food services; Food banks; Food services, congregate meals; Nutrition; Agriculture/food; Youth development, agriculture; Children/youth, services.
Program:
Nourish Today, Flourish Tomorrow Grants: Through the Nourish Today, Flourish Tomorrow Grants program, the foundation invests in partnerships with high-impact, nonprofit organizations, as well as pilot programs that take an innovative approach to addressing needs in the core areas of child hunger and nutrition education.
Type of support: In-kind gifts; Program development; Program evaluation; Research; Technical assistance.
Geographic limitations: Giving primarily in Washington, DC, and Chicago, IL; giving also to national organizations.
Support limitations: No support for religious organizations not of direct benefit to the entire community, fraternal, social, labor, veteran, or alumni organizations, exclusive membership clubs, professional and amateur sports organizations and teams, terrorist organizations or those not compliant with the USA Patriot Act, athletic events and programs, capital campaigns (unless solicited at the funder's discretion), or memorial campaigns. No grants to individuals, or for fundraising, travel, or advertising.

Application information: Applications not accepted. Contributes only to pre-selected organizations.
Officers: Christopher P. Kircher, Chair.; Kori E. Reed, Pres.; Colleen Batcheler, Secy.; Robert G. Wise, Treas.
EIN: 470824577
Selected grants: The following grants are a representative sample of this grantmaker's funding activity:
$1,500,000 to Share Our Strength, Washington, DC, 2008. For Operation Frontline.
$192,334 to Feeding America, Chicago, IL, 2008. For Kid's Cafe Program.
$178,125 to Feeding America, Chicago, IL, 2008. For Kid's Cafe Program.
$178,125 to Feeding America, Chicago, IL, 2008. For Kid's Cafe Program.
$178,125 to Feeding America, Chicago, IL, 2008. For Kid's Cafe Program.
$178,125 to Feeding America, Chicago, IL, 2008. For Kid's Cafe Program.
$178,125 to Feeding America, Chicago, IL, 2008. For Kid's Cafe Program.
$178,125 to Feeding America, Chicago, IL, 2008. For Kid's Cafe Program.
$178,125 to Feeding America, Chicago, IL, 2008. For Kid's Cafe Program.
$178,125 to Feeding America, Chicago, IL, 2008. For Kid's Cafe Program.

ConAgra Foods Foundation

(formerly The ConAgra Foundation, Inc.)
1 ConAgra Dr.
Omaha, NE 68102-5001
FAX: (402) 595-4595;
E-mail: foundation@conagrafoods.com; URL: http://www.nourishkidstoday.org

Establishment information: Established in 1977.
Donors: ConAgra, Inc.; ConAgra Foods, Inc.; Barbara Rodkin; Gary M. Rodkin.
Contact: Candy Becker, Fdn. Coord.
Financial data (yr. ended 05/31/12): Assets, $9,624,424 (M); gifts received, $5,153,934; expenditures, $2,238,438; qualifying distributions, $2,238,438; giving activities include $1,986,758 for 61 grants (high: $500,000; low: $250).
Purpose and activities: The foundation supports programs designed to provide solutions for child hunger and nutrition education. Special emphasis is directed toward programs designed to help children in need.
Fields of interest: Public health, physical fitness; Health organizations, research; Health organizations, public education; Agriculture/food, public policy; Agriculture/food, public education; Food services; Food banks; Food services, congregate meals; Nutrition; Agriculture/food; Youth development, agriculture Children.
Programs:

Child Hunger Corps: Through Child Hunger Corps, the foundation and Feeding America select individuals to provide on-the-ground support in communities across America to advance child hunger programs. Child Hunger Corps members have two-year placements within food banks to increase access to nutritious food for children in need, develop the food bank's capacity, and create and implement programs that help alleviate child hunger.

Community Impact Grants: The foundation awards grants to grassroots organizations with programs designed to leverage innovation and creativity to address childhood hunger and nutrition in communities where ConAgra Foods' employees live and work, in states where food insecurity affects at least 22% of children. Grants range from $10,000 to $75,000.

Cooking Matters: Through Cooking Matters, the foundation and other partners provide access to food and facts about food choices so that kids can eat nutritiously, live balanced lifestyles, and succeed in school. The program includes workshops led by expert culinary and nutrition volunteers who teach families how to prepare healthy and affordable meals. The program is administered by Share Our Strength. Visit URL: http://cookingmatters.org/ for more information.

Employee Matching Gifts: The foundation matches contributions made by part-time and full-time employees and directors of ConAgra Foods, Inc. to any tax-exempt U.S. public charity on a one-for-one basis up to $1,000, per contributor, per institution, per year.

Employee-Related Scholarships: The foundation awards college scholarships to children of ConAgra Foods employees. The program is administered by Merit Scholarship Corporation and Scholarship America, Inc.

Hunger Free Summer: The foundation, in partnership with Feeding America, supports and expands the base of existing summer feeding programs for children. The initiative is designed to feed kids who struggle with hunger during the summer months, and will take place in food banks and through mobile "kid's meals" delivery in rural areas.

Nourish Our Community Grants: The foundation awards grants of $5,000 to $25,000 to nonprofit organizations recommended by employees of ConAgra Foods. Special emphasis is directed toward organizations designed to provide children and their families with access to food and nutrition education.

Nourish Today, Flourish Tomorrow Initiative: The foundation supports programs designed to raise awareness about children in America who are at risk of hunger and don't have enough food to live active and healthful lives. The initiative is designed to pursue sustainable solutions in the fight against child hunger, and includes Kids Cafe's, summer feeding programs, and Cooking Matters that feed and educate those in need; and capacity building in leading nonprofits to serve more people and create and bring to life innovative solutions to end child hunger.
Type of support: Donated products; Employee matching gifts; Employee-related scholarships; In-kind gifts; Management development/capacity building; Program development; Research.
Geographic limitations: Giving on a national basis in areas of company operations, with emphasis on AR, AZ, CA, CO, FL, GA, ID, IL, IN, LA, MA, MI, MS, NE, OH, OR, PA, TN, TX, and WA.
Support limitations: No support for religious organizations not of direct benefit to the entire community, fraternal, social, labor, veteran, or alumni organizations, exclusive membership clubs, professional or amateur sports organizations or teams, political organizations, terrorist organizations or those not compliant with the USA Patriot Act, or elementary or secondary schools. No grants to individuals (except for scholarships), or for fundraising or testimonial events or dinners, travel or tours, advertising, endowments, capital campaigns (unless solicited at the funders discretion), memorial campaigns, conferences, seminars, workshops, symposia, or publication of proceedings, radio or television programming underwriting, emergency needs, or athletic events; no loans or debt reduction.
Publications: Application guidelines; Program policy statement.
Application information: Applications accepted. A full proposal may be requested at a later date for Community Impact Grants. Organizations receiving support are asked to submit interim reports and a final report. National partnerships are solicited only at the discretion of ConAgra Foods staff. Application form required.
Initial approach: Complete online eligibility survey and letter of intent for Community Impact Grants
Deadline(s): Jan. 7 to Jan 28 for Community Impact Grants
Officers: Christopher P. Kircher, Chair.; Kori E. Reed, Pres.; Colleen R. Batcheler, Secy.; Robert G. Wise, Treas.
Number of staff: 2 full-time professional.
EIN: 362899320
Selected grants: The following grants are a representative sample of this grantmaker's funding activity:
$400,000 to Donors Trust, Omaha, NE, 2011.
$310,800 to United Way of the Midlands, Omaha, NE, 2011.
$310,500 to Scholarship America, Saint Peter, MN, 2011.
$124,347 to JK Group, Plainsboro, NJ, 2011.
$25,000 to Alameda County Community Food Bank, Oakland, CA, 2011.
$25,000 to Kids Food Basket, Grand Rapids, MI, 2011.
$25,000 to South Central Community Action Partnership, Twin Falls, ID, 2011. For hunger relief progams.
$16,360 to National Merit Scholarship Corporation, Evanston, IL, 2011.
$15,000 to United Way of Metropolitan Chicago, Chicago, IL, 2011.

905
Concept Mining, Inc.

(also known as Ridge Land Company, Inc.)
215 Industrial Park Rd.
P.O. Box 1335
Bluefield, VA 24605-9362 (276) 322-5334

Establishment information: Established in 1989.
Company type: Private company
Business activities: Mines coal and coal products.
Business type (SIC): Mining services/coal
Corporate officer: William Skewes, Owner
Giving statement: Giving through the Skewes Family Foundation.

Skewes Family Foundation

P.O. Box 1014
Bluefield, WV 24701-1014 (276) 326-1418

Establishment information: Established in 2004 in WV.
Donors: Ridgeland Company, Inc.; William G. Skewes†; Concept Mining, Inc.
Contact: Connie Boardwine
Financial data (yr. ended 12/31/11): Assets, $5,664,286 (M); expenditures, $302,250; qualifying distributions, $296,783; giving activities include $278,792 for 45 grants (high: $31,667; low: $425).
Purpose and activities: The foundation supports museums and community foundations and organizations involved with education and recreation.
Fields of interest: Museums; Elementary school/education; Secondary school/education; Higher education; Libraries (public); Education; Recreation, parks/playgrounds; Athletics/sports, school programs; Recreation; YM/YWCAs & YM/YWHAs; Foundations (community).

Type of support: Building/renovation; General/operating support; Program development; Scholarship funds.
Geographic limitations: Giving primarily in VA, WV, and WY.
Application information: Applications accepted. Application form not required.
Initial approach: Proposal
Deadline(s): None
Directors: Jennifer Austin; Jack Caffrey; Ronald Campbell; James C. Mulkey.
Officer: William G. Skewes, Jr., Chair.
EIN: 201978793
Selected grants: The following grants are a representative sample of this grantmaker's funding activity:
$20,000 to Wyoming East Foundation, New Richmond, WV, 2010.
$16,000 to McDowell Public Library, Welch, WV, 2010. For operating fund.
$10,000 to Bluefield College, Bluefield, VA, 2010.
$7,000 to Bluefield State College Foundation, Bluefield, WV, 2010.
$5,000 to Hargrave Military Academy, Chatham, VA, 2010.
$1,000 to Graham High School, Bluefield, VA, 2010.
$1,000 to Pikeview High School, Princeton, WV, 2010.
$1,000 to Princeton Community Hospital Foundation, Princeton, WV, 2010.

906
Conditioned Air Systems, Inc.
2410 Hilton Way, S.W.
Gainesville, GA 30501 (678) 561-4997

Company URL: http://www.conditionedairsystems.com
Establishment information: Established in 1983.
Company type: Private company
Business activities: Provides general contract heating, ventilating, and air conditioning services.
Business type (SIC): Contractors/plumbing, heating, and air-conditioning
Corporate officers: Doug Magnus, Pres.; Kenny Gee, V.P., Opers.; Baya M. Pruitt, Corp. Secy.-Treas.; Teresa Woods, Cont.
Giving statement: Giving through the James D. and Diane S. Magnus Foundation Inc.

James D. and Diane S. Magnus Foundation Inc.
2410 Hilton Way S.W.
Gainesville, GA 30501-6192

Establishment information: Established in GA.
Donor: Conditioned Air Systems, Inc.
Financial data (yr. ended 12/31/11): Assets, $1,588,061 (M); expenditures, $45,838; qualifying distributions, $40,500; giving activities include $40,500 for 12 grants (high: $12,000; low: $1,000).
Purpose and activities: The foundation supports organizations involved with K-12 education, health, children services, residential care, and Christianity.
Fields of interest: Elementary/secondary education; Health care; YM/YWCAs & YM/YWHAs; Children, services; Residential/custodial care; Christian agencies & churches.
Type of support: Annual campaigns; Continuing support; General/operating support; Program development; Scholarship funds; Scholarships—to individuals.
Geographic limitations: Giving primarily in Gainesville, GA.
Application information: Applications not accepted. Unsolicited requests for funds not accepted.
Trustees: Brooke Kalinauskas; Diane S. Magnus; James D. Magnus; Matthew Magnus; Baya M. Pruitt.
EIN: 600000489

907
Cone Denim LLC
(formerly Cone Mills Corporation)
804 Green Valley Rd., Ste. 300
Greensboro, NC 27408-7020
(336) 379-6220

Company URL: http://www.cone.com
Establishment information: Established in 1891.
Company type: Subsidiary of a public company
Business activities: Manufactures bleached, dyed, and printed textiles and polyurethane foam products.
Business type (SIC): Fabrics/broadwoven natural cotton; fabric finishing; plastics and synthetics; plastic products/miscellaneous
Corporate officer: Thomas E. McKenna, Pres.
Giving statement: Giving through the ABC Foundation.

ABC Foundation
804 Green Valley Rd., Ste. 300
Greensboro, NC 27408-7039

Establishment information: Trust established in 1944 in NC.
Donor: Cone Mills Corp.
Financial data (yr. ended 10/31/09): Assets, $0; expenditures, $3,488,156; qualifying distributions, $3,469,473; giving activities include $3,411,543 for 20 grants (high: $3,272,043; low: $500) and $45,000 for 18 grants to individuals (high: $2,500; low: $2,500).
Purpose and activities: The foundation supports hospices and organizations involved with higher education, business education, and community economic development.
Fields of interest: Higher education; Business school/education; Residential/custodial care, hospices; Community/economic development; United Ways and Federated Giving Programs.
Program:
Cone Mills Scholarship Program: The foundation awards college scholarships to children of employees of Cone Mills and International Textile Group. The program is administered by the Center for Scholarship Administration, Inc.
Type of support: Employee-related scholarships; General/operating support.
Geographic limitations: Giving limited to areas of company operations in NC.
Application information: Applications not accepted.
Officers: John L. Bakane, Pres.; Neil W. Koonce, V.P.; Gary L. Smith, V.P.; Terry L. Weatherford*, Secy.-Treas.
Trustee: Bank of America, N.A.
EIN: 581504894
Selected grants: The following grants are a representative sample of this grantmaker's funding activity:
$3,272,043 to Community Foundation of Greater Greensboro, Greensboro, NC, 2009.
$72,000 to United Way of Greater Greensboro, Greensboro, NC, 2009.
$12,000 to United Way of Rutherford County, Spindale, NC, 2009.

908
Conn Appliance, Inc.
22719 Coriander Dr.
Magnolia, TX 77355-3923 (281) 802-7169

Establishment information: Established in 1890.
Company type: Private company
Business activities: Operates household appliance stores.
Business type (SIC): Appliance stores/household
Financial profile for 2010: Number of employees, 25
Corporate officer: C. Conn, Owner
Giving statement: Giving through the Conn Appliances Charitable Foundation Inc.

Conn Appliances Charitable Foundation Inc.
3295 College St.
Beaumont, TX 77701-4611

Establishment information: Established in 1976 in TX.
Donor: Conn Appliances, Inc.
Financial data (yr. ended 11/30/11): Assets, $4,867 (M); expenditures, $0; qualifying distributions, $0.
Purpose and activities: The foundation supports organizations involved with higher education.
Fields of interest: Higher education.
Type of support: General/operating support; Scholarship funds.
Geographic limitations: Giving primarily in TX.
Application information: Applications not accepted. Unsolicited requests for funds not accepted.
Officers: Theodore Wright, C.E.O. and Pres.; Mike Poppe, C.F.O.
EIN: 741884559

910
Connecticut Attorneys Title Insurance Company
(also known as CATIC)
101 Corporate Pl., Fl. 2
Rocky Hill, CT 06067-1853 (860) 257-0606

Company URL: http://www.catic-e.com
Establishment information: Established in 1965.
Company type: Private company
Business activities: Sells title insurance.
Business type (SIC): Insurance/title
Financial profile for 2010: Assets, $76,386,304; sales volume, $98,321,009; liabilities, $32,895,438
Corporate officers: Richard J. Patterson, Pres. and C.E.O.; Richard A. Lawrence, Sr. V.P., Finance, C.F.O., and Treas.; Anne G. Csuka, Sr. V.P., Opers.; Catherine A. Loveland, Secy.
Board of directors: Charles R. Ebersol, Jr., Chair.; Robert S. Carey, Jr.; Leo P. Carroll; Gregory J. Cava; Patricia C. Farrell; Robert L. Fisher; Scott B. Franklin; Joseph W. Flynn; Craig T. Hoekenga; Peter W. Hoops; Leonard Jacobs; Kay Parker Jex; Tony E. Jorgensen; Thomas B. Kane; Ann Farrell Leslie; Joan C. Molloy; Thomas D. Murphy, Jr.; Richard J. Patterson; Keith S. Shaw; E. Jack Shorr; Denise D. Trevenen; William W. Weber
Subsidiary: Vermont Attorneys Title Corp., Burlington, VT
Offices: Norwalk, CT; Holyoke, Wellesley, MA; Manchester, NH; West Warwick, RI
Giving statement: Giving through the CATIC Foundation, Inc.

The CATIC Foundation, Inc.

c/o CT Attorneys Title Ins-R Lawrence
101 Corporate Pl.
Rocky Hill, CT 06067-1895
E-mail: dicklawrence@catic-e.com

Establishment information: Established in 1999 in CT.
Donor: Connecticut Attorneys Title Insurance Co.
Financial data (yr. ended 12/31/11): Assets, $945,199 (M); expenditures, $53,946; qualifying distributions, $49,184; giving activities include $40,500 for 13 grants (high: $10,000; low: $500).
Purpose and activities: The foundation supports organizations involved with legal education, legal aid, and law research.
Fields of interest: Education; Crime/law enforcement; Agriculture/food.
Type of support: Conferences/seminars; Continuing support; Endowments; General/operating support; Research; Scholarship funds.
Support limitations: No support for religious or political organizations. No grants to individuals.
Publications: Biennial report.
Application information: Applications not accepted. Unsolicited requests for funds not accepted.
Board meeting date(s): Spring, Fall, and as needed
Officers and Directors:* Robert S. Carey, Jr.*, Pres.; Leonard Jacobs*, Secy.; Richard A. Lawrence, Treas.; Giacomo T. Guarnaccia, Jr.; Kay P. Jex; Joseph Flynn.
Number of staff: 1 part-time professional.
EIN: 061566677

911
The Connecticut Light and Power Company

(also known as CL&P)
107 Selden St.
Berlin, CT 06037-1616 (860) 665-2944

Company URL: http://www.cl-p.com
Establishment information: Established in 1917.
Company type: Subsidiary of a public company
Business activities: Generates, transmits, and distributes electricity.
Business type (SIC): Electric services
Financial profile for 2010: Number of employees, 1,870; sales volume, $3,000,000,000
Corporate officer: William P. Herdegen, Pres. and C.O.O.
Giving statement: Giving through the CL&P Corporate Giving Program.

CL&P Corporate Giving Program

P.O. Box 270
Hartford, CT 06141-0270 (860) 665-3355
FAX: (860) 665-2666; E-mail: thayejd@nu.com; Additional contact: Lindsay Parke, Connecticut Contributions Administrator, tel.: (860) 665-3306, e-mail: parkelw@un.com; URL: http://www.cl-p.com/Home/Community/Support/CharitableContributions.aspx

Contact: Janet Thayer, Connecticut Contributions Processor Northeast Utilities
Purpose and activities: CL&P makes charitable contributions to nonprofit organizations involved with education, the environment, workforce development, and community development. Support is limited to areas of company operations in Connecticut.
Fields of interest: Vocational education; Education; Environment; Human services; Community/economic development.
Type of support: Employee volunteer services; General/operating support; In-kind gifts; Loaned talent; Program development.
Geographic limitations: Giving limited to areas of company operations in CT.
Support limitations: No support for United Way-supported organizations, combined health charities, art councils or federated funds, private foundations, religious, fraternal, political, or similar organizations, scouting groups, bands, little leagues, or similar groups, or health care organizations. No grants to individuals, or for athletic outings, debt reduction, endowments, or advertising.
Publications: Application guidelines.
Application information: Applications accepted. Applicants are asked to submit one proposal per year and include all requests for funding in that proposal. Organizations receiving support are asked to provide periodic progress reports and a final report. Application form required. Applicants should submit the following:
1) results expected from proposed grant
2) population served
3) name, address and phone number of organization
4) geographic area to be served
5) detailed description of project and amount of funding requested
6) plans for cooperation with other organizations, if any
7) contact person
8) copy of current year's organizational budget and/or project budget
9) listing of additional sources and amount of support

Applications should include the organization's Tax ID Number.
Initial approach: Complete online application
Committee meeting date(s): Quarterly
Deadline(s): Jan. 24 for 1st Quarter; Apr. 4 for 2nd Quarter; Aug. 1 for 3rd Quarter; Oct. 24 for 4th Quarter
Final notification: Apr. 4 for 1st Quarter; June 27 for 2nd Quarter; Oct. 3 for 3rd Quarter; Dec. 19 for 4th Quarter

912
Connecticut Natural Gas Corporation

100 Columbus Blvd., Ste. 400
P.O. Box 1500
Hartford, CT 06144-1500 (860) 727-3000

Company URL: http://www.cngcorp.com
Establishment information: Established in 1848.
Company type: Subsidiary of a public company
Business activities: Transmits and distributes natural gas.
Business type (SIC): Gas production and distribution
Financial profile for 2010: Number of employees, 14; assets, $876,366,000; liabilities, $485,641,000
Corporate officers: Robert M. Allessio, Pres. and C.E.O.; James E. Earley, V.P., Cont., and Treas.; William Reis, V.P., Admin.
Giving statement: Giving through the Connecticut Natural Gas Corporation Contributions Program and the Connecticut Energy Foundation Inc.

Connecticut Natural Gas Corporation Contributions Program

76 Meadow St.
East Hartford, CT 06108-3218 (203) 869-6900
E-mail: cvillano@soconngas.com

Contact: Cherlynn Villano, Public Affairs
Purpose and activities: As a complement to its foundation, Connecticut Natural Gas also makes charitable contributions to nonprofit organizations directly. Support is given primarily in areas of company operations in Connecticut.
Fields of interest: Education; Environment; General charitable giving.
Type of support: Employee volunteer services; General/operating support.
Geographic limitations: Giving primarily in areas of company operations in CT.
Application information: Applications accepted. Proposal should be submitted using organization letterhead. Application form not required.
Initial approach: E-mail proposal to headquarters

Connecticut Energy Foundation Inc.

P.O. Box 1500
Hartford, CT 06144-1500

Establishment information: Established in 1984 in CT.
Donor: Connecticut Natural Gas Corp.
Contact: Shelly Saczynaki
Financial data (yr. ended 06/30/12): Assets, $1,414,193 (M); expenditures, $251,507; qualifying distributions, $250,000; giving activities include $250,000 for 1 grant.
Purpose and activities: The foundation supports programs designed to help low-income people meet their energy needs.
Type of support: Building/renovation; Equipment; Program development; Research.
Geographic limitations: Giving limited to areas of company operations in CT.
Publications: Application guidelines.
Application information: Applications accepted. Application form required. Applicants should submit the following:
1) copy of IRS Determination Letter
2) brief history of organization and description of its mission
3) copy of most recent annual report/audited financial statement/990
4) listing of board of directors, trustees, officers and other key people and their affiliations
5) detailed description of project and amount of funding requested
6) copy of current year's organizational budget and/or project budget

Requests should include documentation as to the expected energy savings.
Initial approach: Contact foundation for application form
Copies of proposal: 1
Deadline(s): None
Trustees: Robert M. Alessio; John A. Dobos; Thomas J. Donohue, Jr.; James Earley; Chris Malone; William Reis.
EIN: 222546022
Selected grants: The following grants are a representative sample of this grantmaker's funding activity:
$35,000 to Rebuilding Together Hartford, Hartford, CT, 2009.

909
Conn-Selmer, Inc.

600 Industrial Pkwy.
P.O. Box 310
Elkhart, IN 46515-0310 (574) 522-1675

Company URL: http://www.conn-selmer.com
Establishment information: Established in 2002.
Company type: Subsidiary of a public company
Business activities: Manufactures musical instruments.
Business type (SIC): Musical instruments
Corporate officers: John M. Stoner, Jr., Pres. and C.E.O.; Robert Speed, V.P., Opers.; Judy Schuchart, V.P., Finance and C.F.O.; Roberta Imel, V.P., Human Resources; Jeffrey Digby, Cont.
Giving statement: Giving through the Conn-Selmer, Inc. Corporate Giving Program.

Conn-Selmer, Inc. Corporate Giving Program

600 Industrial Pkwy.
Elkhart, IN 46516-5414 (574) 523-0657
E-mail: rbreske@conn-selmer.com

Contact: Richard Breske, Dir., Institution Rels.
Financial data (yr. ended 12/31/08): Total giving, $743,000, including $743,000 for 5 in-kind gifts.
Purpose and activities: Conn-Selmer makes in-kind charitable contributions to nonprofit organizations involved with music education.
Fields of interest: Performing arts, education.
Type of support: In-kind gifts; Program development.
Publications: Informational brochure.
Application information: Applications accepted. The Institution Relations Department handles giving. Application form not required. Applicants should submit the following:
1) detailed description of project and amount of funding requested

Initial approach: Proposal to headquarters
Copies of proposal: 1
Deadline(s): None
Final notification: 1 week

Number of staff: 1 full-time professional.

913
ConocoPhillips

(formerly Corvetteporsche Corp.)
600 N. Dairy Ashford
P.O. Box 2197
Houston, TX 77079-1175 (281) 293-1000
FAX: (302) 636-5454

Company URL: http://www.conocophillips.com
Establishment information: Established in 2001.
Company type: Public company
Company ticker symbol and exchange: COP/NYSE
International Securities Identification Number: US20825C1045
Business activities: Conducts crude oil, natural gas, and natural gas liquids exploration and production activities; refines and markets crude oil and petroleum products; manufactures and markets petrochemicals and plastics.
Business type (SIC): Petroleum refining; extraction/oil and gas; extraction/natural gas liquids; chemicals and allied products; plastics and synthetics
Financial profile for 2012: Number of employees, 16,900; assets, $117,144,000,000; sales volume, $62,004,000,000; pre-tax net income, $15,423,000,000; expenses, $46,581,000,000; liabilities, $69,157,000,000
Fortune 1000 ranking: 2012—45th in revenues, 21st in profits, and 57th in assets
Forbes 2000 ranking: 2012—139th in sales, 53rd in profits, and 219th in assets
Corporate officers: Ryan M. Lance, Chair. and C.E.O.; Jeff Sheets, Exec. V.P., Finance and C.F.O.; Janet Langford Kelly, Sr. V.P., Genl. Counsel, and Corp. Secy.; Ellen DeSanctis, V.P., Comms.; Sheila Feldman, V.P., Human Resources
Board of directors: Ryan M. Lance, Chair.; Richard Lee Armitage; Richard H. Auchinleck; James E. Copeland, Jr.; Gay Huey Evans; Jody Freeman; Tan Sri Mohd Hassan Marican; Robert A. Niblock; Harald Norvik; William E. Wade, Jr.
Subsidiaries: Calcasieu Shipping Corp., Sulphur, LA; Phillips Alaska Natural Gas Corp., Anchorage, AK; Tosco Corporation, Old Greenwich, CT
International operations: Australia; Austria; Bahamas; Bermuda; British Virgin Islands; Canada; Cayman Islands; Czech Republic; Denmark; England; Germany; Indonesia; Ireland; Liberia; Luxembourg; Netherlands; Nigeria; Norway; Poland; Russia; Scotland; Sweden; Switzerland; United Arab Emirates; United Kingdom; Venezuela; Vietnam
Historic mergers: Burlington Resources Inc. (March 31, 2006)
Giving statement: Giving through the ConocoPhillips Corporate Giving Program and the ConocoPhillips Dependent Scholarship Program Trust.
Company EIN: 010562944

ConocoPhillips Corporate Giving Program

(formerly Conoco Inc. Corporate Giving Program)
c/o Corp. Contribs., 3132 Marland Bldg.
600 N. Dairy Ashford Rd.
Houston, TX 77079-1100 (281) 293-1000
URL: http://www.conocophillips.com/in-communities/Pages/default.aspx

Purpose and activities: ConocoPhillips makes charitable contributions to nonprofit organizations involved with education and youth programs, health and social services, civic programs and the arts, and the environment. Support is given on a national and international basis.
Fields of interest: Arts; Education; Environment; Health care; Safety, education; Youth development; Public affairs.
Programs:

Dependent Scholarship Program: ConocoPhillips annually awards $3,000 college scholarships to children of ConocoPhillips employees, renewable yearly (for a total of 4 years) based on scholastic achievement.

Employee Volunteer Grant Program: U.S. employees and retirees can apply for up to two individual grants of $500 for every 20 hours volunteered with an eligible 501(c)(3) non-profit organization.

Matching Gift Program: Eligible contributions from employees are matched dollar-for-dollar to an annual maximum of $15,000 per employee. Eligible retiree contributions are matched to an annual maximum of $7,500 per retiree.

Type of support: Emergency funds; Employee matching gifts; Employee volunteer services; Employee-related scholarships; General/operating support.
Geographic limitations: Giving on a national and international basis in areas of company operations, with emphasis on AK, NM, OK, and TX.
Support limitations: No support for sectarian or religious organizations. No grants to individuals (except for employee-related scholarships), or for sponsorships or advertising or endowments.
Publications: Application guidelines.
Application information: Application form required. Applicants should submit the following:
1) results expected from proposed grant
2) copy of IRS Determination Letter
3) detailed description of project and amount of funding requested
4) copy of current year's organizational budget and/or project budget
5) listing of additional sources and amount of support

Initial approach: Complete online application; send to nearest company facility for organizations located outside the U.S.
Copies of proposal: 1
Deadline(s): June 1 to Aug. 1

ConocoPhillips Dependent Scholarship Program Trust

(formerly Educational Fund for Children of Phillips Petroleum Company Employees)
700 Plaza Office Building
Bartlesville, OK 74004

Establishment information: Established in 1939 in OK.
Donors: Phillips Petroleum Co.; ConocoPhillips Co.
Contact: C.G. Bradley, Dir., Corp. Contribs.
Financial data (yr. ended 08/31/10): Assets, $25,500 (M); gifts received, $788,384; expenditures, $771,884; qualifying distributions, $771,884; giving activities include $768,500 for 247 grants to individuals (high: $4,000; low: $1,500).
Purpose and activities: The foundation awards college scholarships to children, adopted children, stepchildren, and fully-dependent wards of present, permanently disabled, and deceased full-time employees of ConocoPhillips and its domestic subsidiaries.
Fields of interest: Higher education.
Type of support: Employee-related scholarships.
Geographic limitations: Giving primarily in areas of company operations, with emphasis on LA, OK, PA, TX, and UT.
Application information: Applications not accepted. Contributes only through employee-related scholarships.
Officer: C.G. Bradley, Admin.
Selection Committee: Urton Anderson; Karl Reid; Roger Blais.
EIN: 736095141

914
Conrail Inc.

1717 Arch St., 32nd Fl.
Philadelphia, PA 19103-2827
(215) 209-2000

Company URL: http://www.conrail.com
Establishment information: Established in 1976.
Company type: Private company
Business activities: Provides railroad transportation services.
Business type (SIC): Transportation/railroad
Corporate officers: Ronald L. Batory, Pres. and C.O.O.; Joseph Rogers, C.F.O.; Anthony Carlini, C.A.O.; Ronald J. Conway, Sr. V.P., Opers.; Joseph Rogers, V.P., Finance
Subsidiary: Consolidated Rail Corp., Philadelphia, PA

Giving statement: Giving through the Women's Aid of Penn Central School IAS.

Women's Aid of Penn Central School IAS

(formerly Women's Aid Scholarship)
1525 W. W.T. Harris Blvd.
Charlotte, NC 28288-5709 (866) 608-0001

Establishment information: Established in 1957.
Donor: Conrail Inc.
Financial data (yr. ended 12/31/11): Assets, $1,589,238 (M); expenditures, $91,675; qualifying distributions, $64,500; giving activities include $64,500 for grants.
Purpose and activities: The foundation awards college scholarships to children of employees and retirees of Conrail and its predecessor railroads. The program is administered through the Center for Scholarship Administration.
Fields of interest: Education.
Type of support: Employee-related scholarships.
Geographic limitations: Giving primarily in areas of company operations in NC.
Application information: Applications accepted. Application form required.
Initial approach: See website www.csascholars.org
Deadline(s): Apr. 1
EIN: 236232572

915
Consolidated Container Company LLC

(formerly Franklin Holdings, Inc.)
3101 Towercreek Pkwy., Ste. 300
Atlanta, GA 30339 (678) 742-4600

Company URL: http://www.ccclic.com
Establishment information: Established in 1999.
Company type: Subsidiary of a private company
Business activities: Manufactures metal cans and plastic containers.
Business type (SIC): Metal containers; plastic products/miscellaneous
Corporate officers: James P. Kelley, Chair.; B. Joseph Rokus, Vice-Chair.; Jeffrey M. Greene, Pres. and C.E.O.; Robert H. Walton, C.O.O.; Louis Lettes, Sr. V.P., Genl. Counsel, and Secy.; Laura Fee, Sr. V.P., Human Resources; Richard P. Sehring, C.F.O.; Jim Beck, C.I.O.; Brad Newman, V.P., Human Resources
Board of directors: James P. Kelley, Chair.; B. Joseph Rokus, Vice-Chair.; Jeffrey M. Greene
Subsidiaries: Continental Bondware, Inc., Rolling Meadows, IL; Continental Container Systems, West Chicago, IL; Continental White Cap, Inc., Northbrook, IL
Giving statement: Giving through the Carle C. Conway Scholarship Foundation, Inc.

Carle C. Conway Scholarship Foundation, Inc.

95 Alexandra Dr.
Stamford, CT 06903-1731
Application address: Carle C. Conway Scholarship Program, P.O. Box 6731, Princeton, NJ 08541

Establishment information: Established in 1950.
Donors: Continental Can Co., Inc.; Franklin Holdings, Inc.
Contact: Marsha L. Colton, V.P. and Treas.
Financial data (yr. ended 06/30/12): Assets, $3,934,461 (M); expenditures, $343,270; qualifying distributions, $294,461; giving activities include $100,000 for 1 grant and $194,461 for 23 grants to individuals (high: $10,000; low: $2,055).
Purpose and activities: The foundation supports organizations involved with higher education.
Fields of interest: Higher education.
Type of support: Employee-related scholarships; General/operating support; Scholarship funds.
Geographic limitations: Giving primarily in areas of company operations in FL, IL, NY, KS, and PA.
Application information: Applications not accepted. Contributes only through employee-related scholarships and to pre-selected organizations.
Board meeting date(s): Usually May
Officers and Director: Stephen Bermas, Pres.; Marsha L. Colten, V.P. and Treas.; Patricia DelTorro Heck, Secy.; Robert S. Cohen.
EIN: 136088936

916
Consolidated Edison Company of New York, Inc.

(also known as Con Edison)
4 Irving Pl.
New York, NY 10003 (212) 460-4600

Company URL: http://www.coned.com
Establishment information: Established in 1884.
Company type: Subsidiary of a public company
International Securities Identification Number: US2091151041
Business activities: Generates, transmits, and distributes electricity; transmits and distributes natural gas; produces and distributes steam.
Business type (SIC): Combination utility services; steam and air-conditioning supply services
Financial profile for 2011: Number of employees, 15,180; assets, $36,146,000,000; sales volume, $13,325,000,000
Corporate officers: Kevin Burke, Chair. and C.E.O.; Craig S. Ivey, Pres.; Robert N. Hoglund, Sr. V.P. and C.F.O.; John D. McMahon, Sr. V.P. and Genl. Counsel; Frances A. Resheske, Sr. V.P., Public Affairs; Robert Stelben, V.P. and Treas.
Board of director: Kevin Burke, Chair.
Giving statement: Giving through the Con Edison Corporate Giving Program.

Con Edison Corporate Giving Program

c/o Strategic Partnerships Program
4 Irving Pl., Rm. 1650-S
New York, NY 10003-3502 (212) 460-4277
FAX: (212) 460-3730;
E-mail: mcmillans@coned.com; Additional e-mail: powerofgiving@coned.com; URL: http://www.coned.com/Partnerships/application_guidelines.asp

Contact: Susan McMillan, Section Mgr., Strategic Partnerships
Purpose and activities: Con Edison makes charitable contributions to community-based, nonprofit organizations involved with community development, arts and culture, education, the environment, health and human services, and civic affairs. Support is given primarily in New York City and Westchester County.
Fields of interest: Arts; Education; Environment.
Type of support: Employee matching gifts; Employee volunteer services; In-kind gifts; Sponsorships.
Geographic limitations: Giving primarily in New York, NY and Westchester County; giving on a national basis to universities.
Support limitations: No support for labor organizations, houses of worship, K-12 schools, or private foundations. No grants to individuals, or for endowments, general operating support, debt reduction, or to cover deficits.
Publications: Application guidelines.
Application information: Applications accepted. Support is limited to 1 contribution per organization during any given year. Multi-year funding is not automatic. Cover letters should be no more than 2 pages in length. Submission of videos, audio tapes, CDs, electronic file storage media, or computer programs are not accepted. The Strategic Partnerships Department handles giving. Application form not required. Applicants should submit the following:
1) population served
2) name, address and phone number of organization
3) copy of IRS Determination Letter
4) brief history of organization and description of its mission
5) geographic area to be served
6) copy of most recent annual report/audited financial statement/990
7) listing of board of directors, trustees, officers and other key people and their affiliations
8) detailed description of project and amount of funding requested
9) contact person
10) copy of current year's organizational budget and/or project budget
11) listing of additional sources and amount of support
12) additional materials/documentation
Initial approach: Proposal to headquarters for organizations that serve general populations throughout several city boroughs and Westchester. If the organization serves a target group within one borough or exclusively within Westchester, send application to appropriate local Con Edison Public Affairs office. See website for addresses of local Con Edison Public Affairs offices
Copies of proposal: 1
Deadline(s): Mar. 1 to Oct. 1
Final notification: Following review

917
Consolidated Electrical Distributors, Inc.

31356 Via Colinas, Ste. 107
Westlake Village, CA 91362
(818) 597-3050

Company URL: http://www.cedcareers.com/company.html
Establishment information: Established in 1913.
Company type: Private company
Business activities: Sells electrical equipment wholesale.
Business type (SIC): Electrical goods—wholesale
Financial profile for 2011: Number of employees, 6,200; sales volume, $3,800,000,000
Corporate officers: Keith W. Colburn, Chair.; H. Dean Bursch, Pres.; David T. Bradford, V.P., Secy., and Genl. Counsel
Board of director: Keith W. Colburn, Chair.
Giving statement: Giving through the Dunard Fund USA, Ltd.

Dunard Fund USA, Ltd.
555 Skokie Blvd., Ste. 555
Northbrook, IL 60062-2845

Establishment information: Established around 1993 in IL.
Donors: Consolidated Electrical Distributors, Inc.; LCR-M Corp.; Carol C. Hogel.
Financial data (yr. ended 12/31/11): Assets, $19,977,846 (M); gifts received, $3,140,000; expenditures, $3,633,031; qualifying distributions, $3,408,711; giving activities include $3,390,836 for 29 grants (high: $1,000,000; low: $420).
Purpose and activities: The foundation supports organizations involved with arts and culture and education.
Fields of interest: Museums; Performing arts, music; Performing arts, orchestras; Performing arts, opera; Performing arts, education; Arts; Higher education.
Type of support: Annual campaigns; Continuing support; Endowments; General/operating support; Program development; Scholarship funds.
Geographic limitations: Giving primarily in CA, New York, NY, and Philadelphia, PA.
Support limitations: No grants to individuals.
Application information: Applications not accepted. Contributes only to organizations referred by known and highly respected figures.
Board meeting date(s): Weekly
Officers and Directors:* Carol C. Hogel*, Pres. and Treas.; David T. Bradford, Secy.; Catherine C. Hogel; Elisabeth Hogel.
EIN: 980087034
Selected grants: The following grants are a representative sample of this grantmaker's funding activity:
$2,123,200 to Colburn School of the Performing Arts, Los Angeles, CA, 2009. For operating endowment.
$790,000 to Los Angeles Philharmonic, Los Angeles, CA, 2009. For annual support.
$500,000 to Americans for Oxford, New York, NY, 2009. For endowment.
$500,000 to Los Angeles Philharmonic, Los Angeles, CA, 2009. For operating endowment.
$125,000 to Los Angeles Opera Company, Los Angeles, CA, 2009. For endowment.
$98,605 to Metropolitan Opera, New York, NY, 2009. For annual support.
$40,000 to Los Angeles Philharmonic, Los Angeles, CA, 2009. For Board of Directors annual fund.
$25,000 to Beginning with Children Foundation, New York, NY, 2009. For annual support.
$25,000 to University of Southern California, Los Angeles, CA, 2009. For endowment.
$17,000 to New School, New York, NY, 2009. For endowment and general support.

918
Consolidated Systems, Inc.
(also known as Consolidated Metal Products)
650 Rosewood Dr.
Columbia, SC 29201-4671 (803) 771-7920

Company URL: http://www.csisteel.com
Establishment information: Established in 1954.
Company type: Private company
Business activities: Manufactures steel products.
Business type (SIC): Fabricated metal products (except machinery and transportation equipment)
Corporate officers: Louise Slator Brownley, Chair.; Brad Pemberton, Co-Pres.; William Strom, Co-Pres.; Ross Bagley, C.I.O. and C.O.O.
Board of director: Louise Slator Brownley, Chair.
Subsidiaries: Consolidated Cargo Carriers, Inc., Columbia, SC; Doublecoat, L.L.C., Jackson, MS; Southeastern Coated Products, Columbia, SC
Giving statement: Giving through the Thomas C. Meredith, Jr. Foundation.

Thomas C. Meredith, Jr. Foundation
1525 W. W.T Harris Blvd. D1114-044
Charlotte, NC 28288-1161 (866) 608-0001
E-mail: michael.boyles@wachovia.com

Establishment information: Established in 1994 in SC.
Donor: Consolidated Systems, Inc.
Financial data (yr. ended 12/31/11): Assets, $50,976 (M); gifts received, $12,000; expenditures, $11,327; qualifying distributions, $10,721; giving activities include $10,000 for 1 grant.
Purpose and activities: The foundation awards college scholarships to children of full-time employees of Consolidated Systems Inc. The program is administered by the Center for Scholarship Administration.
Fields of interest: Higher education.
Type of support: Employee-related scholarships.
Geographic limitations: Giving primarily in SC.
Application information: Applications accepted. Application form required.
Initial approach: See Website
Deadline(s): Feb. 15
Trustee: Wells Fargo.
EIN: 566455071

919
Constellation Brands, Inc.
207 High Point Dr., Bldg. 100
Victor, NY 14564 (585) 678-7100
FAX: (302) 655-5049

Company URL: http://www.cbrands.com
Establishment information: Established in 1945.
Company type: Public company
Company ticker symbol and exchange: STZ/NYSE
International Securities Identification Number: US21036P1084
Business activities: Operates wine company.
Business type (SIC): Beverages
Financial profile for 2013: Number of employees, 4,500; assets, $7,638,100,000; sales volume, $2,796,100,000; pre-tax net income, $516,400,000; expenses, $2,285,700,000; liabilities, $4,777,800,000
Fortune 1000 ranking: 2012—779th in revenues, 361st in profits, and 485th in assets
Forbes 2000 ranking: 2012—1650th in sales, 1226th in profits, and 1594th in assets
Corporate officers: Richard Sands, Chair.; Robert Sands, Pres. and C.E.O.; Robert Ryder, Exec. V.P. and C.F.O.; Thomas J. Mullin, Exec. V.P. and Genl. Counsel
Board of directors: Richard Sands, Chair.; Jerry Fowden; Barry A. Fromberg; Robert L. Hanson; Jeananne K. Hauswald; James A. Locke III; Robert Sands; Judy A. Schmeling; Paul L. Smith; Keith Wandell; Mark Zupan, Ph.D.
Subsidiary: Crown Imports, LLC, Chicago, IL
International operations: Canada; New Zealand
Giving statement: Giving through the Constellation Brands, Inc. Contributions Program.
Company EIN: 160716709

Constellation Brands, Inc. Contributions Program
207 High Point Dr., Bldg. 100
Victor, NY 14564-1061 (585) 678-7100
URL: http://www.cbrands.com/corporate-social-responsibility/giving

920
Conston, Inc.
41 Conshohocken State Rd., Ste. 612
Bala Cynwyd, PA 19004-2438
(610) 664-7898

Company type: Private company
Business activities: Operates women's, children's, and infant's clothing stores.
Business type (SIC): Women's apparel stores
Corporate officers: Charles Conston, Pres.; John Cebulon, Secy.; John Cebular, Treas.
Giving statement: Giving through the Conston Foundation.

Conston Foundation
751 Righters Mill Rd.
Narberth, PA 19072
Application address: 7959 L'Aquila Way, Delray Beach, FL 33446

Establishment information: Established in 1959 in PA.
Donor: Conston, Inc.
Contact: Shirley Conston, Tr.
Financial data (yr. ended 12/31/11): Assets, $1,784,055 (M); expenditures, $123,506; qualifying distributions, $100,950; giving activities include $99,750 for 37 grants (high: $25,500; low: $250).
Purpose and activities: The foundation supports community centers and organizations involved with education and Judaism.
Fields of interest: Education; Human services; Religion.
Type of support: Annual campaigns; Capital campaigns; General/operating support; Scholarship funds.
Support limitations: No grants to individuals.
Application information: Applications accepted. Application form required.
Initial approach: Letter
Deadline(s): None
Trustees: Elizabeth Conston; Shirley Conston; Stuart Conston; Cynthia Savett.
EIN: 236297587

921
Consumers Energy Company
(formerly Consumers Power Company)
1 Energy Plz.
Jackson, MI 49201 (517) 788-0550

Company URL: http://www.consumersenergy.com/
Establishment information: Established in 1886.
Company type: Subsidiary of a public company
Company ticker symbol and exchange: CMS-A/NYSE
Business activities: Generates, transmits, and distributes electricity; transmits and distributes natural gas.
Business type (SIC): Combination utility services
Financial profile for 2012: Number of employees, 7,514; assets, $16,275,000,000; sales volume,

$6,013,000,000; pre-tax net income, $736,000,000; expenses, $5,029,000,000; liabilities, $11,693,000,000
Corporate officers: David W. Joos, Chair.; John G. Russell, Pres. and C.E.O.; Thomas J. Webb, Exec. V.P. and C.F.O.; James E. Brunner, Sr. V.P. and Genl. Counsel; Glenn P. Barba, V.P., Cont., and C.A.O.; Mamatha Chamarthi, V.P. and C.I.O.; Catherine M. Reynolds, V.P. and Corp. Secy.; Venkat Dhenuvakonda Rao, V.P. and Treas.
Board of directors: David W. Joos, Chair.; Merribel S. Ayres; Jon E. Barfield; Stephen E. Ewing; Richard M. Gabrys; William D. Harvey; Philip R. Lochner, Jr.; Michael T. Monahan; John G. Russell; Kenneth L. Way; Laura H. Wright; John B. Yasinsky
Subsidiaries: Huron Hydrocarbons, Inc., Jackson, MI; Michigan Gas Storage Co., Jackson, MI
Giving statement: Giving through the Consumers Energy Company Contributions Program and the Consumers Energy Foundation.
Company EIN: 380442310

Consumers Energy Company Contributions Program

(formerly Consumers Power Company Contributions Program)
1 Energy Plz., EP8-210
Jackson, MI 49201-2276
URL: http://www.consumersenergy.com/content.aspx?id=3221

Purpose and activities: As a complement to its foundation, Consumers Energy also makes charitable contributions to nonprofit organizations directly. Support is given primarily in Michigan, with emphasis on the Lower Peninsula.
Fields of interest: Human services; Salvation Army; United Ways and Federated Giving Programs; Utilities; General charitable giving.
Type of support: Donated products; Equipment; General/operating support; In-kind gifts; Program development.
Geographic limitations: Giving primarily in MI, with emphasis on the Lower Peninsula.
Support limitations: No grants to individuals.
Publications: Application guidelines.
Application information: Applications accepted. Telephone calls, faxes, and e-mails are not encouraged. Video and computer disk submissions are not accepted. Application form required.
Applicants should submit the following:
1) timetable for implementation and evaluation of project
2) how project will be sustained once grantmaker support is completed
3) qualifications of key personnel
4) geographic area to be served
5) how project's results will be evaluated or measured
6) list of company employees involved with the organization
7) listing of board of directors, trustees, officers and other key people and their affiliations
8) detailed description of project and amount of funding requested
9) contact person
10) copy of current year's organizational budget and/or project budget
11) additional materials/documentation

Applications should include a description of past support by Consumer Energy with the organization, the amounts requested of other funders, and priority items in the budget; and include an annual report, if available.
Initial approach: Download application form and mail to headquarters; mail letter of inquiry to headquarters for product donations
Copies of proposal: 1
Committee meeting date(s): Quarterly
Deadline(s): None
Final notification: 6 to 8 weeks
Number of staff: 1 full-time professional; 1 full-time support.

Consumers Energy Foundation

(formerly Consumers Power Foundation)
1 Energy Plz., Rm. EP8-210
Jackson, MI 49201-2276 (517) 788-0432
FAX: (517) 788-2281;
E-mail: foundation@consumersenergy.com;
Additional tel.: (877) 501-4952; URL: http://www.consumersenergy.com/foundation

Establishment information: Established in 1990 in MI.
Donors: Consumers Power Co.; Consumers Energy Co.
Contact: Carolyn A. Bloodworth, Secy.-Treas.
Financial data (yr. ended 12/31/11): Assets, $13,674,517 (M); gifts received, $5,999,996; expenditures, $1,121,536; qualifying distributions, $1,104,157; giving activities include $1,104,157 for grants.
Purpose and activities: The foundation supports programs designed to promote social welfare; Michigan growth and environmental enhancement; education; community and civic development; and culture and the arts.
Fields of interest: Performing arts; Arts; Education, early childhood education; Higher education; Business school/education; Libraries (public); Education; Environment, natural resources; Environment, water resources; Environment, land resources; Environment, energy; Environmental education; Environment; Zoos/zoological societies; Food services; Food banks; Recreation, parks/playgrounds; Boys & girls clubs; Salvation Army; Family services; Family services, domestic violence; Developmentally disabled, centers & services; Homeless, human services; Human services; Community development, neighborhood development; Community development, civic centers; Community/economic development; Foundations (community); United Ways and Federated Giving Programs; Mathematics; Engineering/technology; Science; Economics; Political science; Leadership development.
Programs:
CEEPSACER Program: Through CEEPSACER, Consumers Energy Employees Providing Service Around Children's Essential Resources, the foundation supports America's Promise Alliance, where communities and partners help fulfill five promises for every young person in America: caring adults, safe places, a healthy start, marketable skills, and opportunities to serve. The foundation awards double Volunteer Investment Program (VIP) grants when volunteers and the nonprofit organizations provide at least two of the five promises on an ongoing basis.
Community and Civic Development: The foundation supports programs designed to promote economic development at the local, regional, or statewide level; and supports public parks, convention centers, and neighborhood revitalizations projects.
Culture and the Arts: The foundation supports programs designed to increase awareness of artistic and cultural achievements and encourage its growth for regions or populations that would otherwise be unable to participate; and supports library expansion and renovation, art museums, zoos, symphony orchestras, musical productions, theater, art, and dance.
Education: The foundation supports programs designed to serve schools of higher learning with emphasis on curricula and capital improvements in the study of business, political science, economics, engineering, and natural/physical sciences as they related to energy; and projects designed to enhance leaderships and learning for careers in science, technology, engineering, and mathematics.
Employee Matching Gifts: The foundation matches contributions made by employees and retirees of CMS Energy Corporation to colleges, universities, vocational and technical institutions, community foundations, food banks, pantries, and homeless shelters on a one-for-one basis from $25 to $1,000 per contributor, per year.
Michigan Growth and Environmental Enhancement: The foundation supports preservation, environmental education, and stewardship of Michigan's land, water, and air, including habitat and riverbank preservation, water conservation, watershed education, and brownfield redevelopment. Special emphasis is directed toward programs designed to strengthen the ties between businesses and communities.
Social Welfare: The foundation supports programs designed to help individuals and families to meet the challenges of everyday living, including hunger, poverty, domestic violence, homelessness, and disabilities.
Volunteer Investment Program (VIP): The foundation awards grants of $100 to $500 to nonprofit organizations with which employees and retirees of CMS Energy Corporation volunteer.
Type of support: Building/renovation; Capital campaigns; Continuing support; Curriculum development; Employee matching gifts; Employee volunteer services; Equipment; General/operating support; Scholarship funds.
Geographic limitations: Giving primarily in areas of company operations in MI.
Support limitations: No support for discriminatory organizations, United Way supported organizations, political, labor, or veterans' organizations, religious organizations not of direct benefit to the entire community, fraternal orders, or social clubs. No grants to individuals, or for fundraising, endowments, political campaigns, sports tournaments, talent or beauty contests, or debt reduction; no loans for small businesses.
Publications: Annual report; Annual report (including application guidelines); Program policy statement.
Application information: Applications accepted. The CMF Common Grant Application Form is required. Video and audio submissions are not accepted. Telephone, e-mail, or faxed requests are not accepted. Additional information may be requested at a later date. Application form required. Applicants should submit the following:
1) copy of IRS Determination Letter
2) how project's results will be evaluated or measured
3) explanation of why grantmaker is considered an appropriate donor for project
4) listing of board of directors, trustees, officers and other key people and their affiliations
5) detailed description of project and amount of funding requested
6) contact person
7) copy of current year's organizational budget and/or project budget
8) listing of additional sources and amount of support

Initial approach: Download application form and mail proposal and application form to foundation
Copies of proposal: 1
Board meeting date(s): Quarterly
Deadline(s): None
Final notification: 6 to 8 weeks

Officers and Directors:* John G. Russell*, Chair.; David G. Mengebier*, Pres.; Carolyn A. Bloodworth, Secy.-Treas.; James E. Brunner; John M. Butler; Debra A. Harmon; Nancy A. Popa; Thomas J. Webb; Leeroy Wells, Jr.
Number of staff: 2 full-time professional; 2 full-time support.
EIN: 382935534

922
Continental Development Corporation

2041 Rosecrans Ave., Ste. 200
El Segundo, CA 90245-4707
(310) 640-1520

Company URL: http://www.continentaldevelopment.com
Establishment information: Established in 1969.
Company type: Private company
Business activities: Develops real estate; operates nonresidential buildings.
Business type (SIC): Real estate subdividers and developers; real estate operators and lessors
Corporate officers: Richard C. Lundquist, Pres.; Leonard E. Blakesley, Exec. V.P. and Genl. Counsel; Michael H. Curran, C.F.O. and Treas.; Marcia J. Helfer, Sr. V.P., Admin.
Giving statement: Giving through the Richard C. and Melanie F. Lundquist Family Foundation.

The Richard C. and Melanie F. Lundquist Family Foundation

2041 E. Rosecrans Ave., Ste. 200
El Segundo, CA 90245-4792

Establishment information: Established in 2001 in CA.
Donor: Continental Development Corporation.
Financial data (yr. ended 12/31/11): Assets, $1,571 (M); gifts received, $10,000; expenditures, $9,460; qualifying distributions, $9,430; giving activities include $9,430 for grants.
Purpose and activities: The foundation supports organizations involved with arts and culture, K-12 and higher education, and human services.
Fields of interest: Education; Environment; Youth development.
Type of support: General/operating support; Program development.
Geographic limitations: Giving primarily in CA, with emphasis on Los Angeles.
Support limitations: No grants to individuals.
Application information: Applications not accepted. Unsolicited requests for funds not accepted.
Officers: Melanie F. Lundquist, Pres.; Richard C. Lundquist, Secy.-Treas.
EIN: 954872582

923
Continental Divide Electric Cooperative, Inc.

200 E. High St.
P.O. Box 1087
Grants, NM 87020 (505) 285-6656

Company URL: http://www.cdec.coop
Establishment information: Established in 1945.
Company type: Cooperative
Business activities: Generates, transmits, and distributes electricity.
Business type (SIC): Electric services
Corporate officers: Lynn Head, Chair.; Keith Gottlieb, Pres.; Arsenio Salazar, Secy.-Treas.; Richard Shirley, Admin.
Board of directors: Lynn Head, Chair.; Lyle Adair; Grant Clawson; Keith Gottlieb; Alex Griego; Joe Hoskins; Claudio Romero; Alfred Saavedra; Arsenio Salazar
Giving statement: Giving through the Continental Divide Electric Education Foundation.

Continental Divide Electric Education Foundation

P.O. Box 1087
Grants, NM 87020-1087
FAX: (505) 287-2234; URL: http://www.cdec.coop/content/scholarships

Establishment information: Established in 1988 in NM.
Donor: Continental Divide Electric Cooperative, Inc.
Financial data (yr. ended 12/31/11): Assets, $3,067,306 (M); gifts received, $18,654; expenditures, $319,241; qualifying distributions, $205,500; giving activities include $205,500 for 136 grants to individuals (high: $1,500; low: $1,500).
Purpose and activities: The foundation awards college scholarships to active members and the immediate family members of active members of Continental Divide Electric Cooperative, Inc. attending an institution in Arizona or New Mexico.
Fields of interest: Scholarships/financial aid; Education.
Type of support: Scholarships—to individuals.
Geographic limitations: Giving primarily in AZ and NM.
Publications: Application guidelines.
Application information: Applications accepted. Grants of up to $3,000 are awarded each year. Application form required.
Applications should include official transcripts which states your GPA and 3 letters of recommendation. Letters should state why the applicant is college material and needs financial assistance.
Initial approach: Download application form and mail to foundation
Board meeting date(s): 2nd Thurs. of each month
Deadline(s): May 1
Final notification: Within 30 days
Officers: Lynn Head, Pres.; Keith Gottlieb, V.P.; Arsenio Salazar, Secy.-Treas.
EIN: 850365720

924
Continental Electric Construction Company

815 Commerce Dr., Ste. 100
Oak Brook, IL 60523 (630) 288-0188

Company URL: http://www.cecco.com
Establishment information: Established in 1912.
Company type: Private company
Business activities: Provides general contract electrical services.
Business type (SIC): Contractors/electrical work
Corporate officers: David Witz, Pres. and C.E.O.; Neil Harris, C.F.O.; Mike Hanek, C.I.O.
Giving statement: Giving through the Witz Family Foundation.

The Witz Family Foundation

(formerly Continental Charitable Foundation)
5900 W. Howard St.
Skokie, IL 60077 (847) 677-1600

Establishment information: Established in 1960.
Donors: Continental Electric Construction Co.; Eugene Witz; Leo Witz; William M. Witz; Barbara Witz.
Financial data (yr. ended 01/31/12): Assets, $1,589,567 (M); expenditures, $88,412; qualifying distributions, $86,500; giving activities include $86,500 for grants.
Purpose and activities: The foundation supports music festivals and organizations involved with education, health, skiing, and human services.
Fields of interest: Education; Health care; Human services.
Type of support: Annual campaigns; General/operating support.
Support limitations: No grants to individuals.
Application information: Applications accepted. Application form required.
Initial approach: Letter
Deadline(s): None
Officers: David Witz, Pres.; Steven Witz, Secy.; Neil S. Harris, Treas.
EIN: 366047700

925
Continental Food Management, Inc.

(doing business as Wendy's)
32 Edelman
Irvine, CA 92618-4312 (949) 701-4960

Establishment information: Established in 1992.
Company type: Private company
Business activities: Operates fast-food restaurant chain.
Business type (SIC): Restaurants and drinking places
Corporate officer: Amer A. Boukai, Pres.
Giving statement: Giving through the Boukai Family Foundation.

Boukai Family Foundation

7 Chaparral Ct.
Rancho Santa Margarita, CA 92688-5553

Establishment information: Established in 2003 in CA.
Donors: Continental Food Mgmt.; Global Link Solutions, Inc.; Amer Boukai; Ziad Bouki; Amer Bouki; General Procument Inc.; Issam Bouki.
Financial data (yr. ended 12/31/11): Assets, $37,985 (L); gifts received, $155,416; expenditures, $173,721; qualifying distributions, $172,575; giving activities include $172,575 for 12 grants (high: $35,000; low: $125).
Purpose and activities: The foundation supports organizations involved with education, adoption, Muslim rights, and Islam.
Fields of interest: Elementary school/education; Education; Children, adoption; Civil/human rights; Islam.
Type of support: General/operating support.
Geographic limitations: Giving primarily in CA.
Support limitations: No grants to individuals.
Application information: Applications not accepted. Contributes only to pre-selected organizations.
Officers: Ziad Boukai, Pres.; Amer A. Boukai, Treas.
Director: Akhram Boukai.
EIN: 010788855

Selected grants: The following grants are a representative sample of this grantmaker's funding activity:
$37,500 to Council on American-Islamic Relations-California, Anaheim, CA, 2010.
$20,000 to Islamic Center of Irvine, Irvine, CA, 2010.
$8,125 to Islamic Relief USA, Buena Park, CA, 2010.
$1,000 to William J. Clinton Foundation, Little Rock, AR, 2010.

926
Continental Grain Company Corp.

(formerly ContiGroup Companies, Inc.)
277 Park Ave.
New York, NY 10172-0003 (212) 207-5930

Company URL: http://www.contigroup.com
Establishment information: Established in 1813.
Company type: Private company
Business activities: Produces pork and poultry; produces beef; produces seafood.
Business type (SIC): Farms/livestock; farms/poultry and egg; fish hatcheries and preserves
Financial profile for 2010: Number of employees, 65
Corporate officers: Paul J. Fribourg, Chair. and C.E.O.; Michael J. Zimmerman, Vice-Chair.; Frank W. Baier, Exec. V.P. and C.F.O.; Teresa E. McCaslin, Exec. V.P. and C.A.O.
Board of directors: Paul J. Fribourg, Chair.; Michael J. Zimmerman, Vice-Chair.; Alan H. Fishman; Charles A. Fribourg; Henry Kissinger; Jim P. Manzi; Gerald Rosenfeld; Morton Sosland; Stephen R. Volk; James D. Wolfensohn
International operations: Switzerland
Giving statement: Giving through the Continental Grain Foundation.

Continental Grain Foundation

(formerly ContiGroup Companies Foundation)
277 Park Ave., 50th Fl.
New York, NY 10172-0003
E-mail: Susan.McIntyre@conti.com; URL: http://www.contigroup.com/continentalGrainCompany/CGCFoundation.aspx

Establishment information: Incorporated in 1961 in NY.
Donors: Continental Grain Co.; ContiGroup Cos., Inc.
Contact: Susan McIntyre, Asst. Secy.
Financial data (yr. ended 01/31/12): Assets, $2,945 (M); gifts received, $344,065; expenditures, $341,554; qualifying distributions, $341,404; giving activities include $341,404 for grants.
Purpose and activities: The foundation supports organizations involved with education, conservation, agriculture, human services, community development, leadership development, and economically disadvantaged people.
Fields of interest: Secondary school/education; Higher education; Education, ESL programs; Education, reading; Education; Environment, natural resources; Agriculture; Human services; Community/economic development; Leadership development Economically disadvantaged.
Programs:
Continental Grain Foundation Scholarship: The foundation awards two four-year college scholarships up to $5,000 to children of employees of ContiGroup or one of its businesses. The program is administered by National Merit Scholarship Corp.
Matching Gift Program: The foundation matches contributions made by employees of ContiGroup Companies to institutions of higher education on a one-for-one basis from $100 to $2,000 per employer, per year.
Type of support: Employee matching gifts; Employee-related scholarships; General/operating support; Scholarship funds.
Geographic limitations: Giving primarily in areas of company operations, with emphasis on NY.
Support limitations: No grants to individuals (except for employee-related scholarships).
Application information:
Initial approach: Contact foundation for application information
Officers and Director:* Paul J. Fribourg*, Pres.; Richard Anderson, Treas.; Teresa E. McCaslin.
EIN: 136160912
Selected grants: The following grants are a representative sample of this grantmaker's funding activity:
$25,000 to Appeal of Conscience Foundation, New York, NY, 2009.
$25,000 to Young Womens Leadership Foundation, New York, NY, 2009.
$20,000 to Julie Foudy Leadership Foundation, San Clemente, CA, 2009.
$18,285 to National Merit Scholarship Corporation, Evanston, IL, 2009.
$12,500 to Police Athletic League, New York, NY, 2009.
$10,000 to China Institute in America, New York, NY, 2009.
$10,000 to Cooke Center for Learning and Development, New York, NY, 2009.
$10,000 to Human Rights First, New York, NY, 2009.
$10,000 to Mizel Museum, Denver, CO, 2009.
$10,000 to Public Theater, New York, NY, 2009.

927
Continental Tire North America, Inc.

(formerly Continental General Tire, Inc.)
1800 Continental Blvd.
Charlotte, NC 28273-6388 (704) 588-5895

Company URL: http://www.continentaltire.com
Establishment information: Established in 1915.
Company type: Subsidiary of a foreign company
Business activities: Manufactures tires.
Business type (SIC): Tires and inner tubes
Corporate officer: Matthias Schonberg, C.E.O.
Plants: Mount Vernon, IL; Mayfield, KY; Bryan, OH
Giving statement: Giving through the Continental General Tire Foundation.

Continental General Tire Foundation

1830 MacMillan Park Dr.
Fort Mill, SC 29707-7712 (704) 583-3900

Establishment information: Established in 1996 in NC.
Donors: Continental General Tire, Inc.; Continental Tire North America, Inc.
Financial data (yr. ended 12/31/11): Assets, $23,058 (M); expenditures, $0; qualifying distributions, $0.
Purpose and activities: The foundation supports organizations involved with education.
Type of support: General/operating support.
Geographic limitations: Giving primarily in Charlotte, NC.
Application information: Applications accepted. Application form not required. Applicants should submit the following:
1) name, address and phone number of organization
2) copy of IRS Determination Letter
3) brief history of organization and description of its mission
4) detailed description of project and amount of funding requested

Initial approach: Proposal
Deadline(s): Prior to Dec. 1

Trustees: Rick Ledsinger; Re Racer; Timothy Rogers; Michael Worthington.
EIN: 561960645

928
Contran Corporation

3 Lincoln Ctr.
5430 LBJ Fwy., Ste. 1700
Dallas, TX 75240 (972) 233-1700
FAX: (972) 448-1445

Company URL: http://www.valhi.net
Establishment information: Established in 1944.
Company type: Private company
Business activities: Operates holding company; manufactures and markets titanium dioxide pigments; manufactures ball bearing slides, locks and security products, and ergonomic computer support systems; provides hazardous, toxic, and radioactive waste processing, treatment, storage, and disposal services; produces titanium sponge and melted and mill products.
Business type (SIC): Chemicals/industrial inorganic; metal refining/primary nonferrous; metal refining/secondary nonferrous; cutlery, hand and edge tools, and hardware; machinery/general industry; computer and office equipment; sanitary services; holding company
Financial profile for 2009: Number of employees, 7,175
Corporate officers: Harold C. Simmons, Chair.; Glenn Simmons, Vice-Chair.; Steven L. Watson, Pres.; Bobby D. O'Brien, V.P. and C.F.O.; J. Mark Hollingsworth, V.P. and Genl. Counsel
Board of directors: Harold C. Simmons, Chair.; Glenn Simmons, Vice-Chair.; Steven L. Watson
Subsidiaries: NL Industries, Inc., Houston, TX; Valhi, Inc., Dallas, TX
Giving statement: Giving through the Harold Simmons Foundation.

Harold Simmons Foundation

Three Lincoln Centre
5430 LBJ Fwy., Ste. 1700
Dallas, TX 75240-2697 (972) 233-1700
URL: http://www.haroldsimmonsfoundation.org/

Establishment information: Incorporated in 1988 in TX.
Donors: Contran Corp.; NL Industries, Inc.
Contact: Lisa Simmons Epstein, Pres.
Financial data (yr. ended 12/31/11): Assets, $67,742,483 (M); gifts received, $9,815,000; expenditures, $17,493,467; qualifying distributions, $17,366,971; giving activities include $10,372,110 for grants and $6,994,861 for in-kind gifts.
Purpose and activities: The foundation supports programs designed to promote education; health care; social welfare including human rights; civic improvement; and culture and the arts.

Fields of interest: Museums (art); Performing arts, dance; Performing arts, theater; Arts; Elementary/secondary education; Higher education; Education, services; Education; Environment, natural resources; Zoos/zoological societies; Hospitals (general); Health care, clinics/centers; Health care; Disasters, preparedness/services; YM/YWCAs & YM/YWHAs; Children/youth, services; Youth, services; Women, centers/services; Homeless, human services; Human services; Civil/human rights; Community/economic development; United Ways and Federated Giving Programs; Public affairs.
Type of support: Annual campaigns; Building/renovation; Capital campaigns; Conferences/seminars; Continuing support; Curriculum development; Emergency funds; Employee matching gifts; Equipment; General/operating support; In-kind gifts; Matching/challenge support; Program development; Publication; Research; Scholarship funds.
Geographic limitations: Giving primarily in the Dallas, TX.
Support limitations: No grants to individuals, or for endowments, debt reduction, or discriminatory organizations; no loans.
Publications: Application guidelines.
Application information: Applications accepted. Grants range from $5,000 to $20,000. Collaborations with other agencies and public entities are encouraged. Support is limited to 1 contribution per organization during any given year. Application form not required. Applicants should submit the following:
1) copy of IRS Determination Letter
2) brief history of organization and description of its mission
3) copy of most recent annual report/audited financial statement/990
4) how project's results will be evaluated or measured
5) listing of board of directors, trustees, officers and other key people and their affiliations
6) detailed description of project and amount of funding requested
7) copy of current year's organizational budget and/or project budget
8) listing of additional sources and amount of support

Initial approach: Proposal
Copies of proposal: 1
Board meeting date(s): As needed
Deadline(s): None
Final notification: 3 months

Officers and Directors:* Harold C. Simmons*, Chair.; Lisa K. Simmons*, Pres.; Serena Simmons Connelly, V.P.; A. Andrew R. Louis, Secy.; John A. St. Wrba, Treas.; J. Mark Hollingsworth, Genl. Counsel.
Number of staff: 2 full-time professional; 1 part-time professional; 1 full-time support.
EIN: 752222091
Selected grants: The following grants are a representative sample of this grantmaker's funding activity:
$5,037,750 to Parkland Foundation, Dallas, TX, 2011. For challenge grant for construction of new Women and Infants' Specialty Health Hospital.
$1,157,112 to Dallas Zoological Society, Dallas Zoo, Dallas, TX, 2011. For four-year pledge for the Giants of the Savanna capital campaign.
$1,047,200 to Alba-Golden Independent School District, Alba, TX, 2011. For operating expenses.
$1,002,800 to Dallas Arboretum and Botanical Society, Dallas, TX, 2011. For five-year pledge for Children's Exploration Garden.
$1,000,000 to Crystal Charity Ball, Dallas, TX, 2011. For Dallas Mission for Life $289,573, Los Barrios Unidos Community Clinic, $383,150, Trinity River Mission 327,277.
$1,000,000 to State Fair of Texas, Dallas, TX, 2011. For Livestock Center.
$250,000 to Big Thought, Dallas, TX, 2011. For two-year pledge for Thriving Minds program.
$20,000 to Lutheran Social Service of the South, Austin, TX, 2011. For Trauma-Informed Care for foster children.
$20,000 to Mission East Dallas, Dallas, TX, 2011. For operating expenses for medical clinic.
$20,000 to Operation LIFT, Dallas, TX, 2011. For operating expenses.

929
Control Air Conditioning Corp.

5200 E. La Palma Ave.
Anaheim, CA 92807-2019 (714) 777-8600

Company URL: http://www.controlaircorp.com
Establishment information: Established in 1978.
Company type: Private company
Business activities: Operates commercial and industrial air conditioning installation and services company.
Business type (SIC): Contractors/plumbing, heating, and air-conditioning
Corporate officers: Kendrick G. Ellis, Pres.; Greg Rummler, C.F.O.; Eileen Ellis, Secy.-Treas.
Giving statement: Giving through the Ellis Family Charitable Foundation.

Ellis Family Charitable Foundation

5200 E. La Palma Ave.
Anaheim, CA 92807-2019

Establishment information: Established in 2006 in CA.
Donors: Ellis Real Estate Holdings, LLC; Eco Duct, Inc.; Control Air Conditioning Corp.
Financial data (yr. ended 12/31/11): Assets, $3,303,301 (M); gifts received, $593,900; expenditures, $1,244,252; qualifying distributions, $1,216,013; giving activities include $1,206,839 for 37 grants (high: $107,600; low: $250).
Purpose and activities: The foundation supports camps and ranches and organizations involved with substance abuse, youth development, youth, and Christianity.
Fields of interest: Substance abuse, services; Recreation, camps; Athletics/sports, equestrianism; Youth development, business; Youth, services; Christian agencies & churches.
Type of support: Building/renovation; General/operating support; Program development; Publication.
Geographic limitations: Giving primarily in CA.
Application information: Applications accepted. Application form not required. Applicants should submit the following:
1) results expected from proposed grant
2) population served
3) copy of IRS Determination Letter
4) brief history of organization and description of its mission
5) copy of most recent annual report/audited financial statement/990
6) descriptive literature about organization
7) listing of board of directors, trustees, officers and other key people and their affiliations
8) detailed description of project and amount of funding requested
9) copy of current year's organizational budget and/or project budget
10) listing of additional sources and amount of support

Initial approach: Proposal
Deadline(s): None

Officers: Kendrick G. Ellis, C.E.O. and Pres.; Gregory S. Ellis, V.P.; Kenneth M. Ellis, V.P.; Stanley J. Ellis, V.P.; Jon S. Ellis, Secy.; Greg S. Rummler, C.F.O. and Treas.
EIN: 020788743
Selected grants: The following grants are a representative sample of this grantmaker's funding activity:
$15,000 to Frontier Project Foundation, Rancho Cucamonga, CA, 2010.
$9,500 to Torrance Memorial Medical Center, Torrance, CA, 2010.
$3,500 to Autism Speaks, Los Angeles, CA, 2010.
$3,040 to Community Service Programs, Santa Ana, CA, 2010.
$2,000 to Calicinto Ranch, San Jacinto, CA, 2010.
$1,179 to Saddleback Valley Community Church, Lake Forest, CA, 2010.
$1,000 to Leukemia & Lymphoma Society, Pittsfield, MA, 2010.
$1,000 to Royal Family Kids Camp, Costa Mesa, CA, 2010.

930
Control Systems International, Inc.

8040 Nieman Rd.
Lenexa, KS 66214-1523 (913) 599-5010

Company URL: http://www.csiks.com
Establishment information: Established in 1968.
Company type: Private company
Business activities: Provides automated computer system design services.
Business type (SIC): Computer services
Corporate officers: Kevin McGlensey, Pres. and C.E.O.; James J. Buri, C.O.O.; Thomas W. Marincel, C.F.O.
Giving statement: Giving through the Badger Creek Corporation.

Badger Creek Corporation

(formerly Wildlands Restoration Corporation)
8040 Nieman Rd.
Lenexa, KS 66214-1523

Establishment information: Established in 2004 in KS.
Donors: Control Systems International, Inc.; Defenders of Wildlife.
Financial data (yr. ended 12/31/11): Assets, $16,674,816 (M); gifts received, $5,004,000; expenditures, $1,038,288; qualifying distributions, $2,500; giving activities include $2,500 for grants.
Purpose and activities: The foundation preserves and protects biodiversity of wildlands.
Fields of interest: Environment.
Support limitations: No grants to individuals.
Application information: Applications not accepted. Unsolicited request for funds are not accepted.
Officers: Nelson D. Shirley, Pres.; James N. Shirley, V.P. and Secy.
Director: Lori A. Siebert.
EIN: 201210921

931
Convalescent Services, Inc.

(doing business as Sun Terrace Health Care Center)
(also known as Lake Towers Retirement Community)
105 Trinity Lakes Dr.
Sun City Center, FL 33573-5728
(813) 634-3324

Establishment information: Established in 1980.
Company type: Private company
Business activities: Operates apartment building; operates intermediate care facility.
Business type (SIC): Real estate operators and lessors; nursing and personal care facilities
Corporate officer: Stiles A. Kellett, Pres.
Giving statement: Giving through the Sun Towers Residents Association, Inc.

Sun Towers Residents Association, Inc.

(formerly Lake Towers Residents Good Samaritan Fund)
101 Trinity Lakes Dr., Ste. 667
Sun City Center, FL 33573-5736 (813) 634-4810

Establishment information: Established in 1999.
Donor: Convalescent Services, Inc.
Contact: Robert L. McCroskey, Treas.
Financial data (yr. ended 12/31/11): Assets, $147,760 (M); expenditures, $0; qualifying distributions, $0.
Purpose and activities: The purpose of the foundation is to provide support to employees and children of employees of Lake Towers Retirement Complex to further their education.
Fields of interest: Education.
Geographic limitations: Giving limited to residents of Sun City Center, FL.
Application information: Applications accepted. Application form required.
Initial approach: Contact foundation for application form
Deadline(s): None
Officers: Robert Whitney, Pres.; Audrey Hammond-Whitney, Secy.; Robert L. McCroskey, Treas.
EIN: 596777442

932
ConvaTec Inc.

200 Headquarters Park Dr.
Skillman, NJ 08558 (908) 904-2500

Company URL: wwwhttp://www.convatec.com
Establishment information: Established in 1978.
Company type: Subsidiary of a private company
Business activities: Develop and market new medical technologies designed to meet the needs of ostomy and wound patients.
Business type (SIC): Medical instruments and supplies
Corporate officers: David I. Johnson, C.E.O.; Bradford Barton, Pres.; George Kegler, C.F.O.

ConvaTec Inc. Corporate Giving Program

c/o Ethics and Compliance Office
100 Headquarters Park Dr.
Skillman, NJ 08558 (877) 259-6303
E-mail: grants.charitables@convatec.com;
URL: http://www.convateccorporate.com/corporate-responsibility/

Purpose and activities: ConvaTec makes charitable contributions to nonprofit organizations involved with science and health care education.
Fields of interest: Education; Health care; Health organizations, formal/general education; Science.
Type of support: Donated products; Employee volunteer services; General/operating support.
Support limitations: No grants to individuals.
Application information: Applications accepted. An independent committee oversees the application process.
Initial approach: E-mail or call the Ethics and Compliance Office with questions regarding grant or charitable giving requests

933
Convergys Corporation

201 E. 4th St.
P.O. Box 1895
Cincinnati, OH 45202 (513) 723-7000
FAX: (513) 723-2048

Company URL: http://www.convergys.com
Establishment information: Established in 1998.
Company type: Public company
Company ticker symbol and exchange: CVG/NYSE
Business activities: Develops and provides outsourced information and customer management products and services.
Business type (SIC): Computer services
Financial profile for 2012: Number of employees, 77,000; assets, $2,037,900,000; sales volume, $2,005,000,000; pre-tax net income, $29,300,000; expenses, $1,966,400,000; liabilities, $666,000,000
Fortune 1000 ranking: 2012—906th in revenues, 739th in profits, and 848th in assets
Corporate officers: Philip A. Odeen, Chair.; Andrea J. Ayers, Pres. and C.E.O.; Andre S. Valentine, C.F.O.; Jim Goetz, C.I.O.; Claudia Cline, Sr. V.P. and Genl. Counsel
Board of directors: Philip A. Odeen, Chair.; Andrea J. Ayers; John F. Barrett; Richard R. Devenuti; Jeffrey H. Fox; Joseph E. Gibbs; Joan E. Herman; Thomas L. Monahan III; Ronald L. Nelson; Richard F. Wallman
International operations: China; Israel; Singapore
Giving statement: Giving through the Convergys Foundation, Inc.
Company EIN: 311598292

The Convergys Foundation, Inc.

201 E. 4th St., Ste. 102-1400
Cincinnati, OH 45202-4122
URL: http://www.convergys.com/company/corporate-responsibility/our-communities.php

Establishment information: Established in 1999 in OH.
Donor: Convergys Corp.
Financial data (yr. ended 12/31/11): Assets, $34,096 (M); gifts received, $607,500; expenditures, $576,994; qualifying distributions, $576,994; giving activities include $576,994 for grants.
Purpose and activities: The foundation supports organizations involved with arts and culture and programs designed to enhance community stability through literacy and workforce readiness.
Fields of interest: Arts; Higher education; Education, reading; Education; Employment, services; Boy scouts; Children/youth, services; Human services; Community/economic development; United Ways and Federated Giving Programs.
International interests: Asia; Canada; Europe; India; Latin America; Oceania.
Type of support: Building/renovation; Capital campaigns; Employee matching gifts; Endowments; Internship funds; Research; Seed money; Sponsorships.
Geographic limitations: Giving primarily in Jacksonville and Orlando, FL, Cincinnati, OH, TX, Salt Lake City, UT, and on an international basis in Asia, Canada, Europe, India, Latin America, and Oceania.
Support limitations: No support for political or religious organizations. No grants to individuals.
Application information: Applications not accepted. Unsolicited applications for funding are currently not accepted.
Board meeting date(s): Spring and fall
Officers and Trustees:* Jeffrey H. Fox*, Pres.; Tammy L. Rohrer, Secy.; Taylor J. Greenwald, Treas.; Andrea J. Ayers*, Exec. Dir.; David F. Dougherty; Julia A. Houston; Sajid Malhorta; Earl C. Shanks.
EIN: 311619871
Selected grants: The following grants are a representative sample of this grantmaker's funding activity:
$468,468 to United Way of Greater Cincinnati, Cincinnati, OH, 2010.
$153,182 to ArtsWave, Cincinnati, OH, 2010.
$50,000 to Boy Scouts of America, Dan Beard Council, Cincinnati, OH, 2010.
$13,282 to United Way of South Texas, McAllen, TX, 2010.
$11,808 to United Way of Central Oklahoma, Oklahoma City, OK, 2010.
$11,230 to United Way of Northeast Florida, Jacksonville, FL, 2010.
$4,024 to United Way of Greater Saint Louis, Saint Louis, MO, 2010.
$2,713 to United Way of the Midlands, Omaha, NE, 2010.
$2,051 to United Way, Tulsa Area, Tulsa, OK, 2010.
$1,995 to United Way of the Plains, Wichita, KS, 2010.

903
Con-way Inc.

(formerly CNF Inc.)
2211 Old Earhart Rd., Ste. 100
Ann Arbor, MI 48105-2751 (734) 757-1444
FAX: (734) 757-1158

Company URL: http://www.con-way.com
Establishment information: Established in 1929.
Company type: Public company
Company ticker symbol and exchange: CNW/NYSE
Business activities: Provides trucking services and supply chain management services.
Business type (SIC): Trucking and courier services, except by air; transportation services/freight
Financial profile for 2012: Number of employees, 29,100; assets, $3,141,460,000; sales volume, $5,580,250,000; pre-tax net income, $170,950,000; expenses, $5,351,410,000; liabilities, $2,303,080,000

Fortune 1000 ranking: 2012—450th in revenues, 728th in profits, and 738th in assets
Corporate officers: W. Keith Kennedy, Jr., Chair.; Douglas W. Stotlar, Pres., C.E.O., and C.A.O.; Stephen L. Bruffett, Exec. V.P. and C.F.O.; Stephen K. Krull, Exec. V.P., Genl. Counsel, and Corp. Secy.; Michael J. Morris, Sr. V.P., Finance, and Treas.; Kevin S. Coel, Sr. V.P. and Corp. Cont.; Leslie P. Lundberg, Sr. V.P., Human Resources; C. Randal Mullett, V.P., Public Affairs
Board of directors: W. Keith Kennedy, Jr., Chair.; John J. Anton; William R. Corbin; Michael J. Murray; Edith R. Perez; John C. Pope; William J. Schroeder; Douglas Stotlar; Peter W. Stott; Chelsea C. White III
Giving statement: Giving through the Con-way Inc. Corporate Giving Program.
Company EIN: 941444798

Con-way Inc. Corporate Giving Program

(formerly CNF Inc. Corporate Giving Program)
2211 Old Earhart Rd., Ste. 100
Ann Arbor, MI 48105-2751 (734) 757-1444
URL: http://www.con-way.com/en/about_con_way/corporate_social_responsibility/

Purpose and activities: Con-way makes charitable contributions to nonprofit organizations involved with children, education, health, and motor vehicle safety. Support is given primarily in areas of company operations.
Fields of interest: Education; Health care; Safety, automotive safety; Children, services.
Type of support: Employee volunteer services; Employee-related scholarships; General/operating support.
Geographic limitations: Giving primarily in areas of company operations.
Application information: Applications accepted.
Initial approach: Complete online application

934
Cook Inlet Region, Inc.

(also known as CIRI)
2525 C St., Ste. 500
P.O. Box 93330
Anchorage, AK 99503 (907) 274-8638

Company URL: http://www.ciri.com
Establishment information: Established in 1972.
Company type: Native corporation
Business activities: Operates native corporation.
Business type (SIC): Nonclassifiable establishments
Corporate officers: Charles G. Anderson, Chair.; Patrick M. Marrs, Vice-Chair.; Sophie Minich, Pres. and C.E.O.; Stig Colberg, C.F.O.; Bruce Anders, V.P. and Genl. Counsel; Thomas P. Huhndorf, Secy.; Michael R. Boling, Treas.; Roy M. Huhndorf, Chair. Emeritus
Board of directors: Charles G. Anderson, Chair.; Patrick M. Marrs, Vice-Chair.; Hallie L. Bissett; Michael R. Boling; Penny L. Carty; Rolf A. Dagg; Douglas W. Fifer; Erik I. Frostad; Jeffrey A. Gonnason; Robert E. Harris; Thomas P. Huhndorf; Roy M. Huhndorf; Katrina M. Jacuk; Ted. S. Kroto, Sr.; Louis Nagy, Jr.
Giving statement: Giving through the CIRI Foundation.

The CIRI Foundation

(also known as The Cook Inlet Region, Inc. Foundation)
3600 San Jeronimo Dr., Ste. 256
Anchorage, AK 99508-2870 (907) 793-3575
FAX: (907) 793-3585;
E-mail: tcf@thecirifoundation.org; Additional tel.: (800) 764-3382; URL: http://www.thecirifoundation.org

Establishment information: Established in 1982 in AK.
Donors: CIRI, Inc.; CITC; Salamatof Native Association; AK Villiage Initiatives; Tyonek Native Corp.; Southcentral Foundation.
Financial data (yr. ended 12/31/11): Assets, $47,994,646 (M); gifts received, $335,425; expenditures, $2,923,653; qualifying distributions, $2,509,598; giving activities include $347,021 for 12+ grants (high: $50,000) and $1,441,363 for 579 grants to individuals (high: $10,000).
Purpose and activities: The foundation supports organizations involved with Alaska Native heritage and education, and awards scholarships, grants, and fellowships to Alaska Natives to promote individual self-development and economic self-sufficiency.
Fields of interest: Arts, cultural/ethnic awareness; Visual arts; Performing arts; History/archaeology; Literature; Philosophy/ethics; Historic preservation/historical societies; Arts; Vocational education; Higher education; Graduate/professional education; Business school/education; Engineering school/education; Health sciences school/education; Scholarships/financial aid; Education; Employment, services; Employment, training; Employment; Mathematics Native Americans/American Indians.

Programs:
Achievement Annual Scholarships: The foundation annually awards college and graduate scholarships of up to $8,000 to Alaska Natives maintaining a 3.0 GPA who are original enrollees and the direct lineal descendants of original enrollees of Cook Inlet Region, Inc.
Cap Lathrop Endowment Scholarship Fund: Through the Cap Lathrop Endowment Scholarship Fund, the foundation awards college scholarships to Alaska Natives who are original enrollees and the direct lineal descendants of original enrollees of ANCSA regional or village corporations majoring in broadcasting, telecommunications, business, engineering, journalism, and other media-related fields.
Career Upgrade Grants: The foundation awards grants of up to $4,500 to Alaska Natives who are original enrollees and the direct lineal descendants of original enrollees of Cook Inlet Region, Inc. to enroll in a course of study that contributes to potential employment or employment upgrade.
Carl H. Marrs Scholarship Fund: Through the Carl H. Marrs Scholarship Fund, the foundation awards college and graduate scholarships to Alaska Natives who are original enrollees and the direct lineal descendants of original enrollees of Cook Inlet Region, Inc. for studies in business administration, economics, finance, organizational management, accounting, and similar fields.
Daniel Alex Scholarship Fund: Through the Daniel Alex Scholarship Fund, the foundation awards college scholarships and vocational training grants to Alaska Natives who are original enrollees and the direct lineal descendants of original enrollees of Cook Inlet Region, Inc., Eklutna, Inc., or the Native Village of Eklutna for studies in physics, mathematics, business management, and education.
Education Project Grants: The foundation supports programs designed to promote quality of learning and educational experiences for Alaska Natives from the early school years through adulthood; examine educational issues and opportunities and identify possible solutions to eliminate those factors that hinder successful achievement by Alaska Natives in their educational pursuits; and foster educational enrichment programs that improve the quality of life for Alaska Natives.
Eklutna, Inc. Scholarship and Grant Program: The foundation awards scholarships and grants to original Eklutna Inc. shareholders and their lineal descendants. The foundation awards up to $1,000 for scholarships, vocational training, or career upgrades; up to $500 for general, cultural fellowship, or urgent need; and up to $300 for early childhood and K-12 development.
Excellence Annual Scholarships: The foundation annually awards college and graduate scholarships of up to $10,000 to Alaska Natives maintaining a 3.5 GPA who are original enrollees and the direct lineal descendants of original enrollees of Cook Inlet Region, Inc.
General and Cultural Heritage Fellowships: The foundation awards general fellowships of up to $250 for non-credit workshops or seminars to improve employment skills; and cultural heritage fellowships of up to $250 for the study of visual, literary, and performing arts of Alaska Natives. Fellowships are limited to Alaska Natives maintaining a 2.5 GPA who are original enrollees and the direct lineal descendants of original enrollees of Cook Inlet Region, Inc.
General Semester Scholarships: The foundation awards college and graduate scholarships of up to $2,500 per semester to Alaska Natives maintaining a 2.5 GPA who are original enrollees and the direct lineal descendants of original enrollees of Cook Inlet Region, Inc.
George Miller, Jr. Management Leadership Endowment Fund: Through the George Miller, Jr. Management Leadership Endowment Fund, the foundation awards fellowships of up to $6,000 to Alaska Natives who are original enrollees and the direct lineal descendants of original enrollees of Cook Inlet Region, Inc. to foster improvement of tribal/cultural and corporate management skills for career advancement.
Heritage Project Grants: The foundation supports programs designed to enhance the understanding and appreciation by Alaska Natives and the general public about traditional and contemporary Alaska Native history, ethnology, anthropology, philosophy, literature, arts, and other related fields; promote cultural traditions of Alaska Natives of the Cook Inlet Region and encourage contemporary Alaska Native tradition bearers in the pursuit of their works; foster the identification, preservation, curation, and interpretation of traditional and contemporary Alaska Native cultural resource materials of the Cook Inlet Region; encourage excellence in the development and exhibition of traditional and contemporary Alaska Native art, music, literature, and other works for appreciation by the general public; protect traditional and cultural values ascribed to Alaska Native lands in the Cook Inlet Region; and promote cooperation and involvement of Alaska Natives within the Cook Inlet Region as well as with civic and private organizations to accomplish the foundation's heritage goals.
Howard Rock Foundation Scholarship Program: Through the Howard Rock Foundation Scholarship Program, the foundation awards college and graduate scholarships to Alaska Natives who are original enrollees and the direct lineal descendants of original enrollees of ANCSA regional or village

corporations or members of a tribal or other organization. Special emphasis is directed toward junior and senior students.

Internship Program: The foundation supports individuals obtaining temporary, supervised, and on-the-job training to develop employment skills and gain practical work experience. The program is limited to Alaska Natives maintaining a 2.5 GPA who are original enrollees and the direct lineal descendants of original enrollees of Cook Inlet Region, Inc.

John N. Colberg Scholarship Fund: Through the John N. Colberg Scholarship Fund, the foundation awards college and graduate scholarships to Alaska Natives who are original enrollees and the direct lineal descendants of original enrollees of Cook Inlet Region, Inc. for studies in law.

Keck/Westmin Endowment Scholarship Fund: Through the Keck/Westmin Endowment Scholarship Fund, the foundation awards college and graduate scholarships to Alaska Natives who are original enrollees and the direct lineal descendants of original enrollees of Cook Inlet Region, Inc. for all fields of study.

Kirby McDonald Education Endowment Fund: Through the Kirby McDonald Education Endowment Fund, the foundation awards college and graduate scholarships to Alaska Natives who are original enrollees and the direct lineal descendants of original enrollees of Cook Inlet Region, Inc. for studies in culinary arts, business administration, and engineering.

Lawrence Matson Memorial Endowment Scholarship Fund: Through the Lawrence Matson Memorial Endowment Scholarship Fund, the foundation awards college and graduate scholarships to Alaska Natives who are original enrollees and the direct lineal descendants of original enrollees of Cook Inlet Region, Inc. for studies in language, education, social sciences, arts, communications, and law.

Ninilchik Native Association, Inc. Scholarship and Vocational Grant Fund: The foundation awards college and graduate scholarships and vocational training grants to Alaska Natives maintaining a 2.5 GPA who are original enrollees and the direct lineal descendants of original enrollees of Ninilchik Native Association, Inc.

Peter Kalifornsky Memorial Endowment Scholarship Fund: Through the Peter Kalifornsky Memorial Endowment Scholarship Fund, the foundation awards college and graduate scholarships to Alaska Natives who are original enrollees and the direct lineal descendants of original enrollees of Cook Inlet Region, Inc. for studies in Alaska Native issues.

Roy M. Huhndorf Endowment Scholarship Fund: Through the Roy M. Huhndorf Endowment Scholarship Fund, the foundation awards college and graduate scholarships to Alaska Natives who are original enrollees and the direct lineal descendants of original enrollees of Cook Inlet Region, Inc. for studies in health science.

Salamatof Native Association, Inc. Scholarship and Grant Program: The foundation annually awards college and graduate scholarships or education grants to Alaska Natives maintaining a 2.5 GPA who are original enrollees and the direct lineal descendants, spouses, or adopted children of original enrollees of Salamatof Native Association, Inc.

Special Excellence Annual Scholarships: The foundation awards college and graduate scholarships of up to $20,000 to Alaska Natives maintaining a 3.7 GPA who are original enrollees and the direct lineal descendants of original enrollees of Cook Inlet Region, Inc. Special emphasis is directed toward students studying business, education, math, science, health service, and engineering.

Susie Qimmiqsak Bevins Endowment Scholarship Fund: Through the Susie Qimmiqsak Bevins Endowment Scholarship Fund, the foundation awards college and graduate scholarships of up to $2,000 per semester to Alaska Natives who are original enrollees and the direct lineal descendants of original enrollees of Cook Inlet Region, Inc. for studies in visual, performing, and literary arts.

Vocational Training Grants: The foundation awards grants of up to $4,500 to Alaska Natives who are original enrollees and the direct lineal descendants of original enrollees of Cook Inlet Region, Inc. to attend a vocational training program or obtain a technical skills certificate.

William D. Phillips Scholarship Fund: Through the William D. Philips Scholarship Fund, the foundation annually awards college and graduate scholarships to Alaska Natives who are original enrollees and the direct lineal descendants of original enrollees of Cook Inlet Region, Inc. for studies government and public policy, public administration, budget and public finance, social policy, education policy, or related fields.

Type of support: Conferences/seminars; Continuing support; Fellowships; General/operating support; Grants to individuals; Internship funds; Program development; Research; Scholarship funds; Scholarships—to individuals.

Geographic limitations: Giving primarily in the Cook Inlet Region, AK.

Support limitations: No grants for endowments, buildings or equipment, completed projects, re-granting, or lobbying or propaganda efforts; no loans.

Publications: Application guidelines; Grants list; Program policy statement.

Application information: Applications accepted. Visit website for scholarship endowment funds and named scholarship funds. Additional information may be requested at a later date for project grants. Organizations receiving project grants are asked to submit a final report. Application form required.

Applicants should submit the following:

1) timetable for implementation and evaluation of project
2) results expected from proposed grant
3) statement of problem project will address
4) population served
5) copy of IRS Determination Letter
6) copy of most recent annual report/audited financial statement/990
7) how project's results will be evaluated or measured
8) listing of board of directors, trustees, officers and other key people and their affiliations
9) detailed description of project and amount of funding requested
10) copy of current year's organizational budget and/or project budget
11) listing of additional sources and amount of support

Requests for scholarships and education grants should include proof of eligibility, a letter of reference, transcripts or certificates of completion, a statement of purpose, proof of school acceptance, and a description of courses or seminars. Proposals for project grants should indicate how the project will impact and involve Alaska Native original enrollees and/or lineal descendants of Cook Inlet Region; and should include three letters of support.

Initial approach: Complete online application; download application form and mail proposal and application to foundation for General and Cultural Heritage Fellowships and project grants

Copies of proposal: 1

Board meeting date(s): Quarterly

Deadline(s): Mar. 31, June 30, Sept. 30, and Dec. 1 for Vocational Training Grants, Career Upgrade Grants, General and Cultural Heritage Fellowships, and internships; June 1 for Achievement Annual, Excellence Annual, and Special Excellence Annual Scholarships; June 1 and Dec. 1 for General Semester Scholarships; Mar. 1, June 1, Sept. 1, and Nov. 1 for project grants

Final notification: 30 to 60 days for project grants

Officers and Directors:* Jeff Gonnason*, Chair.; Louis Nagy, Jr.*, Vice-Chair.; Susan A. Anderson, C.E.O. and Pres.; Patrick Duke, Secy.-Treas.; Hallie Bissett; Rayna Duenas; Shirley Holloway, Ph.D.; Deanna Sackett; Jaclyn Sallee; David Wright.

Number of staff: 6

EIN: 920087914

935
Cooper Industries plc

(formerly Cooper Industries, Ltd.)
600 Travis, Ste. 5600
P.O. Box 4446
Houston, TX 77002-1001 (713) 209-8400

Company URL: http://www.cooperindustries.com

Establishment information: Established in 1833.

Company type: Subsidiary of a foreign company

Business activities: Manufactures electrical products and tools and hardware. At press time, the company is in the process of merging with Eaton Corp.

Business type (SIC): Lighting and wiring equipment/electric; cutlery, hand and edge tools, and hardware

Financial profile for 2011: Number of employees, 25,786; assets, $6,447,600,000; sales volume, $5,409,400,000; pre-tax net income, $757,200,000; expenses, $4,589,000,000; liabilities, $2,911,600,000

Corporate officers: Kirk S. Hachigian, Chair., Pres., and C.E.O.; David A. Barta, Sr. V.P. and C.F.O.; Bruce M. Taten, Sr. V.P. and Genl. Counsel; Tyler W. Johnson, V.P. and Treas.; Rick L. Johnson, V.P., Cont., and C.A.O.; Heath B. Monesmith, V.P., Human Resources; Terrance V. Helz, Secy.

Board of directors: Kirk S. Hachigian, Chair.; Stephen G. Butler; Ivor J. Evans; Linda A. Hill; Lawrence D. Kingsley; James J. Postl; Dan F. Smith; Gerald B. Smith; Mark S. Thompson

International operations: Australia; Bermuda; Brazil; British Virgin Islands; China; Colombia; France; Germany; Gibraltar; Hungary; India; Ireland; Italy; Luxembourg; Malaysia; Mexico; Netherlands; Norway; Portugal; Romania; Russia; Singapore; Spain; Sweden; Switzerland; Taiwan; United Kingdom

Giving statement: Giving through the Cooper Industries, Inc. Corporate Giving Program and the Cooper Industries Foundation.

Company EIN: 980632292

Cooper Industries, Inc. Corporate Giving Program

P.O. Box 4446
Houston, TX 77210-4446 (713) 209-8400
E-mail: info@cooperindustries.com; URL: http://www.cooperindustries.com/content/public/en/company/corporate_giving.html

Purpose and activities: As a complement to its foundation, Cooper Industries also makes charitable contributions to nonprofit organizations

directly. Support is given in areas of company operations.
Fields of interest: Arts; Vocational education; Higher education; Education; Environment; Health care; Recreation, parks/playgrounds; Recreation, fairs/festivals; Human services; Community/economic development.
International interests: China; Mexico; United Kingdom.
Program:
Scholarship Program: Cooper Industries awards college scholarships to children of employees in Mexico and the United States. The scholarships are based on academic merit, demonstration of financial need, evidence of outstanding character, and extracurricular activities.
Type of support: Donated equipment; Donated products; Employee volunteer services; Employee-related scholarships; General/operating support; In-kind gifts; Loaned talent; Sponsorships.
Geographic limitations: Giving on a national and international basis in areas of company operations, with emphasis on Peachtree, GA, Highland, IL, St. Louis, MO, Syracuse, NY, Houston, TX, and Waukesha, WI, and China, Mexico, and the United Kingdom.
Support limitations: No support for discriminatory, religious, veterans', or political organizations. No grants to individuals (except for employee-related scholarships).
Application information:
Initial approach: Contact nearest facility for application information
Administrator: Victoria B. Guennewig, V.P., Public Affairs.
Number of staff: 1 full-time professional; 1 full-time support.

Cooper Industries Foundation

P.O. Box 4446
Houston, TX 77210-4446 (713) 209-8400
FAX: (713) 209-8982;
E-mail: info@cooperindustries.com; Additional address: c/o Cooper US, 600 Travis, Ste. 5600, Houston, TX 77002; URL: http://www.cooperindustries.com/content/public/en/company/corporate_giving.html

Establishment information: Incorporated in 1964; absorbed Crouse-Hinds Foundation in 1982; absorbed McGraw-Edison Foundation in 1985.
Donors: Cooper Industries, Inc.; Gerda Kaudisch†.
Contact: Rosemary K. Martone, Secy.
Financial data (yr. ended 12/31/11): Assets, $1,560,316 (M); expenditures, $1,113,111; qualifying distributions, $1,104,975; giving activities include $1,104,975 for grants.
Purpose and activities: The foundation supports organizations involved with arts and culture, education, the environment, health, human services, and community development.
Fields of interest: Arts; Vocational education; Higher education; Education; Environment; Health care; Food banks; Boys & girls clubs; Youth, services; Human services; Community/economic development; United Ways and Federated Giving Programs.
Program:
Employee Matching Gifts: The foundation matches contributions made by employees of Cooper Industries to institutions of higher education on a two-for-one basis from $35 to $2,000 per employee, per year and to nonprofit organizations on a one-for-one basis.
Type of support: Annual campaigns; Building/renovation; Capital campaigns; Continuing support; Emergency funds; Employee matching gifts; Employee volunteer services; General/operating support; Program development; Scholarship funds.
Geographic limitations: Giving primarily in areas of company operations in CA, FL, GA, IL, MO, MS, NC, NY, OH, PA, SC, TN, TX, WI, and Mexico, with emphasis on Houston, TX.
Support limitations: No support for United Way-supported organizations, national or state organizations, religious, veterans', political, labor, or lobbying organizations, hospitals, or primary or secondary schools. No grants to individuals.
Publications: Application guidelines; Corporate giving report.
Application information: Applications accepted. Requests may be forwarded by the foundation to other Cooper Industries locations when appropriate. Application form not required. Applicants should submit the following:
1) copy of IRS Determination Letter
2) brief history of organization and description of its mission
3) listing of board of directors, trustees, officers and other key people and their affiliations
4) detailed description of project and amount of funding requested
5) copy of current year's organizational budget and/or project budget
6) listing of additional sources and amount of support

Initial approach: Proposal to nearest company division; proposal to foundation for organizations located in the Houston, TX, metropolitan area
Copies of proposal: 1
Board meeting date(s): Feb. and Nov.
Deadline(s): None
Final notification: Within 90 days

Officers and Trustees:* Kirk S. Hachigian*, Pres.; Heath B. Monesmith*, V.P.; Terrence V. Helz, Secy.; David A. Barta*, Treas.; Stephen G. Butler; Robert M. Devlin; Ivor J. Evans; Linda A. Hill; Lawrence D. Kingsley; James J. Postl; Dan F. Smith; Gerald B. Smith; Mark S. Thompson.
Number of staff: 1 full-time support.
EIN: 316060698
Selected grants: The following grants are a representative sample of this grantmaker's funding activity:
$80,000 to University of California, Berkeley, CA, 2010.
$71,013 to United Way of Greater Houston, Houston, TX, 2010.
$46,558 to United Way of Central New York, Syracuse, NY, 2010.
$40,280 to United Way in Waukesha County, Waukesha, WI, 2010.
$29,222 to United Way of Greater Saint Louis, Saint Louis, MO, 2010.
$20,000 to Rice University, Houston, TX, 2010.
$13,161 to United Way of Greater Milwaukee, Milwaukee, WI, 2010.
$10,000 to Rice University, Houston, TX, 2010.
$10,000 to University of Pennsylvania, Philadelphia, PA, 2010.
$5,000 to Rockhurst High School, Kansas City, MO, 2010.

936
Cooper Tire & Rubber Company

701 Lima Ave.
Findlay, OH 45840-2315 (419) 423-1321

Company URL: http://www.coopertire.com
Establishment information: Established in 1914.
Company type: Public company
Company ticker symbol and exchange: CTB/NYSE
Business activities: Manufactures tires, tubes, and industrial rubber products.
Business type (SIC): Tires and inner tubes; gaskets, packing and sealing devices, and rubber hose and belting; rubber products/fabricated
Financial profile for 2012: Number of employees, 13,550; assets, $2,801,160,000; sales volume, $4,200,840,000; pre-tax net income, $368,450,000; expenses, $3,803,870,000; liabilities, $2,043,540,000
Fortune 1000 ranking: 2012—560th in revenues, 551st in profits, and 772nd in assets
Corporate officers: Roy V. Armes, Chair., Pres., and C.E.O.; Bradley E. Hughes, V.P. and C.F.O.; Steve Zamansky, V.P., Genl. Counsel, and Secy.
Board of directors: Roy V. Armes, Chair.; Thomas P. Capo; Steven M. Chapman; John J. Holland; John F. Meier; Cynthia Niekamp; John H. Shuey; Richard L. Wambold; Robert D. Welding
Plants: Texarkana, AR; Albany, GA; Clarksdale, Tupelo, MS
International operations: Barbados; Bermuda; Cayman Islands; China; England; Netherlands; United Kingdom
Giving statement: Giving through the Cooper Tire & Rubber Foundation and the Sage Cleveland Foundation.
Company EIN: 344297750

Cooper Tire & Rubber Foundation

701 Lima Ave.
Findlay, OH 45840-2315
Application address: c/o Cooper Tire & Rubber Co., Lima & Western Aves., Findlay, OH 45840, tel.: (419) 423-1321

Establishment information: Established in 1953 in OH.
Donor: Cooper Tire & Rubber Co.
Contact: Patricia Brown, V.P., Global Branding amd Comms.
Financial data (yr. ended 12/31/11): Assets, $6,049 (M); gifts received, $292,102; expenditures, $299,878; qualifying distributions, $297,035; giving activities include $297,035 for grants.
Purpose and activities: The foundation supports organizations involved with arts and culture, education, health, and youth development.
Fields of interest: Museums; Museums (art); Arts; Elementary/secondary education; Higher education; Education; Health care; Boy scouts; Youth development; YM/YWCAs & YM/YWHAs.
Type of support: Capital campaigns; Employee matching gifts; General/operating support.
Geographic limitations: Giving primarily in areas of company operations in IN, OH, and TX.
Application information: Applications accepted. Application form not required. Applicants should submit the following:
1) brief history of organization and description of its mission
2) detailed description of project and amount of funding requested

Initial approach: Proposal
Deadline(s): None

Trustees: C. F. Nagy; Stephen O. Schroeder; Bradley E. Hughes.
EIN: 237025013
Selected grants: The following grants are a representative sample of this grantmaker's funding activity:
$3,200 to Ohio State University, Columbus, OH, 2011.
$2,500 to Miami University, Oxford, OH, 2011.

The Sage Cleveland Foundation

(formerly The Standard Products Foundation)
c/o William Culbertson
3200 National City Ctr.
Cleveland, OH 44114-3485

Establishment information: Incorporated in 1953 in OH.
Donor: The Standard Products Co.
Financial data (yr. ended 12/31/11): Assets, $4,328,256 (M); expenditures, $586,991; qualifying distributions, $554,000; giving activities include $554,000 for grants.
Purpose and activities: The foundation supports health clinics and organizations involved with arts and culture, higher education, and substance abuse.
Fields of interest: Museums (art); Performing arts, theater; Performing arts, orchestras; Arts; Higher education; Health care, clinics/centers; Substance abuse, services; United Ways and Federated Giving Programs.
Type of support: Capital campaigns; General/operating support; Sponsorships.
Geographic limitations: Giving primarily in Cleveland, OH.
Support limitations: No grants to individuals.
Application information: Applications not accepted. Contributes only to pre-selected organizations.
Officers and Trustees:* J. S. Reid, Jr.*, Pres.; R. Steven Kestner*, Secy.; Edward B. Brandon; Sarah S. Cutler; John D. Sigel.
EIN: 346525047
Selected grants: The following grants are a representative sample of this grantmaker's funding activity:
$250,000 to Musical Arts Association, Cleveland, OH, 2011.
$235,000 to Cleveland Museum of Art, Cleveland, OH, 2011.
$15,000 to Playhouse Square Foundation, Cleveland, OH, 2011. For operating fund.
$5,000 to John Carroll University, University Heights, OH, 2011. For operating fund.
$4,000 to Laurel School, Shaker Heights, OH, 2011. For Annual Fund.
$2,500 to Franconia Sculpture Park, Franconia, MN, 2011.
$2,500 to Public Art Saint Paul, Saint Paul, MN, 2011.
$1,000 to PM Foundation, Cleveland, OH, 2011. For Annual Fund.
$1,000 to Saint Martin de Porres High School, Cleveland, OH, 2011. For Annual Fund.

937
COPIC Insurance Company

7351 E. Lowry Blvd.
Denver, CO 80230-6902 (720) 858-6000
FAX: (877) 263-6665

Company URL: http://www.callcopic.com
Establishment information: Established in 1981.
Company type: Subsidiary of a private company
Business activities: Sells property and casualty insurance.
Business type (SIC): Insurance/fire, marine, and casualty
Corporate officers: Theodore J. Clarke, M.D., Chair. and C.E.O.; Steven A. Rubin, Pres. and C.O.O.; Marv Ostermiller, C.F.O.; Kathy Brown, V.P., Corp. Mktg., and Comms.; Mark Fogg, Genl. Counsel
Board of directors: Theodore J. Clarke, M.D., Chair.; Ray N. Blum, M.D.; Linda Ann Clark; Matthew Fleishman, M.D.; Ray J. Groves; Brian C. Harrington, M.D.; Steven A. Rubin; Stephen R. Hoffenberg, M.D.; Roberto Masferrer, M.D.; Richard K. Parker, M.D.; Kathryn A. Paul; Jennifer A. Roller, M.D.; Walter K. Rush III, C.P.A.; John F. Wolz, M.D.; Peter J. Whitted, M.D.; Gerald Zarlengo, M.D.
Subsidiary: COPIC Financial Service Group, Ltd., Denver, CO
Giving statement: Giving through the COPIC Medical Foundation.

COPIC Medical Foundation

7351 Lowry Blvd.
Denver, CO 80230-6082 (720) 858-6071
E-mail: lsidener@copic.com; URL: https://www.callcopic.com/who-we-are/copic-medical/Pages/default.aspx

Establishment information: Established in 1992 in CO.
Donor: COPIC Insurance Company.
Contact: Lindsey Sidener, Mktg. Coord.
Financial data (yr. ended 12/31/11): Assets, $10,351,548 (M); gifts received, $590,429; expenditures, $292,740; qualifying distributions, $291,356; giving activities include $268,000 for 53 grants (high: $75,500; low: $500).
Purpose and activities: The foundation supports programs designed to improve patient safety, quality of care, disease management, and transitions in care and to reduce medical errors. Special emphasis is directed toward educating and training health care professionals; system changes and improvements; pilot programs designed to improve medicine; and the development and implementation of checklists and other tools.
Fields of interest: Medical school/education; Health care, clinics/centers; Dental care; Health care, blood supply; Public health; Health care, patient services; Health care; Cerebral palsy; Medical research; Human services.
Program:
Howard A. Williamson Award: The foundation annually honors one Colorado physician and one Nebraska physician for volunteer medical service and contributions to the community. The honor includes a $10,000 grant to a nonprofit organization of the recipient's choice.
Type of support: Conferences/seminars; Employee volunteer services; Equipment; Program development; Scholarship funds.
Geographic limitations: Giving primarily in CO and NE.
Support limitations: No support for political organizations, religious organizations, societies, or fraternal organizations. No grants to individuals, or for political campaigns or lobbying, endowments, telephone solicitations, ongoing general operating support, construction or repair of facilities, or capital campaigns.
Publications: Application guidelines; Informational brochure.
Application information: Applications accepted. Applications for general grants are currently not accepted for 2012. Visit website for updated guidelines. Application form required.
Initial approach: Download nomination form and mail to foundation for Harold E. Williamson Award
Deadline(s): June 20 for Nebraska Harold E. Williamson Award and Aug. 31 for Colorado Harold E. Williamson Award
Officers and Directors: Theodore J. Clarke, M.D., C.E.O.; Steven A. Rubin, C.O.O.; Ray Blum; Linda A. Clark; James Dreisbach, M.D.; Ray J. Groves; Brian C. Harrington, M.D.; Steven Hoffenberg, M.D.; Roberto Masferrer, M.D.; Richard K. Parker, M.D.; Kathryn Paul; Jennifer A. Roller, M.D.; Walter K. Rush III; Peter Whittied, M.D.; John F. Wolz, M.D.; Gerald V. Zarlengo, M.D.
EIN: 841197083
Selected grants: The following grants are a representative sample of this grantmaker's funding activity:
$40,000 to University of Colorado, Denver, CO, 2011. For general program support.
$15,000 to Cerebral Palsy of Colorado, Denver, CO, 2011. For general program support.
$15,000 to Colorado Nonprofit Development Center, Denver, CO, 2011. For general program support.
$10,000 to Bonfils Blood Center Foundation, Denver, CO, 2011. For general program support.
$10,000 to Colorado Mission of Mercy, Denver, CO, 2011. For general program support.
$10,000 to Regis University, Denver, CO, 2011. For general program support.
$10,000 to Stapleton 2040, Denver, CO, 2011. For general program support.
$5,000 to MDS Counseling Center, Denver, CO, 2011. For general program support.
$3,000 to Childrens Museum of Denver, Denver, CO, 2011. For general program support.
$1,750 to Alzheimers Association, Denver, CO, 2011. For general program support.

938
The Copley Press, Inc.

7776 Ivanhoe Ave.
La Jolla, CA 92037-4520 (858) 454-0411

Company URL: http://www.copleynewspapers.com/
Establishment information: Established in 1905.
Company type: Private company
Business activities: Publishes newspapers.
Business type (SIC): Newspaper publishing and/or printing
Corporate officers: David C. Copley, Chair., Pres., and C.E.O.; Charles F. Patrick, Exec. V.P. and C.O.O.; Dean P. Dwyer, V.P., C.F.O., and Treas.
Board of director: David C. Copley, Chair.
Subsidiaries: Daily Breeze, Torrance, CA; Daily Courier-News, Elgin, IL; The Herald News, Joliet, IL; Journal Star, Peoria, IL; Lincoln Courier, Lincoln, IL; The Register-Mail, Galesburg, IL; State Journal-Register, Springfield, IL; Union Tribune Publishing Co., San Diego, CA
Giving statement: Giving through the Helen K. and James S. Copley Foundation.

Helen K. and James S. Copley Foundation

(formerly James S. Copley Foundation)
7776 Ivanhoe Ave.
P.O. Box 1530
La Jolla, CA 92038-1530 (858) 454-0411

Establishment information: Incorporated in 1953 in CA.
Donors: The Copley Press Inc.; San Diego Union Shoe Fund; Helen K. Copley†.
Contact: Kim Koch, Secy.
Financial data (yr. ended 12/31/11): Assets, $5,556,920 (M); expenditures, $1,867,971; qualifying distributions, $1,853,142; giving activities include $1,853,142 for 20 grants (high: $666,667; low: $125).
Purpose and activities: The foundation supports organizations involved with arts and culture, education, animals and wildlife, health, recreation, and human services.

Fields of interest: Museums; Performing arts, theater; Performing arts, orchestras; Arts; Elementary/secondary education; Higher education; Libraries (special); Education; Animals/wildlife, special services; Hospitals (general); Health care; Athletics/sports, water sports; Recreation; Big Brothers/Big Sisters; Children/youth, services; Human services.

Program:

Employee Matching Gifts: The foundation matches contributions made by employees, directors, retirees, the spouses of employees, directors, and retirees, and the widows and widowers of retirees of the Copley Press to educational institutions on a one-for-one basis from $200 to $1,000 per contributor, per institution, per year.

Type of support: Building/renovation; Capital campaigns; Employee matching gifts; Endowments; Equipment; Scholarship funds.

Geographic limitations: Giving primarily in areas of company operations in CA, IL, and OH.

Support limitations: No support for religious, fraternal, or athletic organizations, government agencies, local chapters of national organizations, public elementary or secondary schools, or public broadcasting systems. No grants to individuals, or for research, publications, conferences, general operating support, or large campaigns; no loans.

Publications: Informational brochure (including application guidelines).

Application information: Applications accepted. Application form not required. Applicants should submit the following:

1) copy of IRS Determination Letter
2) listing of board of directors, trustees, officers and other key people and their affiliations
3) detailed description of project and amount of funding requested
4) copy of current year's organizational budget and/or project budget

Initial approach: Proposal
Copies of proposal: 1
Board meeting date(s): Feb.
Deadline(s): Jan. 2
Final notification: Following board meeting

Officers: David C. Copley, Pres.; Robert F. Crouch, V.P.; Charles F. Patrick, V.P.; Kim Koch, Secy.; Dean P. Dwyer, Treas.

EIN: 956051770

Selected grants: The following grants are a representative sample of this grantmaker's funding activity:

$3,000,000 to UCLA Foundation, Los Angeles, CA, 2010. For David C. Copley Center and Chair.
$666,667 to San Diego Public Library Foundation, San Diego, CA, 2010. For central library building project.
$500,000 to Sharp HealthCare, San Diego, CA, 2010. For campaign.
$428,600 to Museum of Contemporary Art San Diego, La Jolla, CA, 2010. For 21st Century Campaign-Downtown.
$300,000 to Theater and Arts Foundation of San Diego County, La Jolla, CA, 2010. For Artistic Innovative Initiative.
$200,000 to Abraham Lincoln Presidential Library Foundation, Springfield, IL, 2010. For museum support.
$200,000 to Old Globe Theater, San Diego, CA, 2010. To secure San Diego Landmark.
$100,000 to New Childrens Museum, San Diego, CA, 2010. For capital support and program support.
$50,000 to San Diego Opera Association, San Diego, CA, 2010. For Student Night at the Opera.
$20,000 to Monarch School Project, San Diego, CA, 2010. For after school program.

939
Coquille Economic Development Corporation

(also known as CEDCO)
3201 Tremont Ave.
North Bend, OR 97459-3062
(541) 756-0662

Company URL: http://www.cedco.net
Establishment information: Established in 1992.
Company type: Tribal corporation
Business activities: Operates casino hotel; produces cranberries; operates assisted-living facilities; provides broadband communications services.
Business type (SIC): Amusement and recreation services/miscellaneous; farms/fruit and nut; telephone communications; hotels and motels; nursing and personal care facilities
Corporate officers: Calvin Mukumoto, Chair. and C.E.O.; Robert Shreve, C.F.O.; Sharon Parrish, Secy.-Treas.
Board of directors: Calvin Mukumoto, Chair.; Gary Anderson; Bruce Didesch; Donald Garrett; Randy Hunter; Christine Keenan; Chris Severson
Giving statement: Giving through the CEDCO Corporate Giving Program and the Coquille Tribal Community Fund.

CEDCO Corporate Giving Program

c/o Mill Casino Hotel, Mktg. Donations
3201 Tremont Ave.
North Bend, OR 97459-3062 (541) 756-8800
E-mail: donations@themillcasino.com; URL: http://www.themillcasino.com/about/communityinvolvement.cfm

Purpose and activities: CEDCO makes charitable contributions to nonprofit organizations on a case by case basis. Support is given primarily in the Coos Bay, Oregon, area.
Fields of interest: General charitable giving Native Americans/American Indians.
Type of support: General/operating support.
Geographic limitations: Giving primarily in the Coos Bay, OR, area.
Support limitations: No support for religious organizations, sports teams, or school-related clubs. No grants to individuals.
Publications: Application guidelines.
Application information: Applications accepted. Support is limited to 1 contribution per organization during any given year. Telephone calls are not encouraged. Application form required. Applications should specifically note the nature of the request being made, and the event name and date, if applicable.

Initial approach: Complete online application form
Deadline(s): 2 months prior to need

Coquille Tribal Community Fund

3201 Tremont
North Bend, OR 97459-3062
FAX: (541) 756-0847;
E-mail: info@coquilletribalfund.org; Requests for donations of less than $1,000 should be directed to: The Mill Casino at donations@themillcasino.com; URL: http://www.coquilletribalfund.org/

Purpose and activities: The fund makes charitable donations to organizations involved with education, health, public safety, problem gaming, the environment, arts and culture, and historic preservation. Support is given primarily to non-governmental organizations in Coos, Curry, Douglas, Jackson, and Lane counties in southwestern Oregon.
Fields of interest: Historic preservation/historical societies; Arts; Education; Environment; Health care; Mental health, gambling addiction; Crime/violence prevention; Crime/law enforcement, police agencies; Disasters, fire prevention/control; Safety/disasters Native Americans/American Indians.
Type of support: Program development.
Geographic limitations: Giving primarily in Coos, Curry, Douglas, Jackson, and Lane counties in OR.
Support limitations: No support for medical clinics. No grants to individuals, or for fundraising benefits or program advertising, endowments, medical or scientific research, general operating support, recreation or sporting program sponsorships, religious programs, residential care, or scholarships or fellowships.
Publications: Application guidelines.
Application information: Applications accepted. Applicants must reapply annually for continued funding. Applicants who do not receive a reply in response to their letter of inquiry in 2 days should check their e-mail spam box or call the Fund Administrator at 541-756-0904 ext. 10236. Applicants should submit the following:

1) statement of problem project will address
2) name, address and phone number of organization
3) brief history of organization and description of its mission
4) detailed description of project and amount of funding requested
5) contact person

Initial approach: Complete online letter of inquiry form or mail or e-mail letter of inquiry to fund two weeks before deadline
Copies of proposal: 1
Committee meeting date(s): Jan. 2014
Deadline(s): Aug. 31, 2013
Final notification: Feb. 2014

Officer and Trustees:* Michele Burnette*, Chair.; Frank Amatisto; Joe Benetti; Carole Dawson; John Griffith; Gladys Ivy; Judy Rocha.

940
Coral Chemical Company

1915 Industrial Ave.
Zion, IL 60099 (847) 246-6666

Company URL: http://www.coral.com
Establishment information: Established in 1953.
Company type: Private company
Business activities: Manufactures industrial chemical products.
Business type (SIC): Chemicals/industrial inorganic
Corporate officers: John E. Schueneman, Pres.; Michael Stark, C.O.O. and C.F.O.
Plants: Paramount, CA; Lithonia, GA; Garland, TX
Giving statement: Giving through the Coral Foundation.

Coral Foundation

1915 Industrial Ave.
Zion, IL 60099-1435

Establishment information: Established as a company-sponsored operating foundation in 1966.
Donors: Coral International, Inc.; John E. Schueneman; Coral Chemical Co.; Natural Chemistry, Inc.
Financial data (yr. ended 12/31/11): Assets, $154,437 (M); gifts received, $250; expenditures,

$44,511; qualifying distributions, $41,945; giving activities include $41,945 for 9 grants (high: $30,000; low: $250).
Purpose and activities: The foundation supports organizations involved with arts and culture, secondary education, medical research, recreation, and human services.
Fields of interest: Health organizations; Recreation; Human services.
Type of support: General/operating support; Program development; Scholarship funds.
Geographic limitations: Giving limited to IL.
Support limitations: No grants to individuals.
Application information: Applications not accepted. Unsolicited requests for funds not accepted.
Officers and Directors:* Daniel J. Schueneman*, Pres.; John E. Schueneman*, V.P.; Shane Schueneman, Secy.-Treas.
EIN: 366149159

941
CORE Construction Group, Ltd.

(also known as Core Construction Services Of Illinois, Inc.)
(formerly Diversified Buildings, Inc.)
866 N. Main St.
P.O. Box 160
Morton, IL 61550-1602 (309) 263-0808

Company URL: http://www.coreconstruct.com
Establishment information: Established in 1979.
Company type: Subsidiary of a private company
Business activities: Provides general contract construction services.
Business type (SIC): Building construction general contractors and operative builders
Corporate officers: Wayne Baum, Chair.; Terry Baum, Co-Pres.; Mark Steffen, Co-Pres.; Kathreen List, Cont.
Board of director: Wayne Baum, Chair.
Subsidiaries: CORE Construction Services of Arizona, Inc., Phoenix, AZ; CORE Construction Services of Illinois, Inc., Morton, IL; CORE Construction Services of Nevada, Inc., Las Vegas, NV; CORE Construction Services of Texas, Inc., Frisco, TX; CORE Construction Services, Southeast, Inc., Naples, FL
Office: Peoria, IL
Giving statement: Giving through the CORE Construction Foundation.

CORE Construction Foundation

(formerly Diversified Buildings, Inc. Foundation)
866 N. Main St.
Morton, IL 61550-1602

Establishment information: Established in 1998 in IL.
Donors: Diversified Buildings, Inc.; CORE Construction Services of Illinois, Inc.
Financial data (yr. ended 12/31/11): Assets, $47,795 (M); gifts received, $25,000; expenditures, $23,959; qualifying distributions, $23,925; giving activities include $23,900 for 14 grants (high: $7,500; low: $100).
Purpose and activities: The foundation supports museums and organizations involved with television, education, leukemia, human services, and Christianity.
Fields of interest: Education; Youth development; Human services.
Type of support: General/operating support.
Geographic limitations: Giving limited to the Peoria, IL, area.
Support limitations: No grants to individuals.
Application information: Applications not accepted. Contributes only to pre-selected organizations.
Officers and Directors:* Wayne E. Baum*, Pres.; Kenneth D. Baum*, V.P.; Craig R. Baum*, Secy.; Terry L. Baum*, Treas.
EIN: 371376986

942
Cornerstone Bancshares, Inc.

835 Georgia Ave.
Chattanooga, TN 37402 (423) 385-3000

Company URL: http://www.cscbank.com/
Establishment information: Established in 1983.
Company type: Public company
Company ticker symbol and exchange: CSBQ/OTC
Business activities: Operates retail and commercial banks.
Business type (SIC): Banks/commercial
Financial profile for 2012: Number of employees, 105; assets, $440,460,000; pre-tax net income, $1,980,000; liabilities, $399,570,000
Corporate officers: Wesley Miller Welborn, Chair.; Nathaniel F. Hughes, Pres. and C.E.O.
Board of directors: Wesley Miller Welborn, Chair.; B. Kenneth Driver; Karl Fillauer; David G. Fussell; Nathaniel F. Hughes; Lawrence D. Levine; Frank S. McDonald; Doyce G. Payne, M.D.; Billy G. Wiggins; Marsha Yessick
Giving statement: Giving through the Cornerstone Bancshares Foundation.
Company EIN: 621175427

Cornerstone Bancshares Foundation

6401 Lee Hwy., Ste. 119
Chattanooga, TN 37402-2214
E-mail: cornerstonefoundation@cscbank.com; Application address: 835 Georgia Ave., Chattanooga, TN 37402; URL: http://www.thecornerstonefoundation.org

Establishment information: Established in 2007 in TN.
Donor: Cornerstone Bank, N.A.
Contact: Charlotte Lindeman
Financial data (yr. ended 12/31/11): Assets, $384,188 (M); gifts received, $451; expenditures, $29,804; qualifying distributions, $25,000; giving activities include $25,000 for grants.
Purpose and activities: Giving primarily to organizations within the communities served by the foundation involved with at-risk youth, elementary education and economic development.
Fields of interest: Education; Agriculture/food; Human services.
Application information: Applications accepted. Application form required.
Initial approach: Letter
Deadline(s): None
Directors: Frank Hughes; Jerry D. Lee; Lawrence Levine; Doyce Payne; Turner Smith; Miller Wellborn; Marsha Yessick.
EIN: 208115548

943
Cornerstone Bank, N.A.

529 Lincoln Ave.
P.O. Box 69
York, NE 68467-2944 (402) 363-7411

Company URL: http://www.cornerstoneconnect.com
Establishment information: Established in 1882.
Company type: Private company
Business activities: Operates commercial bank.
Business type (SIC): Banks/commercial
Financial profile for 2010: Assets, $1,000,000,000
Corporate officers: Kelly Holthus, Pres.; Frank Roach, Exec. V.P. and C.F.O.
Giving statement: Giving through the Holthus Foundation.

Holthus Foundation

529 Lincoln Ave.
York, NE 68467-2944 (402) 363-7409

Establishment information: Established in 2001 in NE.
Donors: Cornerstone Bank, N.A.; Tom Holthus; Marcy Holthus; C.G. Holthus; Kristie Holthus; Kendell Holthus; Beth Godbout.
Contact: C.G. Holthus, Dir.
Financial data (yr. ended 12/31/12): Assets, $3,667,941 (M); gifts received, $1,538,000; expenditures, $27,968; qualifying distributions, $26,000; giving activities include $26,000 for 2 grants (high: $21,000; low: $5,000).
Purpose and activities: The foundation supports nonprofit organizations in Nebraska, with emphasis on Boone and York counties.
Fields of interest: Health care; Housing/shelter.
Type of support: General/operating support.
Geographic limitations: Giving primarily in Boone and York counties, NE.
Application information: Applications accepted. Application form required.
Initial approach: Letter
Deadline(s): None
Directors: Kristie Holoch; C.G. Holthus; Virginia Holthus.
EIN: 470807361

944
Cornerstone Holdings, LLC

385 Interlocken Crescent, Ste. 250
Broomfield, CO 80021 (303) 410-2510

Company URL: http://www.cstoneholdings.com
Establishment information: Established in 1998.
Company type: Private company
Business activities: investment management and real estate development company.
Business type (SIC): Investors/miscellaneous; real estate subdividers and developers
Corporate officers: Thomas McCloskey, Chair. and C.E.O.; Neville Vere Nicoll, Pres.; John Ord, C.F.O.
Board of director: Tom McCloskey, Chair.
Subsidiaries: Cornerstone Aviation Services, Broomfield, CO; Kauai Ranch, Anahola, HI; McCloskey and Company, Anahola, HI; Urban Green Investments, San Francisco, CA
Giving statement: Giving through the Cornerstone Community Foundation.

Cornerstone Community Foundation

11001 W. 120th Ave., Ste. 310
Broomfield, CO 80021-3493

Establishment information: Established in 2004 in CO.
Donor: Cornerstone Winter Park Holdings, LLC.
Financial data (yr. ended 12/31/11): Assets, $508,059 (M); gifts received, $21,713; expenditures, $27,405; qualifying distributions, $23,300; giving activities include $23,300 for grants.
Purpose and activities: The foundation supports community service clubs and community foundations.
Fields of interest: Education; Health care; Recreation.
Type of support: Sponsorships.
Geographic limitations: Giving primarily in Winter Park, CO.
Application information: Applications not accepted. Unsolicited requests for funds not accepted.
Officers: Thomas D. McCloskey, Jr., Pres.; John Ord, Treas.
Director: C. Clark Lipscomb.
EIN: 364553494

945
Corning Incorporated

1 Riverfront Plz.
Corning, NY 14831-0001 (607) 974-9000
FAX: (607) 974-8091

Company URL: http://www.corning.com
Establishment information: Established in 1851.
Company type: Public company
Company ticker symbol and exchange: GLW/NYSE
International Securities Identification Number: US2193501051
Business activities: Manufactures optical fiber and cable, optical hardware and equipment, and telecommunications photonic modules and components; manufactures glass, glass ceramic, and polymer products.
Business type (SIC): Communications equipment; glass/pressed or blown; metal rolling and drawing/nonferrous
Financial profile for 2012: Number of employees, 28,700; assets, $29,375,000,000; sales volume, $8,012,000,000; pre-tax net income, $2,117,000,000; expenses, $6,717,000,000; liabilities, $7,889,000,000
Fortune 1000 ranking: 2012—326th in revenues, 121st in profits, and 190th in assets
Forbes 2000 ranking: 2012—1093rd in sales, 375th in profits, and 750th in assets
Corporate officers: Wendell P. Weeks, Chair., Pres., and C.E.O.; James B. Flaws, Vice-Chair. and C.F.O.; Kirk P. Gregg, Exec. V.P. and C.A.O.; Jeffrey Evenson, Sr. V.P., Opers.
Board of directors: Wendell P. Weeks, Chair.; James B. Flaws, Vice-Chair.; John Seely Brown; Stephanie A. Burns; John A. Canning, Jr.; Richard T. Clark; Robert F. Cummings, Jr.; James B. Flaws; Kurt M. Landgraf; Deborah D. Rieman; Hansel E. Tookes II; Mark S. Wrighton; Wendell P. Weeks
Subsidiaries: Corning Asahi Video Products Co., Corning, NY; Corning Cable Systems LLC, Hickory, NC; Corning Gilbert Inc., Glendale, AZ; Corning NetOptix, Inc., Keene, NH; Corning Tropel Corp., Fairport, NY
Plants: Harrodsburg, KY; Kennebunk, ME; Acton, MA; Troy, MI; Big Flats, Canton, Horseheads, Oneonta, Painted Post, NY; Concord, Wilmington, NC; Wilkes Barre, PA; Christiansburg, VA
Offices: Washington, DC; New York, NY
Joint Ventures: Cormetech, Inc., Durham, NC; Dow Corning Corporation, Midland, MI; Eurokera North America, Inc., Fountain Inn, SC; Pittsburgh Corning Corp., Pittsburgh, PA
International operations: Australia; Belgium; Cayman Islands; China; France; Germany; Hungary; Japan; Luxembourg; Mauritius; South Korea; Taiwan
Giving statement: Giving through the Corning Incorporated Foundation and the Corning Museum of Glass.
Company EIN: 160393470

Corning Incorporated Foundation

(formerly Corning Glass Works Foundation)
MP-BH-07
Corning, NY 14831-0001
FAX: (607) 974-4756;
E-mail: martinkc@corning.com; Additional contact: Joy M. Huth, Admin. Asst., tel. (607) 974-8722, e-mail: huthjm@corning.com; URL: http://www.corninginc foundation.org

Establishment information: Incorporated in 1952 in NY.
Donor: Corning Inc.
Contact: Karen C. Martin, Pres.
Financial data (yr. ended 12/31/11): Assets, $5,804,520 (M); gifts received, $6,781,531; expenditures, $8,062,712; qualifying distributions, $8,044,466; giving activities include $6,746,939 for 147 grants (high: $2,143,000; low: $700) and $573,686 for 1,285 employee matching gifts.
Purpose and activities: The Corning Incorporated Foundation is dedicated to improving the quality of life in communities where Corning Incorporated is an active corporate citizen. Grants from the foundation to local organizations and to national institutions support programs and projects in the sectors of education, arts and culture, and health and human services.
Fields of interest: Media/communications; Museums; Arts; Elementary/secondary education; Higher education; Libraries/library science; Education; Hospitals (general); Disasters, preparedness/services; YM/YWCAs & YM/YWHAs; Youth, services; Residential/custodial care, hospices; Human services; Foundations (community); United Ways and Federated Giving Programs.
Program:
Employee Matching Gifts Program: The foundation matches contributions made by employees of Corning to educational institutions, hospitals, nursing homes, hospices, performing and visual arts organizations, museums, libraries, public radio and television stations, historical societies, nature centers, and botanical and zoological gardens on a one-for-one basis up to $5,000 per employee, per year.
Type of support: Building/renovation; Capital campaigns; Curriculum development; Employee matching gifts; Equipment; Fellowships; General/operating support; Management development/capacity building; Program development; Program evaluation; Seed money; Technical assistance.
Geographic limitations: Giving primarily in areas of company operations; giving also to national organizations.
Support limitations: No support for political parties, labor or veterans' organizations, religious or fraternal organizations, or volunteer emergency squads. No grants to individuals, or for political campaigns or causes, athletic activities, courtesy advertising, or fundraising.
Publications: Application guidelines; Financial statement; Grants list.
Application information: Applications accepted. Letters of inquiry should be no longer than 2 to 3 pages. Grantmakers Forum of New York's Common Grant Application Form accepted. A full proposal may be requested at a later date. Application form not required. Applicants should submit the following:
1) timetable for implementation and evaluation of project
2) how project will be sustained once grantmaker support is completed
3) copy of most recent annual report/audited financial statement/990
4) how project's results will be evaluated or measured
5) explanation of why grantmaker is considered an appropriate donor for project
6) listing of board of directors, trustees, officers and other key people and their affiliations
7) detailed description of project and amount of funding requested
8) plans for cooperation with other organizations, if any
9) copy of current year's organizational budget and/or project budget

Initial approach: Letter of inquiry
Copies of proposal: 1
Board meeting date(s): Mar., June, Sept., and Nov.
Deadline(s): None
Final notification: 6 weeks

Officers and Trustees:* E. Marie McKee*, Chair.; Karen C. Martin, Pres.; Linda E. Jolly, Secy.; Mark S. Rogus*, Treas.; Jeffrey W. Evenson; James B. Flaws; Kirk P. Gregg; Vincent P. Hatton; James R. Houghton; Lawrence D. McRae; David L. Morse; Christine M. Pambianchi; Wendell P. Weeks.
Number of staff: 2 full-time professional; 1 full-time support.
EIN: 166051394
Selected grants: The following grants are a representative sample of this grantmaker's funding activity:
$2,143,000 to Corning-Painted Post Area School District, Painted Post, NY, 2011. For elementary and secondary programs.
$650,000 to Corning-Painted Post Area School District, Painted Post, NY, 2011. For secondary school curriculum development.
$410,000 to United Way of the Southern Tier, Corning, NY, 2011. For program support.
$390,000 to United Way of the Southern Tier, Corning, NY, 2010. For general program support.
$355,025 to Give2Asia, San Francisco, CA, 2011. For disaster relief.
$350,641 to American Red Cross National Headquarters, Washington, DC, 2011. For disaster relief.
$350,000 to Corning-Painted Post Area School District, Painted Post, NY, 2010. For secondary school curriculum development.
$250,000 to Food Bank of the Southern Tier, Elmira, NY, 2010. For new facility and program expansion.
$200,000 to Chemung County Performing Arts, Elmira, NY, 2010. For facility improvement.
$110,000 to Regional Science and Discovery Center, Corning, NY, 2011. For program support.
$75,000 to Southern Tier Hospice and Palliative Care, Corning, NY, 2010. For Out-Patient Palliative Care Program.
$50,000 to American Red Cross, Corning, NY, 2011. For disaster relief.
$28,750 to Massachusetts Institute of Technology, Cambridge, MA, 2010. For Science Fellowship.
$27,570 to United Way of Catawba County, Hickory, NC, 2011. For program support.
$27,000 to W S K G Public Telecommunications Council, Binghamton, NY, 2011. For broadcast underwriting.

$10,000 to Arnot Art Museum, Elmira, NY, 2010. For Centennial Exhibitions.
$10,000 to Food Bank of Central and Eastern North Carolina, Raleigh, NC, 2010. For general program support.
$6,574 to United Way of Forsyth County, Winston-Salem, NC, 2010. For general program support.
$6,000 to Monroe Community College Foundation, Rochester, NY, 2010. For Career Path Project.

The Corning Museum of Glass

1 Museum Way
Corning, NY 14830-2253 (800) 732-6845
FAX: (607) 974-8470;
E-mail: whitehoudb@cmog.org; URL: http://www.cmog.org

Establishment information: Established as a company-sponsored operating foundation in 1952.
Donors: Corning Inc.; Elaine Steppa; Stanford Steppa; Royal Caribbean International Celebrity cruises; Dorothy Lee-Jones; James B. Flaws; Marcia D. Weber; James R. Houghton; Carl H. Pforzheimer III; Emhart Glass Sweden AB; Jack Wax; The Greenberg Foundation; Daniel Greenberg; Susan Steinhauser; Nancy Bowen; Wendel P. Weeks.
Financial data (yr. ended 12/31/11): Assets, $33,792,834 (M); gifts received, $30,865,522; expenditures, $35,644,073; qualifying distributions, $30,378,953; giving activities include $20,000 for 4 grants (high: $10,000; low: $2,000).
Purpose and activities: The foundation promotes the history of glass and glassmaking and operates an art museum.
Fields of interest: Visual arts; Museums (specialized); Arts.
Programs:

Rakow Grant for Glass Research: Corning Museum of Glass awards grants of up to $10,000 to foster research in the history of glass and glassmaking. Special preference is given to projects that will bring researchers to Corning to study the museum's collections or to use its library. Projects are selected based on merit, the nature and contribution to glass studies, and the ability of the applicant to accomplish the goals as stated. Grants may be used to cover travel, living expenses, or other expenditures necessary to conduct the research or to publish it.

Residency Programs: Corning Museum of Glass offers an artist-in-residence and researcher-in-residence program at the Studio. Artists and researchers are invited to spend a month at The Studio to explore glass art or expand on their current bodies of work. The residency offers transportation, room and board, basic supplies, and the facility will be made available whenever classes are not in session. Residencies are held in March, April, May, October, and November.

Type of support: Scholarships—to individuals.
Geographic limitations: Giving on a national and international basis, including in Paris, France, and the United Kingdom.
Publications: Annual report; Newsletter.
Application information: Applications accepted. Application form required.
Proposals for residencies should include 10 slides or digital images on CD of applicant's work, 2 letters of recommendation, and a resume.
Initial approach: Download application form and mail to foundation for Rakow Grant for Glass Research; proposal for residencies
Deadline(s): Feb. 1 for Rakow Grant for Glass Research; Feb. 1 and Oct. 31 for residencies
Final notification: Apr. 1 for Rakow Grant for Glass Research
Officers and Directors:* E. Marie McKee*, Pres.; James R. Houghton*, V.P.; Amory Houghton, Jr.*, V.P.; Denise A. Hauselt*, Secy.; James B. Flaws, Treas.; David Whitehouse, Exec. Dir.; Robert K. Cassetti; Nancy J. Earley.
EIN: 160764349

946
CORT Business Services Corporation

(also known as CORT Furniture Rental Corporation)
11250 Waples Mill Rd., Ste. 500
Fairfax, VA 22030 (703) 968-8500

Company URL: http://www.cort1.com
Establishment information: Established in 1959.
Company type: Subsidiary of a public company
Business activities: Rents furniture.
Business type (SIC): Equipment rental and leasing/miscellaneous
Corporate officers: Jeff Pederson, Pres. and C.E.O.; Debbie Rosenberg, C.F.O.; Donna Anderson, Cont.
Giving statement: Giving through the CORT Foundation.

CORT Foundation

11250 Waples Mill Rd., Ste. 500
Fairfax, VA 22030-7400

Establishment information: Established in 1991 in VA.
Donor: Mohasco Foundation, Inc.
Contact: Vicky Stiles, V.P.
Financial data (yr. ended 12/31/11): Assets, $0 (M); expenditures, $401; qualifying distributions, $200; giving activities include $200 for grants.
Purpose and activities: The foundation supports organizations involved with higher education and kidney disease.
Fields of interest: Education; Housing/shelter.
Type of support: General/operating support.
Application information: Applications accepted. Application form not required.
Initial approach: Proposal
Deadline(s): None
Officers: Paul N. Arnold, Pres.; Vicky Stiles*, V.P.
Director: Jeffery Pederson.
EIN: 541566234

947
The Corvallis Clinic, P.C.

(formerly Corvallis Clinic, P.C.)
444 N.W. Elks Dr.
Corvallis, OR 97330 (541) 754-1150

Company URL: https://www.corvallisclinic.com/
Establishment information: Established in 1947.
Company type: Private company
Business activities: Operates medical clinic.
Business type (SIC): Offices and clinics/doctors'; drug stores and proprietary stores; laboratories/medical and dental
Corporate officers: Andrew Perry, C.E.O.; Douglas Bourdo, C.F.O.; Rod Aust, C.O.O.
Giving statement: Giving through the Corvallis Clinic Foundation, Inc.

The Corvallis Clinic Foundation, Inc.

444 N.W. Elks Dr.
Corvallis, OR 97330-3744 (541) 754-1374
FAX: (541) 757-1847; URL: http://www.corvallisclinicfoundation.org/

Donors: Corvallis Clinic, P.C.; David Cutsforth, M.D.; Life Wise; The Susan G. Komen Breast Cancer Foundation, Inc.; James R. Naibert, M.D.; Buzz Wheeler; Barker Uerlings Insurance; Hsichao Chow, M.D., Ph.D.; Eric Bunn; Georgia Bunn; Citizens Bank; Corvallis Radiology, PC; Design One One; Karla S. Chambers; Carvallis Gazette-Times; Steve Yutzie Floral; Visual People.
Financial data (yr. ended 12/31/10): Assets, $298,758 (M); gifts received, $147,918; expenditures, $134,513; qualifying distributions, $84,212; giving activities include $23,732 for 10 grants (high: $8,334; low: $250) and $60,480 for foundation-administered programs.
Purpose and activities: The foundation supports programs designed to promote health education; preventative health care; and the delivery of health care to the medically underserved; and awards college scholarships to students to study in health-related fields or in humanities.
Fields of interest: Humanities; Higher education; Medical school/education; Nursing school/education; Education; Nursing care; Health care; Cancer Economically disadvantaged.
Programs:

Corvalis Clinic Health Occupations Scholarships: The foundation awards scholarships to five area high school students who have decided to pursue a career in a health-related field.

Employee Emergency Fund: The foundation awards grants to employees of Corvallis Clinic during times of crisis that results in unexpected financial need.

George W. Knox Memorial Scholarship: The foundation, in partnership with the George W. Knox family, awards $500 scholarships to Corvallis area high school students who express an interest in entering a health-related career field or the humanities.

James A. Riley Health Occupation Scholarship: The foundation awards scholarships to Oregon State University students in the College of Science and the College of Health and Human Sciences who have decided to pursue a career in a health-related field. The scholarship is named in honor of a former clinic physician and founder of the foundation, Dr. James A. Riley. The program is administered through the respective OSU colleges.

James R. Naibert Health Occupation Scholarship: The foundation awards a $1,000 scholarship to a college sophomore or above who demonstrates an interest in a health-related profession that involves direct patient care, including physician, nursing, technical profession, or pharmaceutical studies. The scholarship is named in honor of James R. Naibert, a family physician at The Corvallis Clinic's Waverly Drive facility.

Type of support: General/operating support; Grants to individuals; Program development; Scholarship funds; Sponsorships.
Geographic limitations: Giving limited to the Mid-Willamette Valley and Central Coast, OR.
Publications: Application guidelines; Newsletter.
Application information: Applications accepted. Application form required. Applicants should submit the following:
1) detailed description of project and amount of funding requested
Applications for the James R. Naibert Scholarship should include official transcripts, a 1,000 word essay, and references.

Initial approach: Letter
Deadline(s): 90 days prior to funding
Trustees: Bruce Bynum; John Erkkila, M.D.; Lorri Hendon; Steve Kunke; Fred Koontz; Robin Lannan, M.D.; Robert Poole, M.D.; Alice Rampton; Lark Wysham.
EIN: 936021898

948
Costco Wholesale Corporation

(formerly Costco Companies, Inc.)
999 Lake Dr.
Issaquah, WA 98027-8990 (425) 313-8100
FAX: (425) 313-8103

Company URL: http://www.costco.com
Establishment information: Established in 1976.
Company type: Public company
Company ticker symbol and exchange: COST/NASDAQ
International Securities Identification Number: US22160K1051
Business activities: Operates membership-based warehouse stores.
Business type (SIC): Variety stores
Financial profile for 2012: Number of employees, 174,000; assets, $27,140,000,000; sales volume, $99,137,000,000; pre-tax net income, $2,767,000,000; expenses, $96,378,000,000; liabilities, $14,779,000,000
Fortune 1000 ranking: 2012—22nd in revenues, 123rd in profits, and 202nd in assets
Forbes 2000 ranking: 2012—57th in sales, 306th in profits, and 755th in assets
Corporate officers: Jeffrey H. Brotman, Chair.; W. Craig Jelinek, Pres. and C.E.O.; Richard A. Galanti, Exec. V.P. and C.F.O.; Franz Lazarus, Exec V.P., Admin and Human Resources; Paul G. Moulton, Exec. V.P., Inf. Systems; David S. Petterson, Sr. V.P. and Corp. Cont.; Joel Benoliel, Sr. V.P., Admin.; John Matthews, Sr. V.P., Human Resources
Board of directors: Jeffrey H. Brotman, Chair.; Benjamin S. Carson, Sr.; Susan L. Decker; Daniel J. Evans; Richard A. Galanti; William H. Gates, Sr.; Hamilton E. James; W. Craig Jelinek; Richard M. Libenson; John W. Meisenbach; Charles T. Munger; Jeff Raikes; Jill S. Ruckelshaus; James D. Sinegal
Offices: Garden Grove, Livermore, San Diego, CA; Sterling, VA
International operations: Bermuda; Canada
Giving statement: Giving through the Costco Wholesale Corporation Contributions Program and the Costco Foundation.
Company EIN: 911223280

Costco Wholesale Corporation Contributions Program

(formerly Costco Companies, Inc. Corporate Giving Program)
c/o Community Rels. Dept.
999 Lake Dr.
Issaquah, WA 98027-8990 (425) 313-8100
URL: http://www.costco.com/charitable-giving.html

Purpose and activities: Costco makes charitable contributions to nonprofit organizations involved with education, health, and human services. Special emphasis is directed towards programs designed to promote quality education and health care for children. Support is given primarily in areas of company operations, with some emphasis on Washington.
Fields of interest: Education; Health care; Human services Children.
Type of support: Employee volunteer services; General/operating support; In-kind gifts; Scholarship funds.
Geographic limitations: Giving primarily in areas of company operations, with some emphasis on WA; giving also to national organizations.
Publications: Application guidelines.
Application information: Proposals should be submitted using organization letterhead and be no longer than 2 pages. Support is limited to 1 contribution per organization during any given year. The Community Relations Department handles giving. A charitable committee reviews all requests. Applicants should submit the following:
1) results expected from proposed grant
2) name, address and phone number of organization
3) copy of IRS Determination Letter
4) brief history of organization and description of its mission
5) copy of most recent annual report/audited financial statement/990
6) how project's results will be evaluated or measured
7) list of company employees involved with the organization
8) listing of board of directors, trustees, officers and other key people and their affiliations
9) detailed description of project and amount of funding requested
10) contact person
11) copy of current year's organizational budget and/or project budget
12) listing of additional sources and amount of support
13) additional materials/documentation

Proposals should include a description of past support by Costco with the organization; contact information for the organization's president/CEO; the name and date of the event, if applicable; and indicate specifically how the funds will be used.
Initial approach: Proposal to nearest Costco Warehouse Manager for local in-kind donations; proposal to nearest regional office for in-kind donations impacting a broader community or region; download application form and mail with proposal to headquarters for monetary contributions
Deadline(s): 3 months prior to need
Final notification: 4 weeks
Number of staff: 9 full-time professional.

The Costco Foundation

999 Lake Dr.
Issaquah, WA 98027-8990

Establishment information: Established as a company-sponsored operating foundation in 1997.
Donor: Costco Wholesale Corp.
Contact: John Matthews, Pres.
Financial data (yr. ended 08/28/11): Assets, $3,785 (M); gifts received, $44,000; expenditures, $45,670; qualifying distributions, $45,670; giving activities include $45,660 for 16 grants to individuals (high: $7,415; low: $1,000).
Purpose and activities: The foundation awards grants for emergency assistance to employees of Costco Wholesale and its subsidiaries.
Fields of interest: Disasters, preparedness/services; Human services, emergency aid.
Type of support: Grants to individuals.
Geographic limitations: Giving limited to areas of company operations.
Application information: Applications not accepted. Contributes only through employee-related emergency grants.
Officers and Directors:* John Matthews*, Pres.; Monica Smith*, V.P.; Richard A. Galanti*, Treas.
EIN: 911799391

949
Cotton, Driggs, Walch, Kearney, Holley, Woloson & Thompson

(formerly Santoro, Driggs, Walch, Kearney, Holley & Thompson)
400 South 4th St., 3rd Fl.
Las Vegas, NV 89101-6202
(702) 791-0308

Company URL: http://www.cottondriggs.com
Establishment information: Established in 1996.
Company type: Private company
Business activities: Operates law firm.
Business type (SIC): Legal services
Offices: Las Vegas, Reno, NV
Giving statement: Giving through the Cotton, Driggs, Walch, Kearney, Holley, Woloson & Thompson.

Cotton, Driggs, Walch, Kearney, Holley, Woloson & Thompson

(formerly Santoro, Driggs, Walch, Kearney, Holley & Thompson Pro Bono Program)
400 South 4th St., 3rd Fl.
Las Vegas, NV 89101-6202 (702) 791-0308
FAX: (702) 791-1912;
E-mail: RThompson@nevadafirm.com; URL: http://www.cottondriggs.com/community-service/legal-aid-center/

Contact: Ronald J. Thompson, Managing Shareholder
Fields of interest: Legal services.
Type of support: Pro bono services - legal.

950
Coty Inc.

2 Park Ave., 17th Fl.
New York, NY 10016 (212) 479-4300
FAX: (866) 336-6064

Company URL: http://www.coty.com
Establishment information: Established in 1904.
Company type: Subsidiary of a foreign company
Business activities: Operates fragrance company.
Business type (SIC): Soaps, cleaners, and toiletries
Financial profile for 2010: Number of employees, 5,075; sales volume, $3,500,000,000
Corporate officers: Bart Becht, Chair.; Michele Scannavini, C.E.O.; Darryl McCall, Exec. V.P., Opers.; Sergio Pedreiro, C.F.O.; Jules Kaufman, Sr. V.P., Secy., and Genl. Counsel; Geraud-Marie Lacassagne, Sr. V.P., Human Resources
Board of director: Bart Becht, Chair.
Giving statement: Giving through the Coty Inc. Contributions Program.

Coty Inc. Contributions Program

2 Park Ave.
New York, NY 10016 (212) 479-4300
URL: http://www.coty.com/coty-cares/coty-cares-about-giving-back

951
Country Life Insurance Company
1701 N. Towanda Ave.
P.O. Box 2000
Bloomington, IL 61701-2057
(309) 821-3000

Company URL: http://www.countryfinancial.com
Establishment information: Established in 1929.
Company type: Private company
Business activities: Sells life insurance; sells health insurance; provides investment advisory services.
Business type (SIC): Insurance/life; security and commodity services; insurance/accident and health
Financial profile for 2010: Number of employees, 4,988; assets, $11,906,600,000; sales volume, $3,246,700,000
Corporate officers: Kurt F. Bock, C.E.O.; Barbara A. Baurer, C.O.O.; David A. Magers, C.F.O.
Giving statement: Giving through the Country Life Insurance Company Contributions Program.

Country Life Insurance Company Contributions Program
1701 N. Towanda Ave.
Bloomington, IL 61701-2057
FAX: (309) 820-4744;
E-mail: donations@countryfinancial.com;
URL: http://www.countryfinancial.com/SiteController?url=/whyChooseCountry/countryInYourCommunity

Purpose and activities: Country Life makes charitable contributions to nonprofit organizations involved with agriculture, housing, financial services education, human services, and community development. Support is given primarily in areas of company operations in Alaska, Arizona, Colorado, Illinois, Iowa, Kansas, Minnesota, Missouri, Nevada, North Dakota, Oklahoma, Oregon, Wisconsin, and Washington.
Fields of interest: Agriculture; Housing/shelter; Human services, financial counseling; Human services; Community/economic development.
Programs:
Count on Country Grant Program: Through the Count on Country Grant program, Country annually awards grants of $20,000 to organizations which provide educational opportunities and resources to help families achieve financial security.
Financial Security in Your Community Initiative: The company partners with organizations that provide financial security education for children and adults in order to manage their money effectively, protect their assets, save for special milestones in life like college and retirement, and achieve their full financial potential.
Type of support: Employee volunteer services; General/operating support; Sponsorships.
Geographic limitations: Giving primarily in areas of company operations in AK, AZ, CO, IA, IL, KS, MN, MO, ND, NV, OK, OR, WA, and WI, with emphasis on the greater Chicago, IL, area.
Support limitations: No support for political or religious organizations. No grants to individuals, or for teams.
Publications: Application guidelines.
Application information: Applications accepted. Application form required. Applicants should submit the following:
1) timetable for implementation and evaluation of project
2) population served
3) name, address and phone number of organization
4) geographic area to be served
5) copy of most recent annual report/audited financial statement/990
6) how project's results will be evaluated or measured
7) list of company employees involved with the organization
8) detailed description of project and amount of funding requested
9) contact person

Applications should include a description of past support by Country Life with the organization.
Initial approach: Download application form and e-mail or fax to headquarters for Financial Security in Your Community Initiative
Committee meeting date(s): Quarterly for larger requests
Final notification: 2 weeks

952
Countybank
(formerly The County Bank)
419 Main St.
Greenwood, SC 29648-3129
(864) 942-1500

Company URL: http://www.ecountybank.com
Establishment information: Established in 1933.
Company type: Private company
Business activities: Operates commercial bank.
Business type (SIC): Banks/commercial
Financial profile for 2009: Number of employees, 70
Corporate officers: R. Thornwell Dunlap III, Co-Pres. and C.E.O.; Claude Robinson, Co-Pres.
Giving statement: Giving through the CountyBank Foundation.

CountyBank Foundation
P.O. Box 3129
Greenwood, SC 29648-3129

Establishment information: Established in 1971 in SC.
Donors: The County Bank; R.T. Dunlap, Jr.
Financial data (yr. ended 08/31/11): Assets, $62 (M); gifts received, $22,150; expenditures, $22,150; qualifying distributions, $22,150; giving activities include $22,150 for 5 grants (high: $10,000; low: $250).
Purpose and activities: The foundation supports organizations involved with heart disease and community economic development.
Fields of interest: Heart & circulatory diseases; Community/economic development; United Ways and Federated Giving Programs.
Type of support: Employee volunteer services; Endowments; General/operating support; Program development; Scholarship funds.
Geographic limitations: Giving primarily in Greenwood, SC.
Support limitations: No grants to individuals.
Application information: Applications not accepted. Unsolicited requests for funds not accepted.
Trustees: R.T. Dunlap III; M. John Heydel; W.B. Patrick, Jr.
EIN: 237128545

953
Cousins Real Estate Corp.
191 Peachtree St., N.E., Ste. 500
Atlanta, GA 30303-1740 (404) 407-1000

Company URL: http://www.cousinsproperties.com/
Establishment information: Established in 1986.
Company type: Subsidiary of a public company
Business activities: Operates real estate investment company.
Business type (SIC): Real estate agents and managers
Financial profile for 2010: Number of employees, 30
Corporate officers: Lawrence L. Gellerstedt III, Pres. and C.E.O.; Gregg Adzema, Exec. V.P. and C.F.O.; Pamela F. Roper, Sr. V.P., Genl. Counsel, and Corp. Secy.
Board of director: Lawrence L. Gellerstedt III
Giving statement: Giving through the Cousins Properties Foundation, Inc.

Cousins Properties Foundation, Inc.
c/o Cousins Properties, Inc.
191 Peachtree St., Ste. 3600
Atlanta, GA 30303-1757

Establishment information: Established in 2005 in GA.
Donor: Cousins Real Estate Corp.
Contact: Robert M. Jackson, Sr. V.P., Secy., and Genl. Counsel
Financial data (yr. ended 12/31/11): Assets, $4,428,398 (M); expenditures, $313,583; qualifying distributions, $303,250; giving activities include $303,250 for grants.
Purpose and activities: The foundation supports community foundations and organizations involved with arts and culture, education, health, cancer, and community economic development.
Fields of interest: Arts; Higher education; Education; Health care; Cancer; Boys & girls clubs; Community development, business promotion; Community/economic development; Foundations (community); United Ways and Federated Giving Programs.
Type of support: General/operating support; Program development.
Geographic limitations: Giving primarily in the Atlanta, GA, area; giving also in other parts of southeast and southwest.
Support limitations: No grants to individuals.
Application information: Applications accepted. Application form not required.
Initial approach: Proposal
Deadline(s): None
Officers and Directors:* Larry L. Gellerstedt III*, C.E.O. and Pres.; James A. Fleming*, Exec. V.P. and C.F.O.; Craig B. Jones, Exec. V.P. and C.I.O.; Robert M. Jackson, Sr. V.P., Secy., and Genl. Counsel; Molly Faircloth, V.P. and Treas.
EIN: 203982777
Selected grants: The following grants are a representative sample of this grantmaker's funding activity:
$50,000 to East Lake Foundation, Atlanta, GA, 2010.
$50,000 to Forward Atlanta, Atlanta, GA, 2010.
$20,000 to Georgians for Passenger Rail, Atlanta, GA, 2010.
$15,000 to Robert W. Woodruff Arts Center, Atlanta, GA, 2010.
$12,500 to American Cancer Society, Atlanta, GA, 2010.
$12,500 to Georgia State University Foundation, Atlanta, GA, 2010.

$10,000 to Atlanta Police Foundation, Atlanta, GA, 2010.
$10,000 to Camp Twin Lakes, Atlanta, GA, 2010.
$10,000 to Childrens Healthcare of Atlanta, Atlanta, GA, 2010.
$5,000 to Sheltering Arms Early Education and Family Centers, Atlanta, GA, 2010.

954
Cousins Submarines, Inc.

N83 W13400 Leon Rd.
Menomonee Falls, WI 53051-3306
(262) 253-7700

Company URL: http://www.cousinssubs.com
Establishment information: Established in 1972.
Company type: Private company
Business activities: Operates submarine sandwich shops.
Business type (SIC): Restaurants and drinking places
Corporate officers: William F. Specht, C.E.O.; Kendall Richmond, C.F.O.; Kim Kofler, V.P., Opers.
Subsidiary: Cousins Subs Systems, Inc., Menomonee Falls, WI
Giving statement: Giving through the Cousins Submarines, Inc. Foundation.

Cousins Submarines, Inc. Foundation

N83 W13400 Leon Rd.
Menomonee Falls, WI 53051-3306

Establishment information: Established in 1999 in WI.
Donor: Cousins Submarines, Inc.
Financial data (yr. ended 12/31/11): Assets, $230,891 (M); expenditures, $13,938; qualifying distributions, $12,275; giving activities include $12,275 for grants.
Purpose and activities: The foundation supports hospitals and organizations involved with special education, higher education, and cancer.
Fields of interest: Education; Human services.
Type of support: General/operating support.
Support limitations: No grants to individuals.
Application information: Applications not accepted. Unsolicited requests for funds not accepted.
Officers and Directors: William Specht*, Pres.; Sandy Specht*, V.P.; James Sheppard*, Secy.; Kendall Richmond, Treas.
EIN: 391980576

955
Covance Inc.

210 Carnegie Ctr.
Princeton, NJ 08540 (609) 452-4440
FAX: (302) 655-5049

Company URL: http://www.covance.com
Establishment information: Established in 1987.
Company type: Public company
Company ticker symbol and exchange: CVD/NYSE
Business activities: Provides drug development services; provides laboratory testing services.
Business type (SIC): Research, development, and testing services
Financial profile for 2012: Number of employees, 11,790; assets, $2,288,340,000; sales volume, $2,365,760,000; pre-tax net income, $104,810,000; expenses, $2,257,260,000; liabilities, $981,150,000
Fortune 1000 ranking: 2012—844th in revenues, 750th in profits, and 822nd in assets
Corporate officers: Joseph L. Herring, Chair. and C.E.O.; William E. Klitgaard, Corp. Sr. V.P. and C.I.O.; James W. Lovett, Corp. Sr. V.P., Genl. Counsel, and Secy.; Alison A. Cornell, Corp. V.P. and C.F.O.; Lisa Uthgenannt, Corp. V.P., Human Resources
Board of directors: Joseph L. Herring, Chair.; Robert L. Barchi, M.D., Ph.D.; Gary E. Costley, Ph.D.; Sandra L. Helton; John McCartney; Joseph Scodari; Bradley T. Sheares, Ph.D.
Subsidiaries: Covance Central Laboratory Services, Inc., Indianapolis, IN; Covance Clinical Research Unit, Inc., Madison, WI; Covance Health Economics & Outcome Services, Inc., Gaithersburg, MD; Covance Periapproval Services, Inc., Radnor, PA; Covance Preclinical Corp., Vienna, VA
International operations: Argentina; Australia; Belgium; Canada; France; Germany; Hong Kong; Hungary; Japan; Netherlands; Poland; Singapore; Sweden; Switzerland; United Kingdom
Giving statement: Giving through the Covance Charitable Foundation.
Company EIN: 223265977

Covance Charitable Foundation

210 Carnegie Ctr.
Princeton, NJ 08540-6233

Establishment information: Established in 2002 in DE and NJ.
Donor: Covance Inc.
Financial data (yr. ended 12/31/11): Assets, $536,064 (M); gifts received, $600,100; expenditures, $66,153; qualifying distributions, $66,153; giving activities include $66,153 for 6 grants (high: $23,548; low: $1,105).
Purpose and activities: The foundation supports hospitals and organizations involved with birth defects, cancer, diabetes, medical research, children services, and economically disadvantaged people.
Fields of interest: Health care; Health organizations.
Type of support: General/operating support; Research.
Application information: Applications not accepted. Unsolicited requests for funds not accepted.
Officers: Joseph L. Herring, Pres.; James W. Lovett, V.P. and Secy.; William E. Klitgaard, V.P.; Michele D. Peterson, V.P.; Robert S. Pringle, Treas.
EIN: 810587320
Selected grants: The following grants are a representative sample of this grantmaker's funding activity:
$20,000 to American Association for Laboratory Animal Science Foundation, Memphis, TN, 2009.
$5,000 to Pennsylvania Society for Biomedical Research, Camp Hill, PA, 2009.
$5,000 to Pennsylvania Society for Biomedical Research, Camp Hill, PA, 2009.
$3,500 to Rider University, Lawrenceville, NJ, 2009.
$3,500 to Womanspace, Trenton, NJ, 2009.

956
Covidien

(formerly Tyco Healthcare/Mallinckrodt)
15 Hampshire St.
Mansfield, MA 02048 (508) 261-8000

Company URL: http://www.covidien.com
Establishment information: Established in 1909.
Company type: Public company
Company ticker symbol and exchange: COV/NYSE
Business activities: Operates health care products company.
Business type (SIC): Medical instruments and supplies; drugs
Financial profile for 2012: Number of employees, 43,400; assets, $22,257,000,000; sales volume, $11,852,000,000; pre-tax net income, $2,249,000,000; expenses, $9,411,000,000; liabilities, $11,692,000,000
Corporate officers: Jose E. Almeida, Chair., Pres., and C.E.O.; Charles J. Dockendorff, Exec. V.P. and C.F.O.; John H. Masterson, Sr. V.P. and Genl. Counsel; Michael Sgirgnari, Sr. V.P., Opers.; Eric A. Kraus, Sr. V.P., Corp. Comms. and Public Affairs; Jacqueline F. Strayer, Sr. V.P., Corp. Comms.; Michael P. Dunford, Sr. V.P., Human Resources; Richard G. Brown, Jr., V.P., C.A.O., and Corp. Cont.; Gregory S. Andrulonis, V.P. and Treas.
Board of directors: Jose E. Almeida, Chair.; Joy A. Amundson; Craig Arnold; Robert H. Brust; John M. Connors, Jr.; Christopher J. Coughlin; Randall J. Hogan III; Martin D. Madaus; Dennis H. Reilley; Joseph A. Zaccagnino
Giving statement: Giving through the Covidien Corporate Giving Program.

Covidien Corporate Giving Program

(formerly Tyco Healthcare/Mallinckrodt Corporate Giving Program)
c/o Covidien Partnership for Neighborhood Wellness
15 Hampshire St.
Mansfield, MA 02048-1113 (508) 261-8000
URL: http://www.covidien.com/covidien/pages.aspx?page=AboutUs/socialresponsibility

Purpose and activities: Covidien makes charitable contributions to nonprofit organizations involved with increasing access to quality, affordable healthcare; providing prevention, care, and treatment strategies for obesity, with emphasis on children; and addressing specific needs within the community. Support is given primarily in areas of company operations in California, Colorado, Connecticut, Florida, Georgia, Illinois, Indiana, Massachusetts, Minnesota, Missouri, Nebraska, New York, North Carolina, Ohio, Rhode Island, and South Carolina.
Fields of interest: Hospitals (general); Public health; Public health, obesity; Health care; Health organizations; Children, services Economically disadvantaged.
Programs:
Covidien Matching Gifts: Covidien matches contributions made by its employees to nonprofit organizations on a one-for-one basis, up to $10,000 per employee year.
Covidien Volunteer Incentive Program (VIP): Covidien makes charitable contributions to nonprofit organizations with which employees volunteer.
Type of support: Building/renovation; Capital campaigns; Donated products; Employee matching gifts; Employee volunteer services; General/operating support; In-kind gifts; Management development/capacity building; Program development; Sponsorships.
Geographic limitations: Giving limited to areas of company operations in CA, CO, CT, FL, GA, IL, IN, MA, MN, MO, NC, NE, NY, OH, RI, and SC.
Support limitations: No support for discriminatory organizations, political, lobbying, or religious organizations, organizations seeking advertisements for promotional support, fraternal, social, or labor organizations, or community sports organizations. No grants to individuals, or for endowments, capital campaigns (except for building clinics or healthcare facilities in impoverished communities), multi-year funding, gala dinners, golf fundraisers, or similar events.

Publications: Application guidelines.
Application information: Applications accepted. Brochures, pamphlets, annual reports, and video submissions are not encouraged. Additional information may be requested at a later date. A site visit may be requested. The Civic Affairs Department handles giving. Application form required. Applicants should submit the following:
1) name, address and phone number of organization
2) copy of IRS Determination Letter
3) how company employees can become involved with the organization
4) brief history of organization and description of its mission
5) copy of most recent annual report/audited financial statement/990
6) how project's results will be evaluated or measured
7) list of company employees involved with the organization
8) explanation of why grantmaker is considered an appropriate donor for project
9) listing of board of directors, trustees, officers and other key people and their affiliations
10) detailed description of project and amount of funding requested
11) contact person

Applications should include a description of past support by Covidien with the organization.
Initial approach: Complete online application form; contact local Community Liaison for organizations located outside the U.S.
Committee meeting date(s): Semi-annually
Deadline(s): Sept. 30 to Nov. 30 and Jan. 31 to Mar. 31
Final notification: Jan. 31 and May 31

957
Cow Creek Band of Umpqua Tribe of Indians

(also known as Cow Creek Gamining)
2371 N.E. Stephens St., Ste. 100
Roseburg, OR 97470-1372 (541) 672-9405

Company URL: http://www.cowcreek.com
Establishment information: Established in 1981.
Company type: Native corporation
Business activities: Operates casino hotel; operates truck stop; produces jerky and meat snacks; provides commercial printing services; provides local and long distance telephone communications services; provides broadband communications services; provides self-storage warehousing services; operates motels; sells health insurance; transmits and distributes electricity.
Business type (SIC): Amusement and recreation services/miscellaneous; meat packing plants and prepared meats and poultry; printing/commercial; warehousing and storage; telephone communications; electric services; gasoline service stations; insurance/accident and health; hotels and motels
Corporate officers: Dan Courtney, Chair.; Gary Jackson, Vice-Chair.; Yvonne Dumont-McCafferty, Secy.; Robert VanNorman, Treas.
Board of directors: Dan Courtney, Chair.; Gary Jackson, Vice-Chair.; Jessica Bochart; Tom Cox; Yvonne Dumont-McCafferty; Robert Easterbrook; Steve Jackson; Shirley Roane; George T. Rondeau; Luann Urban; Robert VanNorman
Giving statement: Giving through the Cow Creek Umpqua Indian Foundation.

Cow Creek Umpqua Indian Foundation

(formerly Cow Creek Seven Feathers Foundation)
2371 N.E. Stephens St., Ste. 100
Roseburg, OR 97470-1399 (541) 957-8945
FAX: (541) 677-5574; URL: http://www.cowcreekfoundation.org/

Contact: Carma Mornarich, Dir.
Purpose and activities: The foundation supports organizations involved with K-12 education, youth development, and families. Grants range from $100 to $15,000.
Fields of interest: Elementary/secondary education; Crime/violence prevention, child abuse; Youth development; Children, services; Family services Infants/toddlers; Children; Adults; Native Americans/American Indians.
Type of support: Building/renovation; Capital campaigns; Equipment; General/operating support; Matching/challenge support; Program development; Technical assistance.
Geographic limitations: Giving limited to Coos, Deschutes, Douglas, Jackson, Josephine, Klamath, and Lane counties, OR; giving limited to Douglas County for nonprofit governmental agencies.
Support limitations: No support for sectarian or religious organizations or pass-through organizations. No grants to individuals, or for projects not of direct benefit to the entire community, lobbying, debt reduction, or general fund drives or annual campaigns.
Publications: Application guidelines; Grants list.
Application information: Applications accepted. Organizations receiving support are asked to provide a final report. The foundation may request additional information at a later date. Extraneous proposal materials are not encouraged. Application form required. Applicants should submit the following:
1) copy of IRS Determination Letter
2) copy of most recent annual report/audited financial statement/990
3) listing of board of directors, trustees, officers and other key people and their affiliations
4) copy of current year's organizational budget and/or project budget

Proposals should include the telephone numbers of the organization's board of directors and the organization's brochure, if available.
Initial approach: Telephone foundation; complete online application and upload requested supporting documents
Deadline(s): Mar. 1 and Sept. 1
Final notification: 12 to 16 weeks
Officers and Directors:* Dan Courtney, Chair.; Norm Gershon, Vice-Chair.; Carma Mornarich, Exec. Dir.; Chris Davidson; Jacky Hagan-Sohn; Carol McKinney; Lee Paterson; Delbert Rainville; Tom Rondeau.
Selected grants: The following grants are a representative sample of this grantmaker's funding activity:
$12,555 to Jackson County Child Abuse Task Force, Childrens Advocacy Center, Medford, OR, 2009. For medical assessment and treatment for abused children.
$10,000 to Interact, Bend, OR, 2009. For in-home safety assessments and accessibility upgrades for low-income seniors and disabled adults.
$10,000 to Southwestern Oregon Community Action Committee, Coos Bay, OR, 2009. For preschool and infant center programs providing enrichment services for families.
$5,000 to Deschutes County Healthy Beginnings, Bend, OR, 2009. For health screenings for children.
$5,000 to Patrick McCurdy Education Foundation, Pleasant Hill, OR, 2009. For operating support for Reaching Out Mentoring Program for youth.

958
Cox Communications, Inc.

1400 Lake Hearn Dr., N.E.
Atlanta, GA 30319 (404) 843-5000

Company URL: http://www.cox.com
Establishment information: Established in 1898.
Company type: Subsidiary of a private company
Business activities: Operates cable television and telecommunications company.
Business type (SIC): Communications services/miscellaneous
Financial profile for 2010: Number of employees, 1,000; sales volume, $9,100,000,000
Corporate officers: James C. Kennedy, Chair.; Patrick J. Esser, Pres.; Jill Campbell, Exec. V.P., Sr. V.P., Opers., and C.O.O.; Mark F. Bowser, Exec. V.P. and C.F.O.; David Pugliese, Sr. V.P., Mktg.
Board of director: James C. Kennedy, Chair.
Subsidiaries: CableRep, Inc., Atlanta, GA; Cox Cable Greater Ocala, Inc., Ocala, FL; Cox Cable Hampton Roads, Inc., Virginia Beach, VA; Cox Cable University City, Inc., Gainesville, FL; TWC Cable Partners, Fort Walton Beach, FL; Video Service Co., Atlanta, GA
Divisions: Cox Communications-Amherst, Amherst, MA; Cox Communications-Ashland, Ashland, KY; Cox Communications-Bakersfield, Bakersfield, CA; Cox Communications-Cedar Rapids, Cedar Rapids, IA; Cox Communications-Cleveland, Cleveland, OH; Cox Communications-Coshocton, Coshocton, OH; Cox Communications-Defiance, Defiance, OH; Cox Communications-Gainesville/Ocala, Gainesville, FL; Cox Communications-Greater Hartford, Manchester, CT; Cox Communications-Humboldt Bay, Eureka, CA; Cox Communications-Jefferson Parish Office, Harahan, LA; Cox Communications-Lafayette, Lafayette, IN; Cox Communications-Lubbock, Lubbock, TX; Cox Communications-Meriden, Meriden, CT; Cox Communications-Middle Georgia, Macon, GA; Cox Communications-Midland, Midland, TX; Cox Communications-Myrtle Beach, Myrtle Beach, SC; Cox Communications-New Orleans, New Orleans, LA; Cox Communications-Newark, Newark, OH; Cox Communications-Oklahoma City, Oklahoma City, OK; Cox Communications-Omaha, Omaha, NE; Cox Communications-Orange County, San Juan Capistrano, CA; Cox Communications-Palos Verdes, Rolling Hills Estates, CA; Cox Communications-Pensacola/Fort Walton, Pensacola, FL; Cox Communications-Phoenix, Phoenix, AZ; Cox Communications-Providence/Weymouth, West Warwick, RI; Cox Communications-Quad Cities, Moline, IL; Cox Communications-Rhode Island, Cranston, RI; Cox Communications-Roanoke, Roanoke, VA; Cox Communications-Saginaw, Saginaw, MI; Cox Communications-San Diego, San Diego, CA; Cox Communications-Santa Barbara, Goleta, CA; Cox Communications-Spokane, Spokane, WA; Cox Communications-Springfield, Springfield, IL; Cox Communications-Vista, Vista, CA; Cox Communications-Washington, Washington, PA; Cox Communications-Williamsport, Williamsport, PA
Joint Venture: Emerald Coast Cable Television, Fort Walton Beach, FL
Giving statement: Giving through the Cox Communications, Inc., Corporate Giving program.

Cox Communications, Inc., Corporate Giving program

621 William St.
East Orange, NJ 07017 (973) 677-0529
URL: http://ww2.cox.com/aboutus/our-story/in-the-community.cox

Purpose and activities: Cox Communications makes charitable contributions to organizations involved with youth and education, diversity, and environmental issues. Support is given primarily in areas of company operations.
Fields of interest: Arts; Education; Environment; Youth development; Community/economic development Youth; Minorities; Women.
Type of support: Donated products; General/operating support; In-kind gifts; Sponsorships.
Geographic limitations: Giving primarily in areas of company operations in AK, AZ, CA, CT, FL, GA, KS, OH, LA, NE, RI, and VA.
Support limitations: No support for religious, political, sports, or discriminatory organizations, or foundations. No grants to individuals, or for endowment funds, or travel.
Publications: Application guidelines.
Application information: Applications accepted. Application form required.
Initial approach: Complete online application for appropriate state or region
Deadline(s): None
Final notification: 30 days

959
Cox Enterprises, Inc.

6205 Peachtree Dunwoody Rd.
Atlanta, GA 30328 (678) 645-0000

Company URL: http://www.coxenterprises.com
Establishment information: Established in 1898.
Company type: Private company
Business activities: Provides cable television services; publishes newspapers; broadcasts television; broadcasts radio; provides automobile auction services.
Business type (SIC): Cable and other pay television services; newspaper publishing and/or printing; radio and television broadcasting; retail stores/miscellaneous
Financial profile for 2011: Number of employees, 60,000; sales volume, $15,000,000,000
Corporate officers: James C. Kennedy, Chair.; Dennis Berry, Vice-Chair; Jimmy W. Hayes, Pres. and C.E.O.; John M. Dyer, Exec. V.P. and C.F.O.; Marybeth N. Leamer, Exec. V.P., Human Resources and Admin.; Gregory B. Morrison, Sr. V.P. and C.I.O.; J. Lacey Lewis, Sr. V.P., Finance; Shauna Sullivan Muhl, V.P., Genl. Counsel, and Corp. Secy.; Kathy Decker, V.P. and Treas.; Jack Polish, V.P. and Cont.; Roberto I. Jimenez, V.P., Corp. Comms. and Public Affairs; Robert Cahn, V.P., Human Resources, Devel., and Diversity
Board of directors: James C. Kennedy, Chair.; S. Taylor Glover, Vice-Chair; Michael J. Ahearn; Arthur M. Blank; Anne Cox Chambers; Janet Morrison Clarke; Jimmy W. Hayes; Brady L. Rackley; Christopher Williams
International operations: Canada
Giving statement: Giving through the Cox Enterprises, Inc. Corporate Giving Program, the James M. Cox Foundation, the James M. Cox Foundation of Georgia, Inc., and the Cox Employee Disaster Relief Fund, Inc.

Cox Enterprises, Inc. Corporate Giving Program

6205 Peachtree Dunwoody Rd.
Atlanta, GA 30328-4524 (678) 645-0000
E-mail: CorporateGiving@coxinc.com; URL: http://share.coxenterprises.com/

Contact: Roberto I. Jiminez, V.P., Corp. Comms. and Public Affairs
Purpose and activities: Cox Enterprises makes charitable contributions to nonprofit organizations involved with preserving the environment; empowering individuals, families, and communities; and promoting diversity and inclusion. Support is given primarily in Atlanta, Georgia.
Fields of interest: Environment; Family services; Civil/human rights, equal rights; Community/economic development.
Type of support: General/operating support; Sponsorships.
Geographic limitations: Giving primarily in Atlanta, GA.
Application information: Application form not required.
Initial approach: E-mail proposal
Copies of proposal: 1
Number of staff: 2 full-time professional; 1 full-time support.

James M. Cox Foundation

1700 Farnam St., Ste. 1500
Omaha, NE 68102-2022
URL: http://coxenterprises.com/corporate-responsibility/giving/foundations.aspx#.UZzMJoe84Qo

Establishment information: Established in 1989 in NE.
Donor: James M. Cox†.
Contact: Ronald C. Jensen, Secy.
Financial data (yr. ended 12/31/11): Assets, $1,985,430 (M); expenditures, $185,300; qualifying distributions, $160,249; giving activities include $42,500 for 10 grants (high: $5,000; low: $500) and $105,000 for 28 grants to individuals (high: $30,000; low: $500).
Purpose and activities: Assisting needy children to become productive adults through scholarships, grants to charitable organizations who have a similar purpose, and other methods of assistance.
Fields of interest: Higher education; Education; Children/youth, services.
Type of support: Emergency funds; Matching/challenge support; Scholarship funds; Scholarships—to individuals.
Geographic limitations: Giving restricted to residents of eastern NE.
Publications: Application guidelines.
Application information: Applications accepted. Application form not required.
Initial approach: Letter
Copies of proposal: 1
Board meeting date(s): Varies
Deadline(s): Nov. 30 for non-scholarship grants
Final notification: Feb. for non-scholarship grants
Officers and Trustees:* Norman A. Otto*, Pres.; Kathleen Sites, V.P. and Treas.; Ronald C. Jensen*, Secy.
EIN: 470719195
Selected grants: The following grants are a representative sample of this grantmaker's funding activity:
$5,000 to Boys and Girls Clubs of the Midlands, Omaha, NE, 2005.
$5,000 to Hamilton Community Foundation, Hamilton, OH, 2005.

The James M. Cox Foundation of Georgia, Inc.

6205 Peachtree Dunwoody Rd.
Atlanta, GA 30328 (678) 645-0929
FAX: (678) 645-1708;
E-mail: coxfoundation@coxinc.om; URL: http://coxenterprises.com/corporate-responsibility/giving/foundations.aspx

Establishment information: Incorporated in 1957 in GA.
Donor: Cox Enterprises, Inc.
Contact: Nancy K. Rigby, Treas.
Financial data (yr. ended 12/31/11): Assets, $171,589,881 (M); gifts received, $80,000,000; expenditures, $5,882,286; qualifying distributions, $4,594,750; giving activities include $4,593,000 for 49 grants (high: $1,000,000; low: $5,000).
Purpose and activities: The James M. Cox Foundation provides funding for capital campaigns and special projects in communities where Cox Enterprises Inc. does business. The Foundation concentrates its community support in several priority areas: Conservation and Environment; Early Childhood Education; Empowering Families and Individuals for Success; and Health.
Fields of interest: Education, early childhood education; Environment, natural resources; Environment, beautification programs; Public health, physical fitness; Health care; Medical research; Recreation, parks/playgrounds; Human services.
Type of support: Capital campaigns; Program development.
Geographic limitations: Giving primarily in areas of company operations, with emphasis on Atlanta, GA.
Support limitations: No support for religious, political, or discriminatory organizations. No grants to individuals, or for general operating purposes, seed money, endowment funds, events, or sponsorships.
Publications: Application guidelines.
Application information: Applications accepted. If located outside metropolitan Atlanta, a letter of support from general manager (or equivalent) at local Cox business is required. Application form required. Applicants should submit the following:
1) copy of most recent annual report/audited financial statement/990
2) how project's results will be evaluated or measured
3) listing of board of directors, trustees, officers and other key people and their affiliations
4) detailed description of project and amount of funding requested
5) copy of current year's organizational budget and/or project budget
6) listing of additional sources and amount of support

Initial approach: Complete online eligibility quiz and application
Copies of proposal: 1
Board meeting date(s): Apr., Aug., and Dec.
Deadline(s): Mar. 1, June 1, and Nov. 1
Final notification: May, Aug., and Dec.
Officers and Trustees:* Anne Cox Chambers*, Chair.; James C. Kennedy*, Pres.; James C. Kennedy, Jr.*, V.P.; Alexander C. Taylor*, V.P.; Shauna Sullivan Muhl, Secy.; Nancy K. Rigby, Treas.
EIN: 586032469
Selected grants: The following grants are a representative sample of this grantmaker's funding activity:
$500,000 to Henry W. Grady Health System Foundation, Atlanta, GA, 2011. For capital campaign.
$300,000 to Teach for America, Atlanta, GA, 2011. For special program.
$250,000 to Nature Conservancy, Georgia Office, Atlanta, GA, 2011. For capital campaign.
$100,000 to Big Brothers Big Sisters of Metro Atlanta, Atlanta, GA, 2011. For capital campaign.
$50,000 to Latin American Association, Atlanta, GA, 2011. For Latin Family Self-Sufficient Project.
$25,000 to Palm Beach County Literacy Coalition, Delray Beach, FL, 2011. For capital campaign.

$25,000 to Ronald McDonald House Charities of North Central Florida, Gainesville, FL, 2011. For capital campaign for 30th Anniversary Bedroom Upgrade/Redecoration Project.
$25,000 to Upper Chattahoochee Riverkeeper Fund, Atlanta, GA, 2011. For Clean Water for Healthy Future.
$25,000 to YWCA of Northwest Georgia, Marietta, GA, 2011. For capital campaign.
$10,000 to Genesis Shelter, Atlanta, GA, 2011. For child development classroom.

Cox Employee Disaster Relief Fund, Inc.

6205 Peachtree Dunwoody Rd.
Atlanta, GA 30328-4524 (202) 776-2728

Financial data (yr. ended 12/31/11): Revenue, $3,970,403; assets, $7,667,559 (M); gifts received, $3,858,520; expenditures, $100,058; giving activities include $59,650 for grants to individuals.
Purpose and activities: The fund seeks to provide relief to the victims of natural disasters.
Fields of interest: Disasters, Hurricane Katrina; Safety/disasters.
Type of support: Grants to individuals.
Officers: Leigh Ann Launius, Pres.; Shauna J. Sullivan, Secy.; Carol L. Larner, Treas.
Directors: Becky M. Greenhill; Alan Hicks; Ming Yao.
EIN: 203401306

960
Cox Smith Matthews, Inc

(formerly Cox & Smith Inc.)
112 E. Pecan St., Ste. 1800
San Antonio, TX 78205 (210) 554-5500

Company URL: http://www.coxsmith.com/
Establishment information: Established in 1939.
Company type: Private company
Business activities: Provides legal services.
Business type (SIC): Legal services
Financial profile for 2010: Number of employees, 160
Corporate officer: George H. Casbeer, C.O.O.
Giving statement: Giving through the Cox Smith Matthews Foundation.

Cox Smith Matthews Foundation

(formerly Cox & Smith Foundation)
112 E. Pecan St., Ste. 1800
San Antonio, TX 78205-1521 (210) 554-5500

Establishment information: Established in 1989 in TX.
Donors: Cox Smith Matthews Incorporated; Cox & Smith Inc.
Financial data (yr. ended 12/31/11): Assets, $56,786 (M); gifts received, $66,750; expenditures, $75,965; qualifying distributions, $71,795; giving activities include $71,795 for grants.
Purpose and activities: The foundation supports organizations involved with education, health, youth development, and human services.
Fields of interest: Recreation; Human services; Community/economic development.
Support limitations: No grants to individuals.
Application information: Applications accepted. Application form not required. Applicants should submit the following:
1) copy of IRS Determination Letter
Initial approach: Proposal
Deadline(s): None
Officer: George Casbeer, C.O.O.
Directors: J. Daniel Harkins; Mary Potter; James B. Smith, Jr.
EIN: 742524104

961
Cox Smith Matthews Inc.

112 E. Pecan St., Ste. 1800
San Antonio, TX 78205-1521
(210) 554-5500

Company URL: http://www.coxsmith.com
Establishment information: Established in 1939.
Company type: Private company
Business activities: Operates law firm.
Business type (SIC): Legal services
Corporate officer: George H. Casbeer, C.O.O.
Offices: Austin, Dallas, El Paso, McAllen, San Antonio, TX
Giving statement: Giving through the Cox Smith Matthews Inc. Pro Bono Program.

Cox Smith Matthews Inc. Pro Bono Program

112 E. Pecan St., Ste. 1800
San Antonio, TX 78205-1521 (210) 554-5500
FAX: (210) 226-8395; URL: http://www.coxsmith.com/AboutCoxSmith/ProBono

Fields of interest: Legal services.
Type of support: Pro bono services - legal.
Geographic limitations: Giving primarily in areas of company operations in Austin, Dallas, El Paso, McAllen, and San Antonio, TX.
Application information: Department Leaders manage the pro-bono program.

962
Cox Wood Preserving Co.

860 Cannon Bridge Rd.
P.O. Box 1124
Orangeburg, SC 29115-7284
(803) 534-7467

Company URL: http://www.coxwood.com
Establishment information: Established in 1954.
Company type: Subsidiary of a private company
Business activities: Manufactures outdoor wood products.
Business type (SIC): Lumber and wood products (except furniture); furniture and fixtures
Financial profile for 2010: Number of employees, 150
Corporate officers: Bill Cox, Jr., Chair.; Michael R. Johnson, C.E.O.; Dave Lewis, C.F.O.; Richard Lackey, V.P., Genl. Counsel, and Human Resources; Brian Hayson, V.P., Sales; Keith Harris, V.P., Mktg.
Board of director: Bill Cox, Jr., Chair.
Subsidiaries: Augusta Wood Preserving, Augusta, GA; Cove City Wood Preserving, Cove City, NC; Structual Wood Preserving, Coleridge, NC; Sumter Wood Preserving, Sumter, SC
Giving statement: Giving through the Cox Foundation.

Cox Foundation

c/o Cox Wood Preserving Co.
P.O. Box 1124
Orangeburg, SC 29116-1124 (803) 534-7467

Establishment information: Established in 1986 in SC.
Donors: Cox Wood Preserving Co.; William B. Cox; Arch Chemicals, Inc.
Contact: Cathy C. Yeadon, Dir.
Financial data (yr. ended 04/30/12): Assets, $1,009,680 (M); gifts received, $16,263; expenditures, $43,724; qualifying distributions, $43,724; giving activities include $43,724 for grants to individuals.
Purpose and activities: The foundation awards college scholarships to children and dependents of employees of Cox Wood Preserving Co. and affiliated companies.
Type of support: Employee-related scholarships.
Geographic limitations: Giving limited to NC and SC.
Application information: Applications accepted. Application form required.
Initial approach: Proposal
Deadline(s): Jan. 31
Directors: Pat Black; Elizabeth B. Malinder; Carol H. Riley; Cathy C. Yeadon.
EIN: 570823753

963
Coyotes Hockey, LLC

(also known as Phoenix Coyotes)
6751 N. Sunset Blvd., Ste. 200
Glendale, AZ 85305 (623) 772-3200

Company URL: http://www.phoenixcoyotes.com
Establishment information: Established in 1996.
Company type: Private company
Business activities: Operates professional ice hockey club.
Business type (SIC): Commercial sports
Corporate officers: Mike Nealy, Pres. and C.O.O.; Joe Leibfried, Sr. V.P., Finance; Brad Treliving, V.P., Opers.
Giving statement: Giving through the Phoenix Coyotes Corporate Giving Program and the Coyotes Charities.

Phoenix Coyotes Corporate Giving Program

c/o Phoenix Coyotes Hockey Club
6751 N. Sunset Blvd., #200
Glendale, AZ 85305-3124 (623) 772-3200
FAX: (623) 872-2000;
E-mail: coyotes.charities@phoenixcoyotes.com; URL: http://coyotes.nhl.com/club/page.htm?id=32786

Purpose and activities: The Phoenix Coyotes make charitable contributions of autographed memorabilia and tickets to nonprofit organizations. Support is limited to organizations in Arizona. Donations must be used to raise additional funds for that organization.
Fields of interest: Arts, cultural/ethnic awareness; Education; Health care; Athletics/sports, school programs; Urban/community development.
Type of support: Donated products; In-kind gifts.
Geographic limitations: Giving is limited to organizations in AZ.
Support limitations: No support for religious, political, or labor organizations. No item donations to companies holding organizational campaigns for nonprofit organizations, or for use as door prizes, incentives, or giveaways, school raffles, carnivals, fundraisers, or festivals, school athletic organizations without official nonprofit status, or individual fundraising initiatives such as walk teams, marathons, or Team-in-Training.

Publications: Application guidelines.
Application information: Applications accepted. Requests should be limited to 1 application per organization during any given year. Applications are not accepted by mail, e-mail, fax, or phone. No telephone or email follow-ups will be accepted. Items are not accepted for autograph and will not be returned. Monetary donations are made once a year. Application form required. Applicants should submit the following:
1) name, address and phone number of organization
2) contact person
3) copy of IRS Determination Letter
Initial approach: Complete online application form
Deadline(s): 6 weeks prior to event
Final notification: 2 weeks to one month prior to event, by mail

Coyotes Charities
6751 N. White Out Way, Ste. 200
Glendale, AZ 85305-3153 (623) 463-8800
FAX: (623) 463-8810; URL: http://coyotes.nhl.com/club/page.htm?id=32664

Establishment information: Established in 2001 in AZ.
Contact: John Breslow, Exec. Dir.
Financial data (yr. ended 12/31/11): Revenue, $327,473; assets, $176,976 (M); gifts received, $229,680; expenditures, $296,627; giving activities include $291,205 for grants.
Purpose and activities: The organization seeks to enhance the quality of life throughout Arizona communities by supporting youth and adult education programs, prevention and wellness programs, and cultural arts.
Fields of interest: Arts; Youth development, adult & child programs.
Program:
Program Grants: The program provides grants, generally ranging from $1,000 to $5,000, for programs addressing the areas of healthcare, education, cultural arts, and youth sports. Eligible applicants must have had 501(c)(3) status for at least two years prior to application, and must focus on improving the lives of children in Arizona.
Geographic limitations: Giving limited to AZ.
Support limitations: No support for religious, fraternal, educational, or political institutions, governmental municipalities, or environmental groups. No grants to individuals.
Publications: Application guidelines.
Application information: Applications accepted. Application form required. Applicants should submit the following:
1) qualifications of key personnel
2) statement of problem project will address
3) population served
4) name, address and phone number of organization
5) copy of IRS Determination Letter
6) brief history of organization and description of its mission
7) geographic area to be served
8) copy of most recent annual report/audited financial statement/990
9) how project's results will be evaluated or measured
10) descriptive literature about organization
11) what distinguishes project from others in its field
12) listing of board of directors, trustees, officers and other key people and their affiliations
13) detailed description of project and amount of funding requested
14) organization's charter and by-laws
15) copy of current year's organizational budget and/or project budget
Initial approach: Download application form
Deadline(s): June 18

Officers: Doug Moss, Pres.; Robert Kaufman, V.P.; Andrea Doan, Secy.; Mike Nealy, Treas.; John Breslow, Exec. Dir.
EIN: 861021459

964
Cozen O'Connor
1900 Market St.
Philadelphia, PA 19103 (215) 665-2000

Company URL: http://www.cozen.com
Establishment information: Established in 1970.
Company type: Private company
Business activities: Operates law firm.
Business type (SIC): Legal services
Corporate officers: Stephen A. Cozen, Chair.; Thomas A. Decker, Pres. and C.E.O.
Board of director: Stephen A. Cozen, Chair.
Offices: Los Angeles, San Diego, CA; Denver, CO; Wilmington, DE; Washington, DC; Miami, FL; Atlanta, GA; Chicago, IL; Cherry Hill, NJ; Santa Fe, NM; New York, NY; Charlotte, NC; Harrisburg, Philadelphia, West Conshohocken, Wilkes Barre, PA; Dallas, Houston, TX; Seattle, WA
International operations: Canada; United Kingdom
Giving statement: Giving through the Cozen O'Connor Pro Bono Program and the Cozen O'Connor Foundation, Inc.

Cozen O'Connor Pro Bono Program
1900 Market St., Fl. 3
Philadelphia, PA 19103-3572 (215) 665-4734
E-mail: hhunt@cozen.com; URL: http://www.cozen.com/firm.asp?d=1&fpid=8#

Contact: Hayes Hunt, Chair of the Pro Bono Initiative and Advanced Advocacy Program
Fields of interest: Legal services.
Type of support: Pro bono services - legal.
Geographic limitations: Giving primarily in areas of company operations in Los Angeles, and San Diego, CA, Denver, CO, Washington, DC, Wilmington, DE, Miami, FL, Atlanta, GA, Chicago, IL, Charlotte, NC, Cherry Hill, NJ, Santa Fe, NM, New York, NY, Harrisburg, Philadelphia, West Conshohocken, and Wilkes-Barre, PA, Dallas, and Houston, TX, Seattle, WA, Canada, and the United Kingdom.
Application information: The Pro Bono Committee manages the pro-bono program.

The Cozen O'Connor Foundation, Inc.
1900 Market St.
Philadelphia, PA 19103-3527
URL: http://www.cozen.com/firm.asp?d=1&fpid=6

Financial data (yr. ended 01/31/11): Revenue, $1,450,984; assets, $67,121 (M); gifts received, $1,450,984; expenditures, $1,241,311; giving activities include $1,230,015 for grants.
Purpose and activities: The organization supports various charities and non-profit organizations in the communities in which it practices law.
Officers and Directors:* Harmon Spolan, Chair.; Stephen A. Cozen, Pres.; Thomas A. Decker, V.P.; Patrick J O'Connor, V.P.; Henry A. Gladstone, Secy.; David W. Ellman, Treas.; Dennis Cohen; Gerard Harney.
EIN: 200074096

965
CPI Corp.
1706 Washington Ave.
St. Louis, MO 63103 (314) 231-1575
FAX: (302) 655-5049

Company URL: http://www.cpicorp.com
Establishment information: Established in 1942.
Company type: Public company
Company ticker symbol and exchange: CPICQ/Pink Sheets
Business activities: Operates portrait photography studios and photofinishing laboratories.
Business type (SIC): Photographic portrait studios; business services/miscellaneous
Financial profile for 2012: Number of employees, 11,900; assets, $94,530,000; sales volume, $361,680,000; pre-tax net income, -$43,790,000; expenses, $401,820,000; liabilities, $153,190,000
Corporate officers: David M. Meyer, Chair.; James J. Abel, Pres. and C.E.O.; Dale E. Heins, Sr. V.P., Finance and C.F.O.
Board of directors: David M. Meyer, Chair.; James J. Abel; Michael Glazer; Michael S. Koeneke; Eric Salus; John Turner White IV
Subsidiary: Sears Portrait Studios, St. Louis, MO
International operations: Mexico
Giving statement: Giving through the CPI Corp. Contributions Program and the CPI Corp. Philanthropic Trust.
Company EIN: 431256674

CPI Corp. Philanthropic Trust
1706 Washington Ave.
St. Louis, MO 63103-1717 (314) 231-1575

Establishment information: Established in 1984 in MO.
Donor: CPI Corp.
Contact: Jane E. Nelson
Financial data (yr. ended 01/31/11): Assets, $2,876 (M); expenditures, $2,150; qualifying distributions, $2,000; giving activities include $2,000 for grants.
Purpose and activities: The foundation primarily supports organizations involved with human services.
Fields of interest: Education; Human services.
Type of support: General/operating support.
Geographic limitations: Giving primarily in areas of company operations in MO.
Support limitations: No grants to individuals.
Publications: Application guidelines.
Application information: Applications accepted. Application form required.
Initial approach: Contact foundation for application form
Copies of proposal: 1
Deadline(s): None
Number of staff: 1 part-time professional; 1 part-time support.
EIN: 431334012

966
Cracker Barrel Old Country Store, Inc.
305 Hartmann Dr.
P.O. Box 787
Lebanon, TN 37087-0787 (615) 444-5533
FAX: (615) 443-9818

Company URL: http://www.crackerbarrel.com
Establishment information: Established in 1969.
Company type: Public company
Company ticker symbol and exchange: CBRL/NASDAQ
Business activities: Owns and operates restaurants.
Business type (SIC): Restaurants and drinking places
Financial profile for 2012: Number of employees, 70,000; assets, $1,418,990,000; sales volume, $2,580,200,000; pre-tax net income, $146,290,000; expenses, $2,389,220,000; liabilities, $1,036,320,000
Fortune 1000 ranking: 2012—793rd in revenues, 732nd in profits, and 928th in assets
Corporate officers: Sandra B. Cochran, Pres. and C.E.O.; Lawrence E. Hyatt, Sr. V.P. and C.F.O.; Nicholas V. Flanagan, Sr. V.P., Opers.; Christopher A. Ciavarra, Sr. V.P., Mktg.
Board of directors: Tom Barr; James W. Bradford; Sandra B. Cochran; Glenn Davenport; Richard J. Dobkin; Norman E. Johnson; William W. McCarten; Martha M. Mitchell; Coleman H. Peterson; Andrea M. Weiss
Giving statement: Giving through the Cracker Barrel Old Country Store Foundation.
Company EIN: 621749513

Cracker Barrel Old Country Store Foundation
P.O. Box 787
Lebanon, TN 37088-0787 (615) 443-5533
FAX: (615) 443-9874;
E-mail: pcarroll@crackerbarrel.com; URL: http://www.crackerbarrel.com/foundation/

Establishment information: Established around 1996.
Donor: Cracker Barrel Old Country Store, Inc.
Contact: Penny Carroll, Secy.
Financial data (yr. ended 07/31/11): Assets, $4,725,813 (M); gifts received, $578,545; expenditures, $413,924; qualifying distributions, $413,899; giving activities include $318,375 for 89 grants (high: $20,000; low: $500) and $81,000 for 54 grants to individuals (high: $1,500; low: $1,500).
Purpose and activities: The foundation supports organizations involved with arts and culture, education, the environment, and human services. Special emphasis is directed toward programs designed to address children, youth, and family issues and emphasize hard work, education, and self-reliance.
Fields of interest: Arts; Education; Environment; Children/youth, services; Family services; Human services.
Programs:
Cracker Barrel Foundation Scholarship: The foundation awards 55 $1,500 college scholarships to employees and children of employees of Cracker Barrel Old Country Store. Applicants must enroll in an accredited, not-for-profit college, university, vocational or technical institute as a full time student in the fall of the same calendar year that the scholarship is awarded.
Cultural and Environmental Issues: The foundation supports programs designed to encourage environmental education; preserve and establish historic monuments, natural sites, and parks; and provide arts education.
Education: The foundation supports programs designed to strengthen higher education and increase its availability; increase adult literacy; and improve the quality of education.
Human Services: The foundation supports programs designed to enable individuals to become self-sufficient; and address child and family issues.
Type of support: Employee-related scholarships; Equipment; General/operating support; Matching/challenge support; Program development; Scholarship funds.
Geographic limitations: Giving primarily in Lebanon and Nashville, TN.
Support limitations: No support for religious, political, fraternal, athletic, or veterans' organizations. No grants to individuals (except employee-related scholarships), or for fundraising activities such as benefits, charitable dinners, or sporting events.
Publications: Application guidelines; Informational brochure (including application guidelines); Program policy statement.
Application information: Applications accepted. Application form not required. Applicants should submit the following:
1) results expected from proposed grant
2) qualifications of key personnel
3) name, address and phone number of organization
4) copy of IRS Determination Letter
5) brief history of organization and description of its mission
6) geographic area to be served
7) copy of most recent annual report/audited financial statement/990
8) how project's results will be evaluated or measured
9) descriptive literature about organization
10) listing of board of directors, trustees, officers and other key people and their affiliations
11) detailed description of project and amount of funding requested
12) listing of additional sources and amount of support

Proposals should include a history of previous support from Cracker Barrel Foundation, if applicable.
Initial approach: Proposal
Board meeting date(s): Quarterly
Deadline(s): None
Officers and Directors:* Norman J. Hill*, Chair. and Pres.; Penny Carroll, Secy.; Patrick A. Scruggs, Treas.; Robert V. Dale; Michael A. Woodhouse.
Number of staff: 2 full-time professional.
EIN: 621577717
Selected grants: The following grants are a representative sample of this grantmaker's funding activity:
$20,000 to Sphinx Organization, Detroit, MI, 2010.
$10,300 to Boy Scouts of America, Nashville, TN, 2010.
$10,000 to Canine Companions for Independence, Orlando, FL, 2010.
$10,000 to HandsOn Nashville, Nashville, TN, 2010.
$10,000 to National Trust for Historic Preservation, Washington, DC, 2010.
$8,000 to Cumberland University, Lebanon, TN, 2010.
$6,000 to Nashville Ballet, Nashville, TN, 2010.
$2,000 to New Opportunity School for Women, Berea, KY, 2010. For program support.
$2,000 to Youth Life Foundation of Tennessee, Nashville, TN, 2010.
$1,500 to Vanderbilt University, Nashville, TN, 2010.

967
Craft Brothers Company, Inc.
925 N. 28th St.
Birmingham, AL 35203 (205) 251-8873

Company URL: http://
Establishment information: Established in 1987.
Company type: Private company
Business activities: Provides general contract construction services.
Business type (SIC): Building construction general contractors and operative builders
Giving statement: Giving through the Servants of Christ Ministries, Inc.

Servants of Christ Ministries, Inc.
925 N. 28th St.
Birmingham, AL 35203-1222

Establishment information: Established in 1999 in AL.
Donors: Craft Brothers Co., Inc.; Dale C. Cathey.
Financial data (yr. ended 12/31/11): Assets, $7,466 (M); gifts received, $16,874; expenditures, $19,125; qualifying distributions, $18,535; giving activities include $4,560 for 4 grants (high: $3,600; low: $240).
Purpose and activities: The foundation supports Christian agencies and churches and awards grants to individuals who spread gospel.
Fields of interest: Christian agencies & churches.
Type of support: General/operating support; Grants to individuals.
Geographic limitations: Giving primarily in Birmingham, AL.
Application information: Applications not accepted. Unsolicited requests for funds not accepted.
Officer: Dale C. Cathey, Pres.
EIN: 631227105

968
Craigslist, Inc.
1381 9th Ave.
San Francisco, CA 94122-2308
(415) 566-6394
FAX: (415) 504-6394

Company URL: http://www.craigslist.org
Establishment information: Established in 1995.
Company type: Private company
Business activities: Operates online community bulletin board.
Business type (SIC): Communications services/miscellaneous
Corporate officers: Craig Alexander Newmark, Chair.; Jim Buckmaster, Pres. and C.E.O.
Board of director: Craig Newmark, Chair.
Giving statement: Giving through the Craigslist Charitable Fund.

Craigslist Charitable Fund
1381 9th Ave.
San Francisco, CA 94122-2308

Donor: Craigslist, Inc.
Financial data (yr. ended 12/31/11): Assets, $8,076,589 (M); gifts received, $3,600,000; expenditures, $2,122,515; qualifying distributions,

$2,122,515; giving activities include $2,098,767 for 100 grants (high: $250,150; low: $150).
Fields of interest: Higher education; Education; Boys & girls clubs; Human services; Children/youth, services; Women, centers/services.
Geographic limitations: Giving primarily in CA and NY.
Application information: Applications not accepted. Contributes only to pre-selected organizations.
Officers and Directors:* James Buckmaster*, Pres.; Craig Newmark*, Secy. and C.F.O.
EIN: 263823367

969
Crane & Co., Inc.

30 South St.
Dalton, MA 01226 (413) 684-2600
FAX: (413) 684-0817

Company URL: http://www.crane.com
Establishment information: Established in 1801.
Company type: Private company
Business activities: Manufactures business, social, banknote, and industrial papers.
Business type (SIC): Paper mills
Financial profile for 2010: Number of employees, 1,378
Corporate officers: Charles J. Kittredge, Chair.; Stephen DeFalco, C.E.O.; Scott Parkinson, C.F.O.; Augustus Dupont, V.P., Genl. Counsel and Secy.; Richard C. Kendall, V.P. Human Resources; Tim Erwin, V.P., Opers.; Oz Levia, V.P., Mktg.; George Scimone, V.P., Finance
Board of director: Charles J. Kittredge, Chair.
Giving statement: Giving through the Crane & Co. Fund.
Company EIN: 041215780

Crane & Co. Fund

c/o Elizabeth M. Pomeroy
30 South St.
Dalton, MA 01226-1751

Establishment information: Established in 1953 in MA.
Donors: Crane & Co., Inc.; Byron-Weston Co.
Contact: Richard C. Kendall
Financial data (yr. ended 12/31/11): Assets, $1 (M); gifts received, $602,435; expenditures, $602,435; qualifying distributions, $602,200; giving activities include $602,200 for grants.
Purpose and activities: The foundation supports organizations involved with arts and culture, education, environmental conservation, health, human services, and government and public administration. Support is limited to Berkshire County, Massachusetts.
Fields of interest: Museums; Arts; Education; Environment, natural resources; Health care; Human services; United Ways and Federated Giving Programs; Government/public administration.
Type of support: Annual campaigns; Capital campaigns; General/operating support.
Geographic limitations: Giving limited to Berkshire County, MA.
Support limitations: No grants to individuals, or for scholarships.
Application information: Applications accepted. Application form not required.
Initial approach: Letter of inquiry
Officers and Trustee: Charles J. Kittredge, Pres.; Richard C. Kendall, Treas.; John Kittredge.
EIN: 046057388
Selected grants: The following grants are a representative sample of this grantmaker's funding activity:
$35,000 to Berkshire Medical Center, Pittsfield, MA, 2009.
$1,000 to Housatonic Valley Association, Cornwall Bridge, CT, 2009.

970
Crane Co.

100 1st Stamford Pl.
Stamford, CT 06902-6740 (203) 363-7300
FAX: (302) 655-5049

Company URL: http://www.craneco.com
Establishment information: Established in 1855.
Company type: Public company
Company ticker symbol and exchange: CR/NYSE
Business activities: Manufactures engineered industrial products.
Business type (SIC): Metal products/fabricated
Financial profile for 2012: Number of employees, 10,500; assets, $2,889,880,000; sales volume, $2,579,070,000; pre-tax net income, $284,610,000; expenses, $2,268,630,000; liabilities, $1,971,490,000
Fortune 1000 ranking: 2012—786th in revenues, 553rd in profits, and 760th in assets
Corporate officers: Robert S. Evans, Chair.; Eric C. Fast, Pres. and C.E.O.; Max H. Mitchell, Exec. V.P. and C.O.O.; Andrew L. Krawitt, V.P. and Treas.; Curtis A. Baron, Jr., V.P. and Cont.; Augustus I. DuPont, V.P., Genl. Counsel, and Secy.; Elise M. Kopczick, V.P., Human Resources
Board of directors: Robert S. Evans, Chair.; E. Thayer Bigelow; Donald G. Cook; Eric C. Fast; Richard S. Forte; Philip R. Lochner, Jr.; Ronald F. McKenna; James L.L. Tullis
Plants: Burbank, CA; Elyria, OH; King of Prussia, Warrington, PA
International operations: Germany
Giving statement: Giving through the Crane Foundation, Inc. and the Crane Fund for Widows and Children.
Company EIN: 131952290

Crane Foundation, Inc.

140 Sylvan Ave., Ste. 4
Englewood Cliffs, NJ 07632

Establishment information: Established in 1951 in MO.
Donor: Crane Co.
Financial data (yr. ended 12/31/11): Assets, $5,234,074 (M); expenditures, $245,555; qualifying distributions, $227,955; giving activities include $158,800 for 76 grants (high: $10,000; low: $50).
Purpose and activities: The foundation supports organizations involved with performing arts, K-12 and higher education, health, recreation, human services, philanthropy and voluntarism, and minorities.
Fields of interest: Performing arts; Elementary/secondary education; Higher education; Health care; Recreation; Children/youth, services; Child development, services; Family services; Human services; Philanthropy/voluntarism Minorities.
International interests: Canada.
Type of support: Annual campaigns; Continuing support; Employee matching gifts; General/operating support; Scholarship funds.
Application information: Applications not accepted. Unsolicited requests for funds not accepted.
Officers and Directors:* Eric C. Fast*, Pres.; Augustus I. DuPont*, V.P., Secy., and Genl. Counsel; Andrew L. Krawitt*, V.P. and Treas.; Richard A. Maue*, V.P.; Elise M. Kopczick, V.P.; T.M. Noonan, V.P.; Robert S. Evans*.
EIN: 436051752
Selected grants: The following grants are a representative sample of this grantmaker's funding activity:
$10,000 to Atlantic Legal Foundation, Larchmont, NY, 2010.
$10,000 to Prostate Cancer Foundation, Santa Monica, CA, 2010.
$1,000 to Partnership for a Drug-Free America, New York, NY, 2010.

Crane Fund for Widows and Children

140 Sylvan Ave.
Englewood Cliffs, NJ 07632
E-mail: cfwc@craneco.com; URL: http://www.craneco.com/Category/34/Crane-Fund-for-Widows-and-Children.html

Establishment information: Established in 1914 in IL.
Contact: M. Gellineau
Financial data (yr. ended 12/31/11): Assets, $31,476,929 (M); expenditures, $1,438,868; qualifying distributions, $1,244,200; giving activities include $1,244,200 for grants.
Purpose and activities: Support for community funds, hospitals, and higher education for the needy; limited support also to organizations in Canada.
Fields of interest: Elementary/secondary education; Higher education; Hospitals (general); Human services; United Ways and Federated Giving Programs Economically disadvantaged.
Type of support: Annual campaigns; Continuing support; Scholarship funds.
Geographic limitations: Giving primarily in the U.S.; some giving also in Canada and the U.K.
Support limitations: No grants to individuals.
Application information: Applications not accepted. Unsolicited requests for funds not accepted.
Trustees: A.I. duPont; E.M. Kopczick; A.L. Krawitt.
EIN: 366116543
Selected grants: The following grants are a representative sample of this grantmaker's funding activity:
$25,000 to Eaglebrook School, Deerfield, MA, 2010.
$10,000 to Indiana University Foundation, Bloomington, IN, 2010.
$10,000 to United Way of Greater Cincinnati, Cincinnati, OH, 2010.
$10,000 to University of Pittsburgh, Pittsburgh, PA, 2010.
$5,000 to A Better Chance, New York, NY, 2010.
$5,000 to Brown University, Providence, RI, 2010.
$5,000 to Duke University, Durham, NC, 2010.
$5,000 to Stanford University, Stanford, CA, 2010.
$3,125 to Hospice of Cincinnati, Cincinnati, OH, 2010.
$3,000 to Make-A-Wish Foundation of Greater Los Angeles, Los Angeles, CA, 2010.

971
Cranfill Sumner & Hartzog LLP

5420 Wade Park Blvd., Ste. 300
P.O. Box 27808
Raleigh, NC 27607-4189 (919) 828-5100

Company URL: http://www.cshlaw.com
Establishment information: Established in 1992.

Company type: Private company
Business activities: Operates law firm.
Business type (SIC): Legal services
Corporate officer: Dan M. Hartzog, Managing Partner
Offices: Charlotte, Raleigh, Wilmington, NC
Giving statement: Giving through the Cranfill Sumner & Hartzog LLP Corporate Giving Program.

Cranfill Sumner & Hartzog LLP Corporate Giving Program

5420 Wade Park Blvd., Ste. 300
Raleigh, NC 27607-4189 (919) 828-5100
FAX: (919) 828-2277; URL: http://www.cshlaw.com/community.asp

Purpose and activities: Cranfill Sumner & Hartzog makes charitable contributions to nonprofit organizations involved with arts and culture, health, and human services.
Fields of interest: Arts; Health organizations; Legal services; Human services; Law/international law.
Type of support: Donated equipment; Employee volunteer services; Pro bono services - legal; Sponsorships.

972
Cranston Print Works Company

1381 Cranston St.
Cranston, RI 02920-6789 (401) 943-4800
FAX: (401) 275-9333

Company URL: http://www.cpw.com/
Establishment information: Established in 1807.
Company type: Private company
Business activities: Provides dyeing and fabric finishing services.
Business type (SIC): Fabric finishing; machinery/special industry
Financial profile for 2009: Number of employees, 50
Corporate officers: Ferderic Rockefeller, Pres. and C.E.O.; George W. Shuster, Co-Pres.; Herb Gray, V.P., Human Resources
Subsidiaries: Bercen Inc., Cranston, RI; Cranston Trucking, Cranston, RI; Universal Engravers, Cranston, RI
Plant: Webster, MA
Giving statement: Giving through the Cranston Foundation.

The Cranston Foundation

c/o The Cranston Fdn. Trustees
1381 Cranston St.
Cranston, RI 02920-6739 (401) 943-4800

Establishment information: Trust established in 1960 in RI.
Donor: Cranston Print Works Co.
Financial data (yr. ended 06/30/10): Assets, $2,777 (M); gifts received, $110,820; expenditures, $112,371; qualifying distributions, $112,371; giving activities include $78,962 for 41 grants (high: $5,000; low: $200), $2,476 for 5 grants to individuals (high: $810; low: $207) and $30,933 for employee matching gifts.
Purpose and activities: The foundation supports hospitals and organizations involved with arts and culture, higher education, and the textile industry.
Fields of interest: Arts education; Visual arts, design; Visual arts, textile/fiber arts; Historic preservation/historical societies; Arts; Higher education; Hospitals (general); YM/YWCAs & YM/YWHAs; Business/industry; United Ways and Federated Giving Programs.
Type of support: Employee matching gifts; Employee-related scholarships; General/operating support; Scholarship funds.
Geographic limitations: Giving primarily in MA, ME, NY, and RI.
Application information: Applications accepted. Application form not required. Applicants should submit the following:
1) statement of problem project will address
2) copy of IRS Determination Letter
3) brief history of organization and description of its mission
4) detailed description of project and amount of funding requested
5) copy of current year's organizational budget and/or project budget

Initial approach: Proposal
Copies of proposal: 1
Board meeting date(s): Quarterly
Deadline(s): May 15
Final notification: Sept. 30

Trustees: Gary Nickerson; Lynn Rathburn; Frederic Rockefeller; George W. Shuster; James Thorpe.
Number of staff: 1 full-time professional.
EIN: 056015348
Selected grants: The following grants are a representative sample of this grantmaker's funding activity:
$11,000 to Bryant University, Smithfield, RI, 2009.
$8,000 to University of Connecticut, Storrs, CT, 2009.
$7,000 to Rhode Island School of Design, Providence, RI, 2009.
$5,161 to Worcester State College, Worcester, MA, 2009.
$4,000 to College of the Holy Cross, Worcester, MA, 2009.
$4,000 to Sacred Heart University, Fairfield, CT, 2009.
$4,000 to University of Maine, Orono, ME, 2009.
$4,000 to University of Massachusetts, Amherst, MA, 2009.
$2,500 to University of Rhode Island, Kingston, RI, 2009.
$2,044 to Quinsigamond Community College, Worcester, MA, 2009.

973
Crayola LLC

(formerly Binney & Smith, Inc.)
1100 Church Ln.
Easton, PA 18044-0431 (610) 253-6271

Company URL: http://www.crayola.com
Establishment information: Established in 1885.
Company type: Subsidiary of a private company
Business activities: Manufactures art supplies and drawing materials.
Business type (SIC): Pens, pencils, and art supplies
Corporate officers: Mike Perry, Pres. and C.E.O.; Smith Holland, Exec. V.P. and C.F.O.; Peter S. Ruggerio, Exec. V.P., Opers.; Michelle Powers, Exec. V.P., Human Resources and Admin.
Giving statement: Giving through the Crayola LLC Corporate Giving Program and the Silly Putty Charitable Trust.

Crayola LLC Corporate Giving Program

(formerly Binney & Smith, Inc. Corporate Giving Program)
c/o Public Affairs Dept.
1100 Church Ln., P.O. Box 431
Easton, PA 18044-0431
URL: http://www.crayola.com/corporate/index.cfm?id=6&n_id=68

Purpose and activities: Crayola makes charitable contributions to nonprofit organizations involved with visual arts, early childhood education, disadvantaged children, the aging, and disabled people. Support is limited to Lehigh and Northampton Counties and Kutztown, Pennsylvania, and Phillipsburg, New Jersey.
Fields of interest: Arts education; Visual arts; Arts; Education, early childhood education; Health care; Children, services; Aging, centers/services; Human services; Public affairs Disabilities, people with.
Type of support: Capital campaigns; Donated products; Employee matching gifts; Employee volunteer services; Program development.
Geographic limitations: Giving limited to Kutztown, PA; Lehigh and Northampton Counties, PA; and Phillipsburg, NJ.
Support limitations: No support for religious, veterans', or fraternal organizations, political or labor organizations, schools, government agencies, national or international organizations, individual child care centers, nursing or convalescent homes, hospitals, social clubs, veterans' organizations, or athletic organizations, or United Way-supported organizations. No grants to individuals or prisoners, or for conventions, seminars, or conferences, endowments, debt reduction, travel, advertising, tickets for or tables to special events, .
Publications: Application guidelines.
Application information: Applications accepted. Proposals should be submitted using organization letterhead. The Public Affairs Department handles giving. Proposals should be no longer than 4 pages. Organizations receiving support are asked to provide a final report. Application form not required.
Applicants should submit the following:
1) timetable for implementation and evaluation of project
2) qualifications of key personnel
3) population served
4) copy of IRS Determination Letter
5) brief history of organization and description of its mission
6) list of company employees involved with the organization
7) listing of board of directors, trustees, officers and other key people and their affiliations
8) detailed description of project and amount of funding requested
9) contact person
10) copy of current year's organizational budget and/or project budget
11) listing of additional sources and amount of support

Initial approach: Proposal to headquarters
Copies of proposal: 1
Committee meeting date(s): Annually
Deadline(s): Dec. 1
Final notification: Mar.

Number of staff: 10 full-time professional; 1 part-time professional; 1 part-time support.

Silly Putty Charitable Trust

c/o Wells Fargo Bank, N.A.
101N Independence Mall E., MAC Y1372-062
Philadelphia, PA 19106-2112

Donors: Binney & Smith, Inc.; F. Reid Buckley.

Financial data (yr. ended 12/31/11): Assets, $86,851 (M); gifts received, $3,500; expenditures, $5,568; qualifying distributions, $4,180; giving activities include $3,801 for 21 grants (high: $808; low: $36).
Purpose and activities: The trust supports organizations involved with Catholicism and other areas.
Fields of interest: Catholic agencies & churches; General charitable giving.
Type of support: General/operating support.
Geographic limitations: Giving limited to the Camden, SC, area.
Application information: Applications not accepted. Unsolicited requests for funds not accepted.
Trustee: Wells Fargo Bank, N.A.
EIN: 576071454

974
J. Fletcher Creamer & Son, Inc.

101 E. Broadway
Hackensack, NJ 07601-6851
(201) 488-9800

Company URL: http://www.jfcson.com
Establishment information: Established in 1923.
Company type: Private company
Business activities: Provides general contract excavation services.
Business type (SIC): Contractors/miscellaneous special trade
Corporate officer: J. Fletcher Creamer, Jr., Chair. and C.E.O.
Board of director: J. Fletcher Creamer, Jr., Chair.
Giving statement: Giving through the J. Fletcher Creamer & Son Scholarship Foundation and the J. Fletcher Creamer Foundation.

J. Fletcher Creamer & Son Scholarship Foundation

101 E. Broadway
Hackensack, NJ 07601-6832 (201) 488-9800

Establishment information: Established in 1988 in NJ.
Donor: J. Fletcher Creamer & Son, Inc.
Contact: Estelle R. Marafino, Tr.
Financial data (yr. ended 11/30/12): Assets, $2,055 (M); gifts received, $10,000; expenditures, $10,105; qualifying distributions, $10,000; giving activities include $10,000 for 4 grants to individuals (high: $2,500; low: $2,500).
Purpose and activities: The foundation awards scholarships to children and grandchildren of current employees of J. Fletcher Creamer & Son, Inc., Creamer Bros. Inc., and Signs of Safety.
Type of support: Employee-related scholarships.
Geographic limitations: Giving primarily in areas of company and subsidiary operations.
Application information: Applications accepted. Application form required.
Initial approach: Proposal
Deadline(s): Mar. 1
Trustees: Estelle R. Marafino; Richard D. McLaughlin; Glenn M. Rocca.
EIN: 222870454

J. Fletcher Creamer Foundation

101 E. Broadway
Hackensack, NJ 07601-6851 (201) 488-9800

Establishment information: Established in 1980 in NJ.
Donor: J. Fletcher Creamer & Son, Inc.
Contact: J. Fletcher Creamer, Tr.
Financial data (yr. ended 03/31/12): Assets, $1,358,040 (M); gifts received, $915,403; expenditures, $358,417; qualifying distributions, $352,015; giving activities include $352,015 for grants.
Purpose and activities: Giving primarily for higher education, human services, hospitals, and Roman Catholic agencies and churches.
Fields of interest: Higher education; Hospitals (general); Human services; Catholic agencies & churches.
Geographic limitations: Giving primarily in NJ.
Support limitations: No grants to individuals.
Application information: Applications not accepted. Contributes only to pre-selected organizations.
Trustees: Dale A. Creamer; J. Fletcher Creamer; J. Fletcher Creamer, Jr.
EIN: 222335557
Selected grants: The following grants are a representative sample of this grantmaker's funding activity:
$25,000 to Drug Abuse Resistance Education New Jersey, Cranbury, NJ, 2010.
$25,000 to Hackensack University Medical Center Foundation, Hackensack, NJ, 2010.
$25,000 to Holy Name Health Care Foundation, Teaneck, NJ, 2010.
$15,000 to Hackensack University Medical Center Foundation, Hackensack, NJ, 2010.
$15,000 to Holy Name Health Care Foundation, Teaneck, NJ, 2010.
$10,000 to Boy Scouts of America, Florham Park, NJ, 2010.
$10,000 to Holy Name Health Care Foundation, Teaneck, NJ, 2010.
$5,000 to Boys Town of Italy, New York, NY, 2010.
$5,000 to Integrity, Newark, NJ, 2010.
$2,500 to American Red Cross of Metropolitan New Jersey, Fairfield, NJ, 2010.

975
Creative Artists Agency, LLC

(also known as CAA)
2000 Ave. of the Stars
Los Angeles, CA 90067 (424) 288-2000

Company URL: http://www.caatouring.com/Default.aspx?Page=contact
Establishment information: Established in 1975.
Company type: Private company
Business activities: Operates literary and talent agency.
Business type (SIC): Bands, orchestras, and entertainers
Corporate officers: Bryan Lourd, Co-Chair; Richard Lovett, Pres.; Michael Rubel, C.O.O. and Genl. Counsel.; Jeff M. Berry, C.F.O
Board of director: Lourd Bryan, Co-Chair.
Giving statement: Giving through the CAA Foundation.

CAA Foundation

c/o Bruce E. King
2000 Ave. of the Stars
Los Angeles, CA 90067-4700
URL: http://foundation.caa.com/

Establishment information: Established in 1995 in CA.
Donors: Creative Artists Agency, LLC; Robert Goldman; Bruce King; Richard Lovett; Musictoday, LLC; David O'Connor.
Financial data (yr. ended 11/30/11): Assets, $625,892 (M); gifts received, $832,743; expenditures, $652,550; qualifying distributions, $494,738; giving activities include $494,738 for grants.
Purpose and activities: The foundation supports organizations involved with arts and culture, education, health, human services, and voluntarism promotion.
Fields of interest: Media, film/video; Performing arts, theater; Arts; Education, public education; Elementary/secondary education; Elementary school/education; Education; Health care; Human services; Voluntarism promotion.
Type of support: Cause-related marketing; Employee volunteer services; General/operating support; In-kind gifts; Program development; Scholarship funds.
Geographic limitations: Giving primarily in area of company operations in Los Angeles, CA, New York, NY, and Nashville, TN.
Support limitations: No grants to individuals.
Application information: Applications not accepted. Contributes only to pre-selected organizations.
Officers and Directors:* Richard Lovett*, Pres.; Michelle Kydd*, Secy.; Bruce E. King*, C.F.O.
EIN: 954556189
Selected grants: The following grants are a representative sample of this grantmaker's funding activity:
$37,000 to Lollipop Theater Network, Los Angeles, CA, 2010.
$27,874 to One Voice, Santa Monica, CA, 2010.
$19,950 to Inner-City Filmmakers, Santa Monica, CA, 2010.
$17,900 to ICEF Public Schools, Los Angeles, CA, 2010.
$11,149 to PENCIL Foundation, Nashville, TN, 2010.
$11,111 to HandsOn Nashville, Nashville, TN, 2010.
$8,783 to Remote Area Medical Foundation, Knoxville, TN, 2010.
$2,273 to UNICEF, New York, NY, 2010.
$2,000 to Be the Change, Cambridge, MA, 2010.
$1,000 to MusiCares Foundation, Nashville, TN, 2010.

976
Creative Financial Group, Ltd.

1000 Abernathy Rd., Bldg. 400, Ste. 1500
Atlanta, GA 30328-5606 (770) 913-9704

Company URL: http://www.cfgltd.com
Establishment information: Established in 1988.
Company type: Subsidiary of a public company
Business activities: Provides investment advisory services.
Business type (SIC): Security and commodity services
Corporate officer: Robert "Buzz" Law, Pres.
Giving statement: Giving through the Creative Financial Group, Ltd. Charitable Foundation.

The Creative Financial Group, Ltd. Charitable Foundation

16 Campus Blvd., Ste. 200
Newtown Square, PA 19073-3229 (610) 325-6100

Establishment information: Established in 1993 in PA.
Donors: Creative Financial Group, Ltd.; CFPO, Inc.
Contact: Gary E. Daniels, Pres.
Financial data (yr. ended 12/31/11): Assets, $80,073 (M); gifts received, $100,000; expenditures, $128,887; qualifying distributions,

$128,847; giving activities include $128,847 for 41 grants (high: $35,000; low: $100).
Purpose and activities: The foundation supports historical societies and health clinics and organizations involved with historic preservation, education, animal welfare, cancer, human services, and Catholicism.
Fields of interest: Historic preservation/historical societies; Secondary school/education; Higher education; Teacher school/education; Education; Animal welfare; Health care, clinics/centers; Cancer; Children, services; Residential/custodial care; Human services; Catholic agencies & churches.
Type of support: Annual campaigns; General/ operating support; Grants to individuals; Scholarship funds.
Geographic limitations: Giving primarily in PA.
Application information: Applications accepted. Application form required. Applicants should submit the following:
1) copy of IRS Determination Letter
Initial approach: Proposal
Deadline(s): None
Officers: Gary E. Daniels, Pres.; Joseph V. Naselli, Secy.-Treas.
Trustees: Claire Daniels; Diana Naselli.
EIN: 232705803
Selected grants: The following grants are a representative sample of this grantmaker's funding activity:
$15,000 to American College, Bryn Mawr, PA, 2009.
$14,067 to Academy of Notre Dame de Namur, Villanova, PA, 2009.
$10,000 to Teach for America, Philadelphia, PA, 2009.
$6,000 to Chester County Historical Society, West Chester, PA, 2009.
$5,000 to Community Volunteers in Medicine, West Chester, PA, 2009.
$1,750 to Abraham Lincoln Foundation, Philadelphia, PA, 2009.
$1,000 to Chosen 300 Ministries, Ardmore, PA, 2009.
$1,000 to Immaculata University, Immaculata, PA, 2009.
$1,000 to La Salle Academy, Philadelphia, PA, 2009.
$1,000 to World Impact, Chester, PA, 2009.

977
Credit Bureau of Baton Rouge, Inc.

9489 Interline Ave.
P.O. Box 82724
Baton Rouge, LA 70809-1912
(225) 926-6161

Establishment information: Established in 1923.
Company type: Private company
Business activities: Operates a credit reporting company.
Business type (SIC): Credit reporting and collection agencies
Corporate officers: J. Terrell Brown, Chair.; Steven L. Uffman, Pres. and C.E.O.; Kenneth E. Uffman, Secy.; William G. Lockwood, Treas.
Board of director: J.Terrell Brown, Chair.
Giving statement: Giving through the Credit Bureau of Baton Rouge Foundation.

The Credit Bureau of Baton Rouge Foundation

(formerly 1427 Foundation)
P.O. Box 82724
Baton Rouge, LA 70884-2724
Application address: 402 N. 4th Street, Baton Rouge, LA 70802; URL: http://www.braf.org/index.cfm/page/5

Establishment information: Established in 2004 in LA.
Donor: Credit Bureau of Baton Rouge.
Financial data (yr. ended 12/31/11): Assets, $20,739,031 (M); expenditures, $1,021,607; qualifying distributions, $780,000; giving activities include $780,000 for grants.
Purpose and activities: The foundation supports programs designed to educate the public about the consumer credit system, the prudent use of consumer credit, and how the public should manage their individual finances.
Fields of interest: Human services, financial counseling; Economic development.
Type of support: Building/renovation; Capital campaigns; Equipment; Program development.
Geographic limitations: Giving primarily in Baton Rouge, LA.
Support limitations: No support for private business ventures or political organizations. No grants to individuals or for start-up costs or new organizations.
Publications: Application guidelines.
Application information: Applications accepted. Grants range from $2,500 to $50,000. Organizations receiving support are asked to submit a final report within 60 days of project completion. Grants are administered by the Baton Rouge Area Foundation. Application form required. Applicants should submit the following:
1) qualifications of key personnel
2) statement of problem project will address
3) population served
4) copy of IRS Determination Letter
5) brief history of organization and description of its mission
6) copy of most recent annual report/audited financial statement/990
7) how project's results will be evaluated or measured
8) listing of board of directors, trustees, officers and other key people and their affiliations
9) detailed description of project and amount of funding requested
10) plans for cooperation with other organizations, if any
11) copy of current year's organizational budget and/or project budget
Initial approach: Complete online application
Deadline(s): Feb. 15
Final notification: May 15
Officer and Directors: Layne R. McDaniel, Pres.; Ralph Bender; J. Terrell Brown; Bob Greer, Jr.; Brian Harris; A. Jackson Huff; Byron Kantrow, Jr.; Rhonda Linzy; W.J. "Dub" Noel, Jr.; Beau Olinde; Norman Thompson; Steve Uffman.
EIN: 200665987
Selected grants: The following grants are a representative sample of this grantmaker's funding activity:
$32,196 to Baton Rouge Area Foundation, Baton Rouge, LA, 2010. For general support.
$30,000 to Baton Rouge Area Foundation, Baton Rouge, LA, 2010. For general support.
$26,628 to Baton Rouge Area Foundation, Baton Rouge, LA, 2010. For general support.
$25,000 to Baton Rouge Area Foundation, Baton Rouge, LA, 2010. For general support.
$15,000 to Baton Rouge Area Foundation, Baton Rouge, LA, 2010. For general support.
$13,020 to Baton Rouge Area Foundation, Baton Rouge, LA, 2010. For general support.
$10,296 to Baton Rouge Area Foundation, Baton Rouge, LA, 2010. For general support.
$6,910 to Baton Rouge Area Foundation, Baton Rouge, LA, 2010. For general support.
$5,200 to Baton Rouge Area Foundation, Baton Rouge, LA, 2010. For general support.
$5,000 to Baton Rouge Area Foundation, Baton Rouge, LA, 2010.

978
Credit Bureau Of Clarksville

529 N. 2nd St.
Clarksville, TN 37040-1915 (931) 647-6521

Establishment information: Established in 1925.
Company type: Private company
Business activities: Provides credit reporting services.
Business type (SIC): Credit reporting and collection agencies
Corporate officer: Toni Hoard, Mgr.
Giving statement: Giving through the Clarksville Charitable and Educational Foundation, Inc.

Clarksville Charitable and Educational Foundation, Inc.

P.O. Box 351
Clarksville, TN 37041-0351

Establishment information: Established in 2004 in TN.
Donor: Credit Bureau of Clarksville.
Financial data (yr. ended 12/31/11): Assets, $1,738,911 (M); expenditures, $57,784; qualifying distributions, $39,000; giving activities include $39,000 for grants.
Fields of interest: Recreation; Youth development; Public affairs.
Application information: Applications not accepted. Unsolicited requests for funds not accepted.
Directors: Toni Hoard; David McWhorter; Kris Newsome; Bill Ogles, Jr.; Mike Griffey; Howard Poff; Patrick Sawyer.
EIN: 201679314

979
Credit Marketing & Management Association

5240 Valleypark Dr.
Roanoke, VA 24019 (540) 265-3700

Company type: Private company
Business activities: Provides credit reporting services.
Business type (SIC): Credit reporting and collection agencies
Giving statement: Giving through the Investco Foundation.

Investco Foundation

(formerly Credit Marketing & Management Association Foundation)
P.O. Box 680
Vinton, VA 24179-0680 (540) 265-3740

Establishment information: Established in 1996 in VA.

Donor: Credit Marketing & Management Assn.
Contact: Ronald W. Ernest, Pres.
Financial data (yr. ended 12/31/11): Assets, $143,602 (M); expenditures, $12,860; qualifying distributions, $8,000; giving activities include $8,000 for grants.
Purpose and activities: The foundation supports health clinics and food banks and organizations involved with media, higher education, housing development, and human services.
Fields of interest: Health care; Agriculture/food; Human services.
Type of support: General/operating support; Scholarship funds.
Support limitations: No grants to individuals.
Application information: Applications accepted. Application form required.
Initial approach: Letter
Deadline(s): None
Officers: Ronald W. Ernest, Pres.; T. M. Flinchum, Secy.; Doug W. Densmore, Treas.
Directors: Garland Kidd; Dan Overstreet; Wylie Walton.
EIN: 541779684

980
Credit Suisse (USA), Inc.

(formerly Credit Suisse First Boston LLC)
11 Madison Ave.
New York, NY 10010-3629 (212) 325-2000

Company URL: http://www.credit-suisse.com/us/en/
Establishment information: Established in 1856.
Company type: Subsidiary of a foreign company
Business activities: Operates investment bank.
Business type (SIC): Brokers and dealers/security
Financial profile for 2009: Number of employees, 10,899; sales volume, $13,259,270,000
Corporate officers: Robert S. Shafir, C.E.O.; Paul J. O'Keefe, C.F.O.; Lewis H. Wirshba, C.O.O.; D. Neil Radey, Genl. Counsel; Joe L. Roby, Chair. Emeritus
Offices: Los Angeles, Palo Alto, San Francisco, CA; Miami, FL; Atlanta, GA; Chicago, IL; Boston, MA; Philadelphia, PA; Houston, TX
International operations: Australia; Bahamas; Belgium; Brazil; Canada; China; France; Germany; Italy; Japan; Luxembourg; Netherlands; Panama; Russia; Singapore; United Kingdom; Uruguay
Giving statement: Giving through the Credit Suisse Americas Foundation.

Credit Suisse Americas Foundation

(formerly Credit Suisse First Boston Foundation Trust)
11 Madison Ave., 10th Fl.
New York, NY 10010-3629 (212) 325-2389
FAX: (212) 538-8347;
E-mail: americas.corporatecitizenship@credit-suisse.com; Additional tel.: (212) 325-5260;
URL: https://www.credit-suisse.com/citizenship/en/philantropy_americas.jsp

Establishment information: Established in 1959 in MA.
Donors: Credit Suisse First Boston Corp.; Credit Suisse First Boston LLC; Credit Suisse USA.
Contact: Anne Marie Fell, Dir. of Grantmaking & Comms.
Financial data (yr. ended 12/31/11): Assets, $28,305,928 (M); gifts received, $4,585,623; expenditures, $6,526,875; qualifying distributions, $6,334,977; giving activities include $6,314,977 for 489 grants (high: $366,182; low: $500).
Purpose and activities: The foundation supports organizations that have the greatest impact on local communities in areas of company operations. Special emphasis is directed toward programs that leverage employee volunteerism.
Fields of interest: Elementary school/education; Secondary school/education; Teacher school/education; Education; Health care, clinics/centers; Food services; Food banks; Housing/shelter, development; Disasters, preparedness/services; Recreation, parks/playgrounds; Youth development, centers/clubs; Big Brothers/Big Sisters; Youth development, business; American Red Cross; Family services; Human services; Microfinance/microlending; Voluntarism promotion; United Ways and Federated Giving Programs Economically disadvantaged.
Programs:
Americas Education Program: The foundation supports high performing schools; programs designed to help develop teachers and school leaders; and human capital programs.
Core Engagement Grants: The foundation awards grants to nonprofit organizations with which Credit Suisse employees are personally engaged and where the foundation and the charity organization work in partnership.
Type of support: Employee volunteer services; General/operating support; Management development/capacity building; Matching/challenge support; Program development.
Geographic limitations: Giving primarily in areas of company operations, with emphasis on New York, NY; giving also in Los Angeles and San Francisco, CA, Washington, DC, Miami, FL, Atlanta, GA, Boston, MA, Baltimore, MD, Chicago, IL, Raleigh-Durham, NC, Princeton, NJ, Conshohocken, PA, Dallas and Houston, TX, and in Nassau, Bahamas, Sao Paulo, Brazil, and Toronto, Canada.
Support limitations: No support for religious organizations not of direct benefit to the entire community, veterans', fraternal, or political organizations, private or grantmaking foundations, colleges or universities, or K-12 schools. No grants to individuals, or for scholarships, capital campaigns, endowments, dinners or events, medical research, political causes, or sponsorships; no matching gifts.
Application information: Applications not accepted. Unsolicited applications are currently not accepted.
Board meeting date(s): Quarterly
Officer and Trustees:* Antonio Quintella*, Chair.; Douglas L. Paul, Vice-Chair.; Kathryn M. Quigley, Pres.; Eric Eckholdt, Exec. Dir.; Nicole Arnaboldi; Marc D. Granetz; Kris Klein; Grace J. Koo; Tim O'Hare; Mike Paliotta; D. Neil Radey; Robert S. Shafir; Peter Skoglund; Lewis H. Wirshba; Richard P. Zaloom.
Number of staff: 6 full-time professional.
EIN: 900647568
Selected grants: The following grants are a representative sample of this grantmaker's funding activity:
$779,890 to Robin Hood Foundation, New York, NY, 2009. For general operating support.
$200,000 to City Year New York, New York, NY, 2009. For the East Harlem teams.
$200,000 to Habitat for Humanity New York City, New York, NY, 2009. For general operating support.
$180,000 to Henry Street Settlement, New York, NY, 2009. For general operating support.
$150,000 to City Harvest, New York, NY, 2009. For Gala Event.
$135,000 to Student Sponsor Partners, New York, NY, 2009. For general operating support.
$85,000 to Points of Light Institute, Atlanta, GA, 2009. For HandsOn affiliate projects in Atlanta, Boston.
$37,500 to Per Scholas, Bronx, NY, 2009. For general operating support.
$30,000 to iMentor, New York, NY, 2009. For general operating support.
$20,000 to Open Hand, San Francisco, CA, 2009. For general operating support.

981
Crescent Electric Supply Company

7750 Dunleith Dr.
P.O. Box 500
East Dubuque, IL 61025-4420
(815) 747-3145
FAX: (815) 747-7720

Company URL: http://www.cesco.com/
Establishment information: Established in 1919.
Company type: Private company
Business activities: Sells electrical equipment wholesale.
Business type (SIC): Electrical goods—wholesale
Financial profile for 2012: Number of employees, 1,400
Corporate officers: Martin S. Burbridge, Pres. and C.E.O.; Chris Breslin, Sr. V.P. and C.O.O.; James R. Etheredge, Sr. V.P. and C.F.O.; Ron Schlader, V.P., Opers.; Alice Vontalge, V.P., Finance; Bob Settle, V.P., Mktg.; Dan Philippi, V.P., Human Resources; Carol Hoffman, Secy.-Treas.
Giving statement: Giving through the Crescent Electric Charitable Foundation.

Crescent Electric Charitable Foundation

7750 Dunleith Dr.
East Dubuque, IL 61025-1357

Establishment information: Established in 2003 in IL.
Donor: Crescent Electric Supply Co.
Contact: James R. Etheredge, Sr. V.P. and C.F.O.
Financial data (yr. ended 12/31/11): Assets, $1,412,305 (M); expenditures, $88,303; qualifying distributions, $73,476; giving activities include $73,476 for grants.
Purpose and activities: The foundation supports fire departments and community foundations and organizations involved with arts and culture, education, health, Alzheimer's disease, and the electricity industry.
Fields of interest: Education; Health care; Human services.
Type of support: General/operating support.
Geographic limitations: Giving primarily in Dubuque, IA.
Application information: Applications accepted. Application form not required.
Initial approach: Proposal
Deadline(s): None
Officers: Martin S. Burbridge, Pres.; James R. Etheredge, Sr. V.P. and C.F.O.; Alice Vontalge, V.P., Finance; Carol Hoffman, Secy.
EIN: 680539603

982
Crescent Iron Works
4901 Grays Ave.
Philadelphia, PA 19143-5891
(215) 729-1204

Company URL: http://www.crescentironworks.com
Establishment information: Established in 1931.
Company type: Private company
Business activities: Manufactures structural steel and ornamental metal products.
Business type (SIC): Metal products/structural
Corporate officer: Joseph Milani, Pres.
Giving statement: Giving through the Ulderico & Anna C. Milani Charitable Foundation.

Ulderico & Anna C. Milani Charitable Foundation
4901 Grays Ave.
Philadelphia, PA 19143-5810

Establishment information: Established in 1998.
Donors: Crescent Iron Works Inc.; CDM Holdings, Inc.; PBA Construction, Inc.
Financial data (yr. ended 12/31/11): Assets, $277,690 (M); expenditures, $10,643; qualifying distributions, $7,075; giving activities include $7,075 for 22 grants (high: $1,000; low: $100).
Purpose and activities: The foundation supports organizations involved with education, art therapy, human services, and Catholicism.
Fields of interest: Secondary school/education; Education; Art & music therapy; Human services; Catholic agencies & churches.
Type of support: General/operating support.
Geographic limitations: Giving primarily in Philadelphia, PA.
Support limitations: No grants to individuals.
Application information: Applications not accepted. Unsolicited requests for funds not accepted.
Trustee: Joseph W. Milani.
EIN: 237948901

983
Crescent Plastics, Inc.
955 E. Diamond Ave.
Evansville, IN 47711-3400 (812) 428-9305

Company URL: http://www.crescentplastics.com/
Establishment information: Established in 1949.
Company type: Private company
Business activities: Manufactures molded plastic parts.
Business type (SIC): Plastic products/miscellaneous
Financial profile for 2010: Number of employees, 100
Corporate officer: John C. Schroeder, Pres.
Giving statement: Giving through the Crescent Cresline Wabash Plastics Foundation, Inc.

Crescent Cresline Wabash Plastics Foundation, Inc.
600 Cross Pointe Blvd.
Evansville, IN 47715-9119

Establishment information: Established in 1986 in IN.
Donors: Crescent Plastics, Inc.; Wabash Plastics, Inc.; Cresline Plastics Pipe Co., Inc.
Financial data (yr. ended 12/31/11): Assets, $3,981,118 (M); expenditures, $182,305; qualifying distributions, $177,150; giving activities include $177,150 for 79 grants (high: $10,000; low: $25).
Purpose and activities: The foundation supports museums and organizations involved with performing arts, education, and youth development.
Fields of interest: Museums; Performing arts; Performing arts, orchestras; Higher education; Education; Boy scouts; Youth development, business; Youth development; United Ways and Federated Giving Programs.
Type of support: General/operating support.
Geographic limitations: Giving primarily in areas of company operations in Evansville, IN.
Support limitations: No grants to individuals.
Application information: Applications not accepted. Contributes only to pre-selected organizations.
Officer: Belle Fahrer, Secy.
Directors: John C. Schroeder; Richard A. Schroeder.
EIN: 311196890
Selected grants: The following grants are a representative sample of this grantmaker's funding activity:
$20,000 to Wabash College, Crawfordsville, IN, 2010.
$15,000 to Evansville Philharmonic Orchestra, Evansville, IN, 2010.
$10,000 to Signature School Foundation, Evansville, IN, 2010.
$7,500 to Evansville Vanderburgh School Corporation Foundation, Evansville, IN, 2010.
$7,500 to United Way of Southwestern Indiana, Evansville, IN, 2010.
$2,500 to Wabash College, Crawfordsville, IN, 2010.
$2,400 to United Way of Southwestern Indiana, Evansville, IN, 2010.
$1,500 to University of Evansville, Evansville, IN, 2010.
$1,000 to Arts Council of Southwestern Indiana, Evansville, IN, 2010.
$1,000 to Evansville Philharmonic Orchestra, Evansville, IN, 2010.

984
Crocs, Inc.
7477 E. Dry Creek Pkwy.
Niwot, CO 80503 (303) 848-7000
FAX: (303) 655-5049

Company URL: http://www.crocs.com
Establishment information: Established in 2002.
Company type: Public company
Company ticker symbol and exchange: CROX/NASDAQ
Business activities: Operate footwear company.
Business type (SIC): Footwear/rubber and plastic
Financial profile for 2012: Number of employees, 4,157; assets, $829,640,000; sales volume, $1,123,300,000; pre-tax net income, $145,550,000; expenses, $977,130,000; liabilities, $212,240,000
Corporate officers: Thomas Smach, Chair.; John McCarvel, Pres. and C.E.O.; Scott Crutchfield, C.O.O.; Jeff Lasher, Sr. V.P. Finance and C.F.O.
Board of directors: Thomas Smach, Chair.; Stephen Cannon; Raymond Croghan; Ronald Frasch; Peter Jacobi; Doreen Wright
Giving statement: Giving through the Crocs Cares.
Company EIN: 202164234

Crocs Cares
7477 E. Dry Creek Pkwy.
Niwot, CO 80503 (303) 848-7000
URL: http://company.crocs.com/our-company/crocs-cares/

985
Croft Leominister, Inc.
(also known as Croft Value Fund)
300 Water St., 4th Fl.
Baltimore, MD 21202-3234
(410) 576-0100

Company URL: http://www.croftleo.com/about.html
Establishment information: Established in 1989.
Company type: Private company
Business activities: Provides investment advisory services.
Business type (SIC): Security and commodity services
Corporate officers: Kent G. Croft, Pres.; Phillip Vong, C.F.O. and Treas.
Giving statement: Giving through the Gordon Croft Foundation, Inc.

Gordon Croft Foundation, Inc.
(formerly Leominster-Croft Foundation, Inc.)
Canton House
300 Water St.
Baltimore, MD 21202-3330

Establishment information: Established in 1990 in MD.
Donors: Leominster, Inc.; L. Gordon Croft.
Contact: L. Gordon Croft, V.P.
Financial data (yr. ended 12/31/11): Assets, $5,041,817 (M); expenditures, $231,179; qualifying distributions, $208,880; giving activities include $208,880 for grants.
Purpose and activities: The foundation supports organizations involved with education, the environment, health, human services, economically disadvantaged people, and homeless people.
Fields of interest: Elementary/secondary education; Secondary school/education; Higher education; Education; Botanical gardens; Environmental education; Environment; Health care; Christian agencies & churches Economically disadvantaged; Homeless.
Type of support: Building/renovation; General/operating support.
Geographic limitations: Giving primarily in MD.
Application information: Applications accepted. Application form not required. Applicants should submit the following:
1) detailed description of project and amount of funding requested
Initial approach: Proposal
Deadline(s): None
Officers: Kent Gordon Croft, Pres.; L. Gordon Croft, V.P.; Jane Aurell Croft, Secy.
EIN: 521682796
Selected grants: The following grants are a representative sample of this grantmaker's funding activity:
$15,000 to Saint Ignatius Church, Baltimore, MD, 2009.
$5,200 to Friends of Dickie, Stevenson, MD, 2009.
$4,800 to Dartmouth College, Hanover, NH, 2009.
$2,000 to Adkins Arboretum, Ridgely, MD, 2009.
$1,500 to Gilman School, Baltimore, MD, 2009.
$1,100 to Baltimore Community Foundation, Baltimore, MD, 2009.

$1,000 to Saint Vincent de Paul Church, Baltimore, MD, 2009.

986
Crowell & Moring LLP

1001 Pennsylvania Ave., N.W.
Washington, DC 20004-2595
(202) 624-2500

Company URL: http://www.crowell.com
Establishment information: Established in 1979.
Company type: Private company
Business activities: Operates law firm.
Business type (SIC): Legal services
Corporate officers: Kent Gardiner, Chair.; Ellen Dwyer, Managing Partner; John Oliverio, C.F.O.
Offices: Anchorage, AK; Irvine, Los Angeles, San Francisco, CA; Washington, DC; New York, NY
International operations: Belgium; Egypt; Saudi Arabia; United Kingdom
Giving statement: Giving through the Crowell & Moring LLP Pro Bono Program and the Crowell & Moring Foundation.

Crowell & Moring LLP Pro Bono Program

1001 Pennsylvania Ave., N.W.
Washington, DC 20004-2595 (202) 624-2500
FAX: (202) 628-5116;
E-mail: shoffman@crowell.com; Contact for Pro Bono program: Susie Hoffman, Pro Bono Partner, tel.: (202) 624-2591, e-mail: shoffman@crowell.com; URL: http://www.crowell.com/Pro-Bono#.UcS6Fvm84Qo

Contact: Susie Hoffman, Pro Bono Partner
Purpose and activities: As a complement to its foundation, Crowell & Moring also makes charitable contributions to nonprofit organizations directly.
Fields of interest: Law school/education; Legal services; Minorities/immigrants, centers/services; Civil/human rights, equal rights; Civil/human rights, immigrants.
Type of support: Employee volunteer services; Pro bono services - legal.

Crowell & Moring Foundation

1001 Pennsylvania Ave. N.W.
Washington, DC 20004-2543

Establishment information: Established in DC.
Donors: David Naseman; Wm. Randolph Smith; Crowell & Moring LLP.
Financial data (yr. ended 12/31/11): Assets, $352,397 (M); gifts received, $57,571; expenditures, $212,594; qualifying distributions, $212,500; giving activities include $212,500 for grants.
Purpose and activities: The foundation supports organizations involved with education, legal aid, youth development, human services, Asian-American's, and African-American's.
Fields of interest: Elementary/secondary education; Middle schools/education; Charter schools; Higher education; Scholarships/financial aid; Education; Legal services; Youth development; Homeless, human services; Human services Asians/Pacific Islanders; African Americans/ Blacks.
Type of support: Conferences/seminars; General/ operating support; Program development.
Geographic limitations: Giving primarily in Washington, DC.
Support limitations: No grants to individuals.
Application information: Applications not accepted. Contributes only to pre-selected organizations.
Officers and Directors:* Susan Hoffman*, Pres.; George Ruttinger*, Secy.; Kent Morrison*, Treas.; Deborah E. Arbabi; John T. Brennan, Jr.; Gary R. Edwards; Trina Fairley-Barlow; Clifford Hendler; Andy Liu; Michael L. Martinez; Monica G. Parham; Nicole Quigley; Luther Ziegler.
EIN: 522207644
Selected grants: The following grants are a representative sample of this grantmaker's funding activity:
$45,000 to Equal Justice Works, Washington, DC, 2011. For general support.
$10,000 to Capital Partners for Education, Washington, DC, 2011. For general support.
$10,000 to Washington Jesuit Academy, Washington, DC, 2011. For general support.
$10,000 to Washington Middle School for Girls, Washington, DC, 2011. For general support.
$7,500 to Black Student Fund, Washington, DC, 2011. For general support.
$5,000 to Homeless Childrens Playtime Project, Washington, DC, 2011. For general support.
$5,000 to Septima Clark Public Charter School, Washington, DC, 2011. For general support.
$5,000 to Young Audiences New York, New York, NY, 2011. For general support.
$3,500 to Mentors of Minorities in Education, Washington, DC, 2011. For general support.
$3,500 to Sexual Minority Youth Assistance League, Washington, DC, 2011. For general support.

987
Crown Equipment Corporation

44 S. Washington St.
New Bremen, OH 45869 (419) 629-2311

Company URL: http://www.crown.com
Establishment information: Established in 1945.
Company type: Private company
Business activities: Manufactures heavy-duty electric lift trucks.
Business type (SIC): Machinery/construction, mining, and materials handling
Corporate officers: James F. Dicke II, Chair. and C.E.O.; James F. Dicke III, Pres.; Kent W. Spille, V.P. and C.F.O.; David C. Moran, V.P., Opers.; John G. Maxa, V.P. and Genl. Counsel; Randall W. Niekamp, V.P., Human Resources; James F. Dicke, Chair. Emeritus
Board of director: James F. Dicke II, Chair.
Giving statement: Giving through the Crown Equipment Corporation Contributions Program.

Crown Equipment Corporation Contributions Program

44 S. Washington St.
New Bremen, OH 45869-1247 (419) 629-2311
FAX: (419) 629-2900

Purpose and activities: Crown makes charitable contributions to nonprofit organizations involved with arts and culture, education, and on a case by case basis. Support is given on a national basis, with emphasis on New Bremen, Ohio.
Fields of interest: Arts; Education.
Type of support: Donated equipment; General/ operating support; In-kind gifts.
Geographic limitations: Giving on a national basis, with emphasis on New Bremen, OH.

988
Crown Holdings, Inc.

1 Crown Way
Philadelphia, PA 19154-4599
(215) 698-5100
FAX: (215) 698-7050

Company URL: http://www.crowncork.com
Establishment information: Established in 1892.
Company type: Public company
Company ticker symbol and exchange: CCK/NYSE
Business activities: Operates holding company; designs, manufactures, and sells consumer goods packaging products.
Business type (SIC): Metal containers
Financial profile for 2012: Number of employees, 21,900; assets, $7,490,000,000; sales volume, $8,470,000,000; pre-tax net income, $636,000,000; expenses, $7,834,000,000; liabilities, $7,652,000,000
Fortune 1000 ranking: 2012—312th in revenues, 311th in profits, and 469th in assets
Forbes 2000 ranking: 2012—1044th in sales, 964th in profits, and 1630th in assets
Corporate officers: John W. Conway, Chair. and C.E.O.; Timothy J. Donahue, Pres. and C.O.O.; Thomas A. Kelly, Sr. V.P. and C.F.O.; William T. Gallagher, Sr. V.P., Genl. Counsel, and Secy.; Michael B. Burns, V.P. and Treas.; Kevin C. Clothier, V.P. and Corp. Cont.; Michael F. Dunleavy, V.P., Corp. Affairs & Public Rels.
Board of directors: John W. Conway, Chair.; Jenne K. Britell; Arnold W. Donald; William G. Little; Hans J. Loliger; James H. Miller; Josef M. Mueller; Thomas A. Ralph; Hugues du Rouret; Jim L. Turner; William S. Urkiel
Subsidiary: Crown Cork & Seal Company, Inc., Philadelphia, PA
International operations: Barbados; Belgium; Brazil; British Virgin Islands; Cambodia; Canada; China; Colombia; Finland; France; Germany; Ghana; Greece; Hong Kong; Hungary; Ireland; Italy; Ivory Coast; Jordan; Madagascar; Malaysia; Mexico; Morocco and the Western Sahara; Netherlands; Poland; Portugal; Russia; Saudi Arabia; Singapore; Slovakia; South Africa; Spain; Switzerland; Thailand; Tunisia; Turkey; United Kingdom; Vietnam
Giving statement: Giving through the Crown Holdings, Inc. Corporate Giving Program.
Company EIN: 753099507

Crown Holdings, Inc. Corporate Giving Program

1 Crown Way
Philadelphia, PA 19154-4501

Contact: Michael F. Dunleavy, V.P., Corp. Affairs & Public Rels.
Purpose and activities: Crown makes charitable contributions to nonprofit organizations on a case by case basis. Support is given primarily in Pennsylvania.
Fields of interest: General charitable giving.
Type of support: Employee-related scholarships; General/operating support.
Geographic limitations: Giving primarily in PA.
Application information: Applications accepted. Application form not required. Applicants should submit the following:
1) copy of IRS Determination Letter
2) detailed description of project and amount of funding requested
3) listing of additional sources and amount of support

Initial approach: Proposal to headquarters
Copies of proposal: 1

Deadline(s): Quarterly
Final notification: Following review

989
Crown Roofing Services, Inc.
5 E. 3rd St.
Kenner, LA 70062-7032 (504) 464-4644

Company URL: http://
Establishment information: Established in 1989.
Company type: Private company
Business activities: Operates roofing company.
Business type (SIC): Contractors/roofing, siding, and sheet metal work
Corporate officer: Ray Palmer, Pres.
Board of director: Ray Palmer
Giving statement: Giving through the Crown Group Scholarship Foundation.

The Crown Group Scholarship Foundation
5 E. 3rd St.
Kenner, LA 70062-7032 (504) 464-4644
E-mail: chatmonk@bellsouth.net

Establishment information: Established in 2006 in LA.
Donors: Crown Roofing Services, Inc.; RL Campbell Management Services, Inc.; Thomco Enterprises, Inc.; Rycars Construction, LLC; RoofTech; R.D. & Katie Chatmon; Ray Palmer; Myrtle Palmer.
Financial data (yr. ended 12/31/11): Assets, $74,359 (M); expenditures, $26,928; qualifying distributions, $25,000; giving activities include $25,000 for 10 grants to individuals (high: $2,500; low: $2,500).
Purpose and activities: The foundation awards $2,500 college scholarships to Louisiana high school students.
Type of support: Scholarships—to individuals.
Geographic limitations: Giving primarily in LA.
Application information: Applications accepted. Application form required.
Applications must include official transcripts; a minimum of 30 hours of community service documented on official letterhead; financial information; 3 letters of recommendation; and an essay. A personal interview may be requested for scholarship finalists.
Initial approach: Letter
Deadline(s): None
Trustees: Katie Chatmon; R.D. Chatmon; Calandria Palmer; Myrtle Palmer; Ray Palmer.
EIN: 870788876

990
CryoLife, Inc.
1655 Roberts Blvd., N.W.
Kennesaw, GA 30144-3632
(770) 419-3355
FAX: (770) 426-0031

Company URL: http://www.cryolife.com/
Establishment information: Established in 1984.
Company type: Public company
Company ticker symbol and exchange: CRY/NYSE
Business activities: Markets cryopreserved human cardiovascular, vascular, and orthopedic transplant tissue; develops and markets implant products.
Business type (SIC): Miscellaneous health services; medical instruments and supplies
Financial profile for 2012: Number of employees, 488; assets, $157,160,000; sales volume, $131,720,000; pre-tax net income, $12,050,000; expenses, $119,450,000; liabilities, $29,040,000
Corporate officers: Steven G. Anderson, Chair., Pres., and C.E.O.; D. Ashley Lee, Exec. V.P., Treas., C.O.O., and C.F.O.; Amy D. Horton, C.A.O.; Jeffrey W. Burris, Esq., V.P. and Genl. Counsel; Suzanne K. Gabbert, Secy.
Board of directors: Steven G. Anderson, Chair.; Thomas F. Ackerman; Daniel J. Bevevino; James S. Benson; Ronald Charles Elkins, M.D.; Harvey Morgan; Ronald D. McCall, Esq.; Jon W. Salveson
International operations: United Kingdom
Giving statement: Giving through the CryoLife, Inc. Corporate Giving Program.
Company EIN: 592417093

CryoLife, Inc. Corporate Giving Program
c/o Corp. Contribs.
1655 Roberts Blvd., N.W.
Kennesaw, GA 30144-3632 (678) 290-4390
FAX: (770) 590-3742; URL: http://www.cryolife.com/about/outreach

Purpose and activities: CryoLife makes charitable contributions of cryopreserved human heart valves to nonprofit organizations involved with pediatric reconstructive surgery. Support is given on a national and international basis.
Fields of interest: Heart & circulatory diseases; Pediatrics; Surgery; Children, services; Human services, gift distribution.
Program:
CryoKids Program: CryoLife provides funding for children needing cardiac reconstruction who do not have access to advanced surgical care or the funds to access advanced surgical care. CryoLife works with health organizations, charity groups, and surgeons to donate and transport cryopreserved human heart valves to children in need.
Type of support: Conferences/seminars; Donated products; Program development; Sponsorships; Use of facilities.
Geographic limitations: Giving on a national and international basis.

991
Crystal Print, Inc.
500 Hart Ct.
Little Chute, WI 54140-1938
(920) 739-9135

Establishment information: Established in 1949.
Company type: Private company
Business activities: Provides commercial printing services.
Business type (SIC): Printing/commercial
Corporate officers: Chris J. Hartwig, Pres.; Dennis Howen, Cont.
Board of director: Bob Crosby
Giving statement: Giving through the Crystal Print Foundation, Inc.

Crystal Print Foundation, Inc.
500 Hart Ct.
Little Chute, WI 54140-1938

Establishment information: Established in 1993 in WI.
Donor: Crystal Print, Inc.
Financial data (yr. ended 06/30/12): Assets, $1,599,087 (M); gifts received, $100,000; expenditures, $60,675; qualifying distributions, $53,000; giving activities include $53,000 for 16 grants (high: $10,000; low: $1,000).
Purpose and activities: The foundation supports hospitals and organizations involved with arts and culture and youth development.
Type of support: General/operating support.
Application information: Applications not accepted. Unsolicited requests for funds not accepted.
Officers: Dan Gavronski, Pres.; James Miller, V.P.; Paul Mahlberg, Secy.-Treas.
Directors: Reed Bamke; Dawn Day; Penny Fisch; Evelyn Hartwig; Tricia Korth; Kevin Newhouse; Diane Reynolds; Mark Van Handel; Tim Voissem.
EIN: 391764046

992
Crystal Window & Door Systems, Ltd.
31-10 Whitestone Expwy.
Flushing, NY 11354-2531 (718) 961-7300
FAX: (718) 460-4594

Company URL: http://www.crystalwindows.com
Establishment information: Established in 1990.
Company type: Private company
Business activities: Manufactures vinyl and aluminum windows and doors.
Business type (SIC): Plastic products/ miscellaneous; metal products/structural
Financial profile for 2010: Number of employees, 343
Corporate officer: Thomas Chen, Pres. and C.E.O.
Subsidiary: Diamond Windows & Doors, Brighton, MA
Plants: Milford, CT; Chicago, IL; Rockville, MD; Manlius, New York, NY; Parma, OH; Allentown, Lemoyne, PA; Richmond, VA
Giving statement: Giving through the Crystal Foundation.

Crystal Foundation
31-10 Whitestone Expwy.
Flushing, NY 11354-2531 (718) 961-7300
URL: http://www.crystalwindows.com/corp-phila.html

Establishment information: Established in 2000 in NY.
Donor: Crystal Window & Door Systems, Ltd.
Contact: Thomas Chen, Pres.
Financial data (yr. ended 12/31/11): Assets, $208,509 (M); gifts received, $13,700; expenditures, $14,313; qualifying distributions, $10,000; giving activities include $10,000 for grants.
Purpose and activities: The foundation supports programs designed to foster education and the advancement of Asian art and culture.
Fields of interest: Museums (art); Arts; Higher education; Education; Children, services Asians/ Pacific Islanders.
Type of support: General/operating support; Program development; Scholarship funds.
Geographic limitations: Giving primarily in areas of company operations in NY.
Support limitations: No grants to individuals.
Application information: Applications accepted. Application form not required.
Initial approach: Proposal
Deadline(s): None
Officer and Director:* Thomas Chen*, Pres.
EIN: 113540759

993
CSL Behring, LLC
1020 1st Ave.
P.O. Box 61501
King of Prussia, PA 19406-0901
(610) 878-4000

Company URL: http://www.cslbehring.com
Establishment information: Established in 1904.
Company type: Subsidiary of a foreign company
Business activities: Manufactures plasma-derived and recombinant products.
Business type (SIC): Drugs
Corporate officers: Paul R. Perreault, Pres.; John A. Newsom, C.I.O.; Mary Sontrop, Exec. V.P., Opers.; Karen Neave, Sr. V.P. and C.F.O.; Greg Boss, Sr. V.P. and Genl. Counsel; Dennis Jackman, Sr. V.P., Public Affairs; Laurie Cowan, V.P., Human Resources; Kelly Fox, Corp. Comms.
Giving statement: Giving through the CSL Behring Foundation for Research and Advancement of Patient Health.

CSL Behring Foundation for Research and Advancement of Patient Health
(formerly ZLB Behring Foundation for Research and Advancement of Patient Health)
1020 1st Ave.
P.O. Box 61501
King of Prussia, PA 19406-0901 (866) 963-2566
E-mail: CB.Foundation@cslbehring.com;
URL: http://www.cslbehringfoundation.com

Establishment information: Established in 2001 in PA.
Donor: CSL Behring.
Contact: Garret E. Bergman, Exec. Dir.
Financial data (yr. ended 09/30/11): Assets, $689,772 (M); expenditures, $267,999; qualifying distributions, $264,141; giving activities include $264,141 for grants.
Purpose and activities: The foundation provides funding for research projects and community initiatives designed to advance the standard of care for people with bleeding disorders.
Fields of interest: Hemophilia research; Medical research; Hematology research.
Programs:
General Grants: The foundation awards up to $100,000 for projects that demonstrate medical, scientific and/or humanitarian significance and, without exception, demonstrate that the proposed work will benefit the bleeding disorders community. Eligible applicants must be hemophilia treatment centers or healthcare professionals dedicated to the treatment of people with bleeding disorders; or hemophilia foundations, chapters, associations, and/or other nonprofit organizations that address the needs of the bleeding disorders community. Grant requests must be between $10,000 and $100,000.
Unrestricted Grants: The foundation awards up to five $10,000 grants to assist small, community-based organizations in delivering their many valuable services to the communities they serve. Eligible organizations must be recognized 501(c)(3) patient organizations for persons with bleeding disorders that have an annual operating budget of less than $100,000, provide payment for staff services to two or fewer people, and have not received unrestricted grant support from the foundation previously.
Type of support: Research.
Geographic limitations: Giving primarily in CA, IL, NY, PA, TX, and VA.
Publications: Application guidelines; Grants list.
Application information: The foundation is in the process of establishing new application guidelines for general grants. Visit website for more information.
Officers and Advisory Council Members:* Richard Vogel*, Chair.; Beatrice Pierce*, Vice-Chair.; Greg Boss, Secy.; Jason Mugride, Treas.; Garrett E. Bergman, M.D., Exec. Dir.; Dana Francis, M.S.W.; Susan Geraghty, R.N., M.B.A.; Vicki Jacobs-Pratt; Peter A. Kouides, M.D.; Cindy Leissenger; Rajiv K. Pruthi, M.B.B.S.; Leonard A. Valentino, M.D.
EIN: 311807278
Selected grants: The following grants are a representative sample of this grantmaker's funding activity:
$100,000 to Emory University, Atlanta, GA, 2010. For research.
$86,904 to University of North Carolina, Chapel Hill, NC, 2010. For research.
$45,270 to University of Pennsylvania, Philadelphia, PA, 2010. For research.
$39,847 to University of Colorado, Denver, CO, 2010. For research.
$38,852 to Massachusetts General Hospital, Boston, MA, 2010. For research.
$37,724 to Virginia Commonwealth University, Richmond, VA, 2010. For research.
$20,000 to Puget Sound Blood Center, Seattle, WA, 2010. For research.
$10,000 to Hemophilia and Bleeding Disorders of Alabama, Montgomery, AL, 2010. For research.
$10,000 to Texas Central Hemophilia Association, Dallas, TX, 2010. For research.
$6,498 to Hemophilia of Georgia, Atlanta, GA, 2010. For research.

994
CSRHUB
P.O. Box 28
New Paltz, NY 12561-0028 (646) 321-2755

Company URL: http://www.csrhub.com
Establishment information: Established in 2007.
Company type: Private company
Business type (SIC): Business services/ miscellaneous
Corporate officers: Bahar Gidwani, C.E.O.; Cynthia Figge, C.O.O.
Giving statement: Giving through the CSRHUB Corporate Giving Program.

CSRHUB Corporate Giving Program
P.O. Box 28
New Paltz, NY 12561-0028 (646) 321-2755
E-mail: info@csrhub.com; URL: http://www.csrhub.com

Purpose and activities: CSRHUB is a certified B Corporation that donates a percentage of net profits to charitable organizations.

995
CSRwire, LLC
250 Albany St.
Springfield, MA 01105-1018
(802) 251-0110

Company URL: http://www.csrwire.com
Establishment information: Established in 1999.
Company type: Private company
Business type (SIC): Business services/ miscellaneous
Corporate officer: Aman Singh, Owner
Giving statement: Giving through the CSRwire, LLC Contributions Program.

CSRwire, LLC Contributions Program
250 Albany St.
Springfield, MA 01105-1018 (802) 251-0110
E-mail: help@csrwire.com; URL: http://www.csrwire.com

Purpose and activities: CSRwire is a certified B Corporation that donates a percentage of net profits to charitable organizations. Support is given primarily in Springfield, Massachusetts.
Fields of interest: Youth development; Community development, neighborhood development; Social entrepreneurship.
Type of support: General/operating support.
Geographic limitations: Giving primarily in Springfield, MA.

996
CSS Industries, Inc.
(formerly Philadelphia Industries, Inc.)
1845 Walnut St., Ste. 800
Philadelphia, PA 19103-4755
(215) 569-9900
FAX: (215) 569-9979

Company URL: http://www.cssindustries.com
Establishment information: Established in 1945.
Company type: Public company
Company ticker symbol and exchange: CSS/NYSE
Business activities: Designs, manufactures, distributes, and sells seasonal and social expression products; sells seasonal and social expression products wholesale.
Business type (SIC): Greeting cards; paper and allied products; paper and paper products—wholesale
Financial profile for 2013: Number of employees, 1,200; assets, $289,180,000; sales volume, $364,190,000; pre-tax net income, $22,640,000; expenses, $341,560,000; liabilities, $40,200,000
Corporate officers: Jack Farber, Chair.; Christopher J. Munyan, Pres. and C.E.O.; Vincent A. Paccapaniccia, V.P., Finance and C.F.O.; Lois B. Karpinski, V.P. and C.I.O.; David F. McHugh, V.P., Finance.; William G. Kiesling, V.P. and Genl. Counsel; Denise Andahazy, V.P., Human Resources; Michael A. Santivasci, Secy.; Stefanie L. Smoke, Corp. Cont. and Treas.
Board of directors: Jack Farber, Chair.; Scott A. Beaumont; James H. Bromley; Robert E. Chappell; John J. Gavin; Rebecca C. Matthias; Christopher J. Munyan
Subsidiaries: Berwick Industries, Inc., Berwick, PA; Cleo Inc., Memphis, TN; The Paper Magic Group, Inc., Scranton, PA; Rapidforms, Inc., Thorofare, NJ
Giving statement: Giving through the Farber Foundation, Inc.
Company EIN: 131920657

Farber Foundation, Inc.
1845 Walnut St., Ste. 800
Philadelphia, PA 19103-4711

Establishment information: Established in 1949.
Donor: CSS Industries, Inc.
Contact: Jacqueline A. Tully, Coord., Scholarship Prog.

Financial data (yr. ended 12/31/11): Assets, $871,355 (M); expenditures, $282,735; qualifying distributions, $279,670; giving activities include $279,670 for grants.
Purpose and activities: The foundation supports art museums and organizations involved with education, health, employment services, human services, and Judaism.
Fields of interest: Museums (art); Higher education; Education; Health care; Employment, services; Children/youth, services; Human services; United Ways and Federated Giving Programs; Jewish agencies & synagogues.
Program:
Faber Foundation Scholarship Program: The foundation awards $2,000 college scholarships to high school seniors who are children of employees of CSS Industries or one of its subsidiaries. Scholarships are awarded based on academic performance, SAT/ACT scores, participation in community and extracurricular activities, and financial need. The foundation also awards a $10,000 scholarship to a top-ranking scholarship recipient who exemplifies the academic ability and personality traits of Jacqueline A. Tully, a coordinator of the Faber Foundation Scholarship who died of ovarian cancer.
Type of support: Employee-related scholarships; General/operating support.
Geographic limitations: Giving primarily in PA, with emphasis on Philadelphia.
Officers: Jack Farber, Chair.; Christopher J. Munyan, Pres.; Clifford E. Pietrafitta, V.P.; Stefanie L. Smoke, Treas.
EIN: 236254221
Selected grants: The following grants are a representative sample of this grantmaker's funding activity:
$30,000 to Thomas Jefferson University, Philadelphia, PA, 2011. For general support.
$10,000 to American Jewish Committee, New York, NY, 2011. For general support.
$6,000 to Agnes Scott College, Decatur, GA, 2011.
$6,000 to Clemson University, Clemson, SC, 2011.
$6,000 to Harding University, Searcy, AR, 2011.
$6,000 to Indiana University of Pennsylvania, Indiana, PA, 2011.
$6,000 to Marywood University, Scranton, PA, 2011.
$5,000 to Village Productions, Pottstown, PA, 2011.
$4,000 to Eagles Charitable Foundation, Philadelphia, PA, 2011. For general support.
$3,000 to American Red Cross, Levittown, PA, 2011. For general support.

997
CSX Corporation
500 Water St., 15th Fl.
Jacksonville, FL 32202 (904) 359-3200
FAX: (804) 782-1409

Company URL: http://www.csx.com/
Establishment information: Established in 1978.
Company type: Public company
Company ticker symbol and exchange: CSX/NYSE
International Securities Identification Number: US1264081035
Business activities: Provides railroad transportation services; provides trucking services; operates hotel.
Business type (SIC): Transportation/railroad; trucking and courier services, except by air; hotels and motels
Financial profile for 2012: Number of employees, 32,000; assets, $30,571,000,000; sales volume, $11,756,000,000; pre-tax net income, $2,964,000,000; expenses, $8,299,000,000; liabilities, $21,583,000,000
Fortune 1000 ranking: 2012—231st in revenues, 113th in profits, and 184th in assets
Forbes 2000 ranking: 2012—819th in sales, 328th in profits, and 727th in assets
Corporate officers: Michael J. Ward, Chair., Pres., and C.E.O.; Oscar Munoz, Exec. V.P. and C.O.O.; Fredrik Eliason, Exec. V.P. and C.F.O.; Ellen M. Fitzsimmons, Exec. V.P., Public Affairs, Genl. Counsel, and Corp. Secy.; Clarence W. Gooden, Exec. V.P., Sales and Mktg.; Lisa A. Mancini, Sr. V.P. and C.A.O.; David A. Boor, V.P. and Treas.; Carolyn T. Sizemore, V.P. and Cont.
Board of directors: Michael J. Ward, Chair.; Donna M. Alvarado; Senator John B. Breaux; Pamela L. Carter; Steven T. Halverson; Edward J. Kelly III; Gilbert H. Lamphere; John D. McPherson; Timothy T. O'Toole; David M. Ratcliffe; Donald J. Shepard; Congressman J.C. Watts, Jr.; J. Steven Whisler
Subsidiaries: CSX Intermodal, Inc., Hunt Valley, MD; CSX Transportation, Inc., Jacksonville, FL
Giving statement: Giving through the CSX Corporation Contributions Program.
Company EIN: 621051971

CSX Corporation Contributions Program
500 Water St., 15th Fl.
Jacksonville, FL 32202-4423
E-mail: csx@easymatch.com; URL: http://www.beyondourrails.org/giving

Financial data (yr. ended 12/31/12): Total giving, $14,000,000, including $14,000,000 for grants.
Purpose and activities: CSX makes charitable contributions to nonprofit organizations involved with safety education, community safety, and the environment. Support is given primarily in areas of company operations in Alabama, Connecticut, Washington, DC, Delaware, Florida, Georgia, Illinois, Indiana, Louisiana, Maryland, Massachusetts, Michigan, Mississippi, Missouri, New Jersey, New York, North Carolina, Ohio, Pennsylvania, South Carolina, Tennessee, Virginia, and West Virginia.
Fields of interest: Environment; Safety/disasters, formal/general education; Safety/disasters; Children/youth, services; Family services, domestic violence.
Program:
Dollars for Doers Program: CSX makes charitable contributions of $10 per hour to nonprofit organizations and schools with which its employees volunteer 15 to 40 hours.
Type of support: Employee volunteer services; General/operating support; In-kind gifts; Program development.
Geographic limitations: Giving primarily in areas of company operations in AL, Washington, DC, DE, FL, GA, IL, IN, LA, MA, MD, MI, MO, MS, NC, NJ, NY, OH, PA, SC, TN, VA, and WV; giving also to national organizations.
Support limitations: No support for religious organizations not of direct benefit to the entire community, discriminatory organizations, anti-business groups, or political candidates or lobbying organizations. No grants to individuals, or for endowments or foundations, national conferences, sponsorships or advertising, team sponsorships, athletic scholarships, or travel.
Publications: Application guidelines; Corporate giving report.
Application information: Applications accepted. Multi-year funding is not automatic. Application form required.
Initial approach: Complete online application form
Deadline(s): None
Final notification: 90 days

998
CTSI Logistics, Inc.
1451 W. Knox St.
Torrance, CA 90501-1356 (310) 320-0818
FAX: (310) 320-0688

Company URL: http://www.ctsi-logistics.com/usa/index.aspx
Establishment information: Established in 1991.
Company type: Subsidiary of a foreign company
Business activities: Operates freight forwarding company.
Business type (SIC): Transportation/water freight
Corporate officers: Cho Yee Tan, C.E.O.; Frank Camacho, Co-Pres.; Jerry Tan, Co-Pres.; Maria Capati, Secy.
Giving statement: Giving through the CTSI Logistics, Inc. Contributions Program.

CTSI Logistics, Inc. Contributions Program
451 W. Knox St.
Torrance, CA 90501-1356 (310) 320-0818
URL: http://www.ctsi-logistics.com/aboutus.aspx

999
Cubist Pharmaceuticals, Inc.
65 Hayden Ave.
Lexington, MA 02421 (781) 860-8660
FAX: (302) 655-5049

Company URL: http://www.cubist.com
Establishment information: Established in 1992.
Company type: Public company
Company ticker symbol and exchange: CBST/NASDAQ
Business activities: Operates a biopharmaceutical company.
Business type (SIC): Drugs
Financial profile for 2011: Number of employees, 762; assets, $1,932,380,000; sales volume, $926,360,000; pre-tax net income, $199,600,000; expenses, $689,250,000; liabilities, $941,640,000
Corporate officers: Kenneth M. Bate, Chair.; Robert J. Perez, Pres. and C.O.O.; Michael W. Bonney, C.E.O.; Michael Tomsicek, Sr. V.P., C.F.O., and Treas.; Thomas J. DesRosier, Sr. V.P. and Secy.; Gregory Stea, Sr. V.P., Opers.; Timothy D. Hunt, Sr. V.P., Public Affairs; Maureen Powers, Sr. V.P., Human Resouces
Board of directors: Kenneth M. Bate, Chair.; Michael W. Bonney; Mark H. Corrigan, M.D.; Jane E. Henney, M.D.; Nancy J. Hutson, Ph.D; Alison Lawton; Leon O. Moulder, Jr.; Martin Rosenberg, Ph.D; J. Matthew Singleton, C.P.A.; Martin H. Soeters; Michael B. Wood, M.D.
Giving statement: Giving through the Cubist Pharmaceuticals, Inc. Corporate Giving Program.
Company EIN: 223192085

Cubist Pharmaceuticals, Inc. Corporate Giving Program
65 Hayden Ave.
Lexington, MA 02421-7994 (781) 860-8660
URL: http://www.cubist.com/about/community_outreach

Purpose and activities: Cubist Pharmaceuticals makes charitable contributions to nonprofit organizations that promote an educated workforce in the areas of science and math. Support is given primarily in areas of company operations in Massachusetts.
Fields of interest: Elementary/secondary education; Mathematics; Science.
Type of support: Employee volunteer services; General/operating support.
Geographic limitations: Giving primarily in areas of company operations in MA.

1000
J. P. Cullen & Sons, Inc.

330 E. Delavan Dr.
Janesville, WI 53547-1957 (608) 754-6601
FAX: (608) 754-9171

Company URL: http://www.jpcullen.com
Establishment information: Established in 1892.
Company type: Private company
Business activities: Provides nonresidential general contract construction services.
Business type (SIC): Contractors/general nonresidential building
Corporate officers: Mark A. Cullen, Chair.; David J. Cullen, Pres. and C.E.O.; Stephen P. Wisnefsky, C.F.O.; Richard F. Cullen, V.P., Opers.
Board of director: Mark A. Cullen, Chair.
Giving statement: Giving through the J.P.C. Foundation.

J.P.C. Foundation

c/o Stephen Wisnefsky
P.O. Box 1957
Janesville, WI 53547-1957
URL: http://www.jpcullen.com/AboutCullen/CommunityInvolvement.aspx

Establishment information: Established in 1991 in WI.
Donors: J.P. Cullen & Sons, Inc.; John P. Cullen.
Financial data (yr. ended 05/31/12): Assets, $2,231,736 (M); gifts received, $250,000; expenditures, $145,394; qualifying distributions, $136,266; giving activities include $136,266 for 26 grants (high: $40,000; low: $250).
Purpose and activities: The foundation supports organizations involved with arts and culture, education, health, human services, and Catholicism.
Fields of interest: Arts; Health care; Human services.
Type of support: Building/renovation; General/operating support; Scholarship funds.
Geographic limitations: Giving primarily in WI; some giving also in Honolulu, HI.
Support limitations: No grants to individuals.
Application information: Applications not accepted. Contributes only to pre-selected organizations.
Trustees: John P. Cullen; Mark A. Cullen.
EIN: 391703739
Selected grants: The following grants are a representative sample of this grantmaker's funding activity:
$25,500 to University of Wisconsin Foundation, Madison, WI, 2011.
$16,667 to Forward Foundation, Honolulu, HI, 2011.
$15,000 to Cedar Crest, Janesville, WI, 2011.
$10,000 to Froedtert Hospital Foundation, Milwaukee, WI, 2011.
$10,000 to Porchlight, Inc., Madison, WI, 2011.
$5,500 to Fort Memorial Hospital Foundation, Fort Atkinson, WI, 2011.
$5,000 to YMCA of Metropolitan Milwaukee, Milwaukee, WI, 2011.
$3,500 to Delmarva Christian Schools, Georgetown, DE, 2011.
$3,000 to University of Wisconsin-Platteville, Platteville, WI, 2011. For scholarships.
$2,500 to Gildas Club Madison Wisconsin, Middleton, WI, 2011.

1001
Cullman Savings Bank

(formerly Cullman Savings & Loan)
316 2nd Ave. S.W.
Cullman, AL 35055-4117 (256) 734-1740

Company URL: http://www.cullmansavingsbank.com
Establishment information: Established in 1887 as Cullman Building & Loan.
Company type: Private company
Business activities: Operates savings bank.
Business type (SIC): Savings institutions
Corporate officers: John A. Riley III, Pres. and C.E.O.; Mike Duke, Sr. V.P. and C.F.O.; Robin O'Berry, Sr. V.P. and Secy.; Ginger Guinn, Cont.
Board of directors: Paul D. Bussman; Kim J. Chaney; Nancy McClellan; William F. Peinhardt; John A. Riley III
Giving statement: Giving through the Cullman Savings Bank Foundation.

Cullman Savings Bank Foundation

316 Second Ave., S.W.
Cullman, AL 35055

Donor: Cullman Savings Bank.
Financial data (yr. ended 12/31/11): Assets, $1,103,100 (M); expenditures, $35,299; qualifying distributions, $28,600; giving activities include $28,600 for 7 grants (high: $15,000; low: $100).
Fields of interest: Arts; Education; Human services.
Application information: Applications not accepted. Unsolicited requests for funds not accepted.
Directors: Greg Barksdale; Nancy McCllelan; John A. Riley III.
EIN: 270667288

1002
Culver Franchising System, Inc.

1240 Water St.
Prairie du Sac, WI 53578 (608) 643-7980
FAX: (608) 643-7982

Company URL: http://www.culvers.com
Establishment information: Established in 1984.
Company type: Private company
Business activities: Operates and franchises restaurants.
Business type (SIC): Restaurants and drinking places
Financial profile for 2010: Number of employees, 290
Corporate officers: Craig C. Culver, Chair. and C.E.O.; Philip E. Keiser, Pres. and C.O.O.; Joseph Koss, C.F.O.; Karen Stoll, C.A.O.; David Stidham, V.P., Mktg.; Tom Hendericks, V.P., Inf. Systems; Steve Anderson, Genl. Counsel
Board of director: Craig C. Culver, Chair.
Giving statement: Giving through the Culver's V.I.P. Foundation, Inc.

Culver's V.I.P. Foundation, Inc.

1240 Water Street
Prairie du Sac, WI 53578-1091
URL: http://www.culvers.com/inside-culvers/vip-foundation/

Establishment information: Established in 2001 in WI.
Donors: Culver Franchising System Inc.; PepsiCo, Inc.
Financial data (yr. ended 10/31/11): Assets, $1,707,140 (M); gifts received, $531,171; expenditures, $517,824; qualifying distributions, $459,487; giving activities include $459,487 for grants.
Purpose and activities: The foundation awards college scholarships to children of employees of Culver Franchising System and awards grants to various local organizations.
Fields of interest: Higher education; General charitable giving.
Type of support: Employee-related scholarships.
Application information: Applications not accepted. Contributes only through employee-related scholarships and to pre-selected organizations.
Officers and Directors:* Leola Culver*, Pres. and Treas.; Craig C. Culver*, V.P. and Secy.; Joseph Koss.
EIN: 392042139

1003
Cumberland Farms, Inc.

100 Crossing Blvd.
Framingham, MA 01702 (508) 270-1400

Company URL: http://www.cumberlandfarms.com
Establishment information: Established in 1939.
Company type: Private company
Business activities: Operates convenience stores; operates gasoline service stations.
Business type (SIC): Groceries—retail; gasoline service stations
Financial profile for 2011: Number of employees, 6,500; sales volume, $8,020,000,000
Corporate officers: Lily Haseotes Bentas, Chair.; Ari N. Haseotes, Pres. and C.O.O.; Joseph Petrowski, C.E.O.; Howard Rosenstein, Sr. V.P. and C.F.O.; Gwen Forman, V.P., Mktg.
Board of director: Lily Haseotes Bentas, Chair.
Subsidiary: Gulf Oil L.P., Chelsea, MA
Giving statement: Giving through the Cumberland Farms Inc. Corporate Giving Program.

Cumberland Farms Inc. Corporate Giving Program

100 Crossing Blvd.
Framingham, MA 01702-5401 (800) 225-9702
URL: http://www.cumberlandfarms.com/DoingGood/default.aspx

Purpose and activities: Cumberland Farms makes charitable contributions to nonprofit organizations involved with youth education and sports, hospitals and pediatric care, breast cancer, food distribution to people who are economically disadvantaged, disability issues, human services, and family services. Support is given primarily in areas of company operations, and to national organizations.
Fields of interest: Elementary/secondary education; Hospitals (general); Health care; Breast cancer; Pediatrics; Food services, commodity distribution; Athletics/sports, amateur leagues; Youth development, services; Human services, fund

raising/fund distribution; Family services; Family resources and services, disability; Human services.

Programs:

4-H Youth in Action Grants Program: Cumberland Farms awards mini-grants to local 4-H clubs and after-school sites to implement service learning projects. The program is designed to help young people learn leadership, citizenship, and life skills while benefiting communities in which they live.

Believe and Achieve Scholarship Program: Cumberland Farms awards $1,000 college scholarships to high school students who live within 30 miles of any Cumberland Farms outlet.

Type of support: Annual campaigns; Cause-related marketing; Continuing support; General/operating support; Scholarship funds; Sponsorships.

Geographic limitations: Giving primarily in areas of company operations, and to national organizations.

1004
Cummings & Lockwood LLC

6 Landmark Sq.
Stamford, CT 06901-2704 (203) 327-1700

Company URL: http://www.cl-law.com
Establishment information: Established in 1909.
Company type: Private company
Business activities: Operates law firm.
Business type (SIC): Legal services
Corporate officers: Jonathan B. Mills, Chair.; J. Robert Merola, C.F.O.
Board of director: Jonathan B. Mills, Chair.
Offices: Greenwich, Stamford, West Hartford, CT; Bonita Springs, Naples, Palm Beach Gardens, FL
Giving statement: Giving through the Cummings & Lockwood LLC Pro Bono Program and the Cummings & Lockwood Foundation, Inc.

Cummings & Lockwood Foundation, Inc.

6 Landmark Sq.
Stamford, CT 06901-2704 (203) 327-1700

Establishment information: Established in 1995 in CT.
Donor: Cummings & Lockwood.
Contact: B. Merola
Financial data (yr. ended 12/31/11): Assets, $67,096 (M); gifts received, $45,000; expenditures, $39,653; qualifying distributions, $39,620; giving activities include $39,620 for grants.
Purpose and activities: The foundation supports community foundations and organizations involved with orchestras, conservation, and legal services.
Fields of interest: Crime/law enforcement; Human services; Public affairs.
Type of support: General/operating support.
Geographic limitations: Giving primarily in CT.
Support limitations: No grants to individuals.
Application information: Applications accepted. Application form not required. Applicants should submit the following:
1) copy of IRS Determination Letter
2) detailed description of project and amount of funding requested

Initial approach: Proposal
Deadline(s): None

Officers: Jonathan B. Mills, Pres.; Michael J. Hinton, Secy.
EIN: 061426176

1005
The Cummins Construction Company, Inc.

1420 W. Chestnut
P.O. Box 748
Enid, OK 73703-4307 (800) 375-6001
FAX: (800) 375-9858

Company URL: http://www.cumminsasphalt.com/
Establishment information: Established in 1955.
Company type: Private company
Business activities: Provides highway and street general contract construction services.
Business type (SIC): Construction/highway and street (except elevated)
Financial profile for 2009: Number of employees, 125
Corporate officer: Robert L. Cummins, Jr., Pres.
Giving statement: Giving through the Robert Cummins Family Foundation, Inc.

Robert Cummins Family Foundation, Inc.

1420 W. Chestnut Ave.
Enid, OK 73703-4307 (580) 233-6000

Establishment information: Established in 1996 in OK.
Donors: The Cummins Construction Co., Inc.; Robert L. Cummins; Robert L. Cummins, Jr.; Willa Jane Cummins.
Contact: Ray Feightner, Jr.
Financial data (yr. ended 11/30/12): Assets, $605,592 (M); expenditures, $65,952; qualifying distributions, $50,174; giving activities include $48,766 for 11 grants (high: $16,666; low: $750).
Purpose and activities: The foundation supports parks and playgrounds and organizations involved with historic preservation, baseball, and other areas.
Fields of interest: Recreation; Youth development; Religion.
Type of support: General/operating support.
Geographic limitations: Giving primarily in Enid, OK.
Application information: Applications accepted. Application form required.

Initial approach: Proposal
Deadline(s): None

Officer: Coni Blankenship, Pres.
EIN: 731486208

1006
Cummins Filtration Inc.

(formerly Fleetguard, Inc.)
2931 Elm Hill Pike
Nashville, TN 37214-3719 (615) 367-0040

Company URL: http://www.cumminsfiltration.com
Establishment information: Established in 1958.
Company type: Subsidiary of a public company
Business activities: Designs and manufactures diesel powered equipment filtration products and exhaust systems.
Business type (SIC): Motor vehicles and equipment
Corporate officer: Joseph Saoud, Pres. and C.E.O.
Plants: Lake Mills, IA; Cookeville, TN
Giving statement: Giving through the Nelson Foundation, Inc.

Nelson Foundation, Inc.

(formerly NMC Projects, Inc.)
1801 Hwy. 51/138
Stoughton, WI 53589-0428

Establishment information: Established in 1959 in WI.
Donors: Nelson Industries, Inc.; Fleetguard, Inc.; Cummins Filtration.
Financial data (yr. ended 07/31/11): Assets, $37,375 (M); expenditures, $59,742; qualifying distributions, $55,120; giving activities include $23,670 for 9 grants (high: $20,000; low: $250) and $31,450 for grants to individuals.
Purpose and activities: The foundation supports fire departments and parks and organizations involved with historic preservation, higher education, cancer, multiple sclerosis, and human services and awards college scholarships to high school students.
Fields of interest: Historic preservation/historical societies; Higher education; Cancer; Multiple sclerosis; Disasters, fire prevention/control; Recreation, parks/playgrounds; Children/youth, services; Human services.

Program:

Scholarships: The foundation awards college scholarships to students attending high school in Arcadia, Black River Falls, Bloomer, Mineral Point, Muscoda, Neillsville, Stoughton, Viroqua, Wautoma, and Waynesboro, Wisconsin.

Type of support: Building/renovation; Continuing support; Equipment; Program development; Scholarship funds; Scholarships—to individuals.
Geographic limitations: Giving primarily in WI.
Application information: Applications accepted. Application form required.

Initial approach: Contact high school principal for application information for scholarships
Deadline(s): None

Officers and Trustees: Tim Rusch*, Pres.; Wayne Ziegler*, V.P.; Darcy Prokopec*, Secy.; Michael Schumacher*, Treas.
EIN: 396043256

1007
Cummins Inc.

(formerly Cummins Engine Company, Inc.)
500 Jackson St.
P.O. Box 3005
Columbus, IN 47202-3005 (812) 377-5000
FAX: (812) 377-3334

Company URL: http://www.cummins.com
Establishment information: Established in 1919.
Company type: Public company
Company ticker symbol and exchange: CMI/NYSE
International Securities Identification Number: US2310211063
Business activities: Designs, manufactures, distributes, and services electric power generation systems, engines, and related products.
Business type (SIC): Engines and turbines
Financial profile for 2012: Number of employees, 46,000; assets, $12,548,000,000; sales volume, $17,334,000,000; pre-tax net income, $2,271,000,000; expenses, $15,080,000,000; liabilities, $5,945,000,000
Fortune 1000 ranking: 2012—160th in revenues, 126th in profits, and 339th in assets
Forbes 2000 ranking: 2012—542nd in sales, 414th in profits, and 1310th in assets
Corporate officers: Norman Thomas Linebarger, Chair. and C.E.O.; Patrick J. Ward, V.P. and C.F.O.; Marya M. Rose, C.A.O.; Marsha L. Hunt, V.P. and Corp. Cont.; Sharon R. Barner, V.P., Genl. Counsel,

and Corp. Secy.; Jill E. Cook, V.P., Human Resources
Board of directors: Norman Thomas Lineberger, Chair.; Robert J. Bernhard; Franklin R. Chang-Diaz; Stephen B. Dobbs; Robert K. Herdman; Alexis M. Herman; William I. Miller; Georgia R. Nelson; Carl Ware
Subsidiaries: Cummins Filtration Inc., Nashville, TN; Cummins Natural Gas Engines, Inc., Fort Worth, TX; Kuss Corp., Findlay, OH; Onan Corporation, Minneapolis, MN
Plants: Seymour, IN; Fridley, MN; Jamestown, NY; Rocky Mount, NC; Charleston, SC; Memphis, TN; El Paso, TX
International operations: Argentina; Australia; Austria; Barbados; Belgium; Botswana; Brazil; Canada; Chile; China; Costa Rica; Czech Republic; France; Germany; Ghana; Hong Kong; India; Italy; Japan; Lebanon; Mexico; Netherlands; New Zealand; Norway; Philippines; Romania; Russia; Singapore; South Africa; South Korea; Spain; Thailand; Turkey; United Kingdom; Zambia; Zimbabwe
Giving statement: Giving through the Cummins Inc. Corporate Giving Program and the Cummins Foundation.
Company EIN: 350257090

Cummins Inc. Corporate Giving Program

(formerly Cummins Engine Company, Inc. Corporate Giving Program)
500 Jackson St.
Columbus, IN 47201-6258 (812) 377-5000
URL: http://www.cummins.com/cmi/sustainabilityDisplayAction.do

Purpose and activities: As a complement to its foundation, Cummins also makes charitable contributions to nonprofit organizations directly. Support is given on an international basis in areas of company operations.
Fields of interest: Education; Environment; Human services; Civil/human rights, equal rights; Community/economic development.
International interests: Africa; Australia; Brazil; China; India; Mexico; Russia; United Kingdom.
Type of support: Employee volunteer services; General/operating support; Sponsorships.
Geographic limitations: Giving on an international basis in areas of company operations, including in Africa, Australia, Brazil, China, India, Mexico, and the United Kingdom.
Publications: Grants list.

The Cummins Foundation

(formerly Cummins Engine Foundation)
500 Jackson St.
M.C. 60633
Columbus, IN 47201 (812) 377-3114
FAX: (812) 377-7897;
E-mail: Cummins.Foundation@cummins.com; Additional tel.: (812) 377-3746; URL: http://www.cummins.com/cmi/navigationAction.do?nodeId=1003&siteId=1&nodeName=Corporate+Responsibility&menuId=1003

Establishment information: Incorporated in 1954 in IN.
Donors: Cummins Engine Co., Inc.; Fleetguard, Inc.; Cummins Inc.
Financial data (yr. ended 12/31/11): Assets, $37,669,587 (M); gifts received, $25,880,100; expenditures, $11,976,563; qualifying distributions, $11,036,907; giving activities include $11,036,907 for 180 grants (high: $2,000,000; low: $24).
Purpose and activities: The foundation supports programs designed to promote education, the environment, and social justice; and programs designed to improve communities in which Cummins does business.
Fields of interest: Elementary/secondary education; Higher education; Engineering school/education; Education, services; Education; Environment, climate change/global warming; Environment, natural resources; Environment, energy; Environment; Employment, services; Disasters, preparedness/services; Youth, services; Human services; Civil/human rights; Business/industry; Community/economic development; United Ways and Federated Giving Programs; Mathematics; Engineering/technology; Science Economically disadvantaged.
International interests: Brazil; China; India; Mexico; South Africa.
Type of support: Annual campaigns; Building/renovation; Continuing support; Curriculum development; Emergency funds; Employee matching gifts; Endowments; Equipment; General/operating support; Matching/challenge support; Program development; Publication; Scholarship funds; Sponsorships; Technical assistance.
Geographic limitations: Giving primarily in areas of company operations, with emphasis on Lake Mills, IA, the Columbus and Seymour, IN, areas, Fridley, MN, Jamestown, NY, Rocky Mount, NC, Findlay, OH, Charleston, SC, Cookeville, Memphis, and Nashville, TN, El Paso, TX, Stoughton, WI and in Brazil, China, India, Mexico, and South Africa; giving also to national organizations.
Support limitations: No support for sectarian religious organizations, political candidates, or medical or disease-related organizations. No grants to individuals, or for capital campaigns, business start-up needs or political causes; no loans or product donations.
Publications: Application guidelines; Corporate giving report; Grants list; IRS Form 990 or 990-PF printed copy available upon request.
Application information: Applications accepted. Additional information may be requested at a later date. Organizations receiving support are asked to submit a final report. Applicants should submit the following:
1) results expected from proposed grant
2) qualifications of key personnel
3) statement of problem project will address
4) copy of IRS Determination Letter
5) how project's results will be evaluated or measured
6) listing of board of directors, trustees, officers and other key people and their affiliations
7) detailed description of project and amount of funding requested
8) copy of current year's organizational budget and/or project budget

Initial approach: Proposal
Copies of proposal: 1
Board meeting date(s): Quarterly
Deadline(s): None
Final notification: Varies by board meeting cycle

Officers and Directors:* Theodore M. Solso*, Chair.; Mark Levett, C.E.O.; Mary Chandler, Secy.; Marsha Allamanno, Treas.; Thomas Linebarger; William I. Miller; Marya M. Rose; Patrick J. Ward.
Number of staff: 2 full-time professional; 1 full-time support.
EIN: 356042373
Selected grants: The following grants are a representative sample of this grantmaker's funding activity:
$2,000,000 to EARTH University Foundation, Atlanta, GA, 2011. For release of funds under the current grant agreement based on satisfaction of the conditions met.
$1,107,891 to United Way of Bartholomew County, Columbus, IN, 2011. For campaign contribution based on employee pledges Bartholomew County.
$800,000 to EARTH University Foundation, Atlanta, GA, 2011. For release of funds under the current grant agreement based on satisfaction of the conditions met.
$500,000 to EARTH University Foundation, Atlanta, GA, 2011. For endowed scholarship.
$500,000 to Indianapolis Zoological Society, Indianapolis Zoo, Indianapolis, IN, 2011. For the Orangutan Center, the first component of the new International Great Ape Center.
$237,367 to United Way, Greater Twin Cities, Minneapolis, MN, 2011. For campaign match for Fridley, MN.
$235,153 to United Way, Rocky Mount Area, Rocky Mount, NC, 2011. For campaign match and Rocky Mount Challenge.
$176,000 to Royal School for Deaf Children Margate, Margate, England, 2011. To implement a Visitor Education Centre with Tea Rooms. Grant made through GlobalGiving.
$42,870 to Dandelion School, Beijing, China, 2011. To provide desks, chairs and teaching materials, improve outdoor activity area, repair roof in teacher's living quarters and pay for transportation to participate in activities at CES. Grant made through GlobalGiving.
$26,661 to United Fund of Warren County, Warren, PA, 2011. For campaign match for Warren County.

1008
CUNA Mutual Insurance Society

(also known as CUNA Mutual Group)
5910 Mineral Point Rd.
Madison, WI 53705-4456 (608) 238-5851

Company URL: http://www.cunamutual.com
Establishment information: Established in 1935.
Company type: Mutual company
Business activities: Operates holding company; sells life and health insurance.
Business type (SIC): Holding company; insurance/life; insurance/accident and health
Financial profile for 2011: Number of employees, 4,100; assets, $15,385,800,000; sales volume, $2,876,000,000
Corporate officers: C. Alan Peppers, Chair.; Joseph J. Gasper, Vice-Chair.; Jeff H. Post, Pres. and C.E.O.; Robert Trunzo, Exec. V.P. and C.O.O.; Rick R. Roy, Sr. V.P. and C.I.O.
Board of directors: C. Alan Peppers, Chair.; Joseph J. Gasper, Vice-Chair.; Eldon R. Arnold; Loretta M. Burd; Bert J. Hash, Jr.; Robert J. Marzec; M. Victoria Wood Miller; Jeff Post; Randy M. Smith; Farouk D.G. Wang; Larry T. Wilson; James W. Zilinski
Subsidiaries: CMCI Corp., Madison, WI; CUDIS Insurance Society, Inc., Madison, WI; CUNA Mutual Investment Corp., Madison, WI; CUNA Mutual Life Insurance Company, Waverly, IA; League Life Insurance Co., Southfield, MI
Offices: Atlanta, GA; Lynnfield, MA; Southfield, MI; Jackson, MS; Harrisburg, PA; Chattanooga, TN; Salt Lake City, UT
Giving statement: Giving through the CUNA Mutual Group Foundation, Inc.

CUNA Mutual Group Foundation, Inc.

(formerly CUNA Mutual Insurance Group Charitable Foundation, Inc.)
5910 Mineral Point Rd.
Madison, WI 53705-4456 (800) 356-2644
FAX: (608) 236-7755;
E-mail: Foundation@cunamutual.com; E-mail for Steven A. Goldberg: steven.goldberg@cunamutual.com; Additional address: P.O. Box 391, Madison, WI 53701; URL: http://www.cunamutual.com/portal/server.pt/community/community_involvement/728

Establishment information: Incorporated in 1967 in WI.
Donor: CUNA Mutual Insurance Society.
Contact: Steven A. Goldberg, Exec. Dir.
Financial data (yr. ended 12/31/11): Assets, $28,689 (M); gifts received, $652,200; expenditures, $644,053; qualifying distributions, $643,950; giving activities include $643,950 for grants.
Purpose and activities: The foundation supports organizations involved with arts and culture, education, health, mental health, human services, and community development. Special emphasis is directed toward programs designed to serve at-risk youth.
Fields of interest: Museums (art); Arts; Secondary school/education; Charter schools; Higher education; Libraries (public); Education; Health care, clinics/centers; Health care; Mental health/crisis services; Boys & girls clubs; Big Brothers/Big Sisters; YM/YWCAs & YM/YWHAs; Family services; Family services, domestic violence; Human services; Community/economic development; United Ways and Federated Giving Programs Youth.
Program:
Dollars for Doers: The foundation awards $500 grants to nonprofit organizations with which employees, directors, and retirees of CUNA volunteer 50 hours within a 12-month period.
Type of support: Building/renovation; Capital campaigns; Continuing support; Employee matching gifts; Employee volunteer services; General/operating support; Program development; Scholarship funds.
Geographic limitations: Giving primarily in areas of company operations in Waverly, IA, Fort Worth, TX, and Madison, WI.
Support limitations: No support for political parties or candidates, professional associations, religious organizations, or labor unions. No grants to individuals, or for political campaigns, tickets or items for fundraising events, or endowments.
Publications: Application guidelines.
Application information: Applications accepted. Organizations receiving support are asked to submit a final report. Application form not required.
Applicants should submit the following:
1) detailed description of project and amount of funding requested
Initial approach: E-mail letter of inquiry
Deadline(s): None
Officers and Directors: Faye A. Patzer, Pres.; James H. Metz, V.P.; Steven A. Goldberg, Secy.-Treas. and Exec. Dir.; Gerald W. Pavelich; James M. Power; Steven R. Suleski.
EIN: 396105418
Selected grants: The following grants are a representative sample of this grantmaker's funding activity:
$50,000 to Childrens Service Society of Wisconsin, Milwaukee, WI, 2010.
$50,000 to Childrens Service Society of Wisconsin, Milwaukee, WI, 2010.
$50,000 to Childrens Service Society of Wisconsin, Milwaukee, WI, 2010.
$35,000 to Childrens Service Society of Wisconsin, Milwaukee, WI, 2010.
$2,500 to Cystic Fibrosis Foundation, Bethesda, MD, 2010.

1009
Cupertino Electric, Inc.

1132 N. 7th St.
San Jose, CA 95112 (408) 808-8000
FAX: (408) 275-8575

Company URL: http://www.cei.com
Establishment information: Established in 1954.
Company type: Private company
Business activities: Provides electrical construction services.
Business type (SIC): Contractors/electrical work
Financial profile for 2010: Number of employees, 1,400
Corporate officers: James S. Ryley, Chair.; John Boncher, Pres. and C.E.O.; Tom Schott, C.O.O; Marjorie Goss, Treas. and C.F.O.; Eileen Nelson, Sr. V.P., Human Resources; Jan Kang, V.P., Genl. Counsel, and Secy.; John Sales, V.P., Opers.; Michael Garner, V.P., Sales
Board of director: John S. Ryley, Chair.
Giving statement: Giving through the Cupertino Electric Trust.

Cupertino Electric Trust

300 S. San Antonio Rd.
Los Altos, CA 94022

Donors: Cupertino Electric, Inc.; Cascade Controls, Inc.
Contact: Eugene A. Ravizza, Tr.
Financial data (yr. ended 12/31/11): Assets, $407,140 (M); expenditures, $20,904; qualifying distributions, $17,100; giving activities include $17,100 for grants.
Purpose and activities: The trust supports organizations involved with education, youth development, children and youth, and human services.
Fields of interest: Education; Agriculture/food; Human services.
Type of support: General/operating support.
Geographic limitations: Giving primarily in CA.
Support limitations: No grants to individuals.
Application information: Applications accepted. Application form required.
Initial approach: Letter
Deadline(s): Nov. 1
Trustees: Claranne R. Long; Dianne Ravizza; Eugene A. Ravizza; James S. Ryley.
EIN: 942702210

1010
Curtis, Mallet-Prevost, Colt & Mosle LLP

101 Park Ave.
New York, NY 10178-0061 (212) 696-6121

Company URL: http://www.curtis.com
Establishment information: Established in 1830.
Company type: Private company
Business activities: Operates law firm.
Business type (SIC): Legal services
Corporate officer: J. Dinsmore Adams, Jr., Partner
Offices: Washington, DC; New York, NY; Houston, TX
International operations: France; Germany; Italy; Kazakhstan; Mexico; Oman; Turkey; Turkmenistan; United Arab Emirates; United Kingdom
Giving statement: Giving through the Curtis, Mallet-Prevost, Colt & Mosle LLP Pro Bono Program.

Curtis, Mallet-Prevost, Colt & Mosle LLP Pro Bono Program

101 Park Ave.
New York, NY 10178-0061 (212) 696-6121
E-mail: tsmith@curtis.com; Additional tel.: (212) 696-6000; URL: http://www.curtis.com/sitecontent.cfm?pageid=4

Contact: Turner Smith, Partner
Fields of interest: Legal services.
Type of support: Pro bono services - legal.
Geographic limitations: Giving primarily in areas of company operations in Washington, DC, New York, NY, Houston, TX, and in France, Germany, Kazakhstan, Italy, Mexico, Oman, Turkey, Turkmenistan, United Arab Emirates, and United Kingdom.
Application information: The Pro Bono Committee manages the pro-bono program.

1011
Curves International, Inc.

(also known as Curves for Women)
100 Ritchie Rd.
Waco, TX 76712 (254) 399-9285
FAX: (254) 399-6623

Company URL: http://www.curvesinternational.com
Establishment information: Established in 1995.
Company type: Private company
Business activities: Franchises physical fitness facilities.
Business type (SIC): Amusement and recreation services/miscellaneous; investors/miscellaneous
Corporate officers: H. Gary Heavin, C.E.O.; Christina Kay Russel, V.P., Opers.; Jim Johnson, C.O.O.
Giving statement: Giving through the Gary & Diane Heavin Community Fund Inc.

The Gary & Diane Heavin Community Fund Inc.

(formerly The Curves Community Fund, Inc.)
c/o Ronnie Glaesmann
100 Ritchie Rd.
Waco, TX 76712-8544

Establishment information: Established in 2001 in TX.
Donors: Curves International, Inc.; Gary Heavin; Diane Heaven.
Financial data (yr. ended 12/31/11): Assets, $17,946,615 (M); gifts received, $3,000,000; expenditures, $1,981,457; qualifying distributions, $1,768,502; giving activities include $1,768,502 for grants.
Purpose and activities: The fund supports organizations involved with television, radio, education, health, human services, and Christianity.
Fields of interest: Media, television; Media, radio; Higher education; Education; Hospitals (general); Health care; Salvation Army; Family services; Family services, domestic violence; Aging, centers/services; Developmentally disabled, centers & services; Human services; Christian agencies & churches.
Type of support: General/operating support.
Geographic limitations: Giving primarily in Waco, TX.

Application information: Applications not accepted. Contributes only to pre-selected organizations.
Officers: Gary H. Heavin, Pres.; Diane Heavin, V.P.
EIN: 743003293

1012
Cutco Cutlery Corporation

1116 E. State St.
Olean, NY 14760-3814 (716) 372-3111

Company URL: http://www.cutco.com
Establishment information: Established in 1990.
Company type: Subsidiary of a private company
Business activities: Manufactures kitchen cutlery and accessories and sporting and pocket knives.
Business type (SIC): Cutlery, hand and edge tools, and hardware
Corporate officers: James E. Stitt, Pres.; David J. Koebelin, V.P., Human Resources
Giving statement: Giving through the Cutco Foundation, Inc.

Cutco Foundation, Inc.

1116 E. State St.
Olean, NY 14760-3814

Establishment information: Established in 1995 in NY.
Donors: Cutco Cutlery Corp.; Alcas Corp.; Vector Marketing Corp.; Cutco Cutlery; Mike Lancellot; Cutco Corporation.
Contact: James M. Stitt, Jr., Treas.
Financial data (yr. ended 12/31/11): Assets, $3,386,187 (M); gifts received, $627,100; expenditures, $271,351; qualifying distributions, $268,270; giving activities include $268,270 for grants.
Purpose and activities: The foundation supports hospitals and community foundations and organizations involved with higher education.
Fields of interest: Higher education; Hospitals (general); Foundations (community).
Type of support: Building/renovation; Capital campaigns; Endowments; Matching/challenge support; Scholarship funds.
Geographic limitations: Giving primarily in Olean, NY.
Support limitations: No grants to individuals.
Application information: Applications accepted. Application form required.
Initial approach: Letter
Deadline(s): None
Officers: James E. Stitt, Chair.; John Whelpley, Secy.; James Stitt, Jr., Treas.
Directors: Brent Driscoll; Erick Laine; John Stitt.
EIN: 161491450

1013
Cutie Pie Baby, Inc.

34 W. 33rd St., S., 5th Fl.
New York, NY 10001-3304 (212) 279-0022

Company URL: http://www.cutiepiebaby.com/
Establishment information: Established in 1988.
Company type: Private company
Business activities: Sells baby accessories wholesale.
Business type (SIC): Apparel, piece goods, and notions—wholesale
Corporate officers: Jack Yedid, C.E.O.; Eli Yedid, Pres.; Jerry Yaskowitz, C.F.O.
Giving statement: Giving through the Yedid Charitable Foundation.

Yedid Charitable Foundation

34 W. 33rd St., 9th Fl.
New York, NY 10001-3304

Establishment information: Established in 2003 in NY.
Donor: Cutie Pie Baby Inc.
Financial data (yr. ended 09/30/12): Assets, $10,417 (M); gifts received, $115,000; expenditures, $113,464; qualifying distributions, $113,418; giving activities include $113,418 for 33 grants (high: $65,246; low: $101).
Purpose and activities: The foundation supports organizations involved with education and Judaism.
Fields of interest: Education; Jewish agencies & synagogues.
Type of support: General/operating support.
Geographic limitations: Giving limited to NJ and NY.
Application information: Applications not accepted. Unsolicited requests for funds not accepted.
Officer and Directors:* Simon Yedid*, Pres.; Eli Yedid; Jack Yedid.
EIN: 920188428

1014
CVS Caremark Corporation

(doing business as CVS)
(formerly CVS Corporation)
1 CVS Dr.
Woonsocket, RI 02895-6146
(401) 765-1500
FAX: (302) 655-5049

Company URL: http://info.cvscaremark.com/
Establishment information: Established in 1963.
Company type: Public company
Company ticker symbol and exchange: CVS/NYSE
International Securities Identification Number: US1266501006
Business activities: Operates drug stores.
Business type (SIC): Drug stores and proprietary stores
Financial profile for 2012: Number of employees, 203,000; assets, $65,912,000,000; sales volume, $123,133,000,000; pre-tax net income, $6,323,000,000; expenses, $116,253,000,000; liabilities, $28,208,000,000
Fortune 1000 ranking: 2012—13th in revenues, 51st in profits, and 87th in assets
Forbes 2000 ranking: 2012—38th in sales, 147th in profits, and 356th in assets
Corporate officers: David W. Dorman, Chair.; Larry J. Merlo, Pres. and C.E.O.; David M. Denton, Exec. V.P., C.F.O., C.A.O., and Cont.; Thomas M. Moriarty, Exec. V.P., Genl. Counsel; Laird K. Daniels, Sr. V.P., Finance, Cont., and C.A.O.; Stephen J. Gold, Sr. V.P. and C.I.O.
Board of directors: David W. Dorman, Chair.; C. David Brown II; Anne M. Finucane; Larry J. Merlo; Jean-Pierre Millon; Richard J. Swift; Tony L. White; Kristen Gibney Williams; William C. Weldon
Subsidiary: CVS Revco D.S., Inc., Twinsburg, OH
Historic mergers: Caremark Rx, Inc. (March 22, 2007); Longs Drug Stores Corporation (October 30, 2008)
Giving statement: Giving through the CVS Caremark Corporation Contributions Program and the CVS Caremark Charitable Trust, Inc.
Company EIN: 050494040

CVS Caremark Corporation Contributions Program

(formerly CVS/pharmacy Corporate Giving Program)
One CVS Dr.
Woonsocket, RI 02895-6146 (401) 765-1500
E-mail: communitymailbox@cvs.com; East Region: communitymailbox@cvs.com; Gwen McKenzie: gwendolyn.mckenzie@cvscaremark.com; Karen Ramos: kramos@cvs.com; Massachusetts/Rhode Island: communitymailbox@cvs.com; URL: http://www.cvscaremark.com/community

Financial data (yr. ended 12/31/11): Total giving, $42,700,000, including $22,700,000 for grants and $20,000,000 for in-kind gifts.
Purpose and activities: As a complement to its foundation, CVS/pharmacy also makes charitable contributions to nonprofit organizations directly. Support is limited to states where company operations are located.
Fields of interest: Education, public education; Elementary/secondary education; Environment, natural resources; Health care, fund raising/fund distribution; Medical care, community health systems; Hospitals (general); Physical therapy; Speech/hearing centers; Public health, occupational health; Health care; ALS; Recreation; Children/youth, services; Family services; Independent living, disability; Assistive technology; Military/veterans' organizations Economically disadvantaged.
Type of support: Donated products; Employee volunteer services; General/operating support; In-kind gifts.
Geographic limitations: Giving is limited to states where company operations are located.
Publications: Application guidelines.
Application information: Applications accepted. Grants are limited to $5,000 or less. Calls and emails during the application process are not encouraged. Organizations that receive funding will be asked to post volunteer opportunities on the CVS/pharmacy website so local associates can participate. Application form required. Applicants should submit the following:
1) brief history of organization and description of its mission
2) name, address and phone number of organization
Organizations that are applying for grants must provide an EIN number to begin the eligibility quiz, with the exception of public schools.
Initial approach: Complete eligibility quiz and online application
Deadline(s): Jan. 1 to Oct. 31 for grant applications
Final notification: 4 to 6 weeks for grants and gift cards

CVS Caremark Charitable Trust, Inc.

(formerly CVS/pharmacy Charitable Trust, Inc.)
1 CVS Dr.
Woonsocket, RI 02895-6146 (401) 770-4561
E-mail: Joanne.Dwyer@cvscaremark.com; General Community Rels. Inquiries: CommunityMailbox@cvscaremark.com; URL: http://www.cvscaremark.com/community/our-impact/charitable-trust

Establishment information: Established in 1992 in DE and MA.
Donors: Melville Corp.; CVS Corp.; CVS Pharmacy, Inc.
Contact: Joanne Dwyer, Dir., Corporate Comms. & Community Relas.
Financial data (yr. ended 12/31/11): Assets, $50,545,944 (M); expenditures, $6,050,716; qualifying distributions, $6,055,691; giving

activities include $5,862,123 for 604 grants (high: $500,000; low: $500).
Purpose and activities: The trust supports programs designed to promote access to health care; wellness and prevention initiatives to help people achieve their best health; and programs designed to help all kids in their path to better health.
Fields of interest: Visual arts; Higher education; Medical school/education; Health care, equal rights; Medicine/medical care, public education; Hospitals (general); Health care, clinics/centers; Medical care, rehabilitation; Physical therapy; Art & music therapy; Pharmacy/prescriptions; Public health, physical fitness; Health care, patient services; Health care; Heart & circulatory diseases; Asthma; Diabetes; Pediatrics; Disasters, preparedness/services; Recreation, camps; Recreation, parks/playgrounds; Athletics/sports, school programs; Recreation; Youth development; Family services, parent education; Independent living, disability; Assistive technology Children; Disabilities, people with; Physically disabled; Blind/visually impaired; Deaf/hearing impaired; Mentally disabled; Economically disadvantaged.
Programs:

Access to Health Care: The trust supports programs designed to expand access to health care for underserved populations and promote wellness and prevention, including support for mobile health innovations that provide health care services to locations in need.

All Kids Can CREATE: The trust in partnership with VSA, the International Organization on Arts and Disability sponsors a national campaign to promote inclusive arts education and increased public awareness of the arts for young people with disabilities. The campaign invites students ages 5 to 15 with or without disabilities to respond to the theme "What Inspires Me" through art. Submitted work will be featured in an online gallery and two pieces from every state will be on display at the Martin Luther King Jr. Library. Selected student artists are invited to an all expense paid trip and reception in Washington, D.C. and teachers who submit their students work are eligible to receive $1,500 cash award for use in their classroom.

CVS Caremark All Kids Can: Through the All Kids Can initiative, the trust supports programs designed to increase access to specialized medical and rehabilitation services; and help children with disabilities engage in physical activity, play, and social enrichment. learn, play, and succeed in life. Special emphasis is directed toward coordinated care; early intervention; and inclusion. Visit URL: http://www.cvscaremarkallkidscan.com/ for more information.

CVS Caremark Scholarship Program: The trust awards college scholarships to children of employees of CVS Caremark. Recipients are selected based on academic achievement, extracurricular activities, work experience, community service, and school recommendations. This program will reopen in January 2014.

Pharmacy School Scholarships: The trust awards scholarship funds to institutions and nonprofit organizations to advance the business of pharmacy and support pharmacists as they complete their education.

Volunteer Challenge Grants: The trust awards grants of $500 to $2,500 to nonprofit organizations with which employees or teams of employees of CVS volunteer. Individual employees must volunteer 25 hours of service and teams of employees must volunteer 50 hours of service.
Type of support: Building/renovation; Continuing support; Employee volunteer services; Employee-related scholarships; Management development/capacity building; Program development; Scholarship funds.
Geographic limitations: Giving primarily in areas of company operations in the U.S. and Puerto Rico.
Support limitations: No grants for general operating support, direct healthcare services, staff salaries (unless it's needed to create or enhance a program or increase the number of people or geographic areas served), fundraising events, sponsorships, scholarships (except for employee-related and pharmacy scholarships), endowments, or capital campaigns.
Publications: Application guidelines; Grants list; Program policy statement.
Application information: Applications accepted. Grants range from $10,000 to $50,000. A full proposal may be requested at a later date. Support is limited to 1 contribution per organization during any given year. Application form required. Applicants should submit the following:
1) results expected from proposed grant
2) statement of problem project will address
3) population served
4) copy of IRS Determination Letter
5) geographic area to be served
6) detailed description of project and amount of funding requested
7) contact person
8) copy of current year's organizational budget and/or project budget
9) listing of additional sources and amount of support

Initial approach: Visit website for application guidelines for general grants; complete online application for pharmacy school scholarships

Deadline(s): Visit website for application deadline for general grants; None for pharmacy school scholarships

Officers and Directors:* Eileen Howard Boone*, Pres.; David M. Denton*, V.P. and Treas.; Carol A. DeNale, V.P.
EIN: 223206973
Selected grants: The following grants are a representative sample of this grantmaker's funding activity:
$1,000,000 to Rhode Island Quality Institute, Providence, RI, 2010.
$572,261 to Boundless Playgrounds, New Haven, CT, 2010.
$208,070 to VSA Arts, Washington, DC, 2010.
$200,000 to Big Picture Company, Providence, RI, 2010.
$150,000 to Emma Pendleton Bradley Hospital, East Providence, RI, 2010.
$138,542 to American Red Cross National Headquarters, Washington, DC, 2010.
$30,000 to AccesSport America, Acton, MA, 2010.
$30,000 to Center for the Visually Impaired, Atlanta, GA, 2010.
$25,000 to Women and Infants Hospital of Rhode Island, Providence, RI, 2010.
$5,000 to College of Notre Dame of Maryland, Baltimore, MD, 2010.

1015
Cyan Worlds, Inc.
(formerly Cyan, Inc.)
14617 Newport Hwy.
Mead, WA 99021-9378 (509) 468-0807

Company URL: http://www.cyan.com
Establishment information: Established in 1987.
Company type: Private company
Business activities: Develops computer software.
Business type (SIC): Computer services
Corporate officers: Rand K. Miller, C.E.O.; Tony Fryman, Pres.; Mark Klammer, C.F.O.
Giving statement: Giving through the Azure Group, Inc.

Azure Group, Inc.
14617 N. Newport Hwy.
Mead, WA 99021-9394 (509) 464-0105

Establishment information: Established in 1995 in GA.
Donors: Cyan, Inc.; Cyan Worlds, Inc.
Contact: Ronald K. Miller, V.P.
Financial data (yr. ended 11/30/11): Assets, $11,067 (M); expenditures, $3,842; qualifying distributions, $2,950; giving activities include $2,950 for 3 grants (high: $2,000; low: $250).
Purpose and activities: The foundation supports organizations involved with health, human services, international development, and Christianity.
Fields of interest: Religion.
Type of support: General/operating support.
Application information: Applications accepted. Application form required. Applicants should submit the following:
1) timetable for implementation and evaluation of project
2) name, address and phone number of organization
3) copy of IRS Determination Letter
4) brief history of organization and description of its mission
5) detailed description of project and amount of funding requested

Initial approach: Letter

Deadline(s): None

Officers and Directors:* Rand K. Miller*, Pres.; Robyn C. Miller*, C.F.O.; Ronald K. Miller*, V.P.
EIN: 582239780

1016
Cymer, Inc.
17075 Thornmint Ct.
San Diego, CA 92127 (858) 385-7300
FAX: (858) 385-7100

Company URL: http://www.cymer.com
Establishment information: Established in 1986.
Company type: Public company
Company ticker symbol and exchange: CYMI/NASDAQ
Business activities: Manufactures excimer lasers used in deep ultraviolet photolithography systems.
Business type (SIC): Machinery/special industry
Financial profile for 2012: Number of employees, 1,100; assets, $1,023,230,000; sales volume, $538,620,000; pre-tax net income, -$43,100,000; expenses, $580,990,000; liabilities, $273,450,000
Corporate officers: Robert P. Akins, Ph.D., Chair. and C.E.O.; Edward J. Brown, Jr., Pres. and C.O.O.; Paul B. Bowman, Sr. V.P., C.F.O., and Secy.; Karen K. McGinnis, V.P., Corp. Cont., and C.A.O.
Board of directors: Robert P. Akins, Ph.D., Chair.; Charles J. Abbe; Edward H. Braun; Michael R. Gaulke; William G. Oldham, Ph.D.; Eric M. Ruttenberg; Peter J. Simone; Young K. Sohn; Jon D. Tompkins
Giving statement: Giving through the Cymer, Inc. Corporate Giving Program.
Company EIN: 330175463

Cymer, Inc. Corporate Giving Program

c/o Community Rels.
17075 Thornmint Ct.
San Diego, CA 92127-2413 (858) 385-7300
FAX: (858) 385-7100;
E-mail: CymerCommunity@cymer.com; URL: http://www.cymer.com/about/community/index.htm

Purpose and activities: Cymer makes charitable contributions to nonprofit organizations involved with culture, education, the environment, health, and civic affairs. Support is given primarily in areas of company operations, with emphasis on San Diego, California.
Fields of interest: Arts; Education; Environment; Health care; Public affairs.
Type of support: Continuing support; Employee volunteer services; General/operating support; Program development; Scholarship funds.
Geographic limitations: Giving primarily in areas of company operations, with emphasis on San Diego, CA.
Support limitations: No support for discriminatory, political, or religious organizations. No grants to individuals.
Publications: Application guidelines.
Application information: Applications accepted. The San Diego Common Grant Application is accepted. Qualified applicants who do not receive funding may re-apply 4 months after the initial proposal. A maximum of five organizational reviews, videos, or articles concerning the proposed funding program will be accepted. The Community Relations Department handles giving. A contributions committee reviews all requests. Application form required. Applicants should submit the following:
1) copy of IRS Determination Letter
2) how company employees can become involved with the organization

Applications should include a description of past support by Cymer with the organization, and the number of full-time paid staff, part-time paid staff, and volunteers. Additional requirements noted in the San Diego Common Grant Application.
Initial approach: Download San Diego Common Grant Application and mail to headquarters
Committee meeting date(s): Monthly
Deadline(s): None
Final notification: 3 weeks following contributions committee meeting

1018
D.C. United Holdings

(also known as D.C. United)
(formerly Anschutz D.C. Soccer, LLC)
2400 E. Capitol St., S.E.
Washington, DC 20003 (202) 587-5000

Company URL: http://www.dcunited.com/
Establishment information: Established in 1996.
Company type: Subsidiary of a private company
Business activities: Operates professional soccer club.
Business type (SIC): Commercial sports
Corporate officers: Kevin J. Payne, Pres. and C.E.O.; Michael Williamson, C.O.O. and C.F.O.; Doug Hicks, Sr. V.P., Mktg. and Comms.
Giving statement: Giving through the D.C. United Corporate Giving Program and the United for D.C.

D.C. United Corporate Giving Program

RFK Stadium
2400 E. Capitol St., S.E.
Washington, DC 20003 (202) 587-5453
E-mail: apritchet@dcunited.com; URL: http://www.dcunited.com/community

Contact: Aprile Pritchet, Community Rels.
Purpose and activities: The D.C. United makes charitable contributions to nonprofit organizations on a case by case basis. Support is given primarily in the Washington, DC, area.
Fields of interest: Housing/shelter, development; Athletics/sports, soccer; Youth development; General charitable giving.
Programs:
D.C. United Community Stars: D.C. United honors individuals in the Washington, DC area who demonstrates leadership, compassion, dedication, and a commitment to make their community a better place. Honorees are chosen for each D.C. United home game and winners receive four game tickets, a fan pack including D.C. United promotional items, and an on-field recognition for their community contributions.
United Builds: Through United Builds, D.C. United Staff, players, and fans volunteer together for community projects that benefit nonprofit organizations. Projects range from volunteering with the homeless to holding various community drives for local causes.
United Drives Initiative: D.C. United supports nonprofit organizations by collecting items to help with each beneficiary's mission. The program assigns a different charity drive for each month of the MLS regular season, including the collection of soccer equipment, food, children's books, and school supplies. Individuals who donate four items receive a "United Drives Buy One, Get One Free" ticket voucher. D.C. United also sponsors a competition between D.C. area youth soccer teams to collect the greatest amount of United Drives items each month. The monthly winners receive a Pizza Party with a D.C. United Player.
Type of support: Donated products; Employee volunteer services; In-kind gifts; Income development; Loaned talent.
Geographic limitations: Giving primarily in areas of company operations in the Washington, DC, area, southern MD, and northern VA.
Support limitations: No support for religious organizations not of direct benefit to the entire community.
Publications: Application guidelines.
Application information: Applications accepted. Support is limited to 1 contribution per organization during any given year. Telephone calls during the application process are not encouraged. The Community Relations Department handles giving. Application form required. Applicants should submit the following:
1) name, address and phone number of organization
2) copy of IRS Determination Letter
3) detailed description of project and amount of funding requested
4) contact person

Initial approach: Complete online application for donations and player/coach appearances; complete online nomination for D.C. United Community Stars
Deadline(s): 6 weeks prior to need; none for D.C. United Community Stars
Final notification: 3 weeks

United for D.C.

c/o RFK Stadium
2400 E. Capitol St. S.E.
Washington, DC 20003-1734 (202) 587-5000
FAX: (202) 587-5400;
E-mail: unitedfordc@dcunited.com; URL: http://www.unitedfordc.org

Establishment information: Established in 2002 in DC.
Donor: Anschutz D.C. Soccer, LLC.
Financial data (yr. ended 12/31/11): Revenue, $497,126; assets, $285,599 (M); gifts received, $497,119; expenditures, $466,791.
Purpose and activities: The organization works to serve the Washington, DC community through the creation or support of programs, events, and organizations that advance the educational and social welfare opportunities (primarily health and recreational) for the area's youth, particularly those who may be economically, physically, or mentally disadvantaged.
Fields of interest: Athletics/sports, soccer; Human services Children/youth; Economically disadvantaged.
Programs:
Kicks for Kids: The organization provides qualified nonprofit organizations with access to tickets to United D.C. games free-of-charge. In addition to complimentary tickets, these organizations will also receive free meal vouchers, special give-away items, and access to transportation funding assistance.
United Reads: The organization works to encourage area youth to fall in love with the practice of reading, providing books and other resources to the community, and promoting literacy amongst children and families. To support this, the program will support programs that utilize the sport of soccer to emphasize the importance of reading.
United Soccer Club: The organization partners with the United Soccer Club to create after-school programs that introduce the sport of soccer to youth in the inner-city communities of Washington, D.C.
Geographic limitations: Giving limited to the greater metropolitan Washington, DC, area.
Support limitations: No support for faith-based organizations for sectarian religious purposes. No grants to individuals, or for annual campaigns, fundraising/one-time events, or multi-year projects.
Publications: Informational brochure; Newsletter; Occasional report.
Application information: Applications not accepted. Contributes only to pre-selected organizations.
Officers and Directors:* Kevin J. Payne*, Pres.; Doug Hicks, Sr. V.P.; Stephen Zack*, Exec. V.P.; Dawn Ridley*, V.P.; Michael Williamson, C.F.O.; Alex Caulfield; Amanda Farina; Adam Hoyt; Dave Kasper; Andrew Minucci.
EIN: 010616118

1019
Daffy's, Inc.

(formerly Daffy Dan's Holding Co., Inc.)
1 Daffy's Way
Secaucus, NJ 07094-2120 (201) 902-1455

Company URL: http://www.daffys.com
Establishment information: Established in 1961.
Company type: Private company
Business activities: Operates clothing stores.
Business type (SIC): Family apparel and accessory stores
Corporate officers: Marcia Wilson, Pres. and C.E.O.; Richard Krammer, V.P. and C.F.O.; Cheryl Jascha, C.I.O; Allen Gross, Cont.

Giving statement: Giving through the Daffy's Foundation, Inc.

Daffy's Foundation, Inc.

Daffy's Way
Secaucus, NJ 07094

Establishment information: Established in 1993 in NJ.
Donor: Daffy's, Inc.
Financial data (yr. ended 12/31/11): Assets, $378,147 (M); expenditures, $20,425; qualifying distributions, $19,800; giving activities include $19,800 for grants.
Purpose and activities: The foundation supports organizations involved with theater, education, the environment, health, counseling, employment services, hunger, human services, international affairs, and Judaism.
Fields of interest: Health care; Human services.
Type of support: General/operating support; Scholarship funds.
Support limitations: No grants to individuals.
Application information: Applications not accepted. Unsolicited requests for funds not accepted.
Officers and Trustees:* Marcia Wilson*, Pres.; Irving J. Shulman.
EIN: 223221093

1020
Daiwa Securities America, Inc.

Financial Square, 32 Old Slip, 14th Fl.
New York, NY 10005-3538 (212) 612-7000

Company URL: http://www.us.daiwacm.com
Establishment information: Established in 1964.
Company type: Subsidiary of a foreign company
Business activities: Provides securities brokerage services.
Business type (SIC): Brokers and dealers/security
Financial profile for 2012: Assets, $229,900,000,000; sales volume, $5,100,000,000
Forbes 2000 ranking: 2012—1378th in sales, 1892nd in profits, and 118th in assets
Corporate officers: Masamichi Yokoi, Chair. and C.E.O.; Richard Beggs, Vice-Chair.; Shuji Nishiyama, C.E.O.; Mori Takeaki, Pres.; Ed Towers, C.F.O.
Board of directors: Masamichi Yokoi, Chair.; Richard Beggs, Vice-Chair.
Giving statement: Giving through the Daiwa Securities America Inc. Corporate Giving Program and the Daiwa Securities America Foundation.

Daiwa Securities America Inc. Corporate Giving Program

c/o Human Resources
Financial Sq.
32 Old Slip
New York, NY 10005-3538 (212) 612-7000

Purpose and activities: As a complement to its foundation, Daiwa also makes charitable contributions to nonprofit organizations directly. Support is given primarily in areas of company operations.
Fields of interest: General charitable giving.
Type of support: General/operating support.
Geographic limitations: Giving primarily in areas of company operations.
Support limitations: No grants to individuals or families.
Application information: Applications not accepted. Contributes only to pre-selected organizations.

Daiwa Securities America Foundation

Financial Sq., 32 Old Slip, 14th Fl.
New York, NY 10005-3504 (212) 612-7000
E-mail: christine.shapiro@daiwausa.com

Establishment information: Established in 1993 in NY.
Donor: Daiwa Securities America Inc.
Contact: Gary Mass, Dir.
Financial data (yr. ended 02/28/12): Assets, $442,135 (M); expenditures, $20,226; qualifying distributions, $20,000; giving activities include $20,000 for grants.
Purpose and activities: The foundation supports performing arts centers and organizations involved with health, birth defects, cancer research, and safety.
Type of support: Annual campaigns; Consulting services; Employee matching gifts; Employee-related scholarships; General/operating support; Grants to individuals; Scholarships—to individuals.
Geographic limitations: Giving limited to areas of company and affiliate operations.
Application information: Applications accepted. Application form required.
Initial approach: Letter
Deadline(s): None
Directors: Richard Beggs; Masaaki Goto; Hideki Hemmi; Gary Mass; Hironori Oka; Alexander Yannotti.
EIN: 133637516

1021
Dallas Basketball Limited

(also known as Dallas Mavericks)
2909 Taylor St.
Dallas, TX 75226-1909 (214) 747-6287

Company URL: http://www.mavs.com
Establishment information: Established in 1980.
Company type: Private company
Business activities: Operates professional basketball club.
Business type (SIC): Commercial sports
Corporate officers: Terdema L. Ussery, Pres. and C.E.O.; Buddy Pittman, Sr. V.P., Human Resources; Floyd Jahner, V.P. and C.F.O.; Steve Letson, V.P., Opers.; George Prokos, V.P., Sales; Paul Monroe, V.P., Mktg. and Comms.; Ronnie Fauss, Cont.
Giving statement: Giving through the Dallas Mavericks Corporate Giving Program and the Dallas Mavericks Foundation.

Dallas Mavericks Corporate Giving Program

c/o Donations/Community Svcs.
2909 Taylor St.
Dallas, TX 75226-1909
FAX: (214) 752-3860; Contact for the Mavs Reading Challenge: Gina Calvert, E-mail: gina.calvert@dallasmavs.com; URL: http://www.nba.com/mavericks/community/community_corner.html

Purpose and activities: The Dallas Mavericks make charitable contributions of memorabilia to nonprofit organizations on a case by case basis. Support is given primarily within a 70-mile radius of the Dallas-Fort Worth, Texas, Metroplex area.
Fields of interest: Elementary school/education; Education, reading; Education; Athletics/sports, basketball; General charitable giving.
Programs:
Academic All-Stars: The Dallas Mavericks, in partnership with Flowserve, honors elementary and middle school students who are either excelling or have made significant improvements between grading periods. The program honors 30 students who receive a Mavs goody bag, 2 tickets to a Mavs game, and an invitation to participate in an Academic All-Star field trip with a Mavs player.
Math Matters to the Mavs: The Dallas Mavericks, in partnership with ExxonMobil, provides Mavs prizes and tickets to students in grades 6 to 8 who create word problems using anything related to the Mavs including player stats, ticket pricing, game attendance, player salary, exercise regime, etc. The six most creative word problems will be selected as the winners, and each student will receive an 8X10 autographed photo and replica jersey of their favorite player, $50 Mavs Ultimate Fan Shop gift card, and two tickets to a Mavs game where they will be recognized on court at halftime.
Mavs Reading Challenge: The Dallas Mavericks annually promotes the value of reading and encourages families and adults to read regularly with youth children through the Mavs Reading Challenge. The two month program is designed to encourage students in grades 2 to 5 to read in their leisure time and prizes are awarded based on the number of minutes a student reads. The participating school that reads the most overall minutes receives pep rally from a Mavericks player.
Measure Up to the Mavs: The Dallas Mavericks, in partnership with ExxonMobil and the Museum of Nature & Science, provides a free 50 minute hands-on science program designed to educate students in grades 4-6 on mechanics and levers as it relates to basketball. Students build catapults and shoot miniature basketballs to compare catapults to the structure of the human arm. The program includes a field trip to the museum or a visit by the museum staff, a curriculum guide tailored to specific ages, and a Mavs item for students to take home. The program is administered by The Museum of Nature & Science.
Teacher Recognition Program: The Dallas Mavericks, in partnership with the UPS Store, awards $2,000 to 10 Metroplex teachers for their hard work and efforts in the classroom.
Type of support: Curriculum development; Donated products; In-kind gifts; Income development.
Geographic limitations: Giving primarily in areas of company operations within a 75-mile radius of the Dallas-Fort Worth, TX, Metroplex area.
Support limitations: No grants for general operating support or sponsorships.
Publications: Application guidelines.
Application information: Applications accepted. Support is limited to 1 contribution per organization during any given year. Proposals should be submitted using organization letterhead. Autographed memorabilia is limited to auction and/or raffle to raise funds for non-profit organizations in the Dallas and Fort Worth area. Organizations receiving support are asked to submit a follow-up report specifying the amount raised by the donation and the amount raised through the fundraising event. The Community Relations Department handles giving. Application form not required.
Applicants should submit the following:
1) name, address and phone number of organization
2) copy of IRS Determination Letter
3) brief history of organization and description of its mission
4) detailed description of project and amount of funding requested
5) contact person
Initial approach: Mail or fax proposal to headquarters; download nomination form and

mail or fax to headquarters for Academic All-Stars and Teacher Recognition Program
Copies of proposal: 1
Deadline(s): 60 days prior to need; Feb. 19 for Academic All-Stars; Mar. 19 for Teacher Recognition Program

Dallas Mavericks Foundation

(formerly The New Mavericks Foundation)
2909 Taylor St.
Dallas, TX 75226-1909 (214) 747-6287
FAX: (214) 752-3860; URL: http://www.mavsfoundation.com

Establishment information: Established in 2000 in TX as successor to the first Dallas Mavericks Foundation, established in 1996.
Donors: The Dallas Mavericks Foundation; Minyard Food Stores, Inc.; Dallas Basketball Ltd.; The Michael Finley Foundation; Once Upon A Time Foundation; Ed Ewing.
Financial data (yr. ended 06/30/11): Assets, $1,956,200 (M); gifts received, $233,214; expenditures, $245,316; qualifying distributions, $216,487; giving activities include $216,487 for grants.
Purpose and activities: The foundation supports programs designed to assist young people through programs stressing education, good health, and skills necessary for their future success.
Fields of interest: Elementary/secondary education; Health care; Youth development Youth.
Geographic limitations: Giving primarily in the metropolitan Dallas/Fort Worth, TX, area.
Support limitations: No support for churches, public or private schools, or national organizations without locally, financially independent chapters. No grants to individuals, or for multi-year support, medical research, travel, salaries, general operating support for established organizations, political campaigns or fundraising events, continuing support of programs lasting more than one year, endowments, administrative costs, advertising or fundraising, or research.
Publications: Application guidelines; Grants list.
Application information: Applications accepted. Application form required. Applicants should submit the following:
1) timetable for implementation and evaluation of project
2) copy of IRS Determination Letter
3) listing of board of directors, trustees, officers and other key people and their affiliations
4) detailed description of project and amount of funding requested
5) copy of current year's organizational budget and/or project budget

Initial approach: Download application form and mail to foundation
Copies of proposal: 15
Board meeting date(s): Sept.
Deadline(s): June 30
Final notification: Sept.

Officers and Trustees:* Terdema L. Ussery*, Pres.; Cheryl Karalla*, Secy.; Floyd Jahner*, Treas.; Brian Cuban; Jeff Cuban; Kim Cuban; Tiffany Stewart Cuban; Gretchen Minyard Williams; Martin Woodall.
EIN: 311767408
Selected grants: The following grants are a representative sample of this grantmaker's funding activity:
$25,000 to Captain Hopes Kids, Dallas, TX, 2011.
$25,000 to CONTACT Crisis Line, Dallas, TX, 2011.
$25,000 to Essilor Vision Foundation, Dallas, TX, 2011.
$25,000 to Irving CARES, Irving, TX, 2011.
$19,288 to Family Place, Dallas, TX, 2011.
$11,075 to Dallas Bethlehem Center, Dallas, TX, 2011.
$10,000 to S. M. Wright Foundation, Dallas, TX, 2011.

1022
Dallas Cowboys Football Club, Ltd.

Cowboys Ctr.
1 Cowboys Pkwy.
Irving, TX 75063 (972) 556-9900

Company URL: http://www.dallascowboys.com
Establishment information: Established in 1960.
Company type: Private company
Business activities: Operates professional football club.
Business type (SIC): Commercial sports
Corporate officers: Jerry Jones, Pres.; Stephen Jones, Exec. V.P. and C.O.O.
Giving statement: Giving through the Dallas Cowboys Football Club, Ltd. Corporate Giving Program and the Gene and Jerry Jones Family/Dallas Cowboys Charities.

Dallas Cowboys Football Club, Ltd. Corporate Giving Program

1 Cowboys Pkwy.
Irving, TX 75063-4924 (972) 556-9959
FAX: (972) 556-9304;
E-mail: crelations@dallascowboys.net; E-mail for NFL Play 60 Challenge: nflplay60challenge@heart.org; Contact for Dallas Cowboys/Gatorade Junior Training Camps: Whitney Brandon, Community Relations, tel.: (972) 556-9955, fax: (972) 556-9918, E-mail: wbrandon@dallascowboys.net; URL: http://www.dallascowboys.com/community/community_home.cfm

Purpose and activities: The Dallas Cowboys make charitable contributions to nonprofit organizations involved with education, obesity, physical fitness, breast cancer, football, and youth development. Support is given primarily in Dallas and Fort Worth, Texas.
Fields of interest: Education; Public health, obesity; Public health, physical fitness; Breast cancer; Athletics/sports, football; Youth development; Salvation Army; Community/economic development.
Programs:

Community Quarterback Award: The Dallas Cowboys, in partnership with the Gene and Jerry Jones Family Charities and the NFL, honors a local volunteer who demonstrates leadership, dedication, and a commitment to bettering the Dallas-Fort Worth community. The award includes a $10,000 grant donated to the recipients nonprofit organization and a pre-game ceremony held during a Dallas Cowboys game. Two charities of the runners-up will receive a $1,500 grant for their charity, a runners-up trophy, and a certificate of apperception.

Cowboys/Gatorade Junior Training Camps: The Dallas Cowboys, in partnership with Gatorade and the Gene and Jerry Jones Family Charities, offers a complimentary football clinic for elementary students ages 7 and 14 as part of the NFL Play 60 program. The JTC features a 25-minute assembly featuring Rowdy, the Cowboys mascot and the JTC staff speaking on S.W.E.A.T., Safety, Will to Win, Energy, Attitude, and Training; and a 60-minute Non-Contact Football Camp featuring 6 football drill stations run by school volunteers and JTC staff.

NFL Play 60 Challenge: Through the NFL Play 60 Challenge, the Dallas Cowboys and the American Heart Association, provides a curriculum-based program that inspires kids to get the recommended 60 minutes of physical activity a day at school and at home. The initiative is designed to combat childhood obesity in Dallas-Fort Worth area middle schools and includes an in-school activity kit created for teachers with curriculum-based activity sheets, learning materials and school promotional materials, and an interactive fitness-focused website for children.

U.S. Army/Dallas Cowboys Coach of the Week: The Dallas Cowboys, in partnership with the U.S. Army and the Gene and Jerry Jones Family Charities, honors 10 Dallas/Fort Worth area high school coaches for high level of service during regular football season. The program is designed to promote the development of youth football and help high schools maintain and upgrade their football programs. The coaches school receives a $2,000 grant; and each coach of the week is recognized during an in-school presentation, are given a one-of-a -kind framed certificate, and is invited along with a guest to attend a Dallas Cowboys vs. Baltimore Ravens game.

Type of support: Curriculum development; Donated products; In-kind gifts.
Geographic limitations: Giving primarily in areas of company operations in the Dallas, TX area.
Publications: Application guidelines.
Application information: Applications accepted. The Community Relations Department handles giving. Application form not required.

Initial approach: Contact headquarters for Dallas Cowboys/Gatorade Junior Training Camps
Copies of proposal: 1
Deadline(s): None

Gene and Jerry Jones Family/Dallas Cowboys Charities

1 Cowboys Pkwy.
Irving, TX 75063-4924 (972) 556-9367
URL: http://www.dallascowboys.com/community/community_jones.cfm

Establishment information: Established in TX as a public charity. Status changed to a company-sponsored foundation in 2006.
Donors: Dallas Cowboys Football Club, Ltd.; Texas Stadium Corp; NFL Charities; NFL Youth Football; Dallas Cowboys Merchandising; Cowboys Wives Association.
Contact: Charlotte Jones Anderson, Pres.
Financial data (yr. ended 12/31/11): Assets, $1,390,231 (M); gifts received, $4,819,875; expenditures, $2,039,281; qualifying distributions, $2,038,372; giving activities include $2,036,677 for grants.
Purpose and activities: The foundation supports organizations involved with arts and culture, education, heart disease, athletics and sports, human services, and Christianity.
Fields of interest: Museums; Museums (art); Performing arts centers; Performing arts, orchestras; Arts; Elementary/secondary education; Libraries (special); Students, sororities/fraternities; Education; Heart & circulatory diseases; Athletics/sports, amateur leagues; Boys & girls clubs; Salvation Army; Children/youth, services; Human services; Christian agencies & churches.
Type of support: General/operating support.
Geographic limitations: Giving primarily in Dallas, TX.
Application information: Applications not accepted. Contributes only to pre-selected organizations.

Officers: Charlotte Jones Anderson*, Pres.; Jerral W. Jones, V.P.; John Stephen Jones*, V.P.; Jerral W. Jones, Jr.*, Secy.; George Mitchell, Treas.
EIN: 752808490
Selected grants: The following grants are a representative sample of this grantmaker's funding activity:
$60,000 to George W. Bush Foundation, Dallas, TX, 2010. For general purpose.
$45,000 to Crystal Charity Ball, Dallas, TX, 2010. For general purpose.
$25,000 to Museum of Nature and Science, Dallas, TX, 2010. For general purpose.
$25,000 to Sweetheart Ball, Dallas, TX, 2010. For general purpose.
$10,000 to American Cancer Society, Dallas, TX, 2010. For general purpose.
$10,000 to Dallas Museum of Art, Dallas, TX, 2010. For general purpose.
$10,000 to Family Gateway, Dallas, TX, 2010. For general purpose.
$10,000 to Family Place, Dallas, TX, 2010. For general purpose.
$5,000 to Elisa Project, Dallas, TX, 2010. For general purpose.
$2,000 to Midlothian High School, Midlothian, TX, 2010. For general purpose.

1023
Dallas Stars, L.P.
2601 Ave. of the Stars
Frisco, TX 75034 (214) 387-5500

Company URL: http://www.dallasstars.com
Establishment information: Established in 1967.
Company type: Subsidiary of a private company
Business activities: Operates professional ice hockey club.
Business type (SIC): Commercial sports
Corporate officers: Thomas O. Hicks, Chair.; James R. Lites, Pres. and C.E.O.; Robert Hutson, Exec. V.P., Finance, and C.F.O.; Geoff Moore, Exec. V.P., Sales and Mktg.; Randy Locey, Exec. V.P., Opers.; Colin Faulkner, Sr. V.P., Mktg.; Daniel Doggendorf, V.P. and C.I.O.; Melissa Embry, Cont.
Board of director: Thomas O. Hicks, Chair.
Giving statement: Giving through the Dallas Stars Corporate Giving Program and the Dallas Stars Foundation, Inc.

Dallas Stars Corporate Giving Program
c/o Community Rels.
2601 Ave. of the Stars
Frisco, TX 75034-9015
FAX: (214) 387-5599;
E-mail: starscommunity@dallasstars.com;
URL: http://stars.nhl.com/club/page.htm?id=39297

Purpose and activities: The Dallas Stars make charitable contributions of memorabilia to nonprofit organizations on a case by case basis. Support is given primarily in Texas.
Fields of interest: Education; Cancer; Cancer, leukemia; Athletics/sports, winter sports; Youth, services; General charitable giving.
Type of support: Donated products; In-kind gifts; Income development.
Geographic limitations: Giving primarily in areas of company operations in TX.
Support limitations: No grants to individuals, or for general operating support.
Publications: Application guidelines.
Application information: Applications accepted. Proposals should be submitted using organization letterhead. Support is limited to 1 contribution per organization during any given year. Application form not required. Applicants should submit the following:
1) name, address and phone number of organization
2) detailed description of project and amount of funding requested

Proposals should indicate the date of the event.
Initial approach: E-mail or fax proposal to headquarters for memorabilia donations
Copies of proposal: 1
Deadline(s): 6 weeks prior to need for memorabilia donations
Final notification: 1 to 2 weeks prior to need for memorabilia donations

Dallas Stars Foundation, Inc.
2601 Ave. of the Stars
Frisco, TX 75034-9015 (214) 387-5500
FAX: (214) 387-5610; URL: http://stars.nhl.com/club/page.htm?id=39286
E-mail address for scholarships: starscommunity@dallasstars.com

Establishment information: Established in 1998 in TX.
Contact: Lora Farris, Exec. Dir.
Financial data (yr. ended 06/30/11): Revenue, $548,631; assets, $818,157 (M); gifts received, $359,834; expenditures, $475,230; program services expenses, $301,017; giving activities include $285,346 for 18 grants (high: $25,000).
Purpose and activities: The foundation provides support to the children of the community so they may lead quality lives and develop into contributing members of society.
Fields of interest: Arts; Children, services; Community/economic development.
Programs:
Bob Gainey Honorary Scholarship: Scholarship in the amount of $1,250 per year for a maximum of $5,000 over four years is awarded to a Metroplex high school senior athlete. Applicant must plan to attend an accredited two- or four-year U.S. college or university as a full-time student. The scholarship is based on academic achievement, community and extracurricular involvement, and financial need.
Dallas Stars Foundation Grant: The organization provides support to local organizations that give aid to the Dallas-area community in youth sports, children's healthcare, family support, and education.
Hockey and Figure Skating Scholarships: Dr. Pepper StarCenter athletes are eligible for hockey and figure skating scholarships. Applicants must exhibit strong academic performance, financial need, involvement in extracurricular and/or community activities, and exemplary conduct during practices, games, and competitions.
Type of support: Scholarships—to individuals.
Geographic limitations: Giving primarily in the Dallas/Fort Worth, TX, area.
Application information: Applications accepted. See web site for additional application guidelines. Application form required. Applicants should submit the following:
1) copy of IRS Determination Letter
2) descriptive literature about organization
3) listing of board of directors, trustees, officers and other key people and their affiliations
4) copy of current year's organizational budget and/or project budget

Initial approach: Download application form and mail to foundation
Board meeting date(s): Quarterly
Deadline(s): May 1
Final notification: Apr. 20
Officers and Directors:* Jeff Cogen, Chair.; Geoff Moore*, Exec. V.P.; Casey Coffman*, Secy.; Robert Hutson*, Treas.; Lora Farris, Exec. Dir.; Carla Rosenberg, Exec. Dir.; Brett Hull; Kristin Reaugh; Rob Scichili; Kelly Turco.
EIN: 752780401

1024
Damar Machine Company, Inc.
14767 172nd Dr., S.E.
Monroe, WA 98272-1033 (360) 794-4448

Company URL: http://www.damarmachine.com
Establishment information: Established in 1973.
Company type: Subsidiary of a foreign company
Business activities: Manufactures industrial metal parts.
Business type (SIC): Industrial and commercial machinery and computer equipment
Financial profile for 2011: Number of employees, 225
Corporate officers: M. Thomas Kroon, Chair. and C.E.O.; John Gavaert, C.O.O.and C.F.O.
Board of director: M. Thomas Kroon, Chair.
Giving statement: Giving through the Kedge Foundation.

Kedge Foundation
31620 23rd Ave., S., No. 218
Federal Way, WA 98003

Establishment information: Established in 2000 in WA.
Donor: Damar Machine Co., Inc.
Financial data (yr. ended 12/31/11): Assets, $31,677 (M); gifts received, $100,000; expenditures, $80,787; qualifying distributions, $79,583; giving activities include $79,583 for grants.
Purpose and activities: The foundation supports food banks and organizations involved with education, multiple sclerosis, housing, and military and veterans.
Fields of interest: Health care; Human services; Community/economic development.
Type of support: Employee-related scholarships; General/operating support; Scholarship funds.
Application information: Applications not accepted. Unsolicited requests for funds not accepted.
Trustees: Gwenann Kroon; M. Thomas Kroon; Bonnie K. Roulstone; Douglas R. Roulstone.
EIN: 916506503

1026
Dana Holding Corporation
3939 Technology Dr.
Maumee, OH 43537 (419) 535-4500
FAX: (419) 887-5961

Company URL: http://www.dana.com
Establishment information: Established in 1904.
Company type: Public company
Company ticker symbol and exchange: DAN/NYSE
Business activities: Manufactures automotive parts and industrial components and systems.
Business type (SIC): Motor vehicles and equipment; gaskets, packing and sealing devices, and rubber hose and belting; metal products/fabricated; machinery/general industry; machinery/industrial and commercial
Financial profile for 2012: Assets, $5,144,000,000; sales volume, $7,224,000,000;

pre-tax net income, $364,000,000; expenses, $6,860,000,000; liabilities, $3,301,000,000
Fortune 1000 ranking: 2012—356th in revenues, 471st in profits, and 584th in assets
Corporate officers: Keith E. Wandell, Chair.; Roger J. Wood, Pres. and C.E.O.; William G. Quigley, Exec. V.P. and C.F.O.; Jeffrey Bowen, C.A.O.; Marc S. Levin, Sr. V.P., Genl. Counsel, and Secy.
Board of directors: Keith E. Wandell, Chair.; Mark T. Gallogly; Virginia A. Kamsky; Terrence J. Keating; Brandt F. McKee; Joseph C. Muscari; Mark A. Schulz; Steve Schwarzwaelder; Richard F. Wallman; Roger J. Wood
Plant: Bristol, VA
International operations: Argentina; Australia; Bermuda; Brazil; British Virgin Islands; Canada; China; Colombia; France; Germany; Hong Kong; Hungary; India; Ireland; Italy; Luxembourg; Mauritius; Mexico; South Africa; South Korea; Spain; Switzerland; Taiwan; Thailand; United Kingdom; Uruguay; Venezuela
Giving statement: Giving through the Dana Holding Corporation Contributions Program and the Dana Corporation Foundation.
Company EIN: 261531856

Dana Corporation Foundation

1 Village Center Dr.
Van Buren Township, MI 48111
Application address: Attn: Joe Stancati, P.O. Box 1000, Maumee, OH 43537, tel.: (419) 887-5141

Establishment information: Incorporated in 1956 in OH.
Donor: Dana Corporation.
Contact: Joe Stancati, Secy.
Financial data (yr. ended 03/31/12): Assets, $317,293 (M); gifts received, $200,000; expenditures, $351,119; qualifying distributions, $345,430; giving activities include $345,430 for grants.
Purpose and activities: The foundation supports organizations involved with arts and culture, education, cancer, food distribution, and human services.
Fields of interest: Museums (art); Performing arts, theater; Performing arts, orchestras; Arts; Education; Cancer; Food distribution, meals on wheels; Boys & girls clubs; Youth development, business; American Red Cross; Children/youth, services; Human services; United Ways and Federated Giving Programs.
Program:
Employee Matching Gifts: The foundation matches contributions made by employees, directors, and retirees of Dana to educational institutions from $25 to $5,000 per contributor, per year.
Type of support: Annual campaigns; Building/renovation; Capital campaigns; Continuing support; Emergency funds; Employee matching gifts; Employee-related scholarships; Equipment; General/operating support.
Geographic limitations: Giving primarily in areas of company operations in KY and OH.
Support limitations: No grants to individuals (except for the Driveshaft Scholarship Fund), or for fellowships; no loans.
Application information: Applications accepted. Application form not required.
Initial approach: Proposal
Copies of proposal: 1
Board meeting date(s): Apr., Aug., and Dec. or May, Sept., and Jan.
Deadline(s): None
Officers and Directors:* Robert Marcin*, Pres.; Ralph Than*, V.P.; Joe Stancati*, Secy.; Rick Dyer, Treas.; Cindy Simon, Treas.; David Benson.
Number of staff: 1 part-time professional.
EIN: 346544909
Selected grants: The following grants are a representative sample of this grantmaker's funding activity:
$50,000 to Toledo Museum of Art, Toledo, OH, 2011.
$50,000 to United Way of Greater Toledo, Toledo, OH, 2011.
$20,000 to Toledo Museum of Art, Toledo, OH, 2011.
$10,000 to Junior Achievement of Northwestern Ohio, Toledo, OH, 2011.
$10,000 to Toledo Symphony, Toledo, OH, 2011.
$4,500 to Coyote Hill Christian Childrens Home, Harrisburg, MO, 2011.
$3,500 to United Fund of Cumberland County, Crossville, TN, 2011.
$3,250 to Genesis House, Cookeville, TN, 2011.
$2,000 to United Way of West Tennessee, Jackson, TN, 2011.
$1,000 to Toledo Day Nursery, Toledo, OH, 2011.

1027
Danaher Corporation

2200 Pennsylvania Ave., N.W., Ste. 800W
Washington, DC 20037 (202) 828-0850
FAX: (202) 828-0860

Company URL: http://www.danaher.com
Establishment information: Established in 1969.
Company type: Public company
Company ticker symbol and exchange: DHR/NYSE
Business activities: Operates a science and technology company that designs, manufactures, and markets products and services to professional, medical, industrial, and commercial customers.
Business type (SIC): Laboratory apparatus; electrical industrial apparatus; communications equipment; medical instruments and supplies
Financial profile for 2012: Number of employees, 63,000; assets, $32,941,000,000; sales volume, $18,260,400,000; pre-tax net income, $3,010,800,000; expenses, $15,095,300,000; liabilities, $13,924,500,000
Fortune 1000 ranking: 2012—152nd in revenues, 83rd in profits, and 170th in assets
Forbes 2000 ranking: 2012—503rd in sales, 237th in profits, and 685th in assets
Corporate officers: Steven M. Rales, Chair.; H. Lawrence Culp, Jr., Pres. and C.E.O.; Daniel L. Comas, Exec. V.P. and C.F.O.; Robert S. Lutz, Sr. V.P. and C.A.O.; Jonathan P. Graham, Sr. V.P. and Genl. Counsel; James H. Ditkoff, Sr. V.P., Finance; Angela S. Lalor, Sr. V.P., Human Resources
Board of directors: Steven M. Rales, Chair.; Mortimer M. Caplin; H. Lawrence Culp, Jr.; Donald J. Ehrlich; Linda P. Hefner; Teri List-Stoll; Walter G. Lohr, Jr.; Mitchell P. Rales; John T. Schwieters; Alan G. Spoon; Elias A. Zerhouni, M.D.
Subsidiaries: ABEK, L.L.C., Unionville, CT; ACME-Cleveland Corp., Pepper Pike, OH; American Precision Industries, Inc., Amherst, NY; American Thermocraft Corp., Somerset, NJ; Anderson Instrument Company, Inc., Fultonville, NY; Api Development Corp., Worcester, MA; Aquafine Corp., Valencia, CA; Armstrong Tools, Inc., Lancaster, PA; Assembly Technologies, L.L.C., Chattanooga, TN; Attachments International, Inc., San Mateo, CA; Aviation Mobility, L.L.C., Charlotte, NC; Ball Screws and Actuators Company, Inc., San Jose, CA; Beckman Coulter, Inc., Brea, CA; ChemTreat, Inc., Ashland, VA; Comark Instruments, Inc., Portland, OR; Danaher Foundation, Cleveland, OH; Danaher Motion, L.L.C., Ronkonkoma, NY; Danaher Motion Technology, L.L.C., Mayfield Heights, OH; DCI Consolidated Industries, Inc., Raleigh, NC; Delta Consolidated Industries, Inc., Sparks, MD; Dental Equipment, L.L.C., Charlotte, NC; DEXIS, L.L.C., Alpharetta, GA; DH Holdings Corp., Washington, DC; Diesel Engine Retarders, Inc., Wilmington, DE; DMG Partners, Fort Collins, CO; Dolan-Jenner Industries, Inc., Lawrence, MA; Dynapar Corp., Gurnee, IL; Easco Hand Tools Inc., Simsbury, CT; ELE International, L.L.C., Pelham, AL; EXE International Inc., Princeton, NJ; FJ 900, Inc., Washington, DC; Fluke Corp., Everett, WA; Fluke Electronics Corp., Everett, WA; G&L Motion Control Inc., Fond du Lac, WI; Gems Sensors Inc., Plainville, CT; Gendex Corp., Des Plaines, IL; Gilbarco Inc., Greensboro, NC; Great Plains Meter, Inc., Aurora, NE; Hach Company, Loveland, CO; Hach Ultra Analytics Inc., Grants Pass, OR; Hart Scientific, L.L.C., American Fork, UT; Hawk IR International, Inc., Charlotte, NC; Hennessy Industries, Inc., La Vergne, TN; Hennessy Industries Inc., La Vergne, TN; Jacobs Vehicle Systems Inc., Bloomfield, CT; Kollmorgen Corporation, Waltham, MA; Matco Tools Corp., Stow, OH; Pacific Scientific Co., Newport Beach, CA; Veeder-Root Co., Slimsbury, CT; Western Pacific Industries Inc., Terryville, CT
Plant: Gurnee, IL
International operations: Argentina; Australia; Austria; Barbados; Belgium; Brazil; Bulgaria; Canada; Cayman Islands; Chile; China; Cyprus; Czech Republic; Denmark; Dominican Republic; Estonia; Finland; France; Georgia (Republic of); Germany; Greece; Hong Kong; Hungary; India; Ireland; Israel; Italy; Jamaica; Japan; Latvia; Luxembourg; Malaysia; Mauritius; Mexico; Moldova; Netherlands; Netherlands Antilles; New Zealand; Norway; Poland; Portugal; Russia; Scotland; Singapore; Slovakia; Slovenia; South Africa; Spain; Sweden; Switzerland; Taiwan; Thailand; Turkey; United Kingdom; Uruguay; Venezuela; Vietnam
Giving statement: Giving through the Danaher Corporation Contributions Program and the Danaher Foundation.
Company EIN: 591995548

Danaher Foundation

6095 Parkland Blvd., Ste. 310
Mayfield Heights, OH 44124-6140

Establishment information: Established in 1952 in IL.
Donors: Joslyn Corp.; Steven M. Rales.
Financial data (yr. ended 12/31/11): Assets, $761,033 (M); gifts received, $1,000,151; expenditures, $376,992; qualifying distributions, $338,402; giving activities include $338,402 for grants.
Purpose and activities: The foundation supports organizations involved with arts and culture, higher education, health, cancer, kidney disease, international relief, philanthropy, and women.
Fields of interest: Media, print publishing; Visual arts; Arts; Higher education; Health care; Cancer; Cancer, leukemia; Kidney diseases; International relief; Philanthropy/voluntarism Women.
Type of support: General/operating support.
Geographic limitations: Giving primarily in areas of company operations, with emphasis on Washington, DC, MD, PA, and VA.
Support limitations: No grants to individuals.
Application information: Applications not accepted. Contributes only to pre-selected organizations.
Officers and Directors:* Robert S. Lutz*, Pres.; James F. O'Reilly, V.P. and Treas.; Laurence S. Smith, V.P.
EIN: 366042871

Selected grants: The following grants are a representative sample of this grantmaker's funding activity:
$150,000 to American Red Cross National Headquarters, Washington, DC, 2011.
$37,260 to Network for Good, Bethesda, MD, 2011.
$13,900 to National Kidney Foundation of the National Capital Area, Washington, DC, 2011.
$10,000 to Boys and Girls Clubs of Greater Washington, Washington, DC, 2011.
$5,000 to California State University at Northridge Foundation, Northridge, CA, 2011.
$5,000 to National Braille Press, Boston, MA, 2011.
$2,842 to Susan G. Komen for the Cure, Dallas, TX, 2011.
$2,400 to Washington Humane Society, Washington, DC, 2011.

1028
John W. Danforth Company

300 Colvin Woods Pkwy.
Tonawanda, NY 14150-6976
(716) 832-1940

Company URL: http://www.jwdanforth.com
Establishment information: Established in 1884.
Company type: Private company
Business activities: Provides contract mechanical services.
Business type (SIC): Contractors/plumbing, heating, and air-conditioning; contractors/miscellaneous special trade
Corporate officers: Kevin G. Reilly, Chair. and C.E.O.; Patrick J. Reilly, Pres.
Board of director: Kevin G. Reilly, Chair.
Giving statement: Giving through the John W. Danforth Company Foundation, Inc.

John W. Danforth Company Foundation, Inc.

300 Colvin Woods Pkwy.
Tonawanda, NY 14150-6976 (716) 832-1940

Establishment information: Established in NY.
Donor: John W. Danforth Co.
Contact: Kevin G. Reilly, Dir.
Financial data (yr. ended 12/31/11): Assets, $142,399 (M); gifts received, $181,438; expenditures, $213,992; qualifying distributions, $213,767; giving activities include $213,767 for grants.
Purpose and activities: The foundation supports organizations involved with education, health, cancer, Krabbe disease research, recreation, human services, community development, and Judaism.
Fields of interest: Higher education; Education; Health care; Cancer; Medical research; Athletics/sports, soccer; Athletics/sports, winter sports; Recreation; Human services; Community/economic development; United Ways and Federated Giving Programs; Jewish agencies & synagogues.
Type of support: General/operating support.
Geographic limitations: Giving primarily in the western NY area.
Support limitations: No grants to individuals.
Application information: Applications accepted. Application form not required. Applicants should submit the following:
1) detailed description of project and amount of funding requested
Initial approach: Proposal
Deadline(s): None
Directors: Emmitt Reilly; Kevin G. Reilly; Patrick Reilly.
EIN: 166027290
Selected grants: The following grants are a representative sample of this grantmaker's funding activity:
$10,600 to National Kidney Foundation, New York, NY, 2010.

1029
Danis Building Construction Company

3233 Newmark Dr.
Miamisburg, OH 45342 (937) 228-1225

Company URL: http://www.danisbuilding.com
Establishment information: Established in 1916.
Company type: Private company
Business activities: Provides nonresidential general contract construction services.
Business type (SIC): Contractors/general nonresidential building
Corporate officers: Tom Danis, Chair. and C.E.O.; Tom Hammelrath, Pres.; Mark R. Graeser, V.P., Mktg.; Tim Carlson, Cont.
Board of director: Tom Danis, Chair.
Giving statement: Giving through the Danis Foundation, Inc.

The Danis Foundation, Inc.

3233 Newmark Dr.
Miamisburg, OH 45342-5422

Establishment information: Established in 1957 in OH.
Donor: Danis Building Construction Co.
Contact: Karen Applegarth
Financial data (yr. ended 12/31/11): Assets, $621,400 (M); gifts received, $20,000; expenditures, $111,834; qualifying distributions, $108,425; giving activities include $108,425 for 23 grants (high: $32,130; low: $473).
Purpose and activities: The foundation supports food banks and organizations involved with education, health, heart disease, and human services.
Fields of interest: Higher education; Education; Health care, clinics/centers; Heart & circulatory diseases; Food banks; Salvation Army; Human services.
Type of support: Building/renovation; Capital campaigns; Employee-related scholarships; General/operating support; Program development.
Geographic limitations: Giving primarily in the Dayton, OH, area.
Application information: Applications accepted.
Initial approach: Contact foundation for application information for general grants
Officers: John Danis, Pres. and Secy.-Treas.; Thomas P. Hammelrath, V.P.
Number of staff: 1 part-time professional.
EIN: 316041012

1030
The Dannon Company, Inc.

100 Hillside Ave., Ste.3
White Plains, NY 10603 (914) 872-8400

Company URL: http://www.dannon.com
Establishment information: Established in 1919.
Company type: Subsidiary of a foreign company
Business activities: Produces yogurt.
Business type (SIC): Dairy products
Financial profile for 2010: Number of employees, 200
Corporate officers: Gustavo Valle, Pres. and C.E.O.; Timothy Weaver, C.I.O.; Lucho Lopez-May, Sr. V.P., Sales; Sergio Fuster, Sr. V.P., Mktg.; Antoine Remy, V.P., Finance and C.F.O.; Tony Cicio, V.P., Human Resources; Fernando Lafuente, V.P., Opers.
Plants: Naperville, IL; Minster, OH; Arlington, Fort Worth, TX; West Jordan, UT
Giving statement: Giving through the Dannon Company, Inc. Corporate Giving Program and the Dannon Research Institute, Inc.

The Dannon Company, Inc. Corporate Giving Program

c/o Dannon Donation Request
100 Hillside Ave.
White Plains, NY 10603
FAX: (610) 231-8597; E-mail for Dannon Next Generation Nutrition Grant: DannonNutritionGrant@dannon.com

Purpose and activities: As a complement to its foundation, The Dannon Company also makes charitable contributions to nonprofit organizations directly. Special emphasis is directed toward programs that nurture healthy eating habits among children or promote children's nutrition education. Support is given in areas of company operations in New York, Ohio, Texas, and Utah.
Fields of interest: Child development, education; Nutrition; General charitable giving.
Programs:
Dannon Children of Employees Scholarship Program: The Dannon Company awards 15 scholarships of $1,500 each to the children of its employees to help with costs at any accredited two or four-year college, university or vocational school.
Dannon Next Generation Nutrition Grant: The Dannon Company annually awards single grants of $30,000 to programs nurturing healthy eating habits among children in each the four areas of company operations. To qualify, organizations must need funding for a current nutrition education program for children up to age 18 or be able to launch such an initiative.
Partnership in Giving: The Dannon Company matches contributions made by its part-time and full-time employees to nonprofit organizations on a one-for-one basis from $25 to $5,000 per employee, per year.
Type of support: Donated products; Employee matching gifts; Employee volunteer services; Employee-related scholarships; General/operating support.
Geographic limitations: Giving in areas of company operations in Westchester County, NY, Auglaize, Darke, Mercer, and Shelby counties, OH, Tarrant County, TX, and Salt Lake County, UT.
Support limitations: No support for non-501(c)(3) organizations, religious organizations not of direct benefit to the entire community, political, fraternal, veteran, membership, or discriminatory organizations, sports teams, or film or video projects. No grants to individuals, or for capital campaigns, construction or renovation projects, advertisements or marketing projects, raffles, sporting events, testimonial dinners, or endowments, professorships or scholarships sponsored by academic institutions.
Publications: Application guidelines.
Application information: Applications accepted. Application form required.
Initial approach: Download application form and e-mail or fax to headquarters

Deadline(s): 60 days prior to event for product donations
Final notification: 2 weeks

The Dannon Research Institute, Inc.

c/o Dannon Tax Dept.
100 Hillside Ave.
White Plains, NY 10603-2861 (914) 872-8578
E-mail: dannon.institute@dannon.com; URL: http://www.dannon-institute.org/

Establishment information: Established in 1996 in DE and NY; status changed to company-sponsored operating foundation in 2004.
Donor: The Dannon Co., Inc.
Financial data (yr. ended 12/31/11): Assets, $175,041 (M); gifts received, $474,887; expenditures, $536,396; qualifying distributions, $413,515; giving activities include $10,000 for 2 grants (high: $5,000; low: $5,000) and $460,245 for 4 foundation-administered programs.
Purpose and activities: The foundation supports programs designed to promote nutrition. Special emphasis is directed toward children's nutrition and fostering the growth of tomorrow's leaders in the field of nutrition.
Fields of interest: Health care; Nutrition Children.
Type of support: General/operating support; Program development; Research; Sponsorships.
Geographic limitations: Giving on a national basis.
Support limitations: No grants to individuals.
Application information: Applications not accepted. Contributes only to pre-selected organizations.
Officers and Directors:* Virginia A. Stallings, M.D.*, Pres.; Douglas Heimmburger, M.D., V.P.; Gustavo Valle, V.P.; Antoine Remy*, Treas.; Philippe Caradec; Eileen T. Kennedy; Leslie Lytle, Ph.D.
EIN: 133889717

1017
D'Annunzio & Sons, Inc.

136 Central Ave., Ste. 102
Clark, NJ 07066-1142 (732) 574-1300
FAX: (732) 574-1244

Company URL: http://www.dannunziocorp.com/
Establishment information: Established in 1981.
Company type: Private company
Business activities: Operates construction company.
Business type (SIC): Construction/highway and street (except elevated)
Corporate officers: Michael D'Annunzio, Pres.; James D'Annunzio, Treas.; Robert McMaster, Cont.
Giving statement: Giving through the D'Annunzio Family Foundation, Inc.

D'Annunzio Family Foundation, Inc.

136 Central Ave.
Clark, NJ 07066-1142 (732) 574-1300

Establishment information: Established in 2007 in NJ.
Donor: D'Annunzio & Sons, Inc.
Contact: Michael A. D'Annunzio, Pres.
Financial data (yr. ended 12/31/11): Assets, $4,378 (M); expenditures, $0; qualifying distributions, $0.
Purpose and activities: Scholarship awards to family members of a deceased or injured construction worker.
Type of support: Scholarships—to individuals.
Geographic limitations: Giving primarily in PA.
Application information: Applications accepted. Application form not required.
Initial approach: Proposal
Deadline(s): None
Officers and Trustees:* Michael A. D'Annunzio*, Pres.; Joseph P. D'Annunzio*, V.P.; Stephen D. D'Annunzio*, Secy.; James J. D'Annunzio, Treas.
EIN: 352305027

1025
Dan's Supreme Supermarkets, Inc.

474 Fulton Ave.
Hempstead, NY 11550-4101
(516) 483-2400

Establishment information: Established in 1948.
Company type: Subsidiary of a cooperative
Business activities: Operates grocery stores.
Business type (SIC): Groceries—retail
Corporate officers: Donald Gross, Chair.; Richard Grobman, Pres. and C.E.O.; Steve Decarlo, C.O.O.; Sam Cardiello, C.F.O. and Cont.; Dodie Redman, C.I.O.
Board of director: Donald Gross, Chair.
Giving statement: Giving through the Donald & Linda Gross Foundation, Inc.

Donald & Linda Gross Foundation, Inc.

c/o Dans Supreme Supermarkets Inc.
474 Fulton Ave.
Hempstead, NY 11550-4134

Establishment information: Established in 1996 in NY.
Donor: Dan's Supreme Supermarkets, Inc.
Financial data (yr. ended 12/31/11): Assets, $828,725 (M); expenditures, $37,138; qualifying distributions, $36,605; giving activities include $36,605 for 3 grants (high: $23,455; low: $6,000).
Purpose and activities: The foundation supports Jewish federated giving programs and organizations involved with other areas.
Fields of interest: Jewish federated giving programs; General charitable giving.
Type of support: General/operating support.
Geographic limitations: Giving primarily in NY.
Support limitations: No grants to individuals.
Application information: Applications not accepted. Unsolicited requests for funds not accepted.
Directors: Donald Gross; Kenneth Gross; Linda Gross.
EIN: 113352790

1031
Dansko, Inc.

8 Federal Rd.
West Grove, PA 19390 (610) 869-8335

Company URL: http://www.dansko.com
Establishment information: Established in 1990.
Company type: Private company
Business activities: Operates footwear company.
Business type (SIC): Apparel, piece goods, and notions—wholesale
Corporate officers: Amanda Cabot, C.E.O.; Mimi Curry, C.O.O.; James Fox, C.F.O.
Giving statement: Giving through the Dansko Foundation, Inc.

The Dansko Foundation, Inc.

8 Federal Rd.
West Grove, PA 19390-9182

Establishment information: Established in 2002 in PA.
Donor: Dansko, LLC.
Contact: Dave Murphy, Pres.
Financial data (yr. ended 12/31/11): Assets, $985,578 (M); gifts received, $368,900; expenditures, $91,679; qualifying distributions, $91,288; giving activities include $91,288 for grants.
Fields of interest: Animals/wildlife; Health organizations; Human services.
Application information: Applications accepted. Application form required.
Initial approach: Proposal
Deadline(s): None
Officers: David Murphy, Pres.; Nicole Addis, Secy.; Jamey Mullin, Treas.
Directors: Jessica Brown; Wendy Covington; Philomena Curry; Holly Davies; Tara Eggers; Richard Hull; Tanya Mackeand; Marc Vettori.
EIN: 562306394

1032
Darden Restaurants, Inc.

1000 Darden Center Dr.
PO Box 695011
Orlando, FL 32809-4634 (407) 245-4000

Company URL: http://www.darden.com
Establishment information: Established in 1938.
Company type: Public company
Company ticker symbol and exchange: DRI/NYSE
International Securities Identification Number: US2371941053
Business activities: Operates restaurants.
Business type (SIC): Restaurants and drinking places
Financial profile for 2012: Number of employees, 180,000; assets, $5,944,200,000; sales volume, $7,998,700,000; pre-tax net income, $638,000,000; expenses, $7,360,700,000; liabilities, $4,102,200,000
Fortune 1000 ranking: 2012—328th in revenues, 346th in profits, and 543rd in assets
Forbes 2000 ranking: 2012—1065th in sales, 1163rd in profits, and 1674th in assets
Corporate officers: Clarence Otis, Jr., Chair. and C.E.O.; Andrew H. Madsen, Pres. and C.O.O.; C. Bradford Richmond, Sr. V.P. and C.F.O.; Patti Reilly-White, Sr. V.P. and C.I.O.; Teresa Sebastian, Sr. V.P., Genl. Counsel, and Secy.; Dave Lothrop, Sr. V.P. and Corp. Cont.; Ronald Bojalad, Sr. V.P., Human Resources
Board of directors: Clarence Otis, Jr., Chair.; Michael W. Barnes; Leonard L. Berry, Ph.D.; Christopher J. Fraleigh; Victoria D. Harker; David H. Hughes; Charles A. Ledsinger, Jr.; William M. Lewis, Jr.; Connie Mack III; Andrew H. Madsen; Michael D. Rose; Maria A. Sastre; William S. Simon
Subsidiary: GMRI, Inc., Orlando, FL
Giving statement: Giving through the Darden Restaurants, Inc. Corporate Giving Program and the Darden Restaurants, Inc. Foundation.
Company EIN: 593305930

Darden Restaurants, Inc. Corporate Giving Program

P.O. Box 695011
Orlando, FL 32869-5011 (407) 245-4000
E-mail: dardeninthecommunity@darden.com;
URL: http://www.generationcommitment.com/

Purpose and activities: As a complement to its foundation, Darden also makes charitable contributions to nonprofit organizations directly. Support is given primarily in areas of company operations in the U.S. and Canada.
Fields of interest: Higher education; Education; Environment, natural resources; Food services.
Type of support: Employee volunteer services; General/operating support.
Geographic limitations: Giving primarily in areas of company operations in the U.S. and Canada.
Support limitations: No support for discriminatory organizations.
Publications: Corporate giving report.
Application information: Applications accepted. Application information will be available on the company's website in the fall. Questions should be e-mailed with "Restaurants Community Grants" in the subject line.

Darden Restaurants, Inc. Foundation

P.O. Box 695011
Orlando, FL 32869-5011 (407) 245-5366
FAX: (407) 245-4462;
E-mail: communityaffairs@darden.com; URL: http://www.darden.com/commitment/community.asp

Establishment information: Established in 1995 in FL.
Donor: Darden Restaurants, Inc.
Financial data (yr. ended 05/29/11): Assets, $2,965,025 (M); gifts received, $408; expenditures, $5,673,006; qualifying distributions, $5,669,309; giving activities include $5,669,309 for 165 grants (high: $693,000; low: $100).
Purpose and activities: The foundation supports organizations involved with arts and culture, education, the environment, animal welfare, hunger, and human services.
Fields of interest: Performing arts, ballet; Arts; Education, fund raising/fund distribution; Secondary school/education; Higher education; Education, services; Education; Environment, natural resources; Environment, water resources; Environment, land resources; Environmental education; Environment; Animal welfare; Food services; Food banks; Recreation, parks/playgrounds; Boys & girls clubs; American Red Cross; Children/youth, services; Human services; United Ways and Federated Giving Programs.
Programs:

Access to Postsecondary Education: Recipe for Success: The foundation supports programs designed to positively impact the educational prospects of underserved youth ages 14 to 18 through access to the tools and information needed to pursue higher education.

Darden Restaurants Community Grant Program: The foundation, in partnership with every restaurant in the Darden family, awards $1,000 grants to nonprofit organizations in its local community. The program supports access to postsecondary education, preservation of natural resource, and hunger.

Education Gift Matching Program: The foundation matches contributions made by employees of Darden Restaurants to nonprofit organizations involved with education.

Good Neighbor Grants: The foundation supports organizations involved with arts, education, and social services and organizations based in Central Florida; and supports local food banks in communities across the United States.

Preservation of Natural Resources: The foundation supports programs designed protect wildlife; restore and preserve ecosystems and natural resources; and teach environmental sustainability.
Type of support: Conferences/seminars; Employee matching gifts; Employee volunteer services; General/operating support; In-kind gifts; Matching/challenge support; Program development; Scholarship funds.
Geographic limitations: Giving primarily in areas of company operations, with some emphasis on central FL; giving also to national organizations.
Support limitations: No support for discriminatory organizations, religious organizations not of direct benefit to the entire community, or political, lobbying, anti-business, international, or disease-specific organizations, fraternities, or sororities. No grants to individuals, or for event sponsorships, health-related funding, national conferences, capital campaigns, travel, athletic team sponsorships or scholarships, fundraising, galas, benefits, dinners, or sporting events, goodwill advertising, souvenir journals, or dinner programs.
Publications: Application guidelines; Corporate giving report.
Application information: Applications accepted. Organizations receiving support of $5,000 or more are asked to submit a grant report. Application form required. Applicants should submit the following:
1) timetable for implementation and evaluation of project
2) how project will be sustained once grantmaker support is completed
3) qualifications of key personnel
4) statement of problem project will address
5) name, address and phone number of organization
6) copy of IRS Determination Letter
7) brief history of organization and description of its mission
8) geographic area to be served
9) copy of most recent annual report/audited financial statement/990
10) how project's results will be evaluated or measured
11) listing of board of directors, trustees, officers and other key people and their affiliations
12) detailed description of project and amount of funding requested
13) contact person
14) copy of current year's organizational budget and/or project budget
15) listing of additional sources and amount of support

Initial approach: Complete online application form
Copies of proposal: 1
Board meeting date(s): Feb., May, Sept., and Nov.
Deadline(s): Jan. 1, Apr. 1, July 1, and Oct. 1
Final notification: 30 days following quarterly board meeting

Officers and Trustees:* Clarence Otis, Jr.*, Chair. and Pres.; Robert S. McAdam*, V.P.; Bradford C. Richmond, Treas.; Laurie Burns; Mary Darden; Tom Gathers; Valerie L. Insignares; Andrew H. Madsen; Teresa Sebastian.
Number of staff: 1 full-time professional.
EIN: 593332929
Selected grants: The following grants are a representative sample of this grantmaker's funding activity:
$693,000 to College Summit, Washington, DC, 2011. For Recipe for Success.
$545,000 to Boys and Girls Clubs of America, National Headquarters, Atlanta, GA, 2011. For Recipe for Success.
$500,000 to Dr. Phillips Center for the Performing Arts, Orlando, FL, 2011. For Good Neighbor.
$500,000 to Second Harvest Food Bank of Central Florida, Orlando, FL, 2011. For Good Neighbor.
$350,518 to United Way, Heart of Florida, Orlando, FL, 2011. For Good Neighbor.
$230,639 to American Red Cross National Headquarters, Washington, DC, 2011. For Good Neighbor.
$50,000 to Boys and Girls Clubs of Central Florida, Orlando, FL, 2011. For Good Neighbor.
$50,000 to Orlando Philharmonic Orchestra, Orlando, FL, 2011. For Good Neighbor.
$30,000 to Coalition for the Homeless of Central Florida, Orlando, FL, 2011. For Good Neighbor.
$3,000 to Indiana University of Pennsylvania, Indiana, PA, 2011. For education gift matching.

1033
Dart Container Corporation

500 Hogsback Rd.
Mason, MI 48854 (517) 676-3800
FAX: (517) 676-3883

Company URL: http://www.dartcontainer.com
Establishment information: Established in 1937.
Company type: Private company
Business activities: Produces cups, lids, dinnerware, and cutlery; manufactures foam products and containers.
Business type (SIC): Paperboard containers
Financial profile for 2010: Number of employees, 1,250
Corporate officers: William A. Dart, Chair.; Robert C. Dart, C.E.O.; Kenneth B. Dart, Pres.; James D. Lammers, V.P., Admin. and Genl. Counsel
Board of director: William A. Dart, Chair.
Offices: Corona, Lodi, CA; Plant City, FL; Lithonia, GA; North Aurora, IL; Horse Cave, KY; Mason, MI; Quitman, MS; Randleman, NC; Leola, PA; Waxahachie, TX; Tumwater, WA
International operations: Argentina; Australia; Canada; Mexico; United Kingdom
Giving statement: Giving through the Robert C. Dart Foundation.

Robert C. Dart Foundation

500 Hogsback Rd.
Mason, MI 48854-9541

Establishment information: Established in 2006 in MI.
Donors: Robert C. Dart; Dart Container Corporation; Dart Container Sales Co., LLC; Dart Container Corporation of Georgia; Dart Container Corporation of Kentucky.
Financial data (yr. ended 10/31/11): Assets, $28,308,488 (M); gifts received, $12,000,000; expenditures, $2,207,081; qualifying distributions, $2,207,081; giving activities include $2,207,000 for 2 grants (high: $2,000,000; low: $207,000).
Purpose and activities: The foundation supports the Dart Foundation in Mason, Michigan.
Fields of interest: Foundations (private grantmaking); General charitable giving.
Type of support: General/operating support.
Geographic limitations: Giving limited to Mason, MI.
Support limitations: No grants to individuals.
Application information: Applications not accepted. Contributes only to a pre-selected organization.
Officers and Director: Robert C. Dart, Pres. and Treas.; James D. Lammers, Secy.; Ariane Dart.
EIN: 205973757

1034
Dart Energy Corporation
600 Dart Rd.
P.O. Box 177
Mason, MI 48854-9327 (517) 676-2900

Company URL: http://www.dartenergy.com
Establishment information: Established in 1976.
Company type: Private company
Business activities: Conducts crude oil and natural gas exploration and production activities.
Business type (SIC): Extraction/oil and gas
Financial profile for 2010: Number of employees, 50; assets, $107,392,000; liabilities, $6,926,000
Corporate officers: Phil Leece, Pres.; Jim Weigand, C.F.O.
Subsidiary: Beckman Production Services, Inc., Kalkaska, MI
Giving statement: Giving through the Dart Energy Foundation, Inc.

The Dart Energy Foundation, Inc.
600 Dart Rd.
Mason, MI 48854-1077 (517) 676-2900
URL: http://www.dartenergyfoundation.org/

Establishment information: Established in 2006 in MI.
Contact: Joanne Wiliams, Secy.
Financial data (yr. ended 12/31/11): Assets, $1,403,978 (M); expenditures, $85,298; qualifying distributions, $37,754; giving activities include $37,754 for 4 grants (high: $30,000; low: $754).
Purpose and activities: The foundation supports organizations involved with education, employment training, housing development, sports, and human services.
Fields of interest: Higher education; Education; Employment, training; Housing/shelter, development; Athletics/sports, amateur leagues; Children/youth, services; Human services.
Program:
Sons and Daughters Scholarship Program: The foundation awards scholarships to children of employees of Dart Energy. The scholarships are for college or vocational school programs. The program is administered by Scholarship America.
Type of support: Employee-related scholarships; General/operating support; Scholarship funds.
Geographic limitations: Giving primarily in KS, MI, TX, and WY.
Publications: Application guidelines.
Application information: Applications accepted. Application form not required.
Initial approach: Letter
Deadline(s): None
Officers and Directors:* Justin M. Dart*, Pres.; Joanne Williams*, Secy.; Phillip Leece, Treas.; Alexis A. Learmond.
EIN: 204580958

1035
The Davey Tree Expert Company
1500 N. Mantua St.
P.O. Box 5193
Kent, OH 44240-5193 (330) 673-9511
FAX: (330) 673-9843

Company URL: http://www.davey.com
Establishment information: Established in 1880.
Company type: Private company
Business activities: Provides tree planting, pruning, spraying, and clearing and lawn care fertilization and weed control services.
Business type (SIC): Landscape and horticultural services
Corporate officers: Karl J. Warnke, Chair., Pres., and C.E.O.; Patrick M. Covey, C.O.O.; Tom Countryman, C.I.O.; David E. Adante, Exec. V.P., C.F.O., and Secy.; Steven A. Marshall, Exec. V.P., Opers.; Nicholas R. Sucic, V.P. and Cont.; Joseph R. Paul, V.P. and Treas.
Board of directors: Karl J. Warnke, Chair.; R. Douglas Cowan; J. Dawson Cunningham; William J. Ginn; Douglas K. Hall; Sandra W. Harbrecht; John E. Warfel
Subsidiary: The Davey Tree Surgery Co., Livermore, CA
International operations: Canada
Giving statement: Giving through the Davey Company Foundation.

Davey Company Foundation
1500 N. Mantua St.
P.O. Box 5193
Kent, OH 44240-5193 (330) 673-9511
FAX: (330) 673-7089

Establishment information: Established in 1957 in OH.
Donor: The Davey Tree Expert Co.
Contact: David E. Adante, V.P.
Financial data (yr. ended 12/31/11): Assets, $884,029 (M); gifts received, $200,000; expenditures, $187,502; qualifying distributions, $184,307; giving activities include $182,333 for grants.
Purpose and activities: The foundation supports organizations involved with higher education, health, and arboriculture.
Fields of interest: Higher education; Environment, forests; Hospitals (general); Health care.
Type of support: Employee matching gifts; Employee-related scholarships; General/operating support; Research.
Geographic limitations: Giving primarily in CA and OH.
Support limitations: No grants to individuals (except for employee-related scholarships).
Application information: Applications accepted. Application form required.
Initial approach: Letter
Copies of proposal: 1
Deadline(s): None
Officers: Karl J. Warnke, Pres.; David E. Adante, V.P.; Patrick M. Covey, V.P.; Steven A. Marshal, V.P.; Joseph R. Paul, V.P.; Marjorie L. Conner, Secy.
Trustees: R. Douglas Cowan; J. Dawson Cunningham.
EIN: 346555132

1036
Davies Ward Phillips & Vineberg LLP
625 Madison Ave., 12th Fl.
New York, NY 10022-1801 (212) 308-8866

Company URL: http://www.dwpv.com
Establishment information: Established in 2001.
Company type: Private company
Business activities: Operates law firm.
Business type (SIC): Legal services
Corporate officer: Richard Cherney, Partner
Office: New York, NY
International operations: Canada
Giving statement: Giving through the Davies Ward Phillips & Vineberg LLP Pro Bono Program.

Davies Ward Phillips & Vineberg LLP Pro Bono Program
625 Madison Ave., 12th Fl.
New York, NY 10022-1801 (212) 308-8866
FAX: (212) 308-0132; URL: http://www.dwpv.com

Fields of interest: Legal services.
Type of support: Pro bono services - legal.
Geographic limitations: Giving primarily in areas of company operations in New York, NY, and in Canada.

1037
Don Davis Auto World Inc.
2277 Niagara Falls Blvd.
Amherst, NY 14228-3523 (716) 691-7800
FAX: (716) 691-4893

Company URL: http://www.dondavis.com
Establishment information: Established in 1958.
Company type: Private company
Business activities: Operates auto dealership.
Business type (SIC): Motor vehicles—retail
Corporate officers: John Davis, Pres.; Donna Yox, Secy.-Treas.
Giving statement: Giving through the Don Davis Auto World Charitable Foundation.

The Don Davis Auto World Charitable Foundation
(formerly Donald L. Davis Foundation)
2277 Niagara Falls Blvd.
Amherst, NY 14228-3523

Establishment information: Established in NY.
Donors: Donald L. Davis; Don Davis Auto World, Inc.
Financial data (yr. ended 12/31/11): Assets, $46,364 (M); expenditures, $14,865; qualifying distributions, $11,670; giving activities include $11,670 for 22 grants (high: $2,000; low: $50).
Purpose and activities: The foundation supports performing arts centers and organizations involved with education, cancer, medical research, children's services, and the disabled.
Fields of interest: Performing arts centers; Secondary school/education; Higher education; Education; Cancer; Medical research; Children, services; Developmentally disabled, centers & services.
Type of support: Annual campaigns; General/operating support; Scholarship funds.
Geographic limitations: Giving primarily in NY.
Support limitations: No grants to individuals.
Application information: Applications not accepted. Contributes only to pre-selected organizations.
Trustees: John Davis; Matthew Davis.
EIN: 166065355

1038
Davis Brown Law Firm
215 10th St., Ste. 1300
Des Moines, IA 50309-3616
(515) 288-2500

Company URL: http://www.davisbrownlaw.com
Establishment information: Established in 1929.
Company type: Private company
Business activities: Operates law firm.

Business type (SIC): Legal services
Corporate officer: Jeffrey A. Baker, Mgr.
Offices: Des Moines, West Des Moines, IA
Giving statement: Giving through the Davis Brown Law Firm Pro Bono Program.

Davis Brown Law Firm Pro Bono Program

215 10th St., Ste. 1300
Des Moines, IA 50309-3616 (515) 288-2500
E-mail: ScottBrennan@davisbrownlaw.com; URL: http://www.davisbrownlaw.com

Contact: Scott Brennan, V.P.
Fields of interest: Legal services.
Type of support: Pro bono services - legal.
Geographic limitations: Giving primarily in areas of company operations in Des Moines, and West Des Moines, IA.
Application information: An attorney coordinates pro bono projects.

1039
Davis Graham & Stubbs LLP

1550 17th St., Ste. 500
Denver, CO 80202-1500 (303) 892-9400

Company URL: http://www.dgslaw.com
Establishment information: Establsihed in 1915.
Company type: Private company
Business activities: Operates law firm.
Business type (SIC): Legal services
Corporate officer: Chris Richardson, C.E.O.
Giving statement: Giving through the Davis Graham & Stubbs LLP Pro Bono Program.

Davis Graham & Stubbs LLP Pro Bono Program

1550 17th St., Ste. 500
Denver, CO 80202-1500 (303) 892-9400
FAX: (303) 893-1379; URL: http://www.dgslaw.com/about/CommunityService/Pages/default.aspx

Fields of interest: Legal services.
Type of support: Pro bono services - legal.
Geographic limitations: Giving primarily in areas of company operations in Denver, CO.
Application information: An attorney coordinates pro bono projects.

1040
Davis Polk & Wardwell LLP

450 Lexington Ave.
New York, NY 10017-3904 (212) 450-4000

Company URL: http://www.davispolk.com
Establishment information: Established in 1849.
Company type: Private company
Business activities: Operates law firm.
Business type (SIC): Legal services
Giving statement: Giving through the Davis Polk & Wardwell LLP Pro Bono Program.

Davis Polk & Wardwell LLP Pro Bono Program

450 Lexington Ave.
New York, NY 10017-3904 (212) 450-4000
E-mail: sharon.katz@davispolk.com; URL: http://www.davispolk.com/pro-bono/recognition/

Contact: Sharon Katz, Special Counsel for Pro Bono
Fields of interest: Legal services.
Type of support: Pro bono services - legal.
Geographic limitations: Giving primarily in areas of company operations in Menlo Park, CA, Washington, DC, New York, NY, Brazil, China, France, Hong Kong, Japan, Spain, and the United Kingdom.
Application information: The Pro Bono Committee manages the pro-bono program.

1041
Davis Wright Tremaine LLP

1201 Third Ave., Ste. 2200
Seattle, WA 98101-3045 (206) 622-3150

Company URL: http://www.dwt.com
Establishment information: Established in 1908.
Company type: Private company
Business activities: Operates law firm.
Business type (SIC): Legal services
Corporate officer: Dave Baca, Managing Partner
Offices: Anchorage, AK; Los Angeles, San Francisco, CA; Washington, DC; New York, NY; Portland, OR; Bellevue, Seattle, WA
International operations: China
Giving statement: Giving through the Davis Wright Tremaine LLP Corporate Giving Program.

Davis Wright Tremaine LLP Corporate Giving Program

1201 Third Ave., Ste. 2200
Seattle, WA 98101-3045 (206) 622-3150
FAX: (206) 757-7700; E-mail: julieorr@dwt.com; Contact for Pro Bono program: Julie Orr, Pro Bono Coord., tel.: (206) 757-8586, e-mail: julieorr@dwt.com; Contact for Anchorage, Alaska: Diane Pennington, tel.: (907) 257-5300; Contact for Los Angeles, California: Susan Seales or Michael Hensinger, tel.: (213) 633-6800; Contact for San Francisco, California: Karen Baltier-Long or Cassie Widay, tel.: (415) 276-6500; Contact for Washington, DC: Sally Linzau, tel.: (202) 973-4200; Contact for Portland, Maine: Margaret Cicchetti or Hadewych Verlinden, tel.: (503) 241-2300; Contact for New York, New York: Marie Claire Correa, tel.: (212) 489-8230; Contact for Bellevue and Seattle, Washington: Barrie Handy, tel.: (425) 646-6100; URL: http://www.dwt.com/GivingBack/CommunityInvolvement

Contact: Julie Orr, Pro Bono Coord.
Purpose and activities: Davis Wright Tremaine makes charitable contributions to nonprofit organizations involved with arts and culture, health, children services, and human services.
Fields of interest: Arts; Health organizations; Legal services; Children, services; Family services; Human services; Public affairs.
Type of support: Employee volunteer services; General/operating support; Pro bono services - legal.

1042
Davison Iron Works, Inc.

8845 Elder Creek Rd., Ste. A
Sacramento, CA 95828-1835
(916) 381-2121

Company URL: http://www.davisoniron.com
Establishment information: Established in 1959.
Company type: Private company
Business activities: Operates fabricated structural metal manufacturing company.
Business type (SIC): Metal products/structural
Corporate officer: Andrew F. Peszynski, Pres.
Giving statement: Giving through the Peszynski Foundation.

The Peszynski Foundation

8845 Elder Creek Rd.
Sacramento, CA 95828-1835

Establishment information: Established in 2007 in CA.
Donors: Andrew F. Peszynski; Davison Iron Works, Inc.; Loretto High School.
Financial data (yr. ended 12/31/11): Assets, $3,544,169 (M); gifts received, $139,447; expenditures, $202,709; qualifying distributions, $175,000; giving activities include $175,000 for 16 grants (high: $23,000; low: $2,000).
Purpose and activities: The foundation supports organizations involved with K-12 and higher education, human services, and Catholicism.
Fields of interest: Elementary/secondary education; Higher education; Salvation Army; Women, centers/services; Human services; Catholic agencies & churches.
Type of support: Building/renovation; General/operating support.
Geographic limitations: Giving primarily in CA; limited giving in Poland and the United Kingdom.
Support limitations: No grants to individuals.
Application information: Applications not accepted. Contributes only to pre-selected organizations.
Officers and Directors:* Andrew F. Peszynski*, Pres.; Helena Szmit*, V.P.; Elizabeth Perschevitch*, Secy.; I.G. Peszynski*, C.F.O.
EIN: 261349949
Selected grants: The following grants are a representative sample of this grantmaker's funding activity:
$5,000 to Wellspring Womens Center, Sacramento, CA, 2010.
$2,000 to Saint Michaels Episcopal Day School, Carmichael, CA, 2010.
$1,000 to Sacramento Childrens Home, Sacramento, CA, 2010.

1043
davistudio

486 Pratt Hill Rd.
Chatham, NY 12037-2512 (518) 392-7308
FAX: 518-392-8018

Company URL: http://www.davistudio.com
Company type: Private company
Business type (SIC): Business services/miscellaneous
Corporate officer: Mary Anne Davis, Owner
Giving statement: Giving through the davistudio Corporate Giving Program.

davistudio Corporate Giving Program

486 Pratt Hill Rd.
Chatham, NY 12037-2512 (518) 392-7308
E-mail: maryanne@davistudio.com; URL: http://www.davistudio.com

Purpose and activities: davistudio is a certified B Corporation that donates a percentage of profits to charitable organizations. Support is given primarily in Columbia County, New York.
Fields of interest: Historic preservation/historical societies; Arts; Environment; Animal welfare.

Type of support: General/operating support.
Geographic limitations: Giving primarily in Columbia County, NY.

1044
DaVita HealthCare Partners Inc.

(formerly DaVita Inc.)
2000 16th St.
Denver, CO 80202 (303) 405-2100

Company URL: http://www.davita.com
Establishment information: Established in 1995.
Company type: Public company
Company ticker symbol and exchange: DVA/NYSE
Business activities: Provides kidney dialysis services.
Business type (SIC): Miscellaneous health services
Financial profile for 2012: Number of employees, 53,400; assets, $16,004,360,000; sales volume, $8,186,280,000; pre-tax net income, $1,001,300,000; expenses, $6,889,200,000; liabilities, $12,241,230,000
Fortune 1000 ranking: 2012—311th in revenues, 319th in profits, and 284th in assets
Corporate officers: Kent J. Thiry, Co-Chair. and C.E.O.; Robert J. Margolis, M.D., Co-Chair.; Javier J. Rodriguez, Pres.; Dennis L. Kogod, C.O.O.; James K. Hilger, C.F.O. and C.A.O.
Board of directors: Kent J. Thiry, Co-Chair.; Robert J. Margolis, M.D., Co-Chair.; Pamela M. Arway; Charles G. Berg; Carol Anthony Davidson; Paul J. Diaz; Peter T. Grauer; John M. Nehra; William L. Roper; Roger J. Valine
Office: Berwyn, PA
Giving statement: Giving through the DaVita Children's Foundation.
Company EIN: 510354549

DaVita Children's Foundation

c/o Tax Dept.
1423 Pacific Ave.
Tacoma, WA 98401-2076 (815) 675-2405

Establishment information: Established in 2000 in CA and WA.
Donor: DaVita Inc.
Contact: Kay Kargul
Financial data (yr. ended 12/31/11): Assets, $286,049 (M); expenditures, $78,010; qualifying distributions, $78,000; giving activities include $78,000 for 39 grants to individuals (high: $2,000; low: $2,000).
Purpose and activities: The foundation awards college scholarships to children and grandchildren of employees of DaVita Inc.
Type of support: Employee-related scholarships.
Geographic limitations: Giving limited to Tacoma, WA.
Application information: Applications accepted. Application form required.
Initial approach: Letter
Deadline(s): Nov. 1
Officers: Kent Thiry, Pres.; Lin Whatcott, C.F.O. and Treas.
Trustees: Mary Beth Hagey; Peter Koenig; Robert Johnston; Paul Nichols; Odetter Pura; Bill Shannon.
EIN: 330932587

1045
Day Management Corp.

(doing business as Day Wireless)
4700 S.E. International Way
Milwaukie, OR 97222-4657 (503) 659-1240

Company URL: http://www.daywireless.com/
Establishment information: Established in 1969.
Company type: Private company
Business activities: Provides telephone communications services; provides cable television services; provides Internet access services.
Business type (SIC): Telephone communications; cable and other pay television services; repair shops/electrical
Financial profile for 2012: Number of employees, 300
Giving statement: Giving through the Day Management Educational Foundation.

Day Management Educational Foundation

P.O. Box 189
Estacada, OR 97023-0189 (503) 630-4202

Establishment information: Established as a company-sponsored operating foundation in 1996 in OR.
Donors: Rio Virgin Telephone Co.; Cascade Utilities; Ducap Electronics, Inc.; Day Management Corp.
Financial data (yr. ended 06/30/11): Assets, $577,962 (M); expenditures, $26,105; qualifying distributions, $22,655; giving activities include $20,667 for 13 grants to individuals (high: $3,000; low: $667).
Purpose and activities: The foundation awards college scholarships to children of employees of Day Management Corporation.
Type of support: Employee-related scholarships.
Application information: Applications accepted. Application form required.
Initial approach: Proposal
Deadline(s): May 31, Jun. 30, Sept. 30 and Dec. 1
Officers: Matt Enser, Pres.; Dennis Anderson, Secy.; Brooke Wheeler, Treas.
Trustees: Cindy Biama; Michael Daversa.
EIN: 931188551

1046
Day Pitney LLP

242 Trumbull St.
Hartford, CT 06103-1213 (860) 275-0100

Company URL: http://www.daypitney.com
Establishment information: Established in 1902.
Company type: Private company
Business activities: Operates law firm.
Business type (SIC): Legal services
Corporate officers: Kirk R. Rossi, C.O.O. and C.F.O.; Nabil Mughal, C.I.O.; Paul P. Lach, Cont.
Offices: Greenwich, Hartford, New Haven, Stamford, West Hartford, CT; Washington, DC; Boston, MA; Parsippany, NJ; New York, NY
Giving statement: Giving through the Day Pitney LLP Pro Bono Program and the Day Pitney Foundation, Inc.

Day Pitney LLP Pro Bono Program

242 Trumbull St.
Hartford, CT 06103-1213 (203) 977-7418
FAX: (203) 977-7301;
E-mail: hharris@daypitney.com; Additional tel.: (860) 275-0100; URL: http://www.daypitney.com/about/probono/

Contact: Helen Harris, Partner
Fields of interest: Legal services.
Type of support: Pro bono services - legal.
Geographic limitations: Giving primarily in areas of company operations in Greenwich, Hartford, New Haven, Stamford, and West Hartford, CT, Washington, DC, Boston, MA, Parsippany, NJ, and New York, NY.
Application information: The Pro Bono Committee manages the pro-bono program.

Day Pitney Foundation, Inc.

(formerly The Day, Berry & Howard Foundation)
1 E. Putnam Ave.
Greenwich, CT 06830-5429
URL: http://www.daypitneyfoundation.org/

Establishment information: Established in 1986.
Financial data (yr. ended 12/31/11): Assets, $152,968 (M); expenditures, $14,568; qualifying distributions, $14,550; giving activities include $14,500 for 3 grants (high: $10,000; low: $2,000).
Purpose and activities: The foundation supports programs designed to promote diversity in the legal professions; and legal and educational initiatives targeting lawyers, future lawyers, and other professionals.
Fields of interest: Law school/education; Crime/law enforcement.
Type of support: In-kind gifts; Sponsorships.
Geographic limitations: Giving primarily in CT.
Application information: Applications not accepted. Unsolicited requests for funds not accepted.
Officers and Directors:* Peter Chadwick*, Pres.; Linda S. Dalby*, V.P.; Andrew P. Gallard*, V.P.; Dina Kapur Sanna*, V.P.; Jennifer M. Pagnillo, Secy.; David A. White, Treas.
EIN: 061199583

1047
The Dayton Power and Light Company

1065 Woodman Dr.
Dayton, OH 45432 (937) 224-6000

Company URL: http://www.dpandl.com/
Establishment information: Established in 1911.
Company type: Subsidiary of a public company
Business activities: Generates, transmits, and distributes electricity; transmits and distributes natural gas.
Business type (SIC): Combination utility services
Corporate officers: W. August Hillenbrand, Co-Chair.; Robert D. Briggs, Co-Chair.; Philip Herrington, Pres. and C.E.O.; Gary G. Stephenson, Exec. V.P., Opers; Frederick J. Boyle, Sr. V.P., C.F.O., and Treas.; Miggie E. Cramblit, V.P. and Secy.; Arthur G. Meyer, V.P. and Genl. Counsel; Patricia K. Swanke, V.P., Opers.
Board of directors: W. August Hillenbrand, Co-Chair.; Robert D. Briggs, Co-Chair.; Paul R. Bishop; James V. Mahoney
Giving statement: Giving through the Dayton Power and Light Company Contributions Program and the Dayton Power and Light Company Foundation.
Company EIN: 310258470

The Dayton Power and Light Company Foundation

1065 Woodman Dr.
Dayton, OH 45432-1423 (937) 259-7925
FAX: (937) 259-7923; URL: http://www.dpandl.com/about-dpl/who-we-are/community-investments/

Establishment information: Established in 1985 in OH.
Donor: The Dayton Power and Light Co.
Financial data (yr. ended 12/31/11): Assets, $26,437,864 (M); expenditures, $1,325,131; qualifying distributions, $1,219,000; giving activities include $1,219,000 for grants.
Purpose and activities: The foundation supports food banks and festivals and organizations involved with arts and culture, health, human services, community economic development, civic affairs, and youth.
Fields of interest: Performing arts; Arts; Secondary school/education; Higher education; Education; Health care; Food banks; Recreation, fairs/festivals; Big Brothers/Big Sisters; Boy scouts; Girl scouts; American Red Cross; Salvation Army; Human services; Community development, business promotion; Community/economic development; United Ways and Federated Giving Programs; Public affairs Youth.
Type of support: Continuing support; Employee volunteer services; General/operating support; Program development.
Geographic limitations: Giving in areas of company operations in west central OH.
Support limitations: No support for religious, fraternal, labor, or veterans' organizations, national organizations, or sports leagues. No grants to individuals, or for capital campaigns, endowments or development campaigns, general operating support for hospitals, or telephone or mass mail solicitations.
Publications: Application guidelines; Informational brochure (including application guidelines).
Application information: Applications accepted. Application form not required. Applicants should submit the following:
1) copy of IRS Determination Letter
2) brief history of organization and description of its mission
3) copy of most recent annual report/audited financial statement/990
4) detailed description of project and amount of funding requested
5) copy of current year's organizational budget and/or project budget
6) listing of additional sources and amount of support

Initial approach: Proposal
Copies of proposal: 1
Board meeting date(s): Quarterly
Deadline(s): None

Officers and Directors:* Daniel J. McCabe, Pres.; Joe Mulpas, Treas.; Tom Raga, Exec. Dir.; Paul R. Bishop; Scott J. Kelly; Tim Rice; Ned J. Sifferlen.
Number of staff: 1 full-time professional.
EIN: 311138883

1048
DCH Auto Group

955 Rte. 9 N.
South Amboy, NJ 08879 (732) 727-9168
FAX: (732) 727-8373

Company URL: http://www.dchautogroup.com/
Establishment information: Established in 1948.
Company type: Private company
Business activities: Operates auto dealerships.
Business type (SIC): Business services/miscellaneous
Corporate officers: Shau-wai Lam, Chair.; Susan Scarola, Vice-Chair.; George Liang, Pres.; T.Y. Lai, Sr. V.P. and C.O.O.; Mark Slosberg, V.P. and C.F.O.; Rita P. Campanile, V.P., Genl. Counsel, and Secy.
Board of directors: Shau-wai Lam, Chair.; Susan Scarola, Vice-Chair.
Giving statement: Giving through the DCH Auto Group Corporate Giving Program.

DCH Auto Group Corporate Giving Program

955 Rte. 9 North
South Amboy, NJ 08879 (732) 727-9168
URL: http://www.dchautogroup.com/community_focus.aspx

1049
DCI Holdings, Inc.

(doing business as DCI International)
305 N. Springbrook Rd.
Newberg, OR 97132-9263 (503) 538-8343

Company URL: http://www.dcionline.com
Establishment information: Established in 1983.
Company type: Private company
Business activities: Manufactures and distributes dental equipment and supplies.
Business type (SIC): Medical instruments and supplies
Corporate officers: John W. Spencer, Co-Pres.; Darrell McGiveren, Co-Pres.; Janelle Spencer, Secy.
Giving statement: Giving through the Spencer Family Foundation.

Spencer Family Foundation

5665 S.W. Meadows Rd., Ste. 310
Lake Oswego, OR 97035-3192

Establishment information: Established in 2005 in OR.
Donors: Dental Components, Inc.; John Spencer; Janelle Spencer; Joseph Braet; Christine Braet.
Financial data (yr. ended 06/30/11): Assets, $5,460,044 (M); gifts received, $7,000; expenditures, $273,163; qualifying distributions, $273,163; giving activities include $108,761 for 12 grants (high: $36,111; low: $500).
Purpose and activities: The foundation supports camps and organizations involved with education, dental care, cystic fibrosis, child welfare, human services, and Christianity.
Fields of interest: Secondary school/education; Education; Dental care; Cystic fibrosis; Crime/violence prevention, child abuse; Recreation, camps; Developmentally disabled, centers & services; Women, centers/services; Human services; Christian agencies & churches.
Type of support: General/operating support.
Geographic limitations: Giving primarily in OR; giving also to national organizations.
Support limitations: No grants to individuals.
Application information: Applications not accepted. Contributes only to pre-selected organizations.
Officers: John Spencer, Pres.; Janelle Spencer, Secy.-Treas.
Directors: Amy Spencer; Jason Spencer; Laura Spencer.
EIN: 203401912
Selected grants: The following grants are a representative sample of this grantmaker's funding activity:
$25,000 to Bighorn Golf Club Charities, Palm Desert, CA, 2011.
$25,000 to Miracle Corners of the World, New York, NY, 2011.
$4,850 to Cystic Fibrosis Foundation, Bethesda, MD, 2011.
$2,000 to Smile Train, New York, NY, 2011.
$1,500 to Global Health and Education Foundation, Danville, CA, 2011.
$1,500 to Portland Art Museum, Portland, OR, 2011.

1050
S.D. Deacon Corp.

901 N.E. Glisan St., Ste. 100
Portland, OR 97232 (503) 297-8791
FAX: (503) 297-8997

Company URL: http://www.deacon.com/
Establishment information: Established in 1981.
Company type: Private company
Business activities: Operates commercial construction company.
Business type (SIC): Contractors/general nonresidential building
Corporate officers: Steven D. Deacon, Co-Pres. and C.E.O.; Bob Dacy, Co-Pres.; Bill Townsend, C.O.O.
Giving statement: Giving through the Deacon Charitable Foundation.

Deacon Charitable Foundation

901 N.E. Glisan St., Ste. 100
Portland, OR 97232-2730 (503) 297-8791
E-mail: susan.phelps@deacon.com; Charity Committee Liaisons: Seattle, WA: Barbara Keele, e-mail: barbara.keeler@deacon.com; Portland, OR: Kathy Ballard, e-mail: kathy.ballard@deacon.com; Sacramento, CA: Catherine Adamson, e-mail: cynthia.adamson@deacon.com; Irvine, CA: Veronica Wences, e-mail: veronica.wences@deacon.com; URL: http://www.deaconcharitablefoundation.org

Establishment information: Established in 2006 in CA.
Donor: S.D. Deacon of California.
Contact: Susan Bender Phelps, Exec. Dir.
Financial data (yr. ended 09/30/11): Assets, $235,602 (M); gifts received, $250; expenditures, $254,400; qualifying distributions, $254,400; giving activities include $215,958 for 138 grants (high: $10,000; low: $25).
Purpose and activities: The foundation supports organizations involved with the environment, animal welfare, and human services.
Fields of interest: Environment; Animal welfare; Children/youth, services; Human services.
Type of support: Employee matching gifts; General/operating support.
Geographic limitations: Giving primarily in areas of company operations Irvine and Sacramento, CA, Portland, OR and Seattle, WA.
Publications: Application guidelines.
Application information: Applications accepted.

Initial approach: Contact nearest Charity Committee Liaison for proposal guidelines
Deadline(s): None

Officers and Directors:* Steven D. Deacon*, Pres.; Richard Smith*, V.P. and Secy.; Susan Bender Phelps, Exec. Dir.; Paul Cunha; Jarrod Fogle; Kendra Howell; Anke Rind.
EIN: 205702192

Selected grants: The following grants are a representative sample of this grantmaker's funding activity:
$10,000 to Childrens Relief Nursery, Portland, OR, 2011.
$10,000 to Friendship Club, Nevada City, CA, 2011.
$5,000 to Court Appointed Special Advocates for Children, Portland, OR, 2011.
$3,000 to Loaves and Fishes Centers, Portland, OR, 2011.
$3,000 to My Fathers House Community Shelter, Gresham, OR, 2011.
$2,500 to Childrens Cancer Association, Portland, OR, 2011.
$2,500 to DoveLewis Emergency Animal Hospital, Portland, OR, 2011.
$2,000 to Northwest Burn Foundation, Seattle, WA, 2011.
$2,000 to YMCA of Greater Seattle, Seattle, WA, 2011.
$1,500 to Freshwater Trust, Portland, OR, 2011.

1051
Dead River Company

80 Exchange St., Ste. 300
Bangor, ME 04401-6588 (207) 827-5001

Company URL: http://www.deadriver.com
Establishment information: Established in 1909.
Company type: Private company
Business activities: Distributes home heating oil, propane, and other petroleum products.
Business type (SIC): Petroleum and coal products/miscellaneous
Financial profile for 2010: Number of employees, 52
Corporate officers: P. Andrews Nixon, Chair. and C.E.O.; Robert A. Moore, Pres.
Board of directors: P. Andrews Nixon, Chair.; Susannah M. Swihart
Giving statement: Giving through the Mimi Foundation.

The Mimi Foundation

(formerly Dead River Foundation)
80 Exchange St.
P.O. Box 1427
Bangor, ME 04402-1427 (207) 947-8641

Establishment information: Established in 2005 in ME.
Donor: Dead River Co.
Financial data (yr. ended 12/31/11): Assets, $2,290,797 (M); gifts received, $175,000; expenditures, $178,537; qualifying distributions, $204,550; giving activities include $158,500 for 25 grants (high: $67,500; low: $1,000).
Purpose and activities: The foundation supports health centers and organizations involved with education, the environment, and youth development.
Fields of interest: Higher education; Theological school/education; Education; Environment; Health care, clinics/centers; Youth development; YM/YWCAs & YM/YWHAs; United Ways and Federated Giving Programs.
Type of support: General/operating support.
Geographic limitations: Giving primarily in ME.
Application information: Applications accepted. Application form required.
Initial approach: Proposal
Deadline(s): None
Officers: Julie H. Bracken, Pres.; Courtney M. Doherty, V.P.; Calvin E. True, Esq., Secy.; Karen K. Schacht*, Treas.
Director: Deanna S. Sherman.
EIN: 203957984
Selected grants: The following grants are a representative sample of this grantmaker's funding activity:
$35,000 to Bangor Theological Seminary, Bangor, ME, 2010.
$25,000 to LearningWorks, Portland, ME, 2010. For general support.
$25,000 to Western Mountains Charitable Foundation, Kingfield, ME, 2010. For general support.
$11,250 to Maine Sea Coast Missionary Society, Bar Harbor, ME, 2010. For general support.
$10,000 to Mabel Wadsworth Womens Health Center, Bangor, ME, 2010. For general support.
$10,000 to Maine Association of Nonprofits, Portland, ME, 2010. For general support.
$5,000 to University of Maine, Orono, ME, 2010. For general support.
$2,500 to YMCA of Mount Desert Island, Bar Harbor, ME, 2010. For general support.
$1,000 to Husson University, Bangor, ME, 2010.

1052
Dealer Computer Services, Inc.

6700 Hollister St.
Houston, TX 77040-5331 (713) 718-1800
FAX: (713) 718-1473

Company type: Subsidiary of a private company
Business activities: Provides integrated computer system design services.
Business type (SIC): Computer services
Corporate officers: Robert T. Brockman, Chair.; Robert M. Nalley, Pres.; Kenneth E. Bunney, Secy.; Robert D. Burnett, Treas.
Board of director: Robert T. Brockman, Chair.
Giving statement: Giving through the Brockman Foundation.

The Brockman Foundation

(formerly The Robert T. Brockman Charitable Foundation)
c/o Tax Dept.
P.O. Box 2608
Dayton, OH 45401-2608

Establishment information: Established in 1987 in TX.
Donors: Universal Computer Systems, Inc.; Universal Computer Consulting, Inc.; Universal Computer Network, Inc.; Dealer Computer Services, Inc.; Robert T. Brockman.
Financial data (yr. ended 12/31/11): Assets, $1,347,087 (M); expenditures, $1,078; qualifying distributions, $350; giving activities include $200 for 1 grant.
Purpose and activities: The foundation supports organizations involved with health and education.
Fields of interest: Education; Health care; Health organizations.
Type of support: Equipment; General/operating support; Scholarship funds.
Support limitations: No grants to individuals.
Application information: Applications not accepted. Unsolicited requests for funds not accepted.
Officers and Directors:* Robert T. Brockman*, Pres.; Dorothy K. Brockman*, V.P.; Robert Burnett, Secy.-Treas.
EIN: 760239422

1053
Dean Dorton Ford, P.S.C.

106 W. Vine St., Ste. 600
Lexington, KY 40507 (859) 255-2341

Company URL: http://www.ddfky.com
Establishment information: Established in 1979.
Company type: Private company
Business activities: Provides accounting, auditing, tax, and management consulting services.
Business type (SIC): Accounting, auditing, and bookkeeping services
Financial profile for 2010: Number of employees, 91
Corporate officers: Richard O. Dorton, Co-Pres. and C.E.O.; Douglas P. Dean, Co-Pres.
Board of directors: Danielle Adair; Phil Amshoff; John J. Balbach; David C. Bundy; Faith H. Crump; Douglas P. Dean; Melissa G. DeArk; Richard O. Dorton; Gary J. Ermers; Crissy R. Fiscus; Travis C. Frick; James E. Green; Paula C. Hanson; Michael R. Harbold; John W. Herring; Melissa Hicks; Martha E. Jones; Simon M. Keemer; William J. Kohm; Lance Mann; Brandi N. Marcum; Leigh McKee; Jason D. Miller; C. Robert Montgomery; Joseph Overhults; David A. Parks; David W. Richard; Allison Rogers; Gary R. Roth; Jen Shah; Michael T. Shepherd; Adam Shewmaker; James J. Tencza; Gwen E. Tilton; Mike Wade; Elizabeth Z. Woodward
Giving statement: Giving through the Dean Dorton Allen Ford Charitable Foundation, Inc.

Dean Dorton Allen Ford Charitable Foundation, Inc.

(formerly Dean, Dorton & Ford Charitable Foundation, Inc.)
106 W. Vine St., Ste. 600
Lexington, KY 40507-1679
URL: http://www.ddafcpa.com/Community-Involvement.html

Establishment information: Established in 2005 in KY.
Donors: Dean, Dorton & Ford; Mike Shepherd; Crissy Fiscus; David Bundy; Doughlas Dean; Richard O. Dorton; Paula C. Hanson.
Financial data (yr. ended 06/30/11): Assets, $15,649 (M); gifts received, $40,175; expenditures, $34,589; qualifying distributions, $34,589; giving activities include $32,795 for 42 grants (high: $10,000; low: $50).
Purpose and activities: The foundation supports organizations involved with arts and culture, education, cancer, heart disease, human services, and Christianity.
Fields of interest: Museums; Arts; Libraries (public); Education, PTA groups; Education; Cancer; Cancer, leukemia; Heart & circulatory diseases; American Red Cross; YM/YWCAs & YM/YWHAs; Human services; United Ways and Federated Giving Programs; Christian agencies & churches.
Type of support: General/operating support; Program development.
Geographic limitations: Giving primarily in KY.
Support limitations: No grants to individuals.
Application information: Applications not accepted. Unsolicited requests for funds not accepted.
Officers and Directors:* Richard O. Dorton, Pres.; Gwen E. Tilton*, V.P.; James E. Green, Secy.; Michael T. Shepherd*, Treas.; Douglas P. Dean; Paula C. Hanson; Janson D. Miller; James J. Tencza.
EIN: 611497062

1054
Dean Foods Company

(formerly Suiza Foods Corporation)
2711 N. Haskell Ave., Ste. 3400
Dallas, TX 75204 (214) 303-3400
FAX: (302) 655-5049

Company URL: http://www.deanfoods.com
Establishment information: Established in 1925.
Company type: Public company
Company ticker symbol and exchange: DF/NYSE
International Securities Identification Number: US2423701042
Business activities: Produces and sells dairy products.
Business type (SIC): Dairy products
Financial profile for 2012: Number of employees, 21,915; assets, $5,687,090,000; sales volume, $11,462,280,000; pre-tax net income, $263,920,000; expenses, $11,034,490,000; liabilities, $5,329,000,000
Fortune 1000 ranking: 2012—217th in revenues, 639th in profits, and 555th in assets
Forbes 2000 ranking: 2012—771st in sales, 1635th in profits, and 1772nd in assets
Corporate officers: Thomas C. Davis, Chair.; Gregg A. Tanner, C.E.O.; Marty Devine, C.O.O.; Chris Bellairs, Jr., Exec. V.P. and C.F.O.; Rachel Gonzalez, Exec. V.P., Genl. Counsel, and Corp. Secy.; Kim Warmbier, Exec. V.P., Human Resources; Barbara D. Carlini, Sr. V.P. and C.I.O.
Board of directors: Thomas C. Davis, Chair.; V. Janet Hill; J. Wayne Mailloux; John R. Muse; Hector M. Nevares-La Costa; Gregg A. Tanner; Jim L. Turner; Robert T. Wiseman
Subsidiaries: Consolidated Container Company LLC, Atlanta, GA; Dean Holding Co., Dallas, TX; T. G. Lee Foods, Inc., Orlando, FL; WhiteWave Foods Company, Broomfield, CO
International operations: Mexico; United Kingdom
Historic mergers: Dean Foods Company (December 21, 2001)
Giving statement: Giving through the Dean Foods Company Contributions Program and the Dean Foods Foundation.
Company EIN: 752559681

Dean Foods Company Contributions Program

(formerly Suiza Foods Corporation Contributions Program)
c/o Corp. Contribs.
2711 N. Haskell Ave., Ste. 3400
Dallas, TX 75204-2928 (214) 303-3400
E-mail: giving@deanfoods.com; URL: http://responsibility.deanfoods.com/social-responsibility/

Contact: Amy Barker, Mgr., Comms.
Purpose and activities: As a complement to its foundation, Dean Foods also makes charitable contributions to nonprofit organizations directly. Special emphasis is directed toward programs designed to prevent childhood hunger and teach at-risk youth and children about the importance of nutrition. Support is given on a national and international basis in areas of company operations with some emphasis on Dallas, Texas.
Fields of interest: Agriculture, sustainable programs; Food services; Food banks; Nutrition; Disasters, preparedness/services; Children/youth, services; Community/economic development Children.
Program:
Matching Gifts Program: Dean Foods matches contributions made by its employees to disaster relief organizations on a one-for-one basis.
Type of support: Donated products; Employee volunteer services; General/operating support.
Geographic limitations: Giving on a national and international basis in areas of company operations, with some emphasis on Dallas, TX; giving also to national organizations.
Application information: Applications accepted. Application form not required.
Initial approach: Proposal to nearest company facility
Copies of proposal: 1

Dean Foods Foundation

2711 N. Haskell Ave., 34th Fl.
Dallas, TX 75204-2911
E-mail: giving@deanfoods.com; URL: http://responsibility.deanfoods.com/

Establishment information: Established in 1993 in IL.
Donors: Dean Foods Corporation; Dean Management Corp.
Financial data (yr. ended 12/31/11): Assets, $1,488,661 (M); gifts received, $700,000; expenditures, $677,206; qualifying distributions, $677,206; giving activities include $674,772 for 14 grants (high: $250,000; low: $2,500).
Purpose and activities: The foundation supports programs designed to promote childhood hunger prevention; nutrition education for at-risk youth; responsible agriculture; and disaster relief.
Fields of interest: Education; Health care, clinics/centers; Agriculture; Agriculture, farmlands; Food services; Food banks; Nutrition; Disasters, preparedness/services; American Red Cross Children; Youth.
Type of support: Continuing support; General/operating support; Program development.
Geographic limitations: Giving primarily in areas of company operations in Dallas, TX; giving also to national organizations.
Support limitations: No support for religious or faith-based organizations not of direct benefit to the entire community, athletic teams, fraternal, veterans', social, alumni, or labor organizations, political or lobbying organizations, or disease-focused organizations. No grants to individuals, or for travel, film, music, television, video or media productions, or broadcast underwriting, capital campaigns, endowments, general operating support for schools, colleges, or universities, sponsorship of fundraising events, benefit dinners, auctions, sports competitions, or goodwill advertising.
Publications: Application guidelines.
Application information: Applications accepted. A full proposal may be requested at a later date. Organizations applying for support must have been operating and providing relevant services for a least 3 years. Unsolicited applications for disaster relief grants are not accepted. Telephone calls during the application process are not encouraged. Applicants should submit the following:
1) detailed description of project and amount of funding requested
2) name, address and phone number of organization
3) contact person
4) population served
5) listing of additional sources and amount of support
Initial approach: Download letter of inquiry form and e-mail to foundation
Deadline(s): Mar. 31 and Sept. 30
Final notification: Apr. 15 and Oct. 15
Officers and Directors:* Gregg L. Engles*, Chair.; Liliana M. Esposito, Pres.; Timothy A. Smith, Sr. V.P. and Treas.; Kristen N. Cunningham, V.P. and Secy.; Shannon D. Luton*, V.P.; Deborah E. Sutton*, V.P.; H. Shephard Bailey, V.P.; Amy N. Barker*, V.P.
EIN: 363845182

1055
Debevoise & Plimpton LLP

919 3rd Ave.
New York, NY 10022-3902 (212) 909-6000

Company URL: http://www.debevoise.com
Establishment information: Established in 1931.
Company type: Private company
Business activities: Operates law firm.
Business type (SIC): Legal services
Corporate officer: Michael W. Blair, Presiding Partner
Offices: Washington, DC; New York, NY
International operations: China; France; Germany; Hong Kong; Russia; United Kingdom
Giving statement: Giving through the Debevoise & Plimpton LLP Pro Bono Program.

Debevoise & Plimpton LLP Pro Bono Program

919 3rd Ave.
New York, NY 10022-3902 (212) 909-6832
E-mail: mjmenza@debevoise.com; Additional tel.: (212) 909-6000; URL: http://www.debevoise.com/pro_bono/

Contact: Marjorie J. Menza Esq., Pro Bono Mgr.
Fields of interest: Legal services.
Type of support: Pro bono services - legal.
Geographic limitations: Giving primarily in areas of company operations in Washington, DC, New York, NY, and in China, France, Germany, Hong Kong, Russia, and United Kingdom.

1056
DeBlois Oil Company

141 Knight St.
Warwick, RI 02886-1227 (401) 732-2880

Establishment information: Established in 2001.
Company type: Subsidiary of a public company
Business activities: Transmits and distributes natural gas.
Business type (SIC): Gas production and distribution
Corporate officers: James de Metro, Co-Pres.; William Powers, Co-Pres.
Giving statement: Giving through the R. E. DeBlois Family Foundation.

The R. E. DeBlois Family Foundation

(formerly The DeBlois Foundation)
455 Narragansett Bay Ave.
Warwick, RI 02889 (401) 737-5288

Establishment information: Established in 1988 in RI.
Donor: DeBlois Oil Co.
Contact: Robert E. DeBlois, Tr.
Financial data (yr. ended 12/31/11): Assets, $176,156 (M); expenditures, $21,634; qualifying distributions, $19,500; giving activities include $19,500 for grants.
Purpose and activities: The foundation supports hospitals and organizations involved with education.
Fields of interest: Education; Health care; Human services.

Type of support: Capital campaigns; Endowments.
Geographic limitations: Giving primarily in RI.
Application information: Applications accepted. Application form not required.
Initial approach: Proposal
Deadline(s): None
Trustees: Constance A. DeBlois; Robert E. DeBlois.
EIN: 222887276

1057
DeBruce Grain, Inc.

4100 N. Mulberry Dr.
Kansas City, MO 64116 (816) 421-8182
FAX: (816) 584-2350

Company URL: http://
Establishment information: Established in 1978.
Company type: Private company
Business activities: Sells grain wholesale.
Business type (SIC): Farm-product raw materials—wholesale
Financial profile for 2010: Number of employees, 530
Corporate officers: Paul E. DeBruce, C.E.O.; Larry T. Kittoe, Pres. and C.O.O.; Curtis M. Heinz, C.F.O. and Secy.
Giving statement: Giving through the DeBruce Foundation.

The DeBruce Foundation

4100 N. Mulberry Dr.
Kansas City, MO 64116-1696

Establishment information: Established in 1987 in MO.
Donor: DeBruce Grain, Inc.
Contact: Sandy Smith, Dir., Human Resources
Financial data (yr. ended 03/31/12): Assets, $1,946,267 (M); expenditures, $108,009; qualifying distributions, $99,700; giving activities include $99,700 for grants.
Purpose and activities: The foundation supports community foundations and organizations involved with arts and culture, education, and domestic violence.
Fields of interest: Museums (art); Performing arts centers; Performing arts, theater; Arts; Higher education; Business school/education; Education; Boys & girls clubs; Family services, domestic violence; Foundations (community).
Type of support: General/operating support; Program development; Scholarship funds; Sponsorships.
Geographic limitations: Giving primarily in Kansas City, MO.
Support limitations: No grants to individuals, or for political campaigns.
Publications: Application guidelines.
Application information: Applications accepted. Support is limited to 1 contribution per organization during any given year. Organizations receiving support are asked to submit progress reports and a final report. Application form not required. Applicants should submit the following:
1) timetable for implementation and evaluation of project
2) statement of problem project will address
3) name, address and phone number of organization
4) copy of IRS Determination Letter
5) brief history of organization and description of its mission
6) detailed description of project and amount of funding requested
7) contact person
8) copy of current year's organizational budget and/or project budget
9) listing of additional sources and amount of support
Initial approach: Proposal
Board meeting date(s): Annually
Deadline(s): Dec. 31
Officers: Paul E. DeBruce, Pres.; Larry T. Kittoe, V.P.; Patricia L. Piburn, Secy.; Curtis M. Heinz, Treas.
EIN: 431484142
Selected grants: The following grants are a representative sample of this grantmaker's funding activity:
$20,000 to DeLaSalle Education Center, Kansas City, MO, 2011.
$5,000 to Rose Brooks Center, Kansas City, MO, 2011.
$2,500 to Kansas City Art Institute, Kansas City, MO, 2011.
$2,500 to Kansas City Art Institute, Kansas City, MO, 2011.
$2,500 to Kansas City Symphony, Kansas City, MO, 2011.
$2,000 to Operation Breakthrough, Kansas City, MO, 2011.
$1,000 to American Red Cross, Kansas City, MO, 2011.
$1,000 to Kansas City Art Institute, Kansas City, MO, 2011.

1058
Dechert LLP

Cira Centre
2929 Arch St.
Philadelphia, PA 19104-2808
(215) 994-4000

Company URL: http://www.dechert.com
Establishment information: Established in 1875.
Company type: Private company
Business activities: Operates law firm.
Business type (SIC): Legal services
Corporate officer: Joseph Patrick Archie, Partner
Offices: Irvine, Los Angeles, Mountain View, San Francisco, CA; Hartford, CT; Washington, DC; Boston, MA; Princeton, NJ; New York, NY; Charlotte, NC; Philadelphia, PA; Austin, TX
International operations: Belgium; China; France; Germany; Hong Kong; Ireland; Luxembourg; Russia; United Kingdom
Giving statement: Giving through the Dechert LLP Pro Bono Program.

Dechert LLP Pro Bono Program

Circa Centre
2929 Arch St.
Philadelphia, PA 19104-2808 (202) 261-3361
E-mail: suzanne.turner@dechert.com; Additional tel.: (215) 994-4000; URL: http://www.dechert.com/pro_bono/

Contact: Suzanne Turner, Pro Bono Partner
Fields of interest: Legal services.
Type of support: Pro bono services - legal.
Geographic limitations: Giving primarily in areas of company operations in Irvine, Los Angeles, Mountain View, and San Francisco, CA, Hartford, CT, Washington, DC, Boston, MA, Charlotte, NC, Princeton, NJ, New York, NY, Philadelphia, PA, Austin, TX, Belgium, China, France, Germany, Hong Kong, Ireland, Luxembourg, Russia, and the United Kingdom.
Application information: The Pro Bono Committee manages the pro-bono program.

1059
Deckers Outdoor Corporation

495-A S. Fairview Ave.
Goleta, CA 93117 (805) 967-7611
FAX: (302) 636-5454

Company URL: http://www.deckers.com
Establishment information: Established in 1973.
Company type: Public company
Company ticker symbol and exchange: DECK/NASDAQ
Business activities: Operates footwear company.
Business type (SIC): Apparel, piece goods, and notions—wholesale
Financial profile for 2012: Number of employees, 2,300; assets, $1,068,060,000; sales volume, $1,414,400,000; pre-tax net income, $184,120,000; expenses, $1,227,450,000; liabilities, $329,260,000
Corporate officers: Angel R. Martinez, Chair., Pres., and C.E.O.; Zohar Ziv, C.O.O.; Thomas A. George, C.F.O.; George Troy, V.P., Opers.; Graciela Montgomery, V.P., Human Resources
Board of directors: Angel R. Martinez, Chair.; Karyn O. Barsa; Maureen Conners; Michael F. Devine III; John M. Gibbons; Rex A. Licklider; John G. Perenchio; James E. Quinn; Lauri Shanahan
International operations: China; France; Hong Kong; Japan; Netherlands; United Kingdom
Giving statement: Giving through the Deckers Outdoor Corporation Contributions Program.
Company EIN: 953015862

Deckers Outdoor Corporation Contributions Program

495-A S. Fairview Ave.
Goleta, CA 93117-3681 (805) 967-7611
E-mail: corporate.responsibility@deckers.com; URL: http://www.deckers.com/company/corporate-responsibility

Financial data (yr. ended 12/31/10): Total giving, $700,000, including $700,000 for grants.
Purpose and activities: Decker Outdoor Corporation makes charitable contributions to nonprofit organizations involved with human rights, the environment, and community development. Support is limited to Santa Barbara County, California.
Fields of interest: Environment; Civil/human rights; Community/economic development.
Type of support: Donated products; Employee matching gifts; Employee volunteer services; General/operating support.
Geographic limitations: Giving limited to areas of company operations in Santa Barbara County, CA.
Support limitations: No support for organizations that are focused on medical, religious, political or sexual orientation issues.
Publications: Application guidelines.
Application information: Applications accepted. Application form required. Applicants should submit the following:
1) copy of IRS Determination Letter
2) brief history of organization and description of its mission
3) detailed description of project and amount of funding requested
4) population served
5) name, address and phone number of organization
Initial approach: E-mail completed form and supporting documents to Deckers Corporate Responsibility
Deadline(s): None

1060
Dedham Institution for Savings
55 Elm St.
Dedham, MA 02026-5996 (781) 329-6700

Company URL: http://www.dedhamsavings.com
Establishment information: Established in 1831.
Company type: Private company
Business activities: Operates savings bank.
Business type (SIC): Savings institutions
Financial profile for 2011: Assets, $1,087,680,000; liabilities, $981,239,000
Corporate officers: Peter G. Brown, Pres. and C.E.O.; Mark C. Ingalls, Exec. V.P., C.F.O., and Treas.; Gerard R. Lavoie, Exec. V.P. and C.O.O.; Mark A. McKinnon, Exec. V.P and C.I.O.; Thomas J. Filbin, Exec. V.P. and Genl. Counsel; Jean M. Tennihan, Sr. V.P., Human Resources
Giving statement: Giving through the Dedham Institution for Savings Foundation.

The Dedham Institution for Savings Foundation
45 School St., 5th Fl.
Boston, MA 02108-3204 (781) 461-0163
E-mail: glavoie@dedhamsavings.com; Application address: 55 Elm St., Dedham, MA 02026;
URL: http://www.dedhamsavings.com/news-events-community-involvement.htm

Establishment information: Established in 1998 in MA.
Donor: Dedham Institution for Savings.
Contact: Gerard R. Lavoie, Tr.
Financial data (yr. ended 12/31/11): Assets, $2,506,869 (M); expenditures, $334,285; qualifying distributions, $304,575; giving activities include $304,575 for grants.
Purpose and activities: The foundation supports organizations involved with arts and culture, education, health, recreation, and human services.
Fields of interest: Performing arts, theater; Historical activities; Historic preservation/historical societies; Arts; Secondary school/education; Libraries (public); Education; Health care; Athletics/sports, baseball; Recreation; Youth, services; Aging, centers/services; Developmentally disabled, centers & services; Human services.
Type of support: Annual campaigns; Building/renovation; Capital campaigns; Equipment; Program development; Sponsorships.
Geographic limitations: Giving primarily in areas of company operations in Dedham, Needham, Norwood, Sharon, and Westwood, MA.
Support limitations: No support for political or religious organizations. No grants to individuals.
Publications: Application guidelines.
Application information: Applications accepted. Application form required.
Initial approach: Contact foundation for application form
Board meeting date(s): May and Nov.
Deadline(s): Apr. 30 and Oct. 31
Final notification: June and Dec.
Trustees: Peter G. Brown; Judith G. Carver; Thomas J. Filbin; William G. Gothorpe; Robert B. Hanson; Juanita Allen Kingsley; Gerard R. Lavoie; Dean P. Plakias; Margot C. Pyle.
EIN: 043423462
Selected grants: The following grants are a representative sample of this grantmaker's funding activity:
$10,000 to Boston Symphony Orchestra, Boston, MA, 2009.
$8,000 to Education Cooperative, Dedham, MA, 2009.
$8,000 to Westwood Public Schools, Westwood, MA, 2009.
$7,500 to Hale Reservation, Westwood, MA, 2009.
$7,000 to Charles River Center, Needham, MA, 2009.
$5,000 to Home for Little Wanderers, Boston, MA, 2009.
$5,000 to Westwood Historical Society, Westwood, MA, 2009.
$2,500 to Junior Achievement of Northern New England, Waltham, MA, 2009.

1061
Deere & Company
(also known as John Deere)
1 John Deere Pl.
Moline, IL 61265-8098 (309) 765-8000
FAX: (309) 765-8000

Company URL: http://www.deere.com
Establishment information: Established in 1837.
Company type: Public company
Company ticker symbol and exchange: DE/NYSE
International Securities Identification Number: US2441991054
Business activities: Manufactures and distributes farm equipment; manufactures and distributes commercial and residential lawn and garden equipment; manufactures and distributes construction, earthmoving, materials handling, and timber harvesting machines; provides consumer and commercial loans.
Business type (SIC): Machinery/farm and garden; credit institutions/personal; credit institutions/business
Financial profile for 2012: Number of employees, 66,900; assets, $56,265,800,000; sales volume, $36,157,100,000; pre-tax net income, $4,734,400,000; expenses, $31,422,700,000; liabilities, $49,423,700,000
Fortune 1000 ranking: 2012—85th in revenues, 58th in profits, and 98th in assets
Forbes 2000 ranking: 2012—260th in sales, 178th in profits, and 421st in assets
Corporate officers: Samuel R. Allen, Chair. and C.E.O.; Rajesh Kalathur, Sr. V.P. and C.F.O.; Mary K. W. Jones, Sr. V.P. and Genl. Counsel; Max A. Guinn, Sr. V.P., Human Resources; Jenny R. Kimball, V.P. and Treas.; James E. Temperly, V.P. and Compt.; Charles R. Stamp, Jr., V.P., Public Affairs; Gregory R. Noe, Corp. Secy.
Board of directors: Samuel R. Allen, Chair.; Crandall C. Bowles; Vance D. Coffman; Charles O. Holliday, Jr.; Dipak C. Jain; Clayton M. Jones; Joachim Milberg; Richard B. Myers; Thomas H. Patrick; Aulana L. Peters; Sherry M. Smith
Subsidiaries: John Deere Capital Corp., Reno, NV; Deere Credit, Inc., Des Moines, IA; John Deere Credit Co., Moline, IL; Deere Credit Services, Inc., Madison, WI; John Deere Funding Corp., Reno, NV; John Deere Receivables, Inc., Reno, NV
Plants: Augusta, GA; East Moline, Milan, Silvis, IL; Ankeny, Davenport, Dubuque, Ottumwa, Waterloo, IA; Coffeyville, KS; Thibodaux, LA; Fargo, Valley City, ND; Greeneville, TN; Horicon, WI
Offices: Denver, CO; Alpharetta, GA; Lenexa, KS; Cary, Charlotte, NC; Seattle, WA
International operations: Argentina; Australia; Brazil; Canada; China; Finland; France; Germany; India; Italy; Jamaica; Luxembourg; Mexico; Netherlands; New Zealand; Poland; Russia; South Africa; Spain; Sweden; Switzerland; United Kingdom
Giving statement: Giving through the John Deere Corporate Giving Program and the John Deere Foundation.
Company EIN: 362382580

John Deere Corporate Giving Program
(also known as Corporate Citizenship Center of Excellence)
1 John Deere Pl.
Moline, IL 61265-8010
URL: http://www.deere.com/en_US/globalcitizenship/socialinvestment/community/index.html

Purpose and activities: As a complement to its foundation, John Deere also makes charitable contributions to nonprofit organizations involved with arts and culture, education, human services, community development, food service, and disaster relief. Support is given on a national and international basis in areas of company operations, with emphasis on Atlanta, and Augusta, Georgia, Quad Cities, Illinois, Des Moines, Dubuque, Greater Cedar Valley, Ottumwa, Quad Cities, and Waterloo, Iowa, Coffeyville, and Lenexa, Kansas, Thibodaux, Louisiana, Cary, and Fuquay-Varina, North Carolina, Fargo, North Dakota, Greeneville, Tennessee, and Horicon, and Madison, Wisconsin. Giving also in Germany.
Fields of interest: Arts; Higher education, college; Education, computer literacy/technology training; Education; Food services; Safety/disasters, volunteer services; Human services; Community/economic development; United Ways and Federated Giving Programs; Science, formal/general education.
Type of support: Continuing support; Employee matching gifts; Employee volunteer services; In-kind gifts; Program development; Sponsorships.
Geographic limitations: Giving primarily in areas of company operations, with emphasis on Atlanta, and Augusta, GA, Des Moines, Dubuque, Greater Cedar Valley, Ottumwa, Quad Cities, and Waterloo, IA, Quad Cities, IL, Coffeyville, and Lenexa, KS, Thibodaux, LA, Cary, and Fuquay-Varina, NC, Fargo, ND, Greeneville, TN, and Horicon, and Madison, WI.
Support limitations: No support for sports teams, religious, or political organizations, private clubs, fraternities or sororities, or tax-supported entities. No grants to individuals, or for athletic scholarships, building endowments, or capital campaigns.
Publications: Application guidelines; Corporate report.
Application information: Applications accepted. Application form required.
Initial approach: Complete online eligibility quiz and application form
Copies of proposal: 1
Deadline(s): None
Administrators: Cheryl A. Ashcroft, Div. Mgr., Corp. Citizenship.
Number of staff: 6 full-time professional; 2 full-time support.

John Deere Foundation
1 John Deere Pl.
Moline, IL 61265-8010
FAX: (309) 748-7953;
E-mail: bustlejohnw@johndeere.com; URL: http://www.deere.com/en_US/globalcitizenship/socialinvestment/index.html

Establishment information: Incorporated in 1948 in IL.
Donor: Deere & Co.
Contact: John W. Bustle, V.P.
Financial data (yr. ended 12/31/11): Assets, $150,305,334 (M); gifts received, $35,000,000; expenditures, $14,017,133; qualifying distributions, $13,930,897; giving activities include

$13,930,897 for 599 grants (high: $1,250,000; low: $50) and $195,448 for foundation-administered programs.
Purpose and activities: The foundation supports programs designed to promote education; community betterment through community development, human services, and arts and culture; and solutions for world hunger through agricultural development that results in sustainable food supplies and economic growth in underdeveloped countries.
Fields of interest: Arts; Higher education; Education; Agriculture, sustainable programs; Food services; Food banks; Agriculture/food; Disasters, preparedness/services; Youth development, business; American Red Cross; Human services; Community development, business promotion; Community development, small businesses; Community/economic development; Mathematics; Engineering/technology; Science Minorities; Economically disadvantaged.
International interests: Africa; Global programs; India.
Program:
Matching Gift Program: The foundation matches contributions made by employees of Deere & Co. to educational institutions and to Kickstart, a nonprofit organization designed to help farmers in Kenya, Tanzania, and Mali get out of poverty, on a one-for-one basis, from $50 to $1,000 per employee, per year.
Type of support: Annual campaigns; Building/renovation; Continuing support; Emergency funds; Employee matching gifts; Employee volunteer services; General/operating support; Program development; Research; Scholarship funds.
Geographic limitations: Giving primarily in areas of company operations in Atlanta and Augusta, GA, Des Moines, Dubuque, Iowa Quad cities, Ottumwa, and Waterloo, IA, Quad City Region, IL, Coffeyville and Greater Kansas City, KS, Thibodaux, LA, Cary and Fuquay-Varina, NC, Fargo, ND, Greeneville, TN, and Horicon and Madison, WI; giving also to Africa and global programs.
Support limitations: No support for religious organizations, athletic organizations, political organizations, foundations, tax-supported organizations, or fraternal organizations or sororities. No grants to individuals, or for sports programs, political campaigns, advertising, or marketing; no loans; no in-kind equipment donations.
Publications: Application guidelines; Corporate report.
Application information: Applications accepted. Application form required. Applicants should submit the following:
1) results expected from proposed grant
2) statement of problem project will address
3) population served
4) copy of IRS Determination Letter
5) brief history of organization and description of its mission
6) geographic area to be served
7) copy of most recent annual report/audited financial statement/990
8) how project's results will be evaluated or measured
9) detailed description of project and amount of funding requested
10) copy of current year's organizational budget and/or project budget
11) listing of additional sources and amount of support

Initial approach: Complete online eligibility quiz and application
Board meeting date(s): Quarterly
Deadline(s): None
Final notification: 30 days following board meetings

Officers and Directors:* Samuel R. Allen*, Chair.; Mara L. Sovey*, Pres.; John W. Bustle, V.P.; Gregory R. Noe, Secy.; Dennis R. Schwartz, Treas.; Frances B. Emerson; David C. Everitt; James M. Field; James R. Jenkins; Marie Z. Ziegler.
Number of staff: 2.5 full-time professional.
EIN: 366051024
Selected grants: The following grants are a representative sample of this grantmaker's funding activity:
$1,000,000 to American Red Cross of the Quad Cities Area, Moline, IL, 2011. For Disaster Relief.
$1,000,000 to Waterloo Development Corporation, Waterloo, IA, 2011. For Community Betterment.
$500,000 to Augustana College, Rock Island, IL, 2011.
$500,000 to Quad Cities Cultural and Educational Charitable Trust, Davenport, IA, 2011. For Community Betterment.
$250,000 to American Red Cross of the Quad Cities Area, Moline, IL, 2011. For Disaster Relief.
$225,000 to Food Bank of Iowa, Des Moines, IA, 2011. For Solutions for World Hunger.
$27,000 to United Fund of Coffeyville, Coffeyville, KS, 2011. For Community Betterment.
$4,000 to Purdue University, West Lafayette, IN, 2011.

1062
Deerfield Management Company, LP

780 3rd Ave., 37th Fl.
New York, NY 10017-2024 (212) 551-1600

Establishment information: Established in 1993.
Company type: Private company
Business activities: Operates security brokerage.
Business type (SIC): Brokers and dealers/security
Corporate officers: James Edward Flynn, Pres.; Jonathan David Isler, C.F.O.
Giving statement: Giving through the Deerfield Partnership Foundation.

The Deerfield Partnership Foundation

780 3rd Ave., 37th Fl.
New York, NY 10017-2024

Establishment information: Established in 2005 in NY.
Donor: Deerfield Management Company.
Financial data (yr. ended 12/31/11): Assets, $2,000,487 (M); gifts received, $2,333,633; expenditures, $2,109,498; qualifying distributions, $1,949,690; giving activities include $1,945,860 for 10 grants (high: $750,000; low: $50,000).
Purpose and activities: The foundation supports organizations involved with education, health, human services, and economically disadvantaged people. Special emphasis is directed toward programs that benefit children.
Fields of interest: Education; Health care; Children/youth, services; Family services; Human services Children; Economically disadvantaged.
Type of support: General/operating support.
Geographic limitations: Giving primarily in New York, NY.
Application information: Applications not accepted. Contributes only to pre-selected organizations.
Officers and Directors: Alex Karnal*, Chair.; April Tubbs, Pres.; Jordan Fogel, V.P.; Bernadette Haken, V.P.; Leslie Henshaw, V.P.; Jean Kim, V.P.; Ted Huber, Secy.; Kevin Berg, Treas.
EIN: 050618950
Selected grants: The following grants are a representative sample of this grantmaker's funding activity:
$750,000 to Childrens Health Fund, New York, NY, 2011. For general operations.
$550,000 to Partners in Health, Boston, MA, 2011. For general operations.
$125,000 to Family Center, New York, NY, 2011. For general operations.
$120,000 to Little Sisters of the Assumption Family Health Service, New York, NY, 2011.
$65,000 to Coalition for the Homeless, New York, NY, 2011. For general operations.
$52,000 to American Jewish Joint Distribution Committee, New York, NY, 2011. For general operations.

1063
The Defiance Publishing Company

624 W. 2nd St.
Defiance, OH 43512-2161 (419) 784-5441

Establishment information: Established in 1888.
Company type: Private company
Business activities: Publishes newspapers.
Business type (SIC): Newspaper publishing and/or printing
Corporate officer: Albert E. Dix, Pres.
Giving statement: Giving through the Dix Foundation.

Dix Foundation

212 E. Liberty St.
Wooster, OH 44691-4348 (330) 264-3511

Donors: Defiance Publishing Company, LLC; Wooster Republican Printing Co.
Contact: G. Charles Dix II, Tr.
Financial data (yr. ended 12/31/11): Assets, $2,283 (M); gifts received, $6,300; expenditures, $4,655; qualifying distributions, $4,655; giving activities include $4,390 for 4 grants (high: $2,500; low: $390).
Purpose and activities: The foundation supports organizations involved with higher education and economic development.
Fields of interest: Higher education; YM/YWCAs & YM/YWHAs; Economic development.
Type of support: General/operating support.
Geographic limitations: Giving limited to Defiance, OH.
Support limitations: No grants to individuals.
Application information: Applications accepted. Application form required. Applicants should submit the following:
1) detailed description of project and amount of funding requested
2) copy of current year's organizational budget and/or project budget

Initial approach: Letter
Deadline(s): None

Trustees: David E. Dix; G. Charles Dix II; R. Victor Dix; Robert C. Dix, Jr.
EIN: 346554966

1064
Marcel Dekker, Inc.
270 Madison Ave.
New York, NY 10016-0601 (212) 696-9000

Establishment information: Established in 1963.
Company type: Subsidiary of a private company
Business activities: Publishes scientific, technical, and medical publications.
Business type (SIC): Book publishing and/or printing
Financial profile for 2010: Number of employees, 140
Corporate officers: Marcel Dekker, Pres. and C.E.O.; James Clifford, Genl. Counsel
Giving statement: Giving through the Dekker Foundation.

Dekker Foundation
8 Wells Hill Rd.
Weston, CT 06883-2624 (203) 226-3152

Establishment information: Established in 1997 in CT.
Donors: Marcel Dekker, Inc.; Harriett Dekker; David Dekker; Russell Dekker.
Financial data (yr. ended 12/31/11): Assets, $107,414 (M); expenditures, $130,800; qualifying distributions, $130,500; giving activities include $130,500 for 3 grants (high: $62,500; low: $18,000).
Purpose and activities: The foundation supports organizations involved with health, Parkinson's disease, disabled people, and other areas.
Fields of interest: Education; Crime/law enforcement; Human services.
Type of support: General/operating support.
Geographic limitations: Giving primarily in CT and NY.
Support limitations: No grants to individuals.
Application information: Applications accepted. Application form required.
Initial approach: Proposal
Deadline(s): None
Trustee: David Dekker; Harriett Dekker; Marcell Dekker; Russell Dekker.
EIN: 061479508

1065
Del Monte Foods Company
1 Maritime Plz.
San Francisco, CA 94111-3410
(415) 247-3000

Company URL: http://www.delmonte.com/
Establishment information: Established in 1916.
Company type: Private company
Business activities: Produces, distributes, and markets branded food and pet products.
Business type (SIC): Specialty foods/canned, frozen, and preserved
Financial profile for 2012: Number of employees, 5,200
Corporate officers: James M. Kilts, Chair.; Neil Harrison, Vice Chair.; David J. West, Pres. and C.E.O.; Nils Lommerin, Exec. V.P. and C.O.O.; Larry E. Bodner, Exec. V.P., C.F.O., and Treas.; Timothy A. Cole, Exec. V.P., Sales
Board of directors: James M. Kilts, Chair.; Neil Harrison, Vice-Chair.; Max V. Alper; Simon E. Brown; Richard Dunne; David Hopper; James P. Kelley; Kevin Mundt; Dean B. Nelson; David J. West
Giving statement: Giving through the Del Monte Foods Company Contributions Program.
Company EIN: 133542950

Del Monte Foods Company Contributions Program
1 Maritime Plz.
San Francisco, CA 94111-3404
URL: http://www.delmontefoods.com/cr/

Financial data (yr. ended 12/31/10): Total giving, $3,600,000, including $3,600,000 for grants.
Purpose and activities: Del Monte makes charitable contributions to nonprofit organizations involved with animal welfare, public health, food services, and on a case by case basis. Support is given primarily in areas of company operations, with emphasis on Pittsburgh, Pennsylvania.
Fields of interest: Animal welfare; Public health; Food services.
Type of support: Donated products; Employee volunteer services; General/operating support; Sponsorships.
Geographic limitations: Giving primarily in areas of company operations, with emphasis on Pittsburgh, PA, and San Francisco, CA.
Application information: Applications accepted. Application form required.
Initial approach: Complete online application form

1066
Delaware North Companies, Inc.
40 Fountain Plz.
Buffalo, NY 14202 (716) 858-5000
FAX: (716) 858-5479

Company URL: http://www.delawarenorth.com/
Establishment information: Established in 1915.
Company type: Private company
Business activities: Operates restaurants; provides concession services; operates professional ice hockey club; operates arena; provides facilities management services; operates retail shops.
Business type (SIC): Restaurants and drinking places; general merchandise stores; commercial sports; management and public relations services
Financial profile for 2011: Number of employees, 55,000; sales volume, $2,200,000,000
Corporate officers: Jeremy M. Jacobs, Chair. and C.E.O.; Charles E. Moran, Jr., Pres. and C.O.O.; Christopher J. Feeney, C.F.O.; Kevin Quinlivan, C.I.O.; Scott Socha, V.P. and Treas.; Rajat Shah, V.P., Genl. Counsel, and Secy.; Jim Houser, V.P., Admin.; Dan Zimmer, V.P., Finance; Wendy Watkins, V.P., Corp. Comms.; Eileen Morgan, V.P., Human Resources
Board of director: Jeremy M. Jacobs, Chair.
Subsidiaries: Air Terminal Services, Inc., Buffalo, NY; APCOA, Cleveland, OH; Arrow Typographers, Inc., Newark, NJ; Greyhound Racehorses, Buffalo, NY; Sportservice Corporation, Buffalo, NY
Giving statement: Giving through the Delaware North Companies Incorporated Corporate Giving Program.

Delaware North Companies Incorporated Corporate Giving Program
40 Fountain Plz.
Buffalo, NY 14202 (716) 858-5000
FAX: (716) 858-5187; E-mail: webinfo@dncinc.com; URL: http://www.delawarenorth.com/Value-Global-Stewardship.aspx

Purpose and activities: Delaware North makes charitable contributions to museums and nonprofit organizations involved with education, youth development and recreation, the environment, hunger relief, community support, national parks, Special Olympics, and historical preservation. Support is given primarily in areas of company operations on a national basis, and in Australia, Canada, New Zealand, and United Kingdom.
Fields of interest: Museums; Historic preservation/historical societies; Education; Environment; Food services; Recreation, camps; Recreation, parks/playgrounds; Athletics/sports, Special Olympics; Boys & girls clubs; Human services, fund raising/fund distribution; Youth, services; Community/economic development; United Ways and Federated Giving Programs Economically disadvantaged.
Type of support: Donated products; Employee volunteer services; General/operating support; In-kind gifts; Scholarship funds; Sponsorships.
Geographic limitations: Giving primarily in areas of company operations on a national basis, and in Australia, Canada, New Zealand, and United Kingdom.
Support limitations: No grants to individuals, or for religious or political purposes, capital campaigns, sponsorship advertising, research programs, endowments, or any for-profit ventures.
Publications: Application guidelines; Corporate giving report.
Application information: Applications accepted. Application form not required.
Initial approach: Proposal to headquarters for donation requests; contact nearest company location for volunteer requests
Deadline(s): 6 months prior to event

1067
Dell Corning Corporation
575 John Dodd Rd.
Spartanburg, SC 29303-6313
(864) 578-5552

Company URL: http://www.dellcorning.com
Establishment information: Established in 1974.
Company type: Private company
Business activities: Operates automotive interior protective products company.
Business type (SIC): Metal products/structural
Corporate officer: Sam Sebair, Pres.
Giving statement: Giving through the Dell Corning Corporation Contributions Program.

Dell Corning Corporation Contributions Program
575 John Dodd Rd.
Spartanburg, SC 29303 (864) 578-5552
E-mail: dellcorning@dellcorning.com; URL: http://www.dellcorning.com/index-2.html

Purpose and activities: Dell Corning Corporation makes charitable contributions to nonprofit organizations in areas of company operations. Emphasis is given to organizations that encourage the development of educational, social welfare and health, cultural, and civic institutions.
Fields of interest: Arts, cultural/ethnic awareness; Education; Health care; Community development, civic centers; Community/economic development; Public affairs.
Type of support: General/operating support.
Geographic limitations: Giving primarily in areas of company operations.

1068
Dell Inc.

(formerly Dell Computer Corporation)
1 Dell Way
Round Rock, TX 78682-7000
(512) 338-4400

Company URL: http://www.dell.com
Establishment information: Established in 1984.
Company type: Public company
Company ticker symbol and exchange: DELL/NASDAQ
International Securities Identification Number: US24702R1014
Business activities: Manufactures and distributes personal computers.
Business type (SIC): Computer and office equipment; professional and commercial equipment—wholesale; nonstore retailers
Financial profile for 2013: Number of employees, 111,300; assets, $47,540,000,000; sales volume, $56,940,000,000; pre-tax net income, $2,841,000,000; expenses, $53,928,000,000; liabilities, $36,860,000,000
Fortune 1000 ranking: 2012—51st in revenues, 85th in profits, and 116th in assets
Forbes 2000 ranking: 2012—143rd in sales, 242nd in profits, and 482nd in assets
Corporate officers: Michael S. Dell, Chair. and C.E.O.; Jeffrey W. Clarke, Vice-Chair.; Stephen J. Felice, Pres.; Brian T. Gladden, Sr. V.P. and C.F.O.; Lawrence P. Tu, Sr. V.P., Secy., and Genl. Counsel; Steve H. Price, Sr. V.P., Human Resources
Board of directors: Michael S. Dell, Chair.; Jeffrey W. Clarke, Vice-Chair.; James W. Breyer; Donald J. Carty; Janet F. Clark; Laura Conigliaro; Kenneth M. Duberstein; William H. Gray III; Gerard J. Kleisterlee; Klaus S. Luft; Alex J. Mandl; Shantanu Narayen; Ross Perot, Jr.
Subsidiary: Dell Marketing Corp., Austin, TX
International operations: Argentina; Australia; Austria; Bahrain; Barbados; Belgium; Brazil; Bulgaria; Canada; Cayman Islands; Chile; China; Colombia; Costa Rica; Croatia; Czech Republic; Denmark; Ecuador; Egypt; El Salvador; Finland; France; Germany; Ghana; Greece; Guatemala; Honduras; Hong Kong; Hungary; India; Indonesia; Ireland; Israel; Italy; Jamaica; Japan; Jordan; Kazakhstan; Lebanon; Luxembourg; Malaysia; Mexico; Morocco and the Western Sahara; Netherlands; New Zealand; Nigeria; Northern Ireland; Norway; Panama; Peru; Philippines; Poland; Portugal; Romania; Russia; Saudi Arabia; Singapore; Slovakia; South Africa; South Korea; Spain; Sweden; Switzerland; Taiwan; Thailand; Trinidad & Tobago; Turkey; Uganda; Ukraine; United Arab Emirates; United Kingdom; Venezuela; Vietnam
Giving statement: Giving through the Dell Inc. Corporate Giving Program.
Company EIN: 742487834

Dell Inc. Corporate Giving Program

1 Dell Way
Round Rock, TX 78682-7000 (512) 338-4400
E-mail: dell-support@yourcause.com; URL: http://content.dell.com/us/en/corp/cr.aspx?c=us&l=en&s=gen

Financial data (yr. ended 12/31/12): Total giving, $44,100,000, including $33,400,000 for grants and $10,700,000 for in-kind gifts.
Purpose and activities: As a complement to its foundation, Dell also makes charitable contributions to nonprofit organizations directly. Support is given on a national and international basis primarily in areas of company operations.
Fields of interest: Elementary/secondary education; Education, computer literacy/technology training; Cancer; Breast cancer; Food services; Safety/disasters; Youth development; Children, services; Family resources and services, disability; Economic development; Community development, small businesses Economically disadvantaged.
Programs:
Dell YouthConnect: Through the Dell YouthConnect program, the company awards grants to charitable organizations in key emerging countries that have a strong need for both humanitarian aid and technology access. The cash and in-kind grants support technology education for youths up to 17-years-old, and promote math, science, and technology skills.
Matching Donations Program: Dell team members around the world are given the chance to contribute their monies and have Dell match their contribution dollar for dollar, up to $10,000 per employee, per calendar year.
Team-Member Recognition Programs: Through Dell's team-member recognition programs, employees are given the chance to give back by doubling their impact through their recognition. For every recorded 10-plus hours of volunteer service per quarter, team members are given a $150 cause card (in U.S. dollars) to redeem in Dell's Make a Difference online community, which gives them the option to donate to a qualified charity of their choice.
Type of support: Donated products; Employee matching gifts; Employee volunteer services; General/operating support; In-kind gifts.
Geographic limitations: Giving on a national and international basis primarily in areas of company operations.
Application information: Applications accepted.
Initial approach: E-mail proposal for requests for volunteers

1069
Delmarva Power & Light Company

P.O. Box 231
Wilmington, DE 19899-0231
(302) 761-7000

Company URL: http://www.delmarva.com
Establishment information: Established in 1909.
Company type: Subsidiary of a public company
Ultimate parent company: Pepco Holdings, Inc.
Business activities: Generates, transmits, and distributes electricity; transmits and distributes natural gas.
Business type (SIC): Combination utility services
Financial profile for 2010: Number of employees, 905
Corporate officer: John Vanroden, C.F.O.
Giving statement: Giving through the Delmarva Power & Light Company Contributions Program.

Delmarva Power & Light Company Contributions Program

(formerly Conectiv Corporate Giving Program)
P.O. Box 17000
Wilmington, DE 19886-7000
URL: http://www.delmarva.com/welcome/community

Purpose and activities: Delmarva makes charitable contributions to nonprofit organizations involved with education, the environment, health care, housing, public safety, youth development, and the military. Support is given primarily in areas of company operations in Maryland and Delaware.
Fields of interest: Education; Environment; Health care; Heart & circulatory diseases; Housing/shelter; Safety/disasters; Boy scouts; Girl scouts; Youth development; Utilities Military/veterans.
Program:
Education Mini-Grant Program: Through the Education Mini-Grant Program, Delmarva provides classroom teachers with grants of up to $500 to support innovative projects that are geared toward energy-related issues, such as wise energy use, local conventional and alternative energy resources, energy-related science content and electric safety. Grants can be used for purchasing materials, conducting special lessons, taking field trips and implementing special classroom projects that are not usually funded by school districts. Grants are available to public and private school teachers in kindergarten through twelfth grade and special education in Kent and Sussex counties in Delaware and in Cecil, Harford, and the Eastern Shore counties in Maryland.
Type of support: Donated products; Employee volunteer services; General/operating support; Grants to individuals; In-kind gifts; Sponsorships.
Geographic limitations: Giving primarily in areas of company operations in Delaware and Maryland; giving also to national organizations.

1070
Deloitte & Touche LLP

Paramount Bldg., 1633 Broadway
New York, NY 10019-6754 (212) 489-1600

Company URL: http://www.deloitte.com
Establishment information: Established in 1895.
Company type: Subsidiary of a private company
Business activities: Provides accounting, auditing, tax, and management consulting services.
Business type (SIC): Accounting, auditing, and bookkeeping services; management and public relations services
Financial profile for 2009: Number of employees, 44,375; sales volume, $10,980,000,000
Corporate officers: Sharon L. Allen, Chair.; Barry Salzberg, C.E.O.; John Zamora, Chief Diversity Off.
Board of director: Sharon L. Allen, Chair.
Giving statement: Giving through the Deloitte & Touche LLP Corporate Giving Program and the Deloitte Foundation.

Deloitte & Touche LLP Corporate Giving Program

1633 Broadway
New York, NY 10019-6754 (212) 489-1600
Additional address: Laura Eilts, Central Region Community Involvement Leader, Deloitte Services LP, 111 S. Wacker Dr., Chicago, IL 60606-4301, tel.: (312) 486-3190, fax: (312) 247-3190, e-mail: leilts@deloitte.com; URL: http://www.deloitte.com/view/en_US/us/About/Community-Involvement/index.htm

Contact: Holly Cook, Natl. Mgr., Community Rels.
Purpose and activities: As a complement to its foundation, Deloitte & Touche also makes charitable contributions to nonprofit organizations on a case by case basis. Special emphasis is directed toward organizations with which employees are involved. Support is given primarily in areas of company operations.
Fields of interest: General charitable giving.

Type of support: Employee volunteer services; General/operating support; In-kind gifts; Loaned talent; Sponsorships.
Geographic limitations: Giving primarily in areas of company operations.
Application information: Applications accepted. Application form not required.
Initial approach: Proposal to headquarters

Deloitte Foundation

(formerly Deloitte & Touche Foundation)
10 Westport Rd.
P.O. Box 820
Wilton, CT 06897-0820
Contact for Doctoral Fellowship Program: Peg Levine, tel.: (203) 761-3413, e-mail: plevine@deloitte.com; URL: http://www.deloitte.com/us/df

Establishment information: Incorporated in 1928 in NY.
Donors: Deloitte LLP; Deloitte Haskins & Sells; Deloitte & Touche LLP; Charles Stewart Ludlam†; Charles C. Croggon†; Weldon Powell†; Deloitte & Touche USA LLP; Wayne Williamson.
Financial data (yr. ended 06/02/12): Assets, $14,867,614 (M); gifts received, $7,865,552; expenditures, $8,303,444; qualifying distributions, $8,301,273; giving activities include $3,017,012 for 20+ grants (high: $500,000) and $5,179,515 for 340 employee matching gifts.
Purpose and activities: The foundation supports organizations involved with accounting and business education and awards fellowships to doctoral accounting students.
Fields of interest: Higher education; Business school/education; Education.
Programs:
AAA/Deloitte Wildman Medal: The foundation, in partnership with the American Accounting Association, honors an author or co-authors whose article, book, monograph, or other work published has made a highly significant contribution to the practice of public accounting. The $5,000 honorarium is awarded to support research that advances the theory and practice of accounting. The award is administered by the American Accounting Association. See web site, http://aaahq.org/awards/award1.htm for additional information.
AAA/Deloitte/J. Michael Cook Doctoral Consortium: The foundation, in partnership with the American Accounting Association (AAA), gives advanced doctoral students a chance to meet with distinguished faculty through a consortium. The consortium targets issues that are pressing to faculty and to students who are about to become professors, including theoretical and applied research, teaching, and career development.
Accounting Doctoral Scholars: The foundation, in partnership with the AICPA Foundation, awards grants to accountants with public accounting experience in auditing and tax to help them transition into academic roles at the university level. The program includes an annual stipend of $30,000 for a maximum of four years to pursue a Ph.D. and career in academia. The program is administered by the AICPA Foundation. See web site, http://www.adsphd.org/ for additional information.
ATA Teachers Innovation Award: The foundation, in partnership with the American Taxation Association, awards a $5,000 grant to tax professors to develop new teaching methods designed to stimulate students' critical thinking skills and enhance the learning experience. The award is administered by the American Taxation Association. Visit http://aaahq.org/ata/_ATAMenu/CallAwards.html for additional information.
Doctoral Fellowship Program: The foundation annually awards up to ten $25,000 fellowships to doctoral accounting students. Fellowships are disbursed in four payments over two years to help cover expenses during the final year of coursework and during the subsequent year of writing a dissertation.
Employee Matching Gifts-Education: The foundation matches contributions made by employees of Deloitte & Touche to nonprofit organizations on a one-for-one basis from $50 to $5,000 per employee, per year.
Type of support: Conferences/seminars; Curriculum development; Employee matching gifts; Fellowships; Professorships; Research; Scholarship funds; Sponsorships.
Geographic limitations: Giving primarily in Washington, DC, FL, IL, KS, TX, and VA; giving on a national basis for fellowships.
Support limitations: No grants for general operating support, capital campaigns, special programs, or publications; no loans; no matching support.
Publications: Application guidelines; Grants list; Informational brochure.
Application information: Applications accepted. An application form is required for Doctoral Fellowships.
Initial approach: Contact foundation or accounting department head at educational institution for application form for Doctoral Fellowships
Copies of proposal: 1
Board meeting date(s): 3 times per year
Deadline(s): Oct. 15 for Doctoral Fellowships
Final notification: Jan. for Doctoral Fellowships
Officers and Directors:* Punit Renjen, Chair.; Shaun L. Budnik, Pres.; Jennifer Steinmann, Secy.-Treas.; Nathan Andrews; Philip Brunson; Amy Chronis; Tonie Leatherberry; Lissa Perez; John Sizer; Sylvia Smyth.
EIN: 136400341

1071
Delphi Automotive, LLP

(formerly Delphi Corporation)
5725 Delphi Dr.
Troy, MI 48098-2815 (248) 813-2000

Company URL: http://www.delphi.com
Establishment information: Established in 1999.
Company type: Private company
Business activities: Manufactures vehicle electronics, transportation components, integrated systems and modules, and other electronic technology.
Business type (SIC): Motor vehicles and equipment; electronic and other electrical equipment and components
Financial profile for 2012: Assets, $10,200,000,000; sales volume, $15,500,000,000
Forbes 2000 ranking: 2012—609th in sales, 515th in profits, and 1461st in assets
Corporate officers: John A Krol, Chair.; Rodney O'Neal, Pres. and C.E.O.; Kevin P. Clark, C.F.O.; Timothy C. McCabe, V.P. and C.I.O.; David M. Sherbin, V.P., Genl. Counsel, and Secy.; Eleanor E. Mascheroni, V.P., Mktg.; Kevin M. Butler, V.P., Human Resources; Keith D. Stipp, Treas.
Board of directors: John A. Krol, Chair.; Gary L. Cowger; Nicholas M. Donofrio; Mark P. Frissora; Rajiv L. Gupta; J. Randall MacDonald; Sean O. Mahoney; Michael McNamara; Rodney O'Neal; Thomas W. SidlikThomas W. Sidlik; Bernd Wiedemann; Lawrence A. Zimmerman
Divisions: Electrical and Electronic Architecture, Warren, OH; Electronics & Safety Div., Kokomo, IN; Product and Services Solutions, Troy, MI; Thermal Systems, Auburn Hills, MI
International operations: Luxembourg
Giving statement: Giving through the Delphi Corporation Contributions Program and the Delphi Foundation, Inc.

Delphi Corporation Contributions Program

(formerly Delphi Automotive Systems Corporation Contributions Program)
c/o Community Rels.
5725 Delphi Dr.
Troy, MI 48098-2815
URL: http://delphi.com/about/social

Purpose and activities: As a complement to its foundation, Delphi also makes charitable contributions to nonprofit organizations directly. Support is given on a national and international basis in areas of company operations.
Fields of interest: Education; Disasters, preparedness/services; American Red Cross; United Ways and Federated Giving Programs; Science; Engineering/technology; General charitable giving.
Type of support: Employee volunteer services; General/operating support.
Geographic limitations: Giving on a national and international basis in areas of company operations.
Number of staff: 4 part-time professional; 1 part-time support.

Delphi Foundation, Inc.

5725 Delphi Dr., M.C. 483-400-501
Troy, MI 48098-2815
E-mail: ronald.l.beeber@delphi.com; URL: http://delphi.com/about/social/delphifoundation

Establishment information: Established in 1998 in MI.
Donors: General Motors Foundation, Inc.; Delphi Automotive Systems Corp.; Delphi Corp.
Financial data (yr. ended 12/31/11): Assets, $15,546,511 (M); expenditures, $877,724; qualifying distributions, $821,350; giving activities include $821,350 for grants.
Purpose and activities: The foundation supports organizations involved with science and technology education.
Fields of interest: Elementary/secondary education; Higher education; Education; Science, formal/general education; Engineering/technology Youth.
Type of support: Program development.
Geographic limitations: Giving primarily in areas of company operations in IL, IN, MI, NY, PA, and VA.
Support limitations: No support for political, lobbying, or fraternal organizations, private foundations, hospitals, health care institutions, or religious organizations. No grants to individuals, or for endowments, capital campaigns, construction, general operating support, debt reduction, or conferences, workshops, or seminars not directly related to Delphi's business interests.
Publications: IRS Form 990 or 990-PF printed copy available upon request.
Application information: Applications not accepted. The foundation utilizes an invitation only Request For Proposal (RFP) process. Unsolicited requests are not accepted.
Officers and Trustees:* Karen L. Healy*, Chair.; Nancy Moss, Secy.; Keith D. Stipp*, Treas.; James P. Whitson*, Chief Tax Off.; Ronald L. Beeber; Tracy Hensler.
Number of staff: None.
EIN: 383442971

1072
The Delphos Herald, Inc.
405 N. Main St.
Delphos, OH 45833-1577 (419) 695-0015

Company URL: http://www.delphosherald.com
Establishment information: Established in 1960.
Company type: Private company
Business activities: Publishes newspapers.
Business type (SIC): Newspaper publishing and/or printing
Corporate officer: Murray Cohen, Chair.
Board of director: Murray Cohen, Chair.
Giving statement: Giving through the Ethel and Nathan Cohen Foundation Inc.

Ethel and Nathan Cohen Foundation Inc.
6230 A Wilshire Blvd., Ste. 1137
Los Angeles, CA 90048

Establishment information: Established in 2003 in OH.
Donors: Delphos Herald, Inc.; Murray Cohen.
Financial data (yr. ended 12/31/11): Assets, $11,474 (M); gifts received, $25,285; expenditures, $30,856; qualifying distributions, $25,480; giving activities include $25,480 for grants.
Purpose and activities: The foundation supports organizations involved with arts and culture, education, health, human services, and Judaism.
Fields of interest: Education; Housing/shelter; Religion.
Type of support: General/operating support; Program development.
Support limitations: No grants to individuals.
Application information: Applications not accepted. Contributes only to pre-selected organizations.
Trustees: Murray Cohen; Roberta Cohen; Jennifer Shneiderman.
EIN: 450512626

1073
Delta Air Lines, Inc.
1030 Delta Blvd.
P.O. Box 20706
Atlanta, GA 30320-6001 (404) 715-2600
FAX: (404) 677-3851

Company URL: http://www.delta.com
Establishment information: Established in 1924.
Company type: Public company
Company ticker symbol and exchange: DAL/NYSE
Business activities: Provides passenger and freight air transportation services.
Business type (SIC): Transportation/scheduled air
Financial profile for 2012: Number of employees, 74,000; assets, $44,550,000,000; sales volume, $36,670,000,000; pre-tax net income, $1,025,000,000; expenses, $34,613,000,000; liabilities, $46,681,000,000
Fortune 1000 ranking: 2012—83rd in revenues, 197th in profits, and 120th in assets
Forbes 2000 ranking: 2012—261st in sales, 603rd in profits, and 516th in assets
Corporate officers: Daniel A. Carp, Chair.; Roy J. Bostock, Vice-Chair.; Richard H. Anderson, C.E.O.; Edward H. Bastian, Pres.; Stephen E. Gorman, Exec. V.P. and C.O.O.; Michael H. Campbell, Exec. V.P., Human Resources; Paul Jacobson, Sr. V.P. and C.F.O.; Theresa Wise, Sr. V.P. and C.I.O.; John E. Walker, Sr. V.P., Corp. Comms.
Board of directors: Daniel A. Carp, Chair.; Roy J. Bostock, Vice-Chair.; Richard H. Anderson; Edward H. Bastian; John S. Brinzo; David G. DeWatt; Mickey P. Foret; Shirley C. Franklin; David R. Goode; George N. Mattson; Paula Rosput Reynolds; Kenneth C. Rogers; Kenneth B. Woodrow
Subsidiaries: Delta Air Lines Holding, Inc., Atlanta, GA; Western Airlines, Inc., Los Angeles, CA
International operations: Bermuda; Canada; Cayman Islands; France; Germany; India; Ireland; Japan; United Kingdom
Historic mergers: Northwest Airlines Corporation (October 29, 2008)
Giving statement: Giving through the Delta Air Lines, Inc. Corporate Giving Program and the Delta Air Lines Foundation.
Company EIN: 580218548

Delta Air Lines, Inc. Corporate Giving Program
c/o Community Relations
1050 Delta Blvd.
Atlanta, GA 30354-1989
URL: http://www.delta.com/content/www/en_US/about-delta.html

Contact: Scarlet Pressley-Brown, Dir., External Affairs & Community Rels.
Purpose and activities: As a complement to its foundation, Delta also makes charitable contributions to nonprofit organizations directly. Support is given on a national and international basis.
Fields of interest: Museums; Performing arts; Performing arts, orchestras; Historic preservation/historical societies; Arts; Education, fund raising/fund distribution; Higher education; Environment, natural resources; Hospitals (general); Health care, patient services; Health care; Cancer; Breast cancer; Diabetes; Housing/shelter, development; Athletics/sports, baseball; Salvation Army; Children/youth, services; Human services; Civil/human rights, equal rights Economically disadvantaged.
International interests: India; Japan.
Program:
Delta Force For Global Good: Through Delta Force for Global Good, Delta and community partners promote positive local and global change. Special emphasis is directed toward advancing global diversity; improving global wellness; improving the environment; and promoting arts and culture.
Type of support: Building/renovation; Continuing support; Donated equipment; Donated products; Employee volunteer services; General/operating support; In-kind gifts; Research; Scholarship funds; Sponsorships.
Geographic limitations: Giving primarily on a national and international basis in areas of company operations, with emphasis on Washington, DC, Atlanta, GA, Minneapolis, MN, VA, India, and Japan; giving also to national organizations.
Support limitations: No support for partisan political organizations, sectarian, religious, or denominational organizations, tax-supported city, county, or state organizations, or local sports organizations. No grants to individuals, or for local events in areas without Delta facilities, academic or medical research, or fundraisers.
Publications: Application guidelines.
Application information: Applications accepted. Application form required.
Initial approach: Complete online proposal for sponsorships
Deadline(s): 90 days prior to need for sponsorships
Final notification: 4 weeks for sponsorships
Number of staff: 1 full-time support.

The Delta Air Lines Foundation
1525 W. W.T. Harris Blvd., D1114-044
Charlotte, NC 28288-1161 (404) 715-5487
FAX: (404) 715-3267;
E-mail: foundation.delta@delta.com; Application address: Community Affairs, Dept. 979, P.O. Box 20706, Atlanta, GA 30320-6001; URL: http://www.delta.com/about_delta/global_good/

Establishment information: Established in 1968 in DE.
Donor: Delta Air Lines, Inc.
Contact: Scarlett Pressley-Brown, Sr. V.P.
Financial data (yr. ended 12/31/11): Assets, $19,405,104 (M); expenditures, $1,260,378; qualifying distributions, $850,000; giving activities include $850,000 for grants.
Purpose and activities: The foundation and Delta Air Lines supports the Delta's Force for Global Good initiative designed to advance global diversity; improve global wellness; improve the environment; and promote arts and culture.
Fields of interest: Historical activities; Historical activities, centennials; Arts; Education, fund raising/fund distribution; Higher education; Environment; Health care; American Red Cross; Civil/human rights, equal rights; Foundations (community).
Program:
Matching Grants to Education: The foundation matches contributions made by employees and directors of Delta Air Lines to institutions of higher education on a one-for-two basis from $25 to $2,000 per contributor, per year.
Type of support: Continuing support; Employee matching gifts; General/operating support; Program development; Sponsorships.
Geographic limitations: Giving primarily in areas of company operations, with emphasis on Washington, DC, Atlanta, GA, and Fairfax, VA.
Support limitations: No support for political organizations, sectarian, religious, denominational organizations, tax-supported city, county or state organizations, fraternal organizations, professional associations, membership groups, or sports organizations. No grants to individuals, or for academic or medical research, or fundraising.
Publications: Application guidelines.
Application information: Applications accepted. Funding for new proposals for cash or in-kind support are currently limited. Application form required.
Initial approach: Complete online application for sponsorships
Board meeting date(s): Mar., June, Sept., and Nov.
Deadline(s): 90 days prior to need for sponsorships
Final notification: 4 weeks for sponsorships
Officers and Trustees:* Timothy W. Mapes, Pres.; Scarlet Pressley-Brown, Sr. V.P.; Andrew Nelson, V.P. and Treas.; Frank Wrenn, V.P., Opers.; Julie Young, Secy.; Richard H. Anderson; Edward H. Bastian; Michael H. Campbell; Stephen E. Gorman; Glen W. Hauenstein.
EIN: 586073119

1074
Delta Dental of Kansas, Inc.

1619 N. Waterfront Pkwy.
P.O. Box 789769
Wichita, KS 67278-9769 (316) 264-1099

Company URL: http://www.deltadentalks.com
Establishment information: Established in 1972.
Company type: Private company
Business activities: Sells dental insurance.
Business type (SIC): Insurance/accident and health
Corporate officers: Ronald R. Davis, Chair.; Brad Clothier, Vice-Chair.; Linda L. Branter, Pres. and C.E.O.; Jon Carlson, C.O.O.; Michael J. Herbert, C.F.O.; Amy Ellison, V.P., Human Resources
Board of directors: Ronald R. Davis, Chair.; Brad Clothier, Vice-Chair.; Linda Brantner; Hugh Bruner; Jerry Goforth; Elizabeth Kinch; Greg Peppes; Jill Quigley; Brick Sheer; Stanley Wint
Offices: Overland Park, Wichita, KS
Giving statement: Giving through the Delta Dental of Kansas Foundation, Inc.

Delta Dental of Kansas Foundation, Inc.

(formerly Delta Dental Plan of Kansas Foundation)
9300 W. 110th St., Bldg. 55, Ste. 450
Overland Park, KS 66210-1403 (913) 327-3727
FAX: (913) 696-1114;
E-mail: kfinstad@deltadentalks.com; Additional contact: Tammy Penrow, Fdn. Asst., tel.: (913) 327-3728, e-mail: tpenrow@deltadentalks.com;
URL: http://www.deltadentalksfoundation.org

Establishment information: Established in 2004 in KS.
Donor: Delta Dental Plan of Kansas, Inc.
Contact: Karen Finstad, Exec. Dir.
Financial data (yr. ended 12/31/11): Assets, $2,133,299 (M); gifts received, $1,463,699; expenditures, $514,020; qualifying distributions, $386,390; giving activities include $386,390 for grants.
Purpose and activities: The foundation supports programs designed to increase access to dental care by underserved populations; build the capacity to provide dental care; increase public awareness of oral health; and promote the prevention of oral disease. Special emphasis is directed toward programs that emphasize prevention; have significant and/or large impact; and are sustainable solutions.
Fields of interest: Dental school/education; Health care, clinics/centers; Dental care; Employment, training Children; Aging; Economically disadvantaged.
Programs:
Community Dental Health Grants: The foundation award grants of up to $20,000 to programs designed to improve oral health. Special emphasis is directed toward prevention, including intervention with early care, partnering with existing networks, and oral health education; significant or large impact, including services that will affect large numbers and address the oral health needs for the underserved; and sustainable solutions, including building a trained workforce, sustainable sources of support, and infusing new providers in existing networks. Grants are awarded for new initiatives, existing programs, start-up funding, and one-time events.
Matching Gift Program: The foundation matches contributions made by employees of Delta Dental Plan of Kansas to nonprofit organizations on a one-for-one basis up to $100 per employee, per year.
Toothbrush Kit Program: The foundation provides toothbrush kits for new initiatives, new components of existing programs, or one-time events that promote prevention; have significant or large impact; or provides sustainable solutions. Toothbrush kits include a toothbrush, paste, and floss.
Type of support: Building/renovation; Donated products; Employee matching gifts; Equipment; Program development; Program evaluation; Scholarship funds; Seed money.
Geographic limitations: Giving limited to areas of company operations in KS.
Support limitations: No support for political, lobbying, or religious organizations. No grants or dental treatment funds for individuals, or for administrative costs, salaries, fundraising events, ongoing programs, general operating expenses, or existing deficits.
Publications: Annual report; Annual report (including application guidelines); Application guidelines; Grants list.
Application information: Applications accepted. Faxed or e-mailed applications are not accepted. Additional information may be requested at a later date. Organizations receiving support are asked to provide periodic reports. Application form required.
Applicants should submit the following:
1) how project will be sustained once grantmaker support is completed
2) qualifications of key personnel
3) statement of problem project will address
4) population served
5) copy of IRS Determination Letter
6) brief history of organization and description of its mission
7) geographic area to be served
8) copy of most recent annual report/audited financial statement/990
9) how project's results will be evaluated or measured
10) listing of board of directors, trustees, officers and other key people and their affiliations
11) detailed description of project and amount of funding requested
12) contact person
13) copy of current year's organizational budget and/or project budget
14) plans for acknowledgement
15) additional materials/documentation

Initial approach: Download application form and mail proposal and application form to foundation for Community Dental Health Grants and Toothbrush Kit Program
Copies of proposal: 10
Board meeting date(s): Apr. to Dec.
Deadline(s): May 1 for Community Dental Health Grants; Aug. 27 for Toothbrush Kit Program
Final notification: June for Community Dental Health Grants

Officers and Directors:* Brad Clothier*, Chair.; Stanley Wint*, Vice-Chair.; Darlene Harrell, Secy.; Michael Herbert*, Treas.; Karen Finstad*, Exec. Dir.; Linda Branter; Hugh Brunner; Elizabeth Kinch; Greg Peppes; Jill Quigley; Lucynda Raben; Brick Scheer.
Number of staff: 1 full-time professional; 1 part-time professional.
EIN: 680554527
Selected grants: The following grants are a representative sample of this grantmaker's funding activity:
$250,000 to Wichita State University, Wichita, KS, 2009.
$123,305 to Johnson County Community College, Overland Park, KS, 2009.
$30,944 to Kansas Department of Corrections, Topeka, KS, 2009.
$15,000 to Kansas Dental Charitable Foundation, Topeka, KS, 2009.
$1,022 to Salina Family Healthcare Center, Salina, KS, 2009.

1075
Delta Dental of New Jersey, Inc.

1639 State Rte. 10
P.O. Box 222
Parsippany, NJ 07054-4506
(973) 285-4001

Company URL: http://www.deltadentalct.com/
Establishment information: Established in 1969.
Company type: Private company
Business activities: Sells dental insurance.
Business type (SIC): Insurance/accident and health
Corporate officers: Gerald A. Sydell, Chair.; Walter VanBrunt, Pres. and C.E.O.; Bruce Silverman, Sr. V.P. and C.O.O.; Diane Belle, V.P., Corp. Comms.; Deborah Rybicki Dietz, Cont.
Board of director: Gerald A. Sydell, Chair.
Giving statement: Giving through the Delta Dental of New Jersey Foundation, Inc.

The Delta Dental of New Jersey Foundation, Inc.

(formerly Delta Dental Plan of New Jersey Foundation, Inc.)
1639 Rte. 10
P.O. Box 222
Parsippany, NJ 07054-0222 (973) 285-4029
URL: http://www.deltadentalnj.com/foundation/foundation.html

Establishment information: Established in 1986 in NJ; supporting organization of Delta Dental of New Jersey, Inc.
Financial data (yr. ended 12/31/10): Revenue, $1,033,080; assets, $1,174,551 (M); gifts received, $1,000,000; expenditures, $902,251; program services expenses, $840,074; giving activities include $840,074 for 29 grants (high: $74,000; low: $6,000).
Purpose and activities: The foundation promotes and assists educational projects devoted to the enhancement of dental health, as well as research programs designed to increase public awareness of the general benefits of good oral health, and to the improvement of dental health through the science of dentistry.
Fields of interest: Dental care Economically disadvantaged.
Programs:
Grants: The foundation annually provides financial support to community clinics and facilities that help underserved populations gain access to dental care, facilities that provide dental treatment to physically- and developmentally-disabled children and adults, dental education programs, dental research projects, and Head Start programs. Applicants must be nonprofit 501(c)(3) organizations or government entities based in New Jersey and Connecticut. The foundation awards grants for one-time projects, as well as for multiple-year programs, depending on funds available and the success of the program.
Oral Health Education Initiative Grants: The foundation will make grants of up to $5,000 each available to elementary schools in New Jersey's Abbott school districts (including charter schools

located in Abbott school districts) to initiate oral health education programs in their third-grade classes.
Type of support: In-kind gifts; Research; Scholarship funds.
Geographic limitations: Giving primarily in CT and NJ.
Publications: Application guidelines.
Application information: Applications accepted. Application form required.
Initial approach: Download application form
Board meeting date(s): Four times per year
Deadline(s): June 15 for Oral Health Education Initiative Grants; Aug. 17 for Grants
Officers and Trustees:* Gene F. Napoliello, D.D.S.*, Pres.; Diane Belle, M.A.*, V.P.; James Suleski*, V.P.; Gerald A. Sydell, D.D.S.*, V.P.; Walter VanBrunt*, V.P.; Carl Chaityn, D.D.S.*, Secy.; Henry F. Henderson, Jr.*, Treas.; and 6 additional trustees.
EIN: 222764745

1076
Delta Dental of Wisconsin, Inc.

2801 Hoover Rd.
P.O. Box 828
Stevens Point, WI 54481-7100
(715) 344-6087
FAX: (715) 344-2446

Company URL: http://www.deltadentalwi.com
Establishment information: Established in 1962.
Company type: Private company
Business activities: Sells dental insurance.
Business type (SIC): Insurance/accident and health
Financial profile for 2011: Assets, $157,576,610; liabilities, $28,650,057
Corporate officers: Chuck Nason, Chair.; Dennis Brown, Pres. and C.E.O.; Gillian Myers, V.P. and Secy.; Pamela Gartmann, V.P., Admin.; Gary Rogers, V.P., Sales and Mktg.
Board of director: Chuck Nason, Chair.
Giving statement: Giving through the Delta Dental Plan of Wisconsin, Inc. Corporate Giving Program.

Delta Dental Plan of Wisconsin, Inc. Corporate Giving Program

P.O. Box 828
Stevens Point, WI 54481-0828 (800) 236-3713
E-mail: hfischer@deltadentalwi.com; URL: http://www.deltadentalwi.com/about-delta-dental/community/

Contact: Heidi Fischer
Purpose and activities: Delta Dental Plan of Wisconsin makes charitable contributions to nonprofit organizations involved with oral health. Special emphasis is directed toward programs that promote prevention, target underserved populations, and advance the science of dentistry. Support is limited to Wisconsin.
Fields of interest: Dental school/education; Dental care Economically disadvantaged.
Type of support: Employee volunteer services; General/operating support; Program development.
Geographic limitations: Giving limited to WI.
Support limitations: No support for political or discriminatory organizations. No grants to individuals (except for scholarships), or for loans, or projects developed for commercial and proprietary purposes.
Application information: Applications accepted. Application form required. Applicants should submit the following:
1) how project will be sustained once grantmaker support is completed
2) results expected from proposed grant
3) qualifications of key personnel
4) statement of problem project will address
5) population served
6) name, address and phone number of organization
7) how project's results will be evaluated or measured
8) detailed description of project and amount of funding requested
9) plans for cooperation with other organizations, if any
10) contact person
11) copy of current year's organizational budget and/or project budget
12) listing of additional sources and amount of support

Applications should include the Tax ID Number of the organization; and indicate any applicable deadlines; and whether the program will receive Medicaid reimbursements.
Initial approach: Download application form and mail to headquarters

1077
Delta Dental Plan of Arizona, Inc.

15648 N. 35th Ave., Ste. 111
Phoenix, AZ 85053 (602) 938-3131

Company URL: http://www.deltadentalaz.com
Establishment information: Established in 1972.
Company type: Private company
Business activities: Sells dental insurance.
Business type (SIC): Insurance/accident and health
Corporate officers: Joyce A. Rosenthal, Chair.; David M. Day, Vice-Chair.; David Hurley, V.P., Sales; Philip Stoker, Secy.-Treas.
Board of directors: Joyce A. Rosenthal, Chair.; David M. Day, Vice-Chair.; Donald Baker; Wilford A. Cardon; Jason Dittberner; Dale R. Hallberg; Brien V. Harvey; Alvin Matthews; William L. Putnam; Frederick Olsen; Phillip J. Santucci; Philip Stoker; Brian J. Wilson
Giving statement: Giving through the Delta Dental of Arizona Foundation.

Delta Dental of Arizona Foundation

5656 W. Talavi Blvd.
Glendale, AZ 85306-1876 (602) 588-3922
FAX: (602) 548-5023;
E-mail: dlorenzo@deltadentalaz.com; Contact for Community Grants Program: Dr. Sandi Perez, Ph.D., V.P., Communications and Community Benefit, E-mail: sperez@deltadentalaz.com; URL: http://www.deltadentalaz.com/foundation/index.asp

Establishment information: Established in 1996 in AZ.
Donor: Arizona Dental Insurance Services, Inc., Inc.
Contact: Dawn Lorenzo, Dir., Philanthropy
Financial data (yr. ended 12/31/11): Assets, $2,728,379 (M); gifts received, $1,750,196; expenditures, $605,626; qualifying distributions, $420,668; giving activities include $420,668 for grants.
Purpose and activities: The foundation supports organizations involved with dental care, oral health, and human services. Special emphasis is directed toward underserved and uninsured populations.
Fields of interest: Health care, clinics/centers; Dental care; Children/youth, services; Human services Economically disadvantaged.
Programs:
Community Grants Program: The foundation supports programs designed to promote oral health and dental disease prevention for children and youth. Special emphasis is directed toward programs designed to increase access to preventative dental health services through oral health instruction, screenings, exams, education, and/or training. The foundation also supports local community-based groups, coalitions, and community partnerships that address local oral health projects, including staffing needs and costs for oral health community activities. Grants range from $1,000 to $15,000.
Delta Dental Sealant Program: The foundation provides dental sealants, plastic-like material that creates a barrier protecting a tooth from the plaque and acids that cause decay, to second and sixth grade children. The program is designed to primarily serve children without insurance at no charge to their families. The program solicits schools each summer and each child receives toothbrushes, floss, and toothpaste. Participating schools also receives Teeth on the Go, an oral health curriculum kit.
Fluoride Varnish Program - Varnish Today, Vanish Decay: The foundation operates fluoride varnish clinics which provides pre-school children with oral screenings, fluoride varnish, dental supplies, and referrals for children with special dental needs. The program is designed to give preschool children the best chance to enter grade school cavity-free.
Type of support: Donated products; In-kind gifts; Matching/challenge support; Program development; Seed money; Sponsorships.
Geographic limitations: Giving primarily in areas of company operations in Phoenix, AZ.
Support limitations: No support for religious organizations not of direct benefit to the entire community or lobbying organizations. No grants to individuals, or sponsorships or attendance at conferences, debt reduction, or fundraising.
Publications: Application guidelines; Newsletter.
Application information: Applications accepted. Letters of inquiry should be no longer than 1 page. A full application may be requested for Community Grants Program. Additional information and a site visit may be requested. Application form required. Applicants should submit the following:
1) detailed description of project and amount of funding requested
2) statement of problem project will address
3) explanation of why grantmaker is considered an appropriate donor for project
4) copy of current year's organizational budget and/or project budget
5) contact person
6) name, address and phone number of organization

Initial approach: E-mail letter of inquiry for Community Grants Program; contact foundation for Fluoride Varnish Program
Board meeting date(s): Quarterly
Deadline(s): Oct. 1 to Nov. 1 for letters of inquiry for Community Grants Program; Dec. 1 for full application for Community Grants Program; None for Fluoride Varnish Program
Final notification: Feb. for Community Grants Program
Officers and Directors:* James P. Davis, D.D.S.*, Chair.; Karen Berrigan, D.M.D.*, Vice-Chair.; Rebecca Kenyon*, Secy.; Felix Durazo*, Treas.; Allan Allford; Alisa Diggs; Susan Fry; Keith Guazza; Don Henninger; Kathy LaVoy; Alison Lund; Kendis

Muscheid; Fred Olson; Xavier Ortega; Philip Stoker; Tim Wilson, D.D.S.
EIN: 860842694
Selected grants: The following grants are a representative sample of this grantmaker's funding activity:
$49,847 to Childrens Museum of Phoenix, Phoenix, AZ, 2009.
$5,579 to Back to School Clothing Drive Association, Glendale, AZ, 2009.
$5,000 to Homeward Bound, Phoenix, AZ, 2009.
$3,990 to Esperanca, Phoenix, AZ, 2009.
$3,500 to Arizona Foundation for Women, Phoenix, AZ, 2009.
$3,080 to Childrens Action Alliance, Phoenix, AZ, 2009.
$2,375 to Wellcare Foundation, Phoenix, AZ, 2009.
$1,777 to Interfaith Cooperative Ministries, Phoenix, AZ, 2009.
$1,502 to Healthy Smile Foundation, Phoenix, AZ, 2009.

1078
Delta Dental Plan of Michigan, Inc.

4100 Okemos Rd.
P.O. Box 9085
Okemos, MI 48864-3215 (517) 349-6000
FAX: (517) 347-5499

Company URL: http://www.deltadentalmi.com
Establishment information: Established in 1957.
Company type: Private company
Business activities: Sells dental insurance.
Business type (SIC): Insurance/accident and health
Financial profile for 2010: Number of employees, 520; assets, $672,361,000; sales volume, $2,247,217,000
Corporate officers: Laura L. Czelada, C.P.A., Pres. and C.E.O.; Edward J. Zobeck, Exec. V.P. and C.A.O.; Brenda Laird, Exec. V.P. and C.I.O.; Goran Jurcuvic, C.P.A., Sr. V.P. and C.F.O.; Jonathan S. Groat, V.P. and Genl. Counsel; Anthony Robinson, V.P., Sales; Joseph Harris, Secy.; Bruce Smith, Treas.
Board of directors: Douglas R. Anderson; Bruce C. Baird; Fr. Jack H. Baker; Terrence R. Comar; Todd V. Ester; Thomas J. Fleszar; Rory Gamble; James P. Hallan; Joseph C. Harris; Jed J. Jacobson; Jeffrey A. Keller; Terri A. Miller; Timothy E. Moffit; C. Richard Seitz; Bruce R. Smith
Giving statement: Giving through the Delta Dental Foundation.

Delta Dental Foundation

(formerly Delta Dental Fund)
P.O. Box 30416
Lansing, MI 48909-7916 (517) 349-6000
E-mail: ddfund@ddpmi.com; URL: http://www.deltadentalmi.com/About/Giving-Back/Delta-Dental-Foundation.aspx
Application address: P.O. Box 293, Okemos, MI 48805-0293, tel.: (517) 347-5333, fax: (517) 347-5320,
e-mail: DeltaDentalFund@deltadentalmi.com

Establishment information: Established in 1980 in MI; supporting organization of Delta Dental Plan of Michigan, Inc.
Contact: Penelope K. Majeske Ph.D., Vice-Chair.
Financial data (yr. ended 12/31/11): Revenue, $10,926,886; assets, $37,489,864 (M); gifts received, $10,006,453; expenditures, $1,514,443; program services expenses, $1,282,652; giving activities include $942,850 for 7 grants (high: $450,000; low: $6,000) and $154,469 for grants to individuals.
Purpose and activities: The fund supports education and research for the advancement of dental science and promotes the oral health of the public through education and service activities, particularly for those with special needs.
Fields of interest: Dental school/education; Dental care; Cancer; Cancer research Economically disadvantaged.
Programs:
Community Mini-Grants: Grants of up to $5,000 are available for programs or projects that help develop and heighten dental awareness among the public and that offer continuing dental education. Special consideration with be given to projects that promote and/or improve the oral health of underserved children in at-risk populations. Grants must be dedicated to local nonprofit programs designed to promote oral health in communities in Michigan, Ohio, or Indiana.
Dental Master's Thesis Award Program: This program is intended to encourage thesis research that is of direct relevance to the costs or outcomes of dental care. The award offers up to $3,000 to cover costs associated with conducting master's thesis research.
Research Grant: Awards up to $30,000 to researchers from dental schools in Indiana, Michigan, and Ohio. Priority will be given to projects that focus on issues related to the delivery and financing of oral health care, including those which could have direct clinical application with significant potential for reducing treatment costs along with improving oral health.
Scholarships and Student Leadership Awards: Awards and scholarships to students who demonstrate excellent academic and leadership skills, and who exhibit a passion for dentistry. Two students from each dental school in MI, OH, and IN are awarded a foundation scholarship and one graduating dental student from each school is awarded a Student Leadership Award. Recipients are selected by the dean of their school of dentistry.
Thomas P. Moore II Memorial Grant Program: This annual program will award up to $25,000 for programs that help conduct oral cancer research, offer oral cancer education, or develop and heighten oral cancer awareness among the public. Only nonprofit programs in Michigan, Ohio, and Indiana may apply for the grant.
Type of support: Conferences/seminars; Fellowships; Research; Scholarship funds.
Geographic limitations: Giving limited to IN, MI, and OH.
Support limitations: No support for political, or discriminatory organizations. No grants for capital campaigns, overhead or administrative expenses, endowments, advertising, fundraising activates, or projects developed for commercial and proprietary purposes; no loans.
Publications: Application guidelines; Biennial report (including application guidelines).
Application information: Applications accepted. Application form required.
Initial approach: Download application form
Deadline(s): Apr. 15 and Oct. 15 for Research Grants; Sept. 30 for Thomas P. Moore II Memorial Grant; Nov. 1 for Community Mini-Grants
Final notification: Nov. for Community Mini-Grants and Thomas P. Moore II Memorial Grant
Officers and Trustees:* James P. Hallan*, Chair.; Penelope K. Majeske, Ph.D.*, Vice-Chair.; Thomas J. Fleszar, D.D.S.*, Pres. and C.E.O.; C. Richard Seitz*, Secy.; John A. Breza, D.D.S.*, Treas.; Goran Jurkovic*, C.F.O.; Colleen G. Vienna, D.D.S.; Lonny E. Zietz; and 4 additional trustees.
EIN: 382337000

1079
Delta Dental Plan of Oklahoma, Inc.

16 N.W. 63rd St., Ste. 301
P.O. Box 54709
Oklahoma City, OK 73116-9115
(405) 607-2100

Company URL: http://www.deltadentalok.org/
Establishment information: Established in 1973.
Company type: Private company
Business activities: Sells dental insurance.
Business type (SIC): Insurance/accident and health
Corporate officers: Mike Howl, Chair.; John E. Gladden, Pres. and C.E.O.; Barbara Fennell, C.O.O.; Stephanie Leigh H. Elliott, C.F.O. and Cont.; James H. Hampton, Secy.; Sandy P. Bjornson, Treas.
Board of directors: Mike Howl, Chair.; Sandy Bjornsonc; Debbie Corwin; Colin Foster; Stephen Glenn; Jim Hampton; Homer Hilst; Brad Hogan; Mitchell Kramer; Tommy Mayhue; Alan McCormick; Mike McLeod; Vincent Montgomery; G. Ken Rains; Bryan Reusser; John Shearing; Roger Webb
Giving statement: Giving through the Delta Dental of Oklahoma Oral Health Foundation.

Delta Dental of Oklahoma Oral Health Foundation

(formerly Delta Dental Plan of Oklahoma Charitable Foundation)
16 N.W. 63rd St., Ste. 201
Oklahoma City, OK 73116-9116 (405) 607-4771
FAX: (405) 607-4768;
E-mail: foundation@DeltaDentalOK.org; E-mail for Terrisa Singleton: tsingleton@DeltaDentalOK.org; Additional tel.: (800) 522-0188, ext. 771; Captain Supertooth Program: tel.: (405) 607-4788, (800) 522-0188, ext. 788; e-mail: CaptainSupertooth@DeltaDentalOK.org; URL: http://www.deltadentalok.org/communityservice/index.asp

Donor: Delta Dental Plan of Oklahoma, Inc.
Contact: Terrisa Singleton, Fdn. Specialist
Financial data (yr. ended 12/31/10): Assets, $18,664 (M); gifts received, $1,422,609; expenditures, $1,443,921; qualifying distributions, $1,443,921; giving activities include $1,335,545 for 27 grants (high: $410,000; low: $750).
Purpose and activities: The foundation supports programs designed to promote oral health; advance dental education and research; and provide access to dental care. Special emphasis is directed toward programs designed to provide free dental care services or education to indigent or underserved populations; and utilize volunteer dental professionals.
Fields of interest: Dental school/education; Health care, clinics/centers; Dental care Economically disadvantaged.
Programs:
Captain Supertooth: Through the Captain Supertooth program, the foundation teaches students in grades K-3 the benefits of good oral hygiene. The program includes educational presentations and a complimentary toothbrush and tooth brushing chart. Visit URL http://www.captainsupertooth.com/ for more information.

Delta Distinguished Service Award: The foundation, in partnership with the Dental Assistants Association, recognizes a dental assistant for outstanding volunteerism and leadership. The award includes a plaque and a prize package of items to facilitate educational outreach and volunteer work including a $200 gift certificate to Praction, and 200 Captain Supertooth brush charts and brushes.

OU College of Dentistry Delta Dental Scholarship Fund: The foundation annually awards eleven $5,000 scholarships to dental students from the Oklahoma University College of Dentistry who demonstrate outstanding academic performance, financial need, and a commitment to practice in Oklahoma. The program is administered by the OU College of Dentistry.

Type of support: Equipment; General/operating support; Program development; Research; Scholarship funds; Sponsorships.
Geographic limitations: Giving primarily in areas of company operations in OK.
Support limitations: No grants to individuals.
Publications: Application guidelines; Grants list; Newsletter.
Application information: Applications accepted. Organizations receiving support are asked to submit periodic reports. Application form not required.
Applicants should submit the following:
1) role played by volunteers
2) results expected from proposed grant
3) population served
4) name, address and phone number of organization
5) copy of IRS Determination Letter
6) brief history of organization and description of its mission
7) geographic area to be served
8) copy of most recent annual report/audited financial statement/990
9) how project's results will be evaluated or measured
10) listing of board of directors, trustees, officers and other key people and their affiliations
11) detailed description of project and amount of funding requested
12) contact person
13) copy of current year's organizational budget and/or project budget
14) listing of additional sources and amount of support

Applicants should also submit an IRS W-9 Form.
Initial approach: Complete online application; complete online request form for Captain Supertooth
Deadline(s): Sept. 20; None for Captain Supertooth
Final notification: Dec.

Officers and Trustees:* Mitchell Kramer*, Chair.; W. Roger Webb*, Vice-Chair.; John E. Gladden*, Secy.-Treas.; L. Colin Foster; Stephen Glenn; Jim Hampton; C. Alan McCormick; Michael Preston McLeod.
EIN: 731547145
Selected grants: The following grants are a representative sample of this grantmaker's funding activity:
$300,000 to University of Oklahoma, College of Dentistry, Oklahoma City, OK, 2010. For general support.
$101,025 to Dentists for the Disabled and Elderly in Need of Treatment, Oklahoma City, OK, 2010. For general support.
$63,075 to Neighborhood Services Organization, Oklahoma City, OK, 2010. For general support.
$60,000 to Neighbor for Neighbor, Tulsa, OK, 2010. For general support.
$25,000 to Ministries of Jesus, Edmond, OK, 2010. For general support.
$24,393 to City Rescue Mission, Oklahoma City, OK, 2010. For general support.
$20,000 to Catholic Charities, Tulsa, OK, 2010. For general support.
$17,500 to Health for Friends, Norman, OK, 2010. For general support.

1080
Delta Dental Plan of South Dakota

720 N. Euclid Ave.
P.O. Box 1157
Pierre, SD 57501-1717 (605) 224-7345

Company URL: http://www.deltadentalsd.com
Establishment information: Established in 1963.
Company type: Private company
Business activities: Sells dental insurance.
Business type (SIC): Insurance/accident and health
Financial profile for 2010: Number of employees, 32; assets, $37,651,000; expenses, $6,744,000; liabilities, $7,453,000
Corporate officers: Dale Gibson, Chair.; Monty Bechtold, Vice-Chair; Scott O. Jones, Pres. and C.E.O.; Mick Heckenlaible, V.P., Opers.; Kirby Scott, V.P., Finance; Greg Gertsen, Secy.; John Clausen, Treas.
Board of directors: Dale Gibson, Chair.; Monty Bechtold, Vice-Chair.; John Clausen; Steve Culhane; Greg Gertsen; G. Verne Goodsell; Greg Hanson; Pat Hermanson; Mary Hitzemann; Mike Houk; Paul Rezich; Anlee Rola; Jim Russell; Ryan Van Laecken
Giving statement: Giving through the Delta Dental Philanthropic Fund.
Company EIN: 460309258

Delta Dental Philanthropic Fund

P.O. Box 1157
Pierre, SD 57501-1157 (605) 224-0909
E-mail: sales@deltadentalsd.com; Toll Free tel. : (800)-627-3961; URL: http://www.deltadentalsd.com/webpage/About_the_Fund.jsp?DView=AbouttheFund

Establishment information: Established in 1996 in SD; supporting organization of the Delta Dental Plan of South Dakota.
Contact: Scott Jones, Pres.
Financial data (yr. ended 12/31/11): Revenue, $3,232,111; assets, $7,582,114 (M); gifts received, $2,326,055; expenditures, $2,454,689; giving activities include $294,403 for grants and $274,839 for grants to individuals.
Purpose and activities: The fund sponsors educational programs for advancement of dentistry and promotion of dental health.
Fields of interest: Dental school/education; Dental care.
Type of support: Conferences/seminars; Curriculum development; Debt reduction; Equipment; Grants to individuals; In-kind gifts; Program development.
Geographic limitations: Giving limited to SD.
Support limitations: No support for religious or political organizations.
Officers and Directors:* Dale Gibson, D.D.S., Chair.; Monty Bechtold, D.D.S., Vice-Chair.; Scott Jones*, Pres.; Greg Gertsen, D.D.S.*, Secy.; John Clausen*, Treas.; Steve Buechler, D.D.S.; Pat Hermanson, D.D.S.; Mike Houk, D.D.S.; Paul Rezich, D.D.S.; and 6 additional directors.
EIN: 911776857

1081
Delta Dental Washington Dental Service

(also known as Washington Dental Service)
9706 4th Ave., N.E.
Seattle, WA 98115-2157 (206) 522-1300

Establishment information: Established in 1954.
Company type: Private company
Business activities: Sells dental insurance.
Business type (SIC): Insurance/accident and health
Corporate officers: Joanna Lohkamp, Chair.; G. Douglas Beck, Vice-Chair.; Jim Dwyer, Pres. and C.E.O.; Brad Berg, C.F.O. and C.O.O.; C.J. Venkataraman, C.I.O.; Kristin Merlo, V.P., Sales and Mktg.
Board of directors: Joanna Lohkamp, Chair; G. Douglas Beck, Vice-Chair.; David W. Branch; Patrick J. Dineen; James Dwyer; Janis Harwell; Jack E. Neal; Gerald S. Phipps; Allen W. Puckett; Kristin H. Stred; James F. Tune
Giving statement: Giving through the Washington Dental Service Foundation.
Company EIN: 910621480

Washington Dental Service Foundation

(also known as WDS Foundation)
9706 4th Ave. N.E.
Seattle, WA 98115-2157 (206) 528-2337
FAX: (206) 985-4876;
E-mail: foundation@deltadentalwa.com; Toll-free tel.: (800) 572-7835, ext. 2337, E-mail for Laura Smith: lsmith@deltadentalwa.com; URL: http://www.deltadentalwa.com/Guest/Public/AboutUs/WDS%20Foundation.aspx
Application address: P.O. Box 75983, Seattle, WA 98175-0983, toll free tel.: (800) 572-7835, ext. 5494

Establishment information: Established in 2004 in WA; supporting organization of the Washington Dental Service.
Donor: Delta Dental Washington Dental Svc.
Contact: Laura Smith, Pres. and C.E.O.
Financial data (yr. ended 12/31/11): Revenue, $17,584; assets, $242,762 (M); gifts received, $16,890; expenditures, $32,187; program services expenses, $32,187; giving activities include $30,617 for 2 grants (high: $20,480; low: $10,137) and $1,570 for grants to individuals.
Purpose and activities: The foundation works to promote social welfare (including promoting the oral health of the public), and to sponsor and advocate for the advancement of oral health, through supporting the mission of Washington Dental Service.
Fields of interest: Dental care.
Programs:

Access to Baby and Child Dentistry Growth Grant: Grants ranging from $10,000 to $75,000 are awarded to organization to increase utilization in a mature Washington Access to Baby and Child Dentistry (A.B.C.D.) program beyond current levels by: building the capacity to reach higher client utilization rates; addressing challenges to reaching the full utilization potential of A.B.C.D. programs; and by fostering new partnerships and creative thinking.

Dental Team Scholarships: The foundation offers scholarships for underrepresented minority students who are interested in careers as dental hygienists, dental assistants, and laboratory technicians. Applicants must be Washington state residents and be part of an underrepresented minority group.

Grants: Grants are made to eligible organizations for projects that support one or more of the foundation's strategies for improving oral health: engage dentists in seeing young children; engage physicians and other professionals in preventing oral disease; fluoridate drinking water; increase services for underserved populations; increase community orientation of dental professional schools, including efforts that diversify the dental work force; build a constituency for oral health to affect public policy and create a supportive climate; or advocate for oral improvements for seniors. Highest priority is given to long-term efforts that improve policies and change systems while addressing the immediate needs of the underserved.

Loan Repayment Program: The program is designed to recruit dentists to join or to establish private practices in Washington's rural and underserved areas. Under the program, applicants may receive up to $25,000 per year for up to three years for qualified education loans. In return, applicants are required to make a three-year commitment to practice in areas where there is a shortage of dental care and at least 35 percent of patients are Medicaid-insured.

Type of support: Building/renovation; Capital campaigns; Equipment; Matching/challenge support; Scholarship funds; Sponsorships.
Geographic limitations: Giving primarily in WA.
Support limitations: No support for projects not related to oral health, or non-501(c)(3) organizations. No grants to individuals (except for loans), or for ongoing general operating expenses, fundraising events, existing deficits, or research projects.
Publications: Application guidelines; Grants list; Newsletter.
Application information: Applications accepted. Faxed or emailed applications will not be accepted. Application form required.
Initial approach: Contact foundation and download application form
Copies of proposal: 3
Deadline(s): Mar. 15 and Sept. 15 for Grants
Final notification: Late June and late Dec. for Grants
Officers and Trustees:* Eve Rutherford*, Chair.; G. Douglas Beck, D.D.S.*, Treas.; Laura Smith*, Pres. and C.E.O.; David Branch, D.D.S.; Frederick C. Kiga, J.D., M.B.A.; Thomas Locke, M.D., M.P.H.; Alejandro Narvaez, D.D.S.; Gerald Phipps, D.M.D.; R. Gary Schweikhardt; and 6 additional trustees.
Number of staff: 8 full-time professional; 1 part-time professional; 1 full-time support; 1 part-time support.
EIN: 911281990

1082
Delta Industries, Inc.

100 W. Woodrow Wilson Dr.
Jackson, MS 39215 (601) 354-3801

Company URL: http://www.delta-ind.com
Establishment information: Established in 1945.
Company type: Private company
Business activities: Manufactures concrete and masonry products.
Business type (SIC): Concrete, gypsum, and plaster products
Corporate officers: David Robinson, Pres. and C.E.O.; Tom Evans, Exec. V.P. and C.O.O.; Pete Hays, C.F.O. and Secy.-Treas.; Paul Duff, V.P. and C.I.O.
Subsidiary: Pine Belt Ready Mix Concrete Inc., Laurel, MS
Giving statement: Giving through the Delta Industries Foundation, Inc.

Delta Industries Foundation, Inc.

100 W. Woodrow Wilson Dr.
Jackson, MS 39213-7643 (601) 969-1365

Donor: Delta Industries, Inc.
Contact: David Robison, Pres.
Financial data (yr. ended 12/31/11): Assets, $33,647 (M); expenditures, $5,700; qualifying distributions, $5,700; giving activities include $5,700 for grants.
Purpose and activities: The foundation supports organizations involved with ballet, education, health, youth development, and economic development.
Fields of interest: Arts; Education; Youth development.
Type of support: General/operating support; Program development; Scholarship funds.
Geographic limitations: Giving primarily in MS.
Support limitations: No grants to individuals.
Application information: Applications accepted. Application form not required.
Initial approach: Proposal
Deadline(s): None
Officers and Directors:* David Robinson*, Pres.; J. Thomas Evans, V.P.; Pete Hays, Secy.-Treas.; Travis W. Bain II; Bruce J. Brumfield; W. D. Mounger; Leland R. Speed; Cornelius Turner; James Yagow.
EIN: 640611001

1083
Delta Service of Massachusetts, Inc.

(doing business as Delta Dental of Massachusetts)
465 Medford St.
P.O. Box 249
Boston, MA 02129-1454 (617) 886-1000

Company URL: http://www.deltamass.com
Company type: Private company
Business activities: Sells dental insurance.
Business type (SIC): Insurance/accident and health
Corporate officers: H. Jay Sarles, Chair.; Ann Page Palmer, Vice-Chair.; Fay Donohue, Pres. and C.E.O.; M. James Collins, M.D., C.F.O.; Gary Guengerich, V.P. and Treas.; Jack Sheean, Cont.
Board of directors: H. Jay Sarles, Chair.; Ann Page Palmer, Vice-Chair.; Terry Conner; Fay Donohue; Thomas Galligan III; Raul Garcia; John Gusha; Edward Hjerpe III; Marion Kane; Karen Kaplan; Donald Kenney; Donald LeClair; Linda Niesen; Walter Owens; Pamela Reeve; Leslie Zide
Giving statement: Giving through the DentaQuest Foundation.

DentaQuest Foundation

(formerly Oral Health Services Foundation, Inc.)
465 Medford St.
Boston, MA 02129-1454 (617) 886-1760
FAX: (617) 886-1799;
E-mail: andrea.forscht@dentaquestfoundation.org; Contact for Community Response Fund: Michael Monopoli, Dir., Policy and Progs., e-mail: michael.monopoli@dentaquestfoundation.org; Contact for NCC Oral Health Initiative: Mathew Bond, Grants and Progs. Assoc., tel.: (617) 886-1599, e-mail: mathew.bond@dentaquestfoundation.org; Contacts for Oral Health 2014: Patrick Finnerty, Sr. Advisor for State Oral Health Progs., tel.: (804) 929-3318, e-mail: pat.finnerty@dentaquest.com, Carmen Fields, Assoc. Dir. of Natl. Progs., tel.: (617) 886-1344, e-mail: carmen.fields@dentaquestfoundation.org; URL: http://www.dentaquestfoundation.org/

Establishment information: Established in 2000 in MA.
Donors: Dental Services of Massachusetts Inc.; Delta Dental Plan of Massachusetts.
Contact: Andrea Forscht, Grants and Progs. Assoc.
Financial data (yr. ended 12/31/11): Assets, $65,725,927 (M); gifts received, $12,125,000; expenditures, $9,903,509; qualifying distributions, $9,692,117; giving activities include $7,297,267 for 93 grants (high: $276,327; low: $911).
Purpose and activities: The foundation supports programs designed to improve oral health. Special emphasis is directed toward public policy that improves oral health; increased public and private funding for oral health initiatives; improved delivery of oral health care and prevention; and community engagement on oral health issues.
Fields of interest: Dental school/education; Health care, management/technical assistance; Health care, public policy; Health care, equal rights; Medicine/medical care, public education; Health care, clinics/centers; Dental care; Health care Children; Economically disadvantaged.

Programs:

Community Response Fund - Missions of Mercy: The foundation supports initiatives designed to preserve clinical capacity of safety net clinics and community programs that provide access to care for underserved populations. The fund supports specific equipment or staff needed to maintain access to care. The fund also supports Missions of Mercy clinics who have a plan to increase awareness among policy makers and the public of the need for longer-term solutions to access to care programs. The foundation supports one Missions of Mercy request per organization every three years.

Community Water Fluoridation Initiative: The foundation supports community-based strategies to promote community water fluoridation, a cost-effective way to prevent dental caries, infection, pain, suffering, loss of teeth, and other negative effects to overall health. The program is by invitation only.

Demonstration Fund for Oral Health: The foundation supports programs designed to improve the systems that impact oral health though innovative solutions. The fund is designed to support organizations, engage key stakeholder, remove barriers to care, improve infrastructure, and bridge the gap between medical and dental health.

Disease Prevention Campaign: Through the Disease Prevention Campaign, the foundation partners with large national organizations to develop and launch an oral disease prevention campaign. This program is by invitation only.

National Community Committee Oral Health Initiative: The foundation, in partnership with the NCC of the Centers for Disease Control and Prevention, supports local and national capacity for community engagement on oral health issues. The foundation awards grants of up to $125,000 to four partner Community-Based Organizations (CBOs) to integrate oral health into their Prevention Research Center's Core Research Projects or to develop new oral health projects. Grant awards are to develop a two-year plan to implement an intervention strategy within their community. At the end of the year, projects will be considered for first-year implementation grants of up to an additional $125,000.

Oral Health 2014: Through Oral Health 2014 multi-year initiative, the foundation builds leadership and promotes strong community partnerships to eliminate system barriers that limit access to oral health care. Special emphasis is directed toward the U.S. National Oral Health Alliance focus areas: prevention and the public health infrastructure; oral health literacy; medical and dental collaboration; metrics for improving oral health; financing models; and strengthening the dental care delivery system. The foundation awarded grants to 20 state-level organizations as partners, and will select up to 17 to receive up to $150,000 to implement plans.

President's Fund: Through the President's Fund, the foundation awards small grants and sponsorships to initiatives that eliminate disparities and promote health equity and to initiatives that fall outside other priorities and funds.

Strengthening the Oral Health Safety Net Initiative: The foundation supports programs designed to build oral health capacity on the national, state/regional, and community levels. The initiative awards up to $100,000 to four state/regional Primary Care Associations (PCA's) to build their capacity to promote oral health and address issues of oral health for safety net providers across the state. PCA's work with the National Association of Community Health Centers to promote interprofessional activities among dental and medical programs; elevate the importance of oral health within the PCA; develop executive leadership at community health centers to promote optimal oral health; and promote safety net oral health needs at the state level. Selected PCA's work with DentaQuest Institute to select up to five FQHC affiliated safety net dental programs to receive technical assistance from the Institute's Safety Net Solutions Program.

Venture Fund for Oral Health: Through the Venture Fund, the foundation supports oral health programs that have demonstrated positive outcomes and have the potential for expansion. The fund provides financial support and technical assistance to build organizational and technical capacity.

Type of support: Building/renovation; Continuing support; Equipment; Management development/ capacity building; Program development; Sponsorships; Technical assistance.

Geographic limitations: Giving primarily in areas of company operations, with emphasis on FL, IL, MA, and MD; giving also to national organizations.

Support limitations: No support for lobbying organizations. No grants to individuals, or for scholarships, general overhead or indirect costs, capital campaigns, debt reduction, or endowments.

Publications: Annual report; Application guidelines; Grants list; Program policy statement.

Application information: Applications accepted. Applying organizations will be expected to develop metrics and monitor/measure their direct impact on one or more key systems for the Demonstration Fund for Oral Health.

Initial approach: Complete online application; contact foundation for Community Response Fund, President's Fund, and Venture Fund for Oral Health

Deadline(s): July 18 for NCC Oral Health Initiative; Aug. 3 for Strengthening the Oral Health Safety Net; Aug. 15 for Oral Health 2014; May 30 and Sept. 30 for Demonstration Fund for Oral Health

Final notification: Aug. for NCC Oral Health Initiative and Strengthening the Oral Health Safety Net; Sept. 28 for Oral Health 2014; June 28 and Nov. 22 for Demonstration Fund for Oral Health

Officers and Directors:* Marylou Sudders*, Chair.; Caswell A. Evans, Jr., D.D.S., MPH, Vice-Chair.; Ralph Fuccillo, MA*, Pres.; Myra Green, Clerk; Scott Frock, Treas.; Harold D. Cox, MSW; Fay Donohue; Chester W. Douglas, DMD, Ph.D.; Shephard Goldstein, DMD; Leslie E. Grant, D.D.S., MSPA; Marion Kane; Donald J. Kenney; Roderick K. King, M.D., MPH, FAAP; Michael McPherson; Linda C. Niessen, DMD, MPH, MPP; Norman A. Tinanoff, D.D.S.

EIN: 043265080

1084
Deluxe Corporation

3680 Victoria St. N.
Shoreview, MN 55126-2966
(651) 483-7111
FAX: (651) 481-4371

Company URL: http://www.deluxe.com
Establishment information: Established in 1915.
Company type: Public company
Company ticker symbol and exchange: DLX/NYSE
Business activities: Prints checks; prints checkbook covers, business forms, and address labels; manufactures self-inking stamps.
Business type (SIC): Blankbooks, bookbinding, and looseleaf binders; printing/commercial; business forms/manifold; pens, pencils, and art supplies
Financial profile for 2012: Number of employees, 4,881; assets, $1,412,440,000; sales volume, $1,514,920,000; pre-tax net income, $250,750,000; expenses, $1,218,150,000; liabilities, $979,500,000
Corporate officers: Martyn R. Redgrave, Chair.; Lee J. Schram, C.E.O.; Terry D. Peterson, Sr. V.P. and C.F.O.; Anthony C. Scarfone, Sr. V.P., Genl. Counsel, and Secy.; Julie M. Loosbrock, Sr. V.P., Human Resources; R. Wayne Glaus, V.P. and C.I.O.
Board of directors: Martyn R. Redgrave, Chair.; Ronald C. Baldwin; Charles A. Haggerty; Cheryl E. Mayberry McKissack; Don J. McGrath; Neil J. Metviner; Stephen P. Nachtsheim; Mary Ann O'Dwyer; Lee J. Schram
Plants: Phoenix, AZ; Antelope Valley, Chatsworth, CA; Colorado Springs, CO; Des Plaines, IL; Kansas City, KS; Shoreview, MN; Mountain Lakes, NJ; Syracuse, NY; Greensboro, NC; Streetsboro, OH; Salt Lake City, UT
International operations: Canada; United Kingdom
Historic mergers: New England Business Service, Inc. (June 25, 2004)
Giving statement: Giving through the Deluxe Corporation Contributions Program and the Deluxe Corporation Foundation.
Company EIN: 410216800

Deluxe Corporation Contributions Program

3680 Victoria St. N.
Shoreview, MN 55126-2966 (651) 483-7111
URL: http://www.deluxe.com/about-deluxe/community.jsp?locid=DLX:lnv_abtdlx-comm-serv

Purpose and activities: As a complement to its foundation, Deluxe also makes charitable contributions to nonprofit organizations directly. Support is given primarily in areas of company operations.
Fields of interest: Health care, blood supply; Food services; Aging, centers/services; General charitable giving Military/veterans.
Type of support: Employee volunteer services.
Geographic limitations: Giving primarily in areas of company operations.
Publications: Application guidelines.
Application information: Applications accepted. Contact headquarters for nearest application address. Application form not required. Applicants should submit the following:
1) statement of problem project will address
2) copy of IRS Determination Letter
3) detailed description of project and amount of funding requested

Initial approach: Proposal to nearest company facility
Deadline(s): None
Final notification: Following review

Deluxe Corporation Foundation

(formerly Deluxe Check Printers Foundation)
3680 Victoria St. N.
Shoreview, MN 55126-2966 (651) 483-7111
E-mail: Jenny.Anderson@deluxe.com; Application contact for organizations outside of MN: Pamela Bridger, Foundation and Community Affairs Admin., tel.: (651) 787-5124, e-mail: pam.bridger@deluxe.com; URL: http://www.deluxe.com/dlxab/deluxe-foundation.jsp

Establishment information: Incorporated in 1952 in MN.
Donor: Deluxe Corp.
Contact: Jennifer A. Anderson, Dir., Foundations & Community Affairs
Financial data (yr. ended 12/31/11): Assets, $23,643,087 (M); expenditures, $2,799,228; qualifying distributions, $2,698,924; giving activities include $2,345,738 for 300 grants (high: $170,000; low: $5) and $203,970 for 421 employee matching gifts.
Purpose and activities: The foundation supports programs designed to invest in tomorrow through education; address transitional and youth services; and promote community enrichment through the arts. Special emphasis is directed toward partnerships to help people, businesses, and communities grow.
Fields of interest: Museums; Performing arts; Business school/education; Education, services; Education, reading; Mental health/crisis services; Boys & girls clubs; Youth development, adult & child programs; YM/YWCAs & YM/YWHAs; Human services; Community development, small businesses; United Ways and Federated Giving Programs Youth.

Programs:

Communities Enrichment through the Arts: The foundation supports museums and professional arts groups including orchestras, theaters, choral groups, and dance companies.

Employee Matching Gifts: The foundation matches contributions made by employees, retirees, and directors of Deluxe to accredited schools, professional arts organizations, historical societies and museums, and public educational TV and radio on a two-for-one basis from $10 to $500 and on a one-for-one basis from $500 to $2,500 per contributor, per institution, per year up to $3,000 per contributor, per year.

Investing In Tomorrow Through Education: The foundation supports programs designed to promote after-school academic initiatives; business education; and programs designed to partner with business schools.

Time Is Money Program: The foundation awards $200 grants to qualifying non-profits with which employees of Deluxe volunteer 16 or more hours during a calendar year. Employees who serve as nonprofit board members, and donate at least 40 hours during a calendar year, receive a $500 match.

Transitional and Youth Services: The foundation supports programs designed to serve at-risk youth; help at-risk high school students prepare for post-secondary education; promote self-sufficiency; provide small business coaching; and promote crisis response and intervention.
Type of support: Annual campaigns; Building/renovation; Capital campaigns; Continuing support; Emergency funds; Employee matching gifts; Employee volunteer services; Equipment; General/operating support; Program development.
Geographic limitations: Giving on a national basis in areas of company operations, with emphasis on MN; giving also to national organizations.
Support limitations: No support for national, religious, health, political, or lobbying organizations, fraternal organizations, start-up organizations, civic organizations, or organizations supported by government sources. No grants to individuals, or for event sponsorships, conferences, fundraisers, advertising, research projects, travel, athletic events, start-up needs, or long-term housing; no loans.
Publications: Application guidelines; Grants list.
Application information: Applications accepted. Application form not required. Applicants should submit the following:
1) population served
2) copy of IRS Determination Letter
3) brief history of organization and description of its mission
4) geographic area to be served
5) copy of most recent annual report/audited financial statement/990
6) listing of board of directors, trustees, officers and other key people and their affiliations
7) detailed description of project and amount of funding requested
8) copy of current year's organizational budget and/or project budget
9) listing of additional sources and amount of support

Initial approach: Letter of inquiry to foundation for first-time applicants in MN; proposal to foundation for previous grantees in MN; e-mail letter of inquiry to application address for organizations located outside of MN
Copies of proposal: 1
Board meeting date(s): Feb.
Deadline(s): Mar. 1 to Apr. 15 for arts organizations in MN; May 1 to June 30 for youth organizations in MN; July 1 to Oct. 15 for all other organizations in MN; Apr. 1 to Oct. 1 for organizations located outside of MN
Final notification: 3 months

Officers and Directors:* Lee J. Schramm*, Pres.; Jennifer A. Anderson*, V.P. and. Secy.; Julie M. Loosbruck; Terry D. Peterson; Anthony C. Scarfone.
Number of staff: 1 full-time professional; 1 full-time support.
EIN: 416034786

1085
Demoulas Super Markets, Inc.

875 East St.
Tewksbury, MA 01876 (978) 851-8000
FAX: (978) 640-8390

Company URL: http://supportmarketbasket.org
Establishment information: Established in 1917.
Company type: Private company
Business activities: Operates grocery stores.
Business type (SIC): Groceries—retail
Financial profile for 2011: Number of employees, 19,000; sales volume, $3,200,000,000
Corporate officers: Arthur T. Demoulas, Pres. and C.E.O.; Julien Lacourse, Exec. V.P., Mktg.; Donald T. Mulligan, V.P., C.F.O., and Treas.; Michael King, V.P. and Cont.
Board of director: Arthur T. Demoulas
Giving statement: Giving through the Demoulas Foundation.

Demoulas Foundation

286 Chelmsford St.
Chelmsford, MA 01824-2403 (978) 244-1024

Establishment information: Established in 1964 in MA.
Donors: Demoulas Super Markets, Inc.; Members of the Demoulas family.
Contact: Arthur T. Demoulas, Tr.
Financial data (yr. ended 12/31/11): Assets, $31,846,119 (M); expenditures, $1,730,513; qualifying distributions, $1,639,965; giving activities include $1,639,965 for grants.
Purpose and activities: The foundation supports hospitals and organizations involved with arts and culture, education, conservation, cancer, cardiac amyloidosis, human services, community development, and religion.
Fields of interest: Performing arts, opera; Arts; Secondary school/education; Higher education; Education; Hospitals (general); Health care; Cancer; Heart & circulatory diseases; Boys & girls clubs; YM/YWCAs & YM/YWHAs; Children, services; Human services; Community/economic development; Orthodox agencies & churches; Religion.
Type of support: Annual campaigns; Endowments; General/operating support; Program development; Scholarship funds.
Geographic limitations: Giving primarily in MA.
Application information: Applications accepted. Application form not required. Applicants should submit the following:
1) detailed description of project and amount of funding requested

Initial approach: Letter of inquiry
Deadline(s): None

Trustee: Arthur T. Demoulas.
EIN: 042723441
Selected grants: The following grants are a representative sample of this grantmaker's funding activity:
$20,000 to Boston College, Chestnut Hill, MA, 2011.
$10,000 to University of Massachusetts, Lowell, MA, 2011.
$7,500 to United Negro College Fund, Fairfax, VA, 2011.
$2,500 to American Heart Association, Dallas, TX, 2011.

1086
DeniseLawrence.Com

800 Belle Terre Pkwy., Ste. 200-177
Palm Coast, CA 32136 (386) 259-1192

Company URL: http://www.deniselawrence.com
Establishment information: Established in 2005.
Company type: Private company
Business type (SIC): Business services/miscellaneous
Corporate officer: Denise Baraka Lawrence, C.E.O.
Giving statement: Giving through the DeniseLawrence.Com, LLC Contributions Program.

DeniseLawrence.Com, LLC Contributions Program

800 Belle Terre, Pkwy. #200
Palm Coast, FL 32164-2316 (386) 259-1192
E-mail: denise@deniselawrence.com; URL: http://www.deniselawrence.com

Purpose and activities: DeniseLawrence.Com is a certified B Corporation that donates a percentage of profits to charitable organizations.
Fields of interest: Arts; Education; Food services; Housing/shelter.
Type of support: Cause-related marketing.

1087
Denny's Corporation

(formerly Advantica Restaurant Group, Inc.)
203 E. Main St.
Spartanburg, SC 29319-9966
(864) 597-8000
FAX: (302) 655-5049

Company URL: http://www.dennys.com
Establishment information: Established in 1953.
Company type: Public company
Company ticker symbol and exchange: DENN/NASDAQ
Business activities: Operates restaurants.
Business type (SIC): Restaurants and drinking places
Financial profile for 2012: Number of employees, 8,000; assets, $324,880,000; sales volume, $488,360,000; pre-tax net income, $35,090,000; expenses, $439,870,000; liabilities, $329,350,000
Corporate officers: Debra Smithart-Oglesby, Chair.; John C. Miller, Pres. and C.E.O.; F. Mark Wolfinger, Exec. V.P., C.A.O., and C.F.O.; Timothy E. Flemming, Sr. V.P. and Genl. Counsel; Christopher D. Bode, Sr. V.P., Opers.; S. Alex Lewis, V.P. and C.I.O.; Jay C. Gilmore, V.P. and Corp. Cont.; Ross B. Nell, V.P. and Treas.; John W. Dillon, V.P., Mktg.; Jill A. Van Pelt, V.P., Human Resources
Board of directors: Debra Smithart-Oglesby, Chair.; Gregg R. Dedrick; Jose M. Gutierrez; George W. Haywood; Brenda J. Lauderback; Robert E. Marks; John C. Miller; Louis P. Neeb; Donald C. Robinson; Laysha Ward; F. Mark Wolfinger
Subsidiary: Denny's Inc., Spartanburg, SC
International operations: Canada
Giving statement: Giving through the Denny's Corporation Contributions Program.
Company EIN: 133487402

Denny's Corporation Contributions Program

(formerly Advantica Restaurant Group, Inc. Corporate Giving Program)
203 E. Main St., P15-02
Spartanburg, SC 29319-9966
URL: http://dennysdiversity.com/site/pages/community.html

Purpose and activities: Denny's makes charitable contributions to nonprofit organizations on a case by case basis. Support is given in areas of company operations.
Fields of interest: Scholarships/financial aid; Education; Muscular dystrophy; Athletics/sports, Special Olympics; Children, services; Human services, gift distribution; Civil/human rights; General charitable giving.

Type of support: Donated products; Employee volunteer services; General/operating support; Scholarship funds; Sponsorships.
Geographic limitations: Giving primarily in areas of company operations on a national basis and in Canada.

1088
DENSO International America, Inc.

24777 Denso Dr.
P.O. Box 5047
Southfield, MI 48033 (248) 350-7500

Company URL: http://www.densocorp-na.com
Establishment information: Established in 1985.
Company type: Subsidiary of a foreign company
Business activities: Manufactures automotive technology, systems, and components.
Business type (SIC): Motor vehicles and equipment
Financial profile for 2012: Number of employees, 751
Corporate officers: Hikaru Sugi, Pres. and C.E.O.; Kazumasa Kimura, C.O.O.; Terry Helgesen, Sr. V.P., Sales and Mktg.
Plants: Vista, CA; Waterloo, IA; Erlanger, KY; Dublin, OH
Giving statement: Giving through the DENSO International America, Inc. Corporate Giving Program and the DENSO North America Foundation.

DENSO International America, Inc. Corporate Giving Program

24777 Denso Dr.
P.O. Box 5133, M.C. 4610
Southfield, MI 48086-5047 (248) 350-7500
URL: http://www.densocorp-na.com/about_us/community_support

Purpose and activities: As a complement to its foundation, DENSO International also makes charitable contributions to nonprofit organizations directly. Support is given primarily in areas of company operations in California, Iowa, and Ohio, with emphasis on southeast Michigan.
Fields of interest: Arts; Higher education; Environment, air pollution; Environment, water pollution; Environment, land resources; Environment; Human services; Science; Engineering.
Type of support: Employee volunteer services; General/operating support.
Geographic limitations: Giving primarily in areas of company operations in CA, IA, and OH, with emphasis on southeast MI.
Support limitations: No support for discriminatory organizations, religious, political, veterans', or labor organizations, or social clubs. No grants to individuals, or for endowments, dinners or fundraisers, political campaigns, capital campaigns, conferences, trips, or similar events, or advertising.
Publications: Application guidelines.
Application information: Applications accepted. Application form required. Applicants should submit the following:
1) name, address and phone number of organization
2) brief history of organization and description of its mission
3) listing of board of directors, trustees, officers and other key people and their affiliations
4) copy of current year's organizational budget and/or project budget

Applications should include the organization's Tax ID Number and web site, and indicate whether any previous grant applications have been submitted.
Initial approach: Complete online application form
Contributions Committee: William Steffan, Chair.; Barbara Wertheimer, Prog. Coord.
Number of staff: 1 part-time professional.

DENSO North America Foundation

24777 DENSO Dr., MC 4610
Southfield, MI 48086-5047 (248) 372-8225
FAX: (248) 213-2551;
E-mail: densofoundation@denso-diam.com;
Additional tel.: (248) 372-8250; URL: http://www.densofoundation.org

Establishment information: Established in 2001 in MI.
Donor: DENSO International America, Inc.
Financial data (yr. ended 12/31/11): Assets, $11,650,338 (M); gifts received, $3,004,911; expenditures, $605,434; qualifying distributions, $604,609; giving activities include $604,609 for grants.
Purpose and activities: The foundation supports organizations involved with engineering education and related business areas. Special emphasis is directed toward programs designed to demonstrate technological innovation and automotive engineering.
Fields of interest: Business school/education; Engineering school/education; Engineering/technology.
International interests: Canada; Mexico.
Type of support: Building/renovation; Capital campaigns; Equipment; Program development.
Geographic limitations: Giving primarily in CA, MI, MS, OH, and TN, and in Canada and Mexico.
Support limitations: No grants to individuals, or for administrative costs, stipends, trips, conferences, or travel expenses.
Publications: Application guidelines; Grants list.
Application information: Applications accepted. The foundation considers proposals on an invitation and request basis. If applicants are approved, they will be asked to submit a 1 page concept paper. Application form not required.
Initial approach: Telephone foundation to discuss possible funding
Board meeting date(s): May and Oct.
Deadline(s): None
Officers and Directors: Dennis Dawson*, Pres.; Robert Townsend, V.P.; Sharon Brosch, Secy.; Kim Madaj, Treas.; Hugh Cantrell; David Cole; Karen Cooper-Boyer; Douglas Patton; Richard Shiozaki.
Agent: JPMorgan Chase Bank, N.A.
Number of staff: 1 full-time professional.
EIN: 383547055

1089
DENTSPLY International Inc.

Susquehanna Commerce Ctr.-St. 60W
221 W. Philadelphia St., 872
York, PA 17405-0872 (717) 845-7511
FAX: (302) 655-5049

Company URL: http://www.dentsply.com
Establishment information: Established in 1988.
Company type: Public company
Company ticker symbol and exchange: XRAY/NASDAQ
Business activities: Designs, develops, manufactures, and markets dental products.
Business type (SIC): Medical instruments and supplies
Financial profile for 2012: Number of employees, 11,900; assets, $4,972,300,000; sales volume, $2,928,430,000; pre-tax net income, $330,680,000; expenses, $2,546,490,000; liabilities, $2,763,600,000
Fortune 1000 ranking: 2012—724th in revenues, 454th in profits, and 597th in assets
Corporate officers: Bret W. Wise, Chair. and C.E.O.; Christopher T. Clark, Pres. and C.F.O.; James G. Mosch, Exec. V.P. and C.O.O; William E. Reardon, V.P. and Treas.; Richard M. Wagner, V.P. and Corp. Cont.; Deborah M. Rasin, V.P., Genl. Counsel, and Secy.; Maureen J. MacInnis, V.P., Human Resources
Board of directors: Bret W. Wise, Chair.; Michael C. Alfano, Ph.D.; Eric K. Brandt; Paula H.J. Cholmondeley; Michael J. Coleman; Willie A. Deese; William F. Hecht; Leslie A. Jones; Francis J. Lunger; John Miclot; John C. Miles II
Subsidiary: Ceramco Inc., Burlington, NJ
International operations: Argentina; Brazil; Canada; Cayman Islands; China; India; Mexico; Philippines; Spain; Switzerland; Thailand; United Kingdom
Giving statement: Giving through the DENTSPLY International Foundation.
Company EIN: 391434669

DENTSPLY International Foundation

c/o Tax Dept.
221 W. Philadelphia St., Rm. 60W
York, PA 17401-2991 (717) 845-7511

Establishment information: Established in 1955 in PA.
Donor: DENTSPLY International Inc.
Financial data (yr. ended 12/31/11): Assets, $705,017 (M); expenditures, $296,102; qualifying distributions, $296,000; giving activities include $296,000 for grants.
Purpose and activities: The foundation supports organizations involved with higher education, health, and human services.
Fields of interest: Higher education; Dental school/education; Hospitals (general); Dental care; Health care; American Red Cross; Human services; United Ways and Federated Giving Programs.
Type of support: General/operating support; Scholarship funds.
Geographic limitations: Giving primarily in DE and PA.
Application information: Applications accepted. Application form not required.
Initial approach: Letter
Copies of proposal: 1
Board meeting date(s): Nov. and Dec.
Deadline(s): None
Officer: Brian M. Addison, Secy.
Trustees: Linda Niessen; William E. Reardon; Leslie A. Satfin; Bret W. Wise.
Number of staff: None.
EIN: 236297307
Selected grants: The following grants are a representative sample of this grantmaker's funding activity:
$100,000 to Oral Health America, Chicago, IL, 2010.
$31,500 to United Way of York County, York, PA, 2010.
$2,500 to York Health Foundation, York, PA, 2010.
$1,500 to Multiple Sclerosis Society, National, New York, NY, 2010.

1090
Denver Nuggets L.P.

1000 Chopper Cir.
Denver, CO 80204-5809 (303) 405-1100
FAX: (303) 575-1920

Company URL: http://www.nba.com/nuggets
Establishment information: Established in 1967.
Company type: Subsidiary of a private company
Business activities: Operates professional basketball club.
Business type (SIC): Commercial sports
Corporate officers: Josh Kroenke, Pres.; Masai Ujiri, Exec. V.P., Opers; Stephen Stieneker, V.P. and Genl. Counsel
Giving statement: Giving through the Denver Nuggets L.P. Corporate Giving Program.

Denver Nuggets L.P. Corporate Giving Program

Pepsi Ctr.
1000 Chopper Cir.
Denver, CO 80204-5805 (303) 405-1104
FAX: (720) 931-2022;
E-mail: llinscott@pepsicenter.com; Additional contacts: For Quality Time and Team Fit: Katie Wolfe, tel.: (303) 405-1351, e-mail: kwolfe@pepsicenter.com; For Nugget for a Day: Doug Fulton, tel.: (303) 405-1107, e-mail: dfulton@pepsicenter.com; URL: http://www.nba.com/nuggets/community/index.html

Contact: Lesley Linscott
Purpose and activities: The Denver Nuggets make charitable contributions of memorabilia and tickets to nonprofit organizations on a case by case basis. Support is given primarily in Colorado.
Fields of interest: Elementary/secondary education; Education, reading; Education; Public health, physical fitness; Health care; Nutrition; Athletics/sports, amateur leagues; Athletics/sports, basketball; Youth development; YM/YWCAs & YM/YWHAs; Children/youth, services; General charitable giving.
Programs:

Community Ambassadors: Through the Denver Nuggets Community Ambassadors program, past NBA players, coaches, and referees visit classrooms, community events, and organizations in Denver to encourage students to embrace learning, respect others, value good sportsmanship, and achieve excellence.

High School Athletic Training Awards: The Denver Nuggets honors high school certified athletic trainers and athletic training programs in Colorado. The program provides a $2,000 grant to 3 high school athletic training programs at Nuggets game and 5 $200 scholarships to student athletic trainers to be used for workshops at the National Athletic Training Association Board of Certifications schools.

KSE Ticket Donation Program: Kroenke Sports Enterprises (KSE) on behalf of the Denver Nuggets provides game tickets to home games at the Pepsi Center and Dick's Sporting Goods Park to nonprofit organizations.

Nugget for a Day: The Denver Nuggets honors kids who are not Straight-A students or All-State athletes, but demonstrate academic achievement, positive attitude, good citizenship, good behavior, and community involvement. Winners receive an official game-day itinerary, a visit to a Nuggets practice, game tickets, a dinner inside the Conoco suite a Pepsi Center, and in-game recognition.

Nuggets Program Sales: The Denver Nuggets provides area youth basketball teams the opportunity to fundraise during home games. Youth sell game programs and keep 100% of the profits. Participants are also given game tickets for players and chaperones.

Quality Time: Through Quality Time, the Denver Nuggets encourages parents and children from elementary, middle, and high schools, nonprofit organizations, and youth programs to spend an evening together at a Nuggets home game. The program includes round-trip transportation in a 55-passenger bus, game tickets, concession vouchers, Quality Time shits, and other team related gifts.

Quest Leadership Challenge: Kroenke Sports, the parent company of the Denver Nuggets, provides scholarships and Denver Nuggets game tickets to high school varsity athletes who demonstrate exemplary service, leadership, and commitment to their community. Applicants must complete a community-based leadership service project that includes 30 volunteer hours to a non-profit or school related cause. Twelve finalists will be awarded scholarships of up to $10,000 and will receive 3 tickets to a Denver Nuggets game, a ceremony on the Nuggets' home court, and an invitation to a private V.I.P. reception.

Team Fit: The Denver Nuggets, in partnership with The Children's Hospital, teaches kids grade 3 to 8 about nutrition and fitness fundamentals through Team Fit. Each class receives fitness tips from Nuggets Strength and Conditioning coaches, a Nuggets health and wellness poster for each child, activity worksheets, and fitness logs to be completed to win Nuggets prizes.

Type of support: Cause-related marketing; Donated products; In-kind gifts; Loaned talent.
Geographic limitations: Giving primarily in areas of company operations in CO.
Publications: Application guidelines; Corporate giving report.
Application information: Applications accepted. The Community Relations Department handles giving. Support is limited to 1 contribution per organization during any given year. Telephone calls are not encouraged. Application form required. Applicants should submit the following:
1) population served
2) name, address and phone number of organization
3) brief history of organization and description of its mission
4) contact person

Initial approach: Complete online application form for ticket and memorabilia donations and Nugget for a Day; register online for Team Fit
Deadline(s): 6 weeks prior to need for memorabilia donations; Sept. 1 for ticket donations; Mar. 2 for Nugget for a Day; Sept. 15 for Team Fit

1091
Dethmers Manufacturing Co.

4010 320th St.
P.O. Box 189
Boyden, IA 51234 (712) 725-2311
FAX: (712) 725-2380

Company URL: http://www.demco-products.com/
Establishment information: Established in 1934.
Company type: Private company
Business activities: Manufactures agricultural equipment, including chemical sprayers, liquid fertilizer applicators, harvest boxes; tow-trailers for recreation vehicles; one-way truck rental; commercial lithographic printing.
Business type (SIC): Printing/commercial; plastic products/miscellaneous; machinery/farm and garden; machinery/general industry; motor vehicles and equipment; transportation equipment/miscellaneous; motor vehicle rentals and leasing
Corporate officers: James E. Koerselman, Pres.; Douglas Beukelman, C.E.O.; Jason Teraherk, C.F.O.; Ken Streff, V.P., Sales and Mktg.
Giving statement: Giving through the Demco Charitable Foundation.

Demco Charitable Foundation

Hwy. 18 E.
Boyden, IA 51234-0189 (712) 725-2311

Establishment information: Established in 1988 in IA.
Donors: Dethmers Manufacturing Co.; James E. Koerselman; Maurere Mfg.
Contact: James E. Koerselman, Pres.
Financial data (yr. ended 06/30/12): Assets, $1,544,214 (M); gifts received, $292,000; expenditures, $187,024; qualifying distributions, $174,452; giving activities include $174,452 for grants.
Fields of interest: Education; Youth development; Human services.
Type of support: Annual campaigns; Building/renovation; General/operating support; Program development; Scholarship funds.
Geographic limitations: Giving primarily in northwestern IA.
Support limitations: No grants to individuals.
Application information: Applications accepted. Application form required. Applicants should submit the following:
1) copy of IRS Determination Letter
2) detailed description of project and amount of funding requested

Initial approach: Letter
Deadline(s): None

Officers: James E. Koerselman, Pres. and Treas.; Robert Koerselman, V.P. and Secy.
EIN: 421322684

1092
Detour Agency, Inc.

16204 Payton
Irvine, CA 92620-3471 (714) 253-7890

Company URL: http://www.detour.co
Establishment information: Established in 2009.
Company type: Private company
Business type (SIC): Business services/miscellaneous
Corporate officer: Gueri Segura, Mgr.
Giving statement: Giving through the Detour Agency, Inc. Corporate Giving Program.

Detour Agency, Inc. Corporate Giving Program

16204 Payton
Irvine, CA 92620-3471 (714) 371-6968
E-mail: hello@detour.co; URL: http://www.detour.co

Purpose and activities: Detour Agency is a certified B Corporation that donates a percentage of net profits to charitable organizations.

1093
Detroit Diesel Corporation
13400 Outer Dr. W.
Detroit, MI 48239-4001 (313) 592-5000
FAX: (313) 592-7288

Company URL: http://www.detroitdiesel.com
Establishment information: Established in 1938.
Company type: Subsidiary of a foreign company
Business activities: Designs, manufactures, sells, and services diesel engines.
Business type (SIC): Engines and turbines
Financial profile for 2010: Number of employees, 6,660
Corporate officers: Martin Daum, Pres. and C.E.O.; Robert E. Belts, C.F.O.
Giving statement: Giving through the Detroit Diesel Scholarship Foundation, Inc.

Detroit Diesel Scholarship Foundation, Inc.
13400 Outer Dr., W.
Detroit, MI 48239-4001
URL: http://www.demanddetroit.com/

Establishment information: Established in 1990 in MI.
Donor: Detroit Diesel Corp.
Contact: Cyril Yuergens
Financial data (yr. ended 12/31/11): Assets, $0 (M); expenditures, $0; qualifying distributions, $0.
Purpose and activities: The foundation awards college and vocational scholarships to spouses, children, and grandchildren of employees of Detroit Diesel Corp.
Fields of interest: Education.
Type of support: Employee-related scholarships.
Geographic limitations: Giving limited to Detroit, MI.
Application information: Applications not accepted. Contributes only through employee-related scholarships.
Officers and Directors: Philip Bezaire*, Pres.; Joseph M. Herrick, Secy.; Joseph B. Street.
EIN: 382964503

1094
The Detroit Lions, Inc.
222 Republic Dr.
Allen Park, MI 48101 (313) 216-4000
FAX: (313) 216-4226

Company URL: http://www.detroitlions.com
Establishment information: Established in 1930.
Company type: Private company
Business activities: Operates professional football club.
Business type (SIC): Commercial sports
Corporate officers: William Clay Ford, Chair.; William Clay Ford, Jr., Vice-Chair.; Tom Lewand, Pres.; Luis Perez, Sr. V.P. and C.F.O.; Bill Keenist, Sr. V.P., Comms.; Allison Maki, V.P., Finance and Admin.; Charles Cusick, V.P., Opers.; David Hempstead, Corp. Secy.
Board of directors: William Clay Ford, Chair.; William Clay Ford, Jr., Vice-Chair.
Giving statement: Giving through the Detroit Lions, Inc. Corporate Giving Program and the Detroit Lions Charities.

The Detroit Lions, Inc. Corporate Giving Program
222 Republic Dr.
Allen Park, MI 48101-3650
URL: http://www.detroitlions.com/community/index.html

Purpose and activities: The Detroit Lions make charitable contributions of memorabilia to nonprofit organizations on a case by case basis. Support is given primarily in areas of company operations in Michigan.
Fields of interest: General charitable giving.
Type of support: In-kind gifts; Loaned talent.
Geographic limitations: Giving primarily in areas of company operations in MI.
Support limitations: No game ticket donations.
Publications: Application guidelines.
Application information: Applications accepted. Proposals should be submitted using organization letterhead. Telephone calls, faxes, mail, and e-mail messages are not encouraged. Application form required. Applicants should submit the following:
1) name, address and phone number of organization
2) detailed description of project and amount of funding requested
3) contact person

Applications should indicate the name, date, location, and expected attendance of the event; the intended use of the donation; and the referral name, if applicable.
Initial approach: Complete online application form and upload proposal
Deadline(s): 6 weeks prior to need

Detroit Lions Charities
222 Republic Dr.
Allen Park, MI 48101-3650 (313) 216-4050
URL: http://www.detroitlions.com/document_display.cfm?document_id=3588

Establishment information: Established in 1990 in MI.
Contact: William Clay Ford, Pres.
Financial data (yr. ended 02/28/11): Revenue, $367,225; assets, $1,118,895 (M); gifts received, $344,207; expenditures, $368,193; program services expenses, $352,174; giving activities include $352,174 for 6 grants (high: $85,229; low: $10,000).
Purpose and activities: The organization assists charitable and worthwhile causes in Michigan, and supports activities and programs that benefit all age groups in education, civic affairs, and health and human services.
Fields of interest: Education; Health care; Human services; Community/economic development.
Program:
Grants: The program awards grants to 501(c)(3) public charities to benefit education, civic affairs, health services, and human services.
Geographic limitations: Giving primarily in Detroit, MI.
Support limitations: No support for political campaigns or activities. No grants to individuals (including loans and scholarships), or for building, raffles, banquets, advertising, equipment, or endowments.
Publications: Application guidelines.
Application information: Applications accepted. Applicants should submit the following:
1) copy of IRS Determination Letter
2) detailed description of project and amount of funding requested
3) copy of current year's organizational budget and/or project budget
4) listing of additional sources and amount of support

Initial approach: Letter (no more than two pages)
Board meeting date(s): Feb.
Deadline(s): Between Oct. 1 and Dec. 31
Final notification: Mar.
Officers: William Clay Ford*, Pres.; William Clay Ford, Jr.*, V.P.; J. Thomas Lesnau*, Treas.
Trustee: William Keenist; Thomas J. Lesnau; Timothy A. Pendell.
EIN: 382945709

1095
Detroit Pistons Basketball Company
6 Championship Dr.
Auburn Hills, MI 48326-1753
(248) 377-0100
FAX: (248) 377-3260

Company URL: http://www.nba.com
Establishment information: Established in 1941.
Company type: Subsidiary of a private company
Business activities: Operates professional basketball club.
Business type (SIC): Commercial sports
Financial profile for 2010: Number of employees, 250
Corporate officers: Alan Ostfield, Pres. and C.E.O.; John O'Reilly, Exec. V.P. and C.F.O.; Dan Hauser, Exec. V.P., Corp. Mktg.; John Ciszewski, Exec. V.P., Corp. Sales; Jim Summers, V.P., Opers.; Michelle Foley, V.P., Human Resources
Giving statement: Giving through the Detroit Pistons Basketball Company Contributions Program and the Pistons-Palace Foundation.

Detroit Pistons Basketball Company Contributions Program
c/o Community Rels.
6 Championship Dr.
Auburn Hills, MI 48326-9906 (248) 377-8637
FAX: (248) 377-0309; URL: http://www.nba.com/pistons/community/

Purpose and activities: The Detroit Pistons make charitable contributions of game tickets and memorabilia to nonprofit organizations involved with youth development, and on a case by case basis. Support is limited to Michigan.
Fields of interest: Education; Tropical diseases; Breast cancer research; Autism research; Food services; Boys & girls clubs; Youth development; Children/youth, services; General charitable giving Military/veterans; Economically disadvantaged.
Program:
Player Ticket Sections: Through the Player Ticket Sections program, Detroit Pistons players, along with coaching staff, purchase tickets to every home game to be donated to nonprofit organizations involved with disadvantaged youths.
Type of support: Building/renovation; In-kind gifts; Income development; Scholarship funds.
Geographic limitations: Giving limited to MI.
Support limitations: No support for political organizations or candidates. No grants to individuals, or for general operating support, political campaigns, trips or tours, or seminars; no in-kind gifts for prizes, recognition gifts, or giveaways.
Publications: Application guidelines; Corporate giving report; Newsletter.
Application information: Applications accepted. Proposals should be submitted using organization

letterhead, and be brief. Support is limited to 1 contribution per organization during any given year. The Community Relations Department handles giving. Application form required. Applicants should submit the following:
1) name, address and phone number of organization
2) brief history of organization and description of its mission
3) contact person
Proposals should include the organization's Tax ID Number, the item requested, and a brief description of the event.
Initial approach: Proposal to headquarters or complete online form for product and ticket donations; fax letter of inquiry for Player Ticket Sections
Deadline(s): 6 weeks prior to need; none for Player Ticket Sections
Final notification: 1 to 2 weeks prior to need

The Pistons-Palace Foundation

6 Championship Dr.
Auburn Hills, MI 48326-1753 (248) 377-0100
FAX: (248) 377-0309; URL: http://www.nba.com/pistons/community/

Establishment information: Established in 1989 in MI.
Donors: Detroit Pistons Basketball Co.; The Palace of Auburn Hills; Guardian Industries Corp.; Bank One, N.A.; Palace Sports & Entertainment, Inc.; Ticketmaster Group, Inc.; Belle Tire; National Basketball Association; Pricewaterhouse Coopers LLP; Quicken Loans; Morgan Bradley LLC.
Contact: Dennis Sampier
Financial data (yr. ended 02/29/12): Assets, $812,106 (M); gifts received, $57,444; expenditures, $79,646; qualifying distributions, $88,135; giving activities include $54,434 for 16 grants (high: $23,159; low: $150).
Purpose and activities: The foundation supports programs designed to promote education, recreation, and healthy lifestyles. Special emphasis is directed toward programs serving youth and adults.
Fields of interest: Elementary school/education; Secondary school/education; Education, reading; Education; Health care; Recreation; Boys & girls clubs Youth.
Programs:
Gift of Reading Scholarship Contest: The foundation, in partnership with Detroit Free Press, annually awards scholarships to K-12 students as part of the "Read to Achieve" tour and online contest. Students submit an essay or short story of up to 2,000 words on the importance of good sportsmanship. Submissions are judged on originality, writing style, grammar, content, and overall message and eight grand-prize winners receive scholarships of up to $2,500 at a Pistons home game.
Know Your Black History Tour and Contest: The foundation, in partnership with Quicken Loans and Fathead.com, annually hosts a Black history tour with which three students from Detroit schools perform a three-minute interpretation on the importance of knowing your Black history in the art form of their choice. Winners receive scholarships of up to $10,000, a Pistons Flathead wall graphic, four tickets to a Pistons game, and participating schools receive five laptops. The foundation also sponsors an online contest which awards a $2,500 scholarship and tickets to a Piston's home game to a high school student who demonstrates extensive knowledge of Black history. The program is limited to high school students in Michigan.
Type of support: Annual campaigns; Building/renovation; General/operating support; In-kind gifts; Program development; Scholarship funds; Scholarships—to individuals; Sponsorships.
Geographic limitations: Giving primarily in areas of company operations in the tri-county metropolitan Detroit area and southeastern MI.
Support limitations: No grants to individuals (except for scholarships).
Publications: Annual report.
Application information: Applications accepted. Application form required.
Initial approach: Contact foundation for application form
Copies of proposal: 1
Deadline(s): Aug. 1
Officers: Mary Ann Sigler, Chair.; Eva M. Kalawski, Vice Chair. and Secy.-Treas.
Directors: Adam Cooper; Bryan Kellen; Dan Krasner; Johnny O. Lopez; Philip Evan Norment; Michael Scott; Stepheanie Smith; Robert J. Wentworth; Sally A. Ward.
Number of staff: 3 full-time professional.
EIN: 382858649

1096
Detroit Red Wings, Inc.

Joe Louis Arena
600 Civic Center Dr.
Detroit, MI 48226 (313) 396-7544

Company URL: http://www.detroitredwings.com
Establishment information: Established in 1926.
Company type: Subsidiary of a private company
Business activities: Operates professional ice hockey club.
Business type (SIC): Commercial sports
Corporate officers: Craig Turnbull, Sr. V.P., Mktg. and Comms.; Robert E. Carr, Sr. V.P., Opers.; John Ciszewski, Sr. V.P., Sales; Paul McDonald, V.P., Finance; Rob Mattina, V.P., Mktg.; Marian Ilitch, Secy.-Treas.
Giving statement: Giving through the Detroit Red Wings, Inc. Corporate Giving Program.

Detroit Red Wings, Inc. Corporate Giving Program

19 Steve Yzerman Dr.
Detroit, MI 48226-4428 (313) 396-7524
FAX: (313) 567-0296; URL: http://redwings.nhl.com/club/page.htm?bcid=com_default

Purpose and activities: The Detroit Red Wings make charitable contributions of memorabilia to nonprofit organizations on a case by case basis. Support is given primarily in Michigan.
Fields of interest: General charitable giving.
Type of support: In-kind gifts; Loaned talent.
Geographic limitations: Giving primarily in MI.
Support limitations: No game ticket donations.
Publications: Application guidelines.
Application information: Applications accepted. Proposals should be submitted using organization letterhead. Support is limited to 1 contribution per organization during any given year. Application form not required. Applicants should submit the following:
1) name, address and phone number of organization
2) copy of IRS Determination Letter
3) contact person
Initial approach: Download application form and mail or fax with proposal to headquarters
Deadline(s): 4 weeks prior to need

1097
Detroit Tigers, Inc.

Comerica Pk., 2100 Woodward Ave.
Detroit, MI 48201-3470 (313) 962-4000

Company URL: http://detroit.tigers.mlb.com
Establishment information: Established in 1901.
Company type: Subsidiary of a private company
Business activities: Operates professional baseball club.
Business type (SIC): Commercial sports
Corporate officers: David Dombrowski, Pres. and C.E.O.; Duane McLean, Sr. V.P., Opers.; Stephen D. Quinn, V.P., Finance, Admin., and C.F.O.; Ellen Hill Zeringue, V.P., Mktg.; Ron Colangelo, V.P., Comms.; Elaine Lewis, V.P., Public Affairs
Board of director: Michael Ilitch
Giving statement: Giving through the Tigers Care Program.

Tigers Care Program

Comerica Park
2100 Woodward
Detroit, MI 48201-3470
URL: http://detroit.tigers.mlb.com/det/community/index.jsp

Purpose and activities: As a complement to its foundation, the Detroit Tigers also make charitable contributions to nonprofit organizations directly. Special emphasis is directed towards youth sports and recreation. Support is given primarily in Michigan.
Fields of interest: Education; Athletics/sports, baseball; Recreation; Youth development.
Type of support: Donated equipment; Equipment; General/operating support; In-kind gifts; Loaned talent; Scholarship funds.
Geographic limitations: Giving primarily in MI.
Publications: Corporate giving report.

1098
The Deutsch Company, Inc.

2444 Wilshire Blvd., Ste. 600
Santa Monica, CA 90403-5819
(310) 453-0055

Establishment information: Established in 1938.
Company type: Private company
Business activities: Manufactures hydraulic and pneumatic components.
Business type (SIC): Machinery/industrial and commercial
Corporate officer: Theodore K. Long, Jr., Pres.
Subsidiaries: Deutsch Co. Metal Components, Gardena, CA; Deutsch Engineered Connecting Devices Co., Banning, CA; Deutsch Engineered Connecting Devices Co., Hemet, CA
Divisions: Deutsch Engineered Connecting Device Div., Calimesa, CA; Deutsch Industrial Products Div., Hemet, CA
Giving statement: Giving through the Three Sisters Foundation.

The Three Sisters Foundation

(formerly The Deutsch Foundation)
c/o Foundation Source
501 Silverside Rd., Ste. 123
Wilmington, DE 19809-1377

Establishment information: Incorporated in 1947 in CA.

Donors: The Deutsch Co.; Carl Deutsch; Eleanor Deutsch; Lester Deutsch; Dworman Foundation, Inc.; Alexis Deutsch-Adler; Gina Deutsch-Zakarin; Victoria D. Sutherland.
Financial data (yr. ended 12/31/11): Assets, $4,752,751 (M); expenditures, $243,199; qualifying distributions, $214,716; giving activities include $194,200 for 11 grants (high: $75,000; low: $1,200).
Purpose and activities: The foundation supports organizations involved with elementary education, health, human services, and international relief.
Fields of interest: Elementary school/education; Health care; Children/youth, services; Children, services; Aging, centers/services; Human services; International relief; Jewish federated giving programs.
Type of support: General/operating support.
Geographic limitations: Giving primarily in CA.
Support limitations: No grants to individuals.
Application information: Applications not accepted. Contributes only to pre-selected organizations.
Officers and Directors:* Gina Deutsche-Zakarin, Pres.; Victoria D. Sutherland, C.F.O.; Alexis Deutsch-Adler*, Secy.; Lester Deutsch; Leslie Lichtenstein.
EIN: 956027369
Selected grants: The following grants are a representative sample of this grantmaker's funding activity:
$15,000 to Everychild Foundation, Pacific Palisades, CA, 2009.
$5,000 to American Film Institute, Los Angeles, CA, 2009.
$5,000 to Childrens Hospital Los Angeles, Los Angeles, CA, 2009.
$5,000 to Mirman School for Gifted Children, Los Angeles, CA, 2009.
$5,000 to Painted Turtle Gang Camp Foundation, Santa Monica, CA, 2009.
$5,000 to Planned Parenthood Los Angeles, Los Angeles, CA, 2009.
$5,000 to Venice Family Clinic, Venice, CA, 2009.
$5,000 to Vista del Mar Child and Family Services, Los Angeles, CA, 2009.
$5,000 to Westside Center for Independent Living, Los Angeles, CA, 2009.
$3,000 to Inner-City Arts, Los Angeles, CA, 2009.

1099
Deutsche Bank Americas Holding Corp.

(formerly Deutsche Bank North America Holding Corp.)
60 Wall St.
New York, NY 10005 (212) 250-5591

Company URL: http://www.db.com/usa/
Establishment information: Established in 1872.
Company type: Subsidiary of a foreign company
Business activities: Operates commercial bank.
Business type (SIC): Banks/foreign; holding company
Financial profile for 2009: Number of employees, 3,031
Corporate officers: Juergen Fitschen, Co-Chair.; Anshu Jain, Co-Chair.; John O. Utendahl, Vice-Chair.; Seth Waugh, C.E.O.; Henry Ritchotte, C.O.O.; Stefan Krause, C.F.O.
Board of directors: Jurgen Fitschen, Co-Chair.; Anshu Jain, Co-Chair.; John O. Utendahl, Vice-Chair.
Subsidiaries: Sharps Pixley Brokers Inc., New York, NY; Sharps Pixley Inc., New York, NY
Giving statement: Giving through the Deutsche Bank North America Holding Corp. Contributions Program, the Deutsche Bank Americas Foundation, and the Deutsche Bank Microcredit Development Fund, Inc.

Deutsche Bank North America Holding Corp. Contributions Program

60 Wall St.
New York, NY 10005 (212) 250-2500
URL: https://www.db.com/usa/content/en/social_responsibility.html

Application information: The company has a staff that only handles contributions. Application form not required.
Deadline(s): None
Final notification: About 2 weeks

Deutsche Bank Americas Foundation

(formerly BT Foundation)
60 Wall St., NYC60-2112
New York, NY 10005-2858
FAX: (212) 797-2255; URL: http://www.db.com/us/content/en/1066.html

Establishment information: Established in 1986 in NY.
Donors: Bankers Trust Co.; BT Capital Corp.; Deutsche Bank Americas Holding Corp.
Financial data (yr. ended 12/31/11): Assets, $24,863,267 (M); gifts received, $11,041,561; expenditures, $11,405,392; qualifying distributions, $12,848,469; giving activities include $7,775,483 for 255 grants (high: $250,000; low: $500), $3,561,078 for 2,290 employee matching gifts and $1,503,935 for loans/program-related investments.
Purpose and activities: The foundation supports organizations involved with arts and culture, education, the environment, health, employment, affordable housing, disaster relief, human services, community economic development, youth, minorities, immigrants, and economically disadvantaged people.
Fields of interest: Visual arts; Museums; Museums (art); Performing arts, music; Arts; Elementary/secondary education; Higher education; Education, services; Education, e-learning; Education; Environment, climate change/global warming; Environment, energy; Environment; Hospitals (general); Optometry/vision screening; Employment, training; Employment; Housing/shelter, development; Housing/shelter; Disasters, preparedness/services; YM/YWCAs & YM/YWHAs; Children/youth, services; Human services, financial counseling; Homeless, human services; Human services; Community development, neighborhood development; Business/industry; Community development, small businesses; Community/economic development; Mathematics; Engineering/technology; Science Youth; Minorities; Immigrants/refugees; Economically disadvantaged.
International interests: Canada; Latin America.
Programs:
Arts & Enterprise Grants Program: The foundation supports cultural institutions that are critical in the revitalization of transitional neighborhoods through a Request for Proposal (RFP) process. The program supports arts, culture, and design as tools for the economic development of distressed communities, and as an opportunity for new employment, and career, and entrepreneurial opportunities for neighborhood residents. The foundation's most recent RFP, Arts & Emerging Technology, supports arts and technology projects that use emerging technologies to further educational programming, reach new audiences, engage new artists, and maximize efficiency.
College Ready Communities: Through College Ready Communities, the foundation partners with Community Development Corporations, education advocacy organizations, and public middle and high schools in low-to-moderate income neighborhoods to improve student academic outcomes. The program includes Student Success Centers where recent high school graduates and current seniors guide younger peers through the college admissions process; professional development for teachers; interaction with parents to discuss college savings and financial aid; and curricular support for students.
DB Share: Through Deutsche Bank Supportive Housing Acquisition and Rehabilitation Effort (DB SHARE), the foundation supports developers of new permanent housing for homeless New Yorkers with special needs. The program is administered through a Request for Proposal (RFP) process and grant recipients receive a three-year award of $75,000 per year for a total of $225,000.
DB Working Capital: Through DB Capital, the foundation funds early state predevelopment activities by community-based organizations to start housing, commercial, or community facility developments. The program is administered through a Request for Proposal (RFP) process and grants are awarded every three years.
Employee Matching Gifts: The foundation matches contributions made by full-time employees and directors of Deutsche Bank Americas to nonprofit organizations involved with community development and social services, education, arts and culture, hospitals and health care, and the environment on a one-for-one basis from $25 to $5,000 per contributor, per year.
Social Investments - Community Development: The foundation supports programs designed to develop affordable housing; generate employment opportunities; and address critical service needs through a Request for Proposal (RFP) process. Special emphasis is directed toward affordable housing and economic development projects in low- and moderate-income neighborhoods.
Teachers as Leaders: Through Teachers as Leaders, the foundation, the City University of New York Black Male Initiative, and the Schott Foundation for Public Education works to increase the number of Black males serving as New York City public school teachers. The program is designed to promote teaching as a preferred career path and includes apprenticeships, mentoring, skills development, and scholarships for participating students.
The New Initiatives Fund: Through the New Initiatives Fund (NIF), the foundation provides financing for community development projects developed by nonprofits, NGOs, and the private sector to serve the needs of poor and disadvantaged communities in the United States and the developing world. The fund was created as a financial product that could be deployed at a larger scale than a typical philanthropic grant, with the ability to assume greater risk and lower returns than conventional bank financing. All foundation commitments through the fund are treated as program-related investments (PRIs). Special emphasis is directed toward projects that offer the opportunity to bring an innovation to scale, have the potential to be replicated, and have realistic plans to graduate from subsidized financing sources to access conventional capital markets.
THRIVE: The foundation, in partnership with New York City Economic Development Corporation and Baruch College, supports the competition To Help Reach Immigrant Ventures and Entrepreneurs (THRIVE). The competition is designed to support sustainable business plans that address challenges

faced by immigrant entrepreneurs in New York City, including access to credit, financial management, language barriers, and access to business networks. Proposals are judged on feasibility, applicability, scalability, and sustainability. The program is administered by Baruch College's Lawrence N. Field Center for Entrepreneurship.
Type of support: Building/renovation; Continuing support; Curriculum development; Employee matching gifts; Employee volunteer services; General/operating support; Management development/capacity building; Matching/challenge support; Mission-related investments/loans; Program development; Program-related investments/loans; Seed money; Sponsorships; Technical assistance.
Geographic limitations: Giving on a national basis in areas of company operations with emphasis on NY, Argentina, Brazil, Canada, Chile, Latin America, Mexico, and Peru.
Support limitations: No support for political candidates, veterans', military, or fraternal organizations, United Way agencies not providing a fundraising waiver, professional or trade associations, discriminatory organizations, organizations that employ adversarial and/or confrontational tactics, or organizations that are not in full compliance with anti-terrorism laws. No grants to individuals, or for endowments, capital campaigns, legal advocacy, or religious purposes.
Publications: Application guidelines; Corporate giving report; Newsletter.
Application information: Applications accepted. Letters of intent should not exceed 3 pages in length. A full proposal may be requested at a later date. The foundation utilizes a Request for Proposal (RFP) process for most programs. Support is limited to 3 years in length. Application form not required. Applicants should submit the following:
1) copy of IRS Determination Letter
2) brief history of organization and description of its mission
3) detailed description of project and amount of funding requested
4) results expected from proposed grant
Initial approach: Letter of intent
Deadline(s): None
Officers and Directors:* Seth Waugh*, Chair.; Gary S. Hattem*, Pres.; Alessandra Digiusto, Secy.-Treas. and C.A.O.; Jorge Arce; Gary Beyer; Jacques Brand; Christopher Habig; Frank Kelly; Roelfien Kuijpers; Erich Mauff; Jeffrey Mayer; Richard Walker.
Number of staff: 3 full-time professional; 3 full-time support.
EIN: 133321736
Selected grants: The following grants are a representative sample of this grantmaker's funding activity:
$300,000 to Asian Americans for Equality, New York, NY, 2010. For College Ready Communities - Collaboration with The Brotherhood Sister Sol/ Coalition for Education Justice.
$200,000 to Association for Neighborhood and Housing Development, New York, NY, 2010. For Neighborhood Opportunities Fund.
$100,000 to Enterprise Community Partners, New York, NY, 2010. For general support.
$100,000 to Resource Foundation, New York, NY, 2010. To build housing through CasaBasica as part of Chile Disaster Relief Program.
$75,000 to Harlem Stage, Aaron Davis Hall, New York, NY, 2010. For Art and Enterprise Stabilization Program.
$30,000 to Corporation for Supportive Housing, New York, NY, 2010. For general operating support.
$25,000 to City Limits, New York, NY, 2010. For Center for Urban Future.
$25,000 to Staten Island Institute of Arts and Sciences, Staten Island, NY, 2010. For Arts and Enterprise Stabilization Program.
$20,000 to Jewish Child Care Association of New York, New York, NY, 2010. For Two Together Program.

Deutsche Bank Microcredit Development Fund, Inc.

c/o Deutsche Bank
60 Wall St., MS NYC60-2110
New York, NY 10005-2836
E-mail for Asad Mahmood: asad.mahmood@db.com;
URL: http://www.db.com/us/content/en/1173.html

Establishment information: Established in 1997 in DE.
Contact: Asad Mahmood, Mgr.
Financial data (yr. ended 12/31/11): Revenue, $140,397; assets, $3,480,430 (M); gifts received, $30,225; expenditures, $58,807.
Purpose and activities: The fund provides loans to nonprofit microcredit lending institutions or nonprofits that are evolving into regulated entities.
Fields of interest: Business/industry.
Program:
Loans: The fund makes loans, ranging from $25,000 to $250,000, to help registered nonprofits reach scale and long-term sustainability by encouraging relationships with local financial institutions. Loans are typically given for a period of one to five years.
Type of support: Program-related investments/loans.
Officers and Directors:* Scott Reardon*, Chair.; Gary S. Hattem*, Pres.; Michael Rauenhorst*, Secy.-Treas.; Paul Dileo; Matthew McConnell; Robert A. Patillo.
EIN: 133957277

1100
Robert J. Devereaux Corp.

10 Emerson Pl., Ste. 2E
Boston, MA 02114-2218 (617) 742-3830

Company URL: http://
Establishment information: Established in 1969.
Company type: Private company
Business activities: Provides single-family home construction services.
Business type (SIC): Contractors/general residential building
Corporate officers: Robert J. Devereaux, Chair., C.E.O., and Co-Pres.; Michael F. Devereaux, Co-Pres.; Owen Lynch, Clerk; Eleanor F. Brennan, Treas.; Eleanor Gillette, Human Resources
Board of directors: Robert J. Devereaux, Chair.; Eleanor Brennan; Michael F. Devereaux
Giving statement: Giving through the Devereaux Charitable Foundation Trust.

The Devereaux Charitable Foundation Trust

10 Emerson Pl.
Charles River Park
Boston, MA 02114-2204 (617) 742-3830

Establishment information: Established in 1985 in MA.
Donors: Robert J. Devereaux Corp.; Robert J. Devereaux.
Contact: Robert J. Devereaux, Tr.
Financial data (yr. ended 03/31/12): Assets, $203,820 (M); gifts received, $225,000; expenditures, $64,594; qualifying distributions, $64,594; giving activities include $64,475 for 41 grants (high: $12,000; low: $100).
Purpose and activities: The trust supports organizations involved with education, athletics, human services, and religion.
Fields of interest: Secondary school/education; Higher education; Education; Athletics/sports, amateur leagues; Athletics/sports, basketball; Athletics/sports, water sports; Athletics/sports, golf; Children/youth, services; Human services; Religion.
Type of support: General/operating support; Scholarship funds.
Support limitations: No grants to individuals.
Application information: Applications accepted. Application form required. Applicants should submit the following:
1) brief history of organization and description of its mission
2) detailed description of project and amount of funding requested
Initial approach: Proposal
Deadline(s): None
Trustee: Robert J. Devereaux.
EIN: 222708298

1101
Dick DeVoe Buick Cadillac Inc.

(doing business as Devoe Buick Gmc)
4100 Tamiami Trail N.
Naples, FL 34103-3197 (239) 261-1234

Company URL: http://www.devoeauto.com
Establishment information: Established in 1968.
Company type: Subsidiary of a private company
Business activities: Operates car dealership.
Business type (SIC): Motor vehicles—retail
Corporate officers: Mark A. DeVoe, Pres.; William Gresh, C.F.O.; Barbara J. DeVoe, Secy.-Treas.
Board of directors: Richard H. Devoe; Charles M. Kelly; Steven R. Whitley
Giving statement: Giving through the Dick DeVoe Buick Cadillac Scholarship Trust.

Dick DeVoe Buick Cadillac Scholarship Trust

c/o William Gresh
4035 10th St. N.
Naples, FL 34103-2304 (239) 261-3538
Application address: 1100 Golden Eagle Cir., Naples, FL 34102, tel.: (239) 261-3538

Establishment information: Established around 1969.
Donors: Dick DeVoe Buick Cadillac Inc.; Richard H. Devoe.
Financial data (yr. ended 12/31/11): Assets, $20,767 (M); gifts received, $100,000; expenditures, $114,315; qualifying distributions, $113,246; giving activities include $113,246 for grants to individuals.
Purpose and activities: The foundation awards college scholarships to graduates of Naples, Collier County, and Estero high schools in Florida.
Fields of interest: Higher education.
Type of support: Scholarships—to individuals.
Geographic limitations: Giving limited to Naples, FL.
Application information: Applications accepted. Application form required.
Applications must include a description of extracurricular activities, honors and awards, state

testing scores, GPA, rank in class, and demonstration of need.
Initial approach: Letter
Deadline(s): Contact foundation for deadlines
Trustee: Richard H. Devoe.
EIN: 237296264

1102
Devon Energy Corporation

333 N. Sheridan Ave.
Oklahoma City, OK 73102-8260
(405) 235-3611

Company URL: http://www.devonenergy.com
Establishment information: Established in 1971.
Company type: Public company
Company ticker symbol and exchange: DVN/NYSE
International Securities Identification Number: US25179M1036
Business activities: Conducts oil and gas exploration, development, and production activities.
Business type (SIC): Extraction/oil and gas
Financial profile for 2012: Number of employees, 5,700; assets, $43,326,000,000; sales volume, $9,502,000,000; pre-tax net income, -$317,000,000; expenses, $9,819,000,000; liabilities, $22,048,000,000
Fortune 1000 ranking: 2012—284th in revenues, 940th in profits, and 128th in assets
Forbes 2000 ranking: 2012—966th in sales, 1864th in profits, and 532nd in assets
Corporate officers: J. Larry Nichols, Chair.; John Richels, Pres. and C.E.O.; David A. Hager, C.O.O.; Jeffrey A. Agosta, Exec. V.P. and C.F.O.; Lyndon C. Taylor, Exec. V.P. and Genl. Counsel; R. Alan Marcum, Exec. V.P., Admin.; William F. Whitsitt, Exec. V.P., Public Affairs; Frank W. Rudolph, Exec. V.P., Human Resources; Bradley A. Foster, Sr. V.P., Opers.; Sue Alberti, Sr. V.P., Mktg.; David G. Harris, V.P., Finance and Treas.; Carla Brockman, Secy.; Gregg L. Henson, Cont.
Board of directors: J. Larry Nichols, Chair.; Robert H. Henry; John A. Hill; Michael M. Kanovsky; Robert A. Mosbacher, Jr.; Duane C. Radtke; Mary P. Ricciardello; John Richels
International operations: Brazil; British Virgin Islands; Canada
Historic mergers: Mitchell Energy & Development Corp. (January 24, 2002)
Giving statement: Giving through the Devon Energy Corporation Contributions Program.
Company EIN: 731567067

Devon Energy Corporation Contributions Program

c/o Community Rels.
20 N. Broadway
Oklahoma City, OK 73102-8260 (405) 235-3611
FAX: (405) 552-4550;
E-mail: christina.rehkop@dvn.com; For organizations located in Canada: Paula King, e-mail: paula.king@dvn.com; URL: http://www.dvn.com/CommunityRelations/Pages/Overview.aspx

Contact: Christina Rehkop
Purpose and activities: Devon Energy makes charitable contributions to nonprofit organizations involved with arts and culture, education, health, the environment, youth development, emergency response, human services, community development, and civic affairs. Support is given primarily in areas of significant company operations in Louisiana, Montana, New Mexico, Oklahoma, Texas, Utah, and Wyoming, and in Canada.
Fields of interest: Arts; Education; Environment; Health care; Disasters, preparedness/services; Youth development; Human services; Community/economic development; Science, formal/general education; Public affairs.
International interests: Canada.
Type of support: Curriculum development; Employee volunteer services; In-kind gifts; Program development; Sponsorships.
Geographic limitations: Giving primarily in areas of significant company operations in LA, MT, NM, OK, TX, UT, and WY, and in Canada.
Support limitations: No support for religious or political organizations, fraternal or partisan organizations, or disease-specific organizations. No grants to individuals, or for team sports, or sporting events.
Application information: Applications accepted. Application form required. Applicants should submit the following:
1) name, address and phone number of organization
2) detailed description of project and amount of funding requested
3) contact person
4) copy of current year's organizational budget and/or project budget
5) listing of additional sources and amount of support
6) plans for acknowledgement

Proposals should include the Tax ID Number of the organization and any applicable deadlines.
Initial approach: Complete online application form

1103
Dexter-Russell, Inc.

(formerly Russell Harrington Cutlery, Inc.)
44 River St.
Southbridge, MA 01550-1834
(508) 764-4344
FAX: (508) 764-2897

Company URL: http://www.dexter-russell.com
Establishment information: Established in 1818.
Company type: Subsidiary of a private company
Business activities: Manufactures cutlery and tools.
Business type (SIC): Cutlery, hand and edge tools, and hardware
Financial profile for 2009: Number of employees, 235
Corporate officers: Richard B. Hardy, Chair.; Alan Peppel, Pres. and C.E.O.; Craig Giguere, C.F.O. and Treas.
Board of director: Richard B. Hardy, Chair.
Subsidiary: Hyde Tools, Inc., Southbridge, MA
Giving statement: Giving through the Hyde Charitable Foundation.

Hyde Charitable Foundation

54 Eastford Rd.
Southbridge, MA 01550-1875 (508) 764-4344

Establishment information: Established in 1982 in MA.
Donors: Dexter-Russell Inc.; Hyde Manufacturing Co.; Russell Harrington Cutlery, Inc.; Dexter-Russell, Inc.
Contact: Richard B. Hardy, Tr.
Financial data (yr. ended 12/31/11): Assets, $3,684,585 (M); expenditures, $213,129; qualifying distributions, $177,994; giving activities include $170,700 for 38 grants (high: $10,000; low: $500).
Purpose and activities: The foundation supports organizations involved with education, human services, and community development.
Fields of interest: Higher education; Education; Hospitals (general); Human services; Community/economic development.
Type of support: Annual campaigns; Building/renovation; Capital campaigns; Emergency funds; Endowments; Equipment; General/operating support.
Geographic limitations: Giving primarily in Worcester County, MA.
Application information: Applications accepted. Application form required. Applicants should submit the following:
1) copy of IRS Determination Letter
2) detailed description of project and amount of funding requested
3) copy of current year's organizational budget and/or project budget

Initial approach: Letter
Board meeting date(s): Mar.
Deadline(s): None
Final notification: Apr.
Trustees: Ronald P. Carlson; Richard R. Clemence; Richard B. Hardy; Susan H. Tretter.
EIN: 042752893

1104
DFS Group LP

525 Market St., 31st Fl., Ste. 3300
San Francisco, CA 94105-2769
(415) 977-2700

Company URL: http://www.dfsgalleria.com
Establishment information: Established in 1961.
Company type: Subsidiary of a foreign company
Business activities: Owns and operates duty-free shops.
Business type (SIC): Variety stores
Corporate officers: Edward J. Brennan, Chair. and C.E.O.; Michael Schriver, Pres.
Board of director: Edward J. Brennan, Chair.
Office: Honolulu, HI
Giving statement: Giving through the DFS Group LP Corporate Giving Program.

DFS Group LP Corporate Giving Program

525 Market St., 33rd Fl.
San Francisco, CA 94105-2708 (415) 977-2700
FAX: (415) 348-3194

Purpose and activities: DFS matches contributions made by its employees to nonprofit organizations.
Fields of interest: General charitable giving.
Type of support: Employee matching gifts.
Application information: Applications not accepted. Contributes only through employee matching gifts.

1105
Dharma Merchant Services

100 Bush St., Ste. 1580
San Francisco, CA 94104 (415) 632-1920

Company URL: http://www.dharmamerchantservices.com
Establishment information: Established in 2007.
Company type: Private company
Business activities: Operates credit card processing company.

Business type (SIC): Business services/ miscellaneous
Corporate officers: Jeffrey Smith, Co-Founder and C.E.O; Jeff Marcous, Co-Founder and Pres.
Giving statement: Giving through the Dharma Merchant Services Corporate Giving Program.

Dharma Merchant Services Corporate Giving Program

353 Kearny St., Ste. 32
San Francisco, CA 94108-3236 (415) 632-1920
FAX: (415) 632-1921; URL: http://www.dharmamerchantservices.com/GivingBack.html

Purpose and activities: Dharma Merchant Services is a certified B Corporation that donates a percentage of profits to nonprofit organizations.
Fields of interest: Arts; Education; Environment; Animal welfare; Animals/wildlife, preservation/protection; Health care; Human services; International development; Public affairs; Religion.
Type of support: Cause-related marketing.

1106
DHL Holdings (USA), Inc.

(formerly DHL Worldwide Express Inc.)
1210 S. Pine Island Rd., Ste. 600
Plantation, FL 33324 (954) 888-7000

Company URL: http://www.dhl-usa.com
Establishment information: Established in 1969.
Company type: Subsidiary of a foreign company
Business activities: Provides air courier services.
Business type (SIC): Transportation/scheduled air
Financial profile for 2010: Number of employees, 350; sales volume, $2,790,000,000
Corporate officers: Ian D. Clough, C.E.O.; Hank Gibson, C.I.O; Keith E. Lovetro, Exec. V.P., Sales
Giving statement: Giving through the DHL Holdings (USA), Inc. Corporate Giving Program.

DHL Holdings (USA), Inc. Corporate Giving Program

c/o Corp. Citizenship Dept.
1200 S. Pine Island Rd., Ste 600
Plantation, FL 33324-4465

Purpose and activities: DHL makes charitable contributions to nonprofit organizations involved with baseball and the fashion industry.
Fields of interest: Athletics/sports, baseball; Business/industry.
Programs:
Delivery Man of the Month: DHL, in collaboration with Major League Baseball, honors the most outstanding relief pitcher each month of the regular season. The honor includes a congratulatory advertisement in USA Today, an on-field ceremony at each winner's ball park, and a $1,500 grant to the winner's local baseball charity.
Delivery Man of the Year: DHL, in collaboration with Major League Baseball, honors the most outstanding relief pitcher of the season. The honor includes a $10,000 grant made in the winners name to the Baseball Tomorrow Fund (BTF), a joint initiative of Major League Baseball and the Major League Baseball Players Association.
Type of support: Employee volunteer services; In-kind gifts; Sponsorships.
Geographic limitations: Giving on a national basis.
Publications: Application guidelines.
Application information: Applications accepted. The Corporate Citizenship Department handles giving. Application form required. Applicants should submit the following:
1) population served
2) name, address and phone number of organization
3) detailed description of project and amount of funding requested
Initial approach: Complete online questionnaire
Deadline(s): None
Final notification: 30 days

1107
Diageo North America, Inc.

(formerly Guinness UDV North America, Inc.)
801 Main Ave.
Norwalk, CT 06851-1127 (203) 229-2100

Company URL: http://www.diageo.com
Establishment information: Established in 1997.
Company type: Subsidiary of a foreign company
Business activities: Sells spirits, wine, and brandy.
Business type (SIC): Beverages; beer, wine, and distilled beverages—wholesale
Financial profile for 2009: Number of employees, 8,040; sales volume, $6,371,870,000
Corporate officers: Franz Humer, Chair.; Ivan M. Menezes, Pres. and C.E.O.; Chris Jessup, C.F.O.; Barbara D. Carlini, C.I.O.
Board of director: Franz Humer, Chair.
Subsidiaries: Beaulieu Vineyard, Rutherford, CA; Palace Brands, Farmington, CT
Giving statement: Giving through the Diageo North America, Inc. and the Diageo North America Foundation, Inc.

Diageo North America Foundation, Inc.

(formerly UDV North America Foundation, Inc.)
801 Main Ave., 4th Fl.
Norwalk, CT 06851-1127

Establishment information: Incorporated in 1960 in DE.
Donors: Heublein, Inc.; United Distillers & Vintners North America, Inc.; Guinness UDV North America, Inc.; Diageo North America, Inc.
Financial data (yr. ended 12/31/11): Assets, $299,120 (M); gifts received, $427,717; expenditures, $414,340; qualifying distributions, $408,883; giving activities include $408,883 for grants.
Purpose and activities: The foundation supports organizations involved with education, health, cancer, human services, religion, and economically disadvantaged people.
Fields of interest: Secondary school/education; Higher education; Business school/education; Education; Health care, patient services; Health care; Cancer; Cancer, leukemia; Children/youth, services; Aging, centers/services; Human services; United Ways and Federated Giving Programs; Christian agencies & churches; Religion Economically disadvantaged.
Programs:
Diageo Foundation Scholarship Program: The foundation awards college scholarships to the children of employees of Diageo North America, Inc. The program is administered by the College Scholarship Service of Princeton, New Jersey.
Employee Matching Gifts: The foundation matches contributions made by employees of Diageo North America, Inc. to nonprofit organizations on a one-for-one basis from $25 to $5,000 per employee, per year.
Type of support: Employee matching gifts; Employee-related scholarships; General/operating support.
Geographic limitations: Giving limited to areas of company operations.
Support limitations: No grants to individuals (except for employee-related scholarships), or for endowments.
Application information: Applications not accepted. Contributes only through employee-related scholarships and to pre-selected organizations.
Board meeting date(s): As required
Officers: Ivan M. Menezes*, Chair.; Guy Smith, Pres.; Gabriel Bisio, Secy.
EIN: 066051280
Selected grants: The following grants are a representative sample of this grantmaker's funding activity:
$2,925 to Leukemia & Lymphoma Society, White Plains, NY, 2010.
$1,050 to Brown University, Providence, RI, 2010.

1108
Diagnos-Techs Inc.c

6620 S. 192nd Pl., Ste. J106
Kent, WA 98032-1157 (425) 251-0596
FAX: (425) 251-0637

Company URL: http://www.diagnostechs.com
Establishment information: Established in 1989.
Company type: Private company
Business activities: Operates medical laboratory.
Business type (SIC): Laboratories/medical and dental
Corporate officer: Elias Ilyia, Pres.
Giving statement: Giving through the Spektamur Agendo Foundation.

Spektamur Agendo Foundation

6620 S. 192nd St., Ste. J105
Kent, WA 98032-1157

Establishment information: Established in 2003 in WA.
Donor: Diagnos-Techs., Inc.
Financial data (yr. ended 12/31/10): Assets, $689,924 (M); gifts received, $500,000; expenditures, $525,406; qualifying distributions, $525,000; giving activities include $465,000 for 8 grants (high: $150,000; low: $10,000) and $60,000 for 1 grant to an individual.
Purpose and activities: The foundation supports organizations involved with education, health, children, and residential care.
Fields of interest: Secondary school/education; Higher education; Education; Health care, association; Health care, clinics/centers; Health care; Children, services; Family services, single parents; Residential/custodial care.
Type of support: General/operating support; Grants to individuals; Program development; Research; Scholarship funds.
Geographic limitations: Giving primarily in CA, Washington, DC, MD, PA, and Seattle, WA.
Application information: Applications not accepted. Contributes only to pre-selected organizations and individuals.
Directors: Shalal Alnoor; Joseph Forde; Elias Ilya.
EIN: 200521846
Selected grants: The following grants are a representative sample of this grantmaker's funding activity:

$150,000 to Bishop Blanchet High School, Seattle, WA, 2010.
$150,000 to Fulcrum Foundation, Seattle, WA, 2010.
$25,000 to Providence General Foundation, Everett, WA, 2010.
$10,000 to Sound Choice Pharmaceutical Institute, Seattle, WA, 2010.

1109
Diamonds International

38 W 48th St., 3rd Fl.
New York, NY 10036-1805 (212) 764-6900

Company URL: http://www.diamonds-international.com
Establishment information: Established in 1986.
Company type: Private company
Business activities: Operates fine jewelry retail stores.
Business type (SIC): Jewelry/precious metal
Corporate officer: Albert Gad, Pres.
Giving statement: Giving through the Diamonds International Corporate Giving Program.

Diamonds International Corporate Giving Program

38 W 48th St.
New York, NY 10036-1805
URL: http://www.diamondsinternational.org/

Purpose and activities: Diamonds International makes charitable contributions to nonprofit organizations on a case by case basis. Support is given primarily in areas of company operations in Antigua, the Bahamas, Barbados, the Cayman Islands, Cancun and Cozumel, Mexico, and St. Lucia.
Fields of interest: Health care; Health organizations, research; Youth development; Children/youth, services; Human services.
International interests: Antigua & Barbuda; Bahamas; Barbados; Cayman Islands; Mexico; Saint Lucia.
Type of support: Cause-related marketing; Continuing support; Employee volunteer services; General/operating support; In-kind gifts; Sponsorships.
Geographic limitations: Giving primarily in areas of company operations in Antigua, the Bahamas, Barbados, the Cayman Islands, Cancun and Cozumel, Mexico, and St. Lucia; giving also to national and international organizations.

1110
Dick's Sporting Goods, Inc.

345 Court St.
Coraopolis, PA 15108 (724) 273-3400
FAX: (302) 636-5454

Company URL: http://www.dickssportinggoods.com
Establishment information: Established in 1948.
Company type: Public company
Company ticker symbol and exchange: DKS/NYSE
Business activities: Operates sporting goods stores.
Business type (SIC): Shopping goods stores/miscellaneous
Financial profile for 2013: Number of employees, 29,800; assets, $2,887,810,000; sales volume, $5,836,120,000; pre-tax net income, $489,820,000; expenses, $5,344,810,000; liabilities, $1,300,480,000
Fortune 1000 ranking: 2012—437th in revenues, 482nd in profits, and 761st in assets
Forbes 2000 ranking: 2012—1304th in sales, 1433rd in profits, and 1942nd in assets
Corporate officers: Edward W. Stack, Chair. and C.E.O.; William J. Colombo, Vice-Chair.; Joseph H. Schmidt, Pres. and C.O.O.; Timothy E. Kullman, Exec. V.P., Finance, Admin., and C.F.O.; Joe Oliver, Sr. V.P. and C.A.O.; Matthew J. Lynch, Sr. V.P. and C.I.O.; Don Germano, Sr. V.P., Opers.; Kathy Sutter, Sr. V.P., Human Resources; David I. Mosse, Genl. Counsel
Board of directors: Edward W. Stack, Chair.; William J. Colombo, Vice-Chair.; Vincent C. Byrd; Emanuel Chirico; Jacqualyn A. Fouse; Walter Rossi; Lawrence J. Schorr; Larry D. Stone; Allen Weiss
Giving statement: Giving through the Dick's Sporting Goods, Inc. Corporate Giving Program, the Dick's Sporting Goods Foundation, and the Dick Stack Memorial Scholarship Fund.
Company EIN: 161241537

Dick's Sporting Goods, Inc. Corporate Giving Program

300 Industry Dr., RIDC Park W.
Pittsburgh, PA 15275
URL: http://dickssportinggoods.sponsorport.com/Home.aspx

Purpose and activities: As a complement to its foundation, Dick's Sporting Goods also makes charitable contributions to nonprofit organizations directly. Support is limited to areas of company operations.
Fields of interest: Athletics/sports, amateur leagues; Youth development.
Type of support: Donated products; Sponsorships.
Geographic limitations: Giving limited to areas of company operations.
Support limitations: No support for religious organizations. No grants to individuals, or for scholarships, or political causes, campaigns, or candidates.
Publications: Application guidelines.
Application information: Applications accepted.
Initial approach: Complete online application
Deadline(s): 3 months prior to need
Final notification: 15 to 30 days

Dick's Sporting Goods Foundation

345 Court St.
Coraopolis, PA 15108-3817

Establishment information: Established in PA.
Donor: Dick's Sporting Goods, Inc.
Financial data (yr. ended 01/31/12): Assets, $3,210,753 (M); gifts received, $1,000,000; expenditures, $789,247; qualifying distributions, $789,247; giving activities include $702,450 for 575 grants (high: $250,000; low: $100).
Purpose and activities: Giving primarily for professional, as well as youth and school-related sports teams and associations.
Fields of interest: Recreation, association; Athletics/sports, amateur leagues; Athletics/sports, professional leagues; Recreation; Human services Youth.
Program:
Protecting Athletes through Concussion Education (PACE): With its partners, the foundation supports what is currently the nation's largest baseline concussion screening initiative.
Geographic limitations: Giving on a national basis.
Application information:
Initial approach: Letter
Deadline(s): None
Officers: Tim Kullman, Pres.; David Mosse, Secy.; Todd Hipwell, Treas.; Elizabeth Baran, Co-Exec. Dir.; Scott Rolf, Co-Exec. Dir.
EIN: 274516157

Dick Stack Memorial Scholarship Fund

209 Southwood Dr.
Vestal, NY 13850

Establishment information: Established in 2000 in NY.
Donors: Dick's Sporting Goods, Inc.; Kim Myers; Nancy Heichemer.
Financial data (yr. ended 09/30/12): Assets, $101,838 (M); gifts received, $10,000; expenditures, $931; qualifying distributions, $0.
Purpose and activities: The foundation awards college scholarships to individuals.
Type of support: Scholarships—to individuals.
Application information: Applications not accepted. Unsolicited requests for funds not accepted.
Officers: Kim Myers, Pres.; Nancy Heichemer, V.P.
EIN: 161555913

1111
Dickstein Shapiro LLP

1825 Eye St., N.W.
Washington, DC 20006-5403
(202) 420-2200

Company URL: http://www.dicksteinshapiro.com
Establishment information: Established in 1953.
Company type: Private company
Business activities: Operates law firm.
Business type (SIC): Legal services
Corporate officers: Michael E. Nannes, Chair.; Richard J. Leveridge, Managing Partner
Offices: Irvine, Los Angeles, Redwood City, CA; Stamford, CT; Washington, DC; New York, NY
Giving statement: Giving through the Dickstein Shapiro LLP Pro Bono Program.

Dickstein Shapiro LLP Pro Bono Program

1825 Eye St., N.W.
Washington, DC 20006-5403 (202) 420-4851
E-mail: arabatzise@dicksteinshapiro.com; Additional tel.: (202) 420-2200; URL: http://www.dicksteinshapiro.com/firmoverview/probono/

Contact: Elaine Arabatzis, Diversity/Pro Bono Counsel
Fields of interest: Legal services.
Type of support: Pro bono services - legal.
Geographic limitations: Giving primarily in areas of company operations in Irvine, Los Angeles, and Palo Alto, CA, Stamford, CT, Washington, DC, and New York, NY.
Application information: The Pro Bono Committee manages the pro-bono program.

1112
Diebold, Inc.

5995 Mayfair Rd.
P.O. Box 3077
North Canton, OH 44720-8077
(330) 490-4000
FAX: (330) 490-3794

Company URL: http://www.diebold.com
Establishment information: Established in 1859.
Company type: Public company
Company ticker symbol and exchange: DBD/NYSE
Business activities: Manufactures, sells, installs, and services automated self-service transaction systems, electronic and physical security products, and election systems; develops computer software.
Business type (SIC): Computer and office equipment; metal products/fabricated; computer services
Financial profile for 2011: Number of employees, 16,751; assets, $2,592,990,000; sales volume, $2,991,690,000; pre-tax net income, $117,430,000; expenses, $2,866,980,000; liabilities, $1,783,020,000
Fortune 1000 ranking: 2012—716th in revenues, 776th in profits, and 794th in assets
Corporate officers: Henry D. G. Wallace, Chair.; Bradley C. Richardson, Exec. V.P. and C.F.O.; Frank A. Natoli, Jr., Exec. V.P. and C.I.O.; George S. Mayes, Jr., Exec. V.P. and C.O.O; David Ramsey, V.P. and C.I.O.; M. Scott Hunter, V.P. and Treas.; Christopher Macey, V.P. and Corp. Cont.; Chad F. Hesse, V.P., Genl. Counsel, and Secy.
Board of directors: Henry D. G. Wallace, Chair.; Bruce L. Byrnes; Phillip R. Cox; Richard L. Crandall; Gale S. Fitzgerald; Rajesh K. Soin; Thomas W. Swidarski; Henry D.G. Wallace; Alan J. Weber
Subsidiaries: ATM Finance, Inc., Canton, OH; DBD Investment Management Co., Canton, OH; Diebold Credit Corp., Canton, OH; Diebold Finance Co., Inc., Canton, OH; Diebold Foreign Sales Corp., Canton, OH; Diebold International Ltd., Canton, OH; Diebold Investment Co., Canton, OH; Diebold Latin America Holding Co., Inc., Canton, OH; Diebold Mexico Holding Co., Inc., Canton, OH; Diebold of Nevada, Inc., Sparks, NV; Diebold Pacific, Ltd., Canton, OH; VDM Holding Co., Canton, OH
Joint Venture: InterBold, Canton, OH
International operations: Argentina; Australia; Austria; Barbados; Belgium; Bolivia; Brazil; Canada; Chile; China; Colombia; Costa Rica; Czech Republic; Dominican Republic; Ecuador; El Salvador; France; Guatemala; Honduras; Hong Kong; Hungary; India; Indonesia; Ireland; Italy; Kazakhstan; Luxembourg; Malaysia; Mexico; Netherlands; Nicaragua; Panama; Paraguay; Peru; Philippines; Poland; Portugal; Russia; Singapore; Slovakia; South Africa; Spain; Switzerland; Thailand; Turkey; United Kingdom; Uruguay; Venezuela
Giving statement: Giving through the Diebold, Incorporated Corporate Giving Program, the Diebold Employees Charitable Fund, and the Diebold Foundation.
Company EIN: 340183970

Diebold, Incorporated Corporate Giving Program

5995 Mayfair Rd.
P.O. Box 8230
Canton, OH 44720-8230 (330) 490-5050
FAX: (216) 490-4549

Purpose and activities: As a complement to its foundation, Diebold also makes charitable contributions to nonprofit organizations directly. Support is given primarily in areas of company operations.
Fields of interest: Elementary/secondary education; General charitable giving.
Type of support: Capital campaigns; Continuing support; Donated equipment; Employee volunteer services; Equipment; General/operating support.
Geographic limitations: Giving primarily in areas of company operations, with emphasis on Canton, OH.
Application information: Applications accepted. Application form not required. Applicants should submit the following:
1) detailed description of project and amount of funding requested
Initial approach: Proposal to headquarters
Deadline(s): None

Diebold Employees Charitable Fund

c/o KeyBank N.A.
4900 Tiedeman Rd. OH-01-49-0150
Brooklyn, OH 44144-2338 (216) 689-7663
Application address: 127 Public Sq., 16th Fl., Cleveland, OH 44114, tel.: (216) 689-7663

Establishment information: Established around 1977.
Donors: Diebold, Inc.; Employees of Diebold Corp.
Contact: Kathy Mabin
Financial data (yr. ended 10/31/12): Assets, $463,317 (M); gifts received, $23,614; expenditures, $18,848; qualifying distributions, $11,648; giving activities include $10,000 for 1 grant.
Purpose and activities: The foundation supports hospitals and organizations involved with arts and culture, education, Alzheimer's disease, employment, hunger, and human services.
Fields of interest: Arts; Human services.
Type of support: General/operating support.
Geographic limitations: Giving primarily in OH.
Support limitations: No grants to individuals.
Application information: Applications accepted. Application form required. Applicants should submit the following:
1) detailed description of project and amount of funding requested
Initial approach: Letter
Deadline(s): None
Trustee: KeyBank, N.A.
EIN: 346734175

Diebold Foundation

c/o Tax Dept.
P.O. Box 3077
North Canton, OH 44720-8077
Application address: c/o Michael E. Ziarko, 5995 Mayfair Rd., North Canton, OH 44720, tel.: (330) 490-6134

Establishment information: Established in 1993 in OH.
Donor: Diebold, Inc.
Contact: Micheal E. Ziarko
Financial data (yr. ended 12/31/11): Assets, $6,749,303 (M); expenditures, $583,814; qualifying distributions, $531,100; giving activities include $531,100 for grants.
Purpose and activities: The foundation supports food banks and organizations involved with arts and culture, education, human services, and community development.
Fields of interest: Arts; Higher education; Education; Food banks; Youth development, business; Children/youth, services; Human services; Business/industry; Community development, business promotion; Community/economic development; United Ways and Federated Giving Programs.
Type of support: Annual campaigns; Capital campaigns; Emergency funds; Equipment; General/operating support; Program development; Sponsorships.
Geographic limitations: Giving primarily in OH.
Support limitations: No support for religious, political, or fraternal organizations, athletic teams, or discriminatory organizations. No grants to individuals, or for sponsorships of conventions or conferences, or athletic fundraising events not associated with schools.
Publications: Application guidelines.
Application information: Applications accepted. Proposals should be submitted using organization letterhead. Organizations receiving support are asked to submit a follow-up evaluation report. Application form not required. Applicants should submit the following:
1) copy of IRS Determination Letter
Initial approach: Proposal
Deadline(s): 2 months prior to need
Officers and Trustee: Kevin J. Krakora, Pres.; Sheila Rutt, V.P. and Treas.; Ted Watko, Secy.; Timothy J. McDannold.
EIN: 341757351
Selected grants: The following grants are a representative sample of this grantmaker's funding activity:
$245,000 to United Way of Greater Stark County, Canton, OH, 2011. For general operations.
$38,650 to Scholarship America, Saint Peter, MN, 2011. For general operations.
$25,000 to Goodwill Industries of Greater Cleveland and East Central Ohio, Canton, OH, 2011. For general operations.
$25,000 to Stark State College Foundation, Canton, OH, 2011. For general operations.
$18,334 to Stark Development Board, Canton, OH, 2011. For general operations.
$10,375 to American Heart Association, Canton, OH, 2011. For general operations.
$8,000 to Urban League, Greater Stark County, Canton, OH, 2011. For general operations.
$7,500 to Arts in Stark, Canton, OH, 2011. For general operations.
$5,000 to Akron-Canton Regional Foodbank, Akron, OH, 2011. For general operations.
$1,140 to Miami University, Oxford, OH, 2011. For general operations.

1113
Diemolding Corp.

125 Rasbach St.
Canastota, NY 13032-1430
(315) 697-2221
FAX: (315) 697-8083

Company URL: http://www.diemolding.com/
Establishment information: Established in 1920.
Company type: Subsidiary of a foreign company
Business activities: Manufactures plastics products.
Business type (SIC): Plastic products/miscellaneous
Corporate officers: Donald H. Dew, C.E.O.; Dennis O'Brien, Pres.; Bernadette Buell, Exec. V.P., Corp. Comms.; Michael Pendleton, Sr. V.P., Sales; Dennis P. Costanzo, Cont.
Giving statement: Giving through the Donald Hicks Dew Foundation.

Donald Hicks Dew Foundation
544 Florence Ave.
Oneida, NY 13421-2229

Donors: Diemolding Corp.; Lois Brooks; Donald F. Dew, Sr.; Donald H. Dew; Thomas H. Dew.
Financial data (yr. ended 12/31/11): Assets, $35,556 (M); gifts received, $30,000; expenditures, $46,112; qualifying distributions, $45,077; giving activities include $45,077 for grants.
Purpose and activities: The foundation supports art councils and fire departments and organizations involved with health, heart disease, and human services.
Fields of interest: Health care; Safety/disasters; Human services.
Type of support: General/operating support.
Geographic limitations: Giving primarily in the Canastota and Oneida, NY, area.
Application information: Applications not accepted. Unsolicited requests for funds not accepted.
Trustees: Bruce J. Dew, Jr.; Donald F. Dew; Donald H. Dew.
EIN: 166062084

1114
Dietz & Watson, Inc.
5701 Tacony St.
Philadelphia, PA 19135-4394
(215) 831-9000

Company URL: http://www.dietzandwatson.com
Establishment information: Established in 1939.
Company type: Private company
Business activities: Produces deli meats.
Business type (SIC): Meat packing plants and prepared meats and poultry
Corporate officers: Ruth Dietz Eni, Chair.; Louis Eni, Pres. and C.E.O.; Christopher W. Eni, C.O.O.; Cindy Eni Yingling, C.F.O.; Christopher Yingling, Treas.
Board of director: Ruth Deitz Eni, Chair.
Giving statement: Giving through the Dietz & Watson Foundation.

Dietz & Watson Foundation
c/o Glenmede Trust Co.
1650 Market St., Ste. 1200
Philadelphia, PA 19103-7391

Establishment information: Established in 2001 in PA.
Donor: Dietz & Watson, Inc.
Contact: Cynthia Eni Yingling, Pres.
Financial data (yr. ended 12/31/11): Assets, $7,779,722 (M); gifts received, $100,000; expenditures, $386,882; qualifying distributions, $347,389; giving activities include $347,389 for grants.
Purpose and activities: The foundation supports organizations involved with education, health, cancer, Tourette's syndrome, digestive diseases, sports, and human services.
Fields of interest: Higher education; Medical school/education; Education; Hospitals (general); Health care; Cancer; Breast cancer; Nerve, muscle & bone diseases; Digestive diseases; Athletics/sports, amateur leagues; Athletics/sports, golf; Children/youth, services; Human services.
Type of support: General/operating support; Scholarship funds.
Geographic limitations: Giving primarily in MD, NJ, NY, and Philadelphia, PA.
Support limitations: No grants to individuals.
Application information: Applications not accepted. Contributes only to pre-selected organizations.
Officers and Trustees:* Cynthia Eni Yingling*, Pres.; Ruth Eni*, Secy.-Treas.; Christopher W. Eni; Louis J. Eni, Jr.
EIN: 233028685
Selected grants: The following grants are a representative sample of this grantmaker's funding activity:
$31,000 to Crohns and Colitis Foundation of America, New York, NY, 2010. For general purposes.
$25,000 to Drexel University, College of Medicine, Philadelphia, PA, 2010. For general purposes.
$10,000 to Moorestown Friends School, Moorestown, NJ, 2010. For general purposes.
$10,000 to University of Pennsylvania, Philadelphia, PA, 2010. For general purposes.
$5,000 to Heart of Camden, Camden, NJ, 2010. For general purposes.
$5,000 to Shore Memorial Health Foundation, Somers Point, NJ, 2010. For general purposes.
$3,900 to New England Food Foundation, Boston, MA, 2010. For general purposes.
$2,500 to Deborah Hospital Foundation, Browns Mills, NJ, 2010. For general purposes.
$2,500 to SCARC Foundation, Augusta, NJ, 2010. For general purposes.
$2,200 to Center for Family Services, Camden, NJ, 2010. For general purposes.

1115
Digi-Block, Inc.
12 Elliot St.
P.O. Box 380247
Cambridge, MA 02138-5706
(617) 661-0100

Company URL: http://www.digi-block.com
Establishment information: Established in 1997.
Company type: Private company
Business activities: Manufactures mathematics learning system.
Business type (SIC): Games, toys, and sporting and athletic goods
Corporate officers: Elon Kohlberg, Ph.D., Chair.; Steve D. Smith, C.E.O.; Janie Rosenthal, V.P., Sales
Board of director: Elon Kohlberg, Ph.D., Chair.
Giving statement: Giving through the Digi-Block Grant Program.

Digi-Block Grant Program
c/o Grant Dept.
P.O. Box 380247
Cambridge, MA 02238-0247 (617) 661-0100
FAX: (617) 661-3310;
E-mail: grants@digi-block.com; URL: http://digiblock.com/teachers/grants/

Purpose and activities: Digi-Block makes charitable contributions to nonprofit organizations involved with education.
Fields of interest: Elementary school/education; Mathematics.
Program:
Digi-Block Annual Grant Program: Digi-Block awards grants of up to $5,000 to teachers and teacher groups for materials and training for school and classroom use, curriculum development and implementation projects, staff development and training, after-school programs or co-curricular activities, and innovative assessment techniques using the Digi-Block Program.
Type of support: Curriculum development; Donated products; Program development.
Application information: Applications accepted.
Initial approach: Visit website for application information

1116
Dilbeck, Inc.
(also known as Dilbeck GMAC Real Estate)
1030 Foothill Blvd.
La Canada, CA 91011-3241
(818) 790-6774

Company URL: http://www.dilbeck.com
Establishment information: Established in 1950.
Company type: Private company
Business activities: Operates real estate agency.
Business type (SIC): Real estate agents and managers
Corporate officers: Mark Dilbeck, Pres.; Lynn Kornmann, C.F.O.; Richard Seccombe, C.I.O.; Mona Leigh Rose, V.P. and Genl. Counsel
Offices: Arcadia, Burbank, Eagle Rock, Glendale, La Canada Flintridge, La Crescenta, Pasadena, San Marino, South Pasadena, Valencia, Westlake Village, Woodland Hills, CA
Giving statement: Giving through the Dilbeck Realtors & Associates Charitable Foundation.

Dilbeck Realtors & Associates Charitable Foundation
1030 Foothill Blvd.
La Canada, CA 91011-3241
URL: http://www.dilbeck.com/v2pages/foundation/index.cfm

Donors: Dilbeck, Inc.; Community Service Foundation.
Financial data (yr. ended 12/31/12): Assets, $26,159 (M); gifts received, $1,487; expenditures, $11,044; qualifying distributions, $10,777; giving activities include $10,250 for 10 grants (high: $1,000; low: $500).
Purpose and activities: The foundation supports organizations involved with arts and culture, education, health, human services, and civic affairs.
Fields of interest: Arts; Education; Health care; Boys & girls clubs; American Red Cross; YM/YWCAs & YM/YWHAs; Children/youth, services; Developmentally disabled, centers & services; Human services; Public affairs.
Type of support: Annual campaigns; General/operating support; Program development.
Geographic limitations: Giving limited to CA.
Support limitations: No grants to individuals.
Application information: Applications not accepted. Unsolicited requests for funds not accepted.
Officers: Mark Dilbeck, C.E.O.; Lynn Kornmann, C.F.O.; Dennis Falsetti, Secy.
EIN: 954691602

1117
Diller Telephone Company
318 Commercial St.
P.O. Box 218
Diller, NE 68342-4094 (402) 793-5330
FAX: (402) 793-5139

Company URL: http://www.diodecom.net
Establishment information: Established in 1899.
Company type: Private company

Business activities: Provides local telephone communications services; provides Internet access services.
Business type (SIC): Telephone communications
Corporate officers: Randy Sandman, Co-Pres. and C.E.O.; William P. Sandman, Co-Pres.; Gladys Sandman, Secy.
Giving statement: Giving through the Sandman Family Foundation.

Sandman Family Foundation

318 Commercial St.
Diller, NE 68342-4094

Establishment information: Established in 2004 in NE.
Donor: Diller Telephone Co.
Financial data (yr. ended 12/31/11): Assets, $777,575 (M); expenditures, $57,283; qualifying distributions, $39,775; giving activities include $39,775 for grants.
Support limitations: No grants to individuals.
Application information: Applications not accepted. Unsolicited requests for funds not accepted.
Officers: Steve Sandman, Pres.; Randy Sandman, Secy.; Bill Sandman, Treas.
EIN: 201612327

1118
Dime Savings Bank of Norwich

290 Salem Tpke.
Norwich, CT 06360-6494 (860) 859-4300

Company URL: http://www.dimesavingsbank.com
Establishment information: Established in 1869.
Company type: Subsidiary of a private company
Business activities: Operates savings bank.
Financial profile for 2011: Assets, $707,183,135; pre-tax net income, $5,843,106; liabilities, $70,183,135
Corporate officers: Nicholas Caplanson, Pres. and C.E.O.; David J. Stanland, Sr. V.P., C.F.O., and Treas.; Cheryl A. Calderado, Sr. V.P., Admin; Deborah L. Malone, V.P and Cont.; Shawn J. Pishka, V.P., Opers.
Board of directors: Nicholas Caplanson; Lee-Ann Gomes; Ronald J. Harris; James M. Kirker; Linda L. Mariani; Vincent J. Naccarota; Robert A. Staley; Mark E. Tramontozzi, M.D.
Giving statement: Giving through the Dime Bank Foundation, Inc.

Dime Bank Foundation, Inc.

(formerly The Dime Savings Bank Foundation, Inc.)
290 Salem Tpke.
Norwich, CT 06360-6456 (860) 859-4300
E-mail: ccalderado@dime-bank.com; URL: https://dime-bank.com/dime-foundation.php

Establishment information: Established in 1998 in CT.
Donors: Dime Savings Bank of Norwich; Dime Bank.
Contact: Cheryl A. Calderado, Secy.
Financial data (yr. ended 12/31/11): Assets, $2,961,763 (M); expenditures, $169,493; qualifying distributions, $159,501; giving activities include $159,501 for 45 grants (high: $5,000; low: $2,000).
Purpose and activities: The foundation supports organizations involved with arts and culture, education, health, substance abuse services, employment, hunger, affordable housing, and human services.
Fields of interest: Performing arts; Arts; Libraries (public); Education, reading; Education; Hospitals (general); Health care; Substance abuse, services; Employment, training; Employment; Food services; Housing/shelter; YM/YWCAs & YM/YWHAs; Children/youth, services; Family services; Aging, centers/services; Homeless, human services; Human services; United Ways and Federated Giving Programs Economically disadvantaged.
Type of support: Building/renovation; Capital campaigns; Equipment; General/operating support; Matching/challenge support; Program development; Scholarship funds.
Geographic limitations: Giving primarily in areas of company operations in Baltic, Bozrah, East Lyme, Franklin, Gales Ferry, Griswold, Groton, Jewett City, Ledyard, Lisbon, Mystic, Montville, New London, Niantic, North Stonington, Norwich, Oakdale, Pawcatuck, Preston, Sprague, Stonington, Taftville, Uncasville, Voluntown, Waterford, West Mystic, and Yantic, CT, and Hopkinton, Richmond, and Westerly, RI.
Support limitations: No grants to individuals.
Publications: Application guidelines; Grants list.
Application information: Applications accepted. Organizations receiving support are asked to submit a final report. Application form required. Applicants should submit the following:
1) timetable for implementation and evaluation of project
2) results expected from proposed grant
3) population served
4) copy of IRS Determination Letter
5) brief history of organization and description of its mission
6) copy of most recent annual report/audited financial statement/990
7) descriptive literature about organization
8) listing of board of directors, trustees, officers and other key people and their affiliations
9) detailed description of project and amount of funding requested
10) copy of current year's organizational budget and/or project budget

Applications should include 2 copies of the most recent financial statement and program brochure.
Initial approach: Letter
Board meeting date(s): Quarterly
Deadline(s): None
Officers: Nicholas Caplanson, Pres.; Charles O. Treat, V.P.; Cheryl Calderado, Secy.; David Standland, Treas.
Directors: Michael G. Betten, M.D.; Roladn J. Harris; James M. Kirker; Linda L. Mariani; Vincent J. Naccarato; Robert A. Stanley; Mark Tramontozzi.
EIN: 061507800
Selected grants: The following grants are a representative sample of this grantmaker's funding activity:
$5,000 to Catholic Charities, Norwich, CT, 2009.
$5,000 to Habitat for Humanity of Southeastern Connecticut, New London, CT, 2009.
$5,000 to Hartford Hospital, Hartford, CT, 2009.
$5,000 to Westerly Area Rest Meals, Westerly, RI, 2009.
$5,000 to Womens Center of Southeastern Connecticut, New London, CT, 2009.
$5,000 to YMCA, Ocean Community, Westerly, RI, 2009.
$4,500 to Sea Research Foundation, Mystic, CT, 2009.
$4,000 to Bethsaida Community, Norwich, CT, 2009.
$3,520 to Martin House, Norwich, CT, 2009.
$3,000 to Madonna Place, Norwich, CT, 2009.

1119
Dimeo Construction Company

75 Chapman St.
Providence, RI 02905-5405 (401) 781-9800
FAX: 401-461-4580

Company URL: http://www.dimeo.com
Establishment information: Established in 1930.
Company type: Private company
Business activities: Provides construction management services.
Business type (SIC): Management and public relations services
Corporate officers: Bradford S. Dimeo, Pres. and C.E.O.; Stephen F. Rutledge, Exec. V.P. and C.O.O.; Steven B. Avery, C.P.A., C.F.O.; Paul G. Aballo, V.P., Opers.
Division: Dimeo Properties, Warwick, RI
Giving statement: Giving through the Dimeo Construction Company Contributions Program.

Dimeo Construction Company Contributions Program

75 Chapman St.
Providence, RI 02905-5405 (401) 781-9800
FAX: (401) 461-4580; URL: http://www.dimeo.com/community-involvement

Purpose and activities: Dimeo makes charitable contributions to nonprofit organizations. Support is given primarily in Rhode Island.
Fields of interest: Food services.
Type of support: General/operating support.
Geographic limitations: Giving primarily in RI.

1120
DineEquity, Inc.

(doing business as IHOP)
(formerly IHOP Corp.)
450 N. Brand Blvd., 7th Fl.
Glendale, CA 91203-4415 (818) 240-6055
FAX: (302) 636-5454

Company URL: http://dineequity.com/
Establishment information: Established in 1958.
Company type: Public company
Company ticker symbol and exchange: DIN/NYSE
Business activities: Develops, operates, and franchises pancake restaurants.
Business type (SIC): Investors/miscellaneous; restaurants and drinking places
Financial profile for 2012: Number of employees, 2,450; assets, $2,415,400,000; sales volume, $849,930,000; pre-tax net income, $194,920,000; expenses, $655,000,000; liabilities, $2,106,590,000
Corporate officers: Julia A. Stewart, Chair., Pres., and C.E.O.; Tom Emrey, C.F.O.; Bryan R. Adel, Sr. V.P., Genl. Counsel, and Secy.; Greggory Kalvin, C.P.A., Sr. V.P. and Corp. Cont.; Tod MacKenzie, Sr. V.P., Comms., and Public Affairs; John Jakubek, Sr. V.P., Human Resources
Board of directors: Julia A. Stewart, Chair.; Daniel J. Brestle; Howard M. Berk; Richard J. Dahl; Michael S. Gordon; Stephen P. Joyce; Larry Alan Kay; Caroline W. Nahas; Douglas M. Pasquale; Gilbert T. Ray; Patrick W. Rose
Subsidiaries: Applebee's International, Inc., Overland Park, KS; IHOP Realty Corp., Glendale, CA; International House of Pancakes, Inc., Glendale, CA
Giving statement: Giving through the DineEquity, Inc. Corporate Giving Program.
Company EIN: 953038279

DineEquity, Inc. Corporate Giving Program

(formerly IHOP Corp. Contributions Program)
450 N. Brand Blvd., 7th Fl.
Glendale, CA 91203-4415 (866) 995-3463
URL: http://dineequity.com/socialresponsibility.html

Purpose and activities: DineEquity, Inc. makes charitable contributions to nonprofit organizations involved with children and education, and for fundraising events. Support is given primarily in areas of company operations; giving also to national organizations.
Fields of interest: Education; Human services, fund raising/fund distribution; Children, services.
Type of support: Annual campaigns; Employee volunteer services.
Geographic limitations: Giving primarily in areas of company operations; giving also to national organizations.
Application information:
Copies of proposal: 1

1121
Dinsmore & Shohl LLP

255 E. 5th St., Ste. 1900
Cincinnati, OH 45202-4720 (513) 977-8200

Company URL: http://www.dinslaw.com/
Establishment information: Established in 1897.
Company type: Private company
Business activities: Operates law firm.
Business type (SIC): Legal services
Corporate officers: George H. Vincent, Chair.; Suellen Young, C.F.O.; Juanene L. Wong, C.I.O.
Board of director: George H. Vincent, Chair.
Giving statement: Giving through the Dinsmore & Shohl LLP Pro Bono Program.

Dinsmore & Shohl LLP Pro Bono Program

255 E. 5th St., Ste. 1900
Cincinnati, OH 45202-4720
E-mail: alan.abes@dinsmore.com; Additional tel.: (513) 977-8200; URL: http://www.dinslaw.com/

Contact: Alan H. Abes, Partner
Geographic limitations: Giving primarily in areas of company operations in Washington, DC, Frankfort, Lexington, and Louisville, KY, Cincinnati, Columbus, and Dayton, OH, Pittsburgh, PA, Charleston, SC, Lewisburg, Morgantown, and Wheeling, WV.
Application information: A Department Chair coordinates the pro-bono program.
Initial approach: Written application accompanied by confirmation of 501(c)(3) status
Deadline(s): December 31 of each calendar year

1122
Dippin' Dots, Inc.

5101 Charter Oak Dr.
Paducah, KY 42001 (270) 443-8994

Company URL: http://www.dippindots.com
Establishment information: Established in 1988.
Company type: Private company
Business activities: Manufactures ice cream; operates chain of franchised locations selling ice cream, frozen yogurt, and frozen ice.
Business type (SIC): Restaurants and drinking places
Corporate officers: Curt D. Jones, Chair. and C.E.O.; Tom Leonard, Pres.; Michael Barrette, V.P., Sales and Mktg.; Michael Milner, Cont.
Board of director: Curt D. Jones, Chair.
Giving statement: Giving through the Dippin' Dots Foundation, Inc.

Dippin' Dots Foundation, Inc.

5101 Charter Oak Dr.
Paducah, KY 42001-5209 (270) 443-8994

Establishment information: Established in KY.
Donors: Eric Patton; Dippin Dots Franchising, Inc.
Contact: Steve Heisner, Treas.
Financial data (yr. ended 12/31/11): Assets, $38,307 (M); gifts received, $19,056; expenditures, $111,492; qualifying distributions, $111,492; giving activities include $25,998 for 4 grants (high: $21,498; low: $1,000) and $500 for 1 grant to an individual.
Purpose and activities: The foundation supports organizations involved with education and provides for employees of Dippin' Dots Inc. and its affiliates in times of financial hardship.
Fields of interest: Higher education; Education.
Type of support: General/operating support; Grants to individuals; Scholarship funds.
Geographic limitations: Giving primarily in areas of company operations in CA, IL, and KY.
Application information: Applications accepted. Application form required.
Initial approach: Letter
Deadline(s): None
Officers: Kay Jones, Pres.; Marilyn Phillips, V.P.; Tracey Jones, Secy.; Steve Heisner, Treas.; Jeanette Jones; Tracy Jones; Harry Junkerman; Lisa Ulrich.
EIN: 203097061

1123
Direct Dental Administrators, LLC

P.O. Box 2667
San Anselmo, CA 94979-0542
(415) 457-2836
FAX: (415) 454-2928

Company URL: http://www.directdentalplans.com
Establishment information: Established in 1998.
Company type: Private company
Business type (SIC): Business services/miscellaneous
Corporate officers: John Cunningham, President; Ryan Gomes, V.P., Finance
Giving statement: Giving through the Direct Dental Administrators, LLC Contributions Program.

Direct Dental Administrators, LLC Contributions Program

P.O. Box 542
San Anselmo, CA 94979-0542 (415) 457-2836
E-mail: info@directdentalplans.com; URL: http://www.directdentalplans.com

Purpose and activities: Direct Dental Administrators is a certified B Corporation that donates a percentage of profits to charitable organizations.

1124
The DIRECTV Group, Inc.

(formerly Hughes Electronics Corporation)
2230 E. Imperial Hwy.
El Segundo, CA 90245-0956
(310) 964-5000
FAX: (302) 636-5454

Company URL: http://www.directv.com
Establishment information: Established in 1985.
Company type: Private company
Company ticker symbol and exchange: DTV/NASDAQ
Business activities: Provides satellite television services; provides satellite business network services; provides broadband Internet access services.
Business type (SIC): Cable and other pay television services; telephone communications
Financial profile for 2012: Number of employees, 16,200; assets, $20,600,000,000; sales volume, $29,700,000,000; pre-tax net income, $4,442,000,000; expenses, $24,719,000,000; liabilities, $25,986,000,000
Fortune 1000 ranking: 2012—102nd in revenues, 64th in profits, and 235th in assets
Forbes 2000 ranking: 2012—318th in sales, 197th in profits, and 957th in assets
Corporate officers: Michael D. White, Chair., Pres., and C.E.O.; Patrick T. Doyle, Exec. V.P. and C.F.O.; Larry D. Hunter, Exec. V.P. and Genl. Counsel; John F. Murphy, Sr. V.P., Cont., and C.A.O.; Fazal Merchant, Sr. V.P. and Treas.
Board of directors: Michael D. White, Chair.; Neil R. Austrian; Ralph F. Boyd, Jr.; Abelardo E. Bru; David B. Dillon; Samuel A. DiPiazza, Jr.; Dixon Doll; Charles R. Lee; Peter A. Lund; Nancy S. Newcomb; Lorrie Norrington
Divisions: Hughes Aircraft Alabama, Foley, AL; Hughes Aircraft Mississippi, Inc., Forest, MS; Hughes Georgia, Inc., LaGrange, GA; Hughes Optical Products, Inc., Des Plaines, IL; Hughes Research Laboratories, Malibu, CA; Hughes Santa Barbara Research Center, Goleta, CA; Hughes Spectrolab, Inc., Sylmar, CA
International operations: Argentina; Brazil; British Virgin Islands; Cayman Islands; Chile; Colombia; Curacao; Ecuador; India; Mauritius; Mexico; Netherlands; Netherlands Antilles; Paraguay; Peru; Trinidad & Tobago; United Kingdom; Uruguay; Venezuela
Giving statement: Giving through the DIRECTV Group, Inc. Corporate Giving Program and the Gregory B. Jarvis Memorial Scholarship Foundation.
Company EIN: 521106564

The DIRECTV Group, Inc. Corporate Giving Program

c/o Corp. Citizenship
2330 E. Imperial Hwy.
El Segundo, CA 90245-3504 (310) 964-5000
E-mail: CorporateCitizenship@directv.com.; URL: http://www.directv.com/DTVAPP/global/contentPage.jsp?assetId=P4310192
Additional URL: http://www.directv4schools.com/

Purpose and activities: DIRECTV Group makes charitable contributions to nonprofit organizations involved with education, public health, and disaster relief. Support is given primarily in areas of company operations in Alabama, California, Colorado, Georgia, Idaho, Illinois, Montana, New York, and Oklahoma.
Fields of interest: Education; Public health; Disasters, preparedness/services.

Programs:

DIRECTV Goes to School: DIRECTV Group provides a 75-channel School Choice programming package and a four-room DIRECTV system for free to eligible K-12 schools. The program is designed to encourage teachers to use TV as an educational tool.

DIRECTV4Schools: DIRECTV Group awards grants to schools on behalf of each new customer who registers for a year of DIRECTV service and existing customers who extends their DIRECTV service. The company awards a $100 grant for new customers and a $50 grant for existing customers to the school of their choice.

Employee Gift Matching: DIRECTV Group matches contributions made by its employees to nonprofit organizations on a one-for-one basis up to $20,000 per employee, per year.

Type of support: Cause-related marketing; Curriculum development; Donated products; Employee matching gifts; Equipment; General/operating support; In-kind gifts.
Geographic limitations: Giving primarily in areas of company operations in AL, CA, CO, GA, ID, IL, MT, NY, and OK; giving also to national organizations.
Support limitations: No support for non-tax-exempt organizations, for-profit ventures, discriminatory organizations, or sports teams. No grants for discounted or temporary DIRECTV programming, hardware, installation, or televisions (except for DIRECTV Goes to School), sponsorships, conferences, seminars, contests, fundraising activities, or sports events.
Application information: Applications not accepted. Unsolicited requests for funding are not accepted. The Corporate Citizenship Department handles giving.

Gregory B. Jarvis Memorial Scholarship Foundation

2250 E. Imperial Hwy.
El Segundo, CA 90245-0956

Donors: Hughes Electronics Corp.; The DIRECTV Group, Inc.
Financial data (yr. ended 12/31/11): Assets, $111,415 (M); expenditures, $6,000; qualifying distributions, $6,000; giving activities include $6,000 for grants to individuals.
Purpose and activities: The foundation awards $6,000 college scholarships to high school seniors who are dependents of employees of DIRECTV or its subsidiaries and affiliates and planning to pursue a technical degree in engineering, computer science, mathematics, physics, or chemistry.
Type of support: Employee-related scholarships.
Geographic limitations: Giving primarily in areas of company operations.
Application information: Applications not accepted. Unsolicited requests for funds not accepted.
Trustees: Patrick Doyle; Joseph A. Bosch; J. William Little.
EIN: 954089695

1125
Discover Financial Services

2500 Lake Cook Rd.
Riverwoods, IL 60015 (224) 405-0900
FAX: (302) 655-5049

Company URL: http://www.discoverfinancial.com
Establishment information: Established in 1986.
Company type: Public company
Company ticker symbol and exchange: DFS/NYSE
Business activities: Operates credit card issuer and electronic payment services company.
Business type (SIC): Credit institutions/personal
Financial profile for 2012: Number of employees, 13,009; assets, $73,491,000,000; pre-tax net income, $274,000,000; liabilities, $63,618,000,000
Fortune 1000 ranking: 2012—294th in revenues, 87th in profits, and 79th in assets
Forbes 2000 ranking: 2012—1000th in sales, 246th in profits, and 328th in assets
Corporate officers: David W. Nelms, Chair. and C.E.O.; Roger C. Hochschild, Pres. and C.O.O.; Mark R. Graf, Exec. V.P. and C.F.O.; Kathryn McNamara Corley, Exec. V.P., Genl. Counsel, and Secy.; Glenn Schneider, Sr. V.P. and C.I.O
Board of directors: David W. Nelms, Chair.; Jeffrey S. Aronin; Mary K. Bush; Gregory C. Case; Cynthia A. Glassman, Ph.D.; Richard H. Lenny; Thomas G. Maheras; Michael H. Moskow, Ph.D.; E. Follin Smith; Mark A. Thierer; Lawrence A. Weinbach
Giving statement: Giving through the Discover Financial Services Corporate Giving Program.
Company EIN: 362517428

Discover Financial Services Corporate Giving Program

2500 Lake Cook Rd.
Riverwoods, IL 60015-3851 (224) 405-0900
E-mail: communityaffairs@discover.com; Tel. for grant application questions: (877) 807-0203. E-mail for Pathway to Financial Success, for applicants who do not receive a response within 60 days: pathway@discover.com.; URL: http://www.discoverfinancial.com/community/index.shtml

Purpose and activities: Discover Financial Services supports nonprofit organizations involved with education and financial literacy. Emphasis is given to programs that include employee involvement. Support is given primarily in areas of company operations in Arizona, California, Delaware, Illinois, Kentucky, Ohio, and Utah.
Fields of interest: Elementary/secondary education; Education; Environment, beautification programs; Animal welfare; Hospitals (specialty); Cancer; Diabetes; Safety/disasters; Big Brothers/Big Sisters; Children/youth, services; Human services, financial counseling; Military/veterans' organizations.

Programs:

Discover Cares Month: Discover Cares Month is a volunteer initiative that takes place in September. Business units throughout the company participate in large-scale projects such as building playgrounds, painting school hallways and classrooms, and filling backpacks with school supplies. During the month of September, thousands of employees volunteer tens of thousands of hours to help organizations nationwide.

Junior Achievement: Each year, Discover employee volunteers reach more than 500,000 students and their families through the company's partnership with Junior Achievement, which shows young people how money is generated, managed, and used to create jobs, and encourages entrepreneurial thinking. The partnership includes sponsorship of programs that allow students to spend the day in a virtual city learning how to manage a job and balance a budget. In addition, Discover designed a mock debit card program that is incorporated in these virtual cities to teach the importance of money management. The partnership also involves a workplace mentoring program at Discover locations where employee volunteers teach local high school students how to build a business from start to finish: from selling stock and raising capital to marketing and selling a product.

Pathway to Financial Success: Discover is investing up to $10 million in financial education. Any public high school in the U.S. can apply for a grant toward a financial education curriculum if they meet the following criteria: The school has implemented or is looking to implement a financial education curriculum; a measurement tool is or will be in place to assess participation in and comprehension of the financial education curriculum; and the school agrees to share overall results of the measurement tool's pre and post-curriculum testing with Discover upon the program's completion. Special consideration is given to first time applicants and schools that have a stand alone curriculum.

Success in Schools: Through the Success in Schools program, Discover adopts a school in each of the communities where the company does business. Each adopted school receives financial support to fund academic programs and resources. In addition, company employees have the opportunity to participate in volunteer activities such as tutoring, mentoring, and interior and exterior beautification projects at those schools.

You Care, We Share Employee Giving Program: Each year, employees donate to thousands of nonprofit organizations across the country and Discover provides a match for employee donations.

Type of support: Annual campaigns; Employee matching gifts; Employee volunteer services; General/operating support; Sponsorships.
Geographic limitations: Giving primarily in areas of company operations in AZ, CA, DE, IL, KY, OH, and UT.
Support limitations: No support for political, religious, or discriminatory organizations. No grants to individuals, or for endowments, capital campaigns, fundraising activities, such as galas, benefits, dinners and sporting events, goodwill advertising, souvenir journals or dinner programs, travel, or books, magazines, or articles in professional journals.
Publications: Application guidelines.
Application information: Applications accepted. Limited funding for unsolicited proposals. Application form required. Applicants should submit the following:
1) results expected from proposed grant
2) population served
3) geographic area to be served
4) how project's results will be evaluated or measured
5) descriptive literature about organization
6) detailed description of project and amount of funding requested

Organizations that are selected must allow Discover Financial Services to use its name and/or logo in communication materials. Any use of Discover Financial Services' name/logo by the recipient must be approved by Community Affairs.
Initial approach: Complete online application
Final notification: 60 days for Pathway to Financial Success

1126
Discovery Communications, Inc.

1 Discovery Pl.
Silver Spring, MD 80112 (240) 662-2000
FAX: (302) 636-5454

Company URL: http://corporate.discovery.com
Establishment information: Established in 1985.
Company type: Public company

Company ticker symbol and exchange: DISCA/NASDAQ
Business activities: Produces television programming.
Business type (SIC): Motion pictures/production and services allied to
Financial profile for 2012: Number of employees, 4,600; assets, $12,930,000,000; sales volume, $4,487,000,000; pre-tax net income, $1,518,000,000; expenses, $2,632,000,000; liabilities, $6,639,000,000
Forbes 2000 ranking: 2012—1453rd in sales, 644th in profits, and 1281st in assets
Corporate officers: John S. Hendricks, Chair.; David M. Zaslav, Pres. and C.E.O.; Andrew Warren, Sr. Exec. V.P. and C.F.O.; Adria Alpert Romm, Sr. Exec. V.P., Human Resources; Bruce L. Campbell, Genl. Counsel
Board of directors: John S. Hendricks, Chair.; Robert R. Beck; Robert R. Bennett; Paul A. Gould; John C. Malone; Robert J. Miron; Steven A. Miron; M. LaVoy Robison; J. David Wargo; David M. Zaslav
Subsidiaries: Animal Planet, New York, NY; Discovery Networks, Inc., Bethesda, MD; Discovery People, Bethesda, MD; DiscoveryHealth.com, Bethesda, MD; The Nature Co., Berkeley, CA; The Travel Channel, Bethesda, MD
Giving statement: Giving through the Discovery Communications, Inc. Corporate Giving Program, the Discovery Channel Global Education Partnership, and the Petfinder.com Foundation.
Company EIN: 352333914

Discovery Communications, Inc. Corporate Giving Program

1 Discovery Pl.
Silver Spring, MD 20910-3354 (240) 662-2000
URL: http://impact.discovery.com/

Purpose and activities: Discovery Communications makes charitable contributions to programs designed to make a positive impact in local communities; and programs designed to foster curiosity and help people explore, understand, and enjoy the world. Support is given on a national basis in areas of company operations.
Fields of interest: Media, film/video; Historic preservation/historical societies; Scholarships/financial aid; Education, reading; Education; Environment; AIDS; Autism; Food services; Disasters, preparedness/services; American Red Cross; Human services, gift distribution; Human services; Community/economic development; Science; Military/veterans' organizations; General charitable giving.
Programs:
Discovery Education 3M Young Scientist Challenge: Through the Discovery Education 3M Young Scientist Challenge, the company annually awards cash prizes and trips to middle school students in grades 5-8 competing in a nationwide science competition. The program is designed to encourage exploration of science and innovation among youth and promote the importance of science communication. Ten finalists are awarded an all-expense paid trip to competition finals, $1,000, a contest medal or trophy, a chance to win a trip from Discovery Student Adventures, and participation in a summer mentorship program. The first place winner is awarded $25,000, a trip from Discovery Student Adventures, a contest trophy, and the title of "America's Top Young Scientist".
Discovery Gets Packing: It's What's Inside That Counts: The company, in partnership with Discovery employees, provides elementary school students with recycled backpacks filled with back-to-school supplies. The backpacks are made from recycled network billboard advertisements and the program is designed to help kids start the upcoming school year in eco-friendly style.
Discovery Impact: Creating Change: Through Discovery Impact: Creating Change pro-bono initiative, the company and its employees provides full design, marketing, and communications work on behalf of local nonprofit organizations. Pro-bono work includes social media training, event concepting, promotional materials, websites, pamphlets, logos, PSAs, press kits, and mission statements.
Type of support: Annual campaigns; Employee matching gifts; Employee volunteer services; Grants to individuals; In-kind gifts; Pro bono services; Pro bono services - marketing/branding; Program development.
Geographic limitations: Giving on a national and international basis.
Application information:
Parents or guardians must complete online parental consent form for Discovery Education 3M Young Scientist Challenge.
Initial approach: Complete online registration and submit video entry for Discovery Education 3M Young Scientist Challenge
Deadline(s): Apr. 15 for Discovery Education 3M Young Scientist Challenge

Discovery Channel Global Education Partnership

(formerly Discovery Channel Global Education Fund)
1 Discovery Pl.
Silver Spring, MD 20910-3354 (240) 662-2986
E-mail: partnership_info@discoveryglobaled.org; URL: http://www.discoveryglobaled.org

Establishment information: Established in 1997 in DE.
Donor: Discovery Communications, Inc.
Financial data (yr. ended 12/31/11): Revenue, $6,078,232; assets, $12,868,997 (M); gifts received, $5,997,830; expenditures, $4,545,322.
Purpose and activities: The fund works to use the power of television as a tool for development and education in communities with limited resources around the world.
Fields of interest: Media, film/video; Education; Science.
Type of support: Scholarships—to individuals.
Geographic limitations: Giving on a national and international basis.
Officer and Directors:* John Hendricks, Chair.; William Asiko; Hon. Jack Fields; Willard O. Freeman; Mark Hollinger; Aric Noboa; William Irwin; Anthony V. Lupo; Donald M. Payne; Carol Wainaina.
EIN: 522043740

Petfinder.com Foundation

4729 E. Sunrise Dr., Ste. 119
Tucson, AZ 85718-4534 (520) 207-0626
E-mail: foundation@petfinder.com; E-Mail for Lisa Robinson: lisa@petfinderfoundation.com; URL: http://www.petfinder.com/foundation

Establishment information: Established in 2003 in AZ.
Contact: Lisa Robinson, Exec. Dir.
Financial data (yr. ended 12/31/11): Revenue, $7,063,307; assets, $2,154,133 (M); gifts received, $7,069,885; expenditures, $6,625,517; giving activities include $6,209,323 for grants.
Purpose and activities: The foundation works to help homeless pets by saving lives through adoptions, helping shelters prepare for and recover from disaster, and working to make shelters across the country more sustainable.
Fields of interest: Animal welfare; Disasters, preparedness/services.
Program:
Disaster Recovery & Emergency Response Grants: Grants, typically ranging from $500 to $5,000, are available to animal rescue and shelter organizations devastated by hurricanes, tornadoes, fires, floods, earthquakes, or other events. Grants are intended to support: emergency equipment or supplies, including communications and technological equipment; emergency animal transport and housing; information management systems to enable operations during and after disasters; and equipment and training for critical responders (including command and/or emergency training activities).
Geographic limitations: Giving on a national basis.
Publications: Application guidelines.
Application information: Applications accepted. Application form required. Applicants should submit the following:
1) copy of IRS Determination Letter
Initial approach: Download application form
Deadline(s): None
Officers: Betsy Saul*, Chair.; Jared Saul*, Pres.; Dan Cohen*, V.P.; Rob Rauh*, Secy.-Treas.; Lisa Robinson, Exec. Dir.
Trustees: Greg Hesgerberg; Jim Morris; Amanda Sumner.
EIN: 870694641

1127
The Walt Disney Company

500 S. Buena Vista St., MC 9722
Burbank, CA 91521-0001 (818) 560-1000
FAX: (302) 636-5454

Company URL: http://corporate.disney.go.com
Establishment information: Established in 1923.
Company type: Public company
Company ticker symbol and exchange: DIS/NYSE
Business activities: operates radio and television networks; produces motion pictures; operates theme parks and resorts; licenses consumer products; provides Internet information services; provides catalog shopping services.
Business type (SIC): Amusement and recreation services/miscellaneous; radio and television broadcasting; investors/miscellaneous; hotels and motels; computer services; motion pictures
Financial profile for 2012: Number of employees, 166,000; assets, $74,898,000,000; sales volume, $42,278,000,000; pre-tax net income, $9,260,000,000; expenses, $33,018,000,000; liabilities, $35,139,000,000
Fortune 1000 ranking: 2012—66th in revenues, 32nd in profits, and 80th in assets
Forbes 2000 ranking: 2012—213th in sales, 100th in profits, and 304th in assets
Corporate officers: Robert A. Iger, Chair. and C.E.O.; Jay Rasulo, Sr. Exec. V.P. and C.F.O.; Alan Braverman, Sr. Exec. V.P., Genl. Counsel, and Secy.; Christine M. McCarthy, Exec. V.P. and Treas.; Zenia Mucha, Exec. V.P., Corp. Comms.
Board of directors: Robert A. Iger, Chair.; Susan E. Arnold; John S. Chen; Judith L. Estrin; Fred H. Langhammer; Aylwin B. Lewis; Monica C. Lozano; Robert W. Matschullat; Sheryl Sandberg; Orin C. Smith
Subsidiaries: ABC, Inc., New York, NY; Walt Disney World Co., Lake Buena Vista, FL; Fort Worth Star-Telegram, Fort Worth, TX; Miramax Film Corp., New York, NY
Offices: Santa Ana, CA; Minneapolis, MN

International operations: British Virgin Islands; Canada; England; France; Germany; Hong Kong; Italy; Japan; Netherlands; Singapore; Switzerland; United Kingdom
Historic mergers: Capital Cities/ABC, Inc. (February 9, 1996)
Giving statement: Giving through the Walt Disney Company Contributions Program and the Walt Disney Company Foundation.
Company EIN: 954545390

The Walt Disney Company Contributions Program

500 S. Buena Vista St.
Burbank, CA 91521-0001 (877) 282-8322
URL: http://corporate.disney.go.com/citizenship/community.html

Purpose and activities: As a complement to its foundation, Disney also makes charitable contributions to nonprofit organizations, K-12 public schools, and public school districts. Giving primarily in areas of company operations; giving also on a national and international basis, including in Argentina, Australia, Canada, China, Hong Kong, India, Korea, Japan, and the United Kingdom.
Fields of interest: Media, film/video; Education; Environment, natural resources; Medical research, fund raising/fund distribution; Employment, management/technical assistance; Employment; Children/youth, services; Family services; Community/economic development; Science.
Program:
Matching Gift Program: Disney matches up to $15,000 per employee contribution per calendar year to any eligible organization.
Type of support: Curriculum development; Donated products; Employee matching gifts; Employee volunteer services; General/operating support; In-kind gifts; Program development.
Geographic limitations: Giving primarily in areas of company operations; giving also on a national and international basis, including in Argentina, Australia, Canada, China, Hong Kong, India, Korea, Japan, and the United Kingdom.
Support limitations: No support for organizations that do not comply with the U.S. Patriot Act, discriminatory organizations, organizations with controversial issues or tactics, organizations that operate or support activities that are counter to Disney policies, labor, or political organizations, or fraternal, athletic, or social clubs. No grants to individuals, or families, or individuals or organizations raising funds on behalf of another group, or for online auctions or broadcast promotions, competitions, recognition events, holiday parties, door prizes, giveaways, or rewards or other incentive programs, sponsorships or donations for individuals or teams, such as walk-a-thons, contests, pageants, scholarships, or ambassador programs.
Publications: Application guidelines.
Application information: Applications accepted. Applications from organizations that have received a donation from Disney, ABC, or ESPN in the last 12 months are not accepted. The standard donation is four, one-day Park Hopper tickets. Ticket contributions must be used for fundraising efforts only. No complimentary hotel or cruise accommodations, travel arrangements, merchandise items, or other forms of donations are available. Application form required. Applicants should submit the following:
1) contact person
2) detailed description of project and amount of funding requested
3) copy of IRS Determination Letter
4) name, address and phone number of organization
Initial approach: Complete online eligibility quiz and application form
Deadline(s): 60 days to 6 months prior to need

The Walt Disney Company Foundation

500 S. Buena Vista St.
Burbank, CA 91521-6444
URL: http://corporate.disney.go.com/responsibility/index.html

Establishment information: Incorporated in 1951 in CA.
Donor: The Walt Disney Co.
Financial data (yr. ended 10/01/11): Assets, $6,724,245 (M); gifts received, $4,000,000; expenditures, $2,787,753; qualifying distributions, $2,641,727; giving activities include $2,392,174 for 8 grants (high: $898,288; low: $6,000) and $207,513 for 257 employee matching gifts.
Purpose and activities: The foundation supports organizations involved with arts and culture, education, the environment, and programs involved with the health and well-being of children and youth.
Fields of interest: Media/communications; Media, film/video; Media, television; Arts; Scholarships/financial aid; Education; Environment, land resources; Environment; Health care, clinics/centers; Health care; Children/youth, services.
Programs:
Disney Scholars Program: The foundation awards 50 college scholarships of $20,000 to high school seniors who are children of employees of Walt Disney Company and its subsidiaries or affiliated companies. Scholarships are awarded based on academic and extracurricular achievement. The program is administered by the Educational Testing Service.
Educational Matching Gifts: The foundation matches contributions made by full-time employees of Walt Disney to institutions of higher education on a one-for-one basis up to $2,000 per employee, per year.
Type of support: Annual campaigns; Capital campaigns; Continuing support; Employee matching gifts; Employee-related scholarships; General/operating support; Program development; Scholarship funds.
Geographic limitations: Giving primarily in CA, DC, FL, NJ, and NY.
Support limitations: No support for public agencies or tax-supported organizations.
Application information: Applications not accepted. Contributes only to pre-selected organizations.
Officers: Robert A. Iger, Pres.; Christine M. McCarthy, Treas.; Jay Rasulo, Sr. Exec. V.P.; Marsha Reed.
EIN: 956037079

1128
Walt Disney World Co.

P.O. Box 10000
Lake Buena Vista, FL 32830-1000
(407) 824-2222

Company URL: http://disneyworld.disney.go.com
Establishment information: Established in 1971.
Company type: Subsidiary of a public company
Business activities: Operates resorts; operates cruise line.
Business type (SIC): Hotels and motels; transportation/water passenger
Corporate officer: Robert A. Iger, Chair. and C.E.O.
Board of director: Robert A. Iger, Chair.
Giving statement: Giving through the Walt Disney World Co. Contributions Program.

Walt Disney World Co. Contributions Program

c/o Community Rels.
P.O. Box 10000
Lake Buena Vista, FL 32830-1000 (407) 828-3453
URL: http://www.wdwpublicaffairs.com/

Purpose and activities: Walt Disney World makes charitable contributions to nonprofit organizations involved with helping children in need. Support is limited to Orange, Osceola, Lake, Polk, and Seminole counties, Florida for monetary contributions; giving in the eastern and central states for theme park ticket donations.
Fields of interest: Children.
Type of support: Donated products; Employee volunteer services; General/operating support; In-kind gifts.
Geographic limitations: Giving limited to Orange, Osceola, Lake, Polk, and Seminole counties, FL for monetary contributions; giving in the eastern and central states for theme park ticket donations.
Support limitations: No theme park ticket donations for incentives.
Publications: Application guidelines; Corporate giving report.
Application information: Applications accepted. Ticket donations are limited to one contribution per organization during any given year. Application form required. Applicants should submit the following:
1) name, address and phone number of organization
2) brief history of organization and description of its mission
3) detailed description of project and amount of funding requested
Ticket donation requests should include the organization's Tax ID Number; the name, date, and a description of the event; details of the event budget and the expected revenue; and the name of the organization's Executive Director, CEO, or Principal.
Initial approach: Contact headquarters for application information for monetary contributions; complete online application form for ticket donations
Deadline(s): 6 to 8 weeks prior to need for ticket donations
Final notification: 6 to 8 weeks for ticket donations

1129
The Dispatch Printing Company

34 S. 3rd St.
Columbus, OH 43215-4201
(614) 461-5000

Company URL: http://www.dispatch.com
Establishment information: Established in 1871.
Company type: Private company
Business activities: Publishes newspapers.
Business type (SIC): Newspaper publishing and/or printing
Corporate officers: John F. Wolfe, Chair. and C.E.O.; Michael J. Fiorile, Pres. and C.O.O.; Joseph Y. Gallo, Exec. V.P. and C.I.O.; Poe A. Timmons, C.F.O.
Board of director: John F. Wolfe, Chair.
Subsidiaries: CNS-Community News Service Weekly Newspapers, Columbus, OH; Dispatch Consumer Svcs., Westerville, OH; Video Indiana-WTHR, Indianapolis, IN; WBNS Television & Radio, Columbus, OH

Giving statement: Giving through the Wolfe Associates, Inc.

Wolfe Associates, Inc.

34 S. 3rd St.
Columbus, OH 43215-4201 (614) 460-3782

Establishment information: Incorporated in 1973 in OH.
Donors: The Dispatch Printing Co.; The Ohio Co.; WBNS-TV, Inc.; RadiOhio, Inc.; Video Indiana, Inc.
Contact: Rita J. Wolfe, V.P.
Financial data (yr. ended 12/31/11): Assets, $14,828,977 (M); gifts received, $586,136; expenditures, $1,017,590; qualifying distributions, $928,950; giving activities include $928,950 for grants.
Purpose and activities: The foundation supports organizations involved with arts and culture, education, health, youth development, human services, community development, and religion.
Fields of interest: Arts; Elementary/secondary education; Higher education; Education; Hospitals (general); Health care; Goodwill Industries; Youth development; Children/youth, services; Human services; Business/industry; Community/economic development; United Ways and Federated Giving Programs; Religion.
Type of support: Annual campaigns; Building/renovation; Continuing support; Equipment; General/operating support; Matching/challenge support; Scholarship funds.
Geographic limitations: Giving primarily in Columbus, OH.
Support limitations: No grants to individuals, or for research, demonstration projects, publications, or conferences.
Publications: Application guidelines; Program policy statement.
Application information: Applications accepted. Application form not required. Applicants should submit the following:
1) population served
2) copy of IRS Determination Letter
3) copy of most recent annual report/audited financial statement/990
4) detailed description of project and amount of funding requested
5) listing of additional sources and amount of support

Initial approach: Letter of inquiry
Copies of proposal: 1
Board meeting date(s): Mar., June, Sept., and Dec.
Deadline(s): None
Final notification: Following board meetings

Officers and Trustees:* John F. Wolfe*, Chair. and Pres.; Poe A. Timmons*, V.P. and Treas.; Michael F. Curtin*, V.P.; Michael J. Fiorile*, V.P.; Nancy Wolfe Lane*, V.P.; Sara Wolfe Perrini*, V.P.; Katherine Wolfe*, V.P.; Rita J. Wolfe*, V.P.; Sherry L. Lewis, Secy.
EIN: 237303111
Selected grants: The following grants are a representative sample of this grantmaker's funding activity:
$15,000 to Columbus Foundation, Columbus, OH, 2010.
$15,000 to Columbus Foundation, Columbus, OH, 2010.
$10,000 to Nationwide Childrens Hospital Foundation, Columbus, OH, 2010.
$6,000 to Childhood League Center, Columbus, OH, 2010.
$5,000 to A Kid Again, Columbus, OH, 2010.
$5,000 to Boy Scouts of America, Columbus, OH, 2010.
$2,500 to Columbus School for Girls, Columbus, OH, 2010.
$2,500 to Mid-Ohio Foodbank, Grove City, OH, 2010.
$2,500 to Nationwide Childrens Hospital Foundation, Columbus, OH, 2010.
$2,500 to Ohio Historical Society, Columbus, OH, 2010.

1130
Diversey, Inc.

(formerly S. C. JohnsonDiversey, Inc.)
8310 16th St.
P.O. Box 902
Sturtevant, WI 53177-0902 (262) 631-4001
FAX: (262) 631-4282

Company URL: http://www.diversey.com/home
Establishment information: Established in 1997.
Company type: Private company
Business activities: Manufactures and provides floor care, carpet care, housekeeping, foodservice, sanitation, and restroom hygiene products and services.
Business type (SIC): Soaps, cleaners, and toiletries
Financial profile for 2010: Number of employees, 10,170; assets, $3,284,000,000; sales volume, $3,127,700,000
Corporate officers: Helen P. Johnson-Leipold, Chair.; Scott D. Russell, Exec. V.P., Genl. Counsel, and Secy.; Brent Hoag, V.P. and C.I.O.
Board of directors: Helen P. Johnson-Leipold III, Chair.; Manvinder S. Banga; Todd C. Brown; Robert M. Howe; George K. Jaquette; Philip W. Knisely; Edward Lonergan; Clifton D. Louis; Winifred Johnson Marquart; Richard J. Schnall
International operations: Argentina; Australia; Austria; Barbados; Belgium; Brazil; Canada; Cayman Islands; Chile; China; Colombia; Costa Rica; Czech Republic; Dominican Republic; Egypt; France; Germany; Greece; Guatemala; Hong Kong; Hungary; India; Indonesia; Ireland; Israel; Italy; Jamaica; Japan; Kenya; Malaysia; Mexico; Morocco and the Western Sahara; Netherlands; New Zealand; Niger; Pakistan; Paraguay; Peru; Philippines; Poland; Portugal; Romania; Russia; Singapore; Slovakia; Slovenia; South Africa; South Korea; Spain; Sweden; Taiwan; Thailand; Turkey; United Arab Emirates; United Kingdom; Uruguay; Venezuela
Giving statement: Giving through the Diversey, Inc. Corporate Giving Program.
Company EIN: 391877511

Diversey, Inc. Corporate Giving Program

(formerly JohnsonDiversey, Inc. Corporate Giving Program)
8310 16th St.
Sturtevant, WI 53177-1964 (262) 631-4000
URL: http://www.diversey.com/sustainability

Purpose and activities: JohnsonDiversey makes charitable contributions to K-12 schools and nonprofit organizations involved with children's hygiene and safety. Support is given on a national and international basis in areas of company operations.
Fields of interest: Public health, hygiene; Employment, training; Housing/shelter; Safety/disasters, public education; Disasters, preparedness/services Children; Women.
Type of support: Building/renovation; Employee matching gifts; Employee volunteer services; Equipment; In-kind gifts; Loaned talent.
Geographic limitations: Giving on a national and international basis in areas of company operations.

1131
Diversityinc Media LLC

570 Broad St., 15th Fl.
Newark, NJ 07102-4560 (973) 494-0500
FAX: (973) 494-0525

Company URL: http://www.diversityinc.com
Establishment information: Established in 1998.
Company type: Private company
Business activities: Publishes magazine and newsletters.
Business type (SIC): Periodical publishing and/or printing
Corporate officers: Luke Visconti, C.E.O.; Clark S. Arnold, C.O.O.
Giving statement: Giving through the DiversityInc Foundation.

DiversityInc Foundation

342 Nassau St.
Princeton, NJ 08540
E-mail for Maria Auciello: MAuciello@DiversityInc.com; URL: http://www.diversityinc.com/diversityincfoundation/

Establishment information: Established in 2006 in NJ.
Donors: Country Financial; Daimler Chrysler; Diversityinc Media; Grand Rapids Area Chamber of Commerce; Harrahs Entertainment; Online Testing Exchange; The Pepsi Bottling Group, Inc.; SC Johnson; Spherion; Trinity Health.
Contact: Maria Auciello
Financial data (yr. ended 12/31/10): Assets, $145,580 (M); expenditures, $85,108; qualifying distributions, $0.
Purpose and activities: The mission of the foundation is to fund scholarships for financially-disadvantaged students.
Type of support: General/operating support; Scholarship funds.
Support limitations: No grants to individuals directly.
Application information: Applications not accepted. Unsolicited requests for funds not accepted.
Officers: Lucas Visconti, Pres.; Carolyn Johnson, V.P.; Barbara Frankel, C.F.O.
EIN: 204664985

1132
The Dixie Group, Inc.

(formerly Dixie Yarns, Inc.)
104 Nowlin Lane, Ste. 101
Chattanooga, TN 37421 (423) 510-7000

Company URL: http://www.thedixiegroup.com
Establishment information: Established in 1920.
Company type: Public company
Company ticker symbol and exchange: DXYN/NASDAQ
Business activities: Manufactures, markets, and sells carpets and rugs.
Business type (SIC): Carpets and rugs; yarn and thread mills
Financial profile for 2012: Number of employees, 1,171; assets, $201,770,000; sales volume, $266,370,000; pre-tax net income, -$1,050,000; expenses, $264,560,000; liabilities, $137,720,000

Corporate officers: Daniel K. Frierson, Chair. and C.E.O.; D. Kennedy Frierson, Jr., V.P. and C.O.O.; Jon A. Faulkner, V.P. and C.F.O.; W. Derek Davis, V.P., Human Resources; Starr T. Klein, Secy.; D. Eugene Lasater, Cont.
Board of directors: Daniel K. Frierson, Chair.; Charles E. Brock; J. Don Brock, Ph.D.; D. Kennedy Frierson, Jr.; Paul K. Frierson; Walter W. Hubbard; Lowry F. Kline; Hilda S. Murray; John W. Murrey III
Subsidiaries: Fabrica Intl., Santa Ana, CA; Masland Carpets, LLC, Mobile, AL
Plants: Atmore, Roanoke, Saraland, AL
Giving statement: Giving through the Dixie Group Corporate Giving Program and the Dixie Group Foundation, Inc.
Company EIN: 620183370

The Dixie Group Foundation, Inc.

(formerly Dixie Yarns Foundation, Inc.)
P.O. Box 25107
Chattanooga, TN 37422-5107 (423) 510-7005

Establishment information: Established in 1944 in DE.
Donors: Dixie Yarns, Inc.; The Dixie Group, Inc.
Contact: Starr T. Klein, Secy.-Treas.
Financial data (yr. ended 12/31/11): Assets, $728,701 (M); gifts received, $40,000; expenditures, $68,011; qualifying distributions, $62,350; giving activities include $62,350 for 38 grants (high: $15,000; low: $250).
Purpose and activities: The foundation supports organizations involved with education and human services and awards grants to employees and former employees, and scholarships to the children of employees of the Dixie Group.
Type of support: Annual campaigns; Capital campaigns; Continuing support; Emergency funds; Employee-related scholarships; Endowments; General/operating support; Grants to individuals; Scholarships—to individuals.
Application information: Applications accepted. Application form required.
Initial approach: Proposal
Deadline(s): None
Officers and Trustees:* Daniel K. Frierson*, Pres.; W. Derek Davis*, V.P.; Starr T. Klein, Secy.-Treas.
EIN: 620645090

1133
Dixon Hughes Goodman LLP

(formerly Goodman & Company, L.L.P.)
6525 Morrison Blvd., Ste. 500
Charlotte, NC 28211 (704) 367-7020

Company URL: http://www.dhgllp.com/
Company type: Private company
Business activities: Provides accounting, consulting, and technology services.
Business type (SIC): Accounting, auditing, and bookkeeping services; management and public relations services
Corporate officers: Charles Edgar Sams, Jr., Chair.; Thomas H. Wilson, Dept. Chair. and C.O.O.; Kenneth M. Hughes, C.E.O.
Board of director: Jacques Marmier
Offices: Birmingham, AL; Washington, DC; Jacksonville, FL; Atlanta, GA; Rockville, MD; Asheville, Greenville, Hendersonville, High Point, Pinehurst, Raleigh, Winston-Salem, NC; Hudson, OH; Charleston, Greenville, Spartanburg, Summerville, SC; Memphis, Nashville, TN; Dallas, TX; Chester, Danville, Newport News, Richmond, Roanoke, Tysons, Virginia Beach, VA; Charleston, Morgantown, WV
Giving statement: Giving through the Goodman & Company, CPA's Foundation Honoring Retired Partners, Inc.

Goodman & Company, CPA's Foundation Honoring Retired Partners, Inc.

Fountain Plz. 1, 701 Ctr. Dr., Ste. 700
Newport News, VA 23606-4295

Establishment information: Established in 1997 in VA.
Donors: Goodman & Company, L.L.P.; Dixon Hughes Goodman, LLP; Wallace Dunn; Joel Flax.
Financial data (yr. ended 06/30/12): Assets, $228,895 (M); gifts received, $33,263; expenditures, $26,414; qualifying distributions, $25,091; giving activities include $25,091 for 13 grants (high: $11,200; low: $100).
Purpose and activities: The foundation supports organizations involved with higher education.
Fields of interest: Education.
Type of support: General/operating support; Scholarship funds.
Geographic limitations: Giving limited to VA.
Support limitations: No grants to individuals.
Application information: Applications not accepted. Unsolicited requests for funds not accepted.
Officers: Charles Sams, Jr., Chair.; James Haggard, Pres.; L. Kent Satterfield, Secy.-Treas.
EIN: 541847474

1134
DJO Incorporated

1430 Decision St.
Vista, CA 92081 (760) 727-1280

Company URL: http://www.djoglobal.com
Establishment information: Established in 1978.
Company type: Private company
Business activities: Provides orthopedic devices and surgical reconstructive implant products.
Business type (SIC): Medical instruments and supplies
Corporate officers: Mike S. Zafirovski, Chair.; Michael P. Mogul, Pres. and C.E.O.; Vickie L. Capps, Exec. V.P., C.F.O., and Treas.; Donald M. Roberts, Exec. V.P., Genl. Counsel, and Secy.; Stephen Murphy, Exec. V.P., Sales and Mktg.; Tom Capizzi, Exec. V.P., Human Resources
Board of directors: Mike S. Zafirovski, Chair.; Sidney Braginsky; John Chiminski; Chinh E. Chu; Leslie H. Cross; John R. Murphy; James R. Lawson; Julia Kahr; James A. Quella
Giving statement: Giving through the DJO Incorporated Corporate Giving Program.

DJO Incorporated Corporate Giving Program

1430 Decision St.
Vista, CA 92081
URL: http://www.djoglobal.com/en_US/Corporate_Citizenship.html

Purpose and activities: DJO Incorporated makes charitable contributions to nonprofit organizations on a case by case basis. Support is given primarily in areas of company operations, with emphasis on California.
Fields of interest: Hospitals (specialty); Arthritis; Spine disorders; Disasters, preparedness/services; Boys & girls clubs; Children, services; Homeless, human services.
Type of support: Donated products; Employee volunteer services; General/operating support; Sponsorships.
Geographic limitations: Giving primarily in areas of company operations, with emphasis on CA.

1135
Djr Holding Corporation

(doing business as Schiebout Tire Company)
815 W. 10th St.
Pella, IA 50219-7859 (641) 628-3153

Establishment information: Established in 1983.
Company type: Private company
Business activities: Manufactures tires.
Business type (SIC): Motor vehicles, parts, and supplies—wholesale
Corporate officer: Travis Thompson, Pres. and C.E.O.
Board of director: Wilma Veenstra
Giving statement: Giving through the Schiebout Charitable Foundation.

Schiebout Charitable Foundation

815 W. 10th St.
Pella, IA 50219-2003

Establishment information: Established in IA.
Donor: DJR Holding Corp.
Financial data (yr. ended 12/31/11): Assets, $120 (M); gifts received, $50,000; expenditures, $49,904; qualifying distributions, $49,904; giving activities include $49,904 for grants.
Purpose and activities: The foundation supports hospitals and organizations involved with education and Christianity.
Type of support: General/operating support.
Geographic limitations: Giving primarily in areas of company operations in Pella, IA.
Support limitations: No grants to individuals.
Application information: Applications not accepted. Unsolicited requests for funds not accepted.
Directors: John Veenstra; Kevin Veenstra.
EIN: 510196278

1136
Do it Best Corp.

6502 Nelson Rd.
Fort Wayne, IN 46803-1920
(260) 748-5300

Company URL: http://www.doitbestcorp.com
Establishment information: Established in 1945.
Company type: Cooperative
Business activities: A hardware and building materials buying cooperative offering products and retail services to independent hardware, home center, and lumberyard member-owners.
Business type (SIC): Hardware, plumbing, and heating equipment—wholesale; lumber and construction materials—wholesale; electrical goods—wholesale; durable goods—wholesale
Corporate officers: Mike Fujimoto, Chair.; Pat Sullivan, Vice-Chair.; Bob Taylor, Pres. and C.E.O.; Dan Starr, Exec. V.P. and C.O.O.; Doug Roth, V.P., Finance and C.F.O.; Tim Miller, V.P., Mktg.; Jay Brown, V.P., Sales; Gury Furst, V.P., Human Resources and Genl. Counsel.
Board of directors: Mike Fujimoto, Chair.; Pat Sullivan, Vice-Chair.; Robert Ashley; Frank Blair; Tom Brown; Tom Lamberth; Jim Lehrer; Howard Miller; J. Johnson; Randy Skinner

Offices: Fort Wayne, IN; Burnsville, MN; Montgomery, NY; Woodburn, OR; Lexington, SC
Giving statement: Giving through the Do it Best Corp. Contributions Program.

Do it Best Corp. Contributions Program

Nelson Rd.
P.O. Box 868
Fort Wayne, IN 46801-0868 (260) 748-5300

Contact: Bob Taylor, Pres.
Purpose and activities: Do it Best makes charitable contributions to nonprofit organizations involved with youth development and community development. Support is given primarily in areas of company operations.
Fields of interest: Youth development; Community/economic development.
Type of support: General/operating support; In-kind gifts; Sponsorships.
Geographic limitations: Giving primarily in areas of company operations.
Application information: Application form not required. Applicants should submit the following:
1) detailed description of project and amount of funding requested
Initial approach: Proposal to headquarters
Copies of proposal: 1
Final notification: Following review

1137
Dobson Telephone Company, Inc.

14101 Wireless Way, Ste. 300
Oklahoma City, OK 73134-2514
(405) 391-8400

Company URL: http://www.dobsonteleco.com/
Establishment information: Established in 1935.
Company type: Private company
Business activities: Operates telephone company.
Business type (SIC): Telephone communications
Financial profile for 2011: Number of employees, 18
Corporate officer: James R. Rutherford, Pres. and C.O.O.
Giving statement: Giving through the Continue Learning and Strive for Success Foundation.

Continue Learning and Strive for Success Foundation

13900 North Portland
Oklahoma City, OK 73134-4042
URL: http://www.dobsonteleco.com/community/scholarship
Scholarship address: Dobson Telephone Co., Attn. Scholarship Comm., 402 E. Broadway Ave., McLoud, OK 74851

Establishment information: Established in 2005 in OK.
Donor: Dobson Telephone Co.
Financial data (yr. ended 12/31/11): Assets, $7,682 (M); expenditures, $12,423; qualifying distributions, $12,423; giving activities include $10,000 for 10 grants (high: $1,000; low: $1,000).
Purpose and activities: The foundation awards scholarships to students who are customers of Dobson Telephone Company or the affiliates Intelleq and Dobson Technologies to attend an Oklahoma institute of higher learning.
Fields of interest: Higher education.
Program:
CLASS Scholarship Program: The foundation annually awards $1,000 scholarships to high school seniors who are customers or in the household of customers of Dobson Telephone Company or affiliates Intelleq or Dobson Technologies. Applicants must have a GPA of 3.0 and plan to attend an Oklahoma Institute of higher learning.
Type of support: Scholarships—to individuals.
Geographic limitations: Giving primarily in areas of company operations in OK.
Publications: Application guidelines.
Application information: Applications accepted. Application form required.
Applications should include a notarized letter or transcripts, a wallet-sized professional photo, 200-word essay, and a copy of the latest local phone service invoice to provide proof of service.
Initial approach: Download application form and mail to application address
Deadline(s): Apr. 15
Final notification: May
Directors: Robert Dean Hill; James W. Rutherford; Donna Wynn.
EIN: 203393143

1138
Doctor's Associates, Inc.

(also known as Subway)
325 Bic Dr.
Milford, CT 06461-3059 (203) 877-4281

Company URL: http://www.subway.com
Establishment information: Established in 1965.
Company type: Private company
Business activities: Franchises submarine sandwich shops.
Business type (SIC): Investors/miscellaneous
Corporate officers: Frederick A. DeLuca, Pres. and C.E.O.; Thys Van Hout, C.I.O.; David Worroll, Cont.
Giving statement: Giving through the Subway Corporate Giving Program.

Subway Corporate Giving Program

325 Bic Dr.
Milford, CT 06461-3072 (203) 877-4281
URL: http://www.subway.com/subwayroot/about_us/Social_Responsibility/default.aspx

Purpose and activities: Subway makes charitable contributions to nonprofit organizations involved with education and health and on a case by case basis. Support is given primarily in areas of company operations.
Fields of interest: Secondary school/education; Education; Health care; Heart & circulatory diseases; Athletics/sports, baseball; American Red Cross; General charitable giving.
Program:
Hispanic Heritage Youth Sports Awards: Subway awards college scholarships to graduating Latino high school seniors with a 3.0 GPA. The program is limited to Phoenix, AZ, Los Angeles, San Diego, San Francisco, and San Jose, CA, Washington, DC, Miami, FL, Chicago, IL, NJ, New York, NY, Philadelphia, PA, and Dallas, Houston, and San Antonio, TX.
Type of support: Donated products; In-kind gifts; Scholarships—to individuals; Sponsorships.
Geographic limitations: Giving primarily in areas of company operations, with emphasis on Phoenix, AZ, Los Angeles, San Diego, San Francisco, and San Jose, CA, Washington, DC, Miami, FL, Chicago, IL, NJ, New York, NY, Philadelphia, PA, and Dallas, Houston, and San Antonio, TX; giving also to national organizations.
Publications: Application guidelines.
Application information: Applications accepted. Applicants should submit the following:
1) name, address and phone number of organization
2) detailed description of project and amount of funding requested
3) contact person
Initial approach: Complete online application; contact nearest company store for application information for Heritage Youth Sports Awards
Deadline(s): None

1139
The Doctors Company

185 Greenwood Rd.
P.O. Box 2900
Napa, CA 94558-0900 (707) 226-0100
FAX: (707) 226-0111

Company URL: http://www.thedoctors.com
Establishment information: Established in 1976.
Company type: Subsidiary of a private company
Business activities: Operates physician-owned and -operated provider of medical malpractice insurance.
Business type (SIC): Insurance/fire, marine, and casualty
Financial profile for 2011: Assets, $3,955,287,000; liabilities, $2,720,618,000
Corporate officers: Richard E. Anderson, M.D., Chair. and C.E.O.; Robert D. Francis, C.O.O.; David A. McHale, Sr. V.P. and Genl. Counsel
Board of directors: Richard E. Anderson, M.D., Chair.; James P. Bagian, M.D.; Eugene M. Bullis, C.P.A.; David M. Charles, M.D.; Kenneth R. Chrisman; William J. Gallagher, M.D.; Charles R. Kossman, Ph.D., M.D.; Bryan Lawton, Ph.D.; Donald J. Palmisano, M.D.; Robert W. Pike, Esq.; Kathleen D. Ricord; Mary Ann Thode; David B. Troxel, M.D.; Ronald H. Wender, M.D.
Giving statement: Giving through the Doctors Company Foundation.

The Doctors Company Foundation

185 Greenwood Rd.
Napa, CA 94558-6270 (707) 226-0373
FAX: (707) 226-0153;
E-mail: apply@tdcfoundation.com; URL: http://www.tdcfoundation.com

Establishment information: Established in 2007 in CA.
Donor: The Doctors Co.
Contact: Leona Egeland Siadek, Exec. Dir.
Financial data (yr. ended 12/31/11): Assets, $1,467,108 (M); gifts received, $2,000,000; expenditures, $756,411; qualifying distributions, $752,366; giving activities include $752,366 for grants.
Purpose and activities: The foundation supports programs designed to advance and protect the practice of good medicine. Special emphasis is directed toward patient safety research, forums, and pilot programs; patient safety education; and medical liability research.
Fields of interest: Health care, clinics/centers; Health care, patient services; Health care; Medical research.
Program:
Vanguard Award for the Advancement of Patient Safety: Through the Vanguard Award for the Advancement of Patient Safety, the foundation

honors individual physicians for their leadership contributions to the national patient safety movement. The award is designed to draw public and industry attention to the importance of patient safety within the medical profession and to recognize physicians who demonstrate leadership in this area.
Type of support: Conferences/seminars; Continuing support; General/operating support; Grants to individuals; Program development; Sponsorships.
Geographic limitations: Giving primarily in CA, IL, MA, OH, OR, VA, and WA.
Publications: Application guidelines; Grants list.
Application information: Applications accepted. Additional information may be requested at a later date. Organizations receiving support are asked to submit a final report. Applicants should submit the following:

1) timetable for implementation and evaluation of project
2) signature and title of chief executive officer
3) copy of IRS Determination Letter
4) brief history of organization and description of its mission
5) explanation of why grantmaker is considered an appropriate donor for project
6) detailed description of project and amount of funding requested
7) copy of current year's organizational budget and/or project budget

Initial approach: Mail or e-mail proposal, including cover letter signed by authorized officer of organization
Deadline(s): None; proposals received after Oct. 1 may be reviewed the following year

Officers and Directors:* David B. Troxel, M.D.*, Chair.; Robert D. Francis, Vice-Chair.; David G. Preimesberger*, Secy.-Treas.; Leona Egeland Siadek, Exec. Dir.; Richard E. Anderson, M.D.; Robin Diamond; Charles R. Kossman, M.D.; Donald J. Palisano, M.D.; Kathleen D. Ricord.
EIN: 261636256
Selected grants: The following grants are a representative sample of this grantmaker's funding activity:
$100,719 to Cleveland Clinic Foundation, Cleveland, OH, 2010.
$85,100 to National Patient Safety Foundation, North Adams, MA, 2010.
$50,000 to Institute for Healthcare Improvement, Cambridge, MA, 2010.
$44,747 to University of Washington, Seattle, WA, 2010.
$5,000 to Scripps Health Foundation, San Diego, CA, 2010.

1140
The Dolan Company

(formerly Dolan Media Company)
222 S. 9th St., Ste. 2300
Minneapolis, MN 55402 (612) 317-9420

Company URL: http://www.dolanmedia.com/
Establishment information: Established in 1992.
Company type: Public company
Company ticker symbol and exchange: DM/NYSE
Business activities: Provides business information and professional services to legal, financial and real estate sectors.
Financial profile for 2009: Number of employees, 1,903; assets, $528,290,000; sales volume, $262,920,000; pre-tax net income, $53,170,000; expenses, $212,140,000; liabilities, $279,430,000
Corporate officers: James P. Dolan, Chair., Pres., and C.E.O.; Scott J. Pollei, Exec. V.P. and C.O.O.; Vicki J. Duncomb, V.P., C.F.O., and Secy.; Renee Jackson, V.P. and Genl. Counsel
Board of directors: James P. Dolan, Chair.; John C. Bergstrom; Anton J. Christianson; Lauren Rich Fine; Arthur F. Kingsbury; Jacques Massicotte; George J. Rossi; Gary H. Stern
Giving statement: Giving through the Dolan Media Foundation.
Company EIN: 522065604

Dolan Media Foundation

222 S. 9th St., Ste. 2300
Minneapolis, MN 55402-3363

Establishment information: Established in 2005 in MN.
Donors: Jim Dolan; Cherrytree Investments; David Michael Winton; Abry Partners, LLC.
Contact: Scott J. Pollei, Dir.
Financial data (yr. ended 12/31/11): Assets, $6,186 (M); gifts received, $4,175; expenditures, $5,525; qualifying distributions, $5,500; giving activities include $5,500 for grants to individuals.
Purpose and activities: The foundation awards relief grants to individuals for domestic abuse, tornado damage, and home foreclosures.
Type of support: Grants to individuals.
Geographic limitations: Giving primarily in MN.
Application information: Applications accepted. Proposals should detail financial hardship. Application form required.
Initial approach: Proposal
Deadline(s): None
Directors: James P. Dolan; Scott J. Pollei.
EIN: 204000022

1141
Dole Food Company, Inc.

1 Dole Dr.
Westlake Village, CA 91362-7300
(818) 879-6600
FAX: (302) 655-5049

Company URL: http://www.dole.com
Establishment information: Established in 1851.
Company type: Public company
Company ticker symbol and exchange: DOLE/NYSE
Business activities: Produces and markets fresh fruits, vegetables, and packaged foods.
Business type (SIC): Farms/fruit and nut; farms/vegetable and melon; specialty foods/canned, frozen, and preserved; groceries—wholesale
Financial profile for 2012: Number of employees, 34,800; assets, $4,229,770,000; sales volume, $4,246,710,000; pre-tax net income, $5,900,000; expenses, $4,230,120,000; liabilities, $3,543,640,000
Fortune 1000 ranking: 2012—372nd in revenues, 935th in profits, and 644th in assets
Corporate officers: David H. Murdock, Chair.; David A. DeLorenzo, Co-Pres. and C.E.O.; C. Michael Carter, Co-Pres. and C.O.O.; Joseph S. Tesoriero, Exec. V.P. and C.F.O.; Sue Hagen, Sr. V.P., Human Resources; Yoon J. Hugh, V.P., Cont., and C.A.O.
Board of directors: David H. Murdock, Chair.; C. Michael Carter; Elaine L. Chao; Andrew J. Conrad, Ph.D.; David A. DeLorenzo; E. Rolland Dickson, M.D.; Sherry Lansing; Justin Murdock; Dennis M. Weinberg
Subsidiaries: Dole Citrus & Deciduous Fruit, Bakersfield, CA; Dole Food Co., Honolulu, HI; Dole Food Co., Inc., Los Angeles, CA; Dole Fresh Fruit Co., Westlake Village, CA; Dole Fresh Vegetables, Salinas, CA; Dole Northwest, Wenatchee, WA; Dole Packaged Food Co., Westlake Village, CA
International operations: Bermuda; Canada; Chile; Costa Rica; Czech Republic; Ecuador; France; Germany; Honduras; Italy; Japan; Panama; South Africa; South Korea; Spain; Sweden; Thailand; United Kingdom
Giving statement: Giving through the Dole Food Company, Inc. Corporate Giving Program and the LG Corp.
Company EIN: 990035300

Dole Food Company, Inc. Corporate Giving Program

1 Dole Dr.
Westlake Village, CA 91362-7300 (818) 879-6600
URL: http://dolecrs.com/corporate-responsibility/

Purpose and activities: Dole Food Company makes charitable contributions to nonprofit organizations involved with nutrition education for children. Support is given to national organizations.
Fields of interest: Elementary/secondary education; Agriculture; Nutrition Children/youth.
Type of support: Donated products; General/operating support; In-kind gifts.
Geographic limitations: Giving to national organizations.
Support limitations: No support for political, religious, fraternal, lobbying, or athletic organizations. No grants to individuals, or for sponsorships or sporting events.
Application information: Applications accepted. Application form not required. Applicants should submit the following:

1) copy of IRS Determination Letter

Initial approach: Proposal to headquarters

1142
Dollar Bank, FSB

3 Gateway Ctr.
401 Liberty Ave., 9th Fl.
Pittsburgh, PA 15222 (412) 261-3098

Company URL: http://www.dollarbank.com
Establishment information: Established in 1855.
Company type: Private company
Business activities: Operates savings bank.
Business type (SIC): Savings institutions
Corporate officers: Robert P. Oeler, Pres. and C.E.O.; Joseph B. Smith, Sr. V.P., Mktg.
Giving statement: Giving through the Dollar Bank Foundation.

Dollar Bank Foundation

c/o Dollar Bank, Public Affairs Dept.
3 Gateway Ctr., Rm. 1E
Pittsburgh, PA 15222-1094

Establishment information: Established in 1998 in PA.
Donor: Dollar Bank, FSB.
Financial data (yr. ended 11/30/11): Assets, $6,295,907 (M); gifts received, $2,000,000; expenditures, $404,954; qualifying distributions, $397,721; giving activities include $397,721 for grants.
Purpose and activities: The foundation supports community foundations and organizations involved with arts and culture, education, water conservation, housing, human services, and community economic development.

Fields of interest: Museums; Performing arts, orchestras; Arts; Higher education; Education; Environment, water resources; Housing/shelter; Human services; Community development, neighborhood development; Community/economic development; Foundations (community); United Ways and Federated Giving Programs.
Type of support: Continuing support; General/operating support; Program development; Scholarship funds.
Geographic limitations: Giving primarily in areas of company operations in Cleveland, OH and Pittsburgh, PA.
Support limitations: No support for political, veterans', fraternal, labor, or religious organizations, hospitals, or health care delivery facilities. No grants to individuals, or for non-academic efforts at the elementary or high school level.
Publications: Application guidelines.
Application information: Applications accepted. Multi-year funding is not automatic. Application form not required. Applicants should submit the following:
1) principal source of support for project in the past
2) copy of IRS Determination Letter
3) explanation of why grantmaker is considered an appropriate donor for project
4) descriptive literature about organization
5) detailed description of project and amount of funding requested
6) copy of current year's organizational budget and/or project budget

Initial approach: Proposal
Deadline(s): None

Officers: Thomas A. Kobus, Pres.; James Carroll, V.P.; C. Andrew McGhee, Secy.; James T. Jurcic, Treas.
EIN: 251822243
Selected grants: The following grants are a representative sample of this grantmaker's funding activity:
$65,000 to United Way of Allegheny County, Pittsburgh, PA, 2010.
$50,000 to Pittsburgh Partnership for Neighborhood Development, Pittsburgh, PA, 2010.
$25,000 to Chatham University, Pittsburgh, PA, 2010.
$25,000 to Hill House Association, Pittsburgh, PA, 2010.
$20,000 to Pittsburgh Community Reinvestment Group, Pittsburgh, PA, 2010.
$12,500 to Cleveland Foundation, Cleveland, OH, 2010.
$10,000 to Cleveland Housing Network, Cleveland, OH, 2010.
$10,000 to Pittsburgh Symphony, Pittsburgh, PA, 2010.
$10,000 to Riverlife, Pittsburgh, PA, 2010.
$5,000 to Cleveland Zoological Society, Cleveland, OH, 2010.

1143
Dollar General Corporation

100 Mission Ridge
Goodlettsville, TN 37072-2171
(615) 855-4000
FAX: (615) 386-9936

Company URL: http://www.dollargeneral.com
Establishment information: Established in 1955.
Company type: Public company
Company ticker symbol and exchange: DG/NYSE
Business activities: Operates discount stores.
Business type (SIC): Apparel, piece goods, and notions—wholesale; appliances/household; auto and home supplies—retail; shoe stores; furniture and home furnishing stores
Financial profile for 2013: Number of employees, 90,500; assets, $10,367,680,000; sales volume, $16,022,130,000; pre-tax net income, $1,497,390,000; expenses, $14,366,850,000; liabilities, $5,382,350,000
Fortune 1000 ranking: 2012—175th in revenues, 206th in profits, and 376th in assets
Forbes 2000 ranking: 2012—588th in sales, 577th in profits, and 1445th in assets
Corporate officers: Richard W. Dreiling, Chair. and C.E.O.; David M. Tehle, Exec. V.P. and C.F.O.; Susan S. Lanigan, Exec. V.P. and Genl. Counsel; Anita C. Elliott, Sr. V.P. and Cont.
Board of directors: Richard W. Dreiling, Chair.; Raj Kumar Agrawal; Warren F. Bryant; Michael M. Calbert; Sandra B. Cochran; Patricia.D Fili-Krushel; Adrian M. Jones; William C. Rhodes III; David B. Rickard
International operations: Hong Kong
Giving statement: Giving through the Dollar General Corporation Contributions Program, the Dollar General Employee Assistance Foundation, and the Dollar General Literacy Foundation.
Company EIN: 610502302

Dollar General Corporation Contributions Program

100 Mission Ridge
Goodlettsville, TN 37072-2171 (615) 855-4000
URL: http://www2.dollargeneral.com/About-Us/Serving-Others/pages/DG-cares.aspx

Purpose and activities: As a complement to its foundation, Dollar General also makes charitable contributions to nonprofit organizations directly. Support is given primarily in areas of company operations.
Fields of interest: Health care; Disasters, preparedness/services; American Red Cross Military/veterans.
Type of support: Cause-related marketing; General/operating support; In-kind gifts.
Geographic limitations: Giving primarily in areas of company operations; giving also to national organizations.

Dollar General Employee Assistance Foundation

c/o Denine Torr
100 Mission Ridge
Goodlettsville, TN 37072-2171 (615) 855-5208

Establishment information: Established in 2006 in TN.
Donors: Dollar General Corp.; William Bass.
Financial data (yr. ended 01/31/10): Assets, $751,131 (M); gifts received, $483,545; expenditures, $339,697; qualifying distributions, $328,814; giving activities include $321,314 for 217 grants to individuals (high: $5,000; low: $214).
Purpose and activities: The foundation provides grants to general employees and their families who are experiencing financial hardship due to circumstances beyond their control.
Fields of interest: Economically disadvantaged.
Type of support: Emergency funds; Grants to individuals.
Application information: Applications not accepted. Contributes only through employee-related disaster relief grants.
Officers: Susan S. Lanigan, Pres.; Jeffrey Rice, Secy.; Anita C. Elliott, Treas.
Director: Kathleen Guion.
EIN: 611492355

Dollar General Literacy Foundation

100 Mission Ridge
Goodlettsville, TN 37072-2170 (615) 855-5208
URL: http://www.dgliteracy.com/mission/

Establishment information: Established in 1993 in TN.
Financial data (yr. ended 01/31/12): Revenue, $12,649,349; assets, $28,497,964 (M); gifts received, $12,575,824; expenditures, $11,599,812; program services expenses, $11,512,946; giving activities include $11,503,872 for grants.
Purpose and activities: The foundation fosters the advancement of adult literacy.
Fields of interest: Adult education—literacy, basic skills & GED.

Programs:

Adult Literacy Grants Program: Through this program, the foundation supports programs designed to provide direct service to adults in need of literacy assistance in the instructional areas of adult basic education, general education diploma preparation, or English for speakers of other languages. Grants will be awarded for up to $20,000.

Back-to-School Grants: These grants provide funding of up to $5,000 to assist schools in meeting some of the financial challenges they face in implementing new programs or purchasing new equipment, materials, or software for their school library or literacy program. Funds must be used to enhance or expand the school's library, media center, or literacy programs. Eligible programs or projects may target new readers, below-grade-level readers, readers with learning disabilities, or general literacy.

Beyond Words: The Dollar General School Library Relief Program: In collaboration with the American Library Association, the American Association of School Librarians and the National Education Association, the foundation operates a school library disaster relief fund for public school libraries in the states served by Dollar General. The fund will provide grants to public schools whose school library program has been affected by a disaster. Grants are to replace or supplement books, media, and/or library equipment in the school library setting. For more information, visit http://www.ala.org/ala/aasl/aaslawards/dollargeneral/disasterrelief.cfm.

Family Literacy Grants Program: Through this program, the foundation will award grants to direct family literacy service providers. Eligible family literacy programs must have the following four components: adult education instruction; children's education; parent and child together time (PACT); and parenting classes that teach parents to be the primary teacher for their child. Grants of up to $20,000 will be awarded.

Waiting List Reduction Grants: This program provides funding of up to $10,000 to adult literacy organizations to address student waiting list reduction efforts. Eligible nonprofit organizations must provide direct services to adults in need of literacy assistance in one of the following instructional areas: adult basic education, general educational development (GED) diploma preparation, and English as a second language. Applicants must be a qualified 501(c)(3) organization with a valid IRS tax ID, a K-12 private or public school, a college or university, or a public library.

Youth Literacy Grants: These grants provide funding to schools, public libraries, and nonprofit organizations to help with the implementation or expansion of literacy programs for students who are below grade level or experiencing difficulty reading. Grants of up to $3,000 will be awarded.

Geographic limitations: Giving on a national basis.
Support limitations: No support for political candidates or organizations, or private charities or foundations. No grants to individuals, or for endowments, capital campaigns, film or video projects, the purchase of vehicles, advertising, construction or building costs, general fundraising events, or political causes or campaigns.
Publications: Application guidelines.
Application information: Applications accepted. Application form required.
Deadline(s): Varies
Final notification: Feb. 29 and Oct. 30 for Youth Literacy Grants; within eight weeks for School Library Relief Program
Officers: Cal Turner, Pres.; Jeffrey Rice, V.P.; Susan Lanigan, Secy. and Genl. Counsel; Barbara Springer, Treas.
EIN: 621546736

1144
Dollar Thrifty Automotive Group, Inc.

5330 E. 31st St.
Tulsa, OK 74135 (918) 660-7700
FAX: (302) 655-5049

Company URL: http://www.dtag.com
Establishment information: Established in 1997.
Company type: Public company
Company ticker symbol and exchange: DTG/NYSE
Business activities: Rents automobiles. The company is in the process of merging with Hertz Global Holdings, Inc.
Business type (SIC): Motor vehicle rentals and leasing
Financial profile for 2011: Number of employees, 5,900; assets, $2,615,670,000; sales volume, $1,548,930,000; pre-tax net income, $261,240,000; expenses, $1,287,690,000; liabilities, $2,007,990,000
Corporate officers: Scott L. Thompson, Chair., Pres., and C.E.O.; H. Clifford Buster III, Sr. Exec. V.P., C.F.O., and Treas.; Rick Morris, Exec. V.P. and C.I.O.; Vicki J. Vaniman, Exec. V.P., Genl. Counsel, and Secy.
Board of directors: Scott L. Thompson, Chair.; Thomas P. Capo; Maryann N. Keller; Edward C. Lumley; Richard W. Neu; John C. Pope
Subsidiaries: Dollar Rent A Car Systems, Inc., Tulsa, OK; Thrifty, Inc., Tulsa, OK
Giving statement: Giving through the Dollar Thrifty Community Driven.
Company EIN: 731356520

Dollar Thrifty Community Driven

5330 E. 31st St.
Tulsa, OK 74135-5076
URL: http://www.dtag.com/phoenix.zhtml?c=71946&p=irol-communitydriven

Purpose and activities: Dollar Thrifty makes charitable contributions to organizations involved with education, healthcare, food services, housing, youth development, and senior citizen services. Support is given primarily in areas of company operations, with some emphasis on Oklahoma.
Fields of interest: Education, alliance/advocacy; Health care, blood supply; Food banks; Housing/shelter; Athletics/sports, Special Olympics; Big Brothers/Big Sisters; Boy scouts; Girl scouts; Youth development, business; American Red Cross; YM/YWCAs & YM/YWHAs; Aging, centers/services; Human services; General charitable giving.
Type of support: Employee volunteer services; General/operating support.
Geographic limitations: Giving primarily in areas of company operations, with some emphasis on OK; giving also to national organizations.

1145
Dollar Tree, Inc.

(formerly Dollar Tree Stores, Inc.)
500 Volvo Pkwy.
Chesapeake, VA 23320 (757) 321-5000
FAX: (757) 855-5555

Company URL: http://www.dollartree.com
Establishment information: Established in 1953.
Company type: Public company
Company ticker symbol and exchange: DLTR/NASDAQ
Business activities: Operates discount stores.
Business type (SIC): Variety stores
Financial profile for 2013: Number of employees, 81,920; assets, $2,752,000,000; sales volume, $7,394,500,000; pre-tax net income, $978,900,000; expenses, $6,474,400,000; liabilities, $1,084,700,000
Fortune 1000 ranking: 2012—346th in revenues, 285th in profits, and 781st in assets
Forbes 2000 ranking: 2012—1151st in sales, 975th in profits, and 1948th in assets
Corporate officers: Macon F. Brock, Jr., Chair.; Bob Sasser, Pres. and C.E.O.; Gary M. Philbin, C.O.O.; Kevin S. Wampler, C.F.O.; James A. Gorry III, Genl. Counsel and Corp. Secy.; J. Douglas Perry, Chair. Emeritus
Board of directors: Macon F. Brock, Jr., Chair.; Arnold S. Barron; Mary Anne Citrino; H. Ray Compton; Conrad M. Hall; Lemuel E. Lewis; J. Douglas Perry; Bob Sasser; Thomas A. Saunders III; Thomas E. Whiddon; Carl P. Zeithaml
Giving statement: Giving through the Dollar Tree, Inc. Corporate Giving Program.
Company EIN: 262018846

Dollar Tree, Inc. Corporate Giving Program

c/o Corp. Giving
500 Volvo Pkwy.
Chesapeake, VA 23320-1604
URL: http://www.dollartree.com/custserv/custserv.jsp?pageName=Corporate_Giving&parentName=About

Purpose and activities: Dollar Tree makes charitable contributions to nonprofit organizations involved with arts and culture, education, the environment, children, military organizations, gift distribution, and the economically disadvantaged. Support is given primarily in areas of company operations, with emphasis on Chesapeake, Hampton, Newport News, Norfolk, Portsmouth, Suffolk, and Virginia Beach, Virginia.
Fields of interest: Arts; Child development, education; Environmental education; Environment; Children, services; Human services, gift distribution; Military/veterans' organizations Economically disadvantaged.
Type of support: Employee volunteer services; General/operating support; Scholarship funds.
Geographic limitations: Giving primarily in areas of company operations, with emphasis on Chesapeake, Hampton, Newport News, Norfolk, Portsmouth, Suffolk, and Virginia Beach, VA.
Support limitations: No support for individual K-12 schools, or for membership, religious, political, labor, international, or fraternal organizations. No grants to individuals, including student exchange programs, family reunions, memorials, or benefits, or for merchandise, discounts, gift certificates, or giveaways, donations of returned, damaged, or excess merchandise, sponsorship, or fundraising for special events such as auctions, raffles, luncheons and dinners, carnivals, or sporting events, individual K-12 school events such as proms, graduations, or PTO/PTA groups, conferences, seminars, capital campaigns, construction, or renovation projects, international projects, or film, video, or research projects.
Publications: Application guidelines.
Application information: Applications accepted. No telephoned, faxed, or e-mailed requests will be considered. Proposals should be submitted using organization letterhead. No merchandise donations, discounts, or gift certificates. Application form not required. Applicants should submit the following:
1) name, address and phone number of organization
2) copy of IRS Determination Letter
3) brief history of organization and description of its mission
4) explanation of why grantmaker is considered an appropriate donor for project
5) detailed description of project and amount of funding requested
6) contact person
7) copy of current year's organizational budget and/or project budget
8) listing of additional sources and amount of support

Proposals should include fax number, and website address.
Initial approach: Mail completed proposal to headquarters
Final notification: Only successful applicants will be notified

1146
The Dollywood Company

2700 Dollywood Parks Blvd.
Pigeon Forge, TN 37863-4102
(865) 428-9890

Company URL: http://www.dollywood.com
Establishment information: Established in 1986.
Company type: Subsidiary of a private company
Business activities: Operates theme park.
Business type (SIC): Amusement and recreation services/miscellaneous
Corporate officers: Ken Bell, Pres.; Rick Baker, V.P., Mktg.
Giving statement: Giving through the Dollywood Foundation.

The Dollywood Foundation

2700 Dollywood Parks Blvd.
Pigeon Forge, TN 37863-4113 (865) 428-9606
FAX: (865) 428-9612;
E-mail: ddotson@dollyfoundation.com; URL: http://www.imaginationlibrary.com/

Establishment information: Established in 1988 in TN.
Contact: David C. Dotson, Pres.
Financial data (yr. ended 12/31/11): Revenue, $1,736,176; assets, $9,817,530 (M); gifts received, $1,345,979; expenditures, $1,150,815; program services expenses, $984,574; giving activities include $34,390 for grants and $61,875 for 16 grants to individuals.
Purpose and activities: The foundation develops and administers educational programs for the

children of Sevier County to inspire them to dream more, learn more, do more, and be more.
Fields of interest: Education, early childhood education.
Program:
Dollywood Foundation Scholarships: Nine college scholarships, three per each Sevier County high school (Gatlinburg-Pitman High School, Sevier County High School, and Seymour High School), are awarded annually to graduating seniors in the following areas: music ($1,500), academic achievement ($1,200), and environment ($1,000). A faculty committee at each high school selects the winners among their students.
Type of support: Scholarships—to individuals.
Geographic limitations: Giving limited to Sevier County, TN.
Publications: Annual report.
Application information: Applications not accepted. Contributes only to pre-selected organizations.
Board meeting date(s): Quarterly
Officers and Directors:* Dolly Parton*, Chair.; Ted C. Miller*, Vice-Chair.; David C. Dotson*, Pres. and Exec. Dir.; Ken Bell*, V.P.; Barbara Joines*, Secy.-Treas..; Jo Blalock; Charles W. Kite; Edna Rogers; Ann Warden.
Number of staff: 3 full-time professional.
EIN: 621348105

1147
Dolphins Enterprises, LLC

(also known as Miami Dolphins)
7500 S.W. 30th St.
Davie, FL 33314-1020 (954) 452-7000

Company URL: http://www.miamidolphins.com
Establishment information: Established in 1965.
Company type: Private company
Business activities: Operates professional football club.
Business type (SIC): Commercial sports
Corporate officers: Stephen M. Ross, Chair.; Jorge Perez, Co-Vice-Chair.; Donald F. Shula, Co-Vice-Chair.; Mike Dee, C.E.O.; Mark Brockelman, Sr. V.P., C.F.O., and C.A.O.; Bill Galante, Sr. V.P., Opers.; George Torres, V.P., Sales
Board of directors: Stephen M. Ross, Chair.; Jorge Perez, Co-Vice-Chair.; Donald F. Shula, Co-Vice-Chair.
Giving statement: Giving through the Miami Dolphins Corporate Giving Program and the South Florida Sports Foundation, Inc.

Miami Dolphins Corporate Giving Program

c/o Community Rels. Dept.
7500 S.W. 30th St.
Fort Lauderdale, FL 33314-1020
URL: http://prod.www.dolphins.clubs.nfl.com/community/foundation.html

Purpose and activities: As a complement to its foundation, the Miami Dolphins also make charitable contributions to nonprofit organizations involved with children and on a case by case basis. Support is given primarily in Florida.
Fields of interest: Elementary/secondary education; Child development, education; Education, reading; Youth, services; Community/economic development; General charitable giving.
Type of support: In-kind gifts.
Geographic limitations: Giving primarily in FL.
Application information: Applications accepted. Proposals should be submitted using organization letterhead. Support is limited to 1 contribution per organization during any given year. Application form not required. Applicants should submit the following:
1) population served
2) geographic area to be served
Proposals should indicate the date, time, and location of the event; and specifically note the nature of the request being made.
Initial approach: Proposal to headquarters
Copies of proposal: 1
Deadline(s): 6 to 8 weeks prior to need

South Florida Sports Foundation, Inc.

(doing business as Miami Dolphins Foundation)
347 Don Shula Dr.
Miami Gardens, FL 33056 (305) 943-8000

Establishment information: Established in 1995 in FL.
Financial data (yr. ended 12/31/11): Revenue, $2,364,675; assets, $3,097,166 (M); gifts received, $1,027,948; expenditures, $2,042,941; giving activities include $1,562,940 for grants.
Purpose and activities: The foundation is committed to the betterment of south Florida youth through a direct focus on, but not limited to, educational, health, social, and community service issues.
Fields of interest: Education; Health care; Boys & girls clubs; Urban League; United Ways and Federated Giving Programs.
Geographic limitations: Giving limited to south FL.
Officers: Stephen M. Ross*, Chair.; Martin Edelman*, V.P.; Ronald Katz*, V.P. and Secy.-Treas.; Kara Ross*, V.P.
EIN: 650575416

1148
Dominion Chevrolet Company

12050 W. Broad St.
Richmond, VA 23233 (804) 364-4500
FAX: (804) 524-3540

Company URL: http://www.dominionautogroup.com
Establishment information: Established in 1973.
Company type: Private company
Business activities: Operates car dealership.
Business type (SIC): Motor vehicles—retail
Corporate officers: J. Ted Linhart, Chair. and C.E.O.; Clements W. John, Pres.; Barbara Angelotti, C.F.O. and Cont.
Board of director: J. Ted Linhart, Chair.
Giving statement: Giving through the Linhart Foundation.

The Linhart Foundation

c/o J. Theodore Linhart
12050 W. Broad St.
Richmond, VA 23233-1001

Establishment information: Established in DE and VA.
Donors: Thelma K. Lindemann†; Dominion Chevrolet Co.; The Linhart Co.
Financial data (yr. ended 12/31/11): Assets, $1,035,102 (M); gifts received, $10,000; expenditures, $80,665; qualifying distributions, $67,500; giving activities include $67,500 for grants.
Purpose and activities: The foundation supports orchestras, food banks, and police agencies and organizations involved with animal welfare, cancer, diabetes, and human services and awards college scholarships to high school seniors attending Douglas Southall Freeman and John Randolph Tucker high schools in Richmond, Virginia.
Fields of interest: Education; Human services; Religion.
Type of support: General/operating support; Program development; Scholarships—to individuals.
Geographic limitations: Giving primarily in Richmond, VA.
Application information: Applications accepted. Application form required.
Initial approach: Letter
Deadline(s): None
Officer: J. Theodore Linhart, Pres. and Secy.
Directors: C.F. Johnson; E.K. Johnson; Marilyn Moses.
EIN: 540846082

1149
Dominion Homes, Inc.

4900 Tuttle Crossing Blvd.
Dublin, OH 43016-5555 (614) 356-5000
FAX: (614) 356-6010

Company URL: http://www.dominionhomes.com
Establishment information: Established in 1955.
Company type: Private company
Business activities: Builds houses.
Business type (SIC): Contractors/general residential building
Financial profile for 2010: Number of employees, 193
Corporate officers: Douglas D. Borror, Chair.; David Borror, Vice-Chair.; William G. Cornely, Pres., and C.E.O.; Michael A. Archer, Sr. V.P., Sales and Opers.; Terry E. George, Sr. V.P. and Treas.; Beth A Patton, V.P., Admin.
Board of directors: Douglas D. Borror, Chair.; David Borror, Vice-Chair.
Giving statement: Giving through the Dominion Homes-Borror Family Foundation.
Company EIN: 311393233

Dominion Homes-Borror Family Foundation

c/o The Columbus Fdn.
1234 E. Broad St.
Columbus, OH 43205-1453 (614) 251-4000
URL: http://columbusfoundation.org/giving/foundations/dominion-homes-borror/

Establishment information: Established in 2004 in OH; supporting organization of the Columbus Foundation.
Financial data (yr. ended 12/31/11): Revenue, $34,520; assets, $987,928 (M); expenditures, $47,063; giving activities include $18,900 for grants.
Fields of interest: Education; Public health; Youth development; Human services; Urban/community development; Social entrepreneurship; Community/economic development.
Geographic limitations: Giving limited to Ashley and Columbus, OH.
Application information: Applications not accepted. Contributes only to pre-selected organizations; unsolicited requests for funds not considered or acknowledged.
Trustees: Douglas G. Borror; Stephen P. Close; Denis Connor; Jodi Larson; John S. Sokol.
EIN: 200523484

1150
Dominion Resources, Inc.
120 Tredegar St.
Richmond, VA 23219-4306 (804) 819-2000
FAX: (804) 775-5819

Company URL: http://www.dom.com
Establishment information: Established in 1983.
Company type: Public company
Company ticker symbol and exchange: D/NYSE
International Securities Identification Number: US25746U1097
Business activities: Operates holding company; generates, transmits, and distributes electricity; transmits and distributes natural gas.
Business type (SIC): Combination utility services; electric services
Financial profile for 2012: Number of employees, 15,500; assets, $46,838,000,000; sales volume, $13,093,000,000; pre-tax net income, $497,000,000; expenses, $11,937,000,000; liabilities, $36,013,000,000
Fortune 1000 ranking: 2012—210th in revenues, 467th in profits, and 119th in assets
Forbes 2000 ranking: 2012—741st in sales, 1494th in profits, and 491st in assets
Corporate officers: Thomas F. Farrell II, Chair., Pres., and C.E.O.; Mark F. McGettrick, Exec. V.P. and C.F.O.; Steven A. Rogers, Sr. V.P. and C.I.O.; G. Scott Hetzer, Sr. V.P. and Treas.; Carter M. Reid, V.P., Gen. Counsel, and Corp. Secy.; Ashwini Sawhney, V.P. and Cont.
Board of directors: Thomas E. Farrell II, Chair.; William P. Barr; Peter W. Brown, M.D.; Helen E. Dragas; James O. Ellis; John W. Harris; Robert S. Jepson, Jr.; Mark J. Kington; Pamela J. Royal, M.D.; Robert H. Spilman, Jr.; Michael E. Szymanczyk; David A. Wollard
Subsidiaries: Consolidated Natural Gas Company, Pittsburgh, PA; Dominion Capital, Inc., Richmond, VA; Dominion Energy, Inc., Richmond, VA; The East Ohio Gas Company, Cleveland, OH; Virginia Electric and Power Company, Richmond, VA
Giving statement: Giving through the Dominion Resources, Inc. Corporate Giving Program and the Dominion Foundation.
Company EIN: 541229715

Dominion Resources, Inc. Corporate Giving Program
P.O. Box 26532
Richmond, VA 23261-6532 (804) 771-4795
URL: http://www.dom.com/about/community/index.jsp

Purpose and activities: As a complement to its foundation, Dominion Resources also makes charitable contributions to nonprofit organizations directly. Support is given primarily in areas of company operations in northeastern North Carolina, Ohio, Virginia, and West Virginia, and in select locations in New England, the Midwest, and the Mid-Atlantic.
Fields of interest: Arts, cultural/ethnic awareness; Education; Environment, natural resources; Environment, energy; Health care, clinics/centers; Health care; Food services; Housing/shelter, services; Housing/shelter, repairs; Human services; Aging, centers/services; Civil/human rights, equal rights; Community development, neighborhood development; United Ways and Federated Giving Programs Economically disadvantaged.
Programs:
Dominion Memorial Scholarship Fund: Dominion awards six college scholarships of up to $5,000 to children or grandchildren of employees of Dominion. The awards are given in honor of the Virginia Tech shootings which claimed the lives of three college students whose parents or grandparents worked for Dominion.
EnergyShare: Dominion provides heating assistance in the winter months and cooling assistance in the summer for the elderly, the ill, and anyone who faces financial hardships from unemployment or family crisis. The company provides a one-time payment for any heating source, including oil, gas, kerosene, wood, and electricity. The program is limited to North Carolina, Ohio, and Virginia.
Strong Men and Women: Excellence in Leadership: Dominion supports an educational series to provide youth with positive role models, African-American men and women whose accomplishments and determination demonstrates excellence in leadership. The company annually distributes curriculum sets during Black History Month to schools and libraries located in areas of company operations. The program also includes a writing contest for high school juniors and seniors in Dominion's North Carolina, Ohio, and Virginia operating regions, who submit essays on the achievements of outstanding African-Americans featured in the series. Student winners receive a commemorative plaque of the essay and a laptop computer. In addition, each winner's school receives a $1,000 cash award. The "Strong Men and Women: Excellence in Leadership" series will become part of a new partnership with the Library of Virginia's Black History program "African American Trailblazers in Virginia History" in 2013.
Type of support: Curriculum development; Employee volunteer services; General/operating support; Program development; Technical assistance.
Geographic limitations: Giving primarily in areas of company operations in northeastern NC, OH, VA, and WV, and in select locations in New England, the Midwest, and the Mid-Atlantic.

Dominion Foundation
(formerly Consolidated Natural Gas Company Foundation)
501 Martindale St., Ste. 400
Pittsburgh, PA 15212-5835 (412) 237-2973
FAX: (412) 690-7608; Tel. for Dominion Educational Partnership: (800) 730-7217, e-mail: Educational_Grants@dom.com; URL: http://www.dom.com/about/community/charitable-giving-and-the-dominion-foundation.jsp

Establishment information: Established about 1985 in PA.
Donors: Consolidated Natural Gas Co.; Dominion Resources, Inc.; Peoples Natural Gas Co.; Dominion Energy, Inc.; Dominion Energy New England; Dominion Transmission.
Contact: James C. Mesloh, Exec. Dir.
Financial data (yr. ended 12/31/11): Assets, $36,273,623 (M); expenditures, $15,624,115; qualifying distributions, $15,140,383; giving activities include $13,572,135 for 1,270 grants (high: $500,000; low: $500) and $1,568,248 for 1,487 employee matching gifts.
Purpose and activities: The foundation supports organizations involved with arts and culture, education, the environment, health, human services, community development, and civic affairs.
Fields of interest: Museums; Performing arts, dance; Performing arts, theater; Arts; Elementary/secondary education; Business school/education; Engineering school/education; Libraries (public); Education; Environment, natural resources; Environment, energy; Environmental education; Environment; Health care; Food services; Food banks; Recreation, parks/playgrounds; Homeless, human services; Human services; Civil/human rights, equal rights; Economic development; Business/industry; Community/economic development; Science, formal/general education; Mathematics; Engineering/technology; Engineering; Economics; Public affairs.
Programs:
Civic and Community Development: The foundation supports programs designed to improve the amenities that make a place livable; create an environment for new business development; foster appreciation of diversity; and stimulate neighborhood revitalization.
Community Impact Awards: The foundation, in partnership with Inside Business Magazine, recognizes organizations that have made major contributions to the economic and social revitalization of communities within the Dominion East Ohio service area. The award includes a cash grant and winners will be featured in an issue of Inside Business Magazine.
Culture and the Arts: The foundation supports programs designed to promote a wide range of cultural activities, including music, theater, dance, libraries, parks, and museums to enrich the mind and improve the quality of life within communities.
Dominion Higher Educational Partnership: The foundation awards grants of up to $50,000 to post-secondary programs designed to develop a skilled workforce in areas critical to Dominion. Special emphasis directed toward projects designed to address business, including business practices, accounting, finance, or accounting; craft, including welding trades, power line, or pipeline construction or maintenance; engineering, including chemical, civil, electrical, mechanical, petroleum and natural gas, or nuclear engineering; environment, including environmental sciences and study; energy, including exploration of alternative energies or student-led conservation; and technical, including information systems, electronics, control trades, power plant operations, and electrical technicians.
Dominion K-12 Educational Partnership: The foundation awards grants to programs designed to strengthen K-12 math and science education through the study of energy and the environment. Grants are awarded for environmental education projects designed to develop math and/or science skills through the study of the environment; and energy projects designed to increase student's awareness of energy efficiency and conservation, energy sources, or other energy-related topics. Grants range from $1,000 to $10,000 depending on project scope and focus and the number of children and/or classes involved.
Education: The foundation supports programs designed to promote quality education to ensure a strong successful education system; and programs designed to promote youth, society's most valuable natural resource.
Employee Matching Gifts: The foundation matches contributions made by full-time employees, directors, and retirees of Dominion Resources to nonprofit organizations on a one-for-one basis, up to $5,000 per donor, per year. The foundation also provides a once-a-year two-for-one volunteer match for employees who serve on the board of a qualified charity or have volunteered 50 hours on the organization's behalf during the previous 12 months.
Environment: The foundation supports programs designed to engage in environmental stewardship and education; and protect natural resources.
Health and Human Services: The foundation supports programs designed to meet critical needs at the local level and strengthen the community through health and human services.

Type of support: Annual campaigns; Building/renovation; Capital campaigns; Conferences/seminars; Continuing support; Curriculum development; Employee matching gifts; Equipment; General/operating support; In-kind gifts; Matching/challenge support; Program development.
Geographic limitations: Giving primarily in areas of company operations in Colchester, East Lyme, Groton, Ledyard, Montville, New London, North Stonington, Norwich, Old Lyme, Salem, Stonington, and Waterford, CT, Christian, Montgomery, Sangamon and Will, IL, Lake County, IN, Fall River, Lynn, Marblehead, Salem, Somerset, Swansea, and Westport, MA, Calvert, Charles, Prince George's, and St. Mary's counties, MD, Beaufort, Bertie, Camden, Chowan, Currituck, Dare, Edgecombe, Gates, Halifax, Hertford, Hyde, Martin, Nash, Northampton, Pasquotank, Perquimans, Pitt, Tyrell, Warren, and Washington counties, and the cities of Roanoke Rapids and Weldon, NC, Allegany, St. Lawrence, and Oneida, NY, Allen, Ashland, Ashtabula, Auglaize, Belmont, Carroll, Columbiana, Cuyahoga, Geauga, Guernsey, Jefferson, Hardin, Harrison, Holmes, Knox, Lake, Mahoning, Medina, Mercer, Monroe, Noble, Paulding, Portage, Putman, Shelby, Stark, Summit, Trumbull, Tuscarawas, Van Wert, Washington, and Wayne, OH, Allegheny, Armstrong, Beaver, Berks, Blair, Bucks, Butler, Cambria, Cameron, Carbon, Centre, Chester, Clarion, Clearfield, Clinton, Columbia, Crawford, Cumberland, Dauphin, Delaware, Elk, Fayette, Franklin, Greene, Huntingdon, Indiana, Jefferson, Juniata, Lackawanna, Lancaster, Lawrence, Lebanon, Lehigh, Luzerne, Lycoming, McKean, Mercer, Mifflin, Monroe, Montgomery, Montour, Northampton, Northumberland, Perry, Philadelphia, Pike, Potter, Schuylkill, Snyder, Somerset, Tioga, Union, Venango, Washington, Wayne, Westmoreland, and York, PA, Bristol, Cranston, Kingston, Providence, and Pawtucket, RI, VA, Brown, Kewaunee, and Manitowoc, WI, and WV.
Support limitations: No support for churches or other sectarian organizations, fraternal, political, advocacy, or labor organizations, or discriminatory organizations. No grants to individuals, or for religious programs, general operating support for individual United Way agencies, fundraising events, golf tournaments or other sporting events, benefit or courtesy advertising, travel or student trips or tours, or memorial campaigns; no university research projects or endowed chairs.
Publications: Application guidelines; Program policy statement.
Application information: Applications accepted. Grants generally range from $1,000 to $15,000, however higher amounts may be awarded. A password to access an online application form will be sent following receipt of a passing eligibility quiz. Proposals should be no longer than 3 pages for Dominion Educational Partnership. Funding requests are reviewed and approved by regional committees. Multi-year funding is not automatic. Organizations receiving support are asked to provide a final report. Applicants should submit the following:
1) how project will be sustained once grantmaker support is completed
2) results expected from proposed grant
3) population served
4) copy of IRS Determination Letter
5) copy of most recent annual report/audited financial statement/990
6) how project's results will be evaluated or measured
7) listing of board of directors, trustees, officers and other key people and their affiliations
8) listing of additional sources and amount of support

Visit website for detailed contact and application information.
Initial approach: Complete online eligibility quiz; complete online application and proposal for Dominion Educational Partnership
Copies of proposal: 1
Board meeting date(s): Quarterly
Deadline(s): None; May 1 for Dominion Educational Partnership
Final notification: 2 to 6 months; July 16 for Dominion Educational Partnership
Officers and Directors:* Virginia M. Board*, Pres.; Marjorie N. Grier*, V.P.; James C. Mesloh*, Exec. Dir.; Robert M. Blue; David A. Christian; William C. Hall, Jr.; Paul D. Koonce; Mark F. McGettrick; S. A. Rogers; Gary L. Sypolt.
Trustee: The Bank of New York Mellon.
Number of staff: 6 full-time professional; 3 full-time support.
EIN: 136077762
Selected grants: The following grants are a representative sample of this grantmaker's funding activity:
$500,000 to Virginia Museum of Fine Arts Foundation, Richmond, VA, 2011. For Top Ten Fund.
$250,000 to Nature Conservancy, Virginia Office, Charlottesville, VA, 2011.
$250,000 to State Fair of Virginia, Doswell, VA, 2011. For SFVA Campaign for The Meadow.
$250,000 to Virginia Union University, Richmond, VA, 2011. For Agenda for a New Era of Excellence Campaign.
$200,000 to United Way of Greater Richmond and Petersburg, Richmond, VA, 2011. For Annual Community Support.
$150,000 to SeniorNavigator.com, Richmond, VA, 2011. For disAbilityNavigator Statewide Expansion.
$125,000 to Metropolitan Richmond Sports Backers, Richmond, VA, 2011. For Dominion Riverrock.
$10,000 to Progressive Arts Alliance, Cleveland, OH, 2011. For Energy PSAs Project.
$5,000 to Southwest Virginia Community College Educational Foundation, Richlands, VA, 2011. For Scholarships for the Future.
$5,000 to U.S.S. Massachusetts Memorial Committee, Fall River, MA, 2011. For Battleship Cove Community Boating.

1151
Domino's Pizza, Inc.

30 Frank Lloyd Wright Dr.
P.O. Box 997
Ann Arbor, MI 48106-0997 (734) 930-3030
FAX: (734) 930-4346

Company URL: http://www.dominosbiz.com
Establishment information: Established in 1960.
Company type: Public company
Company ticker symbol and exchange: DPZ/NYSE
Business activities: Operates pizza delivery shops.
Business type (SIC): Restaurants and drinking places
Financial profile for 2012: Number of employees, 10,000; assets, $478,200,000; sales volume, $1,678,440,000; pre-tax net income, $181,190,000; expenses, $1,396,110,000; liabilities, $1,813,720,000
Corporate officers: David A. Brandon, Chair.; J. Patrick Doyle, Pres. and C.E.O.; Michael Lawton, Exec. V.P. and C.F.O.; Kevin Vasconi, Exec. V.P. and C.I.O.; Kenneth B. Rollin, Exec. V.P. and Genl. Counsel; Lynn M. Liddle, Exec. V.P., Comms.
Board of directors: David A. Brandon, Chair.; Andrew B. Balson; Diana F. Cantor; J. Patrick Doyle; Richard A. Federico; James A. Goldman; Bud O. Hamilton; Gregory A. Trojan
Subsidiaries: Domino's, Inc., Ann Arbor, MI; Domino's Pizza LLC, Ann Arbor, MI
Giving statement: Giving through the Domino's Pizza, Inc. Corporate Giving Program and the Domino's Pizza Partners Foundation.
Company EIN: 382511577

Domino's Pizza, Inc. Corporate Giving Program

c/o Community Rels.
30 Frank Lloyd Wright Dr.
P.O. Box 997
Ann Arbor, MI 48106-0997 (734) 930-3030
FAX: (734) 930-4346;
E-mail: communitygiving@dominos.com;
URL: http://www.dominosbiz.com/Biz-Public-EN/Site+Content/Secondary/About+Dominos/Community/

Purpose and activities: Domino's makes charitable contributions of pizza to nonprofit organizations on a case by case basis. Support is given primarily in areas of company operations, with emphasis on southeastern Michigan.
Fields of interest: General charitable giving.
Type of support: Donated products.
Geographic limitations: Giving primarily in areas of company operations, with emphasis on southeastern MI.
Application information: Applications accepted. Application form not required.
Proposals should include the date, time, location, and expected attendance of the event.
Initial approach: Mail proposal to nearest company store; for organizations located in the southeastern MI area, e-mail or fax proposal to headquarters
Deadline(s): 1 month prior to event
Final notification: 2 weeks

Domino's Pizza Partners Foundation

30 Frank Lloyd Wright Dr.
Ann Arbor, MI 48106-0997 (734) 930-3297
E-mail: partners@dominos.com; Toll-free fax: (800) 253-8182; URL: http://www.dominosbiz.com/Biz-Public-EN/Site+Content/Secondary/About+Dominos/Community/

Establishment information: Established in 1986 in GA.
Financial data (yr. ended 12/31/11): Revenue, $1,327,669; assets, $3,627,285 (M); gifts received, $1,171,446; expenditures, $1,209,264; program services expenses, $1,036,157; giving activities include $850,382 for grants to individuals.
Purpose and activities: The foundation was established to assist Domino's Pizza team members in time of special need or tragedy as a result of natural disaster, unexpected afflictions, on-the-job accidents, and other emergencies.
Fields of interest: Employment; Human services, emergency aid.
Type of support: Grants to individuals.
Geographic limitations: Giving on a worldwide basis.
Application information: Applications not accepted. Contributes only through employee-related emergency grants.
Officers and Trustees:* Jim Stansik*, Chair.; Dana Stearns, Exec. Dir.; Julie Hepler; Ray Montez; Alan Murph; Mike Orcutt; Anthony Osani; Osman Qasim; George Ralph; Cory Whittle.
EIN: 581703733

1152
Don McGill Toyota, Inc.
21555 Katy Freeway
Katy, TX 77450-1802 (832) 772-1000
FAX: (832) 772-1097

Company URL: http://www.donmcgilltoyotakaty.com
Establishment information: Established in 1970.
Company type: Private company
Business activities: Operates auto dealerships.
Business type (SIC): Motor vehicles—retail
Corporate officers: Raymond Lott, Mgr.; Allen Simmer, Mgr.; Brandon Sine, Mgr.
Giving statement: Giving through the Donald Ray McGill, Jr. Agape Foundation.

The Donald Ray McGill, Jr. Agape Foundation
21555 Katy Freeway
Katy, TX 77450-1802

Donor: Don McGill Toyota, Inc.
Financial data (yr. ended 12/31/11): Assets, $18,659 (M); gifts received, $25,000; expenditures, $33,060; qualifying distributions, $33,060; giving activities include $33,000 for 3 grants to individuals (high: $11,000; low: $11,000).
International interests: Romania.
Geographic limitations: Giving primarily in TX.
Application information: Applications not accepted. Unsolicited requests for funds not accepted.
Directors: Donald R. McGill; John O. McGill.
EIN: 760671332

1153
Donaldson Company, Inc.
1400 W. 94th St.
Minneapolis, MN 55431-2370
(952) 887-3131

Company URL: http://www.donaldson.com
Establishment information: Established in 1915.
Company type: Public company
Company ticker symbol and exchange: DCI/NYSE
Business activities: Manufactures pollution control and filtration equipment.
Business type (SIC): Machinery/industrial and commercial
Financial profile for 2012: Number of employees, 13,000; assets, $1,730,080,000; sales volume, $2,493,250,000; pre-tax net income, $370,780,000; expenses, $2,130,230,000; liabilities, $820,070,000
Fortune 1000 ranking: 2012—812th in revenues, 508th in profits, and 887th in assets
Corporate officers: William M. Cook, Chair., Pres., and C.E.O.; Charles J. McMurray, Sr. V.P. and C.A.O.; James F. Shaw, V.P. and C.F.O.; Mary Lynne Perushek, V.P. and C.I.O.; Norman C. Linnell, V.P., Genl. Counsel, and Secy.; Joseph E. Lehman, V.P., Opers.; Sandra N. Joppa, V.P., Human Resources
Board of directors: William M. Cook, Chair.; F. Guillaume Bastiaens; Janet M. Dolan; Michael J. Hoffman; Paul David Miller; Jeffrey Noddle; Willard Oberton; James J. Owens; Ajita G. Rajendra; John P. Wiehoff
Plants: Auburn, AL; Ontario, CA; Norcross, GA; Dixon, IL; Frankfort, Monticello, Rensselaer, IN; Cresco, Grinnell, Oelwein, IA; Nicholasville, KY; Chillicothe, MO; Greeneville, Maryville, TN; Baldwin, Stevens Point, WI
Joint Venture: Advanced Filtration Systems, Inc., Champaign, IL
International operations: Australia; Austria; Belgium; Brazil; China; Czech Republic; Denmark; France; Germany; India; Indonesia; Italy; Japan; Luxembourg; Malaysia; Mexico; Netherlands; Norway; Philippines; Poland; Saudi Arabia; Singapore; Slovakia; South Africa; South Korea; Spain; Switzerland; Taiwan; Thailand; Turkey; United Kingdom
Giving statement: Giving through the Donaldson Foundation.
Company EIN: 410222640

The Donaldson Foundation
P.O. Box 1299, M.S. 100
Minneapolis, MN 55440-1299 (952) 703-4999
FAX: (952) 887-3005;
E-mail: donaldsonfoundation@donaldson.com;
URL: http://www.donaldson.com/en/about/community/foundation.html

Establishment information: Established in 1966 in MN.
Donor: Donaldson Co., Inc.
Contact: Kristine Graham, Pres.
Financial data (yr. ended 07/31/12): Assets, $3,661,943 (M); gifts received, $750,000; expenditures, $1,100,025; qualifying distributions, $1,093,250; giving activities include $1,093,250 for grants.
Purpose and activities: The foundation supports organizations involved with education.
Fields of interest: Education; United Ways and Federated Giving Programs.
Program:
Donaldson Scholars: The foundation awards college scholarships to children of employees of Donaldson Company. The program is administered by Scholarship America, Inc.
Type of support: Annual campaigns; Building/renovation; Capital campaigns; Continuing support; Employee matching gifts; Employee-related scholarships; Scholarship funds.
Geographic limitations: Giving on a national basis in areas of company operations.
Support limitations: No support for religious organizations. No grants to individuals (except for employee-related scholarships).
Publications: Annual report (including application guidelines); Application guidelines; Informational brochure (including application guidelines).
Application information: Applications accepted. Application form not required. Applicants should submit the following:
1) detailed description of project and amount of funding requested
Initial approach: Letter of inquiry
Copies of proposal: 1
Board meeting date(s): Bi-monthly
Deadline(s): None
Officer and Directors: Kristine Graham, Pres.; Jessica Exely; Cory Gunderson; Steve Johnson; Tamara Keeler; Jeff May.
EIN: 416052950

1154
Dondlinger and Sons Construction Co., Inc.
2656 S. Sheridan St.
P.O. Box 398
Wichita, KS 67201-0398 (316) 945-0555

Company URL: http://www.dondlinger.biz/
Establishment information: Established in 1898.
Company type: Private company
Business activities: Provides industrial and private construction services.
Business type (SIC): Contractors/general nonresidential building; construction/miscellaneous heavy
Corporate officers: Tom E. Dondlinger, Pres.; Gregory D. Phillips, Secy.-Treas. and Cont.
Giving statement: Giving through the Dondlinger Foundation, Inc.

Dondlinger Foundation, Inc.
P.O. Box 398
Wichita, KS 67201-0398 (316) 945-0555
Application address: 2656 S. Sheridan, Wichita, KS 67217

Donor: Dondlinger and Sons Construction Co., Inc.
Contact: Thomas E. Dondlinger, Pres.
Financial data (yr. ended 06/30/12): Assets, $603,279 (M); expenditures, $52,626; qualifying distributions, $52,626; giving activities include $51,500 for 8 grants (high: $11,000; low: $500).
Purpose and activities: The foundation supports organizations involved with arts and culture, secondary and higher education, employment, and Catholicism.
Fields of interest: Museums (science/technology); Performing arts, opera; Arts; Secondary school/education; Higher education; Goodwill Industries; Catholic agencies & churches.
Type of support: General/operating support.
Geographic limitations: Giving primarily in Wichita, KS.
Application information: Applications accepted. Application form not required.
Initial approach: Proposal
Deadline(s): None
Final notification: Within 3 days
Officers and Trustee:* Thomas E. Dondlinger*, Pres.; James M. Dondlinger, V.P. and Secy.-Treas.
EIN: 480698333

1155
R. R. Donnelley & Sons Company
111 S. Wacker Dr.
Chicago, IL 60606-4301 (312) 326-8000
FAX: (312) 326-8001

Company URL: http://www.rrdonnelley.com
Establishment information: Established in 1864.
Company type: Public company
Company ticker symbol and exchange: RRD/NASDAQ
Business activities: Provides commercial printing, information, and logistics services.
Business type (SIC): Printing/commercial; management and public relations services
Financial profile for 2012: Number of employees, 57,000; assets, $7,262,700,000; sales volume, $10,221,900,000; pre-tax net

income, -$640,000,000; expenses, $10,611,900,000; liabilities, $7,209,900,000
Fortune 1000 ranking: 2012—264th in revenues, 965th in profits, and 479th in assets
Corporate officers: Stephen M. Wolf, Chair.; Thomas J. Quinlan III, Pres. and C.E.O.; Daniel L. Knotts, C.O.O.; Suzanne S. Bettman, Exec. V.P., Genl. Counsel, and Corp. Secy.; Doug Fitzgerald, Exec. V.P., Comms.; Andrew B. Coxhead, Sr. V.P., C.A.O., and Cont.; Daniel N. Leib, Sr. V.P. and Treas.
Board of directors: Stephen M. Wolf, Chair.; Susan M. Cameron; Lee A. Chaden; Richard L. Crandall; Judith H. Hamilton; Thomas S. Johnson; Richard K. Palmer; John C. Pope; Thomas J. Quinlan III; Michael T. Riordan; Oliver R. Sockwell
Subsidiaries: R.R. Donnelley Norwest Inc., Portland, OR; Mobium Corp., Chicago, IL
Plants: Los Angeles, CA; Dwight, Elgin, Mattoon, Mendota, Pontiac, Wheeling, IL; Crawfordsville, Seymour, Warsaw, IN; Danville, Glasgow, KY; Hudson, MA; Senatobia, MS; Reno, NV; New York, NY; Newark, Willard, OH; Lancaster, Pittsburgh, PA; Spartanburg, SC; Gallatin, TN; McAllen, TX; Harrisonburg, Lynchburg, Salem, VA
Office: Nashville, TN
International operations: Argentina; Barbados; Belgium; Brazil; British Virgin Islands; Canada; Cayman Islands; Chile; China; Costa Rica; Cyprus; Czech Republic; El Salvador; England; France; Germany; Guatemala; Honduras; Hong Kong; Hungary; India; Ireland; Italy; Mauritius; Mexico; Netherlands; Poland; Singapore; Spain; Sri Lanka; Switzerland; Trinidad & Tobago; United Kingdom; Venezuela; Wales
Historic mergers: Banta Corporation (October 31, 2006)
Giving statement: Giving through the R. R. Donnelley Foundation.
Company EIN: 361004130

R. R. Donnelley Foundation

111 S. Wacker Dr., 38th Fl
Chicago, IL 60601-4301 (312) 322-6946
E-mail: communityrelations@rrd.com; Application address: 3075 Highland Pkwy., Downers Grove, IL 60515; URL: http://www.rrdonnelley.com/about/external-affairs/community-relations.aspx

Establishment information: Established in 2000 in IL.
Donor: R.R. Donnelley & Sons Co.
Contact: Kamala L. Martinez, Mgr., Community Rels.
Financial data (yr. ended 12/31/10): Assets, $1,379,777 (M); gifts received, $1,250,000; expenditures, $877,848; qualifying distributions, $877,848; giving activities include $854,026 for 59 grants (high: $193,250; low: $500).
Purpose and activities: The foundation supports programs designed to promote youth, education, inclusion, and diversity.
Fields of interest: Museums; Secondary school/education; Higher education; Libraries (public); Education, reading; Education; Boys & girls clubs; YM/YWCAs & YM/YWHAs; Children/youth, services; Human services; Civil/human rights, equal rights; United Ways and Federated Giving Programs Youth.
Programs:
Dollars for Doers: The foundation awards $100 grants to nonprofit organizations with which employees of R.R. Donnelley volunteer 36 to 60 hours during the course of a year, and $250 for over 60 hours of volunteer service.
Scholarship Program: The foundation awards college scholarships to children of employees of R.R. Donnelley. The program is administered by the National Merit Scholarship Corporation.
Type of support: Employee volunteer services; Employee-related scholarships; General/operating support; Sponsorships.
Geographic limitations: Giving in areas of company operations, with emphasis on Bolingbrook and Chicago, IL, Reno, NV, and New York, NY; giving also to national organizations.
Support limitations: No support for religious or political organizations or hospitals. No grants to individuals (except for employee-related scholarships), or for printing, television, radio, film, video, clinical care, medical research, or equipment.
Publications: Application guidelines.
Application information: Applications accepted. Application form not required. Applicants should submit the following:
1) copy of IRS Determination Letter
2) copy of most recent annual report/audited financial statement/990
3) listing of board of directors, trustees, officers and other key people and their affiliations
4) detailed description of project and amount of funding requested

Initial approach: Download application form and e-mail to foundation
Copies of proposal: 1
Board meeting date(s): Quarterly
Deadline(s): None

Officers and Directors:* Damayanti P. Vasudevan*, Pres.; Suzanne S. Bettman*, Secy.; Daniel N. Leib, Treas.; Thomas J. Quinlan.
EIN: 364398696
Selected grants: The following grants are a representative sample of this grantmaker's funding activity:
$50,000 to United Way of Metropolitan Chicago, Chicago, IL, 2010.
$42,200 to Chicago Public Library Foundation, Chicago, IL, 2010.
$40,000 to National Minority Supplier Development Council, New York, NY, 2010.
$25,000 to Autism Speaks, New York, NY, 2010.
$24,300 to Girls Incorporated, New York, NY, 2010.
$14,150 to Girl Scouts of the U.S.A., Chicago, IL, 2010.
$10,000 to Jumpstart for Young Children, Boston, MA, 2010.
$10,000 to University of Chicago, Chicago, IL, 2010.
$5,000 to Chicago Youth Centers, Chicago, IL, 2010.
$5,000 to University of Cincinnati Foundation, Cincinnati, OH, 2010.

1156
Donovan Marine, Inc.

6316 Humphreys St.
New Orleans, LA 70123-3159
(504) 488-5731

Company URL: http://www.donovanmarine.com
Establishment information: Established in 1984.
Company type: Private company
Business activities: Operates marine equipment distribution company.
Business type (SIC): Industrial machinery and equipment—wholesale
Corporate officer: Benton Smallpage, Owner
Giving statement: Giving through the Smallpage Family Foundation.

Smallpage Family Foundation

6316 Humphreys St.
Harahan, LA 70123-3159 (504) 729-2520

Establishment information: Established in 1995 in LA.
Donors: Donovan Marine, Inc.; Thomas B. Favrot Fund.
Contact: John Benton Smallpage, Jr., Pres.
Financial data (yr. ended 03/31/12): Assets, $1,941,710 (M); gifts received, $775; expenditures, $136,870; qualifying distributions, $137,025; giving activities include $137,025 for 32 grants (high: $30,000; low: $75).
Purpose and activities: The foundation supports organizations involved with education, crime and violence prevention, human services, community economic development, and public policy research.
Fields of interest: Education; Human services; Public affairs.
Type of support: General/operating support.
Geographic limitations: Giving primarily in LA.
Support limitations: No grants to individuals.
Application information: Applications accepted. Application form not required.
Initial approach: Proposal
Deadline(s): None
Directors: Charlotte Favrot Smallpage; Jack L. Smallpage; John Benton Smallpage III; Kathryn Carrere Smallpage.
Officers: John Benton Smallpage, Jr., Pres.; Kathryn F. Smallpage, V.P.; David G. Bailey, Secy.
Number of staff: 1 part-time support.
EIN: 721295264

1157
Dorsey & Whitney LLP

50 S. 6th St., Ste. 1500
Minneapolis, MN 55402-1498
(612) 340-2600

Company URL: http://www.dorsey.com
Establishment information: Established in 1912.
Company type: Private company
Business activities: Operates law firm.
Business type (SIC): Legal services
Corporate officer: Marianne D. Short, Managing Partner
Offices: Anchorage, AK; Irvine, Palo Alto, CA; Denver, CO; Wilmington, DE; Washington, DC; Des Moines, IA; Minneapolis, MN; Missoula, MT; New York, NY; Fargo, ND; Salt Lake City, UT; Seattle, WA
International operations: Australia; Canada; China; Hong Kong; United Kingdom
Giving statement: Giving through the Dorsey & Whitney LLP Pro Bono Program.

Dorsey & Whitney LLP Pro Bono Program

50 S. 6th St., Ste. 1500
Minneapolis, MN 55402-1498 (612) 340-8722
E-mail: Wilson.Perry@dorsey.com; Additional tel.: (612) 340-2600; URL: http://www.dorsey.com/probono/overview/

Contact: Perry Wilson, Pro Bono Partner
Fields of interest: Legal services.
Type of support: Pro bono services - legal.
Geographic limitations: Giving primarily in areas of company operations in Anchorage, AK, Costa Mesa, and Palo Alto, CA, Denver, CO, Washington, DC, Wilmington, DE, Des Moines, IA, Minneapolis, MN, Missoula, MT, Fargo, ND, New York, NY, Salt Lake City, UT, and Seattle, WA, and in Australia, Canada, China, Hong Kong, and United Kingdom.
Application information: A Pro Bono Committee manages the pro bono program.

1158
Dot Foods, Inc.

1 Dot Way
P.O. Box 192
Mount Sterling, IL 62353 (217) 773-4411
FAX: (217) 773-3321

Company URL: http://www.dotfoods.com
Establishment information: Established in 1960.
Company type: Private company
Business activities: Sells food wholesale.
Business type (SIC): Groceries—wholesale
Financial profile for 2011: Number of employees, 3,300; sales volume, $3,600,000,000
Corporate officers: Patrick F. Tracy, Chair.; John Tracy, C.E.O.; Joe Tracy, Pres. and C.O.O.; Bob Metzinger, C.F.O.; Jim Tracy, Sr. V.P. and Genl. Counsel; Michael Duggan, V.P., Sales; Matt Holt, V.P., Human Resources; Thomas L. Tracy, Cont.
Board of director: Patrick Tracy, Chair.
Giving statement: Giving through the Dot Foods, Inc. Corporate Giving Program and the Tracy Family Foundation.

Dot Foods, Inc. Corporate Giving Program

1 Dot Way
P.O. Box 192
Mount Sterling, IL 62353-1664 (217) 773-4411
FAX: (217) 773-3321;
E-mail: pperry@dotfoods.com; Contact for California: Becky Shokraii, tel.: (800) 366-6569, e-mail: bshokraii@dotfoods.com; Contact for Georgia: Jennifer Evans, tel.: (800) 379-6591 jevans@dotfoods.com; Contact for Idaho: Terry Andrew, tel.: (877) 812-7192, e-mail: tandrew@dotfoods.com; Contact for Indiana: Gina Ruffcorn, tel.: (888) 735-0411, e-mail: gruffcorn@dotfoods; Contact for Maryland: Wendy Young, tel.: (800) 366-5670, e-mail: wyoung@dotfoods.com; Contact for Missouri: Cathie Cooke, tel.: (800) 366-5666, e-mail: ccooke@dotfoods.com; Contact for New York: Molly Barber, tel.: 800.962.3668 mbarber@dotfoods.com; Contact for Oklahoma: Penni Wilson, tel.: (800) 2180-1448, e-mail: pwilson@dotfoods.com;; URL: http://www.dotfoods.com/about-dot/corporate-responsibility/

Contact: Peggy Perry
Purpose and activities: As a complement to its foundation, Dot Foods also makes charitable contributions to nonprofit organizations directly. Giving limited to areas of company operations, with emphasis on a 60-mile radius of Mount Sterling, Illinois, and in Adams, Brown, Cass, Fulton, Hancock, McDonough, Morgan, Pike, and Schuyler counties, Illinois.
Fields of interest: Secondary school/education; Public health; Health care; Community/economic development.
Type of support: Donated products; Employee-related scholarships; General/operating support; Scholarship funds.
Geographic limitations: Giving limited to areas of company operations, with emphasis on a 60-mile radius of Mount Sterling, IL, and in Adams, Brown, Cass, Fulton, Hancock, McDonough, Morgan, Pike, and Schuyler counties, IL; giving also in distribution facility areas in CA, GA, ID, MD, MO, NY, and OK.
Application information: Applications accepted. A committee of employees at each facility reviews applications and awards grants. Application form not required.
Initial approach: For requests of $200 and under, or for requests for food product from the Dot Country Store, contact Peggy Perry; For requests above $200, complete online eligibility quiz; For application information from local facilities, telephone or e-mail nearest community contact

Tracy Family Foundation

P.O. Box 25, Highway 99 South
Mount Sterling, IL 62353-0025 (217) 773-4411
FAX: (217) 773-4205;
E-mail: kblielik@dotfoods.com; Additional contact: Jean Buckley, Pres., e-mail: jbuckley@tracyfoundation.org; URL: http://www.tracyfoundation.org

Establishment information: Established in 1997 in IL.
Donor: Dot Foods, Inc.
Contact: Kim Bielik, Admin.
Financial data (yr. ended 12/31/11): Assets, $7,510,035 (M); gifts received, $2,867,500; expenditures, $1,758,459; qualifying distributions, $1,444,824; giving activities include $1,444,824 for grants.
Purpose and activities: The foundation supports organizations involved with education, youth development, and programs designed to strengthen the family unit.
Fields of interest: Elementary/secondary education; Education, early childhood education; Education; Youth development; YM/YWCAs & YM/YWHAs; Children/youth, services; Family services; Human services; Community/economic development; Leadership development; Catholic agencies & churches.
Programs:
Brown County T.E.A.C.H.E.R. Fund: The foundation awards grants to teachers and administrators of Brown County K-12 schools to support programs designed to address improvements needed and identified within the School Improvement Plan; best teaching practices identified by the school's Instructional Leadership Team; and instructional focus of the school.
Capacity Building Grant Program: The foundation awards grants of up to $2,000 for projects and activities designed to increase organizational effectiveness of an agency due to improvements made in management, leadership, and board governance. Special emphasis is directed toward strategic planning; staff training; professional development conferences; Center for Effective Nonprofits workshops and Institute for Excellence in Leadership certificate program; and consultants. Only organizations who have received prior funding through the Formal Funding Grant Program may apply.
Formal Funding Grant Program: The foundation supports programs designed to promote education, families, and youth. Special emphasis is directed toward preK-12 catholic school education; capacity building of nonprofits; community centers; education and curriculum support for pre-school-grade 12 academics; youth development in the areas of leadership, character, and spiritual development; and unmet needs of at-risk families.
Matching Grants: The foundation matches contributions made by Tracey Family Foundation trustees and Tracey family members to nonprofit organizations on a one-for-one basis or two-for-one basis.
The Tracy Family Foundation College Scholarship Fund: The foundation annually awards up to 10 renewable college scholarships to Brown County High School seniors who have earned at least one "Ready for College, Ready for Work" certificate. Recipients are selected based on their Ready for College, Ready for Work score, demonstration of financial need, academic preparation and college plan, and the quality of the submitted essay. The program is administered by ACT, Inc.
Third Generation Grants: The foundation awards grants of up to $2,000 to nonprofit organizations on behalf of third generation Tracy family members between the ages of 5 and 39. The program is designed to educate third generations on the issues in their communities.
Type of support: Annual campaigns; Capital campaigns; Curriculum development; Employee matching gifts; General/operating support; Management development/capacity building; Program development; Scholarship funds.
Geographic limitations: Giving primarily in Adams, Brown, Cass, Greene, Hancock, McDonough, Morgan, Pike, Schuyler, and Scott County, IL.
Support limitations: No grants to individuals.
Publications: Application guidelines; IRS Form 990 or 990-PF printed copy available upon request.
Application information: Applications accepted. Organizations may be invited to submit a formal application for the Formal Funding Grant Program and the Brown County T.E.A.C.H.E.R. Fund. Support is limited to 1 contribution per organization during any given year. Organizations receiving support are asked to submit a final report. Application form required. Applicants should submit the following:
1) timetable for implementation and evaluation of project
2) population served
3) copy of most recent annual report/audited financial statement/990
4) how project's results will be evaluated or measured
5) listing of board of directors, trustees, officers and other key people and their affiliations
6) detailed description of project and amount of funding requested
7) copy of current year's organizational budget and/or project budget
8) listing of additional sources and amount of support

Initial approach: Complete online pre-application for Formal Funding Grant Program and Brown County T.E.A.C.H.E.R. Fund; complete online application for Capacity Building Grant
Board meeting date(s): Mar., July, and Nov.
Deadline(s): Jan 1, May 1, and Sept. 1 for Formal Funding Grant Program and Brown County T.E.A.C.H.E.R. Fund; None for Capacity Building Grant
Final notification: Apr., Aug., and Nov. for Formal Funding Grant Program and Brown County T.E.A.C.H.E.R. Fund

Officers and Trustees:* Jean C. Buckley*, Pres.; Pat Smith, V.P.; David Slocum*, Secy.; Rob Tracy*, Treas.; John Buckley; Mary Sullivan; Linda Tracy; Jaclyn Tracy; Jane Tracy; Don Tracy; Tom Tracy.
EIN: 364163760
Selected grants: The following grants are a representative sample of this grantmaker's funding activity:
$20,000 to Whole Kids Outreach, Ellington, MO, 2010.
$17,000 to Cheerful Home, Quincy, IL, 2010. For program support.
$15,000 to Community Foundation of the Quincy Area, Quincy, IL, 2010. For program support.
$15,000 to Community Foundation of the Quincy Area, Quincy, IL, 2010. For program support.
$10,000 to Dominican Academy, New York, NY, 2010. For program support.

$8,850 to Quincy Notre Dame High School, Quincy, IL, 2010. For program support.
$8,000 to Quincy Notre Dame High School, Quincy, IL, 2010. For program support.
$5,000 to Community Foundation of the Quincy Area, Quincy, IL, 2010.
$3,400 to Teach for America, Saint Louis, MO, 2010. For program support.
$1,000 to Madonna House, Quincy, IL, 2010.

1159
Douglas Corporation

9650 Valley View Rd.
Eden Prairie, MN 55344-3507
(952) 941-2944

Company URL: http://www.douglascorp.com
Establishment information: Established in 1933.
Company type: Private company
Business activities: Manufactures injection molded plastic nameplates, chrome and gold electroplated nameplates, injection molded plastic bezels and faceplates, membrane switches and graphic overlays, flexible circuits, poured polyurethane urocals, individual letter graphics, screen printed decals, and decorative trim and parts.
Business type (SIC): Plastic products/ miscellaneous; electronic components and accessories; manufacturing/miscellaneous
Corporate officers: Douglas R. Skanse, Pres. and Treas.; Joseph L. Hamelin, V.P., Sales; Carol A. Skanse, Secy.
Giving statement: Giving through the Douglas Foundation.

Douglas Foundation

9650 Valley View Rd.
Eden Prairie, MN 55344-3507 (952) 941-2944

Establishment information: Established in 1980 in MN.
Donor: Douglas Corp.
Financial data (yr. ended 09/30/12): Assets, $42,955 (M); gifts received, $90,000; expenditures, $118,064; qualifying distributions, $118,064; giving activities include $118,000 for 44 grants (high: $8,000; low: $1,000).
Purpose and activities: The foundation supports health centers and organizations involved with arts and culture, education, human services, and Christianity.
Fields of interest: Education; Health organizations; Human services.
Type of support: General/operating support.
Geographic limitations: Giving primarily in MN.
Support limitations: No grants to individuals.
Application information: Applications accepted. Application form not required.
Initial approach: Proposal
Deadline(s): None
Officers: Douglas R. Skanse, Pres.; C.A. Skanse, V.P.; Ronald D. Skanse, Secy.
EIN: 411385064

1160
Dow AgroSciences LLC

(formerly DowElanco LLC)
9330 Zionsville Rd.
Indianapolis, IN 46268-1053
(317) 337-3000

Company URL: http://www.dowagro.com
Establishment information: Established in 1989.
Company type: Subsidiary of a public company
Ultimate parent company: The Dow Chemical Company
Business activities: Manufactures pest management, agricultural, and biotechnology products.
Business type (SIC): Fertilizers and agricultural chemicals
Corporate officers: Andrew N. Liveris, Chair., Pres. and C.E.O.; Bill Wales, Exec. V.P. and C.F.O.; Charles J. Kalil, Exec. V.P., Genl. Counsel, and Corp.Secy.
Board of directors: Andrew N. Liverls, Chair.; Arnold A. Allemang; Ajay Banga; Jacqueline K. Barton; James A. Bell; Jeff M. Fettig; John B. Hess; Paul Polman; Dennis H. Reilley; James M. Ringier; Ruth G. Shaw
International operations: China; India; Netherlands; South Africa
Giving statement: Giving through the Dow AgroSciences LLC Corporate Giving Program.

Dow AgroSciences LLC Corporate Giving Program

9330 Zionsville Rd.
Indianapolis, IN 46268-1053 (317) 337-3000
FAX: (317) 337-4096; URL: http://www.dowagro.com/sustainability/commitments/

Purpose and activities: Dow AgroSciences makes charitable contributions to nonprofit organizations involved with science education, environmental preservation, and housing. Support is given primarily in areas of company operations, and to national and international organizations.
Fields of interest: Elementary/secondary education; Health sciences school/education; Environment, natural resources; Animals/wildlife, preservation/protection; Housing/shelter, volunteer services.
Type of support: Employee volunteer services; General/operating support.
Geographic limitations: Giving primarily in areas of company operations, and to national and international organizations.

1161
The Dow Chemical Company

2030 Willard H. Dow Ctr.
Midland, MI 48674-0001 (989) 636-1000
FAX: (989) 832-1556

Company URL: http://www.dow.com
Establishment information: Established in 1897.
Company type: Public company
Company ticker symbol and exchange: DOW/NYSE
Business activities: Manufactures and sells chemicals, plastic materials, and agricultural products.
Business type (SIC): Chemicals and allied products; plastics and synthetics; fertilizers and agricultural chemicals
Financial profile for 2012: Number of employees, 54,000; assets, $69,605,000,000; sales volume, $56,786,000,000; pre-tax net income, $1,665,000,000; expenses, $55,121,000,000; liabilities, $48,728,000,000
Fortune 1000 ranking: 2012—52nd in revenues, 169th in profits, and 83rd in assets
Forbes 2000 ranking: 2012—145th in sales, 502nd in profits, and 342nd in assets
Corporate officers: Andrew N. Liveris, Chair., Pres., and C.E.O.; William H. Weideman, Exec. V.P. and C.F.O.; David E. Kepler, Exec. V.P. and C.I.O.; Charles J. Kalil, Exec. V.P., Genl. Counsel, and Corp. Secy.; Gregory M. Freiwald, Exec. V.P., Human Resources; Fernando Ruiz, Corp. V.P. and Treas.; Ron Edmonds, V.P. and Cont.
Board of directors: Andrew N. Liveris, Chair.; Arnold A. Allemang; Ajay Banga; Jacqueline K. Barton; James A. Bell; Jeff M. Fettig; Paul Polman; Dennis H. Reilley; James M. Ringler; Ruth G. Shaw
Subsidiaries: Dow AgroSciences LLC, Indianapolis, IN; DowBrands Inc., Indianapolis, IN; Essex Chemical Corp., Clifton, NJ; FilmTec Corp., Minneapolis, MN; Rohm and Haas Company, Philadelphia, PA; Union Carbide Corporation, Danbury, CT
Plants: Pittsburg, CA; Plaquemine, LA; Strongsville, OH; Freeport, Houston, TX
Joint Venture: Dow Corning Corporation, Midland, MI
International operations: Argentina; Australia; Chile; China; Colombia; Germany; Hong Kong; Indonesia; Ireland; Japan; Malaysia; Mexico; Netherlands; New Zealand; Peru; Singapore; South Africa; South Korea; Switzerland; Taiwan; Thailand; United Kingdom; Venezuela
Giving statement: Giving through the Dow Chemical Company Contributions Program and the Dow Chemical Company Foundation.
Company EIN: 381285128

The Dow Chemical Company Contributions Program

2030 Dow Ctr.
Midland, MI 48674-0001 (989) 636-1000
URL: http://www.dow.com/company/sponsorship/

The Dow Chemical Company Foundation

2030 Dow Ctr.
Midland, MI 48674-0001
FAX: (989) 636-3518; E-mail: bomiller@dow.com; URL: http://www.dow.com/about/sponsorship/

Establishment information: Established in 1979 in MI.
Donor: The Dow Chemical Co.
Contact: R.N. "Bo" Miller, Pres. and Exec. Dir.
Financial data (yr. ended 12/31/11): Assets, $14,366,007 (M); gifts received, $24,900,000; expenditures, $24,866,980; qualifying distributions, $24,864,323; giving activities include $24,864,323 for grants.
Purpose and activities: The foundation supports organizations involved with K-12 education, the environment, community development, and chemical research.
Fields of interest: Elementary/secondary education; Environment; Community/economic development; United Ways and Federated Giving Programs; Chemistry.
Program:
Employee Matching Gifts: The foundation matches contributions made by full-time employees, retirees, and directors of Dow Chemical to institutions of higher education on a one-for-one basis from $250 to $10,000 per contributor, per year.

Type of support: Donated products; Employee matching gifts; Equipment; In-kind gifts; Program development; Seed money.
Geographic limitations: Giving on a national and international basis primarily in areas of company operations.
Support limitations: No support for political or religious organizations. No grants for travel or administrative costs.
Application information: Applications accepted. Application form not required. Applicants should submit the following:
1) geographic area to be served
2) detailed description of project and amount of funding requested

Initial approach: Letter of inquiry
Copies of proposal: 1
Board meeting date(s): 4 times per year
Deadline(s): None
Final notification: 2 to 3 months

Officers and Trustees:* Dave E. Kepler, Chair.; R.N. "Bo" Miller*, Pres. and Exec. Dir.; Nancy Logan, Secy.; Colleen W. Kay, Treas.; Bill Banholzer; Gregory M. Freiwald; Geoffery E. Merszei; William H. Weideman.
Number of staff: 1 full-time professional; 7 part-time professional.
EIN: 382314603
Selected grants: The following grants are a representative sample of this grantmaker's funding activity:
$1,500,000 to YMCA, Bay Area Family, Bay City, MI, 2010.
$1,250,000 to University of California, Center for Responsible Business, Berkeley, CA, 2011.
$1,000,000 to Michigan Molecular Institute, Midland, MI, 2010.
$1,000,000 to Michigan Molecular Institute, Midland, MI, 2011.
$1,000,000 to National Science Teachers Association, Arlington, VA, 2011.
$1,000,000 to University of California, Haas School of Business, Center for Responsible Business, Berkeley, CA, 2010.
$1,000,000 to YMCA, Bay Area Family, Bay City, MI, 2011.
$828,630 to Resource Foundation, New York, NY, 2010.
$761,500 to United Way of Midland County, Midland, MI, 2010.
$751,911 to United Way of Midland County, Midland, MI, 2011.
$41,512 to Associacao Cultural Brasil-Estados Unidos, Salvador, Brazil, 2010.
$23,000 to United Way of Northeast Louisiana, Monroe, LA, 2011.
$22,000 to United Way of Northeast Louisiana, Monroe, LA, 2010.
$20,000 to Buena Vista High School, Saginaw, MI, 2010. For FIRST Robotics Program.
$20,000 to Delaware Valley Science Fairs, Philadelphia, PA, 2011.
$19,000 to Clinton Global Initiative, New York, NY, 2011.
$5,000 to Assistance League of Indianapolis, Indianapolis, IN, 2010.
$5,000 to Oakland University, Rochester, MI, 2011.
$4,829 to La Marque Independent School District, La Marque, TX, 2010.

1162
Dow Corning Corporation

2200 W. Salzburg Rd.
P.O. Box 994
Midland, MI 48686 (989) 496-4400

Company URL: http://www.dowcorning.com
Establishment information: Established in 1943.
Company type: Joint venture
Business activities: Manufactures and provides silicon-based technologies and solutions.
Business type (SIC): Plastics and synthetics
Financial profile for 2009: Number of employees, 10,000; sales volume, $5,450,000,000
Corporate officers: Robert D. Hansen, Pres. and C.E.O.; Joseph D. Sheets, Exec. V.P. and C.F.O.; N. Cornell Boggs III, Sr. V.P., Genl. Counsel, and Corp. Secy.; Kristy Folkwein, V.P. and C.I.O.
Plants: Auburn, MI; Greensboro, NC
Joint Venture: Hemlock Semiconductor Corp., Hemlock, MI
International operations: Australia
Giving statement: Giving through the Dow Corning Corporation Contributions Program and the Dow Corning Foundation.

Dow Corning Corporation Contributions Program

P.O. Box 994
Midland, MI 48686-0994 (989) 496-4400
E-mail: community@dowcorning.com; URL: http://www.dowcorning.com/content/about/aboutcomm/?e=About+Dow+Corning

Purpose and activities: As a complement to its foundation, Dow Corning also makes charitable contributions to nonprofit organizations directly. Support is given primarily in Seneffe, Belgium, Campinas, Brazil, Songjiang, China, Saint-Laurent-du-Pont, France, Wiesbaden, Germany, Fukui and Yamakita, Japan, Jincheon, South Korea, and Barry, Wales.
Fields of interest: Community/economic development; Mathematics; Science.
International interests: Belgium; Brazil; China; France; Germany; Japan; South Korea; Wales.
Program:
Employee Matching Gift Program: Dow Corning matches contributions made by its employees to colleges and universities on a one-for-one basis up to $10,000 per employee and $3,000 for retirees, per year. For cultural arts organizations, Dow Corning matches contributions made by its employees on a one-for-two basis up to $1,000 per employee, per year.
Type of support: Donated equipment; Donated products; Employee matching gifts; General/operating support.
Geographic limitations: Giving primarily in Seneffe, Belgium, Campinas, Brazil, Songjiang, China, Saint-Laurent-du-Pont, France, Wiesbaden, Germany, Fukui and Yamakita, Japan, Jincheon, South Korea, and Barry, Wales.
Support limitations: No support for political, veterans', religious, or government-funded organizations. No grants to individuals, or for fundraising, collegiate athletic activities, scholarships, conferences, or travel.
Publications: Application guidelines.
Application information: Applications accepted. Organizations receiving support are asked to provide a final report. Application form not required.
Initial approach: E-mail letter of inquiry to headquarters

Dow Corning Foundation

c/o Dow Corning Corp.
Coporate Center
P.O. Box 994
Midland, MI 48686-0994
E-mail: foundation@dowcorning.com; URL: http://www.dowcorning.com/content/about/aboutcomm/dowcorningfoundation.aspx

Establishment information: Established in 1982 in MI.
Donors: Dow Corning Corp.; Hemlock Semiconductor Corp.
Contact: Kathryn Curtiss Spence, Dir.
Financial data (yr. ended 12/31/11): Assets, $27,862,161 (M); gifts received, $1,300,000; expenditures, $1,297,213; qualifying distributions, $1,150,927; giving activities include $1,150,927 for 48 grants (high: $200,000).
Purpose and activities: The foundation supports programs designed to increase access to science, technology, engineering and math (STEM) education; improve community vitality; and increase awareness and use of innovative and sustainable technology.
Fields of interest: Museums; Elementary/secondary education; Higher education; Environment, natural resources; Environment; Hospitals (general); Health care; Food services; Recreation, parks/playgrounds; Boy scouts; Youth development, business; Community/economic development; Foundations (community); United Ways and Federated Giving Programs; Science, formal/general education; Mathematics; Engineering/technology.
Programs:
Community Vitality Grants: The foundation supports programs designed to leverage volunteerism and citizenship to improve local quality of life; sustainable projects designed to continue beyond a funding period and demonstrate a positive impact on a broad segment of the community; and projects with multiple funders.
Donor Advised Funds: The foundation established donor advised funds with community foundations in Bay, Midland, and Saginaw to support regional project and programs that align with Dow Corning's mission.
STEM Education Grants: The foundation supports Science, Technology, Engineering, and Math (STEM) projects designed to increase access to STEM educational opportunities for those who currently have little or no access due to economics, gender, racial bias, or other factors.
Sustainability: The foundation supports programs designed to conserve natural resources and reduce the negative impact of human lifestyles on the environment through innovative technologies.
Type of support: Building/renovation; Capital campaigns; Continuing support; Curriculum development; Equipment; Matching/challenge support; Program development; Scholarship funds; Seed money.
Geographic limitations: Giving in areas of company operations, with emphasis on Kendallville, IN, Carrollton and Elizabethtown, KY, Bay, Midland, and Saginaw counties, MI, and Greensboro, NC.
Support limitations: No support for veterans', political, or religious groups or athletic leagues. No grants to individuals, or for scholarships, conferences, travel costs of groups, dinners, fundraising events, projects normally funded by government taxation, or personal needs; no research or international grants.
Publications: Application guidelines.
Application information: Applications accepted. Organizations receiving support are asked to submit annual progress reports and a final report.

Application form required. Applicants should submit the following:
1) copy of IRS Determination Letter
Initial approach: Complete online application
Board meeting date(s): Quarterly
Deadline(s): STEM grants reviewed in Mar.; Quality-of-life grants reviewed in June; Innovative technology grants reviewed in Sept.; All types of grants reviewed in Dec.
Officers and Trustees:* Mary Lou Benecke*, Chair.; Kimberly R. Houston-Philpot*, Pres.; Mathew J. Nolan*, Secy.; Ronald G. Thompson*, Treas.; Jeanne D. Dodd*; Robert L. Kain; Thomas H. Lane; Christopher C. Shirk; Christian A. Velasquez.
Number of staff: 1 part-time professional; 1 part-time support.
EIN: 382376485

1163
Dow Jones & Company, Inc.

1211 Ave. of the Americas
New York, NY 10036 (212) 416-2000

Company URL: http://www.dj.com/
Establishment information: Established in 1882.
Company type: Subsidiary of a foreign company
Business activities: Publishes financial periodicals and newspapers; provides news services.
Business type (SIC): Newspaper publishing and/or printing; business services/miscellaneous
Corporate officers: Rupert Murdoch, Chair.; Lex Fenwick, C.E.O.; William T. Kennedy, C.O.O.; Mark H. Jackson, Exec. V.P. and Genl. Counsel; Kevin P. Halpin, C.F.O.; Patricia Gatto, V.P., Human Resources
Board of director: Rupert Murdoch, Chair.
International operations: China; Germany; United Kingdom
Giving statement: Giving through the Dow Jones & Company, Inc. Corporate Giving Program and the Dow Jones Foundation.
Company EIN: 135034940

Dow Jones & Company, Inc. Corporate Giving Program

1 World Financial Ctr.
200 Liberty St.
New York, NY 10281-1000 (212) 416-2000
E-mail: tom.mcguirl@dowjones.com; Additional tel.: (609) 520-5145

Contact: Thomas W. McGuirl, V.P., Tax
Purpose and activities: As a complement to its foundation, Dow Jones also makes charitable contributions to nonprofit organizations directly. Support is given on a national and international basis in areas of company operations.
Fields of interest: Media, print publishing; Higher education; Community/economic development.
Program:
Dow Jones Volunteer Support Program: Dow Jones awards grants of up to $500 to nonprofit organizations with which employees of Dow Jones volunteers up to 100 hours.
Type of support: Employee volunteer services; General/operating support; Scholarship funds.
Geographic limitations: Giving on a national and international basis in areas of company operations.
Application information: Applications accepted. Application form not required.
Initial approach: Proposal to headquarters
Copies of proposal: 1
Deadline(s): Nov. 1
Final notification: Following review

Dow Jones Foundation

P.O. Box 1802
Providence, RI 02901-1802
Mailing address: P.O. Box 300, Princeton, NJ 08543, tel.: (609) 520-5145

Establishment information: Established in 1954 in NY.
Donor: Dow Jones & Co., Inc.
Contact: Thomas McGuirl
Financial data (yr. ended 12/31/11): Assets, $127,208 (M); expenditures, $735; qualifying distributions, $214.
Purpose and activities: The foundation supports organizations involved with journalism and higher education.
Fields of interest: Media, print publishing; Higher education; United Ways and Federated Giving Programs.
Type of support: Annual campaigns; Continuing support; General/operating support; Internship funds; Scholarship funds.
Geographic limitations: Giving primarily in areas of company operations, with emphasis on CA, Washington, DC, NJ, and NY.
Support limitations: No grants to individuals, or for medical or scientific research.
Application information: Applications accepted. Application form required.
Initial approach: Letter
Board meeting date(s): Usually in the last quarter
Deadline(s): None
Trustee: Bank of America, N.A.
EIN: 136070158
Selected grants: The following grants are a representative sample of this grantmaker's funding activity:
$160,921 to Literacy Partners, New York, NY, 2009.
$110,000 to California Polytechnic State University, San Luis Obispo, CA, 2009.
$36,000 to New York University, New York, NY, 2009.
$25,000 to Reporters Committee for Freedom of the Press, Arlington, VA, 2009.
$24,150 to Institute of International Education, New York, NY, 2009.
$10,000 to Asian American Journalists Association, San Francisco, CA, 2009.
$10,000 to Columbia University, School of Journalism, New York, NY, 2009.
$10,000 to Inner-City Scholarship Fund, New York, NY, 2009.
$10,000 to National Association of Black Journalists, College Park, MD, 2009.
$10,000 to National Association of Hispanic Journalists, Washington, DC, 2009.

1164
Dow Lohnes PLLC

1200 New Hampshire Ave., N.W., Ste. 800
Washington, DC 20036-6802
(202) 776-2000

Company URL: http://www.dowlohnes.com
Establishment information: Established in 1918.
Company type: Private company
Business activities: Operates law firm.
Business type (SIC): Legal services
Corporate officer: Leonard J. Baxt, Chair.
Board of director: Leonard J. Baxt, Chair.
Offices: Washington, DC; Atlanta, GA; Greenville, SC
Giving statement: Giving through the Dow Lohnes PLLC Pro Bono Program.

Dow Lohnes PLLC Pro Bono Program

1200 New Hampshire Ave., N.W., Ste. 800
Washington, DC 20036-6802 (202) 776-2545
E-mail: jgwadz@dowlohnes.com; URL: http://www.dowlohnes.com/firmoverview/probono/

Contact: Joyce T. Gwadz, Partner
Fields of interest: Legal services.
Type of support: Pro bono services - legal.
Geographic limitations: Giving primarily in areas of company operations in Washington, DC, and Atlanta, GA.
Application information: An attorney coordinates pro bono projects.

1165
Dowling & Partners Securities, LLC

190 Farmington Ave.
Farmington, CT 06032-1713
(860) 676-8600
FAX: (860) 676-8617

Company URL: http://www.dowling.com
Establishment information: Established in 1990.
Company type: Private company
Business activities: Provides investment advisory services.
Business type (SIC): Security and commodity services
Corporate officers: Mark Haushill, Exec. V.P. and C.F.O.; Geoffrey Dunn, C.I.O.
Giving statement: Giving through the Dowling & Partners Charitable Foundation, Inc.

The Dowling & Partners Charitable Foundation, Inc.

c/o Foundation Source
501 Silverside Rd., Ste. 123
Wilmington, DE 19809-1377

Establishment information: Established in 2004 in DE.
Donors: Dowling & Partners Securities, LLC; Acuity, A Mutual Insurance Co.; Great American Insurance Co.
Financial data (yr. ended 12/31/11): Assets, $403,003 (M); gifts received, $68,015; expenditures, $81,120; qualifying distributions, $77,500; giving activities include $77,500 for grants.
Purpose and activities: The foundation supports hospitals and organizations involved with medical education, cancer, autism, children services, and homelessness.
Fields of interest: Health care; Health organizations; Human services.
Type of support: General/operating support; Scholarship funds.
Geographic limitations: Giving primarily in CA, FL, MA, and NY.
Application information: Applications not accepted. Unsolicited requests for funds not accepted.
Officers and Directors:* Vincent J. Dowling, Jr.*, Pres. and Secy.; Mark Galiette, V.P.; Barbara C. Howard, V.P.; Kevin O'Shea, V.P.; Rachel Rhine, V.P.; Brenna Sullivan-Lent*, V.P.; Frank Wetchler, V.P.; Caroline D. Klotz.
EIN: 200856682

1166
Downey Brand LLP
621 Capitol Mall, Fl. 18
Sacramento, CA 95814-4731
(916) 444-1000

Company URL: http://www.downeybrand.com
Establishment information: Established in 1926.
Company type: Private company
Business activities: Operates law firm.
Business type (SIC): Legal services
Financial profile for 2010: Number of employees, 133
Corporate officer: David R.E. Aladjem, Partner
Offices: Roseville, Sacramento, San Francisco, Stockton, CA; Reno, NV
Giving statement: Giving through the Downey Brand LLP Pro Bono Program.

Downey Brand LLP Pro Bono Program
621 Capitol Mall, Fl. 18
Sacramento, CA 95814-4731 (916) 444-1000
E-mail: jgalvin@downeybrand.com; URL: http://www.downeybrand.com

Contact: Jeff Galvin, Partner
Fields of interest: Legal services.
Type of support: Pro bono services - legal.
Geographic limitations: Giving primarily in areas of company operations in Roseville, Sacramento, San Francisco, and Stockton, CA, and Reno, NV.
Application information: The Pro Bono Coordinator manages the pro-bono program.

1167
Doyon Ltd.
1 Doyon Pl., Ste. 300
Fairbanks, AK 99701-2941 (907) 459-2000

Company URL: http://www.doyon.com
Establishment information: Established in 1971.
Company type: Native corporation
Business activities: Operates native corporation.
Business type (SIC): Nonclassifiable establishments
Corporate officers: Orie G. Williams, Chair.; Victor Nicholas, Vice-Chair.; Aaron M. Schutt, Pres. and C.E.O.; Roberta Quintavell, Sr. V.P. and C.O.O.; Patrick W. Duke, Sr. V.P. and C.F.O.; Geraldine Simon, Sr. V.P., Admin.; Kelly Brooks, V.P., Finance; Sharon McConnell, V.P., Comms.; Robin Renfroe, V.P., Human Resources; Michael R. Fleagle, Secy.; Miranda Wright, Treas.; Karen A. Clark, Corp. Cont.; Allen Todd, Genl. Counsel
Board of directors: Orie G. Williams, Chair.; Victor Nicholas, Vice-Chair.; Walter Carlo; Jennifer Fate; Michael R. Fleagle; Andrew Jimmie; Georgianna Lincoln; Josephine Malemute; Esther McCarty; Cheryl Northway Silas; Teisha Simmons; Christopher Simon; Miranda Wright
Giving statement: Giving through the Doyon Foundation.

The Doyon Foundation
615 Bidwell, Ste. 101
Fairbanks, AK 99701-7580 (907) 459-2048
FAX: (905) 459-2065;
E-mail: foundation@doyon.com; E-mail for Doris Miller: millerd@doyon.com; Additional tel.: (888) 478-4755; URL: http://www.doyonfoundation.com/
Tel. for Tonya. Garnett; (907) 459-2049, e-mail: garnett@doyon.com

Establishment information: Established in 1988 in AK.
Donor: Doyon Ltd.
Contact: Doris Miller, Exec. Dir.
Financial data (yr. ended 06/30/11): Assets, $13,362,919 (M); gifts received, $1,308,495; expenditures, $1,283,466; qualifying distributions, $631,815; giving activities include $631,815 for grants to individuals.
Purpose and activities: The foundation supports programs designed to improve educational, career, and cultural opportunities for Dayan shareholders. Special emphasis is directed toward programs designed to strengthen Native culture and heritage through education.
Fields of interest: Arts, cultural/ethnic awareness; Elementary/secondary education; Vocational education; Higher education; Education Native Americans/American Indians.
Program:
Scholarship Program: The foundation awards college scholarships ranging from $400 to $7,000 to shareholders and descendants of shareholders of Doyon, Ltd., enrolled in a part-time or full-time degree program, or enrolled in a vocational program. The foundation awards competitive scholarships of up to $7,000; basic scholarships of up $400 for part-time students and $800 for full-time students; short-term vocational scholarships of up to $400; and advanced college credit scholarships of up $400 for high school students taking college courses.
Type of support: General/operating support; Internship funds; Scholarships—to individuals.
Geographic limitations: Giving primarily in AK.
Publications: Annual report; Application guidelines; Informational brochure; Newsletter.
Application information: Applications accepted. Application form required.
Requests for Competitive Scholarships should include a letter of acceptance, high school or college transcripts, a personal essay, and two letters of recommendation.
Initial approach: Complete online application or download application and mail
Board meeting date(s): Quarterly
Deadline(s): Apr. 15 for Competitive Scholarships; Mar. 15, Apr. 15, and Nov. 15 for Basic Scholarships; Mar. 15, Apr. 15, Sept. 15, and Nov. 15 for Vocational Scholarships
Officers and Directors:* Mark Holmgren, C.E.O.; Julie Anderson, Pres.; Wesley Roberts Dalton, V.P.; Lorraine B. David, Secy.-Treas.; Doris Miller, Exec. Dir.; Shane Derendoff; Paul Mountain; Victor Nicholas; Teisha M. Simmons.
Number of staff: 2 full-time professional.
EIN: 943089624

1168
DP Partners
5500 Equity Ave.
Reno, NV 89502 (775) 858-8080

Company URL: http://www.dermody-properties.com/
Establishment information: Established in 1960.
Company type: Private company
Business activities: Develops industrial real estate; provides property management services; provides construction management services.
Business type (SIC): Real estate subdividers and developers; real estate agents and managers; management and public relations services
Financial profile for 2010: Number of employees, 44
Corporate officers: Michael C. Dermody, Chair. and C.E.O.; Douglas A. Kiersey, Jr., Pres.; John Atwell, C.O.O.; C. Douglas Lanning, C.F.O.
Board of directors: Michael C. Dermody, Chair.; Heidi Evans; Doug Kiersey; James V. Mascaro; Sharon Mills; Kirk Olsen; Bruce D. Storey; Alice Swanson; Elizabeth Teske
Plant: Philadelphia, PA
Offices: Chicago, IL; Portland, OR
Giving statement: Giving through the DP Partners Corporate Giving Program and the Dermody Properties Foundation.

Dermody Properties Foundation
5500 Equity Ave.
Reno, NV 89502-2343 (775) 858-8080
FAX: (775) 856-0831;
E-mail: cmartin@dermody-properties.com; URL: http://www.dermody-properties.com/dp_foundation

Establishment information: Established in 1987 in NV.
Donors: Dermody Properties, Inc.; DP Advisors LLC; DP Homes LLC; Michael C. Dermody.
Contact: Carol Martin, Admin.
Financial data (yr. ended 12/31/11): Assets, $10,497 (M); gifts received, $223,617; expenditures, $214,375; qualifying distributions, $199,752; giving activities include $199,752 for 111 grants (high: $25,000; low: $250).
Purpose and activities: The foundation supports organizations involved with arts and culture, education, and family services. Special emphasis is directed toward children and the elderly.
Fields of interest: Arts; Education; Food services; Food banks; Family services Children; Aging.
Program:
Capstone Award: Through the Capstone Award, the foundation annually awards grants to one or more nonprofits to help them continue good work throughout the Thanksgiving holiday season.
Type of support: Conferences/seminars; Continuing support; Equipment; General/operating support; Program development; Scholarship funds; Sponsorships.
Geographic limitations: Giving primarily in Rochelle, IL, Las Vegas and Reno, NV, and Harrisburg, PA.
Support limitations: No grants to individuals, or for endowments or capital campaigns.
Publications: Application guidelines; Grants list.
Application information: Applications accepted. Grants range from $500 to $3,000. Application form required. Applicants should submit the following:
1) copy of IRS Determination Letter
2) brief history of organization and description of its mission
3) listing of board of directors, trustees, officers and other key people and their affiliations
4) copy of current year's organizational budget and/or project budget

Initial approach: E-mail or call foundation for application form
Copies of proposal: 1
Board meeting date(s): Quarterly
Deadline(s): Mid-Aug.
Final notification: Following review
Directors: Heidi Evans; Douglas A, Kiersey, Jr.; James Mascaro; Sharon Mills; Kirk Olsen; Alice Swanson; Elizabeth Teske.
Number of staff: 1 part-time support.
EIN: 943086271
Selected grants: The following grants are a representative sample of this grantmaker's funding activity:
$25,000 to Food Bank of Northern Nevada, McCarran, NV, 2010.

$25,000 to Washoe County School District, Reno, NV, 2010.
$3,500 to Catholic Charities of Northern Nevada, Reno, NV, 2010.
$3,240 to Step 2, Reno, NV, 2010.
$3,000 to Loaves and Fishes Centers, Portland, OR, 2010.
$2,500 to Appel Farm Arts and Music Center, Elmer, NJ, 2010.
$2,500 to Boys and Girls Clubs of Portland Metropolitan Area, Portland, OR, 2010.
$1,500 to Portland YouthBuilders, Portland, OR, 2010.
$1,500 to University of Nevada at Las Vegas Foundation, Las Vegas, NV, 2010.
$1,000 to Domestic Violence Services of Cumberland and Perry Counties, Carlisle, PA, 2010.

1169
Dr Pepper Snapple Group, Inc.

(also known as Snapple)
(formerly Cadbury Schweppes Americas Beverages, Inc.)
5301 Legacy Dr.
Plano, TX 75024-3109 (972) 673-7000

Company URL: http://www.drpeppersnapplegroup.com
Establishment information: Established in 2007.
Company type: Public company
Company ticker symbol and exchange: DPS/NYSE
International Securities Identification Number: US26138E1091
Business activities: Produces soft drinks.
Business type (SIC): Beverages
Financial profile for 2012: Number of employees, 19,000; assets, $8,928,000,000; sales volume, $5,995,000,000; pre-tax net income, $978,000,000; expenses, $4,903,000,000; liabilities, $6,648,000,000
Fortune 1000 ranking: 2012—427th in revenues, 283rd in profits, and 427th in assets
Forbes 2000 ranking: 2012—1284th in sales, 971st in profits, and 1551st in assets
Corporate officers: Wayne R. Sanders, Chair.; Larry D. Young, Pres. and C.E.O.; Martin M. Ellen, C.F.O.; James L. Baldwin, Jr., Exec. V.P. and Genl. Counsel; James R. Trebilcock, Exec. V.P., Mktg.; Lain Hancock, Exec. V.P., Human Resources
Board of directors: Wayne R. Sanders, Chair.; John L. Adams; David E. Alexander; Terence D. Martin; Pamela H. Patsley; Joyce Roche; Ronald G. Rogers; Jack J. Stahl; M. Anne Szostak; Larry D. Young
Giving statement: Giving through the Dr Pepper Snapple Group, Inc. Corporate Giving Program and the Cadbury Schweppes Americas Emergency Relief Fund.
Company EIN: 980517725

Dr Pepper Snapple Group, Inc. Corporate Giving Program

(also known as ACTION Nation)
(formerly Dr Pepper/Seven Up, Inc. Corporate Giving Program)
5301 Legacy Dr.
Plano, TX 75024-3109 (972) 673-7000
URL: http://www.drpeppersnapplegroup.com/values/sustainability/corporate-philanthropy/

Financial data (yr. ended 12/31/11): Total giving, $13,400,000, including $11,600,000 for grants and $1,800,000 for in-kind gifts.
Purpose and activities: Dr Pepper Snapple Group makes charitable contributions to nonprofit organizations for programs that promote fit and active lifestyles, environmental initiatives, emergency relief, and community celebrations. Support is given primarily in areas of company operations in the U.S., with emphasis on Texas, and in Mexico.
Fields of interest: Environment, natural resources; Environmental education; Environment; Hospitals (specialty); Public health, physical fitness; Cerebral palsy; Muscular dystrophy; Food banks; Safety/disasters; Recreation, community; Recreation, fairs/festivals; Boys clubs; Girls clubs; Youth, services; Community/economic development; Military/veterans' organizations.
Program:
Let's Play: Let's Play is a community partnership led by Dr Pepper Snapple Group to get kids and families active nationwide. The first Let's Play initiative is a $15 million, three-year commitment to KaBOOM!, a national nonprofit that works to ensure that children have places to play within walking distance. Working with local nonprofits, beverage associations, legislators, and customers, company employees built 20 playgrounds across the U.S. and Mexico in 2011, giving an estimated 50,000 children a great place to play. Together, through Let's Play, Dr Pepper Snapple Group and KaBOOM! aim to build or fix up to 2,000 playgrounds by the end of 2013, benefiting an estimated five million children.
Type of support: Cause-related marketing; Donated products; Employee volunteer services; General/operating support; In-kind gifts; Sponsorships.
Geographic limitations: Giving primarily in areas of company operations, with emphasis on TX, and in Mexico.
Support limitations: No support for membership organizations, labor groups, churches or religious organizations, organizations located outside the U.S., United Way-supported organizations, political organizations, fraternal or veterans' organizations, or sports teams. No grants to individuals.
Publications: Corporate report.
Application information: Applications accepted. Applications are not accepted via e-mail, fax, mail, or phone.
Initial approach: Complete online application

Cadbury Schweppes Americas Emergency Relief Fund

P.O. Box 259199
Plano, TX 75025-9199 (972) 673-8088

Financial data (yr. ended 12/31/11): Revenue, $75,259; assets, $72,553 (M); gifts received, $75,259; expenditures, $61,104; program services expenses, $60,275; giving activities include $60,275 for grants.
Purpose and activities: The fund works to provide relief in response to disasters and emergency hardships suffered by current and future employees of CBI Holdings, Inc. and subsidiaries.
Fields of interest: Human services, emergency aid.
Type of support: Grants to individuals.
Officers and Director:* Vicki Draughn*, V.P.; Terri Harrell*, V.P.; Laurie Huebner*, V.P.; Ivan Thompsn*, V.P.; Janet Barrett*, Secy.; Lisa Papageorge*, Treas.; Tina Barry.
EIN: 412184477

1170
Draper and Kramer, Inc.

33 W. Monroe, 19th Fl.
Chicago, IL 60603 (312) 346-8600

Company URL: http://www.draperandkramer.com
Establishment information: Established in 1893.
Company type: Subsidiary of a private company
Business activities: Operates property and financial services company.
Business type (SIC): Real estate agents and managers
Corporate officers: Forrest D. Bailey, Pres. and C.E.O.; Anthony F. Kramer, Exec. V.P. and C.A.O.; James Hayes, Sr. V.P. and C.F.O.; Gail Eubanks, V.P., Human Resources; Gordon Ziegenhagen, V.P., Opers.
Board of director: Douglas Kramer, Chair.
Giving statement: Giving through the D & K Foundation.

D & K Foundation

33 W. Monroe St.
Chicago, IL 60603-5486 (312) 346-8600

Donors: D & K Insurance Agency; Ferdinand Kramer†; Draper & Kramer, Inc.
Contact: Forrest D. Bailey, Pres.
Financial data (yr. ended 12/31/11): Assets, $23,825 (M); gifts received, $25,000; expenditures, $21,438; qualifying distributions, $21,000; giving activities include $21,000 for grants.
Purpose and activities: The foundation supports museums and organizations involved with performing arts, secondary and higher education, birth defects, disability services, and civic affairs.
Type of support: General/operating support.
Support limitations: No grants to individuals.
Application information: Applications accepted. Application form required. Applicants should submit the following:
1) copy of IRS Determination Letter
2) detailed description of project and amount of funding requested
Initial approach: Proposal
Deadline(s): None
Officers and Directors:* Forrest D. Bailey*, Pres.; Frederick C. Ford, V.P. and Treas.; Douglas Kramer*, V.P.; Lorraine N. Madsen, Secy.
EIN: 237044259

1171
The Charles Stark Draper Laboratory, Inc.

(doing business as Draper Laboratory)
555 Technology Sq.
Cambridge, MA 02139-3563
(617) 258-1000

Company URL: http://www.draper.com
Establishment information: Established in 1973.
Company type: Private company
Business activities: Operates a research and development company.
Business type (SIC): Research, development, and testing services
Corporate officers: John A. Gordon, Chair.; James D. Shields, Pres. and C.E.O.; Elizabeth Mora, C.F.O.; Len Polizzotto, V.P., Mktg.; Melinda J. Brown, Secy. and Genl Counsel
Board of directors: John A. Gordon, Chair.; Frank H. Akers, Jr.; William F. Ballhaus, Jr.; Delores M. Etter;

Sherwin Greenblatt; Daniel E. Hastings; Miriam E. John; Franklin C. Miller; George M. Milne, Jr.; M. Elisabeth Pate-Cornell; Richard T. Roca; James D. Shields; Peter B. Teets; Richard D. White
Offices: Huntsville, AL; Cape Canaveral, St. Petersburg, Tampa, FL; Pittsfield, MA; Houston, TX; Arlington, VA
Giving statement: Giving through the Charles Stark Draper Laboratory, Inc. Corporate Giving Program.

The Charles Stark Draper Laboratory, Inc. Corporate Giving Program

555 Technology Sq., MS 75
Cambridge, MA 02139-3563 (617) 258-2196
E-mail: communications@draper.com; Contact info. for Ellen Avery: e-mail: eavery@draper.com; tel.: (617) 258-2196; URL: http://www.draper.com/community_outreach.html

Contact: Ellen Avery, Mgr., Community Rels.
Purpose and activities: The Charles Stark Draper Laboratory makes charitable contributions to nonprofit organizations involved with education and community development. Special emphasis is directed toward programs that support engineering, mathematics, and science education. Support is limited to areas of company operations.
Fields of interest: Arts; Education; Human services; Mathematics; Engineering/technology; Science.
Type of support: General/operating support; In-kind gifts; Sponsorships.
Geographic limitations: Giving limited to areas of company operations in Huntsville, AL, Washington, DC, St. Petersburg and Tampa, FL, Cambridge, MA, and Houston, TX.
Support limitations: No support for political, religious, or discriminatory organizations, or agencies or organizations that do not directly serve the Cambridge community. No grants to individuals, or for academic research, underwriting of film, video, or television productions, conferences, trips, or tours, advertising, or membership fees or association fees.
Publications: Application guidelines.
Application information: Applications accepted. Sponsorships are granted to organizations engaged in the provision of events that give students, families and the community the chance to engage in STEM-related activities. Application form required.
Initial approach: E-mail Ellen Avery for sponsorship requests; Complete online application for grants
Deadline(s): Oct. 31 for grants
Final notification: First week of December

1172
DreamWorks Animation SKG, Inc.

Campanile Bldg.
1000 Flower St.
Glendale, CA 91201 (818) 695-5000
FAX: (800) 989-4671

Company URL: http://www.dreamworksanimation.com
Establishment information: Established in 1994.
Company type: Public company
Company ticker symbol and exchange: DWA/NASDAQ
Business activities: Produces computer generated animated motion pictures.
Business type (SIC): Motion pictures/production and services allied to
Financial profile for 2012: Number of employees, 2,400; assets, $1,944,890,000; sales volume, $749,840,000; pre-tax net income, -$53,640,000; expenses, $812,240,000; liabilities, $599,280,000
Corporate officers: Roger A. Enrico, Chair.; Jeffrey Katzenberg, C.E.O.; Lewis W. Coleman, Pres. and C.F.O.; Ann Daly, C.O.O.; Heather O'Connor, C.A.O.; Andrew Chang, Genl. Counsel and Corp. Secy.
Board of directors: Roger A. Enrico, Chair.; Harry M. Brittenham; Lewis W. Coleman; Thomas E. Freston; Mellody L. Hobson; Jeffrey Katzenberg; Michael J. Montgomery; Nathan Myhrvold; Richard Sherman
Giving statement: Giving through the DreamWorks Animation SKG, Inc. Contributions Program and the DreamWorks Animation Charitable Foundation, Inc.
Company EIN: 680589190

DreamWorks Animation SKG, Inc. Contributions Program

1000 Flower St.
Glendale, CA 91201-3007 (818) 695-5000
URL: http://www.dreamworksanimation.com/

DreamWorks Animation Charitable Foundation, Inc.

1000 Flower St.
Glendale, CA 91201-3007

Establishment information: Established in 2004 in CA.
Donor: DreamWorks Animation SKG, Inc.
Financial data (yr. ended 12/31/11): Assets, $3,073,997 (M); expenditures, $13,510; qualifying distributions, $13,430.
Purpose and activities: The foundation supports organizations involved with secondary and higher education, children, family services, and international relief.
Fields of interest: Elementary/secondary education; Higher education; American Red Cross; Children, services; Family services; International relief; International relief, 2004 tsunami.
Type of support: General/operating support.
Geographic limitations: Giving limited to CA.
Application information: Applications not accepted. Unsolicited requests for funds not accepted.
Officers: Heather O'Connor, Pres. and Treas.; Robert Kelly, V.P. and Secy.
EIN: 270111348

1173
Dresser, Inc.

15455 Dallas Pkwy., Ste. 1100
Addison, TX 75001 (972) 361-9800

Company URL: http://www.dresser.com
Establishment information: Established in 2001.
Company type: Subsidiary of a private company
Business activities: Designs, manufactures, and markets energy industry equipment and services.
Business type (SIC): Laboratory apparatus
Corporate officers: John P. Ryan, Pres. and C.E.O.; Linda Rutherford, Sr. V.P. and Genl. Counsel.; Darrin F. Whitney, V.P. and C.I.O.; Robbie Marshall, V.P., Human Resources; Richard T. Kernan, Treas.
Divisions: Dresser Wayne Div., Austin, TX; Waukesha Engine Div., Waukesha, WI
Giving statement: Giving through the James E. DeLong Foundation, Inc.

James E. DeLong Foundation, Inc.

1101 W. St. Paul Ave.
Waukesha, WI 53188-4961

Donors: Dresser Industries, Inc.; Halliburton Co.; Dresser, Inc.
Financial data (yr. ended 09/30/12): Assets, $115,472 (M); gifts received, $8,500; expenditures, $11,850; qualifying distributions, $11,750; giving activities include $11,750 for 10 grants to individuals (high: $2,250; low: $500).
Purpose and activities: The foundation awards college scholarships to children of employees of the Waukesha, Wisconsin, division of Dressner, Inc.
Fields of interest: Education.
Type of support: Employee-related scholarships.
Geographic limitations: Giving limited to Waukesha, WI.
Application information: Applications not accepted. Contributes only through employee-related scholarships.
Officers: Brian White, Pres.; Dan Hansen, V.P., Finance.
EIN: 396050331

1174
Dreyer's Grand Ice Cream Holdings, Inc.

5929 College Ave.
Oakland, CA 94618-1325 (510) 652-8187

Company URL: http://www.dreyersinc.com
Establishment information: Established in 1928.
Company type: Subsidiary of a foreign company
Business activities: Produces and sells ice cream products.
Business type (SIC): Dairy products; groceries—wholesale
Corporate officers: Mike Mitchell, Pres. and C.E.O.; Steve Barbour, Exec. V.P. and C.F.O.; Tony Sarsam, Exec. V.P., Sales and Opers.; William R. Oldenburg, Exec. V.P., Opers.; Bob Estes, C.I.O.; William C. Collett, Treas.
Plants: City of Commerce, Union City, CA; Lakewood, CO; Tampa, FL; Glendale Heights, IL; Gaithersburg, MD; Rockaway, NJ
Giving statement: Giving through the Dreyer's Grand Ice Cream Charitable Foundation.

Dreyer's Grand Ice Cream Charitable Foundation

5929 College Ave.
Oakland, CA 94618-1325 (510) 652-8187
FAX: (510) 610-4400; URL: http://www.nestleusa.com/Creating-Shared-Value/Community.aspx

Establishment information: Established in 1987 as a company-sponsored operating foundation.
Donor: Dreyer's Grand Ice Cream, Inc.
Contact: Kelly M. Su'a, Secy.
Financial data (yr. ended 12/25/10): Assets, $8,048 (M); gifts received, $405,025; expenditures, $400,276; qualifying distributions, $401,237; giving activities include $252,943 for 185 grants (high: $20,000; low: $40) and $61,900 for 1 foundation-administered program.
Purpose and activities: The foundation supports programs designed to promote family, school, and community environments that build skills and foster talents in young people.
Fields of interest: Elementary/secondary education; Vocational education; Higher education; Education, services; Education Youth.

Type of support: Capital campaigns; Continuing support; Donated products; Employee volunteer services; Equipment; General/operating support; Program development.
Geographic limitations: Giving primarily in the East Bay, Oakland, and Pleasanton CA, area.
Support limitations: No support for religious organizations not of direct benefit to the entire community or political organizations or candidates. No grants to individuals, or for raffle tickets, one-time conventions or meetings, scholarships, athletic sponsorships, benefit advertising, field trips or tours, independent film or video productions, or endowment projects.
Publications: Application guidelines.
Application information: Applications accepted. The foundation awards small grants of up to $1,000. Letters of inquiry should be submitted using organization letterhead and should be no longer than 1 page. Telephone calls during the application process are not encouraged. Application form not required. Applicants should submit the following:
1) name, address and phone number of organization
2) brief history of organization and description of its mission
3) detailed description of project and amount of funding requested
4) contact person

Initial approach: Letter of inquiry for small grants and product donations
Copies of proposal: 1
Board meeting date(s): 3rd Friday of the month
Deadline(s): 8 weeks prior to need for small grants and product donations
Final notification: 2 weeks following board meeting for small grants and product donations

Officers and Directors: Diane McIntyre, Pres.; David Bennett, V.P.; Dave Moirao, V.P.; Kelly M. Su'a, Secy.; Steve Robinson, Treas.; Geoff Fisher; Patricia J. Marino.
EIN: 943006987
Selected grants: The following grants are a representative sample of this grantmaker's funding activity:
$80,000 to Teach for America, New York, NY, 2009.
$40,000 to New Leaders for New Schools, New York, NY, 2009.
$35,000 to College Track, Oakland, CA, 2009.
$7,500 to Oakland Museum of California, Oakland, CA, 2009.
$5,000 to Reading Partners, Milpitas, CA, 2009.
$2,692 to Delancey Street Foundation, San Francisco, CA, 2009.

1175
Drinker Biddle & Reath LLP
1 Logan Sq., Ste. 2000
Philadelphia, PA 19103-6996
(215) 988-2700

Company URL: http://www.drinkerbiddle.com
Establishment information: Established in 1849.
Company type: Private company
Business activities: Operates law firm.
Business type (SIC): Legal services
Offices: Los Angeles, San Francisco, CA; Wilmington, DE; Washington, DC; Chicago, IL; Florham Park, Princeton, NJ; Albany, New York, NY; Philadelphia, PA; Milwaukee, WI
Giving statement: Giving through the Drinker Biddle & Reath LLP Pro Bono Program.

Drinker Biddle & Reath LLP Pro Bono Program
1 Logan Sq., Ste. 2000
Philadelphia, PA 19103-6996 (973) 549-7180
E-mail: Paul.Nittoly@dbr.com; Additional tel.: (215) 988-2700; URL: http://www.drinkerbiddle.com/about-us

Contact: Paul Nittoly, Partner; Pro Bono Comm. Co-Chair
Fields of interest: Legal services.
Type of support: Pro bono services - legal.
Geographic limitations: Giving primarily in areas of company operations in Los Angeles, and San Francisco, CA, Washington, DC, Wilmington, DE, Chicago, IL, Florham Park, and Princeton, NJ, Albany and New York, NY, Philadelphia, PA, and Milwaukee, WI.
Application information: The Pro Bono Committee manages the pro-bono program.

1176
L. F. Driscoll Co., LLC
9 Presidential Blvd.
P.O. Box 468
Bala Cynwyd, PA 19004-1003
(610) 668-0950

Company URL: http://www.lfdriscoll.com
Establishment information: Established in 1929.
Company type: Private company
Business activities: Provides construction management services.
Business type (SIC): Management and public relations services
Corporate officers: John J. Donnelly, C.E.O.; Frank M. Stulb, Pres.
Giving statement: Giving through the L. F. Driscoll Company Contributions Program.

L. F. Driscoll Company Contributions Program
9 Presidential Blvd.
Bala Cynwyd, PA 19004-1003
URL: http://www.lfdriscoll.com/web2013/our-company/community-involvement/

Purpose and activities: L.F. Driscoll makes charitable contributions to nonprofit organizations on a case by case basis. Support is given primarily in the Delaware Valley, Delaware, Maryland, New Jersey, and Pennsylvania area.
Fields of interest: Alzheimer's disease; Disasters, preparedness/services Children.
Type of support: Employee volunteer services.
Geographic limitations: Giving primarily in the Delaware Valley, DE, MD, NJ, and PA area.

1177
Drive Financial Services, LP
8585 N. Stemmons Fwy., Ste. 900
Dallas, TX 75247 (214) 634-1110

Company URL: http://www.drivefinancial.com
Establishment information: Established in 1992.
Company type: Subsidiary of a foreign company
Business activities: Provides consumer loans.
Business type (SIC): Credit institutions/personal
Corporate officer: Don Goin, C.I.O.
Giving statement: Giving through the Santander Consumer USA Inc. Foundation.

Santander Consumer USA Inc. Foundation
(formerly Drive With A Heart Foundation)
8585 N. Stemmons Fwy., Ste. 1100
Dallas, TX 75247-3836 (888) 222-4227
FAX: (214) 237-0533; URL: http://www.santanderconsumerusa.com/about/drive_w_heart.aspx

Establishment information: Established in 2004 in TX.
Donors: Scot A. Foith; Drive Financial Services LP; Santander Consumer Inc.; Blake Bozman; Concorde Group Corp.
Financial data (yr. ended 12/31/11): Assets, $243,866 (M); gifts received, $145,144; expenditures, $55,564; qualifying distributions, $55,265; giving activities include $55,265 for grants.
Purpose and activities: The foundation supports organizations involved with education, health, and poverty and awards college scholarships to K-12 and GED students.
Fields of interest: Education; Health care Economically disadvantaged.
Program:
Scholarship Program: The foundation awards college scholarships to K-12 and GED students residing in the Turner Courts housing development in Dallas, Texas.
Type of support: General/operating support; Scholarships—to individuals.
Geographic limitations: Giving primarily in Dallas, TX.
Application information: Applications not accepted. Contributes only to pre-selected organizations and individuals.
Officers: Thomas Dundon, Pres.; Jason Kulas, Treas.
EIN: 201519185
Selected grants: The following grants are a representative sample of this grantmaker's funding activity:
$5,000 to YWCA of Metropolitan Dallas, Dallas, TX, 2009.
$3,225 to Boys and Girls Clubs of Monterey County, Seaside, CA, 2009.
$1,000 to Cystic Fibrosis Foundation, Dallas, TX, 2009.

1178
Drop Down Deals, LLC
2701 Loker Ave. W., Ste. 200
Carlsbad, CA 92010 (760) 266-5090

Establishment information: Established in 2010.
Company type: Private company
Business activities: Operates coupon web site and browser shopping app development company.
Business type (SIC): Computer services
Corporate officer: Aaron Mendes, C.E.O.
Giving statement: Giving through the Drop Down Deals, LLC Contributions Program.

Drop Down Deals, LLC Contributions Program
2701 Loker Ave. W., Ste. 200
Carlsbad, CA 92010-6639
URL: http://www.dropdowndeals.com

1179
DRS Technologies, Inc.
5 Sylvan Way
Parsippany, NJ 07054 (973) 898-1500
FAX: (973) 898-4730

Company URL: http://www.drs.com
Establishment information: Established in 1968.
Company type: Subsidiary of a foreign company
Business activities: Manufactures and provides defense electronic products and systems and military support services.
Business type (SIC): Search and navigation equipment
Financial profile for 2010: Number of employees, 10,200
Corporate officers: William J. Lynn III, C.E.O.; Robert F. Mehmel, Pres. and C.O.O.; Richard A. Schneider, Exec. V.P. and C.F.O.; Mark A. Dorfman, Exec. V.P., Genl. Counsel, and Secy.; Allen H. Golland, Sr. V.P. and C.I.O.; Thomas P. Crimmins, Sr. V.P. and Corp. Cont.; Robert Russo, Sr. V.P., Opers.; Joseph Militano, Sr. V.P., Public Affairs and Comms.; Andrea J. Mandel, Sr. V.P., Human Resources; Donald G. Hardman, Treas.
Subsidiaries: DRS Data & Imaging Systems, Inc., Oakland, NJ; DRS Infrared Technologies, LP, Dallas, TX; DRS Optronics, Inc., Palm Bay, FL; DRS Sensors & Targeting Systems, Inc., Cypress, CA; DRS Surveillance Support Systems, Inc., Largo, FL; DRS Tactical Systems, Inc., West Palm Beach, FL; DRS Test & Energy Management, Inc., Huntsville, AL; Engineered Support Systems, Inc., St. Louis, MO; Night Vision Equipment Co., Inc., Emmaus, PA
Plant: Buffalo, NY
Joint Venture: Laurel Technologies Partnership, Johnstown, PA
International operations: Canada; United Kingdom
Giving statement: Giving through the DRS Technologies Charitable Foundation, Inc.
Company EIN: 132632319

DRS Technologies Charitable Foundation, Inc.
5 Sylvan Way
Parsippany, NJ 07054-3818 (973) 451-3584
FAX: (973) 898-7184; URL: http://www.drs.com/corporateinfo/corporategiving.aspx

Establishment information: Established in 2005 in NJ.
Donor: DRS Technologies Inc.
Contact: Richard Goldberg, Pres.
Financial data (yr. ended 12/31/11): Assets, $96,776 (M); gifts received, $1,058,850; expenditures, $1,029,279; qualifying distributions, $1,020,569; giving activities include $1,020,569 for grants.
Purpose and activities: The foundation supports organizations involved with education, health, disaster relief, human services, community development, civic affairs, children, and the military.
Fields of interest: Elementary/secondary education; Education; Health care; Disasters, preparedness/services; American Red Cross; Human services; Community/economic development; Military/veterans' organizations; Public affairs Children; Military/veterans.
Type of support: Continuing support; Employee-related scholarships; Program development; Scholarship funds.
Geographic limitations: Giving on a national basis in areas of company operations, with emphasis on Washington, DC, FL, MD, NY, PA, and VA; giving also to regional organizations active in areas of company operations.
Support limitations: No support for discriminatory organizations, religious, fraternal, political, or athletic organizations, school-affiliated orchestras, bands, choirs, or drama groups, or organizations operating solely outside of the U.S. No grants to individuals (except for employee-related scholarships) or families, or for basic research projects, endowments, general operating support, school-affiliated sports, or yearbooks.
Publications: Application guidelines.
Application information: Applications accepted. Proposals should be submitted using organization letterhead. Telephone calls during the application process are not encouraged. Multi-year funding is not automatic. Organizations receiving support are asked to submit a Form W-9. Application form not required. Applicants should submit the following:
1) results expected from proposed grant
2) population served
3) copy of IRS Determination Letter
4) brief history of organization and description of its mission
5) how project's results will be evaluated or measured
6) listing of board of directors, trustees, officers and other key people and their affiliations
7) detailed description of project and amount of funding requested
8) listing of additional sources and amount of support

Initial approach: Mail or e-mail proposal to foundation
Copies of proposal: 1
Deadline(s): None
Final notification: 4 to 6 weeks

Officers and Trustees: Richard Goldberg, Pres.; Richard A. Schneider, Secy.; Donald G. Hardman, Treas.; Larry Brewer; Robert Dann; Mark A. Dorfman; Andrea J. Mandel; Jason Rinsky.
EIN: 204025605
Selected grants: The following grants are a representative sample of this grantmaker's funding activity:
$300,000 to Army Distaff Foundation, Washington, DC, 2010.
$200,000 to Intrepid Relief Fund, New York, NY, 2010.
$38,700 to Community Hope, Parsippany, NJ, 2010.
$30,000 to Morristown Memorial Health Foundation, Morristown, NJ, 2010.
$24,000 to Intrepid Museum Foundation, New York, NY, 2010.
$10,000 to Project Healing Waters, La Plata, MD, 2010.
$9,400 to Navy Marine Coast Guard Residence Foundation, McLean, VA, 2010.
$8,800 to United States Navy Memorial Foundation, Washington, DC, 2010.
$5,000 to National Maritime Historical Society, Peekskill, NY, 2010.
$4,360 to Saint Louis ARC, Saint Louis, MO, 2010.

1180
Drugstore.com, Inc.
411 108th Ave. N.E., Ste. 1400
Bellevue, WA 98004 (425) 372-3200
FAX: (425) 372-3800

Company URL: http://www.drugstore.com
Establishment information: Established in 1998.
Company type: Subsidiary of a public company
Business activities: Provides Internet shopping and information services; operates online drug store; operates online beauty products store. At press time, the company is in the process of merging with Walgreen Co.
Business type (SIC): Drug stores and proprietary stores; computer services
Corporate officers: Dawn G. Lepore, Chair., Pres., and C.E.O.; Tracy Wright, V.P. and C.F.O.; Robert Potter, V.P. and C.A.O.; Jon Axelsson, V.P., Opers.
Board of director: Dawn G. Lepore, Chair.
Subsidiary: Beauty.com, Inc., Bellevue, WA
International operations: Australia; Canada; United Kingdom
Giving statement: Giving through the drugstore.com Foundation.
Company EIN: 043416255

drugstore.com Foundation
411 108th Ave. N.E., Ste. 1400
Bellevue, WA 98004-8417
E-mail: foundation@drugstore.com; URL: http://www.drugstore.com/green-commitment/qxc149848

Establishment information: Established in 1999 in WA.
Donor: drugstore.com, inc.
Financial data (yr. ended 06/30/12): Assets, $284,097 (M); expenditures, $7,842; qualifying distributions, $6,556; giving activities include $5,000 for 1 grant.
Purpose and activities: The foundation supports programs designed to facilitate emotional and economic self-sufficiency and improve the health, dignity, and well-being of people in need.
Fields of interest: Health care; Human services Economically disadvantaged.
Application information: Applications not accepted. Unsolicited requests for funds not accepted.
Officers and Directors:* Amy Reischauer, Pres.; Cabrelle Abel, V.P. and Secy.; Julie A. Johnston, V.P.; Jonnell Quarrie, Treas.
EIN: 943341248

1181
DRW Holdings, LLC
(also known as DRW Trading Group)
540 W. Madison St., Ste. 2500
Chicago, IL 60661-2555 (312) 542-1000

Company URL: http://www.drwtrading.com
Establishment information: Established in 1992.
Company type: Private company
Business activities: Provides financial market making services.
Business type (SIC): Brokers and dealers/security
Corporate officers: Donald R. Wilson, Jr., C.E.O.; James Lange, C.F.O.; Donald Wilson, Genl. Counsel
Giving statement: Giving through the DRW Trading Group Foundation.

DRW Trading Group Foundation
540 W. Madison St., Ste. 2500
Chicago, IL 60661-2555

Establishment information: Established in 2004 in IL.
Donor: DRW Holdings LLC.
Financial data (yr. ended 12/31/11): Assets, $1,309,625 (M); gifts received, $750,000; expenditures, $357,479; qualifying distributions, $357,282; giving activities include $352,118 for 27 grants (high: $52,188; low: $50).
Purpose and activities: The foundation supports food banks and organizations involved with

education, health, spine disorders, medical research, recreation, and human services.
Fields of interest: Charter schools; Education, reading; Education; Health care; Spine disorders; Medical research; Food services; Athletics/sports, golf; Recreation; Human services.
Type of support: General/operating support; Program development.
Application information: Applications not accepted. Contributes only to pre-selected organizations.
Officers: Jeffery Levoff, Pres.; Donald R. Wilson, Jr., V.P. and Secy.; Kevin Kroger, Treas.
EIN: 201734765

1182
DS Waters of America, Inc.

(formerly Suntory Water Group, Inc.)
5660 New Northside Dr., Ste. 500
Atlanta, GA 30328 (770) 933-1400

Company URL: http://www.water.com
Establishment information: Established in 1985.
Company type: Private company
Business activities: Operates water-cooler delivery company; also operates a national coffee and tea delivery service.
Business type (SIC): Beverages
Financial profile for 2010: Number of employees, 4,820
Corporate officers: Dillon K. Schickli, C.E.O.; Pete MacLean, Pres.; Tom Harrington, C.O.O.
Subsidiary: Hinckley & Schmitt, Inc., Chicago, IL
Giving statement: Giving through the DS Waters of America, Inc. Corporate Giving Program.

DS Waters of America, Inc. Corporate Giving Program

(formerly Suntory Water Group, Inc. Corporate Giving Program)
c/o Corp. Contribs.
5660 New Northside Dr., Ste. 500
Atlanta, GA 30328-5826

Purpose and activities: DS Waters of America makes charitable contributions to zoos and nonprofit organizations involved with cancer, disaster relief, recreation, and other areas on a case by case basis. Support is given primarily in areas of company operations.
Fields of interest: Zoos/zoological societies; Cancer, leukemia; Breast cancer; Disasters, fire prevention/control; Recreation, fairs/festivals; Athletics/sports, amateur leagues; Recreation; General charitable giving.
Type of support: Donated products; In-kind gifts; Sponsorships.
Geographic limitations: Giving primarily in areas of company operations.
Application information: Applications accepted. Application form required. Applicants should submit the following:
1) detailed description of project and amount of funding requested
2) contact person
3) name, address and phone number of organization
4) plans for acknowledgement

Initial approach: Complete online application form
Copies of proposal: 1
Deadline(s): 30 days prior to need for water donations; 45 days prior to need for sponsorships
Final notification: Following review

1183
DTE Energy Company

1 Energy Plz.
Detroit, MI 48226-1279 (313) 235-4000
FAX: (313) 235-6743

Company URL: http://www.dteenergy.com
Establishment information: Established in 1996.
Company type: Public company
Company ticker symbol and exchange: DTE/NYSE
International Securities Identification Number: US2333311072
Business activities: Operates holding company; generates, transmits, and distributes electricity; transmits and distributes natural gas.
Business type (SIC): Electric services; gas production and distribution; holding company
Financial profile for 2012: Number of employees, 9,900; assets, $26,339,000,000; sales volume, $8,791,000,000; pre-tax net income, $960,000,000; expenses, $7,512,000,000; liabilities, $18,966,000,000
Fortune 1000 ranking: 2012—299th in revenues, 288th in profits, and 207th in assets
Forbes 2000 ranking: 2012—1014th in sales, 937th in profits, and 823rd in assets
Corporate officers: Gerard M. Anderson, Chair., Pres., and C.E.O.; David E. Meador, Exec. V.P. and C.F.O.; Bruce D. Peterson, Sr. V.P. and Genl. Counsel; Larry E. Steward, V.P., Human Resources; Sandy Ennis, V.P., Corp. Comms.; Lisa A. Muschong, Corp. Secy.
Board of directors: Gerald M. Anderson, Chair.; Lillian Bauder; David Brandon; W. Frank Fountain, Jr.; Charles G. McClure, Jr.; Gail J. McGovern; Mark A. Murray; James B. Nicholson; Charles W. Pryor, Jr.; Josue Robles, Jr.; Ruth G. Shaw; James H. Vandenberghe
Subsidiary: The Detroit Edison Company, Detroit, MI
Giving statement: Giving through the DTE Energy Company Contributions Program and the DTE Energy Foundation.
Company EIN: 383217752

DTE Energy Company Contributions Program

1 Energy Plz.
Detroit, MI 48226-1221
URL: http://www.dteenergy.com/dteEnergyCompany/community/

Purpose and activities: As a complement to its foundation, DTE also makes charitable contributions to nonprofit organizations directly. Support is given primarily in Michigan.
Fields of interest: Education; Environment; Animals/wildlife; Public health; Food banks; Food distribution, meals on wheels; Nutrition; Safety/disasters, public education; Aging, centers/services; Homeless, human services; Human services; Civil/human rights, equal rights.
Type of support: Employee volunteer services; In-kind gifts; Sponsorships.
Geographic limitations: Giving primarily in Michigan.
Application information:
Number of staff: 3 full-time professional; 2 full-time support.

DTE Energy Foundation

(formerly Detroit Edison Foundation)
1 Energy Plz., 1578 WCB
Detroit, MI 48226-1279 (313) 235-9271
E-mail: foundation@dteenergy.com; URL: http://www.dteenergy.com/dteEnergyCompany/community/

Establishment information: Established in 1986 in MI.
Donors: The Detroit Edison Co.; DTE Energy Ventures, Inc.
Contact: Karla Hall, V.P. and Secy.
Financial data (yr. ended 12/31/11): Assets, $50,208,564 (M); gifts received, $21,010,031; expenditures, $9,839,384; qualifying distributions, $9,786,284; giving activities include $9,560,208 for 549 grants (high: $530,000; low: $25).
Purpose and activities: The foundation supports programs designed to promote LEAD initiatives including, leadership, education, environment, achievement, development, and diversity in DTE Energy service territories.
Fields of interest: Arts, cultural/ethnic awareness; Performing arts; Arts; Elementary/secondary education; Higher education; Business school/education; Engineering school/education; Education, services; Education; Environment, natural resources; Environment, energy; Environment, forests; Environmental education; Environment; Employment; Food distribution, meals on wheels; Youth development; American Red Cross; Human services; Civil/human rights, equal rights; Community development, neighborhood development; Urban/community development; Business/industry; Community/economic development; Mathematics; Engineering/technology; Science; Leadership development Minorities; Women.

Programs:

Development: The foundation supports transformational projects located in DTE Energy's urban core cities designed to demonstrate significant economic impact.

Diversity: The foundation supports programs and organizations designed to promote personal understanding and inclusiveness; encourage and advocate for effective, positive change to combat discrimination; and celebrate and enhance awareness of different cultures.

Education - Higher Learning: The foundation supports specific academic departments of engineering, science, and business designed to prepare students to enter the workforce; institutions designed to prepare students for technical and skilled trade careers in the energy industry; and programs designed to increase student retention and success in engineering, the sciences, and business with a focus on women and minorities.

Education - K-12: The foundation supports programs designed to increase the number of college undergraduates entering the STEM (Science, Technology, Engineering, and Math) disciplines, to expand the STEM workforce pipeline. Special emphasis is directed toward programs designed to demonstrate proven effectiveness with increasing the number of college undergraduates in the STEM disciplines; provide an opportunity to improve skills in more than one STEM discipline; target high school age children; serve underserved communities of DTE Energy's service area; serve a large number of students (district-wide, multiple cities); and academic tutorial and enhancement programs designed to advance student achievement.

Environment: The foundation supports programs designed to protect and restore the environment and enhance quality of life; and build understanding of the environment and promote the links between environmental stewardship and sustainable development, including education about renewable energy and energy efficiency that reaches a broad audience.

Human Needs: The foundation supports initiatives that are in the forefront of addressing critical and acute human needs of citizens in DTE

Energy's customer service area brought on by the economic downturn.

Leadership: The foundation supports programs designed to provide unique experiences to equip individuals with leadership skills.

Type of support: Capital campaigns; Continuing support; Curriculum development; Employee matching gifts; Employee volunteer services; General/operating support; Program development; Sponsorships.

Geographic limitations: Giving primarily in areas of company operations in MI.

Support limitations: No support for political parties or organizations, religious organizations not of direct benefit to the entire community, discriminatory organizations, national or international organizations (unless they provide benefits directly to DTE Energy service areas), single purpose health organizations, or hospitals for building or equipment needs. No grants to individuals, or for political activities, student group trips, conferences, or building or equipment needs for hospitals.

Publications: Application guidelines; Program policy statement.

Application information: Applications accepted. Telephone calls and video submissions are not encouraged. Organizations receiving support are asked to provide a final report. Application form required. Applicants should submit the following:

1) role played by volunteers
2) timetable for implementation and evaluation of project
3) signature and title of chief executive officer
4) statement of problem project will address
5) population served
6) copy of IRS Determination Letter
7) brief history of organization and description of its mission
8) copy of most recent annual report/audited financial statement/990
9) how project's results will be evaluated or measured
10) explanation of why grantmaker is considered an appropriate donor for project
11) listing of board of directors, trustees, officers and other key people and their affiliations
12) detailed description of project and amount of funding requested
13) plans for cooperation with other organizations, if any
14) copy of current year's organizational budget and/or project budget
15) listing of additional sources and amount of support

Initial approach: Download application form and E-mail proposal and application form to foundation

Copies of proposal: 1

Board meeting date(s): Quarterly

Deadline(s): Jan. 2 to Feb. 15; Apr. 22 to May 3; July 15 to July 26; and Oct. 14 to Oct. 25

Final notification: Apr. 19, July 12, Oct. 11, and Dec. 27

Officers and Directors:* Joyce V. Hayes-Giles*, Chair.; Frederick E. Shell, Pres.; Karla D. Hall*, V.P. and Secy.; Naif A. Khouri*, Treas.; Lynne Ellyn; Paul C. Hillegonds; Bruce D. Peterson; Michael C. Porter; Larry E. Steward.

Number of staff: 1 full-time professional; 2 full-time support.

EIN: 382708636

Selected grants: The following grants are a representative sample of this grantmaker's funding activity:

$718,180 to United Way for Southeastern Michigan, Detroit, MI, 2010.
$530,000 to City Connect Detroit, Detroit, MI, 2011.
$475,100 to United Way for Southeastern Michigan, Detroit, MI, 2011.
$418,521 to Detroit Institute of Arts, Detroit, MI, 2011.
$275,000 to Business Leaders for Michigan Foundation, Detroit, MI, 2010.
$260,602 to University of Michigan, Ann Arbor, MI, 2010.
$257,050 to University of Michigan, Office of the President, Ann Arbor, MI, 2011.
$252,545 to Detroit Symphony Orchestra, Max M. Fisher Music Center, Detroit, MI, 2010.
$250,000 to Nature Conservancy, Michigan Chapter, Lansing, MI, 2011.
$125,000 to Detroit 300 Conservancy, Detroit, MI, 2010.
$102,500 to Womens Caring Program, Ann Arbor, MI, 2011.
$50,000 to Arab-American and Chaldean Council, Lathrup Village, MI, 2010.
$20,000 to One of Us, Detroit, MI, 2011.
$12,500 to Metropolitan Affairs Coalition, Detroit, MI, 2010.
$10,030 to Michigan History Foundation, Lansing, MI, 2010.
$10,000 to Woodward Avenue Action Association, Royal Oak, MI, 2011.
$7,425 to Calvin College, Grand Rapids, MI, 2010.
$5,733 to United Way of the Lakeshore, Muskegon, MI, 2010.
$5,500 to United Way of Gratiot County, Alma, MI, 2011.
$5,000 to Virginia Tech Foundation, Blacksburg, VA, 2011.

1184
E. I. du Pont de Nemours and Company

(also known as DuPont)
1007 Market St.
Wilmington, DE 19898-0001
(302) 774-1000
FAX: (302) 351-6454

Company URL: http://www2.dupont.com
Establishment information: Established in 1802.
Company type: Public company
Company ticker symbol and exchange: DD/NYSE
Business activities: Manufactures and sells high performance materials, specialty chemicals, pharmaceuticals, and biotechnology products.
Business type (SIC): Plastics and synthetics; chemicals and allied products; drugs
Financial profile for 2012: Assets, $49,736,000,000; sales volume, $35,310,000,000; pre-tax net income, $3,115,000,000; expenses, $32,195,000,000; liabilities, $39,648,000,000
Fortune 1000 ranking: 2012—72nd in revenues, 69th in profits, and 112th in assets
Forbes 2000 ranking: 2012—268th in sales, 210th in profits, and 463rd in assets
Corporate officers: Ellen J. Kullman, Chair. and C.E.O.; Nicholas C. Fanandakis, Exec. V.P. and C.F.O.; Thomas M. Connelly, Jr., Exec. V.P. and C.I.O.; Thomas L. Sager, Sr. V.P. and Genl. Counsel; Benito Cachinero-Sanchez, Sr. V.P., Human Resources; Scott Coleman, V.P., Sales and Mktg.
Board of directors: Ellen J. Kullman, Chair.; Lamberto Andreotti; Richard H. Brown; Robert A. Brown; Bertrand P. Collomb; Curtis J. Crawford; Alexander M. Cutler; Eleuthere I. Du Pont; Cornel B. Fuerer; Marillyn Hewson; Ellen Kullman; Lois D. Juliber; Lee M. Thomas
Subsidiaries: ChemFirst Inc., Jackson, MS; DuPont Agrichemicals Caribe, Inc., Manati, PR; Pioneer Hi-Bred International, Inc., Johnston, IA
International operations: Argentina; Australia; Belgium; Brazil; Canada; China; Colombia; France; Germany; Italy; Luxembourg; Mexico; Netherlands; Singapore; Spain; Sweden; Switzerland; Taiwan; United Kingdom; Venezuela
Giving statement: Giving through the DuPont Corporate Giving Program.
Company EIN: 510014090

DuPont Corporate Giving Program

c/o Corp. Contribs. Office
1007 N. Market St.
Wilmington, DE 19898-0001 (302) 774-1000
Application address for education: c/o DuPont Center for Collaborative Research and Education, P.O. Box 80357, Wilmington, DE 19880-0357;
URL: http://www2.dupont.com/Social_Commitment/en_US/outreach/index.html

Purpose and activities: DuPont makes charitable contributions to nonprofit organizations involved with arts and culture, education, the environment, health and human services, increasing access to opportunity, civic and community services, self-sufficiency, quality of life, and services for youth, children, and families. Support is given on a national and international basis, with emphasis on Wilmington, Delaware.

Fields of interest: Arts, cultural/ethnic awareness; Arts; Elementary/secondary education; Higher education; Education; Environment; Health care; Children/youth, services; Family services; Human services; Civil rights, race/intergroup relations; Community/economic development; Mathematics; Engineering/technology; Science; Public affairs.

Type of support: Employee volunteer services; Fellowships; General/operating support; Scholarship funds.

Geographic limitations: Giving on a national and international basis in areas of company operations, with emphasis on Wilmington, DE.

Support limitations: No support for disease-specific organizations, fraternal or veterans' organizations, political organizations or campaigns, sectarian organizations not of direct benefit to the entire community, or discriminatory organizations. No grants to individuals, or for endowments, political campaigns, curriculum development or assessment, or capital campaigns.

Publications: Application guidelines.

Application information: The DuPont Contributions and Memberships Team is responsible for non-education-related financial contributions. Proposals should be limited to 2 pages and should include an explanation of how the program relates to the DuPont philosophy of community sustainability. Application form not required. Applicants should submit the following:

1) explanation of why grantmaker is considered an appropriate donor for project
2) descriptive literature about organization
3) detailed description of project and amount of funding requested

Proposals should include the organization's e-mail address.

Initial approach: Proposal to headquarters; proposal to application address for education

Copies of proposal: 1

Committee meeting date(s): May and Sept.

Deadline(s): None

1185
Duane Morris LLP

30 S. 17th St
Philadelphia, PA 19103 (215) 979-1000

Company URL: http://www.duanemorris.com
Establishment information: Established in 1904.
Company type: Private company
Business activities: Operates law firm.
Business type (SIC): Legal services
Offices: Los Angeles, San Diego, San Francisco, Truckee, CA; Wilmington, DE; Washington, DC; Boca Raton, Miami, FL; Atlanta, GA; Chicago, IL; Baltimore, MD; Boston, MA; Las Vegas, NV; Cherry Hill, Newark, Princeton, NJ; New York, NY; Philadelphia, Pittsburgh, PA; Houston, TX
International operations: Singapore; United Kingdom; Vietnam
Giving statement: Giving through the Duane Morris LLP Pro Bono Program.

Duane Morris LLP Pro Bono Program

30 S. 17th St
Philadelphia, PA 19103-4196 (215) 979-1835
E-mail: anfriant@duanemorris.com; Additional tel.: (215) 979-1000; URL: http://www.duanemorris.com/site/probono.html

Contact: A. Nicole Friant, Esq., Pro Bono Counsel
Fields of interest: Legal services.
Type of support: Pro bono services - legal.
Geographic limitations: Giving primarily in areas of company operations in Los Angeles, San Diego, San Francisco, and Truckee, CA, Washington, DC, Wilmington, DE, Boca Raton, and Miami, FL, Atlanta, GA, Chicago, IL, Baltimore, MD, Cherry Hill, and Newark, NJ, New York, NY, Las Vegas, NV, Philadelphia, and Pittsburgh, PA, Houston, TX, and in Singapore, United Kingdom, Vietnam.
Application information: The Pro Bono Committee coordinates the pro-bono program.

1186
Duane Reade Holdings, Inc.

440 9th Ave.
New York, NY 10001-1640 (212) 273-5700

Company URL: http://www.duanereade.com
Establishment information: Established in 1960.
Company type: Subsidiary of a public company
Business activities: Operates drug store chain.
Business type (SIC): Drug stores and proprietary stores
Corporate officers: John A. Lederer, Chair. and C.E.O.; John K. Henry, Sr. V.P. and C.F.O.; Phillip A. Bradley, Sr. V.P., Genl. Counsel, and Secy.; Vincent A. Scarfone, Sr. V.P., Human Resources and Admin.
Board of directors: John A. Lederer, Chair.; Michael S. Green; John P. Malfettone
Giving statement: Giving through the Duane Reade Charitable Foundation.
Company EIN: 050599589

Duane Reade Charitable Foundation

440 9th Ave.
New York, NY 10001-1620 (212) 356-5241
E-mail: Drcharity@duanereade.com; E-mail for Cedar Scarlett-Lyon: scarletc@duanereade.com; URL: http://www.duanereade.com/CharitableFoundation.aspx

Establishment information: Established in 2007 in DE and NJ.
Donors: Beyer Farms, Inc.; Proctor and Gamble; Coca Cola Bottling Company NY; Graphics Atlanta Inc; Interactive Communications Intl Inc.; Johnson & Johnson; Kimberly-Clark; Kiss Products; L'Oreal Paris Division; Maybelline; Nature's Bounty Inc.; Novartis Consumer Health; Oak Hill Capital Management LLC; Paul, Weiss, Rifkind, Wharton & Garrison LLP; Steiner Foods Inc.; The American Bottling Company; The Michael Alan Group; The Walking Man Inc.; Tropical Foods; UTZ Quality Foods, Inc; Winick Realty Group, LLC; Wrigley.
Contact: Cedar Scarlett-Lyon
Financial data (yr. ended 12/31/11): Assets, $781,769 (M); gifts received, $568,168; expenditures, $350,000; qualifying distributions, $350,600; giving activities include $286,510 for 17 grants (high: $132,010; low: $500).
Purpose and activities: The foundation supports programs designed to promote health and wellness; address local community needs; and promote growth and development of communities in the New York Metro area.
Fields of interest: Health care, clinics/centers; Health care, patient services; Health care; Breast cancer; ALS; AIDS; Diabetes; Food services; Children/youth, services; Human services.
Type of support: General/operating support; Program development; Scholarship funds; Sponsorships.
Geographic limitations: Giving primarily in areas of store operations in NY.
Support limitations: No grants to individuals.
Publications: Application guidelines.
Application information: Applications accepted. Application form not required. Applicants should submit the following:
1) timetable for implementation and evaluation of project
2) copy of IRS Determination Letter
3) brief history of organization and description of its mission
4) detailed description of project and amount of funding requested

Initial approach: E-mail letter of inquiry to foundation
Board meeting date(s): Monthly
Deadline(s): 1 month prior to need

Officers and Directors:* Gregory Calvano, V.P.; Chris Darrow*, V.P.; Jeffrey Koziel, V.P.; Joseph Magnacca*, V.P.; Charles Newsom, V.P.; Aileen Rodriguez, V.P.; Paul Tiberio*, V.P.; Kenneth Wistreich, V.P.
EIN: 208607795
Selected grants: The following grants are a representative sample of this grantmaker's funding activity:
$135,059 to Susan G. Komen for the Cure, New York, NY, 2010.
$115,063 to Gay Mens Health Crisis, New York, NY, 2010.
$50,000 to American Diabetes Association, New York, NY, 2010.
$1,000 to Leukemia & Lymphoma Society, White Plains, NY, 2010.
$1,000 to New York Families for Autistic Children, Ozone Park, NY, 2010.

1187
The Duchossois Industries, Inc.

845 Larch Ave.
Elmhurst, IL 60126-1114 (630) 279-3600

Company URL: http://www.duch.com/
Establishment information: Established in 1916.
Company type: Private company
Business activities: Manufactures railroad equipment and artillery; broadcasts television and radio.
Business type (SIC): Railroad equipment; ammunition, ordinance, and accessories; radio and television broadcasting
Financial profile for 2010: Number of employees, 6,222; sales volume, $1,300,000,000
Corporate officers: Richard L. Duchossois, Chair.; Craig J. Duchossois, C.E.O.; Robert L. Fealy, Pres. and C.O.O.; Michael E. Flannery, Exec. V.P. and C.F.O.; Colleen M. O'Connor, V.P. and Treas.; Eric A. Reeves, V.P. and Genl. Counsel; William J. Connell, V.P. and Cont.
Board of directors: Richard L. Duchossois, Chair.; Robert L. Fealy
Subsidiaries: The Chamberlain Group, Inc., Elmhurst, IL; Chamberlain Manufacturing Corp., Elmhurst, IL; Thrall Car Manufacturing Co., Chicago Heights, IL; Transportation Corp. of America, Chicago Heights, IL
Giving statement: Giving through the Duchossois Family Foundation.

The Duchossois Family Foundation

(formerly The Duchossois Foundation)
333 N. Michigan Ave., Ste. 510
Chicago, IL 60601-3934 (312) 641-5765
E-mail: iriskrieg1@aol.com

Establishment information: Established in 1984 in IL.
Donors: Duchossois Industries, Inc.; Thrall Car Manufacturing Co.; Duchossois Technology Partners, LLC; Chamberlain Group, Inc.
Contact: Iris Krieg, Exec. Dir.
Financial data (yr. ended 12/31/11): Assets, $1,021,020 (M); gifts received, $1,000,000; expenditures, $1,818,882; qualifying distributions, $1,813,925; giving activities include $1,614,773 for 58 grants (high: $1,000,000; low: $5) and $60,410 for 7 employee matching gifts.
Purpose and activities: The foundation supports organizations involved with mental health, cancer, and human services.
Fields of interest: Mental health/crisis services; Cancer; Cancer research; Human services.
Type of support: Annual campaigns; Capital campaigns; Employee matching gifts; General/operating support; Research.
Geographic limitations: Giving primarily in the metropolitan Chicago, IL, area.
Application information: Applications not accepted. Contributes only to pre-selected organizations.
Board meeting date(s): 4 times per year
Officers and Directors:* Kimberly Duchossois*, Pres.; Craig J. Duchossois*, V.P. and Treas.; Richard L. Duchossois*, Secy.; Iris Krieg, Exec. Dir.; R. Bruce Duchossois; Dayle Fortino-Duchossois.
Number of staff: 1 part-time professional; 1 part-time support.
EIN: 363327987
Selected grants: The following grants are a representative sample of this grantmaker's funding activity:
$1,025,000 to Culver Educational Foundation, Culver, IN, 2010.
$1,000,000 to American Cancer Society, Chicago, IL, 2010.
$1,000,000 to University of Chicago, Chicago, IL, 2010. For metastases research.
$60,000 to Metropolitan Family Services, Chicago, IL, 2010.
$50,000 to American Cancer Society, Chicago, IL, 2010.
$15,000 to Hospice Foundation of Northeastern Illinois, Barrington, IL, 2010.

$5,000 to Hospice Foundation of Northeastern Illinois, Barrington, IL, 2010.

1188
A. Duda & Sons, Inc.

1200 Duda Trail
P.O. Box 620257
Oviedo, FL 32765-4507 (407) 365-2111

Company URL: http://www.duda.com
Establishment information: Established in 1926.
Company type: Private company
Business activities: Produces and markets fruits and vegetables; produces canned and frozen vegetables; produces frozen juice concentrate; produces sod; produces sugarcane; produces cattle; develops real estate.
Business type (SIC): Farms/vegetable and melon; farms, except cash grains/field crop; farms/fruit and nut; horticultural specialties; farms/livestock; specialty foods/canned, frozen, and preserved; real estate subdividers and developers
Corporate officers: Ferdinand S. Duda, Chair.; David J. Duda, C.E.O.; P. Barton Weeks, C.O.O.; Mark Engwall, C.F.O.; Tracy Duda-Chapman, Sr. V.P., Genl. Counsel; Dan Duda, Sr. V.P., Opers.
Board of directors: Ferdinand S. Duda, Chair.; Charles E. Adams; Richard A. Beard III; Andy Duda, Jr.; Andy L. Duda; Joseph A. Duda; Sammy Duda; Debbie Martell; Ernest M. Millet, Jr.; Mark J. O'Brien
Subsidiaries: Gene Jackson Farms, Oxnard, CA; Valley Onions, McAllen, TX; The Viera Co., Melbourne, FL
Giving statement: Giving through the John & Katherine Duda Foundation, Inc.

The John & Katherine Duda Foundation, Inc.

(formerly The John Duda Foundation, Inc.)
P.O. Box 620257
Oviedo, FL 32762-0257

Establishment information: Established in 1991 in FL as partial successor to the Duda Foundation.
Donors: A. Duda & Sons, Inc.; A. Duda & Sons, Inc.
Financial data (yr. ended 12/31/11): Assets, $2,428,578 (M); gifts received, $183,100; expenditures, $147,634; qualifying distributions, $118,855; giving activities include $115,700 for 27 grants (high: $17,400; low: $500).
Purpose and activities: The foundation supports organizations involved with education, human services, and Christianity.
Fields of interest: Education; Human services; Religion.
Type of support: Building/renovation; General/operating support.
Support limitations: No grants to individuals.
Application information: Applications not accepted. Contributes only to pre-selected organizations.
Officers: Linda Duda Nichols, Pres.; Diane Duda Miller, V.P.; Audrey Stinson, Secy.; Lisa Duda Bocchino, Treas.
Director: Mark Edward Dingwell.
EIN: 593041359

1189
Duke Energy Corporation

(formerly Duke Power Company)
526 South Church St.
Charlotte, NC 28202-1803 (704) 594-6200

Company URL: http://www.duke-energy.com
Establishment information: Established in 1916.
Company type: Public company
Company ticker symbol and exchange: DUK/NYSE
International Securities Identification Number: US26441C1053
Business activities: Generates, transmits, and distributes electricity.
Business type (SIC): Electric services
Financial profile for 2012: Number of employees, 27,885; assets, $113,856,000,000; sales volume, $19,624,000,000; pre-tax net income, $2,451,000,000; expenses, $16,514,000,000; liabilities, $72,993,000,000
Fortune 1000 ranking: 2012—145th in revenues, 116th in profits, and 59th in assets
Forbes 2000 ranking: 2012—480th in sales, 349th in profits, and 225th in assets
Corporate officers: James E. Rogers, Chair., Pres., and C.E.O.; Lynn J. Good, Exec. V.P. and C.F.O.; Jennifer L. Weber, Exec. V.P., Human Resources; A.R. Mullinax, V.P. and C.I.O.; Steven K. Young, V.P., Cont., and C.A.O.; Stephen G. De May, V.P. and Treas.
Board of directors: James E. Rogers, Chair.; William Barnet III; G. Alex Bernhardt, Sr.; Michael G. Browning; Harris E. DeLoach, Jr.; Daniel R. DiMicco; John H. Forsgren; Ann Maynard Gray; James H. Hance, Jr.; John T. Herron; James B. Hyler, Jr.; E. Marie McKee; E. James Reinsch; James T. Rhodes; Carlos A. Saladrigas; Philip R. Sharp
Subsidiaries: Cinergy Corp., Cincinnati, OH; PanEnergy Corp, Houston, TX
International operations: Argentina; Australia; Bermuda; Bolivia; Canada; Cayman Islands; Denmark; Ecuador; El Salvador; England; Greece; Guatemala; India; Ireland; Mauritius; Mexico; Netherlands; Nigeria; Panama; Peru; Saudi Arabia; South Africa; Spain; Trinidad & Tobago; United Kingdom; Uruguay
Historic mergers: Progress Energy, Inc. (July 2, 2012)
Giving statement: Giving through the Duke Energy Foundation and the Progress Energy Foundation, Inc.
Company EIN: 202777218

Duke Energy Foundation

(formerly Duke Power Company Foundation)
400 South Tryon St.
P.O. Box 1007
Charlotte, NC 28201-1007 (704) 382-7200
FAX: (704) 382-7600; Address for Share the Warmth Fund: Duke Energy Foundation, P.O. Box 35469, Charlotte, NC 28254; URL: http://www.duke-energy.com/community/foundation.asp

Establishment information: Established in 1984 in NC.
Donors: Duke Power Co.; Duke Energy Corp.; Duke Energy Field Services, LP; Duke Energy Business Services; DPC Midstream; Cinergy Foundation.
Contact: Alisa McDonald, V.P.
Financial data (yr. ended 12/31/11): Assets, $24,822,225 (M); gifts received, $707,911; expenditures, $16,892,151; qualifying distributions, $16,892,151; giving activities include $15,530,693 for 1,757 grants (high: $625,000; low: $80) and $1,358,853 for 2,409 employee matching gifts.
Purpose and activities: The foundation supports organizations involved with arts and culture, education, the environment, health, employment, safety, human services, community development, science, leadership development, senior citizens, and economically disadvantaged people.
Fields of interest: Arts; Elementary/secondary education; Vocational education; Higher education; Higher education, college (community/junior); Education; Environment, research; Environment, natural resources; Environment, energy; Environment; Employment, training; Employment, retraining; Employment; Safety/disasters; American Red Cross; Human services; Economic development; Business/industry; United Ways and Federated Giving Programs; Mathematics; Engineering/technology; Science; Leadership development Aging; Economically disadvantaged.
Programs:

Community Vitality: The foundation supports programs designed to promote human services, arts, cultural, and community safety; and foster community leadership.

Cooling Assistance: The foundation and Duke Energy provides financial assistance to the handicapped, elderly, and/or low-income families during the summer months to help with extreme temperatures. The program is administered by select social service agencies.

Duke Energy Matching Gifts Program: The foundation matches contributions made by employees and retirees of Duke Energy to educational institutions on a one-for-one basis up to $5,000 per employee, per year and to nonprofit organizations on a one-for-two basis up to $5,000 per employee, per year.

Duke Energy Scholars: The foundation annually awards 15 college scholarships of up to $5,000 to children of employees and retirees of Duke Energy. The program is administered by Scholarship America, Inc.

Economic Development: The foundation supports programs designed to promote economic development strategies; and skills and workforce development.

Education: The foundation supports programs designed to promote K-12 education, including science, technology, engineering, and math; and higher education including STEM and environment related initiatives.

Environment: The foundation supports programs designed to promote conservation, training, and research around environmental initiatives; and the efficient use of energy that doesn't create a conflict with approved jurisdictions.

Fan-Heat Relief: The foundation provides financial assistance to purchase fans for senior citizens during the summer months. The program is administered by the N.C. Department of Human Resources, Division of Aging and the State of South Carolina Office of the Governor.

Share the Warmth Fund: The foundation, in partnership with Duke Energy customers and Duke Energy's Bulk Power Marketing (BPM), provides financial assistance for heating bills during the winter season for low-income families. Duke Energy customers receive bill inserts about the Share the Warmth program, and the foundation matches contributions made by customers, up to $50 per customer.

Type of support: Annual campaigns; Building/renovation; Employee matching gifts; Employee volunteer services; Employee-related scholarships; General/operating support; In-kind gifts; Management development/capacity building; Matching/challenge support; Program development; Research; Scholarship funds.

Geographic limitations: Giving primarily in areas of company operations in FL, IN, KY, OH, NC, and SC.
Support limitations: No support for discriminatory organizations, political organizations or candidates, sports or all-star teams, elementary, secondary, or private schools, parent-teacher associations, religious organizations, or fraternal, veterans', or labor groups. No grants to individuals (except for employee-related scholarships), or for political activities or campaigns, fundraisers, uniforms, religious activities, general operating support, debt reduction, films, video, or television productions, membership or association fees, capital campaigns, investments, or improvements, endowments, conferences, trips, or tours, advertising, dinners, tables, walks, or runs; no utility service reduction.
Publications: Application guidelines; Informational brochure; IRS Form 990 or 990-PF printed copy available upon request; Program policy statement.
Application information: Applications accepted. Organizations receiving support are asked to submit periodic reports. Application form required.
Initial approach: Complete online application form
Board meeting date(s): Quarterly
Deadline(s): None
Officers and Trustees: Richard T. Williams, Pres.; Alisa McDonald, V.P.; Janet Robinson, Secy.; Kalyn Matthews, Treas.; Lynn J. Good; Dhiaa M. Jamil; Marc E. Manly; Keith B. Trent; Jennifer L. Weber.
Number of staff: 2 full-time professional.
EIN: 581586283
Selected grants: The following grants are a representative sample of this grantmaker's funding activity:
$625,000 to Queens University of Charlotte, Charlotte, NC, 2011.
$500,000 to Foundation for the Carolinas, Charlotte, NC, 2011.
$500,000 to Foundation for the Carolinas, Charlotte, NC, 2011.
$500,000 to University of North Carolina at Charlotte Foundation, Charlotte, NC, 2011.
$333,000 to North Carolina Museum of Natural Sciences, Friends of the, Raleigh, NC, 2011.
$175,000 to Chamber of Commerce Foundation of Greater Cincinnati, Cincinnati, OH, 2011.
$5,000 to Hendricks County Community Foundation, Avon, IN, 2011.
$4,000 to Executive Service Corps of Cincinnati, Cincinnati, OH, 2011.
$4,000 to Tippecanoe Arts Federation, Lafayette, IN, 2011.
$3,500 to National Black MBA Association, Chicago, IL, 2011.

Progress Energy Foundation, Inc.

(formerly CP&L Foundation, Inc.)
P.O. Box 2591
Raleigh, NC 27602-2591 (919) 546-2207
FAX: (919) 546-4338;
E-mail: jennifer.pittman@pgnmail.com; Additional e-mail: grants@pgnmail.com; URL: https://www.progress-energy.com/commitment/community/index.page?

Establishment information: Established in 1990 in NC.
Donors: Carolina Power & Light Co.; Progress Energy, Inc.; Florida Progress Corp.
Contact: Jennifer Pittman, Contribs. Specialist
Financial data (yr. ended 12/31/11): Assets, $1,636,876 (M); expenditures, $6,173,054; qualifying distributions, $6,148,219; giving activities include $6,137,941 for 503 grants (high: $225,500; low: $8).
Purpose and activities: The foundation supports programs designed to help communities understand and adapt to the new realities posed by the shifting energy landscape. Special emphasis is directed toward programs designed to promote energy education, workforce development, and the environment.
Fields of interest: Arts; Elementary/secondary education; Higher education; Teacher school/education; Engineering school/education; Education; Environment, climate change/global warming; Environment, natural resources; Environment, energy; Environment; Employment, services; Employment, training; Employment; Economic development; Engineering/technology.
Programs:
Economic Vitality: The foundation supports major arts organizations that make a significant contribution to the economic vitality of Progress Energy headquarter cites of Raleigh, North Carolina and St. Petersburg, Florida.
Energy Education: The foundation supports programs designed to promote energy literacy in K-12 schools through teacher education, curriculum development, and experiential learning opportunities for students; and to encourage K-12 career academies and other K-12 education programs to raise awareness and interest in energy careers.
Energy Neighbor Fund: Through the Energy Neighbor Fund, Progress Energy provides assistance to low-income individuals and families for home energy bills. The fund collects donations from customers and Progress Energy employees and distributes them locally through social service agencies, community action agencies, and United Way organizations to help those experiencing hardship. Donations to the fund are matched on a one-for-one basis up to $1 million by the Progress Energy Foundation.
Environmental Stewardship: The foundation supports programs designed to advance technologies relating to greenhouse gas reduction and avoidance, alternative and renewable energy, and energy efficiency and conservation.
Workforce Development: The foundation supports programs designed to provide an adequately trained and diverse workforce to secure an energy future; promote workforce development for the energy industry through grants to targeted universities and community colleges in Progress Energy's service territory; establish or expand degree and certificate programs to develop skills and competencies that are in demand by the energy industry; and recruit and retain underrepresented groups in engineering schools through initiatives and scholarships.
Type of support: Annual campaigns; Conferences/seminars; Continuing support; Curriculum development; Employee matching gifts; General/operating support; Matching/challenge support; Program development; Research; Scholarship funds; Sponsorships.
Geographic limitations: Giving limited to areas of company operations in FL, NC, and SC.
Support limitations: No support for religious organizations not of direct benefit to the entire community, political candidates or organizations, lobbying organizations, athletic, labor, or fraternal groups, or individual K-12 schools. No grants to individuals, or for political causes or campaigns, endowments, or capital campaigns.
Publications: Application guidelines; Program policy statement.
Application information: Applications accepted. Additional information may be requested at a later date. Application form required. Applicants should submit the following:
1) statement of problem project will address
2) listing of board of directors, trustees, officers and other key people and their affiliations
3) detailed description of project and amount of funding requested
4) additional materials/documentation
Initial approach: Complete online application form
Board meeting date(s): Quarterly
Deadline(s): Feb. 1 for Energy Education; May 1 for Economic Vitality; Aug. 1 for Environmental Stewardship; Oct. 1 for Workforce Development
Final notification: Within 2 weeks following board meetings
Officers and Directors:* William D. Johnson*, Pres.; Vincent M. Dolan*, V.P.; John R. McArthur*, V.P.; Paula J. Sims*, V.P.; Lloyd M. Yates*, V.P.; Mary Woodley Dicus, Secy.; Mark F. Mulhern*, Treas.
Trustee: Wells Fargo Bank, N.A.
EIN: 561720636
Selected grants: The following grants are a representative sample of this grantmaker's funding activity:
$260,000 to University of Florida Foundation, Gainesville, FL, 2010.
$225,500 to University of Florida Foundation, Gainesville, FL, 2011.
$210,000 to North Carolina State University, Raleigh, NC, 2011.
$200,000 to Carolina Ballet, Raleigh, NC, 2010.
$200,000 to Carolina Ballet, Raleigh, NC, 2011.
$200,000 to North Carolina Symphony Foundation, Raleigh, NC, 2011.
$112,614 to United Way of the Greater Triangle, Morrisville, NC, 2011.
$100,000 to American Red Cross, Raleigh, NC, 2011.
$97,378 to United Way of the Greater Triangle, Morrisville, NC, 2010. For eGiving Campaign.
$71,674 to North Carolina Division of Social Services, Raleigh, NC, 2010. For Energy Neighbor Fund (Assistance program for low-income families, covering home energy bills).
$60,000 to Opera Company of North Carolina, Raleigh, NC, 2010.
$50,000 to Orlando Science Center, Orlando, FL, 2011.
$38,462 to North Carolina Division of Social Services, Raleigh, NC, 2010.
$30,433 to North Carolina Division of Social Services, Raleigh, NC, 2010. For Energy Neighbor Fund (Assistance program for low-income families, covering home energy bills).
$25,000 to Lake Sumter Community College Foundation, Leesburg, FL, 2011.
$25,000 to South Carolina State University, Orangeburg, SC, 2010.
$15,062 to Make-A-Wish Foundation of Central and Western North Carolina, Charlotte, NC, 2011.
$6,181 to Make-A-Wish Foundation of America, Phoenix, AZ, 2010. For eGiving Campaign.
$3,122 to United Way of Volusia-Flagler Counties, Daytona Beach, FL, 2010. For Energy Neighbor Fund.
$2,949 to United Way of Pasco County, Port Richey, FL, 2011. For the Energy Neighbor Fund and Special Medical Needs Programs in Florida.

1190

The Dun & Bradstreet Corporation

(also known as D & B)
103 JFK Pkwy.
Short Hills, NJ 07078 (973) 921-5500
FAX: (866) 560-7035

Company URL: http://www.dnb.com
Establishment information: Established in 1841.
Company type: Public company
Company ticker symbol and exchange: DNB/NYSE
Business activities: Provides business information services.
Business type (SIC): Credit reporting and collection agencies
Financial profile for 2012: Number of employees, 4,600; assets, $1,991,800,000; sales volume, $1,663,000,000; pre-tax net income, $295,200,000; expenses, $1,230,900,000; liabilities, $3,009,200,000
Corporate officers: Sara Mathew, Chair. and C.E.O.; Emanuele A. Conti, Pres.; Richard H. Veldran, Sr. V.P. and C.F.O.; Bruce R. Sink, Sr. V.P. and C.I.O.; Christie A. Hill, Sr. V.P., Genl. Counsel, and Corp. Secy.; Michael Sabin, Sr. V.P., Sales
Board of directors: Sara Mathew, Chair.; Austin A. Adams; John W. Alden; Christopher J. Coughlin; James N. Fernandez; Paul R. Garcia; Sandra E. Peterson; Michael J. Winkler
International operations: Argentina; Belgium; Brazil; Canada; China; Cyprus; England; France; Germany; Hong Kong; India; Ireland; Italy; Japan; Malaysia; Mauritius; Mexico; Netherlands; Peru; Singapore; Taiwan; Uruguay; Venezuela
Giving statement: Giving through the Dun & Bradstreet Corporation Foundation.
Company EIN: 223725387

The Dun & Bradstreet Corporation Foundation

1 Penn Plz.
New York, NY 10119-2100

Establishment information: Incorporated in 1953 in DE.
Donor: The Dun & Bradstreet Corp.
Financial data (yr. ended 12/31/11): Assets, $0 (M); expenditures, $0; qualifying distributions, $0.
Purpose and activities: The foundation supports organizations involved with disadvantaged youth. Special emphasis is directed toward organizations with which D&B employees are involved.
Fields of interest: Youth development.
Program:
Employee Matching Gifts: The foundation matches contributions made by full-time employees and directors of D&B to institutions of higher education on a one-for-one basis from $25 to $4,000 per contributor, per year.
Type of support: Annual campaigns; Continuing support; Employee matching gifts; General/operating support.
Application information: Applications not accepted. Unsolicited requests for funds not accepted.
Officers: Richard Veldran, V.P.; John Cinque, Co-Secy.; Richard Mattessich, Co-Secy.; Kathleen Guinnessey, Co-Treas.; Michael Muller, Co-Treas.
Trustees: Susan Beriont; Christie Hill.
Number of staff: 2
EIN: 136148188

1191

Dunkin' Brands Group Inc.

(formerly Dunkin' Brands, Inc.)
130 Royall St.
Canton, MA 02021 (781) 737-3000
FAX: (302) 636-5454

Company URL: http://www.dunkinbrands.com
Establishment information: Established in 1946.
Company type: Public company
Company ticker symbol and exchange: DNKN/NASDAQ
Business activities: Operates quick-service restaurant franchisor company.
Business type (SIC): Restaurants and drinking places
Financial profile for 2012: Number of employees, 1,104; assets, $3,217,510,000; sales volume, $658,180,000; pre-tax net income, $162,000,000; expenses, $422,710,000; liabilities, $2,870,860,000
Corporate officers: Nigel Travis, Chair. and C.E.O.; Giorgio Minardi, Pres.; Paul Twohig, C.O.O.; Paul Carbone, C.F.O.; Jack Clare, C.I.O.; Richard Emmett, Sr. V.P. and Genl. Counsel
Board of directors: Nigel Travis, Chair.; Raul Alvarez; Anthony DiNovi; Michael Hines; Sandra Horbach; Mark Nunnelly; Joseph Uva
Subsidiaries: Baskin-Robbins, Inc., Canton, MA; Dunkin' Donuts Incorporated, Canton, MA
Giving statement: Giving through the Dunkin' Brands Group Inc. Contributions Program, the Dunkin' Brands Charitable Trust, and the Dunkin' Donuts & Baskin-Robbins Community Foundation, Inc.
Company EIN: 204145825

Dunkin' Brands Group Inc. Contributions Program

130 Royall St.
Canton, MA 02021-1010 (781) 737-3000
FAX: (781) 737-4000;
E-mail: CSR@dunkinbrands.com; URL: http://www.dunkinbrands.com/Responsibility/

Financial data (yr. ended 12/31/10): Total giving, $242,766, including $242,766 for grants.
Purpose and activities: As a complement to its foundation, Dunkin' Brands Group also makes charitable contributions to nonprofit organizations directly. Support is given primarily in areas of company areas; giving also to national organizations.
Fields of interest: Environment, water pollution; Hospitals (general); Health care, blood supply; Health care; Cancer; Autism; Food services; Food banks; Recreation, parks/playgrounds; Athletics/sports, Special Olympics; American Red Cross; Children, services; Family resources and services, disability; Human services, gift distribution.
Type of support: Donated products; Employee volunteer services; General/operating support; In-kind gifts.
Geographic limitations: Giving primarily in areas of company operations.

Dunkin' Brands Charitable Trust

(formerly Dunkin' Donuts Charitable Trust)
c/o Dunkin Brands, Inc.
130 Royall St., Ste. 3WB
Canton, MA 02021-1010 (781) 961-4000

Donor: Dunkin' Donuts Inc.
Financial data (yr. ended 12/31/11): Assets, $115,410 (M); expenditures, $18,034; qualifying distributions, $16,000; giving activities include $16,000 for 8 grants to individuals (high: $2,000; low: $2,000).
Purpose and activities: The trust awards college scholarships to children of employees and franchise owners of Dunkin' Donuts, Baskin-Robbins, and Togo's Franchises. The program is administered by Scholarship America, Inc.
Fields of interest: Higher education.
Type of support: Employee-related scholarships.
Geographic limitations: Giving primarily in areas of company operations.
Application information: Applications not accepted. Contributes only through employee-related scholarships.
Trustees: Kate Lavelle; Jon Luther; Karen Raskopf.
EIN: 042733961

The Dunkin' Donuts & Baskin-Robbins Community Foundation, Inc.

(formerly Dunkin' Brands Community Foundation)
c/o CSR Dept.
130 Royall St.
2 West A
Canton, MA 02021-1010 (781) 737-3946
E-mail: foundation@dunkinbrands.com; URL: http://www.dunkinbrands.com/Foundation/

Donors: Ashapura, Inc., Inc.; Dunkin Brands Inc.
Contact: Christine Riley, Dir.
Financial data (yr. ended 12/31/11): Assets, $2,440,623 (M); gifts received, $1,719,552; expenditures, $1,179,873; qualifying distributions, $773,321; giving activities include $773,321 for grants.
Purpose and activities: The foundation supports programs designed to serve the basic needs of the community. Special emphasis is directed toward programs designed to address food, safety, and children's health.
Fields of interest: Hospitals (general); Health care; Food services; Food banks; Disasters, fire prevention/control; Safety/disasters; Children, services; Human services; Military/veterans' organizations Children.
Programs:
Food for Our Hungry: The foundation addresses critical hunger needs in the community through partnerships with local food banks and hunger relief organizations.
Health for Our Children: The foundation supports programs designed to improve the health and wellness of children. Special emphasis is directed toward children's hospitals and organizations that support research and treatment of children's diseases and illnesses.
Safety for Our Neighborhoods: The foundation supports programs designed to ensure neighborhood safety. Special emphasis is directed toward organizations that support firefighters, public safety officers, and troops at home and abroad.
Type of support: General/operating support; Scholarship funds.
Geographic limitations: Giving primarily in areas of company operations in AZ, CA, Washington, DC, FL, MA, MD, NY, and PA; giving also to national organizations.
Support limitations: No support for organizations lacking 501(c)(3) status.
Application information: Applications not accepted. Contributes only to pre-selected organizations.
Officers and Directors:* Mitch Cohen, Co-Chair.; Karen Raskopf, Co-Chair.; Jeff Miller, Secy.; Jim Damicone, Treas.; Frank Basier; Gary Heckel; Steven Kim; Dominic Laskero; Jon L. Luther; Sheila Patel; Joseph Prazeres; Christine Riley; Dan Saia; Alex Smigelski; Rod Valencia.
EIN: 260593784

Selected grants: The following grants are a representative sample of this grantmaker's funding activity:
$178,061 to Hasbro Childrens Hospital, Providence, RI, 2010. For operating support.
$16,913 to Phoenix Childrens Hospital, Phoenix, AZ, 2010. For operating support.
$10,642 to Jimmy Fund, Brookline, MA, 2010. For operating support.
$7,087 to Childrens Hospital, New Orleans, LA, 2010. For operating support.
$5,000 to RAW Art Works, Lynn, MA, 2010. For operating support.
$2,754 to Bakersfield Memorial Hospital Foundation, Bakersfield, CA, 2010. For operating support.

1192
Dunn Investment Company

3900 Airport Hwy.
Birmingham, AL 35222-1420
(205) 592-8908

Establishment information: Established in 1977.
Company type: Private company
Business activities: Operates non-residential construction company and manufactures ready-mixed concrete.
Business type (SIC): Contractors/general nonresidential building
Corporate officers: James S. M. French, Chair.; Danny Rogers, Pres.; William French, V.P. and C.F.O.
Board of director: James S. M. French, Chair.
Giving statement: Giving through the Dunn-French Foundation.

Dunn-French Foundation

P.O. Box 247
Birmingham, AL 35201-0247

Establishment information: Established in 1999 in AL.
Donor: Dunn Investment Company.
Financial data (yr. ended 12/31/11): Assets, $1,941,596 (M); gifts received, $240,675; expenditures, $104,796; qualifying distributions, $91,250; giving activities include $91,250 for grants.
Fields of interest: Education; Health care; Human services.
Support limitations: No grants to individuals.
Application information: Applications not accepted. Unsolicited requests for funds not accepted.
Officers: William D. French, Pres.; Joe French, V.P.; Mary Dunn French, V.P.; Beverley Hoyt, V.P.; James Overstreet, V.P.; Lucy Spann, V.P.; Stephen Spann, V.P.; Judy Martin, Secy.-Treas.
EIN: 631234807

1193
Dupps Company

548 N. Cherry St.
Germantown, OH 45327-0189
(937) 855-6555

Company URL: http://www.dupps.com
Establishment information: Established in 1935.
Company type: Private company
Business activities: Manufactures meat packing and processing equipment.
Business type (SIC): Machinery/special industry
Corporate officers: John Dupps, Chair.; Frank Dupps, Jr., Pres.; Steve Bray, C.I.O.
Board of director: John Dupps, Chair.
Giving statement: Giving through the Dupps Company Charitable Foundation.
Company EIN: 000000000

The Dupps Company Charitable Foundation

548 N. Cherry St.
P.O. Box 189
Germantown, OH 45327-1108

Establishment information: Established in 1996 in OH.
Donor: Dupps Co.
Financial data (yr. ended 12/31/11): Assets, $101,519 (M); gifts received, $75,000; expenditures, $38,730; qualifying distributions, $36,680; giving activities include $36,680 for grants.
Purpose and activities: The foundation supports organizations involved with education, human services, and business.
Fields of interest: Education; Environment.
Type of support: General/operating support; Program development.
Geographic limitations: Giving primarily in OH.
Support limitations: No grants to individuals.
Application information: Applications not accepted. Unsolicited requests for funds not accepted.
Trustees: David M. Dupps; Frank N. Dupps; John A. Dupps, Jr.
EIN: 311450495

1194
Duquesne Light Company

411 7th Ave.
Pittsburgh, PA 15219-1919 (412) 393-6000
FAX: (412) 393-5517

Company URL: http://www.duquesnelight.com
Establishment information: Established in 1912.
Company type: Private company
Company ticker symbol and exchange: DQUEO/ Pink Sheets
Business activities: Generates, transmits, and distributes electricity.
Business type (SIC): Electric services
Corporate officers: Morgan K. O'Brien, Pres. and C.E.O.; Mark E. Kaplan, C.P.A., Sr. V.P., C.F.O., and Co-Treas.; Joseph G. Belechak, Sr. V.P. and C.O.O.; William F. Fields, V.P. and Co-Treas.
Subsidiaries: DQEnergy Partners, Pittsburgh, PA; DQEnergy Services, Pittsburgh, PA; Duquesne Enterprises, Pittsburgh, PA; Montauk, Pittsburgh, PA
Giving statement: Giving through the Duquesne Light Company Contributions Program.

Duquesne Light Company Contributions Program

c/o Power of Light
411 7th Ave., MD 6-3
Pittsburgh, PA 15219-1919 (412) 393-6000
E-mail: communityrelations@duqlight.com;
URL: https://www.duquesnelight.com/insideDuquesneLight/community/default.cfm

Purpose and activities: Duquesne Light makes charitable contributions to nonprofit organizations involved with illuminating regional and neighborhood landmarks, recreational lighting, and lighting initiatives promoting economic vitality, safety, and security in the community. Support is limited to Allegheny and Beaver counties, Pennsylvania.
Fields of interest: Safety/disasters; Recreation, community; Community/economic development; Utilities Economically disadvantaged.
Type of support: In-kind gifts; Program development.
Geographic limitations: Giving limited to Allegheny and Beaver counties, PA.
Support limitations: No support for tax-supported organizations, political organizations, or fraternal organizations. No grants to individuals, or for capital campaigns, operating expenses, salaries, travel, specific arts performances or openings, fundraising dinners, luncheons, or events, golf outings, or healthcare or medical research.
Publications: Application guidelines.
Application information: Applications accepted. Proposals should be no longer than 3 pages. Submissions over the phone are not accepted. Application form not required. Applicants should submit the following:
1) timetable for implementation and evaluation of project
2) results expected from proposed grant
3) qualifications of key personnel
4) statement of problem project will address
5) population served
6) copy of IRS Determination Letter
7) brief history of organization and description of its mission
8) copy of most recent annual report/audited financial statement/990
9) how project's results will be evaluated or measured
10) listing of board of directors, trustees, officers and other key people and their affiliations
11) copy of current year's organizational budget and/or project budget
12) listing of additional sources and amount of support

Proposals should include financial statements for the past two years; and indicate how the project promotes economic development, enhances the quality of life, supports the wise use of energy, or assists low-income customers.
Initial approach: Mail proposal to headquarters or complete online application form
Deadline(s): None

1195
Dura Automotive Systems, Inc.

2791 Research Dr.
Rochester Hills, MI 48309-3575
(248) 299-7500

Company URL: http://www.duraauto.com
Establishment information: Established in 1990.
Company type: Private company
Business activities: Designs and manufactures automotive cockpit sub-systems, door modules, glass systems, seat mechanisms and structures, and engineered assemblies.
Business type (SIC): Motor vehicles and equipment
Financial profile for 2009: Number of employees, 15,350
Corporate officers: Jeffrey M. Stafeil, C.E.O.; Martin Becker, Exec. V.P. and C.O.O.; Jim Gregor, Exec. V.P. and C.F.O.; Sabine Urselmann, V.P., Human Resources
Board of director: Peter Hollex
Subsidiary: Universal Tool & Stamping Co., Inc., Butler, IN
Office: Elkhart, IN
International operations: Canada

Giving statement: Giving through the Dura Automotive Systems, Inc. Charitable Foundation.
Company EIN: 383185711

Dura Automotive Systems, Inc. Charitable Foundation
(formerly Excel Industries, Inc. Charitable Foundation)
2791 Research Dr.
Rochester Hills, MI 48309-3575

Establishment information: Established in 1988 in IN.
Donor: Excel Industries, Inc.
Financial data (yr. ended 12/31/11): Assets, $56,799 (M); expenditures, $31,967; qualifying distributions, $28,442; giving activities include $28,442 for grants.
Purpose and activities: The foundation supports the United Way.
Type of support: General/operating support.
Geographic limitations: Giving primarily in areas of company operations.
Support limitations: No grants to individuals.
Application information: Applications not accepted. Unsolicited requests for funds not accepted.
Trustee: Key Trust Company of Indiana, N.A.
EIN: 311243165

1196
Duro-Last Roofing, Inc.
525 Morley Dr.
Saginaw, MI 48601 (800) 248-0280
FAX: (800) 432-9331

Company URL: http://www.duro-last.com/
Establishment information: Established in 1978.
Company type: Private company
Business activities: Manufactures and installs prefabricated plastic roofing systems for commercial and industrial buildings.
Business type (SIC): Contractors/roofing, siding, and sheet metal work
Financial profile for 2010: Number of employees, 525
Corporate officers: Thomas Hollingsworth, Pres.; Steve Ruth, V.P. of Sales and Mktg.; Kelth Bowler, V.P., Human Services; Debbie Beirlein, Cont.
Giving statement: Giving through the John R. & Mildred B. Burt Charitable Foundation.

John R. & Mildred B. Burt Charitable Foundation
525 W. Morley Dr.
Saginaw, MI 48601-9485
E-mail: ssny@duro-last.com

Establishment information: Established in 2002 in MI.
Donors: Duro-Last Roofing; Plastatech Engineering; Oscoda Plastics; Tip Top Screw.
Financial data (yr. ended 12/31/11): Assets, $1,569,096 (M); gifts received, $196,977; expenditures, $69,172; qualifying distributions, $64,000; giving activities include $64,000 for grants.
Purpose and activities: The foundation supports organizations involved with education.
Fields of interest: Education.
Type of support: Scholarship funds.
Application information: Applications not accepted. Unsolicited requests for funds not accepted.
Officers: Jason Tunney, Pres.; Matthew Moeller, V.P.; Shawn Sny, Secy.
EIN: 300081622

1197
Dutch Gold Honey, Inc.
2220 Dutch Gold Dr.
Lancaster, PA 17601 (717) 393-1716
FAX: (717) 393-8687

Company URL: http://www.dutchgoldhoney.com
Establishment information: Established in 1946.
Company type: Private company
Business activities: Produces honey.
Business type (SIC): Miscellaneous prepared foods
Corporate officers: Nancy Gamber, Pres. and C.E.O.; Joe Semmelman, V.P., Opers.; Charles Schatzman, V.P., Admin. and Finance
Giving statement: Giving through the Gamber Foundation.

Gamber Foundation
2220 Dutch Gold Dr.
Lancaster, PA 17601-1997 (717) 393-1716

Establishment information: Established in 1984 in PA.
Donors: Dutch Gold Honey, Inc.; Luella M. Gamber; W. Ralph Gamber‡; Gamber Glass Container, Inc.
Contact: Michael T. Kane, Pres.
Financial data (yr. ended 09/30/12): Assets, $2,820,527 (M); gifts received, $124,000; expenditures, $171,133; qualifying distributions, $167,750; giving activities include $167,000 for 28 grants (high: $25,000; low: $1,000).
Purpose and activities: The foundation supports organizations involved with higher education, health, birth defects, housing development, and human services.
Fields of interest: Education; Health care; Human services.
Type of support: Capital campaigns; Employee-related scholarships; Endowments; Equipment; General/operating support; Program development; Scholarship funds.
Geographic limitations: Giving primarily in Lancaster, PA.
Application information: Applications accepted. Application form not required.
Initial approach: Proposal
Deadline(s): None
Officers: Michael T. Kane, Pres.; Julie A. Good, Secy.; Nancy J. Gamber, Treas.
Directors: Kitty L. Gamber; Luella M. Gamber; Marianne M. Gamber; W.R. Gamber II; Steven E. Kane; Christopher Markley; Timothy M. Zimmerman.
EIN: 232331958

1198
DVK, Inc.
1110 Albany Pl., S.E.
Orange City, IA 51041-1982
(712) 737-8880

Company type: Private company
Business activities: Rents equipment.
Business type (SIC): Equipment rental and leasing/miscellaneous
Giving statement: Giving through the Vogel Foundation.

The Vogel Foundation
(formerly Sinapi Aba Family Foundation)
P.O. Box 440
Orange City, IA 51041-0440

Establishment information: Established in 2000 in IA.
Donors: Van Sickle Paint Manufacturing Co., Inc.; DVK, Inc.; Diamond Vogel North, Inc.; Vogel Paint & Wax Co., Inc.
Financial data (yr. ended 12/31/11): Assets, $1,345,406 (M); gifts received, $523,000; expenditures, $264,154; qualifying distributions, $263,279; giving activities include $263,279 for grants.
Purpose and activities: The foundation supports environmental beautification programs and organizations involved with health, housing, human services, and Christianity.
Fields of interest: Environment, beautification programs; Health care; Housing/shelter; YM/YWCAs & YM/YWHAs; Children, day care; Aging, centers/services; Developmentally disabled, centers & services; Human services; United Ways and Federated Giving Programs; Christian agencies & churches.
Type of support: Building/renovation; General/operating support; Scholarship funds.
Geographic limitations: Giving primarily in Orange City, IA.
Support limitations: No grants to individuals.
Application information: Applications not accepted. Contributes only to pre-selected organizations.
Officers: Drew F. Vogel, Chair. and Pres.; Jean E. Vogel, Vice-Chair. and V.P.; Bert Aarsen, Secy.
EIN: 912068867
Selected grants: The following grants are a representative sample of this grantmaker's funding activity:
$5,000 to Brush Up Nebraska, Omaha, NE, 2011.
$3,000 to Bethany Christian Services, Grand Rapids, MI, 2011.

1199
Dykema Gossett PLLC
400 Renaissance Ctr.
Detroit, MI 48243 (313) 568-6800

Company URL: http://www.dykema.com/
Establishment information: Established in 1926.
Company type: Private company
Business activities: Operates law firm.
Business type (SIC): Legal services
Corporate officer: Rex E. Schlaybaugh, Jr., Chair.
Giving statement: Giving through the Dykema Gossett PLLC Pro Bono Program.

Dykema Gossett PLLC Pro Bono Program
400 Renaissance Ctr.
Detroit, MI 48243-1502 (734) 214-7710
E-mail: hnaasko@dykema.com; Additional tel.: (313) 568-6800; URL: http://www.dykema.com/probono.html

Contact: Heidi Naasko, Pro Bono Counsel
Fields of interest: Legal services.
Type of support: Pro bono services - legal.
Geographic limitations: Giving primarily in areas of company operations in Los Angeles, CA, Washington, DC, Bloomfield Hills, Chicago, and Lisle, IL, Ann Arbor, Detroit, Grand Rapids, and Lansing, MI, Charlotte, NC, and Dallas, TX.

Application information: The Pro Bono Committee manages the pro-bono program.

1200
Dynamet Inc.

195 Museum Rd.
Washington, PA 15301-6135
(724) 228-1000

Establishment information: Established in 1967.
Company type: Subsidiary of a public company
Business activities: Manufactures titanium and nickel based alloys, wire, bar, coil, forged parts, and machined parts.
Business type (SIC): Metal rolling and drawing/nonferrous; metal forgings and stampings; machinery/industrial and commercial
Corporate officers: Mark S. Kamon, Pres.; David L. Smith, V.P., Mktg. and Sales
Giving statement: Giving through the Rossin Foundation.

Rossin Foundation

(formerly Dynamet Foundation)
P.O. Box 1225
McMurray, PA 15317-4225 (412) 746-3401

Establishment information: Established in 1989 in PA.
Donors: Dynamet Inc.; Peter C. Rossin; Ada E. Rossin.
Contact: Viola G. Taboni, Treas.
Financial data (yr. ended 12/31/11): Assets, $15,481,671 (M); expenditures, $576,092; qualifying distributions, $362,388; giving activities include $362,388 for grants.
Purpose and activities: The foundation supports hospitals and organizations involved with arts and culture, patient services, and senior citizens.
Fields of interest: Museums (art); Arts; Hospitals (general); Health care, patient services; YM/YWCAs & YM/YWHAs; Aging, centers/services.
Type of support: Building/renovation; General/operating support; Program development; Research.
Geographic limitations: Giving primarily in PA, with some emphasis on Pittsburgh.
Support limitations: No grants to individuals.
Application information: Applications accepted. Application form not required. Applicants should submit the following:
1) detailed description of project and amount of funding requested
Initial approach: Proposal
Deadline(s): None
Officers and Trustees:* Ada E. Rossin*, Chair.; Peter N. Stephans*, Pres.; Joan R. Stephans*, Co-Treas.; Viola G. Taboni*, Co-Treas.; Katherine Dec; John Campbell Harmon; Elizabeth Lee Stephans-Baker.
EIN: 256327217
Selected grants: The following grants are a representative sample of this grantmaker's funding activity:
$300,000 to Saint Clair Memorial Hospital Foundation, Pittsburgh, PA, 2010. For general purpose.
$75,000 to Coalition for Christian Outreach, Pittsburgh, PA, 2010. For general purpose.
$12,000 to Washington and Jefferson College, Washington, PA, 2010. For general purpose.
$5,000 to Coalition for Christian Outreach, Pittsburgh, PA, 2010.
$4,000 to Washington Hospital Foundation, Washington, PA, 2010.
$2,500 to W Q E D Multimedia, Pittsburgh, PA, 2010.
$1,000 to Blind and Vision Rehabilitation Services of Pittsburgh, Homestead, PA, 2010.
$1,000 to Pressley Ridge Foundation, Pittsburgh, PA, 2010.
$1,000 to YMCA of Greater Pittsburgh, Pittsburgh, PA, 2010.

1201
Eagle Publishing, Inc.

(formerly Phillips International, Inc.)
1 Massachusetts Ave. N.W., Ste. 610
Washington, DC 20001 (202) 216-0600

Company URL: http://www.eaglepub.com
Establishment information: Established in 1993.
Company type: Private company
Business activities: Provides consumer and business information and solutions.
Business type (SIC): Business services/miscellaneous
Corporate officers: Thomas L. Phillips, Chair.; Jeffrey J. Carneal, Pres.; Jon A. Heimerman, V.P., Opers. and C.F.O.; Bob Austen, V.P., Mktg.
Board of directors: Thomas L. Phillips, Chair.; Jeffrey J. Carneal
Giving statement: Giving through the Phillips Foundation, Inc.

The Phillips Foundation, Inc.

1 Massachusetts Ave. N.W., Ste. 620
Washington, DC 20001-1401
FAX: (202) 216-9188;
E-mail: jfarley@thephillipsfoundation.org;
URL: http://www.thephillipsfoundation.org/#about.cfm
Contact for scholarships: c/o D. Jeffrey Hollingsworth, tel.: (202) 250-3887, ext. 628, e-mail: jhollingsworth@thephillipsfoundation.org

Establishment information: Established in 1990 in MD.
Donors: The Lynde and Harry Bradley Foundation, Inc.; Ann M. Corkery; Shelby Cullum Davis Foundation; Shelby Cullum Davis Foundation; Koch Foundation; Law Enforcement Legal Defense Fund; The Lehrman Institute; Lew Lehrman; Fred Malik Family; News Corporation; Robert Novak†; Pfizer; Phillips International, Inc.; Phillips Publishing International, Inc.; John William Pope Foundation; The Lesly & Pat Sajak Foundation; Tom Phillips Revocable Trust.
Contact: John W. Farley, Exec. Dir.
Financial data (yr. ended 09/30/11): Assets, $392,603 (M); gifts received, $280,302; expenditures, $962,790; qualifying distributions, $925,668; giving activities include $25,000 for 4 grants (high: $20,000; low: $1,000) and $378,500 for 83 grants to individuals (high: $30,000; low: $1,000).
Purpose and activities: The foundation awards college scholarships to college undergraduates, and fellowships to working print and online journalists.
Fields of interest: Higher education; Journalism school/education.
Programs:
Diana Davis Spencer Fellowship: The foundation awards fellowships to working journalists with less than ten years of professional experience in print and online journalism for writing projects focusing on the impact of free enterprise on society.
Environmental Fellowship: The foundation awards fellowships to working journalists with less than ten years of professional experience in print and online journalism for writing projects focusing on the environment from a free market perspective.
Law Enforcement Fellowship: The foundation awards fellowships to working journalists with less than ten years of professional experience in print and online journalism for writing projects focusing on some aspect of law enforcement in the U.S.
Robert Novak Journalism Fellowship Program: The foundation awards $50,000 full-time fellowships and $25,000 part-time fellowships to working journalists with less than ten years of professional experience in print and online journalism. Fellowships are comprised of a one-year writing project on a topic of the applicants choosing, focusing on journalism supportive of American culture and a free society.
Ronald Reagan College Leaders Scholarship Program: The foundation awards four-year renewable scholarships to college undergraduates who demonstrate leadership on behalf of freedom, American values, and constitutional principles. Scholarships range from $1,000 to $10,000.
Type of support: Fellowships; Scholarships—to individuals.
Geographic limitations: Giving on a national basis, with emphasis on CA, DC, MD, NJ, NY, PA, and VA.
Application information: Applications not accepted. Visit website for more information.
Officers and Trustees:* Thomas L. Phillips*, Chair.; Jon Heimerman, Treas.; John W. Farley, Exec. Dir.; Kellyanne E. Conway; Becky Norton Dunlop; Thomas A. Fuentes; Alfred S. Regnery; Ronald E. Robinson.
Number of staff: 2 part-time professional; 2 part-time support.
EIN: 521707001

1202
Eagle Tech International Inc.

44238 Fremont Blvd.
Fremont, CA 94538-6000 (510) 623-8481

Establishment information: Established in 1985.
Company type: Private company
Business activities: Manufactures general industrial engineered products and specialty systems.
Business type (SIC): Machinery/general industry
Corporate officer: Charles K. Chang, Owner
Giving statement: Giving through the Freshwind Foundation.

Freshwind Foundation

44238 Fremont Blvd.
Fremont, CA 94538-6000

Establishment information: Established in CA.
Donors: Eagletech International, Inc.; Charles K. Chang; Grace T. Wu.
Financial data (yr. ended 12/31/11): Assets, $2,156,759 (M); expenditures, $161,353; qualifying distributions, $133,200; giving activities include $133,200 for 10 grants (high: $50,000; low: $200).
Purpose and activities: The foundation supports organizations involved with historic preservation, education, and religion.
Fields of interest: Historic preservation/historical societies; Education; Christian agencies & churches; Religion.
Type of support: General/operating support.
Geographic limitations: Giving primarily in CA.
Application information: Applications not accepted. Contributes only to pre-selected organizations.

Officers: Charles K. Chang, Pres.; Grace T. Wu, Secy.
EIN: 202031040

1203
Eagle West, LLC
4611 Ivey Dr., Ste. 450
Macon, GA 31206-8814 (478) 745-7111

Establishment information: Established in 2003.
Company type: Private company
Business activities: Provides nonresidential general contract construction services.
Business type (SIC): Contractors/general nonresidential building
Corporate officers: Beckie Adams, Co-Pres.; Jed Renfroe, Co-Pres.
Giving statement: Giving through the Renfroe Family Foundation, Inc.

Renfroe Family Foundation, Inc.
125 Westridge Industrial Blvd., Ste. 101
McDonough, GA 30253-9098

Establishment information: Established in 2002 in GA.
Donor: Eagle West, LLC.
Financial data (yr. ended 12/31/11): Assets, $1,037 (M); gifts received, $17,874; expenditures, $18,655; qualifying distributions, $18,300; giving activities include $18,300 for grants.
Purpose and activities: The foundation supports organizations involved with higher education, athletics, children services, residential care, and Christianity.
Type of support: General/operating support; Program development; Scholarship funds.
Geographic limitations: Giving primarily in GA.
Support limitations: No grants to individuals.
Application information: Applications not accepted. Unsolicited requests for funds not accepted.
Officers: Charles Hartley Renfroe, Pres.; Debra Shoaf, C.F.O.; Patricia Renfroe, Secy.
Director: Christa Hurley.
EIN: 020545623

1204
EAP Lifestyle Management, LLC
1605 Main St.
Daphne, AL 36526-4463 (251) 621-5360
FAX: (251) 621-5361

Company URL: http://eaplifestyle.com/
Establishment information: Established in 1994.
Company type: Private company
Business activities: Operates employee assistance and work/life services company.
Business type (SIC): Personnel supply services
Corporate officer: Patty Vanderpool, Pres.
Giving statement: Giving through the EAP Lifestyle Management, LLC Contributions Program.

EAP Lifestyle Management, LLC Contributions Program
1605 Main St.
Daphne, AL 36526-4463 (251) 621-5360
URL: http://eaplifestyle.com/about.html

Fields of interest: Disasters, preparedness/services.
Type of support: Donated products.

1205
Dale Earnhardt, Inc.
1675 Dale Earnhardt Hwy., Ste. 3
Mooresville, NC 28115-8330
(704) 662-8000

Company URL: http://www.daleearnhardtinc.com
Establishment information: Established in 1980.
Company type: Private company
Business activities: Races cars; licenses intellectual property rights.
Business type (SIC): Commercial sports; investors/miscellaneous
Corporate officers: Teresa Earnhardt, Pres. and C.E.O.; Richie Gilmore, C.O.O.; Judy Queen, V.P., Opers.; Dale Frazer, Cont.
Giving statement: Giving through the Dale Earnhardt Foundation, Inc.

The Dale Earnhardt Foundation, Inc.
1675 Dale Earnhardt Hwy., No. 3
Mooresville, NC 28115-8330
FAX: (704) 663-7945;
E-mail: foundation@dei-zone.com; Toll-free tel.: (877) 334-3253; URL: http://www.daleearnhardtinc.com/foundation/index.php

Establishment information: Established in 2002 in NC.
Contact: Teresa Earnhardt, Chair.
Financial data (yr. ended 12/31/11): Revenue, $394,072; assets, $3,924,190 (M); gifts received, $54,319; expenditures, $182,605; giving activities include $7,000 for grants to individuals.
Purpose and activities: The mission of The Dale Earnhardt Foundation is to "continue the legend" and legacy of Dale Earnhardt through charitable programs and grants that sustain his lifelong commitment to children, education, and environmental/wildlife preservation.
Fields of interest: Child development, education; Higher education; Education; Environmental education; Animals/wildlife, preservation/protection; Community/economic development, public education; Community development, public/private ventures; Leadership development.
Program:
Legend Leadership Award: Grants of $7,000 each are available to individuals who demonstrate creativity and skills to bring bridges across boundaries (geographic, religious, ethnic, and philosophical) and bring together broad and increasingly diverse constituencies.
Type of support: Grants to individuals; Program development; Scholarship funds; Scholarships—to individuals.
Geographic limitations: Giving on a national basis.
Application information: Applications accepted. Application must include a copy of IRS Determination Letter. Application form required.
Initial approach: Download application form and mail to foundation for Legend Leadership Award with supporting document.
Copies of proposal: 1
Deadline(s): Postmarked by Dec. 31 for Legend Leadership Award
Officer and Directors:* Teresa Earnhardt*, Chair.; Pat LeGare; Judy Queen.
EIN: 510421279

1206
Earthquakes Soccer, LLC
(also known as San Jose Earthquakes)
(formerly Anschutz San Jose Soccer, Inc.)
451 El Camino Real, Ste. 220
Santa Clara, CA 95050 (408) 556-7700

Company URL: http://www.sjearthquakes.com/
Establishment information: Established in 2007.
Company type: Subsidiary of a private company
Business activities: Operates professional soccer club.
Business type (SIC): Commercial sports
Corporate officers: Dave Kaval, Pres.; Jared Shawlee, V.P., Sales
Giving statement: Giving through the San Jose Earthquakes Corporate Giving Program.

San Jose Earthquakes Corporate Giving Program
c/o Community Rels. Dept., Donations
451 El Camino Real
Santa Clara, CA 95050 (408) 556-7700
E-mail: jmettee@sjearthquakes.com; URL: http://www.sjearthquakes.com/community/quakes-contributions

Purpose and activities: The San Jose Earthquakes make charitable contributions of memorabilia to nonprofit organizations involved with education, youth soccer, and community development. Support is given primarily in northern California.
Fields of interest: Education; Athletics/sports, soccer; Youth development; Community/economic development.
Type of support: In-kind gifts.
Geographic limitations: Giving primarily in northern CA.
Application information: Applications accepted. Support is limited to 1 contribution per organization during any given year. Proposals should be submitted using organization letterhead. Application form not required. Applicants should submit the following:
1) name, address and phone number of organization
2) copy of IRS Determination Letter
3) detailed description of project and amount of funding requested
4) contact person

Proposals should indicate the date and location of the event and the type of fundraiser.
Initial approach: Proposal to headquarters
Copies of proposal: 1
Deadline(s): 1 month prior to need

1207
East Boston Savings Bank
67 Prospect St.
Peabody, MA 01960 (978) 977-2200

Company URL: http://www.ebsb.com
Establishment information: Established in 1848.
Company type: Subsidiary of a private company
Business activities: Operates savings bank.
Business type (SIC): Savings institutions
Corporate officers: Richard J. Gavegnano, Chair.; Deborah J. Jackson, Pres. and C.O.O.; Mark L. Abbate, C.F.O.; John A. Carroll, Sr. V.P. and C.I.O.; Paula M. Cotter, Sr. V.P., Opers.; Eric M. Heath, Sr. V.P., Human Resources
Board of director: Richard J. Gavegnano, Chair.
Giving statement: Giving through the East Boston Savings Charitable Foundation, Inc.

East Boston Savings Charitable Foundation, Inc.

(formerly Meridian Charitable Foundation, Inc.)
c/o East Boston Savings Bank
67 Prospect St.
Peabody, MA 01960-1604 (978) 977-2201
Additional tel.: (617) 567-1500; URL: http://www.ebsb.com/about-us/community/default.aspx

Establishment information: Established in 1998 in MA.
Donors: East Boston Savings Bank; Ralph R. Bagley, Esq.
Contact: Deborah J. Jackson, Treas.
Financial data (yr. ended 12/31/11): Assets, $3,972,945 (M); expenditures, $154,481; qualifying distributions, $153,511; giving activities include $153,511 for grants.
Purpose and activities: The foundation supports camps and organizations involved with education, health, hunger, housing, human services, and community development.
Fields of interest: Secondary school/education; Education; Health care; Food services; Housing/shelter, homeless; Housing/shelter; Recreation, camps; YM/YWCAs & YM/YWHAs; Youth, services; Family services; Residential/custodial care, hospices; Aging, centers/services; Developmentally disabled, centers & services; Homeless, human services; Human services; Community/economic development.
Type of support: Capital campaigns; Equipment; General/operating support; Program development; Scholarship funds.
Geographic limitations: Giving limited to East Boston, Everett, Lynn, Lynnfield, Melrose, Peabody, Revere, Saugus, Wakefield, and Winthrop, MA, and other North Shore, MA, areas.
Support limitations: No support for national organizations or city, town, state, or federal agencies. No grants to individuals or for annual campaigns or salaries.
Publications: Application guidelines; Grants list.
Application information: Applications accepted. Grants range from $1,000 to $5,000. Proposal narratives should be no longer than 3 pages. If brochures or pamphlets are included with the application, the applicant must provide 10 copies of each. Support is limited to 1 contribution per organization during any given year. Application form required. Applicants should submit the following:
1) role played by volunteers
2) timetable for implementation and evaluation of project
3) statement of problem project will address
4) population served
5) principal source of support for project in the past
6) name, address and phone number of organization
7) copy of IRS Determination Letter
8) brief history of organization and description of its mission
9) geographic area to be served
10) copy of most recent annual report/audited financial statement/990
11) descriptive literature about organization
12) listing of board of directors, trustees, officers and other key people and their affiliations
13) detailed description of project and amount of funding requested
14) plans for cooperation with other organizations, if any
15) contact person
16) organization's charter and by-laws
17) copy of current year's organizational budget and/or project budget

Initial approach: Download application form and mail proposal and form to foundation
Deadline(s): July
Final notification: 60 to 90 days

Officers and Directors: Richard J. Gavegnano, Pres.; Deborah J. Jackson, Treas.; Martha R. Bagley, Esq.; Paula M. Cotter; Grace Previte Magoon; Peter F. Scolaro; Ruth A. Sheets.
EIN: 043406328
Selected grants: The following grants are a representative sample of this grantmaker's funding activity:
$7,500 to Dimock Community Health Center, Roxbury, MA, 2009.
$6,200 to Boys and Girls Club of Lynn, Lynn, MA, 2009.
$5,750 to East Boston Social Centers, East Boston, MA, 2009.
$5,000 to HarborCOV, Chelsea, MA, 2009.
$5,000 to Mental Health Association, North Suffolk, Chelsea, MA, 2009.
$5,000 to Neighborhood House Charter School, Dorchester, MA, 2009.
$5,000 to Neighborhood of Affordable Housing, East Boston, MA, 2009.
$5,000 to Piers Park Sailing Center, East Boston, MA, 2009.
$5,000 to Pine Street Inn, Boston, MA, 2009.
$5,000 to Wellspring House, Gloucester, MA, 2009.

1208
East Cambridge Savings Bank

292 Cambridge St.
Cambridge, MA 02141-1263
(617) 354-7700

Company URL: http://www.ecsb.com
Establishment information: Established in 1854.
Company type: Private company
Business activities: Operates savings bank.
Business type (SIC): Savings institutions
Corporate officers: Lee C. Craig, Chair.; Gilda M. Nogueira, Pres. and C.O.O.; Gisella L. Margotta, Sr. V.P. and Treas.; Francesca DeFabrizio, Sr. V.P., Human Resources; Michael F. Ferreer, V.P., Mktg.
Board of director: Lee C. Craig, Chair.
Giving statement: Giving through the East Cambridge Savings Charitable Foundation, Inc.

East Cambridge Savings Charitable Foundation, Inc.

292 Cambridge St.
East Cambridge, MA 02141-1203 (617) 354-7700

Establishment information: Established in 1997 in MA.
Donor: East Cambridge Savings Bank.
Financial data (yr. ended 12/31/11): Assets, $168,364 (M); gifts received, $228,645; expenditures, $85,604; qualifying distributions, $84,010; giving activities include $84,010 for grants.
Purpose and activities: The foundation supports organizations involved with arts and culture, education, housing, and human services.
Fields of interest: Arts; Education; Human services.
Type of support: Employee-related scholarships; General/operating support; Program development.
Geographic limitations: Giving primarily in the Cambridge, MA, area.
Application information: Applications accepted. Application form required.
Initial approach: Proposal
Deadline(s): None

Officers and Directors:* Arthur C. Spears*, Pres.; Janine Mahoney, V.P.; Gisella L. Margotta, Treas.; Gilda M. Nogueira, Clerk; Joseph A. Amoroso, Jr.; Charles Aufiero; Lee C. Craig; Daniel A. Leone; Albert M. Pacheco; George E. Wilson.
EIN: 043399319

1209
Eastern Bank

265 Franklin St.
Boston, MA 02110-3113 (617) 897-1100

Company URL: http://www.easternbank.com
Establishment information: Established in 1818.
Company type: Subsidiary of a mutual company
Business activities: Operates mutual bank.
Business type (SIC): Savings institutions
Corporate officers: Richard E. Holbrook, Chair. and C.E.O.; Robert F. Rivers, Vice-Chair.; Jan A. Miller, Pres.; James B. Fitzgerald, C.F.O.; Terence A. McGinnis, Secy. and Genl. Counsel
Board of directors: Richard E. Holbrook, Chair.; Robert F. Rivers, Vice-Chair.; Richard C. Bane; Deborah H. Bornheimer; Paul M. Connolly; Robert A. Glassman; Daryl A. Hellman; Deborah C. Jackson; Wendell C. Knox; Peter K. Markell; George E. Massaro; John M. Plukas; Roger D. Scoville; Michael B. Sherman
Historic mergers: Plymouth Savings Bank (January 1, 2005); Wainwright Bank & Trust Company (December 17, 2010)
Giving statement: Giving through the Eastern Bank Charitable Foundation.

Eastern Bank Charitable Foundation

195 Market St., EP5-02
Lynn, MA 01901-1508 (781) 598-7595
FAX: (781) 596-4445;
E-mail: l.kurzrok@easternbk.com; TDD/TTY tel.: (781) 596-4408; URL: https://www.easternbank.com/foundation

Establishment information: Established in 1994 in MA.
Donor: Eastern Bank.
Contact: Laura Kurzrok, Exec. Dir.; Cindy Ciman, Fdn. Admin.
Financial data (yr. ended 12/31/11): Assets, $54,853,563 (M); gifts received, $5,000,000; expenditures, $3,135,624; qualifying distributions, $2,827,581; giving activities include $2,692,876 for 1,337 grants (high: $100,000; low: $40).
Purpose and activities: The foundation supports organizations involved with education, the environment, health, employment, affordable housing, children and families, human services, immigration, civil liberties, and economic revitalization. Special emphasis is directed toward programs designed to promote health and vitality in eastern Massachusetts.
Fields of interest: Higher education; Education; Environment; Health care, clinics/centers; Health care; Employment, services; Employment, training; Food banks; Nutrition; Housing/shelter; Boys & girls clubs; Youth development; Children, services; Family services; Family services, domestic violence; Human services, financial counseling; Minorities/immigrants, centers/services; Homeless, human services; Human services; Civil/human rights; Economic development; United Ways and Federated Giving Programs.
Program:
Eastern Bank Matching Gift Program: The foundation matches charitable contributions made by employees, trustees, and directors of Eastern

Bank to nonprofit organizations on a one-for-one basis from $50 to $1,000 per employee, per year.
Type of support: Annual campaigns; Building/renovation; Capital campaigns; Employee matching gifts; Endowments; General/operating support; Program development; Scholarship funds; Sponsorships.
Geographic limitations: Giving primarily in areas of company operations in eastern MA.
Publications: Annual report (including application guidelines); Application guidelines.
Application information: Applications accepted. Community Grants are less than $10,000. Partnership Grants range from $10,000 to $50,000. Partnership Grants are limited to 1 contribution per organization during any 3-year period. Organizations that do not meet the eligibility requirements for Community Grants or Partnership Grants may apply for Neighborhood Support. The average grant for Neighborhood Support is $500. Application form required. Applicants should submit the following:
1) name, address and phone number of organization
2) copy of IRS Determination Letter
3) brief history of organization and description of its mission
4) copy of most recent annual report/audited financial statement/990
5) detailed description of project and amount of funding requested
6) contact person
7) copy of current year's organizational budget and/or project budget

Initial approach: Complete online application
Board meeting date(s): Monthly for Community Grants and Neighborhood Support; Semi-annually for Partnership Grants
Deadline(s): None for Community Grants; Mar. 1 and Sept. 1 for Partnership Grants; None for Neighborhood Support
Final notification: 60 days for Community Grants; May and Nov. for Partnership Grants; 60 days for Neighborhood Support

Trustees: Richard C. Bane; Deborah Hill Bornheimer; Paul M. Connolly; Robert A. Glassman; Daryl A. Hellman; Richard E. Holbrook; Deborah C. Jackson; Wendell J. Knox; Stanley J. Lukowski; Peter K. Markell; George A. Massaro; Henry L. Murphy, Jr., Esq.; E. Joel Peterson; John M. Plukas; Roger D. Scoville; Michael B. Sherman.
Number of staff: 1 full-time professional; 2 part-time support.
EIN: 223317340
Selected grants: The following grants are a representative sample of this grantmaker's funding activity:
$2,500 to Action for Boston Community Development, Boston, MA, 2011.
$1,000 to Boy Scouts of America, Boston, MA, 2011.

1210
Eastern Federal Bank

(formerly Federal Bank)
257 W. Main St., Ste. 1
P.O. Box 709
Norwich, CT 06360-0709 (860) 889-7381

Company URL: http://www.easternfederalbank.com
Establishment information: Established in 1915.
Company type: Private company
Business activities: Operates savings bank.
Business type (SIC): Savings institutions
Corporate officers: Andre J. Messier, Jr., Chair.; Linda M. Adelman, Vice-Chair.; Gerald D. Coia, Pres. and C.E.O.; Brian J. Hennessey, C.F.O.; Richard K. Kreh, V.P. and Cont.
Board of directors: Andre J. Messier, Jr., Chair.; Linda M. Adelman, Vice-Chair.; Gerald D. Coia; Judy S. Jackson; Charles Seeman; Peter H. Shea
Offices: Colchester, Jewett City, Plainfield, CT
Giving statement: Giving through the Eastern Federal Bank Foundation, Inc.

Eastern Federal Bank Foundation, Inc.

(formerly Eastern Savings and Loan Foundation, Inc.)
257 Main St.
Norwich, CT 06360-0709 (860) 425-0145
E-mail: tschmitt@bankefb.com; Application contact: Christi A. Hallstrom, tel.: (860) 889-7381 ext. 145, fax: (860) 859-4489, e-mail: cah@easternfederalbank.com; URL: https://www.bankefb.com/index.asp?pID=aboutus&sID=efb

Establishment information: Established in 1998 in CT.
Donors: Eastern Savings and Loan Assn.; Eastern Federal Bank.
Contact: Tina Schmitt
Financial data (yr. ended 09/30/11): Assets, $313,961 (M); expenditures, $26,413; qualifying distributions, $24,500; giving activities include $24,500 for 31 grants (high: $1,000; low: $500).
Purpose and activities: The foundation supports hospitals and organizations involved with education, housing development, and human services.
Fields of interest: Libraries (public); Education; Housing/shelter, development; Big Brothers/Big Sisters; Family services; Aging, centers/services; Developmentally disabled, centers & services; Women, centers/services; Human services.
Type of support: Building/renovation; Curriculum development; Equipment; Management development/capacity building; Program development; Research; Scholarship funds; Technical assistance.
Geographic limitations: Giving primarily in areas of company operations in eastern CT.
Support limitations: No grants to individuals, or for general operating support.
Publications: Application guidelines.
Application information: Applications accepted. Grants range from $500 to $2,000. Application form required. Applicants should submit the following:
1) name, address and phone number of organization
2) contact person
3) detailed description of project and amount of funding requested
4) copy of current year's organizational budget and/or project budget
5) listing of additional sources and amount of support
6) timetable for implementation and evaluation of project
7) copy of IRS Determination Letter
8) listing of board of directors, trustees, officers and other key people and their affiliations
9) copy of most recent annual report/audited financial statement/990

Initial approach: Download application form and mail to foundation
Copies of proposal: 1
Deadline(s): Nov. 1 to Mar. 31
Final notification: June

Officers and Directors:* Gerald D. Coia, Pres.; Lisa Griffin, Sr. V.P.; Linda M. Adelman*, Secy.; Judy S. Jackson; Andre J. Messier, Jr.; Charles A. Seeman; Peter Shea, M.D.
EIN: 061539443

1211
Eastern New Mexico Rural Telephone Cooperative

(also known as ENMR-Plateau)
7111 N. Prince St.
P.O. Box 1947
Clovis, NM 88102-1947 (575) 389-8328

Company URL: http://www.plateautel.com
Establishment information: Established in 1949.
Company type: Cooperative
Business activities: Provides local, cellular, long distance, and data telephone communications services.
Business type (SIC): Telephone communications
Corporate officers: Tom Phelps, C.E.O.; Frank Blackburn, Pres.; Powhatan Carter, Secy.-Treas.
Board of directors: Frank Blackburn; Powhatan Carter; Kenny Wilhite
Subsidiary: Plateau Telecommunications, Inc., Clovis, NM
Giving statement: Giving through the ENMR-Plateau Corporate Giving Program and the ENMR Education Foundation.

ENMR-Plateau Corporate Giving Program

c/o Office of Public Affairs
P.O. Box 1947
Clovis, NM 88102-1947 (575) 389-4241
FAX: (575) 389-5255; E-mail: jrj@plateautel.com; Additional contact: Launa Waller, Dir., Economic Devel./Govt. Rels.: tel.: (505) 389-4211, fax: (505) 389-5103, e-mail: lwaller@plateautel.com; URL: http://www.enmr.com/donations.asp
Address for Higher Education Grant Program: ENMR-Plateau Telecommunications, P.O. Box 1947, 7111 N. Prince St., Clovis, NM 88102

Purpose and activities: As a complement to its foundation, ENMR-Plateau also makes charitable contributions to nonprofit organizations directly. Special emphasis is directed towards programs designed to promote education and economic development. Support is limited to ENMR-Plateau's service area in Arizona and New Mexico.
Fields of interest: Medical school/education; Health sciences school/education; Education; Agriculture/food, management/technical assistance; Disasters, preparedness/services; Safety/disasters; Athletics/sports, school programs; Community/economic development.
Program:
Higher Education Grant Program: ENMR-Plateau awards grants of up to $3,200 to undergraduate and graduate students who are members of the telephone cooperative or is the dependent of a cooperative member. The program is designed to off-set the costs of higher education including costs such as tuition, books, fees, temporary housing, or other educational expenses. All applicants must be employed while either residing full-time or working full-time in one or more of the telephone exchanges served by EMNR-Plateau.
Type of support: Employee-related scholarships; General/operating support; In-kind gifts; Matching/challenge support; Research; Scholarships—to individuals; Sponsorships.
Geographic limitations: Giving limited to ENMR-Plateau's service area in AZ and NM.
Support limitations: No support for religious or discriminatory organizations, or political organizations or candidates. No grants for individual sports teams or travel.
Publications: Application guidelines.

Application information: Applications accepted. Application form required. Applicants should submit the following:
1) name, address and phone number of organization
2) brief history of organization and description of its mission
3) detailed description of project and amount of funding requested
4) contact person
5) listing of additional sources and amount of support
6) plans for acknowledgement
Applications should specifically note the nature of the request being made, and any applicable deadlines.
Initial approach: Download application form and mail with proposal to headquarters; download application and mail to application address for Higher Education Grant Program
Deadline(s): 2 weeks prior to need; none for Higher Education Grant Program
Number of staff: 1 part-time professional; 1 full-time support.

ENMR Education Foundation

(formerly ENMR Telephone Education Foundation)
P.O. Box 1947
Clovis, NM 88102-1947 (575) 389-5100

Establishment information: Established in 1992 in NM.
Donor: Eastern New Mexico Rural Telephone Cooperative.
Financial data (yr. ended 12/31/11): Assets, $2,289,676 (M); gifts received, $245,105; expenditures, $98,307; qualifying distributions, $88,789; giving activities include $28,381 for 8 grants (high: $7,202; low: $1,650) and $59,525 for 70 grants to individuals (high: $1,600; low: $500).
Purpose and activities: The foundation supports organizations involved with education and public safety and awards scholarships to active members and the immediate family members and dependents of active members of ENMR-Plateau.
Fields of interest: Higher education; Education; Health care, EMS; Crime/law enforcement, police agencies; Disasters, fire prevention/control; Safety/disasters; Engineering/technology.
Programs:
Committed to Excellence Endowment Fund Scholarships: Through the Committed to Excellence Endowment Fund, the foundation awards $1,000 scholarships to high school seniors and returning college students. Applicants must hold a membership in the Cooperative and reside within one of the ENMR Telephone Cooperative exchange areas. High school applicants must have a 19 ACT score or a 1350 SAT score and returning college students must have a cumulative GPA of 2.5 or higher.
Education Foundation School Grant Program: The foundation awards grants of up to $5,000 to schools and school personnel to improve teaching and learning activities. The program is designed to encourage innovation in teaching with emphasis on learning through internet as a tool. Grants can be used for materials, consulting fees, equipment, travel, or other approved purchases and applicants must demonstrate how broadband internet access will be utilized to improve educational opportunities. The program is limited to Plateau Landline Members.
Public Safety Education Grants: The foundation awards grants of up to $5,000 to rural communities, municipalities, and pubic safety departments to assist with training and educational costs with maintaining well-trained and certified law enforcement and fire protection officers.
Type of support: Computer technology; Equipment; General/operating support; Scholarships—to individuals; Travel awards.
Geographic limitations: Giving limited to areas of company operations in NM.
Publications: Application guidelines; Informational brochure; Program policy statement.
Application information: Applications accepted. Applications for School Grant Program should include a brief narrative. Application form required. Applicants should submit the following:
1) statement of problem project will address
2) detailed description of project and amount of funding requested
Committed to Excellence Endowment Fund Scholarships applications should include GPA, ACT/SAT scores, 2 letters of recommendation, and a copy of the applicants current year FAFSA.
Initial approach: Download application form and mail to foundation
Copies of proposal: 1
Board meeting date(s): 4th Thurs. of each month
Deadline(s): None for School Grant Program and Public Safety Education Grants; 30 days prior to the academic year enrollment period for Committed to Excellence Endowment Fund Scholarships
Officer: Kenny Wilhite, Chair.
Trustees: Ismael Aragon; Mable Flores.
Number of staff: 1 full-time support.
EIN: 850385194

1212
Easthampton Savings Bank

36 Main St.
Easthampton, MA 01027-2050
(413) 527-4111

Company URL: http://www.bankesb.com
Establishment information: Established in 1869.
Company type: Private company
Business activities: Operates savings bank.
Business type (SIC): Savings institutions
Corporate officers: John Martin, Chair.; William S. Hogan, Jr., Pres. and C.E.O.; Bozena Dabek, Sr. V.P. and C.F.O.; Holly J. Fuller, Treas.
Board of director: John Martin, Chair.
Giving statement: Giving through the Easthampton Savings Foundation.

Easthampton Savings Foundation

36 Main St.
Easthampton, MA 01027-2050 (413) 779-2296

Establishment information: Established in 1997 in MA.
Donors: Easthampton Savings Bank; ESB Securities Corp.
Contact: Bozena Dabek, Treas.
Financial data (yr. ended 12/31/11): Assets, $1,675,863 (M); gifts received, $787,631; expenditures, $187,292; qualifying distributions, $187,292; giving activities include $187,167 for 36 grants (high: $20,000; low: $1,000).
Purpose and activities: The foundation supports food banks and organizations involved with education, health, housing development, golf, and community economic development.
Fields of interest: Higher education; Libraries (public); Education; Hospitals (general); Health care; Food banks; Housing/shelter, development; Athletics/sports, golf; Boys & girls clubs; YM/YWCAs & YM/YWHAs; Community/economic development; United Ways and Federated Giving Programs.
Type of support: Annual campaigns; Building/renovation; Capital campaigns; Continuing support; Endowments; General/operating support; Program development; Sponsorships.
Geographic limitations: Giving primarily in MA.
Application information: Applications accepted. Application form required.
Initial approach: Contact foundation for application form
Deadline(s): Varies
Officers: William S. Horgan, Jr., Pres.; Bozena Dabek*, Treas.
Directors: Kenneth S. Cernak; Peter Degrandpre; James G. Hayden, D.V.M; Joseph R. Maziarz.
EIN: 043371592
Selected grants: The following grants are a representative sample of this grantmaker's funding activity:
$1,000 to American Cancer Society, Atlanta, GA, 2010.

1213
Eastman Chemical Company

200 S. Wilcox Dr.
P.O. Box 431
Kingsport, TN 37660-5147 (423) 229-2000
FAX: (423) 229-8280

Company URL: http://www.eastman.com
Establishment information: Established in 1920.
Company type: Public company
Company ticker symbol and exchange: EMN/NYSE
International Securities Identification Number: US2774321002
Business activities: Manufactures and sells chemicals, plastics, and fibers.
Business type (SIC): Plastics and synthetics; chemicals and allied products
Financial profile for 2012: Number of employees, 13,500; assets, $11,619,000,000; sales volume, $8,102,000,000; pre-tax net income, $649,000,000; expenses, $7,302,000,000; liabilities, $8,676,000,000
Fortune 1000 ranking: 2012—324th in revenues, 364th in profits, and 355th in assets
Forbes 2000 ranking: 2012—1089th in sales, 1317th in profits, and 1373rd in assets
Corporate officers: James P. Rogers, Chair. and C.E.O.; Mark J. Costa, Pres.; Curt E. Espeland, Sr. V.P. and C.F.O.; David A. Golden, Sr. V.P. and Corp. Secy.; Perry Stuckey, Sr. V.P., HUman Resources
Board of directors: James P. Rogers, Chair.; Humberto P. Alfonso; Gary E. Anderson; Brett D. Begemann; Michael P. Connors; Stephen R. Demeritt; Robert M. Hernandez; Julie F. Holder; Renee J. Hornbaker; Lewis M. Kling; Howard L. Lance; David W. Raisbeck
International operations: Argentina; Australia; Belgium; Brazil; China; Denmark; Estonia; France; Germany; Hong Kong; Hungary; India; Indonesia; Italy; Japan; Malaysia; Mexico; Netherlands; Poland; Russia; Singapore; South Africa; South Korea; Spain; Switzerland; Taiwan; Thailand; Turkey; United Arab Emirates; United Kingdom
Giving statement: Giving through the Eastman Chemical Company Contributions Program and the Eastman Chemical Company Foundation, Inc.
Company EIN: 621539359

Eastman Chemical Company Contributions Program

P.O. Box 431
Kingsport, TN 37662-0431
FAX: (423) 229-8280;
E-mail: angieb@eastman.com; Pennsylvania application address: c/o Gerald Kuhn, Jefferson Site Mgr., Eastman Chemical Co., P.O. Box 567, West Elizabeth, PA 15088, fax: (412) 384-7311; Texas: c/o Sally Azbell, Eastman Chemical Co., P.O. Box 7444, Longview, TX 75607, fax: (903) 237-5799; URL: http://www.eastman.com/Company/Sustainability/Social_Responsibility/communities/Pages/Communities.aspx

Contact: Angie Jobe, Contribs Coord.; George Decroes, Cummunity Rels. Mgr.
Financial data (yr. ended 12/31/12): Total giving, $448,504, including $448,504 for grants.
Purpose and activities: As a complement to its foundation, Eastman Chemical also makes charitable contributions to nonprofit organizations on a case by case basis. Support is given primarily in areas of company operations.
Fields of interest: Arts; Education; Health care; Human services; Community/economic development; General charitable giving.
Type of support: Employee volunteer services; Employee-related scholarships; General/operating support; Sponsorships.
Geographic limitations: Giving primarily in areas of company operations in AL, MA, MD, MO, PA, TN, and TX.
Support limitations: No grants to individuals (except for scholarships), or for travel or tours.
Publications: Application guidelines.
Application information: Applications accepted. Multi-year funding is not automatic. The Community & Public Affairs Department handles giving. A contributions committee reviews all requests. Application form required.
Initial approach: Download online application and mail or fax to corporate headquarters, or Maryland, Pennsylvania, or Texas facilities
Copies of proposal: 1
Committee meeting date(s): Monthly
Deadline(s): None
Final notification: 1 to 2 months
Number of staff: 1 part-time professional; 1 part-time support.
Selected grants: The following grants are a representative sample of this grantmaker's funding activity:
$4,000 to FIRST LEGO League, Manchester, NH, 2012. For Robotics Competition.
$2,500 to Court Appointed Special Advocates Sullivan County, Kingsport, TN, 2012. For Red Shoe Gala.
$2,500 to Umoja Unity Committee, Johnson City, TN, 2012. For Umoja Unity Festival.
$1,500 to good Sports Always Recycle, Knoxville, TN, 2012. For Sustainability Steward Award.
$1,500 to Literacy Council of Kingsport, Kingsport, TN, 2012. For luncheon.
$1,500 to Salvation Army of Johnson City, Johnson City, TN, 2012. For Super Bowl sponsorship.
$1,000 to Food City, Kingsport, TN, 2012. For Santa Train scholarship.
$1,000 to Ronald McDonald House, Johnson City, TN, 2012. For golf tournament.
$700 to Big Brothers Big Sisters of Greater Tri-Cities, Kingsport, TN, 2012. For Bowl for Kids Sake.
$500 to Juvenile Diabetes Research Foundation International, Knoxville, TN, 2012. For Walk to Cure Diabetes.

Eastman Chemical Company Foundation, Inc.

c/o Bank One Trust Co.
P.O. Box 511
Kingsport, TN 37662-5000 (423) 229-1413
Application address: Pennsylvania: c/o Ron Lerario, NA Adhesives and Polymers Mfg. Dir., Eastman Chemical Co., P.O. Box 567, West Elizabeth, PA 15088, fax: (412) 384-7311; Tennessee and National Organizations: c/o Angie Jobe, Eastman Chemical Co., P.O. Box 431, Kingsport, TN 37662, fax: (423) 229-8280; and Texas: c/o Sally Azbell, Eastman Chemical Co., P.O. Box 7444, Longview, TX 75607, fax: (903) 237-5799; URL: http://www.eastman.com/company/sustainability/social_responsibility/communities/philanthropy/Pages/Eastman_Foundation.aspx

Establishment information: Established in 1996 in TN.
Donor: Eastman Chemical Co.
Contact: Paul Montgomery, Dir.
Financial data (yr. ended 12/31/11): Assets, $4,426,932 (M); gifts received, $305,550; expenditures, $2,509,503; qualifying distributions, $2,490,589; giving activities include $2,490,589 for grants.
Purpose and activities: The foundation supports programs designed to promote arts and culture, education, health, human services, community development, and civic affairs. Special emphasis is directed toward programs designed to improve the quality of life in communities where Eastman employees live and work.
Fields of interest: Arts; Health care; Human services; Community/economic development; Public affairs.
Type of support: Capital campaigns; Continuing support; Endowments; General/operating support; Program development; Scholarship funds.
Geographic limitations: Giving in areas of company operations, with emphasis on PA, SC, TN, and TX; giving also to national organizations.
Support limitations: No support for athletic teams, choirs, bands, drill teams, labor, veterans', fraternal, social, or political organizations, United Way-supported agencies (except for capital fund drives), discriminatory organizations, or religious organizations not of direct benefit to the entire community. No grants to individuals, or for travel, student trips, or tours.
Publications: Application guidelines.
Application information: Applications accepted. Support is limited to 1 contribution per organization during any given year. Multi-year funding is not automatic. Application form required. Applicants should submit the following:
1) name, address and phone number of organization
2) copy of IRS Determination Letter
3) brief history of organization and description of its mission
4) geographic area to be served
5) copy of most recent annual report/audited financial statement/990
6) how project's results will be evaluated or measured
7) list of company employees involved with the organization
8) detailed description of project and amount of funding requested
9) contact person
10) copy of current year's organizational budget and/or project budget
11) listing of additional sources and amount of support
Initial approach: Complete online application or download application form and mail or fax to nearest application address
Deadline(s): None
Officers and Directors:* Norris P. Sneed*, Pres.; Etta Clark*, V.P.; Brian L. Henry, Secy.; Mary Hall*, Treas.; Curtis E. Espeland; Paul Montgomery.
EIN: 621614800
Selected grants: The following grants are a representative sample of this grantmaker's funding activity:
$300,000 to Wellmont Foundation, Kingsport, TN, 2010.
$200,000 to University of Tennessee, Knoxville, TN, 2010.
$200,000 to YMCA, Greater Kingsport Family, Kingsport, TN, 2010.
$130,414 to East Tennessee State University, Johnson City, TN, 2010.
$125,000 to Boys and Girls Club of Greater Kingsport, Kingsport, TN, 2010.
$33,470 to United Way of Greater Kingsport, Kingsport, TN, 2010.
$8,000 to Palmetto Health Foundation, Columbia, SC, 2010.
$5,000 to American Red Cross, Columbia, SC, 2010.
$5,000 to Challenge Program, Johnstown, PA, 2010.
$4,000 to University of Alabama, Tuscaloosa, AL, 2010.

1214
Eastman Kodak Company

343 State St.
Rochester, NY 14650-0001 (585) 724-4000
FAX: 9585) 724-0663

Company URL: http://www.kodak.com
Establishment information: Established in 1880.
Company type: Public company
Company ticker symbol and exchange: EK/NYSE
Business activities: Develops, manufactures, and markets traditional and digital imaging products, services, and solutions.
Business type (SIC): Photographic equipment and supplies
Financial profile for 2011: Number of employees, 17,100; assets, $4,678,000,000; sales volume, $6,022,000,000; pre-tax net income, -$758,000,000; expenses, $6,780,000,000; liabilities, $7,030,000,000
Corporate officers: Antonio M. Perez, Chair. and C.E.O.; Philip J. Faraci, Pres.; Eric H. Samuels, C.A.O. and Corp. Cont.; Patrick M. Sheller, Sr. V.P., Secy., Genl. Counsel, and C.A.O.; Kim VanGelder, V.P. and C.I.O; William G. Love, Treas.
Board of directors: Antonio M. Perez, Chair.; Richard S. Braddock; Timothy M. Donahue; Michael Hawley; William H. Hernandez; Douglas R. Lebda; Kyle P. Leeg; Delano E. Lewis; William G. Parrett; Joel Seligman; Dennis F. Strigl
Subsidiaries: Cinesite, Inc., Hollywood, CA; Eastman Kodak International Capital Co., Inc., Rochester, NY; Eastman Software Inc., Rochester, NY; FPC Inc., Hollywood, CA; The Image Bank, Inc., Dallas, TX; Jamieson Film Co., Dallas, TX; Kodak (Near East), Inc., Rochester, NY; Kodak Americas, Ltd., Carolina, PR; Kodak Far East Purchasing, Inc., Rochester, NY; Qualex Inc., Durham, NC; Sterling Winthrop, Inc., New York, NY; Torrey Pines Realty Co., Inc., San Diego, CA
International operations: Argentina; Barbados; Belgium; Canada; Chile; China; Czech Republic; Egypt; England; Finland; France; Germany; Hungary;

India; Japan; Malaysia; Netherlands; New Zealand; Poland; Russia; Singapore; South Korea; Switzerland; Thailand; Venezuela
Giving statement: Giving through the Eastman Kodak Company Contributions Program and the Eastman Kodak Charitable Trust.
Company EIN: 160417150

Eastman Kodak Company Contributions Program

c/o Mgr., Community Affairs
343 State St.
Rochester, NY 14650-0552
URL: http://www.kodak.com/US/en/corp/communityAffairs/index.jhtml?pq-path=2879/2219

Purpose and activities: As a complement to its foundation, Eastman Kodak also makes charitable contributions to nonprofit organizations directly. Support is given primarily in areas of company operations in San Diego, California, Windsor, Colorado, Columbus, Georgia, Rochester, New York, and Dayton, Ohio.
Fields of interest: Arts; Education; Environment; Health care; Employment, training; Human services; Community/economic development Minorities; Economically disadvantaged.
Type of support: Donated equipment; Donated products; General/operating support; In-kind gifts; Research.
Geographic limitations: Giving primarily in areas of company operations in San Diego, CA, Windsor, CO, Columbus, GA, Rochester, NY, and Dayton, OH; giving also to national organizations.
Support limitations: No support for sectarian organizations, political organizations, or United Way-supported organizations. No grants to individuals or legislators, or for endowed chairs, university capital campaigns, event sponsorships, or political campaigns.
Application information: Applications not accepted. Grantmaking is currently suspended.

Eastman Kodak Charitable Trust

c/o JPMorgan Chase Bank
10 S. Dearborn St. 2
Chicago, IL 60605
Application address: Essie Calhoun, Dir., Corp. Contribs., 343 State St., Rochester, NY 14650, tel.: (585) 724-2434

Establishment information: Trust established in 1952 in NY.
Donor: Eastman Kodak Co.
Financial data (yr. ended 12/31/11): Assets, $232,806 (M); expenditures, $1,048,270; qualifying distributions, $1,011,000; giving activities include $1,011,000 for grants.
Purpose and activities: The trust supports organizations involved with education, health, asthma, human services, international relief, and community development.
Fields of interest: Higher education; Education; Hospitals (general); Health care; Asthma; Children/youth, services; Family services; Human services; International relief; Community/economic development.
Type of support: Conferences/seminars; Continuing support; Equipment; General/operating support; Program development; Scholarship funds.
Geographic limitations: Giving primarily in areas of company operations in Canada, China, Japan, Mexico, and the United Kingdom.
Support limitations: No grants to individuals; low priority for building or endowments; no loans; no matching gifts.
Publications: Corporate giving report.
Application information: Applications accepted. Application form not required. Applicants should submit the following:
1) copy of IRS Determination Letter
2) copy of current year's organizational budget and/or project budget
3) listing of additional sources and amount of support
Initial approach: Proposal
Board meeting date(s): Monthly
Deadline(s): None
Trustee: JPMorgan Chase Bank, N.A.
EIN: 166015274

1215
Easton-Bell Sports, Inc.

(formerly Easton Sports, Inc.)
7855 Haskell Ave., Ste. 200
Van Nuys, CA 91406-1902 (818) 902-5800
FAX: (646) 572-6336

Company URL: http://www.eastonbellsports.com/
Establishment information: Established in 1929.
Company type: Subsidiary of a private company
Business activities: Manufactures sporting goods and equipment.
Business type (SIC): Games, toys, and sporting and athletic goods
Corporate officers: Terry G. Lee, Chair. and C.E.O.; Donna L. Flood, C.O.O.; Mark A. Tripp, Sr. V.P., Finance, Secy.-Treas., and C.F.O.
Board of director: Terry G. Lee, Chair.
Giving statement: Giving through the Easton Sports Development Foundation.

Easton Sports Development Foundation

7855 Haskell Ave., Ste. 350
Van Nuys, CA 91406-1902
E-mail: csawyer@jasdeaston.com; URL: http://www.esdf.org/

Establishment information: Established as a company-sponsored operating foundation in 1982.
Donors: Easton Aluminum, Inc.; The National Archery Association Foundation, Inc.; Easton Technical Products, Inc.; Easton Development, Inc.
Financial data (yr. ended 11/30/11): Assets, $23,923,934 (M); gifts received, $28,070; expenditures, $3,321,440; qualifying distributions, $2,247,092; giving activities include $500 for 1 grant and $1,319,651 for 4 foundation-administered programs.
Purpose and activities: The foundation supports programs designed to benefit archery and/or bow hunting.
Fields of interest: Recreation.
Type of support: General/operating support; Scholarship funds.
Application information: Applications not accepted. Unsolicited requests for funds not accepted.
Officers and Directors:* James L. Easton*, Pres.; Caren Sawyer*, C.F.O. and Treas.; Gregory J. Easton*, V.P. and Secy.; Don Rabska, V.P.; Daren Cottle; Lynn E. Easton; Randy Walk.
EIN: 953750153

1216
Eaton Corporation

Eaton Ctr.
Cleveland, OH 44114-2584 (216) 523-5000

Company URL: http://www.eaton.com
Establishment information: Established in 1911.
Company type: Public company
Company ticker symbol and exchange: ETN/NYSE
International Securities Identification Number: US2780581029
Business activities: Designs and manufactures fluid power systems, electrical power quality, distribution, and control products, automotive engine air management and fuel economy products, and truck fuel economy and safety systems.
Business type (SIC): Motor vehicles and equipment; machinery/industrial and commercial; electronic and other electrical equipment and components
Financial profile for 2011: Number of employees, 73,000; assets, $17,873,000,000; sales volume, $16,049,000,000; pre-tax net income, $1,553,000,000; expenses, $14,496,000,000; liabilities, $10,404,000,000
Corporate officers: Alexander M. Cutler, Chair., Pres., and C.E.O.; Craig Arnold, Co-Vice-Chair. and Co-C.O.O.; Thomas S. Gross, Co-Vice-Chair. and Co-C.O.O.; Richard H. Fearon, Co-Vice-Chair. and C.F.O.; Mark M. McGuire, Exec. V.P. and Genl. Counsel; William W. Blausey, Sr. V.P. and C.I.O.; Thomas E. Moran, Sr. V.P. and Secy.; Billie K. Rawot, Sr. V.P. and Cont.; Steven M. Boccadoro, Sr. V.P., Sales and Mktg.; Donald J. McGrath, Sr. V.P., Comms.; William B. Doggett, Sr. V.P., Public Affairs
Board of directors: Alexander M. Cutler, Chair.; Craig Arnold, Co-Vice-Chair.; Richard H. Fearon, Co-Vice-Chair.; Thomas S. Gross, Co-Vice-Chair.; George Barrett; Todd Bluedorn; Christopher M. Connor; Michael J. Critelli; Charles E. Golden; Arthur E. Johnson; Ned C. Lautenbach; Deborah L. McCoy; Gregory R. Page
Subsidiaries: Aeroquip-Vickers, Inc., Maumee, OH; Cutler-Hammer Inc., Pittsburgh, PA
International operations: Argentina; Australia; Austria; Belgium; Brazil; Bulgaria; Canada; China; Czech Republic; Denmark; Dominican Republic; Finland; France; Germany; Hong Kong; Hungary; India; Indonesia; Italy; Japan; Malaysia; Mexico; Netherlands; New Zealand; Norway; Poland; Romania; Russia; Singapore; South Africa; Spain; Sweden; Switzerland; Taiwan; Thailand; United Arab Emirates; United Kingdom; Venezuela
Giving statement: Giving through the Eaton Corporation Contributions Program and the Eaton Charitable Fund.
Company EIN: 340196300

Eaton Corporation Contributions Program

1111 Superior Ave., N.E.
Eaton Ctr.
Cleveland, OH 44114-2584 (216) 523-4944
FAX: (216) 479-7013;
E-mail: barrydoggett@eaton.com

Contact: William B. Doggett, Sr. V.P., Public and Community Affairs
Purpose and activities: As a complement to its foundation, Eaton also makes charitable contributions to nonprofit organizations directly. Support is given on a national and international basis.
Fields of interest: Arts; Elementary/secondary education; Vocational education; Higher education; Engineering school/education; Education, drop-out

prevention; Education; Health care; Disasters, preparedness/services; Family services; Human services; Urban/community development; Community/economic development; Public affairs.
International interests: Argentina; Australia; Belgium; Brazil; Canada; Chile; China; Colombia; Czech Republic; Denmark; Dominican Republic; Finland; France; Germany; Hungary; India; Indonesia; Ireland; Kenya; Mexico; Netherlands; Norway; Peru; Poland; Russia; Singapore; South Africa; Sweden; Taiwan; United Kingdom.
Type of support: Capital campaigns; Donated products; Employee volunteer services; In-kind gifts; Matching/challenge support; Program-related investments/loans.
Geographic limitations: Giving on a national and international basis in areas of company operations.
Support limitations: No support for religious, fraternal, political, or labor organizations. No grants to individuals, or for endowments, debt reduction, or general operating support.
Publications: Application guidelines; Corporate giving report.
Application information: Applications accepted. The Public and Community Affairs Department handles giving. A contributions committee reviews all requests. Application form not required. Applicants should submit the following:
1) results expected from proposed grant
2) copy of IRS Determination Letter
3) brief history of organization and description of its mission
4) copy of most recent annual report/audited financial statement/990
5) how project's results will be evaluated or measured
6) list of company employees involved with the organization
7) listing of board of directors, trustees, officers and other key people and their affiliations
8) detailed description of project and amount of funding requested
9) copy of current year's organizational budget and/or project budget
10) listing of additional sources and amount of support

Initial approach: Proposal to nearest company facility
Copies of proposal: 1
Committee meeting date(s): Bimonthly
Deadline(s): None
Final notification: Following review

Corporate Contributions Committee: Alexander M. Cutler, Chair., Pres., and C.E.O.; Craig Arnold, Vice-Chair. and C.O.O.; Susan J. Cook, Exec. V.P., Human Resources; William W. Blausey, Jr., Sr. V.P. and C.I.O.; Ken D. Semelsberger, Sr. V.P., Finance and Planning; William B. Doggett, V.P., Public and Community Affairs; James E. Sweetnam.
Number of staff: 2 part-time professional; 1 part-time support.

The Eaton Charitable Fund

c/o Eaton Corp.
1111 Superior Ave.
Cleveland, OH 44114-2584 (216) 523-4944
FAX: (216) 479-7013;
E-mail: barrydoggett@eaton.com; URL: http://www.eaton.com/Eaton/OurCompany/Sustainability/SustainablePractices/Community/index.htm

Establishment information: Trust established in 1953 in OH.
Donor: Eaton Corp.
Contact: William B. Doggett, Sr. V.P., Public and Community Affairs
Financial data (yr. ended 12/31/11): Assets, $2,342,713 (M); expenditures, $6,687,920; qualifying distributions, $6,680,349; giving activities include $6,674,039 for 1,503 grants (high: $112,360; low: $25).
Purpose and activities: The fund supports organizations involved with arts and culture, education, health, cancer, housing, disaster relief, human services, and community development. Special emphasis is directed toward organizations with which employees of Eaton are involved.
Fields of interest: Museums (art); Performing arts, theater; Performing arts, orchestras; Arts; Secondary school/education; Higher education; Education; Hospitals (general); Health care, patient services; Health care; Cancer; Housing/shelter, development; Housing/shelter; Disasters, preparedness/services; Youth development, business; American Red Cross; Salvation Army; YM/YWCAs & YM/YWHAs; Children/youth, services; Family services; Human services; Community/economic development; United Ways and Federated Giving Programs.
Program:
Employee Matching Gifts: The fund matches contributions made by full-time employees, retirees, and directors of Eaton and its wholly-owned subsidiaries in the U.S. and Canada to Red Cross and Salvation Army disaster relief funds, K-12 schools, institutions of higher education, and organizations involved with arts and cultural institutions on a one-for-one basis from $25 to $5,000 per contributor, per year.
Type of support: Building/renovation; Capital campaigns; Continuing support; Employee matching gifts; Employee volunteer services; Equipment; General/operating support; In-kind gifts; Matching/challenge support; Program development; Scholarship funds.
Geographic limitations: Giving on a national and international basis in areas of company operations.
Support limitations: No support for religious organizations not of direct benefit to the entire community; fraternal or labor organizations. No grants to individuals, or for endowments, medical research, general operating support for United Way agencies or hospitals, or debt reduction, fundraising events, or sponsorships; no loans.
Publications: Application guidelines; Corporate giving report; Informational brochure (including application guidelines).
Application information: Applications accepted. Cover letter should be submitted using organization letterhead. Proposals should be no longer than 1 to 3 pages. Support is limited to 1 contribution per organization during any given year. Multi-year funding is not automatic. Video and audio submissions are not encouraged. Application form not required. Applicants should submit the following:
1) population served
2) copy of IRS Determination Letter
3) brief history of organization and description of its mission
4) copy of most recent annual report/audited financial statement/990
5) list of company employees involved with the organization
6) explanation of why grantmaker is considered an appropriate donor for project
7) listing of board of directors, trustees, officers and other key people and their affiliations
8) listing of additional sources and amount of support
9) detailed description of project and amount of funding requested
10) copy of current year's organizational budget and/or project budget

Initial approach: Cover letter and proposal to nearest company facility
Copies of proposal: 1
Board meeting date(s): Bimonthly
Deadline(s): None
Final notification: 2 to 3 months

Corporate Contributions Committee: William B. Doggett, Chair.; Craig Arnold; William W. Blausey, Jr.; Alexander M. Cutler; Thomas S. Gross; James W. McGill; Kurt B. McMaken.
Trustee: KeyBank N.A.
Number of staff: None.
EIN: 346501856
Selected grants: The following grants are a representative sample of this grantmaker's funding activity:
$250,000 to University Hospitals Cleveland Medical Center, Cleveland, OH, 2010. For Vision 2010 Capital Campaign.
$200,000 to Economic Growth Foundation, Tower City Center, Cleveland, OH, 2010. For STEM High School.
$144,181 to United Way of Greater Cleveland, Cleveland, OH, 2010. For corporate gift.
$50,000 to Cleveland Orchestra, Cleveland, OH, 2010. For direct contribution.
$50,000 to Make-A-Wish Foundation of Michigan, Brighton, MI, 2010. For program support.
$15,000 to Abraham Lincoln Memorial Hospital, Lincoln, IL, 2010. For capital campaign.
$15,000 to Great Lakes Theater Festival, Cleveland, OH, 2010. For arts awareness.
$10,000 to Union Rescue Mission, Los Angeles, CA, 2010. For families and children.
$5,366 to United Way of Cumberland County, Fayetteville, NC, 2010. For corporate gift.
$5,000 to California Polytechnic State University, San Luis Obispo, CA, 2010. For student activities.

1217
eBay Inc.

2145 Hamilton Ave.
San Jose, CA 95125-5905 (408) 376-7400

Company URL: http://www.ebay.com/
Establishment information: Established in 1995.
Company type: Public company
Company ticker symbol and exchange: EBAY/NASDAQ
International Securities Identification Number: US2786421030
Business activities: Provides Internet marketplace services; provides Internet payment services.
Business type (SIC): Business services/miscellaneous; computer services
Financial profile for 2012: Number of employees, 31,500; assets, $37,074,000,000; sales volume, $14,072,000,000; pre-tax net income, $3,084,000,000; expenses, $11,184,000,000; liabilities, $16,209,000,000
Fortune 1000 ranking: 2012—196th in revenues, 75th in profits, and 152nd in assets
Forbes 2000 ranking: 2012—681st in sales, 222nd in profits, and 610th in assets
Corporate officers: Pierre M. Omidyar, Chair.; John J. Donohoe, Pres. and C.E.O.; Bob Swan, Sr. V.P., Finance and C.F.O.; Michael R. Jacobson, Sr. V.P., Genl. Counsel, and Secy.; Alan L. Marks, Sr. V.P., Corp. Comms.
Board of directors: Pierre M. Omidyar, Chair.; Fred D. Anderson; Marc L. Andreessen; Edward W. Barnholt; Scott D. Cook; John J. Donahoe; William C. Ford, Jr.; Kathleen C. Miltic; David M. Moffett; Richard T. Schlosberg III; Thomas J. Tierney

Subsidiaries: Half.com, Inc., Plymouth Meeting, PA; Paypal, Inc., Mountain View, CA; Shopping.com Inc., Brisbane, CA
International operations: Australia; Austria; Bahamas; Belgium; British Virgin Islands; Canada; Cayman Islands; China; Czech Republic; Denmark; Estonia; France; Germany; Hong Kong; India; Ireland; Israel; Italy; Japan; Luxembourg; Malaysia; Mauritius; Netherlands; Norway; Poland; Portugal; Singapore; South Korea; Spain; Sweden; Switzerland; Taiwan; Turkey; United Kingdom
Giving statement: Giving through the eBay Foundation.
Company EIN: 770430924

eBay Foundation

c/o Silicon Valley Community Foundation
2440 W. El Camino Real, No. 300
Mountain View, CA 94040-1498 (650) 450-5400
E-mail: ebayfoundation@ebay.com; Additional address: 2065 Hamilton Ave., San Jose, CA 95125; URL: http://www.ebayinc.com/profile/ebay_foundation

Establishment information: Established in 1998 in CA; supporting organization of the Community Foundation of Silicon Valley; changed to a private foundation in 2009.
Donor: eBay Inc.
Financial data (yr. ended 12/31/11): Assets, $28,105,495 (M); gifts received, $750,000; expenditures, $3,026,144; qualifying distributions, $2,056,520; giving activities include $2,056,520 for grants.
Purpose and activities: The foundation supports programs designed to improve the economic and social well-being of local communities.
Fields of interest: Employment; Disasters, preparedness/services; Economic development; Business/industry; Social entrepreneurship; Microfinance/microlending; Community/economic development; Foundations (community) Economically disadvantaged.
Programs:
The GIVE Team Program: Through the GIVE Team Program, eBay employees around the world support local communities through volunteerism, drives, and fundraisers. The foundation awards grants to nonprofit organizations recommended by GIVE Teams.
The Opportunity Project: The foundation, in partnership with Ashoka Changemakers, awards grants through an open competition to entrepreneurs who find innovative solutions to issues that challenges the world's vulnerable communities. The program supports projects designed to generate employment; provide and improve job placement; create access to markets; and provide vulnerable individuals with the ability to earn a fair wage and be self-sufficient. Winners of the competition are awarded $50,000 to invest in scaling their solutions. Visit URL: http://www.theopportunityproject.org/ for more information.
Type of support: Emergency funds; Employee volunteer services; General/operating support; Program development.
Geographic limitations: Giving on a national basis in areas of company operations, with emphasis on CA.
Application information: Applications not accepted. Unsolicited requests for funds not considered or acknowledged. The foundation awards grants to organizations recommended by employee GIVE Teams. Grants are administered by the Silicon Valley Community Foundation.
Officers and Directors:* Elizabeth Axelrod*, Chair.; Lauren Moore, Pres. and Exec. Dir.; Amyn Thawer, Secy.; Jennifer Ceran, C.F.O.; Bill Barmeier; Alan Marks.
EIN: 020605596

1218
Eberhard Equipment

2506 S. Harbor Blvd.
Santa Ana, CA 92704-5241
(714) 957-1111

Company URL: http://www.eberhardequipment.com
Establishment information: Established in 1945.
Company type: Private company
Business activities: Operates construction equipment dealership.
Business type (SIC): Industrial machinery and equipment—wholesale
Corporate officer: Ken D. Eberhard, Pres. and C.E.O.
Giving statement: Giving through the Eberhard Foundation.

The Eberhard Foundation

2506 S. Harbor Blvd.
Santa Ana, CA 92704-5241 (714) 957-1111

Establishment information: Established in 1990 in CA.
Donor: Eberhard Equipment.
Financial data (yr. ended 06/30/12): Assets, $184,926 (M); gifts received, $7,696; expenditures, $36,798; qualifying distributions, $36,600; giving activities include $36,600 for grants.
Purpose and activities: The foundation supports organizations involved with higher education, employment training, housing development, human services, and homeless people.
Fields of interest: Housing/shelter; Human services; Religion.
Type of support: General/operating support.
Geographic limitations: Giving primarily in CA.
Application information: Applications not accepted. Unsolicited requests for funds not accepted.
Officers: Ken D. Eberhard, Pres.; Sandra Eberhard, Secy.
EIN: 330476660

1219
Eclipse, Inc.

1665 Elmwood Rd.
Rockford, IL 61103-1211 (815) 877-3031
FAX: (815) 877-2656

Company URL: http://www.eclipsenet.com
Establishment information: Established in 1908.
Company type: Private company
Business activities: Manufactures and provides industrial process heating products, systems, and services.
Business type (SIC): Metal plumbing fixtures and heating equipment/nonelectric
Financial profile for 2010: Number of employees, 520
Corporate officers: Douglas C. Perks, Chair. and C.E.O.; Harry Steltmann, Vice-Chair.; Lachlan L. Perks, Pres. and C.O.O.; Gregory Bubp, V.P. and C.F.O.; June Lindquist, V.P., Human Resources
Board of directors: Douglas C. Perks, Chair.; Harry Steltmann, Vice-Chair.; Barry S. Cain; Joel W. Chemers; Wendy Perks Fisher; Lachlan L. Perks; John Scales; Paul G. Shelton
Subsidiaries: Eclipse-Combustion, Rockford, IL; Exothermics-Eclipse, Inc., Toledo, OH; SDI, Seattle, WA
Division: Combustion Tec Div., Apopka, FL
International operations: Argentina; Brazil; Canada; Chile; China; Colombia; Denmark; Finland; France; Germany; Greece; India; Indonesia; Italy; Japan; Malaysia; Mexico; Netherlands; New Zealand; Peru; Philippines; Poland; Russia; Slovenia; South Africa; South Korea; Spain; Sweden; Taiwan; Thailand; United Kingdom
Giving statement: Giving through the Eclipse, Inc. Corporate Giving Program and the Eclipse Foundation, Inc.

Eclipse Foundation, Inc.

1665 Elmwood Rd.
Rockford, IL 61103-1211 (815) 877-3031

Establishment information: Established in 1960.
Donors: Eclipse, Inc.; A. C. Perks†; ACP Loan Repayment; Blackman Kallick.
Contact: Wendy Perks Fisher, Pres.
Financial data (yr. ended 03/31/12): Assets, $995,788 (M); gifts received, $120,971; expenditures, $131,364; qualifying distributions, $122,400; giving activities include $122,400 for grants.
Purpose and activities: The foundation supports museums and conservatories and organizations involved with secondary education and homelessness.
Fields of interest: Education; Recreation; Human services.
Type of support: General/operating support.
Geographic limitations: Giving primarily in Rockford and Winnebago County, IL, and surrounding areas.
Support limitations: No grants to individuals.
Application information: Applications accepted. Application form not required. Applicants should submit the following:
1) copy of most recent annual report/audited financial statement/990
2) listing of board of directors, trustees, officers and other key people and their affiliations
3) detailed description of project and amount of funding requested
Initial approach: Proposal
Copies of proposal: 1
Board meeting date(s): June
Deadline(s): None
Officers: Wendy Perks Fisher, Pres.; Douglas C. Perks, V.P.; Harry F. Steltmann, Secy.-Treas.
EIN: 366056968
Selected grants: The following grants are a representative sample of this grantmaker's funding activity:
$25,000 to YMCA of Rock River Valley, Rockford, IL, 2009.
$16,500 to United Way of Rock River Valley, Rockford, IL, 2009.
$7,000 to Rockford Art Museum, Rockford, IL, 2009.
$1,000 to Rockford Symphony Orchestra, Rockford, IL, 2009.

1220
Ecolab Inc.

Ecolab Ctr., 370 Wabasha St. N.
St. Paul, MN 55102-2233 (651) 292-2233
FAX: (302) 655-5049

Company URL: http://www.ecolab.com
Establishment information: Established in 1923.
Company type: Public company
Company ticker symbol and exchange: ECL/NYSE
International Securities Identification Number: US2788651006
Business activities: Develops and markets cleaning, sanitizing, pest elimination, maintenance, and repair products, systems, and services.
Business type (SIC): Soaps, cleaners, and toiletries; fertilizers and agricultural chemicals
Financial profile for 2012: Number of employees, 40,860; assets, $17,572,300,000; sales volume, $11,838,700,000; pre-tax net income, $1,012,600,000; expenses, $10,549,400,000; liabilities, $11,495,300,000
Fortune 1000 ranking: 2012—229th in revenues, 263rd in profits, and 259th in assets
Forbes 2000 ranking: 2012—815th in sales, 772nd in profits, and 1051st in assets
Corporate officers: Douglas M. Baker, Jr., Chair. and C.E.O.; Thomas W. Handley, Pres. and C.O.O.; Daniel J. Schmechel, C.F.O.; James J. Siefert, Exec. V.P., Genl. Counsel, and Secy.; Stewart H. McCutcheon, Exec. V.P. and C.I.O.; Michael L. Meyer, Exec. V.P., Human Resources; John J. Corkrean, Sr. V.P. and Corp. Cont.; Heidi K. Thom, Sr. V.P., Mktg. and Comms.
Board of directors: Douglas M. Baker, Jr., Chair.; Barbara J. Beck; Leslie S. Biller; Jerry A. Grundhofer; Arthur J. Higgins; Joel W. Johnson; Jerry W. Levin; Michael Larson; Robert L. Lumpkins; C. Scott O'Hara; Victoria J. Reich; Daniel S. Sanders; Mary M. VanDeWeghe; John J. Zillmer
Subsidiaries: Kay Chemical Co., Greensboro, NC; Nalco Company, Naperville, IL
Plants: San Jose, CA; Atlanta, GA; Elk Grove Village, Joliet, IL; Grand Forks, ND; Hebron, OH; Garland, TX; Beloit, WI
International operations: Antigua & Barbuda; Argentina; Aruba; Australia; Austria; Bahamas; Barbados; Belgium; Brazil; Bulgaria; Canada; Cayman Islands; Chile; China; Colombia; Costa Rica; Croatia; Cyprus; Czech Republic; Denmark; Dominica; Ecuador; El Salvador; Finland; France; Germany; Greece; Guatemala; Guernsey; Honduras; Hong Kong; Hungary; India; Indonesia; Ireland; Israel; Italy; Jamaica; Japan; Kenya; Latvia; Luxembourg; Macau; Malaysia; Malta; Mexico; Morocco and the Western Sahara; Netherlands; Netherlands Antilles; New Zealand; Nicaragua; Norway; Panama; Peru; Philippines; Poland; Romania; Russia; Serbia; Singapore; Slovakia; Slovenia; South Africa; South Korea; Spain; Sweden; Switzerland; Taiwan; Tanzania, Zanzibar and Pemba; Thailand; Trinidad & Tobago; Turkey; Uganda; Ukraine; United Arab Emirates; United Kingdom; Uruguay; Venezuela
Giving statement: Giving through the Ecolab Inc. Corporate Giving Program and the Ecolab Foundation.
Company EIN: 410231510

Ecolab Foundation

(also known as Ecolab Industry Foundation)
370 Wabasha St. N.
St. Paul, MN 55102-1323 (651) 293-2923
FAX: (651) 225-3193;
E-mail: ecolabfoundation@ecolab.com; Additional tel.: (651) 293-2259; URL: http://www.ecolab.com/our-story/our-company/community-involvement

Establishment information: Established in 1982 in MN.
Donor: Ecolab Inc.
Contact: Kris J. Taylor, V.P.
Financial data (yr. ended 12/31/11): Assets, $6,167,408 (M); gifts received, $7,019,073; expenditures, $4,883,727; qualifying distributions, $4,883,727; giving activities include $4,060,814 for 898 grants (high: $145,000; low: $25).
Purpose and activities: The foundation supports organizations involved with arts and culture, education, the environment, health, employment, hunger, housing, youth, community development, civic affairs, and economically disadvantaged people.
Fields of interest: Arts education; Performing arts, orchestras; Arts; Elementary/secondary education; Higher education; Education; Environment, natural resources; Environmental education; Environment; Health care, patient services; Health care; Employment; Food services; Food banks; Housing/shelter; Youth, services; Community/economic development; United Ways and Federated Giving Programs; Public affairs Economically disadvantaged.

Program:

Visions for Learning: Through the Visions for Learning program, the foundation awards grants of up to $3,000 to teachers to enhance their curriculum by providing more exciting, challenging, and accessible ways to learn. The program is designed to increase understanding of academic content, raise student achievement, and emphasize the connection between school and life.

Type of support: Curriculum development; Emergency funds; Employee matching gifts; General/operating support; Grants to individuals; Program development.
Geographic limitations: Giving primarily in areas of company operations in City of Industry and San Jose, CA, McDonough, GA, Elk Grove Village and Joliet, IL, Huntington, IN, Greensboro, NC, Grand Forks, ND, Garland, TX, Beloit, WI, and Martinsburg, WV, with emphasis on St. Paul, MN.
Support limitations: No support for sectarian or denominational religious organizations not of direct benefit to the entire community, political or lobbying organizations, or disease-specific organizations. No grants to individuals (except for Visions for Learning), or for industry, trade, or professional association memberships, sports or athletic programs or facilities, or fundraising events or sponsorships; no loans or program-related investments.
Publications: Application guidelines.
Application information: Applications accepted. Applicants should submit the following:

1) detailed description of project and amount of funding requested
2) brief history of organization and description of its mission
3) copy of current year's organizational budget and/or project budget
4) geographic area to be served
5) listing of board of directors, trustees, officers and other key people and their affiliations
6) statement of problem project will address
7) timetable for implementation and evaluation of project
8) how project's results will be evaluated or measured

Initial approach: Complete online application form for organizations located in St. Paul, MN; telephone or e-mail foundation for application information for organizations located outside St. Paul, MN; e-mail foundation for Visions for Learning
Board meeting date(s): Quarterly
Deadline(s): Dec. 1 for organizations located in St. Paul, MN; all other communities email or call foundation for deadline; varies per location for Visions for Learning
Final notification: 3 to 4 months

Officers and Directors:* Michael J. Monahan*, Pres.; Kris J. Taylor*, V.P.; David F. Duvick, Secy.; Ching-Meng Chew, Treas.; Douglas M. Baker, Jr.
Number of staff: 2 full-time professional.
EIN: 411372157
Selected grants: The following grants are a representative sample of this grantmaker's funding activity:
$250,000 to Ronald McDonald House Charities, Oak Brook, IL, 2009.
$215,000 to Association for Professionals in Infection Control and Epidemiology, Washington, DC, 2009.
$200,000 to Johnson and Wales University, Providence, RI, 2009.
$75,000 to Share Our Strength, Washington, DC, 2009.
$72,500 to United Way, Greater Twin Cities, Minneapolis, MN, 2009.
$50,000 to Saint Paul Chamber Orchestra Society, Saint Paul, MN, 2009.
$12,500 to Lifetrack Resources, Saint Paul, MN, 2009.
$10,000 to Minnesota Opera, Minneapolis, MN, 2009.
$4,500 to YMCA, 2009.
$3,000 to East Lake Elementary School, Chattanooga, TN, 2009.

1221
EcoNexus

5071 Rodeo Cir.
Antioch, CA 94531-8106 (925) 348-9450

Company URL: http://www.econexusinc.com/
Company type: Private company
Business type (SIC): Business services/miscellaneous
Giving statement: Giving through the EcoNexus Corporate Giving Program.

EcoNexus Corporate Giving Program

5071 Rodeo Cir.
Antioch, CA 94531-8106 (925) 348-9450
URL: http://www.econexus.info/

Purpose and activities: EcoNexus is a certified B Corporation that donates a percentage of profits to charitable organizations.

1222
Econoco Corporation

300 Karin Ln.
Hicksville, NY 11801-5358 (516) 935-7700

Company URL: http://www.econoco.com
Establishment information: Established in 1925.
Company type: Subsidiary of a private company
Business activities: Manufactures commercial equipment, partitions, signs and specialty packaging paper.
Business type (SIC): Professional and commercial equipment—wholesale

Corporate officers: Barry A. Rosenberg, C.E.O.; Mark Zelniker, Pres.; Ron Mayer, V.P., Sales; Lynne Forrest, Cont.
Giving statement: Giving through the Rosenberg Foundation, Inc.

The Rosenberg Foundation, Inc.

(formerly The Rosenberg Zelniker Foundation)
c/o Barry Rosenberg
300 Karin Ln.
Hicksville, NY 11801

Establishment information: Established in 1945 in NY.
Donor: Econoco Corp.
Financial data (yr. ended 12/31/11): Assets, $132,689 (M); expenditures, $13,718; qualifying distributions, $9,110; giving activities include $9,110 for grants.
Purpose and activities: Giving to medical funds for children, health associations, Jewish agencies, hospitals, and colleges.
Fields of interest: Museums; Higher education; Hospitals (general); Jewish federated giving programs; Jewish agencies & synagogues.
Type of support: Capital campaigns; General/operating support; Scholarship funds.
Geographic limitations: Giving primarily in Nassau County and New York, NY.
Support limitations: No grants to individuals.
Application information: Applications not accepted. Contributes only to pre-selected organizations.
Officer and Director: Barry Rosenberg, Pres.; Marjorie Rosenberg.
EIN: 136160042

1223
Econscious Market

603 Alpine Ave.
Boulder, CO 80304 (303) 444-4144

Establishment information: Established in 2007.
Company type: Private company
Business activities: Operates online commerce web site.
Business type (SIC): Nonstore retailers
Corporate officers: Mathew Gerson, Co-Founder; Pippa Sorley, Co-Founder
Giving statement: Giving through the Econscious Market Corporate Giving Program.

Econscious Market Corporate Giving Program

603 Alpine Dr.
Boulder, CO 80304-3211 (303) 444-4144

Purpose and activities: Econscious Market donates a percentage of each online transaction to nonprofit organizations.
Fields of interest: Environmental education; Environment; Animal welfare; Food services; Children/youth, services; International economic development; International human rights.
Type of support: Cause-related marketing; General/operating support.

1224
Daniel J. Edelman, Inc.

(doing business as Edelman)
200 E. Randolph St., 63rd. Fl.
Chicago, IL 60601 (312) 240-3000
FAX: (312) 240-2900

Company URL: http://www.edelman.com
Establishment information: Established in 1952.
Company type: Private company
Business activities: Operates public relations firm.
Business type (SIC): Management and public relations services
Corporate officers: Daniel J. Edelman, Chair.; Alan Vandermolen, Vice-Chair.; Richard Edelman, Pres. and C.E.O.; Matthew Harrington, C.O.O.; Victor Malanga, Exec. V.P. and C.F.O.
Board of directors: Daniel J. Edelman, Chair.; Alen Vandermolen, Vice-Chair.
Offices: Los Angeles, Sacramento, San Francisco, CA; Washington, DC; Orlando, FL; Atlanta, GA; New York, NY; Portland, OR; Austin, Dallas, Houston, TX; Seattle, WA
International operations: Argentina; Australia; Belgium; Brazil; Canada; China; France; Germany; Hong Kong; India; Indonesia; Ireland; Italy; Japan; Malaysia; Mexico; Netherlands; Poland; Russia; Singapore; South Korea; Spain; Sweden; Switzerland; Taiwan; United Arab Emirates; United Kingdom; Vietnam
Giving statement: Giving through the Edelman, Inc. Contributions Program.

Edelman, Inc. Contributions Program

200 E. Randolph St., 63rd Fl.
Chicago, IL 60601 (312) 240-2626
E-mail: john.edelman@edelman.com; URL: http://www.edelman.com/who-we-are/global-citizenship/

Contact: John Edelman, Managing Dir., Global Engagement
Financial data (yr. ended 12/31/11): Total giving, $143,650, including $143,650 for grants.
Purpose and activities: Edelman makes charitable contributions to nonprofit organizations and nongovernmental organizations (NGOs) involved with eradicating hunger and poverty, strengthening communities, education and youth, culture and arts, animal welfare, the environment, and health. Support is given primarily in areas of company operations, on a national and international basis.
Fields of interest: Arts; Education; Environment; Animal welfare; Health care; Breast cancer; Food services; Youth development; Human services; Community/economic development Economically disadvantaged.
Program:
Community Investment Grant Programs: In FY2011, Edelman launched its first Community Investment Grant program. The program gives Edelman employees the chance to receive up to $2,500 of funding for the organizations with which they are engaged as board members or volunteers. In its inaugural year, approximately $150,000 was awarded to employees across all regions. In FY2012, the program awarded $143,650 to 64 organizations worldwide in the following categories: animal welfare, community development, culture and arts, education, environment, health, poverty and hunger, and social services and youth.
Type of support: Advocacy; Employee matching gifts; Employee volunteer services; General/operating support; In-kind gifts; Loaned talent; Pro bono services; Public relations services.
Geographic limitations: Giving primarily in areas of company operations, on a national and international basis.

1225
The Edgar County Bank & Trust Company

177 W. Wood St.
P.O. Box 400
Paris, IL 61944-1737 (217) 465-4154

Company URL: http://www.edgarcountybank.com
Establishment information: Established in 1873.
Company type: Private company
Business activities: Operates commercial bank.
Business type (SIC): Banks/commercial
Corporate officers: Robert Morgan, Chair.; William L. Milbourn, Vice-Chair.; W. Eric Volkmann, Pres. and C.E.O.; Sharon S. Hornbrook, Sr. V.P. and Co-C.O.O.; Donna Gragg, Co-C.O.O.
Board of directors: Robert Morgan, Chair.; William L. Milbourn, Vice-Chair.; John S. Blair; Robert E. Colvin; Charles B. Jared; Michael A. Maggert; Richard J. O'Neill; W. Eric Volkmann
Giving statement: Giving through the Edgar County Bank & Trust Foundation.

Edgar County Bank & Trust Foundation

P.O. Box 400
Paris, IL 61944-0400

Establishment information: Established in 1991 in IL.
Donor: Edgar County Bank & Trust Co.
Contact: John D. Carrington, Secy.-Treas.
Financial data (yr. ended 07/31/12): Assets, $22,502 (M); gifts received, $49,000; expenditures, $29,550; qualifying distributions, $29,550; giving activities include $28,707 for 43 grants (high: $3,500; low: $75).
Purpose and activities: The foundation supports police agencies and organizations involved with education, wildlife preservation, health, and cancer and awards college scholarships to high school students located in Edgar County, Illinois, and contiguous counties in Illinois and Indiana.
Fields of interest: Elementary/secondary education; Education; Animals/wildlife, preservation/protection; Hospitals (general); Reproductive health, family planning; Health care; Cancer; Crime/law enforcement, police agencies; YM/YWCAs & YM/YWHAs.
Type of support: General/operating support; Scholarships—to individuals.
Geographic limitations: Giving limited to Edgar county, IL, and contiguous counties in IL and IN.
Application information: Applications accepted. Application form required.
Initial approach: Contact Foundation for application form
Deadline(s): None
Officers: Robert Morgan, Pres.; Cathy Morgan, V.P.; John D. Carrington, Secy.-Treas.
EIN: 371286227

1226
Edible Arrangements International, Inc.

(formerly Edible Arrangements, LLC)
95 Barnes Rd.
Wallingford, CT 06492-1800
(203) 774-8000

Company URL: http://www.ediblearrangements.com/
Establishment information: Established in 1999.
Company type: Private company
Business activities: Produces edible fruit arrangements.
Business type (SIC): Shopping goods stores/miscellaneous
Corporate officers: Tariq Farid, C.E.O.; Kamran Farid, C.O.O.; Stephen Thomas, V.P., Mktg.
Giving statement: Giving through the Edible Arrangements, LLC Corporate Giving Program and the Farid Foundation.

Edible Arrangements, LLC Corporate Giving Program

95 Barnes Rd.
Wallingford, CT 06492 (203) 774-8000
URL: http://www.ediblearrangements.com/About/Donations.aspx

Purpose and activities: As a complement to its foundation, Edible Arrangements makes charitable contributions to nonprofit organizations directly. Support is given primarily in areas of company operations; giving also to national organizations.
Fields of interest: Breast cancer; Breast cancer research.
Type of support: General/operating support; Sponsorships.
Geographic limitations: Giving primarily in areas of company operations; giving also to national organizations.
Application information: Applications accepted.
Initial approach: Contact a local store

Farid Foundation

95 Barnes Rd.
Wallingford, CT 06492-1800 (203) 774-8000

Establishment information: Established in 2005 in CT.
Donor: Edible Arrangements Franchise Group, Inc.
Contact: Tariq Farid, Tr.
Financial data (yr. ended 12/31/11): Assets, $773,941 (M); gifts received, $370,861; expenditures, $411,950; qualifying distributions, $383,230; giving activities include $383,230 for grants.
Purpose and activities: The foundation supports organizations involved with education and Islam.
Fields of interest: Education; Islam.
Type of support: General/operating support.
Geographic limitations: Giving primarily in CT.
Application information: Applications accepted. Application form not required.
Initial approach: Proposal
Deadline(s): None
Trustees: Kamran Farid; Tariq Farid.
EIN: 203096696
Selected grants: The following grants are a representative sample of this grantmaker's funding activity:
$20,000 to Catholic Relief Services, Baltimore, MD, 2010. For general support.
$20,000 to Inner-City Muslim Action Network, Chicago, IL, 2010. For general support.
$12,000 to Columbus House, New Haven, CT, 2010. For general support.
$12,000 to Downtown Evening Soup Kitchen, New Haven, CT, 2010. For general support.

1227
Edina Realty, Inc.

(also known as Edina Realty Home Services)
6800 France Ave. S., Ste. 625
Minneapolis, MN 55435-1988
(952) 928-5900

Company URL: http://www.edinarealty.com
Establishment information: Established in 1955.
Company type: Subsidiary of a public company
Ultimate parent company: Berkshire Hathaway Inc.
Business activities: Provides real estate brokerage services; provides mortgages; provides real estate title services; sells property insurance.
Business type (SIC): Insurance agents, brokers, and services; brokers and bankers/mortgage; insurance/fire, marine, and casualty; real estate agents and managers; real estate title abstract offices
Corporate officer: Robert Peltier, Pres. and C.E.O.
Subsidiaries: Edina Realty Mortgage, Edina, MN; Edina Realty Title, Edina, MN
Giving statement: Giving through the Edina Realty Foundation.

Edina Realty Foundation

6800 France Ave. S., Ste. 600
Edina, MN 55435-2017
Additional tel.: (952) 928-5356; URL: http://www.edinarealty.com/Content/Content.aspx?ContentID=187015

Establishment information: Established in 1996 in MN.
Donor: Edina Realty, Inc.
Contact: Susan Cowsert, Dir.
Financial data (yr. ended 09/30/11): Assets, $319,334 (M); gifts received, $276,687; expenditures, $351,307; qualifying distributions, $340,036; giving activities include $340,036 for grants.
Purpose and activities: The foundation supports programs designed to provide housing and related services to homeless individuals and families.
Fields of interest: Health care, infants; Health care; Employment, job counseling; Housing/shelter, homeless; Housing/shelter, expense aid; Family services; Family services, domestic violence; Homeless, human services; Human services Homeless.
Type of support: Building/renovation; Capital campaigns; Curriculum development; Emergency funds; General/operating support; Program development; Research.
Geographic limitations: Giving primarily in MN.
Support limitations: No grants to individuals.
Publications: Annual report; Application guidelines; Program policy statement.
Application information: Applications accepted. Application form required. Applicants should submit the following:
1) copy of IRS Determination Letter
2) detailed description of project and amount of funding requested
3) explanation of why grantmaker is considered an appropriate donor for project
4) timetable for implementation and evaluation of project
5) additional materials/documentation

Initial approach: Download application form and mail to nearest company facility
Copies of proposal: 1
Board meeting date(s): Quarterly
Deadline(s): None
Officer and Directors:* Michele Fremming*, V.P. and C.F.O.; Mark Christopherson; Susan Cowsert; Scott Harris; Todd Johnson; Amy Kleinschmidt; Marc Kuhnley; Deb Stumne.
Number of staff: 1 full-time support; 1 part-time support.
EIN: 411826980
Selected grants: The following grants are a representative sample of this grantmaker's funding activity:
$1,000 to Vail Place, Hopkins, MN, 2011.

1228
Edison International

(formerly SCEcorp)
2244 Walnut Grove Ave.
P.O. Box 976
Rosemead, CA 91770-3714
(626) 302-2222
FAX: (626) 302-4815

Company URL: http://www.edison.com/
Establishment information: Established in 1886.
Company type: Public company
Company ticker symbol and exchange: EIX/NYSE
Business activities: Operates holding company; generates, transmits, and distributes electricity.
Business type (SIC): Holding company; electric services
Financial profile for 2012: Number of employees, 16,593; assets, $44,394,000,000; sales volume, $11,862,000,000; pre-tax net income, $1,861,000,000; expenses, $9,577,000,000; liabilities, $33,203,000,000
Forbes 2000 ranking: 2012—808th in sales, 1846th in profits, and 519th in assets
Corporate officers: Theodore F. Craver, Jr., Chair., Pres., and C.E.O.; William J. Scilacci, Exec. V.P., C.F.O., and Treas.; Robert L. Adler, Exec. V.P. and Genl. Counsel; Polly L. Gault, Exec. V.P., Public Affairs; Janet Clayton, Sr. V.P., Corp. Comms.; Barbara E. Mathews, V.P. and Corp. Secy.; Mark Clarke, V.P. and Cont.
Board of directors: Theodore F. Craver, Jr., Chair.; Jagjeet S. Bindra; Vanessa C.L. Chang; France A. Cordova; Bradford M. Freeman; Luis G. Nogales; Ronald L. Olson; Richard T. Schlosberg III; Thomas C. Sutton; Peter J. Taylor; W. Brett White
Subsidiaries: The Mission Group, Irvine, CA; Southern California Edison Company, Rosemead, CA
Plants: Sacramento, CA; Washington, DC
International operations: Canada; United Kingdom
Giving statement: Giving through the Edison International Corporate Giving Program and the Edison International Foundation.
Company EIN: 954137452

Edison International Corporate Giving Program

(formerly SCEcorp Contributions Program)
2244 Walnut Grove Ave., Ste. 369
Rosemead, CA 91770-3714 (800) 347-8625
E-mail: edison.gifts@sce.com; URL: http://www.edison.com/community/default.asp

Purpose and activities: As a complement to its foundation, Edison International also makes charitable contributions to nonprofit organizations

directly. Emphasis is given to organizations that have a strong commitment to diversity and the underserved. Support is given primarily in areas of company operations.
Fields of interest: Elementary/secondary education; Higher education; Education; Environment, natural resources; Environment, water resources; Environment, energy; Environmental education; Environment; Animals/wildlife, preservation/protection; Animals/wildlife, endangered species; Employment, services; Employment; Disasters, preparedness/services; Community/economic development; Science, formal/general education; Mathematics; Engineering/technology; Public affairs Economically disadvantaged.
Programs:
Computers for the Community: The Computers for the Community program is open to public and private schools serving K-12 student populations and nonprofit organizations located in areas of company operations. To apply, schools should be state-accredited and not for profit. Donations are limited to a maximum of five computers for nonprofits or ten computers for schools (laptop and/ or desktop, in any combination) every two years. All computer donations are subject to equipment inventory availability.
Edison Scholars Program: The Edison Scholars Program provides students with financial assistance to achieve a college education. This program also helps the company foster its workforce for tomorrow by supporting students pursuing higher education in the areas of math, physics, chemistry, engineering, materials science, computer science, or information systems. This program is currently being re-conceived to better meet the needs of the college students of the future. Interested students should check the website in Fall 2012 for the 2013-2014 academic years. Information on awards, eligibility and how to apply will be available then.
Employee Volunteer Program: Edison awards grants of up to $200 to nonprofit organizations with which its employees volunteer.
Type of support: Annual campaigns; Employee volunteer services; General/operating support; In-kind gifts; Program development; Scholarships—to individuals; Sponsorships.
Geographic limitations: Giving primarily in areas of company operations in southern CA.
Support limitations: No support for American youth soccer organizations, cheer teams, or school sports leagues. No grants to individuals (except for financial assistance for energy bills), or for capital campaigns or projects, festivals, carnivals, or parties; no in-kind electrical services.
Publications: Application guidelines.
Application information: Applications accepted. Most grants range from $1,000 to $5,000. Application form required.
Initial approach: Complete online application
Deadline(s): Feb. 1 to 28; May 1 to May 31; and Aug. 1 to Aug. 31
Final notification: 6 to 8 weeks

Edison International Foundation

(formerly SCEcorp Foundation)
2244 Walnut Grove Ave.
Rosemead, CA 91770-3714 (626) 302-7900

Establishment information: Established in 1992 in CA.
Donors: SCEcorp; Edison Intl.
Contact: Darla Vasquez
Financial data (yr. ended 12/31/11): Assets, $62,628 (M); expenditures, $5,016; qualifying distributions, $5,000; giving activities include $5,000 for 1 grant.
Purpose and activities: The foundation supports organizations involved with arts and culture, higher education, and community development.
Fields of interest: Arts; Higher education; Community/economic development.
Type of support: Annual campaigns; Employee matching gifts; General/operating support; In-kind gifts; Program development; Sponsorships.
Geographic limitations: Giving limited to southern CA.
Support limitations: No support for religious or political organizations. No grants to individuals.
Publications: Annual report; Application guidelines.
Application information: Applications accepted. Application form not required.
Initial approach: Proposal
Deadline(s): None
Officers: Janet Clayton*, Pres.; Michael A. Henry, Secy.; Jeffrey L. Barnett*, Treas.
EIN: 954383002

1229
Edison Properties, LLC

100 Washington St.
Newark, NJ 07102 (973) 643-7700

Company URL: http://www.edisonproperties.com/
Establishment information: Established in 1956.
Company type: Private company
Business activities: Provides parking services; provides storage services; provides building management services.
Business type (SIC): Motor vehicle parking; warehousing and storage; management and public relations services
Corporate officer: Gary DeBode, Pres.
Giving statement: Giving through the Edison Properties Charitable Trust of Newark.

Edison Properties Charitable Trust of Newark

c/o Edison Properties, LLC
100 Washington St.
Newark, NJ 07102-3024

Establishment information: Established in 2000.
Donor: JWG Equipment Assocs.
Contact: Margery Gottesman, Tr.
Financial data (yr. ended 12/31/10): Assets, $6,061,880 (M); expenditures, $271,285; qualifying distributions, $269,035; giving activities include $269,035 for grants.
Purpose and activities: The foundation supports organizations involved with arts and culture, education, human services, and community development. Special emphasis is directed toward programs designed to improve the quality of life in Newark, New Jersey.
Fields of interest: Museums; Performing arts centers; Arts; Elementary/secondary education; Libraries (public); Education; Salvation Army; Children/youth, services; Human services; Community/economic development; United Ways and Federated Giving Programs.
Type of support: General/operating support.
Geographic limitations: Giving primarily in Newark, NJ.
Support limitations: No grants to individuals.
Application information: Applications not accepted.
Trustees: Gary Debode; Jerome Gottesman; Margery Gottesman.
EIN: 226872667
Selected grants: The following grants are a representative sample of this grantmaker's funding activity:
$49,500 to New Jersey Performing Arts Center, Newark, NJ, 2010.
$25,000 to GlassRoots, Newark, NJ, 2010.
$25,000 to Saint Philips Academy, Newark, NJ, 2010.
$25,000 to Trust for Public Land, San Francisco, CA, 2010.
$20,000 to Newark Museum, Newark, NJ, 2010.
$20,000 to Uncommon Schools, New York, NY, 2010.
$7,500 to Newark Now, Newark, NJ, 2010.
$5,000 to Integrity, Newark, NJ, 2010.
$5,000 to Ironbound Community Corporation, Newark, NJ, 2010.
$5,000 to Saint Benedicts Preparatory School, Newark, NJ, 2010.

1230
Edsim Leather Co., Inc.

131 W. 35th St., 14th Fl.
New York, NY 10001-2111 (212) 695-8500

Company URL: http://www.edsim.com
Establishment information: Established in 1981.
Company type: Private company
Business activities: Supplies leather for apparel, outerwear, handbag, footwear, upholstery, and accessories.
Business type (SIC): Leather tanning and finishing
Corporate officer: Simone Kamali, Pres. and C.E.O.
Giving statement: Giving through the Mousa Kamali Charitable Trust.

The Mousa Kamali Charitable Trust

131 W. 35 St., 14 Fl.
New York, NY 10001

Establishment information: Established in 2005 in NY.
Donor: Edsim Leather Co., Inc.
Financial data (yr. ended 12/31/11): Assets, $111,806 (M); gifts received, $60,000; expenditures, $23,345; qualifying distributions, $23,294; giving activities include $23,294 for grants.
Fields of interest: Arts; Human services; Religion.
Support limitations: No grants to individuals.
Application information: Applications not accepted. Unsolicited requests for funds not accepted.
Trustees: Edmond Kamali; Simone Kamali.
EIN: 204005078

1231
EduCare Education Inc

12809 Glendale Ct.
Fredericksburg, VA 22407-2060
(866) 338-7217

Company URL: http://www.educarelab.com
Establishment information: Established in 2010.
Company type: Private company
Business activities: Operates online education company.
Business type (SIC): Business services/ miscellaneous
Corporate officer: Piyush Mangukiya, Owner
Giving statement: Giving through the EduCare Education Inc. Contributions Program.

EduCare Education Inc. Contributions Program

12809 Glendale Ct
Fredericksburg, VA 22407-2060
E-mail: info@educatencare.com; URL: http://www.educarelab.com/our-movement/#.URP1D6W7MQp

Purpose and activities: EduCare is a certified B Corporation that donates a percentage of net profits to charitable organizations. Support is given primarily in Africa and Asia.
Fields of interest: Elementary/secondary education Economically disadvantaged.
International interests: Africa; Asia.
Type of support: General/operating support.
Geographic limitations: Giving primarily in Africa and Asia.

1232
Education Lending Group, Inc.

12680 High Bluff Dr., Ste. 400
San Diego, CA 92130-2017
(858) 617-6080
FAX: (858) 617-6079

Company URL: http://
Establishment information: Established in 1986.
Company type: Subsidiary of a private company
Business activities: Provides student loans.
Business type (SIC): Credit institutions/personal; credit institutions/federal and federally-sponsored
Corporate officers: Robert DeRose, Chair. and C.E.O.; Donald Erickson, Co-Pres.; Anne Ciolek, Co-Pres.
Board of director: Robert DeRose, Chair.
Subsidiaries: Financialaid.com, LLC, San Diego, CA; Student Loan Xpress, Inc., San Diego, CA
Giving statement: Giving through the Student Loan Express Foundation.
Company EIN: 330851387

The Student Loan Express Foundation

(formerly Education Lending Group Foundation)
1 CIT Dr., MS No. 2108-A
Livingston, NJ 07039-5703

Establishment information: Established in 2004 in CA.
Donor: Education Lending Group, Inc.
Financial data (yr. ended 12/31/09): Assets, $0; expenditures, $36; qualifying distributions, $23,437; giving activities include $23,437 for 4 grants (high: $10,000; low: $1,437).
Purpose and activities: The foundation supports organizations involved with education and youth development.
Fields of interest: Education.
Type of support: General/operating support.
Geographic limitations: Giving primarily in VA; giving also to national organizations.
Application information: Applications not accepted. Unsolicited requests for funds not accepted.
Officers and Director: Randall M. Chesler, C.E.O. and Pres.; Eric S. Mandelbaum, Secy.; Glenn A. Votek, Treas.; Robert J. Ingato.
EIN: 061730618

1233
Educational Communications, Inc.

(also known as Merit Publishing Company)
7211 Circle S. Rd., Bldg. A
Austin, TX 78745-6603 (512) 444-0571

Establishment information: Established in 1967.
Company type: Private company
Business activities: Publishes educational directories.
Business type (SIC): Book publishing and/or printing
Corporate officer: Paul Krouse, Pres.
Giving statement: Giving through the Balfour Communications Scholarships Foundation.

Balfour Communications Scholarships Foundation

(also known as ECI Scholarship Foundation)
(formerly Educational Communications Scholarship Foundation)
1701 Directors Blvd., Ste. 920
Austin, TX 78744-1098
Application address: 7211 Circle S Rd., Austin, TX 78745

Establishment information: Established in 1968 in IL; reincorporated in 2003 in TX.
Donor: Educational Communications, Inc.
Contact: Steve Bauer
Financial data (yr. ended 03/31/11): Assets, $5,067 (M); expenditures, $3,920; qualifying distributions, $3,500; giving activities include $3,500 for grants.
Purpose and activities: The foundation provides scholarship funds to college and universities.
Fields of interest: Higher education.
Type of support: Scholarship funds; Scholarships—to individuals.
Geographic limitations: Giving on a national basis.
Support limitations: No grants to individuals (except for scholarships).
Application information: Applications accepted. Application form not required.
Initial approach: Contact foundation for application information
Deadline(s): None
Officers: Alyce Alston, Pres.; Sherice P. Bench, V.P. and Secy.-Treas.
Number of staff: 1 full-time support.
EIN: 470947697

1234
Edvisors, Inc.

(also known as Student Loan Network)
1250 Hancock St., Ste. 703N
Quincy, MA 02169 (617) 328-1565

Company URL: http://www.edvisors.com/
Establishment information: Established in 1997.
Company type: Private company
Business activities: Operates higher education marketing and college financial aid company.
Business type (SIC): Colleges, universities, and professional schools
Corporate officers: Joe Kakaty, C.E.O.; Geoffrey Willison, Pres.
Giving statement: Giving through the Edvisors Foundation, Inc.

Edvisors Foundation, Inc.

1250 Hancock St., Ste. 703N
Quincy, MA 02169-4337
URL: http://www.edvisors.org/

Establishment information: Established in 2005 in MA.
Donors: Edvisors Network, Inc.; Joseph M. Cronin; Joseph Cronin, Jr.
Financial data (yr. ended 12/31/11): Assets, $774,537 (M); gifts received, $110,000; expenditures, $39,945; qualifying distributions, $39,400; giving activities include $39,400 for 8 grants (high: $12,500; low: $400).
Purpose and activities: The foundation supports organizations involved with arts and culture and education.
Fields of interest: Historical activities; Arts; Secondary school/education; Education.
Type of support: Program development; Scholarship funds.
Geographic limitations: Giving primarily in Boston, MA.
Support limitations: No grants to individuals.
Application information: Applications not accepted. Unsolicited requests for funds not accepted.
Officers and Directors:* Joseph Cronin*, Pres.; Moria Duncan*, Clerk; Joseph Cronin, Jr.*, Treas.
EIN: 753201618

1235
Edwards Industries, Inc.

495 S. High St., Ste. 150
Columbus, OH 43215-5695
(614) 241-2070

Establishment information: Established in 1978.
Company type: Private company
Business activities: Operates holding company; leases rental property.
Business type (SIC): Holding company; steel mill products
Corporate officers: Peter H Edwards, Jr., M.D., Chair.; Gwen Carmack, C.E.O.; Douglas A. Hill, C.F.O.; Tom Markworth, Secy.
Board of director: Peter H. Edwards, M.D., Chair.
Giving statement: Giving through the Edwards Foundation, Inc.

The Edwards Foundation, Inc.

(formerly J. T. Edwards Company Foundation)
495 S. High St., Ste. 150
Columbus, OH 43215-5695

Establishment information: Established in 1964 in OH.
Donors: Edwards Industries, Inc.; Ross Willoughby Co.; Edwards Insulation; Duffy Homes; Swan Manufacturing Co.; Mooney and Moses of Ohio, Inc.; Jeffrey W. Edwards; Multicon Builders, Inc.; F.A. Kohler, Inc.; Peter H. Edwards.
Financial data (yr. ended 06/30/12): Assets, $3,666 (M); gifts received, $100,000; expenditures, $120,598; qualifying distributions, $120,500; giving activities include $120,500 for 5 grants (high: $100,000; low: $500).
Purpose and activities: The foundation supports organizations involved with arts and culture, education, and human services.
Fields of interest: Education.
Type of support: General/operating support.
Support limitations: No grants to individuals; no loans or program-related investments.
Application information: Applications not accepted. Unsolicited requests for funds not accepted.

Trustees: Paula Cochran; Jeffrey W. Edwards; Peter H. Edwards; Judith Sandbo.
Officer: John A. Leibold, Treas.
EIN: 237447588

1236
EFC Holdings, Inc.
5960 S.W. 57th Ave.
Miami, FL 33143-2345 (305) 860-0116

Company type: Private company
Business activities: Operates luxury real estate construction company.
Business type (SIC): Real estate subdividers and developers
Corporate officer: Ella Fontanals-Cisneros, C.E.O.
Giving statement: Giving through the Cisneros Fontanals Foundation for the Arts.

Cisneros Fontanals Foundation for the Arts
5960 S.W. 57th Ave.
Miami, FL 33143-2345 (305) 455-3333
FAX: (305) 860-9401; E-mail: info@cifo.org; Additional address: 1018 N. Miami Ave., Miami, FL 33136, tel.: (305) 455-3335; URL: http://www.cifo.org/index.php

Establishment information: Established in 2002 in DE.
Donors: EFC Holdings, Inc.; Swift Limited Company; NYCRE Bond Inc.; Bayside Development of Miami; Red Rainbow Corp.; Sirius Realty Development LLC; The Clositers Donations; Northern Trust.
Contact: Patricia Garcia-Velez
Financial data (yr. ended 12/31/11): Assets, $54,683 (M); gifts received, $880,400; expenditures, $1,003,028; qualifying distributions, $982,298; giving activities include $41,038 for 1 grant, $65,000 for 10 grants to individuals (high: $10,000; low: $5,000) and $305,432 for foundation-administered programs.
Purpose and activities: The foundation supports programs designed to foster culture and education exchange through arts and culture projects; grants to emerging and mid-career visual artists from Latin America; exhibitions from Latin American artists and international contemporary art from the Ella Fontanals-Cisneros Collection; and bilingual publications.
Fields of interest: Arts, cultural/ethnic awareness; Visual arts; Museums (art); Arts.
Type of support: General/operating support; Program development; Publication; Scholarships—to individuals.
Geographic limitations: Giving primarily in Los Angeles, CA, Miami, FL, New York, NY, Brazil, Chile, Colombia, Latin America, Spain, and Venezuela.
Publications: Grants list.
Application information: Applications not accepted. Unsolicited applications are not accepted. Artists are nominated by CIFO's honorary Advisory Committee.
Officer and Directors: Ella Fontanals-Cisneros, Pres.; Claudia Cisnero; Anilu Gomez; Manuel E. Gonzalez; Guillermo Kuitca; Guido Albi Marini; Anna Maria Maiolino; Cuauhtemoc Medina; Solita Cohen de Mishaan; Lisa Philips; Marisa Cisneros Rizzon; Manuel De Santaren.
EIN: 542081286

1237
EI Technologies, LLC
19750 E. Parker Square Dr., Ste. 100
Parker, CO 80134-7303 (720) 851-1717

Company URL: http://www.eitek.com
Establishment information: Established in 1992.
Company type: Private company
Business activities: Provides Internet and mobile Geographic Information System solutions.
Business type (SIC): Computer services
Corporate officers: Nirav Shah, Pres.; Bill Schlanger, V.P., Finance
Giving statement: Giving through the EI Charitable Foundation.

EI Charitable Foundation
19750 E. Parker Square Dr., Ste. 100
Parker, CO 80134-7302 (720) 851-1717
E-mail: info@eitek.com; URL: http://www.eicharity.org/

Establishment information: Established in 2000 in CO.
Donors: EI Technologies, LLC; Nirav Shah; Vipul Kachhia.
Contact: Nirav Shah, Pres.
Financial data (yr. ended 09/30/11): Assets, $147,999 (M); gifts received, $25,000; expenditures, $2,951; qualifying distributions, $2,927; giving activities include $2,927 for 4 grants (high: $1,825; low: $100).
Purpose and activities: The foundation supports organizations involved with education, HIV/AIDS, and human services and awards college scholarships to students and grants to economically disadvantaged people.
Fields of interest: Human services; Religion.
Type of support: General/operating support; Grants to individuals; Scholarships—to individuals.
Geographic limitations: Giving primarily in Denver, CO.
Application information: Applications accepted. Application form not required.
Initial approach: Proposal
Deadline(s): None
Officer: Nirav Shah, Pres.
EIN: 841569279

1238
El Dorado Motors, Inc.
2300 N. Central Expwy.
McKinney, TX 75070 (972) 569-0101
FAX: (972) 569-0199

Company URL: http://www.eldoradomotors.com
Establishment information: Established in 1991.
Company type: Private company
Business activities: Operates automobile dealership.
Business type (SIC): Motor vehicles—retail
Financial profile for 2009: Number of employees, 190
Corporate officers: Stanley V. Graff, Pres.; Row Alenese, C.F.O.; Terry Watwood, Cont.
Giving statement: Giving through the Graff Educational Foundation, Inc.

Graff Educational Foundation, Inc.
1405 E. Main St.
Grand Prairie, TX 75050-5939 (972) 264-0700

Establishment information: Established in 2000 in TX.
Donors: El Dorado Motors, Inc.; Graff Chevrolet, Inc.
Contact: Roland Alaniz
Financial data (yr. ended 11/30/11): Assets, $226,171 (M); expenditures, $2,327; qualifying distributions, $0.
Purpose and activities: The foundation supports organizations involved with education and awards college scholarships to students from the Grand Prairie, Texas, area.
Type of support: General/operating support; Scholarships—to individuals.
Application information: Applications accepted. Application form required.
Initial approach: Letter
Deadline(s): None
Officers: Stanley V. Graff, Pres.; Clayton Sawyers, V.P.; Mark Welch, Secy.-Treas.
Directors: Jennifer Solis; Terri Watwood.
EIN: 752913161

1239
El Paso Corporation
1001 Louisiana St.
P.O. Box 2511
Houston, TX 77252-2511 (713) 420-2600

Company URL: http://www.elpaso.com
Establishment information: Established in 1928.
Company type: Public company
Company ticker symbol and exchange: EP/NYSE
Business activities: Transmits natural gas; conducts natural gas exploration and production activities; generates electricity.
Business type (SIC): Gas production and distribution; extraction/oil and gas; electric services
Financial profile for 2011: Number of employees, 4,937; assets, $24,314,000,000; sales volume, $4,860,000,000; pre-tax net income, $377,000,000; expenses, $3,895,000,000; liabilities, $19,960,000,000
Corporate officers: Douglas L. Foshee, Chair., Pres., and C.E.O.; John R. Sult, Exec. V.P. and C.F.O.; Susan B. Ortenstone, Exec. V.P. and C.A.O.; Robert W. Baker, Exec. V.P. and Genl. Counsel
Board of directors: Douglas L. Foshee, Chair.; Juan Carlos Braniff; David W. Crane; Robert W. Goldman; Anthony W. Hall, Jr.; Thomas R. Hix; Ferrell P. McClean; Timothy J. Probert; Steven J. Shapiro; J. Michael Talbert; Robert F. Vagt; John L. Whitmire
Subsidiaries: Colorado Interstate Gas Company, Colorado Springs, CO; El Paso CGP Co., Houston, TX; El Paso Natural Gas Company, Houston, TX; El Paso Tennessee Pipeline Co., Houston, TX; Southern Natural Gas Co., Birmingham, AL
Office: Colorado Springs, CO
International operations: Argentina; Aruba; Bermuda; Bolivia; Brazil; Cayman Islands; Chile; India; Malaysia; Mauritius; Pakistan; Panama; Philippines; Scotland; United Kingdom
Giving statement: Giving through the El Paso Corporation Contributions Program and the El Paso Corporate Foundation.
Company EIN: 760568816

El Paso Corporate Foundation
(formerly El Paso Energy Foundation)
P.O. Box 2511
Houston, TX 77252-2511 (713) 420-2600
E-mail: community@elpaso.com; URL: http://www.elpaso.com/community

Establishment information: Established in 1992 in TX.

Donors: El Paso Natural Gas Co.; El Paso Energy Corp.; El Paso Corp.
Financial data (yr. ended 12/31/11): Assets, $393,014 (M); gifts received, $100,000; expenditures, $90,000; qualifying distributions, $100,000; giving activities include $100,000 for 1 grant.
Purpose and activities: The foundation supports organizations involved with arts and culture; education; the environment; health and human services; and civic and community.
Fields of interest: Arts; Elementary/secondary education; Vocational education; Higher education; Business school/education; Education, reading; Education; Environment, natural resources; Environmental education; Health care; Youth development, business; Children/youth, services; Aging, centers/services; Developmentally disabled, centers & services; Human services; Community development, neighborhood development; Community/economic development; United Ways and Federated Giving Programs; Science, formal/general education; Mathematics; Engineering/technology; Public affairs Economically disadvantaged.
Programs:
Education: The foundation supports district and regional endorsed programs and programs designed to educate youth in the fields of science, technology, engineering, and mathematics (STEM). Special emphasis is directed toward pre-K-12 initiatives, including the developmental needs of children, college preparation for underserved populations, teacher development and support across STEM curriculum, and youth programs that promote awareness of the free enterprise marketplace; accredited four-year university and college programs designed to increase pool of graduates from which El Paso can recruit and promote STEM, accounting, and business disciplines; and trade schools and two-year colleges, with concentration on technical training of skills including, but not limited to, plant operations, controls, welding, and gas measurement.
Environment: The foundation supports programs designed to prepare and educate youth to be effective stewards of the environment through increased access to environmental education and experiences. Special emphasis is directed toward programs designed to protect and preserve natural resources; and educate and equip youth to understand and address environmental issues through hands-on service.
Give Where You Live: The foundation matches contributions made by employees of El Paso to nonprofit organizations designed to enhance quality of life and improve academic achievement.
Scholarship Program: The foundation awards $8,000 college scholarships to children of employees of El Paso. The program is administered by the National Merit Scholarship Corporation.
Type of support: Annual campaigns; Building/renovation; Continuing support; Curriculum development; Donated equipment; Employee matching gifts; Employee volunteer services; Employee-related scholarships; General/operating support; Program development; Scholarship funds; Sponsorships.
Geographic limitations: Giving limited to areas of company operations, with emphasis on AL, CO, and TX.
Support limitations: No support for religious organizations not of direct benefit to the entire community, hospitals, youth sports organizations, war veterans' or fraternal service organizations, pass-through organizations, or political organizations or candidates. No grants to individuals (except for scholarships), or for capital campaigns, multi-year commitments, medical research, athletics, endowments, fundraising events such as dinners, luncheons, or golf tournaments, political campaigns, national or statewide initiatives, computers, or computer-related projects; no loans.
Publications: Application guidelines; Program policy statement.
Application information: Applications accepted. Letters of inquiry should be no longer than 2 pages. Additional information may be requested at a later date. Application form not required. Applicants should submit the following:
1) name, address and phone number of organization
2) copy of IRS Determination Letter
3) geographic area to be served
4) listing of board of directors, trustees, officers and other key people and their affiliations
5) detailed description of project and amount of funding requested
6) contact person
7) copy of current year's organizational budget and/or project budget
8) listing of additional sources and amount of support

Initial approach: Letter of inquiry
Deadline(s): None
Final notification: 45 days

Officers and Directors:* Douglas L. Foshee*, Chair. and C.E.O.; John P. Sousa II, Pres.; Robert W. Baker*, Exec. V.P. and Genl. Counsel; D. Mark Leland*, Exec. V.P.; John R. Sult*, Sr. V.P. and C.F.O.; Katherine A. Murray, Sr. V.P.; Susan B. Ortenstone*, Sr. V.P.; Marguerite Wong-Chapman, V.P. and Secy.; John J. Hopper, V.P. and Treas.; Frances C. Olmsted III, V.P. and Cont.; Faye L. Stallings, V.P.; James J. Cleary; Brent J. Smolik; Dane E. Whitehead; James C. Yardley.
Number of staff: 2 full-time professional; 1 full-time support.
EIN: 742638185

1240
Electric Power Equipment Company

P.O. Box 6034
Hilliard, OH 43026

Business activities: Provides electrical construction and maintenance services.
Business type (SIC): Electrical industrial apparatus; contractors/electrical work
Giving statement: Giving through the Electric Power Equipment Company Foundation.

Electric Power Equipment Company Foundation

3986 Main St.
Hilliard, OH 43026-6034 (614) 527-1295
Application address: P.O. Box 6034, Hilliard OH 43026

Establishment information: Established in 1956 in OH.
Donor: Electric Power Equipment Co.
Contact: James C. McAtee, Tr.
Financial data (yr. ended 09/30/12): Assets, $123,934 (M); expenditures, $29,095; qualifying distributions, $29,095; giving activities include $1,675 for 30 grants (high: $350; low: $25).
Purpose and activities: The foundation supports food banks and organizations involved with higher education, health, youth development, and philanthropy.
Fields of interest: Education; Human services; Religion.
Type of support: Annual campaigns; General/operating support.
Application information: Applications accepted. Application form required.
Initial approach: Letter
Deadline(s): None
Trustees: Kathy Lower; James C. McAtee; Amanda Paisley.
EIN: 316035112

1241
Electrolux Major Appliances, North America

10200 David Taylor Dr.
Charlotte, NC 28262 (980) 236-2000

Company URL: http://www.eureka.com
Establishment information: Established in 1909.
Company type: Subsidiary of a foreign company
Business activities: Operates vacuum cleaner company.
Business type (SIC): Appliances/household
Corporate officer: Jack Truong, C.E.O.

Electrolux Major Appliances, North America Corporate Giving Program

10200 David Taylor Dr.
Charlotte, NC 28262 (980) 236-2000
URL: http://www.eureka.com/en-US/About-Eureka/Company-Information/

1242
Electronic Arts Inc.

209 Redwood Shores Pkwy.
Redwood City, CA 94065-1175
(650) 628-1500
FAX: (302) 655-5049

Company URL: http://www.ea.com
Establishment information: Established in 1982.
Company type: Public company
Company ticker symbol and exchange: EA/NASDAQ
Business activities: Operates game software and content company.
Business type (SIC): Computer services
Financial profile for 2013: Number of employees, 9,300; assets, $5,070,000,000; sales volume, $3,797,000,000; pre-tax net income, $139,000,000; expenses, $3,676,000,000; liabilities, $2,803,000,000
Fortune 1000 ranking: 2012—565th in revenues, 777th in profits, and 566th in assets
Corporate officers: Lawrence F. Probst III, Chair.; John Riccitiello, C.E.O.; Peter Moore, C.O.O.; Blake Jorgensen, C.F.O.; Ken Barker, Sr. V.P. and C.A.O.; Stephen G. Bene, Sr. V.P., Genl. Counsel, and Corp. Secy.
Board of directors: Lawrence F. Probst III, Chair.; Leonard S. Coleman; Jay C. Hoag; Jeffrey T. Huber; Gregory B. Maffei; Vivek Paul; Richard A. Simonson; Luis Ubinas; Denise F. Warren
Offices: Los Angeles, San Francisco, CA; Orlando, FL; Austin, TX; Salt Lake City, UT; Fairfax, VA
International operations: Canada; Germany; India; Romania; Singapore; South Korea; Sweden; Switzerland; United Kingdom
Giving statement: Giving through the Electronic Arts Inc. Contributions Program.

Company EIN: 942838567

Electronic Arts Inc. Contributions Program
209 Redwood Shores Pkwy.
Redwood City, CA 94065-1175 (650) 628-1500
URL: http://aboutus.ea.com/ea_outreach.action

Purpose and activities: Electronic Arts makes charitable contributions to inspire and encourage the pursuit of math, computer science, music and the arts. Support is given primarily in areas of company operations.
Fields of interest: Arts; Education; Mathematics; Computer science.
Type of support: Donated products; Employee matching gifts; Employee volunteer services; General/operating support.
Geographic limitations: Giving primarily in areas of company operations in CA, CT, FL, TX, UT, and in Canada.

1243
Eleek, Inc.
2326 N. Flint Ave.
Portland, OR 97227-1905 (503) 232-5526
FAX: (503) 232-5527

Company URL: http://www.eleekinc.com/
Establishment information: Established in 2000.
Company type: Private company
Business type (SIC): Business services/ miscellaneous
Corporate officers: Sattie Clark, Owner; Eric Kaster, Owner
Giving statement: Giving through the Eleek, Inc. Contributions Program.

Eleek, Inc. Contributions Program
2326 N. Flint Ave.
Portland, OR 97227-1905 (503) 232-5526
E-mail: info@eleekinc.com; URL: http://www.eleekinc.com/

Purpose and activities: Eleek is a certified B Corporation that donates a percentage of profits to charitable organizations.

1244
Elemental Herbs
1281 3rd St.
Los Osos, CA 93443 (805) 528-4000

Company URL: http://www.elementalherbs.com
Establishment information: Established in 2005.
Company type: Private company
Business activities: Manufactures organic herbal body care products.
Business type (SIC): Soaps, cleaners, and toiletries
Corporate officers: Caroline Duell, Pres.; Burr Purnell, Co-Owner; Ryan Rich, Co-Owner
Giving statement: Giving through the Elemental Herbs Corporate Giving Program.

Elemental Herbs Corporate Giving Program
1281 3rd St.
Los Osos, CA 93443-1115 (805) 464-0464
URL: http://elementalherbs.com/about/our-commitment

Purpose and activities: Elemental Herbs is a certified B Corporation that donates a percentage of profits to nonprofit organizations. Special emphasis is directed toward organizations and programs that promote environmental, social, and economic health.
Fields of interest: Environment; Animal welfare; Consumer protection.
Type of support: General/operating support; Sponsorships.

1245
Elevation Group, LLC
1718 M St. N.W.
Washington, DC 20036 (800) 475-4590

Company URL: http://www.elevationweb.org
Establishment information: Established in 2002.
Company type: Private company
Business activities: Operates web solution firm for non-profit organizations.
Business type (SIC): Computer services
Corporate officer: Joe Bertolo, Acct. Mgr.
Offices: Boca Raton, FL; Chicago, IL; Boston, MA; New York, NY; Philadelphia, PA
Giving statement: Giving through the Elevation Group, LLC Corporate Giving Program.

Elevation Group, LLC Corporate Giving Program
1718 M St. N.W.
Washington, DC 20036-4504
E-mail: info@elevationweb.org; E-mail for RFP's: rfps@elevationweb.org; URL: http://www.elevationweb.org/one_for_one.php?utm_source=GSCA+21&utm_medium=email&utm_campaign=1+for+1+Grant+Match+2012+-+J

Contact: Joe Bertolo, Acct. Mgr.
Financial data (yr. ended 12/31/11): Total giving, $450,000, including $450,000 for 125 in-kind gifts.
Purpose and activities: Elevation Group will match every dollar spent on web design, programming, or other media-related work on a one-for-one basis up to $500,000.
Fields of interest: Nonprofit management; Philanthropy/voluntarism, management/technical assistance.
Type of support: In-kind gifts; Matching/challenge support; Technical assistance.
Geographic limitations: Giving on a national basis.
Publications: Application guidelines.
Application information: Applications accepted. Funds will be allocated on a first come, first served basis. Application form required.
Initial approach: Complete online application or e-mail RFP
Deadline(s): None

1246
Elgin Sweeper Company
1300 W. Bartlett Rd.
Elgin, IL 60120-7529 (847) 741-5370

Company URL: http://www.elginsweeper.com
Establishment information: Established in 1914.
Company type: Subsidiary of a public company
Business activities: Manufactures motorized street-cleaning equipment.
Business type (SIC): Motor vehicles and equipment
Corporate officers: Mark D. Weber, Pres.; Chip Avery, V.P., Finance; Michael Higgins, V.P., Sales and Mktg.
Giving statement: Giving through the Elgin Sweeper Foundation.

Elgin Sweeper Foundation
1300 W. Bartlett Rd.
Elgin, IL 60120-7528 (847) 741-5370

Donor: Elgin Sweeper Co.
Contact: Mark Weber, Pres.
Financial data (yr. ended 12/31/11): Assets, $177,042 (M); expenditures, $27,216; qualifying distributions, $27,000; giving activities include $27,000 for grants.
Purpose and activities: The foundation supports Elgin Community College and the United Way of Elgin in Elgin, Illinois.
Fields of interest: Education.
Geographic limitations: Giving limited to the Elgin, IL.
Application information: Applications accepted. Application form required. Applicants should submit the following:
1) brief history of organization and description of its mission
2) geographic area to be served
3) detailed description of project and amount of funding requested

Initial approach: Proposal
Deadline(s): Apr. 1

Officers: Mark D. Weber, Pres.; Dan Des Rochers, Secy.; Kevin Pfau, Treas.
EIN: 366078209

1247
Elias Industries, Inc.
605 Epsilon Dr.
Pittsburgh, PA 15238-2807 (412) 782-4300

Company type: Private company
Business activities: Sells plumbing equipment wholesale.
Business type (SIC): Hardware, plumbing, and heating equipment—wholesale
Corporate officer: Norman Elias, Pres.
Giving statement: Giving through the Joseph Elias Charitable Trust.

Joseph Elias Charitable Trust
P.O. Box 2812
Pittsburgh, PA 15230-2812 (412) 963-1306

Establishment information: Established in 1987 in PA.
Donors: Norman Elias; Tap South, Inc.; Elias Industries, Inc.
Contact: Slyvia M. Elias, Tr.
Financial data (yr. ended 12/31/11): Assets, $463,913 (M); gifts received, $203,450; expenditures, $67,137; qualifying distributions, $66,832; giving activities include $66,817 for 22 grants (high: $50,572; low: $40).
Purpose and activities: The foundation supports organizations involved with hunger, human services, and Judaism.
Fields of interest: Food services; Children, services; Family services; Human services; Jewish federated giving programs; Jewish agencies & synagogues.
Type of support: Capital campaigns; General/operating support; Program development.
Geographic limitations: Giving primarily in Pittsburgh, PA.

Support limitations: No grants to individuals.
Application information: Applications accepted. Application form not required.
Initial approach: Proposal
Deadline(s): None
Trustees: Norman Elias; Sylvia M. Elias.
EIN: 256284538

1248
Eliason, Corp.

9229 Shaver Rd.
Kalamazoo, MI 49024 (269) 327-7003

Company URL: http://www.eliasoncorp.com/about.htm
Establishment information: Established in 1952.
Company type: Private company
Business activities: Manufactures doors and freezers.
Business type (SIC): Metal products/structural; appliances/household
Corporate officers: Jeffrey S. Stark, Pres. and C.E.O.; Kyle Dekema, C.F.O.; Anthony Sommer, V.P. and C.F.O; Timothy St. Onge, V.P., Opers.; Mike Evans, V.P., Sales and Mktg.
Board of director: Roger A. Knight
Giving statement: Giving through the Eleanor's Pantry Inc.

Eleanor's Pantry Inc.

(formerly Eliason Foundation)
P.O. Box 64
Paw Paw, MI 49079

Donors: Eliason Corp.; Wanda M. Eliason.
Financial data (yr. ended 11/30/11): Assets, $26,880 (M); gifts received, $44,539; expenditures, $46,465.
Purpose and activities: The foundation supports art museums, botanical gardens, and hospitals and organizations involved with higher education, cancer, human services, and Christianity.
Fields of interest: Museums (art); Higher education; Botanical gardens; Hospitals (general); Health care, clinics/centers; Cancer; Children/youth, services; Human services; United Ways and Federated Giving Programs; Christian agencies & churches.
Type of support: General/operating support.
Geographic limitations: Giving primarily in MI.
Support limitations: No grants to individuals.
Application information: Applications not accepted. Unsolicited requests for funds not accepted.
Officers: Don Prediger, Chair.; Tom Abbott, Pres.; Eleanor Dunlop, Secy.; Leah Baldwin, Treas.
Board Members: Ben Bowater; Sue Danielson; Bill Grevelding; Pat Mickinney; Sue Miller; Bill Stembaugh; Doris Stembaugh.
EIN: 382364961

1249
Elite Spice, Inc.

7151 Montevideo Rd.
Jessup, MD 20794-9308 (410) 796-1900
FAX: (410) 379-6933

Company URL: http://www.elitespice.com
Establishment information: Established in 1988.
Company type: Private company
Business activities: Operates a commercial food preparation company.
Business type (SIC): Miscellaneous prepared foods
Corporate officers: Isaac Samuel, Pres.; Paul Kurpe, V.P., Sales; Debbie Ingle, Cont.
Giving statement: Giving through the Anton Samuel Family Foundation, Inc.

Anton Samuel Family Foundation, Inc.

8 Branchwood Ct.
Baltimore, MD 21208-3301

Establishment information: Established in 2003 in MD.
Donor: Elite Spice, Inc.
Financial data (yr. ended 12/31/11): Assets, $278,325 (M); gifts received, $75,000; expenditures, $80,290; qualifying distributions, $80,290; giving activities include $80,290 for grants.
Fields of interest: Theological school/education; Jewish agencies & synagogues.
Type of support: General/operating support.
Geographic limitations: Giving primarily in IL and MD; some giving in Israel.
Support limitations: No grants to individuals.
Application information: Applications not accepted. Unsolicited requests for funds not accepted.
Directors: Anton Samuel; Isaac Samuel; Tamara Samuel.
EIN: 020649804

1250
Elizabeth Nursing and Rehab Center

1048 Grove St.
Elizabeth, NJ 07202 (908) 354-0002

Company URL: http://www.elizabethnursingrehab.com/
Establishment information: Established in 1993.
Company type: Private company
Business activities: Operates skilled nursing facility.
Business type (SIC): Nursing and personal care facilities
Giving statement: Giving through the Z.B.F. Foundation, Inc.

Z.B.F. Foundation, Inc.

4600 14th Ave., Ste. 3E
Brooklyn, NY 11219-2605

Establishment information: Established in 1999 in NY.
Donors: Zev Fishman; Moses Elias; Elizabeth Nursing Home; Plaza Nursing & Convalescent Center, Inc.
Financial data (yr. ended 06/30/11): Assets, $723,050 (M); gifts received, $5,200; expenditures, $101,658; qualifying distributions, $77,400; giving activities include $77,200 for 15 grants (high: $17,000; low: $1,000).
Purpose and activities: The foundation supports organizations involved with Judaism.
Fields of interest: Religion.
Application information: Applications not accepted. Unsolicited requests for funds not accepted.
Officers: Zev Fishman, Mgr.; Blimie Fishman, Mgr.
EIN: 311676062

1251
Ellin & Tucker, Chartered

Bank of America Bldg.
100 S. Charles St., Ste. 1300
Baltimore, MD 21201-2714
(410) 727-5735
FAX: (410) 727-1405

Company URL: http://www.etnet.com
Establishment information: Established in 1946.
Company type: Private company
Business activities: Provides consulting services; provides accounting services.
Business type (SIC): Management and public relations services; accounting, auditing, and bookkeeping services
Financial profile for 2011: Number of employees, 3,130
Corporate officers: Edwin R. Brake, C.E.O.; Aileen M. Eskildsen, C.P.A., Principal; Jane Schoeder, C.P.A., Cont.
Offices: Washington, DC; Belcamp, Frederick, MD
Giving statement: Giving through the Lester Ellin Scholarship Fund, Inc.
Company EIN: 520959934

The Lester Ellin Scholarship Fund, Inc.

100 S. Charles St., Ste. 1300
Baltimore, MD 21201-2727
URL: http://www.etnet.com/overview/lester_ellin.htm

Establishment information: Established in 2001 in MD.
Donors: Ellin & Tucker, Chartered; Joshua Kaufman; Silberstein Insurance Group.
Financial data (yr. ended 12/31/11): Assets, $17,483 (M); expenditures, $1,000; qualifying distributions, $1,000; giving activities include $1,000 for grants.
Purpose and activities: The foundation awards college scholarships to students attending Loyola College and Towson University majoring in accounting.
Type of support: Scholarships—to individuals.
Application information: Applications not accepted. Unsolicited requests for funds not accepted.
Officers and Directors:* Harold I. Hackerman, Pres.; Todd A. Feuerman, V.P.; Steven King, V.P.; Edwin R. Brake, Secy.-Treas.
EIN: 522300553

1252
Ellucian, Inc.

(formerly Datatel, Inc.)
4375 Fair Lakes Ct.
Fairfax, VA 22033 (610) 647-5930
FAX: (610) 578-5102

Company URL: http://www.datatel.com
Establishment information: Established in 1968.
Company type: Private company
Business activities: Develops computer software; provides integrated computer software and service solutions.
Business type (SIC): Computer services
Corporate officers: John F. Speer III, Pres. and C.E.O.; Kevin M. Boyce, Sr. V.P. and C.F.O.; Jim Bennett, Sr. V.P. and Genl. Counsel; Barbara Polk, V.P., Admin. and Human Resources
Giving statement: Giving through the Datatel Scholars Foundation.

Datatel Scholars Foundation
4375 Fair Lakes Ct.
Fairfax, VA 22033-4234 (800) 486-4332
FAX: (703) 968-4625; Additional tel.: (703) 968-9000

Establishment information: Established in 1990 in VA.
Donors: Datatel, Inc.; Marriott International.
Contact: Jane H. Roth, Exec. Dir.
Financial data (yr. ended 12/31/11): Assets, $133,665 (M); gifts received, $11,406; expenditures, $364; qualifying distributions, $0.
Purpose and activities: The foundation awards college and graduate scholarships to students attending an institution of higher learning that uses Datatel's software.
Fields of interest: Higher education; Education.
Programs:
Angelfire Scholarship: The foundation awards $1,700 scholarships to outstanding graduate and undergraduate students currently attending an eligible Datatel client institution who served the U.S. military or is a child or spouse of a veteran.
Datatel Scholars Foundation Scholarship: The foundation awards scholarships of up to $2,400 to undergraduate and graduate students currently attending an eligible Datatel client institution. Applicants must have a GPA of 3.50 or higher and should apply to their educational institutions. Each participating school may nominate two of their most outstanding students for scholarship consideration.
Russ Griffith Memorial Scholarship: The foundation awards $2,000 scholarships to outstanding graduates and undergraduate students currently attending an eligible Datatel client institution who have returned to school after an absence of five years or longer.
Type of support: Scholarships—to individuals.
Geographic limitations: Giving on a national basis; giving also in American Samoa, Bermuda, Canada, Guam, and Puerto Rico.
Application information: Applications not accepted. The scholarship program is currently on hiatus. The foundation will distribute information when grantmaking resumes.
Officers and Directors:* Jane H. Roth, Exec. Dir. and Secy.; Kevin M. Boyce; John F. Speer III.
Number of staff: None.
EIN: 541604129

1253
EMC Corporation
176 South St.
Hopkinton, MA 01748 (508) 435-1000
FAX: (508) 435-5222

Company URL: http://www.emc.com/index.htm?fromGlobalSiteSelect
Establishment information: Established in 1979.
Company type: Public company
Company ticker symbol and exchange: EMC/NYSE
International Securities Identification Number: US2686481027
Business activities: Designs, manufactures, markets, and supports computer hardware and software products; provides electronic information storage, management, protection, and sharing services.
Business type (SIC): Computer and office equipment; management and public relations services
Financial profile for 2012: Number of employees, 60,000; assets, $38,068,680,000; sales volume, $21,713,900,000; pre-tax net income, $3,803,610,000; expenses, $17,752,850,000; liabilities, $15,711,540,000
Fortune 1000 ranking: 2012—133rd in revenues, 72nd in profits, and 148th in assets
Forbes 2000 ranking: 2012—435th in sales, 213th in profits, and 598th in assets
Corporate officers: Joseph M. Tucci, Chair. and C.E.O.; William J. Tueber, Jr., Vice-Chair.; David I. Goulden, Pres. and C.O.O.; Paul T. Dacier, Exec. V.P. and Genl. Counsel; Mary Louise Krakauer, Exec. V.P., Human Resources
Board of directors: Joseph M. Tucci, Chair.; William J. Teuber, Jr., Vice-Chair.; Michael W. Brown; Randolph L. Cowen; Gail Deegan; James S. DiStasio; John R. Egan; Edmund F. Kelly; Jami Miscik; Windle B. Priem; Paul Sagan; David N. Strohm
Plants: Santa Clara, CA; Englewood, Louisville, CO; Westborough, MA
International operations: Ireland; Netherlands
Giving statement: Giving through the EMC Corporation Contributions Program.
Company EIN: 042680009

EMC Corporation Contributions Program
176 South St.
Hopkinton, MA 01748-2209
E-mail: CommunityInvolvement@emc.com;
URL: http://www.emc.com/social-emc/index.htm#social-community

Purpose and activities: EMC makes charitable contributions to nonprofit organizations involved with the arts, education, health, disaster relief, and human services. Support is given on a national and international basis in areas of company operations.
Fields of interest: Arts; Education, reading; Education; Health care; Disasters, preparedness/services; Human services; Science, formal/general education; Mathematics; Engineering/technology; General charitable giving.
Type of support: Donated products; Employee volunteer services; General/operating support; In-kind gifts; Sponsorships.
Geographic limitations: Giving on a national and international basis in areas of company operations.
Support limitations: No support for organizations with overhead expenses exceeding 25 percent of the total operating budget, religious, veterans', or fraternal organizations or political candidates, or discriminatory organizations. No grants to individuals, or for political causes, direct mail solicitations, advertising, endowments, tickets for contests, or debt reduction.
Publications: Application guidelines.
Application information: Applications accepted. The company may request additional information at a later date. Organizations receiving support are asked to provide a final report. Application form required. Applicants should submit the following:
1) timetable for implementation and evaluation of project
2) results expected from proposed grant
3) name, address and phone number of organization
4) brief history of organization and description of its mission
5) how project's results will be evaluated or measured
6) listing of board of directors, trustees, officers and other key people and their affiliations
7) detailed description of project and amount of funding requested
8) contact person
9) copy of current year's organizational budget and/or project budget
10) listing of additional sources and amount of support

Applications should include a description of past support by EMC with the organization.
Initial approach: Download application form and e-mail to headquarters
Committee meeting date(s): Bi-monthly
Final notification: 8 weeks

1254
EMCO Chemical Distributors, Inc.
2100 Commonwealth Ave.
North Chicago, IL 60064 (847) 689-2200

Company URL: http://www.emcochem.com/
Establishment information: Established in 1971.
Company type: Private company
Business activities: Distributes chemicals that include acids, alcohols, surfactants, solvents, and other industrial and specialty chemicals.
Business type (SIC): Chemicals and allied products—wholesale
Corporate officers: Edward Polen, Pres.; Igor Roitman, C.I.O.; Randall Polen, Secy.; David Sigafus, Cont.
Giving statement: Giving through the Polen Family Foundation.

Polen Family Foundation
c/o Edward Polen
2780 Ridge Rd.
Highland Park, IL 60035-1532

Establishment information: Established in 2005 in IL.
Donor: Emco Chemical Distributions, Inc.
Financial data (yr. ended 12/31/11): Assets, $198,347 (M); expenditures, $38,576; qualifying distributions, $36,125; giving activities include $36,125 for grants.
Fields of interest: Education; Recreation; Human services.
Support limitations: No grants to individuals.
Application information: Applications not accepted. Unsolicited requests for funds not accepted.
Officers and Directors:* Edward Polen*, Pres. and Secy.; Tamra Polen*, Treas.; Bernard A. Schlifke.
EIN: 203970463

1255
EMCOR Group, Inc.
301 Merritt Seven Corp. Park
Norwalk, CT 06851-1060 (203) 849-7800
FAX: (203) 849-7900

Company URL: http://www.emcorgroup.com
Establishment information: Established in 1966.
Company type: Public company
Company ticker symbol and exchange: EME/NYSE
Business activities: Operates electrical and mechanical construction company.
Business type (SIC): Contractors/electrical work
Financial profile for 2012: Number of employees, 26,000; assets, $3,107,070,000; sales volume, $6,346,680,000; pre-tax net income, $244,250,000; expenses, $6,096,710,000; liabilities, $1,760,990,000
Fortune 1000 ranking: 2012—399th in revenues, 654th in profits, and 741st in assets
Corporate officers: Frank T. MacInnis, Chair.; Anthony J. Guzzi, Pres. and C.E.O.; Mark A. Pompa, Exec. V.P. and C.F.O.; Sheldon I. Cammaker, Esq.,

Exec. V.P., Genl. Counsel, and Secy.; Mava K. Heffler, V.P., Mktg. and Comms.; Paul J. Fracassini, V.P. and Cont.; Lisa Haight, V.P., Human Resources; Joseph A. Serino, Treas.
Board of directors: Frank T. MacInnis, Chair.; Stephen W. Bershad; David A. B. Brown; Larry J. Bump; Albert Fried, Jr.; Anthony J. Guzzi; Richard F. Hamm, Jr.; David H. Laidley; Jerry E. Ryan; Michael T. Yonker
Giving statement: Giving through the EMCOR Group, Inc. Corporate Giving Program.
Company EIN: 842725338

EMCOR Group, Inc. Corporate Giving Program

(also known as Touching Lives)
301 Merritt Seven, 6th Fl.
Norwalk, CT 06851-1060
E-mail: jawolfe@emcor.net; URL: http://www.emcorgroup.com/508

Purpose and activities: EMCOR makes charitable contributions to nonprofit organizations on a case by case basis. Support is given primarily in areas of company operations.
Fields of interest: Children; Military/veterans.
Type of support: Employee volunteer services; General/operating support.
Geographic limitations: Giving primarily in areas of company operations.
Application information: Applications not accepted. Contributes only to pre-selected organizations.

1256
EMD Serono, Inc.

(formerly Serono Laboratories, Inc.)
1 Technology Pl.
Rockland, MA 02370 (781) 982-9000

Company URL: http://www.emdserono.com/
Company type: Subsidiary of a foreign company
Business activities: Develops, manufactures, and markets pharmaceuticals.
Business type (SIC): Drugs
Corporate officers: Fereydoun Firouz, Pres. and C.E.O.; Stefan Rupp, C.F.O.; Tom Gunning, V.P. and Genl. Counsel; Megan Wherry, V.P., Human Resources
Giving statement: Giving through the Serono, Inc. Corporate Giving Program and the Foundation of Advanced Reproductive Sciences, Inc.

Foundation of Advanced Reproductive Sciences, Inc.

111 Madison Ave., Rm. 100
Morristown, NJ 07960-6083 (973) 971-4600

Establishment information: Established in 2005 in NJ.
Donor: Serono, Inc.
Financial data (yr. ended 12/31/10): Revenue, $260,560; gifts received, $10,500; expenditures, $577,593; giving activities include $429,240 for grants.
Purpose and activities: Giving for research and education on all aspects of reproduction.
Fields of interest: Medical research; Obstetrics/gynecology research.
Support limitations: No grants to individuals.
Application information: Applications not accepted. Contributes only to pre-selected organization.
Officers: Richard T. Scott, M.D., Pres.; Kathy Miller, V.P.; Brad Miller, M.D., Corporate Secy.; David Balser, Treas.
Trustees: William Chow; Robin Mangieri; Edwin Robins, M.D.
EIN: 202005980

1257
Emerson Electric Co.

8000 W. Florissant Ave.
P.O. Box 4100
St. Louis, MO 63136-1494 (314) 553-2000
FAX: (314) 553-3527

Company URL: http://www.emerson.com
Establishment information: Established in 1890.
Company type: Public company
Company ticker symbol and exchange: EMR/NYSE
International Securities Identification Number: US2910111044
Business activities: Designs, manufactures, and sells electrical and electronic products and systems.
Business type (SIC): Electrical industrial apparatus; machinery/general industry; machinery/refrigeration and service industry; communications equipment; repair shops/electrical
Financial profile for 2012: Number of employees, 134,900; assets, $23,818,000,000; sales volume, $24,412,000,000; pre-tax net income, $3,115,000,000; expenses, $21,297,000,000; liabilities, $13,523,000,000
Fortune 1000 ranking: 2012—123rd in revenues, 104th in profits, and 214th in assets
Forbes 2000 ranking: 2012—378th in sales, 274th in profits, and 881st in assets
Corporate officers: David N. Farr, Chair. and C.E.O.; Edward L. Monser, Pres. and C.O.O.; Frank L. Steeves, Exec. V.P., Genl. Counsel, and Secy.; Frank J. Dellaquilla, Sr. V.P. and C.F.O.; Richard J. Schlueter, V.P., C.A.O., and Cont.
Board of directors: David N. Farr, Chair.; Clemens A.H. Boersig; August A. Busch III; Joshua B. Bolten; Carlos Fernandez G.; Arthur F. Golden; Harriet Green; William R. Johnson; Matthew S. Levatich; Charles A. Peters; Joseph W. Prueher; Randall L. Stephenson
Subsidiaries: ACDC Electronics, Oceanside, CA; Beckman Industrial Corp., Fullerton, CA; Branson Corp., Newtown, CT; Chance Load Management Systems, Hazelwood, MO; Computer Powers Systems Corp., Carson, CA; Doerr Electric Corp., Cedarburg, WI; Hurst Manufacturing, Princeton, IN; In-Sink-Erator, Racine, WI; Liebert Corp., Columbus, OH; E.L. Wiegand, Pittsburgh, PA
Plants: Calabasas, CA; Maysville, KY; Honeoye Falls, Ithaca, NY; Cincinnati, Mansfield, Sidney, OH; Bennettsville, SC
International operations: Belgium; Bermuda; Canada; Colombia; France; Hong Kong; India; Italy; Mauritius; Mexico; Morocco and the Western Sahara; Netherlands; Spain; Switzerland; Taiwan; United Kingdom; Venezuela
Giving statement: Giving through the Emerson Electric Co. Contributions Program, the Emerson Charitable Trust, and the EMR Foundation Inc.
Company EIN: 430259330

Emerson Electric Co. Contributions Program

8000 W. Florissant Ave., M.S. 2015
St. Louis, MO 63136-1414 (314) 553-2000
FAX: (314) 553-1605; Contact for Emerson Gold Star Grants: Barrett Hadican, tel.: (314) 982-9101, e-mail: barrett.hadican@fleishman.com; URL: http://www.emerson.com/en-us/about_emerson/company_overview/pages/community_involvement.aspx

Contact: Robert M. Cox, Sr. V.P., Admin.
Purpose and activities: As a complement to its foundation, Emerson also makes charitable contributions to nonprofit organizations directly. Support is given in areas of company operations.
Fields of interest: Arts; Higher education; Education; Health care; Disasters, preparedness/services; Boys & girls clubs; Big Brothers/Big Sisters; Family services; Human services; Community/economic development; United Ways and Federated Giving Programs; Public affairs Youth.
Programs:
Emerson Excellence in Teaching Awards: Emerson annually recognizes outstanding classroom educators from elementary and secondary schools and higher education institutions in the bi-state St. Louis metropolitan area. All honorees and their school's are administrators are invited to participate in a awards ceremony held every November.
Emerson Excellence in Teaching Gold Star Grants: Emerson awards grants to support the professional and personal development goals of elementary and secondary school teachers in St. Louis who are current or past recipients of the Emerson Excellence Teaching Award. Each cash grant awarded to a teacher, or team of teachers, will be matched with a grant to the teachers' employing educational institution. Two $2,500 cash grants will be awarded in the individual teacher category for grades K-12, and one $10,000 cash grant will be awarded in the teamwork category to a teaching team of two or more teachers. Grants will be awarded for supplementary curriculum materials; classroom or school equipment; team building activities; parent and/or community outreach and support activities; student field trips; post-graduate study, research, or academic development activities; professional certifications; and life experience activities that contribute to professional and personal growth.
Type of support: Employee volunteer services; General/operating support; Matching/challenge support; Program development; Scholarship funds; Sponsorships.
Geographic limitations: Giving on a national basis in areas of company operations, with emphasis on St. Louis, MO.
Publications: Application guidelines.
Application information: Applications accepted. Proposals for Emerson Gold Star Grants should be no longer than 3 pages. Application form required. Applicants should submit the following:
1) how project's results will be evaluated or measured
2) explanation of why grantmaker is considered an appropriate donor for project
3) detailed description of project and amount of funding requested
4) copy of current year's organizational budget and/or project budget

Initial approach: Download application form and mail proposal and application form to headquarters for Emerson Gold Star Grants
Copies of proposal: 1
Deadline(s): Feb. 6 for Emerson Gold Star Grants
Final notification: Apr. for Emerson Gold Star Grants

Emerson Charitable Trust

8000 W. Florissant Ave.
P.O. Box 4100
St. Louis, MO 63136-8506
URL: http://www.emerson.com/en-US/about_emerson/company_overview/pages/emerson_charitable_trust.aspx

Establishment information: Established in 1944 in MO as Emerson Electric Manufacturing Company Charitable Trust; current name adopted in 1981.
Donors: Emerson Electric Co.; Daniel Industries, Inc.; Astec America Inc.; Emerson Ventures.
Financial data (yr. ended 09/30/11): Assets, $20,328,617 (M); gifts received, $23,000,000; expenditures, $24,612,742; qualifying distributions, $24,591,286; giving activities include $24,588,902 for grants.
Purpose and activities: The foundation supports programs designed promote arts and culture; education; health and human services; civic affairs; and youth.
Fields of interest: Media/communications; Museums; Performing arts; Arts; Elementary/secondary education; Higher education; Libraries (public); Education; Environment, natural resources; Zoos/zoological societies; Hospitals (general); Health care, EMS; Health care; Health organizations; Medical research; Crime/violence prevention; Crime/law enforcement, police agencies; Crime/violence prevention, domestic violence; Crime/violence prevention, child abuse; Employment, training; Employment; Housing/shelter, development; Housing/shelter; Disasters, preparedness/services; Disasters, fire prevention/control; Recreation, parks/playgrounds; Youth development, adult & child programs; Youth development; American Red Cross; Salvation Army; Family services; Residential/custodial care, hospices; Human services; United Ways and Federated Giving Programs; Public affairs Youth.
Programs:
Arts and Culture: The foundation supports organizations designed to enrich the diversity, creativity, and liveliness of the community, including dance, music, and theater groups, educational television, public radio, libraries, museums, zoos, and science centers.
Civic: The foundation supports programs designed to provide stability, safety, and protection within the community, including public service organizations like local police, fire, and rescue squads; housing assistance organizations; local conservation groups; and parks.
Education: The foundation supports programs designed to promote educational systems at all levels to create leaders, business managers, and skilled individuals who can thrive in a changing world.
Employee Matching Gifts: The foundation matches contributions made by full-time employees and directors of Emerson Electric and its wholly-owned subsidiaries and divisions to institutions of higher education and arts and cultural nonprofit organizations.
Health and Human Services: The foundation supports international health organizations, medical research initiatives, hospitals, care centers, and hospices; and supports special initiatives including the treatment of medical disorders, domestic abuse shelters, and employment and job training.
Youth: The foundation supports programs designed to instill character and values in young people in their developmental years, including mentors, advocates, and skill development programs; child abuse prevention; and providing care for terminally ill children.
Type of support: Employee matching gifts; Employee volunteer services; Employee-related scholarships; General/operating support; Program development; Sponsorships.
Geographic limitations: Giving primarily on a national basis areas of company operations, with emphasis on St. Louis, MO.
Publications: Corporate giving report.
Application information: Applications not accepted.
Trustees: Emerson Electric Co.; The Northern Trust Co.
EIN: 526200123
Selected grants: The following grants are a representative sample of this grantmaker's funding activity:
$1,400,000 to United Way of Greater Saint Louis, Saint Louis, MO, 2011. For general support.
$660,000 to Washington University, Saint Louis, MO, 2011. For general support.
$625,000 to American Red Cross National Headquarters, Washington, DC, 2011. For general support.
$500,000 to Saint Louis Science Center Foundation, Saint Louis, MO, 2011. For general support.
$437,500 to Boy Scouts of America, Area Council, Saint Louis, MO, 2011. For general support.
$25,000 to Center of Creative Arts, Saint Louis, MO, 2011. For general support.
$25,000 to Girls Inc. of Saint Louis, Saint Louis, MO, 2011. For general support.
$20,000 to United Way of Greater Saint Louis, Saint Louis, MO, 2011. For general support.
$15,000 to YMCA, Valley of the Sun, Phoenix, AZ, 2011. For general support.
$12,600 to Cornell University, Ithaca, NY, 2011. For general support.

EMR Foundation Inc.

c/o The Northern Trust Co.
P.O. Box 803878
Chicago, IL 60680-3878

Establishment information: Established in 1992.
Donor: Emerson Electric Co.
Financial data (yr. ended 09/30/11): Assets, $3,129 (M); expenditures, $0; qualifying distributions, $0.
Purpose and activities: The foundation supports the American Diabetes Association.
Fields of interest: Diabetes; Health organizations.
Type of support: General/operating support.
Application information: Applications not accepted. Unsolicited requests for funds not accepted.
Officers: Robert M. Cox, Jr., Pres.; Phillip G. Conrad, V.P.; Timothy G. Westman, Secy.-Treas.
EIN: 431598144

1258
EMI Christian Music Group, Inc.

101 Winners Cir., N.
P.O. Box 5084
Brentwood, TN 37027 (615) 371-6800

Company URL: http://www.emicmg.com
Establishment information: Established in 1992.
Company type: Subsidiary of a foreign company
Business activities: Operates record labels.
Business type (SIC): Audio and video equipment/household
Financial profile for 2010: Number of employees, 100
Corporate officers: Billy Ray Hearn, Chair.; Bill Hearn, Co-Pres. and C.E.O.; Bruce Lundvall, Co-Pres.; Rick Horne, C.F.O.; Troy Vest, C.I.O.
Board of director: Billy Ray Hearn, Chair.
Giving statement: Giving through the Sparrow Foundation.

The Sparrow Foundation

101 Winners Cir.
Brentwood, TN 37024-5085

Establishment information: Established in 1992 in TN.
Donors: EMI Christian Music Group, Inc.; First American National Bank; Craig Phillips; Dean Phillips.
Financial data (yr. ended 06/30/11): Assets, $1 (M); expenditures, $5,338; qualifying distributions, $1,260.
Purpose and activities: The foundation supports organizations involved with Christian music and music education.
Fields of interest: Performing arts, music; Performing arts, education; Higher education; Christian agencies & churches.
Type of support: Conferences/seminars; Curriculum development; Endowments; Equipment; General/operating support; Grants to individuals; Program development; Scholarship funds; Sponsorships.
Geographic limitations: Giving primarily in TN.
Support limitations: No grants for non-music programs.
Application information: Applications not accepted. Unsolicited requests for funds not accepted.
Officers: Billy Ray Hearn, Pres.; Rick Horne, Secy.-Treas.; Holly Hearn-Whaley, Exec. Dir.
Directors: Margaret Becker; Richard Green; Steve Green; Bill Hearn; Vicki Horne.
Number of staff: 1 part-time professional.
EIN: 621516024

1259
Emmis Communications Corporation

(formerly Emmis Broadcasting)
1 Emmis Plz., 40 Monument Cir., Ste. 700
Indianapolis, IN 46204-3011
(317) 266-0100
FAX: (317) 684-5583

Company URL: http://www.emmis.com
Establishment information: Established in 1979.
Company type: Public company
Company ticker symbol and exchange: EMMS/NASDAQ
Business activities: Broadcasts radio; broadcasts television; publishes magazines.
Business type (SIC): Radio and television broadcasting; periodical publishing and/or printing
Financial profile for 2012: Number of employees, 1,140; assets, $340,770,000; sales volume, $236,010,000; pre-tax net income, -$590,000; expenses, $223,880,000; liabilities, $395,120,000
Corporate officers: Jeffrey H. Smulyan, Chair., Pres., and C.E.O.; Patrick Walsh, Exec. V.P., C.F.O., and C.O.O.; J. Scott Enright, Exec. V.P. and Genl. Counsel; Ryan A. Hornaday, Sr. V.P., Finance and Treas.; Traci L. Thomson, V.P., Human Resources
Board of directors: Jeffrey H. Smulyan, Chair.; Susan B. Bayh; James Dubin; Gary L. Kaseff; Richard A. Leventhal; Peter A. Lund; Greg A. Nathanson; Lawrence B. Sorrel; Patrick M. Walsh
Subsidiaries: Emmis Indiana Broadcasting, L.P., Indianapolis, IN; Emmis Publishing, L.P., Indianapolis, IN; Emmis Radio, LLC, Indianapolis, IN; Emmis Television Broadcasting, L.P., Indianapolis, IN; Los Angeles Magazine Holding Co., Inc., Los Angeles, CA; SJL of Kansas Corp., Wichita, KS; Topeka Television Corp., Topeka, KS
Giving statement: Giving through the Emmis Community Fund, Inc.
Company EIN: 351542018

Emmis Community Fund, Inc.

40 Monument Cir., Ste. 700
Indianapolis, IN 46204-3011 (317) 266-0100

Contact: Tom Severino, Pres.
Financial data (yr. ended 02/28/11): Revenue, $11,047; assets, $206,171 (M); expenditures, $40,431; program services expenses, $40,000; giving activities include $40,000 for grants.
Purpose and activities: The fund provides support for charitable purposes, particularly in dealing with people in need in the Emmis broadcasting communities.
Fields of interest: Education.
Geographic limitations: Giving primarily in AZ.
Officers and Directors:* Tom Severino, Pres.; Val Maki, V.P.; Scott Gillmore*, V.P.; Ryan Hornaday, V.P.-Accounting; Erika Richey*, Treas.; Carrie Wolf, Asst. Treas.; Karen Paul, Asst. Trea.; Tom Severino; J. Scott Enright; Lindy Richman.
EIN: 351968698

1260
Emmis Radio, LLC

(formerly Emmis Radio Corporation)
1 Emmis Plz.
40 Monument Cir., Ste. 700
Indianapolis, IN 46204 (317) 266-0100

Company URL: http://www.emmis.com
Establishment information: Established in 1986.
Company type: Subsidiary of a public company
Business activities: Broadcasts radio.
Business type (SIC): Radio and television broadcasting
Corporate officers: Richard F. Cummings, Pres.; Scott Enright, Exec. V.P. and Genl. Counsel
Giving statement: Giving through the KISS Cares Foundation, Inc.

KISS Cares Foundation, Inc.

(formerly Kiss Kares Fund, Inc.)
c/o Emmis Communications Corp.
40 Monument Cir.
Indianapolis, IN 46204-3019
Additional address: 395 Hudson Street, 7th Fl., New York, NY 10014; URL: http://www.987kissfm.com/KISSCares/

Establishment information: Established in 1995 in NY.
Donors: Emmis Radio Corp.; Emmis Radio, LLC; IAG Entertainment, Inc.
Contact: Brian D'Aurelio, Pres.
Financial data (yr. ended 12/31/11): Assets, $5,856 (M); expenditures, $4,300; qualifying distributions, $4,300; giving activities include $4,300 for 5 grants (high: $1,100; low: $200).
Purpose and activities: The foundation supports programs designed to improve quality of life in the community through family services, youth initiatives, health initiatives, and financial well-being.
Fields of interest: Health care; Boys & girls clubs; Youth development; Youth, services; Family services; Human services, financial counseling; Economic development.
Type of support: General/operating support; Program development; Scholarship funds.
Geographic limitations: Giving limited to New York, NY.
Application information: Applications accepted. Application form required.
Initial approach: Contact foundation for application form
Deadline(s): None
Officers: Brian D'Aurelio, Pres.; Dan Halyburton, V.P.; Kharisman Gooden-Mitchell*, Secy.; Robert Finley, Treas.
EIN: 061424235

1261
Empire Resorts, Inc.

c/o Monticello Casino and Raceway, 204 Rte. 17B
P.O. Box 5013
Monticello, NY 12701 (845) 807-0001
FAX: (302) 655-5049

Company URL: http://www.empireresorts.com
Establishment information: Established in 1993.
Company type: Public company
Company ticker symbol and exchange: NYNY/NASDAQ
Business activities: Operates a hospitality and gaming company.
Business type (SIC): Amusement and recreation services/miscellaneous
Financial profile for 2012: Number of employees, 310; assets, $52,449,000; sales volume, $71,973,000; pre-tax net income, -$697,000; liabilities, $27,636,000
Corporate officers: Emanuel R. Pearlman, Chair.; Joseph A. D'Amato, C.E.O.; Clifford A. Ehrlich, Pres.; Charles A. Degliomini, Exec. V.P., Corp. Comms.; Laurette J. Pitts, Sr. V.P. and C.F.O.
Board of directors: Emanuel R. Pearlman, Chair.; Fook Yew Au; Joseph D'Amato; Gregg Polle; Nancy Palumbo; James Simon
Giving statement: Giving through the Empire Resorts, Inc. Contributions Program.
Company EIN: 133714474

Empire Resorts, Inc. Contributions Program

c/o Monticello Casino and Race
Rte. 17B
P.O. Box 5013
Monticello, NY 12701-5193 (845) 807-0001
URL: http://www.empireresorts.com/about-empire/corp-social-resp.php

1262
Empire Southwest, LLC

(formerly Empire Southwest Company)
1725 S. Country Club Dr.
Mesa, AZ 85210-6003 (480) 633-4000
FAX: (480) 633-4489

Company URL: http://empirecat.com
Establishment information: Established in 1950.
Company type: Private company
Business activities: Operates heavy equipment and engine dealership.
Business type (SIC): Equipment rental and leasing/miscellaneous
Corporate officers: Jeffrey S. Whiteman, Chair. and C.E.O.; John Helms, C.F.O.; David Wise, C.I.O; Jan Holland, V.P., Human Resources
Board of director: Jeffrey S. Whiteman, Chair.
Giving statement: Giving through the Whiteman Foundation.

The Whiteman Foundation

(formerly Edna Rider Whiteman Foundation)
1725 South Country Club Dr.
Mesa, AZ 85210-6003 (480) 633-4413
E-mail: mtrivers@empire-cat.com; URL: http://whitemanfoundation.com

Establishment information: Established in 1961 in AZ.
Donors: Empire Southwest Co.; C. O. Whiteman‡; Jack W. Whiteman‡; Empire Southwest, LLC; John O. Whiteman.
Contact: Mollie C. Trivers, Exec. Dir.
Financial data (yr. ended 12/31/11): Assets, $3,389,890 (M); gifts received, $364,950; expenditures, $1,852,207; qualifying distributions, $1,804,249; giving activities include $1,782,249 for 3 grants (high: $1,702,249; low: $5,000).
Purpose and activities: The foundation supports programs designed to promote the health, education, and welfare of children. Special emphasis is directed toward early childhood development.
Fields of interest: Museums; Education, early childhood education; Education; Health care; Child development, services Children; Economically disadvantaged.
Type of support: Annual campaigns; Building/renovation; Capital campaigns; Continuing support; General/operating support; Matching/challenge support; Program development; Research; Seed money.
Geographic limitations: Giving primarily in the metropolitan Maricopa County and Phoenix, AZ, area.
Support limitations: No support for religious, athletic, or fraternal organizations or largely tax-supported organizations. No grants to individuals.
Publications: Application guidelines.
Application information: Applications accepted. Applicants should submit the following:
1) copy of IRS Determination Letter
2) brief history of organization and description of its mission
3) detailed description of project and amount of funding requested
4) copy of current year's organizational budget and/or project budget

Initial approach: Contact foundation to discuss project; complete online application
Deadline(s): None
Officers and Directors: John O. Whiteman, Pres. and Treas.; Anne C. Wilson, V.P. and Secy.; Eric Whiteman, V.P.; Jeff Whiteman, V.P.; Mollie C. Trivers, Exec. Dir.; LouElla Kleinz; Chrisy Whiteman Wilson.
Number of staff: 1 part-time professional.
EIN: 866052816
Selected grants: The following grants are a representative sample of this grantmaker's funding activity:
$30,000 to Museum of Contemporary Craft, Portland, OR, 2010.
$20,000 to Center for the Future of Arizona, Phoenix, AZ, 2010.
$5,000 to Arizona Foundation for Women, Phoenix, AZ, 2010.
$5,000 to United Way, Valley of the Sun, Phoenix, AZ, 2010.
$2,800 to Rodel Charitable Foundation of Arizona, Scottsdale, AZ, 2010.

1263
Employers Insurance Company of Wausau

(also known as Wausau Insurance Companies)
2000 Westwood Dr.
Wausau, WI 54401-7802 (715) 845-5211

Company URL: http://
Establishment information: Established in 1911.
Company type: Private company
Business activities: Sells insurance.
Business type (SIC): Insurance carriers
Corporate officers: Susan M. Doyle, Pres. and C.E.O.; Joe Gilles, C.O.O.
Giving statement: Giving through the Wausau Insurance Companies Contributions Program.

Wausau Insurance Companies Contributions Program

c/o Corp. Contribs.
2000 Westwood Dr.
Wausau, WI 54401-7881

Purpose and activities: Wausau Insurance makes charitable contributions to nonprofit organizations involved with business education and athletics. Support is given primarily in Wausau, Wisconsin.
Fields of interest: Business school/education; Athletics/sports, school programs; Athletics/sports, football; Athletics/sports, golf.
Type of support: Sponsorships.
Geographic limitations: Giving primarily in Wausau, WI.

1264
Employers Mutual Casualty Company

(also known as EMC Insurance Companies)
717 Mulberry St.
P.O. Box 712
Des Moines, IA 50309-3810
(515) 280-2511

Company URL: http://www.emcins.com
Establishment information: Established in 1911.
Company type: Subsidiary of a public company
Business activities: Sells property and casualty insurance.
Business type (SIC): Insurance/fire, marine, and casualty
Financial profile for 2011: Assets, $1,230,459,000; sales volume, $472,644,000; liabilities, $871,690,567
Corporate officers: George C. Carpenter III, Chair.; Bruce G. Kelley, Pres. and C.E.O.; Kevin J. Hovick, Exec. V.P. and C.O.O.; Mark E. Reese, Sr. V.P. and C.F.O.; Lisa A. Stange, V.P., Treas., and C.I.O.; Richard W. Hoffmann, V.P., Genl. Counsel, and Corp. Secy.; Elizabeth A. Nigut, V.P., Human Resources
Board of directors: George C. Carpenter III, Chair.; Stephen A. Crane; Jonathan R. Fletcher; Robert L. Howe; Bruce G. Kelley; Gretchen H. Tegeler
Subsidiary: EMC Insurance Group Inc., Des Moines, IA
Giving statement: Giving through the EMC Insurance Foundation.

EMC Insurance Foundation

(formerly Employers Mutual Charitable Foundation)
P.O. Box 712
Des Moines, IA 50303-0712
URL: http://www.emcins.com/AboutEMC/Community_Involvement.aspx

Establishment information: Established in 1989 in IA.
Donor: Employers Mutual Casualty Co.
Contact: Robert Morlan, Mgr. and Exec. Dir.
Financial data (yr. ended 12/31/12): Assets, $6,904,534 (M); gifts received, $1,474,752; expenditures, $1,065,130; qualifying distributions, $1,058,780; giving activities include $1,058,780 for 90 grants (high: $250,250; low: $20).
Purpose and activities: The foundation supports organizations involved with arts and culture, education, health, human services, and insurance education.
Fields of interest: Performing arts, orchestras; Arts; Elementary/secondary education; Higher education; Education; Health care; American Red Cross; Children/youth, services; Human services; Community development, civic centers; Business/industry; United Ways and Federated Giving Programs.
Type of support: General/operating support.
Geographic limitations: Giving primarily in areas of company operations in IA.
Support limitations: No grants to individuals.
Application information: Applications accepted. Application form not required. Applicants should submit the following:
1) copy of IRS Determination Letter
2) listing of additional sources and amount of support
3) detailed description of project and amount of funding requested

Initial approach: Proposal
Deadline(s): None

Officers and Directors:* Bruce G. Kelley*, C.E.O. and Pres.; John C. Burgeson, V.P.; Richard Hoffmann, Secy.; Ronald D. Herman, Treas.; Robert C. Morlan*, Mgr. and Exec. Dir.; David J. Fischer; John H. Kelley; Frederick Schiek.
EIN: 421343474
Selected grants: The following grants are a representative sample of this grantmaker's funding activity:
$252,590 to Drake University, Des Moines, IA, 2011. For general support.
$60,000 to Iowa Historical Foundation, Des Moines, IA, 2011. For general support.
$26,000 to Hospice of Central Michigan, Mount Pleasant, MI, 2011. For general support.
$26,000 to Special Olympics Iowa, Grimes, IA, 2011. For general support.
$20,000 to Science Center of Iowa, Des Moines, IA, 2011. For general support.
$14,000 to Civic Center of Greater Des Moines, Des Moines, IA, 2011. For general support.
$10,000 to Iowa Health Foundation, Des Moines, IA, 2011. For general support.
$7,000 to American Lung Association of Illinois-Iowa, Des Moines, IA, 2011. For general support.
$6,720 to Iowa State University, Ames, IA, 2011. For general support.
$5,000 to Habitat for Humanity, Greater Des Moines, Des Moines, IA, 2011. For general support.

1265
Enbridge Energy Partners, L.P.

1100 Louisiana St., Ste. 3300
Houston, TX 77002 (713) 821-2000
FAX: (713) 821-2230

Company URL: http://www.enbridgepartners.com
Establishment information: Established in 1991.
Company type: Public company
Company ticker symbol and exchange: EEP/NYSE
Business activities: Operates crude oil, liquid petroleum, and natural gas transportation and storage assets.
Business type (SIC): Pipelines (except natural gas/operation of)
Financial profile for 2012: Assets, $12,796,800,000; sales volume, $6,706,100,000; pre-tax net income, $558,200,000; expenses, $5,812,900,000; liabilities, $8,342,400,000
Fortune 1000 ranking: 2012—381st in revenues, 338th in profits, and 333rd in assets
Corporate officers: Jeffrey A. Connelly, Chair.; Terrance L. McGill, Pres.; Stephen J. Neyland, V.P., Finance
Board of directors: Jeffery A. Connelly, Chair.; J. Richard Bird; J. Herb England; Mark A. Maki; Terrance L. McGill; Rebecca B. Roberts; Dan Westbrook; Stephen J. Wuori
Giving statement: Giving through the Enbridge Energy Partners, L.P. Corporate Giving Program.
Company EIN: 391715850

Enbridge Energy Partners, L.P. Corporate Giving Program

1100 Louisiana St., Ste. 3300
Houston, TX 77002-5216 (832) 914-9461
FAX: (713) 821-2230; URL: http://www.enbridgeus.com/Main.aspx?id=309&tmi=135&tmt=4

Purpose and activities: Enbridge makes charitable contributions to nonprofit organizations involved with arts and culture, health and safety, education, the environment, and community development. Support is given primarily in areas of company operations.
Fields of interest: Arts; Education; Environment; Public health; Health care; Safety/disasters; American Red Cross; Human services, emergency aid; Community/economic development.
Type of support: Employee volunteer services; General/operating support.
Geographic limitations: Giving primarily in areas of company operations.
Support limitations: No support for religious, lobbying, political, or fraternal organizations, or K-12 schools. No grants to individuals, or for advertising, memberships, ticket sales, or lotteries, mass-mailed or non-addressed solicitations, pass-through organizations, or trips or tours.
Publications: Application guidelines.
Application information: Applications accepted.

Initial approach: Complete online application form or mail proposal to headquarters
Copies of proposal: 1
Deadline(s): None
Final notification: 60 days

1266
Encana Oil & Gas (USA), Inc.
370 - 17 St., Ste. 1700
Denver, CO 80202-5632 (303) 623-2300

Company URL: http://www.encana.com
Establishment information: Established in 1987.
Company type: Subsidiary of a foreign company
Business activities: Operates natural gas producing company.
Business type (SIC): Extraction/oil and gas
Corporate officer: Jeff Wojahn, Pres.
Giving statement: Giving through the Ecofund Foundation Ecuador and the EnCana Cares (USA) Foundation.

Ecofund Foundation Ecuador
c/o The Corporation Trust Co.
1209 N. Orange St.
Wilmington, DE 19801
E-mail: ecofondoecuador@ecofondoecuador.org; URL: http://en.powerstats.net/index.php?lang=en

Establishment information: Established in 2004 in DE.
Donor: Encana Corporation.
Financial data (yr. ended 12/31/11): Assets, $1,935,395 (M); expenditures, $21,668; qualifying distributions, $16,658.
Purpose and activities: Giving to promote the conservation of the watersheds, ecosystems, native vegetation types, and species found primarily in the zone of the influence of Oleoducto de Crudos Pesados, for the long-term benefit of the Ecuadorian people.
Fields of interest: Environment.
Geographic limitations: Giving on an international basis, primarily in Ecuador.
Support limitations: No grants to individuals.
Application information: Applications not accepted. Unsolicted requests for funds not accepted.
Officers: Andres Mendizabal, Pres.; Ximena Cabezas, Secy.; Alonso Colina, Treas.; Danilo Silva, Exec. Dir.
Directors: Rocio Alarcon; Susana Cabeza de Vaca; Carmen Josse; Wong Loon; Domingo Paredes; Marlo Raynolds.
EIN: 200642904

EnCana Cares (USA) Foundation
370 17th St., Ste. 1700
Denver, CO 80202-5632

Establishment information: Established in 2006 in CO.
Donors: Galen Archer; Clark L. Vickers; Julia Gwaltney; Lisa Mallin; David Smith II; John Holmberg; Encana Oil & Gas (USA), Inc.
Financial data (yr. ended 12/31/11): Assets, $1 (M); gifts received, $1,814,324; expenditures, $1,814,324; qualifying distributions, $1,814,324; giving activities include $1,814,324 for grants.
Purpose and activities: The foundation matches contributions made by employees of EnCana to nonprofit organizations.
Fields of interest: General charitable giving.
Type of support: Employee matching gifts.
Geographic limitations: Giving primarily in CO and TX.
Application information: Applications not accepted. Contributes only through employee matching gifts.
Officers and Directors:* Jeff Wojahn*, Pres.; Don McClure*, V.P. and Treas.; Doug Hock*, Secy.
EIN: 205064193

1267
The Endeavor Agency, LLC
9701 Wilshire Blvd., 3rd Fl.
Beverly Hills, CA 90212-5219
(310) 248-2000
FAX: (310) 248-2020

Establishment information: Established in 1995.
Company type: Private company
Business activities: Operates talent agency.
Business type (SIC): Bands, orchestras, and entertainers
Corporate officers: Areil Z. Emanuel, Owner; Robin Davis, Cont.
Giving statement: Giving through the William Morris Endeavor Entertainment Foundation.

The William Morris Endeavor Entertainment Foundation
(formerly The Endeavor Foundation: A California Nonprofit Public Benefit Co.)
c/o TMG
9100 Wilshire Blvd., #400W
Beverly Hills, CA 90212-3481

Establishment information: Established in 2000 in CA.
Donors: The Endeavor Agency, L.L.C.; William Morris Endeavor Agency.
Financial data (yr. ended 12/31/11): Assets, $1,281,015 (M); gifts received, $9,437; expenditures, $339,044; qualifying distributions, $338,299; giving activities include $338,299 for grants.
Purpose and activities: The foundation supports organizations involved with arts and culture, education, children and youth, and family services.
Fields of interest: Museums; Arts; Education, services; Education; Children/youth, services; Family services.
Type of support: General/operating support; Program development.
Geographic limitations: Giving primarily in CA.
Application information: Applications not accepted. Contributes only to pre-selected organizations.
Officers and Directors:* Richard Weitz*, Chair.; Michael Donkis, Pres.; Lisa Harrison*, V.P.; Melissa Myers, V.P.; Anna Du Val, Secy.; Jason Lublin, C.F.O.; Adriana Alberghetti; Chris Donnelly.
EIN: 954823036
Selected grants: The following grants are a representative sample of this grantmaker's funding activity:
$25,000 to LACER Afterschool Programs, Hollywood, CA, 2010.
$25,000 to Los Angeles Leadership Academy, Los Angeles, CA, 2010.
$17,500 to Museum of Contemporary Art, Los Angeles, CA, 2010.
$15,000 to Aviva Family and Childrens Services, Los Angeles, CA, 2010.
$12,500 to City Hearts: Kids Say Yes to the Arts, Topanga, CA, 2010.
$5,000 to Street Poets, Los Angeles, CA, 2010.
$3,500 to Hawn Foundation, Santa Monica, CA, 2010.

1268
Endo Health Solutions Inc
(formerly Endo Pharmaceuticals Holdings Inc)
1400 Atwater Dr.
Malvern, PA 19355 (484) 216-0000
FAX: (302) 655-5049

Company URL: http://www.endo.com
Establishment information: Established in 1997.
Company type: Public company
Company ticker symbol and exchange: ENDP/NASDAQ
Business activities: Operates healthcare solutions company.
Business type (SIC): Drugs
Financial profile for 2012: Number of employees, 4,629; assets, $6,568,560,000; sales volume, $3,027,360,000; pre-tax net income, -$741,580,000; expenses, $3,586,300,000; liabilities, $5,495,700,000
Fortune 1000 ranking: 2012—708th in revenues, 972nd in profits, and 509th in assets
Corporate officers: Roger H. Kimmel, Chair.; Rajiv De Silva, Pres. and C.E.O.; Julie H. McHugh, C.O.O.; Alan G. Levin, Exec. V.P. and C.F.O.; Caroline B. Manogue, Exec. V.P. and Secy.; Larry Cunningham, Exec. V.P., Human Resources
Board of directors: Roger H. Kimmel, Chair.; John J. Delucca; Michael Hyatt; Nancy J. Hutson, Ph.D.; William P. Montague; David B. Nash, M.D.,M.B.A.; Joseph C. Scodari; Rajiv De Silva; Jill D. Smith; William F. Spengler
Subsidiary: American Medical Systems Holdings, Inc., Minnetonka, MN
Giving statement: Giving through the Endo Pharmaceuticals Holdings Inc. Contributions Program.
Company EIN: 134022871

Endo Pharmaceuticals Holdings Inc. Contributions Program
100 Endo Blvd.
Chadds Ford, PA 19317 (610) 558-9800
E-mail: External.Affairs@endo.com; URL: http://www.endo.com/about-us/our-commitment

Purpose and activities: Endo Pharmaceuticals supports initiatives that improve communities located in areas of company operations, provide better access to care for patients, improve patient outcomes by supporting education for healthcare professionals, and support research that will advance scientific knowledge about its products to generate new medical interventions.
Fields of interest: Health care, research; Health care, patient services; Health care; Human services; Patients' rights.
Program:
U.S. Patient Assistance Program: The Endo Pharmaceuticals Inc., patient assistance program offers free medication to people who otherwise cannot afford their medications. Patients must meet financial and other program specific criteria to be eligible for assistance.
Type of support: Donated products; Employee matching gifts; Employee volunteer services; General/operating support; Research.
Geographic limitations: Giving primarily in areas of company operations in Huntsville, AL, San Jose, CA, Augusta, GA, Minnetonka, MN, Charlotte, NC, Cranbury, NJ, Westbury, NY, Chadds Ford and Malvern, PA, and Austin, TX.
Support limitations: No support for sectarian, religious, labor, or discriminatory organizations; private foundations, or sports teams. No grants to

individuals, or for memorial funds, medical conferences, or symposiums.
Publications: Application guidelines.
Application information: Applications accepted. Requests are limited to 1 application per organization during any given year. Multi-year funding is not automatic. Application form required.
Initial approach: Complete online application
Deadline(s): None

1269
Endres Manufacturing Company

802 S. Century Ave.
Waunakee, WI 53597-1608 (608) 849-4143
FAX: (608) 849-7903

Company URL: http://www.endresmfg.com
Establishment information: Established in 1926.
Company type: Private company
Business activities: Manufactures structural steel products.
Business type (SIC): Metal products/structural
Corporate officers: Diane Endres-Ballweg, Pres.; Annie Ballweg, Secy.; Mike Steinl, Treas.
Giving statement: Giving through the Endres Manufacturing Foundation Inc.

Endres Manufacturing Foundation Inc.

350 S. Hamilton St., Ste. 701
Madison, WI 53703-4187 (608) 836-1751
E-mail: Foundation@EndresMfg.com; Tel.: (608) 836-1751; URL: http://www.endresmfg.com/foundation.htm

Establishment information: Established in 1995 in WI.
Donors: Gordy Acker; Jean Acker; Annie Ballweg; Ben Ballweg; Diane Ballweg; Jackie Ballweg; Ken Ballweg; Nick Ballweg; Sam Ballweg; Endres Manufacturing Co.; Charlie Endres; Laura Endres; Tracy Hellenbrand; Wayne Hellenbrand; Bob Kopp; Shirley Kopp; Ross Kuehn; Connie Lange; Tom Lange; Charlie Oldroyd; Nancy Oldroyd; Debra Palm; Mike Palm; Karen Ripp; Kevin Ripp; Elaine Wolfe; Cubby Wolfe.
Contact: Diane Ballweg, Pres.
Financial data (yr. ended 12/31/11): Assets, $1,340,257 (M); gifts received, $14,226; expenditures, $90,475; qualifying distributions, $80,940; giving activities include $80,430 for grants.
Purpose and activities: The foundation supports camps and organizations involved with arts and culture, education, hunger, human services, and Christianity.
Fields of interest: Performing arts, theater; Arts; Elementary/secondary education; Education; Food services; Recreation, camps; Children/youth, services; Human services; Christian agencies & churches.
Type of support: Employee matching gifts; General/operating support; Matching/challenge support; Scholarship funds.
Geographic limitations: Giving primarily in the south central WI area, with emphasis on Dane County.
Support limitations: No grants to individuals.
Publications: Application guidelines; Grants list; Informational brochure (including application guidelines).
Application information: Applications accepted. Support is limited to 1 contribution per organization during any given year. Organizations receiving support are asked to provide a final report. Application form required. Applicants should submit the following:
1) timetable for implementation and evaluation of project
2) statement of problem project will address
3) copy of IRS Determination Letter
4) copy of most recent annual report/audited financial statement/990
5) listing of board of directors, trustees, officers and other key people and their affiliations
6) detailed description of project and amount of funding requested
7) copy of current year's organizational budget and/or project budget

Initial approach: Download application form and mail proposal and application form to foundation
Copies of proposal: 6
Board meeting date(s): May 15 and Nov. 15
Deadline(s): May 1 and Nov. 1
Final notification: Within 2 weeks of board meeting

Officers: Diane Ballweg, Pres.; Gordy Acker, V.P.; Annie Ballweg, Secy.; Michael Steinl, Treas.
Directors: Cari Joseph; Bob Kopp; Alan Wolfe.
Number of staff: None.
EIN: 391839327

1270
Energen Corporation

605 Richard Arrington, Jr. Blvd. N.
Birmingham, AL 35203-2707
(205) 326-2700
FAX: (205) 326-2704

Company URL: http://www.energen.com
Establishment information: Established in 1985.
Company type: Public company
Company ticker symbol and exchange: EGN/NYSE
Business activities: Operates oil and gas exploration and production company.
Business type (SIC): Gas production and distribution
Financial profile for 2012: Number of employees, 1,575; assets, $6,175,890,000; sales volume, $1,617,170,000; pre-tax net income, $397,380,000; expenses, $1,157,780,000; liabilities, $3,499,200,000
Corporate officers: James T. McManus II, Chair. and C.E.O.; Charles W. Porter, Jr., V.P., C.F.O., and Treas.; J. David Woodruff, V.P., Genl. Counsel, and Secy.; Russell E. Lynch, Jr., V.P. and Cont.; William K. Bibb, V.P., Human Resources
Board of directors: James T. McManus II, Chair.; Stephen D. Ban, Ph.D.; Julian W. Banton; Kenneth W. Dewey; T. Michael Goodrich; Jay Grinney; Judy M. Merritt; Stephen A. Snider; David W. Wilson; Gary C. Youngblood
Giving statement: Giving through the Energen Corporation Contributions Program and the Energen Foundation.
Company EIN: 630757759

Energen Corporation Contributions Program

605 Richard Arrington, Jr. Blvd. N.
Birmingham, AL 35203-2707 (205) 326-2700
URL: http://www.energen.com/About-Energen/In-the-Community-178.html

Purpose and activities: Energen makes charitable contributions involved with the arts, education, healthcare, human services, community development, and civic affairs. Support is given primarily in areas of company operations, with emphasis on Alabama.
Fields of interest: Arts; Higher education; Health care; Human services; Community/economic development; United Ways and Federated Giving Programs; Public affairs.
Type of support: Donated equipment; Employee matching gifts; Employee volunteer services; General/operating support; Scholarship funds.
Geographic limitations: Giving primarily in areas of company operations, with emphasis on AL.

Energen Foundation

605 Richard Arrington Jr. Blvd. N.
Birmingham, AL 35203-2707

Donor: Energen Corporation.
Financial data (yr. ended 12/31/11): Assets, $3,235,002 (M); gifts received, $1,250,000; expenditures, $904,016; qualifying distributions, $897,529; giving activities include $897,529 for grants.
Application information: Applications not accepted. Unsolicited requests for funds not accepted.
Officers and Directors:* James T. McManus II*, Pres.; Dudley C. Reynolds*, V.P.; Robert S. Mcannally*, Secy.; Charles W. Porter, Jr.*, Treas.; William K. Bibb.
EIN: 261678215
Selected grants: The following grants are a representative sample of this grantmaker's funding activity:
$25,000 to Jefferson County Committee for Economic Opportunity, Birmingham, AL, 2010.
$22,000 to Greater Birmingham Ministries, Birmingham, AL, 2010.
$10,000 to American Red Cross, Birmingham, AL, 2010.
$10,000 to McWane Science Center, Birmingham, AL, 2010.
$10,000 to Petroleum Museum, Midland, TX, 2010.
$9,876 to United Way, San Juan, Farmington, NM, 2010.
$7,800 to United Way of West Alabama, Tuscaloosa, AL, 2010.

1271
Energizer Holdings, Inc.

533 Maryville University Dr.
St. Louis, MO 63141 (314) 985-2000
FAX: (314) 985-2000

Company URL: http://www.energizer.com
Establishment information: Established in 1999.
Company type: Public company
Company ticker symbol and exchange: ENR/NYSE
Business activities: Manufactures primary batteries, flashlights, and men's and women's wet-shave products.
Business type (SIC): Electrical equipment and supplies; cutlery, hand and edge tools, and hardware; lighting and wiring equipment/electric
Financial profile for 2012: Number of employees, 14,800; assets, $6,731,200,000; sales volume, $4,567,200,000; pre-tax net income, $565,400,000; expenses, $4,001,800,000; liabilities, $4,661,700,000
Fortune 1000 ranking: 2012—525th in revenues, 390th in profits, and 502nd in assets
Forbes 2000 ranking: 2012—1449th in sales, 1256th in profits, and 1700th in assets
Corporate officers: J. Patrick Mulcahy, Chair.; Ward M. Klein, C.E.O.; Daniel J. Sescleifer, Exec. V.P. and C.F.O.; Mark S. Lavigne, V.P. and Genl. Counsel; Peter J. Conrad, V.P., Human Resources

Board of directors: J. Patrick Mulcahy, Chair.; Bill G. Armstrong; Daniel J. Heinrich; R. David Hoover; John C. Hunter III; John E. Klein; W. Patrick McGinnis; Pamela M. Nicholson; John R. Roberts
Subsidiary: Schick Manufacturing, Inc., Milford, CT
International operations: Argentina; Australia; Austria; Barbados; Belgium; Bermuda; Brazil; Canada; Cayman Islands; Chile; China; Colombia; Czech Republic; Dominican Republic; Ecuador; Egypt; France; Germany; Greece; Hong Kong; Hungary; India; Indonesia; Ireland; Italy; Japan; Kenya; Malaysia; Mexico; Netherlands; New Zealand; North Korea; Peru; Philippines; Poland; Portugal; Russia; Singapore; Slovakia; Spain; Sri Lanka; Sweden; Switzerland; Thailand; Turkey; United Kingdom; Uruguay; Venezuela
Giving statement: Giving through the Energizer Charitable Trust.
Company EIN: 431863181

Energizer Charitable Trust

c/o The Northern Trust Co.
P.O. Box 803878
Chicago, IL 60680-3878
Application address: c/o Barb LeClere, Energizer Charitable Trust, 533 Maryville University Dr., St. Louis, MO 63141

Establishment information: Established in 2000 in MO.
Donors: Ralston Purina Trust Fund; Energizer Holdings, Inc.
Financial data (yr. ended 09/30/11): Assets, $10,419,752 (M); gifts received, $3,000,000; expenditures, $1,444,694; qualifying distributions, $1,441,694; giving activities include $1,441,694 for grants.
Purpose and activities: The trust supports museums and organizations involved with education, animal welfare, diabetes, housing development, youth development, human services, and economically disadvantaged people.
Fields of interest: Museums; Museums (art); Elementary/secondary education; Education, special; Higher education; Libraries (public); Scholarships/financial aid; Education, services; Education; Animal welfare; Diabetes; Housing/shelter, development; Boys & girls clubs; Youth development, business; Youth development; Children/youth, services; Human services; United Ways and Federated Giving Programs Economically disadvantaged.
Program:
Employee Matching Gifts: The foundation matches contributions made by employees of Energizer to nonprofit organizations on a one-for-one basis from $25 to $1,000 per employee, per year.
Type of support: Continuing support; Employee matching gifts; General/operating support; Program development; Scholarship funds.
Geographic limitations: Giving primarily in St. Louis, MO and other areas of company operations in CT, IL, KY, NC, NY, and OH.
Support limitations: No support for veterans' or fraternal organizations not of direct benefit to the entire community. No grants to individuals, or for religious or politically partisan purposes, investment funds, tickets for dinners, benefits, exhibits, conferences, sports events, or other short term activities, advertisements, or debt reduction or post-event needs; no loans.
Application information: Applications accepted. Application form not required. Applicants should submit the following:
1) timetable for implementation and evaluation of project
2) qualifications of key personnel
3) copy of IRS Determination Letter
4) brief history of organization and description of its mission
5) copy of most recent annual report/audited financial statement/990
6) how project's results will be evaluated or measured
7) detailed description of project and amount of funding requested
8) copy of current year's organizational budget and/or project budget

Initial approach: Proposal
Board meeting date(s): Quarterly
Deadline(s): None

Trustees: Buron Buffkin; Jacqueline E. Burwitz; Dan Carpenter; William C. Fox; Mark A. Schafale; Joseph J. Tisone; Jeff Ziminski.
EIN: 367324191
Selected grants: The following grants are a representative sample of this grantmaker's funding activity:
$140,000 to United Way of Milford, Milford, CT, 2010.
$106,207 to United Way of Delaware, Wilmington, DE, 2010.
$99,475 to United Way of Delaware, Wilmington, DE, 2010.
$75,000 to Teach for America, New York, NY, 2010.
$16,644 to United Way, Shelby County, Sidney, OH, 2010.
$16,222 to United Way, Shelby County, Sidney, OH, 2010.
$15,279 to United Way of Bergen County, Paramus, NJ, 2010.
$7,660 to United Way of Volusia-Flagler Counties, Daytona Beach, FL, 2010.
$4,228 to United Way of Volusia-Flagler Counties, Daytona Beach, FL, 2010.
$2,500 to Ready Readers, Saint Louis, MO, 2010.

1272
Energy Corporation of America

(also known as ECA)
4643 S. Ulster St., Ste. 1100
Denver, CO 80237-2867 (303) 694-2667

Company URL: http://www.energycorporationofamerica.com
Establishment information: Established in 1963.
Company type: Private company
Business activities: Conducts crude oil and natural gas exploration, development, and production activities.
Business type (SIC): Extraction/oil and gas
Corporate officers: Thomas R. Goodwin, Chair.; John F. Mork, Pres. and C.E.O.; Kyle M. Mork, C.O.O.; Michael S. Fletcher, C.F.O.; Donald C. Supcoe, Exec. V.P. and Genl. Counsel; J. Michael Forbes, V.P. and Treas.; Randall Farkosh, V.P., Mktg.
Board of directors: Thomas R. Goodwin, Chair.; W. Gaston Caperton III; Peter H. Coors; L.B. Curtis; John Fischer; James Markowsky; F.H. McCullough III; John F. Mork; Julie M. Mork; Kyl Mork; Jerry Neely; Jay S. Pifer; Donald C. Supcoe
Subsidiaries: Eastern American Energy Corp., Charleston, WV; Eastern Marketing Corp., Charleston, WV; Eastern Pipeline Corp., Charleston, WV; Westech Energy Corp., Denver, CO
Giving statement: Giving through the ECA Foundation, Inc.
Company EIN: 841235822

ECA Foundation, Inc.

4643 S. Ulster, Ste. 1100
Denver, CO 80237-2867 (303) 694-2667
FAX: (303) 694-2763;
E-mail: sara@energycorporationofamerica.com;
URL: http://www.ecafoundation.org/

Establishment information: Established in 1996 in CO.
Donors: Eastern American Energy Corp.; Mountaineer Gas Co.; Energy Corp. of America.
Contact: Sara DiManna, Prog. Admin.
Financial data (yr. ended 06/30/11): Assets, $1,952,540 (M); gifts received, $1,304,415; expenditures, $1,370,352; qualifying distributions, $1,359,327; giving activities include $1,258,426 for 78 grants (high: $350,000; low: $1,000) and $100,901 for 15 employee matching gifts.
Purpose and activities: The foundation supports programs designed to maximize the development and potential of youth academically, physically, and spiritually.
Fields of interest: Elementary/secondary education; Education; Health care; Children/youth, services Children/youth; Children; Youth.
Type of support: Curriculum development; Employee matching gifts; Management development/capacity building; Matching/challenge support; Program development; Scholarship funds.
Geographic limitations: Giving primarily in areas of company operations in the metropolitan Denver, CO, area, metropolitan Houston, TX, area, PA and WV.
Support limitations: No support for political organizations or discriminatory organizations. No grants to individuals, or for publications, films, media projects, seminars, conferences, events, or meetings travel, start-up needs, research, general operating support, capital campaigns or acquisitions, construction or renovation, debt reduction, endowments, or recruiting or training.
Publications: Application guidelines; Grants list; Informational brochure (including application guidelines).
Application information: Applications accepted. Proposals may be submitted using the Colorado Common Grant Format. Hardcopy submission only; e-mail submissions not accepted. Support is limited to 1 contribution per organization during any given year. A site visit may be requested. Organizations receiving support are asked to provide a final report. Application form not required. Applicants should submit the following:
1) signature and title of chief executive officer
2) results expected from proposed grant
3) qualifications of key personnel
4) statement of problem project will address
5) name, address and phone number of organization
6) copy of IRS Determination Letter
7) brief history of organization and description of its mission
8) copy of most recent annual report/audited financial statement/990
9) listing of board of directors, trustees, officers and other key people and their affiliations
10) detailed description of project and amount of funding requested
11) contact person
12) copy of current year's organizational budget and/or project budget
13) listing of additional sources and amount of support

Proposals should indicate the percentage of funds budgeted for fundraising, administrative costs, and programs.

Initial approach: Proposal to foundation or telephone foundation
Copies of proposal: 1

Board meeting date(s): Mar., June, Sept., and Dec.
Deadline(s): Feb. 1, May 1, Aug. 1, and Nov. 1
Final notification: Approximately 6 to 8 weeks
Officers and Directors: Sara E. DiManna, Secy. and Prog. Admin.; Michael S. Fletcher, Treas.; Joseph E. Casabona; J. Michael Forbes; Frank H. McCullough III; John F. Mork; Julie M. Mork; Kyle M. Mork; Donald C. Supcoe.
Number of staff: 2 part-time professional.
EIN: 841349588
Selected grants: The following grants are a representative sample of this grantmaker's funding activity:
$25,000 to Read Aloud West Virginia of Kanawha County, Charleston, WV, 2009. For capacity building.
$20,000 to Community Resource Center, Denver, CO, 2009. For job training.
$20,000 to Goodwill Industries of Denver, Denver, CO, 2009. For STEM Educaiian.
$20,000 to YWCA of Charleston, Charleston, WV, 2009. For job training for the homeless.
$15,000 to CASA, Denver, Denver, CO, 2009.
$15,000 to Whiz Kids Tutoring, Denver, CO, 2009. For tutoring for at-risk elementary students.
$10,000 to Denver Public Library, Denver, CO, 2009. For summer reading.
$10,000 to Work Options for Women, Denver, CO, 2009. To train women for stable careers.
$7,500 to Junior Achievement of West Virginia and the Advantage Valley, Charleston, WV, 2009. For educational programs.
$5,000 to I Have A Dream Foundation, Denver, CO, 2009. To follow at-risk students to graduation.

1273
Energy Future Holdings Corp.

(formerly TXU Corp.)
1601 Bryan St.
Dallas, TX 75201-3411 (214) 812-4600

Company URL: http://www.energyfutureholdings.com/
Establishment information: Established in 1945.
Company type: Private company
Business activities: Operates holding company; generates, transmits, and distributes electricity; provides communications services; distributes natural gas.
Business type (SIC): Electric services; communications; gas production and distribution; holding company
Financial profile for 2011: Number of employees, 9,200; assets, $46,388,000,000; sales volume, $8,235,000,000
Fortune 1000 ranking: 2012—447th in revenues, 996th in profits, and 138th in assets
Corporate officers: Donald L. Evans, Chair.; John F. Young, Pres. and C.E.O.; Paul M. Keglevic, Exec. V.P. and C.F.O.; Robert C. Walters, Exec. V.P. and Genl. Counsel; Richard Landy, Exec. V.P., Human Resources; Tom Baker, Chair. Emeritus
Board of directors: Donald L. Evans, Chair.; Arcilia C. Acosta; David Bonderman; Thomas D. Ferguson; Frederick M. Goltz; James R. Huffines; Scott Lebovitz; Jeffrey Liaw; Marc S. Lipschultz; Michael MacDougal; Amb. Lyndon L. Olson, Jr.; Kenneth Pontarelli; William R. Reilly; Jonathan D. Smidt; John F. Young; Kneeland Youngblood
International operations: Australia
Giving statement: Giving through the Energy Future Holdings Corp. Contributions Program.
Company EIN: 752669310

Energy Future Holdings Corp. Contributions Program

(formerly Energy Future Holdings Corp.)
Energy Plz.
1601 Bryan St.
Dallas, TX 75201-3411 (214) 812-4600

Purpose and activities: Energy Future Holdings makes charitable contributions to nonprofit organizations on a case by case basis. Support is given primarily in Texas.
Fields of interest: General charitable giving.
Type of support: Employee matching gifts; General/operating support.
Geographic limitations: Giving primarily in TX; giving also to national organizations.
Number of staff: 4 full-time professional.

1274
EnMark Gas Gathering, L.P.

1700 Pacific Ave., Ste. 4500
Dallas, TX 75201 (214) 965-9580

Company URL: http://www.enmarkservices.com/about/
Company type: Private company
Business activities: Sells gas wholesale; develops real estate.
Business type (SIC): Petroleum and petroleum products—wholesale; real estate subdividers and developers
Corporate officer: Spencer Falls, Pres.
Giving statement: Giving through the Miller Foundation, Inc.

The Miller Foundation, Inc.

17341 Remington Park Cir.
Dallas, TX 75252-5358

Establishment information: Established in 1994 in TX.
Donor: EnMark Gas Gathering, L.P.
Financial data (yr. ended 12/31/11): Assets, $150,313 (M); gifts received, $750,000; expenditures, $47,154; qualifying distributions, $46,000; giving activities include $46,000 for grants.
Purpose and activities: The foundation supports organizations involved with Christianity and other areas.
Fields of interest: Arts; Youth development; Human services.
Type of support: General/operating support.
Geographic limitations: Giving primarily in Orlando, FL and Plano, TX.
Support limitations: No grants to individuals.
Application information: Applications not accepted. Unsolicited requests for funds not accepted.
Officers: Rodney G. Miller, Pres.; Olivia A. Miller, Secy.
Directors: Melissa K. Sloan; Tracy D. Stringfield.
EIN: 752518345

1275
The Ensign Group, Inc.

27101 Puerta Real, Ste. 450
Mission Viejo, CA 92691-8566
(949) 487-9500
FAX: (302) 674-5266

Company URL: http://www.ensigngroup.net/
Establishment information: Established in 1999.
Company type: Public company
Company ticker symbol and exchange: ENSG/NASDAQ
Business activities: Operates assisted-living facilities.
Business type (SIC): Nursing and personal care facilities
Financial profile for 2012: Number of employees, 10,371; assets, $690,860,000; sales volume, $824,720,000; pre-tax net income, $64,070,000; expenses, $748,670,000; liabilities, $364,390,000
Corporate officers: Roy E. Christensen, Chair.; Christopher R. Christensen, Pres. and C.E.O.; Suzanne D. Snapper, C.P.A., C.F.O.; Gregory K. Stapley, Exec. V.P. and Secy.; Beverly B. Wittekind, V.P. and Genl. Counsel
Board of directors: Roy E. Christensen, Chair.; Christopher R. Christensen; Antoinette T. Hubenette, M.D.; Van R. Johnson; Thomas A. Maloof; John G. Nackel, Ph.D.; Daren Shaw
Giving statement: Giving through the Ensign Foundation.
Company EIN: 330861263

The Ensign Foundation

27101 Puerta Real, Ste. 450
Mission Viejo, CA 92691 (949) 487-9500
URL: http://ensignfoundation.org

Donors: Ensign Facility Services, Inc.; GE Capital Corp.; LTC Properties, Inc.; Medline Industries, Inc.; National Purchasing Corp.; Innovatix, LLC; Blue Shield of California.
Financial data (yr. ended 12/31/11): Assets, $229,221 (M); gifts received, $153,495; expenditures, $126,124; qualifying distributions, $69,250; giving activities include $69,250 for grants.
Fields of interest: Health organizations; Community/economic development; Religion.
Application information: Applications accepted. Application form required.
Initial approach: Proposal
Deadline(s): None
Directors: Ramona Ayers; Christie Bohnsack; Maya Castillo.
EIN: 263458040

1276
Ensign-Bickford Industries, Inc.

125 Powder Forest Dr., 3rd Fl.
P.O. Box 7
Simsbury, CT 06070-2429 (860) 843-2000

Company URL: http://www.e-bind.com
Establishment information: Established in 1836.
Company type: Private company
Business activities: Manufactures caulks, tapes and fibers, and fiber optics.
Business type (SIC): Chemical preparations/miscellaneous; plastics and synthetics
Financial profile for 2009: Number of employees, 1,600

Corporate officers: Caleb White, C.E.O.; Denise M. Grant, C.F.O.; Genevieve Defelice, C.I.O.; Michael J. Butler, V.P., Human Resources; Kevin Schultz, V.P., Human Resources
Giving statement: Giving through the Ensign-Bickford Foundation, Inc.

The Ensign-Bickford Foundation, Inc.

125 Powder Forest Dr.
P.O. Box 7
Simsbury, CT 06070-9658 (860) 843-2384

Establishment information: Incorporated in 1952 in CT.
Donor: Ensign-Bickford Industries, Inc.
Contact: Richard Roberts
Financial data (yr. ended 12/31/11): Assets, $88 (M); gifts received, $175,000; expenditures, $179,956; qualifying distributions, $179,956; giving activities include $179,856 for 129 grants (high: $15,000; low: $100).
Purpose and activities: The foundation supports zoos and organizations involved with arts and culture, education, animal welfare, housing, youth development, business promotion, and military and veterans.
Fields of interest: Performing arts; Performing arts, theater; Performing arts, music; Arts; Elementary/secondary education; Higher education; Education; Animal welfare; Zoos/zoological societies; Housing/shelter; Boys & girls clubs; Community development, business promotion; United Ways and Federated Giving Programs; Military/veterans' organizations.
Type of support: General/operating support; Program development; Research; Scholarship funds.
Geographic limitations: Giving primarily in areas of company operations in CT, with emphasis on the Avon and Simsbury areas.
Support limitations: No grants to individuals (except for employee-related scholarships), or for endowments, general operating support, emergency needs, or debt reduction; no loans.
Application information: Applications accepted. Application form not required. Applicants should submit the following:
1) geographic area to be served
2) copy of current year's organizational budget and/or project budget
3) listing of additional sources and amount of support
4) detailed description of project and amount of funding requested

Initial approach: Proposal
Board meeting date(s): Approximately every 2 months
Deadline(s): None
Final notification: 3 months

Officers and Directors:* Joan D. Lovejoy*, Chair.; Denise M. Grant, Treas.; Jacquelyn A. Levin; Michael L. Pitcher; Richard Roberts; Caleb E. White.
Number of staff: 1 part-time professional.
EIN: 066041097
Selected grants: The following grants are a representative sample of this grantmaker's funding activity:
$2,000 to Conservation Law Foundation, Boston, MA, 2011.
$1,286 to Leukemia & Lymphoma Society, White Plains, NY, 2011.
$1,200 to American Kidney Fund, Rockville, MD, 2011.
$1,000 to American Cancer Society, Atlanta, GA, 2011.
$1,000 to Gideons International, Nashville, TN, 2011.
$1,000 to Heartbeat International, Columbus, OH, 2011.
$1,000 to Student Conservation Association, Charlestown, NH, 2011.

1277
Entelco Corporation

132 W. 2nd St., Ste. B
Perrysburg, OH 43551-7632
(419) 872-4620
FAX: (419) 872-4623

Establishment information: Established in 1981.
Company type: Private company
Business activities: Conducts investment activities.
Business type (SIC): Investors/miscellaneous
Corporate officers: Stephen Stranahan, Pres.; Thomas L. Reed, Treas.
Giving statement: Giving through the Entelco Foundation.

Entelco Foundation

132 W. 2nd St., Ste. B
Perrysburg, OH 43551-7632
FAX: (419) 872-4623;
E-mail: sstranahan@entelcocorp.com

Establishment information: Established in 1979 in OH.
Donors: Entelco Corp.; Stephen Stranahan.
Financial data (yr. ended 12/31/11): Assets, $4,165,549 (M); expenditures, $250,553; qualifying distributions, $197,340; giving activities include $195,965 for 52 grants (high: $95,000; low: $100).
Purpose and activities: The foundation supports organizations involved with arts and culture, education, human services, community development, and other areas.
Fields of interest: Arts; Education; Human services; Community/economic development; General charitable giving.
Programs:
Community Fund: Through the Community Fund, the foundation supports organizations involved with arts and culture, education, human services, and other areas.
Entelco Fund: Through the Entelco Fund, the foundation supports organizations with which employees of Entelco are interested and involved.
Special Projects Fund: Through the Special Projects Fund, the foundation supports programs designed to work together to build positive community change. Special emphasis is directed toward programs designed to encourage members to become actively involved "from the bottom up" in problem-solving, goal-setting, and leadership; take calculated risks; and implement an innovative, non-traditional approach to problem-solving.
Type of support: Capital campaigns; Employee volunteer services; General/operating support; Program development.
Geographic limitations: Giving primarily in the Toledo and northwestern OH area, and areas where Entelco Corporation, its founders and stockholders have charitable interests.
Support limitations: No grants to individuals, or for endowments, publications, debt reduction, film or video production, or land acquisition.
Publications: Application guidelines.
Application information: Applications accepted. The foundation is not accepting new proposals until further notice. Application form required. Applicants should submit the following:
1) detailed description of project and amount of funding requested
2) copy of current year's organizational budget and/or project budget

Initial approach: Letter
Copies of proposal: 1
Board meeting date(s): May and Nov.
Deadline(s): Mar. 31 and Sept. 30
Final notification: 2 months

Trustees: Ann A. Stranahan; Stephen Stranahan.
Director: Louise Jackson.
Number of staff: 1 part-time support.
EIN: 341288595
Selected grants: The following grants are a representative sample of this grantmaker's funding activity:
$10,000 to Maumee Valley Country Day School, Toledo, OH, 2009.
$7,500 to Trinity Episcopal Church, Toledo, OH, 2009.
$5,000 to American Farmland Trust, Washington, DC, 2009.
$5,000 to American Farmland Trust, Washington, DC, 2009.
$5,000 to Amos House, Providence, RI, 2009.
$5,000 to Community MusicWorks, Providence, RI, 2009.
$5,000 to Wheeler School, Providence, RI, 2009.
$2,500 to Maumee Valley Country Day School, Toledo, OH, 2009.
$2,500 to Northwest School of Wooden Boatbuilding, Port Hadlock, WA, 2009.
$2,000 to Black Swamp Conservancy, Perrysburg, OH, 2009.

1278
Entergy Arkansas, Inc.

(formerly Arkansas Power & Light Company)
425 W. Capitol Ave., 27th Fl.
P.O. Box 551
Little Rock, AR 72201 (501) 377-4434

Company URL: http://www.entergy-arkansas.com
Establishment information: Established in 1926.
Company type: Subsidiary of a public company
Business activities: Generates, transmits, and distributes electricity.
Business type (SIC): Electric services
Financial profile for 2011: Number of employees, 3,500
Corporate officers: Leo P. Denault, Chair. and C.E.O.; Hugh T. McDonald, Pres.; Andrew Marsh, Exec. V.P. and C.F.O.; Theodore Bunting, Jr., Sr. V.P. and C.A.O.
Board of directors: Leo P. Denault, Chair.; Hugh T. McDonald
Giving statement: Giving through the Entergy Arkansas, Inc. Corporate Giving Program.

Entergy Arkansas, Inc. Corporate Giving Program

(formerly Arkansas Power & Light Company Contributions Program)
P.O. Box 551
Little Rock, AR 72203-0551 (501) 377-0551
FAX: (501) 377-4448;
E-mail: smcdonn@entergy.com; URL: http://www.entergy-arkansas.com/economic_development/tmar_dept_programs.aspx

Contact: Sherry McDonnell, Community Devel. Coord.
Purpose and activities: Entergy Arkansas makes charitable contributions to programs designed to

promote community economic development. Support is given primarily in areas of company operations in Arkansas.

Fields of interest: Economic development; Business/industry; Community development, business promotion; Community/economic development; Leadership development.

Program:

Community Development Program: Entergy Arkansas supports programs designed to provide communities with the tools necessary to move forward with economic development; and inform them of the process involved in retaining existing business and recruiting new business. The company supports these programs through awareness, consulting, contributions, and connections.

Type of support: Conferences/seminars; Consulting services; General/operating support; Program development; Sponsorships; Technical assistance.

Geographic limitations: Giving primarily in areas of company operations in AR.

Application information: Applications accepted.

Initial approach: Contact Teamwork Arkansas Staff for application information

Teamwork Arkansas Staff: Flave Carpenter, Community Devel. Consultant; Sherry McDonnell, Community Devel. Consultant.

1279
Entergy Corporation

639 Loyola Ave.
New Orleans, LA 70113 (504) 576-4000
FAX: (504) 569-4063

Company URL: http://www.entergy.com
Establishment information: Established in 1989.
Company type: Public company
Company ticker symbol and exchange: ETR/NYSE
International Securities Identification Number: US29364G1031
Business activities: Operates holding company; generates, transmits, and distributes electricity.
Business type (SIC): Electric services; holding company
Financial profile for 2012: Number of employees, 15,000; assets, $43,202,500,000; sales volume, $10,302,080,000; pre-tax net income, $899,220,000; expenses, $9,000,900,000; liabilities, $33,724,900,000
Fortune 1000 ranking: 2012—261st in revenues, 229th in profits, and 129th in assets
Forbes 2000 ranking: 2012—908th in sales, 653rd in profits, and 535th in assets
Corporate officers: Leo Denault, Chair. and C.E.O.; Mark T. Savoff, Exec. V.P. and C.O.O.; Andrew Marsh, Exec. V.P. and C.F.O.; Rod K. West, Exec. V.P. and C.A.O.; Renae Conley, Exec. V.P., Human Resources and Admin.; Marcus V. Brown, Sr. V.P. and Genl. Counsel
Board of directors: Leo P. Denault, Chair.; Maureen S. Bateman; Gary W. Edwards; Alexis M. Herman; Donald C. Hintz; Stuart L. Levenick; Blanche Lambert Lincoln; Stewart C. Myers; W.J. Billy Tauzin; Steven V. Wilkinson
Subsidiaries: Entergy Arkansas, Inc., Little Rock, AR; Entergy Gulf States, Inc., Beaumont, TX; Entergy Mississippi, Inc., Jackson, MS; Entergy New Orleans, Inc., New Orleans, LA
Plant: Pine Bluff, AR
Giving statement: Giving through the Entergy Corporation Contributions Program, the Entergy Charitable Foundation, and the Monroe Chamber Foundation.
Company EIN: 710005900

Entergy Corporation Contributions Program

639 Loyola Ave.
New Orleans, LA 70161-1000 (504) 576-6980
URL: http://www.entergy.com/our_community

Contact: Patty Riddlebarger, Dir., Corp. Social Responsibility
Purpose and activities: As a complement to its foundation, Entergy also makes charitable contributions to nonprofit organizations directly. Support is given primarily in areas of company operations.
Fields of interest: Arts, cultural/ethnic awareness; Performing arts; Arts; Education, reading; Education; Environment; Housing/shelter; Disasters, preparedness/services; Children, services; Family services; Human services; Community development, neighborhood development; Economic development; United Ways and Federated Giving Programs Economically disadvantaged.

Programs:

Community Connectors Volunteer Program: The company awards grants to nonprofit organizations with which its employees and retirees volunteer. Individual volunteers receive $100 for 50 hours of service and $250 for 100 hours of service. Volunteer teams of up to 3 hours receive $250 for 150 hours or service and $500 for 300 hours of service.

Community Partnership Grants: The company awards grants of up to $1,000 to projects designed to impact arts and culture; community improvement/enrichment; education/ literacy; or healthy families.

Community Power Scholarship: The company awards scholarships to children and dependents of its employees to pursue college or vocational school programming.

Matching Educational Gifts: The company matches contributions made by its employees and retirees to secondary schools and institutions of higher education on a one-for-one basis from $25 to $3,000 per contributor, per year.

Micro Grants: The company awards grants of up to $1,000 to programs designed to promote arts and culture; community improvement/enrichment; economic development; education/literacy; environment; and healthy families.

Open Grants: The company supports programs designed to promote arts and culture; community improvement and enrichment; and healthily families.

Power to Care Facebook Challenge: The company awards $145,000 to community partner nonprofit organizations located in an Entergy service territory. The public is invited to vote for their nonprofit organization on Facebook and the top 5 organizations with the most votes is awarded $25,000. Four finalists in each service area is awarded $1,000 and organizations who post news, updates, and success stories on Facebook is also eligible for a monthly random drawing for $1,000.

The Power to Care: The company provides emergency bill payment assistance to seniors and disabled individuals in crisis. The company also doubles contributions from the public with matching shareholder contributions of up to $500,000 per year.

Type of support: Annual campaigns; Donated equipment; Emergency funds; Employee matching gifts; Employee volunteer services; Employee-related scholarships; In-kind gifts; Program development; Scholarship funds; Use of facilities.

Geographic limitations: Giving primarily in areas of company operations in AR, LA, MA, MI, MS, NH, NY, TX, and VT.

Support limitations: No support for political organizations, or candidates or sectarian religious organizations, organizations owned or operated by an employee of Entergy, or amateur sports teams. No grants to individuals, or for general operating support, consultant fees, administrative expenses, capital campaigns, or purchase of uniforms or trips for school-related organizations.

Publications: Application guidelines; Corporate report.

Application information: Applications accepted. The Corporate Contributions Department handles giving. The company has a staff that only handles contributions. A contributions committee reviews all requests. Support is limited to 1 contribution per organization during any given year. Application form required.

Initial approach: Complete online application form
Committee meeting date(s): Quarterly
Deadline(s): None for Open Grants and Micro Grants; Jan to Apr. for Community Partnership Grants; Complete online application at least 3 months before funding is needed
Final notification: 6 to 8 weeks

Number of staff: 3 full-time professional; 1 full-time support.

Entergy Charitable Foundation

639 Loyola Ave.
New Orleans, LA 70113-3125 (504) 576-6980
Additional address: P.O. Box 61000, New Orleans, LA 70161, tel.: (504) 576-2674; URL: http://www.entergy.com/our_community/ECF_grant_guidelines.aspx

Establishment information: Established in 2000 in AR and LA.
Donor: Entergy Corp.
Financial data (yr. ended 12/31/11): Assets, $1,496,948 (M); gifts received, $3,011,025; expenditures, $3,080,975; qualifying distributions, $3,080,975; giving activities include $3,076,475 for 158+ grants (high: $200,000).
Purpose and activities: The foundation supports programs designed to create and sustain thriving communities. Special emphasis is directed toward programs designed to promote low-income initiatives and solutions; and education and literacy.
Fields of interest: Museums; Education, reading; Education; Environment, energy; Housing/shelter, development; Housing/shelter; Disasters, fire prevention/control; Family services; Human services, financial counseling; Community/economic development, management/technical assistance; United Ways and Federated Giving Programs Children; Aging; Economically disadvantaged.

Programs:

Education and Literacy: The foundation supports programs designed to promote effective knowledge within the community. Special emphasis is directed toward programs designed to eliminate illiteracy.

Low-Income Initiatives and Solutions: The foundation supports programs designed to provide innovative and measurable ways to positively impact families and their ability to support children and the elderly. Special emphasis is directed toward programs designed to help sustain families and teach self-sufficiency; provide housing; provide technical assistance and training for nonprofits; provide home-ownership preparation services; promote energy management and awareness; and promote alternative sources of energy.

Type of support: Building/renovation; Program development; Scholarship funds.

Geographic limitations: Giving primarily in areas of company operations in AR, LA, MA, MS, NH, NY, TX, and VT, with emphasis on New Orleans.
Support limitations: No support for political organizations, religious organizations not of direct benefit to the entire community, or organizations owned or operated by an employee of Entergy. No grants to individuals, or for utility bills, administrative expenses or recurring expenses exceeding 15 percent of the requested amount, capital campaigns, gala events, testimonials, or fundraising meals, advertisements, or uniforms, equipment, or trips for school-related organizations or amateur sports teams; no loans.
Publications: Application guidelines.
Application information: Applications accepted. Visit website for contact information for contributions coordinators in each state. Application form required.
Initial approach: Complete online application form
Board meeting date(s): 3 times per year
Deadline(s): Feb. 1, May 1, and Aug. 1
Final notification: 3 months
Officers and Directors:* Kim Despeaux, Pres.; Kay Kelley Arnold, V.P.; Leo P. Denault*, Treas.; Renea Conley; Haley R. Fisackerly; John Herron; William Mohl; Gary J. Taylor; Rod K. West.
EIN: 710845366

Monroe Chamber Foundation

212 Walnut St., Ste. 100
Monroe, LA 71201-6707

Establishment information: Established in LA.
Donors: Entergy, Corp.; T.H. and Mayme P. Scott Foundation; J.P. Morgan Chase Foundation.
Financial data (yr. ended 12/31/11): Assets, $662 (M); gifts received, $70,900; expenditures, $70,900; qualifying distributions, $70,900; giving activities include $70,900 for grants.
Fields of interest: Public affairs.
Type of support: General/operating support.
Support limitations: No grants to individuals.
Application information: Applications not accepted. Unsolicited requests for funds not accepted.
Officers: Terry Baugh, Chair.; Sue Nicholson*, Pres.; Chuck Bradshaw, V.P.; Tom Deal, V.P.; Cindy Rogers, V.P.; Doug Salter, V.P.; LJ Holland, Treas.
EIN: 720914245

1280
Entergy Mississippi, Inc.

(formerly Mississippi Power & Light Company)
308 E. Pearl St.
Jackson, MS 39201 (601) 368-5000

Company URL: http://www.entergy-mississippi.com
Establishment information: Established in 1927.
Company type: Subsidiary of a public company
Business activities: Generates, transmits, and distributes electricity.
Business type (SIC): Electric services
Corporate officers: Haley R. Fisackerly, Chair., Pres. and C.E.O.; Robert Sloan, Exec. V.P. and Genl. Counsel; Theodore H. Bunting, Jr., Sr. V.P. and C.A.O.
Board of directors: Haley R. Fisackerly, Chair.; Joseph F. Domino; Daniel Jones; Rhonda Keenum; Billy McCain; Tom Pittman; Bill Sones
Giving statement: Giving through the Entergy Mississippi, Inc. Corporate Giving Program.

Entergy Mississippi, Inc. Corporate Giving Program

(formerly Mississippi Power & Light Company Contributions Program)
308 E. Pearl St.
Jackson, MS 39201-3419 (601) 969-2440
URL: http://www.entergy.com/our_community/giving.aspx

Contact: Elizabeth Brister, Contribs. Coord.
Purpose and activities: Entergy Mississippi makes charitable contributions to nonprofit organizations involved with arts and culture, community improvement and enrichment, economic development, education and literacy, the environment, and healthy families. Support is limited to areas of company operations in Mississippi.
Fields of interest: Arts; Child development, education; Education, reading; Environment; Public health; Family services; Community/economic development.
Type of support: Employee matching gifts; Employee volunteer services; General/operating support; Program development; Sponsorships.
Geographic limitations: Giving limited to areas of company operations in MS.
Support limitations: No support for political or religious organizations not of direct benefit to the entire community, amateur sports teams, or organizations owned or operated by an employee of Entergy. No grants to individuals, or for administrative expenses, capital campaigns, purchase of uniforms or travel expenses for school-related organizations, or recurring expenses that exceed 15% of the amount requested; no loans.
Publications: Application guidelines.
Application information: Applications accepted. Application form required.
Initial approach: Complete online application form
Deadline(s): 3 months prior to need
Final notification: 6 to 8 weeks
Number of staff: 1 full-time professional.

1281
Enterprise Rent-A-Car Company

600 Corporate Park Dr.
St. Louis, MO 63105-4211 (314) 512-5000

Company URL: http://www.enterprise.com
Establishment information: Established in 1957.
Company type: Private company
Business activities: Rents and leases automobiles.
Business type (SIC): Motor vehicle rentals and leasing
Financial profile for 2011: Number of employees, 70,000; sales volume, $14,100,000,000
Corporate officers: Andrew C. Taylor, Chair. and C.E.O.; Donald L. Ross, Vice-Chair.; Pamela M. Nicholson, Pres. and C.O.O.; William W. Snyder, Exec. V.P. and C.F.O.; Lee Kaplan, Sr. V.P. and C.A.O.; Craig Kennedy, Sr. V.P. and C.I.O.; Edward Adams, Sr. V.P., Human Resources; Rose Langhorst, Sr. V.P. and Treas.
Board of directors: Andrew C. Taylor, Chair.; Donald L. Ross, Vice Chair.
Giving statement: Giving through the Enterprise Holdings Foundation.

Enterprise Holdings Foundation

(formerly Enterprise Rent-A-Car Foundation)
600 Corporate Park Dr.
St. Louis, MO 63105-4204 (314) 512-5000
FAX: (314) 512-4754; E-mail: foundation@ehi.com; URL: http://www.enterpriseholdings.com/about-us/corporate-citizenship/

Establishment information: Established in 1982 in MO.
Donors: Enterprise Holdings, Inc.; Enterprise Rent-A-Car Co.; Jack C. Taylor.
Contact: Jo Ann Taylor Kindle, Pres.
Financial data (yr. ended 07/31/12): Assets, $169,511,078 (M); gifts received, $39,002,530; expenditures, $16,495,432; qualifying distributions, $16,410,618; giving activities include $16,410,618 for 3,196 grants (high: $1,000,000; low: $26).
Purpose and activities: The foundation supports organizations with which employees, family members of employees, and established customers of Enterprise Rent-A-Car are involved, and organizations involved with education, reforestation, disaster relief, minorities, and economically disadvantaged people.
Fields of interest: Higher education; Environment, land resources; Environment, forests; Employment, training; Disasters, preparedness/services; United Ways and Federated Giving Programs; General charitable giving Minorities; Economically disadvantaged.
International interests: Canada; United Kingdom.
Programs:
Employee Matching Contribution Program: The foundation matches contributions made by employees of Enterprise Rent-A-Car to the United Way on a one-for-two basis in U.S. and Canada and in the "Give As You Earn" program in the United Kingdom.
Jack Taylor Founding Values Award: Through the Jack Taylor Founding Values Award program, the foundation awards grants to nonprofit organizations chosen by regional Enterprise Rent-A-Car Groups that exemplify excellence in living the values that were set in motion by the company's founder, Jack Taylor.
Type of support: Building/renovation; Capital campaigns; Emergency funds; Equipment; General/operating support; Program development; Research; Scholarship funds.
Geographic limitations: Giving on a national basis in areas of company operations, with emphasis on CA, MO, NE, TX, Canada, and the United Kingdom.
Support limitations: No support for religious, political, or labor organizations, or sports teams. No grants to individuals, or for ongoing operating support, salary costs, debt reduction, sponsorships, tuition, fees, memberships, dues, tickets, subscriptions, telethons, or beauty pageants; no vehicle or rental donations.
Publications: Application guidelines.
Application information: Applications accepted. Support is limited to 1 contribution per organization during any given year. Unsolicited requests are accepted from employees and their spouses, and established customers of Enterprise Rent-A-Car on behalf of nonprofit organizations with which there is an established connection. Annual reports, videos, DVDs, CD's and other extraneous materials are not encouraged. The average amount for a first-time request is usually up to $1,500. Grants range from $2,500 to $5,000. Application form not required. Applicants should submit the following:
1) name, address and phone number of organization
2) copy of IRS Determination Letter
3) brief history of organization and description of its mission

4) listing of board of directors, trustees, officers and other key people and their affiliations
5) detailed description of project and amount of funding requested

Applications should include a Customer Confirmation Letter from the Enterprise Holdings entity of which the applicant is a customer.

Initial approach: Complete online application for customers/employees
Copies of proposal: 1
Board meeting date(s): Jan. 24, May 2, and Oct. 24
Deadline(s): Mar. 1, Aug. 1, and Dec. 1
Final notification: 3 to 4 weeks following board meetings

Officers and Directors:* Jo Ann Taylor Kindle*, Pres.; Rick A. Short*, V.P. and Treas.; Carolyn Kindle, V.P. and Exec. Dir.; Mathew G. Darrah*, V.P.; Jack C. Taylor.
EIN: 431262762
Selected grants: The following grants are a representative sample of this grantmaker's funding activity:
$1,500,000 to University of Missouri, Saint Louis, MO, 2011. For Enterprise Opportunity Driver Scholarship.
$1,000,000 to National Arbor Day Foundation, Lincoln, NE, 2011. For 50-year commitment, 1 million per year.
$1,000,000 to Urban League, National, New York, NY, 2011. For Whitney M. Young, Jr. Center for Urban Leadership.
$715,000 to United Way of Greater Saint Louis, Saint Louis, MO, 2011. For annual United Way employee match for Saint Louis.
$613,294 to United Way of Greater Los Angeles, Los Angeles, CA, 2011. For campaign.
$34,100 to United Way, Greater Twin Cities, Minneapolis, MN, 2011. For campaign.
$20,000 to Urban League, Greater Washington, Washington, DC, 2011. For annual Whitney M. Young Gala.
$13,390 to Sustainable Travel International, Boulder, CO, 2011. For Carbon Offset Program.
$10,000 to Marine Corps Scholarship Foundation, Alexandria, VA, 2011. For Saint Louis Marine Week.

1282
EOG Resources, Inc.

1111 Bagby, Sky Lobby 2
Houston, TX 77002 (713) 651-7000
FAX: (713) 651-6995

Company URL: http://www.eogresources.com
Establishment information: Established in 1985.
Company type: Public company
Company ticker symbol and exchange: EOG/NYSE
Business activities: Conducts natural gas and crude oil exploration, development, production, and marketing activities.
Business type (SIC): Extraction/oil and gas
Financial profile for 2012: Number of employees, 2,650; assets, $27,336,580,000; sales volume, $11,682,640,000; pre-tax net income, $1,280,740,000; expenses, $10,202,840,000; liabilities, $14,051,810,000
Fortune 1000 ranking: 2012—233rd in revenues, 304th in profits, and 198th in assets
Forbes 2000 ranking: 2012—830th in sales, 909th in profits, and 790th in assets
Corporate officers: Mark G. Papa, Chair. and C.E.O.; William R. Thomas, Pres.; Gary L. Thomas, C.O.O.; Lloyd W. Helms, Jr., Exec. V.P., Opers.; Timothy K. Driggers, V.P. and C.F.O.; Sandeep Bhakhri, V.P. and C.I.O.; Michael P. Donaldson II, V.P., Genl. Counsel, and Corp. Secy.; Helen Y. Lim, V.P. and Treas.; Marc R. Eschenburg, V.P., Mktg.; Patricia L. Edwards, V.P., Human Resources and Admin.
Board of directors: Mark G. Papa, Chair.; Charles R. Crisp; James C. Day; H. Leighton Steward; Donald F. Textor; Thomas R. William; Frank G. Wisner
International operations: Canada; Cayman Islands; Netherlands; Poland; Trinidad & Tobago; United Kingdom
Giving statement: Giving through the EOG Resources, Inc. Corporate Giving Program.
Company EIN: 470684736

EOG Resources, Inc. Corporate Giving Program

1111 Bagby, Sky Lobby 2
Houston, TX 77002 (713) 651-7000
FAX: (713) 651-6995; URL: http://www.eogresources.com/responsibility/communities.html

Purpose and activities: EOG Resources makes charitable contributions to nonprofit organizations on a case by case basis. Support is given in areas of company operations.
Fields of interest: General charitable giving.
Program:
Employee Matching Gifts Program: EOG Resources matches contributions made by its employees to nonprofit organizations on a one-for-one basis up to $60,000 per employee, per year. The company provides a three-to-one dollar match on employee contributions to hurricane relief efforts.
Type of support: Employee matching gifts; Employee volunteer services.
Geographic limitations: Giving primarily in areas of company operations in CO, OK, PA, TX, and WY; giving also to national organizations.
Application information: Applications not accepted. Contributes only to pre-selected organizations.

1283
EPES Carriers Inc.

3400 Edgefield Ct.
Greensboro, NC 27409 (336) 668-3358
FAX: (336) 668-7008

Company URL: http://www.epescarriers.com
Establishment information: Established in 1931.
Company type: Private company
Business activities: Operates trucking company.
Business type (SIC): Transportation services/miscellaneous
Corporate officers: Alvin Bodford, Chair. and C.E.O.; Britt Coley, Pres.; Michael Dunlap, Exec. V.P. and C.F.O.; Michael Hamilton, V.P., Human Resources
Board of director: Alvin Bodford, Chair.
Giving statement: Giving through the Bodford Family Foundation.

The Bodford Family Foundation

3400 Edgefield Ct.
Greensboro, NC 27409-9663

Establishment information: Established in 1998 in NC.
Donors: Epes Carriers, Inc.; Alvin M. Bodford; Jason M. Bodford.
Financial data (yr. ended 04/30/12): Assets, $903,173 (M); expenditures, $47,977; qualifying distributions, $46,100; giving activities include $46,100 for grants.
Fields of interest: Health organizations; Human services; Religion.
Application information: Applications not accepted. Unsolicited requests for funds not accepted.
Officers: Amy Bodford Poteat, Pres.; Alvin M. Bodford, Secy.-Treas.
Directors: Brenda S. Bodford; Jason M. Bodford.
EIN: 562099865

1284
Epiphany Farms Enterprise

23676 E. 800 N. Rd.
P.O. Box 178
Downs, IL 61736-7541 (702) 672-5459

Company URL: http://www.epiphanyfarms.com
Establishment information: Established in 2009.
Company type: Private company
Business type (SIC): Business services/miscellaneous
Corporate officer: Ken Myszka, Owner
Giving statement: Giving through the Epiphany Farms Enterprise Corporate Giving Program.

Epiphany Farms Enterprise Corporate Giving Program

23676 800 N.
Downs, IL 61736-7541 (702) 672-5459
E-mail: info@epiphanyfarms.com; URL: http://www.epiphanyfarms.com

Purpose and activities: Epiphany Farms is a certified B Corporation that donates a percentage of profits to charitable organizations.

1285
Eppstein Uhen Architects, Inc.

333 E. Chicago St., Stop 1
Milwaukee, WI 53202-5881
(414) 271-5350

Company URL: http://www.eppsteinuhen.com
Establishment information: Established in 1907.
Company type: Private company
Business activities: Operates architectural design firm.
Business type (SIC): Engineering, architectural, and surveying services
Corporate officer: Samuel Eppstein, Chair.
Board of director: Samuel Eppstein, Chair.
Giving statement: Giving through the Eppstein Uhen Foundation, Inc.

The Eppstein Uhen Foundation, Inc.

333 E. Chicago St.
Milwaukee, WI 53202

Establishment information: Established in 2006 in WI.
Donors: Eppstein Uhen Architects, Inc.; Deltek Systems, Inc.; Newforma, Inc.; C.G. Schmidt.
Financial data (yr. ended 12/31/11): Assets, $189,887 (M); gifts received, $65,259; expenditures, $65,978; qualifying distributions, $24,205; giving activities include $24,205 for grants.
Fields of interest: Human services.
Geographic limitations: Giving primarily in WI.
Support limitations: No grants to individuals.
Application information: Applications not accepted. Unsolicited requests for funds not accepted.

Officers and Directors:* Greg Uhen*, Pres.; Rich Tennessen*, V.P.; Matthew Hall*, Secy.-Treas.; Sam Eppstein.
EIN: 208080585

1286
Epson America, Inc.

3840 Kilroy Airport Way
Long Beach, CA 90806-2469
(562) 981-3840

Company URL: http://www.epson.com/
Establishment information: Established in 1975.
Company type: Subsidiary of a foreign company
Business activities: Manufactures digital imaging products.
Business type (SIC): Computer and office equipment
Financial profile for 2005: Number of employees, 832; sales volume, $2,645,400,000
Corporate officers: John D. Lang, Pres. and C.E.O.; Alan Pound, C.F.O.; Jim Marshall, Sr. V.P., Sales and Mktg.; Judith S. Bain, V.P. and Genl. Counsel; Genevieve Walker, V.P., Admin.; Miko Sion, V.P., Inf. Systems
Giving statement: Giving through the Epson America, Inc. Corporate Giving Program.

Epson America, Inc. Corporate Giving Program

3840 Kilroy Airport Way
Long Beach, CA 90806-2452
URL: http://www.epson.com/cgi-bin/Store/AboutFocusedGivingProgram.jsp?BV_UseBVCookie=yes

Contact: Kelly J. Pierce, Mgr., Branded Events and Community Rels.
Purpose and activities: Epson makes charitable contributions to nonprofit organizations involved with education, digital arts, and environmental stewardship. Special emphasis is directed towards programs that involve K-12 youth. Support is limited to the Long Beach and the greater Los Angeles areas of California, San Francisco, Washington, DC, Miami, Florida, Chicago, Illinois, Indianapolis, Indiana, and New York, New York.
Fields of interest: Arts; Elementary/secondary education; Education; Youth development; Human services; Public affairs.
Type of support: Donated products; General/operating support; In-kind gifts; Program development; Sponsorships.
Geographic limitations: Giving primarily in Support is limited to the Long Beach and the greater Los Angeles areas of CA, San Francisco, CA, Washington, DC, Miami, FL, Chicago, IL, Indianapolis, IN, and New York, NY.
Support limitations: No support for sectarian organizations, fraternal, political, labor, or social organizations, government agencies, organizations located outside the U.S., or correctional facilities. No grants to individuals or inmates.
Publications: Application guidelines.
Application information: Applications accepted. Proposals should be submitted using organization letterhead. Grants do not generally exceed $5,000. Support is limited to 1 contribution per organization during any given year. Application form not required. Applicants should submit the following:
1) statement of problem project will address
2) population served
3) copy of IRS Determination Letter
4) brief history of organization and description of its mission
5) listing of board of directors, trustees, officers and other key people and their affiliations
6) detailed description of project and amount of funding requested
7) contact person
8) listing of additional sources and amount of support
9) plans for cooperation with other organizations, if any
10) additional materials/documentation

Requests for product donations should indicate the items being requested and the quantity of each item.
Initial approach: Proposal to headquarters
Copies of proposal: 1
Deadline(s): None
Final notification: 2 months

1287
EQT Corporation

(formerly Equitable Resources, Inc.)
625 Liberty Ave., Ste. 1700
EQT Plz.
Pittsburgh, PA 15222 (412) 553-5700
FAX: (412) 553-5757

Company URL: http://www.eqt.com
Establishment information: Established in 1888.
Company type: Public company
Company ticker symbol and exchange: EQT/NYSE
Business activities: Provides natural gas and energy solutions.
Business type (SIC): Gas production and distribution
Financial profile for 2012: Number of employees, 1,873; assets, $8,849,860,000; sales volume, $1,641,610,000; pre-tax net income, $301,710,000; expenses, $1,171,080,000; liabilities, $5,246,040,000
Corporate officers: David L. Porges, Chair., Pres., and C.E.O.; Philip P. Conti, Sr. V.P. and C.F.O.; Lewis B. Gardner, V.P. and Genl. Counsel; Theresa Z. Bone, V.P. and Corp. Cont.
Board of directors: David L. Porges, Chair.; Vicky A. Bailey; Philip G. Behrman, Ph.D.; Kenneth M. Burke; A. Bray Cary, Jr.; Margaret K. Dorman; George L. Miles, Jr.; James E. Rohr; David S. Shapira; Stephen A. Thorington; Lee T. Todd, Jr., Ph.D.
Divisions: ERI Services, Pittsburgh, PA; ERI Supply and Logistics, Houston, TX; ERI Utilities, Pittsburgh, PA
Giving statement: Giving through the EQT Foundation, Inc.
Company EIN: 250464690

EQT Foundation, Inc.

(formerly Equitable Resources Foundation, Inc.)
2 PNC Plaza
620 Liberty Ave., 30th Fl.
Pittsburgh, PA 15222-2719 (412) 762-3502
E-mail: bruce.bickel@pncadvisors.com; URL: http://www.eqt.com/commlnit/foundation.aspx
Application address: 625 Liberty Ave., Pittsburgh, PA 15222, e-mail: aspire@egt.com

Establishment information: Established in 2003 in PA.
Donors: Equitable Production Co.; EQD Holdings Co., LLC.
Contact: Bruce Bickel, Exec. Dir.
Financial data (yr. ended 12/31/11): Assets, $25,156,956 (M); expenditures, $4,327,162; qualifying distributions, $4,139,536; giving activities include $2,848,016 for 61 grants (high: $275,569; low: $450), $125,740 for 74 grants to individuals (high: $7,500; low: $740) and $1,083,124 for 158 employee matching gifts.
Purpose and activities: The foundation supports programs designed to promote arts and culture; education; the environment; and community economic development. Special emphasis is directed toward programs designed to promote education, with a focus on K-12 and academic activities, including reading, writing, math, and science initiatives that impact students directly and senior citizens habitually.
Fields of interest: Arts, cultural/ethnic awareness; Museums; Performing arts; Arts; Elementary/secondary education; Higher education; Adult/continuing education; Libraries (public); Education, reading; Education; Environment, recycling; Environment, natural resources; Environment, energy; Environmental education; Housing/shelter, development; Youth development, adult & child programs; Youth development, business; Business/industry; Community/economic development; Mathematics; Engineering/technology; Science Aging; Economically disadvantaged.
Program:
ASPIRE (Area Students Participating in Rewarding Education): Through ASPIRE, college-bound juniors and seniors are provided with one-on-one mentoring and scholarships. EQT employees volunteer their time to help students and assist them with life choices, career development, and personal direction. The program awards five $2,500 scholarships which are renewable for up to six years. Scholarship recipients are selected based on essay and presentation, participation, and mentor partnership. The program is limited to Charleston and Pittsburgh, PA.
Type of support: Employee volunteer services; In-kind gifts; Matching/challenge support; Program development; Scholarship funds; Scholarships—to individuals; Seed money; Sponsorships.
Geographic limitations: Giving primarily in areas of company operations in KY, Pittsburgh, PA, VA, and WV.
Support limitations: No support for churches or religious organizations, political parties, candidates, or public policy advocates, for-profit businesses or associations, tax-supported entities (except for public schools), or fraternal, social, union, or hobby/recreational clubs or organizations. No grants to individuals (except for ASPIRE), or for capital campaigns, endowments, new construction or building renovations, mortgage/rent/insurance/utility costs, vehicle purchases or repairs, infrastructure improvements, sporting events including golf outings, travel to conferences, workshops, seminars, competitions, or emergency or stop-gap funding.
Publications: Application guidelines.
Application information: Applications accepted. Proposals should be no longer than 6 pages. Application form required. Applicants should submit the following:
1) role played by volunteers
2) statement of problem project will address
3) copy of IRS Determination Letter
4) copy of most recent annual report/audited financial statement/990
5) how project's results will be evaluated or measured
6) listing of board of directors, trustees, officers and other key people and their affiliations
7) detailed description of project and amount of funding requested
8) plans for cooperation with other organizations, if any
9) copy of current year's organizational budget and/or project budget

10) listing of additional sources and amount of support
11) plans for acknowledgement
Initial approach: Download application form and mail proposal and application form to foundation; complete application form during enrollment period for ASPIRE
Copies of proposal: 1
Board meeting date(s): Mar., June, Sept., and Dec.
Deadline(s): Feb. 1, May 1, Aug. 1, and Nov. 1; Varies for ASPIRE

Officers and Directors:* Charlene G. Petrelli*, Pres.; Pamela Coates, V.P., Community Rels.; Patrick J. Kane, V.P., Finance; John Kevin West, V.P., Public Affairs; Christopher T. Akers, V.P.; Kenneth C. Kirk, V.P.; John H. Obrist, Secy.; James E. Crockard III, Treas.; Bruce Bickel, Exec. Dir.; Martin A. Fritz, Esq.; Lewis B. Gardner; David L. Porges; Steven T. Schlotterbeck.
EIN: 043747289
Selected grants: The following grants are a representative sample of this grantmaker's funding activity:
$110,000 to Allegheny Conference on Community Development, Pittsburgh, PA, 2009.
$100,000 to Hill House Association, Pittsburgh, PA, 2009.
$100,000 to Pittsburgh Symphony, Pittsburgh, PA, 2009.
$95,004 to American Heart Association, Pittsburgh, PA, 2009.
$40,000 to Greater Pittsburgh Literacy Council, Pittsburgh, PA, 2009.
$15,000 to Allegheny Conference on Community Development, Pittsburgh, PA, 2009.
$15,000 to Vintage, Pittsburgh, PA, 2009.
$5,000 to Duquesne University, Pittsburgh, PA, 2009.
$4,895 to Multiple Sclerosis Society, National, Pittsburgh, PA, 2009.
$3,000 to Pittsburgh Public Theater, Pittsburgh, PA, 2009.

1288
Equifax Inc.

1550 Peachtree St., N.W., Ste. H46
Atlanta, GA 30309-2468 (404) 885-8000
FAX: (404) 885-8682

Company URL: http://www.equifax.com
Establishment information: Established in 1899.
Company type: Public company
Company ticker symbol and exchange: EFX/NYSE
Business activities: Provides information, transaction processing, and Internet information services.
Business type (SIC): Credit reporting and collection agencies; computer services; business services/ miscellaneous
Financial profile for 2012: Number of employees, 7,000; assets, $4,511,100,000; sales volume, $2,160,500,000; pre-tax net income, $440,200,000; expenses, $1,671,500,000; liabilities, $2,577,900,000
Fortune 1000 ranking: 2012—895th in revenues, 501st in profits, and 625th in assets
Corporate officers: Richard F. Smith, Chair. and C.E.O.; David Webb, C.I.O.; Lee Adrean, Corp. V.P. and C.F.O.
Board of directors: Richard F. Smith, Chair.; James E. Copeland, Jr.; Robert D. Daleo; Walter W. Driver, Jr.; Mark L. Feidler; L. Phillip Humann; Siri S. Marshall; John A. McKinley, Jr.; Mark B. Templeton
Subsidiaries: Equifax Information Technology, Inc., Atlanta, GA; TALX Corporation, St. Louis, MO
International operations: Brazil; Canada; Chile; Costa Rica; England; Ireland; Luxembourg; Mauritius; Netherlands; Peru; United Kingdom; Uruguay
Giving statement: Giving through the Equifax Foundation.
Company EIN: 580401110

Equifax Foundation

1550 Peachtree St. N.W.
Atlanta, GA 30309-2468

Establishment information: Trust established in 1978 in GA.
Donors: Retail Credit Co.; Equifax Inc.
Contact: Robert W. Kamerschen, Sr. V.P.; Ann Chakales
Financial data (yr. ended 12/31/11): Assets, $5,075,091 (M); expenditures, $1,272,023; qualifying distributions, $1,269,371; giving activities include $1,015,435 for 217 grants and $253,936 for 569 employee matching gifts.
Purpose and activities: The foundation supports organizations involved with arts and culture, education, economics, civic affairs, and youth. Special emphasis is directed toward programs that serve the needy, and K-12 education for underserved youth.
Fields of interest: Arts; Education; Human services; Economics Children/youth; Youth; Economically disadvantaged.
Program:
Matching Gift Program: The foundation matches contributions made by employees of Equifax to nonprofit organizations on a one-for-one basis from $50 to $5,000 per employee, per year.
Type of support: Building/renovation; Capital campaigns; Employee matching gifts; General/ operating support; Land acquisition; Management development/capacity building; Matching/ challenge support; Scholarship funds; Technical assistance.
Geographic limitations: Giving primarily in Atlanta, GA; limited giving in cities with field offices.
Support limitations: No support for religious, political, fraternal, or social organizations. No grants to individuals, or for debt reduction, fellowships, publications, or travel.
Publications: Corporate report.
Application information: Applications accepted. Application form not required. Applicants should submit the following:
1) copy of IRS Determination Letter
2) listing of board of directors, trustees, officers and other key people and their affiliations
3) copy of current year's organizational budget and/ or project budget
Initial approach: Proposal; letter of inquiry
Copies of proposal: 1
Board meeting date(s): Quarterly
Deadline(s): Rolling
Final notification: 60 days

Officer and Trustees:* Robert W. Kamerschen*, Secy.; J. Dann Adams; Lee Adrean; Kent Mast; Coretha Rushing; Richard F. Smith.
Number of staff: 1 part-time professional; 1 part-time support.
EIN: 581296807
Selected grants: The following grants are a representative sample of this grantmaker's funding activity:
$227,024 to United Way of Metropolitan Atlanta, Atlanta, GA, 2011.
$37,500 to Habitat for Humanity in Atlanta, Atlanta, GA, 2011.
$25,000 to KIPP Metro Atlanta Collaborative, Atlanta, GA, 2011.
$25,000 to Teach for America, Atlanta, GA, 2011.
$15,000 to Atlanta Community Food Bank, Atlanta, GA, 2011.
$15,000 to Breakthrough Atlanta, Atlanta, GA, 2011.
$2,000 to Families First, Atlanta, GA, 2011.
$1,000 to Georgia Center for Nonprofits, Atlanta, GA, 2011.
$1,000 to Georgia Consortium for Personal Financial Literacy, Atlanta, GA, 2011.

1289
Ergon, Inc.

2829 Lakeland Dr., Ste. 2000
P.O. Box 1639
Jackson, MS 39215-1639 (601) 933-3000
FAX: (601) 933-3350

Company URL: http://www.ergon.com
Establishment information: Established in 1954.
Company type: Private company
Business activities: Refines and markets crude oil; manufactures asphalt and emulsions; manufactures information technology products; develops real estate; conducts crude oil and natural gas exploration activities.
Business type (SIC): Petroleum refining; extraction/ oil and gas; asphalt and roofing materials; electronic components and accessories; real estate subdividers and developers
Financial profile for 2009: Number of employees, 3,000; sales volume, $3,830,000,000
Corporate officers: Leslie B. Lampton, Sr., C.E.O.; A. Patrick Busby, C.F.O.; Kathryn W. Stone, Treas.
Subsidiaries: Crafco, Inc., Chandler, AZ; Diversified Technology, Inc., Ridgeland, MS; Ergon Asphalt & Emulsions, Inc., Chandler, AZ; Ergon-West Virginia, Inc., Newell, WV; Lampton-Love, Inc., Jackson, MS; Lion Oil Co., El Dorado, AR; Magnolia Gas Inc., Poplarville, MS; Natchez Butane Inc., Natchez, MS; Southern Propane Inc., Taylorsville, MS; Starkville LP Gas Inc., Starkville, MS
Giving statement: Giving through the Ergon Foundation, Inc.

Ergon Foundation, Inc.

P.O. Drawer 1639
Jackson, MS 39215-1639

Establishment information: Established in 1980.
Donors: Diversified Technology, Inc.; Ergon Exploration, Inc.; Ergon Nonwovens, Inc.; Ergon Refining, Inc.; Ergon, Inc.; Magnolia Marine Transport Co.; Ergon Asphalt & Emulsions, Inc.; Ergon-West Virginia, Inc.
Financial data (yr. ended 06/30/12): Assets, $34,159,685 (M); expenditures, $882,729; qualifying distributions, $857,400; giving activities include $857,400 for grants.
Purpose and activities: The foundation supports organizations involved with education, health, cancer, human services, and Christianity.
Fields of interest: Elementary/secondary education; Education, special; Higher education; Theological school/education; Health sciences school/education; Education; Hospitals (general); Health care; Cancer; Salvation Army; Children/ youth, services; Family services; Residential/ custodial care, group home; Homeless, human services; Human services; Christian agencies & churches.
Type of support: Annual campaigns; General/ operating support.

Geographic limitations: Giving primarily in MS.
Support limitations: No grants to individuals.
Application information: Applications not accepted. Contributes only to pre-selected organizations.
Officers and Directors:* Leslie B. Lampton*, Pres.; Dorothy Lee Lampton*, V.P.; Lee C. Lampton*, V.P.; Leslie B. Lampton III, V.P.; Robert H. Lampton*, V.P.; William W. Lampton*, V.P.; Kathryn W. Stone*, Secy.-Treas.
EIN: 640656341
Selected grants: The following grants are a representative sample of this grantmaker's funding activity:
$2,110,207 to University of Mississippi Medical Center, Jackson, MS, 2009. For endowment for cancer research.
$200,000 to Mississippi Childrens Home Services, Jackson, MS, 2009. For capital campaign.
$75,000 to Little Light House - Central Mississippi, Brandon, MS, 2009. For general support.
$65,000 to Jackson Preparatory School, Jackson, MS, 2009. For general support.
$50,000 to French Camp Academy, French Camp, MS, 2009. For general support.
$45,000 to Palmer Home for Children, Columbus, MS, 2009. For general support.
$35,000 to Jackson Academy, Jackson, MS, 2009. For general support.
$35,000 to Saint Richard Catholic School, Jackson, MS, 2009. For general support.
$25,000 to Salvation Army Divisional Headquarters, Jackson, MS, 2009. For general support.
$22,000 to Southern Christian Services for Children and Youth, Jackson, MS, 2009. For general support.

1290
C. Erickson and Sons

2200 Arch St., Ste. 200
Philadelphia, PA 19103-1315
(215) 568-3120
FAX: (215) 496-9460

Company URL: http://www.cerickson.com
Establishment information: Established in 1954.
Company type: Private company
Business activities: Provides nonresidential construction services company.
Business type (SIC): Contractors/general nonresidential building
Corporate officers: Charles G. Erickson III, Pres.; Suzanne Erickson, Secy.
Giving statement: Giving through the Chinese Church Planting Partners.

Chinese Church Planting Partners

2200 Arch St., Ste. 200
Philadelphia, PA 19103-1315 (215) 568-3120

Establishment information: Established in 2004 in PA.
Donors: C. Erickson & Sons, Inc.; Joshua Mooney; Wayne Hayashi; Nancy Hayashi; Trinity Presbyterian Church; Taipei Hope Christian Association; Allen Quillen; Lois Quillen.
Contact: Charles Erickson, Dir.
Financial data (yr. ended 05/31/10): Assets, $8,226 (M); gifts received, $103,494; expenditures, $105,085; qualifying distributions, $100,407; giving activities include $100,407 for 3 grants to individuals (high: $35,972; low: $30,340).
Purpose and activities: Giving to support foreign missionaries in China and Taiwan.
Type of support: Grants to individuals.
Geographic limitations: Giving primarily in China.
Application information: Applications accepted. Application form required.
Initial approach: Letter
Deadline(s): None
Director: Charles Erickson.
EIN: 201590078

1291
Erie Indemnity Company

100 Erie Insurance Pl.
Erie, PA 16530-1104 (814) 870-2000
FAX: (814) 870-4040

Company URL: http://www.erieinsurance.com
Establishment information: Established in 1925.
Company type: Public company
Company ticker symbol and exchange: ERIE/NASDAQ
Business activities: Sells property and casualty insurance.
Business type (SIC): Insurance/fire, marine, and casualty
Financial profile for 2012: Number of employees, 4,400; assets, $15,400,000,000; sales volume, $5,400,000,000; pre-tax net income, $899,000,000; expenses, $4,613,000,000; liabilities, $14,799,000,000
Fortune 1000 ranking: 2012—455th in revenues, 634th in profits, and 294th in assets
Forbes 2000 ranking: 2012—1339th in sales, 1617th in profits, and 1160th in assets
Corporate officers: Thomas B. Hagen, Chair.; Terrence W. Cavanaugh, Pres. and C.E.O.; Marcia A. Dall, Exec. V.P. and C.F.O.; Robert Ingram, Exec. V.P. and C.I.O.; James J. Tanous, Exec. V.P., Secy., and Genl. Counsel; John F. Kearns, Exec. V.P., Sales and Mktg.
Board of directors: Thomas B. Hagen, Chair.; J. Ralph Borneman, Jr.; Terrence W. Cavanaugh; Jonathan Hirt Hagen; Susan Hirt Hagen; C. Scott Hartz; Claude C. Lilly III; Lucian L. Morrison, Esq.; Thomas W. Palmer, Esq.; Martin P. Sheffield; Richard L. Stover; Elizabeth Hirt Vorsheck; Robert C. Wilburn, Ph.D.
Giving statement: Giving through the Erie Insurance Group Corporate Giving Program.
Company EIN: 250466020

Erie Insurance Group Corporate Giving Program

100 Erie Insurance Pl.
Erie, PA 16530-1104 (814) 870-7403
E-mail: GivingNetwork@erieinsurance.com; URL: http://www.erieinsurance.com/GivingNetwork/funding.htm

Geographic limitations: Giving primarily in areas of company operations in DC, IL, IN, MD, NC, NY, OH, PA, TN, VA, WI, and WV.
Support limitations: No support for religious, political, labor, national, or discriminatory organizations. No grants to individuals, or for endowments.
Publications: Application guidelines.
Application information: Applications accepted. Application form required.
Initial approach: Complete online application
Deadline(s): Jan. 13, Mar. 8, June 21, Sept. 15, and Oct. 25
Final notification: 4 to 8 weeks

1292
ERM Group, Inc.

350 Eagleview Blvd., Ste. 200
Exton, PA 19341-1155 (610) 524-3500

Company URL: http://www.erm.com/
Establishment information: Established in 1977.
Company type: Subsidiary of a foreign company
Business activities: Provides environmental, health and safety, risk, and social consulting services.
Business type (SIC): Engineering, architectural, and surveying services; management and public relations services
Corporate officers: David McArthur, C.E.O.; John C. Stipa, C.F.O.; Patrick J. Brennan, Cont.
Giving statement: Giving through the ERM Group Foundation, Inc.

The ERM Group Foundation, Inc.

350 Eagleview Blvd., Ste. 200
Exton, PA 19341-1180 (610) 524-3630
FAX: (610) 524-3858;
E-mail: janice.taplar@erm.com; URL: http://www.erm.com/foundation

Establishment information: Established in 1994 in PA.
Financial data (yr. ended 12/31/11): Revenue, $305,058; assets, $221,979 (M); gifts received, $303,264; expenditures, $256,655; giving activities include $200,400 for grants and $15,000 for grants to individuals.
Purpose and activities: The mission of the foundation is to provide human resources and/or financial assistance to projects that contribute to the improvement of the earth's environment, the quality of life, and sustainable development throughout the world through appropriate charitable, scientific, and educational endeavors.
Fields of interest: Environment.
Programs:
ERM Foundation Sustainability Fellowship: The foundation supports entrepreneurial graduate students who want to implement their visions for a more sustainable world. In addition to a monetary stipend of up to $15,000 for the selected fellow, the top five fellowship finalists will be given an opportunity to interview for a compensated internship position in one of ERM's global offices (in Annapolis, MD; Houston, TX; London, UK; or Sydney, Australia). Eligible applicants must be enrolled in a U.S.-based tax-exempt educational organization during the current academic year.
Grants: The foundation awards grants, ranging from $5,000 to $30,000, to projects that work to make a significant difference in the environment and/or quality of life. Eligible projects must make a positive impact on the environment, include an educational component related to the environment (including health, safety, or sustainability), and contribute to the improvement in the quality of life of individuals or a community by reducing impacts and/or promoting sustainable resource management.
Type of support: Annual campaigns; Matching/challenge support.
Geographic limitations: Giving on a national and international basis.
Publications: Annual report; Application guidelines; Grants list; Informational brochure; Newsletter.
Application information: Applications accepted. See web site for additional application information and guidelines. Application form required.
Initial approach: Download application form
Copies of proposal: 2

Board meeting date(s): Jan., Mar., June, Sept., and Nov.
Deadline(s): Dec. 16 for ERM Foundation Sustainability Fellowship; Dec. 31 for Grants
Officers and Directors:* John Alexander*, C.E.O.; Roy Burrows; Barrett Cieutat; Shawn Doherty; Keryn James; David McArthur; Steve McGrory; Andrew Silverbeck; John Simonson; Julio Torti.
Number of staff: 1 part-time professional.
EIN: 232792333

1293
Ernst & Young LLP

5 Times Sq., 14th Fl.
New York, NY 10036-6530 (212) 773-3000

Company URL: http://www.ey.com
Establishment information: Established in 1903.
Company type: Private company
Business activities: Provides auditing, accounting, tax, and management consulting services.
Business type (SIC): Accounting, auditing, and bookkeeping services; management and public relations services
Financial profile for 2011: Number of employees, 152,000; sales volume, $22,880,000,000
Corporate officers: James Turley, Chair. and C.E.O.; John Ferraro, C.O.O.; Beth Brooke, Vice-Chair.; Billie Williamson, Americas Inclusiveness Officer
Board of directors: James Turley, Chair.; Beth Brooke, Vice-Chair.
Giving statement: Giving through the Ernst & Young Foundation.

Ernst & Young Foundation

5 Times Sq.
New York, NY 10036-6523 (212) 773-3000
FAX: (212) 773-6504

Establishment information: Established in 1937 in NY due to the merger of the Arthur Young Foundation and the Ernst & Whinney Foundation.
Contact: Ellen Glazerman, Exec. Dir.
Financial data (yr. ended 06/30/11): Revenue, $11,993,466; assets, $22,926,591 (M); gifts received, $11,727,859; expenditures, $10,559,599; giving activities include $10,357,702 for grants.
Purpose and activities: The foundation provides support to higher education institutions, including business education, legal education, and education for minorities, with emphasis on accounting; the foundation also provides support for mathematics, educational research, and lectureships, and provides fellowships to faculty.
Fields of interest: Higher education; Business school/education; Law school/education; Education; Mathematics.
Type of support: Curriculum development; Employee matching gifts; Fellowships; Research.
Geographic limitations: Giving on a national basis.
Application information: Applications not accepted. Contributes only to pre-selected organizations.
Board meeting date(s): Quarterly
Officers and Directors:* Nancy A. Altobello*, Pres.; Timothy T. Griffy*, Treas.; Ellan Glazerman, Exec. Dir.; Beth A. Brooke; Malcomb D. Coley; Howard A. Levenson; Allen W. Mark; Michael S. Solender.
Number of staff: 2 full-time professional; 1 full-time support.
EIN: 136094489

1294
Erving Paper Mills, Inc.

97 E. Main St.
Erving, MA 01344-9717 (413) 422-2700

Company URL: http://ervingpaper.com/
Establishment information: Established in 1993.
Company type: Subsidiary of a private company
Business activities: Manufactures paper products; provides printing services.
Business type (SIC): Paper and paperboard/coated, converted, and laminated; paper mills
Corporate officers: Charles B. Housen, Chair.; Morris Housen, Pres. and C.E.O.; Thomas Newton, C.O.O.; Denis Emmett, Treas. and C.F.O.
Board of director: Charles B. Housen, Chair.
Giving statement: Giving through the Housen Foundation, Inc.

Housen Foundation, Inc.

97 E. Main St.
Erving, MA 01344-9756

Establishment information: Incorporated in 1968 in MA.
Donors: Erving Paper Mills, Inc.; Brattleboro Paper Products, Inc.; Erving Industries, Inc.
Financial data (yr. ended 12/31/11): Assets, $1,898 (M); expenditures, $311; qualifying distributions, $250; giving activities include $250 for grants.
Purpose and activities: The foundation supports organizations involved with elementary education.
Fields of interest: Education.
Type of support: Employee-related scholarships; General/operating support.
Geographic limitations: Giving limited to Erving, MA.
Support limitations: No grants to individuals (except for employee-related scholarships).
Application information: Applications not accepted. Unsolicited requests for funds not accepted.
Officers and Directors:* Charles B. Housen*, Pres.; Morris Housen*, V.P. and Clerk; Denis L. Emmett*, Treas.; Majorie G. Housen.
EIN: 046183673

1295
Esbenshade's Greenhouses, Inc.

546A E. 28th Division Hwy., Ste. A
Lititz, PA 17543-9766 (717) 626-7007

Company URL: http://www.esbenshades.com
Establishment information: Established in 1960.
Company type: Private company
Business activities: Operates garden centers.
Business type (SIC): Garden supplies—retail
Financial profile for 2010: Number of employees, 75
Corporate officers: Roger Esbenshade, Pres.; Terry Esbenshade, Secy.; Fred Esbenshade, Treas.; Pat Steele, Cont.
Giving statement: Giving through the Triple H Foundation.

Triple H Foundation

1755 Bowmansville Rd.
Mohnton, PA 19540-9444

Establishment information: Established in 1997 in PA.
Donor: Esbenshade's Greenhouses, Inc.
Financial data (yr. ended 11/30/12): Assets, $238,300 (M); expenditures, $81,451; qualifying distributions, $80,740; giving activities include $80,740 for 13 grants (high: $15,000; low: $160).
Purpose and activities: The foundation supports organizations involved with disaster response, human services, business, Christianity, and economically disadvantaged people.
Fields of interest: Youth development; Human services; Religion.
Type of support: General/operating support.
Geographic limitations: Giving limited to PA.
Support limitations: No grants to individuals.
Application information: Applications not accepted. Unsolicited requests for funds not accepted.
Board Members: Fred Esbenshade; Roger Esbenshade; Scott Esbenshade.
Officer: Terry Esbenshade, Pres.
EIN: 232986164

1296
ESCO Technologies Inc.

9900 A Clayton Rd.
St. Louis, MO 63124-1186 (314) 213-7200
FAX: (314) 213-7250

Company URL: http://www.escotechnologies.com
Establishment information: Established in 1990.
Company type: Public company
Company ticker symbol and exchange: ESE/NYSE
Business activities: Produces engineered products and systems for utility, industrial and commercial applications.
Business type (SIC): Communications equipment
Financial profile for 2012: Number of employees, 2,690; assets, $1,033,750,000; sales volume, $688,400,000; pre-tax net income, $71,680,000; expenses, $616,720,000; liabilities, $402,440,000
Corporate officers: Vic Richey, Jr., Chair., Pres., and C.E.O.; Gary E. Muenster, Exec. V.P. and C.F.O.; Alyson Schlinger Barclay, Sr. V.P., Genl. Counsel, and Secy.
Board of directors: Victor L. Richey, Jr., Chair.; G.E. Muenster; L.W. Solley; James M. Stolze, C.P.A.; Donald C. Trauscht; James D. Woods
Giving statement: Giving through the ESCO Technologies Foundation.
Company EIN: 431554045

ESCO Technologies Foundation

9900A Clayton Rd.
St. Louis, MO 63124-1186 (314) 213-7277
E-mail: info@escotechnologiesfoundation.org; URL: http://www.escotechnologiesfoundation.org/

Establishment information: Established in 2005 in MO.
Donors: J. Joe Adorjan; Wendall Blanton; Mr. Mark Griesman; Mrs. Mark Griesman; Stephen B. Guy; National City.
Financial data (yr. ended 09/30/11): Revenue, $276,286; assets, $270,223 (M); gifts received, $276,279; expenditures, $225,839; giving activities include $200,600 for grants and $23,450 for grants to individuals.
Purpose and activities: The foundation's funding is focused primarily on providing assistance to charities that work with children and families.
Fields of interest: Housing/shelter; Youth development; Children/youth, services; Family services Homeless.

Programs:
Emergency Hardship Assistance Program: Support through this program is available to employees of ESCO Technologies Inc. and its subsidiaries.
Scholarship Program: The foundation awards scholarships to college-age children of U.S. ESCO Technologies Inc. employees. Candidates must be enrolled for a minimum of 12 hours and accepted at an accredited technical school, college, university, or graduate school. Selection criteria include community involvement, academics, work experience, participation in the arts, and sports activities.
Type of support: Employee-related scholarships.
Geographic limitations: Giving primarily in areas of company operations, with emphasis on CA, IL, MO, and TX.
Application information: Applications accepted.
Initial approach: E-mail
Officers and Directors:* Kathleen "Kate" Lowrey*, Chair.; Jennifer Tilly*, Secy.; Matthew Mainer*, Treas.; Charles Kretschmer; Heather Moler; David Schatz; Diane Williams; James Wojtila; and 4 additional directors.
EIN: 203192719

1297
Essa Bancorp, Inc.

200 Palmer St.
Stroudsburg, PA 18360-1645
(570) 421-0531
FAX: (570) 421-7158

Company URL: https://www.essabank.com
Establishment information: Established in 1916.
Company type: Public company
Company ticker symbol and exchange: ESSA/NASDAQ
Business activities: Operates savings bank.
Business type (SIC): Savings institutions
Financial profile for 2012: Number of employees, 270; assets, $1,418,790,000; pre-tax net income, $250,000; liabilities, $1,243,380,000
Corporate officers: John E. Burrus, Chair.; Gary S. Olson, Pres. and C.E.O.; Allan A. Muto, Exec. V.P. and C.F.O.
Board of directors: John E. Burrus, Chair.; William P. Douglass; Daniel J. Henning; Frederick E. Kutteroff; Gary S. Olson; Brian T. Regan; John S. Schoonover, Jr.; Robert C. Selig, Jr.; William A. Viechnicki; Elizabeth Bensinger Weekes, Esq.
Giving statement: Giving through the ESSA Bank & Trust Foundation.
Company EIN: 208023072

ESSA Bank & Trust Foundation

200 Palmer St., P.O. Box L
Stroudsburg, PA 18360-0160 (570) 422-0182
URL: https://www.essabank.com/html/essa_foundation1.html

Establishment information: Established in 2007 in PA.
Donor: ESSA Bancorp, Inc.
Contact: Suzie T. Farley, V.P. and Secy.-Treas.
Financial data (yr. ended 12/31/11): Assets, $11,212,703 (M); gifts received, $1,171; expenditures, $693,714; qualifying distributions, $673,920; giving activities include $673,920 for grants.
Purpose and activities: The foundation supports fire departments and organizations involved with arts and culture, education, health, housing, recreation, human services, and community development.
Fields of interest: Arts; Higher education; Libraries (public); Education; Health care, clinics/centers; Health care; Housing/shelter; Disasters, fire prevention/control; Recreation, parks/playgrounds; Athletics/sports, baseball; Recreation; Boy scouts; YM/YWCAs & YM/YWHAs; Children/youth, services; Family services; Residential/custodial care, hospices; Human services; Community/economic development.
Type of support: Capital campaigns; Equipment; General/operating support.
Geographic limitations: Giving limited to areas of company operations in Monroe County, PA.
Publications: Application guidelines; Grants list.
Application information: Applications accepted. Support is limited 1 contribution per organization during a three year period. Application form not required. Applicants should submit the following:
1) copy of IRS Determination Letter
2) copy of most recent annual report/audited financial statement/990
3) copy of current year's organizational budget and/or project budget
Initial approach: Letter of inquiry
Deadline(s): None
Officers and Directors:* John E. Burrus*, Pres.; Suzie T. Farley*, V.P. and Secy.-Treas.; Lois B. Heckman; Gary S. Olson; Elizabeth B. Weekes.
EIN: 208227643
Selected grants: The following grants are a representative sample of this grantmaker's funding activity:
$20,000 to Boy Scouts of America, Lehigh Valley, PA, 2010.
$20,000 to Salvation Army of East Stroudsburg, East Stroudsburg, PA, 2010.
$8,425 to East Stroudsburg University Foundation, East Stroudsburg, PA, 2010.
$6,000 to Northampton Community College Foundation, Bethlehem, PA, 2010.

1298
Esurance Inc.

650 Davis St.
San Francisco, CA 94111 (415) 875-4500

Company URL: http://www.esurance.com
Establishment information: Established in 1998.
Company type: Subsidiary of a public company
Business activities: Sells online auto insurance policies.
Business type (SIC): Insurance/fire, marine, and casualty
Corporate officers: Gary C. Tolman, Pres. and C.E.O.; Jonathan Adkisson, C.F.O.; Elinor MacKinnon, C.I.O.; Kerian Bunch, Genl. Counsel and Corp. Secy.
Giving statement: Giving through the Esurance Inc. Corporate Giving Program.

Esurance Inc. Corporate Giving Program

650 Davis St.
San Francisco, CA 94111-1904
URL: http://www.esurance.com/community

Purpose and activities: Esurance supports nonprofit organizations involved with youth development, health care, LGBTQ rights, disabilities, food banks, education, and the environment. Giving also to national organizations.
Fields of interest: Environment, beautification programs; Environment; Health care; Mental health/crisis services, suicide; Food banks; Athletics/sports, Special Olympics; Boys & girls clubs; Youth development; Independent living, disability; Civil/human rights, LGBTQ.
Type of support: Employee volunteer services; General/operating support; In-kind gifts; Income development; Sponsorships.
Geographic limitations: Giving primarily in areas of company operations.
Application information: Applications accepted. Requests are not accepted via e-mail, fax, mail, or phone.
Initial approach: Complete online application for donation and sponsorship requests

1299
Ethicon Endo-Surgery, Inc.

4545 Creek Rd.
Cincinnati, OH 45242-2803 (513) 337-7000

Company URL: http://www.ethiconendo.com
Establishment information: Established in 1992.
Company type: Subsidiary of a public company
Business activities: Manufactures surgical instruments.
Business type (SIC): Medical instruments and supplies
Corporate officers: Kevin Lobo, Pres.; Thomas Rochon, V.P., Human Resources; M. R. McGranaghan, V.P., Finance
International operations: Germany
Giving statement: Giving through the Ethicon Endo-Surgery, Inc. Corporate Giving Program.

Ethicon Endo-Surgery, Inc. Corporate Giving Program

4545 Creek Rd.
Cincinnati, OH 45242-2803 (513) 337-7000
E-mail: fundingrequests@eesus.jnj.com;
URL: http://www.ethiconendosurgery.com/Corporate/ourconnections/funding

Purpose and activities: Ethicon Endo-Surgery makes charitable contributions to nonprofit organizations involved with disease prevention through early detection and prevention of childhood obesity, colorectal cancer, breast cancer, and diabetes. Support is given primarily in areas of company operations, with emphasis on the greater Cincinnati, Ohio, area, and in Brazil, China, Germany, India, Japan, and Russia.
Fields of interest: Public health, obesity; Health care; Cancer; Breast cancer; Diabetes; Pediatrics; Surgery.
International interests: Brazil; China; Germany; India; Japan; Russia.
Type of support: Conferences/seminars; Donated products; Employee volunteer services; Faculty/staff development; General/operating support; Program development; Research; Sponsorships.
Geographic limitations: Giving primarily in areas of company operations, with emphasis on the greater Cincinnati, OH, area, and in Brazil, China, Germany, India, Japan, and Russia; giving also to national and international organizations.
Support limitations: No support for religious or political organizations. No grants for "bricks-and-mortar" projects.
Application information: Applications accepted. Application form required. Applicants should submit the following:
1) name, address and phone number of organization
2) copy of IRS Determination Letter
3) detailed description of project and amount of funding requested
4) contact person

Applications should indicate the date of the event, if applicable. Requests for product donations should indicate any applicable deadlines, and specify the products needed by product code and in single instrument quantities.
Initial approach: Complete online application form
Deadline(s): None

1300
Bob Evans Farms, Inc.
3776 S. High St.
Columbus, OH 43207-4012
(614) 491-2225

Company URL: http://www.bobevans.com
Establishment information: Established in 1948.
Company type: Public company
Company ticker symbol and exchange: BOBE/NASDAQ
Business activities: Operates restaurants; produces food products.
Business type (SIC): Restaurants and drinking places; food and kindred products
Financial profile for 2012: Number of employees, 46,818; assets, $1,065,780,000; sales volume, $1,654,410,000; pre-tax net income, $99,990,000; expenses, $1,546,540,000; liabilities, $409,190,000
Corporate officers: Steven A. Davis, Chair. and C.E.O.; Randall L. Hicks, Pres.; Joseph Eulberg, Exec. V.P., Human Resource; Paul F. DeSantis, C.F.O. and Treas.; Colin Daly, Sr. V.P., Genl. Counsel, and Corp. Secy.; Edward Mitchell, C.P.A., V.P. and Corp. Cont.; Michael Doty, V.P., Finance
Board of directors: Steven A. Davis, Chair.; Larry C. Corbin; Michael J. Gasser; E. Gordon Gee; Mary Kay Haben; E. William Ingram III; Cheryl L. Krueger; G. Robert Lucas; Eileen A. Mallesch; Paul S. Williams
Subsidiaries: Hickory Specialties, Inc., Crossville, TN; Owens Country Sausage, Inc., Richardson, TX
Plants: Galva, IL; Hillsdale, MI; Bidwell, Springfield, Xenia, OH
Giving statement: Giving through the Bob Evans Farms, Inc. Corporate Giving Program.
Company EIN: 314421866

Bob Evans Farms, Inc. Corporate Giving Program
3776 S. High St.
Columbus, OH 43207-4012 (800) 272-7675
URL: http://www.bobevans.com/ourcompany/philanthropy.aspx

Purpose and activities: Bob Evans Farms makes charitable contributions to nonprofit organizations involved with education, health and wellness, and food and nutrition. Support is given primarily in Ohio.
Fields of interest: Education; Public health; Health care; Food services; Nutrition; Agriculture/food.
Type of support: Continuing support; General/operating support; Sponsorships.
Geographic limitations: Giving primarily in OH; giving also to national organizations.
Application information: Applications accepted.
Initial approach: Complete online letter of inquiry form

1301
Evans Landscaping Inc.
3700 Round Bottom Rd.
Cincinnati, OH 45244-2413 (513) 271-1119

Company URL: http://www.evanslandscaping.com
Company type: Private company
Business activities: Operates landscaping and demolition contracting company.
Business type (SIC): Landscape and horticultural services
Giving statement: Giving through the BLR Foundation, Inc.

BLR Foundation, Inc.
c/o Douglas L. Evans
4229 Roundbottom Rd.
Cincinnati, OH 45244-1629 (513) 361-0444
Application address: 537 E. Pete Rose Way, Cincinnati, OH 45202

Establishment information: Established in 2005 in OH.
Contact: Robert Edmiston
Financial data (yr. ended 12/31/11): Assets, $604,456 (M); expenditures, $10,124; qualifying distributions, $1,000; giving activities include $1,000 for grants.
Fields of interest: Education.
Application information: Applications accepted. Application form required.
Initial approach: Letter
Deadline(s): None
Officers: Douglas L. Evans, Pres.; Richard A. Evans, M.D., V.P.; Anthony E. Schweier, Secy.-Treas.
EIN: 203936633

1302
Evening Post Publishing Company
134 Columbus St.
Charleston, SC 29403-4809
(843) 577-7111

Company URL: http://www.evepost.com
Establishment information: Established in 1894.
Company type: Private company
Business activities: Publishes newspapers; broadcasts television.
Business type (SIC): Newspaper publishing and/or printing; radio and television broadcasting
Corporate officers: Pierre Manigault, Chair.; John P. Barnwell, Co.-Vice-Chair. and C.E.O.; Edward M. Gilbreth, Co.-Vice-Chair.; Travis O. Rockey, Pres. and C.O.O.; Roger A. Berardinis, V.P. and C.F.O.; Arthur M. Wilcox, Secy.
Board of directors: Pierre Manigault, Chair.; John P. Barnwell, Co.-Vice-Chair.; Edward M. Gilbreth, Co.-Vice-Chair.
Subsidiaries: Aiken Communications, Inc., Aiken, SC; Editors Press Service, New York, NY; Georgetown Communications, Inc., Georgetown, SC; KCTZ Communications, Inc., Bozeman, MT; Kingstree Communications, Kingstree, SC; KPAX Communications, Inc., Missoula, MT; KRTV Communications, Inc., Great Falls, MT; KTVQ Communications, Inc., Billings, MT; KVOA Communications, Inc., Tucson, AZ; KXLF Communications, Inc., Butte, MT; Sangre de Cristo Communications, Inc., Pueblo, CO; Sawtooth Communications, Inc., Nampa, ID
Giving statement: Giving through the Post and Courier Foundation.

Post and Courier Foundation
134 Columbus St.
Charleston, SC 29403-4800 (843) 937-5605

Establishment information: Incorporated in 1951 in SC.
Donors: Evening Post Publishing Co.; Blackbaud, Inc.
Contact: Susan N. Sanders, Secy.
Financial data (yr. ended 12/31/11): Assets, $2,938,768 (M); gifts received, $329,808; expenditures, $933,300; qualifying distributions, $891,340; giving activities include $891,340 for grants.
Purpose and activities: The foundation supports food banks and youth development centers and organizations involved with arts and culture, education, conservation, animal welfare, human services, and the visually impaired.
Fields of interest: Arts education; Museums; Historic preservation/historical societies; Arts; Higher education; Medical school/education; Libraries (public); Education; Environment, natural resources; Animals/wildlife, preservation/protection; Health care; Food banks; Youth development, centers/clubs; Salvation Army; Human services; United Ways and Federated Giving Programs Blind/visually impaired.
Type of support: Annual campaigns; Building/renovation; Capital campaigns; Continuing support; General/operating support; Scholarship funds; Sponsorships.
Geographic limitations: Giving primarily in Charleston, SC.
Support limitations: No grants to individuals.
Application information: Applications accepted. Application form not required.
Initial approach: Proposal
Board meeting date(s): As needed, usually twice annually
Deadline(s): July 30
Officers: Rebecca Gilbreth Herres, Pres.; Pierre Manigault, V.P.; Susan N. Sanders, Secy.; Roger A. Berardinis, Treas.
Number of staff: 1 part-time professional.
EIN: 576020356

1303
Ewing Irrigation Products, Inc.
3441 E. Harbour Dr.
Phoenix, AZ 85034-7229 (602) 437-9530
FAX: (602) 431-9067

Company URL: http://www.ewing1.com
Establishment information: Established in 1922.
Company type: Private company
Business activities: Wholesale distributor of commercial and residential irrigation supplies.
Business type (SIC): Irrigation systems services
Corporate officers: Susan E. York, Chair.; Douglas W. York, Pres. and C.E.O.
Board of director: Susan E. York, Chair.
Giving statement: Giving through the Ewing Employee Assistance Foundation and the Ewing York Foundation.

Ewing Employee Assistance Foundation
3441 E. Harbour Dr.
Phoenix, AZ 85034-7229

Establishment information: Established in 2007 in AZ.
Donor: Ewing Irrigation, Inc.

Financial data (yr. ended 06/30/11): Assets, $50,723 (M); gifts received, $25,000; expenditures, $0; qualifying distributions, $0.
Fields of interest: Community/economic development.
Support limitations: No grants to individuals.
Application information: Applications not accepted. Unsolicited requests for funds not accepted.
Officers: Susan York, Chair.; Kelli York, Pres.; Victoria York, V.P.
EIN: 753226421

The Ewing York Foundation

3441 E. Harbour Dr.
Phoenix, AZ 85034-7935

Establishment information: Established in 2007 in AZ.
Donor: Ewing Irrigation, Inc.
Financial data (yr. ended 06/30/11): Assets, $238,035 (M); gifts received, $100,000; expenditures, $101,780; qualifying distributions, $101,500; giving activities include $101,500 for 3 grants (high: $100,000; low: $500).
Fields of interest: Education.
Geographic limitations: Giving primarily in AZ.
Support limitations: No grants to individuals.
Application information: Applications not accepted. Unsolicited requests for funds not accepted.
Officers: Susan York, Chair.; Kelli York, Pres.; Victoria York, V.P.
EIN: 753226420

1304
Excell Marketing, L.C.

(formerly Iowa Periodicals, Inc.)
5501 Park Ave.
P.O. Box 1297
Des Moines, IA 50321-1206
(515) 244-0300

Company URL: http://www.excellmktg.com
Establishment information: Established in 1996.
Company type: Private company
Business activities: Distributes products to create a complete gaming, trading card and collectables department in retail stores.
Business type (SIC): Non-durable goods—wholesale
Corporate officers: Stan Seidler, Pres.; Patrick Burton, C.F.O.; Steve Jones, V.P., Mktg.; Mark Den Adel, Cont.
Giving statement: Giving through the Seidler Foundation.

The Seidler Foundation

P.O. Box 1297
Des Moines, IA 50305-1297

Establishment information: Established in 1982 in IA.
Donors: Iowa Periodicals, Inc.; Stanley B. Seidler; Excell Mktg.
Contact: Stanley B. Seidler, Pres.
Financial data (yr. ended 12/31/11): Assets, $8,131,571 (M); gifts received, $450,000; expenditures, $419,505; qualifying distributions, $411,563; giving activities include $411,563 for grants.
Purpose and activities: The foundation supports organizations involved with arts and culture, higher education, education services, children, and Judaism.
Fields of interest: Performing arts, music; Arts; Higher education; Education, services; Children, services; United Ways and Federated Giving Programs; Jewish federated giving programs; Jewish agencies & synagogues.
Type of support: General/operating support; Scholarship funds; Scholarships—to individuals.
Geographic limitations: Giving primarily in IA and WY.
Application information: Applications accepted. Application form not required.
Initial approach: Proposal
Deadline(s): None
Officer and Directors: Stanley B. Seidler, Pres.; Carol Seidler Mavrakis; Susan Seidler Newman.
EIN: 421209825
Selected grants: The following grants are a representative sample of this grantmaker's funding activity:
$76,700 to Grand Teton Music Festival, Wilson, WY, 2010. For general support.
$52,500 to Jewish Federation of Greater Des Moines, Des Moines, IA, 2010. For general support.
$30,000 to Cornell College, Mount Vernon, IA, 2010. For general support.
$22,800 to Des Moines Art Center, Des Moines, IA, 2010.
$15,000 to United Way of Central Iowa, Des Moines, IA, 2010. For general support.
$7,500 to Lyric Opera of Chicago, Chicago, IL, 2010. For general support.
$5,000 to Northwestern University, Evanston, IL, 2010. For general support.
$3,500 to Kansas City Art Institute, Kansas City, MO, 2010. For general support.
$3,000 to Wildlife of the American West, Jackson, WY, 2010. For general support.
$2,500 to Des Moines Symphony, Des Moines, IA, 2010. For general support.

1305
Excellium Pharmaceutical, Inc.

3-G Oak Rd.
Fairfield, NJ 07004-2903 (973) 276-9600

Company URL: http://www.excellium.com/
Establishment information: Established in 1996.
Company type: Private company
Business activities: Manufactures pharmaceuticals.
Business type (SIC): Drugs
Corporate officer: Hasmukh M. Doshi, Pres.
Giving statement: Giving through the Hasmukh & Chandrika Doshi Foundation.

Hasmukh & Chandrika Doshi Foundation

14 Liberty Ct.
Fairfield, NJ 07004-1588

Establishment information: Established in 2003 in NJ.
Donor: Excellium Pharmaceutical, Inc.
Financial data (yr. ended 12/31/11): Assets, $314,001 (M); gifts received, $565; expenditures, $16,600; qualifying distributions, $15,011; giving activities include $15,011 for grants.
Purpose and activities: The foundation supports organizations involved with blindness and Hinduism.
Fields of interest: Community/economic development; Religion.
International interests: India.
Type of support: General/operating support.
Geographic limitations: Giving primarily in CA, IL, KS, NJ, NY, and PA.
Support limitations: No grants to individuals.
Application information: Applications accepted. Application form required. Applicants should submit the following:
1) copy of IRS Determination Letter
Initial approach: Letter
Deadline(s): None
Officers: Hasmukh M. Doshi, Pres.; Vashal Doshi, V.P.; Chandrika Doshi, Secy.
EIN: 562399451

1306
Exchange Bank Santa Rosa

545 4th St.
P.O. Box 403
Santa Rosa, CA 95402-0403
(707) 524-3111

Company URL: http://www.exchangebank.com
Establishment information: Established in 1890.
Company type: Public company
Company ticker symbol and exchange: EXSR/OTC
Business activities: Operates commercial bank.
Financial profile for 2011: Assets, $1,600,403,000; pre-tax net income, $17,613,000; liabilities, $1,437,384,000
Corporate officers: C. William Reinking, Chair.; William R. Schrader, Pres. and C.E.O.; Bruce E. DeCrona, Exec. V.P. and C.O.O.; Greg Jahn, Sr. V.P. and C.F.O.; Shauna R. Lorenzen, V.P. and Cont.; Marlene K. Soiland, Corp. Secy.
Board of directors: C. William Reinking, Chair.; Richard W. Abbey; Dante B. Benedetti; Daniel G. Libarle; James M. Ryan; William R. Schrader; Marlene K. Soiland; Carlos G. Tamayo
Subsidiary: Dumac Leasing, Santa Rosa, CA
Offices: Bennett Valley, Cloverdale, Coddingtown, College, Cotati, Dutton, Healdsburg, Larkfield, Montgomery Village, Petaluma, Rohnert Park, Sebastopol, Sonoma, St. Francis, Stony Point, Windsor, CA
Giving statement: Giving through the Exchange Bank Foundation.

Exchange Bank Foundation

P.O. Box 403
Santa Rosa, CA 95402-0403 (707) 524-3109

Establishment information: Established in 1979 in CA.
Donor: Exchange Bank.
Contact: C. William Reinking, Chair.
Financial data (yr. ended 12/31/11): Assets, $76,808 (M); gifts received, $50,000; expenditures, $45,381; qualifying distributions, $45,380; giving activities include $45,380 for grants.
Purpose and activities: The foundation supports organizations involved with arts and culture, higher education, parks and playgrounds, human services, and Judaism.
Fields of interest: Education; Health care; Youth development.
Type of support: Building/renovation; Equipment; General/operating support; Program development.
Geographic limitations: Giving primarily in Sonoma County, CA.
Publications: Application guidelines.
Application information: Applications accepted. Application form not required. Applicants should submit the following:
1) role played by volunteers
2) population served
3) copy of IRS Determination Letter
4) geographic area to be served

5) copy of most recent annual report/audited financial statement/990
6) listing of board of directors, trustees, officers and other key people and their affiliations
7) detailed description of project and amount of funding requested
8) organization's charter and by-laws
9) copy of current year's organizational budget and/ or project budget
10) listing of additional sources and amount of support

Proposals should indicate the organization's membership structure, including fees, dues, and total number of members, if applicable.

Initial approach: Proposal
Copies of proposal: 1
Board meeting date(s): Varies
Deadline(s): None
Final notification: 90 to 120 days

Officers: C. William Reinking, Chair.; James M. Ryan, Vice-Chair.
Trustees: Richard W. Abbey; Dante B. Benedetti; Daniel G. Libarle; William R. Schrader; Marlene K. Soiland; Carlos G. Tamayo.
Number of staff: 1 part-time professional; 1 part-time support.
EIN: 942576480

1307
Exchange National Bank and Trust Company
600 Commercial St.
Atchison, KS 66002-2405 (913) 367-6000

Company URL: http://www.exchangebankonline.com
Establishment information: Established in 1857.
Company type: Private company
Business activities: Operates commercial bank.
Business type (SIC): Banks/commercial; trusts
Corporate officers: Paul H. Adair, Chair.; Richard R. Dickason, Pres.
Board of director: Paul H. Adair, Chair.
Giving statement: Giving through the Adair—Exchange Bank Foundation.

Adair—Exchange Bank Foundation
P.O. Box 189
Atchison, KS 66002-0189

Donors: Exchange National Bank & Trust Co.; First National Bank; Exchange Bankshares Corp.
Financial data (yr. ended 12/31/11): Assets, $707,955 (M); gifts received, $90,000; expenditures, $77,517; qualifying distributions, $74,500; giving activities include $74,500 for grants.
Purpose and activities: The foundation supports organizations involved with education, animal welfare, human services, and religion.
Fields of interest: Elementary/secondary education; Education; Animal welfare; Big Brothers/ Big Sisters; Human services; Catholic agencies & churches; Religion.
Type of support: General/operating support.
Geographic limitations: Giving primarily in KS.
Support limitations: No grants to individuals.
Application information: Applications not accepted. Unsolicited requests for funds not accepted.
Officers and Directors:* Paul H. Adair*, Pres.; Richard R. Dickason*, V.P.; Sharon Baldridge*, Secy.; Marsha A. Adair*, Treas.
EIN: 237389214

1308
Executive Lodging Ltd. Inc.
1827 Sage Rd.
P.O. Box 571208
Houston, TX 77056-3502 (713) 552-9852

Company URL: http://www.executivelodging.net
Establishment information: Established in 1983.
Company type: Private company
Business activities: Provides corporate lodging solutions.
Business type (SIC): Real estate operators and lessors
Corporate officer: Candice Noll, Pres.
Giving statement: Giving through the Everest Foundation.

The Everest Foundation
P.O. Box 28
Caldwell, TX 77836-0028

Establishment information: Established in 2005 in TX.
Donors: Executive Lodging Ltd., Inc.; Jack W. Parks III.
Financial data (yr. ended 12/31/11): Assets, $233,519 (M); gifts received, $24,900; expenditures, $80,592; qualifying distributions, $80,147; giving activities include $80,147 for grants.
Fields of interest: Agriculture/food; Human services; Religion.
Geographic limitations: Giving primarily in TX; some giving in Italy.
Support limitations: No grants to individuals.
Application information: Applications not accepted. Contributes only to pre-selected organizations.
Directors: Joe Milyasevich; Jack W. Parks, Jr.; Jack W. Parks III.
EIN: 201032167

1309
Exelon Corporation
10 S. Dearborn St., 48th Fl.
P.O. Box 805398
Chicago, IL 60680-5398 (312) 394-7398

Company URL: http://www.exeloncorp.com
Establishment information: Established in 1887.
Company type: Public company
Company ticker symbol and exchange: EXC/NYSE
International Securities Identification Number: US30161N1019
Business activities: Operates public utility holding company; generates, transmits, and distributes electricity; distributes natural gas.
Business type (SIC): Combination utility services; holding company
Financial profile for 2012: Number of employees, 26,057; assets, $78,600,000,000; sales volume, $23,500,000,000; pre-tax net income, $1,798,000,000; expenses, $21,018,000,000; liabilities, $56,930,000,000
Fortune 1000 ranking: 2012—129th in revenues, 176th in profits, and 76th in assets
Forbes 2000 ranking: 2012—405th in sales, 504th in profits, and 313th in assets
Corporate officers: Mayo Shattuck III, Chair.; Christopher M. Crane, Pres. and C.E.O.; Jonathan W. Thayer, Exec. V.P. and C.F.O.; Ruth Ann M. Gillis, Exec. V.P. and C.A.O.; Darryl M. Bradford, Sr. V.P. and Genl. Counsel; James D. Firth, Sr. V.P., Comms.
Board of directors: Mayo Shattuck III, Chair.; Ann C. Berzin; John A. Canning, Jr.; Christopher M. Crane; Yves C. deBalmann; Nicholas DeBenedictis; Nelson A. Diaz; Sue Ling Gin; Paul L. Joskow, Ph.D.; Robert J. Lawless; William C. Richardson, Ph.D.; Thomas J. Ridge; John W. Rogers, Jr.; Stephen D. Steinour
Subsidiaries: AmerGen Energy Co., LLC, Kennett Square, PA; Commonwealth Edison Company, Chicago, IL; Exelon Energy Co., Westchester, IL; Exelon Enterprises Co., LLC, Chicago, IL; Exelon Generation Co., LLC, Kennett Square, PA; PECO Energy Power Co., Philadelphia, PA; Susquehanna Electric Co., Darlington, MD; Susquehanna Power Co., Darlington, MD
Historic mergers: Constellation Energy Group, Inc. (March 12, 2012)
Giving statement: Giving through the Exelon Corporation Contributions Program, the Constellation Energy Group Foundation, Inc., and the Exelon Foundation.
Company EIN: 232990190

Exelon Corporation Contributions Program
(formerly ComEd Corporate Giving Program)
10 S. Dearborn St., 48th Fl.
P.O. Box 805398
Chicago, IL 60680-5398 (800) 483-3220
E-mail: corporaterelations@exeloncorp.com;
URL: http://www.exeloncorp.com/community/givingandgrants/givingandgrants.aspx

Purpose and activities: As a complement to its foundation, Exelon also makes charitable contributions to nonprofit organizations directly. Emphasis is given to organizations involved with arts and culture, education, the environment, and neighborhood development. Support is limited to areas of company operations in California, Illinois, Iowa, Maryland, Massachusetts, New Jersey, Pennsylvania, and Texas.
Fields of interest: Arts; Scholarships/financial aid; Education; Environment, natural resources; Environment, energy; Environment, beautification programs; Environmental education; Environment; Health care; Employment, training; Youth development, adult & child programs; Human services; Community/economic development; United Ways and Federated Giving Programs; Science, formal/general education; Mathematics.
Program:
Dollars for Doers: Employees who volunteer 25 hours or more at a single nonprofit organization in one year can apply for a $250 grant for that organization. Exelon doubles grants for those volunteering at environmental organizations in order to support the Exelon 2020 goal of helping local communities reduce their carbon footprints. In 2011, over 2,400 employees served over 61,000 hours as volunteers at various organizations in Exelon's service areas. The company's senior management team and other employees serve on the boards of more than 350 nonprofit organizations throughout the Chicago and Philadelphia areas. In 2011, they helped 12 organizations raise in excess of $900,000. Exelon employees also pledged over $4 million in 2011 toward the annual United Way campaign.
Type of support: Employee volunteer services; General/operating support; In-kind gifts; Program development; Sponsorships.
Geographic limitations: Giving is limited to areas of company operations in CA, IA, IL, MA, MD, NJ, PA, TX.
Support limitations: No support for discriminatory organizations. No grants to individuals.
Publications: Application guidelines; Corporate giving report.

Application information: Applications accepted. Support is limited to 1 contribution per organization during any given year. Application form required.
Initial approach: Complete online application form

Constellation Energy Group Foundation, Inc.

(formerly Baltimore Gas and Electric Foundation, Inc.)
c/o Community Partnerships
100 Constellation Way, Ste. 600C
Baltimore, MD 21202-6302 (888) 460-2002
FAX: (410) 470-4098;
E-mail: exeloncorporatecontributions@exeloncorp.com; URL: http://www.constellation.com/SocialResponsibility/Community/Pages/CommunityOverview.aspx

Establishment information: Established in 1986 in MD.
Donors: Baltimore Gas and Electric Co.; Constellation Energy Group, Inc.
Contact: Barbara Shortridge, Coord., Community Partnerships
Financial data (yr. ended 12/31/11): Assets, $28,595,330 (M); expenditures, $8,026,787; qualifying distributions, $8,005,421; giving activities include $6,047,064 for 1,044 grants (high: $1,000,000; low: $100) and $1,958,357 for employee matching gifts.
Purpose and activities: The foundation supports organizations involved with education, energy assistance, the environment, and economic growth.
Fields of interest: Higher education; Education; Environment, pollution control; Environment, natural resources; Environment, land resources; Environmental education; Environment; Housing/shelter, development; Recreation, parks/playgrounds; Athletics/sports, golf; Youth development, business; Children/youth, services; Economic development; United Ways and Federated Giving Programs; Mathematics; Engineering/technology Youth; Economically disadvantaged.
Programs:
E2 Energy to Educate: The foundation awards grants to projects that reach and inspire students to think differently about energy and builds on student knowledge and application of science, technology, engineering, and math (STEM). Projects must be aligned with one of three focuses: basic science and engineering needed to address energy challenges; new energy technologies entering the marketplace; and the expanding role of information technology. Grants of up to $25,000 for partner grades 6-12 are awarded and up to $50,000 for 2 and 4 year colleges and universities.
Economic Development: The foundation supports programs designed to stimulate business growth and vibrant neighborhoods in the communities where Constellation Energy operates.
EcoStar Grants: The foundation awards grants of up to $5,000 to support local community environmental stewardship projects. Special emphasis is directed toward pollution prevention, education, energy efficiency, preservation, and community activism.
Education: The foundation supports programs designed to prepare graduating high school students for the workforce or higher education to maximize their potential for success.
Energy Initiatives: The foundation supports programs designed to promote increased access to emergency energy assistance and related services to promote future self reliance.
Environment: The foundation supports programs designed to create environmental stewardship between citizens, business, and government for the preservation of the natural environment.
Matching Gift Program: The foundation matches contributions made by employees and retirees of Constellation to the United Way and to institutions of higher education.
Type of support: Building/renovation; Capital campaigns; Conferences/seminars; Continuing support; Employee matching gifts; Employee volunteer services; General/operating support; Matching/challenge support; Program development; Scholarship funds.
Geographic limitations: Giving primarily in areas of company operations, with emphasis on DE, KY, central MD, NJ, NY, PA, TX,.
Support limitations: No support for churches not of direct benefit to the entire community, organizations actively opposing Constellation's position on issues, individual schools, or sports teams. No grants to individuals, or for general operating or program development support for United Way agencies, start-up needs, or hospital capital campaigns.
Publications: Application guidelines.
Application information: Applications accepted. Preference is given to organizations that have Constellation Energy employees on their boards and as volunteers. Support is limited to 1 contribution per organization during any given year. Organizations receiving support are asked to provide a final report. Application form required. Applicants should submit the following:
1) role played by volunteers
2) timetable for implementation and evaluation of project
3) how project will be sustained once grantmaker support is completed
4) results expected from proposed grant
5) qualifications of key personnel
6) statement of problem project will address
7) population served
8) copy of IRS Determination Letter
9) brief history of organization and description of its mission
10) geographic area to be served
11) copy of most recent annual report/audited financial statement/990
12) how project's results will be evaluated or measured
13) explanation of why grantmaker is considered an appropriate donor for project
14) listing of board of directors, trustees, officers and other key people and their affiliations
15) detailed description of project and amount of funding requested
16) plans for cooperation with other organizations, if any
17) copy of current year's organizational budget and/or project budget
18) listing of additional sources and amount of support
19) plans for acknowledgement
Initial approach: Complete online application
Board meeting date(s): June and Oct.
Deadline(s): May 1 and Sept. 1 for Community Grants; Mar. 1 for EcoStar Grants; Sept. 15 for E2 Energy to Educate
Final notification: June 20 and Oct. 15 for Community Grants; Apr. 22 for EcoStar Grants; Nov. 19 for E2 Energy to Educate
Officers and Directors:* Mayo A. Shattuck II*, Chair. and Pres.; Charles A. Berardesco*, V.P. and Secy.; S. M. Ulrich, V.P.; Reese K. Feuerman, Co-Treas.; J. E. Lowry, Co-Treas.; James L. Connaughton.
Number of staff: None.
EIN: 521452037

Selected grants: The following grants are a representative sample of this grantmaker's funding activity:
$25,000 to Humanim, Columbia, MD, 2007.
$25,000 to Living Classrooms Foundation, Baltimore, MD, 2007.
$25,000 to Stevenson University, Stevenson, MD, 2007.
$20,000 to Business Volunteers Unlimited Maryland, Baltimore, MD, 2007.
$20,000 to Stevenson University, Stevenson, MD, 2007.
$17,916 to Loyola University Maryland, Baltimore, MD, 2007.
$10,000 to Teach for America, Baltimore, MD, 2007.
$7,500 to Trust for Public Land, Washington, DC, 2007.
$5,000 to Resources for the Future, Washington, DC, 2007.
$5,000 to Volunteers for Medical Engineering, Baltimore, MD, 2007.

Exelon Foundation

P.O. Box 5408
Chicago, IL 60680-5408 (312) 394-2200
E-mail: exelonfoundation@exeloncorp.com;
URL: http://www.exelonfoundation.org

Establishment information: Established in 2007 in IL.
Donor: Exelon Corporation.
Financial data (yr. ended 12/31/11): Assets, $64,732,137 (M); gifts received, $12,000; expenditures, $3,432,287; qualifying distributions, $3,150,000; giving activities include $3,150,000 for grants.
Purpose and activities: The foundation supports programs designed to promote the environment and conservation; innovative math and science education; and diversity and tolerance.
Fields of interest: Education; Environment, natural resources; Environment, land resources; Environment, energy; Environment; Recreation, parks/playgrounds; Civil/human rights, equal rights; Mathematics; Science; Public affairs.
Programs:
Diversity and Tolerance: The foundation supports programs designed to educate and create awareness of the civic and social aspects of diversity and the importance tolerance.
Environment and Conservation: The foundation supports programs designed to promote environmental stewardship and energy efficiency; and partnerships focused on preservation and conservation of open lands, wildlife habitats, parks, trail systems, and recreational areas.
Innovative Math and Science Education: The foundation supports programs designed to incorporate the relationship between preserving the environment and using energy wisely.
Type of support: Program development.
Geographic limitations: Giving primarily in areas of company operations in IL, MA, MD, PA, and TX.
Support limitations: No grants to individuals.
Publications: Application guidelines.
Application information: Letters of inquiry should be brief. Generally, the foundation does not accept unsolicited proposals. Full proposals are accepted by invitation only. Applicants should submit the following:
1) detailed description of project and amount of funding requested
Initial approach: E-mail letter of inquiry
Board meeting date(s): Quarterly
Deadline(s): None
Officers and Directors:* John W. Rowe*, Chair.; Steven J. Solomon, Pres.; Joseph Dominquez, V.P.;

James Firth*, V.P.; Michelle McConnell, Secy.; Matthew F. Hilzinger*, Treas.; Douglass J. Brown; Frank Clark; Katherine Combs; Christopher M. Crane; Ruth Ann M. Gillis; Denis O'Brien; John M. Palms, Ph.D.; Williamson C. Richardson, Ph.D.; William A. Van Hoene, Jr.; Andrea Zopp.
EIN: 830499473
Selected grants: The following grants are a representative sample of this grantmaker's funding activity:
$200,000 to Museum of Science and Industry, Chicago, IL, 2010.
$125,000 to African American Museum in Philadelphia, Philadelphia, PA, 2010.
$125,000 to Drexel University, Philadelphia, PA, 2010.
$100,000 to Chicago Community Trust, Chicago, IL, 2010.
$100,000 to DePaul University, Chicago, IL, 2010.
$100,000 to Franklin Institute Science Museum, Philadelphia, PA, 2010.
$75,000 to Civil War and Underground Railroad Museum of Philadelphia, Philadelphia, PA, 2010.
$50,000 to Morton Arboretum, Lisle, IL, 2010.
$50,000 to Student Conservation Association, Oakland, CA, 2010.
$50,000 to Student Conservation Association, Charlestown, NH, 2010.

1310
Exotic Metals Forming Company LLC

5411 S. 226th St.
Kent, WA 98032-1891 (253) 395-3710

Company URL: http://www.exoticmetals.com
Establishment information: Established in 1963.
Company type: Private company
Business activities: Operates high-temperature, high-strength sheet metal forming and assembly company serving the aerospace industry.
Business type (SIC): Aircraft and parts
Corporate officers: Bill Binder, Co-Pres. and C.E.O.; Katherine A Binder, Co-Pres.; Karl D'Ambrosio, C.I.O.
Giving statement: Giving through the Lochland Foundation.

The Lochland Foundation

P.O. Box 90016
Bellevue, WA 98009-9016
Contact for scholarships: James K. McBain, c/o Inslee Best Doezie & Ryder PS, 777 108th Ave. N.E., Ste. 190, Bellevue, WA 98004, tel.: (425) 455-1234, e-mail: jmcbain@insleebest.com

Establishment information: Established in 2002 in WA.
Donors: Phyllis Lindsey; Exotic Metals Forming Co., LLC.
Financial data (yr. ended 12/31/11): Assets, $5,976,888 (M); gifts received, $750,000; expenditures, $490,986; qualifying distributions, $472,098; giving activities include $472,098 for grants.
Purpose and activities: The foundation supports flight museums and organizations involved with education, animal welfare, and Christianity and awards college scholarships to high school students in the Seattle area.
Fields of interest: Museums (specialized); Education, public education; Secondary school/ education; Higher education; Education; Animal welfare; YM/YWCAs & YM/YWHAs; Christian agencies & churches.
Program:
Irene and Anna Scholarship Fund: The foundation awards college scholarships to high schools students in the Seattle area with demonstrated financial need, academic achievement, and appropriate teacher recommendations.
Type of support: General/operating support; Scholarship funds; Scholarships—to individuals.
Geographic limitations: Giving primarily in WA.
Application information: Applications accepted. Application form required.
Scholarship applications should include financial information, transcripts, essay, and recommendations.
Initial approach: Contact foundation for application form for Irene and Anna Scholarship Fund
Deadline(s): At the discretion of the board for Irene and Anna Scholarship Fund
Officers: Phyllis Lindsey, Pres.; Mark Lindsey, V.P.; Katherine A. Binder, Secy.-Treas.
EIN: 510420961
Selected grants: The following grants are a representative sample of this grantmaker's funding activity:
$100,000 to League of Education Voters Foundation, Seattle, WA, 2011. For general fund.
$100,000 to Montana State University, Bozeman, MT, 2011. For scholarships.
$55,000 to First Presbyterian Church of Bellevue, Bellevue, WA, 2011. For general fund.
$27,500 to CRISTA Ministries, Seattle, WA, 2011.
$22,000 to Museum of Flight Foundation, Seattle, WA, 2011. For general fund.
$2,500 to Center for New Creation, Seattle, WA, 2011. For general fund.
$2,000 to K C T S Television, Seattle, WA, 2011. For general fund.

1311
Expedia, Inc.

333 108th Ave. N.E.
Bellevue, WA 98004 (425) 679-7200

Company URL: http://www.expediainc.com
Establishment information: Established in 2005.
Company type: Public company
Company ticker symbol and exchange: EXPE/ NASDAQ
Business activities: Operates online travel company.
Business type (SIC): Transportation services
Financial profile for 2012: Number of employees, 12,330; assets, $7,085,190,000; sales volume, $4,030,350,000; pre-tax net income, $350,060,000; expenses, $3,598,620,000; liabilities, $4,804,940,000
Fortune 1000 ranking: 2012—583rd in revenues, 494th in profits, and 486th in assets
Forbes 2000 ranking: 2012—1516th in sales, 1425th in profits, and 1662nd in assets
Corporate officers: Barry Diller, Chair.; Victor A. Kaufman, Vice-Chair.; Dara Khosrowshahi, Pres. and C.E.O.; Mark D. Okerstrom, Exec. V.P. and C.F.O.; Robert Dzielak, Exec. V.P., Genl. Counsel, and Secy.; Lance A. Soliday, V.P., C.A.O., and Cont.
Board of directors: Barry Diller, Chair.; Victor A. Kaufman, Vice-Chair.; A. George Battle; Jonathan L. Dolgen; William R. Fitzgerald; Craig A. Jacobson; Peter M. Kern; Dara Khosrowshahi; John C. Malone; Jose A. Tazon
Giving statement: Giving through the Expedia, Inc. Corporate Giving Program.
Company EIN: 202705720

Expedia, Inc. Corporate Giving Program

3150 139th Ave. S.E.
Bellevue, WA 98005 (425) 679-7200
E-mail: expcomre@expedia.com

Purpose and activities: Expedia matches charitable contributions made by its employees to nonprofit organizations involved with environmental awareness and responsibility. Special emphasis is directed toward organizations with which employees of Expedia volunteer.
Fields of interest: Historic preservation/historical societies; Environment, volunteer services; Environment; Community/economic development.
Type of support: Employee matching gifts; Employee volunteer services; General/operating support.
Geographic limitations: Giving on a national and international basis primarily in areas of company operations.
Application information: Applications not accepted. Contributes only to pre-selected organizations.

1312
Exponential, Inc.

2100 Riveredge Pkwy., Ste. 1100
Atlanta, GA 30328

Company type: Private company
Business activities: Publishes books.
Business type (SIC): Book publishing and/or printing
Corporate officers: Bruce Wilkinson, C.E.O. and C.F.O.; Darlene Wilkinson, Secy.
Giving statement: Giving through the Global Vision Resources, Inc.

Global Vision Resources, Inc.

11801 Broadwater LN
Charlotte, NC 28273

Establishment information: Established in 2001 in GA as a company-sponsored operating foundation.
Donors: Exponential, Inc.; Walk Thru the Bible.
Financial data (yr. ended 12/31/11): Assets, $27,718 (M); expenditures, $19,702; qualifying distributions, $4,715; giving activities include $3,050 for 2+ grants (high: $2,900).
Purpose and activities: The foundation supports Walk Thru the Bible in Johannesburg, South Africa.
Fields of interest: Religion.
International interests: South Africa.
Type of support: Equipment.
Geographic limitations: Giving limited to Johannesburg, South Africa.
Application information: Applications not accepted. Unsolicited requests for funds not accepted.
Officers: Jim Milligan, Pres.; Joel Milligan, Secy.-Treas.
Director: Tom Bowers.
EIN: 582660997

1313
Express Scripts Holding Company

(formerly Express Scripts, Inc.)
1 Express Way
St. Louis, MO 63121 (314) 996-0900

Company URL: http://www.express-scripts.com
Establishment information: Established in 1986.
Company type: Public company
Company ticker symbol and exchange: ESRX/ NASDAQ
International Securities Identification Number: US58405U1025
Business activities: Provides pharmacy benefit management services.
Business type (SIC): Miscellaneous health services
Financial profile for 2012: Number of employees, 30,215; assets, $15,607,000,000; sales volume, $46,128,300,000; pre-tax net income, $2,024,400,000
Fortune 1000 ranking: 2012—24th in revenues, 154th in profits, and 95th in assets
Forbes 2000 ranking: 2012—71st in sales, 459th in profits, and 407th in assets
Corporate officers: George Paz, Chair. and C.E.O.; Patrick McNamee, Exec. V.P. and C.O.O.; Jeffrey Hall, Exec. V.P. and C.F.O.; Keith J. Ebling, Exec. V.P. and Genl. Counsel; Edward B. Ignaczak, Exec. V.P., Sales and Mktg.; Gary Wimberly, Sr. V.P. and C.I.O.
Board of directors: George Paz, Chair.; Gary G. Benanav; Maura C. Breen; William J. DeLaney; Nicholas J. LaHowchic; Thomas P. Mac Mahon; Frank Mergenthaler; Woodrow A. Myers, Jr., M.D.; John O. Parker, Jr.; William L. Roper, M.D.; Samuel Skinner; Seymour Sternberg
International operations: Canada
Historic mergers: Medco Health Solutions, Inc. (April 2, 2012)
Giving statement: Giving through the Express Scripts Foundation.
Company EIN: 452884094

Express Scripts Foundation

1 Express Way
St. Louis, MO 63121-1824
E-mail: ExpressScriptsCares@easymatch.com; URL: http://www.express-scripts.com/aboutus/ citizenship/corp_giving.shtml

Establishment information: Established in 2002 in MO.
Donor: Express Scripts, Inc.
Financial data (yr. ended 12/31/11): Assets, $16,520,347 (M); expenditures, $1,285,044; qualifying distributions, $1,146,015; giving activities include $1,146,015 for grants.
Purpose and activities: The foundation supports programs designed to provide access to health and medical services for those in need; educate underserved youth to prepare them for success; provide services to U.S. military troops and their families; strengthen communities by aiding youth and families in need; and support education programs designed to prepare students for careers in pharmacy.
Fields of interest: Arts; Elementary/secondary education; Higher education; Medical school/ education; Education, reading; Education; Medicine/medical care, public education; Pharmacy/prescriptions; Public health; Health care, insurance; Health care, patient services; Health care; Children/youth, services; Children, services; Family services; Mathematics; Science; Military/ veterans' organizations Children; Military/veterans.
Program:
Employee Matching Gifts: The foundation matches contributions made by employees of Express Scripts to educational institutions up to $1,000 per employee, per year.
Type of support: Capital campaigns; Continuing support; Employee matching gifts; General/ operating support; Program development.
Geographic limitations: Giving primarily in areas of company operations, with emphasis on St. Louis, MO.
Support limitations: No support for discriminatory organizations, political candidates or organizations, social clubs, or athletic teams. No grants to individuals, or for political causes or campaigns, fundraising activities, benefits, charitable dinners, galas, or endowments or capital campaigns.
Publications: Annual report; Application guidelines; Program policy statement.
Application information: Applications accepted. Support is limited to 1 contribution per organization during any given year. Multi-year funding is not automatic. Organizations receiving support are asked to provide status reports and a final report. Application form required.
Initial approach: Complete online application form
Deadline(s): None
Officers and Directors:* James E. McCleod, Ph.D., Chair. and Pres.; Larry Zarin*, V.P.; Martin P. Akins, Secy.; Matt Harper, Treas.; Susan Schlichter, Exec. Dir.; Chip Casteel; Mimi Hirshberg; Susan Lang.
Number of staff: 1 part-time support.
EIN: 020566229
Selected grants: The following grants are a representative sample of this grantmaker's funding activity:
$119,960 to University of Missouri, Saint Louis, MO, 2010.
$100,000 to University of Missouri, Saint Louis, MO, 2010. For capital campaign.
$88,632 to American Red Cross, Saint Louis, MO, 2010. To match donations for Haiti.
$75,000 to March of Dimes Birth Defects Foundation, Saint Louis, MO, 2010.
$50,000 to Parents as Teachers National Center, Saint Louis, MO, 2010.
$50,000 to YMCA of Greater Saint Louis, Saint Louis, MO, 2010.
$40,000 to Operation Food Search, Saint Louis, MO, 2010.
$39,300 to American Heart Association, Saint Louis, MO, 2010.
$35,000 to Family Support Network, Saint Louis, MO, 2010.
$30,000 to Christian Hospital Foundation, Saint Louis, MO, 2010.

1314
Extendicare Health Services, Inc.

111 W. Michigan St.
Milwaukee, WI 53203-2903
(414) 908-8000

Company URL: http://www.extendicare.com/ index.aspx
Establishment information: Established in 1985.
Company type: Subsidiary of a foreign company
Business activities: Provides nursing and personal care services.
Business type (SIC): Nursing and personal care facilities
Corporate officers: Timothy L. Lukenda, Chair. and C.E.O.; Douglas J. Harris, Sr. V.P., Treas., and C.F.O.; David Pearce, V.P. and Genl. Counsel; Jillian E. Fountain, Corp. Secy.
Board of director: Timothy L. Lukenda, Chair.
Giving statement: Giving through the Extendicare Foundation, Inc.

Extendicare Foundation, Inc.

(formerly Unicare Foundation, Inc.)
c/o Tax Dept.
111 W. Michigan St.
Milwaukee, WI 53203-2903 (414) 908-8230
E-mail: lnelson@extendicare.com; URL: http:// www.extendicarefoundation.org/index.html

Establishment information: Established in 1985 in WI.
Donors: Extendicare Health Services, Inc.; Action Building Contractors; Paramount Painting & Services, Inc.; Service Painting Corporation; US Bank; Health Care Services Group; KCI; Walker Dunlop.
Contact: LaRae Nelson, Pres. and Dir.
Financial data (yr. ended 12/31/11): Assets, $889,321 (M); gifts received, $333,464; expenditures, $171,070; qualifying distributions, $167,320; giving activities include $162,478 for grants.
Purpose and activities: The foundation supports programs designed to address Alzheimer's, including research, education, and informational services; improve the quality of life or quality of care within nursing and rehabilitation centers; and educate caregivers on long-term care.
Fields of interest: Health care, management/ technical assistance; Health care, patient services; Alzheimer's disease; Alzheimer's disease research.
Type of support: Curriculum development; Program development; Research; Seed money.
Geographic limitations: Giving primarily in areas of company operations in MN and WI.
Support limitations: No support for political organizations or for-profit organizations. No grants to individuals, or for capital campaigns, fundraising, administrative or overhead costs, or general operating support.
Publications: Application guidelines.
Application information: Applications accepted. Application form required. Applicants should submit the following:
1) results expected from proposed grant
2) statement of problem project will address
3) population served
4) copy of IRS Determination Letter
5) brief history of organization and description of its mission
6) copy of most recent annual report/audited financial statement/990
7) how project's results will be evaluated or measured
8) listing of board of directors, trustees, officers and other key people and their affiliations
9) detailed description of project and amount of funding requested
10) copy of current year's organizational budget and/or project budget

Initial approach: Request application form
Copies of proposal: 1
Board meeting date(s): Quarterly
Deadline(s): Request application form
Officers and Directors:* LaRae Nelson*, Pres.; Lisa Behling*, Secy.; Scott Miller*, Treas.; Sandy Cunningham; Tony Evers; Patti Roche; Mary Spinella; Peter Swenson; Janet Watton; Kay Weidner.
EIN: 391549381
Selected grants: The following grants are a representative sample of this grantmaker's funding activity:

$40,895 to Medical College of Wisconsin, Milwaukee, WI, 2010.
$11,000 to Alzheimers Foundation of America, New York, NY, 2010.
$10,000 to Medical College of Wisconsin, Milwaukee, WI, 2010.
$7,500 to National Alliance on Mental Illness Minnesota, Saint Paul, MN, 2010.
$3,500 to Amery Area Senior Citizens, Amery, WI, 2010.

1315
Exxon Mobil Corporation

(formerly Exxon Corporation)
5959 Las Colinas Blvd.
Irving, TX 75039-2298 (972) 444-1000
FAX: (972) 444-1505

Company URL: http://www.exxonmobil.com
Establishment information: Established in 1882.
Company type: Public company
Company ticker symbol and exchange: XOM/NYSE
International Securities Identification Number: US30231G1022
Business activities: Conducts crude oil and natural gas exploration and production activities; manufactures petroleum products; operates crude oil, natural gas, and petroleum product pipelines; manufactures and markets commodity petrochemicals; generates electricity.
Business type (SIC): Petroleum refining; extraction/oil and gas; plastics and synthetics; pipelines (except natural gas/operation of); electric services; gas production and distribution
Financial profile for 2012: Number of employees, 76,900; assets, $333,795,000,000; sales volume, $467,285,000,000; pre-tax net income, $78,726,000,000; expenses, $403,242,000,000; liabilities, $167,932,000,000
Fortune 1000 ranking: 2012—2nd in revenues, 1st in profits, and 17th in assets
Forbes 2000 ranking: 2012—3rd in sales, 1st in profits, and 91st in assets
Corporate officers: Rex W. Tillerson, Chair. and C.E.O.; David. S. Rosenthal, V.P. and Secy.; Robert N. Schleckser, V.P. and Treas.; S. Jack Balagia, V.P. and Genl. Counsel; Patrick T. Mulva, V.P. and Cont.; M. A. Farrant, V.P., Human Resources; K. P. Cohen, V.P., Public Affairs
Board of directors: Rex W. Tillerson, Chair.; Michael J. Boskin; Peter Brabeck-Letmathe; Ursala M. Burns; Larry R. Faulkner; Jay S. Fishman; Henrietta H. Fore; Kenneth C. Frazier; William W. George; Samuel J. Palmisano; Steven S. Reinemund; William C. Weldon; Edward E. Whitacre, Jr.
Subsidiary: Mobil Corporation, Fairfax, VA
Plants: Torrance, CA; Joliet, IL; Baton Rouge, Chalmette, LA; Billings, MT; Baytown, Beaumont, TX
Offices: Houston, TX; Fairfax, VA
International operations: Africa; Argentina; Australia; Austria; Bahamas; Belgium; Brazil; Cameroon; Canada; Cayman Islands; Chad; Chile; China; Colombia; Czech Republic; Ecuador; Egypt; Finland; France; Germany; Guatemala; Guyana; Hong Kong; Hungary; India; Indonesia; Ireland; Italy; Japan; Kazakhstan; Kuwait; Luxembourg; Malaysia; Mexico; Middle East; Netherlands; New Zealand; Nigeria; Norway; Paraguay; Peru; Philippines; Poland; Portugal; Qatar; Russia; Saudi Arabia; Singapore; Slovakia; Spain; Suriname; Sweden; Switzerland; Thailand; Turkey; United Kingdom
Historic mergers: XTO Energy Inc. (June 25, 2010)
Giving statement: Giving through the Exxon Mobil Corporation Contributions Program and the ExxonMobil Foundation.
Company EIN: 135409005

Exxon Mobil Corporation Contributions Program

(formerly Exxon Corporation Contributions Program)
c/o Corp. Contribs.
5959 Las Colinas Blvd.
Irving, TX 75039-2298 (972) 444-1106
FAX: (972) 444-1405; URL: http://www.exxonmobil.com/community

Contact: Bill Carpenter, Budget and Fdn. Support Analyst
Financial data (yr. ended 12/31/10): Total giving, $126,845,437, including $126,845,437 for grants.
Purpose and activities: As a complement to its foundation, Exxon Mobil also makes charitable contributions to nonprofit organizations directly. Support is given on a national and international basis.
Fields of interest: Elementary/secondary education; Higher education; Education; Environment; Health care Minorities; Women; Girls.
International interests: Africa; Asia; Canada; Caribbean; Europe; Latin America; Middle East.
Type of support: Employee matching gifts; Employee volunteer services; Fellowships; General/operating support; Sponsorships.
Geographic limitations: Giving on a national and international basis in areas of company operations, with emphasis on Baldwin and Mobile County, AL, Anchorage, AK, Torrance, CA, Cortez, CO, Washington, DC, Joliet, IL, Kingman, KS, Baton Rouge and Chalmette, LA, Billings, MT, Clinton, Edison, Paulsboro, and the Linden, NJ, area, Rochester, NY, Baytown, Dallas, Fort Worth, Longview, Midland, Odessa, and the Houston, TX, area, Fairfax County, VA, Lincoln, Sublette, and Sweetwater counties, WY, and in Africa, Canada, the Caribbean, Europe, the Far East, Latin America, and the Middle East; giving also to national organizations.
Support limitations: No support for political or religious organizations or United Way-supported organizations; low priority for disease-specific organizations. No grants to individuals, or for endowments.
Publications: Annual report; Corporate giving report; Grants list.
Application information: Applications not accepted. Contributes only to pre-selected organizations. The Public Affairs Department handles giving. The company has a staff that only handles contributions.
Number of staff: 6 full-time professional; 4 full-time support.

ExxonMobil Foundation

5959 Las Colinas Blvd.
Irving, TX 75039-2298
URL: http://www.exxonmobil.com/Corporate/community_foundation.aspx

Establishment information: Incorporated in 1955 in NJ as Esso Education Foundation; name changed to Exxon Education Foundation in 1972; name changed to ExxonMobil Foundation in 1999.
Donors: Exxon Corp.; Exxon Mobil Corp.
Contact: Patrick McCarthy, Exec. Dir.
Financial data (yr. ended 12/31/11): Assets, $67,519,757 (M); gifts received, $67,988,677; expenditures, $74,767,234; qualifying distributions, $74,749,355; giving activities include $44,132,359 for grants and $30,375,238 for employee matching gifts.
Purpose and activities: The foundation supports organizations involved with education, the environment, endangered species and habitats, health, medical research, human services, community development, civic affairs, and women. Special emphasis is directed toward programs designed to provide mathematics, engineering, science, and technology education. Support is given primarily in areas of company operations; giving also to national and international organizations.
Fields of interest: Higher education; Engineering school/education; Education; Environment, natural resources; Environment; Animals/wildlife, endangered species; Health care; Parasitic diseases; Medical research; Human services; Economic development; Business/industry; Community/economic development; Science, formal/general education; Mathematics; Public policy, research; Public affairs Women.
International interests: Africa; Developing countries.

Programs:

Cultural Matching Gift Program: The foundation matches contributions made by employees, retirees, directors, and widowed spouses of former employees of Exxon Mobil to nonprofit organizations involved with arts and culture on a one-for-one basis from $20 to $2,000 per contributor, per year.

Education: The foundation supports programs designed to provide fundamental education and literacy in developing countries; and improve science, technology, engineering, and mathematics education in countries where basic education levels have been achieved.

Educational Matching Gift Program: The foundation matches contributions made by employees and annuitants of Exxon Mobil and certain of its consolidated affiliates to institutions of higher education, the United Negro College Fund, the American Indian College Fund, and the National Hispanic Scholarship Fund on a three-for-one basis up to $7,500 per contributor, per year.

Environment: The foundation supports programs designed to encourage informed public discussion of sound environmental policy alternatives and the study and preservation of endangered species and habitats.

ExxonMobil Malaria Initiative: The foundation, in partnership with Exxon Mobil, local institutions, and international NGOs supports programs designed to fight malaria. Special emphasis is directed toward programs designed to improve the delivery and use of prevention tools such as bed nets; provide technical assistance to help countries increase their capacity to control malaria; and facilitate the monitoring and progress through integrated communications.

ExxonMobil Women's Economic Opportunity: The foundation, in partnership with ExxonMobil, supports programs designed to help women fulfill their economic potential and create economic and social change in their communities. Special emphasis is directed toward programs designed to develop women entrepreneurs and business leaders through skills development training, mentoring, and businesswomen's networks; create opportunities for women's economic participation through advocacy and research initiatives; and identify and deploy technologies that accelerate women's economic advancement through high-impact and sustainable innovations, research, and sharing best practices.

Volunteer Involvement Program (VIP): The foundation awards $500 grants to nonprofit organizations with which employees and retirees of Exxon Mobil volunteer at least 20 hours per year.

Type of support: Employee matching gifts; Employee volunteer services; General/operating support; Program development.
Geographic limitations: Giving on national and international basis, primarily in areas of company

operations in Baldwin and Mobile counties, AL, Anchorage, Fairbanks, and North Slope, AK, Santa Barbara County and Torrance, CA, Cortez and Rio Blanco County, CO, Washington, DC, LaGrange, GA, Joliet, IL, Baton Rouge, Chalmette, and Grand Isle, LA, Billings, MT, Clinton and Paulsboro, NJ, Rochester, NY, Akron, OH, Shawnee and Texas County, OK, Baytown, Beaumont, Dallas, Fort Worth, Houston, Midland, Odessa, and Tyler, TX, San Juan County, UT, Fairfax County and northern VA, and Lincoln, Sublette, and Sweetwater counties, WY; giving also to national and international organizations.
Support limitations: No support for political or religious organizations or youth sports organizations. No grants to individuals, or for institutional scholarship or fellowship programs, capital campaigns, land acquisition, equipment, renovation projects, endowments, athletics, or scholarships; no loans.
Publications: Annual report; Corporate giving report; Grants list.
Application information: Applications not accepted. Contributes only to pre-selected organizations.
Officers and Trustees:* K. P. Cohen*, Chair.; Suzanne M. McCarron, Pres.; N. H. Jenkins, Secy.; L. M. Rubin, Treas.; B. A. Babock, Cont.; Patrick McCarthy, Exec. Dir.; L. M. Lachenmyer; J. M. Spellings; E. White; J. J. Woodbury.
Number of staff: 5 part-time professional; 3 part-time support.
EIN: 136082357
Selected grants: The following grants are a representative sample of this grantmaker's funding activity:
$1,750,000 to National Science Teachers Association, Arlington, VA, 2011. For Mickelson ExxonMobil (EM) Teachers Academies designed to provide third- through fifth-grade teachers with the knowledge and skills necessary to motivate students to pursue careers in science and math.
$1,655,000 to Centre for Development and Population Activities, Washington, DC, 2011. For Global Women in Management Initiative, which strengthens women's management, leadership and technical skills to enhance and bring to scale programs that advance women's economic opportunities and build the next generation of women business leaders and entrepreneurs.
$1,500,000 to Cherie Blair Foundation for Women, London, England, 2011. For Mobil Phone Technology Study in Nigeria, Saudi Arabia and Indonesia.
$1,000,000 to Malaria No More, New York, NY, 2011. For malaria advocacy and prevention work in Chad and Cameroon.
$653,850 to MediSend International, Dallas, TX, 2011. To provide biomedical training.
$600,000 to Harris Foundation, Houston, TX, 2011. For administration of Bernard Harris Summer Science Camp.
$300,000 to Harvard University, Cambridge, MA, 2011. For Closing the Global Gender Gap.
$250,000 to Business Coalition Against Malaria, Tuberculosis and HIV/AIDS in Cameroon, Douala, Cameroon, 2011. For malaria prevention in the workplace.
$35,000 to Houston Museum of Natural Science, Houston, TX, 2011. For ExxonMobil Teacher Tuesday.
$25,000 to Vital Voices Global Partnership, Washington, DC, 2011. To support La Pietra Coalition, initiative to advance women and the world.

1316
Exygy, LLC

576 Natoma
San Francisco, CA 94103-2825
(415) 992-7251
FAX: (415) 723-7899

Company URL: http://exygy.com/partners/
Company type: Private company
Business type (SIC): Business services/ miscellaneous
Corporate officer: Zachary Berke, C.E.O.
Giving statement: Giving through the Exygy, LLC Contributions Program.

Exygy, LLC Contributions Program

576 Natoma
San Francisco, CA 94103-2825
E-mail: hello.there@exygy.com; URL: http://exygy.com/partners/

Purpose and activities: Exygy, is a certified B Corporation that donates a percentage of profits to charitable organizations.

1317
The Eyak Corporation

901 LeFevre St.
P.O. Box 340
Cordova, AK 99574 (907) 424-7161

Company URL: http://www.eyakcorporation.com
Establishment information: Established in 1973.
Company type: Native corporation
Business activities: Operates native corporation.
Business type (SIC): Nonclassifiable establishments
Financial profile for 2009: Number of employees, 270
Corporate officers: Jim Ujioka, Chair.; Rod Worl, C.E.O.; Nancy Barnes, Pres.; Brennan Cain, V.P. and Genl. Counsel; Tor Daley, V.P., Finance; Steve Donaldson, Treas.; Mark Truog, Cont.
Board of directors: Jim Ujioka, Chair.; Nancy Barnes; Jason Barnes; Roxanne Dolfi; Steve Donaldson; Sylvia Lange; Jim McDaniel; Jerry O'Brien, Jr.; Martin Parsons
Office: Anchorage, AK
Giving statement: Giving through the Eyak Foundation.

The Eyak Foundation

(formerly Cordova Native Foundation)
360 W. Benson Blvd., Ste. 210
Anchorage, AK 99503-3953 (907) 334-3940
E-mail: info@eyakfoundation.org; URL: http://www.eyakfoundation.org/

Establishment information: Established in 1997 in AK.
Donors: The Eyak Corp.; Eyak Technology, LLC.
Financial data (yr. ended 12/31/11): Assets, $1,096,220 (M); gifts received, $452,856; expenditures, $85,614; qualifying distributions, $41,775; giving activities include $41,775 for grants.
Purpose and activities: The foundation awards scholarships for college and vocational training to Alaska Native shareholders and lineal descendants of shareholders of Eyak Corporation.
Fields of interest: Higher education.
Type of support: Scholarships—to individuals.
Geographic limitations: Giving primarily in Cordova, AK.
Publications: Application guidelines; Grants list.
Application information: Applications accepted. Application form required.
Requests should include proof of lineal descent of a original Eyak Corp. shareholder, 2 letters of reference, high school or college transcripts, typed personal history and education goal essay, a letter of acceptance to a two- or four-year college or graduate degree program, course description and requirements of institution for full-time students, and a recent wallet size photo.
Initial approach: Download application form and mail to foundation
Deadline(s): Mar. 15 for spring; Oct. 31 for fall
Officers and Directors: Jim Ujioka, Pres.; Melissa Zelinger, V.P.; Barbara Sappah, Secy.; Bernice Smith-Galloway, Treas.; Glen Buchta; Steve Donaldson.
EIN: 920161386

1318
F.N.B. Corporation

(formerly Omega Financial Corporation)
1 F.N.B. Blvd.
Hermitage, PA 16148 (724) 981-6000

Company URL: http://www.fnbcorporation.com/corporateHome/
Establishment information: Established in 1974.
Company type: Public company
Company ticker symbol and exchange: FNB/NYSE
Business activities: Operates financial holding company; provides community banking, wealth management, insurance, and consumer finance products and services to consumers and small businesses.
Business type (SIC): Banks/commercial; holding company
Financial profile for 2012: Number of employees, 3,015; assets, $12,023,980,000; pre-tax net income, $154,180,000; liabilities, $10,621,910,000
Corporate officers: Stephen J. Gurgovits, Sr., Chair.; Vincent J. Delie, Jr., Pres. and C.E.O.; Vincent J. Calabrese, C.F.O.; David B. Mogle, Sr. V.P. and Secy.; Scott D. Free, Sr. V.P. and Treas.; Timothy G. Rubritz, Sr. V.P. and Corp. Cont.
Board of directors: Stephen J. Gurgovits, Sr., Chair.; William B. Campbell; Vincent J. Delie, Jr.; Philip E. Gingerich; Robert B. Goldstein; Dawne S. Hickton; David J. Malone; D. Stephen Martz; Robert J. McCarthy, Jr.; Harry F. Radcliffe; Arthur J. Rooney II; John W. Rose; Stanton R. Sheetz; William J. Strimbu; Earl K. Wahl, Jr.
Giving statement: Giving through the Omega Financial Corporation Charitable Foundation.
Company EIN: 251255406

Omega Financial Corporation Charitable Foundation

c/o First National Bank Of Pennsylvania
1 F.N.B. Blvd.
Hermitage, PA 16148 (814) 272-4113

Establishment information: Established in 2002 in PA.
Donors: Omega Financial Corp.; Central Pennsylvania Investment Company.
Contact: Kelly Camden
Financial data (yr. ended 12/31/11): Assets, $41,169 (M); expenditures, $1,500; qualifying distributions, $0.

Purpose and activities: The foundation supports history museums and libraries and organizations involved with performing arts, higher education, and health.
Fields of interest: Museums (natural history); Performing arts; Performing arts, theater; Higher education; Libraries (public); Libraries (school); Hospitals (general); Health care, EMS; Health care.
Type of support: Capital campaigns; General/operating support.
Geographic limitations: Giving primarily in the State College, PA, area.
Support limitations: No grants to individuals.
Application information: Applications accepted. Application form required. Applicants should submit the following:
1) name, address and phone number of organization
2) brief history of organization and description of its mission
3) detailed description of project and amount of funding requested
Initial approach: Proposal
Deadline(s): None
Board Member: Bruce ERB; Kim Graig; Bob Heiple; Matt Stever.
EIN: 756672711

1319
Faber Brothers, Inc.
4141 S. Pulaski Rd.
Chicago, IL 60632 (773) 376-9300
FAX: (773) 376-0732

Establishment information: Established in 1959.
Company type: Private company
Business activities: Sells sporting goods wholesale.
Business type (SIC): Durable goods—wholesale
Corporate officers: Arthur Shapiro, Co-Chair.; Lois Shapiro, Co-Chair.; Wayne J. Kozlowski, Pres.; Mark Davis, C.F.O.; Mishka Snowsky, V.P. and Secy.-Treas.
Board of directors: Arthur Shapiro, Co-Chair.; Lois Shapiro, Co-Chair.
Giving statement: Giving through the Faber Foundation.

Faber Foundation
1000 Lake Shore Plaza, 26A
Chicago, IL 60611-5149 (312) 280-0086

Donors: Faber Brother, Inc.; Shapiro Family, L.P.
Contact: Lois Shapiro, Pres.
Financial data (yr. ended 12/31/11): Assets, $92,561 (M); gifts received, $5,000; expenditures, $16,189; qualifying distributions, $15,315; giving activities include $15,315 for grants.
Purpose and activities: The foundation supports organizations involved with arts and culture, conservation, and Judaism.
Fields of interest: Arts; Human services; Religion.
Type of support: General/operating support.
Geographic limitations: Giving primarily in Chicago, IL.
Support limitations: No grants to individuals.
Application information: Applications accepted. Application form not required. Applicants should submit the following:
1) copy of IRS Determination Letter
2) brief history of organization and description of its mission
3) detailed description of project and amount of funding requested
Initial approach: Letter
Deadline(s): None
Officers: Lois Shapiro, Pres.; Arthur Shapiro, Treas.
Director: Mishka Snowsky.
EIN: 366150287

1320
Fabiano Brothers, Inc.
1219 N. Mission Rd.
Mount Pleasant, MI 48858-4690
(989) 773-3605

Company URL: http://www.fabianobrothers.com
Establishment information: Established in 1969.
Company type: Private company
Business activities: Sells alcoholic beverages wholesale.
Business type (SIC): Beer, wine, and distilled beverages—wholesale
Corporate officers: James C. Fabiano, Pres.; Gerard Witte, C.F.O.; Wendy Shugert, Human Resources
Giving statement: Giving through the Fabiano Foundation.

Fabiano Foundation
1885 Bevanda Ct.
Bay City, MI 48706

Establishment information: Established in 1997 in MI.
Donor: Fabiano Brothers, Inc.
Financial data (yr. ended 12/31/11): Assets, $1,272,655 (M); gifts received, $100,000; expenditures, $237,400; qualifying distributions, $237,000; giving activities include $237,000 for grants.
Purpose and activities: The foundation supports organizations involved with historical activities, education, children services, and Catholicism.
Fields of interest: Historical activities; Secondary school/education; Higher education; Education; YM/YWCAs & YM/YWHAs; Children, services; Catholic agencies & churches.
Type of support: Capital campaigns; General/operating support.
Geographic limitations: Giving primarily in areas of company operations in MI.
Support limitations: No grants to individuals.
Application information: Applications not accepted. Contributes only to pre-selected organizations.
Officers: James C. Fabiano, Pres. and Treas.; James C. Fabiano II, V.P.; Joseph R. Fabiano II, V.P.; Evangeline L. Fabiano, Secy.
EIN: 383324462
Selected grants: The following grants are a representative sample of this grantmaker's funding activity:
$50,000 to Northwood University, Midland, MI, 2010.

1321
John Fabick Tractor Company
1 Fabick Dr.
Fenton, MO 63026-2928 (636) 343-5900

Company URL: http://www.fabickcat.com
Establishment information: Established in 1917.
Company type: Private company
Business activities: Sells construction and mining equipment.
Business type (SIC): Industrial machinery and equipment—wholesale
Financial profile for 2010: Number of employees, 380
Corporate officers: Harry Fabick, Chair. and C.E.O.; Douglas R. Fabick, Pres.; Scott R. Borlinghaus, V.P. and C.F.O.; Dave Kramer, Secy.-Treas.
Board of director: Harry Fabick, Chair.
Subsidiaries: Fabick & Co., Fenton, MO; Fabick Brothers Equipment, Fenton, MO; Fabick Machinery, Fenton, MO; Fabick Tractor, Fenton, MO
Giving statement: Giving through the Fabick Charitable Trust, Inc.

Fabick Charitable Trust, Inc.
1 Fabick Dr.
Fenton, MO 63026-2928 (636) 343-5900

Establishment information: Incorporated in 1969 in MO.
Donor: John Fabick Tractor Co.
Contact: David Kramer
Financial data (yr. ended 12/31/11): Assets, $12,703 (M); gifts received, $275,000; expenditures, $267,772; qualifying distributions, $267,700; giving activities include $267,700 for grants.
Purpose and activities: The foundation supports hospitals and organizations involved with education, disaster relief, human services, and Christianity.
Fields of interest: Theological school/education; Education; Hospitals (general); Disasters, preparedness/services; Boy scouts; Salvation Army; Children/youth, services; Homeless, human services; Human services; Christian agencies & churches; Catholic agencies & churches.
Type of support: General/operating support.
Geographic limitations: Giving primarily in St. Louis, MO.
Support limitations: No grants to individuals.
Application information: Applications accepted. Application form not required. Applicants should submit the following:
1) detailed description of project and amount of funding requested
Initial approach: Letter of inquiry
Copies of proposal: 1
Deadline(s): Oct. 15
Officers: Harry Fabick, Pres.; Scott R. Borlinghaus, Secy.
EIN: 237013262
Selected grants: The following grants are a representative sample of this grantmaker's funding activity:
$50,000 to Cardinal Glennon Childrens Hospital, Saint Louis, MO, 2010. For general support.
$20,000 to Boy Scouts of America, Saint Louis, MO, 2010. For general support.
$20,000 to Catholic Relief Services, Baltimore, MD, 2010. For general support.
$10,200 to Missionaries of the Holy Family, Saint Louis, MO, 2010. For general support.
$5,500 to Little Sisters of the Poor, Saint Louis, MO, 2010. For general support.
$5,000 to Boy Scouts of America, Saint Louis, MO, 2010. For general support.
$3,000 to Holy Childhood Church, Mascoutah, IL, 2010. For general support.
$1,000 to United Way of Greater Saint Louis, Saint Louis, MO, 2010. For general support.

1322
Fabri-Kal Corporation
600 Plastics Pl.
Kalamazoo, MI 49001 (269) 385-5050

Company URL: http://www.fabri-kal.com/
Establishment information: Established in 1950.
Company type: Private company

Business activities: Manufactures plastic food and food service containers.
Business type (SIC): Plastic products/ miscellaneous; manufacturing/miscellaneous
Financial profile for 2010: Number of employees, 190
Corporate officers: Robert P. Kittredge, Chair. and C.E.O.; Mike Roeder, Pres. and C.O.O.; Gary C. Galia, Exec. V.P., Finance and C.F.O.
Board of director: Robert P. Kittredge, Chair.
Giving statement: Giving through the Fabri-Kal Foundation.

Fabri-Kal Foundation

600 Plastics Pl.
Kalamazoo, MI 49001-4882 (269) 385-5050
URL: http://www.fabri-kal.com/why-fabri-kal/foundation/

Establishment information: Established in 1969 in MI.
Donor: Fabri-Kal Corp.
Contact: Robert P. Kittredge, Pres.
Financial data (yr. ended 12/31/11): Assets, $47 (M); gifts received, $705,797; expenditures, $705,797; qualifying distributions, $705,664; giving activities include $705,664 for grants.
Purpose and activities: The foundation supports health clinics and organizations involved with trailways, family planning, human services, and neighborhood development. Special emphasis is directed toward cultural and educational causes.
Fields of interest: Performing arts, theater; Arts; Higher education; Education; Environment, land resources; Health care, clinics/centers; Reproductive health, family planning; Goodwill Industries; Girl scouts; YM/YWCAs & YM/YWHAs; Aging, centers/services; Human services; Community development, neighborhood development; United Ways and Federated Giving Programs.
Type of support: Building/renovation; Capital campaigns; Employee-related scholarships; Equipment.
Geographic limitations: Giving limited to areas of company operations in Kalamazoo, MI, Hazleton, PA, and Greenville, SC.
Publications: Application guidelines; Grants list.
Application information: Applications accepted. Application form not required.
Initial approach: Proposal
Board meeting date(s): May
Deadline(s): None
Officers: Robert P. Kittredge, Pres.; Gary C. Galia, Exec. V.P., Finance; Bob Weyhing, Secy.
EIN: 237003366
Selected grants: The following grants are a representative sample of this grantmaker's funding activity:
$38,444 to United Way of Greater Hazleton, Hazleton, PA, 2011.
$28,930 to United Way of Greenville County, Greenville, SC, 2011.
$7,500 to Arts Council of Greater Kalamazoo, Kalamazoo, MI, 2011.
$5,000 to YMCA and Outdoor Center, Sherman Lake, Augusta, MI, 2011.
$4,000 to Residential Opportunities, Kalamazoo, MI, 2011.
$2,000 to MRC Industries, Kalamazoo, MI, 2011.
$1,000 to Heritage Community of Kalamazoo, Kalamazoo, MI, 2011.

1323
Factory Mutual Insurance Company

(doing business as FM Global)
270 Central Ave.
P.O. Box 7500
Johnston, RI 02919-4923 (401) 275-3000

Company URL: http://www.fmglobal.com
Establishment information: Established in 1835.
Company type: Mutual company
Business activities: Provides engineering and research services.
Business type (SIC): Engineering, architectural, and surveying services; professional membership organization; research, development, and testing services
Financial profile for 2011: Number of employees, 5,152; assets, $14,258,200,000; sales volume, $3,658,400,000
Fortune 1000 ranking: 2012—541st in revenues, 247th in profits, and 278th in assets
Corporate officers: Shivan S. Subramaniam, Chair. and C.E.O.; Ruud H. Bosman, Vice-Chair.; Jefferey A. Burchilli, Sr. V.P., Finance; Enzo Rebula, Sr. V.P., Human Resources; William A. Merkrut, V.P. and Treas.
Board of directors: Shivan S. Subramaniam, Chair.; Ruud H. Bosman, Vice-Chair.; Walter J. Galvin; Mary L. Howell; John A. Luke, Jr.; Gracia C. Martore; Robert J. O'Toole; Christine M. McCarthy; Jonathan D. Mariner; John R. Paloian; David Pulman; Edward J. Rapp; Elisabeth M. Struckell; James C. Thyen; Alfred J. Verrecchia
Offices: Concord, Orange, CA; Norcross, GA; Hoffman Estates, IL; Livonia, MI; Minneapolis, MN; Earth City, MO; Florham Park, NJ; Charlotte, NC; North Olmstead, OH; Bala Cynwyd, Pittsburgh, PA; Dallas, TX; Bellevue, WA; Milwaukee, WI
International operations: Canada; United Kingdom
Giving statement: Giving through the FM Global Corporate Giving Program and the FM Global Foundation.

FM Global Corporate Giving Program

c/o Fire Prevention Grants
270 Central Ave.
P.O. Box 7500
Johnston, RI 02919-4923
E-mail: firepreventiongrants@fmglobal.com;
URL: http://www.fmglobal.com/page.aspx?id=01060200

Purpose and activities: As a complement to its foundation, FM Global also makes charitable contributions to nonprofit organizations directly. Support is given on a national and international basis.
Fields of interest: Disasters, fire prevention/ control.
Program:
FM Global Fire Prevention Grant Program: FM Global supports programs designed to combat fire. Special emphasis is directed toward a wide array of fire prevention, preparedness, and control efforts, including: 1) Pre-fire planning for commercial, industrial and institutional facilities; 2) Fire and arson prevention and investigation; and 3) Fire prevention education and training programs.
Type of support: Seed money.
Geographic limitations: Giving on a national and international basis.
Application information: Applications accepted. Application form required.
Initial approach: Download application form and mail to headquarters
Deadline(s): None

FM Global Foundation

(formerly Allendale Insurance Foundation)
270 Central Ave.
P.O. Box 7500
Johnston, RI 02919-4923
URL: http://www.fmglobal.com/page.aspx?id=01060100

Establishment information: Established in 1986 in RI.
Donors: Allendale Mutual Insurance Co.; Factory Mutual Insurance Co.
Financial data (yr. ended 12/31/11): Assets, $9,224,016 (M); gifts received, $42,000; expenditures, $3,891,876; qualifying distributions, $3,733,624; giving activities include $2,357,006 for 23 grants (high: $876,971) and $1,349,044 for 1,508 foundation-administered programs.
Purpose and activities: The foundation supports museums and organizations involved with education, human services, community development, and public policy research.
Fields of interest: Museums; Elementary/ secondary education; Scholarships/financial aid; Education; Human services; Economic development, visitors/convention bureau/tourism promotion; Community/economic development; United Ways and Federated Giving Programs; Public policy, research.
International interests: Canada.
Program:
Employee Matching Gift Program: The foundation matches contributions made by employees of FM to eligible charities and other organizations.
Type of support: Employee matching gifts; Employee volunteer services; General/operating support; Scholarship funds.
Geographic limitations: Giving primarily in NJ, RI, WA, and Canada.
Support limitations: No grants to individuals.
Application information: Applications not accepted. Contributes only to pre-selected organizations.
Officers and Directors: Shivan S. Subramaniam*, Chair., C.E.O., and Pres.; Paul E. LaFleche, Sr. V.P., Investments; Nelson G. Wester, V.P. and Secy.; William A. Mekrut*, V.P. and Treas.; John N. Lemieux, V.P.
Trustee: JPMorgan Chase Bank, N.A.
Number of staff: 1
EIN: 222773230
Selected grants: The following grants are a representative sample of this grantmaker's funding activity:
$874,851 to United Way of Rhode Island, Providence, RI, 2010.
$485,284 to United Way of King County, Seattle, WA, 2010.
$364,407 to Educational Testing Service, Ewing, NJ, 2010.
$165,368 to United Ways of New England, Boston, MA, 2010.
$64,638 to United Way of Metropolitan Dallas, Dallas, TX, 2010.
$25,000 to United Way of Rhode Island, Providence, RI, 2010.
$21,400 to University of Notre Dame, Notre Dame, IN, 2010.
$20,000 to Boston Conservatory of Music, Boston, MA, 2010.
$15,100 to North Central College, Naperville, IL, 2010.
$11,500 to Saint Mary Academy-Bay View, Riverside, RI, 2010.

1324
Faegre Baker Daniels LLP
(formerly Baker & Daniels, LLC)
2200 Wells Fargo Ctr.
Minneapolis, MN 55402 (612) 766-7000

Company URL: http://www.faegrebd.com
Establishment information: Established in 1863.
Company type: Private company
Business activities: Operates law firm.
Business type (SIC): Legal services
Corporate officers: Andrew Humphrey, C.E.O.; Thomas Froehle, Jr., C.O.O.
Offices: Washington, DC; Chicago, IL; Fort Wayne, Indianapolis, South Bend, IN
International operations: China
Giving statement: Giving through the Faegre Baker Daniels LLP Corporate Giving Program and the Faegre and Benson Foundation.

Faegre Baker Daniels LLP Corporate Giving Program
(formerly Baker & Daniels LLP Corporate Giving Program)
2200 Wells Fargo Ctr.
90 S. 7th St.
Minneapolis, MN 55402 (612) 766-7000
FAX: (612) 766-1600; Contact for Pro Bono program: Dianne C. Heins, Pro Bono Counsel & Dir. of Pro Bono and Community Service, tel.: (612) 766-7000, e-mail: dianne.heins@FaegreBD.com; URL: http://www.faegrebd.com/Connected-to-the-Community

Fields of interest: Legal services.
Type of support: Employee volunteer services; Pro bono services - legal.
Application information: A Pro Bono Committee manages the pro bono program.

Faegre and Benson Foundation
c/o Michael A. Ponto
90 S. 7th St., Ste. 2200
Minneapolis, MN 55402-3901 (612) 766-7000
URL: http://www.faegre.com/11574

Establishment information: Established in 1993 in MN.
Contact: Michael A. Ponto, Treas.
Financial data (yr. ended 12/31/11): Revenue, $398,500; assets, $2,392 (M); gifts received, $398,500; expenditures, $888,390; giving activities include $872,770 for grants.
Purpose and activities: The foundation supports organizations involved with the judicial system.
Fields of interest: Law school/education; Education; Legal services; Children's rights; United Ways and Federated Giving Programs.
Type of support: Annual campaigns; General/operating support.
Geographic limitations: Giving primarily in areas of company operations, with some emphasis on the Twin Cities metropolitan area; giving also to national organizations.
Support limitations: No support for religious, neighborhood, or lobbying organizations, or service clubs. No grants to individuals, or for fundraising benefits or events.
Publications: Application guidelines.
Application information: Applications accepted. Application form not required. Applicants should submit the following:
1) copy of current year's organizational budget and/or project budget
2) copy of most recent annual report/audited financial statement/990

Initial approach: Proposal
Deadline(s): Early Nov.
Final notification: Dec.

Officers and Directors:* Peggy S. Abram*, Pres.; Richard A. Forschler*, Secy.; Michael A. Ponto*, Treas.; Michael S. McCarthy; Thomas G. Morgan.
EIN: 411766405

1325
Fairfax State Savings Bank
409 Vanderbilt St.
P.O. Box 277
Fairfax, IA 52228-9508 (319) 846-2300

Company URL: http://www.thebankhere.com/a_about.htm
Establishment information: Established in 1924.
Company type: Private company
Business activities: Operates savings bank.
Business type (SIC): Banks/commercial
Corporate officer: David C. Neuhaus, Chair., Pres., and C.E.O.
Board of director: David C. Neuhaus, Chair.
Giving statement: Giving through the Fairfax State Savings Bank Charitable Trust.

Fairfax State Savings Bank Charitable Trust
409 Vanderbilt St.
Fairfax, IA 52228-9508

Establishment information: Established in 1988 in IA.
Donor: Fairfax State Savings Bank.
Financial data (yr. ended 11/30/12): Assets, $604,289 (M); expenditures, $47,932; qualifying distributions, $47,255; giving activities include $47,030 for 19 grants (high: $14,150; low: $500).
Purpose and activities: The trust supports organizations involved with education, health, and human services.
Fields of interest: Education; Health care; Human services.
Type of support: General/operating support.
Geographic limitations: Giving primarily in Cedar Rapids, IA.
Support limitations: No grants to individuals.
Application information: Applications not accepted. Unsolicited requests for funds not accepted.
Trustees: William E. Boland, Jr.; David Neuhaus.
EIN: 421356335

1326
Fairfield National Bank
220 E. Main St.
P.O. Box 429
Fairfield, IL 62837-2002 (618) 842-2107

Company URL: http://www.fairfieldnb.com
Establishment information: Established in 1903.
Company type: Subsidiary of a private company
Business activities: Operates commercial bank.
Business type (SIC): Banks/commercial
Corporate officers: Laurie McClellan, Chair.; Carrie Wick, C.E.O.; Larry Rost, Pres. and C.F.O.
Board of directors: Laurie McClellan, Chair.; Michael Copeland; Richard Curd; Todd Davis; Neal Laws, Jr.; Preston Mathews; Dimitri Monge; Diane Robinson; Larry Rost; William L. Taylor; Kent Vinson
Giving statement: Giving through the Fairfield National Bank Community Foundation.

Fairfield National Bank Community Foundation
P.O. Box 279
Fairfield, IL 62837-0279

Establishment information: Established in 1998 in IL.
Donors: Fairfield National Bank; Mike Copeland.
Financial data (yr. ended 12/31/11): Assets, $667,417 (M); gifts received, $54,050; expenditures, $31,555; qualifying distributions, $30,204; giving activities include $30,204 for grants.
Purpose and activities: The foundation supports hospitals and organizations involved with education, reproductive health, youth development, and day care.
Fields of interest: Education; Health care; Human services.
Type of support: General/operating support; Scholarship funds.
Geographic limitations: Giving limited to Fairfield, IL.
Support limitations: No grants to individuals.
Application information: Applications not accepted. Unsolicited requests for funds not accepted.
Officers and Directors:* Linda Vinson*, Pres.; Linda Monge*, V.P.; Sue Davis*, Secy.-Treas.
EIN: 371379680

1327
Fairmont Speciality
(formerly Ranger Insurance Company)
10350 Richmond Ave., Ste. 300
P.O. Box 2807
Houston, TX 77042 (713) 954-8100

Company URL: http://specialty.fairmontspecialty.com
Company type: Private company
Business activities: Sells property and casualty insurance.
Business type (SIC): Insurance/fire, marine, and casualty
Corporate officers: Marc Adee, Pres.; Nicole Bennett-Smith, C.I.O
Giving statement: Giving through the Ranger-Ryan Scholarship Foundation.

Ranger-Ryan Scholarship Foundation
2850 Lake Vista Dr., Ste. 150
Lewisville, TX 75067 (713) 954-8372

Establishment information: Established in 1990.
Donors: Ranger Insurance Co.; The Sixty Four Foundation.
Financial data (yr. ended 12/31/11): Assets, $88,502 (M); expenditures, $3,000; qualifying distributions, $3,000; giving activities include $3,000 for 6 grants to individuals (high: $500; low: $500).
Purpose and activities: The foundation awards college scholarships to high school graduates who have graduated from Ryan Middle School in Houston, Texas.
Fields of interest: Higher education.
Program:
Scholarships: The foundation awards four-year $1,000 college scholarships to high school graduates who have graduated from Ryan Middle School in Houston, Texas.
Type of support: Scholarships—to individuals.
Geographic limitations: Giving limited to Houston, TX.

Application information: Applications not accepted. Unsolicited requests for funds not accepted.
Officers and Directors:* Marc J. Adee*, Pres.; Loyd R. Godbold, V.P. and Secy.-Treas.; Janelle Hungate.
EIN: 760266492

1328
Fairmount Tire & Rubber, Inc.
618 E. 61st St.
Los Angeles, CA 90001-1021
(323) 750-2840

Company URL: http://www.fairmounttire.com/home.html
Establishment information: Established in 1958.
Company type: Private company
Business activities: Sells automobile tires and allied products.
Business type (SIC): Auto and home supplies—retail
Corporate officer: Gerald A. Sraberg, Pres.
Giving statement: Giving through the Fairmount Tire Charitable Foundation, Inc.

Fairmount Tire Charitable Foundation, Inc.
10960 Wilshire Blvd., Ste. 1100
Los Angeles, CA 90024 (559) 542-2639
Application address: 56816 Aspen Dr., Springville, CA 93265, tel.: (559) 542-2639

Establishment information: Established in 1993 in CA.
Donors: Fairmount Tire & Rubber Inc.; Gerald Sraberg.
Contact: Alvie Kracik
Financial data (yr. ended 12/31/11): Assets, $31,740 (M); expenditures, $4,569; qualifying distributions, $4,569; giving activities include $4,569 for 1 grant.
Purpose and activities: The foundation promotes health and welfare of youth through scholarships to low income students, with emphasis on scholarships to students pursuing a career in nursing.
Fields of interest: Nursing school/education.
Type of support: Scholarship funds; Scholarships—to individuals.
Geographic limitations: Giving limited to the greater Los Angeles, CA, area.
Application information: Applications accepted. Application form required.
Initial approach: Proposal
Deadline(s): None
Officers and Directors:* Gerald Sraberg*, C.E.O.; Ilene Sraberg*, C.F.O.; Bradley Sraberg*, Secy.; Candace M. Sraberg.
EIN: 954424035

1329
The Fallon Company, LLC
1 Marina Park Dr.
Boston, MA 02210-2079 (617) 737-4100

Company URL: http://www.falloncompany.com
Establishment information: Established in 1993.
Company type: Private company
Business activities: Operates commercial real estate development company.
Business type (SIC): Real estate subdividers and developers
Corporate officers: Joseph F. Fallon, Pres. and C.E.O.; Neil F. Abbott, Secy.; Susan G. Fallon, Treas.
Giving statement: Giving through the Fallon Family Charitable Foundation.

Fallon Family Charitable Foundation
c/o The Fallon Co., LLC
1 Marina Park Dr.
Boston, MA 02210

Establishment information: Established in 2007 in MA.
Donor: The Fallon Co., LLC.
Financial data (yr. ended 12/31/11): Assets, $139 (M); gifts received, $51,500; expenditures, $52,040; qualifying distributions, $48,000; giving activities include $45,500 for 4 grants (high: $30,000; low: $500) and $2,500 for 1 grant to an individual.
Fields of interest: Health care.
Type of support: Grants to individuals.
Application information: Applications not accepted. Unsolicited requests for funds not accepted.
Trustees: Graceann B. Cirame; Elizabeth J. Fallon; Michael J. Fallon; Susan G. Fallon.
EIN: 207489163

1330
Family Dollar Stores, Inc.
10401 Monroe Rd.
Matthews, NC 28105 (704) 847-6961

Company URL: http://www.familydollar.com
Establishment information: Established in 1959.
Company type: Public company
Company ticker symbol and exchange: FDO/NYSE
Business activities: Operates a chain of general merchandise retail discount stores.
Business type (SIC): General merchandise stores
Financial profile for 2012: Number of employees, 55,000; assets, $3,373,070,000; sales volume, $9,331,000,000; pre-tax net income, $663,940,000; expenses, $8,642,900,000; liabilities, $2,075,440,000
Fortune 1000 ranking: 2012—287th in revenues, 376th in profits, and 715th in assets
Forbes 2000 ranking: 2012—960th in sales, 1339th in profits, and 1894th in assets
Corporate officers: Howard R. Levine, Chair. and C.E.O.; Michael K. Bloom, Pres. and C.O.O.; Mary A. Winston, Exec. V.P. and C.F.O.; Joshua R. Jewett, Sr. V.P. and C.I.O.; James C. Snyder, Jr., Sr. V.P., Genl. Counsel, and Secy.; Bryan E. Venberg, Sr. V.P., Human Resources
Board of directors: Howard R. Levine, Chair.; Mark R. Bernstein; Pamela L. Davies; Sharon Allred Decker; Edward C. Dolby; Glenn A. Eisenberg; Edward P. Garden; George R. Mahoney, Jr.; James G. Martin; Harvey Morgan; Dale C. Pond
Giving statement: Giving through the Family Dollar Stores, Inc. Corporate Giving Program.
Company EIN: 560942963

Family Dollar Stores, Inc. Corporate Giving Program
10401 Monroe Rd.
Matthews, NC 28105-5349
URL: http://www.familydollar.com/givingback.aspx

Purpose and activities: Family Dollar Stores makes charitable contributions to nonprofit organizations involved with education and health care. Special emphasis is directed toward programs that target low-income and low-middle income families, including senior citizens, minorities and at-risk youth. Support is limited to areas of company operations.
Fields of interest: Food services; Youth development; Youth, services; Family services; Aging, centers/services; Human services Minorities; Economically disadvantaged.
Type of support: General/operating support; Sponsorships.
Geographic limitations: Giving limited to areas of company operations.
Support limitations: No support for religious organizations. No grants to individuals, or for ads in programs, yearbooks or other fundraising vehicles, conferences, seminars, or gala fundraisers.
Publications: Application guidelines.
Application information: Applications accepted. The typical grant is $250 or less. Support is limited to 1 contribution per organization during any given fiscal year (Sept. to Aug.). Family Dollar will not offer additional discounts on its merchandise. Application form required. Applicants should submit the following:
1) name, address and phone number of organization
2) contact person
Applications should include the Tax ID Number of the organization and any applicable guidelines.
Initial approach: Complete online application
Deadline(s): None
Final notification: 6 to 8 weeks

1331
Farella Braun + Martel LLP
Russ Bldg.
235 Montgomery St., 17th Fl.
San Francisco, CA 94104 (415) 954-4400

Company URL: http://www.fbm.com
Establishment information: Established in 1962.
Company type: Private company
Business activities: Operates law firm.
Business type (SIC): Legal services
Offices: Saint Helena, San Francisco, CA
Giving statement: Giving through the Farella Braun + Martel LLP Pro Bono Program.

Farella Braun + Martel LLP Pro Bono Program
Russ Bldg.
235 Montgomery St., 17th Fl.
San Francisco, CA 94104-2902 (415) 954-4400
E-mail: gwon@fbm.com; Additional tel.: (415) 954-4400; URL: http://www.fbm.com/index.cfm/fuseaction/about.probono/probono.cfm

Contact: Grace Won, Pro Bono Partner
Fields of interest: Legal services.
Type of support: Pro bono services - legal.
Geographic limitations: Giving primarily in areas of company operations in Saint Helena and San Francisco, CA.
Application information: An attorney coordinates pro bono projects.

1332
Faribault Foods, Inc.
Campbell Mithun Twr., Ste. 3380
222 S. 9th St.
Minneapolis, MN 55402 (612) 333-6461
FAX: (612) 342-2908

Company URL: http://www.faribaultfoods.com
Establishment information: Established in 1895.
Company type: Private company
Business activities: Produces and markets canned vegetables, dry beans, pastas, and prepared foods.
Business type (SIC): Specialty foods/canned, frozen, and preserved; food and kindred products; miscellaneous prepared foods
Financial profile for 2010: Number of employees, 510
Corporate officers: Reid V. MacDonald, Pres. and C.E.O.; Scott King, Exec. V.P., Opers.; Frank Lynch, Exec. V.P., Sales and Mktg.; Mark Hentges, C.F.O.; Jim Lear, V.P., Finance; Jim Noonan, V.P., Sales
Subsidiaries: Butter Kernel Products, Faribault, MN; Kuner-Empson Co., Brighton, CO; Mrs. Grimes Foods, Grimes, IA
Giving statement: Giving through the Faribault Foods, Inc. Corporate Giving Program.

Faribault Foods, Inc. Corporate Giving Program
Campbell Mithum Tower, Ste. 3380
Minneapolis, MN 55402 (612) 333-6461
URL: http://www.faribaultfoods.com/news

Purpose and activities: Faribault Foods makes charitable contributions to nonprofit organizations involved with hunger. Support is given primarily in areas of company operations in Minnesota, and to national organizations.
Fields of interest: Breast cancer; Food services; Food banks.
Type of support: Annual campaigns; Continuing support; Donated products; In-kind gifts; Sponsorships.
Geographic limitations: Giving primarily in areas of company operations in MN; giving also to national organizations.

1333
Farm Capital Services, LLC
63 Indian Pipe Ln.
Concord, MA 01742-4768 (978) 371-7111

Company URL: http://www.farmcapitalservices.com
Establishment information: Established in 1988.
Company type: Private company
Business type (SIC): Business services/miscellaneous
Corporate officers: Thomas W. Bird, Partner; Ken Saxon, Partner
Giving statement: Giving through the Farm Capital Services, LLC Contributions Program.

Farm Capital Services, LLC Contributions Program
63 Indian Pipe Ln.
Concord, MA 01742-4768 (978) 371-7111
URL: http://www.farmcapitalservices.com

Purpose and activities: Farm Capital Services is a certified B Corporation that donates a percentage of profits to charitable organizations. Support is given primarily in California and Massachusetts.
Fields of interest: Higher education; Social entrepreneurship; Foundations (community); Venture philanthropy.
Type of support: General/operating support; Pro bono services - strategic management.
Geographic limitations: Giving primarily in CA and MA.

1334
Farmers & Merchants State Bank
101 W. Jefferson
P.O. Box 29
Winterset, IA 50273 (515) 462-4242
FAX: (515) 462-4246

Company URL: http://www.fmsbiowa.com
Establishment information: Established in 1934.
Company type: Private company
Business activities: Operates commercial bank.
Business type (SIC): Savings institutions
Corporate officer: Shane Pashek, Pres.
Giving statement: Giving through the Farmers & Merchants Development Fund.

Farmers & Merchants Development Fund
c/o Jerrold B. Oliver
P.O. Box 230
Winterset, IA 50273-0230

Donor: Farmers and Merchants Bank & Trust Co.
Financial data (yr. ended 12/31/11): Assets, $1 (M); gifts received, $5,000; expenditures, $2,950; qualifying distributions, $2,600; giving activities include $2,600 for grants.
Purpose and activities: The foundation supports camps and organizations involved with education, diabetes, children, and business promotion.
Type of support: General/operating support.
Geographic limitations: Giving primarily in St. Charles and Winterset, IA.
Support limitations: No grants to individuals.
Application information: Applications not accepted. Unsolicited requests for funds not accepted.
Trustees: Jerrold B. Oliver; Farmers Merchants Bank.
EIN: 421266563

1335
Farmers Alliance Mutual Insurance Co.
(also known as Farmers Alliance Companies)
1122 N. Main St.
P.O. Box 1401
McPherson, KS 67460-1401
(620) 241-2200

Company URL: http://www.fami.com
Establishment information: Established in 1888.
Company type: Mutual company
Business activities: Sells property and casualty insurance.
Business type (SIC): Insurance/fire, marine, and casualty
Corporate officers: L. Keith Birkhead, Chair., Pres., and C.E.O.; John M. Rader, Exec. V.P. and C.O.O.; Andy Edwardson, V.P. and C.I.O.; Greg McCullough, V.P., Human Resources; Paul Taliaferro, V.P. and Treas.
Board of directors: L. Keith Birkhead, Chair.; Robert M. Alexander; R. J. Breidenthal, Jr.; Sheila Frahm; Joe F. Jenkins II; Joseph W. Jeter; James L. Ketcherside; Eric J. Larson; Marilyn Pauly; Brett A. Reber; Harold W. Walters; Larry E. Williams
Subsidiaries: Alliance Indemnity Co., McPherson, KS; Alliance Insurance Co., Inc., McPherson, KS; Blakely Crop Hail Inc., Topeka, KS; North Central Crop Insurance, Inc., Eau Claire, WI
Giving statement: Giving through the Farmers Alliance Companies Charitable Foundation.

Farmers Alliance Companies Charitable Foundation
(formerly Alliance Companies Charitable Foundation)
1122 N. Main St.
McPherson, KS 67460-2846 (620) 241-2200

Establishment information: Established in 1996 in KS.
Donors: Farmers Alliance Mutual Insurance Company; Joe F. Jenkins II; Dale J. Sondergard.
Contact: L. Keith Birkhead, Pres.
Financial data (yr. ended 12/31/11): Assets, $936,837 (M); gifts received, $196,500; expenditures, $38,696; qualifying distributions, $35,400; giving activities include $35,400 for grants.
Purpose and activities: The foundation supports organizations involved with higher education, insurance education, health, and human services.
Fields of interest: Higher education; Health care; American Red Cross; YM/YWCAs & YM/YWHAs; Business/industry.
Type of support: General/operating support; Scholarship funds.
Geographic limitations: Giving primarily in KS.
Application information: Applications accepted. Additional information may be required at a later date. Application form required.
Initial approach: Letter of inquiry
Deadline(s): None
Officers: L. Keith Birkhead, Pres.; Sue A. Howard, Secy.; W. Paul Taliaferro, Treas.
EIN: 481172871

1336
Farmers and Merchants Trust Company of Chambersburg
(also known as F & M Trust Company)
20 S. Main St.
P.O. Box 6010
Chambersburg, PA 17201-2202
(717) 264-6116

Company URL: http://www.fmtrustonline.com
Establishment information: Established in 1906.
Company type: Subsidiary of a public company
Business activities: Operates commercial bank.
Business type (SIC): Banks/commercial
Corporate officers: G. Warren Elliott, Chair.; William E. Snell, Jr., Pres. and C.E.O.; Mark R. Hollar, Sr. V.P. and C.F.O.
Board of director: G. Warren Elliott, Chair.
Giving statement: Giving through the F & M Trust Company Scholarship Program Trust.

F & M Trust Company Scholarship Program Trust

P.O. Box 6010
Chambersburg, PA 17201-6010 (717) 264-6116

Establishment information: Established in 2004 in PA.
Financial data (yr. ended 12/31/11): Assets, $137,455 (M); expenditures, $4,709; qualifying distributions, $3,227; giving activities include $2,900 for 3 grants (high: $1,500; low: $700).
Purpose and activities: The foundation awards college scholarships to children of employees of Farmers & Merchants Trust Co.
Fields of interest: Higher education.
Type of support: Employee-related scholarships.
Geographic limitations: Giving primarily in PA.
Application information: Applications not accepted. Contributes only through employee-related scholarships.
Trustee: Farmers & Merchants Trust Company of Chambersburg.
EIN: 256823291

1337
Farmers Electric Cooperative, Inc. of New Mexico

(also known as FEC)
3701 N. Thornton St.
P.O. Box 550
Clovis, NM 88101-3452 (505) 762-4466

Company URL: http://www.fecnm.org
Establishment information: Established in 1938.
Company type: Cooperative
Business activities: Generates, transmits, and distributes electricity.
Business type (SIC): Electric services
Corporate officers: Michael B. West, Pres.; Ernest Riley, Secy.-Treas.
Board of directors: Donnie Bidegain; George Dodge, Jr.; Earnest Riley; Billy Tate; Thom Moore; Michael B. West; Pat Woods; Paul Quintana
Giving statement: Giving through the Farmers' Electric Education Foundation.

Farmers' Electric Education Foundation

P.O. Box 550
Clovis, NM 88102-0550 (505) 762-4466
E-mail: thom@fecnm.org; Tel. for Youth Tour Program: (800) 445-8541; URL: http://fecnm.coopwebbuilder.com/content/farmers-electric-education-foundation

Donor: Farmers' Electric Cooperative, Inc. of New Mexico.
Contact: Lance R. Adkins
Financial data (yr. ended 12/31/11): Assets, $781,883 (M); gifts received, $21,908; expenditures, $46,846; qualifying distributions, $45,750; giving activities include $45,750 for grants.
Purpose and activities: The foundation awards college scholarships to members and immediate family members of members of Farmers' Electric Cooperative, Inc. of New Mexico.
Fields of interest: Vocational education; Higher education; Education; Government/public administration.
Programs:
Farmers' Electric Education Foundation Scholarship Fund: The foundation annually awards one-time scholarships of $500 to $750 to active members and the immediate family of active members receiving services from Farmers' Electric Cooperative. Applicants must plan to attend a vocational school, technical school, college, or university and maintain a 2.5 GPA.
Youth Tour: The foundation annually sponsors a contest for high school seniors who are dependents of active members of the cooperative to attend the Government In Action Youth Tour in Washington, DC held in June. The foundation selects two individuals a year and selection is based on series of questions and essay response. Farmers' Electric provides transportation, lodging, meals, and tour expenses.
Type of support: Conferences/seminars; Scholarships—to individuals.
Geographic limitations: Giving primarily in areas of company operations in NM.
Publications: Application guidelines; Grants list.
Application information: Applications accepted. Application form required.
Requests should include transcripts and 2 letters of recommendation.
Initial approach: Download application form and mail to foundation for scholarships; download contest form and e-mail to foundation for Youth Tour
Deadline(s): Feb. 1
Final notification: 60 days
Officers: Michael B. West, Pres.; George Dodge, Jr., V.P.; Ernest Riley, Secy.-Treas.
Directors: Jerry Franklin; Paul Quintana; Billy Tate; Pat Woods.
EIN: 850348498

1338
Farmers Group, Inc.

4680 Wilshire Blvd.
Los Angeles, CA 90010-3807
(208) 239-8400

Company URL: http://www.farmersinsurance.com
Establishment information: Established in 1928.
Company type: Subsidiary of a foreign company
Business activities: Insurance and financial services provider.
Business type (SIC): Insurance/life; insurance/accident and health; insurance/fire, marine, and casualty
Financial profile for 2010: Number of employees, 2,100; sales volume, $5,520,000,000
Corporate officers: Axel P. Lehmann, Chair.; Jeffrey John Dailey, Pres., C.O.O., and C.E.O.; Scott R. Lindquest, C.P.A., Exec. V.P. and C.F.O.; David Tavers, Exec. V.P., Opers.
Board of director: Axel P. Lehmann, Chair.
Subsidiaries: Civic Property and Casualty Co., Los Angeles, CA; Exact Property and Casualty Co., Los Angeles, CA; Farmers Insurance Co., Inc., Mission, KS; Farmers Insurance Co. of Arizona, Phoenix, AZ; Farmers Insurance Co. of Idaho, Pocatello, ID; Farmers Insurance Co. of Oregon, Tigard, OR; Farmers Insurance Co. of Washington, Vancouver, WA; Farmers Insurance Exchange, Los Angeles, CA; Farmers Insurance of Columbus, Inc., Columbus, OH; Farmers New World Life Insurance Co., Mercer Island, WA; Farmers Texas County Mutual Insurance Co., Austin, TX; Fire Insurance Exchange, Los Angeles, CA; Illinois Farmers Insurance Co., Aurora, IL; Mid Century Insurance Co. of Texas, Austin, TX; Mid-Century Insurance Co., Los Angeles, CA; Neighborhood Spirit Property and Casualty, Los Angeles, CA; Texas Farmers Insurance Co., Austin, TX; Truck Insurance Exchange, Los Angeles, CA
Offices: Simi Valley, CA; North Aurora, IL; Overland Park, KS; Hillsboro, OR; Austin, TX
Giving statement: Giving through the Farmers Group, Inc. Corporate Giving Program and the Farmers Insurance Group Safety Foundation.

Farmers Group, Inc. Corporate Giving Program

4680 Wilshire Blvd.
Los Angeles, CA 90010-3807
URL: http://www.farmers.com/FarmComm/farmers_community.html

Purpose and activities: As a complement to its foundation, Farmers makes charitable contributions to nonprofit organizations. Support is given primarily in areas of company operations. Giving also to national organizations.
Fields of interest: Secondary school/education; Health care, fund raising/fund distribution; Health care, infants; Cancer; Housing/shelter, volunteer services; Safety/disasters, public education; Athletics/sports, school programs; Athletics/sports, amateur leagues.
Programs:
Agents' Community Sponsorship Fund: Through the Agents' Community Sponsorship Fund, Farmers makes charitable contributions to nonprofit organizations involved with community development with which company agents and district managers volunteer.
Aid to Education: Through the Aid to Education program, Farmers makes annual contributions to institutions of higher education attended by company employees with four or more years of service.
Employee Matching Gifts: Farmers matches contributions made by its employees to institutions of higher education.
Type of support: Curriculum development; Employee volunteer services; Film/video/radio; General/operating support; Scholarship funds; Sponsorships.
Geographic limitations: Giving primarily in areas of company operations; giving also to national organizations.
Application information:
Number of staff: 1 part-time professional; 1 part-time support.

Farmers Insurance Group Safety Foundation

4680 Wilshire Blvd.
Los Angeles, CA 90010-3863 (323) 932-7183

Establishment information: Established in 1950.
Donor: Farmers Group, Inc.
Contact: Doren E. Hohl, Secy.
Financial data (yr. ended 12/31/11): Assets, $711,682 (M); expenditures, $263,155; qualifying distributions, $263,145; giving activities include $263,145 for grants.
Purpose and activities: The foundation supports police agencies and organizations involved with disaster relief and fire safety.
Fields of interest: Crime/law enforcement, police agencies; Disasters, preparedness/services; Disasters, fire prevention/control; American Red Cross.
Type of support: Emergency funds; Equipment; General/operating support; Program development; Sponsorships.
Geographic limitations: Giving limited to areas of company operations in CA and OR.

Support limitations: No support for religious, political, or international organizations. No grants to individuals, or for construction projects.
Application information: Applications accepted. Application form not required. Applicants should submit the following:
1) copy of IRS Determination Letter
2) brief history of organization and description of its mission
3) copy of most recent annual report/audited financial statement/990
4) detailed description of project and amount of funding requested
5) copy of current year's organizational budget and/or project budget
Initial approach: Proposal
Deadline(s): 2 months prior to need
Officers: F. Robert Woudstra, Pres.; Dons L. Dunn, V.P. and Treas.; Frank J. Ceglar, Jr., V.P.; Jeffrey J. Dailey, V.P.; Scott R. Lindquist, V.P.; Ronald G. Myhan, V.P.; Denise E. Ruggiero, V.P.; Doren E. Hohl, Secy.
EIN: 956016633

1339
Farmers Union Marketing & Processing Association

(also known as FUMPA)
590 W. Park Rd.
P.O. Box 319
Redwood Falls, MN 56283-1431
(507) 637-2938

Company URL: http://www.fumpa.com
Establishment information: Established in 1929.
Company type: Private company
Business activities: Produces and markets animal and poultry by-products; produces pet food ingredients; provides restaurant grease collection services.
Business type (SIC): Fats and oils; business services
Corporate officer: Don W. Davis, Pres. and C.E.O.
Subsidiaries: Central Bi-Products, Redwood Falls, MN; MidWest Grease, Redwood Falls, MN; Nortland Choice, Redwood Falls, MN
Giving statement: Giving through the Farmers Union Marketing & Processing Foundation.

Farmers Union Marketing & Processing Foundation

P.O. Box 319
Redwood Falls, MN 56283-0319
E-mail: danderson@centralbi.com
Application address: Dave Velde, 1118 Broadway, Alexander, MN 56308, tel.: (320) 763-6561

Establishment information: Established in 1998 in MN.
Donor: Farmers Union Marketing & Processing Assoc.
Contact: Dwight Bassingthwaite, Pres.
Financial data (yr. ended 06/30/12): Assets, $2,871,169 (M); expenditures, $346,328; qualifying distributions, $260,100; giving activities include $251,600 for 18 grants (high: $50,000; low: $900) and $8,500 for 7 grants to individuals (high: $1,500; low: $1,000).
Purpose and activities: The foundation supports research and education programs designed to promote agriculture production, management, and cooperative ventures.
Fields of interest: Higher education; Education; Agriculture; Agriculture, sustainable programs; Agriculture, farmlands; Agriculture/food.
Programs:
David Morman Scholarship: The foundation annually awards scholarships to children of FUMPA employees to attend an accredited two or four year college, university, or technical program for any field of study. FUMPA is an association made up of five companies including Central Bi-Products, Northland Choice, Midwest Grease, and Pet Care Systems.
FUMP Stanley Moore Scholarship: The foundation awards $1,000 scholarships to Farmers Union members and their children who plan to pursue agricultural study at an institute of higher education. Recipients are selected based on academic record, social and community involvement, personal/professional goals, and applicants involvement with the Farmers Union.
Type of support: Conferences/seminars; Employee-related scholarships; Equipment; Program development; Research; Seed money; Sponsorships.
Geographic limitations: Giving primarily in MN, MT, ND, SD, and WI.
Publications: Annual report; Informational brochure.
Application information: Applications accepted. Application form required.
Initial approach: Contact foundation for application form
Copies of proposal: 3
Board meeting date(s): Bimonthly
Deadline(s): None
Final notification: 2 months
Officers and Directors: Dwight Bassingthwaite, Pres.; Dennis Rosen, Secy.-Treas.; Robert Carlson; Doug Peterson; Doug Somke; Paul Symens.
EIN: 311634460
Selected grants: The following grants are a representative sample of this grantmaker's funding activity:
$50,000 to Cooperative Education Corporation, Great Falls, MT, 2011.
$30,000 to Minnesota Farmers Union Foundation, Saint Paul, MN, 2011.
$12,500 to Cooperative Education Corporation, Great Falls, MT, 2011.
$5,000 to Cooperative Education Corporation, Great Falls, MT, 2011.
$3,500 to Cooperative Education Corporation, Great Falls, MT, 2011.
$2,500 to Cooperative Education Corporation, Great Falls, MT, 2011.

1340
Farmland LP

1 Market
Spear Tower, Ste. 3600
San Francisco, CA 94105 (415) 465-2400
FAX: (415) 634-3205

Company URL: http://www.farmlandlp.com/
Establishment information: Established in 2009.
Company type: Private company
Business type (SIC): Business services/miscellaneous
Corporate officers: Greyson Colvin, Partner; Craig Wichner, Partner
Giving statement: Giving through the Farmland LP Contributions Program.

Farmland LP Contributions Program

Spear Tower, Ste. 3600
San Francisco, CA 94105 (415) 465-2400
URL: http://www.farmlandlp.com

Purpose and activities: Farmland LP is a certified B Corporation that donates a percentage of profits to charitable organizations.

1341
Farrell & Co.

1200 Reedsdale St., Ste. 2
Pittsburgh, PA 15233-2117 (412) 237-2260

Establishment information: Established in 1982.
Company type: Private company
Business activities: Operates investment bank.
Business type (SIC): Brokers and dealers/security
Corporate officers: Larry C. Farrell, Chair.; Michael J. Farrell, Pres. and C.E.O.
Board of director: Larry C. Farrell, Chair.
Giving statement: Giving through the Reinecke Family Charitable Foundation.

Reinecke Family Charitable Foundation

c/o PNC Bank, N.A.
620 Liberty Ave., 10th Fl.
Pittsburgh, PA 15222-2705 (412) 437-2260
Application address: c/o Farrell & Co., 1200 Reedsdale St., Pittsburgh, PA 15233, tel.: (412) 237-2260

Establishment information: Established in 1998 in PA.
Donor: Farrell & Co.
Financial data (yr. ended 12/31/11): Assets, $265,672 (M); expenditures, $34,195; qualifying distributions, $31,664; giving activities include $31,664 for grants.
Purpose and activities: The foundation supports organizations involved with K-12 and higher education and human services and awards college scholarships to individuals.
Fields of interest: Education; Human services.
Type of support: Annual campaigns; Program development; Scholarships—to individuals.
Geographic limitations: Giving primarily in Pittsburgh, PA.
Application information: Applications accepted. Application form required.
Initial approach: Letter
Deadline(s): None
Trustee: PNC Bank, N.A.
EIN: 232937856

1342
Fashion Trend LLC

1407 Broadway, Ste. 2704
New York, NY 10018-2588 (212) 575-6556

Establishment information: Established in 1997.
Company type: Private company
Business activities: Manufactures women's apparel.
Business type (SIC): Apparel—women's outerwear
Corporate officers: Albert Cohen, Pres.; Leonard Kopolovitz, Cont.
Giving statement: Giving through the Fashion Trend Foundation, Inc.

Fashion Trend Foundation, Inc.

1407 Broadway, Ste. 2704
New York, NY 10018-2588

Establishment information: Established in 2002 in NY.
Donor: Fashion Trend LLC.
Contact: Albert Cohen
Financial data (yr. ended 12/31/10): Assets, $29,523 (M); gifts received, $40,000; expenditures, $56,746; qualifying distributions, $56,746; giving activities include $56,721 for 43 grants (high: $19,000; low: $52).
Purpose and activities: The foundation supports organizations involved with education and Judaism.
Fields of interest: Education; Jewish agencies & synagogues.
International interests: Israel.
Type of support: General/operating support.
Geographic limitations: Giving primarily in New York and in Jerusalem, Israel.
Application information: Applications accepted. Application form not required.
Initial approach: Proposal
Deadline(s): None
Directors: Abraham Cohen; Moshe Cohen; Raymond Cohen.
EIN: 331022893

1343
Fast Retailing USA, Inc.

101 Avenue of the Americas, 11th Fl.
New York, NY 10013-1941 (212) 221-9037

Company URL: http://www.fastretailing.com
Establishment information: Established in 2004.
Company type: Subsidiary of a foreign company
Business activities: Operates retail clothing stores.
Business type (SIC): Family apparel and accessory stores
Corporate officers: Tadashi Yanai, Chair., Pres. and C.E.O.; Shin Odake, C.O.O.
Board of director: Tadashi Yanai, Chair.
Giving statement: Giving through the Fast Retailing USA, Inc.Corporate Giving Program.

Fast Retailing USA, Inc.Corporate Giving Program

101 Avenue of the Americas, 11th Fl.
New York, NY 10013 (212) 221-9037
E-mail: marketing@uniqlo-usa.com; URL: http://www.fastretailing.com/eng/csr/

Purpose and activities: Fast Retailing USA makes charitable contributions to nonprofit organizations involved with the environment, international refugees, and disaster relief.
Fields of interest: Environment; Disasters, preparedness/services; Athletics/sports, Special Olympics; International migration/refugee issues.
Type of support: Cause-related marketing; Donated products; Employee volunteer services; General/operating support.

1344
Fast Trac Buildings, Inc.

65 Invemess Dr. E., Ste. 500
Englewood, CO 80112-5141
(303) 797-0991

Company URL: http://www.fasttracbldgs.com
Establishment information: Established in 1997.
Company type: Private company
Business activities: Manufactures steel frame and steel arch buildings.
Business type (SIC): Metal products/structural
Corporate officers: Dale Schamel, C.E.O; Dan Baerg, Cont.

Buildings for Babies, Inc.

7344 S. Alton Way, Unit 8F
Centennial, CO 80112
URL: http://www.buildings4babies.com

Establishment information: Established as a company-sponsored operating foundation in 2003; status changed to public charity in 2004.
Donors: Fast Trac Buildings, Inc.; Precision Components, Inc.; Colorado Steel Contractors; V. Dale Schamel; Colorado Steel Systems; Jannice Schamel.
Financial data (yr. ended 12/31/11): Assets, $2,527,443 (M); gifts received, $266,837; expenditures, $251,875; qualifying distributions, $56,098; giving activities include $56,098 for grants.
Purpose and activities: The foundation is committed to supporting children from newborn to 12 years old through different organizations and sponsors.
Fields of interest: Religion.
Type of support: Grants to individuals.
Geographic limitations: Giving on a national basis.
Application information: Applications not accepted. Unsolicited requests for funds not accepted.
Officers: Jannice Schamel, Pres.; V. Dale Schamel, C.F.O.
EIN: 270049020

1345
FBR Capital Markets & Co.

(also known as FBRC)
(formerly Friedman, Billings, Ramsey & Co., Inc.)
1001 19th St. N., Ste. 1100
Arlington, VA 22209 (703) 312-9500

Company URL: http://www.fbr.com
Establishment information: Established in 1989.
Company type: Subsidiary of a public company
Business activities: Operates investment bank; provides securities brokerage services; provides investment advisory services; conducts investment activities.
Business type (SIC): Brokers and dealers/security; security and commodity services; investors/miscellaneous
Corporate officers: Richard J. Hendrix, Chair. and C.E.O.; Bradley J. Wright, Exec. V.P., C.F.O., and C.A.O.; James C. Neuhauser, Exec. V. P. and C.I.O; William J. Ginivan, Exec. V.P. and Genl. Counsel
Board of directors: Richard J. Hendrix, Chair.; Reena Aggarwal; Thomas J. Hynes, Jr.; Adam J. Klein; Richard A. Kraemer; Ralph S. Michael III; Thomas S. Murphy, Jr.; Arthur J. Reimers
Giving statement: Giving through the FBR Capital Markets Charitable Foundation, Inc.

FBR Capital Markets Charitable Foundation, Inc.

(formerly Friedman, Billings, Ramsey & Co. Charitable Foundation, Inc.)
1001 19th St. N., 18th Fl.
Arlington, VA 22209
E-mail: dwalker@fbr.com; URL: http://www.fbr.com/en/Company/Corporate-Giving.aspx

Establishment information: Established in 1992 in DC and DE.
Donors: Friedman, Billings, Ramsey & Co., Inc.; Emanuel Friedman; Kindy French; Eric Billings; Marianne Billings; Eric Generous; Thunderbirds Charities; Dayton Foundation; Edward Wheeler; Kurt Harrington; J. Rock Tonkel, Jr.; FBR Capital Markets, Inc.; Ed Wheeler.
Financial data (yr. ended 12/31/10): Assets, $41,510 (M); gifts received, $101,282; expenditures, $98,540; qualifying distributions, $78,465; giving activities include $78,465 for 135 grants (high: $5,396; low: $20).
Purpose and activities: The foundation supports organizations involved with arts and culture, education, health, disaster relief, human services, philanthropy, and African-Americans. Special emphasis is directed toward programs designed to promote education for disadvantaged and at-risk youth and families.
Fields of interest: Arts; Education; Human services.
Type of support: Program development; Scholarship funds.
Geographic limitations: Giving primarily in the Washington, DC, area, including MD and VA.
Support limitations: No support for labor, religious, veterans', or fraternal organizations, sports groups, discriminatory organizations, political parties or candidates, United Way agencies, veterans' organizations, or professional or trade associations. No grants to individuals, or for endowments, capital campaigns, general operating support, fundraising events, conferences, symposiums, or sports competitions, religious activities, courtesy advertising, films, or the performing arts.
Application information: Applications not accepted. Grantmaking is currently suspended.
Officers and Directors:* Richard J. Hendrix, Chair.; William K. Stephens, Pres.; Ann Marie Pulsch, Secy.; Robert Kiernan, Treas.; William J. Ginivan; Bradley J. Wright.
EIN: 521802675
Selected grants: The following grants are a representative sample of this grantmaker's funding activity:
$104,750 to Cystic Fibrosis Foundation, Bethesda, MD, 2009.
$30,250 to Washington Scholarship Fund, Washington, DC, 2009.
$27,561 to Imagination Stage, Bethesda, MD, 2009.
$7,675 to University of Southern California, Los Angeles, CA, 2009.
$1,000 to Alzheimers Association, Fairfax, VA, 2009.
$1,000 to American Sudden Infant Death Syndrome Institute, Marietta, GA, 2009.
$1,000 to Harvard College Fund, Cambridge, MA, 2009.
$1,000 to Montgomery College Foundation, Rockville, MD, 2009.
$1,000 to Randolph-Macon College, Ashland, VA, 2009.
$1,000 to University of Alabama, Tuscaloosa, AL, 2009.

1346
FDI Holdings, Inc.
(formerly Finkle Distributors, Inc.)
160 Enterprise Rd.
P.O. Box 689
Johnstown, NY 12095-3328
(518) 762-3446

Establishment information: Established in 1928.
Company type: Private company
Business activities: Sells tobacco products, confectionery products, and groceries wholesale.
Business type (SIC): Non-durable goods—wholesale; groceries—wholesale
Corporate officers: Leon Finkle, Chair.; Dan Finkle, Pres.; Dave Groff, V.P., Opers.; Marian Finkle, Treas.; Janine Brooks, Co-Cont.; Tom O'Donnell, Co-Cont.
Board of director: Leon Finkle, Chair.
Giving statement: Giving through the Marian & Leon Finkle Foundation, Inc.

Marian & Leon Finkle Foundation, Inc.
40 Autumn Dr., Apt. 256
Slingerlands, NY 12159-9356

Establishment information: Established as a company-sponsored operating foundation in 1986.
Donors: Finkle Distributors, Inc.; Leon Finkle; Marian Finkle.
Financial data (yr. ended 12/31/11): Assets, $66,965 (M); expenditures, $54,705; qualifying distributions, $54,500; giving activities include $54,500 for 7 grants (high: $30,000; low: $1,500).
Purpose and activities: The foundation supports camps and organizations involved with radio, performing arts, education, health, cancer, and children services.
Fields of interest: Arts; Education; Religion.
Type of support: General/operating support; Scholarship funds.
Geographic limitations: Giving primarily in NY.
Support limitations: No grants to individuals.
Application information: Applications not accepted. Unsolicited requests for funds not accepted.
Officers: Marian Finkle, Pres. and Treas.; Dan Finkle, V.P.; Linda Finkle, Secy.
EIN: 222582643

1347
Federal Home Loan Bank of Dallas
8500 Freeport Pkwy. S., Ste. 600
P.O. Box 619026
Irving, TX 75063-2547 (214) 441-8500
FAX: (214) 441-8552

Company URL: http://www.fhlb.com
Company type: Cooperative
Business activities: Provides loans wholesale.
Business type (SIC): Credit institutions/federal and federally-sponsored
Corporate officers: Lee R. Gibson, Chair.; Mary E. Ceverha, Vice-Chair.; Terry Smith, Pres. and C.E.O.; Nancy J. Parker, Exec. V.P., Opers. and Co-C.O.O.; Michael Sims, Exec. V.P., Finance and Co-C.O.O.; Tom Lewis, Sr. V.P. and C.A.O.; Bre Chapman, Sr. V.P., Corp. Secy., and Corp. Comms.; Sandra Damholt, V.P. and Genl. Counsel
Board of directors: Lee R. Gibson, Chair.; Mary E. Ceverha, Vice-Chair.; Dianne Bolen; Patricia Brister; Tim Carter; James H. Clayton; C.Kent Conine; Julie Cripe; W.Wesley Hoskins; Charles G. Morgan, Jr.; James Pate II; Joseph F. Quinlan, Jr.; R. Michael Rigby; John Salazer; Margo Scholin; Anthony S. Sciortino; Ron Wiser
Giving statement: Giving through the Federal Home Loan Bank of Dallas Corporate Giving Program.
Company EIN: 716013989

Federal Home Loan Bank of Dallas Corporate Giving Program
P.O. Box 619026
Dallas, TX 75261-9026

Purpose and activities: Federal Home Loan Bank of Dallas makes charitable contributions to nonprofit organizations involved with community development and housing. Support is given primarily in areas of member institution operations in Arkansas, Louisiana, Mississippi, New Mexico, and Texas.
Fields of interest: Housing/shelter; Economic development.
Type of support: General/operating support.
Geographic limitations: Giving primarily in areas of member institution operations in AR, LA, MS, NM, and TX.

1348
Federal Home Loan Mortgage Corporation
(also known as Freddie Mac)
8200 Jones Branch Dr.
McLean, VA 22102-3110 (703) 903-2000
FAX: (703) 903-2759

Company URL: http://www.freddiemac.com
Establishment information: Established in 1970.
Company type: Public company
Company ticker symbol and exchange: FMCC/OTC
Business activities: Provides mortgages.
Business type (SIC): Brokers and dealers/security
Financial profile for 2012: Number of employees, 4,961; assets, $1,989,856,000,000; sales volume, $80,635,000,000; pre-tax net income, $9,445,000,000; expenses, $71,190,000,000; liabilities, $1,981,029,000,000
Fortune 1000 ranking: 2012—31st in revenues, 14th in profits, and 4th in assets
Forbes 2000 ranking: 2012—86th in sales, 33rd in profits, and 16th in assets
Corporate officers: Christopher S. Lynch, Chair.; Donald H. Layton, C.E.O.; Ross J. Kari, Exec. V.P. and C.F.O.; Jerry Weiss, Exec. V.P. and C.A.O.; William McDavid, Exec. V.P., Secy., and Genl. Counsel; Robert Lux, Sr. V.P. and C.I.O.; Hollis McLoughlin, Sr. V.P., Corp. Comms.
Board of directors: Christopher S. Lynch, Chair.; Linda B. Bammann; Carolyn H. Byrd; Donald H. Layton; Nicolas P. Retsinas; Eugene B. Shanks, Jr.; Anthony A. Williams
Offices: Woodland Hills, CA; Atlanta, GA; Chicago, IL; New York, NY; Dallas, TX
Giving statement: Giving through the Freddie Mac Corporate Giving Program and the Freddie Mac Foundation.

Freddie Mac Corporate Giving Program
8250 Jones Branch Dr.
McLean, VA 22102-3107
E-mail: mike_schwartz@freddiemac.com;
URL: http://www.freddiemac.com/corporate/communities/

Contact: Mike Schwartz, Dir., Corp. Giving and Employee Involvement
Purpose and activities: As a complement to its foundation, Freddie Mac also makes charitable contributions to nonprofit organizations directly. Emphasis is given to organizations involved with home preservation, education, housing opportunities, and outreach and diversity. Support is given primarily in areas of company operations.
Fields of interest: Education; Housing/shelter, volunteer services; Housing/shelter, home owners; Housing/shelter; Safety/disasters; Human services, financial counseling; Civil/human rights, equal rights; Community/economic development.
Type of support: Continuing support; Employee volunteer services; General/operating support; Program development.
Geographic limitations: Giving primarily in areas of company operations.
Application information:
Administrators: Mike Schwartz, Dir., Community Rels.
Number of staff: 1 full-time professional; 1 full-time support.

Freddie Mac Foundation
c/o Grants Mgr.
8250 Jones Branch Dr., M.S. A-40
McLean, VA 22102-3110 (703) 918-8888
FAX: (703) 918-8895;
E-mail: freddiemac_foundation@freddiemac.com;
URL: http://www.freddiemacfoundation.org

Establishment information: Established in 1991 in VA.
Donor: Federal Home Loan Mortgage Corp.
Financial data (yr. ended 12/31/11): Assets, $107,329,000 (M); expenditures, $25,824,062; qualifying distributions, $24,696,023; giving activities include $19,655,912 for 231 grants (high: $1,050,000; low: $2,000), $1,741,420 for 1,292 employee matching gifts and $2,874,531 for 3 foundation-administered programs.
Purpose and activities: The foundation supports programs designed to make home a place where vulnerable children and their families can thrive. Special emphasis is directed toward programs designed to create stable homes and families; find adoptive homes for foster children; and help youth improve their academic achievement and achieve career success.
Fields of interest: Education, early childhood education; Elementary school/education; Secondary school/education; Education, services; Education; Employment, training; Housing/shelter, temporary shelter; Housing/shelter, homeless; Housing/shelter; Youth development; Children/youth, services; Children, adoption; Children, foster care; Family services Economically disadvantaged; Homeless.
Programs:
Academic and Career Success: The foundation supports programs designed to help vulnerable young people in low-income communities achieve academically and succeed in their careers. Special emphasis is directed toward childhood education; academic achievement for school-age children; and college preparation and career training with the goal of preparing young people to become self-sufficient.
Employee Matching Gifts Program: The foundation matches contributions made by employees and directors of Freddie Mac to nonprofit organizations on a one-for-one basis from $25 to $10,000 per contributor, per year.
Foster Care and Adoption: The foundation supports programs designed to improve the lives of foster children by promoting adoption from foster care; providing pre-and post-adoption resources;

and helping teens transition out of the foster care system.

J.C. Nalle Community School: The foundation, in partnership with J. C. Elementary School, supports programs and activities for students living in Southeast Washington, DC. The foundation awards grants and volunteer hours from Freddie Mac employees to bring an array of support services to the children and families of J.C. Nalle, to transform the school into a full service community school.

Stable Homes, Stable Families: The foundation supports programs designed to help families in crises secure vital services to meet their immediate needs, including emergency shelter and transitional housing; and programs designed to address long-term needs by supporting residential services so that families become more self-sufficient. Special emphasis is directed toward families who are homeless and those who are participating in housing-based service programs.

Wednesday's Child: Through the Wednesday's Child program, the foundation increases the number of children being adopted across the country. The foundation partners with local news stations and child welfare organizations for televised news segments that profile children waiting to be adopted. The news program highlights each child's special qualities and interests, and each child is also featured on the National Adoption Center's Web site.

Type of support: Capital campaigns; Conferences/seminars; Consulting services; Continuing support; Employee matching gifts; Employee volunteer services; General/operating support; Management development/capacity building; Program development; Publication; Research; Sponsorships; Technical assistance.

Geographic limitations: Giving primarily in the metropolitan Washington, DC, area, with emphasis on the District of Columbia, Charles, Frederick, Howard, Montgomery, and Prince George's counties, MD, and Alexandria, Arlington County, Fairfax County, Falls Church, Leesburg, Loudoun County, Manassas Park, and Prince William County, VA; giving also to statewide organizations in MD and VA and national organizations.

Support limitations: No support for discriminatory organizations. No grants to individuals, or for training in or promotion of religious doctrine, debt reduction, endowments, or lobbying or political activity.

Publications: Annual report; Grants list; Informational brochure.

Application information: Applications not accepted. The foundation is winding down its giving and plans to conclude its grantmaking in 2014. Grant applications are accepted from current grantees only. Unsolicited applications to support new programs or projects are not accepted.

Board meeting date(s): 1st Thurs. in Mar., June, Sept., and Dec.

Officers and Directors:* Ronald F. Poe*, Chair.; Ralph F. Boyd, Jr., C.E.O. and Pres.; Margaret Meiers, V.P. and Prog. Dir.; Alicia Myara, Secy.; Adel Antoun, Treas and C.F.O.; Wendell J. Chambliss, Exec. Dir.; Carolyn Byrd; Paul E. Mullings; Nicolas Retsinas; Dwight Robinson; Clarice Dibble Walker.

Number of staff: 11 full-time professional.

EIN: 541573760

Selected grants: The following grants are a representative sample of this grantmaker's funding activity:

$1,050,000 to National Alliance to End Homelessness, Washington, DC, 2011. For family stability through housing.

$1,025,000 to Bright Beginnings, Washington, DC, 2011. For family stability through housing.

$1,000,000 to Local Initiatives Support Corporation, Washington, DC, 2011. For family stability through housing.

$650,000 to Northern Virginia Family Service, Oakton, VA, 2011. For family stability through housing.

$450,000 to Montgomery County Coalition for the Homeless, Rockville, MD, 2011. For family stability through housing.

$445,000 to National Center for Children and Families, Bethesda, MD, 2011. For academic and career success.

$340,000 to DC Public Education Fund, Washington, DC, 2011. For academic and career success.

$60,000 to Transitional Housing BARN, Bristow, VA, 2011. For family stability through housing.

$40,000 to Hortons Kids, Washington, DC, 2011. For academic and career success.

$35,000 to Main Street Child Development Center, Fairfax, VA, 2011. For academic and career success.

1349
Federal National Mortgage Association

(also known as Fannie Mae)
3900 Wisconsin Ave., N.W.
Washington, DC 20016-2892
(202) 752-7000
FAX: (202) 752-4447

Company URL: http://www.fanniemae.com
Establishment information: Established in 1938.
Company type: Public company
Company ticker symbol and exchange: FNMA/OTC
Business activities: Provides mortgages.
Business type (SIC): Credit institutions/federal and federally-sponsored
Financial profile for 2012: Number of employees, 7,200; assets, $3,226,200,000,000; sales volume, $131,900,000,000; pre-tax net income, $17,220,000,000; expenses, $111,970,000,000; liabilities, $3,215,239,000,000
Fortune 1000 ranking: 2012—12th in revenues, 6th in profits, and 1st in assets
Forbes 2000 ranking: 2012—29th in sales, 67th in profits, and 1st in assets
Corporate officers: Philip A. Laskawy, Chair.; Timothy J. Mayopoulos, Pres. and C.E.O.; David Benson, Exec. V.P. and C.F.O.; Bradley Lerman, Exec. V.P., Genl. Counsel and Corp. Secy.; Pascal Boillat, Sr. V.P., Opers. and Tech.
Board of directors: Philip A. Laskawy, Chair.; William Thomas Forrester; Brenda J. Gaines; Charlynn Goins; Frederick B. Harvey III; Robert H. Herz; Timothy J. Mayopoulos; Egbert L. J. Perry; Jonathan Plutzik; David H. Sidwell
Offices: Birmingham, AL; Phoenix, AZ; Los Angeles, Pasadena, CA; Denver, CO; Hartford, CT; Miami, Orlando, FL; Atlanta, GA; Chicago, IL; Des Moines, IA; New Orleans, LA; Baltimore, MD; Boston, MA; Detroit, MI; St. Paul, MN; Jackson, MS; Kansas City, St. Louis, MO; Lincoln, NE; Las Vegas, NV; Albuquerque, NM; Buffalo, New York, NY; Charlotte, NC; Cleveland, Columbus, OH; Oklahoma City, OK; Portland, OR; Philadelphia, PA; Dallas, Houston, San Antonio, TX; Seattle, WA
Giving statement: Giving through the Fannie Mae Corporate Giving Program.
Company EIN: 520883107

Fannie Mae Corporate Giving Program

c/o Community and Charitable Giving
3900 Wisconsin Ave., N.W.
Washington, DC 20016-2806
URL: http://www.fanniemae.com/portal/about-us/company-overview/about-fm.html?

Purpose and activities: Fannie Mae makes charitable contributions to organizations involved with community development, housing, and homelessness. Special emphasis is directed toward initiatives that help families achieve homeownership and affordable rental housing. Support is given on a national basis, with emphasis on Washington, DC.
Fields of interest: Housing/shelter; Homeless, human services; Urban/community development; Community/economic development.
Type of support: Employee matching gifts; Employee volunteer services; General/operating support.
Geographic limitations: Giving on a national basis, with emphasis on Washington, DC.
Publications: Corporate giving report; Grants list.
Application information: Applications not accepted. Unsolicited applications are not accepted. The Office of Community and Charitable Giving handles giving.

1350
Federal Screw Works

20229 9 Mile Rd., Ste. 2400
Saint Clair Shores, MI 48080-1775
(586) 443-4200
FAX: (586) 443-4210

Company URL: http://www.federalscrew.com/
Establishment information: Established in 1917.
Company type: Public company
Company ticker symbol and exchange: FSCR/Pink Sheets
Business activities: Manufactures screws, bolts, screw machines, and industrial component parts.
Business type (SIC): Screw machine products
Financial profile for 2012: Number of employees, 183; assets, $46,370,000; sales volume, $58,650,000; pre-tax net income, -$1; expenses, $59,330,000; liabilities, $50,900,000
Corporate officers: W.T. ZurSchmiede, Jr., Chair., C.F.O., and Secy.-Treas.; Thomas ZurSchmiede, Pres. and C.E.O.; Robert F. ZurSchmiede, Exec. V.P. and C.O.O.; John M. O'Brien, V.P., Sales and Mktg.
Board of directors: W.T. ZurSchmiede, Jr., Chair.; David W. Ayriss, Sr.; Thomas W. Butler, Jr.; Frank S. Galgan; Hugh G. Harness; F.D. Tennent; Aaron ZurSchmiede; Robert F. Zurschmiede; Thomas Zurschmiede
Divisions: Big Rapids Div., Big Rapids, MI; Chelsea Div., Chelsea, MI; Novex Tool Div., Brighton, MI; Romulus Div., Romulus, MI; Steel Processing Div., Romulus, MI
Giving statement: Giving through the Federal Screw Works Foundation, Inc.
Company EIN: 380533740

Federal Screw Works Foundation, Inc.

20229 Nine Mile Rd.
St. Clair Shores, MI 48080-1775 (586) 443-4200

Establishment information: Established in 1953 in MI.
Donor: Federal Screw Works.
Contact: W. Thomas Zurschmiede, Jr., Tr.
Financial data (yr. ended 06/30/12): Assets, $84,137 (M); expenditures, $3,740; qualifying

distributions, $3,544; giving activities include $3,100 for 10 grants (high: $1,600; low: $150).
Purpose and activities: The foundation supports organizations involved with opera, higher education, health, cancer, hunger, children and youth, and economic development.
Fields of interest: Education; Health organizations; Human services.
Type of support: General/operating support.
Geographic limitations: Giving primarily in Detroit, MI.
Support limitations: No grants to individuals.
Application information: Applications accepted. Application form required. Applicants should submit the following:
1) copy of IRS Determination Letter
2) brief history of organization and description of its mission

Initial approach: Letter
Copies of proposal: 1
Deadline(s): None

Officer: Jan Buckler, Treas.
Trustees: Wade C. Plaskey; Tom Zurschmiede; W.T. Zurschmiede, Jr.
EIN: 386088208

1351
Federated Investors, Inc.

Federated Investors Tower
1001 Liberty Ave.
Pittsburgh, PA 15222-3779 (412) 288-1900
FAX: (412) 288-6823

Company URL: http://www.federatedinvestors.com
Establishment information: Established in 1955.
Company type: Public company
Company ticker symbol and exchange: FII/NYSE
Business activities: Provides investment advisory services.
Business type (SIC): Security and commodity services
Financial profile for 2012: Number of employees, 1,402; assets, $1,090,060,000; sales volume, $945,710,000; pre-tax net income, $308,510,000; expenses, $633,110,000; liabilities, $594,630,000
Corporate officers: John F. Donahue, Chair.; John W. McGonigle, Co-Vice-Chair., Exec. V.P., and Secy.; Gordon J. Ceresino, Co-Vice-Chair.; Richard B. Fisher, Co-Vice-Chair.; J. Christopher Donahue, Pres. and C.E.O.; Thomas R. Donahue, Treas. and C.F.O.
Board of directors: John F. Donahue, Chair.; Gordon J. Ceresino, Co-Vice-Chair.; Richard B. Fisher, Co-Vice-Chair.; John W. McGonigle, Co-Vice-Chair.; J. Christopher Donahue; Michael J. Farrell; David M. Kelly; Edward G. O'Connor
Subsidiary: Investlink Technologies, Inc., New York, NY
Giving statement: Giving through the Federated Investors Foundation, Inc.
Company EIN: 251111467

Federated Investors Foundation, Inc.

1001 Liberty Avenue, 21st Fl.
Pittsburgh, PA 15222-3779

Establishment information: Established in 1997.
Donor: Federated Investors, Inc.
Financial data (yr. ended 04/30/12): Assets, $650,252 (M); expenditures, $593,069; qualifying distributions, $592,900; giving activities include $592,900 for grants.
Purpose and activities: The foundation supports organizations involved with arts and culture, education, crime and law enforcement, human services, civil liberties, public affairs, and Christianity.
Fields of interest: Arts, cultural/ethnic awareness; Media/communications; Museums; Performing arts, opera; Historic preservation/historical societies; Arts; Elementary school/education; Secondary school/education; Higher education; Education; Crime/law enforcement; Children, services; Human services; Civil liberties, advocacy; Civil liberties, right to life; United Ways and Federated Giving Programs; Public affairs, alliance/advocacy; Christian agencies & churches.
Type of support: Annual campaigns; Building/renovation; Capital campaigns; General/operating support; Program development; Scholarship funds.
Geographic limitations: Giving primarily in Pittsburgh, PA.
Support limitations: No grants to individuals.
Application information: Applications not accepted. Contributes only to pre-selected organizations.
Officers and Directors:* J. Christopher Donahue*, Pres.; John W. McGonigle, Secy.; Thomas R. Donahue, Treas.; John F. Donahue.
EIN: 232913182
Selected grants: The following grants are a representative sample of this grantmaker's funding activity:
$78,000 to United Way of Allegheny County, Pittsburgh, PA, 2011.
$50,000 to Columbus Citizens Foundation, New York, NY, 2011.
$40,000 to Oakland Catholic High School, Pittsburgh, PA, 2011.
$25,000 to Becket Fund for Religious Liberty, Washington, DC, 2011.
$25,000 to Catholic Charities of the Diocese of Pittsburgh, Pittsburgh, PA, 2011.
$6,000 to River City Brass Band, Pittsburgh, PA, 2011.
$5,500 to Pittsburgh Parks Conservancy, Pittsburgh, PA, 2011.
$5,000 to Jewish National Fund, New York, NY, 2011.
$5,000 to National Flag Foundation, Pittsburgh, PA, 2011.
$5,000 to Society of Jesus of New England, Watertown, MA, 2011.

1352
FedEx Corporation

(formerly FDX Corporation)
942 S. Shady Grove Rd., 2nd Fl.
Memphis, TN 38120 (901) 818-7500

Company URL: http://www.fedex.com
Establishment information: Established in 1998 from the merger of Caliber System, Inc. with Federal Express Corp.
Company type: Public company
Company ticker symbol and exchange: FDX/NYSE
International Securities Identification Number: US31428X1063
Business activities: Provides express, ground, and freight delivery services; provides logistics, supply chain management, and electronic commerce services and solutions.
Business type (SIC): Transportation/scheduled air; trucking and courier services, except by air; management and public relations services
Financial profile for 2012: Number of employees, 149,000; assets, $29,903,000,000; sales volume, $42,680,000,000; pre-tax net income, $3,141,000,000; expenses, $39,494,000,000; liabilities, $15,176,000,000
Fortune 1000 ranking: 2012—63rd in revenues, 98th in profits, and 187th in assets
Forbes 2000 ranking: 2012—205th in sales, 339th in profits, and 704th in assets
Corporate officers: Frederick W. Smith, Chair. and Co-C.E.O.; Robert B. Carter, Co-C.E.O. and C.I.O.; Alan B. Graf, Jr., Exec. V.P. and C.F.O.; Christine P. Richards, Exec. V.P., Genl. Counsel, and Secy.; T. Michael Glenn, Exec. V.P., Corp. Comms.
Board of directors: James L. Barksdale; John A. Edwardson; Shirley Ann Jackson, Ph.D.; Steven R. Loranger; Gary W. Loveman, Ph.D.; R. Brad Martin; Joshua Cooper Ramo; Susan C. Schwab; Joshua I. Smith; David P. Steiner; Paul S. Walsh
Subsidiaries: FDX Global Logistics, Inc., Memphis, TN; Federal Express Corporation, Memphis, TN
International operations: Canada
Giving statement: Giving through the FedEx Corporation Contributions Program.
Company EIN: 621721435

FedEx Corporation Contributions Program

(formerly FDX Corporation Contributions Program)
c/o Global Citizenship
3610 Hacks Cross Rd.
Bldg. A
Memphis, TN 38125-8800
E-mail: communityrelations@fedex.com;
URL: http://about.van.fedex.com/corporate_responsibility

Purpose and activities: FedEx makes charitable contributions to nonprofit organizations involved with disaster relief, child pedestrian safety, and environmental sustainability. Support is on a national and international basis.
Fields of interest: Environment; Safety/disasters, public education; Disasters, preparedness/services; Safety, automotive safety; Safety/disasters; American Red Cross; Salvation Army; International relief Children.
Type of support: Continuing support; Employee volunteer services; General/operating support; In-kind gifts; Program development.
Geographic limitations: Giving on a national and international basis.
Support limitations: Generally, no support for athletic organizations, exclusively tax-supported educational institutions, labor or political organizations, public or private elementary or secondary schools or colleges, sectarian or religious organizations, or discriminatory organizations. Generally, no grants to individuals, or for athletic activities, beauty contests, endowments or memorials, scholarships, membership dues, general operating support for United Way-associated organizations, or travel; no shipping donations for items sold through fundraisers; no FedEx promotional merchandise donations.
Publications: Application guidelines.
Application information: Applications accepted. Application form required. Applicants should submit the following:
1) timetable for implementation and evaluation of project
2) statement of problem project will address
3) population served
4) geographic area to be served
5) how project's results will be evaluated or measured
6) list of company employees involved with the organization
7) detailed description of project and amount of funding requested
8) copy of current year's organizational budget and/or project budget

9) listing of additional sources and amount of support
Initial approach: Complete online eligibility quiz and application form

1353
FEECO International, Inc.
3913 Algoma Rd.
Green Bay, WI 54311-9707 (920) 468-1000

Company URL: http://www.feeco.com
Establishment information: Established in 1951.
Company type: Private company
Business activities: Designs, engineers, manufactures, and installs material handling and waste recovery systems and equipment.
Business type (SIC): Machinery/construction, mining, and materials handling
Corporate officers: Daniel Madigan, Pres.; Craig Johnson, Cont.; Debbie Johnson, Human Resources
Giving statement: Giving through the FEECO International Foundation, Inc.

FEECO International Foundation, Inc.
3913 Algoma Rd.
Green Bay, WI 54311-9707 (920) 469-5100

Establishment information: Established in 1997 in WI.
Donors: FEECO International, Inc.; Daniel Madigan.
Contact: Daniel Madigan, Pres.
Financial data (yr. ended 06/30/12): Assets, $632,696 (M); gifts received, $100,007; expenditures, $14,505; qualifying distributions, $14,470; giving activities include $14,470 for grants.
Purpose and activities: The foundation supports hospitals and organizations involved with education, health, recreation, youth development, and human services.
Fields of interest: Education; Human services; Public affairs.
Type of support: General/operating support.
Support limitations: No grants to individuals.
Application information: Applications accepted. Application form not required.
Initial approach: Proposal
Deadline(s): None
Officers and Directors:* Daniel P. Madigan*, Pres. and Treas.; Laura Madigan*, V.P. and Secy.; Justin Madigan.
EIN: 391916022

1354
Feelgoodz, LLC
6320 Cartwright Dr.
New Orleans, LA 70122 (504) 283-2403

Company URL: http://www.feelgoodz.com
Establishment information: Established in 2007.
Company type: Private company
Business type (SIC): Business services/miscellaneous
Corporate officer: Kyle R. Berner, C.E.O.
Giving statement: Giving through the Feelgoodz Corporate Giving Program.

Feelgoodz Corporate Giving Program
6320 Cartwright Dr.
New Orleans, LA 70122-2806 (504) 283-2403
E-mail: kyle.berner@feelgoodz.com; URL: http://www.feelgoodz.com

Purpose and activities: Feelgoodz is a certified B Corporation that donates a percentage of profits to charitable organizations.
Fields of interest: Education; Environment; Social entrepreneurship.
Type of support: General/operating support.

1355
Feld Entertainment, Inc.
8607 Westwood Center Dr.
Vienna, VA 22182 (703) 448-4000

Company URL: http://www.feldentertainment.com
Establishment information: Established in 1967.
Company type: Private company
Business activities: Provides live entertainment.
Business type (SIC): Amusement and recreation services/miscellaneous
Corporate officers: Kenneth Feld, Chair. and C.E.O.; Michael Shannon, Pres. and C.O.O.; Jerome Sowalsky, Exec. V.P. and Genl. Counsel; Keith Senglamb, C.F.O.; Jeff Meyer, Sr. V.P., Mktg. and Sales; Emily Roisman, V.P. and Corp. Counsel; Casey Rodgers, V.P., Finance; Stephen Payne, V.P., Corp. Comms.; Kirk McCoy, V.P., Human Resources
Board of directors: Kenneth Feld, Chair.; Keith Senglaub; Michael Shannon
Subsidiary: Ringling Bros., Barnum & Bailey Combined Shows, Inc., Vienna, VA
Giving statement: Giving through the Feld Entertainment, Inc. Corporate Giving Program.

Feld Entertainment, Inc. Corporate Giving Program
8607 Westwood Center Dr.
Vienna, VA 22182-7506 (703) 448-4000

Purpose and activities: Feld Entertainment makes charitable contributions of show tickets to nonprofit organizations on a case by case basis. Support is given on a national and international basis.
Fields of interest: General charitable giving.
Type of support: Donated products.
Geographic limitations: Giving on a national and international basis in areas of company operations.
Application information: Applications accepted. Application form not required.
Initial approach: Mail or fax proposal to headquarters
Copies of proposal: 1
Deadline(s): None

1356
Felhaber, Larson, Fenlon & Vogt, P.A.
US Bank Plz.
220 S. 6th St., Ste. 2200
Minneapolis, MN 55402-4504
(612) 339-6321

Company URL: http://www.felhaber.com
Establishment information: Established in 1943.
Company type: Private company
Business activities: Operates law firm.
Business type (SIC): Legal services
Corporate officers: Thomas J. Doyle, Chair.; Christopher S. Hayhoe, Pres.; Richard C. Salmen, V.P.
Offices: Minneapolis, Saint Paul, MN
Giving statement: Giving through the Felhaber, Larson, Fenlon & Vogt, P.A. Pro Bono Program.

Felhaber, Larson, Fenlon & Vogt, P.A. Pro Bono Program
US Bank Plz.
220 S. 6th St., Ste. 2200
Minneapolis, MN 55402-4504 (612) 373-8478
E-mail: kdyck@felhaber.com; Additional tel.: (612) 339-6321; URL: http://www.felhaber.com

Contact: Karen Dyck, Mktg. Dir.
Fields of interest: Legal services.
Type of support: Pro bono services - legal.
Geographic limitations: Giving primarily in areas of company operations in Minneapolis, and St. Paul, MN.
Application information: A non-attorney administrator manages the pro bono program.

1357
Fellowes, Inc.
(formerly Fellowes Manufacturing Company)
1789 Norwood Ave.
Itasca, IL 60143-1095 (630) 893-1600
FAX: (630) 893-1683

Company URL: http://www.fellowes.com
Establishment information: Established in 1917.
Company type: Private company
Business activities: Manufactures office, travel, and leisure products.
Business type (SIC): Computer and office equipment
Corporate officers: James E. Fellowes, Chair. and C.E.O.; John E. Fellowes II, Pres.; Mike Parker, Exec. V.P., Sales; Lyn Bulman, Exec. V.P., Human Resources
Board of directors: James E. Fellowes, Chair.; John E. Fellowes II
Giving statement: Giving through the Fellowes, Inc. Corporate Giving Program.

Fellowes, Inc. Corporate Giving Program
(formerly Fellowes Manufacturing Company Contributions Program)
1789 Norwood Ave.
Itasca, IL 60143-1095 (630) 893-1600
URL: http://www.fellowes.com/Fellowes/site/aboutus/about_missions.aspx

Purpose and activities: Fellowes makes charitable contributions to the City of Hope in Duarte, California.
Fields of interest: Cancer; Cancer research; Medical research.
Type of support: General/operating support.

1358
Fema Electronics Corporation
17815 Newhope St., Ste. G
Fountain Valley, CA 92708 (714) 825-0140
FAX: (714) 825-0210

Company URL: http://www.femacorp.com
Establishment information: Established in 1980.

Company type: Private company
Business activities: Manufactures liquid crystal display products.
Business type (SIC): Electrical equipment and supplies
Corporate officers: Bob Cheng, Co-Pres.; Clifford Cheng, Co-Pres.
Giving statement: Giving through the Jatain Charitable Foundation.

Jatain Charitable Foundation

58 Archipelago Dr.
Newport Coast, CA 92657-2106 (714) 825-0140

Establishment information: Established as a company-sponsored foundation in 2000 in NJ.
Donor: Fema Electronics Corp.
Contact: Bob Cheng, Tr.
Financial data (yr. ended 12/31/11): Assets, $6,049,793 (M); gifts received, $1,038,030; expenditures, $380,015; qualifying distributions, $223,400; giving activities include $223,400 for 10 grants (high: $210,000; low: $500).
Purpose and activities: The foundation supports organizations involved with cultural and ethnic awareness, higher education, and Taiwanese heritage.
Fields of interest: Arts, cultural/ethnic awareness; Higher education Asians/Pacific Islanders.
Type of support: General/operating support.
Geographic limitations: Giving primarily CA, NJ, and PA.
Application information: Applications accepted. Application form not required.
Initial approach: Proposal
Deadline(s): None
Trustees: Bob Cheng; Clifford Cheng; George Cheng; Jean Cheng.
EIN: 226824275

1359
Fender Musical Instruments Corporation

17600 N. Perimeter Dr., Ste. 100
Scottsdale, AZ 85255 (480) 596-9690
FAX: (480) 596-1384

Company URL: http://www.fender.com
Establishment information: Established in 1943.
Company type: Private company
Business activities: Manufactures guitars.
Business type (SIC): Musical instruments
Financial profile for 2010: Number of employees, 3,186
Corporate officers: Mark H. Fukunaga, Co-Chair.; Michael P. Lazarus, Co-Chair.; Larry E. Thomas, C.E.O.; James S. Broenen, C.F.O.; Michael Spandau, C.I.O.
Board of directors: Mark H. Fukunaga, Co-Chair.; Michael P. Lazarus, Co-Chair.; Larry E. Thomas
Giving statement: Giving through the Fender Music Foundation.

The Fender Music Foundation

(formerly The Guitar Center Music Foundation)
28118 Agoura Rd., Ste. 105
P.O. Box 67
Agoura Hills, CA 91301-2443
FAX: (818) 735-7518;
E-mail: info@fendermusicfoundation.org;
URL: http://www.fendermusicfoundation.org/

Establishment information: Established in 2005 in CA.
Financial data (yr. ended 12/31/11): Revenue, $472,427; assets, $452,961 (M); gifts received, $453,098; expenditures, $201,935; program services expenses, $112,746; giving activities include $39,308 for grants.
Purpose and activities: The foundation provides funding and resources for music programs across America so that kids and adults alike will have an opportunity to experience the joys of music.
Fields of interest: Arts education; Performing arts, music; Arts; Education.
Program:
Grants Program: This program provides instruments and equipment for eligible nonprofit music instruction programs. Awarded items are lightly used, blemished, or otherwise imperfect and have been collected by the foundation from manufacturers and retailers. The foundation is currently awarding acoustic guitars, electric guitars, acoustic-electric guitars, bass guitars, and the equipment necessary to play them. However, other traditional music instruments, including string, woodwind, brass, and percussion instruments, as well as keyboards, are sometimes available. The foundation awards instruments only to music instruction programs offered by public schools or 501(c)(3) tax-exempt organizations. To qualify as a music instruction program, participants must be learning how to make music. Music appreciation or entertainment programs do not qualify, and the participants may not be professional or career musicians.
Type of support: In-kind gifts; Program development.
Geographic limitations: Giving primarily in CA.
Support limitations: No support for for-profit enterprises, entertainment, event sponsorship, artists in school assemblies, school-owned after-school assemblies, music appreciation, music production, recording studios, instrument repairs, or beginning a school band program. No grants to individuals, or for general operating expenses, sheet music, uniforms, or salaries.
Publications: Application guidelines.
Application information: Applications accepted.
Initial approach: Online grant application form
Deadline(s): None
Officer and Directors:* Larry E. Thomas*, Chair.; Gina Atton-Thomas; Cathy Genzler; Greg Grunberg; Allen Kepler; JoAnn Kepler; Robert Knight; Don Lombardi; Tim Pohlman; Daniel Smith; Mike Vizvary; Dave Weiderman; Rich Winer.
EIN: 203436786

1360
Fennemore Craig, P.C.

3003 N. Central Ave., Ste. 2600
Phoenix, AZ 85012-2913 (602) 916-5000

Company URL: http://www.fclaw.com
Establishment information: Established in 1884.
Company type: Private company
Business activities: Operates law firm.
Business type (SIC): Legal services
Offices: Nogales, Phoenix, Tucson, AZ; Denver, CO; Las Vegas, NV
Giving statement: Giving through the Fennemore Craig, P.C. Pro Bono Program and the Fennemore Craig Foundation.

Fennemore Craig, P.C. Pro Bono Program

3003 N. Central Ave., Ste. 2600
Phoenix, AZ 85012-2913 (602) 916-5319
E-mail: swissink@fclaw.com; Additional tel.: (602) 916-5000; URL: http://www.fclaw.com/pro-bono/

Contact: Susan M. Wissink, Dir.
Fields of interest: Legal services.
Type of support: Pro bono services - legal.
Geographic limitations: Giving primarily in areas of company operations in Nogales, Phoenix, and Tucson, AZ, Denver, CO, and Las Vegas, NV.
Application information: The Pro Bono Committee coordinates the pro-bono program.

Fennemore Craig Foundation

3003 N. Central Ave., Ste. 2600
Phoenix, AZ 85012-2913 (602) 916-5000
URL: http://www.fennemorecraigfoundation.com/index.cfm

Financial data (yr. ended 12/31/11): Revenue, $38,586; assets, $31,189 (M); gifts received, $38,193; expenditures, $37,334; program services expenses, $35,354; giving activities include $35,195 for grants.
Purpose and activities: The foundation works to involve Fennemore Craig employees, their families, and clients in civic and charitable events in the Phoenix community.
Fields of interest: Community/economic development.
Type of support: In-kind gifts.
Geographic limitations: Giving limited to Phoenix, AZ.
Officers and Director:* Jay S. Kramer*, Pres.; Phillip F. Fargotstein*, Secy.; Susan M. Ciupak.
EIN: 860980784

1361
Fenton Art Glass Company

700 Elizabeth St.
Williamstown, WV 26187-1028
(304) 375-6122
FAX: (304) 375-7833

Company URL: http://www.fentonartglass.com
Establishment information: Established in 1905.
Company type: Private company
Business activities: Manufactures colored glass.
Business type (SIC): Glass/flat
Corporate officers: George W. Fenton, Pres. and C.E.O.; Scott K. Fenton, V.P., Sales
Giving statement: Giving through the Fenton Foundation Inc.

Fenton Foundation Inc.

700 Elizabeth St.
Williamstown, WV 26187-1028

Establishment information: Established in 1955 in WV.
Donors: Fenton Art Glass Co.; Fenton Gift Shops, Inc.; Thomas K. Fenton; Harold Swartz; Neva Swartz; Martin Land Co.
Contact: Thomas K. Fenton, Pres. and Treas.
Financial data (yr. ended 12/31/11): Assets, $3,184,679 (M); gifts received, $4,000; expenditures, $172,004; qualifying distributions, $145,757; giving activities include $145,620 for 44 grants (high: $22,000; low: $120).
Purpose and activities: The foundation supports organizations involved with arts and culture,

elementary and higher education, health, human services, community development, and Christianity.
Fields of interest: Performing arts, theater; Arts; Elementary school/education; Higher education; Human services; Community/economic development; United Ways and Federated Giving Programs; Christian agencies & churches.
Type of support: Capital campaigns; General/operating support.
Geographic limitations: Giving primarily in the William County, OH and Williamstown, WV, area.
Support limitations: No grants to individuals.
Application information: Applications accepted. Application form not required. Applicants should submit the following:
1) detailed description of project and amount of funding requested
Initial approach: Letter of inquiry
Copies of proposal: 1
Deadline(s): None
Officers: Thomas K. Fenton, Pres. and Treas.; Randall R. Fenton, V.P.; Lynn F. Erb, Secy.
Directors: Michael D. Fenton; Scott K. Fenton.
EIN: 556017260
Selected grants: The following grants are a representative sample of this grantmaker's funding activity:
$20,000 to Marietta College, Marietta, OH, 2010. For capital campaign.
$12,000 to Artsbridge, Parkersburg, WV, 2010.
$4,000 to First Baptist Church, Williamstown, WV, 2010.
$3,000 to Williamstown, City of, Williamstown, WV, 2010.
$2,000 to Friends of the Museum, Marietta, OH, 2010.
$1,000 to Boy Scouts of America, Parkersburg, WV, 2010.

1362
Fenwick & West LLP
Silicon Valley Ctr.
801 California St.
Mountain View, CA 94041-1990
(650) 335-7244

Company URL: http://www.fenwick.com
Establishment information: Established in 1972.
Company type: Private company
Business activities: Operates law firm.
Business type (SIC): Legal services
Corporate officer: Gordon K. Davidson, Chair.
Offices: Mountain View, San Francisco, CA; Boise, ID; Seattle, WA
Giving statement: Giving through the Fenwick & West LLP Pro Bono Program.

Fenwick & West LLP Pro Bono Program
Silicon Valley Ctr.
801 California St.
Mountain View, CA 94041-1990 (650) 335-7244
E-mail: jjpark@fenwick.com; Additional tel.: (650) 988-8500; URL: http://www.fenwick.com/community/8.1.0.asp

Contact: Julie Park, Dir. of Pro Bono
Fields of interest: Legal services.
Type of support: Pro bono services - legal.
Geographic limitations: Giving primarily in areas of company operations in Mountain View, and San Francisco, CA, Boise, ID, and Seattle, WA.
Application information: The Pro Bono Committee manages the pro-bono program.

1363
Ferguson Electric Construction Co., Inc.
333 Ellicott St.
Buffalo, NY 14203-1618 (716) 852-2010
FAX: (716) 852-4887

Company URL: http://www.fergusonelectric.com/
Establishment information: Established in 1935.
Company type: Private company
Business activities: Provides general contract electric services.
Business type (SIC): Contractors/electrical work
Corporate officers: Angelo A. Veanes, Pres.; Jeffrey H. Lattimer, C.F.O.; Kevin M. Mislin, V.P., Mktg.
Subsidiary: Ferguson Electric Service Corp., Buffalo, NY
Giving statement: Giving through the Ferguson Electric Foundation.

Ferguson Electric Foundation
333 Ellicott St.
Buffalo, NY 14203-1618 (716) 852-2010

Establishment information: Established in 2004 in NY.
Donors: Ferguson Family Foundation, Inc.; Ferguson Electric Construction Co., Inc.; Ferguson Electric Service Co., Inc.
Contact: Jeffrey H. Lattimer, Secy.-Treas.
Financial data (yr. ended 12/31/11): Assets, $475,730 (M); gifts received, $90,000; expenditures, $97,953; qualifying distributions, $89,000; giving activities include $89,000 for grants.
Purpose and activities: The foundation supports hospitals and organizations involved with performing arts, zoology, medical research, and parks and playgrounds.
Fields of interest: Arts; Education; Health care.
Type of support: General/operating support.
Geographic limitations: Giving primarily in the Buffalo, NY, area.
Application information: Applications accepted. Application form required. Applicants should submit the following:
1) detailed description of project and amount of funding requested
Initial approach: Letter
Deadline(s): None
Officers: Paul C. Reilly, Pres.; Angelo A. Veanes, V.P.; Jeffrey H. Lattimer, Secy.-Treas.
EIN: 201084040

1364
Ferrara Pan Candy Company
7301 W. Harrison St.
Forest Park, IL 60130-2016
(708) 366-0500

Company URL: http://www.ferrarapan.com
Establishment information: Established in 1908.
Company type: Private company
Business activities: Produces candy.
Business type (SIC): Sugar, candy, and salted/roasted nut production
Corporate officers: Nello V. Ferrara, Chair.; Salvatore Ferrara II, Pres. and C.E.O.; Thomas P. Polke, C.O.O.; James S. Buffardi, Secy.-Treas.
Board of director: Nello V. Ferrara, Chair.
Giving statement: Giving through the Ferrara Pan Foundation.

Ferrara Pan Foundation
c/o Nello Ferrara
7301 W. Harrison St.
Forest Park, IL 60130-2083

Establishment information: Established in 1992 in IL.
Donor: Ferrara Pan Candy Company.
Financial data (yr. ended 12/31/11): Assets, $67,231 (M); gifts received, $10,000; expenditures, $12,085; qualifying distributions, $12,000; giving activities include $12,000 for grants.
Purpose and activities: The foundation supports organizations involved with health and Catholicism.
Fields of interest: Health organizations; Youth development; Religion.
Type of support: General/operating support.
Geographic limitations: Giving primarily in IL.
Support limitations: No grants to individuals.
Application information: Applications not accepted. Unsolicited requests for funds not accepted.
Directors: James S. Buffardi; Louis J. Buffardi; Nello V. Ferrara; Salvatore Ferrara II; Louis V. Pagano; Thomas A. Pagano.
EIN: 363870512

1365
Ferrellgas Partners, L.P.
7500 College Blvd., Ste. 1000
Overland Park, KS 66210 (913) 661-1500

Company URL: http://www.ferrellgas.com
Establishment information: Established in 1939.
Company type: Public company
Company ticker symbol and exchange: FGP/NYSE
Business activities: Operates holding company; distributes propane.
Business type (SIC): Fuel dealers—retail; holding company
Financial profile for 2012: Number of employees, 3,470; assets, $1,397,280,000; sales volume, $2,339,090,000; pre-tax net income, -$9,770,000; expenses, $2,256,110,000; liabilities, $1,426,370,000
Fortune 1000 ranking: 2012—850th in revenues, 892nd in profits, and 930th in assets
Corporate officers: James E. Ferrell, Chair.; Stephen L. Wambold, Pres. and C.E.O.; Boyd H. McGathey, Exec. V.P. and C.O.O.; James Ryan VanWinkle, Exec. V.P. and C.F.O.; Randy Schott, Co-Sr. V.P., Opers.; Jay Werner, Co-Sr. V.P., Opers.; Al Heitmann, Sr. V.P., Finance; Scott Brockelmeyer, V.P., Corp. Comms. and Mktg.; Cathy Brown, V.P., Human Resources
Board of directors: James E. Ferrell, Chair.; A. Andrew Levison; John R. Lowden; Michael F. Morrissey; Daniel G. Kaye, CPA; Stephen L. Wambold
Subsidiaries: Ferrellgas, L.P., Liberty, MO; Ferrellgas Partners Finance Corp., Liberty, MO
Giving statement: Giving through the Ferrellgas Partners, L.P. Corporate Giving Program.
Company EIN: 431698480

Ferrellgas Partners, L.P. Corporate Giving Program

7500 College Blvd., Ste. 1000
Overland Park, KS 66210-4098 (913) 661-1500
URL: http://www.ferrellgas.com/Our-Company/Community-Involvement

Purpose and activities: Ferrellgas makes charitable contributions to nonprofit organizations involved with cancer research, food services, and the military and their families. Support is given primarily in areas of company operations.
Fields of interest: Cancer research; Food services; General charitable giving Military/veterans.
Type of support: Cause-related marketing; General/operating support; In-kind gifts.
Geographic limitations: Giving primarily in areas of company operations; giving also to national organizations.

1366
Ferro Corporation

6060 Parkland Blvd.
Mayfield Heights, OH 44124
(216) 875-5600
FAX: (216) 875-5627

Company URL: http://www.ferro.com
Establishment information: Established in 1919.
Company type: Public company
Company ticker symbol and exchange: FOE/NYSE
Business activities: Manufactures specialty chemicals and materials.
Business type (SIC): Chemical preparations/miscellaneous; chemicals/industrial organic
Financial profile for 2012: Number of employees, 4,948; assets, $1,079,100,000; sales volume, $1,768,630,000; pre-tax net income, -$263,550,000; expenses, $2,032,180,000; liabilities, $885,580,000
Corporate officers: William B. Lawrence, Chair.; Peter T. Thomas, Pres. and C.E.O.; Jeffrey L. Rutherford, V.P. and C.F.O.; Mark H. Duesenberg, V.P., Genl. Counsel, and Secy.; Ann E. Killian, V.P., Human Resources
Board of directors: William B. Lawrence, Chair.; Richard C. Brown; Sandra Austin Crayton; Richard J. Hipple; Jennie S. Hwang; Gregory E. Hyland; Peter T. Kong; Timothy K. Pistell; Ronald P. Vargo
Subsidiary: Ferro Electronic Materials Inc., Santa Barbara, CA
Plants: Evansville, Plymouth, IN; Zachary, LA; Penn Yan, NY; Stryker, Walton Hills, OH
International operations: Argentina; Australia; Brazil; Canada; China; Ecuador; Germany; Hong Kong; Indonesia; Japan; Mexico; Netherlands; South Korea; Spain; Taiwan; Thailand; United Kingdom; Venezuela
Giving statement: Giving through the Ferro Corporation Contributions Program and the Ferro Foundation.
Company EIN: 340217820

Ferro Corporation Contributions Program

1000 Lakeside Ave.
Cleveland, OH 44114-7000 (216) 641-8580
URL: http://www.ferro.com/About/Social+Responsibility/

Purpose and activities: As a complement to its foundation, Ferro also makes charitable contributions to nonprofit organizations directly. Support is given primarily in the Cleveland, Ohio, area.
Fields of interest: Museums (science/technology); Elementary/secondary education; Environment, energy; Environment; Community/economic development; United Ways and Federated Giving Programs; Science; General charitable giving.
Type of support: Annual campaigns; Employee volunteer services; General/operating support; Sponsorships.
Geographic limitations: Giving primarily in the Cleveland, OH, area.
Application information: Applications not accepted. Contributes only to pre-selected organizations.

Ferro Foundation

6060 Parkland Blvd.
Mayfield Heights, OH 44124 (216) 641-8580
URL: http://www.ferro.com/About/Social+Responsibility/Philanthropy.htm

Establishment information: Incorporated in 1959 in OH.
Donor: Ferro Corp.
Financial data (yr. ended 04/30/11): Assets, $62,624 (M); gifts received, $200,000; expenditures, $196,542; qualifying distributions, $193,492; giving activities include $193,492 for 35 grants (high: $60,000; low: $150).
Purpose and activities: The foundation supports organizations involved with arts and culture, education, health and welfare, and community development. Special emphasis is directed toward programs designed to promote human services and civic development.
Fields of interest: Arts; Higher education; Education; Health care; Human services; Community/economic development; United Ways and Federated Giving Programs; Public affairs.
Type of support: Annual campaigns; Building/renovation; Capital campaigns; General/operating support; Program development.
Geographic limitations: Giving primarily in areas of company operations, with emphasis on the greater Cleveland, OH area.
Support limitations: No support for religious, political, lobbying, or labor organizations. No grants to individuals.
Publications: Application guidelines.
Application information: Applications accepted. Application form required. Applicants should submit the following:
1) role played by volunteers
2) statement of problem project will address
3) copy of IRS Determination Letter
4) brief history of organization and description of its mission
5) list of company employees involved with the organization
6) explanation of why grantmaker is considered an appropriate donor for project
7) detailed description of project and amount of funding requested
8) listing of additional sources and amount of support
Initial approach: Proposal
Board meeting date(s): Quarterly
Deadline(s): None
Officers: James F. Kirsch*, Pres.; Don E. Katchman, V.P.; M. Abood, Secy.; D. R. Knapp, Treas.
Trustees: Mark H. Duesenberg; Ann E. Killian.
EIN: 346554832
Selected grants: The following grants are a representative sample of this grantmaker's funding activity:
$25,000 to Great Lakes Museum of Science, Environment and Technology, Cleveland, OH, 2010.
$5,000 to John Carroll University, University Heights, OH, 2010.
$2,500 to Hunger Network of Greater Cleveland, Cleveland, OH, 2010.
$2,000 to American Heart Association, Cleveland, OH, 2010.
$2,000 to Cleveland Zoological Society, Cleveland, OH, 2010.
$2,000 to Hiram House, Chagrin Falls, OH, 2010.
$1,500 to Towards Employment, Cleveland, OH, 2010.
$1,000 to Law Enforcement Foundation, Dublin, OH, 2010.
$1,000 to Ohio Cancer Research Associates, Columbus, OH, 2010.
$1,000 to Recovery Resources, Cleveland, OH, 2010.

1367
The Scott Fetzer Company

28800 Clemens Rd.
Westlake, OH 44145-1197 (440) 892-3000

Establishment information: Established in 1914.
Company type: Subsidiary of a public company
Business activities: Manufactures and markets cleaning systems and household products, commercial and industrial accessories, and education and information systems.
Business type (SIC): Appliances/household; plastic products/miscellaneous; cutlery, hand and edge tools, and hardware; machinery/general industry
Corporate officers: Kenneth J. Semelsberger, Chair.; Robert D. McBride, Pres. and C.E.O.; William W. T. Stephans, C.F.O.; Patricia M. Scanlon, Genl. Counsel
Board of director: Kenneth J. Semelsberger, Chair.
Giving statement: Giving through the Scott & Fetzer Foundation.

The Scott & Fetzer Foundation

28800 Clemens Rd.
Westlake, OH 44145-1134 (440) 892-3000

Establishment information: Established in 1967 in OH.
Donor: The Scott Fetzer Co.
Financial data (yr. ended 12/31/11): Assets, $120,743 (M); gifts received, $65,000; expenditures, $83,277; qualifying distributions, $83,000; giving activities include $83,000 for 11 grants (high: $18,000; low: $500).
Purpose and activities: The foundation supports organizations involved with education, health, heart disease, human services, and community economic development.
Fields of interest: Secondary school/education; Higher education; Education; Health care; Salvation Army; Aging, centers/services; Human services; Community/economic development; United Ways and Federated Giving Programs.
Type of support: General/operating support.
Geographic limitations: Giving primarily in OH, with emphasis on Cleveland.
Support limitations: No grants to individuals.
Application information: Applications accepted. Application form not required. Applicants should submit the following:
1) copy of IRS Determination Letter
Initial approach: Letter
Deadline(s): None
Officers: Robert D. McBride, Pres.; Patricia M. Scanlon, V.P. and Secy.; John W. Gretta, Treas.
EIN: 346596076

1368
FHC Health Systems, Inc.

(formerly First Hospital Corporation)
1100 First Colonial Rd.
Virginia Beach, VA 23454-2403
(757) 496-6000

Company URL: http://www.valueoptions.com/
Establishment information: Established in 1983.
Company type: Subsidiary of a private company
Business activities: Provides mental health services.
Business type (SIC): Hospitals
Financial profile for 2010: Number of employees, 250
Corporate officers: Ronald I. Dozoretz, M.D., Chair.; Barbara B. Hill, C.E.O.; Michele D. Alfonsa, C.O.O.; E. Paul Dunn, Jr., C.F.O.; Paul Rosenberg, Genl. Counsel
Board of director: Ronald I. Dozoretz, M.D., Chair.
Giving statement: Giving through the First Hospital Corporation Private Foundation.

First Hospital Corporation Private Foundation

240 Corporate Blvd., Ste. 400
Norfolk, VA 23502-4948 (757) 459-5100

Establishment information: Established in 1992 in VA.
Donors: First Hospital Corp.; FHC Options, Inc.; FHC Health Systems, Inc.; Ronald I. Dozoretz, M.D.
Contact: Ronald I. Dozoretz M.D., Pres.
Financial data (yr. ended 06/30/12): Assets, $755,444 (M); expenditures, $6,126; qualifying distributions, $3,000; giving activities include $3,000 for 1 grant.
Purpose and activities: The foundation supports organizations involved with performing arts, education, health, children and youth, civic affairs, and Judaism.
Fields of interest: Medical research; Human services.
Type of support: General/operating support.
Geographic limitations: Giving primarily in Washington, DC, and VA.
Application information: Applications accepted. Application form required. Applicants should submit the following:
1) brief history of organization and description of its mission
2) detailed description of project and amount of funding requested
Initial approach: Letter
Deadline(s): None
Officers: Ronald I. Dozoretz, M.D., Pres.; Beth Dozoretz, V.P.; Shari D. Friedman, V.P.; Renee D. Strelitz, V.P.; Michael Smith, Secy.
EIN: 541674740

1369
Fibre Converters, Inc.

1 Industrial Park Dr.
P.O. Box 130
Constantine, MI 49042-8735
(269) 279-1700

Company URL: http://www.fibreconverters.com
Establishment information: Established in 1949.
Company type: Private company
Business activities: Manufactures laminated and vinyl coated paper and paperboard.
Business type (SIC): Paper and paperboard/coated, converted, and laminated
Financial profile for 2010: Number of employees, 48
Corporate officers: James D. Stuck, Pres. and C.E.O.; Stephen N. Reed, V.P., Opers.; David M. Posey, Cont.
Board of director: David C. Lushin
Giving statement: Giving through the Fibre Converters Foundation, Inc.

Fibre Converters Foundation, Inc.

1 Industrial Ave.
P.O. Box 130
Constantine, MI 49042-0248 (269) 279-1700

Establishment information: Incorporated in 1957 in MI.
Donor: Fibre Converters, Inc.
Contact: David T. Stuck, Dir.
Financial data (yr. ended 03/31/12): Assets, $1,013,336 (M); expenditures, $49,714; qualifying distributions, $39,200; giving activities include $39,200 for grants.
Purpose and activities: The foundation supports organizations involved with education, health, and Christianity.
Fields of interest: Education; Health care; Religion.
Type of support: General/operating support.
Application information: Applications accepted. Application form required. Applicants should submit the following:
1) name, address and phone number of organization
2) copy of IRS Determination Letter
3) brief history of organization and description of its mission
4) detailed description of project and amount of funding requested
Initial approach: Proposal
Deadline(s): None
Directors: David T. Stuck; James D. Stuck.
EIN: 386081026

1370
FIDELIO Insurance Company, Inc.

2826 Mt. Carmel Ave.
Glenside, PA 19038-2245 (215) 885-2443

Company URL: https://www.fideliodental.com
Establishment information: Established in 1986.
Company type: Subsidiary of a private company
Business activities: Provides insurance brokerage services.
Business type (SIC): Insurance agents, brokers, and services
Corporate officers: Mike Mele, C.E.O.; Mario V. Mele, Pres.; Dorothy Gentilcore, Secy.; Frank Mele, Treas.
Giving statement: Giving through the FIDELIO Foundation.

The FIDELIO Foundation

2826 Mt. Carmel Ave.
Glenside, PA 19038-2245

Establishment information: Established in 2001 in PA.
Donors: FIDELIO Insurance, Inc.; Dental Delivery, Inc.; Mario V. Mele; Salvatore Mele; Mutual Fire Foundation; Mario Mele; Fidelio Insurance Company; Dental Delivery Systems, Inc.
Financial data (yr. ended 12/31/11): Assets, $820,538 (M); gifts received, $60,000; expenditures, $51,802; qualifying distributions, $40,000; giving activities include $40,000 for grants.
Purpose and activities: The foundation supports organizations involved with Christianity.
Fields of interest: Arts; Religion.
Geographic limitations: Giving limited to Philadelphia, PA.
Support limitations: No grants to individuals.
Application information: Applications not accepted. Unsolicited requests for funds not accepted.
Trustee: Caroline D. Bratic; Mario V. Mele.
EIN: 036074145

1371
Fidelity National Information Services, Inc.

(also known as FIS)
601 Riverside Ave.
Jacksonville, FL 32204 (904) 854-5000
FAX: (904) 357-1105

Company URL: http://www.fisglobal.com
Establishment information: Established in 1968.
Company type: Public company
Company ticker symbol and exchange: FIS/NYSE
Business activities: Operates financial services technology company.
Business type (SIC): Computer services
Financial profile for 2012: Number of employees, 35,000; assets, $13,549,700,000; sales volume, $5,807,600,000; pre-tax net income, $831,200,000; expenses, $4,728,400,000; liabilities, $6,908,800,000
Fortune 1000 ranking: 2012—434th in revenues, 351st in profits, and 317th in assets
Forbes 2000 ranking: 2012—1301st in sales, 1118th in profits, and 1248th in assets
Corporate officers: Frank R. Martire, Chair. and C.E.O.; Gary Norcross, Pres. and C.O.O.; Michael D. Hayford, Exec. V.P. and C.F.O.; Greg Schaffer, Exec. V.P. and C.I.O.; Michael Gravelle, Exec. V.P. and Secy.; James Woodall, Sr. V.P., C.A.O., and Cont.; Kirk Larsen, Sr. V.P. and Treas.
Board of directors: Frank R. Martire, Chair.; William P. Foley II; Thomas M. Hagerty; Keith W. Hughes; David K. Hunt; Stephan A. James; Richard N. Massey; James C. Neary
Giving statement: Giving through the FIS Foundation, Inc.
Company EIN: 371490331

FIS Foundation, Inc.

(formerly Metavante Technologies Foundation, Inc.)
601 Riverside Ave., Corp. Tax Dept.
Jacksonville, FL 32204-2901

Establishment information: Established in 2007 in WI.
Donor: Metavante Technologies, Inc.
Contact: Donald W. Layden, Jr., Secy.
Financial data (yr. ended 12/31/11): Assets, $851,241 (M); gifts received, $606,000; expenditures, $958,365; qualifying distributions, $958,305; giving activities include $958,305 for 158 grants (high: $150,000; low: $100).
Purpose and activities: The foundation supports organizations involved with arts and culture, education, health, cancer, cancer research, and children services.
Fields of interest: Museums; Performing arts; Arts; Higher education; Scholarships/financial aid; Education; Hospitals (general); Health care, patient services; Health care; Cancer; Cancer, leukemia;

Cancer research; Big Brothers/Big Sisters; Youth development, business; American Red Cross; Children, services.
Type of support: General/operating support; Program development.
Geographic limitations: Giving primarily in FL.
Application information: Applications not accepted. Contributes only to pre-selected organizations.
Officers: Frank R. Martire, Pres.; Michael D. Hayford, V.P. and Treas.; Michael Oates, Secy.
EIN: 261628191
Selected grants: The following grants are a representative sample of this grantmaker's funding activity:
$200,000 to United Way of Greater Milwaukee, Milwaukee, WI, 2010.
$50,000 to United Way of Greater Milwaukee, Milwaukee, WI, 2010.
$32,500 to Cathedral Arts Project, Jacksonville, FL, 2010.
$10,000 to American Diabetes Association, Milwaukee, WI, 2010.
$10,000 to Childrens Hospital and Health System Foundation, Milwaukee, WI, 2010.
$10,000 to Notre Dame Middle School, Milwaukee, WI, 2010.
$5,000 to Alliance for Children and Families, Milwaukee, WI, 2010.
$5,000 to American Diabetes Association, Jacksonville, FL, 2010.
$5,000 to Museum of Science and History, Jacksonville, FL, 2010.
$5,000 to Special Olympics Wisconsin, Milwaukee, WI, 2010.

1372
Fidelity Products Company

(formerly Fidelity File Box, Inc.)
5601 International Pkwy.
Minneapolis, MN 55428-3046
(612) 536-6500

Establishment information: Established in 2004.
Company type: Private company
Business activities: Distributes office and industrial supplies and equipment.
Business type (SIC): Paper and paper products—wholesale; furniture/office; fixtures/office and store; furniture and fixtures/miscellaneous; furniture and home furnishings—wholesale; industrial machinery and equipment—wholesale
Giving statement: Giving through the Mike and Linda Fiterman Family Foundation.

Mike and Linda Fiterman Family Foundation

(formerly The Jack and Bessie Fiterman Foundation)
5500 Wayzata Blvd., Ste. 1015
Minneapolis, MN 55416-1255 (763) 971-1904

Establishment information: Established in 1966 in MN.
Donors: Fidelity Products Co.; Liberty Carton Co.; Safco Products Co.; Shamrock Industries, Inc.; FLS Properties; B&B Lease Co.; Liberty Diversified Industries, Inc.
Contact: Linda Fiterman, Treas.
Financial data (yr. ended 05/31/12): Assets, $12,230,134 (M); gifts received, $1,100,000; expenditures, $1,076,139; qualifying distributions, $994,450; giving activities include $994,450 for grants.
Purpose and activities: The foundation supports hospitals and clinics and organizations involved with education, employment, housing development, human services, and religion.
Fields of interest: Education, early childhood education; Elementary school/education; Education; Hospitals (general); Health care, clinics/centers; Employment, services; Housing/shelter, development; YM/YWCAs & YM/YWHAs; Children/youth, services; Family services; Developmentally disabled, centers & services; Human services; Catholic agencies & churches; Jewish agencies & synagogues; Religion.
Type of support: General/operating support.
Geographic limitations: Giving primarily in MN.
Support limitations: No support for lobbying or advocacy groups. No grants to individuals.
Application information: Applications accepted. Application form required.
Initial approach: Contact foundation for application form
Deadline(s): None
Officers: Michael Fiterman, Pres.; David Lenzen, Secy.; Linda Fiterman, Treas.
EIN: 416058465
Selected grants: The following grants are a representative sample of this grantmaker's funding activity:
$102,500 to Herzl Camp, Saint Louis Park, MN, 2009.
$25,000 to Minneapolis Foundation, Minneapolis, MN, 2009.
$15,000 to Minnesota Early Learning Foundation, Minneapolis, MN, 2009.
$10,000 to Twin Cities RISE, Minneapolis, MN, 2009.
$8,500 to YouthCARE, Minneapolis, MN, 2009.
$3,500 to Saint Louis Park Emergency Program, Saint Louis Park, MN, 2009.
$2,500 to Sharing and Caring Hands, Minneapolis, MN, 2009.
$1,000 to Bridging, Inc., Bloomington, MN, 2009.
$1,000 to Nash Avery Foundation, Minneapolis, MN, 2009.
$1,000 to Working Family Resource Center, Saint Paul, MN, 2009.

1373
Fieldale Farms Corporation

555 Broiler Blvd.
P.O. Box 558
Baldwin, GA 30511-0558 (706) 778-5100

Company URL: http://www.fieldale.com
Establishment information: Established in 1972.
Company type: Private company
Business activities: Produces poultry.
Business type (SIC): Farms/poultry and egg
Corporate officers: Thomas Hensley, Pres.; Joseph M. Hatfield, Exec. V.P., Opers.
Giving statement: Giving through the Fieldale Farms Foundation.

Fieldale Farms Foundation

P.O. Box 558
Baldwin, GA 30511-0558

Establishment information: Established in GA.
Financial data (yr. ended 12/31/12): Assets, $119,818 (M); expenditures, $9,306; qualifying distributions, $9,250; giving activities include $9,250 for 7 grants (high: $2,500; low: $250).
Purpose and activities: The foundation supports health clinics and organizations involved with higher education and counseling.
Fields of interest: Education; Public affairs.
Type of support: General/operating support; Scholarship funds.
Geographic limitations: Giving primarily in GA.
Application information: Applications not accepted. Unsolicited requests for funds not accepted.
Officers: Thomas M. Hensley, Jr., Pres.; Joe M. Hatfield, V.P.; Thomas A. Arrendale III, V.P.
EIN: 582511834

1374
Fieldstone Communities, Inc.

30 Fairbanks, Ste. 100
Irvine, CA 92618 (949) 790-5400
FAX: (949) 453-0944

Company URL: http://www.fieldstone-homes.com
Establishment information: Established in 1981.
Company type: Private company
Business activities: Builds houses.
Business type (SIC): Operative builders
Financial profile for 2010: Number of employees, 150
Corporate officers: Peter M. Ochs, Chair.; Keith A. Johnson, Vice-Chair.; William H. McFarland, C.E.O.; C. Alan Arthur, Pres. and C.F.O.
Board of directors: Peter M. Ochs, Chair.; Keith Johnson, Vice-Chair.
Offices: San Diego, CA; San Antonio, TX; Salt Lake City, UT
Giving statement: Giving through the Fieldstone Foundation.

The Fieldstone Foundation

14 Corporate Plz., Ste. 100
Newport Beach, CA 92660-7995 (949) 873-2717
FAX: (949) 453-0944; URL: http://fieldstonefoundation.org/

Establishment information: Established in 1983 in CA.
Donor: Fieldstone Communities, Inc.
Contact: Janine Mason, Secy.
Financial data (yr. ended 12/31/11): Assets, $3,977,997 (M); expenditures, $535,355; qualifying distributions, $509,499; giving activities include $168,850 for 88 grants (high: $8,500; low: $50).
Purpose and activities: The foundation supports programs designed to address humanitarian issues; community and education; cultural arts; and Christian ministries. Special emphasis is directed toward programs designed to serve children and families.
Fields of interest: Arts, cultural/ethnic awareness; Arts education; Arts; Child development, education; Education, reading; Education; Substance abuse, services; Crime/violence prevention, abuse prevention; Crime/violence prevention, domestic violence; Crime/violence prevention, child abuse; Housing/shelter; Youth development; Children/youth, services; Children, foster care; Family services; Human services; Community/economic development; Leadership development; Public affairs; Christian agencies & churches.
Programs:
Christian Ministries: The foundation supports programs designed to promote Christianity, Christian leadership, and Christian values.
Community and Education: The foundation supports programs designed to promote literacy; youth character building and personal development; after-school programs; crime and community violence prevention; and community empowerment to deal with local issues.

Cultural Arts: The foundation supports programs designed to promote arts education; cultural awareness, understanding, and participation of children and families in the arts; art as a mechanism to address community issues; and art as a tool to deal with abuse, trauma, and loss.

Humanitarian: The foundation supports programs designed to promote affordable housing; family violence prevention through domestic violence prevention, battered women services, and child abuse or neglect prevention; emergency assistance and crisis prevention for families with children; foster care and youth emancipation; and substance abuse prevention.

Type of support: Employee matching gifts; General/operating support; Management development/capacity building; Matching/challenge support; Program development; Scholarship funds.
Geographic limitations: Giving primarily in areas of company operations in San Diego and Orange Counties, CA.
Support limitations: No support for political parties or candidates, veterans', labor, fraternal, or athletic organizations not of direct benefit to the entire community, or individual churches. No grants to individuals, or for advertising, continuing support, or capital campaigns.
Publications: Grants list.
Application information: Applications accepted. Application form not required. Applicants should submit the following:
1) copy of IRS Determination Letter
2) detailed description of project and amount of funding requested

Initial approach: Request application
Deadline(s): None

Officers: Peter M. Ochs, Chair.; Keith A. Johnson, Pres.; Rick Haugen, Treas.; Janine Mason, Secy.
Number of staff: 1 full-time professional; 1 part-time professional; 1 part-time support.
EIN: 330103025
Selected grants: The following grants are a representative sample of this grantmaker's funding activity:
$9,250 to National Network of Youth Ministries, San Diego, CA, 2009.
$7,500 to Families Forward, Irvine, CA, 2009. For program support.
$5,000 to Center for Family Relations, San Antonio, TX, 2009. For scholarships.
$5,000 to Laguna Playhouse, Laguna Beach, CA, 2009.
$5,000 to Make-A-Wish Foundation of Utah, Murray, UT, 2009.
$5,000 to Moolelo Performing Arts Company, San Diego, CA, 2009.
$5,000 to University of San Diego, San Diego, CA, 2009.
$4,000 to Boy Scouts of America, Santa Ana, CA, 2009.
$3,000 to El Viento Foundation, Huntington Beach, CA, 2009. For program support.
$3,000 to San Diego Council on Literacy, San Diego, CA, 2009. For general support.

1375
Fiesta Mart, Inc.

5235 Katy Fwy.
Houston, TX 77007-2210 (713) 869-5060

Company URL: http://www.fiestamart.com
Establishment information: Established in 1972.
Company type: Subsidiary of a private company
Business activities: Operates grocery stores.
Business type (SIC): Groceries—retail
Corporate officers: Louis Katopodis, Pres. and C.E.O.; Stacey Walker, C.F.O.; Charles H. Carmouche, Genl. Counsel
Giving statement: Giving through the Fiesta Mart, Inc. Corporate Giving Program.

Fiesta Mart, Inc. Corporate Giving Program

5235 Katy Fwy.
Houston, TX 77007-2210 (713) 869-5060

Purpose and activities: Fiesta Mart makes charitable contributions to nonprofit organizations involved with education, sports, and on a case by case basis. Support is given primarily in areas of company store operations.
Fields of interest: Education; Recreation; General charitable giving.
Type of support: Donated products; General/operating support.
Geographic limitations: Giving primarily in areas of company store operations.

1376
Fifth & Pacific Companies, Inc.

(formerly Liz Clairborne, Inc.)
1441 Broadway
New York, NY 10018-1805 (212) 354-4900
FAX: (212) 626-1800

Company URL: http://fifthandpacific.com
Establishment information: Established in 1976.
Company type: Public company
Company ticker symbol and exchange: FNP/NYSE
Business activities: Designs and markets women's and men's clothing and accessories.
Business type (SIC): Apparel—women's outerwear; apparel, piece goods, and notions—wholesale
Financial profile for 2012: Number of employees, 5,800; assets, $902,520,000; sales volume, $1,505,090,000; pre-tax net income, -$55,990,000; expenses, $1,549,300,000; liabilities, $1,029,450,000
Corporate officers: Nancy J. Karch, Chair.; William L. McComb, C.E.O.; George M. Carrara, Exec. V.P., C.O.O., and C.F.O.; Nicholas Rubino, Sr. V.P., Genl. Counsel, and Corp. Secy.; Linda Yanussi, Sr. V.P., Opers.; Robert J. Vill, Sr. V.P., Finance and Treas.; Jane Randel, Sr. V.P., Corp. Comms.; William Higley, Sr. V.P., Human Resources.; Michael Rinaldo, V.P., Corp. Cont., and C.A.O.
Board of directors: Nancy J. Karch, Chair.; Bernard W. Aronson; Lawrence S. Benjamin; Raul J. Fernandez; Kenneth B. Gilman; Kenneth P. Kopelman; Kay Koplovitz; Arthur C. Martinez; William L. McComb; Doreen A. Toben
Plants: North Bergen, NJ; New York, NY
International operations: Austria; Belgium; Brazil; Canada; China; Colombia; Costa Rica; Czech Republic; El Salvador; Finland; France; Germany; Greece; Hong Kong; Hungary; Ireland; Israel; Italy; Luxembourg; Malaysia; Mexico; Netherlands; Norway; Poland; Portugal; Spain; Sweden; Switzerland; United Kingdom
Giving statement: Giving through the Fifth & Pacific Foundation.
Company EIN: 132842791

Fifth & Pacific Foundation

(formerly Liz Claiborne Foundation)
1441 Broadway
New York, NY 10018-1805 (212) 626-5704
FAX: (212) 626-1841;
E-mail: Foundation@fnpc.com; URL: http://www.fifthandpacific.com/web/guest/foundation

Establishment information: Established in 1981 in NY.
Donors: Liz Claiborne Inc.; Fifth & Pacific Companies, Inc.
Contact: Sheila M. Renovitch, Dir.; Alison Mathias, Prog. Off.
Financial data (yr. ended 12/31/10): Assets, $25,677,162 (M); expenditures, $1,438,776; qualifying distributions, $1,240,854; giving activities include $1,240,853 for 37+ grants (high: $50,000).
Purpose and activities: The foundation supports programs designed to promote women's economic self-sufficiency. Special emphasis is directed toward women affected by domestic violence who are transitioning from poverty into successful independent living.
Fields of interest: Employment, services; Employment, training; Family services, domestic violence; Human services; Economic development Women.
Program:

Matching Gift Program: The foundation matches contributions made by full-time employees of Fifth & Pacific to nonprofit organizations on a one-for-one basis from $25 to $10,000 per employee, per year and to nonprofit organizations with which employees serve on the board of directors, on a two-for-one basis.

Type of support: Annual campaigns; Employee matching gifts; General/operating support; Matching/challenge support; Program development; Technical assistance.
Geographic limitations: Giving primarily in areas of company operations with emphasis on Los Angeles County, CA, Hudson County, NJ, and New York, NY; limited giving also to national organizations.
Support limitations: No support for political organizations, or religious, fraternal, or veterans' organizations. No grants to individuals, or for capital campaigns, equipment, professional meetings, conferences, or symposia, endowments, research, technical assistance, media projects, fundraising events, sponsorships, or journal advertisements.
Publications: Application guidelines.
Application information: Applications accepted. Application form not required. Applicants should submit the following:
1) qualifications of key personnel
2) copy of IRS Determination Letter
3) brief history of organization and description of its mission
4) copy of most recent annual report/audited financial statement/990
5) how project's results will be evaluated or measured
6) listing of board of directors, trustees, officers and other key people and their affiliations
7) detailed description of project and amount of funding requested
8) copy of current year's organizational budget and/or project budget
9) listing of additional sources and amount of support

Applications should also include a description of how the program or project is to be carried out; the number of professional and support staff, their titles, and qualifications; number of clients to be served for the upcoming grant period; measurable outcomes for the upcoming grant period; program sources of income and revenue for each fiscal year for which a budget is submitted; actual, pledged, and pending grants for each fiscal year for which a budget is submitted; and any shortfalls between the expenses and anticipated income in the year for which the grant is requested and an explanation of how the remaining amount will be covered.

Initial approach: Download proposal cover sheet and mail proposal and cover sheet to foundation

Copies of proposal: 1

Board meeting date(s): Quarterly

Deadline(s): None

Final notification: 5 days following board meetings

Officers and Directors :* John Moroz*, Chair.; Alison Mathias, Secy. and Prog. Off.; John Engeman, Treas.; Sheila Renovitch, Fdn. Dir.; Diana Buchman; Jerome Chazen; Elaine Goodell; Evon Jones; Roberta Karp; Craig Leavitt; William McComb; John Moroz; Jane Randel; Nick Rubino.

Number of staff: 2 full-time professional.

EIN: 133060673

Selected grants: The following grants are a representative sample of this grantmaker's funding activity:

$75,000 to Joyful Heart Foundation, New York, NY, 2012. For No More Project.

$65,000 to Sanctuary for Families, New York, NY, 2011.

$50,000 to Rising Tide Capital, Jersey City, NJ, 2011.

$50,000 to Womens Initiative for Self Employment, San Francisco, CA, 2011. For Women's Initiative in the New York City metropolitan area.

$45,000 to Hot Bread Kitchen, Brooklyn, NY, 2012.

$30,000 to Women in Nontraditional Employment Roles, Long Beach, CA, 2011.

1377
Fifth Third Bank

38 Fountain Sq. Plz.
Fifth 3rd Ctr.
Cincinnati, OH 45263-0001 (513) 579-5300

Company URL: http://www.53.com
Establishment information: Established in 1858.
Company type: Subsidiary of a public company
Ultimate parent company: Fifth Third Bancorp
International Securities Identification Number: US3167731005
Business activities: Operates commercial bank.
Business type (SIC): Banks/commercial
Corporate officers: Kevin T. Kabat, Vice-Chair. and C.E.O.; Greg D. Carmichael, Pres. and C.O.O.; Daniel T. Poston, Exec. V.P. and C.F.O.; Todd Clossin, Exec. V.P. and C.A.O.; Joseph R. Robinson, Exec. V.P. and C.I.O.; Paul L. Reynolds, Exec. V.P. and Secy.; Tayfun Tuzun, Sr. V.P. and Treas.; Mark D. Hazel, Sr. V.P. and Cont.
Board of director: Kevin T. Kabat, Vice-Chair.
Giving statement: Giving through the Fifth Third Bank Corporate Giving Program and the Fifth Third Foundation.
Company EIN: 621376024

Fifth Third Bank Corporate Giving Program

c/o Community Affairs
Fifth Third Ctr.
Cincinnati, OH 45263-0001 (513) 534-8525
URL: https://www.53.com/site/about/in-the-community/index.html

Purpose and activities: As a complement to its foundation, Fifth Third also makes charitable contributions to nonprofit organizations directly. Support is given primarily in areas of company operations in Florida, Georgia, Illinois, Indiana, Kentucky, Michigan, Missouri, North Carolina, Ohio, Pennsylvania, Tennessee, and Virginia.
Fields of interest: Education; Youth development; Human services, financial counseling; Community/economic development; Financial services.
Type of support: Employee volunteer services; Program development; Sponsorships.
Geographic limitations: Giving primarily in areas of company operations in FL, GA, IL, IN, KY, MI, MO, NC, OH, PA, TN, and VA.
Publications: Corporate giving report.
Application information: The Community Affairs Department handles giving.

The Fifth Third Foundation

38 Fountain Square Plz., M.D. 1090CA
Cincinnati, OH 45263 (513) 534-4397
FAX: (513) 534-0960; Additional tel.: (513) 534-7001; URL: https://www.53.com/wps/portal/av/?New_WCM_Context=/wps/wcm/connect/FifthThirdSite/About+53/In+the+Community

Establishment information: Trust established in 1948 in OH.
Donor: Fifth Third Bank.
Contact: Heidi B. Jark, Managing Dir.
Financial data (yr. ended 09/30/12): Assets, $9,924,821 (M); gifts received, $6,000,000; expenditures, $4,649,679; qualifying distributions, $4,599,210; giving activities include $4,571,877 for 599 grants (high: $500,000; low: $25).
Purpose and activities: The foundation supports organizations involved with arts and culture, education, health, human services, and community development.
Fields of interest: Arts; Higher education; Business school/education; Education; Health care; Housing/shelter; American Red Cross; Human services; Community/economic development; United Ways and Federated Giving Programs.
Programs:

Employee Matching Gifts: The foundation matches contributions made by full-time employees of Fifth Third to educational institutions on a one-for-one basis from $25 to $500 per employee, per institution.

Fifth Third Scholarship Program: The foundation annually awards 17 $2,500 college scholarships to children of employees of Fifth Third. The program is administered by the National Merit Scholarship Corporation.

Type of support: Annual campaigns; Building/renovation; Capital campaigns; Continuing support; Employee-related scholarships; Equipment; General/operating support; Program development; Scholarship funds.
Geographic limitations: Giving primarily in areas of company operations in FL, GA, IL, IN, KY, MI, MO, NC, OH, PA, TN, and WV.
Support limitations: No support for individual churches or publicly-supported organizations or government agencies; generally, no support for elementary or middle schools. No grants to individuals (except for employee-related scholarships).
Publications: Application guidelines; Corporate giving report.
Application information: Applications accepted. Visit website for nearest company facility address. A full proposal may be requested. A site visit may be requested. Support is limited to 1 contribution per organization during any given year. Support is limited to 3 years for multi-year grants. Applicants seeking multi-year funding must meet additional requirements. Organizations receiving support are asked to submit a written evaluation. Application form not required. Applicants should submit the following:

1) brief history of organization and description of its mission
2) detailed description of project and amount of funding requested

Initial approach: Letter of inquiry to nearest company facility; contact foundation for major campaign requests

Board meeting date(s): Jan., Mar., June, and Sept.

Deadline(s): None

Final notification: 6 months

Trustee: Fifth Third Bank.
EIN: 316024135

1378
Figari & Davenport, L.L.P.

3400 Bank of America Plz., 901 Main St.
Dallas, TX 75202-3776 (214) 939-2000

Company URL: http://www.figdav.com
Establishment information: Established in 1986.
Company type: Private company
Business activities: Operates law firm.
Business type (SIC): Legal services
Corporate officer: Michael G. Brown, Partner
Giving statement: Giving through the Figari & Davenport, L.L.P. Pro Bono Program.

Figari & Davenport, L.L.P. Pro Bono Program

901 Main St., Ste. 3400
Dallas, TX 75202-3776 (214) 939-2000
FAX: (214) 939-2090; URL: http://www.figdav.com

Fields of interest: Legal services.
Type of support: Pro bono services - legal.
Geographic limitations: Giving primarily in areas of company operations in Dallas, TX.

1379
Fila USA Inc.

1 Fila Way
Sparks, MD 21152-3000 (410) 773-3000

Company URL: http://www.fila.com
Establishment information: Established in 1923.
Company type: Subsidiary of a private company
Business activities: Manufactures and distributes footwear.
Business type (SIC): Leather footwear; apparel, piece goods, and notions—wholesale
Corporate officers: Gene Y.S. Yoon, Chair.; Jonathan G. Epstein, Pres.; Young-Chan Cho, C.F.O.
Board of director: Gene Y.S. Yoon, Chair.
Giving statement: Giving through the Fila USA Inc. Corporate Giving Program.

Fila USA Inc. Corporate Giving Program

c/o Community Rels.
930 Ridgebrook Rd., Ste. 200
Sparks, MD 21152-9390 (410) 773-3000
E-mail: lmellon@fila.com; Additional tel.: (410) 773-3236; URL: http://www.fila.com/us/eng/corporate/sponsorships

Contact: Lauren Mallon, Mgr., Global Mktg.
Purpose and activities: Fila makes charitable contributions to nonprofit organizations on a case by

case basis. Support is given on a national basis, primarily to a preferred partner.
Fields of interest: General charitable giving.
Type of support: Donated products; General/operating support; In-kind gifts; Sponsorships.
Geographic limitations: Giving on a national basis.
Application information: Applications accepted. Proposals should be submitted using organization letterhead. Most giving through pre-selected organizations. Application form not required.
Initial approach: Proposal to headquarters
Deadline(s): None

1380
FileMaker, Inc.
5201 Patrick Henry Dr.
Santa Clara, CA 95054-1171
(408) 987-7000

Company URL: http://www.filemaker.com
Establishment information: Established in 1998.
Company type: Subsidiary of a public company
Business activities: Develops database solution computer software.
Business type (SIC): Computer services
Corporate officers: Dominique Philippe Goupil, Pres.; Bill Epling, Sr. V.P., Finance, and Opers.; Dave Williams, V.P., Finance; Ryan Rosenberg, V.P., Mktg.; John Pinheiro, V.P., Human Resources, and Genl. Counsel; Scott Lewis, V.P., Opers. and Inf. Systems
Giving statement: Giving through the FileMaker, Inc. Corporate Giving Program.

FileMaker, Inc. Corporate Giving Program
5201 Patrick Henry Dr.
Santa Clara, CA 95054-1164 (408) 987-7000
Application address: Good360, 1330 Braddock Pl., Ste. 600, Alexandria, VA 22314; URL: http://www.good360.org/; URL: http://www.filemaker.com/company/donations.html

Purpose and activities: FileMaker makes charitable contributions of software licenses to nonprofit organizations on a case by case basis. Support is given on a national and international basis.
Fields of interest: General charitable giving.
Type of support: Donated products.
Geographic limitations: Giving on a national and international basis.
Application information: Applications accepted. Application form required.
Initial approach: Visit Good360 website for application details

1381
Finance Factors Limited
1164 Bishop St., Ste. 100
P.O. Box 3979
Honolulu, HI 96813 (808) 548-3311
FAX: (808) 548-4959

Company URL: http://www.financefactors.com
Establishment information: Established in 1952.
Company type: Private company
Business activities: Provides mortgages.
Business type (SIC): Brokers and bankers/mortgage
Corporate officers: Russell J. Lau, Vice-Chair. and C.E.O.; Steven J. Teruya, Pres. and C.O.O.; Aaron Sato, Sr. V.P. and Co-C.F.O.; Jed Sueoka, V.P. and Co-C.F.O.
Board of director: Russell J. Lau, Vice-Chair.
Giving statement: Giving through the Finance Factors Foundation.

Finance Factors Foundation
1164 Bishop St., Ste. 1089
Honolulu, HI 96813-2810 (808) 548-3393
E-mail: info@financefactors.com; URL: http://www.financefactors.com/community.html

Establishment information: Established in 1998 in HI as successor to the original Finance Factors Foundation, established in 1958.
Donor: Finance Factors, Ltd.
Contact: June Yip
Financial data (yr. ended 12/31/11): Assets, $1,373,571 (M); gifts received, $1,382; expenditures, $72,597; qualifying distributions, $67,814; giving activities include $67,814 for grants.
Purpose and activities: The foundation supports organizations involved with arts and culture, education, health, multiple sclerosis, hunger, human services, community development, and civic affairs.
Fields of interest: Education; Environment; Human services.
Type of support: Employee matching gifts; General/operating support.
Geographic limitations: Giving primarily in HI.
Support limitations: No grants to individuals.
Application information: Applications accepted. Application form required. Applicants should submit the following:
1) brief history of organization and description of its mission
2) detailed description of project and amount of funding requested
Initial approach: Letter
Deadline(s): None
Officers and Directors:* Daniel B.T. Lau*, Pres. and Secy.; Russell J. Lau*, V.P. and Treas.; Patrick Chun*, V.P.; Jeffrey D. Lau, V.P.; June Yip, V.P.; Jennifer Chapman; Date Fong; Pearl Fong; Daniel B.T. lau; Russell J. Lau.
EIN: 311642776

1382
Financial Industry Regulatory Authority, Inc.
(formerly National Association of Securities Dealers, Inc.)
1735 K St. N.W.
Washington, DC 20006-1516
(301) 590-6500

Company URL: http://www.nasd.com
Establishment information: Established in 1939.
Company type: Private company
Business activities: Provides financial regulatory services; operates stock exchange.
Business type (SIC): Security and commodity brokers, dealers, exchanges, and services; security and commodity exchange
Corporate officers: Richard G. Ketchum, Chair. and C.E.O.; Stephen Luparello, Vice-Chair.; Todd T. DiGanci, Exec. V.P. and C.F.O.; Grant Gallery, Exec. V.P. and Genl. Counsel; Gregory Ahern, Exec. V.P., Corp. Comms.; Marcia E. Asquith, Sr. V.P. and Corp. Secy.; Tracy Johnson, Sr. V.P., Human Resources
Board of directors: Richard G. Ketchum, Chair.; Stephen Luparello, Vice-Chair.; Jed Bandes; Joel R. Blumenschein; Charles A. Bowsher; John J. Brennan; Ellyn L. Brown; Richard F. Brueckner; James E. Burton; Mark S. Casady; John F. X. Dolan; W. Dennis Ferguson; Harvey J. Goldschmid; William H. Heyman; Shirley Ann Jackson; Ken Norensberg; Richard S. Pechter; John W. Schmidlin; Joel Seligman; Gary H. Stern; Kurt P. Stocker; Seth H. Waugh; James D. Weddle
Subsidiaries: American Stock Exchange LLC, New York, NY; NASD Regulation, Inc., Rockville, MD
Giving statement: Giving through the FINRA Investor Education Foundation.

FINRA Investor Education Foundation
(formerly NASD Investor Education Foundation)
1735 K St., N.W.
Washington, DC 20006-1506 (202) 728-6964
FAX: (202) 728-8149; URL: http://www.finrafoundation.org

Establishment information: Established in 2004 in DE as the NASD Investor Education Foundation; current name adopted in 2007.
Donor: National Association of Securities Dealers, Inc.
Contact: John M. Gannon, Secy.
Financial data (yr. ended 12/31/11): Revenue, $2,385,831; assets, $51,238,393 (M); gifts received, $1,500,000; expenditures, $12,512,892; giving activities include $5,105,343 for grants.
Purpose and activities: The foundation seeks to support financial education and provide investors with high quality, easily accessible information and tools to better understand investing and the markets; the foundation is also interested in programs and research to help older Americans handle their finances during retirement.
Fields of interest: Education; Economics; Public affairs, finance; Financial services Aging.
Program:
General Grant Program: Through its grant program, the foundation funds research and/or educational projects that support its mission of providing underserved Americans with the knowledge, skills, and tools necessary for financial success throughout life. The foundation is interested in funding projects that will reach and actively engage at-risk audiences, such as seniors and first-time investors, by offering them access to unbiased information about the markets and fundamental financial issues. There is no set minimum or maximum for the number of grants to be funded or for the amounts of the grants awarded. Each year, the foundation chooses specific targets with which to focus its grantmaking.
Type of support: Program development; Research.
Geographic limitations: Giving on a national basis.
Support limitations: No grants to individuals.
Publications: Grants list; Newsletter.
Application information: Applications accepted. The foundation accepts three-page project concept forms at any time during the year; the foundation will respond to a completed project concept form within one month of receipt and either decline the request or invite a full proposal. Full proposals will be reviewed three times a year, though concept forms are accepted anytime. Contact organization for current grantmaking priorities. Application form required.
Initial approach: Submit project concept form online
Deadline(s): Feb. 8, Apr. 11, and July 12
Final notification: June, Oct., and Dec.
Officers and Directors:* Richard G. Ketchum*, Chair.; Geraldine M. Walsh, Pres.; Marcia E. Asquith, Secy.; Eileen M. Famiglietti, Treas.; Jayne Barnard;

Idalia P. Fernandez; John T. Dooley; Sharon P. Smith; G. Donald Steel.
EIN: 200863779

1383
The Finish Line, Inc.

3308 N. Mitthoeffer Rd.
Indianapolis, IN 46235 (317) 899-1022
FAX: (317) 899-0237

Company URL: http://www.finishline.com
Establishment information: Established in 1976.
Company type: Public company
Company ticker symbol and exchange: FINL/NASDAQ
Business activities: Operates athletic and lifestyle footwear, activewear, and accessories stores.
Business type (SIC): Shoe stores
Financial profile for 2013: Number of employees, 11,900; assets, $706,420,000; sales volume, $1,443,370,000; pre-tax net income, $112,500,000; expenses, $1,331,070,000; liabilities, $181,560,000
Corporate officers: Glenn S. Lyon, Chair. and C.E.O.; Steven J. Schneider, Pres. and C.O.O.; Edward W. Wilhelm, Exec. V.P. and C.F.O.
Board of directors: Glenn S. Lyon, Chair.; Torrence Boone; William P. Carmichael; Richard P. Crystal; Stephen Goldsmith; Norman H. Gurwitz; Bill Kirkendall; Dolores A. Kunda; Catherine A. Langham
Giving statement: Giving through the Finish Line Youth Foundation, Inc.
Company EIN: 351537210

Finish Line Youth Foundation, Inc.

3308 N. Mitthoeffer Rd.
Indianapolis, IN 46235-2332
E-mail: Youthfoundation@finishline.com;
URL: http://www.finishline.com/store/youthfoundation/youthfoundation.jsp

Establishment information: Established in 1998 in IN.
Donors: The Finish Line, Inc.; The Sablosky Family Foundation, Inc.; Reebok International Ltd.; The Cohen Family Foundation, Inc.; Adidas; Nike; PUMA; GE.
Contact: Micca Leppert, Prog. Dir.
Financial data (yr. ended 12/31/11): Assets, $7,211,828 (M); gifts received, $2,077,710; expenditures, $962,468; qualifying distributions, $626,110; giving activities include $626,110 for grants.
Purpose and activities: The foundation supports organizations involved with athletics and youth development. Special emphasis is directed toward programs designed to promote active lifestyles and team building skills; and camps designed to promote sports and active lifestyles, and serve disadvantaged and special needs kids.
Fields of interest: Recreation, camps; Athletics/sports, amateur leagues; Youth development Youth; Disabilities, people with; Economically disadvantaged.
Programs:

Founder's Grant: The foundation awards grants of up to $25,000 to nonprofit organizations that have an emergency need that would somehow be keeping the organization from providing current services.

Legacy Grant: The foundation awards grants of up to $75,000 to nonprofit organizations that need improvement and/or renovations to existing buildings, grounds, property, or for facilities and/or grounds.

Type of support: Building/renovation; Capital campaigns; Emergency funds; Equipment; Program development; Scholarship funds.
Geographic limitations: Giving on a national basis in areas of company operations.
Support limitations: No support for discriminatory organizations, religious organizations not of direct benefit to the entire community, fraternal, veterans', or labor organizations, or foundations affiliated with a for-profit entity. No grants to individuals, or for political campaigns, endowments, general operating support, start-up needs, debt reduction, beauty or talent contests, team sponsorships, special events, or fundraising activities, medical, scientific, or academic research, or travel.
Publications: Application guidelines.
Application information: Applications accepted. Application form required.
Initial approach: Complete online application
Board meeting date(s): Jan., Apr., July, and Oct.,
Deadline(s): Mar. 31, June 30, Sept. 30, and Dec. 31
Final notification: Mar. 1, June 1, Sept. 1, and Dec. 1
Officers and Directors:* Bob Edwards*, Pres.; Roger C. Underwood, V.P.; Mark Vlark, Secy.; Linda Disher, Treas.; Greg Davis; Danny Dean; Jenni Dillon; Chad Edmundson; Cindie Norris; Mike Northrop; Lisa Robinson; Curt Simc; Ed Wihelm.
EIN: 352059749
Selected grants: The following grants are a representative sample of this grantmaker's funding activity:
$40,000 to Gleaners Food Bank of Indiana, Indianapolis, IN, 2010.
$10,000 to Friendship Ventures, Annandale, MN, 2010.
$10,000 to Harpeth Youth Soccer Association, Nashville, TN, 2010.
$10,000 to Indianapolis Parks Foundation, Indianapolis, IN, 2010.
$7,500 to Dragonfly Forest, Conshohocken, PA, 2010.
$5,000 to American Diabetes Association, Bala Cynwyd, PA, 2010.
$5,000 to American Lung Association, Washington, DC, 2010.
$5,000 to Amputee Coalition of America, Knoxville, TN, 2010.
$5,000 to Green Hill Therapy, Louisville, KY, 2010.
$3,000 to Zina Garrison All Court Tennis Academy, Houston, TX, 2010.

1384
Finnegan, Henderson, Farabow, Garrett & Dunner, L.L.P.

901 New York Ave., N.W.
Washington, DC 20001-4413
(202) 408-4000

Company URL: http://www.finnegan.com
Establishment information: Established in 1965.
Company type: Private company
Business activities: Operates law firm.
Business type (SIC): Legal services
Offices: Palo Alto, CA; Washington, DC; Atlanta, GA; Cambridge, MA; Reston, VA
International operations: Belgium; China; Japan; Taiwan
Giving statement: Giving through the Finnegan, Henderson, Farabow, Garrett & Dunner, L.L.P. Pro Bono Program.

Finnegan, Henderson, Farabow, Garrett & Dunner, L.L.P. Pro Bono Program

901 New York Ave., N.W.
Washington, DC 20001-4413 (202) 408-4000
E-mail: christine.lehman@finnegan.com;
URL: http://www.finnegan.com/probono/

Contact: Christine Lehman, Chair, Pro Bono Comm.
Fields of interest: Legal services.
Type of support: Pro bono services - legal.
Geographic limitations: Giving primarily in Palo Alto, CA, Washington, DC, Atlanta, GA, Cambridge, MA, and Reston, VA, and in Belgium, China, Japan, and Taiwan.
Application information: The Pro Bono Committee manages the pro-bono program.

1385
Fireman's Fund Insurance Company

777 San Marin Dr.
Novato, CA 94998 (415) 899-3600

Company URL: http://www.firemansfund.com
Establishment information: Established in 1863.
Company type: Subsidiary of a foreign company
Business activities: Sells insurance.
Business type (SIC): Insurance carriers
Corporate officers: Gary Bhojwani, Chair.; Michael LaRocco, Pres. and C.E.O.; Jill Patterson, Exec. V.P. and C.F.O.; Antonio Derossi, C.O.O.; Gregory Tacchetti, Sr. V.P. and C.A.O.; Sally Narey, Corp. Secy.
Board of directors: Jan Carendi, Chair.; Michael LaRocco; Jill Paterson
Giving statement: Giving through the Fireman's Fund Foundation.

Fireman's Fund Foundation

(formerly Fireman's Fund Insurance Company Foundation)
777 San Marin Dr.
Novato, CA 94998-1320 (415) 899-2757
E-mail: gberg@ffic.com

Establishment information: Incorporated in 1953 in CA. Status changed to company-sponsored operating foundation in 2004.
Donor: Fireman's Fund Insurance Co.
Financial data (yr. ended 12/31/11): Assets, $3,181 (M); expenditures, $0; qualifying distributions, $0.
Purpose and activities: The foundation supports hospices and organizations involved with education, substance abuse, crime and violence, human services, civil rights, youth, senior citizens, mentally disabled people, women, economically disadvantaged people, and homeless people. Support is given primarily in areas of company operations.
Programs:

Education: The foundation supports programs designed to provide access to education for all segments of society; and promote knowledge with an emphasis on academic improvement, support of families, diversity, and tolerance.

Human Needs: The foundation supports programs designed to assist the elderly, mentally ill, and developmentally challenged; and provide prevention, education, and rehabilitation programs to combat various forms of abuse.

Type of support: Employee matching gifts; Program development; Sponsorships.
Geographic limitations: Giving primarily in areas of company operations in East Bay, Marin, and Sonoma counties, CA.
Support limitations: No support for religious organizations not of direct benefit to the entire community, fraternal, veterans', sectarian, political, health, or national organizations, other grantmaking bodies, or organizations not registered with Guidestar.org. No grants to individuals, or for scholarships, capital campaigns, endowments, medical research, travel, advertising, subscription fees, admissions tickets, sporting events, benefit events, video or film production, or general operating support; no loans.
Application information: Applications accepted. Application form required. Applicants should submit the following:
1) copy of IRS Determination Letter
2) copy of most recent annual report/audited financial statement/990
3) listing of board of directors, trustees, officers and other key people and their affiliations
4) copy of current year's organizational budget and/ or project budget
5) listing of additional sources and amount of support

Initial approach: Proposal
Deadline(s): None

Officers and Directors:* Paul Stachura*, Chair. and Pres.; Douglas E. Franklin*, Treas.
Number of staff: 1 full-time professional.
EIN: 946078025

1386
Firestone Building Products Company, LLC

250 W. 96th St.
Indianapolis, IN 46260 (317) 575-7000
FAX: (317) 575-7100

Company URL: http://www.firestonebpco.com
Establishment information: Established in 1900.
Company type: Subsidiary of a private company
Business activities: Manufactures commercial roofing systems.
Business type (SIC): Asphalt and roofing materials
Corporate officers: Kenneth Weaver, Chair., Pres., and C.E.O.; Michael Vall, C.O.O.; Clair McCloy, C.F.O.
Board of director: Kenneth Weaver, Chair.
Giving statement: Giving through the Firestone Prescott Community Fund.

Firestone Prescott Community Fund

P.O. Box 710
Prescott, AR 71857-0710 (870) 887-2673

Financial data (yr. ended 12/31/11): Revenue, $23,568; assets, $11,839 (M); gifts received, $23,559; expenditures, $20,590; giving activities include $20,330 for grants.
Purpose and activities: The fund provides grants to nonprofit and disaster relief organizations in the surrounding communities where employees of the Firestone Company reside.
Fields of interest: Safety/disasters; Community/ economic development.
Geographic limitations: Giving primarily in AR.
Officers: Susan Powell, Pres.; Felix Wiley, V.P.; Eric Pate, Secy.; Jeff McKnight, Treas.
EIN: 710613928

1387
Firestone Polymers, LLC

381 W. Wilbeth Rd.
Akron, OH 44301-2465 (330) 379-7000
FAX: (330) 379-7483

Company URL: http://www.firesyn.com
Establishment information: Established in 2001.
Company type: Subsidiary of a foreign company
Business activities: Operates synthetic and thermoplastic rubber company.
Business type (SIC): Rubber products/fabricated
Financial profile for 2010: Number of employees, 567
Corporate officer: John S. Vincent, Pres.
Giving statement: Giving through the Firestone Polymers, LLC Contributions Program.

Firestone Polymers, LLC Contributions Program

381 W. Wilbeth Rd.
Akron, OH 44301-2465 (330) 379-7000
URL: http://www.firesyn.com

1388
First American Bank, N.A.

114 N. 27th St.
Fort Dodge, IA 50501-4322 (515) 573-2154
FAX: (515) 573-5454

Company URL: http://www.bankfirstamerican.com
Establishment information: Established in 1934.
Company type: Subsidiary of a private company
Business activities: Operates commercial bank.
Business type (SIC): Banks/commercial
Corporate officer: Joseph D. Lawler, Pres.
Giving statement: Giving through the Stark Group Charitable Foundation, Inc.

Stark Group Charitable Foundation, Inc.

(formerly First American Bank Charitable Foundation, Inc.)
1207 Central Ave., Ste. 200
Fort Dodge, IA 50501-4245

Establishment information: Established in 2003 in IA.
Donor: First American Bank of Fort Dodge.
Financial data (yr. ended 12/31/11): Assets, $372,095 (M); expenditures, $19,641; qualifying distributions, $16,750; giving activities include $16,750 for grants.
Purpose and activities: The foundation supports parks and playgrounds and organizations involved with arts and culture, education, housing rehabilitation, human services, community development, and religion.
Type of support: General/operating support; Scholarship funds.
Support limitations: No grants to.
Application information: Applications not accepted. Unsolicited requests for funds not accepted.
Officers: C. Richard Stark, Jr., Chair.; Thomas G. Schnurr, Pres. and C.E.O.; Cindy S. Burke, Treas.
Directors: Kristin Gose; Jennifer Mortimer; Steven Risdal; Howard Stearns; Lisa Wilson.
EIN: 721558992

1389
The First American Financial Corporation

(also known as First American Financial)
(formerly The First American Corporation)
1 First American Way
Santa Ana, CA 92707-5913
(714) 250-3000

Company URL: http://www.firstam.com
Establishment information: Established in 1889.
Company type: Public company
Company ticker symbol and exchange: FAF/NYSE
Business activities: Sells title insurance; provides real estate transfer and closing services.
Business type (SIC): Insurance/title
Financial profile for 2012: Number of employees, 17,312; assets, $6,050,850,000; sales volume, $4,541,820,000; pre-tax net income, $467,410,000; expenses, $4,074,410,000; liabilities, $3,702,780,000
Fortune 1000 ranking: 2012—527th in revenues, 470th in profits, and 539th in assets
Corporate officers: Parker S. Kennedy, Chair.; Dennis J. Gilmore, C.E.O.; Mark E. Seaton, C.F.O; Mark E. Rutherford, Sr. V.P., Human Resources
Board of directors: Parker S. Kennedy, Chair.; Anthony K. Anderson; George L. Argyros; James L. Doti; Dennis J. Gilmore; Michael D. McKee; Thomas V. McKernan; Mark Oman; Herbert B. Tasker; Virginia M. Ueberroth
Subsidiaries: C.I.C., Inc., Largo, FL; Contour Software, Inc., Campbell, CA; First American Capital Management, Inc., Newport Beach, CA; First American Real Estate Information Services, Inc., St. Petersburg, FL; First American Registry, Inc., Rockville, MD; First American Title Insurance Co., Santa Ana, CA; First American Title Insurance Company, Santa Ana, CA; SMS Settlement Services, Inc., Orange, CA
International operations: Australia; British Virgin Islands; Canada; Cayman Islands; Chile; China; England; Hungary; India; Japan; New Zealand; Philippines; Poland; Singapore; South Korea; Turkey; United Kingdom
Giving statement: Giving through the First American Financial Foundation.
Company EIN: 951068610

First American Financial Foundation

1 First American Way
Santa Ana, CA 92707-5913
URL: http://www.firstam.com

Establishment information: Established in 1985 in CA.
Donors: The First American Corp.; Parker S. Kennedy.
Financial data (yr. ended 10/31/11): Assets, $192,431 (M); gifts received, $80,000; expenditures, $84,464; qualifying distributions, $83,450; giving activities include $83,450 for 12 grants (high: $25,000; low: $100).
Purpose and activities: The foundation supports police officers and firefighters and organizations involved with education, Alzheimer's disease, employment, football, and military and veterans.
Fields of interest: Higher education; Education; Alzheimer's disease; Crime/law enforcement, police agencies; Goodwill Industries; Disasters, fire prevention/control; Athletics/sports, football; United Ways and Federated Giving Programs; Military/veterans' organizations.
Type of support: Annual campaigns; General/ operating support; Program development; Scholarship funds; Sponsorships.

Geographic limitations: Giving primarily in areas of company operations in Costa Mesa, Irvine, Los Angeles, Newport Beach, Orange, and Santa Ana, CA.
Support limitations: No grants to individuals.
Application information: Applications not accepted. Contributes only to pre-selected organizations.
Officers: Parker S. Kennedy, Pres.; Max O. Valdes, C.F.O.; Colleen Suiste Kennedy, Secy.
EIN: 330148572
Selected grants: The following grants are a representative sample of this grantmaker's funding activity:
$25,000 to Business Committee for the Arts, Costa Mesa, CA, 2009.
$20,000 to Americans for the Arts, Washington, DC, 2009.
$15,000 to Chapman University, Orange, CA, 2009.
$10,000 to United Way, Orange County, Irvine, CA, 2009.
$5,000 to Business Committee for the Arts, Costa Mesa, CA, 2009.
$5,000 to Lestonnac Free Clinic, Orange, CA, 2009.
$5,000 to Santa Ana College Foundation, Santa Ana, CA, 2009.
$5,000 to WomanSage, Irvine, CA, 2009.

1390
First American Title Insurance Company

1 First American Way
Santa Ana, CA 92707 (714) 250-3000

Company URL: http://www.firstam.com
Establishment information: Established in 1889.
Company type: Subsidiary of a public company
Business activities: Sells title insurance; provides real estate transfer and closing services.
Business type (SIC): Insurance/title
Corporate officers: Parker S. Kennedy, Chair.; Curt G. Johnson, Vice-Chair. and Pres.; Dennis J. Gilmore, C.E.O.; Thomas R. Wawersich, V.P. and C.F.O.
Board of directors: Parker S. Kennedy, Chair.; Curt G. Johnson, Vice-Chair.; Dennis J. Gilmore
Giving statement: Giving through the CoreLogic Foundation.

CoreLogic Foundation

(formerly First American Homeownership Foundation)
4 First American Way
Santa Ana, CA 92707-5913 (714) 250-3788
FAX: (714) 250-3618

Establishment information: Established in 2006 in CA.
Donors: First American Title Insurance Company; First American Real Estate Solutions, LLC.
Financial data (yr. ended 12/31/10): Assets, $0; gifts received, $310,000; expenditures, $431,120; qualifying distributions, $415,998; giving activities include $415,998 for 8 grants (high: $243,750; low: $3,709).
Purpose and activities: The foundation supports programs designed to increase housing development, housing education, and neighborhood revitalization through financial literacy, responsible housing, and community intelligence initiatives.
Fields of interest: Housing/shelter, public education; Housing/shelter, formal/general education; Housing/shelter, home owners; Housing/shelter; Human services, financial counseling; Community development, neighborhood development Economically disadvantaged.
Type of support: Continuing support; General/operating support; Program development.
Geographic limitations: Giving primarily in AZ, CA, Washington, DC, IL and TX; giving also to regional and national programs.
Support limitations: No support for religious organizations, political groups, or fraternal organizations. No grants to individuals, or for travel, sporting events, conferences, advertising, or event sponsorships.
Application information: Applications not accepted. Contributes only to pre-selected organizations.
Officers: Karen Jones Collins, Pres.; Corina Polk Cherian, Secy.
EIN: 204330935
Selected grants: The following grants are a representative sample of this grantmaker's funding activity:
$243,750 to Operation Hope, Los Angeles, CA, 2010.
$82,289 to Childrens Medical Center Foundation, Dallas, TX, 2010.
$50,000 to Social Compact, Washington, DC, 2010.
$10,000 to Ronald McDonald House of Dallas, Dallas, TX, 2010.
$3,709 to Montebello Housing Development Corporation, Montebello, CA, 2010.

1391
The First Bancorp, Inc.

(formerly First National Lincoln Corporation)
223 Main St.
P.O. Box 940
Damariscotta, ME 04543 (207) 563-3195
FAX: (207) 563-3225

Company URL: https://www.thefirstbancorp.com
Establishment information: Established in 1985.
Company type: Public company
Company ticker symbol and exchange: FNLC/NASDAQ
Business activities: Operates bank holding company; operates commercial bank.
Business type (SIC): Banks/commercial; holding company
Financial profile for 2012: Number of employees, 228; assets, $1,415,000,000; pre-tax net income, $16,060,000; liabilities, $1,258,680,000
Corporate officers: Stuart G. Smith, Chair.; Daniel R. Daigneault, Pres. and C.E.O.; Tony C. McKim, Exec. V.P. and C.O.O.; F. Stephen Ward, Exec. V.P., C.F.O., and Treas.
Board of directors: Stuart G. Smith, Chair.; Katherine M. Boyd; Daniel R. Daigneault; Robert B. Gregory; Tony C. McKim; Carl S. Poole, Jr.; Mark N. Rosborough; David B. Soule, Jr.; Bruce B. Tindal
Subsidiary: The First National Bank of Damariscotta, Damariscotta, ME
Giving statement: Giving through the First Bancorp, Inc. Contributions Program.
Company EIN: 010404322

The First Bancorp, Inc. Contributions Program

(formerly First National Lincoln Corporation Contributions Program)
223 Main St.
P. O. Box 940
Damariscotta, ME 04543-0940 (207) 563-3195
FAX: (207) 563-3356; URL: https://www.thefirst.com/Content.aspx?Id=44
Additional URL: http://www.the1st.com/about/community/community-involvement.asp

Purpose and activities: First National Lincoln makes charitable contributions to nonprofit organizations involved with arts and culture, K-12 education, youth development, health care, economic development, and civic affairs. Support is limited to areas of company operations in coastal Maine.
Fields of interest: Arts; Elementary/secondary education; Health care; Youth development; Human services; Community/economic development; Public affairs.
Type of support: Capital campaigns; Employee volunteer services; Program development; Sponsorships.
Geographic limitations: Giving limited to areas of company operations in coastal ME.
Support limitations: No grants for general operating support.
Application information: Applications accepted. Support is limited to 1 program development contribution per organization during any given year. A contributions committee reviews all program development and capital campaign requests. Application form not required. Applicants should submit the following:
1) copy of IRS Determination Letter
2) brief history of organization and description of its mission
3) list of company employees involved with the organization
4) listing of board of directors, trustees, officers and other key people and their affiliations
5) detailed description of project and amount of funding requested
6) listing of additional sources and amount of support

Proposals should indicate whether any First Bancorp employee, board member, or shareholder endorses the request.
Initial approach: Proposal to headquarters
Copies of proposal: 1
Deadline(s): None

1392
First Bank & Trust, s.b.

101 S. Central Ave.
P.O. Box 880
Paris, IL 61944-1728 (217) 465-6381

Company URL: http://www.firstbanktrust.com
Establishment information: Established in 1887.
Company type: Subsidiary of a public company
Business activities: Operates savings bank.
Business type (SIC): Savings institutions
Corporate officers: Jack R. Franklin, Pres. and C.E.O.; Jean Galloway, Sr. V.P. and C.F.O.
Giving statement: Giving through the BancTrust Opportunity Foundation.

BancTrust Opportunity Foundation

101 S. Central Ave.
P.O. Box 880
Paris, IL 61944-1728 (217) 465-6381

Establishment information: Established in 2002 in IL.
Donor: First Bank & Trust Co.
Contact: Sarah Handley
Financial data (yr. ended 12/31/11): Assets, $56,201 (M); gifts received, $84,000; expenditures, $32,386; qualifying distributions, $31,646; giving activities include $31,646 for 20 grants to individuals (high: $2,000; low: $316).

Purpose and activities: The foundation awards college scholarships to students at Clark and Edgar counties, Illinois, high schools.
Type of support: Scholarships—to individuals.
Geographic limitations: Giving limited to Clark and Edgar counties, IL.
Publications: Application guidelines.
Application information: Applications accepted. Application form required.
Applications should include a cover sheet, academic information, extracurricular activities, 2 letters of reference, and a statement by the applicant.
Initial approach: Contact participating high schools for application form
Deadline(s): Mar. 1
Officers: Mary Ann Tucker, Pres.; Robert E. Sprague, V.P.; Robert W. Hodge, Secy.; C. Kenneth Bridwell, Treas.
EIN: 300109336

1393
First Banks, Inc.
135 N. Meramec Ave.
Clayton, MO 63105 (314) 854-4600
FAX: (314) 592-6840

Company URL: http://www.firstbanks.com
Establishment information: Established in 1910.
Company type: Private company
Business activities: Operates bank holding company; operates commercial bank.
Business type (SIC): Banks/commercial; holding company
Corporate officers: James F. Dierberg, Chair.; Michael J. Dierberg, Vice-Chair.; Terrance M. McCarthy, Pres. and C.E.O.; Lisa K. Vansickle, Exec. V.P. and C.F.O.; Peter D. Wimmer, Sr. V.P., Genl. Counsel, and Corp. Secy.; Michael J. Normile, Sr. V.P. and Cont.
Board of directors: James F. Dierberg, Chair.; Michael J. Dierberg, Vice-Chair.; Allen H. Blake; James A. Cooper; Terrance M. McCarthy; John S. Poelker; Guy Rounsaville, Jr.; David L. Steward; Douglas H. Yaeger
Giving statement: Giving through the Dierberg Foundation.
Company EIN: 431175538

The Dierberg Foundation
c/o Tax Dept., M.C. 019
600 James S. McDonnell Blvd.
Hazelwood, MO 63042-2302

Establishment information: Established in 2003 in MO.
Donor: First Banks, Inc.
Financial data (yr. ended 12/31/11): Assets, $8,840,374 (M); expenditures, $421,874; qualifying distributions, $419,500; giving activities include $419,500 for grants.
Purpose and activities: The foundation supports museums and hospitals and organizations involved with historic preservation, higher education, human services, and Catholicism.
Fields of interest: Museums; Historic preservation/historical societies; Higher education; Hospitals (general); Boys & girls clubs; Human services; United Ways and Federated Giving Programs; Catholic agencies & churches.
Type of support: Annual campaigns; Building/renovation; General/operating support.
Geographic limitations: Giving primarily in St. Louis, MO.
Application information: Applications not accepted. Contributes only to pre-selected organizations.
Trustees: James F. Dierberg; James F. Dierberg II; Mary W. Dierberg; Michael J. Dierberg; Ellen Dierberg Schepman.
EIN: 436897690
Selected grants: The following grants are a representative sample of this grantmaker's funding activity:
$12,000 to CRUDEM Foundation, Ludlow, MA, 2010.
$7,000 to Annunziata Catholic Church, Saint Louis, MO, 2010. For annual fundraiser.
$4,000 to Vitae Caring Foundation, Jefferson City, MO, 2010. For annual fundraiser.
$1,000 to Community School, Saint Louis, MO, 2010. For annual fundraiser.
$1,000 to Saint Louis Art Museum, Saint Louis, MO, 2010. For annual appeal.
$1,000 to Saint Louis Zoo, Saint Louis, MO, 2010. For annual fundraiser.

1394
First Business Bank
401 Charmany Dr.
P.O. Box 44961
Madison, WI 53744 (608) 238-8008

Company URL: http://www.firstbusiness.com/about/madison
Establishment information: Established in 1990.
Company type: Subsidiary of a private company
Business activities: Operates commercial bank.
Business type (SIC): Banks/commercial
Corporate officers: Gerald Kilcoyne, Chair.; Mark J. Meloy, Pres. and C.E.O.; Barbara Conley, Sr. V.P., Corp. Secy., and Genl. Counsel; Tom Rude, 1st V.P., Finance
Board of directors: Gerald Kilcoyne, Chair.; Laurie Benson; Ralph Kauten; Sandra Lampman; Mark J. Meloy; Steven Mixtacki, C.P.A.; Daniel Olszewski; Audrey L. Polencheck; Mark Winter
Giving statement: Giving through the First Business Charitable Foundation, Inc.

First Business Charitable Foundation, Inc.
401 Charmany Dr.
Madison, WI 53719-1272 (608) 232-5970
URL: http://www.firstbusiness.com/about/madison/community/contributions/

Establishment information: Established in 2003 in WI.
Donor: First Business Bank.
Contact: James F. Ropella, C.F.O.
Financial data (yr. ended 12/31/11): Assets, $3,951 (M); gifts received, $32,000; expenditures, $28,600; qualifying distributions, $28,600; giving activities include $28,600 for grants.
Purpose and activities: The foundation supports organizations involved with early childhood education, housing development, human services, and community development.
Fields of interest: Education, early childhood education; Housing/shelter, development; Salvation Army; Homeless, human services; Human services; Community development, civic centers; Community/economic development.
Type of support: General/operating support.
Geographic limitations: Giving primarily in Madison, WI.
Application information: Applications accepted. Application form required. Applicants should submit the following:
1) contact person
Initial approach: Letter of inquiry
Deadline(s): None
Officer: James F. Rogella, C.F.O.
EIN: 421614475

1395
First Citizens Bancorporation, Inc.
(formerly First Citizens Bancorporation of South Carolina, Inc.)
1230 Main St.
Columbia, SC 29201-3210 (803) 733-3456

Company URL: http://www.firstcitizensonline.com
Establishment information: Established in 1913.
Company type: Public company
Company ticker symbol and exchange: FCBN/OTC
Business activities: Operates commercial bank.
Business type (SIC): Banks/commercial
Financial profile for 2011: Assets, $8,153,895,000; liabilities, $7,413,397,000
Corporate officers: Jim B. Apple, Chair., Pres., and C.E.O.; Frank B. Holding, Vice-Chair.; Peter M. Bristow, Exec. V.P. and C.O.O.; Craig L. Nix, Exec. V.P., C.F.O., and Treas.; William A. Loadholdt, Exec. V.P. and C.I.O.; Charles D. Cook, Secy.
Board of directors: Jim B. Apple, Chair.; Frank B. Holding, Vice-Chair.; Carmen Holding Ames; Peter M. Bristow; Richard W. Blackmon; Walter C. Cottingham; David E. Dukes; M. Craig Garner, Jr.; William E. Hancock III; Robert B. Haynes; Wycliffe E. Haynes; Lewis M. Henderson; Kevin B. Marsh; Charles S. McLaurin III; N. Welch Morrisette; E. Perry Palmer; William E. Sellars; Henry F. Sherrill; Tommy Wessinger
Subsidiaries: Exchange Bank of South Carolina, Kingstree, SC; First Citizens Bank & Trust Company of South Carolina, Columbia, SC; Wateree Life Insurance, Columbia, SC
Giving statement: Giving through the First Citizens Foundation, Inc.
Company EIN: 570738665

First Citizens Foundation, Inc.
1230 Main St.
Columbia, SC 29201-3210 (803) 733-2020

Establishment information: Established in 2000 in SC.
Donors: First Citizens Bancorporation of South Carolina, Inc.; First Citizens Bancorporation, Inc.
Contact: Peter Bristow, V.P.
Financial data (yr. ended 12/31/11): Assets, $10,869,811 (M); expenditures, $707,524; qualifying distributions, $661,801; giving activities include $661,801 for grants.
Purpose and activities: The foundation supports zoos and festivals and organizations involved with arts and culture, education, human services, and community development.
Fields of interest: Museums; Arts; Secondary school/education; Higher education; Business school/education; Education; Zoos/zoological societies; Recreation, fairs/festivals; YM/YWCAs & YM/YWHAs; Children/youth, services; Developmentally disabled, centers & services; Human services; Community/economic development; United Ways and Federated Giving Programs.
Type of support: Annual campaigns; Building/renovation; Capital campaigns; Endowments; Equipment; General/operating support; Program development; Scholarship funds; Sponsorships.

Geographic limitations: Giving primarily in SC, with emphasis on Columbia.
Application information: Applications accepted. Application form required.
Initial approach: Contact foundation for application form
Deadline(s): None
Officers and Directors:* Frank B. Holding*, Chair.; Jim B. Apple*, Pres.; Peter M. Bristow*, V.P.; Charles D. Cook, Secy.; Craig L. Nix, Treas.
EIN: 571108547
Selected grants: The following grants are a representative sample of this grantmaker's funding activity:
$50,000 to Columbia College, Columbia, SC, 2010.
$40,000 to United Way of the Midlands, Columbia, SC, 2010.
$35,000 to United Way of the Midlands, Columbia, SC, 2010.
$25,000 to Claflin University, Orangeburg, SC, 2010.
$25,000 to Spoleto Festival USA, Charleston, SC, 2010.
$20,000 to Cultural Council of Richland and Lexington Counties, Columbia, SC, 2010.
$20,000 to Lancaster County Educational Foundation, Lancaster, SC, 2010.
$15,000 to Disabilities Foundation of Charleston County, Charleston, SC, 2010.
$10,000 to Childrens Museum of the Upstate, Greenville, SC, 2010.
$10,000 to Richland School District Two, Columbia, SC, 2010.

1396
First Citizens BancShares, Inc.

4300 Six Forks Rd.
P.O. Box 27131
Raleigh, NC 27609 (919) 716-7000
FAX: (302) 655-5049

Company URL: http://www.firstcitizens.com
Establishment information: Established in 1986.
Company type: Public company
Company ticker symbol and exchange: FCNCA/NASDAQ
Business activities: Operates bank holding company; operates commercial bank.
Business type (SIC): Holding company; banks/commercial
Financial profile for 2012: Number of employees, 4,821; assets, $21,283,650,000; pre-tax net income, $194,170,000; liabilities, $19,419,650,000
Corporate officers: Frank B. Holding, Jr., Chair. and C.E.O.; Hope Holding Connell, Co-Vice-Chair.; Frank B. Holding, Sr., Co-Vice-Chair.; Edward L. Willingham IV, Pres.; Kenneth A. Black, V.P., Treas., and C.F.O.; James E. Creekman, Secy.
Board of directors: Frank B. Holding, Jr., Chair.; Hope Holding Connell, Co-Vice-Chair; Frank B. Holding, Sr., Co-Vice-Chair.; John M. Alexander, Jr.; Victor E. Bell III; Hubert M. Craig III; H. Lee Durham, Jr.; Daniel L. Heavner; Lucius S. Jones; Robert E. Mason IV; Robert T. Newcomb; James M. Parker; Ralph K. Shelton
Subsidiary: First-Citizens Bank & Trust Company, Raleigh, NC
Giving statement: Giving through the First Citizens BancShares, Inc. Corporate Giving Program and the First Citizens Foundation, Inc.
Company EIN: 561528994

First Citizens BancShares, Inc. Corporate Giving Program

P.O. Box 151
Raleigh, NC 27602-0151 (919) 755-7000
URL: https://www.firstcitizens.com/meet-first-citizens/our-commitments/community/

Purpose and activities: As a complement to its foundation, First Citizens also makes charitable contributions to nonprofit organizations directly. Support is given primarily in areas of company operations.
Fields of interest: Arts; Education; Health care; Human services, financial counseling; Human services; Economic development; Community/economic development; United Ways and Federated Giving Programs.
Type of support: Employee volunteer services; General/operating support; Sponsorships.
Geographic limitations: Giving primarily in areas of company operations in CA, CO, DC, FL, MD, NC, TN, VA, WA, and WV.

First Citizens Foundation, Inc.

P.O. Box 1377
Smithfield, NC 27577-1377

Establishment information: Established in 1957 in NC.
Donor: First Citizens BancShares, Inc.
Financial data (yr. ended 12/31/11): Assets, $482,906 (M); expenditures, $24,754; qualifying distributions, $23,350; giving activities include $23,350 for grants.
Purpose and activities: The foundation supports organizations involved with arts and culture, higher education, and human services.
Fields of interest: Arts; Education.
Type of support: General/operating support; Scholarship funds.
Geographic limitations: Giving primarily in NC.
Application information: Applications not accepted. Unsolicited requests for funds not accepted.
Officers: Frank B. Holding, Pres.; Hope H. Honnell, V.P. and Secy.; Virginia Hopkins, Co-Treas.; T.E. Williams, Co-Treas.
EIN: 566044206

1397
First Citizens National Bank

2601 4th St. S.W.
Mason City, IA 50401-4650
(641) 423-1600

Company URL: http://www.firstcitizensnb.com
Establishment information: Established in 1892.
Company type: Private company
Business activities: Operates commercial bank.
Business type (SIC): Banks/commercial
Corporate officers: O. Jay Tomson, Chair.; Marti T. Rodamaker, Pres. and C.E.O.; Connie Anderson, V.P., Mktg.
Board of director: O. Jay Tomson, Chair.
Offices: Alta Vista, Clarion, Kanawha, Latimer, New Hampton, Osage, IA
Giving statement: Giving through the First Citizens National Bank Charitable Foundation, Inc.

First Citizens National Bank Charitable Foundation, Inc.

2601 4th St. S.W.
P.O. Box 1708
Mason City, IA 50402-1708 (641) 423-1600
E-mail: ojt2@mchsi.com; URL: http://www.firstcitizensnb.com/asp/general_4.asp

Establishment information: Established in 1996 in IA.
Donors: First Citizens National Bank; O. Jay Tomson; First Citizens Financial Corp.
Contact: Patricia A. Tomson, Exec. Dir.
Financial data (yr. ended 12/31/11): Assets, $953,296 (M); gifts received, $400,000; expenditures, $324,364; qualifying distributions, $313,350; giving activities include $313,350 for grants.
Purpose and activities: The foundation supports fire departments and organizations involved with arts and culture, education, animal welfare, health, human services, community development, and low-to-moderate income individuals.
Fields of interest: Arts; Higher education; Education; Animal welfare; Health care, clinics/centers; Health care; Disasters, fire prevention/control; Salvation Army; YM/YWCAs & YM/YWHAs; Children/youth, services; Human services; Community/economic development Economically disadvantaged.
Type of support: Annual campaigns; Building/renovation; Capital campaigns; Curriculum development; Debt reduction; Emergency funds; Equipment; General/operating support; Program development; Scholarship funds; Sponsorships.
Geographic limitations: Giving primarily in areas of company operations in North IA, with emphasis on Chickasaw, Cerro Gordo, Floyd, Franklin, Hancock, Mitchell, and Wright.
Support limitations: No grants for endowments.
Publications: Application guidelines.
Application information: Applications accepted. Application form required. Applicants should submit the following:
1) statement of problem project will address
2) copy of IRS Determination Letter
3) detailed description of project and amount of funding requested
4) copy of current year's organizational budget and/or project budget
5) contact person
6) additional materials/documentation
Initial approach: Complete online application or download application form and mail to foundation
Board meeting date(s): June and Nov.
Deadline(s): None
Officers and Directors: O. Jay Tomson, Pres.; Patricia A. Tomson, Exec. Dir.; Gordon Anderson; Marti T. Rodamaker; Cathy Rottinghaus; Kris Schultz.
Number of staff: 1 part-time professional.
EIN: 421451615

1398
First Commercial Bank, N.A.

Little Rock, AR

Business activities: Operates commercial bank.
Business type (SIC): Banks/commercial
Subsidiaries: Financial Fleet Services, Inc., Little Rock, AR; First Commercial, Inc., Little Rock, AR; First Commercial Investments, Inc., Little Rock, AR; First Commercial Mortgage Co., Little Rock, AR

Giving statement: Giving through the Actelion Pharmaceuticals Ltd Corporate Giving Program, the Advantest Corporation Contributions Program, the Aird & Berlis LLP Pro Bono Program, the Alibaba.com Corporate Giving Program, the All Nippon Airways Co., Ltd. Contributions Program, the APP Japan Ltd. Corporate Giving Program, the Astellas Pharma Inc. Corporate Giving Program, the Autoliv, Inc., the AXA Life Insurance Company Limited Contributions Program, the Baker & McKenzie LLP Pro Bono Program, the BASF SE Corporate Giving Program, the Fogg & Powers LLC Pro Bono Program, the Forman Perry Watkins Krutz & Tardy LLP Pro Bono Program, the Foulston Siefkin LLP Pro Bono Program, the Hyatt Hotels Corporation Contributions Program, the Hyundai Motor Manufacturing Alabama, LLC Contributions Program, the Purdue Pharma L.P. Contributions Program, the Renasant Corporation Contributions Program, the Rent-A-Center, Inc. Contributions Program, the SCA Americas Inc. Contributions Program, the Shiseido Corporate Giving Program, the T. Marzetti Company Contributions Program, the ThyssenKrupp Steel USA, LLC Contributions Program, the United Furniture Industries, Inc. Contributions Program, the Volkswagen Group of America Corporate Giving Program, and the Make Life Better Foundation.

Hyatt Hotels Corporation Contributions Program

71 S. Wacker Dr., 12th Fl.
Chicago, IL 60606 (312) 750-1234
URL: http://www.hyatt.com/hyatt/about/social-responsibility/our-commitment.jsp

Type of support: Employee volunteer services; General/operating support; Loaned talent; Program development.

Volkswagen Group of America Corporate Giving Program

2200 Ferdinand Porsche Dr.
Herndon, VA 20171-5884 (703) 364-7000
URL: http://www.volkswagengroupamerica.com/community/philanthropy.htm

Purpose and activities: Support is given primarily in areas of company operations, with emphasis on Washington, DC, Tennessee, and Virginia.
Fields of interest: Arts; Vocational education; Health care; Youth development; Human services; Community/economic development; General charitable giving Minorities.
Type of support: Employee matching gifts; Employee volunteer services; General/operating support; Sponsorships.
Geographic limitations: Giving primarily in areas of company operations, with emphasis on Washington, DC, TN, and VA.

Hyundai Motor Manufacturing Alabama, LLC Contributions Program

700 Hyundai Blvd.
Montgomery, AL 36105-9622 (334) 387-8000
URL: http://www.hmmausa.com/?page_id=119

Purpose and activities: Hyundai Motor Manufacturing Alabama makes charitable contributions to nonprofit organizations involved with education, health and recreation, diversity, cultural arts, and the environment.
Fields of interest: Arts; Education; Environment; Recreation.
Type of support: Employee volunteer services; General/operating support; Program development; Sponsorships.
Geographic limitations: Giving limited to AL.

Purdue Pharma L.P. Contributions Program

1 Stamford Forum
201 Tresser Blvd.
Stamford, CT 06901-3431 (203) 588-8000
URL: http://www.purduepharma.com/About/Community/Pages/default.aspx

Purpose and activities: Purdue makes charitable contributions to nonprofit organizations involved with arts and culture, education, the environment, healthcare, and community and economic development. Support is given primarily in the greater Stamford, Connecticut, and Wilson, North Carolina, areas.
Fields of interest: Arts; Education; Environment; Health care; Disasters, preparedness/services; Community/economic development.
Type of support: Advocacy; Continuing support; Curriculum development; Employee volunteer services; Fellowships; General/operating support; In-kind gifts; Program development; Research; Scholarship funds.
Geographic limitations: Giving primarily in the greater Stamford, CT, and Wilson, NC, areas.

Renasant Corporation Contributions Program

209 Troy St.
Tupelo, MS 38802-4827 (662) 680-1001
URL: http://www.renasantbank.com

Rent-A-Center, Inc. Contributions Program

5501 Headquarters Dr.
Plano, TX 75024-3556 (972) 801-1100
URL: http://www6.rentacenter.com/RACommunity.html

Purpose and activities: Rent-A-Center makes charitable contributions to nonprofit organizations involved with education, food services, and youth development. Support is given on a national basis in areas of company operations, with emphasis on Texas.
Fields of interest: Education; Food services; Youth development; General charitable giving.
Type of support: Computer technology; General/operating support; Scholarships—to individuals.
Geographic limitations: Giving on a national basis in areas of company operations, with emphasis on TX; giving also to national organizations.
Application information: Applications not accepted. Contributes only to pre-selected organizations.

SCA Americas Inc. Contributions Program

2929 Arch St., Ste. 2600
Philadelphia, PA 19104-2863 (610) 499-3700
E-mail: americas@sca.com; URL: http://www.sca.com/en/us/Sustainability1/Corporate-Social-Responsibility/

Purpose and activities: SCA Americas makes charitable contributions to nonprofit organizations involved with the environment, healthcare, youth development, human services, and on a case by case basis. Support is given primarily in areas of company operations in Barton, Alabama, Bellemont and Flagstaff, Arizona, Bowling Green, Kentucky, South Glens Falls and Greenwich, New York, Philadelphia, Pennsylvania, and Neenah and Menasha, Wisconsin.
Fields of interest: Environment; Health care; Disasters, preparedness/services; Youth development; Human services; United Ways and Federated Giving Programs; General charitable giving.
Type of support: Continuing support; Donated products; Employee volunteer services; General/operating support.
Geographic limitations: Giving primarily in areas of company operations in Barton, AL, Bellemont and Flagstaff, AZ, Bowling Green, KY, South Glens Falls and Greenwich, NY, Philadelphia, PA, and Neenah and Menasha, WI.

T. Marzetti Company Contributions Program

37 W. Broad St.
Columbus, OH 43215 (614) 846-2232
URL: http://www.marzetti.com

Type of support: In-kind gifts.

ThyssenKrupp Steel USA, LLC Contributions Program

1 ThyssenKrupp Dr.
P. O. Box 456
Calvert, AL 36513-0456 (251) 289-3000

Purpose and activities: ThyssenKrupp Steel makes charitable contributions to educational institutions and nonprofit organizations on a case by case basis.
Fields of interest: Education; Community/economic development; General charitable giving.
Type of support: General/operating support.
Geographic limitations: Giving primarily in Mobile, AL.

United Furniture Industries, Inc. Contributions Program

431 Highway 41 E.
P.O. Box 308
Okolona, MS 38860-9792 (662) 447-5504
URL: http://www.unitedfurnitureindustries.com

Purpose and activities: United Furniture Industries makes charitable contributions to nonprofit organizations involved with providing camps and programs for children with serious medical conditions.
Fields of interest: Health care, patient services; Recreation, camps; Children, services.
Type of support: Continuing support; General/operating support.

1399
The First County Bank Inc.

1042 High Ridge Rd.
Stamford, CT 06905-1122 (203) 323-3423

Company URL: http://www.firstcountybank.com
Establishment information: Established in 1851.
Company type: Private company
Business activities: Operates savings bank.
Business type (SIC): Savings institutions
Financial profile for 2011: Assets, $1,319,140,000; liabilities, $1,319,140,000
Corporate officers: Reyno A. Giallongo, Jr., Chair. and C.E.O.; Katherine A. Harris, Pres. and C.O.O.; Peter C. Rugen, Sr. V.P. and C.A.O.; Diane L. Tenney, Corp. Secy.
Board of directors: Reyno A. Giallongo, Jr., Chair.; Thomas L. Bartram; Denise C. Doria, C.P.A.; Nicholas DuBiago, C.P.A.; Robert D. Emslie; Reyno

A. Giallongo, Jr.; David W. Hopper, Esq.; Mark A. Lapine; James B. McArdle, Jr.; Gerald A. Nielsen, Jr.; Richard E. Taber
Giving statement: Giving through the First County Bank Foundation, Inc.

First County Bank Foundation, Inc.

100 Prospect St., 4th Fl.
Stamford, CT 06901-1201 (203) 462-4858
FAX: (203) 462-4442;
E-mail: foundation@firstcountybank.com; Additional contact: RoseMary Ogden; URL: https://www.firstcountybank.com/first-county-bank-foundation-inc

Establishment information: Established in 2000 in CT.
Donor: First County Bank.
Contact: Katherine A. Harris, V.P.
Financial data (yr. ended 12/31/11): Assets, $3,375,331 (M); expenditures, $632,141; qualifying distributions, $591,267; giving activities include $591,267 for grants.
Purpose and activities: The foundation supports programs designed to address community economic development and children and families. Special emphasis is directed toward programs designed to serve low-to-moderate income populations.
Fields of interest: Higher education; Education; Health care; Food services; Housing/shelter; Boys & girls clubs; Salvation Army; Children/youth, services; Family services; Homeless, human services; Human services; Community/economic development; United Ways and Federated Giving Programs Economically disadvantaged.
Program:
Richard E. Taber Citizenship Award: The foundation awards $5,000 college scholarships to three high school seniors living in the Fairfield County area. Applicants must demonstrate and excel in citizenship, leadership, academics, service, and sportsmanship. In addition to the scholarships, honorees receive a personalized certificate or plaque honoring the recipient, a congratulatory ad in the local newspaper with a photo, and a mention and photo on the First County Bank Foundation web site.
Type of support: Continuing support; Equipment; General/operating support; Program development; Scholarship funds; Scholarships—to individuals.
Geographic limitations: Giving limited to areas of company operations in Darien, Greenwich, New Canaan, Norwalk, Stamford, and Westport, CT.
Support limitations: No support for religious organizations not of direct benefit to the entire community, private or parochial schools, discriminatory organizations, or organizations not open to the public. No grants to individuals (except for the Richard E. Taber Citizenship Award), or for capital or endowment campaigns, fundraising events, trips, tours, or conferences, debt spending or liquidation, or political causes.
Publications: Application guidelines.
Application information: Applications accepted. CommunityFirst Grant Program are for requests of $2,500 and under if your organization supports community or economic development or children and families; and for requests of $1,000 and under if your organization falls outside of the grant parameters. Application form required. Applicants should submit the following:
1) results expected from proposed grant
2) qualifications of key personnel
3) statement of problem project will address
4) population served
5) name, address and phone number of organization
6) copy of IRS Determination Letter
7) brief history of organization and description of its mission
8) copy of most recent annual report/audited financial statement/990
9) listing of board of directors, trustees, officers and other key people and their affiliations
10) detailed description of project and amount of funding requested
11) plans for cooperation with other organizations, if any
12) contact person
13) copy of current year's organizational budget and/or project budget
14) listing of additional sources and amount of support

Applications for the Richard E. Taber Citizenship Award must include reference letters from three individuals, an official high school transcript, and a brief essay.
Initial approach: Download application form and mail proposal and application form to foundation; complete online application form for the Richard E. Taber Citizenship Award
Deadline(s): Jan. 1 to Mar. 31 for Standard Grant Applications; Jan. 1 to Dec. 31 for CommunityFirst Grant Program and Richard E. Taber Citizenship Award
Final notification: End of June for Richard E. Taber Citizenship Award
Officers and Directors:* Reyno A. Giallongo, Jr.*, Pres.; Katherine Harris, V.P.; Ronald Holbert, Treas.; Thomas L. Bartram; Robert A. Beer; Dr. Marcia Bull; Francis DeLuca; Nicholas Dubiago; Robert Emslie; Mark Lapine; James McArdle, Jr.; Alphonse Palmer.
EIN: 061604469

1400
First Data Corporation

5565 Glenridge Connector, N.E.
Atlanta, GA 30342-4756 (303) 967-8000

Company URL: http://www.firstdata.com
Establishment information: Established in 1964.
Company type: Private company
Business activities: Provides money transfer and bill payment services; provides electronic commerce services.
Business type (SIC): Depository banking/functions related to; computer services
Financial profile for 2011: Number of employees, 24,500; assets, $9,790,000,000; sales volume, $10,380,000,000
Corporate officers: Frank J. Bisignano, C.E.O.; Ray Winborne, Exec. V.P. and C.F.O.; David R. Money, Exec. V.P. and Genl. Counsel; Kevin Kern, Exec. V.P., Opers.; Peter Boucher, Exec. V.P., Human Resources
Board of directors: James R. Fisher; Joe W. Forehand; Henry R. Kravis; Scott C. Nuttall; Tagar C. Olson
Subsidiaries: Cardservice International, Inc., Simi Valley, CA; E Commerce Group, Inc., New York, NY; eONE Global, LP, Napa, CA; First Data Merchant Services Corp., Coral Springs, FL; First Data Resources Inc., Omaha, NE; First Data Technologies, Inc., Englewood, CO; First Data Voice Svcs., Omaha, NE; Integrated Payment Systems Inc., Englewood, CO; Linkpoint International, Inc., Agoura Hills, CA; Orlandi Valuta, Cerritos, CA; Paymap Inc., San Francisco, CA; PaySys International, Inc., Orlando, FL; REMITCO LLC, Englewood, CO; TASQ Corp., Rocklin, CA; Taxware, LP, Salem, MA; TeleCheck Services, Inc., Houston, TX; ValueLink, LLC, Englewood, CO
Office: Maitland, FL
International operations: Argentina; Australia; Austria; Bangladesh; Belgium; Bermuda; Brazil; Brunei; Canada; China; Colombia; Costa Rica; Croatia; Czech Republic; Estonia; France; Germany; Greece; Hong Kong; Hungary; India; Ireland; Italy; Japan; Latvia; Lithuania; Luxembourg; Macau; Malaysia; Mauritius; Mexico; Netherlands; New Zealand; Norway; Pakistan; Panama; Poland; Romania; Russia; Serbia; Singapore; Slovakia; South Africa; South Korea; Spain; Sri Lanka; Turkey; United Arab Emirates; United Kingdom; Uruguay
Giving statement: Giving through the First Data Foundation.

First Data Foundation

6200 S. Quebec St., Ste. 330
Greenwood Village, CO 80111-4729 (303) 967-7700
FAX: (954) 509-2842;
E-mail: ellen.sandberg@firstdata.com; URL: http://www.firstdata.com/en_us/about-first-data/corporate-responsibility/foundation

Establishment information: Established in 2006 in CO.
Donor: First Data Corp.
Contact: Ellen Y. Sandberg, Pres.
Financial data (yr. ended 12/31/11): Assets, $13,897 (M); gifts received, $703,934; expenditures, $711,649; qualifying distributions, $711,223; giving activities include $711,223 for grants.
Purpose and activities: The foundation supports food banks and organizations involved with education, health, housing, disaster relief, human services, economically disadvantaged people and other areas. Special emphasis is directed toward programs designed to promote financial literacy and employee engagement.
Fields of interest: Education; Health care; Food banks; Housing/shelter; Disasters, preparedness/services; American Red Cross; Children/youth, services; Human services, financial counseling; Homeless, human services; Human services; United Ways and Federated Giving Programs; General charitable giving Economically disadvantaged.
International interests: Argentina; Australia; Germany; Greece; United Kingdom.
Programs:
Donations for Doers Program: The foundation awards $500 grants to nonprofit organizations with which employees of First Data volunteers 50 hours in a year.
Employee Gift Matching: The foundation matches contributions made by employees of First Data to nonprofit organizations on a one-for-two basis up to $5,000 per employee, per year.
Type of support: Employee matching gifts; Employee volunteer services; General/operating support.
Geographic limitations: Giving primarily in CA, Denver, CO, GA, Omaha, NE, and Long Island, NY, giving also in Australia, Argentina, Germany, Greece, and the United Kingdom.
Support limitations: No support for religious or political organizations. No grants for films.
Publications: Corporate report.
Application information: Applications not accepted. Contributes only to pre-selected organizations.
Board meeting date(s): Jan., Apr., July, and Oct.
Officers and Directors:* Ed Labry*, Chair.; Joe Samuel*, Vice-Chair.; Ellen Sanderg, Pres.; Alan Bethscheider, Secy.; Barry Cooper, Treas.
Number of staff: 2 full-time professional.
EIN: 205626313
Selected grants: The following grants are a representative sample of this grantmaker's funding activity:
$302,520 to United States Fund for UNICEF, New York, NY, 2010.

$50,000 to Habitat for Humanity International, Americus, GA, 2010.
$25,372 to United Way of the Midlands, Omaha, NE, 2010.
$8,825 to Hope Center, Omaha, NE, 2010.
$5,000 to Washington University, Saint Louis, MO, 2010.
$3,000 to Entertainment Industry Foundation, Los Angeles, CA, 2010.
$1,500 to Roncalli High School, Omaha, NE, 2010.
$1,320 to Hope Center, Omaha, NE, 2010.
$1,300 to Love146, New Haven, CT, 2010.
$1,000 to Avenues for Homeless Youth, Minneapolis, MN, 2010.

1401
First Federal Community Bank

630 Clarksville St.
Paris, TX 75460-5934 (903) 784-0881

Company URL: http://www.1st-fed.com/
Establishment information: Established in 1934.
Company type: Private company
Business activities: Operates federal savings bank.
Business type (SIC): Savings institutions
Corporate officers: Richard M. Amis, Pres. and C.E.O.; Gordon Hogue, Sr. V.P. and C.O.O.; Jeff Wright, Sr. V.P. and C.F.O.; Robert Slider, V.P., Opers.
Giving statement: Giving through the First Federal Community Foundation.

First Federal Community Foundation

630 Clarksville St.
Paris, TX 75460-5934

Establishment information: Established in 1997 in TX.
Donor: First Federal Community Bank.
Contact: Richard M. Amis, Tr.
Financial data (yr. ended 12/31/11): Assets, $1,862,837 (M); expenditures, $101,808; qualifying distributions, $98,140; giving activities include $98,140 for grants.
Purpose and activities: The foundation supports organizations involved with education, patient services, youth development, human services, and community development.
Fields of interest: Education; Health care, patient services; Big Brothers/Big Sisters; Boy scouts; Youth development; Children/youth, services; Human services; Community/economic development.
Type of support: General/operating support.
Geographic limitations: Giving limited to the greater Clarksville, Mt. Pleasant, and Paris, TX areas.
Application information: Applications accepted. Application form required. Applicants should submit the following:
1) copy of IRS Determination Letter
2) detailed description of project and amount of funding requested

Initial approach: Proposal
Deadline(s): Sept. 30

Trustees: Richard M. Amis; E. Sims Norment; Tim Taylor.
EIN: 752716310

1402
First Federal of Northern Michigan Bancorp, Inc.

100 S. 2nd Ave.
Alpena, MI 49707-2814 (989) 356-9041
FAX: (989) 354-8671

Company URL: http://www.first-federal.com
Establishment information: Established in 1957.
Company type: Public company
Company ticker symbol and exchange: FFNM/NASDAQ
Business activities: Operates bank holding company; operates commercial bank.
Business type (SIC): Banks/commercial; holding company
Financial profile for 2011: Number of employees, 93; assets, $217,040,000; pre-tax net income, $740,000; liabilities, $192,480,000
Corporate officers: Martin A. Thomson, Chair.; Michael W. Mahler, Pres. and C.E.O.
Board of directors: Martin Thomson, Chair.; Michael Mahler; Thomas Townsend; Gary VanMassenhove; Keith D. Wallace
Subsidiary: First Federal of Northern Michigan, Alpena, MI
Giving statement: Giving through the First Federal Community Foundation.
Company EIN: 320135202

First Federal Community Foundation

100 S. 2nd Ave.
Alpena, MI 49707-2814 (989) 354-7319
Tel.: (989) 354-7319; URL: http://www.first-federal.com/about-us/our-community-foundation.html

Establishment information: Established in 2005 in MI.
Donor: First Federal of Northern Michigan Bancorp, Inc.
Contact: Michael W. Mahler, Pres.
Financial data (yr. ended 12/31/11): Assets, $297,929 (M); expenditures, $20,143; qualifying distributions, $218,752; giving activities include $17,096 for 30 grants (high: $3,000; low: $58).
Purpose and activities: The foundation supports programs designed to enhance the relationship between First Federal of Northern Michigan and the communities in which it operates and enable its communities to share in its long-term growth.
Fields of interest: Museums; Secondary school/education; Higher education; Education; Health care, clinics/centers; Food banks; Human services; Community/economic development; United Ways and Federated Giving Programs; General charitable giving.
Type of support: Building/renovation; Capital campaigns; Equipment; Program development; Scholarship funds; Seed money.
Geographic limitations: Giving limited to areas of company operations in Alcona, Alpena, Cheboygan, Charlevoix, Crawford, Emmet, Iosco, Montmorency, Ogemaw, Oscoda, Otsego, and Presque Isle counties, MI.
Support limitations: No support for religious organizations not of direct benefit to the entire community. No grants to individuals, or for general operating support or debt reduction.
Publications: Application guidelines.
Application information: Applications accepted. The foundation currently accepts two types of applications. The Mini-Grant Application is available for grant requests of up to $250, and the Common Grant Application is available for grant requests of $250 to $1,500. Application form required. Applicants should submit the following:
1) role played by volunteers
2) population served
3) copy of IRS Determination Letter
4) how project's results will be evaluated or measured
5) listing of board of directors, trustees, officers and other key people and their affiliations
6) detailed description of project and amount of funding requested
7) copy of current year's organizational budget and/or project budget
8) listing of additional sources and amount of support

Initial approach: Letter
Board meeting date(s): Mar., June, Sept., and Dec.
Deadline(s): 1st regular workday of the month

Officers: Gary C. VanMassenhove, Chair.; Michael W. Mahler, Pres.; Amy E. Essex, V.P. and Treas.; Daniel J. Florip, Co-secy.; Lora Greene, Co-Secy.
EIN: 202531733

1403
First Federal Savings Bank

383 Shoshone St., N.
P.O. Box 249
Twin Falls, ID 83301-6152 (208) 733-4222

Company URL: http://www.firstfd.com
Establishment information: Established in 1889.
Company type: Private company
Business activities: Operates savings bank.
Business type (SIC): Savings institutions
Corporate officers: C. Alan Horner, Chair., Pres., and C.E.O.; Jay P. Dodds, Exec. V.P., C.F.O., and Corp. Treas.; Jason A. Meyerhoeffer, Exec. V.P. and Corp. Secy.; Michael D. Traveller, Sr. V.P. and Cont.; Gregory P. Edson, V.P., Mktg.
Board of directors: C. Alan Horner, Chair.; Tom Ashenbrener; Jay P. Dodds; Rex E. Lytle; Jason A. Meyerhoeffer; G. Alex Sinclair; Stephen Westfall
Offices: Buhl, Burley, Jerome, Rupert, ID
Giving statement: Giving through the First Federal Foundation, Inc.

First Federal Foundation, Inc.

1329 Albion Ave.
Burley, ID 83318-1817
URL: http://www.firstfd.com/2062/mirror/a-foundation.htm

Establishment information: Established as a company-sponsored operating foundation in 2003 in ID.
Donor: First Federal Savings Bank.
Financial data (yr. ended 12/31/11): Assets, $1,222,032 (M); gifts received, $22,432; expenditures, $60,574; qualifying distributions, $59,974; giving activities include $59,974 for 23 grants (high: $5,000; low: $1,000).
Purpose and activities: The foundation supports organizations involved with arts and culture, education, health, human services, community development, and civic affairs.
Fields of interest: Arts; Elementary school/education; Education; Health care; Recreation; Salvation Army; Children/youth, services; Aging, centers/services; Human services; Community/economic development; Public affairs.
Type of support: Building/renovation; Capital campaigns; Equipment; Matching/challenge support; Sponsorships.

Geographic limitations: Giving primarily in Cassia, Gooding, Jerome, Lincoln, Minidoka, and Twin Falls counties, ID.
Support limitations: No support for religious organizations or private clubs. No grants to individuals or for political causes.
Application information: Applications not accepted. Unsolicited requests for funds not accepted.
Directors: Barbara Geitzen; Jan McBride; Rob Newman; Ron Rasmussen; Linda Watkins; Kevin Welch; Brian Williams.
Officers: Rex Lytle, Pres.; Becky Curtis, Secy.
EIN: 571141539

1404
First Financial Northwest, Inc.

201 Wells Ave. S.
P.O. Box 360
Renton, WA 98057 (425) 255-4400
FAX: (425) 228-7227

Company URL: http://www.fsbnw.com/
Establishment information: Established in 1923.
Company type: Public company
Company ticker symbol and exchange: FFNW/NASDAQ
Business activities: Operates savings bank.
Business type (SIC): Savings institutions
Financial profile for 2012: Number of employees, 113; assets, $942,650,000; pre-tax net income, $1,710,000; liabilities, $755,540,000
Corporate officers: Victor Karpiak, Chair., Pres., and C.E.O.; Roger Elmore, Sr. V.P. and C.A.O.; Kari A. Stenslie, V.P. and C.F.O.; Lorna K. Reggio, V.P. and Cont.
Board of directors: Victor Karpiak, Chair.; Robert L. Anderson; Gary F. Faull; Joseph W. "Joe" Kiley III; Gary F. Kohlwes; Joann E. Lee; Kevin D. Padrick; Daniel L. Stevens
Giving statement: Giving through the First Financial Northwest Foundation.
Company EIN: 260610707

First Financial Northwest Foundation

c/o Joann E. Lee
201 Wells Ave. S.
Renton, WA 98057-2131

Establishment information: Established in 2007 in WA.
Donor: First Financial Northwest, Inc.
Financial data (yr. ended 12/31/11): Assets, $9,158,230 (M); expenditures, $459,974; qualifying distributions, $410,862; giving activities include $410,862 for grants.
Purpose and activities: The foundation supports community foundations and organizations involved with human services.
Fields of interest: American Red Cross; Human services; Foundations (community).
Type of support: General/operating support.
Geographic limitations: Giving primarily in Renton, WA.
Support limitations: No grants for individuals.
Application information: Applications not accepted. Contributes only to pre-selected organizations.
Officers and Trustees:* Charles J. Delaurenti II*, Chair.; Gary F. Faull, Secy.; Joann E. Lee, Treas.; Gary F. Kohlwes, Exec. Dir.; Harry A. Blencoe.
EIN: 261421623
Selected grants: The following grants are a representative sample of this grantmaker's funding activity:
$500,000 to Renton Community Foundation, Renton, WA, 2010.
$130,000 to Renton Community Foundation, Renton, WA, 2010.

1405
First Hawaiian Bank

999 Bishop St., 29th Fl.
P.O. Box 29450
Honolulu, HI 96813-4423 (808) 525-7000

Company URL: http://www.fhb.com
Establishment information: Established in 1933.
Company type: Subsidiary of a foreign company
Business activities: Operates commercial bank.
Business type (SIC): Banks/commercial
Financial profile for 2011: Assets, $15,830,240,000
Corporate officers: Donald G. Horner, C.E.O. and Pres.; Albert M. Yamada, C.F.O.; William E. Atwater III, Exec. V.P., Genl. Counsel, and Secy.; Gerald J. Keir, Exec. V.P., Corp. Comms.; Iris Y. Matsumoto, Exec. V.P., Human Resources; Sheila M. Sumida, Exec. V.P., Human Resources; Kristi L. Maynard, Sr. V.P. and Treas.; Glen R. Okazaki, Sr. V.P. and Cont.; Sharon Shiroma Brown, Sr. V.P., Sales
Board of directors: Donald G. Horner; Robin K. Campaniano; W. Allen Doane; Julia Ann Frohlich; Michael K. Fujimoto; Robert S. Harrison; Warren H. Haruki; Robert P. Hiam; John A. Hoag; David C. Hulihee; Richard R. Kelley; Bert T. Kobayashi, Jr.; Faye Watanabe Kurren; Dee Jay A. Mailer; Richard T. Mamiya; Fujio Matsuda; Leighton S.L. Mau; Wesley T. Park; John K. Tsui; Allen B. Uyeda; Jenai Sullivan Wall; James C. Wo; Robert C. Wo; Albert M. Yamada
Giving statement: Giving through the First Hawaiian Bank Foundation.

First Hawaiian Bank Foundation

(formerly First Hawaiian Foundation)
999 Bishop St.
Honolulu, HI 96813-4423 (808) 525-7777
FAX: (808) 525-8708;
E-mail: fhbfoundation@fhb.com; URL: http://www.fhb.com/about-corp-giving.htm

Establishment information: Established in 1975 in HI.
Donors: First Hawaiian Bank; BancWest Corp.
Contact: Sharon Shiroma Brown, Pres.
Financial data (yr. ended 12/31/11): Assets, $11,648,248 (M); gifts received, $2,004; expenditures, $1,467,194; qualifying distributions, $1,454,268; giving activities include $1,454,268 for 62 grants (high: $200,000; low: $1,000).
Purpose and activities: The foundation supports programs designed to meet community needs; improve access to health care; provide educational opportunities; serve youth and children; and enrich life through culture and the arts.
Fields of interest: Arts; Education; Hospitals (general); Health care; Children/youth, services; Human services; Community/economic development; United Ways and Federated Giving Programs; Religion.
Type of support: Annual campaigns; Building/renovation; Capital campaigns; Continuing support; Employee volunteer services; Endowments; Equipment; Program development; Sponsorships.
Geographic limitations: Giving primarily in areas of company operations in Honolulu, HI.
Support limitations: No grants for ongoing general operating support, endowments, sponsorships, or conferences.
Publications: Application guidelines.
Application information: Applications accepted. Application form required.
Initial approach: Complete online application
Board meeting date(s): Quarterly
Deadline(s): E-mail foundation for deadline dates
Officers and Directors:* Donald G. Horner*, Chair.; Sharon Shiroma Brown*, Pres.; Gary L. Caulfield*, V.P.; Robert S. Harrison*, V.P.; William E. Atwater III*, Secy.; Albert M. Yamada*, Treas.; Alan H. Arisumi; Winston K.H. Chow; Brandt G. Farias; Robert T. Fujioka; Anthony R. Guerrero, Jr.; Corbett A.K. Kalama; Iris Y. Matsumoto; Kristi L. Maynard; Robin S. Midkiff; James W. Mills; Raymond S. Ono; Curt T. Otaguro; Lily K. Yao.
EIN: 237437822
Selected grants: The following grants are a representative sample of this grantmaker's funding activity:
$250,000 to United Way, Aloha, Honolulu, HI, 2009. For corporate pledge.
$108,053 to Moanalua High School, Honolulu, HI, 2009. For study of the major administrative and support functions within Hawaii Department of Education.
$100,000 to Hawaii High School Athletic Association, Honolulu, HI, 2009. To cover budget cut for Hawaii's high school athletic programs.
$40,000 to Mid-Pacific Institute, Honolulu, HI, 2009. For construction of new elementary school.
$40,000 to Sacred Hearts Academy, Honolulu, HI, 2009. For capital campaign for Student Center.
$33,000 to United Way, Hawaii Island, Hilo, HI, 2009. For corporate pledge.
$28,800 to United Way, Maui, Wailuku, HI, 2009. For corporate pledge.
$25,000 to American Red Cross, Hawaii State Chapter, Honolulu, HI, 2009. To assist in preventing/alleviating suffering in disasters/emergencies.
$25,000 to Friends of the 50th State Commemoration, Honolulu, HI, 2009. For statehood anniversary conference to discuss Hawaii's history and future.
$20,000 to Hanalani Schools, Mililani, HI, 2009. For capital campaign to add classrooms and make upgrades.

1406
First Horizon National Corporation

(formerly First Tennessee National Corporation)
165 Madison Ave.
Memphis, TN 38103-2723 (901) 523-4444

Company URL: http://www.firsthorizon.com
Establishment information: Established in 1864.
Company type: Public company
Company ticker symbol and exchange: FHN/NYSE
International Securities Identification Number: US3205171057
Business activities: Operates financial holding company; operates commercial bank.
Business type (SIC): Banks/commercial; holding company
Financial profile for 2012: Number of employees, 4,514; assets, $25,520,140,000; pre-tax net income, -$101,700,000; liabilities, $23,306,100,000
Forbes 2000 ranking: 2012—1841st in sales, 1781st in profits, and 837th in assets
Corporate officers: D. Bryan Jordan, Chair., Pres., and C.E.O.; William C. Losch III, Exec. V.P. and C.F.O.; Bruce A. Livesay, Exec. V.P. and C.I.O.; Thomas C. Adams, Jr., Exec. V.P. and Corp. Treas.;

Charles T. Tuggle, Jr., Exec. V.P. and Genl. Counsel; Kimberley C. Cherry, Exec. V.P., Corp. Comms.
Board of directors: D. Bryan Jordan, Chair.; Robert B. Carter; John C. Compton; Mark A. Emkes; Corydon J. Gilchrist; Vicky B. Gregg; R. Brad Martin; Scott M. Niswonger; Vicki R. Palmer; Colin V. Reed; Luke Yancy III
Subsidiaries: First Tennessee Bank N.A., Southaven, MS; Highland Capital Management Corp., Memphis, TN
Giving statement: Giving through the First Horizon National Corporation Contributions Program and the First Horizon Foundation.
Company EIN: 620803242

First Horizon National Corporation Contributions Program

(formerly First Tennessee National Corporation Contributions Program)
165 Madison Ave.
P.O. Box 84
Memphis, TN 38103-2723
E-mail: PWAviotti@FirstTennessee.com;
URL: http://www.fhnc.com/index.cfm?Fuseaction=Community.Main

Contact: Penny Aviotti
Purpose and activities: As a complement to its foundation, First Horizon also makes charitable contributions to nonprofit organizations directly. Support is given primarily in areas of company operations.
Fields of interest: Arts; Education; Health care; Housing/shelter; Youth development, business; Youth, services; Human services, financial counseling; Human services; Community development, business promotion; Community/economic development; United Ways and Federated Giving Programs; Public affairs.
Type of support: Annual campaigns; Continuing support; Employee volunteer services; General/operating support; Program development; Sponsorships.
Geographic limitations: Giving primarily in areas of company operations in TN, with emphasis on Memphis.
Support limitations: No support for bank "clearinghouse" organizations, charities supported solely by a single civic organization, pass through organizations, religious, veterans', social, athletic, or fraternal organizations, or political organizations. No grants to individuals, or for trips or tours or debt reduction.
Publications: Application guidelines.
Application information: Applications accepted. Support is limited to 3 years in length. The Corporate Communications Department handles giving. Application form not required. Applicants should submit the following:
1) copy of IRS Determination Letter
2) brief history of organization and description of its mission
3) copy of most recent annual report/audited financial statement/990
4) list of company employees involved with the organization
5) listing of board of directors, trustees, officers and other key people and their affiliations
6) detailed description of project and amount of funding requested
7) copy of current year's organizational budget and/or project budget

Initial approach: Proposal to nearest community investment manager
Copies of proposal: 1
Deadline(s): None

Administrator: Terry Lee, Sr. V.P. and Mgr., Corp. Comms.

First Horizon Foundation

(formerly First Tennessee Foundation)
c/o First Horizon National Corp.
165 Madison Ave., 8th. Fl.
Memphis, TN 38103-2723 (901) 532-4357
FAX: (901) 523-4354;
E-mail: PWAviotti@firsthorizon.com; Contact for Leadership Grants Program: Erica Wilkins, e-mail: EEWilkins@firsthorizon.com; Additional tel.: (901) 523-4291; Contact for Award for Innovation in the Arts: Lizzy Haymond, Corp. Comms., tel.: (901) 523-4291, e-mail: emhaymond@firsthorizon.com;
URL: http://www.firsttennesseefoundation.com/

Establishment information: Established in 1993 in TN.
Donors: First Tennessee National Corp.; First Horizon National Corp.
Contact: Penny Aviotti
Financial data (yr. ended 12/31/11): Assets, $46,781,394 (M); expenditures, $5,392,065; qualifying distributions, $5,102,850; giving activities include $5,102,850 for 1,081 grants (high: $400,000; low: $25).
Purpose and activities: The foundation supports programs designed to promote arts and culture; education and youth; affordable housing; health and human services; and economic development. Special emphasis is directed toward programs designed to promote financial literacy.
Fields of interest: Visual arts; Museums; Performing arts, orchestras; Arts; Higher education; Education; Hospitals (general); Health care, clinics/centers; Health care; Cancer; Housing/shelter, development; Housing/shelter; Athletics/sports, amateur leagues; Salvation Army; Youth, services; Human services, financial counseling; Human services; Economic development; United Ways and Federated Giving Programs.
Programs:

Award for Innovation in the Arts: The foundation supports a competition for art groups designed to promote artistic excellence. Qualifying organizations must focus on the arts, support the Memphis market, and be eligible for funds from ArtsMemphis.

Employee Matching Gifts: The foundation matches contributions made by employees of First Horizon Foundation to nonprofit organizations on a 2-for-1 basis from $50 to $2,000 per employee, per year.

Leadership Grants Program: The foundation awards grants to nonprofit organizations with which employees of First Horizon volunteer and have become leaders. Leaders may request grants of up to $1,000 on behalf of their nonprofit organization.

Type of support: Annual campaigns; Building/renovation; Capital campaigns; Conferences/seminars; Employee matching gifts; Employee volunteer services; Endowments; Equipment; General/operating support; Professorships; Program development; Scholarship funds; Sponsorships.
Geographic limitations: Giving primarily in areas of company operations in TN.
Support limitations: No support for bank clearinghouse organizations, charities sponsored solely by a single civic organization, pass through organizations, religious, veterans', social, or fraternal organizations, or political organizations. No grants to individuals, or for trips or tours, or debt reduction.
Publications: Application guidelines.
Application information: Applications accepted. Proposals for Innovation in the Arts should not exceed 3 pages. Applicants for the Award for Innovation in the Arts should submit nine copies of the proposal. Applicants should submit the following:
1) copy of IRS Determination Letter
2) brief history of organization and description of its mission
3) copy of most recent annual report/audited financial statement/990
4) listing of board of directors, trustees, officers and other key people and their affiliations
5) detailed description of project and amount of funding requested
6) copy of current year's organizational budget and/or project budget
7) additional materials/documentation

Initial approach: Cover letter and proposal to nearest community investment manager; download application form and mail proposal and application form to foundation for Award for Innovation in the Arts
Deadline(s): None; Jan. 28 for Award for Innovation in the Arts

Officers and Directors:* Charles T. Tuggle, Jr.*, Chair.; Gregg I. Lansky*, Pres., C.F.O, and Treas.; Clyde A. Billings, Jr.*, V.P. and Secy.; Charles G. Burkett; Kim Cherry; Mike Edwards; Herb H. Hilliard; William C. Losch III.
EIN: 621533987
Selected grants: The following grants are a representative sample of this grantmaker's funding activity:
$400,000 to Memphis Tomorrow, Memphis, TN, 2010. For general operating support.
$244,061 to United Way of the Mid-South, Memphis, TN, 2010. For general operating support.
$225,000 to University of Memphis Foundation, Memphis, TN, 2010. For general operating support.
$211,134 to American Red Cross National Headquarters, Washington, DC, 2010. For general operating support.
$105,000 to Saint Jude Childrens Research Hospital, Memphis, TN, 2010. For general operating support.
$100,000 to ArtsMemphis, Memphis, TN, 2010. For general operating support.
$13,193 to United Way of Williamson County, Franklin, TN, 2010. For general operating support.
$8,500 to Fort Sanders Foundation, Knoxville, TN, 2010. For general operating support.
$5,000 to Advance Memphis, Memphis, TN, 2010. For general operating support.
$2,500 to Presbyterian Day School, Memphis, TN, 2010. For general operating support.

1407
First Housing Development Corporation of Florida

107 S. Willow Ave.
Tampa, FL 33606-1945 (813) 289-9410

Company URL: http://www.firsthousingfl.com
Establishment information: Established in 1979.
Company type: Private company
Business activities: Provides mortgages.
Business type (SIC): Brokers and bankers/mortgage
Financial profile for 2010: Number of employees, 41
Corporate officers: Douglas I. McCree, Pres. and C.E.O.; Randall J. Enders, C.F.O. and Treas.; Anne Gehlsen, Corp. Secy.; Julie Carr, Cont.
Office: Garland, TX
Giving statement: Giving through the First Housing Foundation, Inc.

First Housing Foundation, Inc.

107 S. Willow Ave.
Tampa, FL 33606

Establishment information: Established as a company-sponsored operating foundation in 2000 in FL.
Donor: First Housing Development Corp. of Florida.
Financial data (yr. ended 12/31/10): Assets, $419,986 (M); gifts received, $105,200; expenditures, $37,269; qualifying distributions, $32,000; giving activities include $32,000 for 8 grants (high: $4,000; low: $4,000).
Purpose and activities: The foundation supports organizations involved with abuse prevention, affordable housing, residential care, and human services.
Fields of interest: Housing/shelter; Human services.
Type of support: General/operating support.
Support limitations: No grants to individuals.
Publications: Grants list.
Application information: Applications not accepted. Contributes only to pre-selected organizations.
Officers: Steve Cohen, Chair.; Carlos Noble, Vice-Chair.; Douglas McCree, Pres.; Anne Gehlsen, Secy.; Randall J. Enders, Treas.
Directors: Barton Goldberg; Bob Kramer.
EIN: 593690741

1408
First Insurance Company of Hawaii, Ltd.

1100 Ward Ave.
P.O. Box 2866
Honolulu, HI 96814-1600 (808) 527-7777

Company URL: http://www.ficoh.com
Establishment information: Established in 1911.
Company type: Subsidiary of a foreign company
Business activities: Sells insurance.
Business type (SIC): Insurance carriers
Financial profile for 2010: Number of employees, 310
Corporate officers: Allen Bruce Uyeda, Pres. and C.E.O.; Jeffrey Shonka, Sr. V.P., Treas. and C.O.O.; David Disera, V.P. and C.I.O.; Steve Tabussi, V.P., Mktg.
Board of director: Marie Weite
Giving statement: Giving through the First Insurance Company of Hawaii, Ltd. Corporate Giving Program and the First Insurance Company of Hawaii Charitable Foundation.

First Insurance Company of Hawaii, Ltd. Corporate Giving Program

1100 Ward Ave.
Honolulu, HI 96814-1600 (808) 527-7777
FAX: (808) 543-3200

Purpose and activities: As a complement to its foundation, First Insurance Company of Hawaii also makes charitable contributions to nonprofit organizations directly. Support is given primarily in Hawaii.
Fields of interest: General charitable giving.
Type of support: Cause-related marketing.
Geographic limitations: Giving primarily in HI.
Support limitations: No grants to individuals.

First Insurance Company of Hawaii Charitable Foundation

1100 Ward Ave.
Honolulu, HI 96814-1600 (808) 527-7616

Establishment information: Established in 1998 in HI.
Donor: First Insurance Co. of Hawaii, Ltd.
Contact: Allen B. Uyeda, Tr.
Financial data (yr. ended 12/31/11): Assets, $6,890,912 (M); expenditures, $389,570; qualifying distributions, $350,650; giving activities include $350,650 for 63 grants (high: $40,000; low: $100).
Purpose and activities: The foundation supports organizations involved with arts and culture, education, human services, goodwill promotion, and community economic development.
Fields of interest: Arts, cultural/ethnic awareness; Performing arts, orchestras; Arts; Education, early childhood education; Higher education; Education; Hospitals (general); Genetic diseases and disorders; American Red Cross; Children/youth, services; Human services; International affairs, goodwill promotion; Business/industry; Community/economic development; United Ways and Federated Giving Programs.
Type of support: General/operating support.
Geographic limitations: Giving limited to HI.
Support limitations: No grants to individuals.
Application information: Applications accepted. Application form not required. Applicants should submit the following:
1) detailed description of project and amount of funding requested
Initial approach: Letter of inquiry
Deadline(s): None
Trustees: Faye W. Kurren; Jeffrey A. Shonka; Stephen J. Tabussi; Allen B. Uyeda; Jeffrey N. Watanabe.
EIN: 990339536
Selected grants: The following grants are a representative sample of this grantmaker's funding activity:
$25,000 to Enterprise Honolulu, Honolulu, HI, 2010.
$25,000 to Enterprise Honolulu, Honolulu, HI, 2010.
$25,000 to Enterprise Honolulu, Honolulu, HI, 2010.
$10,000 to Enterprise Honolulu, Honolulu, HI, 2010.
$5,000 to Teach for America, New York, NY, 2010.
$5,000 to Teach for America, New York, NY, 2010.
$2,500 to American Diabetes Association, Alexandria, VA, 2010.
$2,000 to Executive Women International, Salt Lake City, UT, 2010.
$1,000 to Muscular Dystrophy Association, Tucson, AZ, 2010.

1409
First Interstate Bank

104 S. Wolcott St., Ste. 602
Casper, WY 82601-2553 (307) 235-4201

Establishment information: Established in 1968.
Company type: Subsidiary of a private company
Business activities: Operates commercial bank.
Business type (SIC): Banks/commercial
Financial profile for 2010: Number of employees, 80
Corporate officers: Randy Scott, Chair.; Ron J. Pascoe, Pres.
Board of directors: Randy Scott, Co-Chair.; Tom Scott, Co-Chair.; James Scott, Vice-Chair.; Ka Alberts; Sara Flitner; Ed Garding; Charles Heyneman; Mike Huston; Susan Humble; Donovan McComb; Shawn Rost; Risa Scott; Lynette Scott; Steve Wheeler
Giving statement: Giving through the First Interstate BancSystem Foundation, Inc. and the First Interstate Bank of Commerce Centennial Youth Foundation.

First Interstate BancSystem Foundation, Inc.

401 N. 31st St., Ste. 700
Billings, MT 59101-1285
FAX: (406) 255-5311; E-mail: foundation@fib.com; Application address: P.O. Box 7113, Billings, MT 59103-7113; URL: https://www.firstinterstatebank.com/company/commitment/foundation/

Establishment information: Established in 1990 in MT.
Donors: First Interstate Bank of Commerce; Wells Fargo Bank, N.A.; First Interstate Bank.
Contact: Kelly Bruggeman, Exec. Dir.
Financial data (yr. ended 12/31/11): Assets, $1,619,572 (M); gifts received, $719,000; expenditures, $1,227,103; qualifying distributions, $1,195,075; giving activities include $1,195,075 for grants.
Purpose and activities: The foundation supports organizations involved with arts and culture, education, health, hunger, housing, human services, community development, leadership development, and economically disadvantaged people. Support is given primarily in areas of company operations.
Fields of interest: Arts; Secondary school/education; Higher education; Education; Health care; Food services; Housing/shelter; Human services; Community development, neighborhood development; Economic development; Community/economic development; Leadership development Economically disadvantaged.

Programs:

Community Development: The foundation supports programs designed to promote community development. Special emphasis is directed toward programs designed to promote affordable housing for low and moderate income individuals; services targeting low and moderate income individuals; activities that revitalize or stabilize low and moderate income geographies; and activities that foster economic development.

Employee Matching Program: The foundation matches contributions made by employees of First Interstate BancSystem to nonprofit organizations on a one-for-one basis.

Leadership Grants: The foundation supports programs recommended by local branch leadership to meet the needs of their prospective communities.

Mini Banks: The foundation, in partnership with community schools and local First Interstate branches, promotes financial literacy and asset building in students, schools, families, and communities through student-operated savings banks. All students have their own savings account and each Mini Bank account earns 4% interest.

Neighbors Feeding Neighbors: The foundation matches contributions made by employees and directors of First Interstate to nonprofit organizations that has established a food program during July, August, and September on a two-for-one basis.

Volunteer Matching Program: The foundation awards grants to nonprofit organizations with which

employees of First Interstate BancSystem volunteers. The foundation awards $8 dollars for every hour donated, with a 20 hour minimum.
Type of support: Building/renovation; Capital campaigns; Employee matching gifts; Employee volunteer services; Equipment; Matching/challenge support; Program development; Scholarship funds.
Geographic limitations: Giving primarily in areas of company operations in MT, western SD, and WY.
Support limitations: No support for lobbying or political organizations, sectarian or religious organizations not of direct benefit to the entire community, or discriminatory organizations. No grants to individuals, or for endowments, or general operating support for established organizations.
Publications: Application guidelines; Grants list; Program policy statement.
Application information: Applications accepted. The First Interstate BancSystem Foundation only awards grants to organizations recommended by local First Interstate Bank branches. Applying organizations must apply to the nearest branch. Visit website for branch location address. Additional information may be requested at a later date. Application form required. Applicants should submit the following:
1) timetable for implementation and evaluation of project
2) results expected from proposed grant
3) statement of problem project will address
4) population served
5) name, address and phone number of organization
6) copy of IRS Determination Letter
7) brief history of organization and description of its mission
8) geographic area to be served
9) copy of most recent annual report/audited financial statement/990
10) how project's results will be evaluated or measured
11) descriptive literature about organization
12) listing of board of directors, trustees, officers and other key people and their affiliations
13) detailed description of project and amount of funding requested
14) contact person
15) copy of current year's organizational budget and/or project budget
16) listing of additional sources and amount of support
17) additional materials/documentation

Initial approach: Download application and mail to nearest branch location
Board meeting date(s): Quarterly
Deadline(s): None

Officer and Directors:* Randy Scott*, Chair. and Pres.; Kelly Bruggeman, Exec. Dir.; Ka Alberts; Sara Flitner; Ed Garding; Charles Heyneman; Susan Humble; Mike Huston; Donovan McComb; Shawn Rost; James Scott; Lynette Scott; Risa Scott; Thomas Scott; Steve Wheeler.
Trustee Bank: First Interstate Bank.
Number of staff: 3 full-time professional.
EIN: 810465899

First Interstate Bank of Commerce Centennial Youth Foundation

(formerly First Interstate Bank of Billings Centennial Youth Foundation)
401 N. 31st St., Ste. 700
Billings, MT 59101-1256
Application address: c/o First Interstate Bank, P.O. Box 30918, Billings, MT 59116, tel.: (406) 255-5317

Establishment information: Established around 1982.
Donors: First Interstate Bank of Commerce; Wells Fargo Bank, N.A.; First Interstate Bank.
Contact: Michelle Boucher
Financial data (yr. ended 12/31/11): Assets, $7 (M); gifts received, $20,001; expenditures, $20,000; qualifying distributions, $20,000; giving activities include $20,000 for grants.
Purpose and activities: The foundation supports youth-oriented organizations. Support is limited to Yellowstone County, Montana.
Fields of interest: Education; Recreation; Human services.
Type of support: Building/renovation; Equipment; General/operating support; Program development; Scholarship funds.
Geographic limitations: Giving limited to Yellowstone County, MT.
Support limitations: No grants to individuals.
Application information: Applications accepted. Application form required. Applicants should submit the following:
1) copy of IRS Determination Letter
2) copy of most recent annual report/audited financial statement/990
3) listing of board of directors, trustees, officers and other key people and their affiliations
4) copy of current year's organizational budget and/or project budget
5) listing of additional sources and amount of support

Initial approach: Contact nearest company bank for application form and mail to foundation
Copies of proposal: 6
Deadline(s): Varies

Directors: Dana Bishop; Lisa Posada Griffin; Vicki Olson Johnson; Marilynn Miller; Fr. Steve Tokarski.
EIN: 742265711

1410
First Merchants Corporation

200 E. Jackson St.
Muncie, IN 47305-2835 (765) 747-1500
FAX: (765) 282-6304

Company URL: http://www.firstmerchants.com
Establishment information: Established in 1893.
Company type: Public company
Company ticker symbol and exchange: FRME/NASDAQ
Business activities: Operates commercial bank.
Business type (SIC): Banks/commercial
Financial profile for 2012: Number of employees, 1,149; assets, $4,304,080,000; pre-tax net income, $60,990,000; liabilities, $3,752,590,000
Corporate officers: Charles E. Schalliol, Chair.; Michael C. Rechin, Pres. and C.E.O.; Mark K. Hardwick, Exec. V.P. and C.F.O.; Jami L. Bradshaw, Sr. V.P. and C.A.O.; Robert R. Connors, Sr. V.P., Opers.
Board of directors: Charles E. Schalliol, Chair.; Michael R. Becher; Roderick English; Jo Ann M. Gora; William L. Hoy; Gary J. Lehman; Michael C. Rechin; Patrick A. Sherman; Terry L. Walker; Jean L. Wojtowicz
Giving statement: Giving through the First Merchants Corporation Contributions Program and the First Merchants Charitable Foundation, Inc.
Company EIN: 351544218

First Merchants Charitable Foundation, Inc.

(formerly Lincoln Charitable Foundation, Inc.)
1121 E. Main St.
Plainfield, IN 46168-1760 (317) 844-2097

Establishment information: Established in 1999 in IN.
Donor: Lincoln Bank.
Contact: David Mansfield, Dir.
Financial data (yr. ended 12/31/11): Assets, $977,001 (M); expenditures, $7,984; qualifying distributions, $5,000; giving activities include $5,000 for 8 grants (high: $1,000; low: $250).
Purpose and activities: The foundation provides funds to charitable organizations providing services within the geographic locations of the foundation's primary contributor, Lincoln Bank.
Fields of interest: Housing/shelter; Human services; Religion.
Type of support: Endowments; General/operating support.
Geographic limitations: Giving limited to Brown, Clinton, Hendricks, Johnson, Montgomery, and Morgan counties, IN.
Support limitations: No grants to individuals.
Application information: Applications accepted. Application form required.

Initial approach: Letter
Copies of proposal: 1
Board meeting date(s): Semi-annually, or as needed
Deadline(s): Feb. 1; grants selection completed by May

Officer: David E. Mansfield, Pres.
Directors: Patrick A. Sherman; Beth Ann Leach*; John M. Baer; Lester N. Bergum; Jerry R. Engle; W. Thomas Harmon; Jerry Holifield; R.J. McConnell; John Milholland; John L. Wyatt.
EIN: 352052344

1411
First Mid-Illinois Bancshares, Inc.

1515 Charleston Ave.
P.O. Box 499
Mattoon, IL 61938 (217) 234-7454
FAX: (217) 258-0426

Company URL: http://www.firstmid.com
Establishment information: Established in 1865.
Company type: Public company
Company ticker symbol and exchange: FMBH/OTCB
Business activities: Operates bank holding company; operates commercial bank; sells insurance.
Business type (SIC): Banks/commercial; insurance carriers; holding company
Financial profile for 2012: Number of employees, 400; assets, $1,578,030,000; pre-tax net income, $22,430,000; liabilities, $1,421,350,000
Corporate officers: William S. Rowland, Chair. and C.E.O.; Michael L. Taylor, Exec. V.P. and C.F.O.
Board of directors: William S. Rowland, Chair.; Holly A. Bailey; Joseph R. Dively; Steven L. Grissom; Benjamin I. Lumpkin; Gary W. Melvin; Ray Anthony Sparks
Subsidiary: First Mid-Illinois Bank & Trust, N.A., Mattoon, IL
Giving statement: Giving through the First Mid-Illinois Bancshares, Inc.
Company EIN: 371103704

First Mid-Illinois Bancshares, Inc.

P.O. Box 499
Mattoon, IL 61938-0499

Establishment information: Established in 1994.

Donors: First Mid-Illinois Bancshares, Inc.; First Mid-Illinois Bank & Trust.
Contact: William S. Rowland
Financial data (yr. ended 12/31/11): Assets, $390,730 (M); gifts received, $60,036; expenditures, $49,829; qualifying distributions, $43,400; giving activities include $43,400 for grants.
Purpose and activities: The foundation supports community foundations and organizations involved with higher education and senior citizens.
Fields of interest: Human services; Community/economic development.
Type of support: General/operating support.
Geographic limitations: Giving primarily in Mattoon, IL.
Support limitations: No grants to individuals.
Application information: Applications accepted. Application form required. Applicants should submit the following:
1) brief history of organization and description of its mission
2) detailed description of project and amount of funding requested
Initial approach: Letter
Deadline(s): None
Trustee: First Mid-Illinois Bank & Trust.
EIN: 371339718

1412
First Mid-Illinois Bank & Trust, N.A.
1515 Charleston Ave.
Mattoon, IL 61938 (217) 258-0653

Company URL: https://www.firstmid.com/
Establishment information: Established in 1981.
Company type: Subsidiary of a public company
Business activities: Operates commercial bank.
Business type (SIC): Banks/commercial
Corporate officers: William S. Rowland, Chair and C.E.O.; Joseph R. Dively, Pres.; Michael L. Taylor, Exec. V.P. and C.F.O.
Board of director: William S. Rowland, Chair.
Giving statement: Giving through the First Mid-Illinois Bank & Trust, Trust.

First Mid-Illinois Bank & Trust, Trust
P.O. Box 529
Mattoon, IL 61938-0499 (217) 258-0633

Establishment information: Established in 1993 in IL.
Donors: First Mid-Illinois Bank & Trust; Genevieve Daily; Elgin Daily.
Contact: Laura Walk
Financial data (yr. ended 07/31/11): Assets, $1,271,138 (M); expenditures, $132,732; qualifying distributions, $65,252; giving activities include $52,000 for 11 grants (high: $9,096; low: $2,274) and $11,370 for 2 grants to individuals (high: $8,000; low: $2,500).
Purpose and activities: The foundation awards college scholarships to residents of Coles County, Illinois, who are studying in the field of agriculture.
Fields of interest: Education; Religion.
Type of support: Scholarships—to individuals.
Geographic limitations: Giving primarily in Coles County, IL.
Application information: Applications accepted. Application form required.
Initial approach: Contact foundation or Coles County High School for application form
Deadline(s): Apr. 15
Trustee: First Mid-Illinois Bank & Trust.
EIN: 376314454

1413
First Midwest Bancorp, Inc.
1 Pierce Pl., Ste. 1500
P.O. Box 459
Itasca, IL 60143-9768 (630) 875-7450

Company URL: http://www.firstmidwest.com
Establishment information: Established in 1983.
Company type: Public company
Company ticker symbol and exchange: FMBI/NASDAQ
Business activities: Operates bank holding company; operates commercial bank.
Business type (SIC): Banks/commercial; holding company
Financial profile for 2012: Number of employees, 1,707; assets, $8,009,840,000; pre-tax net income, -$49,940,000; liabilities, $7,158,950,000
Corporate officers: Robert P. O'Meara, Chair.; Michael L. Scudder, Pres. and C.E.O.; Mark G. Sander, Sr. Exec. V.P. and C.O.O.; Paul F. Clemens, Exec. V.P. and C.F.O.; James P. Hotchkiss, Exec. V.P. and Treas.
Board of directors: Robert P. O'Meara, Chair.; Barbara A. Boigegrain; John F. Chlebowski, Jr.; James Gaffney; Phupinder S. Gill; Peter J. Henseler; Patrick J. McDonnell; Ellen A. Rudnick; Michael L. Scudder; Michael J. Small; John L. Sterling; J. Stephen Vanderwoude
Subsidiaries: First Midwest Bank, Itasca, IL; First Midwest Insurance Co., Itasca, IL
Historic mergers: Palos Bank & Trust, Co. (August 13, 2010)
Giving statement: Giving through the First Midwest Charitable Foundation and the Palos Bank Foundation, Inc.
Company EIN: 363161078

First Midwest Charitable Foundation
c/o First Midwest Bank
1 Pierce Pl., Ste. 1500
Itasca, IL 60143-1253

Establishment information: Established in 2002 in IL.
Donors: First Midwest Bancorp, Inc.; First Midwest Bank.
Financial data (yr. ended 12/31/11): Assets, $1,997,470 (M); expenditures, $105,401; qualifying distributions, $102,629; giving activities include $102,500 for 23 grants (high: $5,000; low: $2,500).
Purpose and activities: The foundation supports organizations involved with child welfare and human services.
Fields of interest: Crime/violence prevention, child abuse; Children, services; Family services; Family services, domestic violence; Human services.
Type of support: General/operating support; Program development.
Geographic limitations: Giving limited to IL.
Support limitations: No grants to individuals.
Application information: Applications not accepted. Unsolicited requests for funds not accepted.
Officers: Michael L. Scudder, Pres. and Secy.; Sharon Carnaghi, Treas.
EIN: 050545258
Selected grants: The following grants are a representative sample of this grantmaker's funding activity:
$5,000 to Allendale Association, Lake Villa, IL, 2011.
$5,000 to Blessings in a Backpack, Louisville, KY, 2011.
$5,000 to Childrens Memorial Foundation, Chicago, IL, 2011.
$5,000 to Cornerstone Services, Joliet, IL, 2011.
$5,000 to Crisis Center for South Suburbia, Tinley Park, IL, 2011.
$5,000 to Mothers Trust Foundation, Lake Forest, IL, 2011.
$5,000 to Pediatric Oncology Treasure Chest Foundation, Orland Park, IL, 2011.
$5,000 to SOS Childrens Villages Illinois, Chicago, IL, 2011.
$2,500 to Saint Jude House, Crown Point, IN, 2011.
$2,500 to YWCA Lake County, Waukegan, IL, 2011.

Palos Bank Foundation, Inc.
c/o Gregory J. Paetow
12600 S. Harlem Ave.
Palos Heights, IL 60463-0927

Establishment information: Established in 2001 in IL; status changed to company-sponsored operating foundation in 2002.
Donor: Palos Bank & Trust Co.
Financial data (yr. ended 12/31/10): Assets, $223 (M); gifts received, $22,000; expenditures, $22,025; qualifying distributions, $22,000; giving activities include $22,000 for 11 grants to individuals (high: $2,000; low: $2,000).
Purpose and activities: The foundation awards college scholarships to high school seniors attending Alan B. Shepard, Amos Alonzo Stagg, Carl Sandburg, Chicago Christian, Lincoln-Way East, Lincoln-Way Central, Lockport, Marist, Mother McAuley, and Providence Catholic high schools in Illinois.
Fields of interest: Higher education.
Type of support: Scholarships—to individuals.
Geographic limitations: Giving primarily in IL.
Application information: Applications accepted. Application form required.
Initial approach: Contact high school for application form
Deadline(s): Mar. 1
Final notification: By Apr. 16
Officers and Directors:* Georgeann M. Iles*, Co-Pres.; Gregory J. Paetow*, Co-Pres.; Rodney D. Stickle*, Treas.; William J. Paetow.
EIN: 364443693

1414
First National Bank
202 E. 11th St.
P.O. Box 570
Goodland, KS 67735-3006 (785) 890-2000

Company URL: http://www.fnb.com
Establishment information: Established in 1886.
Company type: Private company
Business activities: Operates bank holding company; operates commercial bank.
Business type (SIC): Holding company; banks/commercial
Corporate officer: Dwane L. Timm, Chair.
Board of directors: Dwane L. Timm, Chair.; Larry Evans; Peggy Hanke; Larry Ihrig; Ralph A. Jensen; Perry Keller; Tim Livengood; Victor Nemechek; Lyle Saddler
Giving statement: Giving through the First National Bank Charitable Trust.

First National Bank Charitable Trust

P.O. Box 570
Goodland, KS 67735-0570

Donors: First National Bank; Wright Farms, Inc.; Carol Sanders; Ole R. Cram; Betsy C. Cram.
Financial data (yr. ended 12/31/11): Assets, $1,595,876 (M); gifts received, $14,358; expenditures, $100,103; qualifying distributions, $46,172; giving activities include $46,172 for grants.
Purpose and activities: The trust supports recreation centers and organizations involved with education.
Fields of interest: Education; Community/economic development.
Type of support: General/operating support; Scholarship funds.
Geographic limitations: Giving primarily in KS.
Support limitations: No grants to individuals.
Application information: Applications accepted. Application form required. Applicants should submit the following:
1) copy of most recent annual report/audited financial statement/990
2) detailed description of project and amount of funding requested

Initial approach: Letter
Deadline(s): None

Trustee: First National Bank.
EIN: 486133921

1415
First National Bank Alaska

101 W. 36th Ave.
P.O. Box 100720
Anchorage, AK 99510 (907) 777-4362
FAX: (907) 777-4569

Company URL: http://www.fnbalaska.com/
Establishment information: Established in 1922.
Company type: Public company
Company ticker symbol and exchange: FBAK/OTC
Business activities: Operates a commercial bank.
Business type (SIC): Banks/commercial
Financial profile for 2011: Number of employees, 662; assets, $2,870,170,000; pre-tax net income, $51,110,000; liabilities, $2,425,910,000
Corporate officers: Daniel H. Cuddy, Chair. and Pres.; Betsy Lawer, Vice-Chair.; Michele Schuh, Sr. V.P. and C.F.O.; Phil Griffin, Sr. V.P. and C.I.O.
Board of directors: Daniel H. Cuddy, Chair.; Betsy Lawer, Vice-Chair.; Maurice J. Coyle; Perry Eaton; George E. Gordon; Margy K. Johnson; Jane Klopfer; Loren H. Lounsbury; Lucy Mahan
Giving statement: Giving through the First National Bank Alaska Corporate Giving Program.

First National Bank Alaska Corporate Giving Program

c/o Mktg. Dept.
101 W. 36th Ave., Ste. 207
P.O. Box 100720
Anchorage, AK 99510-0720 (907) 777-4362
URL: http://www.fnbalaska.com/412.cfm

Financial data (yr. ended 12/31/11): Total giving, $996,000, including $996,000 for grants.
Purpose and activities: First National Bank Alaska makes charitable contributions to nonprofit organizations involved with arts and culture, education, health, community and public service, and youth and senior citizens. Support is limited to Alaska.
Fields of interest: Arts; Education; Health care; Youth development; Aging, centers/services; Human services; Community/economic development; Public affairs.
Type of support: Employee volunteer services; General/operating support.
Geographic limitations: Giving limited to AK.
Support limitations: No support for religious or political organizations. No grants to individuals, or for travel expenses.
Publications: Application guidelines.
Application information: Applications accepted. A contributions committee reviews all requests. Application form required. Applicants should submit the following:
1) timetable for implementation and evaluation of project
2) population served
3) name, address and phone number of organization
4) copy of IRS Determination Letter
5) brief history of organization and description of its mission
6) copy of most recent annual report/audited financial statement/990
7) listing of board of directors, trustees, officers and other key people and their affiliations
8) detailed description of project and amount of funding requested
9) contact person
10) copy of current year's organizational budget and/or project budget
11) listing of additional sources and amount of support
12) plans for acknowledgement

Applications should include a statement demonstrating broad community support for and involvement in the project and the organization.

Initial approach: Download application form and mail to headquarters
Copies of proposal: 1
Committee meeting date(s): Monthly
Deadline(s): 2 months prior to need
Final notification: Following board meetings

1416
First National Bank Bemidji

1600 Paul Bunyan Dr., N.W.
P.O. Box 670
Bemidji, MN 56601-3060 (218) 751-2430

Company URL: http://www.fnbbemidji.com
Establishment information: Established in 1897.
Company type: Private company
Business activities: Operates commercial bank.
Business type (SIC): Banks/commercial
Corporate officer: Thomas E. Welle, Chair. and Pres.
Board of director: Thomas E. Welle, Chair.
Giving statement: Giving through the First National Bank Bemidji Corporate Giving Program and the First National Bank of Bemidji Foundation.

First National Bank Bemidji Corporate Giving Program

P.O. Box 670
Bemidji, MN 56619-0670
URL: http://www.fnbbemidji.com/aboutcomm.htm

Purpose and activities: As a complement to its foundation, the First National Bank Bemidji also makes charitable contributions to nonprofit organizations directly. Support is given primarily in areas of company operations in Bemidji, Minnesota.
Fields of interest: Arts; Health organizations; Youth development; Human services; Community/economic development; General charitable giving.
Type of support: Employee volunteer services; General/operating support.
Geographic limitations: Giving primarily in areas of company operations in Bemidji, MN.

First National Bank of Bemidji Foundation

P.O. Box 670
Bemidji, MN 56619-0670 (218) 751-2430
URL: https://www.fnbbemidji.com/aboutcomm.htm

Establishment information: Established in 1993 in MN.
Donor: First National Bank Bemidji.
Contact: Paul N. Welle, Pres.
Financial data (yr. ended 12/31/11): Assets, $1,041,315 (M); gifts received, $52,500; expenditures, $51,274; qualifying distributions, $50,475; giving activities include $50,000 for 9 grants (high: $12,500; low: $500).
Purpose and activities: The foundation supports programs designed to enrich the lives of children and their families.
Fields of interest: Performing arts, theater; Performing arts, orchestras; Historic preservation/historical societies; Arts; Education; Boys & girls clubs; Children, services; Family services.
Type of support: Capital campaigns; General/operating support; Program development; Scholarship funds.
Geographic limitations: Giving primarily in areas of company operations in MN.
Publications: Application guidelines; Grants list.
Application information: Applications accepted. Application form required. Applicants should submit the following:
1) name, address and phone number of organization
2) brief history of organization and description of its mission
3) how project's results will be evaluated or measured
4) copy of current year's organizational budget and/or project budget
5) listing of additional sources and amount of support

Initial approach: Proposal
Board meeting date(s): Annually
Deadline(s): None

Directors: Ron Cuperus; B. Scott Curb; Joseph Lueken; Dean Thompson; Robert Welle; Kyle Young.
Officers: Paul N. Welle, Pres.; E. Joseph Welle, V.P.; Susan S. Engel, Secy.-Treas.
EIN: 411765936

1417
The First National Bank of Pawnee

601 Harrison St.
Pawnee, OK 74058-2001 (918) 762-2503

Company URL: http://www.fnbpawnee.com
Establishment information: Established in 1894.
Company type: Private company
Business activities: Operates commercial bank.
Business type (SIC): Banks/commercial
Financial profile for 2011: Assets, $63,355,695
Corporate officer: Clark L. Shouse, Jr., Chair. and Pres.
Board of directors: Clark L. Shouse, Chair.; Debbie Branch; Lynn Mennem; James S. Plaxico; Robert J. Scott; Clark Shouse, Jr.

Giving statement: Giving through the First National of Pawnee Foundation.

The First National of Pawnee Foundation

601 Harrison St.
Pawnee, OK 74058-2520

Donor: The First National Bank of Pawnee.
Financial data (yr. ended 12/31/11): Assets, $13,557 (M); expenditures, $6,160; qualifying distributions, $5,585; giving activities include $5,585 for grants.
Purpose and activities: The foundation supports organizations involved with arts and culture, education, health, recreation, and community development.
Fields of interest: Education.
Type of support: General/operating support.
Geographic limitations: Giving limited to Pawnee, OK.
Support limitations: No grants to individuals.
Application information: Applications not accepted. Unsolicited requests for funds not accepted.
Officers: Clark L. Shouse, Pres.; Lewis Bryant, Secy.
Director: Robert J. Scott.
EIN: 731622017

1418
First Newton National Bank

100 N. 2nd Ave. W.
P.O. Box 489
Newton, IA 50208-3246 (641) 792-3010

Company URL: http://www.firstnnb.com
Establishment information: Established in 1882.
Company type: Private company
Business activities: Operates commercial bank.
Business type (SIC): Banks/commercial
Corporate officers: Gary Kahn, C.E.O.; Dan Clark, Pres.
Board of directors: Ronald W. Helms; Willard Russell
Giving statement: Giving through the First Newton National Foundation.

First Newton National Foundation

c/o Gary S. Kahn
100 N. 2nd Ave. W.
Newton, IA 50208-3246 (641) 792-3010
URL: http://www.firstnnb.com/

Establishment information: Established in 2002 in IA.
Donor: First Newton National Bank.
Contact: Gary S. Kahn, Dir.
Financial data (yr. ended 12/31/11): Assets, $60,706 (M); gifts received, $15,000; expenditures, $24,085; qualifying distributions, $23,710; giving activities include $23,335 for 19 grants (high: $9,900; low: $100).
Purpose and activities: The foundation supports organizations involved with higher education, health, housing development, and recreation.
Fields of interest: Health care; Medical research; Recreation.
Type of support: General/operating support.
Geographic limitations: Giving limited to IA.
Application information: Applications accepted. Telephone calls during the application process are not encouraged. Application form required.
Applicants should submit the following:
1) detailed description of project and amount of funding requested

Initial approach: Letter
Deadline(s): None

Directors: Crystal Failor; Gary S. Kahn; Jane B. Kahn; Rob Khan; James E. Willemsen.
EIN: 680512765

1419
First Niagara Financial Group, Inc.

(also known as First Niagara)
(formerly Niagara Bancorp, Inc.)
726 Exchange St., Ste. 618
Buffalo, NY 14210 (716) 819-5600
FAX: (302) 655-5049

Company URL: http://www.fnfg.com
Establishment information: Established in 1870.
Company type: Public company
Company ticker symbol and exchange: FNFG/NASDAQ
Business activities: Operates bank holding company; operates savings bank.
Business type (SIC): Savings institutions; holding company
Financial profile for 2012: Number of employees, 6,191; assets, $36,809,000,000; pre-tax net income, $239,362,000; liabilities, $31,881,000,000
Forbes 2000 ranking: 2012—1849th in sales, 1551st in profits, and 615th in assets
Corporate officers: Gary M. Crosby, Pres. and C.E.O.; Gregory W. Norwood, Sr. Exec. V.P. and C.F.O.; Richard M. Barry, Exec. V.P. and Chief Risk Off.; Andrew Fornarola, Exec. V.P., Consumer Finance; Mark Rendulic, Exec. V.P., Retail Banking
Board of directors: G. Thomas Bowers, Chair.; Thomas E. Baker; Roxanne J. Coady; Carl A. Florio; Carlton L. Highsmith; George M. Philip; Peter B. Robinson; Nathaniel D. Woodson
Historic mergers: NewAlliance Bancshares, Inc. (April 15, 2011)
Giving statement: Giving through the Cohoes Savings Foundation, the First Niagara Foundation, the Hudson River Bancorp, Inc. Foundation, and the Willow Grove Foundation.
Company EIN: 421556195

Cohoes Savings Foundation

60 Remsen St.
P.O. Box 230
Cohoes, NY 12047-2833
E-mail: brennaja@nycap.rr.com; URL: http://www.cohoessavingsfoundation.org/

Establishment information: Established in 1998.
Donors: Cohoes Savings Bank; Hudson River Bank & Trust Co.
Financial data (yr. ended 12/31/11): Assets, $3,689,118 (M); expenditures, $289,376; qualifying distributions, $253,597; giving activities include $158,750 for grants.
Purpose and activities: The foundation supports organizations involved with arts and culture, health, human services, community development, and religion. Special emphasis is directed toward programs designed to promote self-help and self-sufficiency.
Fields of interest: Arts; Health care; Developmentally disabled, centers & services; Human services; Community/economic development; General charitable giving.
Type of support: Curriculum development; Program development; Research; Scholarship funds; Sponsorships.
Geographic limitations: Giving primarily in Albany, Rensselaer, Saratoga, Schenectady, and Warren counties, NY.
Support limitations: No support for religious organizations. No grants to individuals.
Publications: Application guidelines.
Application information: Applications accepted. Application form required. Applicants should submit the following:
1) how project will be sustained once grantmaker support is completed
2) signature and title of chief executive officer
3) results expected from proposed grant
4) qualifications of key personnel
5) copy of IRS Determination Letter
6) geographic area to be served
7) copy of most recent annual report/audited financial statement/990
8) how project's results will be evaluated or measured
9) listing of board of directors, trustees, officers and other key people and their affiliations
10) detailed description of project and amount of funding requested
11) copy of current year's organizational budget and/or project budget
12) listing of additional sources and amount of support

Initial approach: Download application form and mail to foundation
Copies of proposal: 1
Board meeting date(s): Quarterly
Deadline(s): None
Final notification: Varies

Officers and Directors:* Harry L. Robinson*, Chair.; Frank D. Colaruotolo*, Secy.; Chester C. DeLaMater*, Treas.; Jacqueline E. Brennan, Exec. Dir.
Number of staff: 1 full-time professional.
EIN: 141809837
Selected grants: The following grants are a representative sample of this grantmaker's funding activity:
$23,375 to Cohoes Community Center, Cohoes, NY, 2007.
$9,500 to C-R Productions, Cohoes, NY, 2007.
$5,000 to Northeast Health Foundation, Troy, NY, 2007.
$3,000 to Parsons Child and Family Center, Albany, NY, 2007.
$3,000 to Regional Food Bank of Northeastern New York, Latham, NY, 2007.
$2,500 to Literacy Volunteers of Rensselaer County, Troy, NY, 2007.
$1,300 to Cystic Fibrosis Foundation, Northeastern New York Chapter, Latham Office, Latham, NY, 2007.
$1,000 to Arthritis Foundation, Northeastern New York Chapter, Albany, NY, 2007.
$600 to Hispanic Outreach Services, Albany, NY, 2007.
$500 to Little Sisters of the Poor, Latham, NY, 2007.

First Niagara Foundation

(formerly First Niagara Bank Foundation)
726 Exchange St., Ste. 900
Buffalo, NY 14210-1452 (716) 270-8675
FAX: (716) 819-5160; E-mail: florine.luhr@fnfg.com; URL: https://www.firstniagara.com/About_Us/Community_Commitment/Community_Commitment.aspx

Establishment information: Established in 1998 in NY.
Donors: Niagara Bancorp, Inc.; First Niagara Financial Group, Inc.; Lockport Savings Bank; First Niagara Bank.

Contact: Elizabeth S. Gurney, Exec. Dir.; Florine Luhr, Fdn. Admin.
Financial data (yr. ended 12/31/12): Assets, $35,782,860 (M); gifts received, $10,010,000; expenditures, $10,643,712; qualifying distributions, $10,511,659; giving activities include $10,237,761 for 794 grants and $568,789 for 2 in-kind gifts.
Purpose and activities: The foundation supports organizations involved with mentoring and children and youth. Giving is limited to areas of company operations.
Fields of interest: Arts, single organization support; Arts education; Education, single organization support; Higher education; Adult education—literacy, basic skills & GED; Education; Health care; Food banks; Food distribution, meals on wheels; Housing/shelter, management/technical assistance; Housing/shelter, single organization support; Housing/shelter, information services; Housing/shelter, public education; Housing/shelter, formal/general education; Housing/shelter, development; Housing/shelter, rehabilitation; Housing/shelter, home owners; Recreation, community; Youth development, alliance/advocacy; Youth development, single organization support; Boys & girls clubs; Youth development, adult & child programs; Big Brothers/Big Sisters; Youth development; Children/youth, services; Residential/custodial care; Community development, neighborhood development; Economic development; Community development, small businesses Children/youth; Children; Youth; Young adults; Economically disadvantaged.
Programs:
Mentoring Matters: Mentoring Matters provides monetary and employee volunteer support to organized mentoring initiatives. The program reinforces the importance of mentoring and the positive impact that it has on young adults. Special emphasis is directed toward organizations with which employees of First Niagara volunteer. The grant program is administered each year in the 3rd and 4th quarters.
Regional Community Grants: Regional Community Grants support programs of nonprofit organizations, which include program support and special projects. To apply for a Regional Charitable Grant, the applicant organization must be a charitable, nonprofit organization as defined by section 501(c) 3 of the IRS tax code.
Type of support: Employee volunteer services; Program development; Sponsorships.
Geographic limitations: Giving limited to areas of company operations in CT, Western MA, Upstate and Hudson Valley NY, and PA.
Support limitations: No support for organizations with limited availability to the general public; political organizations, candidates or lobbying efforts; national or international organizations, unless their programs have significant local impact; organizations that discriminate based on: age, race, color, sex, religion, national origin, disability, marital status, receipt of public assistance, sexual orientation, or military status. No grants to individuals or programs that benefit specific individuals.
Publications: Application guidelines; Corporate giving report.
Application information: Applications accepted. Contributions are limited to one donation per organization in any given year. Organizations receiving Mentoring Matters support are asked to submit a final report. Application form required. Applicants should submit the following:
1) timetable for implementation and evaluation of project
2) results expected from proposed grant
3) qualifications of key personnel
4) statement of problem project will address
5) population served
6) name, address and phone number of organization
7) copy of IRS Determination Letter
8) how company employees can become involved with the organization
9) brief history of organization and description of its mission
10) geographic area to be served
11) copy of most recent annual report/audited financial statement/990
12) how project's results will be evaluated or measured
13) list of company employees involved with the organization
14) listing of board of directors, trustees, officers and other key people and their affiliations
15) detailed description of project and amount of funding requested
16) contact person
17) copy of current year's organizational budget and/or project budget
18) listing of additional sources and amount of support
19) plans for acknowledgement
20) additional materials/documentation

Initial approach: Complete online application at www.firstniagara.com
Copies of proposal: 1
Board meeting date(s): Quarterly
Deadline(s): 90 days prior to need

Officers and Directors:* w Mark Rendulic, Pres.; Rose Melisz, Secy.; Ann Segarra, Treas.; Daniel E. Cantara; Peter Cosgrove; Robert Kane; Robert MacDonald; Paul McCraven; Todd Moules; David Ring; Cathie Schaffer.
Number of staff: 2 full-time professional.
EIN: 161549641
Selected grants: The following grants are a representative sample of this grantmaker's funding activity:
$125,000 to Big Brothers Big Sisters Southeastern Pennsylvania, Philadelphia, PA, 2012. For mentoring program.
$125,000 to United Way of Allegheny County, Pittsburgh, PA, 2012. For Be a 6th Grade Mentor program.
$100,000 to Central New York Community Foundation, Syracuse, NY, 2012. For Say Yes Syracuse mentoring program.
$100,000 to Zoological Society of Philadelphia, Philadelphia, PA, 2012. For Big Cat Falls.
$50,000 to Be A Friend Program, Buffalo, NY, 2012. For Tranforming Buffalo Through Mentoring and Education Program.
$50,000 to Mass Mentoring Partnership, Boston, MA, 2012. For youth mentoring.
$48,150 to Urban League of Pittsburgh, Pittsburgh, PA, 2012. For education and youth development programs.
$45,000 to Women's Business Development Council, Stamford, CT, 2012. For financial clinics opportunity fund and programs.
$27,000 to Saint John Fisher College, Rochester, NY, 2012. For World of Inquiry School students mentoring program.
$25,000 to Junior Achievement of Northeastern New York, Latham, NY, 2012. For Mentoring Matters.
$25,000 to Pottstown Cluster of Religious Communities, Pottstown, PA, 2012. For Getting Ahead Initiative.
$20,000 to Habitat for Humanity, Capital District, Albany, NY, 2012. For Fox Hollow at Burden and Cross.
$20,000 to Milton J. Rubenstein Museum of Science and Technology, Syracuse, NY, 2012. For Ice Age Mammoths Exhibit.
$10,000 to Joseph Avenue Business Association, Rochester, NY, 2012.
$25 to State University of New York at Buffalo, Center for Entrepreneurial Leadership, Buffalo, NY, 2012. For program support.

Hudson River Bancorp, Inc. Foundation

P.O. Box 76
Hudson, NY 12534-0076 (518) 671-6226
FAX: (518) 822-1419;
E-mail: hrappleyea@hrbtfoundation.com; Additional address: P.O. Box 1189, Hudson, NY 12534;
URL: http://www.hrbtfoundation.com

Establishment information: Established in 1998 in NY.
Donors: Hudson River Bank & Trust Co.; Carl Florio.
Contact: Holly Rappleyea, Secy.
Financial data (yr. ended 03/31/12): Assets, $13,609,808 (M); gifts received, $11,580; expenditures, $878,052; qualifying distributions, $745,244; giving activities include $715,244 for grants.
Purpose and activities: The foundation supports programs designed to address healthcare; community development; education and youth; arts and culture; historic preservation; and environmental protection.
Fields of interest: Historic preservation/historical societies; Arts; Education; Environment, natural resources; Hospitals (general); Health care; Youth, services; Community/economic development.
Type of support: Building/renovation; Capital campaigns; Equipment; General/operating support; Program development; Scholarship funds.
Geographic limitations: Giving primarily in upstate NY.
Support limitations: No support for political groups or religious groups for sectarian purposes. No grants to individuals or for debt liquidation.
Publications: Application guidelines.
Application information: Applications accepted. Support is limited to 1 contribution per organization during any given year. Organizations receiving support are asked to submit a grantee report. Application form not required. Applicants should submit the following:
1) name, address and phone number of organization
2) copy of IRS Determination Letter
3) brief history of organization and description of its mission
4) listing of board of directors, trustees, officers and other key people and their affiliations
5) detailed description of project and amount of funding requested
6) contact person
7) copy of current year's organizational budget and/or project budget
8) listing of additional sources and amount of support

Initial approach: Letter of inquiry for grant requests of up to $1,000; telephone foundation for requests over $1,000
Board meeting date(s): 4th week of the month
Deadline(s): None

Officers and Directors: Marilyn A. Herrington, Pres.; Tony (William H.) Jones, V.P.; Holly Rappleyea, Secy.; Carl A. Florio, Treas.; Joseph Phelan; Sid Richter.
EIN: 223595668
Selected grants: The following grants are a representative sample of this grantmaker's funding activity:

$100,000 to Columbia-Greene Hospital Foundation, Hudson, NY, 2011.
$20,000 to Columbia Opportunities, Hudson, NY, 2011.
$10,000 to Columbia Land Conservancy, Chatham, NY, 2011.
$10,000 to Equine Advocates, Chatham, NY, 2011.
$10,000 to Hawthorne Valley School, Ghent, NY, 2011.
$7,500 to Northeast Parent and Child Society, Schenectady, NY, 2011.
$7,500 to Northern Dutchess Hospital Foundation, Rhinebeck, NY, 2011.
$5,000 to Germantown Library, Germantown, NY, 2011.
$5,000 to Proctors Theater, Schenectady, NY, 2011.
$4,500 to STRIDE, Inc., Rensselaer, NY, 2011.

Willow Grove Foundation

1837 Harte Rd.
Jenkintown, PA 19046 (215) 886-0607
FAX: (215) 886-0637; E-mail: lkremp@comcast.net; URL: http://www.willowgrovefoundation.com

Establishment information: Established in 1998 in PA.
Donors: Willow Grove Bank; Willow Financial Bank.
Contact: Laura Kremp, Exec. Dir.
Financial data (yr. ended 06/30/11): Assets, $733,153 (M); expenditures, $66,195; qualifying distributions, $54,311; giving activities include $41,250 for 39 grants (high: $4,000; low: $250).
Purpose and activities: The foundation supports organizations involved with arts and culture, education, the environment, health, employment training, housing, recreation, and human services.
Fields of interest: Arts; Education; Environment.
Programs:
Community Service: The foundation supports organizations involved with arts and culture, the environment, health, recreation, and human services.
Education: The foundation supports programs designed to improve life options through education and the enhancement of work skills.
Housing: The foundation supports programs designed to expand home ownership and rental housing opportunities for at-risk populations.
Type of support: Building/renovation; Capital campaigns; Equipment; General/operating support; Matching/challenge support; Program development; Seed money.
Geographic limitations: Giving primarily in the greater Willow Grove, PA, area.
Support limitations: No support for fraternal or professional organizations, political candidates or organizations, or discriminatory organizations. No grants to individuals, or for religious activities, raffles, telethons, benefit dinners, auctions, or advertising.
Publications: Application guidelines.
Application information: Applications accepted. Application form required. Applicants should submit the following:
1) results expected from proposed grant
2) statement of problem project will address
3) copy of IRS Determination Letter
4) brief history of organization and description of its mission
5) copy of most recent annual report/audited financial statement/990
6) how project's results will be evaluated or measured
7) descriptive literature about organization
8) detailed description of project and amount of funding requested
9) contact person
10) copy of current year's organizational budget and/or project budget
11) listing of additional sources and amount of support
12) plans for acknowledgement
Initial approach: Proposal
Copies of proposal: 1
Board meeting date(s): Jan., Apr., July, and Oct.
Deadline(s): 15th of the month prior to board meetings

Officers and Directors:* Charles F. Kremp III, Chair.; William B. Weihenmayer, Vice-Chair.; Frederick A. Marcell, Jr.*, Secy.-Treas.; Laura Kremp, Exec. Dir.; Donald L. Clark; Shirley M. Dennis; Stewart J. Greenleaf; J. Ellwood Kirk.
EIN: 233002286
Selected grants: The following grants are a representative sample of this grantmaker's funding activity:
$12,500 to Pennsylvania Citizens for Better Libraries, Horsham, PA, 2005.
$5,000 to Abington Memorial Hospital Foundation, Abington, PA, 2005.
$5,000 to American Red Cross, Philadelphia, PA, 2005.
$5,000 to Montgomery County Association for the Blind, North Wales, PA, 2005.
$5,000 to Willow Grove Community Development Corporation, Willow Grove, PA, 2005.
$3,000 to Womens Center of Montgomery County, Elkins Park, PA, 2005.
$2,500 to American Red Cross, Philadelphia, PA, 2005.
$2,000 to Abington Art Center, Jenkintown, PA, 2005.
$2,000 to Quaker School at Horsham, Horsham, PA, 2005.
$1,000 to Fox Chase Cancer Center, Philadelphia, PA, 2005.

1420
First Place Financial Corp.

185 E. Market St.
Warren, OH 44481 (330) 373-1221
FAX: (302) 655-5049

Company URL: https://www.firstplacebank.com/
Establishment information: Established in 1998.
Company type: Public company
Company ticker symbol and exchange: FPFC/Pink Sheets
Business activities: Operates bank holding company; operates savings bank.
Business type (SIC): Savings institutions; holding company
Financial profile for 2010: Number of employees, 950; assets, $3,152,640,000; pre-tax net income, -$39,030,000; liabilities, $2,900,170,000
Corporate officers: Samuel A. Roth, Chair.; J. Craig Carr, Exec. V.P., Genl. Counsel, and Secy.; David W. Gifford, C.F.O.; Robert J. Kowalski, Corp. Exec. V.P., Human Resources
Subsidiary: First Place Bank, Warren, OH
Giving statement: Giving through the First Place Bank Community Foundation.
Company EIN: 341880130

First Place Bank Community Foundation

(formerly First Federal of Warren Community Foundation)
P.O. Box 551
185 E. Market St.
Warren, OH 44482-0551

Establishment information: Established in 1998 in DE.
Donor: First Place Financial Corp.
Contact: David J. Jenkins, Secy. and Exec. Dir.
Financial data (yr. ended 06/30/12): Assets, $1,453,810 (M); expenditures, $161,901; qualifying distributions, $133,919; giving activities include $133,919 for grants.
Purpose and activities: The foundation supports organizations involved with arts and culture, education, health, human services, urban affairs and economic development.
Fields of interest: Humanities; Arts; Education; Health care; Human services; Urban/community development.
Type of support: Annual campaigns; Building/renovation; Capital campaigns; Continuing support; Curriculum development; Employee matching gifts; Equipment; General/operating support; Matching/challenge support; Program development; Scholarship funds.
Geographic limitations: Giving primarily in areas of company retail operations.
Support limitations: No support for political organizations or religious organizations.
Publications: Application guidelines.
Application information: Applications accepted. Telephone calls are not encouraged. Application form required. Applicants should submit the following:
1) results expected from proposed grant
2) statement of problem project will address
3) population served
4) copy of IRS Determination Letter
5) brief history of organization and description of its mission
6) copy of most recent annual report/audited financial statement/990
7) listing of board of directors, trustees, officers and other key people and their affiliations
Proposal should include the percentage of clients at or below the low-to-moderate income level.
Initial approach: Write or e-mail foundation for application form
Copies of proposal: 1
Board meeting date(s): 4th Thurs. of Jan., Apr., July, and Oct.
Deadline(s): Dec. 31, Mar. 31, June 30, and Sept. 30
Final notification: End of month following board meetings

Officers and Directors:* Robert S. McGeough, Chair.; Steven R. Lewis*, Pres.; Robert P. Grace; David J. Jenkins, Secy. and Exec. Dir.; E. Jeffrey Rossi.
Number of staff: 2 part-time professional.
EIN: 341879025

1421
First Savings Bank of Perkasie

219 S. 9th St.
Perkasie, PA 18944-0176 (215) 257-5035
FAX: (215) 453-2332

Company URL: http://www.fsbperkasie.com
Establishment information: Established in 1922.
Company type: Private company
Business activities: Operates savings bank.
Business type (SIC): Savings institutions
Corporate officers: Walter H. Cressman, Chair.; Frederick E. Schea, Pres. and C.E.O.; Todd Hurley, Exec. V.P. and C.O.O.; Jerome P. Arrison, Exec. V.P., C.F.O., and Treas.; Michael Postorino, C.I.O.; Shari Miller, Sr. V.P., Opers.; Jason Hiestand, Cont.

Board of directors: Walter H. Cressman, Chair.; Richard E. Aichele III; Robert L. Byers; Gerald Soulder; Richard Hendricks; Jeffrey A. Naugle; Frederick E. Schea; Vernon C. Wehrung
Offices: Bedminster, Dublin, Milford Square, Pipersville, Quakertown, Richlandtown, Riegelsville, PA
Giving statement: Giving through the First Savings Community Foundation.

First Savings Community Foundation

219 S. 9th St.
P.O. Box 176
Perkasie, PA 18944-0176 (215) 257-5035
E-mail: fschea@fsbperkasie.com; URL: https://www.firstsavingsonline.com/top_about_community.php

Establishment information: Established in 1998.
Donor: First Savings Bank of Perkasie.
Contact: Frederick E. Schea, Pres. and C.E.O.
Financial data (yr. ended 12/31/11): Assets, $2,424,351 (M); expenditures, $184,579; qualifying distributions, $177,975; giving activities include $177,975 for 71 grants (high: $15,000; low: $100).
Purpose and activities: The foundation supports museums, hospitals, and fire departments and organizations involved with mental health, housing development, youth development, and human services.
Fields of interest: Museums; Museums (art); Higher education; Hospitals (general); Mental health/crisis services; Housing/shelter, development; Disasters, fire prevention/control; Youth development; YM/YWCAs & YM/YWHAs; Human services.
Type of support: Annual campaigns; Capital campaigns; Employee matching gifts; General/operating support; Program development.
Geographic limitations: Giving limited to Bethlehem, Bucks, Lehigh, and Montgomery counties, PA.
Support limitations: No grants to individuals.
Application information: Applications accepted. Application form required. Applicants should submit the following:
1) copy of IRS Determination Letter
2) detailed description of project and amount of funding requested

Initial approach: Letter
Deadline(s): None

Directors: E. Richard Aichele III; Robert L. Byers, Jr.; Walter H. Cressman; Thomas W. Lomax; Jeffrey A. Naugle.
Officers: Frederick E. Schea, Pres. and C.E.O.; Todd Hurley, Secy. and C.O.O.; Jerry P. Arrison, C.F.O.
EIN: 232984663
Selected grants: The following grants are a representative sample of this grantmaker's funding activity:
$16,000 to YMCA, Central Bucks Family, Doylestown, PA, 2010. For capital campaign.
$10,500 to Bucks County Community College, Newtown, PA, 2010.
$10,000 to Doylestown Hospital, Doylestown, PA, 2010.
$5,500 to Pearl S. Buck International, Perkasie, PA, 2010.
$5,000 to Grand View Hospital, Sellersville, PA, 2010. For capital campaign.
$2,500 to A Womans Place, Doylestown, PA, 2010.
$1,500 to Boy Scouts of America, Bucks County Council, Doylestown, PA, 2010.
$1,250 to Multiple Sclerosis Society, National, Philadelphia, PA, 2010.

1422
First Security Federal Savings Bank

936 N. Western Ave.
Chicago, IL 60622-4695 (773) 772-4500

Establishment information: Established in 1922.
Company type: Private company
Business activities: Operates savings bank.
Business type (SIC): Savings institutions
Corporate officers: Julian Kulas, C.E.O.; Pavlo T. Bandriwsky, C.O.O.
Giving statement: Giving through the Heritage Foundation of First Security Federal Savings Bank, Inc.

The Heritage Foundation of First Security Federal Savings Bank, Inc.

2329 W. Chicago Ave.
Chicago, IL 60622-4723 (773) 486-6645

Establishment information: Established in 1997 in IL.
Donors: First Security Federal Savings Bank; Maria Olijnyk.
Contact: Julian E. Kulas, Pres.
Financial data (yr. ended 12/31/11): Assets, $12,129,870 (M); expenditures, $582,971; qualifying distributions, $470,450; giving activities include $470,450 for grants.
Purpose and activities: The foundation supports programs designed to preserve Ukrainian culture and heritage; and promote democracy and a free market economy.
Fields of interest: Arts, alliance/advocacy; Arts, cultural/ethnic awareness; Museums; Arts; Higher education; Education; International affairs, foreign policy; Public affairs, alliance/advocacy; Catholic agencies & churches.
International interests: Ukraine.
Type of support: Conferences/seminars; General/operating support; Program development; Publication.
Geographic limitations: Giving primarily in IL.
Support limitations: No grants to individuals.
Application information: Applications accepted. Application form not required.

Initial approach: Proposal
Deadline(s): None

Officers and Trustees:* Julian E. Kulas, Pres.; Paul Nadzikewycz, V.P.; Terry Gawryk, Secy.; Taras Drozd; Dmytro Shtohryn; Chrysta Wereszczak.
Number of staff: 1 part-time support.
EIN: 364135415
Selected grants: The following grants are a representative sample of this grantmaker's funding activity:
$60,000 to American Ukrainian Youth Association, Chicago, IL, 2011.
$25,000 to Ukrainian Institute of Modern Art, Chicago, IL, 2011.
$25,000 to Ukrainian National Museum, Chicago, IL, 2011.
$10,000 to American Foreign Policy Council, Washington, DC, 2011.
$5,000 to Ukrainian Catholic Archdiocese of Philadelphia, Philadelphia, PA, 2011.
$5,000 to Ukrainian Museum-Archives, Cleveland, OH, 2011.
$3,550 to Ukrainian National Womens League of America, New York, NY, 2011.
$2,500 to Columbia University, New York, NY, 2011.

1423
First State Bank of Newcastle

24 N. Sumner Ave.
P.O. Box 910
Newcastle, WY 82701-2138
(307) 746-4411

Company URL: https://www.fsbnewcastle.com
Establishment information: Established in 1924.
Company type: Private company
Business activities: Operates commercial bank.
Business type (SIC): Banks/commercial
Corporate officers: John C. Sullivan, Chair.; Leonard E. Nack, Pres.
Board of directors: John C. Sullivan, Chair.; Robert Gersack; Donna Baldwin Hunt; Donald J. Jording; Michael Jording; Leonard Nack; Alan Roberts
Giving statement: Giving through the Homestead Foundation, Inc.

The Homestead Foundation, Inc.

P.O. Box 1283
Livingston, MT 59047-1283

Establishment information: Established in 2002 in MT.
Donors: John Sullivan; Northeastern Wyoming Bank Corp.; First State Bank of Newcastle.
Financial data (yr. ended 12/31/11): Assets, $1,076,666 (M); gifts received, $250,000; expenditures, $37,473; qualifying distributions, $31,300; giving activities include $31,300 for grants.
Fields of interest: Arts; Education; Agriculture/food.
Support limitations: No grants to individuals.
Application information: Applications not accepted. Unsolicited requests for funds not accepted.

Board meeting date(s): Unsolicited requests for funds not accepted

Officers: John Sullivan, Pres.; Meredith Key Sullivan, V.P.
Director: Mike Waters.
EIN: 522389050

1424
FirstEnergy Corp.

76 S. Main St.
Akron, OH 44308-1890 (330) 761-7837

Company URL: http://www.firstenergycorp.com
Establishment information: Established in 1997 from the merger of Centerior Energy Corp. with Ohio Edison Co.
Company type: Public company
Company ticker symbol and exchange: FE/NYSE
Business activities: Operates holding company; generates, transmits, and distributes electricity.
Business type (SIC): Electric services; holding company
Financial profile for 2012: Number of employees, 16,500; assets, $50,000,000,000; sales volume, $15,000,000,000; pre-tax net income, $1,324,000,000; expenses, $13,127,000,000; liabilities, $35,877,000,000
Fortune 1000 ranking: 2012—181st in revenues, 249th in profits, and 110th in assets
Forbes 2000 ranking: 2012—619th in sales, 706th in profits, and 457th in assets
Corporate officers: George M. Smart, Chair.; Anthony J. Alexander, Pres. and C.E.O.; Mark T. Clark, Exec. V.P., Finance and Strategy; James F. Pearson, Sr. V.P. and C.F.O.; Leila L. Vespoli, Exec. V.P. and Genl. Counsel; Lynn M. Cavalier, Sr. V.P., Human Resources

Board of directors: George M. Smart, Chair.; Paul T. Addison; Anthony J. Alexander; Michael J. Anderson; Carol A. Cartwright; William T. Cottle; Robert B. Heisler, Jr.; Julia L. Johnson; Ted J. Kleisner; Donald T. Misheff; Ernest J. Novak, Jr.; Christopher D. Pappas; Catherine A. Rein; Wesley M. Taylor
Subsidiaries: The Cleveland Electric Illuminating Co., Cleveland, OH; FirstEnergy Nuclear Operating Co., Akron, OH; FIRSTENERGY SERVICE COMPANY, Akron, OH; FirstEnergy Solutions Corp., Akron, OH; Jersey Central Power & Light Company, Reading, PA; Metropolitan Edison Co., Reading, PA; Ohio Edison Company, Akron, OH; Pennsylvania Electric Co., Erie, PA; The Toledo Edison Co., Toledo, OH
Historic mergers: Allegheny Energy, Inc. (February 25, 2011)
Giving statement: Giving through the FirstEnergy Corp. Contributions Program and the FirstEnergy Foundation.
Company EIN: 341843785

FirstEnergy Corp. Contributions Program

(formerly Centerior Energy Corporation Contributions Program)
76 S. Main St.
Akron, OH 44308-1817 (800) 984-9480
URL: https://www.firstenergycorp.com/content/fecorp/community.html

Purpose and activities: As a complement to its foundation, FirstEnergy also makes charitable contributions to nonprofit organizations directly. Support is limited to areas of company operations, with emphasis on New Jersey, Ohio, and Pennsylvania. Emphasis is given to organizations with significant employee volunteerism, including leadership roles.
Fields of interest: Arts; Elementary/secondary education; Higher education; Adult education—literacy, basic skills & GED; Education; Environment; Health care; Cancer; Food banks; Food services, commodity distribution; Housing/shelter, volunteer services; Housing/shelter; Safety/disasters; Human services, fund raising/fund distribution; Human services; Community/economic development; United Ways and Federated Giving Programs; Public affairs.
Program:
Mathematics, Science, and Technology Education Grants: FirstEnergy awards grants of up to $500 for classroom projects and teacher professional development initiatives focusing on mathematics, science, and technology. The program is designed for Pre-K-12 educators and youth-group leaders located in areas of company operations. Special emphasis is directed toward projects designed to clearly explain how the items requested for funding are vital to the project's successful completion; focus on electricity and electricity production; improve, advance, and enrich student learning; have one-time, one-year implementation and evaluation; are flexible and appropriate for targeted stage of student development; range from formative ideas that explore learning concepts to fully tested models that are ready to be adopted and disseminated; include additional support from other sources for larger projects; and projects that provide networking, mentoring, interdisciplinary or team-teaching, and teacher training/professional development.
Type of support: Annual campaigns; Employee volunteer services; Equipment; General/operating support.
Geographic limitations: Giving limited to areas of company operations, with emphasis on NJ, OH, and PA.
Support limitations: No support for organizations that receive significant public tax funding, organizations already supported by federal campaigns such as United Way, fraternal, religious, labor, athletic, social, or veterans' organizations not of direct benefit to the entire community, national or international organizations, foundations, or pre-K, elementary, or secondary schools. No grants to individuals, or for political or legislative activities, research, equipment purchases, loans, or second-party giving, such as endowments, or debt retirement.
Publications: Application guidelines; Informational brochure.
Application information: Applications accepted. A Contributions Committee handles giving. Proposals are evaluated by Sept. 1 for the next calendar year. Applicants should submit the following:
1) copy of IRS Determination Letter
2) brief history of organization and description of its mission
3) geographic area to be served
4) how project's results will be evaluated or measured
5) explanation of why grantmaker is considered an appropriate donor for project
6) listing of board of directors, trustees, officers and other key people and their affiliations
7) detailed description of project and amount of funding requested

Grant proposals should include a one to two-page profile of the organization.
Initial approach: Proposal letter to local facility for grant requests. Check website for applications for mathematics, science, engineering, and technology education grants
Deadline(s): None for grant requests
Final notification: 12 weeks for grant requests

FirstEnergy Foundation

76 S. Main St.
Akron, OH 44308-1890 (330) 384-5022
For PA and WV, call: (724) 838-3082; for NJ and MD, call (732) 212-4147.; URL: https://www.firstenergycorp.com/community/firstenergy_foundation.html

Establishment information: Incorporated in 1961 in OH.
Donors: Centerior Energy Corp.; The Cleveland Electric Illuminating Co.; FirstEnergy Corp.; GPU Service, Inc.; Jersey Central Power & Light Co.; Metropolitan Edison Co.; Ohio Edison Co.; Pennsylvania Electric Co.; Potomic Edison; The Toledo Edison Co.; West Penn Power; UM Power.
Contact: Delores J. Lowery, Pres.; Terry Gilman, Mgr., Community Initiatives and Contribs.
Financial data (yr. ended 12/31/12): Assets, $43,782,988 (M); expenditures, $4,384,317; qualifying distributions, $4,384,927; giving activities include $3,869,161 for 340 grants (high: $500,000; low: $340) and $136,766 for 493 employee matching gifts.
Purpose and activities: The foundation supports programs designed to improve the vitality of the community and promote key safety initiatives; promote local and regional economic development and revitalization efforts; and programs designed to support FirstEnergy employees' community leadership and volunteer interests; advance an educated workforce by supporting professional development, literacy, and science, technology, and mathematics education initiatives.
Fields of interest: Arts; Higher education; Education; Health care; Employment; Youth, services; Human services; Community/economic development; United Ways and Federated Giving Programs; Mathematics; Engineering/technology; Science; Public affairs.
Program:
Matching Gifts Program: The foundation matches contributions made by full-time employees of FirstEnergy to institutions of higher education and organizations involved with arts and culture, health, youth, and civic affairs on a one-for-one basis from $50 to $5,000 per employee, per year.
Type of support: Annual campaigns; Building/renovation; Capital campaigns; Employee matching gifts; General/operating support; Program development.
Geographic limitations: Giving primarily in areas of company operations in MD, NJ, OH, PA, and WV.
Support limitations: No support for largely tax-supported organizations, fraternal, religious, labor, athletic, social, or veterans' organizations not of direct benefit to the entire community, national or international organizations, United Way-supported organizations, or public or private Pre-K, elementary, or secondary schools. No grants to individuals, or for political or legislative activities, research, equipment, endowments, or debt reduction; no loans.
Publications: Informational brochure.
Application information: Unsolicited grant applications are not accepted at this time. Grant inquiries should be discussed with the local management of FirstEnergy companies and the staff of the foundation.
Board meeting date(s): Rolling
Officers and Trustees:* Leila L. Vespoli, Chair.; Dolores J. Lowery, Pres.; Rhonda S. Ferguson, Secy.; James F. Pearson, Treas.; Mark T. Clark; Charles E. Jones.
Number of staff: 1 full-time professional; 3 part-time professional; 1 full-time support; 1 part-time support.
EIN: 346514181

1425
Firstmerit Bank, N.A.

106 S. Main St.
Akron, OH 44308-1417 (330) 384-7093

Company URL: https://www.firstmerit.com/personal/index.aspx
Establishment information: Established in 1981.
Company type: Subsidiary of a public company
Business activities: Operates commercial bank.
Business type (SIC): Banks/commercial
Corporate officers: John R. Cochran, Chair.; Paul G. Greig, Pres. and C.E.O.
Board of directors: John R. Cochran, Chair.; Paul G. Greig
Giving statement: Giving through the FirstMerit Foundation.

FirstMerit Foundation

3 Cascade Plz., CAS 50
Akron, OH 44308-1124 (330) 996-6444

Donor: FirstMerit Bank, N.A.
Contact: Jane Litz
Financial data (yr. ended 12/31/11): Assets, $252,255 (M); expenditures, $775,700; qualifying distributions, $775,700; giving activities include $775,700 for grants.
Purpose and activities: The foundation supports organizations involved with performing arts, education, health, and community economic development.

Fields of interest: Performing arts; Performing arts, orchestras; Higher education; Education; Hospitals (general); Health care; YM/YWCAs & YM/YWHAs; Community development, neighborhood development; Community development, service clubs; Community/economic development; United Ways and Federated Giving Programs.
Type of support: Annual campaigns; Building/renovation; Capital campaigns; Continuing support; Equipment; General/operating support; Program development; Sponsorships.
Geographic limitations: Giving primarily in areas of company operations in OH.
Application information: Applications accepted. Application form required.
Initial approach: Contact foundation for application form
Deadline(s): None
Officers and Directors:* Nancy H. Worman*, Pres.; Judith Steiner*, Secy.; Michael E. Miller*, Treas.
EIN: 205608263
Selected grants: The following grants are a representative sample of this grantmaker's funding activity:
$100,000 to United Way of Summit County, Akron, OH, 2010.
$100,000 to University of Akron Foundation, Akron, OH, 2010.
$40,000 to United Way of Greater Stark County, Canton, OH, 2010.
$15,000 to Ohio Foundation of Independent Colleges, Columbus, OH, 2010.
$15,000 to United Way of Greater Cleveland, Cleveland, OH, 2010.
$15,000 to United Way of Greater Lorain County, Lorain, OH, 2010.
$6,800 to United Way of Central Ohio, Columbus, OH, 2010.
$5,000 to El Centro de Servicios Sociales, Lorain, OH, 2010.
$5,000 to Pathway Caring for Children, North Canton, OH, 2010.
$2,000 to Salvation Army, Columbus, OH, 2010.

1426
FirstService Residential Management
1815 Griffin Rd., Ste. 404
Dania Beach, FL 33004 (866) 522-3671

Company URL: http://www.fsresidential.com
Company type: Subsidiary of a foreign company
Business activities: Operates residential management services company.
Business type (SIC): Real estate agents and managers
Corporate officers: Gene Gomberg, Chair.; Mike Natale, C.F.O.; Bruno Sperduti, C.I.O.; David Diestel, Sr. V.P., Opers.

FirstService Residential Management Corporate Giving Program
1815 Griffin Rd., Ste. 404
Dania Beach, FL 33004 (866) 522-3671
URL: http://www.fsresidential.com/green-and-sustainability/

1427
Fiserv, Inc.
255 Fiserv Dr.
Brookfield, WI 53045-5815 (262) 879-5000
FAX: (262) 879-5275

Company URL: http://www.fiserv.com
Establishment information: Established in 1984.
Company type: Public company
Company ticker symbol and exchange: FISV/NASDAQ
Business activities: Provides financial data processing services; develops information management computer software.
Business type (SIC): Computer services
Financial profile for 2012: Number of employees, 20,000; assets, $8,500,000,000; sales volume, $4,500,000,000; pre-tax net income, $889,000,000; expenses, $3,426,000,000; liabilities, $5,080,000,000
Fortune 1000 ranking: 2012—532nd in revenues, 287th in profits, and 441st in assets
Forbes 2000 ranking: 2012—1451st in sales, 903rd in profits, and 1580th in assets
Corporate officers: Donald F. Dillon, Chair.; Jeffrey W. Yabuki, Pres. and C.E.O.; Thomas J. Hirsch, Exec. V.P., C.F.O., and Treas.; Mark A. Ernst, Exec. V.P. and C.O.O.; Clifford A. Skelton, Exec. V.P. and C.I.O.; Charles W. Sprague, Exec. V.P., Genl. Counsel, and Secy.; Kevin Pennington, Exec. V.P., Human Resources
Board of directors: Donald F. Dillon, Chair.; Christopher M. Flink; Daniel P. Kearney; Dennis F. Lynch; Denis J. O'Leary; Glenn M. Renwick; Kim M. Robak; Doyle R. Simons; Thomas C. Wertheimer; Jeffrey W. Yabuki
Subsidiaries: Aspen Investment Alliance, Inc., Denver, CO; Benefit Planners Ltd., L.L.P., Boerne, TX; BeneSight, Inc., Lake Mary, FL; EPSIIA Corp., Austin, TX; First Trust Corp., Denver, CO; Fiserv CIR, Inc., Brookfield, WI; Fiserv Clearing, Inc., Philadelphia, PA; Fiserv CSW, Inc., Cambridge, MA; Fiserv FSC, Inc., Agoura Hills, CA; Fiserv Investor Services, Inc., Houston, TX; Fiserv LeMans, Inc., King of Prussia, PA; Fiserv NCSI, Inc., Rockville, MD; Fiserv Securities, Inc., Philadelphia, PA; General American Corp., Pittsburgh, PA; Harrington Benefit Services, Inc., Westerville, OH; ILS Title Agency, LLC, Rocky Hill, CT; Information Technology, Inc., Lincoln, NE; Insurance Management Solutions Group, Inc., St. Petersburg, FL; Lenders Financial Services, LLC, Agoura Hills, CA; Lincoln Trust Co., Englewood, CO; National Flood Services, Inc., Kalispell, MT; Precision Direct, Inc., Kent, WA; Remarketing Services of America, Inc., Amherst, NY; RemitStream Solutions, LLC, Chicago, IL; TradeStar Investments, Inc., Houston, TX; USERS Inc., Valley Forge, PA; XP Systems Corp., Moorpark, CA
Offices: South Bend, IN; Dallas, TX
International operations: Australia; France; India; Luxembourg; Malaysia; United Kingdom
Historic mergers: CheckFree Corporation (December 4, 2007)
Giving statement: Giving through the Fiserv Foundation.
Company EIN: 391506125

Fiserv Foundation
(formerly The Trust Foundation)
4400 Westown Pkwy.
West Des Moines, IA 50266-6751 (515) 224-8295
Tel: (515) 224-8295

Establishment information: Established in 1988 in IA.
Donors: Financial Information Trust; Fiserv.
Contact: Adam Wood, Treas.
Financial data (yr. ended 12/31/11): Assets, $7,080 (M); gifts received, $12,273; expenditures, $13,849; qualifying distributions, $13,735; giving activities include $13,735 for grants.
Purpose and activities: The foundation supports civic centers and organizations involved with media, education, animals, health, and human services.
Fields of interest: Media/communications; Higher education; Education; Animals/wildlife; Hospitals (general); Health care, patient services; Health care; Salvation Army; Children/youth, services; Residential/custodial care, hospices; Human services; Community development, civic centers.
Type of support: General/operating support.
Geographic limitations: Giving primarily in areas of company operations in Des Moines, IA.
Support limitations: No grants to individuals.
Application information: Applications accepted. Application form required. Applicants should submit the following:
1) brief history of organization and description of its mission
2) copy of most recent annual report/audited financial statement/990
3) contact person
Initial approach: Letter or telephone call
Deadline(s): None
Officers: Jim Pech, Chair.; Bill Stuart, Vice-Chair.; Adam Wood, Treas.
Board Members: Maria Bales; Elizabeth Bauman; Pat Carroll; Theresa Flactiff.
EIN: 421313172

1428
Fish & Richardson P.C.
1 Marina Park Dr., Ste. 1700
Boston, MA 02210-1878 (617) 542-5070

Company URL: http://www.fr.com
Establishment information: Established in 1878.
Company type: Private company
Business activities: Operates law firm.
Business type (SIC): Legal services
Offices: Redwood City, San Diego, CA; Wilmington, DE; Washington, DC; Atlanta, GA; Boston, MA; Minneapolis, MN; New York, NY; Austin, Dallas, Houston, TX
International operations: Switzerland
Giving statement: Giving through the Fish & Richardson P.C. Pro Bono Program.

Fish & Richardson P.C. Pro Bono Program
1 Marina Park Dr., Ste. 1700
Boston, MA 02210-1878 (617) 542-5070
E-mail: kolodney@fr.com; URL: http://www.fr.com/pro-bono-about/

Contact: Lawrence Kolodney, Principal; Pro Bono Chair
Fields of interest: Legal services.
Type of support: Pro bono services - legal.
Geographic limitations: Giving primarily in areas of company operations in Redwood City, and San Diego, CA, Washington, DC, Wilmington, DE, Atlanta, GA, Boston, MA, Minneapolis, MN, New York, NY, and Austin, Dallas, and Houston, TX, and in Germany.
Application information: The Pro Bono Committee manages the pro-bono program.

1429
The Fishel Company
1366 Dublin Rd.
Columbus, OH 43215 (614) 274-8100
FAX: (614) 274-6794

Company URL: http://www.fishelco.com
Establishment information: Established in 1936.
Company type: Private company
Business activities: Provides nonresidential general contract construction services.
Business type (SIC): Contractors/general nonresidential building
Corporate officers: Diane Fishel Keeler, Chair.; John Phillips, Pres. and C.E.O.; Randy Blair, Exec. V.P. and C.O.O.; Paul R. Riewe, V.P. and C.F.O.; Ken Katz, V.P., Tech.; Greg R. Grabovac, V.P. and Genl. Counsel
Board of director: Diane Fishel Keeler, Chair.
Division: Professional Services Group, Columbus, OH
Offices: Chandler, Dewey, Mesa, Phoenix, AZ; Lake Forest, Oceanside, CA; Broomfield, CO; Deland, Winter Garden, FL; Albany, Duluth, Lithonia, GA; Vincennes, Yorktown, IN; Bowling Green, Lexington, Louisville, KY; Artesia, Las Cruces, NM; Cincinnati, Dayton, OH; Memphis, Nashville, TN; Houston, Southlake, TX; Manassas, VA
Giving statement: Giving through the Fishel Foundation.

Fishel Foundation
1366 Dublin Road
Columbus, OH 43215-1093

Establishment information: Established in 1993 in OH.
Donors: The Fishel Co.; Diane L. Keeler.
Financial data (yr. ended 02/28/12): Assets, $1,595,065 (M); gifts received, $785,522; expenditures, $222,151; qualifying distributions, $215,042; giving activities include $215,042 for grants.
Purpose and activities: The foundation supports organizations involved with higher education, health, children, Christianity, and refugees.
Fields of interest: Education; Health care; Religion.
Type of support: General/operating support.
Geographic limitations: Giving primarily in Columbus, OH.
Support limitations: No grants to individuals.
Application information: Applications not accepted. Unsolicited requests for funds not accepted.
Officer: Kathy C. Blackstone, Treas.
Trustee: Diane L. Keeler.
EIN: 316063414
Selected grants: The following grants are a representative sample of this grantmaker's funding activity:
$57,875 to First Community Church, Columbus, OH, 2012.
$35,000 to United Way of Central Ohio, Columbus, OH, 2012.
$20,000 to Denison University, Granville, OH, 2012.
$10,000 to Childhood League Center, Columbus, OH, 2012.
$10,000 to Lifecare Alliance, Columbus, OH, 2012.
$10,000 to Nationwide Childrens Hospital, Columbus, OH, 2012.
$6,667 to Columbus Museum of Art, Columbus, OH, 2012.

1430
Fisher Broadcasting Company
(formerly Fisher Broadcasting Inc.)
140 4th Ave. N., Ste. 500
Seattle, WA 98109 (206) 404-7000

Company URL: http://www.fsci.com
Establishment information: Established in 1926.
Company type: Subsidiary of a public company
Business activities: Broadcasts radio and television.
Business type (SIC): Radio and television broadcasting
Corporate officers: Paul A. Bible, Chair.; Colleen B. Brown, Pres. and C.E.O.
Board of director: Paul A. Bible, Chair.
Subsidiary: Fisher Radio Regional Group Inc., Spokane, WA
Giving statement: Giving through the Thomas R. Dargan Minority Scholarship Fund and the Fisher Broadcasting Inc. Minority Scholarship Fund.

Thomas R. Dargan Minority Scholarship Fund
(formerly KATU Thomas R. Dargan Minority Scholarship Fund)
P.O. Box 2
Portland, OR 97207-0002 (503) 231-4222
URL: http://www.katu.com/about/scholarship

Establishment information: Established in 1989 in OR.
Donors: Fisher Broadcasting Inc.; Fisher Broadcasting Co.
Financial data (yr. ended 03/31/12): Assets, $201,359 (M); expenditures, $10,216; qualifying distributions, $10,000; giving activities include $10,000 for 2 grants to individuals (high: $5,000; low: $5,000).
Purpose and activities: The foundation awards college scholarships to minority students studying communications or broadcasting.
Fields of interest: Media/communications; Media, television; Media, radio; Web-based media Minorities.
Program:
KATU Thomas R. Dargan Scholarship: The foundation awards $6,000 scholarships to minority sophomore students who are enrolled in a broadcast, communications, or multi-media curriculum at an institution of higher education in Oregon or Washington or are permanent residents of Oregon or Washington attending an out-of-state institution. Applicants must have a GPA of 3.0 and winners are eligible to receive a paid internship in selected departments at Fisher Broadcasting/KATU.
Type of support: Scholarships—to individuals.
Geographic limitations: Giving limited to OR and WA.
Support limitations: No scholarships to non-minority students or students not majoring in communications.
Publications: Application guidelines; Informational brochure (including application guidelines).
Application information: Applications accepted. Application form required.
Applications should include a statement of need, official transcripts, 3 letters of recommendation, and an essay.
Initial approach: Letter
Board meeting date(s): Quarterly
Deadline(s): Apr. 30
Final notification: July 1
Trustees: Coleen Brown; Anna Canzano; Tracey Lam; Betty Jean Lee; Paul Mai; Bev Pratt Miller; Rhonda Shelby; John Tamerlano.
Number of staff: None.
EIN: 943101223

Fisher Broadcasting Inc. Minority Scholarship Fund
(formerly KOMO Radio and Television Minority Scholarship Fund)
140 4th Ave. N., Ste. 500
Seattle, WA 98109-4983 (206) 404-4000
FAX: (206) 404-6013; E-mail: jendejan@fsci.com; URL: http://fsci.com/careers/scholarships-for-minorities/

Establishment information: Established in 1990 in WA.
Donors: Fisher Broadcasting Inc.; Fisher Broadcasting Co.
Contact: Karen Aliabadi, Chair.
Financial data (yr. ended 12/31/11): Assets, $284,375 (M); expenditures, $18,116; qualifying distributions, $18,000; giving activities include $18,000 for 6 grants to individuals (high: $4,000; low: $1,500).
Purpose and activities: The foundation awards college scholarships to minority students pursuing careers in broadcasting, marketing, or journalism.
Fields of interest: Media/communications; Media, television; Media, radio; Media, journalism Minorities.
Program:
Scholarships for Minorities: The foundation annually awards college scholarships to minority students enrolled in a broadcast oriented curriculum focusing on radio, television, marketing, or broadcast technology. Students must be at the sophomore level or above and have a minimum GPA of 2.5. Scholarships are awarded based on need, academic achievement, and personal qualities.
Type of support: Scholarships—to individuals.
Geographic limitations: Giving limited to CA, ID, MT, OR, and WA.
Publications: Application guidelines; Informational brochure; IRS Form 990 or 990-PF printed copy available upon request.
Application information: Applications accepted. Application form required.
Applications should include official transcripts, 2 letters of recommendation, an essay, estimated expense/income spreadsheet, and proof of citizenship.
Initial approach: Letter
Board meeting date(s): Annually
Deadline(s): Apr. 30
Officers and Trustees:* Karen Aliabadi*, Chair.; Laurie Anderson*, Treas.; James A. Clayton.
EIN: 911500276

1431
Fisher Brothers
299 Park Ave.
New York, NY 10171-0002 (212) 752-5000

Company URL: http://www.fisherbrothers.com
Company type: Private company
Business activities: Develops real estate.
Business type (SIC): Real estate subdividers and developers
Corporate officers: Samuel Rosenberg, C.F.O.; Douglas A. Raelson, Genl. Counsel
Giving statement: Giving through the Fisher Brothers Foundation, Inc.

The Fisher Brothers Foundation, Inc.

c/o Fisher Brothers
299 Park Ave.
New York, NY 10171-0001
URL: http://www.fisherbrothers.com/philanthropy/fisher-brothers-foundation

Establishment information: Established in 1981 in NY.
Donors: Fisher Brothers; Fisher Park Lane Co.; Fisher Capital Assets; 1345 Cleaning Service Co. II LP; 299 Cleaning Service Co. II LP; Plaza Cleaning Service Co. II LP; 605 Cleaning Service Co. II LP; Columbia Cleaning; Fisher 120 Wall; Fisher 92nd St.; FSAR Fee Associates; Rancho Road Development; Park Clipper Leasing Associates; Sandhurst Associates; Zachary & Elizabeth Fisher Charitable Trust.
Financial data (yr. ended 12/31/11): Assets, $263,118 (M); gifts received, $2,700,000; expenditures, $2,466,780; qualifying distributions, $2,434,388; giving activities include $2,434,388 for grants.
Purpose and activities: The foundation supports police agencies and fire departments and organizations involved with arts and culture, health, golf, military and veterans, and Judaism.
Fields of interest: Museums; Performing arts centers; Arts; Hospitals (general); Health care; Crime/law enforcement, police agencies; Disasters, fire prevention/control; Athletics/sports, golf; Jewish federated giving programs; Military/veterans' organizations; Jewish agencies & synagogues.
Type of support: Annual campaigns; General/operating support; Program development; Scholarship funds.
Geographic limitations: Giving limited to New York, NY.
Support limitations: No grants to individuals.
Application information: Applications not accepted. Contributes only to pre-selected organizations.
Directors: Arnold Fisher; Kenneth Fisher; Winston C. Fisher.
EIN: 133118286
Selected grants: The following grants are a representative sample of this grantmaker's funding activity:
$810,000 to UJA-Federation of New York, New York, NY, 2009.
$500,000 to Intrepid Fallen Heroes Fund, New York, NY, 2009.
$326,000 to Intrepid Museum Foundation, New York, NY, 2009.
$125,000 to New York-Presbyterian Hospital, New York, NY, 2009.
$110,000 to Lincoln Center for the Performing Arts, New York, NY, 2009.
$25,000 to Wounded Warrior Project, Jacksonville, FL, 2009.
$21,000 to Metropolitan Museum of Art, New York, NY, 2009.
$12,500 to Boys Town New York, New York, NY, 2009.
$10,000 to THIRTEEN, New York, NY, 2009.
$10,000 to USO of Metropolitan New York, New York, NY, 2009.

1432
The Fisher Housing Companies, Inc.

(doing business as Home Headquarters)
1390 N. Wesleyan Blvd.
Rocky Mount, NC 27804-1816
(252) 442-3700

Company URL: http://homeheadquarters.net/
Establishment information: Established in 2001.
Company type: Private company
Business activities: Provides general contract modular house construction services.
Business type (SIC): Contractors/general residential building
Corporate officers: Donald Fisher, Pres.; Mary A. Fisher, Secy.
Giving statement: Giving through the Scholarship Headquarters, Inc.

Scholarship Headquarters, Inc.

1390 N. Wesleyan Blvd.
Rocky Mount, NC 27804-1816 (252) 443-9520

Establishment information: Established as a company-sponsored operating foundation in 2002.
Donor: The Fisher Housing Cos., Inc.
Contact: Don Fisher, Dir.
Financial data (yr. ended 12/31/11): Assets, $10,230 (M); gifts received, $6,653; expenditures, $7,911; qualifying distributions, $7,600; giving activities include $7,600 for 4 grants to individuals (high: $3,200).
Purpose and activities: The foundation awards college scholarships and student loans to Christian students in the Rocky Mount, North Carolina, area to attend Christian colleges and universities.
Fields of interest: Higher education; Education.
Type of support: Scholarships—to individuals; Student loans—to individuals.
Geographic limitations: Giving limited to the Rocky Mount, NC, area.
Application information: Applications accepted. Application form required.
Initial approach: Contact foundation for application form
Board meeting date(s): Quarterly
Deadline(s): None
Final notification: Within 1 month following board meetings
Directors: Gerry Carlson; Brian Carruthers; Finley Cutshaw; Don Fisher; Frank Hamrick; Monty Kaufman.
EIN: 331038618

1433
Eileen Fisher Inc.

2 Bridge St., Ste. 230
Irvington, NY 10533-1527 (914) 591-5700

Company URL: http://www.eileenfisher.com
Establishment information: Established in 1984.
Company type: Private company
Business activities: Manufactures women's apparel; operates women's apparel stores.
Business type (SIC): Apparel—women's outerwear
Corporate officers: Eileen Fisher, Pres.; Kenneth Pollack, C.F.O.; Hayley Gluck, Cont.
Offices: Los Angeles, CA; Atlanta, GA; Secaucus, NJ; Irvington, New York, NY
Giving statement: Giving through the Eileen Fisher Inc. Corporate Giving Program.

Eileen Fisher Inc. Corporate Giving Program

2 Bridge St.
Irvington, NY 10533-1527
FAX: (914) 789-2285;
E-mail: socialconsciousness@eileenfisher.com;
URL: http://www.eileenfisher.com/EileenFisherCompany/CompanyGeneralContentPages/SocialConciousness.jsp?bmLocale=en_US

Contact: Reisa Brafman, Social Consciousness Assc.
Financial data (yr. ended 12/31/08): Total giving, $1,207,006, including $1,056,266 for 212 grants, $52,000 for 9 grants to individuals, $38,000 for 245 employee matching gifts and $60,740 for 62 in-kind gifts.
Purpose and activities: Eileen Fisher makes charitable contributions to nonprofit organizations involved with women's and girl's empowerment and women entrepreneurs. Support is given primarily in areas of company operations.
Fields of interest: Health care; Youth development, services; Human services, mind/body enrichment; Business/industry; Leadership development; General charitable giving Women; Girls; Adults, women; Young adults, female; Economically disadvantaged.
Programs:
Activating Leadership Grant Program for Women and Girls: Eileen Fisher annually awards grants of $5,000 or more to programs designed to activate leadership qualities in women and girls. Special emphasis is directed toward programs designed to foster self-discovery and personal transformation; help women and/or girls find their inner strength and trust their intuition; and address any phase of a woman's and/or girl's life.
Business Grant Program for Women Entrepreneurs: Eileen Fisher annually awards five $12,500 grants to women entrepreneurs with established businesses and start-up businesses. Businesses must be innovative, 100% women owned, and produce products that foster environmental and economical health in the community.
Community Partnership Grants: Eileen Fisher supports organizations in areas of company operations with in-kind gifts, event tickets, gift certificates of up to $250, items for gift bags, merchandise, and grants of up to $2,500. Special emphasis is directed toward organizations that work to address local issues with core services that focus on strengthening the community; demonstrate long-term viability and sustainability; and keeps with Eileen Fisher's mission.
Employee Matching Gift Program: Eileen Fisher matches contributions made by its employees to nonprofit organizations on a one-for-one basis up to $1,000 per employee, per year.
Type of support: Annual campaigns; Conferences/seminars; Continuing support; Donated products; Emergency funds; Employee matching gifts; Employee volunteer services; General/operating support; Grants to individuals; In-kind gifts; Program development; Seed money; Sponsorships.
Geographic limitations: Giving primarily in areas of company operations; giving also to U.S.-based international organizations active in developing nations abroad.
Support limitations: No support for political, religious, or research organizations. No grants to individuals (except for the Business Grant Program for Women Entrepreneurs).
Publications: Application guidelines; Corporate giving report (including application guidelines); Grants list.

Application information: Applications accepted. Support is limited to 1 contribution per organization during any given year. The Social Consciousness Department handles giving. The company has a staff that only handles contributions. A contributions committee reviews all requests. Application form required. Applicants should submit the following:
1) copy of IRS Determination Letter
2) copy of current year's organizational budget and/or project budget
3) additional materials/documentation
Initial approach: Complete online application form
Copies of proposal: 1
Committee meeting date(s): Feb. 17, Apr. 27, June 16, Aug. 18, Oct. 12, and Nov. 17
Deadline(s): 1 week before committee meeting for Community Partnership Grants; 1 and Aug. 1; Mar. 15 for Activating Leadership Grant Program for Women & Girls; May 15 for Business Grant Program for Women Entrepreneurs
Final notification: 8 weeks following committee meetings
Administrators: Amy Hall, Dir., Social Consciousness; Cheryl Campbell, Business Grant Coord.; Reisa Brafman, Social Consciousness Assoc.
Number of staff: 2 full-time professional; 1 part-time support.

1434
Fitzpatrick, Cella, Harper & Scinto
1290 Ave. of the Americas
New York, NY 10104-3800 (212) 218-2100

Company URL: http://www.fitzpatrickcella.com/?p=2534
Establishment information: Established in 1971.
Company type: Private company
Business activities: Operates law firm.
Business type (SIC): Legal services
Corporate officers: Colleen Tracy, Firm Managing Partner; Brian L. Klock, Managing Partner; Michael K. I O'Neil, Managing Partner
Offices: Costa Mesa, CA; Washington, DC; New York, NY
Giving statement: Giving through the Fitzpatrick, Cella, Harper & Scinto Pro Bono Program.

Fitzpatrick, Cella, Harper & Scinto Pro Bono Program
1290 Ave. of the Americas
New York, NY 10104-3800 (212) 218-2100
FAX: (212) 218-2200; URL: http://www.fitzpatrickcella.com/?p=2534

Contact: Donald J. Curry, Partner
Fields of interest: Legal services.
Type of support: Pro bono services - legal.
Geographic limitations: Giving primarily in areas of company operations in Costa Mesa, CA, Washington, DC, and New York, NY.
Application information: An attorney coordinates pro bono projects.

1435
Fleck Company, Inc.
2040 15th Ave., W.
Seattle, WA 98119 (206) 284-2200

Company type: Private company
Business activities: Designs and engineers plastic moldings and products.
Business type (SIC): Plastic products/miscellaneous
Giving statement: Giving through the Fleck Family Foundation.

Fleck Family Foundation
14655 S.E. 267th St.
Kent, WA 98042

Establishment information: Established in 1989 in WA.
Donors: Fleck Co., Inc.; Duane Fleck; Lorraine D. Fleck; Peter J. Fleck; Sandra Fleck; and other members of the Fleck family.
Financial data (yr. ended 12/31/11): Assets, $1,470,813 (M); gifts received, $1,600; expenditures, $76,435; qualifying distributions, $76,435; giving activities include $76,000 for 14 grants (high: $10,000; low: $4,000).
Purpose and activities: The foundation supports organizations involved with mental health, Alzheimer's disease, recreation, and human services.
Fields of interest: Youth development; Human services; Religion.
Type of support: General/operating support; Scholarship funds.
Application information: Applications not accepted. Unsolicited requests for funds not accepted.
Officers: Duane Fleck, Pres.; Brian Fleck, V.P.; Sandra Fleck, Secy.
EIN: 911460966

1436
Flexcon Company, Inc.
2021 E. 23rd St.
Columbus, NE 68601-3404 (402) 562-6131

Company URL: http://www.flexcon.com
Establishment information: Established in 1956.
Company type: Private company
Business activities: Manufactures films and plastic products.
Business type (SIC): Plastic products/miscellaneous
Financial profile for 2010: Number of employees, 125
Corporate officer: Neil McDonough, Pres. and C.E.O.
Giving statement: Giving through the C. Jean and Myles McDonough Charitable Foundation.

The C. Jean and Myles McDonough Charitable Foundation
8 Westwood Dr.
Worcester, MA 01609-1243

Establishment information: Established in 1986 in MA.
Donors: C. Jean McDonough; Myles McDonough; Flexcon Co., Inc.
Financial data (yr. ended 11/30/11): Assets, $656,305 (M); expenditures, $482,649; qualifying distributions, $477,150; giving activities include $477,150 for grants.
Purpose and activities: The foundation supports museums and organizations involved with historic preservation, higher education, the environment, and human services.
Fields of interest: Museums (art); Museums (history); Museums (science/technology); Historic preservation/historical societies; Higher education; Environment; Children/youth, services; Human services.
Geographic limitations: Giving primarily in Worcester, MA.
Support limitations: No grants to individuals.
Application information: Applications not accepted. Contributes only to pre-selected organizations.
Trustees: C. Jean McDonough; Myles McDonough.
EIN: 042947391
Selected grants: The following grants are a representative sample of this grantmaker's funding activity:
$160,000 to Worcester Art Museum, Worcester, MA, 2010.
$5,000 to Abbys House, Worcester, MA, 2010.
$3,000 to Music Worcester, Worcester, MA, 2010.
$2,500 to American Antiquarian Society, Worcester, MA, 2010.
$2,500 to W G B H Educational Foundation, Boston, MA, 2010.

1437
Flextronics International U.S.A., Inc.
6201 America Center Dr.
San Jose, CA 95002 (408) 576-7000

Company URL: http://www.flextronics.com
Establishment information: Established in 1986.
Company type: Subsidiary of a foreign company
Business activities: Designs, engineers, and manufactures electronics products.
Business type (SIC): Electronic components and accessories; electronic and other electrical equipment and components
Corporate officers: H. Raymond Bingham, Chair.; Mike McNamara, C.E.O.; Francois Barbier, Pres., Opers.; Christopher Collier, Sr. V.P., Finance and C.A.O.; David E. Smoley, Sr. V.P. and C.I.O.; Jonathan S. Hoak, Sr. V.P. and Genl. Counsel; Paul Read, Exec. V.P. and C.F.O.
Board of director: H. Raymond Bingham, Chair.
International operations: Brazil; Mexico
Historic mergers: Solectron Corporation (October 1, 2007)
Giving statement: Giving through the Flextronics Foundation.

Flextronics Foundation
847 Gibraltar Dr.
Milpitas, CA 95035-6332 (408) 576-7528
Regional Contact for Asia Pacific: Tony Khaw, 1 Kallang Pl., 339211 Singapore, tel.: +65.6854.3737; Regional Contact for Europe: Roy Scott, Unit 10, Keypoint Business Centre, Dublin 11, Lincester, Ireland, tel.: +52.449.9107125; URL: http://www.flextronics.com/social_resp/Flextronics_Foundation/default.aspx

Establishment information: Established in 2001 in CA.
Donors: Flextronics International U.S.A., Inc.; Richard Sharp; Michael Marks.
Contact: Lori Kenepp, Community Rels. Mgr.
Financial data (yr. ended 12/31/11): Assets, $7,790,401 (M); gifts received, $400,000;

expenditures, $500,482; qualifying distributions, $500,272; giving activities include $500,272 for grants.
Purpose and activities: The foundation supports programs designed to address disaster relief; provide medical relief and health; and promote education. Special emphasis is directed toward programs designed to serve communities where Flextronics employees, suppliers, and customers live and work.
Fields of interest: Education, special; Higher education; Education; Health care; Disasters, preparedness/services; Business/industry; Community/economic development; Mathematics; Engineering/technology; Science Economically disadvantaged.
Programs:
Disaster Relief: The foundation provides aid to relieve human suffering caused by a natural or civil disaster or emergency hardship, including floods, fires, riots, storms, earthquakes, or similar large-scale adversities.
Educational Programs: The foundation supports educational programs designed to benefit students with socioeconomic issues, learning disabilities or handicaps; and promote electronic manufacturing and the betterment of disadvantaged students. Special emphasis is directed toward educational programs where Flextronics employees volunteer their time.
Medical Relief and Heath Programs: The foundation supports programs designed to promote health and provide medical relief to communities where Flextronics employees live and work. Special emphasis is directed toward organizations with which employees of Flextronics volunteers.
Type of support: Continuing support; Emergency funds; Employee volunteer services; General/operating support; Program development; Scholarship funds.
Geographic limitations: Giving primarily in areas of company operations in CA, and in Asia, Europe, and Mexico.
Support limitations: No support for religious, political, discriminatory, or for-profit organizations. No grants to individuals, or for advertising, athletic events or league sponsorships, conventions, conferences, meetings or seminars, clubs, contests, field trips, film and/or video projects, fundraising activities, marketing, sponsorships, or travel or similar activities.
Publications: Application guidelines; IRS Form 990 or 990-PF printed copy available upon request; Program policy statement.
Application information: Applications accepted. Multi-year funding is not automatic. Application form required.
Initial approach: Contact a regional representative for application form
Board meeting date(s): Mar., June, Sept., and Dec.
Deadline(s): None
Officers: Paul Humphries, Pres.; Tim Stewart, Secy.; Chris Collier, C.F.O.; Don Standley, Treas.
EIN: 770567788
Selected grants: The following grants are a representative sample of this grantmaker's funding activity:
$35,000 to Silicon Valley Education Foundation, San Jose, CA, 2009.
$31,000 to Red Cross Society of China, Beijing, China, 2009.
$15,000 to San Jose State University, San Jose, CA, 2009.
$10,000 to Aim High for High School, San Francisco, CA, 2009.
$10,000 to Childrens Museum of Memphis, Memphis, TN, 2009.
$10,000 to Tech Museum of Innovation, San Jose, CA, 2009.
$5,000 to Plano Independent School District Education Foundation, Plano, TX, 2009.
$5,000 to United Way of the Greater Triangle, Morrisville, NC, 2009.
$5,000 to United Way, Montgomery County, The Woodlands, TX, 2009.
$1,978 to Granville Education Foundation, Oxford, NC, 2009.

1438
Flint Association of Plumbing and Mechanical Contractors, Inc.

(also known as Flint Association PMC)
58 Parkland Plz., Ste. 600
Ann Arbor, MI 48103-6209 (734) 665-2207

Company URL: http://www.flintpmc.org
Establishment information: Established in 1920.
Company type: Business league
Business activities: Operates business association.
Business type (SIC): Business association
Financial profile for 2010: Number of employees, 10
Corporate officers: Curt LaLonde, Pres.; Chad Miller, Secy.-Treas.
Board of directors: Ken Coon; Gary Dickerson; Dominic Goyette; Curt LaLonde; Tom Long; Chad Miller; Sandra Miller; Greg Pfeiffer; John Walter; Doug Wyrwicki
Giving statement: Giving through the Scholarship Fund of Flint Plumbing and Pipefitting Industry.

Scholarship Fund of Flint Plumbing and Pipefitting Industry

6525 Centurion Dr.
Lansing, MI 48917-9275 (810) 720-5243

Establishment information: Established in 1987 in MI.
Donor: Flint Plumbers & Pipefitting.
Contact: Mike Tomaszewski, Tr.
Financial data (yr. ended 04/30/12): Assets, $13,673 (M); gifts received, $18,884; expenditures, $17,273; qualifying distributions, $17,273; giving activities include $16,000 for 16 grants to individuals (high: $1,000; low: $1,000).
Purpose and activities: The foundation awards scholarships to children of active or deceased members of Flint Plumbing and Pipefitting Industry.
Fields of interest: Higher education.
Type of support: Employee-related scholarships.
Geographic limitations: Giving primarily in MI.
Application information: Applications accepted. Application form required.
Initial approach: Proposal
Deadline(s): Mar. 1
Trustees: Dominic Goyette; Mike Tomaszewski; John D. Walter; Dave Worthing, Jr.
EIN: 386522581

1439
Flint Hills Resources, LP

4111 E. 37th St. N.
Wichita, KS 67220-3203 (316) 828-3477

Company URL: http://www.fhr.com
Establishment information: Established in 1940.
Company type: Subsidiary of a private company
Business activities: Refines petroleum; manufactures petrochemicals and chemical intermediates.
Business type (SIC): Petroleum refining; chemicals and allied products
Financial profile for 2009: Number of employees, 3,500
Corporate officers: Bradley J. Razook, Pres. and C.E.O.; Anthony J. Sementelli, Exec. V.P. and C.F.O.; Jeff Wilkes, Exec. V.P., Opers.
Giving statement: Giving through the Flint Hills Resources, LP Corporate Giving Program.

Flint Hills Resources, LP Corporate Giving Program

4111 E. 37th St. N.
Wichita, KS 67220-3203
Application addresses: For Alaska: 1100 H & H Ln., North Pole, AL, 99705; For Illinois, Michigan, and Minnesota: P.O. Box 64596, St. Paul, MN, 55164-0596; For Texas: P.O. Box 2608, Corpus Christi, TX, 78403; URL: http://www.fhr.com/community/default.aspx

Purpose and activities: Flint Hills Resources makes charitable contributions to nonprofit organizations involved with K-12 education, children's services, natural resource preservation, environmental safety and health, and services for disadvantaged groups. Support is given primarily in Alaska, Illinois, Kansas, Minnesota, and Texas.
Fields of interest: Elementary/secondary education; Environment, natural resources; Public health; Safety/disasters; Children, services; Human services; Science, public education; Mathematics Economically disadvantaged.
Program:
Flint Hills Resources Scholar Recognition: For more than 18 years, the company has honored Corpus Christi-area students for their athletic and academic achievements through the Flint Hills Resources Scholar Recognition. Each student is selected by a panel of school administrators and teachers, receives a plaque, attends a banquet and appears in a television and radio spot. Since 1995, more than 500 students from 40 Coastal Bend schools have been recognized.
Type of support: Donated equipment; Employee volunteer services; General/operating support.
Application information: Applications accepted. Application form not required.
Initial approach: Mail proposal to appropriate regional office

1440
Flir Advanced Imaging Systems, Inc.

(doing business as Salvador Imaging Inc.)
(formerly Salvador Imaging, Inc.)
5061 N. 30th St., Ste. 103
Colorado Springs, CO 80919-3248
(719) 598-6006

Company URL: http://www.salvadorimaging.com/
Establishment information: Established in 2004.

Company type: Subsidiary of a public company
Business activities: Manufactures photographic equipment and supplies.
Business type (SIC): Photographic equipment and supplies
Corporate officer: David Wayne Gardner, Chair. and Pres.
Board of director: David Wayne Gardner, Chair.
Giving statement: Giving through the Salvador Foundation.

The Salvador Foundation

5061 N. 30th St., Ste. 103
Colorado Springs, CO 80919-3248 (719) 598-6006
FAX: (719) 598-6556;
E-mail: info@salvadorfoundation.org; E-mail address for applications: grants@salvadorfoundation.org; URL: http://www.salvadorfoundation.org/

Establishment information: Established in 2005 in CO.
Donor: Salvador Imaging, Inc.
Financial data (yr. ended 12/31/11): Assets, $19,503,386 (M); gifts received, $620; expenditures, $1,135,946; qualifying distributions, $945,386; giving activities include $945,386 for grants.
Purpose and activities: The foundation supports programs designed empower individuals, organizations, and communities through Christianity. Special emphasis is directed toward helping people who are truly in need.
Fields of interest: Education; Environment, water resources; Health care; Agriculture; Human services; Economic development; Microfinance/microlending; Christian agencies & churches Economically disadvantaged.
International interests: Latin America.
Type of support: General/operating support.
Geographic limitations: Giving primarily in Miami, FL, and in Latin America.
Support limitations: No support for organizations that advocate abortion or the taking of human life. No grants to individuals, or for sports activities (unless participants are mentally or physically handicapped), general operating support of K-12 schools or colleges, or mission trips.
Publications: Application guidelines; Newsletter.
Application information: Applications accepted. Applicants should submit the following:
1) copy of IRS Determination Letter
2) brief history of organization and description of its mission
3) detailed description of project and amount of funding requested

Initial approach: Download application form and e-mail to foundation
Deadline(s): None

Officers: H. William Mahaffey, Chair.; David W. Gardner, Pres.; Mary Gardner, Secy.-Treas.
Director: Nick Gonzales.
EIN: 202760889
Selected grants: The following grants are a representative sample of this grantmaker's funding activity:
$100,000 to Florida Institute of Technology, Melbourne, FL, 2010.

1441
Florence Savings Bank

(also known as FSB)
85 Main St.
Florence, MA 01062-1400 (413) 586-1300

Company URL: http://www.florencesavings.com
Establishment information: Established in 1873.
Company type: Private company
Business activities: Operates savings bank.
Business type (SIC): Savings institutions
Corporate officers: John F. Heaps, Jr., Pres.; Thomas Cynical, C.F.O.; A.E. Putnam, Treas.
Giving statement: Giving through the Florence Savings/Easthampton Branch Charitable Foundation, Inc.

Florence Savings/Easthampton Branch Charitable Foundation, Inc.

85 Main St.
Florence, MA 01062-1400 (413) 587-1761

Establishment information: Established in 1999 in MA.
Donor: Florence Securities Corp.
Contact: Sara E. Darling
Financial data (yr. ended 12/31/11): Assets, $679,840 (M); expenditures, $45,570; qualifying distributions, $30,000; giving activities include $30,000 for grants.
Purpose and activities: The foundation supports organizations involved with arts and culture, education, sports, and children services.
Fields of interest: Arts; Secondary school/education; Scholarships/financial aid; Education; Athletics/sports, baseball; Athletics/sports, soccer; Children, foster care; Children, services.
Type of support: Annual campaigns; Building/renovation; Endowments; Equipment; Program development; Scholarship funds; Sponsorships.
Geographic limitations: Giving primarily in the Easthampton, MA, area.
Support limitations: No grants to individuals.
Application information: Applications accepted. Application form required.

Initial approach: Contact foundation for application form

Officers: John F. Heaps, Jr., Pres.; Douglas H. Burr, Clerk; Kevin R. Day, Treas.
Directors: Nancy Labom Bard; Robert F. Ebert; Thomas C. McCarthy; Donald Laplante; Irving R. Rosazza; Virginia L. Smith; Thomas Whiteley.
EIN: 043484588

1442
Florida Panthers Hockey Club, Ltd.

1 Panther Pkwy.
Sunrise, FL 33323-5315 (954) 835-7000

Company URL: http://www.floridapanthers.com
Establishment information: Established in 1993.
Company type: Private company
Business activities: Operates professional ice hockey club.
Business type (SIC): Commercial sports
Corporate officers: Clifford G. Viner, Chair. and C.E.O.; Michael Yormark, Pres.; Louis Partenza, Exec. V.P. and C.F.O.; Steve Ziff, V.P., Mktg.; Ryan McCoy, V.P., Sales; Matthew F. Sacco, V.P., Comms. and Public Affairs; Elisa Hernandez, V.P., Human Resources
Board of director: Clifford G. Viner, Chair.
Giving statement: Giving through the Florida Panthers Hockey Club, Ltd. Corporate Giving Program and the Florida Panthers Foundation, Inc.

Florida Panthers Hockey Club, Ltd. Corporate Giving Program

c/o Community Devel. Dept.
1 Panther Pkwy.
Sunrise, FL 33323-5315 (954) 835-7720
URL: http://panthers.nhl.com/club/page.htm?id=37211

Contact: Jean Marshall
Purpose and activities: The Florida Panthers make charitable contributions to nonprofit organizations that benefit children's healthcare, education, and cultural needs. Support is given primarily in areas of company operations.
Fields of interest: Arts; Education; Health care; Children, services; General charitable giving.
Type of support: Donated products; Employee volunteer services; In-kind gifts; Income development; Loaned talent.
Geographic limitations: Giving primarily in areas of company operations in Broward, Miami-Dade, and Palm Beach, FL; giving also to national organizations.
Publications: Application guidelines.
Application information: Applications accepted. Proposals should be submitted using organization letterhead. Telephone calls during the application process are not encouraged. The Community Development Department handles giving. Application form not required. Applicants should submit the following:
1) name, address and phone number of organization
2) copy of IRS Determination Letter
3) detailed description of project and amount of funding requested

Letters of inquiry should list date and time of the event, location, and the cause that the event benefits.

Initial approach: Mail proposal to headquarters for memorabilia or tickets; letter of inquiry to headquarters for player appearances
Copies of proposal: 1
Deadline(s): 6 weeks prior to need

Florida Panthers Foundation, Inc.

1 Panther Pkwy.
Sunrise, FL 33323-5315 (954) 835-7612
URL: http://panthers.nhl.com/club/page.htm?id=37211

Establishment information: Established in 2003 in FL.
Financial data (yr. ended 12/31/10): Revenue, $272,861; assets, $198,016 (M); gifts received, $82,743; expenditures, $365,151; program services expenses, $214,659; giving activities include $114,194 for 6 grants (high: $19,600; low: $8,000).
Purpose and activities: The foundation's mission is to assist nonprofit organizations that focus on family health care, medical research, children's education, and cultural needs through corporate partnerships, philanthropic grants, and unique resources.
Fields of interest: Education; Health care; Medical research; Youth development; Youth, services Economically disadvantaged.
Geographic limitations: Giving primarily in FL.
Directors: Evelyn Lopez; Randy Moller.
EIN: 300176325

1443
Florida Power & Light Company

700 Universe Blvd.
Juno Beach, FL 33408-2657
(561) 694-4000
FAX: (561) 694-4718

Company URL: http://www.fpl.com
Establishment information: Established in 1925.
Company type: Subsidiary of a public company
Business activities: Generates, transmits, and distributes electricity.
Business type (SIC): Electric services
Financial profile for 2009: Number of employees, 5,930; sales volume, $11,491,000,000
Corporate officers: Lewis Hay III, Chair.; Eric Silagy, Pres.; Kimberly Ousdahl, V.P., C.A.O. and Cont.; Lakshman Charanjiva, V.P. and C.I.O.; Robert E. Barrett, Jr., V.P., Finance; Timothy Fitzpatrick, V.P., Mktg. and Comms.; Wade Litchfield, Genl. Counsel
Board of director: Lewis Hay III, Chair.
Giving statement: Giving through the Florida Power & Light Company Contributions Program and the NextEra Energy Foundation, Inc.

Florida Power & Light Company Contributions Program

700 Universe Blvd.
Juno Beach, FL 33408-2657
FAX: (561) 694-4718;
E-mail: antonia.toomey@fpl.com; URL: http://www.fpl.com/community/index.shtml

Contact: Antonia Toomey
Financial data (yr. ended 12/31/09): Total giving, $5,832,923, including $5,642,079 for 1,119 grants and $190,844 for 273 employee matching gifts.
Purpose and activities: As a complement to its foundation, Florida Power & Light also makes charitable contributions to nonprofit organizations directly. Support is given primarily in areas of company operations in Florida.
Fields of interest: Arts; Elementary/secondary education; Higher education; Education; Environment, energy; Environmental education; Environment; Disasters, preparedness/services; Safety/disasters; Human services Aging.
Programs:
FPL Care to Share: Florida Power & Light Company provides emergency assistance funds of up to $500 to customers who have experienced a personal or family crisis and are unable to pay their electric bills.
Power in Knowledge: Florida Power & Light Company supports educational outreach programs for students, parents, and educators to promote energy, electrical safety, and energy conservation. The program includes activities within the classroom, science fairs, field trips, career development, workshops, and interactive web resources.
Solar Stations Program: Through the Solar Stations Program, Florida Power & Light donates 5 kw solar arrays to schools in its Florida service territory. The company also supports teacher training and awards project grants.
Type of support: Building/renovation; Conferences/seminars; Emergency funds; Employee matching gifts; Employee volunteer services; In-kind gifts; Internship funds; Program development; Scholarship funds; Sponsorships.
Geographic limitations: Giving primarily in areas of company operations in FL.
Support limitations: No support for religious, political, or discriminatory organizations, or for sports teams.
Publications: Application guidelines.
Application information: Applications accepted. The Community Relations Department handles giving. Application form not required. Applicants should submit the following:
1) listing of additional sources and amount of support
2) copy of IRS Determination Letter
3) listing of board of directors, trustees, officers and other key people and their affiliations
Initial approach: Send completed form to headquarters
Copies of proposal: 1
Deadline(s): None
Final notification: 2 to 3 weeks
Number of staff: 2 full-time professional.
Selected grants: The following grants are a representative sample of this grantmaker's funding activity:
$500,000 to Camillus House, Miami, FL, 2010.
$50,000 to Audubon Society, National, Miami, FL, 2010.

NextEra Energy Foundation, Inc.

(formerly FPL Group Foundation, Inc.)
700 Universe Blvd.
Juno Beach, FL 33408-2683
FAX: (561) 694-4718;
E-mail: Antonia.Toomey@fpl.com; Application address: P.O. Box 029100, Miami, FL 33102, tel. (305) 552-4090; URL: http://www.fpl.com/community/community_programs.shtml

Establishment information: Established in 1987 in FL.
Donor: Florida Power & Light Co.
Contact: Antonia Toomey, Community Rels. Specialist
Financial data (yr. ended 12/31/11): Assets, $7,165,193 (M); gifts received, $20,007; expenditures, $1,696,800; qualifying distributions, $1,664,778; giving activities include $1,664,778 for grants.
Purpose and activities: The foundation supports organizations involved with arts and culture, education, the environment, health, animals and wildlife, affordable housing, human services, neighborhood development, economic development, government administration, and economically disadvantaged people.
Fields of interest: Arts; Higher education; Education; Environment, energy; Environmental education; Environment; Animal welfare; Animals/wildlife; Health care; Housing/shelter; Salvation Army; Aging, centers/services; Homeless, human services; Human services; Community development, neighborhood development; Economic development; United Ways and Federated Giving Programs; Government/public administration Economically disadvantaged.
Programs:
Community Development: The foundation supports programs designed to enhance the overall quality of life and aesthetics within the community through affordable housing, arts and culture, economic development, and government initiatives.
Education: The foundation supports programs designed to promote energy-related projects or curriculum.
Employee Matching Gift Program: The foundation matches contributions made by employees and directors of NextEra Energy to educational institutions on a one-for-one basis from $50 to $10,000 per contributor, per year.
Health and Human Services: The foundation supports programs designed to provide for the needs of NextEra Energy's diverse customer base, with emphasis on the elderly and low-income customers.
The Environment: The foundation supports programs designed to preserve the natural environment and provide environmental education.
Type of support: Capital campaigns; Curriculum development; Employee matching gifts; Endowments.
Geographic limitations: Giving primarily in areas of company operations, with emphasis on the east coast of FL and the west coast from Bradenton to Naples.
Support limitations: No support for religious organizations, political or lobbying groups, United Way-affiliated agencies, or discriminatory organizations. No grants to individuals, or for school events, travel, or conferences, or endowments.
Publications: Application guidelines.
Application information: Applications accepted. Application form required. Applicants should submit the following:
1) copy of IRS Determination Letter
2) copy of most recent annual report/audited financial statement/990
3) copy of current year's organizational budget and/or project budget
Initial approach: Contact foundation for application form and mail to application address
Copies of proposal: 1
Deadline(s): Aug.
Final notification: 4 to 6 weeks
Officers and Directors:* Lewis Hay III*, Chair.; Armando J. Olivera*, Pres. and Treas.; James W. Poppell, V.P.; Alissa E. Ballot, Secy.; James L. Robo; Charles E. Sieving; T.J. Tuscai.
Number of staff: 2 part-time support.
EIN: 650031452
Selected grants: The following grants are a representative sample of this grantmaker's funding activity:
$1,000 to University of Miami, Miami, FL, 2008.

1444
Florida Rock & Tank Lines, Inc.

200 W. Forsyth St., 7th Fl.
Jacksonville, FL 32202-4936
(904) 396-5733

Company URL: http://www.floridarockandtanklines.com/about.html
Establishment information: Established in 1962.
Company type: Subsidiary of a public company
Business activities: Provides trucking services; conducts investment activities.
Business type (SIC): Trucking and courier services, except by air; pipelines (except natural gas/operation of); investors/miscellaneous
Corporate officers: Robert E. Sandlin, Pres. and C.E.O.; Ray M. Van Landingham, C.F.O.; John D. Klopfenstein, C.A.O. and Cont.; Michael Gilbertstein, C.I.O.
Subsidiaries: The Aurundel Corp., Sparks, MD; Cardinal Concrete Co., Springfield, VA
Plants: Estero, Gainesville, Holiday, Orlando, FL
Giving statement: Giving through the Florida Rock & Tank Lines Foundation.

Florida Rock & Tank Lines Foundation

200 W. Forsyth St., 7th Fl.
Jacksonville, FL 32202 (904) 396-5733

Donors: Florida Rock & Tank Lines, Inc.; Patriot Transportation Holding, Inc.
Contact: John Milton, Treas.

Financial data (yr. ended 09/30/12): Assets, $851,375 (M); expenditures, $64,227; qualifying distributions, $59,603; giving activities include $59,603 for 14 grants (high: $20,000; low: $400).
Purpose and activities: The foundation supports health clinics and organizations involved with arts education, cerebral palsy, muscular dystrophy, human services, and civic affairs.
Fields of interest: Education; Health care; Human services.
Type of support: General/operating support.
Application information: Applications accepted. Application form required.
Initial approach: Letter
Deadline(s): None
Officers: Edward L. Baker, Pres.; John Baker, V.P.; John Milton, Treas.
EIN: 593050577

1445
Florsheim Brothers

(also known as Florsheim Homes)
1701 W. March Ln., Ste. D
Stockton, CA 95207-6416 (209) 473-1106

Company URL: http://www.florsheimhomes.com
Establishment information: Established in 1983.
Company type: Subsidiary of a private company
Business activities: Builds single-family houses.
Business type (SIC): Operative builders
Corporate officers: Robert H. Florsheim, Pres.; Suzanne M. Candini, C.O.O.
Giving statement: Giving through the Florsheim Brothers, A California Non-Profit Benefit Corporation.

Florsheim Brothers, A California Non-Profit Benefit Corporation

1701 W. March Ln., Ste. D
Stockton, CA 95207-6416 (209) 473-1106

Establishment information: Established in 1997 in CA.
Donors: Florsheim Brothers; Delhi Harmony Ranch; Florsheim Homes, LLC; Florsheim Land, LLC.
Contact: David Florsheim, Pres.
Financial data (yr. ended 12/31/11): Revenue, $77,071; assets, $721,129 (M); gifts received, $27,000; expenditures, $123,441; giving activities include $118,309 for grants to individuals.
Purpose and activities: The foundation supports organizations involved with education and human services.
Fields of interest: Education; Children/youth, services; Family services; Human services.
Type of support: General/operating support; Scholarship funds; Sponsorships.
Geographic limitations: Giving primarily in CA.
Application information: Applications accepted. Application form not required.
Initial approach: Proposal
Deadline(s): None
Officers and Directors:* David Florsheim, Pres.; Robert Florsheim, V.P.; Joseph Anfuso; Jim Dyson; Diane Florsheim; Lissa Heaton; Melody Martinez; Dennis Oliveria; John Vosbein; Ralph Yasin.
EIN: 911775773

1446
Flowers Foods, Inc.

(formerly Flowers Industries)
1919 Flowers Cir.
Thomasville, GA 31757 (229) 226-9110
FAX: (229) 225-3816

Company URL: http://www.flowersfoods.com
Establishment information: Established in 1919.
Company type: Public company
Company ticker symbol and exchange: FLO/NYSE
Business activities: Producer and marketer of bakery products.
Business type (SIC): Food and kindred products
Financial profile for 2012: Number of employees, 9,800; assets, $1,995,850,000; sales volume, $3,046,490,000; pre-tax net income, $208,770,000; expenses, $2,827,980,000; liabilities, $1,137,230,000
Fortune 1000 ranking: 2012—703rd in revenues, 676th in profits, and 854th in assets
Corporate officers: George E. Deese, Chair. and C.E.O.; Allen L. Shiver, Pres. and C.E.O; Gene D. Lord, Exec. V.P. and C.O.O.; R. Steven Kinsey, Exec. V.P. and C.F.O.; Stephen R. Avera, Exec. V.P., Genl. Counsel, and Secy.; Karyl H. Lauder, Sr. V.P. and C.A.O.; David A. Hubbard, Sr. V.P. and C.I.O.; H. Mark Courtney, Sr. V.P., Sales and Mktg.; Donald A. Thriffiley, Jr., Sr. V.P., Human Resources
Board of directors: George E. Deese, Chair.; Joe E. Beverly; Franklin L. Burke; Manuel A. Fernandez; Benjamin H. Griswold IV; Amos R. McMullian; J.V. Shields, Jr.; Allen L. Shiver; David V. Singer; Melvin T. Stith, Ph.D.; Jacquelyn M. Ward; C. Martin Wood III
Subsidiary: Tasty Baking Company, Philadelphia, PA
Giving statement: Giving through the Flowers Foods, Inc. Corporate Giving Program.
Company EIN: 582582379

Flowers Foods, Inc. Corporate Giving Program

c/o Marta J. Turner, Exec. V.P., Corp. Rels.
1919 Flowers Cir.
Thomasville, GA 31757-1137
FAX: (229) 225-3816; URL: http://www.flowersfoods.com/FFC_CorporateGiving/index.cfm

Contact: Marta J. Turner, Sr. V.P., Corp. Rels.
Purpose and activities: Flowers Foods makes charitable contributions to nonprofit organizations and national charities. Support is given on a national basis, and in areas of company operations, with an emphasis on Thomasville, Georgia.
Fields of interest: General charitable giving.
Program:
The Flowers Foods Sons & Daughters Scholarship Program: Through The Flowers Foods Sons & Daughters Scholarship Program, the company awards scholarships to help finance higher education for children of employees of Flowers Foods and its subsidiaries. The program is independently managed by Scholarship America. Applicants must be children of full-time employees who have a minimum of two years employment with the company as of the application deadline. For more information on this program, employees may contact their human resources department or call Scholarship America at 800-537-4180.
Type of support: Donated products; Employee-related scholarships; In-kind gifts.
Geographic limitations: Giving on a national basis, and in areas of company operations, with an emphasis on Thomasville, GA.
Application information: Applications accepted. Application form not required. Applicants should submit the following:
1) brief history of organization and description of its mission
Initial approach: Contact regional branch when possible; or mail or fax request to headquarters
Deadline(s): None

1447
Flowserve Corporation

(formerly Durco International Inc.)
5215 N. O'Connor Blvd., Ste. 2300
Irving, TX 75039 (972) 443-6500
FAX: (972) 443-6800

Company URL: http://www.flowserve.com
Establishment information: Established in 1912.
Company type: Public company
Company ticker symbol and exchange: FLS/NYSE
Business activities: Operates flow control equipment manufacturing company.
Business type (SIC): Machinery/general industry; metal products/fabricated; machinery/special industry; machinery/industrial and commercial
Financial profile for 2012: Number of employees, 17,000; assets, $4,810,960,000; sales volume, $4,751,340,000; pre-tax net income, $611,570,000; expenses, $4,075,560,000; liabilities, $2,920,740,000
Fortune 1000 ranking: 2012—508th in revenues, 358th in profits, and 604th in assets
Forbes 2000 ranking: 2012—1412th in sales, 1281st in profits, and 1823rd in assets
Corporate officers: James O. Rollans, Chair.; Mark A. Blinn, Pres. and C.E.O.; Thomas L. Pajonas, Sr. V.P. and C.O.O.; Michael S. Taff, Sr. V.P. and C.F.O.; Mark D. Dailey, Sr. V.P. and C.A.O.; Carey A. O'Connor, Sr. V.P., Genl. Counsel and Secy.
Board of directors: James O. Rollans, Chair.; Mark A. Blinn; Gayla J. Delly; Roger L. Fix; John R. Friedery; Joseph E. Harlan; Michael F. Johnston; Rick J. Mills; Charles M. Rampacek; David E. Roberts; William C. Rusnack
Subsidiaries: Automax, Inc., Cincinnati, OH; Durametallic Corp., Kalamazoo, MI; Metal Fab Corp., Ormond Beach, FL; Valtek International, Springville, UT
Divisions: Engineered Plastic Products Div., Springboro, OH; Filtration Systems Div., Filtration Products, Angola, NY; Filtration Systems, DurcoMeter Products, Angola, NY; The Duriron Co., Inc. Foundry Div., Dayton, OH; The Duriron Co., Inc. Rotating Equipment Grp., Dayton, OH; The Duriron Co., Inc. Valve Div., Cookeville, TN
Giving statement: Giving through the Flowserve Corporation Contributions Program.
Company EIN: 310267900

Flowserve Corporation Contributions Program

5215 N. O'Connor Blvd., Ste. 2300
Irving, TX 75039-3726 (972) 443-6500
URL: http://www.flowserve.com/About-Flowserve/Corporate-Sustainability

Purpose and activities: Flowserve Corporation makes charitable contributions to nonprofit organizations involved with children and education. Support is given on a national and international basis in areas of company operations.
Fields of interest: Education Children.

Type of support: Donated equipment; Employee volunteer services; General/operating support; In-kind gifts; Sponsorships.
Geographic limitations: Giving on a national and international basis in areas of company operations.

1448
Fluor Corporation

6700 Las Colinas Blvd.
Irving, TX 75039 (469) 398-7000
FAX: (469) 398-7255

Company URL: http://www.fluor.com
Establishment information: Established in 1912.
Company type: Public company
Company ticker symbol and exchange: FLR/NYSE
International Securities Identification Number: US3434121022
Business activities: Operates holding company; provides engineering, procurement, construction, and maintenance services.
Business type (SIC): Heavy construction other than building construction contractors; holding company; engineering, architectural, and surveying services
Financial profile for 2012: Number of employees, 32,592; assets, $8,276,040,000; sales volume, $27,577,130,000; pre-tax net income, $733,500,000; expenses, $26,843,630,000; liabilities, $4,934,750,000
Fortune 1000 ranking: 2012—110th in revenues, 356th in profits, and 446th in assets
Forbes 2000 ranking: 2012—343rd in sales, 1067th in profits, and 1594th in assets
Corporate officers: David Thomas Seaton, Chair. and C.E.O.; Biggs C. Porter, Sr. V.P. and C.F.O.; Carlos M. Hernandez, Sr. V.P. and Secy.; James M. Lucas, Sr. V.P. and Treas.; Gary Smalley, Sr. V.P. and Cont.; Glenn C. Gilkey, Sr. V.P., Human Resources and Admin.; Kenneth H. Lockwood, V.P., Finance
Board of directors: David T. Seaton, Chair.; Peter K. Barker; Rosemary T. Berkery; Alan M. Bennett; Peter J. Fluor; James T. Hackett; Kent Kresa; Dean R. O'Hare; Armando J. Olivera; Adm. Joseph Wilson Prueher; Nader H. Sultan; Suzanne H. Woolsey, Ph.D.
Giving statement: Giving through the Fluor Corporation Contributions Program and the Fluor Foundation.
Company EIN: 330927079

Fluor Corporation Contributions Program

6700 Las Colinas Blvd.
Irving, TX 75039-2902
URL: http://www.fluor.com/sustainability/community/fluor_giving/Pages/default.aspx

Contact: Suzanne Huffmon Esber, Dir., Community Rels.
Purpose and activities: As a complement to its foundation, Fluor also makes charitable contributions to nonprofit organizations directly. Emphasis is given to organizations involved with education, social services, community and economic development, and the environment. Support is given on a national and international basis.
Fields of interest: Education; Environment; Human services; Community/economic development; United Ways and Federated Giving Programs.
International interests: Australia; Canada; Chile; China; India; Netherlands; Philippines; Poland; South Africa; Spain; United Kingdom.
Type of support: Annual campaigns; Building/renovation; Employee volunteer services; General/operating support; Loaned talent; Program development; Use of facilities.
Geographic limitations: Giving on a national and international basis in areas of company operations, with emphasis on Orange County, CA, Fernald, OH, Greenville, SC, Fort Bend County, TX, Richland, WA, and in Australia, Canada, Chile, China, India, the Netherlands, the Philippines, Poland, South Africa, Spain, and the United Kingdom.
Support limitations: No support for religious, political, fraternal, or labor organizations. No grants to individuals, or for entertainment events, school-related bands and events, freelance films, video tapes, or audio productions, or courtesy advertising, including program books and yearbooks.
Publications: Application guidelines.
Application information: The Community Relations Department handles giving. Letter of inquiry should be limited to 2-3 pages. Application form not required. Applicants should submit the following:
1) role played by volunteers
2) name, address and phone number of organization
3) copy of IRS Determination Letter
4) brief history of organization and description of its mission
5) descriptive literature about organization
6) listing of board of directors, trustees, officers and other key people and their affiliations
7) detailed description of project and amount of funding requested
8) contact person

Letter of inquiry should include previous support by Fluor, if applicable.
Initial approach: Letter of inquiry to headquarters
Copies of proposal: 1
Deadline(s): None
Final notification: 2 months
Number of staff: 7 full-time professional; 2 full-time support.

The Fluor Foundation

6700 Las Colina Blvd.
Irving, TX 75039-2902 (469) 398-7000
E-mail: community.relations@fluor.com;
URL: http://www.fluor.com/sustainability/community/Pages/default.aspx

Establishment information: Incorporated in 1952 in CA.
Donor: Fluor Corp.
Contact: Terence H. Robinson, Sr. Dir., Community Affairs & Fluor Fdn.
Financial data (yr. ended 12/31/11): Assets, $13,117,277 (M); gifts received, $4,363,593; expenditures, $4,401,411; qualifying distributions, $4,363,593; giving activities include $4,362,647 for 505 grants (high: $605,466; low: $50).
Purpose and activities: The foundation supports organizations involved with arts and culture, education, hunger, housing, youth development, human services, community development, volunteerism, and civic affairs.
Fields of interest: Arts education; Arts councils; Media, television; Media, radio; Visual arts; Museums; Performing arts; Performing arts, orchestras; Arts; Elementary/secondary education; Higher education; Business school/education; Engineering school/education; Education; Food services; Housing/shelter; Youth development, adult & child programs; Youth, services; Family services; Human services, financial counseling; Human services, emergency aid; Human services; Economic development; Community/economic development; Voluntarism promotion; Science, formal/general education; Mathematics; Engineering/technology; Public policy, research; Public affairs.
Programs:
Culture: The foundation supports arts funds and councils, museums, symphonies, and community art festivals and organizations involved with arts education, public radio and television, and visual and performing arts.
Education: The foundation supports programs designed to encourage elementary and secondary students to pursue higher education and training with emphasis on engineering; improve and enhance math and science curriculum; provide teacher training in math and science; and promote mentoring programs and economic literacy.
Fluor Aggie Scholarship Fund: The foundation annually awards college scholarships to Texas A&M University students pursuing degrees in engineering, construction science, or business. The scholarships are administered by Texas A&M University.
Fluor Foundation Job Corps Scholarship Program: The foundation annually awards seven $5,000 college scholarships to students attending Job Corps Centers located in Arkansas, Florida, Kentucky, Mississippi, and New Mexico. The program is administered by Scholarship America.
Fluor Scholarship Program: The foundation annually awards renewable college scholarships of $1,000 to $3,000 to children of employees of Fluor. The program is designed to acknowledge student accomplishments and support their goals to obtain degrees or certificates at universities, colleges, and vocational or technical schools.
Human Services: The foundation supports programs designed to provide community services such as food, shelter, and family assistance, emergency relief, and youth services.
Matching Gift Program for Colleges and Universities: The foundation matches contributions made by full-time employees of Fluor to institutions of higher education on a one-for-one basis from $25 to $5,000 per employee, per year.
Public and Civic Affairs: The foundation supports organizations involved with economic and community development, volunteerism, and public policy.
Type of support: Annual campaigns; Building/renovation; Capital campaigns; Curriculum development; Employee matching gifts; Employee volunteer services; Employee-related scholarships; Endowments; Equipment; General/operating support; Program development; Research; Scholarship funds.
Geographic limitations: Giving primarily in areas of company operations, with some emphasis on AK, Aliso Viejo, CA, FL, KY, MS, NM, Greenville, SC, Irving and Sugar Land, TX, and Richland, WA.
Support limitations: No support for sports organizations, veterans', fraternal, labor, or religious organizations, or lobbying or political organizations. No grants to individuals (except for employee scholarships), or for film production, publishing activities, sports programs, or lobbying or political campaigns.
Publications: Application guidelines; Financial statement; Informational brochure; IRS Form 990 or 990-PF printed copy available upon request; Program policy statement.
Application information: Applications accepted. Proposals should be no longer than 2 to 3 pages. Additional information may be requested at a later date. Application form not required. Applicants should submit the following:
1) name, address and phone number of organization
2) copy of IRS Determination Letter
3) brief history of organization and description of its mission

4) copy of most recent annual report/audited financial statement/990
5) list of company employees involved with the organization
6) listing of board of directors, trustees, officers and other key people and their affiliations
7) detailed description of project and amount of funding requested
8) contact person
9) copy of current year's organizational budget and/or project budget
10) listing of additional sources and amount of support

Proposals should include the organization's e-mail address, if available, and a description of past involvement by the foundation with the organization.

Initial approach: Proposal to nearest company facility
Copies of proposal: 1
Board meeting date(s): Apr. and Oct.
Deadline(s): None
Final notification: Within 2 months

Officers and Directors:* Lee C. Tashjian*, Pres.; Carlos M. Hernandez, Secy.; E. J. Kowalchuk, Treas.; Ray F. Barnard; David E. Constable; S. B. Dobbs; Glenn C. Gilkey; David T. Seaton; D. Michael Steuert; Dwayne A. Wilson.
EIN: 510196032

1449
FMC Corporation

1735 Market St.
Philadelphia, PA 19103-7501
(215) 299-6000
FAX: (215) 299-6140

Company URL: http://www.fmc.com
Establishment information: Established in 1928.
Company type: Public company
Company ticker symbol and exchange: FMC/NYSE
Business activities: Manufactures industrial and military machinery; produces chemicals; assembles automobiles.
Business type (SIC): Machinery/general industry; chemicals/industrial inorganic; fertilizers and agricultural chemicals; ammunition, ordinance, and accessories; motor vehicles and equipment
Financial profile for 2012: Number of employees, 5,700; assets, $4,373,900,000; sales volume, $3,748,000,000; pre-tax net income, $612,600,000; expenses, $3,090,100,000; liabilities, $2,893,600,000
Fortune 1000 ranking: 2012—617th in revenues, 385th in profits, and 631st in assets
Corporate officers: Pierre R. Brondeau, Ph.D., Chair., Pres., and C.E.O.; Paul Graves, Exec. V.P. and C.F.O.; Andrea E. Utecht, Exec. V.P., Genl. Counsel, and Secy.; Kenneth R. Garnett, Exec. V.P., Human Resources; Barry Crawford, V.P., Opers.; Kenneth A. Gedaka, V.P., Comms. and Public Affairs
Board of directors: Pierre Brondeau, Chair.; Eduardo E. Cordeiro; G. Peter D'Aloia; C. Scott Greer; Dirk A. Kempthorne; Edward J. Mooney; Paul J. Norris; Robert C. Pallash; William H. Powell; Vincent R. Volpe, Jr.
Subsidiaries: FMC Gold Co., Chicago, IL; FMC Paradise Peak Corp., Reno, NV; FMC Wyoming Corp., Green River, WY; Lithium Corp., Gastonia, NC; Moorco International Inc., Houston, TX
Plants: Anniston, AL; Conway, Jonesboro, AR; Fresno, Madera, Riverside, Santa Clara, CA; Denver, CO; Newark, DE; Lakeland, Orlando, FL; Pocatello, ID; Chicago, Hoopeston, IL; Lawrence, KS; Baltimore, MD; Minneapolis, MN; Tupelo, MS; Reno, NV; Carteret, Princeton, NJ; Buffalo, Middleport, NY; Aberdeen, Gastonia, NC; Chalfont, Homer City, Philadelphia, PA; Aiken, SC; Dallas, Houston, Stephenville, TX; Institute, South Charleston, WV; Green Bay, WI
Offices: Rentha, MA; Erie, PA; Houston, TX
International operations: Australia; Belgium; Brazil; Canada; China; France; Germany; Iceland; India; Indonesia; Ireland; Italy; Japan; Malaysia; Mexico; Netherlands; Norway; Pakistan; South Korea; Spain; Switzerland; Thailand; United Kingdom
Giving statement: Giving through the FMC Corporation Contributions Program.
Company EIN: 940479804

FMC Corporation Contributions Program

1735 Market St.
Philadelphia, PA 19103 (215) 299-6000
URL: http://www.fmc.com/corporateresponsibility/CivicInvolvement/tabid/60/Default.aspx

Contact: Judy Smeltzer, Dir., State Govt. Rels.
Purpose and activities: As a complement to its foundation, FMC makes charitable contributions to nonprofit organizations involved with arts and culture, education, tsunami relief, and community economic development, and to the United Way. Support is given primarily in areas of company operations.
Fields of interest: Arts; Education; Community/economic development; United Ways and Federated Giving Programs.

Programs:

Dollars for Doers: FMC supports "Dollars for Doers" programs to recognize and encourage community service, matching employees' volunteer service hours with qualifying organizations up to $500.

Matching Gifts to United Way: FMC matches contributions made by its employees to the United Way up to 60 percent on the dollar, based on the percentage of participating employees.

National Merit Scholarship Program: FMC supports the National Merit Scholarship Program each year, providing three-year scholarships to qualifying children of active employees.

Type of support: Employee matching gifts; Employee volunteer services; Employee-related scholarships; General/operating support.
Geographic limitations: Giving primarily in areas of company operations.

1450
FMR Corp.

(also known as Fidelity Investments)
82 Devonshire St.
Boston, MA 02109-3605 (617) 563-7000

Company URL: http://www.fidelity.com
Establishment information: Established in 1946.
Company type: Private company
Business activities: Provides investment advisory services; provides securities brokerage services; sells life insurance.
Business type (SIC): Security and commodity services; brokers and dealers/security; insurance/life
Financial profile for 2011: Number of employees, 37,600; sales volume, $12,260,000,000
Corporate officers: Edward C. "Ned" Johnson III, Chair. and C.E.O.; Stephen A. Scullen III, Pres. and C.I.O.; Robert J. Chersi, C.F.O.
Board of director: Edward C. Johnson III, Chair.
International operations: Canada
Giving statement: Giving through the Fidelity Investments Corporate Giving Program, the Fidelity Foundation, and the Fidelity Charitable Gift Fund.

Fidelity Investments Corporate Giving Program

(formerly Fidelity Cares)
155 Congress St.
Boston, MA 02110-2511 (800) 343-3548
URL: http://www.fidelity.com/inside-fidelity/community/corporate-citizen

Purpose and activities: As a complement to its foundation, Fidelity also makes charitable contributions to nonprofit organizations directly. Emphasis is given to organizations involved with education and the arts. Support is given on a national basis in areas of company operations.
Fields of interest: Performing arts, music; Arts; Elementary/secondary education; Education, drop-out prevention; Education, reading; Education; Environment; Heart & circulatory diseases; Human services, financial counseling; Human services, gift distribution Economically disadvantaged.
Type of support: Employee volunteer services; General/operating support; Sponsorships.
Geographic limitations: Giving on a national basis in areas of company operations.
Publications: Application guidelines.
Application information: Applications accepted. Proposals are not accepted via phone, mail, fax, or e-mail. Application form required. Applicants should submit the following:
1) copy of IRS Determination Letter
2) brief history of organization and description of its mission
3) copy of most recent annual report/audited financial statement/990
4) detailed description of project and amount of funding requested

Initial approach: Complete online application
Copies of proposal: 1
Deadline(s): 90 days prior to event
Final notification: 30 days

Fidelity Foundation

11 Keewaydin Dr., Ste. 100
Salem, NH 03079-2999
E-mail: info@FidelityFoundation.org; URL: http://www.fidelityfoundation.org

Establishment information: Trust established in 1965 in MA.
Donors: FMR Corp.; Fidelity Ventures Ltd.; FMR Capital; The Colt, Inc.
Financial data (yr. ended 12/31/11): Assets, $310,227,743 (M); expenditures, $19,719,663; qualifying distributions, $18,612,873; giving activities include $14,890,246 for 104 grants (high: $3,025,000; low: $1,850) and $2,217,296 for 1,139 employee matching gifts.
Purpose and activities: The foundation supports organizations involved with arts and culture, education, health, human services, and community development. Special emphasis is directed toward programs designed to strengthen long-term effectiveness of nonprofit institutions.
Fields of interest: Arts; Education; Health care; Human services; Community/economic development.
International interests: Canada.

Program:

Employee Matching Gifts to Education Program: The foundation matches contributions made by full-time employees of FMR to educational institutions on a two-for-one basis from $50 to

$1,000 and on a one-for-one basis up to $3,000 per employee, per year.
Type of support: Building/renovation; Capital campaigns; Conferences/seminars; Consulting services; Curriculum development; Employee matching gifts; Equipment; Faculty/staff development; Management development/capacity building; Matching/challenge support; Program development; Publication; Technical assistance.
Geographic limitations: Giving primarily in areas of company operations in the Northeast and Middle Atlantic, with emphasis on Jacksonville, FL, New York, NY, Cincinnati, OH, RI, Dallas, Fort Worth and northern TX, Salt Lake City, UT, and Toronto, Canada; giving also to regional and national organizations.
Support limitations: No support for start-up, sectarian, or civic organizations, public school systems, or disease-specific organizations. No grants to individuals, or for general operating support, sponsorships, scholarships, galas or benefits, corporate memberships, or video or film projects.
Publications: Application guidelines.
Application information: Applications accepted. Grants are generally made to organizations with operating budgets of $500,000 or more. Letters of inquiry should be no longer than 3 pages. A full proposal may be requested at later date. A site visit may be requested. Organizations receiving support are asked submit a six-month progress report and a final report. Application form required. Applicants should submit the following:
1) brief history of organization and description of its mission
2) copy of most recent annual report/audited financial statement/990
3) detailed description of project and amount of funding requested
4) contact person
5) copy of current year's organizational budget and/ or project budget
6) listing of additional sources and amount of support

Applying organizations should request funding for planning initiatives, technology projects, capital improvements, or organizational development. Letters of inquiry for capital campaigns should include progress toward a fundraising goal.
Initial approach: E-mail letter of inquiry
Deadline(s): None
Final notification: 4 to 6 months
Officers and Trustees:* Anne-Marie Soulliere*, Pres.; Desiree Caldwell, C.O.O.; Paul Kuenstner, V.P.; Tom Lewis, V.P.; Mary Sullivan, Cont.; Abigail P. Johnson; Edward C. Johnson III; Edward C. Johnson IV; Ross E. Sherbrooke.
Number of staff: 4 full-time professional; 3 full-time support.
EIN: 046131201
Selected grants: The following grants are a representative sample of this grantmaker's funding activity:
$3,025,000 to Cherokee Ranch and Castle Foundation, Sedalia, CO, 2011. For land acquisition.
$750,000 to National Arts Strategies, Alexandria, VA, 2010. For program development.
$750,000 to National Arts Strategies, Alexandria, VA, 2011. For pilot program development.
$500,000 to Cathedral High School, Boston, MA, 2011. For construction.
$500,000 to Feeding America, Chicago, IL, 2011. For technology.
$500,000 to New-York Historical Society, New York, NY, 2010. For technology.
$475,000 to Cherokee Ranch and Castle Foundation, Sedalia, CO, 2011. For land acquisition.
$300,000 to Nantucket Dreamland Foundation, Nantucket, MA, 2010. For construction.
$300,000 to Salvation Army, Canton, MA, 2011. For construction.
$250,000 to University of Utah, Salt Lake City, UT, 2010. For construction.
$200,000 to Westminster College, Salt Lake City, UT, 2010. For construction.
$137,734 to Utah Food Bank, Salt Lake City, UT, 2010. For technology.
$100,000 to Boston Modern Orchestra Project, Malden, MA, 2011. For organizational development.
$100,000 to Cummer Museum of Art and Gardens, Jacksonville, FL, 2010. For consulting.
$100,000 to Rhode Island Community Food Bank Association, Providence, RI, 2011. For construction.
$89,590 to AppleTree Institute for Education Innovation, Washington, DC, 2011. For consulting.
$85,000 to Food Bank of Central and Eastern North Carolina, Raleigh, NC, 2010. For equipment.
$81,000 to Rhode Island Community Food Bank Association, Providence, RI, 2010. For technology.
$75,000 to Friends of Choice in Urban Schools, Washington, DC, 2010. For technology.
$62,200 to New Beginning Center, Garland, TX, 2011. For technology.

Fidelity Charitable Gift Fund

P.O. Box 770001
Cincinnati, OH 45277-0053
FAX: (617) 476-7206; Toll-free tels.: (800) 952-4438, (800) 262-6039; toll-free fax: (877) 665-4274; additional address: 100 Crosby Pkwy., Mail Zone KC1D-FCS, Covington, KY 41015-9325; URL: http://www.fidelitycharitable.org/

Establishment information: Established in 1991 in MA as a donor-advised fund.
Contact: Janice Dolnick, Electronic Mktg. Consul.
Financial data (yr. ended 06/30/11): Revenue, $1,874,887,580; assets, $5,615,146,363 (M); gifts received, $1,735,234,386; expenditures, $1,275,762,649; giving activities include $1,250,208,282 for 67,804 grants.
Purpose and activities: The fund makes donor-advised grants primarily to U.S. tax-exempt charitable organizations.
Fields of interest: Philanthropy/voluntarism.
Geographic limitations: Giving on a national basis.
Publications: Annual report; Financial statement; Grants list; Newsletter.
Application information: Applications not accepted. Contributes only to pre-selected organizations; unsolicited requests for funds not considered or acknowledged.
Board meeting date(s): Feb., June, and Oct.
Officers and Trustees:* Scott Bergeson*, Chair.; David L. Giunta, Pres.; Rudman J. Ham; Audrey McNiff; Kristin W. Mugford; Anna Spangler Nelson; Alfred E. Osborne, Jr.; Thomas R. Powers; Melvin R. Seiden; Anne-Marie Soulliere; Richard Tadler.
Number of staff: 50 full-time professional.
EIN: 110303001

1451
Focus Point Media, Inc.

(doing business as CharityAdvantage, Inc.)
(formerly Net Cruiser Technologies, Inc.)
425 E. Alvarado St., Ste. E
Fallbrook, CA 92028 (800) 677-4180

Company URL: http://www.charityadvantage.com
Company type: Private company
Business activities: Provides Internet fundraising services.
Business type (SIC): Computer services
Giving statement: Giving through the Focus Point Media, Inc. Corporate Giving Program.

Focus Point Media, Inc. Corporate Giving Program

(doing business as CharityAdvantage, Inc. Corporate Giving Program)
(formerly The TechAdvantage Program)
c/o CharityAdvantage
425 East Alvarado St., Ste. A201
Fallbrook, CA 92028 (800) 677-4180
URL: http://www.charityadvantage.com

Purpose and activities: CharityAdvantage provides technology consulting and website building services to nonprofit organizations and churches. Support is given on a national basis.
Fields of interest: Education, computer literacy/ technology training; Engineering/technology; Electronic communications/Internet.
Type of support: Computer technology; Consulting services; Loaned talent; Technical assistance.
Geographic limitations: Giving on a national basis.
Application information: Applications accepted. Application form required.
Initial approach: Complete online application form

1452
Foldcraft Co.

615 Centennial Dr.
Kenyon, MN 55946 (507) 789-5111

Company URL: http://www.foldcraft.com
Establishment information: Established in 1947.
Company type: Private company
Business activities: Manufactures restaurant furnishings.
Business type (SIC): Fixtures/office and store
Corporate officers: Chuck Mayhew, Pres. and C.E.O.; Doug Westra, C.F.O.
Giving statement: Giving through the Foldcraft Foundation.

Foldcraft Foundation

615 Centennial Dr.
Kenyon, MN 55946-1252

Establishment information: Established in 1997 in MN.
Donor: Foldcraft, Co.
Financial data (yr. ended 12/31/11): Assets, $104,644 (M); gifts received, $22,500; expenditures, $26,634; qualifying distributions, $19,600; giving activities include $19,600 for grants.
Fields of interest: Religion.
Geographic limitations: Giving primarily in Minneapolis, MN.
Support limitations: No grants to individuals.
Application information: Applications not accepted. Unsolicited requests for funds not accepted.

Officers: Dennis Blackmer, Pres.; Dawn Rohl, V.P.; Annette Bjork, Secy.; Randy Dessner, Treas.
EIN: 411872480

1453
Foley & Lardner LLP

U.S. Bank Center
777 E. Wisconsin Ave.
Milwaukee, WI 53202-5306
(407) 244-3268

Company URL: http://apps.foley.com/students/landing.aspx
Company type: Private company
Business activities: Operates law firm.
Business type (SIC): Legal services
Offices: Los Angeles, Palo Alto, Sacramento, San Diego, San Francisco, CA; Washington, DC; Jacksonville, Miami, Orlando, Tallahassee, Tampa, FL; Chicago, IL; Boston, MA; Detroit, MI; New York, NY; Madison, Milwaukee, WI
Giving statement: Giving through the Foley & Lardner LLP Pro Bono Program.

Foley & Lardner LLP Pro Bono Program

US Bank Center
777 E. Wisconsin Ave.
Milwaukee, WI 53202-5306 (202) 295-4067
E-mail: slambert@foley.com; Additional tel.: (414) 271-2400; URL: http://www.foley.com/probono/

Contact: Steven C. Lambert, Vice-Chair, Pro Bono Svcs. Committee
Fields of interest: Legal services.
Type of support: Pro bono services - legal.
Geographic limitations: Giving primarily in areas of company operations in Los Angeles, Palo Alto, Sacramento, and San Diego, CA, Washington, DC, Jacksonville, Miami, Orlando, Tallahassee, and Tampa, FL, Chicago, IL, Boston, MA, Detroit, MI, New York, NY, and Madison, WI.
Application information: The Pro Bono Committee manages the pro-bono program.

1454
Foley Hoag LLP

(formerly Foley, Hoag & Eliot LLP)
Seaport World Trade Center West
155 Seaport Blvd., Ste. 1600
Boston, MA 02210-2600 (617) 832-1000

Company URL: http://www.foleyhoag.com/
Establishment information: Established in 1943.
Company type: Private company
Business activities: Provides legal services.
Business type (SIC): Legal services
Corporate officers: Tom Block, C.O.O.; Kevin Smith, C.F.O.
Offices: Washington, DC; Boston, Waltham, MA
International operations: France
Giving statement: Giving through the Foley Hoag LLP Pro Bono Program and the Foley Hoag Foundation.

Foley Hoag LLP Pro Bono Program

Seaport West
155 Seaport Blvd.
Boston, MA 02210-2600 (617) 832-1755
E-mail: rcazabon@foleyhoag.com; Additional tel.: (617) 832-1000; URL: http://www.foleyhoag.com/practices/litigation/pro-bono

Contact: Rebecca Cazabon, Pro Bono Managing Attorney
Fields of interest: Legal services.
Type of support: Pro bono services - legal.
Geographic limitations: Giving primarily in areas of company operations in Washington, DC, Boston, and Waltham, MA, and in France.
Application information: The Pro Bono Coordinator manages the pro-bono program.

Foley Hoag Foundation

155 Seaport Blvd.
Boston, MA 02210-2697 (617) 426-7172

Establishment information: Established in 1980 in MA.
Donors: Foley, Hoag & Eliot LLP; Foley Hoag LLP.
Financial data (yr. ended 12/31/11): Assets, $36,622 (M); gifts received, $8,800; expenditures, $83,898; qualifying distributions, $83,500; giving activities include $83,500 for 22 grants (high: $4,000; low: $2,500).
Purpose and activities: The foundation supports programs designed to advance racial harmony, civil rights, and intercultural relations in Boston, Massachusetts. Special emphasis is directed toward programs designed to focus on youth.
Fields of interest: Arts; Education; Recreation; Youth development; Civil/human rights, equal rights; Civil rights, race/intergroup relations; Civil/human rights.
Type of support: Continuing support; General/operating support; Matching/challenge support; Program development; Seed money.
Geographic limitations: Giving limited to Boston, MA.
Support limitations: No grants to individuals, or for general operating support.
Publications: Annual report; Application guidelines; Grants list.
Application information: Applications accepted. Grants range from $2,000 to $10,000. Support is limited to 1 contribution per organization during any given year. Multi-year funding is not automatic. Organizations receiving support are asked to submit an evaluation report. Application form required.
Applicants should submit the following:
1) name, address and phone number of organization
2) brief history of organization and description of its mission
3) detailed description of project and amount of funding requested
4) contact person

Initial approach: Request application form
Board meeting date(s): June and Dec.
Deadline(s): None

Trustees: Mossik Hacobian; Michael B. Keating; Jeanne Pinado.
Number of staff: 2 part-time professional.
EIN: 042716893

1455
Follett Corporation

2233 W. St.
River Grove, IL 60171-1895
(708) 583-2000
FAX: (708) 452-9347

Company URL: http://www.follett.com
Establishment information: Established in 1873.
Company type: Private company
Business activities: Operates bookstores; sells books wholesale; develops computer software.
Business type (SIC): Shopping goods stores/miscellaneous; non-durable goods—wholesale; computer services
Financial profile for 2012: Number of employees, 10,000; sales volume, $2,700,000,000
Corporate officers: Alison E. O'Hara, Chair.; Mary Lee Schneider, Jr., Pres. and C.E.O.; Kathryn A. Stanton, Exec. V.P., Finance and C.F.O.; Doug Thompson, Sr. V.P. and C.I.O.; Michael Flaherty, V.P., Opers.; Thomas Kline, V.P., Corp. Comms.; Patrick Rivers, Treas.
Board of director: Alison E. O'Hara, Chair.
Subsidiary: Follett College Stores Corp., Elmhurst, IL
Divisions: Follett Campus Resources, River Grove, IL; Follett Collegiate Graphics, River Grove, IL; Follett Education Services, Chicago, IL; Follett Library Resources, Crystal Lake, IL; Follett Software Co., McHenry, IL
Giving statement: Giving through the Follett Corporation Contributions Program and the Follett Educational Foundation.

Follett Corporation Contributions Program

2233 West St.
River Grove, IL 60171-1817 (708) 583-2000
URL: http://www.follett.com/CommunityCommitment.cfm

Purpose and activities: As a complement to its foundation, Follett Corporation also makes charitable contributions to nonprofit organizations directly. Support is given primarily in areas of company operations in Illinois.
Fields of interest: Education, reading; General charitable giving.
Type of support: Donated products; Employee matching gifts; In-kind gifts; Sponsorships.
Geographic limitations: Giving primarily in areas of company operations in IL.

Follett Educational Foundation

c/o Follett Corp., Human Resources
2233 West St.
River Grove, IL 60171-1817 (708) 437-2402
URL: http://www.follett.com/CommunityCommitment.cfm

Establishment information: Established in 1964 in IL.
Donors: Follett Corp.; Dwight W. Follett†; Mildred Follett.
Financial data (yr. ended 07/31/11): Assets, $3,136,594 (M); gifts received, $325,281; expenditures, $386,735; qualifying distributions, $376,662; giving activities include $376,662 for grants.
Purpose and activities: The foundation awards college scholarships to children of employees of Follett Corporation.
Fields of interest: Higher education.
Type of support: Employee-related scholarships.
Geographic limitations: Giving limited to areas of company operations, with emphasis on IL.
Application information: Applications not accepted. Contributes only through employee-related scholarships.

Board meeting date(s): June

Officers and Trustees:* Richard Ellspermann*, Pres.; Keith O'Hara, V.P.; Doug Thompson, Secy.; Themis G. Galanis*, Treas.; Cliff Ewert; R. Mark Litzsinger; Lisa McManaman; Christopher D. Traut; Richard A. Waichler.
EIN: 366104348

1456
Fonville & Co.
4450 South Boulevard
Charlotte, NC 28209 (704) 525-9990

Establishment information: Established in 1972.
Company type: Private company
Business activities: Remanufactures and distributes automotive products.
Business type (SIC): Motor vehicles and equipment
Corporate officers: Charles L. Fonville, Pres.; Charles Fonville, V.P., Sales; Susan Nunnery, Cont.
Giving statement: Giving through the Charles L. & Doris M. Fonville Foundation.

Charles L. & Doris M. Fonville Foundation
P.O. Box 11309
Charlotte, NC 28220-1309

Establishment information: Established around 1995 in NC.
Donor: Fonville & Co.
Financial data (yr. ended 12/31/11): Assets, $1,081,690 (M); expenditures, $70,204; qualifying distributions, $65,000; giving activities include $65,000 for grants.
Purpose and activities: The foundation supports organizations involved with education and human services.
Fields of interest: Education; Youth development; Human services.
Type of support: General/operating support; Scholarship funds.
Geographic limitations: Giving primarily in Charlotte, NC.
Support limitations: No grants to individuals.
Application information: Applications not accepted. Unsolicited requests for funds not accepted.
Officer: Charles L. Fonville, Chair.
Trustee: Doris Fonville.
EIN: 561896989

1457
Food Emporium, Inc.
(doing business as The Great Atlantic & Pacific Tea Company)
(formerly Shopwell, Inc.)
2 Paragon Dr.
Montvale, NJ 07645 (866) 443-7374

Company URL: http://www.thefoodemporium.com
Establishment information: Established in 1979.
Company type: Subsidiary of a foreign company
Business activities: Operates supermarkets.
Business type (SIC): Groceries—retail
Corporate officers: Sam Martin, Pres. and C.E.O.; Chris McGarry, Exec. V.P. and Genl. Counsel; Paul Hertz, Exec. V.P., Opers.; Frederic F. Brace, C.A.O.; Krystyna Lack, V.P. and Treas.
Giving statement: Giving through the Food Emporium Corporate Giving Program.

Food Emporium Corporate Giving Program
2 Paragon Dr.
Montvale, NJ 07645-1718 (866) 443-7374
URL: http://www.thefoodemporium.com/pages_aboutUs_CO.asp

Purpose and activities: The Food Emporium makes charitable contributions of gift cards to organizations involved with the education, health, and welfare of children. Support is given primarily in Manhattan, New York.
Fields of interest: Elementary/secondary education; Health care; Children, services Children.
Type of support: Donated products.
Geographic limitations: Giving primarily in Manhattan, NY.
Support limitations: No support for political or discriminatory organizations. No grants to individuals.
Application information: Applications accepted. Proposals should be submitted using organization letterhead. Application form required. Applicants should submit the following:
1) name, address and phone number of organization
2) brief history of organization and description of its mission
3) detailed description of project and amount of funding requested
4) contact person
5) plans for acknowledgement

Proposals should include the organization's Tax ID Number and any deadlines.
Initial approach: Contact manager at nearest store for application
Final notification: 4 weeks

1458
Food Lion, LLC
2110 Executive Dr.
P.O. Box 1330
Salisbury, NC 28145-1330 (704) 633-8250

Company URL: http://www.foodlion.com
Establishment information: Established in 1957.
Company type: Subsidiary of a foreign company
Business activities: Operates grocery stores.
Business type (SIC): Groceries—retail
Financial profile for 2010: Number of employees, 200; sales volume, $2,161,100,000
Corporate officers: Mats Jansson, Chair.; Roland Smith, Pres. and C.E.O.; Pierre Bouchut, Exec. V.P. and C.F.O.; Michael R. Waller, Exec. V.P., Genl. Counsel, and Secy.; Nicolas Hollanders, Exec. V.P., Human Resources; Terry E. Morgan, Sr. V.P. and C.I.O.; Ken Mills, V.P., Sales and Mktg.
Board of directors: Mats Jansson, Chair.; Claire Babrowski; Shari L. Ballard; Pierre-Olivier Beckers; Jacques de Vaucleroy; Hugh G. Farrington; Jean-Pierre Hansen; Bill McEwan; Didier Smits; Jack L. Stahl; Baron Vansteenkiste
Giving statement: Giving through the Food Lion, LLC Corporate Giving Program, the Food Lion Charitable Foundation, Inc., and the Lion's Pride Foundation, Inc.

Food Lion, LLC Corporate Giving Program
(formerly Food Lion, Inc. Corporate Giving Program)
P.O. Box 1330
Salisbury, NC 28145-1330 (800) 210-9569
URL: http://www.foodlion.com/CommunityOutreach

Purpose and activities: As a complement to its foundation, Food Lion also makes charitable contributions to nonprofit organizations directly. Support is limited to areas of company operations.
Fields of interest: Arts, cultural/ethnic awareness; Museums; Elementary school/education; Education, reading; Health care; Food services; Nutrition; Athletics/sports, school programs; Recreation, fairs/festivals; Athletics/sports, amateur leagues; Children, services; Women, centers/services; Community development, civic centers; Military/veterans' organizations.
Programs:
Lion Shop and Share: Food Lion supports local communities through Lion Shop & Share, a program in which local customers raise money for nonprofit organizations such as schools, churches, and civic groups. Customers link their MVP Food Lion card to the charity of their choice, and every time they shop a portion of their total grocery purchase is donated to their organization.
Roaring to Read: Food Lion, in partnership with Weekly Reader Corporation Consumer & Custom Publishing, supports children's literacy through educational program guides designed for grades K-1, 2-3, and 4-6. The program is designed to enhance language arts curriculum and reward students for extracurricular reading. Upon completion of program, students receive a Certificate of Achievement and a gift from Food Lion.
Type of support: General/operating support; In-kind gifts; Sponsorships.
Geographic limitations: Giving limited to areas of company operations.
Support limitations: No grants to individuals, or for endowment funds, scholarships, pageants or contests, student trips, general operating budgets, political causes, campaigns or candidates, fundraisers for national organizations, projects that send products or people for relief efforts to a foreign country, church or faith-based organizations to purchase real estate, or supplies; or programs to benefit only the organization or its members (including youth groups, mission trips, or Sunday school supplies).
Publications: Application guidelines.
Application information: Applications accepted.
Initial approach: Contact store manager at nearest Food Lion store for local donation and sponsorship requests

Food Lion Charitable Foundation, Inc.
2110 Executive Dr.
Salisbury, NC 28147-9007 (704) 633-8250
FAX: (704) 638-1988; E-mail: flcf@foodlion.com; Application address: Community Rels. Dept., P.O. Box 1330, Salisbury, NC 28145-1330; URL: http://charitablefoundation.foodlion.org

Establishment information: Established as a company-sponsored operating foundation in 2001 in NC.
Donor: Food Lion LLC.
Contact: Denise Hill, Chair.
Financial data (yr. ended 12/31/10): Assets, $452,333 (M); gifts received, $1,103,804; expenditures, $707,164; qualifying distributions, $560,300; giving activities include $560,300 for 149 grants (high: $100,000; low: $1,000).
Purpose and activities: The foundation supports programs and agencies designed to feed the hungry with a focus on eliminating hunger.
Fields of interest: Food services; Food banks; Food distribution, meals on wheels; United Ways and Federated Giving Programs.
Type of support: Continuing support; Program development.
Geographic limitations: Giving primarily in areas of company operations in DE, FL, GA, KY, MD, NC, PA, SC, TN, VA. and WV.
Support limitations: No grants to individuals, or for administrative costs.
Publications: Application guidelines.
Application information: Applications accepted. Grants range from $2,500 to $5,000. Preference is given to organizations that involve Food Lion associates. Support is limited to 1 contribution per organization during any given year. Organizations

receiving support are asked to submit information regarding grant success and outcomes. Application form required. Applicants should submit the following:
1) population served
2) copy of IRS Determination Letter
3) brief history of organization and description of its mission
4) detailed description of project and amount of funding requested
5) listing of additional sources and amount of support
Applications should include a W-9 form and a statement from agency CEO certifying Feeding America or United Way affiliation in good standing.
Initial approach: Download application form and mail to foundation
Board meeting date(s): Jan., Apr., July, and Oct.
Deadline(s): Mar. 15 and Sept. 15
Final notification: May and Nov.
Officers: Denise Hill, Chair.; Lou Delorenzo, V.P.; Chris Dove, Secy.-Treas.
EIN: 562279572
Selected grants: The following grants are a representative sample of this grantmaker's funding activity:
$20,000 to Medical University of South Carolina, Charleston, SC, 2010.
$6,000 to Senior Resources of Guilford, Greensboro, NC, 2010.
$5,000 to City Rescue Mission, Fayetteville, NC, 2010.
$5,000 to Food Bank of Greenwood County, Greenwood, SC, 2010.
$5,000 to Golden Harvest Food Bank, Augusta, GA, 2010.
$5,000 to Greenhouse Ministries, Murfreesboro, TN, 2010.
$5,000 to Lutheran Community Services, Wilmington, DE, 2010.
$5,000 to Meals on Wheels of Rowan, Salisbury, NC, 2010.
$5,000 to Salvation Army of Durham, Durham, NC, 2010.
$3,000 to Rescue Mission of Roanoke, Roanoke, VA, 2010.

The Lion's Pride Foundation, Inc.

P.O. Box 1330
Salisbury, NC 28145-1330 (704) 633-8250
FAX: (704) 656-4162

Establishment information: Established in 1994 in NC.
Financial data (yr. ended 12/31/11): Revenue, $174,250; assets, $847,223 (M); gifts received, $150,966; expenditures, $224,735; giving activities include $187,306 for grants to individuals.
Purpose and activities: The foundation assists individuals in times of crisis through grants.
Fields of interest: Human services.
Program:
Emergency Assistance Grants: Awards of up to $500 per year are given to individuals who provide sufficient evidence of need (e.g., water, electricity, mortgage bills).
Type of support: Grants to individuals; In-kind gifts.
Geographic limitations: Giving on a national basis.
Application information: Applications accepted. Applications and supporting documents will be subject to verification. Application form required.
Initial approach: Applications for grants are available at all store locations
Copies of proposal: 1
Board meeting date(s): Weekly
Deadline(s): None
Officers: Jason Ramsey, Pres.; Maria Lowder, 1st V.P.; Maxine Barnes, 2nd V.P.; Jon Corriher, Secy.; Craig Coghill, Treas.
Number of staff: 10 full-time professional.
EIN: 561895601

1459
Foot Locker, Inc.

(formerly Venator Group, Inc.)
112 W. 34th St.
New York, NY 10120-0101 (212) 720-3700
FAX: (212) 553-7026

Company URL: http://www.footlocker-inc.com
Establishment information: Established in 1879.
Company type: Public company
Company ticker symbol and exchange: FL/NYSE
Business activities: Operates athletic footwear and apparel stores.
Business type (SIC): Shoe stores; men's and boys' apparel and accessory stores; women's apparel stores
Financial profile for 2013: Number of employees, 40,639; assets, $3,367,000,000; sales volume, $6,182,000,000; pre-tax net income, $607,000,000; expenses, $5,575,000,000; liabilities, $990,000,000
Fortune 1000 ranking: 2012—413th in revenues, 401st in profits, and 717th in assets
Forbes 2000 ranking: 2012—1265th in sales, 1191st in profits, and 1912th in assets
Corporate officers: Ken C. Hicks, Chair., Pres., and C.E.O.; Lauren B. Peters, Exec. V.P. and C.F.O.; Richard A. Johnson, Exec. V.P. and C.O.O.; Giovanna Cipriano, Sr. V.P. and C.A.O.; Peter D. Brown, Sr. V.P. and C.I.O.; Gary M. Bahler, Sr. V.P., Genl. Counsel, and Secy.; Laurie J. Petrucci, Sr. V.P., Human Resources; John A. Maurer, V.P. and Treas.
Board of directors: Ken C. Hicks, Chair.; Maxine Clark; Nicholas DiPaolo; Alan D. Feldman; Jarobin Gilbert, Jr.; Guillermo G. Marmol; Matthew M. McKenna; Cheryl Nido Turpin; Dona D. Young
International operations: Austria; Belgium; Canada; Denmark; France; Germany; Greece; Hungary; Ireland; Italy; Netherlands; Portugal; Spain; Turkey; United Kingdom
Giving statement: Giving through the Foot Locker, Inc. Corporate Giving Program and the Foot Locker Foundation, Inc.
Company EIN: 133513936

Foot Locker, Inc. Corporate Giving Program

(formerly Venator Group, Inc. Corporate Giving Program)
112 W. 34th St.
New York, NY 10120-0101 (212) 720-3700
URL: http://www.footlocker-inc.com/community.cfm?page=community

Purpose and activities: As a complement to its foundation, Foot Locker also makes charitable contributions to nonprofit organizations directly. Support is given in areas of company operations.
Fields of interest: Education; Cancer; Breast cancer; Athletics/sports, amateur leagues; Recreation; Youth development, services.
Type of support: Program development; Sponsorships.
Geographic limitations: Giving primarily in areas of company operations; giving also to national organizations.

Foot Locker Foundation, Inc.

112 W. 34th St.
New York, NY 10120-0101 (212) 720-3961

Establishment information: Established in 2001 in DE.
Financial data (yr. ended 01/31/12): Revenue, $2,157,591; assets, $1,775,860 (M); gifts received, $2,219,017; expenditures, $1,703,301; giving activities include $1,414,699 for grants.
Fields of interest: Education; Recreation; Youth development.
Officers: Ken Hicks*, Pres.; Peter D. Brown*, Sr. V.P.; Robert W. Mchugh*, Sr. V.P.; Laurie J. Petrucci, Sr. V.P.; Giovanna Cipriano, V.P.; John A. Maurer, V.P. and Treas.; Jeremy L. Nowak, V.P.; Sheilagh M. Clarke*, Secy.
EIN: 522348625

1460
Football Northwest, LLC

(doing business as Seattle Seahawks)
12 Seahawks Way
Renton, WA 98056-1572 (425) 203-8000

Company URL: http://www.seahawks.com
Establishment information: Established in 1976.
Company type: Subsidiary of a private company
Business activities: Operates professional football club.
Business type (SIC): Commercial sports
Corporate officers: Paul G. Allen, Chair.; Peter McLoughlin, Pres.; Karen Beckman, V.P., Finance and C.F.O.; Cindy Kelley, V.P., Admin. and Human Resources; Chuck Arnold, V.P., Sales and Mktg.; Dave Pearson, V.P., Comms.
Board of director: Paul G. Allen, Chair.
Giving statement: Giving through the Seattle Seahawks Corporate Giving Program and the Seattle Seahawks Charitable Foundation.

Seattle Seahawks Corporate Giving Program

c/o Donations
12 Seahawks Way
Renton, WA 98056-1572
URL: http://www.seahawks.com/community/community.aspx?id=34910

Purpose and activities: As a complement to its foundation, the Seattle Seahawks also make charitable contributions of memorabilia to nonprofit organizations directly. Special emphasis is directed towards programs designed to focus on education and youth athletics. Support is limited to the Pacific Northwest.
Fields of interest: Education; Athletics/sports, amateur competition; Youth development.
Type of support: In-kind gifts.
Geographic limitations: Giving limited to the Pacific Northwest, including AK, ID, MT, OR, and WA.
Support limitations: No game ticket donations.
Publications: Application guidelines.
Application information: Applications accepted. Donation requests are not accepted via telephone, fax, or e-mail. Application form required. Applicants should submit the following:
1) name, address and phone number of organization
2) contact person
Applications should include the Tax ID Number of the organization, and the name, date, location, and a description of the event.
Initial approach: Complete online application form
Deadline(s): 6 weeks prior to need

Seattle Seahawks Charitable Foundation

505 5th Ave. S., Ste. 900
Seattle, WA 98104-3821 (206) 342-2000
URL: http://www.seahawks.com/community/foundation.html

Contact: Jo Allen Patton, Pres.
Financial data (yr. ended 12/31/11): Revenue, $205,631; assets, $438,383 (M); gifts received, $205,107; expenditures, $173,768; giving activities include $142,595 for grants.
Purpose and activities: The foundation provides access for youth and young adults to academic, athletic, and health programs that improve their quality of life and improve their prospects for the future.
Fields of interest: Elementary/secondary education; Education; Health care; Health organizations; Youth development; Children, services; Youth, services.
Geographic limitations: Giving primarily in OR and WA.
Support limitations: No support for sectarian or religious organizations. No grants to individuals, or for fund drives or capital expenditures.
Application information: Applications accepted. Application form required.
Copies of proposal: 3
Officers and Directors:* Paul G. Allen*, Chair.; Peter McLoughlin, Pres.; Lance Lopes, Sr., V.P.; Chuck Arnold*, V.P. and Sales & Marketing; Susan Darrington, V.P. and Facility Operations & Services; Karen Beckman, V.P. and Finance & CFO; Mike Flood, V.P. and Community Relations & Special Projects; John Idzik, V.P. and Football Administration; Ron Jenkins, V.P. and Corporate Partnerships; Cindy Kelley, V.P. and Human Resources & Administration; Will Lewis, V.P. and Football Operations; Dave Pearson, V.P. and Communications, Broadcasting & Website Content; addistional 16 directors.
EIN: 911680811

1461
ForceBrain.com

1920 Leslie St.
San Mateo, CA 94403-1325
(650) 513-1668
FAX: (800) 609-4072

Company URL: http://www.ForceBrain.com
Establishment information: Established in 2008.
Company type: Private company
Business type (SIC): Business services/miscellaneous
Corporate officer: Jason Foster North, Pres.
Giving statement: Giving through the ForceBrain.com Contributions Program.

ForceBrain.com Contributions Program

1920 Leslie St.
San Mateo, CA 94403-1325 (650) 513-1668
URL: http://www.ForceBrain.com

Purpose and activities: ForceBrain.com is a certified B Corporation that donates a percentage of profits to charitable organizations. Support is given primarily in areas of company operations in Georgia, Illinois, Massachusetts, Minnesota, Nevada, New York, Pennsylvania, Texas, and Washington, with emphasis on California, and in Argentina, Canada, England, India, Ireland, Mexico, and the Philippines.
International interests: Argentina; Canada; England; India; Ireland; Mexico; Philippines.
Type of support: General/operating support; In-kind gifts.
Geographic limitations: Giving primarily in areas of company operations in GA, IL, MA, MN, NV, NY, PA, TX, and WA, with emphasis on CA, and in Argentina, Canada, England, India, Ireland, Mexico, and the Philippines.

1462
Ford & Harrison LLP

271 17th St., N.W., Ste. 1900
Atlanta, GA 30363-6202 (404) 888-3800

Company URL: http://www.fordharrison.com/about.aspx?Show=3114
Establishment information: Established in 1978.
Company type: Private company
Business activities: Operates law firm.
Business type (SIC): Legal services
Corporate officer: C. Lash Harrison, Firm Managing Partner
Offices: Birmingham, AL; Phoenix, AZ; Los Angeles, San Francisco, CA; Denver, CO; Washington, DC; Jacksonville, Miami, Orlando, Tampa, FL; Atlanta, GA; Chicago, IL; Minneapolis, MN; New York, NY; Asheville, NC; Akron, OH; Spartanburg, SC; Memphis, TN; Dallas, TX
International operations: Australia
Giving statement: Giving through the Ford & Harrison LLP Pro Bono Program.

Ford & Harrison LLP Pro Bono Program

271 17th St., N.W., Ste. 1900
Atlanta, GA 30363-6202 (404) 888-3824
E-mail: mparker@fordharrison.com; URL: http://www.fordharrison.com/about.aspx?Show=3114

Contact: Monica Parker, Mgr. of Professional Devel.
Fields of interest: Legal services.
Type of support: Pro bono services - legal.
Geographic limitations: Giving primarily in areas of company operations in Birmingham, AL, Phoenix, AZ, Los Angeles, and San Francisco, CA, Denver, CO, Washington, DC, Jacksonville, Melbourne, Miami, Orlando, and Tampa, FL, Atlanta, GA, Chicago, IL, Minneapolis, MN, Asheville, NC, New York, NY, Akron, OH, Spartanburg, SC, Memphis, TN, and Dallas, TX.
Application information: The Pro Bono Coordinator manages the pro-bono program.

1463
The Ford Meter Box Company, Inc.

775 Manchester Ave.
P.O. Box 443
Wabash, IN 46992-0443 (260) 563-3171

Company URL: http://www.fordmeterbox.com
Establishment information: Established in 1898.
Company type: Private company
Business activities: Manufactures brass water works valves and fittings, water meter setting equipment, water meter testing equipment, and pipeline maintenance and restraint products.
Business type (SIC): Metal products/fabricated; machinery/general industry; laboratory apparatus
Financial profile for 2010: Number of employees, 550
Corporate officers: Hendry A. Lender, Chair.; Steven R. Ford, Pres.; John Philippsen, C.F.O.; Carl Doran, Sr. V.P., Sales
Board of director: Hendry A. Lender, Chair.
Giving statement: Giving through the Ford Meter Box Foundation, Inc.

Ford Meter Box Foundation, Inc.

775 Manchester Ave.
P.O. Box 443
Wabash, IN 46992-0443

Establishment information: Established in 1988 in IN.
Donor: The Ford Meter Box Co., Inc.
Contact: Marta D. Gidley, Secy.
Financial data (yr. ended 12/31/11): Assets, $1,251,702 (M); gifts received, $250,000; expenditures, $436,819; qualifying distributions, $436,725; giving activities include $436,725 for grants.
Purpose and activities: The foundation supports organizations involved with arts and culture, education, health, youth development, children and youth, family services, residential care, and community development.
Fields of interest: Museums (history); Arts; Higher education; Education; Health care; Youth development, business; Youth development; Children/youth, services; Family services; Residential/custodial care; Community/economic development.
Type of support: Annual campaigns; Building/renovation; Capital campaigns; Endowments; General/operating support.
Geographic limitations: Giving primarily in Wabash County, IN.
Publications: Application guidelines.
Application information: Applications accepted. Application form not required.
Initial approach: Proposal
Copies of proposal: 1
Deadline(s): None
Officers and Directors:* Thomas G. Vanosdol*, Chair.; Daniel H. Ford*, Vice-Chair.; Marta D. Gidley*, Secy.; Mark S. Ford*, Treas.
EIN: 351253080
Selected grants: The following grants are a representative sample of this grantmaker's funding activity:
$100,000 to Wabash County Historical Museum, Wabash, IN, 2010. For general fund.
$40,000 to United Fund, Wabash County, Wabash, IN, 2010. For annual fund drive.
$31,000 to Independent Colleges of Indiana, Indianapolis, IN, 2010. For general fund.
$1,100 to Wabash Valley Music Association, Wabash, IN, 2010.
$1,000 to North Manchester Historical Society, North Manchester, IN, 2010. For general fund.
$1,000 to Wabash Area Community Theater, Wabash, IN, 2010.
$1,000 to Wabash County Arts Council, Wabash, IN, 2010. For general fund.
$1,000 to Wabash Valley Dance Theater, Wabash, IN, 2010.

1464
Ford Motor Company

1 American Rd., Ste. 1026
Dearborn, MI 48126-2798 (313) 322-3000

Company URL: http://www.ford.com
Establishment information: Established in 1903.
Company type: Public company

Company ticker symbol and exchange: F/NYSE
International Securities Identification Number: US3453708600
Business activities: Manufactures automobiles and trucks; provides consumer loans; rents vehicles and equipment.
Business type (SIC): Motor vehicles and equipment; credit institutions/personal; motor vehicle rentals and leasing
Financial profile for 2012: Number of employees, 171,000; assets, $190,554,000,000; sales volume, $134,252,000,000; pre-tax net income, $7,720,000,000; expenses, $127,975,000,000; liabilities, $174,607,000,000
Fortune 1000 ranking: 2012—10th in revenues, 34th in profits, and 32nd in assets
Forbes 2000 ranking: 2012—27th in sales, 96th in profits, and 143rd in assets
Corporate officers: William Clay Ford, Jr., Chair.; Alan R. Mullaly, Pres. and C.E.O.; Mark Fields, C.O.O.; Robert L. Shanks, Exec. V.P. and C.F.O.; Nicholas J. Smither, Group V.P. and C.I.O.; David G. Leitch, Group V.P. and Genl. Counsel; Felicia J. Fields, Group V.P., Human Resources; Neil M. Schloss, V.P. and Treas.; Stuart Rowley, V.P. and Cont.; Raymond F. Day, V.P., Comms.
Board of directors: William Clay Ford, Jr., Chair.; Stephen G. Butler; Kimberly A. Casiano; Anthony F. Earley, Jr.; Edsel B. Ford II; Richard A. Gephardt; James H. Hance, Jr.; William W. Helman IV; Irvine O. Hockaday, Jr.; Jon M. Huntsman, Jr.; Richard A. Manoogian; Ellen R. Marram; Alan Mulally; Homer A. Neal; Gerald L. Shaheen; John L. Thornton
Subsidiaries: Ford Motor Credit Company, Dearborn, MI; USL Capital, San Francisco, CA; Volvo Cars of North America, LLC, Rockleigh, NJ
International operations: Bermuda; Canada; Czech Republic; India; Netherlands; Portugal; Russia; South Africa; Spain; Switzerland; Turkey; Venezuela
Giving statement: Giving through the Ford Motor Company Contributions Program, the El Paso County Salute to Education Inc, the Ford Motor Company Fund, and the UAW-Ford National Programs.
Company EIN: 380549190

Ford Motor Company Contributions Program

P.O. Box 1899
Dearborn, MI 48121-1899 (888) 313-0102
URL: http://www.ford.com/our-values/ford-fund-community-service

Purpose and activities: As a complement to its foundation, Ford also makes charitable contributions to nonprofit organizations directly. Support is given on a national and international basis in areas of company operations.
Fields of interest: Education; Breast cancer research; Diabetes research; Agriculture; Disasters, preparedness/services; Safety, automotive safety; Youth development; United Ways and Federated Giving Programs Physically disabled; Military/veterans.
Type of support: Employee volunteer services; General/operating support; In-kind gifts; Sponsorships.
Geographic limitations: Giving on a national and international basis in areas of company operations.
Publications: Corporate giving report.
Application information:
Number of staff: 9 full-time professional; 7 full-time support.

El Paso County Salute to Education Inc

124 W. Castellano
El Paso, TX 79912-7444 (915) 309-6444
Application address: 1808 Arnold Palmer, El Paso, TX 79935

Establishment information: Established in 1998 in TX.
Donors: Ford Motor Credit Co.; Ford Motor Co.; Casa Ford, Inc.; Shamaley Ford, L.P.; Mesa Ford, L.P.
Contact: Christina Sandavol
Financial data (yr. ended 12/31/10): Assets, $15,954 (M); expenditures, $5,772; qualifying distributions, $0.
Purpose and activities: The foundation awards college scholarships to graduating high school seniors located in El Paso and Hudspeth counties, Texas.
Type of support: Scholarships—to individuals.
Geographic limitations: Giving limited to El Paso and Hudspeth counties, TX.
Application information: Applications accepted. Application form required.
Initial approach: Proposal
Deadline(s): 1st quarter of calendar year
Officers: Clay Lowenfield, Chair. and Pres.; Maurine Cox, Secy.-Treas.
Director: Jimmy Dick IV.
EIN: 742871171

Ford Motor Company Fund

1 American Rd.
P.O. Box 1899
Dearborn, MI 48126-2798 (888) 313-0102
FAX: (313) 594-7001; E-mail: fordfund@ford.com; Contact for Ford Driving Dreams through Education: David Perez, Devel. Dir., LULAC, tel.: (202) 833-6130, ext. 12, e-mail: DPerez@LULAC.org; E-mail for Belt It Out Contest: FordDSFL@ford.com; URL: http://corporate.ford.com/about-ford/community

Establishment information: Incorporated in 1949 in MI.
Donors: Ford Motor Co.; Ford Motor Credit Co.
Financial data (yr. ended 12/31/11): Assets, $64,531,767 (M); gifts received, $35,052,250; expenditures, $20,983,492; qualifying distributions, $20,955,096; giving activities include $19,480,363 for 391 grants (high: $2,666,121; low: $1,000).
Purpose and activities: The fund supports programs designed to promote innovation and education; community development and American heritage and diversity; and auto-related safety education.
Fields of interest: Museums; Performing arts; Performing arts, music; Performing arts, orchestras; Historical activities; Arts; Elementary/secondary education; Charter schools; Higher education; Engineering school/education; Scholarships/financial aid; Education, drop-out prevention; Education; Environment; Food services; Food banks; Safety, automotive safety; Civil/human rights, equal rights; Community/economic development; United Ways and Federated Giving Programs Minorities; African Americans/Blacks; Hispanics/Latinos.
Programs:

Alliance for Women in Media Scholarship Competition: The fund, in partnership with the Alliance for Women in Media, invites female undergraduates to submit a creative and thought-provoking concept paper and a three-to-five minute video celebrating inspiring women from American history. Selected applicants receive $2,500. The program is administered by the Alliance for Women in Media.

Driving Skills for Life: The fund, in partnership with the Governors Highway Safety Association, promotes teen safe driving though a safe-driving curriculum aimed at teens, parents, and the drivers education community. The program targets four skill areas: hazard recognition, vehicle handling, space management, and speed management; and educates teens through educational materials, courses and workshops, public service announcements, exhibits, ride-and-drive events, customized in-school events, and an interactive website.

Ford Blue Oval Scholars Program: The fund awards scholarships to high school seniors through partnerships with the Hispanic College Fund, the American Indian College Fund, the United Negro College Fund, the Disabled American Veterans Jesse Brown Memorial Youth Scholarship Program, the Society for Automotive Engineers Education Foundation, and other community organizations. The program is administered by participating organizations.

Ford College Community Challenge (Ford C3): The fund invites partner universities and colleges to develop and utilize school resources to address an urgent community need related to sustainability. Projects must have significant student input, involvement, and leadership. Five winners are awarded $50,000 to build sustainable communities.

Ford Driving Dreams through Education: The fund, in partnership with the League of United Latin American Citizens (LULAC), awards grants of up to $20,000 to 10 LULAC councils to address the high school dropout rate among Latino students. Special emphasis is directed toward programs designed to build student support systems through mentorship, after school activities, and academic re-enforcement programs and tutoring; parental engagement programs; programs aimed at older youths; and leadership development programs. The program is administered by the LULAC National Office.

Ford Freedom Award: The fund, in partnership with the Charles H. Wright Museum of African-American History, honors posthumously an individual whose achievements have promoted positive change for African-Americans and the world through their chosen field. The program also includes the Ford Freedom Award Scholar, which honors a living scholar who is continuing the legacy of improving the world for African-Americans.

Ford Fund/Detroit Free Press Journalism Scholarship: The fund, in partnership with Detroit Free Press, annually awards one $24,000 scholarship to one Detroit high school senior to help the student pursue his/her aspirations in journalism. The program is administered by the Detroit Free Press.

Ford Next Generation Learning (Ford NGL): Through Ford NGL, the fund supports a network of communities committed to transforming high school into career academies where students learn their academics. The program is designed to increase graduation and college-going rates; and prepare students for high-skilled careers in their careers. Visit URL http://fordpas.org/ for more information.

Heart Behind the Oval Scholarship Contest: The fund awards scholarships to high school and college students who describe via essay what they are doing to make a positive impact in their communities through volunteering, mentoring, and working. Ten students are selected as semi-finalists and are awarded Flip Cams to produce short videos showing the positive impact of their projects in the communities. Videos are posted on the Ford Scholars website and the public, along with a judging panel, select three winners to receive scholarships of up to $5,000.

Smithsonian Latino Center Young Ambassadors Program: The fund sponsors 24 graduating high school Latino seniors who are gifted in the arts, sciences, or the humanities with a leadership program at the Smithsonian Institution. The training program includes a week-long trip to Washington, DC, seminars, a four-week internship, a stipend, and a $2,000 scholarship for higher education. The program is administered by the Smithsonian.

Type of support: Annual campaigns; Building/renovation; Capital campaigns; Continuing support; Curriculum development; Emergency funds; Employee matching gifts; Employee volunteer services; Employee-related scholarships; Equipment; Grants to individuals; Internship funds; Program development; Publication; Scholarship funds; Sponsorships.

Geographic limitations: Giving primarily in areas of company operations, with emphasis on southeastern MI; giving also in Phoenix, AZ, San Diego, CA, Miami, FL, Chicago, IL, Detroit, MI, Nashville, TN, and San Antonio, TX.

Support limitations: No support for animal-rights, lobbying, political, or fraternal organizations, labor groups, private K-12 schools, profit-making enterprises, religious organizations not of direct benefit to the entire community, species-specific organizations, or sports teams. No grants to individuals (except for scholarships), or for advocacy-directed programs, beauty or talent contests, general operating support, debt reduction, endowments, or sponsorships related to fundraising activities; no loans for small businesses or program-related investments; no vehicle donations.

Publications: Annual report; Application guidelines; Corporate giving report; Newsletter.

Application information: Applications accepted. Application form required. Applicants should submit the following:

1) detailed description of project and amount of funding requested
2) copy of current year's organizational budget and/or project budget

Initial approach: Complete online application
Board meeting date(s): Apr. and Oct.
Deadline(s): None; visit website for Community Challenge grants and scholarship programs
Final notification: Within 8 weeks

Officers and Trustees:* James G. Vella*, Chair. and Pres.; Neil M. Schloss, V.P. and Secy.; Michael Banister; Steve Biegun; Susan M. Cischke; Alfred B. Ford; Sheila Ford Hamp; David G. Leitch; Martin J. Mulloy; Ziad S. Ojakli.

Number of staff: 11 full-time professional; 10 full-time support.

EIN: 381459376

Selected grants: The following grants are a representative sample of this grantmaker's funding activity:

$1,862,461 to Governors Highway Safety Association, Washington, DC, 2010. For Driving Skills for Life Program.
$1,250,000 to United Way for Southeastern Michigan, Detroit, MI, 2010. For Annual Campaign Supporting Agenda for Change.
$1,000,000 to Henry Ford Learning Institute, Dearborn, MI, 2010. For Henry Ford Learning Institute.
$720,000 to Wayne State University, College of Engineering, Detroit, MI, 2010. For capital campaign.
$600,000 to Michigan Opera Theater, Detroit, MI, 2010. For Crowning Achievement Campaign.
$325,000 to Focus: HOPE, Detroit, MI, 2010. For Hope Village Initiative.
$35,000 to National Association of Hispanic Journalists, Washington, DC, 2010. For NAHJ/NAHP Ford Blue Oval Journalism Internship.
$30,000 to Detroit Lions Charities, Allen Park, MI, 2010. For Detroit Lions Charities.
$15,000 to Silicon Valley Community Foundation, Mountain View, CA, 2010. For San Bruno Fire Fund.
$10,000 to Boys and Girls Clubs of Southeastern Michigan, Farmington Hills, MI, 2010. For Power Hour.

UAW-Ford National Programs

151 West Jefferson Ave.
P.O. Box 33009
Detroit, MI 48232-5009 (313) 392-7100
URL: http://www.uawford.com

Establishment information: Established in 1982 in MI.

Contact: Jimmy Settles, Co.-Chair. and Co.-Pres.

Financial data (yr. ended 12/31/11): Revenue, $21,340,226; assets, $29,344,949 (M); gifts received, $21,723,362; expenditures, $25,457,434; program services expenses, $18,770,424; giving activities include $1,167,077 for grants to individuals.

Purpose and activities: The organization provides career, health and safety, quality, and employee involvement training to represented Ford Motor Company hourly employees who are represented by the United Auto Workers (UAW).

Fields of interest: Employment, training; Employment.

Type of support: Scholarships—to individuals.

Geographic limitations: Giving on a national basis.

Publications: Newsletter.

Application information: Applications not accepted. Unsolicited requests for funds will not considered or acknowledged.

Officers: Jimmy Settles*, Co-Chair. and Co-Pres.; Marty Mulloy*, Co-Chair. and Co-Pres.; Jack Halverson*, Treas.

Trustees: James Brown; Bill Dirksen; Wendy Fields-Jacobs; Darryl Nolen.

EIN: 382416006

1465
Foreman Architects Engineers, Inc.

525 W. New Castle St.
P.O. Box 189
Zelienople, PA 16063-1048 (724) 452-9690

Company URL: http://www.foremangroup.com
Establishment information: Established in 1956.
Company type: Private company
Business activities: Provides architectural and engineering services; provides construction management services.
Business type (SIC): Engineering, architectural, and surveying services; management and public relations services
Financial profile for 2010: Number of employees, 75
Corporate officers: Phillip G. Foreman, Pres. and C.E.O.; Michael J. Arnold, V.P., Opers.
Giving statement: Giving through the Foreman Foundation.

The Foreman Foundation

525 W. New Castle St.
P.O. Box 189
Zelienople, PA 16063-0189 (724) 452-9690
FAX: (724) 452-5054;
E-mail: ffinfo@foremangroup.com; URL: http://www.foremangroup.com/FF/home.asp

Establishment information: Established in 1995 in PA.

Contact: Julianne Rogozewicz, Exec. Dir.

Financial data (yr. ended 12/31/11): Revenue, $45,614; assets, $32,391 (M); gifts received, $68,307; expenditures, $38,738; giving activities include $26,000 for grants.

Purpose and activities: The foundation seeks to raise funds for medical research that will lead to a cure for melanoma cancer, while heightening awareness.

Fields of interest: Cancer; Cancer research.

Program:

Foreman Foundation Scholarship Fund: Awards $1,000 for four years to honor one Upper St. Claire High School senior student/athlete who is pursuing athletics at the collegiate level to perpetuate the memory of John Bruno, Jr.

Type of support: Research; Scholarships—to individuals.

Application information: Applications accepted. Application form required.

Initial approach: Request application form

Officers and Directors:* Phillip G. Foreman*, Chair.; David A. DeGol, Pres.; Albert D. Emerick, V.P.; Julianne Rogozewicz, Exec. Dir.; Michael J. Arnold; Joseph C. Herrle; William M. Gallagher; Drew McCausland; Anthony J. Mauriello; Annette M. van Eeden.

EIN: 541801519

1466
Foremost Farms USA

E. 10889A Penny Ln.
P.O. Box 111
Baraboo, WI 53913-9419 (608) 355-8700

Company URL: http://www.foremostfarms.com
Establishment information: Established in 1995.
Company type: Cooperative
Business activities: Sells dairy products wholesale.
Business type (SIC): Groceries—wholesale
Corporate officers: David Scheevel, Chair.; Bob Topel, 1st Vice-Chair.; Frank Trierweiler, 2nd Vice-Chair.; David E. Fuhrmann, Pres.; Michael Doyle, V.P., Finance, and C.F.O.; Douglas Wilke, V.P., Mktg.; Michael McDonald, V.P., Human Resources and Comms.
Board of directors: David Scheevel, Chair.; Bob Topel, 1st Vice-Chair.; Frank Trierweiler, 2nd Vice-Chair.; Rick Burkhamer; Bob Clason; Tom Crosby; James Dague; Doug Danielson; Dale Drendel; Dale Hackman; Dave Kyle; James Lepich; Troy Madland; Steven Menting; Randy Mouw; Jeff Notstad; Jon Pesko; Steve Phares; Tom Troxel; Kevin Udelhoven; Jon Wagner
Division: Foremost Ingredient Group, Baraboo, WI
Giving statement: Giving through the Foremost Farms USA Corporate Giving Program.

Foremost Farms USA Corporate Giving Program

E10889 Penny Ln.
Baraboo, WI 53913-8115 (608) 355-8700
E-mail: laura.mihm@foremostfarms.com; E-mail for event brochures:

Communications@ForemostFarms.com;
URL: http://www.foremostfarms.com/About-Us/Responsibility.php

Purpose and activities: Foremost Farms makes charitable contributions to nonprofit organizations involved with food and agriculture, community development, and to hospitals, with an emphasis on dairy-related issues. Support is given primarily in Illinois, Indiana, Iowa, Minnesota, and Wisconsin.
Fields of interest: Elementary/secondary education; Medical care, in-patient care; Hospitals (general); Agriculture/food; Disasters, fire prevention/control; Recreation, fairs/festivals; Community/economic development.
Type of support: Donated products; General/operating support; In-kind gifts.
Geographic limitations: Giving primarily in areas of company operations.
Publications: Application guidelines.
Application information: Applications accepted. Applicants who do not receive a reply one week after submitting a proposal should submit their request again. Application form required. Applicants should submit the following:
1) name, address and phone number of organization
2) contact person
3) plans for acknowledgement
Proposals should include event date and description, expected attendance, and the quantity of cash, cheese, or butter requested.
Initial approach: Complete online application form

1467
Forest City Enterprises, Inc.

50 Public Sq., Ste. 1100
Cleveland, OH 44113 (216) 621-6060

Company URL: http://www.fceinc.com
Establishment information: Established in 1920.
Company type: Public company
Company ticker symbol and exchange: FCE.A/NYSE
Business activities: Engages in the ownership, development, management and acquisition of commercial and residential real estate.
Business type (SIC): Real estate operators and lessors; real estate subdividers and developers
Financial profile for 2012: Number of employees, 2,914; assets, $10,612,432,000; sales volume, $1,134,687,000; expenses, $1,214,446,000; liabilities, $8,634,735,000
Corporate officers: Charles A. Ratner, Chair.; David J. LaRue, Pres. and C.E.O.; Robert G. O'Brien, Exec. V.P. and C.F.O.; Geralyn M. Presti, Exec. V.P., Genl. Counsel, and Secy.; Andrew J. Passen, Exec. V.P., Human Resources; Charles D. Obert, Sr. V.P., C.A.O., and Cont.; Linda M. Kane, Sr. V.P. and Treas.; Jeffrey B. Linton, Sr. V.P., Corp. Comms.
Board of directors: Charles A. Ratner, Chair.; Arthur F. Anton; Kenneth J. Bacon; Scott S. Cowen; Michael P. Esposito, Jr.; Deborah L. Harmon; David J. LaRue; Brian J. Ratner; Bruce C. Ratner; Ronald A. Ratner; Deborah Ratner Salzberg; Stan Ross; Louis Stokes
Giving statement: Giving through the Forest City Enterprises, Inc. Charitable Giving Program.
Company EIN: 340863886

Forest City Enterprises, Inc. Charitable Giving Program

50 Public Sq., Ste. 1405
Cleveland, OH 44113-2202 (216) 621-6060
E-mail: lindakane@forestcity.net; URL: http://www.forestcity.net/company/core_values/Pages/default.aspx

Contact: Linda Kane, Sr. V.P. and Treas.
Purpose and activities: Forest City Enterprises supports nonprofit organizations involved with equality of education, workforce training, economic development, health & welfare, and arts & culture. Special emphasis is directed toward organizations that demonstrate good practices in the areas of diversity, inclusion, and sustainability, while managing overhead effectively to ensure the maximum benefit to those they serve. Support is limited to areas of company operations in headquarters city of Cleveland and core markets of Los Angeles and San Francisco, California, Denver, Colorado, Washington, D.C., Boston, Massachusetts, New York, New York, and Dallas, Texas.
Fields of interest: Museums (art); Performing arts, theater; Performing arts, orchestras; Arts; Elementary/secondary education; Education; Health care, clinics/centers; Mental health/crisis services; Children/youth, services; Human services; Urban/community development; Community/economic development; United Ways and Federated Giving Programs.
Type of support: Annual campaigns; Building/renovation; Capital campaigns; General/operating support; Program development.
Geographic limitations: Giving limited to areas of company operations in headquarters city of Cleveland, OH, and core markets of Los Angeles and San Francisco, CA, Denver, CO, Washington, D.C., Boston, MA, New York, NY, and Dallas, TX.
Support limitations: No grants to individuals.
Application information: Applications accepted.
Initial approach: Letter or email
Copies of proposal: 1
Committee meeting date(s): Quarterly
Deadline(s): None
Final notification: 3 to 6 months
Officers: Charles A. Ratner, Chair.; David J. LaRue, Pres. and C.E.O.; Linda Kane, Sr. V.P. and Treas.

1468
Forest Pharmaceuticals, Inc.

13600 Shoreline Dr.
St. Louis, MO 63045 (314) 493-7000

Company URL: http://www.forestpharm.com/
Establishment information: Established in 1984.
Company type: Subsidiary of a public company
Business activities: Develops, manufactures, and distributes prescription and over-the-counter pharmaceutical products.
Business type (SIC): Drugs
Corporate officers: Howard Solomon, Chair. and C.E.O.; Terry J. Howell, Sr. V.P., Opers.; C. Douglas Glidewell, Sr. V.P., Finance; Gerard J. Azzari, Sr. V.P., Sales
Board of director: Howard Solomon, Chair.
Giving statement: Giving through the Forest Pharmaceuticals, Inc. Patient Assistance Program.

Forest Pharmaceuticals, Inc. Patient Assistance Program

c/o Forest Pharmaceuticals, Inc.
13645 Shoreline Dr.
Earth City, MO 63045-1241 (800) 851-0758
URL: http://www.forestpharm.com/pap/

Purpose and activities: The Forest Pharmaceuticals, Inc. Patient Assistance Program provides specified medications or devices to patients who are unable to afford them.
Fields of interest: Pharmacy/prescriptions; Health care, patient services; Health care Economically disadvantaged.
Type of support: Donated products; In-kind gifts.
Publications: Application guidelines.
Application information: Applications accepted. Qualified applicants receive up to a three-month supply of the Forest product they need, mailed to their licensed practitioner's office. If the applicant is a Medicare Part D enrollee, he or she must also have applied for and been denied the Low-Income Subsidy from the Social Security Administration. Applicants must meet income guidelines to qualify. Application form required. Applicants should submit the following:
1) name, address and phone number of organization
2) contact person
Applications must include a photocopy of an LIS denial letter, a valid prescription, household income, e-mail address, number of people in household, and Medicare and Medicaid enrollment information.
Initial approach: Download application form, complete form with licensed subscriber, and mail to headquarters.
Final notification: 4 weeks

1469
Forever 21, Inc.

2001 S. Alameda St.
Los Angeles, CA 90058 (213) 741-5100
FAX: (213) 741-5161

Company URL: http://www.forever21.com/
Establishment information: Established in 1984.
Company type: Private company
Business activities: Operates retail clothing stores.
Business type (SIC): Women's apparel stores
Financial profile for 2011: Number of employees, 27,228; assets, $1,400,000,000; sales volume, $2,600,000,000
Corporate officers: Do Won Chang, Pres. and C.E.O.; Lawrence Meyer, Sr. V.P. and Co-C.F.O.; Elizabeth Jain, Cont. and Co-C.F.O.
Giving statement: Giving through the Forever 21, Inc. Contributions Program.

Forever 21, Inc. Contributions Program

2001 S. Alameda St.
Los Angeles, CA 90058-1015 (213) 741-5100
URL: http://www.forever21.com

1470
Formosa Plastics Corporation, U.S.A.

9 Peach Tree Hill Rd.
Livingston, NJ 07039-5702 (973) 992-2090

Company URL: http://www.fpcusa.com/
Establishment information: Established in 1980.
Company type: Subsidiary of a foreign company
Business activities: Manufactures petrochemicals and plastic resins.
Business type (SIC): Plastics and synthetics
Corporate officers: Chih-Tsun Lee, Pres.; D. Lin, C.F.O.; H. Lie, Cont.; Steve Rice, Corp. Comms.
Plants: Delaware City, DE; Baton Rouge, LA; Point Comfort, TX
Giving statement: Giving through the Formosa Plastics Corporation, Texas—Calhoun High School Scholarship Foundation, the Formosa Plastics

Environmental Trust, the Formosa Plastics Memorial Medical Trust, and the Formosa Plastics Religious Trust.

Formosa Plastics Corporation, Texas —Calhoun High School Scholarship Foundation

525 N. Commerce St.
Port Lavaca, TX 77979-3034 (361) 552-9728

Establishment information: Established in 1992 in TX.
Donor: Formosa Plastics Corp., Texas.
Financial data (yr. ended 12/31/11): Assets, $1,001,673 (M); expenditures, $45,159; qualifying distributions, $44,000; giving activities include $44,000 for grants.
Purpose and activities: The foundation awards college scholarships to graduates of Calhoun High School in Texas.
Fields of interest: Higher education.
Type of support: Scholarships—to individuals.
Geographic limitations: Giving limited to Calhoun County, TX.
Application information: Applications accepted. Application form required.
Initial approach: Contact foundation for application form
Deadline(s): Varies
Officers: Richard Bothe, Pres.; Randy Smith, V.P.; Dee Harkey, Secy.-Treas.
Directors: Annette Alonzo; Debbie Boyd; Jesse Briseno; Pat Herren; Steven Marwitz; Brandon Stiewig; Deborah Swope; Brenda Wilson.
EIN: 742634043

Formosa Plastics Environmental Trust

c/o First National Bank
P.O. Drawer 7
Port Lavaca, TX 77979-0007 (361) 552-6726

Establishment information: Established around 1992.
Donor: Formosa Plastics Corp., Texas.
Contact: Dee Harkey
Financial data (yr. ended 12/31/11): Assets, $993,691 (M); expenditures, $59,425; qualifying distributions, $54,000; giving activities include $54,000 for grants.
Purpose and activities: The fund supports organizations involved with the environment. Support is limited to Calhoun County, Texas.
Fields of interest: Recreation.
Type of support: Equipment; Program development; Research.
Geographic limitations: Giving limited to Calhoun County, TX.
Application information: Applications accepted. Application form required. Applicants should submit the following:
1) results expected from proposed grant
2) copy of IRS Determination Letter
3) detailed description of project and amount of funding requested
4) copy of current year's organizational budget and/ or project budget
Initial approach: Letter
Deadline(s): Sept. 30
Trustees: William H. Bauer, Jr.; Jack Wu.
EIN: 746388418

Formosa Plastics Religious Trust

c/o First National Bank
P.O. Drawer 7
Port Lavaca, TX 77979 (361) 552-6726

Establishment information: Established in 1995 in TX.
Donor: Formosa Plastics Corp., Texas.
Financial data (yr. ended 12/31/11): Assets, $987,544 (M); expenditures, $59,416; qualifying distributions, $54,000; giving activities include $54,000 for grants.
Purpose and activities: The trust supports organizations involved with human services and Christianity.
Fields of interest: Human services; Religion.
Type of support: Equipment; Program development.
Geographic limitations: Giving limited to Calhoun, Jackson, and Victoria counties, TX.
Support limitations: No grants to individuals.
Application information: Applications accepted. Application form required. Applicants should submit the following:
1) results expected from proposed grant
2) copy of IRS Determination Letter
3) detailed description of project and amount of funding requested
4) copy of current year's organizational budget and/ or project budget
Initial approach: Letter
Deadline(s): Sept. 30
Trustees: William H. Bauer, Jr.; Jack Wu.
EIN: 746432974

1471
Fort Myer Construction Corporation

2237 33rd St. N.E.
Washington, DC 20018 (202) 636-9535
FAX: (202) 526-8572

Company URL: http://fortmyer.com
Establishment information: Established in 1972.
Company type: Private company
Business activities: Provides general contract street, road, bridge, and underground utility construction services.
Business type (SIC): Construction/highway and street (except elevated); construction/ miscellaneous heavy
Corporate officers: Jose Rodriguez, Pres.; Christopher Kerns, V.P. and Genl. Counsel; Harry New, Cont.
Giving statement: Giving through the Fort Myer Construction Corporation Charitable Foundation, Inc.

The Fort Myer Construction Corporation Charitable Foundation, Inc.

2237 33rd St. N.E.
Washington, DC 20018-1594

Establishment information: Established in 2002 in DC.
Donor: Fort Myer Construction Corporation.
Financial data (yr. ended 12/31/11): Assets, $184 (M); gifts received, $25,033; expenditures, $25,783; qualifying distributions, $25,033; giving activities include $25,033 for grants.
Purpose and activities: The foundation supports the FBI Citizens Academy Alumni Association in Washington, DC.
Fields of interest: Education.
Type of support: General/operating support.
Geographic limitations: Giving primarily in Washington, DC.
Application information: Applications not accepted. Unsolicited requests for funds not accepted.
Directors: Ralph Kew-Prince; Jose Rodriguez; Lewis F. Shrensky.
EIN: 311784737

1472
Fort Worth Star-Telegram

400 W. 7th St.
Fort Worth, TX 76102 (817) 390-7400

Company URL: http://www.star-telegram.com/
Establishment information: Established in 1849.
Company type: Subsidiary of a private company
Ultimate parent company: The Walt Disney Company
Business activities: Publishes newspapers.
Business type (SIC): Newspaper publishing and/or printing
Corporate officers: Wesley R. Turner, Co-Pres.; Gary Wortel, Co-Pres.; Roger Provost, V.P. and C.F.O.; Chet Wakefield, Sr. V.P., Opers.; Jerry Scott, V.P., Mktg.
Giving statement: Giving through the Amon G. Carter Star-Telegram Employees Fund.

Amon G. Carter Star-Telegram Employees Fund

P.O. Box 17480
Fort Worth, TX 76102-0480 (817) 332-3535

Establishment information: Established in 1945 in TX.
Donors: Fort Worth Star-Telegram; Amon G. Carter†; KXAS-TV; WBAP Radio.
Contact: Nenetta Carter Tatum, Pres.
Financial data (yr. ended 04/30/11): Assets, $27,471,166 (M); expenditures, $1,215,228; qualifying distributions, $1,059,739; giving activities include $1,059,739 for grants.
Purpose and activities: The foundation supports organizations involved with arts and culture, education, health, breast cancer, housing development, and human services and awards pension, medical, and hardship assistance to employees and scholarships to children of employees.
Fields of interest: Museums; Performing arts; Performing arts, opera; Secondary school/ education; Higher education; Education; Health care, blood supply; Health care; Breast cancer; Housing/shelter, development; Camp Fire; YM/ YWCAs & YM/YWHAs; Children, services; Homeless, human services; Human services.
Type of support: Employee-related scholarships; General/operating support; Grants to individuals.
Geographic limitations: Giving primarily in Arlington, Bedford, Burleson, Cleburne, and Fort Worth, TX.
Support limitations: No grants to individuals (except for employee-related scholarships and employee assistance grants).
Application information: Applications accepted. Application form not required.
Initial approach: Proposal
Copies of proposal: 1
Board meeting date(s): Apr. and June
Deadline(s): None
Officers: Nenetta Carter Tatum, Pres.; Mark L. Johnson, V.P.; John H. Robinson, Secy.-Treas.
Number of staff: 1 part-time professional; 1 part-time support.
EIN: 756014850
Selected grants: The following grants are a representative sample of this grantmaker's funding activity:
$55,000 to All Saints Health Foundation, Fort Worth, TX, 2011.

$50,000 to ACH Child and Family Services, Fort Worth, TX, 2011.
$35,500 to Texas Christian University, Fort Worth, TX, 2011.
$20,000 to Amon Carter Museum of Western Art, Fort Worth, TX, 2011.
$10,000 to Arlington Life Shelter, Arlington, TX, 2011.
$10,000 to Boys and Girls Clubs of America, Dallas, TX, 2011.
$10,000 to Prevent Blindness Texas, Fort Worth, TX, 2011.
$5,000 to CASA of Tarrant County, Fort Worth, TX, 2011.
$5,000 to Mayfest, Fort Worth, TX, 2011.
$5,000 to Meals on Wheels of Tarrant County, Fort Worth, TX, 2011.

1473
Fortis Benefits Insurance Company

(also known as Assurant Employee Benefits)
2323 Grand Blvd.
Kansas City, MO 64108-2670
(816) 474-2345

Company URL: http://www.assurantemployeebenefits.com/
Establishment information: Established in 1977.
Company type: Subsidiary of a public company
Ultimate parent company: Assurant, Inc.
Business activities: Sells dental, disability, and life insurance.
Business type (SIC): Insurance/accident and health; insurance/life
Corporate officer: John S. Roberts, Pres. and C.E.O.
Subsidiary: United Family Life Insurance Company, Atlanta, GA
Giving statement: Giving through the Assurant Employee Benefits Corporate Giving Program.

Assurant Employee Benefits Corporate Giving Program

(formerly Fortis Benefits Insurance Company Contributions Program)
c/o Employee Comm.
2323 Grand Blvd.
Kansas City, MO 64108-2670
E-mail: KansasCityCommunityRelations@assurant.com; URL: http://www.assurantemployeebenefits.com/wps/portal/!ut/p/.cmd/cs/.ce/7_0_A/.s/7_0_D2/_s.7_0_A/7_0_D2
Additional URL: http://www.assurant.com/inc/assurant/community/benefits.html

Purpose and activities: Assurant Employee Benefits makes charitable contributions to nonprofit organizations involved with education, health and human services, and neighborhood preservation. Support is given primarily in areas of company operations.
Fields of interest: Education, services; Education; Environment; Health care; Crime/violence prevention; Recreation; Youth development, adult & child programs; Youth, services; Human services, financial counseling; Developmentally disabled, centers & services; Human services; Civil/human rights, equal rights; Civil rights, race/intergroup relations; Community/economic development.

Programs:

Education: Assurant Employee Benefits supports programs designed to provide alternative education, retraining, and mentoring and tutoring.

Health and Social Welfare: Assurant Employee Benefits supports programs designed to assist disabled or displaced workers, their families, and people with special needs.

Matching Gifts Program: Assurant Employee Benefits matches contributions made by its employees to educational institutions and nonprofit organizations.

Neighborhood Preservation: Assurant Employee Benefits supports programs designed to promote crime prevention; revitalization and environmental projects; neighborhood and youth initiatives; recreational projects; financial education; race relations; and sensitivity to cultural differences.
Type of support: Employee matching gifts; Employee volunteer services; General/operating support; Program development.
Geographic limitations: Giving primarily in areas of company operations, with emphasis on Kansas City, MO, metropolitan areas; giving also to national organizations.
Support limitations: No support for religious organizations not of direct benefit to the entire community, fraternal, membership, or veterans organizations, or political action or advocacy groups. No grants to individuals, or for conferences, research, start-up projects, or capital campaigns; no multi-year or challenge grants.
Publications: Application guidelines; Program policy statement.
Application information: Applications accepted. The Employee Communications Department handles giving. A contributions committee reviews all requests. Application form not required. Applicants should submit the following:
1) timetable for implementation and evaluation of project
2) statement of problem project will address
3) name, address and phone number of organization
4) copy of IRS Determination Letter
5) detailed description of project and amount of funding requested
6) contact person

Initial approach: Proposal to headquarters
Copies of proposal: 1
Committee meeting date(s): Monthly
Deadline(s): None
Final notification: 4 weeks

1474
Fortune Brands Home & Security, Inc.

(formerly Fortune Brands, Inc.)
520 Lake Cook Rd.
Deerfield, IL 60015-5611 (847) 484-4400
FAX: (302) 636-5454

Company URL: http://www.fortunebrands.com
Establishment information: Established in 1904.
Company type: Public company
Company ticker symbol and exchange: FBHS/NYSE
Business activities: Operates home and security products company.
Business type (SIC): Metal products/fabricated
Financial profile for 2012: Number of employees, 16,100; assets, $3,637,900,000; sales volume, $3,873,700,000; pre-tax net income, $154,000,000; expenses, $3,429,400,000; liabilities, $1,492,600,000
Fortune 1000 ranking: 2012—630th in revenues, 705th in profits, and 674th in assets
Corporate officers: David Thomas, Chair.; Christopher Klein, C.E.O.; E. Lee Wyatt, Sr. V.P. and C.F.O.; Lauren Tashma, Sr. V.P., Genl. Counsel, and Secy.; Elizabeth R. Lane, Sr. V.P., Human Resources; Edward Wiertel, Sr. V.P., Finance
Board of directors: David Thomas, Chair.; Richard A. Goldstein; Ann Fritz Hackett; Christopher J. Klein; A.D. David Mackay; John G. Morikis; Ronald V. Waters III; Norman H. Wesley
International operations: Barbados; Canada; China; France; Hong Kong; Mexico
Giving statement: Giving through the Fortune Brands Home & Security, Inc. Contributions Program.
Company EIN: 621411546

Fortune Brands Home & Security, Inc. Contributions Program

(formerly Fortune Brands, Inc. Corporate Giving Program)
520 Lake Cook Rd.
Deerfield, IL 60015-5611 (847) 484-4400
URL: http://www.fbhs.com/corporate-responsibility

Purpose and activities: Fortune Brands makes charitable contributions to nonprofit organizations involved with the environment, medical research, youth development, family services, and on a case by case basis. Support is given primarily in areas of company operations.
Fields of interest: Environment; Substance abuse, services; Medical research; Youth development; Family services; General charitable giving.
Type of support: Employee volunteer services; General/operating support.
Geographic limitations: Giving primarily in areas of company operations.

1475
Foster Pepper PLLC

1111 3rd Ave., Ste. 3400
Seattle, WA 98101-3299 (206) 447-4400

Company URL: http://www.foster.com
Company type: Private company
Business activities: Operates law firm.
Business type (SIC): Legal services
Offices: Seattle, Spokane, WA
Giving statement: Giving through the Foster Pepper PLLC Pro Bono Program.

Foster Pepper PLLC Pro Bono Program

1111 3rd Ave., Ste. 3400
Seattle, WA 98101-3299 (206) 447-5144
E-mail: boisj@foster.com; Additional tel.: (206) 447-4400; URL: http://www.foster.com/probono.aspx?pid=4

Contact: Joanna Plichta Boisen, Pro Bono Counsel
Fields of interest: Legal services.
Type of support: Pro bono services - legal.
Application information: The Pro Bono Committee manages the pro-bono program.

1476
Four Seasons Hotels (U.S.) Inc.

160 E. Pearson St.
Water Tower Pl.
Chicago, IL 60611-2308 (312) 266-1000

Company URL: http://www.fourseasons.com/about_us/
Establishment information: Established in 1960.
Company type: Subsidiary of a foreign company

Business activities: Operates hotel.
Business type (SIC): Hotels and motels
Corporate officers: Isadore Sharp, Chair.; Kathleen Taylor, Pres. and C.E.O; John Davison, Exec V.P. and C.F.O.; Susan Helstab, Exec. V.P., Mktg.; Nick Mutton, Exec. V.P., Human Resources, and Admin.
Board of director: Isadore Sharp, Chair.
Giving statement: Giving through the Four Seasons Hotels (U.S.) Inc. Corporate Giving Program.

Four Seasons Hotels (U.S.) Inc. Corporate Giving Program

160 E. Pearson St.
Chicago, IL 60611-2308 (312) 266-1000

Contact: Gloria Quezada, Asst. Genl. Mgr.
Purpose and activities: Four Seasons Hotels (U.S.) makes charitable contributions of hotel rooms and gift certificates to nonprofit organizations on a case by case basis. Support is given primarily in Illinois.
Fields of interest: General charitable giving.
Type of support: Donated products.
Geographic limitations: Giving primarily in IL, with emphasis on the Chicago area.
Support limitations: No support for political or religious organizations. No grants to individuals.
Application information: Applications accepted. Support is limited to 1 contribution per organization during any given year. Application form not required. Applicants should submit the following:
1) detailed description of project and amount of funding requested
Initial approach: Proposal to headquarters

1477
Four Winds Casino Resort

11111 Wilson Rd.
New Buffalo, MI 49117 (866) 494-6371

Company URL: http://www.fourwindscasino.com
Establishment information: Established in 2009.
Company type: Private company
Business activities: Operates casino resort.
Business type (SIC): Amusement and recreation services/miscellaneous; hotels and motels
Corporate officer: Matt Harkness, Mgr.
Giving statement: Giving through the Pokagon Fund, Inc.

The Pokagon Fund, Inc.

821 E. Buffalo St.
New Buffalo, MI 49117-1522 (269) 469-9322
E-mail: info@pokagonfund.org; E-mail address for applications: grants@pokagonfund.org; URL: http://www.pokagonfund.org/
E-mail address for scholarships: scholarships@pokagonfund.org

Establishment information: Established in 2007 in MI.
Donor: Four Winds Casino Resort.
Contact: Mary L. Dunbar, Exec. Dir.
Financial data (yr. ended 06/30/12): Assets, $10,129,849 (M); gifts received, $2,849,005; expenditures, $3,519,027; qualifying distributions, $3,468,222; giving activities include $3,191,126 for 137 grants (high: $340,000; low: -$18,380).
Purpose and activities: The fund supports programs designed to enhance the lives of residents in the New Buffalo, Michigan, region and the communities where the Pokagon Band of Potawatomi Indians own land. Special emphasis is directed toward arts and culture, education, the environment, health, recreation, and human services.
Fields of interest: Performing arts; Arts; Libraries (public); Education, reading; Education; Environment, recycling; Environment, land resources; Environment; Health care; Recreation, parks/playgrounds; Recreation, fairs/festivals; Recreation; Residential/custodial care, hospices; Human services; Community/economic development Native Americans/American Indians.
Program:
Scholarships: The fund awards college scholarships to graduating high school seniors from River Valley or New Buffalo High Schools. The fund awards $2,500 per year for study at a two-year vocational or technical school (total $5,000), and $2,500 per year for study at a four-year college or university (total $10,000). Scholarships are renewable if the student maintains a 3.0 GPA. Applicants must be residents of the townships of New Buffalo, Chikaming, or Three Oaks, and the cities and villages within those townships.
Type of support: Building/renovation; Conferences/seminars; Consulting services; Continuing support; Curriculum development; Emergency funds; Equipment; Film/video/radio; General/operating support; Land acquisition; Management development/capacity building; Matching/challenge support; Program development; Program-related investments/loans; Research; Scholarship funds; Scholarships—to individuals.
Geographic limitations: Giving in primarily in New Buffalo, MI, region, including the townships of Chikaming, Grand Beach, Michiana, and Three Oaks; some giving also in South Bend, IN, and Dowagia and Hartford MI.
Support limitations: No support for political candidates, political advocacy, or religious organizations not of direct benefit to the entire community. No grants to individuals (except for scholarships), or for endowments.
Publications: Annual report (including application guidelines); Application guidelines; Financial statement; Grants list.
Application information: Applications accepted. The foundation supports municipalities, nonprofit organizations, and charities in areas where the Pokagon Band of Potawatomi Indians are located, and other organizations. An application form is available for each type of organization. Application form required. Applicants should submit the following:
1) timetable for implementation and evaluation of project
2) how project will be sustained once grantmaker support is completed
3) results expected from proposed grant
4) qualifications of key personnel
5) statement of problem project will address
6) copy of most recent annual report/audited financial statement/990
7) listing of board of directors, trustees, officers and other key people and their affiliations
8) detailed description of project and amount of funding requested
9) copy of current year's organizational budget and/or project budget
10) listing of additional sources and amount of support
11) plans for acknowledgement
Scholarship applications should include high school transcripts; a copy of the vocational/technical school or university/college acceptance letter; a copy of a current 1040 tax return for applicant and guardians; letters of recommendation; a 350 word mini autobiography; and a 500 to 800 word essay on the Pokagon Band of Potawatomi Indians.
Initial approach: Complete online application
Board meeting date(s): Second Thurs. of each month
Deadline(s): 90 days prior to need; Mar. 15 for scholarships
Final notification: Within 90 days; May for scholarships
Officers and Directors:* Rose Dudiak*, Chair.; Margaret Murray, Vice-Chair.; Viki Gudas*, Secy.; Michaelina Magnuson, Treas.; Mary L. Dunbar, Exec. Dir.; Rob Carpenter; Alice Overly; Vickie Wagner.
Number of staff: 1 full-time professional; 1 full-time support.
EIN: 300130499

1478
Fowler Packing Company, Inc.

(also known as Parnagian Enterprises)
8570 S. Cedar Ave.
Fresno, CA 93725-8905 (559) 834-5911

Company URL: http://www.fowlerpacking.com
Establishment information: Established in 1950.
Company type: Private company
Business activities: Produces fruit.
Business type (SIC): Farms/fruit and nut
Corporate officers: Dennis Parnagian, Pres.; James Bates, C.F.O.
Giving statement: Giving through the Parnagian Foundation.

Parnagian Foundation

8570 S. Cedar Ave.
Fresno, CA 93725-8905

Establishment information: Established in 2000 in CA.
Donor: Fowler Packing Co.
Financial data (yr. ended 12/31/11): Assets, $116,337 (M); expenditures, $10,180; qualifying distributions, $10,000; giving activities include $10,000 for 2 grants (high: $5,000; low: $5,000).
Purpose and activities: The foundation supports the California Agricultural Leadership Foundation.
Fields of interest: Religion.
Type of support: General/operating support.
Geographic limitations: Giving primarily in CA.
Application information: Applications not accepted. Unsolicited requests for funds not accepted.
Officers: Dennis Parnagian, C.E.O.; Philip Parnagian, Secy.; Randy Parnagian, Treas.
Director: Ken Parnagian.
EIN: 770541025

1479
Fowler White Boggs P.A

501 E. Kennedy Blvd., Ste. 1700
Tampa, FL 33602-5239 (813) 228-7411

Company URL: http://www.fowlerwhite.com
Establishment information: Established in 1943.
Company type: Private company
Business activities: Operates law firm.
Business type (SIC): Legal services
Corporate officers: E. Jackson Boggs, Chair.; Rhea F. Law, Chair. and C.E.O.; C. Joseph Coleman, Pres.
Offices: Fort Lauderdale, Fort Myers, Jacksonville, Tallahassee, Tampa, FL
Giving statement: Giving through the Fowler White Boggs P.A. Pro Bono Program.

Fowler White Boggs P.A. Pro Bono Program

501 E. Kennedy Blvd., Ste. 1700
Tampa, FL 33602-5239 (813) 222-7849
FAX: (813) 229-8313;
E-mail: sarah.amine@fowlerwhite.com; Additional Tel.: (813) 228-7411; URL: http://www.fowlerwhite.com/why-probono.html

Contact: Sarah Lahlou-Amine, Pro Bono Chair
Fields of interest: Legal services.
Type of support: Pro bono services - legal.
Application information: The Pro Bono Committee manages the pro-bono program.

1480
Fox Entertainment Group, Inc.

1211 Ave. of the Americas, 16th Fl.
New York, NY 10036-8701 (212) 556-2560

Company URL: http://www.fox.com
Establishment information: Established in 1985.
Company type: Subsidiary of a public company
Business activities: Produces motion pictures; broadcasts television; provides cable television services.
Business type (SIC): Motion pictures/production and services allied to; radio and television broadcasting; cable and other pay television services
Corporate officers: Anthony J. Vinciquerra, Chair; Keith Rupert Murdoch, C.E.O.; Kevin Reilly, Pres.; David F. DeVoe, C.F.O.
Board of director: Anthony J. Vinciquerra, Chair.
Subsidiaries: Fox Broadcasting Co., Beverly Hills, CA; Twentieth Century Fox Film Corp., Los Angeles, CA
Giving statement: Giving through the Fox Entertainment Group, Inc. Corporate Giving Program.
Company EIN: 954066193

Fox Entertainment Group, Inc. Corporate Giving Program

c/o Corp. Contribs.
1211 Ave. of the Americas
New York, NY 10036 (212) 852-7017
URL: http://www.fox.com/foxgives/

Purpose and activities: Fox makes charitable contributions to nonprofit organizations involved with the underprivileged, the environment, and youth. Support is given in areas of company operations, with emphasis on California; giving also on a national and international basis.
Fields of interest: Environment; Youth, services Economically disadvantaged.
Type of support: Continuing support; Employee volunteer services; General/operating support; In-kind gifts; Sponsorships.
Geographic limitations: Giving on a national basis in areas of company operations, with emphasis on CA; giving also on a national and international basis.

1481
Framingham Co-Operative Bank

828 Concord St.
Framingham, MA 01701-4695
(508) 820-4000
FAX: 508-620-7058

Company URL: http://www.framinghambank.com
Establishment information: Established in 1889.
Company type: Private company
Business activities: Operates commercial bank.
Business type (SIC): Banks/commercial
Financial profile for 2010: Assets, $376,479,434; liabilities, $300,419,023
Corporate officers: Robert P. Lamprey, Chair., C.E.O., and Treas.; Mark R. Haranas, Pres. and C.E.O.; Joseph M. Vincent, Sr. V.P. and Cont.
Board of directors: Robert P. Lamprey, Chair.; Susan E. Acton; Paul V. Galvani; Mark R. Haranas; Robert J. Harrington; Charles W. Hickson; Richard D. Karb; Clement T. Lambert; Paul R. Romeo; James P. Shay; Joseph F. Shay; William R. Swanson
Giving statement: Giving through the MutualOne Charitable Foundation.

The MutualOne Charitable Foundation

(formerly Framingham Co-Operative Bank Charitable Foundation)
828 Concord St.
Framingham, MA 01701-4611 (508) 820-4000
FAX: (508) 872-1768; Application addresses: 160 Cochituate Rd., Framingham, MA 01701; Rachel Stewart, Admin. Dir., MutualOne Charitable Foundation, 49 Main St., Natick, MA 01760; URL: http://www.mutualone.com/client_services_charitable_foundation.html

Establishment information: Established in 1998 in MA.
Donor: Framingham Co-Operative Bank.
Contact: Robert P. Lamprey, Chair.
Financial data (yr. ended 12/31/11): Assets, $5,867,006 (M); expenditures, $242,270; qualifying distributions, $239,295; giving activities include $235,900 for grants.
Purpose and activities: The foundation supports organizations involved with arts and culture, education, the environment, health, workforce development, housing, and community development. Special emphasis is directed toward programs designed to focus on disadvantaged and/or underserved citizens of Framingham and Natick.
Fields of interest: Arts; Secondary school/education; Education; Environment; Health care; Employment, services; Employment, training; Food banks; Housing/shelter; Boys & girls clubs; Children/youth, services; Human services; Community/economic development Economically disadvantaged.
Type of support: Capital campaigns; Matching/challenge support; Program development; Seed money.
Geographic limitations: Giving primarily in areas of company operations in Framingham and Natick, MA, area.
Support limitations: No grants to individuals, or for political or sectarian activities.
Publications: Application guidelines.
Application information: Applications accepted. The foundation awards grants of up to $10,000. Proposals should be no longer than 5 to 6 pages. Application form required. Applicants should submit the following:
1) timetable for implementation and evaluation of project
2) how project will be sustained once grantmaker support is completed
3) statement of problem project will address
4) population served
5) copy of IRS Determination Letter
6) brief history of organization and description of its mission
7) copy of most recent annual report/audited financial statement/990
8) how project's results will be evaluated or measured
9) listing of board of directors, trustees, officers and other key people and their affiliations
10) detailed description of project and amount of funding requested
11) copy of current year's organizational budget and/or project budget
12) geographic area to be served
13) explanation of why grantmaker is considered an appropriate donor for project

Initial approach: Download application form and mail proposal and application form to foundation
Copies of proposal: 3
Deadline(s): None

Officer and Trustees:* Robert P. Lamprey*, Chair.; Susan E. Acton; Paul V. Galvani; Mark R. Haranas; Clement T. Lambert; Steven M. Sousa.
EIN: 311595107
Selected grants: The following grants are a representative sample of this grantmaker's funding activity:
$15,000 to United Way of Tri-County, Framingham, MA, 2010.
$10,000 to Framingham, Town of, Framingham, MA, 2010.
$10,000 to Friends of Resiliency for Life, Framingham, MA, 2010.
$10,000 to Project Just Because, Hopkinton, MA, 2010.
$8,000 to Framingham High School, Framingham, MA, 2010.
$6,000 to John Andrew Mazie Memorial Foundation, Wayland, MA, 2010.
$5,000 to Metrowest Outreach Connection, Framingham, MA, 2010.
$3,000 to Summit Montessori School, Framingham, MA, 2010.
$1,200 to Association of Small Foundations, Washington, DC, 2010.
$1,000 to Framingham State University Foundation, Framingham, MA, 2010.

1482
Sidney Frank Importing Company, Inc.

20 Cedar St.
New Rochelle, NY 10801-5247
(914) 637-5700
FAX: (914) 633-5637

Company URL: http://www.sidneyfrank.com
Establishment information: Established in 1972.
Company type: Private company
Business activities: Imports and distributes premium liquor and spirits.
Business type (SIC): Beer, wine, and distilled beverages—wholesale
Financial profile for 2010: Number of employees, 150
Corporate officers: Catherine Frank Halstead, Chair.; John Frank, Vice-Chair.; Lee R. Einsidler, C.E.O.; Eugene D. Frank, Pres.; William Henderson, Exec. V.P., Mktg.; Stuart W. Moselman, C.F.O.; David Zucker, V.P. and Cont.; William Presti, Genl. Counsel

Board of directors: Catherine Frank Halstead, Chair.; John Frank, Vice-Chair.
Giving statement: Giving through the Sidney Frank Importing Company, Inc. Contributions Program.

Sidney Frank Importing Company, Inc. Contributions Program

20 Cedar St.
New Rochelle, NY 10801 (914) 637-5752
E-mail: klaufer@sidneyfrank.com; URL: http://www.sidneyfrank.com/

1483
The Frankel Organization, L.L.C.

(doing business as Simwood Company)
3200 Legacy Ct.
West Bloomfield, MI 48323-3634
(248) 626-3150

Company URL: http://www.frankelhomes.com
Establishment information: Established in 2008.
Company type: Private company
Business activities: Develops real estate.
Business type (SIC): Real estate subdividers and developers
Corporate officers: Mark Frick, Co-Owner; Laurie Frankel, Co-Owner
Giving statement: Giving through the Herman and Sharon Frankel Foundation.

Herman and Sharon Frankel Foundation

535 Sanctury Dr., Rm. 808C
LongBoat Key, FL 34228-3852

Establishment information: Established in 1993 in MI.
Donors: Simwood Co.; Herman Frankel; Suburban Communities, LLC.
Financial data (yr. ended 12/31/11): Assets, $2,329,975 (M); expenditures, $130,238; qualifying distributions, $130,087; giving activities include $130,086 for 30 grants (high: $60,000; low: $100).
Purpose and activities: The foundation supports organizations involved with performing arts, education, health, children and youth, family services, and Judaism.
Fields of interest: Performing arts; Performing arts, theater; Performing arts, orchestras; Performing arts, opera; Education; Hospitals (general); Health care; Children/youth, services; Family services; United Ways and Federated Giving Programs; Jewish federated giving programs; Jewish agencies & synagogues.
Type of support: General/operating support.
Geographic limitations: Giving primarily in FL and MI.
Support limitations: No grants to individuals.
Application information: Applications not accepted. Contributes only to pre-selected organizations.
Trustee: Herman Frankel.
EIN: 383149105
Selected grants: The following grants are a representative sample of this grantmaker's funding activity:
$200,000 to Gulf Coast Community Foundation of Venice, Venice, FL, 2010.
$20,000 to Michigan Opera Theater, Detroit, MI, 2010.
$11,195 to Detroit Symphony Orchestra, Detroit, MI, 2010.
$10,000 to Henry Ford Health System, Detroit, MI, 2010.
$9,886 to Temple Israel, West Bloomfield, MI, 2010.
$6,350 to Asolo Theater, Sarasota, FL, 2010.
$5,000 to Cranbrook Schools, Bloomfield Hills, MI, 2010.
$5,000 to Mayo Foundation, Rochester, MN, 2010.
$2,500 to Detroit Institute of Arts, Detroit, MI, 2010.

1484
Franklin Electric Company, Inc.

400 E. Spring St.
Bluffton, IN 46714 (260) 824-2900
FAX: (260) 824-2909

Company URL: http://www.franklin-electric.com
Establishment information: Established in 1944.
Company type: Public company
Company ticker symbol and exchange: FELE/NASDAQ
Business activities: Manufactures electric motors.
Business type (SIC): Electrical industrial apparatus
Financial profile for 2012: Number of employees, 4,200; assets, $976,380,000; sales volume, $891,350,000; pre-tax net income, $115,990,000; expenses, $766,190,000; liabilities, $461,970,000
Corporate officers: R. Scott Trumbull, Chair. and C.E.O.; Gregg C. Sengstack, Pres. and C.O.O.; John J. Haines, V.P., Secy., and C.F.O.; Thomas J. Strupp, V.P., Human Resources
Board of directors: R. Scott Trumbull, Chair.; Jerome D. Brady; David T. Brown; David A. Roberts; Thomas R. VerHage; David M. Wathen; Thomas L. Young
Subsidiary: Oil Dynamics, Inc., Tulsa, OK
Giving statement: Giving through the Franklin Electric Charitable & Educational Foundation.
Company EIN: 350827455

The Franklin Electric Charitable & Educational Foundation

(formerly The Franklin Electric—Edward J. Schaefer and T. W. Kehoe Charitable and Educational Foundation, Inc.)
400 E. Spring St.
Bluffton, IN 46714-3798 (260) 824-2900
URL: http://www.franklin-electric.com/corporate/careers/community.aspx

Establishment information: Established in 1964 in IN.
Donor: Franklin Electric Co., Inc.
Contact: R. Scott Trumbull, Pres.
Financial data (yr. ended 12/31/11): Assets, $10,386 (M); gifts received, $162,600; expenditures, $168,693; qualifying distributions, $167,428; giving activities include $141,178 for 32 grants (high: $20,738; low: $100) and $25,000 for 16 grants to individuals (high: $3,000; low: $1,000).
Purpose and activities: The foundation supports orchestras and organizations involved with television, education, and youth development.
Fields of interest: Media, television; Performing arts, orchestras; Elementary/secondary education; Higher education; Education; Boys & girls clubs; United Ways and Federated Giving Programs.
Type of support: Employee-related scholarships; General/operating support; Scholarship funds.
Geographic limitations: Giving primarily in areas of company operations, with emphasis on AR, IN, and OK.
Application information: Applications accepted. Application form required.
Initial approach: Letter
Deadline(s): None
Officers: R. Scott Trumbull, Pres. and C.E.O.; Thomas J. Strupp, V.P.; John J. Haines, Co-Secy.; Angela M. Hughes, Co-Secy.
EIN: 237399324
Selected grants: The following grants are a representative sample of this grantmaker's funding activity:
$29,210 to United Way of Central Oklahoma, Oklahoma City, OK, 2010. For general operations.
$21,684 to Canterbury School, Fort Wayne, IN, 2010. For general operations.
$19,856 to United Way of Wells County, Bluffton, IN, 2010. For general operations.
$5,000 to American Red Cross, Fort Wayne, IN, 2010. For general operations.
$2,500 to Manchester College, North Manchester, IN, 2010. For general operations.
$2,500 to United Way of Dane County, Madison, WI, 2010. For general operations.
$2,125 to Big Brothers Big Sisters of Northeast Indiana, Fort Wayne, IN, 2010. For general operations.
$1,000 to Bucknell University, Lewisburg, PA, 2010. For general operations.
$1,000 to Community Harvest Food Bank of Northeast Indiana, Fort Wayne, IN, 2010. For general operations.

1485
Franklin Federal Savings Bank

(formerly Franklin Federal Savings & Loan Association of Richmond)
4501 Cox Rd.
P.O. Box 5310
Glen Allen, VA 23060-3381 (804) 967-7000

Company URL: http://www.franklinfederal.com/
Establishment information: Established in 1933.
Company type: Subsidiary of a public company
Business activities: Operates federal savings institutions.
Business type (SIC): Savings institutions
Corporate officers: Richard T. Wheeler, Jr., Chair., Pres., and C.E.O.; Donald F. Marker, Exec. V.P., C.F.O., and Secy.-Treas.; Melissa M. Fergel, Sr. V.P. and Cont.
Board of directors: Richard T. Wheeler, Jr., Chair.; Hugh T. Harrison II; Warren A. Mackey; L. Gerald Roach; Elizabeth W. Robertson; George L. Scott; Richard W. Wiltshire, Jr.; Percy Wootton
Giving statement: Giving through the Franklin Federal Foundation.

The Franklin Federal Foundation

4501 Cox Rd.
Glen Allen, VA 23060-3381

Establishment information: Established in 2000 in VA.
Donors: Franklin Federal Savings & Loan; Franklin Financial Corporation.
Financial data (yr. ended 09/30/11): Assets, $6,765,055 (M); gifts received, $5,554,505; expenditures, $209,305; qualifying distributions, $195,908; giving activities include $195,908 for 128 grants (high: $15,000; low: $25).
Purpose and activities: The foundation supports hospitals and organizations involved with arts and

culture, education, hunger, school athletics, human services, and the banking industry.
Fields of interest: Museums (art); Performing arts, orchestras; Arts; Higher education; Education; Hospitals (general); Food banks; Food distribution, meals on wheels; Athletics/sports, school programs; American Red Cross; Salvation Army; Human services, financial counseling; Human services; Business/industry.
Type of support: Employee matching gifts; General/operating support.
Geographic limitations: Giving primarily in VA.
Support limitations: No grants to individuals.
Application information: Applications not accepted. Contributes only to pre-selected organizations.
Officers and Directors:* Richard T. Wheeler, Jr.*, Pres.; William E. W. Frayser, Jr., V.P.; Jennifer R. Merritt, V.P.; Donald F. Marker, Secy.-Treas.; George C. Freeman III; Hugh T. Harrison II; Ern S. Jewett; L. Gerald Roach.
Number of staff: None.
EIN: 541996321
Selected grants: The following grants are a representative sample of this grantmaker's funding activity:
$15,000 to American Red Cross, Richmond, VA, 2011.
$6,000 to University of Virginia, Charlottesville, VA, 2011.
$5,000 to Richmond Symphony, Richmond, VA, 2011.
$5,000 to University of Richmond, Development Office, Richmond, VA, 2011.
$2,270 to VCU Massey Cancer Center, Richmond, VA, 2011.
$2,000 to Better Housing Coalition, Richmond, VA, 2011.
$2,000 to Lewis Ginter Botanical Gardens, Richmond, VA, 2011.
$1,500 to American Cancer Society, Glen Allen, VA, 2011.
$1,000 to Comfort Zone Camp, Richmond, VA, 2011.
$1,000 to Hospital Hospitality House of Richmond, Richmond, VA, 2011.

1486
The Franklin Mutual Insurance Company

(also known as FMI)
5 Broad St.
Branchville, NJ 07826-5601
(973) 948-3120

Company URL: http://www.fmiweb.com
Establishment information: Established in 1879.
Company type: Mutual company
Business activities: Sells property and casualty insurance.
Business type (SIC): Insurance/fire, marine, and casualty
Corporate officers: George H. Guptill, Jr., Chair.; James Ayers, Pres.; Gary J. Capone, V.P., Mktg.; Howard Aldin, V.P., Human Resources
Board of director: George H. Guptill, Jr., Chair.
Giving statement: Giving through the FMI Scholarship Foundation, Inc.

FMI Scholarship Foundation, Inc.

(formerly Franklin Mutual Insurance Scholarship Foundation, Inc.)
P.O. Box 400
Branchville, NJ 07826-0400

Donors: The Franklin Mutual Insurance Co.; Fore John Committee.
Financial data (yr. ended 12/31/11): Assets, $22,268 (M); gifts received, $72,500; expenditures, $70,300; qualifying distributions, $68,500; giving activities include $68,500 for grants.
Purpose and activities: The foundation awards college scholarships to high school students.
Fields of interest: Higher education.
Type of support: Scholarships—to individuals.
Geographic limitations: Giving limited to NJ.
Application information: Applications not accepted. Contributes only to pre-selected individuals.
Trustees: James P. Ayers; George H. Guptill, Jr.; Richard H. Harris; Charles G. Ort.
EIN: 223394738

1487
Franklin Resources, Inc.

1 Franklin Pkwy.
San Mateo, CA 94403 (650) 312-2000
FAX: (650) 312-3655

Company URL: http://www.franklinresources.com
Establishment information: Established in 1947.
Company type: Public company
Company ticker symbol and exchange: BEN/NYSE
International Securities Identification Number: US3546131018
Business activities: Provides investment advisory services.
Business type (SIC): Security and commodity services
Financial profile for 2012: Number of employees, 8,600; assets, $14,751,500,000; sales volume, $7,101,000,000; pre-tax net income, $2,678,200,000; expenses, $4,585,800,000; liabilities, $5,550,200,000
Fortune 1000 ranking: 2012—362nd in revenues, 108th in profits, and 300th in assets
Forbes 2000 ranking: 2012—1153rd in sales, 295th in profits, and 1213th in assets
Corporate officers: Charles B. Johnson, Chair.; Rupert H. Johnson, Jr., Vice-Chair.; Gregory E. Johnson, Pres. and C.E.O.; Jennifer M. Johnson, Exec. V.P. and C.O.O.; Kenneth A. Lewis, Exec. V.P. and C.F.O.; Craig Steven Tyle, Exec. V.P. and Genl. Counsel
Board of directors: Charles B. Johnson, Chair.; Rupert H. Johnson, Jr., Vice-Chair.; Samuel H. Armacost; Peter K. Barker; Charles Crocker; Gregory E. Johnson; Mark C. Pigott; Chutta Ratnathicam; Laura Stein; Anne M. Tatlock; Geoffrey Y. Yang
Subsidiaries: Franklin Advisors, Inc., San Mateo, CA; Franklin Advisory Services, LLC, Fort Lee, NJ; Franklin Investment Advisory Services, Inc., Norwalk, CT; Franklin Mutual Advisors, LLC, Short Hills, NJ; Franklin Properties, Inc., San Mateo, CA; Franklin Templeton Bank & Trust, F.S.B., San Mateo, CA; Franklin Templeton Cos., Inc., San Mateo, CA; Franklin Templeton Services, Inc., San Mateo, CA; Franklin/Templeton Distributors, Inc., San Mateo, CA; Franklin/Templeton Investor Services, Inc., San Mateo, CA; Templeton Investment Counsel, Inc., Fort Lauderdale, FL
International operations: Austria; Brazil; British Virgin Islands; Canada; Cayman Islands; England; France; Germany; Hong Kong; India; Ireland; Luxembourg; Mauritius; North Korea; Poland; Switzerland; United Kingdom
Giving statement: Giving through the Franklin Resources, Inc. Corporate Giving Program.
Company EIN: 132670991

Franklin Resources, Inc. Corporate Giving Program

1 Franklin Pkwy.
San Mateo, CA 94403-1906 (650) 312-2000
FAX: (650) 312-5606; E-mail: giving@frk.com; E-mail for volunteer requests: involved@frk.com;
URL: http://www.franklinresources.com/corp/pages/carousel/about_us/corpCitizenship.jsf

Purpose and activities: Franklin Resources makes charitable contributions to nonprofit organizations on a national and international basis. Support is given in areas of company operations.
Fields of interest: Education; Employment, public education; Human services, financial counseling; Community development, business promotion.
Program:
Employee Matching Gifts Program: Franklin Resources matches contributions made by its employees to nonprofit organizations.
Type of support: Employee matching gifts; Employee volunteer services; General/operating support; Sponsorships.
Geographic limitations: Giving in areas of company operations on a national and international basis.
Application information: Applications accepted. Franklin Templeton's corporate giving program conducts two funding cycles per year in February and August. Unsolicited proposals are not accepted for grants or sponsorships; volunteer requests are accepted. Applicants should submit the following:
1) explanation of why grantmaker is considered an appropriate donor for project
2) detailed description of project and amount of funding requested
Letters of inquiry for grants and sponsorships should be limited to 2 pages.
Initial approach: E-mail letter of inquiry for grants and sponsorships; E-mail details for volunteer requests

1488
Franklin Savings Bank

198 Front St.
P.O. Box 825
Farmington, ME 04938-0825
(207) 778-3339

Company URL: http://www.franklinebranch.com
Establishment information: Established in 1868.
Company type: Private company
Business activities: Operates savings bank.
Business type (SIC): Savings institutions
Financial profile for 2011: Assets, $325,684,968; pre-tax net income, $2,964,020; liabilities, $246,150,233
Corporate officers: William J. Bernard, Chair.; Peter L. Judkins, Pres. and C.E.O.; Timothy J. Thompson, Sr. V.P. and C.F.O; Shelley W. Deane, Sr. V.P., Human Resources, and Admin.
Board of directors: William J. Bernard, Chair.; Bradford S. Adley; Mary Ellen Carpenter; Guthrie S. Colpitts; C. Clinton Knapp; Peter L. Judkins; Michael A. Luciano; Richard H. Smith; Richard M. Walker
Offices: Jay, Mexico, Rangeley, Rumford, Skowhegan, Wilton, ME
Giving statement: Giving through the Franklin Savings Bank Community Development Foundation.

Franklin Savings Bank Community Development Foundation

198 Front St.
P.O. Box 825
Farmington, ME 04938-0825 (207) 778-3339

Establishment information: Established in 2000 in ME.
Donor: Franklin Savings Bank.
Contact: Peter Judkins, Pres.
Financial data (yr. ended 12/31/11): Assets, $2,354,088 (M); expenditures, $193,360; qualifying distributions, $192,050; giving activities include $192,050 for 133 grants (high: $34,000; low: $25).
Purpose and activities: The foundation supports health centers and organizations involved with arts and culture, education, recreation, children services, and community economic development.
Fields of interest: Historic preservation/historical societies; Arts; Secondary school/education; Education; Health care, clinics/centers; Athletics/sports, winter sports; Recreation; Salvation Army; Children, services; Economic development; Community/economic development; United Ways and Federated Giving Programs.
Program:
Franklin Scholars: The foundation awards 10 college scholarships to graduating seniors of Mt. Blue, Mountain Valley, Mt. Abram, Dirigo, Jay, Livermore Falls, Madison, Skowhegan, and Rangeley Lakes Regional High School who plan to attend a 4-year college with a concentration in accounting, finance, computer science, marketing, or majoring in other business-related courses.
Type of support: Annual campaigns; General/operating support; Program development; Scholarships—to individuals; Sponsorships.
Geographic limitations: Giving limited to western central ME.
Publications: Application guidelines.
Application information: Applications accepted. An application form is required for scholarships. Application form required.
Initial approach: Letter
Deadline(s): None
Officers: William J. Bernard, Chair.; Peter Judkins, Pres.; Shelley W. Deane, Secy.; Timothy J. Thompson, Treas.
Directors: C. Clinton Knapp; Richard H. Smith; Richard M. Walker.
EIN: 311719226
Selected grants: The following grants are a representative sample of this grantmaker's funding activity:
$6,000 to Mount Blue High School, Farmington, ME, 2011. For scholarship.
$5,000 to Somerset Economic Development Corporation, Skowhegan, ME, 2011.
$3,000 to Carrabec High School, North Anson, ME, 2011. For scholarship.
$2,534 to Summer Camp, Bridgton, ME, 2011.
$2,000 to Franklin County Childrens Task Force, Farmington, ME, 2011.
$2,000 to United Way of the Tri-Valley Area, Farmington, ME, 2011.
$1,500 to American Cancer Society, Topsham, ME, 2011.
$1,500 to Rangeley Lakes Region Historical Society, Rangeley, ME, 2011.
$1,000 to Good Shepherd Food-Bank, Auburn, ME, 2011.
$1,000 to Gulf of Maine Research Institute, Portland, ME, 2011.

1489
Franshaw, Inc.
112 W. 34th St., Ste. 1515
New York, NY 10120-1515 (212) 719-2222

Establishment information: Established in 1941.
Company type: Private company
Business activities: Sells women's sportswear wholesale.
Business type (SIC): Apparel, piece goods, and notions—wholesale
Corporate officers: Abraham Shamah, Pres.; Ezra Shamah, V.P., Sales and Mktg.; Ezra Tawil, Secy.; Murray Mizrachi, Treas.
Giving statement: Giving through the Rachel & Ezra Shamah Foundation.

Rachel & Ezra Shamah Foundation
c/o Franshaw, Inc.
112 W. 34th St., Ste. 1515
New York, NY 10120-1515 (212) 719-2222

Establishment information: Established in 1991 in NY.
Donor: Franshaw, Inc.
Contact: Ezra Shamah, Tr.
Financial data (yr. ended 12/31/10): Assets, $431 (M); gifts received, $14,500; expenditures, $14,333; qualifying distributions, $13,878; giving activities include $13,878 for 3 grants (high: $8,600; low: $1,000).
Purpose and activities: The foundation supports organizations involved with arts and culture, culinary education, and Judaism.
Fields of interest: Arts education; Arts; Education; Jewish agencies & synagogues.
Type of support: General/operating support.
Geographic limitations: Giving primarily in NY.
Support limitations: No grants to individuals.
Application information: Applications accepted. Application form not required.
Initial approach: Proposal
Deadline(s): None
Trustees: Ezra Shamah; Rachel Shamah.
EIN: 133613890

1490
Fredericksburg Area Association of Realtors Inc.
2050 Gordon W. Shelton Blvd.
Fredericksburg, VA 22401 (540) 373-7711

Company URL: http://www.faarmembers.com
Establishment information: Established in 1957.
Company type: Business league
Business activities: Operates real estate agency for affordable housing.
Business type (SIC): Business association
Corporate officers: Patricia Breme, C.E.O.; Suzanne M. Brady, Pres.; Christine Singhass, Secy.; Linda Fosdick, Treas.
Board of directors: Sabrina Anderson; Linda Fosdick; Bob Mecurio; Jorge Robert; Sarah Stelmok; Michelle Wilson
Giving statement: Giving through the Fredericksburg Realtors Foundation, Inc.

Fredericksburg Realtors Foundation, Inc.
2050 Gordon W. Shelton Blvd.
Fredericksburg, VA 22401-4980 (540) 373-7711
FAX: (540) 736-0301; Application address: c/o Fredericksburg Realtors Foundation, Inc., P.O. Box 3625, Fredericksburg, VA 22401-3625; URL: http://www.faarmembers.com/foundation.asp

Establishment information: Established in 1991 in VA.
Donors: Fredericksburg Area Association of Realtors; National Association of Realtors.
Contact: Pamela Wharton
Financial data (yr. ended 12/31/11): Assets, $6,914 (M); gifts received, $13,800; expenditures, $13,594; qualifying distributions, $11,800; giving activities include $11,800 for 6 grants (high: $3,300; low: $1,000).
Purpose and activities: The foundation supports programs designed to assist area residents struggling with hardships that threaten their ability to secure and retain shelter.
Fields of interest: Education; Housing/shelter; American Red Cross; Human services.
Type of support: General/operating support; Grants to individuals.
Geographic limitations: Giving limited to the Fredericksburg, VA, area.
Application information: Applications accepted. Application form required. Applicants should submit the following:
1) detailed description of project and amount of funding requested
Initial approach: Letter
Deadline(s): None
Officer: Drew Fristoe, Chair.
Directors: Kim Bland; Jeanette Y. Browne; Claire Forcier-Rowe; Carolyn Liddell; Relda M. Shick.
EIN: 541564756

1491
Fredrikson & Byron, P.A.
200 South Sixth St., Ste. 4000
Minneapolis, MN 55402 (612) 492-7141

Company URL: http://www.fredlaw.com
Establishment information: Established in 1948.
Company type: Private company
Business activities: Operates law firm.
Business type (SIC): Legal services
Corporate officer: John M. Koneck, Pres.
Offices: West Des Moines, IA; Minneapolis, MN; Bismarck, Fargo, ND
International operations: China; Mexico
Giving statement: Giving through the Fredrikson & Byron, P.A. Pro Bono Program and the Fredrikson & Byron Foundation.

Fredrikson & Byron, P.A. Pro Bono Program
200 S. 6th St., Ste. 4000
Minneapolis, MN 55402-1425 (612) 492-7608
E-mail: pwandzel@fredlaw.com; Additional tel.: (612) 492-7141; URL: http://www.fredlaw.com/probono/

Contact: Pamela J. Wandzel, Pro Bono Coord.
Fields of interest: Legal services.
Type of support: Pro bono services - legal.
Geographic limitations: Giving primarily in areas of company operations in West Des Moines, IA,

Minneapolis, MN, Bismarck, and Fargo, ND, and in China, and Mexico.
Application information: The Pro Bono Committee manages the pro-bono program.

Fredrikson & Byron Foundation

200 South 6th St., Ste. 4000
Minneapolis, MN 55402-1425 (612) 492-7000
FAX: (612) 492-7077; E-mail: jkoneck@fredlaw.com; URL: http://www.fredlaw.com/firm/foundation.html
Scholarship e-mail: glarson@fredlaw.com

Financial data (yr. ended 05/31/12): Revenue, $485,641; assets, $136,138 (M); gifts received, $485,526; expenditures, $442,309; giving activities include $430,954 for grants and $10,000 for grants to individuals.
Purpose and activities: The foundation supports law-related institutions and events, organizations that complement the rule of law, and a small number of cultural activities that are of special interest to the lawyers of Fredrikson & Byron, P.A.
Fields of interest: Law school/education.
Program:
Minority Scholarship Program: This program sponsors educational opportunities for currently-enrolled, first-year law students of diverse backgrounds by providing one $10,000 scholarship.
Type of support: Scholarships—to individuals.
Publications: Application guidelines.
Application information: Applications accepted. All scholarship applications must be accompanied by two letters of recommendation (one from a law school professor and one from an employer or other reference), one writing sample from a first-year legal writing course, a current law school transcript, an undergraduate transcript, and a resume.
Initial approach: Download application
Copies of proposal: 1
Deadline(s): Sept. 30
Final notification: Dec.
Officers and Directors: Todd A. Wind*, Pres.; Susan D. Steinwall*, V.P. and Secy.; Ronalee Haugen*, Treas.; James Dorsey; Adonis Neblett; Robert Ranum.
EIN: 237401456

1492
Free Range Studios

1605 Connecticut Ave., N.W., 4th Fl.
Washington, DC 20009 (202) 234-5613
FAX: (202) 318-3037

Company URL: http://freerangestudios.com
Establishment information: Established in 1999.
Company type: Private company
Business type (SIC): Business services/miscellaneous
Corporate officer: Jonah Sachs, Owner
Giving statement: Giving through the Free Range Studios Corporate Giving Program.

Free Range Studios Corporate Giving Program

1605 Connecticut Ave., NW, 4th Fl.
Washington, DC 20009 (202) 234-5613
URL: http://freerangestudios.com

Purpose and activities: Free Range Studios is a certified B Corporation that donates a percentage of profits to charitable organizations.
Fields of interest: Environment; Public affairs.
Type of support: Employee volunteer services; Pro bono services - communications/public relations; Pro bono services - interactive/website technology; Pro bono services - marketing/branding.

1493
S. Freedman & Sons, Inc.

3322 Pennsy Dr.
P.O. Box 1418
Landover, MD 20785-1604 (301) 322-5000

Company URL: http://www.sfreedman.com
Establishment information: Established in 1907.
Company type: Private company
Business activities: Sells office supplies wholesale.
Business type (SIC): Paper and paper products—wholesale; industrial machinery and equipment—wholesale; shopping goods stores/miscellaneous
Corporate officers: Mark Freedman, C.E.O.; Louis Sacks, Treas.
Giving statement: Giving through the S-F Foundation, Inc.

S-F Foundation, Inc.

3322 Pennsy Dr.
Landover, MD 20785-0418 (301) 322-5000

Donor: S. Freedman & Sons, Inc.
Contact: Mark S. Freedman, Pres.
Financial data (yr. ended 01/31/12): Assets, $6,856 (M); gifts received, $20,000; expenditures, $22,903; qualifying distributions, $22,030; giving activities include $22,030 for grants.
Purpose and activities: The foundation supports organizations involved with radio, higher education, health, human services, and Judaism.
Fields of interest: Education; Health care; Religion.
Type of support: Annual campaigns; General/operating support; Program development.
Application information: Applications accepted. Application form required.
Initial approach: Proposal
Deadline(s): None
Officer: Mark S. Freedman, Pres.
EIN: 526054184

1494
Freeport-McMoRan Copper & Gold Inc.

333 N. Central Ave.
Phoenix, AZ 85004-2189 (602) 366-8100
FAX: (302) 636-5454

Company URL: http://www.fcx.com
Establishment information: Established in 1987.
Company type: Public company
Company ticker symbol and exchange: FCX/NYSE
International Securities Identification Number: US35671D8570
Business activities: Conducts copper, gold, and silver exploration, mining, and milling activities.
Business type (SIC): Mining/copper; mining/gold and silver; mining/ferroalloys (except vanadium)
Financial profile for 2012: Number of employees, 34,000; assets, $42,588,000,000; sales volume, $4,583,000,000; pre-tax net income, $1,250,000,000; expenses, $3,273,000,000; liabilities, $24,648,000,000
Fortune 1000 ranking: 2012—156th in revenues, 59th in profits, and 158th in assets
Forbes 2000 ranking: 2012—518th in sales, 193rd in profits, and 635th in assets
Corporate officers: James R. Moffett, Chair.; B.M. Rankin, Jr., Vice-Chair.; Richard C. Adkerson, Pres. and C.E.O.; Kathleen L. Quirk, Exec. V.P., C.F.O., and Treas.; Michael J. Arnold, Exec. V.P. and C.A.O.
Board of directors: James R. Moffett, Chair.; B.M. Rankin, Jr., Vice-Chair.; Richard C. Adkerson; Robert J. Allison, Jr.; Robert A. Day; Gerald J. Ford; H. Devon Graham, Jr.; Charles C. Krulak; Bobby Lee Lackey; Jon C. Madonna; Dustan E. McCoy; Stephen H. Siegele
Subsidiaries: Cyprus Amax Minerals Company, Englewood, CO; P.T. Freeport Indonesia Co., New Orleans, LA
International operations: Bermuda; Chile; Indonesia; Peru; Spain
Historic mergers: Phelps Dodge Corporation (March 19, 2007)
Giving statement: Giving through the Freeport-McMoRan Copper & Gold Foundation.
Company EIN: 742480931

Freeport-McMoRan Copper & Gold Foundation

(formerly Phelps Dodge Foundation)
333 N. Central Ave.
Phoenix, AZ 85004-2189 (602) 366-8116
FAX: (602) 366-7305; E-mail: foundation@fmi.com; Additional tel.: (800) 528-1182, ext. 8116; fax: (602) 366-7323; e-mail: communitydevelopment@fmi.com; URL: http://www.freeportinmycommunity.com/
Contact for Scholarship Program: Brittany Watkins, e-mail: brittany_watkins@fmi.com

Establishment information: Incorporated in 1953 in NY.
Donor: Phelps Dodge Corp.
Financial data (yr. ended 12/31/11): Assets, $3,332,162 (M); gifts received, $13,700,000; expenditures, $15,493,727; qualifying distributions, $15,493,199; giving activities include $13,861,235 for 170 grants (high: $1,487,130; low: $400) and $1,631,964 for employee matching gifts.
Purpose and activities: The foundation supports organizations involved with arts and culture, education, the environment, health, mental health, crime and violence prevention, employment, nutrition, housing, safety, recreation, human services, community development, science, civic affairs, and economically disadvantaged people.
Fields of interest: Arts, cultural/ethnic awareness; Arts; Elementary/secondary education; Education, early childhood education; Vocational education; Higher education; Teacher school/education; Adult/continuing education; Education, reading; Education; Environment, natural resources; Environment, water resources; Environment, land resources; Environment, forests; Environmental education; Environment; Hospitals (general); Public health, physical fitness; Health care; Substance abuse, prevention; Mental health/crisis services; Crime/violence prevention, domestic violence; Crime/violence prevention, child abuse; Employment, training; Employment; Nutrition; Housing/shelter; Disasters, preparedness/services; Safety/disasters; Recreation; Youth development, adult & child programs; Children/youth, services; Family services; Family services, domestic violence; Human services; Economic development; Economic development, visitors/convention bureau/tourism promotion; Business/industry; Community development, small businesses; Community/economic development; United Ways and Federated Giving Programs; Science, formal/general education; Physical/earth

sciences; Mathematics; Geology; Engineering/technology; Science; Transportation; Leadership development; Public affairs Native Americans/American Indians; Women; Girls; Economically disadvantaged.

Programs:

Community Investments Funds (CIFs): Through Community Investment Funds, the foundation supports programs designed to promote local capacity-building, community development, and sustainability. The CIFs are governed by community representatives who cultivate and address projects that serve priority needs of the community and the foundation funds those projects that have a positive, sustainable impact. CIFs are limited to Graham County, Greenlee, Green Valley, and Sahuarita AZ, Climax Area, CO, and Grant County, NM.

Employee Matching Gifts Program: The foundation matches contributions made by employees and directors of Freeport-McMoRan to nonprofits, civic, health, social welfare, educational, cultural, environmental or other community organizations that provide a public service. The foundation matches contributions from $25 up to an annual maximum of $40,000. The first $1,000 contributed per institution well be double matched, and any amount above $1,000 will be single matched.

Employee Volunteer Fund: The foundation awards a $250 or $500 grant to nonprofit organizations with which employees of Freeport-McMoRan volunteer a year.

Employee-related Scholarships: The foundation awards college scholarships to children of domestic and international Freeport-McMoRan employees. The program is administered by the National Merit Scholarship Corp. and the International Institute of Education (IIE).

General Social Investment Program: The foundation supports programs designed to ensure that resources are used to address high-priority needs and community development. Special emphasis is directed toward programs designed to address education and training; economic and community development; community safety, health, and wellness; the environment; and cultural heritage and the arts.

Mini Grants for Education: The foundation awards grants to K-12 schools and teachers to strengthen and expand opportunities for young people to learn and excel in education. Special emphasis is directed toward projects designed to promote the environment; mining, mineral, and natural resources; reading and literacy; and Science, Technology, Engineering, and Math (STEM). Grants range from $100 to $500.

Native American Partnership Fund: The foundation supports programs designed to address priority issues and needs in the Native American reservation communities and tribal leaders. Special emphasis is directed toward education and training; health and wellness; cultural preservation; women's development; and elder engagement. The program is limited to the Hualapai, San Carlos Apache, Tohono O'odham, and White Mountain Apache tribes. Grants range from $10,000 to $75,000.

Scholarship Program: The foundation awards scholarships to students pursuing a degree in engineering or mining at select colleges and universities. Special emphasis is directed towards students entering their junior or senior year studying engineering, sustainability, geology, chemistry, environmental sciences, health and safety, or business. Applicants must apply through participating schools. Scholarship recipients are also encouraged to apply for a 10 to 14 week summer internship following each year in which a scholarship is awarded.

STEM Innovation Grants: The foundation awards grants of up to $5,000 to K-12 teachers and schools to develop, improve, and expand innovative instructional programs in science, technology, engineering, and math (STEM).

Women's Development: The foundation supports programs designed to provide women and/or girls opportunities to reach their full potential and achieve economic success, including education, physical/mental health and wellness, entrepreneurship/employment, and mentoring or leadership development, with a goal of increasing access to key services critical to women's equal participation and success in their communities.

Type of support: Annual campaigns; Continuing support; Curriculum development; Employee matching gifts; Employee volunteer services; Employee-related scholarships; Equipment; General/operating support; Internship funds; Management development/capacity building; Matching/challenge support; Research; Scholarship funds; Scholarships—to individuals.

Geographic limitations: Giving primarily in areas of company operations in Ajo, Bagdad, Bisbee Area, Clarkdale, Globe, Graham County, Green Valley, Greenlee County, Jerome, Miami, Phoenix, Sahuarita, Tucson, AZ, Chafee County, Clear Creek County, Denver, Eagle County, Grand County, Lake County, and Summit County, CO, Norwich, CT, Ft. Madison, IA, Jefferson Parish, Lafayette Parish, New Orleans, Plaquemines Parish, St. Bernard Parish, St. Charles Parish, St. John the Baptist Parish, St. Tammany Parish, and Tangipahoa Parish, LA, Elizabeth, NJ, Grant County, NM, and El Paso and Houston, TX.

Support limitations: No support for discriminatory organizations, fraternal, veterans', or labor organizations, churches or religious organizations not of direct benefit to the entire community, political or lobbying organizations, pass-through foundations, or auxiliary organizations. No grants to individuals (except for scholarships), or for travel, conference fees, medical procedures, advertising, religious activities, or debt reduction or operational deficits.

Publications: Application guidelines; Corporate report; Grants list; Informational brochure (including application guidelines); Program policy statement.

Application information: Applications accepted. Organizations receiving STEM Innovation Grants are required to submit a final report. An application form is required for scholarships. Application form required. Applicants should submit the following:

1) timetable for implementation and evaluation of project
2) results expected from proposed grant
3) population served
4) name, address and phone number of organization
5) copy of IRS Determination Letter
6) copy of most recent annual report/audited financial statement/990
7) how project's results will be evaluated or measured
8) explanation of why grantmaker is considered an appropriate donor for project
9) detailed description of project and amount of funding requested
10) copy of current year's organizational budget and/or project budget
11) listing of additional sources and amount of support

Scholarship applications should include an essay, resume, letters of recommendation, and official transcripts.

Initial approach: Complete online application; download application form and mail to participating schools for scholarships
Copies of proposal: 1
Board meeting date(s): May
Deadline(s): Mar. 1 to Aug. 30 for General Social Investment Program; May 1 to Oct. 30 for Mini Grants for Education; Sept. 15 to Mar. 15 for STEM Innovation Grants; Mar. 30, June 30, and Sept. 30 for Native American Partnership Fund; Nov. 30 for Women's Development; Mar. 30 for scholarships; Varies for Community Investment Funds
Final notification: Jan. for General Social Investment Program; Jan. 15 for Mini Grants for Education; May 15 for STEM Innovation Grants; May 30, Aug. 30, and Nov. 30 for Native American Partnership Fund; Dec. 30 for Women's Development; Apr. 20 for scholarships

Officers and Directors:* Tracy L. Bame*, Pres.; Michael J. Arnold*, V.P.; Dean T. Falgoust, V.P.; Catherine R. Hardwick, Secy.; Kathleen L. Quirk*, Treas.; Pamela Q. Masson, Exec. Dir.; Richard C. Adkerson; L. Richards McMillan II.

Number of staff: 2 part-time professional; 1 part-time support.

EIN: 136077350

Selected grants: The following grants are a representative sample of this grantmaker's funding activity:

$1,457,130 to Thunderbird, The Garvin School of International Management, Glendale, AZ, 2011. For Freeport-McMoRan Women's Empowerment Institute.
$1,000,000 to University of Arizona, Institute for Mineral Resources, Tucson, AZ, 2011. For Sustainability, Research and Training Program.
$700,000 to Science Foundation Arizona, Phoenix, AZ, 2011. For STEM Initiative.
$300,000 to Baton Rouge Area Foundation, Baton Rouge, LA, 2011. For City-Wide Renewal Program.
$300,000 to New Mexico State University Foundation, Las Cruces, NM, 2011. For Freeport-McMoRan Water Quality Laboratory.
$250,000 to United Community Health Center, Sahuarita, AZ, 2011. For The Expansion of the Continental Campus.
$150,000 to Advocates of Lake County, Leadville, CO, 2011. For Family Crisis Center.
$50,000 to Nature Conservancy, Baton Rouge, LA, 2011. For Louisiana/Gulf of Mexico Restoration Initiative.
$15,000 to Phoenix Indian Center, Phoenix, AZ, 2011. For Programs and Services.
$10,000 to Arizona Quest for Kids, Phoenix, AZ, 2011. For Quest for College/Baghdad Tour.

1495
Freescale Semiconductor, Inc.

6501 W. William Cannon Dr. W.
Austin, TX 78735 (512) 895-2000

Company URL: http://www.freescale.com
Establishment information: Established in 1965.
Company type: Subsidiary of a private company
Business activities: Designs and manufactures semiconductors.
Business type (SIC): Electronic components and accessories
Financial profile for 2009: Number of employees, 18,000; sales volume, $3,508,000,000
Corporate officers: John Daniel McCranie, Chair.; Gregg A. Lowe, Pres. and C.E.O.; Alan Campbell, Sr. V.P. and C.F.O.; Jonathan Greenberg, Sr. V.P. and Genl. Counsel; Henri Pascal Richard, Sr., V.P., Sales and Mktg.; Jeff Elson, Sr. V.P., Human Resources; Sam Coursen, V.P. and C.I.O.; David Stasse, V.P. and C.I.O.

Board of directors: John Daniel McCranie, Chair.; Richard M. Beyer
Plant: Raleigh, NC
International operations: Germany; Hong Kong; Japan; Singapore
Giving statement: Giving through the Freescale Semiconductor, Inc. Corporate Giving Program.
Company EIN: 200443182

Freescale Semiconductor, Inc. Corporate Giving Program

6501 William Cannon Dr. W.
Austin, TX 78735-8523
E-mail: tamika.hickstubbs@freescale.com; For Asia Pacific and Japan: gloria.shiu@freescale.com; For Europe, the Middle East, and Africa: michel.abitteboul@freescale.com; URL: http://www.freescale.com/webapp/sps/site/homepage.jsp?nodeId=06PfBm

Contact: Tamika Hickstubbs
Purpose and activities: Freescale makes charitable contributions to nonprofit organizations involved with education, the environment, health, and human services. Support is given primarily in areas of company operations in Arizona and Texas, and in Brazil, Canada, the Czech Republic, Denmark, Finland, France, Germany, Hong Kong, India, Israel, Italy, Japan, Korea, Malaysia, Mexico, the Netherlands, Romania, Russia, Singapore, South Korea, Spain, Sweden, Switzerland, Taiwan, and the United Kingdom.
Fields of interest: Elementary/secondary education; Environment; Health care; Human services; Science; Mathematics; Engineering/technology.
International interests: Brazil; Canada; Czech Republic; Denmark; Finland; France; Germany; Hong Kong; India; Israel; Italy; Japan; Malaysia; Mexico; Netherlands; Romania; Russia; Scotland; Singapore; Spain; Sweden; Switzerland; Taiwan; United Kingdom.
Type of support: Employee volunteer services; General/operating support; Program development; Sponsorships.
Geographic limitations: Giving primarily in areas of company operations in AZ and TX, and in Brazil, Canada, the Czech Republic, Denmark, Finland, France, Germany, Hong Kong, India, Israel, Italy, Japan, Malaysia, Mexico, the Netherlands, Romania, Russia, Singapore, South Korea, Spain, Sweden, Switzerland, Taiwan, and the United Kingdom.
Application information: Applications accepted. Application form required. Applicants should submit the following:
1) population served
2) name, address and phone number of organization
3) copy of IRS Determination Letter
4) copy of most recent annual report/audited financial statement/990
5) listing of board of directors, trustees, officers and other key people and their affiliations
6) detailed description of project and amount of funding requested
7) contact person
8) copy of current year's organizational budget and/or project budget
9) listing of additional sources and amount of support
10) plans for acknowledgement

Requests for sponsorships should include a description of past support by Freescale with the organization; the percentage of funding that will go to administrative costs; all sponsorship levels; any deadlines; and the name, date, and location of the event, if applicable.
Initial approach: Download online application form and e-mail with required attachments to Community Contact
Deadline(s): June 1 and Dec. 1

1496
Fremont Bank

39150 Fremont Blvd.
Fremont, CA 94538-1316 (510) 792-2300

Company URL: http://www.fremontbank.com
Establishment information: Established in 1964.
Company type: Subsidiary of a private company
Business activities: Operates commercial bank.
Business type (SIC): Banks/commercial
Corporate officers: Michael J. Wallace, Chair.; Alan L. Hyman, Vice-Chair.; Bradford L. Anderson, C.E.O.; Andrew Mastorakis, Pres.; Ron Wagner, C.F.O.; Howard L. Hyman, Exec. V.P. and Treas.
Board of directors: Michael Wallace, Chair.; Alan L. Hyman, Vice-Chair.
Giving statement: Giving through the Fremont Bank Corporate Giving Program and the Fremont Bank Foundation.

Fremont Bank Corporate Giving Program

c/o Nonprofit Group
39150 Fremont Blvd.
Fremont, CA 94538
FAX: (510) 505-5322;
E-mail: Community@fremontbank.com; URL: http://www.fremontbank.com/communityrelations/

Purpose and activities: As a complement to its foundation, Fremont Bank also sponsors events that raise funds for nonprofit organizations. Support is given primarily in areas of company operations in California.
Fields of interest: General charitable giving.
Type of support: Sponsorships.
Geographic limitations: Giving primarily in cities where the company has a physical presence.
Support limitations: No support for political organizations or activities, individual sports teams, individual public educational institutions (except for in-kind donations or placement of advertisement via the Marketing Sponsorships program), or national or international organizations (except for local chapters in communities served by Fremont Bank). No grants to individuals, or for development or production of books, films, video or television programs, or walks or races, trips or tours, endowments, operating deficits or debt payment programs, membership fees or dues, in-kind or promotional merchandise, conferences or seminars, advertisements, or golf outings, or tournaments, or festivals not associated with a nonprofit organization or cause.
Publications: Application guidelines.
Application information: Applications accepted. The Nonprofit Group handles giving. The company has a staff that only handles contributions. A contributions committee reviews all requests. Multi-year funding is not automatic. Application form required. Applicants should submit the following:
1) copy of IRS Determination Letter
2) listing of board of directors, trustees, officers and other key people and their affiliations

Proposal should include, if applicable and not included in the application, a list of sponsorship levels and benefits, and a list of Fremont Bank clients or associates involved with the event.
Initial approach: Download application form and e-mail
Copies of proposal: 1
Committee meeting date(s): Monthly
Deadline(s): 8 weeks prior to artwork need or 60 days prior to event for sponsorships, whichever is sooner.
Final notification: 2 weeks following committee meetings
Administrator: Marie-Pascale Peterson, Dir., Community Outreach.
Number of staff: 1 full-time professional.

The Fremont Bank Foundation

39150 Fremont Blvd.
Fremont, CA 94538-1316
E-mail: foundation@fremontbank.com; URL: http://www.fremontbank.com/communityrelations/fremontbankfoundation.asp

Establishment information: Established as a company-sponsored operating foundation in 1996 in CA.
Donor: Fremont Bank.
Contact: Marie-Pascale Peterson
Financial data (yr. ended 12/31/11): Assets, $5,204,831 (M); gifts received, $1,964,260; expenditures, $349,187; qualifying distributions, $345,297; giving activities include $345,297 for grants.
Purpose and activities: The Fremont Bank Foundation provides financial assistance to nonprofit organizations for the implementation of series and programs that enhance the quality of life for all people in the communities served by Fremont Bank.
Fields of interest: Performing arts; Arts; Education; Environment; Public health; Health care; Mental health/crisis services; Health organizations; Crime/violence prevention, abuse prevention; Crime/violence prevention, domestic violence; Crime/violence prevention, child abuse; Nutrition; Children/youth, services; Human services, financial counseling; Homeless, human services; Human services.
Programs:
Arts and Culture: The foundation supports programs designed to promote music, dance, theater, and arts to enrich the community; and programs designed to provide a forum for people of all ages to develop talents in creative arts.
Education and Youth: The foundation supports programs designed to teach children and young adults life skills, such as money management, communication, parenting, nutrition, and social skills; and to inspire children to become productive, healthy, and responsible adults.
Health and Wellness: The foundation supports programs designed to promote physical and mental wellness for people of all ages; foster essential fundamental medical care; and address cure and prevention of life-threatening disease.
Social and Human Care: The foundation supports programs designed address social issues such as homelessness, criminal activities, child abuse, and domestic violence; protect the environment; and improve quality of life for all people in the community.
Type of support: Building/renovation; Capital campaigns; Endowments; Equipment; General/operating support; Program development; Research; Scholarship funds.
Geographic limitations: Giving primarily in San Francisco Bay Area, CA in areas of company operations.
Support limitations: No support for private foundations or pass-through organizations. No grants to individuals, or for political or labor activities, or debt reduction.
Publications: Grants list.

Application information: Applications not accepted. Contributes only to pre-selected organizations.
Board meeting date(s): Annually
Officers and Directors: Hattie Hyman Hughes, Pres.; Howard L. Hyman, V.P.; Chris Chenoweth, Secy.; Bradford L. Anderson, C.F.O; Sharon Belshaw-Jones; Brian Hughes; Alan L. Hyman; Michael J. Wallace.
EIN: 943170075
Selected grants: The following grants are a representative sample of this grantmaker's funding activity:
$50,000 to Abode Services, Fremont, CA, 2011.
$25,000 to Holy Spirit Church, Fremont, CA, 2011.
$20,000 to Spectrum Community Services, Hayward, CA, 2011.
$15,000 to Tiburcio Vasquez Health Center, Union City, CA, 2011.
$11,250 to Holy Names University, Oakland, CA, 2011.
$7,500 to Fremont Symphony Orchestra, Fremont, CA, 2011.
$5,000 to Boy Scouts of America, San Leandro, CA, 2011.
$5,000 to Taylor Family Foundation, Livermore, CA, 2011.
$2,500 to Food Bank for Monterey County, Salinas, CA, 2011.
$2,500 to Tri-City Volunteers, Fremont, CA, 2011.

1497
Fremont Group, LLC
199 Fremont St., Ste. 2400
San Francisco, CA 94105-2261
(415) 284-8500

Company URL: http://www.fremontgroup.com
Establishment information: Established in 1986.
Company type: Private company
Business activities: Provides investment advisory services.
Business type (SIC): Security and commodity services
Corporate officers: Alan M. Dachs, Pres. and C.E.O.; Deborah L. Duncan, Exec. V.P. and C.F.O.; Richard S. Kopf, Genl. Counsel and Secy.
Subsidiaries: Freemont Public Opportunities, San Francisco, CA; Fremont Realty Capital, San Francisco, CA
Giving statement: Giving through the Fremont Group Foundation.

The Fremont Group Foundation
P.O. Box 193809
San Francisco, CA 94119-3809
FAX: (415) 284-8128;
E-mail: nhair@fremontgroup.com; URL: http://www.fremontgroup.com/values/commitment.html

Establishment information: Established in 1996 in CA.
Donor: Fremont Sequoia Holding, L.P.
Contact: Nancy Hair
Financial data (yr. ended 12/31/11): Assets, $8,075,607 (M); expenditures, $463,713; qualifying distributions, $378,543; giving activities include $378,543 for grants.
Purpose and activities: The foundation supports food banks and organizations involved with education, the environment, animal welfare, child welfare, human services, and international affairs and matches contributions made by its employees.
Fields of interest: Elementary/secondary education; Education, early childhood education; Higher education; Education; Environment, natural resources; Environment; Animal welfare; Crime/violence prevention, child abuse; Food banks; Boy scouts; Human services; International affairs.
Type of support: Annual campaigns; Employee matching gifts; Employee volunteer services; General/operating support; Program development; Scholarship funds.
Geographic limitations: Giving primarily in CA.
Support limitations: No support for political or religious organizations or organizations involved with reproductive issues. No grants to individuals.
Application information: Applications not accepted. Contributes only to pre-selected organizations.
Board meeting date(s): Twice per year
Officers and Directors:* Alan M. Dachs*, Pres.; Richard S. Kopf*, V.P. and Secy.; Deborah L. Duncan*, V.P. and Treas.
Number of staff: 1 part-time support.
EIN: 333255428
Selected grants: The following grants are a representative sample of this grantmaker's funding activity:
$20,000 to Head-Royce School, Oakland, CA, 2009.
$15,000 to Boy Scouts of America, San Leandro, CA, 2009.
$15,000 to Boy Scouts of America, San Leandro, CA, 2009.
$15,000 to United Negro College Fund, San Francisco, CA, 2009.
$10,000 to Boys and Girls Clubs of Oakland, Oakland, CA, 2009.
$10,000 to Boys and Girls Clubs of San Francisco, San Francisco, CA, 2009.
$10,000 to Head-Royce School, Oakland, CA, 2009.
$10,000 to Trips for Kids, Mill Valley, CA, 2009.
$10,000 to Wesleyan University, Middletown, CT, 2009.
$3,000 to University of California San Francisco Foundation, San Francisco, CA, 2009.

1498
Freres Lumber Co., Inc.
141 14th St.
P.O. Box 276
Lyons, OR 97358-2348 (503) 859-2121

Company URL: http://www.frereslumber.com
Establishment information: Established in 1922.
Company type: Private company
Business activities: Produces softwood lumber and veneer stock.
Business type (SIC): Wood millwork; lumber and wood products
Financial profile for 2010: Number of employees, 410
Corporate officers: Robert T. Freres, Sr., C.E.O.; Theodore F. Freres, Pres.; William M. Smith, Secy.
Giving statement: Giving through the Freres Foundation.

Freres Foundation
c/o Freres Lumber Co., Inc.
P.O. Box 276
Lyons, OR 97358-0276

Donors: Freres Lumber Co., Inc.; Freres Timber Co.
Financial data (yr. ended 09/30/12): Assets, $2,333,042 (M); gifts received, $100,000; expenditures, $117,144; qualifying distributions, $106,550; giving activities include $106,550 for 24 grants (high: $53,000; low: $100).
Purpose and activities: The foundation supports fire departments and organizations involved with education, hunger, community development, and Catholicism.
Fields of interest: Education; Health care; Human services.
Type of support: General/operating support.
Geographic limitations: Giving primarily in OR.
Support limitations: No grants to individuals.
Application information: Applications not accepted. Unsolicited requests for funds not accepted.
Officers: Robert T. Freres, Pres.; Robert T. Freres, Jr., V.P.; Theodore F. Freres, V.P.; William M. Smith, Secy.
EIN: 936027213

1499
Fresh Mark, Inc.
1888 Southway St. S.W.
Massillon, OH 44646-9429 (330) 832-7491

Company URL: http://www.freshmark.com
Establishment information: Established in 1920.
Company type: Private company
Business activities: Produces ham, deli meat, wieners, smoked sausage, and deli products.
Business type (SIC): Meat packing plants and prepared meats and poultry
Corporate officers: Neil Genshaft, Chair. and C.E.O.; Harry Valentino, Pres. and C.O.O.; David Cochenour, V.P., Admin., C.F.O., and Treas.
Board of director: Neil Genshaft, Chair.
Divisions: Carriage Hill Div., Salem, OR; Sugardale Foods Div., Canton, OH; Superior's Brand Div., Massillon, OH
Giving statement: Giving through the Genshaft Family Foundation.

Genshaft Family Foundation
5353 Laurel Dr. N.W.
Canton, OH 44718-1664

Establishment information: Established in 1969 in OH.
Donors: Fresh Mark, Inc.; Leona Genshaft Trust.
Financial data (yr. ended 12/31/11): Assets, $4,342,724 (M); gifts received, $4,000,000; expenditures, $76,024; qualifying distributions, $75,650; giving activities include $75,200 for 3 grants (high: $60,000; low: $200).
Purpose and activities: The foundation supports organizations involved with higher education, health, youth business development, and Judaism.
Fields of interest: Higher education; Health care; Youth development, business; Jewish federated giving programs; Jewish agencies & synagogues.
Type of support: General/operating support.
Geographic limitations: Giving limited to MN and OH.
Support limitations: No grants to individuals.
Application information: Applications not accepted. Contributes only to pre-selected organizations.
EIN: 237008748
Selected grants: The following grants are a representative sample of this grantmaker's funding activity:
$85,000 to Canton Jewish Community Federation, Canton, OH, 2009. For general support.
$35,000 to Mayo Foundation, Rochester, MN, 2009. For general support.

1500
Freshfields Bruckhaus Deringer US LLP
601 Lexington Ave., 31st Fl.
New York, NY 10022-4611 (212) 277-4072

Company URL: http://www.freshfields.com/aboutus/csr/accessible/index.html#
Company type: Private company
Business activities: Operates law firm.
Business type (SIC): Legal services
International operations: Australia; Bahrain; Belgium; China; France; Germany; Italy; Japan; Netherlands; Russia; Saudi Arabia; Spain; United Arab Emirates; United Kingdom; Vietnam
Giving statement: Giving through the Freshfields Bruckhaus Deringer US LLP Pro Bono Program.

Freshfields Bruckhaus Deringer US LLP Pro Bono Program
601 Lexington Ave., 31st Fl.
New York, NY 10022-4611 (212) 277-4085
E-mail: viren.mascarenhas@freshfields.com; URL: http://www.freshfields.com/aboutus/csr/accessible/probono.html

Contact: Viren Mascarenhas, Assoc.
Fields of interest: Legal services.
Type of support: Pro bono services - legal.
Geographic limitations: Giving primarily in areas of company operations in Washington, DC, and New York, NY, and in Austria, Bahrain, Belgium, China, France, Germany, Italy, Japan, the Netherlands, Russia, Saudi Arabia, Spain, United Arab Emirates, United Kingdom, and Vietnam.
Application information: A Pro Bono Committee manages the pro bono program.

1501
Friday, Eldredge & Clark, LLP
400 W. Capitol Ave., Ste. 2000
Little Rock, AR 72201-3522
(501) 376-2011

Company URL: http://www.fridayfirm.com
Establishment information: Established in 1871.
Company type: Private company
Business activities: Provides legal services.
Business type (SIC): Legal services
Corporate officer: Byron Eiseman, Partner
Giving statement: Giving through the Friday, Eldredge & Clark Foundation.

Friday, Eldredge & Clark Foundation
400 W. Capitol Ave., Ste. 2000
Little Rock, AR 72201-3493

Donor: Friday, Eldredge & Clark, LLP.
Financial data (yr. ended 12/31/11): Assets, $79,257 (M); expenditures, $0; qualifying distributions, $0.
Purpose and activities: The foundation supports the Arkansas Sports Hall of Fame in North Little Rock, Arkansas.
Fields of interest: Athletics/sports, amateur leagues.
Type of support: General/operating support.
Geographic limitations: Giving limited to Little Rock, AR.
Support limitations: No grants to individuals.
Application information: Applications not accepted. Unsolicited requests for funds not accepted.
Officers and Directors:* Byron M. Eiseman, Jr.*, Pres.; J. Shephard Russell, III*, V.P.; James E. Harris*, Secy.
EIN: 716050584

1502
Fried, Frank, Harris, Shriver & Jacobson LLP
1 New York Plz.
New York, NY 10004-1980 (212) 859-8285

Company URL: http://www.friedfrank.com/index.cfm
Establishment information: Established in 1971.
Company type: Private company
Business activities: Operates law firm.
Business type (SIC): Legal services
Offices: Washington, DC; New York, NY
International operations: China; France; Germany; Hong Kong; United Kingdom
Giving statement: Giving through the Fried, Frank, Harris, Shriver & Jacobson LLP Pro Bono Program.

Fried, Frank, Harris, Shriver & Jacobson LLP Pro Bono Program
1 New York Plz.
New York, NY 10004-1980 (212) 859-8000
E-mail: jennifer.colyer@friedfrank.com; Additional tel.: (212) 859-8000; URL: http://www.friedfrank.com/index.cfm?pageID=55

Contact: Jennifer Colyer, Litigation Special Counsel
Fields of interest: Legal services.
Type of support: Pro bono services - legal.
Geographic limitations: Giving primarily in areas of company operations in Washington, DC, New York, NY, and in China, France, Germany, Hong Kong, and United Kingdom.
Application information: A Pro Bono Committee manages the pro bono program.

1503
Friedland Realty, Inc.
656 Central Park Ave.
Yonkers, NY 10704-2090 (914) 968-8500

Company URL: http://www.friedlandrealty.com
Establishment information: Established in 1970.
Company type: Private company
Business activities: Provides real estate brokerage services.
Business type (SIC): Real estate agents and managers
Corporate officers: Robert L. Friedland, Pres.; Tony Lembeck, C.E.O.
Office: New York, NY
Giving statement: Giving through the Bob and Sheila Friedland Foundation.

Bob and Sheila Friedland Foundation
656 Central Park Ave.
Yonkers, NY 10704-2019

Establishment information: Established in 1986 in DE and NY.
Donors: Friedland Realty, Inc.; Robert Friedland; Sheila Freidland.
Financial data (yr. ended 11/30/11): Assets, $1,706 (M); expenditures, $161; qualifying distributions, $0.
Purpose and activities: The foundation supports organizations involved with education, women's services, international peace, leadership development, and Judaism.
Fields of interest: Education; Women, centers/services; International peace/security; Jewish federated giving programs; Leadership development; Jewish agencies & synagogues.
Type of support: General/operating support; Program development.
Geographic limitations: Giving primarily in Rockville, MD and New York, NY.
Support limitations: No grants to individuals.
Application information: Applications not accepted. Contributes only to pre-selected organizations.
Officers: Robert Friedland, Pres. and Treas.; Sheila G. Friedland, Secy.
EIN: 133442016

1504
Friedman Kaplan Seiler & Adelman LLP
1633 Broadway, 46th Fl.
New York, NY 10019-6708 (212) 833-1100

Company URL: http://www.fklaw.com/
Establishment information: Established in 1986.
Company type: Private company
Business activities: Operates law firm.
Business type (SIC): Legal services
Offices: Newark, NJ; New York, NY
Giving statement: Giving through the Friedman Kaplan Seiler & Adelman LLP Pro Bono Program.

Friedman Kaplan Seiler & Adelman LLP Pro Bono Program
1633 Broadway, 46th Fl.
New York, NY 10019-6708 (212) 833-1164
E-mail: elosey@fklaw.com; Additional Pro Bono Contact: Benjamin Holzer, Pro Bono Coord., e-mail: bholzer@fklaw.com; URL: http://www.fklaw.com/

Contact: Elizabeth Losey, Pro Bono Coord.
Fields of interest: Legal services.
Type of support: Pro bono services - legal.
Geographic limitations: Giving primarily in areas of company operations in Newark, NJ, and New York, NY.
Application information: A Pro Bono Committee manages the pro bono program.

1505
Friesen Lumber Co.
1155 Deer Island Rd.
P.O. Box 479
Saint Helens, OR 97051-1046
(503) 397-1700

Company URL: http://www.flco.com/
Establishment information: Established in 1993.
Company type: Private company
Business activities: Operates sawmills.
Business type (SIC): Lumber and wood products
Financial profile for 2010: Number of employees, 120
Corporate officers: Jon T. Friesen, Pres.; Aaron Wilson, Cont.
Board of director: Scott Swanson
Giving statement: Giving through the Friesen Foundation, Inc.

Friesen Foundation, Inc.
P.O. Box 3525
Portland, OR 97208-3525

Establishment information: Established in 1990 in OR.
Donors: Friesen Lumber Co.; Friesen Timber, LLC.
Financial data (yr. ended 02/28/12): Assets, $1,373,607 (M); expenditures, $72,926; qualifying distributions, $50,336; giving activities include $47,150 for 22 grants (high: $5,000; low: $350).
Purpose and activities: The foundation supports animal hospitals and organizations involved with arts and culture, education, heart disease, youth services, and Christianity.
Fields of interest: Arts councils; Museums; Performing arts, ballet; Arts; Secondary school/ education; Education; Animal welfare; Hospitals (specialty); Heart & circulatory diseases; Youth, services; Christian agencies & churches.
Type of support: General/operating support; Program development.
Geographic limitations: Giving limited to Portland, OR and VA.
Support limitations: No grants to individuals.
Application information: Applications not accepted. Unsolicited requests for funds not accepted.
Officers and Directors:* Jon Friesen*, Pres.; Lex F. Page*, Secy.; Harlan Friesen*, Treas.
EIN: 931024760

1506
Frito-Lay, Inc.
7701 Legacy Dr.
P.O. Box 660634
Plano, TX 75024-4002 (972) 334-7000

Company URL: http://www.fritolay.com/
Establishment information: Established in 1932.
Company type: Subsidiary of a public company
Business activities: Manufactures snack foods.
Business type (SIC): Miscellaneous prepared foods; bakery products
Financial profile for 2010: Number of employees, 3,000
Corporate officers: Tom R. Greco, Pres.; George Legge, Sr. V.P. and C.F.O.; Jaime Montemayor, Sr. V.P. and C.I.O.; Marc Kesselman, Sr. V.P. and Genl. Counsel; Patrick McLaughlin, Sr. V.P., Human Resources; Christopher Wyse, V.P., Comms.
Plants: Charlotte, NC; Beloit, WI
Giving statement: Giving through the Frito-Lay, Inc. Corporate Giving Program.

Frito-Lay, Inc. Corporate Giving Program
P.O. Box 660634
Dallas, TX 75266-0634
URL: http://www.fritolay.com/about-us/community-information.html

Purpose and activities: Frito-Lay makes charitable contributions to nonprofit organizations involved with human services. Special emphasis is directed towards programs designed to help at-risk children. Support is given on a national basis.
Fields of interest: Human services; Children/youth, services; General charitable giving.
Type of support: General/operating support.
Geographic limitations: Giving on a national basis.
Application information: Applications not accepted. Contributes only to pre-selected organizations.

1507
Frommer Lawrence & Haug LLP
745 5th Ave.
New York, NY 10151-0099 (212) 588-0800

Company URL: http://www.flhlaw.com/
Company type: Private company
Business activities: Operates law firm.
Business type (SIC): Legal services
Offices: Washington, DC; New York, NY; Seattle, WA
International operations: Japan
Giving statement: Giving through the Frommer Lawrence & Haug LLP Pro Bono Program.

Frommer Lawrence & Haug LLP Pro Bono Program
745 5th Ave.
New York, NY 10151-0099 (206) 336-5690
E-mail: mwalters@flhlaw.com; URL: http://www.flhlaw.com/probono/xprGeneralContent2.aspx?xpST=ProBono

Contact: Mark P. Walters, Partner
Fields of interest: Legal services.
Type of support: Pro bono services - legal.
Geographic limitations: Giving primarily in Washington, DC, New York, NY, and Seattle, WA, and in Japan.
Application information: A Pro Bono Committee manages the pro bono program.

1508
Frontier Communications Corporation
(formerly Citizens Communications Company)
3 High Ridge Park
Stamford, CT 06905-1390 (203) 614-5600
FAX: (203) 260-2640

Company URL: http://www.frontier.com/
Establishment information: Established in 1927.
Company type: Public company
Company ticker symbol and exchange: FTR/NYSE
Business activities: Provides local telephone communications services.
Business type (SIC): Telephone communications
Financial profile for 2012: Number of employees, 14,700; assets, $17,733,630,000; sales volume, $5,011,850,000; pre-tax net income, $228,950,000; expenses, $4,106,400,000; liabilities, $13,626,030,000
Fortune 1000 ranking: 2012—492nd in revenues, 675th in profits, and 258th in assets
Forbes 2000 ranking: 2012—1394th in sales, 1669th in profits, and 1046th in assets
Corporate officers: Mary Agnes Wilderotter, Chair. and C.E.O.; Daniel J. McCarthy, Pres. and C.O.O.; John M. Jureller, Exec. V.P. and C.F.O.; Cecilia K. McKenney, Exec. V.P., Human Resources; Susana D'Emic, Sr. V.P. and Cont.; Andrew Crain, Sr. V.P. and Genl. Counsel
Board of directors: Mary Agnes Wilderotter, Chair.; Leroy T. Barnes, Jr.; Peter C.B. Bynoe; Jeri B. Finard; Edward D. Fraioli; James S. Kahan; Pamela D. Reeve; Howard L. Schrott; Larraine D. Segil; Mark Shapiro; Myron A. Wick III
Subsidiary: Frontier Communications of Rochester, Inc., Rochester, NY
Giving statement: Giving through the Frontier Communications Corporation Contributions Program.
Company EIN: 060619596

Frontier Communications Corporation Contributions Program
(formerly Citizens Communications Company Contributions Program)
3 High Ridge Park
Stamford, CT 06905-1337 (203) 614-5600
FAX: (203) 260-2640; For the Great Frontier Donate: Ali Buchanan, tel.: (952) 435-4629, e-mail: Alexandra.Buchanan@FTR.com; URL: http://www.frontier.com/customerservice/media-relations

Purpose and activities: Frontier Communications makes charitable contributions to nonprofit organizations on a case by case basis. Support is given primarily in areas of company operations.
Fields of interest: General charitable giving.
Program:
Great Frontier Donate: Through the Great Frontier Donate program, Frontier Communications makes charitable contributions of up to $85 to enrolled nonprofit organizations when a new residential or business customer purchases qualifying Frontier services.
Type of support: Cause-related marketing; Sponsorships.
Geographic limitations: Giving primarily in areas of company operations.

1509
Frontier Communications of Rochester, Inc.
180 S. Clinton Ave.
Rochester, NY 14646-0002 (585) 777-2000

Company URL: http://www.frontier.com/
Establishment information: Established in 1994.
Company type: Subsidiary of a public company
Business activities: Provides local telephone communications services.
Business type (SIC): Telephone communications
Corporate officer: Corey Hewitt, Mgr.
Giving statement: Giving through the Frontier Communications of Rochester, Inc. Corporate Giving Program.

Frontier Communications of Rochester, Inc. Corporate Giving Program
(formerly Global Crossing North America, Inc. Corporate Giving Program)
180 S. Clinton Ave.
Rochester, NY 14646-0001 (845) 344-9416
E-mail: Karen.Miller@frontiercorp.com; Additional contacts: Pennsylvania: Patricia Amendola, tel.: (570) 631-6013; e-mail: Patricia.Amendola@ftr.com; New York and Pennsylvania: Stephanie Schifano, tel.: (585) 777-7083; e-mail: Stephanie.Schifano@ftr.com; North Carolina, South Carolina, and West Virginia: Dan Page, tel.: (304) 344-7463; e-mail: Dan.Page@ftr.com; Illinois, Minnesota, and Ohio: Patricia Amendola, tel.: (570) 631-6013; e-mail: Patricia.Amendola@ftr.com; Michigan: Matt Kelley, tel.: (260) 461-2325; e-mail: Matt.Kelley@ftr.com; Indiana: Roscoe Spencer, tel.: (317) 208-3383, e-mail: Roscoe.Spencer@ftr.com; Alabama, Arizona, Florida, Georgia, Idaho, Iowa, Mississippi, Montana, Nebraska, Nevada, New Mexico, Tennessee, Utah, and Wisconsin: Karen Miller, tel.: (845) 344-9416, e-mail: Karen.Miller@ftr.com; California, Oregon, and Washington: Steven Crosby, tel.: (916) 686-3333, e-mail: Steven.Crosby@ftr.com;

URL: http://www.frontier.com/corporate_communications/
Additional URL: http://www.frontieronline.com/sponsorship.asp

Purpose and activities: Frontier makes charitable contributions to nonprofit organizations in areas of company operations.
Fields of interest: General charitable giving.
Type of support: General/operating support.
Geographic limitations: Giving primarily in areas of company operations.
Application information: The Community Relations and Outreach and Education teams oversees giving.
Copies of proposal: 1

1510
Frontier Partners, Inc.
400 Skokie Blvd., Ste. 500
Northbrook, IL 60062-2815 (847) 509-9860

Company URL: http://www.frontierpartners.com
Establishment information: Established in 1993.
Company type: Private company
Business activities: Provides marketing and business development consulting services.
Business type (SIC): Management and public relations services
Corporate officers: William D. Forsyth, Pres.; Patrick C. Magner, Partner
Giving statement: Giving through the New Frontiers Foundation.

New Frontiers Foundation
400 Skokie Blvd., Ste. 500
Northbrook, IL 60062-7905 (847) 509-9860
FAX: (847) 509-9845;
E-mail: bforsyth@frontier-partners.com; URL: http://www.frontierpartners.com/foundation.html

Establishment information: Established in 1996 in IL.
Donor: Frontier Partners, Inc.
Contact: William D. Forsyth III, Pres. and Secy.
Financial data (yr. ended 12/31/11): Assets, $1,403,540 (M); expenditures, $90,449; qualifying distributions, $88,000; giving activities include $88,000 for 26 grants (high: $10,000; low: $1,000).
Purpose and activities: The foundation supports programs designed to improve the lives of underprivileged youth through education and social development.
Fields of interest: Education; Youth development Youth; Economically disadvantaged.
Type of support: Continuing support; General/operating support; Program development.
Geographic limitations: Giving primarily in Chicago, IL.
Publications: Grants list.
Application information: Applications accepted. Application form not required.
Initial approach: Proposal
Deadline(s): None
Officer: William D. Forsyth III, Pres. and Secy.
Director: Arnold M. Berlin.
EIN: 364112843

1511
Frost Brown Todd LLC
2200 PNC Ctr.
201 E. 5th St.
Cincinnati, OH 45202-4182 (502) 589-5400

Company URL: http://www.frostbrowntodd.com/
Establishment information: Established in 1919.
Company type: Private company
Business activities: Operates law firm.
Business type (SIC): Legal services
Corporate officers: John R. Crockett III, Chair.; Frank Szabo, C.F.O.; Paul Bromwell, C.I.O.
Offices: Indianapolis, IN; Florence, Lexington, Louisville, KY; Cincinnati, Columbus, West Chester, OH; Nashville, TN; Charleston, WV
Historic mergers: MGLAW, PPLC (June 1, 2012)
Giving statement: Giving through the Frost Brown Todd LLC Pro Bono Program.

Frost Brown Todd LLC Pro Bono Program
2200 PNC Ctr.
201 E. 5th St.
Cincinnati, OH 45202-4182 (502) 589-5400
E-mail: jbyrne@fbtlaw.com; URL: http://www.frostbrowntodd.com/firm-responsibility.html

Contact: Jeremiah A. Byrne, Member
Fields of interest: Legal services.
Type of support: Pro bono services - legal.
Geographic limitations: Giving primarily in areas of company operations in Indianapolis, IN, Florence, Lexington, and Louisville, KY, Cincinnati, Columbus, and West Chester, OH, Nashville, TN, and Charleston, WV.
Application information: A Pro Bono Committee manages the pro bono program.

1512
The Frost National Bank
100 W. Houston St., Ste. 100
San Antonio, TX 78205 (210) 220-4011

Company URL: http://www.frostbank.com
Establishment information: Established in 1868.
Company type: Subsidiary of a public company
Business activities: Operates commercial bank.
Business type (SIC): Banks/commercial
Corporate officers: Richard W. Evans, Jr., Chair. and C.E.O.; David Beck, Pres.; Phillip D. Green, Exec. V.P. and C.F.O.
Board of directors: Richard W. Evans, Jr., Chair.; Royce S. Caldwell; Ruben M. Escobedo; Philip D. Green; Richard M. Kleberg III; Ida Clement Steen
Giving statement: Giving through the Frost National Bank Corporate Giving Program and the Charitable Foundation Frost.

Charitable Foundation Frost
c/o Frost National Bank
P.O. Box 2950
San Antonio, TX 78299-2950

Establishment information: Established around 1979 in TX.
Donor: Frost National Bank.
Financial data (yr. ended 12/31/11): Assets, $2,142,155 (M); gifts received, $2,000,000; expenditures, $2,249; qualifying distributions, $0.
Purpose and activities: The foundation supports organizations involved with arts and culture, education, medical research, and human services.
Geographic limitations: Giving primarily in San Antonio, TX.
Support limitations: No grants to individuals.
Application information: Applications accepted. Proposals should be submitted using organization letterhead. Application form required. Applicants should submit the following:
1) signature and title of chief executive officer
2) name, address and phone number of organization
3) copy of IRS Determination Letter
4) copy of most recent annual report/audited financial statement/990
5) detailed description of project and amount of funding requested
6) organization's charter and by-laws
Initial approach: Proposal
Copies of proposal: 1
Deadline(s): None
Trustee: Frost National Bank.
EIN: 742058155

1513
Fru-Con Construction Corporation
15933 Clayton Rd.
Ballwin, MO 63011-2146 (636) 391-6700

Company URL: http://www.frucon.com
Establishment information: Established in 1872.
Company type: Subsidiary of a foreign company
Business activities: Provides general contract construction services.
Business type (SIC): Building construction general contractors and operative builders
Corporate officers: Ray Bond, Pres. and C.E.O.; Ralf-Rainer Fuchs, Exec. V.P. and C.F.O.; Michael R. Fischer, V.P., Opers.; Eric J. Anderson, Cont.
Giving statement: Giving through the Fruin-Colnon Foundation Trust.

Fruin-Colnon Foundation Trust
P.O. Box 387
St. Louis, MO 63166-0387
Application address: Charles R. Weeks, 15933 Clayton Rd., Ballwin, MO 63011, tel.: (636) 391-6700

Donors: Fruin & Co. General Contractors; Fruin-Colnon Contracting Co.; Fru-Con Corp.
Contact: Charles R. Weeks
Financial data (yr. ended 12/31/11): Assets, $631,611 (M); expenditures, $39,073; qualifying distributions, $24,000; giving activities include $24,000 for grants.
Purpose and activities: The foundation supports organizations involved with education, health, children and youth services, family services, and military and veterans.
Fields of interest: Health care; Health organizations; Religion.
Type of support: General/operating support.
Geographic limitations: Giving primarily in St. Louis, MO.
Support limitations: No grants to individuals.
Application information: Applications accepted. Application form required.
Initial approach: Letter of Inquiry
Deadline(s): None
Trustee: U.S. Bank, N.A.
EIN: 436020406

1514
Fuji Photo Film U.S.A., Inc.
200 Summit Lake Dr., 2nd Fl.
Valhalla, NY 10595-1356 (914) 789-8100

Company URL: http://www.fujifilm.com
Establishment information: Established in 1934.
Company type: Subsidiary of a foreign company
Business activities: Manufactures cameras, film, videotapes, cassettes, floppy disks, and photofinishing supplies.
Business type (SIC): Professional and commercial equipment—wholesale; electrical goods—wholesale
Corporate officers: Stanley E. Freimuth, Chair., Pres., and C.E.O.; Camilla Jenkins, V.P., Corp. Comms.; Joseph Convery, V.P., Human Resources
Board of director: Stanley E. Freimuth, Chair.
Subsidiaries: Fuji Hunt Photographic Chemicals, Inc., Paramus, NJ; Fuji Medical Systems USA, Inc., Stamford, CT; Fuji Photo Film, Inc., Greenwood, SC; Fuji Photo Film Hawaii, Inc., Honolulu, HI
Divisions: Fuji Computer Media Div., Elmsford, NY; Fuji Graphic Arts Div., Itasca, IL; Fuji Industrial Photo Products Div., Elmsford, NY; Fuji Magnetic Products Div., Elmsford, NY; Fuji Micrographics Div., Elmsford, NY; Fuji Photo Finishing Products Div., Elmsford, NY; Fuji Photographic Products Div., Elmsford, NY
Giving statement: Giving through the Fuji Photo Film U.S.A., Inc. Corporate Giving Program.

Fuji Photo Film U.S.A., Inc. Corporate Giving Program
200 Summit Lake Dr., 2nd Fl.
Valhalla, NY 10595-1360
URL: http://www.fujifilmusa.com/about/sustainability/local_commitment/index.html

Purpose and activities: Fuji Photo Film U.S.A. makes charitable contributions to nonprofit organizations on a case by case basis. Support is given primarily in areas of company operations.
Fields of interest: General charitable giving.
Type of support: Donated products.
Geographic limitations: Giving primarily in areas of company operations.
Application information: Applications not accepted. Contributes only to pre-selected organizations.
Number of staff: 1 full-time professional; 1 full-time support.

1515
Fujisankei Communications International, Inc.
150 E. 52nd St., 34th Fl.
New York, NY 10022-6227 (212) 753-8100

Company URL: http://www.fujisankei.com
Establishment information: Established in 1986.
Company type: Subsidiary of a foreign company
Business activities: Broadcasts television.
Business type (SIC): Radio and television broadcasting
Corporate officers: Hisoshi Hieda, Chair.; Takashi Hoga, C.E.O.; Hiroshi Oto, Pres.
Board of directors: Hisoshi Hieda, Chair.; Teruko Secor
Giving statement: Giving through the Society of International Cultural Exchange (SICE), Inc.

Society of International Cultural Exchange (SICE), Inc.
150 E. 52nd St., 34th Fl.
New York, NY 10022-6227 (212) 702-0572

Establishment information: Established in 1994 in FL and NY.
Donor: Fujisankei Communications International, Inc.
Contact: Jiro Saito, Secy.
Financial data (yr. ended 03/31/12): Assets, $824,128 (M); gifts received, $50,000; expenditures, $90,567; qualifying distributions, $90,567; giving activities include $70,450 for 1 grant.
Purpose and activities: The foundation supports the Japan Art Association in Tokyo, Japan.
Fields of interest: Museums (art); Arts.
International interests: Japan.
Type of support: General/operating support.
Geographic limitations: Giving primarily in Tokyo, Japan.
Application information: Applications accepted. Application form not required.
Initial approach: Proposal
Deadline(s): None
Officers: Takashi Hoga, Pres.; Hiroshi Oto, V.P.; Jiro Saito, Secy.; Kiyoshi Onoe, Treas.
Directors: Hisashi Hieda; Kim Marie Parker; Kou Toyoda.
EIN: 133244953

1516
Fulbright & Jaworski L.L.P
1301 McKinney, Ste. 5100
Houston, TX 77010-3095 (713) 651-5151

Company URL: http://www.fulbright.com/
Establishment information: Established in 1919.
Company type: Private company
Business activities: Operates law firm.
Business type (SIC): Legal services
Offices: Los Angeles, CA; Denver, CO; Washington, DC; Minneapolis, MN; Saint Louis, MO; New York, NY; Canonsburg, PA; Austin, Dallas, Houston, San Antonio, TX
International operations: China; Germany; Hong Kong; Saudi Arabia; United Arab Emirates; United Kingdom
Giving statement: Giving through the Fulbright & Jaworski L.L.P. Pro Bono Program.

Fulbright & Jaworski L.L.P. Pro Bono Program
1301 McKinney, Ste. 5100
Houston, TX 77010-3095 (713) 651-5151
E-mail: sgagnon@fulbright.com; URL: http://www.fulbright.com/index.cfm?fuseaction=home.594

Contact: Stewart Gagnon, Partner
Fields of interest: Legal services.
Type of support: Pro bono services - legal.
Application information: The Pro Bono Committee manages the pro-bono program.

1517
H.B. Fuller Company
1200 Willow Lake Blvd.
P.O. Box 64683
St. Paul, MN 55164-0683 (651) 236-5900
FAX: (651) 236-5426

Company URL: http://www.hbfuller.com
Establishment information: Established in 1887.
Company type: Public company
Company ticker symbol and exchange: FUL/NYSE
Business activities: Manufactures and markets adhesives, sealants, coatings, paints, and specialty chemical products.
Business type (SIC): Chemical preparations/miscellaneous; chemicals and allied products; paints and allied products
Financial profile for 2012: Number of employees, 3,700; assets, $1,786,320,000; sales volume, $1,886,240,000; pre-tax net income, $89,550,000; expenses, $1,777,680,000; liabilities, $1,008,050,000
Fortune 1000 ranking: 2012—955th in revenues, 692nd in profits, and 880th in assets
Corporate officers: Lee R. Mitau, Chair.; Jim Owens, Pres. and C.E.O.; James R. Giertz, Sr. V.P. and C.F.O.; Timothy J. Keenan, V.P., Genl. Counsel, and Corp. Secy.; Cheryl Reinitz, V.P. and Treas.; James C. McCreary, Jr., V.P. and Cont.; Kevin Gilligan, V.P., Opers.; Ann B. Parriott, V.P., Human Resources
Board of directors: Lee R. Mitau, Chair.; Thomas W. Handley; J. Michael Losh; Jim Owens; Dante Parrini; Alfredo L. Rovira; John C. Van Roden, Jr.; R. William Van Sant
Plants: Roseville, CA; Gainesville, FL; Covington, Tucker, GA; Palatine, Tinley Park, IL; Elkhart, IN; Paducah, KY; Grand Rapids, MI; Fridley, Oakdale, MN; Cincinnati, OH; Dallas, TX; Vancouver, WA
Giving statement: Giving through the H. B. Fuller Company Contributions Program and the H. B. Fuller Company Foundation.
Company EIN: 410268370

H. B. Fuller Company Contributions Program
1200 Willow Lake Blvd.
P.O. Box 64683
St. Paul, MN 55164-0683 (651) 236-5900
URL: http://phx.corporate-ir.net/phoenix.zhtml?c=203756&p=irol-CorporateContributions

Financial data (yr. ended 12/31/10): Total giving, $179,934, including $179,934 for grants.
Purpose and activities: As a complement to its foundation, H.B. Fuller also makes charitable contributions to nonprofit organizations directly. Support is given on a national and international basis.
Fields of interest: Arts; Education; Environment, public education; Environment, beautification programs; Environmental education; Disasters, fire prevention/control; Recreation; Children, day care; Independent living, disability; Science, public education; Mathematics; Engineering/technology.
International interests: Asia; Canada; Europe; Latin America.
Type of support: Employee volunteer services; General/operating support; Scholarship funds.
Geographic limitations: Giving on a national and international basis in areas of company operations, including St. Paul, MN, and Asia, Canada, Europe, and Latin America.
Application information: Giving is coordinated by 28 employee-directed Community Affairs Councils (CAC) worldwide.

Community Affairs Department: Keralyn Gross, Dir., Community Affairs; Christine Meyer, Community Affairs Rep.
Number of staff: 2 full-time professional.

H. B. Fuller Company Foundation

P.O. Box 64683
St. Paul, MN 55164-0683 (651) 236-5217
FAX: (651) 236-5056;
E-mail: hbfullerfoundation@hbfuller.com;
URL: http://www.hbfuller.com/north-america/about-us/community-responsibility

Establishment information: Established in 1986 in MN.
Donor: H.B. Fuller Co.
Financial data (yr. ended 11/30/11): Assets, $2,232,826 (M); expenditures, $623,213; qualifying distributions, $609; giving activities include $609 for grants.
Purpose and activities: The foundation supports youth education initiatives in areas of science, technology, engineering, and math (STEM); and programs designed to promote leadership development for youth.
Fields of interest: Arts; Elementary/secondary education; Education; Health care; Disasters, preparedness/services; Youth development; Children/youth, services; Human services; Mathematics; Engineering/technology; Science; Leadership development Youth.
Type of support: Annual campaigns; Building/renovation; Employee matching gifts; Equipment; General/operating support; Matching/challenge support; Program development.
Geographic limitations: Giving primarily in areas of company operations in Roseville, CA, Covington, GA, Aurora and Palatine, IL, Paducah, KY, St. Paul, MN, and Vancouver, WA, and China.
Support limitations: No support for religious, fraternal, or veterans' organizations, political or lobbying organizations, national organizations, or disease-specific organizations. No grants to individuals, or for capital campaigns, endowments, travel, basic or applied research, advertising, fundraising events or sponsorships, or general support of educational institutions.
Publications: Application guidelines; Corporate giving report.
Application information: Applications accepted. Proposals should be no longer than five pages. Funding decisions are made by Community Affairs Councils at each facility location. The Minnesota Common Grant Application Form is accepted. Applications from organizations located outside of the U.S. are by invitation only. Application form required. Applicants should submit the following:
1) timetable for implementation and evaluation of project
2) qualifications of key personnel
3) copy of IRS Determination Letter
4) brief history of organization and description of its mission
5) geographic area to be served
6) copy of most recent annual report/audited financial statement/990
7) how project's results will be evaluated or measured
8) list of company employees involved with the organization
9) listing of board of directors, trustees, officers and other key people and their affiliations
10) detailed description of project and amount of funding requested
11) copy of current year's organizational budget and/or project budget
12) listing of additional sources and amount of support

Initial approach: Download application form and e-mail, fax, or mail proposal and application form to foundation
Deadline(s): Postmarked by Mar. 31 and Aug. 31

Officers and Directors:* Richard Kastner*, Pres.; Joel Hedberg, V.P.; Rachel Hart, Secy.; Jodie Monson, Treas.; Kimberlee Sinclair, Exec. Dir.; Traci Jensen; Jim Owens; Wes Oren; Nathan Weaver; Jeff Wroblewski.
EIN: 363500811
Selected grants: The following grants are a representative sample of this grantmaker's funding activity:
$50,000 to Minneapolis Society of Fine Arts, Minneapolis, MN, 2010.
$25,000 to Population Council, New York, NY, 2010.
$7,500 to Saint Catherine University, Saint Paul, MN, 2010.
$7,500 to University of Saint Thomas, Saint Paul, MN, 2010.
$1,000 to DePauw University, Greencastle, IN, 2010.
$1,000 to University of Massachusetts, Amherst, MA, 2010.
$1,000 to University of Saint Thomas, Saint Paul, MN, 2010.

1518
Fulton Financial Corporation

1 Penn Sq.
P.O. Box 4887
Lancaster, PA 17604 (717) 291-2411
FAX: (717) 291-2695

Company URL: http://www.fult.com
Establishment information: Established in 1982.
Company type: Public company
Company ticker symbol and exchange: FULT/NASDAQ
Business activities: Operates bank holding company; operates commercial bank.
Business type (SIC): Banks/commercial; holding company
Financial profile for 2012: Number of employees, 3,570; assets, $16,528,150,000; pre-tax net income, $217,450,000; liabilities, $14,377,970,000
Corporate officers: E. Philip Wenger, Chair., Pres., and C.E.O.; Charles J. Nugent, Sr. Exec. V.P. and C.F.O.; Craig H. Hill, Sr. Exec. V.P., Human Resources
Board of directors: E. Philip Wenger, Chair.; Jeffrey G. Albertson; Joe N. Ballard; John M. Bond, Jr.; Craig A. Dally; Patrick J. Freer; Rufus Ayers Fulton, Jr.; George W. Hodges; Donald W. Lesher, Jr.; Albert Morrison III; Gary A. Stewart
Subsidiaries: The Bank of Gloucester County, Woodbury, NJ; Central Pennsylvania Financial Corp., Lancaster, PA; FFC Management, Inc., Wilmington, DE; First Washington State Bank, Windsor, NJ; FNB Bank, N.A., Danville, PA; Fulton Bank, Lancaster, PA; Fulton Financial Advisors, N.A., Lancaster, PA; Fulton Financial Realty Co., Lancaster, PA; Fulton Insurance Services Group, Inc., Lancaster, PA; Fulton Life Insurance Co., Lancaster, PA; Hagerstown Trust Co., Hagerstown, MD; Lafayette Ambassador Bank, Easton, PA; Lebanon Valley Farmers Bank, Lebanon, PA; The Peoples Bank of Elkton, Elkton, MD; Skylands Community Bank, Hackettstown, NJ; Swineford National Bank, Middleburg, PA; The Woodstown National Bank and Trust Co., Woodstown, NJ
Historic mergers: Premier Bancorp, Inc. (August 1, 2003); Delaware National Bank (December 4, 2010)
Giving statement: Giving through the Fulton Financial Corporation Contributions Program, the Delaware National Bank of Delhi Corporate Charitable Trust, and the Fulton Bank Scholarship Foundation.
Company EIN: 232195389

Fulton Financial Corporation Contributions Program

1 Penn Sq.
Lancaster, PA 17602 (717) 291-2411
URL: http://www.fult.com/aboutus/inthecommunity.asp

Purpose and activities: As a complement to its foundation, Fulton Financial Corporation makes charitable contributions to nonprofit organizations involved with the arts, health and human services, economic development, and education. Support is given primarily in areas of company operations in Delaware, Maryland, New Jersey, Pennsylvania, and Virginia; giving also to national organizations.
Fields of interest: Arts; Education; Health care; Human services; Community/economic development Economically disadvantaged.
Type of support: Employee volunteer services; General/operating support; Sponsorships.
Geographic limitations: Giving primarily in areas of company operations in DE, MD, NJ, PA, and VA; giving also to national organizations.

Delaware National Bank of Delhi Corporate Charitable Trust

124 Main St.
Delhi, NY 13753-1266

Establishment information: Established in 1996 in NY.
Donor: The Delaware National Bank of Delhi.
Financial data (yr. ended 12/31/11): Assets, $218,511 (M); gifts received, $100,000; expenditures, $39,612; qualifying distributions, $39,500; giving activities include $39,500 for 57 grants (high: $10,000; low: $25).
Purpose and activities: The foundation supports hospitals and police agencies and organizations involved with arts and culture, education, cancer, athletics, and community development.
Fields of interest: Media, print publishing; Historic preservation/historical societies; Arts; Higher education; Education; Hospitals (general); Cancer; Crime/law enforcement, police agencies; Athletics/sports, amateur leagues; Community/economic development.
Type of support: Annual campaigns; Capital campaigns; General/operating support; Program development; Scholarship funds; Sponsorships.
Geographic limitations: Giving limited to Delaware County, NY.
Support limitations: No grants to individuals.
Application information: Applications not accepted. Unsolicited requests for funds not accepted.
Trustee: The Delaware National Bank of Delhi.
EIN: 166447080

Fulton Bank Scholarship Foundation

P.O. Box 3215
Lancaster, PA 17604-3215

Donor: Fulton Financial Corp.
Financial data (yr. ended 12/31/11): Assets, $236 (M); gifts received, $37,500; expenditures, $37,500; qualifying distributions, $37,500; giving activities include $37,500 for 25 grants to individuals (high: $1,500; low: $1,500).

Purpose and activities: The foundation awards college scholarships to children of employees of Fulton Financial.
Fields of interest: Higher education.
Type of support: Employee-related scholarships.
Geographic limitations: Giving limited to areas of company and affiliate operations.
Application information: Applications not accepted. Unsolicited requests for funds not accepted.
Trustee: Fulton Financial Advisors.
EIN: 236769593

1519
Furniture Brands International, Inc.

(formerly Interco Inc.)
1 N. Brentwood Blvd., 15th Fl.
St. Louis, MO 63105 (314) 863-1100
FAX: (302) 636-5454

Company URL: http://www.furniturebrands.com
Establishment information: Established in 1921.
Company type: Public company
Company ticker symbol and exchange: FBN/NYSE
Business activities: Manufactures and markets residential furniture.
Business type (SIC): Furniture/household
Financial profile for 2012: Number of employees, 5,600; assets, $618,440,000; sales volume, $1,072,320,000; pre-tax net income, -$49,040,000; expenses, $1,116,400,000; liabilities, $563,640,000
Corporate officers: Ralph P. Scozzafava, Chair. and C.E.O.; Vance C. Johnston, Sr. V.P. and C.F.O.; Meredith M. Graham, Sr. V.P., Genl. Counsel, and Corp. Secy.; Mary E. Sweetman, Sr. V.P., Human Resources; Richard R. Isaak, V.P., C.A.O., and Cont.
Board of directors: Ralph P. Scozzafava, Chair.; Kent J. Hussey; Ira D. Kaplan; Ann Spector Lieff; Aubrey B. Patterson; George E. Ross
Subsidiaries: Broyhill Furniture Industries, Inc., Lenoir, NC; The Lane Company, Incorporated, Tupelo, MS; Thomasville Furniture Industries, Inc., Thomasville, NC
International operations: China; Hong Kong; Indonesia; Malaysia; Philippines; Vanuatu
Giving statement: Giving through the Interco Charitable Trust.
Company EIN: 430337683

Interco Charitable Trust

13321 N. Outer Forty Rd., Ste. 100
St. Louis, MO 63017-5945
FAX: (314) 786-1201; Additional tel.: (314) 786-1200

Establishment information: Trust established in 1944 in MO.
Donor: Furniture Brands International, Inc.
Contact: Michael R. Loynd, Exec. Dir.
Financial data (yr. ended 12/31/11): Assets, $30,051,004 (M); expenditures, $1,946,126; qualifying distributions, $1,309,369; giving activities include $1,309,369 for grants.
Purpose and activities: The foundation supports organizations involved with arts and culture, education, health, youth development, human services, science, and religion. Support is given primarily in the greater St. Louis, Missouri, area.
Fields of interest: Museums (art); Arts; Higher education; Education; Health care; Boys & girls clubs; Youth development; American Red Cross; Youth, services; Homeless, human services; Human services; United Ways and Federated Giving Programs; Science; Religion.
Type of support: Continuing support; General/operating support; Scholarship funds.
Geographic limitations: Giving primarily in St. Louis, MO.
Support limitations: No grants to individuals.
Publications: Annual report; Application guidelines.
Application information: Applications accepted. Application form not required.
Initial approach: Proposal
Board meeting date(s): Apr., July, Oct., and Dec.
Deadline(s): None
Officer and Trustees:* Michael R. Loynd, Exec. Dir.; Donald E. Lasater; Lee M. Liberman; Richard B. Loynd; Robert H. Quenon.
Number of staff: 1 full-time professional.
EIN: 311593436
Selected grants: The following grants are a representative sample of this grantmaker's funding activity:
$100,000 to Boys and Girls Club, Mathews-Dickey, Saint Louis, MO, 2010.
$100,000 to Washington University, Saint Louis, MO, 2010.
$50,000 to American Red Cross, Saint Louis Chapter, Saint Louis, MO, 2010.
$50,000 to Donald Danforth Plant Science Center, Saint Louis, MO, 2010.
$50,000 to Forest Park Forever, Saint Louis, MO, 2010.
$50,000 to Saint Louis Art Museum, Saint Louis, MO, 2010.
$50,000 to Saint Louis University, Saint Louis, MO, 2010.
$50,000 to Saint Patrick Center, Saint Louis, MO, 2010.
$50,000 to Washington University, Saint Louis, MO, 2010.
$30,000 to Today and Tomorrow Educational Foundation, Saint Louis, MO, 2010.

1520
Furr Investments, Ltd.

5150 Broadway St., Upper 601
San Antonio, TX 78209-5710

Company type: Private company
Business activities: Operates holding company.
Business type (SIC): Holding company
Giving statement: Giving through the Hand in Hand Foundation.

Hand in Hand Foundation

2313 Lockhill Selma Rd., PMB 238
San Antonio, TX 78230-3003

Establishment information: Established in 1998 in TX.
Donors: Darla Barger; John Barger; Furr Investments, Ltd.; John Furr; Paula Furr; Timothy Graham, M.D; Bobby Ray; Bonnie Ray; Rifle Church of Christ; SFJTD Charitable Fund; Sunset Ridge Church.
Financial data (yr. ended 12/31/11): Assets, $148,861 (M); gifts received, $66,194; expenditures, $125,525; qualifying distributions, $113,477; giving activities include $113,477 for grants.
Purpose and activities: The foundation supports organizations involved with Christianity.
Fields of interest: Christian agencies & churches.
Type of support: Building/renovation; General/operating support; Program development; Scholarship funds.
Geographic limitations: Giving primarily in FL, IL, and TX.
Application information: Applications not accepted. Contributes only to pre-selected organizations.
Officers: John Furr, Pres. and Treas.; Dean Smith, V.P.; Paula Furr, Secy.
EIN: 742878386

1521
Further The Work

855 Meadow View Dr.
Richmond, CA 94806-6109 (510) 243-0122

Company URL: http://furtherthework.com
Establishment information: Established in 2002.
Company type: Private company
Business activities: Operates boutique consultancy serving nonprofit organizations, educational institutions, and philanthropies.
Business type (SIC): Management and public relations services
Corporate officers: Rebecca Brown, Pres.; Glenn Miller, C.O.O.
Giving statement: Giving through the Further The Work Corporate Giving Program.

Further The Work Corporate Giving Program

855 Meadow View Dr.
Richmond, CA 94806 (510) 243-0122
E-mail: rebecca@FurtherTheWork.com; URL: http://furtherthework.com

Purpose and activities: Further The Work is a certified B Corporation that donates a percentage of profits to nonprofit organizations.

1522
FXDD

7 World Trade Ctr., 32nd Fl.
New York, NY 10007 (212) 791-3933
FAX: (212) 937-3845

Company URL: http://www.fxdd.com
Establishment information: Established in 2002.
Company type: Private company
Business activities: Operates foreign exchange trading company.
Business type (SIC): Brokers and dealers/security
Corporate officer: Lubomir Kaneti, C.O.O.
Giving statement: Giving through the FXDD Corporate Giving Program.

FXDD Corporate Giving Program

7 World Trade Ctr., 32nd Fl.
New York, NY 10007 (212) 791-3933
URL: http://www.fxdd.com

1523
G & R Felpausch Company

(also known as Felpausch)
127 S. Michigan Ave.
Hastings, MI 49058-1830 (269) 945-3485

Company URL: http://www.felpausch.com
Establishment information: Established in 1933.
Company type: Private company
Business activities: Operates grocery stores.

Business type (SIC): Groceries—retail
Corporate officers: Mark S. Feldpausch, Chair., C.E.O., and Co-Pres.; James Feldpausch, Co-Pres.
Board of director: Mark S. Feldpausch, Chair. and Pres.
Giving statement: Giving through the Felpausch Foundation.

Felpausch Foundation

21425 St. Mary's Way
Battle Creek, MI 49017

Establishment information: Established in 1998 in MI.
Donors: G&R Felpausch Co.; T&D Parker Investments, LLC; Parker T. Feldpausch.
Financial data (yr. ended 12/31/11): Assets, $1,680,863 (M); gifts received, $26,412; expenditures, $58,038; qualifying distributions, $39,162; giving activities include $39,162 for grants.
Purpose and activities: The foundation supports art councils, hospitals, and community foundations and organizations involved with science and math education.
Fields of interest: Arts; Education; Health care.
Type of support: Annual campaigns.
Geographic limitations: Giving primarily in MI.
Support limitations: No grants to individuals.
Application information: Applications not accepted. Unsolicited requests for funds not accepted.
Officers: Parker T. Feldpausch, Pres.; Mark S. Feldpausch, Secy.; Keith R. Tolger, Treas.
Directors: Kimberly A. Brubaker; Corey Lagro.
EIN: 383417534

1524
G&K Services, Inc.

5995 Opus Pkwy.
Minnetonka, MN 55343-9078
(952) 912-5500
FAX: (952) 912-5999

Company URL: http://www.gkservices.com/
Establishment information: Established in 1902.
Company type: Public company
Company ticker symbol and exchange: GK/NASDAQ
Business activities: Provides branded identity apparel and facility services programs.
Business type (SIC): Laundry, cleaning, and garment services; business services/miscellaneous
Financial profile for 2012: Number of employees, 6,500; assets, $873,730,000; sales volume, $869,940,000; pre-tax net income, $36,190,000; expenses, $827,670,000; liabilities, $470,670,000
Corporate officers: M. Lenny Pippin, Chair.; Douglas A. Milroy, C.E.O.; Jeffrey L. Wright, Exec. V.P. and C.F.O.; Richard J. Stutz, Sr. V.P., Opers.; Jeffrey Louis Cotter, V.P., Genl. Counsel, and Corp. Secy.; David A. Euson, V.P., Mktg. and Sales; Randall R. Ross, V.P., Human Resources
Board of directors: M. Lenny Pippin, Chair.; John S. Bronson; Lynn Crump-Caine; J. Patrick Doyle; Wayne M. Fortun; Douglas A. Milroy; Ernest Mrozek; Alice M. Richter; Jeffrey L. Wright
Giving statement: Giving through the G&K Services Foundation.
Company EIN: 410449530

G&K Services Foundation

5995 Opus Pkwy., Ste. 500
Minnetonka, MN 55343-8387 (952) 912-5958
E-mail: lgallmeyer@gkservices.com; URL: http://www.gkservices.com/about/foundation.html

Establishment information: Established in 2005 in MN.
Donor: G&K Services.
Contact: Lisa Gallmeyer
Financial data (yr. ended 12/31/11): Assets, $352,418 (M); gifts received, $150,000; expenditures, $86,039; qualifying distributions, $86,014; giving activities include $86,014 for grants.
Purpose and activities: The foundation supports organizations involved with education, employment, disaster relief, youth development, human services, and leadership development.
Fields of interest: Vocational education; Higher education; Adult education—literacy, basic skills & GED; Education, ESL programs; Education, reading; Education; Employment, training; Employment, vocational rehabilitation; Employment; Disasters, preparedness/services; Youth development; Children/youth, services; Human services, personal services; Human services; Leadership development.
Programs:
Education: The foundation supports programs designed to promote higher education, vocational/technical education, and youth/adult leadership development.
Human Services: The foundation supports programs designed to provide human services, including clothing for education, employment, and disaster relief.
Self-Sufficiency: The foundation supports programs designed to promote self-sufficiency through employment procurement/job training, and vocational rehabilitation.
Skills Development: The foundation supports programs designed to promote skills development, including GED, ESL, and literacy.
Type of support: General/operating support; Program development.
Geographic limitations: Giving primarily in areas of company operations in Minneapolis, MN.
Support limitations: No support for political, lobbying, or advocacy organizations or candidates, fraternal, social, labor, veterans', or alumni organizations, athletic groups, religious organizations not of direct benefit to the entire community, pre-schools, nursery schools, or K-12 public or private educational institutions. No grants for scholarships, or for travel, conferences, conventions, sponsorships, recreation, sporting events, advertising, multi-year commitments, capital campaigns, endowments, academic, medical, or scientific research, or daycare programs.
Application information: Applications not accepted. The foundation is accepts proposals through an invitation only process and from existing grantees only.
Board meeting date(s): Semi-annually
Officers: Jeffrey L. Wright, Pres.; Jacqueline T. Punch, V.P.; Jeffrey Louis Cotter, Secy.-Treas.
EIN: 743152076
Selected grants: The following grants are a representative sample of this grantmaker's funding activity:
$49,791 to United Way, Greater Twin Cities, Minneapolis, MN, 2010. For general operating support.
$6,500 to Emergency Foodshelf Network, New Hope, MN, 2010.
$6,000 to Minneapolis Society of Fine Arts, Minneapolis, MN, 2010.
$4,813 to K T C A/K T C I Twin Cities Public Television, Saint Paul, MN, 2010.
$4,000 to Minnesota Orchestral Association, Minneapolis, MN, 2010.
$4,000 to Minnesota Public Radio, Saint Paul, MN, 2010. For general operating support.
$3,780 to YMCA of Greater Saint Paul, Minneapolis, MN, 2010.
$2,970 to University of Saint Thomas, Saint Paul, MN, 2010.
$2,475 to Hennepin County Library, Friends of the, Minneapolis, MN, 2010.
$2,475 to House of Charity, Minneapolis, MN, 2010. For general operating support.

1525
Gable & Gotwals P.C.

1100 ONEOK Plz.
100 W. 5th St., Ste. 1100
Tulsa, OK 74103-4217 (918) 595-4800

Company URL: http://www.gablelaw.com
Establishment information: Established in 1919.
Company type: Private company
Business activities: Provides legal services.
Business type (SIC): Legal services
Office: Oklahoma City, OK
Giving statement: Giving through the Gable & Gotwals Foundation.

Gable & Gotwals Foundation

(formerly Gable & Gotwals Mock Schwabe Kible Gaberino Foundation)
100 W. 5th St., Ste. 1100
Tulsa, OK 74103-4217 (918) 595-4800
URL: http://www.gablelaw.com/about_us/foundation.html

Establishment information: Established in 1992 in OK.
Donors: Gable & Gotwals P.C.; James M. Sturdivant.
Contact: Amy Fogelman, Chair.
Financial data (yr. ended 10/31/12): Assets, $1,041 (M); gifts received, $40,000; expenditures, $42,648; qualifying distributions, $42,648; giving activities include $42,648 for grants.
Purpose and activities: The foundation supports organizations involved with arts and culture, education, health, legal services, youth, social services, and other areas.
Fields of interest: Museums (art); Performing arts, orchestras; Historic preservation/historical societies; Arts; Higher education; Education; Health care; Legal services; Youth, services; Human services; General charitable giving.
Type of support: General/operating support.
Geographic limitations: Giving primarily in the Tulsa, OK, area.
Application information: Applications accepted. Application form required. Applicants should submit the following:
1) copy of IRS Determination Letter
2) detailed description of project and amount of funding requested
Initial approach: Letter
Copies of proposal: 1
Board meeting date(s): Monthly
Deadline(s): None
Officer: Amy Fogelman, Chair.
Trustees: Ellen Adams; Steven L. Barghols; Dennis Cameron; Rob Carlson.
EIN: 731413740

1526
Gable Gotwals
1100 ONEOK Plz.
100 W. 5th St.
Tulsa, OK 74103-4217 (918) 595-4800

Company URL: http://www.gablelaw.com
Company type: Private company
Business activities: Operates law firm.
Business type (SIC): Legal services
Offices: Oklahoma City, Tulsa, OK
Giving statement: Giving through the Gable Gotwals Pro Bono Program.

Gable Gotwals Pro Bono Program
1100 ONEOK Plz.
100 W. 5th St.
Tulsa, OK 74103-4217 (918) 595-4800
E-mail: tcarnery@gablelaw.com; URL: http://www.gablelaw.com/about_us/pro-bono-work.html

Contact: Timothy A. Carney, Shareholder
Fields of interest: Legal services.
Type of support: Pro bono services - legal.
Geographic limitations: Giving primarily in areas of company operations in Oklahoma City, and Tulsa, OK.
Application information: The Pro Bono Committee manages the pro-bono program.

1527
Gaiam, Inc.
833 W. S. Boulder Rd.
P.O. Box 3095
Boulder, CO 80307-3095 (303) 222-3600
FAX: (303) 464-3700

Company URL: http://www.gaiam.com
Establishment information: Established in 1988.
Company type: Public company
Company ticker symbol and exchange: GAIA/NASDAQ
Business activities: Provides catalog shopping services; provides Internet shopping services; sells lifestyle products wholesale; produces television programming.
Business type (SIC): Nonstore retailers; wholesale trade—durable goods; computer services; motion pictures/production and services allied to
Financial profile for 2012: Number of employees, 345; assets, $193,860,000; sales volume, $202,470,000; pre-tax net income, -$18,250,000; expenses, $201,880,000; liabilities, $77,790,000
Corporate officers: Jirka Rysavy, Chair.; Lynn Powers, C.E.O.; William S. Sondheim, Pres.; John Jackson, Secy.; Stephen J. Thomas, Cont., C.A.O., and C.F.O.
Board of directors: Jirka Rysavy, Chair.; James Argyropolous; Barnet M. Feinblum; Barbara Mowry; Lynn Powers; Paul H. Ray; Paul Sutherland
Subsidiary: Real Goods Trading Corp., Inc., Ukiah, CA
Giving statement: Giving through the Gaiam, Inc. Corporate Giving Program.
Company EIN: 841113527

Gaiam, Inc. Corporate Giving Program
c/o Donation Requests
360 Interlocken Blvd.
Broomfield, CO 80021-3496 (303) 222-3608

Purpose and activities: Gaiam makes charitable contributions of lifestyle products to nonprofit organizations on a case by case basis. Support is given primarily in areas of company operations.
Fields of interest: General charitable giving.
Type of support: Donated products.
Geographic limitations: Giving primarily in areas of company operations.
Application information: Applications accepted. Unsolicited requests for general operating support are not accepted. Application form not required. Applicants should submit the following:
1) copy of IRS Determination Letter
2) brief history of organization and description of its mission
3) detailed description of project and amount of funding requested

Initial approach: Mail or fax proposal to headquarters
Copies of proposal: 1
Deadline(s): Early in the year is preferred; 4 months prior to need
Final notification: Following review

1528
Gallagher Koster
(formerly Koster Insurance Agency, Inc.)
500 Victory Rd., Ste. 12
Quincy, MA 02171-3132 (617) 770-9889
FAX: (617) 479-0860

Company URL: https://www.gallagherkoster.com/
Establishment information: Established in 1994.
Company type: Subsidiary of a private company
Business activities: Sells health insurance solutions to educational institutions and students.
Business type (SIC): Insurance/accident and health
Corporate officers: J. Patrick Gallagher, Chair.; Terasa Koster, Pres.; Richard Wallace, V.P. and C.F.O.
Board of director: J. Patrick Gallagher, Chair.
Giving statement: Giving through the Koster Insurance Scholarship Fund, Inc.

Koster Insurance Scholarship Fund, Inc.
500 Victory Rd.
Quincy, MA 02171-3139 (617) 770-9889
FAX: (617) 479-0860;
E-mail: scholarship@gallagherkoster.com;
URL: https://www.gallagherkoster.com/scholarship/

Establishment information: Established in 2000 in MA; classified as a company-sponsored operating foundation in 2001.
Donors: Koster Insurance Agency, Inc.; Gallagher Koster; Arthur J. Gallagher.
Financial data (yr. ended 12/31/10): Assets, $62,219 (M); gifts received, $24,500; expenditures, $29,326; qualifying distributions, $25,000; giving activities include $25,000 for 10 grants to individuals (high: $2,500; low: $2,500).
Purpose and activities: The foundation awards college scholarships to students studying for a career in the healthcare field.
Fields of interest: Health care.
Program:
Health Careers Scholarship Program: The foundation annually awards college scholarships to students in their junior or senior year of undergraduate study at an accredited institution that prepares them for a career in healthcare. Qualifying degree programs include pre-medicine, nursing, public/community health, physical therapy, occupational therapy, pharmacy, biology, chemistry, psychology, social work, dentistry, and optometry. Recipients are selected based on academic excellence, motivation to pursue a healthcare career, dedication to community service, and financial need.
Type of support: Scholarships—to individuals.
Geographic limitations: Giving primarily in CT, HI, ID, IL, MA, MD, MI, NH, and NY.
Publications: Application guidelines.
Application information: Applications accepted. Application form required.
Applications should include a financial aid form, two letters of recommendation, official transcripts, and an essay.
Initial approach: Complete online application
Deadline(s): May 18
Final notification: Aug.
Officer and Directors:* Teresa K. Koster*, Pres., Clerk, and Treas.; Vanessa Britto; Clantha Carrigan-McCurdy; Jack Eiferman; Ted Grace.
EIN: 043542547

1529
E. & J. Gallo Winery
600 Yosemite Blvd.
Modesto, CA 95354-2760 (209) 341-3111

Company URL: http://www.gallo.com
Establishment information: Established in 1933.
Company type: Private company
Business activities: Operates winery.
Business type (SIC): Beverages; farms/fruit and nut; beer, wine, and distilled beverages—wholesale
Financial profile for 2011: Number of employees, 5,000; sales volume, $3,400,000,000
Corporate officers: Ernest Gallo, Chair.; Joseph E. Gallo, Co-Pres. and C.E.O.; James E. Coleman, Co-Pres.
Board of director: Ernest Gallo, Chair.
Divisions: Ballatore Champagne Cellars, Modesto, CA; E & J Distillers Brandy, Modesto, CA; E & J Gallo, Modesto, CA; Tott's Champagne Cellars, Modesto, CA
Giving statement: Giving through the E. & J. Gallo Winery Corporate Giving Program.

E. & J. Gallo Winery Corporate Giving Program
600 Yosemite Blvd.
Modesto, CA 95354-2760 (209) 341-3111
URL: http://www.gallo.com/family/Community/Community.html

Purpose and activities: Gallo makes charitable contributions to nonprofit organizations on a case by case basis. Support is given primarily in areas of company operations in California.
Fields of interest: Arts; Education; Youth development; General charitable giving.
Type of support: Employee matching gifts; Employee volunteer services; General/operating support; In-kind gifts; Scholarship funds; Sponsorships.
Geographic limitations: Giving primarily in areas of company operations in CA.

1530
GameStop Corp.
625 Westport Pkwy.
Grapevine, TX 76051 (817) 424-2000
FAX: (817) 424-2062

Company URL: http://www.gamestopcorp.com
Establishment information: Established in 1994.
Company type: Public company
Company ticker symbol and exchange: GME/NYSE
Business activities: Operates video game products and PC entertainment software stores; provides Internet shopping services; publishes magazine.
Business type (SIC): Consumer electronics and music stores; periodical publishing and/or printing; computer services
Financial profile for 2012: Number of employees, 17,000; assets, $4,133,600,000; sales volume, $8,886,700,000; pre-tax net income, -$44,900,000; expenses, $8,928,300,000; liabilities, $1,847,300,000
Fortune 1000 ranking: 2012—298th in revenues, 947th in profits, and 653rd in assets
Corporate officers: Daniel A. DeMatteo, Chair.; Julian Paul Raines, C.E.O.; Tony D. Bartel, Pres.; Robert A. Lloyd, C.P.A., C.F.O.
Board of directors: Daniel A. Dematteo, Chair.; Jerome L. Davis; R. Richard Fontaine; Thomas Kelly; Shane S. Kim; Steven R. Koonin; J. Paul Raines; Stephanie M. Shern; Gerald R. Szczepanski; Kathy Vrabeck; Larry S. Zilavy
International operations: Australia; Austria; Canada; Denmark; Finland; France; Germany; Italy; Luxembourg; Norway; Spain; Sweden; Switzerland; United Kingdom
Giving statement: Giving through the GameStop Corp. Contributions Program.
Company EIN: 202733559

GameStop Corp. Contributions Program
625 Westport Pkwy.
Grapevine, TX 76051-6740 (817) 424-2000
URL: http://www.gamestopcorp.com/community.aspx

Purpose and activities: GameStop makes charitable contributions to Make-A-Wish Foundation and to nonprofit organizations involved with local communities. Support is given primarily in areas of company operations.
Fields of interest: Health care, patient services; Children/youth, services; General charitable giving Youth.
Type of support: Employee volunteer services; General/operating support.
Geographic limitations: Giving primarily in areas of company operations; giving also to national organizations.
Application information: Applications not accepted. Contributes only to pre-selected organizations.

1531
Gammage & Burnham PLC
2 North Central Ave., 15th, Fl.
Phoenix, AZ 85004 (602) 256-0566

Company URL: http://www.gblaw.com
Establishment information: Established in 1983.
Company type: Private company
Business activities: Operates law firm.
Business type (SIC): Legal services
Corporate officers: Richard B. Burnham, Partner; Grady Gammage, Jr., Partner; Michael R. King, Partner
Giving statement: Giving through the Gammage & Burnham PLC Pro Bono Program.

Gammage & Burnham PLC Pro Bono Program
2 North Central Ave., 15th Fl.
Phoenix, AZ 85004 (602) 256-0566
E-mail: jcraft@gblaw.com; URL: http://www.gblaw.com/community/

Contact: Jim Craft
Fields of interest: Legal services.
Type of support: Pro bono services - legal.

1532
Gannett Company, Inc.
7950 Jones Branch Dr.
McLean, VA 22107-0150 (703) 854-6000
FAX: (302) 655-5049

Company URL: http://www.gannett.com
Establishment information: Established in 1906.
Company type: Public company
Company ticker symbol and exchange: GCI/NYSE
Business activities: Publishes newspapers; broadcasts television; provides marketing, commercial printing, newswire, database, and news programming services.
Business type (SIC): Newspaper publishing and/or printing; printing/commercial; radio and television broadcasting; computer services; business services/miscellaneous
Financial profile for 2012: Assets, $6,379,890,000; sales volume, $5,353,200,000; pre-tax net income, $670,410,000; expenses, $4,563,440,000; liabilities, $4,029,270,000
Fortune 1000 ranking: 2012—467th in revenues, 373rd in profits, and 520th in assets
Forbes 2000 ranking: 2012—1346th in sales, 1279th in profits, and 1723rd in assets
Corporate officers: Marjorie Magner, Chair.; Gracia C. Martore, Pres. and C.E.O.; Victoria D. Harker, C.F.O.; Todd A. Mayman, Sr. V.P., Genl. Counsel, and Secy.; Kevin Lord, Sr. V.P., Human Resources; George R. Gavagan, V.P. and Cont.
Board of directors: Marjorie Magner, Chair.; John E. Cody; Howard D. Elias; Arthur H. Harper; John Jeffry Louis; Gracia C. Martore; Scott K. McCune; Duncan M. McFarland; Susan Ness; Neal Shapiro
Subsidiaries: Baxter County Newspapers, Inc., Mountain Home, AR; Central Newspapers, Inc., Phoenix, AZ; The Courier-Journal, Louisville, KY; Des Moines Register and Tribune Co., Des Moines, IA; The Desert Sun Publishing Co., Palm Springs, CA; The Detroit News, Inc., Detroit, MI; Gannett Direct Marketing Services, Inc., Louisville, KY; Gannett Retail Advertising Group, Inc, Chicago, IL; Gannett Satellite Information Network, Inc., Arlington, VA; Indiana Newspapers, Inc., Indianapolis, IN; Reno Newspapers, Inc., Reno, NV; Salinas Newspapers Inc., Salinas, CA; The Times Herald Co., Port Huron, MI; Visalia Newspapers Inc., Visalia, CA; WFMY Television Corp., Greensboro, NC; WKYC-TV, Inc., Cleveland, OH
International operations: Canada; United Kingdom
Giving statement: Giving through the Cincinnati Enquirer Foundation, the Gannett Foundation, Inc., and the Neediest Kids of All.
Company EIN: 160442930

Cincinnati Enquirer Foundation
312 Elm St.
Cincinnati, OH 45202-2739

Establishment information: Established in 1959.
Donors: Gannett Co., Inc.; The Cincinnati Enquirer.
Financial data (yr. ended 06/30/12): Assets, $72,203 (M); gifts received, $50,004; expenditures, $49,314; qualifying distributions, $49,000; giving activities include $49,000 for 9 grants (high: $40,000; low: $1,000).
Purpose and activities: The foundation supports organizations involved with higher education.
Fields of interest: Education.
Type of support: Employee-related scholarships; General/operating support.
Geographic limitations: Giving limited to OH.
Application information: Applications not accepted. Unsolicited requests for funds not accepted.
Officer: Margaret E. Buchanan, Pres.
EIN: 316037926
Selected grants: The following grants are a representative sample of this grantmaker's funding activity:
$20,000 to United Way of Greater Cincinnati, Cincinnati, OH, 2007.
$20,000 to United Way of Greater Cincinnati, Cincinnati, OH, 2007.

Gannett Foundation, Inc.
7950 Jones Branch Dr.
McLean, VA 22107-0001 (703) 854-6000
FAX: (703) 854-2167;
E-mail: foundation@gannett.com; URL: http://www.gannettfoundation.org

Establishment information: Established in 1991 in VA.
Donor: Gannett Co., Inc.
Contact: Pat Lyle, Mgr.
Financial data (yr. ended 12/31/11): Assets, $12,852,709 (M); gifts received, $8,297,202; expenditures, $5,569,890; qualifying distributions, $5,501,864; giving activities include $4,085,700 for 92 grants (high: $2,700,000; low: $250) and $1,290,404 for 3,914 employee matching gifts.
Purpose and activities: The foundation supports organizations involved with arts and culture, media and journalism, education, conservation, health, youth development, human services, diversity, community development, minorities, women, and economically disadvantaged people.
Fields of interest: Arts, cultural/ethnic awareness; Media/communications; Media, print publishing; Arts; Journalism school/education; Education; Environment, natural resources; Health care; Disasters, preparedness/services; Youth development; Human services; Civil/human rights, equal rights; Civil liberties, first amendment; Community development, neighborhood development; Economic development; Community/economic development Minorities; Women; Economically disadvantaged.
International interests: United Kingdom.
Programs:
Community Action Grants: The foundation supports programs designed to promote education, neighborhood improvement, economic development, youth development, community problem-solving, assistance to disadvantaged people, environmental conservation, and cultural enrichment. Grants range from $1,000 to $5,000.
GannettMatch: The foundation matches contributions made by part-time and full-time employees and directors of Gannett to educational institutions, hospitals, and medical centers on a

one-for-one basis from $25 to $10,000 per contributor, per year.

Madelyn P. Jennings Scholarship Awards: The foundation annually awards $3,000 college scholarships to children of full-time employees of Gannett. The scholarship is named in honor of Madelyn P. Jennings, who served as Gannett's Senior Human Resources Executive. The program is administered by the National Merit Scholarship Corp.

Media Grants: The foundation supports programs designed to promote media education, technological advances in the industry, and the study of journalism, with particular attention to the First Amendment and its responsibilities. Special emphasis is directed toward programs designed to promote diversity in Gannett newsrooms and media coverage; encourage women, minorities, and students to enter the field of journalism; and promote innovative training approaches for mid-career journalists.

Newsquest Grants: The foundation awards grants to local organizations in areas where Newsquest operates in the United Kingdom. Special emphasis is directed toward programs designed to promote education, neighborhood improvement, economic development, youth development, community problem solving, assistance to disadvantaged people, environmental conservation, and cultural enrichment. Grants range from 5,000 to 10,000.

VolunteerMatch: The foundation awards $100 grants to nonprofit organizations with which employees of Gannett volunteer at least 10 hours a year. Each employee may submit 2 requests a year.

Type of support: Capital campaigns; Conferences/seminars; Employee matching gifts; Equipment; Program development; Scholarship funds.

Geographic limitations: Giving on a national and international basis in areas of company operations, with emphasis on AZ, Washington DC, FL, IN, MI, NY, OH, VA, and the United Kingdom.

Support limitations: No support for private foundations, regional or national organizations not addressing local needs, elementary or secondary schools (except for special initiatives not provided by regular school budgets), political action or legislative advocacy groups, medical or research organizations, fraternal groups, athletic teams, bands, veterans' organizations, or volunteer firefighters. No grants to individuals (except for employee-related scholarships), or for religious programs or initiatives, endowments, or multi-year pledge campaigns.

Publications: Annual report; Application guidelines; Informational brochure; IRS Form 990 or 990-PF printed copy available upon request; Program policy statement.

Application information: Applications accepted. Grants range from $1,000 to $5,000; Newsquest grants range from 5,000 to 10,000. Proposals should be no longer than 5 pages. Telephone calls during the application process are not encouraged. Visit website to confirm application deadline for specific areas. Application form required. Applicants should submit the following:

1) role played by volunteers
2) how project will be sustained once grantmaker support is completed
3) qualifications of key personnel
4) population served
5) copy of IRS Determination Letter
6) how project's results will be evaluated or measured
7) descriptive literature about organization
8) detailed description of project and amount of funding requested
9) copy of current year's organizational budget and/or project budget
10) listing of additional sources and amount of support
11) additional materials/documentation

Initial approach: Download application form and mail proposal and form to the company's nearest daily newspaper or broadcast station; download application form and mail proposal and form to foundation for organizations located in the Washington, DC metropolitan area

Copies of proposal: 1

Board meeting date(s): 3 times per year from Feb. to Oct.

Deadline(s): Feb. 15 and Aug. 15 for Community Action Grants; Mar. 1, July 15, and Nov. 1 for Media Grants; Autumn for Newsquest Grants

Final notification: 90 to 120 days

Officers and Directors:* Craig A. Dubow*, Chair. and Pres.; Daniel S. Ehrman, V.P.; Gracia C. Martore*, V.P.; Todd A. Mayman*, Secy.; Michael A. Hart, Treas.; Robin Pence, Exec. Dir.

Number of staff: 1 full-time professional; 1 full-time support.

EIN: 541568843

Selected grants: The following grants are a representative sample of this grantmaker's funding activity:

$590,000 to Quartet Community Foundation, Bristol, England, 2011. For grants recommended by Newsquest.

$540,000 to Quartet Community Foundation, Bristol, England, 2012. For grants recommended by Newsquest Media Group.

$302,000 to Arizona Community Foundation, Phoenix, AZ, 2011. To match donations from readers of The Republic's annual Season for Sharing campaign that benefits local nonprofit agencies.

$302,000 to Arizona Community Foundation, Phoenix, AZ, 2012. For community donations to holiday program, Season for Sharing. Donations are matched up to $400,000 and granted to local non-profit agencies.

$88,000 to Online News Association, Washington, DC, 2012. For sponsorship of Digital training camp ($50,000), Excellence in Journalism Awards ($23,000) to be presented at annual convention and $15,000 for sponsorship of Job Fair/Career/Day at convention.

$85,000 to Unity: Journalists of Color, McLean, VA, 2011. To support of convention held every four years. UNITY 2012 will be in August in Las Vegas and is a collaborative meeting of AAJA, NAHJ, NAJA, and NLGJA members..

$75,000 to Central Indiana Community Foundation, Indianapolis, IN, 2012. To match community donations to annual Season for Sharing Holiday Program campaign that benefits local non-profit agencies.

$72,500 to United Way for Southeastern Michigan, Detroit, MI, 2011. For general support for programming in Southeastern Michigan.

$72,500 to United Way for Southeastern Michigan, Detroit, MI, 2012. For general campaign support.

$48,000 to Arizona Community Foundation, Phoenix, AZ, 2011. To match donations for Season For Sharing campaign that benefits local non-profit agencies.

$40,000 to Public Schools of Hawaii Foundation, Honolulu, HI, 2011. For general support.

$25,000 to Des Moines Public Library Foundation, Des Moines, IA, 2012. To support capital campaign to update and expand branch libraries.

$5,000 to Asian American Journalists Association, San Francisco, CA, 2011. For Gannett Foundation Award for Innovation in Watchdog Journalism.

$5,000 to United Way, Fond du Lac Area, Fond du Lac, WI, 2012. For program support to help the community in three impact areas.

$4,000 to Urban Arts Academy, Minneapolis, MN, 2012. For a neighborhood free art program for youth in both Spanish and English.

$3,800 to United Way, Oshkosh Area, Oshkosh, WI, 2011. For programs that provide solutions to community needs.

$3,000 to Heritage University, Toppenish, WA, 2012. For general support.

$3,000 to Tubman, Minneapolis, MN, 2011. For Peace Camp for child victims of domestic violence includes recreation and violence prevention skill building.

$2,500 to Guiding Light Mission, Grand Rapids, MI, 2012. To support the housing of 110 men every night and serving 350 meals per day.

$2,500 to Literacy Volunteers of America, Morris County Affiliate, Morristown, NJ, 2011. To recruit volunteers for tutoring.

Neediest Kids of All

c/o Juliana F. Wales
312 Elm St.
Cincinnati, OH 45202-2739 (513) 768-8549
E-mail: neediestkidsofall@gmail.com; URL: http://www.cincinnati.com/nkoa/

Establishment information: Established in 1964.

Donor: Gannett Co., Inc.

Contact: J.J. Wales, Exec. Dir.

Financial data (yr. ended 02/28/12): Revenue, $548,390; assets, $1,655,941 (M); gifts received, $513,989; expenditures, $509,228; giving activities include $421,824 for grants.

Purpose and activities: The organization provides basic necessities and educational experiences for needy school children in the greater Cincinnati, Ohio, area.

Fields of interest: Visual arts, sculpture; Human services.

Geographic limitations: Giving primarily in the greater Cincinnati, OH, area.

Officer and Trustees:* J.J. Wales*, Exec. Dir.; Jeanette M. Altenau; Keith D. Bulling; Martha L. Flanagan; Charles J. Fredrick; James C. Jackson; Gerald T. Silvers; Robert P. Temmen; Kirk Varner; and 4 additional trustees.

EIN: 316052858

1533
The Gap, Inc.

2 Folsom St.
San Francisco, CA 94105 (650) 952-4400

Company URL: http://www.gapinc.com

Establishment information: Established in 1969.

Company type: Public company

Company ticker symbol and exchange: GPS/NYSE

Business activities: Operates men's, women's, and children's apparel, personal care, and accessories stores.

Business type (SIC): Family apparel and accessory stores; apparel and accessory stores/miscellaneous

Financial profile for 2013: Number of employees, 136,000; assets, $7,470,000,000; sales volume, $15,651,000,000; pre-tax net income, $1,861,000,000; expenses, $13,709,000,000; liabilities, $4,576,000,000

Fortune 1000 ranking: 2012—179th in revenues, 180th in profits, and 470th in assets

Forbes 2000 ranking: 2012—599th in sales, 530th in profits, and 1630th in assets

Corporate officers: Glenn K. Murphy, Chair. and C.E.O.; Sabrina Simmons, Exec. V.P. and C.F.O.; Tom Keiser, Exec. V.P. and C.I.O.; Michelle Banks,

Exec. V.P., Genl. Counsel, and Corp. Secy.; Eva Sage-Gavin, Exec. V.P., Human Resources
Board of directors: Glenn K. Murphy, Chair.; Adrian D.P. Bellamy; Domenico De Sole; Robert J. Fisher; William S. Fisher; Bella Goren; Bob L. Martin; Jorge P. Montoya; Mayo A. Shattuck III; Katherine Tsang
Subsidiaries: Banana Republic, Inc., San Francisco, CA; Old Navy Inc., San Francisco, CA
International operations: Bermuda; Canada; England; Honduras; Hong Kong; India; Ireland; Italy; Japan; Netherlands; Singapore; South Africa; Thailand; United Arab Emirates; Wales
Giving statement: Giving through the Gap Foundation.
Company EIN: 941697231

The Gap Foundation

2 Folsom St.
15th Fl.
San Francisco, CA 94105-1205
E-mail: gap_foundation@gap.com; URL: http://www.gapinc.com/content/gapinc/html/csr.html

Establishment information: Established in 1977 in CA.
Donor: The Gap, Inc.
Financial data (yr. ended 01/31/12): Assets, $14,919,534 (M); gifts received, $2,305,079; expenditures, $3,524,231; qualifying distributions, $3,523,724; giving activities include $3,523,724 for 57 grants (high: $416,000; low: $3,000).
Purpose and activities: The foundation supports programs designed to reach underserved youth in the developed world and women in the developing world.
Fields of interest: Secondary school/education; Education; Employment, services; Employment, training; Employment; Boys & girls clubs; Youth development, adult & child programs; Youth development; Human services; International affairs Youth; Women; Economically disadvantaged.

Programs:

Board Service Grants: The foundation awards grants to nonprofit organizations with which leaders of Gap serve as board members. This program is limited to Senior Directors and above. Grants range from $1,000 to $10,000.

Field Team Grants: The foundation awards grants to target-aligned nonprofit organizations with which teams of three or more Gap employees volunteer. The foundation awards $250 for 25 volunteer hours, $500 for 50 volunteer hours, and $750 for 75 volunteer hours. Target-aligned nonprofit organizations must help undeserved youth ages 12-18 with a focus on career readiness, job skill training, and mentoring.

Gift Match: The foundation matches contributions made by employees of the Gap to nonprofit organizations on a one-for-one basis up to $1,000 for part-time employees, $2,500 for full-time employees, $5,000 for Directors to Vice Presidents, and $10,000 for Senior Vice Presidents and above.

In-Kind Gifts: The foundation provides merchandise samples, fabric, furniture, and fixtures to nonprofit organizations involved with human services. The program is administered by Good360 (formerly known as Gifts In Kind International).

Money for Time: The foundation awards grants to nonprofit organizations with which employees of the Gap volunteer. The foundation awards $150 for every 15 hours of volunteer service.

Type of support: Donated equipment; Donated products; Employee matching gifts; Employee volunteer services; General/operating support; In-kind gifts; Management development/capacity building; Program development; Scholarship funds; Sponsorships.
Geographic limitations: Giving primarily in areas of company operations, with emphasis on San Francisco, CA, Chicago, IL, New York, NY.
Support limitations: No support for religious, political, or discriminatory organizations. No grants to individuals, or for scholarships, conferences, travel, films, videos, or fundraisers (except for gift card donations).
Application information: Applications not accepted. The foundation does not accept unsolicited proposals for grants or event sponsorships.
Officers and Trustees: Bobbi Silten, Pres.; Forrest Bryant, Treas.; Doris F. Fisher; Marka Hansen; Dan Henkle; Art Peck; Liz O'Neill; Stan Raggio; Steve Stickel; Tom Wyatt.
EIN: 942474426

1534
Garden Fresh Restaurant Corp.

(also known as Garden Fresh Holdings, Inc.)
15822 Bernardo Center Dr., Ste. A
San Diego, CA 92127-2320
(858) 675-1600

Company URL: http://www.souplantation.com
Establishment information: Established in 1983.
Company type: Subsidiary of a private company
Business activities: Operates salad buffet restaurants.
Business type (SIC): Restaurants and drinking places
Corporate officers: Robert A. Gunst, Chair.; Michael P. Mack, C.E.O.; R. Gregory Keller, Co-Pres.; Kenneth Keane, Co-Pres.; Yan Zeng, C.F.O.; Eric Rosenzweig, C.I.O.
Board of director: Robert A. Gunst, Chair.
Giving statement: Giving through the Garden Fresh Restaurant Corp. Contributions Program.

Garden Fresh Restaurant Corp. Contributions Program

c/o Donation/Sponsorship Dept.
15822 Bernardo Center Dr., Ste. A
San Diego, CA 92127-2320 (858) 675-1600
URL: http://www.souplantation.com/communityspirit/

Purpose and activities: Garden Fresh makes charitable contributions of gift cards and food to nonprofit organizations on a case by case basis. Support is limited to areas of company operations in Arizona, California, Colorado, Florida, Georgia, Illinois, Kansas, Missouri, Nevada, New Mexico, North Carolina, Oregon, Texas, Utah, and Washington.
Fields of interest: General charitable giving.
Type of support: Cause-related marketing; Donated products; Sponsorships.
Geographic limitations: Giving limited to areas of company operations in AZ, CA, CO, FL, GA, IL, KS, MO, NC, NM, NV, OR, TX, UT, and WA.
Support limitations: No monetary donations.
Application information: Applications accepted. Proposals should be submitted using organization letterhead. Application form not required. Applicants should submit the following:
1) name, address and phone number of organization
2) descriptive literature about organization
3) contact person
4) plans for acknowledgement
Applications should specifically note the nature of the request being made and how a contribution will be used; and include the date and location of the event, and any applicable deadlines.
Initial approach: Proposal to nearest company restaurant or headquarters
Copies of proposal: 1
Final notification: 30 days

1535
Garden Valley Telephone Company

201 E. Ross Ave.
P.O. Box 259
Erskine, MN 56535 (218) 687-5251

Company URL: http://www.gvtel.com
Establishment information: Established in 1906.
Company type: Private company
Business activities: Provides telephone communications services.
Business type (SIC): Telephone communications
Corporate officers: Vernon Hamnes, Pres.; Byron V. Ness, Secy.; Joe O. Sandberg, Treas.
Board of directors: Ronald E. Engelstad; Jerry T. Freitag; Vernon Hamnes; Warren C. Larson; Byron V. Ness; Arlene J. Novak; Edgar L. Olson; Joe O. Sandberg; Jason L. Smeby
Giving statement: Giving through the Garden Valley Education Foundation.

Garden Valley Education Foundation

201 Ross Ave.
Erskine, MN 56535
URL: http://www.gvtel.com/about_communityinvolvement.html

Establishment information: Established as a company-sponsored operating foundation in 1991.
Donor: Garden Valley Telephone Co.
Financial data (yr. ended 12/31/11): Assets, $67,050 (M); gifts received, $11,336; expenditures, $50,034; qualifying distributions, $50,000; giving activities include $50,000 for grants.
Purpose and activities: The foundation awards technology grants to school districts to aid in the purchase of technology-related services and products.
Type of support: General/operating support; Program development.
Application information: Applications not accepted. Unsolicited requests for funds not accepted.
Officers: Edgar L. Olson, Pres.; Jason L. Smeby, V.P.; Ronald E. Engelstad, Secy.; Arlene J. Novak, Treas.
Directors: Jerry T. Freitag; Vernon Hamnes; Warren C. Larson; Byron V. Ness; Joe O. Sandberg.
EIN: 411682056

1536
Donald A. Gardner Architects, Inc.

86 Villa Rd.
P.O. Box 26178
Greenville, SC 29615 (864) 288-7580

Company URL: http://www.dongardner.com
Establishment information: Established in 1978.
Company type: Private company
Business activities: Provides pre-designed house plans.
Business type (SIC): Engineering, architectural, and surveying services

Corporate officers: Donald A. Gardner, C.E.O.; William Santerini, C.F.O.
Giving statement: Giving through the Gardner-Santerini-Gardner-Rudisill Foundation.

Gardner-Santerini-Gardner-Rudisill Foundation

P.O. Box 25593
Greenville, SC 29616
URL: http://www.gsgrfoundation.org/

Establishment information: Established in 2002 in SC.
Donors: Donald A. Gardner Interactive, LLC; Donald A. Gardner, Inc.; Donald A. Gardner Architects, Inc.; Donald A. Gardner Designs, LLC; Infringement Solutions, Inc.
Financial data (yr. ended 12/31/11): Assets, $228,871 (M); gifts received, $1,000; expenditures, $12,521; qualifying distributions, $11,119; giving activities include $11,119 for grants.
Purpose and activities: The foundation supports programs that encourage and nurture children and families who are affected by medical disorders, illness, or poverty.
Fields of interest: Health organizations; Human services.
Type of support: Continuing support; General/operating support; Scholarship funds.
Support limitations: No grants to individuals.
Application information: Applications not accepted. Contributes only to pre-selected organizations.
Trustees: Sonia G. Rudisill; Angela G. Santerini; William A. Santerini III.
EIN: 161643801

1537
Garelick Manufacturing Co.

644 2nd St.
P.O. Box 8
St. Paul Park, MN 55071-0008
(651) 459-9795
FAX: (651) 459-8269

Company URL: http://www.garelick.com
Establishment information: Established in 1956.
Company type: Private company
Business activities: Manufactures metal lawn and marine furniture and supplies; manufactures surgical and hospital supplies.
Business type (SIC): Metal products/fabricated; medical instruments and supplies
Financial profile for 2009: Number of employees, 130
Corporate officer: Kenneth D. Garelick, C.E.O. and Secy.
Giving statement: Giving through the Garelick Family Foundation.

Garelick Family Foundation

644 2nd St.
St. Paul Park, MN 55071-1852

Donors: Garelick Manufacturing Co., Inc.; Herbert Garelick; Saul S. Garelick; Kenneth D. Garelick; David Garelick; Richard Garelick.
Financial data (yr. ended 10/31/11): Assets, $15 (M); gifts received, $45,100; expenditures, $45,125; qualifying distributions, $45,113; giving activities include $45,100 for 4 grants (high: $25,000; low: $50).
Purpose and activities: The foundation supports organizations involved with education, health, government and public administration, and Judaism.
Fields of interest: Education; Health care; Jewish federated giving programs; Government/public administration; Jewish agencies & synagogues.
Geographic limitations: Giving primarily in the Minneapolis and St. Paul, MN, areas.
Support limitations: No grants to individuals.
Application information: Applications not accepted. Unsolicited requests for funds not accepted.
Directors: Kenneth D. Garelick; Richard J. Garelick.
EIN: 411400379

1538
Garff Enterprises, Inc.

(also known as Ken Garff Automotive Group)
405 S. Main St., Ste. 1200
Salt Lake City, UT 84111-3412
(801) 257-3400

Company URL: http://www.kengarff.com
Establishment information: Established in 1949.
Company type: Private company
Business activities: Operates car dealerships.
Business type (SIC): Motor vehicles—retail
Corporate officers: Robert H. Garff, Chair.; John K. Garff, C.E.O.; Mark Boehlen, C.I.O.
Board of director: Robert H. Garff, Chair.
Giving statement: Giving through the Robert H. & Katharine B. Garff Foundation.

Robert H. & Katharine B. Garff Foundation

405 S. Main St., Ste. 1200
Salt Lake City, UT 84111-3412 (801) 257-3400

Establishment information: Established in 2004 in UT.
Donors: Garff Enterprises, Inc.; Jane F. McCarthey Charitable Trust; JP Morgan Chase Foundation; Walmart; Church of Jesus Christ of LDS; O.C. Tanner; Target Corporation; Sam's Club Foundation; Eccles Foundation; American Express; Garff Enterprises, Inc.; Utah Valley University; Shiela Flanagan; Walmart; Church of Jesus Christ of LDS; O.C. Tanner; Zions Bank; Nissan North America, Inc.; Eagle Gate College; Weber Schoold District Foundation; Sam's Club Foundation; Slcap Head Start; Eccles Foundation; Utah Community Credir Union; Brasher's Salt Lake Auto Auction; US Synthetic; Wasatch Acquisitions & Capital; Ashton Family; Leucadia National Corporation; Burton Foundation; Dee Foundation; Enterprise Holdings Foundation; Newspaper Agency Corp.
Contact: Matthew B. Garff, Pres.
Financial data (yr. ended 12/31/11): Assets, $132,035 (M); gifts received, $374,859; expenditures, $402,165; qualifying distributions, $397,612.
Purpose and activities: The foundation supports zoos and organizations involved with disaster relief and the military.
Fields of interest: Zoos/zoological societies; Disasters, Hurricane Katrina; Military/veterans' organizations.
Type of support: General/operating support.
Application information: Applications accepted. Application form required.
Initial approach: Letter
Deadline(s): None
Officers and Directors:* Matthew B. Garff*, Pres.; Melissa G. Ballard*, V.P.; John K. Garff*, V.P.; Richard Folkerson, Secy.; Mary G. Menlove*, Treas.; Jennifer G. Folkerson; Katherine B. Garff; Robert H. Garff.
EIN: 201412845

1539
Garvey Schubert Barer

1191 2nd Ave., Ste. 1800
Seattle, WA 98101-2996 (202) 298-1789

Company URL: http://www.gsblaw.com
Establishment information: Established in 1966.
Company type: Private company
Business activities: Operates law firm.
Business type (SIC): Legal services
Corporate officers: Anne F. Preston, Chair.; Erle Cohen, C.O.O.; Cindy Tatko, Cont.
Offices: Washington, DC; New York, NY; Portland, OR; Seattle, WA
International operations: China
Giving statement: Giving through the Garvey Schubert Barer Pro Bono Program.

Garvey Schubert Barer Pro Bono Program

1191 2nd Ave., Ste. 1800
Seattle, WA 98101-2996 (206) 816-1356
E-mail: rknox@gsblaw.com; URL: http://www.gsblaw.com/overview/probono.cfm

Contact: Ron Knox, Chair, Public Svc. Comm.
Fields of interest: Legal services.
Type of support: Pro bono services - legal.
Geographic limitations: Giving primarily in areas of company operations in Washington, DC, New York, NY, Portland, OR, and Seattle, WA, and in China.
Application information: A Pro Bono Committee manages the pro bono program.

1540
Gates Corp.

(also known as Gates Winhere, LLC)
1551 Wewatta St.
Denver, CO 80202-6173 (303) 744-1911

Company URL: http://www.gates.com
Establishment information: Established in 1911.
Company type: Subsidiary of a foreign company
Business activities: Manufactures industrial and automotive belts and hoses.
Business type (SIC): Gaskets, packing and sealing devices, and rubber hose and belting
Corporate officers: James Nicol, Chair. and C.E.O.; Alan J. Power, Pres. and C.O.O.; John Zimmerman, C.F.O.; Stacy Winsett, V.P., Human Resources; Margaret Meg Vanderlaan, V.P., Corp. Comms.
Board of directors: James Nicol, Chair. and C.E.O.; Todd Sellden
Subsidiaries: The Gates Rubber Co., Denver, CO; Standard-Thomson Corp., Waltham, MA; Stant Manufacturing Inc., Connersville, IN; Trico Products Corp., Rochester Hills, MI
Division: Ideal Div., St. Augustine, FL
Plants: Dixon, IL; Charleston, Poplar Bluff, MO
International operations: Belgium; Mexico
Giving statement: Giving through the Gates Corporation Contributions Program.

Gates Corporation Contributions Program

1551 Wewatta St.
Denver, CO 80202-6173 (303) 744-1911

Purpose and activities: Gates makes charitable contributions to nonprofit organizations on a case by case basis. Support is given primarily in areas of company operations.
Fields of interest: General charitable giving.
Type of support: In-kind gifts.
Geographic limitations: Giving primarily in areas of company operations.

1541
Gateway, Inc.

(formerly Gateway 2000, Inc.)
7565 Irvine Center Dr.
P.O. Box 6137
Irvine, CA 92618-2930 (949) 471-7000

Company URL: http://www.gateway.com
Establishment information: Established in 1985.
Company type: Subsidiary of a foreign company
Business activities: Manufactures and markets personal computer systems.
Business type (SIC): Computer and office equipment
Corporate officers: Richard D. Snyder, Chair.; Rudi Schmidleithner, C.E.O.; John P. Goldsberry, Sr. V.P. and C.F.O.; Michael R. Tyler, Exec. V.P., Genl. Counsel, and Secy.; Bart R. Brown, Sr. V.P., Mktg.; Lazane M. Smith, Sr. V.P., Human Resources; Craig Calle, V.P., Finance and Treas.
Board of directors: Richard D. Snyder, Chair.; Quincy L. Allen; Janet M. Clarke; Scott Galloway; George H. Krauss; Douglas L. Lacey; Joseph G. Parham, Jr.; Dave E. Russell; Paul E. Weaver
Giving statement: Giving through the Gateway, Inc. Corporate Giving Program and the Gateway Foundation.

Gateway Foundation

(formerly Gateway 2000 Foundation, Inc.)
7565 Irvine Ctr. Dr.
Irvine, CA 92618-2930
E-mail: gatewayfoundation@gateway.com;
URL: http://us.gateway.com/gw/en/US/content/gateway-foundation

Establishment information: Established in 1994 in SD.
Donors: Gateway 2000, Inc.; Gateway, Inc.; TAG; Don M. Forsyth; Center for Siouxland.
Financial data (yr. ended 12/31/11): Assets, $377,489 (M); expenditures, $43,751; qualifying distributions, $42,709; giving activities include $42,709 for grants.
Purpose and activities: The foundation supports organizations involved with education and youth.
Fields of interest: Health care; Human services.
Type of support: Technical assistance.
Geographic limitations: Giving primarily within a 50 mile radius of company locations in Irvine, CA and North Sioux City, SD.
Support limitations: No grants to individuals, or for scholarships, stipends, or fellowships, building or renovation projects, general operating support, annual or capital campaigns, endowments, research, conferences or seminars, or sports programs or competitions; no product donations or premiums for raffles door prizes, auctions, banquets, or any other form of fundraiser or giveaway.
Application information: Applications not accepted. Unsolicited requests for funds not accepted.
Officer: Michael Barry, Secy.
Directors: John W. King; Carol Telgue Jean Thomas.
EIN: 460434986

1542
GATX Corporation

222 W. Adams St.
Chicago, IL 60606-5314 (312) 621-6200
FAX: (312) 621-6648

Company URL: http://www.gatx.com
Establishment information: Established in 1898.
Company type: Public company
Company ticker symbol and exchange: GMT/NYSE
Business activities: Leases railcars and locomotives, aircraft, and information technology equipment.
Business type (SIC): Transportation services; railroad car rental; equipment rental and leasing/ miscellaneous
Financial profile for 2012: Number of employees, 2,046; assets, $6,055,400,000; sales volume, $1,243,200,000; pre-tax net income, $143,800,000; expenses, $1,099,400,000; liabilities, $4,811,200,000
Corporate officers: Brian A. Kenney, Chair., Pres., and C.E.O.; Robert C. Lyons, Exec. V.P. and C.F.O.; Deborah A. Golden, Exec. V.P., Genl. Counsel, and Corp. Secy.; Michael T. Brooks, Sr. V.P. and C.I.O.; William M. Muckian, Sr. V.P., Cont., and C.A.O.; Mary K. Lawler, Sr. V.P., Human Resources
Board of directors: Brian A. Kenney, Chair.; Anne L. Arvia; Ernst A. Haberli; Mark G. McGrath; James B. Ream; Robert J. Ritchie; David S. Sutherland; Casey J. Sylla; Paul G. Yovovich
Subsidiaries: American Steamship Co., Williamsville, NY; General American Transportation Corporation, Chicago, IL
Divisions: Financial Services Div., San Francisco, CA; GATX Rail Div., Chicago, IL
Offices: Mobile, AL; Colton, Lafayette, Valencia, CA; Farmington, CT; Lake City, Tampa, FL; Alpharetta, Macon, Waycross, GA; Terre Haute, IN; Geismar, Norco, Plaquemine, LA; Midland, MI; Marlton, NJ; Las Cruces, NM; Albany, NY; Cincinnati, Masury, Toledo, OH; Catoosa, OK; Copper Hill, TN; Freeport, Galena Park, Hearne, Houston, Nederland, TX; Olympia, Seattle, WA
Giving statement: Giving through the GATX Corporation Contributions Program and the GATX Foundation.
Company EIN: 361124040

GATX Corporation Contributions Program

222 W. Adams St.
Chicago, IL 60606 (312) 621-6200
FAX: (312) 621-6648;
E-mail: contactgatx@gatx.com; URL: http://www.gatx.com/wps/wcm/connect/GATX/GATX_SITE/Home/About/Community+Affairs/

Purpose and activities: As a complement to its foundation, GATX also makes charitable contributions to nonprofit organizations directly. Emphasis is given to organizations involved with cultural, educational, environmental, family, health care and social service issues. Support is given primarily in areas of company operations.
Fields of interest: Education; Environment; Health care; Food services; Food banks; Recreation, parks/ playgrounds; Children/youth, services; Family services; Human services, gift distribution.
Type of support: Annual campaigns; Donated equipment; Donated products; Employee matching gifts; Employee volunteer services; General/ operating support; In-kind gifts; Loaned talent; Matching/challenge support.
Geographic limitations: Giving primarily in areas of company operations in San Francisco, CA, Chicago, IL, and Buffalo, NY.
Support limitations: No support for political, labor, athletic, veterans', fraternal, or sectarian religious organizations, private foundations, individual public or private K-12 schools, United Way-supported organizations, or local chapters of national organizations. No grants to individuals, or for trips, tours, conferences, advertising, tickets, capital campaigns, endowments, land acquisition, debt reduction, or health research.
Publications: Application guidelines.
Application information: Applications accepted. Donations are given primarily by invitation only but unsolicited applications are also accepted.
Initial approach: Proposal
Deadline(s): None
Number of staff: 1 full-time professional.

GATX Foundation

222 W. Adams St.
Chicago, IL 60606-5312

Donor: GATX Corp.
Financial data (yr. ended 12/31/11): Assets, $247,081 (M); expenditures, $278; qualifying distributions, $0.
Purpose and activities: The foundation supports the GATX Scholars scholarship program.
Type of support: Scholarship funds.
Geographic limitations: Giving primarily in Chicago, IL.
Support limitations: No grants to individuals.
Application information: Applications not accepted. Unsolicited requests for funds not accepted.
Officers: Brian A Kennedy, Pres.; Katie Lawler, V.P.; Robert C. Lyons, V.P.; Deborah A. Golden, V.P.; Lisa M. Ibarra, Secy.; William Hasek, Treas.; William M. Muckian, Compt.
EIN: 366059339

1543
Gaunce Management Inc.

113 W. Public Sq., Ste. 200
Glasgow, KY 42141-2438 (270) 651-9302
FAX: (270) 651-6080

Establishment information: Established in 1993.
Company type: Private company
Business activities: Operates restaurants.
Business type (SIC): Restaurants and drinking places
Corporate officers: Wayne Gaunce, Pres.; Patrick Gaunce, Secy.; Peter Morgan, V.P., Opers.
Giving statement: Giving through the GHH Charitable Foundation.

The GHH Charitable Foundation

113 W. Public Sq., Ste. 200
Glasgow, KY 42141-2438

Establishment information: Established in 2002 in KY.
Donors: Gaunce Management Inc.; Wayne Gaunce.
Financial data (yr. ended 12/31/11): Assets, $656,327 (M); gifts received, $100,000;

expenditures, $90,500; qualifying distributions, $90,500; giving activities include $90,500 for grants.
Purpose and activities: The foundation supports hospices and organizations involved with theological education and Christianity.
Fields of interest: Theological school/education; Residential/custodial care, hospices; Christian agencies & churches.
Type of support: General/operating support.
Support limitations: No grants to individuals.
Application information: Applications not accepted. Unsolicited requests for funds not accepted.
Trustees: Chapatcha Gaunce; Wayne Gaunce; Nell Houchens; Ruel Houchens; Jean Hunsaker.
EIN: 320048907

1544
Gear Motions Inc.
1750 Milton Ave.
Syracuse, NY 13209-1626 (315) 488-0100

Company URL: http://www.gearmotions.com/index.htm
Establishment information: Established in 1920.
Company type: Private company
Business activities: Manufactures speed changers and gears.
Business type (SIC): Machinery/general industry
Corporate officer: Samuel R. Haines, Chair. and C.E.O.
Board of director: Samuel R. Haines, Chair.
Subsidiary: Olive Gear, Inc., Buffalo, NY
Giving statement: Giving through the Gear Motions Foundation.

Gear Motions Foundation
1750 Milton Ave.
Syracuse, NY 13209-1686

Donor: Gear Motions Inc.
Financial data (yr. ended 12/31/11): Assets, $71,282 (M); expenditures, $42,291; qualifying distributions, $42,237; giving activities include $42,187 for 19 grants (high: $11,257; low: $50).
Purpose and activities: The foundation supports organizations involved with education, home healthcare, cancer, disability services, the manufacturing industry, robotics, and leadership development.
Fields of interest: Education; Health care, home services; Cancer; Developmentally disabled, centers & services; Business/industry; United Ways and Federated Giving Programs; Engineering/technology; Leadership development.
Type of support: Program development.
Geographic limitations: Giving primarily in Syracuse, NY.
Support limitations: No grants to individuals.
Application information: Applications not accepted. Contributes only to pre-selected organizations.
Trustee: Samuel R. Haines.
EIN: 042724256

1545
Gehl Company
One Gehl Way
P.O. Box 179
West Bend, WI 53095 (262) 334-9461
FAX: (262) 338-7517

Company URL: http://www.gehl.com
Establishment information: Established in 1859.
Company type: Subsidiary of a foreign company
Business activities: Manufactures agricultural and construction equipment.
Business type (SIC): Machinery/farm and garden; machinery/construction, mining, and materials handling
Financial profile for 2010: Number of employees, 848
Corporate officers: Malcolm F. Moore, Pres. and C.E.O.; Brian Pearlman, V.P., Human Resources
Subsidiaries: Gehl Power Products, Inc., Yankton, SD; Hedlund-Martin Inc., Lebanon, PA
Plants: Owatonna, MN; Madison, SD
International operations: Germany
Giving statement: Giving through the Gehl Foundation.
Company EIN: 390300430

Gehl Foundation
1 Gehl Way
West Bend, WI 53095-3415 (262) 334-9461

Establishment information: Established in 1964 in WI.
Donor: Gehl Co.
Contact: Christie Martin
Financial data (yr. ended 12/31/11): Assets, $592,016 (M); gifts received, $12,970; expenditures, $63,180; qualifying distributions, $58,000; giving activities include $58,000 for 8 grants to individuals (high: $8,000; low: $5,000).
Purpose and activities: The foundation awards college scholarships to children of employees of Gehl Company.
Type of support: Employee-related scholarships.
Geographic limitations: Giving primarily in areas of company operations in WI.
Application information: Applications not accepted. Contributes only through employee-related scholarships.
Officers: Dan Miller, Pres.; Steve Lohr, V.P.; James Green, Secy.; Shannon Van Dyke, Treas.
EIN: 391039217

1546
Gelco Construction Inc.
1745 Salem Industrial Dr., NE
Salem, OR 97301-0377 (503) 364-2638

Company URL: http://www.gelcoconstruction.com/
Establishment information: Established in 1976.
Company type: Private company
Business activities: Operates commercial concrete construction company.
Business type (SIC): Contractors/concrete work
Corporate officers: James D. Monaghan, C.E.O.; C. Raffensperger, Secy.
Giving statement: Giving through the Gelco Charitable Foundation.

Gelco Charitable Foundation
c/o Foundation Source
501 Silverside Rd., Ste. 123
Wilmington, DE 19809-1377

Establishment information: Established in 2005 in DE.
Donors: Windsor Rock Products; Lorna Monaghan; Gelco Construction; Gelco Supply, Inc.; Onesource Software, Inc.
Financial data (yr. ended 12/31/11): Assets, $2,523,577 (M); gifts received, $350,000; expenditures, $105,563; qualifying distributions, $73,700; giving activities include $73,700 for grants.
Fields of interest: Human services; Religion.
Support limitations: No grants to individuals.
Application information: Applications not accepted. Unsolicited requests for funds not accepted.
Officers and Director:* James D. Monaghan*, Pres. and Secy.; Kelly Keudell, V.P.; Kristin McCall, V.P.; Kevin Monaghan, V.P.; Lorna Monaghan, V.P.; Corinne Raffensperger, V.P.
EIN: 203818744

1547
Gemini Industries, Inc.
421 S.E. 27th St.
El Reno, OK 73036-5773 (405) 262-5710

Company URL: http://www.geminicoatings.com/p/11776/Default.aspx
Establishment information: Established in 1964.
Company type: Private company
Business activities: Manufactures wood coatings.
Business type (SIC): Paints and allied products
Corporate officer: Roger L. Woolery, Pres.
Giving statement: Giving through the Gemini Industries, Inc., Foundation.

Gemini Industries, Inc., Foundation
2300 Holloway Dr.
P.O. Box 699
El Reno, OK 73036-5773

Establishment information: Established in 1995 in OK.
Donor: Gemini Industries, Inc.
Financial data (yr. ended 12/31/11): Assets, $5,147 (M); gifts received, $24,850; expenditures, $20,112; qualifying distributions, $20,112; giving activities include $20,112 for grants.
Purpose and activities: The foundation supports organizations involved with human services and Christianity.
Fields of interest: Youth development; Human services; Religion.
Type of support: General/operating support; Program development.
Geographic limitations: Giving primarily in OK.
Support limitations: No grants to individuals.
Application information: Applications not accepted. Unsolicited requests for funds not accepted.
Trustee: Rick McGee.
EIN: 736282301

1548
GenCorp Inc.
2001 Aerojet Rd.
P.O. Box 537012
Rancho Cordova, CA 95742-6418
(916) 355-4000

Company URL: http://www.gencorp.com
Establishment information: Established in 1915.
Company type: Public company
Company ticker symbol and exchange: GY/NYSE

Business activities: Develops and manufactures space electronics, smart munitions, and solid and liquid rocket propulsion systems; manufactures chemical intermediates and active pharmaceutical ingredients; develops, manufactures, and sells extruded and molded automotive rubber sealing systems.
Business type (SIC): Motor vehicles and equipment; chemicals and allied products; guided missiles and space vehicles
Financial profile for 2012: Number of employees, 3,391; assets, $919,300,000; sales volume, $994,900,000; pre-tax net income, $13,200,000; expenses, $960,000,000; liabilities, $1,308,100,000
Corporate officers: James R. Henderson, Chair.; Scott J. Seymour, Pres. and C.E.O.; Kathleen E. Redd, V.P. and C.F.O.; Christopher C. Cambria, V.P., Genl. Counsel, and Secy.
Board of directors: James R. Henderson, Chair.; Thomas A. Corcoran; Warren G. Lichtenstein; David A. Lorber; James H. Perry; Scott J. Seymour; Martin Turchin; Robert C. Woods
Subsidiary: Aerojet-General Corp., Sacramento, CA
Plants: Camden, AR; Socorro, NM; Jonesborough, TN; Culpeper, VA; Redmond, WA
International operations: Argentina; Bermuda; Czech Republic; France
Giving statement: Giving through the GenCorp Foundation, Incorporated.
Company EIN: 340244000

GenCorp Foundation, Incorporated

P.O. Box 15619
Sacramento, CA 95852-0619
FAX: (916) 355-2515;
E-mail: gencorp.foundation@gencorp.com;
URL: http://www.gencorp.com/pages/gcfound.html

Establishment information: Incorporated in 1999 in CA as successor to the GenCorp Foundation Inc., established in 1961 in OH.
Donor: GenCorp Foundation Inc.
Contact: Juanita Garcia, Exec. Dir.
Financial data (yr. ended 11/30/12): Assets, $16,225,000 (M); expenditures, $798,985; qualifying distributions, $685,798; giving activities include $577,926 for 256 grants and $107,872 for 191 employee matching gifts.
Purpose and activities: The GenCorp Foundation supports the communities where GenCorp has a business presence. The foundation's primary giving focus is education with emphasis on STEM - science, technology, engineering, and mathematics. The foundation may also fund health and social services, arts organizations, and civic and environmental projects.
Fields of interest: Museums; Elementary/secondary education; Higher education; Engineering school/education; Education; American Red Cross; Mathematics; Engineering/technology; Science Children/youth; Minorities; Girls; Economically disadvantaged.

Programs:

Aerojet Community Scholarships: The foundation awards $1,000 scholarships to local high school seniors who plan to pursue college study in science, technology, engineering, or math. Applicants are selected based on academic ability and economic need.

Aerojet Delivers: Through Aerojet Delivers, employees make charitable contributions to schools and nonprofit organizations through payroll deductions. The foundation pays the administrative fees associated with processing the donations so that 100% of employees' gifts go directly to the charity or school of their choice.

Educational Dollars for Doers Program: The foundation awards grants to schools where GenCorp employees volunteer time in the classroom.

GenCorp Educational Matching Gift Program: The foundation matches contributions made by full-time employees and company directors of GenCorp to educational institutions on a one-for-one basis from $25 to $3,000 per donor per year.

GenCorp Scholarship Program: The foundation offers four-year college scholarships to the children of GenCorp employees. The program is administered by the National Merit Scholarship Corporation.

Type of support: Curriculum development; Employee matching gifts; Employee volunteer services; Employee-related scholarships; Equipment; Program development; Scholarship funds.
Geographic limitations: Giving primarily in Funds primarily in the communities where the company operates: Huntsville, AL, Camden, AR, Sacramento and Vernon, CA, Washington, DC, Socorro, NM, Jonesborough, TN, Clearfield, UT, Gainesville and Orange, VA, and Redmond, WA.
Support limitations: No support for private foundations, religious organizations, or fraternal, athletic, social, political, or disease-specific organizations. No grants to individuals (except for scholarships), or for general operating support, capital campaigns, courtesy advertising, benefits, raffle tickets, golf tournaments, or other fundraising events, research, or conferences; no loans.
Publications: Annual report; Application guidelines; Informational brochure (including application guidelines); Occasional report.
Application information: Applications accepted. Letters of inquiry should be no longer than 1 to 2 pages and should be submitted using organization letterhead. A full proposal may be requested at a later date. Funding cycles are Apr., July, and Oct. Application form not required. Applicants should submit the following:

1) brief history of organization and description of its mission
2) detailed description of project and amount of funding requested

Initial approach: Letter of inquiry; contact foundation or participating schools for Aerojet Community Scholarships
Copies of proposal: 1
Board meeting date(s): As required
Deadline(s): None
Final notification: 30 days

Officers and Trustees:* Chris W. Conely*, Pres.; Jennifer Goolis*, Secy.; David Fox*, Treas.; Dave Hatch*; Roger M. Myers; Ronald Samborsky; Robert Shenton.
Number of staff: 1 full-time professional; 1 part-time support.
EIN: 680441559
Selected grants: The following grants are a representative sample of this grantmaker's funding activity:
$150,000 to Aviation High School, Seattle, WA, 2012. For science laboratory equipment for new STEM high school.
$50,000 to Southern Arkansas University, Magnolia, AR, 2012. For Engineering Preceptor Program.
$45,000 to Northern Virginia Community College, Annandale, VA, 2012. For SySTEMic Solutions Program, STEM-based K-12 curriculum, developed through public-private partnership.
$25,000 to K V I E Public Television, Sacramento, CA, 2012. To underwrite science program, NOVA.
$20,700 to National Merit Scholarship Corporation, Evanston, IL, 2012. For scholarships.
$20,000 to Powerhouse Science Center, Sacramento, CA, 2012. For scholarships for Challenger Learning Center.
$10,275 to Arkansas School for Mathematics, Sciences and the Arts, Hot Springs, AR, 2012. For science program.
$10,000 to Aerospace Museum of California, North Highlands, CA, 2012. For Project Lead the Way.
$10,000 to San Juan Education Foundation, Carmichael, CA, 2012. For elementary school literacy program.
$10,000 to Soil Born Farm Urban Agriculture Project, Sacramento, CA, 2012. For youth environmental education and stewardship program.

1549
Genentech, Inc.

1 DNA Way
South San Francisco, CA 94080-4918
(650) 225-1000

Company URL: http://www.gene.com
Establishment information: Established in 1976.
Company type: Subsidiary of a foreign company
Business activities: Discovers, develops, manufactures, commercializes, and licenses biotherapeutics.
Business type (SIC): Drugs
Financial profile for 2008: Number of employees, 11,186; assets, $21,787,000,000; sales volume, $13,418,000,000; pre-tax net income, $5,431,000,000; expenses, $8,172,000,000; liabilities, $6,116,000,000
Corporate officers: Arthur D. Levinson, Ph.D., Chair.; Ian T. Clark, C.E.O.; Steve Krognes, Sr. V.P. and C.F.O.; Frederick C. Kentz III, Sr. V.P. and Secy.; Denise Smith-Hams, Sr. V.P., Human Resources
Board of directors: Arthur D. Levinson, Ph.D., Chair.; John Irving Bell; William M. Burns; Ian T. Clark; Alan Hippe; Andre Hoffmann; Daniel O'Day; Severin Schwan
Giving statement: Giving through the Genentech, Inc. Corporate Giving Program, the Genentech Access To Care Foundation, the Genentech Foundation, and the Thomas and Gerd Perkins Foundation.

Genentech, Inc. Corporate Giving Program

c/o Mgr., Contribs.
1 DNA Way
South San Francisco, CA 94080-4918 (650) 225-1000
FAX: (650) 225-2021; E-mail: give@gene.com;
URL: http://www.gene.com/gene/about/community

Purpose and activities: As a complement to its foundation, Genentech also makes charitable contributions to nonprofit organizations directly. Special emphasis is directed toward programs designed to promote health science education, patient education and advocacy, and community development. Support is given primarily in Oceanside, South San Francisco and Vacaville, California, Lexington, Kentucky, and Hillsboro, Oregon, and on a national basis for health and science.
Fields of interest: Health care, formal/general education; Health care; Cancer; Patients' rights; Community/economic development; Science; General charitable giving.
Type of support: Conferences/seminars; Donated products; Employee matching gifts; Employee

volunteer services; General/operating support; Research; Scholarship funds; Sponsorships.
Geographic limitations: Giving primarily in Oceanside, South San Francisco, and Vacaville, CA, Lexington, KY, and Hillsboro, OR; giving on a national basis for health and science.
Support limitations: No support for religious, political, sectarian, or discriminatory organizations. No grants for advertising journals or booklets, alumni drives, capital campaigns, building funds, continuing medical education, infrastructural requests (e.g. salaries, equipment), memorial funds, memberships, professional sports events or athletes, scholarships, or yearbooks.
Publications: Application guidelines.
Application information: Applications accepted. The company has a staff that only handles contributions. A contributions committee reviews all requests. Application form required. Applicants should submit the following:
1) copy of IRS Determination Letter
2) brief history of organization and description of its mission
Proposals should include valid e-mail for communications, and program and/or event details.
Initial approach: Complete online application
Deadline(s): None
Final notification: 60 days

Genentech Access To Care Foundation

1 DNA Way, M.S. #858A
South San Francisco, CA 94080-4918
FAX: (650) 335-1366;
E-mail: info@genentech-access.com; URL: http://www.genentech-access.com/hcp

Establishment information: Established in 2002 as a company-sponsored operating foundation.
Donor: Genentech, Inc.
Financial data (yr. ended 12/31/11): Assets, $59,788,925 (M); gifts received, $577,763,551; expenditures, $579,501,968; qualifying distributions, $579,501,968; giving activities include $553,352,278 for grants to individuals.
Purpose and activities: The foundation provides prescription medication to economically disadvantaged patients.
Fields of interest: Health care Economically disadvantaged.
Type of support: Donated products.
Geographic limitations: Giving on a national basis.
Publications: Application guidelines.
Application information: Applications accepted. The application requires medical information from the patient's physician and financial information from the patient to determine eligibility. Application form required.
Initial approach: Complete online application
Deadline(s): None
Officers and Trustees:* Steve Krognes*, Pres.; Renee Shiota, Secy.; Jane Michan, C.F.O.; Louis Dombrowski; Alexander Hardy; Sandra Horning; Sean Johnson; Mary Sliwkowski; Geoff Teeter; Carol Zigulis.
EIN: 460500266

Genentech Foundation

1 DNA Way, M.S. 24
South San Francisco, CA 94080-4918 (877) 313-5778
E-mail: foundation@gene.com; Additional tel.: (650) 467-0805; URL: http://www.genentechfoundation.com/index.html

Establishment information: Established in 2002.
Donor: Genentech, Inc.
Financial data (yr. ended 12/31/11): Assets, $32,720,575 (M); gifts received, $3,000,234; expenditures, $3,215,443; qualifying distributions, $3,185,331; giving activities include $3,185,331 for grants.
Purpose and activities: The foundation supports programs designed to promote health science education; community-wide civic initiatives; and national patient education and advocacy efforts.
Fields of interest: Higher education; Graduate/professional education; Medical school/education; Libraries (public); Education; Health care, patient services; Health care; Cancer; Pediatrics; Employment, services; Employment, training; Food services; Food banks; Housing/shelter; Community/economic development; Science, formal/general education; Public affairs.
Programs:
Community Support: The foundation supports programs designed to enhance, enrich, and support those living in Genentech communities. Special emphasis is directed toward programs designed to address hunger and access to food; help individuals and families obtain access to permanent housing; and promote job training and job creation.
Everyday Needs Assistance Program: The foundation awards grants to organizations that support families with children facing cancer. The program is designed to ease the financial burden of families while they seek care for their child. The program is administered by the Family Reach Foundation, Jake Owen Raborn Foundation, and Mission4Maureen.
Health Science Education: The foundation supports schools, universities, and programs designed to promote health science education to help develop the next generation of scientists. Special emphasis is directed toward programs designed to provide pre- and post-doctoral research fellowships; and promote undergraduate research at U.S. universities.
Patient Education and Advocacy: The foundation supports programs designed to enhance patients' understanding of disease; provide support through diagnosis and treatment of disease; and improve patients' ability to obtain appropriate healthcare for serious illnesses. Special emphasis is directed toward programs designed to provide support and education to pediatric cancer patients.
Type of support: Continuing support; Curriculum development; Fellowships; General/operating support; Program development; Research.
Geographic limitations: Giving primarily in areas of company operations in North San Diego County, Oceanside, South San Francisco, San Francisco County, San Mateo County, Solano County, and Vacaville, CA, Jefferson County, KY, and Washington County, OR; giving also to national organizations.
Support limitations: No support for discriminatory organizations, professional sports athletes, religious organizations not of direct benefit to the entire community, or political organizations. No grants to individuals, or for alumni drives, capital campaigns or building funds, infrastructural requests including salary or equipment, memorial funds, professional sports events, sponsorships, or yearbooks.
Publications: Application guidelines; Grants list; Informational brochure; Program policy statement.
Application information: Applications accepted. A site visit may be requested. Application form required. Applicants should submit the following:
1) statement of problem project will address
2) population served
3) name, address and phone number of organization
4) copy of IRS Determination Letter
5) brief history of organization and description of its mission
6) copy of most recent annual report/audited financial statement/990
7) explanation of why grantmaker is considered an appropriate donor for project
8) detailed description of project and amount of funding requested
9) contact person
10) copy of current year's organizational budget and/or project budget
11) listing of additional sources and amount of support
Initial approach: Complete online application
Copies of proposal: 1
Board meeting date(s): Mar., June, Sept., and Dec.
Deadline(s): Jan. 27, Apr. 6, July 6, and Sept. 28
Officers and Directors:* Richard H. Scheller, Ph.D.*, Chair.; Ashraf Hanna, C.F.O.; Colleen Wilson, Exec. Dir.; Sunil Agarwal, M.D.; Vishva Dixit, M.D.; Markus Gemuend; Denise Smith-Hams; Nancy Oaks; Michelle Rohrer, Ph.D.; Mary B. Silwkowski, Ph.D.; Geoff Teeter.
EIN: 460500264
Selected grants: The following grants are a representative sample of this grantmaker's funding activity:
$330,000 to University of California, San Francisco, CA, 2008.
$250,000 to Multiple Sclerosis Association of America, Cherry Hill, NJ, 2008.
$175,000 to StarVista, San Carlos, CA, 2008.
$109,400 to San Francisco State University, San Francisco, CA, 2008.
$92,547 to Stanford University, Bio X, Stanford, CA, 2008.
$82,500 to Stanford University, Stanford, CA, 2008.
$82,500 to Stanford University, Stanford, CA, 2008.
$66,395 to Stanford University, Stanford, CA, 2008.
$50,000 to Community Overcoming Relationship Abuse, Burlingame, CA, 2008.
$12,000 to Johns Hopkins University, Baltimore, MD, 2008.

Thomas and Gerd Perkins Foundation

4 Embarcadero Ctr., Ste. 3620
San Francisco, CA 94111-4155

Establishment information: Established in 1997.
Donor: Genentech, Inc.
Financial data (yr. ended 12/31/11): Assets, $417,797 (M); expenditures, $263,175; qualifying distributions, $250,000; giving activities include $250,000 for grants.
Purpose and activities: The foundation supports organizations involved with health, leukemia, and other areas.
Fields of interest: Health care; Cancer, leukemia; General charitable giving.
Type of support: Equipment; General/operating support.
Geographic limitations: Giving primarily in San Francisco, CA, Centennial, CO, and White Plains, NY.
Support limitations: No grants to individuals.
Application information: Applications not accepted. Contributes only to pre-selected organizations.
Officer: Thomas J. Perkins, Pres.
EIN: 680134693
Selected grants: The following grants are a representative sample of this grantmaker's funding activity:
$250,000 to Leukemia & Lymphoma Society, White Plains, NY, 2010. For general purpose.
$100,000 to Cleveland Clinic Foundation, Cleveland, OH, 2010.

1550
General Communication, Inc.
(also known as GCI)
2550 Denali St., Ste. 1000
Anchorage, AK 99503-2751
(907) 868-5600
FAX: (907) 868-5676

Company URL: http://www.gci.com/about
Establishment information: Established in 1979.
Company type: Public company
Company ticker symbol and exchange: GNCMA/NASDAQ
Business activities: Operates holding company; provides long distance telephone communications services; provides cable television services; provides Internet access services; provides wireless services.
Business type (SIC): Telephone communications; cable and other pay television services; holding company
Financial profile for 2012: Number of employees, 1,734; assets, $1,506,520,000; sales volume, $710,180,000; pre-tax net income, $21,250,000; expenses, $621,200,000; liabilities, $1,349,340,000
Corporate officers: Stephen M. Brett, Chair.; Ronald A. Duncan, Pres. and C.E.O.; John Lowber, Sr. V.P., and C.F.O.; Tina Pidgeon, Sr. V.P. and Genl. Counsel
Board of directors: Stephen M. Brett, Chair.; Ronald A. Duncan; Jerry A. Edgerton; Scott M. Fisher; William P. Glasgow; Mark Kroloff; Stephen R. Mooney; James M. Schneider
Giving statement: Giving through the GCI Corporate Giving Program.
Company EIN: 920072737

GCI Corporate Giving Program
c/o Corp. Contribs. Prog., Attn: Pebbles Harris
2550 Denali St., Ste. 1000
Anchorage, AK 99503-2751
FAX: (907) 265-5676; URL: http://www.gci.com/connect

Purpose and activities: GCI makes charitable contributions to nonprofit organizations involved with encouraging individual growth and positive decision-making. Special emphasis is directed towards programs that afford opportunities to youth. Support is given primarily in Alaska.
Fields of interest: Youth development.
Type of support: General/operating support; In-kind gifts; Sponsorships.
Geographic limitations: Giving primarily in AK.
Support limitations: No support for religious or political organizations or discriminatory organizations. No grants to individuals or for travel.
Application information: Applications accepted. Proposals should be no longer than 2 pages and include a cover sheet with a 50-word abstract of the proposal and contact information. Attachments should be limited to 3 pages. Contributions generally do not exceed $500. Application form not required. Applicants should submit the following:
1) name, address and phone number of organization
2) brief history of organization and description of its mission
3) list of company employees involved with the organization
4) explanation of why grantmaker is considered an appropriate donor for project
5) detailed description of project and amount of funding requested
6) contact person

Proposals should include a description of past support by GCI with the organization.
Initial approach: Proposal to headquarters
Copies of proposal: 1
Deadline(s): None
Final notification: Following review

1551
General Dynamics Corporation
2941 Fairview Park Dr., Ste. 100
Falls Church, VA 22042-4513
(703) 876-3000
FAX: (703) 876-3125

Company URL: http://www.generaldynamics.com
Establishment information: Established in 1952.
Company type: Public company
Company ticker symbol and exchange: GD/NYSE
Business activities: Manufactures submarines and tanks.
Business type (SIC): Transportation equipment/miscellaneous; ship and boat building and repair
Financial profile for 2012: Number of employees, 92,200; assets, $34,309,000,000; sales volume, $31,513,000,000; pre-tax net income, $541,000,000; expenses, $30,680,000,000; liabilities, $22,919,000,000
Fortune 1000 ranking: 2012—98th in revenues, 950th in profits, and 164th in assets
Forbes 2000 ranking: 2012—300th in sales, 1875th in profits, and 662nd in assets
Corporate officers: Phebe N. Novakovic, Chair. and C.E.O.; L. Hugh Redd, Sr. V.P. and C.F.O.; Gregory Gallopoulos, Sr. V.P., Genl. Counsel, and Secy.; Walter M. Oliver, Sr. V.P., Human Resources and Admin.; David H. Fogg, V.P. and Treas.; Kimberly A. Kuryea, V.P., Cont.
Board of directors: Phebe N. Novakovic, Chair.; Mary T. Barra; Nicholas D. Chabraja; James S. Crown; William P. Fricks; Paul G. Kaminski; John M. Keane; Lester L. Lyles; William A. Osborn; Robert Walmsley
Subsidiaries: American Overseas Marine Corp., Quincy, MA; General Dynamics Land Systems Inc., Sterling Heights, MI; Gulfstream Aerospace Corporation, Savannah, GA; Material Service Corporation, Chicago, IL; Material Service Resources Co., Chicago, IL
Divisions: Armament Systems Div., Burlington, VT; Defense Systems Div., Pittsfield, MA; Electric Boat Div., Groton, CT
Plants: Rancho Cucamonga, San Diego, CA; Fort Worth, TX
International operations: Australia; Austria; Brazil; Canada; Cyprus; Czech Republic; England; France; Germany; Gibraltar; Hong Kong; India; Italy; Lebanon; Mexico; Netherlands; Russia; Saudi Arabia; Singapore; South Korea; Spain; Switzerland; Turkey; United Arab Emirates; United Kingdom; Venezuela; Wales
Giving statement: Giving through the General Dynamics Corporation Contributions Program and the L. Y. Spear Foundation.
Company EIN: 131673581

General Dynamics Corporation Contributions Program
2941 Fairview Park Dr., Ste. 100
Falls Church, VA 22042-4513 (703) 876-3000
FAX: (703) 876-3125; URL: http://www.generaldynamics.com/

Purpose and activities: General Dynamics makes charitable contributions to nonprofit organizations involved with arts and culture, education, human services, and civic affairs. Special emphasis is directed towards programs designed to help the military and their families. Support is given primarily in areas of company operations.
Fields of interest: Arts; Education; Family services; Human services; Public affairs; General charitable giving Military/veterans.
Type of support: Employee volunteer services; General/operating support; Sponsorships.
Geographic limitations: Giving primarily in areas of company operations; giving also to national organizations.
Application information:

L. Y. Spear Foundation
Eastern Point Rd., Electric Boat
Groton, CT 06340-4947

Donor: General Dynamics Corp.
Financial data (yr. ended 12/31/11): Assets, $39,300 (M); gifts received, $2,000; expenditures, $3,843; qualifying distributions, $3,340; giving activities include $3,265 for 1 grant to an individual.
Purpose and activities: The foundation awards grants to graduates of each officer class of the U.S. Naval Submarine School in Groton, Connecticut.
Fields of interest: Education.
Type of support: Grants to individuals.
Geographic limitations: Giving limited to Groton, CT.
Application information: Applications not accepted. Unsolicited requests for funds not accepted.
Trustees: David M. Goebel; Frederick R. Haberlandt; David M. McCall; William A. Miller; Henry J. Nardone; Thomas F. Olson; John Padgett III.
EIN: 066026051

1552
General Electric Company
(also known as GE)
3135 Easton Tpke.
Fairfield, CT 06828-0001 (203) 373-2211
FAX: (203) 373-3131

Company URL: http://www.ge.com
Establishment information: Established in 1892.
Company type: Public company
Company ticker symbol and exchange: GE/NYSE
International Securities Identification Number: US3696041033
Business activities: Develops, manufactures, and markets electricity generation, transmission, distribution, control, and utilization products.
Business type (SIC): Electronic and other electrical equipment and components
Financial profile for 2012: Number of employees, 305,000; assets, $685,328,000,000; sales volume, $147,359,000,000; pre-tax net income, $17,406,000,000; expenses, $129,953,000,000; liabilities, $562,302,000,000
Fortune 1000 ranking: 2012—8th in revenues, 12th in profits, and 11th in assets
Forbes 2000 ranking: 2012—21st in sales, 24th in profits, and 44th in assets
Corporate officers: Jeffrey R. Immelt, Chair. and C.E.O.; Keith S. Sherin, Co.-Vice-Chair. and C.F.O.; John Krenicki, Jr., Co.-Vice-Chair.; Michael A. Neal, Co.-Vice-Chair.; John G. Rice, Co.-Vice-Chair.; Kathryn A. Cassidy, Sr. V.P. and Treas.; Brackett B. Denniston III, Sr. V.P. and Genl. Counsel; John F. Lynch, Sr. V.P., Human Resources
Board of directors: Jeffrey R. Immelt, Chair.; W. Geofrey Beattie; John J. Brennan; James I. Cash, Jr.; Marijn E. Dekkers; Ann M. Fudge; Susan Hockfield; Andrea Jung; Alan G. Lafley; Robert W. Lane; Ralph S. Larsen; Rochelle B. Lazarus; James J. Mulva;

Sam Nunn; Roger S. Penske; Robert J. Swieringa; James S. Tisch; Douglas A. Warner III
Subsidiaries: GE Information Services, Inc., Rockville, MD; General Electric Capital Services, Inc., Stamford, CT; iVillage Inc., New York, NY; Universal Studios, Inc., Universal City, CA
Divisions: GE Aircraft Engines Div., Cincinnati, OH; GE Appliances Div., Louisville, KY; GE Industrial Systems Div., Plainville, CT; GE Lighting Div., Cleveland, OH; GE Medical Systems Div., Milwaukee, WI; GE Plastics Div., Pittsfield, MA; GE Power Systems Div., Atlanta, GA; GE Transportation Systems Div., Erie, PA; Research and Development Div., Schenectady, NY
International operations: Austria; Belgium; Bermuda; Brazil; Canada; China; Finland; France; Germany; Hungary; Ireland; Italy; Japan; Luxembourg; Mexico; Netherlands; Norway; Philippines; Saudi Arabia; Singapore; Sweden; United Kingdom
Historic mergers: Heller Financial, Inc. (October 24, 2001)
Giving statement: Giving through the GE Corporate Giving Program, the GE Foundation, and the GE Consumer & Industrial Employee Community Fund.
Company EIN: 140689340

GE Corporate Giving Program

3135 Easton Tpke.
Fairfield, CT 06828-0001 (203) 373-2211
URL: http://www.gecitizenship.com/

Financial data (yr. ended 12/31/10): Total giving, $97,000,000, including $97,000,000 for grants.
Purpose and activities: As a complement to its foundation, GE also makes charitable contributions to nonprofit organizations directly. Support is given primarily in areas of company operations.
Fields of interest: Education; Environment; Health care; Safety/disasters; Community/economic development.
Type of support: Donated products; Employee volunteer services; General/operating support.
Geographic limitations: Giving primarily in areas of company operations.

GE Foundation

(formerly GE Fund)
3135 Easton Tpke.
Fairfield, CT 06828-0001 (203) 373-3216
FAX: (203) 373-3029;
E-mail: gefoundation@ge.com; E-mail for Corporate Citizenship Team: citizenship@ge.com; E-mail for Developing Health: developing.health@ge.com; URL: http://www.gefoundation.com

Establishment information: Trust established in 1952 in NY.
Donor: General Electric Co.
Contact: Robert L. Corcoran, Chair. and Pres.
Financial data (yr. ended 12/31/11): Assets, $21,352,303 (M); gifts received, $122,587,600; expenditures, $118,720,583; qualifying distributions, $118,787,783; giving activities include $80,598,978 for 422 grants (high: $3,159,566; low: $25) and $35,116,667 for 19,349 employee matching gifts.
Purpose and activities: The foundation supports organizations involved with education, the environment, health, diseases, disaster relief, human services, international affairs, human rights, community development, science, public policy, and leadership development.
Fields of interest: Education, reform; Elementary/secondary education; Middle schools/education; Higher education; Business school/education; Scholarships/financial aid; Education; Environment, climate change/global warming; Environment, water resources; Environment; Health care, clinics/centers; Health care, infants; Reproductive health; Public health, clean water supply; Public health, sanitation; Health care, patient services; Health care; Heart & circulatory diseases; Asthma; Diabetes; Tropical diseases; Surgery; Legal services; Legal services, public interest law; Disasters, preparedness/services; Youth development, business; Human services; International affairs, U.N.; International economics/trade policy; International affairs; Civil/human rights; Community/economic development; United Ways and Federated Giving Programs; Mathematics; Engineering/technology; Science; Public policy, research; Leadership development Girls; Economically disadvantaged.
International interests: Africa; China; Europe; India; Latin America; Middle East; Southeast Asia; Sub-Saharan Africa.
Programs:

Developing Futures in Education: The foundation supports programs designed to improve the equity and quality of public education through collaboration and innovation to ensure that young Americans are prepared for careers in a global economy. Special emphasis is directed toward implementation of the Common Core State Standards for College and Career Readiness.

Developing Health: The foundation, in partnership with the GE Corporate Diversity Council and healthymagination, supports programs designed to increase access to primary care for underserved populations in targeted communities. The program is administered by GE's Affinity Networks and employee groups and supports selected nonprofit health centers based on leadership, accountability, community impact, and willingness to partner with GE volunteers.

Developing Health Globally: The foundation supports programs designed to improve healthcare delivery for the world's most vulnerable populations in Africa, Latin America, and Southeast Asia. Special emphasis is directed toward maternal and infant care; emergency care; surgical care; biomedical practice; safe water; and education.

Disaster Relief: The foundation matches GE employee and retiree gifts and awards grants to select relief organizations to help communities affected by humanitarian and natural disasters. Current partners include GE employees, International Red Cross, UNICEF, AmeriCares, and Save the Children.

Employee Matching Gift Program: The foundation matches contributions made by employees and retirees of GE to schools and nonprofit organizations on a one-for-one basis from $25 to $50,000 per employee, per year.

GE STAR Awards: The foundation awards college scholarships of $500 to $3,500 to children of employees of GE. Winners are selected based on academic record, extracurricular activities, community service, personal experiences, and goals described in a written statement. The program is administered by the Institute of International Education.

Public Policy: The foundation supports programs designed to address public policy in the global business community. Special emphasis is directed toward human rights; rule of law; the environment; and international trade.

Scholar Leaders Program: The foundation, in partnership with the Institute of International Education, provides scholarships to 200 low-income students to attend universities in Canada, the Czech Republic, Hungary, India, Indonesia, Korea, Poland, Romania, Thailand, and Vietnam. The program also includes "leadership in service," a development initiative with community development projects, mentoring, and networking opportunities for students with GE businesses in the region.

Type of support: Continuing support; Curriculum development; Employee matching gifts; Employee-related scholarships; Faculty/staff development; Management development/capacity building; Program development; Publication; Research; Scholarship funds.
Geographic limitations: Giving on a national and international basis, with emphasis on Los Angeles, CA, Stamford, CT, Washington, DC, Chicago, IL, Atlanta, GA, Jefferson County and Louisville, KY, New Orleans, LA, Baltimore, MD, New York and Schenectady, NY, Cincinnati, OH, Erie, PA, Houston, TX, VA, Milwaukee, WI, Africa, Canada, China, Europe, India, Latin America, the Middle East, and Southeast Asia.
Support limitations: No support for religious or political organizations. No grants to individuals (except for employee-related scholarships), or for capital campaigns, endowments, or other special purpose campaigns; no loans; no equipment donations.
Publications: Grants list; Program policy statement.
Application information: Applications not accepted. The foundation practices an invitation only process for giving. The foundation does not encourage unsolicited proposals.

Board meeting date(s): Quarterly

Officers and Directors:* Robert L. Corcoran*, Chair. and Pres.; Janine Rouson, Secy.; Michael J. Cosgrove, Treas.; Donna Granfors, Cont.; Paul Bueker, Secy. and Cont.; E. W. Fraser, Genl. Counsel; Alfredo Arguello; Nani Beccalli; Pamela Daley; Brackett Denniston; Nancy Dorn; John F. Lynch; John G. Rice; Keith S. Sherin; Dmitri Stockton.
Number of staff: 6 full-time professional; 1 part-time professional; 4 full-time support.
EIN: 222621967
Selected grants: The following grants are a representative sample of this grantmaker's funding activity:
$3,942,067 to Student Achievement Partners, New York, NY, 2011.
$1,708,758 to United Way of Greater Cincinnati, Cincinnati, OH, 2011.
$1,087,425 to Institute of International Education, New York, NY, 2011.
$1,084,746 to Health Choice Network, Miami, FL, 2011.
$176,740 to Duke University, Durham, NC, 2011.
$127,500 to Global Reporting Initiative, Amsterdam, Netherlands, 2011.
$100,000 to Whitney M. Young Jr. Health Center, Albany, NY, 2011.
$9,718 to United Way of San Diego County, San Diego, CA, 2011.

GE Consumer & Industrial Employee Community Fund

(formerly General Electric Employees Community Fund)
Appliance Park, AP6-237 A
Louisville, KY 40225-0001 (502) 452-7144
FAX: (502) 452-0257;
E-mail: megan.robison@ge.com; URL: http://www.gelouisville.com/ecf

Establishment information: Established in 1965 in KY.
Donor: General Electric Co.
Contact: Megan Robison, Chair.
Financial data (yr. ended 12/31/11): Revenue, $424,758; assets, $179,971 (M); gifts received, $420,919; expenditures, $852,779; giving activities include $852,779 for grants.

Purpose and activities: The fund supports charitable organizations of interest to employees of GE with a focus on health care and human services in metro Louisville and surrounding areas.
Fields of interest: Education; Health care; Human services; Community development, neighborhood development.
Program:
Grants: The fund provides grants (ranging from $2,500 to $5,000) to nonprofit organizations in the metropolitan Louisville area that benefit children, the elderly, and the needy. Eligible applicants have 501(c)(3) status and support individuals who reside within 125 miles of the metropolitan Louisville area.
Type of support: Continuing support; General/operating support.
Geographic limitations: Giving primarily in KY.
Support limitations: No support for religious or political organizations. No grants to individuals, or for capital campaigns; no product donations.
Publications: Application guidelines; Grants list.
Application information: Applications accepted. Application form required.
Initial approach: Online application
Copies of proposal: 1
Board meeting date(s): Monthly
Deadline(s): None
Final notification: One to three months
Officers and Board Members:* Megan Robison*, Chair.; Michelle Coomes*, Secy.; Adam Kuhn*, Treas.; Joan Burkhart; Kellie Cundiff; Greg Finnicum; Allison Gatta; Marie Geary; Gerard Gephart; and 10 additional board members.
EIN: 616035835

1553
General Iron Industries, Inc.

1909 N. Clifton Ave.
Chicago, IL 60614-4803 (773) 327-9600

Establishment information: Established in 1910.
Company type: Private company
Business activities: Operates scrap metal company.
Business type (SIC): Durable goods—wholesale
Corporate officer: Adam Labkon, Partner
Giving statement: Giving through the Lee and Nathan Rosenmutter Family Foundation.

Lee and Nathan Rosenmutter Family Foundation

(formerly Rosenmutter Foundation)
1909 N. Clifton Ave.
Chicago, IL 60614-4803

Establishment information: Established in IL.
Donors: General Iron Industries, Inc.; Price Watson.
Financial data (yr. ended 01/31/12): Assets, $906,274 (M); expenditures, $40,611; qualifying distributions, $40,170; giving activities include $40,170 for 23 grants (high: $5,400; low: $100).
Purpose and activities: The foundation supports organizations involved with film, education, human services, military and veterans, and Judaism.
Fields of interest: Media, film/video; Secondary school/education; Theological school/education; Education; Developmentally disabled, centers & services; Human services; Military/veterans' organizations; Jewish agencies & synagogues.
International interests: Israel.
Type of support: General/operating support.
Support limitations: No grants to individuals.
Application information: Applications not accepted. Unsolicited requests for funds not accepted.
Officer: Beverly Braverman, Pres.
Directors: Eva Braverman; Adam Labkon; Howard Labkon; Marilyn Labkon.
EIN: 366110084

1554
General Mills, Inc.

1 General Mills Blvd.
Minneapolis, MN 55426 (763) 764-7600
FAX: (763) 764-8330

Company URL: http://www.genmills.com
Establishment information: Established in 1928.
Company type: Public company
Company ticker symbol and exchange: GIS/NYSE
International Securities Identification Number: US3703341046
Business activities: Produces packaged consumer foods.
Business type (SIC): Grain mill products, including pet food
Financial profile for 2012: Number of employees, 35,000; assets, $21,096,800,000; sales volume, $16,657,900,000; pre-tax net income, $2,210,500,000; expenses, $14,095,500,000; liabilities, $14,675,100,000
Fortune 1000 ranking: 2012—169th in revenues, 135th in profits, and 232nd in assets
Forbes 2000 ranking: 2012—539th in sales, 338th in profits, and 903rd in assets
Corporate officers: Kendall J. Powell, Chair. and C.E.O.; Ian R. Friendly, Exec. V.P. and C.O.O., U.S.; Christopher O'Leary, Exec. V.P. and C.O.O., International; Donal Leo Mulligan, Exec. V.P. and C.F.O.; Roderick A. Palmore, Exec. V.P., Genl. Counsel, and Secy.; Michael L. Davis, Sr. V.P., Human Resources; Kofi Bruce, V.P. and Treas.; Jerry Young, V.P. and Cont.
Board of directors: Kendall J. Powell, Chair.; Bradbury H. Anderson; R. Kerry Clark; Paul Danos, Ph.D.; William T. Esrey; Raymond V. Gilmartin; Judith Richards Hope; Heidi G. Miller; Hilda Ochoa-Brillembourg; Steve Odland; Michael D. Rose; Robert L. Ryan; Dorothy A. Terrell
Subsidiaries: Gold Medal Insurance Co., Minneapolis, MN; The Pillsbury Company, Minneapolis, MN; Small Planet Foods, Inc., Sedro Woolley, WA; Yoplait USA, Inc., Minneapolis, MN
Plants: Bakersfield, Carson, Lodi, CA; Covington, GA; Belvidere, West Chicago, IL; New Albany, IN; Carlisle, Cedar Rapids, IA; Methuen, MA; Reed City, MI; Duluth, MN; Hannibal, Joplin, Kansas City, MO; Great Falls, MT; Vineland, NJ; Albuquerque, NM; Buffalo, NY; Cincinnati, Martel, Wellston, OH; Vinita, OK; Allentown, PA; Murfreesboro, TN; Sedro-Woolley, WA; Milwaukee, WI
International operations: Argentina; Australia; Austria; Belgium; Bermuda; Bolivia; Brazil; British Virgin Islands; Canada; Chile; China; Colombia; Czech Republic; Dominican Republic; Ecuador; France; Germany; Gibraltar; Greece; Hong Kong; Hungary; India; Indonesia; Israel; Italy; Japan; Lebanon; Luxembourg; Malaysia; Mauritius; Mexico; Morocco and the Western Sahara; Netherlands; Panama; Paraguay; Peru; Philippines; Poland; Portugal; Romania; Russia; Scotland; Singapore; Slovakia; South Africa; Spain; Sweden; Switzerland; Taiwan; Thailand; Trinidad & Tobago; Turkey; United Arab Emirates; United Kingdom; Uruguay; Venezuela
Giving statement: Giving through the General Mills, Inc. Corporate Giving Program and the General Mills Foundation.
Company EIN: 410274440

General Mills, Inc. Corporate Giving Program

P.O. Box 9452
Minneapolis, MN 55440-9452 (763) 764-7600
URL: http://www.generalmills.com/corporate/commitment/community.aspx

Contact: Ellen Luger, Exec. Dir., General Mills Foundation
Financial data (yr. ended 05/31/12): Total giving, $115,600,000, including $77,900,000 for grants and $37,700,000 for in-kind gifts.
Purpose and activities: As a complement to its foundation, General Mills also makes charitable contributions to nonprofit organizations directly. Support is given primarily in areas of company operations and to national and international organizations.
Fields of interest: Arts; Education; Food services; Food banks; Nutrition; Safety/disasters; Recreation; Women, centers/services; Human services Youth.
Program:
Join My Village: Join My Village is an online giving program that promotes education and economic development for girls and women in Malawi. Visitors to JoinMyVillage.com can instantly activate a contribution from General Mills and partnering companies like Merck by watching a video or reading a story about a girl's future. All personal donations made to Join My Village are matched dollar-for-dollar, up to this year's maximum gift of $900,000. The program, in partnership with the humanitarian organization CARE, funds scholarships for girls and lends money to women.
Type of support: Advocacy; Donated products; Employee matching gifts; Employee volunteer services; General/operating support; In-kind gifts; Loaned talent; Program development.
Geographic limitations: Giving primarily in areas of company operations and to national and international organizations.
Publications: Corporate giving report.
Application information: Applications not accepted. Contributes only to pre-selected organizations. The Community Action Department handles giving.
Number of staff: 5 full-time professional; 4 full-time support.

General Mills Foundation

1 General Mills Blvd.
MS CC-01
Minneapolis, MN 55426-1347
FAX: (763) 764-4114;
E-mail: CommunityActionQA@genmills.com;
URL: http://www.genmills.com/en/Responsibility/Community_Engagement.aspx

Establishment information: Incorporated in 1954 in MN.
Donor: General Mills, Inc.
Contact: Ellen Luger, Exec. Dir.
Financial data (yr. ended 05/31/12): Assets, $98,486,863 (M); gifts received, $63,048,573; expenditures, $28,372,710; qualifying distributions, $28,249,277; giving activities include $25,764,318 for 721 grants (high: $4,366,876; low: $1,000) and $1,836,386 for employee matching gifts.
Purpose and activities: The foundation supports programs designed to support hunger and nutrition wellness; education; and arts and culture.
Fields of interest: Performing arts; Arts; Elementary/secondary education; Education; Public health, physical fitness; Food services; Food banks; Nutrition; Disasters, preparedness/services; YM/YWCAs & YM/YWHAs; Family services; Human

services; United Ways and Federated Giving Programs Children/youth; Minorities; Economically disadvantaged.

Programs:

Celebrating Communities of Color: The foundation annually awards 50 $10,000 grants to nonprofit organizations in the Twin Cities, MN 7-county metro area, with programs designed to serve communities of color. Special emphasis is directed toward programs designed to promote hunger and nutrition wellness; education; family services; and arts and culture.

Community Action Council Program: The foundation awards grants to General Mills 24 manufacturing communities and its surrounding areas of up to 50 miles in the areas of hunger and nutrition wellness, education, family services, and arts and culture. The program is administered by Community Action Councils, groups of General Mills employees who volunteer their time. The program is invitation only.

Employee Gift-Matching: The foundation matches contributions made by employees, retirees, and directors of General Mills to the United Way, educational institutions, and organizations involved with arts and culture on a one-for-one basis.

General Mills Champions for Healthy Kids: The foundation annually awards 50 $10,000 grants to organizations and community-based groups with programs designed to develop creative ways to help young people ages 2 to 18 adopt a balanced diet and physically active lifestyle.

General Mills Foundation Merit Scholarship Program: The foundation awards four-year college scholarships of $500 to $3,000 to children of employees of General Mills and its subsidiaries. The program is administered by the National Merit Scholarship Corporation.

Post-High School Scholarship Program: The foundation awards college scholarships of $500 to $2,500 to children of employees of General Mills and its subsidiaries. The program is administered by Scholarship America, Inc.

Twin Cities - Arts and Culture: The foundation supports organizations designed to provide innovative performing arts and cultural programs through innovation, program quality, and contribution to their community. The program is limited to the Twin Cities, MN 7-county metro area.

Twin Cities - Hunger and Nutrition Wellness: The foundation supports programs designed to promote healthy children and families through providing food to those in need; developing and sharing food solutions; helping families make nutritious food choices; and integrating food with physical fitness. The program is limited to the Twin Cities, MN 7-county metro area.

Twin Cities - Youth Education and Enrichment: The foundation supports programs designed to emphasize student achievement and advancement, particularly at the K-12 level. Special emphasis is directed toward the need and return on effective teacher and administrator training and development; complimenting the classroom experience with proven strategies that keep parenting and caring adults engaged in a child's educational success; and partnering with organizations that provide secondary education pathways and scholarships to at-risk students. The program is limited to the Twin Cities, MN 7-county metro area.

Type of support: Capital campaigns; Employee matching gifts; Employee volunteer services; Employee-related scholarships; General/operating support; Program development; Scholarship funds.

Geographic limitations: Giving primarily in areas of major company operations and headquarters of Twin Cities, MN area; giving also in CA, GA, IA, IL, IN, MA, MD, MI, MO, MT, NJ, NM, NY, OH, TN, WA, and WI for the Community Action Councils Program; limited giving in Malawi and Tanzania.

Support limitations: No support for discriminatory organizations, religious, political, social, labor, veterans', alumni, or fraternal organizations, disease-specific organizations, or athletic associations. No grants to individuals, or for endowments, annual appeals, federated campaigns, fund drives, recreational or sporting events, healthcare, research, advertising, political causes, travel, emergency funding, debt reduction or operating deficits, conferences, seminars or workshops, publications, film, or television, sponsorships, special events, or fundraisers; no loans.

Publications: Application guidelines; Corporate giving report; Corporate report; Financial statement; Grants list.

Application information: Applications accepted. Applications for Community Action Council grants are available by invitation only. A full proposal may be requested at a later date for Twin Cities grants. E-mail letter of inquiry to foundation for capital requests. A site visit may be requested for Celebrating Communities of Color. Telephone calls and personal visits are not encouraged. Support is limited to 1 contribution per organization during any given year. Organizations receiving support may be asked to submit an evaluation report. Application form required. Applicants should submit the following:

1) population served
2) principal source of support for project in the past
3) copy of IRS Determination Letter
4) brief history of organization and description of its mission
5) copy of most recent annual report/audited financial statement/990
6) listing of board of directors, trustees, officers and other key people and their affiliations
7) detailed description of project and amount of funding requested
8) copy of current year's organizational budget and/or project budget
9) listing of additional sources and amount of support

Initial approach: Complete online letter of inquiry for Twin Cities grants; complete online application for Celebrating Communities of Color

Board meeting date(s): Ongoing

Deadline(s): None for Twin Cities grants; Dec. 3 to Feb. 1 for Celebrating Communities of Color

Final notification: May for Celebrating Communities of Color

Officers and Trustees:* Kendall J. Powell*, Chair.; Kimberly A. Nelson*, Pres.; Ellen Goldberg Luger, V.P., Secy., and Exec. Dir.; Marie Pillai, Treas.; Marc Belton; John R. Church; Michael L. Davis; Peter C. Erickson; Ian R. Friendly; Donal Leo Mulligan*; Shawn O'Grady; Christopher O'Leary; Roderick A. Palmore.

Number of staff: 7 full-time professional; 2 full-time support.

EIN: 416018495

Selected grants: The following grants are a representative sample of this grantmaker's funding activity:

$508,750 to Scholarship America, Saint Peter, MN, 2011. For Post High School Scholarship Program.
$450,000 to Amateur Athletic Union of the United States, Lake Buena Vista, FL, 2011. For One Million PALA Campaign.
$334,000 to Second Harvest Heartland, Saint Paul, MN, 2011. For Hunger-Free Minnesota.
$333,000 to Minnesota Orchestral Association, Minnesota Orchestra, Minneapolis, MN, 2011. For Building for the Future Campaign.
$250,000 to Search Institute, Minneapolis, MN, 2011. For The General Mills Report on American Family Strengths.
$137,500 to Interfaith Outreach and Community Partners, Plymouth, MN, 2011. For operating support and capital.
$10,000 to Buffalo Fine Arts Academy, Buffalo, NY, 2011. For Program Operating Support for monthly Free Family Programs at the Albright-Knox Art Gallery.
$10,000 to Volunteers of America of Minnesota, Minneapolis, MN, 2011. For Experience Corps.

1555
General Motors Company

(also known as GM)
(formerly General Motors Corporation)
300 Renaissance Ctr.
P.O. Box 300
Detroit, MI 48265-3000 (313) 556-5000

Company URL: http://www.gm.com
Establishment information: Established in 1908.
Company type: Public company
Company ticker symbol and exchange: GM/NYSE
Business activities: Designs, manufactures, and markets motor vehicles; designs, manufactures, and markets locomotives; provides consumer and business loans; provides mortgages; sells automobile insurance.
Business type (SIC): Motor vehicles and equipment; railroad equipment; credit institutions/personal; credit institutions/business; brokers and bankers/mortgage; insurance/fire, marine, and casualty
Financial profile for 2012: Number of employees, 213,000; assets, $149,422,000,000; sales volume, $152,256,000,000; pre-tax net income, -$30,257,000,000; expenses, $182,869,000,000; liabilities, $113,178,000,000
Fortune 1000 ranking: 2012—7th in revenues, 27th in profits, and 43rd in assets
Forbes 2000 ranking: 2012—18th in sales, 81st in profits, and 180th in assets
Corporate officers: Daniel F. Akerson, Jr., Chair. and C.E.O.; Stephen J. Girsky, Vice-Chair.; Daniel Ammann, Sr. V.P. and C.F.O.; Michael P. Millikin, Sr. V.P. and Genl. Counsel; Thomas S. Timko, V.P., Cont., and C.A.O.; Randall D. Mott, V.P. and C.I.O.; James A. Davlin, V.P., Finance and Treas.; Melissa Howell, V.P., Human Resources; Anne T. Larin, Corp. Secy.
Board of directors: Daniel Akerson, Jr., Chair.; Stephen J. Girsky, Vice-Chair.; David Bonderman; Erroll B. Davis, Jr.; E. Neville Isdell; Robert D. Krebs; Philip A. Laskawy; Kathryn V. Marinello; Michael G. Mullen; James J. Mulva; Patricia F. Russo; Thomas M. Schoewe; Theodore M. Solso; Carol M. Stephenson; Cynthia A. Telles
Subsidiaries: General Motors Financial Company, Inc., Fort Worth, TX; GMAC Mortgage Group, Inc., Horsham, PA; Saturn Corp., Detroit, MI
Joint Venture: New United Motor Manufacturing, Inc., Fremont, CA
International operations: Argentina; Austria; Belgium; Bermuda; Brazil; Canada; Chile; China; Colombia; Germany; Indonesia; Italy; Japan; Kenya; Mexico; New Zealand; Philippines; Singapore; South Africa; South Korea; Spain; United Kingdom; Venezuela
Giving statement: Giving through the GM Corporate Giving Program, the General Motors Foundation,

Inc., and the Indianapolis Motor Speedway Foundation, Inc.
Company EIN: 380572515

GM Corporate Giving Program

300 Renaissance Ctr.
Detroit, MI 48265-3000 (313) 556-5000
URL: http://www.gm.com/corporate/responsibility/community

Purpose and activities: As a complement to its foundation, GM also makes charitable contributions to nonprofit organizations directly. Support is given primarily in areas of company operations.
Fields of interest: Vocational education; Education; Heart & circulatory diseases; Disasters, preparedness/services; Safety, automotive safety.
Type of support: Donated products; Employee volunteer services; General/operating support; In-kind gifts.
Geographic limitations: Giving primarily in areas of company operations.
Application information:
Number of staff: 3 full-time professional; 3 full-time support.

General Motors Foundation, Inc.

(also known as GM Foundation)
300 Renaissance Ctr., M.C. 482-C27-D76
Detroit, MI 48265-3000
E-mail: ann.kihn@gm.com; URL: http://www.gm.com/company/aboutGM/gm_foundation.html

Establishment information: Incorporated in 1976 in MI.
Donor: General Motors Corp.
Contact: Ann Kihn
Financial data (yr. ended 12/31/11): Assets, $136,742,660 (M); expenditures, $25,540,503; qualifying distributions, $24,285,283; giving activities include $23,591,224 for 316 grants (high: $3,274,000; low: $1,000).
Purpose and activities: The foundation supports programs designed to promote education; health and human services; environment and energy; and community development.
Fields of interest: Museums; Education, early childhood education; Secondary school/education; Higher education; Engineering school/education; Education; Environment, natural resources; Environment, energy; Environmental education; Environment; Health care; Cancer research; Heart & circulatory research; Diabetes research; Medical research; Food services; Food banks; Housing/shelter, development; Disasters, preparedness/services; Safety, automotive safety; American Red Cross; Children/youth, services; Human services; Civil/human rights; Community development, civic centers; Business/industry; Community/economic development; United Ways and Federated Giving Programs; Mathematics; Engineering/technology; Science; Military/veterans' organizations.
Programs:
Buick Achievers Scholarship Program: The foundation awards renewable scholarships of up to $25,000 a year for 100 first-time freshman, and $2,000 year for an additional 1,000 incoming students. Applicants must plan to enroll at an institution of higher education; study STEM (science, technology, engineering, or math), design, marketing, accounting, finance, or business; and must demonstrate an interest in pursuing a career in the automotive or related industry. Visit URL http://www.buickachievers.com/ for more information. The program is administered by Scholarship America.
Chevrolet GREEN Educator Award: The foundation, in partnership with Earth Force, honors educators who engage youth in innovative and interactive learning. Special emphasis is directed toward educators who encourage youth to lead the learning process; encourage youth to take their learning beyond the classroom and impact their community; create and sustain local partnerships that connect youth to their community; provide professional expertise to mentor youth; and encourage others to teach about the environment. Visit URL http://www.greeneducator.org/ for more information.
Community Development: The foundation supports programs designed to promote economic development; social action; and improved communities where General Motors has operations. Special emphasis is directed toward the Martin Luther King, Jr. National Memorial; plant city grants to nonprofit organizations located near General Motors faculties; community centers; military and veteran support; and other initiatives designed to serve the community.
Education: The foundation supports programs designed to promote education. Special emphasis is directed toward programs designed to help small children enter school with the skills they need to succeed; increase high school graduation rate; and provide financial assistance for higher education.
Environment and Energy: The foundation supports programs designed to foster responsible management of the environment; and promote environmental sustainability, conservation, and protection as good citizenship.
Health and Human Services: The foundation supports programs designed promote healthcare, disaster relief, and wellness; and research on the causes, prevention, and treatment of various disease including cancer, heart disease, and diabetes.
Networks of Excellence: The foundation, in partnership with the United Way for Southeastern Michigan, creates networks of excellence in seven metro-Detroit high schools. The initiative is designed to increase graduation rates and prepare students for leadership roles and the workforce. The program includes the creation of smaller classrooms; personalized attention for high school students; and early learning centers for children up to age 5 to ensure preparation for first grade.
Safe Kids Buckle Up: The foundation, in partnership with Safe Kids USA, operates a child safety program to give parents and caregivers hands-on instruction about safety inside the car. The initiative includes educational information on car seats, booster seats, safety belts, Spot the Tot program, "Never Leave Your Child Alone in a Car" program, and the "Countdown2Drive" pre-teen safe driving program; grants; and support to Safe Kids coalitions to conduct safety programs at the local level.
Type of support: Annual campaigns; Continuing support; Emergency funds; Employee matching gifts; Employee volunteer services; Equipment; General/operating support; Matching/challenge support; Program development; Research; Scholarship funds; Sponsorships.
Geographic limitations: Giving primarily in areas of company operations, with emphasis on MI.
Support limitations: No support for discriminatory organizations, religious organizations, or political parties or candidates. No grants to individuals (except for the Buick Scholarship Program), or for capital campaigns, endowments, general operating support for U.S. hospitals or health care institutions, conferences, workshops, or seminars not directly related to GM's business interests; no vehicle donations.
Publications: Annual report (including application guidelines); Application guidelines; Corporate giving report; Informational brochure; Program policy statement.
Application information: Applications accepted. Multi-year requests are not encouraged. Additional information may be requested at a later date. Application form required. Applicants should submit the following:
1) timetable for implementation and evaluation of project
2) results expected from proposed grant
3) population served
4) name, address and phone number of organization
5) brief history of organization and description of its mission
6) geographic area to be served
7) how project's results will be evaluated or measured
8) detailed description of project and amount of funding requested
9) contact person
10) copy of current year's organizational budget and/or project budget
11) listing of additional sources and amount of support
12) plans for acknowledgement

Initial approach: Complete online eligibility quiz and application form; complete online application for Buick Scholarship Program
Board meeting date(s): Quarterly
Deadline(s): None; Feb. 28 for Buick Scholarship Program
Final notification: 4 to 8 weeks

Officers and Directors:* Selim Bingol*, Chair.; Mark Reuss*, Vice-Chair.; Vivian R. Pickard, Pres.; Lori Wingerter, V.P.; Kevin W. Cobb, Secy.; Mary Williams, Treas.; Tom P. Gaff, C.F.O.; Daniel Ammann; Lori Arpin; Susan E. Docherty; Stephen J. Girsky; Kathryn M. McBride; Christopher J. Perry; Michael J. Robinson; John F. Smith; Diane D. Tremblay; Janice K. Uhlig; Edward T. Welburn, Jr.
Number of staff: 3 full-time professional; 2 full-time support.
EIN: 382132136
Selected grants: The following grants are a representative sample of this grantmaker's funding activity:
$5,545,000 to United Way for Southeastern Michigan, Detroit, MI, 2011. For general support.
$3,274,000 to Scholarship America, Saint Peter, MN, 2011. For Scholarships.
$2,000,000 to Detroit Economic Growth Association, Detroit, MI, 2011. For general support.
$1,700,000 to Safe Kids Worldwide, Washington, DC, 2011. For general support.
$1,000,000 to American Red Cross National Headquarters, Washington, DC, 2011. For general support.
$450,000 to Arts League of Michigan, Detroit, MI, 2011. For general support.
$50,000 to Michigan Economic Development Foundation, Lansing, MI, 2011. For general support.
$50,000 to Virginia Tech Foundation, Blacksburg, VA, 2011. For general support.
$40,000 to Dallas Film Society, Dallas, TX, 2011. For general support.
$17,500 to United Way of Greater Saint Louis, Saint Louis, MO, 2011. For general support.

Indianapolis Motor Speedway Foundation, Inc.

4790 W. 16th St.
Indianapolis, IN 46222-2550
URL: http://www.indianapolismotorspeedway.com/museum/

Establishment information: Established in 1957 in IN.
Donors: General Motors Corp.; Indianapolis Motor Speedway.
Financial data (yr. ended 12/31/10): Assets, $1,540,449 (M); gifts received, $121,827; expenditures, $1,254,268; qualifying distributions, $1,142,244; giving activities include $10,000 for 1 grant and $1,141,283 for 1 foundation-administered program.
Purpose and activities: The foundation operates the Indianapolis Motor Speedway Hall of Fame Museum.
Fields of interest: Museums (sports/hobby); Foundations (community).
Type of support: General/operating support.
Support limitations: No grants to individuals.
Application information: Applications not accepted. Contributes only to a pre-selected organization.
Officers and Directors:* Anton Hulman George*, Pres.; Mari Hulman George*, V.P.; W. Curtis Brighton, Secy.; Jeffrey G. Belskus, Treas.
Board Members: Howard Shearon; Donald E. Smith.
EIN: 356013771

1556
General Motors Financial Company, Inc.

(formerly AmeriCredit Corp.)
801 Cherry Street, Ste. 3500
Fort Worth, TX 76102 (817) 302-7000
FAX: (817) 302-7897

Company URL: http://www.gmfinancial.com/
Establishment information: Established in 1988.
Company type: Subsidiary of a public company
Business activities: Operates auto finance company.
Business type (SIC): Credit institutions/personal
Corporate officers: Clifton H. Morris, Jr., Chair.; Daniel E. Berce, Pres. and C.E.O.; Chris A. Choate, Exec. V.P., C.F.O., and Treas.; Patrick Rayball, Exec. V.P., and C.I.O.; J. Michael May, Exec. V.P. and Secy.; Connie Coffey, Exec. V.P. and Cont.; Susan Sheffield, Exec. V.P., Finance
Board of director: Clifton H. Morris, Jr., Chair.
Giving statement: Giving through the General Motors Financial Company, Inc. Contributions Program.
Company EIN: 752291093

General Motors Financial Company, Inc. Contributions Program

(formerly AmeriCredit Corp. Contributions Program)
801 Cherry St., Ste. 3500
Fort Worth, TX 76102-6854
URL: http://www.americredit.com/Customers/About/community_involvement.asp

Purpose and activities: AmeriCredit makes charitable contributions to nonprofit organizations involved with health, human services, and on a case by case basis. Support is given primarily in areas of company operations in Chandler, Arizona, Charlotte, North Carolina, and Arlington and Fortworth, Texas, and in Ontario, Canada; giving also to national organizations.
Fields of interest: Genetic diseases and disorders; Health organizations; Salvation Army; United Ways and Federated Giving Programs; General charitable giving.
International interests: Canada.
Type of support: Employee volunteer services; General/operating support.
Geographic limitations: Giving primarily in areas of company operations in Chandler, AZ, Charlotte, NC, and Fortworth, TX, and in Canada; giving also to national organizations.
Application information: National organizations are chosen for Signature Events based on employee interest, number of people and communities served, and availability of volunteer opportunities for AmeriCredit employees.

1557
General Railway Signal Corporation

801 West Ave.
P.O. Box 20600
Rochester, NY 14602-0600 (716) 436-2020

Establishment information: Established in 1904.
Company type: Private company
Business activities: Manufactures signaling systems and devices and steel and aluminum castings.
Business type (SIC): Communications equipment
Giving statement: Giving through the ALSTOM Signaling Foundation, Inc.

ALSTOM Signaling Foundation, Inc.

(formerly General Railway Signal Foundation, Inc.)
1025 John St.
West Henrietta, NY 14586-0600 (585) 279-2300

Establishment information: Established in 1952 in NY.
Donor: General Railway Signal Corp.
Contact: Rhonda DiCiaccio, Secy.-Treas.
Financial data (yr. ended 09/30/12): Assets, $808,416 (M); gifts received, $3,311; expenditures, $65,141; qualifying distributions, $51,700; giving activities include $51,700 for 55 grants (high: $2,000; low: $500).
Purpose and activities: The foundation supports organizations involved with arts and culture, education, health, and human services.
Fields of interest: Arts; Human services; Religion.
Type of support: Annual campaigns; Capital campaigns; Scholarship funds.
Application information: Applications accepted. Application form required.
Initial approach: Letter
Deadline(s): None
Officers: Ellen O'Neill, Pres.; Thomas Lijko, V.P.; Rhonda DiCiaccio, Secy.-Treas.
EIN: 237447593

1558
General Reinsurance Corporation

695 E. Main St.
Stamford, CT 06904-2141 (203) 328-5000

Company URL: http://www.genre.com
Establishment information: Established in 1980.
Company type: Subsidiary of a public company
Business activities: Sells reinsurance.
Business type (SIC): Insurance/accident and health
Financial profile for 2010: Number of employees, 63
Corporate officers: Ted Montross, Chair. and C.E.O.; I. John Cholnoky, Pres.; William Gasdaska, Jr., Sr. V.P., Treas., and C.F.O.; Damon N. Vocke, Sr. V.P., Genl. Counsel, and Secy.
Board of director: Ted Montross, Chair.
International operations: Luxembourg; United Kingdom
Giving statement: Giving through the General Reinsurance Corporation Contributions Program.

General Reinsurance Corporation Contributions Program

120 Long Ridge Rd.
Stamford, CT 06902-1839 (203) 328-5000
FAX: (203) 328-6423; URL: http://www.genre.com/page/0,,ref=CSR-en,00.html

Purpose and activities: Gen Re makes charitable contributions to nonprofit organizations involved with social services and culture. Support is given primarily in areas of company operations.
Fields of interest: Performing arts, music; Arts; Human services.
Program:
Matching Gifts Program: Gen Re has a 100% matching program for the private donations of the company's North American and German staff members.
Type of support: Employee matching gifts; General/operating support; Scholarship funds.
Geographic limitations: Giving primarily in areas of company operations.

1559
Genesco Inc.

1415 Murfreesboro Rd., Ste. 264
P.O. Box 731
Nashville, TN 37202-0731 (615) 367-7000
FAX: (615) 367-8278

Company URL: http://www.genesco.com
Establishment information: Established in 1924.
Company type: Public company
Company ticker symbol and exchange: GCO/NYSE
Business activities: Manufactures and sells footwear.
Business type (SIC): Leather footwear; apparel—men's and boys' coats and suits; apparel—women's outerwear; apparel, piece goods, and notions—wholesale
Financial profile for 2013: Number of employees, 22,700; assets, $1,333,790,000; sales volume, $2,604,820,000; pre-tax net income, $162,940,000; expenses, $2,436,850,000; liabilities, $525,200,000
Fortune 1000 ranking: 2012—785th in revenues, 717th in profits, and 936th in assets
Corporate officers: Robert J. Dennis, Chair., Pres., and C.E.O.; James S. Gulmi, Sr. V.P., Finance, and C.F.O.; Roger G. Sisson, Sr. V.P., Genl. Counsel, and Secy.; Paul D. Williams, V.P. and C.A.O.; Matthew N. Johnson, V.P. and Treas.
Board of directors: Robert J. Dennis, Chair.; James S. Beard; Leonard L. Berry, Ph.D.; William F. Blaufuss, Jr.; James W. Bradford; Matthew C. Diamond; Marty G. Dickens; Thurgood Marshall, Jr.; Kathleen Mason
Subsidiaries: Jarman Shoe Co., Nashville, TN; Johnston & Murphy Shoe Co., Nashville, TN; Laredo Boot Co., Nashville, TN; Volunteer Leather, Nashville, TN
Giving statement: Giving through the Genesco Inc. Corporate Giving Program.
Company EIN: 620211340

Genesco Inc. Corporate Giving Program

P.O. Box 731, Ste. 490
Nashville, TN 37202-0731
FAX: (615) 367-8278;
E-mail: contributions@genesco.com; URL: http://www.genesco.com/community-involvement/

Contact: Claire S. McCall, Dir., Corp. Rels.
Purpose and activities: Genesco makes charitable contributions to nonprofit organizations involved with arts and culture, education, health, children, human services, leadership development, and civic affairs. Support is given primarily in areas of significant company operations, with emphasis on Nashville, Tennessee.
Fields of interest: Arts; Education; Health care; Athletics/sports, amateur leagues; Youth development; Children/youth, services; Human services; Leadership development; Public affairs.
Programs:
Cold Feet, Warm Shoes: Genesco provides needy men, women, and children with a new pair of shoes for the winter. The company creates a mock shoe store staffed by Genesco employees where recipients are given the power of choice and respect to pick the items they need. At other company locations the program has extended to include socks for the homeless, and new hats for disadvantaged youth.
Employee Matching Gift Program: Genesco matches charitable contributions made by its employees to nonprofit organizations up to $1,000 per employee, per year.
Employee Scholarship Fund: The company awards college scholarships to employees and children of employees of Genesco. The program is administered by The Community Foundation of Middle Tennessee.
Type of support: Donated products; Employee matching gifts; Employee volunteer services; Employee-related scholarships; General/operating support; In-kind gifts.
Geographic limitations: Giving primarily in areas of significant company operations, with emphasis on Nashville, TN.
Support limitations: No support for schools below the college level (except matching gifts to annual funds), day care centers, disease-specific organizations, hospitals, or religious, fraternal, athletic, or veterans' groups not of direct benefit to the entire community. No grants to individuals (except for employee-related scholarships) or for scholarships, biomedical or clinical research, newsletters, magazines, or books, trips or tours, endowments, or pledges or payments for walks or telethons.
Publications: Application guidelines.
Application information: Applications accepted. Proposals should be no longer than 3 pages. The Corporate Relations Department handles giving. Application form not required. Applicants should submit the following:
1) timetable for implementation and evaluation of project
2) statement of problem project will address
3) population served
4) name, address and phone number of organization
5) copy of IRS Determination Letter
6) brief history of organization and description of its mission
7) how project's results will be evaluated or measured
8) detailed description of project and amount of funding requested
9) listing of additional sources and amount of support

Initial approach: Proposal to headquarters
Copies of proposal: 1
Deadline(s): None
Final notification: 6 to 8 weeks

1560
Geneseo Communications, Inc.

111 E. 1st St.
Geneseo, IL 61254-2123 (309) 944-2103

Company URL: http://www.geneseotelephone.com
Establishment information: Established in 1905.
Company type: Private company
Business activities: Operates holding company; provides telephone communications services.
Business type (SIC): Telephone communications
Corporate officers: Scott Rubins, Pres. and C.E.O.; Rick Trueblood, C.O.O.; Judi Denys, V.P., Finance
Giving statement: Giving through the Geneseo Communications Charitable Foundation.

Geneseo Communications Charitable Foundation

111 E. 1st St.
Geneseo, IL 61254-2123
URL: http://geneseotelephone.com/pages/community%20involvement.html

Establishment information: Established in 2001 in IL.
Donor: Geneseo Communications, Inc.
Financial data (yr. ended 12/31/11): Assets, $1,997,054 (M); gifts received, $1,352; expenditures, $131,338; qualifying distributions, $109,150; giving activities include $109,150 for grants.
Purpose and activities: The foundation supports hospitals and day care centers and organizations involved with historic preservation, education, and recreation.
Fields of interest: Education; Health care; Human services.
Type of support: General/operating support.
Geographic limitations: Giving primarily in areas of company operations in Geneseo, IL.
Application information: Applications accepted. Application form required. Applicants should submit the following:
1) copy of IRS Determination Letter
2) listing of board of directors, trustees, officers and other key people and their affiliations
3) detailed description of project and amount of funding requested
4) copy of current year's organizational budget and/or project budget

Initial approach: Download application form and mail to foundation
Copies of proposal: 1
Board meeting date(s): Quarterly
Deadline(s): None; applications are reviewed quarterly

EIN: 260001189

1561
Genesis HealthCare Corporation

101 E. State St.
Kennett Square, PA 19348 (610) 444-6350
FAX: (610) 925-4000

Company URL: http://www.genesishcc.com/
Establishment information: Established in 2003.
Company type: Private company
Business activities: Operates assisted living and skilled nursing facilities.
Business type (SIC): Nursing and personal care facilities
Financial profile for 2011: Number of employees, 34,000; sales volume, $2,550,000,000
Corporate officers: George V. Hager, Jr., C.E.O.; Robert A. Reitz, Exec. V.P. and C.O.O.; Tom DiVittorio, Sr. V.P. and C.F.O.; Richard L. Castor, Sr. V.P. and C.I.O.; Michael Sherman, Sr. V.P. and Genl. Counsel; Richard Pell, Jr., Sr. V.P., Admin.
Giving statement: Giving through the Genesis Employee Foundation.

Genesis Employee Foundation

101 E. State St.
Kennett Square, PA 19348-3109 (610) 444-6350
FAX: (610) 347-6217;
E-mail: genesis.employee.foundation@genesishcc.com

Establishment information: Established in 2005 in PA.
Financial data (yr. ended 12/31/11): Revenue, $813,969; assets, $342,859 (M); gifts received, $668,967; expenditures, $807,795; giving activities include $784,864 for grants to individuals.
Purpose and activities: The foundation's mission is to support Genesis HealthCare employees affected by severe financial hardship due to unforeseeable circumstances such as natural disasters.
Fields of interest: Adults; Aging; Young adults; Disabilities, people with; Physically disabled; Blind/visually impaired; Deaf/hearing impaired; Mentally disabled; Minorities; Asians/Pacific Islanders; African Americans/Blacks; Hispanics/Latinos; Native Americans/American Indians; Women; Adults, women; Young adults, female; Men; Adults, men; Young adults, male; Military/veterans; AIDS, people with; Single parents; Crime/abuse victims; Terminal illness, people with; Economically disadvantaged; Homeless.
Type of support: Annual campaigns; Continuing support; Emergency funds; Grants to individuals.
Support limitations: No support for any individuals outside of Genesis Health Care.
Publications: Occasional report.
Application information: Applications not accepted. Contributes only to employees of Genesis Healthcare; unsolicited requests for funds not otherwise considered or acknowledged.
Officers: Robert A. Reitz*, Pres.; Elizabeth Miller*, V.P.; Jeanne M. Phillips*, V.P.; Michael Sherman*, V.P.; Walter Kielar*, Treas.
EIN: 202301122

1562
Genji, Inc.

2 Penn Ctr.
1500 JFK Blvd., Ste. 725
Philadelphia, PA 19102-1747
(215) 523-5782
FAX: (215) 523-6280

Company URL: http://www.genjiweb.com
Establishment information: Established in 1997.
Company type: Private company
Business activities: Operates sushi bars.
Business type (SIC): Restaurants and drinking places
Corporate officer: Shingo Kanai, Pres. and C.E.O.
Giving statement: Giving through the Genji, Inc. Contributions Program.

Genji, Inc. Contributions Program
Penn Ctr., 1500 JFK Blvd., Ste. 725
Philadelphia, PA 19102-1747 (215) 523-5782
URL: http://www.genjiweb.com

1563
GenOn Energy, Inc.
(formerly RRI Energy, Inc.)
1000 Main St.
Houston, TX 77002 (832) 357-3000

Company URL: http://www.genon.com/
Establishment information: Established in 2000.
Company type: Public company
Company ticker symbol and exchange: GEN/NYSE
Business activities: Provides electricity and energy services.
Business type (SIC): Electric services
Financial profile for 2011: Number of employees, 3,487; assets, $12,269,000,000; sales volume, $3,614,000,000; pre-tax net income, -$189,000,000; expenses, $3,405,000,000; liabilities, $7,152,000,000
Corporate officers: Edward R. Muller, Chair. and C.E.O.; William J. Holden III, Exec. V.P. and C.F.O.; Michael L. Jines, Exec. V.P., Genl. Counsel., and Corp. Secy.
Board of directors: Edward R. Muller, Chair.; Spencer Abraham; Terry G. Dallas; Thomas H. Johnson; Steven L. Miller; Elizabeth A. Moller; Robert C. Murray; Laree E. Perez; Evan J. Silverstein; William L. Thacker
International operations: Canada; Netherlands
Historic mergers: Mirant Corporation (December 3, 2010)
Giving statement: Giving through the Don D. Jordan Scholarship Foundation and the RRI Energy Foundation.
Company EIN: 760655566

Don D. Jordan Scholarship Foundation
(formerly Chairman's Award Foundation)
P.O. Box 4567
Houston, TX 77210-4567 (713) 256-9557
Application address: 1111 Nantucket Dr., Houston, TX, 77057, tel.: (713) 256-9557

Donor: Reliant Energy Ventures, Inc.
Contact: Dayle Blake
Financial data (yr. ended 12/31/11): Assets, $1,068,888 (M); gifts received, $91,718; expenditures, $75,979; qualifying distributions, $72,000; giving activities include $72,000 for 24 grants to individuals (high: $3,000; low: $3,000).
Purpose and activities: The foundation awards college scholarships to children of employees of Reliant Energy Ventures.
Type of support: Employee-related scholarships.
Application information: Applications accepted. Application form required.
Initial approach: Proposal
Deadline(s): Jan. 31
Trustee: Charles Dean Woods.
EIN: 760321771

RRI Energy Foundation
(formerly Reliant Energy Foundation)
P.O. Box 3795
Houston, TX 77002-0148 (832) 397-5328
Application address: 1000 Main St., Houston, TX 77002

Establishment information: Established in 1997 in TX.
Donors: Reliant Energy, Inc.; Reliant Energy Ventures, Inc.; Lynn Culmer; Mark M. Jacobs; Shawn McFarlane; Carla Mitcham.
Contact: Lara Gladney
Financial data (yr. ended 12/31/10): Assets, $17,901 (M); expenditures, $543,753; qualifying distributions, $542,686; giving activities include $542,686 for 66 grants (high: $89,250; low: $76).
Purpose and activities: The foundation supports organizations involved with education, conservation, animals and wildlife, health, housing development, and human services.
Fields of interest: Higher education; Education; Environment, natural resources; Environment, water resources; Animals/wildlife, fisheries; Animals/wildlife; Health care; Housing/shelter, development; Boys & girls clubs; American Red Cross; Children/youth, services; Human services; United Ways and Federated Giving Programs.
Type of support: General/operating support; Program development.
Geographic limitations: Giving primarily in CA, FL, PA, and TX.
Support limitations: No grants to individuals.
Application information: Applications accepted. Application form not required. Applicants should submit the following:
1) name, address and phone number of organization
2) copy of IRS Determination Letter
3) copy of most recent annual report/audited financial statement/990
4) listing of board of directors, trustees, officers and other key people and their affiliations
5) detailed description of project and amount of funding requested
6) contact person
Initial approach: Proposal
Deadline(s): None
Officers and Directors:* Michael T. Kuznar*, Pres.; Michael L. Jines, V.P. and Secy.; Albert Myres*, V.P.; Karen D. Taylor*, V.P.; Andrew C. Johannesen, Treas.; Tracy Carmen-Jones.
EIN: 760537222

1564
GenRad, Inc.
(formerly General Radio Corp.)
7 Technology Park Dr.
Westford, MA 01886-3141 (978) 589-7000

Establishment information: Established in 1915.
Company type: Subsidiary of a public company
Business activities: Manufactures electronic test equipment and systems.
Business type (SIC): Laboratory apparatus; computer services
Corporate officers: Walter A. Shephard, C.F.O.; Lori B. Hannay, V.P., Human Resources
Board of director: Robert Dutkowsky, Chair.
Giving statement: Giving through the GenRad Foundation.

GenRad Foundation
P.O. Box 444
West Groton, MA 01472-0444 (978) 448-8942

Establishment information: Established in 1934 in MA.
Donors: GenRad, Inc.; Henry Shaw†.
Contact: Linda B. Schuler, Tr.
Financial data (yr. ended 12/31/11): Assets, $9,700 (M); expenditures, $2,563; qualifying distributions, $0.
Purpose and activities: The foundation supports organizations involved with arts and culture, education, the environment, health, and human services.
Fields of interest: Museums (art); Arts; Education; Environment; Hospitals (general); Health care; Children/youth, services; Aging, centers/services; Human services.
Type of support: Continuing support; Emergency funds; Equipment; General/operating support; Program development.
Geographic limitations: Giving primarily in areas of company operations, with emphasis on Boston, Shirley, and West Groton, MA.
Support limitations: No grants to individuals.
Application information: Applications accepted. Application form not required. Applicants should submit the following:
1) detailed description of project and amount of funding requested
2) geographic area to be served
3) how project's results will be evaluated or measured
4) qualifications of key personnel
5) copy of current year's organizational budget and/or project budget
6) copy of IRS Determination Letter
7) listing of board of directors, trustees, officers and other key people and their affiliations
Initial approach: Proposal
Deadline(s): None
Trustees: Linda B. Schuler; Robert C. Schuler.
Number of staff: 1 full-time professional; 1 part-time support.
EIN: 046043570

1565
Genworth Financial, Inc.
6620 W. Broad St.
Richmond, VA 23230 (804) 281-6000
FAX: (302) 636-5454

Company URL: http://www.genworth.com
Establishment information: Established in 1871.
Company type: Public company
Company ticker symbol and exchange: GNW/NYSE
International Securities Identification Number: US37247D1063
Business activities: Sells life, long-term care, and health insurance; provides investment advisory services; sells mortgage insurance.
Business type (SIC): Insurance/life; security and commodity services; insurance/accident and health; insurance/surety
Financial profile for 2012: Number of employees, 6,300; assets, $113,312,000,000; sales volume, $9,640,000,000; pre-tax net income, $606,000,000; expenses, $9,034,000,000; liabilities, $96,819,000,000
Fortune 1000 ranking: 2012—271st in revenues, 445th in profits, and 60th in assets
Forbes 2000 ranking: 2012—933rd in sales, 1394th in profits, and 227th in assets
Corporate officers: James S. Riepe, Chair.; Martin P. Klein, Pres., C.E.O., Sr. V.P., and C.F.O.; Scott J. McKay, Sr. V.P. and C.I.O.; Daniel J. Sheehan IV, Sr. V.P. and C.I.O.; Leon E. Roday, Sr. V.P., Genl. Counsel, and Secy.; Michael S. Laming, Sr. V.P., Human Resources
Board of directors: James S. Riepe, Chair.; Steven W. Alesio; William H. Bolinder; Nancy J. Karch; Christine B. Mead; Thomas E. Moloney; James A. Parke
Subsidiaries: First Colony Life Insurance Co., Lynchburg, VA; Genworth Life and Annuity Insurance Co., Richmond, VA

International operations: Australia; Bermuda; Canada; Cayman Islands; France; Guernsey; Hong Kong; India; Ireland; Mauritius; Mexico; South Korea; Spain; Turkey; United Kingdom
Giving statement: Giving through the Genworth Foundation.
Company EIN: 331073076

Genworth Foundation

c/o Community Rels. Dept.
6620 W. Broad St.
Richmond, VA 23230-1716
URL: http://www.genworth.com/foundation

Establishment information: Established in 2005 in VA.
Donor: Genworth Financial, Inc.
Contact: Heidi Crapol, Secy.
Financial data (yr. ended 12/31/11): Assets, $4,961,450 (M); gifts received, $4,500,000; expenditures, $3,540,125; qualifying distributions, $3,534,203; giving activities include $2,714,231 for 131 grants (high: $314,778; low: $300) and $811,816 for employee matching gifts.
Purpose and activities: The foundation supports organizations involved with K-12 education, health, hunger, housing, human services, and senior citizens.
Fields of interest: Elementary/secondary education; Education, services; Education; Health care; Alzheimer's disease; Food services; Housing/shelter, development; Housing/shelter, aging; Housing/shelter, temporary shelter; Housing/shelter; Youth, services; Human services, financial counseling; Aging, centers/services; Human services Aging.
Programs:
Basic Needs: The foundation supports the delivery of temporary food, shelter, and clothing; partnerships that keep families in their homes; and programs designed to prevent foreclosures during times of economic distress.
Education: The foundation supports programs designed to strengthen student performance, build life skills for underserved youth, and improve students' financial literacy.
Employee Volunteer Grants: The foundation awards grants to nonprofit organizations with which employees and retirees of Genworth volunteer their time.
Matching Gifts: The foundation matches contributions made by U.S. employees and retirees of Genworth Financial and it's majority-owned subsidiaries and directors of Genworth Financial to nonprofit organizations.
Supporting Seniors: The foundation supports programs designed to prepare local communities for a growing senior population. Special emphasis is directed toward programs designed to provide access to information on health and aging, support family caregivers, and enable independent living.
Type of support: Employee matching gifts; Employee volunteer services; Management development/capacity building; Program development.
Geographic limitations: Giving on a national and international basis in areas of company operations, with emphasis on Raleigh, NC, Lynchburg and Richmond, VA, Australia, Canada, and Europe.
Support limitations: No support for political, labor, fraternal, or social organizations, civic clubs, religious organizations not of direct benefit to the entire community, pass-through or third party organizations; sports, athletic, recreational, or little leagues, or private corporate or family foundations. No grants to individuals, or for advertising, development, or production of books, films, videos, radio, or television programs, endowments, or memorials.
Publications: Annual report; Application guidelines.
Application information: Applications accepted. Letters of intent are required for organizations that have not previously received funding from the Genworth Foundation or have not received funding within the prior calendar year. Grants range from $5,000 to $25,0000. A full proposal may be requested at a later date. Application form required. Applicants should submit the following:
1) detailed description of project and amount of funding requested
Initial approach: Complete online letter of intent
Copies of proposal: 1
Board meeting date(s): Quarterly
Deadline(s): None
Officers and Directors:* Leon E. Roday*, Chair.; Heidi Crapol, Secy.; Megan Dorn, Treas.; Kurt Arehart; Linda Belanger; Elena Edwards; Barbara Faurot; Guy Genney; Daniel P. Healy; Michael S. Laming.
EIN: 203370235

1566
Genzyme Corporation

500 Kendall St.
Cambridge, MA 02142 (617) 252-7500

Company URL: http://www.genzyme.com
Establishment information: Established in 1981.
Company type: Subsidiary of a foreign company
Business activities: Develops, manufactures, and distributes biotechnology pharmaceutical products and in vitro diagnostics products; provides laboratory testing services.
Business type (SIC): Drugs; laboratories/medical and dental
Financial profile for 2011: Assets, $4,900,000,000; sales volume, $2,200,000,000
Corporate officers: Christopher A. Viehbacher, Chair.; David Meeker, Pres. and C.E.O.; Marc Esteva, C.F.O.; Tracey L. Quarles, Sr. V.P. and Genl. Counsel; Jayne M. Gansler, Sr. V.P., Human Resources
Board of directors: Christopher A. Viehbacher, Chair.; David Meeker
Divisions: Diagnostic Products Div., San Carlos, CA; Therapeutics and Genetics Div., Santa Fe, NM
International operations: Belgium; England; France; Ireland; Japan; Luxembourg; Netherlands; Switzerland; United Kingdom
Giving statement: Giving through the Genzyme Charitable Foundation, Inc.
Company EIN: 061047163

Genzyme Charitable Foundation, Inc.

500 Kendall St.
Cambridge, MA 02142-1108
E-mail: CharitableAccessProgram@genzyme.com; Additional tel.: (617) 768-9009; URL: http://www.genzyme.com/commitment/patients/free_programs.asp

Establishment information: Established as a company-sponsored operating foundation in 1997 in MA.
Donor: Genzyme Corp.
Financial data (yr. ended 12/31/11): Assets, $11,036 (M); gifts received, $103,695,242; expenditures, $103,695,242; qualifying distributions, $103,693,242; giving activities include $103,693,242 for grants to individuals.
Purpose and activities: The foundation provides prescription medication to economically disadvantaged individuals lacking prescription drug coverage.
Fields of interest: Health care Economically disadvantaged.
Program:
Charitable Access Program (CAP): The foundation provides prescription medication to people who are uninsured and lack the financial means to purchase treatment. The program currently provides Cerezyme for Gaucher disease, Myozyme for Pompe disease, Aldurazyme for MPS I disease, Leukine to help increase white blood cells, Clolar for Leukemia; Fabrazyme for Fabry disease, Campath to patients suffering from B-CLL, Fludara for B-Cell chronic lymphocytic leukemia (CLL), Thyrogen for Hypothyroidism, and Mozobil for non-Hodgkin's Lymphoma or multiple myeloma. This program is designed to be a temporary measure and patients are expected to explore alternative resources for funding in the future.
Type of support: Donated products; Grants to individuals.
Geographic limitations: Giving on a national basis.
Application information: Applications accepted. Application form required.
Applications should include financial information, a letter of intent to treat from a physician, and a statement of medical necessity from a physician.
Initial approach: Telephone foundation for application form
Board meeting date(s): Monthly
Deadline(s): None
Officer and Director: David Meeker, Pres.
EIN: 043236375

1567
Georgia Power Company

241 Ralph McGill Blvd., N.E.
Atlanta, GA 30308-3374 (404) 506-6526

Company URL: http://www.georgiapower.com
Establishment information: Established in 1927.
Company type: Subsidiary of a public company
Business activities: Generates, transmits, and distributes electricity.
Business type (SIC): Electric services
Financial profile for 2011: Number of employees, 8,310; assets, $27,151,000,000; sales volume, $8,800,000,000; expenses, $6,753,000,000; liabilities, $17,862,000,000
Corporate officers: W. Paul Bowers, Pres. and C.E.O.; Ronnie R. Labrato, Exec. V.P., C.F.O., and Treas.; Anthony Wilson, Exec. V.P., Opers.; Thomas P. Bishop, Sr. V.P., Genl. Counsel, and Secy.; Leonard Owens, V.P., Human Resources
Board of directors: W. Paul Bowers; Robert L. Brown, Jr.; Anna R. Cablik; Thomas A. Fanning; Stephen S. Green; Jimmy C. Tallent; Charles K. Tarbutton; Beverly Daniel Tatum; D. Gary Thompson; Clyde C. Tuggle; Richard W. Ussery
Giving statement: Giving through the Georgia Power Company Contributions Program, the Georgia Power Foundation, Inc., and the Club of Hearts, Inc.
Company EIN: 580257110

Georgia Power Foundation, Inc.

241 Ralph McGill Blvd., N.E., Bin 10131
Atlanta, GA 30308-3374 (404) 506-6784
FAX: (404) 506-1485;
E-mail: gpfoundation@southernco.com; URL: http://www.georgiapower.com/in-your-community/charitable-giving/overview-and-focus.cshtml

Establishment information: Established in 1986 in GA.
Donors: Georgia Power Co.; Savannah Electric Foundation, Inc.

Contact: Susan M. Carter, Secy. and Exec. Dir.
Financial data (yr. ended 12/31/11): Assets, $114,268,693 (M); expenditures, $8,661,812; qualifying distributions, $7,981,330; giving activities include $7,981,330 for 530 grants.
Purpose and activities: The foundation supports organizations involved with arts and culture, education, the environment, cancer, diversity, and workforce planning.
Fields of interest: Arts; Higher education; Education; Environment, air pollution; Environment, water pollution; Environment, natural resources; Environment; Health care; Cancer; Salvation Army; Human services; Community development, neighborhood development.
Program:
Employee Matching Gifts: The foundation matches contributions made by employees and retirees of Georgia Power to institutions of higher education on a one-for-one basis up to $5,000 per contributor, per year.
Type of support: Annual campaigns; Capital campaigns; Conferences/seminars; Continuing support; Emergency funds; Employee matching gifts; Equipment; General/operating support; Program development; Scholarship funds; Sponsorships.
Geographic limitations: Giving primarily in GA.
Support limitations: No support for private foundations, political or religious organizations, private elementary or secondary schools, or non-public charities. No grants to individuals, or for political campaigns or causes.
Publications: Application guidelines; Informational brochure (including application guidelines).
Application information: Applications accepted. Support is limited to 1 contribution per organization during any given year. Multi-year funding is not automatic. Video submissions are not encouraged. Application form not required. Applicants should submit the following:
1) copy of IRS Determination Letter
2) copy of most recent annual report/audited financial statement/990
3) list of company employees involved with the organization
4) listing of board of directors, trustees, officers and other key people and their affiliations
5) detailed description of project and amount of funding requested
6) listing of additional sources and amount of support

Initial approach: Mail proposal to foundation or complete online application form
Copies of proposal: 1
Board meeting date(s): Mar., June, Sept., and Dec.
Deadline(s): Feb. 15, May 15, Aug. 15, and Nov. 15 for requests over $25,000
Final notification: 1 month following board meetings for requests over $25,000

Officers and Directors:* Michael K. Anderson*, Pres. and C.E.O.; Susan M. Carter, Secy. and Exec. Dir.; Roger S. Steffens, Treas.; W. Ron Hinson, C.F.O.; Ronnie R. Labrato*, C.F.O.; W. Craig Barrs; Brad J. Gates; Valerie D. Searcy; Anthony L. Wilson.
EIN: 581709417
Selected grants: The following grants are a representative sample of this grantmaker's funding activity:
$1,330,000 to United Way of Metropolitan Atlanta, Atlanta, GA, 2010. For annual campaign.
$750,000 to Grady Memorial Hospital Corporation, Grady Health System, Atlanta, GA, 2010. For Greater Grady Campaign.
$750,000 to Grady Memorial Hospital Corporation, Grady Health System, Atlanta, GA, 2011. For future payment - final payment of 2 year pledge - $325M Greater Grady Campaign.
$450,000 to Robert W. Woodruff Arts Center, Atlanta, GA, 2010. For annual campaign and corporate challenge.
$250,000 to National Center for Civil and Human Rights, Atlanta, GA, 2010. For future payment - final of two year pledge for design and construction campaign.
$222,223 to Zoo Atlanta, Atlanta, GA, 2011. For capital campaign for Zoo renovations and expansion of the Amphibian and Reptile Complex and the Animal Health Complex.
$130,000 to University of Georgia Foundation, Athens, GA, 2011. For Georgia Power Developing Scholar Program ($80K) and support for relocation of Public Health to Health Sciences Campus ($50K).
$125,000 to Arch Foundation for the University of Georgia, Athens, GA, 2010. For UGA needs based undergraduate scholarship program and Terry College of Business programs.
$125,000 to Community Foundation for Greater Atlanta, Atlanta, GA, 2010. For City of Atlanta Financial Panels Review Fund.
$105,000 to United Way of the Coastal Empire, Savannah, GA, 2010. For annual campaign.
$100,000 to Communities in Schools of Georgia, Atlanta, GA, 2010. To support local affiliates, Performance Learning Centers, and graduation coaches.
$100,000 to Georgia Partnership for Excellence in Education, Atlanta, GA, 2010. For operating expenses.
$100,000 to United Negro College Fund, Atlanta, GA, 2010. For corporate campaign.
$80,000 to Nature Conservancy, Atlanta, GA, 2011. To support conservation work in Georgia.

Club of Hearts, Inc.

241 Ralph McGill Blvd., Bin 10230
Atlanta, GA 30308-3374 (404) 506-3030
E-mail: clubhear@southernco.com

Establishment information: Established in 1956 in GA.
Financial data (yr. ended 12/31/11): Revenue, $959,651; assets, $292,374 (M); gifts received, $957,654; expenditures, $957,654; giving activities include $877,863 for grants and $79,791 for grants to individuals.
Purpose and activities: The organization provides grants to charitable organizations, as well as to Georgia Power Company employees and their families.
Fields of interest: Human services.
Program:
Grants: Funding is available to organizations in the metropolitan Atlanta area that provide direct support and/or relief for health and human suffering to its residents. Applicants must be able to obtain financial support from at least ten Georgia Power/Southern Company Services (GA) employees and/or retirees during the companies' annual employee giving campaign, not be a recipient of United Way of Metropolitan Atlanta funding, and have 501(c)(3) status.
Type of support: Grants to individuals; Program development.
Geographic limitations: Giving primarily in GA.
Application information: Applications accepted. See http://www.georgiapower.com/community/coh.asp for an application and more complete guidelines. Application form required.

Initial approach: Download application
Copies of proposal: 1
Deadline(s): Mar. 31
Final notification: One month

Officers: Jenny Rice*, Chair.; Lolita Jackson*, Vice-Chair.; Al Martin*, Vice-Chair.; Jane Sanders*, Secy.; Cindy Petersen*, Treas.
Directors: Shane Baker; Billy Cole; Magda Gonzalez; Lola Olabode; Sylmarie Ortiz; Sylvester Toe.
EIN: 586056698

1568
Georgia-Pacific Corporation

133 Peachtree St. N.E.
P.O. Box 105605
Atlanta, GA 30303-1808 (404) 652-4000
FAX: (404) 230-7052

Company URL: http://www.gp.com
Establishment information: Established in 1927.
Company type: Subsidiary of a private company
Business activities: Manufactures and sells pulp, paper, and consumer products and building products; conducts logging activities.
Business type (SIC): Lumber and wood products (except furniture); logging; pulp mills; paper mills
Financial profile for 2009: Number of employees, 45,000; sales volume, $12,584,000,000
Corporate officers: James Hannan, Pres. and C.E.O.; Tyler Woolson, Sr. V.P. and C.F.O.; Randal Robison, Sr. V.P. and C.I.O.; Tye Darland, Sr. V.P. and Genl. Counsel; W. Wesley Jones, Exec. V.P., Opers.; Sheila M. Weidman, Sr. V.P., Comms. and Public Affairs; Julie Brehm, Sr. V.P., Human Resources
Subsidiaries: Amador Central Railroad Co., Jackson, CA; Ashley, Drew & Northern Railway Co., Crossett, AR; Brunswick Pulp & Paper Co., Brunswick, GA; Fort James Corporation, Deerfield, IL; Great Northern Nekoosa Corp., Norwalk, CT; Great Southern Paper, Cedar Springs, GA; Nekoosa Packinging Co., Toledo, OH; Northern Paper, Portland, ME; St. Croix Water Power, Woodland, ME; Superwood, Inc., Duluth, MN
Plants: Modesto, CA; Wilmington, DE; Jacksonville, FL; Marietta, Norcross, GA; Dubuque, Monticello, IA; Blue Rapids, KS; West Monroe, LA; Owosso, MI; Taylorsville, MS; Cuba, MO; Buffalo, NY; Asheboro, NC; Canton, OH; Pryor, OK; Pittsburgh, PA; Spartanburg, SC; Plano, TX; Sigurd, UT; Big Island, Milford, VA; Olympia, WA; Grafton, Mount Hope, WV; Oshkosh, WI; Lovell, WY
International operations: Belgium; Canada; France; Germany; Japan; Switzerland; United Kingdom
Giving statement: Giving through the Georgia-Pacific Corporation Contributions Program and the Georgia-Pacific Foundation, Inc.
Company EIN: 930432081

Georgia-Pacific Corporation Contributions Program

133 Peachtree St. N.E.
Atlanta, GA 30303-1808
E-mail: gpbucketbrigade@gapac.com; URL: http://www.gp.com/aboutus/community/index.html
Awards Program Contact: Caitlin Allen, tel.: (312) 988-2310, E-mail: callen@webershandwick.com

Purpose and activities: As a complement to its foundation, Georgia-Pacific also makes charitable contributions to volunteer fire units directly through its Bucket Brigade grant program. Support is given on a national basis in areas of company operations.
Fields of interest: Disasters, fire prevention/control; Safety, education.
Program:
Georgia-Pacific Bucket Bridge: Georgia-Pacific, in partnership with Georgia-Pacific foundation, provides basic need supplies and resources to local

fire departments to help make families, homes, and workplaces safer. The company provides firefighters and rescuers with "turn-out gear" including helmets, boots, gloves, and fireproof coats and pants; and partners with school districts to help teachers train students on fire safety.
Type of support: Donated products; Employee volunteer services; General/operating support.
Geographic limitations: Giving in areas of company operations.
Publications: Application guidelines; Corporate giving report.
Application information: Applications accepted. Applications for Georgia-Pacific Bucket Brigade must be approved by a facility manger before being submitted. Application form required.
Initial approach: Download application form and mail to headquarters for Georgia-Pacific Bucket Brigade
Deadline(s): Aug. 1 for Georgia-Pacific Bucket Brigade
Final notification: Oct. for Georgia-Pacific Bucket Brigade

Georgia-Pacific Foundation, Inc.

133 Peachtree St. N.E., 39th FL
Atlanta, GA 30303-1808 (404) 652-4581
FAX: (404) 749-2754; Additional contact: Charmaine Ward, Dir., Community Affairs, tel.: (404) 652-5302; URL: http://www.gp.com/gpfoundation/index.html

Establishment information: Incorporated in 1958 in OR.
Donor: Georgia-Pacific Corp.
Contact: Curley M. Dossman, Jr., Chair. and Pres.
Financial data (yr. ended 12/31/11): Assets, $416,226 (M); gifts received, $3,400,034; expenditures, $3,358,131; qualifying distributions, $3,358,131; giving activities include $3,322,393 for 397 grants (high: $396,203; low: $100).
Purpose and activities: The foundation supports programs designed to promote education; environment; community enrichment; and entrepreneurship.
Fields of interest: Historic preservation/historical societies; Arts; Elementary/secondary education; Higher education; Education, reading; Education; Environment, air pollution; Environment, recycling; Environment, natural resources; Environment, land resources; Environmental education; Environment; Employment, training; Employment; Housing/shelter, development; Housing/shelter; Disasters, preparedness/services; Disasters, fire prevention/control; Safety/disasters; Youth development, business; Youth development; Social entrepreneurship; Community development, small businesses; Community/economic development; United Ways and Federated Giving Programs Youth; Minorities; Women.
Programs:
Education: The foundation supports programs designed to provide job training; promote literacy; and provide scholarships.
Employee Scholarships: The foundation awards college scholarships to children of employees of Georgia-Pacific. The program is administered by the National Merit Scholarship Corp.
Enrichment: The foundation supports programs designed to promote affordable housing; arts and culture; community safety; youth enrichment; and employee volunteerism.
Entrepreneurship: The foundation supports programs designed to promote youth entrepreneurship; and women and minority entrepreneurship.
Environment: The foundation supports programs designed to promote clean air, clean water, and recycling; environmental education; land conservation; and resource conservation.
Georgia-Pacific Bucket Brigade: The foundation, in partnership with Georgia-Pacific facilities, provides basic need supplies and resources to local fire departments to help make families, homes, and workplaces safer. The foundation provides firefighters and rescuers with "turn-out gear" including helmets, boots, gloves, and fireproof coats and pants; and partners with school districts to help teachers train students on fire safety.
Waymon Powell Scholarship Program: The foundation awards $2,000 college scholarships to high school seniors located in areas of major company operations.
Type of support: Annual campaigns; Building/renovation; Capital campaigns; Conferences/seminars; Continuing support; Employee volunteer services; Employee-related scholarships; Equipment; General/operating support; In-kind gifts; Program development; Scholarship funds; Scholarships—to individuals; Sponsorships.
Geographic limitations: Giving limited to areas of company operations in AL, AR, AZ, CA, Washington, DC, DE, FL, GA, IA, IL, IN, KS, KY, LA, MA, MI, MN, MO, MS, NH, NJ, NM, NV, NY, NC, OH, OK, OR, PA, SC, TN, VA, WA, WI, WV, WY, and Africa, Asia, Europe, and South America.
Support limitations: No support for discriminatory organizations, political candidates, churches or religious denominations, religious or theological schools, social, labor, veterans', alumni, or fraternal organizations not of direct benefit to the entire community, athletic associations, national organizations with local chapters already receiving support, medical or nursing schools, or pass-through organizations. No grants to individuals (except for scholarships), or for emergency needs for general operating support, political causes, legislative lobbying, or advocacy efforts, goodwill advertising, sporting events, general operating support for United Way member agencies, tickets or tables for testimonials or similar benefit events, named academic chairs, social sciences or health science programs, fundraising events, or trips or tours.
Publications: Application guidelines; Program policy statement.
Application information: Applications accepted. Extraneous proposal materials are not encouraged. Electronic or faxed proposals are not accepted. Application form not required. Applicants should submit the following:
1) results expected from proposed grant
2) qualifications of key personnel
3) statement of problem project will address
4) population served
5) name, address and phone number of organization
6) copy of IRS Determination Letter
7) brief history of organization and description of its mission
8) how project's results will be evaluated or measured
9) explanation of why grantmaker is considered an appropriate donor for project
10) listing of board of directors, trustees, officers and other key people and their affiliations
11) detailed description of project and amount of funding requested
12) copy of current year's organizational budget and/or project budget
Initial approach: Proposal; contact foundation for Waymon Powell Scholarships
Copies of proposal: 1
Board meeting date(s): As required
Deadline(s): Between Jan. 1 and Oct. 31
Final notification: Within 60 days

Officers: Curley M. Dossman, Jr.*, Chair. and Pres.; Tye Darland, V.P. and Secy.; Tyler Woolson, C.F.O.; Marty Agard, Treas.
Number of staff: 5 full-time professional; 1 full-time support.
EIN: 936023726

1569
Getty Images, Inc.

605 5th Ave. S., Ste. 400
Seattle, WA 98104-3887 (206) 925-5000

Company URL: http://www.gettyimages.com
Establishment information: Established in 1995.
Company type: Subsidiary of a private company
Business activities: Supplies stock and editorial still and moving images and illustrations.
Business type (SIC): Business services/miscellaneous
Corporate officers: Mark Getty, Chair.; Jonathan Klein, C.E.O.; Nicholas Evans-Lombe, C.O.O.; Bart Catalane, Sr. V.P. and C.F.O.; John Lapham, Sr. V.P. and Genl. Counsel; James C. Gurke, Sr. V.P., Mktg.; Lisa Calvert, Sr. V.P., Human Resources; Steve Heck, Sr. V.P., Tech.
Board of director: Mark Getty, Chair.
Offices: Los Angeles, CA; Chicago, IL; New York, NY
Giving statement: Giving through the Getty Images, Inc. Corporate Giving Program.

Getty Images, Inc. Corporate Giving Program

601 N. 34th St.
Seattle, WA 98103 (206) 925-5000
E-mail: giving@gettyimages.com; Additional e-mail: grants2@gettyimages.com; URL: http://company.gettyimages.com/community.cfm?isource=corporate_website_community_involvement

Purpose and activities: Getty Images, Inc. makes charitable contributions to nonprofit organizations involved with photography, photojournalism, and filmmaking.
Fields of interest: Media, film/video; Visual arts; Visual arts, photography; Education; AIDS.
Programs:
Grants for Editorial Photography: Through the Grants for Editorial Photography program, Getty Images awards $20,000, plus editorial, logistical and promotional support to professional photojournalists. The company also awards 4 student grants of $5,000 per year to photojournalism students at accredited schools.
Grants for Good: Grants for Good provide 2 grants of $15,000 annually, to cover photographer, filmmaker and agency costs as they create new imagery for the nonprofit of their choice. Grants recipients may use the entire award to offset shoot expenses, or choose to donate all or part of it directly to their charity and contribute their own time and resources. The photographer and the nonprofit as well as the communications agency involved will be showcased to the media and to Getty Images customers.
Type of support: Cause-related marketing; Donated products; Employee matching gifts; Employee volunteer services; Film/video/radio; Grants to individuals; Use of facilities.
Publications: Application guidelines; Corporate giving report.
Application information: Applications accepted.
Initial approach: Complete online applications

Deadline(s): Mar. 1 for Grants for Good; May 1 for Grants for Editorial Photography
Final notification: June for Grants for Good; Sept. for Grants for Editorial Photography

1570
Ghilotti Brothers Construction, Inc.
525 Jacoby St.
San Rafael, CA 94901 (415) 454-7011

Company URL: http://www.ghilotti.com
Establishment information: Established in 1914.
Company type: Private company
Business activities: Provides general contract street construction services.
Business type (SIC): Construction/highway and street (except elevated)
Corporate officers: Eva Ghilotti, Chair.; Dante Ghilotti, C.E.O. and Secy.; Richard Dick Ghilotti, Pres. and Treas.; Daniel Chin, C.F.O; Dominic Nuccio, V.P., Opers.
Board of director: Eva Ghilotti, Chair
Giving statement: Giving through the Mario Ghilotti Family Foundation.

Mario Ghilotti Family Foundation
(formerly William A. & Dino J. Ghilotti Memorial Foundation)
525 Jacoby St.
San Rafael, CA 94901

Donors: Ghilotti Brothers Construction, Inc.; D&M Equipment Co.; Michael Ghilotti; Dante Ghilotti; Ghilotti Brothers, Inc.; Ghilotti Construction Co.; Maggiora & Ghilotti, Inc.; Bass Electric; Ghilotti Construction, Inc.; St. Francis Electric; Environova, LLC; R&W Concrete Contractors, Inc; In Memoriam Donations.
Financial data (yr. ended 06/30/12): Assets, $796,258 (M); gifts received, $2,350; expenditures, $86,473; qualifying distributions, $86,300; giving activities include $86,300 for grants.
Purpose and activities: The foundation supports organizations involved with education.
Fields of interest: Education; Recreation; Religion.
Type of support: General/operating support; Scholarship funds.
Application information: Applications not accepted. Unsolicited requests for funds not accepted.
Officers: Eva R. Ghilotti, Pres.; Michael M. Ghilotti, C.F.O.; Dante W. Ghilotti, Secy.
EIN: 946182691

1571
Giant Eagle, Inc.
101 Kappa Dr.
Pittsburgh, PA 15238-2833 (412) 963-6200
FAX: (412) 968-1617

Company URL: http://www.gianteagle.com
Establishment information: Established in 1931.
Company type: Private company
Business activities: Operates supermarkets; sells food wholesale.
Business type (SIC): Groceries—retail; groceries—wholesale
Financial profile for 2011: Number of employees, 36,000; sales volume, $9,300,000,000
Corporate officers: David S. Shapira, Chair.; John R. Lucot, Pres. and C.O.O.; Laura S. Karet, C.E.O.; Mary Winston, Sr. V.P. and C.F.O.; Russell Ross, Sr. V.P. and C.I.O.; Kevin Srigley, Sr. V.P., Sales and Mktg.; Stephanie White, V.P., Opers.; Christopher Haver, V.P., Human Resources
Board of director: David S. Shapira, Chair.
Subsidiary: Riser Foods, Inc., Bedford Heights, OH
Giving statement: Giving through the Giant Eagle, Inc. Corporate Giving Program and the Beacon Foundation Inc.

Giant Eagle, Inc. Corporate Giving Program
101 Kappa Dr.
Pittsburgh, PA 15238-2809 (412) 963-6200
Apples for the Students tel.: (800) 474-4777 for registration; (800) 742-7753 to become a coordinator.; URL: http://www.gianteagle.com/About/Corporate-Responsibility-Annual-Report/

Purpose and activities: As a complement to its foundation, Giant Eagle also makes charitable contributions to nonprofit organizations directly. Special emphasis is directed toward K-12 education, cancer research, blood banks, food banks, children's hospitals, and arts and entertainment venues such as museums, zoos, theaters, symphonies, and amusement parks. Support is limited to areas of company operations in Maryland, Ohio, Pennsylvania, and West Virginia.
Fields of interest: Museums; Performing arts; Performing arts, theater; Performing arts, orchestras; Arts; Elementary/secondary education; Zoos/zoological societies; Hospitals (specialty); Health care, blood supply; Breast cancer; Cancer research; Food banks; Children, services Children.
Programs:
Apples for the Students: Through the Apples for the Students program, Giant Eagle customers have the opportunity to earn benefits for the school(s) of their choice every time they shop. When customers use a Giant Eagle Advantage Card with each purchase (during the program), the designated school(s) will earn points that can be redeemed for classroom items such as computer equipment, software, and other learning tools.
Bonus eBoxTops: Students can earn cash for their school through the Bonus eBoxTops program, a collaborative effort by the Box Tops for Education program and Giant Eagle. The program works by awarding 10 cents for the purchase of each Box Top prooduct purchased online using a Giant Eagle Advantage Card.
Type of support: Donated products; Employee volunteer services; General/operating support; In-kind gifts; Sponsorships.
Geographic limitations: Giving limited to areas of company operations in MD, OH, PA, and WV.

Beacon Foundation Inc.
(formerly The Giant Eagle Foundation)
101 Kappa Dr.
Pittsburgh, PA 15238-2809 (412) 963-6200

Establishment information: Established in PA.
Donor: Giant Eagle, Inc.
Contact: David S. Shapira, Dir.
Financial data (yr. ended 06/30/12): Assets, $45,995,018 (M); gifts received, $3,597,726; expenditures, $5,059,901; qualifying distributions, $4,905,036; giving activities include $4,905,036 for 159 grants (high: $2,288,747; low: $180).
Purpose and activities: The foundation supports children's hospitals and food banks and organizations involved with arts and culture, education, human services, and Judaism.
Fields of interest: Museums (ethnic/folk arts); Performing arts, theater; Performing arts, orchestras; Arts; Elementary/secondary education; Secondary school/education; Higher education; Theological school/education; Education; Hospitals (general); Food banks; Big Brothers/Big Sisters; Salvation Army; YM/YWCAs & YM/YWHAs; Children/youth, services; Human services; Jewish federated giving programs; Jewish agencies & synagogues.
Type of support: Continuing support; General/operating support; Program development.
Geographic limitations: Giving primarily in OH, with emphasis on Cleveland, and PA, with emphasis on Pittsburgh.
Application information: Applications accepted. Application form not required. Applicants should submit the following:
1) copy of IRS Determination Letter
Initial approach: Letter of inquiry
Deadline(s): None
Directors: Gerald Chait; Edward Moravitz; Louis Plung; Charles Porter; David S. Shapira; Norman Weizenbaum.
EIN: 202734721
Selected grants: The following grants are a representative sample of this grantmaker's funding activity:
$162,250 to University of Pittsburgh, Pittsburgh, PA, 2009.
$58,334 to Catholic Diocese of Cleveland, Cleveland, OH, 2009.
$50,000 to Jewish Community Center of Greater Pittsburgh, Pittsburgh, PA, 2009.
$40,000 to YMCA of Greater Pittsburgh, Pittsburgh, PA, 2009.
$30,000 to Community Day School, Pittsburgh, PA, 2009.
$30,000 to Pittsburgh Opera, Pittsburgh, PA, 2009.
$25,000 to Hillel Jewish University Center, Pittsburgh, PA, 2009.
$7,500 to Pittsburgh Public Theater, Pittsburgh, PA, 2009.
$5,000 to Seton Hill University, Greensburg, PA, 2009.
$5,000 to West Side Catholic Center, Cleveland, OH, 2009.

1572
Giant Food Stores, LLC
(doing business as Martin's Food Market)
(also known as Giant-Carlisle)
(formerly Giant Food Stores, Inc.)
1149 Harrisburg Pike
P.O. Box 249
Carlisle, PA 17013 (717) 249-4000

Company URL: http://www.giantpa.com
Establishment information: Established in 1923.
Company type: Subsidiary of a foreign company
Business activities: Operates grocery stores.
Business type (SIC): Groceries—retail
Financial profile for 2010: Number of employees, 550; sales volume, $3,190,000,000
Corporate officers: Carl Schlicker, Pres. and C.E.O.; Jeff Martin, Exec. V.P., Sales; John Bussenger, Exec. V.P., Human Resources; Erik Keptner, Sr. V.P., Mktg.; Jim Saccary, V.P., Human Resources
Board of directors: Todd Robinson; Joseph LaCagnina; Juan-Carlos Vivas
Giving statement: Giving through the Giant Food Stores, LLC Corporate Giving Program.

Giant Food Stores, LLC Corporate Giving Program

(formerly Giant Food Stores, Inc. Corporate Giving Program)
c/o Community Rels.
P.O. Box 249
Carlisle, PA 17013-0249 (717) 249-4000
URL: http://www.giantfoodstores.com/shareddev/sharedcontent/Community/

Purpose and activities: Giant Food makes charitable contributions to nonprofit organizations involved with hunger, children, education, and health. Support is given primarily in areas of company operations.
Fields of interest: Education; Health care; Multiple sclerosis; Pediatrics; Cancer research; Food services Children; Military/veterans.
Type of support: Donated products; General/operating support; In-kind gifts; Sponsorships.
Geographic limitations: Giving primarily in areas of company operations.
Support limitations: No grants to individuals or for travel expenses or third party donations.
Publications: Application guidelines.
Application information: Applications accepted. Proposals should be submitted using organization letterhead. Applicants should submit the following:
1) name, address and phone number of organization
2) copy of IRS Determination Letter
3) detailed description of project and amount of funding requested
4) contact person
5) additional materials/documentation
Deadline(s): 6 weeks in advance for events; 3 months for major sponsorship or partnership development

1573
Giant of Maryland, LLC

(formerly Giant Food LLC)
8301 Professional Pl., Ste. 115
Landover, MD 20785-4303 (301) 341-4100

Company URL: http://www.giantfood.com
Establishment information: Established in 1936.
Company type: Subsidiary of a foreign company
Business activities: Operates grocery stores.
Business type (SIC): Groceries—retail
Financial profile for 2010: Number of employees, 600; sales volume, $4,270,000,000
Corporate officers: Dick Baird, Pres. and C.E.O.; Jim Lawler, Exec. V.P., Human Resources; Bill Holmes, Exec. V.P. and Genl. Counsel
Subsidiaries: Bayside Traffic Services of Maryland, Inc., Fresno, CA; Bursil, Inc., Landover, MD
Plants: Eldersburg, MD; Cherry Hill, Gloucester City, Mount Laurel, Sicklerville, Township of Washington, NJ; Hilltown, PA; Alexandria, VA
Giving statement: Giving through the Giant of Maryland, LLC Corporate Giving Program.

Giant of Maryland, LLC Corporate Giving Program

(formerly Giant Food LLC Corporate Giving Program)
8301 Professional Pl., Ste. 115
Landover, MD 20785-2531
URL: http://www.giantfood.com/about_us/community/index.htm

Contact: Jamie Miller
Purpose and activities: Giant of Maryland makes charitable contributions to nonprofit organizations involved with education, health, and hunger. Support is given primarily in areas of company operations in Washington, DC, Delaware, Maryland, and Virginia.
Fields of interest: Elementary/secondary education; Education; Public health; Food services.
Program:
A+ Rewards Program: Through the A+ School Rewards Program, Giant gives cash grants and educational equipment to local schools.
Type of support: Donated products; General/operating support; In-kind gifts; Sponsorships.
Geographic limitations: Giving primarily in areas of company operations in Washington, DC, DE, MD, and VA.
Publications: Application guidelines.
Application information: Applications accepted. Proposals should be submitted using organization letterhead; no faxes or e-mails. Application form not required. Applicants should submit the following:
1) name, address and phone number of organization
2) copy of IRS Determination Letter
3) detailed description of project and amount of funding requested
4) contact person
Proposals should indicate the date of the event, if applicable.
Initial approach: Mail proposal to headquarters; visit website for A+ rewards program
Copies of proposal: 1
Final notification: 10 to 14 days

1574
Gibbons P.C

1 Gateway Ctr.
Newark, NJ 07102-5310 (973) 596-4500

Company URL: http://www.gibbonslaw.com/
Establishment information: Established in 1926.
Company type: Private company
Business activities: Operates law firm.
Business type (SIC): Legal services
Offices: Wilmington, DE; Newark, NH; Trenton, NJ; New York, NY; Philadelphia, PA
Giving statement: Giving through the Gibbons P.C. Corporate Giving Program.

Gibbons P.C. Corporate Giving Program

1 Gateway Ctr.
Newark, NJ 07102-5310
E-mail: llustberg@gibbonslaw.com; Contact for Pro Bono program: Mara E. Zazzali-Hogan, Dir., tel.: (973) 596-4723, fax: (973) 639-8331, e-mail: mzazzali-hogan@gibbonslaw.com; URL: http://www.gibbonslaw.com/about/index.php?view_page=30

Contact: Lawrence S. Lustberg, Dir., John J. Gibbons Fellowship in Public Interest and Constitutional Law, and Chair, Criminal Defense Dept.
Purpose and activities: Gibbons makes charitable contributions to nonprofit organizations involved with arts and culture, education, health, children, and human services.
Fields of interest: Arts; Education; Health organizations; Legal services; Children, services; Human services; General charitable giving.
Type of support: Employee volunteer services; General/operating support; Pro bono services - legal.

1575
Gibbs & Bruns LLP

1100 Louisiana, Ste. 5300
Houston, TX 77002-5215 (713) 751-5258

Company URL: http://www.gibbsbruns.com/thefirm/
Establishment information: Established in 1983.
Company type: Private company
Business activities: Operates law firm.
Business type (SIC): Legal services
Corporate officer: Scott A. Humphries, Managing Partner
Giving statement: Giving through the Gibbs & Bruns LLP Pro Bono Program.

Gibbs & Bruns LLP Pro Bono Program

1100 Louisiana, Ste. 5300
Houston, TX 77002-5215 (713) 751-5258
E-mail: agulley@gibbsbruns.com; Additional tel.: (713) 650-8805; URL: http://www.gibbsbruns.com/thefirm/

Contact: Aundrea Gulley, Partner
Fields of interest: Legal services.
Type of support: Pro bono services - legal.
Geographic limitations: Giving primarily in areas of company operations in Houston, TX.
Application information: The Partnership decides pro bono work assignments on a case-by-case basis.

1576
Gibbs International, Inc.

9855 Warren H. Abernathy Hwy.
P.O. Box 1727
Spartanburg, SC 29301-5205
(864) 439-8752

Company URL: http://www.gibbsinternational.com
Establishment information: Established in 1972.
Company type: Private company
Business activities: Sells textile equipment; appraises, liquidates and finances textile plants.
Business type (SIC): Industrial machinery and equipment—wholesale
Corporate officers: Jimmy I. Gibbs, Chair.; Ken Compton, Pres. and C.E.O.; Greg Boozer, C.O.O.; Tom Newell, V.P. and Genl. Counsel
Board of director: Jimmy I. Gibbs, Chair.
Giving statement: Giving through the Gibbs Charitable Foundation.

Gibbs Charitable Foundation

P.O. Box 1727
Spartanburg, SC 29304-1727

Establishment information: Established in 2002 in SC.
Donors: Jimmy I. Gibbs; Marsha H. Gibbs; Gibbs International, Inc.
Financial data (yr. ended 12/31/11): Assets, $14,869 (M); gifts received, $275,000; expenditures, $1,249,556; qualifying distributions, $1,249,547; giving activities include $1,249,547 for 44 grants (high: $265,000; low: $100).
Purpose and activities: The foundation supports organizations involved with radio, higher education, health, hunger, sports, human services, and Christianity.
Fields of interest: Media, radio; Higher education; Health care; Cancer; Athletics/sports, amateur leagues; Developmentally disabled, centers &

services; Human services; United Ways and Federated Giving Programs; Christian agencies & churches.
Type of support: Capital campaigns; Endowments; General/operating support; Program development; Scholarship funds.
Geographic limitations: Giving primarily in SC, with emphasis on Spartanburg.
Support limitations: No grants to individuals.
Application information: Applications not accepted. Contributes only to pre-selected organizations.
Trustees: Allen O. Clark; Jimmy I. Gibbs; Marsha H. Gibbs; J. Brian Honeycutt; Joe Lesesne; Sidney H. Walker.
EIN: 571111450
Selected grants: The following grants are a representative sample of this grantmaker's funding activity:
$400,000 to Spartanburg Regional Healthcare System Foundation, Cancer Board, Spartanburg, SC, 2010.
$250,000 to Wofford College, Spartanburg, SC, 2010. For scoreboard.
$244,000 to First Baptist Church, Spartanburg, SC, 2010. For Encouraging Word Ministries.
$210,464 to First Baptist Church, Spartanburg, SC, 2010.
$105,500 to Converse College, Spartanburg, SC, 2010.
$100,000 to Wofford College, Spartanburg, SC, 2010. For Deans Home.
$55,000 to Wofford College, Spartanburg, SC, 2010. For athletic scholarships.
$50,000 to Miracle Hill Ministries, Greenville, SC, 2010.
$25,000 to AnGeL Ministries, Raleigh, NC, 2010.
$20,000 to Glenn Springs Academy, Pauline, SC, 2010.

1577
Gibraltar Material Distribution, LP

320 Southland Dr.
Burnet, TX 78611-9792 (512) 715-9650

Company URL: http://www.gibraltarmaterials.com/
Establishment information: Established in 2006.
Company type: Private company
Business activities: Operates fence and gate security systems company.
Business type (SIC): Steel mill products
Corporate officers: Kaye Givens, Cont.; Bill Neusch, Managing Partner
Giving statement: Giving through the Sparrows' Home Foundation, Inc.

Sparrows' Home Foundation, Inc.

4303 Innovation Loop
Marble Falls, TX 78654-9792 (830) 798-5446
FAX: (830) 798-5447;
E-mail: sue@sparrowshomeadoptions.org;
URL: http://sparrowshomeadoptions.org

Establishment information: Established in 2007 in TX.
Donors: National Christian Foundation; Gibraltar Material Distribution, LP; Foundation Fence, Inc.; Gibraltar Cable Barrier Systems, LP.
Financial data (yr. ended 12/31/11): Assets, $6,864,513 (M); gifts received, $165,000; expenditures, $1,474,926; qualifying distributions, $1,466,604; giving activities include $1,053,465 for 10 grants (high: $526,065; low: $10,000).
Purpose and activities: The foundation supports programs designed to alleviate spiritual, physical, and economic suffering for orphans and widows in distress.
Fields of interest: Education; Children, adoption; Human services; Christian agencies & churches Children; Economically disadvantaged.
Program:
Adoption Fund: The foundation, in partnership with Share Adoptions, provides subsidies to help with the high costs of adoption. The program is designed to help orphaned children become adopted into Christian families. The amount awarded for adoption fees varies per family.
Type of support: General/operating support; Program development; Sponsorships.
Geographic limitations: Giving primarily in CA, CO, NE, TX, Asia, and North Korea.
Support limitations: No grants to individuals.
Application information: Applications accepted. Unsolicited applications for general funding are not accepted. Application form required.
Applications for Adoption Fund must include demonstrated financial need with tax statements; approved and current Home Study; and a letter of recommendation from a church pastor.
Initial approach: Download application form and mail to foundation for Adoption Fund
Deadline(s): None for Adoption Fund
Officers and Directors: William H. Neusch, Pres.; Agnes Neusch, V.P. and Secy.; Regina Ahn, Genl. Counsel; Sarah Neusch*, Prog. Coord.
EIN: 261571372
Selected grants: The following grants are a representative sample of this grantmaker's funding activity:
$1,000 to Antioch Ministries International, Waco, TX, 2010.

1578
Gibson Guitar Corp.

309 Plus Park Blvd.
Nashville, TN 37217 (615) 871-4500
FAX: (615) 889-5509

Company URL: http://www2.gibson.com
Establishment information: Established in 1894.
Company type: Private company
Business activities: Manufactures guitars, pianos, drums, amplifiers, vending machines and jukeboxes.
Business type (SIC): Musical instruments
Financial profile for 2010: Number of employees, 2,800
Corporate officers: Henry E. Juszkiewicz, Chair. and C.E.O.; David Haney, C.I.O.; David H. Berryman, Pres.; Reggie Mebane, C.O.O.; Dave Rodems, C.F.O.
Board of director: Henry E. Juszkiewicz, Chair.
Giving statement: Giving through the Gibson Foundation.

The Gibson Foundation

309 Plus Park Blvd.
Nashville, TN 37217-1005 (615) 871-4500
E-mail: nina.miller@gibson.com; URL: http://www.gibson.com/en-us/Lifestyle/GibsonFoundation/

Establishment information: Established in 2002 in DE.
Contact: Nina Miller, Exec. Dir.
Financial data (yr. ended 12/31/10): Revenue, $1,229,272; assets, $1,373,067 (M); gifts received, $1,226,558; expenditures, $2,029,653; giving activities include $1,941,566 for grants.
Purpose and activities: The foundation is committed to making the world a better place for children by creating, developing, and supporting programs and other nonprofit organizations in their efforts to advance education, music and the arts, the environment, and health and welfare causes.
Fields of interest: Performing arts, music; Arts; Education; Environment; Health care Children.
Program:
Donation Program: The foundation provides support (both cash and in-kind) to 501(c)(3) organizations whose programs and projects align with its mission.
Type of support: In-kind gifts.
Geographic limitations: Giving on a national and international basis.
Support limitations: No support for organizations with religious or political affiliations. No grants to individuals, or for individual scholarships.
Publications: Application guidelines; Financial statement.
Application information:
Initial approach: Submit donation request form
Deadline(s): At least eight weeks before program aid is needed
Officer: Nina Miller, Exec. Dir.
Board Members: Dave Berryman; John Breaux; Karen Giberson; Orrin Hatch; Henry Juszkiewicz; Daniel Katz; Frank Luntz.
EIN: 200832563

1579
Gibson Plumbing, Heating & Air Conditioning, Inc.

11703-U.S. Hwy. 87
Lubbock, TX 79423 (806) 744-2766

Company URL: http://www.gibsononline.com
Establishment information: Established in 1957.
Company type: Private company
Business activities: Operates plumbing, heating and air conditioning contracting company.
Business type (SIC): Contractors/plumbing, heating, and air-conditioning
Corporate officer: Scott Gibson, Pres. and Secy.-Treas.
Giving statement: Giving through the Bill and Pam Gibson Family Foundation.

The Bill and Pam Gibson Family Foundation

8308 34th St.
Lubbock, TX 79407

Establishment information: Established in 2002 in TX.
Donors: Gibson Plumbing Co., Inc.; Bill Gibson; Pam Gibson.
Financial data (yr. ended 12/31/11): Assets, $694,707 (M); gifts received, $200; expenditures, $35,122; qualifying distributions, $33,800; giving activities include $33,800 for grants.
Purpose and activities: The foundation supports churches and nonprofit organizations in the state of Texas. Special emphasis is directed toward programs that promote the advancement of the Christian religion.
Fields of interest: Human services; Religion.
Type of support: General/operating support.
Geographic limitations: Giving primarily in TX.
Support limitations: No grants to individuals.
Application information: Applications accepted. Application form required.

Initial approach: E-mail
Deadline(s): None
Officers: Bill Gibson, Pres.; Pam Gibson, Secy.
Director: Pamela Denise Scott.
EIN: 752954478

1580
Gibson, Dunn & Crutcher LLP

333 S. Grand Ave.
Los Angeles, CA 90071-3197
(213) 229-7686

Company URL: http://www.gibsondunn.com/default.aspx
Company type: Private company
Business activities: Operates law firm.
Business type (SIC): Legal services
Offices: Irvine, Los Angeles, Palo Alto, San Francisco, CA; Denver, CO; Washington, DC; Dallas, TX
International operations: Belgium; Brazil; France; Hong Kong; Singapore; Switzerland; United Arab Emirates; United Kingdom
Giving statement: Giving through the Gibson, Dunn & Crutcher LLP Pro Bono Program.

Gibson, Dunn & Crutcher LLP Pro Bono Program

333 S. Grand Ave.
Los Angeles, CA 90071-3197 (310) 557-8061
E-mail: SEdelman@gibsondunn.com; Additional tel.: (213) 229-7000; URL: http://www.gibsondunn.com/probono/default.aspx

Contact: Scott Edelman, National Pro Bono Chair
Fields of interest: Legal services.
Type of support: Pro bono services - legal.
Geographic limitations: Giving primarily in areas of company operations in Irvine, Los Angeles, Palo Alto, and San Francisco, CA, Denver, CO, Washington, DC, New York, NY, and Dallas, TX, and in Belgium, Brazil, France, Germany, Hong Kong, Singapore, United Arab Emirates, United Kingdom.
Application information: A Pro Bono Committee manages the pro bono program.

1581
Gilbane Building Company

7 Jackson Walkway
Providence, RI 02903 (401) 456-5800
FAX: (401) 456-5962

Company URL: http://www.gilbaneco.com
Establishment information: Established in 1873.
Company type: Subsidiary of a private company
Business activities: Provides nonresidential general contract construction services.
Business type (SIC): Contractors/general nonresidential building
Financial profile for 2011: Number of employees, 2,200; sales volume, $4,300,000,000
Corporate officers: Thomas F. Gilbane, Jr., Chair. and C.E.O.; Paul J. Choquette, Jr., Vice-Chair.; William J. Gilbane, Jr., Pres. and C.O.O.; John T. Ruggieri, Sr. V.P. and C.F.O.
Board of directors: Thomas F. Gilbane, Jr., Chair.; Paul J. Choquette, Jr., Vice-Chair.; Franz F. Colloredo-Mansfeld; Edward J. Cooney; John P. Fowler; Robert V. Gilbane; Thomas F. Gilbane III; William J. Gilbane, Jr.; Frank MacInnis; J. Bonnie Newman; Ronald L. Skates
Subsidiary: Gilbane Properties, Inc., Providence, RI
Giving statement: Giving through the Gilbane Building Company Contributions Program.

Gilbane Building Company Contributions Program

7 Jackson Walkway
Providence, RI 02903-3623
URL: http://www.gilbaneco.com/AboutGilbane.aspx

Purpose and activities: Gilbane makes charitable contributions to nonprofit organizations on a case by case basis. Support is given primarily in areas of company operations.
Fields of interest: Education; Health care; Housing/shelter; Boys & girls clubs; Community/economic development Mentally disabled; Substance abusers.
Type of support: Employee matching gifts; Employee volunteer services; General/operating support; Scholarships—to individuals.
Geographic limitations: Giving primarily in areas of company operations.

1582
Gilead Sciences, Inc.

333 Lakeside Dr.
Foster City, CA 94404-1147
(650) 574-3000
FAX: (650) 578-9264

Company URL: http://www.gilead.com/
Establishment information: Established in 1987.
Company type: Public company
Company ticker symbol and exchange: GILD/NASDAQ
International Securities Identification Number: US3755581036
Business activities: Discovers, develops and commercializes therapeutic drugs for underserved communities around the world.
Business type (SIC): Drugs
Financial profile for 2012: Number of employees, 5,000; assets, $21,239,840,000; sales volume, $9,702,520,000; pre-tax net income, $3,611,980,000; expenses, $5,692,340,000; liabilities, $11,930,100,000
Fortune 1000 ranking: 2012—280th in revenues, 76th in profits, and 230th in assets
Forbes 2000 ranking: 2012—953rd in sales, 220th in profits, and 945th in assets
Corporate officers: John C. Martin, Ph.D., Chair. and C.E.O.; John F. Milligan, Ph.D., Pres. and C.O.O.; Robin L. Washington, Sr. V.P. and C.F.O.; Katie L. Watson, Sr. V.P., Human Resources
Board of directors: John C. Martin, Ph.D., Chair.; John F. Cogan, Ph.D.; Etienne F. Davignon; Carla A. Hills; Kevin E. Lofton; John W. Madigan; Nicholas G. Moore; George P. Shultz; Richard J. Whitley, M.D.; Gayle Edlund Wilson; Per Wold-Olsen
International operations: Australia; Austria; Belgium; Bermuda; Canada; Denmark; Finland; France; Germany; Greece; Hong Kong; Ireland; Italy; Luxembourg; Netherlands; New Zealand; Norway; Portugal; Spain; Sweden; Switzerland; Turkey; United Kingdom
Giving statement: Giving through the Gilead Sciences, Inc. Contributions Program and the Gilead Foundation.
Company EIN: 943047598

Gilead Sciences, Inc. Contributions Program

c/o Grants Coordinator
333 Lakeside Dr.
Foster City, CA 94404-1147 (650) 522-1696
FAX: (650) 522-1707; E-mail: grants@gilead.com; URL: https://grants.gilead.com/

Purpose and activities: As a complement to its foundation, Gilead Sciences also makes charitable contributions to nonprofit organizations directly. Grant funds must enhance patient care or patient community interests. Special emphasis is directed toward programs related to the therapeutic areas in which Gilead has expertise - cystic fibrosis, hepatitis, HIV/AIDS, influenza, pulmonary arterial hypertension and chronic angina.
Fields of interest: Medical school/education; Public health, communicable diseases; Health care; Cystic fibrosis; Heart & circulatory diseases; AIDS; Pathology; Science.
Type of support: Conferences/seminars; Curriculum development; General/operating support; Program development.
Support limitations: No support for No support given to for-profit physician group practices. No grants to individual healthcare professionals, or for travel or registration fees, operating expenses, acquisition of standard equipment or hardware, clinical studies, events that are closed to healthcare professionals in the broader community, grand rounds meetings in which the principal speaker is employed by, and the audience is limited to, the requesting institution, or honoraria for speakers to talk to their own institution. No grants for purposes that reward, influence, or require an organization's purchase, prescription, or recommendation of Gilead's products. No grants to be used in lieu of a discount or price concession, or as part of a contract negotiation, or to compensate individuals who provide services to Gilead, such as speaking or advising directly for the company.
Publications: Application guidelines.
Application information: A Grant Review Committee handles giving. Recipient organizations must acknowledge Gilead's support at the event. Funds not used for the stated purpose must be returned within 30 days from the program date. The organization may be required to document event results and the specific use of funds. Applications for programs intended for broader audiences with a national or regional reach, or for clinical studies, must be submitted to the Gilead Independent Medical Education Department. Applicants should submit the following:
1) copy of IRS Determination Letter
2) detailed description of project and amount of funding requested
3) contact person
4) copy of current year's organizational budget and/or project budget
5) listing of additional sources and amount of support

Requests must include a description of how the audience will be identified and recruited to participate in the project; the accreditation number, if applicable; the number of credits offered; the names, affiliations, and the honoraria requested for all involved speakers; an e-mail address; event location, date, and agenda, if applicable; and the name of a Gilead contact, if applicable.
Initial approach: Complete online application; contact local facility for exhibit requests
Deadline(s): Ongoing
Final notification: Approximately 6 to 12 weeks

Gilead Foundation

333 Lakeside Dr.
Foster City, CA 94404-1147
URL: http://www.gilead.com/corporate_responsibility

Establishment information: Established in 2004 in CA.
Donor: Gilead Sciences, Inc.
Financial data (yr. ended 12/31/11): Assets, $2,532,912 (M); gifts received, $5,009,779; expenditures, $4,976,565; qualifying distributions, $4,975,965; giving activities include $4,950,480 for 46 grants (high: $1,000,000; low: $10,000).
Purpose and activities: The foundation supports organizations involved with improving the health and well-being of underserved communities around the world. Special emphasis is directed toward programs designed to expand access to HIV and hepatitis B education, outreach, prevention, and health services.
Fields of interest: Medical school/education; Health care, formal/general education; Hospitals (general); Health care, clinics/centers; Health care, patient services; Health care; AIDS; AIDS research Economically disadvantaged.
Type of support: Conferences/seminars; Curriculum development; General/operating support; Management development/capacity building; Program development.
Geographic limitations: Giving primarily in CA, CT, Washington, DC, Honolulu, HI, NY, TX, and VA; giving also to international organizations in Africa, Kenya, Mozambique, South Africa, and Zimbabwe.
Support limitations: No support for for-profit physician group practices. No grants to individuals, or for standard equipment, or clinical studies.
Publications: Grants list.
Application information: Applications not accepted. Contributes only to pre-selected organizations.
Officers and Directors:* Howard Jaffe, Chair. and Pres.; Amy Flood, Secy.; Andrew Cheng, Treas.; Gregg H. Alton; Jim Meyers; Coy Stout; Michael Wulfsohn.
EIN: 201042419
Selected grants: The following grants are a representative sample of this grantmaker's funding activity:
$1,000,000 to AIDS Healthcare Foundation, Los Angeles, CA, 2010. For ART Treatment in Care Program in Africa, Asia, Latin America, Caribbean and Eastern Europe.
$1,000,000 to AIDS Healthcare Foundation, Los Angeles, CA, 2010. For ART Treatment and Care Program in Africa, Asia, Latin America, Caribbean and Eastern Europe.
$225,000 to Accordia Global Health Foundation, Washington, DC, 2010. For Gilead Infectious Disease Scholarship Program.
$200,000 to Pangaea Global AIDS Foundation, Oakland, CA, 2010. For detention center treatment program.
$200,000 to Yale University, School of Medicine, New Haven, CT, 2010. To confront XDR TB and HIV in rural South Africa.
$200,000 to Yale University, New Haven, CT, 2010. For HIV/AIDS Prevention Initiative as part of International Elective Program.
$150,000 to Yale University, School of Medicine, New Haven, CT, 2010. For Community Health Care Van program (CHCV).
$143,735 to Association of Asian-Pacific Community Health Organizations, Oakland, CA, 2010. For hepatitis B policy fellowship.
$50,000 to Hepatitis Support Network, Honolulu, HI, 2010. For HBV screening and medical care management in Hawaii.
$50,000 to Pangaea Global AIDS Foundation, Oakland, CA, 2010. For strategic development.

1583
Give Something Back, Inc.

(doing business as Give Something Back Business Products, Inc.)
(also known as GSB)
7730 Pardee Ln., Ste. A
Oakland, CA 94621 (800) 261-2619

Company URL: http://www.givesomethingback.com
Establishment information: Established in 1991.
Company type: Private company
Business activities: Provides office supplies catalog shopping services; provides Internet shopping services.
Business type (SIC): Nonstore retailers; computer services
Corporate officers: Sean Marx, C.E.O.; Mike Hannigan, Pres.
Giving statement: Giving through the Give Something Back, Inc., Corporate Giving Program.

Give Something Back, Inc., Corporate Giving Program

7730 Pardee Ln.
Oakland, CA 94621 (800) 261-2619
FAX: (888) 461-2619;
E-mail: communityfund@givesomethingback.com; For San Francisco Bay & San Diego areas: East Bay Community Foundation/Give Something Back Community Fund, 200 Frank H Ogawa Plz., Oakland, CA 94612; tel.: 510-836-3223. For the greater Sacramento area: Sacramento Region Community Foundation/Give Something Back Community Fund, 995 University Ave., Ste. A, Sacramento, CA 95825; tel.: 916-921-7723. Community Rels. Office tel.: 510-635-5500; URL: http://www.givesomethingback.com/CustomLandingPage.aspx?cpi=Community

Purpose and activities: Give Something Back is a certified B Corporation that donates a percentage of profits to nonprofit organizations involved with arts and culture, education, the environment, health care, and community services. Support is given primarily in areas of company operations in California.
Fields of interest: Arts, cultural/ethnic awareness; Elementary/secondary education; Education; Environment; Health care; Food banks; Youth development; Human services, fund raising/fund distribution; Human services Economically disadvantaged.
Type of support: Cause-related marketing; Donated products; Employee volunteer services; Equipment; General/operating support; In-kind gifts.
Geographic limitations: Giving primarily in areas of company operations in CA.
Support limitations: No support for religious groups or organizations. No grants for political or lobbying purposes.
Publications: Application guidelines.
Application information: Applications accepted. Regional foundations determine if a community-based organization meets the grant criteria and makes recommendations on the groups that appear on the company's donation ballots. Contributions are made primarily through the Give Something Back Customer Ballot, a list of qualifying nonprofit organizations, which is presented once a year to the company's customers. Those organizations which receive the highest number of votes get the largest contributions. Application form required. Applicants should submit the following:
1) name, address and phone number of organization
2) brief history of organization and description of its mission
3) contact person
4) copy of current year's organizational budget and/or project budget
5) copy of IRS Determination Letter
6) population served
Proposals should include a list of the organization's major projects, programs, or services.
Initial approach: Download application form and send completed application to regional foundation
Copies of proposal: 1
Deadline(s): May 30

1584
GJF Construction Corp.

50 Broad St., Fl. 6
New York, NY 10004-2333 (212) 635-0760

Establishment information: Established in 2002.
Company type: Private company
Business activities: Provides general contract construction services.
Business type (SIC): Building construction general contractors and operative builders
Corporate officer: George J. Figliolia, Pres. and C.E.O.
Giving statement: Giving through the Figliolia Foundation Trust.

Figliolia Foundation Trust

45 Broadway St.
New York, NY 10006 (212) 635-0760

Donors: GJF Construction Corp.; George Figliolia.
Contact: George J. Figliolia, Tr.
Financial data (yr. ended 12/31/11): Assets, $131,659 (M); expenditures, $1,778; qualifying distributions, $1,778.
Purpose and activities: The trust awards scholarships to individuals recommended by a Builders Group employee for high school and college education.
Fields of interest: Secondary school/education; Higher education; Education.
Type of support: Employee-related scholarships; Scholarships—to individuals.
Geographic limitations: Giving primarily in the greater metropolitan New York, NY, area.
Application information: Applications accepted. Applicants must be recommended by a Builders Group employee. Application form required.
Initial approach: Proposal
Deadline(s): None
Trustees: George J. Figliolia; Ronald Figliolia.
EIN: 133922569

1585
GKN America Corp.

(formerly The Interlake Corporation)
550 Warrenville Rd., Ste. 400
Lisle, IL 60532-4308 (630) 719-7204

Company URL: http://
Establishment information: Established in 2001.
Company type: Subsidiary of a foreign company

Business activities: Manufactures flat float glass and other automotive components.
Business type (SIC): Motor vehicles and equipment
Corporate officer: Grey Denham, Pres.
Subsidiaries: Chem-Tronics, Inc., El Cajon, CA; Hoeganaes Corp., Riverton, NJ; Interlake Material Handling, Lodi, CA; Interlake Packaging Corp., Racine, WI
Plants: Pontiac, IL; Milton, PA; Fountain Inn, Sumter, SC; Gallatin, TN
Giving statement: Giving through the GKN Foundation.

GKN Foundation

(formerly Interlake Foundation)
550 Warrenville Rd., Ste. 400
Lisle, IL 60532-4387 (630) 737-1456

Establishment information: Incorporated in 1951 in IL.
Donor: The Interlake Corp.
Contact: Hugo Perez, Treas.
Financial data (yr. ended 12/31/11): Assets, $4,244,766 (M); expenditures, $705,434; qualifying distributions, $691,090; giving activities include $691,090 for grants.
Purpose and activities: The foundation supports community foundations and organizations involved with arts and culture, education, health, cancer, diabetes, human services, and community economic development.
Fields of interest: Arts; Higher education; Education; Health care, clinics/centers; Health care, patient services; Health care; Cancer; Diabetes; Youth development, business; American Red Cross; Children/youth, services; Residential/custodial care, hospices; Human services; Community/economic development; Foundations (community); United Ways and Federated Giving Programs.
Type of support: Capital campaigns; Continuing support; Employee matching gifts; Employee-related scholarships; Endowments; General/operating support.
Geographic limitations: Giving primarily in areas of company operations, with emphasis on IL.
Support limitations: No support for political, religious, or athletics organizations.
Application information: Applications accepted. Applicants should submit the following:
1) copy of IRS Determination Letter
2) brief history of organization and description of its mission
3) detailed description of project and amount of funding requested

Initial approach: Letter of inquiry
Deadline(s): None

Officers and Directors:* Paul J. Westman*, Pres.; John M. O'Donnell, V.P. and Genl. Counsel; Barbara A. Gustafson, Secy.; Hugo Perez*, Treas.
EIN: 362590617
Selected grants: The following grants are a representative sample of this grantmaker's funding activity:
$10,000 to Salesmanship Club of Dallas, Dallas, TX, 2011.
$5,000 to American Cancer Society, Atlanta, GA, 2011.
$5,000 to Childrens Hospital Medical Center, Cincinnati, OH, 2011.
$5,000 to College of DuPage Foundation, Glen Ellyn, IL, 2011.
$5,000 to Orangewood Childrens Foundation, Santa Ana, CA, 2011.
$5,000 to United Way of Long Island, Deer Park, NY, 2011.
$2,500 to Hospice of Cincinnati, Cincinnati, OH, 2011.
$2,500 to Safe Kids Worldwide, Washington, DC, 2011.
$2,000 to Hunger Task Force, Milwaukee, WI, 2011.
$1,000 to Art Institute of Chicago, Chicago, IL, 2011.

1586
Glacier Fish Company, LLC

1200 Westlake Ave. N., Ste. 900
Seattle, WA 98109-3543 (206) 298-1200

Company URL: http://www.glacierfish.com
Establishment information: Established in 1982.
Company type: Private company
Business activities: Manufactures canned fish and seafood.
Business type (SIC): Fishing/commercial
Corporate officers: Mike Breivik, C.E.O.; John Bundy, Co-Pres.; Jim Johnson, Co-Pres.; Rob Wood, C.F.O.; Merle Knapp, V.P., Sales and Mktg.
Giving statement: Giving through the Norton Sound Fund.

Norton Sound Fund

420 L St., Ste. 310
Anchorage, AK 99501-1971 (907) 274-2248

Establishment information: Established in 1999 in AK.
Donors: Glacier Fish Company, LLC; American Seafoods Company.
Contact: Simon Kinneen, Pres.
Financial data (yr. ended 12/31/11): Assets, $1,159,924 (M); gifts received, $132,900; expenditures, $44,220; qualifying distributions, $44,200; giving activities include $44,200 for 2 grants (high: $39,200; low: $5,000).
Fields of interest: Employment.
Geographic limitations: Giving primarily in AK.
Application information: Applications accepted. Application form required.

Initial approach: Proposal
Deadline(s): None

Officers: Simon Kinneen, Pres.; Janis Ivanoff, Secy.; Richard Tremaine, Treas.
EIN: 920166389

1587
Glades Electric Cooperative, Inc.

1190 S. U.S. Hwy. 27 E.
Moore Haven, FL 33471-6226
(863) 946-0061

Company URL: http://www.gladesec.com
Establishment information: Established in 1945.
Company type: Cooperative
Business activities: Distributes electricity.
Business type (SIC): Electric services
Corporate officers: L. Tommy Todd, C.E.O.; John Coxe, Pres.; Jeff Brewington, C.O.O.; Jennifer Manning, C.F.O.; Russell Henderson, Secy.-Treas.
Board of directors: James Aul; Ladd Bass; John Coxe; Barney Goodman; Shannon Hall; Lee Henderson; Russell Henderson; Irene Lofton; R.D. Lundy, Jr.
Giving statement: Giving through the Glades Electric Educational Foundation, Inc.

Glades Electric Educational Foundation, Inc.

P.O. Box 519
Moore Haven, FL 33471-0519 (863) 946-0061

Establishment information: Established in 2001 in FL.
Donor: Glades Electric Cooperative, Inc.
Financial data (yr. ended 12/31/11): Assets, $334,014 (M); gifts received, $73,174; expenditures, $29,036; qualifying distributions, $24,000; giving activities include $24,000 for grants to individuals.
Purpose and activities: The foundation awards college scholarships to students with a legal permanent residence served directly or indirectly by Glades Electric Cooperative.
Type of support: Scholarships—to individuals.
Geographic limitations: Giving limited to areas of company operations.
Application information: Applications accepted. Application form required.

Initial approach: Contact foundation for application form
Deadline(s): Mar. 17
Final notification: Within 30 days

Officers: John Coxe, Pres.; C. Russell Henderson, V.P.; Jeffrey R. Brewington, Secy.-Treas.
Directors: Barney Goodman; Irene Lofton.
EIN: 651083705

1588
GlaxoSmithKline

5 Moore Dr.
P.O. Box 13398
Research Triangle Park, NC 27709-3398
(919) 483-2140

Company URL: http://us.gsk.com
Establishment information: Established in 1999.
Company type: Subsidiary of a foreign company
Business activities: Researches, develops, and manufactures pharmaceuticals.
Business type (SIC): Drugs
Financial profile for 2011: Assets, $59,400,000,000; sales volume, $42,500,000,000
Corporate officers: Andrew Witty, C.E.O.; Simon Dingemans, C.F.O.; Bill Louv, C.I.O.
Plant: Zebulon, NC
Office: Philadelphia, PA
Giving statement: Giving through the GlaxoSmithKline Corporate Giving Program, the GlaxoSmithKline Foundation, the GlaxoSmithKline Patient Access Programs Foundation, and the North Carolina GlaxoSmithKline Foundation, Inc.

GlaxoSmithKline Corporate Giving Program

c/o U.S. Community Partnerships
D234.2C
P.O. Box 13398
Research Triangle Park, NC 27709-3398
FAX: (919) 483-8765;
E-mail: community.partnership@gsk.com; Additional application addresses: Philadelphia, PA: Philadelphia Community Partnerships, 1 Franklin Plz., FP2130, P.O. Box 7929, Philadelphia, PA 19101-7929, fax: (215) 751-4046, national organizations: U.S. Community Partnerships, D234.2C, P.O. Box 13398, Research Triangle Park, NC 27709-3398, fax: (919) 483-8765; URL: http://us.gsk.com/html/community/index.html

Contact: William A. Shore, Dir., U.S. Community Partnerships
Purpose and activities: As a complement to its foundation, GlaxoSmithKline Holdings (Americas) also makes charitable contributions to nonprofit organizations directly. Special emphasis is directed toward programs that target underserved and diverse populations. Support is given primarily in North Carolina and the greater Philadelphia, Pennsylvania, area.
Fields of interest: Arts education; Arts; Elementary/secondary education; Education, reading; Education; Health care; Community/economic development; Science, formal/general education; Mathematics Children.
Program:
IMPACT Awards: GlaxoSmithKline Holdings (Americas) annually awards up to ten $40,000 grants to small and mid-sized nonprofit organizations involved with health located in each of two locations; Research Triangle Park, North Carolina, and the greater Philadelphia, Pennsylvania, area in acknowledgement of programs that demonstrate Innovation, Management, Partnership, Achievement, Community Focus, and Targeting Need (IMPACT). Call for applications is on web site during first quarter.
Type of support: Curriculum development; Donated equipment; Donated products; Employee matching gifts; Employee volunteer services; In-kind gifts; Program development; Seed money.
Geographic limitations: Giving primarily in NC, with emphasis on Research Triangle Park, and the greater Philadelphia, PA, area; giving also to national organizations.
Support limitations: No support for political, religious, fraternal, discriminatory, hobby-oriented, or tax-subsidized organizations. No grants to individuals, or for capital campaigns, or general operating support (except for IMPACT Awards).
Publications: Annual report; Application guidelines; Corporate giving report.
Application information: Applications accepted. The U.S. Community Partnerships Department handles giving. The company has a staff that only handles contributions. A contributions committee reviews all requests. E-mails to U.S. Community Partnerships should have "U.S." in the subject line. Application form required. Applicants should submit the following:
1) copy of IRS Determination Letter
Proposals should include program evaluations for the past three years, if applicable.
Initial approach: Download application form and mail or fax to one of the addresses listed in the U.S. Community Partnerships Funding Guidelines and Application located on the company website
Copies of proposal: 1
Committee meeting date(s): Jan., June, and Nov.
Deadline(s): None
Final notification: 8 weeks
Number of staff: 5 full-time professional; 2 part-time support.

GlaxoSmithKline Foundation

(formerly SmithKline Beecham Foundation)
1 Franklin Plz., FP2335
P.O. Box 7929
Philadelphia, PA 19102-1225

Establishment information: Established in 1967 in DE.
Donors: GlaxoSmithKline LLC F.K.A. SmithKline; SmithKline Beecham Corp.
Financial data (yr. ended 12/31/11): Assets, $749,758 (M); gifts received, $2,931,151; expenditures, $3,088,380; qualifying distributions, $3,088,380; giving activities include $3,088,310 for 11,093 employee matching gifts.
Purpose and activities: The foundation matches contributions made by part-time and full-time employees, directors, and retirees of GlaxoSmithKline to nonprofit organizations.
Fields of interest: General charitable giving.
Program:
Employee Matching Gifts: The foundation matches contributions made by part-time and full-time employees, directors, and retirees of GlaxoSmithKline to nonprofit organizations involved with arts and culture, education, health, and human services from $25 to $10,000 per contributor, per year.
Type of support: Employee matching gifts.
Geographic limitations: Giving primarily in Philadelphia, PA.
Support limitations: No grants to individuals.
Application information: Applications not accepted. Contributes only through employee matching gifts.
Officers and Directors:* Eleanor Barger*, Chair.; Judith Lynch*, Secy.-Treas.; Mary Linda Andrews; William Shore.
EIN: 232120418

GlaxoSmithKline Patient Access Programs Foundation

1 Franklin Plaza, Rm. 2335
Philadelphia, PA 19101 (888) 825-5249
Additional address: Frank Barrett, 200 N. 16th St., Philadelphia, PA 19102; Tel. for Bridges to Access: (866) 728-4368; Tel. for Commitment to Access: (866) 265-6491; URL: http://www.gskforyou.com/

Establishment information: Established as a company-sponsored operating foundation in 2003 in NC.
Donor: SmithKline Beecham Corp.
Financial data (yr. ended 12/31/11): Assets, $49,458,764 (L); gifts received, $627,235,271; expenditures, $627,235,271; qualifying distributions, $627,235,271; giving activities include $605,399,422 for grants to individuals.
Purpose and activities: The foundation provides for non-oncology prescription medication to economically disadvantaged patients without prescription drug benefits.
Fields of interest: Health care Economically disadvantaged.
Programs:
Bridges To Access: Through the Bridges to Access program, the foundation provides non-oncology GSK prescription medicines to eligible low-income U.S. patients without prescription drug benefits. URL: http://www.bridgestoaccess.com/ for additional information.
Commitment to Access: Through the Commitment to Access program, the foundation provides oncology and specialty pharmacy products, at little or no cost, to patients who qualify. URL: http://www.gskcta.com/ for additional information.
Type of support: Donated products; Grants to individuals.
Publications: Application guidelines.
Application information: Applications accepted. Applications should include proof of income. Application form required.
Initial approach: Download application and mail to foundation
Deadline(s): None
Officers and Directors:* Lesley A. Tewnion*, Chair.; Mary Linda Andrews*, Secy.-Treas; Frank Barrett, Exec. Dir.; Eric Dube; Nancy J. Pekarek; William Shore.
EIN: 200031992

The North Carolina GlaxoSmithKline Foundation, Inc.

(formerly The Glaxo Wellcome Foundation)
5 Moore Dr.
P.O. Box 13398
Research Triangle Park, NC 27709-3398 (919) 483-2140
FAX: (919) 315-3015;
E-mail: community.partnership@gsk.com; Contact for Ribbon of Hope: Carrie Germeroth, tel.: (303) 632-5578, e-mail: ribbonofhope@mcrel.org; URL: http://www.mcrel.org/GSKRibbonOfHope

Establishment information: Established in 1986 in NC.
Donors: Glaxo Wellcome Americas Inc.; GlaxoSmithKline Holdings (Americas) Inc.
Contact: Marilyn E. Foote-Hudson, Exec. Dir.
Financial data (yr. ended 12/31/11): Assets, $55,489,199 (M); gifts received, $304,509; expenditures, $4,232,831; qualifying distributions, $4,145,737; giving activities include $3,043,840 for 27 grants (high: $1,104,840; low: $24,000).
Purpose and activities: The foundation supports programs designed to promote education, health, and science.
Fields of interest: Museums; Museums (art); Elementary/secondary education; Higher education; Higher education, college (community/junior); Education, reading; Education; Health care, association; Public health; Health care; Children/youth, services; Science Children/youth; Adults; Minorities.
Programs:
GlaxoSmithKline Child Health Recognition Awards Program: The foundation recognizes public health workers and programs that improve the health status of children. The program honors public health professionals and departments for innovative, creative, and successful approaches to improving the lives of the younger generation. The program includes lifetime achievement awards, individual recognition awards, public health staff recognition awards, and local health department awards. The program is administered by the North Carolina Public Health Association.
Ribbon of Hope: The foundation, in partnership with McRel and the North Carolina Center for Nonprofits, awards $25,000 grants to nonprofits organizations to establish or expand local programs in health, science, and education. The initiative is designed to serve identified needs of local communities and includes technical assistance by the North Carolina Center for Nonprofits. Visit URL: http://www.mcrel.org/gskribbonofhope/ for more information.
Traditional Grants: The foundation awards single and multi-year grants to programs designed to advance health, science, and education.
Women in Science Scholars Program: The foundation provides two female undergraduates at select schools with scholarship funds, internships, and mentoring by professional women scientists.
Type of support: Capital campaigns; Curriculum development; Internship funds; Matching/challenge support; Professorships; Program development; Scholarship funds; Seed money.
Geographic limitations: Giving primarily in NC.
Support limitations: No support for religious, political, or international organizations. No grants to individuals, or for construction, restoration projects, or for general operating costs.

Publications: Annual report (including application guidelines); Grants list.
Application information: Applications accepted. Proposals for Ribbon of Hope should be no longer than 10 pages. Support is limited to 1 contribution per organization during any given year. Organizations receiving support are asked to provide interim reports and a final report. Application form not required. Applicants should submit the following:
1) timetable for implementation and evaluation of project
2) how project will be sustained once grantmaker support is completed
3) signature and title of chief executive officer
4) results expected from proposed grant
5) qualifications of key personnel
6) statement of problem project will address
7) population served
8) copy of IRS Determination Letter
9) copy of most recent annual report/audited financial statement/990
10) how project's results will be evaluated or measured
11) detailed description of project and amount of funding requested
12) plans for cooperation with other organizations, if any
13) copy of current year's organizational budget and/or project budget
14) listing of additional sources and amount of support
15) additional materials/documentation
Submission should also include a communications plan.
Initial approach: Proposal for Traditional Grants; download application form and e-mail or mail proposal and application form for Ribbon of Hope
Copies of proposal: 1
Board meeting date(s): Mar., June, Sept., and Dec.
Deadline(s): Jan. 1, Apr. 1, July 1, and Oct. 1 for Traditional Grants; Apr. 1 and Oct. 1 for Ribbon of Hope
Final notification: Within 15 days following board meetings for Traditional Grants; Apr. and Nov. for Ribbon of Hope
Officers and Directors:* Robert A. Ingram*, Chair.; Margaret B. Dardess*, Pres.; Paul A. Holcombe, Jr.*, Secy.; Marilyn E. Foote-Hudson, Exec. Dir.; Mark Werner, Legal Counsel; Julius L. Chambers; Diedre P. Connelly; W. Robert Connor; Shirley T. Frye; Thomas R. Haber; Charles A. Sanders, M.D.; Janice M. Whitaker.
Number of staff: 2 full-time professional; 1 part-time professional; 1 full-time support.
EIN: 581698610
Selected grants: The following grants are a representative sample of this grantmaker's funding activity:
$500,000 to North Carolina Museum of Natural Sciences, Friends of the, Raleigh, NC, 2010. To develop and create Micro Investigations Center.
$135,000 to North Carolina Healthy Start Foundation, Raleigh, NC, 2010. To expand RICHES Program.
$100,000 to North Carolina Museum of Art Foundation, Raleigh, NC, 2010. For teacher training program for art education enhancement.
$100,000 to North Carolina Science, Mathematics and Technology Education Center, Research Triangle Park, NC, 2010. To implement comprehensive, research-based science program.
$100,000 to North Carolina Symphony, Raleigh, NC, 2010. For music education program and ensemble in the schools.
$75,628 to Center for Child and Family Health, Durham, NC, 2010. For Baby College: First Step Project.
$67,500 to Pamlico Community College, Grantsboro, NC, 2010. For Pamlico Model Program Academic Support Center.
$53,360 to Forsyth Medical Center Foundation, Winston-Salem, NC, 2010. For AAS degree in Pharmacy Technology.
$50,000 to North Carolina Museum of Life and Science, Durham, NC, 2010. For BioQuest Project.
$44,525 to North Carolina Coastal Federation, Newport, NC, 2010. For Coastal Habitat Education Program.

1589
Gleacher & Company, Inc.

(formerly Broadpoint Securities Group, Inc.)
12 E. 49th St., 31st Fl.
1290 Ave. of the Americas
New York, NY 10104 (212) 273-7100
FAX: (212) 273-7178

Company URL: http://www.gleacher.com/
Establishment information: Established in 1985.
Company type: Public company
Company ticker symbol and exchange: GLCH/NASDAQ
Business activities: Provides securities brokerage services.
Business type (SIC): Brokers and dealers/security; security and commodity services
Financial profile for 2012: Number of employees, 220; assets, $1,229,640,000; sales volume, $216,420,000; pre-tax net income, -$53,350,000; expenses, $269,770,000; liabilities, $1,048,640,000
Corporate officers: Thomas Hughes, C.E.O.; John Griff, C.O.O.; Patricia A. Arciero-Craig, Genl. Counsel and Secy.
Board of directors: Henry Bienen; Marshall Cohen; Robert Gerard; Thomas Hughes; Mark Patterson; Christopher R. Pechock; Bruce Rohde; Robert S. Yingling
Subsidiary: First Albany Corp., Inc., Albany, NY
Offices: Los Angeles, San Francisco, CA; Greenwich, CT; Atlanta, GA; Chicago, IL; Boston, MA; Roseland, NJ; Albany, NY
Giving statement: Giving through the Broadpoint Foundation, Inc.
Company EIN: 222655804

Broadpoint Foundation, Inc.

(formerly First Albany Foundation, Inc.)
1290 Avenue of the Americas, 4th Fl.
New York, NY 10104-0101

Establishment information: Established in 1993 in NY.
Donors: First Albany Cos. Inc.; First Albany Corp.; First Albany Capital, Inc.
Financial data (yr. ended 12/31/11): Assets, $10,440 (M); gifts received, $15,288; expenditures, $20,000; qualifying distributions, $20,000; giving activities include $20,000 for 1 grant.
Purpose and activities: The foundation supports organizations involved with hunger.
Fields of interest: Food banks; Food distribution, meals on wheels.
Type of support: General/operating support.
Geographic limitations: Giving primarily in NY.
Support limitations: No grants to individuals.
Application information: Applications not accepted. Unsolicited requests for funds not accepted.
Officers and Director:* Thomas Hughes*, C.E.O.; Brain Leegan, V.P.; Eric Gleacher.
EIN: 141749789

1590
Gleaner Life Insurance Society

5200 W. U.S. Hwy. 223
P.O. Box 1894
Adrian, MI 49221-9461 (517) 263-2244

Company URL: http://www.gleanerlife.com
Establishment information: Established in 1894.
Company type: Fraternal benefit society
Business activities: Sells life insurance; provides investment advisory services.
Business type (SIC): Insurance/life; security and commodity services
Corporate officers: Bill Warner, Chair.; David E. Sutton, Vice-Chair.; Kevin A. Marti, Pres. and C.E.O.; Jeffrey S. Patterson, Sr. V.P., Secy.-Treas., and C.F.O.; Daniel L. Gordon, V.P., Mktg.; Janet A. Goulart, V.P., Human Resources; Frank Dick, Chair. Emeritus
Board of directors: Bill Warner, Chair.; David E. Sutton, Vice-Chair.; Richard J. Bennett; Dudley L. Dauterman; Frank Dick; Terry L. Garner; Suann D. Hammersmith; Mark A. Wills
Giving statement: Giving through the Gleaner Life Insurance Society Corporate Giving Program and the Gleaner Life Insurance Society Scholarship Foundation.

Gleaner Life Insurance Society Corporate Giving Program

5200 W. U.S. Hwy. 223
Adrian, MI 49221-9461
URL: http://www.gleanerlife.org/Home.aspx?aud=Member

Purpose and activities: As a complement to its foundation, Gleaner Life Insurance Society also makes charitable contributions to nonprofit organizations directly. Support is given primarily in areas of company operations in Arizona, Florida, Iowa, Illinois, Indiana, Kansas, Kentucky, Michigan, Missouri, Nebraska, Ohio, Tennessee, and Virginia.
Fields of interest: Youth development; Human services, emergency aid; Human services.
Type of support: Employee volunteer services.
Geographic limitations: Giving primarily in areas of company operations in AZ, FL, IA, IL, IN, KS, KY, MI, MO, NE, OH, TN, and VA.

Gleaner Life Insurance Society Scholarship Foundation

5200 W. U.S. Hwy. 223
Adrian, MI 49221-9461 (517) 263-2244
FAX: (517) 265-7745;
E-mail: scholarships@gleanerlife.org; Additional tel.: (800) 992-1894; URL: http://www.gleanerlife.org/PreviewNewsMore.aspx?NewsArticleID=352

Establishment information: Established as a company-sponsored operating foundation in 1992 in MI.
Donors: Gleaner Life Insurance Society; Laura Viers; Charles E. Banner†; Margaret Banner; Frank Dick.
Financial data (yr. ended 06/30/12): Assets, $737,684 (M); gifts received, $115,884; expenditures, $50,993; qualifying distributions, $50,589; giving activities include $48,489 for 4 grants to individuals (high: $41,000; low: $1,000).
Purpose and activities: The foundation awards college scholarships to high school seniors or

graduates who are members of Gleaner Life Insurance Society.
Fields of interest: Higher education.
Type of support: Scholarships—to individuals.
Geographic limitations: Giving primarily in IN, MI, NE, and OH.
Publications: Application guidelines; Informational brochure.
Application information: Applications accepted. Application form required.
Applications should include official transcripts, results of aptitude tests, and 3 letters of recommendation.
Initial approach: Download application form and mail to foundation
Deadline(s): Mar. 1st
Officers: Bill B. Warner, Chair.; Kevin Marti, Pres. and Secy-Treas.
Directors: Richard J. Bennett; Dudley Dauterman; Frank Dick; Terry Garner; Suann A. Hammersmith; Bill B. Warner; Mark A. Wills.
EIN: 383006741

1591
Gleason Corporation

1000 University Ave.
P.O. Box 22970
Rochester, NY 14692-2970 (585) 473-1000

Company URL: http://www.gleason.com
Establishment information: Established in 1865.
Company type: Private company
Business activities: Manufactures gearing technology equipment.
Business type (SIC): Machinery/metalworking
Corporate officers: James S. Gleason, Chair.; John J. Perrotti, Pres. and C.E.O.; Edward J. Pelta, V.P., Genl. Counsel, and Secy.; John W. Pysnack, V.P., Finance, and Treas.; Udo Stolz, V.P., Sales and Mktg.; Brian M. Perry, V.P., Opers.; Nanci Malin-Peck, V.P., Corp. Human Resources
Board of directors: James S. Gleason, Chair.; Gerald R. Adamski; Thomas P. Courtney; Randall P. Terho
Subsidiary: Gleason Works, Rochester, NY
Plant: Troy, MI
International operations: Germany; India; Switzerland; United Kingdom
Giving statement: Giving through the Gleason Works Foundation, Inc.

Gleason Works Foundation, Inc.

P.O. Box 22970
Rochester, NY 14692-2970 (585) 256-8760

Donors: Gleason Corp.; Gleason Foundation.
Contact: Edward J. Pelta, Secy.-Treas.
Financial data (yr. ended 12/31/11): Assets, $145,203 (M); expenditures, $8,022; qualifying distributions, $7,000; giving activities include $7,000 for 5 grants (high: $4,000; low: $250).
Purpose and activities: The foundation supports service clubs and organizations involved with patient services, children and youth, and Protestantism.
Fields of interest: Human services; Religion.
Type of support: General/operating support.
Geographic limitations: Giving primarily in Rochester, NY.
Support limitations: No grants to individuals.
Application information: Applications accepted. Application form required. Applicants should submit the following:
1) detailed description of project and amount of funding requested
Initial approach: Letter
Deadline(s): None
Officers: John T. Perrotti, Pres.; John W. Pysnack, V.P.; Edward J. Pelta, Secy.-Treas.
EIN: 166023236

1592
Global Aviation Holdings Inc.

(formerly Global Aero Logistics, Inc.)
101 World Dr.
Peachtree City, GA 30269-6965
(770) 632-8000

Company URL: http://www.glah.com
Establishment information: Established in 1948.
Company type: Private company
Business activities: Provides passenger and cargo air charter transportation services.
Business type (SIC): Transportation/nonscheduled air
Financial profile for 2009: Number of employees, 2,130; assets, $679,530,000; sales volume, $1,042,580,000
Corporate officers: Robert R. Binns, Chair. and C.E.O.; Charles P. McDonald, Pres.; William A. Garrett, C.F.O.; Brian Gillman, Sr. V.P., Genl. Counsel, and Corp. Secy.
Board of director: Robert R. Binns, Chair.
Subsidiaries: North American Airlines, Inc., Jamaica, NY; World Airways, Inc., Peachtree City, GA
Giving statement: Giving through the Global Aviation Holdings Inc. Corporate Giving Program.

Global Aviation Holdings Inc. Corporate Giving Program

(formerly Global Aero Logistics Corporate Giving Program, Inc.)
101 World Dr.
Peachtree City, GA 30269-6965
FAX: (770) 632-8055; E-mail: sforsyth@glah.com

Contact: Steven E. Forsyth, Dir., Corp. Comms.
Financial data (yr. ended 12/31/10): Total giving, $208,400, including $77,800 for 28 grants (high: $10,400; low: $400), $30,600 for 200 employee matching gifts and $100,000 for 1 in-kind gift.
Purpose and activities: Global Aviation Holdings makes charitable contributions to nonprofit organizations involved with human services, international affairs, and military interests. Support is given on a national basis in areas of company operations, with emphasis on Fayette County, Georgia.
Fields of interest: Human services; Military/veterans' organizations.
International interests: Afghanistan.
Type of support: Annual campaigns; Continuing support; Emergency funds; Employee volunteer services; General/operating support.
Geographic limitations: Giving on a national basis in areas of company operations, with emphasis on Fayette County, GA.
Support limitations: No support for political organizations.
Application information: Applications not accepted. The Corporate Communications Department handles giving.
Number of staff: 1 full-time professional.
Selected grants: The following grants are a representative sample of this grantmaker's funding activity:
$12,500 to American Cancer Society, Atlanta, GA, 2010.
$12,000 to Fayette Fund, Atlanta, GA, 2010.
$9,000 to Humana People to People in South Africa, Johannesburg, South Africa, 2010. For Childrens Town in Caxito, Angola.
$6,500 to Great Georgia Airshow, Peachtree City, GA, 2010.
$5,000 to Carter Center, Atlanta, GA, 2010.
$2,000 to Alzheimers Association National Headquarters, Chicago, IL, 2010.
$2,000 to American Red Cross National Headquarters, Washington, DC, 2010.
$2,000 to Fayette County Education Foundation, Peachtree City, GA, 2010.
$1,600 to Boy Scouts of America, Atlanta Area Council, Atlanta, GA, 2010.
$1,200 to United Service Organization Council of Georgia, Atlanta, GA, 2010.
$400 to American Legion Boys State, GA, 2010.

1593
Global Partners LP

(formerly Global Petroleum Corporation)
800 S. St., Ste. 200
P.O. Box 9161
Waltham, MA 02454-9161 (781) 894-8800
FAX: (302) 636-5454

Company URL: http://www.globalp.com/
Establishment information: Established in 1933.
Company type: Public company
Company ticker symbol and exchange: GLP/NYSE
Business activities: Manufactures fuel oil; distributes natural gas.
Business type (SIC): Gas production and distribution; petroleum and petroleum products—wholesale
Financial profile for 2012: Number of employees, 788; assets, $2,329,750,000; sales volume, $17,626,000,000; pre-tax net income, $48,320,000; expenses, $17,541,410,000; liabilities, $1,893,290,000
Fortune 1000 ranking: 2012—157th in revenues, 829th in profits, and 818th in assets
Corporate officers: Alfred A. Slifka, Chair.; Richard Slifka, Vice-Chair.; Eric Slifka, Pres. and C.E.O.; Thomas J. Hollister, C.O.O. and C.F.O.; Charles A. Rudinsky, Exec. V.P. and C.A.O.; Edward J. Faneuil, Exec. V.P., Genl. Counsel, and Secy.
Board of directors: Alfred A. Slifka, Chair.; Richard Slifka, Vice-Chair.; Thomas J. Hollister; Robert J. McCool; David K. McKown; Andrew Slifka; Eric Slifka; Kenneth I. Watchmaker
Giving statement: Giving through the First Petroleum Corporation Charitable Trust.
Company EIN: 743140887

First Petroleum Corporation Charitable Trust

800 South St.
P.O. Box 9161
Waltham, MA 02453-1478
Application address: 776 Boylston St, Boston, MA 02199

Establishment information: Established in 1986 in MA.
Donor: Global Petroleum Corp.
Contact: Richard Slifka, Tr.
Financial data (yr. ended 12/31/10): Assets, $23,324 (M); expenditures, $2; qualifying distributions, $0.
Purpose and activities: The foundation supports art museums and hospitals and organizations involved with multiple sclerosis, homelessness, and Judaism.

Fields of interest: Museums (art); Hospitals (general); Multiple sclerosis; Homeless, human services; Jewish agencies & synagogues.
Type of support: General/operating support; Program development.
Geographic limitations: Giving primarily in MA and NY.
Application information: Application form not required.
Deadline(s): None
Trustees: Alfred A. Slifka; Richard Slifka.
EIN: 046549918

1594
Globe Newspaper Company, Inc.

135 Morrissey Blvd.
P.O. Box 55819
Boston, MA 02205-5819

Company URL: http://www.boston.com/globe
Establishment information: Established in 1872.
Company type: Private company
Business activities: Publishes newspapers, specialty books, and magazines.
Business type (SIC): Newspaper publishing and/or printing; periodical publishing and/or printing
Corporate officers: Benjamin B. Taylor, Chair.; Christopher Mayer, C.E.O.; Alfred S. Larkin, Jr., Sr. V.P., Human Resources
Board of director: Benjamin B. Taylor, Chair.
Subsidiaries: The Boston Globe, Boston, MA; Community Newsdealers, Inc., Waltham, MA; Wilson Tisdale Co., Boston, MA
Giving statement: Giving through the Boston Globe Foundation, Inc.

The Boston Globe Foundation, Inc.

135 Morrissey Blvd.
Boston, MA 02125-3310 (617) 929-2092
E-mail: foundation@globe.com

Establishment information: Incorporated in 1982 in MA.
Contact: Leah P. Bailey
Financial data (yr. ended 12/31/11): Revenue, $1,303,096; assets, $1,837,052 (M); gifts received, $1,274,705; expenditures, $1,278,621; program services expenses, $1,253,704; giving activities include $1,081,952 for grants to individuals.
Purpose and activities: The foundation assists the next generation of youth to become educated, employable, and responsible citizens; and supports programs that build youth leadership, support education, and forge friendships across racial, cultural, and neighborhood boundaries.
Fields of interest: Education; Youth, services; Family services Disabilities, people with; Minorities; Women; Economically disadvantaged; LGBTQ.
Programs:
Boston Globe Scholars Program: Each year, the foundation makes it possible for several graduates of public high schools in Boston, Massachusetts, to attend the University of Massachusetts, Boston. The students are part of a Learning Community of Globe Scholars that provides direct support and guidance to the students, many of whom are the first generation in their families to attend college. Through the program, the students receive support and guidance from the Globe Scholars Coordinator, and they have access to special programs, events, and activities as a group, including field trips, programs at the Globe, and an annual Globe Scholars Reception held at the Globe recognizing the graduates of the program.
Neighbor to Neighbor Initiative: The initiative targets organizations whose primary service area is Dorchester, Massachusetts. Nonprofits are selected that are doing exceptional work addressing community needs in this area. Grants range from $2,000 to $15,000.
Type of support: General/operating support; Matching/challenge support; Scholarships—to individuals; Seed money; Technical assistance.
Geographic limitations: Giving primarily in the greater Boston, MA area.
Support limitations: No support for religious institutions for sectarian causes. No grants to individuals (except for scholarships), or for the purchase of advertisements or tables.
Publications: Informational brochure.
Application information: Applications not accepted. Unsolicited requests for funds not considered or acknowledged.
Board meeting date(s): Biannually
Officers and Director:* Christopher M. Mayer*, Chair. and Pres.; James F. Follo*, V.P., Finance; Christopher Pircio*, Treas.; Diane McNulty.
Number of staff: 1 full-time professional; 1 part-time support.
EIN: 042731195

1595
The Go Daddy Group, Inc.

14455 N. Hayden Rd., Ste. 226
Scottsdale, AZ 85260-6947
(480) 505-8800

Company URL: http://www.godaddy.com
Establishment information: Established in 1997.
Company type: Private company
Business activities: Operates domain name registrar and related services group of companies.
Business type (SIC): Computer services
Corporate officers: Robert R. Parsons, Chair.; Blake Irving, C.E.O.; Michael J. Zimmerman, Exec. V.P. and C.F.O.; Ronald Hertz, V.P. and Corp. Cont.; Nima Kelly, Genl. Counsel
Board of director: Robert R. Parsons, Chair.
Giving statement: Giving through the Go Daddy Group, Inc. Corporate Giving Program.

The Go Daddy Group, Inc. Corporate Giving Program

(also known as Go Daddy Cares)
14455 N. Hayden Rd., Ste. 219
Scottsdale, AZ 85260-6947 (480) 505-8800
URL: https://www.godaddy.com/gdshop/gd_charity.asp

Purpose and activities: Go Daddy makes charitable contributions to nonprofit organizations involved with domestic violence, child abuse, and animal welfare. Support is given primarily in areas of company operations, with emphasis on Phoenix, Arizona.
Fields of interest: Animal welfare; Health care; Disasters, preparedness/services; Human services; Children/youth, services; Family services, domestic violence.
Type of support: General/operating support.
Geographic limitations: Giving primarily in areas of company operations, with emphasis on Phoenix, AZ; giving also to national organizations.
Publications: Application guidelines.
Application information: Applications accepted. Application form required.
Initial approach: Complete online application

1596
Godfrey & Kahn, S.C.

780 N. Water St.
Milwaukee, WI 53202-3512
(414) 273-3500

Company URL: http://www.gklaw.com/index.cfm
Establishment information: Established in 1957.
Company type: Private company
Business activities: Operates law firm.
Business type (SIC): Legal services
Offices: Washington, DC; Appleton, Green Bay, Madison, Milwaukee, Waukesha, WI
Giving statement: Giving through the Godfrey & Kahn, S.C. Pro Bono Program.

Godfrey & Kahn, S.C. Pro Bono Program

780 N. Water St.
Milwaukee, WI 53202-3512 (414) 273-3500
E-mail: sbosack@gklaw.com; URL: http://www.gklaw.com/about.cfm?action=pro_bono

Contact: Sean O. Bosack, Shareholder
Fields of interest: Legal services.
Type of support: Pro bono services - legal.
Geographic limitations: Giving primarily in areas of company operations in Washington, DC, and in Appleton, Green Bay, Madison, Milwaukee, Waukesha, WI.
Application information: A Pro Bono Committee manages the pro bono program.

1597
Godiva Chocolatier, Inc.

355 Lexington Ave., 16th Fl.
New York, NY 10017 (212) 984-5901

Company URL: http://www.godiva.com
Establishment information: Established in 1926.
Company type: Subsidiary of a foreign company
Business activities: Operates chocolate products company.
Business type (SIC): Sugar, candy, and salted/roasted nut production
Corporate officer: James Goldman, Pres. and C.E.O.
Giving statement: Giving through the Godiva Chocolatier, Inc. Contributions Program.

Godiva Chocolatier, Inc. Contributions Program

355 Lexington Ave., 16th Fl.
New York, NY 10017 (212) 984-5900
URL: http://www.godiva.com

1598
Gold, Inc.

(also known as Goldbug)
18245 E. 40th Ave.
Aurora, CO 80011-0805 (303) 371-2535

Company URL: http://www.goldbug.com
Establishment information: Established in 1968.
Company type: Private company
Business activities: Manufactures children's footwear and accessories.
Business type (SIC): Leather footwear
Corporate officers: Katherine Gold, Co-Pres.; Will Gold, Co-Pres.
Giving statement: Giving through the Gold Family Foundation.

The Gold Family Foundation

18245 E. 40th Ave.
Aurora, CO 80011-0805 (303) 371-2535

Establishment information: Established in 1992 in CO.
Donors: Gold, Inc.; William Gold II.
Contact: William Gold III, Treas.
Financial data (yr. ended 06/30/12): Assets, $1,004,141 (M); gifts received, $100,000; expenditures, $55,802; qualifying distributions, $44,400; giving activities include $44,400 for grants.
Purpose and activities: The foundation supports science museums and organizations involved with education, health, cystic fibrosis, and children's services.
Fields of interest: Health care; Civil/human rights; Religion.
Type of support: General/operating support.
Geographic limitations: Giving primarily in CO.
Application information: Applications accepted. Application form required. Applicants should submit the following:
1) copy of IRS Determination Letter
2) detailed description of project and amount of funding requested
Initial approach: Letter
Deadline(s): None
Officers: William Gold II, Pres.; Elizabeth Gold Duggal, V.P.; Bei-Lee Gold, V.P.; Katherine Gold, Secy.; William Gold III, Treas.
EIN: 850418759

1599
Goldberg Kohn Ltd.

55 E. Monroe St., Ste. 3300
Chicago, IL 60603-5792 (312) 201-3938

Company URL: http://www.goldbergkohn.com/
Company type: Private company
Business activities: Operates law firm.
Business type (SIC): Legal services
Corporate officer: Wendy L. Schlossberg, Cont.
Giving statement: Giving through the Goldberg Kohn Ltd. Pro Bono Program.

Goldberg Kohn Ltd. Pro Bono Program

55 E. Monroe St., Ste. 3300
Chicago, IL 60603-5792 (312) 201-3981
E-mail: roger.lewis@goldbergkohn.com; Additional tel.: (312) 201-4000; URL: http://www.goldbergkohn.com/about-probono.html

Contact: Roger A. Lewis, Principal
Fields of interest: Legal services.
Type of support: Pro bono services - legal.
Geographic limitations: Giving primarily in areas of company operations in Chicago, IL.

1600
GOLDEN Artist Colors, Inc.

188 Bell Rd.
New Berlin, NY 13411-9527
(607) 847-6154

Company URL: http://www.goldenpaints.com
Establishment information: Established in 1980.
Company type: Private company
Business activities: Manufactures and provides art supplies and services.
Business type (SIC): Pens, pencils, and art supplies
Corporate officers: Mark Golden, Chair. and C.E.O.; Barbara J. Schindler, Pres. and C.O.O.; James E. Henderson, C.F.O.
Board of director: Mark Golden, Chair.
Giving statement: Giving through the Sam and Adele Golden Foundation for the Arts.

Sam and Adele Golden Foundation for the Arts

237 Bell Rd.
New Berlin, NY 13411-3616
E-mail: contact@goldenfoundation.org; URL: http://www.goldenfoundation.org

Establishment information: Established in 1997 in NY.
Donors: GOLDEN Artist Colors, Inc.; Mark Golden; Barbara Golden; Anna Marshall.
Financial data (yr. ended 12/31/11): Assets, $1,974,689 (M); gifts received, $258,762; expenditures, $38,597; qualifying distributions, $538,907.
Purpose and activities: The foundation supports programs designed to serve visual artists working in paint and awards fellowships to professional visual artists working in paint.
Fields of interest: Visual arts, painting.
Program:
The Exploratory Residency: The foundation awards artist residencies to assist the professional visual artist in discovering the innovative use of new materials and technologies. Residencies are four weeks in length and includes a range of acrylic and oil paints and mediums, custom and experimental acrylic products, an introduction to the Golden Artist Colors laboratories and manufacturing facilities, consultations with paint technicians, 24/7 access to open studio space, and a private apartment.
Type of support: Fellowships; Grants to individuals.
Geographic limitations: Giving primarily in Sausalito, CA, New Smyrna Beach, FL, Omaha, NE, NY, and Johnson, VT.
Support limitations: No grants to commercial artists or students, or for academic study or travel expenses, photography or installations, or projects ordered by others.
Application information: Applications not accepted. Unsolicited requests for funds not accepted.
Officers: Mark Golden, Pres.; Thomas Golden, V.P.; Barbara Golden, Secy.-Treas.
Number of staff: 1 part-time professional.
EIN: 161523983

1601
Golden Enterprises, Inc.

1 Golden Flake Dr.
Birmingham, AL 35205 (205) 458-7316
FAX: (302) 655-5049

Company URL: http://www.goldenflake.com
Establishment information: Established in 1946.
Company type: Public company
Company ticker symbol and exchange: GLDC/NASDAQ
Business activities: Produces and distributes salted snack items; sells cakes and cookie items, canned dips, pretzels, peanut butter crackers, cheese crackers, dried meat products, and nuts wholesale.
Business type (SIC): Miscellaneous prepared foods; groceries—wholesale
Financial profile for 2012: Number of employees, 795; assets, $48,750,000; sales volume, $136,190,000; pre-tax net income, $3,950,000; expenses, $132,230,000; liabilities, $24,360,000
Corporate officers: Mark W. McCutcheon, Chair., Pres., and C.E.O.; David A. Jones, Exec. V.P., Opers. and Human Resources; Paul R. Bates, Exec. V.P., Sales and Mktg.; Patty Townsend, V.P., C.F.O., and Secy.
Board of directors: Mark W. McCutcheon, Chair.; Joann F. Bashinsky; Paul Bates; David Jones; John P. McKleroy, Jr.; William B. Morton, Jr.; J. Wallace Nall, Jr.; Edward R. Pascoe; F. Wayne Pate; John S. P. Samford; John S. Stein III
Giving statement: Giving through the Bashinsky Foundation, Inc.
Company EIN: 630250005

Bashinsky Foundation, Inc.

3432 E. Briarcliff Rd.
Birmingham, AL 35223-1309 (205) 326-0402
Application address: UAB Office of Student Financial Aid, Joann Bashinsky Scholarship, HUC 17, 1530 3rd Ave. S, Birmingham, AL 35294-1150

Establishment information: Established in 1988 in AL.
Donors: SYB, Inc.; Joann Bashinsky; Sloan Y. Bashinsky, Sr.
Financial data (yr. ended 12/31/11): Assets, $9,336,786 (M); gifts received, $100,000; expenditures, $561,720; qualifying distributions, $501,611; giving activities include $501,611 for 8 grants (high: $150,000; low: $2,500).
Purpose and activities: The foundation supports hospitals and organizations involved with education and equestrianism; and awards scholarships to children of employees of Golden Flakes and to students attending the University of Alabama.
Fields of interest: Elementary/secondary education; Higher education; Education; Hospitals (general); Athletics/sports, equestrianism.
Programs:
Employee-Related Scholarships: The foundation awards college scholarships to dependents of employees of Golden Enterprises, Inc. and Golden Flake Snack Foods, Inc. The program is administered by Scholarship America, Inc.
Joann F. Bashinsky Scholarship: The foundation awards scholarships to students who are currently enrolled in or admitted to a degree granting program at the University of Alabama. Applicants must demonstrate solid academic progress and achievement.
Type of support: Employee-related scholarships; General/operating support; Scholarships—to individuals.
Geographic limitations: Giving primarily in AL.

Support limitations: No grants to individuals (except for employee-related scholarships).
Application information: Applications accepted. Application form required.
Scholarship applications should include a one page essay outlining career goals and why the applicant has chosen a particular field; and 2 letters of recommendation.
Initial approach: Contact the University of Alabama for application form for Joann F. Bashinsky Scholarships
Deadline(s): Varies for Joann F. Bashinsky Scholarships
Officers: Joann Bashinsky, Chair. and C.E.O.; John S. Stein, Pres.; John P. McKleroy, Jr., Secy.
EIN: 630968201
Selected grants: The following grants are a representative sample of this grantmaker's funding activity:
$150,000 to Samford University, Birmingham, AL, 2010.
$150,000 to University of Alabama, Tuscaloosa, AL, 2010.
$100,000 to Saint Vincents Foundation, Birmingham, AL, 2010.
$62,000 to Big Oak Ranch, Springville, AL, 2010.

1602
Golden State Foods Corporation

18301 Von Karman Ave., Ste. 1100
Irvine, CA 92612-1009 (949) 252-2000
FAX: (949) 252-2080

Company URL: http://www.goldenstatefoods.com
Establishment information: Established in 1947.
Company type: Private company
Business activities: Produces and sells foodservice industry food products.
Business type (SIC): Groceries—wholesale
Financial profile for 2011: Number of employees, 4,000; sales volume, $4,600,000,000
Corporate officers: Mark S. Wetterau, Chair. and C.E.O.; Michael Waitukaitis, Vice-Chair.; Neil Cracknell, Exec. V.P. and C.O.O.; Bill Sanderson, Sr. V.P. and C.F.O.; Ken Wolinsky, C.I.O.; Steve Becker, Sr. V.P., Human Resources; John Page, V.P. and Genl. Counsel; Joe Heffington, V.P., Finance; Amy Zurborg, Group V.P., Sales and Mktg.; Shellie Frey, Corp. Comms.
Board of directors: Mark S. Wetterau, Chair.; Michael Waitukaitis, Vice-Chair.
Plants: Phoenix, AZ; City of Industry, CA; Conyers, GA; Waipahu, HI; Oak Brook, IL; Rochester, NY; Greensboro, NC; Lexington, SC; Suffolk, VA; Sumner, WA
Giving statement: Giving through the GSF Foundation.

GSF Foundation

18301 Von Karman Ave., Ste. 1100
Irvine, CA 92612-0133 (949) 252-2000
E-mail: HelpKids.Irvine@GSFFoundation.org; Additional tel.: (877) 473-5437; URL: http://www.gsffoundation.org

Establishment information: Established in 2002 in CA and OR.
Donors: Mark S. Wetterau; Golden State Foods Corp.; Mike Echolds; Leslie Echolds; Orange Wood Children's Fdn.
Financial data (yr. ended 12/31/11): Assets, $1,087,716 (M); gifts received, $3,390,854; expenditures, $4,323,085; qualifying distributions, $2,906,799; giving activities include $2,906,799 for grants.
Purpose and activities: The foundation supports programs designed to improve the lives of children and families. Special emphasis is directed toward programs designed to serve children with various needs, including food, shelter, clothes, medical treatment, and social activities.
Fields of interest: Arts; Education; Health care, patient services; Health care; Food services; Food banks; Housing/shelter; Big Brothers/Big Sisters; Boy scouts; Children, services; Family services; Developmentally disabled, centers & services.
Program:
Time Is Money: The foundation awards grants to nonprofit organizations with which employees of GSF volunteer.
Type of support: Building/renovation; Capital campaigns; Employee volunteer services; Equipment; General/operating support; Program development; Sponsorships.
Geographic limitations: Giving primarily in areas of company operations in AR, CA, GA, IL, MO, NC, NY, OR, SC, VA, WA, and WI.
Support limitations: No support for political organizations or candidates, religious, veterans', or fraternal organizations, or sports teams. No grants for individuals, or for sponsorships of fundraising events, tickets or tables, academic or medical research, political causes, sporting events, trips or travel, festivals or parades, or advertising.
Publications: Annual report; Application guidelines; Newsletter.
Application information: Applications accepted. Unsolicited applications must be nominated by a GSF associate who is currently employed. The associate must be personally affiliated with the organization he or she is nominating. Proposals should be submitted using organization letterhead. Support is limited to 1 contribution per organization during any given year. Faxed, e-mailed, or videotaped applications are not accepted. Application form required. Applicants should submit the following:
1) results expected from proposed grant
2) principal source of support for project in the past
3) copy of IRS Determination Letter
4) brief history of organization and description of its mission
5) copy of most recent annual report/audited financial statement/990
6) list of company employees involved with the organization
7) explanation of why grantmaker is considered an appropriate donor for project
8) descriptive literature about organization
9) listing of board of directors, trustees, officers and other key people and their affiliations
10) detailed description of project and amount of funding requested
11) copy of current year's organizational budget and/or project budget
12) listing of additional sources and amount of support
Initial approach: Download application form and mail proposal and application form to nearest company facility
Deadline(s): None; 60 days prior to need for project grants
Final notification: 30 days
Officers and Directors:* Mark S. Wetterau*, Chair. and C.E.O.; Catherine Duffy, Secy.; Michael Waitukaitis*, Treas. and C.F.O.; Chuck Browne*, Exec. Dir.; Steve Becker; Bob Jorge; Frank Listi; Glenn Parish.
EIN: 460501728
Selected grants: The following grants are a representative sample of this grantmaker's funding activity:
$280,000 to Orangewood Childrens Foundation, Santa Ana, CA, 2010. For general support.
$137,780 to Boy Scouts of America, Los Angeles, CA, 2010. For general support.
$33,745 to Shoes That Fit, Claremont, CA, 2010. For general support.
$25,000 to Foundation for the Children of the Californias, San Diego, CA, 2010. For general support.
$13,908 to Operation Warm, Chadds Ford, PA, 2010. For general support.
$10,200 to Citrus Valley Health Foundation, West Covina, CA, 2010. For general support.
$6,000 to Hillview Acres Childrens Home, Chino, CA, 2010. For general support.
$5,000 to Boys Haven, Louisville, KY, 2010. For general support.
$5,000 to Serving People in Need, Costa Mesa, CA, 2010. For general support.
$2,500 to East Los Angeles Community Youth Center, Los Angeles, CA, 2010. For general support.

1603
The Goldman Sachs Group, Inc.

200 W. St., 29th Fl.
New York, NY 10282 (212) 902-0300
FAX: (312) 655-4458

Company URL: http://www.goldmansachs.com
Establishment information: Established in 1869.
Company type: Public company
Company ticker symbol and exchange: GS/NYSE
Business activities: Operates bank holding company.
Business type (SIC): Holding company; brokers and dealers/security; security and commodity services
Financial profile for 2012: Number of employees, 32,400; assets, $938,600,000,000; sales volume, $41,700,000,000; pre-tax net income, $11,207,000,000; expenses, $30,457,000,000; liabilities, $862,839,000,000
Fortune 1000 ranking: 2012—68th in revenues, 24th in profits, and 7th in assets
Forbes 2000 ranking: 2012—220th in sales, 59th in profits, and 28th in assets
Corporate officers: Lloyd C. Blankfein, Chair. and C.E.O.; Michael S. Sherwood, Co-Vice-Chair.; John S. Weinberg, Co-Vice-Chair.; Gary D. Cohn, Pres. and C.O.O.; Harvey M. Schwartz, Exec. V.P. and C.F.O.; Gregory K. Palm, Exec. V.P., Genl. Counsel, and Secy.
Board of directors: Lloyd C. Blankfein, Chair.; Michael S. Sherwood, Co-Vice-Chair.; John S. Weinberg, Co-Vice-Chair.; M. Michael Burns; Gary D. Cohn; Claes Dahlback; Stephen Friedman; William W. George; James A. Johnson; Lakshmi N. Mittal; Adebayo O. Ogunlesi; James J. Schiro; Debora L. Spar; Mark Edward Tucker
Subsidiaries: BPC Holding Corporation, Evansville, IN; Goldman, Sachs & Co., New York, NY; Kerr Group, Inc., Lancaster, PA
International operations: British Virgin Islands; Cayman Islands; Germany; Hong Kong; Ireland; Mauritius
Giving statement: Giving through the Goldman Sachs Group, Inc. Corporate Giving Program, the Goldman Sachs Charitable Gift Fund, and the Goldman Sachs Philanthropy Fund.
Company EIN: 134019460

The Goldman Sachs Group, Inc. Corporate Giving Program

200 West St., 29th Fl.
New York, NY 10282-2198 (212) 902-0300

Purpose and activities: As a complement to its foundation, Goldman Sachs matches charitable contributions of its employees to nonprofit organizations.
Fields of interest: General charitable giving.
Programs:
10,000 Women: Goldman Sachs provides women in developing countries and targeted areas in developed countries access to business and management education to reduce inequality and to ensure shared economic growth. The program is designed to serve 10,000 women over five years with business and management education; build quality and capacity through global business sister school partnerships; establish mentoring and post-graduation support for women entrepreneurs; work with leading research and women's development organizations; develop partnerships in the United States to help disadvantaged women; and commit the time and dedication of Goldman Sachs people.
Employee Matching Gifts: Goldman Sachs matches contributions made by its employees to colleges and universities, public and private elementary and secondary schools, civic, arts, and culture organizations, health and human service agencies, and environmental organizations on a one-for-one basis up to $20,000 per employee, per year.
The Capacity Building Initiative: Goldman Sachs helps nonprofit organizations increase their impact through capacity building assistance, with emphasis on leadership development, strategic planning, financial management, and technology. Goldman Sachs supports the Capacity Building Initiative Academy where organizations in Chicago, New York, and London receive educational support through organizational assessments and workshops; and the Capacity Building Initiative Grant Program where select organizations receive funding to support the infrastructure and development of their organization.
Type of support: Employee matching gifts.
Geographic limitations: Giving primarily in areas of company operations.
Application information: Applications not accepted. Contributes only through employee matching gifts.

The Goldman Sachs Charitable Gift Fund

(also known as Goldman Sachs Gives)
200 West St., 29th Fl.
New York, NY 10282-2198 (212) 902-4223
URL: http://www.goldmansachs.com/citizenship/index.html

Establishment information: Established in 2007 in DE by Goldman Sachs Group, Inc.
Donor: Goldman Sachs Group, Inc.
Financial data (yr. ended 06/30/11): Revenue, $278,004,921; assets, $474,516,118 (M); gifts received, $275,210,431; expenditures, $222,262,124; giving activities include $210,665,640 for grants.
Purpose and activities: The fund is organized and operated to exclusively encourage and promote philanthropy and charitable giving.
Fields of interest: General charitable giving.
Geographic limitations: Giving on a national and international basis.
Officers: John F.W. Rogers*, Chair.; Dina H. Powell*, Pres.; Kim K. Azzarelli*, V.P.; Russel A. Broome*, V.P.; Nancy D. Browne*, V.P.; Steven M. Bunson*, V.P.; Michael J. Civitella*, V.P.; Richard M. Cundiff*, V.P.; Eileen M. Dillon*, V.P.; Beverly L. O'Toole*, Secy.; Emmett C. St. John*, Treas.
Directors: Peter M. Fahey; Lawton Fitt; Robert J. Katz; Muneer A. Satter; Benjamin J. Rader.
EIN: 113813663

Goldman Sachs Philanthropy Fund

25 British American Blvd.
Latham, NY 12110-1405 (212) 357-1889
FAX: (518) 640-5548;
E-mail: gspf-administration@gs.com; Mailing address: P.O. Box 15203, Albany, NY 12212-5203; toll-free tel.: (800) 787-3000; URL: https://gspf.goldman.com/gspf/ContactUs/tabid/112/Default.aspx

Establishment information: Established in 2001 in NY.
Contact: Karey D. Dye
Financial data (yr. ended 12/31/11): Revenue, $175,980,409; assets, $426,562,541 (M); gifts received, $172,604,510; expenditures, $97,850,267; program services expenses, $97,109,615; giving activities include $96,701,615 for 818 grants (high: $16,800,000; low: $5,250).
Purpose and activities: The fund encourages and promotes philanthropy and charitable giving.
Fields of interest: General charitable giving.
Geographic limitations: Giving on a national basis.
Officers: Karey D. Dye*, Pres.; Gretchen Clayton*, V.P.; Donald Irons*, V.P.; Kathleen Kinne*, V.P.
EIN: 311774905

1604
Goldman, Sachs & Co.

200 West St.
New York, NY 10282 (212) 902-1000

Company URL: http://www.goldmansachs.com
Establishment information: Established in 1869.
Company type: Subsidiary of a public company
International Securities Identification Number: US38141G1040
Business activities: Operates bank holding company.
Business type (SIC): Holding company
Financial profile for 2009: Number of employees, 19,476
Corporate officers: Lloyd C. Blankfein, Chair. and C.E.O.; John S. Weinberg, Vice-Chair.; Michael S. Sherwood, Vice-Chair.; Gary D. Cohn, Pres. and C.O.O.; David A. Viniar, Exec. V.P. and C.F.O.; Gregory K. Palm, Exec. V.P., Genl. Counsel, and Secy.
Board of directors: Lloyd C. Blankfein, Chair.; M. Michele Burns; Gary D. Cohn; Claes Dahlback; Stephen Friedman; William W. George; James A. Johnson; Lakshmi N. Mittal; Adebayo O. Ogunlesi; Debora L. Spar; Mark Edward Tucker
Giving statement: Giving through the Goldman Sachs Foundation.

The Goldman Sachs Foundation

(formerly Goldman Sachs Charitable Fund)
200 West St., 29th Fl.
New York, NY 10282-2198 (212) 902-3246
E-mail: gsfoundation@gs.com; E-mail for 10,000 Small Businesses: 10000SmallBusinesses@gs.com; URL: http://www.goldmansachs.com/citizenship/index.html

Establishment information: Established in 1999 in NY.
Donors: Goldman, Sachs & Co.; MTGLQ Investors, L.P.; Goldman Sachs Group, Inc.
Contact: Brenda Lee, Grants Admin.
Financial data (yr. ended 12/31/11): Assets, $560,669,732 (M); gifts received, $25,242,000; expenditures, $33,966,908; qualifying distributions, $30,822,580; giving activities include $29,237,825 for 97 grants (high: $1,287,196; low: $3,483).
Purpose and activities: The foundation supports strategic programs that include 10,000 Women and 10,000 Small Businesses.
Fields of interest: Education; Community development, small businesses; Community/economic development.
International interests: Africa; Asia; Europe; Middle East; United Kingdom.
Programs:
10,000 Small Businesses: Through 10,000 Small Businesses, the foundation provides underserved small business owners in the United States with access to capital, business education mentors, and networks. The program is designed to help local businesses create new jobs and achieve real growth. The foundation awards grants to community colleges, universities, and community and business development organizations.
10,000 Women: Through the 10,000 Women initiative, the foundation fosters shared economic growth by providing 10,000 underserved women around the world with business and management education. The foundation awards grants to business schools and universities in the United States, Europe, business schools in developing and emerging economies, and research and development organizations.
Type of support: Continuing support; Program development.
Geographic limitations: Giving on a national and international basis primarily in areas of company operations in Asia, Africa, the Middle East, and the United Kingdom.
Support limitations: No support for political causes, campaigns, or candidates. No grants for political fundraising events.
Publications: Informational brochure.
Application information: Applications not accepted. Contributes only to pre-selected organizations and individuals.
Officers and Directors:* John F.W. Rogers*, Chair.; Dina H. Powell, Pres.; Peter M. Fahey*, V.P.; Robert J. Katz*, V.P.; Eileen M. Dillion; Lisa D. Hancock; Katherine Jollon; Matthew LoCurto; Noa Meyer; Beverly L. O'Toole; Benjamin J. Radar; Emmett St. John.
EIN: 311678646
Selected grants: The following grants are a representative sample of this grantmaker's funding activity:
$2,435,746 to Babson College, Babson Park, MA, 2010. To develop, implement and deliver the 10,000 Small Businesses curriculum nationally and to train faculty across the initiative.
$2,000,000 to World Trade Center Memorial Foundation, New York, NY, 2010. To support the construction of a Memorial and Memorial Museum at Ground Zero.
$1,761,253 to LaGuardia Community College of the City University of New York, Long Island City, NY, 2010. For the 10,000 Small Businesses initiative in the greater New York area.
$1,074,184 to Indian School of Business, Hyderabad, India, 2010. For the 10,000 Women Certificate Program for Women Entrepreneurs in India.
$930,567 to Yale University, School of Public Health, New Haven, CT, 2010. For the 10,000 Women Yale-Tsinghua Certificate Program in collaboration with Tsinghua University in China.

$915,479 to Oxford University, Oxford, England, 2010. For the 10,000 Women Entrepreneurship Certificate Program in collaboration with the Global Entrepreneurship Research Center, Zhejiang University in China.
$708,977 to Initiative for a Competitive Inner-City, Boston, MA, 2010. To manage the participant recruitment and selection process nationally.
$392,780 to TechnoServe, Washington, DC, 2010. To enhance business support services in India, China and Brazil.
$375,000 to Delgado Community College Foundation, New Orleans, LA, 2010. For the 10,000 Small Businesses initiative in the New Orleans area.
$120,000 to Center for Global Development, Washington, DC, 2010. To produce a background paper on access to financing for small- and medium-sized enterprises (SME).

1605
The Goldmark Group, Inc.

1155 Bloomfield Ave.
Clifton, NJ 07012 (973) 777-5720
FAX: (973) 777-2390

Company URL: http://www.goldmarkgroup.com
Establishment information: Established in 1974.
Company type: Private company
Business activities: Provides graphic design services; provides commercial printing services.
Business type (SIC): Mailing, reproduction, commercial art, photography, and stenographic service; printing/commercial
Corporate officers: Eugene Markowitz, Pres. and C.E.O.; Joseph Goldbrenner, Secy.-Treas.; Jack Adler, Cont.
Giving statement: Giving through the Markowitz Family Foundation and the Nubren Charitable Foundation.

Markowitz Family Foundation

c/o Goldmark Group
1155 Bloomfield Ave.
Clifton, NJ 07012-2308

Establishment information: Established in 1999 in NY.
Donors: The Goldmark Group, Inc.; Eugene Markowitz; Mark Gold L.P.; Renee Markowitz.
Financial data (yr. ended 06/30/11): Assets, $189,835 (M); gifts received, $94,050; expenditures, $71,481; qualifying distributions, $71,481; giving activities include $44,093 for 25 grants (high: $18,000; low: $500).
Purpose and activities: The foundation supports organizations involved with Judaism.
Fields of interest: Religion.
Type of support: General/operating support.
Support limitations: No grants to individuals.
Application information: Applications not accepted. Unsolicited requests for funds not accepted.
EIN: 134035030

Nubren Charitable Foundation

c/o Goldmark Group
1155 Bloomfield Ave.
Clifton, NJ 07012-2308

Establishment information: Established in 1998 in NY.
Donors: Brenda Goldbrenner; Joseph Goldbrenner; The Goldmark Group, Inc.; Markgold, LP.
Financial data (yr. ended 06/30/12): Assets, $68,908 (M); gifts received, $75,000; expenditures, $35,140; qualifying distributions, $35,013; giving activities include $35,013 for 22 grants (high: $8,725; low: $250).
Purpose and activities: The foundation supports organizations involved with Judaism.
Fields of interest: Religion.
Type of support: General/operating support.
Geographic limitations: Giving primarily in NJ.
Support limitations: No grants to individuals.
Application information: Applications not accepted. Unsolicited requests for funds not accepted.
Trustees: Brenda Goldbrenner; Joseph Goldbrenner.
EIN: 134011269

1606
GoLite, LLC

6325 Gunpark Dr., Ste. 102
Boulder, CO 80301-3593 (303) 546-6000

Company URL: http://www.golite.com
Establishment information: Established in 1998.
Company type: Private company
Business activities: Produces light-weight clothing and equipment for active, outdoor sports.
Business type (SIC): Shopping goods stores/miscellaneous
Corporate officers: Kim Riether Coupounas, Chair.; Demetrios G. C. Coupounas, Pres.
Board of director: Kim Reither Coupounas, Chair.
Giving statement: Giving through the GoLite, LLC Corporate Giving Program.

GoLite, LLC Corporate Giving Program

6325 Gunpark Dr., Ste. 102
Boulder, CO 80301-3593 (303) 546-6000
URL: http://www.golite.com/Info/Meaning-Of-Lite/Giving-Back.aspx

Purpose and activities: GoLite is a certified B Corporation that donates a percentage of profits to nonprofit organizations. Support is given primarily in areas of company operations in Colorado; giving also to national organizations.
Fields of interest: Environment, natural resources; Environment, beautification programs; Environment; Transportation.
Type of support: Donated products; Employee volunteer services; General/operating support.
Geographic limitations: Giving primarily in areas of company operations in CO.

1607
Golub Corporation

(doing business as Price Chopper Supermarkets)
461 Nott St.
Schenectady, NY 12308 (518) 355-5000
FAX: (518) 356-9595

Company URL: http://www.pricechopper.com
Establishment information: Established in 1932.
Company type: Private company
Business activities: Operates grocery stores.
Business type (SIC): Groceries—retail; hardware, plumbing, and heating equipment—wholesale; gasoline service stations
Financial profile for 2011: Number of employees, 22,666; sales volume, $3,420,000,000
Corporate officers: Neil M. Golub, Chair. and C.E.O.; Jerel T. Golub, Pres. and C.O.O.; John J. Endres, Sr. V.P., Finance, C.F.O., and Treas.; Dick Bauer, Sr. V.P., Inf. Systems and C.I.O.; William J. Kenneally, Sr. V.P., Genl. Counsel and Secy.; David Golub, V.P., Admin.
Board of director: Neil M. Golub, Chair.
Subsidiaries: Cengo Construction Corp., Schenectady, NY; Central Distributors, Inc., Schenectady, NY; Golub Service Stations, Inc., Schenectady, NY; Price Chopper Operating Co., Inc., Schenectady, NY
Giving statement: Giving through the Price Chopper's Golub Foundation.

Price Chopper's Golub Foundation

(formerly Golub Foundation)
461 Nott St.
Schenectady, NY 12308-1812 (518) 356-9450
FAX: (518) 374-4259; Application address: P.O. Box 1074, Schenectady, NY 12301; Additional tel.: (877) 877-0870; URL: http://www.pricechopper.com/community/golub-foundation

Establishment information: Established in 1981 in NY.
Donors: Jane Golub; Neil M. Golub; Golub Corp.
Financial data (yr. ended 03/31/12): Assets, $174,794 (M); gifts received, $1,500,000; expenditures, $1,328,637; qualifying distributions, $1,253,742; giving activities include $1,253,742 for grants.
Purpose and activities: The foundation supports organizations involved with arts and culture, education, health, youth development, and human services and awards college scholarships to students located in areas of company operations.
Fields of interest: Museums; Arts; Higher education; Education; Hospitals (general); Health care; Youth development; YM/YWCAs & YM/YWHAs; Human services; United Ways and Federated Giving Programs Minorities.
Programs:

Charlie Pierce Memorial Scholarship: The foundation annually awards a four-year $2,000 college employee-related scholarship to a graduating high school senior who has demonstrated scholastic ability. The scholarship is limited to an active Price Chopper associate, children of employees of Price Chopper, and children of employees of Grocery Manufacturers' Representatives.

Computer Studies Scholarship: The foundation annually awards one $8,000 college scholarship to a graduating high school senior who has demonstrated scholastic ability and is planning to enter the computer sciences, computer information systems, electronic arts, or graphic design field.

Founder's Scholarships: The foundation annually awards two $8,000 college scholarships to graduating high school seniors who have demonstrated outstanding leadership and scholastic abilities.

Graduate or Professional School Scholarship: The foundation annually awards one $4,000 scholarship to a graduating college senior or college graduate who has demonstrated scholastic ability.

Junior College Transfer Scholarship: The foundation annually awards one $4,000 college scholarship to a graduating community or junior college student or community or junior college graduate who has demonstrated scholastic ability.

Lewis Golub Scholarship for Entrepreneurial Sprit: The foundation annually awards one $8,000 college scholarship to a graduating high school senior who has demonstrated scholastic ability and entrepreneurial sprit.

Lotte Meers Memorial Scholarship for Educators: The foundation annually awards one $8,000 college scholarship to a graduating high school senior who has demonstrated scholastic ability and has chosen to enter the field of education.

Tillie Golub-Schwartz Memorial Scholarship for Minorities: The foundation annually awards one $8,000 college scholarship to a minority graduating high school senior who has shown a commitment to humanity through demonstrated activities in school, community, or religious organizations.

Two-Year Health Care Scholarship: The foundation annually awards a $2,000 college scholarship to a graduating high school senior planning to study health care at a degree-granting community or junior college.

Two-Year Scholarship: The foundation annually awards a $2,000 college scholarship to a graduating high school senior planning to attend a degree-granting community or junior college.

Type of support: Annual campaigns; Building/renovation; Capital campaigns; Continuing support; Donated products; Employee matching gifts; General/operating support; Program development; Scholarship funds; Scholarships—to individuals; Sponsorships.

Geographic limitations: Giving limited to areas of company operations in CT, MA, NH, NY, PA, and VT.

Support limitations: No grants to individuals (except for scholarships), or for annual meetings, endowments, film or video projects, advertising, travel, conferences, conventions, or symposiums, publishing, or capital campaigns of national, religious, or political organizations.

Publications: Application guidelines; Informational brochure (including application guidelines).

Application information: Applications accepted. Proposals and letters of request should be submitted using organization letterhead. An application form is required for scholarships. A personal interview may be required for scholarships. Support is limited to 1 contribution per organization during any given year. Applicants should submit the following:

1) population served
2) name, address and phone number of organization
3) copy of IRS Determination Letter
4) geographic area to be served
5) detailed description of project and amount of funding requested
6) contact person
7) plans for acknowledgement

Initial approach: Proposal; complete online application for scholarships; letter of request to nearest store facility for product donations

Deadline(s): 6 to 8 weeks prior to need; Mar. 15 for scholarships; 4 to 5 weeks prior to need for product donations

Final notification: 3 to 4 months; Apr. 15 for scholarships

Trustees: Pamela Cerrone; Warren Cressman; Jane Golub; Wes Holloway; Heidi Reali.

EIN: 222341421

Selected grants: The following grants are a representative sample of this grantmaker's funding activity:

$250,000 to Breast Cancer Research Foundation, New York, NY, 2011.
$59,500 to United Way of the Greater Capital Region, Albany, NY, 2011.
$35,000 to YMCA of the Capital District, Albany, NY, 2011.
$25,000 to American Red Cross of Northeastern New York, Albany, NY, 2011.
$25,000 to Schenectady Light Opera Company, Schenectady, NY, 2011.
$11,550 to Muscular Dystrophy Association, Albany, NY, 2011.
$10,000 to College of Saint Rose, Albany, NY, 2011.
$10,000 to Saint Peters Hospital Foundation, Albany, NY, 2011.
$2,000 to Shakespeare and Company, Lenox, MA, 2011.
$1,500 to YMCA of the Capital District, Albany, NY, 2011.

1608
Gon-Rey, L.L.C.

230 N. Harbor Blvd.
Santa Ana, CA 92703-3337
(714) 265-9394

Establishment information: Established in 1994.
Company type: Private company
Business activities: Operates grocery stores.
Business type (SIC): Groceries—retail
Corporate officer: Oscar Gonzalez, Pres.
Giving statement: Giving through the Familia Gonzalez Reynoso Foundation.

Familia Gonzalez Reynoso Foundation

P.O. Box 1449
Anaheim, CA 92815-1449

Establishment information: Established in 2000 in CA.
Donors: Gon-Rey, LLC; Northgate Gonzalez, LLC.
Financial data (yr. ended 12/31/11): Assets, $140,671 (M); gifts received, $181,301; expenditures, $349,361; qualifying distributions, $89,958; giving activities include $41,100 for 9 grants (high: $30,000; low: $350) and $45,027 for 62 grants to individuals (high: $1,000; low: $291).
Purpose and activities: The foundation supports organizations involved with higher education, human services, and Latinos and awards scholarships and grants for funeral assistance to individuals.
Fields of interest: Higher education; Family services; Human services Hispanics/Latinos.
Type of support: General/operating support; Grants to individuals; Program development; Scholarships—to individuals.
Geographic limitations: Giving primarily in Santa Ana, CA and Mexico.
Application information: Applications not accepted. Contributes only to pre-selected organizations and individuals.
Officers and Directors:* Maria Teresa Reynoso*, Pres.; Oswaldo Gutierrez*, Secy.; Miguel Gonzalez Reynoso*, C.F.O.; Maria Teresa Alvarado; Ana Rosa Gonzalez; Francisco Gonzalez; Jose Jesus Gonzalez; Marco Antonio Gonzalez; Oscar Gonzalez; Ramon Gonzalez; Victor Manuel Gonzalez; Oscar Nunez; Maria Ester Ortiz; Hector Gonzalez Reynoso; Maria Teresa Reynoso; Miguel Gonzalez Reynoso; Richard E. Streza.
EIN: 330912834

1609
Sheldon Good & Company Auctions, LLC

488 Madison Ave., Ste. 201
New York, NY 10022 (212) 213-9770

Company URL: http://www.sheldongood.com
Establishment information: Established in 1965.
Company type: Private company
Business activities: Operates real estate auction firm; provides real estate brokerage, financial and consulting services.
Business type (SIC): Real estate agents and managers
Corporate officers: John J. Cuticelli, Jr., C.E.O.; Mark L. Troen, C.O.O.; Aaron S. Perl, M.D., Corp. Counsel; Carole Gulay, Compt.; Lauren Patton, Human Resources
Offices: San Francisco, CA; Chicago, IL; New York, NY
Giving statement: Giving through the Sheldon F. Good Family Foundation.

Sheldon F. Good Family Foundation

180 E. Pearson St., Ste. 7104
Chicago, IL 60611

Establishment information: Established in 1970.
Donors: Sheldon F. Good; Sheldon Good & Co. International, LLC.
Contact: Sheldon F. Good, Pres. and Treas.
Financial data (yr. ended 12/31/11): Assets, $12,677 (M); gifts received, $42,446; expenditures, $35,257; qualifying distributions, $34,690; giving activities include $34,690 for grants.
Purpose and activities: The foundation supports organizations involved with arts and culture, education, Alzheimer's disease, children and youth, and Judaism.
Fields of interest: Arts; Education; Health organizations.
Type of support: General/operating support; Scholarship funds.
Geographic limitations: Giving primarily in Palm Springs, CA and Chicago, IL.
Support limitations: No grants to individuals.
Application information: Applications accepted. Application form not required.

Initial approach: Letter
Deadline(s): None

Officers: Sheldon F. Good, Pres. and Treas.; Fern Stone, Secy.
Directors: Howard L. Stone; Susan Good.
EIN: 237072959

1610
I. B. Goodman Manufacturing Co., Inc.

120 E. 3rd St., Ste. B
Newport, KY 41071-1610 (859) 261-2086

Company URL: http://www.ibgoodman.com/company.php
Establishment information: Established in 1937.
Company type: Private company
Business activities: Manufactures jewelry.
Business type (SIC): Jewelry/precious metal
Financial profile for 2010: Number of employees, 65
Corporate officers: Babette Goodman Cohen, Chair.; Jonathan Goodman Cohen, Pres. and C.E.O.; Gregory Everett, C.F.O.
Board of director: Babette Goodman Cohen, Chair.
Giving statement: Giving through the I. B. Goodman Foundation.

The I. B. Goodman Foundation

120 E. 3rd St.
Newport, KY 41071-1691

Establishment information: Established in 1983 in OH.
Donor: I.B. Goodman Manufacturing Co., Inc.
Financial data (yr. ended 12/31/11): Assets, $23,151 (M); expenditures, $6,250; qualifying

distributions, $6,250; giving activities include $6,250 for 5 grants (high: $2,500; low: $250).
Purpose and activities: The foundation supports orchestras and organizations involved with cancer, children services, and Judaism.
Fields of interest: Health organizations; Human services; Religion.
Type of support: General/operating support.
Support limitations: No grants to individuals.
Application information: Applications not accepted. Unsolicited requests for funds not accepted.
Trustees: Jane Goodman Baum; Babette Goodman Cohen; Jonathan Cohen.
EIN: 311082135

1611
Goodwin Procter LLP

Exchange Pl.
53 State St.
Boston, MA 02109-2802 (617) 570-1481

Company URL: http://www.goodwinprocter.com
Establishment information: Established in 1912.
Company type: Private company
Business activities: Operates law firm.
Business type (SIC): Legal services
Offices: Los Angeles, Menlo Park, San Diego, San Francisco, CA; Washington, DC; Boston, MA; New York, NY
International operations: Hong Kong; United Kingdom
Giving statement: Giving through the Goodwin Procter LLP Pro Bono Program.

Goodwin Procter LLP Pro Bono Program

Exchange Pl.
53 State St.
Boston, MA 02109-2802 (617) 570-1481
E-mail: crosenthal@goodwinprocter.com; Additional tel.: (617) 570-1000; URL: http://www.goodwinprocter.com/Home/Careers/Pro%20Bono.aspx

Contact: Carolyn Rosenthal, Pro Bono Mgr.
Fields of interest: Legal services.
Type of support: Pro bono services - legal.
Geographic limitations: Giving primarily in areas of company operations in Los Angeles, Menlo Park, San Diego, and San Francisco, CA, Washington, DC, Boston, MA, New York, NY, and in Hong Kong, and United Kingdom.
Application information: The Pro Bono Committee manages the pro-bono program.

1612
The Goodyear Tire & Rubber Company

200 Innovation Way
Akron, OH 44316-0001 (330) 796-2121
FAX: (330) 796-2222

Company URL: http://www.goodyear.com
Establishment information: Established in 1898.
Company type: Public company
Company ticker symbol and exchange: GT/NYSE
Business activities: Manufactures tires and rubber products.
Business type (SIC): Tires and inner tubes; rubber and miscellaneous plastics products
Financial profile for 2012: Number of employees, 69,000; assets, $16,973,000,000; sales volume, $20,992,000,000; pre-tax net income, $440,000,000; expenses, $20,552,000,000; liabilities, $16,603,000,000
Fortune 1000 ranking: 2012—137th in revenues, 561st in profits, and 269th in assets
Forbes 2000 ranking: 2012—447th in sales, 1637th in profits, and 1076th in assets
Corporate officers: Richard J. Kramer, Chair., Pres., and C.E.O.; Darren R. Wells, Exec. V.P. and C.F.O.; David L. Bialosky, Sr. V.P., Genl. Counsel, and Secy.; Gregory L. Smith, Sr. V.P., Opers.; Joseph B. Ruocco, Sr. V.P., Human Resources; Scott Honnold, V.P. and Treas.; Richard J. Noechel, V.P. and Cont.
Board of directors: Richard J. Kramer, Chair.; William J. Conaty; James A. Firestone; Werner Geissler; Peter S. Hellman; W. Alan McCollough; John E. McGlade; Roderick A. Palmore; Shirley D. Peterson; Stephanie A. Streeter; Thomas H. Weidemeyer; Michael R. Wessel
Plants: Gadsden, AL; Social Circle, GA; Topeka, KS; Niagara Falls, NY; Asheboro, Fayetteville, Statesville, NC; Lawton, OK; Union City, TN; Beaumont, Houston, San Angelo, TX; Danville, VA
International operations: Belgium; Brazil; Canada; Chile; Colombia; France; Germany; India; Indonesia; Japan; Luxembourg; Malawi; Netherlands; Peru; Poland; Singapore; Slovenia; Taiwan; Thailand; Turkey; United Arab Emirates; United Kingdom; Venezuela
Giving statement: Giving through the Goodyear Tire & Rubber Company Contributions Program and the Goodyear Tire & Rubber Company Fund.
Company EIN: 340253240

The Goodyear Tire & Rubber Company Contributions Program

200 Innovation Way
Akron, OH 44316-0001
E-mail: community-outreach@goodyear.com; URL: http://www.goodyear.com/corporate/about/about_community.html

Contact: Faith S. Stewart, Dir., Community Affairs
Purpose and activities: Goodyear makes charitable contributions to nonprofit organizations involved with safety for children and families, safe transportation, education, health and human services, community development, and civic affairs. Support is limited to communities where the company has plants and offices.
Fields of interest: Higher education; Education; Health care; Safety, education; Human services; Community/economic development Children/youth; Children.
Type of support: General/operating support.
Geographic limitations: Giving limited to communities where the company has plants and offices.
Support limitations: No support for United Way-supported organizations located in areas of company operations, or for national, political, labor, fraternal, or social organizations. No grants to individuals, or for endorsements, endowments, athletics, extracurricular activities, travel, or debt reduction.
Publications: Application guidelines; Corporate report.
Application information: Applications accepted. The Community Affairs Department handles giving. A contributions committee reviews all requests. Support is limited to 1 contribution per organization during any given year; grant recipients must re-apply for consideration in future years. Application form not required. Applicants should submit the following:
1) signature and title of chief executive officer
2) copy of IRS Determination Letter
3) listing of board of directors, trustees, officers and other key people and their affiliations
4) detailed description of project and amount of funding requested
5) copy of current year's organizational budget and/or project budget
6) listing of additional sources and amount of support

Initial approach: Proposal to nearest company facility by mail or e-mail
Copies of proposal: 1
Committee meeting date(s): Quarterly
Deadline(s): Nov. 15 for following year
Final notification: 2 months

Number of staff: 1 full-time professional; 1 part-time support.

Goodyear Tire & Rubber Company Fund

1144 E. Market St. D/616
Akron, OH 44316-0001 (330) 796-2408

Establishment information: Incorporated in 1945 in DE.
Donor: The Goodyear Tire & Rubber Co.
Contact: David. L. Bialosky, V.P. and Secy.
Financial data (yr. ended 12/31/11): Assets, $6,862 (M); expenditures, $0; qualifying distributions, $0.
Purpose and activities: The foundation supports organizations involved with higher education.
Fields of interest: Higher education; United Ways and Federated Giving Programs.
Type of support: General/operating support.
Geographic limitations: Giving primarily in areas of company operations in OH.
Support limitations: No grants to individuals or for endowments; no loans; no matching gifts.
Application information: Applications accepted. Application form required.
Initial approach: Letter
Deadline(s): None
Officers and Trustees:* Richard J. Kramer*, Chair. and Pres.; David L. Bialosky*, V.P. and Secy.; Scott A. Honnold*, V.P. and Treas.; Edward Markey; Joseph B. Ruocco; Darren R. Wells.
Number of staff: 2
EIN: 346522959

1613
Google Inc.

1600 Amphitheatre Pkwy.
Mountain View, CA 94043 (650) 253-0000
FAX: (650) 253-0001

Company URL: http://www.google.com
Establishment information: Established in 1998.
Company type: Public company
Company ticker symbol and exchange: GOOG/NASDAQ
International Securities Identification Number: US38259P5089
Business activities: Provides Internet search and advertising services.
Business type (SIC): Computer services
Financial profile for 2012: Number of employees, 53,861; assets, $93,798,000,000; sales volume, $50,175,000,000; pre-tax net income, $13,386,000,000; expenses, $37,415,000,000; liabilities, $22,083,000,000
Fortune 1000 ranking: 2012—55th in revenues, 17th in profits, and 65th in assets
Forbes 2000 ranking: 2012—176th in sales, 39th in profits, and 263rd in assets

Corporate officers: Eric E. Schmidt, Ph.D., Chair.; Larry Page, C.E.O.; Patrick Pichette, Sr. V.P. and C.F.O.; David C. Drummond, Secy.
Board of directors: Eric E. Schmidt, Ph.D., Chair.; Sergey Brin; L. John Doerr; Diane B. Greene; John L. Hennessy; Ann Mather; Paul S. Otellini; Larry Page; Eric E. Schmidt; K. Ram Shriram; Shirley M. Tilghman
Subsidiaries: DoubleClick Inc., New York, NY; Motorola Mobility Holdings, Inc., Libertyville, IL
Offices: Newport Beach, Santa Monica, CA; Englewood, CO; Atlanta, GA; Chicago, IL; Boston, MA; Novi, MI; New York, NY; Irving, TX; Seattle, WA
International operations: Argentina; Australia; Austria; Belgium; Bermuda; Brazil; Canada; Chile; China; Czech Republic; Denmark; Egypt; Finland; France; Germany; Hong Kong; Hungary; India; Ireland; Israel; Italy; Japan; Netherlands; Netherlands Antilles; New Zealand; Norway; Russia; Singapore; South Africa; South Korea; Spain; Sweden; Switzerland; Turkey; United Arab Emirates; United Kingdom
Giving statement: Giving through the Google.org and the Google Foundation.
Company EIN: 770493581

Google.org

1600 Amphitheatre Pkwy.
Mountain View, CA 94043-1351 (650) 253-0000
FAX: (650) 253-0001; Google will provide limited e-mail support via: research-awards@google.com; Additional website: Google Gives, www.google.com/giving/index.html; URL: http://www.google.com/landing/givesback/2011/

Financial data (yr. ended 12/31/10): Total giving, $183,100,000, including $183,100,000 for grants.
Purpose and activities: As a complement to its foundation, Google makes charitable contributions to nonprofit organizations directly. Support is given to organizations involved with science, technology, engineering, and math (STEM) education; girls' education; empowerment through technology; and fighting human trafficking and modern-day slavery. Support is given on a national and international basis in areas of company operations.
Fields of interest: Education; Environment; Animals/wildlife, endangered species; Animals/wildlife; Public health; Public health, clean water supply; Safety/disasters, information services; Youth development; Civil/human rights; Community/economic development, fund raising/fund distribution; Mathematics; Engineering/technology; Computer science; Science Economically disadvantaged.
Programs:

Google Checkout for Non-Profits: Google Checkout for Non-Profits is a fast, convenient donation process that helps organizations attract more donors and increase online giving to their organization.

Google Earth Outreach: Google Earth Outreach gives nonprofits and public benefit organizations the knowledge and resources they need to visualize their cause and tell their story in Google Earth & Maps to hundreds of millions of people.

Google Grants: Google Grants is the nonprofit edition of AdWords, Google's online advertising tool. Google Grants empowers nonprofit organizations, through $10,000 per month in in-kind AdWords advertising, to promote their missions and initiatives on Google.com.

Google's Global Impact Awards: Global Impact Awards support organizations using technology and innovative approaches to tackle some of the world's toughest human challenges. Google looks for nimble, entrepreneurial organizations that have a specific project that tests a big idea and a brilliant team. From real-time sensors that monitor clean water to DNA barcoding that stops wildlife trafficking, the first round of awards provides $23 million to seven organizations changing the world.
Type of support: Donated products; Employee matching gifts; Employee volunteer services; Fellowships; In-kind gifts; Technical assistance.
Geographic limitations: Giving on a national and international basis in areas of company operations.
Support limitations: No grants for administrative, indirect, or overhead costs, or salaries for full-time researchers or non-student researchers employed by the university, from Research Awards.
Publications: Application guidelines.
Application information: Applications accepted. Applications for Research Awards are restricted to full-time university professors and professors at research institutions that award research degrees to PhD students. Applicants who receive funding are asked to wait one year before applying again. Research Awards are designed to support one year of work. Proposals should have a minimum 10-point font size and 1-inch (2.5-cm) margins. Application form required. Applicants should submit the following:
1) listing of additional sources and amount of support
2) copy of current year's organizational budget and/or project budget
3) detailed description of project and amount of funding requested
4) name, address and phone number of organization
5) contact person
6) statement of problem project will address
7) results expected from proposed grant

Proposals for Research Awards should include the names of two potential Google sponsors, references, where applicable, results from past projects, and a CV for the Principal Investigator.
Initial approach: Visit website by Apr. 1 for application information on Research Awards
Deadline(s): Apr. 15, 2013 and Oct. 15, 2013 for Research Awards
Final notification: 4 months for Research Awards

Google Foundation

1600 Amphitheatre Pkwy.
Mountain View, CA 94043-1351
URL: http://www.google.org/foundation.html

Establishment information: Established in 2004 in CA.
Donor: Google Inc.
Financial data (yr. ended 12/31/10): Assets, $83,106,960 (M); expenditures, $1,211,472; qualifying distributions, $1,090,160; giving activities include $1,075,000 for 4 grants (high: $500,000; low: $50,000).
Purpose and activities: The foundation supports venture philanthropy funds and organizations involved with climate change, poverty, and emerging disease.
Fields of interest: Higher education; Education; Environment, climate change/global warming; Environment, water resources; Disasters, preparedness/services; Civil/human rights Economically disadvantaged.
Type of support: General/operating support; Program development.
Geographic limitations: Giving primarily in CA; giving also to international organizations in India and Tanzania.
Publications: Financial statement; IRS Form 990 or 990-PF printed copy available upon request.
Application information: Applications not accepted. Contributes only to pre-selected organizations.
Officers and Directors:* Megan Smith, Pres.; Luis Arbulu, Secy.-Treas.; Sergey Brin; Lawrence Page; Alfred Spector.
EIN: 201548253

1614
Ryan Gootee General Contractors LLC

1100 Ridgewood Dr.
P.O. Box 56253
Metairie, LA 70001-6100 (504) 832-1282

Company URL: http://www.rggc.com/
Establishment information: Established in 2005.
Company type: Private company
Business activities: Operates general contracting company.
Business type (SIC): Contractors/general nonresidential building
Corporate officers: Ryan P. Gootee, Pres. and C.E.O.; Derek Gardes, C.F.O.; Ronald J. Schellinger, V.P., Opers.
Giving statement: Giving through the Ryan P. Gootee Family Foundation.

Ryan P. Gootee Family Foundation

1100 Ridgewood Dr.
Metairie, LA 70001-7208

Establishment information: Established in 2006 in LA.
Donors: Ryan Gootee General Contractors, LLC; Ryan P. Gootee.
Financial data (yr. ended 12/31/11): Assets, $726,939 (M); gifts received, $102,000; expenditures, $45,642; qualifying distributions, $45,000; giving activities include $45,000 for grants.
Fields of interest: Education.
Geographic limitations: Giving primarily in New Orleans, LA.
Support limitations: No grants to individuals.
Application information: Applications not accepted. Unsolicited requests for funds not accepted.
Officers: Ryan P. Gootee, Pres.; Sara M. Gootee, V.P. and Secy.-Treas.
EIN: 205910512

1615
Gordon Food Service, Inc.

333 50th St., S.W.
P.O. Box 1787
Grand Rapids, MI 49501 (616) 530-7000
FAX: (616) 717-7600

Company URL: http://www.gfs.com
Establishment information: Established in 1897.
Company type: Private company
Business activities: Sells groceries wholesale.
Business type (SIC): Groceries—wholesale
Financial profile for 2011: Number of employees, 12,000; sales volume, $7,700,000,000
Corporate officers: Dan Gordon, Chair.; John M. Gordon, Vice-Chair.; Jim Gordon, C.E.O.; Jeff Maddox, C.F.O.
Board of directors: Dan Gordon, Chair.; John Gordon, Vice-Chair.
Giving statement: Giving through the Gordon Food Service, Inc. Corporate Giving Program.

Gordon Food Service, Inc. Corporate Giving Program

c/o Donation Comm.
P.O. Box 1787
Grand Rapids, MI 49501-1787
URL: http://www.gfs.com/en/about-us/donations.page?

Purpose and activities: Gordon Food Service makes charitable contributions to nonprofit organizations on a case by case basis. Support is given primarily in areas of company operations, with emphasis on Michigan.
Fields of interest: General charitable giving.
Type of support: Donated products; Sponsorships.
Geographic limitations: Giving primarily in areas of company operations, with emphasis on MI.
Application information: Applications accepted. Proposals should be submitted using organization letterhead. Faxes and e-mail messages are not encouraged. Application form not required.
Applicants should submit the following:
1) population served
2) name, address and phone number of organization
3) brief history of organization and description of its mission
4) detailed description of project and amount of funding requested
Proposals should specifically note the nature of the request being made.
Initial approach: Proposal to headquarters
Copies of proposal: 1
Deadline(s): None
Final notification: 3 weeks

1616
Gordon, Feinblatt, Rothman, Hoffberger & Hollander, LLC

Garrett Bldg.
233 E. Redwood St.
Baltimore, MD 21202-3332
(410) 576-4198

Company URL: http://www.gfrlaw.com/
Establishment information: Established in 1946.
Company type: Private company
Business activities: Operates law firm.
Business type (SIC): Legal services
Corporate officer: Barry F. Rosen, Chair. and C.E.O.
Giving statement: Giving through the Gordon, Feinblatt, Rothman, Hoffberger & Hollander, LLC Pro Bono Program.

Gordon, Feinblatt, Rothman, Hoffberger & Hollander, LLC Pro Bono Program

Garrett Bldg.
233 E. Redwood St.
Baltimore, MD 21202-3332 (410) 576-4198
E-mail: cbledsoe@gfrlaw.com; URL: http://www.gfrlaw.com/probono/xprGeneralContent2.aspx?xpST=ProBono

Contact: Catherine Bledsoe, Member
Fields of interest: Legal services.
Type of support: Pro bono services - legal.
Geographic limitations: Giving primarily in areas of company operations in Baltimore, MD.
Application information: An attorney coordinates pro bono projects.

1617
Gosiger, Inc.

108 McDonough St.
Dayton, OH 45402-2246 (877) 288-1538

Company URL: http://www.gosiger.com/
Establishment information: Established in 1922.
Company type: Private company
Business activities: Sells machinery and machine tools wholesale.
Business type (SIC): Industrial machinery and equipment—wholesale
Corporate officers: Jane Gosiger Haley, Chair. and C.E.O.; Brent Sheerer, Pres.; Bill Glaser, V.P., Finance
Board of director: Jane Gosiger Haley, Chair.
Giving statement: Giving through the Gosiger Foundation.

Gosiger Foundation

108 McDonough St.
Dayton, OH 45402-2246

Establishment information: Established in 1992 in OH.
Donor: Gosiger, Inc.
Financial data (yr. ended 12/31/11): Assets, $1,969,572 (M); gifts received, $1,450,000; expenditures, $482,276; qualifying distributions, $471,000; giving activities include $471,000 for grants.
Purpose and activities: The foundation supports organizations involved with arts and culture, education, conservation, human services, and Catholicism.
Fields of interest: Performing arts, orchestras; Performing arts, opera; Arts; Secondary school/education; Higher education; Theological school/education; Environment, natural resources; Human services; United Ways and Federated Giving Programs; Catholic agencies & churches.
Type of support: General/operating support; Scholarship funds.
Geographic limitations: Giving primarily in Dayton, OH.
Support limitations: No grants to individuals.
Application information: Applications not accepted. Contributes only to pre-selected organizations.
Officers and Trustees:* Jane Gosiger Haley*, Pres.; John R. Haley*, V.P.; Peter G. Haley*, V.P.; Hugh E. Wall III, Secy.; Jerry R. Pressel, Treas.
EIN: 311365457
Selected grants: The following grants are a representative sample of this grantmaker's funding activity:
$65,000 to University of Notre Dame, Notre Dame, IN, 2011.
$12,500 to University of Dayton, Dayton, OH, 2011.

1618
Gould Electronics Inc.

2555 W. Fairview St., Ste. 103
Chandler, AZ 85224 (480) 223-0870

Company URL: http://www.gould.com
Establishment information: Established in 1884.
Company type: Subsidiary of a foreign company
Business activities: Manufactures electronic products and systems.
Business type (SIC): Computer and office equipment; electronic components and accessories
Corporate officer: John P. Callahan, Pres.
Board of directors: Mike Hayes; Rolland D. Savage
Divisions: Gould Electronics Inc.-Fiber Optics Div., Millersville, MD; Gould Electronics Inc.-Foil Div., Eastlake, OH; Gould Electronics Inc.-Shawmut Circuit Protection Div., Newburyport, MA
Giving statement: Giving through the Gould Inc. Foundation.

Gould Inc. Foundation

c/o Thomas N. Rich
34929 Curtis Blvd.
Eastlake, OH 44095-4006

Establishment information: Incorporated in 1951 in OH.
Donor: Gould Electronics Inc.
Financial data (yr. ended 12/31/11): Assets, $2,074,402 (M); expenditures, $112,610; qualifying distributions, $109,500; giving activities include $109,500 for 43 grants (high: $34,500; low: $200).
Purpose and activities: The foundation supports food banks and fire departments and organizations involved with arts and culture, education, cancer, heart disease, Alzheimer's, baseball, and human services.
Fields of interest: Museums; Performing arts; Arts; Education; Cancer; Heart & circulatory diseases; Alzheimer's disease; Food banks; Disasters, fire prevention/control; Athletics/sports, baseball; Salvation Army; Human services; United Ways and Federated Giving Programs.
Type of support: Annual campaigns; General/operating support.
Geographic limitations: Giving primarily in OH.
Application information: Applications not accepted. Unsolicited requests for funds not accepted.
Officers: Thomas N. Rich, Pres. and Treas.; Sharon Roach, Secy.
EIN: 346525555

1619
Goulds Pumps, Inc

240 Fall St.
Seneca Falls, NY 13148-1590
(315) 568-2811

Company URL: http://www.gouldspumps.com
Establishment information: Established in 1848.
Company type: Subsidiary of a public company
Business activities: Manufactures centrifugal pumps and water systems.
Business type (SIC): Machinery/general industry; laboratory apparatus
Corporate officers: Ken Napolitano, Pres.; Tom C. Wu, V.P., Finance and Cont.; Ron Golumbeck, V.P., Human Resources
Subsidiary: Oil Dynamics, Inc., Tulsa, OK
Plants: City of Industry, CA; Baldwinsville, NY; Ashland, PA; Lubbock, TX
International operations: Canada
Giving statement: Giving through the Goulds Pumps, Incorporated Corporate Giving Program and the Gould Scholarship Fund.

Gould Scholarship Fund

(formerly Norman J. and Anna B. Gould Scholarship Fund)
P.O. Box 1802
Providence, RI 02901-1802
Application address: 240 Fall St., Seneca Falls, NY 13148-8745

Donor: Goulds Pumps, Inc.
Contact: M.J. Catoe

Financial data (yr. ended 12/31/11): Assets, $169,664 (M); expenditures, $7,812; qualifying distributions, $6,009; giving activities include $5,100 for 5 grants (high: $1,100; low: $1,000).
Purpose and activities: The foundation awards college scholarships to employees of Goulds Pumps and residents of Seneca Falls, New York.
Fields of interest: Higher education.
Type of support: Employee-related scholarships; Scholarships—to individuals.
Geographic limitations: Giving primarily in areas of company operations, with emphasis on Seneca Falls, NY.
Application information: Applications accepted. Application form required.
Initial approach: Proposal
Deadline(s): None
Trustee: Bank of America, N.A.
EIN: 166051306

1620
Government Employees Benefit Association Inc.

P.O. Box 206
Annapolis Junction, MD 20701-0206
(301) 688-7912

Company URL: http://www.geba.com
Establishment information: Established in 1957.
Company type: Private company
Business activities: Provides health, life, and disability insurance.
Business type (SIC): Insurance agents, brokers, and services
Financial profile for 2011: Assets, $10,192,104
Corporate officers: Gil Dipietro, Chair.; Linda B. Hart, Pres.; John D. Long, Secy.; John Yelnosky, Treas.
Board of directors: Gil DiPietro, Chair.; Dominic Aello; Robert Arsenault; Cathleen Civiello; Bruce Leuthold; Joe Talieri; Kimberly Wroten
Giving statement: Giving through the Government Employees Benefit Association Scholarship Foundation, Inc.

Government Employees Benefit Association Scholarship Foundation, Inc.

P.O. Box 206
Annapolis Junction, MD 20701-0206 (301) 688-7912
URL: http://www.geba.com

Establishment information: Established in 2005 in MD.
Donor: Government Employees Benefit Assoc., Inc.
Financial data (yr. ended 12/31/11): Assets, $13,200 (M); gifts received, $58,060; expenditures, $54,117; qualifying distributions, $54,117; giving activities include $44,000 for 22 grants to individuals (high: $2,000; low: $2,000).
Purpose and activities: Grant awards to members of GEBA or a member's spouse, child or grandchild, and a GEBA member for 3 full calendar years.
Type of support: Scholarships—to individuals.
Geographic limitations: Giving primarily in Columbia, MD.
Application information: Applications accepted. Application form required.
Initial approach: See Foundation website
Deadline(s): Apr. 14
Officers and Directors:* Bruce Leuthold*, Chair.; John Delong*, Pres.; Joseph Talieri*, Secy.; Robert Arsenault*, Treas.; Catheen Civiello; Carolyn Crooks*; Gilbert Dipietro; Murray Kenyon; Terry Santivicca; John Yelnosky.
EIN: 320143828

1621
Government Employees Insurance Company

(doing business as GEICO Corporation)
(also known as GEICO)
1 Geico Plz.
Washington, DC 20076-0005
(301) 986-3000

Company URL: http://www.geico.com
Establishment information: Established in 1936.
Company type: Subsidiary of a public company
Business activities: Sells automobile insurance.
Business type (SIC): Insurance/fire, marine, and casualty
Corporate officers: Olza M. Nicely, Chair., Pres., and C.E.O.; Mike Campbell, Sr. V.P. and C.F.O.; Greg Kalinsky, Sr. V.P. and C.I.O.
Board of directors: Olza M. Nicely, Chair.; Campbell Mike
Giving statement: Giving through the GEICO Philanthropic Foundation.
Company EIN: 530075853

GEICO Philanthropic Foundation

c/o GEICO Corp.
5260 Western Ave.
Chevy Chase, MD 20815-3701 (301) 986-2750
URL: http://www.geico.com/information/military/service-awards/
Application Address for GEICO Public Service Awards: Federal Dept., Nomination Committee (Federal Program), 1 GEICO Plaza, Washington, DC 20076; Contact for Military Service Awards: Mike Baker, Military Dept., Dir., tel.: (800) 824-5404, ext. 3906, e-mail: mbaker@geico.com

Establishment information: Established in 1980 in DC.
Donor: Government Employees Insurance Co.
Contact: Donald R. Lyons, Chair.
Financial data (yr. ended 12/31/11): Assets, $57,548,339 (M); gifts received, $6,406,397; expenditures, $7,448,203; qualifying distributions, $7,409,617; giving activities include $7,382,117 for 1,674 grants (high: $438,812; low: $15) and $27,500 for 11 grants to individuals (high: $2,500; low: $2,500).
Purpose and activities: The foundation supports organizations involved with serious injury rehabilitation, automotive safety, and children's services, and awards grants to federal employees and active members of the military.
Fields of interest: Hospitals (general); Health care, clinics/centers; Medical care, rehabilitation; Health care; Cancer; Breast cancer; Crime/law enforcement; Safety, automotive safety; Boys & girls clubs; Girl scouts; Children, services; United Ways and Federated Giving Programs; Military/veterans' organizations.
Programs:
Davidson, Snyder, Byrne, and Kreeger Scholarship Programs: The foundation awards college scholarships to dependent children of full-time employees of GEICO. The program is administered by Scholarship America.
GEICO Public Service Awards: The foundation annually awards four $2,500 grants to federal employees who have made outstanding achievements in the following categories: substance abuse prevention and treatment; fire prevention and safety; physical rehabilitation; and traffic safety and accident prevention. One grant in each category is awarded each year. The foundation also awards a $2,500 grant to a retired federal employee honored for contributions made since retirement. This program will terminate in 2012.
GEICO Work-Study and Leo Goodwin Scholarship Program: The foundation awards $2,500 college scholarships to juniors at selected schools. Students must be majoring in business or insurance; recommended by their college or university head; excel in scholastic achievement; and be proficient in quantitative abilities as demonstrated through course work in accounting, math, or statistics. Liberal arts students will also be considered given demonstrated good performance in courses requiring quantitative abilities. The program is administered by Scholarship America.
Military Service Awards: The foundation annually awards six $2,500 grants, one to an enlisted member from each Military service branch, and one to a member of the reserve/national guard component. The award is given to recognize outstanding achievement in the following categories: drug and alcohol abuse prevention; fire safety and fire prevention; and traffic safety and accident prevention.
The Snyder Family Education Assistance Program: The foundation awards scholarships to students in grades 8 to11 who are children of full-time employees of GEICO for study at an accredited private secondary school. The program is administered by Scholarship America.
Type of support: Employee matching gifts; Employee-related scholarships; General/operating support; Grants to individuals; Scholarships—to individuals; Sponsorships.
Geographic limitations: Giving primarily in CA, Washington, DC, FL, GA, MD, NY, TX and VA.
Support limitations: No support for political organizations or religious organizations not of direct benefit to the entire community. No grants to individuals (except for GEICO Public Service Awards, Military Service Awards, and scholarships).
Application information: Applications accepted. Visit website for nomination addresses for Military Service Awards. The foundation primarily supports groups where GEICO associates have significant involvement. Applicants should submit the following:
1) listing of board of directors, trustees, officers and other key people and their affiliations
2) detailed description of project and amount of funding requested
3) copy of current year's organizational budget and/or project budget
4) listing of additional sources and amount of support

Initial approach: Proposal; contact selected military service channels for Military Service Awards
Board meeting date(s): Quarterly
Deadline(s): None; Oct. 31 for Military Service Awards
Officers and Directors:* Donald R. Lyons*, Chair.; Dana K. Proulx*, Pres.; William C. E. Robinson, Secy.; Michael H. Campbell*, Treas.; Stephen C. Parsons; Nancy L. Pierce; Rynthia M. Rost.
Number of staff: 1 full-time professional.
EIN: 521202740
Selected grants: The following grants are a representative sample of this grantmaker's funding activity:
$438,812 to Insurance Institute for Highway Safety, Arlington, VA, 2011.
$438,812 to Insurance Institute for Highway Safety, Arlington, VA, 2011.

$300,000 to Wounded Warrior Project, Jacksonville, FL, 2011.
$197,560 to Scholarship America, Saint Peter, MN, 2011.
$159,000 to United Way of Central Georgia, Macon, GA, 2011.
$150,000 to National Rehabilitation Hospital, Washington, DC, 2011.
$75,000 to Girl Scouts of the U.S.A., Council of the Nations Capital, Washington, DC, 2011.
$55,000 to American Cancer Society, Virginia Beach, VA, 2011.
$50,000 to Wolf Trap Foundation for the Performing Arts, Vienna, VA, 2011.
$18,000 to United Way of the National Capital Area, Vienna, VA, 2011.

1622
Goya Foods Inc.

100 Seaview Dr.
Secaucus, NJ 07096 (201) 348-4900
FAX: (201) 348-6609

Company URL: http://www.goya.com
Establishment information: Established in 1936.
Company type: Private company
Business activities: Distributes food products.
Business type (SIC): Groceries—wholesale
Financial profile for 2010: Number of employees, 3,500; sales volume, $1,700,000,000
Corporate officers: Robert I. Unanue, Pres.; Carlos Ortiz, V.P. and Genl. Counsel; Miguel Lugo, Jr., V.P., Finance
Subsidiaries: Bison Canning Co., Inc., Angola, NY; Goya Foods of Florida, Miami, FL
International operations: Dominican Republic; Spain
Giving statement: Giving through the Goya Foods Inc. Corporate Giving Program.

Goya Foods Inc. Corporate Giving Program

100 Seaview Dr.
Secaucus, NJ 07094-1800 (201) 348-4900
URL: http://www.goya.com

Purpose and activities: Goya Foods makes charitable contributions to nonprofit organizations on a case by case basis. Support is given primarily in areas of company operations.
Fields of interest: General charitable giving.
Type of support: Donated products.
Geographic limitations: Giving primarily in areas of company operations.

1623
W.R. Grace & Co.

7500 Grace Dr.
Columbia, MD 21044-4009 (410) 531-4000
FAX: (410) 531-4367

Company URL: http://www.grace.com
Establishment information: Established in 1854.
Company type: Public company
Company ticker symbol and exchange: GRA/NYSE
Business activities: Manufactures specialty chemicals, construction materials, and container sealants.
Business type (SIC): Chemical preparations/ miscellaneous; chemicals and allied products
Financial profile for 2012: Number of employees, 6,500; assets, $5,090,200,000; sales volume, $3,155,500,000; pre-tax net income, $57,800,000; expenses, $3,097,700,000; liabilities, $4,781,800,000
Fortune 1000 ranking: 2012—683rd in revenues, 751st in profits, and 592nd in assets
Corporate officers: Alfred E. Festa, Chair. and C.E.O.; Gregory E. Poling, Pres. and C.O.O.; Andrew Hudson La Force III, Sr. V.P. and C.F.O.; Mark A. Shelnitz, V.P., Genl. Counsel, and Secy.
Board of directors: Fred E. Festa, Chair.; John F. Akers; H. Furlong Baldwin; Ronald C. Cambre; Mary Anne Fox; Janice K. Henry; Jeffry N. Quinn; Christopher J. Steffen; Mark. E. Tomkins
Subsidiaries: A-1 Bit & Tool Company, Inc., Dallas, TX; Advanced Refining Technologies, Cambridge, MA; Advanced Refining Technologies, L.L.C., Columbia, MD; Alewife Boston Ltd., Cambridge, MA; Alltech Associates, Inc., Deerfield, IL; Amicon, Inc., Beverly, MA; CB Biomedical, Inc., Columbia, MD; Creative Food 'N Fun Co., Dallas, TX; Darex Puerto Rico, Inc., Toa Baja, PR; Five Alewife Boston Limited, Cambridge, MA; G C Management, Inc., San Clemente, CA; GEC Management Corp., Dallas, TX; Grace Chemicals, Inc., Boca Raton, FL; Grace Culinary Systems, Inc., Laurel, MD; Grace Drilling Co., Dallas, TX; Grace Energy Corp., Carthage, MO; Grace Environmental, Inc., Denver, CO; Grace H-G II Inc., Columbia, MD; Grace International Holdings, Inc., Dallas, TX; Grace Management Services, Inc., Lorain, OH; Grace Ventures Corp., Cupertino, CA; Grace Washington, Inc., Washington, DC; Hanover Square Corp., New York, NY; Homco International, Inc., Houston, TX; L B Realty, Inc., Foxboro, MA; Litigation Management, Inc., Cleveland, OH; Monolith Enterprises, Inc., Santa Clarita, CA; MRA Holdings Corp., Columbia, MD; MRA Staffing Systems, Inc., Fort Lauderdale, FL; Remedium Group, Inc., Cambridge, MA; W. R. Grace & Co.-Conn., Los Angeles, CA; W. R. Grace Capital Corp., Columbia, MD
International operations: Argentina; Australia; Belgium; Brazil; Canada; Chile; China; Colombia; Cuba; France; Germany; Greece; Hong Kong; Hungary; India; Indonesia; Ireland; Italy; Japan; Malaysia; Mexico; Netherlands; Netherlands Antilles; New Zealand; Philippines; Poland; Russia; Singapore; South Africa; South Korea; Spain; Sweden; Switzerland; Taiwan; Thailand; United Kingdom; Venezuela; Vietnam
Giving statement: Giving through the W. R. Grace & Co. Contributions Program and the W. R. Grace Foundation, Inc.
Company EIN: 650773649

W. R. Grace & Co. Contributions Program

7500 Grace Dr.
Columbia, MD 21044-4009 (410) 531-4000
FAX: (410) 531-4367; URL: http://www.grace.com/About/CommunityStewardship/default.aspx

Purpose and activities: As a complement to its foundation, W.R. Grace also makes charitable contributions to nonprofit organizations directly. Support is given on a national and international basis in areas of company operations.
Fields of interest: Education; Environmental education; Health care; Youth development.
Type of support: Employee volunteer services; General/operating support; Scholarship funds; Sponsorships.
Geographic limitations: Giving on a national and international basis in areas of company operations.

W. R. Grace Foundation, Inc.

7500 Grace Dr.
Columbia, MD 21044-4009 (410) 531-4000
URL: http://www.grace.com/About/CommunityStewardship/GraceFoundation.aspx

Establishment information: Incorporated in 1996 in FL.
Donor: W.R. Grace & Co.
Contact: Janet Davis
Financial data (yr. ended 12/31/11): Assets, $1,389,345 (M); gifts received, $850,000; expenditures, $732,015; qualifying distributions, $719,899; giving activities include $719,899 for grants.
Purpose and activities: The foundation supports organizations involved with arts and culture, the environment, health, youth development, human services, and civic affairs. Special emphasis is directed toward programs designed to address education and basic needs.
Fields of interest: Museums; Arts; Higher education; Education; Environment, natural resources; Environment; Hospitals (general); Health care; Food services; Youth development; Human services; United Ways and Federated Giving Programs; Public affairs.
Program:
Matching Gift Program: The foundation matches contributions made by employees of W.R. Grace to secondary schools, colleges, and universities on a one-for-one basis.
Type of support: Building/renovation; Capital campaigns; Employee matching gifts; General/operating support; Program development; Scholarship funds.
Geographic limitations: Giving on a national basis in areas of company operations in the U.S. and in Canada.
Publications: Application guidelines.
Application information: Applications accepted. Preference will be given to nonprofit organizations that have a Grace connection such as employee volunteers. Application form not required. Applicants should submit the following:
1) copy of IRS Determination Letter
2) brief history of organization and description of its mission
3) copy of most recent annual report/audited financial statement/990
4) detailed description of project and amount of funding requested
5) listing of additional sources and amount of support

Initial approach: Proposal
Deadline(s): Nov.

Officers and Directors:* W. Brian McGowan*, Chair. and Pres.; Mark A. Shelnitz, Secy.; Andrew Hudson La Force III, Treas.; William M. Corcoran; Alfred E. Festa.
EIN: 650630671

1624
Graco Inc.

88-11th Ave., N.E.
Minneapolis, MN 55413-1829
(612) 623-6000
FAX: (612) 623-6777

Company URL: http://www.graco.com
Establishment information: Established in 1926.
Company type: Public company
Company ticker symbol and exchange: GGG/NYSE
Business activities: Manufactures fluid management equipment.

Business type (SIC): Machinery/general industry
Financial profile for 2012: Number of employees, 2,600; assets, $1,321,730,000; sales volume, $1,012,460,000; pre-tax net income, $217,330,000; expenses, $787,780,000; liabilities, $867,620,000
Corporate officers: Lee R. Mitau, Chair.; Patrick J. McHale, Pres. and C.E.O.; James A. Graner, C.F.O.; Karen Park Gallivan, V.P., Genl. Counsel, and Secy.; Christian E. Rothe, V.P. and Treas.; Caroline M. Chambers, V.P. and Corp. Cont.; David M. Ahlers, V.P., Human Resources and Corp. Comms.
Board of directors: Lee R. Mitau, Chair.; William J. Carroll; Eric P. Etchart; Jack W. Eugster; J. Kevin Gilligan; Patrick J. McHale; Martha A. Morfitt; William G. Van Dyke; R. William Van Sant
Subsidiary: Graco Minnesota Inc., Minneapolis, MN
Plants: Anoka, Rogers, MN; North Canton, OH; Sioux Falls, SD
International operations: Australia; Belgium; Canada; China; India; Japan
Giving statement: Giving through the Graco Foundation.
Company EIN: 410285640

The Graco Foundation

88 11th Ave. N.E.
Minneapolis, MN 55413-1829 (612) 623-6767
FAX: (612) 623-6944; E-mail: Kristi_k_@graco.com; URL: http://www.graco.com/us/en/about-graco/foundation.html

Establishment information: Incorporated in 1956 in MN.
Donor: Graco Inc.
Contact: Kristi Lee, Mgr., Community Rels.
Financial data (yr. ended 12/31/11): Assets, $5,505,131 (M); gifts received, $2,300,000; expenditures, $628,772; qualifying distributions, $613,578; giving activities include $613,578 for grants.
Purpose and activities: The foundation helps organizations serve community needs by expanding or enhancing services to clients, with some emphasis on capital projects and technology needs. Special emphasis is directed toward organizations with a proven track record of enabling self-sufficiency and programs that promote education, workforce development, and youth development. Support is given primarily in areas of company operations, with emphasis on Minnesota.
Fields of interest: Education, early childhood education; Education; Employment, services; Employment; Youth development; Human services; Business/industry; United Ways and Federated Giving Programs Children/youth; Adults; Minorities.
Programs:
Dollars for Doers: The foundation awards $1,000 to nonprofit organizations with which employees, spouses of employees, or dependents of employees of Graco volunteer at least 50 hours per year.
Employee Giving Campaign: The foundation matches contributions made by employees of Graco to eligible nonprofit organizations on a one-for-one basis up to $2,000 per employee, per year.
Type of support: Building/renovation; Capital campaigns; Employee matching gifts; Employee volunteer services; Employee-related scholarships; Equipment; Management development/capacity building; Program development; Scholarship funds; Technical assistance.
Geographic limitations: Giving primarily in areas of company operations, with emphasis on MN, including the northern and northeastern communities in Minneapolis, as well as North Canton, OH and Sioux Falls, SD.
Support limitations: No support for political, religious, or fraternal organizations. No grants to individuals (except for employee-related scholarships), or for start-up needs, emergency needs, debt reduction, land acquisition, endowments, publications, fundraising, travel, conferences, or national or local campaigns for disease research; no loans or product donations.
Application information: Applications not accepted. The foundation is not currently accepting new applications.
Board meeting date(s): June
Officers and Directors:* Patrick J. McHale*, Pres.; Kristin R. Ridley, Secy. and Grants Admin. Mgr.; Janel W. French, Treas.; Karen Park Gallivan; Anthony J. Gargano; Chad L. Hellwig; Beth A. Honzal; Karl A. Hurston; David Lowe; Charles L. Rescorla.
Number of staff: 1 full-time professional.
EIN: 416023537

1625
Graham Capital Co.

1420 Sixth Ave.
P.O. Box 1104
York, PA 17405 (717) 849-4001

Company URL: http://www.thegrahamgroup.com
Establishment information: Established in 1989.
Company type: Private company
Business activities: Operates investment management company.
Business type (SIC): Investors/miscellaneous; investment offices
Financial profile for 2012: Number of employees, 358
Corporate officers: William H. Kerlin, Jr., Chair. and C.E.O.; Paul L. Rudy III, Pres.; Chuck Silverman, V.P., Cont. and Admin.; William J. Scott III, V.P., Human Resources
Board of director: William H. Kerlin, Jr., Chair.
International operations: Argentina; Belgium; Brazil; Canada; Ecuador; England; Finland; France; Italy; Mexico; Netherlands; Poland; Turkey; United Kingdom; Venezuela; Wales
Giving statement: Giving through the Graham Foundation.
Company EIN: 231988068

The Graham Foundation

P.O. Box 1104
York, PA 17405-1104 (717) 849-4001

Establishment information: Established in 1986 in PA.
Donors: Graham Engineering Corp.; Graham Capital Corp.; Donald C. Graham; Graham Packaging Co., L.P.; Graham Packaging Holdings Co.; Graham Architectural Products.
Contact: William H. Kerlin, Jr., Tr.
Financial data (yr. ended 12/31/11): Assets, $16,856,401 (M); gifts received, $120,000; expenditures, $1,065,039; qualifying distributions, $1,053,308; giving activities include $1,052,308 for 67 grants (high: $570,000; low: $100).
Purpose and activities: The foundation supports community foundations and organizations involved with arts and culture, education, land conservation, animals and wildlife, and human services.
Fields of interest: Performing arts centers; Arts; Secondary school/education; Higher education; Education; Environment, land resources; Animals/wildlife; YM/YWCAs & YM/YWHAs; Human services; Foundations (community); United Ways and Federated Giving Programs.
Type of support: Annual campaigns; Building/renovation; Capital campaigns; General/operating support; Program development; Scholarship funds; Sponsorships.
Geographic limitations: Giving primarily in York, PA.
Support limitations: No grants to individuals.
Application information: Applications accepted. Application form not required.
Initial approach: Proposal
Deadline(s): None
Trustees: Donald C. Graham; Ingrid A. Graham; Kristin Graham; William H. Kerlin, Jr.
EIN: 236805421

1626
W.W. Grainger, Inc.

(doing business as Grainger)
100 Grainger Pkwy.
Lake Forest, IL 60045-5201
(847) 535-1000
FAX: (847) 535-0878

Company URL: http://www.grainger.com
Establishment information: Established in 1927.
Company type: Public company
Company ticker symbol and exchange: GWW/NYSE
Business activities: Distributes electric motors, mechanical equipment, and other industrial machinery.
Business type (SIC): Industrial machinery and equipment—wholesale; electrical goods—wholesale; hardware, plumbing, and heating equipment—wholesale
Financial profile for 2012: Number of employees, 22,400; assets, $5,014,600,000; sales volume, $8,950,050,000; pre-tax net income, $1,117,790,000; expenses, $7,818,920,000; liabilities, $1,990,690,000
Fortune 1000 ranking: 2012—295th in revenues, 266th in profits, and 595th in assets
Forbes 2000 ranking: 2012—1002nd in sales, 813th in profits, and 1817th in assets
Corporate officers: James T. Ryan, Chair., Pres., and C.E.O.; Ronald L. Jadin, Sr. V.P. and C.F.O.; Timothy M. Ferrarell, Sr. V.P. and C.I.O.; John L. Howard, Sr. V.P. and Genl. Counsel; Laura D. Brown, Sr. V.P., Comms.; Lawrence J. Pilon, Sr. V.P., Human Resources.
Board of directors: James T. Ryan, Chair.; Brian P. Anderson; Ann V. Hailey; William K. Hall; Stuart L. Levenick; John W. McCarter, Jr.; Neil S. Novich; Michael J. Roberts; Gary L. Rogers; Scott E. Santi; James D. Slavik
International operations: Canada
Giving statement: Giving through the W. W. Grainger, Inc. Corporate Giving Program.
Company EIN: 361150280

W. W. Grainger, Inc. Corporate Giving Program

c/o Company Contribs.
100 Grainger Pkwy.
Lake Forest, IL 60045-5201 (847) 535-1162
URL: http://pressroom.grainger.com/phoenix.zhtml?c=194987&p=irol-products

Contact: Laura Coy, Mgr., Public Affairs
Purpose and activities: Grainger supports disaster preparedness and response through volunteerism, and technical education for students pursuing degrees in the industrial trades at community colleges.
Fields of interest: Vocational education; Vocational education, post-secondary; Disasters, preparedness/services Military/veterans.

Type of support: Employee matching gifts; Scholarship funds.
Geographic limitations: Giving primarily in areas of company operations.
Application information: Applications not accepted. Contributes only through existing partnerships. Additional support is granted through employee matching gifts.

1627
Grand Circle Corporation

(also known as Grand Circle Travel)
347 Congress St.
Boston, MA 02210-1230 (617) 350-7500

Company URL: http://www.gct.com
Establishment information: Established in 1958.
Company type: Private company
Business activities: Operates travel agency.
Business type (SIC): Travel and tour arrangers
Corporate officers: Alan E. Lewis, Chair.; Harriet R. Lewis, Vice-Chair.; Vince Cook, C.E.O.; Sean Stover, C.F.O.; Richard Langerman, Secy.; Eilleen Miquelon, Cont.
Board of directors: Alan E. Lewis, Chair.; Harriet R. Lewis, Vice-Chair.
Giving statement: Giving through the Grand Circle Foundation, Inc.

Grand Circle Foundation, Inc.

347 Congress St.
Boston, MA 02210-1280 (617) 346-6602
FAX: (617) 346-6030;
E-mail: foundation@grandcirclefoundation.org; Contact for Grand Circle Association Fund: Lianne Hughes, Boston Community Initiative Coord., e-mail: LHughes@grandcirclefoundation.org; Additional tel.: (800) 859-0852;; URL: http://www.grandcirclefoundation.org/

Establishment information: Established in 1993 in MA.
Donors: Grand Circle Corp.; Overseas Adventure Travel; Alan E. Lewis; Harriet R. Lewis; Grand Circle Trust; Grand Circle Travel.
Financial data (yr. ended 12/31/11): Assets, $4,254,108 (M); gifts received, $3,862,503; expenditures, $3,028,888; qualifying distributions, $1,651,892; giving activities include $1,651,392 for 174 grants (high: $111,668; low: $75).
Purpose and activities: The foundation supports programs designed to identify and develop gutsy leaders who create social change and economic opportunity; partner with leaders in the villages where Grand Circle members travel, live, and work to create jobs, improve school performance, support small business, and promote the health and safety of citizens; and bring together in dialogue and action Grand Circle associates, travelers, travel partners, and leaders around a shared set of values and goals to create change.
Fields of interest: Arts, cultural/ethnic awareness; Elementary school/education; Education, drop-out prevention; Education, reading; Education; Health care; Employment; Youth development; Human services; Economic development; Rural development; Social entrepreneurship; Community development, small businesses Aging.
International interests: Africa; Asia; Europe; Italy; Mexico; South America; Thailand; Turkey.
Programs:
A Day in the Life of a Village: Through the Day in the Life initiative, the foundation supports travelers and links school visits with hands-on cultural exchange with the community. The program includes a school visit, a walking tour of the village or town, an in-home meal with the students' families, a visit to a local entrepreneur, and a visit to a community or senior center.
CollegeWorks: The foundation, in partnership with Bottom Line and community organizations in Boston's Spine, supports higher education through this five-year initiative. Special emphasis is directed toward partnerships designed to double the number of students from the Spine who receive a 4-year college degree by 2018.
Grand Circle Associates Fund Community Grants Program: The foundation supports programs designed to promote youth education and discovery. Special emphasis is directed toward programs designed to improve the future for children and youth, particularly those who are at-risk; expand horizons for young people and build confidence in their abilities and future; and improve global literacy and promote global citizenship. Grants range from $100 to $10,000.
Invest in a Village: Through the Invest in a Village program, the foundation partners with local communities and villages to identify sustainable entrepreneurial activities that will benefit future generations. Activities range from renovating schools and building electricity and irrigation systems to leadership building for women and agriculture cooperatives. The program is designed to have clear milestones and fundraising goals for each project.
Matching Gift Program: The foundation matches contributions made by U.S. associates of Grand Circle to nonprofit organizations on a one-for-one basis from $25 to $500 per associate, per year.
World Classroom Initiative: The foundation supports programs designed to foster the education of young people around the world and engage the communities in which they live. The program establishes relationships with schools and universities, supports and identifies the community need, and invests in leaders and educators at World Classroom sights to serve those needs.
Type of support: Building/renovation; Continuing support; Curriculum development; Employee matching gifts; Employee volunteer services; Equipment; Program development.
Geographic limitations: Giving primarily in MA, with emphasis on Allston, Dorchester, Mattapan, and Roxbury; some giving in Africa, Asia, Chile, China, Costa Rica, Croatia, Egypt, Europe, Italy, Kenya, Mexico, Namibia, Peru, South America, Tanzania, Thailand, Turkey, and Zimbabwe.
Support limitations: No support for discriminatory, political, or religious organizations. No grants to individuals, or for general operating support, administrative costs, salaries, advertising, or dinner table sponsorship.
Publications: Annual report; Application guidelines; Newsletter.
Application information: Applications accepted. Proposals should be limited to 2 to 3 pages. Support is limited to 1 contribution per organization during any given year. Organizations receiving support are asked to provide a final report. Application form not required. Applicants should submit the following:
1) results expected from proposed grant
2) statement of problem project will address
3) population served
4) copy of IRS Determination Letter
5) brief history of organization and description of its mission
6) copy of most recent annual report/audited financial statement/990
7) how project's results will be evaluated or measured
8) listing of board of directors, trustees, officers and other key people and their affiliations
9) detailed description of project and amount of funding requested
10) contact person
11) copy of current year's organizational budget and/or project budget

Proposals for the Grand Circle Associates Fund should include a W9 Form and a photo in .jpg format that shows your organization at work.
Initial approach: E-mail proposal for Grand Circle Associates Fund
Copies of proposal: 1
Board meeting date(s): May, Aug., and Dec.
Deadline(s): Mar. 25 and Oct. 25 for Grand Circle Associates Fund
Officers and Directors:* Alan E. Lewis*, Co-Chair.; Harriet R. Lewis*, Co-Chair.; Martha Prybylo, V.P.
Number of staff: 2 full-time professional.
EIN: 043175434
Selected grants: The following grants are a representative sample of this grantmaker's funding activity:
$60,000 to Greater Boston Food Bank, Boston, MA, 2010. For general support.
$35,000 to Year Up, Boston, MA, 2010. For general support.
$10,900 to Museum of Fine Arts, Boston, MA, 2010. For general support.
$3,000 to American Diabetes Association, Alexandria, VA, 2010. For general support.
$1,509 to San Francisco School, San Francisco, CA, 2010. For general support.

1628
Grand Rapids Label Co.

2351 Oak Industrial Dr., N.E.
Grand Rapids, MI 49505-6017
(616) 459-8134
FAX: (616) 459-4543

Company URL: http://www.grlabel.com
Establishment information: Established in 1884.
Company type: Private company
Business activities: Provides commercial printing and publishing services.
Business type (SIC): Printing/commercial; publishing/miscellaneous
Financial profile for 2010: Number of employees, 70
Corporate officers: William W. Muir, Pres.; John Laninga, C.F.O.; Brian Gould, C.I.O.; John Crosby, V.P., Sales and Mktg.
Giving statement: Giving through the Grand Rapids Label Foundation.

Grand Rapids Label Foundation

2351 Oak Industrial Dr., N.E.
Grand Rapids, MI 49505-6017

Establishment information: Established in 1979.
Donor: Grand Rapids Label Co.
Financial data (yr. ended 06/30/11): Assets, $81,197 (M); gifts received, $13,099; expenditures, $17,385; qualifying distributions, $17,385; giving activities include $17,365 for 4 grants (high: $9,365; low: $1,000).
Purpose and activities: The foundation supports organizations involved with arts and culture, education, and children and youth.
Fields of interest: Arts; Education; Health care.
Type of support: Annual campaigns; Building/renovation; Capital campaigns; Continuing support; General/operating support; Program development; Scholarship funds.
Geographic limitations: Giving primarily in Kent County, MI.

Support limitations: No support for foundations or religious or political organizations. No grants to individuals, or for fundraising.
Application information: Applications not accepted. Unsolicited requests for funds not accepted.
Officers: Elizabeth J. Crosby, Pres.; William M. Muir, Secy.; James S. Crosby, Treas.
Directors: Martin J. Allen; Michael P. Allen; Stephen Allen; Susan J. Allen; John F. Crosby; Elizabeth M. Muir; David F. Muir; Kathleen K. Muir; Kathleen Olin.
EIN: 382281916

1629
Grand Victoria Casino

250 S. Grove Ave.
Elgin, IL 60120-6447 (847) 468-7000

Company URL: http://www.grandvictoria-elgin.com
Establishment information: Established in 1994.
Company type: Subsidiary of a public company
Business activities: Operates riverboat casinos.
Business type (SIC): Amusement and recreation services/miscellaneous
Corporate officer: Randy Roberts, Mgr.
Board of directors: Dan Edmund; Patrick Kasbar
Giving statement: Giving through the Grand Victoria Foundation.

Grand Victoria Foundation

230 W. Monroe St., Ste. 2530
Chicago, IL 60606-5048 (312) 609-0200
FAX: (312) 658-0738;
E-mail: nancyf@grandvictoriafdn.org; Application address for Elgin Grantworks: 50 S. Grove Ave. Ste. A, Elgin, IL 60120, tel.: (847) 289-8575, fax: (847) 289-8576; Additional e-mail: info@grandvictoriafdn.org; E-mail for Vital Lands Illinois: vitallandsillinois@grandvictoriafdn.org; URL: http://www.grandvictoriafdn.org

Establishment information: Established in 1996 in IL.
Donors: Grand Victoria Casino; Elgin Riverboat Resort.
Contact: Nancy Fishman, Exec. Dir.; Mary Kay Francel, Dir., Opers.
Financial data (yr. ended 12/31/11): Assets, $94,931,177 (M); gifts received, $9,611,396; expenditures, $16,535,573; qualifying distributions, $16,384,197; giving activities include $14,331,232 for 141 grants (high: $1,685,309; low: $250) and $6,650 for 7 employee matching gifts.
Purpose and activities: The foundation supports programs designed to strengthen educational opportunities for children and adults; foster economic vitality of neighborhoods, cities, and regions; and restore and preserve natural resources.
Fields of interest: Education, early childhood education; Elementary/secondary school reform; Environment, air pollution; Environment, natural resources; Environment, water resources; Environment, land resources; Environment, plant conservation; Community/economic development, public policy; Public affairs, reform; Transportation.
Programs:
Core Grants - Economic Development: The foundation supports programs designed to stimulate state and regional economies through education and employment preparedness; move low-wage earners along career pathways to jobs with higher responsibilities, better wages, and good benefits; expand housing options available near public transportation and jobs; and implement regional growth and transportation strategies that promote economic vitality and environmental health.
Core Grants - Education: The foundation supports programs designed to promote equal access to a high quality education that leads to excellent student outcomes. Special emphasis is directed toward strengthening public policies; improving training, effectiveness and continuous development of teachers/staff/administrators; and implementing effective education and management practices.
Core Grants - Enviroment: The foundation supports programs designed to enhance economic vitality and promote land and water health; develop and implement conservation and stewardship plans to enhance ecosystem services; and promote policies and practices that result in clean air.
Elgin Grantworks: The foundation supports organizations headquartered and working in Elgin, IL. Qualified organizations may apply for general operating grants of up to $25,000 per year.
Vital Lands Illinois: This program supports acquisition of vitally important and irreplaceable natural landscapes across Illinois to create a statewide system of permanently protected natural lands, ensure their long-term stewardship, and build public support for conservation.
Type of support: Continuing support; Employee matching gifts; General/operating support; Land acquisition; Management development/capacity building; Program development; Technical assistance.
Geographic limitations: Giving limited to the Chicago metropolitan region, Elgin, and statewide efforts.
Support limitations: No support for religious or political purposes; or to support programs that are beyond the scope of the Foundation's mission and strategies. No grants to individuals, or for endowments, capital campaigns, fundraising events, debt reduction, research, or planning projects.
Publications: Application guidelines; Financial statement; Grants list; Informational brochure; Occasional report; Program policy statement.
Application information: Applications accepted. Application form required. Applicants should submit the following:
1) timetable for implementation and evaluation of project
2) how project will be sustained once grantmaker support is completed
3) signature and title of chief executive officer
4) results expected from proposed grant
5) qualifications of key personnel
6) statement of problem project will address
7) population served
8) name, address and phone number of organization
9) brief history of organization and description of its mission
10) geographic area to be served
11) copy of most recent annual report/audited financial statement/990
12) how project's results will be evaluated or measured
13) list of company employees involved with the organization
14) explanation of why grantmaker is considered an appropriate donor for project
15) listing of board of directors, trustees, officers and other key people and their affiliations
16) detailed description of project and amount of funding requested
17) plans for cooperation with other organizations, if any
18) contact person
19) copy of current year's organizational budget and/or project budget
20) listing of additional sources and amount of support
21) additional materials/documentation

Initial approach: Letter of inquiry; Core Grant Program: Download guidelines, follow instructions, prepare and send letter of inquiry; Elgin Grantworks: download guidelines/ application form and send proposal with application to 50A S. Grove, Elgin, IL 60120; Vital Land Illinois: Download guidelines, prepare application and email to vitallandsillinois@grandvictoriafdn.org
Board meeting date(s): Quarterly
Deadline(s): 1st Fri. in May and Oct. for Education, Economic Development, and Environment; 1st Fri. in Feb., Jun., and Oct. for Elgin Grantworks; None for Vital Lands Illinois
Final notification: 20 working days for letter of inquiry; Elgin Grantworks: 8-10 weeks for grant decision; Vital Lands Illinois: 5-10 weeks from receipt of full proposal

Officers and Directors:* Nicholas J. Pritzker, Pres.; Richard L. Schulze, Exec. V.P.; Daniel Azark*, V.P.; Phyllis James, Secy.; Corey Sanders*, Treas.; Nancy Fishman, Exec. Dir.; Taffy Hoffer; Will Martin; Eric T. McKissack.
Number of staff: 7 full-time professional; 2 full-time support.
EIN: 364107162
Selected grants: The following grants are a representative sample of this grantmaker's funding activity:
$1,685,309 to Oak Park-River Forest Community Foundation, Oak Park, IL, 2011. For challenge grant.
$1,268,254 to DuPage Community Foundation, Wheaton, IL, 2011. For challenge grant.
$666,600 to University of Illinois at Urbana-Champaign, Urbana, IL, 2011. For project support.
$510,000 to HeartLands Conservancy, Mascoutah, IL, 2011. For project support.
$505,970 to Openlands, Chicago, IL, 2011. For project support.
$300,000 to Illinois Action for Children, Chicago, IL, 2011. For project support.
$250,002 to Kankakee River Valley Community Foundation, Kankakee, IL, 2011. For challenge grant.
$38,435 to Clifftop Alliance, Maeystown, IL, 2011. For project support.
$31,000 to Collaboration for Early Childhood Care and Education, Oak Park, IL, 2011. For project support.
$25,000 to One Hope United, Lake Villa, IL, 2011. For general operating support.

1630
Grandma Brown's Beans, Inc.

5837 Scenic Ave.
P.O. Box 230
Mexico, NY 13114-3481 (315) 963-7221

Establishment information: Established in 1990.
Company type: Private company
Business activities: Produces beans and bean products.
Business type (SIC): Specialty foods/canned, frozen, and preserved
Corporate officer: Sandra L. Brown, Chair., Pres., and C.E.O.
Board of director: Sandra L. Brown, Chair.
Giving statement: Giving through the Grandma Brown Foundation, Inc.

Grandma Brown Foundation, Inc.

P.O. Box 230
Mexico, NY 13114-0230 (315) 963-7221

Establishment information: Established in 1961 in NY.
Donors: Grandma Brown's Beans, Inc.; Sandra L. Brown.
Contact: Sandra L. Brown, Tr.
Financial data (yr. ended 12/31/11): Assets, $277,778 (M); gifts received, $50,000; expenditures, $23,127; qualifying distributions, $21,500; giving activities include $21,500 for grants.
Purpose and activities: The foundation supports organizations involved with media, performing arts, medical education, health, and cancer and awards college scholarships to local area residents.
Fields of interest: Education; Human services; Public affairs.
Type of support: General/operating support; Scholarships—to individuals.
Application information: Applications accepted. Application form required. Applicants should submit the following:
1) copy of IRS Determination Letter
2) detailed description of project and amount of funding requested
Initial approach: Letter
Copies of proposal: 1
Deadline(s): None
Trustee: Sandra L. Brown.
EIN: 166052275

1631
Grange Mutual Casualty Company

650 S. Front St.
Columbus, OH 43206 (614) 445-2900

Company URL: http://www.grangeinsurance.com
Establishment information: Established in 1935.
Company type: Mutual company
Business activities: Sells automobile, casualty, and life insurance.
Business type (SIC): Insurance/fire, marine, and casualty; insurance/life
Financial profile for 2010: Number of employees, 850
Corporate officers: Michael V. Parrott, Chair.; Thomas H. Welch, Pres. and C.E.O.; Mark C. Russell, V.P. and C.A.O.; Charles R. Carter, V.P. and C.I.O.; Carol L. Drake, V.P., Mktg.; Robert Holtsberry, V.P., Human Resources; David T. Roark, V.P., Genl. Counsel, and Secy.
Board of directors: Michael V. Parrott, Chair.; Glenn E. Corlett; Robert J. O'Brien; Philip W. Stichter; Philip H. Urban
Subsidiary: Grange Life Insurance Co. Inc., Columbus, OH
Giving statement: Giving through the Grange Mutual Casualty Company Contributions Program.

Grange Mutual Casualty Company Contributions Program

671 S. High St., 11th Fl.
Columbus, OH 43206-1066 (614) 445-2609
FAX: (614) 445-2428; In-kind printing contact: Natalina R. Fickell, Exec. Asst., tel.: (614) 445-2609; e-mail: fickelln@grangeinsurance.com. Volunteer support contact: Sue Ridolfo, Mgr., Assoc. & Community Progs., tel.: (614) 445-2690; e-mail: ridolfos@grangeinsurance.com; URL: https://www.grangeinsurance.com/community.aspx

Contact: Patricia Eshman, Asst. V.P., Comm. Rels.
Purpose and activities: Grange makes charitable contributions to nonprofit organizations involved with arts and culture, education, and on a case by case basis. Support is given primarily in areas of company operations.
Fields of interest: Arts; Education; Health care; Safety/disasters; Human services; Community/economic development; Public affairs.
Type of support: Capital campaigns; Employee matching gifts; Employee volunteer services; General/operating support.
Geographic limitations: Giving primarily in areas of company operations with emphasis on Columbus area and central OH.
Application information: Proposals should be submitted using organization letterhead. Applicants should submit the following:
1) copy of IRS Determination Letter
Initial approach: Proposal to headquarters

1632
Granite Construction Incorporated

585 W. Beach St.
P.O. Box 50085
Watsonville, CA 95076 (831) 724-1011
FAX: (831) 722-9657

Company URL: http://www.graniteconstruction.com
Establishment information: Established in 1922.
Company type: Public company
Company ticker symbol and exchange: GVA/NYSE
Business activities: Operates holding company; provides general contract heavy construction services.
Business type (SIC): Heavy construction other than building construction contractors; holding company
Financial profile for 2012: Number of employees, 1,700; assets, $1,729,490,000; sales volume, $2,083,040,000; pre-tax net income, $81,030,000; expenses, $2,002,200,000; liabilities, $899,530,000
Fortune 1000 ranking: 2012—921st in revenues, 831st in profits, and 888th in assets
Corporate officers: William H. Powell, Chair.; James H. Roberts, Pres. and C.E.O.; Laurel J. Krzeminski, V.P. and C.F.O.; Richard A. Watts, V.P., Genl. Counsel, and Secy.; Philip DeCocco, V.P., Human Resources
Board of directors: William H. Powell, Chair.; Claes G. Bjork; James W. Bradford, Jr.; Gary M. Cusumano; William G. Dorey; David H. Kelsey; Rebecca A. McDonald; James H. Roberts; Gaddi H. Vasquez
Subsidiaries: Granite Halmar Construction Co., Inc., Mount Vernon, NY; Wilder Construction Co., Everett, WA
Division: Heavy Construction Div., Watsonville, CA
Offices: Tucson, AZ; Bakersfield, French Camp, Fresno, Indio, Sacramento, Santa Barbara, Santa Clara, CA; Sparks, NV; Salt Lake City, UT
Giving statement: Giving through the Granite Construction Incorporated Corporate Giving Program.
Company EIN: 770239383

Granite Construction Incorporated Corporate Giving Program

585 W. Beach St.
Box 50085
Watsonville, CA 95076-5123 (916) 855-8868
E-mail: robert.dugan@gcinc.com

Contact: Robert Dugan, Dir., Public and Gov't. Affairs
Purpose and activities: Granite makes charitable contributions to nonprofit organizations involved with arts and culture, education, youth sports, human services, community development, and senior citizens. Support is given primarily in areas of company operations.
Fields of interest: Arts; Education; Recreation; Youth development; Human services; Community/economic development Aging.
Type of support: Employee volunteer services; General/operating support; In-kind gifts.
Geographic limitations: Giving primarily in areas of company operations.

1633
Grant Thornton LLP

175 W. Jackson Blvd., 20th Fl.
Chicago, IL 60604 (312) 856-0200

Company URL: http://www.gti.org
Establishment information: Established in 1924.
Business activities: Provides accounting services.
Business type (SIC): Accounting, auditing, and bookkeeping services
Financial profile for 2009: Number of employees, 11,385; sales volume, $1,690,000,000
Corporate officers: Stephen Chipman, C.E.O.; Thomas G. Rotherham, Pres.; Lou J. Grabowsky, C.O.O.; Russell G. Wieman, C.F.O.; Thomas D. Rafter, Genl. Counsel
Subsidiaries: Grant Thornton Financial Special Services, New York, NY; Grant Thornton International Trade Resources, Washington, DC
Offices: Irvine, Los Angeles, Sacramento, San Francisco, San Jose, Stockton, Woodland Hills, CA; Colorado Springs, Denver, CO; Washington, DC; Fort Lauderdale, Miami, St. Petersburg, Tampa, West Palm Beach, FL; Atlanta, GA; Honolulu, HI; Wichita, KS; Baltimore, MD; Boston, MA; Southfield, MI; Minneapolis, MN; Kansas City, St. Louis, MO; Lincoln, Omaha, NE; Reno, NV; Parsippany, NJ; Melville, New York, NY; Cincinnati, Cleveland, OH; Oklahoma City, OK; Portland, OR; Jenkintown, Philadelphia, PA; Dallas, Houston, TX; Provo, Salt Lake City, UT; Vienna, VA; Seattle, WA; Appleton, Brookfield, Fond du Lac, Madison, WI
Giving statement: Giving through the Grant Thornton Foundation.

Grant Thornton Foundation

175 W. Jackson Blvd.
Chicago, IL 60604

Establishment information: Established in 2007 in IL.
Donor: Grant Thornton LLP.
Financial data (yr. ended 07/31/11): Assets, $1,000 (M); gifts received, $795,751; expenditures, $795,751; qualifying distributions, $784,157; giving activities include $784,157 for grants.
Fields of interest: Higher education.
Type of support: General/operating support.
Geographic limitations: Giving primarily in areas of company operations in AK, AL, AR, AZ, CA, CO, CT, DC, FL, GA, HI, IL, KS, KY, MA, MD, ME, MI, MN, MO, MS, NC, ND, NH, NJ, NM, NY, OH, OK, OR, PA, RI, SC, TN, UT, VA, WA, WI, and WV.
Application information: Applications not accepted. Contributes only to pre-selected organizations.

Officers and Directors:* Stan I. Levy*, Pres.; Margaret M. Zagel, Secy.; Fred K. Walz*, Treas.; Anne Lang.
EIN: 300438415
Selected grants: The following grants are a representative sample of this grantmaker's funding activity:
$101,954 to American Red Cross, Chicago, IL, 2011.
$28,940 to Brigham Young University, Provo, UT, 2011.
$19,050 to University of Utah, Salt Lake City, UT, 2011.
$18,700 to University of Florida Foundation, Gainesville, FL, 2011.
$16,650 to Oklahoma State University Foundation, Stillwater, OK, 2011.
$14,500 to University of Notre Dame Foundation, Notre Dame, IN, 2011.
$14,000 to University of Illinois Foundation, Urbana, IL, 2011.
$11,300 to Save the Children Federation, Westport, CT, 2011.
$6,200 to Loyola University of Chicago, Chicago, IL, 2011.
$1,300 to United States Fund for UNICEF, New York, NY, 2011.

1634
Graphic Arts Show Company, Inc.

1899 Preston White Dr.
Reston, VA 20191-5468 (703) 264-7200

Company URL: http://www.gasc.org
Establishment information: Established in 1982.
Company type: Private company
Business activities: Operates business association serving the graphic communications and converting industries.
Business type (SIC): Business association
Corporate officers: Vince Lapinski, C.E.O.; Ralph Nappi, Pres.
Giving statement: Giving through the Graphic Arts Education and Research Foundation.

Graphic Arts Education and Research Foundation

1899 Preston White Dr.
Reston, VA 20191-4326 (703) 264-7200
FAX: (703) 620-3165; E-mail: gaerf@npes.org; Toll free tel.: (866) 381-9839; E-mail for Eileen Cassidy: ecassidy@npes.org; URL: http://www.gaerf.org

Establishment information: Established in 1984 in VA.
Donors: Graphic Arts Show Co., Inc.; Hilton Chicago; Intercontinental Chicago; Hyatt Regency Chicago; Hyatt Regency McCormick Place; Sheraton Chicago Hotel & Towers; Cygnus Business Media, Inc.
Financial data (yr. ended 12/31/11): Assets, $876,585 (M); gifts received, $239,090; expenditures, $486,208; qualifying distributions, $29,766; giving activities include $29,766 for grants.
Purpose and activities: The foundation supports education and research pertaining to the graphic communications industry.
Fields of interest: Health care; Youth development.
Type of support: Conferences/seminars; Curriculum development; Program development; Publication; Research; Scholarship funds.
Geographic limitations: Giving primarily in NC and NY.
Support limitations: Generally, no grants for equipment, except under rare and extenuating circumstances.
Publications: Annual report; Application guidelines; Informational brochure.
Application information: Applications accepted. Application form required.
Initial approach: Proposal
Copies of proposal: 3
Deadline(s): May 30
Officers and Directors:* Sephen L. Johnson, Chair.; Ralph J. Nappi, Pres.; Michael F. Makin, Secy.; Joseph P. Truncale, Treas.; H.A. Brandtjen III; D.J. Burgess; Randolph W. Camp; William Delgado; Patrick Klarecki; Darren Loken; James H. Mayes.
Number of staff: 2 full-time professional.
EIN: 521321169

1635
Graphic Packaging Holding Company

(formerly Graphic Packaging International, Inc.)
814 Livingston Ct.
Marietta, GA 30067-8940 (770) 644-3000
FAX: (770) 644-2970

Company URL: http://www.graphicpkg.com
Establishment information: Established in 1923.
Company type: Public company
Company ticker symbol and exchange: GPK/NYSE
Business activities: Manufactures and provides paperboard and paperboard packaging solutions; manufactures containerboard.
Business type (SIC): Paperboard mills; paperboard containers
Financial profile for 2012: Number of employees, 13,900; assets, $4,620,800,000; sales volume, $4,337,100,000; pre-tax net income, $200,300,000; expenses, $4,025,700,000; liabilities, $3,646,800,000
Fortune 1000 ranking: 2012—549th in revenues, 698th in profits, and 618th in assets
Corporate officers: John R. Miller, Chair.; David W. Scheible, Pres. and C.E.O.; Daniel J. Blount, Sr. V.P. and C.F.O.; Stephen A. Hellrung, Sr. V.P., Genl. Counsel, and Secy.; Cynthia A. Baerman, Sr. V.P., Human Resources; Deborah R. Frank, V.P. and C.A.O.
Board of directors: John R. Miller, Chair.; George V. Bayly; G. Andrea Botta; David D. Campbell; Kevin J. Conway; Jeffrey H. Coors; Harold R. Logan, Jr.; Michael G. MacDougall; David A. Perdue; David W. Scheible; Robert W. Tieken; Lynn A. Wentworth
Giving statement: Giving through the Graphic Packaging Int'l Philanthropic Fund.

Graphic Packaging Int'l Philanthropic Fund

(formerly Riverwood International Corporation Philanthropic Fund)
814 Livingston Ct.
Marietta, GA 30067

Establishment information: Established in 1993 in GA and DE.
Donors: Riverwood International Corp.; Graphic Packaging International, Inc.
Contact: Lucia Ross
Financial data (yr. ended 12/31/11): Assets, $68,849 (M); gifts received, $100,000; expenditures, $67,025; qualifying distributions, $61,000; giving activities include $61,000 for 1 grant.
Purpose and activities: The foundation awards college scholarships to children and dependents of Graphic Packaging employees. The program is administered by Scholarship America.
Fields of interest: Education.
Programs:
Matching Gifts: The foundation matches contributions made by employees, directors, and retirees of Graphic Packaging International to educational institutions on a one-for-one basis.
Scholarship Grants: The foundation awards college scholarships to children of employees of Graphic Packaging International. The program is administered by Scholarship America, Inc.
Type of support: Employee-related scholarships.
Geographic limitations: Giving primarily in areas of company operations, with emphasis on GA.
Support limitations: No grants to individuals (except for employee-related scholarships).
Application information: Applications accepted. Application form not required.
Initial approach: Proposal
Deadline(s): None
Officers and Trustees:* Cynthia Baerman*, Pres.; Bradford G. Ankerholz, V.P. and Treas.; Stephen A. Hellrung, Secy.; Teresa A. Bishop; Gregory L. Mangum.
EIN: 582059854

1636
The Graphic Printing Company, Inc.

309 W. Main St.
Portland, IN 47371-1803 (260) 726-8141

Establishment information: Established in 1946.
Company type: Private company
Business activities: Provides commercial printing services.
Business type (SIC): Printing/commercial
Corporate officers: John C. Ronald, Pres.; Nyree Lewis, Mgr.
Board of director: Bill Milligan
Giving statement: Giving through the Graphic Printing Company, Inc. Corporate Giving Program.

The Graphic Printing Company, Inc. Corporate Giving Program

309 W. Main St.
Portland, IN 47371-1803

Purpose and activities: Graphic Printing makes charitable contributions to nonprofit organizations on a case by case basis. Support is given primarily in Portland, Indiana.
Fields of interest: General charitable giving.
Type of support: General/operating support.
Geographic limitations: Giving primarily in Portland, IN.

1637
Graphix Unlimited, Inc.

3947 U.S. 106 E.
Bremen, IN 46506-9066 (574) 546-2074

Company URL: http://www.graphixunlimited.com/
Establishment information: Established in 1990.
Company type: Private company
Business activities: Designs screenprinted products.
Business type (SIC): Printing/commercial

Corporate officers: Gregory Erickson, C.E.O.; Bernie Erickson, Pres.; Jerry Anders, Cont.
Giving statement: Giving through the His Hands Foundation, Inc.

His Hands Foundation, Inc.

c/o Graphix Unlimited, Inc.
3947 US 106 E.
Bremen, IN 46506-9066 (574) 546-3770

Establishment information: Established in 1995 in IN.
Donor: Graphix Unlimited, Inc.
Contact: Bernard B. Erickson, Jr., Dir.
Financial data (yr. ended 12/31/11): Assets, $1,050 (M); gifts received, $2,000; expenditures, $1,588; qualifying distributions, $1,083; giving activities include $1,083 for 3 grants (high: $1,000; low: $30).
Purpose and activities: The foundation supports organizations involved with education, cancer, Alzheimer's disease, baseball, human services, and other areas.
Fields of interest: Education; Human services.
Type of support: General/operating support; Scholarship funds.
Geographic limitations: Giving primarily in IN.
Application information: Applications accepted. Application form required.
Initial approach: Contact foundation for application form
Deadline(s): None
Directors: Bernard B. Erickson, Jr.; Gregory Erickson.
EIN: 351948627

1638
Gravel & Shea

76 Saint Paul St., 7th Fl.
Burlington, VT 05402-0369 (802) 658-0220

Company URL: http://www.gravelshea.com/
Establishment information: Established in 1955.
Company type: Private company
Business activities: Operates law firm.
Business type (SIC): Legal services
Giving statement: Giving through the Gravel & Shea Pro Bono Program.

Gravel & Shea Pro Bono Program

76 Saint Paul St., 7th Fl.
Burlington, VT 05402-0369 (802) 658-0220
E-mail: roneill@gravelshea.com; URL: http://www.gravelshea.com/

Contact: Robert F. O'Neill, Partner
Fields of interest: Legal services.
Type of support: Pro bono services - legal.
Geographic limitations: Giving primarily in areas of company operations in Burlington, VT.
Application information: A Department Chair manages the pro bono program.

1639
Gray Ghost Ventures

2200 Century Pkwy., Ste. 100
Atlanta, GA 30345 (678) 365-4700
FAX: (678) 365-4752

Company URL: http://www.grayghostventures.com
Establishment information: Established in 2003.
Company type: Private company
Business type (SIC): Business services/miscellaneous
Corporate officers: Arun Gore, Pres. and C.E.O.; Brenda Bracken, Treas.
Giving statement: Giving through the Gray Ghost Ventures Corporate Giving Program.

Gray Ghost Ventures Corporate Giving Program

2200 Century Pkwy., Ste. 100
Atlanta, GA 30345-3103 (678) 365-4700
E-mail: info@grayghostventures.com; URL: http://www.grayghostventures.com

1640
Graybar Electric Company, Inc.

34 N. Meramec Ave.
St. Louis, MO 63105-3882 (314) 573-9200

Company URL: http://www.graybar.com
Establishment information: Established in 1869.
Company type: Private company
Business activities: Sells electrical, telecommunications, and networking products wholesale.
Business type (SIC): Electrical goods—wholesale
Financial profile for 2011: Number of employees, 7,000; assets, $1,519,400,000; sales volume, $4,616,400,000
Corporate officers: Robert A. Reynolds, Jr., Chair., Pres., and C.E.O.; Kathleen M. Mazzarella, Exec. V.P. and C.O.O.; D. Beatty D'Alessandro, Sr. V.P. and C.F.O.; Matthew W. Geekie, Sr. V.P., Genl. Counsel, and Secy.; Lawrence R. Giglio, Sr. V.P., Opers.; Beverly L. Propst, Sr. V.P., Human Resources
Board of directors: Robert A. Reynolds, Jr., Chair.; Richard A. Cole; D. Beatty D'Alessandro; Matthew W. Geekie; Lawrence R. Giglio; Thomas S. Gurganous; Randall R. Harwood; Frank H. Hughes; Robert C. Lyons; Kathleen M. Mazzarella; Beverly L. Propst
Subsidiaries: Commonwealth Controls Corp., Richmond, VA; Distribution Associates, Inc., Chicago, IL; Graybar Financial Services, Inc., Saint Louis, MO; Graybar International, Inc., Saint Louis, MO; Graybar Services, Inc., Glendale Heights, IL
International operations: Japan
Giving statement: Giving through the Graybar Foundation.
Company EIN: 130794380

Graybar Foundation

34 N. Meramec Ave.
Clayton, MO 63105-3844
Application address: P.O. Box 7231, St. Louis, MO 63177

Establishment information: Established in 1984 in MO.
Donor: Graybar Electric Company, Inc.
Contact: Mathew W. Geekie, Secy.
Financial data (yr. ended 11/30/11): Assets, $3,016,352 (M); gifts received, $173,809; expenditures, $243,615; qualifying distributions, $242,565; giving activities include $218,500 for 32 grants (high: $80,000; low: $1,000) and $24,065 for employee matching gifts.
Purpose and activities: The foundation supports zoos and festivals and organizations involved with arts and culture, youth development, human services, and public policy.
Fields of interest: Performing arts, orchestras; Arts; Zoos/zoological societies; Recreation, fairs/festivals; Boy scouts; Girl scouts; Youth development; Salvation Army; YM/YWCAs & YM/YWHAs; Children/youth, services; Residential/custodial care; Human services; Community/economic development, public policy; United Ways and Federated Giving Programs.
Type of support: Continuing support; Employee matching gifts; General/operating support.
Geographic limitations: Giving primarily in St. Louis, MO.
Application information: Applications accepted. Proposals should be submitted using organization letterhead. Application form required. Applicants should submit the following:
1) brief history of organization and description of its mission
2) copy of most recent annual report/audited financial statement/990
3) descriptive literature about organization
4) detailed description of project and amount of funding requested
5) copy of current year's organizational budget and/or project budget
6) listing of additional sources and amount of support

Initial approach: Proposal
Copies of proposal: 1
Deadline(s): None
Final notification: Usually within 120 days
Officers and Directors:* Robert A. Reynolds, Jr.*, Pres.; Kathleen M. Mazzerella*, V.P.; J. N. Reed, V.P.; Mathew W. Geekie*, Secy.; D. Beatty D'Alessandro*, Treas.; Lawrence R. Giglio; R. C. Lyons; Beverly L. Propst.
EIN: 431301419
Selected grants: The following grants are a representative sample of this grantmaker's funding activity:
$5,000 to Teach for America, New York, NY, 2010.
$2,500 to United Negro College Fund, Fairfax, VA, 2010.
$2,000 to Ronald McDonald House Charities, Oak Brook, IL, 2010.

1641
Graycor Inc.

2 Mid America Plz., Ste. 400
Oakbrook Terrace, IL 60181
(630) 684-7110
FAX: (630) 684-7111

Company URL: http://www.graycor.com/
Establishment information: Established in 1921.
Company type: Private company
Business activities: Manages construction, maintenance, and design/build services of industrial plants, office towers and shopping malls.
Business type (SIC): Contractors/general nonresidential building
Corporate officers: Melvin Gray, Chair. and C.E.O.; Steven F. Gray, Vice-Chair. and C.F.O.; Matthew J. Gray, Pres.; Kenneth A. Isaacs, C.O.O.
Board of directors: Melvin Gray, Chair.; Steven F. Gray, Vice-Chair.; Matthew Gray
Giving statement: Giving through the Sue and Melvin Gray Foundation.

The Sue and Melvin Gray Foundation

(formerly Melvin and Susanne Gray Foundation)
2 Mid America Plz., Ste. 400
Oakbrook Terrace, IL 60181-4714

Establishment information: Established in 1986 in IL.
Donor: Graycor, Inc.
Financial data (yr. ended 12/31/11): Assets, $1,216,558 (M); expenditures, $168,534; qualifying distributions, $157,549; giving activities include $157,500 for grants.
Purpose and activities: The foundation supports organizations involved with arts and culture, education, health, and human services.
Fields of interest: Performing arts, theater; Performing arts, orchestras; Arts; Higher education; Libraries (public); Education; Hospitals (general); Children/youth, services; Human services; Jewish federated giving programs.
Type of support: General/operating support.
Geographic limitations: Giving primarily in Chicago, IL.
Support limitations: No grants to individuals.
Application information: Applications accepted. Application form not required.
Initial approach: Letter of inquiry
Deadline(s): None
Officers: Melvin Gray, Pres.; Susanne Gray, V.P.; Steven F. Gray, Secy.
EIN: 363485579

1642
The Great Atlantic & Pacific Tea Company, Inc.

(also known as A & P)
2 Paragon Dr.
P.O. Box 418
Montvale, NJ 07645-1718 (201) 573-9700
FAX: (201) 930-4079

Company URL: http://www.aptea.com
Establishment information: Established in 1859.
Company type: Public company
Company ticker symbol and exchange: GAPTQ/Pink Sheets
Business activities: Operates and franchises supermarkets.
Business type (SIC): Groceries—retail
Financial profile for 2011: Number of employees, 39,000; assets, $2,644,850,000; sales volume, $8,078,450,000; pre-tax net income, -$677,200,000; expenses, $8,551,060,000; liabilities, $3,642,510,000
Corporate officer: Samuel M. Martin III, Pres. and C.E.O.
Subsidiaries: Compass Foods, Inc., Montvale, NJ; Food Emporium, Inc., Montvale, NJ; Kohl's Food Stores, Inc., Wauwatosa, WI; Pathmark Stores, Inc., Carteret, NJ; Super Fresh Food Markets, Inc., Montvale, NJ; Waldbaum, Inc., Springfield, MA
International operations: Bermuda
Giving statement: Giving through the A & P Corporate Giving Program.

A & P Corporate Giving Program

2 Paragon Dr.
Montvale, NJ 07645-1718
URL: http://www.apsupermarket.com/donation-and-solicitation-requests
Additional URL: http://www.aptea.com/community.asp

Purpose and activities: A&P makes charitable contributions of gift cards to nonprofit organizations involved with the education, health, and welfare of children. Support is limited to areas of company operations in the Connecticut, New Jersey, and New York tri-state area.
Fields of interest: Elementary school/education; Health care Children.
Type of support: In-kind gifts.
Geographic limitations: Giving primarily in areas of company operations in the CT, NJ, and NY tri-state area.
Support limitations: No support for political organizations or discriminatory organizations.
Publications: Application guidelines.
Application information: Applications accepted. Proposals should be submitted using organization letterhead. Support is limited to 1 contribution per organization during any given year. Application form required. Applicants should submit the following:
1) name, address and phone number of organization
2) detailed description of project and amount of funding requested
3) plans for acknowledgement
Applications should include the organization's Tax ID Number, and any deadlines, if applicable.
Initial approach: Download application form and submit with proposal to nearest company store
Deadline(s): 4 weeks prior to need

1643
Great Lakes Castings LLC

(formerly Great Lakes Castings Corporation)
800 N. Washington Ave.
Ludington, MI 49431-2724 (231) 843-2501

Company URL: http://www.greatlakescastings.com
Establishment information: Established in 1945.
Company type: Subsidiary of a private company
Business activities: Manufactures compression bodies, hydraulic valves, pumps, and light automotive and miscellaneous gray iron castings.
Business type (SIC): Iron and steel foundries; metal products/fabricated; machinery/general industry
Corporate officers: Robert E. Killips, Pres. and C.E.O.; Carol Henke, V.P., Finance and Admin.; Eric Bansch, V.P., Sales and Mktg.
Plants: Holland, Ludington, MI
Giving statement: Giving through the Great Lakes Castings Corporation Foundation.

Great Lakes Castings Corporation Foundation

800 N. Washington Ave.
Ludington, MI 49431-2724 (231) 843-2501

Donor: Great Lakes Castings Corp.
Contact: Carol Henke, Tr.
Financial data (yr. ended 12/31/11): Assets, $858,777 (M); gifts received, $3,739; expenditures, $35,631; qualifying distributions, $29,617; giving activities include $29,617 for grants.
Purpose and activities: The foundation supports organizations involved with higher education and awards college scholarships to high school students in Ludington, Michigan, area school districts.
Fields of interest: Health organizations; Human services; Community/economic development.
Type of support: General/operating support; Scholarships—to individuals.
Geographic limitations: Giving limited to the Ludington, MI, area.
Application information: Applications accepted. Application form required.
Initial approach: Contact foundation for application information
Deadline(s): Apr. 1 of applicant's senior year of high school or college for scholarships
Trustees: Tim Fischer; Carol Henke; Rob Killips.
EIN: 382250546

1644
Great Lakes Financial Resources Inc.

(doing business as Great Lakes Bank)
4600 W. Lincoln Hwy.
Matteson, IL 60443-2315 (708) 503-0400

Company URL: https://www.bankofchoice.com
Establishment information: Established in 1896.
Company type: Private company
Business activities: Operates commercial banks.
Business type (SIC): Banks/commercial
Financial profile for 2009: Number of employees, 275
Corporate officers: Thomas S. Agler, Pres., C.E.O., and C.O.O.; Jim Calvert, C.F.O.
Giving statement: Giving through the Great Lakes Bank Foundation.

Great Lakes Bank Foundation

(formerly Great Lakes Financial Resources Charitable Foundation, Inc.)
4600 W. Lincoln Hwy.
Matteson, IL 60443-2315
E-mail: VanZeeP@bankofchoice.com; URL: https://www.bankofchoice.com/foundation.aspx

Establishment information: Established in 1998 in IL.
Donors: Great Lakes Financial Resources; Great Lakes Bank, N.A.
Financial data (yr. ended 12/31/11): Assets, $1,245,151 (M); gifts received, $30,000; expenditures, $46,555; qualifying distributions, $45,000; giving activities include $45,000 for 2 grants (high: $25,000; low: $20,000).
Purpose and activities: The foundation supports nonprofit organizations involved with healthcare and education. Special emphasis is directed toward programs that target children and the economically disadvantaged.
Fields of interest: Education; Health care Children; Economically disadvantaged.
Type of support: Continuing support; Program development.
Geographic limitations: Giving limited to areas of company operations in Alsip, Blue Island, Flossmoor, Hazel Crest, Homewood, Lansing, Matteson, and Mokena, IL.
Support limitations: No support for political, labor, or fraternal organizations, or other private or public foundations that are grant-making bodies. No grants to individuals, or for general operating expenses, or administrative salaries.
Application information: Applications not accepted. Unsolicted requests for funds not accepted.
Directors: Randall J. De Vries; Anita N. Lebowitz; Ronald T. Shropshire.
Officers: Thomas S. Agler, Chair.; Paul S. Van Zee, Secy.-Treas.
EIN: 363925858
Selected grants: The following grants are a representative sample of this grantmaker's funding activity:
$25,000 to Governors State University Foundation, University Park, IL, 2011.

1645
Great Lakes Higher Education Corporation

2401 International Ln.
Madison, WI 53704-3192 (608) 246-1800

Company URL: https://www.mygreatlakes.org
Establishment information: Established in 1967.
Company type: Private company
Business activities: Operates student loan service company and is designated student loan guarantor for Minnesota, Ohio, Wisconsin, Puerto Rico, and the U.S. Virgin Islands.
Business type (SIC): Credit reporting and collection agencies
Corporate officers: Richard Dick George, Pres. and C.E.O.; Nancy Seifert, C.F.O.; Brett Lindquist, Sr. V.P., Sales and Mktg.
Giving statement: Giving through the Great Lakes Higher Education Corporation.

Great Lakes Higher Education Corporation

2401 International Ln.
Madison, WI 53704-3192
URL: https://www.mygreatlakes.org/web/community/index.html

Establishment information: Established in 1967 in WI; supporting organization of Great Lakes Higher Education Guaranty Corporation and Northstar Guarantee, Inc.
Financial data (yr. ended 12/31/11): Revenue, $21,798,418; assets, $555,540,168 (M); expenditures, $54,773.
Fields of interest: Elementary/secondary education; Higher education; Higher education, college (community/junior); Higher education, college; Higher education, university; Education Children/youth; Children; Adults; Minorities; Economically disadvantaged.
Programs:
College Ready Grants: Through this program, grants of up to $300,000 will be awarded to sustain, improve, or replicate college-success programming during the 2013-14 academic year. The program is designed to support efforts to help students from low-income households, students of color, and students who will be first in their family to attend college prepare for academic success. The following outcomes, proven to be strong indicators of college success, will be used to measure student achievement: ACT or SAT scores, grade-point average, or academic performance as indicated by pre- and post-test scores. Community-based organizations and nonprofit colleges and universities in Minnesota and Wisconsin that provide academic-focused services to traditionally underserved students in grades 6-12 and adult learners are encouraged to apply.
College Success Grants: These grants of up to $300,000 are intended to foster programs that connect students of similar backgrounds who are attending two- and four-year colleges and universities, including community and technical colleges, through mentoring and proactive advising services, the development of learning communities, and academic tutoring. To be considered for funding, programs must provide ongoing services designed to increase retention and persistence rates for a defined group of students in collaboration with external or internal partners. Applicants must be nonprofit, Title IV-eligible higher education institutions and community-based organizations with 501(c)(3) tax-exempt status and be located in Iowa, Minnesota, or Wisconsin.
Requests for Proposals: The corporation occasionally puts out requests for proposals (RFPs) that focus on two funding priorities: academic enrichment programs that help students prepare for success in postsecondary education (and that may also include components that provide supporting services such as counseling, mentoring, and parental engagement), and persistence programs that address barriers preventing students enrolled in a postsecondary institution from completing a degree or certificate. Programs must provide baseline data to demonstrate the problem to be solved, and develop data-driven, measurable outcomes for each of the program's activities.
Geographic limitations: Giving limited to WI.
Application information: Applications accepted. See website for request for proposal for specific RFP opportunities. Contributes only to pre-selected organizations; unsolicited requests for funds not considered or acknowledged.
Deadline(s): Mar. 14 for College Success Grants; varies for all others
Officers and Directors:* Richard George*, Chair., Pres., C.E.O., Treas., and Genl. Counsel; David J. Hanson*, Secy.; Nancy Seifert*, C.F.O. and Asst. Secy.; Emerson L. Brumback; James N. Elliott; Janice Hesalroad; Linda Hoeschler; Alex J. Pollock; Richard A. Weiss.
EIN: 391090394

1646
Great West Casualty Company

(also known as GWCC)
1100 W. 29th St.
P.O. Box 277
South Sioux City, NE 68776-3130
(404) 494-2084

Company URL: http://
Establishment information: Established in 1956.
Company type: Subsidiary of a public company
Business activities: Sells property and casualty insurance.
Business type (SIC): Insurance/fire, marine, and casualty
Corporate officers: R. Scott Rager, Chair.; Jim Jensen, C.E.O.; Hugh Fugleberg, Co-Pres. and C.O.O.; Al Johnson, Co-Pres.; Gaylen L. Tenhulzen, Sr. V.P. and C.F.O.
Board of director: R. Scott Rager, Chair.
Giving statement: Giving through the Great West Casualty Company Contributions Program.

Great West Casualty Company Contributions Program

c/o Corp. Human Resources Dept.
1100 W. 29th St., Box 277
South Sioux City, NE 68776-3130 (800) 228-8602

Purpose and activities: Great West makes charitable contributions to nonprofit organizations involved with education. Support is given primarily in the South Sioux City, Nebraska, area.
Fields of interest: Education.
Type of support: Employee volunteer services; General/operating support; Scholarships—to individuals; Sponsorships.
Geographic limitations: Giving primarily in the South Sioux City, NE, area.

1648
The Greater Construction Corp.

(also known as Greater Homes)
1105 Kensington Park Dr.
Altamonte Springs, FL 32714-1939
(407) 869-0300

Establishment information: Established in 1965.
Company type: Subsidiary of a public company
Business activities: Provides commercial and industrial construction services.
Business type (SIC): Real estate operators and lessors; operative builders
Corporate officers: Robert A. Mandell, Chair. and C.E.O.; Charles W. Gregg, Pres.
Board of director: Robert A. Mandell, Chair.
Giving statement: Giving through the Mandell Family Charitable Foundation, Inc.

Mandell Family Charitable Foundation, Inc.

(formerly The Greater Construction Corp. Charitable Foundation, Inc.)
P.O. Box 2106
Winter Park, FL 32790-2106

Establishment information: Established in 1988 in FL.
Donors: The Greater Construction Corp.; Lester Zimmerman; Robert A. Mandell; Maynard Knapp; Allison Knapp.
Financial data (yr. ended 12/31/10): Assets, $0 (M); expenditures, $7,812; qualifying distributions, $6,557; giving activities include $6,557 for 1 grant.
Purpose and activities: The foundation supports organizations involved with secondary and higher education, health, children and youth, and homelessness.
Fields of interest: Health care.
Type of support: General/operating support.
Geographic limitations: Giving limited to Orlando, FL.
Support limitations: No grants to individuals.
Application information: Applications not accepted. Unsolicited requests for funds not accepted.
Officer and Directors:* Robert A. Mandell*, Pres. and Secy.; Zachary H. Mandell.
EIN: 592870807

1649
Greater Omaha Packing Co., Inc.

3001 L St.
Omaha, NE 68107 (402) 731-1700
FAX: (402) 731-8020

Company URL: http://www.greateromaha.com/
Establishment information: Established in 1920.
Company type: Private company
Business activities: Operates beef slaughterhouse and meat packing plant.
Business type (SIC): Meat packing plants and prepared meats and poultry
Financial profile for 2010: Number of employees, 690
Corporate officers: Henry Davis, Pres. and C.E.O.; Daniel Jensen, V.P., Sales
Giving statement: Giving through the Greater Omaha Packing Co. Foundation.

Greater Omaha Packing Co. Foundation

P.O. Box 7566
Omaha, NE 68107-0566

Establishment information: Established in 2003 in NE.
Donor: Greater Omaha Packing Co.
Financial data (yr. ended 08/31/11): Assets, $1,876,977 (M); expenditures, $160,748; qualifying distributions, $149,136; giving activities include $149,136 for 23 grants (high: $66,666; low: $250).
Purpose and activities: The foundation supports organizations involved with education, child welfare, youth development, foster care, beef industry, Catholicism, and Judaism.
Fields of interest: Higher education; Education; Crime/violence prevention, child abuse; Girls clubs; Youth development; American Red Cross; YM/YWCAs & YM/YWHAs; Children, foster care; Business/industry; Catholic agencies & churches; Jewish agencies & synagogues.
Type of support: General/operating support; Scholarship funds.
Geographic limitations: Giving primarily in St. Peter, MN and Omaha, NE.
Support limitations: No grants to individuals.
Application information: Applications not accepted. Contributes only to pre-selected organizations.
Directors: Henry Davis; Angelo Fili.
EIN: 550849849
Selected grants: The following grants are a representative sample of this grantmaker's funding activity:
$24,233 to Scholarship America, Saint Peter, MN, 2009.
$5,000 to American Heart Association, Omaha, NE, 2009.
$5,000 to Girls Inc. of Omaha, Omaha, NE, 2009.
$4,500 to Inclusive Communities, Omaha, NE, 2009.
$3,000 to Iowa Western Community College, Council Bluffs, IA, 2009.
$2,600 to Childrens Hospital and Medical Center Foundation, Omaha, NE, 2009.
$2,000 to Bellevue University, Bellevue, NE, 2009.
$2,000 to Metropolitan Community College, Omaha, NE, 2009.
$1,000 to College of Saint Mary, Omaha, NE, 2009.
$1,000 to University of Nebraska-Omaha, Omaha, NE, 2009.

1647
Great-West Life & Annuity Insurance Company

8515 E. Orchard Rd.
P.O. Box 1700
Greenwood Village, CO 80111-5000
(800) 537-2033

Company URL: http://www.greatwest.com
Establishment information: Established in 1907.
Company type: Subsidiary of a foreign company
Business activities: Sells health, life, and disability insurance; provides investment advisory services.
Business type (SIC): Insurance/accident and health; security and commodity services; insurance/life
Financial profile for 2009: Number of employees, 1,900; assets, $41,800,000,000; sales volume, $2,030,000,000
Corporate officers: Raymond L. McFeetors, Chair.; Mitchell T.G. Graye, Pres. and C.E.O.; S. Mark Corbett, Exec. V.P. and C.I.O.; James L. McCallen, Sr. V.P. and C.F.O.; Scot A. Miller, Sr. V.P. and C.I.O.; Richard G. Schultz, Sr. V.P., Genl. Counsel, and Secy.; James H. Van Harmelen, Sr. V.P. and Corp. Cont.
Board of directors: Raymond L. McFeetors, Chair.; James Balog
Giving statement: Giving through the Great-West Life & Annuity Insurance Company Contributions Program.

Great-West Life & Annuity Insurance Company Contributions Program

8515 E. Orchard Rd.
Greenwood Village, CO 80111-5002
Great-West Great-Teachers URL: http://www.greatwest.com/greatwestgreateachers/index.html; URL: http://www.greatwest.com/social-responsibility.shtml

Purpose and activities: Great-West makes charitable contributions to pre-K-12 public schools and nonprofit organizations involved with financial education, and on a case by case basis. Support is given primarily in areas of company operations, with emphasis on Colorado.
Fields of interest: Education, public education; Elementary/secondary education; Health organizations; Youth development, business; Economics; General charitable giving.
Programs:
Financial Match Program: Great-West matches contributions made by employees to nonprofit organizations on a one-for-one basis up to $5,000 per employee, per year.
Great-West Great-Teachers Financial Literacy Grants: Great-West awards 25 grants of $5,000 to Colorado pre-K-12 public school teachers to assist them with bringing financial education into their classrooms.
Volunteer Match Program: Great-West makes charitable contributions of $8 per hour to nonprofit organizations with which employees volunteer and matches funds raised by employees for nonprofit organizations on a one-for-one basis up to $1,500 per employee, per year.
Type of support: Curriculum development; Employee matching gifts; Employee volunteer services; General/operating support; Sponsorships.
Geographic limitations: Giving primarily in areas of company operations, with emphasis on CO; giving also to national organizations.
Publications: Application guidelines.
Application information: Applications accepted. Application form required.
Visit website for detailed application guidelines for Great-West Great-Teachers Financial Literacy Grants.
Initial approach: Complete online application for Great-West Great-Teachers Financial Literacy Grants
Number of staff: 2 full-time professional.

1650
Green Awakening Coffee

8165 27th St. E.
Sarasota, FL 34243 (941) 803-0610

Company URL: http://www.green-awakening.com
Company type: Cooperative
Business type (SIC): Business services/miscellaneous
Giving statement: Giving through the Green Awakening Coffee Corporate Giving Program.

Green Awakening Coffee Corporate Giving Program

8165 27th St. E.
Sarasota, FL 34243-2874 (941) 803-0610
E-mail: info@green-awakening.com; URL: http://www.green-awakening.com

Purpose and activities: Green Awakening Coffee is a certified B Corporation that donates a percentage of profits to charitable organizations.
Fields of interest: Elementary/secondary education; Environment; Animal welfare; Employment, training; Children, services; Human services.
Type of support: Cause-related marketing; General/operating support.

1651
Green Bay Packers, Inc.

Lambeau Field Atrium, 1265 Lombardi Ave.
P.O. Box 10628
Green Bay, WI 54304-3927 (920) 569-7500

Company URL: http://www.packers.com
Establishment information: Established in 1919.
Company type: Private company
Business activities: Operates professional football club.
Business type (SIC): Commercial sports
Corporate officers: Mark Hodge Murphy, Pres. and C.E.O.; Ed Policy, V.P. and Genl. Counsel; Paul Baniel, V.P., Finance and Admin.; Tim Connolly, V.P., Sales and Mktg.; Carl W. Kuehne, Secy.; Mark J. McMullen, Treas.; Robert E. Harlan, Chair. Emeritus
Board of directors: Daniel T. Ariens; Thomas D. Arndt; John F. Bergstrom; Ave M. Bie; Thomas J. Cardella; Richard J. Chernick; James M. Christensen; Casey Cuene; Valerie Daniels-Carter; Andrew E. Farah; Susan M. Finco; Beverly A. French; Terrence R. Fulwiler; Johnnie L. Gray; George F. Hartmann; Philip J. Hendrickson; Jeffrey A. Joerres; George F. Kerwin; David Kohler; William F. Kress; Carl W. Kuehne; Thomas G. Kunkel; Charles R. Lieb; Thomas J. Lutsey; John N. MacDonough; Edward N. Martin; Michael J. McClone; Mark J. McMullen; John C. Meng; Mark H. Murphy; Thomas M. Olejniczak; Thomas L. Olson; Bryce E. Paup; Michael R. Reese; Pat Richter; Gary M. Rotherham; Diane L. Roundy; Michael D. Simmer; Mark D. Skogen; Albert L. Toon, Jr.; Mike L. Weller; Larry L. Weyers; Michael A. Wier; Donald R. Zuidmulder
Giving statement: Giving through the Green Bay Packers, Inc. Corporate Giving Program and the Green Bay Packers Foundation.

Green Bay Packers, Inc. Corporate Giving Program

c/o Donations
P.O. Box 10628
Green Bay, WI 54307-0628 (920) 569-7500
FAX: (920) 569-7302;
E-mail: IGAMDonations@packers.com; Additional e-mail: donations@packers.com; URL: http://www.packers.com/community/index.html

Purpose and activities: As a complement to its foundation, Green Bay Packers also makes charitable contributions of memorabilia to nonprofit organizations directly. Support is limited to Michigan and Wisconsin.
Fields of interest: General charitable giving.
Type of support: In-kind gifts.
Geographic limitations: Giving limited to MI and WI.
Support limitations: No game ticket donations.

Publications: Corporate giving report.
Application information: Applications accepted. The Community Outreach department handles giving. The company has a staff that only handles contributions. Application form required.
Initial approach: Complete online application form
Deadline(s): 6 to 8 weeks prior to need
Final notification: Following review
Administrators: Julie Broeckel, Community Outreach. Asst.; Cathy A. Dworak, Mgr., Community Outreach and Player/Alumni Rels.; Bobbi Jo Eisenreich, Corp. Donations Supvr.; Sue Zernicke, Community Rels. Asst.
Number of staff: 1 full-time professional; 1 part-time professional; 2 part-time support.

Green Bay Packers Foundation

P.O. Box 10628
1265 Lombardi Ave.
Green Bay, WI 54307-0628 (920) 569-7315
FAX: (920) 569-7309;
E-mail: meyersm@packers.com; Additional e-mail: IGAMFoundation@packers.com; URL: http://www.packers.com/community/packers-foundation.html

Establishment information: Established in 1986 in WI.
Donors: Youth Football Fund, Inc.; Green Bay Packers.
Contact: Margaret J. Meyers, Secy.
Financial data (yr. ended 03/31/12): Assets, $5,927,034 (M); gifts received, $1,363,392; expenditures, $543,683; qualifying distributions, $479,990; giving activities include $479,990 for grants.
Purpose and activities: The foundation supports programs designed to benefit education, health, human services, civic affairs, and youth-related initiatives.
Fields of interest: Secondary school/education; Education; Hospitals (general); Health care; YM/YWCAs & YM/YWHAs; Human services; Foundations (community); Public affairs Youth.
Program:
Under the Packers Scholarship Program: The foundation, in partnership with Scholarships, Inc. and Northeast Wisconsin Technical College, awards college scholarships to students in two-year associate degree or apprentice trades programs. Scholarships are based on community service, involvement in athletic activities, academic achievement of at least a 3.0 grade point average, financial need, and residency in Brown County.
Type of support: Continuing support; Equipment; General/operating support; Program development; Scholarships—to individuals.
Geographic limitations: Giving primarily in WI, with emphasis in Brown County and Green Bay.
Support limitations: No support for political organizations.
Publications: Application guidelines; Grants list.
Application information: Applications accepted. Application form required. Applicants should submit the following:
1) timetable for implementation and evaluation of project
2) results expected from proposed grant
3) population served
4) copy of IRS Determination Letter
5) brief history of organization and description of its mission
6) geographic area to be served
7) copy of most recent annual report/audited financial statement/990
8) descriptive literature about organization
9) listing of board of directors, trustees, officers and other key people and their affiliations
10) detailed description of project and amount of funding requested
11) copy of current year's organizational budget and/or project budget
12) listing of additional sources and amount of support

Initial approach: Compete online application; contact participating administrators for application information for scholarships
Board meeting date(s): Between 6-8 times per year
Deadline(s): Aug. 1
Final notification: Dec.
Officers and Trustees:* Casey Cuene*, Chair.; Margaret J. Meyers*, Secy.; Tom Arndt; Ave M. Bie; Rick Chernick; Johnnie Gray; Charles Lieb; Edward N. Martin; Diane Roundy; Mark Skogen; Associated Bank, N.A.
EIN: 391577137
Selected grants: The following grants are a representative sample of this grantmaker's funding activity:
$52,000 to Saint Vincent Hospital, Green Bay, WI, 2011.
$7,500 to Scholarships Inc., Green Bay, WI, 2011.
$5,000 to Court Appointed Special Advocates of Brown County, Green Bay, WI, 2011.
$5,000 to Family Services of Northeast Wisconsin, Green Bay, WI, 2011.
$5,000 to Growing Power, Milwaukee, WI, 2011.
$4,000 to Einstein Project, Green Bay, WI, 2011.
$3,500 to Big Brothers Big Sisters of Northeastern Wisconsin, Green Bay, WI, 2011.
$2,500 to Milwaukee Kickers Soccer Club, Milwaukee, WI, 2011.
$2,000 to COTS, Appleton, WI, 2011.
$2,000 to Trinity Lutheran Church, Eau Claire, WI, 2011.

1652
Green Building Services, Inc.

421 S.W. 6th Ave., Ste. 200
Portland, OR 97204-1629 (503) 467-4710

Company URL: http://www.greenbuildingservices.com/
Establishment information: Established in 2000.
Company type: Private company
Business type (SIC): Business services/miscellaneous
Corporate officers: Elaine Aye, Principal; Ralph DiNola, Principal; Richard Manning, Principal; Katrina Shum Miller, Principal
Giving statement: Giving through the Green Building Services, Inc. Contributions Program.

Green Building Services, Inc. Contributions Program

421 Southwest 6th Ave., Ste. 200
Portland, OR 97204-1629 (503) 467-4710
URL: http://www.greenbuildingservices.com/AboutUs.asp

Purpose and activities: Green Building Services is a certified B Corporation that donates a percentage of profits to charitable organizations.

1653
Green Mountain Coffee Roasters, Inc.

(formerly Green Mountain Coffee, Inc.)
33 Coffee Ln.
Waterbury, VT 05676-8900 (802) 244-5621
FAX: (914) 949-9618

Company URL: http://www.gmcr.com
Establishment information: Established in 1981.
Company type: Public company
Company ticker symbol and exchange: GMCR/NASDAQ
Business activities: Produces coffee.
Business type (SIC): Miscellaneous prepared foods
Financial profile for 2012: Number of employees, 5,800; assets, $3,500,000,000; sales volume, $4,000,000,000; pre-tax net income, $576,140,000; expenses, $2,281,990,000; liabilities, $1,354,560,000
Fortune 1000 ranking: 2012—605th in revenues, 425th in profits, and 694th in assets
Forbes 2000 ranking: 2012—1507th in sales, 1241st in profits, and 1906th in assets
Corporate officers: Norman H. Wesley, Chair.; Brian Kelley, Pres. and C.E.O.; Frances G. Rathke, C.F.O. and Treas.; Stephen L. Gibbs, V.P. and C.A.O.; Sonia Cudd, V.P., Corp. Genl. Counsel, and Secy.
Board of directors: Norman H. Wesley, Chair.; Michael J. Mardy; Lawrence J. Blanford; Barbara Carlini; Jules A. Del Vecchio; David E. Moran; Hinda Miller; Robert P. Stiller
Giving statement: Giving through the Green Mountain Coffee Roasters, Inc. Corporate Giving Program and the Better and Better Foundation.
Company EIN: 030339228

Green Mountain Coffee Roasters, Inc. Corporate Giving Program

(formerly Green Mountain Coffee, Inc. Corporate Giving Program)
33 Coffee Ln.
Waterbury, VT 05676-8900 (802) 244-5621
E-mail: CSR.Vermont@gmcr.com; For product donations: donations@gmcr.com; URL: http://www.gmcr.com/csr/

Purpose and activities: As a complement to its foundation, Green Mountain Coffee Roasters also makes charitable contributions to nonprofit organizations directly. Support is given in areas of company operations and coffee-growing communities.
Fields of interest: Environment, pollution control; Environment, water pollution; Environmental education; Cancer; Agriculture, sustainable programs; Food banks; Housing/shelter, temporary shelter; Housing/shelter, homeless; Disasters, floods; Recreation, camps; Rural development Economically disadvantaged.
Program:
Employee Matching Gift Program: Green Mountain Coffee Roasters matches all cash donations to U.S. and Canadian non-profits at 100%, up to $1,000 per employee, per year. In certain situations, such as natural disasters or local causes that are particularly meaningful to employees, the annual cap is removed.
Type of support: Donated equipment; Donated products; Employee matching gifts; Employee volunteer services; General/operating support; In-kind gifts; Scholarship funds.
Geographic limitations: Giving limited to areas of company operations, with emphasis on Castroville,

CA, Reading, MA, Knoxville, TN, VT, and Sumner, WA, and in Canada.
Support limitations: No support for discriminatory, lobbying, or political organizations, youth clubs, athletic teams, or troops. No grants for capital expenditures, land acquisition, building purchase or improvement, fixed assets, or sectarian, fraternal, or religious activities not of direct benefit to the entire community, or for sporting events, athletes, class projects, school trips, fundraising dinners, conferences, or other events, advertising, mass market film, video, or television productions, college or university student scholarships, academic research, trips, tours, or travel expenses, or fees for participation in competitive programs.
Publications: Application guidelines; Corporate giving report.
Application information: Applications accepted. Support is limited to 1 contribution per organization during any given year. Applicants should submit the following:
1) copy of IRS Determination Letter
Initial approach: Complete online eligibility quiz and application
Copies of proposal: 1
Committee meeting date(s): Quarterly
Deadline(s): 2 weeks to 3 months prior to need for donation requests
Final notification: Quarterly

Better and Better Foundation

(formerly Green Mountain Coffee Roasters Foundation)
P.O. Box 2263
South Burlington, VT 05407 (802) 244-6193
E-mail: Diane.Davis@GMCR.com; URL: http://www.greenmountaincoffeefoundation.org

Establishment information: Established in 2000 in VT.
Donor: Robert J. Stiller.
Contact: Betsy Stanford
Financial data (yr. ended 09/30/11): Assets, $2,680,092 (M); expenditures, $1,056,310; qualifying distributions, $1,050,128; giving activities include $1,050,128 for 6 grants (high: $466,420; low: $28,880).
Purpose and activities: The foundation supports organizations involved with arts and culture, animal welfare, human services, civil and human rights, and community economic development.
Fields of interest: Arts; Animal welfare; Human services; Civil/human rights; Business/industry; Community development, service clubs; Community/economic development.
Type of support: General/operating support.
Geographic limitations: Giving primarily in VT.
Application information: Applications accepted. Application form not required.
Initial approach: Contact foundation for application information
Deadline(s): None
Officer: Robert Stiller, Pres.
EIN: 030341004

1654
Greenberg Traurig, P.A.

333 S.E. 2nd Ave., Ste. 4400
Miami, FL 33131-2184 (305) 579-0500

Company URL: http://www.gtlaw.com
Establishment information: Established in 1967.
Company type: Private company
Business activities: Operates law firm.
Business type (SIC): Legal services
Corporate officers: Cesar L. Alvarez, Co-Chair.; Larry J. Hoffman, Co-Chair.; Richard A. Rosenbaum, C.E.O.
Board of directors: Cesar L. Alvarez, Co-Chair.; Larry J. Hoffman, Co-Chair.
Offices: Phoenix, AZ; East Palo Alto, Irvine, Los Angeles, Sacramento, San Francisco, CA; Denver, CO; Wilmington, DE; Washington, DC; Boca Raton, Fort Lauderdale, Miami, Orlando, Tallahassee, Tampa, West Palm Beach, FL; Atlanta, GA; Chicago, IL; Boston, MA; Las Vegas, NV; Florham Park, NJ; Albany, White Plains, NY; Philadelphia, PA; Austin, Dallas, Houston, TX; McLean, VA
International operations: China; Netherlands; United Kingdom
Giving statement: Giving through the Greenberg Traurig Fellowship Foundation.

Greenberg Traurig Fellowship Foundation

333 Avenue of the Americans, Ste. 4400
Miami, FL 33131-2184 (212) 801-9200
E-mail: silvermanw@gtlaw.com; Contact for Pro Bono program: Holly R. Skolnick, Pro Bono Shareholder, tel.: (305) 579-0860, e-mail: skolnickh@gtlaw.com; URL: http://www.gtlaw.com/AboutUs/ServeOurCommunities

Contact: William C. Silverman
Purpose and activities: Greenberg Taurig makes charitable contributions to nonprofit organizations on a case by case basis.
Fields of interest: Legal services; General charitable giving.
Type of support: Employee volunteer services; Fellowships; General/operating support; Pro bono services - legal.
Application information: A Pro Bono Committee manages the pro bono program.

1655
GreenChoice Bank

5225 W. 25th St.
Cicero, IL 60804 (708) 656-0100

Company URL: http://www.greenchoicebank.com
Establishment information: Established in 2008.
Company type: Private company
Business type (SIC): Business services/miscellaneous
Corporate officers: Harold L. Sherman, Chair., Pres., and C.E.O.; Steve Sherman, Exec. V.P. and C.O.O.; Kenneth C. Kline, Exec. V.P. and C.F.O.
Board of directors: Harold L. Sherman, Chair.; Robert M. Beavers, Jr.; Robert Gremley; Marc Kahan; Donald Larson; Frank Reid; Samuel Sallerson; Dennis Schueler
Giving statement: Giving through the GreenChoice Bank Corporate Giving Program.

GreenChoice Bank Corporate Giving Program

5225 W. 25th St.
Cicero, IL 60804-3308 (708) 656-0100
URL: http://www.greenchoicebank.com

Purpose and activities: GreenChoice Bank is a certified B Corporation that donates a percentage of net profits to charitable organizations. Support is given primarily in Illinois.
Geographic limitations: Giving primarily in IL.

1656
W. H. Greene & Associates, Inc.

400 Quaker Rd.
East Aurora, NY 14052 (716) 805-1090

Company URL: http://www.whgreene.com
Establishment information: Established in 1986.
Company type: Private company
Business activities: Insurance underwriter specializing in non-standard and high-limit coverage.
Business type (SIC): Insurance agents, brokers, and services
Corporate officers: Bill Greene, Pres.; Terry Greene, C.F.O.
Giving statement: Giving through the W. H. Greene Foundation, Inc.

W. H. Greene Foundation, Inc.

400 Quaker Rd.
East Aurora, NY 14052-2158

Establishment information: Established in 2002.
Donor: W.H. Greene & Assocs., Inc.
Contact: William H. Greene III, Pres.
Financial data (yr. ended 12/31/11): Assets, $1,125,466 (M); gifts received, $113,325; expenditures, $62,904; qualifying distributions, $62,904; giving activities include $60,046 for 35 grants (high: $10,500; low: $160).
Fields of interest: Education; Medical research; Human services.
Geographic limitations: Giving primarily in NY.
Application information: Applications accepted. Application form not required.
Initial approach: Proposal
Deadline(s): None
Officers and Trustees:* William H. Greene III*, Pres.; Mary Jane Greene*, Secy.; Terrence G. Greene*, Treas.; Caitlin E. Greene; Jennifer L. Greene; Kristie A. Greene.
EIN: 331049504

1657
Greene, Tweed & Co., Inc.

2075 Detwiler Rd.
P.O. Box 305
Kulpsville, PA 19443-0305 (215) 256-9521
FAX: (215) 256-0189

Company URL: http://www.gtweed.com
Establishment information: Established in 1863.
Company type: Private company
Business activities: Manufactures specialty seals and engineered plastic components.
Business type (SIC): Gaskets, packing and sealing devices, and rubber hose and belting; plastic products/miscellaneous
Corporate officers: John J. Jorgensen, Pres. and C.E.O.; Kevin Lukiewski, C.F.O.; Paul O'Brlen, Secy.; Mike Brewer, V.P., Sales
Giving statement: Giving through the GT Foundation.

GT Foundation

c/o Michael Delfiner
P.O. Box 305
Kulpsville, PA 19443-0305

Establishment information: Established in 1998 in PA.
Donor: Green, Tweed & Co.
Financial data (yr. ended 12/31/11): Assets, $4,753,850 (M); gifts received, $480,000;

expenditures, $352,929; qualifying distributions, $351,000; giving activities include $351,000 for grants.
Purpose and activities: The foundation supports organizations involved with animals and wildlife, patient services, horses, children and youth, homelessness, and Judaism.
Fields of interest: Animals/wildlife, special services; Health care, patient services; Athletics/sports, equestrianism; Children/youth, services; Homeless, human services; Jewish agencies & synagogues.
Type of support: General/operating support.
Geographic limitations: Giving primarily in CA, MT, NY, and PA.
Support limitations: No grants to individuals.
Application information: Applications not accepted. Contributes only to pre-selected organizations.
Trustees: Hannah Delfiner; Michael Delfiner; Ruth Delfiner; Joan Stanley; Kenneth Stanley; Nancy Stanley.
EIN: 237927474
Selected grants: The following grants are a representative sample of this grantmaker's funding activity:
$15,000 to American Jewish World Service, New York, NY, 2011.
$6,000 to Brigham and Womens Hospital, Boston, MA, 2011.
$6,000 to Interfaith Hospitality Network - Main Line, Norristown, PA, 2011. For general support.

1658
Greenlight Apparel

48521 Warm Springs Blvd., Ste. 317
Fremont, CA 94539 (510) 474-3965
FAX: (510) 405-8913

Company URL: http://www.greenlightapparel.com
Establishment information: Established in 2007.
Company type: Private company
Business activities: Operates ethically sourced apparel manufacturing company.
Business type (SIC): Apparel and accessories/miscellaneous; business services/miscellaneous
Corporate officer: Sonny Aulakh, C.E.O.
Giving statement: Giving through the Greenlight Apparel Corporate Giving Program.

Greenlight Apparel Corporate Giving Program

48521 Warm Springs Blvd.
Fremont, CA 94539-7792 (510) 474-3965
E-mail: info@greenlightapparel.com; URL: http://www.greenlightapparel.com

Purpose and activities: Greenlight Apparel is a certified B Corporation that donates a percentage of profits to charitable organizations.
Fields of interest: Anti-slavery/human trafficking; Children's rights.
Type of support: General/operating support.

1659
Greensfelder, Hemker & Gale, P.C.

10 S. Broadway, Ste. 2000
Saint Louis, MO 63102-1747
(314) 241-9090

Company URL: http://www.greensfelder.com
Establishment information: Established in 1895.
Company type: Private company
Business activities: Operates law firm.
Business type (SIC): Legal services
Offices: Belleville, Chicago, IL; Saint Louis, MO
Giving statement: Giving through the Greensfelder, Hemker & Gale, P.C. Pro Bono Program.

Greensfelder, Hemker & Gale, P.C. Pro Bono Program

10 S. Broadway, Ste. 2000
Saint Louis, MO 63102-1747 (314) 345-4757
E-mail: tda@greensfelder.com; URL: http://www.greensfelder.com/community-investment.aspx

Contact: Ted Agniel
Fields of interest: Legal services.
Type of support: Pro bono services - legal.
Geographic limitations: Giving primarily in areas of company operations in Belleville, and Chicago, IL, and St. Louis, MO.
Application information: An attorney who coordinates pro bono projects as an ancillary duty to other work.

1660
Greenwood Dermatology, Inc.

(also known as Greenwood Dermatology, P.C.)
92 S. Park Blvd.
Greenwood, IN 46143 (317) 889-7546

Establishment information: Established in 2009.
Company type: Private company
Business activities: Provides medical services.
Business type (SIC): Offices and clinics/doctors'
Corporate officer: Thomas Eads, M.D., Owner
Giving statement: Giving through the Ten Talents International Ministries, Inc.

Ten Talents International Ministries, Inc.

1013 Mt. Vernon Dr.
Greenwood, IN 46142-1853
E-mail: info@TenTalentsInt.org; Additional address: P.O. Box 7252, Greenwood, IN 46142-7252; URL: http://www.tentalentsint.org

Establishment information: Established in 2003.
Donor: Greenwood Dermatology, Inc.
Contact: Thomas Eads, Dir.
Financial data (yr. ended 12/31/11): Assets, $114,330 (M); expenditures, $6,680; qualifying distributions, $6,000; giving activities include $6,000 for grants.
Purpose and activities: The foundation supports Christian agencies and churches.
Fields of interest: Christian agencies & churches.
Type of support: General/operating support.
Application information: Applications not accepted. Contributes only to pre-selected organizations.
Officers and Directors:* Thomas Eads*, Pres.; Thomas Redmond, V.P., Exec. Affairs.; James Hughes, V.P., Research; James Livengood, Secy.; Misha Eads, Treas.
EIN: 200513456

1661
Carl Gregory Enterprises Inc.

3000 Northlake Pkwy., Bldg. 100
Columbus, GA 31909 (706) 324-2380

Company URL: http://www.cgcars.com
Establishment information: Established in 1994.
Company type: Private company
Business activities: Operates car dealership.
Business type (SIC): Motor vehicles—retail
Corporate officers: Carl L. Gregory, Chair. and C.E.O.; Jason Gregory, Pres.; C. David Drake, V.P. and Secy.; Beth Lawson, Corp. Cont.
Board of director: Carl L. Gregory, Chair.
Giving statement: Giving through the Carl Gregory Foundation, Inc.

The Carl Gregory Foundation, Inc.

2821 Harley Ct., Ste. 300
Columbus, GA 31909

Establishment information: Established in 1997 in GA.
Donors: Carl Gregory Enterprises Inc.; Carl L. Gregory.
Financial data (yr. ended 12/31/11): Assets, $421 (M); gifts received, $93,786; expenditures, $94,036; qualifying distributions, $94,036; giving activities include $94,036 for 23 grants (high: $25,000; low: $100).
Purpose and activities: The foundation supports organizations involved with arts and culture, education, health, recreation, and human services.
Fields of interest: Arts; Education; Health care; Recreation; Boy scouts; Human services.
Type of support: General/operating support; Program development; Sponsorships.
Geographic limitations: Giving primarily in Columbus, GA.
Application information: Applications not accepted. Unsolicited requests for funds not accepted.
Officers: Carl L. Gregory, Chair.; Jason Gregory, Vice-Chair.; Robert I. Behar, Treas.
EIN: 582358881

1662
Gregory Industries, Inc.

(formerly Gregory Galvanizing & Metal Processing Inc.)
4100 13th St., S.W.
Canton, OH 44710-1464 (330) 477-4800

Company URL: http://www.gregorycorp.com
Establishment information: Established in 1957.
Company type: Private company
Business activities: Provides zinc galvanizing services.
Business type (SIC): Metal coating and plating
Financial profile for 2010: Number of employees, 80
Corporate officers: Raymond T. Gregory, Chair.; T. Stephen Gregory, C.E.O.; Fred T. Zalenski, Pres.; Joseph Weaver, C.F.O.
Board of director: Raymond T. Gregory, Chair.
Giving statement: Giving through the T. Raymond Gregory Family Foundation.

T. Raymond Gregory Family Foundation

P.O. Box 1558 Dept. EA4E86
Columbus, OH 43216 (330) 477-4800
Application address: c/o Gregory Galvanizing & Metal Processing, Inc., 1723 Cleveland Ave. S.W., Canton, OH 44707

Establishment information: Established in 1991 in OH.
Donors: Gregory Galvanizing & Metal Processing, Inc.; Gregory Industries; Huntington Bank.
Contact: T. Raymond Gregory
Financial data (yr. ended 12/31/11): Assets, $1,022,766 (M); expenditures, $83,466; qualifying distributions, $78,000; giving activities include $72,147 for 6 grants (high: $25,000; low: $2,000).
Purpose and activities: The foundation supports service clubs and organizations involved with nursing education and human services.
Fields of interest: Nursing school/education; Salvation Army; Children/youth, services; Family services; Human services; Community development, service clubs.
Type of support: General/operating support.
Support limitations: No grants to individuals.
Application information: Applications accepted. Application form required. Applicants should submit the following:
1) detailed description of project and amount of funding requested
Initial approach: Letter
Deadline(s): None
Trustees: Huntington National Bank.
EIN: 341685584

1663
Greif, Inc.

425 Winter Rd.
Delaware, OH 43015 (740) 549-6000
FAX: (302) 655-5049

Company URL: http://www.greif.com/
Establishment information: Established in 1877.
Company type: Public company
Company ticker symbol and exchange: GEF/NYSE
Business activities: Manufactures industrial packaging products.
Business type (SIC): Paperboard containers
Financial profile for 2012: Number of employees, 13,560; assets, $3,856,900,000; sales volume, $4,269,500,000; pre-tax net income, $187,100,000; expenses, $3,985,000,000; liabilities, $2,656,100,000
Fortune 1000 ranking: 2012—555th in revenues, 691st in profits, and 676th in assets
Corporate officers: Michael J. Gasser, Chair.; David B. Fischer, Pres. and C.E.O.; Gary R. Martz, Exec. V.P. and Genl. Counsel; Robert M. McNutt, Sr. V.P. and C.F.O.; Douglas W. Lingrel, V.P. and C.I.O.; Nadeem S. Ali, V.P. and Treas.; Kenneth B. Andre, V.P. and Corp.Cont.
Board of directors: Michael J. Gasser, Chair.; Vicki L. Avril; Bruce A. Edwards; Mark A. Emkes; John F. Finn; David B. Fischer; Daniel J. Gunsett; Judith D. Hook; John W. McNamara; Patrick J. Norton
International operations: Algeria; Argentina; Belgium; Bermuda; Brazil; Canada; China; Costa Rica; Czech Republic; France; Germany; Hungary; Ireland; Italy; Malaysia; Mexico; Netherlands; Portugal; Russia; Singapore; South Africa; Spain; Sweden; United Kingdom; Venezuela
Giving statement: Giving through the Greif, Inc. Corporate Giving Program.
Company EIN: 314388903

Greif, Inc. Corporate Giving Program

c/o V.P., Comms.
425 Winter Rd.
Delaware, OH 43015-8903 (740) 549-6000
URL: http://www.greif.com/about-greif/default.asp

Purpose and activities: Greif, Inc. makes charitable contributions to nonprofit organizations involved with families, health and human services, education, and youth development. Support is given primarily in areas of company operations, with emphasis on established charitable organizations with minimal administrative overhead.
Fields of interest: Education; Health care; Youth development; Family services; Human services.
Program:
Employee Matching Gift Program: Greif matches contributions made by its employees to nonprofit organizations and educational institutions up to $500 per employee, per year, with a total maximum corporate match of $20,000 per year.
Type of support: Donated products; Employee matching gifts; General/operating support; In-kind gifts.
Geographic limitations: Giving primarily in areas of company operations.
Support limitations: No support for veterans', labor, or discriminatory organizations, fraternal, athletic, or social clubs or programs, individual member agencies of the United Way or United Fund, organizations that charge fees or dues, or athletic foundations, including those supporting university, college, semi- or professional sports teams. Generally no grants to individuals, including requests for awards, sponsorships, or any form of personal financial assistance, or for capital improvement projects, endowments, conferences, seminars, trips, tours, or similar group or individual activities, religious programs, political activities, or one-time, annual, or multiple advertising placements, or direct-mail campaigns, or publication, video, film, or television productions.
Publications: Application guidelines.
Application information: Applications accepted. A contributions committee reviews all requests. Greif will match employee contributions to nonprofit organizations and educational institutions up to $500 per employee, with a total maximum corporate match per year of $20,000. Application form not required. Applicants should submit the following:
1) statement of problem project will address
2) copy of IRS Determination Letter
3) brief history of organization and description of its mission
4) detailed description of project and amount of funding requested

Applications should note if the organization receives funds from the United Way, the United Fund or a regional equivalent.
Initial approach: Submit a proposal and cover letter to headquarters

1664
Greyhound Lines, Inc.

600 Vine St., Ste. 1400
Cincinnati, OH 45202-1491 (513) 241-2200

Company URL: http://www.greyhound.com
Establishment information: Established in 1914.
Company type: Subsidiary of a foreign company
Business activities: Provides intercity bus transportation services.
Business type (SIC): Transportation/intercity and rural bus
Financial profile for 2010: Number of employees, 250
Corporate officers: Dave Leach, Pres. and C.E.O.; Bill Blankenship, C.O.O.; Andrew Kaplinsky, C.F.O.; Rhonda Piar MacAndrew, Sr. V.P., Human Resources; Myron Watkins, V.P., Opers.
Giving statement: Giving through the Greyhound Lines, Inc. Corporate Giving Program.
Company EIN: 860572343

Greyhound Lines, Inc. Corporate Giving Program

c/o Corp. Comms. Dept.
350 N. St. Paul St.
Dallas, TX 75201
FAX: (214) 849-8410;
E-mail: fgacommunications@firstgroup.com;
URL: http://www.greyhound.com/HOME/en/About/InTheCommunity.aspx

Purpose and activities: Greyhound makes charitable contributions to nonprofit organizations involved with the disabled, minorities, women, and the economically disadvantaged. Support is given on a national basis to a select few charitable partners.
Fields of interest: Disabilities, people with; Minorities; Women; Economically disadvantaged.
Type of support: Donated products; Employee volunteer services; General/operating support.
Geographic limitations: Giving on a national basis in areas of company operations; giving also to national organizations.
Support limitations: No support for health or disease-specific organizations, religious, fraternal, political, animal, athletic, or veterans' organizations, private K-12 schools, colleges or universities, or private foundations. No grants to individuals, or for regional, national, or international competitions, conferences, or events for local organizations.
Application information: Applications not accepted. Contributes only to pre-selected organizations. The External Communications Department handles giving. The company has a staff that only handles contributions.
Administrator: Timothy Stokes, Mgr., Media Rels.

1665
Greystone Funding Corporation

152 West 57th St., 60th Fl.
New York, NY 10019 (212) 649-9700

Company URL: http://www.greyco.com
Establishment information: Established in 1988.
Company type: Private company
Business activities: Operates investment company.
Business type (SIC): Investment offices
Corporate officers: Stephen Rosenberg, Pres. and C.E.O.; Robert R. Barolak, Co-C.O.O.; Curtis A. Pollock, Co-C.O.O.; J. Bruce Bolick, C.F.O.; Jonathan Russell, C.I.O.; Lisa Schwartz, Genl. Counsel
Board of director: Arthur Hatzopoulos
Giving statement: Giving through the Murray & Sydell Rosenberg Foundation.

Murray & Sydell Rosenberg Foundation

(formerly Murray M. Rosenberg Foundation)
3330 Cumberland Blvd., Ste. 900
Atlanta, GA 30339-5998

Establishment information: Established in 1991 in GA.
Donor: Greystone Funding Corp.

Financial data (yr. ended 06/30/12): Assets, $15,083 (M); gifts received, $1,645,552; expenditures, $1,671,174; qualifying distributions, $1,667,342; giving activities include $1,667,342 for 51+ grants (high: $428,322).
Purpose and activities: The foundation supports programs designed to help impoverished Jewish families.
Fields of interest: Education; Jewish agencies & synagogues Economically disadvantaged.
International interests: Israel.
Type of support: General/operating support; Grants to individuals.
Geographic limitations: Giving primarily in NJ and NY, and in Israel.
Application information: Applications not accepted. Contributes only to pre-selected organizations and individuals.
Directors: Lisa Lifshitz; Cheryl Rosenberg; Stephen Rosenberg.
Number of staff: 3 full-time professional.
EIN: 581947342

1666
Griffith, Inc.

(doing business as Alpha Systems)
458 Pike Rd.
Huntingdon Valley, PA 19006-1610
(215) 322-8100

Company URL: http://www.alpha-sys.com
Establishment information: Established in 1975.
Company type: Private company
Business activities: Provides document scanning services.
Business type (SIC): Business services/ miscellaneous
Corporate officers: Richard S. Griffith, Sr., Chair.; Dale Dagen, Pres.; David Embry, C.O.O.; Jim Dinges, C.F.O.
Board of director: Richard S. Griffith, Sr., Chair.
Giving statement: Giving through the Faith Foundation.

Faith Foundation

c/o Brett Griffith
458 Pike Rd.
Huntingdon Valley, PA 19006-1610

Establishment information: Established in 1994 in PA.
Donors: Griffith, Inc.; Richard S. Griffith; Helga L. Griffith; Scott M. Griffith; Brett R. Griffith; Alpha Systems; Pike Realty LP.
Financial data (yr. ended 09/30/11): Assets, $3,762,829 (M); gifts received, $300,000; expenditures, $321,020; qualifying distributions, $293,000; giving activities include $293,000 for 6 grants (high: $116,000; low: $2,000).
Purpose and activities: The foundation supports organizations involved with human services and Christianity.
Fields of interest: Human services; Religion.
Type of support: General/operating support.
Geographic limitations: Giving primarily in areas of company operations in CO, FL, MO, and PA.
Support limitations: No grants to individuals.
Application information: Applications not accepted. Unsolicited requests for funds not accepted.
Trustees: Barbara L. Baldwin; Brett R. Griffith; Helga L. Griffith; Richard S. Griffith; Richard S. Griffith, Jr.; Scott M. Griffith.
EIN: 237794551

1667
Griffith Laboratories, Inc.

12200 S. Central Ave.
Alsip, IL 60803 (708) 371-0900

Company URL: http://www.griffithlaboratories.com
Establishment information: Established in 1919.
Company type: Private company
Business activities: Produces condiments, miscellaneous food ingredients, breadings, batters, gravies, and sauces.
Business type (SIC): Miscellaneous prepared foods; specialty foods/canned, frozen, and preserved; drugs; chemical preparations/ miscellaneous; research, development, and testing services
Corporate officers: Dean L. Griffith, Co-Chair.; Lois J. Griffith, Co-Chair.; Herve de la Vauvre, Pres. and C.E.O.; Joseph R. Maslick, Exec. V.P. and C.F.O.
Board of directors: Dean L. Griffith, Co-Chair.; Lois J. Griffith, Co-Chair.
Subsidiary: Custom Food Products Inc., Alsip, IL
International operations: Belgium; Canada; China; Colombia; Costa Rica; Ireland; Italy; Japan; Mexico; Panama; Philippines; Singapore; Spain; Thailand; United Kingdom
Giving statement: Giving through the Griffith Laboratories, Inc. Corporate Giving Program and the Griffith Laboratories Foundation, Inc.

Griffith Laboratories Foundation, Inc.

c/o Griffith Laboratories, Inc.
1 Griffith Ctr.
Alsip, IL 60803-3495 (708) 371-0900

Establishment information: Established in 1976.
Donors: Griffith Laboratories, Inc.; Griffith Laboratories U.S.A., Inc.; Griffith Micro Science, Inc.; Griffith Labs Worldwide.
Contact: Joseph R. Maslick, Jr., V.P. and Treas.
Financial data (yr. ended 09/30/11): Assets, $831,318 (M); gifts received, $678,701; expenditures, $295,357; qualifying distributions, $295,332; giving activities include $295,332 for grants.
Purpose and activities: The foundation supports organizations involved with diabetes, children and youth, and Christianity.
Fields of interest: Diabetes; Children/youth, services; Christian agencies & churches.
Type of support: General/operating support.
Geographic limitations: Giving primarily in GA, IL, and WI.
Support limitations: No grants to individuals.
Application information: Applications accepted. Application form not required. Applicants should submit the following:
1) statement of problem project will address
2) detailed description of project and amount of funding requested

Initial approach: Proposal
Copies of proposal: 1
Deadline(s): July 1

Officers: Dean L. Griffith, Pres.; Joseph R. Maslick, Jr., V.P. and Treas.; James S. Legg, Secy.
EIN: 510195285
Selected grants: The following grants are a representative sample of this grantmaker's funding activity:
$115,700 to Chapel on the Hill, Lake Geneva, WI, 2010.
$30,000 to Full Belly Project, Wilmington, NC, 2010.
$15,000 to Christ for the City International, Omaha, NE, 2010.
$15,000 to International Leadership Institute, Carrollton, GA, 2010.

1668
Grinnell Mutual Reinsurance Company

4215 Hwy. 146 S.
P.O. Box 790
Grinnell, IA 50112 (641) 269-8000

Company URL: http://www.gmrc.com
Establishment information: Established in 1909.
Company type: Mutual company
Business activities: Sells reinsurance and insurance.
Business type (SIC): Insurance carriers
Corporate officers: Michael J. Fordyce, Chair.; Dale R. Bartelt, Vice-Chair.; Tom B. Jones, Vice-Chair.; Steven R. Crawford, Pres. and C.E.O.; Dave Wingert, C.F.O.; Dennis H. Mehmen, V.P. and C.I.O.; Jerry D. Woods, V.P., Finance, Treas., and C.F.O.; Dennis G. Day, V.P., Genl. Counsel, and Secy.; Hutch A. Kracht, Cont.
Board of directors: Michael J. Fordyce, Chair.; Dale R. Bartelt, Vice-Chair.; Tom B. Jones, Vice-Chair.; Linda M. Bernhard; James D. Buch; Charles M. Jones; Thomas G. Knoll; William J. Lampe; Wilbur J. Maas; Wayne L. Roush; Stephen J. Smith; Paul G. Stueven
Giving statement: Giving through the Grinnell Mutual Group Foundation.

Grinnell Mutual Group Foundation

(formerly GMG Foundation)
4215 Hwy. 146
Grinnell, IA 50112-0790
E-mail: jwoods@gmrc.com

Establishment information: Established in 1987 in IA.
Donor: Grinnell Mutual Reinsurance Co.
Contact: Barbara Baker
Financial data (yr. ended 12/31/11): Assets, $17,217 (M); gifts received, $90,000; expenditures, $90,882; qualifying distributions, $90,881; giving activities include $90,881 for grants.
Purpose and activities: The foundation supports organizations involved with education, natural resources, agriculture, community development, and civic affairs.
Fields of interest: Health care; Human services; Community/economic development.
Type of support: Annual campaigns; Employee matching gifts; General/operating support; Program development.
Geographic limitations: Giving primarily in areas of company operations, with emphasis on Grinnell, IA.
Support limitations: No support for religious or political organizations.
Publications: Annual report.
Application information: Applications accepted. Application form required.

Initial approach: Proposal
Deadline(s): None

Officers and Directors:* Dan F. Agnew*, Pres.; Adam Smith, Secy.; Jerry D. Woods*, Treas.; Tom Bachmann; Steve Crawford; Stacy Heinen; Larry Jansen; Brent Larsen; Shawn McKay; Wendy Munyon; Ray Spriggs; Phyllis Steffen.
Number of staff: None.
EIN: 421308146

1669
Griswold Industries, Inc.
(doing business as Cla-Val Co.)
1701 Placentia Ave.
Costa Mesa, CA 92627-4475
(949) 722-4805

Company URL: http://www.cla-val.com
Establishment information: Established in 1936.
Company type: Private company
Business activities: Manufactures automatic control valves.
Business type (SIC): Metal products/fabricated
Financial profile for 2009: Number of employees, 400
Corporate officers: Martin Pickett, Pres. and C.E.O.; Vic Roberts, V.P., Sales and Mktg.
Subsidiary: Soundcast Co., Costa Mesa, CA
Division: CLA-VAL Automatic Control Valves Div., Newport Beach, CA
Giving statement: Giving through the Lilly's Gift Foundation and the Scientific Being Research Foundation Inc.

Lilly's Gift Foundation
c/o Lois G. Ericson
8519 Shady Dell Rd.
MacDoel, CA 96058-9758 (530) 398-4373
Additional tel.: (530) 398-8519

Establishment information: Established in 2000 in CA.
Donor: Griswold Industries, Inc.
Contact: Lois G. Ericson, Pres.
Financial data (yr. ended 12/31/11): Assets, $8,681,682 (M); gifts received, $1,100,165; expenditures, $406,791; qualifying distributions, $360,000; giving activities include $360,000 for grants.
Purpose and activities: The foundation supports food banks and organizations involved with health, birth defects, ALS, fire prevention and control, and human services.
Fields of interest: Health care, emergency transport services; Health care; Genetic diseases and disorders; ALS; Food banks; Disasters, fire prevention/control; YM/YWCAs & YM/YWHAs; Residential/custodial care, hospices; Developmentally disabled, centers & services; Human services.
Type of support: Equipment; General/operating support; Program development.
Geographic limitations: Giving primarily in CA.
Application information: Applications accepted. Application form not required. Applicants should submit the following:
1) detailed description of project and amount of funding requested
Initial approach: Proposal
Deadline(s): None
Officer and Directors:* Lois G. Ericson*, Pres.; Steven L. Ericson; Constance D. Shepherd.
EIN: 680445376
Selected grants: The following grants are a representative sample of this grantmaker's funding activity:
$17,000 to YMCA, Yreka Family, Yreka, CA, 2010.
$15,000 to Stable Hands, Yreka, CA, 2010.
$10,000 to Dorris Volunteer Fire Department, Dorris, CA, 2010.
$10,000 to Human Options, Irvine, CA, 2010.
$10,000 to Madrone Hospice, Yreka, CA, 2010.
$10,000 to Smile Train, New York, NY, 2010.
$8,000 to Klamath Crisis Center, Klamath Falls, OR, 2010.
$7,000 to Guiding Eyes for the Blind, Yorktown Heights, NY, 2010.
$6,000 to Rocky Mountain Elk Foundation, Missoula, MT, 2010.
$5,000 to Asher Student Foundation, Los Angeles, CA, 2010.

Scientific Being Research Foundation Inc.
2803 Barranca Pkwy.
Irvine, CA 92606
URL: http://www.forgoodnesssake.org/

Establishment information: Established in 1999 in CA as a company-sponsored operating foundation.
Donor: Griswold Industries.
Financial data (yr. ended 12/31/10): Assets, $1,040,749 (M); gifts received, $247,161; expenditures, $573,954; qualifying distributions, $516,653; giving activities include $850 for 2 grants (high: $700; low: $150) and $150 for 1 grant to an individual.
Purpose and activities: The foundation provides educational seminars on Christian scientific teachings.
Fields of interest: Human services; Religion.
Type of support: General/operating support.
Support limitations: No grants to individuals.
Application information: Applications not accepted. Unsolicited requests for funds not accepted.
Officers: David E. Griswold, Pres.; Genelle Austin-Lett, Exec. Dir.; Andrew Hill, Exec. Dir.
Director: Marjorie S. Griswold.
EIN: 912026760

1670
Groeniger & Co.
27750 Industrial Blvd.
Hayward, CA 94545-4043 (510) 786-3333

Company URL: http://www.groeniger.com
Establishment information: Established in 1949.
Company type: Private company
Business activities: Sells water works, wastewater, fire protection, and irrigation pipeline equipment wholesale.
Business type (SIC): Hardware, plumbing, and heating equipment—wholesale
Corporate officers: Michael H. Groeniger, Chair.; Michael H. Groeniger, Sr., Pres. and C.E.O.; Richard Alexas, C.O.O.; Beverly J. Groeniger, Treas.
Board of director: Michael H. Groeniger, Chair.
Plants: Bakersfield, Fresno, Modesto, Redding, Roseville, Sacramento, Salinas, San Jose, Santa Maria, Santa Paula, Santa Rosa, CA
Giving statement: Giving through the Mike & Bev Groeniger College Scholarship Fund.

Mike & Bev Groeniger College Scholarship Fund
3854 Bay Center Pl.
Hayward, CA 94545-3629 (510) 786-3333

Establishment information: Established in 2000 in CA.
Donor: Groeniger & Co.
Contact: Richard Groeniger, Tr.
Financial data (yr. ended 12/31/10): Assets, $488,233 (M); gifts received, $3,043; expenditures, $51,329; qualifying distributions, $49,851; giving activities include $48,000 for 11 grants to individuals (high: $5,000; low: $1,500).
Purpose and activities: The foundation awards college scholarships to children of employees of Groeniger & Company.
Fields of interest: Higher education.
Type of support: Employee-related scholarships.
Geographic limitations: Giving limited to CA.
Application information: Applications not accepted. Contributes only through employee-related scholarships.
Trustee: Richard Groeniger.
EIN: 946757910

1671
Groom Law Group
1701 Pennsylvania Ave., N.W.
Washington, DC 20006-5805
(202) 861-5406

Company URL: http://http://www.groom.com/practices-142.html
Company type: Private company
Business activities: Operates law firm.
Business type (SIC): Legal services
Corporate officers: Stephen M. Saxon, Chair.; Jon Breyfogle, Exec. Principal
Giving statement: Giving through the Groom Law Group, Chartered Pro Bono Program.

Groom Law Group, Chartered Pro Bono Program
1701 Pennsylvania Ave., N.W.
Washington, DC 20006-5805 (202) 861-5406
E-mail: etd@groom.com; Additional tel.: (202) 857-0620; URL: http://www.groom.com/practices-142.html

Contact: Elizabeth Dold, Pro Bono Comm. Chair
Fields of interest: Legal services.
Type of support: Pro bono services - legal.
Geographic limitations: Giving primarily in areas of company operations in Washington, DC.
Application information: The Pro Bono Committee manages the pro-bono program.

1672
Grove Farm Company, Inc.
3-1850 Kaumualii Hwy.
P.O. Box 662069
Lihue, HI 96766-8609 (808) 245-3678

Company URL: http://www.grovefarm.com
Establishment information: Established in 1864.
Company type: Private company
Business activities: Provides real estate management services; leases real estate.
Business type (SIC): Real estate agents and managers; real estate operators and lessors
Corporate officers: Daniel Case, Chair.; Warren H. Haruki, Pres. and C.E.O.; Jesse Wipf, C.F.O.; Sharyl E. Lam Yuen, Corp. Secy.
Board of director: Daniel Case, Chair.
Subsidiaries: Puhi Sewer & Water, Lihue, HI; Waiahi Water, Lihue, HI
Giving statement: Giving through the Grove Farm Foundation.
Company EIN: 990039265

Grove Farm Foundation
3-1850 Kaumuali Hwy.
Lihue, HI 96766-7069
FAX: (808) 246-9470; URL: http://www.grovefarm.com/giving
Scholarship Contact: Marissa Sandblom, tel.: (808) 245-3678, ext. 223,
e-mail: msandblom@grovefarm.com

Establishment information: Established in 1992 in HI.
Donor: Grove Farm Co., Inc.
Financial data (yr. ended 12/31/11): Assets, $1,991,058 (M); gifts received, $250,000; expenditures, $88,337; qualifying distributions, $88,837; giving activities include $56,580 for 40 grants (high: $10,000; low: $50) and $31,000 for 7 grants to individuals (high: $5,000; low: $1,000).
Purpose and activities: The foundation supports programs designed to promote educational enrichment; enhance and protect the environment; assist health and human service projects; and create economic opportunities for Kaua'i's future.
Fields of interest: Education; Environment; Health care; Human services; Economic development.

Programs:

Employee Volunteer Grants Program: The foundation awards $500 grants to nonprofit organizations with which employees of Grove Farm volunteer at least 25 hours.

Grove Farm Scholarship Program: Merit-based scholarships to Kauai high school students to pursue higher education. Recipients are selected based on community service, citizenship, academic accomplishments, and quality of character. Scholarships of up to $20,000 are awarded and is limited to students from Kapaa High School, Kauai High School, and Waimea High School. Applicant must be a Hawaii state resident.

Type of support: Employee volunteer services; General/operating support; Scholarships—to individuals.
Geographic limitations: Giving primarily in Kauai, HI.
Application information: Applications accepted. Scholarship applicants must attend Kapaa High, Kauai High, or Waimea High. An interview may be required for scholarships.
Scholarship applications should include three character references.
Initial approach: Download application form and mail for scholarships
Deadline(s): Mar. 1 for scholarships
Officers and Directors:* Marissa Sandblom*, Pres.; Sharyl Lam Yuen*, Secy.; Blanche R. Yoshida*, Treas.; Warren H. Haruki; Alison Moriguchi; Keith Yap.
EIN: 990297416

1673
S. J. Groves and Sons Company

965 Hwy. 169 N.
Plymouth, MN 55441-6405 (763) 546-6943

Establishment information: Established in 1905.
Company type: Private company
Business activities: Conducts mining activities; operates water, sewage, and power plants; provides contract construction services.
Business type (SIC): Construction/miscellaneous heavy; construction/highway and street (except elevated); contractors/miscellaneous special trade
Corporate officers: Franklin N. Groves, Chair. and C.E.O.; Roger J. Ludlam, Pres.; P.A. Seppala, C.F.O.; S.A. Martell, Co-Secy.; T.G. Kost, Co-Secy.-Treas.
Board of director: Franklin N. Groves, Chair.
Giving statement: Giving through the Groves Foundation.

Groves Foundation

P.O. Box 1267
Minneapolis, MN 55440-1267 (763) 546-8323

Establishment information: Incorporated in 1952 in MN.
Donors: S.J. Groves and Sons Co.; Frank N. Groves†.
Contact: David F. Cmiel, Secy.
Financial data (yr. ended 09/30/11): Assets, $9,697,936 (M); expenditures, $464,763; qualifying distributions, $211,500; giving activities include $211,500 for grants.
Purpose and activities: The foundation supports organizations involved with arts and culture, education, animal welfare, heart disease, employment, and athletics.
Fields of interest: Arts; Elementary/secondary education; Education, special; Higher education; Education; Animal welfare; Heart & circulatory diseases; Employment, training; Employment; Athletics/sports, Special Olympics.
Type of support: General/operating support.
Geographic limitations: Giving primarily in the Minneapolis, MN, area.
Support limitations: No grants to individuals or for capital or endowment funds; no loans; no matching gifts.
Application information: Applications accepted. Application form not required. Applicants should submit the following:
1) detailed description of project and amount of funding requested
Initial approach: Letter of inquiry
Deadline(s): None
Officers: Franklin N. Groves, Pres.; C. T. Groves, V.P.; David F. Cmiel, Secy.
Number of staff: 1
EIN: 416038512
Selected grants: The following grants are a representative sample of this grantmaker's funding activity:
$1,000 to American Heart Association, Dallas, TX, 2011.

1674
GROWMARK, Inc.

1701 Towanda Ave.
Bloomington, IL 61701-2090
(309) 557-6000

Company URL: http://www.growmark.com
Establishment information: Established in 1927.
Company type: Cooperative
Business activities: Manufactures and produces livestock and poultry feeds and chemical fertilizers.
Business type (SIC): Grain mill products, including pet food; fertilizers and agricultural chemicals; petroleum refining; farm-product raw materials—wholesale
Financial profile for 2012: Assets, $2,762,630,000
Corporate officers: Daniel Kelley, Chair. and Pres.; Rick Nelson, Co-Vice-Chair.; John Reifsteck, Co-Vice-Chair.; Jeff Solberg, C.E.O.; Marshall Bohbrink, V.P., Finance and C.F.O.; Gary Swango, V.P., Human Resources; Brent Bostrom, V.P. and Genl. Counsel; Chet Esther, Jr., Secy.
Board of directors: Dan Kelley, Chair.; Rick Nelson, Co-Vice-Chair.; John Reifsteck, Co-Vice-Chair.; Ed Benjamins; Chet Esther, Jr.; Bill Hanson; Matt Heitz; Gary Leber; Randy Newcomb; Bob Phelps; Ray Steffens; Allen Tanner; David Watt
Giving statement: Giving through the GROWMARK Foundation.

The GROWMARK Foundation

1701 Towanda Ave.
P.O. Box 2500
Bloomington, IL 61702-2500

Establishment information: Established in IL.
Donor: Growmark, Inc.
Financial data (yr. ended 12/31/11): Assets, $4,124,640 (M); gifts received, $4,806,160; expenditures, $803,969; qualifying distributions, $705,810; giving activities include $705,810 for grants.
Purpose and activities: The foundation supports food banks and organizations involved with higher education, plant conservation, health, and agriculture.
Fields of interest: Higher education; Environment, plant conservation; Health care; Agriculture/food, alliance/advocacy; Agriculture; Food banks; Youth development, agriculture; United Ways and Federated Giving Programs.
Type of support: General/operating support; Scholarship funds.
Geographic limitations: Giving primarily in IL.
Support limitations: No grants to individuals.
Application information: Applications not accepted. Contributes only to pre-selected organizations.
Directors: Davis Anderson; Brent B. Bostrom; B. Stevens Buckalew; Kevin Carroll; Dennis Farmer; Sandra Heissier; James K. Hoyt; Shelly Kruse; Jeff Lynch; Jeffrey M. Solberg; James Spradlin.
EIN: 371401632
Selected grants: The following grants are a representative sample of this grantmaker's funding activity:
$40,200 to University of Illinois at Urbana-Champaign, Urbana, IL, 2010. For student scholarships.
$35,000 to Illinois Agricultural Leadership Foundation, Macomb, IL, 2010.
$30,500 to Illinois State University Foundation, Normal, IL, 2010. For student scholarships.
$25,000 to Midwest Food Bank, Bloomington, IL, 2010.
$22,500 to Future Farmers of America Foundation, Iowa, Mitchellville, IA, 2010.
$10,000 to Iowa State University, Ames, IA, 2010. For student scholarships.
$10,000 to University of Wisconsin-Platteville, Platteville, WI, 2010. For student scholarships.
$8,000 to Western Illinois University, Macomb, IL, 2010. For student scholarships.
$2,000 to Four-H Foundation, Iowa, Ames, IA, 2010.
$1,000 to Agriculture Future of America, Kansas City, MO, 2010.

1675
Stephen R. Grubb Construction, Inc.

475 S. 50th St., Ste. 100
West Des Moines, IA 50265-6980
(515) 327-1700

Establishment information: Established in 1968.
Company type: Private company
Business activities: Builds houses; builds residential buildings; develops land.
Business type (SIC): Contractors/general residential building; real estate subdividers and developers
Corporate officer: Stephen R. Grubb, Pres.
Giving statement: Giving through the Stephen R. Grubb Charitable Foundation Inc.

Stephen R. Grubb Charitable Foundation Inc.

475 S. 50th St., Ste. 100
West Des Moines, IA 50265-6980 (515) 327-1700

Establishment information: Established in 1998 in IA.
Donors: Stephen R. Grubb Construction, Inc.; Stephen R. Grubb; St. Mary's Hispanic Ministry.
Contact: Stephen R. Grubb, Pres.
Financial data (yr. ended 12/31/11): Assets, $10,900 (M); gifts received, $7,500; expenditures, $7,017; qualifying distributions, $6,600; giving activities include $5,100 for 1 grant and $1,500 for 1 grant to an individual.
Purpose and activities: The foundation supports organizations involved with families and Christianity and awards grants to individuals.
Fields of interest: Family services; Christian agencies & churches.
Type of support: Grants to individuals; Program development.
Geographic limitations: Giving primarily in Des Moines, IA.
Application information: Applications accepted. Application form required. Applicants should submit the following:
1) brief history of organization and description of its mission
Initial approach: Letter
Deadline(s): None
Officer: Stephen R. Grubb, Pres.
EIN: 391901112

1676
GSM Industrial, Inc.

3249 Hempland Rd.
Lancaster, PA 17601-6913 (717) 207-8985

Company URL: http://www.gsmindustrial.com
Establishment information: Established in 1946.
Company type: Private company
Business activities: Fabricates sheet metal.
Business type (SIC): Metal products/structural; contractors/roofing, siding, and sheet metal work
Corporate officers: John S. Gooding, Chair.; Jim Towers, Vice-Chair.; Brian Dombach, Pres.; Dana Lichty, Mgr.
Board of directors: John S. Gooding, Chair.; Jim Towers, Vice-Chair.
Giving statement: Giving through the Gooding Group Foundation.

Gooding Group Foundation

345 S. Reading Rd.
Ephrata, PA 17522-1832 (717) 733-1247

Establishment information: Established in 1988 in PA.
Donors: GSM Industrial, Inc.; Gooding, Simpson, and Mackes, Inc.; GSM Roofing.
Contact: John S. Gooding, Pres.
Financial data (yr. ended 12/31/11): Assets, $436,578 (M); gifts received, $9,107; expenditures, $59,993; qualifying distributions, $41,045; giving activities include $41,045 for grants.
Purpose and activities: The foundation supports food banks and organizations involved with performing arts, historic preservation, education, judicial administration, human services, and civic affairs.
Fields of interest: Education; Human services; Public affairs.
Type of support: Employee-related scholarships; General/operating support; Scholarship funds.
Application information: Applications accepted. Application form required. Applicants should submit the following:
1) detailed description of project and amount of funding requested
Initial approach: Letter
Deadline(s): None
Officers: John S. Gooding, Pres.; James K. Towers III, V.P.; William H. Gooding, Secy.-Treas.
EIN: 232516754

1677
GTECH Holdings Corporation

10 Memorial Blvd., Ste 101
Providence, RI 02903-1152 (401) 392-1000

Company URL: http://www.gtech.com
Establishment information: Established in 1981.
Company type: Subsidiary of a foreign company
Business activities: Manufactures and provides computer-based lottery services and equipment.
Business type (SIC): Amusement and recreation services/miscellaneous; computer services
Corporate officers: Donald R. Sweitzer, Chair.; Jaymin Patel, Pres. and C.E.O.; Frank Ward, C.F.O.; Donald Stanford, C.I.O.; Alan Eland, Sr. V.P., and C.O.O.; Michael K. Prescott, Sr. V.P., Genl. Counsel, and Corp. Secy.; Stefano Monterosso, Sr. V.P., Mktg.
Board of directors: Donald R. Sweitzer, Chair.; Jaymin Patel
Subsidiaries: Dreamport, Inc., Coventry, RI; Transactive Corp., Austin, TX; Worldserv, Herndon, VA
Plant: Boca Raton, FL
Giving statement: Giving through the GTECH Holdings Corporation Contributions Program.
Company EIN: 050450121

GTECH Holdings Corporation Contributions Program

c/o Community Rels.
10 Memorial Blvd.
Providence, RI 02903-1152 (401) 392-1000
E-mail: CorporateCommunications@gtech.com; Contact for After School Advantage: Elena Chiaradio, tel.: (401) 392-7705, e-mail: elena.lupinacci@gtech.com; URL: http://www.gtech.com/eng/social/sr.html

Purpose and activities: GTECH makes charitable contributions to nonprofit organizations involved with education and community development and on a case by case basis. Support is given on a national and international basis in areas of company operations.
Fields of interest: Elementary/secondary education; Community/economic development; General charitable giving.
Programs:
After School Advantage: Through the After School Advantage program, GTECH makes charitable contributions of Internet ready computer labs of up to $15,000 in value to inner-city after-school programs. The program is designed to bridge the digital divide among at-risk children.
Dollars for Doers: GTECH makes charitable contributions of $250 to nonprofit organizations with which employees volunteer at least 25 hours per year.
Matching Gifts: GTECH matches contributions made by its employees to educational institutions on a one-for-one basis from $50 to $500 per employee, per year.
Type of support: Employee matching gifts; Employee volunteer services; General/operating support; Program development; Sponsorships.
Geographic limitations: Giving on a national and international basis in areas of company operations.
Support limitations: No support for religious organizations, political candidates or lobbying organizations, labor, fraternal, or veterans' organizations, anti-business or government organizations, national chapters of disease-specific organizations, or private foundations. No grants to individuals, or for monuments or memorials, travel, sporting events, golf tournaments, or team or athletic sponsorships, advertising, annual campaigns or debt reduction, or capital campaigns or endowments.
Publications: Application guidelines.
Application information: Applications accepted. The Community Relations Department handles giving. Application form not required. Applicants should submit the following:
1) name, address and phone number of organization
2) copy of IRS Determination Letter
3) brief history of organization and description of its mission
4) copy of most recent annual report/audited financial statement/990
5) descriptive literature about organization
6) listing of board of directors, trustees, officers and other key people and their affiliations
7) detailed description of project and amount of funding requested
8) contact person
9) copy of current year's organizational budget and/or project budget
10) listing of additional sources and amount of support
11) plans for acknowledgement
Initial approach: Proposal to headquarters for After School Advantage
Copies of proposal: 1
Deadline(s): None for After School Advantage

1678
Guarantee Electric Company Inc.

1524 W. 8th St.
Hastings, NE 68901-4340 (402) 463-4586

Establishment information: Established in 1914.
Company type: Private company
Business activities: Provides general contract electrical services.
Business type (SIC): Contractors/electrical work
Corporate officers: David O. Peterson, Pres.; Gary Anderson, Treas.
Giving statement: Giving through the Family Benevolent Foundation.

Family Benevolent Foundation

1020 W. 8th St.
Hastings, NE 68901-4403

Establishment information: Established in 2002 in NE.
Donors: Mary L. Peterson; Lyle Weitzel; David O. Peterson; Margaret C. Peterson; Guarantee Electric Co.; Mark A. Peterson; Sharon Peterson; Guarantee Electric Co.
Financial data (yr. ended 12/31/11): Assets, $264,213 (M); gifts received, $38,000; expenditures, $14,251; qualifying distributions, $14,000; giving activities include $14,000 for grants.
Fields of interest: Housing/shelter; Human services; Religion.

Geographic limitations: Giving primarily in FL, IL, and NE.
Support limitations: No grants to individuals.
Application information: Applications not accepted. Unsolicited requests for funds not accepted.
Officers and Directors:* David O. Peterson, Pres.; Margaret C. Peterson, V.P.; David A. Peterson*, Secy.; Mark A. Peterson*, Treas.
EIN: 481285065

1679
Guaranty Bank and Trust Company

302 3rd Ave., S.E.
P.O. Box 1807
Cedar Rapids, IA 52401-1507
(319) 286-6200

Company URL: http://www.guaranty-bank.com
Establishment information: Established in 1934.
Company type: Private company
Business activities: Operates commercial bank.
Business type (SIC): Banks/commercial
Corporate officers: Harold M. Becker, Chair.; Robert D. Becker, C.E.O.; Chris Lindell, Pres. and C.O.O.; Todd Kerska, C.F.O.
Board of directors: Harold M. Becker, Chair.; Robert D. Becker; Pat Cobb; Nancy Evans; Jeff Hamilton; Chris Lindell; Cheryle Mitvalsky; Don Nebergall; Doug Olson; John Osako; Amy Reasner
Giving statement: Giving through the Guaranty Bank and Trust Company Charitable Trust.

Guaranty Bank and Trust Company Charitable Trust

P.O. Box 1807
Cedar Rapids, IA 52406-1807
URL: http://www.guaranty-bank.com/

Donors: Guaranty Bank and Trust Co.; AmSouth Bank.
Contact: Robert Becker, Tr.
Financial data (yr. ended 12/31/11): Assets, $1 (M); expenditures, $36,122; qualifying distributions, $35,500; giving activities include $35,500 for grants.
Purpose and activities: The foundation supports organizations involved with arts and culture, health, human services, and diversity.
Fields of interest: Arts; Health care; Human services.
Type of support: General/operating support.
Geographic limitations: Giving primarily in IA.
Application information: Applications accepted. Application form required.
Initial approach: Letter
Deadline(s): None
Trustees: Harold M. Becker; Robert D. Becker; Nancy Evans.
EIN: 510182485

1680
Guard Publishing Company

(doing business as The Register Guard)
3500 Chad Dr.
Eugene, OR 97408-7348 (541) 485-1234

Company URL: http://www.registerguard.com
Establishment information: Established in 1927.
Company type: Private company
Business activities: Publishes newspapers.
Business type (SIC): Newspaper publishing and/or printing
Financial profile for 2011: Number of employees, 270
Corporate officers: Edwin M. Baker, Chair.; Alton Baker, Pres. and C.E.O.; David Pero, C.O.O.; Scott Diehl, C.F.O.; Rick Baker, C.I.O.
Board of director: Edwin M. Baker, Chair.
Giving statement: Giving through the Baker Family Foundation.

Baker Family Foundation

3500 Chad Dr.
Eugene, OR 97408-7348 (541) 338-2700
FAX: (541) 984-4699

Establishment information: Established in 1999 in OR.
Donor: Guard Publishing Co.
Financial data (yr. ended 12/31/11): Assets, $547,193 (M); expenditures, $35,166; qualifying distributions, $27,095; giving activities include $26,600 for 19 grants (high: $5,000; low: $100).
Purpose and activities: The foundation supports organizations involved with arts and culture, health, recreation, human services, and education. Special emphasis is directed toward programs designed to promote journalism, literacy, and citizenship.
Fields of interest: Media, print publishing; Arts; Education, reading; Education; Health care; Recreation; Human services Children; Adults; Young adults.
Type of support: Building/renovation; Capital campaigns; Curriculum development; Donated equipment; Donated products; Emergency funds; Equipment; Management development/capacity building; Program development; Scholarship funds; Seed money.
Geographic limitations: Giving primarily in Eugene, Lane County, and Springfield, OR.
Support limitations: No support for political organizations. No grants to individuals.
Publications: Annual report; Application guidelines.
Application information: Applications accepted. Application form required.
Initial approach: Contact foundation for application form
Copies of proposal: 10
Board meeting date(s): Sept., Oct., and Dec.
Deadline(s): Sept. 1
Final notification: 2 months
Officers: Bridget Baker Kincaid, Pres.; Ann Baker Mack, V.P.; Susan Diamond, Secy.-Treas.
Directors: Alton F. Baker III; Edwin M. Baker; Richard A. Baker, Jr.; David Johnson; R. Fletcher Little; Jeff Rondestvedt.
Number of staff: 1 part-time professional; 1 part-time support.
EIN: 931265230

1681
Guardian Corp.

3801 Sunset Ave., Ste. A
Rocky Mount, NC 27804-3126
(252) 443-4101

Establishment information: Established in 1981.
Company type: Private company
Business activities: Operates restaurants.
Business type (SIC): Restaurants and drinking places
Corporate officers: Vincent C. Andracchio II, Pres.; Debra Williams, C.F.O. and Treas.; Wilma J. Morin, Secy.
Giving statement: Giving through the Leon Algernon, Jr. & Pattie McCay Dunn Family Foundation.

The Leon Algernon, Jr. & Pattie McCay Dunn Family Foundation

P.O. Box 7397
Rocky Mount, NC 27804-7397

Establishment information: Established in 1990 in NC.
Donors: Guardian Corp.; Guardian Holdings, Inc.; Pattie M. Dunn.
Financial data (yr. ended 12/31/11): Assets, $928 (M); gifts received, $40,922; expenditures, $40,172; qualifying distributions, $40,172; giving activities include $40,051 for 21 grants (high: $24,101; low: $100).
Purpose and activities: The foundation supports veteran memorials and organizations involved with K-12 and higher education.
Fields of interest: Historical activities, war memorials; Elementary/secondary education; Higher education.
Type of support: Building/renovation; General/operating support; Scholarship funds.
Geographic limitations: Giving primarily in areas of company operations in Rocky Mount, NC.
Support limitations: No grants to individuals.
Application information: Application form required.
Initial approach: Letter
Deadline(s): Apr. 15th
Officers and Directors:* Eugenie Dunn Andracchio*, Pres.; Debra W. Williams*, Secy.-Treas.; Vincent C. Andracchio II; Jane D. Pittman; Pattie McCay Dunn.
EIN: 561711109

1682
Guardian Industries Corporation

2300 Harmon Rd.
Auburn Hills, MI 48326-1714
(248) 340-1800

Company URL: http://www.guardian.com
Establishment information: Established in 1932.
Company type: Private company
Business activities: Manufactures float glass and fabricated glass products; manufactures exterior automotive products; sells building materials wholesale; manufactures mirrors.
Business type (SIC): Glass/flat; glass/pressed or blown; glass products/miscellaneous; motor vehicles and equipment; lumber and construction materials—wholesale
Financial profile for 2011: Number of employees, 17,000; sales volume, $4,900,000,000
Corporate officers: Charles Croskey, Chair.; Jeffrey A. Knight, C.F.O.; Robert H. Gorlin, V.P. and Genl. Counsel; Bruce Cummings, V.P., Human Resources
Board of director: Charles Croskey, Chair.
Subsidiaries: Guardian Industries Corp., Albion, MI; Guardian Transportation Corp., Milbury, OH
Plants: Rogers, AR; Fullerton, Kingsburg, Los Angeles, CA; Fort Lauderdale, FL; Atlanta, GA; Overland Park, Wichita, KS; Capitol Heights, MD; Boston, Webster, MA; Carleton, Farmington Hills, MI; Columbus, Upper Sandusky, OH; West Elizabeth, PA; Corsicana, TX; Parkersburg, WV
International operations: Thailand
Giving statement: Giving through the Guardian Industries Educational Foundation.

Guardian Industries Educational Foundation

2300 Harmon Rd.
Auburn Hills, MI 48326-1714

Establishment information: Established in 1986 in DE and MI.
Donor: Guardian Industries Corp.
Financial data (yr. ended 12/31/11): Assets, $53,568 (M); gifts received, $858,596; expenditures, $953,011; qualifying distributions, $909,300; giving activities include $909,300 for grants to individuals.
Purpose and activities: The foundation awards college scholarships to children of full-time employees of Guardian Industries and its subsidiaries. The scholarship program is administered by Educational Testing Service.
Fields of interest: Higher education.
Type of support: Employee-related scholarships.
Geographic limitations: Giving primarily in areas of company operations.
Support limitations: No loans or program-related investments.
Application information: Applications not accepted. Contributes only through employee-related scholarships.
Officers and Directors:* Ralph J. Gerson*, Pres.; Bruce Cummings, V.P.; David B. Jaffe, Secy.; Jeffrey A. Knight, Treas.; Russell J. Ebeid.
EIN: 382707035

1683
The Guardian Life Insurance Company of America

7 Hanover Sq.
New York, NY 10004-4025 (212) 598-8000

Company URL: http://www.guardianlife.com
Establishment information: Established in 1860.
Company type: Mutual company
Business activities: Sells life and disability insurance; provides investment advisory services; sells health and dental insurance.
Business type (SIC): Insurance/life; security and commodity services; insurance/accident and health
Financial profile for 2010: Number of employees, 1,200; sales volume, $7,808,000,000
Corporate officers: Dennis J. Manning, Chair.; Deanna M. Mulligan, Pres. and C.E.O.; D. Scott Dolfi, C.O.O.; Robert E. Broatch, C.P.A., Exec. V.P. and C.F.O.; Thomas G. Sorell, Exec. V.P. and C.I.O.; Tracy L. Rich, Exec. V.P., Genl. Counsel, and Corp. Secy.; Brad Thomas, Exec. V.P., Human Resources
Board of directors: Dennis J. Manning, Chair.; John J. Brennan; Robert E. Broatch, C.P.A.; Lloyd E. Campbell; Richard E. Cavanagh; James E. Daley; Deborah L. Duncan; Paul B. Guenther; Deanna M. Mulligan; John A. Somers; Stephen J. Squeri; Donald C. Waite III
Subsidiaries: Berkshire Life Insurance Company of America, Pittsfield, MA; The Guardian Insurance & Annuity Co., Inc., New York, NY; Guardian Investor Services LLC, New York, NY
Giving statement: Giving through the Guardian Life Insurance Company of America Corporate Giving Program and the Edward Kane Guardian Life Welfare Trust.
Company EIN: 061116976

The Guardian Life Insurance Company of America Corporate Giving Program

7 Hanover Sq.
New York, NY 10004-4010
FAX: (212) 919-2944;
E-mail: community_involvement@glic.com; E-mail for Karen L. Olvany: kolvany@glic.com; Contact for Bethlehem, PA region: Karen Warg, Dir., NRO Human Resources, The Guardian Life Insurance Co., Northeast Regional Office, P.O. Box 26250, Lehigh Valley, PA 18003-6250; Appleton, WI region: Jennie Gietman, Admin. Coord., The Guardian Life Insurance Co., 2300 E. Capitol Dr., A1-L, P.O. Box 8011, Appleton, WI 54912; Spokane, WA region: Gloria L. Loeffler, Mgr., Human Resources, The Guardian Life Insurance Co., 777 E. Magnesium Rd., 2-A, Spokane, WA 99208; URL: http://www.guardianlife.com/company_info/community_involvement.html
Application address for Girls Going Places: c/o Girls Going Places, H-25-E, 7 Hanover Sq., New York, NY 10004, e-mail: guardianwomenschannel@glic.com

Contact: Karen L. Olvany, Asst. Corp. Secy.
Financial data (yr. ended 12/31/08): Total giving, $1,747,300, including $1,625,000 for 120 grants (high: $250,000; low: $500) and $122,300 for 340 employee matching gifts.
Purpose and activities: The company's philanthropic focus on affordable housing helps individuals and their families in the local communities in which it operates achieve stable and secure housing. Support is given primarily in areas of company operations.
Fields of interest: Housing/shelter, public policy; Housing/shelter, development; Housing/shelter, rehabilitation; Housing/shelter, homeless; Disasters, preparedness/services; Youth development; Business/industry; Community/economic development Girls; Young adults, female.
Programs:
Girls Going Places Entrepreneurship Award Program: Through the Girls Going Places Entrepreneurship Award Program, Guardian annually awards 15 prizes to girls between 12 and 16 years old who demonstrate budding entrepreneurship, are taking the first steps toward financial independence, and make a difference in their school and community. Three top finalists receive $10,000, $5,000, and $3,000, respectively, and the remaining 12 finalists receive $1,000. The awards are designed to help winners and finalists save for college and continue their entrepreneurial pursuits.
Matching Gift Program for Higher Education: The company matches contributions made by employees, directors, and retirees of The Guardian Life Insurance Company of America to institutions of higher education on a one-for-one basis from $25 to $5,000 per contributor, per year.
Type of support: Emergency funds; Employee matching gifts; Employee volunteer services; General/operating support; Grants to individuals.
Geographic limitations: Giving primarily in areas of company operations, with emphasis on New York, NY, Bethlehem, PA, Spokane, WA, and Appleton, WI; giving on a national basis for Girls Going Places.
Support limitations: No support for organizations located outside the U.S., religious organizations, political organizations, or labor organizations. No grants to individuals (except for Girls Going Places), or for research, endowments, travel, political causes, or capital campaigns.
Publications: Application guidelines; Corporate report; Program policy statement (including application guidelines).
Application information: Applications accepted. The Corporate Secretary in New York handles giving (except for Girls Going Places). Application form required. Applicants should submit the following:
1) results expected from proposed grant
2) qualifications of key personnel
3) copy of IRS Determination Letter
4) brief history of organization and description of its mission
5) copy of most recent annual report/audited financial statement/990
6) how project's results will be evaluated or measured
7) listing of board of directors, trustees, officers and other key people and their affiliations
8) detailed description of project and amount of funding requested
9) copy of current year's organizational budget and/or project budget
10) listing of additional sources and amount of support

Applications for Girls Going Places should include a 250-word personal statement, a 750-word letter of recommendation, and specific examples of how the applicant started their business/service and are financially independent.
Initial approach: Proposal for Affordable Housing Focus to nearest regional contact; download entry form for Girls Going Places and mail to application address
Copies of proposal: 2
Deadline(s): None for Affordable Housing Focus; postmarked Feb. 28 for Girls Going Places
Final notification: Following review; Apr. 25 to May 9 for Girls Going Places
Number of staff: 1 full-time professional; 1 full-time support.

The Edward Kane Guardian Life Welfare Trust

(formerly The Guardian Life Welfare Trust)
7 Hanover Sq., Ste. H21-K
New York, NY 10004-2616
URL: http://www.guardianlife.com/AboutGuardian/CompanyOverview/CorporateCitizenship/EdwardKaneGuardianWelfareTrust/index.htm

Establishment information: Established in 1926.
Donors: The Guardian Life Insurance Co. of America; Cecilia Dunphy; Edward K. Kane; Dennis J. Manning.
Financial data (yr. ended 12/31/11): Assets, $467,975 (M); gifts received, $128,050; expenditures, $74,161; qualifying distributions, $74,161; giving activities include $73,662 for grants.
Purpose and activities: The trust awards grants and loans to needy employees of Guardian Life Insurance Company for catastrophic events when no other resources are available.
Fields of interest: Human services, emergency aid Economically disadvantaged.
Type of support: Grants to individuals; Loans—to individuals.
Geographic limitations: Giving primarily in areas of company operations.
Application information: Applications not accepted. Contributes only through employee-related grants and loans.
Board meeting date(s): Feb., May, Aug., and Nov.
Officers: John Flannigan, Pres.; Richard O'Donnell, V.P. and Treas.; Electra Jacobs, Secy.
Trustees: Luanna Labriola; Virginia Mayora; Thomas Rafferty; Richard Potter; Ruben Serrano.
Number of staff: None.
EIN: 136197206

1684
Gucci America, Inc.
685 5th Ave.
New York, NY 10022-4204 (212) 750-5220

Company URL: http://www.gucci.com
Establishment information: Established in 1953.
Company type: Subsidiary of a foreign company
Business activities: Manufactures shoes and accessories; operates retail stores.
Business type (SIC): Women's apparel stores; women's specialty and accessory stores; shoe stores
Corporate officers: Daniella Vitale, C.E.O.; Tony Mauro, V.P., Opers., and C.O.O.; Susan Chokachi, Sr. V.P., Mktg., and Comms.
Giving statement: Giving through the Gucci America, Inc. Corporate Giving Program and the Gucci Foundation.

The Gucci Foundation
685 5th Ave.
New York, NY 10022-4223

Donor: Gucci America, Inc.
Financial data (yr. ended 12/31/11): Assets, $24,825 (M); expenditures, $11,151; qualifying distributions, $11,151; giving activities include $10,000 for 1 grant.
Purpose and activities: The foundation supports Dignitas International USA.
Fields of interest: AIDS; Medical research.
Type of support: General/operating support.
Geographic limitations: Giving primarily in Canada.
Application information: Applications not accepted. Unsolicited requests for funds not accepted.
Officers: Laura Lendrum, Pres.; Nicole Marra, Secy.; Matteo Mascazzini, Treas.
EIN: 261378939
Selected grants: The following grants are a representative sample of this grantmaker's funding activity:
$900,000 to Film Foundation, Los Angeles, CA, 2010.
$110,000 to Dia Center for the Arts, New York, NY, 2010.
$45,000 to UNICEF, New York, NY, 2010.
$40,000 to Metropolitan Museum of Art, New York, NY, 2010.
$10,000 to San Francisco Film Society, San Francisco, CA, 2010.
$1,308 to American Cancer Society, Brooklyn, NY, 2010.

1685
Guess?, Inc.
1444 S. Alameda St.
Los Angeles, CA 90021-2433
(213) 765-3100

Company URL: http://www.guess.com
Establishment information: Established in 1981.
Company type: Public company
Company ticker symbol and exchange: GES/NYSE
Business activities: Designs, markets, distributes, and licenses casual apparel, accessories, and related consumer products.
Business type (SIC): Apparel—men's and boys' outerwear; apparel—women's outerwear; apparel—women's, girls', and children's undergarments
Financial profile for 2013: Number of employees, 15,200; assets, $1,713,510,000; sales volume, $2,658,610,000; pre-tax net income, $280,610,000; expenses, $2,384,080,000; liabilities, $626,510,000
Fortune 1000 ranking: 2012—778th in revenues, 610th in profits, and 890th in assets
Corporate officers: Maurice Marciano, Chair.; Paul Marciano, Vice-Chair. and C.E.O.; Michael Relich, Exec. V.P. and C.I.O.
Board of directors: Maurice Marciano, Chair.; Paul Marciano, Vice-Chair.; Judith Blumenthal; Gianluca Bolla; Anthony Chidoni; Kay Isaacson-Leibowitz; Alex Yemenidjian
International operations: Bermuda; Canada; France; Germany; Hong Kong; Italy; Macau; Mexico; Netherlands; South Korea; Spain; Switzerland; Taiwan
Giving statement: Giving through the Guess? Foundation.
Company EIN: 953679695

Guess? Foundation
c/o Corporate Citizenship & Philanthropy
1444 S. Alameda St.
Los Angeles, CA 90021-2433
FAX: (213) 774-7844; URL: http://www.guess.com/worldofguess/#/philanthropy

Establishment information: Established in 1994 in CA.
Donor: Guess ?, Inc.
Financial data (yr. ended 12/31/11): Assets, $1,139,346 (M); gifts received, $1,500,000; expenditures, $1,519,650; qualifying distributions, $1,497,490; giving activities include $1,497,490 for grants.
Purpose and activities: The foundation supports organizations involved with education, the environment, health, substance abuse services, heart disease, diabetes, HIV/AIDS research, housing, human services, the fashion industry, and Judaism.
Fields of interest: Education; Environment; Health care; Substance abuse, services; Heart & circulatory diseases; AIDS; Diabetes; AIDS research; Housing/shelter; Recreation, camps; Children/youth, services; Children, foster care; Human services; Business/industry; Jewish agencies & synagogues.
Type of support: General/operating support; Program development; Publication; Scholarship funds; Sponsorships.
Geographic limitations: Giving primarily in the Greater Los Angeles, CA area.
Support limitations: No grants to individuals.
Publications: Application guidelines.
Application information: Applications accepted. Application form not required. Applicants should submit the following:
1) how project will be sustained once grantmaker support is completed
2) results expected from proposed grant
3) copy of IRS Determination Letter
4) detailed description of project and amount of funding requested

Initial approach: Fax proposal to foundation
Deadline(s): 8 weeks prior to need

Officer and Directors: Deborah Siegel, Secy.; Maurice Marciano; Paul Marciano.
EIN: 954500475
Selected grants: The following grants are a representative sample of this grantmaker's funding activity:
$99,002 to Invisible Children, San Diego, CA, 2010.
$80,000 to Miracles and Wonders Foundation, Encino, CA, 2010.
$50,000 to American Jewish Committee, New York, NY, 2010.
$50,000 to Friends of the Israel Defense Forces, New York, NY, 2010.
$25,000 to A Place Called Home, Los Angeles, CA, 2010.
$25,000 to Community Health Charities of California, Sacramento, CA, 2010.
$25,000 to New School, New York, NY, 2010.
$25,000 to Phoenix House Development Fund, New York, NY, 2010.
$25,000 to United Friends of the Children, Los Angeles, CA, 2010.
$10,000 to American Heart Association, Dallas, TX, 2010.

1686
Guided Alliance Healthcare Service Inc.
(also known as Guided Alliance Pharmacy)
34145 Pacific Coast Hwy., Ste. 195
Dana Point, CA 92629-2808
(949) 496-3906

Company URL: http://www.guidedalliance.com
Establishment information: Established in 2002.
Company type: Private company
Business activities: Provides home health care services.
Business type (SIC): Home healthcare services
Corporate officer: Timothy McFadden, Pres. and C.E.O.
Giving statement: Giving through the McFadden Family Foundation.

McFadden Family Foundation
34145 Pacific Coast Hwy., Ste. 195
Dana Point, CA 92629

Establishment information: Established in 2003.
Donors: Global Cornerstone Healthcare Services, Inc.; Guided Alliance Healthcare Services; Timothy McFadden; Mary McFadden.
Financial data (yr. ended 12/31/11): Assets, $293,477 (M); expenditures, $732; qualifying distributions, $0.
Purpose and activities: The foundation supports Junipero Serra High School in San Juan Capistrano, California.
Fields of interest: Secondary school/education.
Type of support: General/operating support.
Support limitations: No grants to individuals.
Application information: Applications not accepted. Contributes only to pre-selected organizations.
Officers: Timothy McFadden, Pres.; Mary McFadden, V.P.
EIN: 200170944

1687
GuideOne Life Insurance Co.
1111 Ashworth Rd.
West Des Moines, IA 50265-3538
(877) 448-4331

Company URL: https://www.guideone.com
Establishment information: Established in 1947.
Company type: Private company
Business activities: Sells insurance.
Business type (SIC): Insurance carriers
Corporate officers: James D. Wallace, Chair., Pres., and C.E.O.; Scott Reddig, Exec. V.P. and C.O.O.; Mark Joos, Sr. V.P. and C.F.O.; Tom Fischer, Sr. V.P. and C.I.O.; Tom Farr, Sr. V.P. and Genl. Counsel; Sarah Buckley, V.P., Corp. Comms and Mktg.; Marq

James, V.P., Sales; Cathy Murray, V.P., Human Resources
Board of directors: James D. Wallace, Chair.; Cara Heiden
Giving statement: Giving through the GuideOne Insurance Foundation, Inc.

The GuideOne Insurance Foundation, Inc.

1111 Ashworth Rd., M.S. A27
West Des Moines, IA 50265-3544
URL: http://www.guideone.com/AboutUs/foundation.htm

Establishment information: Established in 2000 in IA as a company-sponsored operating foundation.
Donor: GuideOne Life Insurance Co.
Contact: Sarah Buckley, V.P., Corp. Comms. and Mktg.
Financial data (yr. ended 12/31/11): Assets, $2,273,366 (M); gifts received, $67,644; expenditures, $425,739; qualifying distributions, $425,739; giving activities include $425,739 for 33 grants (high: $160,410).
Purpose and activities: The foundation supports food banks and organizations involved with housing development, human services, community development, and Christianity. Special emphasis is directed toward programs designed to promote mission and community development; provide assistance for immediate needs; and promote prevention of drinking and driving and underage drinking.
Fields of interest: Crime/law enforcement, DWI; Food banks; Housing/shelter, development; Disasters, preparedness/services; Safety, automotive safety; American Red Cross; Children/youth, services; Human services; Community/economic development; United Ways and Federated Giving Programs; Christian agencies & churches.
Programs:

Drinking and Driving and Underage Drinking Prevention: The foundation supports programs designed to provide alcohol-free community activities such as post prom parties, church overnight lock-ins, and New Year's Eve family events.

Immediate Need Assistance: The foundation supports programs designed to provide disaster relief, as well as food, shelter, clothing, and safe environments for people and families with immediate needs.

Mission and Community Development Organizations: The foundation supports organizations involved with housing development, human services, community development, and Christianity.

Type of support: Emergency funds; General/operating support; Program development; Sponsorships.
Geographic limitations: Giving primarily in IA; giving also to national organizations.
Support limitations: No grants to individuals.
Officers and Directors:* James D. Wallace*, Chair. and Pres.; Brian Hughes, Treas.; Tom Fischer.
EIN: 391910630
Selected grants: The following grants are a representative sample of this grantmaker's funding activity:
$10,000 to Fellowship of Christian Athletes, Kansas City, MO, 2009.
$3,500 to Alzheimers Association, Chicago, IL, 2009.

1688
Gulf Marine Fabricators, LP

1982 FM 2725
P.O. Box 3000
Aransas Pass, TX 78336 (361) 775-4600

Company URL: http://www.gulfisland.com/contact.php
Establishment information: Established in 1985.
Company type: Subsidiary of a foreign company
Business activities: Manufactures structural steel products.
Business type (SIC): Metal products/structural
Corporate officers: Frank A. Smith, Pres. and C.E.O.; Deborah Kern-Knoblock, Corp. Secy.; Jarod P. Richard, Corp. Cont.
Giving statement: Giving through the Gulf Marine Fabricators Employee Foundation.

Gulf Marine Fabricators Employee Foundation

(also known as AGM Employee Foundation)
P.O. Box 310
Houma, LA 70361-0310 (985) 875-2100

Financial data (yr. ended 12/31/11): Revenue, $49,909; assets, $71,074 (M); gifts received, $49,715; expenditures, $93,270; giving activities include $93,225 for grants.
Purpose and activities: The foundation supports organizations involved with health and human services.
Fields of interest: Health care; Human services.
Executive Committee Members: Roy Breerwood; Lety Mora; Frank Smith.
EIN: 742738442

1689
Gulf Power Company

1 Energy Pl.
Pensacola, FL 32520-0001 (850) 969-3111

Company URL: http://www.gulfpower.com/
Establishment information: Established in 1926.
Company type: Subsidiary of a public company
Business activities: Generates, transmits, and distributes electricity.
Business type (SIC): Electric services
Corporate officers: Stan Connally, Pres. and C.E.O.; Susan N. Story, C.E.O.; Scott Teel, V.P. and C.F.O.; P. Bernard Jacob, V.P., Opers.
Board of directors: Allan Bense; Debbie Calder; Stan Connally; William C. Cramer, Jr.; Mort O'Sullivan; Winston E. Scott
Plants: Fort Walton Beach, Panama City, Scholz, Smith, FL
Giving statement: Giving through the Gulf Power Company Contributions Program and the Gulf Power Foundation, Inc.

Gulf Power Company Contributions Program

P.O. Box 830660
Birmingham, AL 35283-0660 (800) 225-5797
URL: http://www.gulfpower.com/community/charity.asp

Purpose and activities: As a complement to its foundation, Gulf Power also makes charitable contributions to nonprofit organizations directly. Support is given primarily in areas of company operations in northwest Florida.
Fields of interest: Education; Cancer; Salvation Army; Children/youth, services; Human services, gift distribution; Aging, centers/services; United Ways and Federated Giving Programs; Utilities Economically disadvantaged.
Program:

Project SHARE: Gulf Power provides emergency assistance to the elderly, the sick, and others who are experiencing financial hardship and need help with energy bills, repairs to heating and air-conditioning equipment, and other energy-related needs. The program is administered by the Salvation Army.

Type of support: Annual campaigns; Employee matching gifts; Employee volunteer services; General/operating support.
Geographic limitations: Giving primarily in areas of company operations in northwest FL.

Gulf Power Foundation, Inc.

1 Energy Pl.
Pensacola, FL 32520-0786 (850) 444-6806
FAX: (850) 444-6026;
E-mail: chklingl@southernco.com; URL: http://www.gulfpower.com/community/charity.asp

Establishment information: Established in 1987 in FL.
Donor: Gulf Power Co.
Contact: Bernard Jacob, Chair.
Financial data (yr. ended 12/31/11): Assets, $3,173,740 (M); gifts received, $500,000; expenditures, $261,431; qualifying distributions, $258,991; giving activities include $258,991 for grants.
Purpose and activities: The foundation supports organizations involved with arts and culture, education, health, human services, community development, and civic affairs.
Fields of interest: Arts; Higher education; Education; Health care; Human services; Community/economic development; Public affairs.
Program:

Matching Educational Program: The foundation matches contributions made by employees, retirees, and directors of Gulf Power to institutions of higher education on a one-for-one basis.

Type of support: Annual campaigns; Building/renovation; Capital campaigns; Continuing support; Emergency funds; Employee matching gifts; Equipment; General/operating support; Program development; Scholarship funds.
Geographic limitations: Giving limited to areas of company operations in northwestern FL.
Support limitations: No support for political or lobbying organizations or arts councils (except for capital campaigns). No grants to individuals.
Publications: Annual report; Informational brochure (including application guidelines).
Application information: Applications accepted. Requests should include a copy of the organization's Florida Solicitation Letter. Application form required. Applicants should submit the following:
1) copy of IRS Determination Letter
2) copy of most recent annual report/audited financial statement/990
3) copy of current year's organizational budget and/or project budget

Initial approach: Contact foundation for application form
Copies of proposal: 1
Board meeting date(s): Quarterly
Deadline(s): Feb. 15, May 15, Aug. 15, and Nov. 15
Final notification: 1 month

Officers and Trustees:* Bernard Jacob, Chair.; Susan D. Ritenour, Secy.-Treas.; Constance Erickson; Theodore J. McCullough; Bentina C. Terry.
EIN: 592817740
Selected grants: The following grants are a representative sample of this grantmaker's funding activity:
$275,000 to University of West Florida, Pensacola, FL, 2010. For capital campaign.
$44,087 to United Way of Escambia County, Pensacola, FL, 2010. For operating funds.
$40,000 to University of West Florida, Pensacola, FL, 2010. For capital campaign.
$15,000 to United Way of Santa Rosa County, Milton, FL, 2010. For operating funds.
$2,000 to Bay Education Foundation, Panama City, FL, 2010. For operating funds.
$2,000 to University of Florida Foundation, Gainesville, FL, 2010. For scholarship.
$2,000 to University of West Florida, Pensacola, FL, 2010. For scholarship.
$1,000 to Chipola Junior College, Marianna, FL, 2010. For scholarship.

1690
Gulfstream Aerospace Corporation

(formerly Gulfstream Aerospace, Corp.)
500 Gulfstream Rd.
P.O. Box 2206
Savannah, GA 31402-2206 (912) 965-3000

Company URL: http://www.gulfstream.com
Establishment information: Established in 1958.
Company type: Subsidiary of a public company
Business activities: Manufactures aircraft.
Business type (SIC): Aircraft and parts
Corporate officers: Larry Flynn, Pres.; Kelvin R. Mason, C.I.O.; Dan Clare, Sr. V.P., Finance and C.F.O.; Jason W. Aiken, Sr. V.P. and C.F.O.
Giving statement: Giving through the Gulfstream Aerospace Corporation Contributions Program.

Gulfstream Aerospace Corporation Contributions Program

P.O. Box 2206
Savannah, GA 31402-2206 (912) 965-3000
URL: http://www.gulfstream.com/careers/our_community.html

Purpose and activities: Gulfstream Aerospace Corporation makes charitable contributions to nonprofit organizations involved with arts and culture, education, and human services. Support is given primarily in areas of company operations in Lincoln and Long Beach, California, West Palm Beach, Florida, Brunswick, Georgia, Westfield, Massachusetts, Dallas, Texas, and Appleton, Wisconsin, with emphasis on Savannah, Georgia.
Fields of interest: Arts; Education; Human services; General charitable giving.
Type of support: Employee volunteer services; General/operating support; In-kind gifts; Loaned talent; Use of facilities.
Geographic limitations: Giving primarily in areas of company operations in Lincoln and Long Beach, CA, West Palm Beach, FL, Brunswick, GA, Westfield, MA, Las Vegas, NV, Dallas, TX, and Appleton, WI, with emphasis on Savannah, GA; also giving to national organizations.

1691
Gust Rosenfeld PLC

1 E. Washington St., Ste. 1600
Phoenix, AZ 85004-2553 (602) 257-7422

Company URL: http://www.gustlaw.com
Establishment information: Established in 1921.
Company type: Private company
Business activities: Operates law firm.
Business type (SIC): Legal services
Offices: Phoenix, Tucson, AZ
Giving statement: Giving through the Gust Rosenfeld PLC Pro Bono Program.

Gust Rosenfeld PLC Pro Bono Program

1 E. Washington St., Ste. 1600
Phoenix, AZ 85004-2553 (602) 257-7422
FAX: (602) 254-4878; URL: http://www.gustlaw.com/community.tpl

Fields of interest: Legal services.
Type of support: Pro bono services - legal.
Geographic limitations: Giving primarily in Phoenix and Tucson, AZ.
Application information: The Executive Committee manages pro bono projects.

1692
Guth Lighting Systems, Inc.

(also known as Guth Lighting Co.)
1324 Washington Ave.
St. Louis, MO 63103-1941 (314) 533-3200

Establishment information: Established in 1985.
Company type: Private company
Business activities: Manufactures commercial and industrial lighting fixtures.
Business type (SIC): Lighting and wiring equipment/electric
Corporate officer: Robert Catone, Mgr.
Giving statement: Giving through the Edwin F. Guth Charitable Trust.

Edwin F. Guth Charitable Trust

(formerly Edwin F. Guth Company Charitable Trust)
231 S. LaSalle St., ILI-231-10-05
Chicago, IL 60697-0001
Application address: c/o 345 E. 47th St., New York, NY 10017

Donor: Guth Lighting Systems, Inc.
Contact: Roger Finch
Financial data (yr. ended 08/31/11): Assets, $207,343 (M); expenditures, $10,652; qualifying distributions, $9,078; giving activities include $7,295 for 1 grant.
Purpose and activities: The foundation supports the Illuminating Engineering Society of North America.
Fields of interest: Engineering school/education; Science.
Type of support: General/operating support.
Geographic limitations: Giving limited to New York, NY.
Support limitations: No grants to individuals.
Application information: Applications accepted. Application form required.
Initial approach: Letter
Deadline(s): None
Trustee: Bank of America, N.A.
EIN: 436057215

1693
The Gymboree Corporation

500 Howard St.
San Francisco, CA 94105-3000
(415) 278-7000

Company URL: http://www.gymboree.com
Establishment information: Established in 1976.
Company type: Subsidiary of a private company
Business activities: Operates children's apparel and accessories stores.
Business type (SIC): Apparel and other finished products made from fabrics and similar materials; children's apparel and accessory stores
Financial profile for 2010: Sales volume, $1,100,000,000
Corporate officers: Matthew K. McCauley, Chair. and C.E.O.; Kip M. Garcia, Pres.; Blair W. Lambert, C.O.O.; Jeffrey P. Harris, C.F.O.; Lynda S. Gustafson, V.P. and Cont.
Board of director: Matthew K. McCauley, Chair.
Giving statement: Giving through the Gymboree Corporation Contributions Program.
Company EIN: 942615258

The Gymboree Corporation Contributions Program

c/o Community Donations
500 Howard St.
San Francisco, CA 94105-3000 (415) 278-7000
FAX: (415) 218-7100; URL: http://www.gymboree.com/our_company/cs_home.jsp?

Purpose and activities: Gymboree makes charitable contributions of gift cards to nonprofit organizations on a case by case basis. Support is given primarily in areas of company operations, with some emphasis on San Francisco, California.
Fields of interest: General charitable giving.
Type of support: In-kind gifts.
Geographic limitations: Giving primarily in areas of company operations, with some emphasis on San Francisco, CA; giving also to national organizations.
Application information: Applications accepted. Support is limited to 1 contribution per organization during any given year. Application form not required. Applicants should submit the following:
1) name, address and phone number of organization
2) contact person
Applications should include the Tax ID Number of the organization; and the name and date of the event.
Initial approach: Proposal to headquarters
Copies of proposal: 1
Deadline(s): None
Final notification: 4 to 6 weeks

1694
H & K Inc.

1210 Dillingham Blvd., Ste. 4
Honolulu, HI 96817-4436 (808) 847-4427

Company URL: http://
Establishment information: Established in 1977.
Company type: Private company
Business activities: Operates grocery stores.
Business type (SIC): Groceries—retail
Corporate officers: Hyo H. Lim, Pres.; Hae Joo Lim, V.P. and Treas.
Giving statement: Giving through the Palama Scholarship Foundation Inc.

Palama Scholarship Foundation Inc.

725 Kapiolani Blvd., Ste. C-110
Honolulu, HI 96813-6012 (808) 847-4427
Application address: 1210 Dillingham Blvd., Honolulu, HI 96817, tel.: (808) 847-4427

Establishment information: Established in 2003 in HI.
Donors: Palama Supermarket; H&K Inc.
Contact: Hyo Kyu Lim, Pres.
Financial data (yr. ended 12/31/11): Assets, $46,602 (M); gifts received, $36,000; expenditures, $52,944; qualifying distributions, $50,000; giving activities include $50,000 for 10 grants to individuals (high: $5,000; low: $5,000).
Purpose and activities: The foundation awards scholarships to residents of Hawaii who have at least 25-percent Korean-American ancestry.
Fields of interest: Higher education.
Type of support: Scholarships—to individuals.
Geographic limitations: Giving primarily in HI.
Application information: Applications accepted. Application form required.
Initial approach: Contact foundation for application form
Deadline(s): Aug. 10
Officers: Hyo Kyu Lim, Pres.; Hae Joo Lim, V.P.; Thomas Kim, Treas.
EIN: 990344016

1695
H & R Block, Inc.

1 H&R Block Way
Kansas City, MO 64105 (816) 854-3000
FAX: (816) 753-5346

Company URL: http://www.hrblock.com
Establishment information: Established in 1955.
Company type: Public company
Company ticker symbol and exchange: HRB/NYSE
Business activities: Operates holding company; provides income tax return preparation and electronic income tax return filing services; provides securities brokerage services; provides mortgages; develops personal productivity software.
Business type (SIC): Personal services; brokers and bankers/mortgage; brokers and dealers/security; holding company; personal services/ miscellaneous; computer services
Financial profile for 2012: Number of employees, 2,500; assets, $4,649,570,000; sales volume, $2,893,770,000; pre-tax net income, $576,070,000; expenses, $2,327,480,000; liabilities, $3,323,680,000
Fortune 1000 ranking: 2012—665th in revenues, 505th in profits, and 615th in assets
Forbes 2000 ranking: 2012—1660th in sales, 1167th in profits, and 1885th in assets
Corporate officers: Robert A. Gerard, Chair.; William C. Cobb, Pres. and C.E.O.; Gregory J. Macfariane, C.F.O.; Richard Agar, C.I.O.
Board of directors: Robert A. Gerard, Chair.; Paul J. Brown; William C. Cobb; Marvin R. Ellison; David Baker Lewis; Victoria J. Reich; Bruce C. Rohde; Tom D. Seip; Christianna Wood; James F. Wright
International operations: Australia; Bahamas; Bermuda; Canada; Hong Kong; India; United Kingdom
Giving statement: Giving through the H & R Block, Inc. Corporate Giving Program and the H & R Block Foundation.
Company EIN: 440607856

H & R Block, Inc. Corporate Giving Program

1 H&R Block Way
Kansas City, MO 64105-1905 (816) 854-3000
E-mail for Dollars & Sense: DollarsandSense@hrblock.com; URL: http://www.hrblock.com/company/community_involvement/index.html

Purpose and activities: As a complement to its foundation, H & R Block also makes charitable contributions to nonprofit organizations directly. Support is given on a national basis.
Fields of interest: Secondary school/education; Youth development, business.
Program:
H & R Block Dollars & Sense: Through the H & R Block Dollars & Sense program, H & R Block awards scholarships and curriculum grants to students and high schools nationwide to develop teens' financial fitness. The program consists of two parts. One is an interactive, simulation-based curriculum taught by high school teachers. The other is the H & R Block Dollars & Sense National Challenge, where high school students nationwide demonstrate their financial skills to win scholarships. Visit URL: http://www.hrblockdollarsandsense.com/ for more information.
Type of support: Curriculum development; Employee volunteer services; In-kind gifts; Scholarships—to individuals.
Geographic limitations: Giving on national basis.
Publications: Application guidelines.
Application information: Applications accepted. Application form required.
Visit Dollars & Sense website for detailed application guidelines.
Initial approach: Complete online application
Deadline(s): Varies for Dollars & Sense Program

The H & R Block Foundation

1 H&R Block Way
Kansas City, MO 64105-1905 (816) 854-4361
FAX: (816) 854-8025;
E-mail: foundation@hrblock.com; Additional contacts: David P. Miles, Pres., tel.: (816) 854-4372, e-mail: davmiles@hrblock.com; Carey Wilkerson Looney, V.P. and Secy., tel.: (816) 854-4373, e-mail: cwilkerson@hrblock.com; Robert Bloch, Prog. Off., tel.: (816) 854-4360, e-mail: rbloch@hrblock.com; Hillary Beuschel, Prog. Off., tel.: (816) 854-4361, e-mail: hillary.beuschel@hrblock.com; Jack Nachman, Prog. Asst., tel.: (816) 854-4363, e-mail: jnachman@hrblock.com; URL: http://www.blockfoundation.org

Establishment information: Incorporated in 1974 in MO.
Donors: H&R Block, Inc.; HRB Management, Inc.
Contact: David P. Miles, Pres.
Financial data (yr. ended 12/31/11): Assets, $55,442,545 (M); gifts received, $893,800; expenditures, $3,239,230; qualifying distributions, $2,587,554; giving activities include $2,587,554 for 382 grants (high: $100,000; low: $100).
Purpose and activities: The foundation supports organizations involved with arts and culture, education, health, mental health, housing, youth development, human services, community development, and economically disadvantaged people.
Fields of interest: Arts; Education, early childhood education; Adult education—literacy, basic skills & GED; Education; Health care; Mental health/crisis services; Housing/shelter; Youth development; Human services; Economic development; Urban/ community development; Community/economic development Economically disadvantaged.
Programs:
Arts and Culture: The foundation supports programs designed to promote classic to contemporary artistic and cultural endeavors; and improve access to the arts for all people.
Cash for Champions: The foundation awards $100 grants to nonprofit organizations with which employees of H&R Block volunteer 50 hours or more.
Community Development: The foundation supports programs designed to promote healthy neighborhoods, urban core revitalization, and economic development.
Education: The foundation supports programs designed to promote quality early-learning and adult literacy.
Health and Human Service: The foundation supports programs designed to promote health and mental health services; shelter for men, women, and children; and youth development.
Henry W. Bloch National Awards for Outstanding Community Service: The foundation awards $5,000 grants to nonprofit organizations selected by employee winners from each H&R Block business unit. The award honors exceptional corporate and volunteer service.
Matching Gift Program: The foundation matches contributions made by employees and directors of H&R Block to educational institutions on a one-for-one basis from $100 to $1,000 per employee, per year.
Type of support: Annual campaigns; Building/ renovation; Capital campaigns; Continuing support; Emergency funds; Employee matching gifts; Employee volunteer services; Employee-related scholarships; Equipment; General/operating support; Matching/challenge support; Program development; Scholarship funds.
Geographic limitations: Giving primarily in Johnson and Wyandotte, KS, and Clay, Jackson, Kansas City, and Platte, MO.
Support limitations: No support for discriminatory organizations, businesses, or disease-specific organizations. No grants to individuals (except for employee-related scholarships), or for publications, travel, conferences, telethons, dinners, advertising, fundraising, animal-related causes, sports programs, or historic preservation projects.
Publications: Application guidelines; Grants list; Program policy statement.
Application information: Applications accepted. Proposals should be no longer than 5 to 6 pages. Application form required. Applicants should submit the following:
1) qualifications of key personnel
2) population served
3) copy of IRS Determination Letter
4) copy of most recent annual report/audited financial statement/990
5) how project's results will be evaluated or measured
6) listing of board of directors, trustees, officers and other key people and their affiliations
7) detailed description of project and amount of funding requested
8) copy of current year's organizational budget and/ or project budget
9) listing of additional sources and amount of support

Initial approach: Download application form and mail proposal and application form to foundation
Copies of proposal: 1
Board meeting date(s): Quarterly
Final notification: 10 weeks following deadlines

Officers and Directors:* Henry W. Bloch*, Chair. and Treas.; Frank L. Salizzoni*, Vice-Chair.; David P. Miles, Pres.; Carey Wilkenson Looney, V.P. and Secy.; William A. Hall; Edward T. Matheny, Jr.; Morton I. Sosland.
Number of staff: 3 full-time professional; 1 part-time professional.
EIN: 237378232

1696
Hachette Book Group USA, Inc.

237 Park Ave.
New York, NY 10017 (212) 364-1200
FAX: (212) 364-0628

Company URL: http://www.hbgusa.com
Establishment information: Established in 2006.
Company type: Subsidiary of a foreign company
Business activities: Publishes books.
Business type (SIC): Book publishing and/or printing
Corporate officers: David Young, Chair.; Michael Pietsch, C.E.O.; Kenneth Michaels, Exec. V.P. and C.O.O.; Tom Maciag, Exec. V.P. and C.F.O.; Carol Ross, Exec. V.P. and Genl. Counsel; Christine Barba, Exec. V.P., Sales and Mktg.; Andrea Weinzimer, Sr. V.P., Human Resources; Christopher Murphy, V.P., Sales; Sophie Cottrell, V.P., Comms.
Board of director: David Young, Chair.
Giving statement: Giving through the Hachette Book Group USA, Inc. Corporate Giving Program.

Hachette Book Group USA, Inc. Corporate Giving Program

c/o Community Affairs Dept.
3 Center Plz., Ste. G
Boston, MA 02108-2083 (617) 227-0730
E-mail: donation.requests@hbgusa.com;
URL: http://www.hachettebookgroup.com/about_CorporateSocialResponsibility.aspx

Purpose and activities: Hachette Book Group USA makes charitable contributions to nonprofit organizations involved with literacy. Support is given primarily in areas of company operations.
Fields of interest: Literature; Education, reading.
Program:
Employee Matching Gift Program: Hachette Book Group matches contributions made by its employees to nonprofit organizations on a two-for-one basis up to $1,000 per employee, per year.
Type of support: Donated products; Employee matching gifts; General/operating support.
Geographic limitations: Giving primarily in areas of company operations.
Application information: Applications accepted.
Initial approach: E-mail proposal to headquarters

1697
Hackstock Properties Inc.

4155 S. University Blvd.
Englewood, CO 80113-4904
(303) 761-6728

Company type: Private company
Business activities: Operates commercial real estate company.
Business type (SIC): Real estate operators and lessors
Corporate officer: Nich J. Hackstock, Principal
Giving statement: Giving through the Hackstock Family Foundation.

Hackstock Family Foundation

4155 S. University Blvd.
Englewood, CO 80110-4904

Establishment information: Established in 2000 in CO.
Donors: NANC Partners, Ltd.; Anne Hackstock; Nick J. Hackstock; Nick J. Hackstock, Inc.
Contact: Nick J. Hackstock, Pres.
Financial data (yr. ended 12/31/11): Assets, $1,261,590 (M); expenditures, $68,122; qualifying distributions, $67,573; giving activities include $67,573 for 29 grants (high: $13,000; low: $100).
Purpose and activities: The foundation supports organizations involved with education, animal welfare, health, cancer, orthopedics, civil liberties, and religion.
Fields of interest: Higher education; Education; Animal welfare; Health care, clinics/centers; Health care; Cancer; Breast cancer; Orthopedics; Boy scouts; Civil liberties, freedom of religion; United Ways and Federated Giving Programs; Social sciences, interdisciplinary studies; Religion.
Type of support: General/operating support; Scholarship funds.
Geographic limitations: Giving primarily in Denver, CO.
Support limitations: No grants to individuals.
Application information: Applications accepted. Application form required. Applicants should submit the following:
1) detailed description of project and amount of funding requested
Initial approach: Letter of inquiry
Deadline(s): None
Officer: Nick J. Hackstock, Pres.
EIN: 841566303

1698
Hagerty Brothers Company

1506 W. Detweiller Dr.
P.O. Box 1500
Peoria, IL 61615-1601 (309) 589-0200

Company URL: http://www.hagertybrothers.com/
Establishment information: Established in 1860.
Company type: Private company
Business activities: Distributes wholesale products.
Business type (SIC): Hardware, plumbing, and heating equipment—wholesale
Financial profile for 2010: Number of employees, 47
Corporate officers: Randy D. Fellerhoff, Pres. and Co-C.E.O.; Nicholas R. Owen, Co-C.E.O; Susan Mahany, C.F.O.; Susan Felerhoff, Secy.
Giving statement: Giving through the Hagerty Brothers Company Foundation.

Hagerty Brothers Company Foundation

1500 W. Detweiller Dr.
P.O. Box 1500
Peoria, IL 61655-1500

Establishment information: Established in IL.
Donor: Hagerty Brothers Company.
Financial data (yr. ended 12/31/11): Assets, $143,924 (M); expenditures, $16,750; qualifying distributions, $12,801; giving activities include $12,801 for 13 grants (high: $8,000; low: $25).
Fields of interest: Higher education; Recreation; Human services; Protestant agencies & churches.
Geographic limitations: Giving primarily in IL.
Support limitations: No grants to individuals.
Application information: Applications not accepted. Unsolicited requests for funds not accepted.
Officers: Randall Fellerhoff, Fdn. Mgr.; Susan Fellerhoff, Fdn. Mgr.
Director: Whitney Vincent.
EIN: 205838347

1699
Haggen, Inc.

2211 Rimland Dr.
P.O. Box 9704
Bellingham, WA 98226 (360) 733-8720
FAX: (360) 650-8235

Company URL: http://www.haggen.com
Establishment information: Established in 1933.
Company type: Private company
Business activities: Operates supermarkets.
Business type (SIC): Groceries—retail
Corporate officers: Clarence J. Gabriel, Jr., Pres. and C.E.O.; Ron Kara, Sr. V.P., Opers.; Harrison Lewis, V.P. and C.I.O.; Derrick Anderson, V.P., Opers; Tom Kenney, V.P., Finance; Scott Smith, V.P., Mktg.
Giving statement: Giving through the Haggen, Inc. Corporate Giving Program.

Haggen, Inc. Corporate Giving Program

P.O. Box 9704
Bellingham, WA 98227-9704 (360) 733-8720
URL: http://www.haggen.com/operation-winter-warmth/

Purpose and activities: Haggen makes charitable contributions to nonprofit organizations involved with K-12 education, animal welfare, pediatrics, multiple sclerosis research, food banks, homeless and economically disadvantaged people, and children services. Support is given primarily in areas of company store operations in Oregon and Washington.
Fields of interest: Elementary/secondary education; Animal welfare; Pediatrics; Multiple sclerosis research; Food banks; Children/youth, services Economically disadvantaged; Homeless.
Type of support: Cause-related marketing; Employee volunteer services; Sponsorships.
Geographic limitations: Giving primarily in areas of company store operations in OR and WA.

1700
Hahn Loeser & Parks LLP

200 Public Sq., Ste. 2800
Cleveland, OH 44114-2306 (216) 621-0150

Company URL: http://www.hahnlaw.com
Establishment information: Established in 1920.
Company type: Private company
Business activities: Operates law firm.
Business type (SIC): Legal services
Offices: Fort Myers, Naples, FL; Indianapolis, IN; Akron, Cleveland, Columbus, OH
Giving statement: Giving through the Hahn Loeser & Parks LLP Pro Bono Program.

Hahn Loeser & Parks LLP Pro Bono Program

200 Public Sq., Ste. 2800
Cleveland, OH 44114-2306 (216) 274-2371
E-mail: jabrauer@hahnlaw.com; URL: http://www.hahnlaw.com/ProBono.aspx

Contact: Jeff Brauer, Partner
Fields of interest: Legal services.
Type of support: Pro bono services - legal.
Geographic limitations: Giving primarily in areas of company operations in Fort Myers, and Naples, FL, Fishers, IN, Akron, Cleveland, and Columbus, OH.
Application information: The Pro Bono Coordinator manages the pro bono program.

1701
Haines & Haines, Inc.

3432 New Gretna Chatsworth Rd.
Chatsworth, NJ 08019-2202
(609) 726-1330

Establishment information: Established in 1988.
Company type: Private company
Business activities: Produces cranberries and blueberries.
Business type (SIC): Farms/fruit and nut
Financial profile for 2010: Number of employees, 2
Corporate officer: William S. Haines, Jr., Pres.
Giving statement: Giving through the Haines Family Foundation, Inc.

The Haines Family Foundation, Inc.

c/o Haines & Haines, Inc.
3432A Rte. 563
Chatsworth, NJ 08019

Establishment information: Established in 1995 in NJ.
Donors: Haines & Haines, Inc.; Pine Island Cranberry Co., Inc.; William S. Haines†; William S. Haines, Jr.
Contact: Holly Haines, Treas.
Financial data (yr. ended 12/31/11): Assets, $9,395,337 (M); gifts received, $50,000; expenditures, $422,577; qualifying distributions, $365,000; giving activities include $365,000 for grants.
Purpose and activities: The foundation supports the Burlington County Institute of Technology in Burlington, New Jersey.
Fields of interest: Higher education.
Geographic limitations: Giving limited to NJ.
Support limitations: No grants to individuals.
Application information: Applications accepted. Application form required. Applicants should submit the following:
1) copy of IRS Determination Letter
Initial approach: Letter or Proposal
Copies of proposal: 1
Deadline(s): Sep. 30th
Officers: William S. Haines, Jr., Pres.; Nadine Haines, Secy.; Holly Haines, Treas.
EIN: 223412616
Selected grants: The following grants are a representative sample of this grantmaker's funding activity:
$150,000 to YMCA Camp Ockanickon, Medford, NJ, 2011.

1702
Edward E. Hall & Company

99 Mill Dam Rd.
Centerport, NY 11721 (631) 547-6003

Company URL: http://www.edwardehall.com/
Establishment information: Established in 1866.
Company type: Private company
Business activities: Operates insurance company.
Business type (SIC): Insurance agents, brokers, and services
Corporate officer: Michael P. Heagerty, Pres.
Giving statement: Giving through the Heagerty Family Foundation, Inc.

Heagerty Family Foundation, Inc.

99 Mill Dam Rd.
Centerport, NY 11721-1502 (631) 547-6003

Establishment information: Established in 2007 in NY.
Donor: Edward E. Hall, Inc.
Contact: Michael Heagerty, Dir.
Financial data (yr. ended 12/31/11): Assets, $12,106 (M); gifts received, $90,233; expenditures, $78,185; qualifying distributions, $77,025; giving activities include $77,025 for grants.
Purpose and activities: The foundation supports hospitals and organizations involved with secondary education, sports, youth, and Catholicism and awards grants to mothers in need.
Fields of interest: Education; Youth development; Religion.
Type of support: General/operating support; Grants to individuals.
Geographic limitations: Giving primarily in NY.
Application information: Applications accepted. Application form not required.
Initial approach: Proposal
Deadline(s): None
Directors: Annie Heagerty; Mary Heagerty; Michael Heagerty; Riley Heagerty.
EIN: 510629883
Selected grants: The following grants are a representative sample of this grantmaker's funding activity:
$20,000 to Companions in Courage Foundation, Huntington, NY, 2009.

1703
Hall & Evans, LLC

1125 17th St., Ste. 600
Denver, CO 80202-2052 (303) 628-3300
FAX: 303-628-3368

Company URL: http://www.hallevans.com
Establishment information: Established in 1932.
Company type: Private company
Business activities: Provides legal services.
Business type (SIC): Legal services
Corporate officers: Kenneth H. Lyman, Chair.; Kevin E. O'Brien, C.E.O.; Sandra S. Daly, C.O.O.
Board of director: Kenneth L. Lyman, Chair.
Giving statement: Giving through the Hall & Evans L.L.C. Foundation.

Hall & Evans L.L.C. Foundation

1125 17th St.
Denver, CO 80202 (303) 628-3300

Establishment information: Established in 1998 in CO.
Donor: Hall & Evans L.L.C.
Contact: Chris McGrath
Financial data (yr. ended 12/31/11): Assets, $63,272 (M); gifts received, $40,650; expenditures, $36,695; qualifying distributions, $34,095; giving activities include $34,095 for grants.
Purpose and activities: The foundation supports organizations involved with higher education, human services, and community development.
Fields of interest: Education; Human services; Community/economic development.
Type of support: Employee matching gifts; General/operating support; Scholarship funds.
Geographic limitations: Giving primarily in CO.
Support limitations: No grants to individuals.
Application information: Applications accepted. Application form required.
Initial approach: Proposal
Deadline(s): None
Trustees: Robert M. Ferm; Kevin E. O'Brien; Andrew D. Ringel.
EIN: 841443224

1704
Hallberg, Inc.

26470 Fallbrook Ln.
P.O. Box 277
Wyoming, MN 55092 (651) 462-4516
FAX: (651) 462-4061

Company URL: http://www.hallbergmarine.com
Establishment information: Established in 1959.
Company type: Private company
Business activities: Provides boat storage and warehousing services; operates boat dealership.
Business type (SIC): Transportation services/water; boats—retail
Corporate officer: Eugene C. Hallberg, Pres.
Giving statement: Giving through the Hallberg Family Foundation.

Hallberg Family Foundation

P.O. Box 130
Forest Lake, MN 55025-0130 (651) 462-4516

Establishment information: Established in 2003.
Donors: Hallberg, Inc.; Hallberg Marine, Inc.; Hallberg Family, L.P.; Eugene C. Hallberg.
Contact: Eugene C. Halberg, Chair.
Financial data (yr. ended 12/31/11): Assets, $901,349 (M); gifts received, $135,000; expenditures, $46,000; qualifying distributions, $46,000; giving activities include $46,000 for grants.
Purpose and activities: The foundation supports fire departments and nonprofit organizations involved with performing arts, education, youth, community development, and Christianity.
Fields of interest: Performing arts; Performing arts, theater; Secondary school/education; Scholarships/financial aid; Education; Disasters, fire prevention/control; Salvation Army; Youth, services; Community development, service clubs; Community/economic development; Christian agencies & churches.
Type of support: Capital campaigns; Equipment; Program development; Research; Scholarship funds.
Geographic limitations: Giving primarily in MN.
Application information: Applications accepted. Application form not required. Applicants should submit the following:
1) detailed description of project and amount of funding requested

Initial approach: Letter
Deadline(s): None
Officer and Directors: Eugene C. Hallberg*, Chair.; Dana Hallberg; Melissa Hallberg; Michael Hallberg; Denise Hallberg Tetrault.
EIN: 411989115

1705
Hallelujah Acres, Inc.
900 S. Post Rd.
P.O. Box 2388
Shelby, NC 28152 (704) 481-1700

Company URL: http://www.hacres.com
Establishment information: Established in 1992.
Company type: Private company
Business activities: Produces natural food products.
Business type (SIC): Food and kindred products
Corporate officers: Paul Malkmus, Pres. and C.E.O.; Robert Pinion, C.F.O.
Giving statement: Giving through the Genesis 1:29 Foundation.

The Genesis 1:29 Foundation
P.O. Box 2388
Shelby, NC 28151

Establishment information: Established in 2001 in NC.
Donors: Hallelujah Acres, Inc.; George Malkmus; Paul Malkmus.
Financial data (yr. ended 08/31/11): Assets, $1,559 (M); gifts received, $84,559; expenditures, $87,421; qualifying distributions, $87,421.
Purpose and activities: The foundation promotes direct research into physiological and other health benefits of vegetarian diet, with an emphasis on raw foods.
Support limitations: No grants to individuals.
Application information: Applications not accepted. Unsolicited requests for funds not accepted.
Officers and Directors:* George Malkmus*, Pres.; Paul H. Malkmus*, Secy.-Treas.; Rhonda Malkmus.
EIN: 562272677

1706
Halliburton Company
3000 N. Sam Houston Pkwy E.
Houston, TX 77032 (281) 871-4000

Company URL: http://www.halliburton.com
Establishment information: Established in 1919.
Company type: Public company
Company ticker symbol and exchange: HAL/NYSE
International Securities Identification Number: US4062161017
Business activities: Provides energy services and engineering and construction services.
Business type (SIC): Oil and gas field services; heavy construction other than building construction contractors
Financial profile for 2012: Number of employees, 73,000; assets, $27,410,000,000; sales volume, $28,503,000,000; pre-tax net income, $3,822,000,000; expenses, $24,344,000,000; liabilities, $11,645,000,000
Fortune 1000 ranking: 2012—106th in revenues, 74th in profits, and 197th in assets
Forbes 2000 ranking: 2012—333rd in sales, 219th in profits, and 787th in assets
Corporate officers: David J. Lesar, Chair., Pres., and C.E.O.; Jeff Miller, Exec. V.P. and C.O.O.; Mark A. McCollum, Exec. V.P. and C.F.O.; Albert O. Cornelison, Jr., Exec. V.P. and Genl. Counsel; Lawrence J. Pope, Exec. V.P., Admin.; Evelyn M. Angelle, Sr. V.P. and C.A.O.; Christian Garcia, Sr. V.P. and Treas.; Christina M. Ibrahim, V.P. and Corp. Secy.
Board of directors: David J. Lesar, Chair.; Alan M. Bennett; James R. Boyd; Milton Carroll; Nance K. Dicciani; Murry S. Gerber; S. Malcom Gillis; Abdallah S. Jum'ah; Robert A. Malone; Landis J. Martin; Debra L. Reed
Subsidiaries: DII Industries, L.L.C., Houston, TX; Halliburton Affiliates, L.L.C., Houston, TX; Halliburton Energy Services, Inc., Midland, TX; Kellogg Energy Services, Inc., Houston, TX; Landmark Graphics Corp., Houston, TX
International operations: Canada; Cayman Islands; Germany; Mexico; Netherlands; Norway; Panama; United Kingdom
Giving statement: Giving through the Halliburton Foundation, Inc.
Company EIN: 752677995

Halliburton Company Contributions Program
10200 Bellaire Blvd.
Houston, TX 77072-5206
URL: http://www.halliburton.com/AboutUs/default.aspx?navid=988&pageid=2274

Financial data (yr. ended 12/31/11): Total giving, $1,400,000, including $1,400,000 for grants.
Purpose and activities: As a complement to its foundation, Halliburton makes charitable contributions to nonprofit organizations directly.
Fields of interest: Arts, cultural/ethnic awareness; Arts; Education; Environment, energy; Environment; Health care, research; Public health; Health care; Housing/shelter, volunteer services; Human services, fund raising/fund distribution; Children/youth, services; Aging, centers/services; Physical/earth sciences; Engineering/technology; Public affairs.
Program:
Giving Choices: Every October, employees in the United States, Canada, Mexico, the United Kingdom, Australia, New Zealand, India, Indonesia, Singapore, and Malaysia pledge money to charities. Halliburton then absorbs any administrative fees to support the campaign, and approved charities are matched with a 10 percent contribution by the company. In 2011, employees pledged more than $3.4 million to assist their local communities.
Type of support: Computer technology; Employee volunteer services; General/operating support; In-kind gifts.
Geographic limitations: Giving in areas of company operations on a national and international basis, including Angola, Australia, Canada, Egypt, India, Indonesia, Malaysia, Mexico, New Zealand, Singapore, the United Kingdom, and Vietnam.
Publications: Application guidelines.
Application information: Applications accepted. The Community Relations Review Board (CRRB) handles all requests.
Initial approach: Mail proposal to application address for operating support and in-kind donations
Committee meeting date(s): Quarterly
Deadline(s): Jan. 31, Apr. 30, July 31, and Oct. 31

Halliburton Foundation, Inc.
P.O. Box 42806
Houston, TX 77242-2806 (281) 575-3558
Application address: 10200 Bellaire Blvd., Houston, TX 77072-5206; Additional address: P.O. Box 4574, Houston, TX 77072-4574; URL: http://www.halliburton.com/AboutUs/default.aspx?navid=992&pageid=2347

Establishment information: Incorporated in 1965 in TX.
Donors: Halliburton Co.; Brown & Root, Inc.
Contact: Brinda Maxwell, Prog. Admin.
Financial data (yr. ended 12/31/11): Assets, $16,126,784 (M); gifts received, $3,000,000; expenditures, $2,553,713; qualifying distributions, $2,527,722; giving activities include $2,527,722 for grants.
Purpose and activities: The foundation supports organizations involved with education, health, and health-related social services.
Fields of interest: Elementary/secondary education; Higher education; Education; Health care; Human services.
Programs:
Employee Matching Gifts: The foundation matches contributions made by employees of Halliburton and its subsidiaries and divisions to junior colleges, colleges, and universities on a two-for-one basis from $10 to $20,000 per employee, per year; and to elementary and secondary schools on a one-for-one basis from $100 to $500 per employee, per year.
Employee-Related Scholarship Program: The foundation awards four-year $1,500 college scholarships to children of employees of Halliburton. The program is administered by the National Merit Scholarship Corporation.
Type of support: Annual campaigns; Conferences/seminars; Continuing support; Curriculum development; Employee matching gifts; Employee volunteer services; Employee-related scholarships; Equipment; General/operating support; Program development.
Geographic limitations: Giving primarily in areas of company operations, with emphasis on KS, LA, OK, PA, and TX.
Support limitations: No support for religious, fraternal, or veterans organizations, athletic organizations, or political or union organizations. No grants to individuals (except for employee-related scholarships), or for trips, sporting events, tours, or transportation, advertising, film, or video projects; no loans.
Publications: Application guidelines.
Application information: Applications accepted. Application form not required. Applicants should submit the following:
1) timetable for implementation and evaluation of project
2) results expected from proposed grant
3) population served
4) copy of IRS Determination Letter
5) copy of most recent annual report/audited financial statement/990
6) listing of board of directors, trustees, officers and other key people and their affiliations
7) detailed description of project and amount of funding requested
8) copy of current year's organizational budget and/or project budget

Initial approach: Proposal
Copies of proposal: 1
Board meeting date(s): Quarterly
Deadline(s): None
Final notification: 3 months

Officers and Trustees: David J. Lesar, Pres.; Cathy Mann, V.P. and Secy.; Craig W. Nunez, Treas.; Lawrence J. Pope; Tim Probert.
EIN: 751212458
Selected grants: The following grants are a representative sample of this grantmaker's funding activity:
$149,374 to Texas A & M Foundation, College Station, TX, 2010.
$100,830 to Stanford University, Stanford, CA, 2010.
$100,000 to Harvard University, Cambridge, MA, 2010.
$80,184 to Oklahoma State University Foundation, Stillwater, OK, 2010.
$80,102 to University of Oklahoma Foundation, Norman, OK, 2010.
$20,000 to Martin Memorial Foundation, Stuart, FL, 2010.
$20,000 to Northeast Foundation, Beverly, MA, 2010.
$10,000 to American Museum of Natural History, New York, NY, 2010.
$6,000 to American Film Institute, Los Angeles, CA, 2010.
$6,000 to University of Illinois Foundation, Urbana, IL, 2010.

1707
Hallmark Cards, Incorporated

2501 McGee St.
Kansas City, MO 64108-2615
(816) 274-5111

Company URL: http://www.hallmark.com
Establishment information: Established in 1910.
Company type: Private company
Business activities: Prints greeting cards; manufactures gifts; manufactures ornaments; manufactures partyware; publishes gift books; manufactures art materials; produces television programming.
Business type (SIC): Greeting cards; paper and paperboard/coated, converted, and laminated; blankbooks, bookbinding, and looseleaf binders; pens, pencils, and art supplies; manufacturing/miscellaneous; motion pictures/production and services allied to
Financial profile for 2011: Number of employees, 13,030; sales volume, $3,810,000,000
Corporate officers: Donald J. Hall, Sr., Chair.; Donald J. Hall, Jr., Vice-Chair., Pres., and C.E.O.; Brian E. Gardner, Exec. V.P. and Genl. Counsel; Ellen Junger, Sr. V.P., Mktg.; Steve Doyal, Sr. V.P., Public Affairs and Comms.; Bob Bloss, Sr. V.P., Human Resources; Jeff McMillen, V.P. and Treas.
Board of directors: Donald J. Hall, Sr., Chair.; Donald J. Hall, Jr., Vice-chair.
Subsidiaries: William Arthur, West Kennebunk, ME; Crayola LLC, Easton, PA; DaySpring, Siloam Springs, AR; Gift Certificate Center, Minneapolis, MN; ImageArts, Marshfield, MA; Irresistible Ink, Two Harbors, MN; Litho-Krome Co., Columbus, GA; Sunrise, Bloomington, IN
Plants: Enfield, CT; Metamora, IL; Lawrence, Leavenworth, Topeka, KS; Liberty, MO; Center, TX
International operations: Australia; Belgium; Canada; Mexico; Monaco; Netherlands; New Zealand; United Kingdom
Giving statement: Giving through the Hallmark Cards, Incorporated Corporate Giving Program and the Hallmark Corporate Foundation.

Hallmark Cards, Incorporated Corporate Giving Program

c/o Corp. Contribs. Mgr.
P.O. Box 419580, M.D. 323
Kansas City, MO 64141-6580 (816) 274-5111
E-mail: contributions@hallmark.com; URL: http://corporate.hallmark.com/Corporate-Citizenship/Community-Involvement

Purpose and activities: As a complement to its foundation, Hallmark Cards, Inc. also makes charitable contributions to nonprofit organizations directly. Support is limited to areas of significant company operations in Enfield, Connecticut; Columbus, Georgia; Lawrence and Metamora, Illinois; Leavenworth and Topeka, Kansas; metropolitan Kansas City and Liberty, Missouri; and Center, Texas. Sponsorships are limited to Kansas City, Missouri.
Fields of interest: Arts; Child development, education; Education; Human services; Community/economic development.
Type of support: Capital campaigns; Continuing support; Donated products; Employee volunteer services; General/operating support; Program development; Sponsorships.
Geographic limitations: Giving primarily in areas of significant company operations, with emphasis on Enfield, CT, Columbus, GA, Metamora, IL, Lawrence, Leavenworth, and Topeka, KS, Kansas City and Liberty, MO, and Center, TX. Sponsorships are limited to Kansas City, MO.
Support limitations: No support for religious organizations not of direct benefit to the entire community, fraternal, international, or veterans organizations, sports teams or athletic associations, individual youth clubs, troops, groups, or school classrooms, social clubs, foundations, or disease-specific organizations whose local chapters primarily raise funds for national research. No grants for debt reduction, scholarships, endowments, travel, conferences, scholarly or health-related research, business start-up purposes, or film, television, or radio programs.
Publications: Application guidelines; Grants list.
Application information: Applications accepted. Support is generally limited to 1 contribution per organization during any given year. Application form required. Applicants should submit the following:
1) timetable for implementation and evaluation of project
2) results expected from proposed grant
3) statement of problem project will address
4) population served
5) name, address and phone number of organization
6) copy of IRS Determination Letter
7) copy of most recent annual report/audited financial statement/990
8) how project's results will be evaluated or measured
9) detailed description of project and amount of funding requested
10) copy of current year's organizational budget and/or project budget
11) listing of additional sources and amount of support

Proposals for sponsorships should include the date, time, location, sponsorship levels, and a description of the event.
Initial approach: Complete online application form
Copies of proposal: 1
Deadline(s): None
Final notification: 6 weeks; 2 weeks for sponsorships
Number of staff: 4 full-time professional; 1 full-time support.

Selected grants: The following grants are a representative sample of this grantmaker's funding activity:
$200,000 to University of Kansas, School of Fine Arts, Lawrence, KS, 2005. For Leadership in Design Education.
$142,120 to American Red Cross National Headquarters, Washington, DC, 2005. For Hurricane Katrina relief.
$45,000 to United Negro College Fund, Saint Louis, MO, 2005. For Kansas City Scholarship Initiative.
$25,000 to Boys and Girls Clubs of Greater Kansas City, Kansas City, MO, 2005. For general support.
$25,000 to Family Service and Guidance Center of Topeka, Topeka, KS, 2005. For capital campaign.
$25,000 to PEN/Faulkner Foundation, Washington, DC, 2005. For Writers in the Schools Program in Kansas City.
$23,000 to Bridge Home for Children, Kansas City, MO, 2005. For environmental and recycling programs.
$20,000 to Guadalupe Centers, Kansas City, MO, 2005. For facility improvements.
$15,000 to Good Samaritan Project, Kansas City, MO, 2005. For technology support for AIDS programming.
$10,000 to Habitat for Humanity, Heartland, Kansas City, KS, 2005. For Youth Home building Program.

Hallmark Corporate Foundation

P.O. Box 419580, M.D. 323
Kansas City, MO 64141-6580
E-mail: contributions@hallmark.com; URL: http://corporate.hallmark.com/Corporate-Citizenship/Community-Involvement

Establishment information: Established in 1983 in MO.
Donors: Hallmark Cards, Inc.; Crayola, LLC.
Contact: Carol Hallquist; Cora Storbeck
Financial data (yr. ended 12/31/11): Assets, $816,038 (M); gifts received, $1,950,000; expenditures, $1,977,274; qualifying distributions, $1,971,887; giving activities include $1,971,887 for grants.
Purpose and activities: The foundation supports organizations involved with arts and culture, education, human services, and urban development.
Fields of interest: Arts; Child development, education; Education; Children/youth, services; Human services; Urban/community development.
Programs:
Employee Matching Gifts: The foundation matches contributions made by full-time employees of Hallmark to institutions of higher education on a one-for-one basis from $20 to $2,000 per employee, per institution, per year up to $6,000 per employee, per year.
Volunteer Involvement Pays (VIP): The foundation awards $200 grants to nonprofit organizations with which employees of Hallmark volunteer at least 25 hours during a six-month period.
Type of support: Building/renovation; Capital campaigns; Continuing support; Employee matching gifts; Employee volunteer services; Equipment; General/operating support; Program development; Program evaluation; Technical assistance.
Geographic limitations: Giving limited to areas of company operations in Columbus, GA, Metamora, IL, Lawrence, Leavenworth, and Topeka, KS, Liberty and the Kansas City, MO, area, and Center, TX.
Support limitations: No support for religious, fraternal, political, international, or veterans' organizations, athletic or labor groups, social clubs, or disease-specific organizations. No grants to individuals, or for scholarships, endowments, debt

reduction, travel, conferences, sponsorships, scholarly or health-related research, advertising, mass media campaigns, or fundraising.
Publications: Application guidelines; Grants list; Informational brochure (including application guidelines).
Application information: Applications accepted. Support is limited to 1 contribution per organization during any given year. Additional information may be requested at a later date. A personal or telephone interview or site visit may be requested. Application form required. Applicants should submit the following:
1) statement of problem project will address
2) population served
3) copy of IRS Determination Letter
4) brief history of organization and description of its mission
5) copy of most recent annual report/audited financial statement/990
6) detailed description of project and amount of funding requested
7) copy of current year's organizational budget and/or project budget
8) listing of additional sources and amount of support

Initial approach: Complete online application form
Copies of proposal: 1
Board meeting date(s): Periodic
Deadline(s): None
Final notification: 4 to 6 weeks

Officers and Directors:* Donald J. Hall, Jr., Chair.; Carol Hallquist, Pres.; Cora Storbeck, V.P.; Al Mauro, Secy.; Terri R. Maybee, Treas.; Steve Doyal; David E. Hall.
Number of staff: 3 full-time professional; 1 full-time support.
EIN: 431303258
Selected grants: The following grants are a representative sample of this grantmaker's funding activity:
$11,260,000 to United Way of Greater Kansas City, Kansas City, MO, 2011. For annual campaign.
$183,400 to Kansas City Symphony, Kansas City, MO, 2011. For general support.
$120,700 to Kansas City Repertory Theater, Kansas City, MO, 2011. For general support.
$115,000 to Kansas City Area Development Council, Kansas City, MO, 2011.
$100,000 to Nelson Gallery Foundation, Kansas City, MO, 2011.
$98,800 to Kansas City Ballet Association, Kansas City, MO, 2011. For general support.
$89,000 to Chamber of Commerce of Greater Kansas City, Kansas City, MO, 2011.
$79,200 to Lyric Opera of Kansas City, Kansas City, MO, 2011.
$67,000 to Civil Council of Greater Kansas City, 2011.
$65,000 to Childrens Mercy Hospital, Kansas City, MO, 2011.
$65,000 to Kansas City Art Institute, Kansas City, MO, 2011.

1708
Halstead Industries, Inc.

1330 Carden Farm Dr.
Clinton, TN 37716-4130 (865) 463-9505

Establishment information: Established in 1906.
Company type: Private company
Business activities: Manufactures copper tubing, foam, and rubber products.
Business type (SIC): Plastic products/miscellaneous; rubber products/fabricated; metal rolling and drawing/nonferrous
Division: Halstead Industrial Prods. Div., Wynne, AR
Plant: Pine Hall, NC
Giving statement: Giving through the Halstead Foundation, Inc.

The Halstead Foundation, Inc.

P.O. Box 9983
Greensboro, NC 27404

Establishment information: Established in 1988 in NC.
Donor: Halstead Industries, Inc.
Financial data (yr. ended 12/31/11): Assets, $1,372,322 (M); expenditures, $105,495; qualifying distributions, $56,677; giving activities include $56,677 for grants.
Purpose and activities: The foundation supports organizations involved with arts and culture, higher education, housing, and children services and awards college scholarships.
Fields of interest: Arts; Education; Environment.
Type of support: General/operating support; Scholarship funds; Scholarships—to individuals.
Geographic limitations: Giving primarily in Greensboro, NC.
Application information: Applications not accepted. Unsolicited requests for funds not accepted.
Officers: William Halstead, Chair.; Martha Halstead, Pres.; Leroy Lintz, V.P.; Peggy Robertson, V.P.
EIN: 581821220

1709
Halton Co.

4421 N.E. Columbia Blvd.
Portland, OR 97218-1338 (503) 288-6411

Establishment information: Established in 1940.
Company type: Private company
Business activities: Operates heavy equipment and engine dealership.
Business type (SIC): Industrial machinery and equipment—wholesale; equipment rental and leasing/miscellaneous
Corporate officers: Edward H. Halton, Jr., Pres.; Mark Fahey, V.P., Treas., and C.F.O.
Offices: Salem, The Dalles, Wilsonville, OR; Longview, WA
Giving statement: Giving through the Halton Foundation.

Halton Foundation

P.O. Box 3377
Portland, OR 97208-3377 (503) 780-0453

Establishment information: Established in 1965 in OR.
Donors: Halton Co.; Kathryn Rebagliati.
Contact: Susan Halton, Mgr.
Financial data (yr. ended 08/31/11): Assets, $1,483,568 (M); gifts received, $310,000; expenditures, $52,036; qualifying distributions, $48,695; giving activities include $48,695 for grants to individuals.
Purpose and activities: The foundation supports organizations involved with education.
Fields of interest: Higher education; Education.
Program:
Halton Scholars: The foundation awards college scholarships to children of employees of Halton Co. and its related companies. Employees must be employed for a period of six months before a child can apply. All applicants must be under 28 years of age and plan to pursue higher education as a full-time student. Applicants are evaluated on the basis of financial need, academic achievement, and participation in extracurricular activities, which include athletics, a part-time job, volunteer work, etc.
Type of support: Employee-related scholarships; General/operating support.
Geographic limitations: Giving limited to areas of company operations in OR, WA and CO.
Application information: Applications accepted. Application form required.
Proposed academic program, statement of extra curricular activities, including any related awards, honors or special recognition received, statement explaining financial need, amount of support applicant furnish to self and efforts made to do so, amount of support provided by parents, financial statement of parents, results of aptitude test taken, transcript of academic work, three references from teachers, employers or other adults.
Initial approach: Proposal
Deadline(s): Feb. 1
Officer: Susan Halton, Mgr.
Trustees: E.H. Halton, Jr.; Kathryn Rebagliati.
EIN: 936036295

1710
Hamilton, Brook, Smith & Reynolds, P.C.

530 Virginia Rd.
P.O. Box 9133
Concord, MA 01742-9133 (978) 341-0036

Company type: Private company
Business activities: Operates law firm.
Business type (SIC): Legal services
Corporate officer: John L. DuPre, Pres. and Principal
Giving statement: Giving through the Hamilton, Brook, Smith & Reynolds, P.C. Pro Bono Program.

Hamilton, Brook, Smith & Reynolds, P.C. Pro Bono Program

530 Virginia Rd.
P.O. Box 9133
Concord, MA 01742-9133 (978) 341-0036
URL: http://www.hbsr.com/about_the_firm/pro-bono

Fields of interest: Legal services.
Type of support: Pro bono services - legal.
Geographic limitations: Giving primarily in areas of company operations in Concord, MA.
Application information: Attorneys generate pro bono projects.

1711
Hammond Machinery, Inc.

1600 Douglas Ave.
Kalamazoo, MI 49007-1630
(269) 345-7151

Company URL: http://www.hammondmach.com
Establishment information: Established in 1881.
Company type: Subsidiary of a private company
Business activities: Manufactures abrasive belt grinders, dust collectors, and polishing and buffing machines.

Business type (SIC): Machinery/metalworking; machinery/general industry
Corporate officer: Robert E. Hammond, Pres.
Giving statement: Giving through the Hammond Foundation.

The Hammond Foundation

P.O. Box 75000
Detroit, MI 48275-3302 (269) 345-7151
Application address: 1600 Douglas Ave., Kalamazoo, MI 49007, tel.:(269) 345-7151

Establishment information: Established in 1952 in MI.
Donor: Hammond Machinery, Inc.
Contact: Christine A. Hammond, Pres. and Treas.
Financial data (yr. ended 12/31/11): Assets, $786,556 (M); expenditures, $68,825; qualifying distributions, $57,925; giving activities include $57,925 for grants.
Purpose and activities: The foundation supports camps and organizations involved with arts and culture, education, the environment, and human services.
Fields of interest: Arts; Education; Community/economic development.
Type of support: General/operating support; Program development.
Geographic limitations: Giving primarily in Kalamazoo, MI.
Support limitations: No grants to individuals; no loans.
Application information: Applications accepted. Application form required.
Initial approach: Letter
Deadline(s): None
Officers: Christine A. Hammond, Pres. and Treas.; Jeremy Hammond, Secy.
Director: Robert Hammond.
Trustee: Comerica Bank.
EIN: 386061610

1712
Hampden Bancorp, Inc.

19 Harrison Ave.
P.O. Box 2048
Springfield, MA 01102-2048
(413) 736-1812
FAX: (302) 655-5049

Company URL: https://www.hampdenbank.com/
Establishment information: Established in 1852.
Company type: Public company
Company ticker symbol and exchange: HBNK/NASDAQ
Business activities: Operates commercial bank.
Business type (SIC): Banks/commercial
Financial profile for 2012: Number of employees, 120; assets, $615,960,000; pre-tax net income, $4,800,000; liabilities, $528,800,000
Corporate officers: Richard J. Kos, Chair.; Glenn S. Welch, Pres. and C.E.O.; Robert A. Massey, Sr. V.P., Treas., and C.F.O.; Richard L. DeBonis, Sr. V.P., Mktg.; Craig W. Kaylor, Genl. Counsel and Secy.
Board of directors: Richard J. Kos, Esq., Chair.; Thomas R. Burton; Judith E. Kennedy; Stanley Kowalski, Jr., Ph.D.; Kathleen O'Brien Moore; Arlene Putnam; Mary Ellen Scott; Richard D. Suski, C.P.A.; Glenn S. Welch; Linda M. Silva Thompson
Giving statement: Giving through the Hampden Bank Charitable Foundation.

Hampden Bank Charitable Foundation

P.O. Box 2048
Springfield, MA 01102-2048 (413) 452-5181

Establishment information: Established in 2006 in DE and MA.
Donor: Hampden Bancorp.
Contact: Robert M. Massey, Treas.
Financial data (yr. ended 10/31/11): Assets, $4,266,531 (M); expenditures, $166,842; qualifying distributions, $161,573; giving activities include $136,000 for 28 grants (high: $20,000; low: $500).
Purpose and activities: The foundation supports organizations involved with arts and culture, education, and human services.
Fields of interest: Performing arts, music; Performing arts, orchestras; Arts; Higher education; YM/YWCAs & YM/YWHAs; Children/youth, services; Aging, centers/services; Developmentally disabled, centers & services; Human services.
Type of support: Continuing support; General/operating support; Program development.
Geographic limitations: Giving primarily in areas of company operations in the Springfield, MA, area.
Support limitations: No grants to individuals.
Application information: Applications accepted. Application form required.
Initial approach: Contact foundation for a formal submission packet
Deadline(s): Varies
Officers and Directors:* Thomas R. Burton*, Pres.; Eddie Wright, Secy.; Robert M. Massey*, Treas.; Lynn S. Bunce.
EIN: 331165388
Selected grants: The following grants are a representative sample of this grantmaker's funding activity:
$5,000 to Rebuilding Together, Washington, DC, 2010.

1713
Hampden Savings Bank

19 Harrison Ave.
P.O. Box 2048
Springfield, MA 01102-2048
(413) 736-1812

Company URL: http://www.hampdenbank.com
Establishment information: Established in 1852.
Company type: Subsidiary of a public company
Business activities: Operates savings bank.
Business type (SIC): Savings institutions
Corporate officers: Glenn S. Welch, Pres. and C.O.O.; Robert A. Massey, Treas. and C.F.O.; Sheryl L. Shinn, Sr. V.P., Opers.; Lynn Stevens Bunce, V.P., Human Resources; Craig W. Kaylor, Esq., Genl. Counsel
Offices: Agawam, Longmeadow, West Springfield, MA
Giving statement: Giving through the Hampden Savings Foundation, Inc.

Hampden Savings Foundation, Inc.

P.O. Box 2048
Springfield, MA 01102-2048
Application address: 19 Harrison Ave., Springfield, MA 01103, tel.: (413) 452-5181

Establishment information: Established in 2001 in MA.
Donor: Hampden Savings Bank.
Contact: Robert A. Massey, Pres. and Treas.
Financial data (yr. ended 10/31/11): Assets, $819,505 (M); expenditures, $340,898; qualifying distributions, $337,771; giving activities include $337,771 for grants.
Purpose and activities: The foundation supports organizations involved with arts and culture, education, children services and community development.
Fields of interest: Arts; Education; Community/economic development.
Type of support: Annual campaigns; Capital campaigns; General/operating support; Scholarship funds; Sponsorships.
Geographic limitations: Giving primarily in areas of company operations in western MA, with emphasis on the greater Springfield area.
Application information: Applications accepted. Application form required.
Initial approach: Contact foundation for application form
Deadline(s): None
Officers and Directors: Robert A. Massey, Pres. and Treas.; Lynn S. Bunce, Secy.; Donald R. Dupree; Nancy D. Mirkin; Eddie Wright.
EIN: 043583365

1714
Hampton Management Company

(also known as Hampton Affiliates)
9600 S.W. Barnes Rd., Ste. 200
Portland, OR 97225-6666 (503) 297-7691

Company URL: http://www.hamptonaffiliates.com
Establishment information: Established in 1942.
Company type: Private company
Business activities: Manufactures lumber; conducts logging activities.
Business type (SIC): Lumber and wood products (except furniture); logging
Corporate officers: Michael P. Hollern, Chair.; Mike Phillips, Pres.; Steven Zika, C.F.O.; Robert L. Bluhm, V.P., Finance, and C.F.O.
Board of director: Michael P. Hollern, Chair.
Subsidiary: Willamina Lumber Co. Inc., Portland, OR
Giving statement: Giving through the Hampton Affiliates Corporate Giving Program.

Hampton Affiliates Corporate Giving Program

c/o Corp. Contribs.
9600 S.W. Barnes Rd., Ste. 200
Portland, OR 97225-6666 (503) 297-7691

Purpose and activities: Hampton Affiliates makes charitable contributions to nonprofit organizations on a case by case basis. Support is given primarily in areas of company operations.
Fields of interest: General charitable giving.
Type of support: General/operating support; In-kind gifts.
Geographic limitations: Giving primarily in areas of company operations in CA, OR, and WA.
Application information: Applications accepted. The company's chairman and president and C.E.O. review all requests. Application form not required. Applicants should submit the following:
1) detailed description of project and amount of funding requested
Initial approach: Proposal to headquarters

1715
Hamrick Mills, Inc.
515 W. Buford St.
P.O. Box 48
Gaffney, SC 29341 (864) 489-4731

Company URL: http://www.hamrickmills.com
Establishment information: Established in 1900.
Company type: Private company
Business activities: Manufactures textiles, print cloths, cotton, yarns, thread, and other materials.
Business type (SIC): Textile goods/miscellaneous; fabrics/broadwoven natural cotton
Corporate officers: Wylie L. Hamrick, Chair.; Carlisle Hamrick, Pres.; David Dorman, Cont.
Board of director: Wylie L. Hamrick, Chair.
Giving statement: Giving through the Hamrick Mills Foundation, Inc.

Hamrick Mills Foundation, Inc.
P.O. Box 48
Gaffney, SC 29342-0048

Establishment information: Established in 1952 in SC.
Donor: Hamrick Mills Inc.
Contact: Charles J. Bonner, Exec. Dir.
Financial data (yr. ended 12/31/11): Assets, $1,478,110 (M); expenditures, $86,219; qualifying distributions, $67,185; giving activities include $67,185 for grants.
Purpose and activities: The foundation supports organizations involved with historic preservation, education, cancer, athletics, human services, and Christianity.
Fields of interest: Education; Human services; Religion.
Type of support: General/operating support; Program development; Scholarship funds.
Geographic limitations: Giving primarily in Cherokee County, SC.
Support limitations: No grants to individuals.
Application information: Applications accepted. Application form required. Applicants should submit the following:
1) copy of IRS Determination Letter
2) brief history of organization and description of its mission
3) copy of most recent annual report/audited financial statement/990
4) detailed description of project and amount of funding requested

Initial approach: Proposal
Deadline(s): None

Officers and Directors:* Lyman W. Hamrick*, Chair.; W. C. Hamrick*, Secy.; C. F. Hamrick II*, Treas.; D. E. Dorman; A. W. Hamrick.
EIN: 576024261

1716
Hancock County Savings Bank, FSB
351 Carolina Ave.
Chester, WV 26034-1127 (304) 387-1620

Company URL: http://www.hcsbank.com
Establishment information: Established in 1899.
Company type: Private company
Business activities: Operates savings bank.
Business type (SIC): Savings institutions
Corporate officers: Harry Comm, Chair.; Jerry Linger, Vice-Chair.; Catherine Ferrari, Pres. and C.E.O.; Mark Eckleberry, Secy.
Board of directors: Harry Comm, Chair.; Jerry Linger, Vice-Chair.; Mark Eckleberry; Catherine Ferrari; John Fitzjohn; Cheryl Schreiber; Suzan Smith; Lee Swearingen; Sandra West
Offices: Chester, New Cumberland, Weirton, WV
Giving statement: Giving through the Hancock County Savings Bank Charitable Foundation.

Hancock County Savings Bank Charitable Foundation
351 Carolina Ave.
P.O. Box 245
Chester, WV 26034-1127 (304) 387-1620

Establishment information: Established in 1999 in WV.
Donor: Hancock County Savings Bank, FSB.
Financial data (yr. ended 12/31/11): Assets, $781,118 (M); expenditures, $46,432; qualifying distributions, $43,500; giving activities include $43,500 for grants.
Purpose and activities: The foundation supports organizations involved with human services. Support is limited to areas of company operations.
Fields of interest: Education; Human services; Religion.
Type of support: General/operating support.
Geographic limitations: Giving limited to areas of company operations in WV.
Application information: Applications accepted. Application form required. Applicants should submit the following:
1) copy of current year's organizational budget and/or project budget
2) descriptive literature about organization

Initial approach: Contact nearest company bank for application form
Board meeting date(s): Fourth Thurs. in Oct.
Deadline(s): Sept. 30

Officers: Harry Comm, Chair.; Steven Cooper, Pres.; Anthony Bernardi, Secy.-Treas.
Trustees: George E. Ash, Sr.; Romie Castelli; Cheryl D. Schreiber; Marvin Six.
EIN: 550767253

1717
John Hancock Financial Services, Inc.
200 Clarendon St., 4th Fl.
Boston, MA 02116-5047 (617) 572-6000

Company URL: http://www.jhancock.com
Establishment information: Established in 1999.
Company type: Subsidiary of a foreign company
Business activities: Sells insurance; provides investment advisory services.
Business type (SIC): Insurance/life; security and commodity services; insurance carriers
Corporate officers: Craig Bromley, Pres.; Steve Finch, Exec. V.P. and C.F.O.; James Gallagher, Exec. V.P., Genl. Counsel, and C.A.O.; Allan T. Hackney, Sr. V.P. and C.I.O.; Diana Scott, Sr. V.P., Human Resources
Subsidiary: John Hancock Life Insurance Co., Boston, MA
Giving statement: Giving through the John Hancock Financial Services, Inc. Corporate Giving Program.

John Hancock Financial Services, Inc. Corporate Giving Program
601 Congress St.
Boston, MA 02117-2806 (617) 663-3000
E-mail: corporatesocialresponsibility@jhancock.com ; URL: http://www.johnhancock.com/corporateresponsibility/index.html

Purpose and activities: John Hancock makes charitable contributions to nonprofit organizations involved with education, health and wellness, youth development, human services, and civic affairs. Support is given primarily in Boston, Massachusetts.
Fields of interest: Education; Public health; Health care; Employment, training; Housing/shelter, homeless; Disasters, preparedness/services; Youth development; Human services; Public affairs; General charitable giving Disabilities, people with.
Type of support: Cause-related marketing; Employee volunteer services; General/operating support; Internship funds; Program development.
Geographic limitations: Giving primarily in Boston, MA.
Application information: Applicants should submit the following:
1) copy of current year's organizational budget and/or project budget
2) detailed description of project and amount of funding requested
3) brief history of organization and description of its mission
4) copy of IRS Determination Letter
5) results expected from proposed grant

Initial approach: E-mail letter of inquiry
Deadline(s): Letters of inquiry should be no longer than 2 pages

Number of staff: 6 full-time professional; 1 full-time support.

1718
Handy & Harman
1133 Westchester Ave., Ste. N222
White Plains, NY 10604 (914) 461-1300

Company URL: http://www.handyharman.com
Establishment information: Established in 1867.
Company type: Subsidiary of a public company
Business activities: Manufactures electronic components, specialty fasteners, engineered materials, specialty wire and tubing, and fabricated precious metal products.
Business type (SIC): Electronic components and accessories; fabricated metal products (except machinery and transportation equipment); cutlery, hand and edge tools, and hardware; metal products/fabricated
Corporate officers: Jack L. Howard, Chair.; Glen M. Kassan, Vice-Chair.; James F. McCabe, Jr., Sr. V.P. and C.F.O.; Michael Macmanus, V.P., Secy., and Genl. Counsel
Board of directors: Jack L. Howard, Chair.; Glen K. Kassan, Vice-Chair.
Subsidiaries: Continental Industries, Inc., Tulsa, OK; Handy & Harman Electronic Materials Corp., East Providence, RI; Handy & Harman Tube Co., Inc., Norristown, PA; Indiana Tube Corp., Evansville, IN; Lucas-Milhaupt, Inc., Cudahy, WI; Olympic Manufacturing Group, Inc., Agawam, MA; Sumco Inc., Indianapolis, IN
International operations: Canada; Denmark; Singapore
Giving statement: Giving through the Handy & Harman Foundation.
Company EIN: 135129420

Handy & Harman Foundation

1133 Westchester Ave., Ste. N222
White Plains, NY 10604

Establishment information: Established in 1974 in NY.
Donor: Handy & Harman.
Financial data (yr. ended 12/31/10): Assets, $0 (M); expenditures, $0; qualifying distributions, $0.
Purpose and activities: The foundation supports organizations involved with education, health, and government and public administration.
Fields of interest: Higher education; Education; Health care; United Ways and Federated Giving Programs; Government/public administration.
Type of support: Annual campaigns; Continuing support.
Geographic limitations: Giving primarily in CT, DC, MA, and NY.
Support limitations: No support for political organizations. No grants to individuals.
Application information: Applications not accepted. Unsolicited requests for funds not accepted.
Officers and Trustees:* Jeffrey A. Svoboda*, Pres.; James F. McCabe, Jr.*, Treas.
EIN: 237408431

1719
Hanes Companies, Inc.

600 W. Northwest Blvd.
P.O. Box 202
Winston-Salem, NC 27101 (336) 747-1600

Company URL: http://www.hanesindustries.com/aboutus.html
Establishment information: Established in 1986.
Company type: Subsidiary of a public company
Business activities: Provides fabric dyeing and finishing services.
Business type (SIC): Fabric finishing
Corporate officers: Ralph Womble, C.E.O.; Randy Snyder, Jr., Pres.; Waller K. Howard, V.P. and C.F.O.; Samantha Howell, V.P., Human Resources; Paul Reid, Cont.
Giving statement: Giving through the Hanes Companies Foundation.

Hanes Companies Foundation

P.O. Box 202
Winston-Salem, NC 27102-0202

Establishment information: Established in 1986 in NC.
Donor: Hanes Cos., Inc.
Financial data (yr. ended 12/31/11): Assets, $77,230 (M); gifts received, $25,000; expenditures, $62,886; qualifying distributions, $62,000; giving activities include $62,000 for grants.
Purpose and activities: The foundation supports organizations involved with arts and culture, secondary and higher education, homeless services, and community economic development.
Fields of interest: Arts; Education; Community/economic development.
Type of support: General/operating support.
Application information: Applications not accepted. Unsolicited requests for funds not accepted.
Officers: Jerry W. Greene, Jr., Pres.; David S. Haffner, V.P.; W. Kim Howard, Secy.-Treas.
Director: Matthew C. Flanigan.
EIN: 581658698

1720
Hanesbrands Inc.

1000 E. Hanes Mill Rd.
Winston-Salem, NC 27105 (336) 519-4400

Company URL: http://www.hanesbrands.com
Establishment information: Established in 1901.
Company type: Public company
Company ticker symbol and exchange: HBI/NYSE
Business activities: Manufactures apparel essentials such as t-shirts, bras, panties, men's underwear, kids' underwear, casualwear, activewear, socks and hosiery.
Business type (SIC): Apparel—women's, girls', and children's undergarments
Financial profile for 2012: Number of employees, 51,500; assets, $3,631,700,000; sales volume, $4,525,720,000; pre-tax net income, $262,940,000; expenses, $4,085,610,000; liabilities, $2,744,830,000
Fortune 1000 ranking: 2012—518th in revenues, 625th in profits, and 692nd in assets
Corporate officers: Richard A. Noll, Chair. and C.E.O.; Gerald W. Evans, Jr., Co-C.O.O.; William J. Nictakis, Co-C.O.O.; Richard D. Moss, Jr., C.F.O.; Joia M. Johnson, Genl. Counsel and Corp. Secy.; Michael S. Ryan, Cont.
Board of directors: Richard A. Noll, Chair.; Lee A. Chaden; Bobby J. Griffin; James C. Johnson; Jessica Tuchman Mathews; J. Patrick Mulcahy; Ronald L. Nelson; Andrew J. Schindler; Ann E. Ziegler
Giving statement: Giving through the Hanesbrands Inc. Corporate Giving Program.
Company EIN: 203552316

Hanesbrands Inc. Corporate Giving Program

1000 E. Hanes Mill Rd.
Winston-Salem, NC 27105-1384
URL: http://www.hanesbrands.com/hbi/templates/OurValues/CommunityService.aspx

Purpose and activities: Hanesbrands makes charitable contributions to nonprofit organizations in areas of company operations; giving also to national and international organizations.
Fields of interest: Disasters, preparedness/services; Community/economic development; General charitable giving.
Type of support: Employee volunteer services; General/operating support; In-kind gifts.
Geographic limitations: Giving primarily in areas of company operations.
Application information: Applications not accepted. Contributes only to pre-selected organizations.

1721
Hangley Aronchick Segal & Pudlin

1 Logan Sq., 27th Fl.
Philadelphia, PA 19103-6933
(215) 568-6200

Company URL: http://www.hangley.com
Establishment information: Established in 1994.
Company type: Private company
Business activities: Operates law firm.
Business type (SIC): Legal services
Offices: Cherry Hill, NJ; Harrisburg, Norristown, Philadelphia, PA
Giving statement: Giving through the Hangley Aronchick Segal & Pudlin Pro Bono Program.

Hangley Aronchick Segal & Pudlin Pro Bono Program

1 Logan Sq., 27th Fl.
Philadelphia, PA 19103-6933 (215) 496-7044
E-mail: acp@hangley.com; URL: http://www.hangley.com/Pro_Bono/

Contact: Alan C. Promer, Attorney
Fields of interest: Legal services.
Type of support: Pro bono services - legal.
Geographic limitations: Giving primarily in areas of company operations in Cherry Hill, NJ, Harrisburg, Norristown, and Philadelphia, PA.

1722
Howard Hanna Company

119 Gamma Dr.
Pittsburgh, PA 15238 (412) 967-9000

Company URL: http://www.howardhanna.com
Establishment information: Established in 1957.
Company type: Private company
Business activities: Operates real estate agency.
Business type (SIC): Real estate agents and managers
Corporate officers: Howard W. Hanna III, Chair. and C.E.O.; Helen Hanna Casey, Pres.; Annie Hanna Cestra, Exec. V.P. and C.O.O.; Tracy Rossetti Delvaux, Sr. V.P. and C.F.O.; Barbara Reynolds, Sr. V.P., Mktg. and Comms.; Jean Hayes, V.P., Opers.; Kelly Silver, V.P., Mktg.
Board of director: Howard W. Hanna III, Chair.
Giving statement: Giving through the Howard Hanna Foundation.

Howard Hanna Foundation

119 Gamma Dr.
Pittsburgh, PA 15238-2919

Establishment information: Established in 1998 in PA.
Donor: Howard Hanna Corporation.
Financial data (yr. ended 12/31/11): Assets, $2,282,279 (M); gifts received, $200,000; expenditures, $97,812; qualifying distributions, $85,000; giving activities include $85,000 for grants.
Purpose and activities: The foundation supports organizations involved with community development and the visually impaired.
Fields of interest: Education; Community/economic development; Public affairs.
Type of support: General/operating support.
Geographic limitations: Giving primarily in Pittsburgh, PA.
Support limitations: No grants to individuals.
Application information: Applications not accepted. Unsolicited requests for funds not accepted.
Officers: Howard W. Hanna, Jr., Chair.; Howard W. Hanna III, Pres.; Helen Hanna Casey, V.P.; Annie H. Cestra, V.P.; Tracy Rossetti-Delvaux, C.F.O. and Treas.
EIN: 311621640

1723
Hannaford Bros. Co.

145 Pleasant Hill Rd.
Scarborough, ME 04074-9309
(207) 883-2911

Company URL: http://www.hannaford.com
Establishment information: Established in 1883.
Company type: Subsidiary of a foreign company
Business activities: Operates supermarkets and drug stores.
Business type (SIC): Groceries—wholesale; groceries—retail; drug stores and proprietary stores; insurance agents, brokers, and services
Financial profile for 2010: Number of employees, 1,262; sales volume, $3,931,200,000
Corporate officers: Beth M. Newlands-Campbell, Pres.; Paul A. Fritzson, Exec. V.P. and C.F.O.
Subsidiary: South Paris Shop 'n Save, Inc., Oxford, ME
Giving statement: Giving through the Hannaford Bros. Co. Contributions Program and the Hannaford Charitable Foundation.

Hannaford Bros. Co. Contributions Program

P.O. Box 1000
Portland, ME 04104-5005 (207) 883-2911
Application addresses for regional or national organizations: For Massachusetts and New Hampshire: Hannaford Community Rels., 108 Lancaster Street, Leominster, MA 01453; For Maine: Hannaford Community Rels., P.O. Box 1000, Portland, ME 04104; For New York and Vermont: Hannaford Community Rels., 970 Route 9, Schodack Landing, NY 12156; Additional e-mail: hannafordhelpsschools@hannaford.com; URL: http://www.hannaford.com/content.jsp?pageName=Community&leftNavArea=AboutLeftNav

Purpose and activities: As a complement to its foundation, Hannaford also makes charitable contributions to nonprofit organizations directly. Special emphasis is directed towards programs that help children and families. Support is given primarily in areas of company operations in Maine, Massachusetts, New Hampshire, New York, and Vermont; giving also to national organizations.
Fields of interest: Elementary/secondary education; Genetic diseases and disorders; Breast cancer; Agriculture, sustainable programs; Food banks; Nutrition; Athletics/sports, winter sports; Children, services; United Ways and Federated Giving Programs.
Type of support: Cause-related marketing; Donated products; General/operating support; Program development; Sponsorships.
Geographic limitations: Giving primarily in areas of company operations in MA, ME, NH, NY, and VT; giving also to national organizations.
Publications: Application guidelines.
Application information: Applications accepted. Support is limited to 1 contribution per organization during any given year. Application form required.
Applicants should submit the following:
1) detailed description of project and amount of funding requested
2) plans for acknowledgement
Applications should include the organization's Tax ID Number, and all levels of sponsorship.
Initial approach: Download application form and mail with proposal to nearest application address; for local support, address requests to Hannaford Supermarket Store Manager
Deadline(s): 6 to 8 weeks prior to the event or print deadlines for regional requests

Hannaford Charitable Foundation

P.O. Box 1000
Portland, ME 04104-5005
URL: http://www.hannaford.com/content.jsp?pageName=charitableFoundation&leftNavArea=AboutLeftNav

Establishment information: Established in 1993 in ME.
Donor: Hannaford Bros. Co.
Financial data (yr. ended 12/31/11): Assets, $1,415,002 (M); gifts received, $1,311,000; expenditures, $1,388,667; qualifying distributions, $1,388,667; giving activities include $1,360,773 for 77 grants (high: $200,000; low: $1,000).
Purpose and activities: The foundation supports organizations involved with arts and culture, education, fisheries, health, human services, marine science, and civic affairs.
Fields of interest: Arts; Higher education; Education; Animals/wildlife, fisheries; Hospitals (general); Health care, clinics/centers; Health care; YM/YWCAs & YM/YWHAs; Children/youth, services; Human services; United Ways and Federated Giving Programs; Marine science; Public affairs.
Type of support: Building/renovation; Capital campaigns; Employee-related scholarships; Program development.
Geographic limitations: Giving primarily in areas of company operations in MA, ME, NH, NY, and VT.
Support limitations: No support for tax-supported organizations or veterans', fraternal, or religious organizations not of direct benefit to the entire community. No grants to individuals (except for employee-related scholarships), or for advertising or general operating support.
Publications: Application guidelines.
Application information: Applications accepted. Proposals should be submitted using organization letterhead. Additional information may be requested at a later date. Application form not required.
Applicants should submit the following:
1) how project will be sustained once grantmaker support is completed
2) statement of problem project will address
3) population served
4) name, address and phone number of organization
5) copy of IRS Determination Letter
6) brief history of organization and description of its mission
7) geographic area to be served
8) copy of most recent annual report/audited financial statement/990
9) detailed description of project and amount of funding requested
10) contact person
11) listing of additional sources and amount of support
Visit website for detailed application guidelines.
Initial approach: Proposal
Copies of proposal: 10
Deadline(s): 6 to 8 weeks prior to need
Final notification: 6 to 8 weeks for requests under $50,000; 3 to 4 months for requests over $50,000
Officers and Directors: Beth Newlands Campbell, Pres.; Donna J. Boyce, Secy.; Jim Kacer, Treas.; Mark Doiron; Tod Pepin; Bob Schools; Tod Pepin.
EIN: 010483892
Selected grants: The following grants are a representative sample of this grantmaker's funding activity:
$200,000 to Scholarship America, Saint Peter, MN, 2010.
$200,000 to University of New England, School of Pharmacy, Portland, ME, 2010.
$200,000 to University of New England, Biddeford, ME, 2011.
$158,093 to United Way of Greater Portland, Portland, ME, 2010.
$125,000 to University of Southern Maine, Portland, ME, 2010.
$101,000 to Maine Medical Center, Portland, ME, 2010.
$100,000 to Foundation for Maines Community Colleges, South Portland, ME, 2011.
$100,000 to Gulf of Maine Research Institute, Portland, ME, 2011.
$100,000 to Maine Medical Center, Portland, ME, 2011. For capital campaign.
$100,000 to Scholarship America, Saint Peter, MN, 2011.
$100,000 to Southern Maine Community College Foundation, South Portland, ME, 2010.
$98,750 to Scholarship America, Saint Peter, MN, 2011.
$50,000 to Mercy Hospital, Portland, ME, 2010.
$50,000 to Mercy Hospital, Portland, ME, 2011.
$39,548 to United Way of Greater Portland, Portland, ME, 2011.
$39,548 to United Way of Greater Portland, Portland, ME, 2011.
$33,200 to United Way of the Greater Capital Region, Albany, NY, 2010.
$26,500 to United Way of Eastern Maine, Bangor, ME, 2011.
$10,000 to Northeast Health, Troy, NY, 2010.
$3,100 to United Way of Tri-County, Framingham, MA, 2010.

1724
The Hanover Insurance Group, Inc.

440 Lincoln St.
Worcester, MA 01653-0002
(508) 855-1000
FAX: (508) 855-8078

Company URL: http://www.hanover.com
Establishment information: Established in 1852.
Company type: Public company
Company ticker symbol and exchange: THG/NYSE
Business activities: Operates property and casualty insurance holding company.
Business type (SIC): Insurance/fire, marine, and casualty
Financial profile for 2012: Number of employees, 5,100; assets, $13,484,900,000; sales volume, $4,590,700,000; pre-tax net income, $28,700,000; expenses, $4,562,000,000; liabilities, $10,889,500,000
Fortune 1000 ranking: 2012—522nd in revenues, 808th in profits, and 319th in assets
Corporate officers: Michael P. Angelini, Chair.; Frederick H. Eppinger, Pres. and C.E.O.; David Greenfield, Exec. V.P. and C.F.O.; Gregory D. Tranter, Exec. V.P., C.I.O., and C.O.O.; J. Kendall Huber, Exec. V.P. and Genl. Counsel
Board of directors: Michael P. Angelini, Chair.; John J. Brennan; P. Kevin Condron; Frederick H. Eppinger; Neal F. Finnegan; David J. Gallitano; Wendell J. Knox; Robert J. Murray; Joseph R. Ramrath; Harriett Tee Taggart
Subsidiaries: Citizens Insurance Company of America, Howell, MI; The Hanover Insurance Company, Worcester, MA
Giving statement: Giving through the Hanover Insurance Group Foundation, Inc.
Company EIN: 043263626

The Hanover Insurance Group Foundation, Inc.

(formerly Allmerica Financial Charitable Foundation, Inc.)
440 Lincoln St., N100
Worcester, MA 01653-0002 (508) 855-2524
E-mail: foundation@hanover.com; Michigan application address: Becky E. Best, Mgr., Corp. Community Rels., Citizens Insurance Co. of America, 808 Highlander Way, HWC340, Howell, MI 48843, tel.: (517) 540-4290, e-mail: bbest@hanover.com; URL: http://www.hanover.com/thg/about/community/grant.htm

Establishment information: Established in 1990 in MA.
Donors: First Allmerica Financial Life Insurance Co.; The Hanover Insurance Co.
Contact: Jennifer Luisa, Asst. V.P., Community Rels.
Financial data (yr. ended 12/31/11): Assets, $3,615,761 (M); gifts received, $500,000; expenditures, $2,605,182; qualifying distributions, $2,544,967; giving activities include $2,514,967 for 377 grants (high: $749,633; low: $50) and $30,000 for loans/program-related investments.
Purpose and activities: The foundation supports organizations involved with arts and culture, health, medical research, hunger, housing, human services, and community development. Special emphasis is directed toward programs designed to build world class public education systems; and inspire and empower youth to achieve their full potential.
Fields of interest: Visual arts; Performing arts; Arts; Higher education; Education; Health care; Medical research; Food services; Housing/shelter; Youth development; Aging, centers/services; Homeless, human services; Human services; Community/economic development Youth.

Programs:

Hanover Scholarship Program: The foundation awards 36 college scholarships of $1,000 up to $2,500 to high school seniors and college freshman from public high schools in the Greater Worcester and Howell areas, and to children of employees of Hanover Insurance Group. The program is administered by Scholarship America.

Volunteer Incentive Program (VIP): The foundation awards $500 grants to nonprofit organizations with which employees of Hanover Insurance Group volunteer.

Type of support: Building/renovation; Employee volunteer services; Employee-related scholarships; General/operating support; Program development; Scholarship funds; Scholarships—to individuals.
Geographic limitations: Giving primarily in areas of company operations in the greater Worcester County, MA, area and the Howell and Livingston County, MI, area.
Support limitations: No support for private schools, amateur or professional sporting groups, or religious, political, professional, fraternal, or labor organizations. No grants to individuals (except for scholarships), or for national fundraising drives, capital campaigns, or beauty or talent contests.
Publications: Application guidelines; Corporate giving report; Program policy statement.
Application information: Applications accepted. Support is limited to 1 contribution per organization during any given year. Organizations receiving support are asked to provide a final report. Application form required. Applicants should submit the following:

1) how project will be sustained once grantmaker support is completed
2) results expected from proposed grant
3) copy of IRS Determination Letter
4) copy of most recent annual report/audited financial statement/990
5) how project's results will be evaluated or measured
6) explanation of why grantmaker is considered an appropriate donor for project
7) listing of board of directors, trustees, officers and other key people and their affiliations
8) detailed description of project and amount of funding requested
9) copy of current year's organizational budget and/or project budget
10) listing of additional sources and amount of support
11) plans for acknowledgement

Initial approach: Download application form and mail to application address
Board meeting date(s): Mar., June, Sept., and Nov.
Deadline(s): Jan. 15, Apr. 15, July 15, and Sept. 15

Officers and Directors:* Jennifer F. Luisa*, Pres.; Charles F. Cronin, Clerk; Celeste J. Nelson, Treas.; Ann K. Tripp, Investment Off.; Bryan D. Allen; Frederick H. Eppinger.
EIN: 043105650
Selected grants: The following grants are a representative sample of this grantmaker's funding activity:
$749,633 to Worcester Center for Performing Arts, Worcester, MA, 2011.
$60,000 to Reading Matters, Boston, MA, 2011.
$55,000 to United Way of Central Massachusetts, Worcester, MA, 2011.
$55,000 to United Way of Central Massachusetts, Worcester, MA, 2011.
$25,000 to YMCA of Central Massachusetts, Worcester, MA, 2011.
$20,000 to Central Massachusetts Housing Alliance, Worcester, MA, 2011.
$13,000 to American Heart Association, Framingham, MA, 2011.
$10,000 to Audubon Society, Massachusetts, Worcester, MA, 2011.
$10,000 to Boys and Girls Club of Worcester, Worcester, MA, 2011.
$5,000 to American Antiquarian Society, Worcester, MA, 2011.

1725
Hanson Bridgett LLP

425 Market St., 26th Fl.
San Francisco, CA 94105-5401
(415) 777-3200

Company URL: http://www.hansonbridgett.com
Establishment information: Established in 1958.
Company type: Private company
Business activities: Operates law firm.
Business type (SIC): Legal services
Corporate officer: Andrew Giacomini, Managing Partner
Offices: Foster City, Larkspur, Sacramento, San Francisco, Walnut Creek, CA
Giving statement: Giving through the Hanson Bridgett LLP Corporate Giving Program.

Hanson Bridgett LLP Corporate Giving Program

425 Market St., 26th Fl.
San Francisco, CA 94105-5401 (415) 777-3200
E-mail: jsherman@hansonbridgett.com; Contact for Pro Bono program: Julie Veit, Sr. Counsel, e-mail: jveit@hansonbridgett.com; URL: http://www.hansonbridgett.com/about_us/community_involvement/index.php

Contact: Julie Sherman, Assoc.
Purpose and activities: Hanson Bridgett is a certified B Corporation that donates a percentage of profits to nonprofit organizations in areas of company operations, with emphasis on San Francisco, California.
Fields of interest: Legal services; Food banks; Human services; Community/economic development.
Type of support: Employee volunteer services; General/operating support; Loaned talent; Pro bono services - legal.
Geographic limitations: Giving primarily in areas of company operations, with emphasis on San Francisco, CA.

1726
Harbert Management Corporation

2100 3rd Ave. N., Ste. 600
Birmingham, AL 35203-3416
(205) 987-5500

Company URL: http://www.harbert.net
Establishment information: Established in 1993.
Company type: Private company
Business activities: Provides investment advisory services.
Business type (SIC): Security and commodity services
Corporate officers: Raymond J. Harbert, Chair. and C.E.O.; Michael D. Luce, Pres. and C.O.O.; David A. Boutwell, Exec. V.P. and Co-C.F.O.; Charlie Miller, Co-C.F.O.; Jeffrey B. Liles, C.I.O.; John W. McCullough, Sr. V.P. and Genl. Counsel
Board of director: Raymond J. Harbert, Chair.
Giving statement: Giving through the Harbert Management Corporation Contributions Program and the Harbert Employees Reaching Out Foundation.

Harbert Employees Reaching Out Foundation

(formerly Hero Foundation)
P.O. Box 1297
Birmingham, AL 35201-1297 (205) 987-5500
FAX: (205) 987-5568; E-mail: skeeton@harbert.net; URL: http://www.harbert.net/company/community-outreach/

Establishment information: Established in 1998 in AL.
Donor: Employees of Harbert Management Corp.
Contact: Liz Deuel, Pres.
Financial data (yr. ended 12/31/11): Revenue, $633,006; assets, $918,759 (M); gifts received, $647,855; expenditures, $750,833; program services expenses, $748,400; giving activities include $27,516 for 2 grants (high: $15,000; low: $12,516) and $720,884 for grants to individuals.
Purpose and activities: The foundation provides direct financial or other appropriate assistance to individuals or families in crisis due to a natural disaster, medical condition, or temporary financial hardship.
Fields of interest: Human services.

Program:

Hero Foundation Grants: Grants averaging $500 to $10,000 are awarded to individuals who have consistently demonstrated responsible financial practices and whose needs are based on

unexpected events or medical conditions causing financial hardship.
Type of support: Grants to individuals.
Geographic limitations: Giving primarily in AL.
Publications: Application guidelines; Financial statement; Newsletter.
Application information: Applications accepted. Applicants must be sponsored by an employee of Harbert before making a formal application to the foundation. Application form required.
Initial approach: Contact chairperson of sponsor committee to receive assignment of a sponsor
Copies of proposal: 1
Board meeting date(s): Annually
Deadline(s): None
Officers: Elizabeth Deuel*, Pres.; Chris Hartin*, V.P.; Trey Ferguson*, V.P.; Melody Lewis*, V.P.; Lindsey McCurdy*, V.P. and Treas.; Margaret Russo*, V.P.; Betsy Lovell*, Secy.
EIN: 631202843

1727
Hard Rock Cafe International, Inc.

(formerly Hard Rock Cafe International (USA) Inc.)
6100 Old Park Ln.
Orlando, FL 32835 (407) 445-7625

Company URL: http://www.hardrock.com
Establishment information: Established in 1971.
Company type: Subsidiary of a tribal corporation
Business activities: Operates restaurants.
Business type (SIC): Restaurants and drinking places
Corporate officers: Hamish A. Dodds, Pres. and C.E.O.; Michael Kneidinger, V.P., Opers.; Thomas Gispanski, V.P., Finance
Giving statement: Giving through the Hard Rock Cafe Foundation, Inc.

Hard Rock Cafe Foundation, Inc.

6100 Old Park Ln.
Orlando, FL 32835-2466

Establishment information: Established in 2000 in FL.
Donors: Hard Rock Cafe International (USA) Inc.; WDI Corporation.
Financial data (yr. ended 12/31/11): Assets, $242 (M); gifts received, $1,451,173; expenditures, $1,447,461; qualifying distributions, $1,446,153; giving activities include $1,446,153 for 19 grants (high: $330,353; low: $3).
Purpose and activities: The foundation supports organizations involved with music, substance abuse services, cancer research, hunger, agriculture, human services, civil and human rights, and economically disadvantaged people.
Fields of interest: Performing arts, music; Substance abuse, services; Cancer research; Breast cancer research; Agriculture; Agriculture, sustainable programs; Food services; Children, services; Family services; Human services; Civil/human rights Economically disadvantaged.
Type of support: General/operating support; Grants to individuals; Program development; Research.
Geographic limitations: Giving limited to Washington, DC and New York, NY.
Application information: Applications not accepted. Contributes only to pre-selected organizations.
Officers and Directors:* Hamish Dodds*, Pres.; Jay Wolszczak*, Secy.; Thomas Gispanski*, Treas.
EIN: 593686985

Selected grants: The following grants are a representative sample of this grantmaker's funding activity:
$550,707 to World Hunger Year, New York, NY, 2010.
$549,764 to Breast Cancer Research Foundation, New York, NY, 2010.
$373,076 to City of Hope, Duarte, CA, 2010.
$106,994 to Wildlife Conservation Society, Bronx, NY, 2010.
$49,405 to Musicians on Call, New York, NY, 2010.
$11,460 to Millennium Promise Alliance, New York, NY, 2010.
$6,032 to Best Friends Animal Society, Kanab, UT, 2010.
$2,868 to Amnesty International USA, New York, NY, 2010.
$1,751 to Broadway Cares/Equity Fights AIDS, New York, NY, 2010.

1728
Harden & Associates, Inc.

501 Riverside Ave., Ste. 1000
Jacksonville, FL 32202 (904) 354-3785
FAX: (904) 634-1302

Company URL: http://www.hardenassociates.com
Establishment information: Established in 1953.
Company type: Private company
Business activities: Operates risk and employee benefits management firm.
Business type (SIC): Insurance agents, brokers, and services
Corporate officers: John Harden, Chair.; Paul Lunetta, Pres. and C.O.O.; Daniel Dieterle, V.P. and C.F.O.
Board of director: John Harden, Chair.
Giving statement: Giving through the Harden & Associates Foundation.

The Harden & Associates Foundation

501 Riverside Ave., Ste. 1000
Jacksonville, FL 32204-4941

Establishment information: Established in 2007 in FL.
Donor: Harden & Assocs., Inc.
Financial data (yr. ended 12/31/11): Assets, $181,556 (M); gifts received, $10,346; expenditures, $66,605; qualifying distributions, $66,575; giving activities include $66,575 for grants.
Fields of interest: Education; Health care; Human services.
Support limitations: No grants to individuals.
Application information: Applications not accepted. Unsolicited requests for funds not accepted.
Trustees: Marvin C. Harden III; Paul J. Lunetta.
EIN: 207205656

1729
Hardinge Inc.

(formerly Hardinge Brothers, Inc.)
1 Hardinge Dr.
Elmira, NY 14902-1507 (607) 734-2281
FAX: (607) 734-3886

Company URL: http://www.hardinge.com
Establishment information: Established in 1890.
Company type: Public company
Company ticker symbol and exchange: HDNG/NASDAQ
Business activities: Manufactures turning machine tools.
Business type (SIC): Machinery/metalworking
Financial profile for 2012: Number of employees, 1,417; assets, $325,650,000; sales volume, $334,410,000; pre-tax net income, $19,340,000; expenses, $314,330,000; liabilities, $164,450,000
Corporate officers: Richard L. Simons, Chair., Pres., and C.E.O.; Douglas C. Tifft, Sr. V.P., Admin.; Edward J. Gaio, V.P. and C.F.O.
Board of directors: Richard L. Simons, Chair.; Daniel J. Burke; Douglas A. Greenlee; J. Philip Hunter; Robert J. Lepofsky; John J. Perrotti; Mitchell I. Quain; Tony Tripeny
International operations: Canada; Germany; Russia; Switzerland; Taiwan; United Kingdom
Giving statement: Giving through the Douglas G. Anderson—Leigh R. Evans Foundation.
Company EIN: 160470200

Douglas G. Anderson—Leigh R. Evans Foundation

1 Hardinge Dr.
Elmira, NY 14902-1507 (607) 378-4217

Establishment information: Incorporated in 1960 in NY.
Donor: Hardinge Inc.
Contact: Douglas Tifft
Financial data (yr. ended 10/31/11): Assets, $1,058,710 (M); expenditures, $54,533; qualifying distributions, $53,325; giving activities include $48,700 for 19 grants (high: $12,000; low: $500).
Purpose and activities: The foundation supports organizations involved with arts and culture, secondary education, literacy, and human services.
Fields of interest: Education; Health care; Human services.
Type of support: Annual campaigns; Building/renovation; Capital campaigns; Continuing support; Equipment; General/operating support; Scholarship funds; Sponsorships.
Geographic limitations: Giving primarily in Chemung County, NY.
Support limitations: No grants to individuals.
Application information: Applications accepted. Application form required. Applicants should submit the following:
1) copy of IRS Determination Letter
2) listing of board of directors, trustees, officers and other key people and their affiliations
3) detailed description of project and amount of funding requested
Initial approach: Letter of inquiry
Deadline(s): Apr. 15 and Oct. 15
Officers and Trustees:* Robert E. Agan*, Pres.; Richard L. Simons*, V.P.; J. Philip Hunter*, Secy.; Douglas C. Tifft*, Treas.; Daniel J. Burke; Richard J. Cole; Douglas A. Greenlee; John Potter.
Number of staff: 1 part-time professional.
EIN: 166024690

1730
Hargray Communications Group

856 William Hilton Pkwy.
P.O. Box 5986
Hilton Head Island, SC 29938
(843) 341-1501

Company URL: http://www.hargray.com
Establishment information: Established in 1947.
Company type: Private company

Business activities: Operates holding company; provides telecommunications services.
Business type (SIC): Communications
Corporate officers: Michael I. Gottdenker, Chair. and C.E.O.; James J. Volk, C.F.O.; Christopher M. McCorkendale, V.P., Opers.; Andrew J. Rein, V.P., Sales and Mktg.; David H. Armistead, Genl. Counsel and Secy.
Board of director: Michael I. Gottdenker, Chair.
Giving statement: Giving through the Hargray Communications Group Corporate Giving Program.

Hargray Communications Group Corporate Giving Program

856 William Hilton Pkwy.
Hilton Head Island, SC 29928-3423
URL: http://www2.hargray.com/company/in-the-community

Purpose and activities: Hargray makes charitable contributions to nonprofit organizations involved with health and youth development. Support is given primarily in Lowcountry, South Carolina.
Fields of interest: Medical research; Youth development.
Type of support: Employee volunteer services; General/operating support.
Geographic limitations: Giving primarily in Lowcountry, SC; giving also to national organizations.
Application information: Applications accepted. Application form not required.

1731
Harken, Inc.

N. 15W 24983 Bluemound Rd.
Pewaukee, WI 53072-3755 (262) 691-3320

Company URL: http://www.harken.com
Establishment information: Established in 1967.
Company type: Private company
Business activities: Manufactures and markets sailboat hardware and accessories.
Business type (SIC): Ship and boat building and repair
Corporate officers: Peter Harken, Pres.; Robert Sweet, C.F.O. and Treas.; Marc Monreal, Corp. Secy.
Giving statement: Giving through the Harken Family Foundation, Inc.

Harken Family Foundation, Inc.

c/o Olaf T. Harken
1251 E. Wisconsin Ave.
Pewaukee, WI 53072

Establishment information: Established in 2002 in WI.
Donor: Harken, Inc.
Financial data (yr. ended 12/31/11): Assets, $173,477 (M); expenditures, $13,161; qualifying distributions, $11,884; giving activities include $11,884 for grants.
Purpose and activities: The foundation supports libraries and organizations involved with television, orchestras, and sailing.
Fields of interest: Media, television; Performing arts, orchestras; Libraries (public); Athletics/sports, water sports.
Type of support: Annual campaigns; General/operating support.
Geographic limitations: Giving primarily in WI.
Support limitations: No grants to individuals.
Application information: Applications not accepted. Unsolicited requests for funds not accepted.
Directors: Olaf T. Harken; Peter O. Harken; Ruth F. Harken.
EIN: 680532306

1732
Harley-Davidson, Inc.

3700 W. Juneau Ave.
Milwaukee, WI 53208 (414) 342-4680
FAX: (414) 343-4621

Company URL: http://www.harley-davidson.com
Establishment information: Established in 1903.
Company type: Public company
Company ticker symbol and exchange: HOG/NYSE
Business activities: Manufactures motorcycles, recreational vehicles, specialized commercial vehicles, and allied parts and accessories.
Business type (SIC): Motorcycles, bicycles, and parts
Financial profile for 2012: Number of employees, 5,800; assets, $9,170,770,000; sales volume, $5,580,510,000; pre-tax net income, $961,510,000; expenses, $4,580,330,000; liabilities, $6,613,150,000
Fortune 1000 ranking: 2012—449th in revenues, 284th in profits, and 416th in assets
Forbes 2000 ranking: 2012—1321st in sales, 982nd in profits, and 1532nd in assets
Corporate officers: Keith E. Wandell, Chair., Pres., and C.E.O.; John A. Olin, Sr. V.P. and C.F.O.; Paul J. Jones, V.P., Genl. Counsel, and Secy.; Joanne M. Bischmann, V.P., Comms.; Tonit M. Calaway, V.P., Human Resources
Board of directors: Keith E. Wandell, Chair.; Berry K. Allen; John R. Anderson; Richard I. Beattie; Martha F. Brooks; George H. Conrades; Donald A. James; Sara L. Levinson; Norman Thomas Linebarger; George L. Miles, Jr.; James A. Norling; Jochen Zeitz
Subsidiaries: Eaglemark Financial Services, Inc., Chicago, IL; H-D Michigan, Inc., Ann Arbor, MI; Holiday Rambler LLC, Wakarusa, IN
Giving statement: Giving through the Harley-Davidson, Inc. Corporate Giving Program and the Harley-Davidson Foundation, Inc.
Company EIN: 391382325

Harley-Davidson, Inc. Corporate Giving Program

3700 W. Juneau Ave.
Milwaukee, WI 53208-2818 (414) 343-4056
URL: http://www.harley-davidson.com/wcm/Content/Pages/Diversity/community.jsp?locale=en_US&bmLocale=en_US

Purpose and activities: As a complement to its foundation, Harley-Davidson also makes charitable contributions to nonprofit organizations directly. Support is given primarily in areas of company operations, and to national organizations. Special emphasis is directed toward muscular dystrophy.
Fields of interest: Health care, research; Muscular dystrophy.
Type of support: Advocacy; Continuing support; Employee volunteer services; General/operating support; Program development; Sponsorships.
Geographic limitations: Giving primarily in areas of company operations, and to national organizations.

Harley-Davidson Foundation, Inc.

3700 W. Juneau Ave.
Milwaukee, WI 53208-2818 (414) 343-4001
Application address: P.O. Box 653, Milwaukee, WI 53201; URL: http://www.harley-davidson.com/en_US/Content/Pages/Foundation/foundation.html?locale=en_US&bmLocale=en_US

Establishment information: Established in 1994 in WI.
Donors: Harley-Davidson, Inc.; Karl Eberle; John Mink.
Contact: Mary Ann Martiny, Secy.
Financial data (yr. ended 12/31/11): Assets, $22,362,077 (M); gifts received, $4,000,577; expenditures, $2,653,449; qualifying distributions, $2,498,923; giving activities include $2,498,923 for grants.
Purpose and activities: The foundation supports organizations involved with arts and culture, the environment, and health. Special emphasis is directed toward programs designed to promote education and community revitalization.
Fields of interest: Arts; Education; Environment; Health care; Employment; Human services; Community development, neighborhood development; Community/economic development; United Ways and Federated Giving Programs.
Programs:
Community Revitalization: The foundation supports programs designed to promote community revitalization. Special emphasis is directed toward programs designed to promote job enablers; neighborhoods; and social services.
Education: The foundation supports programs designed to promote education. Special emphasis is directed toward programs designed to promote core curriculum and academic enhancement.
Education Matching Grants: The foundation matches contributions made by employees of Harley-Davidson to K-12 schools and institutions of higher education on a one-for-two basis per employee, per year.
Employee Volunteer Services: The foundation awards grants to nonprofit organizations with which employees of Harley-Davidson volunteer.
Type of support: Curriculum development; Employee matching gifts; Employee volunteer services; Program development; Scholarship funds.
Geographic limitations: Giving primarily in Kansas City, MO, York, PA, and Milwaukee, Menomonee Falls, Tomahawk, and Wauwatosa, WI; giving also to national organizations.
Support limitations: No support for political candidates, athletic teams, or religious organizations not of direct benefit to the entire community. No grants to individuals, or for political causes, general operating, or endowment funds; generally, no funding for conferences or capital campaigns.
Publications: Application guidelines; Corporate giving report; IRS Form 990 or 990-PF printed copy available upon request.
Application information: Applications accepted. The Wisconsin Common Grant Application Form is accepted. Application form required. Applicants should submit the following:
1) timetable for implementation and evaluation of project
2) how project will be sustained once grantmaker support is completed
3) results expected from proposed grant
4) population served
5) name, address and phone number of organization
6) copy of IRS Determination Letter
7) brief history of organization and description of its mission
8) copy of most recent annual report/audited financial statement/990
9) how project's results will be evaluated or measured
10) listing of board of directors, trustees, officers and other key people and their affiliations

11) detailed description of project and amount of funding requested
12) copy of current year's organizational budget and/or project budget
13) listing of additional sources and amount of support
Initial approach: Download application form and mail to application address
Copies of proposal: 1
Deadline(s): Mar. 9, July 6, and Oct. 12
Officers and Directors:* Tonit M. Calaway*, Pres.; John A. Olin*, V.P. and C.F.O.; J. Darrell Thomas, V.P. and Treas.; Mary Anne Martiny, Secy.; Joanne M. Bischmann; Matthew S. Levatich; Patrick Smith.
EIN: 391769946

1733
Harleysville Group Inc.
355 Maple Ave.
Harleysville, PA 19438-2297
(215) 256-5000
FAX: (302) 655-5049

Company URL: http://www.harleysvillegroup.com
Establishment information: Established in 1979.
Company type: Public company
Company ticker symbol and exchange: HGIC/NASDAQ
Business activities: Operates holding company; sells property and casualty insurance.
Business type (SIC): Insurance/fire, marine, and casualty; holding company
Financial profile for 2011: Number of employees, 1,717; assets, $3,267,070,000; sales volume, $995,160,000; pre-tax net income, $16,260,000; expenses, $978,900,000; liabilities, $2,513,510,000
Corporate officers: William W. Scranton III, Chair.; Michael L. Browne, Pres. and C.E.O.; Mark R. Cummins, Exec. V.P., C.I.O., and Treas.; Arthur E. Chandler, Sr. V.P. and C.F.O.; Robert A. Kauffman, Sr. V.P., Secy., and Genl. Counsel; Beth A. Friel, Sr. V.P., Human Resources
Board of directors: William W. Scranton III, Chair.; Barbara A. Austell; W. Thacher Brown; Michael L. Browne; G. Lawrence Buhl, C.P.A.; Mirian M. Graddick-Weir; Jerry S. Rosenbloom; William E. Storts
Subsidiaries: Great Oaks Insurance Co., Dublin, OH; Harleysville Insurance Co. of New Jersey, Moorestown, NJ; Harleysville-Atlantic Insurance Co., Savannah, GA; Huron Insurance Co., Harleysville, PA; Lake States Insurance Co., Traverse City, MI; Mid-America Insurance Co., Harleysville, PA; Minnesota Fire and Casualty Co., Minnetonka, MN; New York Casualty Insurance Co., Watertown, NY; Worcester Insurance Co., Worcester, MA
Giving statement: Giving through the Care Force.
Company EIN: 510241172

Care Force
355 Maple Ave.
Harleysville, PA 19438-2297 (215) 256-5286
E-mail: information@harleysvillegroup.com;
URL: http://www.harleysvillegroup.com/abo/abo_5_1.html

Purpose and activities: Harleysville makes charitable contributions to nonprofit organizations involved with education, the environment, housing, safety, human services, and community development. Support is given primarily in areas of company operations.
Fields of interest: Education; Environment; Housing/shelter, development; Safety/disasters; Human services; Community development, neighborhood development.
Type of support: Employee volunteer services.
Geographic limitations: Giving primarily in areas of company operations.
Application information: Applications not accepted. Contributes only to pre-selected organizations.

1734
Harnish Group Inc.
17025 W. Valley Hwy.
Tukwila, WA 98188-5519 (425) 251-5800
FAX: (425) 251-5831

Company URL: http://www.ncmachinery.com
Establishment information: Established in 1929.
Company type: Private company
Business activities: Operates equipment dealership; services, rents, and sells new and used Caterpillar machines.
Business type (SIC): Industrial machinery and equipment—wholesale
Financial profile for 2010: Number of employees, 1,000
Corporate officers: John J. Harnish, Chair. and C.E.O.; Richard Bellin, C.F.O.; Steve Wallace, C.I.O.; Troy Hickey, V.P., Sales and Mktg.; Mark Beatty, Cont.
Board of director: John Harnish, Chair.
Giving statement: Giving through the Harnish Foundation.

Harnish Foundation
17035 W. Valley Hwy.
Tukwila, WA 98188-5519

Establishment information: Established in 2005 in WA.
Donors: John J. Harnish; Harnish Group, Inc.
Financial data (yr. ended 12/31/11): Assets, $13,105,038 (M); gifts received, $2,877,298; expenditures, $306,607; qualifying distributions, $305,000; giving activities include $305,000 for grants.
Purpose and activities: The foundation supports camps and organizations involved with secondary education, health, substance abuse treatment, children, and residential care.
Fields of interest: Secondary school/education; Health care; Substance abuse, treatment; Recreation, camps; Children, services; Residential/custodial care.
Type of support: General/operating support.
Geographic limitations: Giving primarily in MN and WA.
Support limitations: No grants to individuals.
Application information: Applications not accepted. Contributes only to pre-selected organizations.
Officers and Directors:* John J. Harnish*, Pres. and Treas.; Richard C. Bellin, V.P.; Katherine A. Harnish*, V.P.; Jennifer C. Harnish*, Secy.; Dean Blackford; John W. Harnish; Troy Hickey.
EIN: 383730146
Selected grants: The following grants are a representative sample of this grantmaker's funding activity:
$50,000 to Eastside Academy, Bellevue, WA, 2011.
$50,000 to Treehouse, Seattle, WA, 2011.
$25,000 to Church of Mary Magdalene, Seattle, WA, 2011.
$25,000 to Eagle Mount Billings, Billings, MT, 2011.
$5,000 to Eagle Mount Bozeman, Bozeman, MT, 2011.

1735
Harper Brush Works, Inc.
400 N. 2nd St.
Fairfield, IA 52556-2416 (800) 223-7894

Company URL: http://www.harperbrush.com
Establishment information: Established in 1900.
Company type: Private company
Business activities: Manufactures commercial and industrial brushes.
Business type (SIC): Manufacturing/miscellaneous
Corporate officers: Barry D. Harper, Pres.; Garry Wells, C.F.O.; Paul Moberg, C.I.O.
Board of director: Wendall King
Offices: Stockton, CA; Greenville, NC
Giving statement: Giving through the Harper Brush Works Foundation, Inc.

Harper Brush Works Foundation, Inc.
402 N. 2nd St.
Fairfield, IA 52556-0608 (641) 472-7876

Donors: Harper Brush Works; Harper Corp.; Texas Feathers, Inc.
Contact: Diana Spates, Pres.
Financial data (yr. ended 08/31/11): Assets, $4,321 (M); expenditures, $4,524; qualifying distributions, $4,250; giving activities include $4,250 for grants.
Purpose and activities: The foundation supports organizations involved with education and Christianity.
Fields of interest: Libraries/library science; Education; Christian agencies & churches.
Type of support: Grants to individuals; Scholarships—to individuals.
Geographic limitations: Giving primarily in Fairfield, IA, and TX.
Application information: Applications accepted. Application form not required.
Initial approach: Proposal
Deadline(s): None
Directors: Barry Harper; Don Cummings; Gary Sparks.
EIN: 421145331

1736
Harris Corporation
1025 W. NASA Blvd.
Melbourne, FL 32919-0001 (321) 727-9100
FAX: (321) 724-3973

Company URL: http://www.harris.com
Establishment information: Established in 1895.
Company type: Public company
Company ticker symbol and exchange: HRS/NYSE
Business activities: Designs, manufactures, distributes, and services electronic systems, semiconductors, communications equipment, and office equipment.
Business type (SIC): Communications equipment; electronic components and accessories; search and navigation equipment
Financial profile for 2012: Number of employees, 15,200; assets, $5,592,800,000; sales volume, $5,451,300,000; pre-tax net income, $841,900,000; expenses, $4,510,200,000; liabilities, $3,653,900,000
Fortune 1000 ranking: 2012—429th in revenues, 849th in profits, and 561st in assets
Corporate officers: Thomas A. Dattilo, Chair.; William M. Brown, Pres. and C.E.O.; Daniel R. Pearson, Exec. V.P. and C.O.O.; Gary L. McArthur, Sr. V.P. and C.F.O.; Robert L. Duffy, Sr. V.P., Human

Resources, and Admin.; Scott T. Mikuen, V.P., Genl. Counsel, and Secy.
Board of directors: Thomas A. Dattilo, Chair.; William M. Brown; Peter W. Chiarelli; Terry D. Growcock; Lewis Hay III; Karen Katen; Stephen P. Kaufman; Leslie F. Kenne; David B. Rickard; James C. Stoffel; Gregory T. Swienton; Hansel E. Tookes II
Plants: Redwood Shores, Sunnyvale, CA; Colorado Springs, Denver, CO; Palm Bay, FL; Quincy, IL; Rochester, NY; Research Triangle Park, NC; Mason, OH; San Antonio, TX
International operations: Argentina; Australia; Austria; Bangladesh; Belgium; Bermuda; Brazil; Canada; Cayman Islands; Chile; China; Denmark; France; Germany; Ghana; Honduras; Hong Kong; Hungary; India; Japan; Kenya; Malaysia; Mauritius; Mexico; Netherlands; New Zealand; Nigeria; Poland; Singapore; South Africa; Thailand; United Kingdom
Giving statement: Giving through the Harris Corporation Contributions Program and the Harris Foundation.
Company EIN: 340276860

Harris Corporation Contributions Program

1025 W. NASA Blvd.
Melbourne, FL 32919-0001 (321) 727-9100
URL: http://harris.com/corporate_responsibility/

Purpose and activities: As a complement to its foundation, Harris also makes charitable contributions to nonprofit organizations directly. Support is given primarily in areas of company operations in the Melbourne, Florida, area.
Fields of interest: Elementary/secondary education; Higher education; Education; Food services; Housing/shelter, development; Disasters, preparedness/services; Human services, fund raising/fund distribution; Community/economic development; United Ways and Federated Giving Programs; Mathematics; Science; Military/veterans' organizations; General charitable giving.
Program:
Merit Scholarship Program: Harris annually awards two college scholarships to children of Harris employees who are selected as National Merit Scholarship winners. Scholarship winners are selected based on PSAT/NMSQT scores and academic achievement. The program is administered by the National Merit Scholarship Corporation.
Type of support: Donated products; Employee volunteer services; Employee-related scholarships; General/operating support; Sponsorships.
Geographic limitations: Giving primarily in areas of company operations in the Melbourne, FL, area.
Publications: Corporate report.
Application information: Applications not accepted. Contributes only to pre-selected organizations.

Harris Foundation

1025 W. NASA Blvd., M.S. A-11P
Melbourne, FL 32919-0002 (321) 724-3167
E-mail: harris.foundation@harris.com; URL: http://harris.com/corporate_responsibility/foundation.aspx

Establishment information: Incorporated in 1958 in OH.
Donor: Harris Corp.
Financial data (yr. ended 06/30/11): Assets, $2,361,321 (M); gifts received, $10,719; expenditures, $1,490,076; qualifying distributions, $1,490,031; giving activities include $1,336,916 for 145 grants (high: $530,000; low: $50) and $136,898 for employee matching gifts.
Purpose and activities: The foundation supports organizations involved with arts and culture, education, health, human services, and civic affairs. Special emphasis is directed toward science, math, engineering, and technology (STEM).
Fields of interest: Arts; Higher education; Education; Health care; Children/youth, services; Human services; United Ways and Federated Giving Programs; Mathematics; Engineering/technology; Science; Public affairs.
Programs:
Harris Aid-to-Education Gift Matching Program: The foundation matches contributions made by employees of Harris to institutions of higher education on a one-for-one basis up to $10,000 per individual, per year.
Harris Community Gift Matching Program: The foundation matches contributions made by employees of Harris to nonprofit organizations involved with charitable, cultural, or civic programs.
Type of support: Capital campaigns; Employee matching gifts; General/operating support.
Geographic limitations: Giving limited to areas of company operations, with emphasis on FL.
Support limitations: No support for discriminatory organizations, school organizations or clubs, radio/TV stations, or Boy & Girl Scout Troops, religious organizations not of direct benefit to the entire community, professional associations, labor organizations, fraternal organizations, or social clubs. No grants to individuals, or for school sponsored events, athletics, home-based child care/educational services, walk-a-thons, ride-a-thons, dance-a-thons, or bowl-a-thons, salaries, travel, accounting, license fees, maintenance or repairs, office expenses, utilities, insurance, or property management or taxes.
Publications: Application guidelines.
Application information: Applications accepted. Support is limited to 1 contribution per organization during any given year. Support for capital campaigns (bricks and mortar) are given priority. Application form not required. Applicants should submit the following:
1) statement of problem project will address
2) population served
3) name, address and phone number of organization
4) copy of IRS Determination Letter
5) list of company employees involved with the organization
6) explanation of why grantmaker is considered an appropriate donor for project
7) detailed description of project and amount of funding requested
8) contact person
9) listing of additional sources and amount of support
10) plans for acknowledgement
11) how project's results will be evaluated or measured
12) copy of most recent annual report/audited financial statement/990
13) listing of board of directors, trustees, officers and other key people and their affiliations
14) copy of current year's organizational budget and/or project budget
Initial approach: E-mail proposal to foundation
Deadline(s): Feb. 1 to 28
Officers and Trustee: Howard L. Lance, Pres.; Jeffrey S. Shuman, V.P.; Scott T. Mikuen, Secy.; Gary L. McArthur, Treas.; Cindy Kane.
EIN: 346520425
Selected grants: The following grants are a representative sample of this grantmaker's funding activity:
$35,000 to North Carolina State University, Raleigh, NC, 2010. For general use.
$25,000 to American Heart Association, Dallas, TX, 2010. For general use.
$14,000 to American Cancer Society, Atlanta, GA, 2010. For general use.
$12,500 to Pennsylvania State University, University Park, PA, 2010. For general use.
$11,115 to Cystic Fibrosis Foundation, Bethesda, MD, 2010. For general use.
$6,540 to Childrens Home Society of Florida, Winter Park, FL, 2010. For general use.
$5,000 to Clemson University, Clemson, SC, 2010. For general use.
$5,000 to University of Michigan, Ann Arbor, MI, 2010. For general use.
$4,779 to Leukemia & Lymphoma Society, White Plains, NY, 2010. For general use.
$2,500 to Soldiers Angels, Pasadena, CA, 2010. For general use.

1737
Harris myCFO, Inc.

1080 Marsh Rd., Ste. 100
Menlo Park, CA 94025-1025
(650) 210-5000

Company URL: https://www.harrismycfo.com
Establishment information: Established in 2003.
Company type: Subsidiary of a private company
Business activities: Operates wealth management company.
Business type (SIC): Security and commodity services
Financial profile for 2009: Number of employees, 130
Corporate officers: Joe Calabrese, Pres.; Carol Flick, C.F.O.
Giving statement: Giving through the Harris myCFO Foundation.

Harris myCFO Foundation

P.O. Box 10196
Palo Alto, CA 94303-0996 (650) 210-5000
FAX: (310) 407-1192;
E-mail: info@mycfofoundation.org; Toll-free tel.: (877) 692-3605; URL: http://www.harrismycfofoundation.org/

Establishment information: Established in 2000 in CA.
Contact: Claudia B. Sangster, Pres. and Exec. Dir.
Financial data (yr. ended 06/30/11): Revenue, $1,079,703; assets, $206,480 (M); expenditures, $91,666,841; giving activities include $91,663,542 for grants.
Purpose and activities: The foundation sponsors donor-advised funds designed to assist individuals in effective charitable giving; and seeks to promote, educate, and facilitate effective giving by its donors in order to positively impact the world.
Fields of interest: Philanthropy/voluntarism.
Application information: Applications not accepted. Contributes only to pre-selected organizations.
Officers: Claudia B. Sangster*, Pres. and Exec. Dir.; Jody Giles*, Secy.; James R. Cody*, Treas.
Directors: Carolyn Aver; Kevin Compton; Cecily Mistarz; Georganne F. Perkins.
EIN: 770558454

1738
Harris Teeter, Inc.
701 Crestdale Rd.
P.O. Box 10100
Matthews, NC 28105 (704) 844-3904

Company URL: http://www.harristeeter.com
Establishment information: Established in 1949.
Company type: Subsidiary of a public company
Business activities: Operates supermarkets.
Business type (SIC): Groceries—retail
Financial profile for 2010: Number of employees, 300; sales volume, $2,450,000,000
Corporate officers: Thomas W. Dickson, Chair. and C.E.O.; Fred J. Morganthall II, Pres. and C.O.O.; John B. Woodlief, Exec. V.P. and C.F.O.; Rodney C. Antolock, Exec. V.P., Opers.; Jeff D. Sherman, Sr. V.P., Finance, and Secy.; Ronald Volger, V.P. and Treas.; Charles F. Corbeil, V.P., Mktg.
Board of director: Thomas W. Dickson, Chair.
Subsidiary: Ruddick Investment Co., Charlotte, NC
Division: Hunter Farms Div., Charlotte, NC
Giving statement: Giving through the Harris Teeter, Inc. Corporate Giving Program.

Harris Teeter, Inc. Corporate Giving Program
701 Crestdale Rd.
Matthews, NC 28105-1700 (704) 844-3100
URL: http://www.harristeeter.com/Default.aspx?pageId=221

Purpose and activities: Harris Teeter makes charitable contributions to food banks and nonprofit organizations involved with K-12 education, youth sports, disaster relief, and on a case by case basis. Support is given primarily in areas of company operations in Washington, DC, Delaware, Florida, Georgia, Maryland, North Carolina, South Carolina, Tennessee, and Virginia.
Fields of interest: Elementary/secondary education; Food banks; Disasters, preparedness/services; Athletics/sports, amateur leagues; Youth development; United Ways and Federated Giving Programs; General charitable giving.
Type of support: Cause-related marketing; Employee-related scholarships; In-kind gifts; Sponsorships.
Geographic limitations: Giving primarily in areas of company operations in Washington, DC, DE, FL, GA, MD, NC, SC, TN, and VA.
Support limitations: No support for political or religious organizations. No grants to individuals (except for employee-related scholarships), or for deficit reduction, operating expenses, trips, tours, or student exchange programs.
Application information: Applications accepted. The Corporate Contributions Committee reviews all requests. Application form required.
Initial approach: Complete online application form
Deadline(s): None
Final notification: 6 weeks

1739
Harris Trust and Savings Bank
111 W. Monroe St., 3rd Fl.
Chicago, IL 60603-4096 (312) 461-2121

Company URL: http://www.harrisbank.com
Establishment information: Established in 1882.
Company type: Subsidiary of a public company
Business activities: Operates commercial bank; provides securities brokerage services.
Business type (SIC): Banks/commercial; brokers and dealers/security
Corporate officers: Peter McNitt, Vice-Chair.; Ellen M. Costello, Pres. and C.E.O.; Pamela Piarowski, Sr. V.P. and C.F.O.; Andy Plews, Sr. V.P., Corp. Comms.
Board of director: Peter McNitt, Vice-Chair.
Subsidiaries: Atlantic Nominees, Chicago, IL; Harris Capital Holdings, Inc., Chicago, IL; Harris Mid-America Holdings, Inc., Chicago, IL; Harris Preferred Capital Corp., Chicago, IL; Harris Processing Corp., Chicago, IL
Historic mergers: AMCORE Financial, Inc. (January 1, 2011)
Giving statement: Giving through the Harris Trust and Savings Bank Corporate Giving Program.

Harris Trust and Savings Bank Corporate Giving Program
c/o Community Affairs and Economic Devel.
111 W. Monroe St.
Chicago, IL 60603-4096 (312) 461-5834
E-mail: community.affairs@harrisbank.com;
URL: https://www4.harrisbank.com/us/about/community?nav=left

Purpose and activities: As a complement to its foundation, Harris Trust and Savings also makes charitable contributions to nonprofit organizations directly. Support is given primarily in areas of company operations in Arizona, Florida, Illinois, Indiana, Kansas, Minnesota, Missouri, Nevada, and Wisconsin.
Fields of interest: Arts; Employment; Housing/shelter; Community/economic development; Financial services Economically disadvantaged.
Type of support: Employee volunteer services; General/operating support; Sponsorships.
Geographic limitations: Giving primarily in areas of company operations in AZ, FL, IL, IN, KS, MN, MO, NV, and WI.
Application information:
Initial approach: E-mail letter of inquiry to headquarters for application information
Contributions Committee: Yasmin Bates, Exec. V.P.; Mary H. Houpt.
Number of staff: 5 full-time professional; 1 full-time support.

1740
Harriss and Covington Hosiery Mills, Inc.
1250 Hickory Chapel Rd.
High Point, NC 27260-7187
(336) 882-6811

Company URL: http://www.harrissandcov.com
Establishment information: Established in 1920.
Company type: Private company
Business activities: Manufactures hosiery.
Business type (SIC): Hosiery and knitted fabrics
Financial profile for 2011: Number of employees, 275
Corporate officers: Ned Covington, Pres. and C.E.O.; Darrell L. Frye, V.P., Finance and Admin.
Giving statement: Giving through the Harriss and Covington Foundation.

The Harriss and Covington Foundation
P.O. Box 1909
High Point, NC 27261-1909

Donor: Harriss and Covington Hosiery Mills, Inc.
Financial data (yr. ended 12/31/11): Assets, $1,667 (M); gifts received, $25,000; expenditures, $228,528; qualifying distributions, $228,190; giving activities include $228,190 for grants.
Purpose and activities: The foundation supports arts councils and organizations involved with human services.
Fields of interest: Arts councils; Boy scouts; Human services.
Type of support: General/operating support.
Geographic limitations: Giving primarily in High Point, NC.
Support limitations: No grants to individuals.
Application information: Applications not accepted. Unsolicited requests for funds not accepted.
Officers and Directors:* Edward H. Covington*, Pres.; Darrell L. Frye*, Secy.
EIN: 582037679

1741
Harsco Corporation
350 Poplar Church Rd.
Camp Hill, PA 17011 (717) 763-7064
FAX: (717) 763-6424

Company URL: http://www.harsco.com
Establishment information: Established in 1853.
Company type: Public company
Company ticker symbol and exchange: HSC/NYSE
Business activities: Manufactures defense, industrial service, building, and engineered products.
Business type (SIC): Metal products/fabricated; asphalt and roofing materials; plastic products/miscellaneous; metal products/structural; motor vehicles and equipment; railroad equipment; transportation equipment/miscellaneous
Financial profile for 2012: Number of employees, 18,500; assets, $2,975,970,000; sales volume, $3,046,020,000; pre-tax net income, -$218,500,000; expenses, $3,220,810,000; liabilities, $2,164,130,000
Fortune 1000 ranking: 2012—704th in revenues, 944th in profits, and 753rd in assets
Corporate officers: Henry W. Knueppel, Chair.; Patrick K. Decker, Pres. and C.E.O.; Stephen J. Schnoor, Sr. V.P., C.F.O., and Treas.; Douglas Eubanks, Sr. V.P. and C.I.O.; Barry E. Malamud, V.P. and Corp. Cont.; Verona A. Dorch, V.P., Genl. Counsel, and Corp. Secy.
Board of directors: Henry W. Knueppel, Chair.; James F. Earl; Kathy G. Eddy; David C. Everitt; Stuart E. Graham; Terry D. Growcock; James M. Loree; Andrew J. Sordoni III; Robert C. Wilburn
Subsidiaries: BMY Co., Bellefontaine, OH; BMY Co., Windsor, PA; BMY Co., York, PA; BMY-Combat Systems, York, PA; BMY-Wheeled Vehicles, Marysville, OH; Capitol Manufacturing Co., Westerville, OH; Fairmont Tamper Co., West Columbia, SC; Heckett MultiServ, Butler, PA; IKG Industries, Clark, NJ; Patent Construction Systems, Paramus, NJ; Patterson-Kelley Co., East Stroudsburg, PA; Reed Minerals, Highland, IN; Sherwood Co., Lockport, NY; Taylor-Wharton Gas Equipment, Camp Hill, PA
International operations: Argentina; Australia; Austria; Bahrain; Belgium; Bermuda; Brazil; Canada; Chile; China; Czech Republic; Denmark; Ecuador; Egypt; Finland; France; Germany; Gibraltar; Greece; Guatemala; Guernsey; Hungary; India; Ireland; Italy; Jersey; Latvia; Luxembourg; Malaysia; Mexico; Netherlands; New Zealand; Norway; Panama; Peru; Poland; Portugal; Qatar; Romania; Russia; Saint Kitts-Nevis; Saudi Arabia; Scotland; Serbia; Singapore; Slovakia; South Africa; Spain; Sweden;

Thailand; Ukraine; United Arab Emirates; United Kingdom
Giving statement: Giving through the Harsco Corporation Fund.
Company EIN: 231483991

Harsco Corporation Fund

c/o Harsco Corp.
350 Poplar Church Rd.
Camp Hill, PA 17001-2521 (717) 763-7064
Application address for charitable gifts: c/o Robert G. Yocum, Chair., Harsco Corporation Fund, P.O. Box 8888, Camp Hill, PA 17001-8888

Establishment information: Established in 1956 in PA.
Donor: Harsco Corp.
Contact: Robert G. Yocum, Chair.
Financial data (yr. ended 12/31/11): Assets, $88,410 (M); expenditures, $392,445; qualifying distributions, $380,385; giving activities include $380,385 for grants.
Purpose and activities: The foundation supports organizations involved with arts and culture, education, health, housing development, human services, and the steel industry.
Fields of interest: Media/communications; Arts; Higher education; Scholarships/financial aid; Education; Health care; Housing/shelter, development; Human services; Business/industry; United Ways and Federated Giving Programs.
Programs:
Harsco Corporation Fund International Scholarship Program: The foundation awards up to 15 college scholarship of $2,000 to $3,500 to children of non-U.S. based employees of Harsco Corporation. The program is administered by the Institute of International Education (IIE).
Harsco Corporation Fund Scholarship Program: The foundation awards up to 12 college scholarships of $2,000 to $3,500 to children of employees of Harsco Corporation. The program is administered by the National Merit Scholarship Corp.
Type of support: Continuing support; Employee matching gifts; Employee-related scholarships; General/operating support.
Geographic limitations: Giving on a national basis in areas of company operations, with some emphasis on NY and PA.
Support limitations: No grants to individuals (except for employee-related scholarships), or for special projects, building or endowments, or research; no loans.
Application information: Applications accepted. Application form not required. Applicants should submit the following:
1) detailed description of project and amount of funding requested
Initial approach: Letter of inquiry
Board meeting date(s): Apr. and as required
Deadline(s): None
Officers and Trustees:* Robert G. Yocum*, Chair.; Salvatore D. Fazzolari*, Secy.-Treas.; D. C. Hathaway.
EIN: 236278376
Selected grants: The following grants are a representative sample of this grantmaker's funding activity:
$147,935 to Institute of International Education, New York, NY, 2011.
$30,000 to United Way of the Capital Region, Enola, PA, 2011.
$10,000 to Cultural Enrichment Fund, Harrisburg, PA, 2011.
$5,000 to Harrisburg Area Community College, Harrisburg, PA, 2011.
$5,000 to Open Stage of Harrisburg, Harrisburg, PA, 2011.
$5,000 to United Way of Mason County, Ludington, MI, 2011.
$5,000 to YMCA, Carlisle Family, Carlisle, PA, 2011.
$2,500 to American Cancer Society, Columbia, SC, 2011.
$2,500 to Foundation for Enhancing Communities, Harrisburg, PA, 2011.
$2,000 to United Way of Monroe County, Tannersville, PA, 2011.

1742
The Hartford Financial Services Group, Inc.

(formerly ITT Hartford Group, Inc.)
1 Hartford Plz.
Hartford, CT 06155 (860) 547-5000
FAX: (888) 322-8444

Company URL: http://www.thehartford.com
Establishment information: Established in 1810.
Company type: Public company
Company ticker symbol and exchange: HIG/NYSE
International Securities Identification Number: US4165151048
Business activities: Provides diversified financial services; sells property, casualty, and life insurance.
Business type (SIC): Insurance/fire, marine, and casualty; insurance/life
Financial profile for 2012: Number of employees, 22,500; assets, $298,513,000,000; sales volume, $26,412,000,000; pre-tax net income, -$527,000,000; expenses, $26,939,000,000; liabilities, $276,066,000,000
Fortune 1000 ranking: 2012—112th in revenues, 901st in profits, and 20th in assets
Forbes 2000 ranking: 2012—355th in sales, 1781st in profits, and 100th in assets
Corporate officers: Liam E. McGee, Chair., Pres., and C.E.O.; Brion Johnson, C.I.O.; Christopher J. Swift, Exec. V.P. and C.F.O.; Alan J. Kreczko, Exec. V.P. and Genl. Counsel; Martha Gervasi, Exec. V.P., Human Resources
Board of directors: Liam E. McGee, Chair.; Robert B. Allardice III; Trevor Fetter; Paul G. Kirk, Jr.; Kathryn Mikells; Michael G. Morris; Thomas A. Renyi; Charles B. Strauss; H. Patrick Swygert
Subsidiaries: First State Insurance Co., Boston, MA; Hartford Fire Insurance Co., Hartford, CT; Hartford Life and Accident Insurance Co., Hartford, CT
International operations: Argentina; Bermuda; Brazil; Canada; Hong Kong; Ireland; Japan; United Kingdom
Giving statement: Giving through the Hartford Financial Services Group, Inc. Corporate Giving Program.
Company EIN: 133317783

The Hartford Financial Services Group, Inc. Corporate Giving Program

(formerly ITT Hartford Group, Inc. Corporate Giving Program)
1 Hartford Plz.
Hartford, CT 06115-0001 (860) 547-5000
E-mail: communityrelations@thehartford.com;
URL: http://www.thehartford.com/utility/about-thehartford/corporate-social-responsibility/

Purpose and activities: The Hartford makes charitable contributions to nonprofit organizations involved with education, the environment, human services, and community development. Support is given primarily in the Hartford, Connecticut, area, with emphasis on Asylum Hill.
Fields of interest: Education; Environment; Human services; Community/economic development.
Type of support: Employee volunteer services; General/operating support; Program development; Sponsorships.
Geographic limitations: Giving primarily in the Hartford, CT, area, with emphasis on Asylum Hill; giving also to national organizations.
Application information: Applications accepted.
Committee meeting date(s): E-mail letter of inquiry to headquarters
Number of staff: 2 full-time professional; 2 part-time professional.

1743
The Hartford Steam Boiler Inspection and Insurance, Co.

(also known as HSB)
1 State St.
Hartford, CT 06103-3199 (860) 722-1866

Company URL: http://www.hsb.com
Establishment information: Established in 1866.
Company type: Subsidiary of a public company
Ultimate parent company: American International Group, Inc.
Business activities: Provides engineering services; sells property insurance.
Business type (SIC): Engineering, architectural, and surveying services; insurance/fire, marine, and casualty
Corporate officers: Anthony J. Kuczinski, Chair.; Greg Barats, Pres. and C.E.O.; Nancy Onken, Exec. V.P., Genl. Counsel, and Corp. Secy.; Peter Richter, C.F.O.; Loren P. Shoemaker, Sr. V.P. and C.O.O.; William J. Rucci, Sr. V.P. and C.I.O.; Susan W. Ahrens, Sr. V.P. and Human Resources
Board of director: Anthony J. Kuczinski, Chair.
Giving statement: Giving through the Hartford Steam Boiler Inspection and Insurance Company Contributions Program.

The Hartford Steam Boiler Inspection and Insurance Company Contributions Program

1 State St.
Hartford, CT 06102-5024 (860) 722-1866
URL: http://www.hsb.com/HSBGroup/HSB_In_The_Community.aspx

Purpose and activities: Hartford Steam Boiler makes charitable contributions to nonprofit organizations involved with the arts, education, health, and civic responsibility; employees also serve on boards of directors. Support is given primarily in the greater Hartford, Connecticut, area.
Fields of interest: Arts, cultural/ethnic awareness; Arts; Education; Health care; Human services, fund raising/fund distribution; Human services; United Ways and Federated Giving Programs; Public affairs.
Program:
Matching Gifts Programs: Hartford Steam Boiler has a matching gift program that doubles its employees' donations to educational and medical organizations and facilities.
Type of support: Employee matching gifts; Employee volunteer services; General/operating support; Loaned talent.
Geographic limitations: Giving primarily in the greater Hartford, CT, area.

Application information:
Initial approach: Proposal to headquarters

1744
The Hartz Mountain Corporation
400 Plaza Dr.
Secaucus, NJ 07094-3605 (201) 348-1200

Company URL: http://www.hartz.com
Establishment information: Established in 1932.
Company type: Subsidiary of a foreign company
Business activities: Manufactures and distributes pet supplies.
Business type (SIC): Grain mill products, including pet food; soaps, cleaners, and toiletries; manufacturing/miscellaneous; groceries—wholesale; non-durable goods—wholesale
Corporate officers: William D. Ecker, Pres. and C.E.O.; Albert Ahn, V.P., Corp. Comms.
Giving statement: Giving through the Hartz Mountain Corporation Contributions Program.

The Hartz Mountain Corporation Contributions Program
400 Plaza Dr.
Secaucus, NJ 07094-3688 (201) 271-4800
URL: http://www.hartz.com/About_Hartzpet/Community%20Outreach.aspx

Purpose and activities: Hartz Mountain makes charitable contributions to programs designed to improve the lives of pets. Support is given on a national basis.
Fields of interest: Animal welfare.
Type of support: Donated products; General/operating support; In-kind gifts; Sponsorships.
Geographic limitations: Giving on a national basis.
Publications: Grants list.

1745
Hartzell Industries, Inc.
1025 S. Roosevelt Ave.
Piqua, OH 45356 (937) 773-7054
FAX: (937) 773-6160

Company URL: http://www.hartzellindustries.com/
Establishment information: Established in 1875.
Company type: Private company
Business activities: Operates holding company; sells walnut lumber and veneer wholesale.
Business type (SIC): Lumber and construction materials—wholesale; wood millwork; holding company
Corporate officers: James Robert Hartzell, Chair.; Jeffery A. Bannister, C.E.O.; Michael C. Bardo, Pres. and Treas.; Jane M. Farley, Corp. Secy.
Board of directors: James Robert Hartzell, Chair.; William Barkalow; Melinda H. Grubbs; Janet Johnston; Julie H. Kaebnick; Michael R. Light; George D. Sumner; Kathleen H. Thorpe
Giving statement: Giving through the Hartzell-Norris Charitable Trust.

Hartzell-Norris Charitable Trust
P.O. Box 630858
Cincinnati, OH 45263-0858
URL: http://www.hartzellindustries.com/careers/community.html

Establishment information: Established in 1943 in OH.
Donor: Hartzell Industries, Inc.
Financial data (yr. ended 10/31/11): Assets, $4,636,358 (M); expenditures, $300,909; qualifying distributions, $232,713; giving activities include $232,513 for 70 grants (high: $16,000; low: $100).
Purpose and activities: The foundation supports organizations involved with arts and culture, education, health, cancer, housing development, human services, and Christianity.
Fields of interest: Arts; Elementary/secondary education; Higher education; Education; Hospitals (general); Health care; Cancer; Housing/shelter, development; Boy scouts; Human services; United Ways and Federated Giving Programs; Christian agencies & churches.
Type of support: General/operating support.
Geographic limitations: Giving primarily in OH.
Application information: Applications not accepted. Unsolicited requests for funds not accepted.
Trustee: Fifth Third Bank of Western Ohio.
EIN: 316024521
Selected grants: The following grants are a representative sample of this grantmaker's funding activity:
$7,500 to Miami University, Oxford, OH, 2009. For scholarship.
$5,000 to University of Toledo, Toledo, OH, 2009. For scholarship.
$5,000 to Xavier University, Cincinnati, OH, 2009. For scholarship.
$4,800 to Adriel School, West Liberty, OH, 2009. For program services.
$4,125 to United Way of Jay County, Portland, IN, 2009. For program services.
$3,600 to Rehabilitation Center for Neurological Development, Piqua, OH, 2009. For program services.
$2,500 to John Jay Center for Learning, Portland, IN, 2009. For program services.
$2,500 to Ohio Northern University, Ada, OH, 2009. For scholarship.
$2,500 to Ohio University, Athens, OH, 2009. For scholarship.
$2,400 to Health Partners of Miami County, Troy, OH, 2009. For program services.

1746
Harvey Construction Company
523 W. Mayes St.
P.O. Box 4648
Jackson, MS 39213-6220 (601) 366-5246

Company URL: http://www.harveyconstructionco.com/
Company type: Private company
Business activities: Provides nonresidential general contract construction services.
Business type (SIC): Contractors/general nonresidential building
Corporate officer: Kevin McIntyre, C.F.O.
Giving statement: Giving through the Lucian A. Harvey and Jerri Jeter Harvey Foundation.

Lucian A. Harvey and Jerri Jeter Harvey Foundation
2222 Eastover Dr.
Jackson, MS 39211-6721

Establishment information: Established in 2001 in MS.
Donor: Harvey Construction Co.
Financial data (yr. ended 12/31/11): Assets, $176,501 (M); expenditures, $10,905; qualifying distributions, $10,305; giving activities include $10,305 for grants.
Purpose and activities: The foundation supports community foundations and museums and organizations involved with performing arts, K-12 education, leukemia, and children services.
Fields of interest: Arts; Education; Human services.
Type of support: Annual campaigns; General/operating support.
Geographic limitations: Giving limited to MS.
Support limitations: No grants to individuals.
Application information: Applications not accepted. Unsolicited requests for funds not accepted.
Officers: Jerri Jeter Harvey, Pres.; Lucia Harvey White, V.P.; Robin L. Harvey, Secy.; Lucian A. Harvey, Treas.
EIN: 010554145

1747
Hasbro, Inc.
1027 Newport Ave.
P.O. Box 1059
Pawtucket, RI 02862-1059 (401) 431-8697
FAX: (401) 727-5544

Company URL: http://www.hasbro.com
Establishment information: Established in 1926.
Company type: Public company
Company ticker symbol and exchange: HAS/NASDAQ
International Securities Identification Number: US4180561072
Business activities: Designs, manufactures, and markets children's and family leisure time and entertainment games, toys, and products.
Business type (SIC): Games, toys, and sporting and athletic goods
Financial profile for 2012: Number of employees, 5,500; assets, $4,325,390,000; sales volume, $4,088,980,000; pre-tax net income, $453,400,000; expenses, $3,537,200,000; liabilities, $2,818,010,000
Fortune 1000 ranking: 2012—576th in revenues, 438th in profits, and 634th in assets
Corporate officers: Alfred J. Verrecchia, Chair.; Brian D. Goldner, Pres. and C.E.O.; Deborah M. Thomas, Sr. V.P. and C.F.O.; Barbara Finigan, Sr. V.P. and Secy.; Martin R. Trueb, Sr. V.P. and Treas.
Board of directors: Alfred J. Verrecchia, Chair.; Basil L. Anderson; Alan R. Batkin; Frank J. Biondi, Jr.; Kenneth A. Bronfin; John M. Connors, Jr.; Michael W.O. Garrett; Lisa Gersh; Brian D. Goldner; Jack M. Greenberg; Alan G. Hassenfeld; Tracy A. Leinbach; Edward M. Philip
Subsidiaries: Cranium, Seattle, WA; Wizards of the Coast, Inc., Seattle, WA
Giving statement: Giving through the Hasbro Gift of Play Program and the Hasbro Children's Fund, Inc.
Company EIN: 050155090

Hasbro Gift of Play Program
(formerly Hasbro, Inc. Corporate Giving Program)
1027 Newport Ave., P.O. Box 1059
Pawtucket, RI 02862-1059 (401) 431-8447
URL: http://www.hasbro.com/corporate/community-relations/gifts-of-play.cfm

Purpose and activities: As a complement to its foundation, Hasbro also makes charitable contributions to nonprofit organizations directly. Support is given on a national basis, with emphasis on areas of company operations. Support for hospital and shelter playrooms is limited to Los Angeles, California, Springfield, Massachusetts, Rhode Island, and Renton, Washington. Support for

holiday giving programs is limited to areas of company operations.
Fields of interest: Medical care, in-patient care; Hospitals (general); Health care; Housing/shelter, homeless; Disasters, preparedness/services; Recreation, camps; Recreation; Children/youth, services; Children, adoption; Military/veterans' organizations Economically disadvantaged.
Type of support: Continuing support; Donated products; General/operating support; In-kind gifts; Program development.
Geographic limitations: Giving on a national basis, with emphasis on areas of company operations. Support for hospital and shelter playrooms is limited to Los Angeles, CA, Springfield, MA, RI, and Renton, WA. Support for holiday giving programs is limited to areas of company operations.
Support limitations: No support for schools. No grants to individuals, or for fundraisers, including carnivals, auctions, and raffles, incentive programs, intermediary donations, or lost or broken pieces to donated games or toys.
Publications: Application guidelines.
Application information: Applications accepted. Unsolicited requests are not accepted for holiday giving programs. Contributes only to pre-selected organizations for hospital playrooms, orphanage programs, and disaster relief services. Application form required.
Initial approach: Complete online application
Deadline(s): June 30 for summer camps; Sept. 1 for non-holiday Fisher House giving, and shelter playrooms; Oct. 1 for holiday parties for children of deployed soldiers, and Fisher House holiday giving

Hasbro Children's Fund, Inc.

(formerly Hasbro Charitable Trust, Inc.)
c/o Hasbro, Inc.
1027 Newport Ave.
Pawtucket, RI 02861-2539 (401) 727-5429
E-mail: kdavis@hasbro.com; URL: http://www.hasbro.org

Establishment information: Established in 1984 in RI.
Donor: Hasbro, Inc.
Contact: Karen Davis, V.P., Community Rels.
Financial data (yr. ended 12/25/11): Assets, $8,946,642 (M); gifts received, $1,527; expenditures, $5,870,228; qualifying distributions, $5,870,102; giving activities include $5,722,733 for 107 grants (high: $1,500,000; low: $90) and $15,560 for 30 employee matching gifts.
Purpose and activities: The fund supports programs designed to assist children in triumphing over critical life obstacles; and bring the joy of play into their lives. Special emphasis is directed toward programs designed to provide hope to children who need it most; play for children who otherwise would not be able to experience that joy; and empowerment of youth through service.
Fields of interest: Elementary/secondary education; Zoos/zoological societies; Hospitals (general); Health care; Mental health/crisis services; Food services; Food banks; Housing/shelter; Disasters, preparedness/services; Recreation, parks/playgrounds; Recreation; Philanthropy/voluntarism Children; Economically disadvantaged.
Programs:
Dollars for Doers: The fund matches contributions made by employees of Hasbro to nonprofit organizations involved with children. The fund matches up to $250 per employee, per year for employees who volunteer at least 48 hours per year with the organization and up to $2,500 per employee, per year for employees who serve on the board of directors or as a member of a capital campaign steering committee of the organization.
Employee Matching Gifts Program: The fund matches contributions made by employees of Hasbro to institutions of higher education from $25 to $2,500 per employee, per year.
Local Grants: The fund supports programs designed to provide stability for children in crisis; pediatric physical and mental health services; hunger security; education in collaboration with state leadership; and quality out of school time initiatives. The primary focus of local grants changes on an annual basis.
Strategic Partnerships: The fund partners with global and national organizations to ensure long-lasting strategic relationships that maximize benefits for children. Partnerships include Operation Smile, World Vision, generationOn, Tragedy Assistance Program for Survivors, SOS Children's Villages, Association of Hole in the Wall Camps, Hasbro Children's Hospital, and Big Apple Circus.
Type of support: Building/renovation; Capital campaigns; Continuing support; Employee matching gifts; Employee volunteer services; General/operating support; Program development.
Geographic limitations: Giving primarily in Los Angeles, CA, Springfield, MA, RI, and Renton, WA; giving also to regional, national, and U.S.-based international organizations through strategic partnership program.
Support limitations: No support for religious organizations, political organizations, or schools. No grants to individuals, or for research, scholarships, travel, endowments, advertising, sponsorship of recreational activities, fundraisers, or auctions; no loans; no cash-free grants.
Publications: Application guidelines; Corporate giving report.
Application information: Applications accepted. The fund awards grants through an RFP process. Visit website for updated guidelines. Unsolicited requests from regional, national, and U.S.-based international organizations are not accepted. Application form required.
Initial approach: Complete online letter of inquiry
Board meeting date(s): Oct./Nov.
Deadline(s): Varies
Officers: David D.R. Hargreaves, C.O.O.; Brian Goldner, Pres.; Barbara Finigan, Sr. V.P. and Secy.; Deborah Thomas, Sr. V.P. and C.F.O.; Martin Trueb, Sr. V.P. and Treas.; Jeffrey Barkan, Sr. V.P and Cont.
Number of staff: 3 full-time professional; 1 full-time support; 1 part-time support.
EIN: 222538470
Selected grants: The following grants are a representative sample of this grantmaker's funding activity:
$1,350,000 to Points of Light Institute, Atlanta, GA, 2010. For generationOn.
$478,662 to Rhode Island Hospital Foundation, Providence, RI, 2010. For GetWellNetwork.
$266,000 to American Lebanese Syrian Associated Charities, Memphis, TN, 2010. For Boundless Playground Built at Target House.
$250,000 to Give Kids the World, Kissimmee, FL, 2010. For Enchanted Castle of Miracles - Star Tower.
$250,000 to Springfield Library and Museums Association, Springfield, MA, 2010. For Hasbro's GameLand.
$50,000 to CIDRZ Foundation, Washington, DC, 2010. For Puppet Therapy for Children Dealing with HIV/AIDS.
$50,000 to Providence Childrens Museum, Providence, RI, 2010. For Capacity Building, The Climber and Underland.
$15,000 to Boys and Girls Club of Pawtucket, Pawtucket, RI, 2010. For Success through After School Programming.
$10,000 to Rhode Island School of Design, Providence, RI, 2010. For Project Open Door (POD).
$10,000 to YMCA of Greater Seattle, Eastside Branch, Bellevue, WA, 2010. For Renton School-aged Child Care.

1748
Haskell Slaughter Young & Rediker, LLC

2001 Park Pl. Tower, Ste. 1400
Birmingham, AL 35203 (205) 251-1000

Company URL: http://www.hsy.com
Establishment information: Established in 1973.
Company type: Private company
Business activities: Provides legal services.
Business type (SIC): Legal services
Corporate officer: J. Michael Rediker, Partner
Board of directors: Deepa Bhate; Carol Clark; Renee Carter; Jesse Hernandez; Larry Harper; Mark Jackson; Bruce Larson; Lyndy Rogers; Judy Merritt; Marianne Prime; Deborah Vance
Subsidiary: Haskell Slaughter Young & Gallion, LLC, Montgomery, AL
Office: New York, NY
Giving statement: Giving through the Haskell, Slaughter & Young Charitable Foundation, Inc.

Haskell, Slaughter & Young Charitable Foundation, Inc.

(formerly Haskell Slaughter Young & Gallion Charitable Foundation, Inc.)
1400 Park Pl. Tower
2001 Park Pl. N.
Birmingham, AL 35203-2700 (205) 251-1000

Establishment information: Established in 1998 in AL.
Financial data (yr. ended 12/31/11): Assets, $118 (M); gifts received, $200; expenditures, $29,540; qualifying distributions, $29,390; giving activities include $29,390 for grants.
Purpose and activities: The foundation supports organizations involved with arts and culture, education, patient services, cancer research, legal aid, human services, and community development.
Fields of interest: Visual arts; Performing arts; Arts; Education, fund raising/fund distribution; Higher education; Law school/education; Health care, patient services; Cancer research; Legal services; Children, services; Developmentally disabled, centers & services; Human services; Community/economic development.
Type of support: Program development.
Geographic limitations: Giving primarily in Birmingham, AL.
Support limitations: No grants to individuals.
Application information: Applications accepted. Application form required. Applicants should submit the following:
1) brief history of organization and description of its mission
2) detailed description of project and amount of funding requested
Initial approach: Proposal
Deadline(s): None
Officers: Ross N. Cohen, Pres.; Thomas L. Krebs, Secy.; Mark E. Ezell, Treas.

Directors: Thomas T. Gallion III; Wyatt R. Haskell; J. Michael Rediker; William M. Slaughter; Frank M. Young III.
EIN: 631193730

1749
Hastings Mutual Insurance Company

404 E. Woodlawn Ave.
Hastings, MI 49058-1091 (269) 945-3405

Company URL: http://www.hastingsmutual.com
Establishment information: Established in 1885 as Michigan Mutual Tornado, Cyclone and Windstorm Insurance Company.
Company type: Mutual company
Business activities: Sells property and casualty insurance.
Business type (SIC): Insurance/fire, marine, and casualty
Corporate officers: Joseph J. Babiak, Jr., Chair., Pres., and C.E.O.; Michael W. Puerner, V.P., Secy., and Genl. Counsel; Michael T. Kinnary, V.P., Treas., and C.F.O.; Keith E. Jandahl, V.P., Mktg.; Dana A. Walters, V.P., Human Resources; Kristy R. Dombkowski, Cont.
Board of directors: Joseph J. Babiak, Jr., Chair.; Douglas J. Finn; Christopher J. Fluke, C.P.A.; Frederic L. Halbert; Kellie M. Haines; John R. Kerschen; Mark A. Kolanowski; Bruce J. Osterink; Norice Thorlund Rasmussen; James R. Toburen, C.P.A.
Giving statement: Giving through the Hastings Mutual Insurance Company Charitable Foundation.

Hastings Mutual Insurance Company Charitable Foundation

404 E. Woodlawn Ave.
Hastings, MI 49058-1005 (269) 945-3405

Establishment information: Established in 2004 in MI.
Donor: Hastings Mutual Insurance Co.
Contact: Cindy Beckwith
Financial data (yr. ended 12/31/11): Assets, $2,523,317 (M); expenditures, $144,686; qualifying distributions, $141,415; giving activities include $141,415 for 45 grants (high: $15,144; low: $500).
Purpose and activities: The foundation supports programs designed to provide for essential needs, including food, clothing, and medical services to at-risk youth and financially challenged families; and programs designed to promote general welfare and betterment of the community.
Fields of interest: Hospitals (general); Health care; Food services; Big Brothers/Big Sisters; Youth, services; Homeless, human services; Human services; Community/economic development.
Type of support: Building/renovation; Equipment; General/operating support; Management development/capacity building; Matching/challenge support; Program development.
Geographic limitations: Giving limited to IL, IN, MI, OH, and WI.
Support limitations: No grants to individuals.
Application information: Applications accepted. Organizations receiving support are asked to submit a final report. Application form required. Applicants should submit the following:
1) name, address and phone number of organization
2) geographic area to be served
3) detailed description of project and amount of funding requested

Initial approach: Contact foundation for application form
Deadline(s): Mar. 31, June 30, Sept. 30, and Dec. 31
Final notification: 45 days

Officers: Joseph Babiak, Pres.; Michael W. Puerner, Secy.; Michael T. Kinnary, Treas.
Directors: Bruce Ostennk; Mark Kolanowski; James Toburen; William H. Wallace.
EIN: 202031029

1750
Hautly Cheese Company, Inc.

251 Axminister Dr.
St. Louis, MO 63026-2932 (636) 533-4400

Company URL: http://www.hautly.com
Establishment information: Established in 1934.
Company type: Private company
Business activities: Sells cheese wholesale.
Business type (SIC): Groceries—wholesale
Corporate officers: Alan C. Hautly, Pres.; Barbara A. Fisher, Secy.
Giving statement: Giving through the Hautly Foundation.

The Hautly Foundation

c/o Alan C. Hautly
251 Axminister Dr.
Fenton, MO 63026

Establishment information: Established in 2001 in MO.
Donor: Hautly Cheese Co., Inc.
Financial data (yr. ended 12/31/11): Assets, $216,184 (M); expenditures, $2,975; qualifying distributions, $0.
Purpose and activities: The foundation supports hospitals and organizations involved with secondary and higher education.
Fields of interest: Secondary school/education; Higher education; Hospitals (general).
Type of support: General/operating support.
Geographic limitations: Giving primarily in St. Louis, MO.
Support limitations: No grants to individuals.
Application information: Applications not accepted. Unsolicited requests for funds not accepted.
Trustees: Barbara Fisher; Alan C. Hautly.
EIN: 431911162

1751
Havana Central

151 W. 46th St.
New York, NY 10036-8512 (212) 398-7440

Company URL: http://www.havanacentral.com
Establishment information: Established in 2002.
Company type: Private company
Business activities: Operates restaurant.
Business type (SIC): Restaurants and drinking places
Corporate officers: Jeremy Merrin, Pres.; Randy Talbot, V.P., Opers.
Giving statement: Giving through the Havana Central Corporate Giving Program.

Havana Central Corporate Giving Program

151 W 46th St.
New York, NY 10036-8512
URL: http://havanacentral.com/about/philanthropy/

Purpose and activities: Havana Central makes charitable contributions to nonprofit organizations involved with education and hunger. Support is given primarily in New York City; giving also to national and international organizations.
Fields of interest: Education; Food services.
Type of support: General/operating support.
Geographic limitations: Giving primarily in areas of company operations in New York, NY; giving also to national and international organizations.

1752
Haviland Plastic Products Co.

100 W. Main St.
P.O. Box 38
Haviland, OH 45851 (419) 622-3110
FAX: (419) 622-6911

Company URL: http://www.havilandplastics.com
Establishment information: Established in 1995.
Company type: Private company
Business activities: Manufactures blow-molded plastic products.
Business type (SIC): Plastic products/miscellaneous
Corporate officers: Craig Stoller, Pres.; Todd Stoller, Secy.-Treas.
Giving statement: Giving through the Samaritan Foundation.

Samaritan Foundation

P.O. Box 97
Haviland, OH 45851-0097 (419) 622-4611

Establishment information: Established in 2002 in OH.
Donor: Haviland Plastic Products Co.
Contact: Todd Stoller, Secy.-Treas.
Financial data (yr. ended 12/31/11): Assets, $4,652,343 (M); gifts received, $562,084; expenditures, $242,436; qualifying distributions, $240,550; giving activities include $240,550 for grants.
Purpose and activities: The foundation supports food banks and organizations involved with education, patient services, disaster relief, human services, and Christianity; awards grants and loans to indigent individuals in economic distress; and awards college scholarships to students located in Paulding County, Ohio.
Fields of interest: Secondary school/education; Education; Health care, patient services; Food banks; Disasters, preparedness/services; American Red Cross; Children/youth, services; Human services; Christian agencies & churches Economically disadvantaged.
Type of support: General/operating support; Grants to individuals; Loans—to individuals; Scholarships—to individuals.
Geographic limitations: Giving primarily in IN, KY, and OH.
Publications: Application guidelines.
Application information: Applications accepted. An application form is required for scholarships. Requests for scholarships should include a copy of the applicant's parents' IRS Form 1040, a photograph, and college transcripts.

Initial approach: Proposal; contact foundation for application form for scholarships
Deadline(s): None
Officers: Russell Stoller, Pres.; Craig Stoller, V.P.; Todd Stoller, Secy.-Treas.
EIN: 341957355
Selected grants: The following grants are a representative sample of this grantmaker's funding activity:
$48,000 to West Ohio Food Bank, Lima, OH, 2010. For general purposes.

1753
Hawaii National Bank

45 N. King St.
Honolulu, HI 96817-5107 (808) 528-7755

Company URL: http://www.hawaiinational.com
Establishment information: Established in 1960.
Company type: Private company
Business activities: Operates commercial bank.
Business type (SIC): Banks/commercial
Corporate officers: Warren K.K. Luke, Chair., Pres., and C.E.O.; Robert Nobriga, Exec. V.P. and C.F.O.
Board of directors: Warren K.K. Luke, Chair.; William S. Chee; Arthur S.K. Fong; Tan Tek Lum; Arthur C. Tokin
Giving statement: Giving through the Hawaii National Foundation.

Hawaii National Foundation

45 N. King St., 7th Fl.
Honolulu, HI 96817

Establishment information: Established in 1988 in HI.
Donor: Hawaii National Bank.
Financial data (yr. ended 12/31/11): Assets, $150,159 (M); expenditures, $8,199; qualifying distributions, $5,500; giving activities include $5,500 for grants.
Purpose and activities: The foundation supports food banks and organizations involved with education, athletics, human services, and public policy research.
Fields of interest: Education; Recreation; Human services.
Type of support: General/operating support.
Geographic limitations: Giving primarily in Honolulu, HI.
Support limitations: No grants to individuals.
Application information: Applications not accepted. Unsolicited requests for funds not accepted.
Officers and Directors:* Warren Kwan Kee Luke, Chair. and Pres.; Robert Nobriga, V.P. and Treas.; Bryan Luke, V.P. and Secy.
EIN: 990268927

1754
Hawaii Planing Mill, Ltd.

16-166 Melekahiwa St.
Keaau, HI 96749-8016 (808) 966-5466

Company URL: http://www.hpmhawaii.com/about
Establishment information: Established in 1921.
Company type: Private company
Business activities: Sells building construction materials wholesale.
Business type (SIC): Lumber and construction materials—wholesale; lumber and other building materials—retail
Corporate officers: Robert M. Fujimoto, Chair.; Jon Y. Miyata, V.P. and C.E.O.
Board of director: Robert M. Fujimoto, Chair.
Giving statement: Giving through the Hawaii Planing Mill Foundation.

Hawaii Planing Mill Foundation

380 Kanoelehua Ave.
Hilo, HI 96720-4618

Donor: Hawaii Planing Mill, Ltd.
Financial data (yr. ended 11/30/11): Assets, $601,606 (M); expenditures, $90,400; qualifying distributions, $90,360; giving activities include $90,360 for 61 grants (high: $10,000; low: $200).
Purpose and activities: The foundation supports food banks and organizations involved with secondary and higher education, conservation, heart disease, youth development, and children services.
Fields of interest: Education; Health care; Health organizations.
Type of support: General/operating support.
Geographic limitations: Giving limited to HI.
Support limitations: No grants to individuals.
Application information: Applications not accepted. Unsolicited requests for funds not accepted.
Officers: Robert M. Fujimoto, Chair. and Treas.; Michael K. Fujimoto, Vice-Chair.; Roberta F. Chu*, Secy.
EIN: 990207048

1755
Hawaiian Electric Industries, Inc.

(also known as HEI, Inc.)
1001 Bishop St., Ste. 2900
P.O. Box 730
Honolulu, HI 96813 (808) 543-5662
FAX: (808) 543-7966

Company URL: http://www.hei.com
Establishment information: Established in 1891.
Company type: Public company
Company ticker symbol and exchange: HE/NYSE
Business activities: Operates holding company; generates, transmits, and distributes electricity; operates savings bank.
Business type (SIC): Electric services; savings institutions; holding company
Financial profile for 2012: Number of employees, 3,870; assets, $10,149,130,000; sales volume, $3,374,990,000; pre-tax net income, $217,410,000; expenses, $3,090,800,000; liabilities, $8,555,270,000
Fortune 1000 ranking: 2012—656th in revenues, 671st in profits, and 386th in assets
Corporate officers: Jeffrey N. Watanabe, Chair.; Constance H. Lau, Pres. and C.E.O.; James A. Ajello, Exec. V.P., C.F.O., and Treas.; Chet A. Richardson, Exec. V.P., Genl. Counsel, Secy., and C.A.O.
Board of directors: Jeffrey N. Watanabe, Chair.; Thomas B. Fargo; Peggy Y. Fowler; Constance H. Lau; A. Maurice Myers; Keith P. Russell; James K. Scott; Kelvin H. Taketa; Barry K. Taniguchi
Subsidiaries: Hawaiian Electric Co., Inc., Honolulu, HI; Hawaiian Tug & Barge Corp., Honolulu, HI; HEI Investment Corp., Honolulu, HI; HEI Power Corp., Honolulu, HI; Malama Pacific Corp., Honolulu, HI
Giving statement: Giving through the Hawaiian Electric Industries, Inc. Corporate Giving Program and the Hawaiian Electric Industries Charitable Foundation.
Company EIN: 990208097

Hawaiian Electric Industries, Inc. Corporate Giving Program

900 Richards St.
Honolulu, HI 96813-2919 (808) 543-5662
URL: http://www.hei.com/

Hawaiian Electric Industries Charitable Foundation

(also known as H.E.I. Charitable Foundation)
P.O. Box 730
Honolulu, HI 96808-0730 (808) 543-7601
FAX: (808) 543-7602; E-mail: heicf@hei.com;
URL: http://www.hei.com/heicf/heicf.html

Establishment information: Established in 1984 in HI.
Donor: Hawaiian Electric Industries, Inc.
Contact: Rena Wang
Financial data (yr. ended 12/31/11): Assets, $3,997,265 (M); gifts received, $3,000,000; expenditures, $1,720,287; qualifying distributions, $1,706,501; giving activities include $1,636,530 for 72 grants and $69,971 for employee matching gifts.
Purpose and activities: The foundation supports organizations involved with education, the environment, family services, and community development.
Fields of interest: Education; Environment; Family services; Community/economic development.
Type of support: Capital campaigns; Continuing support; Employee matching gifts; General/operating support; Program development.
Geographic limitations: Giving limited to HI.
Support limitations: No support for political, religious, veterans', fraternal, or labor organizations. No grants to individuals or for advertising, dinners, or tournaments.
Publications: Annual report; Application guidelines.
Application information: Applications accepted. Support is limited to 1 contribution per organization during any given year. Application form required.
Applicants should submit the following:
1) staff salaries
2) statement of problem project will address
3) population served
4) copy of IRS Determination Letter
5) brief history of organization and description of its mission
6) copy of most recent annual report/audited financial statement/990
7) how project's results will be evaluated or measured
8) listing of board of directors, trustees, officers and other key people and their affiliations
9) detailed description of project and amount of funding requested
10) copy of current year's organizational budget and/or project budget
11) listing of additional sources and amount of support
12) plans for acknowledgement

Initial approach: Download application form and mail proposal and application form to foundation
Copies of proposal: 1
Board meeting date(s): Quarterly
Deadline(s): Jan. 1, Apr. 1, July 1, and Oct. 1

Officers and Directors:* Constance H. Lau*, Pres.; James A. Ajello, V.P., Finance and Treas.; Charles A. Richardson*, Secy.; Jeffrey N. Watanabe; Andrew Chang.
Number of staff: 1 full-time professional; 1 full-time support.
EIN: 990230697

Selected grants: The following grants are a representative sample of this grantmaker's funding activity:
$436,000 to United Way Statewide Association of Hawaii, Honolulu, HI, 2009.
$100,000 to Enterprise Honolulu, Honolulu, HI, 2009.
$55,000 to United Way, Aloha, Honolulu, HI, 2009. For College Connections, Teach for America, Hawaii Alliance for Community Based Economic Development and Honolulu Habitat for Humanity.
$50,000 to Bishop Museum, Honolulu, HI, 2009.
$47,000 to Scholarship America, Saint Peter, MN, 2009.
$25,000 to Friends of the 50th State Commemoration, Honolulu, HI, 2009.
$25,000 to YWCA of Oahu, Honolulu, HI, 2009.
$20,000 to Maui Economic Development Board, Kihei, HI, 2009.
$15,000 to University of Hawaii Foundation, Honolulu, HI, 2009.
$15,000 to YMCA of Honolulu, Honolulu, HI, 2009.

1756
Hawaiian Host, Inc.

500 Alakawa St., Ste. 111
Honolulu, HI 96817 (808) 848-0500

Company URL: http://www.hawaiianhost.com
Establishment information: Established in 1960.
Company type: Private company
Business activities: Produces chocolate candy.
Business type (SIC): Sugar, candy, and salted/roasted nut production
Corporate officers: Dennis Teranishi, Pres. and C.E.O.; Norman Kukino, V.P., Sales
Giving statement: Giving through the Mamoru & Aiko Takitani Foundation, Inc.

Mamoru & Aiko Takitani Foundation, Inc.

(formerly Takitani Foundation, Inc.)
81 S. Hotel St., Ste. 308
Honolulu, HI 96813-3145 (808) 228-0209
Mailing address: P.O. Box 10687, Honolulu, HI 96816-0687; Additional tel.: (808) 247-6085; URL: http://www.hawaiianhost.com/foundation

Establishment information: Established in 1976 in HI.
Donors: Hawaiian Host, Inc.; Aiko Takitani.
Financial data (yr. ended 12/31/11): Assets, $5,675,860 (M); expenditures, $255,965; qualifying distributions, $135,079; giving activities include $10,000 for 2 grants and $125,079 for 77 grants to individuals (high: $5,000; low: $500).
Purpose and activities: The foundation awards college scholarships to high school seniors living in Hawaii.
Fields of interest: Higher education; Boys & girls clubs; Youth, services.
Program:
Scholarships: The foundation annually awards over 50 $1,000 college scholarships to high school seniors living in Hawaii. In addition, ten state finalists receive an additional $2,000, one student receives a $5,000 Outstanding Award, and two students receive $10,000 Distinguished Awards. Awards are based on financial need, community service, and scholastic achievement.
Type of support: Scholarship funds; Scholarships—to individuals.
Geographic limitations: Giving limited to HI.
Application information: Applications accepted. Application form required.
Initial approach: Contact school administrator for an application form
Deadline(s): None
Officers: Michael W. Perry, Chair.; Hideo Kondo, Pres.; Janice Luke Loo, V.P.; Mildred Higashi, Secy.; Stuart Ho, Treas.
Directors: Brett G. Schlemmer; Karen Uno.
EIN: 510212114

1757
Hawkins Construction Company

2516 Deer Park Blvd.
Omaha, NE 68105-3771 (402) 342-1607

Company URL: http://www.hawkins1.com/
Establishment information: Established in 1922.
Company type: Private company
Business activities: Provides construction services for buildings, runways, highways, bridges, and other projects.
Business type (SIC): Construction/miscellaneous heavy; contractors/general residential building
Corporate officers: Fred Hawkins, Jr., C.E.O.; Kim Hawkins, Pres.; Mathew Miller, Exec. V.P. and C.F.O.; Chris Hawkins, V.P. and Genl. Counsel
Giving statement: Giving through the Hawkins Charitable Trust.

Hawkins Charitable Trust

2516 Deer Park Blvd.
Omaha, NE 68105-3771 (402) 342-1607

Establishment information: Established in 1964 in NE.
Donor: Hawkins Construction Co.
Contact: Fred Hawkins Sr., Tr.
Financial data (yr. ended 12/31/11): Assets, $4,194,442 (M); gifts received, $200,000; expenditures, $254,884; qualifying distributions, $253,804; giving activities include $253,804 for grants.
Purpose and activities: The foundation supports organizations involved with education, health, baseball, human services, and business promotion.
Fields of interest: Higher education; Education; Hospitals (specialty); Health care; Athletics/sports, baseball; Boys & girls clubs; Boy scouts; Children/youth, services; Human services; Community development, business promotion; United Ways and Federated Giving Programs.
Type of support: Annual campaigns; Building/renovation; General/operating support; Scholarship funds.
Geographic limitations: Giving primarily in NE.
Support limitations: No grants to individuals.
Application information: Applications accepted. Application form not required. Applicants should submit the following:
1) detailed description of project and amount of funding requested
2) statement of problem project will address
Initial approach: Proposal
Deadline(s): None
Trustees: Chris Hawkins; Kim Hawkins; Fred Hawkins, Jr.; Fred Hawkins, Sr.
EIN: 476041927
Selected grants: The following grants are a representative sample of this grantmaker's funding activity:
$80,000 to University of Nebraska Foundation, Omaha, NE, 2010. For general funding.
$30,000 to Bellevue University, Bellevue, NE, 2010. For general funding.
$6,660 to Metropolitan Entertainment and Convention Authority, Omaha, NE, 2010. For general funding.
$5,000 to Creighton University, Omaha, NE, 2010. For general funding.
$1,500 to Georgia Tech Foundation, Atlanta, GA, 2010. For general funding.

1758
Haworth Inc.

(formerly Modern Products)
1 Haworth Ctr.
Holland, MI 49423-9576 (616) 393-3000

Company URL: http://www.haworth.com
Establishment information: Established in 1948.
Company type: Private company
Business activities: Designs and manufactures office furniture.
Business type (SIC): Furniture/office
Corporate officers: Matthew R. Haworth, Chair.; Franco Bianchi, Pres. and C.E.O.; Ann Harten, V.P., Human Resources; Richard G. Haworth, Chair. Emeritus
Board of director: Matthew R. Haworth, Chair.
International operations: Australia; Belgium; Canada; China; France; Germany; Hungary; India; Japan; Malaysia; Portugal; Singapore; Spain; Switzerland; United Kingdom
Giving statement: Giving through the Haworth Inc. Corporate Giving Program.

Haworth Inc. Corporate Giving Program

1 Haworth Ctr.
Holland, MI 49423-9570
URL: http://www.haworth.com/bottom-nav/company-info/sustainability/people

Contact: Virginia Conklin
Purpose and activities: Haworth makes charitable contributions to nonprofit organizations involved with the sciences, arts, medicine, and environmental preservation. Special emphasis is directed towards education. Support is given on a national and international basis in areas of company operations.
Fields of interest: Arts; Education; Environment; Science; General charitable giving.
Type of support: Donated products; Employee volunteer services; Employee-related scholarships; General/operating support.
Geographic limitations: Giving on a national and international basis in areas of company operations.
Application information: Applications accepted. Executive management handles giving. Application form not required.
Initial approach: Letter
Copies of proposal: 1
Committee meeting date(s): Quarterly
Deadline(s): None
Final notification: 3 months

1759
Haynes and Boone, LLP

2323 Victory Ave., Ste. 700
Dallas, TX 75219 (214) 651-5000

Company URL: http://www.hayboo.com
Establishment information: Established in 1964.

Company type: Private company
Business activities: Provides legal services.
Business type (SIC): Legal services
Corporate officer: Jim Miller, C.F.O.
Offices: Washington, DC; New York, NY; Austin, Fort Worth, Houston, Richardson, San Antonio, TX
Giving statement: Giving through the Haynes & Boone, LLP Pro Bono Program and the Haynes and Boone Foundation.

Haynes and Boone Foundation

2323 Victory Ave., Ste. 700
Dallas, TX 75219

Establishment information: Established in 2000 in TX.
Donor: Haynes and Boone, LLP.
Financial data (yr. ended 12/31/11): Assets, $289,807 (M); gifts received, $200,000; expenditures, $159,495; qualifying distributions, $159,400; giving activities include $159,400 for 16 grants (high: $31,500; low: $2,500).
Purpose and activities: The foundation supports bar associations and organizations involved with child welfare, housing development, safety, human services, social entrepreneurship, and women.
Fields of interest: Crime/violence prevention, child abuse; Legal services; Housing/shelter, development; Safety/disasters; Human services; Social entrepreneurship; United Ways and Federated Giving Programs Women.
Type of support: General/operating support.
Support limitations: No grants to individuals.
Application information: Applications not accepted. Unsolicited requests for funds not accepted.
Officers and Directors:* George W. Bramblett, Pres.; Michael M. Boone, V.P.; Tim Powers, V.P.; Terry W. Conner, Secy.; Barry F. McNeil; Robert E. Wilson.
EIN: 752860846

1760
Haynie & Associates, Inc.

120 Delta Rd., Ste. A
Lafayette, LA 70506-3032 (337) 235-6704

Company URL: http://www.haynieandassociates.com/
Establishment information: Established in 1980.
Company type: Private company
Business activities: Provides public relations services.
Business type (SIC): Management and public relations services
Corporate officers: Randy K. Haynie, Pres.; Ryan K. Haynie, Owner
Giving statement: Giving through the Haynie Family Foundation.

Haynie Family Foundation

108 Waterside Dr.
Lafayette, LA 70503-8407
E-mail: chris@haynie.com

Establishment information: Established in 1995 in LA.
Donors: Randy K. Haynie; Haynie & Associates, Inc.
Financial data (yr. ended 12/31/11): Assets, $961 (M); gifts received, $47,200; expenditures, $66,940; qualifying distributions, $66,940; giving activities include $66,050 for 29 grants (high: $25,000; low: $250).
Purpose and activities: The foundation supports hospices and community foundations and organizations involved with arts and culture, education, health, and Catholicism.
Fields of interest: Arts councils; Museums (art); Arts; Secondary school/education; Health care; Boy scouts; Residential/custodial care, hospices; Foundations (community); United Ways and Federated Giving Programs; Catholic agencies & churches.
Type of support: Capital campaigns; General/operating support.
Geographic limitations: Giving primarily in Lafayette, LA.
Support limitations: No grants to individuals.
Publications: Grants list.
Application information: Applications not accepted. Unsolicited requests for funds not accepted.
Officers: Dayna E. Haynie, Pres.; Ryan K. Haynie, V.P.; Mary Daynese Haynie, Secy.; Randy K. Haynie, Treas.
EIN: 721288377

1761
Hays Companies

IDS Ctr.
80 S. 8th St., Ste. 700
Minneapolis, MN 55402 (612) 333-3323
FAX: (612) 373-7270

Company URL: http://www.haysgroup.com
Establishment information: Established in 1994.
Company type: Private company
Business activities: Provides risk management consulting services; provides insurance brokerage services.
Business type (SIC): Management and public relations services; insurance agents, brokers, and services
Financial profile for 2011: Number of employees, 550
Corporate officers: James C. Hays, Pres. and C.E.O.; Stephen Lerum, Secy.-Treas. and C.F.O.
Offices: Phoenix, AZ; Los Angeles, San Francisco, CA; Denver, CO; Washington, DC; Fort Lauderdale, FL; Chicago, IL; Baltimore, MD; Boston, MA; Kansas City, St. Louis, MO; Morristown, NJ; Lake Success, NY; Portland, OR; Dallas, TX; Salt Lake City, UT; Milwaukee, WI
Giving statement: Giving through the Hays Foundation.

The Hays Foundation

IDS Ctr., 80 S. 8th St., Ste. 700
Minneapolis, MN 55402-2105

Establishment information: Established in 2001 in MN.
Donors: Hays Cos.; The Hays Group.
Financial data (yr. ended 12/31/11): Assets, $5,081 (M); gifts received, $40,000; expenditures, $39,025; qualifying distributions, $39,000; giving activities include $39,000 for grants.
Purpose and activities: The foundation supports organizations involved with education.
Fields of interest: Education.
Type of support: General/operating support; Scholarship funds.
Geographic limitations: Giving primarily in Minneapolis and Minnetonka, MN.
Support limitations: No grants to individuals.
Application information: Applications not accepted. Unsolicited requests for funds not accepted.
Officers: James C. Hays, Chair. and Pres.; William Mershon, V.P.; Stephen Lerum, Secy.-Treas.
EIN: 412021251

1762
HCA Holdings, Inc.

(also known as Hospital Corporation of America)
(formerly HCA, Inc.)
1 Park Plz.
Nashville, TN 37203-6527 (615) 344-9551

Company URL: http://www.hcahealthcare.com
Establishment information: Established in 1968.
Company type: Public company
Business activities: Operates hospitals and surgery centers.
Business type (SIC): Hospitals
Financial profile for 2012: Assets, $28,100,000,000; sales volume, $33,000,000,000
Fortune 1000 ranking: 2012—82nd in revenues, 130th in profits, and 194th in assets
Forbes 2000 ranking: 2012—287th in sales, 399th in profits, and 773rd in assets
Corporate officers: Richard M. Bracken, Chair. and C.E.O.; R. Milton Johnson, Pres. and C.F.O.; Noel Brown Williams, Sr. V.P. and C.I.O.; Donald W. Stinnett, Sr. V.P. and Cont.; Robert A. Waterman, Sr. V.P. and Genl. Counsel; David G. Anderson, Sr. V.P., Finance and Treas.; John M. Steele, Sr. V.P., Human Resources
Board of directors: Richard M. Bracken, Jr., Chair.; John Connaughton; Kenneth W. Freeman; Thomas F. Frist III; William R. Frist; Chris Gordon; R. Milton Johnson; Jay O. Light; Geoffrey G. Meyers; Michael W. Michelson; James C. Momtazee; Stephen G. Pagliuca; Wayne J. Riley, M.D.
Subsidiaries: Athens Community Hospital, Inc., Athens, TN; Center for Advanced Imaging, L.L.C., Roanoke, VA; Central Health Services Hospice, Inc., Atlanta, GA; Chicago Lakeshore Hospital, Chicago, IL; Columbine Psychiatric Center, Inc., Littleton, CO; Far West Division, Inc., Henderson, NV; Galen-Soch, Inc., Louisville, KY; Greenview Hospital, Inc., Bowling Green, KY; Healdsburg General Hospital, Inc., Healdsburg, CA; Hughston Sports Medicine Hospital, Columbus, GA; JFK Medical Center L.P., Atlantis, FL; Las Encinas Hospital, Pasadena, CA; Las Encinas Hospital, Pasadena, CA; Los Robles Regional Medical Center, Thousand Oaks, CA; Los Robles SurgiCenter, L.L.C., Thousand Oaks, CA; MCA Investment Co., Wilmington, DE; Mission Bay Memorial Hospital, Inc., San Diego, CA; Riverside Healthcare System, L.P., Riverside, CA; Riverside Surgicenter, L.P., Riverside, CA; Southwest Surgical Clinic, Inc., Wise, VA; Wesley Medical Center, L.L.C., Wichita, KS
International operations: Bermuda; Cayman Islands; Luxembourg; Switzerland; United Kingdom
Giving statement: Giving through the HCA Corporate Giving Program, the HCA Foundation, and the HCA Hope Fund.
Company EIN: 273865930

The HCA Foundation

(formerly Columbia/HCA Healthcare Foundation, Inc.)
1 Park Plz., 4th Fl. East
Nashville, TN 37203-6527 (615) 344-2390
FAX: (615) 344-5722;
E-mail: lois.abrams@hcahealthcare.com; Tel.: (615) 344-2343; e-mail: Corp.FoundationsGifts@HCAHealthcare.com;
URL: http://www.hcacaring.org/serving/

Establishment information: Established in 1992 in KY.
Donors: Columbia/HCA Healthcare Corp.; HCA—The Healthcare Co.; HCA Inc.
Contact: Lois Abrams, Grants Mgr.

Financial data (yr. ended 12/31/11): Assets, $70,898,318 (M); expenditures, $4,472,214; qualifying distributions, $4,540,580; giving activities include $4,472,214 for 720 grants (high: $300,000; low: $1).
Purpose and activities: The foundation supports organizations involved with education, health, mental health, hunger, housing, family services, and economic development. Special emphasis is directed toward programs designed to promote health and well-being; support childhood and youth development; and foster the arts in middle Tennessee.
Fields of interest: Arts education; Visual arts; Performing arts, opera; Historical activities; Arts; Education; Health care, clinics/centers; Health care; Food services; Housing/shelter, development; Housing/shelter; Youth development, community service clubs; Youth development, business; Youth development; YM/YWCAs & YM/YWHAs; Family services; Economic development; United Ways and Federated Giving Programs.
Programs:
Arts: The foundation supports programs designed to provide community outreach; and serve children and adults in the community through education.
Childhood and Youth Development: The foundation supports programs designed to encourage the positive growth and development of children and youth; and promote success in school, skill-building, character development, responsibility, service, and leadership.
Health and Well-Being: The foundation supports programs designed to promote health and well-being; provide basic health and human needs such as healthcare, housing, and food; and promote higher levels of mental and physical well-being.
Power of One Program: The foundation awards $500 to nonprofit organizations with which employees of HCA volunteer 25 hours. At the end of the year, ten agencies with the most recorded volunteer hours receive $1,000.
Team HCA Grant: The foundation awards up to $500 in material costs to teams of HCA employee volunteers for a service project of their choice.
Type of support: Annual campaigns; Building/renovation; Capital campaigns; Employee matching gifts; Employee volunteer services; Equipment; General/operating support; Matching/challenge support; Program development; Scholarship funds.
Geographic limitations: Giving primarily in middle TN.
Support limitations: No support for political organizations, individual churches or schools, organizations established less than 3 years ago, or arts and culture, athletic, environmental or wildlife, or civic or international affairs organizations. No grants to individuals, or for advertising or sponsorships or social events or similar fundraising activities.
Publications: Corporate giving report; Grants list; Newsletter.
Application information: Applications accepted. Letters of inquiry should be no longer than 1 to 2 pages. A full application may be requested at a later date. Organizations must have a full updated GivingMatters.com profile to be considered for funding. Organizations receiving support are asked to submit interim reports. Unsolicited capital requests are accepted on an exception basis. Application form not required. Applicants should submit the following:
1) copy of IRS Determination Letter
2) copy of most recent annual report/audited financial statement/990
3) how project's results will be evaluated or measured
4) listing of board of directors, trustees, officers and other key people and their affiliations
5) detailed description of project and amount of funding requested
6) copy of current year's organizational budget and/or project budget
7) additional materials/documentation

Initial approach: Letter of inquiry to foundation for new applicants; complete online application for returning grantees
Board meeting date(s): Feb., May, Aug., and Nov.
Deadline(s): Mar. 15, June 14, Sept. 13, and Dec. 14

Officers and Directors:* Richard M. Bracken*, Chair.; R. Milton Johnson, Vice-Chair.; Joanne Pulles*, Pres.; Gary Pack, Secy.; David G. Anderson, Treas.; Peter F. Bird, Jr.; Jana Davis; Ray Monroe; Bruce Moore, Jr.; Cheryl Read; John M. Steele; John Steakley; Noel Brown Williams.
Number of staff: 1 full-time professional; 1 full-time support.
EIN: 611230563
Selected grants: The following grants are a representative sample of this grantmaker's funding activity:
$300,000 to Frist Center for the Visual Arts, Nashville, TN, 2009. For Operational Funding.
$200,000 to Adventure Science Center, Nashville, TN, 2009. For the BodyQuest Exhibit on behalf of TriStar Family of Hospitals.
$154,722 to Habitat for Humanity, Nashville Area, Nashville, TN, 2009. For Capital Funding.
$100,000 to Campus for Human Development, Nashville, TN, 2009. For Capital Funding.
$100,000 to Centerstone Community Mental Health Centers, Nashville, TN, 2009. For Capital Funding.
$68,750 to HCA Hope Fund, Nashville, TN, 2009. For quarterly operational support.
$50,000 to Community Foundation of Middle Tennessee, Nashville, TN, 2009. For Program Funding.
$50,000 to Rutherford County Primary Care, CDB Primary Care and Hope Clinic, Murfreesboro, TN, 2009. For operational support.
$20,000 to Graceworks Health Clinic, Franklin, TN, 2009. For operational support.
$15,000 to Nashville Public Television, Nashville, TN, 2009. For program support.

HCA Hope Fund

P.O. Box 550
Nashville, TN 37202-0550 (877) 857-4673
FAX: (866) 337-4354;
E-mail: hopefund@hcahealthcare.com; URL: http://www.hcahopefund.org

Establishment information: Established in 2005 in TN.
Financial data (yr. ended 12/31/11): Revenue, $4,652,504; assets, $7,932,235 (M); gifts received, $4,631,576; expenditures, $1,434,025; giving activities include $1,179,578 for grants to individuals.
Purpose and activities: The fund provides emergency assistance to employees of the Hospital Corporation of America (HCA).
Fields of interest: Safety/disasters; Human services, emergency aid.
Program:
Emergency Grants: The fund provides grants to HCA employees and their immediate families who were affected by hardship due to an event beyond their control, including disasters, extended illness or injury, and other special situations. Levels of emergency assistance in cases related to a disaster are based on household size and historical levels of emergency assistance provided by disaster relief organizations. Grants in this category will not exceed $2,500. For extended illness/injury and other special circumstances, applicants may receive up to $1,000. Applicants are limited to $5,000 in assistance from the fund over their lifetime.
Type of support: Emergency funds; Grants to individuals.
Publications: Application guidelines.
Application information: Applications accepted. Application form required.
Initial approach: Submit application form along with copies of the bills requesting to be paid to local HCA human resources department
Officers and Directors:* John M. Steele*, Chair.; Joanne Pulles, Pres.; Susan Short Jones, Secy.; David Anderson, Treas.; Lee Adams; Beth Brill; Mike Cassity; Jana Joustra Davis; Sam Hazen; Guy Samuel; Doug Welch; Jeff Whitehorn; and 16 additional directors.
EIN: 470957872

1763
HCR Manor Care

(formerly HCR Manor Care, Inc.)
333 N. Summit St.
P.O. Box 10086
Toledo, OH 43604-2617 (419) 252-5500

Company URL: http://www.hcr-manorcare.com
Establishment information: Established in 1929.
Company type: Private company
Business activities: Provides health care services.
Business type (SIC): Nursing and personal care facilities
Financial profile for 2011: Number of employees, 61,000; sales volume, $4,500,000,000
Corporate officers: Paul A. Ormond, Chair., Pres., and C.E.O.; Steven M. Cavanaugh, Exec. V.P. and C.O.O; Steven M. Cavanaugh, V.P. and C.F.O.
Board of director: Paul A. Ormond, Chair.
Historic mergers: Manor Care, Inc. (September 25, 1998)
Giving statement: Giving through the HCR ManorCare Foundation, Inc.

HCR ManorCare Foundation, Inc.

(formerly Manor Care Foundation, Inc.)
333 N. Summit St.
P.O. Box 10086
Toledo, OH 43699-0086 (419) 252-5578
URL: http://www.hcr-manorcare.org/

Establishment information: Established in 1997 in MD.
Donors: Manor Care, Inc.; HCR Manor Care, Inc.; Virginia Hill Trust; Anna Mae Lee; Mary Louise and Marjori Lord Trust Fund; Elizabeth O'Brien; Florence MacGowen‡.
Contact: William White, Dir.
Financial data (yr. ended 05/31/12): Assets, $1,427,192 (M); expenditures, $171,652; qualifying distributions, $150,400; giving activities include $57,500 for 62 grants (high: $15,000; low: $500).
Purpose and activities: The foundation supports hospices and organizations involved with arts and culture, education, health, and senior citizens.
Fields of interest: Arts; Secondary school/education; Higher education; Nursing school/education; Education; Hospitals (general); End of life care; Palliative care; Nursing care; Health care; Residential/custodial care, hospices; Aging, centers/services Aging.

Programs:
Community Care Fund: The foundation awards $500 to local nonprofit organizations that provide services, support, or education to patients and residents of HCR ManorCare facilities. Organizations are selected by HCR ManorCare employees in select communities. Communities considered for support change regularly.
Corporate Office Charitable Event Giving Program: The foundation awards grants of up to $2,500 to support charitable events organized by HCR ManorCare employees. The event must feature nonprofit organizations that align with the company's focus on healthcare, disease treatment and research, senior care, and end-of-life or palliative care. The program is limited to Ohio.
Employee Matching Gift Program: The foundation matches contributions made by employees of HCR ManorCare to arts and cultural organizations and educational institutions on a one-for-one basis from $25 to $2,000, per employee, per year.
Volunteer Grant Program: The foundation awards $500 grants to nonprofit organizations with which employees of HCR ManorCare volunteer.
Type of support: Employee matching gifts; Employee volunteer services; General/operating support; Matching/challenge support; Program development.
Geographic limitations: Giving on a national basis in areas of company operations in AZ, CA, CO, CT, DE, FL, GA, IA, IL, IN, KS, KY, MD, MI, MN, MO, NC, ND, NJ, NM, NV, OH, OK, PA, SC, SD, TN, TX, UT, VA, WA, WI, and WV.
Support limitations: No support for professional associations, political or lobbying organizations, social organizations, or trade organizations. No grants to individuals, or for building or capital campaigns, endowments, fundraising events, overhead fees, advertising, political purposes, or continuing support.
Publications: Application guidelines.
Application information: Applications accepted. The Community Care Fund is offered in select communities each year. Support is limited to 1 contribution per organization during any given year.
Initial approach: Visit website for Community Care Fund
Board meeting date(s): June and Dec.
Deadline(s): Varies
Officers and Directors:* Rick Rump*, Pres.; Matt O'Connor*, Secy.; Eric Talbert*, Treas.; Martin Allen; Lynn Hood; Carla Hughes; Bruce Schroeder; William White.
Number of staff: 3 full-time professional; 2 full-time support.
EIN: 522031975

1764
Health Care Management Consulting, Inc.

(doing business as Welcome Homecare)
9570 Regency Square Blvd., Ste. 400
Jacksonville, FL 32225-9103
(904) 725-7100

Establishment information: Established in 1982.
Company type: Private company
Business activities: Provides home health care services; provides management consulting services.
Business type (SIC): Home healthcare services; management and public relations services
Corporate officers: Dwight Cenac, Pres.; Connie Cenac, Treas.
Giving statement: Giving through the Seacoast Charter Academy Inc.

Seacoast Charter Academy Inc.

9570 Regency Square Blvd.
Jacksonville, FL 32225-8100

Establishment information: Established as a company-sponsored operating foundation.
Donor: Health Care Management Consulting, Inc.
Contact: Paul Barker, Tr.
Financial data (yr. ended 06/30/11): Assets, $944 (M); gifts received, $1,679; expenditures, $23,488; qualifying distributions, $23,488.
Purpose and activities: The foundation awards grants to indigent individuals.
Fields of interest: Economically disadvantaged.
Application information: Applications accepted. Application form required.
Initial approach: Letter
Deadline(s): None
Officers and Directors:* Deborah L. Barker*, Pres.; Lisa A. Christopherson*, Secy.; Kathy S. Harcourt*, Treas.; Lindsey C. Brock III; Rosellen Gyland; Catherine S. Wolf.
EIN: 593222344

1765
Health Management Associates, Inc.

5811 Pelican Bay Blvd., Ste. 500
Naples, FL 34108-2710 (239) 598-3131
FAX: (302) 655-5049

Company URL: http://www.hma.com
Establishment information: Established in 1977.
Company type: Public company
Company ticker symbol and exchange: HMA/NYSE
Business activities: Operates acute care hospitals.
Business type (SIC): Hospitals
Financial profile for 2012: Number of employees, 40,400; assets, $6,400,790,000; sales volume, $5,878,240,000; pre-tax net income, $301,480,000; expenses, $5,576,760,000; liabilities, $5,396,870,000
Fortune 1000 ranking: 2012—376th in revenues, 626th in profits, and 516th in assets
Corporate officers: William J. Schoen, Chair.; Gary D. Newsome, Pres. and C.E.O.; Kelly E. Curry, Exec. V.P. and C.F.O.; Steven E. Clifton, Sr. V.P. and Genl. Counsel; Robert E. Farnham, Sr. V.P., Finance
Board of directors: William J. Schoen, Chair.; Kent P. Dauten; Pascal J. Goldschmidt; Donald E. Kiernan; Robert A. Knox; Gary D. Newsome; Vicki A. O'Meara; William J. Schoen; William C. Steere, Jr.; Randolph W. Westerfield, Ph.D.
Giving statement: Giving through the HMA Employee Disaster Relief Fund, Inc. and the HMA Foundation, Inc.
Company EIN: 610963645

HMA Employee Disaster Relief Fund, Inc.

5811 Pelican Bay Blvd., Ste. 500
Naples, FL 34108-2711 (239) 598-3131
Application address: c/o Health Management Associates, Inc., 5811 Pelican Bay Blvd., Ste. 500, Naples, FL 34108

Establishment information: Established in 2004 in FL.
Contact: Patrick E. Lombardo, V.P.
Financial data (yr. ended 12/31/11): Assets, $2,976 (M); gifts received, $9,111; expenditures, $8,748; qualifying distributions, $8,748; giving activities include $8,500 for 14 grants to individuals (high: $1,000; low: $500).
Purpose and activities: Giving primarily for hurricane disaster relief.
Application information: Applications accepted. Application form required.
Initial approach: Letter
Deadline(s): 6 months after the president declares the area a disaster
Officers: Patrick E. Lombardo, V.P.; Frederick B. Drow, V.P.; Gary S. Bryant, Treas.
EIN: 201507465

HMA Foundation, Inc.

5811 Pelican Day Blvd., Ste. 500
Naples, FL 34108-2711 (239) 598-3131
Application address: c/o HMA Foundation, Inc., 5811 Pelican Bay Blvd., Ste. 500, Naples, FL 34108

Establishment information: Established in FL.
Donor: Health Management Associates, Inc.
Contact: Mary Pirro
Financial data (yr. ended 12/31/11): Assets, $965,843 (M); gifts received, $2,000; expenditures, $175,333; qualifying distributions, $169,800; giving activities include $169,800 for 6 grants (high: $150,000; low: $1,800).
Purpose and activities: The foundation supports organizations involved with orchestras, higher education, and cancer.
Fields of interest: Arts; Education; Health organizations.
Type of support: Sponsorships.
Geographic limitations: Giving primarily in Ava Maria and Naples, FL.
Application information: Applications accepted. Application form not required.
Initial approach: Proposal
Deadline(s): None
Officers: Gary D. Newsome, Pres.; Robert E. Farnham, V.P.
Director: William J. Schoen.
EIN: 651115909

1766
Health Net, Inc.

(formerly Foundation Health Systems, Inc.)
21650 Oxnard St.
Woodland Hills, CA 91367-6607
(818) 676-6000
FAX: (302) 655-5049

Company URL: http://www.healthnet.com
Establishment information: Established in 1979.
Company type: Public company
Company ticker symbol and exchange: HNT/NYSE
Business activities: Operates medical service plan.
Business type (SIC): Insurance/accident and health
Financial profile for 2012: Number of employees, 7,386; assets, $3,934,390,000; sales volume, $11,289,090,000; pre-tax net income, $3,165,000,000; expenses, $11,257,440,000; liabilities, $2,377,360,000
Fortune 1000 ranking: 2012—236th in revenues, 699th in profits, and 669th in assets
Forbes 2000 ranking: 2012—851st in sales, 1660th in profits, and 1885th in assets
Corporate officers: Roger F. Greaves, Chair.; Jay M. Gellert, Pres. and C.E.O.; James E. Woys, Exec. V.P. and C.O.O.; Joseph C. Capezza, C.P.A., Exec. V.P., Treas., and C.F.O.; Marie Montgomery, Sr. V.P. and Corp. Cont.; Angelee F. Bouchard, Sr. V.P., Genl. Counsel, and Secy.
Board of directors: Roger F. Greaves, Chair.; Mary Anne Citrino; Theodore F. Craver, Jr.; Vicki B. Escarra; Gale S. Fitzgerald; Patrick Foley; Jay M.

Gellert; Douglas M. Mancino; Bruce G. Wilson; Frederick C. Yeager
Subsidiaries: Health Net Federal Services, LLC, Rancho Cordova, CA; Health Net of Arizona, Inc., Tempe, AZ; Health Net of California , Inc., Woodland Hills, CA; Health Net of the Northeast, Inc., Shelton, CT; Health Net Pharmaceutical Services, Rancho Cordova, CA; QualMed, Inc., Pueblo, CO
International operations: Cayman Islands
Giving statement: Giving through the Health Net, Inc. Corporate Giving Program and the Health Net Foundation, Inc.
Company EIN: 954288333

Health Net, Inc. Corporate Giving Program

(formerly Foundation Health Systems, Inc. Corporate Giving Program)
21650 Oxnard St.
Woodland Hills, CA 91367-4901 (818) 676-6000

Purpose and activities: As a complement to its foundation, Health Net also supports initiatives designed to address post-traumatic stress disorder among military service members and veterans and their families. Support is given primarily in areas of company operations.
Fields of interest: Public health; Mental health/crisis services; Family services Military/veterans.
Type of support: Sponsorships.
Geographic limitations: Giving primarily in areas of company operations.
Application information:
Administrators: Pat Johnston; David Olson.

Health Net Foundation, Inc.

21650 Oxnard St., 22nd Fl.
Woodland Hills, CA 91367-7824

Establishment information: Established in 2007 in CA.
Donor: Health Net, Inc.
Financial data (yr. ended 12/31/11): Assets, $2,197,886 (M); gifts received, $259,030; expenditures, $325,690; qualifying distributions, $298,917; giving activities include $298,917 for grants.
Purpose and activities: The foundation programs designed to improve healthcare in communities.
Fields of interest: Health care, clinics/centers; Dental care; Health care; Heart & circulatory diseases.
Type of support: General/operating support.
Geographic limitations: Giving primarily in CA, FL, TX, and WA.
Support limitations: No grants to individuals.
Application information: Applications not accepted. Contributes only to pre-selected organizations.
Officers and Directors: Patricia Clarey, Pres.; Angelee F. Bouchard, Secy.; Joseph C. Capezza, Treas.; Jay M. Gellert; Scott R. Kelly; Karin Mayhew; John Sivori; Linda Tano*; Steve Tough; James E. Woys.
EIN: 412241862

1767
The Heat Group

(also known as Miami Heat)
American Airlines Arena
601 Biscayne Blvd.
Miami, FL 33132-1801 (786) 777-1000

Company URL: http://www.nba.com/heat
Establishment information: Established in 1988.
Company type: Private company
Business activities: Operates professional basketball club.
Business type (SIC): Commercial sports
Corporate officers: Nick Arison, C.E.O.; Pat Riley, Pres.; Sammy Schulman, Exec. V.P. and C.F.O.; Stephen Weber, Exec. V.P., Sales; Tony Coba, Exec. V.P. and C.I.O.; Raquel Libman, Exec. V.P. and Genl. Counsel; Jim Spencer, V.P., Opers.; Jeff Morris, V.P., Finance; Jeff Craney, V.P., Mktg.; Sonia Harty, V.P., Human Resources
Giving statement: Giving through the Miami Heat Corporate Giving Program.

Miami Heat Corporate Giving Program

c/o Community Affairs Dept.
601 Biscayne Blvd.
Miami, FL 33132-1801
URL: http://www.nba.com/heat/community/community_index.html
Contact for Miami Heat Scholarships: Ralph Leon

Purpose and activities: The Miami Heat makes charitable contributions to nonprofit organizations on a case by case basis. Support is given primarily in southern Florida.
Fields of interest: Elementary school/education; Secondary school/education; Education, reading; Education; Athletics/sports, basketball; Athletics/sports, water sports; Youth, services; Human services, gift distribution; Homeless, human services; General charitable giving.
Programs:
Heat Academy: Through the Heat Academy, the Miami Heat and the Miami-Dade County Public Schools provides children with an academic after-school program. The Academy provides economically disadvantaged children who are most at-risk of academic failure or juvenile delinquency with after-school tutoring focusing on reading, writing, math, and science skills.
Heat Learn to Swim: The Miami Heat, in partnership with the Blue Cross Blue Shield of Florida, sponsors a water safety campaign. Through Learn to Swim, the Miami Heat encourages people to receive training in aquatics and water safety. The campaign includes coupons for discount swim lessons and visits by the Miami Heat players to various swim locations.
Heat Scholarships: The Heat annually awards 4 $2,500 scholarships to high school seniors attending a Miami-Dade, Broward, or Palm Beach school based on academic performance and outstanding community service.
Miami Heat Learn and Play Centers: The Miami Heat, in partnership with Blue Cross Blue Shield of Florida, creates Learn and Play Centers to provide a safe place where children can read and play. The Heat renovates an existing room into a Heat-themed area with fresh paint and provides computers, furniture, books, audio/video equipment, and games for children.
Type of support: Building/renovation; Donated products; Employee volunteer services; Equipment; In-kind gifts; Loaned talent; Scholarships—to individuals.
Geographic limitations: Giving primarily in areas of company operations in southern FL.
Publications: Application guidelines.
Application information: Applications accepted. Proposals should be submitted using organization letterhead. Unsolicited autograph requests are not accepted. The Community Affairs Department handles giving. Applicants should submit the following:
1) brief history of organization and description of its mission
2) descriptive literature about organization
3) detailed description of project and amount of funding requested
4) additional materials/documentation
Scholarship applications should include official transcripts, W2 forms, a copy of the last tax filing, 5 letters of recommendation, and a letter of acceptance to a four-year college or university.
Initial approach: Proposal to headquarters for memorabilia, player appearances, and Learn and Play Centers; download application form and mail to headquarters for scholarships
Copies of proposal: 1
Deadline(s): 6 weeks prior to need for memorabilia and player appearances; None for Learn and Play Centers; Apr. 3 for scholarships
Final notification: May for scholarships

1768
B. V. Hedrick Gravel & Sand Company

120 1/2 N. Church St.
Salisbury, NC 28144-4311 (704) 633-5982

Company URL: http://www.hedrickind.com
Establishment information: Established in 1924.
Company type: Private company
Business activities: Operates gravel and sand company.
Business type (SIC): Mining/sand and gravel
Corporate officers: Frances H. Johnson, Chair.; Jeffrey V. Goodman V, Pres.; Joanne Johnson, Secy.-Treas.
Board of director: Frances H. Johnson, Chair.
Subsidiary: Southern Concrete Materials, Inc., Asheville, NC
Giving statement: Giving through the Johnson Foundation, Inc.

The Johnson Foundation, Inc.

P.O. Box 1040
Salisbury, NC 28145-1040

Establishment information: Established in 1954 in NC.
Donors: B.V. Hedrick Gravel & Sand Co.; Frances H. Johnson; Southern Concrete Materials, Inc.; Aggregate Resources; Material Sales Co., Inc.; Cumberland Gravel & Sand Co.
Financial data (yr. ended 12/31/11): Assets, $1,386,793 (M); gifts received, $46,494; expenditures, $10,179; qualifying distributions, $10,000; giving activities include $10,000 for grants.
Purpose and activities: The foundation supports Boy Scouts of America in North Carolina.
Fields of interest: Education; Youth development.
Type of support: General/operating support.
Geographic limitations: Giving limited to Salisbury, NC.
Support limitations: No grants to individuals.
Application information: Applications not accepted. Unsolicited requests for funds not accepted.

Officers: Frances H. Johnson, Pres.; F. Joanne Johnson, V.P.; Judith H. Johnson, Secy.; Kathryn H. Johnson, Treas.
EIN: 566034758

1769
Heffernan Insurance Brokers

1350 Carlback Ave.
Walnut Creek, CA 94596 (925) 934-8500

Company URL: http://www.heffgroup.com/
Establishment information: Established in 1988.
Company type: Private company
Business activities: Operates insurance brokerage.
Business type (SIC): Insurance agents, brokers, and services
Corporate officers: F. Michael Heffernan, Pres. and C.E.O.; Robin Newman, C.O.O.
Giving statement: Giving through the Heffernan Group Foundation.

Heffernan Group Foundation

1350 Carlback Ave., Ste. 350
Walnut Creek, CA 94596-7328
FAX: (925) 934-8278;
E-mail: michellel@heffernanfoundation.com; Tel. for Michelle Lonaker: (925) 295-2575; URL: http://www.heffernanfoundation.com/index.php

Establishment information: Established in 2006 in CA.
Donor: Heffernan Insurance Brokers.
Contact: Michelle Lonaker, Dir.
Financial data (yr. ended 12/31/11): Assets, $344,786 (M); gifts received, $891,984; expenditures, $617,773; qualifying distributions, $613,174; giving activities include $613,174 for 277 grants (high: $100,000; low: $250).
Purpose and activities: The foundation supports programs designed to provide shelter, food, and education; and preserve the environment. Special emphasis is directed toward programs designed to serve families or individuals in need.
Fields of interest: Higher education; Education; Environment, natural resources; Environment; Food services; Food banks; Housing/shelter, development; Housing/shelter; Boys & girls clubs; Children/youth, services; Family services; Family services, domestic violence; Residential/custodial care, hospices; Human services.
Program:
Garee Lee Smith Scholarship Program: The foundation award five $5,000 scholarships to Heffernan Group employees or to children of Heffernan Group employees. Employees must be in good standing and employed on a full-time permanent basis for at least a year.
Type of support: Employee-related scholarships; General/operating support; Program development; Scholarship funds.
Geographic limitations: Giving primarily in areas of company operations, with emphasis on CA.
Publications: Grants list.
Application information: Applications not accepted. Unsolicited applications are not accepted. Grant submissions from local charities are by invitation only. Grants range from $2,500 to $10,000.
Board meeting date(s): Dec.
Officers and Directors:* F. Michael Heffernan*, Chair.; Dan Sebastiani, Treas.; Michelle Lonaker; Kurt Scheidt; Jessica Standiford; Louisa Tallarida.
EIN: 711010693
Selected grants: The following grants are a representative sample of this grantmaker's funding activity:
$10,300 to Giants Community Fund, San Francisco, CA, 2010.
$5,000 to Affordable Housing Associates, Berkeley, CA, 2010.
$5,000 to Aspiranet, South San Francisco, CA, 2010.
$5,000 to University of California at San Diego, La Jolla, CA, 2010.
$5,000 to Walden House, San Francisco, CA, 2010.
$4,000 to Opportunity Fund, San Jose, CA, 2010.
$4,000 to Pathways for Kids, San Francisco, CA, 2010.
$3,000 to Alameda County Community Food Bank, Oakland, CA, 2010.
$3,000 to Breast Friends, Tigard, OR, 2010.
$3,000 to Womens Center of San Joaquin County, Stockton, CA, 2010.

1770
Heidtman Steel Products, Inc.

2401 Front St.
Toledo, OH 43605 (419) 691-4646
FAX: (419) 698-1150

Company URL: http://www.heidtman.com
Establishment information: Established in 1954.
Company type: Private company
Business activities: Manufactures flat-rolled steel products.
Business type (SIC): Steel mill products
Financial profile for 2010: Number of employees, 1,000
Corporate officers: John C. Bates, Co-Pres. and C.E.O.; Tim Berra, Co-Pres.; Mark E. Ridenour, C.F.O.; Tod Gonzales, C.O.O.; Mike Kruse, V.P., Mktg.; Rita Czerniakowski, Cont.
Giving statement: Giving through the John C. Bates Foundation.

The John C. Bates Foundation

2401 Front St.
Toledo, OH 43605-1145

Establishment information: Established in 1993 in OH.
Donors: Heidtman Steel Products, Inc.; Centaur, Inc.; HS Processing, LP.
Financial data (yr. ended 03/31/12): Assets, $1,375,757 (M); gifts received, $1,035,176; expenditures, $296,614; qualifying distributions, $289,293; giving activities include $289,293 for grants.
Purpose and activities: The foundation supports zoological societies, community foundations, and organizations involved with education, health, human services, and Christianity.
Fields of interest: Elementary/secondary education; Higher education; Education; Zoos/zoological societies; Health care; Cancer; Family services; Human services; Foundations (community); Christian agencies & churches.
Type of support: Capital campaigns; Program development; Scholarship funds.
Geographic limitations: Giving primarily in IN, MI, and OH.
Support limitations: No grants to individuals.
Application information: Applications not accepted. Contributes only to pre-selected organizations.
Officers and Trustees:* Darlene B. Dotson*, Pres.; John M. Carey*, Secy.; Mark E. Ridenour*, Treas.; Sarah J. Bates; Debra A. Shinkle.
EIN: 341749094
Selected grants: The following grants are a representative sample of this grantmaker's funding activity:
$50,000 to Saint Johns Jesuit High School, Toledo, OH, 2009.
$18,000 to Saint Ursula Academy, Toledo, OH, 2009.
$5,000 to Toledo Zoological Society, Toledo, OH, 2009.
$2,500 to Ohio State University, Columbus, OH, 2009.
$1,500 to Multiple Sclerosis Society, National, Maumee, OH, 2009.

1771
Heinens, Inc.

4540 Richmond Rd.
Warrensville Heights, OH 44128
(216) 475-2300

Company URL: http://www.heinens.com
Establishment information: Established in 1929.
Company type: Private company
Business activities: Operates grocery stores.
Business type (SIC): Groceries—retail
Corporate officers: Jeffrey J. Heinen, Pres.; Thomas J. Heinen, C.O.O.
Giving statement: Giving through the Heinens, Inc. Corporate Giving Program.

Heinens, Inc. Corporate Giving Program

4540 Richmond Rd.
Warrensville Heights, OH 44128-5757

Contact: Brenda Goad
Purpose and activities: Heinens makes charitable contributions to nonprofit organizations on a case by case basis. Support is given primarily in areas of company operations.
Fields of interest: General charitable giving.
Type of support: Donated products; General/operating support.
Geographic limitations: Giving primarily in areas of company operations.
Support limitations: No grants to individuals.
Application information: Applications accepted. Proposals should be submitted using organization letterhead. Application form not required.
Proposals should include a Preferred Customer Card number, if available.
Initial approach: Proposal to headquarters
Copies of proposal: 1
Deadline(s): None
Final notification: Telephone contact person within 10 days for decision

1772
H.J. Heinz Company

1 PPG Pl., Ste. 1300
P.O. Box 57
Pittsburgh, PA 15222 (412) 456-5700

Company URL: http://www.heinz.com
Establishment information: Established in 1869.
Company type: Private company
Parent company: Berkshire Hathaway Inc.
Business activities: Produces and markets processed food products.
Business type (SIC): Specialty foods/canned, frozen, and preserved
Financial profile for 2012: Number of employees, 32,200; assets, $11,983,290,000; sales volume, $11,649,080,000; pre-tax net income,

$1,183,440,000; expenses, $10,197,910,000; liabilities, $9,224,700,000
Fortune 1000 ranking: 2012—234th in revenues, 215th in profits, and 351st in assets
Corporate officers: Bernardo Hees, C.E.O.; Paulo Basilio, C.F.O.; Theodore N. Bobby, Exec. V.P., Genl. Counsel, and Corp. Secy.; Isobel Thomson, C.I.O.
International operations: Australia; Belgium; Botswana; Canada; China; Cyprus; Egypt; France; Germany; Greece; Indonesia; Ireland; Italy; Netherlands; New Zealand; Poland; Portugal; Russia; South Korea; Spain; Thailand; United Kingdom; Venezuela; Zimbabwe
Giving statement: Giving through the H. J. Heinz Company Contributions Program and the H. J. Heinz Company Foundation.
Company EIN: 250542520

H. J. Heinz Company Contributions Program

1 PPG Place
Pittsburgh, PA 15222 (412) 237-5757
URL: http://www.heinz.com/sustainability.aspx

Purpose and activities: As a complement to its foundation, Heinz also makes charitable contributions to nonprofit organizations directly. Support is given on a national and international basis in areas of company operations, with emphasis on Cambodia, China, Haiti, India, Indonesia, and Tanzania.
Fields of interest: Health care; Nutrition; Children, services.
International interests: Cambodia; China; Haiti; India; Indonesia; Tanzania, Zanzibar and Pemba.
Program:
The Heinz Micronutrient Campaign: Through the Heinz Micronutrient Campaign (HCM), the H.J. Heinz Company and its foundation combat iron-deficiency anemia and vitamin and mineral deficiencies in the developing world, especially as they affect young children, by providing micronutrient assistance to millions of children worldwide at risk of vitamin and mineral malnutrition.
Type of support: Donated products; Employee volunteer services; General/operating support; In-kind gifts.
Geographic limitations: Giving on a national and international basis in areas of company operations, with emphasis on Cambodia, China, Haiti, India, Indonesia, and Tanzania.
Publications: Corporate giving report.

H. J. Heinz Company Foundation

P.O. Box 57
Pittsburgh, PA 15230-0057 (412) 456-5773
FAX: (412) 442-3227;
E-mail: heinz.foundation@us.hjheinz.com;
URL: http://www.heinz.com/sustainability/social/heinz-foundation.aspx

Establishment information: Established in 1951 in PA.
Donor: H.J. Heinz Co.
Contact: Tammy B. Aupperle, Chair.
Financial data (yr. ended 04/29/12): Assets, $14,295,971 (M); gifts received, $5,000,000; expenditures, $3,041,523; qualifying distributions, $2,974,852; giving activities include $2,511,450 for 503 grants (high: $209,000; low: $25).
Purpose and activities: The foundation supports organizations involved with arts and culture, education, human services, diversity, women, and economically disadvantaged people. Special emphasis is directed toward programs designed to promote the health and nutritional needs of children and families.
Fields of interest: Arts; Higher education; Education; Public health, obesity; Health care; Food banks; Nutrition; Big Brothers/Big Sisters; Children/youth, services; Family services; Human services; Civil/human rights, equal rights Minorities; Women; Economically disadvantaged.
Programs:
Community Grants: The foundation, in partnership with Heinz North America, provides grants dollars to Heinz factory locations for community investment in areas of nutrition, diversity, and healthy communities.
Diversity: The foundation supports programs designed to promote the advancement of minority populations and women with focus on development opportunities for girls and minority youth.
Employee Matching Gifts: The foundation matches contributions made by full-time employees, directors, and retirees to nonprofit organizations on a one-for-one basis from $25 to $5,000 per contributor, per year.
Fostering Healhty Communities: The foundation supports programs designed to enhance the quality of life in communities through arts and culture and community. Special emphasis is directed toward children and youth.
Heinz HELPS: Through Heinz Employees Lending Public Service (HELPS), the foundation awards grants of up to $500 to nonprofits with which employees of Heinz volunteer at least 50 hours a year.
Heinz Micronutrient Campaign: Through the Heinz Micronutrient Campaign, Heinz and the H.J., Heinz Company Foundation distributes micronutrient sachets to address the global health threat of iron-deficiency anemia and vitamin and mineral malnutrition in the developing world.
Heinz Scholars Program: The foundation, in collaboration with Washington & Lee University, provides scholarships and internship opportunities to economically disadvantaged students who have distinguished themselves through academic and personal achievements. The program is administered by Washington & Lee University.
Nutrition: The foundation promotes improvements in and a better understanding of nutrition and contributes to the health and well-being of people and communities.
Type of support: Annual campaigns; Building/renovation; Capital campaigns; Emergency funds; Employee matching gifts; Employee volunteer services; Endowments; General/operating support; In-kind gifts; Internship funds; Program development; Scholarship funds; Seed money; Technical assistance.
Geographic limitations: Giving primarily in areas of company operations, with emphasis on Pittsburgh, PA; giving to Africa, Bangladesh, China, India, and Tanzania for Heinz Micronutrient Campaign; giving also to international organizations.
Support limitations: No support for religious or political organizations. No grants to individuals (except for Heinz Scholars), or for political campaigns, debt reduction, land acquisition, equipment, conferences, travel, or unsolicited research projects; no loans.
Publications: Annual report (including application guidelines); Application guidelines; Corporate giving report.
Application information: Applications accepted. An interview may be requested. Multi-year funding is not automatic. Organizations receiving support are asked to provide a final report. Application form not required. Applicants should submit the following:
1) how project will be sustained once grantmaker support is completed
2) results expected from proposed grant
3) statement of problem project will address
4) population served
5) copy of IRS Determination Letter
6) how company employees can become involved with the organization
7) brief history of organization and description of its mission
8) copy of most recent annual report/audited financial statement/990
9) how project's results will be evaluated or measured
10) list of company employees involved with the organization
11) explanation of why grantmaker is considered an appropriate donor for project
12) listing of board of directors, trustees, officers and other key people and their affiliations
13) detailed description of project and amount of funding requested
14) copy of current year's organizational budget and/or project budget
15) listing of additional sources and amount of support

Initial approach: Proposal; letter of inquiry for international organizations
Copies of proposal: 1
Board meeting date(s): Quarterly
Deadline(s): None
Final notification: Varies

Officers and Directors:* Tammy Aupperle*, Chair.; Theodore N. Bobby*, Secy.; Kristen Clark*, Treas.; Michael Okoroafor; Michael Mullen; Sonja Narcisse; John Runkel.
Number of staff: 1 full-time professional; 1 full-time support.
EIN: 300055087

1773
Heller Consulting, Inc.

1736 Franklin St., Ste. 600
Oakland, CA 94612 (510) 841-4222

Company URL: http://www.teamheller.com
Establishment information: Established in 1996.
Company type: Private company
Business activities: Operates consulting firm specializing in fundraising technology and operations.
Business type (SIC): Computer services
Financial profile for 2011: Number of employees, 50
Corporate officers: Keith Heller, Pres. and C.E.O.; Marie Colbert, C.F.O.
Board of director: Jeffrey Appell
Offices: Chicago, IL; New York, NY
Giving statement: Giving through the Heller Consulting, Inc. Corporate Giving Program.

Heller Consulting, Inc. Corporate Giving Program

125 University Ave., Ste. 5
Berkeley, CA 94710-1616 (510) 841-4222
URL: http://www.teamheller.com/index.php?option=com_content&task=view&id=104&Itemid=264

Purpose and activities: Heller Consulting is a certified B Corporation that matches employee contributions to nonprofit organizations.
Fields of interest: General charitable giving.
Type of support: Conferences/seminars; Employee matching gifts.

1774
Helmerich & Payne, Inc.
1437 S. Boulder Ave., Ste. 1400
Tulsa, OK 74119-3623 (918) 742-5531
FAX: (918) 742-0237

Company URL: http://www.hpinc.com
Establishment information: Established in 1920.
Company type: Public company
Company ticker symbol and exchange: HP/NYSE
Business activities: Provides oil and gas well drilling services; develops, owns, and operates commercial real estate.
Business type (SIC): Oil and gas field services; real estate operators and lessors; real estate subdividers and developers
Financial profile for 2012: Number of employees, 8,128; assets, $5,721,090,000; sales volume, $3,151,800,000; pre-tax net income, $902,580,000; expenses, $2,242,200,000; liabilities, $1,886,090,000
Fortune 1000 ranking: 2012—684th in revenues, 301st in profits, and 553rd in assets
Forbes 2000 ranking: 2012—1591st in sales, 905th in profits, and 1757th in assets
Corporate officers: Hans Helmerich, Chair. and C.E.O.; John W. Lindsay, Pres. and C.O.O.; Steven R. Mackey, Exec. V.P., Secy., Genl. Counsel, and C.A.O.; Juan Pablo Tardio, V.P. and C.F.O.
Board of directors: Hans Helmerich, Chair.; William L. Armstrong; Randy A. Foutch; John W. Lindsay; Paula Marshall; Thomas A. Petrie; Donald F. Robillard, Jr.; Edward B. Rust, Jr.; Francis Rooney; John D. Zeglis
Subsidiaries: Helmerich & Payne International Drilling Co., Tulsa, OK; Helmerich & Payne Properties, Inc., Tulsa, OK; Helmerich & Payne Rasco Inc., Tulsa, OK; Natural Gas Odorizing, Baytown, TX; Space Center, Inc., Tulsa, OK; The Tearoom in Utica Square, Inc., Tulsa, OK; Utica Square Shopping Center, Inc., Tulsa, OK
Giving statement: Giving through the Helmerich & Payne, Inc. Corporate Giving Program.
Company EIN: 730679879

Helmerich & Payne, Inc. Corporate Giving Program
1437 S. Boulder St.
Tulsa, OK 74119-3609 (918) 742-5531

Purpose and activities: Helmerich & Payne makes charitable contributions to nonprofit organizations involved with arts and culture, K-12 and higher education, health and human services, and community development. Support is given primarily in the Tulsa, Oklahoma, area.
Fields of interest: Arts; Elementary/secondary education; Higher education; Health care; Human services; Community/economic development.
Type of support: Employee volunteer services; Employee-related scholarships; General/operating support; In-kind gifts; Sponsorships.
Geographic limitations: Giving primarily in the Tulsa, OK, area.
Application information: Applications accepted. Application form not required.
Initial approach: Proposal to headquarters

1775
The Hemmerdinger Corporation
8000 Cooper Ave.
Glendale, NY 11385-7739 (718) 326-3560

Company type: Private company
Business activities: Operates nonresidential buildings.
Business type (SIC): Real estate operators and lessors
Corporate officer: H. Dale Hemmerdinger, Chair.
Board of director: H. Dale Hemmerdinger, Chair.
Giving statement: Giving through the Hemmerdinger Foundation.

The Hemmerdinger Foundation
c/o Atco Properties & Management
70-34 83rd St., Bldg. 19
Glendale, NY 11385-7717

Establishment information: Established in 1959 in DE.
Donors: H. Dale Hemmerdinger; The Hemmerdinger Corp.; 373-381 Park Avenue South, LLC; Hemmerdinger Ventures, LLC; Elizabeth G. Hemmerdinger.
Financial data (yr. ended 12/31/11): Assets, $5,520 (M); gifts received, $85,000; expenditures, $82,949; qualifying distributions, $82,943; giving activities include $82,500 for 7 grants (high: $25,000; low: $2,500).
Purpose and activities: The foundation supports police associations and organizations involved with education, children and youth, civic affairs, and Judaism.
Fields of interest: Higher education; Education; Crime/law enforcement, correctional facilities; Children/youth, services; Public affairs, finance; Public affairs; Jewish agencies & synagogues.
Type of support: General/operating support; Scholarship funds.
Geographic limitations: Giving primarily in New York, NY.
Support limitations: No grants to individuals.
Application information: Applications not accepted. Unsolicited requests for funds not accepted.
Officers: H. Dale Hemmerdinger, Pres.; Elizabeth C. Hemmerdinger, V.P. and Secy.
EIN: 136278506

1776
Hendrick Automotive Group
6000 Monroe Rd., Ste. 100
Charlotte, NC 28212 (704) 568-5550
FAX: (704) 566-3295

Company URL: http://www.hendrickauto.com
Establishment information: Established in 1976.
Company type: Private company
Business activities: Operates car dealerships.
Business type (SIC): Motor vehicles—retail
Financial profile for 2010: Number of employees, 7,500
Corporate officers: Joseph Riddick Hendrick III, Chair.; Edward J. Brown III, Pres. and C.E.O.; James Huzi, Exec. V.P. and C.F.O.
Board of director: Joseph Riddick Hendrick III, Chair.
Subsidiary: Hendrick Motorsports, Inc., Charlotte, NC
Giving statement: Giving through the Hendrick Foundation for Children.

Hendrick Foundation for Children
6000 Monroe Rd.
Charlotte, NC 28212-6119 (704) 568-5550
URL: http://www.thehendrickfoundation.org

Establishment information: Established in 2004 in NC.
Donors: Hendrick Automotive Group; Marrow Foundation; Hendrick Motorsports Inc.; Gems Motorsports; Joe Gibbs Racing; Alesha Gainey; Branch Banking & Trust Co.; Burroughs & Chapin; Cathy Hendrick; Hendrick Honda Easley SC; Hendrick Honda South Blvd.; Honda Cars of Bradenton; Honda Cars of Hickory; J. R. Hendrick III; James & Arlene Swing; JLH Management Corporation; Julian Rawl; Mary Hendrick; Redline Design; Reynolds & Reynolds; Toyota of Wilmington; Phoenix Racing; John Staluppi; Jeanette Stalippi; Sonic Automotive Inc.; Lowe's; Bank of America; Robert C. Rice; Karen Rice; Cathy Hendrick.
Financial data (yr. ended 12/31/11): Assets, $74,043 (M); gifts received, $84,416; expenditures, $33,720; qualifying distributions, $33,750; giving activities include $33,750 for 2 grants (high: $32,250; low: $1,500).
Purpose and activities: The foundation supports programs designed to provide health, medical, social welfare, and educational services to benefit children with illness, disease, injury, pain, disability, incapacity, or other disadvantages; and improve quality of life for children with life-threatening or chronic injuries, illness, and disabilities.
Fields of interest: Elementary/secondary education; Health care; Children, services Physically disabled.
Type of support: Building/renovation; General/operating support; Scholarship funds.
Geographic limitations: Giving primarily in Charlotte, NC.
Application information: Applications accepted. Proposals should be submitted using organization letterhead. Application form required. Applicants should submit the following:
1) copy of IRS Determination Letter
Initial approach: Letter
Deadline(s): None
Officers and Directors:* Charles V. Ricks*, Pres. and Treas.; Gregory H. Gach*, Secy.
EIN: 201786855

1777
Hendrick Manufacturing Company
1 7th Ave.
Carbondale, PA 18407-2251
(570) 282-1010

Company URL: http://www.hendrickmfg.com
Establishment information: Established in 1876.
Company type: Private company
Business activities: Manufactures perforated products.
Business type (SIC): Metal forgings and stampings
Corporate officers: Michael L. Drake, C.E.O.; Ramal Malay, C.I.O.
Giving statement: Giving through the Drake Foundation.

The Drake Foundation
482 Halle Park Dr., Ste. 101
Collierville, TN 38017-7089

Establishment information: Established in 1997 in TN.

Donors: Hendrick Manufacturing Co.; Drake Industries, LLC.
Contact: Pansy L. Drake, Pres. and Dir.
Financial data (yr. ended 12/31/11): Assets, $509,562 (M); gifts received, $324,174; expenditures, $76,000; qualifying distributions, $76,000; giving activities include $76,000 for 8 grants (high: $20,000; low: $1,000).
Purpose and activities: The foundation supports organizations involved with cancer, domestic violence, international relief, leadership development, and Christianity.
Fields of interest: Cancer; YM/YWCAs & YM/YWHAs; Family services, domestic violence; International relief; Leadership development; Christian agencies & churches.
Type of support: General/operating support.
Geographic limitations: Giving primarily in KY, MO, TN, and TX.
Support limitations: No grants to individuals.
Application information: Applications accepted. Application form required.
Initial approach: Letter
Deadline(s): None
Officers and Directors:* Pansy L. Drake, Pres.; Darin Drake, Secy.
EIN: 621684643
Selected grants: The following grants are a representative sample of this grantmaker's funding activity:
$20,000 to YMCA of Carbondale, Carbondale, PA, 2009.
$5,000 to Sharon Reves Foundation, Germantown, TN, 2009.

1778
Henkel Corporation

1001 Trout Brook Crossing
Rocky Hill, CT 06067-3910 (860) 571-5100

Company URL: http://www.henkelcorp.com
Establishment information: Established in 1876.
Company type: Subsidiary of a foreign company
Business activities: Manufactures hair styling products, consumer adhesives, resins and additives, sealants, adhesives, and coatings, and oleochemicals.
Business type (SIC): Soaps, cleaners, and toiletries; paper and paperboard/coated, converted, and laminated; plastics and synthetics; paints and allied products; chemicals/industrial organic
Financial profile for 2009: Number of employees, 4,542
Corporate officer: Jeffrey Piccolomini, Pres.
Divisions: Amchem Prods. Div., Ambler, PA; Chemical Specialties Div., Ambler, PA; Fire Chemicals Div., Minneapolis, MN; Functional Products Div., Minneapolis, MN; International Div., Minneapolis, MN; Leather Chemicals Div., Saugus, MA; Leather Chemicals Div., Oak Creek, WI; Minerals Industry Div., Minneapolis, MN; Polymers Div., Minneapolis, MN; Water Soluble Polymers Div., Minneapolis, MN
Giving statement: Giving through the Henkel Corporation Contributions Program.

Henkel Corporation Contributions Program

1001 Trout Brook Crossing
Rocky Hill, CT 06067-3910 (860) 571-5100

Contact: Judi Brown, Exec., Admin. Asst.
Purpose and activities: Henkel makes charitable contributions to nonprofit organizations involved with arts and culture, education, community development, and civic affairs. Support is given primarily in Montgomery County and the Philadelphia, Pennsylvania, area.
Fields of interest: Arts; Education; Community/economic development; Public affairs.
Type of support: Annual campaigns; General/operating support.
Geographic limitations: Giving primarily in Montgomery County and the Philadelphia, PA, area.
Support limitations: No support for political, religious, or veterans' organizations.
Application information: Applications accepted. Application form not required.
Initial approach: Proposal to headquarters
Copies of proposal: 1
Deadline(s): None
Final notification: Two months

1779
Henkels & McCoy, Inc.

985 Jolly Rd.
Blue Bell, PA 19422-0900 (215) 283-7600
FAX: (215) 283-7659

Company URL: http://www.henkels.com
Establishment information: Established in 1923.
Company type: Private company
Business activities: Provides engineering services; provides general contract construction services.
Business type (SIC): Engineering, architectural, and surveying services; building construction general contractors and operative builders
Corporate officers: Paul M. Henkels, Chair.; Kenneth L. Rose, Vice-Chair.; T. Roderick Henkels, Pres. and C.E.O.; Jonathan C. Schoff, Exec. V.P. and C.O.O.
Board of directors: Paul M. Henkels, Chair.; Kenneth L. Rose, Vice-Chair.
Giving statement: Giving through the Henkels & McCoy, Inc. Corporate Giving Program and the Henkels Foundation.

Henkels & McCoy, Inc. Corporate Giving Program

c/o Corp. Contribs.
985 Jolly Rd.
Blue Bell, PA 19422-0900 (215) 283-7600
FAX: (215) 283-7452

Purpose and activities: As a complement to its foundation, Henkels & McCoy also makes charitable contributions to nonprofit organizations directly. Support is given on a national basis.
Fields of interest: General charitable giving.
Type of support: General/operating support.
Geographic limitations: Giving on a national basis in areas of company operations.
Application information: Applications not accepted. Contributes only to pre-selected organizations.

Henkels Foundation

985 Jolly Rd.
Blue Bell, PA 19422-0900 (215) 283-7628

Establishment information: Established in 1956 in DE and PA.
Donors: Henkels & McCoy, Inc.; Liberty Mutual Group.
Financial data (yr. ended 06/30/11): Assets, $739,955 (M); gifts received, $1,521,832; expenditures, $1,753,512; qualifying distributions, $1,756,968; giving activities include $1,735,475 for 128 grants (high: $410,352; low: $46).
Purpose and activities: The foundation supports organizations involved with education, family planning, human services, and Christianity.
Fields of interest: Secondary school/education; Higher education; Scholarships/financial aid; Education; Reproductive health, family planning; Children, services; Family services; Human services; Christian agencies & churches; Catholic agencies & churches.
Type of support: General/operating support; Program development; Scholarship funds.
Geographic limitations: Giving primarily in PA.
Support limitations: No grants to individuals.
Application information: Applications not accepted. Contributes only to pre-selected organizations.
Officers: Barbara B. Henkels, Pres.; Christopher B. Henkels, V.P.; Paul M. Henkels, Jr., V.P.; Angela Henkels Dale, Secy.-Treas.
EIN: 236235239
Selected grants: The following grants are a representative sample of this grantmaker's funding activity:
$5,000,524 to Ave Maria University, Ave Maria, FL, 2010.
$379,382 to Father Judge High School, Philadelphia, PA, 2010.
$379,381 to Father Judge High School, Philadelphia, PA, 2010.
$124,740 to Holy Name High School, Reading, PA, 2010.
$124,739 to Holy Name High School, Reading, PA, 2010.
$124,483 to Mount Saint Joseph Academy, Flourtown, PA, 2010.
$124,483 to Mount Saint Joseph Academy, Flourtown, PA, 2010.
$89,304 to Roman Catholic High School for Boys, Philadelphia, PA, 2010.
$74,950 to Bishop McDevitt High School, Wyncote, PA, 2010.
$12,825 to Saint Charles Borromeo School, Bensalem, PA, 2010.

1780
The John Henry Company

5800 W. Grand River Ave.
P.O. Box 17099
Lansing, MI 48906-9111 (517) 323-9000
FAX: (800) 968-5646

Company URL: http://www.jhc.com
Establishment information: Established in 1912.
Company type: Subsidiary of a private company
Business activities: Prints and manufactures pharmaceutical and floriculture and horticulture products and packaging products.
Business type (SIC): Printing/commercial; paper and paperboard/coated, converted, and laminated
Financial profile for 2010: Number of employees, 1,800
Corporate officers: Shahriar Ghoddousi, Vice Chair and C.E.O.; Larry Irish, C.F.O.
Board of director: Shahriar Ghoddousi, Vice Chair.
Giving statement: Giving through the John Henry Company—Lou Brand Scholarship Foundation.

The John Henry Company—Lou Brand Scholarship Foundation

10620 Gulf Shore Dr., Ste. 301
Naples, FL 34108

Establishment information: Established in 1995 in MI.

Donors: The John Henry Co.; Floral Innovations, Inc.; Shahriar Ghoddousi.
Contact: Shahriar Ghoddousi, Vice-Chair. and Pres.
Financial data (yr. ended 06/30/12): Assets, $387,116 (M); gifts received, $7,517; expenditures, $22,586; qualifying distributions, $20,050; giving activities include $20,050 for grants to individuals.
Purpose and activities: The foundation awards college scholarships to children of employees of the John Henry Company.
Type of support: Employee-related scholarships.
Geographic limitations: Giving primarily in areas of company operations.
Application information: Applications accepted. Application form required.
Initial approach: Letter
Deadline(s): 3rd Monday of May
Officers and Directors:* Shahriar Ghoddousi, Chair.; Larry G. Irish, Secy.-Treas.; Bruce Harte.
EIN: 383243055

1781
Henry Modell & Company, Inc.

(doing business as Modell's Sporting Goods)
498 7th Ave., 20th Fl.
New York, NY 10018 (212) 822-1000

Company URL: http://www.modells.com
Establishment information: Established in 1889.
Company type: Private company
Business activities: Operates sporting goods stores.
Business type (SIC): Shopping goods stores/ miscellaneous
Corporate officers: William Modell, Chair.; Mitchell B. Modell, C.E.O.; Robert Stevenish, Pres. and C.O.O.; Eric J. Spiel, Exec. V.P. and C.F.O.
Board of directors: William Modell, Chair.; Michael Blitzer; William Kussell

Modell's Sporting Goods Corporate Giving Program

c/o Community Affairs
498 Seventh Ave., 20th Fl.
New York, NY 10018-6738
URL: http://www.modells.com/corp/index.jsp?page=corporategiving

Purpose and activities: Modell's Sporting Good makes charitable contributions to nonprofit organizations involved with families, youth, education, and physical activity. Support is limited to Connecticut, Washington, DC, Delaware, Massachusetts, Maryland, New Hampshire, New Jersey, New York, Pennsylvania, Rhode Island, and Virginia.
Fields of interest: Education; Public health, physical fitness; Athletics/sports, amateur leagues; Youth development; Family services.
Type of support: Donated products; General/ operating support; In-kind gifts; Sponsorships.
Geographic limitations: Giving limited to areas of company operations in CT, Washington, DC, DE, MA, MD, NH, NJ, NY, PA, RI, and VA.
Support limitations: No support for religious organizations not of direct benefit to the entire community, or political, fraternal, lobbying, or discriminatory organizations. No grants to individuals, or for capital campaigns, endowments, or memorials.
Publications: Application guidelines.
Application information: Applications accepted. Proposals should be submitted using organization letterhead. E-mailed or faxed proposals are not accepted. Proposal materials, including photographs, videos, CDs and special binders, cannot be returned. Telephone calls and e-mails during the application process are not encouraged. Application form required. Applicants should submit the following:
1) qualifications of key personnel
2) name, address and phone number of organization
3) geographic area to be served
4) copy of most recent annual report/audited financial statement/990
5) listing of board of directors, trustees, officers and other key people and their affiliations
6) detailed description of project and amount of funding requested
7) contact person
8) copy of current year's organizational budget and/ or project budget

Proposals should specifically note the nature of the request being made; and include the date and location of the event; a description of past support by Modell's Sporting Goods with the organization; and the Tax ID Number of the organization.
Initial approach: Download application form and send with proposal to local Modell's Sporting Goods Store
Copies of proposal: 1
Deadline(s): 8 weeks prior to event; 12 weeks prior to event for product donations
Final notification: 4 weeks; 8 weeks for product donations

1782
Hensyn, Inc.

200 Central Ave., Ste. 200
Mountainside, NJ 07092-1961
(908) 654-4360

Establishment information: Established in 1974.
Company type: Private company
Business activities: Operates residential construction company.
Business type (SIC): Contractors/general residential building
Corporate officers: Henry Schwartz, Pres.; Steven Schwarz, Secy.-Treas.
Giving statement: Giving through the Schwarz Foundation.

Schwarz Foundation

200 Central Ave., Ste. 102
Mountainside, NJ 07092-1691

Establishment information: Established in 1982 in NJ.
Donors: Steven Schwarz; Henryk Schwarz; Brooklawn Gardens, Inc.; East Rock Village, Inc.; Hensyn, Inc.; Greenwood Gardens, Inc.; Oakwood Homes, Inc.; Woodcliff, Inc.
Financial data (yr. ended 06/30/12): Assets, $26,448,051 (M); gifts received, $2,240,000; expenditures, $837,269; qualifying distributions, $830,500; giving activities include $830,500 for grants.
Purpose and activities: The foundation supports hospitals and organizations involved with children and youth, family services, and Judaism.
Fields of interest: Hospitals (general); Children/ youth, services; Family services; Jewish federated giving programs; Jewish agencies & synagogues.
Type of support: General/operating support.
Geographic limitations: Giving primarily in NY; some funding in MA.
Support limitations: No grants to individuals.
Application information: Applications not accepted. Contributes only to pre-selected organizations.
Officers: Steven Schwarz, Pres.; Henryk Schwarz, Secy.
EIN: 222430208
Selected grants: The following grants are a representative sample of this grantmaker's funding activity:
$640,000 to PEF Israel Endowment Funds, New York, NY, 2011.
$200,000 to Beth Israel Deaconess Medical Center, Boston, MA, 2011.
$20,000 to American Society for Yad Vashem, New York, NY, 2011.
$10,000 to Harlem Childrens Zone, New York, NY, 2011.
$5,000 to Anti-Defamation League Foundation, New York, NY, 2011.
$2,500 to Simon Wiesenthal Center, New York, NY, 2011.

1783
Herbalist & Alchemist, Inc.

51 S. Wandling Ave.
Washington, NJ 07882-2192
(908) 689-9020

Company URL: http://www.herbalist-alchemist.com
Establishment information: Established in 1981.
Company type: Private company
Business type (SIC): Business services/ miscellaneous
Corporate officer: David Winston, Pres.
Giving statement: Giving through the Herbalist & Alchemist, Inc. Contributions Program.

Herbalist & Alchemist, Inc. Contributions Program

51 South Wandling Ave.
Washington, NJ 07882 (908) 689-9020
URL: http://www.herbalist-alchemist.com

Purpose and activities: Herbalist & Alchemist is a certified B Corporation that donates a percentage of profits to charitable organizations.

1784
Heritage Imports, Inc.

9808 Reisterstown Rd.
Owings Mills, MD 21117-4137
(410) 363-8300

Establishment information: Established in 1984.
Company type: Subsidiary of a private company
Business activities: Distributes lace fabrics.
Business type (SIC): Apparel, piece goods, and notions—wholesale
Financial profile for 2011: Sales volume, $19,400,000
Corporate officers: Brian Fader, Pres.; Steven B. Fader, C.E.O.
Giving statement: Giving through the Heritage Lace Foundation.

Heritage Lace Foundation

(formerly Heritage Imports Foundation)
309 South St.
Pella, IA 50219-2155

Establishment information: Established in 1989 in IA.

Donors: Heritage Imports, Inc.; J. Mark De Cook; M. Bruce Heerema.
Contact: J. Mark DeCook, Fdn. Mgr.
Financial data (yr. ended 12/31/11): Assets, $52,393 (M); expenditures, $1,667; qualifying distributions, $1,250; giving activities include $1,250 for grants.
Purpose and activities: The foundation supports organizations involved with K-12 and higher education, counseling, and human services.
Fields of interest: Education; Public affairs; Religion.
Type of support: General/operating support.
Geographic limitations: Giving primarily in central IA.
Support limitations: No grants to individuals.
Application information: Applications accepted. Application form required.
Initial approach: Contact foundation for application form
Copies of proposal: 2
Deadline(s): None
Officers: J. Mark DeCook, Fdn. Mgr.; M. Bruce Heerema, Fdn. Mgr.
EIN: 421343484

1785
Heritage Oaks Bancorp

1222 Vine St.
Paso Robles, CA 93446 (805) 369-5200
FAX: (805) 238-6257

Company URL: http://www.heritageoaksbank.com
Establishment information: Established in 1983.
Company type: Public company
Company ticker symbol and exchange: HEOP/NASDAQ
Business activities: Operates bank holding company; operates commercial bank.
Business type (SIC): Banks/commercial; holding company
Financial profile for 2012: Number of employees, 251; assets, $1,097,530,000; pre-tax net income, $11,240,000; liabilities, $952,000,000
Corporate officers: Michael J. Morris, Chair.; Donald H. Campbell, Vice-Chair.; Simone F. Lagomarsino, Pres. and C.E.O.; Mark K. Olson, Exec. V.P. and C.F.O.; William Raver, Exec. V.P., Genl. Counsel
Board of directors: Michael J. Morris, Chair.; Donald Campbell, Vice-Chair.; Michael J. Behrman; Mark C. Fugate; Dee Lacey; Simone F. Lagomarsino; James J. Lynch; Daniel J. O'Hare; Michael E. Pfau; Alexander F. Simas; Lawrence P. Ward
Subsidiary: Heritage Oaks Bank, Paso Robles, CA
Giving statement: Giving through the Heritage Oaks Bancorp Contributions Program.
Company EIN: 770388249

Heritage Oaks Bancorp Contributions Program

P.O. Box 7012
Paso Robles, CA 93447-7012
URL: http://www.heritageoaksbank.com/about_us/community_giving

Purpose and activities: Heritage Oaks makes charitable contributions to nonprofit organizations involved with education, youth development, and community development. Support is given primarily in areas of company operations in the Central Coast, California area.
Fields of interest: Education; Youth development; Community/economic development.
Type of support: Employee volunteer services; Scholarship funds.
Geographic limitations: Giving primarily in areas of company operations in the Central Coast, CA area; giving also to national organizations.
Application information: Applications accepted. Application form required. Applicants should submit the following:
1) name, address and phone number of organization
2) detailed description of project and amount of funding requested
3) contact person
Applications should indicate the event name, date, location, and time, if applicable.
Initial approach: Complete online application form
Deadline(s): 120 days prior to need
Final notification: 45 days

1786
Hermann Companies, Inc.

7701 Forsyth Blvd., 10th Fl.
St. Louis, MO 63105-1818 (314) 863-9200
FAX: (314) 863-9202

Establishment information: Established in 1956.
Company type: Private company
Business activities: Manufactures plastic packaging materials.
Business type (SIC): Plastic products/miscellaneous
Financial profile for 2009: Number of employees, 600
Corporate officers: Robert Ringen Hermann, Jr., Chair. and C.E.O.; Dolores M. Frank, V.P. and Secy.
Board of director: Robert Ringen Hermann, Jr., Chair.
Giving statement: Giving through the Hermann Family Foundation.

Hermann Family Foundation

(formerly The Hermann Foundation)
7701 Forsyth Blvd., 10th Fl.
St. Louis, MO 63105-1818

Establishment information: Established in 1992 in MO.
Donors: Robert R. Hermann; Hermann Cos., Inc.; Jean E. Hermann.
Contact: Robert R. Hermann, Sr. Dir.
Financial data (yr. ended 12/31/11): Assets, $90,660 (M); expenditures, $256,298; qualifying distributions, $252,387; giving activities include $252,387 for grants.
Purpose and activities: The foundation supports botanical gardens and organizations involved with education, wildlife, and recreation. Support is given primarily in the St. Louis, Missouri, area.
Fields of interest: Education; Botanical gardens; Animals/wildlife; Recreation; United Ways and Federated Giving Programs.
Geographic limitations: Giving limited to St. Louis, MO.
Support limitations: No support for political organizations.
Application information: Applications not accepted. Contributes only to pre-selected organizations.
Board meeting date(s): Dec. and June
Directors: Dolores Frank, Secy.; Mary Lee Hermann; Robert R. Hermann, Sr.; Robert R. Hermann, Jr.; Carlota Hermann Holton.
EIN: 431616989
Selected grants: The following grants are a representative sample of this grantmaker's funding activity:
$5,000 to Princeton University, Princeton, NJ, 2009.
$5,000 to Saint Louis Science Center Foundation, Saint Louis, MO, 2009.
$2,500 to Saint Louis Art Museum Foundation, Saint Louis, MO, 2009.

1787
Herr Foods Inc.

20 Herr Dr.
P.O. Box 300
Nottingham, PA 19362-9788
(610) 932-9330
FAX: (610) 932-1190

Company URL: http://www.herrs.com
Establishment information: Established in 1946.
Company type: Private company
Business activities: Produces snack chips.
Business type (SIC): Miscellaneous prepared foods
Financial profile for 2010: Number of employees, 1,500
Corporate officers: James M. Herr, Chair. and C.E.O.; Edwin H. Herr, Pres.; Gerry Kluis, Sr. V.P., Finance, and C.F.O.
Board of director: James M. Herr, Chair.
Giving statement: Giving through the Herr Foods Inc. Corporate Giving Program.

Herr Foods Inc. Corporate Giving Program

c/o Corp. Donations
20 Herr Dr.
P.O. Box 300
Nottingham, PA 19362-9788 (610) 932-9330
For organization names A-K: Maryann Tice, fax: (610) 998-2936, e-mail: maryann.tice@herrs.com; For organization names L-Z: Sherri Ankney, fax: (610) 998-2937, e-mail: sherri.ankney@herrs.com; URL: http://www.herrs.com/AboutHerrs/CharitableGiving.html

Purpose and activities: Herr makes charitable contributions to nonprofit organizations involved with children and youth, health care, human services, and on a case by case basis. Support is given primarily in areas of company operations.
Fields of interest: Health care; Human services; General charitable giving Children/youth.
Type of support: Donated products; General/operating support; Sponsorships.
Geographic limitations: Giving primarily in areas of company operations; giving also to national organizations.
Application information: Applications accepted. Application form not required. Applicants should submit the following:
1) population served
2) name, address and phone number of organization
3) contact person
Product donation requests should include the name, date, location, and a description of the event.
Initial approach: Proposal to headquarters
Deadline(s): 3 weeks prior to need for product donations

1788
Herrick Pacific Corporation
2000 Crow Canyon Pl., Ste. 360
San Ramon, CA 94583-1383
(925) 242-0244

Establishment information: Established in 1969.
Company type: Private company
Business activities: Manufactures fabricated and structured steel products for the automobile industry.
Business type (SIC): Fabricated metal products (except machinery and transportation equipment); manufacturing/miscellaneous
Corporate officers: D.L. Howard, Pres.; Stephen G. Bender, V.P., Finance
Board of director: Frederick M. O'Such
Giving statement: Giving through the Quest Foundation.

Quest Foundation
P.O. Box 339
Danville, CA 94526-0339 (925) 743-1925

Establishment information: Established in 2005 in CA.
Donors: Herrick-Pacific Corporation; Dorothy Jernstedt Trust.
Financial data (yr. ended 12/31/11): Assets, $85,570,117 (M); expenditures, $4,627,290; qualifying distributions, $4,380,964; giving activities include $4,103,400 for 61 grants (high: $2,246,000; low: $3,400).
Purpose and activities: The foundation supports youth development clubs and organizations involved with education, substance abuse services, learning disorders, and human services.
Fields of interest: Secondary school/education; Education, services; Education, reading; Education; Substance abuse, services; Learning disorders; Youth development, centers/clubs; Boys & girls clubs; Children/youth, services; Family services; Women, centers/services; Human services.
Type of support: Continuing support; General/operating support.
Geographic limitations: Giving primarily in CA.
Application information: Applications not accepted. Contributes only to pre-selected organizations.
Officers and Director:* Dorothy Jernstedt*, Pres.; Derek Jernstedt, Secy. and Exec. Dir.; Richard Becher, C.F.O.; Mary Gonup, Mgr.; Jaci Jernstedt.
EIN: 201844715
Selected grants: The following grants are a representative sample of this grantmaker's funding activity:
$130,104 to Teach for America, San Francisco, CA, 2009.
$115,000 to Chartwell School, Seaside, CA, 2009.
$100,000 to Off the Street Club, Chicago, IL, 2009.
$88,000 to Eastside College Preparatory School, East Palo Alto, CA, 2009.
$50,525 to Athenian School, Danville, CA, 2009.
$46,250 to Friends of the Children-Portland, Portland, OR, 2009.
$42,403 to Hanna Boys Center, Sonoma, CA, 2009.
$27,523 to KIPP LA Schools, Los Angeles, CA, 2009.
$20,640 to Bay Area Crisis Nursery, Concord, CA, 2009.
$20,000 to Big Sky Youth Empowerment Project, Bozeman, MT, 2009.

1789
Herrick, Feinstein LLP
2 Park Ave.
New York, NY 10016-5675 (212) 592-1507

Company URL: http://www.herrick.com/index.cfm
Establishment information: Established in 1928.
Company type: Private company
Business activities: Operates law firm.
Business type (SIC): Legal services
Offices: Newark, Princeton, NJ; New York, NY
Giving statement: Giving through the Herrick, Feinstein LLP Pro Bono Program.

Herrick, Feinstein LLP Pro Bono Program
2 Park Ave.
New York, NY 10016-5675 (212) 592-1498
E-mail: lgoldberg@herrick.com; Additional tel.: (212) 592-1400; Additional Pro Bono Contact: Louis Goldberg, Partner, tel.: (212) 592-1498, e-mail: lgoldberg@herrick.com; URL: http://www.herrick.com/sitecontent.cfm?pageid=11&itemid=1447

Contact: Louis Goldberg, Partner
Fields of interest: Legal services.
Type of support: Pro bono services - legal.
Geographic limitations: Giving primarily in areas of company operations in Newark, and Princeton, NJ, and New York, NY.
Application information: The Pro Bono Committee manages the pro bono program.

1790
Herschend Family Entertainment Corporation
(formerly Silver Dollar City, Inc.)
100 Corporate Pl.
Branson, MO 65616-6172 (417) 334-0142

Company URL: http://www.hfecorp.com
Establishment information: Established in 1950.
Company type: Subsidiary of a private company
Business activities: Operates theme park.
Business type (SIC): Amusement and recreation services/miscellaneous
Financial profile for 2009: Number of employees, 1,500
Corporate officers: Joel Manby, Pres. and C.E.O.; Jane Cooper, C.O.O; Andrew Wexler, C.F.O.; Rick Baker, Sr. V.P., Corp. Mktg.; Eric Lent, Sr. V.P., Mktg.; Rick Todd, Sr. V.P., Human Resources; Rhonda Youngblood, V.P. and C.A.O.; Brandon Kenney, V.P. and C.I.O.; Steve Earnest, V.P. and Genl. Counsel; John Carson, V.P., Human Resources
Board of directors: Chuck Bengochea; R.A. Griffin, Jr.; Chris Herschend; Joel Manby; Todd Schurz; Nelson Schwab III; Donna Tuttle
Giving statement: Giving through the Silver Dollar City, Inc. Corporate Giving Program and the Silver Dollar City Foundation, Inc.

Silver Dollar City, Inc. Corporate Giving Program
5445 Triangle Pkwy., Ste. 200
Norcross, GA 30092
URL: http://www.hfecorp.com/commitment/community.php

Purpose and activities: As a complement to its foundation, Silver Dollar City also makes charitable contributions to nonprofit organizations directly. Support is given to national organizations.
Fields of interest: Education, reading; Environment, plant conservation; Animals/wildlife, sanctuaries; Aquariums; Marine science.
Type of support: Employee volunteer services; In-kind gifts.
Geographic limitations: Giving primarily in areas of company operations; giving also to national organizations.

Silver Dollar City Foundation, Inc.
7347 W. Hwy. 76, Ste. A
Branson, MO 65616-7116 (417) 336-7077
FAX: (417) 336-7075;
E-mail: acallison@silverdollarcity.com; Additional tel.: (417) 336-7055; URL: http://www.silverdollarcityfoundation.com/

Establishment information: Established in 1996 in MO.
Donor: Silver Dollar City, Inc.
Contact: Anita Prochnow, Exec. Dir.
Financial data (yr. ended 12/31/10): Assets, $158,154 (M); gifts received, $275,897; expenditures, $321,807; qualifying distributions, $261,400; giving activities include $261,400 for grants.
Purpose and activities: The foundation supports programs designed to actively bring about positive change in the lives of area youth and families with resources that strengthen family relationships while enhancing and growing communities centered in Christian values and ethics.
Fields of interest: Family services; Human services; Christian agencies & churches Youth.
Program:
Care For Kids: The foundation awards grants to area school districts to help meet the basic physical needs of kids where funding is below adequate or nonexistent; promotes in-school mentoring to support kids beyond the physical needs; and provides funding and assistance to area youth ministries that work to meet the spiritual and emotional needs of youth.
Type of support: Building/renovation; General/operating support; Matching/challenge support; Program development.
Geographic limitations: Giving primarily in Stone and Taney counties, MO.
Support limitations: No grants to individuals or for capital campaigns.
Publications: Application guidelines.
Application information: Applications accepted. Letters of inquiry should be no longer than 1 page. Additional information may be requested at a later date. Application form not required. Applicants should submit the following:
1) copy of IRS Determination Letter
2) detailed description of project and amount of funding requested
Initial approach: Letter of inquiry
Board meeting date(s): Mar., June, and Sept.
Deadline(s): None
Officers and Directors:* John Baltes*, Pres.; Brad Thomas, V.P.; Judy Miller, Secy.; Gayle Myer*, Treas.; Anita Prochnow, Exec. Dir.; Tracey Barton; Ted Cunningham; Anne Ficarra; Jim Herschend; Lisa Rau.
Number of staff: 2 full-time professional; 1 part-time professional.
EIN: 431742873
Selected grants: The following grants are a representative sample of this grantmaker's funding activity:

$35,000 to Discipleship Focus, Branson, MO, 2010.

1791
The Hershey Company

(formerly Hershey Foods Corporation)
100 Crystal A Dr.
P.O. Box 810
Hershey, PA 17033-9529 (717) 534-4200
FAX: (717) 534-7873

Company URL: http://www.thehersheycompany.com
Establishment information: Established in 1894.
Company type: Public company
Company ticker symbol and exchange: HSY/NYSE
International Securities Identification Number: US4278661081
Business activities: Produces, distributes, and sells confectionery, snack, refreshment, and grocery products.
Business type (SIC): Sugar, candy, and salted/roasted nut production
Financial profile for 2012: Number of employees, 14,200; assets, $4,754,840,000; sales volume, $6,644,250,000; pre-tax net income, $1,015,580,000; expenses, $5,533,100,000; liabilities, $3,718,090,000
Fortune 1000 ranking: 2012—384th in revenues, 272nd in profits, and 607th in assets
Forbes 2000 ranking: 2012—1215th in sales, 828th in profits, and 1823rd in assets
Corporate officers: James E. Nevels, Chair.; John P. Bilbrey, Pres. and C.E.O.; David W. Tacka, Sr. V.P. and C.F.O.; Leslie M. Turner, Sr. V.P., Genl. Counsel, and Secy.; Waheed Zaman, Sr. V.P. and C.A.O.
Board of directors: James E. Nevels, Chair.; Pamela Arway; John P. Bilbrey; Robert F. Cavanaugh; Charles A. Davis; Robert M. Malcolm; James M. Mead; Anthony J. Palmer; Thomas J. Ridge; David L. Shedlarz
Subsidiaries: Hershey Chocolate & Confectionery Corp., Wheat Ridge, CO; Hershey Chocolate of Virginia, Inc., Stuarts Draft, VA
Plants: Oakdale, CA; Naugatuck, CT; Hilo, HI; Robinson, IL; Hazleton, Lancaster, Palmyra, Pennsburg, Reading, PA; Memphis, TN
International operations: Canada; Mexico; Netherlands
Giving statement: Giving through the Hershey Company Contributions Program.
Company EIN: 230691590

The Hershey Company Contributions Program

(formerly Hershey Foods Corporation Contributions Program)
100 Crystal A Dr., P.O. Box 810
Hershey, PA 17033-0810 (800) 468-1714
URL: http://www.thehersheycompany.com/social-responsibility/community.aspx

Purpose and activities: The Hershey Company makes charitable contributions to organizations involved with arts and culture, education, the environment, health and human services, and civic and community initiatives. Special emphasis is directed towards programs designed to help at-risk children. Support is limited to areas of company operations in Hawaii, Illinois, Pennsylvania, Tennessee, and Virginia, and in Brazil, China, India, and Mexico.
Fields of interest: Arts; Education; Environment; Health care; Children/youth, services; Human services; Community/economic development; Public affairs.
International interests: Brazil; China; India; Mexico.
Program:
Dollars for Doers: Through the Dollars for Doers program, The Hershey Company awards grants of $250 to eligible charities with which employees volunteer at least 50 hours.
Type of support: Continuing support; Donated products; Employee volunteer services; General/operating support; Program development.
Geographic limitations: Giving limited to areas of company operations in HI, IL, PA, TN, and VA, and in Brazil, China, India, and Mexico.
Support limitations: No support for political or lobbying organizations, churches or religious organizations, fraternal organizations, or labor organizations. No grants to individuals, or for political campaigns, or general operating support for Cultural Enrichment Fund- or United Way-supported organizations; no student loans.
Publications: Application guidelines.
Application information: Applications accepted. Proposals should be submitted using organization letterhead. Video and other unsolicited submissions are not encouraged. Application form not required.
Applicants should submit the following:
1) timetable for implementation and evaluation of project
2) name, address and phone number of organization
3) copy of IRS Determination Letter
4) brief history of organization and description of its mission
5) copy of most recent annual report/audited financial statement/990
6) list of company employees involved with the organization
7) listing of board of directors, trustees, officers and other key people and their affiliations
8) detailed description of project and amount of funding requested
9) contact person
10) listing of additional sources and amount of support

Requests for product donations should indicate the intended use of the donation, and the date and a description of the event.
Initial approach: Proposal to nearest company facility
Copies of proposal: 1
Deadline(s): 3 months prior to need for product donations
Administrators: Jennifer M. Goss, Corp. Contribs. and Community Rels. Rep.; John C. Long, V.P., Corp. Affairs.
Number of staff: 2 full-time professional; 1 part-time support.

1792
Hertz Global Holdings, Inc.

225 Brae Blvd.
Park Ridge, NJ 07656-0713
(201) 307-2000

Company URL: http://www.hertz.com
Establishment information: Established in 1918.
Company type: Public company
Company ticker symbol and exchange: HTZ/NYSE
Business activities: Rents and leases automobiles; rents industrial and construction equipment.
Business type (SIC): Motor vehicle rentals and leasing; equipment rental and leasing/miscellaneous
Financial profile for 2012: Number of employees, 30,200; assets, $23,286,040,000; sales volume, $9,020,810,000; pre-tax net income, $450,550,000; expenses, $8,570,260,000; liabilities, $20,778,750,000
Fortune 1000 ranking: 2012—293rd in revenues, 531st in profits, and 217th in assets
Forbes 2000 ranking: 2012—1001st in sales, 1600th in profits, and 891st in assets
Corporate officers: Mark P. Frissora, Chair. and C.E.O.; Elyse Douglas, Exec. V.P. and C.F.O.; Joseph F. Eckroth, Exec. V.P. and C.I.O.; Robert J. Stuart, Exec. V.P., Sales and Mktg.; Jeffrey Zimmerman, Exec. V.P., Genl. Counsel, and Secy.; Scott Massengill, Sr. V.P. and Treas.; Jatindar Kapur, Sr. V.P., Finance and Cont.; Richard Broome, Sr. V.P., Comms.; LeighAnne Baker, Sr. V.P., Human Resources
Board of directors: Mark P. Frissora, Chair.; George W. Tamke; Barry H. Beracha; Brian A. Bernasek; Carl T. Berquist; Michael J. Durham; Carolyn Everson; Debra Kelly-Ennis; Michael F. Koehler; Linda Fayne Levinson; David H. Wasserman; Henry C. Wolf
Giving statement: Giving through the Hertz Corporate Giving Program.
Company EIN: 203530539

Hertz Corporate Giving Program

225 Brae Blvd.
Park Ridge, NJ 07656-1870
E-mail: sustainability@hertz.com; URL: http://www.hertzlivingjourney.com/community

Purpose and activities: Hertz makes charitable contributions to nonprofit organizations on a case by case basis. Support is given on a national basis primarily in areas of company operations.
Fields of interest: Disasters, preparedness/services; General charitable giving.
Type of support: Employee volunteer services; General/operating support; Sponsorships.
Geographic limitations: Giving on a national basis primarily in areas of company operations.
Application information: Application form not required.
Initial approach: Proposal to headquarters

1793
Hess Corporation

(formerly Amerada Hess Corporation)
1185 Ave. of the Americas, 40th Fl.
New York, NY 10036 (212) 997-8500
FAX: (302) 655-5049

Company URL: http://www.hess.com
Establishment information: Established in 1933.
Company type: Public company
Company ticker symbol and exchange: HES/NYSE
International Securities Identification Number: US42809H1077
Business activities: Produces oil, gas, and petroleum products.
Business type (SIC): Extraction/oil and gas; petroleum refining
Financial profile for 2012: Number of employees, 14,775; assets, $43,441,000,000; sales volume, $38,373,000,000; pre-tax net income, $3,738,000,000; expenses, $34,635,000,000; liabilities, $22,351,000,000
Fortune 1000 ranking: 2012—75th in revenues, 99th in profits, and 127th in assets
Forbes 2000 ranking: 2012—253rd in sales, 304th in profits, and 530th in assets
Corporate officers: John B. Hess, Chair. and C.E.O.; John P. Rielly, Sr. V.P. and C.F.O.; Timothy B. Goodell II, Sr. V.P. and Genl. Counsel; John J. Scelfo, Sr. V.P., Finance; Mykel Ziolo, Sr. V.P., Human

Resources; Jeffery L. Steinhorn, V.P. and C.I.O.; George C. Barry, V.P. and Secy.; Robert Biglin, V.P. and Treas.; Kevin B. Wilcox, V.P. and Cont.; Richard J. Lawlor, V.P., Sales; John J. Pepper, V.P., Corp. Comms.
Board of directors: John B. Hess, Chair.; Samuel W. Bodman III; Nicholas F. Brady; Gregory P. Hill; Edith E. Holiday; Thomas H. Kean; Risa J. Lavizzo-Mourey; Craig G. Matthews; John H. Mullin III; Samuel A. Nunn; Frank A. Olson; James H. Quigley; Ernst H. Von Metzsch; Robert N. Wilson
Subsidiaries: Amerada Hess Corp., Woodbridge, NJ; Amerada Hess Corp., Houston, TX; Amerada Hess Pipeline Corp., Woodbridge, NJ; Hess Oil Virgin Islands Corp., St. Croix, VI
International operations: Cayman Islands; Denmark; Gabon; Norway; Russia; United Kingdom
Giving statement: Giving through the Hess Corporation Contributions Program.
Company EIN: 134921002

Hess Corporation Contributions Program

(formerly Amerada Hess Corporation Contributions Program)
1185 Ave. of the Americas
New York, NY 10036-2602 (212) 997-8500
URL: http://www.hess.com/sustainability/socialresponsibility/default.aspx

Purpose and activities: Hess Corporation makes charitable contributions to nonprofit organizations involved with education, health, and the quality of life in communities where Hess Corporation does business. Support is given on a national and international basis.
Fields of interest: Education; Environment; Health care; Housing/shelter, development; Disasters, preparedness/services; Community/economic development.
International interests: Algeria; Azerbaijan; Equatorial Guinea; Gabon; Indonesia; Malaysia; Thailand; United Kingdom.
Type of support: Building/renovation; Donated equipment; Donated products; Emergency funds; Employee volunteer services; Fellowships; General/operating support; Program development; Scholarship funds; Sponsorships.
Geographic limitations: Giving on a national and international basis primarily in areas of company operations, in Europe, The Americas, Africa, Southeast Asia, and the United Kingdom.

1794
Hewlett-Packard Company

(also known as HP)
3000 Hanover St.
Palo Alto, CA 94304-1185 (650) 857-1501
FAX: (650) 857-5518

Company URL: http://www.hp.com
Establishment information: Established in 1939.
Company type: Public company
Company ticker symbol and exchange: HPQ/NYSE
International Securities Identification Number: US4282361033
Business activities: Manufactures and provides computing and imaging products, solutions, and services.
Business type (SIC): Computer and office equipment
Financial profile for 2012: Number of employees, 331,800; assets, $108,766,000,000; sales volume, $120,357,000,000; pre-tax net income, -$11,933,000,000; expenses, $131,414,000,000; liabilities, $86,332,000,000
Fortune 1000 ranking: 2012—15th in revenues, 1000th in profits, and 61st in assets
Forbes 2000 ranking: 2012—39th in sales, 1997th in profits, and 238th in assets
Corporate officers: Ralph V. Whitworth, Chair.; Margaret C. Whitman, Pres. and C.E.O.; Bill Veghte, C.O.O.; Catherine A. Lesjak, Exec. V.P. and C.F.O.; John F. Schultz, Exec. V.P. and Genl. Counsel; John Hinshaw, Exec. V.P., Opers.; Tracy Keogh, Exec. V.P., Human Resources
Board of directors: Ralph V. Whitworth, Chair.; Marc L. Andreessen; Shumeet Banerji; Rajiv L. Gupta; John H. Hammergren; Raymond J. Lane; Ann M. Livermore; Gary M. Reiner; Patricia F. Russo; Kennedy G. Thompson; Margaret C. Whitman
Subsidiary: Compaq Computer Corporation, Houston, TX
Plants: Cupertino, Mountain View, Roseville, San Diego, Sunnyvale, CA; Colorado Springs, Fort Collins, CO; Atlanta, GA; Boise, ID; Littleton, MA; Rockaway, NJ; Cincinnati, OH; Corvallis, OR; Aguadilla, PR; Vancouver, WA
International operations: Argentina; Australia; Belgium; Brazil; Bulgaria; Canada; Chile; China; Colombia; Costa Rica; Croatia; Czech Republic; Denmark; Ecuador; Egypt; Finland; France; Germany; Greece; Guatemala; Hong Kong; Hungary; India; Ireland; Israel; Italy; Japan; Latvia; Lithuania; Malaysia; Mexico; Morocco and the Western Sahara; Netherlands; New Zealand; Nigeria; Norway; Peru; Philippines; Poland; Portugal; Romania; Russia; Singapore; Slovakia; Slovenia; South Africa; South Korea; Spain; Sweden; Switzerland; Taiwan; Thailand; Turkey; United Arab Emirates; United Kingdom; Venezuela; Vietnam
Historic mergers: Electronic Data Systems Corporation (August 26, 2008); Palm, Inc. (July 1, 2010)
Giving statement: Giving through the HP Corporate Giving Program, the Palm Foundation, the TE Connectivity Ltd. Corporate Giving Program, and the Hewlett-Packard Company Foundation.
Company EIN: 941081436

HP Corporate Giving Program

c/o Office of Global Social Innovation
3000 Hanover St.
Palo Alto, CA 94304-1185 (650) 857-1501
FAX: (650) 857-5518; URL: http://www.hp.com/hpinfo/socialinnovation/index.html

Purpose and activities: As a complement to its foundation, HP also makes charitable contributions to nonprofit organizations and education institutions directly. Special emphasis is directed toward programs designed to promote education; entrepreneurship; health; and community development. Support is given on a national and international basis in areas of company operations.
Fields of interest: Elementary/secondary education; Higher education; Engineering school/education; Education; Medical care, community health systems; Health care, clinics/centers; Health care, infants; Pharmacy/prescriptions; Health care; AIDS; Disasters, preparedness/services; Youth development, business; Children/youth, services; Business/industry; Social entrepreneurship; Community development, small businesses; Science; Mathematics; Engineering/technology; Computer science Minorities; African Americans/Blacks; Hispanics/Latinos; Native Americans/American Indians; Economically disadvantaged.
Programs:

Employee Product Gift Matching: Through the Employee Product Giving Program, employees supports nonprofit organizations and educational institutions with equipment donations. Employees pay 25% of the list price of an HP product, and HP pays the remaining 75%.

HP Catalyst Initiative: Through the HP Catalyst Initiative, the company creates a network of educators, education institutions, and key stakeholders in selected countries to explore innovative approaches to STEM education. Each consortium through dialogue and debate focuses on specific opportunities to use technology to enhance STEM teaching and learning to better prepare students to compete in the information economy.

HP Labs Innovation Research Program (IRP): Through IRP, HP Labs annually awards research grants of up to $75,000 to a graduate student to assist the Principal Investigator conduct a collaborative research project. Research topics include cloud and security, information analytics, intelligent infrastructure, mobile and immersive experience, networking and communications, printing and content delivery, services, social computing, and sustainable ecosystems. Awards are renewable up to three years based on research outcomes and HP business needs.

HP Learning Initiative for Entrepreneurs (HP LIFE): Through HP LIFE, the company trains students, entrepreneurs, and small business owners to harness the power of IT to establish and grow their business, build successful companies, and create jobs.

HP Scholars: The company awards scholarships to African-American, Latino, and American Indian high school seniors to complete degrees in computer science, computer engineering, or electrical engineering at a HP Scholar partnership university. Scholarship packages include cash, HP internships, HP equipment, and a paid internship at HP during the three summers between their engineering studies.

Type of support: Computer technology; Donated products; Employee matching gifts; Employee volunteer services; Equipment; General/operating support; In-kind gifts; Pro bono services - interactive/website technology; Pro bono services - legal; Pro bono services - marketing/branding; Pro bono services - strategic management; Program development.
Geographic limitations: Giving on a national and international basis in areas of company operations, with emphasis on CA, Washington, DC, MA, NY, VA, Brazil, China, India, Kenya, Nigeria, Russia, South Africa, and Turkey.
Support limitations: No grants to individuals (except for HP Scholars and HP Labs Research Program), or for scholarships, sponsorships, conferences, contests, door prizes, festivals, fundraising, incentive programs, marketing, promotional items, raffles, registration fees, research, or feasibility studies, or sports events; no loans.
Application information: Unsolicited requests for funds are generally not accepted. Hewlett-Packard creates partnerships with select international leaders to find systemic solutions to global issues.
Deadline(s): Visit website for application deadlines and guidelines for HP Labs Innovation Research Program and HP Scholars
Administrators: Caroline Barlerin, Dir., Comms. and Global Community Involvement; Paul Ellingstad, Dir., Global Health; Jeannette Weisschuh, Dir., Education Initiatives; Gabi Zedlmayer, V.P., Office of Global Social Innovation.
Number of staff: 18 full-time professional; 2 full-time support.

The Palm Foundation
(formerly Palm, Inc. Corporate Giving Program)
950 West Maude Ave.
Sunnyvale, CA 94085-2801
FAX: (408) 224-7563;
E-mail: gisela.bushey@palm.com; URL: http://www.hpwebos.com/us/company/palm-foundation-template.html

Contact: Gisela B. Bushey, Fdn. Mgr.
Purpose and activities: The Palm Foundation makes charitable contributions to nonprofit organizations involved with child and youth development and education. Special emphasis is directed towards programs that demonstrate the innovative use of Palm mobile computing devices. Support is given primarily in areas of company operations in California and Massachusetts, and in Brazil, France, Ireland, Singapore, and the United Kingdom.
Fields of interest: Elementary/secondary education; Child development, education; Education, special; Youth development; Children/youth, services; Children, foster care.
International interests: Brazil; France; Ireland; Singapore; United Kingdom.
Program:
Employee Matching Gift Program: Through the Employee Matching Gift Program, Palm matches cash donations and volunteer time up to $1,000 per employee, per fiscal year.
Type of support: Donated products; Employee matching gifts; Employee volunteer services; General/operating support.
Geographic limitations: Giving primarily in areas of company operations in CA and MA, and in Brazil, France, Ireland, Singapore, and the United Kingdom.
Application information: The foundation is not accepting new proposals until further notice.

Hewlett-Packard Company Foundation
3000 Hanover St.
Palo Alto, CA 94304-1112 (650) 857-4954
E-mail: philanthropy_ed@hp.com; Application address: P.O. Box 10301, Palo Alto, CA 94303; URL: http://www8.hp.com/us/en/hp-information/social-innovation/hp-foundation.html

Establishment information: Established in 1979 in CA.
Donors: Hewlett-Packard Co.; EDS Foundation.
Financial data (yr. ended 10/31/11): Assets, $64,197,524 (M); expenditures, $4,770,346; qualifying distributions, $4,398,276; giving activities include $1,400,000 for 15 grants (high: $525,000; low: $75,000) and $2,998,276 for employee matching gifts.
Purpose and activities: The foundation supports programs designed to promote science and math education; and responds to natural disasters in times of need.
Fields of interest: Education; Health care; Disasters, preparedness/services; Disasters, floods; Disasters, search/rescue; American Red Cross; Human services; United Ways and Federated Giving Programs; Mathematics; Engineering/technology; Science.
Type of support: Building/renovation; Employee matching gifts; Equipment; General/operating support.
Geographic limitations: Giving on a national basis in areas of company operations, with emphasis on Washington, DC; giving also to national organizations.
Support limitations: No support for sectarian or denominational groups or discriminatory or political organizations. No grants to individuals or for research.
Application information: Applications not accepted. Contributes only to pre-selected organizations.
Officers and Directors:* Marcela Perez de Alonso*, Chair.; Michael J. Holston*, Secy.; Catherine A. Lesjak*, C.F.O.
EIN: 942618409
Selected grants: The following grants are a representative sample of this grantmaker's funding activity:
$811,146 to American Red Cross National Headquarters, Washington, DC, 2010. For disaster relief.
$300,000 to Save the Children Federation, Westport, CT, 2010. For disaster relief for floods in Pakistan.
$250,000 to Doctors Without Borders USA, New York, NY, 2010. For disaster relief for Chile Earthquake.
$230,000 to Resource Area for Teaching, San Jose, CA, 2010. To supply teaching resources.
$125,000 to UNICEF, New York, NY, 2010. For disaster relief for China Earthquake.
$125,000 to World Vision International, Monrovia, CA, 2010. For disaster relief for China Earthquake.
$50,000 to World Food Program USA, Washington, DC, 2010. For disaster relief for floods in Pakistan.

1795
Hexcel Corporation
2 Stamford Plz., 16th Fl.
281 Tresser Blvd.
Stamford, CT 06901-3238 (203) 969-0666
FAX: (302) 636-5454

Company URL: http://www.hexcel.com/
Establishment information: Established in 1946.
Company type: Public company
Company ticker symbol and exchange: HXL/NYSE
Business activities: Develops, manufactures, and markets lightweight reinforcement products, composite materials, and composite structures.
Business type (SIC): Plastics and synthetics
Financial profile for 2012: Number of employees, 4,973; assets, $1,603,100,000; sales volume, $1,578,200,000; pre-tax net income, $237,700,000; expenses, $1,329,400,000; liabilities, $609,000,000
Corporate officers: David E. Berges, Chair. and C.E.O.; Nick L. Stanage, Pres. and C.O.O.; Wayne C. Pensky, Sr. V.P. and C.F.O.; Ira J. Krakower, Sr. V.P., Genl. Counsel, and Secy.; Robert G. Hennemuth, Sr. V.P., Human Resources; Kimberly A. Hendricks, V.P., Corp. Cont., and C.A.O.; Michael J. MacIntyre, Treas.
Board of directors: David E. Berges, Chair.; Joel S. Beckman; Lynn Brubaker, Jr.; Jeffrey C. Campbell; Sandra L. Derickson; W. Kim Foster; Thomas A. Gendron; Jeffrey A. Graves; David C. Hill; David L. Pugh
Plants: Casa Grande, Chandler, AZ; Anaheim, Del Mar, Livermore, Newbury Park, Pleasanton, San Francisco, CA; Reno, NV; Lancaster, OH; Pottsville, PA; Graham, Seguin, TX; Burlington, WA
International operations: Austria; Barbados; Belgium; Brazil; Denmark; France; Germany; Hong Kong; Italy; Japan; Luxembourg; Malaysia; Mauritius; Netherlands; Spain; United Kingdom
Giving statement: Giving through the Hexcel Corporation Contributions Program, the Wallace Meschishnick Clackson Zawada Pro Bono Program, and the Hexcel Foundation.
Company EIN: 941109521

Hexcel Foundation
281 Tresser Blvd., 16th Fl.
Stamford, CT 06901-3238 (203) 969-0666
URL: http://hexcel.com/

Establishment information: Established in 1984 in CA.
Donor: Hexcel Corp.
Contact: Michael Bacal, Treas.
Financial data (yr. ended 06/30/12): Assets, $23,205 (M); gifts received, $57,000; expenditures, $59,662; qualifying distributions, $59,600; giving activities include $59,600 for 15 grants (high: $57,000; low: $25).
Purpose and activities: The foundation supports organizations involved with higher education. Special emphasis is directed toward institutions offering degrees in and programs designed to focus on materials science.
Fields of interest: Education.
Type of support: Capital campaigns; General/operating support; Scholarship funds.
Geographic limitations: Giving primarily in CT.
Support limitations: No support for religious organizations, veterans', political, or labor organizations or organizations not of direct benefit to the entire community. No grants to individuals, or for courtesy or journal advertising not of direct benefit to the entire community.
Publications: Application guidelines.
Application information: Applications accepted. Application form required. Applicants should submit the following:
1) copy of IRS Determination Letter
2) list of company employees involved with the organization
3) explanation of why grantmaker is considered an appropriate donor for project
4) detailed description of project and amount of funding requested

Initial approach: Proposal
Deadline(s): None

Officers: Wayne Pensky, Pres.; Michael P. MacIntyre, V.P.; Rodney P. Jenks, Jr., Secy.; Michael Bacal, Treas.
EIN: 942972860

1796
Heyrman Construction Co., Inc.
1030 Waube Ln.
P.O. Box 28046
Green Bay, WI 54324-8046 (920) 499-0827

Company URL: http://www.heyrmanconstruction.com
Establishment information: Established in 1959.
Company type: Private company
Business activities: Provides nonresidential general contract construction services.
Business type (SIC): Contractors/general nonresidential building
Corporate officers: Christopher Heyrman, Pres.; Earl Heyrman, Treas.; Carla Raisleger, Cont.
Giving statement: Giving through the Heyrman Construction Co., Inc. Foundation.

Heyrman Construction Co., Inc. Foundation
P.O. Box 12800
Green Bay, WI 54307-2800
Application address: c/o Heyrman Construction Co., Inc., 1030 Waube Ln., Green Bay, WI 54304

Establishment information: Established in 1995.

Donor: Heyrman Construction Co., Inc.
Contact: Audrey Feldhausen, Tr.
Financial data (yr. ended 12/31/11): Assets, $91,869 (M); expenditures, $6,370; qualifying distributions, $4,700; giving activities include $4,700 for grants.
Purpose and activities: The foundation supports organizations involved with cancer, youth development, and homelessness.
Fields of interest: Youth development; Human services; Community/economic development.
Type of support: General/operating support.
Geographic limitations: Giving primarily in areas of company operations in WI.
Support limitations: No grants to individuals.
Application information: Applications accepted. Application form not required.
Initial approach: Proposal
Deadline(s): None
Trustees: Audry Feldhausen; Earl Heyrman; Lawrence Heyrman; Vernon Heyrman.
EIN: 396615213

1797
Hickory Tech Corporation

221 E. Hickory St.
P.O. Box 3248
Mankato, MN 56002-3248 (507) 387-3355
FAX: (507) 625-9191

Company URL: http://www.hickorytech.com
Establishment information: Established in 1898.
Company type: Public company
Company ticker symbol and exchange: HTCO/NASDAQ
Business activities: Operates holding company; provides telecommunications services.
Business type (SIC): Holding company; telephone communications
Financial profile for 2012: Number of employees, 508; assets, $2,683,000,000; sales volume, $183,200,000; pre-tax net income, $13,680,000; expenses, $163,810,000; liabilities, $2,194,600,000
Corporate officers: Dale Parker, Jr., Chair.; Diane Dewbrey, Vice-Chair.; John W. Finke, Pres. and C.E.O.; David A. Christensen, Sr. V.P. and C.F.O.; Carol Wirsbinski, Corp. V.P. and C.O.O.; Lane Nordquist, Corp. V.P. and C.I.O.; Mary T. Jacobs, Corp. V.P., Human Resources
Board of directors: Diane Dewbrey, Chair.; Myrita Craig, Vice-Chair.; Robert Alton, Jr.; Lyle Bosacker; James Bracke; John W. Finke; R. Wynn Kearney, Jr.; Dale Parker
Subsidiaries: Mankato Citizens Telephone Co., Mankato, MN; Mid-Communications, Inc., Mankato, MN; National Independent Billing, Inc., Mankato, MN
Giving statement: Giving through the Hickory Tech Corporation Foundation.
Company EIN: 411524393

Hickory Tech Corporation Foundation

(formerly Mankato Citizens Telephone Company Foundation)
P.O. Box 3248
Mankato, MN 56002-3248 (507) 387-3355
E-mail: info@hickorytech.com; URL: http://www.hickorytech.com/about-us/foundation.aspx

Establishment information: Established in 1963 in MN.
Donor: Hickory Tech Corp.
Financial data (yr. ended 02/29/12): Assets, $3,110,097 (M); gifts received, $100,500; expenditures, $156,375; qualifying distributions, $143,592; giving activities include $142,787 for 86 grants (high: $10,000; low: $25).
Purpose and activities: The foundation supports programs designed to promote culture, education, and community.
Fields of interest: Arts; Education; Human services.
Type of support: Continuing support; Employee matching gifts; Employee volunteer services; Employee-related scholarships; Scholarship funds.
Geographic limitations: Giving limited to areas of company operations, with emphasis on the Mankato, MN, area.
Support limitations: No support for discriminatory organizations, political organizations, religious organizations not of direct benefit to the entire community, or fraternal, veterans', or labor groups. No grants to individuals (except for employee-related scholarships), or for general operating support, capital campaigns, political activities, special occasion or goodwill advertising, sports programs or events, or cause-related marketing; no loans or loan guarantees.
Publications: Application guidelines.
Application information: Applications accepted. Application form required. Applicants should submit the following:
1) name, address and phone number of organization
2) copy of IRS Determination Letter
3) brief history of organization and description of its mission
4) copy of most recent annual report/audited financial statement/990
5) explanation of why grantmaker is considered an appropriate donor for project
6) listing of board of directors, trustees, officers and other key people and their affiliations
7) detailed description of project and amount of funding requested
8) contact person
9) copy of current year's organizational budget and/or project budget
10) listing of additional sources and amount of support
11) plans for acknowledgement
Initial approach: Request application form
Copies of proposal: 1
Board meeting date(s): Jan.
Deadline(s): Dec. 1st
Officers: Lyle G. Jacobson, Pres.; David A. Christensen, Secy.-Treas.
Directors: Myrita J. Craig; Diane L. Dewbrey; John W. Finke; Mike L. Olsen.
Number of staff: None.
EIN: 416034001

1798
Highland Craftsmen Inc

534 Oak Ave.
Spruce Pine, NC 28777 (828) 765-9010
FAX: (828) 765-9012

Company URL: http://www.BarkHouse.com
Establishment information: Established in 1992.
Company type: Private company
Business type (SIC): Business services/miscellaneous
Financial profile for 2010: Number of employees, 50
Corporate officers: Chris McCurry, Co-founder; Marty McCurry, Co-founder
Giving statement: Giving through the Highland Craftsmen Inc. Contributions Program.

Highland Craftsmen Inc. Contributions Program

534 Oak Ave.
Spruce Pine, NC 28777-2728 (828) 765-9010
URL: http://www.BarkHouse.com

Purpose and activities: Highland Craftsmen is a certified B Corporation that donates a percentage of profits to charitable organizations.

1799
Highmark Inc.

5th Avenue Pl.
120 5th Ave.
Pittsburgh, PA 15222-3099 (412) 544-7000
FAX: (412) 544-8368

Company URL: https://www.highmark.com
Establishment information: Established in 1937.
Company type: Private company
Business activities: Operates medical service plan.
Business type (SIC): Insurance/accident and health
Financial profile for 2009: Number of employees, 20,000; sales volume, $13,694,220,000
Corporate officers: J. Robert Baum, Ph.D., Chair.; William Winkenwerder, Jr., M.D., Pres. and C.E.O.; Nanette P. DeTurk, Exec. V.P., Treas., C.A.O., and C.F.O.; Matthew V. T. Ray, Exec. V.P. and C.I.O.; Thomas L. Vankirk, Exec. V.P. and Corp. Secy.
Board of directors: J. Robert Baum, Ph.D., Chair.; David A. Blandino, M.D.; R. Yvonne Campos; Thomas J. Castellano, M.D.; John H. Damcott; Thomas R. Donahue; Don P. Foster; Rufus A. Fulton, Jr.; William M. George; Joseph C. Guyaux; Steven M. Hoffman; Calvin B. Johnson, M.D.; Mark S. Kamlet, Ph.D.; David J. Malone; David M. Matter; Glen T. Meakem; Kenneth R. Melani; Victor A. Roque; Susan W. Shoval; Doris Carson Williams; William Winkenwerder, Jr.
Subsidiaries: Alliance Ventures , Inc., Pittsburgh, PA; Clarity Vision, Camp Hill, PA; Empire Vision Center Inc., Syracuse, NY; Health Education Center Inc., Pittsburgh, PA; HealthGuard of Lancaster, Lancaster, PA; Highmark Life & Casualty Group , Inc., Pittsburgh, PA; Highmark Life Insurance Co., Pittsburgh, PA; Keystone Health Plan West, Inc., Pittsburgh, PA; Standard Property Corp., Pittsburgh, PA; United Concordia Cos. Inc., Harrisburg, PA
Giving statement: Giving through the Highmark Inc. Corporate Giving Program and the Highmark Foundation.

Highmark Inc. Corporate Giving Program

c/o Community Affairs
120 5th Ave.
Pittsburgh, PA 15222 (412) 544-7000
Central Pennsylvania application address: Susan Hubley, 1800 Center St., CTRST 1B L4, Camp Hill, PA 17089, tel.: (717) 302-3843, e-mail: GrantsCentPAApply@highmark.com; Northwestern Pennsylvania application address: James Martin, 717 State St., Erie, PA 16501, tel.: (814) 871-6778, e-mail: GrantsNWPAApply@highmark.com; Southwestern Pennsylvania application address: Mary Anne Papale, 120 5th Ave., FAP 2585, Pittsburgh, PA, 15222, tel.: (412) 544-4032, e-mail: GrantsSWPAApply@highmark.com; URL: https://www.highmark.com/hmk2/responsibility/commitment/index.shtml

Purpose and activities: As a complement to its foundation, Highmark also makes charitable contributions to nonprofit organizations directly. Support is limited to central and western Pennsylvania.
Fields of interest: Public health, obesity; Public health, physical fitness; Mental health, grief/bereavement counseling; Nutrition; Disasters, preparedness/services; Athletics/sports, water sports; Youth development; Children, services; United Ways and Federated Giving Programs; General charitable giving.
Type of support: Employee matching gifts; Employee volunteer services; General/operating support; Sponsorships.
Geographic limitations: Giving limited to central and western PA.
Support limitations: No support for political, fraternal, start-up, or civic organizations. No grants to individuals, or for capital or building campaigns, endowments, religious programs, political campaigns, multi-year pledges, or seed money.
Publications: Application guidelines.
Application information: Applications accepted. Support is limited to 1 contribution per organization during any given year. Application form not required. Applicants should submit the following:
1) timetable for implementation and evaluation of project
2) results expected from proposed grant
3) population served
4) name, address and phone number of organization
5) copy of IRS Determination Letter
6) brief history of organization and description of its mission
7) geographic area to be served
8) how project's results will be evaluated or measured
9) listing of board of directors, trustees, officers and other key people and their affiliations
10) detailed description of project and amount of funding requested
11) copy of current year's organizational budget and/or project budget
12) listing of additional sources and amount of support
13) plans for acknowledgement

Sponsorship requests should include the date, time, and land location of the event; a description of the event, including the number of years it has been held and past significant or presenting sponsors; sponsorship levels and benefits; confirmed sponsors and other sponsors approached; and the names and backgrounds of any speakers participating in the event.
Initial approach: Proposal
Deadline(s): None for grant requests; 6 to 8 weeks prior to event for sponsorship requests

Selected grants: The following grants are a representative sample of this grantmaker's funding activity:
$50,000 to Center for the Blind and Visually Impaired, Chester, PA, 2007. For statewide Prevention of Blindness program designed to prevent vision loss and impairment in children.
$35,000 to Southeast Lancaster Health Services, Lancaster, PA, 2007. For women's health program to help with cost of prenatal care for uninsured women.
$22,830 to East End United Community Center, Uniontown, PA, 2007. For increased physical activity and nutrition education for Elementary and Middle School After School Program.
$21,500 to Schuylkill Medical Center-South Jackson Street, Pottsville, PA, 2007. Toward Community Health Awareness Talks (CHATS).
$15,000 to Benedictine Sisters, Inner-City Neighborhood Art House, Erie, PA, 2007. To continue fitness, wellness, and nutrition programs for more than 500 of Erie's inner-city children ages 7-18.
$10,000 to Beaver County Career and Technology Center, Monaca, PA, 2007. For enhancing Healthy Hearts program, which addresses issues of obesity, high cholesterol and diabetes in adolescents.
$10,000 to Bethesda Mission, Harrisburg, PA, 2007. To provide dental exams, preventative care, and follow-up to men in need who use organization's shelter.
$7,800 to Childrens Sickle Cell Foundation, Pittsburgh, PA, 2007. For peer education program for sickle cell disease and trait education for teens at 13 YouthPlaces, Inc. sites in Allegheny County.
$5,000 to Adagio Health, Pittsburgh, PA, 2007. For Diaper Incentive Program to reward mothers who quit smoking during pregnancy.
$5,000 to CARE for Children, Bradford, PA, 2007. For Care Kid Fitness Program, which addresses physical, social, and mental well-being of all children, including those with physical and developmental disabilities.

Highmark Foundation

120 5th Ave., Ste. 1733
Pittsburgh, PA 15222-3001 (866) 594-1730
FAX: (412) 544-6120;
E-mail: info@highmarkfoundation.org; Additional tel.: (866) 594-1730; URL: http://www.highmarkfoundation.org/
Additional URL: http://www.highmarkhealthyhigh5.org/index.shtml

Establishment information: Established in 2000 in PA.
Donors: Highmark West Virginia, Inc.; Highmark Inc.
Financial data (yr. ended 12/31/11): Assets, $28,010,601 (M); gifts received, $1,000,000; expenditures, $16,520,798; qualifying distributions, $18,014,943; giving activities include $13,638,548 for 72 grants (high: $3,801,017; low: $5,000).
Purpose and activities: The foundation supports programs designed to address chronic disease, family health, service delivery systems, and healthy communities. Special emphasis is directed toward programs designed to promote lifelong healthy habits in children by addressing bullying and childhood obesity.
Fields of interest: Elementary/secondary education; Education; Health care, equal rights; Hospitals (general); Health care, clinics/centers; Dental care; Reproductive health, prenatal care; Public health; Public health, obesity; Public health, physical fitness; Health care, patient services; Health care; Mental health, grief/bereavement counseling; Mental health/crisis services; Cancer; Heart & circulatory diseases; Nerve, muscle & bone diseases; Diabetes; Health organizations; Crime/violence prevention, youth; Nutrition; Family services Children; Youth; Aging; Disabilities, people with; Minorities; Economically disadvantaged.

Programs:
Chronic Disease: The foundation supports programs designed to address prevalent chronic diseases for at-risk populations, including diabetes, heart disease, cancer, and obesity. Special emphasis is directed toward programs designed to promote intervention, nutrition guidance, physical activity, weight management, and understanding and measuring chronic disease.
Family Health: The foundation supports programs designed to address family health, including childhood obesity and bullying prevention, maternal health, adolescent health, mental health, nutrition and physical activity, and senior care.
Healthy Communities: The foundation supports programs designed to create healthy communities through capacity building and addressing health inequities and interventions. Special emphasis is directed toward programs designed to facilitate a collaborative agenda through community engagement; enhance the capacity and assets needed to improve community health; use data and replicable models; and leverage collaboration to meet the needs of communities.
Highmark Health High 5: Through Highmark Healthy High 5, the foundation promotes lifelong healthy habits in children ages 6-18 by addressing five critical health issues: nutrition, physical activity, bullying prevention, grief, and self-esteem. The program includes a School Challenge Grant Program designed to promote nutrition and physical activity in schools; Health eTools for Schools, a secure web portal for school nurses; SPARK (Sports Play Activity and Recreation for Kids); KidShape, a childhood weight management program, and LearntobeHealthy.org, a wellness website. The initiative concluded at the end of 2011.
Service Delivery Systems: The foundation supports programs designed to help underserved populations gain access to quality health services and retain quality healthcare providers. The foundation supports underserved and uninsured populations, access to care, recruitment of healthcare professionals, community health clinics, and screenings.
Type of support: Continuing support; Curriculum development; Equipment; General/operating support; Management development/capacity building; Matching/challenge support; Program development.
Geographic limitations: Giving primarily in PA.
Support limitations: No support for fraternal or civic groups, discriminatory organizations, or sports teams. No grants to individuals, or for annual fundraising campaigns, capital campaigns, endowment funds, lobbying or political causes or campaigns, debt reduction, sponsorships, clinical research, scholarships, routine operational costs, or overhead costs or direct financial subsidies of health services.
Publications: Application guidelines; Informational brochure (including application guidelines); Program policy statement.
Application information: Applications accepted. Unsolicited proposals are considered on rare occasions. The foundation utilizes invited proposals and a request for proposals (RFP) process. Applicants should submit the following:
1) timetable for implementation and evaluation of project
2) signature and title of chief executive officer
3) qualifications of key personnel
4) statement of problem project will address
5) population served
6) name, address and phone number of organization
7) copy of IRS Determination Letter
8) brief history of organization and description of its mission
9) how project's results will be evaluated or measured
10) detailed description of project and amount of funding requested
11) contact person
12) copy of current year's organizational budget and/or project budget
13) listing of additional sources and amount of support

Initial approach: Proposal
Board meeting date(s): Mar., June, Sept., and Dec.
Deadline(s): None

Officers and Directors:* Doris Carson Williams, Vice-Chair.; Yvonne Cook, Pres.; Melissa M. Anderson*, Treas.; C. Michael Blackwood; Janine Colinear; Don Onorato; Thomas J. Rohner, Jr., M.D.
EIN: 251876666
Selected grants: The following grants are a representative sample of this grantmaker's funding activity:
$3,500,000 to Caring Foundation, Pittsburgh, PA, 2010. To support program and services for Highmark Caring Place, grief counseling facility for children and youth.
$990,627 to Central Susquehanna Intermediate Unit, Milton, PA, 2010. Toward PA Cares (Creating Atmosphere of Respect and Environment for Success) Initiative and to expand access to Olweus Bullying Prevention Program across the Highmark service region.
$750,000 to Susan P. Byrnes Health Education Center, York, PA, 2010. For program activities for Learntobehealthy.org.
$711,112 to Windber Research Institute, Windber, PA, 2010. For HALT Bullying Prevention Program.
$365,000 to Hamilton Health Center, Harrisburg, PA, 2010. For Camp Curtain and Downey Elementary School-Based Health Centers in partnership with Harrisburg School District.
$250,000 to Conemaugh Valley Memorial Hospital, Johnstown, PA, 2010. To establish Center for Health Promotion and Disease Management within the office of Community Health.
$129,815 to Hopeful Hearts, Indiana, PA, 2010. To develop volunteer-based peer support program for grieving children, adolescents and their families at a newly established bereavement center in Indiana County.
$97,460 to Home Nursing Agency and Visiting Nurse Association, Altoona, PA, 2010. For volunteer-based peer support programs for grieving children and their families at two bereavement centers located in Blair and Cambria Counties.
$93,132 to Tides, Inc., State College, PA, 2010. To expand grief support program for children and their families in Centre, Huntingdon and Mifflin Counties.
$34,840 to South Hanover Elementary School, Hershey, PA, 2010. For Moving on Up and Moving Around Program, physical activity for kids in K-5.

1800
Highwoods Realty, LP

3100 Smoketree Ct., Ste. 600
Raleigh, NC 27604-1050 (919) 872-4924

Company URL: http://www.highwoods.com/
Establishment information: Established in 1994.
Company type: Subsidiary of a private company
Business activities: Owns and operates suburban office, industrial, and retail properties.
Business type (SIC): Real estate operators and lessors
Corporate officers: O. Temple Sloan, Jr., Chair.; Edward J. Fritsch, Pres. and C.E.O.; Terry Stevens, Sr. V.P. and C.F.O.; Michael E Harris, Exec. V.P. and C.O.O.; Daniel L. Clemmens, V.P. and C.A.O.; Jeffrey D. Miller, V.P., Genl. Counsel, and Secy.; Art H. McCann, Co.-C.I.O; Theodore J. Klinick, Co.-C.I.O.; S. Hugh Esleeck, Treas.
Board of directors: O. Temple Sloan, Jr., Chair.; Thomas W. Adler; Gene H. Anderson; Edward J. Fritsch; David J. Hartzell; Sherry A. Kellett; Mark F. Mulhern; L. Glenn Orr, Jr.
Giving statement: Giving through the Nichols Company Charitable Trust.

Nichols Company Charitable Trust

4706 Broadway Ave., Ste. 260
Kansas City, MO 64112-1910 (816) 561-3456
Application address: 310 Ward Pkwy., Kansas City, MO 64112; tel.:(816) 561-3456

Establishment information: Trust established in 1952 in MO.
Donors: J.C. Nichols Co.; Highwoods Realty L.P.
Contact: Daniel Hollman, Treas.
Financial data (yr. ended 12/31/11): Assets, $2,995,334 (M); expenditures, $152,077; qualifying distributions, $140,077; giving activities include $137,100 for 54 grants (high: $20,000; low: $100).
Purpose and activities: The foundation supports art museums and hospitals and organizations involved with education, patient services, human services, and the real estate industry.
Fields of interest: Museums (art); Secondary school/education; Higher education; Education; Hospitals (general); Health care, patient services; Food services; Boy scouts; Youth development, business; Salvation Army; Children/youth, services; Human services; Business/industry.
Type of support: General/operating support.
Geographic limitations: Giving primarily in Kansas City, MO.
Support limitations: No grants to individuals.
Application information: Applications accepted. Application form not required. Applicants should submit the following:
1) copy of IRS Determination Letter
2) brief history of organization and description of its mission
3) detailed description of project and amount of funding requested

Initial approach: Letter of inquiry
Deadline(s): None

Officers: Barrett Brady, Pres.; Daniel Hollman, Treas.
EIN: 446015538
Selected grants: The following grants are a representative sample of this grantmaker's funding activity:
$25,000 to Nelson Gallery Foundation, Kansas City, MO, 2009.
$21,000 to Saint Teresas Academy, Kansas City, MO, 2009.
$11,000 to Saint Lukes Hospital Foundation, Kansas City, MO, 2009.
$5,000 to Salvation Army, Kansas City, MO, 2009.
$5,000 to ULI Foundation, Washington, DC, 2009.
$2,500 to Jellybean Conspiracy, Westwood Hills, KS, 2009.
$1,500 to Bishop Ward High School, Kansas City, KS, 2009.
$1,500 to Sherwood Center for the Exceptional Child, Kansas City, MO, 2009.
$1,500 to Synergy Services, Parkville, MO, 2009.

1801
Tommy Hilfiger U.S.A., Inc.

601 W. 26th St., 17th Fl., Ste. 600
New York, NY 10001 (212) 549-6000

Company URL: http://usa.tommy.com
Establishment information: Established in 1985.
Company type: Subsidiary of a foreign company
Business activities: Designs, sources, and markets men's and women's sportswear, jeanswear, and childrenswear.
Business type (SIC): Apparel—men's and boys' outerwear; apparel—women's outerwear
Corporate officers: Fred Gehring, C.E.O.; Ludo Onnink, C.O.O.; Bettina Havrilla, Sr. V.P., Human Resources
Giving statement: Giving through the Tommy Hilfiger Corporate Foundation, Inc.

The Tommy Hilfiger Corporate Foundation, Inc.

601 W. 26th St., 6th Fl.
New York, NY 10001-1101
URL: http://global.tommy.com/int/en/About/philanthropy/corporate-fondation

Establishment information: Established in 1995 in NY.
Donors: Tommy Hilfiger U.S.A., Inc.; Superba, Inc.; VIACOM; L'Oreal USA; Time Warner Inc.
Financial data (yr. ended 03/31/12): Assets, $2,019,314 (M); gifts received, $20,677; expenditures, $0; qualifying distributions, $0.
Purpose and activities: The foundation supports organizations involved with arts and culture, education, health, and international development. Special emphasis is directed toward programs designed to empower youth.
Fields of interest: Historical activities, centennials; Arts; Education; Health care; American Red Cross; International development; Civil/human rights, minorities Youth.
Type of support: General/operating support; Program development; Sponsorships.
Geographic limitations: Giving on a national basis in areas of company operations, with some emphasis on New York, NY.
Support limitations: No support for political parties or discriminatory organizations. No grants to individuals, or for endowments, or film, video, television, or radio projects.
Application information: Applications accepted. Grants range from $10,000 to $25,000. Applicants should submit a separate cover letter summarizing the proposal. Proposals should be no longer than 3 to 5 pages. Telephone calls during the application process are not encouraged. Application form required. Applicants should submit the following:
1) timetable for implementation and evaluation of project
2) how project will be sustained once grantmaker support is completed
3) results expected from proposed grant
4) qualifications of key personnel
5) copy of IRS Determination Letter
6) brief history of organization and description of its mission
7) copy of most recent annual report/audited financial statement/990
8) listing of board of directors, trustees, officers and other key people and their affiliations
9) detailed description of project and amount of funding requested
10) copy of current year's organizational budget and/or project budget
11) listing of additional sources and amount of support

Initial approach: Proposal
Copies of proposal: 1
Deadline(s): Apr. 1 and Oct. 1
Final notification: Following review

Officers and Directors:* Emanuel Chirico*, Chair.; R. Guy Vickers, Pres.; Michael A. Shaffer, Exec. V.P. and C.F.O.; Mark D. Fischer, Sr. V.P. and Secy.; Dana A. Perlman, Sr. V.P. and Treas.; Bruce Goldstein, Sr. V.P.; David F. Kozel, Sr. V.P.; Mathew O'Laughlin, V.P.
EIN: 133856562

1802
Hill Ward Henderson
101 E. Kennedy Blvd., Ste. 3700
Tampa, FL 33602-5195 (813) 221-3900

Company URL: http://www.hwhlaw.com/
Establishment information: Established in 1986.
Company type: Private company
Business activities: Operates law firm.
Business type (SIC): Legal services
Giving statement: Giving through the Hill Ward Henderson Pro Bono Program.

Hill Ward Henderson Pro Bono Program
101 E. Kennedy Blvd., Ste. 3700
Tampa, FL 33602-5195
URL: http://www.hwhlaw.com

Fields of interest: Legal services.
Type of support: Pro bono services - legal.
Application information: The Department Chair manages the pro bono program.

1803
Hill, Holliday, Connors, Cosmopulos, Inc.
53 State St.
Boston, MA 02109 (617) 366-4000

Company URL: http://www.hhcc.com/
Establishment information: Established in 1968.
Company type: Subsidiary of a public company
Business activities: Operates marketing communications and advertising agency.
Business type (SIC): Advertising
Corporate officers: Michael J. Sheehan, C.E.O.; Karen Kaplan, Pres.; Kevin P. Walsh, C.F.O.
Division: Hill, Holliday/New York, New York, NY
Offices: New York, NY; Greenville, SC
Giving statement: Giving through the Hill, Holliday, Connors, Cosmopulos, Inc. Corporate Giving Program.

Hill, Holliday, Connors, Cosmopulos, Inc. Corporate Giving Program
53 State St.
Boston, MA 02109 (617) 366-4000
URL: http://www.hhcc.com/about

Purpose and activities: Hill, Holliday, Connors, and Cosmopulos makes charitable contributions to nonprofit organizations in the greater Boston, Massachusetts, area.
Fields of interest: General charitable giving.
Type of support: Employee volunteer services; General/operating support; In-kind gifts; Pro bono services - marketing/branding; Sponsorships.
Geographic limitations: Giving primarily in the greater Boston, MA, area.
Support limitations: No support for advocacy groups. No grants to individuals.
Application information: Applications accepted. Application form not required.
Initial approach: Proposal to headquarters

1805
The Hilliard Corporation
100 W. 4th St.
Elmira, NY 14902-1504 (607) 733-7121

Company URL: http://www.hilliardcorp.com/
Establishment information: Established in 1905.
Company type: Private company
Business activities: Manufactures engine starters, industrial clutches, and oil purifying equipment.
Business type (SIC): Machinery/general industry; engines and turbines; machinery/industrial and commercial
Corporate officers: Nelson Mooers Van den Blink, Chair. and C.E.O.; Paul D. Webb, Pres.; Gordon Webster, C.F.O.
Board of director: Nelson Mooers Van Den Blink, Chair.
Giving statement: Giving through the Hilliard Foundation, Inc.

Hilliard Foundation, Inc.
100 W. 4th St.
Elmira, NY 14901-2190

Donor: The Hilliard Corp.
Contact: Jan van den Blink, Pres.
Financial data (yr. ended 04/30/12): Assets, $890,597 (M); gifts received, $179,000; expenditures, $100,791; qualifying distributions, $97,609; giving activities include $97,417 for 13 grants (high: $15,000; low: $3,000).
Purpose and activities: The foundation supports history museums and organizations involved with secondary and higher education, health, and community economic development.
Fields of interest: Health care; Youth development; Community/economic development.
Type of support: Capital campaigns.
Geographic limitations: Giving primarily in Elmira, NY.
Support limitations: No grants to individuals.
Application information: Applications accepted. Application form required.
Initial approach: Letter
Deadline(s): None
Officers and Trustees:* Jan Van den Blink*, Pres.; Mary Welles Mooers Smith*, V.P.; Gordon Webster*, Treas.; George L. Howell; Gerald F. Schichtel; Paul H. Schweizer; Allen C. Smith; Finley M. Steele; Richard W. Swan.
EIN: 161176159

1806
Hilliard Farber & Co., Inc.
45 Broadway, 7th Fl.
New York, NY 10006-4009 (212) 797-2115

Company URL: http://www.tradeweb.com/Inter-Dealer/Our-Businesses/
Establishment information: Established in 1975.
Company type: Subsidiary of a foreign company
Business activities: Provides securities brokerage services.
Business type (SIC): Brokers and dealers/security
Corporate officers: Hilliard Farber, Chair., Pres., and C.E.O.; Richard J. Cotter, Exec. V.P. and Cont.
Board of director: Hilliard Farber, Chair.
Office: Murray Hill, NJ
Giving statement: Giving through the Gerald and Carol Galgano Foundation Inc and the Nancy and Thomas Walsh Foundation.

The Gerald and Carol Galgano Foundation Inc
30 Talmadge Ln.
Basking Ridge, NJ 07920-2986

Establishment information: Established in 2002 in NJ.
Donor: Hilliard Farber & Co., Inc.
Financial data (yr. ended 12/31/11): Assets, $699,333 (M); expenditures, $45,807; qualifying distributions, $36,575; giving activities include $36,575 for grants.
Purpose and activities: The foundation supports hospitals and organizations involved with education, counseling and support groups, and children services.
Fields of interest: Education; Human services; Religion.
Type of support: General/operating support; Scholarship funds.
Geographic limitations: Giving primarily in NJ, NY, and PA.
Support limitations: No grants to individuals.
Application information: Applications not accepted. Unsolicited requests for funds not accepted.
Trustees: Carol Galgano; Cheryl A. Galgano; Gerald Galgano; Jim Galgano.
EIN: 522384603

The Nancy and Thomas Walsh Foundation
1030 Clay Ave.
Pelham Manor, NY 10803

Establishment information: Established in 2005 in NY.
Donor: Hilliard Farber & Co., Inc.
Financial data (yr. ended 09/30/11): Assets, $179,744 (M); expenditures, $61,760; qualifying distributions, $57,370; giving activities include $57,370 for 25 grants (high: $25,000; low: $100).
Purpose and activities: The foundation supports organizations involved with education, sports, and children's services.
Fields of interest: Arts; Education; Health care.
Type of support: General/operating support.
Geographic limitations: Giving primarily in NY.
Support limitations: No grants to individuals.
Application information: Applications not accepted. Contributes only to pre-selected organizations.
Directors: Nancy H. Walsh; Sara Ellen Walsh; Thomas C. Walsh, Jr.
EIN: 203987326

1807
Hillis Clark Martin & Peterson P.S.
1221 2nd Ave., Ste. 500
Seattle, WA 98101-2925 (206) 623-1745

Company URL: http://www.hcmp.com/
Establishment information: Established in 1971.
Company type: Private company
Business activities: Operates law firm.
Business type (SIC): Legal services
Giving statement: Giving through the Hillis Clark Martin & Peterson P.S. Pro Bono Program.

Hillis Clark Martin & Peterson P.S. Pro Bono Program
1221 2nd Ave., Ste. 500
Seattle, WA 98101-2925 (206) 623-1745
E-mail: bcf@hcmp.com; URL: http://www.hcmp.com/index.php?p=1_42-community_involvement

Contact: Brian Free, Pro Bono Coord.
Fields of interest: Legal services.
Type of support: Pro bono services - legal.
Geographic limitations: Giving primarily in areas of company operations in Seattle, WA.
Application information: Attorneys pursue pro bono work based on their own personal interests.

1804
Hill-Rom Holdings, Inc.
(formerly Hillenbrand Industries, Inc.)
1069 State Rte. 46 E.
Batesville, IN 47006 (812) 934-7777
FAX: (812) 934-8189

Company URL: http://www.hill-rom.com
Establishment information: Established in 1969.
Company type: Public company
Company ticker symbol and exchange: HRC/NYSE
Business activities: Operates holding company; manufactures and provides medical technologies and related services.
Business type (SIC): Furniture and fixtures/ miscellaneous; medical instruments and supplies; manufacturing/miscellaneous; insurance/life; holding company
Financial profile for 2012: Number of employees, 6,950; assets, $1,627,600,000; sales volume, $1,634,300,000; pre-tax net income, $163,500,000; expenses, $1,465,500,000; liabilities, $815,000,000
Corporate officers: Rolf A. Classon, Chair.; John J. Greisch, Pres. and C.E.O.; Mark Guinan, C.F.O.; Richard G. Keller, V.P., Cont., and C.A.O.; Michael Macek, Treas.
Board of directors: Rolf A. Classon, Chair.; Joanne C. Smith, M.D.; James R. Giertz; Charles E. Golden; John J. Greisch; W. August Hillenbrand; Ronald A. Malone; Eduardo R. Menasce; Katherine S. Napier
Subsidiary: Advanced Respiratory, Inc., St. Paul, MN
Giving statement: Giving through the Hill-Rom Holdings, Inc. Corporate Giving Program and the American Biosystems Vest Foundation.
Company EIN: 351160484

American Biosystems Vest Foundation
(formerly The Vest Foundation)
c/o Corp. Tax Dept.
1020 W. County Rd. F
St. Paul, MN 55126-2910

Donors: American Biosystems; Advanced Respiratory, Inc.
Contact: Pam Strong
Financial data (yr. ended 12/31/11): Assets, $39,029 (M); gifts received, $132; expenditures, $42; qualifying distributions, $0.
Purpose and activities: The foundation donates vest airway clearance devices to economically disadvantaged individuals suffering from acute or chronic respiratory complications.
Fields of interest: Economically disadvantaged.
Type of support: Donated products; Grants to individuals.
Application information: Applications accepted. Application form required.
Initial approach: Letter
Deadline(s): None
Officers: Gregory N. Miller, Chair.; Richard G. Keller, Vice-Chair.; Joyce Hoying, Secy.; Gregory N. Miller, Treas.; Steve Gray, Exec. Dir.
Directors: Patrick D. De Maynadier; Richard G. Keller; Gregory N. Miller.
EIN: 411961092

1808
Hills Bank and Trust Company
131 Main St.
P.O. Box 160
Hills, IA 52235 (319) 679-2291

Company URL: http://www.hillsbank.com
Establishment information: Established in 1904.
Company type: Private company
Business activities: Operates commercial bank.
Business type (SIC): Banks/commercial
Corporate officers: Dwight O. Seegmiller, Pres. and C.E.O.; Shari J. DeMaris, C.F.O. and Secy.-Treas.
Giving statement: Giving through the Hills Bancorporation Foundation.

Hills Bancorporation Foundation
131 Main St.
Hills, IA 52235

Establishment information: Established in 1997.
Donor: Hills Bank and Trust Co.
Financial data (yr. ended 12/31/11): Assets, $1,578,501 (M); gifts received, $200,000; expenditures, $61,101; qualifying distributions, $59,000; giving activities include $59,000 for grants.
Purpose and activities: The foundation supports hospitals and organizations involved with arts and culture, higher education, youth development, and business and industry.
Fields of interest: Arts; Education.
Type of support: General/operating support.
Application information: Applications not accepted. Unsolicited requests for funds not accepted.
Officers: Dwight O. Seegmiller, Pres.; William H. Olin, V.P.; Earlis Rohret, V.P.; John Benson, Secy.; James G. Pratt, Treas.
Directors: Willis M. Bywater; Ann M. Rhodes.
EIN: 391890766

1809
Hillshire Brands Co.
(formerly Sara Lee Corporation)
400 South Jefferson St.
Chicago, IL 60607 (312) 614-6000
FAX: (630) 598-8482

Company URL: http://www.saralee.com
Establishment information: Established in 1939.
Company type: Public company
Company ticker symbol and exchange: HSH/NYSE
International Securities Identification Number: US8031111037
Business activities: Operates food solutions company.
Business type (SIC): Food and kindred products; meat packing plants and prepared meats and poultry
Financial profile for 2012: Number of employees, 9,500; assets, $2,450,000,000; sales volume, $4,094,000,000; pre-tax net income, -$37,000,000; expenses, $4,059,000,000; liabilities, $2,215,000,000
Fortune 1000 ranking: 2012—288th in revenues, 230th in profits, and 808th in assets
Forbes 2000 ranking: 2012—1506th in sales, 858th in profits, and 1961st in assets
Corporate officers: Sean Connolly, Pres. and C.E.O.; Kent Magill, Exec. V.P., Genl. Counsel, and Corp. Secy.; Maria Henry, C.F.O.
Board of directors: Christopher B. Begley; Todd Becker; Ellen L. Brothers; Virgis W. Colbert; Sean Connolly; Laurette T. Koellner; Craig P. Omtvedt; Ian Maurice Gray Prosser; Jonathan P. Ward; James D. White
Plants: Florence, AL; San Lorenzo, CA; Storm Lake, IA; Kansas City, KS; Alexandria, KY; Traverse City, Zeeland, MI; Earth City, St. Joseph, MO; Tarboro, Valdese, NC; Newbern, TN; Haltom City, TX; New London, WI
International operations: Australia; Belgium; Bermuda; Brazil; Canada; China; Czech Republic; Denmark; France; Germany; Greece; Hungary; India; Indonesia; Italy; Kenya; Luxembourg; Malaysia; Mexico; Netherlands; New Zealand; Norway; Philippines; Poland; Portugal; South Africa; Spain; Sri Lanka; Sweden; Switzerland; Thailand; Turkey; United Kingdom; Zimbabwe
Giving statement: Giving through the Hillshire Brands Co. Contributions Program.
Company EIN: 362089049

Hillshire Brands Co. Contributions Program
(formerly Sara Lee Corporation Contributions Program)
400 South Jefferson St.
Chicago, IL 60607 (312) 614-6000
URL: http://www.hillshirebrands.com/Sustainability/CorporateContributions.aspx

Purpose and activities: As a complement to its foundation, Hillshire Brands Co. provides charitable donations to nonprofit organizations directly. Emphasis is given to organizations involved with domestic hunger and promoting healthy weight through energy balance, diet and nutrition education, and physical activity; limited support is also given for new or innovative civic and cultural programs.
Fields of interest: Arts; Public health, obesity; Public health, physical fitness; Food services; Food banks; Nutrition; Public affairs Economically disadvantaged.
Program:
Matching Grants Program: The Hillshire Brands Matching Grants Program is designed to encourage active full-time employees to support eligible nonprofit organizations. Through the program, employees participate in the selection of organizations to be funded by Hillshire Brands. The Matching Grants Program will match contributions made by employees to eligible nonprofit organizatios.
Type of support: Annual campaigns; Donated products; Employee matching gifts; Employee volunteer services; General/operating support; In-kind gifts; Sponsorships.
Geographic limitations: Giving primarily in areas of company operations, with emphasis on Chicago, IL; giving also to national organizations.
Support limitations: No support for organizations whose most recent audit shows an accumulated deficit, organizations with a limited constituency, such as fraternities and veterans groups, religious, discriminatory, or political organizations, single-disease organizations, or government units.

No matching grants for United Way or similar intermediary/re-granting organizations; K-12/ elementary and secondary schools; individual scholarships; discriminatory organizations; political groups; labor organizations; trade or business organizations; fraternal, social or service clubs; PTAs; athletic clubs; athletic boosters; alumni associations; little leagues; churches, religious groups, and associated religious groups that operate nonprofit organizations and represent themselves as having religious backgrounds and ties; fiscal agents; or organizations providing services to domesticated animals such as Anti-Cruelty Societies. No grants to individuals.
Publications: Application guidelines.
Application information: Applications accepted. Requests for Proposals are accepted by invitation only. Hillshire Brands provides United Way Incentive Grants to the local United Way when campaigns are conducted at their facilities. Local United Ways are not eligible to apply using the Letters of Intent feature of the website.
Initial approach: Complete online eligibility quiz and, if applicable, a Letter of Intent; submit online request for event or table support
Administrators: Jason Laws, Volunteer Admin.; Robert Rizzo, Grants Mgr.; Judy E. Schaefer, Dir., Community Investment; Emily Wittenberg, Finance Admin.
Number of staff: 4 full-time professional.

1810
Hillside Capital Incorporated

405 Park Ave., Ste. 1202
New York, NY 10022-4462 (212) 935-6090

Establishment information: Established in 1997.
Company type: Subsidiary of a private company
Business activities: Operates asset management company.
Business type (SIC): Investment offices
Corporate officer: Raymond Weldon, Mgr.
Giving statement: Giving through the JJJ Charitable Foundation.

JJJ Charitable Foundation

c/o Brookside International Inc.
80 Field Point Rd.
Greenwich, CT 06830-6416

Establishment information: Established in 1997 in CT.
Donor: Hillside Capital, Inc.
Financial data (yr. ended 12/31/11): Assets, $12,897,875 (M); expenditures, $1,249,354; qualifying distributions, $1,108,000; giving activities include $1,108,000 for grants.
Purpose and activities: The foundation supports camps and organizations involved with arts and culture, education, wildlife conservation, and health.
Fields of interest: Arts; Education, public policy; Higher education; Education; Animals/wildlife, preservation/protection; Health care, clinics/ centers; Health care; Recreation, camps.
Type of support: Annual campaigns; General/ operating support.
Geographic limitations: Giving primarily in CT and NY.
Support limitations: No grants to individuals.
Application information: Applications not accepted. Contributes only to pre-selected organizations.
Officers and Directors:* John N. Irwin III*, Pres. and Treas.; Raymond F. Weldon, Secy.; Jane W.I. Droppa; Anna M. Irwin; Genevieve T. Irwin; Jeanet H. Irwin.
EIN: 133932002
Selected grants: The following grants are a representative sample of this grantmaker's funding activity:
$150,000 to Wildlife Conservation Society, Bronx, NY, 2010.
$130,000 to Princeton University, Princeton, NJ, 2010.
$50,000 to Wildlife Conservation Society, Bronx, NY, 2010.
$27,000 to American University in Cairo, New York, NY, 2010.
$5,000 to Friends of the National World War II Memorial, Washington, DC, 2010.
$1,000 to Boston University, Boston, MA, 2010.
$1,000 to National Center for Policy Analysis, Dallas, TX, 2010.

1811
Hilo Hattie

1450 Ala Moana Blvd., Ste. 1254
Honolulu, HI 96814 (808) 973-3266
FAX: (808) 973-3277

Company URL: http://www.hilohattie.com
Establishment information: Established in 1963.
Company type: Private company
Business activities: Operates clothing stores.
Business type (SIC): Family apparel and accessory stores
Corporate officers: Donald B.S. Kang, Pres. and C.E.O.; Mark Storfer, Exec. V.P. and C.O.O.; Reid Watanable, V.P. and C.I.O.; Felix Calvo, V.P., Sales and Mktg.
Giving statement: Giving through the Hilo Hattie Corporate Giving Program.

Hilo Hattie Corporate Giving Program

1450 Ala Moana Blvd., Ste. # 1037
Honolulu, HI 96814-4604
E-mail: info@hilohattie.com; URL: http:// www.hilohattie.com

1812
Hilton Worldwide, Inc.

(formerly Hilton Hotels Corporation)
7930 Jones Branch Dr.
McLean, VA 22102 (703) 883-1000

Company URL: http://www.hiltonworldwide.com/
Establishment information: Established in 1919.
Company type: Subsidiary of a private company
Business activities: Operates hotels and resorts.
Business type (SIC): Hotels and motels
Financial profile for 2011: Number of employees, 130,000; sales volume, $8,000,000,000
Corporate officers: Christopher J. Nassetta, Pres. and C.E.O.; Robert Webb, C.I.O.; Thomas C. Kennedy, Exec. V.P. and C.F.O.; Kristin Campbell, Exec. V.P. and Genl. Counsel; Ellen Gonda, Sr. V.P. and Corp. Comms.
International operations: Belgium
Historic mergers: Bally Entertainment Corporation (December 18, 1996)
Giving statement: Giving through the Hilton Worldwide Corporate Giving Program.

Hilton Worldwide Corporate Giving Program

(formerly Hilton Hotels Corporation Contributions Program)
7930 Jones Branch Dr.
McLean, VA 22102 (703) 883-1000
E-mail: corporateresponsibilityinquiries@hilton.com; URL: http://www.hiltonworldwide.com/ corporate-responsibility/

Contact: Kathryn Beiser, Exec. V.P., Corp. Comms.
Purpose and activities: Hilton Worldwide makes charitable contributions to nonprofit organizations involved with sustainability, community, culture, and opportunity. Support is given primarily in areas of company operations.
Fields of interest: Arts, cultural/ethnic awareness; Historic preservation/historical societies; Elementary/secondary education; Education, reading; Environment, natural resources; Employment, training; Food services; Food banks; Housing/shelter; Safety/disasters; Athletics/ sports, Olympics; Athletics/sports, Special Olympics; Youth development; Human services, gift distribution; International human rights; Civil/ human rights, equal rights; Children's rights; Civil rights, race/intergroup relations; Economic development, visitors/convention bureau/tourism promotion; Community/economic development; Public policy, research; Public affairs Economically disadvantaged; Homeless.
Program:
Hilton HHonors Giving Back Program.: Through the Hilton HHonors Giving Back Program, Hilton Worldwide will contribute $25 for every 10,000 HHonor points donated to charitable organizations by card members.
Type of support: Building/renovation; Continuing support; Donated equipment; Donated products; Employee volunteer services; General/operating support; In-kind gifts; Scholarship funds; Sponsorships.
Geographic limitations: Giving primarily in areas of company operations; giving also to national organizations, and in Egypt.
Support limitations: No support for discriminatory organizations, political organizations, candidates, or campaigns, sport teams, or religious organizations not of direct benefit to the entire community. No grants to individuals, or for association membership, sports activities, capital campaigns or endowments, promotional merchandise or tickets, medical research or disease-specific initiatives, medical procedures for individuals, event sponsorship, research studies or video projects, including student films and documentaries (unless related to initiatives Hilton Worldwide is already supporting), or performing arts tours, except on a case by case basis.
Publications: Application guidelines.
Application information: Applications accepted. Proposals are generally accepted by invitation only. The Corporate Responsibility team handles invitations and the Contributions Review Committee evaluates proposals.
Initial approach: E-mail proposal
Administrator: Kathy Shepard, V.P., Corp. Comms.
Number of staff: 2 full-time professional; 2 part-time support.

1813
Hines Interests L.P.
Williams Tower
2800 Post Oak Blvd.
Houston, TX 77056-6118 (713) 621-8000

Company URL: http://www.hines.com
Establishment information: Established in 1957.
Company type: Private company
Business activities: Develops real estate; manages real estate.
Business type (SIC): Real estate subdividers and developers; real estate agents and managers
Corporate officers: Gerald D. Hines, Chair.; C. Hastings Johnson, Vice-Chair. and C.I.O.; Jeffrey C. Hines, Pres. and C.E.O.; Charles M. Baughin, C.F.O.; David LeVrier, Sr. V.P. and C.A.O.; Jesse Carrillo, Sr. V.P. and C.I.O.; George C. Lancaster, Sr. V.P., Corp. Comms.; Stephanie Fore, Sr. V.P., Human Resources; Kay P. Forbes, Treas.
Board of directors: Gerald D. Hines, Chair.; C. Hastings Johnson, Vice-Chair.
Giving statement: Giving through the Hines Interests L.P. Corporate Giving Program.

Hines Interests L.P. Corporate Giving Program
2800 Post Oak Blvd.
Houston, TX 77056-6100 (713) 621-8000
FAX: (713) 966-2636; URL: http://www.hines.com/careers/community.aspx

Purpose and activities: Hines makes charitable contributions to nonprofit organizations involved with arts and culture, the environment, youth development, community development, and on a case by case basis. Support is given primarily in areas of company operations in San Francisco, California, Atlanta, Georgia, Chicago, Illinois, New York, New York, and Houston, Texas, and in Brazil, Canada, China, France, Germany, India, Ireland, Italy, Luxembourg, Mexico, Panama, Poland, Russia, Spain, Turkey, the United Arab Emirates and the United Kingdom.
Fields of interest: Arts; Elementary/secondary education; Environment; Youth development; Community/economic development; General charitable giving.
International interests: Brazil; Canada; China; France; Germany; India; Ireland; Italy; Luxembourg; Mexico; Panama; Poland; Russia; Spain; Turkey; United Arab Emirates; United Kingdom.
Type of support: Employee volunteer services; General/operating support.
Geographic limitations: Giving primarily in areas of company operations in San Francisco, CA, Atlanta, GA, Chicago, IL, New York, NY, and Houston, TX, and in Brazil, Canada, China, France, Germany, India, Ireland, Italy, Luxembourg, Mexico, Panama, Poland, Russia, Spain, Turkey, the United Arab Emirates and the United Kingdom.

1814
Hinshaw & Culbertson LLP
222 North LaSalle St., Ste.300
Chicago, IL 60601 (312) 704-3000

Company URL: http://www.hinshawlaw.com
Establishment information: Established in 1934.
Company type: Private company
Business activities: Operates law firm.
Business type (SIC): Legal services
Financial profile for 2012: Number of employees, 500
Corporate officer: Donald L. Mrozek, Chair.
Giving statement: Giving through the Hinshaw & Culbertson LLP Pro Bono Program.

Hinshaw & Culbertson LLP Pro Bono Program
222 North LaSalle St., Ste. 300
Chicago, IL 60601 (312) 704-3453
E-mail: dboho@hinshawlaw.com; URL: http://www.hinshawlaw.com/probono/

Contact: Dan L. Boho, Capital Partner
Fields of interest: Legal services.
Type of support: Pro bono services - legal.

1815
Hiscock & Barclay, LLP
1 Park Pl.
300 South State St.
Syracuse, NY 13202 (315) 245-2700

Company URL: http://hblaw.com
Establishment information: Established in 1849.
Company type: Private company
Business activities: Operates law firm.
Business type (SIC): Legal services
Financial profile for 2012: Number of employees, 200
Corporate officers: Marjorie Pepe, Pres.; John P. Langan, Managing Partner
Giving statement: Giving through the Hiscock & Barclay, LLP Pro Bono Program.

Hiscock & Barclay, LLP Pro Bono Program
1 Park Pl.
300 South State St.
Syracuse, NY 13202 (315) 425-2700
E-mail: skatzoff@hblaw.com; URL: http://hblaw.com/firm/pro-bono/

Contact: Susan R. Katzoff, Partner
Fields of interest: Legal services.
Type of support: Pro bono services - legal.

1816
Hitachi America, Ltd.
50 Prospect Ave.
Tarrytown, NY 10591 (914) 332-5800

Company URL: http://www.hitachi-america.us/
Establishment information: Established in 1959.
Company type: Subsidiary of a foreign company
Business activities: Manufactures electrical equipment, communications equipment, industrial machinery, automotive parts, rolling stock, semiconductors, computers, electronic components, and motors.
Business type (SIC): Electronic components and accessories; machinery/general industry; computer and office equipment; electric transmission and distribution equipment; electrical industrial apparatus; motor vehicles and equipment; laboratory apparatus
Financial profile for 2010: Number of employees, 125
Corporate officers: Tadahiko Ishigaki, Chair.; Chiaki Fujiwara, Co-Pres. and C.E.O.; Hiroaki Nakanishi, Co-Pres.; Don Kovalsky, C.I.O.
Board of director: Tadahiko Ishigaki, Chair.
Giving statement: Giving through the Hitachi America, Ltd. Corporate Giving Program.

Hitachi America, Ltd. Corporate Giving Program
50 Prospect Ave.
Tarrytown, NY 10591-4698 (914) 332-5800
FAX: (914) 333-2787;
E-mail: lauren.garvey@hal.hitachi.com

Contact: Lauren Garvey, Sr. Mgr.
Purpose and activities: Hitachi America makes charitable contributions to nonprofit organizations involved with education, health care, the environment, arts, vocational training, and literacy, on a case by case basis. Support is given primarily in areas of company operations.
Fields of interest: Arts; Vocational education; Education, reading; Education; Environment; General charitable giving.
Type of support: Emergency funds; Employee volunteer services; Program development.
Geographic limitations: Giving primarily in areas of company operations.
Support limitations: No support for religious, political, labor, or discriminatory organizations. No grants to individuals, or for special events, endowments, general operating costs, or capital improvements.
Application information: Applications accepted. Application form required.
Initial approach: Proposal to nearest company facility
Copies of proposal: 1
Committee meeting date(s): Monthly
Deadline(s): None
Final notification: 2 months following submission
Number of staff: 1 full-time professional.

1817
HNI Corporation
(formerly HON Industries Inc.)
408 E. 2nd St.
P.O. Box 1109
Muscatine, IA 52761-0071 (563) 272-7400
FAX: (563) 272-7655

Company URL: http://www.honi.com
Establishment information: Established in 1944.
Company type: Public company
Company ticker symbol and exchange: HNI/NYSE
Business activities: Manufactures and markets office furniture and hearth products.
Business type (SIC): Furniture/office; metal plumbing fixtures and heating equipment/nonelectric
Financial profile for 2012: Number of employees, 10,400; assets, $1,079,630,000; sales volume, $2,004,000,000; pre-tax net income, $77,600,000; expenses, $1,916,380,000; liabilities, $659,270,000
Fortune 1000 ranking: 2012—946th in revenues, 825th in profits, and 961st in assets
Corporate officers: Stan A. Askren, Chair., Pres., and C.E.O.; Kurt A. Tjaden, V.P. and C.F.O.; Richard ("Rick") Johnson, V.P. and C.I.O.; Steven M. Bradford, V.P., Genl. Counsel, and Secy.; Derek P. Schmidt, V.P., Corp. Finance
Board of directors: Stan A. Askren, Chair.; Mary H. Bell; Miguel M. Calado; Cheryl A. Francis; James R. Jenkins; Dennis J. Martin; Larry B. Porcellato; Abbie J. Smith; Brian E. Stern; Ronald V. Waters III

Subsidiaries: Allsteel Inc, Muscatine, IA; BPI Inc., Kent, WA; The Gunlocke Co., Wayland, NY; Holga Inc., Van Nuys, CA; The HON Co., Muscatine, IA
International operations: Canada; Hong Kong; Mexico
Giving statement: Giving through the HNI Charitable Foundation.
Company EIN: 420617510

HNI Charitable Foundation

(formerly HON INDUSTRIES Charitable Foundation)
P.O. Box 1109
Muscatine, IA 52761-0071 (563) 252-7503
FAX: (563) 264-7217;
E-mail: stelznerd@hnicorp.com; Application address: 408 W. Second St., Muscatine, IA 52761

Establishment information: Established in 1985 in IA.
Donors: HON INDUSTRIES Inc.; HNI Corp.
Contact: Dianna Stelzner, Secy.-Treas.
Financial data (yr. ended 12/31/11): Assets, $2,845,728 (M); gifts received, $171,600; expenditures, $977,126; qualifying distributions, $944,294; giving activities include $944,294 for grants.
Purpose and activities: The foundation supports organizations involved with arts and culture, education, health, disaster preparedness, and human services.
Fields of interest: Historic preservation/historical societies; Arts; Higher education; Libraries (public); Education, services; Education; Hospitals (general); Health care, clinics/centers; Health care; Disasters, preparedness/services; Disasters, fire prevention/control; Boy scouts; YM/YWCAs & YM/YWHAs; Human services; United Ways and Federated Giving Programs.
Type of support: Building/renovation; Capital campaigns; General/operating support.
Geographic limitations: Giving limited to areas of company operations, with emphasis on IA, IL, KY, MN, NC and WA.
Support limitations: No support for national, statewide, or religious organizations. No grants to individuals.
Application information: Applications accepted. Application form not required. Applicants should submit the following:
1) copy of IRS Determination Letter
Initial approach: Proposal
Copies of proposal: 1
Deadline(s): None

Officers: Stan A. Askren, Pres.; Roger R. Behrens, V.P.; Gary L. Carlson, V.P.; Tim Heth, V.P.; Dianna Stelzner, Secy.-Treas.
Number of staff: 1 full-time professional.
EIN: 421246787

1818
Hobart Corporation

701 S. Ridge Ave.
Troy, OH 45374 (937) 332-3000

Company URL: http://www.hobartcorp.com
Establishment information: Established in 1897.
Company type: Subsidiary of a public company
Business activities: Manufactures and provides food equipment, systems, and services.
Business type (SIC): Machinery/special industry
Financial profile for 2010: Number of employees, 100
Corporate officer: Mary Beth Siddons, Pres.
Board of directors: Rob Geile; Paul Kerkhoff; Donald Lewis; Pete Lindeman; Bill Schlieper; Robert Strouse
Giving statement: Giving through the Hobart Corporation Contributions Program.

Hobart Corporation Contributions Program

701 S. Ridge Ave.
Troy, OH 45374-0001

Contact: Kenneth Kessler, V.P., Finance, and C.A.O.
Purpose and activities: Hobart makes charitable contributions to nonprofit organizations with which its employees are involved. Support is limited to areas of significant company operations.
Fields of interest: General charitable giving.
Type of support: Employee matching gifts; General/operating support.
Geographic limitations: Giving limited to areas of significant company operations.
Support limitations: No support for organizations with which employees are not involved.
Application information: Applications accepted. Application form not required. Applicants should submit the following:
1) detailed description of project and amount of funding requested
Initial approach: Proposal to headquarters
Copies of proposal: 1
Final notification: Following review

1819
Hockey Western New York, LLC

(also known as Buffalo Sabres)
First Niagara Ctr.
1 Seymour H. Knox III Plz.
Buffalo, NY 14203-4122 (716) 855-4100

Company URL: http://www.sabres.com
Establishment information: Established in 1970.
Company type: Private company
Business activities: Operates professional ice hockey club.
Business type (SIC): Commercial sports
Corporate officers: Theodore N. Black, Pres.; Chuck Lamattina, V.P., Finance and Opers.; John Livsey, V.P., Sales; Michael Gilbert, V.P., Public Rels.; Kristin Zirnheld, Corp. Cont.
Giving statement: Giving through the Buffalo Sabres Corporate Giving Program.

Buffalo Sabres Corporate Giving Program

HSBC Arena 1
Seymour Knox III Plz.
Buffalo, NY 14203

Purpose and activities: The Buffalo Sabres make charitable contributions of memorabilia to nonprofit organizations on a case by case basis. Support is given on a national basis.
Fields of interest: General charitable giving.
Type of support: In-kind gifts.
Geographic limitations: Giving on a national basis, with emphasis on NY.

1820
Hodgson Russ LLP

The Guaranty Bldg.
140 Pearl St., Ste. 100
Buffalo, NY 14202-4040 (716) 856-4000

Company URL: http://www.hodgsonruss.com/
Establishment information: Established in 1817.
Company type: Private company
Business activities: Operates law firm.
Business type (SIC): Legal services
Corporate officers: Gary M. Schober, Pres. and C.E.O.; Paul R. Comeau, Chair.; Paul V. Hartigan, C.O.O.; Eileen Crotty, C.F.O.
Offices: Palm Beach, FL; Albany, Buffalo, Johnstown, New York, NY
International operations: Canada
Giving statement: Giving through the Hodgson Russ LLP Corporate Giving Program.

Hodgson Russ LLP Corporate Giving Program

The Guaranty Bldg.
140 Pearl St., Ste. 100
Buffalo, NY 14202-4040
URL: http://www.hodgsonruss.com/Home/Our_Firm/CommunityInvolvement

Contact: Joseph Sedita, Pro Bono Partner
Purpose and activities: Hodgson Russ makes charitable contributions to nonprofit organizations involved with arts and culture, healthcare, human services, and civic affairs.
Fields of interest: Arts; Health care; Legal services; Human services; Public affairs.
Type of support: Employee volunteer services; General/operating support; Pro bono services - legal.

1821
Hoffer Plastics Corporation

500 N. Collins St.
South Elgin, IL 60177 (847) 741-5740
FAX: (847) 741-3086

Company URL: http://www.hofferplastics.com
Establishment information: Established in 1953.
Company type: Private company
Business activities: Manufactures plastic products.
Business type (SIC): Plastic products/miscellaneous
Financial profile for 2012: Number of employees, 300
Corporate officers: Robert A. Hoffer, Co-Chair.; Greg Abbott, Co-Chair.; William A. Hoffer, Pres. and C.E.O.; Gerry Krausert, V.P., Opers.; Jack Shedd, V.P., Sales & Mktg.; Mary Eagin, Treas.; Lynn Martino, Cont.
Board of directors: Greg Abbott, Co-Chair.; Robert A. Hoffer, Co-Chair.
Giving statement: Giving through the Hoffer Foundation.

Hoffer Foundation

500 N. Collins St.
South Elgin, IL 60177-1104
URL: http://www.hofferplastics.com/people/the-hoffer-foundation/

Establishment information: Established in 1966 in IL.
Donors: Hoffer Plastics Corp.; Robert A. Hoffer†.
Contact: Gretchen Hoffer Farb, Tr.

Financial data (yr. ended 11/30/11): Assets, $2,657,090 (M); expenditures, $490,665; qualifying distributions, $457,125; giving activities include $457,125 for grants.
Purpose and activities: The foundation supports organizations involved with education, health, and human services.
Fields of interest: Higher education; Education; Hospitals (general); Health care; Boys & girls clubs; YM/YWCAs & YM/YWHAs; Family services, domestic violence; Residential/custodial care, hospices; Human services; United Ways and Federated Giving Programs.
Type of support: General/operating support.
Geographic limitations: Giving primarily in IL, with emphasis on Elgin and South Elgin.
Support limitations: No support for political or religious organizations.
Application information: Applications accepted. Application form not required.
Initial approach: Proposal
Board meeting date(s): Quarterly
Deadline(s): None
Officers and Trustees:* William A. Hoffer*, Pres.; Robert A. Hoffer, Jr.*, V.P.; Mary Hoffer Eagin; Sara Eagin; Gretchen Hoffer Farb; Helen C. Hoffer; Charlotte H. Canning; W. Alex Hoffer.
EIN: 366160991

1822
Hoffman Adjustment Company

3010 Laporte St.
Highland, IN 46322-1429 (219) 838-3318

Establishment information: Established in 1988.
Company type: Private company
Business activities: Provides insurance adjustment services.
Business type (SIC): Insurance agents, brokers, and services
Corporate officer: Joseph A. Hoffman, Pres.
Giving statement: Giving through the Hoffman Charitable Trust.

Hoffman Charitable Trust

P.O. Box 201
LaGrange, IN 46761-0201

Establishment information: Established in 1996 in IN.
Donors: Hoffman Adjustment Inc.; Joseph A. Hoffman.
Financial data (yr. ended 12/31/11): Assets, $836,410 (M); gifts received, $10,000; expenditures, $43,522; qualifying distributions, $23,225; giving activities include $11,100 for 4 grants (high: $5,000; low: $100).
Purpose and activities: The foundation supports food banks and hospices and organizations involved with cancer research, housing development, and Christianity.
Fields of interest: Cancer research; Food banks; Housing/shelter, development; Salvation Army; Residential/custodial care, hospices; Christian agencies & churches.
Type of support: General/operating support.
Geographic limitations: Giving primarily in Gary, Highland, and Munster, IN.
Support limitations: No grants to individuals.
Application information: Applications not accepted. Unsolicited requests for funds not accepted.
Officer: Doris Kennedy, Pres.
Directors: Shay Francis; Brock Hoffman; Kent Hoffman.
EIN: 356624421

1823
Hoffmann-La Roche Inc.

(also known as Roche Nutley)
340 Kingsland St.
Nutley, NJ 07110-1199 (973) 235-5000

Company URL: http://www.rocheusa.com
Establishment information: Established in 1905.
Company type: Subsidiary of a foreign company
Business activities: Manufactures pharmaceuticals, chemicals, vitamins, and diagnostics.
Business type (SIC): Drugs; soaps, cleaners, and toiletries; laboratories/medical and dental; research, development, and testing services
Financial profile for 2010: Number of employees, 3,000
Corporate officer: George Abercrombie, Pres. and C.E.O.
Board of directors: Thomas Doran; John Finn
Subsidiaries: Genentech, Inc., South San Francisco, CA; Roche Carolina Inc., Florence, SC; Roche Colorado Corporation, Boulder, CO; Roche Diagnostics Corporation, Indianapolis, IN; Roche Molecular Systems Inc., Pleasanton, CA; Roche Palo Alto, Palo Alto, CA
Giving statement: Giving through the Hoffmann-La Roche Inc. Corporate Giving Program and the Roche Foundation.

Hoffmann-La Roche Inc. Corporate Giving Program

(formerly Roche Laboratories Inc. Corporate Giving Program)
c/o Corp. Donations and Sponsorship
340 Kingsland St.
Nutley, NJ 07110-1150 (973) 235-5000
URL: http://www.rocheusa.com/portal/usa/corporate_responsibility

Purpose and activities: As a complement to its foundation, Hoffmann-La Roche also makes charitable contributions to nonprofit organizations directly. Support is given on a national and international basis.
Fields of interest: Health care; Disasters, preparedness/services; Human services; International relief; Community/economic development; Science, formal/general education; Science; Science.
Programs:
Education: Roche supports programs designed to promote K-12 science and math education. Special emphasis is directed toward programs designed to focus on teacher enrichment.
Health Promotion and Education: Roche supports programs designed to promote health and provide health education. Special emphasis is directed toward programs designed to address genitourinary disease; infectious diseases; inflammation, metabolic diseases, and neurology; oncology; osteoporosis; transplantation; vascular diseases; and virology.
Type of support: Building/renovation; Fellowships; In-kind gifts; Program development; Research; Seed money; Sponsorships; Technical assistance.
Geographic limitations: Giving primarily in areas of company operations.
Support limitations: No support for political or religious organizations. No grants to individuals, or for mass mails, unsigned requests or broadcast requests throughout the corporation, commercial and/or mainstream entertainment events, fundraising events, third-party organizations, or advertising.
Application information: Applications accepted. The Corporate Communications Department handles giving. Application form not required. Applicants should submit the following:
1) copy of IRS Determination Letter
2) detailed description of project and amount of funding requested
Initial approach: Proposal to local General Manager; proposal to local Roche Research organization for scientific grants

The Roche Foundation

(formerly The Hoffmann-La Roche Foundation)
1 DNA Way, MS #24
South San Francisco, CA 94080-4918 (877) 888-0389
Application address: P.O. Box 278, Nutley, NJ 07110-0278; URL: http://www.rocheusa.com/portal/usa/the_roche_foundation

Establishment information: Trust established in 1945 in NJ.
Donors: Hoffmann-La Roche Inc.; Roche Laboratories Inc.
Contact: Patricia Hughes, Exec. Dir.
Financial data (yr. ended 12/31/11): Assets, $4,541,097 (M); gifts received, $65,000; expenditures, $511,582; qualifying distributions, $508,375; giving activities include $508,375 for grants.
Purpose and activities: The foundation supports organizations involved with arts and culture, education, health, the environment, human services, and science.
Fields of interest: Museums; Arts; Elementary/secondary education; Higher education; Teacher school/education; Education; Environment; Health care; Health organizations; Food banks; Human services; Science, formal/general education; Science.
Type of support: Curriculum development; General/operating support; Program development.
Geographic limitations: Giving primarily in areas of company operations, with emphasis on NJ.
Support limitations: No support for political organizations, candidates, or office holders, sectarian groups (except for education or health programs which serve the general public), or labor or veterans' organizations not of direct benefit to the entire community. No grants to individuals, or for endowments, scholarship funds, purchasing or renovating facilities, equipment, capital campaigns, sponsorships of athletic teams or events, or goodwill advertising.
Publications: Application guidelines.
Application information: Applications accepted. Visit website for online application. Additional information may be requested at a later date. Unsolicited applications for arts and culture and environmental grants are not accepted. Application form required. Applicants should submit the following:
1) results expected from proposed grant
2) copy of IRS Determination Letter
3) brief history of organization and description of its mission
4) copy of most recent annual report/audited financial statement/990
5) listing of board of directors, trustees, officers and other key people and their affiliations
6) detailed description of project and amount of funding requested
7) contact person
8) copy of current year's organizational budget and/or project budget
Initial approach: Complete online application
Copies of proposal: 1
Board meeting date(s): As required

Deadline(s): 60 days prior to need
Final notification: 45 to 60 days
Officers and Trustees:* Frederick C. Kentz III*, Secy.; Patricia Hughes, Exec. Dir.; Jean-Jacques Garaud; Ivor Macleod.
EIN: 226063790

1824
The Hofmann Company

1380 Galaxy Way
Concord, CA 94520 (925) 682-4830

Company URL: http://www.hofmannhomes.com
Establishment information: Established in 1959.
Company type: Private company
Business activities: Builds houses.
Business type (SIC): Operative builders
Corporate officer: Thomas Whalen, Pres.
Board of director: Mark K. Bratlien
Giving statement: Giving through the Hofmann Family Foundation.

The Hofmann Family Foundation

(formerly The K.H. Hofmann Foundation)
P.O. Box 907
Concord, CA 94522-0907 (925) 687-1826
Application address: 3000 Oak Rd., Ste. 360, Walnut Creek, CA 94595

Establishment information: Established in 1963 in CA.
Donors: The Hofmann Co.; New Discovery, Inc.; Kenneth H. Hofmann; Martha J. Hofmann; The Hofmann 1987 Revocable Trust.
Contact: Dennis Costanza, Pres. and Mgr.
Financial data (yr. ended 12/31/11): Assets, $43,241,889 (M); expenditures, $1,757,107; qualifying distributions, $1,205,646; giving activities include $998,150 for 59 grants (high: $250,000; low: $100).
Purpose and activities: The foundation supports organizations involved with secondary and higher education, wildlife protection, health, recreation, human services, and Christianity.
Fields of interest: Secondary school/education; Higher education; Education; Animals/wildlife, preservation/protection; Hospitals (general); Palliative care; Health care; Athletics/sports, baseball; Recreation; Children/youth, services; Human services; Christian agencies & churches.
Type of support: Annual campaigns; Capital campaigns; Employee matching gifts; General/operating support; Sponsorships.
Geographic limitations: Giving primarily in CA; some giving for national organizations.
Application information: Applications accepted. Application form not required. Applicants should submit the following:
1) copy of IRS Determination Letter
2) detailed description of project and amount of funding requested

Initial approach: Proposal
Copies of proposal: 1
Board meeting date(s): Quarterly
Deadline(s): None
Final notification: 3 to 4 months

Officers and Directors:* Kenneth H. Hofmann*, Chair.; Dennis Costanza, Pres. and Mgr.; Lisa A. Hofmann-Morgan, V.P.; John E. Amaral, Secy.; Dennis M. Drew, Treas.; Steve Gonsalves; Richard L. Greene; Martha Jean Hofmann; Vita Sechrest.
Number of staff: 4
EIN: 946108897

Selected grants: The following grants are a representative sample of this grantmaker's funding activity:
$6,000,000 to John Muir Health Foundation, Walnut Creek, CA, 2010.
$3,000,000 to John Muir Health Foundation, Walnut Creek, CA, 2010.
$500,000 to De La Salle High School, Concord, CA, 2010.
$500,000 to De La Salle High School, Concord, CA, 2010.
$500,000 to University of California, San Francisco, CA, 2010.
$240,000 to University of Notre Dame, Notre Dame, IN, 2010.
$125,000 to Childrens Hospital and Research Center at Oakland, Oakland, CA, 2010.
$100,000 to Community Youth Center, Concord, CA, 2010.
$100,000 to Community Youth Center, Concord, CA, 2010.
$80,000 to Community Youth Center, Concord, CA, 2010.

1825
Hogan Lovells US LLP

Columbia Sq.
555 13th St., N.W.
Washington, DC 20004-1109
(202) 637-5600

Company URL: http://www.hoganlovells.com/
Establishment information: Established in 1904.
Company type: Private company
Business activities: Operates law firm.
Business type (SIC): Legal services
Offices: Los Angeles, Palo Alto, San Francisco, CA; Colorado Springs, Denver, CO; Washington, DC; Miami, FL; Baltimore, MD; New York, NY; Philadelphia, PA; Houston, TX; McLean, VA
International operations: Belgium; China; Croatia; Czech Republic; France; Germany; Hong Kong; Hungary; Italy; Japan; Mongolia; Netherlands; Poland; Russia; Saudi Arabia; Singapore; Spain; United Arab Emirates; United Kingdom; Venezuela; Vietnam
Giving statement: Giving through the Hogan Lovells US LLP Corporate Giving Program.

Hogan Lovells US LLP Corporate Giving Program

Columbia Sq.
555 13th St., N.W.
Washington, DC 20004-1109
Contact for Pro Bono program: Patricia A. Brannan, Co-Head, Pro Bono Practice, tel.: (202) 637-8686, fax: (202) 637-5910,
e-mail: patricia.brannan@hoganlovells.com;
URL: http://www.hoganlovells.com/citizenship/

Contact: T. Clark Weymouth, Co-Head, Pro Bono Practice
Purpose and activities: Hogan Lovells matches charitable contributions to nonprofit organizations made by its employees.
Fields of interest: General charitable giving.
Type of support: Employee matching gifts; Employee volunteer services; Pro bono services - legal.

1826
HolacracyOne, LLC

1741 Hilltop Rd., Ste. 200
Spring City, PA 19475 (484) 359-8922

Company URL: http://www.holacracy.org
Establishment information: Established in 2001.
Company type: Private company
Business type (SIC): Business services/miscellaneous
Corporate officers: Brian Robertson, C.E.O.; Tom Thomison, Partner
Giving statement: Giving through the HolacracyOne, LLC Contributions Program.

HolacracyOne, LLC Contributions Program

1741 Hilltop Rd., Ste. 200
Spring City, PA 19475-9512 (484) 359-8922
URL: http://www.holacracy.org

Purpose and activities: HolacracyOne donates a percentage of net profits to charitable organizations.
Fields of interest: Spirituality.
Type of support: In-kind gifts.

1827
Holce Logging Company, Inc.

854 Grant Ave.
Vernonia, OR 97064-1228 (503) 429-6783

Establishment information: Established in 1948.
Company type: Private company
Business activities: Conducts logging activities.
Business type (SIC): Logging
Corporate officers: Randall E. Holce, Pres.; Bonnie J. Holce, Secy.
Giving statement: Giving through the Holce Logging Company Scholarship Foundation Inc.

Holce Logging Company Scholarship Foundation Inc

P.O. Box 127
Vernonia, OR 97064-0127

Establishment information: Established in 1983 in OR.
Financial data (yr. ended 04/30/12): Assets, $258,069 (M); gifts received, $3,000; expenditures, $10,421; qualifying distributions, $10,421; giving activities include $10,334 for 6 grants to individuals (high: $3,000; low: $1,000).
Purpose and activities: The fund awards college scholarships to recent graduates of Vernonia High School in Vernonia, Oregon.
Fields of interest: Education.
Type of support: Scholarships—to individuals.
Geographic limitations: Giving limited to Vernonia, OR.
Application information: Applications accepted. Application form required.

Initial approach: Contact guidance counselor of Vernonia High School for application form
Deadline(s): Apr. 15

Officers: Evelyn L. Holce, Pres.; Randall E. Holce, V.P. and Treas.; Bonnie J. Holce, Secy.
EIN: 930845692

1828
Holcim (US), Inc.
(formerly Holnam Inc.)
201 Jones Rd.
Waltham, MA 02451 (781) 647-2501

Company URL: http://www.holcim.com/USA
Establishment information: Established in 1912.
Company type: Subsidiary of a foreign company
Business activities: Manufactures cement.
Business type (SIC): Cement/hydraulic
Corporate officers: Bernard Terver, Pres. and C.E.O.; Rick Reinhart, Sr. V.P. and C.F.O.; Norman L. Jagger, Sr. V.P., Sales and Mktg.; Russell Wiles, Sr. V.P., Human Resources; Jay Tangney, Sr. V.P and Corp.-Secy.
Subsidiaries: Dundee Cement Co., Dundee, MI; Northwestern States Portland Cement, Mason City, IA; United Cement Co., Artesia, MS
Division: Western Div., Denver, CO
International operations: Canada
Giving statement: Giving through the Holcim (US) Inc. Corporate Giving Program and the Gygi and von Wyss Foundation.

Holcim (US) Inc. Corporate Giving Program
(formerly Holnam Inc. Corporate Giving Program)
201 Jones Rd.
Waltham, MA 02451-1600
URL: http://www.holcim.us/en/in-the-community.html

Purpose and activities: Holcim (US) makes charitable contributions to nonprofit organizations on a case by case basis. Support is given on a national basis in areas of company operations.
Fields of interest: Environment; Disasters, preparedness/services; Recreation, community; Athletics/sports, amateur competition; American Red Cross.
Type of support: Donated land; Donated products; Employee matching gifts; Employee volunteer services; General/operating support; Loaned talent.
Geographic limitations: Giving on a national basis in areas of company operations; giving also to national organizations.

Gygi and von Wyss Foundation
(formerly Hans Gygi Foundation)
201 Jones Rd.
Waltham, MA 02451-1600 (781) 647-2526
FAX: (781) 647-2548

Establishment information: Incorporated in 1983 in MI.
Donors: Holnam Inc.; Holcim (US) Inc.
Contact: Sarah Long, Asst. Secy.
Financial data (yr. ended 12/31/11): Assets, $7,448 (M); gifts received, $160,000; expenditures, $155,091; qualifying distributions, $144,765; giving activities include $144,765 for 26 grants to individuals (high: $8,000).
Purpose and activities: The foundation awards college scholarships to children and step-children of full-time employees of Holcim (US) Inc. and Holcim Texas, LP.
Fields of interest: Higher education.
Type of support: Employee-related scholarships.
Geographic limitations: Giving on a national basis in areas of company operations.
Application information: Applications not accepted. Contributes only through employee-related scholarships.
Board meeting date(s): Jan. 29
Officers: Bernerd Terver, Pres.; Lisa Olsen, V.P.; Russell Wiles, V.P.; Lucy Chadis, Secy.; Mathew Callahoan, Treas.
EIN: 382472472

1829
Holder Construction Co.
3333 Riverwood Pkwy. S.E., Ste. 400
Atlanta, GA 30339-3304 (770) 988-3000

Company URL: http://www.holderconstruction.com
Establishment information: Established in 1960.
Company type: Private company
Business activities: Provides nonresidential general contract construction services.
Business type (SIC): Contractors/general nonresidential building
Corporate officers: Thomas M. Holder, Chair. and C.E.O.; Michael Kennig, Vice-Chair.; David W. Miller, Pres. and C.O.O.; Lee Johnston, Exec. V.P., Human Resources; J.C. Pendrey, Jr., C.F.O.; Ray Riddle, V.P., Sales and Mktg.; Michelle Hahn, V.P., Opers.; Tracy Turner, V.P., Finance
Board of directors: Thomas M. Holder, Chair.; Michael Kennig, Vice-Chair.
Offices: Phoenix, AZ; St. Petersburg, FL; Winston-Salem, NC; Fairfax, VA
Giving statement: Giving through the Holder Construction Foundation.

The Holder Construction Foundation
3333 Riverwood Pkwy., Ste. 400
Atlanta, GA 30339-3304 (770) 988-3280

Donor: Holder Construction Co.
Contact: J.C. Pendrey, Jr., Tr.
Financial data (yr. ended 12/31/11): Assets, $4,631,996 (M); gifts received, $1,500,000; expenditures, $935,670; qualifying distributions, $932,970; giving activities include $932,970 for grants.
Purpose and activities: The foundation supports zoos and organizations involved with arts and culture, education, health, human services, and business.
Fields of interest: Museums (art); Performing arts, ballet; Arts; Elementary/secondary education; Higher education; Education; Zoos/zoological societies; Health care; Children/youth, services; Human services; Business/industry; United Ways and Federated Giving Programs.
Type of support: General/operating support.
Geographic limitations: Giving in the greater metropolitan Atlanta, GA, area.
Application information: Applications accepted. Application form not required.
Initial approach: Proposal or telephone
Deadline(s): None
Distribution Committee: Elizabeth D. Holder; Thomas M. Holder.
Trustee: J.C. Pendrey, Jr.
EIN: 586412965
Selected grants: The following grants are a representative sample of this grantmaker's funding activity:
$150,000 to Atlanta Ballet, Atlanta, GA, 2010.
$25,000 to Savannah College of Art and Design, Savannah, GA, 2010.
$20,000 to Business Executives for National Security, Washington, DC, 2010.
$15,000 to Atlanta Ballet, Atlanta, GA, 2010.
$10,000 to Trust for Public Land, San Francisco, CA, 2010.
$8,500 to University System of Georgia Foundation, Atlanta, GA, 2010.
$7,000 to American Cancer Society, Atlanta, GA, 2010.
$5,000 to American Cancer Society, Atlanta, GA, 2010.
$5,000 to Clemson University Foundation, Clemson, SC, 2010.
$3,500 to Big Brothers Big Sisters of America, Philadelphia, PA, 2010.

1830
Holiday Auto & Truck Inc.
321 N. Rolling Meadows Dr.
Fond du Lac, WI 54937-9726
(920) 921-8898

Company URL: http://www.holidayautomotive.com
Company type: Private company
Business activities: Operates car dealership.
Business type (SIC): Motor vehicles—retail
Corporate officer: Michael E. Shannon, Pres.
Giving statement: Giving through the Holiday Automotive Foundation, Inc.

Holiday Automotive Foundation, Inc.
321 N. Rolling Meadows Dr.
Fond du Lac, WI 54937-9726

Establishment information: Established in 2001 in WI.
Donors: Holiday Auto & Truck Inc.; Mike-Shannon Automotive, Inc.
Financial data (yr. ended 12/31/11): Assets, $519,612 (M); gifts received, $186,000; expenditures, $72,788; qualifying distributions, $71,750; giving activities include $71,750 for grants.
Purpose and activities: The foundation supports fire associations and organizations involved with secondary education, health, ice skating, and youth services.
Fields of interest: Education; Housing/shelter; Human services.
Type of support: General/operating support.
Geographic limitations: Giving primarily in Fond du Lac, WI.
Support limitations: No grants to individuals.
Application information: Applications not accepted. Unsolicited requests for funds not accepted.
Officers: Michael R. Shannon, Pres.; James I. Flood, V.P.; Patrick McCullough, Secy.-Treas.
EIN: 392018969

1831
Holiday Chrysler Dodge Jeep
815 S. Rolling Meadows Dr.
Fond du Lac, WI 54937 (866) 419-2682

Company URL: http://www.holidaycdj.com/
Establishment information: Established in 1959.
Company type: Private company
Business activities: Operates auto dealership.
Business type (SIC): Motor vehicles—retail
Financial profile for 2010: Number of employees, 2
Giving statement: Giving through the Holiday Chrysler Dodge Jeep Foundation Inc.

Holiday Chrysler Dodge Jeep Foundation Inc.
815 S. Rolling Meadows Dr.
Fond Du Lac, WI 54937-8200

Establishment information: Established in WI.
Donor: Holiday Chrysler Dodge Jeep, Inc.
Financial data (yr. ended 12/31/11): Assets, $2,200 (M); gifts received, $6,000; expenditures, $10,260; qualifying distributions, $10,260; giving activities include $10,250 for 6 grants (high: $3,750; low: $500).
Fields of interest: Arts; Human services; Religion.
Geographic limitations: Giving primarily in WI.
Application information: Applications not accepted. Unsolicited requests for funds not accepted.
Officers: James Flood, Pres.; Michael J. Berg, V.P.; Charles Weiland, Secy.-Treas.
Directors: Judy Flood; Nancy McCullough-Berg.
EIN: 202968792

1832
Holiday Companies

4567 American Blvd. W.
P.O. Box 1224
Bloomington, MN 55437-1123
(952) 830-8700

Company URL: http://www.holidaystationstores.com
Establishment information: Established in 1928.
Company type: Subsidiary of a private company
Business activities: Operates convenience stores.
Business type (SIC): Groceries—retail
Financial profile for 2011: Number of employees, 5,000; sales volume, $3,630,000,000
Corporate officers: Ronald A. Erickson, Chair. and C.E.O.; Gerald A. Erickson, Vice-Chair.; Brent G. Blackey, Pres. and C.O.O.; Rick Johnson, Sr. V.P., Opers.; Randy Skare, V.P. and C.I.O.
Board of directors: Ronald A. Erickson, Chair.; Gerald A. Erickson, Vice-Chair.
Giving statement: Giving through the Holiday Stationstores, Inc. Corporate Giving Program and the Arthur T. Erickson Foundation.

Arthur T. Erickson Foundation

P.O. Box 1224
Minneapolis, MN 55440-1224

Donor: Holiday Stationstores, Inc.
Financial data (yr. ended 12/31/11): Assets, $318,821 (M); gifts received, $150,000; expenditures, $153,561; qualifying distributions, $153,475; giving activities include $153,475 for grants.
Purpose and activities: The foundation supports community foundations and organizations involved with arts and culture, K-12 and higher education, horticulture, health, equestrianism, disability services, and religion.
Fields of interest: Education; Health care; Religion.
Type of support: Annual campaigns; General/operating support; Program development; Research.
Geographic limitations: Giving primarily in Minneapolis and St. Paul, MN.
Support limitations: No grants to individuals.
Application information: Applications not accepted. Unsolicited requests for funds not accepted.
Trustees: Gerald A. Erickson; Marjorie J. Pihl.
EIN: 416050855

1833
Holland & Hart LLP

555 17th St., Ste. 3200
Denver, CO 80202-3921 (801) 799-5806

Establishment information: Established in 1947.
Company type: Private company
Business activities: Operates law firm.
Business type (SIC): Legal services
Offices: Aspen, Boulder, Colorado Springs, Denver, Greenwood Village, CO; Washington, DC; Boise, ID; Billings, MT; Carson City, Las Vegas, Reno, NV; Santa Fe, NM; Salt Lake City, UT; Cheyenne, Jackson, WY
Giving statement: Giving through the Holland & Hart LLP Pro Bono Program and the Holland & Hart Foundation.

Holland & Hart Foundation

555 17th St., Ste. 3200
Denver, CO 80202-3921 (303) 295-8000
E-mail: rconnery@hollandhart.com; URL: http://www.hollandhartfoundation.org/

Establishment information: Established in 1998.
Contact: Ashley Wald, Pres.
Financial data (yr. ended 12/31/11): Revenue, $97,214; assets, $131,193 (M); gifts received, $97,214; expenditures, $70,200; giving activities include $57,804 for grants.
Purpose and activities: The organization builds community internally, locally and globally through charitable and educational activities and programs.
Officers and Directors:* Chris Balch*, Co-Chair.; Tom O'Donnell*, Co-Chair.; Ashley Wald*, Pres.; Stephanie Walkenshaw*, V.P., Public Rels.; Sue Combs*, Secy.; Valerie Stephens*, Treas.; Betty Arkell; Greg Austin; Lee Gray; Jean Guyton; Sam Guyton; and 4 additional directors.
Advisory Board: John Castellano; Jean Guyton; Sam Guyton.
EIN: 841482793

1834
Holland & Knight LLP

100 N. Tampa St., Ste. 4100
Tampa, FL 33602-3642 (813) 227-8500

Company URL: http://www.hklaw.com
Establishment information: Established in 1968.
Company type: Private company
Business activities: Operates law firm.
Business type (SIC): Legal services
Corporate officer: Rick Hutchison, Exec. Partner
Offices: Los Angeles, San Francisco, CA; Washington, DC; Fort Lauderdale, Jacksonville, Lakeland, Miami, Orlando, Tallahassee, West Palm Beach, FL; Atlanta, GA; Chicago, IL; Bethesda, MD; Boston, MA; New York, NY; Portland, OR; McLean, VA
International operations: China; Mexico; United Arab Emirates
Giving statement: Giving through the Holland & Knight LLP Pro Bono Program and the Holland & Knight Charitable Foundation, Inc.

Holland & Knight Charitable Foundation, Inc.

P.O. Box 2877
Tampa, FL 33601-2877 (813) 227-8500
FAX: (813) 229-0134;
E-mail: foundation@hklaw.com; Toll-free tel.: (866) 452-2737; E-Mail for Elias Matsakis: elias.matsakis@hklaw.com; URL: http://foundation.hklaw.com
Application address for African American Heritage: Holland & Knight LLP, Attn. Lura Battle, 1201 W. Peachtree St., N.E., 1 Atlantic Ctr., Ste. 2000, Atlanta, GA 30309-3453; E-mail and URL for Holocaust Project: holocaust@hklaw.com, www.holocaust.hklaw.com; E-mail for Young Native Writers' Contest: indian@hklaw.com

Establishment information: Established in 1996 in FL.
Contact: Elias Matsakis, Pres.
Financial data (yr. ended 12/31/10): Revenue, $653,110; assets, $1,068,493 (M); gifts received, $651,841; expenditures, $776,203; program services expenses, $753,399; giving activities include $549,693 for 3 grants (high: $154,901; low: $6,500) and $41,872 for grants to individuals.
Purpose and activities: The foundation provides support to organizations working in the fields of art and science, child services, education, health and disability issues, homelessness assistance, indigent legal services, and international relief and civic causes.
Fields of interest: Arts; Education; Legal services; Housing/shelter; Children, services; Family resources and services, disability; Homeless, human services; International relief; Science African Americans/Blacks; Native Americans/American Indians.
Programs:
Dream Scholarship Program: This program honors the many African Americans who have dreamed for a better America by offering an essay contest and the potential to recieve scholarships to all students age 19 and under who are currently enrolled as juniors or seniors in public high schools in Atlanta and DeKalb counties. The first, second, and third place winners will receive scholarships worth $3,000, $2,000, and $1,000 respectively.
Holocaust Remembrance Project Essay Contest: This program is a national essay contest for high-school students that is designed to encourage and promote the study of the Holocaust. Participation in this project encourages students to think responsibly, be aware of world conditions that undermine human dignity, and make decisions that promote respect for the value inherent in every person. Eligible applicants include high-school students in the U.S. and Mexico. Scholarships for first place begin at $2,500.
Young Native Writers Essay Contest: This contest allows Native American high school students to write about their experiences, inspiring honest portrayals of the richness of Native American life and history. Five first-place winners will be chosen to receive scholarships ranging from $1,000 to $5,000, and to be flown to Washington D.C. to visit the National Museum of the American Indian and other prominent sites. Eligible applicants include Native American Indian and Alaska Native individuals who are enrolled members of a state- or federally-recognized tribe, and who are also enrolled in high schools or alternative schools, or are homeschooled.
Type of support: Grants to individuals.
Geographic limitations: Giving on a national and international basis.
Publications: Application guidelines.
Application information: Applications accepted. Application form required.
Deadline(s): Apr. 15 for Young Native Writers Essay Contest; Dec. 3 for Living the Dream Essay and Scholarship Program
Officers and Directors:* Ralph Lepore*, Chair.; Elias Matsakis*, Pres.; Susanne Judas*, Secy.; Charles L. Stutts*, Treas.; Angela M. Ruth*, Exec.

Dir.; Deborah E. Barnard; Bernard Barton; Christopher Bellows; and 17 additional directors.
EIN: 311472972

1835
Holland America Line Inc.
300 Elliott Ave. W.
Seattle, WA 98119 (206) 281-3535

Company URL: http://www.hollandamerica.com
Establishment information: Established in 1873.
Company type: Subsidiary of a public company
Business activities: Operates cruise ship line.
Business type (SIC): Transportation/water passenger
Corporate officers: Stein Kruse, Pres. and C.E.O.; Richard Meadows, Exec. V.P., Mktg. and Sales; Larry D. Calkins, Sr. V.P., Finance and C.F.O.; Kelly P. W. Clark, V.P. and Genl. Counsel; Sally Andrews, V.P., Public Rels.; Brendan J. Vierra, V.P., Human Resources; Steve Leonard, V.P., Sales
Giving statement: Giving through the Holland America Line Inc. Corporate Giving Program.

Holland America Line Inc. Corporate Giving Program
300 Elliott Ave. West
Seattle, WA 98119 (206) 281-3535

Purpose and activities: As a complement to its foundation, Holland America Line also makes charitable contributions to nonprofit organizations directly. Support is given primarily in areas of company operations in Alaska, San Diego, California, Fort Lauderdale and Tampa, Florida, Seattle, Washington, and in Canada; giving also to national organizations.
Fields of interest: Arts; Environment; Breast cancer research; Disasters, preparedness/services; Marine science.
Type of support: Employee matching gifts; Employee volunteer services; General/operating support; In-kind gifts.
Geographic limitations: Giving primarily in areas of company operations in AK, San Diego, CA, Fort Lauderdale and Tampa, FL, Seattle, WA, and in Canada; giving also to national organizations.
Application information: Applications not accepted. Contributes only to pre-selected organizations.

1836
Hollingsworth LLP
1350 I St., N.W.
Washington, DC 20005-3305
(202) 898-5800

Company URL: http://www.hollingsworthllp.com/home.php
Establishment information: Established in 1982.
Company type: Private company
Business activities: Operates law firm.
Business type (SIC): Legal services
Corporate officer: Donald W. Fowler, Managing Partner
Giving statement: Giving through the Hollingsworth LLP Pro Bono Program.

Hollingsworth LLP Pro Bono Program
1350 I St., N.W.
Washington, DC 20005-3305 (202) 898-5800
E-mail: bberger@hollingsworthllp.com; URL: http://www.hollingsworthllp.com/firm.php?AboutusID=1

Contact: Bruce Berger, Partner
Fields of interest: Legal services.
Type of support: Pro bono services - legal.
Geographic limitations: Giving primarily in areas of company operations in Washington, DC.
Application information: The Pro Bono Coordinator manages the pro bono program.

1837
Holme Roberts & Owen LLP
1700 Lincoln St., Ste. 4100
Denver, CO 80203-4541 (303) 861-7000

Company URL: http://www.hro.com/
Establishment information: Established in 1898.
Company type: Private company
Business activities: Operates law firm.
Business type (SIC): Legal services
Corporate officers: Paul E. Smith, Chair.; Randall H. Miller, Managing Partner
Offices: Los Angeles, San Francisco, CA; Boulder, Colorado Springs, Denver, CO; Salt Lake City, UT
International operations: Ireland; United Kingdom
Giving statement: Giving through the Holme Roberts & Owen LLP Corporate Giving Program.

Holme Roberts & Owen LLP Corporate Giving Program
1700 Lincoln St., Ste. 4100
Denver, CO 80203-4541
Contact for Pro Bono program: Tracy Ashmore, Partner, Chair of the Pro Bono Comm., tel.: (303) 866-0304, e-mail: tracy.ashmore@hro.com; URL: http://www.hro.com/community-investment/

Purpose and activities: Holme Roberts & Owen makes charitable contributions to nonprofit organizations on a case by case basis.
Fields of interest: Legal services; United Ways and Federated Giving Programs; General charitable giving.
Type of support: Employee volunteer services; General/operating support; Pro bono services - legal; Scholarships—to individuals.

1838
Holmes Automotive Group Inc.
11344 Hickman Rd.
Des Moines, IA 50325-3744
(515) 253-3000

Company URL: http://www.holmesauto.com
Establishment information: Established in 1986.
Company type: Subsidiary of a private company
Business activities: Operates automotive repair shops.
Business type (SIC): Motor vehicle repair shops
Corporate officer: Chris Weyer, Mgr.
Giving statement: Giving through the Holmes Foundation.

Holmes Foundation
11206 Hickman Rd.
Clive, IA 50325-3795 (515) 253-3050

Establishment information: Established in 2004 in IA.
Donor: Holmes Automotive Group.
Contact: Max H. Holmes, Dir.
Financial data (yr. ended 12/31/11): Assets, $186 (M); gifts received, $5,000; expenditures, $6,505; qualifying distributions, $6,500; giving activities include $6,500 for grants.
Fields of interest: Education; Human services; Religion.
Application information: Applications accepted. Application form required.
Initial approach: Proposal
Deadline(s): None
Directors: Janelle L. Holmes; Julie Holmes; Max H. Holmes; Max Harvey Holmes; Catherine A. Keylon; Jackie Matt.
EIN: 202047135

1839
Holt & Bugbee Company
1600 Shawsheen St.
P.O. Box 37
Tewksbury, MA 01876 (978) 851-7201
FAX: (978) 851-3941

Company URL: http://www.holtandbugbee.com
Establishment information: Established in 1825.
Company type: Private company
Business activities: Manufactures and sells hardwood and softwood lumber.
Business type (SIC): Lumber and wood products
Financial profile for 2010: Number of employees, 180
Corporate officers: Phillip T. Pierce, Pres.; William Collins, C.F.O.
Giving statement: Giving through the Holt & Bugbee Foundation, Inc.

Holt & Bugbee Foundation, Inc.
1600 Shawsheen St.
Tewksbury, MA 01876-0037

Establishment information: Classified as a company-sponsored operating foundation in 2003 in MA. Reclassified as a company-sponsored independent foundation in 2004.
Donors: Holt & Bugbee Co.; Holt & Bugbee Hardwoods, Inc.
Financial data (yr. ended 12/31/11): Assets, $323,999 (M); expenditures, $16,529; qualifying distributions, $16,529; giving activities include $10,000 for 4 grants to individuals (high: $2,500; low: $2,500).
Purpose and activities: The foundation supports organizations involved with secondary education and awards scholarships.
Fields of interest: Education.
Type of support: Scholarship funds; Scholarships—to individuals.
Geographic limitations: Giving primarily in Tewksbury, MA.
Application information: Applications not accepted. Contributes only to pre-selected organizations and individuals.
Officers and Directors:* Phillip T. Pierce*, Pres.; Rebecca Pierce Herlihy, Clerk; Roger C. Pierce, Jr.*, Treas.
EIN: 200446975

1840
Holtz House of Vehicles Inc.

(also known as John Holtz)
3925 W. Henrietta Rd.
Rochester, NY 14623-3705 (585) 424-2810

Company URL: http://www.johnholtz.com
Establishment information: Established in 1977.
Company type: Private company
Business activities: Operates car dealership.
Business type (SIC): Motor vehicles—retail
Corporate officer: John D. Holtz, Pres. and C.E.O.
Office: East Rochester, NY
Giving statement: Giving through the John D. and Seana L. Holtz Foundation, Inc.

John D. and Seana L. Holtz Foundation, Inc.

3883 W. Henrietta Rd.
Rochester, NY 14623-3700

Establishment information: Established in 2001 in NY.
Donors: Holtz House of Vehicles Inc.; John Holtz Acura; National Auto Care Corp.
Financial data (yr. ended 12/31/11): Assets, $2,002,038 (M); gifts received, $2,023,000; expenditures, $21,390; qualifying distributions, $20,500; giving activities include $20,500 for grants.
Purpose and activities: The foundation supports organizations involved with higher education and cancer.
Fields of interest: Education; Youth development; Human services.
Type of support: General/operating support; Scholarship funds.
Geographic limitations: Giving limited to Rochester, NY.
Support limitations: No grants to individuals.
Application information: Applications not accepted. Unsolicited requests for funds not accepted.
Directors: John D. Holtz; Seana Holtz; William Kreienberg; James Latona, Sr.
EIN: 364490829

1841
Homasote Company

932 Lower Ferry Rd.
P.O. Box 7240
West Trenton, NJ 08628-0240
(609) 883-3300
FAX: (609) 883-3497

Company URL: http://www.homasote.com
Establishment information: Established in 1909.
Company type: Private company
Company ticker symbol and exchange: HMTC/Pink Sheets
Business activities: Manufactures insulated wood fiber board and polyisocyanurate foam products.
Business type (SIC): Lumber and wood products (except furniture); wood products/miscellaneous; plastic products/miscellaneous
Corporate officers: Warren L. Flicker, Chair. and C.E.O.; Craig R. Stiffler, Pres. and C.O.O.; Ronald D. Fasano, C.F.O.
Board of directors: Warren L. Flicker, Chair.; Craig R. Stiffler
Giving statement: Giving through the Homasote Foundation.
Company EIN: 210388986

Homasote Foundation

932 Lower Ferry Rd.
West Trenton, NJ 08628-0240

Donor: Homasote Co.
Financial data (yr. ended 12/31/11): Assets, $263,829 (M); expenditures, $21,643; qualifying distributions, $17,680; giving activities include $17,680 for 27 grants (high: $10,000; low: $25).
Purpose and activities: The foundation supports fire departments and nonprofit organizations involved with media, health, cancer, housing, human services, Judaism, and women.
Fields of interest: Media/communications; Media, print publishing; Health care; Cancer; Housing/shelter; Disasters, fire prevention/control; Human services; United Ways and Federated Giving Programs; Jewish federated giving programs; Jewish agencies & synagogues Women.
Type of support: General/operating support.
Support limitations: No grants to individuals.
Application information: Applications not accepted. Unsolicited requests for funds not accepted.
Officers: Warren L. Flicker, Pres.; Norman Sharlin, V.P.; Jennifer D. Bartkovich, Secy.; James M. Reiser, Treas.
EIN: 216018542

1842
The Home Depot, Inc.

2455 Paces Ferry Rd., N.W.
Atlanta, GA 30339-1834 (770) 433-8211

Company URL: http://www.homedepot.com
Establishment information: Established in 1978.
Company type: Public company
Company ticker symbol and exchange: HD/NYSE
Business activities: Operates home improvement stores; provides catalog shopping services.
Business type (SIC): Lumber and other building materials—retail; nonstore retailers
Financial profile for 2013: Number of employees, 340,000; assets, $41,084,000,000; sales volume, $74,754,000,000; pre-tax net income, $7,221,000,000; expenses, $66,988,000,000; liabilities, $23,307,000,000
Fortune 1000 ranking: 2012—34th in revenues, 40th in profits, and 137th in assets
Forbes 2000 ranking: 2012—97th in sales, 120th in profits, and 566th in assets
Corporate officers: Francis S. Blake, Chair. and C.E.O.; Carol B. Tome, Exec. V.P. and C.F.O.; Matthew A. Carey, Exec. V.P. and C.I.O.; Terda Wynn Roseborough, Exec. V.P., Genl. Counsel, and Secy.; Timothy M. Crow, Exec. V.P., Human Resources; Marc Powers, Sr. V.P., Opers.; Brad Shaw, V.P., Corp. Comms.
Board of directors: Francis S. Blake, Chair.; F. Duane Ackerman; Ari Bousbib; Gregory D. Brenneman; J. Frank Brown; Albert Carey; Armando Codina; Bonnie G. Hill; Karen L. Katen; Mark Vadon
Historic mergers: Hughes Supply, Inc. (March 31, 2006)
Giving statement: Giving through the Home Depot, Inc. Corporate Giving Program and the THDF II, Inc.
Company EIN: 953261426

The Home Depot, Inc. Corporate Giving Program

2455 Paces Ferry Rd. N.W.
Atlanta, GA 30339-1834
URL: http://corporate.homedepot.com/wps/portal/

Purpose and activities: As a complement to its foundation, the Home Depot also makes charitable contributions to nonprofit organizations directly. Support is given on a national basis.
Fields of interest: Vocational education; Housing/shelter, formal/general education; Disasters, preparedness/services; American Red Cross.
Program:
Pro Trade Scholarship Program: Through the Pro Trade Scholarship Program, the Home Depot awards 500 $1,000 scholarships to students currently enrolled in a building and construction trade school program at a vocational/technical school, college, or university.
Type of support: Employee volunteer services; General/operating support; Scholarships—to individuals.
Geographic limitations: Giving on a national basis.
Application information:
Initial approach: Telephone headquarters for application information for Pro Trade Scholarships

THDF II, Inc.

(doing business as Home Depot Foundation)
(formerly The Homer Fund)
2455 Paces Ferry Rd., Ste. C-17
Atlanta, GA 30339-1834 (770) 384-3889
FAX: (770) 384-3908;
E-mail: hd_foundation@homedepot.com; Additional e-mail: small_grants@homedepot.com; contact for The Homer Fund: Erin Cannaday, tel.: (800) 654-0688, ext. 12611, e-mail: Homer_Fund@HomeDepot.com; URL: http://www.homedepotfoundation.org

Establishment information: Established in 1999 in GA.
Financial data (yr. ended 12/31/11): Revenue, $50,856,534; assets, $41,119,012 (M); gifts received, $50,155,563; expenditures, $45,205,678; giving activities include $22,109,016 for grants and $17,144,260 for grants to individuals.
Purpose and activities: The fund provides short-term financial assistance to Home Depot associates and employees who encounter hardship due to catastrophic circumstances beyond their control. The fund also provides Home Depot associates with tips and information on topics such as renter's insurance, health care, and financial preparedness. Scholarships are also available to associates' children to pursue higher education.
Fields of interest: Higher education; Safety/disasters.
Programs:
Community Impact Grants: These grants are being offered as a part of the organization's Celebration of Service initiative to ensure that every United States military veteran has a safe place to call home. These grants may support a range of activities, including repairs, refurbishments, and modifications to low-income and/or transitional veteran's housing or community facilities; weatherizing or projects designed to increase the energy efficiency of low-income and/or transitional veterans' housing or community facilities; and planting trees or community gardens and/or landscaping community facilities that serve veterans. Grants must support work completed by community volunteers in the U.S. Only registered 501(c)(3) nonprofit organizations, tax-exempt public schools, and tax- exempt public agencies in the U.S. are eligible to apply. Grants of up to $5,000 will be provided in the form of Home Depot gift cards for the purchase of tools, materials, or services. Complete program guidelines and the

online grant application are available at the Home Depot Foundation web site.

Scholarship Program: Scholarships, ranging from $1,000 to $2,500 USD ($1,000 USD for Mexico) each, are available to children of Home Depot associates. Eligible applicant must be high school seniors, college freshmen, sophomores, or juniors enrolled as undergraduate students. Parents or legal guardians must be employed by Home Depot for at least one year and still be employed at the time awards are announced. Awards are renewable; recipients and non-recipients are encouraged to reapply each year they are eligible.
Type of support: Emergency funds; Grants to individuals; Scholarships—to individuals.
Geographic limitations: Giving on a national basis, and to Canada and Mexico.
Support limitations: No support for fraternal, political, labor, athletic, social, or religious organizations, or nonprofit organizations that have been in existence for less than one year, or civic clubs, candidates, or projects. No grants for capital campaigns, endowments or endowed chairs, or film, music, television, video or media production projects or broadcast underwriting, or goodwill advertising or marketing, or for sponsorship or prizes for events such as conferences, festivals, dinners, sports competitions, art exhibits, fundraisers (e.g. dinners, walks/runs/relays, golf tournaments and auctions.
Publications: Application guidelines.
Application information: Applications accepted. Application form required.
Initial approach: Complete online application
Deadline(s): Dec. 12
Final notification: Within 6 weeks
Officers and Trustees:* Marvin Ellison*, Pres.; Layne Thome*, Secy.; Brad Shaw, Treas.; Stacie Bearden; Clay Brown; Chris Canoles; John Carr; Jennifer Hepp; Tim Hourigan; Shannon Tucker; Dana Weinman.
EIN: 582491657

1843
Home Federal Bancorp, Inc.

500 12th Ave. S.
Nampa, ID 83651 (208) 466-4634

Company URL: http://www.myhomefed.com
Establishment information: Established in 1920.
Company type: Public company
Company ticker symbol and exchange: HOME/NASDAQ
Business activities: Operates bank holding company; operates savings bank.
Business type (SIC): Savings institutions; holding company
Financial profile for 2011: Number of employees, 395; assets, $1,116,430,000; pre-tax net income, $2,160,000; liabilities, $925,160,000
Corporate officers: Daniel L. Stevens, Chair.; Len E. Williams, Pres. and C.E.O.; Eric S. Nadeau, Exec. V.P., C.F.O., and Secy.-Treas.
Board of directors: Daniel L. Stevens, Chair.; Norman Charles Hedemark; Brad J. Little; Richard J. Navarro; James R. Stamey; Robert A. Tinstman; Len E. Williams
Subsidiary: Home Federal Bank, Nampa, ID
Giving statement: Giving through the Home Federal Foundation, Inc.
Company EIN: 200945587

Home Federal Foundation, Inc.

500 12th Ave. S.
Nampa, ID 83651-4250 (208) 466-4634
URL: http://www.myhomefed.com

Establishment information: Established in 2004 in ID.
Donor: Home Federal Bancorp, Inc.
Contact: Daniel L. Stevens, Dir.
Financial data (yr. ended 09/30/11): Assets, $1,241,813 (M); expenditures, $101,963; qualifying distributions, $100,250; giving activities include $100,250 for grants.
Purpose and activities: The foundation supports organizations involved with arts and culture, education, health, human services, and community development. Support is given Giving primarily in areas of company operations in Ada, Canyon, Elmore and Gem Counties, Idaho.
Fields of interest: Education; Animals/wildlife; Health care; Human services; Community/economic development.
Type of support: General/operating support; Program development.
Geographic limitations: Giving primarily in areas of company operations in Ada, Canyon, Elmore and Gem Counties, ID.
Application information: Applications accepted. Application form required.
Initial approach: Proposal
Deadline(s): None
Directors: N. Charles Hedemark; Fred Helpenstell; Dale G. Peterson; Daniel L. Stevens.
EIN: 202424028

1844
Home Loan Investment Bank

1 Home Loan Plz., Ste. 3
Warwick, RI 02886-1764 (401) 739-8800

Company URL: http://www.homeloanbank.com/
Establishment information: Established in 1959.
Company type: Private company
Business activities: Operates savings bank.
Business type (SIC): Savings institutions
Corporate officers: John M. Murphy, Sr., Chair.; Brian J. Murphy, Pres. and C.E.O.; Eric B. Rose, Exec. V.P. and C.O.O.; Randolph A. Wyrofsky, Exec. V.P. and C.F.O.
Board of director: John M. Murphy, Sr., Chair.
Giving statement: Giving through the Home Loan Investment Bank Corporate Giving Program.

Home Loan Investment Bank Corporate Giving Program

1 Home Loan Plz.
Warwick, RI 02886 (401) 732-1991
URL: http://www.homeloanbank.com/community.aspx

Purpose and activities: Home Loan Investment Bank makes charitable contributions to nonprofit organizations involved with community, health care, housing, youth programs, education, and the environment. Support is given primarily in areas of company operations.
Fields of interest: Arts education; Performing arts, theater; Education; Environment; Hospitals (specialty); Health care; ALS; Housing/shelter; Boys clubs; Girls clubs; Youth development; Children, services; Civil/human rights, equal rights; Community/economic development.
Type of support: Employee volunteer services; General/operating support; Scholarship funds.
Geographic limitations: Giving primarily in areas of company operations.

1845
The Home Savings and Loan Company

275 W. Federal St.
Youngstown, OH 44503-1200
(330) 742-0500

Company URL: http://www.homesavings.com
Establishment information: Established in 1889.
Company type: Subsidiary of a public company
Business activities: Operates savings bank.
Business type (SIC): Savings institutions
Corporate officers: Richard J. Schiraldi, Chair; Patrick W. Bevack, Pres. and C.E.O.; James R. Reske, C.F.O. and Treas.; Jude J. Nohra, Genl. Counsel and Secy.
Board of directors: Richard J. Schiraldi, Chair.; Marty E. Adams; Eugenia C. Atkinson; Patrick W. Bevack; Richard J. Buoncore; Lee J. Burdman; Scott N. Crewson; Scott D. Hunter; David C. Sweet
Giving statement: Giving through the Home Savings Charitable Foundation.

Home Savings Charitable Foundation

P.O. Box 1111
Youngstown, OH 44501-1111 (330) 742-0571
FAX: (330) 742-0532;
E-mail: dpavlock@homesavings.com; Additional fax: (330) 742-0499; URL: https://www.homesavings.com/foundation

Establishment information: Established in 1991 in OH.
Donors: Home Savings and Loan Co.; United Community Financial Corp.
Contact: Darlene Pavlock, Exec. Dir.
Financial data (yr. ended 12/31/11): Assets, $10,730,465 (M); expenditures, $615,582; qualifying distributions, $537,969; giving activities include $537,969 for grants.
Purpose and activities: The foundation supports programs designed to promote education and address the needs of economically disadvantaged children and adults.
Fields of interest: Higher education; Education; Health care; YM/YWCAs & YM/YWHAs; Human services; United Ways and Federated Giving Programs Children; Economically disadvantaged.
Type of support: Annual campaigns; Capital campaigns; Equipment; Program development; Scholarship funds; Sponsorships.
Geographic limitations: Giving primarily in areas of company operations in northeastern, north central, and northwestern OH, with emphasis on Columbiana, Mahoning, and Trumbull counties.
Support limitations: No grants to individuals.
Publications: Application guidelines.
Application information: Applications accepted. Additional information may be requested at a later date. Application form required. Applicants should submit the following:
1) statement of problem project will address
2) copy of IRS Determination Letter
3) brief history of organization and description of its mission
4) copy of most recent annual report/audited financial statement/990
5) how project's results will be evaluated or measured
6) listing of board of directors, trustees, officers and other key people and their affiliations

7) detailed description of project and amount of funding requested
8) contact person
9) copy of current year's organizational budget and/or project budget
Initial approach: Telephone foundation; download application form and mail to foundation
Copies of proposal: 2
Deadline(s): None

Officer: Darlene Pavlock, Exec. Dir.
Trustee: Farmers Trust Co.
Number of staff: 1 full-time professional.
EIN: 341695319
Selected grants: The following grants are a representative sample of this grantmaker's funding activity:
$28,416 to American Cancer Society, Canfield, OH, 2010.
$25,000 to Youngstown Foundation, Youngstown, OH, 2010.
$17,500 to First Tee of Cleveland, Cleveland, OH, 2010.
$10,000 to Boy Scouts of America, Canton, OH, 2010.
$10,000 to Neil Kennedy Recovery Clinic, Youngstown, OH, 2010.
$10,000 to Warren City School District, Warren, OH, 2010.
$10,000 to Youngstown Business Incubator, Youngstown, OH, 2010.
$5,000 to Bellevue United Selective Fund, Bellevue, OH, 2010.
$5,000 to Niles Community Services, Niles, OH, 2010.
$2,000 to Heidelberg University, Tiffin, OH, 2010.

1846
Home State Bank

300 E. 29th St.
P.O. Box 329
Loveland, CO 80537-4337 (970) 203-6100

Company URL: http://www.homestatebank.com
Establishment information: Established in 1950.
Company type: Private company
Business activities: Operates commercial bank.
Business type (SIC): Banks/commercial
Financial profile for 2012: Assets, $67,752,141,427; liabilities, $61,456,106,542
Corporate officers: Jack Devereaux, Jr., Chair.; Harry Devereaux, Pres.; Don Churchwell, C.E.O.; Mark Bower, Exec. V.P., C.O.O., and C.F.O.; Sharon Manago, V.P. Finance
Board of directors: Jack Devereaux, Jr., Chair.; Robert Bisetti; Mark Bower; Don Churchwell; Morrison Heth; Nelse Lundeen; Daniel Mills; Carey Salomonson; Roger Sample; Joe Scherger; Kenneth R. Weedin
Giving statement: Giving through the Home State Bank Charitable Foundation.

Home State Bank Charitable Foundation

115 W. State St.
Jefferson, IA 50129-1911 (515) 386-2131

Establishment information: Established in 1991 in IA.
Donor: Home State Bank.
Contact: Sid Jones, Pres.
Financial data (yr. ended 12/31/11): Assets, $184,394 (M); gifts received, $36,000; expenditures, $35,917; qualifying distributions, $35,600; giving activities include $35,600 for 43 grants (high: $2,890; low: $50).
Purpose and activities: The foundation supports community foundations and organizations involved with media, historic preservation, education, land conservation, cancer, muscular dystrophy, and Catholicism.
Fields of interest: Education; Health organizations; Religion.
Type of support: General/operating support.
Geographic limitations: Giving limited to IA.
Support limitations: No grants to individuals.
Application information: Applications accepted. Application form required. Applicants should submit the following:
1) detailed description of project and amount of funding requested
Initial approach: Letter
Deadline(s): None

Officers and Directors:* Sid Jones*, Pres.; Elizabeth Garst*, Secy.; Mary Garst*, Treas.; Jennifer Garst; Douglas McDermott; Wayne Seaman; Scott Sievers; Susan Tronchetti.
EIN: 421378344

1847
Homecrest Industries, Inc.

1250 Homecrest Ave.
Wadena, MN 56482 (218) 631-1000

Company URL: http://www.homecrest.com
Establishment information: Established in 1953.
Company type: Private company
Business activities: Manufactures casual and outdoor residential furniture; manufactures commercial furniture.
Business type (SIC): Furniture/household; furniture and fixtures/miscellaneous
Corporate officers: Mark Sillhouer, C.E.O.; Joe Kincade, Co.-Pres.; Gene Koontz, Co.-Pres.; Mike Wise, C.F.O.; Scott Coremin, V.P.
Giving statement: Giving through the Bottemiller Family Foundation.

Bottemiller Family Foundation

(formerly Homecrest Foundation)
13995 42nd Ave. N.
Plymouth, MN 55446-3826

Establishment information: Established in 1986 in MN.
Donor: Homecrest Industries, Inc.
Contact: Donald L. Bottemiller, Tr.
Financial data (yr. ended 07/31/11): Assets, $127,691 (M); gifts received, $920; expenditures, $2,655; qualifying distributions, $5,155; giving activities include $2,600 for 4 grants (high: $1,500; low: $250).
Purpose and activities: The foundation supports organizations involved with music and education and awards college scholarships.
Fields of interest: Performing arts, music; Higher education; Education.
Programs:
Employee-Related Scholarships: The foundation awards college scholarships to children of employees of Homecrest Industries.
Scholarships: The foundation annually awards one college scholarship to a senior at Wadena High School in Wadena, Minnesota; and one college scholarship to a senior at Wadena High School in Wadena, Minnesota majoring in business.
Type of support: Employee-related scholarships; General/operating support; Scholarships—to individuals; Sponsorships.
Geographic limitations: Giving primarily in areas of company operations in MN.
Publications: Annual report.
Application information: Applications accepted. Application form required.
Initial approach: Letter
Deadline(s): None

Officer: Mark Bottemiller, Secy.-Treas.
Trustee: Donald L. Bottemiller.
EIN: 411550750

1848
Homestar Bank & Financial Services

(formerly HomeStar Bank)
303 Section Line Rd.
Manteno, IL 60950-1059 (815) 468-2265

Company URL: http://www.homestarbank.com
Establishment information: Established in 1946.
Company type: Private company
Business activities: Operates commercial bank.
Business type (SIC): Banks/commercial
Corporate officers: Patrick M. O'Brien, Pres. and C.E.O.; Debbie Moss, C.F.O.
Offices: Bourbonnais, Bradley, Mokena, Plainfield, IL
Giving statement: Giving through the HomeStar Education Foundation, Inc.

HomeStar Education Foundation, Inc.

3 Diversatech Dr.
Manteno, IL 60950-9201 (815) 468-2357
E-mail: starmail@homestarbank.com; URL: http://www.homestarbank.com/Scholarship.htm
Scholarship application addresses: HomeStar Customer Scholarship Prog.: HomeStar Bank, Mktg. Dept., 435 E. North St., Bradley, IL 60915; HomeStar-NAACP Scholarship Prog.: NAACP Education Comm., P.O. Box 1986, Kankakee, IL 60901

Establishment information: Established in 2001 in IL.
Donor: HomeStar Bank.
Contact: Deborah S. Maw, Treas.
Financial data (yr. ended 12/31/11): Assets, $1 (M); gifts received, $39,500; expenditures, $39,500; qualifying distributions, $39,500; giving activities include $39,500 for grants.
Purpose and activities: The foundation awards college scholarships to children and grandchildren of customers of HomeStar Bank and its affiliates; students in Kankakee County, Illinois, who are members of the Kankakee County branch of the NAACP; and to high school seniors in Kankakee or Iroquois County, Illinois who have Latino heritage.
Type of support: Employee-related scholarships; Scholarships—to individuals.
Geographic limitations: Giving limited to IL.
Publications: Application guidelines.
Application information: Applications accepted. Application form required.
Applications should include two letters of recommendation, official transcripts, and an essay.
Initial approach: Download application form and mail to foundation
Deadline(s): Feb. 6
Final notification: Apr.

Officer and Directors: Madelyn O'Brien, Chair.; Patrick M. O'Brien*, Pres.; Michael P. O'Brien, Secy.; Deborah S. Maw, Treas.; Mark Argyelan; Patrick D. Martin; James Smith.
EIN: 364452037

1849
Homewood Corp.
2700 E. Dublin-Granville Rd., Ste. 300
Columbus, OH 43231 (614) 898-7200

Company URL: http://www.homewood-homes.com
Establishment information: Established in 1963.
Company type: Private company
Business activities: Builds houses.
Business type (SIC): Contractors/general residential building
Corporate officers: John H. Bain, C.E.O.; Joe Merz, Cont.
Giving statement: Giving through the Salem Lutheran Foundation.

Salem Lutheran Foundation
2700 E. Dublin-Granville Rd., Rm. 300
Columbus, OH 43231-4089 (614) 898-7200

Establishment information: Established in 1968 in OH.
Donors: Homewood Corp.; George A. Skestos.
Contact: Terrie L. Rice, Secy.
Financial data (yr. ended 12/31/11): Assets, $3,349,876 (M); expenditures, $157,446; qualifying distributions, $149,800; giving activities include $149,800 for grants.
Purpose and activities: The foundation awards college scholarships to men entering the pastoral ministry and attending Martin Lutheran College in Minnesota and Wisconsin Lutheran Seminary in Wisconsin.
Type of support: Scholarships—to individuals.
Geographic limitations: Giving limited to MN and WI.
Application information: Applications accepted. Application form required.
Requests should include transcripts and a letter of recommendation from a Pastor.
Initial approach: Contact foundation for application form
Deadline(s): July 1
Final notification: After Aug. 1
Officers and Trustees:* William A. Goldman*, Pres.; Terrie L. Rice, Secy.; Adam N. Scott, Treas.; Hagop Mekhjian; James W. Phieffer.
EIN: 316084166

1850
R. L. Honbarrier Company
1321 W. Fairfield Rd., Ste. 101
P.O. Box 7027
High Point, NC 27263 (336) 431-4300

Establishment information: Established in 1997.
Company type: Private company
Business activities: Operates a real estate company.
Business type (SIC): Real estate agents and managers
Corporate officer: Archie L. Honbarrier, Pres.
Giving statement: Giving through the Honbarrier Foundation, Inc.

Honbarrier Foundation, Inc.
P.O. Box 7027
High Point, NC 27264-7027

Establishment information: Established in 2006 in NC.
Donor: R.L. Honbarrier Co.
Financial data (yr. ended 12/31/11): Assets, $521,149 (M); expenditures, $13,206; qualifying distributions, $10,000; giving activities include $10,000 for 1 grant.
Purpose and activities: The foundation supports parks and organizations involved with elementary education.
Fields of interest: Public affairs.
Type of support: General/operating support.
Support limitations: No grants to individuals.
Application information: Applications not accepted. Unsolicited requests for funds not accepted.
Officers: Archie L. Honbarrier*, Pres.; Charles L. Odom, V.P. and Secy.
EIN: 208101796

1851
Honda of America Manufacturing, Inc.
24000 Honda Pkwy.
Marysville, OH 43040 (937) 642-5000

Company URL: http://www.ohio.honda.com
Establishment information: Established in 1979.
Company type: Subsidiary of a foreign company
Business activities: Manufactures motorcycles, cars, and engines.
Business type (SIC): Motorcycles, bicycles, and parts; engines and turbines; motor vehicles and equipment
Corporate officers: Hidenobu Iwata, Pres. and C.E.O.; Harold Brown, Exec. Dir.
Board of director: Hidenobu Iwata
Subsidiary: Honda Manufacturing of Alabama, LLC, Lincoln, AL
Plants: Anna, East Liberty, OH
Giving statement: Giving through the Honda of America Mfg., Inc. Corporate Giving Program and the Honda of America Foundation.

Honda of America Mfg., Inc. Corporate Giving Program
24000 Honda Pkwy.
Marysville, OH 43040-9251
E-mail: grants@ham.honda.com; URL: http://www.ohio.honda.com/community/giving.cfm

Purpose and activities: As a complement to its foundation, Honda of America also makes charitable contributions to nonprofit organizations directly. Support is limited to Allen, Auglaize, Champaign, Clark, Darke, Delaware, Franklin, Hardin, Logan, Madison, Marion, Mercer, Miami, Shelby, and Union, Ohio.
Fields of interest: Arts, cultural/ethnic awareness; Elementary/secondary education; Environment; Safety, automotive safety; Safety/disasters; Human services; United Ways and Federated Giving Programs.
Programs:
Honda Hero Volunteer Program: Through the Honda Hero Volunteer Program, Honda makes charitable contributions of $250 to nonprofit organizations with which its employees and retirees and their spouses volunteer at least 50 hours per year.
Matching Gift Program: Honda matches contributions made by its employees to two and four-year colleges, technical institutes, and nonprofit organizations involved with arts and culture on a one-for-two basis up to $500 per employee, per year.
Type of support: Annual campaigns; Employee matching gifts; Employee volunteer services; General/operating support; In-kind gifts.
Geographic limitations: Giving limited to Allen, Auglaize, Champaign, Clark, Darke, Delaware, Franklin, Hardin, Logan, Madison, Marion, Mercer, Miami, Shelby, and Union, OH.
Support limitations: No support for organizations based outside of Ohio, political candidates, committees or organizations, lobbying organizations or memberships, fraternal, labor, social, or veteran's organizations, churches, religious or sectarian organizations that do not benefit the entire community, or individual K-12 schools. Excluded organizations may still be eligible for support from other Honda programs, such as matching gifts and Honda Hero Dollars for Doers programs. No grants to individuals, or for teams, sporting events, or tournaments, including charity golf tournaments, fundraising events such as telethons or walkathons, fashion shows, beauty pageants, or contestants, or non-academic educational activities such as bands, choirs, proms, after-proms, or graduations. Organizations with excluded purposes may still be eligible for support from other Honda programs, such as matching gifts and Honda Hero Dollars for Doers programs.
Publications: Application guidelines; Informational brochure.
Application information: Applications accepted. Application form required. Applicants should submit the following:
1) listing of additional sources and amount of support
2) copy of current year's organizational budget and/or project budget
3) contact person
4) listing of board of directors, trustees, officers and other key people and their affiliations
5) copy of most recent annual report/audited financial statement/990
6) copy of IRS Determination Letter
7) name, address and phone number of organization

Initial approach: Complete online application form
Copies of proposal: 1
Deadline(s): Sept. 1 to Nov. 30 for grants; 90 days prior to need for events

Honda of America Foundation
c/o Corp. Affairs, Marysville Motorcyle Plant
24000 Honda Pkwy.
Marysville, OH 43040-9251 (937) 644-6412
FAX: (937) 645-8787;
E-mail: nancy_larry@ham.honda.com; URL: http://www.ohio.honda.com/community/giving.cfm

Establishment information: Established in 1981 in OH.
Donor: Honda of America Mfg., Inc.
Contact: Caroline Ramsey, Exec. Dir.
Financial data (yr. ended 12/31/11): Assets, $7,879,136 (M); gifts received, $150,000; expenditures, $641,737; qualifying distributions, $548,500; giving activities include $548,500 for grants.
Purpose and activities: The foundation supports organizations involved with arts and culture, education, the environment, safety, community development, and civic responsibility.
Fields of interest: Arts; Education; Environment; Safety, automotive safety; Community/economic development; Public affairs.
Type of support: Building/renovation; General/operating support; Program development; Scholarship funds.
Geographic limitations: Giving primarily in areas of company operations in west central OH, with emphasis on Allen, Auglaize, Champaign, Clark, Darke, Delaware, Franklin, Hardin, Logan, Madison, Marion, Mercer, Miami, Shelby and Union counties.

Support limitations: No support for religious organizations, national health, fraternal, lobbying, political, or veterans' organizations, or sports teams. No grants to individuals, or for courtesy advertisements, legal advocacy, memberships, conferences, workshops, seminars, pageants, or extracurricular school activities.
Publications: Application guidelines.
Application information: Applications accepted. Application form required.
Initial approach: Complete online application form
Copies of proposal: 1
Board meeting date(s): Quarterly
Deadline(s): None for requests of up to $15,000; Mar. 31, June 30, Sept. 30, and Dec. 31 for requests over $15,000
Final notification: 1 month after board meeting
Officers and Directors: Tom Shoupe, Pres.; Shaun McCloskey, Treas.; Caroline Ramsey, Exec. Dir.; Steve Francis; Jan Gansheimer.
Number of staff: 1 full-time professional.
EIN: 311006130
Selected grants: The following grants are a representative sample of this grantmaker's funding activity:
$275,000 to Nationwide Childrens Hospital Foundation, Columbus, OH, 2010.
$41,667 to Lincoln Theater Association, Columbus, OH, 2010.
$25,000 to Columbus Council on World Affairs, Columbus, OH, 2010.
$25,000 to Columbus Museum of Art, Columbus, OH, 2010.
$20,000 to YWCA Columbus, Columbus, OH, 2010.
$15,000 to Columbus Association for the Performing Arts, Columbus, OH, 2010.

1852
Honeywell International, Inc.

(formerly AlliedSignal Inc.)
101 Columbia Rd.
P.O. Box 4000
Morristown, NJ 07962 (973) 455-2000
FAX: (973) 455-6394

Company URL: http://honeywell.com/
Establishment information: Established in 1920.
Company type: Public company
Company ticker symbol and exchange: HON/NYSE
International Securities Identification Number: US4385161066
Business activities: Manufactures and provides aerospace products and services, control technologies, automotive products, power generation systems, specialty chemicals, fibers, and plastics.
Business type (SIC): Motor vehicles and equipment; chemicals and allied products; plastics and synthetics; electrical industrial apparatus; aircraft and parts; laboratory apparatus
Financial profile for 2012: Number of employees, 132,000; assets, $41,853,000,000; sales volume, $37,665,000,000; pre-tax net income, $3,875,000,000; expenses, $33,790,000,000; liabilities, $28,878,000,000
Fortune 1000 ranking: 2012—78th in revenues, 65th in profits, and 131st in assets
Forbes 2000 ranking: 2012—254th in sales, 196th in profits, and 550th in assets
Corporate officers: David M. Cote, Chair. and C.E.O.; Mark R. James, Sr. V.P., Human Resources, and Comms.; David J. Anderson, Sr. V.P. and C.F.O.; Katherine L. Adams, Sr. V.P. and Genl. Counsel; Krishna Mikkilineni, Sr. V.P., Opers.; Mike Lang, V.P. and C.I.O.
Board of directors: David M. Cote, Chair.; Gordon M. Bethune; Kevin Burke; Jaime Chico Pardo; D. Scott Davis; Linnet F. Deily; Judd Gregg; Clive R. Hollick; Grace D. Lieblein; George Paz; Bradley T. Sheares, Ph.D.; Bradley T. Washington; Robin L. Washington
Plants: Phoenix, AZ; Torrance, CA; Clearwater, FL; South Bend, IN; Olathe, KS; Baton Rouge, LA; Columbia, MD; Kansas City, MO; Columbia, SC; Chesterfield, Hopewell, Petersburg, VA
International operations: Australia; Belgium; Bermuda; Canada; China; Czech Republic; France; Germany; India; Italy; Luxembourg; Netherlands; North Korea; Switzerland; United Kingdom
Giving statement: Giving through the Honeywell Corporate Giving Program.
Company EIN: 222640650

Honeywell Corporate Giving Program

(formerly AlliedSignal Inc. Corporate Giving Program)
101 Columbia Rd.
Morristown, NJ 07962-2245
URL: http://www.honeywell.com/sites/hhs

Purpose and activities: Honeywell makes charitable contributions to nonprofit organizations involved with math and science education, the environment, housing and shelter, and family safety and security. Support is given on a national basis in areas of company operations.
Fields of interest: Education; Environmental education; Environment; Housing/shelter, development; Housing/shelter; Disasters, preparedness/services; Safety/disasters; Family services; Science, formal/general education; Space/aviation; Mathematics; Engineering/technology; Science; Leadership development.
Programs:
Got 2B Safe Safety Contest: Honeywell, in partnership with the National Center for Missing & Exploited Children, rewards teachers for their commitment to child safety. Five grand prize winners receive professional classroom makeovers worth $10,000 and 100 winners receive gift certificates for school supplies worth up to $500. The contest is part of the Got 2B Safe prevention initiative that teaches elementary school children potential life-saving lessons.
Honeywell Educators @ Space Academy: Honeywell, in partnership with the U.S. Space and Rocket Center, annually awards 100 scholarships to middle school science and math teachers to attend a five-day program of intensive classroom, laboratory, and training time focusing on space science and space exploration at the U.S. Space and Rocket Center in Huntsville, Alabama.
Honeywell Institute for Ecosystems Foundation: Honeywell, in partnership with the New Jersey Audubon Society, Montezuma Audubon Center, Onondaga Audubon Society, and the Maryland Science Center, awards stipends and scholarships to middle and high school science and social studies teachers to attend a four-day institute in August to learn about ecosystems. The institute is designed to teach education techniques to integrate environmental science into curriculums.
Honeywell Leadership Challenge Academy: Honeywell, in partnership with the U.S. Space and Rocket Center, provides children of employees of Honeywell with a week-long academy to develop leadership skills through science. The program is designed to encourage high school students to pursue math and science and to promote purposeful leadership, effective communication, integrated planning, team trust and cohesion, and critical thinking. The academy takes place at the U.S. Space and Rocket Center in Huntsville, Alabama.
Type of support: Curriculum development; Employee matching gifts; Employee volunteer services; Employee-related scholarships; General/operating support; Program development; Scholarship funds; Scholarships—to individuals; Sponsorships.
Geographic limitations: Giving on a national basis in areas of company operations, with emphasis on NJ and NY.
Publications: Application guidelines.
Application information: Applications accepted. Application form required.
Applications for the Got 2B Safe Safety Contest must include a one-age lesson plan on demonstrating how you teach Got 2B Safe.
Initial approach: Download application form and e-mail or mail to foundation for Honeywell Educators at Space Academy; complete online registration form for Got 2B Safe Safety Contest; download application form and mail to application address for Honeywell Institute for Ecosystems Education
Deadline(s): Visit website for deadlines for Honeywell Educators at Space Academy and Got 2B Safe Safety Contest; June for Honeywell Institute for Ecosystems Education

1853
Honigman Miller Schwartz & Cohn LLP

2290 1st National Bldg.
660 Woodward Ave.
Detroit, MI 48226-3506 (313) 465-7382

Company URL: http://www.honigman.com/
Establishment information: Established in 1948.
Company type: Private company
Business activities: Operates law firm.
Business type (SIC): Legal services
Corporate officers: David Foltyn, Chair.; Joel S. Adelman, Vice-Chair.; Alan S. Schwartz, Vice-Chair.; Robert D. Kubic, C.O.O.
Giving statement: Giving through the Honigman Miller Schwartz & Cohn LLP Pro Bono Program.

Honigman Miller Schwartz & Cohn LLP Pro Bono Program

2290 1st National Bldg.
660 Woodward Ave.
Detroit, MI 48226-3506 (313) 465-7382
E-mail: jbelveal@honigman.com; Additional tel.: (313) 465-7000, fax: (313) 465-8213; URL: http://www.honigman.com/aboutus/xprCallOut.aspx?xpST=AboutUsCommunity

Contact: Jennifer Belveal, Pro Bono Comm. Chair.
Fields of interest: Legal services.
Type of support: Pro bono services - legal.
Application information: The Pro Bono Coordinator manages the pro bono program.

1854
HP Hood Inc.

90 Everett Ave., Ste. 1
Chelsea, MA 02150-2301 (617) 887-8455
FAX: (617) 241-2165

Company URL: http://www.hphood.com
Establishment information: Established in 1846.
Company type: Subsidiary of a private company

Business activities: Produces dairy, extended shelf-life dairy, frozen dessert, citrus, non-dairy, and specialty food products.
Business type (SIC): Dairy products; specialty foods/canned, frozen, and preserved
Corporate officers: John A. Kaneb, Chair., Pres., and C.E.O.; James F. Walsh, Exec. V.P., Sales; Gary R. Kaneb, C.F.O.; Paul C. Nightingale, Sr. V.P. and Genl. Counsel; H. Scott Blake, Sr. V.P., Opers.; Theresa M. Bresten, V.P. and Treas.; James A. Marcinelli, V.P. and Cont.; Christopher S. Ross, V.P., Mktg.; Bruce W. Bacon, V.P., Human Resources
Board of director: John A. Kaneb, Chair.
Plants: Suffield, CT; Portland, ME; Agawam, MA; Oneida, Vernon, NY; Barre, VT; Winchester, VA
Giving statement: Giving through the HP Hood Inc. Corporate Giving Program.

HP Hood Inc. Corporate Giving Program

c/o Corp. Donations Prog.
6 Kimball Ln.
Lynnfield, MA 01940 (617) 887-3000
URL: http://www.hood.com/About/default.aspx?id=795

Purpose and activities: HP Hood makes charitable contributions to nonprofit organizations involved with health and nutrition for children and families. Support is given primarily in areas of company operations.
Fields of interest: Education; Health care; Food banks; Nutrition; Children, services; Family services; United Ways and Federated Giving Programs.
Program:
Hood Sportsmanship Scholarship Program: Hood is also proud to reward 18 high school student athletes in New England with $5,000 towards furthering their education at a 2- or 4-year accredited college or university through the Hood Sportsmanship Scholarship program, which was launched in 2010.
Type of support: General/operating support; In-kind gifts; Scholarship funds.
Geographic limitations: Giving primarily in areas of company operations.
Support limitations: No support for religious organizations, fraternal or labor organizations, or organizations that pose a conflict with the company's goals, programs, products, or employees. Generally no grants for endowments, sectarian activities, benefit tickets or courtesy advertising, political campaigns, or individual or group travel.
Application information: Telephone calls are not encouraged. Application form not required.
Applicants should submit the following:
1) population served
2) copy of IRS Determination Letter
3) geographic area to be served
4) detailed description of project and amount of funding requested
5) name, address and phone number of organization
Proposals should be submitted using organization letterhead. Proposals should specify the product and quantity the organization is requesting.
Initial approach: Proposal to headquarters
Copies of proposal: 1
Final notification: 4 to 6 weeks

1855
Hooker Furniture Corporation

440 E. Commonwealth Blvd.
P.O. Box 4708
Martinsville, VA 24112-1831
(276) 632-0459

Company URL: http://www.hookerfurniture.com
Establishment information: Established in 1924.
Company type: Public company
Company ticker symbol and exchange: HOFT/NASDAQ
Business activities: Manufactures home and office furniture.
Business type (SIC): Furniture/household; furniture/office; fixtures/office and store
Financial profile for 2013: Number of employees, 600; assets, $155,820,000; sales volume, $218,360,000; pre-tax net income, $12,990,000; expenses, $205,420,000; liabilities, $24,780,000
Corporate officers: Paul B. Toms, Jr., Chair. and C.E.O.; Alan D. Cole, Pres.; Paul A. Huckfeldt, V.P., Finance and C.F.O.
Board of directors: Paul B. Toms, Jr., Chair.; W. Christopher Beeler, Jr.; Alan D. Cole; John L. Gregory III; E. Larry Ryder; Mark F. Schreiber; David G. Sweet; Henry G. Williamson, Jr.
Joint Venture: Triwood, Inc., Ridgeway, VA
Giving statement: Giving through the Hooker Educational Foundation.
Company EIN: 540251350

Hooker Educational Foundation

P.O Box 4708
Martinsville, VA 24112-2040 (276) 632-2133

Establishment information: Established in 1991 in VA.
Donors: Hooker Furniture Corp.; Mabel B. Hooker; J. Clyde Hooker; A. Frank Hooker, Jr.†.
Contact: Debbie T. Lawless, Dir.
Financial data (yr. ended 12/31/11): Assets, $2,042,471 (M); gifts received, $29,225; expenditures, $78,354; qualifying distributions, $49,250; giving activities include $49,250 for 13 grants (high: $5,250; low: $2,500).
Purpose and activities: The foundation awards college scholarships to children of full-time employees of Hooker Furniture Corporation.
Fields of interest: Education.
Type of support: Employee-related scholarships.
Geographic limitations: Giving limited to areas of company operations in CO, NC, TN, and VA.
Application information: Applications accepted. Application form required.
Applications should include school transcripts and letters of recommendation.
Initial approach: Letter
Deadline(s): Apr. 1
Officers: E. Larry Ryder, Pres.; Paul B. Toms, Jr., Secy.
Directors: Carlene Blankenship; Katherine H. Boaz; Anne Jacobson; Deborah T. Lawless.
EIN: 541583948

1856
Hooper, Lundy & Bookman, P.C.

1875 Century Park E., Ste. 1600
Los Angeles, CA 90067-2517
(310) 551-8111

Company URL: http://health-law.com/
Company type: Private company
Business activities: Operates law firm.
Business type (SIC): Legal services
Offices: Los Angeles, San Diego, San Francisco, CA; Washington, DC
Giving statement: Giving through the Hooper, Lundy & Bookman, P.C. Pro Bono Program.

Hooper, Lundy & Bookman, P.C. Pro Bono Program

1875 Century Park E., Ste. 1600
Los Angeles, CA 90067-2517 (310) 551-8111
URL: http://health-law.com/

Contact: Stacie Neroni, Partner, Chair. of Pro Bono Comm.
Fields of interest: Legal services.
Type of support: Pro bono services - legal.
Geographic limitations: Giving primarily in areas of company operations in Los Angeles, San Francisco, and San Diego, CA, and Washington, DC.
Application information: The Pro Bono Committee manages the pro bono program.

1857
Hoops L.P.

(also known as Memphis Grizzlies)
191 Beale St.
Memphis, TN 38103 (901) 888-4667

Company URL: http://www.nba.com/grizzlies
Establishment information: Established in 1995.
Company type: Private company
Business activities: Operates professional basketball club.
Business type (SIC): Commercial sports
Corporate officers: Gene Bartow, Pres.; Don Hardman, V.P., Opers.; Todd Kobus, V.P., Finance
Giving statement: Giving through the Memphis Grizzlies Corporate Giving Program and the Memphis Grizzlies Charitable Foundation.

Memphis Grizzlies Corporate Giving Program

c/o Coord., Charitable Donation Review
191 Beale St.
Memphis, TN 38103-3715
FAX: (901) 205-1444;
E-mail: donations@grizzlies.com; Contact for Tickets for Kids: ticketsforkids@grizzlies.com; URL: http://www.nba.com/grizzlies/community/index.html

Purpose and activities: The Memphis Grizzlies make charitable contributions of game tickets and memorabilia to nonprofit organizations involved with education, basketball development, and youth development. Special emphasis is directed toward programs that serve youth. Support is given primarily in the Mid-South.
Fields of interest: Education, reading; Education; Hospitals (general); Athletics/sports, basketball; Youth development; Children, services; United Ways and Federated Giving Programs; General charitable giving.
Programs:
Educator of the Month: The Grizzlies, in partnership with Ashley Furniture HomeStore, honors outstanding leaders in K-12 education at home games. Teachers are nominated by student essays and winners are selected monthly. The winning teacher and student are featured on the Grizzlies website, receive two tickets to a Grizzlies game, the teacher receives a $1,000 gift card from Ashley Furniture HomeStore, and the student receives a Grizzlies prize pack.

Read to Achieve: Through Read to Achieve, the Grizzlies encourages youth to develop a life-long love of reading through school assemblies with the Grizzlies All-Star Reading Team and the Grizz mascot; and a six-week reading challenge for 3rd, 4th, and 5th graders where top students with the most books read attend the Grizzlies Read to Achieve Celebration.

Stay in School Challenge: Through the Stay in School Challenge, The Grizzlies and Lucite International, sponsors an attendance program designed to increase attendance rates in select schools. Students receive incentives when they maintain a 95% or above attendance rate.

Tickets for Kids Program: The Grizzlies, in partnership with Grizzlies players, coaches, owners, and season ticket holders, provide game tickets to Mid-South charities and youth organizations. The program is designed to provide children who would not otherwise have the opportunity to attend a Grizzlies home basketball game; and to recognize hard work and achievement.

Type of support: Building/renovation; Donated products; In-kind gifts; Income development.
Geographic limitations: Giving primarily in areas of company operations in the Mid-South, with emphasis on the Tri-State area of AR, MS, and TN.
Support limitations: No support for schools for memorabilia donations. No monetary donations or support for general operating expenses.
Publications: Application guidelines.
Application information: Applications accepted. Proposals should be submitted using organization letterhead. Support is limited to 1 contribution per organization during any given year. Telephone calls are not encouraged. Organizations receiving support are asked to submit a follow-up form. The Grizzlies Charitable Review Committee reviews all requests. Applicants should submit the following:
1) population served
2) name, address and phone number of organization
3) copy of IRS Determination Letter
4) detailed description of project and amount of funding requested
5) contact person

Proposals for memorabilia donations should indicate the date of the event. Nominations for Educator of the Month should include a one-page essay explaining how your teacher inspires you to succeed.
Initial approach: Mail, fax, or e-mail proposal to headquarters for memorabilia; download application form and mail, fax, or e-mail to headquarters for Tickets for Kids; download nomination form and mail to headquarters for Educator of the Month
Copies of proposal: 1
Deadline(s): 6 weeks prior to need for memorabilia; None for Tickets for Kids; visit website for Educator of the Month deadlines
Final notification: 2 weeks prior to need for memorabilia donations

Memphis Grizzlies Charitable Foundation

191 Beale St.
Memphis, TN 38103-3715 (901) 205-8326
FAX: (901) 205-1444;
E-mail: foundation@grizzlies.com; E-mail for Tickets for Kids: ticketsforkids@grizzlies.com; Contact for Honoring Our Military Families: Eric Bleier, tel.: (901) 205-1249; URL: http://www.teamupmemphis.org/

Establishment information: Established in 2004 in TN.
Donors: The Poplar Foundation; Hope Christian Community Foundation; Helco Holding, Inc.
Contact: Jenny Koltnow, Exec. Dir.
Financial data (yr. ended 12/31/11): Assets, $395,554 (M); gifts received, $2,714,607; expenditures, $2,485,667; qualifying distributions, $2,483,167; giving activities include $2,342,754 for 25 grants (high: $1,600,000; low: $2,500).
Purpose and activities: The foundation supports programs designed to serve youth through education and mentoring.
Fields of interest: Secondary school/education; Education; Athletics/sports, amateur leagues; Athletics/sports, basketball; Boys & girls clubs; Youth development, adult & child programs; Youth development; Human services.

Programs:
Honoring Our Military Families: The foundation awards ticket packages to returning servicemen and servicewomen and their families, and to families of currently deployed military personnel. The ticket package includes a maximum of 10 tickets, up to two parking passes for the Ford Park Garage, and one $10 concession voucher per person. A member of the family must be aligned with a Mid-South base or unit to qualify.

Tickets for Kids Program: The foundation awards tickets purchased by Grizzlies players, coaches, owners, corporate partners, and season ticket holders to Mid-South charities and youth organizations. The program is designed to reward kids for hard work and achievement.

Type of support: Donated products; General/operating support; In-kind gifts; Program development; Technical assistance.
Geographic limitations: Giving limited to AR, MS, and the Memphis, TN, area.
Publications: Application guidelines.
Application information: Applications accepted. Unsolicited requests for grants are not accepted. Application form required.
Initial approach: Download application form and E-mail or fax to foundation for Tickets for Kids and Honoring Our Military Families
Deadline(s): None
Officers and Directors:* Staley Cates*, Pres.; Elliot Perry, V.P.; Stanley Meadows*, Secy.-Treas.; Jenny Koltnow, Exec. Dir.; Andy Cates; Mike Conley; Charles Ewing, Sr.; Michael Heisley; Barbara Hyde; J. R. Hyde III; Fred Jones, Jr.; Pete Prancia; Sean Tuohy.
EIN: 201356702
Selected grants: The following grants are a representative sample of this grantmaker's funding activity:
$1,000,000 to Memphis Athletic Ministries, Memphis, TN, 2010.
$25,000 to Memphis Child Advocacy Center, Memphis, TN, 2010.
$25,000 to Memphis Leadership Foundation, Memphis, TN, 2010.
$25,000 to Metropolitan Inter-Faith Association, Memphis, TN, 2010.
$25,000 to Streets Ministries, Memphis, TN, 2010.

1858
Hooters of America, Inc.

1815 The Exchange
Atlanta, GA 30339 (770) 951-2040

Company URL: http://www.hooters.com
Establishment information: Established in 1983.
Company type: Private company
Business activities: Owns and franchises restaurants.
Business type (SIC): Restaurants and drinking places; investors/miscellaneous
Corporate officers: Terrance M. Marks, C.E.O.; Sam Rothschild, C.O.O.; Matt Wickesberg, C.F.O.; Chris Duncan, C.I.O.; Chris Duncan, V.P., Admin.; Mike McNeil, V.P., Mktg.; Doug White, V.P., Human Resources; Bryan Struble, Genl. Counsel
Giving statement: Giving through the Hooters Community Endowment Fund, Inc.

Hooters Community Endowment Fund, Inc.

1815 The Exchange
Atlanta, GA 30339-2027 (770) 951-2040

Establishment information: Established in 1992.
Donors: Hooters of America, Inc.; RMD Corp.; Marinos Charity; Heineken; Miller Brewing Co.; Tyson; Sam Adams; McCain Foods; Bacardi; Brown-Forman; Thompson Elaree; ISI International; KPMG; Lamb Weston; Pace Airlines; Pernod Ricard USA; US Foodservice; Vienna Beef; Pepsico; Hootwinc 100; Rocky Mountain Mktg. and Promo.; Wings Investors Co.; Texas Wings.
Financial data (yr. ended 12/31/11): Assets, $311,412 (M); gifts received, $720,427; expenditures, $475,434; qualifying distributions, $433,200; giving activities include $433,200 for grants.
Purpose and activities: The foundation supports organizations involved with health, genetic diseases, cancer, muscular dystrophy, diabetes, cancer research, hunger, athletics, human services, military and veterans, and Christianity.
Fields of interest: Health care; Genetic diseases and disorders; Cancer; Muscular dystrophy; Diabetes; Cancer research; Food services; Athletics/sports, Special Olympics; American Red Cross; Salvation Army; Children/youth, services; Human services; Military/veterans' organizations; Christian agencies & churches.
Type of support: General/operating support.
Geographic limitations: Giving primarily in areas of company operations in FL, GA, NC, and SC.
Support limitations: No grants to individuals.
Application information: Applications accepted.
Initial approach: Contact foundation for application information
Deadline(s): None
Officers: Coby G. Brooks, C.E.O.; Jim Tessmer, C.F.O. and Secy.
EIN: 582006561

1859
Hopkins Federal Savings Bank

134 S. Eaton St.
Baltimore, MD 21224 (410) 675-2828

Company URL: http://www.hopkinsfsb.com
Establishment information: Established in 1921.
Company type: Subsidiary of a private company
Business activities: Operates savings bank.
Business type (SIC): Banks/commercial; savings institutions
Financial profile for 2011: Assets, $350,816,998; liabilities, $350,816,998
Corporate officers: Alvin M. Lapidus, Chair.; Steven A. Cohen, Pres.; Melissa Strohman, Sr. V.P. and Corp. Secy.; Kenneth Ensor, Sr. V.P. and Treas.; W. Benton Knight, C.E.O.
Board of directors: Alvin M. Lapidus, Chair.; Richard Alter; Richard Azrael; Kenneth Ensor; W. Benton Knight; Basil Taibel
Giving statement: Giving through the Hopkins Federal Savings Bank Foundation.

Hopkins Federal Savings Bank Foundation

134 S. Eaton St.
Baltimore, MD 21224-2425

Establishment information: Established in 1993 in MD.
Donor: Hopkins Federal Savings Bank.
Financial data (yr. ended 09/30/12): Assets, $28,181 (M); expenditures, $20,940; qualifying distributions, $20,940; giving activities include $20,935 for 22 grants (high: $5,000; low: $100).
Purpose and activities: The foundation supports organizations involved with arts and culture, education, medical research, and Judaism.
Fields of interest: Historic preservation/historical societies; Arts; Education; Medical research; Jewish agencies & synagogues.
Type of support: General/operating support.
Geographic limitations: Giving primarily in Baltimore, MD.
Support limitations: No grants to individuals.
Application information: Applications not accepted. Unsolicited requests for funds not accepted.
Officers and Directors:* Alvin M. Lapidus, Chair. and Pres.; Steven A. Cohen*, V.P. and Treas.; Nancy L. Oring*, Secy.
EIN: 521842115

1860
Horix Manufacturing Company

1384 Island Ave.
McKees Rocks, PA 15136 (412) 771-1111

Company URL: http://www.horixmfg.com/
Establishment information: Established in 1903.
Company type: Private company
Business activities: Manufactures liquid filling, capping, warming, and cooling machinery.
Business type (SIC): Machinery/general industry
Corporate officer: Linda M. Szramowski, Pres. and C.E.O.
Plant: McKees Rocks, PA
Giving statement: Giving through the Fairbanks-Horix Foundation.

Fairbanks-Horix Foundation

c/o PNC Bank, N.A.
P.O. Box 94651
Cleveland, OH 44101-4651 (412) 768-8538
Application address: 620 Liberty Ave. 7th Fl., Pittsburgh, PA 15222, tel.: (412) 768-8538

Establishment information: Established in 1965 in PA.
Donor: Horix Manufacturing Co.
Contact: John Montoya
Financial data (yr. ended 12/31/11): Assets, $599,379 (M); expenditures, $24,095; qualifying distributions, $19,283; giving activities include $13,000 for 3 grants (high: $5,000; low: $3,000) and $1,000 for grants to individuals.
Purpose and activities: The foundation supports food banks and organizations involved with education and senior citizen services.
Fields of interest: Education; Food banks; Aging, centers/services.
Type of support: Employee-related scholarships; Equipment; General/operating support; Scholarship funds.
Geographic limitations: Giving primarily in areas of company operations in western PA.
Application information: Applications accepted. Application form not required. Applicants should submit the following:
1) copy of IRS Determination Letter
2) detailed description of project and amount of funding requested
Initial approach: Letter
Copies of proposal: 1
Deadline(s): May 1
Trustee: PNC Bank, N.A.
EIN: 256084211

1861
Horizon Air Industries, Inc.

19300 International Blvd.
P.O. Box 68900
Seattle, WA 98188-5402 (206) 241-6757
FAX: 206-4314624

Company URL: http://www.alaskaair.com
Establishment information: Established in 1981.
Company type: Subsidiary of a public company
Business activities: Provides air transportation services.
Business type (SIC): Transportation/scheduled air
Financial profile for 2010: Number of employees, 3,900
Corporate officers: William S. Ayer, Chair.; Bradley D. Tilden, C.E.O.; Glenn S. Johnson, Pres.; Brandon S. Pedersen, C.F.O.; Gene Hahn, Sr. V.P., Opers.; Rudi H. Schmidt, Treas.
Board of director: William S. Ayer, Chair.
Giving statement: Giving through the Horizon Air Industries, Inc. Corporate Giving Program.

Horizon Air Industries, Inc. Corporate Giving Program

19300 International Blvd.
Seattle, WA 98188-5304 (206) 241-6757
For requests benefiting the Lower 48/International: c/o Donna Hartman, Mgr., Community Rels., Alaska Airlines, P.O. Box 68900, Seattle, WA 98168, tel.: (206) 392-5383; For requests benefiting the states of Alaska or Hawaii: c/o Susan Bramstedt, Dir., Public Affairs, Alaska Airlines, 4750 Old International Airport Rd., Anchorage, AK 99502, tel.: (907) 266-7230; URL: http://www.alaskaair.com/content/about-us/social-responsibility/corporate-giving.aspx

Purpose and activities: Horizon Air makes charitable contributions to nonprofit organizations involved with art and culture, education, the environment, health, human services, and community development. Support is given primarily in areas of company operations, with emphasis on Alaska, Oregon, and Washington.
Fields of interest: Arts; Education; Environment; Health care; Human services; Community/economic development.
Programs:
Dollars for Doers: Through the Dollars for Doers Program, Horizon Air makes charitable contributions of $10 per hour to nonprofit organizations with which employees volunteer, up to $1,000 per year, per employee.
Employee Matching Gift Program: Horizon Air matches contributions made by its employees to qualified nonprofit organizations and educational institutions on a one-for-one basis.
Type of support: Employee matching gifts; Employee volunteer services; In-kind gifts; Sponsorships.
Geographic limitations: Giving primarily in areas of company operations, with emphasis on AK, OR, and WA.
Support limitations: No support for private businesses, religious organizations not of direct benefit to the entire community, discriminatory organizations, United Way-supported organizations, or educational institutions (except through the Employee Matching Gift Program). No grants to individuals, or for endowments, pageants, sports teams, United Way campaigns, capital campaigns, or general operating support; no loans.
Publications: Application guidelines.
Application information: Applications accepted. Application form not required. Applicants should submit the following:
1) name, address and phone number of organization
2) copy of IRS Determination Letter
3) how company employees can become involved with the organization
4) brief history of organization and description of its mission
5) geographic area to be served
6) list of company employees involved with the organization
7) listing of board of directors, trustees, officers and other key people and their affiliations
8) contact person
9) listing of additional sources and amount of support
10) plans for acknowledgement
Applications should the organization's Tax ID Number and include a description of past support by Horizon Air with the organization. Ticket donation requests should indicate the number of tickets requested and the intended use of the donation.
Initial approach: Complete online application form
Deadline(s): 6 weeks prior to need
Final notification: 4 weeks

1862
Horizon Beverage Company

80 Stockwell Dr.
Avon, MA 02322-1106 (508) 587-1110
FAX: (508) 587-2714

Company URL: http://www.horizonbeverage.com
Establishment information: Established in 1933.
Company type: Private company
Business activities: Sells spirits, beer, and wine wholesale.
Business type (SIC): Beer, wine, and distilled beverages—wholesale
Financial profile for 2011: Number of employees, 700
Corporate officer: Robert Epstein, Pres.
Giving statement: Giving through the James L. Rubenstein Family Foundation.

James L. Rubenstein Family Foundation

163 Allen's Point
Marion, MA 02738-2301 (508) 587-1110

Establishment information: Established in 1997 in MA.
Donors: Brockton Wholesale Beverage Co., Inc.; Horizon Beverage Co., Inc.
Contact: James L. Rubenstein, Tr.
Financial data (yr. ended 12/31/11): Assets, $586,025 (M); gifts received, $175,000; expenditures, $61,170; qualifying distributions, $60,250; giving activities include $60,250 for grants.

Purpose and activities: The foundation supports organizations involved with education, the environment, health, disaster relief, youth development, human services, community development, and Judaism.
Fields of interest: Education; Health care; Youth development.
Geographic limitations: Giving primarily in MA; giving also to national organizations.
Support limitations: No grants to individuals.
Application information: Applications accepted. Application form not required. Applicants should submit the following:
1) detailed description of project and amount of funding requested
Initial approach: Proposal
Deadline(s): None
Trustees: Benjamin C. Rubenstein; James L. Rubenstein; Samuel R. Rubenstein.
EIN: 046833651

1863
Horizon Blue Cross Blue Shield of New Jersey

(also known as Horizon Healthcare Services, Inc.)
3 Penn Plz. E.
Newark, NJ 07105-2200 (973) 466-4000

Company URL: http://www.horizon-bcbsnj.com
Establishment information: Established in 1932.
Company type: Private company
Business activities: Operates medical service plan.
Business type (SIC): Insurance/accident and health
Financial profile for 2009: Number of employees, 5,200; sales volume, $7,963,000,000
Corporate officers: William J. Marino, Chair., Pres. and C.E.O.; Robert A. Marino, Exec. V.P. and C.O.O.; Robert J. Pures, Sr. V.P., Admin., C.F.O., and Treas.; Mark L. Barnard, Sr. V.P. and C.I.O.; Linda A. Willett, Sr. V.P., Genl. Counsel, and Secy.; David R. Huber, V.P., Finance; Margaret M. Coons, V.P., Human Resources
Board of directors: William J. Marino, Chair.; Lawrence R. Codey, Esq.; Barbara Bell Coleman; Leonard G. Feld; Aristides W. Georgantas; Vincent J. Giblin; Emmanuel A. Kampouris; Alfred C. Koeppe; Barry R. Mandelbaum, Esq.; Robert J. Martin; Daniel J. McCarthy, Esq.; Leo J. Rogers, Jr.; Eric B. Shuffler, Esq.; James A. Skidmore, Jr.; Peter G. Stewart, Esq.
Giving statement: Giving through the Horizon Blue Cross Blue Shield of New Jersey Corporate Giving Program and the Horizon Charitable Foundation, Inc.

Horizon Blue Cross Blue Shield of New Jersey Corporate Giving Program

3 Penn Plz. E.
Newark, NJ 07101 (973) 466-4000
URL: http://www.horizon-bcbsnj.com/community_involvement.html?WT.svl=topnav

Purpose and activities: As a complement to its foundation, Horizon Blue Cross Blue Shield of New Jersey also makes charitable contributions to nonprofit organizations directly. Support is given primarily in areas of company operations.
Fields of interest: Higher education; Health care; Safety/disasters; General charitable giving.

Program:

Horizon Cares: Horizon Cares is the company's employee volunteer program. Since the launch of the program in 2006, employees have donated over 15,000 hours to charitable organizations, higher education institutions, and disaster relief efforts.
Type of support: Employee matching gifts; Employee volunteer services.
Geographic limitations: Giving primarily in areas of company operations in NJ.

Horizon Charitable Foundation, Inc.

(doing business as The Horizon Foundation for New Jersey)
3 Penn Plz. E., PP-M2H
Newark, NJ 07105-2258
E-mail: foundation_info@horizonblue.com; Tel. and e-mail for Michele Berry: (973) 466-5551, Michele_L_Berry@HorizonBlue.com; Additional contact: Filomena Machleder, Prog. Off., tel.: (973) 466-8945, e-mail: filomena_machleder@horizonblue.com;
URL: http://www.horizon-bcbsnj.com/foundation

Establishment information: Established in 2003 in NJ.
Donor: Horizon Healthcare Services, Inc.
Contact: Michele L. Berry, Grants Coord.
Financial data (yr. ended 12/31/11): Assets, $53,214,087 (M); gifts received, $10,122,500; expenditures, $4,021,776; qualifying distributions, $3,665,292; giving activities include $3,434,580 for 117 grants (high: $200,000; low: $4,000) and $230,712 for employee matching gifts.
Purpose and activities: The foundation supports programs designed to enhance arts and cultural opportunities for New Jersey residents; and programs designed to improve the health of New Jersey residents through quality health-related prevention, education, and access to primary health care.
Fields of interest: Arts, cultural/ethnic awareness; Arts education; Performing arts; Arts; Education; Health care, information services; Health care, clinics/centers; Public health; Public health, obesity; Public health, physical fitness; Health care; Mental health, depression; Mental health/crisis services; Cancer; Heart & circulatory diseases; Diabetes; Nutrition; YM/YWCAs & YM/YWHAs; Children, services Children; Aging.

Programs:

Arts: The foundation supports programs designed to promote the arts. Special emphasis is directed toward after-school arts education; arts and cultural programs for families; arts and cultural programs for senior citizens. Grants range from $10,000 to $20,000.

Health: The foundation supports programs designed to promote health prevention, education, and awareness to facilitate good health. Special emphasis is directed toward programs designed to promote prevention and education relating to asthma, cancer, heart disease, diabetes, and obesity; depression and other mental health screening and treatment initiatives; health literacy to help individuals understand basic health information and navigate the health care system; childhood immunizations; and outdoor community spaces that promote health, well-being, or physical activity for residents of all ages. Grants range from $10,000 to $50,000.

Health Center Initiative: The foundation awards grants to New Jersey's independent and Federally Qualified Health Centers, free/volunteer clinics, and independent clinics to increase access to health care services for uninsured and underinsured populations. Grants of up to $125,000 are awarded annually for up to two years.

Healthy U: The foundation, in partnership with New Jersey YMCA State Alliance, promotes institutional behavioral changes in children to combat childhood obesity. The program utilizes nutrition education, increased physical activity, and a focus on family. Visit URL http://www.horizonblue.com/about-us/in-the-community/healthy-u for more information.
Type of support: Continuing support; Curriculum development; Employee matching gifts; Employee volunteer services; General/operating support; Program development; Research; Sponsorships; Technical assistance.
Geographic limitations: Giving limited to areas of company operations in NJ.
Support limitations: No support for hospitals or hospital foundations or political organizations or candidates. No grants to individuals, or for capital campaigns, endowments, or political causes or campaigns.
Publications: Application guidelines; Program policy statement.
Application information: Applications accepted. General operating support is only available for art projects. Support is limited to 1 contribution per organization during any given year. Multi-year funding is not automatic. Organizations receiving support are asked to submit a final report. Application form required. Applicants should submit the following:
1) timetable for implementation and evaluation of project
2) results expected from proposed grant
3) population served
4) name, address and phone number of organization
5) copy of IRS Determination Letter
6) brief history of organization and description of its mission
7) copy of most recent annual report/audited financial statement/990
8) descriptive literature about organization
9) listing of board of directors, trustees, officers and other key people and their affiliations
10) detailed description of project and amount of funding requested
11) contact person
12) copy of current year's organizational budget and/or project budget
13) listing of additional sources and amount of support
Initial approach: Complete online application form
Copies of proposal: 1
Board meeting date(s): Mar. 12, June 4, Sept. 17, and Dec. 10
Deadline(s): Jan. 10, Apr. 4, July 18, and Oct. 3
Final notification: 90 days
Officers and Directors:* Robert A. Marino*, Pres.; Kevin P. Conlin, V.P.; Linda A. Willet, Secy.; David R. Huber, Treas.; Jonathan Pearson, Exec. Dir.
Number of staff: None.
EIN: 200252405

1864
Horizon Cash Management, LLC

325 W. Huron St., Ste. 808
Chicago, IL 60654-3638 (312) 335-8500

Company URL: http://www.horizoncash.com
Establishment information: Established in 1991.
Company type: Private company
Business activities: Provides investment advisory services.
Business type (SIC): Security and commodity services
Corporate officers: Diane Mix, Chair.; Pauline Modjeski, Pres. and C.O.O.; Michael Markowitz, Exec. V.P. and C.I.O.
Board of director: Diane Mix, Chair.

Giving statement: Giving through the Horizon Foundation for Education.

Horizon Foundation for Education

c/o Pauline Modjeski
325 W. Huron St., Ste. 808
Chicago, IL 60654-3636

Establishment information: Established in 2001 in IL.
Donor: Horizon Cash Management, LLC.
Financial data (yr. ended 12/31/11): Assets, $38,166 (M); gifts received, $9,750; expenditures, $1,276; qualifying distributions, $750; giving activities include $750 for 1 grant.
Purpose and activities: The foundation supports organizations involved with K-12 education and children and youth.
Fields of interest: Children/youth, services.
Type of support: General/operating support.
Application information: Applications not accepted. Unsolicited requests for funds not accepted.
Officers: Diane Mix Birnberg, Pres.; Jennifer Wenthen, Secy.; Pauline Modjeski, Treas.
EIN: 311809673

1865
Horizon-Five Star Enterprises, Inc.

1250 E. Diehl Rd., Ste. 404
Naperville, IL 60563-9389 (708) 955-0800

Establishment information: Established in 1990.
Company type: Private company
Business activities: Operates holding company; manufactures polyethylene and polypropylene looseleaf and presentation packaging sheet.
Business type (SIC): Blankbooks, bookbinding, and looseleaf binders; holding company
Corporate officers: George Faulstich, Jr., Chair., Pres., and C.E.O.; Anne S. Faulstich, Secy.
Board of director: George Faulstich, Jr., Chair.
Subsidiary: Crawford Industries, Crawfordsville, IN
Giving statement: Giving through the Faulstich Family Charitable Foundation.

Faulstich Family Charitable Foundation

25 E. Superior, Apt. 3205
Chicago, IL 60611-2591

Establishment information: Established in 2001 in IL.
Donors: Horizon-Five Star Enterprises, Inc.; George L. Faulstich, Jr.; Anne S. Faulstich.
Financial data (yr. ended 12/31/11): Assets, $190,435 (M); gifts received, $7,500; expenditures, $11,220; qualifying distributions, $8,900; giving activities include $8,900 for grants.
Purpose and activities: The foundation supports camps and organizations involved with performing arts, education, and Christianity.
Fields of interest: Arts; Education; Religion.
Type of support: General/operating support.
Geographic limitations: Giving primarily in IL, IN, MO, and NH.
Support limitations: No grants to individuals.
Application information: Applications not accepted. Unsolicited requests for funds not accepted.
Trustees: Amy Lynn Barton; Anne S. Faulstich; Blair D. Faulstich; George L. Faulstich, Jr.; Kendall P. Faulstich.
EIN: 364486386

1866
Hormel Foods Corporation

(formerly Geo. A. Hormel & Company)
1 Hormel Pl.
Austin, MN 55912-3680 (507) 437-5611

Company URL: http://www.hormel.com
Establishment information: Established in 1891.
Company type: Public company
Company ticker symbol and exchange: HRL/NYSE
International Securities Identification Number: US4404521001
Business activities: Produces and markets meat and food products.
Business type (SIC): Meat packing plants and prepared meats and poultry; food and kindred products
Financial profile for 2012: Number of employees, 19,700; assets, $4,563,970,000; sales volume, $8,230,670,000; pre-tax net income, $758,340,000; expenses, $7,466,000,000; liabilities, $1,744,510,000
Fortune 1000 ranking: 2012—319th in revenues, 336th in profits, and 620th in assets
Forbes 2000 ranking: 2012—1061st in sales, 1022nd in profits, and 1839th in assets
Corporate officers: Jeffrey M. Ettinger, Chair., Pres., and C.E.O.; Jody H. Feragen, Exec. V.P. and C.F.O.; Brian D. Johnson, V.P. and Corp. Secy.; James N. Sheehan, V.P. and Cont.; Lori J. Marco, V.P. and Genl. Counsel; Ronald G. Gentzler, V.P., Finance and Treas.; Julie H. Craven, V.P., Corp. Comms.; David P. Juhlke, V.P., Human Resources
Board of directors: Jeffrey M. Ettinger, Chair.; Terrell K. Crews; Jody H. Feragen; Glenn S. Forbes, M.D.; Stephen M. Lacy; Susan I. Marvin; John L. Morrison; Elsa A. Murano, Ph.D.; Robert C. Nakasone; Susan K. Nestegard; Dakota A. Pippins; Christopher J. Policinski
Subsidiaries: Hormel Foods International Corp., Austin, MN; Jennie-O Turkey Store, Inc., Willmar, MN
International operations: Australia; Canada; China; Japan; Netherlands; Spain
Giving statement: Giving through the Hormel Foods Corporation Contributions Program and the Hormel Foods Corporation Charitable Trust.
Company EIN: 410319970

Hormel Foods Corporation Contributions Program

(formerly Geo. A. Hormel & Company Contributions Program)
1 Hormel Pl.
Austin, MN 55912-3673
URL: http://www.hormelfoods.com/responsibility/default.aspx

Purpose and activities: As a complement to its foundation, Hormel also makes charitable contributions to nonprofit organizations directly. Support is given primarily in areas of company operations in California, Georgia, Illinois, Iowa, Kansas, Nebraska, and Wisconsin, with some emphasis on Minnesota.
Fields of interest: Food services; Disasters, preparedness/services; American Red Cross.
Type of support: Employee volunteer services; General/operating support; In-kind gifts; Sponsorships.
Geographic limitations: Giving primarily in areas of company operations in CA, GA, IA, IL, KS, NE, and WI, with some emphasis on MN; giving also to national organizations.

Hormel Foods Corporation Charitable Trust

c/o Corp. Comms.
1 Hormel Pl.
Austin, MN 55912-3673 (507) 437-5233
E-mail: rjsmith@hormel.com; URL: http://www.hormelfoods.com/responsibility/default.aspx

Establishment information: Established in 2003 in MN.
Donor: Hormel Foods Corp.
Financial data (yr. ended 12/31/11): Assets, $1,557,776 (M); gifts received, $1,500,000; expenditures, $1,103,972; qualifying distributions, $1,103,065; giving activities include $1,103,065 for grants.
Purpose and activities: The foundation supports programs designed to promote education; hunger; and quality of life.
Fields of interest: Elementary/secondary education; Higher education; Education; Health care, clinics/centers; Food services; Food banks; Disasters, preparedness/services; Human services; United Ways and Federated Giving Programs.
Programs:
College/University Matching Gift Program: The foundation matches contributions made by employees and retirees of Hormel to institutions of higher education on a one-for-one basis from $25 to $10,000 per contributor, per year up to $15,000 per institution, per year.
K-12 Matching Gift Program: The foundation matches contributions made by employees and retirees of Hormel to K-12 grade schools on a one-for-one basis from $25 to $1,000 per contributor, per year up to $15,000 per school, per year.
Plant Communities: The foundation awards grants through local plants to promote quality of life in areas where Hormel employees work, live, and interact.
Type of support: Annual campaigns; Building/renovation; Continuing support; Donated products; Employee matching gifts; Employee-related scholarships; General/operating support; In-kind gifts; Program development; Scholarship funds; Sponsorships.
Geographic limitations: Giving primarily in areas of company operations, with emphasis on IA, MN, NE, and WI.
Support limitations: No support for political campaigns. No grants to individuals or families.
Publications: Application guidelines.
Application information: Applications accepted. Donations to a single organization do not exceed $15,000. Proposals should be no longer than 1 page. The Hormel Foods Contributions Committee handles giving. Telephone calls during the application process are not encouraged. Applicants should submit the following:
1) brief history of organization and description of its mission
2) list of company employees involved with the organization
3) detailed description of project and amount of funding requested
4) contact person

Proposal should detail the type of award requested including product, merchandise, or monetary.
Initial approach: Proposal
Board meeting date(s): Quarterly
Deadline(s): None
Final notification: Following review
Officers and Director: David P. Juhlke, Pres.; James W. Cavanaugh, Secy.; Roland G. Gentzler, Treas.; Julie H. Craven.
EIN: 010761416

Selected grants: The following grants are a representative sample of this grantmaker's funding activity:
$110,000 to Des Moines Area Religious Council, Des Moines, IA, 2011.
$25,000 to Lakewood Health System, Staples, MN, 2011.
$14,156 to Iowa State University Foundation, Ames, IA, 2011.
$13,338 to Purdue Foundation, West Lafayette, IN, 2011.
$7,500 to Mary Hitchcock Memorial Hospital, Lebanon, NH, 2011.
$5,000 to American Heart Association, Midwest Affiliate, Overland Park, KS, 2011.
$5,000 to Aurora Area Interfaith Food Pantry, Aurora, IL, 2011.
$5,000 to Childrens Association for Maximum Potential, San Antonio, TX, 2011.
$5,000 to United Way of the Plains, Wichita, KS, 2011.
$4,760 to Brigham Young University, Provo, UT, 2011.

1867
Hospira, Inc.

275 N. Field Dr.
Lake Forest, IL 60045 (224) 212-2000
FAX: (302) 655-5049

Company URL: http://www.hospira.com
Establishment information: Established in 2003.
Company type: Public company
Company ticker symbol and exchange: HSP/NYSE
International Securities Identification Number: US4410601003
Business activities: Develops, manufactures, and markets specialty injectable pharmaceuticals and medication delivery systems.
Business type (SIC): Drugs
Financial profile for 2012: Number of employees, 16,000; assets, $6,088,000,000; sales volume, $4,092,100,000; pre-tax net income, -$41,900,000; expenses, $4,033,300,000; liabilities, $3,046,900,000
Fortune 1000 ranking: 2012—575th in revenues, 833rd in profits, and 538th in assets
Corporate officers: John C. Staley, Chair.; F. Michael Ball, C.E.O.; Thomas E. Werner, Sr. V.P., Finance, and C.F.O.; Daphne E. Jones, Sr. V.P. and C.I.O.; John B. Elliot, Sr. V.P., Opers.; Matthew R. Stober, Sr. V.P., Opers.
Board of directors: John C. Staley, Chair.; Irwin W. Bailey II; F. Michael Ball; Barbara L. Bowles; Connie R. Curran; William G. Dempsey; Dennis M. Fenton, Ph.D.; Roger W. Hale; Jacque J. Sokolov, M.D.; Heino von Prondzynski; Mark F. Wheeler, M.D.
Plants: Morgan Hill, San Diego, CA; Buffalo, NY; Austin, TX
International operations: Australia; Bahamas; Belgium; Brazil; Canada; Chile; China; Colombia; Finland; France; Germany; Hong Kong; India; Ireland; Italy; Japan; Malaysia; Mexico; Netherlands; New Zealand; Philippines; Portugal; Singapore; Spain; Sweden; Switzerland; Thailand; United Kingdom
Giving statement: Giving through the Hospira Foundation.
Company EIN: 200504497

Hospira Foundation

275 N. Field Dr., Dept. 051N, Bldg. H-1
Lake Forest, IL 60045-2579 (866) 806-8996
E-mail: HospiraFoundation@easygive.com;
URL: http://www.hospira.com/InTheCommunity/default.aspx

Establishment information: Established in 2004 in IL.
Donor: Hospira, Inc.
Financial data (yr. ended 11/30/12): Assets, $16,444,878 (M); expenditures, $1,266,054; qualifying distributions, $1,172,962; giving activities include $1,054,158 for grants.
Purpose and activities: The foundation supports organizations involved with health and other areas. Special emphasis is directed toward programs designed to advance wellness.
Fields of interest: Public health; Health care; General charitable giving.
Programs:
Advancing Wellness: The foundation supports programs designed to promote health and wellness activities associated with Hospira's core expertise and business objectives and competencies.
Community Investments: The foundation supports programs designed to support community causes in areas of company operations of Hospira. Special emphasis is directed toward programs designed to focus on health and wellness, such as increasing access to and improving the delivery of healthcare.
Employee Matching Gifts: The foundation matches contributions made by employees of Hospira to nonprofit organizations on a one-for-two basis.
Type of support: Donated products; Employee matching gifts; Program development.
Geographic limitations: Giving primarily in Morgan Hill, CA, Boulder, CO, Lake County, IL, McPherson, KS, Buffalo, NY, Clayton and Rocky Mount, NC, Austin, TX, and Kenosha County, WI; giving also to national organizations.
Support limitations: No support for veterans', labor, or political organizations, fraternal, athletic, or social organizations, or organizations posing a conflict of interest with Hospira's code of business conduct or corporate policies. No grants to individuals, or for capital campaigns, endowments, general operating support, equipment, charity event attendance, debt reduction, political campaigns, or religious or sectarian causes; no loans.
Publications: Application guidelines; Corporate giving report; Corporate report.
Application information: Applications accepted. Proposals should be no longer than 2 pages. Multi-year funding is not automatic. Application form not required. Applicants should submit the following:
1) how project will be sustained once grantmaker support is completed
2) results expected from proposed grant
3) statement of problem project will address
4) population served
5) copy of IRS Determination Letter
6) how project's results will be evaluated or measured
7) detailed description of project and amount of funding requested

Initial approach: Complete online application
Copies of proposal: 1
Board meeting date(s): Quarterly
Deadline(s): None
Final notification: 6 weeks for national organizations and organizations located in Lake County, IL, and Kenosha County, WI

Directors: Christopher B. Begley; Lon Carlson; Stacey Eisen; Terrence C. Kearney; Henry Weishaar.
EIN: 202039190

1868
The Hotel Wailea

(formerly Diamond Resort Hawaii)
555 Kaukahi St.
Kihei, HI 96753-5469 (808) 874-0500

Company URL: http://www.hotelwailea.com/
Establishment information: Established in 1988.
Company type: Private company
Business activities: Operates resort.
Business type (SIC): Hotels and motels
Corporate officers: Kimura Kyoko, Pres.; Martin Lunar, Secy.; Malia Quenga, Admin.
Giving statement: Giving through the Diamond Resort Scholarships.

Diamond Resort Scholarships

2200 Main St., Ste. 400
Wailuku, HI 96793-1691 (808) 242-4535

Establishment information: Established in 1988 in HI.
Donor: Diamond Resort Hawaii.
Contact: B. Martin Luna, Tr.
Financial data (yr. ended 12/31/11): Assets, $68,917 (M); expenditures, $9,393; qualifying distributions, $7,000; giving activities include $7,000 for grants.
Purpose and activities: The foundation awards college scholarships to graduating seniors of public high schools in Maui County, Hawaii.
Type of support: Scholarships—to individuals.
Geographic limitations: Giving limited to Maui County, HI.
Application information: Applications accepted. Application form required.
Applications should include official transcripts, SAT scores, and 2 letters of recommendation.
Initial approach: Proposal
Deadline(s): Mar. 1
Final notification: May 1
Trustee: B. Martin Luna.
EIN: 996055912

1869
Houghton Mifflin Harcourt Publishing Company

222 Berkeley St.
Boston, MA 02116-3764 (617) 351-5000

Company URL: http://www.hmco.com
Establishment information: Established in 1832.
Company type: Subsidiary of a private company
Business activities: Publishes educational materials, assessment materials, and supplementary instructional materials; develops and sells multimedia instructional products; develops and sells computer-based testing solutions.
Business type (SIC): Book publishing and/or printing; computer services
Financial profile for 2009: Number of employees, 3,550
Corporate officers: Lawrence K. Fish, Chair.; Linda K. Zecher, Pres. and C.E.O; Eric Shuman, C.F.O.; William Bayers, Exec. V.P. and Genl. Counsel
Board of directors: Lawrence K. Fish, Chair.; Sheru Chowdhry; L. Gordon Crovitz; Jill Greenthal; John F. Killian; John McKernan; Roger Novak; Linda K. Zecher
Subsidiaries: Earobics, Evanston, IL; Edusoft, San Francisco, CA; Great Source Education Group,

Wilmington, MA; McDougal Littell, Evanston, IL; The Riverside Publishing Co., Itasca, IL
Offices: Geneva, IL; New York, NY; Dallas, TX
International operations: United Kingdom
Giving statement: Giving through the Houghton Mifflin Harcourt Publishing Company Contributions Program.
Company EIN: 041456030

Houghton Mifflin Harcourt Publishing Company Contributions Program

222 Berkeley St.
Boston, MA 02116-3748
URL: http://www.hmhco.com/content/corporate-social-responsibility

Purpose and activities: Houghton Mifflin makes charitable contributions to educational institutions and nonprofit organizations involved with improving the quality of K-12 education. Support is given on a national and international basis.
Fields of interest: Elementary/secondary education Economically disadvantaged.
Type of support: Curriculum development; Donated products; Faculty/staff development; General/operating support; Scholarships—to individuals.
Geographic limitations: Giving on a national and international basis.
Administrator: Nicole Peaslee, Admin., Matching Gifts.

1870
A.C. Houston Lumber Company

(also known as Houston Lumber Co.)
2912 E. La Madre Way, N.
North Las Vegas, NV 89031-2628
(702) 633-5100

Company URL: http://www.houstonlumber.com
Establishment information: Established in 1884.
Company type: Private company
Business activities: Operates lumber and building materials company.
Business type (SIC): Lumber and other building materials—retail
Financial profile for 2010: Number of employees, 200
Corporate officers: Robert A. Houston, Chair. and C.E.O.; Ron Mason, Pres. and C.O.O.; Gordon Barclay, C.F.O.
Board of director: Robert A. Houston, Chair.
Giving statement: Giving through the Robert A. and Margaret C. Houston Family Foundation.

The Robert A. and Margaret C. Houston Family Foundation

4848 Lemmon Ave.
Dallas, TX 75219 (214) 450-4850

Establishment information: Established in 2005 in NV.
Donor: AC Houston Lumber Co.
Contact: Kristine H. McCallum, Pres.
Financial data (yr. ended 12/31/11): Assets, $337,433 (M); expenditures, $38,116; qualifying distributions, $15,500; giving activities include $15,500 for grants.
Fields of interest: Health organizations; Human services.
Geographic limitations: Giving primarily in ID and KS.
Application information: Applications accepted. Application form required. Applicants should submit the following:
1) brief history of organization and description of its mission
2) descriptive literature about organization
3) detailed description of project and amount of funding requested

Grants are only made to tax-exempt public charities as defined in section 501(C)(3) of the Internal Revenue Code (IRC).
Initial approach: Letter
Deadline(s): Sep. 1
Officers: Kristine Houston McCallum, Pres.; Margaret C. Houston, V.P.; Robert A. Houston, Exec. Dir.
Directors: Jonathan A. Houston; Robert C. Houston.
EIN: 203844272

1871
Houston McLane Company, Inc.

(also known as Houston Astros)
501 Crawford St., Ste. 500
Houston, TX 77002-2113 (713) 259-8000

Company URL: http://houston.astros.mlb.com
Establishment information: Established in 1962.
Company type: Private company
Business activities: Operates professional baseball club.
Business type (SIC): Commercial sports
Corporate officers: Jim Crane, Chair.; George Postolos, Pres. and C.E.O.; Doug Seckel, V.P., Finance; Larry Stokes, V.P., Human Resources
Board of director: Jim Crane, Chair.
Giving statement: Giving through the Houston Astros Corporate Giving Program and the Astros in Action Foundation—Fielding the Dreams of Houston.

Houston Astros Corporate Giving Program

c/o Community Affairs Dept.
P.O. Box 288
Houston, TX 77001-0288 (713) 259-8000
FAX: (713) 259-8025; URL: http://houston.astros.mlb.com/NASApp/mlb/hou/community/index.jsp

Purpose and activities: The Houston Astros make charitable contributions of game tickets to nonprofit organizations on a case by case basis. Support is given primarily in Texas.
Fields of interest: Elementary school/education; Secondary school/education; Education, reading; Education; Children, services; Family services; General charitable giving.
Programs:
Charity Group Tickets: The Astros awards game tickets to nonprofit organizations and charity groups that serve children and adults who do not have the resources on their own to attend a game.
Honor Roll Ticket Program: The Astros awards game tickets to students in grades 6-12 who make the honor roll during the second semester of the school year.
Perfect Attendance Ticket Program: The Astros awards game tickets to students in grades K-5 who achieve perfect attendance during the second semester of the school year.
Summer Reading Program: The Astros awards game tickets to students in grades K-12 who complete the highest level of each participating library's Summer Reading Program during the months of June through August.
Type of support: Donated products; In-kind gifts; Income development.
Geographic limitations: Giving primarily in areas of company operations within a 150-mile radius of Houston, TX.
Support limitations: No monetary donations.
Publications: Application guidelines.
Application information: Applications accepted. Proposals should be submitted using organization letterhead. Telephone calls during the application process are not encouraged. The Community Affairs Department handles giving. Applicants should submit the following:
1) name, address and phone number of organization
2) copy of IRS Determination Letter
3) contact person

Proposals should indicate the date of the event, if applicable. Visit website for application deadlines for Honor Roll, Perfect Attendance, and Summer Reading Programs.
Initial approach: Mail or fax proposal to headquarters for ticket donations; download application form and mail or fax to headquarters for Charity Group Tickets
Copies of proposal: 1
Deadline(s): 6 weeks prior to need; Mar. 1 to Aug. 31 for Charity Group Tickets

Astros in Action Foundation—Fielding the Dreams of Houston

501 Crawford St., Ste. 500
Houston, TX 77002-2113
E-mail: foundation@astros.com; Additional address: P.O. Box 288, Houston, TX 77001; Additional tel.: (713) 259-8956; URL: http://houston.astros.mlb.com/NASApp/mlb/hou/community/foundation_mission.jsp
E-mail for Grand Slam for Youth Baseball Scholarships: scholarships@gsfyb.org

Establishment information: Established in 2000 in TX.
Donors: Houston McLane Co., Inc.; William L. Berkman; Lance Berkman; Carlos Lee; Drayton McLane, Jr.; Roy Oswalt.
Financial data (yr. ended 12/31/11): Assets, $596,793 (M); gifts received, $199,107; expenditures, $545,615; qualifying distributions, $468,527; giving activities include $468,527 for grants.
Purpose and activities: The foundation supports programs designed to promote literacy; education; scholarship; health; faith-based organizations; and programs designed to revive baseball in the inner city.
Fields of interest: Education, reading; Education; Health care; Cancer; Heart & circulatory diseases; Athletics/sports, baseball; Boys & girls clubs; United Ways and Federated Giving Programs; Christian agencies & churches; Religion.
Programs:
Grand Slam for Youth Baseball Field Makeover: The foundation, in partnership with Minute Maid, pledges to refurbish one youth baseball or softball field each year for the next two decades. Refurbishment includes renovated field surfaces, fencing, covered dugouts, scoreboards, and other needs.
Grand Slam for Youth Baseball Fundraising: The foundation, in partnership with Minute Maid, supports Minute Maid Juice Stands for local youth baseball and softball teams and leagues. Qualifying teams and leagues can earn a minimum of $1,000. The program is designed to support teams and leagues that need to earn extra money for necessary player equipment, umpire fees, field repair/improvements and other related expenses.
Grand Slam for Youth Baseball Scholarships: The foundation, in partnership with Minute Maid, awards

25 $2,500 college scholarships to Houston area high school seniors who have participated in a youth baseball or softball. The program is designed to assist youth with college expenses.

Hometown Heroes: Through Hometown Heroes, the foundation honors an area citizen who has gone over and beyond and performed extraordinary acts within their communities. Winners are chosen monthly to throw out the ceremonial first pitch prior to a game and be a special guest of the Astros for the evening.

Type of support: Building/renovation; Capital campaigns; General/operating support; Grants to individuals; Program development; Scholarship funds; Scholarships—to individuals; Sponsorships.
Geographic limitations: Giving primarily in Houston, TX.
Publications: Application guidelines.
Application information: Applications accepted. A personal interview may be requested for Grand Slam for Youth Baseball Scholarships. Application form required.
Applications for Grand Slam for Youth Baseball Scholarships must include proof of acceptance to a post-secondary college or university and 2 recommendations.

Initial approach: Download application form and mail to foundation for Grand Slam for Youth Baseball Fundraising and Scholarships; download nomination form for Hometown Heroes
Deadline(s): None for Grand Slam for Youth Baseball Fundraising; May 14 for Grand Slam for Youth Baseball Scholarships; None for Hometown Heroes
Final notification: 4 weeks for Grand Slam for Youth Baseball Fundraising; June 17 for Grand Slam for Youth Baseball Scholarships

Officers and Directors:* Drayton McLane, Jr.*, Pres.; Pamela J. Gardner, V.P.; Marian Harper, V.P.; Robert S. McClaren, V.P.; G.W. Sanford, Jr.*, V.P.; Webster F. Stickney, Jr.*, Secy.-Treas.
EIN: 742793078
Selected grants: The following grants are a representative sample of this grantmaker's funding activity:
$15,920 to Special Olympics Texas, Houston, TX, 2009.
$15,000 to Incarnate Word Academy, Houston, TX, 2009.
$10,000 to Texas A & M University, College Station, TX, 2009. For scholarships.
$7,500 to Sam Houston State University, Huntsville, TX, 2009. For scholarships.
$7,000 to Urban League, Houston Area, Houston, TX, 2009.
$5,500 to Literacy Advance of Houston, Houston, TX, 2009.
$5,000 to Alvin Community College, Alvin, TX, 2009. For scholarship.
$5,000 to Texas Southern University, Houston, TX, 2009. For scholarships.
$5,000 to University of Texas, Austin, TX, 2009. For scholarships.
$2,500 to Houston Baptist University, Houston, TX, 2009. For scholarship.

1872
Houston NFL Holdings, LP

(also known as Houston Texans)
2 Reliant Park
Houston, TX 77054-1573 (832) 667-2000

Company URL: http://www.houstontexans.com
Establishment information: Established in 1998.
Company type: Private company
Business activities: Operates professional football club.
Business type (SIC): Commercial sports
Corporate officers: Robert C. McNair, Chair. and Co.-C.E.O.; D. Cal McNair, Co.-Vice-Chair. and Co.-C.E.O.; Philip J. Burguieres, Co.-Vice-Chair.; Jamey Rootes, Pres.; Rick Smith, Exec. V.P., Opers.; Scott E. Schwinger, Sr. V.P., Treas., and C.F.O.; Suzie Thomas, Sr. V.P., Genl. Counsel, and C.A.O.; Greg Watson, V.P., Finance
Board of directors: Robert C. McNair, Chair.; Philip J. Burguieres, Co.-Vice-Chair.; D. Cal McNair, Co.-Vice-Chair.
Giving statement: Giving through the Houston Texans Foundation.

Houston Texans Foundation

109 N. Post Oak Ln., Ste. 600
Houston, TX 77024-7753 (713) 336-7800
Mailing address: Reliant Stadium, 2 Reliant Park, Houston, TX 77054-1573; URL: http://www.houstontexans.com/community/houston-texans-foundation.html

Establishment information: Established in 2002 in TX.
Contact: Joanie Haley, Exec. Dir.
Financial data (yr. ended 12/31/10): Revenue, $359,391; assets, $830,501 (M); gifts received, $346,729; expenditures, $1,146,263; program services expenses, $953,337; giving activities include $953,337 for 51 grants (high: $238,017; low: $335).
Purpose and activities: The foundation encourages and enables all youth and families in Houston, Texas, and the surrounding area to reach their full potential and to achieve success.
Fields of interest: Environment, beautification programs; Youth development; Community/economic development.
Program:
NFL Student All-Star Mini Grant Program: This program awards 25 small grants (up to $200) to young people, 13 years and younger, to help finance community improvement and volunteer projects (such as food/clothing collection drives, community clean-ups, the beautification of youth or senior centers, etc.) within the Houston area. Eligible applicants must be responsible for the creation and execution of a new project-based service or program; projects requiring a sponsoring organization may use a school, religious, or community organization, or other 501(c)(3) group.
Type of support: In-kind gifts.
Geographic limitations: Giving primarily in Houston, TX.
Officers and Directors:* Robert C. McNair*, Pres.; James M. Kendrigan*, V.P.; Daniel C. McNair*, V.P.; Janice S. McNair*, V.P.; Jamey Rootes*, V.P.; Scott E. Schwinger*, V.P.; Suzanne Thomas*, V.P.; Tony Wyllie*, V.P.; Joanie Haley, Exec. Dir.; Melissa M. Reichert; Ruth M. Smith.
EIN: 010572814

1873
Howard Perry & Walston Realty, Inc.

1001 Wade Ave., Ste. 200
Raleigh, NC 27605-3323 (919) 781-4663

Company URL: http://www.hpw.com
Establishment information: Established in 1972.
Company type: Private company
Business activities: Operates full-service residential real estate company.
Business type (SIC): Real estate agents and managers
Financial profile for 2010: Number of employees, 40
Corporate officers: Edward Moore, C.E.O.; Debbie Houston, Pres.; David N. Jones, C.O.O.; Sean Nally, C.I.O.
Giving statement: Giving through the Howard Perry & Walston Foundation.

The Howard Perry & Walston Foundation

1001 Wade Ave.
Raleigh, NC 27605-3322

Establishment information: Established in 1998 in NC.
Contact: Meredith Morgan, Pres.
Financial data (yr. ended 03/31/12): Revenue, $50,715; assets, $65,413 (M); gifts received, $50,715; expenditures, $43,652; giving activities include $19,630 for 6 grants (high: $5,537; low: $1,704) and $20,257 for in-kind gifts.
Purpose and activities: The foundation works to create opportunities for Coldwell Banker Howard Perry and Walston employees and sales associates to support charitable and nonprofit organizations in their local communities.
Fields of interest: Human services, emergency aid; Community/economic development.
Type of support: Grants to individuals.
Geographic limitations: Giving primarily to Cary, Morrisville, Princeton, and Raleigh, NC.
Officers: Meredith Morgan, Pres.; David Jones, V.P.; Kim Gunshinan Byrd, Secy.; M. Paulette Tisdale, Treas.
EIN: 562108108

1874
F. M. Howell & Co.

79 Pennsylvania Ave.
P.O. Box 286
Elmira, NY 14902 (607) 734-6291

Company URL: http://www.howellpkg.com
Establishment information: Established in 1883.
Company type: Private company
Business activities: Manufactures packaging materials.
Business type (SIC): Paperboard containers; printing/commercial; plastic products/miscellaneous; business services/miscellaneous
Corporate officers: George L. Howell, Chair.; Katherine Howell Roehlke, Pres. and C.E.O.; Tim G. Lee, C.E.O.; David J. Sheen, C.I.O.
Board of director: George L Howell, Chair.
Giving statement: Giving through the Lowman-Howell Foundation, Inc.

Lowman-Howell Foundation, Inc.

1 W. Church St.
Elmira, NY 14901-2741

Donors: F.M. Howell & Co.; George L. Howell.
Financial data (yr. ended 03/31/12): Assets, $1,398,430 (M); expenditures, $59,430; qualifying distributions, $50,000; giving activities include $50,000 for grants.
Purpose and activities: The foundation supports historical societies and organizations involved with Protestantism.
Fields of interest: Religion.

Application information: Applications not accepted. Unsolicited requests for funds not accepted.
Officers and Directors:* George L. Howell*, Pres. and Treas.; John R. Alexander*, Secy.; Sarah B. Howell; Katherine H. Roehlke; Thomas L. Roehlke.
EIN: 222537870

1875
Howmedica Osteonics Corp.

(also known as Stryker Orthopaedics)
325 Corporate Dr.
Mahwah, NJ 07430

Company URL: http://www.stryker.com/en-us/corporate/AboutUs/index.htm
Establishment information: Established in 1970.
Company type: Subsidiary of a public company
Business activities: Manufactures orthopedic medical products.
Business type (SIC): Medical instruments and supplies
Giving statement: Giving through the AOC Foundation, Inc.

AOC Foundation, Inc.

1765 Old W. Broad St., Bldg. 2, Ste. 200
Athens, GA 30606-2867 (706) 433-3290

Establishment information: Established in 1998 in GA.
Donors: Howmedica Osteonics Corp.; Stryker Orthopedics; AOC Ambulatory Surgery Center; AM Society for Surgery of the Hand.
Contact: R. Mixon Robinson, C.E.O.
Financial data (yr. ended 08/31/12): Assets, $49,464 (M); gifts received, $158,293; expenditures, $203,296; qualifying distributions, $43,675; giving activities include $43,675 for grants.
Purpose and activities: The AOC Foundation supports research that will improve non-surgical and surgical techniques, reduce post-surgical complications, and speed recovery in conditions involving the musculoskeletal system.
Fields of interest: Medical research; Surgery research.
Application information: Applications not accepted.
Officers: R. Mixon Robinson, M.D., C.E.O.; Cathy Cofer, C.F.O.
EIN: 311630901

1876
HSBC Bank USA, N.A.

(formerly HSBC Bank USA, Inc.)
452 5th Ave., 18th Fl.
New York, NY 10018-2706 (212) 525-5000

Company URL: http://www.us.hsbc.com
Establishment information: Established in 1980.
Company type: Subsidiary of a foreign company
Business activities: Operates commercial bank.
Business type (SIC): Banks/commercial
Corporate officer: Irene Dorner, Chair., Pres., and C.E.O.
Board of director: Irene Dorner, Chair.
International operations: Canada
Giving statement: Giving through the HSBC Bank USA Corporate Giving Program.

HSBC Bank USA Corporate Giving Program

(formerly Republic New York Corporation Contributions Program)
452 Fifth Ave., 13th Fl.
New York, NY 10018-2706 (212) 525-8239
FAX: (212) 525-8239;
E-mail: heather.l.nesle@us.hsbc.com; Tel. for Eileen Turner: (224) 568-1835, e-mail: eileen.j.turner@us.hsbc.com; URL: http://www.hsbcusa.com/corporateresponsibility

Contact: Heather Nesle, V.P., Corporate Sustainability; Eileen Turner, Asst. V.P. and Prog. Mgr.
Purpose and activities: As a complement to its foundation, HSBC also makes charitable contributions to nonprofit organizations directly. Support is given primarily in areas of company operations.
Fields of interest: Scholarships/financial aid; Education; Environment, research; Environment, public policy; Environmental education; Environment; Community/economic development.
Program:
Matching Gift Program: Through the Matching Gift Program, HSBC matches qualified employee contributions, dollar for dollar, of $25 or more to eligible nonprofit organizations, up to $3,500 per employee per year.
Type of support: Conferences/seminars; Curriculum development; Donated equipment; Employee matching gifts; Employee volunteer services; General/operating support; In-kind gifts; Management development/capacity building; Program development; Scholarship funds; Sponsorships; Use of facilities.
Geographic limitations: Giving primarily in areas of company operations, with emphasis on CA, CT, Washington, DC, DE, FL, IL, MD, NJ, NY, OR, VA, and WA.
Support limitations: No support for political, fraternal, veterans', labor, athletic, lobbying, or voter registration organizations. No grants to individuals, or for advertising, travel, or student aid.
Publications: Application guidelines; Informational brochure; Program policy statement.
Application information: Application form not required. Applicants should submit the following:
1) detailed description of project and amount of funding requested
Initial approach: Complete online application
Copies of proposal: 1
Deadline(s): Nov. 1
Final notification: 1 month

1877
Hubbard Broadcasting, Inc.

3415 University Ave.
St. Paul, MN 55114-1019 (651) 646-5555

Establishment information: Established in 1921.
Company type: Private company
Business activities: Broadcasts radio and television; operates motels.
Business type (SIC): Radio and television broadcasting; hotels and motels
Financial profile for 2010: Number of employees, 700
Corporate officers: Stanley S. Hubbard, Chair., Pres., and C.E.O.; Gerald D. Deeney, C.F.O.; Harold Crump, V.P., Public Affairs
Board of director: Stanley S. Hubbard, Chair.
Subsidiaries: CONUS Communication Co., St. Paul, MN; F&F Productions, Inc., St. Petersburg, FL; KOB-TV, Inc., Albuquerque, NM; KSTP-AM Inc., St. Paul, MN; KSTP-FM, Inc., Maplewood, MN; Pan American Ocean Resort Hotel, Miami Beach, FL; WDIO-TV, Duluth, MN
Giving statement: Giving through the Hubbard Broadcasting Foundation.

The Hubbard Broadcasting Foundation

(formerly The Hubbard Foundation)
3415 University Ave.
St. Paul, MN 55114-1019 (651) 642-4305

Establishment information: Incorporated in 1958 in MN.
Donors: Hubbard Broadcasting, Inc.; KSTP, Inc.; Stanley E. Hubbard†.
Contact: Kathryn Hubbard Rominski, Exec. Dir.
Financial data (yr. ended 12/31/11): Assets, $22,569,029 (M); expenditures, $1,554,626; qualifying distributions, $1,265,876; giving activities include $1,163,450 for grants.
Purpose and activities: The foundation supports zoos and organizations involved with arts and culture, education, health, skin disorders, hockey, human services, and leadership development.
Fields of interest: Media, print publishing; Museums; Performing arts, theater; Performing arts, orchestras; Arts; Elementary/secondary education; Education, early childhood education; Higher education; Education; Zoos/zoological societies; Hospitals (general); Health care, clinics/centers; Health care; Skin disorders; Athletics/sports, winter sports; Children/youth, services; Human services; Leadership development.
Type of support: Capital campaigns; General/operating support.
Geographic limitations: Giving primarily in MN.
Support limitations: No grants to individuals.
Application information: Applications accepted. Application form not required. Applicants should submit the following:
1) copy of IRS Determination Letter
2) brief history of organization and description of its mission
3) detailed description of project and amount of funding requested
Initial approach: Proposal
Deadline(s): Prior to end of calendar year
Officers and Directors:* Stanley S. Hubbard*, Pres.; Karen H. Hubbard*, V.P.; Tom Newberry, Secy-Treas.; Kathryn Hubbard Rominski*, Exec. Dir.; Robert W. Hubbard; Stanley E. Hubbard; Virginia H. Morris.
EIN: 416022291
Selected grants: The following grants are a representative sample of this grantmaker's funding activity:
$14,500 to Minneapolis Academy, Minneapolis, MN, 2011.
$10,000 to Lutheran Social Service of Minnesota, Saint Paul, MN, 2011.
$10,000 to Mayo Foundation, Rochester, MN, 2011.
$5,000 to Arthritis Foundation, Atlanta, GA, 2011.
$5,000 to Courage Center, Minneapolis, MN, 2011.
$5,000 to Minneapolis Heart Institute Foundation, Minneapolis, MN, 2011.
$3,500 to Chamber of Commerce of Greater Albuquerque, Albuquerque, NM, 2011.
$2,500 to Minneapolis Society of Fine Arts, Minneapolis, MN, 2011.
$2,000 to University of Saint Thomas, Saint Paul, MN, 2011.
$1,000 to Association of Fundraising Professionals, Arlington, VA, 2011.

1878
Hubbard Farms, Inc.
195 Main St.
P.O. Box 415
Walpole, NH 03608-4516 (603) 756-3311

Company URL: http://www.hubbardbreeders.com/
Establishment information: Established in 1921.
Company type: Private company
Business activities: Operates poultry breeding farms.
Business type (SIC): Farms/poultry and egg
Giving statement: Giving through the Hubbard Farms Charitable Foundation.

Hubbard Farms Charitable Foundation
P.O. Box 505
Walpole, NH 03608-0505 (603) 756-3311

Establishment information: Established around 1966.
Donor: Hubbard Farms, Inc.
Contact: Jane F. Kelly, Clerk
Financial data (yr. ended 12/31/11): Assets, $938,924 (M); expenditures, $55,597; qualifying distributions, $55,431; giving activities include $52,939 for 6 grants (high: $16,500; low: $500).
Purpose and activities: The foundation supports organizations involved with education, health, recreation, youth development, human services, minorities, and economically disadvantaged people; and awards scholarships to financially needy students in the fields of poultry science, genetics, and other life sciences.
Fields of interest: Higher education; Education; Health care; Genetic diseases and disorders; Agriculture, livestock issues; Recreation; Youth development; YM/YWCAs & YM/YWHAs; Aging, centers/services; Human services; United Ways and Federated Giving Programs; Science Minorities; Economically disadvantaged.
Type of support: General/operating support; Program development; Scholarship funds; Scholarships—to individuals.
Geographic limitations: Giving primarily in areas of company operations in AR, NC, NH, TN, and VT.
Publications: Application guidelines.
Application information: Applications accepted. Application form required. Applicants should submit the following:
1) copy of IRS Determination Letter
2) copy of most recent annual report/audited financial statement/990
3) detailed description of project and amount of funding requested

Initial approach: Letter
Deadline(s): Apr. 1 and Oct. 1

Officers: Diana J. Myers-Miller, Chair.; Mark H. Barnes, Vice-Chair.; Jane F. Kelly, Clerk; Paul T. Ledell, Treas.
Trustee: William L. Gibson.
EIN: 026015114

1879
Hubbell Incorporated
40 Waterview Dr.
P.O. Box 1000
Shelton, CT 06484-1000 (475) 882-4000

Company URL: http://www.hubbell.com
Establishment information: Established in 1888.
Company type: Public company
Company ticker symbol and exchange: HUB.B/NYSE
Business activities: Manufactures electrical products.
Business type (SIC): Electronic components and accessories; metal rolling and drawing/nonferrous; machinery/refrigeration and service industry; electric transmission and distribution equipment; electrical equipment and supplies
Financial profile for 2012: Number of employees, 13,600; assets, $2,947,000,000; sales volume, $3,044,400,000; pre-tax net income, $441,800,000; expenses, $2,572,600,000; liabilities, $1,285,800,000
Fortune 1000 ranking: 2012—705th in revenues, 472nd in profits, and 757th in assets
Corporate officers: Timothy H. Powers, Chair.; David G. Nord, Pres. and C.E.O.; W. Robert Murphy, Exec. V.P., Mktg. and Sales; William R. Sperry, Sr. V.P. and C.F.O.; James H. Biggart, Jr., V.P. and Treas.; Darrin S. Wegman, V.P. and Cont.; An-Ping Hsieh, V.P. and Genl. Counsel; Louis G. Pizzoli, V.P., Opers.; Stephen M. Mais, V.P., Human Resources; Megan C. Preneta, Corp. Secy
Board of directors: Timothy H. Powers, Chair.; Lynn J. Good; Anthony J. Guzzi; Neal J. Keating; John F. Malloy; Andrew McNally IV; David G. Nord; G. Jackson Ratcliffe, Jr.; Carlos A. Rodriguez; John G. Russell; Richard J. Swift; Daniel S. Van Riper
Subsidiaries: Hipotronics, Inc., Brewster, NY; Hubbell Industrial Controls, Inc., Madison, OH; Hubbell Lighting, Inc., Christiansburg, VA; The Ohio Brass Co., Wadsworth, OH; Pulse Communications, Inc., Herndon, VA
International operations: Australia; Brazil; Canada; Cayman Islands; Hong Kong; Mexico; Switzerland; United Kingdom
Giving statement: Giving through the Harvey Hubbell Foundation.
Company EIN: 060397030

The Harvey Hubbell Foundation
584 Derby Milford Rd.
P.O. Box 549
Orange, CT 06477-2228

Establishment information: Trust established in 1959 in CT.
Donor: Hubbell Inc.
Financial data (yr. ended 12/31/11): Assets, $8,373,247 (M); gifts received, $200,000; expenditures, $379,020; qualifying distributions, $376,020; giving activities include $376,020 for grants.
Purpose and activities: The foundation supports health centers and organizations involved with performing arts, education, breast cancer, diabetes, safety, youth development, and children services.
Fields of interest: Performing arts; Performing arts centers; Performing arts, theater; Higher education; Libraries (public); Scholarships/financial aid; Education; Health care, clinics/centers; Breast cancer; Diabetes; Safety/disasters; Youth development, adult & child programs; Children, services; United Ways and Federated Giving Programs.
Type of support: Annual campaigns; Building/renovation; Capital campaigns; Employee matching gifts; General/operating support.
Geographic limitations: Giving primarily in areas of company operations in CT.
Support limitations: No grants to individuals.
Application information: Applications not accepted. Contributes only to pre-selected organizations.
Trustees: Stephen M. Mais; David G. Nord; Timothy H. Powers.
EIN: 066078177
Selected grants: The following grants are a representative sample of this grantmaker's funding activity:
$4,000 to Pennsylvania State University, University Park, PA, 2010.
$4,000 to Yale University, New Haven, CT, 2010.
$3,555 to Duke University, Durham, NC, 2010.
$2,000 to University of South Carolina, Columbia, SC, 2010.
$1,250 to Clemson University, Clemson, SC, 2010.
$1,085 to Clemson University, Clemson, SC, 2010.
$1,000 to Leukemia & Lymphoma Society, White Plains, NY, 2010.
$1,000 to Multiple Sclerosis Society, National, New York, NY, 2010.

1880
Hudson City Bancorp, Inc.
80 W. Century Rd.
Paramus, NJ 07652-1405 (201) 967-1900
FAX: (201) 261-1995

Company URL: https://www.hcsbonline.com
Establishment information: Established in 1868.
Company type: Public company
Company ticker symbol and exchange: HCBK/NASDAQ
Business activities: Operates savings bank. At press time, the company is in the process of merging with M&T Bank.
Business type (SIC): Savings institutions
Financial profile for 2012: Number of employees, 1,692; assets, $40,596,340,000; pre-tax net income, $413,780,000; liabilities, $35,896,530,000
Forbes 2000 ranking: 2012—1811th in sales, 1539th in profits, and 569th in assets
Corporate officers: Ronald E. Hermance, Jr., Chair. and C.E.O.; Denis J. Salamone, Pres. and C.O.O.; James C. Kranz, Exec. V.P. and C.F.O.; Veronica A. Olszewski, Sr. V.P., Treas., and Corp. Secy.
Board of directors: Ronald E. Hermance, Jr., Chair.; Michael W. Azzara; William G. Bardel; Scott A. Belair; Victoria H. Bruni; Cornelius E. Golding; Denis J. Salamone; Joseph G. Sponholz; Donald O. Quest, M.D.
Giving statement: Giving through the Hudson City Savings Bank Corporate Giving Program and the Hudson City Savings Charitable Foundation.
Company EIN: 223640393

Hudson City Savings Bank Corporate Giving Program
80 W. Century Rd.
Paramus, NJ 07652 (201) 967-1900
URL: http://www.hcsbonline.com

Hudson City Savings Charitable Foundation
(formerly Sound Federal Savings and Loan Association Charitable Foundation)
80 W. Century Rd.
Paramus, NJ 07652-1405 (201) 967-1900

Establishment information: Established in 1998 in DE.
Donor: Hudson City Savings Bank.
Contact: Lisa Roberts
Financial data (yr. ended 12/31/11): Assets, $1,876,688 (M); gifts received, $90,000; expenditures, $179,627; qualifying distributions, $171,500; giving activities include $171,500 for 58 grants (high: $10,000; low: $2,000).
Purpose and activities: The foundation supports organizations involved with arts and culture,

education, health, hunger, housing, human services, and community development.
Fields of interest: Performing arts; Arts; Higher education; Education; Health care; Food services; Housing/shelter, development; Housing/shelter; YM/YWCAs & YM/YWHAs; Children/youth, services; Residential/custodial care, group home; Homeless, human services; Human services; Community/economic development.
Type of support: Building/renovation; Capital campaigns; General/operating support; Program development; Scholarship funds.
Geographic limitations: Giving limited to areas of company operations in Fairfield County, CT, NJ, and Rockland and Westchester counties, NY.
Support limitations: No grants to individuals.
Application information: Applications accepted. Application form not required. Applicants should submit the following:
1) copy of IRS Determination Letter
2) copy of most recent annual report/audited financial statement/990
3) detailed description of project and amount of funding requested

Initial approach: Proposal
Deadline(s): None

Officers and Directors:* Ronald E. Hermance*, Pres.; Denis J. Salamane*, Secy.; Christopher P. Dooley, Treas.; Donald H. Herthaus.
EIN: 134046178
Selected grants: The following grants are a representative sample of this grantmaker's funding activity:
$10,000 to Table to Table, Englewood Cliffs, NJ, 2010.
$7,500 to Evas Village, Paterson, NJ, 2010.
$7,500 to Housing Partnership for Morris County, Dover, NJ, 2010.
$7,500 to Scholarship Fund for Inner-City Children, Newark, NJ, 2010.
$5,000 to New Jersey Community Development Corporation, Paterson, NJ, 2010.
$2,500 to Blythedale Childrens Hospital, Valhalla, NY, 2010.
$2,500 to Kennedy Dancers, Jersey City, NJ, 2010.
$2,500 to United Way of Greenwich, Greenwich, CT, 2010.
$2,500 to Vantage Health System, Dumont, NJ, 2010.
$2,000 to Leukemia & Lymphoma Society, White Plains, NY, 2010.

1881
Hudson Liquid Asphalts, Inc.
89 Ship St.
Providence, RI 02905 (401) 274-2200
FAX: (401) 274-2220

Company URL: http://www.hudsoncompanies.com
Establishment information: Established in 1955.
Company type: Private company
Business activities: Sells asphalt and paving mixtures.
Business type (SIC): Lumber and construction materials—wholesale
Corporate officers: Thomas Hudson, C.E.O.; Francis J. O'Brien, Co-Pres. and C.O.O.; Matthew J. Gill, Co-Pres.; Douglas E. Scala, C.F.O.; Joseph Murphy, V.P., Opers.; Rick Chagnon, V.P., Sales
Giving statement: Giving through the Thomas F. Hudson Charitable Foundation and the John J. and Nancy E. Hudson Charitable Foundation.

John J. and Nancy E. Hudson Charitable Foundation
89 Ship St.
Providence, RI 02903-4218

Establishment information: Established in 2001 in RI.
Donors: Hudson Liquid Asphalts, Inc.; Lillian V. Hudson†.
Financial data (yr. ended 12/31/11): Assets, $162,963 (M); expenditures, $1,451; qualifying distributions, $1,000; giving activities include $1,000 for 1 grant.
Purpose and activities: The foundation supports organizations involved with education and Catholicism.
Fields of interest: Elementary/secondary education; Education; YM/YWCAs & YM/YWHAs; Catholic agencies & churches.
Type of support: General/operating support; Scholarship funds.
Geographic limitations: Giving primarily in RI.
Support limitations: No grants to individuals.
Application information: Applications not accepted. Unsolicited requests for funds not accepted.
Directors: John J. Hudson; Karen J. Hudson; Nancy E. Hudson; Edward R. Lodge, Jr.
EIN: 050515452

The Thomas F. Hudson Charitable Foundation
89 Ship St.
Providence, RI 02903-4218

Establishment information: Established in 2001 in RI.
Donors: Lillian V. Hudson†; Hudson Liquid Asphalts, Inc.
Financial data (yr. ended 12/31/11): Assets, $173,042 (M); expenditures, $451; qualifying distributions, $0.
Purpose and activities: The foundation supports St. Martha's Church in Rhode Island.
Type of support: General/operating support.
Geographic limitations: Giving primarily in RI.
Support limitations: No grants to individuals.
Application information: Applications not accepted. Unsolicited requests for funds not accepted.
Directors: Ryan M. Hudson; Thomas F. Hudson; Thomas J. Hudson; Edward R. Lodge, Jr.
EIN: 050515296

1882
Hudson Neckwear Company
841 3rd St.
Brooklyn, NY 11220-4727 (212) 689-3244

Company type: Private company
Business activities: Manufactures men's neckwear.
Business type (SIC): Apparel—men's and boys' outerwear
Giving statement: Giving through the Hudson Charitable Foundation, Inc.

The Hudson Charitable Foundation, Inc.
1312-44th St., Ste. 144
Brooklyn, NY 11219

Establishment information: Established in 1983 in NY.
Donors: Hudson Neckwear Co.; Irving Berger; William Berger; Leo Lieber.
Financial data (yr. ended 06/30/11): Assets, $0 (M); expenditures, $0; qualifying distributions, $0.
Purpose and activities: The foundation supports organizations involved with education and Judaism.
Fields of interest: Education; Jewish agencies & synagogues.
Application information: Applications not accepted. Unsolicited requests for funds not accepted.
Director: G. Lindner.
EIN: 133202380

1883
Hufcor, Inc.
2101 Kennedy Rd.
P.O. Box 5591
Janesville, WI 53547-0591 (608) 756-1241

Company URL: http://www.hufcor.com/
Establishment information: Established in 1900.
Company type: Private company
Business activities: Manufactures movable wall systems and room dividers.
Business type (SIC): Fixtures/office and store
Corporate officers: James C. Landherr, Pres.; Michael Borden, C.E.O.; Mark E. Blanchard, V.P., Sales and Mktg.
Giving statement: Giving through the Hufcor Foundation, Inc.

Hufcor Foundation, Inc.
c/o Marshall & Ilsey Trust Company
P.O. Box 5000
Janesville, WI 53547-5000

Establishment information: Established in 1988 in WI.
Donor: Hufcor, Inc.
Financial data (yr. ended 05/31/11): Assets, $736,935 (M); gifts received, $100,000; expenditures, $30,733; qualifying distributions, $29,000; giving activities include $29,000 for 7 grants (high: $5,500; low: $2,000).
Purpose and activities: The foundation supports organizations involved with higher education and human services.
Fields of interest: Higher education; Boys & girls clubs; Salvation Army; YM/YWCAs & YM/YWHAs; Human services.
Type of support: General/operating support.
Geographic limitations: Giving primarily in Janesville, WI.
Support limitations: No grants to individuals.
Application information: Applications not accepted. Unsolicited requests for funds not accepted.
Trustees: Hufcor, Inc.; Marshall & Ilsley Trust Company.
EIN: 391574139

1884
Huhtamaki Consumer Packaging, Inc.
9201 Packaging Dr.
De Soto, KS 66018 (913) 583-3025

Company URL: http://www.us.huhtamaki.com
Establishment information: Established in 1964.
Company type: Subsidiary of a foreign company
Business activities: Manufactures packaging products.

Business type (SIC): Paperboard containers
Corporate officers: Charles F. Marcy, Pres. and C.E.O.; John T. Carper, Sr. V.P., Finance, and C.F.O.; John T. Slattery, V.P. and C.I.O.; J. Patrick Muldoon, V.P., Mktg.; T. Carl Walker, V.P., Human Resources
Board of director: Charles F. Marcy
Subsidiary: Huhtamaki Packaging, Inc., De Soto, KS
Plants: Los Angeles, CA; Fulton, NY
Giving statement: Giving through the Huhtamaki Foundation, Inc.
Company EIN: 160876812

Huhtamaki Foundation, Inc.

(formerly Sealright Foundation, Inc.)
9201 Packaging Dr.
De Soto, KS 66018-9503 (913) 583-3025

Establishment information: Established in 1990 in MO.
Donor: Sealright Co., Inc.
Contact: Jean M. Sumner, Mgr., State and Local Tax Svcs.
Financial data (yr. ended 12/31/11): Assets, $247,420 (M); expenditures, $22,560; qualifying distributions, $22,335; giving activities include $21,325 for 8 grants (high: $10,000; low: $25).
Purpose and activities: The foundation supports organizations involved with education, health, human services, and religion.
Fields of interest: Higher education; Education; Health care; Children/youth, services; Human services; Religion.
Type of support: Annual campaigns; Capital campaigns; Employee matching gifts.
Geographic limitations: Giving on a national basis, with emphasis on areas of company operations.
Support limitations: No support for political organizations. No grants to individuals.
Application information: Applications accepted. Application form not required. Applicants should submit the following:
1) copy of IRS Determination Letter
Initial approach: Proposal
Copies of proposal: 1
Board meeting date(s): Dec.
Deadline(s): None
Final notification: Varies
Officers and Directors:* Clay Dunn, Pres.; John O'Dea*, V.P.; Rochelle Stringer, Secy.; Earlene A. Sells*, Treas.
Number of staff: None.
EIN: 156019087

1885
Hulman & Company

900 Wabash Ave.
P.O. Box 150
Terre Haute, IN 47808-0150
(812) 232-9446

Company URL: http://www.hulman.com
Establishment information: Established in 1850.
Company type: Private company
Business activities: Produces baking powder; operates motor speedway.
Business type (SIC): Miscellaneous prepared foods; commercial sports
Corporate officers: Mark D. Miles, C.E.O.; Jeffrey G. Belskus, Pres.
Giving statement: Giving through the Hulman & Company Foundation, Inc.

Hulman & Company Foundation, Inc.

P.O. Box 150
Terre Haute, IN 47808-0150 (812) 232-9446

Establishment information: Established in 1998 in IN.
Donor: Hulman & Co.
Contact: W. Curtis Brighton, Secy.
Financial data (yr. ended 12/31/11): Assets, $3,391,715 (M); expenditures, $158,190; qualifying distributions, $151,000; giving activities include $151,000 for 9 grants (high: $83,500; low: $5,000).
Purpose and activities: The foundation supports community foundations and organizations involved with engineering education, animal welfare, and youth services.
Fields of interest: Engineering school/education; Animal welfare; American Red Cross; Youth, services; Foundations (community).
Type of support: General/operating support.
Support limitations: No grants to individuals.
Application information: Applications accepted. Application form not required.
Initial approach: Proposal
Deadline(s): None
Officers and Directors: W. Curtis Brighton, Pres.; Gretchen E. Snelling, Secy.; Jeffrey G. Belskus, Treas.; Anton Hulman George; M. Josephine George; Katherine M. George; Mari Hulman George; Nancy L. George.
EIN: 352063427

1886
Humana Inc.

500 W. Main St.
Louisville, KY 40202 (502) 580-1000
FAX: (502) 580-3639

Company URL: http://www.humana.com
Establishment information: Established in 1961.
Company type: Public company
Company ticker symbol and exchange: HUM/NYSE
International Securities Identification Number: US4448591028
Business activities: Operates medical service plan.
Business type (SIC): Insurance/accident and health
Financial profile for 2012: Number of employees, 43,400; assets, $19,979,000,000; sales volume, $39,126,000,000; pre-tax net income, $1,911,000,000; expenses, $37,110,000,000; liabilities, $11,132,000,000
Fortune 1000 ranking: 2012—73rd in revenues, 166th in profits, and 241st in assets
Forbes 2000 ranking: 2012—235th in sales, 511th in profits, and 973rd in assets
Corporate officers: Michael B. McCallister, Jr., Chair.; Bruce D. Broussard, Pres. and C.E.O.; James E. Murray, Exec. V.P. and C.O.O.; James H. Bloem, Sr. V.P., Treas., and C.F.O.; Brain LeClaire, Sr. V.P. and C.I.O.; Christopher M. Todoroff, Sr. V.P. and Genl. Counsel; Heidi S. Margulis, Sr. V.P., Public Affairs; Steven E. McCulley, V.P. and Cont.
Board of directors: Michael B. McCallister, Jr., Chair.; Bruce D. Broussard; Frank A. D'Amelio; W. Roy Dunbar; Kurt J. Hilzinger; David A. Jones, Jr.; William J. McDonald; William E. Mitchell; David B. Nash, M.D.; James J. O'Brien; Marissa T. Peterson
Offices: Anchorage, AK; Phoenix, Tucson, AZ; Denver, CO; Clearwater, Daytona, Fort Lauderdale, Fort Myers, Jacksonville, Miami, Orlando, St. Petersburg, Tampa, West Palm Beach, FL; Atlanta, GA; Chicago, IL; Ft. Wayne, Indianapolis, IN; Lexington, KY; Detroit, Grand Rapids, MI; Kansas City, MO; Charlotte, Raleigh, NC; Cincinnati, OH; Oklahoma City, OK; Mayaguez, Ponce, San Juan, PR; Memphis, TN; Austin, Corpus Christi, Dallas, Houston, San Antonio, TX; Green Bay, Madison, Milwaukee, WI
International operations: England; Wales
Giving statement: Giving through the Humana Foundation, Inc.
Company EIN: 610647538

The Humana Foundation, Inc.

500 W. Main St., Ste. 208
Louisville, KY 40202-2946 (502) 580-4140
FAX: (502) 580-1256;
E-mail: bwright@humana.com; Additional e-mail: HumanaFoundation@humana.com; URL: http://www.humanafoundation.org

Establishment information: Incorporated in 1981 in KY.
Donor: Humana Inc.
Contact: Barbara Wright; Virginia K. Judd, Exec. Dir.
Financial data (yr. ended 12/31/11): Assets, $150,577,206 (M); gifts received, $35,000,000; expenditures, $5,019,418; qualifying distributions, $4,979,925; giving activities include $4,979,925 for grants.
Purpose and activities: The foundation supports programs designed to promote healthy lives and healthy communities, with a focus on the needs of children, families, and seniors. Special emphasis is directed toward programs designed to promote childhood health and education; health literacy; and active lifestyles and wellness.
Fields of interest: Arts; Elementary school/education; Education; Public health, obesity; Public health, physical fitness; Health care; Nutrition; Disasters, preparedness/services; Children, services; Family services; Human services; Public affairs Aging; Economically disadvantaged.

Programs:

Human's Dollars 4 Doers Drawing: The foundation administers a drawing on a quarterly basis for employees of Humana that volunteer at a nonprofit organization for a least 4 hours per month. The winner of the drawing receives $4,000 for his or her nonprofit organization.

Humana Communities Benefit Program: The foundation annually awards one-time $100,000 transformational grants to nonprofit organizations focused on improving health experiences. Special emphasis is directed toward childhood health and education; family wellness and active lifestyles; and health literacy for diverse populations and seniors.

Humana Volunteer of the Year Award: The foundation annually honors a Humana associate who demonstrates an ongoing dedication to his or her community through volunteerism. The associate is awarded a special trip and a $10,000 grant to the nonprofit organization with which he or she volunteers.

Spirit of Philanthropy Award: The foundation honors a department or group of employees who display exceptional commitment to the community. The employees are recognized in a ceremony and a nonprofit organization of their choice is awarded $25,000.

The Humana Foundation Scholarship Program: The foundation annually awards up to 75 college scholarships of up to $3,000 to children of employees of Humana. The program is administered by Scholarship America.

Type of support: Annual campaigns; Building/renovation; Capital campaigns; Continuing support; Curriculum development; Employee matching gifts; Employee volunteer services; Employee-related scholarships; General/operating support;

Matching/challenge support; Professorships; Program development; Scholarship funds.
Geographic limitations: Giving primarily in areas of company operations in Phoenix, AZ, San Diego and San Francisco, CA, Denver, CO, CT, FL, GA, Bloomington, Chicago, Peoria, and Rockford, IL, Indianapolis, IN, Louisville, KY, New Orleans, LA, Boston, MA, Baltimore, MD, Detroit, MI, Kansas City and St. Louis, MO, Charlotte, NC, NJ, Las Vegas, NV, NY, Cincinnati, OH, Philadelphia and Pittsburgh, PA, Columbia, SC, Nashville, TN, Austin, Dallas, and Houston, TX, Salt Lake City, UT, VA, and Green Bay and Milwaukee, WI.
Support limitations: No support for social, labor, political, veterans', or fraternal organizations, lobbying efforts, or mission-focused activities. No grants for start-up needs or seed money, salary expenses or other administrative costs, general operating support for religious organizations, or for construction or renovation of sanctuaries.
Publications: Application guidelines; Grants list; Informational brochure; Newsletter.
Application information: Applications accepted. Support is limited to 1 contribution per organization during any given year. Application form required.
Applicants should submit the following:
1) statement of problem project will address
2) copy of IRS Determination Letter
3) geographic area to be served
4) copy of most recent annual report/audited financial statement/990
5) how project's results will be evaluated or measured
6) listing of board of directors, trustees, officers and other key people and their affiliations
7) detailed description of project and amount of funding requested
8) plans for cooperation with other organizations, if any
9) copy of current year's organizational budget and/or project budget

Initial approach: Complete online application form
Copies of proposal: 1
Board meeting date(s): Every 2 months
Deadline(s): Nov. 1 through Jan. 15 for organizations located in Louisville, KY; Nov. 1 through Aug. 12 for organizations located outside of Louisville, KY. Visit website for specific deadline dates per state
Final notification: Generally, 6 weeks to 2 months

Officers and Directors:* Michael B. McCallister*, Chair., C.E.O., and Pres.; James H. Bloem, Sr. V.P., C.F.O., and Treas.; George G. Bauernfeind, V.P.; Joan O. Lenahan, Secy.; Virginia K. Judd, Exec. Dir.; David A. Jones; David A. Jones, Jr.
EIN: 611004763
Selected grants: The following grants are a representative sample of this grantmaker's funding activity:
$733,935 to Scholarship America, Saint Peter, MN, 2009. For scholarships for children of Humana employees.
$675,000 to Actors Theater of Louisville, Louisville, KY, 2009. For Humana Festival of New American Plays.
$510,000 to United Way, Metro, Louisville, KY, 2009. For annual support.
$320,000 to Fund for the Arts, Louisville, KY, 2009. For campaign.
$177,500 to National Center for Family Literacy, Louisville, KY, 2009. For Health Literacy Project WellZone.
$120,000 to Jefferson County Public Education Foundation, Louisville, KY, 2009. For HealthE Schools Support, promoting student health.
$60,000 to University of Kentucky, College of Public Health, Lexington, KY, 2009.
$50,000 to Hult Center for Health Education, Peoria, IL, 2009. For program support.

1887
Huna Totem Corporation

9301 Glacier Hwy., Ste. 200
Juneau, AK 99801-9380 (907) 523-3670

Company URL: http://www.hunatotem.com
Establishment information: Established in 1971.
Company type: Native corporation
Business activities: Operates native corporation.
Business type (SIC): Nonclassifiable establishments
Corporate officers: Russell Dick, Chair.; Edward Davis, Vice-Chair.; Lawrence Gaffaney, Pres. and C.E.O.; Samuel Feruness, C.F.O.; William O. Sheakley, Secy.; Glory Scarano, Treas.
Board of directors: Russell Dick, Chair.; Edward Davis, Vice-Chair.; Tilli G. Abbott; Will Davis; Bertha M. Franulovich; Harold Houston; Ernest Jack; William O. Sheakley; Paul White, Jr.
Subsidiary: Icy Straits Point, Hoonah, AK
Giving statement: Giving through the Huna Heritage Foundation.

Huna Heritage Foundation

9301 Glacier Hwy., Ste. 210
Juneau, AK 99801-9306 (907) 789-1896
FAX: (907) 789-1896;
E-mail: heritage@hunatotem.com; Tel.: (907) 789-1896; URL: http://www.hunaheritage.org

Establishment information: Established in 1990 in AK.
Donors: Huna Totem Corp.; National Park Service; Sealaska Heritage Institute; Institute of Museum Library Sciences.
Financial data (yr. ended 12/31/11): Assets, $331,261 (M); gifts received, $287,626; expenditures, $280,294; qualifying distributions, $180,878; giving activities include $9,495 for 16 grants (high: $2,200; low: $50) and $64,395 for 50 grants to individuals (high: $2,000; low: $395).
Purpose and activities: The foundation supports programs designed to perpetuate Huna culture and promote education for the Huna people through scholarships, cultural grants, and vocational assistance.
Fields of interest: Arts, cultural/ethnic awareness; Arts; Vocational education; Higher education; Education Native Americans/American Indians.
Programs:
Cultural Education Assistance: The foundation awards grants of up to $300 to Huna Totem shareholders and descendants for instructional activities associated with traditional practices or art forms. The program is designed to assist in preserving, advocating, and learning the history and culture of the Huna people. Applicants must be accepted into a program to learn an art form which is related to the traditional culture of the Huna people.
Education Assistance: The foundation awards grants of up to $2,000 to Huna Totem shareholders and descendants to meet students' financial needs after personal funds and other resources are exhausted. Applicants must have a high school diploma or GED; be accepted by or attending an accredited college or university; enrolled in a minimum of six semester hours; and have good academic standing.
Vocational Education Assistance: The foundation awards grants to Vocational Education and Apprenticeship programs for Huna Totem shareholders or descendants to receive training that leads to gainful employment. Vocational Education courses must be approved by a National Accreditation Association or the Alaska Department of Education's Division of Vocational Education. Apprentice programs must be approved by the U.S. Bureau of Apprenticeship Training. All applicants must be unemployed.
Type of support: General/operating support; In-kind gifts; Program development; Scholarships—to individuals; Sponsorships.
Geographic limitations: Giving primarily in AK, OR, and WA.
Publications: Annual report; Application guidelines; Corporate report; Newsletter.
Application information: Applications accepted. Application form required.

Initial approach: Proposal; download application form and mail for Education Assistance, Vocational Education Assistance, and Cultural Education Assistance
Deadline(s): Jan. 31 and Sept. 30 for Education Assistance; None for Vocational Education Assistance or Cultural Education Assistance
Final notification: 3 to 5 weeks for Education Assistance

Officers: Marlene Johnson, Chair.; Gordon Greenwald, Vice-Chair.; William "Ozzie" Sheakley, Treas.; Kathryn Hurtley, Exec. Dir.
Trustee: Bertha Franlovich.
Number of staff: 1 full-time professional.
EIN: 943113818

1888
The Hunt Corporation

6720 N. Scottsdale Rd., Ste. 300
Scottsdale, AZ 85253-4460
(480) 368-4700
FAX: (480) 368-4747

Company URL: http://www.thehuntcorp.com
Establishment information: Established in 1944.
Company type: Private company
Business activities: Operates holding company; provides general contract construction services.
Business type (SIC): Building construction general contractors and operative builders; holding company
Corporate officers: Robert G. Hunt, Chair. and C.E.O.; Michael Fratianni, C.O.O.; Stephen E. Atkins, Exec. V.P. and C.F.O.; David B. Smith, C.I.O. and Treas.
Board of director: Robert G. Hunt, Chair.
Subsidiaries: Hunt Construction Group, Inc., Indianapolis, IN; The Hunt Paving Co., Inc., Indianapolis, IN; Hunt Sports, Indianapolis, IN
Giving statement: Giving through the Hunt Corporation Contributions Program.

The Hunt Corporation Contributions Program

6720 N. Scottsdale Rd., Ste. 300
Scottsdale, AZ 85253 (480) 368-4700
FAX: (480) 368-4747; URL: http://www.huntconstructiongroup.com/index.php?option=com_content&view=article&id=134&Itemid=150

Purpose and activities: Hunt makes charitable contributions to nonprofit organizations on a case by case basis. Support is given in areas of company operations.
Fields of interest: Health care, blood supply; Recreation, camps; Human services, gift

distribution; United Ways and Federated Giving Programs.
Type of support: Donated products; Employee volunteer services; General/operating support; In-kind gifts; Loaned talent.
Geographic limitations: Giving primarily in areas of company operations.

1889
Hunt Oil Company

1900 N. Akard St.
Dallas, TX 75201-2300 (214) 978-8000
FAX: (214) 978-8888

Company URL: http://www.huntoil.com
Establishment information: Established in 1934.
Company type: Subsidiary of a private company
Business activities: Conducts crude petroleum exploration and production activities.
Business type (SIC): Extraction/oil and gas
Financial profile for 2011: Number of employees, 4,700; sales volume, $4,000,000,000
Corporate officers: Ray L. Hunt, Chair. and C.E.O.; Steve Suellentrop, Pres.; Dennis J. Grindinger, Exec. V.P. and C.F.O.; Mark Gunnin, Sr. V.P. and Genl. Counsel; Jeanne Phillips, Sr. V.P., Corp. Affairs; Bruce Cope, V.P. and C.A.O.; Jim Jennings, Chair. Emeritus
Board of directors: Ray L. Hunt, Chair.; Steve Suellentrop
Subsidiary: Hunt Refining Co., Tuscaloosa, AL
Divisions: Hunt Oil Central Exploration Div., Dallas, TX; Hunt Oil Gulf Coast Exploration Div., Houston, TX
Offices: Cotton Valley, Lafayette, LA; Midland, Poynor, TX; Casper, WY
International operations: Argentina; Canada; Chile; Peru; Singapore; United Kingdom; Yemen
Giving statement: Giving through the Hunt Oil Company Contributions Program.

Hunt Oil Company Contributions Program

1445 Ross Ave., Ste. 1500
Dallas, TX 75202-2751

Contact: Amb. Jeanne Phillips
Purpose and activities: Hunt makes charitable contributions to nonprofit organizations involved with education. Support is given primarily in areas of company operations.
Fields of interest: Education.
Type of support: Employee volunteer services; General/operating support; Scholarship funds; Sponsorships.
Geographic limitations: Giving primarily in areas of company operations.
Application information: Applications accepted. Application form not required.
Initial approach: Proposal to headquarters
Copies of proposal: 1
Deadline(s): None
Final notification: 3 months

1890
Hunt Real Estate Corp.

5570 Main St., Ste. 1
Williamsville, NY 14221-5477
(716) 631-4800

Company URL: http://www.huntrealestate.com
Establishment information: Established in 1911.
Company type: Private company
Business activities: Operates real estate agency.
Business type (SIC): Real estate agents and managers
Financial profile for 2010: Number of employees, 80
Corporate officers: Peter F. Hunt, Chair. and C.E.O.; Louis Izzo, Pres.; Carlos Pegado, C.I.O.; Jennifer Booker, Exec. Secy.
Board of directors: Peter F. Hunt, Chair.; David Hess; C. Stuart Hunt
Giving statement: Giving through the Hunt Charitable Foundation, Inc.

The Hunt Charitable Foundation, Inc.

430 Dick Rd.
Depew, NY 14043

Establishment information: Established in 2001 in NY.
Donors: Hunt Real Estate Corp.; Mary Jo Hunt; Peter F. Hunt.
Financial data (yr. ended 12/31/11): Assets, $1,708 (M); gifts received, $18,500; expenditures, $18,725; qualifying distributions, $18,655; giving activities include $18,655 for grants.
Purpose and activities: The foundation supports organizations involved with arts and culture, education, health, human services, and Christianity.
Fields of interest: Education; Human services; Religion.
Type of support: General/operating support.
Geographic limitations: Giving primarily in Buffalo, NY.
Support limitations: No grants to individuals.
Application information: Applications not accepted. Unsolicited requests for funds not accepted.
Officer and Directors:* Peter F. Hunt*, Pres.; Emily Hunt Forbes; Charles Hunt; Mary Jo Hunt.
EIN: 161584859

1891
Hunt Sports Group, LLC

(doing business as FC Dallas)
1601 Elm St., Ste. 4000
Dallas, TX 75201 (214) 720-1600

Company URL: http://www.huntcapital.com/about.htm
Establishment information: Established in 1993.
Company type: Subsidiary of a private company
Business activities: Operates professional soccer club.
Business type (SIC): Commercial sports
Corporate officers: John A. Wagner, Pres.; Alan W Tompkins, V.P. and Secy.
Giving statement: Giving through the FC Dallas Corporate Giving Program.

FC Dallas Corporate Giving Program

c/o Community Rels.
9200 World Cup Way., Ste. 202
Frisco, TX 75033-4958
URL: http://www.fcdallas.com/community

Purpose and activities: FC Dallas makes charitable contributions of memorabilia to nonprofit organizations involved with youth development. Support is limited to Texas.
Fields of interest: Youth development.
Type of support: In-kind gifts.
Geographic limitations: Giving limited to TX.
Application information: Applications accepted. The Community Relations Department handles giving. Telephone calls are not encouraged. Support is limited to 1 contribution per organization during any given year. Application form required. Applicants should submit the following:
1) name, address and phone number of organization
2) contact person
Applications should include the organization's Tax ID Number; and the name, date, and a description of the event.
Initial approach: Complete online application form
Deadline(s): 6 weeks prior to need
Final notification: 2 weeks

1892
J.B. Hunt Transport Services, Inc.

615 J.B. Hunt Corporate Dr.
Lowell, AR 72745-0130 (479) 820-0000
FAX: (479) 659-6297

Company URL: http://www.jbhunt.com
Establishment information: Established in 1961.
Company type: Public company
Company ticker symbol and exchange: JBHT/NASDAQ
Business activities: Operates holding company; provides trucking services; provides railroad transportation services.
Business type (SIC): Trucking and courier services, except by air; transportation/railroad; holding company
Financial profile for 2012: Number of employees, 16,475; assets, $2,464,640,000; sales volume, $5,054,980,000; pre-tax net income, $504,640,000; expenses, $4,524,780,000; liabilities, $1,672,780,000
Fortune 1000 ranking: 2012—486th in revenues, 460th in profits, and 806th in assets
Corporate officers: Kirk Thompson, Chair.; John N. Roberts III, Pres. and C.E.O.; Craig Harper, Exec. V.P., Opers. and C.O.O.; Kay Johnson Palmer, Exec. V.P. and C.I.O.; David G. Mee, C.P.A., Exec. V.P., Finance, Admin., C.F.O., and Corp. Secy.; David Chelette, Sr. V.P. and Treas.; John Kuhlow, V.P. and Cont.
Board of directors: Kirk Thompson, Chair.; Douglas G. Duncan; Francesca Maher Edwardson; Wayne Garrison; Sharilyn S. Gasaway; Gary C. George; J. Bryan Hunt, Jr.; Coleman H. Peterson; John N. Roberts III; James L. Robo; John A. White
Subsidiary: J.B. Hunt Transport, Inc., Lowell, AR
Plants: Hueytown, AL; Little Rock, AR; South Gate, CA; Atlanta, Carnesville, GA; Springfield, OH; Oklahoma City, OK; Dallas, Houston, TX
International operations: Mexico
Giving statement: Giving through the J. B. Hunt Transport Services, Inc. Corporate Giving Program.
Company EIN: 710335111

J. B. Hunt Transport Services, Inc. Corporate Giving Program

P.O. Box 130
Lowell, AR 72745-0130
E-mail: corporate_giving@jbhunt.com; URL: http://www.jbhunt.com/aboutus/corporategiving.html

Contact: Amy Bain, Mgr., Corp. Giving
Purpose and activities: J.B. Hunt makes charitable contributions to nonprofit organizations involved with K-12 education, youth outreach, and health research. Support is given primarily in areas of company operations. Support is given on a national basis.

Fields of interest: Elementary/secondary education; Education; Medical research; Youth development.
Type of support: General/operating support; Program development.
Geographic limitations: Giving on a national basis.
Support limitations: No support for religious organizations not of direct benefit to the entire community, organizations with overhead expenses exceeding 25 percent of the total operating budget, organizations located outside the U.S., or discriminatory organizations. No grants to individuals, political causes, travel, film or video projects, fashion shows or beauty pageants, program advertising, or recreational sports teams.
Publications: Application guidelines.
Application information: Applications accepted. Letters of inquiry should be submitted using organization letterhead. Applicants should submit the following:
1) statement of problem project will address
2) copy of IRS Determination Letter
3) brief history of organization and description of its mission

Applications should include the Tax ID Number of the organization.

Initial approach: Letter of inquiry
Deadline(s): Dec. 1

1893
Hunter Douglas, Inc.

1 Blue Hill Plz.
Pearl River, NY 10965 (845) 664-7000

Company URL: http://www.hunterdouglas.com
Establishment information: Established in 1951.
Company type: Subsidiary of a foreign company
Business activities: Operates window coverings company.
Business type (SIC): Plastic products/ miscellaneous
Corporate officers: Marvin B. Hopkins, Pres. and C.E.O.; Gordon Khan, Sr. V.P. and C.F.O.; Robert Melen, C.I.O.
Subsidiaries: Carole Fabrics Corp., Martinez, GA; Comfortex Corp., Watervliet, NY; Hunter Douglas Architectural Products Inc., Norcross, GA; Hunter Douglas Fabrication Co., Poway, CA; Hunter Douglas Fashions Inc., Los Angeles, CA; Hunter Douglas Northwest, Renton, WA; Hunter Douglas Pleated Shade Corp., Gastonia, NC; Isoteck Inc., Pompano Beach, FL
Divisions: Hunter Douglas Verticals Div., Fort Lauderdale, FL; Hunter Douglas Window Fashions Div., Broomfield, CO
Giving statement: Giving through the Hunter Douglas, Inc. Contributions Program and the Hunter Douglas Foundation Inc.

Hunter Douglas, Inc. Contributions Program

1 Blue Hill Plz.
Pearl River, NY 10965 (845) 664-7000
URL: http://www.hunterdouglas.com

Hunter Douglas Foundation Inc.

1 Blue Hill Plaza
Pearl River, NY 10965-3104 (845) 664-7000

Establishment information: Established as a company-sponsored operating foundation in 1999 in NJ.
Donor: Hunter Douglas, Inc.
Financial data (yr. ended 12/31/11): Assets, $10,644 (M); gifts received, $197,800; expenditures, $196,866; qualifying distributions, $196,866; giving activities include $193,000 for 81 grants to individuals (high: $5,000; low: $500).
Purpose and activities: The foundation supports organizations involved with the 9/11 disaster and awards college scholarships to children of employees of Hunter Douglas, Inc.
Fields of interest: Education; Disasters, 9/11/01.
Type of support: Employee-related scholarships.
Geographic limitations: Giving limited to Upper Saddle River, NJ and NY.
Application information: Applications accepted. Application form required.

Initial approach: Proposal
Deadline(s): Annually by mid-Sept.

Officers and Directors:* Gordon Khan*, V.P.; Arthur Lorenz*, V.P.; Marvin Hopkins.
EIN: 223694713

1894
Huntington Bancshares Incorporated

Huntington Ctr.
41 S. High St.
Columbus, OH 43287 (614) 480-8300
FAX: (614) 480-3761

Company URL: http://www.huntington.com
Establishment information: Established in 1866.
Company type: Public company
Company ticker symbol and exchange: HBAN/ NASDAQ
International Securities Identification Number: US4461501045
Business activities: Operates bank holding company; operates commercial bank.
Business type (SIC): Holding company; banks/ commercial
Financial profile for 2012: Number of employees, 11,806; assets, $56,153,180,000; pre-tax net income, $825,120,000; liabilities, $50,362,970,000
Fortune 1000 ranking: 2012—707th in revenues, 276th in profits, and 99th in assets
Forbes 2000 ranking: 2012—1624th in sales, 900th in profits, and 415th in assets
Corporate officers: Stephen D. Steinour, Chair., Pres., and C.E.O.; Donald R. Kimble, Sr. Exec. V.P. and C.F.O.; Zahid Afzal, Sr. Exec. V.P. and C.I.O.; Keith Sanders, Sr. Exec. V.P., Human Resources
Board of directors: Stephen D. Steinour, Chair.; Don M. Casto III; Ann B. Crane; Steven Elliott; Michael Endres; John B. Gerlach, Jr.; Peter J. Kight; Jonathan A. Levy; Richard W. Neu; David L. Porteous; Kathleen H. Ransier
Subsidiaries: The Huntington Acceptance Co., Pittsburgh, PA; Huntington Bancshares Indiana, Inc., Indianapolis, IN; The Huntington National Bank, Columbus, OH; The Huntington Savings Bank, Sebring, FL; The Huntington Trust Co. of Florida, Naples, FL
Offices: Covington, Louisville, KY; Warren, MI; Cincinnati, Dover, Lima, OH; Morgantown, WV
International operations: Canada; Cayman Islands; Hong Kong; Luxembourg
Historic mergers: Sky Financial Group, Inc. (July 1, 2007)
Giving statement: Giving through the Huntington Bancshares Incorporated Contributions Program and the Huntington Foundation.
Company EIN: 310724920

Huntington Bancshares Incorporated Contributions Program

Huntington Ctr.
41 S. High St.
Columbus, OH 43287 (614) 480-8300
URL: https://www.huntington.com/regions/

Purpose and activities: As a complement to its foundation, Huntington Bancshares makes charitable contributions to nonprofit organizations directly. Support is given primarily in areas of company operations in Indiana, Kentucky, Michigan, Ohio, Pennsylvania, and West Virginia.
Fields of interest: Housing/shelter; Human services, financial counseling; Human services; Economic development; Community development, small businesses.
Type of support: Employee matching gifts; Employee volunteer services; General/operating support; In-kind gifts; Loaned talent; Sponsorships.
Geographic limitations: Giving primarily in areas of company operations in IN, KY, MI, OH, PA, and WV.

The Huntington Foundation

41 S. High St., HC 0643
Columbus, OH 43215-6101
FAX: (614) 480-4973;
E-mail: steven.fields@huntington.com

Establishment information: Established in 1999 in OH.
Donors: Huntington Bancshares Inc.; The Huntington National Bank.
Contact: Steven Fields, Tr.
Financial data (yr. ended 12/31/11): Assets, $41,996 (M); expenditures, $850,490; qualifying distributions, $850,290; giving activities include $850,290 for 32 grants (high: $250,000; low: $500).
Purpose and activities: The foundation supports organizations involved with arts and culture, education, health, employment, hunger, human services, and community economic development.
Fields of interest: Museums (art); Performing arts; Performing arts, ballet; Performing arts, orchestras; Higher education; Education; Health care, patient services; Health care, home services; Health care; Food services; Food banks; Boys & girls clubs; YM/ YWCAs & YM/YWHAs; Children/youth, services; Family services, domestic violence; Human services; Community/economic development; United Ways and Federated Giving Programs.
Type of support: Capital campaigns.
Geographic limitations: Giving primarily in areas of company operations.
Support limitations: No support for political, religious, ethnic, military, fraternal, or labor organizations. No grants to individuals, or for endowments, research, equipment, or films, videos, or television programs.
Publications: Application guidelines.
Application information: Applications accepted. Application form not required. Applicants should submit the following:
1) timetable for implementation and evaluation of project
2) qualifications of key personnel
3) population served
4) copy of IRS Determination Letter
5) brief history of organization and description of its mission
6) geographic area to be served
7) copy of most recent annual report/audited financial statement/990
8) how project's results will be evaluated or measured

9) listing of board of directors, trustees, officers and other key people and their affiliations
10) detailed description of project and amount of funding requested
11) contact person
12) copy of current year's organizational budget and/or project budget

Initial approach: Complete online application
Deadline(s): Feb. 15, May 15, Aug. 15, and Nov. 15,
Final notification: Within 4 months

Trustees: Steven Fields, Pres.; John Liebersbach, Secy.; Edward J. Kane, Treas.; Eric Stachler.
EIN: 311681542

1895
Huntsman Corporation

500 Huntsman Way
Salt Lake City, UT 84108-1235
(801) 584-5700
FAX: (801) 584-5781

Company URL: http://www.huntsman.com
Establishment information: Established in 1970.
Company type: Public company
Company ticker symbol and exchange: HUN/NYSE
Business activities: Manufactures chemicals.
Business type (SIC): Chemicals and allied products
Financial profile for 2012: Number of employees, 12,000; assets, $8,884,000,000; sales volume, $11,187,000,000; pre-tax net income, $547,000,000; expenses, $10,422,000,000; liabilities, $7,111,000,000
Fortune 1000 ranking: 2012—241st in revenues, 423rd in profits, and 430th in assets
Corporate officers: Jon M. Huntsman, Chair.; Nolan D. Archibald, Vice-Chair.; Peter R. Huntsman, Pres. and C.E.O.; J. Kimo Esplin, Exec. V.P. and C.F.O.; James R. Moore, Exec. V.P., Genl. Counsel, and Secy.; R. Wade Rogers, Sr. V.P., Human Resources; Maria Csiba-Womersley, V.P. and C.I.O.; Randy W. Wright, V.P. and Cont.
Board of directors: Jon M. Huntsman, Chair.; Nolan D. Archibald, Vice-Chair.; Mary C. Beckerle, Ph.D.; M. Anthony Burns; Patrick T. Harker; Jon M. Hunstman, Jr.; Peter R. Huntsman; Robert Margetts; Wayne A. Reaud; Alvin V. Shoemaker
Subsidiary: Huntsman Polymers Corporation, The Woodlands, TX
International operations: Argentina; Armenia; Australia; Austria; Belgium; Brazil; Canada; Cayman Islands; China; Colombia; Czech Republic; Egypt; France; Germany; Guatemala; Hong Kong; Hungary; India; Indonesia; Italy; Japan; Luxembourg; Malaysia; Mexico; Netherlands; New Zealand; Pakistan; Panama; Poland; Russia; Saudi Arabia; Singapore; South Africa; South Korea; Spain; Sweden; Switzerland; Taiwan; Thailand; Turkey; United Arab Emirates; United Kingdom
Giving statement: Giving through the Huntsman Corporation Contributions Program.
Company EIN: 421648585

Huntsman Corporation Contributions Program

10003 Woodloch Forest Dr., Ste. 260
The Woodlands, TX 77380-1955
URL: http://www.huntsman.com/eng/Sustainability/Social_responsibility/Social_responsibility/index.cfm?PageID=8646

Purpose and activities: Huntsman makes charitable contributions to nonprofit organizations involved with education, cancer, international relief, and homeless people. Support is given primarily in areas of company operations, with emphasis on Utah, and in Armenia.
Fields of interest: Education; Cancer; International development; International relief; Economic development; Business/industry; Community/economic development Economically disadvantaged; Homeless.
International interests: Armenia.
Type of support: Employee volunteer services; General/operating support; Grants to individuals; Scholarship funds.
Geographic limitations: Giving primarily in areas of company operations, with emphasis on UT, and in Armenia.

1896
Husch Blackwell LLP

4801 Main St., Ste. 1000
Kansas City, MO 64112-2551
(816) 983-8000

Company URL: http://www.huschblackwell.com
Company type: Private company
Business activities: Operates law firm.
Business type (SIC): Legal services
Offices: Phoenix, AZ; Denver, CO; Washington, DC; Chicago, Peoria, IL; Jefferson City, Kansas City, Saint Louis, Springfield, MO; Omaha, NE; Chattanooga, Memphis, TN
International operations: United Kingdom
Giving statement: Giving through the Husch Blackwell LLP Corporate Giving Program.

Husch Blackwell LLP Corporate Giving Program

4801 Main St., Ste. 1000
Kansas City, MO 64112-2551
E-mail: Jennifer.Schwendemann@huschblackwell.com; Contact for Pro Bono program: Jennifer Schwendemann, Dir. of Risk Mgmt./Pro Bono; URL: http://www.huschblackwell.com/community-leadership/

Contact: Jennifer Schwendemann, Dir. of Risk Mgmt./Pro Bono Svcs.
Fields of interest: Legal services.
Type of support: Pro bono services - legal.

1897
Hutchinson Black & Cook, LLC

921 Walnut St., Ste. 200
Boulder, CO 80302-5173 (303) 442-6514

Company URL: http://www.hbcboulder.com/
Establishment information: Established in 1891.
Company type: Private company
Business activities: Operates law firm.
Business type (SIC): Legal services
Giving statement: Giving through the Hutchinson Black & Cook, LLC Corporate Giving Program.

Hutchinson Black & Cook, LLC Corporate Giving Program

921 Walnut St., Ste. 200
Boulder, CO 80302-5173 (303) 442-6514
FAX: (303) 442-6593; Contact for Pro Bono project: Maureen Eldredge, Attorney, e-mail: eldredge@hbcboulder.com; URL: http://www.hbcboulder.com/community.community.html

Fields of interest: Legal services.
Type of support: Pro bono services - legal.

1898
Hutchison Supply Co.

2425 Brockton St., Ste. 103
San Antonio, TX 78217-4923
(210) 826-6616

Company URL: http://`
Establishment information: Established in 2011.
Company type: Private company
Business activities: Sells steel doors and frames wholesale.
Business type (SIC): Lumber and construction materials—wholesale
Giving statement: Giving through the Mike and Dian Hutchison Family Foundation.

Mike and Dian Hutchison Family Foundation

c/o Wylie Mgmt.
P.O. Box 1131
Dripping Springs, TX 78620-1131

Establishment information: Established in 2000 in TX.
Donors: Hutchison Supply Co.; William M. Hutchison.
Financial data (yr. ended 12/31/11): Assets, $143,820 (M); expenditures, $13,228; qualifying distributions, $11,000; giving activities include $11,000 for grants.
Purpose and activities: The foundation supports the Children's Medical Center Foundation in Austin, Texas.
Fields of interest: Health care; Human services.
Type of support: General/operating support.
Geographic limitations: Giving limited to Austin, TX.
Support limitations: No grants to individuals.
Application information: Applications not accepted. Unsolicited requests for funds not accepted.
Officers and Directors:* William M. Hutchison*, Pres.; Dian D. Hutchison, V.P.; Mike Wylie, Secy.-Treas.; Curtis R. Hutchison; Dian D. Hutchison.
EIN: 742982407

1899
Hutton Financial Advisors

3918 Telephone Rd., Ste. 100
Fort Worth, TX 76135-2933 (817) 238-6995

Company URL: http://www.huttonfinancial.com
Establishment information: Established in 1990.
Company type: Private company
Business activities: Provides investment advisory services.
Business type (SIC): Security and commodity services
Corporate officer: Timothy Hutton, Pres. and C.E.O.
Giving statement: Giving through the Hutton Foundation, Inc.

The Hutton Foundation, Inc.

569 CR 3581
Paradise, TX 76073-3207 (817) 238-6995
Application address: 3980 Boat Club Rd., Ste. 207, Fort Worth, TX 76135 tel: (817) 238-6995

Establishment information: Established in 2003 in TX.
Donor: Hutton Financial Advisors.
Contact: Timothy Hutton, Dir.
Financial data (yr. ended 12/31/11): Assets, $1,713 (M); gifts received, $74,670; expenditures, $74,697; qualifying distributions, $71,360; giving activities include $71,360 for grants.
Purpose and activities: The foundation supports organizations involved with religion and awards grants to individuals located in Fort Worth, Texas.
Fields of interest: Health care; Human services; Religion.
Type of support: General/operating support; Grants to individuals.
Geographic limitations: Giving primarily in Fort Worth, TX.
Application information: Applications accepted. Application form not required.
Initial approach: Letter of inquiry
Deadline(s): None
Directors: Gloria Hutton; Tim Hutton.
EIN: 900122801

1901
Hygeia Dairy Company

(formerly Southern Foods Group, LLC)
525 Beaumont Ave.
McAllen, TX 78501-2737 (956) 686-0511

Establishment information: Established in 1994.
Company type: Private company
Business activities: Produces dairy goods.
Business type (SIC): Dairy products
Corporate officer: Howard Hotcaveg, Mgr.
Giving statement: Giving through the Hygeia Foundation.

Hygeia Foundation

P.O. Box 751
Harlingen, TX 78551-0751 (956) 423-2050
Application address: 720 S. F St., Harlingen, TX 78550

Establishment information: Established in 1953 in TX.
Donor: Hygeia Dairy Co.
Contact: H. Lee Richards
Financial data (yr. ended 03/31/11): Assets, $204,904 (M); expenditures, $33,618; qualifying distributions, $29,050; giving activities include $29,050 for 7 grants (high: $20,000; low: $500).
Purpose and activities: The foundation supports organizations involved with arts and culture, education, health, human services, and Christianity.
Fields of interest: Education; Recreation.
Type of support: Annual campaigns; Capital campaigns; Continuing support; General/operating support; Scholarship funds.
Application information: Applications accepted. Application form required. Applicants should submit the following:
1) copy of IRS Determination Letter
2) copy of most recent annual report/audited financial statement/990
Initial approach: Letter
Deadline(s): None
Trustees: James D. Purl, Jr.; H. Lee Richards; Merry K. Richards.
EIN: 746047054
Selected grants: The following grants are a representative sample of this grantmaker's funding activity:
$5,000 to Texas A & M Foundation, College Station, TX, 2009.
$1,500 to Gladys Porter Zoo, Brownsville, TX, 2009.

1902
Hyundai Motor America

10550 Talbert Ave.
Fountain Valley, CA 92708-6031
(714) 965-3000

Company URL: http://www.hyundaiusa.com
Establishment information: Established in 1985.
Company type: Subsidiary of a foreign company
Business activities: Operates auto company.
Business type (SIC): Motor vehicles and equipment
Financial profile for 2011: Number of employees, 5,000
Corporate officers: John Krafcik, Pres. and C.E.O.; Jerry Flannery, Exec. V.P., Genl. Counsel, and Secy.; David Zuchowski, Exec. V.P., Sales; Kathy Parker, V.P., Human Resources; Steve Shannon, V.P., Mktg.
Giving statement: Giving through the Hope on Wheels Hyundai Dealers.

Hope on Wheels Hyundai Dealers

1875 Century Park E., Ste. 200
Los Angeles, CA 90067-2503 (310) 882-4002
E-mail: info@hopeonwheels.org; URL: http://www.hyundaihopeonwheels.org

Establishment information: Established in 2007 in CA.
Contact: Mickey Pong, Chair.
Financial data (yr. ended 12/31/11): Revenue, $14,528,373; assets, $1,694,272 (M); gifts received, $14,526,761; expenditures, $14,488,971; program services expenses, $14,380,976; giving activities include $12,195,348 for 83 grants (high: $2,050,000; low: $50,000).
Purpose and activities: The organization supports hospitals in their research to cure cancer in children.
Fields of interest: Cancer; Medical research, fund raising/fund distribution Girls; Boys.
Type of support: General/operating support.
Geographic limitations: Giving on a national basis.
Application information: Applications accepted.
Officers and Directors:* Mickey Pong*, Chair.; Scott Stark*, Vice-Chair.; Gary Micallef*, Secy.; Zafar Brooks; Scott Fink; Marc Garvey; Mike Kelly; Don Reilly; Scott Stark; Dave Zuchowski.
EIN: 260628722

1900
Hy-Vee, Inc.

5820 Westown Pkwy.
West Des Moines, IA 50266-8223
(515) 267-2800
FAX: (515) 267-2817

Company URL: http://www.hy-vee.com
Establishment information: Established in 1930.
Company type: Private company
Business activities: Operates supermarkets and drug stores.
Business type (SIC): Groceries—retail; drugs, proprietaries, and sundries—wholesale; groceries—wholesale; drug stores and proprietary stores; liquor stores
Financial profile for 2011: Number of employees, 56,000; sales volume, $6,894,400,000
Corporate officers: Richard N. Jurgens, Chair., Pres., and C.E.O.; Randy B. Edeker, Exec. V.P. and C.O.O.; John C. Briggs, Exec. V.P., Treas., and C.F.O.; Kenneth W. Waller, Exec. V.P. and C.A.O.; Stephen P. Meyer, Sr. V.P. and Secy.; Kevin A. Reeve, Cont.; Ronald D. Pearson, Chair. Emeritus
Board of directors: Richard N. Jurgens, Chair.; Ronald D. Pearson
Subsidiaries: D & D Salads, Inc., Omaha, NE; Florist Distributing, Des Moines, IA; Lomar Distributing, Des Moines, IA; Meyocks & Priebe Advertising, West Des Moines, IA; Midwest Heritage Bank, Chariton, IA; PDI, Ankeny, IA
Giving statement: Giving through the Hy-Vee, Inc. Corporate Giving Program and the Hy-Vee Foundation, Inc.

Hy-Vee, Inc. Corporate Giving Program

5820 Westown Pkwy.
West Des Moines, IA 50266-8223 (515) 267-2800
E-mail for Smart Points: info@hy-veesmartpoints.com.; URL: http://www.hy-vee.com/company/community/default.aspx

Purpose and activities: As a complement to its foundation, Hy-Vee also makes charitable contributions to nonprofit organizations directly. Support is given to organizations involved with health care, education, the arts, leisure and recreation, the environment, economic opportunity, and civic improvement. Support is given primarily in areas of company operations.
Fields of interest: Arts; Education; Environment; Health care; Diabetes; Food services; Recreation; American Red Cross; Children, services; Community/economic development; Military/veterans' organizations; Public affairs.
Program:
Smart Points: For every $20 of Procter & Gamble products purchased at Hy-Vee from September 1, 2012 through November 30, 2012, customers earned 100 SMART Points to donate to the school of their choice using the promotional codes from receipts of purchase. Participants were required to be 18 years of age to donate points.
Type of support: Donated products; Employee volunteer services; General/operating support; In-kind gifts.
Geographic limitations: Giving primarily in areas of company operations.

Hy-Vee Foundation, Inc.

5820 Westown Pkwy.
West Des Moines, IA 50266-8223 (515) 453-2791
E-mail: jclaussen@hy-vee.com; URL: http://www.hy-vee.com/company/scholarships/default.aspx

Establishment information: Established in 1968 in IA.
Donors: Hy-Vee Food Stores, Inc.; Hy-Vee, Inc.
Contact: JoDee Claussen, Recruiting Coord.
Financial data (yr. ended 09/28/11): Assets, $5,450 (M); gifts received, $80,000; expenditures, $75,550; qualifying distributions, $75,550; giving activities include $71,000 for 71 grants to individuals (high: $1,000; low: $1,000).
Purpose and activities: The foundation awards college scholarships to employees and children of employees of Hy-Vee.
Fields of interest: Education.
Type of support: Employee-related scholarships.
Geographic limitations: Giving limited to areas of company operations in IA, IL, KS, MN, MO, NE, and SD.
Application information: Applications accepted. Application form required.

Initial approach: Proposal
Deadline(s): Feb. 10
Officers and Directors:* Denise Broderick*, Pres.; Sheila Laing*, V.P.; Victor Roberts, Secy.-Treas.; Rose Kleyweg Mitchell; Michael Skokan.
EIN: 420942086

1903
IAC/InterActiveCorp

(formerly InterActiveCorp)
555 W. 18th St.
New York, NY 10011 (212) 314-7300
FAX: (212) 314-7309

Company URL: http://www.iac.com
Establishment information: Established in 1986.
Company type: Public company
Company ticker symbol and exchange: IACI/NASDAQ
Business activities: Provides cable television services; produces television programming; provides ticketing services; provides hotel reservation services; provides Internet shopping and information services; produces motion pictures; broadcasts television.
Business type (SIC): Radio and television broadcasting; cable and other pay television services; computer services; business services/miscellaneous; motion pictures/production and services allied to; amusement and recreation services/miscellaneous
Financial profile for 2012: Number of employees, 4,200; assets, $3,805,830,000; sales volume, $2,800,930,000; pre-tax net income, $289,060,000; expenses, $2,486,050,000; liabilities, $2,150,100,000
Fortune 1000 ranking: 2012—748th in revenues, 636th in profits, and 680th in assets
Corporate officers: Barry Diller, Chair.; Victor A. Kaufman, Vice-Chair.; Gregory R. Blatt, C.E.O.; Vincent Luciani, C.I.O.; Jeff Kip, Exec. V.P. and C.F.O.; Jason Stewart, Sr. V.P. and C.A.O.; Nick Stoumpas, Sr. V.P. and Treas.; Michael H. Schwerdtman, Sr. V.P. and Cont.; Gregg Winiarski, Sr. V.P. and Genl. Counsel
Board of directors: Barry Diller, Chair.; Victor A. Kaufman, Vice-Chair.; Gregory R. Blatt; Edgar M. Bronfman, Jr.; Chelsea Clinton; Sonali De Rycker; Michael Eisner; Donald R. Keough; Bryan Lourd; Arthur C. Martinez; David Rosenblatt; Alan G. Spoon; Alexander Von Furstenberg; Richard F. Zannino
Subsidiaries: Home Shopping Network, Inc., St. Petersburg, FL; Ticketmaster Group, Inc., West Hollywood, CA; USA Broadcasting, Inc., New York, NY; USA Network, New York, NY
International operations: Australia; Bermuda; Canada; Cayman Islands; China; England; Germany; Ireland; Italy; Japan; Luxembourg; Mauritius; Netherlands; New Zealand; Spain; United Kingdom; Wales
Giving statement: Giving through the IAC/InterActiveCorp Contributions Program and the IAC Foundation.
Company EIN: 592712887

The IAC Foundation

(formerly USA Networks Foundation, Inc.)
555 W. 18th St.
New York, NY 10011-2822

Establishment information: Established in 1998 in NY.
Donors: USA Networks, Inc.; USA Interactive; InterActiveCorp; IAC/InterActiveCorp.
Financial data (yr. ended 12/31/11): Assets, $0 (M); expenditures, $0; qualifying distributions, $0.
Purpose and activities: The foundation supports organizations involved with arts and culture, education, health, multiple sclerosis, AIDS, human services, and Judaism.
Fields of interest: Media/communications; Performing arts, music; Arts; Higher education; Education, reading; Education; Health care; Multiple sclerosis; AIDS; Human services; Jewish federated giving programs; Jewish agencies & synagogues.
Type of support: Employee matching gifts; General/operating support.
Geographic limitations: Giving on a national basis, with some emphasis on NY.
Application information: Applications not accepted. Unsolicited requests for funds not accepted.
Officers and Directors: Nick Stoumpas, V.P. and Treas.; Thomas J. Mcinerney*, V.P.; Michael H. Schwerdtman, V.P.; Gregory R. Blatt*, Secy.; Victor A. Kaufman.
EIN: 133994361

1904
Iberdrola USA, Inc.

(formerly The Energy East Corporation)
52 Farm View Dr.
New Gloucester, ME 04260-5116
(207) 688-6300

Company URL: http://www.energyeast.com
Establishment information: Established in 1997.
Company type: Subsidiary of a foreign company
Business activities: Operates utility holding company that distributes electricity and natural gas.
Business type (SIC): Combination utility services
Financial profile for 2009: Number of employees, 40; assets, $12,670,000,000; sales volume, $4,361,600,000
Corporate officers: Robert D. Kump, C.E.O.; Kevin E. Walker, C.O.O.; Jose Maria Torres, V.P. and C.F.O.; R. Scott Mahoney, V.P., Genl. Counsel, and Secy.; Jose Maria Cirujano, V.P., Opers.; Sheri Lamoureux, V.P., Human Resources
Office: Greenville, ME
Giving statement: Giving through the Iberdrola USA Foundation, Inc.

The Iberdrola USA Foundation, Inc.

(formerly The Energy East Foundation, Inc.)
52 Farm View Dr.
New Gloucester, ME 04260-5100 (207) 688-4341
FAX: (207) 688-4354;
E-mail: darlene.beach@energyeast.com

Establishment information: Established in 2001 in DE.
Donors: The Union Water-Power Co.; Central Maine Power Co.
Contact: Darlene E. Beach, Treas.
Financial data (yr. ended 12/31/11): Assets, $6,724,801 (M); gifts received, $807,966; expenditures, $1,039,624; qualifying distributions, $734,941; giving activities include $734,941 for grants.
Purpose and activities: The foundation supports organizations involved with education, health, and community development and the environment. Support is given primarily in areas of company operations.
Fields of interest: Higher education, university; Education; Environment; Health care, clinics/centers; End of life care; Health care; Community/economic development Children; Young adults; Physically disabled; Economically disadvantaged; Homeless.
Type of support: Emergency funds; Matching/challenge support; Program development; Sponsorships.
Geographic limitations: Giving primarily in the Northeast, with emphasis on DC, ME, and NY.
Support limitations: No support for political, labor, or fraternal organizations, religious organizations, or organizations with overhead expenses exceeding 25 percent of the total operating budget. No grants to individuals, or for capital campaigns or endowments, conferences, or symposia.
Publications: Informational brochure (including application guidelines).
Application information: Applications accepted. Application form required.
Initial approach: Contact foundation for application form
Copies of proposal: 2
Board meeting date(s): Varies
Deadline(s): None
Final notification: 90 to 120 days
Officers: Robert D. Kump, Pres.; Mark V. Dolan, Secy.; Darlene E. Beach*, Treas.
Number of staff: None.
EIN: 134200689

1905
Ice Miller LLP

1 American Sq., Ste. 2900
Indianapolis, IN 46282-0200
(317) 236-2100

Company URL: http://www.icemiller.com
Establishment information: Established in 1910.
Company type: Private company
Business activities: Operates law firm.
Business type (SIC): Legal services
Corporate officers: Phillip Bayt, Chief Managing Partner; Deb Abbott, Mgr.
Offices: Washington, DC; Chicago, IL; Indianapolis, IN; Cleveland, Columbus, OH
Historic mergers: Schottenstein, Zox & Dunn Co., LPA (January 1, 2012)
Giving statement: Giving through the Ice Miller LLP Pro Bono Program.

Ice Miller LLP Pro Bono Program

1 American Sq., Ste. 2900
Indianapolis, IN 46282-0200 (317) 236-5832
E-mail: thomas.mixdorf@icemiller.com; URL: http://www.icemiller.com/community_involvement.aspx

Contact: Thomas Mixdorf, Partner and Pro Bono Coord.
Fields of interest: Legal services.
Type of support: Pro bono services - legal.
Application information: An attorney coordinates pro bono projects.

1906
ICON Health & Fitness, Inc.

1500 S. 1000 W.
Logan, UT 84321-8206 (435) 750-5000
FAX: (435) 750-3917

Company URL: http://www.iconfitness.com
Establishment information: Established in 1977.
Company type: Private company
Business activities: Manufactures fitness equipment.

Business type (SIC): Games, toys, and sporting and athletic goods
Financial profile for 2010: Number of employees, 2,000
Corporate officers: Scott R. Watterson, Chair. and C.E.O.; Robert C. Gay, Vice-Chair.; David J. Watterson, Pres.; M. Joseph Brough, C.O.O.; S. Fred Beck, C.F.O.
Board of directors: Scott R. Watterson, Chair.; Robert C. Gay, Vice-Chair.
Subsidiary: NordicTrack, Inc., Logan, UT
Giving statement: Giving through the ICON Health & Fitness, Inc. Corporate Giving Program.

ICON Health & Fitness, Inc. Corporate Giving Program

1500 S. 1000 W.
Logan, UT 84321-8206
URL: http://www.iconfitness.com/about/involvement

Purpose and activities: ICON Health & Fitness makes charitable contributions to nonprofit organizations on a case by case basis. Support is given primarily in Utah.
Fields of interest: Education; Health care, patient services; Health care; Medical research, institute; General charitable giving Children/youth.
Type of support: General/operating support; Sponsorships.
Geographic limitations: Giving primarily in UT.

1907
IDACORP, Inc.

1221 W. Idaho St.
P.O. Box 70
Boise, ID 83702-5627 (208) 388-2200
FAX: (208) 388-6916

Company URL: http://www.idacorpinc.com
Establishment information: Established in 1998.
Company type: Public company
Company ticker symbol and exchange: IDA/NYSE
Business activities: Operates holding company; generates, transmits, and distributes electricity; distributes natural gas.
Business type (SIC): Electric services; gas production and distribution; holding company
Financial profile for 2012: Number of employees, 2,079; assets, $5,319,520,000; sales volume, $1,080,660,000; pre-tax net income, $195,050,000; expenses, $838,060,000; liabilities, $3,560,760,000
Corporate officers: Gary G. Michael, Chair.; J. LaMont Keen, Pres. and C.E.O.; Darrel T. Anderson, Exec. V.P. and C.F.O.; Rex Blackburn, Sr. V.P. and Genl. Counsel; Steve R. Keen, V.P., Finance, and Treas.; Jeffrey L. Malmen, V.P., Public Affairs; Patrick A. Harrington, Corp. Secy.; Ken Petersen, Corp. Cont. and C.A.O.
Board of directors: Gary G. Michael, Chair.; C. Stephen Allred; Richard J. Dahl; Judith A. Johansen; Dennis Johnson; J. LaMont Keen; Christine King; Jan B. Packwood; Joan H. Smith; Robert A. Tinstman; Thomas J. Wilford
Subsidiaries: Ida-West Energy Co., Boise, ID; Idaho Power Company, Boise, ID
Giving statement: Giving through the IDACORP, Inc. Corporate Giving Program and the Idaho Power Foundation, Inc.
Company EIN: 820505802

IDACORP, Inc. Corporate Giving Program

c/o Corp. Contribs.
P.O. Box 70
Boise, ID 83707-0070 (208) 388-2477
E-mail: ldodson@idahopower.com; URL: http://www.idahopower.com/NewsCommunity/Community/default.cfm
Application address for Scholarship for Academic Excellence: Idaho Power Scholarship Program, c/o Scholarship Program Administrator, 301 E. Benton, Pocatello, Idaho 83201; Application address for Larry Wimer Memorial Scholarship: Elly Davis, Idaho Community Foundation, 210 W. State St., Boise, ID 83702; Additional scholarship contact: Claudia Tremelling, tel.: (208) 236-7733, e-mail: ctremelling@idahopower.com

Contact: Layne Dodson, Prog. Mgr
Purpose and activities: As a complement to its foundation, IDACORP also makes charitable contributions to nonprofit organizations directly. Support is given primarily in areas of company operations in southern Idaho, northern Nevada, and eastern Oregon.
Fields of interest: Visual arts; Museums; Performing arts; Arts; Secondary school/education; Higher education; Adult/continuing education; Education; Environment, natural resources; Hospitals (general); Health care; Housing/shelter; Safety/disasters; Youth, services; Aging, centers/services; Human services; Community/economic development; United Ways and Federated Giving Programs; Engineering; Public affairs; General charitable giving.
Programs:

Douglas E. Sprenger Memorial Scholarship Fund: The company awards scholarships to high school seniors who are children of employees of Idaho Power. Applicants must plan to enroll full-time at an Idaho or Oregon college, university, or vocational technical school. Scholarships are awarded based on academic achievement, leadership potential, and school and community involvement.

Kevin Whittier Memorial Scholarship Fund: The company awards scholarships to high school seniors who are children of employees of Idaho Power and plan to enroll at an Idaho college, university, or vocational-technical school. Applicants must plan to seek a degree in engineering.

Larry Wimer Memorial Scholarship: The company annually awards $500 scholarships to students who plan to enroll in the University of Idaho's Department of Natural Resources.

Scholarships for Academic Excellence: The company annually awards ten $2,000 scholarships to graduating high school students who live within Idaho Power's service area and are planning to enroll at an accredited Idaho or Oregon college, university, or vocational-technical school. The scholarship honors individual achievement, community awareness and involvement, and academic accomplishment.

Type of support: Capital campaigns; Employee matching gifts; Employee volunteer services; Employee-related scholarships; Fellowships; General/operating support; In-kind gifts; Program development; Public relations services; Publication; Scholarship funds; Scholarships—to individuals; Sponsorships.
Geographic limitations: Giving primarily in areas of company operations in southern ID, northern NV, and eastern OR.
Support limitations: No support for religious organizations not of direct benefit to the entire community, fraternal or labor organizations, individual schools, or discriminatory organizations. No grants to individuals (except for scholarships), or for investments, tickets for contests, raffles, or other prize-oriented activities, or advertising; no loans or investments.
Publications: Application guidelines; Corporate giving report.
Application information: Applications accepted. Applications for Larry Wilmer Memorial scholarships should be no longer than 15 pages. Applications for Scholarship for Academic Excellence should be no longer than 14 pages. The Community Relations Department handles giving. Application form required. Applicants should submit the following:
1) results expected from proposed grant
2) copy of IRS Determination Letter
3) copy of most recent annual report/audited financial statement/990
4) how project's results will be evaluated or measured
5) listing of board of directors, trustees, officers and other key people and their affiliations
6) detailed description of project and amount of funding requested
7) copy of current year's organizational budget and/or project budget
8) listing of additional sources and amount of support

Requests for scholarships must include a statement of 250 to 300 words summarizing curricular and extra-curricular activities, accomplishments, qualifications, goals, and objectives for higher education; official transcripts; copies of ACT and/or SAT scores; and 3 letters of recommendation.

Initial approach: Download application form and mail proposal and application form to headquarters; download application form and mail to application address for Scholarship for Academic Excellence and Larry Wilmer Memorial Scholarship
Copies of proposal: 1
Deadline(s): None; Mar. 1 for Scholarship for Academic Excellence; Apr. 1 for Larry Wilmer Memorial Scholarship
Final notification: Apr. 1 for Scholarship for Academic Excellence; July 1 for Larry Wilmer Memorial Scholarship

Idaho Power Foundation, Inc.

1221 W. Idaho St.
Boise, ID 83702-5627 (208) 388-2530

Establishment information: Established in 2001 in ID.
Donor: IDACORP, Inc.
Contact: Fran Martin
Financial data (yr. ended 12/31/11): Assets, $902,675 (M); expenditures, $206,399; qualifying distributions, $206,128; giving activities include $206,128 for grants.
Purpose and activities: The foundation supports food banks and organizations involved with arts and culture, education, the environment, health, substance abuse prevention, heart disease, and human services.
Fields of interest: Media, television; Arts; Higher education; Education; Environment; Hospitals (general); Health care; Substance abuse, prevention; Heart & circulatory diseases; Food banks; Boys & girls clubs; Salvation Army; Human services.
Type of support: Equipment; General/operating support; Program development; Scholarship funds; Sponsorships.
Geographic limitations: Giving limited to southern ID, northern NV, and eastern OR.
Application information: Applications accepted. Application form required.

Initial approach: Contact foundation for application form
Deadline(s): None
Officers: J. Lamont Keen, Pres.; Darrel T. Anderson, Treas.
EIN: 820530529

1908
Ideal Industries, Inc.
(formerly Ideal Commutator Dresser Company)
Becker Pl.
Sycamore, IL 60178-2938 (815) 895-5181

Company URL: http://www.idealindustries.com
Establishment information: Established in 1916.
Company type: Private company
Business activities: Manufactures industrial tools and supplies.
Business type (SIC): Cutlery, hand and edge tools, and hardware
Corporate officers: Jim James, Pres. and C.E.O.; Roger Smith, C.I.O.; Joe Saganowich, V.P., Sales and Mktg.; Bob Bukowsky, V.P., Sales
International operations: Australia; Brazil; Canada; China; Dominican Republic; France; Germany; Mexico; United Kingdom
Giving statement: Giving through the Ideal Industries Foundation.

Ideal Industries Foundation
Becker Pl.
Sycamore, IL 60178 (815) 895-5181

Establishment information: Established in 1986 in IL.
Donors: Ideal Industries, Inc.; Susan Golding; Dave Juday; Nancy Juday; Patricia Juday; Sally Juday; David W. Juday; Chris Lamb; Roberta McQuade.
Contact: James Pfotenhauer, Treas.
Financial data (yr. ended 12/31/11): Assets, $1,807,973 (M); gifts received, $175,000; expenditures, $189,435; qualifying distributions, $180,900; giving activities include $180,900 for 43 grants (high: $25,000; low: $50).
Purpose and activities: The foundation supports history museums and organizations involved with child welfare, children and youth, disability services, homelessness, and economic development.
Fields of interest: Museums (history); Crime/violence prevention, child abuse; YM/YWCAs & YM/YWHAs; Children/youth, services; Developmentally disabled, centers & services; Homeless, human services; Economic development; United Ways and Federated Giving Programs.
Type of support: Continuing support; General/operating support.
Geographic limitations: Giving primarily in IL.
Application information: Applications accepted. Application form required. Applicants should submit the following:
1) detailed description of project and amount of funding requested
Initial approach: Proposal
Copies of proposal: 1
Deadline(s): None
Officers: David W. Juday, Pres.; Roberta McQuade, V.P. and Secy.; James Pfotenhauer, Treas.
Directors: Jessica Baack; Deanna Cada; Chris Lamb.
EIN: 363449960
Selected grants: The following grants are a representative sample of this grantmaker's funding activity:
$15,000 to American Red Cross, Des Moines, IA, 2010.
$15,000 to Hope Haven of DeKalb County, DeKalb, IL, 2010.
$10,000 to Safe Passage, Yarmouth, ME, 2010.
$7,000 to DeKalb County Youth Service Bureau, DeKalb, IL, 2010.
$6,000 to Kishwaukee College Foundation, Malta, IL, 2010.
$5,500 to Ben Gordon Center, DeKalb, IL, 2010.
$5,000 to Youth Outlook, Naperville, IL, 2010.
$3,000 to DeKalb County Hospice, DeKalb, IL, 2010.
$2,500 to Northern Illinois Food Bank, Geneva, IL, 2010.
$1,500 to Kishwaukee Community Hospital, DeKalb, IL, 2010.

1909
Idealist Consulting
25 N.W. 23rd Pl., Ste. 6
P.O. Box 393
Portland, OR 97210-5599 (503) 889-8832

Company URL: http://www.idealistconsulting.com
Establishment information: Established in 2000.
Company type: Private company
Business activities: Operates database development company serving socially responsible organizations.
Business type (SIC): Computer services
Corporate officer: Robert E. Jordon, Principal
Board of director: Robert E. Jordan
Giving statement: Giving through the Idealist Consulting Corporate Giving Program.

Idealist Consulting Corporate Giving Program
PMB 393
25 N.W. 23rd Pl., Ste. 6
Portland, OR 97210-5599 (503) 889-8832
E-mail: info@idealistconsulting.com; URL: http://www.idealistconsulting.com/ethics/

Purpose and activities: Idealist Consulting is a certified B Corporation that makes annual contributions of consulting time to nonprofit organizations involved with community development, environmental protection, business ethics, philanthropy, education, disaster relief, local government, social services. Support is limited to areas of company operations in Portland Oregon.
Fields of interest: Education; Environment; Disasters, preparedness/services; Human services; Business/industry; Community/economic development; Philanthropy/voluntarism.
Type of support: Loaned talent.
Geographic limitations: Giving limited to areas of company operations in Portland, OR.

1910
IDT Corporation
520 Broad St.
Newark, NJ 07102-3121 (973) 438-1000

Company URL: http://www.idt.net
Establishment information: Established in 1990.
Company type: Public company
Company ticker symbol and exchange: IDT/NYSE
Business activities: Provides long distance telephone communications services.
Business type (SIC): Telephone communications
Financial profile for 2012: Number of employees, 1,280; assets, $451,110,000; sales volume, $1,506,840,000; pre-tax net income, -$6,990,000; expenses, $1,509,080,000; liabilities, $348,880,000
Corporate officers: Howard S. Jonas, Chair. and C.E.O.; Samuel Jonas, C.O.O.; Mitch Silberman, C.A.O. and Cont.; Joyce J. Mason, Exec. V.P., Genl. Counsel, and Corp. Secy.; Marcelo Fischer, Sr. V.P., Finance
Board of directors: Howard S. Jonas, Chair.; Lawrence E. Bathgate II; Eric F. Cosentino; Ira A. Greenstein; Bill Pereira; Judah Schorr
Subsidiary: Winstar Communications, LLC, New York, NY
International operations: Argentina; Australia; Belgium; Brazil; Chile; Denmark; France; Germany; Gibraltar; Hong Kong; Ireland; Italy; Netherlands; Norway; Peru; South Africa; Sweden; Switzerland; United Kingdom
Giving statement: Giving through the IDT Charitable Foundation.
Company EIN: 223415036

The IDT Charitable Foundation
520 Broad St.
Newark, NJ 07102-3121 (973) 438-1000

Establishment information: Established as a company-sponsored operating foundation in 2001.
Donor: IDT Corp.
Contact: Sidney Mehl
Financial data (yr. ended 12/31/11): Assets, $3,969,954 (M); gifts received, $1,883,192; expenditures, $2,902,517; qualifying distributions, $2,902,517; giving activities include $2,764,803 for 125 grants (high: $200,000; low: $100).
Purpose and activities: The foundation supports organizations involved with education, health, cancer, human services, international relief, and Judaism.
Fields of interest: Elementary/secondary education; Higher education; Theological school/education; Libraries (public); Education; Hospitals (general); Health care; Cancer; Children/youth, services; Human services; International relief; Jewish federated giving programs; Jewish agencies & synagogues.
International interests: Israel.
Type of support: Employee matching gifts; General/operating support; Program-related investments/loans; Scholarship funds; Sponsorships.
Geographic limitations: Giving on a national basis in areas of company operations, with emphasis on NJ, NY, and Israel.
Support limitations: No grants to individuals.
Application information: Applications not accepted. Contributes only to pre-selected organizations.
Officers and Directors:* Howard Millendorf*, Pres.; Blake Reiser*, Treas.; Moshe Kaganoff.
EIN: 364450442

1911
IDT Energy, Inc.
550 Broad St.
Newark, NJ 07102 (973) 438-3500

Company URL: http://www.idtenergyinc.com
Establishment information: Established in 2004.
Company type: Subsidiary of a public company
Business activities: Provider of electricity and natural gas.
Business type (SIC): Combination utility services
Corporate officers: Geoffrey Rochwarger, Chair. and C.E.O.; Alan Schwab, C.O.O.; Terrence P. Stronz, Sr. V.P., Finance, and Opers.

IDT Energy, Inc. Contributions Program

550 Broad St.
Newark, NJ 07102 (973) 438-3500
URL: http://www.idtenergy.com

1912
ifPeople

130 Blvd. N.E., Apt. 6
Atlanta, GA 30312-1389 (678) 608-3408

Company URL: http://www.ifpeople.net
Establishment information: Established in 2004.
Company type: Private company
Business type (SIC): Business services/miscellaneous
Corporate officers: Christopher Johnson, C.E.O.; Tirza Hollenhorst, Pres.
Giving statement: Giving through the ifPeople Corporate Giving Program.

ifPeople Corporate Giving Program

130 Blvd. NE, Ste. #6
Atlanta, GA 30312-1389 (678) 608-3408
E-mail: info@ifpeople.net; URL: http://www.ifpeople.net

Purpose and activities: ifPeople is a certified B Corporation that donates a percentage of net profits to charitable organizations.

1913
IHC Construction Companies, LLC

(formerly IHC Group, Inc.)
1500 Executive Dr.
Elgin, IL 60123-9311 (847) 742-1516

Company URL: http://www.ihcconstruction.com/
Establishment information: Established in 1906.
Company type: Private company
Business activities: Provides general contract construction services.
Business type (SIC): Building construction general contractors and operative builders
Corporate officers: Thomas S. Rakow, Chair.; David Rock, Pres.; Alan Orosz, C.F.O.
Board of director: Thomas S. Rakow, Chair.
Giving statement: Giving through the IHC Group Foundation.

The IHC Group Foundation

(formerly Illinois Hydraulic Foundation)
1500 Executive Dr.
Elgin, IL 60123-9311

Donors: Illinois Hydraulic Construction Co.; The IHC Group, Inc.; Thomas S. Rakow; Susan Rakow; May Rakow.
Financial data (yr. ended 08/31/12): Assets, $45,763 (M); gifts received, $3,650; expenditures, $176,080; qualifying distributions, $174,125; giving activities include $172,275 for 48 grants (high: $50,000; low: $100).
Purpose and activities: The foundation supports organizations involved with education, animal welfare, health, youth development, and human services.
Fields of interest: Higher education; Education; Animals/wildlife, preservation/protection; Hospitals (general); Health care; Boys & girls clubs; Youth development; Family services; Human services.
Type of support: Capital campaigns; General/operating support; Program development; Scholarship funds.
Geographic limitations: Giving limited to IL.
Support limitations: No grants to individuals.
Application information: Applications not accepted. Unsolicited requests for funds not accepted.
Officers: Thomas S. Rakow, Pres.; Susan Rakow, V.P.
EIN: 366069769
Selected grants: The following grants are a representative sample of this grantmaker's funding activity:
$50,000 to Gail Borden Public Library Foundation, Elgin, IL, 2011. For general operations.
$13,850 to Boys and Girls Clubs of Elgin, Elgin, IL, 2011.
$10,000 to Wheaton College, Wheaton, IL, 2011.
$5,000 to Max McGraw Wildlife Foundation, Dundee, IL, 2011. For general operations.
$2,950 to YMCA of Elgin, Elgin, IL, 2011. For general operations.
$2,500 to Oak Crest Residence Association, Elgin, IL, 2011. For general operations.
$1,000 to Administer Justice, East Dundee, IL, 2011. For general operations.
$1,000 to Association for Individual Development, Aurora, IL, 2011. For general operations.
$1,000 to Riverwoods Christian Center, Saint Charles, IL, 2011. For general operations.
$1,000 to Salvation Army of Elgin, Elgin, IL, 2011. For general operations.

1914
IKON Office Solutions, Inc.

(formerly Alco Standard Corporation)
70 Valley Stream Pkwy.
Malvern, PA 19355-0989 (610) 296-8000

Company URL: http://www.ikon.com/about/
Establishment information: Established in 1952.
Company type: Subsidiary of a foreign company
Business activities: Provides document management and computer network solutions.
Business type (SIC): Professional and commercial equipment—wholesale
Financial profile for 2010: Number of employees, 300
Corporate officers: Matthew J. Espe, Chair. and C.E.O.; Henry M. Miller, Jr., Sr. V.P. and C.F.O.; Tracey J. Rothenberger, Sr. V.P. and C.I.O.; Mark A. Hershey, Sr. V.P., Genl. Counsel, and Secy.; Donna A. Venable, Sr. V.P., Human Resources
Board of director: Matthew J. Espe, Chair.
International operations: Canada; France
Giving statement: Giving through the IKON Office Solutions Foundation, Inc.

IKON Office Solutions Foundation, Inc.

(formerly Alco Standard Foundation)
P.O. Box 834
Valley Forge, PA 19482-0834

Establishment information: Established in 1974 in PA.
Donor: IKON Office Solutions, Inc.
Financial data (yr. ended 12/31/11): Assets, $1,807,061 (M); expenditures, $267,207; qualifying distributions, $267,207; giving activities include $267,207 for grants.
Purpose and activities: The foundation supports organizations involved with secondary and higher education.
Fields of interest: Secondary school/education; Higher education.
Type of support: Employee matching gifts; General/operating support.
Geographic limitations: Giving primarily in areas of company operations.
Support limitations: No grants to individuals.
Application information: Applications not accepted. Grantmaking suspended until further notice.
Officers: Henry M. Miller, Jr., Pres.; David Digiacomo, V.P. and Treas.; Mark A. Hershey, Secy.
EIN: 237378726
Selected grants: The following grants are a representative sample of this grantmaker's funding activity:
$24,565 to American Cancer Society, Philadelphia, PA, 2010.
$1,500 to Drury University, Springfield, MO, 2010.
$1,500 to Roncalli High School, Manitowoc, WI, 2010.
$1,500 to University of Oregon Foundation, Eugene, OR, 2010.
$1,500 to University of Tennessee Foundation, Knoxville, TN, 2010.
$1,500 to University of Washington Foundation, Seattle, WA, 2010.
$1,500 to Virginia Athletics Foundation, Charlottesville, VA, 2010.
$1,475 to Providence College, Providence, RI, 2010.
$1,468 to University of South Carolina Educational Foundation, Columbia, SC, 2010.
$1,240 to University of Georgia Athletic Association, Athens, GA, 2010.

1915
Ilitch Holdings, Inc.

2211 Woodward Ave.
Detroit, MI 48201-3467 (313) 471-6600

Company URL: http://www.ilitchholdings.com
Establishment information: Established in 1999.
Company type: Private company
Business activities: Operates pizza restaurants; operates professional ice hockey club; operates professional baseball club; operates theaters; operates arenas; operates stadium; sells restaurant supplies wholesale; produces pizza, pizza crusts, and cookie dough.
Business type (SIC): Restaurants and drinking places; specialty foods/canned, frozen, and preserved; grain mill products, including pet food; groceries—wholesale; real estate operators and lessors; motion picture theaters; commercial sports
Financial profile for 2011: Number of employees, 8
Corporate officers: Michael Ilitch, Chair.; Marian Ilitch, Vice-Chair.; Christopher Ilitch, Pres. and C.E.O.; Scott Fisher, C.F.O.; Todd Seroka, C.I.O.; Joni C. Nelson, V.P., Human Resources
Board of directors: Michael Ilitch, Chair.; Marian Ilitch, Vice-Chair.
Subsidiaries: Detroit Red Wings, Inc., Detroit, MI; Detroit Tigers, Inc., Detroit, MI; Little Caesars, Inc., Detroit, MI
Giving statement: Giving through the Ilitch Charities, Inc.

Ilitch Charities, Inc.

(formerly Ilitch Charities for Children, Inc.)
2211 Woodward Ave.
Detroit, MI 48201-3400 (313) 983-6340
URL: http://www.ilitchcharitiesforchildren.com

Establishment information: Established in 2000 in MI.
Contact: Anne Marie Krappmann, V.P.
Financial data (yr. ended 12/31/11): Revenue, $1,633,172; assets, $3,437,177 (M); gifts received, $1,066,791; expenditures, $1,222,162; program services expenses, $908,539; giving activities include $474,616 for grants (high: $52,302), $160,229 for 41 grants to individuals, $161,978 for in-kind gifts and $111,716 for foundation-administered programs.
Purpose and activities: The organization is dedicated to improving the lives of children in the areas of health, education, and recreation.
Fields of interest: Arts, association; Education; Health care; Recreation.
Program:
Little Caesars AAA Hockey Scholarship Program: The program honors an outstanding high school male and female (19 and under) athlete and provides each of them with a $2,500 scholarship toward the college of their choice.
Type of support: Scholarships—to individuals.
Geographic limitations: Giving primarily in the metropolitan Detroit, MI area.
Publications: Application guidelines.
Application information: Applications accepted. See web site for status of grantmaking opportunities.
Initial approach: Letter of inquiry for grants; download application form for Hockey Scholarship
Deadline(s): Four months prior to project start date for letter of inquiry; Apr. 19 for Hockey Scholarship
Officers and Directors:* Christopher Ilitch*, Chair.; Michael J. Healy*, Pres.; Stan Berenbaum*, V.P.; Joan Rivard*, V.P.; Robert Carr*, Secy.; David Agius, Treas.; Rick Fenton; John Hahn; Kelle Illitch; Elaine Lewis; Tim Padgett.
EIN: 383548144

1916
Illinois Tool Works Inc.

(also known as ITW)
3600 W. Lake Ave.
Glenview, IL 60026-1215 (847) 724-7500
FAX: (847) 657-4261

Company URL: http://www.itw.com
Establishment information: Established in 1912.
Company type: Public company
Company ticker symbol and exchange: ITW/NYSE
Business activities: Manufactures general industrial engineered products and specialty systems.
Business type (SIC): Machinery/general industry
Financial profile for 2012: Number of employees, 60,000; assets, $19,300,000,000; sales volume, $17,900,000,000; pre-tax net income, $3,603,000,000; expenses, $15,077,000,000; liabilities, $8,748,000,000
Fortune 1000 ranking: 2012—155th in revenues, 66th in profits, and 250th in assets
Forbes 2000 ranking: 2012—522nd in sales, 202nd in profits, and 999th in assets
Corporate officers: Robert S. Morrison, Chair.; David C. Parry, Vice-Chair.; Scott E. Santi, Pres. and C.E.O.; Ronald D. Kropp, Sr. V.P. and C.F.O.; Maria C. Green, Jr., Sr. V.P., Genl. Counsel, and Secy.; Sharon M. Brady, Sr. V.P., Human Resources
Board of directors: Robert S. Morrison, Chair.; David C. Parry, Vice-Chair.; Daniel J. Brutto; Susan Crown; Don H. Davis, Jr.; James W. Griffith; Robert C. McCormack; E. Scott Santi; James A. Skinner; David B. Smith, Jr.; Pamela B. Strobel; Kevin M. Warren; Anre D. Williams
Subsidiaries: Hobart Brothers Co., Troy, OH; Hobart Corporation, Troy, OH
Plants: Fresno, CA; Colorado Springs, CO; Waterbury, CT; Pompano Beach, FL; Frankfort, Wood Dale, IL; Michigan City, IN; Guthrie Center, IA; Russellville, KY; Sparrows Point, MD; Danvers, MA; Ferndale, MI; Alexandria, MN; Pontotoc, MS; Piscataway, NJ; Orangeburg, NY; Zebulon, NC; Tipp City, OH; Montgomeryville, PA; Mount Pleasant, TN; Seguin, TX; Lynchburg, VA; Weirton, WV; Plymouth, WI
International operations: Argentina; Australia; Austria; Belgium; Bermuda; Brazil; British Virgin Islands; Bulgaria; Canada; Cayman Islands; Chile; China; Colombia; Costa Rica; Croatia; Czech Republic; Denmark; Ecuador; Estonia; Finland; France; Germany; Guatemala; Hong Kong; Hungary; India; Indonesia; Ireland; Italy; Jamaica; Japan; Kenya; Liechtenstein; Luxembourg; Malawi; Malaysia; Malta; Mauritius; Mexico; Morocco and the Western Sahara; Netherlands; Netherlands Antilles; New Zealand; Norway; Philippines; Poland; Portugal; Russia; Singapore; Slovakia; Slovenia; South Africa; South Korea; Spain; Sweden; Switzerland; Taiwan; Thailand; Turkey; United Arab Emirates; United Kingdom
Historic mergers: Premark International, Inc. (November 23, 1999)
Giving statement: Giving through the Illinois Tool Works Foundation.
Company EIN: 361258310

Illinois Tool Works Foundation

3600 W. Lake Ave.
Glenview, IL 60025-5811 (847) 724-7500
FAX: (847) 657-4505; URL: http://www.itw.com/social-responsibility/community-relations/itw-foundation/

Establishment information: Incorporated in 1954 in IL.
Donor: Illinois Tool Works Inc.
Contact: Rosemary Keefe, Secy. and Dir. of Community Rels.
Financial data (yr. ended 12/31/11): Assets, $24,470,858 (M); gifts received, $30,038,534; expenditures, $36,266,852; qualifying distributions, $36,223,303; giving activities include $22,483,495 for 254 grants (high: $6,369,909; low: $75) and $13,692,830 for 13,759 employee matching gifts.
Purpose and activities: The foundation supports organizations involved with arts and culture, education, the environment, health, human services, and youth.
Fields of interest: Media, radio; Museums (history); Museums (science/technology); Planetarium; Performing arts; Performing arts, ballet; Performing arts, orchestras; Arts; Elementary/secondary education; Higher education; Business school/education; Education; Botanical gardens; Environment, beautification programs; Environment; Aquariums; Hospitals (general); Health care, clinics/centers; Health care; Food banks; Boys & girls clubs; Youth development, business; American Red Cross; YM/YWCAs & YM/YWHAs; Residential/custodial care, hospices; Human services; United Ways and Federated Giving Programs; Science Youth.
Programs:
Employee Matching Gifts: The foundation matches contributions made by full-time employees, retirees, and directors of ITW to nonprofit organizations on a three-for-one, up to $5,000 in donations for a total of $15,000 match per person.
ITW Scholarships: The foundation awards scholarships to children of ITW employees for post-secondary education. The program is administered by the National Merit Scholarship Corporation and Scholarship America.
Type of support: Annual campaigns; Building/renovation; Capital campaigns; Continuing support; Employee matching gifts; Employee-related scholarships; General/operating support; Program development; Scholarship funds.
Geographic limitations: Giving primarily in areas of company operations, with emphasis on Chicago, IL; giving also to national organizations.
Support limitations: No support for political organizations or candidates or religious organizations. No grants to individuals (except for employee-related scholarships), or for endowments or research; no loans.
Publications: Application guidelines; Corporate giving report.
Application information: Applications accepted. Preference is given to nonprofit organizations that have an established relationship with an ITW employee or business unit. Application form required. Applicants should submit the following:
1) copy of IRS Determination Letter
2) detailed description of project and amount of funding requested
Initial approach: Complete online application
Board meeting date(s): May and Dec.
Deadline(s): None
Officers and Directors: Sharon M. Brady, Pres.; Rosemary Keefe, Secy. and Dir. of Community Rels.; Leanne Ono, Treas.; Maria C. Green; David C. Parry; Ernest Scott Santi; David B. Speer.
Number of staff: 1 full-time support.
EIN: 366087160
Selected grants: The following grants are a representative sample of this grantmaker's funding activity:
$5,524,085 to United Way of Metropolitan Chicago, Chicago, IL, 2011. For general support.
$850,000 to University of Illinois at Chicago, Chicago, IL, 2011. For general support.
$570,900 to Scholarship America, Saint Peter, MN, 2011. For general support.
$262,415 to National Merit Scholarship Corporation, Evanston, IL, 2011. For general support.
$200,000 to Adler Planetarium, Chicago, IL, 2011. For general support.
$200,000 to Childrens Memorial Foundation, Chicago, IL, 2011. For general support.
$60,000 to Scott and White Memorial Hospital, Temple, TX, 2011. For general support.
$25,000 to Teach for America, Chicago, IL, 2011. For general support.
$25,000 to United Way Fox Cities, Menasha, WI, 2011. For general support.
$10,000 to Hubbard Street Dance Chicago, Chicago, IL, 2011. For general support.

1917
The IMA Financial Group, Inc.

(formerly Insurance Management Associates, Inc.)
8200 E. 32nd St. N., Ste. 100
P.O. Box 2992
Wichita, KS 67226-2606 (316) 266-6574

Company URL: http://www.imacorp.com
Establishment information: Established in 1974.
Company type: Private company
Business activities: Sells insurance.

Business type (SIC): Insurance agents, brokers, and services
Financial profile for 2010: Number of employees, 15
Corporate officers: Robert L. Cohen, Chair. and C.E.O.; Kurt D. Watson, Pres. and C.O.O.
Board of directors: Robert L. Cohen, Chair.; Stephen Patrick Ashcraft; William C. Cohen, Jr.; Gregory Georgieff; Stephen G. McConahey; Bob Reiter; SueAnn Schultz; David L. Strohm; Kurt D. Watson
Subsidiaries: Esix, Atlanta, GA; IMA of Colorado Inc., Denver, CO; IMA of Topeka Inc., Topeka, KS; IMA of Wichita Inc., Wichita, KS; Risk Management Associates Inc., Wichita, KS
Giving statement: Giving through the Insurance Management Associates Foundation.

Insurance Management Associates Foundation

(also known as IMA Foundation)
8200 E. 32nd St., N
Wichita, KS 67226-2606
E-mail: foundation@imacorp.com; Application address: 1150 17th Street, Ste. 600, Denver, CO 80202; URL: http://www.imacorp.com/about/community

Donors: The IMA Financial Group Inc.; Insurance Management Associates, Inc.
Contact: Ruth Rohs, Exec. Dir.
Financial data (yr. ended 12/31/11): Assets, $1,717,643 (M); gifts received, $192,000; expenditures, $255,392; qualifying distributions, $247,239; giving activities include $247,239 for grants.
Purpose and activities: The foundation supports programs designed to advance youth; promote arts and culture; enhance economic vitality; and promote health and wellness.
Fields of interest: Museums (art); Arts; Hospitals (general); Health care; Boy scouts; Children/youth, services; Aging, centers/services; Human services; Community/economic development; United Ways and Federated Giving Programs Youth.
Type of support: Capital campaigns; General/operating support; Program development; Scholarship funds.
Geographic limitations: Giving primarily in areas of company operations in Denver, CO, Kansas City, Topeka, and Wichita, KS, and Dallas TX.
Support limitations: No support for fiscal agents or sponsors. No grants to individuals.
Publications: Application guidelines.
Application information: Applications accepted. Organizations applying for capital support must contact the IMA Foundation staff in advance. Application form required. Applicants should submit the following:
1) role played by volunteers
2) qualifications of key personnel
3) population served
4) copy of IRS Determination Letter
5) brief history of organization and description of its mission
6) copy of most recent annual report/audited financial statement/990
7) how project's results will be evaluated or measured
8) listing of board of directors, trustees, officers and other key people and their affiliations
9) detailed description of project and amount of funding requested
10) plans for cooperation with other organizations, if any
11) copy of current year's organizational budget and/or project budget
12) listing of additional sources and amount of support
Initial approach: Download application form and e-mail or mail proposal and application form to application address
Deadline(s): Apr. 1 and Oct. 1
Officer and Trustees: Ruth Rohs, Exec. Dir.; Anita Bourke; Robert L. Cohen; William C. Cohen, Jr.; Robert Reiter; Kurt D. Watson.
EIN: 237432160
Selected grants: The following grants are a representative sample of this grantmaker's funding activity:
$21,623 to United Way of the Plains, Wichita, KS, 2010.
$12,296 to University of Colorado Hospital Foundation, Aurora, CO, 2010.
$10,000 to Boy Scouts of America, Denver Area Council, Denver, CO, 2010.
$8,750 to Wichita Art Museum, Wichita, KS, 2010.
$7,500 to Wichita Educational Foundation, Wichita, KS, 2010.
$7,150 to National Sports Center for the Disabled, Denver, CO, 2010.
$5,000 to Food Bank of the Rockies, Denver, CO, 2010.
$5,000 to Rainbows United, Wichita, KS, 2010.
$4,800 to Arlington Life Shelter, Arlington, TX, 2010.
$2,500 to Judis House, Denver, CO, 2010.

1918
Imagineers, LLC

635 Farmington Ave.
Hartford, CT 06105-2901 (860) 768-3300

Company URL: http://www.imagineersllc.com
Establishment information: Established in 1973.
Company type: Private company
Business activities: Operates real estate agency.
Business type (SIC): Real estate agents and managers
Corporate officers: Jim Allman, C.F.O.; Patti Sebring, Cont.
Board of director: Arthur T. Anderson
Giving statement: Giving through the Imagineers Foundation, Inc.

The Imagineers Foundation, Inc.

c/o Foundation Source
501 Silverside Rd.
Wilmington, DE 19809-1377

Establishment information: Established in 2004 in DE.
Donors: Vincent J. Dowling, Jr.; Imagineers, LLC; Imagineers Property Mgmt., LLC.
Financial data (yr. ended 12/31/11): Assets, $72,539 (M); gifts received, $17,500; expenditures, $136,927; qualifying distributions, $133,950; giving activities include $133,950 for grants.
Fields of interest: Arts; Education.
Geographic limitations: Giving primarily in CT.
Support limitations: No grants to individuals.
Application information: Applications not accepted. Unsolicited requests for funds not accepted.
Officers and Directors:* Vincent J. Dowling, Jr.*, Pres. and Secy.; Kenneth Schultz, V.P.; Caroline D. Klotz.
EIN: 200856784

1919
Imation Corp.

1 Imation way
Oakdale, MN 55128-3414 (651) 704-4000
FAX: (651) 704-6692

Company URL: http://www.imation.com
Establishment information: Established in 1996.
Company type: Public company
Company ticker symbol and exchange: IMN/NYSE
Business activities: Develops, manufactures, provides, and markets magnetic and optical removable data storage products and services; provides computer hardware field services; sells document imaging consumables and computer hardware systems wholesale.
Business type (SIC): Electrical equipment and supplies; professional and commercial equipment —wholesale; computer services
Financial profile for 2012: Number of employees, 1,230; assets, $793,500,000; sales volume, $1,099,600,000; pre-tax net income, -$341,100,000; expenses, $1,435,700,000; liabilities, $393,100,000
Corporate officers: L. White Matthews, Chair.; Mark E. Lucas, Pres. and C.E.O.; Paul R. Zeller, Sr. V.P. and C.F.O.; John P. Breedlove, V.P., Genl. Counsel, and Corp. Secy.; Scott J. Robinson, V.P., Corp. Cont., and C.A.O.; Patricia Hamm, V.P., Human Resources
Board of directors: L. White Matthews III, Chair.; David P. Berg; Theodore Bunting, Jr.; William LaPerch; Mark E. Lucas; Trudy A. Rautio; David B. Stevens
International operations: Argentina; Canada; Colombia; Ireland; Netherlands; Poland; Singapore; Thailand; United Arab Emirates; United Kingdom
Giving statement: Giving through the Imation Corp. Contributions Program.
Company EIN: 411838504

Imation Corp. Contributions Program

c/o Imation Community Affairs
1 Imation Pl.
Oakdale, MN 55128-3414 (651) 704-3280
FAX: (651) 704-7029; URL: http://www.imationcorp.com/en-US/About-Imation/Corporate-Responsibility/

Contact: Tonnja Magee
Purpose and activities: Imation makes charitable contributions to nonprofit organizations involved with arts and culture, education, and human services. Support is given primarily in Camarillo and Cerritos, California, Westin, Florida, Minneapolis and St. Paul, Minnesota, Southaven, Missouri, Wahpeton, North Dakota, and Weatherford, Oklahoma.
Fields of interest: Arts; Elementary/secondary education; Business school/education; Education; Employment; Food services; Youth, services; Human services; United Ways and Federated Giving Programs; Economics Economically disadvantaged.
Type of support: Annual campaigns; Employee volunteer services; General/operating support; Loaned talent; Sponsorships.
Geographic limitations: Giving primarily in Camarillo and Cerritos, CA, Weston, FL, Minneapolis and St. Paul, MN, Southaven, MS, Wahpeton, ND, and Weatherford, OK; giving on a national basis for scholarships.
Support limitations: No support for political, lobbying, or religious organizations. No grants to individuals, or for loans or investments, endowments, capital campaigns, fundraising, or industry, trade, or professional association memberships.

Publications: Application guidelines.
Application information: Applications accepted. The Community Affairs and Contributions Program handles giving. Application form not required. Events and sponsorships will be considered only if Imation has a strong representation of employee participation and/or a current employee is on the board of directors of the organization.
Initial approach: E-mail, fax, or mail letter of inquiry to headquarters

1920
IMC Financial Markets Chicago

233 South Wacker Dr., Ste. 4300
Chicago, IL 60606 (312) 244-3324
FAX: (312) 244-3301

Company URL: http://www.imc-chicago.com/Financial-markets/Offices/Chicago/
Establishment information: Established in 2000.
Company type: Private company
Business activities: Operates proprietary trading firm.
Business type (SIC): Investors/miscellaneous; investment offices
Corporate officers: Robert H. Defares, Co-C.E.O.; Wiet H.M. Pot, Co-C.E.O.; Osias S. Lilian, C.F.O.
Giving statement: Giving through the IMC Chicago Charitable Foundation.

IMC Chicago Charitable Foundation

233 S. Wacker Dr., Ste. 4300
Chicago, IL 60606
E-mail: lisa.wiersma@imc-charity.org; URL: http://www.imc-chicago.com/Financial-markets/Offices/Chicago/Social-commitment/

Establishment information: Established in 2007.
Financial data (yr. ended 12/31/11): Assets, $1,914,220 (M); gifts received, $945,391; expenditures, $206,373; qualifying distributions, $162,232; giving activities include $162,232 for grants.
Purpose and activities: The foundation supports programs that enrich educational opportunities for students in Chicago public schools. Special emphasis is directed toward programs that promote college readiness, STEM education, and broadening student horizons.
Fields of interest: Education, public education; Elementary school/education Children/youth.
Type of support: Employee volunteer services; General/operating support; Scholarship funds.
Geographic limitations: Giving limited to Chicago, Il.
Support limitations: No support for political organizations. No grants to individuals.
Application information: Applications not accepted. Unsolicited requests for funds not accepted.
Officers and Directors:* Emir Al-Rawi*, Pres.; Khalid Tahiri, Treas.; Andrew Larsen; Carrie O'Brien.
EIN: 261416954

1921
Impact Makers, Inc.

2922 W. Marshall St.
Richmond, VA 23230 (804) 332-6383

Company URL: http://www.impactmakers.org
Establishment information: Established in 2006.
Company type: Private company
Business activities: Operates a professional services consulting company providing information technology and management support for the healthcare industry.
Business type (SIC): Computer services
Corporate officers: Michael I. Pirron, C.E.O.; Carl Miller, Pres.
Board of directors: Michael S. Cousins, Ph.D.; Jeffery S. Cribbs, Sr.; Josh Dare; Nancy K. Eberhardt; David I. Greenberg; Stan A. Maupin; J. Robert Mooney; Michael I. Pirron; Jill Sumner; Robert L. Thalhimer; Marianne Vermeer; David P. Wade
Giving statement: Giving through the Impact Makers, Inc. Corporate Giving Program.

Impact Makers, Inc. Corporate Giving Program

2922 West Marshall St.
Richmond, VA 23230-4811 (804) 212-5056
E-mail: info@impactmakers.org; URL: http://impactmakers.org/community-impact

Purpose and activities: Impact Makers is a certified B Corporation that donates a percentage of profits to local, nonprofit, community organizations. Support is limited to areas of company operations in Virginia.
Fields of interest: Health care, insurance; Health care.
Type of support: General/operating support.
Geographic limitations: Giving limited to areas of company operations in VA.
Support limitations: No support for political or religious organizations. No grants to individuals.

1922
Imperial Sugar Company

(formerly Imperial Holly Corporation)
1 Imperial Sq., 8016 Hwy. 90-A
P.O. Box 9
Sugar Land, TX 77487 (281) 491-9181
FAX: (281) 490-9530

Company URL: http://www.imperialsugar.com
Establishment information: Established in 1843.
Company type: Public company
Company ticker symbol and exchange: IPSU/NASDAQ
Business activities: Refines and markets sugar.
Business type (SIC): Sugar, candy, and salted/roasted nut production
Financial profile for 2011: Number of employees, 530; assets, $490,420,000; sales volume, $847,980,000; pre-tax net income, -$58,890,000; expenses, $898,140,000; liabilities, $328,970,000
Corporate officers: James J. Gaffney, Chair.; John C. Sheptor, Pres. and C.E.O.; Harold P. Mechler, Sr. V.P. and C.F.O.; Louis T. Bolognini, Sr. V.P., Genl. Counsel, and Secy.
Board of directors: James J. Gaffney, Chair.; Gaylord O. Coan; Ronald C. Kesselman; David C. Moran; John C. Sheptor; John E. Stokely; John K. Sweeney
Subsidiary: Savannah Foods & Industries, Inc., Savannah, GA
Giving statement: Giving through the Imperial Sugar Company Contributions Program.
Company EIN: 740704500

Imperial Sugar Company Contributions Program

(formerly Imperial Holly Corporation Contributions Program)
8016 Hwy. 90A
P.O. Box 9
Sugar Land, TX 77478-2961
E-mail: DonationRequests@ImperialSugar.com

Purpose and activities: Imperial Sugar makes charitable contributions to nonprofit organizations involved with children and youth and health care. Support is given primarily in areas of company operations in Port Wentworth, Georgia, Gramercy, Louisiana, and Sugar Land, Texas.
Fields of interest: Museums (children's); Performing arts, music ensembles/groups; Elementary/secondary education; Health care Children/youth.
Type of support: Donated products; Employee volunteer services; General/operating support.
Geographic limitations: Giving primarily in areas of company operations in Port Wentworth, GA, Gramercy, LA, and Sugar Land, TX.
Application information: Applications accepted.
Initial approach: E-mail headquarters for product donations

1923
IMRA America, Inc.

1044 Woodridge Ave.
Ann Arbor, MI 48105 (734) 930-2594
FAX: (734) 930-9957

Company URL: http://www.imra.com/
Establishment information: Established in 1990.
Company type: Subsidiary of a foreign company
Business activities: Operates ultrafast fiber laser company.
Business type (SIC): Research, development, and testing services
Financial profile for 2010: Number of employees, 55
Corporate officers: Takashi Omitsu, Pres.; Makoto Yoshida, Secy.
Giving statement: Giving through the IMRA America, Inc. Contributions Program.

IMRA America, Inc. Contributions Program

1044 Woodridge Ave.
Ann Arbor, MI 48105-9748 (734) 930-2560
URL: http://www.imra.com/

Purpose and activities: IMRA America makes charitable contributions to nonprofit organizations on a case by case basis. Support is given on a national and international basis.
Fields of interest: General charitable giving.
Type of support: General/operating support.
Geographic limitations: Giving on a national and international basis.

1924
IMS Health Incorporated

901 Main Ave., Ste. 612
Norwalk, CT 06851-1187 (203) 845-5200

Company URL: http://www.imshealth.com
Establishment information: Established in 1954.
Company type: Private company

Business activities: Provides market intelligence to the pharmaceutical and healthcare industries.
Business type (SIC): Computer services; research, development, and testing services
Corporate officers: Ari Bousbib, Chair. and C.E.O.; Ronald Bruehlman, Sr. V.P. and C.F.O.; Harvey A. Ashman, Sr. V.P. and Genl. Counsel; Sati Sian, Sr. V.P., Opers.; Paul Thomson, Sr. V.P., Human Resources, and Admin.; Harshan Bhangdia, V.P. and Cont.; Thomas Kinsley, V.P., Finance; Betty Nelson, V.P., Mktg.
Board of director: Ari Bousbib, Chair.
International operations: Canada; Germany; Gibraltar; Hong Kong; Israel; Japan; Philippines; Singapore; Taiwan; United Kingdom
Giving statement: Giving through the IMS Health Incorporated Corporate Giving Program.
Company EIN: 061506026

IMS Health Incorporated Corporate Giving Program

83 Wooster Heights Rd.
Danbury, CT 06810 (203) 448-4600
URL: http://www.imshealth.com

Purpose and activities: IMS Health makes charitable contributions to organizations involved with global health, including cancer prevention, treatment, and research. Support is given primarily in areas of company operations.
Fields of interest: Higher education; Health care; Cancer; Medical research, fund raising/fund distribution; Cancer research; Safety/disasters.
Type of support: Consulting services; Employee matching gifts; Employee volunteer services; General/operating support; In-kind gifts; Pro bono services - medical.
Geographic limitations: Giving primarily in Support is given primarily in areas of company.

1925
Independence Bank

Independence Sq.
2425 Frederica St.
Owensboro, KY 42301 (270) 686-1776

Company URL: http://www.1776bank.com
Establishment information: Established in 1909.
Company type: Private company
Business activities: Operates state commercial bank.
Business type (SIC): Banks/commercial
Corporate officers: Christopher Reid, Pres.; Janet Reid, C.O.O.; Cathy R. Switzer, C.F.O.
Giving statement: Giving through the Independence Foundation, Inc.

Independence Foundation, Inc.

2425 Frederica St.
P.O. Box 988
Owensboro, KY 42302 (270) 686-1776
Additional Contact: Lauren Patton, Charitable Trust Mgr., Independence Fdn., 425 E. 18th St., Owensboro, KY 42301, tel.: (270) 684-3630, e-mail: lpatton@1776bank.com

Contact: Chris Reid
Financial data (yr. ended 12/31/11): Assets, $52,291 (M); gifts received, $331,372; expenditures, $316,003; qualifying distributions, $316,003; giving activities include $316,003 for 325+ grants (high: $25,000; low: $25).
Purpose and activities: The foundation supports service clubs and organizations involved with education, cancer, housing development, recreation, youth, and community development; provides relief grants to employees of Independence Bank; and awards college scholarships to high school seniors from a seven county area.
Fields of interest: Elementary school/education; Secondary school/education; Higher education; Education; Cancer; Agriculture; Housing/shelter, development; Athletics/sports, amateur leagues; Recreation; Boys & girls clubs; Youth, services; Community development, service clubs; Community/economic development.
Type of support: Emergency funds; Equipment; General/operating support; Grants to individuals; Program development; Scholarship funds; Scholarships—to individuals; Sponsorships.
Geographic limitations: Giving primarily in areas of company operations in KY, with emphasis on Daviess, Hancock, Henderson, McLean, McCracken, Warren, and Webster counties.
Application information: Applications accepted. Relief grants are limited to employees of Independence Bank. Employees must have been on the job for 12 months to apply. Application form required.
Scholarship applications must include transcripts, SAT/ACT scores, and essay. Personal interviews may be required for scholarship finalists.
Initial approach: Letter of inquiry
Deadline(s): 20th of each month for general funding; Feb. 15 for scholarships
Directors: Marjorie A. Reid; Christopher Reid; Maurice E. Reisz.
EIN: 261568393

1926
Independence Blue Cross

1901 Market St.
Philadelphia, PA 19103-1480
(215) 241-2920

Company URL: http://www.ibx.com
Establishment information: Established in 1938.
Company type: Private company
Business activities: Operates health insurance company.
Business type (SIC): Insurance/accident and health
Financial profile for 2011: Number of employees, 6,987; assets, $5,346,985,000; sales volume, $9,211,537,000; pre-tax net income, $488,970,000; liabilities, $3,098,568,000
Corporate officers: M. Walter D'Alessio, Chair.; Joseph A. Frick, Vice-Chair.; Charles P. Pizzi, Vice-Chair.; Daniel J. Hilferty, Pres. and C.E.O.
Board of directors: M. Walter D'Alessio, Chair.; Joseph A. Frick, Vice-Chair.; Charles P. Pizzi, Vice-Chair.; Joseph A. Barilotti; Robert W. Bogle; Debra L. Brady; Christopher D. Butler; Edward S. Cooper, M.D.; Edward Coryell; A. Bruce Crawley; Nicholas DeBenedictis; Patrick J. Eiding; Patrick D. Finley; Vail P. Garvin; Patrick B. Gillespie; Nicholas A. Giordano; Hon. James F. Kenney; Anne Kelly King; Thomas A. Leonard, Esq.; Andrew L. Lewis IV; Michael D. Marino, Esq.; J. William Mills III; Alan Paul Novak, Esq.; Denis P. O'Brien; Thomas G. Paese, Esq.; Michael V. Puppio, Jr., Esq.; William R. Sautter; James C. Schwartzman, Esq.; Robert W. Sorrell
Giving statement: Giving through the Independence Blue Cross Foundation.

Independence Blue Cross Foundation

1901 Market St.
Philadelphia, PA 19103-1400 (855) 422-3386
URL: http://www.ibxfoundation.org/

Donor: Independence Blue Cross.
Financial data (yr. ended 12/31/11): Assets, $41,869,017 (M); gifts received, $35,000,000; expenditures, $3,284,579; qualifying distributions, $3,284,579; giving activities include $3,283,095 for 58 grants (high: $226,354; low: $2,856).
Geographic limitations: Giving limited to Bucks, Chester, Delaware, Montgomery, and Philadelphia counties, PA.
Support limitations: No support for political causes, candidates, organizations, or capital campaigns;. No grants to individuals or for endowments, award dinners, fund-raising events, capital construction, conferences, seminars, trips or camps.
Application information: Application guidelines available on foundation web site.
Officers and Directors:* Patrick B. Gillespie*, Chair.; Lorina L. Marshall-Blake, Pres.; Lilton R. Taliaferro, Jr., Esq., Secy.; Alan Krigstein, Treas.; Chistopher Cashman; Joan Hilferty; Plato A. Marinakos; Paul A. Tufano, Esq.; I. Steven Udvarhelyi, M.D.
EIN: 364685801

1927
Independent Bank Corp.

288 Union St.
Rockland, MA 02370 (781) 878-6100

Company URL: http://www.rocklandtrust.com/
Establishment information: Established in 1907.
Company type: Public company
Company ticker symbol and exchange: INDB/ NASDAQ
Business activities: Operates bank holding company and provides investment management services.
Business type (SIC): Banks/commercial
Financial profile for 2012: Number of employees, 998; assets, $5,756,980,000; pre-tax net income, $57,300,000; liabilities, $5,227,660,000
Corporate officers: Donna L. Abelli, Chair.; Christopher Oddleifson, Pres. and C.E.O.; Denis K. Sheahan, C.F.O.; David B. Smith, Sr. V.P. and C.I.O.; Robert D. Cozzone, Sr. V.P. and Treas.; Barry H. Jensen, Sr. V.P. and Cont.; Edward H. Seksay, Genl. Counsel and Corp. Secy.
Board of directors: Donna L. Abelli, Chair.; Richard S. Anderson; William P. Bissonnette; Benjamin A. Gilmore II; Kevin J. Jones; Eileen C. Miskell; John J. Morrissey; Christopher Oddleifson; Daniel F. O'Brien; Carl Ribeiro; Richard H. Sgarzi; John H. Spurr, Jr.; Robert D. Sullivan; Brian S. Tedeschi; Thomas R. Venables
Giving statement: Giving through the Rockland Trust Charitable Foundation.
Company EIN: 042870273

Rockland Trust Charitable Foundation

(formerly Benjamin Franklin Bank Charitable Foundation)
288 Union St.
Rockland, MA 02370 (781) 982-6637
E-mail: Jeanne.Travers@RocklandTrust.com; URL: http://www.rocklandtrust.com/community-focus/rockland-trust-charitable-foundation.aspx

Establishment information: Established in 2005 in MA.

Donor: Benjamin Franklin Bancorp, Inc.
Contact: Jeanne Travers, Clerk
Financial data (yr. ended 12/31/11): Assets, $4,999,842 (M); expenditures, $174,093; qualifying distributions, $158,238; giving activities include $158,238 for grants.
Purpose and activities: The foundation supports organizations involved with performing arts, education, health, human services, and community economic development.
Fields of interest: Performing arts; Secondary school/education; Higher education; Education; Health care; Boy scouts; Youth, services; Family services; Human services; Community/economic development; United Ways and Federated Giving Programs.
Program:
Rockland Trust Charitable Foundation Scholarship Program: The foundation awards a $2,500 scholarship to a graduating senior from Franklin High School, Tri-Country Regional Vocational High School, Bellingham High School, Foxborough High School, Milford High School, Medfield High School, Waltham High School, Newton North High School, Learning Prep School, Blackstone Valley Vocational Regional High School, and a student attending Dean College. The award is based on strong character, community involvement, academic achievement, and financial need.
Type of support: Annual campaigns; Capital campaigns; General/operating support; Program development; Publication; Scholarships—to individuals; Sponsorships.
Geographic limitations: Giving primarily in areas of company operations in Bellingham, Blackstone, Foxboro, Franklin, Hopedale, Medfield, Medway, Mendon, Milford, Millis, Newton, Norfolk, Waltham and Wrentham, MA.
Support limitations: No support for discriminatory organizations, religious organizations, candidates for political office, police or fire organizations, labor or fraternal organizations, or community or school sports teams. No grants to individuals (except for scholarships) or for political or government activities.
Application information: Applications accepted. Support is limited to 1 contribution per organization during any given year. Application form required.
Initial approach: Contact foundation for application form; contact Guidance Department at participating high schools for scholarships
Deadline(s): Varies
Officers and Directors:* Thomas R. Venables*, Pres.; Jeanne L. Travers*, Clerk; Claire Beane, Treas.; Jane Lundquist; Ralph R. Valente; Arthur Viana.
EIN: 202668833
Selected grants: The following grants are a representative sample of this grantmaker's funding activity:
$10,000 to REACH Beyond Domestic Violence, Waltham, MA, 2010.
$10,000 to Waltham Alliance to Create Housing, Waltham, MA, 2010.
$5,000 to Women of Means, Wellesley, MA, 2010.
$4,000 to Project Smile, Hopedale, MA, 2010.
$2,500 to Dean College, Franklin, MA, 2010. For scholarship.
$2,500 to Milford Regional Healthcare Foundation, Milford, MA, 2010.
$2,500 to REACH Beyond Domestic Violence, Waltham, MA, 2010.
$2,500 to Women of Means, Wellesley, MA, 2010.
$2,000 to Home for Little Wanderers, Boston, MA, 2010.
$1,500 to Alternatives Unlimited, Whitinsville, MA, 2010.

1928
Independent Stave Company, Inc.

1078 S. Jefferson Ave.
P.O. Box 104
Lebanon, MO 65536 (417) 588-4151
FAX: (417) 588-3344

Company URL: http://www.americanstavecompany.com/about_asc.html
Establishment information: Established in 1912.
Company type: Subsidiary of a private company
Business activities: Manufactures wood-crafted products and kitchen, bathroom, and household wares.
Business type (SIC): Wood containers; wood products/miscellaneous; shopping goods stores/miscellaneous
Financial profile for 2010: Number of employees, 1,000
Corporate officers: John J. Boswell, Chair. and C.E.O.; Brad Boswell, Pres.; Paul Walker, C.F.O. and Secy.-Treas.
Board of director: John J. Boswell, Chair.
Giving statement: Giving through the Boswell Foundation, Inc.

The Boswell Foundation, Inc.

1078 S. Jefferson
Lebanon, MO 65536-3601 (417) 588-4151

Establishment information: Established in 1985 in MO.
Donors: Independent Stave Co., Inc.; Amie Boswell Foundation; Joe Boswell Foundation; Johnathon Boswell Foundation; Julie Boswell Foundation; The Lois K. Boswell Charitable Lead Trust; ISCO Holding Co., Inc.; LKB Investments, Inc.
Contact: John J. Boswell, Pres.
Financial data (yr. ended 11/30/12): Assets, $43,286 (M); gifts received, $225,000; expenditures, $230,642; qualifying distributions, $223,224; giving activities include $223,224 for 2 grants (high: $203,224; low: $20,000).
Purpose and activities: The foundation supports organizations involved with cancer research and Christianity. Special emphasis is directed toward programs designed to promote education.
Fields of interest: Education; Human services; Religion.
Type of support: General/operating support.
Support limitations: No grants to individuals.
Application information: Applications accepted. Application form required. Applicants should submit the following:
1) copy of IRS Determination Letter
2) brief history of organization and description of its mission
3) detailed description of project and amount of funding requested
Initial approach: Letter
Deadline(s): None
Officer: John J. Boswell, Pres.
Trustee: David Waugh.
EIN: 431409051

1929
Indiana Coated Fabrics, Inc.

102 Enterprise Dr.
P.O. Box 1017
Warsaw, IN 46580-1204 (574) 269-1280
FAX: (574) 269-7747

Company URL: http://www.indianacoatedfabrics.com
Establishment information: Established in 1966.
Company type: Private company
Business activities: Manufactures fabric products.
Business type (SIC): Textile mill products
Corporate officers: William J. Haldewang, Pres.; Tim Foster, Mgr.
Giving statement: Giving through the Haldewang Family Charitable Foundation.

Haldewang Family Charitable Foundation

c/o Harbour Trust
P.O. Box 419
Michigan City, IN 46361-0419 (219) 877-3513

Establishment information: Established in 1996 in IN.
Donors: Indiana Coated Fabrics, Inc.; William J. Haldewang; Mildred M. Haldewang; William A. Haldewang.
Contact: Robert Rose
Financial data (yr. ended 12/31/10): Assets, $280,798 (M); expenditures, $20,499; qualifying distributions, $15,000; giving activities include $15,000 for 4 grants (high: $6,000; low: $1,000).
Purpose and activities: The foundation supports service clubs and organizations involved with medical education, youth development, and youth services.
Fields of interest: Medical school/education; Boy scouts; Youth, services; Community development, service clubs.
Type of support: General/operating support.
Support limitations: No grants to individuals.
Application information: Applications accepted. Application form not required.
Initial approach: Letter
Deadline(s): None
Trustee: Harbour Trust Investment Manangement Fiduciary.
EIN: 352003434

1930
Indiana Knitwear Corporation

230 E. Osage St.
P.O. Box 309
Greenfield, IN 46140-2423 (317) 462-4413
FAX: (317) 462-0994

Establishment information: Established in 1930.
Company type: Private company
Business activities: Manufactures men's, women's, and children's outerwear.
Business type (SIC): Apparel—men's and boys' outerwear
Corporate officers: Eugene Bate, Pres. and C.E.O.; John Kirk, C.I.O.; Alice R. Berkowitz, Secy.
Board of directors: Alice Berkowitz; D. Weirich; Pat Jeffers
Giving statement: Giving through the Leonard and Alice Berkowitz Family Foundation, Inc.

Leonard and Alice Berkowitz Family Foundation, Inc.

3523 E. Carmel Dr.
Carmel, IN 46032-4325 (317) 475-0149

Establishment information: Established in 2004 in IN.
Donors: Indiana Knitwear Corp.; Leonard M. Berkowitz; Alice R. Berkowitz.
Contact: Eugene Bate, Secy.-Treas.
Financial data (yr. ended 12/31/11): Assets, $37,011 (M); gifts received, $65,000; expenditures, $34,053; qualifying distributions, $32,500; giving activities include $32,500 for grants.
Purpose and activities: The foundation supports art museums and organizations involved with Judaism.
Fields of interest: Arts; Religion.
Type of support: General/operating support.
Geographic limitations: Giving primarily in Sarasota, FL and Indianapolis, IN.
Application information: Applications accepted. Application form not required.
Initial approach: Proposal
Deadline(s): None
Officers and Directors:* Alice R. Berkowitz*, Pres.; Eugene Bate, Secy.-Treas.; Patrick Jeffers.
EIN: 202039022

1931
Indiana Plumbing Supply Company, Inc.

(also known as The Plumbers Warehouse)
1161 E. Artesia Blvd.
Carson, CA 90746 (310) 635-6500

Company URL: http://www.eplumbing.com
Establishment information: Established in 1942.
Company type: Subsidiary of a private company
Business activities: Sells plumbing equipment wholesale.
Business type (SIC): Hardware, plumbing, and heating equipment—wholesale
Corporate officer: John Muckel, Pres.
Plants: Carlsbad, Los Angeles, San Gabriel, Santa Ana, Van Nuys, Ventura, CA
Giving statement: Giving through the John and Linda Muckel Foundation.

John and Linda Muckel Foundation

6024 Ocean Terrace Dr.
Rancho Palos Verdes, CA 90275-5755

Establishment information: Established in 1999 in CA.
Donors: Indiana Plumbing Supply Co., Inc.; John Muckel.
Financial data (yr. ended 12/31/11): Assets, $356,878 (M); expenditures, $161,065; qualifying distributions, $160,489; giving activities include $160,489 for 55 grants (high: $54,800; low: $100).
Purpose and activities: The foundation supports organizations involved with historical activities, higher education, animal welfare, human services, and Christianity.
Fields of interest: Historical activities; Higher education; Animal welfare; Homeless, human services; Human services; Christian agencies & churches.
Type of support: General/operating support.
Geographic limitations: Giving primarily in CA, Washington, DC, and VA.
Support limitations: No grants to individuals.
Application information: Applications not accepted. Contributes only to pre-selected organizations.
Officers: John Muckel, Pres.; Linda Muckel, Secy. and C.F.O.
EIN: 330882395
Selected grants: The following grants are a representative sample of this grantmaker's funding activity:
$5,000 to Union Rescue Mission, Los Angeles, CA, 2010.
$4,000 to Yankee Golden Retriever Rescue, Hudson, MA, 2010.
$3,500 to World Vision, Federal Way, WA, 2010.
$3,000 to Bible League, Chicago, IL, 2010.
$3,000 to Within the Walls, Forest, VA, 2010.
$2,000 to Liberty University, Lynchburg, VA, 2010.
$1,550 to Statue of Liberty-Ellis Island Foundation, New York, NY, 2010.
$1,500 to City of Hope, Los Angeles, CA, 2010.
$1,300 to National Park Foundation, Washington, DC, 2010.
$1,000 to YMCA of Metropolitan Los Angeles, Los Angeles, CA, 2010.

1932
Indianapolis Colts, Inc.

7001 W. 56th St.
Indianapolis, IN 46254-9725
(317) 297-2658

Company URL: http://www.colts.com
Establishment information: Established in 1953.
Company type: Private company
Business activities: Operates professional football club.
Business type (SIC): Commercial sports
Corporate officers: Casey Foyt, Vice-Chair.; Carlie Irsay-Gordon, Vice-Chair.; Kalen Irsay, Vice-Chair.; James Irsay, C.E.O.; Pete Ward, C.O.O.; Kurt Humphrey, V.P., Finance; Stacy Johns, Cont.; Dan Emerson, V.P. and Genl. Counsel
Board of directors: Casey Foyt, Vice-Chair.; Carlie Irsay-Gordon, Vice-Chair.; Kalen Irsay, Vice-Chair.
Giving statement: Giving through the Indianapolis Colts, Inc. Corporate Giving Program.

Indianapolis Colts, Inc. Corporate Giving Program

c/o Community Rels. Dept.
P.O. Box 535000
Indianapolis, IN 46253-5000
Contact for Big Blue Football Camps: Phil Andrews, tel.: (317) 808-5322; URL: http://www.colts.com/community/index.html

Purpose and activities: The Indianapolis Colts make charitable contributions to nonprofit organizations on a case by case basis and awards game tickets to nonprofit organizations involved with children. Support is given primarily in Indiana and states lacking an NFL franchise.
Fields of interest: Education, reading; Education; Public health, physical fitness; Nutrition; Athletics/sports, football; Children, services; United Ways and Federated Giving Programs; General charitable giving.
Programs:
Anthem Angels: The Colts, in partnership with Anthem Blue Cross and Blue Shield, honors community members including firefighters, police officers, nurses, emergency medical technicians, social workers, and teachers who have been "First Respondents" in outstanding service to the community through civil or public service. The award includes (4) VIP club seat tickets, a Colts Prize Pack, a gameday parking pass, and feature story with his or her photo on the Colts websites, a feature story in the Colts game-day magazine, and on-field recognition.
Big Blue Football Camps: The Colts, in partnership with Gatorade, conducts free football camps for 2nd to 5th graders at local schools. The program is designed to promote football, education, and recreation in a safe and fun environment.
Coach of the Week: The Colts, in partnership with Anthem Blue Cross Blue Shield, honors outstanding high school coaches for their hard work and success on the field and in the community. Winners receive an on-field ceremony, a certificate signed by the NFL commissioner, and a $2,000 grant for their school's football program.
Colts Fitness Camp: The Colts, in partnership with Riley Hospital for Children, CardioChek, and the Indiana Diary Council, conducts fitness camps for middle school students in grades 6 to 8. The camp teaches kids how to work out and live a healthy lifestyle, and prizes are awarded to the students with the most improvement based on a month-long workout and an essay.
Community Quarterback Award: The Colts honors 25 nominated ticket holders who demonstrate an exceptional commitment to the community through volunteerism.
Indiana Colts Youth Football Fund (ICYFF): Through ICYFF, the Colts awards grants to youth football organizations working with kids ages 12 and under for equipment, referee/coach's training, and/or assistance with player registration fees. The program is designed to support football among youth in the community.
Riley Coin Toss Kids: The Colts, in partnership with Clarian Health, honors pediatric patients from Riley Hospital for Children at home games. The honorees receive 4 game tickets, limousine transportation to and from the game, a Colts/Clarian jersey and hat, and participation in the mid-field ceremonial coin toss with the game's referee and team captains.
Student All Star: The Colts, in partnership with Grange Insurance, awards grants of up to $5,000 to students ages 13 and under to complete a service project in their area. The program is designed to give youth the opportunity to make their community a better place.
Type of support: Building/renovation; Continuing support; Donated products; Equipment; General/operating support; In-kind gifts; Income development.
Geographic limitations: Giving primarily in areas of company operations in IN and to states lacking an NFL franchise.
Support limitations: No grants to individuals or families, or for fundraising for individuals or families.
Publications: Application guidelines.
Application information: Applications accepted. Proposals should be submitted using organization letterhead. Support is limited to 1 contribution per organization during any given year. Multi-year donations are not automatic. The Community Relations Department handles giving. Application form required. Applicants should submit the following:
1) name, address and phone number of organization
2) contact person
3) additional materials/documentation
Proposals for game ticket donations should indicate the number of tickets needed and any special needs requirements.
Initial approach: Download application form and mail proposal and application form to headquarters for player appearances, grants, memorabilia, and ticket donations; visit

website for application information for Student All Star, camps, and ICYFF
Copies of proposal: 1
Deadline(s): 8 weeks prior to need for player appearances; 6 weeks prior to need for grants and memorabilia; July 31 for ticket donations
Final notification: 6 weeks

1933
Indium Corporation of America

34 Robinson Rd.
Clinton, NY 13323-1419 (315) 853-4900
FAX: (315) 853-1000

Company URL: http://www.indium.com
Establishment information: Established in 1934.
Company type: Private company
Business activities: Manufactures specialty alloys and solders.
Business type (SIC): Metal rolling and drawing/nonferrous
Corporate officers: William N. Macartney III, Chair.; Gregory P. Evans, Pres.; Les Schenk, C.F.O.; James A. Slattery, V.P.
Board of director: William N. Macartney III, Chair.
Giving statement: Giving through the B11 Foundation, Inc.

B11 Foundation, Inc.

114 Business Park Dr.
Utica, NY 13502-6302

Establishment information: Established in 2005 in NY.
Donor: Indium Corporation.
Financial data (yr. ended 12/31/11): Assets, $2,982,183 (M); expenditures, $175,969; qualifying distributions, $155,000; giving activities include $155,000 for grants.
Fields of interest: Education; Housing/shelter; Human services.
Support limitations: No grants to individuals.
Application information: Applications not accepted. Unsolicited requests for funds not accepted.
Officers and Directors:* William N. Macartney III*, Pres.; Gregory P. Evans, 1st V.P.; Elizabeth S. Macartney-Mitchell, 2nd V.P.; Linda D. Macartney*, Secy.; Justin Weiler*, Treas.; Melanie Macartney; William N. Macartney IV*; James R. Mitchell; Kelle Wallace; Jamie Weiler.
EIN: 202017908

1934
Indus Capital Partners, LLC

152 W. 57th St., 28th Fl.
New York, NY 10019-3310 (212) 909-2888

Company URL: http://www.induscap.com
Establishment information: Established in 2000.
Company type: Private company
Business activities: Operates investment firm.
Business type (SIC): Brokers and dealers/security
Corporate officer: James Joseph Weiner, C.F.O.
Giving statement: Giving through the Indus Charitable Foundation, Inc.

Indus Charitable Foundation, Inc.

c/o Indus Capital Partners, LLC
888 7th Ave.
New York, NY 10019-3386

Establishment information: Established in 2007 in NY.
Donor: Indus Capital Partners, LLC.
Financial data (yr. ended 12/31/11): Assets, $782,630 (M); gifts received, $310,661; expenditures, $135,115; qualifying distributions, $135,115; giving activities include $134,350 for 15 grants (high: $25,000; low: $250).
Purpose and activities: The foundation supports organizations involved with Japanese culture, education, the environment, baseball, and human services.
Fields of interest: Arts, cultural/ethnic awareness; Higher education; Education; Environment, air pollution; Environment, water pollution; Environment, water resources; Athletics/sports, baseball; Children/youth, services; Human services.
Type of support: General/operating support.
Geographic limitations: Giving primarily in NY.
Application information: Applications not accepted. Unsolicted requests for funds not accepted.
Officers: Michael Ernest Guarasci, Pres.; Brian Guzman, Secy.; James Joseph Weiner, Treas.
Director: Michael Sippel.
EIN: 261496848
Selected grants: The following grants are a representative sample of this grantmaker's funding activity:
$25,000 to Blacksmith Institute, New York, NY, 2010.
$25,000 to Global Fund for Children, Washington, DC, 2010.
$22,719 to Riverkeeper, Ossining, NY, 2010.
$10,000 to Fabretto Childrens Foundation, Arlington, VA, 2010.
$10,000 to Stamford Public Education Foundation, Stamford, CT, 2010.
$2,500 to City Harvest, New York, NY, 2010.

1935
Industrial Manufacturing Company LLC

(formerly Vesper Corporation)
8223 Brecksville Rd., Ste. 100
Brecksville, OH 44141-1361
(440) 838-4700

Establishment information: Established in 2000.
Company type: Subsidiary of a private company
Business activities: Designs and manufactures lockers, shelves, and cabinets, aircraft parts, and industrial products.
Business type (SIC): Fixtures/office and store; metal coating and plating; machinery/general industry; aircraft and parts
Corporate officers: James Benenson, Jr., Chair. and C.E.O.; Clement C. Benenson, Co-Pres.; James Benenson, Co-Pres.; John V. Curci, C.F.O.
Board of director: James Benenson, Jr., Chair.
Giving statement: Giving through the Vesper Foundation.

Vesper Foundation

8223 Brecksville Rd., #100
Brecksville, OH 44141-3184

Establishment information: Established in 1961 in OH.
Donors: Vesper Corp.; Industrial Manufacturing Co.
Financial data (yr. ended 12/31/11): Assets, $10,809,558 (M); gifts received, $1,900,000; expenditures, $911,422; qualifying distributions, $891,000; giving activities include $891,000 for grants.
Purpose and activities: The foundation supports hospitals and organizations involved with arts and culture, education, the environment, and religion.
Fields of interest: Museums; Performing arts, theater; Arts; Elementary school/education; Secondary school/education; Higher education; Libraries (public); Education; Environment, water resources; Environment, land resources; Botanical gardens; Environment; Hospitals (general); Religion.
Type of support: General/operating support; Scholarship funds.
Geographic limitations: Giving primarily in CT, MA, ME, NY, and OH.
Support limitations: No grants to individuals.
Application information: Applications not accepted. Contributes only to pre-selected organizations.
Trustees: Clement Benenson; James Benenson, Jr.; James Benenson III; John V. Curci.
EIN: 236251198
Selected grants: The following grants are a representative sample of this grantmaker's funding activity:
$615,000 to Tulane University, New Orleans, LA, 2010. For general fund.
$100,300 to New York Botanical Garden, Bronx, NY, 2010. For general fund.
$50,000 to Blue Hill Memorial Hospital, Blue Hill, ME, 2010. For general fund.
$41,000 to American Independence Museum, Exeter, NH, 2010. For general fund.
$27,000 to Hotchkiss School, Lakeville, CT, 2010. For general fund.
$11,000 to Grace Church School, New York, NY, 2010. For general fund.
$10,000 to Blue Hill Heritage Trust, Blue Hill, ME, 2010. For general fund.
$10,000 to Center for Fiction, New York, NY, 2010. For general fund.
$5,000 to Metropolitan Museum of Art, New York, NY, 2010. For general fund.
$2,000 to Island Nursing Home, Deer Isle, ME, 2010. For general fund.

1936
InfoSource, Inc.

1300 City View Ctr.
Oviedo, FL 32765-5530 (407) 796-5200
FAX: (407) 796-5190

Company URL: http://www.infosourcelearning.com/
Establishment information: Established in 1983.
Company type: Joint venture
Business activities: Develops and distributes technology-related training products.
Business type (SIC): Computer services
Corporate officers: Michael Werner, C.E.O.; Thomas W. Warner, Pres.; Tom Dalton, V.P., Sales and Mktg.
Giving statement: Giving through the InfoSource, Inc. Corporate Giving Program.

InfoSource, Inc. Corporate Giving Program

6479 University Blvd.
Winter Park, FL 32792-7404 (800) 393-4636
E-mail: itcgrantprogram@howtomaster.com

Purpose and activities: InfoSource makes charitable contributions of training products to K-12 school districts. Support is given on a national basis.

Fields of interest: Elementary/secondary education.
Program:
InfoSource Integrating Technology in the Classroom Grant Program: Through the InfoSource Integrating Technology in the Classroom Grant Program, InfoSource makes charitable contributions of one-year licenses for student and faculty use of the InfoSource Learn It! Build It! Share It! suite of online tools and technology training to K-12 school districts.
Type of support: Donated products.
Application information: Applications accepted. Organizations receiving support are asked to provide regular feedback. A contributions committee reviews all requests. Application form required.
Initial approach: Complete online application form
Copies of proposal: 1
Deadline(s): Dec. 31

1937
ING Bank, fsb

(also known as ING DIRECT)
1 S. Orange St.
Wilmington, DE 19801-5045
(302) 658-2200

Company URL: http://www.ingdirect.com
Establishment information: Established in 2000.
Company type: Subsidiary of a public company
Business activities: Operates online savings bank.
Business type (SIC): Savings institutions
Financial profile for 2010: Number of employees, 2,352; sales volume, $2,710,000,000
Corporate officers: Arkadi Kuhlmann, Chair. and C.E.O.; Jim Kelly, C.O.O.; John C. Mason, Co-C.I.O. and Treas.; Rudy Wolfs, Co-C.I.O.
Board of director: Arkadi Kuhlmann, Chair.
Office: Minneapolis, MN
Giving statement: Giving through the ING DIRECT Corporate Giving Program and the ING DIRECT KIDS Foundation.

ING DIRECT KIDS Foundation

1 S. Orange St.
Wilmington, DE 19801-5006 (302) 255-3117
E-mail: communityaffairs@ingdirect.com;
URL: http://www.savekidsnow.org

Establishment information: Established in 2001 in DE.
Contact: Peter Aceto, Dir., Community Affairs
Financial data (yr. ended 12/31/11): Revenue, $219,643; assets, $3,567 (M); gifts received, $166,618; expenditures, $714,166; giving activities include $710,982 for grants.
Purpose and activities: The foundation seeks to improve the quality of life of children and adolescents from all walks of life.
Fields of interest: Children/youth, services.
Type of support: Program development.
Geographic limitations: Giving on a national and international basis.
Publications: Newsletter.
Officers and Directors:* Arkadi Kuhlmann*, Chair.; Cathy MacFarlane*, Pres.; Margot Williams*, Secy.; Anthony F. Caruso, Jr.*, Treas.; Peter Aceto; Deneen Stewart; Rick Perles.
EIN: 510409045

1938
ING Life Insurance and Annuity Company

(also known as ING)
1 Orange Way
Windsor, CT 06095-4774 (770) 980-5100

Company URL: http://www.ing-usa.com
Company type: Subsidiary of a foreign company
Business activities: Sells life and health insurance.
Business type (SIC): Insurance/life; insurance/accident and health
Corporate officers: Robert G. Leary, Pres. and C.O.O.; Thomas Mcinerney, C.E.O.; Steven T. Pierson, Sr. V.P. and C.A.O.
Giving statement: Giving through the ING Life Insurance and Annuity Company Contributions Program and the ING Foundation.

ING Life Insurance and Annuity Company Contributions Program

1 Orange Way, A3S
Windsor, CT 06095-4774
FAX: (860) 580-1665;
E-mail: diana.crecco@us.ing.com; Application address for ING Unsung Heroes Awards: ING Unsung Heroes Awards Prog., c/o Scholarship America, Inc., 1 Scholarship Way, P.O. Box 297, St. Peter, MN 56082, tel.: (800) 537-4180, e-mail: ing@scholarshipamerica.org; URL: http://ing.us/about-ing/responsibility

Purpose and activities: ING makes charitable contributions to nonprofit organizations involved with education and awards grants to K-12 educators. Support is given on a national basis.
Fields of interest: Elementary/secondary education; Education.
Program:
ING Unsung Heroes Awards Program: Through the ING Unsung Heroes Awards Program, ING annually awards 100 $2,000 grants to K-12 educators pioneering new methods and techniques that improve student learning. Three top winners are awarded additional grants of $5,000, $10,000, and $25,000, respectively. At least one award will be granted in each of the 50 United States, provided one or more qualified applications are received from each state. Each project is judged by its innovative method, creativity, and ability to positively influence the students. This program is administered by ING and Scholarship America. Questions regarding the program should be directed to Scholarship America at (507) 931-1682.
Type of support: General/operating support; Grants to individuals; In-kind gifts.
Geographic limitations: Giving primarily in areas of company operations.
Publications: Informational brochure; Program policy statement.
Application information: An application form is required for ING Unsung Heroes Awards. Completed applications must be mailed; faxed applications are not accepted. Supplementary materials such as tapes, news articles, and scrapbooks, are not accepted. Previous recipients of ING Unsung Heroes awards are not eligible to apply for another award. Application form required.
Initial approach: Download application form for ING Unsung Heroes Awards
Copies of proposal: 1
Deadline(s): Apr. 30 for ING Unsung Heroes Awards
Final notification: Sept. for ING Unsung Heroes Awards

ING Foundation

(formerly ReliaStar Foundation)
5780 Powers Ferry Rd., N.W.
Atlanta, GA 30327-4390 (770) 980-6580
FAX: (770) 980-3302;
E-mail: ingfoundation@us.ing.com; URL: http://ing.us/about-ing/citizenship

Establishment information: Established in 1990 in MN.
Donors: ReliaStar Financial Corp.; Northern Life Insurance Co.; ReliaStar Bankers Security Life Insurance Co.; ReliaStar United Services Life Insurance Co.; ReliaStar Life Insurance Co.
Contact: Luis Abarca, Jr., Mgr., Community Rels.
Financial data (yr. ended 12/31/10): Assets, $4,602,169 (M); gifts received, $390,000; expenditures, $2,180,773; qualifying distributions, $2,174,911; giving activities include $2,158,166 for 1,559+ grants.
Purpose and activities: The foundation supports programs designed to promote financial literacy, children's education, diversity, and environmental sustainability.
Fields of interest: Elementary/secondary education; Education; Environment, natural resources; Environmental education; Environment; Health care; Girls clubs; Youth development, business; Children/youth, services; Family services; Human services, financial counseling; Human services; Civil/human rights, equal rights; Economic development Children/youth; Minorities; Economically disadvantaged.
Programs:
Children's Education: The foundation supports programs designed to improve education for youth in grades K-12. Special emphasis is directed toward children in underserved areas or facing economic disadvantages.
Diversity: The foundation supports diversity initiatives designed to reflect ING's commitment to equity and fairness in societies around the world.
Employee Matching Gifts: The foundation matches contributions made by employees of ING to nonprofit organizations on a one-for-one basis up to $5,000 per employee, per year.
Environmental Sustainability: The foundations supports responsible business and environmental protection around the globe.
Financial Literacy: The foundation supports programs designed to empower individuals to take control of their financial futures through education, financial literacy, and financial planning. Special emphasis is directed toward the needs of young people and minorities.
ING-Girls Inc. Investment Challenge: The foundation, ING U.S., and Girls Inc. provides practical hands-on investing experience to girls and college scholarships. The program is designed to serve Girls 12-18 who will manage diversified real-time portfolios as part of an integrated investment- and economic-literacy curriculum. Gains realized from their investment portfolios translate into real dollars for their education. The program is limited to Girls Inc. locations in Alameda and Los Angeles, CA, Denver, CO, Atlanta, GA, New York, NY, and New England.
Volunteer Matching Gifts: The foundation awards $500 grants to nonprofit organizations with which employees of ING volunteers at least 50 hours per year.
Type of support: Continuing support; Employee matching gifts; Employee volunteer services; In-kind gifts; Program development; Scholarship funds; Sponsorships.
Geographic limitations: Giving on a national basis in areas of company operations, with emphasis on

CA, CO, CT, DE, FL, GA, MA, MN, NY, PA, and TX; giving also to national organizations.
Support limitations: No support for religious organizations not of direct benefit to the entire community, private foundations, fraternal organizations, social clubs, labor organizations, lobbying or political organizations, sports teams, or discriminatory organizations. No grants to individuals, or for capital campaigns, endowments, general or administrative costs, institutional, civic, or commemorative advertising, fashion shows, pageants, golf tournaments, athletic events, conferences, workshops, or other meetings, travel, benefits, performances, testimonial dinners, or other fundraising activities.
Publications: Annual report (including application guidelines); Corporate giving report; Informational brochure; Newsletter.
Application information: Applications accepted. Requests under $2,500 are not considered. Additional information may be requested at a later date. Support is limited to 1 contribution per organization during any given year. Multi-year funding is not automatic. Organizations receiving support are asked to submit an interim impact report and a final report. Application form required.
Applicants should submit the following:
1) population served
2) copy of IRS Determination Letter
3) geographic area to be served
4) copy of most recent annual report/audited financial statement/990
5) how project's results will be evaluated or measured
6) detailed description of project and amount of funding requested
7) copy of current year's organizational budget and/ or project budget
8) listing of additional sources and amount of support

Initial approach: Complete online application form
Board meeting date(s): Feb., May, Aug., and Nov.
Deadline(s): Feb. 15 and May 15
Final notification: June 15 and Sept. 14

Officers and Directors:* Rodney Martin*, Chair.; Rhoda Mims Simpson*, Pres.; Timothy W. Brown, Secy.; David S. Pendergrass, Treas.; Jeffery Becker; Bridget M. Healy; Alain Karaoglan; Robert G. Leary.
Number of staff: 1 full-time professional; 1 full-time support.
EIN: 411682766
Selected grants: The following grants are a representative sample of this grantmaker's funding activity:
$450,000 to United States Fund for UNICEF, New York, NY, 2010.
$425,000 to Council of Chief State School Officers, Washington, DC, 2010.
$300,000 to Operation Hope, Los Angeles, CA, 2010.
$250,000 to ING Community Fund, Atlanta, GA, 2010.
$50,000 to Executive Leadership Foundation, Alexandria, VA, 2010.
$50,000 to Robert W. Woodruff Arts Center, Atlanta, GA, 2010.
$35,000 to Aspen Institute, Washington, DC, 2010.
$30,000 to Bridge Family Center, West Hartford, CT, 2010.
$25,000 to Food and Friends, Washington, DC, 2010.
$15,000 to University of Pennsylvania, Philadelphia, PA, 2010.

1939
Ingersoll-Rand Company

(also known as Ingersoll-Rand International Holding Corp.)
155 Chestnut Ridge Rd.
P.O. Box 0445
Montvale, NJ 07645-1115 (201) 573-3233

Company URL: http://www.ingersollrand.com
Establishment information: Established in 1871.
Company type: Subsidiary of a foreign company
International Securities Identification Number: IE00B6330302
Business activities: Designs, manufactures, sells, and services climate control technologies, compact vehicle technologies, construction technologies, industrial technologies, and security technologies.
Business type (SIC): Machinery/refrigeration and service industry; cutlery, hand and edge tools, and hardware; machinery/construction, mining, and materials handling; machinery/general industry
Financial profile for 2012: Assets, $18,500,000,000; sales volume, $14,000,000,000
Forbes 2000 ranking: 2012—688th in sales, 596th in profits, and 1020th in assets
Corporate officer: Michael W. Lamach, Chair. and C.E.O.
Board of director: Michael W. Lamach, Chair.
Subsidiary: Trane Inc., Piscataway, NJ
Giving statement: Giving through the Ingersoll-Rand Charitable Foundation.

Ingersoll-Rand Charitable Foundation

1 Centennial Ave.
Piscataway, NJ 08854-3921

Establishment information: Established in 2004 in DE.
Donor: Ingersoll-Rand Co.
Financial data (yr. ended 12/31/11): Assets, $627,843 (M); gifts received, $3,036,033; expenditures, $3,362,014; qualifying distributions, $3,361,864; giving activities include $1,232,631 for grants and $2,064,483 for employee matching gifts.
Purpose and activities: The foundation supports organizations involved with television, education, cancer research, hunger, and human services.
Fields of interest: Media, television; Elementary/ secondary education; Higher education; Scholarships/financial aid; Education; Cancer research; Food services; American Red Cross; Human services; United Ways and Federated Giving Programs.
Program:
Matching Gift Program: The foundation matches contributions made by employees of Ingersoll-Rand to educational institutions on a one-for-one basis.
Type of support: Employee matching gifts; General/ operating support; Program development; Scholarship funds.
Geographic limitations: Giving primarily in MO, NC and NJ; giving also to national organizations.
Application information: Applications not accepted. Unsolicited requests for funds not accepted.
Officers and Directors:* Michael Lamach, Pres.; Marcia Avedon*, V.P.; William Gauld, V.P.; Barbara A. Santoro*, Secy.; David S. Kuhl, Treas.; Robert L. Katz.
EIN: 202045897
Selected grants: The following grants are a representative sample of this grantmaker's funding activity:
$84,140 to Scholarship America, Saint Peter, MN, 2011.
$78,500 to Habitat for Humanity of Greater Indianapolis, Indianapolis, IN, 2011.
$50,000 to Purdue University, West Lafayette, IN, 2011.
$10,000 to American Cancer Society, Atlanta, GA, 2011.

1940
Ingles Markets, Incorporated

2913 U.S. Hwy. 70 W.
P.O. Box 6676
Black Mountain, NC 28711-9103
(828) 669-2941
FAX: (828) 669-3678

Company URL: http://www.ingles-markets.com
Establishment information: Established in 1965.
Company type: Public company
Company ticker symbol and exchange: IMKTA/ NASDAQ
Business activities: Operates supermarket chain.
Business type (SIC): Groceries—retail
Financial profile for 2012: Number of employees, 20,800; assets, $1,642,110,000; sales volume, $3,709,430,000; pre-tax net income, $67,350,000; expenses, $3,585,590,000; liabilities, $1,184,700,000
Corporate officers: Robert P. Ingle II, Chair., C.E.O., and V.P., Opers.; James W. Lanning, Pres. and C.O.O.; Ronald B. Freeman, V.P., Finance and C.F.O.
Board of directors: Robert P. Ingle II, Chair.; Fred D. Ayers; Keith L. Collins; Ronald B. Freeman; James W. Lanning; John O. Pollard; Charles E. Russell; Laura Ingle Sharp
Giving statement: Giving through the Ingles Markets, Incorporated Corporate Giving Program.
Company EIN: 560846267

Ingles Markets, Incorporated Corporate Giving Program

c/o Corp. Giving Comm.
P.O. Box 6676
Asheville, NC 28816-6676
URL: http://www.ingles-markets.com/ donations.php

Purpose and activities: Ingles makes charitable contributions to nonprofit organizations involved with the education of children, eliminating hunger, and meeting specific community needs. Support is given primarily in areas of company operations in Alabama, Georgia, North Carolina, South Carolina, and Virginia.
Fields of interest: Elementary/secondary education; Food banks; Community/economic development; General charitable giving.
Type of support: Donated products; Employee volunteer services; Employee-related scholarships; General/operating support.
Geographic limitations: Giving primarily in areas of company operations in AL, GA, NC, SC, TN, and VA.
Publications: Application guidelines.
Application information: Applications accepted. Proposals should be submitted using organization letterhead. A contributions committee reviews all requests. Application form not required. Applicants should submit the following:
1) statement of problem project will address
2) copy of IRS Determination Letter
3) detailed description of project and amount of funding requested

Initial approach: Proposal to headquarters
Copies of proposal: 1

Committee meeting date(s): Quarterly
Deadline(s): None

1941
Ingram Micro Inc.
1600 E. St. Andrew Pl.
P.O. Box 25125
Santa Ana, CA 92705 (714) 566-1000
FAX: (302) 655-5049

Company URL: http://www.ingrammicro.com
Establishment information: Established in 1979.
Company type: Public company
Company ticker symbol and exchange: IM/NYSE
Business activities: Operates technology distribution company.
Business type (SIC): Professional and commercial equipment—wholesale
Financial profile for 2012: Number of employees, 20,800; assets, $11,480,450,000; sales volume, $37,827,300,000; pre-tax net income, $396,180,000; expenses, $37,364,950,000; liabilities, $7,869,190,000
Fortune 1000 ranking: 2012—76th in revenues, 465th in profits, and 356th in assets
Forbes 2000 ranking: 2012—252nd in sales, 1377th in profits, and 1380th in assets
Corporate officers: Dale R. Laurance, Chair.; Alain Monie, Pres. and C.E.O.; William D. Humes, C.O.O. and C.F.O.; Mario F. Leone, Exec. V.P. and C.I.O.; Larry C. Boyd, Exec. V.P., Genl. Counsel, and Secy.; Lynn Jolliffe, Exec. V.P., Human Resources; Gina Mastantuono, Exec. V.P., Finance
Board of directors: Dale R. Laurance, Chair.; Howard I. Atkins; Leslie S. Heisz; John R. Ingram; Orrin H. Ingram II; Linda Fayne Levinson; Scott McGregor; Alain Monie; Paul Read; Michael T. Smith; Joe B. Wyatt
Plants: Miraloma, CA; Carol Stream, IL; Jonestown, PA; Millington, TN; Carrollton, TX
Offices: Santa Ana, CA; Buffalo, NY
International operations: Argentina; Australia; Austria; Barbados; Belgium; Bermuda; Brazil; British Virgin Islands; Canada; Cayman Islands; Chile; China; France; Germany; Hong Kong; Hungary; India; Israel; Italy; Luxembourg; Malaysia; Mauritius; Mexico; Netherlands; New Zealand; Panama; Peru; Philippines; Portugal; Singapore; South Africa; Spain; Sri Lanka; Sweden; Switzerland; Thailand; United Kingdom
Giving statement: Giving through the Ingram Micro Inc. Corporate Giving Program.
Company EIN: 621644402

Ingram Micro Inc. Corporate Giving Program
P.O. Box 25125
Santa Ana, CA 92799-5125
FAX: (714) 382-4978;
E-mail: communityrelations@ingrammicro.com;
URL: http://www.ingrammicro.com/imdocs/display/main/1,,591,00.html

Contact: Nicole Trombly, Specialist, Comm. Rels.
Purpose and activities: Ingram Micro makes charitable contributions to nonprofit organizations involved with arts and culture, education, technology, and health and human services. Support is given primarily in Orange County, California, Carol Stream, Illinois, Buffalo, New York, Harrisburg, Pennsylvania, Memphis and Millington, Tennessee, and Carrollton, Texas.
Fields of interest: Education; Engineering/technology.
International interests: Asia; Canada; Europe; Latin America; Mexico; Oceania.
Type of support: Annual campaigns; Donated products; Employee matching gifts; Employee volunteer services; In-kind gifts; Matching/challenge support; Program development.
Geographic limitations: Giving primarily in Orange County, CA, Carol Stream, IL, Buffalo, NY, Harrisburg, PA, Memphis and Millington, TN, and Carrollton, TX; limited giving in Asia, Canada, Latin America, Mexico, Oceania, and western Europe.
Support limitations: No support for sectarian, denominational, or religious organizations, political candidates, sports or sports-related organizations, organizations not of direct benefit to the entire community, or discriminatory organizations. No grants to individuals, or for fundraising.
Publications: Application guidelines.
Application information: Applications accepted. Faxed requests are not accepted. Unsolicited requests for contributions of $5,000 or more are not accepted. The Community Relations Department handles giving. The company has a staff that only handles contributions. A contributions committee reviews all requests. Application form not required. Applicants should submit the following:
1) copy of IRS Determination Letter
2) brief history of organization and description of its mission
3) copy of most recent annual report/audited financial statement/990
4) descriptive literature about organization
5) listing of board of directors, trustees, officers and other key people and their affiliations
6) detailed description of project and amount of funding requested
7) copy of current year's organizational budget and/or project budget

Initial approach: E-mail proposal to headquarters
Copies of proposal: 1
Committee meeting date(s): Bi-weekly
Deadline(s): None
Final notification: 30 days

Administrators: Nicole Trombly, Specialist, Comm. Rels.

1942
Ingredion, Inc.
(formerly Corn Products International, Inc.)
5 Westbrook Corporate Ctr.
Westchester, IL 60154-5749
(708) 551-2600
FAX: (708) 551-2700

Company URL: http://www.cornproducts.com
Establishment information: Established in 1906.
Company type: Public company
Company ticker symbol and exchange: INGR/NYSE
Business activities: Produces and sells corn- and starch-based food ingredients and industrial products.
Business type (SIC): Specialty foods/canned, frozen, and preserved; grain mill products, including pet food
Financial profile for 2012: Number of employees, 11,200; assets, $5,592,000,000; sales volume, $6,532,000,000; pre-tax net income, $601,000,000; expenses, $5,864,000,000; liabilities, $3,155,000,000
Fortune 1000 ranking: 2012—386th in revenues, 371st in profits, and 562nd in assets
Forbes 2000 ranking: 2012—1225th in sales, 1198th in profits, and 1779th in assets
Corporate officers: Ilene S. Gordon, Chair., Pres., and C.E.O.; Cheryl K. Beebe, Exec. V.P. and C.F.O.; Christine M. Castellano, Sr. V.P., Genl. Counsel, and Corp. Secy.; Diane J. Frisch, Sr. V.P., Human Resources; Matthew R. Galvanoni, V.P. and Corp. Cont.; Kimberly A. Hunter, Corp. Treas.
Board of directors: Ilene S. Gordon, Chair.; Richard J. Almeida; Luis Aranguren-Trellez; Paul T. Hanrahan; Karen L. Hendricks; Wayne M. Hewett; Gregory B. Kenny; Barbara A. Klein; James M. Ringler; Dwayne A. Wilson
International operations: Argentina; Brazil; Canada; Mexico
Giving statement: Giving through the Corn Products International, Inc. Corporate Giving Program and the Corn Products Educational Foundation.
Company EIN: 223514823

Corn Products International, Inc. Corporate Giving Program
5 Westbrook Corporate Ctr.
Westchester, IL 60154-5759 (708) 551-2600
FAX: (708) 551-2700;
E-mail: corpcomm@cornproducts.com; URL: http://www.ingredion.com/corporate_responsibility/sustainability/

Purpose and activities: As a complement to its foundation, Corn Products International also makes charitable contributions to nonprofit organizations directly. Support is given on a national and international basis in areas of company operations.
Fields of interest: Arts; Education; Public health; Safety/disasters; Human services; Community/economic development; Public affairs; General charitable giving.
Type of support: Donated products; Employee matching gifts; Employee volunteer services; General/operating support.
Geographic limitations: Giving on a national and international basis in areas of company operations.

Corn Products Educational Foundation
5 Westbrook Corporate Ctr.
Westchester, IL 60154-5749

Establishment information: Established in 2001 in DE.
Donors: Konrad Schlatter; James W. & Jayne A. McKee Foundation; Best Foods Educational Foundation.
Financial data (yr. ended 12/31/11): Assets, $3,183,954 (M); expenditures, $246,565; qualifying distributions, $206,550; giving activities include $206,550 for grants.
Purpose and activities: The foundation awards college scholarships to children of full-time employees of Corn Products International, Inc. and its affiliates.
Fields of interest: Higher education.
Type of support: Employee-related scholarships.
Geographic limitations: Giving primarily in areas of company operations.
Application information: Applications not accepted. Contributes only through employee-related scholarships.
Officers and Directors:* Diane J. Frisch*, Pres.; Mary Ann Hynes*, Secy.; Cheryl K. Beebe*, Treas.
EIN: 364477522

1943
Inman Mills
(doing business as Inman Holding Company, Inc.)
300 Park Rd.
P.O. Box 207
Inman, SC 29349-1754 (864) 472-2121

Company URL: http://www.inmanmills.com
Establishment information: Established in 1901.
Company type: Private company
Business activities: Manufactures cotton textiles and blends.
Business type (SIC): Fabrics/broadwoven natural cotton; fabrics/broadwoven synthetic and silk
Corporate officers: Robert H. Chapman III, Chair., C.E.O., and Treas.; Norman H. Chapman, Pres. and C.O.O.; James C. Pace, Jr., C.F.O. and Cont.
Board of director: Robert H. Chapman III, Chair.
Giving statement: Giving through the Inman-Riverdale Foundation.

Inman-Riverdale Foundation
P.O. Box 207
Inman, SC 29349-0207

Establishment information: Incorporated in 1946 in SC.
Donors: Inman Mills; Chapman High School.
Financial data (yr. ended 11/30/11): Assets, $2,661,983 (M); gifts received, $990,000; expenditures, $168,052; qualifying distributions, $742,252; giving activities include $674,433 for 43 + grants (high: $545,167; low: $85) and $22,174 for grants to individuals.
Purpose and activities: The foundation supports organizations involved with arts and culture, secondary and higher education, health, hunger, human services, and Christianity.
Fields of interest: Arts; Secondary school/education; Higher education; Health care, clinics/centers; Health care; Food services; Food distribution, meals on wheels; Athletics/sports, school programs; YM/YWCAs & YM/YWHAs; United Ways and Federated Giving Programs; Christian agencies & churches.
Type of support: Employee-related scholarships; General/operating support; Program development.
Geographic limitations: Giving primarily in SC.
Application information: Applications not accepted. Contributes only to pre-selected organizations and individuals.
Officers and Trustees:* Robert H. Chapman III*, Chair.; Patricia H. Robbins, Secy.; John F. Renfro, Jr.*, Treas.; Norman H. Chapman; James C. Pace, Jr.
EIN: 576019736

1944
Insperity, Inc.
(formerly Administaff Inc.)
19001 Crescent Springs Dr.
Kingwood, TX 77339-3802 (281) 358-8986

Company URL: http://www.insperity.com
Establishment information: Established in 1986.
Company type: Public company
Company ticker symbol and exchange: NSP/NYSE
Business activities: Operates professional employer organizations that provides small and midsized companies such services as payroll and benefits administration, workers' compensation programs, personnel records management, and employee recruiting.
Business type (SIC): Personnel supply services
Financial profile for 2012: Number of employees, 2,200; assets, $750,200,000; sales volume, $2,158,820,000; pre-tax net income, $68,290,000; expenses, $2,091,330,000; liabilities, $509,300,000
Fortune 1000 ranking: 2012—897th in revenues, 837th in profits, and 989th in assets
Corporate officers: Paul J. Sarvadi, Chair. and C.E.O.; Richard G. Rawson, Pres.; A. Steve Arizpe, Exec. V.P. and C.O.O.; Jay E. Mincks, Exec. V.P., Sales and Mktg.; Douglas S. Sharp, Sr. V.P., Finance, C.F.O., and Treas.; Daniel D. Herink, Sr. V.P., Genl. Counsel, and Secy.; Jason F. Cutbirth, Sr. V.P., Mktg.; Betty L. Collins, Sr. V.P., Corp. Human Resources
Board of directors: Paul J. Sarvadi, Chair.; Michael W. Brown; Jack M. Fields, Jr.; Eli Jones; Paul S. Lattanzio; Gregory E. Petsch; Richard G. Rawson; Austin P. Young III
Giving statement: Giving through the Insperity, Inc. Corporate Giving Program.
Company EIN: 760479645

Insperity, Inc. Corporate Giving Program
(formerly Administaff, Inc. Corporate Giving Program)
19001 Crescent Springs Dr.
Kingwood, TX 77339-3802 (281) 358-8986
E-mail: community.involvement@insperity.com;
URL: http://www.insperity.com/about-us/about-community/?redirect=true

Financial data (yr. ended 12/31/10): Total giving, $2,400,000, including $2,400,000 for grants.
Purpose and activities: Insperity makes contributions to nonprofit organizations involved with health and human services, education, military and veterans, and animal welfare. Support is limited to areas of company operations.
Fields of interest: Education; Animal welfare; Health care; Human services; Military/veterans' organizations.
Type of support: Donated equipment; Donated products; Employee volunteer services; General/operating support; In-kind gifts; Sponsorships.
Geographic limitations: Giving is limited to areas of company operations.
Publications: Application guidelines.
Application information: Applications accepted. Application form not required. Applicants should submit the following:
1) name, address and phone number of organization
2) brief history of organization and description of its mission
3) detailed description of project and amount of funding requested

Grant requests usually range from $500 to $5,000. Clients and business alliances of Insperity are given priority in funding requests. Proposals should include the organization's website.
Initial approach: Complete online application
Copies of proposal: 1
Deadline(s): None
Final notification: 4 to 6 weeks

1945
Inspire Commerce, Inc.
423 Concord Ave.
Boulder, CO 80304 (303) 800-8434

Company URL: http://www.inspirecommerce.com
Establishment information: Established in 2008.
Company type: Private company
Business activities: Operates merchant services company.
Business type (SIC): Business services/miscellaneous; depository banking/functions related to
Corporate officer: Mark Fischer, C.E.O.
Giving statement: Giving through the Inspire Commerce, Inc. Corporate Giving Program.

Inspire Commerce, Inc. Corporate Giving Program
423 Concord Ave.
Boulder, CO 80304-3918 (800) 261-3173
URL: http://www.inspirecommerce.com

Purpose and activities: Inspire Commerce is a certified B Corporation that donates a percentage of its revenue stream to nonprofit organizations.
Fields of interest: General charitable giving.
Type of support: General/operating support.
Application information: Applications not accepted. Contributes only to pre-selected organizations.

1946
Institution for Savings
93 State St.
P.O. Box 510
Newburyport, MA 01950-6695
(978) 462-3106

Company URL: https://www.institutionforsavings.com
Establishment information: Established in 1820.
Company type: Mutual company
Business activities: Operates savings bank.
Business type (SIC): Savings institutions
Corporate officers: Michael J. Jones, Chair., Pres., and C.E.O.; Kimberly A. Rock, Exec. V.P. and C.O.O.; Robert C. LeGallo, C.P.A., Sr. V.P. and C.F.O.; Patricia A. Ferguson, Sr. V.P., Admin. and Human Resources; Stephen P. Cote, V.P., Cont., and Treas.; Rebecca L. Collins, V.P., Finance; Mary Anne Clancy, V.P., Comms.
Board of directors: Michael J. Jones, Chair.; Kenneth C Barney; Freeman J. Condon; Donald M. Greenough; Cindy M. Johnson; Peter G. Kelly; Mary E. Larnard; John F. Leary; Jeremiah T. Lewis; R. Drew Marc-aurele; Donald D. Mitchell; Ellen Galanis Nich; Kimberly A. Rock; Ellen Mackey Rose; Richard J. Silverman; Thomas L. Strickler; David A. Tibbetts; David M. Tierney; Jonathan J. Woodman
Giving statement: Giving through the Institution for Savings, the 2 Depot Square Ipswich Charitable Foundation, and the Institution for Savings Charitable Foundation.

2 Depot Square Ipswich Charitable Foundation
2 Depot Sq.
Ipswich, MA 01938-1914 (617) 356-3600
E-mail: troeger@institutionforsavings.com;
URL: https://www.institutionforsavings.com/two-depot-square-ipswich.htm

Establishment information: Established in 2005 in MA.
Donors: Ipswich Co-operative Bank; 1820 Security Corporation.
Contact: Stephen R. Cote, Treas.
Financial data (yr. ended 04/30/12): Assets, $1,790,135 (M); gifts received, $370,700; expenditures, $271,831; qualifying distributions, $271,831; giving activities include $270,231 for 39 grants (high: $64,500; low: $500).

Purpose and activities: The foundation supports organizations involved with arts and culture, education, health, housing, athletics, youth development, human services, and community economic development.
Fields of interest: Arts; Secondary school/education; Education; Health care; Housing/shelter; Athletics/sports, amateur leagues; Youth development; YM/YWCAs & YM/YWHAs; Children/youth, services; Family services; Human services; Community development, neighborhood development; Community/economic development.
Programs:
Arts and Culture: The foundation supports initiatives designed to provide arts and culture programs that enrich the community.
Economic and Community Empowerment: The foundation supports programs designed to promote and develop access to safe and affordable housing and promote community revitalization.
Health and Human Services: The foundation supports programs designed to enhance the health and well-being of children and families.
Youth Development: The foundation supports programs designed to promote social, educational, athletic, or cultural initiatives for youth.
Type of support: Capital campaigns; General/operating support; Program development; Scholarship funds.
Geographic limitations: Giving primarily in areas of company operations in Ipswich, MA.
Support limitations: No grants to individuals.
Publications: Application guidelines; Program policy statement.
Application information: Applications accepted. Application form required. Applicants should submit the following:
1) population served
2) name, address and phone number of organization
3) copy of IRS Determination Letter
4) brief history of organization and description of its mission
5) geographic area to be served
6) copy of most recent annual report/audited financial statement/990
7) listing of board of directors, trustees, officers and other key people and their affiliations
8) detailed description of project and amount of funding requested
9) contact person
10) copy of current year's organizational budget and/or project budget
Initial approach: Download application form and mail to foundation
Board meeting date(s): Apr. and Nov.
Deadline(s): Apr. 1 and Nov. 1
Officers and Directors:* Michael J. Jones*, Pres.; Tammy A. Roeger, Clerk; Stephen P. Cote, Treas.; Kenneth C. Barney; Donald M. Greenough; Kimberly A. Rock; R. Drew March-Aurele; Ellen G. Nich; Ellen M. Rose; Richard J. Silverman; Mark F. Welch.
EIN: 203950026
Selected grants: The following grants are a representative sample of this grantmaker's funding activity:
$19,000 to Ipswich Public Schools, Ipswich, MA, 2010.
$7,750 to YMCA of the North Shore, Beverly, MA, 2010.
$4,000 to Music at Edens Edge, Essex, MA, 2010.
$1,000 to Beverly School for the Deaf, Beverly, MA, 2010.
$1,000 to Cuvilly Arts and Earth Center, Ipswich, MA, 2010.
$1,000 to Help for Abused Women and Their Children, Salem, MA, 2010.

Institution for Savings Charitable Foundation

(formerly Institution for Savings in Newburyport & Its Vicinity Charitable Foundation, Inc.)
93 State St.
P.O. Box 510
Newburyport, MA 01950-6618 (978) 462-3106
FAX: (978) 462-1980;
E-mail: pconnelly@institutionforsavings.com;
URL: https://www.institutionforsavings.com/institution-for-savings-grant.htm

Establishment information: Established in 1997 in MA.
Donors: Institution for Savings; 1820 Security Corp.
Contact: Patricia Connelly, Clerk
Financial data (yr. ended 06/30/12): Assets, $6,079,890 (M); gifts received, $977,300; expenditures, $872,691; qualifying distributions, $871,491; giving activities include $869,856 for 98 grants (high: $250,000; low: $300).
Purpose and activities: The foundation supports organizations involved with arts and culture, education, hunger, and human services and awards college scholarships to graduating seniors from Newburyport High School and Triton Regional High School.
Fields of interest: Performing arts; Performing arts, orchestras; Arts; Elementary/secondary education; Higher education; Education; Food services; Boys & girls clubs; American Red Cross; YM/YWCAs & YM/YWHAs; Residential/custodial care, hospices; Aging, centers/services; Human services.
Type of support: Annual campaigns; Building/renovation; Capital campaigns; Continuing support; General/operating support; Program development; Scholarship funds; Scholarships—to individuals; Sponsorships.
Geographic limitations: Giving limited to Newburyport, MA.
Publications: Application guidelines; Grants list.
Application information: Applications accepted. Application form required. Applicants should submit the following:
1) population served
2) copy of IRS Determination Letter
3) brief history of organization and description of its mission
4) geographic area to be served
5) copy of most recent annual report/audited financial statement/990
6) listing of board of directors, trustees, officers and other key people and their affiliations
7) detailed description of project and amount of funding requested
8) listing of additional sources and amount of support
Scholarship applications should include transcripts, financial information, and an essay.
Initial approach: Download application form and mail to foundation
Board meeting date(s): 3rd Mon. of Mar., June, Sept., and Dec.
Deadline(s): Mar. 11, June 10, Sept. 9, and Dec. 9; Apr. 1 for scholarships
Officers and Trustees:* Mark F. Welch*, Pres.; Patricia D. Connelly, Clerk; Michael J. Jones*, Treas.; Thomas G. Ambrosi; Kenneth C. Barney; John F. Bradshaw; Freeman J. Condon; V. James Difazio; Donald M. Greenough; Cindy M. Johnson; Peter G. Kelly; Mary E. Larnard; John F. Leary III; David L. Levesque; Jeremiah T. Lewis; Majorie A. Lynn; Drew Marc-Aurele; Donald D. Mitchell; Ellen G. Nich; Nancy E. Peace; Kimberly A. Rock; Ellen Mackey Rose; Richard J. Silverman; Thomas Stickler; Michael E. Strem; David A. Tibbetts; David M. Tierney; Jonathan J. Woodman.
EIN: 043353621
Selected grants: The following grants are a representative sample of this grantmaker's funding activity:
$15,000 to Harvard University, Cambridge, MA, 2011.

1947
Integra LifeSciences Corporation

311 Enterprise Dr.
Plainsboro, NJ 08536-3344 (609) 275-0500

Company URL: http://www.integralife.com/
Establishment information: Established in 1989.
Company type: Subsidiary of a public company
Business activities: Operates medical device company.
Business type (SIC): Medical instruments and supplies
Corporate officers: Stuart M. Essig, Chair.; Peter J. Arduini, Pres. and C.E.O.; John B. Henneman III, Exec. V.P., Finance, Admin., and C.F.O.; Richard D. Gorelick, Sr. V.P., Genl. Counsel, Admin., and Secy.; Nora Brennan, V.P. and Treas.; Jerry E. Corbin, V.P., Corp. Cont. and C.A.O.
Board of directors: Stuart M. Essig, Chair.; Peter J. Arduini
Giving statement: Giving through the Integra Foundation, Inc.

The Integra Foundation, Inc.

2 Goodyear #A
Irvine, CA 92618-2052 (949) 855-7165
FAX: (949) 595-8703;
E-mail: linda.littlejohns@integralife.com;
URL: http://www.integra-foundation.org

Establishment information: Established in 2002 in NJ.
Donor: Integra LifeSciences Corp.
Contact: Linda Littlejohns, Pres. and Exec. Dir.
Financial data (yr. ended 12/31/10): Assets, $1,240,768 (M); gifts received, $700,000; expenditures, $617,020; qualifying distributions, $616,050; giving activities include $616,050 for 78 grants (high: $350,000; low: $500).
Purpose and activities: The foundation supports programs designed to advance innovative medical and health care research and education, primarily in the areas of neurosurgery, reconstructive surgery, and general surgery, to improve the outcome and quality of life for patients and their communities.
Fields of interest: Medical school/education; Hospitals (general); Health care, clinics/centers; Health care; Neuroscience research; Medical research; Surgery research.
Type of support: Conferences/seminars; Equipment; General/operating support; Program development; Scholarship funds; Sponsorships.
Geographic limitations: Giving primarily in areas of company operations.
Support limitations: No support for political, fraternal, social, veterans', or religious organizations. No grants to individuals, or for programs that directly support marketing or sales objectives of Integra LifeSciences.
Publications: Application guidelines; Grants list; Newsletter.
Application information: Applications accepted. Application form required. Applicants should submit the following:
1) copy of IRS Determination Letter
2) copy of most recent annual report/audited financial statement/990

3) listing of board of directors, trustees, officers and other key people and their affiliations
4) copy of current year's organizational budget and/ or project budget
5) listing of additional sources and amount of support

Initial approach: Download application form and mail or fax to foundation
Copies of proposal: 1
Board meeting date(s): Feb., May, Aug., and Nov.
Deadline(s): None

Officers and Trustees: Linda Littlejohns, Pres. and Exec. Dir.; Simon Archibald, V.P.; JoAnne Harla, V.P.; Karen March, V.P.; Nora Brennan, Treas.; Stuart Essig; Jack Henneman; Judith O'Grady.
Number of staff: 1 part-time professional.
EIN: 522388679
Selected grants: The following grants are a representative sample of this grantmaker's funding activity:
$47,500 to Georgetown University, Washington, DC, 2010.
$7,500 to Duke University, Durham, NC, 2010.
$5,000 to Georgetown University, Washington, DC, 2010.
$1,000 to Accelerate Brain Cancer Cure, Washington, DC, 2010.
$1,000 to Healing the Children, Spokane, WA, 2010.

1948
Integrity Bank & Trust

1275 Village Ridge Pt.
Monument, CO 80132-8996
(719) 484-0077

Company URL: http://www.integritybankandtrust.com
Establishment information: Established in 2003.
Company type: Private company
Business activities: Operates state commercial bank.
Business type (SIC): Banks/commercial
Corporate officer: Jim Wyss, Pres. and C.E.O.
Giving statement: Giving through the Integrity Bank and Trust Charitable Trust.

Integrity Bank and Trust Charitable Trust

5550 Powers Center Pt.
Colorado Springs, CO 80920-7104

Donor: Integrity Bank and Trust.
Financial data (yr. ended 09/30/11): Assets, $49,867 (M); gifts received, $13,500; expenditures, $11,319; qualifying distributions, $10,749; giving activities include $10,749 for 8 grants (high: $7,500; low: $75).
Purpose and activities: The foundation supports organizations involved with education, substance abuse prevention, sports, and religion.
Fields of interest: Education; Substance abuse, prevention; Athletics/sports, amateur leagues; Christian agencies & churches; Religion.
Type of support: Capital campaigns; General/ operating support; Program development.
Geographic limitations: Giving primarily in Colorado Springs, CO.
Application information: Applications not accepted. Unsolicited requests for funds not accepted.
Trustee: Randy Rush.
EIN: 205114651

1949
Integrity Partners

1499 Danville Blvd.
Alamo, CA 94507 (925) 478-4300

Company URL: http://www.integritypartners.com/
Company type: Private company
Business activities: Operates venture capital firm.
Business type (SIC): Investors/miscellaneous; investment offices
Financial profile for 2010: Number of employees, 5
Corporate officer: Stephen Williams, C.O.O.
Giving statement: Giving through the W. Charitable Foundation, Inc.

The W. Charitable Foundation, Inc.

12667 Alcosta Blvd., Ste. 160
San Ramon, CA 94583 (925) 791-6100
FAX: (925) 369-7370;
E-mail: elbert@wcharitable.org; Application address: 1499 Danville Blvd., Alamo, CA 94507 Tel.:(925) 791-6100; URL: http://www.wcharitable.org/

Establishment information: Established in 2006 in CA.
Donors: Scott Walchek; Kelli Walchek; Walchek Integrity, LP; Walchek Family.
Contact: Elbert Paul, Exec. Dir.
Financial data (yr. ended 12/31/11): Assets, $5,778,104 (M); expenditures, $295,790; qualifying distributions, $284,032; giving activities include $6,250 for 2 grants (high: $5,000; low: $1,250).
Purpose and activities: The foundation supports programs designed to communicate God's love by sharing resources with people in need; and programs designed to promote spiritual healing and care.
Fields of interest: Human services; Religion.
Type of support: General/operating support.
Geographic limitations: Giving primarily in CA.
Publications: Application guidelines.
Application information: Applications accepted. Applicants who receive a favorable response to their letter of inquiry will be invited to submit a formal proposal with supporting materials. Application form required.

Initial approach: See Foundation website
Deadline(s): None

Officers and Directors: Scott Walchek, C.E.O and Pres.; Elbert Paul, Exec. Dir.
Director: Kelli Walchek.
EIN: 204266256
Selected grants: The following grants are a representative sample of this grantmaker's funding activity:
$1,500 to National Christian Foundation, Alpharetta, GA, 2010. For general charitable purposes.

1950
Intel Corporation

2200 Mission College Blvd.
Santa Clara, CA 95054-1549
(408) 765-8080
FAX: (302) 655-5049

Company URL: http://www.intel.com
Establishment information: Established in 1968.
Company type: Public company
Company ticker symbol and exchange: INTC/ NASDAQ
International Securities Identification Number: US4581401001
Business activities: Manufactures and develops semiconductor chips, boards, systems, and software.
Business type (SIC): Electronic components and accessories; computer services
Financial profile for 2012: Number of employees, 105,000; assets, $84,351,000,000; sales volume, $53,341,000,000; pre-tax net income, $148,730,000; expenses, $38,703,000,000; liabilities, $33,148,000,000
Fortune 1000 ranking: 2012—54th in revenues, 13th in profits, and 72nd in assets
Forbes 2000 ranking: 2012—160th in sales, 35th in profits, and 288th in assets
Corporate officers: Andy D. Bryant, Chair.; Paul S. Otellini, Pres. and C.E.O.; Stacy J. Smith, Sr. V.P. and C.F.O.; A. Douglas Melamed, Sr. V.P. and Genl. Counsel; Cary I. Klafter, V.P. and Corp. Secy.; Ravi Jacob, V.P. and Treas.; Leslie S. Culbertson, V.P., Finance
Board of directors: Andy D. Bryant, Chair.; Amb. Charlene Barshefsky; Susan L. Decker; John J. Donahoe; Reed E. Hundt; Paul S. Otellini; James D. Plummer; David S. Pottruck; Frank D. Yeary; David B. Yoffie
Subsidiary: McAfee, Inc., Santa Clara, CA
Plants: Livermore, CA; Boca Raton, FL; Mount Prospect, IL; Rio Rancho, NM; Hillsboro, OR
International operations: Argentina; Australia; Bangladesh; Belgium; Brazil; Canada; Cayman Islands; China; Colombia; Costa Rica; Czech Republic; Denmark; England; Finland; France; Germany; Hong Kong; India; Indonesia; Israel; Italy; Japan; Malaysia; Mexico; Netherlands; Philippines; Poland; Romania; Russia; Singapore; South Africa; South Korea; Spain; Sweden; Taiwan; Thailand; Turkey; Ukraine; United Kingdom; Vietnam; Wales
Giving statement: Giving through the Intel Corporation Contributions Program and the Intel Foundation.
Company EIN: 941672743

Intel Corporation Contributions Program

2200 Mission College Blvd.
Santa Clara, CA 95054-1549 (408) 765-8080
URL: http://www.intel.com/community/index.htm

Financial data (yr. ended 12/31/10): Total giving, $77,891,526, including $77,891,526 for grants.
Purpose and activities: As a complement to its foundation, Intel also makes charitable contributions to nonprofit organizations directly. Support is limited to areas of company operations in Arizona, East Palo Alto, El Dorado County, Fremont, Placer County, Sacramento County, and Santa Clara County, California, Fort Collins, Colorado, Massachusetts (with an emphasis on Middlesex and Worcester counties), New Mexico, Clackamas, Multnomah, and Washington counties, Oregon, Pierce and Thurston counties, Washington, and in China, Costa Rica, India, Ireland, Israel, Malaysia, Russia, and Vietnam.
Fields of interest: Elementary/secondary education; Education; Environment, natural resources; Environment; Safety/disasters, management/technical assistance; Disasters, search/rescue; Civil/human rights, equal rights; Engineering/technology; Computer science; Science.
International interests: China; Costa Rica; India; Ireland; Israel; Malaysia; Russia; Vietnam.
Type of support: Continuing support; Employee matching gifts; Employee volunteer services; General/operating support; In-kind gifts; Pro bono services; Technical assistance.
Geographic limitations: Giving on a national and international basis in areas of company operations

in AZ, East Palo Alto, El Dorado County, Fremont, Placer County, Sacramento County, and Santa Clara County, CA, Fort Collins, CO, MA (with an emphasis on Middlesex and Worcester counties), NM, Clackamas, Multnomah, and Washington counties, OR, Pierce and Thurston counties, WA, and in China, Costa Rica, India, Ireland, Israel, Malaysia, Russia, and Vietnam.
Support limitations: No support for foundations that are strictly grantmaking bodies, or for discriminatory organizations, Chamber of Commerce, trader, or business associations, labor unions, fraternal, service or veterans' organizations, health care institutions, or religious organizations not of direct benefit to the entire community. Generally no support for private schools or arts organizations. No grants to individuals, or for fundraising events such as walk-a-thons, jog-a-thons, bike-a-thons, raffles, or giveaways, political, or lobbying activities, advocacy to influence public policy or legislation, endowments, capital campaigns, sporting events or teams, general operating expenses, debt-retirement, travel or tours, scholarship awards in the name of another organization, or special occasion goodwill advertising, including program books and yearbooks. Generally no funding for extracurricular school activities or clubs, or unrestricted gifts to national or international organizations.
Publications: Corporate giving report.
Application information: Applications accepted. Matching grants are limited to $10,000 per organization per year. Applicants should submit the following:
1) timetable for implementation and evaluation of project
2) statement of problem project will address
3) population served
4) name, address and phone number of organization
5) copy of IRS Determination Letter
6) geographic area to be served
7) copy of most recent annual report/audited financial statement/990
8) listing of board of directors, trustees, officers and other key people and their affiliations
9) detailed description of project and amount of funding requested
10) copy of current year's organizational budget and/or project budget
11) listing of additional sources and amount of support

Initial approach: Complete online eligibility quiz for U.S. grants; download application form and mail completed application to national facility for international grants
Copies of proposal: 1
Final notification: Quarterly

Intel Foundation

5200 NE Elam Pkwy.
Hillsboro, OR 97124
E-mail: intel.foundation@intel.com; URL: http://www.intel.com/foundation

Establishment information: Established in 1988 in OR.
Donors: Intel Corp.; Intel Capital Corp.
Contact: Wendy Ramage Hawkins, Exec. Dir.
Financial data (yr. ended 12/31/11): Assets, $67,392,581 (M); gifts received, $56,285,795; expenditures, $43,822,177; qualifying distributions, $43,501,825; giving activities include $43,388,787 for grants.
Purpose and activities: The foundation supports programs designed to advance education and improve communities worldwide. Special emphasis is directed toward programs designed to advance education in math, science, and engineering; promote the entrance of women and under-represented minorities into careers in science and engineering; and enable Intel employees to improve quality of life in their communities.
Fields of interest: Elementary/secondary education; Elementary/secondary school reform; Higher education; Higher education, college; Business school/education; Teacher school/education; Engineering school/education; Education, computer literacy/technology training; Education; Disasters, preparedness/services; Youth development, business; United Ways and Federated Giving Programs; Science, formal/general education; Mathematics; Engineering/technology; Engineering; Science Youth; Minorities; African Americans/Blacks; Hispanics/Latinos; Native Americans/American Indians; Women.
Programs:
Intel Computer Clubhouse Network: The foundation, in partnership with the Boston Museum of Science and MIT Media Lab, operates an after-school technology learning program in underserved communities for youth to use digital technology to develop creative projects inspired by their own ideas. The program is designed to support learning through design experiences; help youth build on their own interests; cultivate an "emergent community" of learners; and create an environment of respect and trust. Visit URL http://www.computerclubhouse.org/ for more information.
Intel Global Challenge: Through the Intel Global Challenge, the foundation in collaboration with University of California (UC) Berkeley promotes entrepreneurship in developing countries. An annual competition is held at the Hass School of Business where teams showcase business opportunities that have the greatest potential for a positive impact on society through technology. Awards range from $50,000 for first prize to $5,000 for special awards. Applicants must compete in regional competitions before winning entries are showcased in the final Intel Global Challenge event.
Intel International Science and Engineering Fair (Intel ISEF): Through the Intel International Science and Engineering Fair, a program of the Society for Science & the Public, students and young scientists come together to share and promote scientific discovery and innovation through competition. Awards are based on students' ability to tackle challenging scientific questions, use authentic research practices, and create solutions for the problems of tomorrow. The top Best in Category winner receives $75,000; two students are awarded an Intel Foundation Young Scientists award of $50,000; and three top seniors are awarded an all expense-paid trip to attend the Stockholm International Youth Science Seminar (SIUSS) and attendance at the Nobel Prize ceremonies in Sweden.
Intel Involved Hero Award Program: Through the Involved Hero Award, the foundation recognizes extraordinary achievement in volunteerism by an Intel employee. The recipient receives $10,000 for the school or nonprofit of his or her choice and is recognized at the Intel Achievement Award banquet in San Francisco, California.
Intel Involved Matching Grant Program (IMGP): The foundation awards grants to educational institutions and 501(c)3 nonprofits with which employees and retirees of Intel volunteer at least 20 hours, up to $10,000 per nonprofit organization, and $15,000 per school, per year.
Intel Involved Matching Seed Grants Program: The foundation awards grants of up to $5,000 to underwrite selected employee-initiated community service projects. The program is designed to help teams of Intel employees get creative volunteer initiatives off the ground.
Intel Matching Gifts to Education: The foundation matches contributions made by employees, directors, and the spouses of employees and retirees of Intel to U.S. K-12 and higher education. The match is done at 50% of the donation and ranges from $25 to $10,000 per contributor, per year.
Intel Science Talent Search: Through the Intel Science Talent Search program, high school seniors enter the pre-college science competition with projects from science, technology, engineering, and math disciplines. Cash prizes are awarded to the top 40 finalists. The grand prize winner is awarded a $100,000 four-year college scholarship; the second place winner receives $75,000; and the third place winner receives $50,000.
Type of support: Conferences/seminars; Curriculum development; Employee matching gifts; Employee volunteer services; General/operating support; Matching/challenge support; Program development; Research; Scholarship funds; Sponsorships.
Geographic limitations: Giving primarily in areas of company operations in Phoenix, AZ, Folsom and Santa Clara, CA, Hudson, MA, Albuquerque, NM, Portland, OR, and DuPont, WA, Sao Paulo, Brazil, China, San Jose, Costa Rica, Egypt, India, Israel, Mexico, Russia, Taiwan, and Istanbul, Turkey; limited giving to select national organizations.
Support limitations: No support for religious, sectarian, fraternal, or political organizations, arts or healthcare organizations, environmental organizations, private schools, or sports teams. No grants to individuals, or for endowments, capital campaigns, general fund drives, annual campaigns, fundraising events, sporting events, television or radio production costs, creation of personal/organization websites, travel or tours, or equipment.
Publications: Annual report; Corporate giving report.
Application information: Applications not accepted. Unsolicited applications are not accepted.
Board meeting date(s): Semiannually
Officers and Directors:* Richard G. A. Taylor, Chair.; Shelly M. Esque, Pres.; Suzan A. Miller, Secy.; Ravi Jacob, Treas.; Wendy Ramage Hawkins*, Exec. Dir.; Deborah S. Conrad; Justin Rattner.
Number of staff: 2 part-time professional; 1 full-time support.
EIN: 943092928
Selected grants: The following grants are a representative sample of this grantmaker's funding activity:
$6,550,000 to Society for Science and the Public, Washington, DC, 2012. For Intel International Science and Engineering Fair (ISEF) Foundation.
$5,150,000 to Society for Science and the Public, Washington, DC, 2012. For Intel Science Talent Search (STS).
$3,222,011 to United Way, Valley of the Sun, Phoenix, AZ, 2012. For matching grant.
$1,083,113 to Scholarship America, Saint Peter, MN, 2012. For student support.
$650,000 to Ashoka: Innovators for the Public, Arlington, VA, 2012. For Technology for Social Innovation.
$130,000 to Fundacja Zaawansowanych Technologii, Warsaw, Poland, 2012. For Intel Business Challenge Europe Event.
$105,000 to Tsinghua University, Beijing, China, 2012. For Entrepreneurship Summer Camp.
$94,737 to Teach for Japan, Tokyo, Japan, 2012. For student assistance following Japan earthquake.
$40,000 to Society of Women Engineers, Chicago, IL, 2012. For Corporate Partnership Council (CPC).
$20,000 to Argentina Ministry of Education, Buenos Aires, Argentina, 2012. For National Science and Technology Fairs.

1951
Intelius Inc.
500 108th Ave., N.E., 25th Fl., Ste.2200
Bellevue, WA 98004-5586 (425) 974-6100

Company URL: http://www.intelius.com
Establishment information: Established in 2003.
Company type: Private company
Business activities: Provides fee-based online intelligence services.
Business type (SIC): Business services/ miscellaneous
Corporate officers: Naveen K. Jain, Co-Chair., Pres. and C.E.O.; William A. Owens, Co-Chair.; Paul T. Cook, C.F.O.; William H. Beaver, Jr., Genl. Counsel
Board of directors: William A. Owens, Co-Chair.; Naveen K. Jain, Co-Chair.; Peter W. Currie; Peter Diamandis; Arthur W. Harrigan; Naveen K. Jain; Richard P. Karlgaard; William R. Kerr; Chris Kitze
Giving statement: Giving through the Intelius Inc. Corporate Giving Program.

Intelius Inc. Corporate Giving Program
500 108th Ave., NE, 25th Fl.
Bellevue, WA 98004 (425) 974-6100
URL: http://corp.intelius.com/ intelius-community-outreach

Purpose and activities: Intelius makes charitable contributions to nonprofit organizations supporting education, healthcare, youth, and family issues. Support is given primarily in Washington State.
Fields of interest: Education; Health care; Family services Youth.
Type of support: Employee matching gifts; Employee volunteer services; General/operating support.
Geographic limitations: Giving primarily in WA.

1952
InterBel Telephone Cooperative, Inc.
300 Dewey Ave.
P.O. Box 648
Eureka, MT 59917 (406) 889-3311

Company URL: http://www.interbel.com
Establishment information: Established in 1962.
Company type: Private company
Business activities: Provides telephone communications services.
Business type (SIC): Telephone communications
Corporate officer: Dale Bjorge, Cont.
Giving statement: Giving through the InterBel Telephone Cooperative Education Foundation.

InterBel Telephone Cooperative Education Foundation
c/o Sallie A. Foley , CPA
P.O. Box 648
Eureka, MT 59917 (406) 889-3311
URL: http://www.interbel.com/

Establishment information: Established in 1989 in MT.
Donor: InterBel Telephone Cooperative Inc.
Financial data (yr. ended 12/31/11): Assets, $123,848 (M); expenditures, $11,804; qualifying distributions, $8,000; giving activities include $8,000 for 5 grants to individuals (high: $3,000; low: $1,000).
Purpose and activities: The foundation awards college scholarships to children whose parents or guardians have been a member of InterBel Telephone Cooperative for two of the last five years.
Type of support: Scholarships—to individuals.
Geographic limitations: Giving limited to areas of company operations in Eureka, MT.
Application information: Applications accepted. Application form required.
Initial approach: Contact foundation for application form
Deadline(s): None
Officer and Trustees:* Joan Lefrancois*, Pres.; Sheila Bartmess; Tanna Chaney; Joel Graves; Tammy Lawler; Bobbie Stoken; Jill Yost; First Interstate Bank, Trust Dept.
EIN: 363684131

1953
Interface, Inc.
2859 Paces Ferry Rd., Ste. 2000
Atlanta, GA 30339-6216 (770) 437-6800
FAX: (770) 319-0070

Company URL: http://www.interfaceinc.com
Establishment information: Established in 1973.
Company type: Private company
Company ticker symbol and exchange: IFSIA/ NASDAQ
Business activities: Manufactures, markets, installs, and services modular carpet, broadloom carpet, interior panel fabrics, upholstery fabrics, and raised/access flooring products.
Business type (SIC): Carpets and rugs; textile mill products
Corporate officers: Daniel T. Hendrix, Chair., Pres. and C.E.O.; Patrick C. Lynch, Sr. V.P. and C.F.O.; Raymond S. Willoch, Sr. V.P., Admin., Genl. Counsel, and Secy.; Sanjay Lall, V.P. and C.I.O; Nigel Stansfield, V.P. and C.I.O.
Board of directors: Daniel T. Hendrix, Chair.; Edward C. Callaway; Diane Dillon-Ridgley; Carl I. Gable; June M. Henton; Christopher G. Kennedy; K. David Kohler; James B. Miller, Jr.; Harold M. Paisner
Subsidiary: Rockland React-Rite, Inc., Chatom, AL
Plants: Chatom, AL; Los Angeles, San Francisco, CA; Washington, DC; LaGrange, Rockmart, West Point, GA; Chicago, IL; Saddle Brook, NJ; New York, NY; Houston, TX
International operations: Australia; Canada; Netherlands; Thailand; United Kingdom
Giving statement: Giving through the Interface, Inc. Corporate Giving Program and the Interface Environmental Foundation, Inc.
Company EIN: 581451243

Interface, Inc. Corporate Giving Program
2859 Paces Ferry Rd., Ste. 2000
Atlanta, GA 30339-6216 (770) 437-6800
FAX: (770) 803-6960

Contact: Mary Ann Lanier
Purpose and activities: As a complement to its foundation, Interface also makes charitable contributions to nonprofit organizations directly. Support is given on a national and international basis primarily in areas of company operations.
Fields of interest: Environment, formal/general education; Environment, recycling; Environment.
Type of support: Annual campaigns; Continuing support; General/operating support; In-kind gifts.
Geographic limitations: Giving on a national and international basis in areas of company operations in CA and GA, and in Australia, Canada, the Netherlands, Thailand, and the United Kingdom.
Application information: Applications not accepted. Contributes only to pre-selected organizations.
Committee meeting date(s): Quarterly

Interface Environmental Foundation, Inc.
2859 Paces Ferry Rd., Ste. 2000
Atlanta, GA 30339-6216

Establishment information: Established in 1999 in GA.
Donors: Dubai Municipality; Interface, Inc.; Brickenden Speakers Bureau, Inc.; Hawaii Nature Center; Mount Sequoyah Conferance & Retreat Center; TMA Systems LLC; Warren Wilson College; Connstep, Inc.; CP Kelco, Inc.; Pratt & Whitney Canada; Valparaiso University; Envirosense Consortium, Inc.
Financial data (yr. ended 12/31/11): Assets, $322,554 (M); gifts received, $12,600; expenditures, $184,335; qualifying distributions, $182,835; giving activities include $174,500 for 34 grants (high: $25,000; low: $1,000).
Purpose and activities: The foundation supports conservation and environmental organizations involved with environmental sustainability.
Fields of interest: Higher education; Education; Environment, natural resources; Environmental education; Animals/wildlife.
Type of support: Curriculum development; General/ operating support; Program development.
Geographic limitations: Giving primarily in GA.
Support limitations: No grants to individuals.
Application information: Applications not accepted. Unsolicited requests for funds not accepted.
Officers and Trustees:* Patrick C. Lynch*, Sr. V.P. and Treas.; Daniel T. Hendrix*, Sr. V.P.; Keith J. Armstrong, V.P.; Michael D. Bertolucci, V.P.; Jim Hartzfeld, V.P.; Erin Meezan, V.P.; Raymond S. Willoch, Secy.; Keith Wright, Treas.
EIN: 582413898

1954
Interlock Industries, Inc.
545 S. 3rd St., Ste. 310
Louisville, KY 40202 (502) 569-2007

Company URL: http:// www.interlockindustries.com/
Establishment information: Established in 1982.
Company type: Private company
Business activities: Manufactures metal building components and aluminum casting and extrusions; transportation.
Business type (SIC): Building construction general contractors and operative builders; manufacturing/ miscellaneous
Corporate officers: Jeffrey L. Mackin, Pres.; Craig L. Mackin, C.F.O.
Board of directors: Jeffrey L. Mackin; Michael J. Mackin; Jay L. Mackin; Craig L. Mackin
Giving statement: Giving through the Mackin Foundation, Inc.

Mackin Foundation, Inc.
545 S. Third St., Ste. 310
Louisville, KY 40202-1838 (502) 569-2007
URL: http://www.interlockindustries.com/ mackin_foundation.php

Establishment information: Established in 1999 in KY.
Donor: Interlock Industries, Inc.

Financial data (yr. ended 12/31/11): Assets, $5,230,238 (L); expenditures, $903,031; qualifying distributions, $842,500; giving activities include $842,500 for 12 grants (high: $250,000; low: $2,500).
Purpose and activities: The foundation supports organizations involved with arts and culture, higher education, health, human services, economic development, civic affairs, and religion.
Fields of interest: Arts; Higher education; Hospitals (general); Health care, patient services; Health care; Children/youth, services; Human services; Economic development; Public affairs; Religion.
Type of support: Building/renovation; Employee-related scholarships; General/operating support.
Geographic limitations: Giving primarily in KY.
Publications: Application guidelines.
Application information: Applications accepted. Special consideration is given to requests that have Interlock Industries team member involvement. Application form not required. Applicants should submit the following:
1) copy of IRS Determination Letter
2) list of company employees involved with the organization
3) detailed description of project and amount of funding requested
Initial approach: Proposal
Deadline(s): None
Officers: Jay Lawrence Mackin, Pres.; Craig L. Mackin, Treas.
Directors: Jeffrey L. Mackin; Kimberly Ann Mackin; Michael J. Mackin.
EIN: 352069109
Selected grants: The following grants are a representative sample of this grantmaker's funding activity:
$200,000 to Bellarmine University, Louisville, KY, 2011.
$200,000 to Kosair Childrens Hospital Foundation, Louisville, KY, 2011.
$100,000 to Cabbage Patch Settlement House, Louisville, KY, 2011.
$35,000 to Louisville Zoological Gardens, Louisville, KY, 2011.
$25,000 to Make-A-Wish Foundation of Kentucky, Louisville, KY, 2011.
$10,000 to Friends School, Louisville, KY, 2011.
$5,000 to Spalding University, Louisville, KY, 2011. For scholarship.
$5,000 to University of Michigan, Ann Arbor, MI, 2011. For scholarship.
$5,000 to University of Wisconsin, Eau Claire, WI, 2011. For scholarship.
$2,500 to Kentucky Christian University, Grayson, KY, 2011. For scholarship.

1955
Intermec, Inc.

(formerly Interface Mechanisms)
6001 36th Ave. W.
Everett, WA 98203-1264 (425) 348-2600
FAX: (425) 355-9551

Company URL: http://www.intermec.com/
Establishment information: Established in 1966.
Company type: Public company
Company ticker symbol and exchange: IN/NYSE
Business activities: Manufactures and supports data collection and mobile computing products.
Business type (SIC): Communications equipment
Financial profile for 2011: Number of employees, 2,214; assets, $556,270,000; sales volume, $790,090,000; pre-tax net income, -$66,460,000; expenses, $853,780,000; liabilities, $429,650,000
Corporate officers: Allen J. Lauer, Chair. and C.E.O.; Robert J. Driessnack, Sr. V.P. and C.F.O.; Yukio Morikubo, Sr. V.P., Genl. Counsel, and Corp. Secy.; Dennis Faerber, Sr. V.P., Opers.; James P. McDonnell, Sr. V.P., Sales and Mktg.; Jeanne Lyon, V.P., Human Resources
Board of directors: Allen J. Lauer, Chair.; Keith Barnes; Eric J. Draut; Gregory K. Hinckley; Lydia H. Kennard; Stephen P. Reynolds; Steven B. Sample; Oren G. Shaffer; Larry D. Yost
Giving statement: Giving through the Intermec Foundation.
Company EIN: 954647021

Intermec Foundation

(formerly The UNOVA Foundation)
6001 36th Ave. W.
Everett, WA 98203-1264

Establishment information: Established in 1993 in CA.
Financial data (yr. ended 06/30/12): Assets, $15,660,313 (M); expenditures, $942,240; qualifying distributions, $845,869; giving activities include $845,869 for grants.
Purpose and activities: The foundation supports organizations involved with arts and culture, education, and hunger.
Fields of interest: Museums; Performing arts, theater; Arts; Elementary/secondary education; Higher education; Education; Food services; Food banks; Big Brothers/Big Sisters; United Ways and Federated Giving Programs; Engineering/ technology; Science.
Type of support: Employee matching gifts; Employee volunteer services; Employee-related scholarships; Equipment.
Geographic limitations: Giving primarily in IA, OH, and WA.
Application information: Applications not accepted. Unsolicited requests for funds not accepted. Employees of Intermec apply for foundation grants on behalf of nonprofit organizations.
Officers and Directors: Sue Taylor, Pres.; Constance Chapman, Secy.; Frank McCallick, Treas.; Robert Driessnack; Douglas Stubsten.
EIN: 954453230
Selected grants: The following grants are a representative sample of this grantmaker's funding activity:
$63,195 to United Way of Snohomish County, Everett, WA, 2011.
$40,000 to Food Lifeline, Shoreline, WA, 2011.
$40,000 to Shared Harvest FoodBank, Fairfield, OH, 2011.
$17,000 to University of Southern California, Los Angeles, CA, 2011.
$16,000 to American Red Cross, Everett, WA, 2011.
$15,000 to University of Illinois Foundation, Urbana, IL, 2011.
$12,000 to Stanford University, Stanford, CA, 2011.
$10,000 to Theater Cedar Rapids, Cedar Rapids, IA, 2011.
$10,000 to Washington High School, Cedar Rapids, IA, 2011.
$2,500 to Bishop Blanchet High School, Seattle, WA, 2011.

1956
Intermountain Gas Company

555 S. Cole Rd.
P.O. Box 64
Boise, ID 83709-0940 (208) 377-6839

Company URL: http://www.intgas.com
Establishment information: Established in 1950.
Company type: Subsidiary of a public company
Business activities: Transmits and distributes natural gas.
Business type (SIC): Gas production and distribution
Corporate officers: Richard Hokin, Chair.; Frank Morehouse, C.E.O.; William C. Glynn, Pres.; Eldon Book, Exec. V.P. and C.O.O.; Paul R. Powell, Exec. V.P. and C.F.O.; Mark Chiles, V.P. and Cont.; Mike Huntington, V.P., Mktg.
Board of director: Richard Hokin, Chair.
Giving statement: Giving through the Intermountain Gas Company Contributions Program.

Intermountain Gas Company Contributions Program

P.O. Box 7608
Boise, ID 83707-1608

Purpose and activities: As a complement to its foundation, Intermountain also makes charitable contributions to nonprofit organizations directly. Support is given primarily in areas of company operations in Idaho.
Fields of interest: Youth development; Community/ economic development; General charitable giving.
Type of support: Employee matching gifts; Employee volunteer services; Employee-related scholarships; General/operating support; In-kind gifts; Sponsorships.
Geographic limitations: Giving primarily in areas of company operations in ID.

1957
Intermountain Industries, Inc.

960 Broadway Ave., Ste. 500
P.O. Box 70019
Boise, ID 83706 (208) 685-7600

Company URL: http://www.intermountainindustries.com
Establishment information: Established in 1977.
Company type: Subsidiary of a private company
Business activities: Produces oil and natural gas deposits through subsidiaries; operates holding company.
Business type (SIC): Gas production and distribution; extraction/oil and gas; holding company
Corporate officers: Richard Hokin, Chair.; William C. Glynn, Pres.; Michael E. Rich, Exec. V.P., C.F.O., and Secy.-Treas.; Richard W. Beath, V.P., C.A.O., and Cont.
Board of directors: Richard Hokin, Chair.; J. Kermit Birchfield; William C. Glynn; Alexandra Hokin; Amy Hokin; Dana Hokin; Justin Hokin; Lauren Hokin; Tom Hokin; William J. Hokin; J. Richard Jordan; James M. Kelly; Paul Powell; A.J. Schwartz; Michael E. Thomas
Subsidiaries: IGI Resources, Inc., Boise, ID; III Exploration Co., Boise, ID
Giving statement: Giving through the Petroglyph Energy Foundation, Inc.

Petroglyph Energy Foundation, Inc.

(formerly Intermountain Gas Industries Foundation, Inc.)
P.O. Box 70019
Boise, ID 83707-1608
Application address: 960 Broadway Ave., Ste. 500 Boise, ID 83706, tel.: (208) 685-7600; URL: http://www.intermountainindustries.com/community.php

Establishment information: Established in 1988 in ID.
Donors: Intermountain Gas Co.; IGI Resources, Inc.; Petroglyph Operating Co.; Intermountain Industries, Inc.
Contact: Nancy Murrin
Financial data (yr. ended 09/30/11): Assets, $436,837 (M); gifts received, $243,700; expenditures, $249,339; qualifying distributions, $249,035; giving activities include $249,035 for grants.
Purpose and activities: The foundation supports organizations involved with arts and culture, education, health, human services, community development, and civic affairs.
Fields of interest: Performing arts, orchestras; Arts; Higher education; Education; Health care; Boys & girls clubs; YM/YWCAs & YM/YWHAs; Human services; Community/economic development; United Ways and Federated Giving Programs; Public affairs.
Type of support: General/operating support; Scholarship funds.
Geographic limitations: Giving primarily in areas of company operations, with emphasis on ID.
Support limitations: No grants to individuals.
Application information: Applications accepted. Application form required.
Initial approach: Proposal
Deadline(s): None
Officers and Directors:* William C. Glynn*, Pres.; Michael E. Rich, V.P. and Secy.-Treas.; Paul Powell*, V.P.; Richard Hokin.
EIN: 820431608
Selected grants: The following grants are a representative sample of this grantmaker's funding activity:
$25,000 to Brown University, Providence, RI, 2010.

1958
International Air Leases, Inc.

8613 N.W. 54th St.
Doral, FL 33166 (305) 444-7433

Company type: Private company
Business activities: Sells and leases commercial jet aircraft.
Business type (SIC): Motor vehicles—retail/miscellaneous; equipment rental and leasing/miscellaneous
Giving statement: Giving through the Batchelor Foundation, Inc.

The Batchelor Foundation, Inc.

1680 Michigan Ave., No. PH 1
Miami Beach, FL 33139-2538 (305) 534-5004

Establishment information: Established in 1990 in FL.
Donors: International Air Leases, Inc.; Batchelor Enterprises; George E. Batchelor†.
Contact: Anne O. Batchelor-Robjohns, Co-C.E.O.
Financial data (yr. ended 06/30/12): Assets, $294,722,269 (M); expenditures, $13,198,297; qualifying distributions, $11,042,868; giving activities include $10,451,744 for 153 grants (high: $1,000,000; low: $1,500).
Purpose and activities: The foundation supports organizations involved with arts and culture, education, animals and wildlife, health, agriculture and food, recreation, human services, and economically disadvantaged people. Special emphasis is directed toward programs designed to engage in medical research and provide care for childhood diseases; and promote study, preservation, and public awareness of the natural environment.
Fields of interest: Museums; Arts; Higher education; Education; Environment, research; Environment, public education; Environment, natural resources; Botanical gardens; Environment; Animals/wildlife, preservation/protection; Zoos/zoological societies; Animals/wildlife; Hospitals (general); Health care; Medical research; Food services; Agriculture/food; Athletics/sports, water sports; Recreation; Boy scouts; YM/YWCAs & YM/YWHAs; Children/youth, services; Developmentally disabled, centers & services; Homeless, human services; Human services; United Ways and Federated Giving Programs Economically disadvantaged.
Type of support: Capital campaigns; Continuing support; Endowments; General/operating support; Program development.
Geographic limitations: Giving primarily in Miami, FL.
Support limitations: No grants to individuals.
Application information: Applications accepted. Application form not required. Applicants should submit the following:
1) detailed description of project and amount of funding requested
Initial approach: Letter of inquiry
Deadline(s): None
Officers and Trustees:* Anne O. Batchelor-Robjohns*, Co-C.E.O.; Daniel J. Ferraresi*, Co-C.E.O.; Jon Batchelor, Exec. V.P.; Nancy Ansley, C.F.O.; Caridad Velasco, Cont.; Jack Falk.
EIN: 650188171
Selected grants: The following grants are a representative sample of this grantmaker's funding activity:
$1,520,000 to Florida International University, Miami, FL, 2011. For general operations and endowment.
$525,000 to Community Television Foundation of South Florida, Miami, FL, 2011. For general operations.
$500,000 to Chapman Partnership, Miami, FL, 2011. For general operations and endowment.
$500,000 to Fairchild Tropical Botanic Garden, Coral Gables, FL, 2011. For general operations.
$285,000 to Easter Seals South Florida, Miami, FL, 2011. For general operations.
$188,000 to D-FY-IT, Miami, FL, 2011. For general operations.
$150,000 to McCarthys Wildlife Sanctuary, West Palm Beach, FL, 2011. For general operations.
$50,000 to Childrens Home Society of Florida, South Coastal Division, Fort Lauderdale, FL, 2011. For general operations.
$20,000 to Clewiston Museum, Clewiston, FL, 2011. For general operations.
$20,000 to Indian Ridge School, West Palm Beach, FL, 2011. For general operations.

1959
International Bank For Reconstruction & Development

(also known as World Bank)
1818 H St. N.W.
Washington, DC 20433 (202) 473-1000

Company URL: http://www.worldbank.org
Establishment information: Established in 1944.
Company type: Private company
Business activities: Operates an international development bank.
Business type (SIC): Banks/foreign
Corporate officers: Jim Young Kim, Pres.; Anne-Marie Leroy, Sr. V.P. and Genl. Counsel; Jorge Familiar Calderon, V.P. and Corp. Secy.; Madelyn Antoncic, V.P. and Treas.; Charles McDonough, V.P. and Cont.; Sean McGrath, V.P., Human Resources
Giving statement: Giving through the World Bank Community Connections Fund.

World Bank Community Connections Fund

1818 H St., N.W.
Washington, DC 20433-0001 (202) 458-1504
E-mail: comoutreach@worldbank.org; URL: http://go.worldbank.org/AOYTPZJ480

Establishment information: Established in 2002in DE.
Contact: Zena Soudah, Grants Admin.
Financial data (yr. ended 06/30/11): Revenue, $3,985,858; assets, $238,029 (M); gifts received, $3,978,643; expenditures, $3,994,100; program services expenses, $3,989,702; giving activities include $3,989,702 for 134 grants (high: $303,846; low: $5,001).
Purpose and activities: The organization provides World Bank employees the opportunity to provide support to nonprofit organization that work to improve the quality of life of people and communities.
Fields of interest: Mental health, association; Cancer; Heart & circulatory diseases; AIDS; Legal services; Housing/shelter, homeless; Housing/shelter; Boys & girls clubs; Big Brothers/Big Sisters; Boy scouts; Girl scouts; Salvation Army; Children, adoption; Residential/custodial care, hospices; Philanthropy/voluntarism; Christian agencies & churches; Jewish agencies & synagogues Children/youth.
Programs:
Community Outreach Grants Program: The program awards grants of up to $25,000 to nonprofit organizations that work to improve the quality of life of the people and communities in metropolitan Washington, DC.
Dollars for Doers: Through the program, the World Bank recognizes the volunteerism of World Bank staff members, retirees, and World Bank Volunteer Services (WBVS) volunteers by awarding $500 grants to nonprofits in which a staff member, retiree, or WBVS volunteer has an active, ongoing volunteer involvement.
Geographic limitations: Giving primarily in the greater metropolitan Washington, DC area.
Support limitations: No support for sectarian purposes, partisan political activity, formal academic training programs, or research programs. No grants to individuals applying on their own behalf (either for scholarships or other forms of financial assistance), or special fundraising events or activities.
Publications: Annual report.

Application information: Applications not accepted. Unsolicited requests for proposals not considered or acknowledged.
Officer: Katherine Marshall, Pres.; Thelma Diaz, Secy.; Robert van Pulley, Treas.
Directors: Callisto Maldavo; Inder Sud.
EIN: 421559999

1960
International Business Machines Corporation

(also known as IBM)
1 New Orchard Rd.
Armonk, NY 10504-1722 (914) 499-1900
FAX: (914) 765-6021

Company URL: http://www.ibm.com
Establishment information: Established in 1911.
Company type: Public company
Company ticker symbol and exchange: IBM/NYSE
International Securities Identification Number: US4592001014
Business activities: Manufactures information technology products; provides business, technology, and consulting services.
Business type (SIC): Computer and office equipment; management and public relations services
Financial profile for 2012: Number of employees, 434,246; assets, $119,213,000,000; sales volume, $104,507,000,000; pre-tax net income, $21,902,000,000; expenses, $82,605,000,000; liabilities, $100,353,000,000
Fortune 1000 ranking: 2012—20th in revenues, 9th in profits, and 56th in assets
Forbes 2000 ranking: 2012—55th in sales, 17th in profits, and 215th in assets
Corporate officers: Virginia M. Rometty, Chair., Pres., and C.E.O.; Mark Loughridge, Sr. V.P. and C.F.O.; Robert C. Weber, Sr. V.P. and Genl. Counsel; Jon C. Iwata, Sr. V.P., Mktg. and Comms.; J. Randall MacDonald, Sr. V.P., Human Resources; Burno V. Di Leo, Sr. V.P., Sales; Michelle H. Browdy, V.P. and Secy.; Robert F. Del Bene, V.P. and Treas.; James J. Kavanaugh, V.P. and Cont.
Board of directors: Virginia M. Rometty, Chair.; Alain J.P. Belda; William R. Brody, Ph.D.; Kenneth I. Chenault; Michael L. Eskew; David N. Farr; Shirley Ann Jackson, Ph.D.; Andrew N. Liveris; W. James McNerney, Jr.; James W. Owens; Joan E. Spero, Ph.D.; Sidney Taurel; Lorenzo H. Zambrano
Subsidiaries: IBM Credit Corp., White Plains, NY; Lotus Development Corporation, Cambridge, MA
International operations: Argentina; Australia; Austria; Bahamas; Barbados; Belgium; Bermuda; Bolivia; Brazil; Bulgaria; Canada; Chile; China; Colombia; Costa Rica; Croatia; Czech Republic; Denmark; Ecuador; Estonia; Finland; France; Germany; Ghana; Greece; Guatemala; Hong Kong; Hungary; India; Indonesia; Ireland; Israel; Italy; Jamaica; Japan; Kenya; Latvia; Lithuania; Luxembourg; Malaysia; Mauritius; Mexico; Morocco and the Western Sahara; Netherlands; Netherlands Antilles; New Zealand; Nigeria; Norway; Peru; Philippines; Poland; Portugal; Romania; Russia; Serbia; Singapore; Slovakia; Slovenia; South Africa; South Korea; Spain; Sweden; Switzerland; Taiwan; Thailand; Tunisia; Turkey; Ukraine; United Arab Emirates; United Kingdom; Uruguay; Venezuela; Vietnam
Historic mergers: Sequent Computer Systems, Inc. (September 24, 1999); Candle Corporation (June 7, 2004)
Giving statement: Giving through the IBM Center for The Business of Government, the IBM Corporate Giving Program, and the IBM International Foundation.
Company EIN: 130871985

IBM Center for The Business of Government

(formerly The IBM Endowment for the Business of Government)
600 14th St., N.W., 2nd Fl.
Washington, DC 20005-2020 (202) 551-9342
E-mail: businessofgovernment@us.ibm.com; Tel. and e-mail for Jonathan Breul: (202) 551-9310, jonathan.d.breul@us.ibm.com; URL: http://www.businessofgovernment.org

Contact: Jonathan D. Breul, Exec. Dir.
Purpose and activities: Through the IBM Center for The Business of Government, a direct corporate giving program, IBM awards research grants to individuals. Support is given on a national and international basis.
Fields of interest: Public affairs, reform.
Program:
Research: IBM awards $20,000 research grants to individuals producing research reports on new approaches to improving the effectiveness of government.
Type of support: Fellowships.
Geographic limitations: Giving on a national and international basis.
Publications: Application guidelines.
Application information: Applications accepted. Proposal should include a cover letter and be no longer than 3 pages. Contributions generally do not exceed $20,000. Application form required.
Applicants should submit the following:
1) results expected from proposed grant
2) name, address and phone number of organization
3) detailed description of project and amount of funding requested
4) contact person
Proposals should include the individual's resume.
Initial approach: Complete online application form and submit with proposal
Copies of proposal: 1
Deadline(s): Oct. 3 and Mar. 1
Final notification: 6 weeks
Executives: Jonathan D. Breul, Exec. Dir.; John Kamensky, Sr. Fellow; Albert Morales, Partner-in charge.

IBM Corporate Giving Program

New Orchard Rd.
Armonk, NY 10504 (914) 499-1900
E-mail: ibmgives@vnet.ibm.com; Additional contact: Katie Kabage, IBM Community Rels., e-mail: kkabage@us.ibm.com; URL: http://www.ibm.com/ibm/responsibility

Contact: Judy Chin, Corp. Citizenship and Corp. Affairs CCCA; Reg Foster, CCCA Regional Mgr.
Purpose and activities: As a complement to its foundation, IBM also makes charitable contributions to nonprofit organizations directly. Support is given on a national and international basis.
Fields of interest: Arts; Adult/continuing education; Education; Employment; Community/economic development Disabilities, people with.
International interests: Africa; Asia; Australia; Canada; Europe; Latin America; Middle East; Oceania.
Type of support: Consulting services; Continuing support; Donated products; Employee matching gifts; Employee volunteer services; In-kind gifts.
Geographic limitations: Giving on a national and international basis in areas of company operations, including in Africa, Asia, Australia, Canada, Europe, Latin America, the Middle East, and Oceania.
Support limitations: No support for political, labor, religious, or fraternal organizations or sports groups or discriminatory organizations. No grants to individuals, or for fundraising, capital campaigns or construction or renovation, chairs, endowments, or scholarships, or special events.
Application information: Applications accepted. Unsolicited requests are accepted but not encouraged. Letters of inquiry should be no longer than 2 pages. Videos and other supplemental material submissions are not encouraged. Application form not required. Applicants should submit the following:
1) results expected from proposed grant
2) statement of problem project will address
3) name, address and phone number of organization
4) copy of IRS Determination Letter
5) brief history of organization and description of its mission
6) how project's results will be evaluated or measured
7) detailed description of project and amount of funding requested
8) contact person
9) copy of current year's organizational budget and/or project budget
10) listing of additional sources and amount of support
Letters of inquiry should indicate how IBM technology and volunteers will be incorporated.
Initial approach: Letter of inquiry to nearest company facility
Copies of proposal: 1
Deadline(s): None
Final notification: 6 weeks

IBM International Foundation

(formerly IBM South Africa Projects Fund)
New Orchard Rd.
Armonk, NY 10504-1709
URL: http://www.ibm.com/ibm/responsibility/
E-mail for IBM Fellowship Grants: phdfellow@us.ibm.com

Establishment information: Established in 1985 in NY.
Donor: International Business Machines Corp.
Contact: Judy Chin, Fdn. Mgr.
Financial data (yr. ended 12/31/11): Assets, $171,386,198 (M); gifts received, $18,587,758; expenditures, $24,836,471; qualifying distributions, $24,769,147; giving activities include $14,357,936 for grants and $8,675,965 for employee matching gifts.
Purpose and activities: The foundation supports organizations involved with arts and culture, K-12 education, the environment, health, employment, human services, diversity, science, public policy research, and minorities.
Fields of interest: Arts; Elementary/secondary education; Education, early childhood education; Education, continuing education; Education, reading; Health care; Human services; Civil/human rights, equal rights; Science, formal/general education; Mathematics; Physics; Engineering/technology; Computer science; Engineering; Science; Public policy, research Disabilities, people with; Minorities.
International interests: Africa; Asia; Canada; Europe; Latin America.
Programs:
Corporate Service Corps (CSC): Since its launch in 2008, the Corporate Service Corps (CSC) program has contributed over 1,200 participants on over 100 teams to more than 20 countries around the world. The participants are from over 50 countries and

have served communities in Brazil, Chile, China, Egypt, Ghana, India, Indonesia, Kazakhstan, Kenya, Malaysia, Morocco, Nigeria, the Philippines, Romania, Russia, South Africa, Sri Lanka, Tanzania, Thailand, Turkey and Vietnam. The program continues to expand to new locations each year.

General Support Grants: The foundation supports organizations involved with arts and culture, education, health, human services, workforce diversity, science and technology, public policy research, and underrepresented people.

IBM Fellowship Grants: The foundation awards Ph.D. fellowships to students with an interest in solving problems that are important to IBM. Academic disciplines and areas of study are computer science and engineering, electrical and mechanical engineering, physical sciences including chemistry, material sciences, and physics, mathematical sciences including analytics, statistics, operations research, and optimization, business sciences including financial services, risk management, marketing, communications, and learning/knowledge management, and service science, management, and engineering (SSME). Ph.D. fellowships include a stipend for one academic year and Ph.D. Fellows are paired with an IBM mentor according to their technical interests. The program is by nomination only.

KidSmart Early Learning Program: The foundation supports programs designed to enable young children to achieve a head start in their education. The program includes the Young Explorer, a computer housed in kid-friendly furniture, with educational software to help children learn math, science, and language, and the KidSmart website to support teachers and parents.

Matching Grants Program: The foundation matches contributions made by employees and retirees of IBM to educational institutions, hospitals, hospices, nursing homes, and cultural and environmental organizations. Recipient organizations receive cash or IBM equipment or software.

Type of support: Employee matching gifts; Fellowships; General/operating support; Program development.

Geographic limitations: Giving on a national and international basis, with some emphasis in CA and NY, and in Africa, Asia, Canada, Europe, and Latin America.

Support limitations: No support for fraternal, labor, political, or religious organizations or private or parochial schools. No grants to individuals (except for fellowships), or for scholarships, capital campaigns, fundraising, construction or renovation projects, chairs, endowments, conferences, symposia, or sports competitions.

Application information: Applications accepted. Proposals should be no longer than 2 pages. Additional information may be requested at a later date. Applicants must be nominated by a faculty member for IBM Fellowship Grants. Application form not required. Applicants should submit the following:

1) statement of problem project will address
2) copy of IRS Determination Letter
3) brief history of organization and description of its mission
4) how project's results will be evaluated or measured
5) descriptive literature about organization
6) detailed description of project and amount of funding requested
7) copy of current year's organizational budget and/or project budget
8) listing of additional sources and amount of support
9) additional materials/documentation

Initial approach: Proposal; complete online nomination form for IBM Fellowship Grants
Copies of proposal: 1
Deadline(s): None; Sept. 22 to Nov. 2 for IBM Fellowship Grants
Final notification: 1 month

Officers and Directors:* Samuel J. Palmisano*, Chair.; John C. Iwata*, Vice-Chair.; Stanley S. Litow*, Pres.; Andrew Bonzani, Secy.; Robert Del Bene, Treas.; Nick D'Anniballe, Cont.; Mark Loughridge; Robin G. Willner.

Number of staff: 1 full-time professional.

EIN: 133267906

Selected grants: The following grants are a representative sample of this grantmaker's funding activity:

$6,558,344 to IBM International Foundation, Armonk, NY, 2009. To provide job training/developmental infrastructure in developing countries.
$4,693,000 to IBM United Kingdom Trust, London, England, 2009. To deliver educational and cultural programs to selected European Countries.
$590,000 to IBM International Foundation, Armonk, NY, 2009. For general support.
$425,000 to IBM Italy Foundation, Milan, Italy, 2009. For educational and cultural initiatives.
$411,866 to KidSmart, Bridgeton, MO, 2009. For educational material to enable young children to achieve a head start in their education.
$360,000 to KidSmart, Bridgeton, MO, 2009. For educational material to enable young children to achieve a head start in their education.
$220,497 to United Way of York Region, Markham, Canada, 2009. For IBM Canadian Matching Grants Program.
$125,000 to United Way/Centraide Ottawa, Ottawa, Canada, 2009. For local social and voluntary initiatives.
$60,574 to Global Netoptex, San Jose, CA, 2009. For China documentary.

1961
International Council of Shopping Centers, Inc.

1221 Ave. of the Americas, 41st Fl.
New York, NY 10020-1099 (646) 728-3800

Company URL: http://www.icsc.org
Establishment information: Established in 1957.
Company type: Business league
Business activities: Operates global trade association for the shopping center industry.
Business type (SIC): Business association
Corporate officers: David B. Henry, Chair.; Michael P. Kercheval, Pres. and C.E.O.; John C. Emmert, Jr., C.O.O.; Malachy Kavanagh, Sr. V.P., Comms.; Denise Adrian, V.P. and Mktg.; Gregory Peterson, V.P. and Genl. Counsel; Glen Hale, V.P., Finance and Cont.; Fran Marmer, V.P., Human Resources; Kieran P. Quinn, Secy.-Treas.
Board of director: David Henry, Chair.
Giving statement: Giving through the International Council of Shopping Centers Educational Foundation, Inc.

International Council of Shopping Centers Educational Foundation, Inc.

1221 Ave. of the Americas, 41st Fl.
New York, NY 10020-1099 (646) 728-3628
FAX: (212) 589-5555; E-mail: icsc@icsc.org;
URL: http://www.icsc.org/foundation/index.php

Establishment information: Established in 1989 in NY,Supporting organization of International Council of Shopping Centers Educational Foundation, Inc.
Donors: International Council of Shopping Centers, Inc.; Matthew Bucksbaum.
Financial data (yr. ended 12/31/11): Revenue, $118,834; assets, $4,164,127 (M); gifts received, $366,348; expenditures, $225,284; giving activities include $129,050 for grants.
Purpose and activities: The foundation carries out educational and charitable initiatives that support the interests of the retail real estate industry and the International Council of Shopping Centers (ICSC).
Fields of interest: Higher education; Business school/education.

Programs:

Charles Grossman Graduate Scholarships: Two $10,000 scholarships are available to full-time graduate students who have selected retail real estate as their career path. Eligible recipients must also be ICSC members.

Harold E. Eisenberg Foundation Scholarship: This scholarship covers tuition, enrollment fees, textbooks, workbooks, airfare, and hotel accommodations for an individual to attend the John T. Riordan School for Professional Development. Areas of concentration include management, marketing, and leasing at a technical or strategic level.

ICSC CenterBuild Scholarship: A scholarship will be made available annually to a graduate student enrolled in its Master of Real Estate Development program, or an undergraduate student majoring in planning, architecture, interior design, construction management, engineering, landscape architecture, or real estate development.

John T. Riordan Professional Education Scholarship: This scholarship covers enrollment feels, textbooks, workbooks, airfare, and hotel accommodations for a recipient to attend the John T. Riordan School for Professional Development. Available areas of concentration include management, marketing, and leasing at a technical or strategic level; and development, design, and construction at a technical level. Applicants may be new to retail real estate and looking to expand his or her knowledge of management, marketing, leasing or development, or design and construction. Eligible applicants must be members of the International Council of Shopping Centers (ICSC), employed by a member company in good standing, and be actively employed in the retail real estate industry for a minimum of one year and/or a recent graduate of a college or university with an emphasis in real estate.

Schurgin Family Foundation Scholarship: This program provides a $5,000 scholarship to an undergraduate student who is studying retail real estate, real estate development, or shopping center leasing. Applicants for this scholarship must demonstrate academic excellence, as the scholarship is intended to help qualified students pursue an education that will lead them into productive careers in commercial real estate.

Undergraduate Real Estate Award: Twenty-five awards of $1,000 are provided annually to juniors and seniors enrolled in a collegiate undergraduate real estate program who demonstrate exceptional potential for a career in retail real estate.

Type of support: Conferences/seminars; In-kind gifts; Publication; Research; Scholarships—to individuals.
Geographic limitations: Giving on a national basis.
Publications: Application guidelines.
Application information: Applications accepted.
Deadline(s): Mar. for John T. Riordan Professional Education Scholarship and Graduate Level

Scholarships; Apr. 15 for Schurgin Family Foundation Scholarship
Officers and Directors:* Kieran Quinn*, Chair.; Valerie Cammiso*, Pres.; Norris R. Eber, S.C.S.M.*, Secy.-Treas.; Malachy Kavanagh, Asst. Treas.-Secy.; Michael P. Kercheral, Asst. Treas.-Secy.; Gary Brown, CLS; Marcelo Baptista Carvalho, C.S.M., C.M.D.; David Henry; Heather L. Herring; and 13 additional trustees.
Number of staff: 1 full-time professional.
EIN: 133525440

1962
International Flavors & Fragrances, Inc.
521 W. 57th St.
New York, NY 10019-2901 (212) 765-5500
FAX: (21) 708-7132

Company URL: http://www.iff.com
Establishment information: Established in 1833.
Company type: Public company
Company ticker symbol and exchange: IFF/NYSE
Business activities: Manufactures flavor and fragrance compounds, extracts, and aroma chemicals.
Business type (SIC): Chemicals/industrial organic; beverages; soaps, cleaners, and toiletries
Financial profile for 2012: Number of employees, 5,700; assets, $3,249,600,000; sales volume, $2,821,450,000; pre-tax net income, $443,420,000; expenses, $2,378,030,000; liabilities, $2,000,790,000
Fortune 1000 ranking: 2012—743rd in revenues, 519th in profits, and 730th in assets
Corporate officers: Douglas Davis Tough, Chair. and C.E.O.; Kevin Berryman, Exec. V.P. and C.F.O.; Anne Chwat, Sr. V.P., Genl. Counsel, and Corp. Secy.; Francisco Fortanet, Sr. V.P., Opers.; Angelica T. Cantlon, Sr. V.P., Human Resources
Board of directors: Douglas D. Tough, Chair.; Marcello Bottoli; Linda B. Buck, Ph.D.; J. Michael Cook; Roger W. Ferguson, Jr.; Andreas Fibig; Alexandra A. Herzan; Henry W. Howell, Jr.; Katherine M. Hudson; Arthur C. Martinez; Dale F. Morrison
Subsidiaries: IFF FSC, Inc., Hazlet, NJ; Kerr Concentrates, Inc., Salem, OR; The Paks Corp., Junction, TX
Plants: Los Angeles, CA; Chicago, IL; South Brunswick, Union Beach, NJ; Woodburn, OR; Menomonee Falls, WI
International operations: Argentina; Australia; Barbados; Bermuda; Brazil; Canada; Chile; China; Colombia; Denmark; Egypt; England; France; Germany; Gibraltar; Hong Kong; Hungary; India; Indonesia; Ireland; Israel; Italy; Jamaica; Japan; Luxembourg; Mauritius; Mexico; Netherlands; New Zealand; Norway; Pakistan; Philippines; Poland; Portugal; Singapore; South Africa; South Korea; Spain; Sweden; Switzerland; Thailand; Turkey; United Kingdom; Venezuela; Zimbabwe
Giving statement: Giving through the IFF Foundation, Inc.
Company EIN: 131432060

The IFF Foundation, Inc.
521 W. 57th St.
New York, NY 10019-2929
URL: http://www.iff.com/company/philanthropy.aspx

Establishment information: Incorporated in 1963 in NY.
Donor: International Flavors & Fragrances, Inc.
Contact: Carol Brys, Corp. Comms.
Financial data (yr. ended 12/31/11): Assets, $61,486 (M); gifts received, $900,000; expenditures, $848,988; qualifying distributions, $848,547; giving activities include $848,547 for grants.
Purpose and activities: The foundation supports police agencies and organizations involved with arts and culture, education, health, genetic diseases, cancer, cancer research, and human services.
Fields of interest: Museums (art); Performing arts centers; Arts; Higher education; Education; Hospitals (general); Health care; Genetic diseases and disorders; Cancer; Cancer, leukemia; Breast cancer; Cancer research; Crime/law enforcement, police agencies; American Red Cross; Children, services; Human services; United Ways and Federated Giving Programs Women.
Type of support: Annual campaigns; Employee matching gifts; Employee volunteer services; General/operating support; Program development; Publication; Sponsorships.
Geographic limitations: Giving limited to areas of company operations in NJ and New York, NY.
Support limitations: No support for sectarian or religious organizations not of direct benefit to the entire community, political, fraternal, social, or other membership organizations, or organizations whose combined administrative, management, and fundraising expenses exceed 30% of the organization's total budget. No grants to individuals, or for capital campaigns or endowments.
Application information: Applications not accepted. Contributes only to pre-selected organizations.
Officers: Robert M. Amen, Pres.; Kevin C. Berryman, V.P.; Richard A. O'Leary, Treas.
EIN: 136159094
Selected grants: The following grants are a representative sample of this grantmaker's funding activity:
$35,000 to American Cancer Society, New York, NY, 2011.
$25,000 to Whitney Museum of American Art, New York, NY, 2011.
$15,000 to PENCIL, New York, NY, 2011.
$15,000 to Posse Foundation, New York, NY, 2011.
$10,000 to Johnson and Wales University, Providence, RI, 2011.
$10,000 to Lycee Francais de New York, New York, NY, 2011.
$10,000 to Muscular Dystrophy Association, West Long Branch, NJ, 2011.
$10,000 to New York City Police Foundation, New York, NY, 2011.
$5,000 to A Better Chance, New York, NY, 2011.
$5,000 to Opportunities for a Better Tomorrow, Brooklyn, NY, 2011.

1963
International Food Products Corp.
150 Larkin Williams Industrial Ct.
P.O. Box 26377
Fenton, MO 63026 (636) 343-4111

Company URL: http://www.ifpc.com
Establishment information: Established in 1974.
Company type: Private company
Business activities: Trades and distributes commodity ingredients and value added products.
Business type (SIC): Fats and oils; farm-product raw materials—wholesale
Corporate officers: Fred E. Brown, Chair.; Clayton Brown, C.E.O.; Bill Holtgrieve, Pres.; Michael Rivard, C.O.O.; Kathy Langan, V.P., Finance; Jamie Moritz, V.P., Sales and Mktg.; Lisa Filkins, V.P., Human Resources
Board of director: Fred E. Brown, Chair.
Giving statement: Giving through the International Distributing Corporation Charitable Foundation.

International Distributing Corporation Charitable Foundation
150 Larkin Williams Industrial Ct.
Fenton, MO 63026

Establishment information: Established in 1997 in MO. Classified as a company-sponsored operating foundation in 2002.
Donors: International Sweeteners Corp.; Dairy House Co.; International Food Products; FEB Investments; CAB; Belvidere.
Financial data (yr. ended 12/31/11): Assets, $572,249 (M); gifts received, $55,000; expenditures, $90,561; qualifying distributions, $90,057; giving activities include $90,057 for 26 grants (high: $11,500; low: $1,000).
Purpose and activities: The foundation supports organizations involved with secondary and higher education, health, Alzheimer's disease, human services, and Catholicism.
Fields of interest: Education; Human services; Religion.
Type of support: Annual campaigns; Building/renovation; General/operating support; Program development; Research; Scholarship funds; Sponsorships.
Support limitations: No grants to individuals.
Application information: Applications not accepted. Contributes only to pre-selected organizations.
Officers: Carole Ann Brown, Pres.; Elizabeth C. Brown, V.P.; Fred E. Brown, Secy.; Fred E. Brown III, Treas.
EIN: 431661290

1964
International Game Technology
6355 S. Buffalo Dr.
Las Vegas, NV 89113-2133
(702) 669-7777

Company URL: http://www.IGT.com
Establishment information: Established in 1981.
Company type: Public company
Company ticker symbol and exchange: IGT/NYSE
Business activities: Manufactures and distributes computer games and software.
Business type (SIC): Professional and commercial equipment—wholesale; electrical equipment and supplies; manufacturing/miscellaneous; telephone communications; durable goods—wholesale
Financial profile for 2012: Number of employees, 4,800; assets, $4,285,100,000; sales volume, $2,150,700,000; pre-tax net income, $342,800,000; expenses, $1,729,000,000; liabilities, $3,087,300,000
Fortune 1000 ranking: 2012—899th in revenues, 527th in profits, and 638th in assets
Corporate officers: Philip G. Satre, Chair.; Patti S. Hart, C.E.O.; Eric A. Berg, C.O.O.; Eric P. Tom, Exec. V.P., Sales; John Vandemore, C.F.O. and Treas.; Paul C. Gracey, Jr., Gen. Counsel and Secy.
Board of directors: Philip G. Satre, Chair.; Paget L. Alves; Janice Chaffin; Greg Creed; Patti S. Hart; Robert J. Miller; Vincent L. Sadusky; Daniel B. Silvers
Plants: Golden, CO; Hialeah, FL; Gulfport, MS; St. Louis, MO; Missoula, MT; Elko, Las Vegas, Laughlin, Stateline, NV; Atlantic City, NJ

International operations: Argentina; Australia; Belgium; Brazil; Chile; Denmark; France; Germany; Gibraltar; Hong Kong; Ireland; Italy; Netherlands; Norway; Peru; South Africa; Sweden; Switzerland; United Kingdom
Giving statement: Giving through the International Game Technology Corporate Giving Program.
Company EIN: 880173041

International Game Technology Corporate Giving Program

9295 Prototype Dr.
Reno, NV 89521-8986 (775) 448-7777
E-mail: CharitableContributions@IGT.com.;
URL: http://www.igt.com/company-information/about-igt/corporate-social-responsibility.aspx

Purpose and activities: IGT makes charitable contributions to nonprofit organizations involved with arts and culture, education, health, human services, and civic affairs. Special emphasis is directed toward programs designed to integrate IGT's business needs, community interest, and employee involvement. Support is given primarily in areas of company operations, with emphasis on Nevada.
Fields of interest: Arts; Higher education; Business school/education; Health care; Youth development; Children/youth, services; Youth, services; Family services; Human services; Public affairs.
Type of support: Donated equipment; Donated products; Employee volunteer services; In-kind gifts; Sponsorships; Use of facilities.
Geographic limitations: Giving primarily in areas of company operations, with emphasis on NV.
Support limitations: No support for churches, synagogues, or religious groups not of direct benefit to the entire community, political parties or organizations, or other foundations. No grants to individuals or for advertising.
Publications: Application guidelines; Program policy statement.
Application information: Applications accepted. The Corporate Contribution Committee handles giving. Telephone calls during the application process are not encouraged. Support is limited to 1 contribution per organization during any given year. Application form required. Applicants should submit the following:
1) name, address and phone number of organization
2) copy of IRS Determination Letter
3) brief history of organization and description of its mission
4) list of company employees involved with the organization
5) listing of board of directors, trustees, officers and other key people and their affiliations
6) detailed description of project and amount of funding requested
7) contact person
8) copy of current year's organizational budget and/or project budget

Applications should include a description of past support by IGT with the organization.
Initial approach: Complete online application form
Committee meeting date(s): Mar., June, Sept., and Dec.
Deadline(s): 90 days prior to need
Final notification: Following review

1965
International Medical and Educational Data Link, Inc.

10401 Old Georgetown Rd.
Bethesda, MD 20814-1911 (301) 530-5567

Establishment information: Established in 1988.
Company type: Private company
Business activities: Provides telemedicine services; develops medical and educational content; develops software; provides computer network solutions.
Business type (SIC): Cable and other pay television services; computer services; education services
Corporate officer: Jerold J. Principato, M.D., Mgr.
Giving statement: Giving through the Jerold J & Marjorie N Principato Foundation, Inc.

The Jerold J & Marjorie N Principato Foundation, Inc.

5315 Kenwood Ave.
Chevy Chase, MD 20815-6601

Establishment information: Established in 1996 in MD.
Donor: International Medical and Educational Data LINK, Inc.
Financial data (yr. ended 12/31/11): Assets, $3,300,961 (M); expenditures, $194,688; qualifying distributions, $132,350; giving activities include $132,350 for grants.
Purpose and activities: The foundation supports cemeteries and organizations involved with arts and culture, education, the environment, health, human services, and Christianity.
Fields of interest: Arts; Education; Environment.
Type of support: Annual campaigns; Capital campaigns.
Support limitations: No grants.
Application information: Applications not accepted. Unsolicited requests for funds not accepted.
Directors: Deborah Lindsey; Jerold Principato; Marjorie Principato.
EIN: 521960863

1966
International Medical Group, Inc.

(also known as IMG)
2960 N. Meridian St.
P.O. Box 88500
Indianapolis, IN 46208-4715
(317) 655-4500

Company URL: http://www.imglobal.com
Establishment information: Established in 1990.
Company type: Private company
Business activities: Provides health insurance brokerage services.
Business type (SIC): Insurance agents, brokers, and services
Corporate officers: Jefferson W. Brougher, Chair.; Joseph L. Brougher, Pres. and C.E.O.; Jeff Nasser, Sr. V.P., Mktg.; Gordon Bruder, C.F.O.
Giving statement: Giving through the IMG Foundation, Inc.

IMG Foundation, Inc.

2960 N. Meridian St.
Indianapolis, IN 46208-4715 (317) 655-4550
FAX: (317) 655-4505;
E-mail: foundation@imglobal.com; URL: http://www.theimgfoundation.com/

Establishment information: Established in 2003 in Indiana.
Donors: IMG; Keller & Keller.
Contact: Thomas Moses, Pres.
Financial data (yr. ended 12/31/11): Assets, $298,013 (M); gifts received, $57,365; expenditures, $88,361; qualifying distributions, $43,538; giving activities include $43,538 for grants.
Purpose and activities: The foundation supports programs designed to provide services for the well-being of children; health care regardless of a patient's ability to pay; research, education, and treatment of illness, injury, or disease; and programs designed to promote educational opportunities for underprivileged children.
Fields of interest: Higher education; Education; Hospitals (general); Health care; Human services Children.
Type of support: General/operating support; Scholarship funds.
Geographic limitations: Giving primarily in Indianapolis, IN.
Publications: Application guidelines; Informational brochure.
Application information: Applications accepted. Application form not required.
Initial approach: Letter of inquiry
Deadline(s): None
Officers and Directors:* Joseph L. Brougher, Chair.; Thomas W. Moses, Pres.; Kathy J. Schutte*, Secy.; Kurt F. Kipfer*, Treas.; R. Brian Barwick; Greg Edwards; Beth A. Madden; Karen A. Maxey.
EIN: 352209280

1967
International Packaging Corporation

(also known as Interpak)
517 Mineral Spring Ave.
Pawtucket, RI 02860-3408 (401) 724-1600

Company URL: http://www.interpak.com
Establishment information: Established in 1957.
Company type: Private company
Business activities: Manufactures jewelry boxes and pouches and displays.
Business type (SIC): Paperboard containers
Corporate officers: John D. Kilmartin III, Pres.; John J. Kilcoyne, Treas.
Giving statement: Giving through the Kilmartin Charitable Corporation.

Kilmartin Charitable Corporation

517 Mineral Spring Ave.
Pawtucket, RI 02860-3408 (401) 724-1600

Establishment information: Established in 1982 in RI.
Donor: International Packaging Corp.
Contact: John J. Kilcoyne, Treas.
Financial data (yr. ended 12/31/11): Assets, $1,592,639 (M); gifts received, $50,000; expenditures, $86,068; qualifying distributions, $73,600; giving activities include $73,600 for grants.

Purpose and activities: The foundation supports food banks and organizations involved with education, cancer, disaster relief, athletics, human services, and Judaism.
Fields of interest: Middle schools/education; Secondary school/education; Education; Cancer; Food banks; Disasters, preparedness/services; Athletics/sports, Special Olympics; Human services; United Ways and Federated Giving Programs; Jewish agencies & synagogues.
Type of support: General/operating support.
Geographic limitations: Giving primarily in RI.
Support limitations: No grants to individuals.
Application information: Applications accepted. Application form not required.
Initial approach: Letter of inquiry
Deadline(s): None
Officers: John D. Kilmartin III, Pres.; Paul F. Kilmartin, Secy.; John J. Kilcoyne, Treas.
EIN: 050398850

1968
International Paper Company

6400 Poplar Ave.
Memphis, TN 38197 (901) 419-9000

Company URL: http://www.internationalpaper.com/
Establishment information: Established in 1898.
Company type: Public company
Company ticker symbol and exchange: IP/NYSE
International Securities Identification Number: US4601461035
Business activities: Produces forest products; manufactures paper and packaging products.
Business type (SIC): Paper mills; logging; paperboard containers
Financial profile for 2012: Number of employees, 70,000; assets, $32,153,000,000; sales volume, $27,833,000,000; pre-tax net income, $1,024,000,000; expenses, $26,809,000,000; liabilities, $25,849,000,000
Fortune 1000 ranking: 2012—107th in revenues, 241st in profits, and 174th in assets
Forbes 2000 ranking: 2012—340th in sales, 723rd in profits, and 698th in assets
Corporate officers: John V. Faraci, Chair. and C.E.O.; Carol L. Roberts, Sr. V.P. and C.F.O.; John N. Balboni, Sr. V.P. and C.I.O.; Sharon R. Ryan, Sr. V.P., Genl. Counsel, and Corp. Secy.; Paul J. Karre, Sr. V.P., Human Resources and Comms.
Board of directors: John V. Faraci, Chair.; David J. Bronczek; Ahmet C. Dorduncu; Ilene S. Gordon; Stacey J. Mobley; Joan E. Spero; John L. Townsend III; John F. Turner; William G. Walter; J. Steven Whisler
Subsidiary: Temple-Inland Inc., Austin, TX
Division: xpedx, Loveland, OH
Plants: Courtland, Prattville, Selma, AL; Pine Bluff, AR; Pensacola, FL; Augusta, Savannah, GA; Terre Haute, IN; Fort Madison, IA; Bastrop, Mansfield, Pineville, LA; Bucksport, Jay, ME; Quinnesec, MI; Sartell, MN; Vicksburg, MS; Ticonderoga, NY; Riegelwood, Roanoke Rapids, NC; Eastover, Georgetown, SC; Texarkana, TX; Franklin, VA
International operations: Brazil; France; Luxembourg; Singapore
Historic mergers: Union Camp Corporation (April 30, 1999); Champion International Corporation (June 20, 2000)
Giving statement: Giving through the International Paper Company Contributions Program, the International Paper Company Foundation, and the International Paper Company Employee Relief Fund.
Company EIN: 130872805

International Paper Company Contributions Program

6400 Poplar Ave.
Memphis, TN 38197 (901) 419-7000
URL: http://www.internationalpaper.com/US/EN/Company/IPGiving/IPGiving.html

Purpose and activities: As a complement to its foundation, International Paper also makes charitable contributions to nonprofit organizations on a case by case basis; giving to national organizations. Support is given primarily in areas of company operations.
Fields of interest: General charitable giving.
Type of support: Donated products; Employee volunteer services; General/operating support; In-kind gifts; Sponsorships.
Geographic limitations: Giving primarily in areas of company operations.
Support limitations: No grants to individuals.
Application information: Application form not required. Applicants should submit the following:
1) detailed description of project and amount of funding requested
Initial approach: Proposal to nearest company facility
Copies of proposal: 1
Deadline(s): Varies
Final notification: Varies

International Paper Company Foundation

6400 Poplar Ave.
Memphis, TN 38197-0100 (800) 236-1996
E-mail: IPFoundation@ipaper.com; E-mail for Coins 4 Kids Program: coins4kids@ipaper.com; URL: http://www.internationalpaper.com/US/EN/Company/IPGiving/IPFoundation.html

Establishment information: Incorporated in 1952 in NY.
Donor: International Paper Co.
Contact: Deano C. Orr, Exec. Dir.
Financial data (yr. ended 12/31/11): Assets, $51,945,249 (M); expenditures, $2,718,130; qualifying distributions, $2,471,198; giving activities include $2,471,198 for 378 grants (high: $650,000; low: $50).
Purpose and activities: The foundation supports organizations involved with literacy, environmental education, and critical community needs.
Fields of interest: Education, ESL programs; Education, reading; Education; Environment, air pollution; Environment, water pollution; Environment, recycling; Environment, forests; Environmental education; Food services; Human services; Science Children; Youth.
International interests: Africa.
Programs:
Coin 4 Kids Program: The foundation, in collaboration with World Food Programme, provides meals in schools for pre-primary and primary-aged children in poverty stricken areas near Nairobi, Kenya.
Employee Involvement: The foundation awards grants nonprofit organizations with which employees of International Paper volunteers or serves as a member of the organization's board of directors.
Environmental Education: The foundation supports programs designed to help generations understand a sustainable approach to business that balances environmental, social, and economic needs. Special emphasis is directed toward National Geographic Kids Magazine subscriptions at schools in local communities; Earth's Birthday Project kits for children; science-based programs targeting children; outdoor classrooms at schools or in communities; outdoor science programs tied to forestry, air, or water; and education-based programs that promote recycling, tree planting, and composting.
Literacy: The foundation supports programs designed to improve literacy. Special emphasis is directed toward programs designed to enhance reading materials at schools and community libraries; enhance reading skills of children; and teach English as a second language.
New Critical Community Needs: The foundation provides seed money to projects designed to improve the welfare of communities where International Paper has operations in response to critical community need. The project must be a new "critical" community initiative; demonstrate the support of the local community and should provide a benefit to the community at large; and the sources of potential funding must be identified.
Type of support: Curriculum development; Employee matching gifts; Employee volunteer services; Equipment; General/operating support; In-kind gifts; Program development; Seed money.
Geographic limitations: Giving on a national basis in areas of company operations, with some emphasis on Memphis, TN; giving also in Africa through the World Food Program.
Support limitations: No support for veterans' or labor groups, religious or political groups, lobbying organizations, discriminatory organizations, or private foundations. No grants to individuals, or for scholarships, salaries, stipends, or other forms of compensation, mortgage, rent, or utilities, endowments, capital campaigns, multi-year commitments, sponsorships, advertising, travel or lodging expenses, national conferences, sporting events, or other one-time events; no loans.
Publications: Application guidelines; Corporate giving report; Program policy statement.
Application information: Applications accepted. All applications are routed to a local IP facility. Please contact the facility for local submission deadlines. Application form required. Applicants should submit the following:
1) copy of IRS Determination Letter
2) brief history of organization and description of its mission
3) copy of most recent annual report/audited financial statement/990
4) listing of board of directors, trustees, officers and other key people and their affiliations
5) detailed description of project and amount of funding requested
6) copy of current year's organizational budget and/or project budget
7) listing of additional sources and amount of support
Initial approach: Complete online eligibility quiz and application
Copies of proposal: 1
Board meeting date(s): Sept.
Deadline(s): Varies
Officers and Directors:* Patricia Neuhoff, Pres.; Marla Adair, Secy.; Carol Tusch, Treas.; Deano C. Orr, Exec. Dir.; Terri Herrington; Paul J. Karre; Franz Marx; Carol L. Roberts; Mark Sutton; Fred Towler.
Number of staff: 3 full-time professional; 1 part-time support.
EIN: 136155080
Selected grants: The following grants are a representative sample of this grantmaker's funding activity:
$375,000 to Friends of the World Food Program, Washington, DC, 2009. For Coins 4 Kids program.
$375,000 to Friends of the World Food Program, Washington, DC, 2009. For Coins 4 Kids.

$250,000 to National Geographic Society, Washington, DC, 2009. For publication of National Geographic Explorer Magazine for Kids.
$100,000 to Memphis Botanic Garden, Memphis, TN, 2009. For My Big Backyard Project.
$100,000 to National Civil Rights Museum, Memphis, TN, 2009. For Freedom Award winner and to assist with programming and education.
$100,000 to Rise Foundation, Memphis, TN, 2009. For IP Goal Card program at College Park.
$50,000 to Kroc Center, Memphis, TN, 2009. For education activities.
$25,000 to Responsible Environmentalism Foundation, Temperate Forest Foundation, Beaverton, OR, 2009. For teacher education projects.
$17,500 to Childrens Museum of Memphis, Memphis, TN, 2009. For environmental education program at the Treehouse.
$15,000 to Net Impact: New Leaders for Better Business, San Francisco, CA, 2009. For International Paper Live Case Competition.

International Paper Company Employee Relief Fund

6400 Poplar Ave.
Memphis, TN 38197-0198 (901) 419-9000
FAX: (901) 419-4092; Toll-free fax: (877)-603-0756; URL: http://www.internationalpaper.com/US/EN/Company/Sustainability/IPGiving.html

Establishment information: Established in 2002 in TN.
Contact: Kim Wirth, Exec. Dir.
Financial data (yr. ended 12/31/10): Revenue, $380,698; assets, $178,865 (M); gifts received, $380,686; expenditures, $224,266; program services expenses, $224,266; giving activities include $150,000 for grants and $23,058 for grants to individuals.
Purpose and activities: The fund provides basic necessities to persons who have encountered financial hardship for reasons beyond their control, and provides temporary relief to meet the necessities of life of persons who are needy and distressed because of a disaster.
Fields of interest: Human services, emergency aid; Economic development; Business/industry.
Program:
Grants: The program is intended to provide basic necessities and temporary relief to meet the necessities of life of persons who are needy as a direct result of a disaster. Any active, full-time employee of International Paper or an affiliated company where International Paper holds a majority interest may apply for an employee relief fund grant. A maximum of three weeks of the applicant's base pay or $2,500, whichever is less, per hardship will be considered for individuals. Actual assistance will depend on need.
Type of support: Emergency funds; Grants to individuals.
Geographic limitations: Giving limited to areas of company operations in AL, AR, GA, NC, SC, TX, and VA.
Support limitations: No grants for medical- or dental-related claims, assistance to individuals experiencing financial difficulties due to poor financial management or judgment or neglect, expenses (including travel) covered by insurance or other sources of income, or funeral expenses.
Application information: Applications accepted.
Initial approach: Download application form
Officers: Patty Neuhoff*, Pres.; Joe Saab*, Secy.; Carol Tusch*, Treas.; Kim Wirth, Exec. Dir.
Directors: Stanley Burton; Terri Herrington; Carol Roberts; John Taylor; Martha Williams.
EIN: 621857413

1969
International Profit Associates, Inc.

1250 Barclay Blvd.
Buffalo Grove, IL 60089 (847) 808-5590
FAX: (847) 808-5599

Company URL: http://www.ipa-iba.com
Establishment information: Established in 1991.
Company type: Private company
Business activities: Provides consulting services to small and medium-size businesses.
Business type (SIC): Management and public relations services
Financial profile for 2010: Number of employees, 300
Corporate officers: Gregg M. Steinberg, Pres.; Larry Lang, Exec. V.P., Human Resources; Howard Regenbaum, C.F.O.
Giving statement: Giving through the IPA Charities, Inc.

IPA Charities, Inc.

1250 Barclay Blvd.
Buffalo Grove, IL 60089-4500
E-mail: dana.burgess@ipa-iba.com; URL: http://www.ipacharities.org

Establishment information: Established in 2006 in IL.
Donors: International Profit Associates, Inc.; Integrated Business Analysis; Strategic Tax Advisors, Inc.; International Services, Inc.
Contact: Dana Burgess, Pres.
Financial data (yr. ended 09/30/11): Assets, $300 (M); gifts received, $48,000; expenditures, $48,686; qualifying distributions, $48,686; giving activities include $44,435 for 16+ grants (high: $30,000).
Purpose and activities: The foundation supports programs designed to improve communities and people's lives around the world. Special emphasis is directed toward civic and community service; global health and medical research; and education.
Fields of interest: Education; Health care; Cancer; Muscular dystrophy; Medical research; Athletics/sports, Special Olympics; Human services; Science, formal/general education; Leadership development; Public affairs.
Type of support: General/operating support.
Geographic limitations: Giving primarily in IL.
Publications: Grants list.
Application information: Applications accepted. Application form required.
Initial approach: Letter
Deadline(s): None
Officers: Ken Sweet, Chair.; Dana Burgess, Pres.; Tyler Burgess, Secy.; David Danzig, Treas.
Directors: Gerald P. Cukierski; Larry Lang.
EIN: 760807973

1970
International Speedway Corporation

1 Daytona Blvd.
Daytona Beach, FL 32114-1252
(386) 254-2700
FAX: (904) 947-6489

Company URL: http://www.iscmotorsports.com
Establishment information: Established in 1953.
Company type: Public company
Company ticker symbol and exchange: ISCA/NASDAQ
Business activities: Operates motorsports entertainment facilities.
Business type (SIC): Commercial sports
Financial profile for 2012: Number of employees, 840; assets, $2,018,660,000; sales volume, $128,550,000; pre-tax net income, $22,230,000; expenses, $103,410,000; liabilities, $755,650,000
Corporate officers: James C. France, Chair.; Lesa France Kennedy, C.E.O.; John Saunders, Pres.; Daniel W. Houser, Sr. V.P., C.F.O., and Treas.; W. Garrett Crotty, Sr. V.P., Genl. Counsel, and Secy.; Craig A. Neeb, V.P. and C.I.O.; Laura Jackson, V.P., Human Resources
Board of directors: James C. France, Chair.; Larry Aiello, Jr.; J. Hyatt Brown; Brian Z. France; Edsel B. Ford II; William P. Graves; Christy Harris; Morteza Hosseini-Kargar; Lesa France Kennedy; Lloyd Reuss
Giving statement: Giving through the International Speedway Corporation Contributions Program.
Company EIN: 590709342

International Speedway Corporation Contributions Program

International Motorsports Ctr.
1 Daytona Blvd.
Daytona Beach, FL 32114 (386) 254-2700
URL: http://www.internationalspeedwaycorporation.com

1971
International Textile Group, Inc.

804 Green Valley Rd., Ste. 300
Greensboro, NC 27408 (336) 379-6220
FAX: (302) 655-5049

Company URL: http://www.itg-global.com
Establishment information: Established in 2004.
Company type: Public company
Company ticker symbol and exchange: ITXN/OTC
Business activities: Manufactures and provides apparel, interior furnishing, and industrial fabrics and textile solutions.
Business type (SIC): Textile mill products
Financial profile for 2011: Number of employees, 7,800; assets, $436,100,000; sales volume, $694,370,000; pre-tax net income, -$67,550,000; expenses, $707,750,000; liabilities, $595,820,000
Corporate officers: Wilbur L. Ross, Jr., Chair.; Joseph L. Gorga, Pres. and C.E.O.; Kenneth T. Kunberger, C.O.O.; Gail A. Kuczkowski, Exec. V.P. and C.F.O.; Craig J. Hart, V.P. and Treas.; Neil W. Koonce, V.P., Genl. Counsel, and Secy.; Robert E. Garren, V.P., Human Resources and Corp. Comms.
Board of directors: Wilbur L. Ross, Jr., Chair.; Stephen W. Bosworth; Michael J. Gibbons; John Gildea; Joseph L. Gorga; David H. Storper, Ph.D.; Daniel D. Tessoni; David L. Wax; Pamela K. Wilson

Giving statement: Giving through the Burlington Industries Foundation.
Company EIN: 330596831

Burlington Industries Foundation

P.O. Box 26540
Greensboro, NC 27415-6540

Establishment information: Established in 1943 in NC.
Donors: Burlington Industries, Inc.; Burlington Industries LLC.
Contact: Delores C. Sides, Exec. Dir.
Financial data (yr. ended 09/30/10): Assets, $1,434,889 (M); expenditures, $192,933; qualifying distributions, $182,185; giving activities include $182,185 for grants.
Purpose and activities: The foundation supports art councils and organizations involved with education, multiple sclerosis, youth development, and business promotion.
Fields of interest: Arts councils; Elementary/ secondary education; Higher education; Education; Multiple sclerosis; Boy scouts; Youth development; Community development, business promotion; United Ways and Federated Giving Programs.
Programs:
Burlington Industries Foundation Scholarships: The foundation awards college scholarships at North Carolina State University and the University of North Carolina-Greensboro to children of employees of International Textile Group.
Employee Matching Gifts: The foundation matches contributions made by full-time employees and directors of International Textile Group to institutions of higher education on a one-for-one basis from $25 to $5,000 per employee, per year and $25 to $7,500 per director, per year.
Hardship Aid Program: The foundation awards grants to employees who have sustained severe losses from disasters.
Type of support: Annual campaigns; Building/ renovation; Capital campaigns; Employee matching gifts; Employee volunteer services; Employee-related scholarships; Grants to individuals; Program development; Scholarship funds.
Geographic limitations: Giving primarily in areas of company operations in NC, SC, and VA.
Support limitations: Generally, no support for sectarian or denominational religious organizations, national organizations, private secondary schools, or historic preservation organizations. No grants to individuals (except for employees in distress), or for conferences, seminars, workshops, endowments, outdoor dramas, films, or documentaries, or medical research; no loans.
Publications: Application guidelines.
Application information: Applications accepted. Application form not required.
Initial approach: Proposal
Copies of proposal: 1
Board meeting date(s): Annually
Deadline(s): None
Final notification: 3 months
Officer and Trustees:* Delores C. Sides*, Exec. Dir.; Park R. Davidson; Joseph L. Gorga; George W. Henderson III; Charles A. McLendon, Jr.
EIN: 566043142
Selected grants: The following grants are a representative sample of this grantmaker's funding activity:
$5,000 to University of North Carolina, Greensboro, NC, 2009.
$5,000 to University of North Carolina, Greensboro, NC, 2009.
$5,000 to University of North Carolina, Greensboro, NC, 2009.
$2,550 to Duke University, Durham, NC, 2009.
$2,500 to Multiple Sclerosis Society National Headquarters, New York, NY, 2009.
$2,500 to University of North Carolina, Greensboro, NC, 2009.
$1,500 to American Heart Association, Mid-Atlantic Affiliate, Dallas, TX, 2009.

1972
International-Matex Tank Terminals

(also known as Consulate General of Denmark)
321 St. Charles Ave., Ste. 900
New Orleans, LA 70130-3145
(504) 586-8300

Company URL: http://www.imtt.com
Establishment information: Established in 1975.
Company type: Private company
Business activities: Provides bulk liquid handling services.
Business type (SIC): Warehousing and storage
Corporate officers: Thomas B. Coleman, C.E.O.; Richard D. Courtney, Pres. and C.O.O.; John Siragusa, Sr. V.P. and C.F.O.
Offices: Richmond, CA; Bayonne, NJ
Giving statement: Giving through the Coleman Family Foundation.

The Coleman Family Foundation

321 St. Charles Ave., 10th Fl.
New Orleans, LA 70130-3145

Establishment information: Established in 2000 in LA.
Donors: International-Matex Tank Terminals; James J. Coleman, Sr.
Financial data (yr. ended 12/31/11): Assets, $1 (M); expenditures, $900; qualifying distributions, $0.
Purpose and activities: The foundation supports organizations involved with Christianity.
Type of support: General/operating support; Publication.
Support limitations: No grants to individuals.
Application information: Applications not accepted. Unsolicited requests for funds not accepted.
Trustees: Dorothy Coleman; James J. Coleman, Jr.; Thomas B. Coleman.
EIN: 721486006

1973
Intero Real Estate Services, Inc.

175 E. Main Ave., Ste. 130
Morgan Hill, CA 95037-7520
(408) 201-0144

Company URL: http://www.interorealestate.com
Establishment information: Established in 2002.
Company type: Private company
Business activities: Operates real estate agency.
Business type (SIC): Real estate agents and managers
Financial profile for 2011: Number of employees, 50
Corporate officers: Robert Moles, Chair.; Gino Blefari, Pres. and C.E.O.; Thomas Tognoli, C.O.O.; Stuart Blomgren, C.F.O. and Secy.-Treas.; Patrick Cardwell, Genl. Counsel
Board of director: Robert Moles, Chair.
Giving statement: Giving through the Intero Foundation, Inc.

The Intero Foundation, Inc.

10275 N. De Anza Blvd.
Cupertino, CA 95014-2045
E-mail: children@interofoundation.org; URL: http://www.interofoundation.org

Establishment information: Established in 2003 in CA.
Contact: David Piazza, Dir.
Financial data (yr. ended 12/31/11): Revenue, $296,112; assets, $439,838 (M); gifts received, $281,867; expenditures, $226,074; giving activities include $205,209 for grants.
Purpose and activities: The foundation aims to positively impact the growth and well-being of children by supporting organizations focused on assisting children in their education and personal development.
Fields of interest: Community/economic development Children.
Program:
General Grants: The foundation provides funding to organizations that work with disadvantaged children through education, counseling, providing food or shelter, or that work with children with life-altering disabilities. Priority is given to smaller non-profit organizations.
Geographic limitations: Giving primarily in CA.
Support limitations: No support for human services programs that don't improve their clients' conditions, organizations that discriminate, professional associations, labor organizations, fraternal organization, social clubs, exhibition groups, political organizations, or religion organizations. No grants for events, athletic programs or sporting events, one-time projects, research studies, reducing debt or past operating deficits, underwriting films, television, or advertising, and pilot programs.
Publications: Application guidelines.
Application information: Applications accepted. Application form required. Applicants should submit the following:
1) role played by volunteers
2) qualifications of key personnel
3) population served
4) name, address and phone number of organization
5) copy of IRS Determination Letter
6) brief history of organization and description of its mission
7) geographic area to be served
8) copy of most recent annual report/audited financial statement/990
9) how project's results will be evaluated or measured
10) listing of board of directors, trustees, officers and other key people and their affiliations
11) detailed description of project and amount of funding requested
12) plans for cooperation with other organizations, if any
13) contact person
14) copy of current year's organizational budget and/or project budget
15) plans for acknowledgement
Initial approach: Submit proposal
Deadline(s): June 1st (for inquiries from the San Francisco Peninsula) and Oct. 1st (for inquiries from Silicon Valley)
Officers and Directors:* Denise Pearson*, Pres.; Sandra Troia*, V.P.; Cathy Jackson, Secy.; Bonnie Wilson*, C.F.O.; Gino Blefari; John Thompson; Tom Tognoli.
EIN: 870688284

1974
The Interpublic Group of Companies, Inc.

1114 Avenue of the Americas
New York, NY 10036 (212) 704-1200
FAX: (212) 704-1201

Company URL: http://www.interpublic.com
Establishment information: Established in 1902.
Company type: Public company
Company ticker symbol and exchange: IPG/NYSE
Business activities: Provides advertising and marketing services.
Business type (SIC): Advertising
Financial profile for 2012: Number of employees, 43,300; assets, $13,493,900,000; sales volume, $6,956,200,000; pre-tax net income, $674,800,000; expenses, $6,277,900,000; liabilities, $11,073,300,000
Fortune 1000 ranking: 2012—366th in revenues, 359th in profits, and 318th in assets
Corporate officers: Michael I. Roth, Chair. and C.E.O.; Frank Mergenthaler, Exec. V.P. and C.F.O.; Christopher F. Carroll, Sr. V.P., Cont., and C.A.O.; Andrew Bonzani, Sr. V.P., Genl. Counsel, and Secy.; Joseph W. Farrelly, Sr. V.P. and C.I.O.; Ellen T. Johnson, Sr. V.P. and Treas.; Raj Singhal, Sr. V.P., Finance
Board of directors: Michael I. Roth, Chair.; Jocelyn Carter-Miller; Jill M. Considine; Richard A. Goldstein; H. John Greeniaus; Dawn Hudson; William T. Kerr; Mary J. Steele Guilfoile; David M. Thomas
International operations: Australia; Bahrain; Belgium; Brazil; Canada; China; Denmark; France; Germany; Greece; India; Israel; Italy; Japan; Mauritius; Netherlands; Norway; Philippines; Poland; Portugal; Romania; South Africa; South Korea; Spain; Sweden; Thailand; Turkey; United Arab Emirates; United Kingdom
Giving statement: Giving through the Interpublic Group of Companies, Inc., Corporate Giving Program.
Company EIN: 131024020

The Interpublic Group of Companies, Inc., Corporate Giving Program

1114 Avenue of the Americas
New York, NY 10036 (212) 704-1200
FAX: (212) 704-1201;
E-mail: tom.cunningham@interpublic.com;
URL: http://www.interpublic.com/corporatecitizenship/communityinvolvement

Contact: Tom Cunningham, Corp. Comms.
Purpose and activities: The Interpublic Group of Companies, Inc., makes charitable contributions to organizations involved with arts and culture, and education. Support is given primarily in areas of company operations.
Fields of interest: Arts; Graduate/professional education; Human services; International relief; General charitable giving.
Type of support: Employee volunteer services; General/operating support; Pro bono services - communications/public relations; Pro bono services - marketing/branding.
Geographic limitations: Giving primarily in areas of company operations.

1975
Interstate Packaging Corporation

2285 Hwy. 47 N.
P.O. Box 789
White Bluff, TN 37187-4126
(615) 797-9000

Company URL: http://www.interstatepkg.com
Establishment information: Established in 1969.
Company type: Private company
Business activities: Manufactures labels and flexible packaging.
Business type (SIC): Paper and paperboard/coated, converted, and laminated; printing/commercial; plastic products/miscellaneous
Financial profile for 2012: Number of employees, 300
Corporate officers: Jerald Doochin, Chair. and Co-Pres.; Michael Doochin, Co-Pres.
Board of director: Jerald Doochin, Chair.
Giving statement: Giving through the Doochin Family Charitable Trust.

Doochin Family Charitable Trust

(formerly Interstate Packaging Foundation Charitable Trust)
P.O. Box 789
White Bluff, TN 37187-0922 (615) 797-9000

Establishment information: Established in 1977.
Donor: Interstate Packaging Corp.
Contact: Jerald Doochin, Tr.
Financial data (yr. ended 04/30/12): Assets, $1,406,586 (M); gifts received, $170,705; expenditures, $273,451; qualifying distributions, $273,451; giving activities include $273,451 for grants.
Purpose and activities: The foundation supports community foundations and organizations involved with arts and culture, education, children and youth, and Judaism.
Fields of interest: Performing arts, theater; Performing arts, orchestras; Arts; Elementary/secondary education; Higher education; Education; Children/youth, services; Foundations (community); Jewish federated giving programs; Jewish agencies & synagogues.
Type of support: General/operating support.
Geographic limitations: Giving primarily in Nashville, TN.
Support limitations: No grants to individuals.
Application information: Applications accepted. Application form not required. Applicants should submit the following:
1) detailed description of project and amount of funding requested
Initial approach: Proposal
Deadline(s): None
Trustees: Jerald Doochin; Michael Doochin.
EIN: 621031459
Selected grants: The following grants are a representative sample of this grantmaker's funding activity:
$40,248 to Congregation Micah, Brentwood, TN, 2010.
$15,600 to Center for Jewish Awareness, Nashville, TN, 2010.
$9,250 to University School of Nashville, Nashville, TN, 2010.
$8,000 to Nashville Childrens Theater, Nashville, TN, 2010.
$7,000 to Vanderbilt University, Nashville, TN, 2010.
$6,000 to American Chestnut Foundation, Bennington, VT, 2010.
$2,750 to Nashville Symphony, Nashville, TN, 2010.
$2,500 to Sierra Club Foundation, San Francisco, CA, 2010.
$1,500 to Nashville Public Library, Nashville, TN, 2010.
$1,000 to Fisk University, Nashville, TN, 2010.

1976
Intertech, Inc.

1020 Discovery Rd., Ste. 145
St. Paul, MN 55121 (651) 454-0013

Company URL: http://www.intertech.com
Establishment information: Established in 1991.
Company type: Private company
Business activities: Provides computer software training services.
Business type (SIC): Vocational schools
Corporate officers: Thomas Salonek, Pres. and C.E.O.; Ryan McCabe, V.P., Sales
Office: Chicago, IL
Giving statement: Giving through the Intertech Foundation.

Intertech Foundation

1575 Thomas Center Dr.
Eagan, MN 55122-2642 (651) 288-7000
FAX: (651) 846-5666;
E-mail: Foundation@intertech.com; Additional tel.: (651) 994-8558; URL: http://www.intertech-inc.com/Foundation/Foundation.aspx

Establishment information: Established in 2003 in MN.
Donors: Intertech, Inc.; Tom Salonek; Linda Salonek; Ryan McCabe.
Contact: Ryan McCabe, Secy.
Financial data (yr. ended 12/31/11): Assets, $139,786 (M); gifts received, $49,500; expenditures, $4,276; qualifying distributions, $3,581; giving activities include $3,581 for 5 grants (high: $750; low: $644).
Purpose and activities: The foundation supports the Ronald McDonald House in Minneapolis, Minnesota and awards grants to Minnesota families with terminally ill children in need of financial assistance.
Fields of interest: Housing/shelter.
Type of support: General/operating support; Grants to individuals.
Geographic limitations: Giving limited to Minneapolis, MN.
Publications: Application guidelines.
Application information: Applications accepted. Applicants must be or have been a resident of Ronald McDonald House in Minneapolis, Minnesota. Individuals may receive up to two grants per year. Application form required.
Initial approach: Download application form and fax or mail to foundation
Deadline(s): None
Officers and Directors:* Tom Salonek*, Pres.; Ryan McCabe*, Secy.; Linda Salonek.
EIN: 200498817

1977
The InterTech Group, Inc.
4838 Jenkins Ave.
P.O. Box 5205
North Charleston, SC 29405-4816
(843) 744-5174

Company URL: http://www.theintertechgroup.com/
Establishment information: Established in 1982.
Company type: Private company
Business activities: Operates holding company; manufactures metalworking machinery.
Business type (SIC): Machinery/metalworking; holding company
Financial profile for 2011: Number of employees, 15,000; sales volume, $3,600,000,000
Corporate officers: Anita Zucker, Chair. and C.E.O.; Jonathan M. Zucker, Pres.; Julian A. Tiedemann, Exec. V.P. and C.O.O.; M. Brice Sweatt, V.P., Finance
Board of director: Anita Zucker, Chair.
Subsidiary: The Rug Barn Inc., Abbeville, SC
Giving statement: Giving through the InterTech Group Foundation, Inc.

The InterTech Group Foundation, Inc.
4838 Jenkins Ave.
North Charleston, SC 29405-4816 (843) 744-5174

Establishment information: Established in 2004 in SC.
Donors: The InterTech Group, Inc.; Anita G. Zucker.
Financial data (yr. ended 12/31/11): Assets, $2,127,994 (M); gifts received, $102,738; expenditures, $102,422; qualifying distributions, $96,858; giving activities include $96,858 for 66 grants (high: $5,000; low: $54).
Purpose and activities: The foundation supports food banks and organizations involved with education, water safety, cancer, housing development, human services, and Christianity.
Fields of interest: Education; Environment; Health organizations.
Type of support: General/operating support.
Geographic limitations: Giving primarily in SC.
Support limitations: No grants to individuals.
Application information: Applications accepted. Contributes only to pre-selected organizations. Application form required.
Initial approach: Check foundation website
Deadline(s): None
Directors: Andrea Z. Zucker; Anita G. Zucker; Jeffrey M. Zucker; Jonathan M. Zucker.
EIN: 201473099

1978
Interthyr Corporation
(also known as Interthyr Research Foundation)
340 W. State St., Unit 36
Athens, OH 45701-1566 (740) 566-6023

Company URL: http://www.interthyr.com/
Establishment information: Established in 1999.
Company type: Private company
Business activities: Develops diagnostic assays and therapeutics for endocrine diseases, autoimmune-inflammatory diseases, and cancer.
Business type (SIC): Research, development, and testing services
Corporate officer: Leonard D. Kohn, Pres. and C.E.O.
Giving statement: Giving through the Interthyr Research Foundation.

Interthyr Research Foundation
18602 N.E. 137th St.
Woodinville, WA 98072-9331 (425) 885-0205

Establishment information: Established in 1983 in WA.
Financial data (yr. ended 12/31/11): Revenue, $81,819; assets, $182 (M); expenditures, $92,589; giving activities include $32,703 for grants.
Purpose and activities: The foundation promotes scientific research in the bio-medical field, particularly research in endocrinology, through grants to researchers located in the U.S. and foreign countries; the foundation also participates in managing and licensing inventions and patents with the objective to make new bio-medical technology available to improve public health and to produce licensing revenue to fund such research.
Fields of interest: Public health; Medical research.
Type of support: Grants to individuals; Research.
Geographic limitations: Giving on a national and international basis.
Officers and Directors:* Dr. William Valente, Pres.; Dr. Salvatore Aloj, V.P.; Dr. S. Ambesi-Impiombato, Secy.; Dr. Leonard D. Kohn, Treas.; Marjory Bundock; Dr. Evelyn Grollman; Dr. P. Vitti.
EIN: 521366806

1979
Intoximeters, Inc.
2081 Craig Rd.
St. Louis, MO 63146-4107 (314) 429-4000

Company URL: http://www.intox.com
Establishment information: Established in 1945.
Company type: Private company
Business activities: Develops, manufactures, and markets alcohol breath testing instruments.
Business type (SIC): Measuring, analyzing, and controlling instruments
Financial profile for 2012: Number of employees, 60
Corporate officers: M. Rankine Forrester, C.E.O.; Christopher Dalton, Pres.; Mark Gilmer, V.P., Mktg.; Kathy Vallmann, Cont.
Giving statement: Giving through the Intoximeters, Inc. Corporate Giving Program.

Intoximeters, Inc. Corporate Giving Program
2081 Craig Rd.
St. Louis, MO 63146-4107
FAX: (314) 429-4170

Contact: Keith Hart, Asst. Cont. and Human Resources Mgr.
Purpose and activities: Intoximeters makes charitable contributions to nonprofit organizations on a case by case basis. Special emphasis is directed toward programs that promote education of youth, human services for economically disadvantaged individuals and families, healthcare in underserved areas, broad-based participation in arts and culture, and the environment. Support is given on a national basis.
Fields of interest: General charitable giving Children/youth; Minorities; African Americans/Blacks; Native Americans/American Indians; Economically disadvantaged.
Type of support: Annual campaigns; Continuing support; Employee matching gifts; General/operating support.
Geographic limitations: Giving on a national basis, with emphasis on areas of company operations.
Support limitations: No support for religious, labor, or political organizations. Generally, no grants to individuals, or for group travel.
Application information: Applications accepted. A contributions committee reviews all requests. Application form not required.
Initial approach: Mail proposal to headquarters
Copies of proposal: 1
Committee meeting date(s): Nov.
Deadline(s): Oct. 10

1980
Intrepid Production Corporation
707 17th St., Ste. 4200
Denver, CO 80202-3432 (303) 296-3006

Establishment information: Established in 1984.
Company type: Private company
Business activities: Operates oil and gas exploration company.
Business type (SIC): Oil and gas field services
Corporate officers: Robert P. Jornayvaz III, Pres.; Louisa Jornayvaz, Corp. Secy.
Board of directors: Terry Considine; Chris A. Elliott; J. Landis Martin; Barth E. Whitham
Giving statement: Giving through the Larrk Foundation.

Larrk Foundation
707 17th St., Ste. 4100
Denver, CO 80202-3404

Establishment information: Established in 2008 in CO.
Donor: Intrepid Production Corp.
Contact: Wendell Fleming, Exec. Dir.
Financial data (yr. ended 12/31/11): Assets, $15,853,190 (M); expenditures, $1,028,057; qualifying distributions, $703,116; giving activities include $703,116 for grants.
Fields of interest: Performing arts, ballet; Education; Hospitals (specialty); Human services.
Geographic limitations: Giving primarily in CO.
Application information: Applications not accepted. Unsolicited requests for funds not accepted.
Officers and Directors:* Robert Jornayvaz*, Pres.; Louisa Craft Jornayvaz*, Secy.; Wendell Fleming, Exec. Dir.
EIN: 263818473

1981
INTRUST Bank, N.A.
(formerly First National Bank in Wichita)
105 N. Main St.
Wichita, KS 67202-1412 (316) 383-1234

Company URL: http://www.intrustbank.com
Establishment information: Established in 1876.
Company type: Subsidiary of a private company
Business activities: Operates commercial bank.
Business type (SIC): Banks/commercial
Financial profile for 2011: Assets, $4,077,238,000; liabilities, $3,814,266,000
Corporate officers: Charles Q. Chandler IV, Chair., Pres., and C.E.O.; J.V. Lentell, Vice-Chair.; Jay Smith, C.O.O.
Board of directors: Charles Q. Chandler IV, Chair.; J.V. Lentell, Vice-Chair.; Rick Beach; C. Robert Buford; Anderson Chandler; Stephen L. Clark; Kenneth Griggs; Richard M. Kerschen; Thomas D.

Kitch; Eric T. Knorr; Charles G. Koch; Kenneth Shannon; Stephen B. Slawson; Jay Smith; John T. Stewart III; Jeffrey L. Turner
Giving statement: Giving through the INTRUST Bank Charitable Trust.

INTRUST Bank Charitable Trust

(formerly First National Bank in Wichita Charitable Trust)
c/o INTRUST Bank, N.A.
P.O. Box 1
105 North Main
Wichita, KS 67201-5001 (316) 383-1489
FAX: (316) 383-5801;
E-mail: Diane.Iseman@intrustbank.com

Establishment information: Established in 1952 in KS.
Donor: INTRUST Bank, N.A.
Contact: Diane Iseman, V.P., Corp. Comms.
Financial data (yr. ended 12/31/11): Assets, $885,778 (M); gifts received, $420,000; expenditures, $394,494; qualifying distributions, $393,819; giving activities include $393,819 for grants.
Purpose and activities: The foundation supports organizations involved with arts and culture, higher education, and human services.
Fields of interest: Arts; Higher education; Children/youth, services; Human services; United Ways and Federated Giving Programs.
Type of support: Building/renovation; Capital campaigns; Continuing support; General/operating support.
Geographic limitations: Giving limited to KS, with emphasis on Wichita.
Publications: Application guidelines.
Application information: Applications accepted. Application form not required. Applicants should submit the following:
1) copy of IRS Determination Letter
2) brief history of organization and description of its mission
3) copy of most recent annual report/audited financial statement/990
4) listing of board of directors, trustees, officers and other key people and their affiliations
5) detailed description of project and amount of funding requested
6) copy of current year's organizational budget and/or project budget
7) listing of additional sources and amount of support

Initial approach: Proposal
Copies of proposal: 1
Deadline(s): None
Final notification: 6 weeks

Trustees: Jill Beckman; Charles Q. Chandler IV; J.V. Lentell; Rodney D. Pitts; Susan Sullivan; Lyndon Wells.
EIN: 486102412

1982
Intuit Inc.

2632 Marine Way
Mountain View, CA 94043 (650) 944-6000
FAX: (650) 944-3060

Company URL: http://www.intuit.com
Establishment information: Established in 1983.
Company type: Public company
Company ticker symbol and exchange: INTU/NASDAQ
International Securities Identification Number: US4612021034
Business activities: Provides business and financial management solutions.
Business type (SIC): Computer services
Financial profile for 2012: Number of employees, 8,500; assets, $4,684,000,000; sales volume, $4,151,000,000; pre-tax net income, $1,151,000,000; expenses, $2,974,000,000; liabilities, $1,940,000,000
Fortune 1000 ranking: 2012—558th in revenues, 242nd in profits, and 611th in assets
Forbes 2000 ranking: 2012—1487th in sales, 686th in profits, and 1810th in assets
Corporate officers: William V. Campbell, Chair.; Brad D. Smith, Pres. and C.E.O.; R. Neil Williams, Sr. V.P. and C.F.O.; Sasan Goodarzi, Sr. V.P. and C.I.O.; Laura A. Fennell, Sr. V.P., Genl. Counsel, and Secy.; Sherry Whiteley, Sr. V.P., Human Resources; Jeffrey Hank, V.P., Finance and C.A.O.
Board of directors: William V. Campbell, Chair.; Christopher W. Brody; Scott D. Cook; Diane B. Greene; Suzanne Nora Johnson; Edward A. Kangas; Dennis D. Powell; Brad D. Smith; Jeffrey Weiner
Subsidiaries: Intuit Insurance Services, Inc., Alexandria, VA; Intuit Lender Services, Inc., Mountain View, CA; Lacerte Educational Services, Inc., Dallas, TX
Offices: Tucson, AZ; Mountain View, San Diego, CA; New York, NY; Orem, UT; Richmond, VA
International operations: Australia; Canada; Hong Kong; India; Mauritius; Singapore; South Africa; United Kingdom
Giving statement: Giving through the Intuit Inc. Corporate Giving Program, the Intuit Foundation, and the Intuit Scholarship Foundation.
Company EIN: 770034661

Intuit Inc. Corporate Giving Program

2632 Marine Way
Mountain View, CA 94043-1126 (650) 944-6000
Contact for product donations: TechSoup, tel.: (800) 659-3579 ext. 700; URL: http://www.intuit.com/about_intuit/philanthropy/donation_about.jsp

Purpose and activities: As a complement to its foundation, Intuit also makes charitable contributions of donated software to nonprofit organizations directly. Special emphasis is directed towards programs designed to support financial literacy or small business development in disadvantaged communities. Support is given primarily in areas of company operations.
Fields of interest: Human services, financial counseling; Economic development; Business/industry; Community/economic development.
Type of support: Donated products; In-kind gifts.
Geographic limitations: Giving primarily in areas of company operations.
Publications: Application guidelines.
Application information: Applications accepted.
Initial approach: Visit website for application guidelines

The Intuit Foundation

P.O. Box 7850, MS MTV-07-02
Mountain View, CA 94039-7850
URL: http://www.intuit.com/about_intuit/philanthropy/how.jsp#Foundation

Establishment information: Established in 2002 in CA.
Donor: Intuit Inc.
Financial data (yr. ended 03/31/12): Assets, $933,395 (M); gifts received, $1,500,000; expenditures, $1,216,792; qualifying distributions, $1,123,037; giving activities include $1,123,037 for grants.
Purpose and activities: The foundation supports organizations involved with education, health, children and youth, human services, community development, and economically disadvantaged people. Special emphasis is directed toward programs designed to foster economic empowerment.
Fields of interest: Education; Health care; Children/youth, services; Human services, financial counseling; Human services; Economic development; Community development, small businesses; Community/economic development Economically disadvantaged.
International interests: Canada.
Programs:
Economic Empowerment: The foundation supports programs designed to cultivate an entrepreneurial spirit among small businesses in disadvantaged communities; help nonprofits do more with their resources; and encourage financial literacy among people in need.
We Care and Give Back Program: The foundation matches contributions made by employees of Intuit to nonprofit organizations on a one-for-one basis up to $2,000 per employee, per year. The foundation also awards grants to nonprofit organizations with which employees volunteer. Special emphasis is directed toward education programs for at-risk children and youth and disadvantaged adults; and antipoverty programs designed to provide health, food, shelter, clothing, gifts and toys, disaster relief, and other social services.
Type of support: Employee matching gifts; Employee volunteer services; General/operating support; Program development.
Geographic limitations: Giving primarily in AZ, CA, Washington, DC, GA, MA, NV, NY, TX, and VA.
Support limitations: No support for religious organizations, political or labor organizations, private foundations, or discriminatory organizations. No grants to individuals, or for fundraising events or sponsorships, advertising, souvenir journals, or dinner programs, or conferences, exhibits, or academic research.
Application information: Applications not accepted. Contributes only to pre-selected organizations.
Officers and Directors:* Sherry Whiteley*, C.E.O. and Pres.; Ken Wach, V.P.; Tyler Cozzens, Secy.; David Merenbach*, Treas.; Scott D. Cook.
EIN: 470860921
Selected grants: The following grants are a representative sample of this grantmaker's funding activity:
$51,700 to African Leadership Foundation, San Francisco, CA, 2011. For general support.
$18,570 to Kiva Microfunds, San Francisco, CA, 2011. For general support.
$9,785 to Second Harvest Food Bank of Santa Clara and San Mateo Counties, San Jose, CA, 2011. For general support.
$9,693 to Leukemia & Lymphoma Society, Los Angeles, CA, 2011. For general support.
$8,825 to Palo Alto Partners in Education, Palo Alto, CA, 2011. For general support.
$8,175 to Doctors Without Borders USA, New York, NY, 2011. For general support.
$6,084 to Marine Toys for Tots Foundation, Triangle, VA, 2011. For general support.
$3,780 to Big Brothers Big Sisters of Northern Nevada, Reno, NV, 2011. For general support.
$2,713 to Aid for AIDS of Nevada, Las Vegas, NV, 2011. For general support.
$1,050 to University of Chicago, Chicago, IL, 2011. For general support.

The Intuit Scholarship Foundation

1015 Middlefield Rd.
Palo Alto, CA 94301-3343 (650) 944-6000
Application address: c/o P.O. Box 7850, Mountain View, CA 94039

Establishment information: Established in 1996 in CA.
Donors: Scott D. Cook; Signey Ostby.
Contact: Noelani Luke
Financial data (yr. ended 07/31/11): Assets, $1,426 (M); gifts received, $95,000; expenditures, $95,305; qualifying distributions, $95,270.
Purpose and activities: The foundation awards college scholarships to children and dependents of employees of Intuit. The program is administered by Scholarship America.
Fields of interest: Higher education.
Type of support: Employee-related scholarships.
Geographic limitations: Giving primarily in areas of company operations, with emphasis on AR, CA, MA, OH, TX, and VA.
Application information: Applications not accepted. Contributes only through employee-related scholarships.
Officers and Directors:* Scott D. Cook*, Pres.; Helen Signe Ostby*, C.F.O.; Bryn Roe Ostby*, Secy.
EIN: 770417277

1983
Invesco AIM Management Group, Inc.

(formerly Aim Management Group Inc.)
11 Greenway Plz., Ste. 2500
Houston, TX 77046-1173 (713) 626-1919

Company URL: https://www.invesco.com/portal/site/us
Establishment information: Established in 1976.
Company type: Subsidiary of a public company
International Securities Identification Number: BMG491BT1088
Business activities: Provides investment advisory services.
Business type (SIC): Security and commodity services
Financial profile for 2009: Number of employees, 2,000
Corporate officers: Robert H. Graham, Chair.; Philip A. Taylor, Pres.
Board of director: Robert H. Graham, Chair.
Giving statement: Giving through the Invesco Ltd. Corporate Giving Program and the AIM Foundation.

Invesco Ltd. Corporate Giving Program

(formerly Invesco AIM Management Group Inc. Corporate Giving Program)
Two Peachtree Pointe
1555 Peachtree St., N.E., Ste. 1800
Atlanta, GA 30309-3142 (404) 479-1095
E-mail: ContactUs@invesco.com; URL: http://www.invesco.com/portal/site/global/CommunityDevelopment

Purpose and activities: As a complement to its foundation, Invesco also makes charitable contributions to nonprofit organizations directly. Support is given primarily in areas of company operations; giving also to national and international organizations.
Fields of interest: Arts; Education; Environment; Recreation; Community/economic development, fund raising/fund distribution; General charitable giving.
Type of support: Employee volunteer services; Sponsorships.
Geographic limitations: Giving primarily in areas of company operations; giving also to national and international organizations.
Application information: Application form not required.
Copies of proposal: 1

AIM Foundation

1555 Peachtree St. N.E., Ste. 1800
Atlanta, GA 30309-2499

Establishment information: Established in 1997 in TX.
Donors: Robert H. Graham; AIM Management Group Inc.; AMVESCAP.
Financial data (yr. ended 12/31/11): Assets, $1,268,573 (M); expenditures, $2,115,012; qualifying distributions, $2,085,720; giving activities include $2,000,000 for 8 grants (high: $250,000; low: $250,000).
Purpose and activities: The foundation supports organizations involved with education.
Fields of interest: Elementary/secondary education; Education, early childhood education; Higher education; Education.
Type of support: General/operating support; Scholarship funds.
Geographic limitations: Giving primarily in TX, with emphasis on Houston.
Support limitations: No support for religious organizations or grantmaking foundations. No grants to individuals, or for benefits, dinners, galas, or special fundraising events, mass appeal solicitations, scientific or medical research projects, feasibility studies, costs for trips, meetings, attendance, conferences, or group competitions or performances, or political candidates; no loans.
Application information: Applications not accepted. Contributes only to pre-selected organizations.
Officers: Robert H. Graham, Pres.; Gary T. Crum, V.P. and Secy.-Treas.
Trustee: John M. Zerr.
EIN: 760522586

1984
Investors Bancorp, Inc.

101 JFK Pkwy.
Short Hills, NJ 07078-2716 (973) 924-5100

Company URL: https://www.isbnj.com
Establishment information: Established in 1926.
Company type: Public company
Company ticker symbol and exchange: ISBC/NASDAQ
Business activities: Operates bank holding company.
Business type (SIC): Holding company; savings institutions
Financial profile for 2012: Number of employees, 1,219; assets, $12,722,570,000; pre-tax net income, $144,850,000; liabilities, $11,655,760,000
Corporate officers: Robert M. Cashill, Chair.; Kevin Cummings, Pres. and C.E.O.; Domenick A. Cama, Sr. V.P. and C.O.O.; Thomas F. Splaine, Jr., Sr. V.P. and C.F.O.
Board of directors: Robert M. Cashill, Chair.; Doreen R. Byrnes; Domenick A. Cama; William V. Cosgrove; Kevin Cummings; Brian D. Dittenhafer; James J. Garibaldi; Vincent D. Manahan III; Stephen J. Szabatin; James H. Ward III
Subsidiary: Investors Savings Bank, Short Hills, NJ
Giving statement: Giving through the Investors Savings Bank Charitable Foundation.
Company EIN: 223493930

Investors Savings Bank Charitable Foundation

101 JFK Pkwy.
Short Hills, NJ 07078-2716
E-mail: rodger@herrigelbolan.com; Additional e-mail address: foundation@isbnj.com; URL: http://www.isbnj.com/home/community/foundation

Establishment information: Established in 2005 in DE.
Donor: Investors Savings Bank.
Contact: Rodger K. Herrigel, Secy. and Exec. Dir.
Financial data (yr. ended 06/30/11): Assets, $20,079,777 (M); expenditures, $951,638; qualifying distributions, $877,950; giving activities include $877,950 for grants.
Purpose and activities: The foundation supports organizations involved with arts and culture, education, health, affordable housing, youth development, and human services. Support is limited to areas of company operations.
Fields of interest: Arts; Education; Health care; Housing/shelter; Youth development; Human services.
Type of support: Capital campaigns; Continuing support; Equipment; General/operating support; Matching/challenge support; Program development; Scholarship funds; Seed money.
Geographic limitations: Giving limited to areas of company operations in NJ.
Support limitations: No support for political organizations. No grants to individuals.
Publications: Application guidelines.
Application information: Applications accepted. Application form required.
Initial approach: Letter
Copies of proposal: 1
Board meeting date(s): Sept., Dec., Mar., and June
Deadline(s): 2 months prior to month of board meetings
Officers and Directors:* Robert M. Cahshill*, Pres.; Kevin Cummings, V.P. and Treas.; Rodger K. Herrigel*, Secy. and Exec. Dir.; Vincent D. Manahan III; Ada Melendez; Rose Sigler; William A. Tansey III.
Number of staff: 1 part-time professional; 1 part-time support.
EIN: 203743857
Selected grants: The following grants are a representative sample of this grantmaker's funding activity:
$5,000 to American Heart Association, Dallas, TX, 2011. For general support.
$5,000 to Garden Conservancy, Cold Spring, NY, 2011. For general support.
$1,000 to United Negro College Fund, Fairfax, VA, 2011. For general support.

1985
Inwood Office Furniture, Inc.

(doing business as Inwood Office Invironments)
1108 E. 15th St.
P.O. Box 646
Jasper, IN 47547-0646 (812) 482-9732

Company URL: http://www.inwood.net/
Establishment information: Established in 1948.
Company type: Private company
Business activities: Manufactures tables.

Business type (SIC): Furniture/household
Corporate officers: Omer Sturm, C.E.O.; Glen Sturm, Pres.; Gregory Sturm, Treas.
Giving statement: Giving through the Inwood Office Furniture Foundation, Inc.

Inwood Office Furniture Foundation, Inc.

(formerly Jasper Table Company Foundation, Inc.)
1108 E. 15th St.
Jasper, IN 47546-2227 (812) 482-6121

Donors: Jasper Table Co.; Inwood Office Furniture, Inc.
Contact: Glen M. Sturm, Pres.
Financial data (yr. ended 06/30/09): Assets, $292,642 (M); expenditures, $12,622; qualifying distributions, $12,134; giving activities include $9,884 for 47 grants (high: $3,000; low: $25) and $2,250 for 6 grants to individuals (high: $375; low: $375).
Purpose and activities: The foundation supports hospitals and organizations involved with education, breast cancer, safety, human services, community economic development, and Catholicism.
Fields of interest: Education; Health care; Religion.
Type of support: Building/renovation; Employee-related scholarships; General/operating support; Program development; Sponsorships.
Geographic limitations: Giving primarily in areas of company operations in Jasper, IN.
Support limitations: No grants to individuals (except for employee-related scholarships).
Application information: Applications accepted. Application form required. Applicants should submit the following:
1) copy of IRS Determination Letter
2) brief history of organization and description of its mission
Initial approach: Proposal
Deadline(s): None
Officers: Glen M. Sturm, Pres.; Thomas Krodel, V.P.; Ron Steffe, Secy.; Greg Sturm, Treas.
EIN: 350984764

1986
Iowa Savings Bank

510 W. U.S. Hwy. 30
P.O. Box 967
Carroll, IA 51401-2248 (712) 792-9772

Company URL: http://www.iowasavingsbank.com
Establishment information: Established in 1902.
Company type: Private company
Business activities: Operates savings bank.
Business type (SIC): Banks/commercial
Corporate officers: Bill Hess, Pres. and C.E.O.; Richard Fulton, C.F.O.; Rose Long, Secy.
Board of directors: Thomas E. Farner; Dierk Halverson; Bill Hess; Ron Juergens; Gene Vincent
Giving statement: Giving through the Iowa Savings Bank Charitable Foundation.

Iowa Savings Bank Charitable Foundation

P.O. Box 967
Carroll, IA 51401-0967 (712) 792-9772

Establishment information: Established in 1988 in IA.
Donor: Iowa Savings Bank.
Contact: William C. Hess, Pres.
Financial data (yr. ended 12/31/11): Assets, $848 (M); gifts received, $35,925; expenditures, $64,239; qualifying distributions, $63,864; giving activities include $63,864 for grants.
Purpose and activities: The foundation supports organizations involved with education, health, substance abuse treatment, human services, business, and religion.
Fields of interest: Education; Agriculture/food; Recreation.
Type of support: Capital campaigns; General/operating support; Program development.
Geographic limitations: Giving primarily in IA.
Support limitations: No grants to individuals.
Application information: Applications accepted. Application form required. Applicants should submit the following:
1) detailed description of project and amount of funding requested
Initial approach: Letter
Deadline(s): None
Officers and Directors:* William C. Hess*, Pres.; Richard Fulton*, Secy.-Treas.; Tom Farner; Dierk Halverson; Ron Juergens; Gene Vincent.
EIN: 421329826

1987
Iowa State Bank

(formerly Sac City State Bank)
500 Audubon St.
P.O. Box 486
Sac City, IA 50583-0486 (712) 662-4721

Company URL: http://www.scsbank.com
Establishment information: Established in 1926.
Company type: Private company
Business activities: Operates commercial bank.
Business type (SIC): Banks/commercial
Corporate officers: William C. Hess, Chair.; Steve Spotts, Pres. and C.E.O.; Annetee Wellington, Secy.; Myra Horton, V.P., Opers.
Board of directors: William C. Hess, Chair.; Duane Herrig; Timothy O. Lee; Don Nadrchal; Charles E. Sayre; Steve Spotts
Giving statement: Giving through the Iowa State Bank Foundation.

Iowa State Bank Foundation

(formerly Sac City State Bank Foundation)
500 Audubon St.
Sac City, IA 50583-2208 (712) 662-4721

Establishment information: Established in 1995 in IA.
Donors: Sac City State Bank; Iowa State Bank.
Contact: Steven Spotts, Pres.
Financial data (yr. ended 12/31/11): Assets, $11,178 (M); gifts received, $24,000; expenditures, $33,912; qualifying distributions, $33,912; giving activities include $33,912 for grants.
Purpose and activities: The foundation supports organizations involved with EMS services, human services, community development, Christianity, and Catholicism.
Fields of interest: Education; Human services; Religion.
Type of support: General/operating support; Scholarship funds.
Geographic limitations: Giving limited to Sac City, IA.
Support limitations: No grants to individuals.
Application information: Applications accepted. Application form not required. Applicants should submit the following:
1) detailed description of project and amount of funding requested
Initial approach: Proposal
Deadline(s): None
Officers: Steve Spotts, Pres.; Frank Strain, Secy.-Treas.
Director: William C. Hess.
EIN: 421448100

1988
IPALCO Enterprises, Inc.

1 Monument Cir.
Indianapolis, IN 46204-2901
(317) 261-8261

Company URL: http://www.iplpower.com/
Establishment information: Established in 1983.
Company type: Subsidiary of a public company
Parent company: The AES Corporation
Business activities: Operates holding company; generates, transmits, and distributes electricity; produces and distributes steam.
Business type (SIC): Holding company; combination utility services
Corporate officers: Ann D. Murtlow, Chair., Pres., and C.E.O.; Hamsa Shadaksharappa, Sr. V.P., Finance; Kirk B. Michael, V.P. and C.F.O.; William P. Marsan, V.P., Genl. Counsel, and Secy.; John R. Brehm, V.P. and Treas.; Edward P. Convery, V.P., Opers.
Board of director: Ann D. Murtlow, Chair.
Subsidiaries: Indianapolis Power & Light Co., Indianapolis, IN; Mid-America Capital Resources, Inc., Indianapolis, IN
Giving statement: Giving through the IPALCO Enterprises, Inc. Corporate Giving Program and the IPALCO Foundation Inc.

IPALCO Enterprises, Inc. Corporate Giving Program

c/o Public Affairs Dept.
1 Monument Cir.
Indianapolis, IN 46204-2901 (317) 261-8213
FAX: (317) 261-8324;
E-mail: publicaffairs.ipl@aes.com; URL: http://www.iplpower.com/Our_Company/Community/Community_Involvement/
Application address for Golden Apple Awards: IPL Golden Apple Awards, c/o Shank Public Rels. Counselors, 2611 Waterfront Pkwy., East Dr., Ste. 310, Indianapolis, IN 46214; Contact for Golden Apple Awards: Marilyn Shank, tel.: (317) 293-5590, e-mail: iplgoldenapple@shrankpr.com

Contact: Cindy Leffler
Purpose and activities: IPALCO Enterprises makes charitable contributions to nonprofit organizations involved with arts and culture, education, the environment, diversity, economic development, and community development. Support is given primarily in areas of company operations.
Fields of interest: Arts; Elementary/secondary education; Education; Environment, natural resources; Environment; Civil/human rights, equal rights; Economic development; Community/economic development; Mathematics; Engineering/technology; Science.
Programs:
Arts and Culture: The company supports programs designed to heighten awareness of the arts and local culture of the community.
Community Enhancement: The company supports programs designed to promote diversity and/or improved quality of life in the community.

Economic Development: The company supports programs designed to encourage economic development within areas served by IPALCO.

Education: The company supports programs designed to promote education. Special emphasis is directed toward math, science, and technology.

Environmental: The company supports programs designed to protect, conserve, and/or improve the environment.

Golden Apple Awards: The company annually awards up to 25 $2,000 grants to central and Pike County, Indiana, K-12 educators who demonstrate creative vision and ability to effectively teach math, science, or technology in the classroom. The school of each winner receives $1,000.

Golden Eagle Environmental Grants: The company supports programs designed to protect, preserve, enhance, and restore Indiana's environment.

IPL Environmentalist of the Year: The company awards a $3,000 grant to an Indiana resident who works or volunteers to improve the environment. The recipient is selected by the Golden Eagle Grant Advisory Panel.

Trees for Tomorrow: Through Trees for Tomorrow, IPALCO, Indy Parks and Keep Indianapolis Beautiful, increases planting of public trees in Indianapolis; provides care to those trees to enhance their longevity; and educates the public about the importance of trees to quality of life. The program is administered by Keep Indianapolis Beautiful, Inc.

Volunteer Involvement Program: The company awards grants to nonprofit organizations with which employees of IPALCO volunteers. The company awards $10 per hour for every hour volunteered, up to 50 hours annually.

Type of support: Continuing support; Employee volunteer services; General/operating support; Grants to individuals; Sponsorships.

Geographic limitations: Giving primarily in areas of company operations, with emphasis on Marion County, the surrounding 7 counties, and Pike County, IN.

Support limitations: No support for political organizations or candidates. No grants to individuals (except for Golden Apple Awards), or for conferences or seminars, political activities, post-event needs, or walks or runs.

Publications: Application guidelines; Program policy statement.

Application information: Applications accepted. Multi-year funding is not automatic. Support is limited to 1 contribution per organization during any given year. Organizations receiving support are asked to provide a final report. The Public Affairs Department handles giving. Applicants should submit the following:

1) statement of problem project will address
2) copy of IRS Determination Letter
3) brief history of organization and description of its mission
4) listing of board of directors, trustees, officers and other key people and their affiliations
5) detailed description of project and amount of funding requested
6) copy of current year's organizational budget and/or project budget
7) listing of additional sources and amount of support

Proposals should include a description of the three possible levels of sponsorship available to IPALCO and indicate how each level would assist the organization and the benefits to IPALCO associated with each level.

Initial approach: Proposal to headquarters; download nomination form for Golden Apple Awards and Environmentalist of the Year

Deadline(s): None; Nov. 5 for Golden Eagle Environmental Grants; Mar. 8 for Golden Apple Awards; Oct. 16 for Environmentalist of the Year

Final notification: 4 weeks

IPALCO Foundation Inc.

1 Monument Cir.
Indianapolis, IN 46204

Establishment information: Established in 1998 in IN.

Donor: IPALCO Enterprises, Inc.

Financial data (yr. ended 12/31/11): Assets, $1,233,191 (M); expenditures, $254,911; qualifying distributions, $142,168.

Purpose and activities: The foundation preserves and maintains the Congressional Medal of Honor Memorial in Indianapolis, Indiana.

Fields of interest: Historical activities, war memorials.

Geographic limitations: Giving primarily in IN.

Support limitations: No grants to individuals.

Application information: Applications not accepted. Unsolicited requests for funds not accepted.

Officers: Greg Fennig, Pres.; Don Hart, Secy.; Dewayne Boyer, Treas.

Directors: Eric Fulford; Susan Hanafee; Bill Marsan.

EIN: 352061820

1989
Ipswich Shellfish Company, Inc.

(also known as Ipswich Shellfish Group)
8 Hayward St.
Ipswich, MA 01938-2012 (978) 356-4371

Company URL: http://www.ipswichshellfish.com

Establishment information: Established in 1935.

Company type: Private company

Business activities: Produces seafood.

Business type (SIC): Fishing/commercial

Corporate officers: Chrissi Pappas, Pres. and Exec. V.P.; James Sactson, C.F.O.

Giving statement: Giving through the Ipswich Shellfish Foundation.

Ipswich Shellfish Foundation

8 Hayward St.
Ipswich, MA 01938-2012 (978) 356-4371

Establishment information: Established in 1998 in MA; classified as a company-sponsored operating foundation in 1999.

Donors: Ipswich Shellfish Co., Inc.; Ipswich Lobster Co., Inc.; Maine Shellfish Co., Inc.; United Shellfish Co., Inc.

Contact: Chrissi Pappas, Pres.

Financial data (yr. ended 12/31/11): Assets, $68,820 (M); expenditures, $3,386; qualifying distributions, $3,250; giving activities include $3,250 for 10 grants to individuals (high: $325; low: $325).

Purpose and activities: The foundation awards college scholarships to children of employees of Ipswich Shellfish.

Fields of interest: Higher education; Education.

Type of support: Employee-related scholarships.

Geographic limitations: Giving limited to residents of Ipswich, MA.

Application information: Applications not accepted. Contributes only through employee-related scholarships.

Officers and Directors:* Chrissi Pappas*, Pres.; Edward J. Michon*, Clerk and Treas.; Peter J. Mandragouras.

EIN: 043412318

1990
Stuart C. Irby, Co.

815 S. State St.
Jackson, MS 39201-5999 (601) 969-1811

Company URL: http://www.irby.com

Establishment information: Established in 1926.

Company type: Subsidiary of a private company

Business activities: Provides power transmission line construction services.

Business type (SIC): Construction/miscellaneous heavy

Corporate officers: Michael C. Wigton, Pres.; Andy Waring, C.O.O.; John Honigfort, C.F.O.; Gary Bodam, V.P., Human Resources

Giving statement: Giving through the Stuart C. Irby Company Contributions Program.

Stuart C. Irby Company Contributions Program

815 S. State St.
Jackson, MS 39201-5908 (601) 960-7304
FAX: (601) 960-7221; E-mail: tremmier@irby.com; URL: http://www.irby.com/about_irby/about_irby_community.asp

Purpose and activities: Irby makes charitable contributions to nonprofit organizations involved with education, safety and disasters, and youth mentoring, and to the United Way. Support is given primarily in areas of company operations.

Fields of interest: Education; Disasters, Hurricane Katrina; Big Brothers/Big Sisters; United Ways and Federated Giving Programs.

Type of support: Employee volunteer services; General/operating support.

Geographic limitations: Giving primarily in areas of company operations.

Application information: Application form not required.

1991
Irell & Manella LLP

1800 Ave. of the Stars, Ste. 900
Los Angeles, CA 90067-4276
(310) 277-1010

Company URL: http://www.irell.com

Establishment information: Established in 1941.

Company type: Private company

Business activities: Operates law firm.

Business type (SIC): Legal services

Offices: Los Angeles, Newport Beach, CA

Giving statement: Giving through the Irell & Manella LLP Pro Bono Program.

Irell & Manella LLP Pro Bono Program

1800 Ave. of the Stars, Ste. 900
Los Angeles, CA 90067-4276 (949) 760-5236
E-mail: mermer@irell.com; Additional tel.: (310) 203-7510; URL: http://www.irell.com/about-probono.html

Contact: Michael Ermer, Partner

Fields of interest: Legal services.

Type of support: Pro bono services - legal.

Geographic limitations: Giving primarily in areas of company operations in Los Angeles, and Newport Beach, CA.

Application information: The Pro Bono Committee manages the pro bono program.

1992
The Irvine Company, LLC

550 Newport Center Dr.
Newport Beach, CA 92660-7011
(949) 720-2000

Company URL: http://www.irvinecompany.com
Establishment information: Established in 1864.
Company type: Private company
Business activities: Builds houses; operates residential and nonresidential buildings.
Business type (SIC): Operative builders; real estate operators and lessors
Corporate officers: Donald L. Bren, Chair.; Kevin Baldridge, Pres.; Gregory Lindstrom, Exec. V.P., Genl. Counsel, and Secy.; Marc Ley, C.F.O.
Board of director: Donald L. Bren, Chair.
Subsidiaries: Irvine Apartment Communities Inc., Newport Beach, CA; Irvine Community Development Co., Newport Beach, CA
Giving statement: Giving through the Irvine Ranch Conservancy.
Company EIN: 133177751

Irvine Ranch Conservancy

(formerly Irvine Ranch Land Reserve Trust)
4727 Portolo Pkwy.
Irvine, CA 92602-1914
URL: http://www.irconservancy.org

Establishment information: Established as a company-sponsored operating foundation in 2003 in CA.
Donors: The Irvine Co. LLC; California Department of Fish and Game; Octa Restoration Grant; Recreational Equipment Inc.; Environmental Systems Research Institute.
Financial data (yr. ended 06/30/11): Assets, $1,042,941 (M); gifts received, $529,618; expenditures, $3,161,799; qualifying distributions, $3,144,647.
Purpose and activities: The trust promotes public access and environmental stewardship of the Irvine Ranch Land Reserve in Orange County, California.
Geographic limitations: Giving primarily in CA.
Application information: Applications not accepted. Unsolicited requests for funds not accepted.
Officers: Donald L. Bren*, Chair.; Michael McKee*, Vice-Chair.; Michael O'Connell*, Pres. and Exec. Dir.; Patricia Frobes, Secy.; John Flynn, Treas.
EIN: 061703160

1993
Isabella Bank and Trust

200 E. Broadway St.
Mount Pleasant, MI 48858-2314
(989) 772-9471

Company URL: http://www.isabellabank.com
Establishment information: Established in 1903.
Company type: Subsidiary of a private company
Business activities: Operates commercial bank.
Business type (SIC): Banks/commercial
Corporate officers: David J. Maness, Chair.; Richard J. Barz, C.E.O.; Dennis P. Angner, Pres. and C.F.O.
Board of director: David J. Maness, Chair.
Giving statement: Giving through the Isabella Bank and Trust Foundation.

Isabella Bank and Trust Foundation

200 E. Broadway
P.O. Box 100
Mount Pleasant, MI 48804-0100 (989) 772-9471

Establishment information: Established in 1997 in MI.
Donor: Isabella Bank and Trust.
Financial data (yr. ended 12/31/11): Assets, $900,095 (M); expenditures, $213,196; qualifying distributions, $209,000; giving activities include $209,000 for grants.
Purpose and activities: The foundation supports hospitals and community foundations and organizations involved with arts and culture, higher education, and human services.
Fields of interest: Education; Community/economic development; Religion.
Type of support: General/operating support; Sponsorships.
Geographic limitations: Giving primarily in Isabella County, MI, with emphasis on the Mt. Pleasant area.
Support limitations: No grants to individuals.
Application information: Applications accepted. Application form required.
Initial approach: Proposal
Deadline(s): None
Officers and Directors:* William J. Strickler*, Chair.; Richard J. Barz*, Pres.; Roxanne Schultz*, Secy.; Steven D. Pung*, Treas.; Dennis P. Angner.
EIN: 383348258

1994
Isaly's Inc.

(formerly Isaly Klondike Company)
141 N. Washington St.,
P.O. Box F
Evans City, PA 16033-2001 (724) 538-9044

Company URL: http://www.isalys.com
Establishment information: Established in 2006.
Company type: Private company
Business activities: Operates dairy and deli products company.
Business type (SIC): Food and kindred products; dairy products
Corporate officer: James T. Deily, Pres.
Giving statement: Giving through the Isaly Dairy Charitable Trust.

Isaly Dairy Charitable Trust

(formerly Isaly Co. Charitable Trust)
c/o PNC Bank
620 Liberty Ave., 10th Fl.
Pittsburgh, PA 15222-2705 (412) 762-3588
Application address: 1730 Arabian Lane, Palm Harbor, FL 34685, tel.: (813) 784-3621

Donors: Isaly Klondike Co.; Isaly Co., Inc.
Contact: H. William Isaly
Financial data (yr. ended 12/31/11): Assets, $233,861 (M); expenditures, $12,442; qualifying distributions, $10,900; giving activities include $10,900 for grants.
Purpose and activities: The foundation supports organizations involved with arts and culture and education.
Fields of interest: Arts; Education; Youth development.
Type of support: General/operating support.
Geographic limitations: Giving primarily in FL.
Support limitations: No grants to individuals.
Application information: Applications accepted. Application form not required. Applicants should submit the following:
1) brief history of organization and description of its mission
2) detailed description of project and amount of funding requested
Initial approach: Letter of inquiry
Deadline(s): None
Trustee: PNC Bank, N.A.
EIN: 256024887

1995
ISGN U.S.

17488 N. Laurel Park Dr.
Livonia, MI 48152 (800) 462-5545

Company URL: http://www.isgn.com/
Establishment information: Established in 2007.
Company type: Subsidiary of a foreign company
Business activities: Operates mortgage technology and services company.
Business type (SIC): Computer services
Corporate officers: Krishna Srinivasan, Vice-Chair.; Ritesh Idnani, C.E.O.; Scott Slifer, Pres., Sales and Mktg.; Amit Kothiyal, C.O.O.; Shailendra Gupta, C.F.O.; Erik Anderson, C.A.O. and Genl. Counsel; Raghavan Tiru, C.I.O.
Board of director: Krishna Srinivasan, Vice-Chair.
Historic mergers: Dynatek, Inc. (May 23, 2007)
Giving statement: Giving through the Luhtanen-Howes Charitable Foundation Inc.

Luhtanen-Howes Charitable Foundation Inc.

40536 N. Northville Trail
Northville, MI 48168-3244

Establishment information: Established in 1999 in MI.
Donor: Dynatek, Inc.
Financial data (yr. ended 12/31/11): Assets, $416,561 (M); expenditures, $31,342; qualifying distributions, $24,000; giving activities include $24,000 for 4 grants (high: $7,000; low: $3,000).
Purpose and activities: The foundation supports hospitals and organizations involved with human services and Christianity.
Fields of interest: Hospitals (general); Boys & girls clubs; Salvation Army; Children/youth, services; Homeless, human services; Human services; Christian agencies & churches.
Type of support: General/operating support.
Geographic limitations: Giving limited to MI.
Application information: Applications not accepted. Unsolicited requests for funds not accepted.
Officers: Todd A. Luhtanan, Pres.; Linda L. Luhtanen, Secy.-Treas.
EIN: 383497266

1996
Island Insurance Company, Ltd.

1022 Bethel St.
P.O. Box 1520
Honolulu, HI 96813 (808) 564-8200

Company URL: http://www.islandinsurance.com
Establishment information: Established in 1939.
Company type: Subsidiary of a private company
Business activities: Sells property and casualty insurance.

Business type (SIC): Insurance/fire, marine, and casualty
Financial profile for 2010: Number of employees, 380
Corporate officers: Colbert M. Matsumoto, Chair. and C.E.O.; John Schapperle, Pres. and C.O.O.; Nolan Kawano, Sr. V.P. and C.F.O.; Jeff Fabry, Sr. V.P. and C.I.O.; Paul Iijima, V.P., Finance and Cont.; Todd Yamanaka, V.P., Mktg.; Lynne Nishiura, V.P., Human Resources
Board of director: Colbert M. Matsumoto, Chair.
Giving statement: Giving through the Island Insurance Foundation.

Island Insurance Foundation

1022 Bethel St.
Honolulu, HI 96813-4302
Additional contact: Tyler M. Tokioka, Pres. and Secy.; URL: http://www.islandinsurance.com/AboutUs/Community.asp

Establishment information: Established in 2002 in HI; classified as a company-sponsored operating foundation in 2003.
Donor: Island Insurance Co., Ltd.
Contact: Franklin M. Tokioka, Chair.
Financial data (yr. ended 12/31/11): Assets, $10,211,252 (M); expenditures, $620,252; qualifying distributions, $620,252; giving activities include $535,883 for 95 grants (high: $54,570; low: $25).
Purpose and activities: The foundation supports organizations involved with arts and culture, K-12 and higher education, health, children and youth, family services, community development, and other areas.
Fields of interest: Arts, cultural/ethnic awareness; Arts; Elementary/secondary education; Higher education; Health care; Boy scouts; American Red Cross; Children/youth, services; Family services; Community/economic development; United Ways and Federated Giving Programs; General charitable giving.
Type of support: Capital campaigns; Continuing support; Employee matching gifts; Matching/challenge support; Program development.
Geographic limitations: Giving primarily in HI.
Application information: Applications accepted. Application form not required. Applicants should submit the following:
1) detailed description of project and amount of funding requested
Initial approach: Proposal
Deadline(s): None
Officers and Directors:* Franklin M. Tokioka*, Chair.; Tyler M. Tokioka*, Pres. and Secy.; Colbert M. Matsumoto*, V.P.; Nolan N. Kawano, Treas.; John F. Schapperle; Lionel Y. Tokioka.
EIN: 710894475
Selected grants: The following grants are a representative sample of this grantmaker's funding activity:
$25,000 to Enterprise Honolulu, Honolulu, HI, 2010.
$10,000 to Teach for America, New York, NY, 2010.
$5,000 to YMCA of Honolulu, Honolulu, HI, 2010.
$2,500 to Mothers Against Drunk Driving, Irving, TX, 2010.

1997
Issa Properties, LLC

341 E. Huron St., Apt. B
Ann Arbor, MI 48104-1908 (734) 662-4446

Company URL: http://www.issaproperties.com
Establishment information: Established in 1994.
Company type: Private company
Business activities: Operates apartment buildings.
Business type (SIC): Real estate operators and lessors
Corporate officer: Mohammad Issa, Owner
Giving statement: Giving through the Issa Foundation.

Issa Foundation

341 E. Huron St.
Ann Arbor, MI 48104-1908

Establishment information: Established in 1997 in MI.
Donors: Issa Properties; Global Education Excellance.
Financial data (yr. ended 12/31/11): Assets, $5,090 (M); gifts received, $27,800; expenditures, $36,020; qualifying distributions, $36,020; giving activities include $36,020 for grants.
Purpose and activities: The foundation supports Islamic agencies and mosques and organizations involved with arts and culture, health, and housing.
Fields of interest: Performing arts, music; Arts; Health care; Housing/shelter; Islam.
Type of support: General/operating support.
Geographic limitations: Giving limited to MI.
Application information: Applications not accepted. Unsolicited requests for funds not accepted.
Directors: Abdulaziz M. Issa; Anwar M. Issa; Mohammad M. Issa; Raed Issa; Said Issa.
EIN: 383379607

1998
ITA Group, Inc.

4800 Westown Pkwy., Ste. 300
West Des Moines, IA 50266-6700
(515) 326-3400
FAX: (515) 326-3589

Company URL: http://www.itagroup.com
Establishment information: Established in 1963.
Company type: Private company
Business activities: Provides human resource consulting services.
Business type (SIC): Management and public relations services
Corporate officers: Steven G. Chapman, Chair.; Thomas J. Mahoney, Jr., Pres. and C.E.O.; Richard A. Rue, Sr. V.P. and C.F.O.; Doug Stine, Sr. V.P., Sales; John Rose, V.P. and C.I.O.; Brent VanderWaal, V.P., Finance and Cont.
Board of directors: Steven G. Chapman, Chair.; Mary Z. Bussone; Thomas J. Mahoney, Jr.; Richard A. Rue
Offices: Irvine, CA; Belleair Bluffs, FL; Atlanta, GA; Hoffman Estates, IL; Indianapolis, IN; Troy, MI; Wayzata, MN; Mount Arlington, NJ; King of Prussia, Newtown, PA; Irving, TX
Giving statement: Giving through the ITA Group Foundation.

ITA Group Foundation

4800 Westown Pkwy., Ste. 300
West Des Moines, IA 50266-6719

Establishment information: Established in 1996 in IA.
Donor: ITA Group Inc.
Financial data (yr. ended 12/31/11): Assets, $284,757 (M); gifts received, $100,000; expenditures, $105,798; qualifying distributions, $105,448; giving activities include $105,125 for 53 grants (high: $30,000; low: $125).
Purpose and activities: The foundation supports public libraries and organizations involved with children and youth.
Fields of interest: Arts; Education; Human services.
Geographic limitations: Giving primarily in IA.
Support limitations: No grants to individuals.
Application information: Applications not accepted. Unsolicited requests for funds not accepted.
Officers: Thomas J. Mahoney, Jr., Pres.; Richard A. Rue, Secy.-Treas.
EIN: 421462086

1999
ITT Corporation

(formerly ITT Industries, Inc.)
1133 Westchester Ave.
White Plains, NY 10604-3516
(914) 641-2000
FAX: (914) 696-2950

Company URL: http://www.itt.com/
Establishment information: Established in 1920.
Company type: Public company
Company ticker symbol and exchange: ITT/NYSE
Business activities: Designs, manufactures, and provides connectors and switches, defense products and services, and pumps and complementary products.
Business type (SIC): Machinery/industrial and commercial; machinery/general industry; electronic components and accessories; search and navigation equipment
Financial profile for 2012: Number of employees, 9,000; assets, $3,386,100,000; sales volume, $2,227,800,000; pre-tax net income, $149,100,000; expenses, $2,076,300,000; liabilities, $2,682,900,000
Fortune 1000 ranking: 2012—861st in revenues, 694th in profits, and 714th in assets
Corporate officers: Frank MacInnis, Chair.; Denise L. Ramos, Pres. and C.E.O.; Tom Scalera, C.F.O.; Burt Fealing, Genl. Counsel and Corp. Secy.
Board of directors: Frank T. MacInnis, Chair.; Orlando D. Ashford; G. Peter D'Aloia; Don DeFosset, Jr., Ph.D.; Christina A. Gold; Richard P. Lavin; Denise L. Ramos; Donald J. Stebbins
Subsidiaries: Goulds Pumps, Inc, Seneca Falls, NY; ITT Automotive, Inc., Auburn Hills, MI; ITT Defense & Electronics, McLean, VA; ITT Fluid Technology, Midland Park, NJ
International operations: Argentina; Australia; Austria; Canada; Cayman Islands; Chile; China; Finland; France; Germany; Greece; Hong Kong; Hungary; India; Indonesia; Ireland; Italy; Japan; Lithuania; Luxembourg; Malaysia; Mexico; New Zealand; Philippines; Portugal; Saudi Arabia; Singapore; South Korea; Spain; Sweden; Thailand; Turkey; United Kingdom; Venezuela
Giving statement: Giving through the ITT Corporation Contributions Program and the Earl J. Gossett Foundation.
Company EIN: 135158950

ITT Corporation Contributions Program

(formerly ITT Industries, Inc. Corporate Giving Program)
1133 Westchester Ave.
White Plains, NY 10604-3516 (914) 641-2000
URL: http://www.itt.com/citizenship/

Purpose and activities: ITT Industries makes charitable contributions to nonprofit organizations involved with education, water conservation, and science. Support is given on a national and international basis in areas of company operations.
Fields of interest: Education, fund raising/fund distribution; Higher education; Education; Environment, water resources; Environment; Physics; Engineering/technology; Science.
Type of support: Building/renovation; Employee volunteer services; Equipment; Scholarship funds; Sponsorships.
Geographic limitations: Giving on a national and international basis in areas of company operations.
Publications: Occasional report.

Earl J. Gossett Foundation

c/o Gloria Walsh
8200 N. Austin Ave.
Morton Grove, IL 60053-3205 (847) 983-5626

Donor: ITT Industries, Inc.
Contact: For loans: Tiffany Mendez
Financial data (yr. ended 04/30/12): Assets, $260,707 (M); expenditures, $55,075; qualifying distributions, $55,000; giving activities include $55,000 for 11 grants to individuals (high: $5,000; low: $5,000).
Purpose and activities: The foundation awards student loans to employees and children of employees of ITT Industries' Bell & Gossett division.
Type of support: Student loans—to individuals.
Geographic limitations: Giving primarily in areas of company operations in IL.
Application information: Applications accepted. Application form required.
Initial approach: Proposal
Deadline(s): Aug. 5
Trustees: Cathy Stone; Gloria Walsh.
EIN: 366084312

2000
ITW Ark-Les Corporation

(formerly Ark-Less Corporation)
95 Mill St.
Stoughton, MA 02072-1422
(781) 297-6000

Company URL: http://www.ark-les.com/
Establishment information: Established in 1937.
Company type: Subsidiary of a public company
Business activities: Supplies engineered user interfaces, and manufactures sensor and control products.
Business type (SIC): Lighting and wiring equipment/electric
Corporate officers: Malcolm F. MacNeil, Pres.; Robert Towers, Exec. V.P., C.O.O., and Treas.
Giving statement: Giving through the Malcolm F. MacNeil Family Foundation II.

Malcolm F. MacNeil Family Foundation II

247 Lincoln Rd.
Lincoln, MA 01773 (781) 297-6000

Establishment information: Established in 1947 in MA.
Donor: Ark-Les Corp.
Contact: Bruce M. MacNeil, Tr.
Financial data (yr. ended 12/31/11): Assets, $1,061,795 (M); expenditures, $75,990; qualifying distributions, $66,500; giving activities include $66,500 for grants.
Purpose and activities: The foundation supports organizations involved with education.
Fields of interest: Higher education; Education.
Type of support: General/operating support.
Geographic limitations: Giving primarily in ME.
Support limitations: No grants to individuals.
Application information: Applications accepted. Application form required.
Initial approach: Letter
Deadline(s): None
Trustee: Bruce M. Macneil.
EIN: 237230620

2001
ITW Sexton, Inc.

(formerly Sexton Can Company, Inc.)
3101 Sexton Rd., S.E.
Decatur, AL 35603-1707 (256) 355-5850

Company URL: http://www.sextoncan.com
Establishment information: Established in 1880.
Company type: Private company
Business activities: Manufactures metal containers.
Business type (SIC): Metal containers
Financial profile for 2010: Number of employees, 82
Giving statement: Giving through the Sexton Can Company Employees Aid Fund.

Sexton Can Company Employees Aid Fund

3101 Sexton Rd., S.E.
Decatur, AL 35603-1707 (256) 355-5850

Donor: Sexton Can Co., Inc.
Contact: Carol Wiley
Financial data (yr. ended 12/31/11): Assets, $0 (M); expenditures, $941; qualifying distributions, $0; giving activities include $0 for grants to individuals.
Purpose and activities: The foundation awards grants to current and former employees and the dependents of current and former employees of Sexton Can Company to assist in the payment of medical expenses.
Type of support: Grants to individuals.
Geographic limitations: Giving primarily in Falkville, AL, and Hedgesville, WV.
Application information: Applications accepted. Application form required.
Initial approach: Letter
Deadline(s): None
Trustee: Yurd Wowczuk.
EIN: 046087676

2002
iVillage Inc.

500 7th Ave., 14th Fl.
New York, NY 10018 (212) 664-4444

Company URL: http://www.ivillage.com
Establishment information: Established in 1995.
Company type: Subsidiary of a private company
Ultimate parent company: General Electric Company
Business activities: Provides Internet information and shopping services.
Business type (SIC): Computer services
Corporate officers: Lauren Zalaznick, Chair.; Douglas W. McCormick, Pres.; Hilary Smith, Sr. V.P., Comms.
Board of director: Lauren Zalaznick, Chair.
Giving statement: Giving through the iVillage Inc. Corporate Giving Program.
Company EIN: 133845162

iVillage Inc. Corporate Giving Program

212 5th Ave.
New York, NY 10010-2103 (212) 600-6000

Purpose and activities: iVillage makes charitable contributions of public relations services to nonprofit organizations involved with women. Support is given on a national basis.
Fields of interest: Women.
Type of support: Employee volunteer services; Public relations services.
Support limitations: No support for partisan political organizations or religious organizations. No grants for general operating support.
Application information: Applications accepted. Telephone calls are not encouraged. Application form not required. Applicants should submit the following:
1) detailed description of project and amount of funding requested
Initial approach: E-mail proposal to headquarters
Final notification: Varies

2003
Iwo Jima, Inc.

45 Sanford St.
Rye, NY 10580 (914) 925-9137

Company URL: http://www.iwojima.com/
Company type: Private company
Business activities: Publishes books.
Business type (SIC): Book publishing and/or printing
Giving statement: Giving through the James Bradley Peace Foundation, Inc.

James Bradley Peace Foundation, Inc.

(formerly Sons of Iwo Jima, Inc.)
c/o Eisikovic
1430 Broadway
New York, NY 10018
URL: http://www.jamesbradley.com/jbpf/

Establishment information: Established in 2000 in WI.
Donor: Iwo Jima, Inc.
Financial data (yr. ended 12/31/11): Assets, $52,025 (M); gifts received, $3,340; expenditures, $28,698; qualifying distributions, $24,250; giving activities include $24,250 for grants.
Purpose and activities: The foundation supports programs designed to provide high school students with international awareness through homestay international exchange, and awards college scholarships.
Fields of interest: Education.
Program:
James Bradley Peace Foundation Scholarship Program: The foundation awards college scholarships to high school students to study in

China and Japan. The program is administered by Youth for Understanding USA.
Type of support: Scholarship funds; Scholarships—to individuals.
Publications: Newsletter.
Application information: Applications not accepted. Unsolicited requests for funds not accepted.
Officer: James Bradley, Pres.
Directors: Alison Bradley; Michelle Bradley.
EIN: 392008597

2004
J & S Precision Products Co., Inc.

16 Evesboro Rd.
Medford, NJ 08055-9592 (609) 654-0900

Company URL: http://www.jsprec.com/about.htm
Establishment information: Established in 1964.
Company type: Private company
Business activities: Manufactures screw machine products.
Business type (SIC): Screw machine products
Corporate officers: Steven Janssen, Pres. and C.E.O.; Barbara Janssen, Secy.-Treas.
Giving statement: Giving through the Donald Janssen, Sr. Memorial Foundation.

Donald Janssen, Sr. Memorial Foundation

16 Evesboro Rd.
Medford, NJ 08055-9592

Establishment information: Established in 2000 in NJ.
Donor: J&S Precision Products Co., Inc.
Financial data (yr. ended 12/31/11): Assets, $244,965 (M); expenditures, $17,443; qualifying distributions, $17,443; giving activities include $17,000 for 17 grants to individuals (high: $1,000; low: $1,000).
Purpose and activities: The foundation awards college scholarships to individuals.
Type of support: Scholarships—to individuals.
Geographic limitations: Giving primarily in NJ.
Application information: Applications not accepted. Unsolicited requests for funds not accepted.
Trustees: Barbara Janssen; David Janssen.
EIN: 223744775

2006
Jabil Circuit, Inc.

10560 Dr. Martin Luther King Jr. St. N.
St. Petersburg, FL 33716-3718
(727) 577-9749
FAX: (302) 655-5049

Company URL: http://www.jabil.com
Establishment information: Established in 1966.
Company type: Public company
Company ticker symbol and exchange: JBL/NYSE
International Securities Identification Number: US4663131039
Business activities: Operates electronics manufacturing services company.
Business type (SIC): Electronic components and accessories
Financial profile for 2012: Number of employees, 141,000; assets, $7,803,100,000; sales volume, $17,151,900,000; pre-tax net income, $508,900,000; expenses, $16,530,010,000; liabilities, $5,698,080,000
Fortune 1000 ranking: 2012—163rd in revenues, 402nd in profits, and 458th in assets
Forbes 2000 ranking: 2012—532nd in sales, 1158th in profits, and 1603rd in assets
Corporate officers: Timothy L. Main, Chair.; Thomas A. Sansone, Vice-Chair.; Mark T. Mondello, C.E.O.; William E. Peters, Pres.; William D. Muir, Jr., Exec. V.P. and C.O.O.; Forbes I.J. Alexander, C.F.O.; Michael K. Dastoor, Sr. V.P. and Cont.; Robert L. Paver, Genl. Counsel and Corp. Secy.; Sergio A. Cadavid, Treas.
Board of directors: Timothy L. Main, Chair.; Thomas A. Sansone, Vice-Chair.; Martha F. Brooks; Mel S. Lavitt; Mark T. Mondello; Lawrence J. Murphy; Frank A. Newman; Steven A. Raymund; David M. Stout
Giving statement: Giving through the Jabil Circuit, Inc. Contributions Program.

Jabil Circuit, Inc. Contributions Program

10560 Dr. Martin Luther King Jr. St. N.
St. Petersburg, FL 33716-3718 (727) 577-9749
URL: http://www.jabil.com/jabil_cares/communities.html

Purpose and activities: Jabil Circuit makes charitable contributions to nonprofit organizations involved with education, the environment, natural disasters, and on a case by case basis. Support is given primarily in areas of company operations in Arizona, California, Colorado, Florida, Kentucky, Michigan, New York, Tennessee, and Texas, and in Austria, Belgium, Brazil, China, England, France, Germany, Hungary, India, Italy, Japan, Malaysia, Mexico, the Netherlands, Poland, Russia, Scotland, Singapore, Taiwan, Ukraine, and Vietnam.
Fields of interest: Education; Environment; Disasters, preparedness/services; General charitable giving.
International interests: Austria; Belgium; Brazil; China; England; France; Germany; Hungary; India; Italy; Japan; Malaysia; Mexico; Netherlands; Poland; Russia; Scotland; Singapore; Taiwan; Ukraine; Vietnam.
Type of support: Employee volunteer services; General/operating support; In-kind gifts; Program development; Scholarships—to individuals.
Geographic limitations: Giving primarily in areas of company operations in AZ, CA, CO, FL, KY, MI, NY, TN, and TX, and in Austria, Belgium, Brazil, China, England, France, Germany, Hungary, India, Italy, Japan, Malaysia, Mexico, the Netherlands, Poland, Russia, Scotland, Singapore, Taiwan, Ukraine, and Vietnam.

2007
Jack in the Box Inc.

(formerly Foodmaker, Inc.)
9330 Balboa Ave.
San Diego, CA 92123-1516
(858) 571-2121
FAX: (302) 674-5266

Company URL: http://www.jackinthebox.com
Establishment information: Established in 1951.
Company type: Public company
Company ticker symbol and exchange: JACK/NASDAQ
Business activities: Owns, operates, and franchises restaurants.
Business type (SIC): Restaurants and drinking places; investors/miscellaneous
Financial profile for 2012: Number of employees, 22,100; assets, $1,463,720,000; sales volume, $1,545,030,000; pre-tax net income, $93,610,000; expenses, $1,432,540,000; liabilities, $1,051,780,000
Fortune 1000 ranking: 2012—894th in revenues, 802nd in profits, and 925th in assets
Corporate officers: Linda A. Lang, Chair. and C.E.O.; Lenny Comma, Pres. and C.O.O.; Phillip H. Rudolph, Exec. V.P., Genl. Counsel, and Secy.; Jerry P. Rebel, Exec. V.P. and C.F.O.; Mark H. Blankenship, Ph.D., Sr. V.P. and C.A.O.; Elana M. Hobson, Sr. V.P., Opers.; Paul D. Melancon, V.P., Finance, Cont., and Treas.; Carol A. DiRaimo, V.P., Corp. Comms.
Board of directors: Linda A. Lang, Chair.; David L. Goebel; Madleine Kleiner; Michael W. Murphy; James M. Myers; David M. Tehle; Wendy M. Webb; John T. Wyatt
Giving statement: Giving through the Jack in the Box Foundation.
Company EIN: 952698708

Jack in the Box Foundation

c/o Tax Dept.
9330 Balboa Ave.
San Diego, CA 92123-1516
E-mail: kathy.kovacevich@jackinthebox.com;
URL: http://www.jackinthebox.com/corporate/corporate-responsibility/

Establishment information: Established in 1998 in CA.
Donors: Foodmaker, Inc.; Jack in the Box Inc.
Contact: Kathy Kovacevich, Secy.
Financial data (yr. ended 09/30/11): Assets, $505,422 (M); gifts received, $1,907,401; expenditures, $1,896,821; qualifying distributions, $1,475,690; giving activities include $1,475,690 for grants.
Purpose and activities: The foundation supports organizations involved with education, health, youth development, human services, children, and economically disadvantaged people. Special emphasis is directed toward programs designed to help children in need.
Fields of interest: Middle schools/education; Secondary school/education; Education; Hospitals (general); Health care; Youth development, adult & child programs; Big Brothers/Big Sisters; Youth development, business; Youth development; Human services; United Ways and Federated Giving Programs Children; Economically disadvantaged.
Type of support: General/operating support; Grants to individuals; Matching/challenge support; Program development; Sponsorships.
Geographic limitations: Giving on a national basis in areas of company operations, with some emphasis on San Diego, CA.
Application information: Applications accepted. Application form not required. Applicants should submit the following:
1) detailed description of project and amount of funding requested
2) listing of board of directors, trustees, officers and other key people and their affiliations
3) brief history of organization and description of its mission

Initial approach: Proposal
Deadline(s): None

Officers and Directors:* Brian Luscomb*, Pres.; Kathy Kovacevich*, Secy.; Mike Bamrick; Mark H. Blankenship, Ph.D.; Terri Graham; Linda A. Lang; Paul Melancon; Phil Rudolph; Eric Tunquist.
EIN: 330776076
Selected grants: The following grants are a representative sample of this grantmaker's funding activity:

$200,000 to Big Brothers Big Sisters of America, Philadelphia, PA, 2009.
$40,143 to Saint Louis Childrens Hospital, Saint Louis, MO, 2009.
$25,000 to San Diego Hospice and Palliative Care, San Diego, CA, 2009.
$25,000 to University of California at San Diego Foundation, La Jolla, CA, 2009.
$16,500 to Classroom of the Future Foundation, San Diego, CA, 2009.
$13,000 to Monarch School, San Diego, CA, 2009.
$10,000 to Big Brothers Big Sisters of Central Texas, Austin, TX, 2009.
$5,000 to YMCA of San Diego County, San Diego, CA, 2009.
$3,769 to Big Brothers Big Sisters of Greater Los Angeles, Los Angeles, CA, 2009.
$1,431 to Cook Childrens Medical Center, Fort Worth, TX, 2009.

2008
Jackson Iron & Metal Co., Inc.

1404 Allen St.
Jackson, MS 39201 (601) 354-7664

Company type: Private company
Business activities: Operates metal scrap disposal company.
Business type (SIC): Durable goods—wholesale
Giving statement: Giving through the Meyer Crystal Family Foundation.

The Meyer Crystal Family Foundation

(formerly Jackson Iron & Metal Company Inc. Charitable Foundation)
P.O. Box 23309
Jackson, MS 39225-3309 (601) 969-6910

Establishment information: Established in MS.
Donors: Jackson Iron & Metal Company, Inc.; Emanuel Crystal.
Financial data (yr. ended 12/31/11): Assets, $114,672 (M); gifts received, $80,000; expenditures, $65,650; qualifying distributions, $64,000; giving activities include $64,000 for 16 grants (high: $20,000; low: $500).
Fields of interest: Arts; Education; Human services; Children/youth, services; Jewish federated giving programs; Jewish agencies & synagogues.
Geographic limitations: Giving primarily in Jackson, MS.
Application information: Applications accepted. Application form required.
Initial approach: Letter
Deadline(s): None
Trustees: Clayton Crystal; Elaine Crystal; Emanuel Crystal; Gerald P. Crystal; Lynn Crystal; Shannon Crystal; Paula Erlich.
EIN: 640851269

2009
Jackson National Life Insurance Company

IMG Service Ctr.
1 Corporate Way
Lansing, MI 48951-0001 (517) 381-5500

Company URL: https://www.jackson.com
Establishment information: Established in 1961.
Company type: Subsidiary of a foreign company
Business activities: Sells life insurance.
Business type (SIC): Insurance/life
Financial profile for 2010: Number of employees, 1,400
Corporate officers: Michael A. Wells, Pres. and C.E.O.; James R. Sopha, C.O.O.; P. Chad Myers, Exec. V.P. and C.F.O.; J. Mark Clark, Sr. V.P. and C.I.O.
Historic mergers: Life Insurance Company of Georgia (May 19, 2005)
Giving statement: Giving through the Jackson National Community Fund.

Jackson National Community Fund

1 Corporate Way
Lansing, MI 48951-0001
E-mail: jncf@jackson.com; URL: https://www.jackson.com/about/Community.jsp?

Purpose and activities: The Jackson National Community Fund makes charitable contributions to educational institutions and nonprofit organizations involved with community enrichment. Special emphasis is directed towards programs designed to enhance the lives of children and the elderly. Support is limited to Denver, Colorado, Chicago, Illinois, Lansing, Michigan, and Nashville, Tennessee.
Fields of interest: Higher education; Children, services; Aging, centers/services; Community/economic development Children; Aging.
Program:
Employee Matching Gifts Program: The Jackson Community Fund matches contributions made by Jackson employees to children and elderly charities on a two-for-one basis up to $10,000 per employee, per year.
Type of support: Employee matching gifts; Employee volunteer services; General/operating support; In-kind gifts; Program development; Sponsorships.
Geographic limitations: Giving limited to Denver, CO, Chicago, IL, Lansing, MI, and Nashville, TN.
Support limitations: No support for private foundations, health clinics, treatment centers or hospitals, political parties or candidates, religious organizations not of benefit to the entire community, elementary or secondary schools, industry or professional organizations, service organizations, or fraternal, labor, or veterans' organizations. No grants to individuals.
Publications: Application guidelines; Corporate giving report.
Application information: Applications accepted. A contributions committee reviews all requests. DVDs, CDs, and other unsolicited materials are not encouraged. Application form required. Applicants should submit the following:
1) timetable for implementation and evaluation of project
2) results expected from proposed grant
3) population served
4) name, address and phone number of organization
5) brief history of organization and description of its mission
6) contact person
7) copy of current year's organizational budget and/or project budget
8) listing of additional sources and amount of support

Applications should include the organization's Tax ID Number and all sponsorship levels, if applicable; and indicate whether the project or program has been conducted in the past, and how its goals were met or exceeded.
Initial approach: Complete online application form
Copies of proposal: 1
Committee meeting date(s): Quarterly
Deadline(s): Nov. 11, Feb. 10, May 26, and Aug. 11
Final notification: Jan 21, March 25, July 8, and Sept. 30
Administrator: Danielle Weller, Corp. Responsibility Specialist.
Number of staff: 1 full-time professional.

2010
Jackson Paper Company

4400-C Mangum Dr.
Flowood, MS 39232-2113 (601) 360-9620

Company URL: http://www.jacksonpaper.com/
Establishment information: Established in 1921.
Company type: Private company
Business activities: Distributes paper products, printing paper, janitorial supplies, cleaning and floor care products.
Business type (SIC): Paper and paper products—wholesale
Corporate officers: Tommy Galyean, Chair.; James Archer, C.E.O.; Scott Garrett, C.F.O.; Dixon Thronton, V.P., Sales; Marty White, Treas.; Ken Densmore, Cont.
Board of director: Tommy Galyean, Chair.
Giving statement: Giving through the Jackson-Newell Foundation, Inc.

Jackson-Newell Foundation, Inc.

1212 Grand Ave.
Meridian, MS 39301-6509 (601) 693-1783
Application address: P.O. Box 631, Meridian, MS 39302-0631, tel.: (601) 693-1783

Establishment information: Established in MS.
Donor: Jackson Paper Co.
Contact: Brenda Bernhard, Dir.
Financial data (yr. ended 12/31/11): Assets, $6,118 (M); gifts received, $15,275; expenditures, $15,127; qualifying distributions, $14,850; giving activities include $14,850 for grants.
Fields of interest: Education; Health care; Human services.
Geographic limitations: Giving primarily in MS.
Support limitations: No grants to individuals.
Application information: Applications accepted. Application form required.
Initial approach: Letter
Deadline(s): None
Directors: William B. Allen; Brenda Bernhard; William Gates; M.D. Huckabee; Noel Machost; James B. Thompson; Dixon Thornton; Mart F. White.
EIN: 640592242

2011
The Jackson Rancheria Band of Miwuk Indians

12222 New York Ranch Rd.
Jackson, CA 95642 (209) 223-8385

Company URL: http://www.jacksoncasino.com
Establishment information: Established in 1898.
Company type: Tribal corporation
Business activities: Operates casino resort.
Business type (SIC): Amusement and recreation services/miscellaneous; hotels and motels
Corporate officers: Irvin Marks, Chair.; Robert Dalton, Jr., Vice-Chair.; Rich Hoffman, C.E.O.

Giving statement: Giving through the Jackson Rancheria Band of Miwuk Indians Corporate Giving Program.

The Jackson Rancheria Band of Miwuk Indians Corporate Giving Program

c/o Grant Application Office
P.O. Box 1090
Jackson, CA 95642-1090
URL: http://www.jacksoncasino.com/tribal/community-involvement

Purpose and activities: The Jackson Rancheria Band of Miwuk Indians makes charitable donations to nonprofit organizations with an emphasis on local community groups, schools, organizations, and projects that benefit children and seniors. Support is given primarily in areas of company operations in Amador County, CA, and to national organizations.
Fields of interest: Safety/disasters; Recreation, parks/playgrounds; American Red Cross; Children, services; Aging, centers/services Economically disadvantaged.
Type of support: General/operating support.
Geographic limitations: Giving primarily in areas of company operations in Amador County, CA, and to national organizations.
Application information: Applications accepted. Proposals are limited to one application per organization in any given year. Phone calls are not encouraged. Application form required. Applicants should submit the following:
1) name, address and phone number of organization
2) copy of IRS Determination Letter
3) detailed description of project and amount of funding requested
4) contact person
5) listing of additional sources and amount of support
Proposals should include the name and date of the event.
Initial approach: Download application form and mail completed form to headquarters
Deadline(s): None; applications must be received by the 15th of the month to be considered for funding at the end of the following month
Final notification: 6 weeks

2012
Jackson Walker L.L.P.

901 Main St., Ste. 6000
Dallas, TX 75202-3748 (214) 953-5933

Company URL: http://www.jw.com
Establishment information: Established in 1887.
Company type: Private company
Business activities: Operates law firm.
Business type (SIC): Legal services
Offices: Austin, Dallas, Fort Worth, Houston, San Angelo, San Antonio, TX
Giving statement: Giving through the Jackson Walker L.L.P. Pro Bono Program.

Jackson Walker L.L.P. Pro Bono Program

901 Main St., Ste. 6000
Dallas, TX 75202-3748 (214) 953-5933
E-mail: bkilpatrick@jw.com; Additional tel.: (214) 953-6000; URL: http://www.jw.com/about/pro_bono

Contact: Brian A. Kilpatrick, Partner
Fields of interest: Legal services.
Type of support: Pro bono services - legal.
Geographic limitations: Giving primarily in area of company operations in Austin, Dallas, Fort Worth, Houston, San Angelo, and San Antonio, TX.
Application information: The Pro Bono Committee manages the pro bono program.

2013
Jackson-Shaw Company

4890 Alpha Rd., Ste. 100
Dallas, TX 75244-4639 (972) 628-7400

Company URL: http://www.jacksonshaw.com
Establishment information: Established in 1972.
Company type: Private company
Business activities: Operates real estate development company.
Business type (SIC): Contractors/general nonresidential building
Corporate officers: Lewis W. Shaw II, Chair. and C.E.O.; Michele Wheeler, Pres. and C.O.O.; John Stone, C.F.O.; Joy Chiles, V.P. and Cont.; Jill Warren, V.P., Admin.
Board of director: Lewis W. Shaw II, Chair.
Giving statement: Giving through the Jackson-Shaw Foundation.

Jackson-Shaw Foundation

4890 Alpha Rd., Ste. 100
Dallas, TX 75244-4639
URL: http://www.jacksonshaw.com

Establishment information: Established in 2007 in TX.
Donor: Jackson-Shaw Company.
Financial data (yr. ended 12/31/11): Assets, $20,305 (M); gifts received, $30,230; expenditures, $14,807; qualifying distributions, $13,000; giving activities include $13,000 for grants.
Fields of interest: Animals/wildlife; Recreation; Youth development.
Geographic limitations: Giving primarily in FL, MD, NV, and TX.
Support limitations: No grants to individuals.
Application information: Applications not accepted. Unsolicited requests for funds not accepted.
Directors: Thomas Aylward; Jason Nunley; M. Jill Warren; Michele Wheeler.
EIN: 208287507

2014
Jacksonville Jaguars, Ltd.

1 EverBank Field Dr.
Jacksonville, FL 32202 (904) 633-6000

Company URL: http://www.jaguars.com
Establishment information: Established in 1993.
Company type: Private company
Business activities: Operates professional football club.
Business type (SIC): Amusement and recreation services/miscellaneous
Corporate officers: Shahid Khan, Chair.; Mark Lamping, Pres.; Bill Prescott, C.F.O.; Dan Edwards, Sr. V.P., Comms.; Megha Parekh, V.P. and Genl. Counsel; Chad Johnson, V.P., Sales
Board of director: Shahid Khan, Chair.
Giving statement: Giving through the Jacksonville Jaguars, Ltd. Corporate Giving Program and the Jacksonville Jaguars Foundation.

Jacksonville Jaguars, Ltd. Corporate Giving Program

c/o Community Rels. Dept.
1 EverBank Field Dr.
Jacksonville, FL 32202-1928
FAX: (914) 633-6055; URL: http://prod.www.jaguars.clubs.nfl.com/foundation-community/community/donation-requests.html

Purpose and activities: The Jacksonville Jaguars make charitable contributions of memorabilia to nonprofit organizations on a case by case basis. Support is limited to Florida and southern Georgia.
Fields of interest: General charitable giving.
Type of support: In-kind gifts; Loaned talent.
Geographic limitations: Giving limited to FL and southern GA.
Application information: Applications accepted. Proposals should be submitted using organization letterhead. Support is limited to 1 contribution per organization during any given year. Application form not required. Applicants should submit the following:
1) population served
2) name, address and phone number of organization
3) copy of IRS Determination Letter
4) detailed description of project and amount of funding requested
5) contact person
Proposals should indicate the date, time, and location of the event.
Initial approach: Mail or fax proposal to headquarters
Copies of proposal: 1
Deadline(s): 8 weeks prior to need
Final notification: 2 weeks prior to need

Jacksonville Jaguars Foundation

1 EverBank Field Dr.
Jacksonville, FL 32202-1920 (904) 633-5437
FAX: (904) 633-5683;
E-mail: sahil@nfl.jaguars.com; E-mail for Peter Racine: racinep@jaguars.nfl.com; Contact for Community Scholars: Heather Burk, University of North Florida, Service Learning Coord., tel.: (904) 620-3922, E-mail: hburk@unf.edu; URL: http://www.jaguars.com/foundation-community/index.html

Establishment information: Established in 1994 in FL.
Donor: Jacksonville Jaguars, Ltd.
Contact: Peter M. Racine, Pres.
Financial data (yr. ended 12/31/11): Assets, $4,895,403 (M); gifts received, $223,967; expenditures, $1,475,298; qualifying distributions, $1,083,450; giving activities include $1,083,450 for grants.
Purpose and activities: The foundation supports programs designed to serve economically and socially disadvantaged youth and families.
Fields of interest: Media/communications; Arts; Education; Public health, STDs; Public health, obesity; Public health, physical fitness; AIDS; Nutrition; Recreation; YM/YWCAs & YM/YWHAs; Youth, pregnancy prevention; Family services; Human services Youth; Economically disadvantaged.
Programs:
Community Scholars: The foundation, in partnership with the University of North Florida, awards scholarships to sophomores and juniors in high school who have participated in the Jaguars Honor Rows program. The students must be nominated by his/her youth agency, committed to a drug-free lifestyle, and demonstrates a commitment to public service. Scholarship recipients receive full

tuition for up to four years and mentorship support from University of North Florida honor students.

Honor Rows: The foundation awards seats to Jaguars home games to nonprofit organizations designed to serve youth. Seats are used as incentives to encourage economically and socially disadvantaged youth between the ages 9 to 17 to set and achieve goals for personal and academic achievement, physical fitness and nutrition, and volunteer service. In addition, all Honor Rows youth pledge to remain free from illegal drugs, alcohol, and tobacco. Organizations applying for the first time may request up to 60 Honor Row seats and the maximum award for large-capacity agencies is 360 seats. At the game, participants receive a meal, Honor Rows t-shirt and hat, and special recognition by the Weavers and fans.

Straight Talk: Through the Straight Talk Program, the foundation reduces teen pregnancy and the spread of AIDS and other sexually transmitted infections (STI) thorough media partnerships. The foundation utilizes radio, newspaper, internet sites, billboard outlets, and local television stations to connect with teens and their parents about the consequences faced by sexually active teenagers. The program also includes public service announcements featuring Jaguar players run on local TV station and the Jumbotron at Jaguars home games. Visit URL: http://straighttalk.jacksonville.com/ for more information.

Type of support: Capital campaigns; Continuing support; General/operating support; In-kind gifts; Matching/challenge support; Program development; Scholarship funds.
Geographic limitations: Giving limited to the greater Jacksonville, FL, area, including Baker, Clay, Duval, Nassau, and St. Johns counties.
Support limitations: No support for schools, religious organizations not of direct benefit to the entire community, or disease-specific organizations. No grants to individuals or for fundraising or sponsorships.
Publications: Application guidelines.
Application information: Applications accepted. A full proposal may be requested at a later date. Multi-year funding is limited to a maximum of 2 to 3 consecutive years. Organizations receiving support are asked to submit a final report. Applicants should submit the following:

1) how project will be sustained once grantmaker support is completed
2) statement of problem project will address
3) population served
4) geographic area to be served
5) detailed description of project and amount of funding requested
6) copy of current year's organizational budget and/or project budget

Initial approach: Complete online eligibility quiz and letter of inquiry for new applicants; complete online application for returning grantees; download application form and mail to foundation for Honor Rows
Board meeting date(s): Generally, summer and winter
Deadline(s): June 12 for new applicants; July 12 for returning grantees; visit website for Honor Rows deadline
Final notification: 30 days; June 1 for Honor Rows

Officers and Directors:* Peter M. Racine, Pres.; Lawrence J. Dubow*, Treas.; Elizabeth P. Petway; J. Wayne Weaver.
Number of staff: 3 full-time professional; 1 full-time support; 1 part-time support.
EIN: 593249687
Selected grants: The following grants are a representative sample of this grantmaker's funding activity:

$72,000 to Bridge of Northeast Florida, Jacksonville, FL, 2010.
$40,750 to PACE Center for Girls of Jacksonville, Jacksonville, FL, 2010.
$35,330 to Local Initiatives Support Corporation, New York, NY, 2010.
$30,000 to Girls on the Run of Northeast Florida, Jacksonville, FL, 2010.
$30,000 to OneJax, Jacksonville, FL, 2010.
$25,000 to Limelight Theater, Saint Augustine, FL, 2010.
$25,000 to Saint Augustine Youth Services, Saint Augustine, FL, 2010.
$25,000 to Student Conservation Association, Charlestown, NH, 2010.
$11,000 to Saint Vincents Foundation, Jacksonville, FL, 2010.
$10,000 to I. M. Sulzbacher Center for the Homeless, Jacksonville, FL, 2010.

2015
Jaclyn, Inc.

197 W. Spring Valley Ave.
Maywood, NJ 07607 (201) 909-6000
FAX: (201) 854-7202

Company URL: http://www.jaclyninc.com/
Establishment information: Established in 1968.
Company type: Public company
Company ticker symbol and exchange: JCLY/Pink Sheets
Business activities: Designs and sells branded and private-label apparel, bags, and related accessories for men, women, and children.
Business type (SIC): Apparel, piece goods, and notions—wholesale
Financial profile for 2012: Number of employees, 182; assets, $50,220,000; sales volume, $195,930,000; pre-tax net income, $5,100,000; expenses, $194,600,000; liabilities, $24,670,000
Corporate officers: Allan Ginsburg, Chair.; Howard Ginsburg, Vice-Chair.; Robert Chestnov, Pres. and C.E.O.; Anthony C. Christon, C.F.O.
Board of directors: Allan Ginsburg, Chair.; Howard Ginsburg, Vice-Chair.; Norman Axelrod; Martin Brody; Richard Chestnov; Robert Chestnov; Abe Ginsburg; Albert Safer; Harold Schechter
Giving statement: Giving through the Abe & Sylvia Ginsburg Foundation.
Company EIN: 221432053

Abe & Sylvia Ginsburg Foundation

197 W. Spring Valley Ave.
Maywood, NJ 07607

Establishment information: Established in 1994 in NJ.
Donors: Jaclyn, Inc.; Abraham Ginsburg; Silvia Gisnburg Trust; Abe Ginsburg Trust.
Financial data (yr. ended 12/31/11): Assets, $1,011,686 (M); gifts received, $64,002; expenditures, $71,018; qualifying distributions, $67,141; giving activities include $67,141 for grants.
Purpose and activities: The foundation supports camps and organizations involved with K-12 and higher education, health, cancer, human services, and Judaism.
Fields of interest: Education; Health care; Human services; Religion.
Type of support: Annual campaigns; General/operating support.
Geographic limitations: Giving primarily in NJ and NY.
Support limitations: No grants to individuals.
Application information: Applications not accepted. Contributes only to pre-selected organizations.
Officers: Jaclyn Hartstein, Pres.; Bernice Gailing Schwartz, V.P. and Treas.; Howard Ginsburg, Secy.
EIN: 237077996

2016
Jacobs Engineering Group Inc.

1111 S. Arroyo Pkwy.
P.O. Box 7084
Pasadena, CA 91105-7084 (626) 578-3500
FAX: (626) 568-7144

Company URL: http://www.jacobs.com
Establishment information: Established in 1947.
Company type: Public company
Company ticker symbol and exchange: JEC/NYSE
International Securities Identification Number: US4698141078
Business activities: Provides engineering, design, and consulting services; provides construction and construction management services; provides process plant maintenance services.
Business type (SIC): Engineering, architectural, and surveying services; heavy construction other than building construction contractors; services to dwellings
Financial profile for 2012: Number of employees, 48,600; assets, $3,839,430,000; sales volume, $10,893,780,000; pre-tax net income, $593,340,000; expenses, $10,291,410,000; liabilities, $3,116,960,000
Fortune 1000 ranking: 2012—249th in revenues, 418th in profits, and 494th in assets
Forbes 2000 ranking: 2012—874th in sales, 1353rd in profits, and 1682nd in assets
Corporate officers: Noel G. Watson, Chair.; Craig L. Martin, Pres. and C.E.O.; John W. Prosser, Jr., Exec. V.P., Finance, Admin., and Treas.; Nazim G. Thawerbhoy, Sr. V.P. and Cont.; Patricia H. Summers, Sr. V.P., Human Resources
Board of directors: Noel G. Watson, Chair.; Joseph R. Bronson; John F. Coyne; Robert C. Davidson, Jr.; Ralph E. Eberhart; Edward V. Fritzky; Linda Fayne Levinson; Craig L. Martin; Benjamin F. Montoya; Peter J. Robertson
Subsidiaries: Carter & Burgess Inc., Fort Worth, TX; Edwards and Kelcey, Inc., Morristown, NJ; Jacobs Civil Consultants, Inc., New York, NY; Jacobs Consultancy, Inc., Houston, TX; Jacobs Engineering, Inc., McClellan, CA; Jacobs Engineering New York, Inc., New York, NY; Jacobs Field Services North America, Inc., Houston, TX; Jacobs Government Services Co., Pasadena, CA; Jacobs Industrial Services Inc., St. Louis, MO; Jacobs Project Management Co., Sacramento, CA; Jacobs Technology, Inc., Tullahoma, TN
Historic mergers: Sverdrup Corporation (January 14, 1999)
Giving statement: Giving through the Jacobs Engineering Group Inc. Corporate Giving Program and the Jacobs Engineering Foundation.
Company EIN: 954081636

Jacobs Engineering Foundation

P.O. Box 7084
Pasadena, CA 91109-7084 (626) 578-3500

Establishment information: Established in 1978 in CA.
Donor: Jacobs Engineering Group Inc.
Contact: John W. Prosser, Jr., Treas.
Financial data (yr. ended 12/31/11): Assets, $2,567,530 (M); gifts received, $731,994; expenditures, $923,836; qualifying distributions,

$923,751; giving activities include $923,751 for grants.
Purpose and activities: The foundation supports museums and organizations involved with education, health, genetic diseases, cancer, golf, human services, engineering, and civic affairs.
Fields of interest: Museums; Higher education; Medical school/education; Education; Hospitals (general); Health care, clinics/centers; Health care; Genetic diseases and disorders; Cancer; Athletics/sports, golf; Boys & girls clubs; American Red Cross; Human services; Engineering; Public affairs, association; Government/public administration; Public affairs.
Type of support: Annual campaigns; Employee-related scholarships; General/operating support; Matching/challenge support; Scholarship funds; Sponsorships.
Geographic limitations: Giving primarily in CA, CO, Washington, DC, IL, MO, NY, TX, and VA.
Application information: Applications accepted. Application form not required. Applicants should submit the following:
1) copy of IRS Determination Letter
2) detailed description of project and amount of funding requested
Initial approach: Proposal
Deadline(s): None
Officers and Directors:* George A. Kunberger*, Chair.; Craig L. Martin*, Pres.; Michael S. Udovic, Secy.; John W. Prosser, Jr.*, Treas.; Nazim G. Thawerbhoy, Cont.
EIN: 953195445
Selected grants: The following grants are a representative sample of this grantmaker's funding activity:
$151,175 to Scholarship America, Saint Peter, MN, 2011.
$30,000 to United Way of Greater Houston, Houston, TX, 2011.
$11,000 to Business Council for International Understanding, New York, NY, 2011.
$10,000 to Houston Ballet, Houston, TX, 2011.
$9,850 to City of Hope, Duarte, CA, 2011.
$8,250 to Scholarship America, Saint Peter, MN, 2011.
$8,000 to United Way of Greater Los Angeles, Los Angeles, CA, 2011.
$7,500 to Boys and Girls Clubs of America, Atlanta, GA, 2011.
$5,000 to National Forum for Black Public Administrators, Washington, DC, 2011.
$2,250 to Urban League of Greater New Orleans, New Orleans, LA, 2011.

2017
Jai Ma Creation Inc.
1400 Broadway, Ste. 1402
New York, NY 10018-5214 (212) 840-2222

Establishment information: Established in 1994.
Company type: Private company
Business activities: Sells apparel wholesale.
Business type (SIC): Apparel, piece goods, and notions—wholesale
Corporate officer: Lisa Gulati, Pres.
Giving statement: Giving through the Mata Ji Foundation.

Mata Ji Foundation
P.O. Box 1359
New York, NY 10018-0019 (212) 840-2222

Establishment information: Established in 2001.
Donor: Jai Ma Creation Inc.
Contact: Anastasios Kopsidas, Secy.
Financial data (yr. ended 12/31/10): Assets, $164,209 (M); gifts received, $100,000; expenditures, $355,826; qualifying distributions, $354,500; giving activities include $354,500 for 5 grants (high: $200,000; low: $4,500).
Purpose and activities: The foundation supports organizations involved with education and religion.
Fields of interest: Higher education; Education; Spirituality; Religion.
International interests: India.
Type of support: General/operating support.
Geographic limitations: Giving primarily in NY and India.
Application information: Applications accepted. Application form not required. Applicants should submit the following:
1) name, address and phone number of organization
2) contact person
3) detailed description of project and amount of funding requested
Initial approach: Letter of inquiry
Deadline(s): None
Officers: Shilpi Kopsidas, Pres.; Satmata Kopsidas, V.P.; Anastasios Kopsidas, Secy.
EIN: 113557588
Selected grants: The following grants are a representative sample of this grantmaker's funding activity:
$4,500 to Educational Foundation for the Fashion Industries, New York, NY, 2010.

2018
Jalapeno Corporation
(also known as Petro Yates, Inc.)
1429 Central Ave., N.W.
Albuquerque, NM 87104-1148
(505) 242-2050

Company URL: http://www.jalapenocorp.com
Establishment information: Established in 1993.
Company type: Private company
Business activities: Operates oil and gas exploration company.
Business type (SIC): Oil and gas field services
Corporate officer: Harvey E. Yates, Jr., Pres. and C.E.O.
Giving statement: Giving through the Adelante Now Foundation.

Adelante Now Foundation
P.O. Box O
Albuquerque, NM 87103-1266

Establishment information: Established in NM.
Donors: Jalapeno Corp.; Harvey E. Yates, Jr.; Yates Petroleum Corp.
Financial data (yr. ended 12/31/11): Assets, $8,523 (M); gifts received, $5,000; expenditures, $17,946; qualifying distributions, $17,206; giving activities include $17,206 for grants.
Fields of interest: Education.
Geographic limitations: Giving primarily in NM.
Support limitations: No grants to individuals.
Application information: Applications not accepted. Unsolicited requests for funds not accepted.
Officers: Harvey E. Yates, Pres.; Barrett E. Yates-Mack, V.P.; Ryan Cangiolosi, Secy.; Bob Davey, Treas.
EIN: 850480126

2019
JAM Securities Company
(formerly JAM Securities Corp.)
166 Geary St., Ste. 702
San Francisco, CA 94108-5618
(415) 392-5248

Establishment information: Established in 1924.
Company type: Private company
Business activities: Conducts investment activities.
Business type (SIC): Investors/miscellaneous
Corporate officers: Douglas G. Moore, Pres.; James R. Moore, Treas.
Giving statement: Giving through the Moore Dry Dock Foundation.

Moore Dry Dock Foundation
166 Geary St., Ste. 702
San Francisco, CA 94108-5618 (415) 392-5248

Donor: JAM Securities Corp.
Contact: Marilyn Boring, Pres.
Financial data (yr. ended 06/30/11): Assets, $474,983 (M); expenditures, $26,671; qualifying distributions, $24,330; giving activities include $17,760 for 26 grants (high: $3,500; low: $100).
Purpose and activities: The foundation supports organizations involved with arts and culture, education, and ALS.
Fields of interest: Arts; Education; Environment.
Type of support: General/operating support.
Geographic limitations: Giving primarily in Oakland and San Francisco, CA.
Support limitations: No grants to individuals.
Application information: Applications accepted. Application form required. Applicants should submit the following:
1) detailed description of project and amount of funding requested
Initial approach: Letter of inquiry
Deadline(s): None
Officers: Marilyn Boring, Pres.; Joseph M. Mock, V.P.; James R. Moore, Jr., V.P.; Douglas G. Moore, Secy.-Treas.
EIN: 941681456

2020
Jamba Juice Company
6475 Christie Ave. Ste. 150
Emeryville, CA 94608 (510) 596-0100

Company URL: http://www.jambajuice.com
Establishment information: Established in 1990.
Company type: Private company
Business activities: Operates juice shops.
Business type (SIC): Restaurants and drinking places
Corporate officers: James D. White, Chair., Pres., and C.E.O.; Bruce E. Schroder, C.O.O.; Karen L. Luey, Exec. V.P., C.F.O., C.A.O., and Secy.
Board of director: James D. White, Chair.
Giving statement: Giving through the Jamba Juice Company Contributions Program.

Jamba Juice Company Contributions Program
6475 Christie Ave., Ste. 150
Emeryville, CA 94608-2259 (510) 596-0100
FAX: (510) 295-2896; URL: http://jambajuice.com/live-fruitfully/community

Purpose and activities: Jamba Juice makes charitable contributions to educational institutions

and nonprofit organizations involved with nutrition and wellness. Support is given primarily in areas of company operations, with some emphasis on California.
Fields of interest: Education; Public health, physical fitness; Nutrition; Athletics/sports, school programs; Youth development; Community development, neighborhood development.
Type of support: Employee volunteer services; Sponsorships.
Geographic limitations: Giving primarily in areas of operations, with some emphasis on CA.
Application information:
Copies of proposal: 1

2021
Raymond James Financial, Inc.

The Raymond James Financial Ctr.
880 Carillon Pkwy.
St. Petersburg, FL 33716-2749
(727) 567-1000

Company URL: http://www.raymondjames.com
Establishment information: Established in 1962.
Company type: Public company
Company ticker symbol and exchange: RJF/NYSE
Business activities: Operates holding company; provides securities brokerage services; provides investment advisory services.
Business type (SIC): Brokers and dealers/security; security and commodity services; holding company
Financial profile for 2012: Number of employees, 10,400; assets, $21,160,260,000; sales volume, $3,897,900,000; pre-tax net income, $467,920,000; expenses, $3,429,980,000; liabilities, $17,891,330,000
Fortune 1000 ranking: 2012—601st in revenues, 477th in profits, and 231st in assets
Forbes 2000 ranking: 2012—1496th in sales, 1495th in profits, and 912th in assets
Corporate officers: Thomas A. James, Chair.; Francis S. Godbold, Vice-Chair.; Paul Reilly, C.E.O.; Dennis Zank, C.O.O.; Jeffrey P. Julien, Exec. V.P., Finance, and C.F.O.
Board of directors: Thomas A. James, Chair.; Francis S. Godbold, Vice-Chair.; Shelley G. Broader; H. William Habermeyer, Jr.; Chester B. Helck; Gordon L. Johnson; Paul C. Reilly; Robert P. Saltzman; Hardwick Simmons; Susan N. Story
Subsidiaries: Eagle Asset Management, Inc., St. Petersburg, FL; Heritage Asset Management, Inc., St. Petersburg, FL; Raymond James & Associates, Inc., St. Petersburg, FL; Raymond James Capital, Inc., St. Petersburg, FL; Raymond James Financial Services, Inc., St. Petersburg, FL; Raymond James Partners, Inc., St. Petersburg, FL; RJ Leasing, Inc., St. Petersburg, FL; RJC Partners, Inc., St. Petersburg, FL
International operations: Argentina; Brazil; British Virgin Islands; Canada; Mauritius; Switzerland; United Kingdom; Uruguay
Giving statement: Giving through the Raymond James Financial, Inc. Corporate Giving Program.
Company EIN: 591517485

Raymond James Financial, Inc. Corporate Giving Program

The Raymond James Financial Ctr.
880 Carillon Pkwy.
St. Petersburg, FL 33716-1102 (727) 567-1000
URL: http://www.raymondjames.com/about/charitable_giving.htm

Purpose and activities: Raymond James Financial makes charitable contributions to nonprofit organizations involved with arts and culture and education. Support is given on a national basis in areas of company operations, with emphasis on Tampa Bay, Florida.
Fields of interest: Visual arts; Performing arts, theater; Performing arts, orchestras; Arts; Education; Disasters, preparedness/services; Youth development, business; Children, services; Human services; United Ways and Federated Giving Programs Disabilities, people with.
Type of support: Employee volunteer services; General/operating support; Sponsorships.
Geographic limitations: Giving on a national basis in areas of company operations, with emphasis on Tampa Bay, FL.

2022
JanPak, Inc.

(formerly Paper Supply Company)
705 Griffith St., Ste. 300
Davidson, NC 28036-9308 (704) 892-0219
FAX: (704) 731-0978

Company URL: http://www.janpak.com
Establishment information: Established in 1945.
Company type: Private company
Business activities: Sells paper and paper products wholesale.
Business type (SIC): Paper and paper products—wholesale
Corporate officers: Tim Feeheley, Pres.; Deborah H. Greer, V.P., Sales; Jo-Anne Williams, Secy.
Giving statement: Giving through the JanPak Charitable Foundation, Inc.

The JanPak Charitable Foundation, Inc.

(formerly The Paper Supply Company Charitable Foundation, Inc.)
100 Bluefield Ave., Ste. 3
Bluefield, WV 24701-2836 (304) 325-3514
Application address: P.O. Box 130, Bluefield, WV 24701

Establishment information: Established in 1996 in WV.
Donors: Paper Supply Co.; Paper Supply Co. of Bristol, Inc.; JanPak, Inc.
Contact: Michael R. Shott, Dir.
Financial data (yr. ended 06/30/12): Assets, $69,481 (M); gifts received, $1,000; expenditures, $64,784; qualifying distributions, $61,250; giving activities include $61,250 for grants.
Purpose and activities: The foundation supports organizations involved with education, health, cancer, recreation, and human services.
Fields of interest: Education; Safety/disasters; Civil/human rights.
Type of support: General/operating support.
Geographic limitations: Giving primarily in NC, SC, TN, VA, and WV.
Support limitations: No grants to individuals.
Application information: Applications accepted. Application form required.
Initial approach: Contact foundation for application information
Deadline(s): None
Directors: Roger Estep; Thomas W. Reef; John C. Shott; Michael R. Shott; Scott H. Shott.
EIN: 550754736

2023
Janssen Pharmaceuticals, Inc.

(formerly Janssen Pharmaceutica Inc.)
1125 Trenton-Harbourton Rd.
P.O. Box 200
Titusville, NJ 08560-0200 (609) 730-2000

Company URL: http://www.janssenpharmaceuticalsinc.com/
Establishment information: Established in 1973.
Company type: Subsidiary of a public company
Business activities: Develops, manufactures, and markets pharmaceutical products and services.
Business type (SIC): Drugs
Corporate officers: Janet N. Vergis, Pres.; John Szabo, Cont.; JoAnn Heffernan Heisen, V.P., Human Resources
Giving statement: Giving through the Janssen Pharmaceuticals, Inc. Contributions Program.

Janssen Pharmaceuticals, Inc. Contributions Program

1125 Trenton-Harbourton Rd.
P.O. Box 200
Titusville, NJ 08560-0200 (609) 730-2000
URL: http://www.janssenpharmaceuticalsinc.com/our-giving

Purpose and activities: Janssen Pharmaceuticals makes charitable contributions to nonprofit organizations in areas of company operations.
Fields of interest: General charitable giving.
Type of support: Employee volunteer services; General/operating support.
Geographic limitations: Giving primarily in areas of company operations.

2024
Janus Capital Management, L.L.C.

(formerly Janus Capital Corporation)
151 Detroit St.
Denver, CO 80206-4921 (303) 333-3863

Company URL: http://www.janus.com
Establishment information: Established in 1969.
Company type: Subsidiary of a public company
Business activities: Provides investment advisory services.
Business type (SIC): Security and commodity services
Corporate officers: Jonathan D. Coleman, Co-C.I.O.; Gibson Smith, Co-C.I.O.; Gregory Alan Frost, Sr. V.P., and C.F.O.; Heidi Walter Hardin, Sr. V.P. and Genl. Counsel
Giving statement: Giving through the Janus Foundation.

The Janus Foundation

151 Detroit St., 4th FL
Denver, CO 80206-4805 (303) 333-3863
FAX: (303) 394-7797;
E-mail: janusfoundation@janus.com; URL: https://ww3.janus.com/community/janus-foundation

Establishment information: Established in 1994 in CO.
Donors: Janus Capital Corp.; Janus Capital Management LLC.
Financial data (yr. ended 12/31/11): Assets, $544,340 (M); gifts received, $1,516,849; expenditures, $1,343,234; qualifying distributions,

$1,316,033; giving activities include $1,316,033 for grants.
Purpose and activities: The foundation supports organizations involved with education.
Fields of interest: Elementary/secondary education; Libraries (public); Education; Children/youth, services Economically disadvantaged.
Program:
Janus Charity Challenge: Through Janus Charity Challenge, Ironman Triathlons athletes use the race to raise money for the charity of their choice. The foundation awards an additional contribution to the beneficiaries of the 50 top fundraisers at each race, 1st place $10,000 donation, 2nd place $8,000 donation, 3rd place $6,000 donation, 4th place $4,000 donation, and 5th place $2,000 donation. The foundation also awards $750 to the next 30 highest fundraisers who have raised a minimum of $750, and $100 to the next 15 highest fundraisers who have raised a minimum of $100.
Type of support: Continuing support; Curriculum development; Employee matching gifts; Program development; Scholarship funds.
Geographic limitations: Giving primarily in areas of company operations in Denver, CO.
Support limitations: No grants to individuals, or for sponsorship events or tables, field trips or tours, recreational activities, conferences, seminars, workshops, annual membership or affiliation campaigns, publication or distribution of books, articles, newsletters, videos, or electronic media, religious or political purposes, health-related programs, or environmental projects.
Application information: Applications not accepted. Contributes only to pre-selected organizations.
Board meeting date(s): 1st week of each month
Officers and Director: Casey Cotese, Pres.; Karlene J. Lacy, V.P., Tax; Curt R. Foust, Secy.; Greg Frost.
Number of staff: 2 part-time professional.
EIN: 841271105

2025
Jasper Desk Company, Inc.

415 E. 6th St.
Jasper, IN 47546 (812) 482-4132

Company URL: http://www.jasperdesk.com
Establishment information: Established in 1876.
Company type: Private company
Business activities: Manufactures wood office furniture.
Business type (SIC): Furniture/office
Corporate officers: James Arvin, Pres.; James Seifert, Treas.
Giving statement: Giving through the Jasper Desk Foundation, Inc.

Jasper Desk Foundation, Inc.

c/o Jasper Desk Co., Inc.
P.O. Box 111
Jasper, IN 47546

Donor: Jasper Desk Co., Inc.
Financial data (yr. ended 12/31/11): Assets, $32,149 (M); expenditures, $4,001; qualifying distributions, $4,000; giving activities include $4,000 for 24 grants (high: $500; low: $50).
Purpose and activities: The foundation supports fire departments and organizations involved with theological education, forest restoration, health, cancer, and religion.
Fields of interest: Theological school/education; Environment, forests; Hospitals (general); Health care; Cancer; Disasters, fire prevention/control; Boy scouts; Religion.
Type of support: Capital campaigns; General/operating support; Program development; Scholarship funds.
Geographic limitations: Giving primarily in Jasper, IN.
Support limitations: No grants to individuals.
Application information: Applications not accepted. Unsolicited requests for funds not accepted.
Officers: James A. Seifert, Pres.; Michael Pfau, Secy.-Treas.
Directors: James Arvin; Phillip Gramelspacher; Eric Olinger; Carole Veatch.
EIN: 356024532

2026
Jasper Group

(formerly Jasper Seating Company, Inc.)
225 S. Clay St.
P.O. Box 231
Jasper, IN 47547 (812) 482-3204

Company URL: http://www.jaspergroup.us.com/
Establishment information: Established in 1929.
Company type: Private company
Business activities: Manufactures chairs.
Business type (SIC): Furniture/office; furniture/public building
Corporate officer: Michael Elliott, Pres. and C.E.O.
Giving statement: Giving through the Jasper Seating Foundation, Inc.

Jasper Seating Foundation, Inc.

c/o Jasper Seating Co., Inc.
P.O. Box 231
Jasper, IN 47546-0231

Donor: Jasper Seating Co., Inc.
Financial data (yr. ended 12/31/11): Assets, $65,261 (M); gifts received, $55,000; expenditures, $18,862; qualifying distributions, $18,862; giving activities include $18,855 for 99 grants (high: $2,500; low: $25).
Purpose and activities: The foundation supports community foundations and organizations involved with education, health, fire safety, human services, community development, and Catholicism.
Fields of interest: Higher education; Theological school/education; Education; Hospitals (general); Health care; Disasters, fire prevention/control; Children/youth, services; Human services; Community/economic development; Foundations (community); Catholic agencies & churches.
Type of support: Annual campaigns; General/operating support; Program development; Scholarship funds.
Geographic limitations: Giving primarily in Jasper, IN.
Application information: Applications accepted. Application form required.
Initial approach: Letter
Deadline(s): None
Officers: Michael Elliott, Pres.; Glenn Gramelspacher II, Secy.; William Rubino, Treas.
Directors: Ronald Beck; Nicholas Gramelspacher.
EIN: 356024534

2027
Jasper Wood Products, LLC

37385 Jasper Lowell Rd.
Jasper, OR 97438 (541) 988-1127

Establishment information: Established in 2001.
Company type: Private company
Business activities: Provides contract wood product manufacturing services.
Business type (SIC): Lumber and wood products (except furniture)
Corporate officer: Douglas Henton, Owner
Giving statement: Giving through the Jasper Wood Products Foundation, Inc.

Jasper Wood Products Foundation, Inc.

(doing business as Gramelspacher Foundation)
P.O. Box 2386
Indianapolis, IN 46206-2386 (317) 423-9800

Establishment information: Established in 1945 in IN.
Donors: Mark B. Gramelspacher; Jasper Wood Products Co., Inc.; CMW Inc.
Contact: Mark B. Gramelspacher, Pres. and Treas.
Financial data (yr. ended 12/31/11): Assets, $270,844 (M); gifts received, $100,800; expenditures, $809; qualifying distributions, $466.
Purpose and activities: The foundation supports organizations involved with health and Protestantism.
Fields of interest: Education; Environment; Health organizations.
Geographic limitations: Giving primarily in IN.
Application information: Applications accepted. Application form required. Applicants should submit the following:
1) statement of problem project will address
2) detailed description of project and amount of funding requested
Initial approach: Letter
Copies of proposal: 1
Board meeting date(s): Dec.
Deadline(s): None
Officer: Mark B. Gramelspacher, Pres. and Treas.
EIN: 356024934

2028
Jazz Basketball Investors, Inc.

(also known as Utah Jazz)
301 W. South Temple
Salt Lake City, UT 84101-1216
(801) 325-2500

Company URL: http://www.nba.com/jazz
Establishment information: Established in 1974.
Company type: Subsidiary of a private company
Business activities: Operates professional basketball club.
Business type (SIC): Commercial sports
Corporate officers: Greg S. Miller, C.E.O.; Randy Rigby, Pres.; Steve Miller, C.O.O.; Robert G. Hyde, Exec. V.P. and C.F.O.; Linda Luchetti, Exec. V.P., Comms.; Robert D. Tingey, Genl. Counsel
Giving statement: Giving through the Larry H. Miller Charities.

Larry H. Miller Charities

301 W. S. Temple
Salt Lake City, UT 84101-1216 (801) 563-4100

Establishment information: Established in 1995.

Contact: Stayner Landward, Pres.
Financial data (yr. ended 12/31/10): Revenue, $467,809; assets, $241,927 (M); gifts received, $349,488; expenditures, $494,508; program services expenses, $489,430; giving activities include $489,430 for 24 grants (high: $35,000; low: $5,920).
Purpose and activities: The organization supports various 501(c)(3) charitable organizations, with an emphasis on education and human services.
Fields of interest: Education; Human services Children/youth; Economically disadvantaged.
Program:
Grants: Funding will be provided to groups whose programs and services benefit those who live in the same communities where Larry H. Miller Companies does business (Arizona, Colorado, Idaho, New Mexico, and Utah). Giving focuses on programs that assist children, with an emphasis on health and education.
Type of support: Building/renovation; Capital campaigns; Conferences/seminars; Continuing support; Curriculum development; Equipment; General/operating support; Program development; Scholarship funds.
Geographic limitations: Giving limited to AZ, CO, ID, NM, OR, and UT.
Support limitations: No support for individuals.
Publications: Application guidelines.
Application information: Applications accepted. Application form not required. Applicants should submit the following:
1) detailed description of project and amount of funding requested
2) copy of current year's organizational budget and/or project budget
3) brief history of organization and description of its mission
4) copy of IRS Determination Letter
5) copy of most recent annual report/audited financial statement/990
Initial approach: Letter
Copies of proposal: 1
Board meeting date(s): Every six to eight weeks
Deadline(s): Applications accepted on a rolling basis
Officers and Trustees:* Stayner Landward*, Pres.; Linda Louise Luchetti*, V.P.; Jay Kent Francis*, V.P.; Karol Sue Elkington*, Secy.; Susan Elizabeth Wood*, Treas.; Libby Arias; Kathryn Ann Farrow; Alan Blaine Fernelius; Pauline E. Lloyd; Stephen F. Miller; Jaymie Osborne; Holly Ann Thunell; Betsy Ward.
EIN: 870541212

2029
Jeffer Mangels Butler & Mitchell LLP

1900 Ave. of the Stars, 7th Fl.
Los Angeles, CA 90067 (312) 203-8080

Company URL: http://www.jmbm.com/
Establishment information: Established in 1981.
Company type: Private company
Business activities: Operates law firm.
Business type (SIC): Legal services
Financial profile for 2012: Number of employees, 125
Corporate officer: Bruce P. Jeffer, Managing Partner
Giving statement: Giving through the Jeffer Mangels Butler & Mitchell LLP Pro Bono Program.

Jeffer Mangels Butler & Mitchell LLP Pro Bono Program

1900 Ave. of the Stars, 7th Fl.
Los Angeles, CA 90067 (310) 201-3548
E-mail: sgibson@jmbm.com; URL: http://www.jmbm.com

Contact: Stan Gibson, Partner
Fields of interest: Legal services.
Type of support: Pro bono services - legal.

2030
Jefferies Group, Inc.

520 Madison Ave., 10th Fl.
New York, NY 10022 (212) 284-2550
FAX: (212) 284-2111

Company URL: http://www.jefco.com
Establishment information: Established in 1962.
Company type: Public company
Company ticker symbol and exchange: JEF/NYSE
Business activities: Operates securities and investment banking firm.
Business type (SIC): Brokers and dealers/security
Financial profile for 2012: Number of employees, 3,804; assets, $36,293,540,000; sales volume, $3,871,200,000; pre-tax net income, $491,800,000; expenses, $3,379,410,000; liabilities, $3,285,753
Corporate officers: Richard B. Handler, Chair. and C.E.O.; Peregrine C. Broadbent, Exec. V.P. and C.F.O.; Michael J. Sharp, Exec. V.P., Genl. Counsel, and Secy.
Board of directors: Richard B. Handler, Chair.; W. Patrick Campbell; Richard G. Dooley; Brian P. Friedman; Robert E. Joyal; Michael T. O'Kane; Joseph S. Steinberg
Subsidiary: Jefferies & Company, Inc., New York, NY
International operations: China; France; Germany; Hong Kong; India; Japan; Singapore; Switzerland; United Kingdom
Giving statement: Giving through the Jefferies Group, Inc. Corporate Giving Program.
Company EIN: 954719745

Jefferies Group, Inc. Corporate Giving Program

520 Madison Avenue, 10th Fl.
New York, NY 10022-4213 (212) 284-2300
URL: http://www.jefferies.com/OurFirm/2/165

Purpose and activities: Jefferies Group makes charitable contributions to nonprofit organizations involved with cancer research and disaster relief, and annually awards educational scholarships to children of Jefferies employees. Support is given on a national and international basis.
Fields of interest: Education; Medical research, fund raising/fund distribution; Cancer research; Disasters, preparedness/services; Safety/disasters.
Type of support: Employee matching gifts; Employee-related scholarships; General/operating support.
Geographic limitations: Giving on a national and international basis.

2031
Jeg's Automotive, Inc.

(also known as JEGS High Performance)
101 Jegs Pl.
Delaware, OH 43015 (614) 294-5050
FAX: (740) 362-7017

Company URL: http://www.jegs.com
Establishment information: Established in 1960.
Company type: Private company
Business activities: Provides catalog shopping services; operates automobile parts stores.
Business type (SIC): Nonstore retailers; auto and home supplies—retail
Financial profile for 2009: Number of employees, 300
Corporate officers: Edward James Coughlin, Pres.; Jeg Coughlin, V.P.; Garry Cook, C.I.O.; George Gow, Cont.
Giving statement: Giving through the Jegs Foundation.

The Jegs Foundation

(formerly Jeg's Quarter Mile Charities)
101 Jegs Pl.
Delaware, OH 43015-9279
URL: http://www.jegs.com/s/customercare/foundation.html

Establishment information: Established in 2000 in OH.
Donor: Jeg's Automotive, Inc.
Financial data (yr. ended 12/31/11): Assets, $4,975,650 (M); gifts received, $17,388; expenditures, $264,157; qualifying distributions, $255,000; giving activities include $255,000 for 2 grants (high: $250,000; low: $5,000).
Purpose and activities: The foundation supports organizations involved with cancer and human services.
Fields of interest: Cancer; Cancer research; Human services.
Type of support: General/operating support; Research.
Geographic limitations: Giving primarily in OH, with emphasis on Columbus.
Support limitations: No grants to individuals.
Application information: Applications not accepted. Unsolicited requests for funds not accepted.
Officers and Trustees:* Phillip Troy Coughlin*, Pres.; Edward John Coughlin*, Secy.-Treas.; Jeg Anthony Coughlin; Michael Allen Coughlin.
EIN: 311731261

2032
Jeld-Wen, Inc.

3250 Lakeport Blvd.
P.O. Box 1329
Klamath Falls, OR 97601 (541) 882-3451
FAX: (541) 885-7403

Company URL: http://www.jeld-wen.com
Establishment information: Established in 1960.
Company type: Private company
Business activities: Manufactures doors, windows, and millwork products.
Business type (SIC): Wood millwork
Financial profile for 2011: Number of employees, 20,000; sales volume, $3,000,000,000
Corporate officers: Robert F. Turner, Chair.; Roderick C. Wendt, Pres. and C.E.O.; Barry Homrighaus, C.O.O.; Scott Todd, C.I.O.; Scott Whitmore, V.P., Mktg.

Board of director: Robert F. Turner, Chair.
Subsidiaries: Frank Paxton Co., Kansas City, MO; Young Door & Challenge Door Co., Plymouth, IN
Giving statement: Giving through the Jeld-Wen Foundation.

The Jeld-Wen Foundation

(formerly Jeld-Wen, Wenco Foundation)
200 SW Market St., Ste. 550
Portland, OR 97201-5727 (503) 417-8096
FAX: (503) 242-3826; Klamath Falls Office: 3250 Lakeport Blvd., Klamath Falls, OR 97601, tel.: (541) 880-2185; URL: http://www.jeld-wenfoundation.org/

Establishment information: Established in 1969.
Donors: Jeld-Wen, Inc.; Jeld-Wen Fiber Products, Inc. of Iowa; Jeld-Wen Co. of Arizona; Wenco, Inc. of North Carolina; Wenco, Inc. of Ohio; Jeld-Wen Holding, Inc.
Contact: Robert Kingzett, Exec. Dir.
Financial data (yr. ended 12/31/11): Assets, $19,752,223 (M); expenditures, $2,350,636; qualifying distributions, $2,064,227; giving activities include $2,064,227 for grants.
Purpose and activities: The foundation supports organizations involved with arts and culture, education, health, human services, community development, and civic affairs. Special emphasis is directed toward programs designed to strengthen families, improve neighborhoods, and build better communities.
Fields of interest: Humanities; Arts; Education; Hospitals (general); Health care; Human services; Community/economic development; United Ways and Federated Giving Programs; Public policy, research; Public affairs.
Type of support: Building/renovation; Capital campaigns; Endowments; Equipment; General/operating support; Matching/challenge support; Program development; Scholarship funds.
Geographic limitations: Giving on a national basis in areas of company operations, with emphasis on OR.
Support limitations: No support for private or religious schools. No grants to individuals, or for religious activities or programs that duplicate services provided by other government or private agencies; no annual support.
Publications: Application guidelines.
Application information: Applications accepted. The foundation requests that applicants involve a Jeld-Wen manager in the application process. A site visit may be requested. Support is limited to 1 contribution per organization during any given year. Application form required. Applicants should submit the following:
1) copy of IRS Determination Letter
2) listing of board of directors, trustees, officers and other key people and their affiliations
3) contact person

Initial approach: Contact foundation or nearest general manager for application form
Board meeting date(s): Quarterly
Deadline(s): Varies, but are scheduled around quarterly meetings

Officers and Trustees:* Roderick C. Wendt*, Secy.; Robert Kingzett, Exec. Dir.; W. B. Early; Robert F. Turner; Nancy J. Wendt.
EIN: 936054272

2033
Jelly Belly Candy Company

1 Jelly Belly Ln.
Fairfield, CA 94533-6741 (707) 399-2390

Company URL: http://www.jellybelly.com
Establishment information: Established in 1869.
Company type: Private company
Business activities: Produces candy.
Business type (SIC): Sugar, candy, and salted/roasted nut production
Corporate officers: Herman Goelitz Rowland, Sr., Chair. and C.E.O.; William H. Kelley, Vice-Chair.; Robert M. Simpson, Pres. and C.O.O.
Board of directors: Herman Goelitz Rowland, Sr., Chair.; William Kelley, Vice-Chair.
Giving statement: Giving through the Jelly Belly Candy Company Contributions Program.

Jelly Belly Candy Company Contributions Program

c/o Event Mktg. Dept.
1 Jelly Belly Ln.
Fairfield, CA 94533-6722
E-mail: EventMarketing@JellyBelly.com; URL: http://www.jellybelly.com/sports_sponsorships/sponsorship_guidelines.aspx

Purpose and activities: Jelly Belly Candy makes charitable contributions to nonprofit organizations on a case by case basis. Support is limited to Contra Costa, Napa, Sacramento, Solano, Sonoma, and Yolo counties, California; Cook and Lake counties, Illinois; and Kenosha, Milwaukee, and Racine counties, Wisconsin.
Fields of interest: General charitable giving.
Type of support: Donated products; In-kind gifts; Sponsorships.
Geographic limitations: Giving limited to Contra Costa, Napa, Sacramento, Solano, Sonoma, and Yolo counties, CA; and Cook and Lake counties, IL; and Kenosha, Milwaukee, and Racine counties, WI.
Support limitations: No support for discriminatory, labor, religious, or political organizations, or fraternal, athletic, or social organizations.
Publications: Application guidelines.
Application information: Applications accepted. The Event Marketing Department handles giving. Application form required. Applicants should submit the following:
1) name, address and phone number of organization
2) brief history of organization and description of its mission
3) geographic area to be served
4) detailed description of project and amount of funding requested
5) contact person

Applications should specifically note the nature of the request being made; and indicate the name, date, expected attendance, and a description of the event. Applications should include the Tax ID Number of the organization.
Initial approach: Complete online application form
Final notification: 90 days prior to need

2034
Jemez Mountains Electric Cooperative, Inc.

19365 State Rd., 84-285
P.O. Box 128
Hernandez, NM 87537 (505) 753-2105

Company URL: http://www.jemezcoop.org/
Establishment information: Established in 1947.
Company type: Cooperative
Business activities: Generates, transmits, and distributes electricity.
Business type (SIC): Electric services
Corporate officers: Levi Valdez, Pres.; David R. Salazar, Secy.; Dolores G. McCoy, Treas.
Board of directors: Kenneth T. Borrego; Lucas Cordova, Jr.; Elias Coriz; Ralph Garcia; Manuel Garcia; Johnny Jaramillo; Ron Lovato; Dolores G. McCoy; Patrick Montoya; David Salazar; Levi Valdez
Giving statement: Giving through the Jemez Mountains Electric Cooperative, Inc.

Jemez Mountains Electric Cooperative, Inc.

(also known as Jemez Mountains Electric Foundation)
P.O. Box 128
Espanola, NM 87532-0128

Donor: Jemez Mountains Electric Cooperative, Inc.
Financial data (yr. ended 12/31/11): Assets, $560,621 (M); gifts received, $43,008; expenditures, $107,124; qualifying distributions, $105,380; giving activities include $105,380 for grants.
Purpose and activities: The foundation awards college scholarships to graduates of high schools in areas of company operations of Jemez Mountains Electric Cooperative.
Type of support: Scholarships—to individuals.
Geographic limitations: Giving limited to areas of company operations.
Application information: Applications not accepted. Unsolicited requests for funds not accepted.
Officers: Levi Valdez, Pres.; Kenny Borrego, V.P.; David Salazar, Secy.; Dolores G. McCoy, Treas.
EIN: 237022094

2035
Jenner & Block LLP

353 N. Clark St.
Chicago, IL 60654-3456 (312) 923-8822

Establishment information: Established in 1914.
Company type: Private company
Business activities: Operates law firm.
Business type (SIC): Legal services
Offices: Los Angeles, CA; Washington, DC; Chicago, IL; New York, NY
Giving statement: Giving through the Jenner & Block LLP Pro Bono Program.

Jenner & Block LLP Pro Bono Program

353 N. Clark St.
Chicago, IL 60654-3456 (312) 923-8822
E-mail: pabrahamson@jenner.com; Additional tel.: (312) 222-9350, fax: (312) 840-7616; URL: http://www.jenner.com/publicservice/called_to_serve

Contact: Pam Abrahamson, Pro Bono Coord.
Fields of interest: Legal services.
Type of support: Pro bono services - legal.

Geographic limitations: Giving primarily in areas of company operations in Los Angeles, CA, Washington, DC, Chicago, IL, and New York, NY.
Application information: The Pro Bono Committee manages the pro bono program.

2036
Jennings, Strouss & Salmon, P.L.C.

1 E. Washington St., Ste. 1900
Phoenix, AZ 85004-2554 (602) 262-5910

Company URL: http://www.jsslaw.com
Establishment information: Established in 1942.
Company type: Private company
Business activities: Operates law firm.
Business type (SIC): Legal services
Corporate officer: Steven Smitham, C.O.O.
Offices: Peoria, Phoenix, AZ; Washington, DC
Giving statement: Giving through the Jennings, Strouss & Salmon, P.L.C. Pro Bono Program.

Jennings, Strouss & Salmon, P.L.C. Pro Bono Program

1 E. Washington St., Ste. 1900
Phoenix, AZ 85004-2554 (602) 262-5911
E-mail: mpalumbo@jsslaw.com; Additional tel.: (602) 262-5910; URL: http://www.jsslaw.com/

Contact: Michael R. Palumbo, Pro Bono Member
Fields of interest: Legal services.
Type of support: Pro bono services - legal.
Geographic limitations: Giving primarily in areas of company operations in Peoria, Phoenix, AZ, and Washington, DC.
Application information: The Pro Bono Coordinator manages the pro bono program.

2037
Jenzabar, Inc.

101 Huntington Ave., Ste. 2200
Boston, MA 02199-7610 (617) 492-9099
FAX: (617) 492.9081

Company URL: http://www.jenzabar.net/
Establishment information: Established in 1998.
Company type: Private company
Business activities: Provides enterprise software and executive services for colleges and universities.
Business type (SIC): Computer services
Corporate officers: Robert A. Maginn, Jr., Chair. and C.E.O.; Ling Chai, Pres. and C.O.O.; Jamison Barr, V.P. and Genl. Counsel; Mimi Jespersen, V.P., Finance; Jayne Edge, V.P., Mktg.; Patricia Barnett, V.P., Human Resources
Board of director: Robert A. Maginn, Jr., Chair.
Giving statement: Giving through the Jenzabar Foundation.

The Jenzabar Foundation

101 Huntington Ave., Ste. 2205
Boston, MA 02199-7603 (617) 492-9099
FAX: (617) 492-9081;
E-mail: info@thejenzabarfoundation.org; Additional e-mail: foundation@jenzabar.net; E-mail for John Beahm: John.Beahm@thejenzabarfoundation.org; URL: http://www.thejenzabarfoundation.org/

Establishment information: Established in 2007 in MA.
Donor: Jenzabar, Inc.
Contact: John Beahm, Exec. Dir.
Financial data (yr. ended 12/31/11): Revenue, $1,185,983; assets, $659,461 (M); gifts received, $1,182,562; expenditures, $766,938; program services expenses, $429,233; giving activities include $429,233 for grants.
Purpose and activities: The mission of the foundation is to recognize and support the good work and humanitarian efforts of student leaders serving others across the globe.
Fields of interest: Higher education; Student services/organizations; Human services; International development; Community/economic development; Electronic communications/Internet; Leadership development.
Programs:
Grants: provides grants to institutions of higher education and nonprofit organizations that support the development of student leaders and the promotion of community service through their missions; service and leadership that benefit the campus community their local community as well as global growth.
Student Leadership Awards: These awards honor student-led campus groups or activities that have made a significant contribution to better the world outside of their institutions of higher education.
Type of support: Program development; Technical assistance.
Geographic limitations: Giving in the U.S.
Publications: Application guidelines.
Application information: Applications accepted. Applicants must first register online with the foundation before accessing application materials; see foundation web site for application guidelines and requirements, including downloadable application form. Application form required.
Applicants should submit the following:
1) copy of IRS Determination Letter
2) descriptive literature about organization
3) detailed description of project and amount of funding requested
Initial approach: Completed application form may be submitted by e-mail, fax, or postal mail.
Copies of proposal: 1
Deadline(s): Mar. 31 for Jenzabar Student Leadership Awards; Grants accepted on a rolling basis
Officers: Robert A. Maginn, Jr.*, Chair.; John Beahm, Exec. Dir.; Chai Ling.
EIN: 261635489

2038
Jeppesen Sanderson, Inc.

55 Inverness Dr. E.
Englewood, CO 80112-5498
(303) 799-9090

Company URL: http://www.jeppesen.com
Establishment information: Established in 1934.
Company type: Subsidiary of a public company
Business activities: Publishes and provides air, sea, and rail navigation and operations management products and services.
Business type (SIC): Book publishing and/or printing; computer services
Financial profile for 2010: Number of employees, 1,400
Corporate officers: Mark Van Tine, Pres. and C.E.O.; Brad Thomann, Sr. V.P. and C.O.O.; Bob Kurtz, Sr. V.P. and C.F.O.; Marilyn Aragon, V.P., Opers.; Mitchell Villanueva, V.P., Human Resources
International operations: Germany
Giving statement: Giving through the Jeppesen Sanderson, Inc. Corporate Giving Program and the Jeppesen Aviation Foundation.

Jeppesen Aviation Foundation

55 Inverness Dr. E.
Englewood, CO 80112-5412 (303) 328-4303

Financial data (yr. ended 12/31/11): Revenue, $13; assets, $40,974 (M); expenditures, $874.
Purpose and activities: The foundation seeks the advancement of opportunities in aviation. The foundation also operates an aviation-related museum at Denver International Airport.
Fields of interest: Museums (specialized); Space/aviation.
Geographic limitations: Giving on a national basis.
Officers: Mark Van Tine, Chair.; Sandy Stedman, V.P.; Suzanne Yeonopolus, Secy.
EIN: 841190173

2039
Jersey Mortgage Company of New Jersey, Inc.

(doing business as Jersey Mortgage Company)
20 Commerce Dr., Ste. 340
Cranford, NJ 07016-3617 (908) 276-2442

Company URL: http://www.jerseymortgage.com/index.htm
Establishment information: Established in 1988.
Company type: Private company
Business activities: Provides mortgages.
Business type (SIC): Brokers and bankers/mortgage
Corporate officer: Eugene Van Note, Pres.
Giving statement: Giving through the Jersey Mortgage Company Foundation, Inc.

Jersey Mortgage Company Foundation, Inc.

20 Commerce Dr., Ste. 340
Cranford, NJ 07016-3617

Establishment information: Established in 2003 in NJ.
Donor: Jersey Mortgage Co. of New Jersey, Inc.
Financial data (yr. ended 12/31/11): Assets, $69,609 (M); expenditures, $9,479; qualifying distributions, $7,600; giving activities include $7,600 for grants.
Purpose and activities: The foundation supports organizations involved with cancer, sports, children services, Christianity, and military and veterans.
Fields of interest: Recreation.
Type of support: General/operating support.
Geographic limitations: Giving limited to NJ.
Application information: Applications not accepted. Unsolicited requests for funds not accepted.
Officers and Directors:* Eugene Van Note*, Pres.; Peter Kenny*, V.P.; Dolores Sullivan*, Secy.
EIN: 651162958

2040
Jesco, Inc.

1275 Bloomfield Ave., Ste. 27C
Fairfield, NJ 07004 (973) 882-8855

Company URL: http://www.jesco.us
Establishment information: Established in 1972.

Company type: Private company
Business activities: Operates construction equipment dealership.
Business type (SIC): Industrial machinery and equipment—wholesale
Corporate officers: Jon Robustelli, Pres.; Greg Blaszka, C.F.O.; Anthony Falzarano, V.P., Sales
Giving statement: Giving through the Robustelli Family Foundation.

Robustelli Family Foundation

c/o Jonathan Robustelli
118 St. Nicholas Ave.
South Plainfield, NJ 07080 (908) 753-8080

Establishment information: Established in 1994 in NJ.
Donor: Jesco, Inc.
Contact: Stacy Robustelli
Financial data (yr. ended 12/31/11): Assets, $125,261 (M); expenditures, $14,745; qualifying distributions, $14,695; giving activities include $2,000 for 1 grant and $12,695 for 5 grants to individuals (high: $5,000; low: $195).
Purpose and activities: The foundation supports organizations involved with education and recreation and awards college scholarships to students located in Mount Holly and Plainfield, New Jersey.
Fields of interest: Education; Health care.
Type of support: General/operating support; Scholarship funds; Scholarships—to individuals.
Geographic limitations: Giving limited to Mount Holly and Plainfield, NJ.
Application information: Applications accepted. Application form required.
Initial approach: Proposal
Deadline(s): End of Nov.
Trustee: Jonathan Robustelli.
EIN: 223341755

2041
JetBlue Airways Corporation

27-01 Queens Plz. N.
Long Island City, NY 11101 (718) 286-7900

Company URL: http://www.jetblue.com
Establishment information: Established in 1999.
Company type: Public company
Company ticker symbol and exchange: JBLU/NASDAQ
Business activities: Operates passenger airline.
Business type (SIC): Transportation/scheduled air
Financial profile for 2012: Number of employees, 14,347; assets, $7,070,000,000; sales volume, $4,982,000,000; pre-tax net income, $209,000,000; expenses, $4,606,000,000; liabilities, $5,182,000,000
Fortune 1000 ranking: 2012—495th in revenues, 689th in profits, and 488th in assets
Corporate officers: Joel C. Peterson, Chair.; Frank V. Sica, Vice-Chair.; David Barger, Pres. and C.E.O.; Robert Maruster, Exec. V.P. and C.O.O.; James Hnat, Exec. V.P., Genl. Counsel, and Corp. Secy.; Mark Powers, C.F.O.; Eash Sundaram, C.I.O.
Board of directors: Joel C. Peterson, Chair.; Frank V. Sica, Vice-Chair.; David Barger; Jens Bischof; Peter Boneparth; David W. Checketts; Virginia Gambale; Stephan Gemkow; Ellen Jewett; Stanley McChrystal; Ann Rhoades
Giving statement: Giving through the JetBlue Airways Corporation Contributions Program.
Company EIN: 870617894

JetBlue Airways Corporation Contributions Program

27-01 Queens Plaza N.
Long Island City, NY 11101
URL: http://www.jetblue.com/about/community/

Purpose and activities: JetBlue Airways Corporation makes charitable contributions to nonprofit organizations involved with health care, education, communities, and the environment. Support is given primarily to areas of company operations, and to national organizations.
Fields of interest: Education; Environment; Health care; Community/economic development.
Type of support: Donated products; Employee volunteer services; General/operating support; Sponsorships.
Geographic limitations: Giving primarily to areas of company operations, and to national organizations.
Publications: Application guidelines.
Application information: Applications accepted. Applicants should submit the following:
1) copy of IRS Determination Letter
Initial approach: Complete online application
Deadline(s): 3 months prior to need
Final notification: 6 weeks

2042
Jewett City Savings Bank

111 Main St.
Jewett City, CT 06351-2259
(860) 376-4444

Company URL: http://www.jcsbank.com
Establishment information: Established in 1873.
Company type: Private company
Business activities: Operates savings bank.
Business type (SIC): Savings institutions
Financial profile for 2011: Assets, $242,417,000; liabilities, $203,842,000
Corporate officers: Louis J. Demicco, Chair.; John E. Burke, Vice-Chair.; Kevin C. Merchant, Pres. and C.E.O.; James A. McDonald, Sr. V.P., C.F.O., and Treas.; Diana L. Rose, V.P. and Corp. Secy.
Board of directors: Louis J. Demicco, Chair.; John E. Burke, Vice-Chair.; Diane L. Manning; Kevin C. Merchant; Eric L. Moore; David T. Panteleakos; Gary W. Peloquin; Gail Rooke-Norman; Phillip E. Tetreault
Giving statement: Giving through the Jewett City Savings Bank Foundation, Inc.

Jewett City Savings Bank Foundation, Inc.

111 Main St.
Jewett City, CT 06351-4444 (860) 376-4444

Establishment information: Established in 2003 in CT.
Donor: Jewett City Savings Bank.
Contact: Kevin C. Merchant, Pres.
Financial data (yr. ended 12/31/11): Assets, $1,044,000 (M); expenditures, $54,100; qualifying distributions, $52,350; giving activities include $52,300 for 52 grants (high: $5,000; low: $500).
Purpose and activities: The foundation supports public libraries, food banks, fire departments, and hospices and organizations involved with music education, health, housing, and economically disadvantaged people.
Fields of interest: Health care; Agriculture/food; Human services.
Type of support: Annual campaigns; Capital campaigns; Continuing support; Equipment; General/operating support; Program development; Scholarship funds; Seed money.
Geographic limitations: Giving limited to areas of company operations in eastern CT.
Support limitations: No support for individual schools or religious groups. No grants to individuals or for sports.
Publications: Application guidelines.
Application information: Applications accepted. The maximum grant amount is $5,000. Application form required. Applicants should submit the following:
1) signature and title of chief executive officer
2) name, address and phone number of organization
3) copy of IRS Determination Letter
4) geographic area to be served
5) detailed description of project and amount of funding requested
6) contact person
7) copy of current year's organizational budget and/or project budget
Initial approach: Download application form and mail application form and cover letter to the foundation
Deadline(s): Aug. 31
Final notification: Dec. 31
Officers and Directors:* Lewis J. Demicco*, Chair.; Kevin C. Merchant*, Pres.; Diana L. Rose, Secy.; James A. McDonald, Treas.; John E. Burke; Diane L. Manning; Eric L. Moore; David T. Panteleakos; Gary W. Peloquin; Gail Rooke-Norman; Phillips E. Tetreault.
EIN: 134242396

2043
Jim's Formal Wear Company

1 Tuxedo Park
P.O. Box 125
Trenton, IL 62293 (618) 224-9211

Company URL: http://www.jimsformalwear.com
Establishment information: Established in 1964.
Company type: Private company
Business activities: Sells men's formalwear wholesale.
Business type (SIC): Apparel, piece goods, and notions—wholesale
Corporate officers: Gary Davis, Chair. and C.E.O.; Steve Davis, Pres. and C.O.O.; Tom Barnett, Sr. V.P., Opers., and Admin.; June Davis, V.P. and Secy.; Kevin Littekin, V.P., Finance
Board of director: Gary Davis, Chair.
Plants: Visalia, CA; Pueblo, CO; Atlanta, GA; Ottawa, IL; Anderson, IN; Salina, KS; Seguin, TX
Giving statement: Giving through the Davis Charitable Foundation.

Davis Charitable Foundation

P.O. Box 125
Trenton, IL 62293-0125

Establishment information: Established in 1990 in IL.
Donors: Jim's Formal Wear Co.; J.F.W., Inc.; James W. Davis; Betty Davis.
Financial data (yr. ended 12/31/11): Assets, $1,704,434 (M); gifts received, $100,000; expenditures, $89,108; qualifying distributions, $74,965; giving activities include $74,965 for grants.
Purpose and activities: The foundation supports organizations involved with education.
Fields of interest: Education.
Type of support: Equipment; General/operating support; Scholarship funds.

Application information: Applications not accepted. Unsolicited requests for funds not accepted.
Trustees: Gary L. Davis; Steven J. Davis.
EIN: 371272682

2044
JM Family Enterprises, Inc.

100 Jim Moran Blvd.
Deerfield Beach, FL 33442-1702
(954) 429-2000
FAX: (954) 429-2300

Company URL: http://www.jmfamily.com
Establishment information: Established in 1968.
Company type: Private company
Business activities: Operates car dealerships; provides automobile loans and warranties; sells automobile insurance.
Business type (SIC): Motor vehicles—retail; credit institutions/personal; insurance/fire, marine, and casualty
Financial profile for 2011: Number of employees, 3,800; sales volume, $9,300,000,000
Corporate officers: Colin Brown, Pres. and C.E.O.; Brent D. Burns, Exec. V.P. and C.F.O.; Ken Yerves, Exec. V.P., C.A.O., and C.I.O.; Carmen Johnson, Exec. V.P. and Genl. Counsel; Ron Coombs, Sr. V.P. and C.O.O.
Giving statement: Giving through the JM Family Enterprises, Inc. Corporate Giving Program and the Jim Moran Foundation, Inc.

JM Family Enterprises, Inc. Corporate Giving Program

111 Jim Moran Blvd.
Deerfield Beach, FL 33442-1701 (954) 429-2000
URL: http://www.jmfamily.com/Community/CorporatePhilanthropy.aspx

Purpose and activities: As a complement to its foundation, JM Family also makes charitable contributions to nonprofit organizations directly. Special emphasis is directed towards programs designed to empower families and nurture children, provide essential needs, promote education, and preserve the environment. Support given primarily in areas of significant company operations.
Fields of interest: Education; Environment; Children, services; Family services; Human services.
Type of support: Employee volunteer services; General/operating support; Program development; Sponsorships.
Geographic limitations: Giving primarily in areas of significant company operations in Mobile, AL; Broward and south Palm Beach Counties and Jacksonville, FL; Alpharetta and Commerce, GA; Beverly, MA; St. Louis, MO; and Solon, OH, and in Montreal and Toronto, Canada.
Support limitations: No support for individual schools. No grants to individuals, or for clubs, troops, or teams; no vehicle donations.
Publications: Application guidelines.
Application information: Applications accepted. Proposals should be submitted using organization letterhead. Additional information may be requested at a later date. The Corporate Philanthropy Department handles giving. Application form not required. Applicants should submit the following:
1) qualifications of key personnel
2) population served
3) name, address and phone number of organization
4) brief history of organization and description of its mission
5) listing of board of directors, trustees, officers and other key people and their affiliations
6) detailed description of project and amount of funding requested
7) contact person

Proposals should include a Form W-9. Applications for event sponsorships should include the name, date, time, location, and purpose of the event, a list of committed sponsors, sponsorship levels, and advertising specifics, and any applicable deadlines.
Initial approach: Proposal to headquarters
Copies of proposal: 1
Final notification: 4 to 6 weeks

The Jim Moran Foundation, Inc.

100 Jim Moran Blvd.
Deerfield Beach, FL 33442-1702 (954) 429-2122
FAX: (954) 429-2699;
E-mail: information@jimmoranfoundation.org;
URL: http://www.jimmoranfoundation.org/

Establishment information: Established in 2000 in FL.
Donors: James M. Moran‡; Janice M. Moran; JM Family Enterprises, Inc.; Jim Moran & Associates, Inc.; Automotive Management Services, Inc.; AutoNation.
Financial data (yr. ended 12/31/11): Assets, $86,973,399 (M); gifts received, $14,117,326; expenditures, $7,733,864; qualifying distributions, $7,368,151; giving activities include $7,368,151 for 88 grants (high: $425,000; low: $3,000).
Purpose and activities: The foundation supports programs designed improve quality of life for youth and families in Florida through initiatives and opportunities that meet ever-changing needs of the community. Special emphasis is directed towards education; elder care; family strengthening; afterschool initiatives; and youth transitional living.
Fields of interest: Secondary school/education; Higher education; Education, services; Education, reading; Education; Big Brothers/Big Sisters; Salvation Army; Children/youth, services; Children, foster care; Family services; Residential/custodial care, group home; Aging, centers/services; Homeless, human services; Human services; Community/economic development Youth; Aging; Economically disadvantaged.
Programs:
Jim Moran Foundation Award: The foundation honors individuals who give back to their community through active service and personal commitment. Honorees must exemplify characteristics of the mission of the Jim Moran Foundation, reflect proven accomplishments that address real community needs and/or concerns, and inspire others to embrace civic and charitable responsibility in meeting the needs of their community. The award includes a $25,000 grant to the charity of the honorees choice.
Youth Achiever Award: The foundation, in partnership with The Jim Moran Institute for Global Entrepreneurship at Florida State University, honors a high school senior who qualifies for financial aid and has applied and received admission to FSU. Recipients are selected based on outstanding academics and leadership.
Type of support: Continuing support; Equipment; General/operating support; Program development; Scholarship funds.
Geographic limitations: Giving primarily in FL, with emphasis on Broward, Palm Beach, and Duval counties.
Support limitations: No grants to individuals, or for administrative or overhead costs, capital campaigns, capacity building, healthcare or medical research.
Publications: Application guidelines; Grants list; Newsletter.
Application information: Applications accepted. A full application may be requested at a later date. No consecutive year funding, except for multi-year grants. Application form required. Applicants should submit the following:
1) population served
2) copy of IRS Determination Letter
3) detailed description of project and amount of funding requested
4) contact person
5) copy of current year's organizational budget and/or project budget

Initial approach: Complete online letter of inquiry form
Deadline(s): None
Final notification: 90 days

Officers and Directors:* Janice M. Moran*, Chair. and Pres.; Larry D. McGinnes*, V.P.; Melanie A. Burgess*, Secy. and Exec. Dir.; Thomas K. Blanton*, Treas.; Irvin A, Kiffin; Lucia C. Lopez; Richard A. Noland; Dom Pino; Melvin T. Stith.
EIN: 651058044
Selected grants: The following grants are a representative sample of this grantmaker's funding activity:
$425,000 to Florida State University Foundation, College of Business, Tallahassee, FL, 2011. To provide expanded outreach of Jim Moran Institute for Global Entrepreneurship into South Florida through Entrepreneurial University Program..
$340,000 to Childrens Services Council of Broward County, Lauderhill, FL, 2011. For collaborative funding to support a holistic system of care in Broward County for at-risk young adults transitioning into independent living from foster care.
$338,768 to Family Central, North Lauderdale, FL, 2011. For Community for Quality Early Learning and Literacy (C-QuELL) Project, which holistically supports children's early learning by engaging the family, child care centers, elementary schools and communities in Broward County..
$225,000 to United Way of Broward County, Fort Lauderdale, FL, 2011. For Project Lifeline, hunger relief initiative which provides for purchase and distribution of nutritious groceries to food pantries throughout Broward County.
$219,960 to Boys and Girls Clubs of Broward County, Fort Lauderdale, FL, 2011. To provides transportation directly from schools to Boys and Girls Clubs throughout Broward County for a safe place to learn with healthy snacks and a nutritious dinner.
$154,616 to Housing Opportunities, Mortgage Assistance, and Effective Neighborhood Solutions, Fort Lauderdale, FL, 2011. For Transition to Independent Living (TIL) Youth Apartment Rental Program, which provides safe housing and compassionate support for former foster-care or kin-care youth transitioning into adulthood in Broward County.
$116,015 to I. M. Sulzbacher Center for the Homeless, Jacksonville, FL, 2011. For Emergency Shelter Services for Homeless Families, program to provide transitional housing, case management and life skills training to equip families for self-sufficiency.
$75,000 to SOS Childrens Village of Florida, Coconut Creek, FL, 2011. For After-Care Program, which provides teens in foster care and transitioning young adults with the tools necessary to improve their life skills, academic outcomes and career development with support and coaching from an after-care coordinator.

$50,000 to Network for Teaching Entrepreneurship, Miami, FL, 2011. For Building the Entrepreneurial Community Program, which provides entrepreneurial training to students at Stranahan and Hallandale high schools in Broward County.
$50,000 to PACE Center for Girls of Palm Beach County, West Palm Beach, FL, 2011. For SPIRITED GIRLS! program which provides young women with academics and essential life skills for more successful futures.

2005
J-M Manufacturing Company, Inc.

(doing business as JM Eagle)
5200 W. Century Blvd.
Los Angeles, CA 90045 (800) 621-4404

Company URL: http://www.jmeagle.com
Establishment information: Established in 1982.
Company type: Subsidiary of a private company
Business activities: Produces polyvinyl chloride and high-density polyethylene pipes, fittings, and tubing products.
Business type (SIC): Plastic products/miscellaneous
Financial profile for 2009: Number of employees, 1,200
Corporate officers: Walter W. Wang, Pres. and C.E.O.; Dennis Campbell, C.O.O.; Kevin Tackaberry, V.P., Human Resources and C.I.O.; Neal Gordon, V.P., Mktg.
Giving statement: Giving through the JMM Charitable Foundation, Inc.

JMM Charitable Foundation, Inc.

5200 W. Century Rd.
Los Angeles, CA 90045-5928

Establishment information: Established in 2006 in NJ.
Donor: J-M Manufacturing Co., Inc.
Financial data (yr. ended 12/31/11): Assets, $12,352,144 (M); expenditures, $745,925; qualifying distributions, $652,775; giving activities include $652,775 for grants.
Purpose and activities: The foundation supports hospitals and organizations involved with legal aid, civil rights, and Christianity.
Fields of interest: Hospitals (general); Legal services; Civil/human rights, minorities; Christian agencies & churches.
Type of support: General/operating support.
Geographic limitations: Giving primarily in Dana Point, Los Angeles, and San Francisco, CA and Plano, TX.
Support limitations: No grants to individuals.
Application information: Applications not accepted. Contributes only to pre-selected organizations.
Officers and Director:* Walter W. Wang*, Pres.; Johnny Mai, Secy.; Shirley W. Wang.
EIN: 204679694
Selected grants: The following grants are a representative sample of this grantmaker's funding activity:
$100,000 to Give2Asia, San Francisco, CA, 2009.
$22,868 to UCLA Foundation, Los Angeles, CA, 2009.
$5,000 to Cancer Research Institute, New York, NY, 2009.

2045
Jockey International, Inc.

2300 60th St.
P.O. Box 1417
Kenosha, WI 53141-1417 (262) 658-8111

Company URL: http://www.jockey.com
Establishment information: Established in 1876.
Company type: Private company
Business activities: Manufactures underwear, loungewear, and sleepwear.
Business type (SIC): Apparel—men's and boys' outerwear; hosiery and knitted fabrics; apparel—women's, girls', and children's undergarments; apparel, piece goods, and notions—wholesale
Corporate officers: Debra Steigerwaldt Waller, Chair. and C.E.O.; Edward C. Emma, Pres. and C.O.O.; Frank Schneider, Sr. V.P., C.F.O., and C.I.O.
Board of director: Debra Steigerwaldt Waller, Chair.
Giving statement: Giving through the Jockey International, Inc. Corporate Giving Program and the Debra Steigerwaldt Waller Foundation for Adoption, Ltd.

Debra Steigerwaldt Waller Foundation for Adoption, Ltd.

(formerly Debra Steigerwaldt Waller Foundation, Ltd.)
2300 60th St.
Kenosha, WI 53140-3822 (262) 653-3273
URL: http://www.jockeybeingfamily.com/

Establishment information: Established in 2005 in WI.
Donor: Jockey International, Inc.
Financial data (yr. ended 12/31/11): Assets, $1,154,832 (M); gifts received, $263,236; expenditures, $127,703; qualifying distributions, $105,340; giving activities include $105,340 for grants.
Purpose and activities: The foundation supports organizations and initiatives designed to promote adoption.
Fields of interest: Children, adoption.
Type of support: Equipment; General/operating support; Program development; Sponsorships.
Geographic limitations: Giving primarily in Washington, DC, MD, OH, WI, and Canada.
Support limitations: No grants to individuals.
Application information: Applications not accepted. Unsolicited requests for funds not accepted.
Officers and Directors:* Debra Steigerwaldt Waller*, Pres. and Treas.; Anne Arbas*, V.P.; William Steigerwaldt*, V.P.; Noreen Wilkinson, Secy.
EIN: 203980156

2046
JOFCO, Inc.

(also known as Jasper Office Furniture Company)
402 E. 13th St.
P.O. Box 71
Jasper, IN 47547-0071 (812) 482-5154

Company URL: http://www.jofco.com
Establishment information: Established in 1922.
Company type: Private company
Business activities: Manufactures wood office furniture.
Business type (SIC): Furniture/office
Financial profile for 2010: Number of employees, 30
Corporate officers: Bill Rubino, Pres. and C.E.O.; Ray Steventon, V.P., Sales and Mktg.; Scott Sturm, Cont.
Giving statement: Giving through the Jasper Office Furniture Foundation, Inc.

Jasper Office Furniture Foundation, Inc.

P.O. Box 71
Jasper, IN 47547
Application address: 13th & Vine Sts., Jasper, IN 47546

Establishment information: Established in 1951 in IN.
Donor: JOFCO, Inc.
Contact: William Rubino, Pres.
Financial data (yr. ended 12/31/11): Assets, $224,568 (M); expenditures, $42,088; qualifying distributions, $42,050; giving activities include $42,050 for grants.
Purpose and activities: The foundation supports fire departments and organizations involved with arts and culture, higher and theological education, human services, and Catholicism.
Type of support: Building/renovation; Equipment; General/operating support; Program development; Scholarship funds; Sponsorships.
Geographic limitations: Giving primarily in IN.
Support limitations: No grants to individuals.
Application information: Applications accepted. Application form required. Applicants should submit the following:
1) copy of IRS Determination Letter
Initial approach: Proposal
Deadline(s): None
Officers: Joseph F. Steurer, Chair.; William Rubino, Pres.; Greg Sturm, V.P. and Secy.
Directors: Kenneth Tretter; Bernard Messmer.
EIN: 356024533

2047
Johns Manville Corporation

(formerly Schuller Corporation)
717 17th St.
P.O. Box 5108
Denver, CO 80202 (303) 978-2000

Company URL: http://www.jm.com
Establishment information: Established in 1858.
Company type: Subsidiary of a public company
Business activities: Manufactures and markets building and specialty products.
Business type (SIC): Abrasive, asbestos, and nonmetallic mineral products; asphalt and roofing materials
Corporate officer: Todd Raba, Chair., Pres., and C.E.O.
Board of director: Todd Raba, Chair., Pres., and C.E.O.
Subsidiaries: Riverwood International Corp., Atlanta, GA; Schuller International Group Inc., Denver, CO
International operations: Canada; Germany
Giving statement: Giving through the Johns Manville Corporation Contributions Program and the Johns Manville Fund, Inc.

Johns Manville Fund, Inc.

(formerly Schuller Fund, Inc.)
717 17th St.
Denver, CO 80202-3330

Establishment information: Incorporated in 1952 in DE; reincorporated in 2005 in CO and DE.
Donors: Schuller Corp.; Johns Manville Corp.
Financial data (yr. ended 12/31/10): Assets, $38,183 (M); gifts received, $25,000; expenditures, $24,177; qualifying distributions, $22,075; giving activities include $22,075 for grants.
Purpose and activities: The fund supports organizations involved with arts and culture, education, health, youth, and human services.
Fields of interest: Arts; Education; Health care; American Red Cross; Youth, services; Human services.
International interests: Canada.

Programs:

Employee-Related Scholarships: The fund awards college scholarships to children of full-time employees of Johns Manville. The program is administered by Scholarship Management Services.

Volunteer Recognition: The foundation awards grants to nonprofit organizations with which employees and retirees of Johns Manville volunteer. A $500 grant is awarded to nonprofit organizations chosen by Johns Manville Most Valuable Volunteer and a $2,500 grant is awarded to nonprofit organizations chosen by Johns Manville Volunteer of the Year.

Type of support: Employee volunteer services; Employee-related scholarships; General/operating support; Program development.
Geographic limitations: Giving primarily in areas of company operations in Denver, CO, Etowah, TN, and in Canada.
Support limitations: No support for religious organizations not of direct benefit to the entire community, hospitals, or non-special needs private educational organizations. No grants for special events.
Application information: Applications accepted. Application form not required.
Initial approach: Proposal
Copies of proposal: 1
Deadline(s): None
Officers and Trustees:* M. Dunbar*, Pres.; Jeanne Mitisek*, Secy.-Treas.
Number of staff: 1 part-time professional; 1 part-time support.
EIN: 840856796

2048
Johnson & Johnson

1 Johnson & Johnson Plz.
New Brunswick, NJ 08933-0001
(732) 524-0400
FAX: (732) 214-0332

Company URL: http://www.jnj.com
Establishment information: Established in 1886.
Company type: Public company
Company ticker symbol and exchange: JNJ/NYSE
International Securities Identification Number: US4781601046
Business activities: Manufactures and sells health care products.
Business type (SIC): Medical instruments and supplies
Financial profile for 2012: Number of employees, 127,600; assets, $121,347,000,000; sales volume, $67,224,000,000; pre-tax net income, $13,775,000,000; expenses, $53,449,000,000; liabilities, $56,521,000,000
Fortune 1000 ranking: 2012—41st in revenues, 15th in profits, and 52nd in assets
Forbes 2000 ranking: 2012—118th in sales, 36th in profits, and 212th in assets
Corporate officers: Alex Gorsky, Chair. and C.E.O.; Dominic J. Caruso, V.P., Finance and C.F.O.; Michael H. Ullmann, V.P. and Genl. Counsel; Peter M. Fasolo, V.P., Human Resources; John A. Papa, Treas.; Stephen J. Cosgrove, Corp. Cont. and C.A.O.; Douglas K. Chia, Corp. Secy.
Board of directors: Alex Gorsky, Chair.; Mary Sue Coleman, Ph.D.; James G. Cullen; Ian E.L. Davis; Michael M.E. Johns, M.D.; Susan L. Lindquist, Ph.D.; Anne M. Mulcahy; Leo F. Mullin; William D. Perez; Charles O. Prince III; A. Eugene Washington, M.D.; Ronald A. Williams
Subsidiaries: ALZA Corporation, Mountain View, CA; Biosense Webster, Inc., Diamond Bar, CA; Centocor, Inc., Horsham, PA; Codman & Shurtleff, Inc., Raynham, MA; Cordis Corp., Miami, FL; DePuy, Inc., Warsaw, IN; DePuy Mitek, Inc., Westwood, MA; DePuy Orthopaedics, Inc., Warsaw, IN; DePuy Spine, Inc., Raynham, MA; Ethicon, Inc., Somerville, NJ; Ethicon Endo-Surgery, Inc., Cincinnati, OH; Independence Technology, L.L.C., Warren, NJ; Janssen Biotech, Inc., Horsham, PA; Janssen Pharmaceutica Products, L.P., Titusville, NJ; Janssen Pharmaceuticals, Inc., Titusville, NJ; Johnson & Johnson Consumer Cos., Inc., Skillman, NJ; Johnson & Johnson Development Corp., New Brunswick, NJ; Johnson & Johnson Finance Corp., New Brunswick, NJ; Johnson & Johnson Health Care Systems Inc., Piscataway, NJ; Johnson & Johnson Pharmaceutical Research & Development, L.L.C., Raritan, NJ; Johnson & Johnson Services, Inc., Raritan, NJ; Johnson & Johnson Vision Care, Inc., Roanoke, VA; Johnson & Johnson-Merck Consumer Pharmaceuticals Co., Fort Washington, PA; LifeScan, Inc., Milpitas, CA; McNEIL-PPC, Inc., Skillman, NJ; Neutrogena Corporation, Los Angeles, CA; Noramco, Inc., Athens, GA; Ortho Biotech Products, L.P., Bridgewater, NJ; Ortho-Clinical Diagnostics, Inc., Rochester, NY; Ortho-McNeil Pharmaceutical, Inc., Raritan, NJ; Scios, Inc., Fremont, CA; Therakos, Inc., Exton, PA
International operations: Argentina; Australia; Austria; Belgium; Brazil; Canada; China; Colombia; Czech Republic; Denmark; Egypt; Finland; France; Germany; Greece; Hong Kong; Hungary; India; Indonesia; Ireland; Israel; Italy; Japan; Luxembourg; Malaysia; Mexico; Netherlands; New Zealand; Pakistan; Panama; Peru; Philippines; Poland; Portugal; Russia; Singapore; Slovakia; Slovenia; South Africa; South Korea; Spain; Sweden; Switzerland; Taiwan; Thailand; United Kingdom; Venezuela
Giving statement: Giving through the Johnson & Johnson Corporate Giving Program, the Blue Ridge Bone & Joint Research Foundation, the Johnson & Johnson Family of Companies Foundation, and the Johnson & Johnson Patient Assistance Foundation, Inc.
Company EIN: 221024240

Johnson & Johnson Corporate Giving Program

1 Johnson & Johnson Plz., WH7143
New Brunswick, NJ 08933-0001
FAX: (732) 524-3564; E-mail: smickus@its.jnj.com; Address for Community Health Care Prog.: Sierra Veale, Johnson & Johnson Community Health Care Prog., 615 N. Wolfe St., Ste. E2100, Baltimore, MD 21205, tel.: (443) 287-5138, fax: (410) 510-1974; Additional contacts: Intl. Progs. and Product Donations: Conrad Person, Dir., Intl. Progs./Product Giving, Arts/Culture, K-12 Education, and Employee Volunteer Services: Michael J. Bzdak, Dir., Corp. Contribs., fax: (732) 524-3300; URL: http://www.jnj.com/caring/corporate-giving

Purpose and activities: As a complement to its foundation, Johnson & Johnson also makes charitable contributions to nonprofit organizations directly. Support is given on a national and international basis.
Fields of interest: Arts; Nursing school/education; Education; Environment; Public health; Health care, cost containment; Health care; AIDS; Employment, services; Disasters, preparedness/services; Children, services; Human services; International relief; Community/economic development Disabilities, people with; Women; Girls.
International interests: Africa; East Asia; Oceania; South America; South Asia; Southeast Asia.
Type of support: Curriculum development; Donated products; Emergency funds; Employee matching gifts; Fellowships; Internship funds; Management development/capacity building; Program development; Program evaluation; Research; Scholarship funds; Sponsorships.
Geographic limitations: Giving on a national and international basis.
Support limitations: No support for religious organizations not of direct benefit to the entire community or political, fraternal, or athletic organizations. No grants to individuals, or for general operating support, scholarships, trips or tours, endowments, or capital campaigns; no loans.
Application information: Applications not accepted. Unsolicited requests are not accepted. The Corporate Contributions department handles giving. The company has a staff that only handles contributions. A contributions committee reviews all requests.
Corporate Contributions Committee: Brian D. Perkins, Chair.; Sharon D'Agostino, V.P., Worldwide Corp. Contribs. and Community Rels.; Colleen A. Goggins; Raymond C. Jordan; Jose Antonio Justino; Donna Malin; David Norton; Jose V. Sartarelli, Ph.D.; Nicholas J. Valeriani.
Number of staff: 19 full-time professional; 1 part-time professional; 1 part-time support.

Blue Ridge Bone & Joint Research Foundation

P.O. Box 21763
Roanoke, VA 24018-0178 (540) 761-5068

Establishment information: Established in 2003 in VA.
Donor: DePuy Orthopaedics, Inc.
Contact: Joseph Moskal, Dir.
Financial data (yr. ended 07/31/11): Assets, $15,694 (M); expenditures, $16,797; qualifying distributions, $16,030; giving activities include $15,937 for 2 grants to individuals (high: $15,147; low: $250).
Purpose and activities: The foundation supports knee, bone, and joint research and awards scholarship funds for students who have completed an orthopedic residency training program.
Type of support: Research; Scholarship funds.
Geographic limitations: Giving primarily in IN and VA.
Application information: Applications accepted. Application form required.
Initial approach: Proposal
Deadline(s): None
Directors: J. Douglas Call; Joseph T. Moskal.
EIN: 200193668

Johnson & Johnson Family of Companies Foundation

(formerly Johnson & Johnson Family of Companies Contribution Fund)
c/o Michele Lee
1 Johnson & Johnson Plz.
New Brunswick, NJ 08933-0001
URL: http://www.jnj.com/connect/caring/

Establishment information: Incorporated in 1953 in NJ.
Donor: Johnson & Johnson.
Financial data (yr. ended 12/31/09): Assets, $8,647,433 (M); gifts received, $52,857,179; expenditures, $49,558,298; qualifying distributions, $49,558,298; giving activities include $38,311,307 for 632 grants and $11,244,991 for 22,567 employee matching gifts.
Purpose and activities: The foundation supports organizations involved with arts and culture, education, health, HIV/AIDS, hunger, human services, international affairs, philanthropy, and economically disadvantaged people.
Fields of interest: Arts; Education, early childhood education; Higher education; Education; Hospitals (general); Health care; AIDS; Food services; American Red Cross; Children, services; Human services; International development; International affairs, U.N.; International affairs; United Ways and Federated Giving Programs; Philanthropy/voluntarism Economically disadvantaged.
Program:
Employee Matching Gifts: The foundation matches contributions made by employees and retirees of Johnson & Johnson to public broadcasting stations, museums, performing arts groups, historical societies, cultural and humanities organizations, institutions of higher education, libraries, hospitals, health care organizations, residential substance abuse treatment centers, and medical research organizations on a two-for-one basis from $25 to $12,500 per contributor, per year.
Type of support: Annual campaigns; Continuing support; Employee matching gifts; General/operating support; Program development; Scholarship funds.
Geographic limitations: Giving on a national basis in areas of company operations; giving also to national and international organizations.
Support limitations: No support for fraternal, political, religious, or athletic organizations. No grants to individuals, or for debt reduction, trips, tours, capital campaigns or endowments, or publications; no loans.
Publications: Corporate giving report.
Application information: Applications not accepted. Contributes only to pre-selected organizations.
Board meeting date(s): Mar., June, Sept., and Dec.
Officers: B.D. Perkins, Pres.; S. Dagostino, V.P.; M.H. Ullmann, Secy.; John A. Papa, Treas.
EIN: 226062811
Selected grants: The following grants are a representative sample of this grantmaker's funding activity:
$1,952,744 to Elizabeth Glaser Pediatric AIDS Foundation, Los Angeles, CA, 2009.
$1,062,758 to United Ways of the Greater New York, New Jersey and Connecticut Tri-State Area, New York, NY, 2009.
$1,033,000 to Dartmouth-Hitchcock Medical Center, Lebanon, NH, 2009.
$716,912 to United Nations Development Fund for Women, New York, NY, 2009.
$710,000 to University of Pennsylvania, Philadelphia, PA, 2009.
$50,000 to Catholic Medical Mission Board, New York, NY, 2009.
$40,000 to NBI Foundation, Valhalla, NY, 2009.
$30,000 to Resource Foundation, New York, NY, 2009.
$25,000 to Boston University, Boston, MA, 2009.
$20,000 to Elizabeth Glaser Pediatric AIDS Foundation, Los Angeles, CA, 2009.

Johnson & Johnson Patient Assistance Foundation, Inc.

(formerly Janssen Ortho Patient Assistance Foundation, Inc.)
1 Johnson & Johnson Plz.
New Brunswick, NJ 08933-0001
FAX: (888) 526-5168; E-mail: dsitarik@jnj.com; Application address: Patient Assistance Program, P.O. Box 221857, Charlotte, NC 28222-1857; Additional tel.: (866) 317-2775, (800) 652-6227; URL: http://www.jjpaf.org/

Establishment information: Established as a company-sponsored operating foundation in 1997 in NJ.
Donors: Janssen Pharmaceutica Inc.; Johnson & Johnson; Ortho Biotech Inc.; Ortho-McNeil Pharmaceutical, Inc.; Vistakon Pharmaceutical; Pricara; Ortho Womens Health & Urology; Neurogena; DePuy Mitek, Inc.; Therakos, Inc.
Contact: Denise Sitarikev, V.P.
Financial data (yr. ended 12/13/11): Assets, $53,367,014 (M); gifts received, $508,461,553; expenditures, $514,027,049; qualifying distributions, $496,523,981; giving activities include $496,523,981 for 156,000 grants to individuals.
Purpose and activities: The foundation provides pharmaceutical products to needy persons who lack prescription drug coverage.
Fields of interest: Health care Economically disadvantaged.
Type of support: Donated products.
Geographic limitations: Giving on a national basis, including U.S. territories and the Virgin Islands.
Support limitations: No support for religious or political organizations.
Publications: Application guidelines; Informational brochure.
Application information: Applications accepted. Application must be completed and signed, and accompanied by proof of income and a HIPAA release form signed by the patient. Application form required.
Initial approach: Complete online eligibility quiz and fax or mail application or apply via phone
Board meeting date(s): Third Thursday of each month
Deadline(s): None
Final notification: Within 24 business hours, expedited same day approval possible if needed
Officers and Directors:* Sharon D'Agostino*, Pres.; Denise Sitarik*, V.P.; Michael McCully*, Secy.; Michael Hepburn*, Treas.; Judith Fernandez; Margaret Forrestel; Irene Infanti; Gwendolyn Miley; Greg Panico; Louise Weingrod.
Number of staff: 5 full-time professional; 1 full-time support.
EIN: 311520982

2049
S. C. Johnson & Son, Inc.

(also known as SC Johnson Wax)
1525 Howe St.
Racine, WI 53403-2237 (262) 260-2000

Company URL: http://www.scjohnson.com
Establishment information: Established in 1886.
Company type: Private company
Business activities: Manufactures home cleaning, home storage, personal care, and insect control products; supplies commercial, industrial, and institutional facility products and services; conducts venture capital investment activities; sells insurance.
Business type (SIC): Soaps, cleaners, and toiletries; paper and paperboard/coated, converted, and laminated; fertilizers and agricultural chemicals; insurance carriers; investment offices; services to dwellings
Financial profile for 2011: Number of employees, 12,000; sales volume, $8,880,000,000
Corporate officers: H. Fisk Johnson, Ph.D., Chair. and C.E.O.; Michael W. Wright, Vice-Chair.; David Hecker, Sr. V.P., Genl. Counsel, and Secy.; Kelly M. Semrau, V.P., Comms.
Board of directors: H. Fisk Johnson, Ph.D., Chair.; Michael W. Wright, Vice-Chair.; Gerard J. Arpey; Robin R. Burns-McNeill; Jan-Michiel Hessels; Helen P. Johnson-Leipold; John Jeffry Louis; Steven S. Rogers; Christine Todd Whitman; Robert B. Willumstad
Subsidiaries: PRISM, Miami, FL; Whitmire Micro-Gen Research Laboratories, Inc., St. Louis, MO
International operations: Argentina; Australia; Belgium; Brazil; Canada; China; Colombia; Costa Rica; Cyprus; Ecuador; Egypt; Germany; Ghana; Greece; Indonesia; Italy; Japan; Kenya; Mexico; New Zealand; Nigeria; Norway; Portugal; Singapore; South Africa; South Korea; Spain; Sweden; Switzerland; Taiwan; Thailand; Ukraine; United Kingdom; Venezuela
Giving statement: Giving through the S. C. Johnson & Son, Inc. Corporate Giving Program, the Johnson Foundation, Inc., and the SC Johnson Fund, Inc.

S. C. Johnson & Son, Inc. Corporate Giving Program

1525 Howe St.
Racine, WI 53403-5011
URL: http://www.scjohnson.com/en/commitment/overview.aspx

Purpose and activities: As a complement to its foundation, S.C. Johnson & Son also makes charitable contributions to nonprofit organizations directly. Support is given on a national and international basis in areas of company operations.
Fields of interest: Education; Environment; Public health; Health care; Disasters, preparedness/services; United Ways and Federated Giving Programs; General charitable giving.
Program:
Employee Volunteer Grants: S.C. Johnson awards $250 grants to nonprofit organizations with which employees or retirees volunteer at least 40 hours per year, up to $2,500 per organization.
Type of support: Building/renovation; Donated products; Employee volunteer services; General/operating support; In-kind gifts; Scholarship funds.
Geographic limitations: Giving on a national and international basis in areas of company operations.

The Johnson Foundation, Inc.

(formerly Wingspread Foundation, Inc.)
33 E. 4 Mile Rd.
Racine, WI 53402-2621
E-mail: bschmidt@johnsonfdn.org; Email for Roger C. Dower, Pres.: rdower@johnsonfdn.org; URL: http://www.johnsonfdn.org

Establishment information: Established in 2003 in WI.
Donors: The Johnson Foundation, Inc.; S.C. Johnson & Son, Inc.; Diversey, Inc.
Contact: Barbara J. Schmidt, Prog. Asst.
Financial data (yr. ended 06/30/11): Assets, $49,393,729 (M); gifts received, $3,619,398; expenditures, $5,987,348; qualifying distributions, $5,268,523; giving activities include $65,000 for 14 grants (high: $10,000; low: $1,000).
Purpose and activities: The foundation supports organizations involved with performing arts, education, and human services; and promotes local conferences and events to gather public opinion on environmental quality and community issues.
Fields of interest: Performing arts; Performing arts, opera; Higher education; Education; Environment; Women, centers/services; Human services.
Type of support: General/operating support; Program development.
Geographic limitations: Giving primarily in IL, PA, and WI.
Support limitations: No grants to individuals.
Publications: Financial statement.
Application information: Applications accepted. Application form not required.
Initial approach: Letter of inquiry
Deadline(s): None
Officers and Trustees:* Helen Johnson-Leipold*, Chair.; Roger C. Dower, Pres.; Imogene Powers Johnson*, V.P.; Michael P. Dombeck; James D. Ericson; Winifred J. Marquart; Paul R. Portney; Paula Wolff; Kate Wolford.
Number of staff: 11 full-time professional; 5 full-time support; 1 part-time support.
EIN: 383675289

SC Johnson Fund, Inc.

(formerly SC Johnson Wax Fund Inc.)
1525 Howe St.
Racine, WI 53403-2237
URL: http://www.scjohnson.com/en/commitment/focus-on/creating/giving-back.aspx

Establishment information: Incorporated in 1959 in WI.
Donors: S.C. Johnson & Son, Inc.; JohnsonDiversey, Inc.
Financial data (yr. ended 06/30/12): Assets, $7,441,019 (M); gifts received, $7,211,000; expenditures, $7,111,427; qualifying distributions, $7,077,834; giving activities include $7,059,234 for 391 grants (high: $2,900,000; low: $25).
Purpose and activities: The foundation supports organizations involved with arts and culture, human services, and community development. Special emphasis is directed toward programs designed to promote the environment, social equity, and economic vitality.
Fields of interest: Museums; Arts; Elementary/secondary education; Higher education; Education; Environment, natural resources; Environment, water resources; Environment; YM/YWCAs & YM/YWHAs; Youth, services; Homeless, human services; Human services; Economic development; Community/economic development; United Ways and Federated Giving Programs.
Program:
Employee Matching Gifts: The foundation matches contributions made by employees of S.C. Johnson & Son to nonprofit organizations and the United Way.
Type of support: Annual campaigns; Building/renovation; Capital campaigns; Employee matching gifts; Employee-related scholarships; Endowments; Equipment; Fellowships; General/operating support; Program development; Scholarship funds; Seed money; Sponsorships.
Geographic limitations: Giving primarily in areas of company operations in Racine, WI.
Support limitations: No support for political, religious, social, athletic, veterans', labor, or fraternal organizations, United Way-supported organizations, or national health organizations. No grants to individuals (except for scholarships and fellowships), or for staff or administrative payrolls or national health fund drives.
Publications: Annual report; Application guidelines.
Application information: Applications accepted. Support is limited to 1 contribution per organization during any given year. Application form not required. Applicants should submit the following:
1) copy of IRS Determination Letter
2) brief history of organization and description of its mission
3) copy of most recent annual report/audited financial statement/990
4) detailed description of project and amount of funding requested
5) copy of current year's organizational budget and/or project budget
6) listing of additional sources and amount of support
Initial approach: Proposal
Copies of proposal: 1
Board meeting date(s): Feb., June, and Oct.
Deadline(s): Varies
Final notification: 4 months
Officers and Trustees:* H. Fisk Johnson III*, Chair. and C.E.O.; Kelly M. Semrau, Vice-Chair. and Pres.; Jeffrey M. Waller, V.P. and Treas.; Gregory L. Anderegg, V.P. and Exec. Dir.
Number of staff: 2 full-time professional; 2 part-time professional; 2 part-time support.
EIN: 396052089
Selected grants: The following grants are a representative sample of this grantmaker's funding activity:
$2,900,000 to Johnson Foundation, Racine, WI, 2011. For unrestricted support.
$899,974 to United Way of Racine County, Racine, WI, 2011. For matching grant for employees and retirees.
$890,454 to Racine Charter One, Racine, WI, 2011. For startup support and payments on loan.
$400,424 to JK Group, Plainsboro, NJ, 2011. For Community Service Dollars.
$300,000 to Conservation International, Arlington, VA, 2011. For unrestricted support.
$295,555 to Scholarship America, Saint Peter, MN, 2011. For Sons' and Daughters' Scholarship Awards.
$277,750 to Scholarship America, Saint Peter, MN, 2011. For Young Leaders' Scholarships.
$150,000 to Prairie School, Racine, WI, 2011. For Prairie Center for Developing Excellence.
$125,000 to Sierra Club, San Francisco, CA, 2011. For Great Lakes Wind Siting Project.
$17,800 to Lakeside Curative Services, Racine, WI, 2011. Toward greenhouse project to be used for horticulture training.

2050
Johnson Controls, Inc.

5757 N. Green Bay Ave.
P.O. Box 591
Milwaukee, WI 53209 (414) 524-1200
FAX: (414) 524-2070

Company URL: http://www.johnsoncontrols.com
Establishment information: Established in 1885.
Company type: Public company
Company ticker symbol and exchange: JCI/NYSE
International Securities Identification Number: US4783661071
Business activities: Manufactures controls and automotive products.
Business type (SIC): Motor vehicles and equipment; furniture/public building
Financial profile for 2012: Number of employees, 170,000; assets, $30,884,000,000; sales volume, $41,955,000,000; pre-tax net income, $1,590,000,000; expenses, $40,365,000,000; liabilities, $19,329,000,000
Fortune 1000 ranking: 2012—67th in revenues, 163rd in profits, and 181st in assets
Forbes 2000 ranking: 2012—218th in sales, 514th in profits, and 718th in assets
Corporate officers: Stephen A. Roell, Chair. Pres., and C.E.O.; Alex A. Molinaroli, Vice Chair.; R. Bruce McDonald, Exec. V.P. and C.F.O.; Susan F. Davis, Exec. V.P., Human Resources; Colin Boyd, V.P. and C.I.O.; Jerome D. Okarma, V.P., Secy., and Genl. Counsel; Frank A. Voltolina, V.P. and Corp. Treas.; Brian J. Stief, V.P. and Corp. Cont.; William C. Jackson, V.P., Opers.; Charles A. Harvey, V.P., Public Affairs
Board of directors: Stephen A. Roell, Chair.; David Abney; Dennis W. Archer; Natalie A. Black; Julie L. Bushman; Richard Goodman; Jeffrey A. Joerres; William H. Lacy; Eugenio Clariond Reyes-Retana; Mark P. Vergnano
Subsidiaries: Trim Masters Inc., Harrodsburg, KY; York International Corporation, York, PA
Giving statement: Giving through the Johnson Controls, Inc. Corporate Giving Program and the Johnson Controls Foundation, Inc.
Company EIN: 390380010

Johnson Controls, Inc. Corporate Giving Program

5757 N. Green Bay Ave.
Glendale, WI 53209-4408 (414) 524-1200
URL: http://www.johnsoncontrols.com/publish/us/en/sustainability/for_our_communities.html
Address for Igniting Creative Energy: National Energy Foundation, 4516 South 700 East, Ste. 100, Murray, UT 84107

Financial data (yr. ended 12/31/10): Total giving, $3,210,000, including $3,210,000 for grants.
Purpose and activities: As a complement to its foundation, Johnson Controls also makes charitable contributions to nonprofit organizations directly.
Fields of interest: Elementary/secondary education; Environment, natural resources; Environment, energy; Environment; Youth development; Human services; Leadership development.
Program:
Igniting Creative Energy Challenge: Johnson Controls, in partnership with the National Energy Foundation, annually invites K-12 students to design and share innovative ways to make a difference in energy, water conservation, and the environment through competition. Five grand prizes are awarded to 4 students and 1 teacher. Prizes include a trip to Washington, DC for 2 and an invitation to participate

in the National Energy Forum in June to share their ideas with energy and government leaders. The highest scoring student in each state will be recognized and participating schools are also eligible to receive a $1,000 grant to beautify their school, educate students, or impact their community.
Type of support: Employee volunteer services; General/operating support; Grants to individuals; Program development; Sponsorships.
Geographic limitations: Giving primarily in areas of company operations; giving on a national basis for Igniting Creative Energy Challenge.
Publications: Corporate giving report.
Application information: Applications accepted. Igniting Creative Energy projects are limited to 500 words or 3 pages for documentation or written entries, a 3 minute limit for audio or music entries, and a 10 minute limit for media or electronic entries. Application form required.
Initial approach: Complete online entry form for Igniting Creative Energy and mail project to application address
Deadline(s): Mar. 4 for Igniting Creative Energy
Number of staff: 1 full-time support.

Johnson Controls Foundation, Inc.

(formerly Johnson Controls Foundation)
5757 N. Green Bay Ave.
P.O. Box 591
Milwaukee, WI 53201-0591 (414) 524-2296
URL: http://www.johnsoncontrols.com/publish/us/en/about/our_community_focus/johnson_controls_foundation.html

Establishment information: Trust established in 1952 in WI.
Donor: Johnson Controls, Inc.
Contact: Valerie Adisek, Coord.
Financial data (yr. ended 12/31/11): Assets, $20,364,457 (M); expenditures, $7,036,781; qualifying distributions, $6,949,528; giving activities include $6,948,028 for 597 grants (high: $2,958,058; low: $35).
Purpose and activities: The foundation supports organizations involved with arts and culture, education, health, human services, and community development.
Fields of interest: Media, television; Media, radio; Visual arts; Museums; Performing arts; Literature; Arts; Higher education; Adult/continuing education; Libraries (public); Scholarships/financial aid; Education; Hospitals (general); Health care; Youth, services; Human services, financial counseling; Human services; Urban/community development; Community/economic development; United Ways and Federated Giving Programs.
Programs:
Arts and Culture: The foundation supports museums, libraries, and programs designed to engage in and promote visual, performing, and literary arts, public radio and television, and other related cultural activities.
Education: The foundation supports organizations involved with higher, adult, and economics education.
Education and Arts Matching Gift Program: The foundation matches contributions made by employees, retirees, and directors of Johnson Controls to institutions of higher education and nonprofit organizations involved with arts and culture on a one-for-one basis from $50 to $5,000 per contributor, per year.
Employee Scholarships: The foundation awards college scholarships to children of employees of Johnson Control. The program is designed to reward students who achieve a balance between academic achievement, leadership, and civic involvement.
Health and Social Service: The foundation supports organizations involved with health and human services, including the United Way.
Type of support: Annual campaigns; Building/renovation; Capital campaigns; Continuing support; Emergency funds; Employee matching gifts; Employee-related scholarships; General/operating support; Program development; Scholarship funds; Seed money.
Geographic limitations: Giving primarily in areas of company operations in Milwaukee, WI.
Support limitations: No support for political or lobbying organizations, public or private pre-schools, elementary or secondary schools, sectarian institutions or organizations not of direct benefit to the entire community, foreign-based institutions, fraternal or veterans' organizations, or private foundations. No grants to individuals (except for employee-related scholarships), or for testimonial dinners, fundraising events, tickets to benefits, shows, advertising, travel or tours, seminars or conferences, book or magazine publication, media productions, specific medical or scientific research projects, or endowments; no equipment, product, or labor donations.
Publications: Application guidelines; Program policy statement.
Application information: Applications accepted. Telephone calls and personal visits are not encouraged. Multi-year funding is not automatic. Additional information may be requested at a later date. Requests to finance office equipment and computer systems receive low priority. Application form not required. Applicants should submit the following:
1) copy of IRS Determination Letter
2) brief history of organization and description of its mission
3) geographic area to be served
4) copy of most recent annual report/audited financial statement/990
5) listing of board of directors, trustees, officers and other key people and their affiliations
6) detailed description of project and amount of funding requested
7) copy of current year's organizational budget and/or project budget
8) listing of additional sources and amount of support

Initial approach: Proposal
Copies of proposal: 1
Board meeting date(s): Usually Mar. and Sept.
Deadline(s): None
Final notification: Up to 120 days
Officers and Directors:* Charles A. Harvey*, Pres.; Susan F. Davis*, Secy.; Stephen A. Roell*, Treas.; Jacqueline F. Stayer.
Trustee: U.S. Bank, N.A.
Number of staff: 1 full-time professional.
EIN: 203510307
Selected grants: The following grants are a representative sample of this grantmaker's funding activity:
$1,852,504 to United Way of Greater Milwaukee, Milwaukee, WI, 2010. For general support.
$618,508 to United Performing Arts Fund, Milwaukee, WI, 2010. For general support.
$143,000 to Boys and Girls Clubs of Greater Milwaukee, Milwaukee, WI, 2010. For general support.
$55,100 to Medical College of Wisconsin, Milwaukee, WI, 2010. For general support.
$50,000 to Childrens Outing Association, Milwaukee, WI, 2010. For general support.
$15,000 to Junior Achievement of Southeastern Michigan, Detroit, MI, 2010. For general support.
$10,000 to American Red Cross in Southeastern Wisconsin, Milwaukee, WI, 2010. For general support.
$5,198 to United Way, Metro, Louisville, KY, 2010. For general support.
$5,000 to Holland Area Arts Council, Holland, MI, 2010. For general support.
$2,800 to University of Illinois Foundation, Urbana, IL, 2010. For general support.

2051
Johnson Investment Counsel, Inc.

3777 W. Fork Rd.
Cincinnati, OH 45247-7545 (513) 661-3100

Company URL: http://www.johnsoninv.com
Establishment information: Established in 1965.
Company type: Private company
Business activities: Operates wealth management firm.
Business type (SIC): Security and commodity services
Corporate officers: Ronald H. McSwain, Chair.; Timothy E. Johnson, Pres. and C.E.O.; Marc E. Figgins, C.F.O and Treas.; Jennifer J. Keihoffer, Secy.; Lisa Oliverio, C.P.A., Cont.
Board of director: Ronald H. McSwain, Chair.
Giving statement: Giving through the Johnson Charitable Gift Fund.

Johnson Charitable Gift Fund

3777 W. Fork Rd.
Cincinnati, OH 45247-7575 (513) 661-3100
FAX: (513) 661-3160; Toll-free tel.: (800) 541-0170; additional address (Columbus office): 100 E. Broad St., Ste. 2300, Columbus, OH 43215-3653, tel.: (614) 365-9103, fax: (614) 365-9943, toll-free tel.: (866) 365-4523; additional address (Dayton office): 40 N. Main St., Ste. 2110, Dayton, OH 45423-1021, tel.: (937) 461-3790, fax: (937) 461-2969, toll-free tel.: (800) 851-9114; URL: http://www.johnsoninv.com/johnsonsharitablegiftfund.aspx

Establishment information: Established in 2003 in OH.
Contact: Michael D. Barnes, Chair. and Pres.
Financial data (yr. ended 06/30/12): Revenue, $13,982,021; assets, $52,076,892 (M); gifts received, $12,841,323; expenditures, $8,710,340; program services expenses, $8,573,371; giving activities include $8,573,371 for 195 grants (high: $1,002,250; low: $5,000).
Purpose and activities: The fund supports and promotes philanthropy by administering a donor-advised fund.
Fields of interest: Philanthropy/voluntarism.
Geographic limitations: Giving on a national basis.
Officers and Directors:* Michael D. Barnes*, Chair. and Pres.; Scott J. Bischoff*, V.P. and Treas.; Marcy Gruen*, Secy.; Todd D. Bacon; Thomas W. Seith.
EIN: 300233491

2052
Johnson Machine Works, Inc.
(formerly Chariton Foundary and Machine Shops)
318 N. 11th St.
Chariton, IA 50049 (641) 774-2191

Company URL: http://www.jmworks.com
Establishment information: Established in 1907 as Chariton Foundary and Machine Shops.
Company type: Private company
Business activities: Manufactures steel products.
Business type (SIC): Fabricated metal products (except machinery and transportation equipment)
Corporate officers: Jeffrey Johnson, Pres.; Brian Franks, C.F.O.
Giving statement: Giving through the Johnson Foundation.

The Johnson Foundation
c/o Shawn Garton
318 N. 11th St.
Chariton, IA 50049-1704

Establishment information: Established in 1957 in IA.
Donor: Johnson Machine Works Inc.
Financial data (yr. ended 11/30/11): Assets, $727,715 (M); gifts received, $80,000; expenditures, $94,431; qualifying distributions, $93,055; giving activities include $93,055 for 4 grants (high: $60,305; low: $2,750).
Purpose and activities: The foundation supports hospitals and community foundations and organizations involved with ballet, higher education, cancer, and Christianity.
Fields of interest: Performing arts, ballet; Higher education; Hospitals (general); Cancer; Foundations (community); Christian agencies & churches.
Type of support: Equipment; General/operating support; Program development; Scholarship funds.
Application information: Applications not accepted. Unsolicited requests for funds not accepted.
Trustees: Aaron Garton; Shawn Garton; Danielle Johnson.
EIN: 426062888

2053
Johnson Ventures, Inc.
417 Washington St.
Columbus, IN 47201-6757 (812) 373-4039

Company URL: http://www.johnsonventures.com
Establishment information: Established in 2002.
Company type: Private company
Business activities: Operates private investment firm.
Corporate officers: Richard L. Johnson, Jr., Pres.; Betty Kelley, Cont.
Giving statement: Giving through the Johnson Charitable Foundation.

Johnson Charitable Foundation
417 Washington St.
Columbus, IN 47201-6757

Establishment information: Established in 2002 in IN.
Donors: Johnson Oil Co., Inc.; Johnson Ventures, Inc.
Financial data (yr. ended 12/31/11): Assets, $39,321 (M); gifts received, $120,000; expenditures, $159,056; qualifying distributions, $157,500; giving activities include $157,500 for 5 grants (high: $120,000; low: $2,500).
Purpose and activities: The foundation supports organizations involved with arts and culture, business education, human services, and business promotion.
Fields of interest: Arts councils; Historic preservation/historical societies; Arts; Business school/education; Family services; Human services; Community development, business promotion.
Type of support: General/operating support; Program development; Sponsorships.
Geographic limitations: Giving primarily in IN.
Support limitations: No grants to individuals.
Application information: Applications not accepted. Contributes only to pre-selected organizations.
Officers: Richard L. Johnson, Jr., Pres.; Kevin Martin, Secy.-Treas.
Directors: Alice Johnson; Jennifer Johnson; Ruth W. Johnson.
EIN: 611415325
Selected grants: The following grants are a representative sample of this grantmaker's funding activity:
$10,000 to Riley Childrens Foundation, Indianapolis, IN, 2010.
$5,000 to Christian Theological Seminary, Indianapolis, IN, 2010.
$5,000 to Hospice of South Central Indiana, Columbus, IN, 2010.

2054
Johnston Textiles, Inc.
(doing business as Southern Phenix Textiles)
300 General Colin Powell Pkwy.
Phenix City, AL 36869 (334) 298-9351

Company URL: http://www.johnstontextiles.com
Establishment information: Established in 1948.
Company type: Private company
Business activities: Manufactures synthetic fabrics.
Business type (SIC): Fabrics/broadwoven synthetic and silk
Corporate officers: Jim Morrelli, Pres. and C.E.O.; James J. Murray, C.F.O.
Giving statement: Giving through the Southern Phenix Textiles Scholarship Fund Inc.

Southern Phenix Textiles Scholarship Fund Inc.
P.O. Box 1108
Phenix City, AL 36868 (334) 664-3367

Establishment information: Established in 1990 in AL.
Donor: Southern Phenix Textiles, Inc.
Contact: Ronnie Brooks, Secy.-Treas.
Financial data (yr. ended 06/30/12): Assets, $3,671 (M); expenditures, $4,500; qualifying distributions, $4,000; giving activities include $4,000 for grants to individuals.
Purpose and activities: The fund awards college scholarships to dependents of employees of Southern Phenix Textiles residing in Phenix City, Alabama, and the surrounding community.
Type of support: Employee-related scholarships.
Geographic limitations: Giving limited to the Phenix City, AL, area.
Application information: Applications not accepted. Contributes only through employee-related scholarships.
Officers: Don Craft, Pres.; Ronnie Brooks, Secy.-Treas.
Director: Lee Tucker.
EIN: 631018039

2055
Edward D. Jones & Co., L.P.
12555 Manchester Rd.
St. Louis, MO 63131-3729 (314) 515-2000
FAX: (314) 515-3269

Company URL: http://www.edwardjones.com
Establishment information: Established in 1922.
Company type: Private company
Business activities: Provides investment advisory services.
Business type (SIC): Security and commodity services
Financial profile for 2012: Number of employees, 38,000; assets, $13,042,000,000; liabilities, $11,059,000,000
Corporate officers: Steve Novik, C.F.O.; Rich Malone, C.I.O.
Giving statement: Giving through the Edward D. Jones & Co. Foundation.

The Edward D. Jones & Co. Foundation
(also known as Edward Jones Foundation)
c/o Edward D. Jones & Co., L.P.
12555 Manchester Rd.
St. Louis, MO 63131-3710
FAX: (314) 515-3331;
E-mail: mary.berry@edwardjones.com

Establishment information: Established in 1991 in MO.
Donor: Edward D. Jones & Co., L.P.
Contact: Mary Berry, Admin., Contribs. Comm.
Financial data (yr. ended 12/31/11): Assets, $14,106,159 (M); gifts received, $7,414,734; expenditures, $5,832,436; qualifying distributions, $5,828,636; giving activities include $5,828,636 for 120 grants (high: $2,427,563; low: $50).
Purpose and activities: The foundation supports zoos and food banks and organizations involved with arts and culture, education, health, human services, community development, and civic affairs.
Fields of interest: Arts councils; Media, radio; Museums (science/technology); Arts; Higher education; Education; Environment, land resources; Zoos/zoological societies; Hospitals (general); Health care, patient services; Health care; Food banks; Disasters, preparedness/services; Big Brothers/Big Sisters; Youth development, business; American Red Cross; Salvation Army; YM/YWCAs & YM/YWHAs; Children/youth, services; Human services; Community/economic development; United Ways and Federated Giving Programs; Public affairs, finance; Public affairs.
Type of support: Capital campaigns; General/operating support.
Geographic limitations: Giving primarily in St. Louis, MO.
Support limitations: No grants to individuals.
Application information: Applications accepted. Priority is given to nonprofit organizations with which Edward D. Jones associates have a financial interest. Application form not required. Applicants should submit the following:
1) copy of most recent annual report/audited financial statement/990
2) copy of current year's organizational budget and/or project budget
3) listing of board of directors, trustees, officers and other key people and their affiliations
4) copy of IRS Determination Letter

5) detailed description of project and amount of funding requested
6) brief history of organization and description of its mission
7) list of company employees involved with the organization
8) timetable for implementation and evaluation of project
9) geographic area to be served
10) population served
11) listing of additional sources and amount of support
12) statement of problem project will address
13) results expected from proposed grant

Proposals should also list the number of people that will benefit from the request; the percentage of contributions used for providing services versus administration; and if there is an event associated with the project, the percentage of total revenue from the event that will go the organization.

Initial approach: Proposal
Deadline(s): None

Officer and Trustee:* Jim Weddle, Chair.; Kevin Bastien.
EIN: 431595600
Selected grants: The following grants are a representative sample of this grantmaker's funding activity:
$2,427,563 to United Way Worldwide, Alexandria, VA, 2011. For disaster relief.
$350,000 to National Chamber Foundation, Washington, DC, 2011.
$312,500 to American Red Cross National Headquarters, Washington, DC, 2011. For disaster relief.
$253,000 to University of Missouri, Saint Louis, MO, 2011.
$200,000 to Saint Louis Science Center, Saint Louis, MO, 2011.
$200,000 to Washington University, Saint Louis, MO, 2011.
$200,000 to Webster University, Saint Louis, MO, 2011.
$100,000 to YMCA of Greater Saint Louis, Saint Louis, MO, 2011.
$60,000 to Claremont Graduate University, Claremont, CA, 2011.
$15,000 to Repertory Theater of Saint Louis, Saint Louis, MO, 2011.

2056
R. A. Jones & Company Inc.

(also known as Oystar Group)
2701 Crescent Springs Rd.
Covington, KY 41017-1504 (859) 341-0400

Company URL: http://www.rajones.com
Establishment information: Established in 1905.
Company type: Subsidiary of a foreign company
Business activities: Manufactures packaging machinery.
Business type (SIC): Machinery/general industry
Corporate officers: Gordon B. Bonfield, Pres. and C.E.O.; Jeff Williams, V.P., Sales and Mktg.; John Tamashasky, V.P., Human Resources
Giving statement: Giving through the Motch Family Foundation Inc.

Motch Family Foundation Inc.

530 Old U.S. Rte. 52
New Richmond, OH 45157

Establishment information: Established in 1962.
Donors: R.A. Jones & Co. Inc.; David W. Motch.
Financial data (yr. ended 11/30/11): Assets, $1,998,181 (M); expenditures, $98,728; qualifying distributions, $87,725; giving activities include $87,500 for 38 grants (high: $6,000; low: $500).
Purpose and activities: The foundation supports organizations involved with arts and culture, education, and health.
Fields of interest: Museums; Performing arts; Performing arts, orchestras; Arts; Elementary/secondary education; Higher education; Education; Hospitals (general); Speech/hearing centers; Health care.
Type of support: Annual campaigns; General/operating support.
Geographic limitations: Giving primarily in Cincinnati, OH.
Support limitations: No grants to individuals.
Application information: Applications not accepted. Unsolicited requests for funds not accepted.
Trustees: Diana T. Dwight; Alan W. Motch; Arthur E. Motch III; David W. Motch; Oliva DeBolt Motch.
EIN: 316032887

2057
Jones Apparel Group, Inc.

1411 Broadway
New York, NY 10018 (212) 642-3860
FAX: (215) 785-1795

Company URL: http://www.jonesgroupinc.com
Establishment information: Established in 1970.
Company type: Public company
Company ticker symbol and exchange: JNY/NYSE
Business activities: Designs, markets, and licenses women's sportswear, suits and dresses, and shoes and accessories, men's, women's, and children's casual sportswear and jeanswear, and costume jewelry.
Business type (SIC): Apparel—women's outerwear; apparel—men's and boys' outerwear; leather footwear; jewelry and notions/costume
Financial profile for 2012: Number of employees, 6,250; assets, $2,595,500,000; sales volume, $3,798,100,000; pre-tax net income, -$67,900,000; expenses, $3,723,400,000; liabilities, $1,590,700,000
Fortune 1000 ranking: 2012—608th in revenues, 909th in profits, and 793rd in assets
Corporate officers: Sidney Kimmel, Chair.; Wesley R. Card, C.E.O.; Christopher R. Cade, Exec. V.P., Cont., and C.A.O.; Ira M. Dansky, Exec. V.P., Genl. Counsel, and Secy.; John T. McClain, C.F.O.; Joseph T. Donnalley, Sr. V.P. and Treas.
Board of directors: Sidney Kimmel, Chair.; Wesley R. Card; Gerald C. Crotty; John D. Demsey; Margaret H. Georgiadis; Matthew H. Kamens; Robert L. Mettler; Jeffrey D. Nuechterlein; Lowell W. Robinson; Ann Marie C. Wilkins
Subsidiaries: Jones Holding Corp., Wilmington, DE; Jones Investment Co. Inc., Wilmington, DE; Melru Corp., Bristol, PA; Nine West Group Inc., White Plains, NY; Sun Apparel, Inc., New York, NY; Victoria +Co Ltd., Warwick, RI
International operations: Canada; Hong Kong; Mexico
Giving statement: Giving through the Jones Apparel Group, Inc. Corporate Giving Program.
Company EIN: 060935166

Jones Apparel Group, Inc. Corporate Giving Program

180 Rittenhouse Cir.
Bristol, PA 19007-1618 (215) 785-4000
FAX: (215) 826-8902

Purpose and activities: Jones makes charitable contributions to nonprofit organizations involved with education, breast cancer research, and on a case by case basis. Support is given on a national basis.
Fields of interest: Education; Breast cancer research; General charitable giving.
Program:
JNY In The Classroom: Jones Apparel Group provides ongoing financial and volunteer support to Jones New York in the Classroom, a program designed to help improve the quality of education for America's children.
Type of support: Employee volunteer services; General/operating support; Sponsorships.
Geographic limitations: Giving primarily in areas of company operations.

2058
Jones Day

(also known as Jones, Day, Reavis & Pogue)
North Point
901 Lakeside Ave.
Cleveland, OH 44114-1190 (216) 586-3939

Company URL: http://www.jonesday.com
Establishment information: Established in 1893.
Company type: Private company
Business activities: Provides legal services.
Business type (SIC): Legal services
Corporate officer: Stephen J. Brogan, Managing Partner
Offices: Irvine, Los Angeles, Menlo Park, Palo Alto, San Diego, San Francisco, CA; Washington, DC; Atlanta, GA; Chicago, IL; New York, NY; Columbus, OH; Pittsburgh, PA; Dallas, Houston, TX
International operations: Australia; Belgium; Brazil; China; France; Germany; Hong Kong; India; Italy; Japan; Mexico; Russia; Saudi Arabia; Singapore; Spain; Taiwan; United Arab Emirates; United Kingdom
Giving statement: Giving through the Jones Day Pro Bono Program and the Jones Day Foundation.

Jones Day Pro Bono Program

North Point, 901 Lakeside Ave.
Cleveland, OH 44114-1190 (202) 879-7648
E-mail: lparcher@jonesday.com; Additional tel.: (202) 586-3939, fax (202) 579-0212; URL: http://www.jonesdayprobono.com/mission/

Contact: Laura Tuell Parcher, Firmwide Partner in Charge of Pro Bono
Fields of interest: Legal services.
Type of support: Pro bono services - legal.
Application information: The Pro Bono Committee manages the pro bono program.

Jones Day Foundation

(formerly Jones, Day, Reavis & Pogue Foundation)
North Point
901 Lakeside Ave.
Cleveland, OH 44114-1163 (216) 586-7028

Establishment information: Established in 1988 in OH.
Financial data (yr. ended 12/31/11): Revenue, $4,032,030; assets, $5,444,472 (M); gifts received, $4,014,442; expenditures, $2,039,596; program services expenses, $2,031,778; giving activities include $1,671,778 for 18 grants (high: $500,000; low: $7,500).
Purpose and activities: The foundation makes grants to selected charitable 501(c)(3)

organizations in which Jones Day lawyers are involved.
Fields of interest: Community/economic development.
Geographic limitations: Giving on a national basis.
Support limitations: No support for organizations lacking 501(c)(3) status and in which Jones Day lawyers are not involved. No grants to individuals.
Officers and Trustees:* Lizanne Thomas*, Pres.; Mary Ellen Powers*, V.P.; Jeffrey S. Leavitt*, Secy.; Paul A. Grater, Treas.; Andrew M. Kramer; Luis Riesgo; Gregory M. Shumaker; Robert L. Thomson.
EIN: 341570455

2059
The Jones Financial Companies, L.L.L.P.

12555 Manchester Rd.
Des Peres, MO 63131 (314) 515-2000

Company URL: http://www.edwardjones.com
Establishment information: Established in 1871.
Company type: Private company
Business activities: Operates investment brokerage network catering to individual investors.
Business type (SIC): Brokers and dealers/security
Financial profile for 2010: Number of employees, 37,000; sales volume, $4,163,100,000
Corporate officers: Kevin Bastien, C.F.O.; Norman Eaker, C.A.O.; Vinny Ferrari, C.I.O.
Giving statement: Giving through the Jones Financial Companies, L.L.L.P. Contributions Program.

The Jones Financial Companies, L.L.L.P. Contributions Program

(also known as Edward Jones)
1245 JJ Kelley Memorial Dr.
St. Louis, MO 63131-3600 (314) 515-2000
URL: http://www.edwardjones.com/en_US/company/community/index.html

Purpose and activities: Edward Jones makes charitable contributions to nonprofit organizations involved with food, blanket, and toy drives, heart disease, breast cancer, arts, education, juvenile diabetes research, and infant medical care, and to the United Way and the American Red Cross. Giving primarily in areas of company operations in St. Louis, Missouri, and to national organizations.
Fields of interest: Arts; Education; Health care, infants; Breast cancer; Heart & circulatory diseases; Diabetes; Medical research, single organization support; Food services; American Red Cross; Children, services; Human services, gift distribution; United Ways and Federated Giving Programs.
Type of support: Employee volunteer services; General/operating support; In-kind gifts.
Geographic limitations: Giving primarily in areas of company operations in St. Louis, MO, and to national organizations.

2060
J. R. Jones Fixture Company

3216 Winnetka Ave. N.
Minneapolis, MN 55427-2018
(763) 398-4300

Company URL: http://www.jonesfixture.com
Establishment information: Established in 1945.
Company type: Private company
Business activities: Manufactures wood partitions and fixtures; manufactures wood millwork products.
Business type (SIC): Fixtures/office and store; wood millwork
Corporate officers: Douglas J. Jones, Pres.; Eric Jones, V.P., Opers.
Giving statement: Giving through the J. R. Jones Fixture Company Foundation.

J. R. Jones Fixture Company Foundation

3216 Winnetka Ave. N.
Golden Valley, MN 55427-2018

Establishment information: Established in 2003 in MN.
Donor: J.R. Jones Fixture Co.
Financial data (yr. ended 12/31/10): Assets, $32,736 (M); gifts received, $25,000; expenditures, $21,829; qualifying distributions, $20,725; giving activities include $20,000 for 1 grant.
Purpose and activities: The foundation supports zoos and organizations involved with K-12 education.
Fields of interest: Education.
Type of support: General/operating support.
Support limitations: No grants to individuals.
Application information: Applications not accepted. Contributes only to pre-selected organizations.
Officers: Douglas J. Jones, Pres.; Eric N. Jones, C.F.O.
Directors: Adam B. Jones; Ashley E. Jones.
EIN: 900124523

2061
Jones Lang LaSalle Incorporated

200 E. Randolph Dr.
Chicago, IL 60601 (312) 782-5800
FAX: (312) 782-4339

Company URL: http://www.joneslanglasalle.com
Establishment information: Established in 1783.
Company type: Public company
Company ticker symbol and exchange: JLL/NYSE
Business activities: Operates a real estate services and investment management company.
Business type (SIC): Real estate operators and lessors
Financial profile for 2012: Number of employees, 48,000; assets, $4,351,500,000; sales volume, $3,932,830,000; pre-tax net income, $278,090,000; expenses, $3,643,430,000; liabilities, $2,400,320,000
Fortune 1000 ranking: 2012—596th in revenues, 567th in profits, and 633rd in assets
Corporate officers: Sheila A. Penrose, Chair.; Colin Dyer, Pres. and C.E.O.; Lauralee E. Martin, C.O.O. and C.F.O.; David B. Johnson, C.I.O.; Mark Ohringer, Genl. Counsel and Corp. Secy.; Joe Romenesko, Treas.; Mark Engel, Cont.
Board of directors: Sheila A. Penrose, Chair.; Hugo Bague; Colin Dyer; Darryl Hartley-Leonard; DeAnne Julius; Ming Lu; Lauralee E. Martin; Martin H. Nesbitt; David B. Rickard; Roger T. Staubach; Thomas C. Theobald
Giving statement: Giving through the Jones Lang LaSalle Incorporated Corporate Giving Program.
Company EIN: 364150422

Jones Lang LaSalle Incorporated Corporate Giving Program

200 East Randolph Dr.
Chicago, IL 60601 (312) 782-5800
URL: http://www.joneslanglasalle.com/Pages/CorporateSocialResponsibility.aspx

Purpose and activities: Jones Lang LaSalle makes charitable contributions to nonprofit organizations on a case by case basis. Support is given on a national and international basis in areas of company operations.
Fields of interest: Disasters, preparedness/services; General charitable giving.
Type of support: Employee matching gifts; Employee volunteer services; General/operating support.
Geographic limitations: Giving on a national and international basis in areas of company operations.

2062
Jordache Enterprises, Inc.

1400 Broadway, 15th Fl.
New York, NY 10018-5336 (212) 944-1330
FAX: (212) 768-5736

Company URL: http://www.jordache.com
Establishment information: Established in 1979.
Company type: Private company
Business activities: Manufactures apparel and accessories.
Business type (SIC): Apparel and other finished products made from fabrics and similar materials
Financial profile for 2010: Number of employees, 8,000
Corporate officers: Joseph Nakash, Chair. and C.E.O.; Liz Berlinger, Pres.; Joe Taylor, C.F.O.; Ralph Nakash, Secy.-Treas.
Board of director: Joseph Nakash, Chair.
Giving statement: Giving through the Nakash Family Foundation.

Nakash Family Foundation

1400 Broadway, 14th Fl.
New York, NY 10018-5300

Establishment information: Established in 1984 in NY.
Donors: Jordache Ltd.; Jordache Enterprises, Inc.
Contact: Joseph Nakash, Pres.; Ralph Nakash, Secy.-Treas.
Financial data (yr. ended 12/31/11): Assets, $1,513,069 (M); gifts received, $735,000; expenditures, $1,566,220; qualifying distributions, $1,509,618; giving activities include $1,509,618 for grants.
Purpose and activities: The foundation supports organizations involved with theological education and Judaism.
Fields of interest: Theological school/education; Jewish agencies & synagogues.
Type of support: General/operating support.
Support limitations: No grants to individuals.
Application information: Applications accepted. Application form not required.
Initial approach: Proposal
Deadline(s): None
Officers: Joseph Nakash, Pres.; Avi Nakash, V.P.; Ralph Nakash, Secy.-Treas.
EIN: 133030267

2063
W. M. Jordan Company, Inc.
11010 Jefferson Ave.
Newport News, VA 23601-0337
(757) 596-6341

Company URL: http://www.wmjordan.com
Establishment information: Established in 1958.
Company type: Private company
Business activities: Provides nonresidential general contract construction services.
Business type (SIC): Contractors/general nonresidential building
Corporate officers: Robert T. Lawson, Chair.; John R. Lawson, Pres. and C.E.O.
Board of director: Robert T. Lawson, Chair.
Office: Richmond, VA
Giving statement: Giving through the W. M. Jordan Company Charitable Foundation.

The W. M. Jordan Company Charitable Foundation
11010 Jefferson Ave.
Newport News, VA 23601-0337 (757) 596-6341

Establishment information: Established in 1996 in VA.
Donor: W.M. Jordan Co., Inc.
Financial data (yr. ended 12/31/11): Assets, $270,562 (M); gifts received, $180,000; expenditures, $116,150; qualifying distributions, $116,150; giving activities include $116,150 for 15 grants (high: $36,000; low: $200).
Purpose and activities: The foundation supports organizations involved with arts and culture, education, health, and human services.
Fields of interest: Arts; Secondary school/education; Higher education; Education; Hospitals (general); Health care; Children/youth, services; Human services; United Ways and Federated Giving Programs.
Type of support: Continuing support; Equipment; General/operating support; Sponsorships.
Geographic limitations: Giving primarily in VA.
Support limitations: No grants to individuals.
Application information: Applications accepted. Application form required. Applicants should submit the following:
1) copy of most recent annual report/audited financial statement/990
Initial approach: Proposal
Deadline(s): None
Trustees: John R. Lawson; Thomas M. Shelton.
EIN: 546407107

2064
Jordan-Kitt Music, Inc.
9520 Baltimore Ave.
College Park, MD 20740-1322
(301) 474-9500

Company URL: http://www.jordankitts.com
Establishment information: Established in 1912.
Company type: Private company
Business activities: Operates piano and organ stores.
Business type (SIC): Consumer electronics and music stores
Corporate officers: Chris Syllaba, Pres. and C.E.O.; David C. Mahoney, V.P., Admin; Ken Saliba, V.P., Sales; Scott Darrow, Cont.
Giving statement: Giving through the William and Mary McCormick Foundation Inc.

William and Mary McCormick Foundation Inc.
(formerly The William McCormick Foundation, Inc.)
9528 Woodington Dr.
Potomac, MD 20854 (301) 299-4412

Establishment information: Established in 1987 in MD.
Donor: Jordan-Kitt Music, Inc.
Financial data (yr. ended 12/31/10): Assets, $280,861 (M); expenditures, $9,978; qualifying distributions, $7,000; giving activities include $7,000 for 2 grants (high: $6,500; low: $500).
Purpose and activities: The foundation supports organizations involved with arts and culture, education, and cancer.
Fields of interest: Education.
Type of support: General/operating support.
Application information: Applications accepted. Application form not required.
Initial approach: Proposal
Deadline(s): None
Officers: Maureen Grant, Pres.; Sally A. Fugere, V.P.; Barbara F. Grace, V.P.
EIN: 521530479

2065
Roy Jorgensen Associates, Inc.
3735 Buckeystown Pike
P.O. Box 70
Buckeystown, MD 21717-0070
(301) 831-1000

Company URL: http://www.royjorgensen.com
Establishment information: Established in 1961.
Company type: Private company
Business activities: Operates highway maintenance company.
Business type (SIC): Construction/highway and street (except elevated)
Corporate officers: John S. Jorgensen, Sr., Pres.; Donna M. Morgan, Cont.
Giving statement: Giving through the Roy Jorgensen Foundation Inc.

The Roy Jorgensen Foundation Inc.
P.O. Box 70
Buckeystown, MD 21717-0070
E-mail: john_jorgenson@royjorgensen.com

Establishment information: Established in 2004 in MD.
Donor: Roy Jorgensen Association, Inc.
Financial data (yr. ended 12/31/11): Assets, $320,267 (M); expenditures, $23,060; qualifying distributions, $22,960; giving activities include $7,000 for 2 grants (high: $5,000; low: $2,000) and $15,000 for 1 grant to an individual.
Purpose and activities: The foundation promotes design excellence in highway maintenance management through scholarships to students pursuing a degree in civil engineering.
Fields of interest: Higher education; Engineering school/education.
Program:
Roy E. Jorgensen Memorial Scholarship: The foundation annually awards a $15,000 scholarship to an undergraduate college senior or graduate student enrolled at an accredited school of engineering in the U.S. Recipients are selected based on academic record, career objectives and life goals, extracurricular activities, and community activities. Preference is given to qualified residents of Maryland. Applicant must be a citizen of the U.S.
Type of support: Scholarship funds; Scholarships—to individuals.
Geographic limitations: Giving primarily in GA, MD, and SC.
Application information: Applications not accepted. Unsolicited requests for funds not accepted.
Officers: John S. Jorgensen, Pres.; John S. Jorgensen, Jr., Secy.; Douglas Selby, Treas.
EIN: 202052767

2066
J. Josephson Inc.
35 Horizon Blvd.
South Hackensack, NJ 07606-1804
(201) 440-7000
FAX: (201) 440-7109

Company URL: http://www.jjosephson.com
Establishment information: Established in 1965.
Company type: Private company
Business activities: Manufactures converted paper products.
Business type (SIC): Paper and paperboard/coated, converted, and laminated
Corporate officers: Mark Goodman, Pres.; Gilbert Goodman, C.E.O.; Stanley Garrett, Secy.
Giving statement: Giving through the Goodman Family Foundation.

The Goodman Family Foundation
134 E. 70th St.
New York, NY 10021-5035

Establishment information: Established in 2003 in NY.
Donor: J. Josephson, Inc.
Financial data (yr. ended 12/31/11): Assets, $1,133,603 (M); gifts received, $150,000; expenditures, $181,594; qualifying distributions, $172,250; giving activities include $172,250 for 15 grants (high: $50,000; low: $250).
Purpose and activities: The foundation supports hospitals and organizations involved with education and Judaism.
Fields of interest: Secondary school/education; Education; Hospitals (general); Jewish federated giving programs; Jewish agencies & synagogues.
Type of support: General/operating support.
Geographic limitations: Giving primarily in NY.
Support limitations: No grants to individuals.
Application information: Applications not accepted. Contributes only to pre-selected organizations.
Officers and Directors:* Mark Goodman*, Pres.; Judith Goodman*, Secy.; Gilbert Goodman.
EIN: 510486580
Selected grants: The following grants are a representative sample of this grantmaker's funding activity:
$50,000 to Mount Sinai Hospital, New York, NY, 2010. For general support.
$35,000 to UJA-Federation of New York, New York, NY, 2010. For general support.
$25,000 to Columbia Grammar and Preparatory School, New York, NY, 2010. For general support.
$23,950 to Park Avenue Synagogue, New York, NY, 2010. For general support.
$15,000 to Washington University, Saint Louis, MO, 2010. For general support.

2067
Jostens, Inc.
3601 Minnesota Dr., Ste. 400
Minneapolis, MN 55435 (952) 830-3300

Company URL: http://www.jostens.com
Establishment information: Established in 1897.
Company type: Subsidiary of a foreign company
Business activities: Manufactures and provides achievement and affiliation products and services.
Business type (SIC): Photographic portrait studios; publishing/miscellaneous; jewelry/precious metal
Corporate officers: Timothy M. Larson, Pres. and C.E.O.; Val Williams, C.O.O.; Jim Simpson, C.F.O.; Scott Henkel, C.I.O.; Keith Kugler, V.P., Finance; Rick Cochran, V.P., Sales; Natalie Stute, V.P., Human Resources
Plants: Visalia, CA; Topeka, KS; Eagan, Owatonna, MN; Winston-Salem, NC; State College, PA; Laurens, SC; Clarksville, Shelbyville, TN; Denton, TX
Giving statement: Giving through the Jostens Foundation, Inc.

The Jostens Foundation, Inc.
3601 Minnesota Dr., Ste. 400
Minneapolis, MN 55435-5281 (952) 830-3235
E-mail: foundation@jostens.com; URL: http://www.jostens.com/misc/aboutus/about_jostens_cp_foundation.html

Establishment information: Established in 1976 in MN.
Donor: Jostens, Inc.
Contact: Teresa Olson
Financial data (yr. ended 12/31/11): Assets, $200,253 (M); expenditures, $477,304; qualifying distributions, $464,670; giving activities include $464,670 for grants.
Purpose and activities: The foundation supports organizations involved with education and youth development.
Fields of interest: Elementary/secondary education; Higher education; Education, drop-out prevention; Education, reading; Education; Youth development.
Programs:
Josten Scholarships: The foundation awards $2,000 college scholarships to dependents of full-time employees and independent sales representatives of Jostens. Winners are eligible for an additional three-year $2,500 scholarship. Recipients are selected based on outstanding community service, academic achievement, and leadership.
Jostens Community Grants: The foundation supports programs designed to help young people acquire the skills they need in school and life. Special emphasis is directed toward early intervention; improving literacy or high school graduation rates; and preparing students for post-secondary education.
Jostens Employee Gift Matching: The foundation matches contributions made by employees and independent sales representatives of Jostens to nonprofit organizations on a one-for-one basis from $25 to $1,000 per contributor, per year.
Type of support: Employee matching gifts; Employee-related scholarships; General/operating support; Program development.
Geographic limitations: Giving in areas of company operations, with emphasis on MN.
Support limitations: No support for schools, school districts, or school foundations, organizations involved with highly political or controversial issues, churches or religious groups, or fraternal, veterans', or professional organizations. No grants to individuals (except for employee-related scholarships), or for personal needs, political campaigns or political lobbying activities, benefit fundraising events or tickets to fundraisers, recognition or testimonial events, disease-specific fundraising campaigns, athletic scholarships or activities, advertising, endowments, or capital campaigns.
Publications: Application guidelines; Informational brochure (including application guidelines); Program policy statement.
Application information: Applications accepted. Requests may be submitted using the Minnesota Common Grant Form. Application form required. Applicants should submit the following:
1) timetable for implementation and evaluation of project
2) how project will be sustained once grantmaker support is completed
3) results expected from proposed grant
4) statement of problem project will address
5) copy of IRS Determination Letter
6) brief history of organization and description of its mission
7) copy of most recent annual report/audited financial statement/990
8) how project's results will be evaluated or measured
9) descriptive literature about organization
10) listing of board of directors, trustees, officers and other key people and their affiliations
11) detailed description of project and amount of funding requested
12) copy of current year's organizational budget and/or project budget

Proposals should indicate the organization's relationship with other organizations working to meet the same needs or providing similar services; the number of full-time paid staff, part-time paid staff, and volunteers; and why the organization is uniquely suited to address the problem.
Initial approach: Proposal
Copies of proposal: 1
Board meeting date(s): Quarterly
Deadline(s): Mar. 5, June 2, Sept. 1, and Nov. 29
Final notification: Within 1 month of board meetings
Officers and Directors:* Charley Nelson, Pres.; Veronica Sanderson, Secy.; Randall Wilson, Treas.; Teresa Olson, Admin.; Norma Christenson; Sheri Hank; Claire Krause; Al Nuness; Kris Thomson.
EIN: 411280587
Selected grants: The following grants are a representative sample of this grantmaker's funding activity:
$25,000 to American Red Cross, Minneapolis, MN, 2010.
$12,500 to Freedom Writers Foundation, Long Beach, CA, 2010.
$12,500 to Freedom Writers Foundation, Long Beach, CA, 2010.
$12,500 to Freedom Writers Foundation, Long Beach, CA, 2010.
$10,000 to Edina ABC Foundation, Edina, MN, 2010. For general operating expense.
$10,000 to La Oportunidad, Minneapolis, MN, 2010.
$8,000 to College Possible, Saint Paul, MN, 2010.
$5,000 to A Chance to Grow, Minneapolis, MN, 2010.
$5,000 to Keystone Community Services, Saint Paul, MN, 2010.
$5,000 to YouthCARE, Minneapolis, MN, 2010.

2068
Journal-Gazette Company
600 W. Main St.
P.O. Box 88
Fort Wayne, IN 46801-0088
(260) 461-8648

Company URL: http://www.journalgazette.net/
Establishment information: Established in 1950.
Company type: Private company
Business activities: Publishes newspapers.
Business type (SIC): Newspaper publishing and/or printing
Corporate officer: Gregory A. A. Johnson, C.F.O.
Giving statement: Giving through the Journal-Gazette Foundation, Inc.

Journal-Gazette Foundation, Inc.
701 S. Clinton St., Ste. 104
Fort Wayne, IN 46802-1883 (260) 424-5257

Establishment information: Established in 1985 in IN.
Donors: Journal-Gazette Co.; Richard G. Inskeep; Harriett J. Inskeep.
Contact: Jerry D. Fox, Secy.-Treas.
Financial data (yr. ended 12/31/11): Assets, $11,129,471 (M); gifts received, $20,000; expenditures, $484,196; qualifying distributions, $479,091; giving activities include $479,091 for grants.
Purpose and activities: The foundation supports zoological societies, parks and playgrounds, and food banks and organizations involved with arts and culture, education, health, cancer, child welfare, and human services.
Fields of interest: Historical activities; Arts; Higher education; Education; Zoos/zoological societies; Health care; Cancer; Crime/violence prevention, child abuse; Food banks; Recreation, parks/playgrounds; YM/YWCAs & YM/YWHAs; Children/youth, services; Human services; United Ways and Federated Giving Programs.
Type of support: Capital campaigns; General/operating support; Scholarship funds.
Geographic limitations: Giving limited to northeastern IN and northeastern OH.
Support limitations: No grants to individuals.
Application information: Applications accepted. Applicants should submit the following:
1) detailed description of project and amount of funding requested
Initial approach: Proposal
Board meeting date(s): Quarterly
Deadline(s): None
Officers and Directors:* Richard G. Inskeep*, Pres.; Jerry D. Fox, Secy.-Treas.; Gilmore S. Haynie, Jr.; Harriett J. Inskeep; Thomas R. Inskeep; Julie Inskeep Simpson.
EIN: 311134237
Selected grants: The following grants are a representative sample of this grantmaker's funding activity:
$11,500 to Indiana University Foundation, Bloomington, IN, 2010.

2069
Jovon Broadcasting Corporation

18600 Oak Park Ave.
Tinley Park, IL 60477-3980 (708) 633-0001

Establishment information: Established in 1981.
Company type: Private company
Business activities: Operates broadcasts television station.
Business type (SIC): Radio and television broadcasting
Corporate officer: Joseph Stroud, Chair. and Pres.
Board of director: Joseph Stroud, Chair.
Giving statement: Giving through the Stroud Foundation.

The Stroud Foundation

1900 Spring Rd.
Oak Brook, IL 60523 (630) 368-0511

Establishment information: Established in 2003.
Donor: Jovon Broadcasting Corporation.
Contact: Joseph A. Stroud, Pres.
Financial data (yr. ended 12/31/11): Assets, $1,143,203 (M); expenditures, $86,413; qualifying distributions, $70,000; giving activities include $70,000 for grants.
Purpose and activities: The foundation supports museums and organizations involved with music, higher education, children, and religion.
Fields of interest: Arts.
Type of support: Building/renovation; General/operating support; Scholarship funds.
Geographic limitations: Giving primarily in Chicago, IL.
Support limitations: No grants to individuals.
Application information: Applications accepted. Application form not required.
Initial approach: Letter of inquiry
Deadline(s): None
Officers: Joseph A. Stroud, Pres.; Yvonne M. Stroud, Secy.-Treas.
Directors: Amber Stroud; Vonesca Stroud.
EIN: 010793830
Selected grants: The following grants are a representative sample of this grantmaker's funding activity:
$5,000 to Chicago Jazz Philharmonic, Chicago, IL, 2009. For general support.

2070
Joy Global Inc.

(formerly Harnischfeger Industries, Inc.)
100 E. Wisconsin Ave., Ste. 2780
P.O. Box 554
Milwaukee, WI 53202-4127
(414) 319-8500
FAX: (302) 655-5049

Company URL: http://www.joyglobal.com
Establishment information: Established in 1884.
Company type: Public company
Company ticker symbol and exchange: JOY/NASDAQ
Business activities: Manufactures and markets underground mining machinery and surface mining equipment.
Business type (SIC): Machinery/construction, mining, and materials handling
Financial profile for 2012: Number of employees, 18,019; assets, $6,142,500,000; sales volume, $5,660,890,000; pre-tax net income, $1,105,130,000; expenses, $4,488,330,000; liabilities, $3,565,310,000
Fortune 1000 ranking: 2012—446th in revenues, 250th in profits, and 534th in assets
Forbes 2000 ranking: 2012—1318th in sales, 743rd in profits, and 1745th in assets
Corporate officers: John Nils Hanson, Chair.; Michael W. Sutherlin, Pres. and C.E.O.; Sean D. Major, Exec. V.P., Genl. Counsel, and Secy.; Dennis R. Winkleman, Exec. V.P., Admin.; Johan Maritz, V.P., Human Resources
Board of directors: John Nils Hanson, Chair.; Steven L. Gerard; John T. Gremp; Gale E. Klappa; Richard B. Loynd; P. Eric Siegert; Michael Sutherlin; James H. Tate
Subsidiaries: Harnischfeger Corp., Milwaukee, WI; Joy Technologies Inc., Warrendale, PA
International operations: China
Giving statement: Giving through the Joy Global Foundation, Inc.
Company EIN: 391566457

Joy Global Foundation, Inc.

(formerly Harnischfeger Industries Foundation)
P.O. Box 554
Milwaukee, WI 53201-0554

Establishment information: Established in 1989 in WI.
Donors: Harnischfeger Industries, Inc.; Joy Global Inc.
Contact: Sandy McKenzie
Financial data (yr. ended 10/31/11): Assets, $8,036,942 (M); expenditures, $650,211; qualifying distributions, $602,836; giving activities include $602,836 for grants.
Purpose and activities: The foundation supports organizations involved with arts and culture, education, health, medical research, and community development.
Fields of interest: Visual arts; Museums; Performing arts; Arts; Libraries/library science; Education; Health care; Medical research; Community development, neighborhood development; Community/economic development; Government/public administration.
Programs:
Civic and Community: The foundation supports programs designed to better the community, urban environment, public safety, and justice and the law; and promote public understanding of and participation in government and civic activities.
Culture and Humanities: The foundation supports programs designed to promote the vitality of the visual and performing arts; and stimulate and enrich the public intellectual experience, including libraries, museums, artistic performances, and other cultural activities.
Education: The foundation supports programs designed to foster and improve the knowledge and skills of individuals of all ages with the objective of enhancing their ability to achieve a better quality of life.
Health and Welfare: The foundation supports organizations involved with health and medical research and supports programs designed to treat and prevent disease; address nutrition, hygiene, and safety; and improve public health.
Type of support: Annual campaigns; Continuing support; General/operating support; Program development.
Geographic limitations: Giving primarily in areas of company operations in WI.
Support limitations: No support for religious organizations or institutions primarily supported by taxes or public lands. No grants to individuals.
Publications: Application guidelines.
Application information: Applications accepted. Personal visits and telephone calls are not encouraged. Application form not required. Applicants should submit the following:
1) statement of problem project will address
2) population served
3) copy of IRS Determination Letter
4) brief history of organization and description of its mission
5) copy of most recent annual report/audited financial statement/990
6) detailed description of project and amount of funding requested
Initial approach: Proposal
Copies of proposal: 1
Board meeting date(s): 2nd Mon. in Dec.
Deadline(s): None
Final notification: 90 days
Officers and Directors:* Michael W. Sutherlin*, Pres.; Dennis R. Winkleman*, V.P.; John D. Major*, Secy.; Kenneth J. Stark, Treas.; Edward I. Doheny II; Terry F. Nicola; Michael S. Olsen.
EIN: 391659070
Selected grants: The following grants are a representative sample of this grantmaker's funding activity:
$90,000 to Junior Achievement of Wisconsin, Milwaukee, WI, 2011.
$60,000 to Milwaukee Symphony Orchestra, Milwaukee, WI, 2011.
$25,000 to Betty Brinn Childrens Museum, Milwaukee, WI, 2011.
$25,000 to Boys and Girls Clubs of Greater Milwaukee, Milwaukee, WI, 2011.
$25,000 to Urban Ecology Center, Milwaukee, WI, 2011.
$20,000 to Childrens Hospital of Pittsburgh Foundation, Pittsburgh, PA, 2011.
$20,000 to Woodlands Foundation, Wexford, PA, 2011.
$14,500 to United Way of Greater Milwaukee, Milwaukee, WI, 2011. For annual campaign.
$14,500 to United Way of Greater Milwaukee, Milwaukee, WI, 2011. For annual campaign.
$10,000 to Lebanon, City of, Lebanon, KY, 2011.

2071
JPMorgan Chase & Co.

(formerly The Chase Manhattan Corporation)
270 Park Ave.
New York, NY 10017-2070 (212) 270-6000
FAX: (212) 270-1648

Company URL: http://www.jpmorganchase.com
Establishment information: Established in 1799.
Company type: Public company
Company ticker symbol and exchange: JPM/NYSE
International Securities Identification Number: US46625H1005
Business activities: Operates financial holding company; operates commercial bank.
Business type (SIC): Banks/commercial; holding company
Financial profile for 2012: Number of employees, 261,453; assets, $2,359,141,000,000; pre-tax net income, $28,917,000,000; liabilities, $2,155,072,000,000
Fortune 1000 ranking: 2012—18th in revenues, 4th in profits, and 2nd in assets
Forbes 2000 ranking: 2012—50th in sales, 12th in profits, and 9th in assets
Corporate officers: James Dimon, Chair., Pres., and C.E.O.; Matthew E. Zames, C.O.O.; Marianne Lake, C.F.O.; Anthony J. Horan, Secy.; Stephen M. Cutler, Genl. Counsel

Board of directors: James Dimon, Chair.; James A. Bell; Crandall C. Bowles; Stephen B. Burke; David M. Cote; James S. Crown; Timothy P. Flynn III; Ellen V. Futter; Laban P. Jackson, Jr.; Lee R. Raymond; William C. Weldon
Subsidiary: JPMorgan Chase Bank, N.A., New York, NY
Offices: Denver, CO; New Orleans, LA; Detroit, MI; Jackson, MS; Dallas, Houston, TX
International operations: Germany; Japan; Mexico; Singapore; Switzerland; United Kingdom
Historic mergers: The Chase Manhattan Corporation (March 31, 1996); J. P. Morgan & Co. Incorporated (December 31, 2000); Bank One Corporation (July 1, 2004)
Giving statement: Giving through the JPMorgan Chase & Co. Corporate Giving Program and the JPMorgan Chase Foundation.
Company EIN: 132624428

JPMorgan Chase & Co. Corporate Giving Program

(formerly The Chase Manhattan Bank Corporate Social Responsibility Program)
1111 Polaris Pkwy.
Columbus, OH 43240-7001
E-mail: corporate.secretary@jpmchase.com; URL: http://www.jpmorganchase.com/corporate/Corporate-Responsibility/corporate-responsibility.htm

Contact: Steven W. Gelston, V.P.
Purpose and activities: As a complement to its foundation, JPMorgan Chase also makes charitable contributions to nonprofit organizations directly. Special emphasis is directed toward organizations involved with community asset development, community life, and youth education.
Fields of interest: Media, film/video; Visual arts; Performing arts; Performing arts, dance; Performing arts, theater; Performing arts, music; Arts; Education, reform; Elementary/secondary education; Education; Employment, training; Employment; Housing/shelter; Human services; Civil rights, race/intergroup relations; Economic development; Nonprofit management; Community/economic development; Public policy, research; Public affairs Minorities; Economically disadvantaged.
Programs:
Arts and Culture: JPMorgan Chase supports programs designed to build arts audiences; promote the creation of new artistic work and encourage emerging artists; and support sustained arts in education programs in public schools.
Chase Community Giving: Through Chase Community Giving campaigns, JPMorgan Chase awards up to $5 million to be shared among 200 charities with grants ranging form $20,000 to $250,000. Charities are chosen and voted on by the public via Facebook.
Community Asset Development: JPMorgan Chase supports programs designed to promote public policies that effect the well-being of the community by stimulating economic growth and community development; and promote the effective management of nonprofits.
Community Development and Human Services: JPMorgan Chase supports programs designed to preserve and expand the supply of affordable housing; promote economic development, entrepreneurship, and the creation of entry-level jobs; and provide direct services to those most in need, especially the homeless, the hungry, the unemployed, and youth at risk.
Employee Matching Gifts: JPMorgan Chase matches contributions made by its employees to nonprofit organizations involved with arts and culture, education, natural resources conservation, health and human services, housing, and economic development on a one-for-one basis.
International Grants: JPMorgan Chase makes charitable contributions to nonprofit organizations located in approximately 50 countries where the company has a business presence involved with international development and relief. Support is also given to U.S.-based international organizations.
Pre-Collegiate Education: JPMorgan Chase supports programs designed to improve educational opportunity for K-12 students, primarily in public schools.
State Committees Program: Through the State Committees Program, JPMorgan Chase makes charitable contributions to nonprofit organizations located outside the Connecticut, New Jersey, and New York tri-state area involved with arts and culture, education, employment training, human services, and community development. Support is given primarily in Arizona, California, Delaware, Florida, Illinois, Louisiana, Massachusetts, and Ohio.
Type of support: Continuing support; Donated equipment; Employee matching gifts; Employee volunteer services; Equipment; General/operating support; In-kind gifts; Program development; Sponsorships; Technical assistance.
Geographic limitations: Giving primarily in the CT, NJ, and NY tri-state area, AZ, CA, CO, DE, FL, IL, IN, KY, LA, MI, OH, OK, TX, UT, WV, WI, and on an international basis in areas of company operations; giving also to national organizations and U.S.-based international organizations.
Support limitations: No support for religious, fraternal, or veterans' organizations, or United Way member organizations. No grants to individuals, or for medical research, fundraising events, debt reduction, deficit financing, capital endowments, scholarships, or tuition; generally no grants for health issues or higher education.
Publications: Application guidelines.
Application information: Applications accepted. Visit corporate website for details. The company has a staff that only handles contributions. A contributions committee at each company location reviews all requests originating from that particular area. Application form required.
Initial approach: Complete online eligibility quiz
Copies of proposal: 1
Deadline(s): Various
Final notification: Following review

The JPMorgan Chase Foundation

(formerly The Chase Manhattan Foundation)
270 Park Ave., 37th Fl.
New York, NY 10017-2014 (212) 270-0471
E-mail address for regional contacts: Asia and Pacific: ashley.lykins@jpmorgan.com; Africa, Europe, and the Middle East: kelly.j.lihaven@jpmchase.com; Argentina: paula.m.albin@jpmorgan.com; Brazil and Latin America: rentata.biselli@jpmorgan.com; Canada: darcy.k.delamere@jpmorgan.com; Chile: alejandra.x.gallo@jpmorgan.com; Colombia: lina.mora@jpmorgan.com; Mexico: olivia.zubieta@jpmorgan.com; and Peru: karla.a.stammer@jpmorgan.com; URL: http://www.jpmorganchase.com/corporate/Corporate-Responsibility/corporate-philanthropy.htm

Establishment information: Incorporated in 1969 in NY; name changed in 2001 as a result of the merger of Chase Manhattan Corp. with J.P. Morgan & Co. Inc.
Donors: The Chase Manhattan Bank; JPMorgan Chase Bank, N.A.; Chatham Ventures, Inc.; CMRCC, Inc.; Chemical Investments, Inc.; Bank One Investment Corp.
Contact: Kimberly B. Davis, Pres.
Financial data (yr. ended 12/31/11): Assets, $276,488,223 (M); gifts received, $214,917,536; expenditures, $139,437,312; qualifying distributions, $137,903,050; giving activities include $136,201,550 for 19,651 grants (high: $6,000,000; low: $1).
Purpose and activities: The foundation supports programs designed to promote affordable housing; economic development; financial empowerment; and workforce readiness. Special emphasis is directed toward neighborhoods located in areas of JPMorgan Chase major operations.
Fields of interest: Arts education; Museums; Museums (art); Arts; Education, reform; Elementary/secondary education; Higher education; Teacher school/education; Adult/continuing education; Education, services; Education, reading; Education; Employment, services; Employment, training; Employment; Food services; Housing/shelter, development; Housing/shelter, home owners; Housing/shelter; Youth development; YM/YWCAs & YM/YWHAs; Children/youth, services; Family services; Human services, financial counseling; Community development, neighborhood development; Economic development; Urban/community development; Community development, small businesses; Microfinance/microlending; Community/economic development; Financial services; Leadership development; Public affairs Economically disadvantaged.
Programs:
Affordable Housing: The foundation supports programs designed to address the need for transitional, permanent supportive, and affordable housing; disaster relief; and community-level models that stabilize neighborhoods, rehabilitate properties, and increase the supply of affordable housing. Special emphasis is directed toward permanent supportive housing, affordable rentals, and homeownership.
Economic Development: The foundation supports programs designed to promote new businesses and sustain existing businesses; promote economic development planning at a regional, state, and local level; and provide assistance to small businesses through incubators and accelerators, microfinance initiatives, and small business technical assistance and training.
Financial Empowerment: The foundation supports programs designed help individuals acquire the knowledge, skills, and tools needed to understand their finances, budget and increase their assets; and promote financial literacy education for young people and financial empowerment for adults, including initiatives that increase access to financial services, benefits utilization, and access to the Earned Income Tax Credit.
Workforce Readiness: The foundation supports programs designed to provide opportunities for individuals and companies to better compete in the global economy, with a focus on engaged youth (14-18 years old), disengaged youth (14-18), and adults (19+). Special emphasis is directed toward programs designed to provide knowledge, skills, and experiences needed to obtain jobs and help employers access skilled employees; STEM teacher training and curriculum development and college preparatory efforts for engaged youth; blended academic, internship, and mentor initiatives for disengaged youth to connect them to education and training pathways; and sector-specific training initiatives and subsidized employment programs to

help adults build the skills needed to find quality jobs.
Type of support: Building/renovation; Conferences/seminars; Continuing support; Curriculum development; Employee matching gifts; Employee volunteer services; General/operating support; Management development/capacity building; Program development; Program-related investments/loans; Sponsorships; Technical assistance.
Geographic limitations: Giving in areas of company operations in AZ, CA, CO, Washington, DC, DE, GA, ID, IL, IN, KY, LA, MI, MN, MO, NJ, NV, OH, OK, OR, PA, TX, UT, WA, WI, and WV, with emphasis on NY; giving also to U.S.-based international organizations active in areas of company operations abroad in Africa, Argentina, Asia, Brazil, Canada, Chile, Columbia, Europe, Latin America, Mexico, the Middle East, and Peru.
Support limitations: No support for religious, fraternal, social, or other membership organizations not of direct benefit to the entire community, athletic teams, health or medical-related organizations, discriminatory organizations, parent teacher associations, private schools, public agencies, or volunteer operated organizations. No grants to individuals, or for capital campaigns or endowments, scholarships or tuition assistance, advertising, fundraising, or debt reduction.
Publications: Application guidelines; Corporate giving report; Newsletter.
Application information: Applications accepted. A full proposal may be requested at a later date. Grants are administered by Community Relations Officers in each market region. Please visit website for regional contact information. Unsolicited applications from organizations in Europe, the Middle East, and Africa are currently not accepted. Application form required. Applicants should submit the following:
1) population served
2) geographic area to be served
3) copy of most recent annual report/audited financial statement/990
4) how project's results will be evaluated or measured
5) listing of board of directors, trustees, officers and other key people and their affiliations
6) detailed description of project and amount of funding requested
7) contact person
8) copy of current year's organizational budget and/or project budget

Initial approach: Complete online letter of inquiry form; non-U.S.-based organizations should e-mail a short preliminary proposal to regional grants coordinator
Deadline(s): None

EIN: 237049738
Selected grants: The following grants are a representative sample of this grantmaker's funding activity:
$5,000,000 to ACCION Texas, San Antonio, TX, 2010.
$2,000,000 to World Trade Center Memorial Foundation, New York, NY, 2010.
$1,100,000 to Enterprise Community Partners, Columbia, MD, 2010.
$1,000,000 to Robin Hood Foundation, New York, NY, 2010.
$605,000 to American Red Cross National Headquarters, Washington, DC, 2010.
$300,000 to Innovations for Learning, Evanston, IL, 2010.
$40,000 to Community Development Technologies Center, Los Angeles, CA, 2010.
$25,000 to Denver Public Schools Foundation, Denver, CO, 2010.
$25,000 to Museum of History and Industry, Seattle, WA, 2010.
$20,000 to Volunteers of America of North Louisiana, Shreveport, LA, 2010.

2072
JPMorgan Chase Bank, N.A.

(formerly The Chase Manhattan Bank)
270 Park Ave., 38th Fl.
New York, NY 10017 (212) 270-6000

Company URL: http://www.jpmorganchase.com
Establishment information: Established in 1799.
Company type: Subsidiary of a public company
Business activities: Operates commercial bank.
Business type (SIC): Banks/commercial
Corporate officers: James Dimon, Chair. and C.E.O.; Frank J. Bisignano, Co-C.O.O.
Board of director: James Dimon, Chair.
Historic mergers: The Bear Stearns Companies Inc. (May 30, 2008)
Giving statement: Giving through the JPMorgan Chase Foundation of Northwest Louisiana.

JPMorgan Chase Foundation of Northwest Louisiana

(formerly The One Foundation)
c/o JPMorgan Chase Bank, N.A.
P.O. Box 3038
Milwaukee, WI 53201-1308 (318) 226-2382
Application address: c/o JPMorgan Chase Bank, N.A., 400 Texas St., Shreveport, LA 71101-3525, tel.: (318) 226-2382

Establishment information: Incorporated in 1955 in LA.
Donors: Premier Bank, N.A.; Bank One, Louisiana, N.A.
Contact: Timothy D. Quinn
Financial data (yr. ended 12/31/11): Assets, $2,561,728 (M); expenditures, $177,955; qualifying distributions, $122,184; giving activities include $115,000 for 21 grants (high: $30,000; low: $1,000).
Purpose and activities: The foundation supports the Biomedical Research Foundation of Northwest in Shreveport, Louisiana.
Fields of interest: Medical research.
Type of support: Program development.
Support limitations: No grants to individuals.
Application information: Applications accepted. Application form not required. Applicants should submit the following:
1) copy of IRS Determination Letter

Initial approach: Proposal
Deadline(s): None

Officers: George D. Nelson, Jr., Pres.; John Peak, V.P.
Trustee: JPMorgan Chase Bank, N.A.
EIN: 726022876

2073
JSJ Corporation

700 Robbins Rd.
Grand Haven, MI 49417-2603
(616) 842-6350

Company URL: http://www.jsjcorp.com
Establishment information: Established in 1919.
Company type: Private company
Business activities: Designs, manufactures, and sells electromechanical products and office furniture.
Business type (SIC): Motor vehicles and equipment; furniture/office
Corporate officers: Nelson C. Jacobson, Chair., Pres., and C.E.O.; Lynne Sherwood, Vice-Chair. and Secy.; Barry Lemay, Sr. V.P. and C.O.O.; Martin R. Jennings, Sr. V.P. and C.F.O.; Dave De Young, V.P. and C.I.O.
Board of directors: Nelson C. Jacobson, Chair.; Lynne Sherwood, Vice-Chair.; Erick P. Johnson; Melinda Johnson, M.D.; David J. Killoran; Douglas A. Milroy; John P. Richardson, Jr.; William J. Schmuhl, Jr.; Ann E. Sherwood
Subsidiaries: Dake, Grand Haven, MI; GHSP Corp., Grand Haven, MI; Hudson Tool & Die Co., Inc., Ormond Beach, FL; izzy+, Spring Lake, MI; Mcloone Metal Graphics Inc., La Crosse, WI; Sparks Belting Co., Grand Rapids, MI
International operations: China; Japan; Mexico
Giving statement: Giving through the JSJ Foundation.

JSJ Foundation

700 Robbins Rd.
Grand Haven, MI 49417-2603 (616) 842-6350
FAX: (616) 847-3112;
E-mail: plowmand@jsjcorp.com; URL: http://www.jsjcorp.com/community/philanthropy/

Establishment information: Established in 1983 in MI.
Donor: JSJ Corp.
Contact: Lynne Sherwood, Chair.
Financial data (yr. ended 12/31/11): Assets, $440,010 (M); gifts received, $50,000; expenditures, $195,828; qualifying distributions, $193,709; giving activities include $193,709 for 37 grants (high: $31,740; low: $500).
Purpose and activities: The foundation supports organizations involved with arts and culture, education, health, human services, and civic affairs.
Fields of interest: Youth development; Human services; Philanthropy/voluntarism.
Type of support: Annual campaigns; Building/renovation; Capital campaigns; Continuing support; Endowments; General/operating support; Program development; Scholarship funds.
Geographic limitations: Giving primarily in areas of company operations in Florence, AL, Ormond Beach, FL, Middleburg, IN, Grand Haven and Grand Rapids, MI, and La Crosse, WI.
Support limitations: No support for political organizations or specific disease-related organizations. No grants to individuals, or for exchange programs, fellowships, internships, lectureships, professorships, or golf outings; no loans.
Publications: Application guidelines.
Application information: Applications accepted. Application form not required. Applicants should submit the following:
1) brief history of organization and description of its mission
2) copy of most recent annual report/audited financial statement/990
3) detailed description of project and amount of funding requested
4) copy of current year's organizational budget and/or project budget
5) listing of additional sources and amount of support

Initial approach: Proposal
Copies of proposal: 1
Board meeting date(s): Nov.
Deadline(s): None

Officers and Trustees:* Lynne Sherwood*, Chair.; Erick P. Johnson*, Secy.-Treas.; Nelson C. Jacobson; Bari S. Johnson; Melinda E. Johnson; Robert J. Mesereau; Mark F. Sherwood.
Number of staff: None.
EIN: 382421508
Selected grants: The following grants are a representative sample of this grantmaker's funding activity:
$24,400 to United Way, Greater Ottawa County, Holland, MI, 2009. For program support.
$16,700 to Loutit District Library, Grand Haven, MI, 2009. For new library.
$10,000 to Grand Haven Schools Foundation, Grand Haven, MI, 2009. For endowment.
$10,000 to Grand Rapids Symphony, Grand Rapids, MI, 2009. For operating support.
$10,000 to Hospice of North Ottawa Community, Spring Lake, MI, 2009.
$10,000 to Kandu, Inc., Holland, MI, 2009. For capital campaign.
$10,000 to Love INC of the Tri-Cities, Grand Haven, MI, 2009.
$10,000 to Tri-Cities Ministries, Grand Haven, MI, 2009.
$6,000 to West Michigan Symphony Orchestra, Muskegon, MI, 2009.

2074
JTB Americas, Ltd.

19700 Mariner Ave.
Torrance, CA 90503-1648 (310) 303-3750

Company URL: http://www.jtbamericas.com/Default.aspx
Establishment information: Established in 1988.
Company type: Subsidiary of a foreign company
Business activities: Operates travel agency; provides freight forwarding services; provides securities brokerage services.
Business type (SIC): Travel and tour arrangers; transportation services/freight; brokers and dealers/security
Financial profile for 2010: Number of employees, 100
Corporate officers: Yoshinori Himeno, Co-Pres. and C.E.O.; Tsuneo Irita, Co-Pres.
Giving statement: Giving through the JTB Cultural Exchange Corp.

JTB Cultural Exchange Corp.

19700 Mariner Ave., 2nd Fl.
Torrance, CA 90503-1648

Establishment information: Established in 1988 in NY.
Donor: JTB Americas, Ltd.
Financial data (yr. ended 12/31/11): Assets, $1,972,808 (M); expenditures, $122,392; qualifying distributions, $122,392; giving activities include $118,996 for 31 grants (high: $40,000; low: $1,000).
Purpose and activities: The foundation supports hospitals and festivals and organizations involved with arts and culture, education, business, and Japanese culture.
Fields of interest: Arts; Education; Agriculture/food.
Type of support: General/operating support.
Support limitations: No grants to individuals.
Application information: Applications not accepted. Unsolicited requests for funds not accepted.
Officers: Santoshi Inoue, Pres.; Francis W. Costello, Secy.; Shinji Nomiyama, Treas.
Director: Kazuharu Abe.
Number of staff: 1 part-time support.
EIN: 133456886

2075
Juniper Networks, Inc.

1194 N. Mathilda Ave.
Sunnyvale, CA 94089-1206 (408) 745-2000
FAX: (408) 745-2100

Company URL: http://www.juniper.net/us/en/
Establishment information: Established in 1996.
Company type: Public company
Company ticker symbol and exchange: JNPR/NYSE
International Securities Identification Number: US48203R1041
Business activities: Operates network infrastructure equipment company.
Business type (SIC): Computer and office equipment
Financial profile for 2012: Number of employees, 9,234; assets, $9,832,100,000; sales volume, $4,365,400,000; pre-tax net income, $291,500,000; expenses, $4,077,300,000; liabilities, $2,833,100,000
Fortune 1000 ranking: 2012—542nd in revenues, 600th in profits, and 393rd in assets
Forbes 2000 ranking: 2012—1463rd in sales, 1642nd in profits, and 1488th in assets
Corporate officers: Scott Kriens, Chair.; Pradeep S. Sindhu, Ph.D., Vice-Chair.; Kevin Johnson, C.E.O.; Robyn Denholm, Exec. V.P. and C.F.O.; Mitchell Gaynor, Exec. V.P., Genl. Counsel, and Secy.; Steven Rice, Exec. V.P., Human Resources
Board of directors: Scott Kriens, Chair.; Pradeep S. Sindhu, Ph.D., Vice-Chair.; Robert M. Calderoni; Mary B. Cranston; Kevin Johnson; Mercedes Johnson; J. Michael Lawrie; William Meehan; David Schlotterbeck; William R. Stensrud
Giving statement: Giving through the Juniper Networks, Inc. Contributions Program.
Company EIN: 770422528

Juniper Networks, Inc. Contributions Program

1194 N. Mathilda Ave.
Sunnyvale, CA 94089-1206 (408) 745-2000
E-mail: community-relations@juniper.net.; URL: http://www.juniper.net/us/en/company/citizenship-sustainability/community/

Purpose and activities: Juniper Networks, Inc. makes charitable contributions to nonprofit organizations directly. Support is given primarily in areas of company operations; giving also to national and international organizations.
Fields of interest: Disasters, preparedness/services; General charitable giving.
Type of support: Employee matching gifts; Employee volunteer services; General/operating support; In-kind gifts.
Geographic limitations: Giving primarily in areas of company operations; giving also to national and international organizations.

2076
Juno Healthcare Staffing System, Inc.

411 5th Ave., Ste. 805
New York, NY 10016 (212) 685-5866

Company URL: http://www.junohealthcare.com
Establishment information: Established in 2001.
Company type: Private company
Business activities: Operates healthcare staffing company.
Business type (SIC): Personnel supply services
Corporate officers: Dante Raul Teodoro, Pres.; Nonette Teodoro, C.E.O.
Giving statement: Giving through the Foundation for God's Glory.

Foundation for God's Glory

411 Fifth Ave., Ste. 805
New York, NY 10016
E-mail: charmaine@fggonline.org; URL: http://www.fggonline.org/

Establishment information: Established in 2005 in NY.
Donor: Juno Healthcare Staffing.
Financial data (yr. ended 12/31/11): Assets, $7,126 (M); gifts received, $1,798; expenditures, $1,917; qualifying distributions, $1,808.
Purpose and activities: The foundation supports organizations involved with education, hunger relief, disaster relief in economically and environmental-distressed communities, and Christianity and awards scholarships to individuals for evangelism study.
Fields of interest: Education; Food services; Disasters, preparedness/services; Christian agencies & churches Economically disadvantaged.
Type of support: General/operating support; Grants to individuals.
Application information: Applications not accepted. Unsolicited requests for funds not accepted.
Directors: Charmaine Teodoro; Dante Teodoro; Nonita Teodoro.
EIN: 571209618

2077
Just Born, Inc.

1300 Stefko Blvd.
Bethlehem, PA 18017 (610) 867-7568
FAX: (610) 867-9931

Company URL: http://www.justborn.com
Establishment information: Established in 1923.
Company type: Private company
Business activities: Produces confectionery products.
Business type (SIC): Sugar, candy, and salted/roasted nut production
Financial profile for 2011: Number of employees, 500
Corporate officers: Ross J. Born, Co-C.E.O.; David N. Shaffer, Co-C.E.O.; David L. Yale, Pres. and C.O.O.; Rob Sweatman, V.P., Opers.; Greg Barratt, V.P., Sales and Mktg.
Plant: Philadelphia, PA
Giving statement: Giving through the Just Born, Inc. Corporate Giving Program.

Just Born, Inc. Corporate Giving Program

c/o Corp. Affairs Dept.
1300 Stefko Blvd.
Bethlehem, PA 18017-6672
FAX: (610) 867-3983; E-mail: grants@justborn.com; E-mail for candy donations: candydonations@justborn.com; URL: http://www.justborn.com/get-to-know-us/corporate-citizenship/donations

Contact: Cindy Glick
Purpose and activities: Just Born makes charitable contributions to nonprofit organizations involved with health and human services, primary and secondary education, arts and cultural events, community development, and environmental education. Special emphasis is directed towards programs designed to promote the health and well-being of children and their families. Support is limited to National Harbor, Maryland, and Lehigh and Northampton counties, Pennsylvania.
Fields of interest: Arts; Elementary/secondary education; Environmental education; Health care; Family services; Human services; Community/economic development; General charitable giving Children.
Type of support: Donated products; Employee volunteer services; General/operating support.
Geographic limitations: Giving limited to National Harbor, MD, and Lehigh and Northampton counties, PA; giving limited to Lehigh and Northampton counties, PA for candy donations.
Support limitations: No support for veterans', labor, or political organizations, fraternal, athletic, social clubs or organizations, churches or religious organizations, or political campaigns. No grants to individuals.
Publications: Application guidelines.
Application information: Applications accepted. The Corporate Affairs Department handles giving. Application form not required. Applicants should submit the following:
1) results expected from proposed grant
2) name, address and phone number of organization
3) copy of IRS Determination Letter
4) brief history of organization and description of its mission
5) how project's results will be evaluated or measured
6) listing of board of directors, trustees, officers and other key people and their affiliations
7) detailed description of project and amount of funding requested
8) contact person
9) copy of current year's organizational budget and/or project budget

Applications for candy donations should indicate the date, purpose, and expected attendance of the event.
Initial approach: Proposal to headquarters; mail or fax proposal to headquarters for candy donations
Copies of proposal: 1
Deadline(s): June 30 and Dec. 4; 4 weeks prior to need for candy donations
Final notification: Sept. and Mar.
Number of staff: 2 full-time professional; 1 full-time support.

2078
Justacip Inc.

(doing business as Nukepills.com)
631 Brawley School Rd., Ste. 407
P.O. Box 165
Mooresville, NC 28117-6204
(866) 283-3986

Establishment information: Established in 1999.
Company type: Private company
Business activities: Operates emergency preparedness retail distribution comapany.
Business type (SIC): Drugs
Corporate officer: Troy Jones, Pres.
Giving statement: Giving through the Justacip Inc. Corporate Giving Program.

Justacip Inc. Corporate Giving Program

(doing business as Nukepills.com Corporate Giving Program)
(also known as Nukepills.com Corporate Giving Program)
PMB #165
631 Brawley School Rd., Ste. 407
Mooresville, NC 28117-6204 (866) 283-3986
E-mail: info@nukepills.com; URL: http://nukepills.com/contact_about.htm

2079
JustNeem, LLC

120 Dry Ave.
Cary, NC 27511 (919) 414-8826

Company URL: http://www.JustNeem.com
Establishment information: Established in 2007.
Company type: Private company
Business type (SIC): Business services/miscellaneous
Corporate officers: Peter Radtke, Chair. and C.E.O.; Magda Radtke, C.O.O.
Board of director: Peter Radtke, Chair.
Giving statement: Giving through the JustNeem, LLC Contributions Program.

JustNeem, LLC Contributions Program

120 Dry Ave.
Cary, NC 27511-3313 (919) 414-8826
E-mail: info@justneem.com; URL: http://www.JustNeem.com

Purpose and activities: JustNeem is a certified B Corporation that donates a percentage of profits to charitable organizations. Support is given primarily in Mauritania, West Africa.
Fields of interest: Community/economic development.
Type of support: General/operating support; Program development.
Geographic limitations: Giving primarily in Mauritania, West Africa.

2080
K&L Gates LLP

K&L Gates Ctr.
210 6th Ave.
Pittsburgh, PA 15222-2613 (412) 355-6500

Company URL: http://www.klgates.com
Company type: Private company
Business activities: Operates law firm.
Business type (SIC): Legal services
Offices: Anchorage, AK; Irvine, Los Angeles, Palo Alto, San Diego, San Francisco, CA; Washington, DC; Miami, FL; Chicago, IL; Boston, MA; Newark, NJ; New York, NY; Charlotte, Morrisville, Raleigh, NC; Portland, OR; Harrisburg, Pittsburgh, PA; Austin, Dallas, Fort Worth, TX; Seattle, Spokane, WA
International operations: Belgium; China; France; Germany; Hong Kong; Japan; Poland; Russia; Singapore; Taiwan; United Arab Emirates; United Kingdom
Giving statement: Giving through the K&L Gates LLP Pro Bono Program.

K&L Gates LLP Pro Bono Program

K&L Gates Ctr.
210 6th Ave.
Pittsburgh, PA 15222-2613 (717) 231-4500
FAX: (717) 231-4501;
E-mail: carleton.strouss@klgates.com; Additional tel.: (412) 355-6500, fax: (412) 355-6501; URL: http://www.klgates.com

Contact: Carleton Strouss, Partner
Fields of interest: Legal services.
Type of support: Pro bono services - legal.
Geographic limitations: Giving primarily in areas of company operations in Anchorage, AK, Irvine, Los Angeles, Palo Alto, San Diego, and San Francisco, CA, Washington, DC, Miami, FL, Chicago, IL, Boston, MA, Charlotte, Morrisville, and Raleigh, NC, Newark, NJ, New York, NY, Portland, OR, Harrisburg and Pittsburgh, PA, Austin, Dallas, and Fort Worth, TX, and Seattle and Spokane, WA, and in Belgium, China, France, Germany, Hong Kong, Japan, Poland, Qatar, Russia, Singapore, Taiwan, United Arab Emirates, and United Kingdom.

2083
Kadant Johnson Inc.

(formerly The Johnson Corporation)
805 Wood St.
Three Rivers, MI 49093-1053
(269) 278-1715

Company URL: http://www.kadant.com/
Establishment information: Established in 1933.
Company type: Subsidiary of a public company
Business activities: Manufactures industrial valves and pipe fittings and other parts, industrial machinery, and process control instruments.
Business type (SIC): Metal products/fabricated; metal products/structural; machinery/general industry; machinery/industrial and commercial; laboratory apparatus
Corporate officers: Jonathan W. Painter, Pres. and C.E.O.; Thomas M. O'Brien, Exec. V.P. and C.F.O.; Eric T. Langevin, Exec. V.P. and C.O.O.; Sandra L. Lambert, V.P., Genl. Counsel, and Secy.; Michael J. McKenney, V.P., Finance and C.A.O.; Wesley A. Martz, V.P., Mktg.; Daniel J. Walsh, Treas.
Subsidiaries: Johnson Export Corp., Three Rivers, MI; Specialty Castings, Inc., Springport, MI
Giving statement: Giving through the Kadant Johnson, Inc. Scholarship Foundation.

Kadant Johnson, Inc. Scholarship Foundation

(formerly Johnson Corporation Scholarship Foundation)
805 Wood St.
Three Rivers, MI 49093-1053
Application address: 700 6th Ave., Three Rivers, MI 49093
Application address: Three Rivers High School Guidance Office, 700 Sixth Ave., Three Rivers, MI 49093

Donors: The Johnson Corp.; Kadant Johnson; Kadant Johnson, Inc.
Financial data (yr. ended 06/30/12): Assets, $206 (M); gifts received, $10,800; expenditures, $10,800; qualifying distributions, $10,800; giving activities include $10,800 for grants to individuals.
Purpose and activities: The foundation awards college scholarships to graduates of Three Rivers High School in Michigan who are planning to attend a Michigan institution to pursue studies in engineering, dentistry, nursing, medicine, teaching, or science.
Fields of interest: Dental school/education; Medical school/education; Nursing school/education; Teacher school/education; Engineering school/education.
Type of support: Scholarships—to individuals.
Geographic limitations: Giving limited to Three Rivers, MI.
Application information: Applications accepted. Application form required.
Initial approach: Proposal
Deadline(s): Apr. 16
Officer: Greg Wedel, Chair.
EIN: 386098327

2084
M. B. Kahn Construction Co., Inc.

101 Flintlake Dr.
P.O. Box 1179
Columbia, SC 29223 (803) 736-2950

Company URL: http://www.mbkahn.com
Establishment information: Established in 1927.
Company type: Private company
Business activities: Provides nonresidential general contract construction services.
Business type (SIC): Contractors/general nonresidential building
Corporate officers: Alan B. Kahn, Chair.; William H. Neely, Pres. and C.E.O.; Robert A. Chisholm, V.P. and C.F.O.; Ronald L. McCall, V.P. and Treas.; L. Davis Petty, Jr., V.P., Opers.
Board of director: Alan B. Kahn, Chair.
Giving statement: Giving through the M. B. Kahn Foundation, Inc.

M. B. Kahn Foundation, Inc.

P.O. Box 1608
Columbia, SC 29202-1608

Establishment information: Established in 1964 in SC.
Donor: M.B. Kahn Construction Co., Inc.
Financial data (yr. ended 09/30/11): Assets, $143,926 (M); gifts received, $190,418; expenditures, $73,845; qualifying distributions, $73,543; giving activities include $73,543 for 40 grants (high: $15,000; low: $100).
Purpose and activities: The foundation supports organizations involved with arts and culture, education, health, diabetes, golf, and Christianity.
Fields of interest: Arts; Higher education; Education; Health care; Diabetes; Athletics/sports, golf; Jewish federated giving programs; Christian agencies & churches.
Type of support: Annual campaigns; Building/renovation; Capital campaigns; Debt reduction; Endowments; General/operating support; Professorships; Research; Scholarship funds; Seed money.
Geographic limitations: Giving primarily in SC; giving also to national organizations on a case by case basis.
Support limitations: No grants to individuals.
Application information: Applications not accepted. Contributes only to pre-selected organizations.
Officer: Alan B. Kahn, Pres.
EIN: 576024465
Selected grants: The following grants are a representative sample of this grantmaker's funding activity:
$10,000 to Healthy Learners, Columbia, SC, 2010. For general use.
$9,000 to Richland School District Two, Columbia, SC, 2010. For general use.
$6,666 to Midlands Housing Alliance, Columbia, SC, 2010. For general use.
$5,000 to River Alliance, Columbia, SC, 2010. For general use.
$4,000 to Epworth Childrens Home, Columbia, SC, 2010. For general use.
$1,000 to Cooperative Ministry, Columbia, SC, 2010. For general use.
$1,000 to Keep the Midlands Beautiful, Columbia, SC, 2010. For general use.
$1,000 to Palmetto Family Council, Columbia, SC, 2010. For general use.
$1,000 to Palmetto Health Foundation, Columbia, SC, 2010. For general use.
$1,000 to Sistercare, Columbia, SC, 2010. For general use.

2085
Kahn-Lucas-Lancaster, Inc.

112 W. 34th St., Ste. 600
New York, NY 10120-0700 (212) 244-4500

Company URL: http://www.kahnlucas.com
Establishment information: Established in 1889.
Company type: Private company
Business activities: Manufactures children's clothing.
Business type (SIC): Apparel—girls' and children's outerwear; apparel—men's and boys' outerwear; apparel—women's outerwear
Financial profile for 2009: Number of employees, 80
Corporate officers: Andrew L. Kahn, Chair.; Howard Kahn, C.E.O.; John Zander, C.F.O.
Board of director: Andrew L. Kahn, Chair.
Giving statement: Giving through the Kahn Foundation, Inc.

Kahn Foundation, Inc.

c/o Kahn Lucas Lancaster
805 Estelle Dr., Ste. 101
Lancaster, PA 17601

Establishment information: Established in 1987 in NY.
Donors: Kahn-Lucas-Lancaster, Inc.; Andrew Kahn.
Financial data (yr. ended 12/31/11): Assets, $204,070 (M); expenditures, $43,806; qualifying distributions, $43,677; giving activities include $43,677 for 10 grants (high: $30,000; low: $200).
Purpose and activities: The foundation supports organizations involved with health, cancer, and human services.
Fields of interest: Hospitals (general); Health care, clinics/centers; Health care; Cancer; Cancer, leukemia; Human services, gift distribution; Human services.
Type of support: General/operating support.
Geographic limitations: Giving primarily in New York, NY.
Support limitations: No grants to individuals.
Application information: Applications not accepted. Unsolicited requests for funds not accepted.
Directors: Andrew Kahn; Peggy Anne Kahn; John Zander.
EIN: 236343794

2086
Kaiser Permanente

1 Kaiser Plz.
21 Bayside
Oakland, CA 94612 (510) 752-1000

Company URL: https://www.kaiserpermanente.org
Establishment information: Established in 1945.
Company type: Private company
Business activities: Operates managed healthcare system.
Business type (SIC): Hospitals; insurance/accident and health
Financial profile for 2009: Number of employees, 164,098; sales volume, $42,100,000,000
Corporate officers: George C. Halvorson, Chair. and C.E.O.; Bernard J. Tyson, Pres. and C.O.O.; Kathy Lancaster, Exec. V.P. and C.F.O.; Philip Fasano, Exec. V.P. and C.I.O.; Mark S. Zemelman, Sr. V.P. and Genl. Counsel
Board of directors: George C. Halvorson, Chair.; Christine K. Cassel, M.D.; Thomas W. Chapman; Daniel P. Garcia; William R. Graber; J. Eugene Grigsby III, Ph.D.; Judith A. Johansen; Kim J. Kaiser; Philip A. Marineau; Jenny J. Ming; Edward Pei; Meg Porfido; Cynthia A. Telles; Bernard J. Tyson
Giving statement: Giving through the Kaiser Permanente Corporate Giving Program, the Kaiser Permanente for the Mid-Atlantic States Corporate Giving Program, the Kaiser Permanente for the Southern California Region, the Kaiser Permanente Northern California Regional Community Grants Program, the Kaiser Permanente of Colorado (Colorado Springs) Corporate Giving Program, the Kaiser Permanente of Colorado (Denver/Boulder) Corporate Giving Program, the Kaiser Permanente of Georgia Community Benefit Program, the Kaiser Permanente of Hawaii Corporate Giving Program, the Kaiser Permanente of Ohio Corporate Giving Program, and the Kaiser Permanente of the Northwest Corporate Giving Program.

Kaiser Permanente Corporate Giving Program

1 Kaiser Plz.
Oakland, CA 94612 (510) 271-5800
URL: http://xnet.kp.org/newscenter/aboutkp/community-benefit.html

Purpose and activities: As a complement to its regional corporate giving programs, Kaiser Permanente also makes charitable contributions to nonprofit organizations directly.
Fields of interest: Public health, obesity; Public health, physical fitness; Health care; Nutrition; Disasters, preparedness/services.

Type of support: Advocacy; General/operating support; Technical assistance.

Kaiser Permanente of the Northwest Corporate Giving Program

c/o Community Benefit
500 N.E. Multnomah St., Ste. 100
Portland, OR 97232-2009 (503) 813-3575
FAX: (503) 813-4235;
E-mail: community.benefit@kp.org; E-mail for Amy Fernandes, Scholarship Prog. Coord.: kpnwscholarship@gmail.com.; URL: http://info.kp.org/communitybenefit/html/our_communities/northwest/our_communities_8.html

Purpose and activities: Kaiser Permanente of the Northwest makes grants and donations to nonprofit organizations that promote physical, mental, and social health through coverage for low-income people, safety net partnerships, community health initiatives, developing and disseminating knowledge, and civic engagement. Emphasis is given to programs that build greater health capacity and sustainability. Support is limited to northwest Oregon and southwest Washington.
Fields of interest: Health care, public policy; Health care, equal rights; Medical care, community health systems; Public health; Health care; Mental health/crisis services; Health organizations, public education; Public affairs Economically disadvantaged.
Programs:
Kaiser Permanente Community Giving Campaign: This program provides matching funds for private donations to any community organization of the employee's choosing - locally, regionally, nationally, or internationally.
Kaiser Permanente Gives-Volunteer Grant Program: This program makes $5,000 to $15,000 in grant funding available to qualified charitable organizations to which Kaiser Permanente employees and clinicians donate their time. Applications for Kaiser Permanente Gives grants are reviewed quarterly by a committee of Kaiser Permanente volunteers. Applications must be submitted by the community organization, not by a Kaiser Permanente employee. Qualification is limited to charitable organizations that facilitate basic needs and self-sufficiency programs and those in which a company employee or employee team has volunteered 25 hours.
The Kaiser Permanente Health Care Career Scholarship Program: Kaiser Permanente, in partnership with Oregon Health Career Center, awards at least one scholarship in the amount of $2,000 to high schools seniors at 113 schools who are pursuing careers in the health care field. Applicants must attend schools located in the Kaiser Permanente Northwest service area, which spans from north of Longview, Washington, to Corvallis, Oregon. Preference is given to students who demonstrate financial need and/or are first-generation college-bound, bilingual, or from an ethnic or racial minority group underrepresented in a health profession.
Type of support: Annual campaigns; Employee volunteer services; Equipment; General/operating support; In-kind gifts.
Geographic limitations: Giving limited to areas of company operations in northwest OR and southwest WA.
Publications: Application guidelines.
Application information: Applications accepted. Applicants should submit the following:
1) copy of IRS Determination Letter
2) brief history of organization and description of its mission
3) copy of most recent annual report/audited financial statement/990
4) listing of board of directors, trustees, officers and other key people and their affiliations
5) detailed description of project and amount of funding requested
6) copy of current year's organizational budget and/or project budget

Recipients of equipment donations are required to sign a bill of sale at the time of donation, and send a letter of acknowledgement within 30 days.
Initial approach: Complete online application for grants and scholarships; E-mail, mail, or fax letter of request (e-mail is preferred) for equipment donations
Deadline(s): Jan. 18 for scholarships; Feb. 6, May 1, Aug. 2, and Oct. 28 for Kaiser Permanente Gives
Final notification: Late April for scholarships; 60 days for Kaiser Permanente Gives; 6 weeks for equipment donations

Kaiser Permanente for the Mid-Atlantic States Corporate Giving Program

(also known as Kaiser Foundation Health Plan of the Mid-Atlantic States, Inc.)
c/o Kaiser Permanente Community Benefit
2101 E. Jefferson St.
Rockville, MD 20852 (301) 816-5879
FAX: (301) 816-7119;
E-mail: MAS-CommunityBenefit@kp.org; Sponsorships: Parveen Burchick, tel.: (301) 816-5879, e-mail: Parveen.K.Burchick@kp.org; Grants: Laura Howard, tel.: (301) 816-6404, e-mail: Laura.J.Howard@kp.org; Community Health Initiatives: Celeste James, tel.: (301) 816-6496, e-mail: Celeste.A.James@kp.org; Care & Coverage Programs: DeShanta Strother, tel.: (301) 816-6417, e-mail: DeShanta.A.Strother@kp.org; Safety Net Partnerships: Mindy Rubin, tel.: (301) 816-6405, e-mail: Mindy.R.Rubin@kp.org; Educational Theater Programs: Michelle Bland, tel.: (301) 902-1210, e-mail: Michelle.L.Bland@kp.org; URL: http://info.kp.org/communitybenefit/html/our_communities/mid-atlantic/our_communities_7_a.html

Purpose and activities: Kaiser Permanente for the Mid-Atlantic States provides charitable donations to nonprofit organizations that work to improve health among individuals by changing the environments in which people live and play. Emphasis is given to programs that work to prevent obesity and chronic illness, bolster community safety net clinics, and encourage research and training. Giving is limited to areas of company operations.
Fields of interest: Public health school/education; Health sciences school/education; Education; Public health; Public health, obesity; Health care; Food banks; Housing/shelter, volunteer services; Residential/custodial care, hospices Economically disadvantaged.
Type of support: Conferences/seminars; Employee volunteer services; General/operating support; Sponsorships; Technical assistance.
Geographic limitations: Giving limited to areas of company operations.
Publications: Application guidelines; Corporate giving report.
Application information: Applications accepted. Mid-Atlantic Medical Centers' Community Service Teams handle volunteer efforts. Application form required.
Initial approach: Complete online application for sponsorships
Committee meeting date(s): Monthly
Deadline(s): 60 days prior to need for sponsorships, and by the end of the last business day of the month; check website for updated information for grants

Kaiser Permanente for the Southern California Region

c/o Community Benefit Grants Prog.
Kaiser Permanente Public Affairs Off.
393 E. Walnut St., 2nd Fl.
Pasadena, CA 91188-0001 (626) 405-5999
E-mail: so.cal.grants@kp.org; CareActors tel.: (818) 546-4447; Educational Theatre Prog. tel.: (818) 546-4470, e-mail: ETPinfo@kp.org, URL: http://www.kp.org/etp; Watts Counseling and Learning Center tel.: (323) 568-2265; Baldwin Park EOP tel.: (626) 851-5183; Medical Financial Assistance tel.: (866) 399-7696; URL: http://info.kp.org/communitybenefit/html/our_communities/southern-california/our_communities_2_a.html

Purpose and activities: Kaiser Permanente of Southern California Region supports nonprofit organizations that offer direct healthcare services or address public policy aimed at improving community health. Emphasis is given to programs that provide care and coverage to low-income families, offer safety net partnerships and community health initiatives, and develop and disseminate knowledge. Support is limited to areas of company operations in Southern California.
Fields of interest: Elementary/secondary education; Health care, public policy; Medical care, community health systems; Public health; Public health, obesity; Health care, financing; Health care; AIDS; Nutrition; Housing/shelter, homeless; Children, services; Aging, centers/services Economically disadvantaged.
Type of support: Capital campaigns; General/operating support; In-kind gifts; Management development/capacity building; Sponsorships.
Geographic limitations: Giving limited to areas of company operations in southern CA.
Support limitations: No support for political or discriminatory organizations. Generally no support for international, social, or recreational clubs. No grants to individuals, or for golf tournaments, sports teams, religious purposes, endowments, or memorials; or for events, programs, or activities that are organized or solely sponsored by alcohol, tobacco, or pharmaceutical companies.
Publications: Application guidelines.
Application information: Applications accepted. The Community Benefit department handles giving. A full proposal may be requested at a later date. Letter of inquiry should be submitted using company letterhead and signed by the chief executive(s), limited to 2 single-spaced pages with 12-point font and 1-inch margins, and submitted by e-mail in PDF format or by mail. Faxes are not accepted. Application form not required. Applicants should submit the following:
1) timetable for implementation and evaluation of project
2) population served
3) name, address and phone number of organization
4) copy of IRS Determination Letter
5) brief history of organization and description of its mission
6) geographic area to be served
7) detailed description of project and amount of funding requested
8) contact person
9) copy of current year's organizational budget and/or project budget

Letters of interest should include a statement of need.

Initial approach: Letter of inquiry
Deadline(s): None
Final notification: 90 days

Kaiser Permanente Northern California Regional Community Grants Program

c/o Community Rels.
Kaiser Permanente Community Involvement Prog., Northern California Region
1950 Franklin St., 3rd Fl.
Oakland, CA 94612-5129 (510) 987-2490
E-mail: NCAL-CB-Programs@kp.org; E-mail for regional sponsorship requests: NCAL-Community-Involvement@kp.org; Kaiser Permanente Community Rels. tel.: (510) 987-2490; URL: http://info.kp.org/communitybenefit/html/our_communities/northern-california/our_communities_1_a.html

Purpose and activities: Kaiser Permanente Northern California supports organizations that provide critical health and human services to vulnerable populations, including the safety net of community clinics, public hospitals, and health care systems, and assist individuals in gaining access to health care and coverage. Support is limited to areas of company operations in northern California.
Fields of interest: Health care, public policy; Health care, equal rights; Public health; Public health, obesity; Health care; Heart & circulatory diseases; Diabetes; Aging, centers/services; Human services Economically disadvantaged.
Type of support: Employee volunteer services; General/operating support; In-kind gifts; Sponsorships.
Geographic limitations: Giving limited to areas of company operations in northern CA.
Support limitations: No support for religious, political, fraternal, athletic, international, or social organizations. No grants to individuals, or for endowments, memorials, or field trips or tours.
Publications: Application guidelines; Corporate giving report.
Application information: Applications accepted. Visit website for links to 13 local Community Benefit programs for grant requests. For regional sponsorships, submit a cover letter on company letterhead stating the project title and amount requested. Application form required. Applicants should submit the following:
1) copy of IRS Determination Letter
2) list of company employees involved with the organization

Regional sponsorship proposals should include a letter from a fiscal agent, if applicable, and state any previous funding from the company.

Initial approach: Letter of inquiry to local center for grants; E-mail or mail proposal for regional event sponsorship requests
Deadline(s): None
Final notification: 4 to 6 months

Kaiser Permanente of Colorado (Colorado Springs) Corporate Giving Program

1975 Research Pkwy., Ste. 250
Colorado Springs, CO 80920-1054 (719) 262-1516
E-mail: mia.n.ramirez@kp.org; Kristi Keolakai, Community and Local Govt. Rels., Grants Coord.: tel.: (303) 344-7352, e-mail: kristi.x.keolakai@kp.org; Kaci Jensen, Community and Local Govt. Rels., Educational Theatre Coord., tel.: (303) 344-7259, e-mail: kaci.l.jensen@kp.org; Russell Taylor, Community and Local Govt. Rels., Volunteer Coord., tel.: (303) 344-7447, e-mail: russell.h.taylor@kp.org; Gordon Loui, Community and Local Govt. Rels., other Kaiser Permanente Colorado community benefit questions, tel.: (303) 344-7252, e-mail: gordon.loui@kp.org.; URL: http://info.kp.org/communitybenefit/html/our_communities/colorado-coloradosprings/our_communities_4.html

Contact: Mia Ramirez, Sr. Community Health Specialist
Purpose and activities: Kaiser Permanente of Colorado Springs supports nonprofit organizations that aim to improve health among individuals by improving community health. Emphasis is given to programs that are evidence, population and/or prevention-based, cost-effective, collaborative, and seek to create sustainable systems improvements. Support is limited to areas of company operations in Colorado.
Fields of interest: Elementary/secondary education; Health care, public policy; Medicine/medical care, public education; Public health; Public health, obesity; Public health, physical fitness; Health care, financing; Health care Economically disadvantaged.
Type of support: Employee volunteer services; General/operating support; In-kind gifts.
Geographic limitations: Giving limited to areas of company operations in CO.
Application information: Applications not accepted. At this time, Kaiser Permanente Colorado's grantmaking is by invitation only or through strategic Request for Proposals.

Kaiser Permanente of Colorado (Denver/Boulder) Corporate Giving Program

c/o Contribs. Coord.
10350 E. Dakota Ave.
Denver, CO 80247-1314 (303) 344-7352
E-mail: kristi.x.keolakai@kp.org; Arlene Rapal, Community Benefit & Rels., Educational Theatre Coordination, tel.: (303) 789-7143; e-mail: arlene.s.rapal@kp.org; Gordon Loui, Community Benefit & Rels., Community Svc. (Volunteer) and Special Events Coord., tel.: (303) 344-7252, e-mail: gordon.loui@kp.org; Russell Taylor, Community Benefit & Rels. Comms. Consultant, General Community Benefit Questions, (303) 344-7447; e-mail: russell.h.taylor@kp.org; URL: http://info.kp.org/communitybenefit/html/our_communities/colorado-denver-boulder/our_communities_3.html

Contact: Kristi Keolakai, Community Benefit & Rels., Grants Coordination
Purpose and activities: Kaiser Permanente of Colorado supports nonprofit organizations that offer direct healthcare services or address public policy aimed at improving community health. Special emphasis is directed toward care and coverage for low-income families, safety net partnerships, community health initiatives, and the development and dissemination of knowledge. Support is limited to areas of company operations in the Boulder, Denver, and Longmont, Colorado metropolitan areas.
Fields of interest: Health care, public policy; Health care, equal rights; Public health; Health care Economically disadvantaged.
Type of support: Conferences/seminars; Employee matching gifts; General/operating support; Sponsorships.
Geographic limitations: Giving limited to areas of company operations in the Boulder, Denver, and Longmont, CO, metropolitan areas.
Application information: Applications not accepted. At this time, Kaiser Permanente Colorado's grantmaking is by invitation only or through strategic Requests for Proposals.

Kaiser Permanente of Georgia Community Benefit Program

(also known as Kaiser Foundation Health Plan of Georgia, Inc. Community Benefit Program)
9 Piedmont Ctr
3495 Piedmont Rd., N.E.
Atlanta, GA 30305-1736 (404) 279-4636
FAX: (404) 364-4797;
E-mail: emily.r.kimble@kp.org; URL: http://www.kpgagives.org

Contact: Emily R. Kimble, Community Benefit
Financial data (yr. ended 12/31/11): Total giving, $12,032,274, including $12,032,274 for grants.
Purpose and activities: Kaiser Permanente of Georgia makes contributions to nonprofit organizations, schools, and government agencies to improve access to healthcare, inform health policy, and implement programs that promote and improve health. Special emphasis is directed toward health-impacting projects that align with funding priorities. Support is limited to areas of company operations in the greater Atlanta, Georgia area.
Fields of interest: Health care; Food services; Nutrition; Human services Economically disadvantaged.
Type of support: Program development.
Geographic limitations: Giving limited to areas of company operations in Barrow, Bartow, Butts, Carroll, Cherokee, Clarke, Clayton, Cobb, Coweta, Dawson, DeKalb, Douglas, Fayette, Forsyth, Fulton, Gwinnett, Hall, Haralson, Heard, Henry, Lamar, Meriwether, Newton, Paulding, Pickens, Pike, Rockdale, Spalding, and Walton counties, GA.
Support limitations: No support for political, religious, or discriminatory organizations, private foundations, or sports teams. No grants to individuals, or for capital campaigns or school yearbook ads.
Publications: Annual report; Application guidelines; Grants list.
Application information: Applications accepted. The Regional Office, Public Affairs Department handles giving. The company has a staff that only handles contributions. A contributions committee reviews all requests. Application form required. Applicants should submit the following:
1) how project will be sustained once grantmaker support is completed
2) results expected from proposed grant
3) statement of problem project will address
4) population served
5) copy of IRS Determination Letter
6) copy of most recent annual report/audited financial statement/990
7) how project's results will be evaluated or measured
8) listing of board of directors, trustees, officers and other key people and their affiliations
9) detailed description of project and amount of funding requested
10) copy of current year's organizational budget and/or project budget

Initial approach: Complete online Letter of Intent (LOI)
Copies of proposal: 1
Committee meeting date(s): Varies
Deadline(s): Varies
Final notification: 3 months

Number of staff: 3 full-time professional.

Kaiser Permanente of Hawaii Corporate Giving Program

c/o Nina Miyata, Community Benefit
2828 Paa St.
Honolulu, HI 96819 (808) 432-5673
E-mail: Nina.Y.Miyata@kp.org; URL: http://info.kp.org/communitybenefit/html/our_communities/hawaii/our_communities_6.html

Contact: Nina Miyata
Purpose and activities: Kaiser Permanente of Hawaii supports nonprofit organizations that work to improve access to health care, influence public policy, and develop programs that promote healthy living. Special emphasis is directed toward care and coverage for low-income families, safety net partnerships, community health initiatives, and the development and dissemination of knowledge. Support is limited to Hawaii.
Fields of interest: Health care, public policy; Medicine/medical care, public education; Health care, formal/general education; Dental care; Public health; Public health, obesity; Public health, physical fitness; Health care, financing; Health care; Food banks; Nutrition; Children, services; Aging, centers/services; Homeless, human services Economically disadvantaged.
Type of support: Employee volunteer services; General/operating support; In-kind gifts; Sponsorships.
Geographic limitations: Giving limited to HI.
Support limitations: No support for political, or religious organizations, or sports teams. No grants to individuals, or for golf tournaments, endowments, memorials, or events or activities sponsored by alcohol or tobacco corporations.
Publications: Application guidelines; Corporate giving report.
Application information: Applications accepted. Application form must be submitted as a PDF document. Application form required. Applicants should submit the following:
1) timetable for implementation and evaluation of project
2) results expected from proposed grant
3) name, address and phone number of organization
4) copy of IRS Determination Letter
5) brief history of organization and description of its mission
6) copy of most recent annual report/audited financial statement/990
7) how project's results will be evaluated or measured
8) listing of board of directors, trustees, officers and other key people and their affiliations
9) detailed description of project and amount of funding requested
10) contact person
11) listing of additional sources and amount of support

Applications should include a copy of the organization's nondiscrimination policy, a statement of need, an explanation of the project's goals, objectives, and activities, potential conflicts of interest, expected number of beneficiaries, and whether the company contributed in the prior year.
Initial approach: Download application and submit completed form with required attachments via e-mail and mail

Kaiser Permanente of Ohio Corporate Giving Program

(also known as Kaiser Permanente of Ohio Thriving Communities Grants Program)
c/o Thriving Communities Grant Program
1001 Lakeside Ave.
Cleveland, OH 44114 (216) 621-5600
E-mail: Jennifer.A.Prather@kp.org; Tel. for Jennifer Prather, Sr. Coord., Charitable Progs. and Grantmaking: (216) 479-5774; Merle R. Gordon, Mgr., Community Benefit, tel.: (216) 479-5532, e-mail: merle.r.gordon@kp.org; Amy Tulenson, Sr. Coord., Community Benefit Progs., tel.: (216) 479-5662, e-mail: amy.tulenson@kp.org; URL: http://info.kp.org/communitybenefit/html/our_communities/ohio/our_communities_9_a.html

Contact: Jennifer A. Prather, Sr. Coord., Charitable Progs. and Grantmaking
Purpose and activities: Kaiser Permanente of Ohio provides charitable donations to nonprofit organizations that work to improve the health and wellness of individuals, families, and communities. Emphasis is given to programs that combat obesity, promote active lifestyles, increase access to healthy food and health care, and impact low-income communities with a history of health disparities. Support is limited to areas of company operations in Cuyahoga, Geauga, Lake, Lorain, Medina, Portage, Stark, Summit, and Wayne counties in northeast OH.
Fields of interest: Health care, public policy; Public health; Public health, physical fitness; Health care; Children, services; Family services Children; Economically disadvantaged.
Type of support: Continuing support; General/operating support; Management development/capacity building; Program development; Seed money.
Geographic limitations: Giving limited to areas of company operations in Cuyahoga, Geauga, Lake, Lorain, Medina, Portage, Stark, Summit, and Wayne counties in northeast OH.
Support limitations: No support for organizations that have been in existence for less than two years, organizations that are out of compliance with registration or financial reporting laws, discriminatory, or political organizations, religious organizations not of direct benefit to the entire community, foundations or organizations that are grantmaking entities, or organizations affiliated with terrorist activities. No grants for contests, raffles, pageants, sports tournaments, or other prize-oriented events, capital campaigns, charitable special events such as luncheons, dinners, or golf outings, individual or team projects, special event advertising, mass mailings or printing, trips or tours, political fundraising events, or endowments.
Publications: Application guidelines.
Application information: Applications accepted. Additional information and/or a site visit may be required. Contributions are limited to one donation per organization during any given year. Grant information for 2013 will be posted in December 2012. Documents must be uploaded in .doc or .xls formats. Application form required. Applicants should submit the following:
1) timetable for implementation and evaluation of project
2) results expected from proposed grant
3) statement of problem project will address
4) population served
5) brief history of organization and description of its mission
6) geographic area to be served
7) how project's results will be evaluated or measured
8) explanation of why grantmaker is considered an appropriate donor for project
9) descriptive literature about organization
10) listing of board of directors, trustees, officers and other key people and their affiliations
11) detailed description of project and amount of funding requested
12) plans for cooperation with other organizations, if any
13) copy of current year's organizational budget and/or project budget

Proposals should include an explanation of the organization's goals, a project title, the number of expected beneficiaries, the program strategy and organizational capacity, anticipated barriers to success, potential conflicts of interest with the company, and the development status of the project. Letters of support are optional.
Deadline(s): Apr. 2, 2012; Aug. 27, 2012

2087
Kajima International, Inc.

3475 Piedmont Rd., N.E., Ste. 1600
Atlanta, GA 30305 (404) 564-3900
FAX: (404) 564-3901

Company URL: http://www.kajimausa.com
Establishment information: Established in 1961.
Company type: Subsidiary of a private company
Business activities: Provides general contract construction services.
Business type (SIC): Contractors/general nonresidential building; contractors/plumbing, heating, and air-conditioning; motion pictures/production and services allied to; engineering, architectural, and surveying services
Corporate officers: Hideya Marugame, Pres. and C.E.O.; Michael Reinhard, V.P., Sales; Sean F. Shinichiro, V.P., Mktg.; Katsushi Norihama, Treas.
Giving statement: Giving through the Kajima Foundation, Inc.

Kajima Foundation, Inc.

3475 Piedmont Rd., Ste. 1600
Atlanta, GA 30305-2993 (404) 564-3900

Establishment information: Established in 1990 in NJ.
Donor: Kajima International, Inc.
Contact: Leia J. Wolfe
Financial data (yr. ended 12/31/11): Assets, $616,477 (M); expenditures, $49,289; qualifying distributions, $46,516; giving activities include $34,500 for 21 grants (high: $3,000; low: $500).
Purpose and activities: The foundation supports organizations involved with Japanese culture, education, leukemia, and children's services, and awards college scholarships.
Fields of interest: Arts, cultural/ethnic awareness; Elementary/secondary education; Higher education; Education; Cancer, leukemia; Children, services Asians/Pacific Islanders.
Program:
Scholarships: The foundation awards college scholarships to students attending the University of Michigan. The program is administered by the National Merit Scholarship Corp.
Type of support: General/operating support; Program development; Scholarship funds; Scholarships—to individuals.
Geographic limitations: Giving primarily in areas of company operations, with emphasis on Atlanta, GA and New York, NY.
Application information: Applications accepted. Application form required.

Initial approach: Proposal
Deadline(s): Bimonthly
Officers: Keisuke Koshijima, Co-Pres.; Noriaki Ohashi, Co-Pres.; Marvin J. Suomi, Secy.; Mitsuyoshi Tamura, Treas.
EIN: 521675796

2088
Kaman Corporation

1332 Blue Hills Ave.
P.O. Box 1
Bloomfield, CT 06002 (860) 243-7100
FAX: (860) 243-6365

Company URL: http://www.kaman.com
Establishment information: Established in 1945.
Company type: Public company
Company ticker symbol and exchange: KAMN/NYSE
Business activities: Manufactures aircraft structures and components, advanced aerospace technology products, and helicopters; sells industrial products wholesale; sells musical instruments and accessories wholesale.
Business type (SIC): Industrial machinery and equipment—wholesale; aircraft and parts; durable goods—wholesale
Financial profile for 2012: Number of employees, 5,007; assets, $1,096,990,000; sales volume, $1,592,830,000; pre-tax net income, $80,830,000; expenses, $1,499,990,000; liabilities, $676,800,000
Corporate officers: Neal J. Keating, Chair., Pres., and C.E.O.; William C. Denninger, Exec. V.P. and C.F.O.; Ronald M. Galla, Sr. V.P. and C.I.O.; Candace A. Clark, Sr. V.P. and Secy.; Shawn G. Lisle, Sr. V.P. and Genl. Counsel; Gregory T. Troy, Sr. V.P., Human Resources; Robert D. Starr, V.P. and Treas.; Michael J. Morneau, V.P. and Cont.; John J. Tedone, V.P., Finance
Board of directors: Neal J. Keating, Chair.; Brian E. Barents; E. Reeves Callaway III; Karen M. Garrison; A. William Higgins; Neal J. Keating; Eileen S. Kraus; Scott E. Kuechle; George E. Minnich, Jr.; Thomas W. Rabaut; Richard J. Swift
Subsidiaries: Kaman Aerospace Group, Inc., Bloomfield, CT; Kaman Industrial Technologies Corp., Bloomfield, CT; Kaman Music Corp., Bloomfield, CT
Giving statement: Giving through the Kaman Corporation Contributions Program and the Fidelco Guide Dog Foundation, Inc.
Company EIN: 060613548

Kaman Corporation Contributions Program

1332 Blue Hills Ave.
Bloomfield, CT 06002-0001
FAX: (860) 243-6365; E-mail: rhj-corp@kaman.com; Mailing address: P.O. Box 1, Bloomfield, CT 06002-0001

Contact: Russell H. Jones, Sr. V.P., Treas., and C.I.O.
Purpose and activities: Kaman makes charitable contributions to nonprofit organizations involved with education, employment, human services, and disabled people. Support is given primarily in the greater Hartford, Connecticut, area.
Fields of interest: Education, reading; Education; Employment; Children/youth, services; Human services Disabilities, people with.
Type of support: Annual campaigns; Building/renovation; Capital campaigns; Continuing support; Employee-related scholarships; General/operating support; Program development.
Geographic limitations: Giving primarily in the greater Hartford, CT, area.
Support limitations: No support for state-supported organizations or United Way-supported organizations. No grants for endowments, galas or events, or advertising.
Application information: Applications not accepted. Contributes only to pre-selected organizations. The Treasury Department handles giving.
Number of staff: 1 part-time professional.

Fidelco Guide Dog Foundation, Inc.

103 Old Iron Ore Rd.
Bloomfield, CT 06002-1424 (860) 243-5200
E-mail: info@fidelco.org; URL: http://www.fidelco.org

Establishment information: Established in 1962 in CT.
Financial data (yr. ended 12/31/11): Revenue, $3,590,473; assets, $20,530,009 (M); gifts received, $2,902,817; expenditures, $4,243,586.
Purpose and activities: The foundation breeds, trains and places German Shepherd guide dogs with people who have visual disabilities.
Fields of interest: Blind/visually impaired.
Program:
Guide Dog Program: Gifts of guide dogs are available to the legally blind. Orientation and mobility training may be required of applicants before they can be considered for a guide dog.
Type of support: Grants to individuals.
Geographic limitations: Giving on a national basis.
Application information: Applications accepted. Interview is required before final approval. Application form required.
Initial approach: Download application online
Deadline(s): Ongoing
Officers and Directors:* Stephen H. Matheson*, Chair.; John H. Gotta*, Vice-Chair.; Eliot D. Russman*, C.E.O.; Glynis Cassis*, Secy.; Mary P. Craig, DVM, MBA*, Treas.; G. Kenneth Bernhard; Mark T. Bertolini; Cindy Cooper; Louise C. England; Pamela K. Goodling; Lillian F. Johnson; Hon. M. Jodi Rell.
EIN: 066060478

2089
Kanaly Trust Co. Inc.

5555 San Felipe, Ste. 200
Houston, TX 77056 (713) 561-9300

Company URL: http://www.kanaly.com
Establishment information: Established in 1975.
Company type: Private company
Business activities: Operates trust company.
Business type (SIC): Trusts
Corporate officers: Drew Kanaly, Chair. and C.E.O.; W. Scott Hill, Sr. V.P. and C.F.O.; James Shelton, C.I.O.
Board of director: Drew Kanaly, Chair.
Giving statement: Giving through the Kanaly Foundation.

The Kanaly Foundation

c/o Kanaly Trust, LTA
5555 San Felipe, Ste. 200
Houston, TX 77056-3143 (713) 626-9483

Establishment information: Established in 1992 in TX.
Donors: Kanaly Trust Co. Inc.; E. Deane Kanaly; Virginia L. Kanaly; Kanaly Family Trust.
Contact: Jeffrey C. Kanaly, Tr.
Financial data (yr. ended 12/31/11): Assets, $967,956 (M); expenditures, $86,423; qualifying distributions, $81,000; giving activities include $81,000 for 4 grants (high: $50,000; low: $1,000).
Purpose and activities: The foundation supports art museums and organizations involved with medical education, multiple sclerosis, and human services.
Fields of interest: Arts; Health organizations; Human services.
Type of support: General/operating support; Scholarship funds.
Geographic limitations: Giving primarily in Houston, TX.
Support limitations: No grants to individuals.
Application information: Applications accepted. Application form not required.
Initial approach: Proposal
Deadline(s): None
Trustees: Andrew D. Kanaly; Jeffrey C. Kanaly; Steven P. Kanaly; Virginia L. Kanaly.
EIN: 760381632

2090
S. Kann Sons Co.

2 Wisconsin Cir., Ste. 630
Chevy Chase, MD 20815-7058
(301) 986-1949

Establishment information: Established in 1893.
Company type: Private company
Business activities: Operates holding company.
Business type (SIC): Holding company
Corporate officer: Bernei Burgunder, Pres.
Giving statement: Giving through the S. Kann Sons Company Foundation, Inc.

S. Kann Sons Company Foundation, Inc.

2 Wisconsin Cir., Ste. 630
Chevy Chase, MD 20815-7058

Establishment information: Established in 1945 in MD.
Donors: S. Kann Sons Co.; B. Bernei Burgunder, Sr.‡; B. Bernei Burgunder, Jr.; Selma K. Burgunder‡; Gertrude Kann‡; Sol Kann‡.
Contact: B. Bernei Burgunder, Jr., Pres.
Financial data (yr. ended 12/31/11): Assets, $1,595,884 (M); expenditures, $113,737; qualifying distributions, $82,950; giving activities include $82,950 for 69 grants (high: $12,000; low: $200).
Purpose and activities: The foundation supports organizations involved with arts and culture, health, human services, international human rights, intergroup and race relations, and Judaism.
Fields of interest: Arts; Hospitals (general); Health care; Children/youth, services; Family services; Human services; International human rights; Civil rights, race/intergroup relations; United Ways and Federated Giving Programs; Jewish federated giving programs; Jewish agencies & synagogues.
Type of support: Annual campaigns; Building/renovation; Capital campaigns; Endowments; General/operating support; Program development.
Geographic limitations: Giving primarily in MD.
Support limitations: No grants to individuals.
Application information: Applications accepted. Application form not required.
Initial approach: Proposal

Board meeting date(s): June and Dec.
Deadline(s): None
Officers: B. Bernei Burgunder, Jr., Pres.; Kay B. Stevens, V.P.; Amelie B. Burgunder, Secy.
EIN: 520794594

2091
Kansas City Chiefs Football Club, Inc.
1 Arrowhead Dr.
Kansas City, MO 64129-1651
(816) 920-9300
FAX: (816) 923-4719

Company URL: http://www.kcchiefs.com
Establishment information: Established in 1959.
Company type: Private company
Business activities: Operates professional football club.
Business type (SIC): Commercial sports
Corporate officers: Clark K. Hunt, Chair. and C.E.O.; Mark Donovan, Pres.; Dan Crumb, C.F.O.; Bill Chapin, Sr. V.P., Opers.
Board of director: Clark K. Hunt, Chair.
Giving statement: Giving through the Kansas City Chiefs Football Club, Inc. Corporate Giving Program and the Hunt Family Foundation.

Kansas City Chiefs Football Club, Inc. Corporate Giving Program
c/o Community Rels. Dept.
1 Arrowhead Dr.
Kansas City, MO 64129-1651 (816) 920-9300
FAX: (816) 923-4719; URL: http://www.kcchiefs.com/community/index.html

Contact: Janet Feltham
Purpose and activities: The Kansas City Chiefs make charitable contributions of memorabilia to nonprofit organizations on a case by case basis. Support is limited to Kansas and Missouri.
Fields of interest: General charitable giving.
Type of support: In-kind gifts.
Geographic limitations: Giving limited to KS and MO.
Support limitations: No monetary contributions, or game tickets, footballs, or team jerseys.
Application information: Applications accepted. Support is limited to 1 contribution per organization during any given year. Application form not required. Applicants should submit the following:
1) name, address and phone number of organization
2) copy of IRS Determination Letter
3) contact person
Applications should include the date and description of the event.
Initial approach: Mail or fax proposal to headquarters
Copies of proposal: 1
Deadline(s): 30 days prior to need

Hunt Family Foundation
1 Arrowhead Dr.
Kansas City, MO 64129-1651 (816) 920-9300

Establishment information: Established in 1983 in MO as a company-sponsored operating fund.
Donors: Kansas City Chiefs Football Club, Inc.; The National Football League; NFL Charities; Youth Football Fund; Chiefs Red Coat / Red Friday; Teammates for Kids Foundation.
Contact: Dan Crumb, V.P. and Treas.
Financial data (yr. ended 01/31/11): Assets, $801,918 (M); gifts received, $86,667; expenditures, $423,232; qualifying distributions, $79,291; giving activities include $55,118 for 30 grants (high: $10,000; low: $500).
Purpose and activities: The foundation supports organizations involved with education, football, and children and youth.
Fields of interest: Education; Human services.
Type of support: General/operating support.
Geographic limitations: Giving limited to the Kansas City, MO area.
Support limitations: No support for private businesses. No support for.
Application information: Applications accepted. Application form required. Applicants should submit the following:
1) copy of IRS Determination Letter
2) detailed description of project and amount of funding requested
Initial approach: Letter
Deadline(s): None
Officers and Directors:* Clark Hunt*, Pres.; Dan Crumb, V.P. and Treas.; James T. Seigfreid*, Secy.; Lee A. Derrough; Lamar Hunt, Jr.
EIN: 431299453

2092
Kansas City Power & Light Company
1200 Main St.
Kansas City, MO 64105-2122
(816) 556-2200

Company URL: http://www.kcpl.com
Establishment information: Established in 1882.
Company type: Subsidiary of a public company
Business activities: Generates, transmits, and distributes electricity.
Business type (SIC): Electric services
Corporate officers: Michael J. Chesser, Chair.; William H. Downey, Pres.; Scott H. Heidtbrink, C.O.O.; James C. Shay, C.F.O.; William G. Riggins, Genl. Counsel
Board of director: Michael J. Chesser, Chair.
Subsidiaries: Red Hill Coal Co., Kansas City, MO; Utility Fuel Co., Kansas City, MO; Wymo Fuels, Inc., Kansas City, MO
Giving statement: Giving through the Kansas City Power & Light Company Contributions Program.
Company EIN: 440308720

Kansas City Power & Light Company Contributions Program
c/o Corp. Contribs.
1200 Main St.
Kansas City, MO 64105-2122 (816) 556-2200
E-mail: comments@kcpl.com; URL: http://www.kcpl.com/community/commun.html

Purpose and activities: Kansas City Power & Light makes charitable contributions to nonprofit organizations involved with at-risk youth, the environment, and economic development. Support is limited to areas of company operations in Kansas and Missouri.
Fields of interest: Environment; Youth development; Community/economic development.
Type of support: Employee volunteer services; General/operating support; Program development.
Geographic limitations: Giving limited to areas of company operations in KS and MO.
Support limitations: No support for athletic organizations or disease-specific organizations. No grants to individuals or for journal advertising.
Publications: Application guidelines.
Application information: Applications accepted. A contributions committee reviews all requests. Application form required. Applicants should submit the following:
1) population served
2) copy of IRS Determination Letter
3) brief history of organization and description of its mission
4) detailed description of project and amount of funding requested
5) contact person
6) copy of current year's organizational budget and/or project budget
7) listing of additional sources and amount of support
Initial approach: Complete online application form
Deadline(s): 3 to 6 months prior to need

2093
Kansas City Royals Baseball Corporation
Kauffman Stadium, 1 Royal Way
Kansas City, MO 64129 (816) 921-8000

Company URL: http://kansascity.royals.mlb.com
Establishment information: Established in 1969.
Company type: Private company
Business activities: Operates professional baseball club.
Business type (SIC): Commercial sports
Corporate officers: David D. Glass, Chair.; Dan Glass, Pres.; Kevin Uhlich, Sr. V.P., Opers.; David Laverentz, V.P., Finance, and Admin.; Michael Bucek, V.P., Mktg.; Michael Swanson, V.P., Comms.; Dan Crabtree, Genl. Counsel
Board of directors: David D. Glass, Chair.; Dan Glass; Ruth Glass; Don Glass; Dayna Martz; Julia Irene Kauffman
Giving statement: Giving through the Kansas City Royals Baseball Corporation Contributions Program.

Kansas City Royals Baseball Corporation Contributions Program
c/o Donations Request
P.O. Box 419969
Kansas City, MO 64141-6969
E-mail: communityrelations@royals.mlb.com; URL: http://kansascity.royals.mlb.com/NASApp/mlb/kc/community/index.jsp

Purpose and activities: The Kansas City Royals make charitable contributions of memorabilia and game tickets to nonprofit organizations involved with underprivileged and at-risk youth, senior citizens, and medically dependent and disabled people. Support is given primarily in the bi-state Kansas City area.
Fields of interest: Breast cancer; Athletics/sports, baseball; Boys & girls clubs; General charitable giving Youth; Aging; Disabilities, people with; Economically disadvantaged.
Programs:
Buck O'Neil Legacy Seat Contest: Through the Buck O'Neil Legacy Seat Contest, the Royals fills a "Buck Seat" for every home game with a member of the community who, on a large or small scale, embodies an aspect of Buck's spirit. Buck Seat honorees will also be featured during the Fox Sports Kansas City broadcasts of home Royals games.

Father of the Year: The Royals, in partnership with the National Center for Fathering, sponsors a "What My Father Means to Me" essay contest in Kansas City schools. The winning authors and their fathers are treated to a game and are recognized during a pre-game ceremony.

Royals Community Ticket Program: The Royals provides game tickets to nonprofit organizations to enhance the lives of underprivileged and at-risk youth, the medically dependent or disabled, and senior citizens.

Royals Speakers Bureau: Through the Royals Speakers Bureau Program, the Royal staff and alumni speak at civic and charitable functions.

Royals Troopers: Through Royal Troopers, the Royals hosts select children who have a parent deployed through the United States military effort overseas. The children join the Royals Ground Crew, help prepare the field prior to the game, and receive game tickets and Royal merchandise.

Type of support: Donated products; In-kind gifts; Income development; Loaned talent.
Geographic limitations: Giving primarily in areas of company operations in the bi-state Kansas City area.
Support limitations: No support for No support in the form of non-fundraising game ticket donations for schools or church groups.
Publications: Application guidelines; Grants list.
Application information: Applications accepted. The Community Relations Department handles giving. Application form required.

Initial approach: Download application form and mail to headquarters for memorabilia and game ticket donations for fundraising, Royals Speakers Bureau, and the Royals Community Ticket Program; complete online nomination form for Buck O'Neil Legacy Seat
Copies of proposal: 1
Deadline(s): 1 month prior to need for memorabilia and game ticket donations for fundraising and the Royals Speakers Bureau; None for Royals Community Ticket Program; Dec. 12 to Sept. 13 for Buck O'Neil Legacy Seat
Final notification: 4 weeks for Royals Community Ticket Program

2094
Kansas City Southern

(formerly Kansas City Southern Industries, Inc.)
427 W. 12th St.
Kansas City, MO 64105 (816) 983-1303

Company URL: http://www.kcsouthern.com
Establishment information: Established in 1887.
Company type: Public company
Company ticker symbol and exchange: KSU/NYSE
Business activities: Operates holding company; provides railroad transportation services.
Business type (SIC): Transportation/railroad; holding company
Financial profile for 2012: Number of employees, 6,110; assets, $6,395,900,000; sales volume, $2,238,600,000; pre-tax net income, $616,400,000; expenses, $1,542,800,000; liabilities, $3,299,300,000
Fortune 1000 ranking: 2012—865th in revenues, 420th in profits, and 518th in assets
Forbes 2000 ranking: 2012—1745th in sales, 1206th in profits, and 1723rd in assets
Corporate officers: Michael R. Haverty, Chair.; David L. Starling, Pres. and C.E.O.; Michael W. Upchurch, Exec. V.P. and C.F.O.; David R. Ebbrecht, Exec. V.P. and C.O.O.; Warren K. Erdman, Exec. V.P., Admin.; Patrick J. Ottensmeyer, Exec. V.P., Sales and Mktg.; Mary K. Stadler, Sr. V.P. and C.A.O.; Michael J. Naatz, Sr. V.P. and C.I.O.; John E. Derry, Sr. V.P., Human Resources; Michael W. Cline, V.P. and Treas.; Adam J. Godderz, Secy.
Board of directors: Michael R. Haverty, Chair.; Lu M. Cordova; Henry R. Davis; Robert J. Druten; Terrence P. Dunn; Antonio O. Garza, Jr.; Thomas A. McDonnell; Rodney E. Slater; David L. Starling
Subsidiary: The Kansas City Southern Railway Co., Kansas City, MO
International operations: Cayman Islands; Mexico; Panama
Giving statement: Giving through the Kansas City Southern Charitable Fund.
Company EIN: 440663509

The Kansas City Southern Charitable Fund

(formerly Kansas City Southern Industries, Inc. Corporate Giving Program)
P.O. Box 219335
Kansas City, MO 64121-9335
FAX: (816) 983-1590;
E-mail: dcarlson@kcsouthern.com; URL: http://www.kcsouthern.com/en-us/AboutKCS/Pages/CharitableGiving.aspx

Contact: C. Doniele Carlson, Asst. V.P., Corp. Comms. and Community Affairs
Purpose and activities: Kansas City Southern makes charitable contributions to nonprofit organizations involved with arts and culture, education, health, human services, community development, and on a case by case basis. Support is given primarily in areas of company operations.
Fields of interest: Arts; Education; Health care; Human services; Community/economic development; General charitable giving.
Program:

Employee Matching Gifts: Kansas City Southern matches contributions made by its employees to nonprofit organizations.

Type of support: Annual campaigns; Capital campaigns; Emergency funds; Employee matching gifts; Employee volunteer services; Equipment; General/operating support; In-kind gifts; Sponsorships.
Geographic limitations: Giving primarily in areas of company operations, with emphasis on Kansas City, MO.
Support limitations: No support for religious, fraternal, or social organizations. No grants to individuals.
Application information: Applications accepted. The Administration and Corporate Affairs Department handles giving. A contributions committee reviews all requests. Application form not required.
Applicants should submit the following:
1) results expected from proposed grant
2) name, address and phone number of organization
3) copy of IRS Determination Letter
4) listing of board of directors, trustees, officers and other key people and their affiliations
5) detailed description of project and amount of funding requested
6) contact person

Proposals should include the organization's fax number, e-mail address, and website address, if available.

Initial approach: Proposal to headquarters
Copies of proposal: 1
Committee meeting date(s): Monthly
Deadline(s): None
Final notification: 1 month

2095
Kappler Safety Group, Inc.

55 Grimes Dr.
P.O. Box 490
Guntersville, AL 35976-9364
(256) 505-4005
FAX: (256) 505-4151

Company URL: http://www.kappler.com/contact_main.html
Establishment information: Established in 1986.
Company type: Private company
Business activities: Manufactures protective garments.
Business type (SIC): Medical instruments and supplies
Corporate officers: George Kappler, C.E.O.; Barbara Stone, C.I.O.
Giving statement: Giving through the Kappler Foundation, Inc.

The Kappler Foundation, Inc.

P.O. Box 490
Guntersville, AL 35976-0490

Establishment information: Established in 1996 in AL.
Donors: Kappler Safety Group, Inc.; Kappler USA, Inc.; Kappler, Inc.
Financial data (yr. ended 12/31/11): Assets, $312 (M); expenditures, $691; qualifying distributions, $0.
Purpose and activities: The foundation supports organizations involved with arts and culture, education, health, substance abuse prevention, housing, and human services.
Type of support: Building/renovation; General/operating support.
Geographic limitations: Giving limited to Guntersville, AL.
Support limitations: No grants to individuals.
Application information: Applications not accepted. Unsolicited requests for funds not accepted.
Officers and Director: George P. Kappler, Jr.*, Pres.; Laura Kappler-Roberts*, Secy.-Treas.; Gale N. Kappler.
EIN: 631131995

2096
KarMART Automotive Group

(also known as KarMart USA Superstores)
660 Auto Blvd.
Burlington, WA 98233 (800) 721-8537

Company URL: http://www.karmart.com
Establishment information: Established in 1985.
Company type: Private company
Business activities: Operates car dealership.
Business type (SIC): Motor vehicles—retail
Corporate officers: Bob Campbell, Pres.; Roxanne Terre Berry, Cont.
Giving statement: Giving through the Karmart for Kids Foundation.

Karmart for Kids Foundation

P.O. Box 570
Burlington, WA 98233-0570 (888) 617-7485
Additional address: 660 Auto Blvd., Burlington, WA 98233; URL: http://www.karmartforkids.com

Establishment information: Established in 2007.
Donors: Cascade Chrysler, Inc.; KarMART Automotive Group.

Financial data (yr. ended 12/31/11): Assets, $5,809 (M); gifts received, $12,500; expenditures, $10,140; qualifying distributions, $8,874; giving activities include $8,874 for grants.
Purpose and activities: The foundation supports organizations involved with education, reproductive health, recreation, and human services.
Fields of interest: Education; Recreation; Religion.
Type of support: General/operating support.
Geographic limitations: Giving primarily in areas of company operations in the western WA region.
Support limitations: No grants to individuals.
Publications: Application guidelines.
Application information: Applications accepted. Application form required. Applicants should submit the following:
1) name, address and phone number of organization
2) copy of IRS Determination Letter
3) brief history of organization and description of its mission
4) explanation of why grantmaker is considered an appropriate donor for project
5) detailed description of project and amount of funding requested
6) contact person
Must include e-mail address of organization.
Initial approach: Contact foundation for application form
Deadline(s): None
Officers: Bob Campbell, Pres.; Tina Campbell, Secy.; Roxanne Terreberry, Treas.
EIN: 260716610

2097
Karr Tuttle Campbell
1201 3rd Ave., Ste. 2900
Seattle, WA 98101-3284 (206) 223-1313

Company URL: http://www.karrtuttle.com
Establishment information: Established in 1904.
Company type: Private company
Business activities: Operates law firm.
Business type (SIC): Legal services
Giving statement: Giving through the Karr Tuttle Campbell Pro Bono Program.

Karr Tuttle Campbell Pro Bono Program
1201 3rd Ave., Ste. 2900
Seattle, WA 98101-3284 (206) 223-1313
E-mail: contact_us@karrtuttle.com; URL: http://www.karrtuttle.com/aboutus/aboutusdesc/id/97/community.aspx

Fields of interest: Legal services.
Type of support: Pro bono services - legal.
Geographic limitations: Giving primarily in areas of company operations in Seattle, WA.

2098
Kasle Steel Corporation
4343 Wyoming St.
Dearborn, MI 48126-3724 (313) 943-2500

Company URL: http://www.steeltechnologies.com/
Establishment information: Established in 1922.
Company type: Subsidiary of a private company
Business activities: Manufactures steel products.
Business type (SIC): Steel mill products; metal forgings and stampings; metals and minerals, except petroleum—wholesale
Financial profile for 2010: Number of employees, 65
Corporate officers: Michael J. Carroll, Pres. and C.E.O.; Michael Ulewicz, C.O.O.; Roger D. Shannon, C.F.O. and Treas.; Rick P. Furber, Exec. V.P., Opers.; Joseph M. Kamer, V.P., Genl. Counsel and Secy.; Patrick M. Flanagan, V.P., Human Resources
Divisions: Auto Blankers, Flint, MI; Quality Coil Processing, Woodhaven, MI
International operations: Canada
Giving statement: Giving through the Kasle Foundation.

The Kasle Foundation
555 Stanley Blvd.
Birmingham, MI 48009-1401

Establishment information: Established in 1945 in MI.
Donors: Kasle Steel Corp.; Roger Kasle; The Kasle Family, LLC.
Financial data (yr. ended 12/31/11): Assets, $28,229 (M); expenditures, $7,670; qualifying distributions, $7,500; giving activities include $7,500 for grants.
Purpose and activities: The foundation supports organizations involved with Alzheimer's disease and international exchange.
Fields of interest: Health care; Human services; International affairs.
Type of support: General/operating support.
Geographic limitations: Giving primarily in MI.
Support limitations: No grants to individuals.
Application information: Applications not accepted. Unsolicited requests for funds not accepted.
Officers and Trustees:* Roger Kasle*, Chair. and Secy.-Treas.; Matthew Kasle*, Pres.; Julie Kasle.
EIN: 386062714

2099
Kasowitz Benson Torres & Friedman LLP
1633 Broadway, 22nd Fl.
New York, NY 10019-6708 (212) 506-1700

Company URL: http://www.kasowitz.com/
Company type: Private company
Business activities: Operates law firm.
Business type (SIC): Legal services
Corporate officers: Mitchell R. Schrage, Managing Partner; Ted Ferguson, C.I.O.
Offices: Redwood Shores, San Francisco, CA; Miami, FL; Atlanta, GA; Newark, NJ; New York, NY; Houston, TX
Giving statement: Giving through the Kasowitz Benson Torres & Friedman LLP Pro Bono Program.

Kasowitz Benson Torres & Friedman LLP Pro Bono Program
1633 Broadway, 22nd Fl.
New York, NY 10019-6708 (212) 506-1701
E-mail: dabrams@kasowitz.com; Additional tel.: (212) 506-1700; URL: http://www.kasowitz.com/pro_bono/

Contact: David J. Abrams, Partner/Pro Bono Coord.
Fields of interest: Legal services.
Type of support: Pro bono services - legal.
Geographic limitations: Giving primarily in areas of company operations in Redwood Shores and San Francisco, CA, Miami, FL, Atlanta, GA, Newark, NJ, New York, NY, and Houston, TX.
Application information: A Pro Bono Coordinator manages the pro-bono program.

2100
Katovich Law Group
436 14th St., Ste. 1120
Oakland, CA 94612-2710 (510) 834-4530

Company URL: http://www.katovichlaw.com
Establishment information: Established in 2001.
Company type: Private company
Business type (SIC): Business services/miscellaneous
Corporate officers: John Katovich, Founder; Angelica Banks, C.O.O.; Zach Cohen, C.F.O.
Giving statement: Giving through the Katovich Law Group Corporate Giving Program.

Katovich Law Group Corporate Giving Program
436 14th St., Ste. 1120
Oakland, CA 94612-2710 (510) 834-4530
E-mail: inquiries@katovichlaw.com; URL: http://www.katovichlaw.com

Purpose and activities: Katovich Law Group is a certified B Corporation that donates a percentage of net profits to charitable organizations. Support is given primarily in Oakland, California.
Geographic limitations: Giving primarily in Oakland, CA.

2101
Katten Muchin Rosenman LLP
(formerly Katten Muchin Zavis Rosenman)
525 W. Monroe St., Ste. 1300
Chicago, IL 60661-3693 (312) 902-5200

Company URL: http://www.kattenlaw.com
Establishment information: Established in 1974.
Company type: Private company
Business activities: Provides legal services.
Business type (SIC): Legal services
Corporate officers: Ellen Wood, C.O.O.; Wayne Richman, C.F.O.
Plants: Irvine, Los Angeles, CA; Washington, DC; Miami, FL; Madison, WI
Offices: Los Angeles, Oakland, CA; Washington, DC; Chicago, IL; New York, NY; Charlotte, NC; Irving, TX
International operations: United Kingdom
Giving statement: Giving through the Katten Muchin Rosenman LLP Pro Bono Program and the Katten Muchin Rosenman Foundation, Inc.

Katten Muchin Rosenman LLP Pro Bono Program
525 W. Monroe St.
Chicago, IL 60661-3693 (312) 902-5479
E-mail: jonathan.baum@kattenlaw.com; Additional tel.: (312) 902-5200; URL: http://www.kattenlaw.com/about/probono/

Contact: Jonathan Baum, Dir. of Pro Bono Svcs.
Fields of interest: Legal services.
Type of support: Pro bono services - legal.
Geographic limitations: Giving primarily in areas of company operations in Los Angeles, and Oakland, CA, Washington, DC, Chicago, IL, Charlotte, NC, New York, NY, and Irving, TX, and in United Kingdom.
Application information: A Pro Bono Committee manages the pro-bono program.

Katten Muchin Rosenman Foundation, Inc.

(formerly Katten Muchin Zavis Rosenman Foundation, Inc.)
525 W. Monroe St., Ste. 1900
Chicago, IL 60661-3693
URL: http://www.kattenlaw.com/about/community/

Establishment information: Established in 1982 in IL.
Donors: Katten Muchin Zavis; Katten Muchin Zavis Rosenman; Katten Muchin Rosenman LLP; Wander Revocable Trust.
Contact: Mark P. Broutman
Financial data (yr. ended 12/31/11): Assets, $402,366 (M); gifts received, $2,203,887; expenditures, $2,067,124; qualifying distributions, $2,066,371; giving activities include $2,066,371 for grants.
Purpose and activities: The foundation supports organizations involved with arts and culture, education, health, cancer, heart disease, legal aid, human services, international relief, civil rights, Judaism, and women.
Fields of interest: Museums; Performing arts; Performing arts, theater; Arts; Higher education; Law school/education; Education; Health care, volunteer services; Hospitals (general); Health care; Cancer; Cancer, leukemia; Heart & circulatory diseases; Legal services; Boys & girls clubs; Children/youth, services; Human services; International relief; Civil/human rights; United Ways and Federated Giving Programs; Jewish agencies & synagogues Women.
Type of support: General/operating support.
Geographic limitations: Giving primarily in the Chicago, IL, area.
Support limitations: No grants to individuals.
Application information: Applications not accepted. Contributes only to pre-selected organizations.
Officers and Directors:* Vincent A.F. Sergi*, Pres.; Herbert S. Wander*, Secy.; Howard S. Lanznar, Treas.; Karen Artz Ash; David J. Bryant; Howard E. Cotton; Arthur W. Hahn; Daniel S. Huffenus; David H. Kistenbroker; Nina B. Matis; Joshua S. Rubenstein; Stuart P. Shulruff; Gail Migdal Title.
EIN: 363165216
Selected grants: The following grants are a representative sample of this grantmaker's funding activity:
$42,455 to American Heart Association, Dallas, TX, 2010.
$25,000 to Legal Assistance Foundation of Metropolitan Chicago, Chicago, IL, 2010.
$24,045 to American Ireland Fund, Boston, MA, 2010.
$23,030 to New Yorkers for Children, New York, NY, 2010.
$20,200 to Boys and Girls Clubs of America, Atlanta, GA, 2010.
$20,000 to Joffrey Ballet, Chicago, IL, 2010.
$20,000 to New York University, New York, NY, 2010.
$13,630 to UJA-Federation of New York, New York, NY, 2010.
$12,000 to University of Chicago Cancer Research Foundation, Chicago, IL, 2010.
$10,200 to HHC Foundation of New York City, New York, NY, 2010.

2102
Kawasaki Motors Corp., U.S.A.

9950 Jeronimo Rd.
P.O. Box 25252
Irvine, CA 92618-2084 (949) 770-0400

Company URL: http://www.kawasaki.com
Establishment information: Established in 1966.
Company type: Subsidiary of a foreign company
Business activities: Manufactures all terrain vehicles, motorcycles, utility vehicles, watercraft, and power products.
Business type (SIC): Transportation equipment/miscellaneous; machinery/farm and garden; ship and boat building and repair; motorcycles, bicycles, and parts
Financial profile for 2010: Number of employees, 480; assets, $1,600,000,000
Corporate officers: Masatoshi Tsurutani, Co-Pres. and C.E.O.; Takeshi Teranishi, Co-Pres.
Giving statement: Giving through the Kawasaki Motors Corp., U.S.A. Corporate Giving Program.

Kawasaki Motors Corp., U.S.A. Corporate Giving Program

P.O. Box 25252
Santa Ana, CA 92799-5252

Purpose and activities: Kawasaki makes charitable contributions to nonprofit organizations on a case by case basis. Support is given primarily in areas of company operations.
Fields of interest: General charitable giving.
Type of support: Donated products; Employee matching gifts; General/operating support.
Geographic limitations: Giving primarily in areas of company operations.

2103
Kawasaki Motors Manufacturing Corp., U.S.A.

6600 N.W. 27th St.
Lincoln, NE 68524-8904 (402) 476-6600

Company URL: http://www.kawasaki.com/OurCompany/kmm.aspx
Establishment information: Established in 1974.
Company type: Subsidiary of a foreign company
Business activities: Manufactures motorcycles, jetskis, and other recreational vehicles.
Business type (SIC): Motorcycles, bicycles, and parts
Corporate officers: Shrio Noiri, Pres.; Matsuhiro Asano, C.E.O.; Paul Kramer, C.I.O.
Giving statement: Giving through the Kawasaki Good Times Foundation.

Kawasaki Good Times Foundation

P.O. Box 81469
Lincoln, NE 68501-1469 (402) 476-6600

Establishment information: Established in 1993 in NE.
Donors: Kawasaki Motors Manufacturing Corp., U.S.A.; Kawasaki Heavy Industries (USA), Inc.; Kawasaki Motors Corp., U.S.A.; Kawasaki Rail Car, Inc.; Kawasaki Robotics (USA) Inc.
Contact: Rob Fairchild
Financial data (yr. ended 12/31/11): Assets, $2,758,978 (M); gifts received, $66,559; expenditures, $179,337; qualifying distributions, $158,250; giving activities include $157,500 for 7 grants (high: $50,000; low: $5,500).
Purpose and activities: The foundation supports museums and organizations involved with Japanese culture, music, and higher education.
Fields of interest: Arts, cultural/ethnic awareness; Museums (art); Museums (specialized); Performing arts, music; Higher education; United Ways and Federated Giving Programs Asians/Pacific Islanders.
Type of support: General/operating support.
Geographic limitations: Giving primarily in NE; some giving also MI and NY.
Application information: Applications accepted. Application form required. Applicants should submit the following:
1) timetable for implementation and evaluation of project
2) results expected from proposed grant
3) detailed description of project and amount of funding requested
4) additional materials/documentation
Initial approach: Letter
Deadline(s): None

Officers and Directors:* Kazushi Hattori*, Pres.; Toshio Kuwata, V.P.; Kazuhiro Kobayashi, Secy.-Treas.; Matsuhiro Asand; Takeshi Teranishi.
EIN: 363879896
Selected grants: The following grants are a representative sample of this grantmaker's funding activity:
$100,000 to University of Nebraska Foundation, Lincoln, NE, 2010.
$50,000 to United States Fund for UNICEF, New York, NY, 2010. For general support.
$40,000 to Metropolitan Museum of Art, New York, NY, 2010. For general support.
$30,000 to University of Nebraska Foundation, Lincoln, NE, 2010.
$10,000 to Carnegie Hall Society, New York, NY, 2010.

2104
Kaytee Products, Inc.

521 Clay St.
P.O. Box 230
Chilton, WI 53014-1477 (920) 849-2321

Company URL: http://www.kaytee.com
Establishment information: Established in 1866.
Company type: Subsidiary of a public company
Business activities: Produces wild bird, companion bird, and small animal food.
Business type (SIC): Grain mill products, including pet food
Corporate officers: Richard W. Best, Jr., Pres. and C.E.O.; Curt Hyzy, C.F.O.; Jim Glassford, V.P., Mktg.
Giving statement: Giving through the Kaytee Avian Foundation, Inc.

Kaytee Avian Foundation, Inc.

521 Clay St.
Chilton, WI 53014-1476 (920) 849-2321

Establishment information: Established in 1995 in WI.
Donors: Kaytee Products, Inc.; Donald Springer†.
Contact: Sue Polzin, Secy.-Treas.
Financial data (yr. ended 12/31/11): Assets, $226,678 (M); gifts received, $60,134; expenditures, $79,790; qualifying distributions, $78,416; giving activities include $78,416 for grants.
Purpose and activities: The foundation supports programs designed to enhance people's knowledge

and enjoyment of birds through education, conservation, and research.
Fields of interest: Environment; Animals/wildlife.
Type of support: General/operating support.
Geographic limitations: Giving primarily in CA, FL, SD, TX, and WI.
Support limitations: No grants to individuals.
Application information: Applications accepted. Application form not required.
Initial approach: Proposal
Deadline(s): None
Officers: Chris Mings, Pres.; Curt Hyzy, Secy.-Treas.
Directors: Susan Clubb; Michelle Goodman; Eric Juergens.
EIN: 391810726

2081
K-B Farms, Inc.

3927 S. Meridian Rd.
Rockford, IL 61102-4010 (815) 962-0099

Establishment information: Established in 1976.
Company type: Private company
Business activities: Operates crop farms.
Business type (SIC): Farms/general crop
Corporate officer: Ronald Groves, Owner
Giving statement: Giving through the Funderburg Foundation.

The Funderburg Foundation

600 S. State St.
Belvidere, IL 61008-4329

Establishment information: Established in 1955 in IL.
Donors: K-B Farms, Inc.; State Bank of Kirkland; Funderburg Farms, Inc.; R. Robert Funderburg†; Barbara F. Warren; Sally D. Funderburg; Henry R. Warren, Jr.; Alpine Bank & Trust Co.; Belvidere National Bank & Trust Co.
Financial data (yr. ended 12/31/11): Assets, $1,503,265 (M); gifts received, $30,500; expenditures, $66,955; qualifying distributions, $59,494; giving activities include $59,494 for grants.
Purpose and activities: The foundation supports organizations involved with arts and culture, education, medical research, hunger, and human services.
Fields of interest: Arts; Education; Youth development.
Type of support: Annual campaigns; Building/renovation; Capital campaigns.
Geographic limitations: Giving primarily in IL.
Support limitations: No grants to individuals.
Application information: Applications not accepted. Unsolicited requests for funds not accepted.
Officers and Directors:* R. Robert Funderburg, Jr.*, Pres. and Treas.; James R. Cox*, V.P.; John K. Funderburg, Jr.*, V.P.; Henry R. Warren, Jr.*, V.P.; Rhonda Harris, Secy.
EIN: 366054385

2105
KB Home

(formerly Kaufman and Broad Home Corporation)
10990 Wilshire Blvd., 7th Fl.
Los Angeles, CA 90024 (310) 231-4000

Company URL: http://www.kbhome.com
Establishment information: Established in 1957.
Company type: Public company
Company ticker symbol and exchange: KBH/NYSE
Business activities: Provides mortgages; builds houses.
Business type (SIC): Brokers and bankers/mortgage; contractors/general residential building; operative builders; wood buildings and mobile homes; holding company
Financial profile for 2010: Number of employees, 1,300; assets, $3,109,750,000; sales volume, $1,590,000,000; pre-tax net income, -$76,370,000; expenses, $1,602,730,000; liabilities, $2,477,870,000
Corporate officers: Stephen F. Bollenbach, Chair.; Jeffrey T. Mezger, Pres. and C.E.O.; Jeff Kaminski, Exec. V.P. and C.F.O.; Brian Woram, Exec. V.P., Genl. Counsel, and Secy.; William R. Hollinger, Sr. V.P. and C.A.O.; Thomas Norton, Sr. V.P., Human Resources
Board of directors: Stephen F. Bollenbach, Chair.; Barabara T. Alexander; Timothy W. Finchem; Kenneth M. Jastrow II; Robert L. Johnson; Melissa Lora; Michael G. McCaffery; Jeffrey T. Mezger; Leslie Moonves; Luis G. Nogales
Subsidiaries: Kaufman and Broad Mortgage Co., Woodland Hills, CA; Lewis Homes Management Corp., Los Angeles, CA
Plants: Anaheim, Dublin, Fremont, Fresno, Modesto, Newport Beach, Palmdale, Roseville, San Diego, CA; Las Vegas, NV
Giving statement: Giving through the KB Home Corporate Giving Program.
Company EIN: 953666267

KB Home Corporate Giving Program

(formerly Kaufman and Broad Home Corporation Contributions Program)
10990 Wilshire Blvd.
Los Angeles, CA 90024-3989 (310) 231-4000

Purpose and activities: KB Home makes charitable contributions to nonprofit organizations involved with shelter-related causes, assistance for children and their families, and community development. Support is given primarily in areas of company operations.
Fields of interest: Housing/shelter; Family services; Community/economic development Children.
Type of support: Employee volunteer services; General/operating support; In-kind gifts; Sponsorships.
Geographic limitations: Giving primarily in areas of company operations.
Application information: Application form not required.
Initial approach: Proposal to headquarters

2106
KBR, Inc.

(formerly Kellogg Brown & Root, Inc.)
601 Jefferson St., Ste. 3400
Houston, TX 77002 (713) 753-2000

Company URL: http://www.kbr.com
Establishment information: Established in 1901.
Company type: Public company
Company ticker symbol and exchange: KBR/NYSE
Business activities: Provides engineering, construction, and project management services supporting the energy, petrochemicals, government services and civil infrastructure sectors.
Business type (SIC): Engineering, architectural, and surveying services; oil and gas field services; contractors/general nonresidential building; construction/highway and street (except elevated); construction/miscellaneous heavy; contractors/miscellaneous special trade
Financial profile for 2012: Number of employees, 27,000; assets, $5,787,000,000; sales volume, $7,921,000,000; pre-tax net income, $288,000,000; expenses, $7,622,000,000; liabilities, $3,225,000,000
Fortune 1000 ranking: 2012—334th in revenues, 662nd in profits, and 549th in assets
Corporate officers: William P. Utt, Chair., Pres., and C.E.O.; John Derbyshire, Pres., Tech.; Sue Carter, Exec. V.P. and C.F.O.; Andrew D. Farley, Exec. V.P. and Genl. Counsel; Farhan Mujib, Exec. V.P., Opers.; Clare Kinahan, Sr. V.P., Human Resources
Board of directors: William P. Utt, Chair.; W. Frank Blount; Loren K. Carroll; Linda Z. Cook; Jeffrey E. Curtiss; John R. Huff; Lester L. Lyles; Jack B. Moore; Richard J. Slater
International operations: Netherlands; United Kingdom; Wales
Giving statement: Giving through the KBR, Inc. Corporate Giving Program.
Company EIN: 204536774

KBR, Inc. Corporate Giving Program

(formerly Kellogg Brown & Root, Inc. Corporate Giving Program)
601 Jefferson St.
Houston, TX 77002-4003 (713) 753-8694
URL: http://www.kbr.com/Social-Responsibility/

Purpose and activities: KBR makes charitable contributions to nonprofit organizations involved with education, health, and the environment. Special emphasis is directed towards programs designed to support STEM (science, technology, engineering, and mathematics) education. Support is given on a national and international basis in areas of company operations.
Fields of interest: Education; Environment; Health care; Science; Mathematics; Engineering/technology.
Type of support: Employee matching gifts; Employee volunteer services; General/operating support; In-kind gifts; Program development.
Geographic limitations: Giving on a national and international basis in areas of company operations.
Support limitations: No support for religious, political, labor, or fraternal organizations, or civic clubs. No grants to individuals, or for athletic or sporting events or programs, capital campaigns, journal advertising, memorial donations, school clubs or events, or development or production of books, films, videos, or radio, or television programs.
Publications: Application guidelines.
Application information: Applications accepted. Proposals should be submitted using organization letterhead. Proposals should include an executive summary no longer than 2 pages. Application form not required. Applicants should submit the following:
1) timetable for implementation and evaluation of project
2) results expected from proposed grant
3) copy of IRS Determination Letter
4) brief history of organization and description of its mission
5) how project's results will be evaluated or measured
6) listing of board of directors, trustees, officers and other key people and their affiliations
7) detailed description of project and amount of funding requested
8) contact person
9) listing of additional sources and amount of support

Applications should include a description of past support by KBR with the organization. In-kind requests should indicate any benefits.
Initial approach: Mail or e-mail proposal to headquarters
Deadline(s): July

2107
A. T. Kearney, Inc.
222 W. Adams St.
Chicago, IL 60606 (312) 648-0111

Company URL: http://www.atkearney.com
Establishment information: Established in 1926.
Company type: Private company
Business activities: Operates management consulting company.
Business type (SIC): Management and public relations services
Corporate officers: Johan Aurik, Chair.; John Yoshimura, C.O.O.; Dan DeCanniere, C.F.O.
Board of director: Johan Aurik, Chair.
Offices: San Francisco, CA; Washington, DC; Atlanta, GA; Detroit, MI; New York, NY; Dallas, Houston, TX
International operations: Australia; Austria; Bahrain; Brazil; Canada; China; Czech Republic; Denmark; Finland; France; Germany; Hong Kong; India; Indonesia; Italy; Japan; Luxembourg; Malaysia; Netherlands; Norway; Poland; Portugal; Romania; Russia; Saudi Arabia; Singapore; South Africa; South Korea; Spain; Sweden; Switzerland; Thailand; Turkey; United Arab Emirates; United Kingdom
Giving statement: Giving through the A. T. Kearney, Inc. Contributions Program.

A. T. Kearney, Inc. Contributions Program
222 W. Adams St.
Chicago, IL 60606
URL: http://www.atkearney.com/index.php/About-us/corporate-social-responsibility.html

Purpose and activities: A. T. Kearney provides pro bono services on a case by case basis in areas of company operations.
Type of support: Pro bono services.
Geographic limitations: Giving on a national and international basis in areas of company operations in CA, DC, GA, IL, MI, NY, and TX.

2108
Kearny Federal Savings Bank
614 Kearny Ave.
Kearny, NJ 07032-2806 (201) 991-4100

Company URL: http://www.kearnyfederalsavings.com
Establishment information: Established in 1884.
Company type: Subsidiary of a public company
Business activities: Operates savings bank.
Business type (SIC): Savings institutions
Corporate officers: John J. Mazur, Jr., Chair.; Craig L. Montanaro, Pres. and C.E.O.; William C. Ledgerwood, Exec. V.P. and C.O.O.; Eric B. Meyer, Sr. V.P. and C.F.O.; Albert E. Gossweiler, Sr. V.P., C.I.O., and Treas.; Sharon Jones, Sr. V.P. and Corp. Secy.
Board of directors: John J. Mazur, Jr., Chair.; Theodore J. Aanensen; John N. Hopkins; Joseph P. Mazza; Matthew T. McClane; John F. McGovern; Craig L. Montanaro; Leopold W. Montanaro; John F. Regan
Giving statement: Giving through the Kearny Federal Savings Charitable Foundation.

Kearny Federal Savings Charitable Foundation
(formerly West Essex Bancorp Charitable Foundation)
120 Passaic Ave.
Fairfield, NJ 07004-3510 (973) 244-4510

Establishment information: Established in 1998 in NJ.
Donor: West Essex Bancorp, Inc.
Contact: Craig Montanaro, Secy.-Treas.
Financial data (yr. ended 12/31/11): Assets, $3,092,126 (M); expenditures, $95,386; qualifying distributions, $84,000; giving activities include $84,000 for grants.
Purpose and activities: The foundation supports camps and organizations involved with secondary education, literacy, human services, community development, and Christianity.
Fields of interest: Education; Human services; Community/economic development.
Type of support: Continuing support; General/operating support.
Geographic limitations: Giving in areas of company operations in NJ.
Support limitations: No grants to individuals.
Application information: Applications accepted. Application form required. Applicants should submit the following:
1) role played by volunteers
2) copy of most recent annual report/audited financial statement/990
3) listing of board of directors, trustees, officers and other key people and their affiliations
4) copy of current year's organizational budget and/or project budget
Initial approach: Contact foundation for application form
Deadline(s): None
Officers and Directors:* John N. Hopkins*, Pres.; Craig Montanaro*, Secy.-Treas.; John McGovern.
EIN: 223597621

2109
Keating Muething & Klekamp PLL
1 E. 4th St., Ste. 1400
Cincinnati, OH 45202-3708 (513) 579-6400

Company URL: http://kmklaw.com
Company type: Private company
Business activities: Operates law firm.
Business type (SIC): Legal services
Corporate officers: Paul V. Muething, Managing Partner; Richard E. Wills, C.I.O.
Giving statement: Giving through the Keating Muething & Klekamp PLL Pro Bono Program.

Keating Muething & Klekamp PLL Pro Bono Program
1 E. 4th St., Ste. 1400
Cincinnati, OH 45202-3708 (513) 639-3928
E-mail: jramsey@kmklaw.com; Additional tel.: (513) 639-3928; URL: http://www.kmklaw.com/careers-service.html

Contact: Jamie M. Ramsey, Partner
Fields of interest: Legal services.
Type of support: Pro bono services - legal.
Application information: A Pro Bono Coordinator manages the pro bono program.

2110
Keefe Real Estate, Inc.
751 Geneva Pkwy. N.
Lake Geneva, WI 53147-4579
(262) 248-4492

Company URL: http://www.keeferealestate.com
Establishment information: Established in 1943.
Company type: Subsidiary of a private company
Business activities: Operates real estate brokerage.
Business type (SIC): Real estate agents and managers
Corporate officers: Stephen Beers, Pres.; Michael Keefe, C.E.O.; Vicki Coe, Cont.
Giving statement: Giving through the Keefe Foundation, Inc.

Keefe Foundation, Inc.
P.O. Box 460
Lake Geneva, WI 53147-0460
URL: http://www.keeferealestate.com/charitable_giving.php

Establishment information: Established in 2006 in WI.
Donors: Keefe Real Estate, Inc.; Keefe & Associates, Inc.; Michael K. Keefe.
Financial data (yr. ended 12/31/11): Assets, $1,202 (M); gifts received, $5,150; expenditures, $4,000; qualifying distributions, $4,000; giving activities include $2,500 for 8 grants (high: $500; low: $50).
Fields of interest: Health organizations; Human services; Civil/human rights.
Support limitations: No grants to individuals.
Application information: Applications not accepted. Unsolicited requests for funds not accepted.
Officers: Michael K. Keefe, Pres.; Robert W. Keefe, V.P.; Dennis L. Carnes, Secy.-Treas.
EIN: 204770988

2111
Keen Transport, Inc.
1951 Harrisburg Pike
Carlisle, PA 17015-7304 (717) 243-6622

Company URL: http://www.keentransport.com
Establishment information: Established in 1968.
Company type: Private company
Business activities: Provides trucking services.
Business type (SIC): Trucking and courier services, except by air
Corporate officers: William R. Keen, C.E.O.; Chris Easter, Pres. and C.O.O.
Subsidiaries: Cressler Trucking Inc., Shippensburg, PA; Hubert Jones Inc., New Kingstown, PA; PDQ Transport Inc., Cheyenne, WY; Vaughan Transport Inc., Lagrange, GA
Offices: Decatur, IL; Skyland, NC
Giving statement: Giving through the Harold and Berta Keen Family Scholarship Foundation.

The Harold and Berta Keen Family Scholarship Foundation
1951 Harrisburg Pike
Carlisle, PA 17013-7304 (717) 243-6622

Donor: Keen Transport, Inc.
Financial data (yr. ended 12/31/11): Assets, $4,546 (M); gifts received, $12,250; expenditures, $12,035; qualifying distributions, $12,000; giving activities include $12,000 for 12 grants to individuals (high: $1,000; low: $1,000).
Purpose and activities: The foundation awards college scholarships to children of employees of Keen Transport, Inc. and residents of central Pennsylvania.
Fields of interest: Higher education; Education.
Type of support: Employee-related scholarships; Scholarships—to individuals.
Geographic limitations: Giving limited to central PA.
Application information: Applications accepted. Application form required.
Initial approach: Contact foundation for application form
Deadline(s): Prior to school term
Officers and Directors:* William R. Keen*, Pres.; Elizabeth A. Keen*, Secy.-Treas.
EIN: 251843433

2112
D.C Keenan Associates, PC
(doing business as The Keenan Law Firm)
The Keenan Bldg.
148 Nassau St., N.W.
Atlanta, GA 30303-2010 (404) 523-2200

Company URL: http://www.keenanlawfirm.com
Establishment information: Established in 1975.
Company type: Private company
Business activities: Operates law firm.
Business type (SIC): Legal services
Corporate officer: Don C. Keenan, Pres., C.E.O., and Secy.
Giving statement: Giving through the Keenan's Kids Foundation, Inc.

Keenan's Kids Foundation, Inc.
148 Nassau St. N.W.
Atlanta, GA 30303-2010 (404) 223-5437
URL: http://www.keenanskidsfoundation.com/

Establishment information: Established in 1993 in GA.
Donors: Don C. Keenan; D.C. Keenan & Assocs., P.C.; Coca-Cola; Fitzerald & Co.; Patrick McGahan.
Contact: Theresa Carter
Financial data (yr. ended 09/30/12): Assets, $1,113,199 (M); gifts received, $31,668; expenditures, $1,359,527; qualifying distributions, $122,038.
Purpose and activities: Giving for the needs of children at-risk in the legal system.
Geographic limitations: Giving primarily in GA.
Support limitations: No grants to individuals.
Application information: Applications accepted. Application form not required.
Initial approach: Proposal
Deadline(s): None
Officer: Don C. Keenan, Mgr.
Directors: Gino Brogdon; Dennis Collins; Joan Dauphinee; David Goo; Shawn Huff; Danica Kombol; John Monaco.
EIN: 582376697

2113
Keeneland Association Inc.
4201 Versailles Rd.
Lexington, KY 40510-9662 (859) 254-3412

Company URL: http://www.keeneland.com
Establishment information: Established in 1936.
Company type: Private company
Business activities: Operates horse racing track; provides race horse auction services; provides horse racing simulcast services.
Business type (SIC): Commercial sports; cable and other pay television services; retail stores/ miscellaneous
Corporate officers: Bill Thomason, Pres. and C.E.O.; Vince Gabbert, V.P. and C.O.O.; Connie van Onselder, V.P. and C.F.O.; Brad Lovell, V.P. and C.I.O.; Walt Robertson, V.P., Sales; Ben Huffman, Secy.
Giving statement: Giving through the Keeneland Foundation, Inc.

Keeneland Foundation, Inc.
4201 Versailles Rd.
P.O. Box 1690
Lexington, KY 40588-1690 (859) 288-4142
FAX: (859) 255-2484;
E-mail: schinn@keeneland.com; Additional tel.: (859) 254-3412; URL: http://www.keeneland.com/ about/keeneland-foundation

Establishment information: Established in 1999 in KY.
Donors: Keeneland Association Inc.; Maker's Mark; Casner Family Fund.
Contact: Sandy Chinn
Financial data (yr. ended 06/30/11): Assets, $177,771 (M); gifts received, $340,867; expenditures, $652,838; qualifying distributions, $625,000; giving activities include $625,000 for 11 grants (high: $500,000; low: $1,000).
Purpose and activities: The foundation supports organizations involved with arts and culture, education, health, human services, and community development. Special emphasis is directed toward programs designed to serve the equine industry, specifically in the areas of thoroughbred breeding and racing.
Fields of interest: Arts; Higher education; Education; Veterinary medicine; Health care; Human services; Community/economic development.
Type of support: Building/renovation; Capital campaigns; Endowments; Equipment; General/ operating support; Program development; Research; Scholarship funds.
Geographic limitations: Giving primarily in central KY.
Support limitations: No support for political organizations, primary or secondary schools, fraternal or veterans' organizations not of direct benefit to the entire community, religious organizations not of direct benefit to the entire community, or youth sports leagues. No grants to individuals, or for courtesy advertising, annual campaigns, general operating support for hospitals or patient care institutions, or tickets or sponsorships; no ticket or dining space contributions.
Publications: Application guidelines.
Application information: Applications accepted. Application form required. Applicants should submit the following:
1) statement of problem project will address
2) population served
3) copy of IRS Determination Letter
4) brief history of organization and description of its mission
5) copy of most recent annual report/audited financial statement/990
6) descriptive literature about organization
7) listing of board of directors, trustees, officers and other key people and their affiliations
8) detailed description of project and amount of funding requested
9) copy of current year's organizational budget and/ or project budget
10) listing of additional sources and amount of support

Initial approach: Download application form and mail or e-mail application form to foundation
Board meeting date(s): Quarterly
Deadline(s): None, but applications are reviewed in Dec.
Officers and Directors: L.L. Haggin III, Pres.; Nick Nicholson, V.P.; Vince Gabbert, Secy.; William Thomason, Treas.; William S. Farish; William M. Lear, Jr.
Number of staff: None.
EIN: 611358165

2114
Kehe Food Distributors, Inc.
900 N. Schmidt Rd.
Romeoville, IL 60446-4056 (630) 343-0000

Company URL: http://www.kehefood.com/
Establishment information: Established in 1952.
Company type: Private company
Business activities: Sells groceries wholesale.
Business type (SIC): Groceries—wholesale
Financial profile for 2010: Number of employees, 500
Corporate officers: Brandon Barnholt, Pres. and C.E.O.; Christopher Meyers, C.F.O.; Scott Cousins, C.I.O.; Jack Porter, Exec. V.P., Sales; Ted Beilman, Exec. V.P., Mktg.; Annette Roder, Sr. V.P., Human Resources
Giving statement: Giving through the A.H.K. Foundation.

A.H.K. Foundation
c/o Jerry Kehe
900 N. Schmidt Rd.
Romeoville, IL 60446-4056 (815) 886-3700

Establishment information: Established in 1994 in IL.
Donors: Kehe Food Distributors, Inc.; Jerald F. Kehe.
Contact: Jerald F. Kehe, Pres. and Secy.-Treas.
Financial data (yr. ended 06/30/12): Assets, $14,089 (M); expenditures, $26,242; qualifying distributions, $25,000; giving activities include $25,000 for grants.
Purpose and activities: The foundation supports organizations involved with Christianity.
Fields of interest: Christian agencies & churches.
Geographic limitations: Giving primarily in La Mirada, CA, Colorado Springs, CO, and IL.
Application information: Applications accepted. Application form required.
Initial approach: Letter
Deadline(s): None
Officer: Jerald F. Kehe, Pres. and Secy.-Treas.
Directors: Edward Amaitis; Janice Kehe; Joseph Shannon.
EIN: 363912532

2115
Keithley Instruments, Inc.
28775 Aurora Rd.
Solon, OH 44139 (440) 248-0400

Company URL: http://www.keithley.com/
Establishment information: Established in 1946.
Company type: Subsidiary of a public company
Business activities: Manufactures complex electronic instruments and systems for high-performance production testing.
Business type (SIC): Laboratory apparatus
Financial profile for 2010: Number of employees, 490; assets, $104,660,000; sales volume, $126,870,000; pre-tax net income, $25,400,000; expenses, $101,550,000; liabilities, $47,720,000
Corporate officers: Joseph P. Keithley, Chair., Co-Pres., and C.E.O.; Linda C. Rae, Co-Pres.
Board of director: Joseph P. Keithley, Chair.
Giving statement: Giving through the Keithley Foundation.
Company EIN: 340794417

Keithley Foundation
28775 Aurora Rd.
Solon, OH 44139-1837

Establishment information: Established in OH.
Donor: Keithley Instruments, Inc.
Financial data (yr. ended 12/31/11): Assets, $1 (M); expenditures, $0; qualifying distributions, $0.
Purpose and activities: The foundation supports the Cleveland Foundation in Cleveland, Ohio.
Fields of interest: Foundations (community); United Ways and Federated Giving Programs.
Type of support: General/operating support.
Geographic limitations: Giving primarily in Cleveland, OH.
Support limitations: No grants to individuals.
Application information: Applications not accepted. Unsolicited requests for funds not accepted.
Officers and Trustees:* Joseph P. Keithley*, Pres.; Mark J. Plush*, Secy.; Linda Rae.
EIN: 341970540

2116
Keller & Heckman
1001 G St., NW, Ste. 500 W.
Washington, DC 20001-4545
(202) 434-4100

Company URL: http://www.khlaw.com
Establishment information: Established in 1962.
Company type: Private company
Business activities: Operates law firm.
Business type (SIC): Legal services
Offices: San Francisco, CA; Washington, DC
International operations: Belgium; China
Giving statement: Giving through the Keller & Heckman Pro Bono Program.

Keller & Heckman Pro Bono Program
1001 G St., NW, Ste. 500 W.
Washington, DC 20001-4545 (202) 434-4100
E-mail: behr@khlaw.com; URL: http://www.khlaw.com/about.aspx?Show=3306

Contact: Douglas J. Behr, Pro Bono Comm. Chair
Fields of interest: Legal services.
Type of support: Pro bono services - legal.
Geographic limitations: Giving primarily in areas of company operations in San Francisco, CA, Washington, DC, and in Belgium and China.
Application information: A Pro Bono Committee manages the pro bono program.

2117
Keller-Crescent Co.
(formerly Westlake Industries, Inc.)
1100 E. Louisiana St.
Evansville, IN 47711-4748 (812) 464-2461
FAX: (812) 426-7704

Company URL: http://www.kellercrescent.com
Establishment information: Established in 1885.
Company type: Subsidiary of a foreign company
Business activities: Manufactures pressure-sensitive roll labels, package outserts and inserts, specialty printing and packaging products, and folding cartons.
Business type (SIC): Paper and paperboard/ coated, converted, and laminated; paperboard containers
Financial profile for 2010: Number of employees, 850
Corporate officers: Peter Weber, Pres. and Co-C.E.O.; Bill Mitchell, Co-C.E.O.; William Mitchell, Co-C.E.O.; Susan Everett, V.P. and C.I.O.; Brad Platts, V.P. and Cont.; Ernest Chaplin, V.P., Mktg.
Subsidiary: Pharmagraphics LLC, Greensboro, NC
Giving statement: Giving through the Richard W. Treleaven Private Foundation.

Richard W. Treleaven Private Foundation
15208 Gulf Blvd., No. 407
Madeira Beach, FL 33708-1860

Establishment information: Established in 1977 in IL.
Donors: Westlake Industries, Inc.; Carl W. Treleaven; Lina Z. Treleaven.
Contact: Carl W. Treleaven, Pres.
Financial data (yr. ended 06/30/12): Assets, $28,470 (M); expenditures, $5,025; qualifying distributions, $5,000; giving activities include $5,000 for grants.
Fields of interest: Human services.
Geographic limitations: Giving primarily in NC.
Support limitations: No grants to individuals.
Application information: Applications accepted. Application form required.
Initial approach: Letter of inquiry
Deadline(s): None
Officers: Carl W. Treleaven, Pres.; Lina Z. Treleaven, V.P. and Secy.; Thomas J. Schultz, Treas.
EIN: 362944336

2118
Kelley Drye & Warren LLP
101 Park Ave.
New York, NY 10178-0002 (212) 808-7800

Company URL: http://www.kelleydrye.com
Establishment information: Established in 1836.
Company type: Private company
Business activities: Operates law firm.
Business type (SIC): Legal services
Offices: Los Angeles, CA; Stamford, CT; Washington, DC; Chicago, IL; Parsippany, NJ; New York, NY
International operations: Belgium
Giving statement: Giving through the Kelley Drye & Warren LLP Pro Bono Program.

Kelley Drye & Warren LLP Pro Bono Program
101 Park Ave.
New York, NY 10178-0002 (212) 808-7711
E-mail: jogara@kelleydrye.com; Additional tel.: (212) 808-7800; URL: http://www.kelleydrye.com/about/pro_bono/index

Contact: James O'Gara Esq, Pro Bono Counsel
Fields of interest: Legal services.
Type of support: Pro bono services - legal.
Geographic limitations: Giving primarily in areas of company operations in Los Angeles, CA, Stamford, CT, Washington, DC, Chicago, IL, Parsippany, NJ, New York, NY, and in Belgium.
Application information: A Pro Bono Committee manages the pro bono program.

2119
Kelley Williamson Company
1132 Harrison Ave.
Rockford, IL 61104-7290 (815) 397-9410

Company URL: http://www.kw-oil.com
Establishment information: Established in 1926.
Company type: Private company
Business activities: Operates gasoline service stations; operates convenience food stores.
Business type (SIC): Gasoline service stations; groceries—retail
Financial profile for 2010: Number of employees, 480
Corporate officers: Polly Griffin, Chair.; John P. Griffin, Pres. and C.O.O.; Kim Griffin, C.F.O.; Greg McKean, C.I.O.
Board of director: Polly Griffin, Chair.
Giving statement: Giving through the Griffin Williamson Foundation.

Griffin Williamson Foundation
c/o Kelley Williamson Co.
1132 Harrison Ave.
Rockford, IL 61104-7290

Establishment information: Established in 2002 in IL.
Donor: Kelley Williamson Co.
Financial data (yr. ended 12/31/11): Assets, $114,180 (M); expenditures, $1,198; qualifying distributions, $15.
Purpose and activities: The foundation supports Roscecrance Health Network in Rockford, Illinois.
Fields of interest: Substance abuse, services.
Type of support: General/operating support.
Geographic limitations: Giving limited to Rockford, IL.
Support limitations: No grants to individuals.
Application information: Applications not accepted. Unsolicited requests for funds not accepted.
Officers and Directors:* John C. Griffin*, Pres.; Wally G. Beville*, V.P.; Cherry J. Beto*, Secy.-Treas.
EIN: 364486091

2120
Kellogg Company
1 Kellogg Sq.
P.O. Box 3599
Battle Creek, MI 49016-3599
(269) 961-2000
FAX: (269) 961-2871

Company URL: http://www.kelloggcompany.com
Establishment information: Established in 1906.
Company type: Public company
Company ticker symbol and exchange: K/NYSE
International Securities Identification Number: US4878361082
Business activities: Produces cereals and other breakfast food products.
Business type (SIC): Grain mill products, including pet food; specialty foods/canned, frozen, and preserved; bakery products
Financial profile for 2012: Number of employees, 31,000; assets, $15,184,000,000; sales volume, $14,197,000,000; pre-tax net income, $1,325,000,000; expenses, $12,635,000,000; liabilities, $12,765,000,000
Fortune 1000 ranking: 2012—192nd in revenues, 204th in profits, and 298th in assets
Forbes 2000 ranking: 2012—675th in sales, 609th in profits, and 1170th in assets
Corporate officers: James M. Jenness, Chair.; John A. Bryant, Pres. and C.E.O.; Ronald L. Dissinger, C.F.O.; Brian S. Rice, Sr. V.P. and C.I.O.; Gary H. Pilnick, Sr. V.P., Genl. Counsel, and Secy.; Sammie Long, Sr. V.P., Human Resources
Board of directors: James M. Jenness, Chair.; John A. Bryant; Benjamin S. Carson, Sr.; John T. Dillon; Gordon Gund; Dorothy A. Johnson; Donald R. Knauss; Ann McLaughlin Korologos; Mary A. Laschinger; Cynthia H. Milligan; Rogelio M. Rebolledo; Sterling K. Speirn; John L. Zabriskie
Subsidiaries: Keebler Foods Company, Elmhurst, IL; Worthington Foods, Inc., Worthington, OH
Plants: San Jose, CA; New Haven, CT; Atlanta, GA; Mattoon, IL; Pikeville, KY; Omaha, NE; Blue Anchor, NJ; West Seneca, NY; Lancaster, Muncy, PA; Memphis, Rossville, TN
International operations: Argentina; Australia; Canada; Colombia; Ecuador; England; Germany; India; Japan; Malaysia; Netherlands; New Zealand; Poland; Singapore; South Korea; Thailand; Venezuela
Historic mergers: Wholesome & Hearty Foods Company (November 5, 2007)
Giving statement: Giving through the Kellogg Company Contributions Program, the Kellogg Company 25-Year Employees Fund, Inc., and the Kellogg's Corporate Citizenship Fund.
Company EIN: 380710690

Kellogg Company Contributions Program
1 Kellogg Sq.
P.O. Box 3599
Battle Creek, MI 49016-3599 (269) 961-2000
URL: http://www.kelloggcompany.com/corporateresponsibility.aspx

Purpose and activities: As a complement to its foundation, Kellogg also makes charitable contributions to nonprofit organizations directly. Special emphasis is directed towards programs that educate children and parents about nutrition and fitness. Support is given on a national and international basis in areas of company operations.
Fields of interest: Elementary/secondary education; Public health; Public health, physical fitness; Food banks; Nutrition; Disasters, Hurricane Katrina; Youth development, services; Civil/human rights, equal rights; United Ways and Federated Giving Programs Children/youth.
Type of support: Donated products; Employee matching gifts; Employee volunteer services; General/operating support; Sponsorships.
Geographic limitations: Giving on a national and international basis in areas of company operations; giving also to national organizations.

Kellogg Company 25-Year Employees Fund, Inc.
c/o Kellogg Co.
1 Kellogg Sq.
P.O. Box 3599
Battle Creek, MI 49016-3599 (269) 961-2000

Establishment information: Established in 1944 in MI.
Donor: W.K. Kellogg†.
Contact: Timothy S. Knowlton, Pres.
Financial data (yr. ended 12/31/11): Assets, $61,012,738 (M); expenditures, $3,981,742; qualifying distributions, $3,946,129; giving activities include $2,500,949 for 2+ grants (high: $2,500,000) and $1,239,585 for 171 grants to individuals (high: $28,750; low: $150).
Purpose and activities: The fund supports retiree associations and awards grants for living and medical expenses to current and former 25-year employees and the dependents of 25-year employees of Kellogg.
Fields of interest: Zoos/zoological societies; Food banks; Community/economic development; United Ways and Federated Giving Programs Economically disadvantaged.
International interests: Australia; Canada; Mexico; United Kingdom.
Type of support: Emergency funds; Grants to individuals.
Geographic limitations: Giving primarily in areas of company operations, with emphasis on Battle Creek, MI; giving also in Australia, Canada, England, Mexico, and the United Kingdom.
Support limitations: No grants to individuals (except for employee-related funds).
Application information: Applications not accepted. Applicants must be employees or dependents of employees at Kellogg or a Kellogg subsidiary for at least 25 years.
Board meeting date(s): Jan., Apr., July, and Oct.
Officers and Directors:* Timothy S. Knowlton*, Pres.; Joel Vanderkooi, Treas.; Margaret Bath; Celeste A. Clark; Ronald L. Dissinger; Ed Rector.
Number of staff: 1 full-time support.
EIN: 386039770
Selected grants: The following grants are a representative sample of this grantmaker's funding activity:
$3,500,000 to Battle Creek Public Schools, Battle Creek, MI, 2006.
$200,000 to YMCA and Outdoor Center, Sherman Lake, Augusta, MI, 2006.

Kellogg's Corporate Citizenship Fund
1 Kellogg Sq.
Battle Creek, MI 49016-3599 (269) 961-2867
E-mail: linda.fields@kelloggs.com; Additional e-mail: corporateresponsibility@kellogg.com; URL: http://www.kelloggcompany.com/corporateresponsibility.aspx?id=659

Establishment information: Established in 1994 in MI.
Donor: Kellogg Co.
Contact: Linda Fields, Secy.
Financial data (yr. ended 12/31/11): Assets, $39,388,513 (M); expenditures, $8,928,845; qualifying distributions, $8,837,335; giving activities include $8,290,435 for 468 grants (high: $3,181,365; low: $25).
Purpose and activities: The fund supports food banks and community foundations and organizations involved with arts and culture, education, fitness and health, hunger, nutrition, athletics, and human services.
Fields of interest: Arts; Elementary/secondary education; Higher education; Education; Public health, obesity; Public health, physical fitness; Health care; Food services; Food banks; Nutrition; Athletics/sports, amateur leagues; Athletics/sports, water sports; American Red Cross; YM/YWCAs & YM/YWHAs; Children/youth, services; Human services; Foundations (community); United Ways and Federated Giving Programs.
Programs:
Breakfast Programs: The fund supports research studying the impact of breakfast and the importance of fiber in encouraging better health; programs designed to improve nutrition and physical activities; and the development and promotion of "breakfast clubs" in schools to serve morning meals to children.
Kellogg Care$: The fund awards $250 grants to nonprofit organizations with which full-time salaried and hourly employees of all Kellogg U.S. Divisions, Kellogg Company retirees, and active Kellogg Company board members have volunteered a minimum of 25 hours in a calendar year.
Matching Grant Program: The fund matches contributions made by employees, retirees, directors, and the surviving spouses of employees, retirees, and directors of Kellogg to educational, cultural, arts, and environmental organizations on a one-for-one basis from $25 to $10,000 per contributor, per year.
Type of support: Building/renovation; Employee matching gifts; Employee volunteer services; General/operating support; Program development; Research; Scholarship funds; Technical assistance.
Geographic limitations: Giving primarily in areas of company operations in CA, Washington, DC, IL, PA, and TX, with emphasis on Battle Creek, MI; some giving also in Australia, Canada, and the United Kingdom.
Application information: Applications not accepted. The foundation practices an invitation only process for giving.
Officers and Directors:* Celeste A. Clark*, Pres.; Gary H. Pilnick, V.P.; Linda Fields, Secy.; Janice L. Perkins*, Treas.; Timothy S. Knowlton*, Exec. Dir.; Kris Charles; Paul Norman; Dennis W. Shuler; Steve Sterling; Mark Wagner.
EIN: 383167772
Selected grants: The following grants are a representative sample of this grantmaker's funding activity:
$3,181,365 to Truist, Washington, DC, 2011. For United Way.
$1,000,000 to Healthy Weight Commitment Foundation, Washington, DC, 2011. For nutrition research.
$900,000 to Community Foundation for Greater Manchester, Manchester, England, 2011.
$550,000 to Resource Foundation, New York, NY, 2011.
$250,000 to American Red Cross National Headquarters, Washington, DC, 2011. For disaster relief.
$250,000 to Global FoodBanking Network, Chicago, IL, 2011.
$100,000 to Action for Healthy Kids, Chicago, IL, 2011.

$72,000 to Baylor College of Medicine, USDA/ARS Children's Nutrition Research Center, Houston, TX, 2011. For nutrition research.
$50,000 to United Way of Quinte, Belleville, Canada, 2011.

2121
Kellwood Company

600 Kellwood Pkwy.
Chesterfield, MO 63017-5800
(314) 576-3100
FAX: (314) 576-3434

Company URL: http://www.kellwood.com
Establishment information: Established in 1961.
Company type: Subsidiary of a private company
Business activities: Manufactures and markets apparel and consumer soft goods.
Business type (SIC): Apparel—women's outerwear
Financial profile for 2010: Number of employees, 3,072
Corporate officers: Michael W. Kramer, Pres. and C.E.O.; Michael M. Saunders III, Sr. V.P. and C.O.O.; Steven Baginski, Sr. V.P. and C.F.O.
Subsidiaries: American Recreation Products, Inc., St. Louis, MO; A.J. Brandon, Vernon, CA; Cricket Lane, West Bridgewater, MA; Crowntuft, New York, NY; David Dart, Inc., Chatsworth, CA; DeCorp, Dallas, TX; E-N-C, City of Commerce, CA; Goodman Knitting, Brockton, MA; Halmode Apparel, Inc., New York, NY; Ivy, Vernon, CA; Kellwood Lingerie/ActiveWear, Summit, MS; Kellwood Sportswear, Rutherford, TN; Melrose, Chatsworth, CA; Sag Harbor, New York, NY; Robert Scott/David Brooks, Dedham, MA; Vintage Blue, Arleta, CA
International operations: Canada; China
Giving statement: Giving through the Kellwood Foundation.

The Kellwood Foundation

P.O. Box 78039
St. Louis, MO 63178-8039 (314) 576-3100
Application address: 600 Kellwood Pkwy., Chesterfield, MO 63017

Establishment information: Established in 1965 in IL.
Donor: Kellwood Co.
Contact: Teri Schmidt
Financial data (yr. ended 12/31/11): Assets, $1,493,147 (M); expenditures, $116,015; qualifying distributions, $115,000; giving activities include $115,000 for 7 grants (high: $50,000; low: $500).
Purpose and activities: The foundation supports organizations involved with education, health, cancer, and human services.
Fields of interest: Higher education; Education; Health care; Cancer; Recreation, camps; Children/youth, services; Human services; United Ways and Federated Giving Programs.
Type of support: Endowments; General/operating support; Matching/challenge support; Program development; Sponsorships.
Geographic limitations: Giving primarily in the greater St. Louis, MO, area.
Support limitations: No grants to individuals.
Application information: Applications accepted. Application form not required. Applicants should submit the following:
1) copy of IRS Determination Letter
2) detailed description of project and amount of funding requested
Initial approach: Proposal
Copies of proposal: 1
Board meeting date(s): Mar., June, Sept., and Dec.
Deadline(s): None
Officers and Directors: Patrick J. Sweeney, Secy.
Trustees: Michael W. Kramer.
Officers and Directors: Brandi Wilson, Treas.; Keith A. Grypp; Scott Mannis; Michael M. Saunders.
EIN: 366141441
Selected grants: The following grants are a representative sample of this grantmaker's funding activity:
$52,000 to Saint Patrick Center, Saint Louis, MO, 2010.
$35,000 to University of Missouri, Columbia, MO, 2010.
$30,100 to United Way of Greater Saint Louis, Saint Louis, MO, 2010.
$10,000 to American Red Cross, Saint Louis, MO, 2010.
$3,000 to Sherwood Forest Camp, Saint Louis, MO, 2010.
$2,250 to Magic House, Saint Louis, MO, 2010.

2122
Kelly Tractor Company

8255 N.W. 58th St.
Miami, FL 33166 (305) 592-5360
FAX: (305) 463-6066

Company URL: http://www.kellytractor.com
Establishment information: Established in 1933.
Company type: Private company
Business activities: Operates construction and industrial equipment dealerships.
Business type (SIC): Industrial machinery and equipment—wholesale; equipment rental and leasing/miscellaneous
Financial profile for 2012: Number of employees, 500
Corporate officers: Lloyd Kelly, Chair.; Fenando Cabrera, C.F.O.; Luis Botas, Pres.; Bridget Downey Duncan, Treas.
Board of director: Lloyd Kelly, Chair.
Giving statement: Giving through the Kelly Foundation, Inc.

Kelly Foundation, Inc.

17225 SW 77th Ct.
Miami, FL 33157-4859 (305) 238-2792
Application address: 801 E. Sugerland Hwy., Clewiston, FL 33440

Establishment information: Established in 1956 in FL.
Donor: Marjorie Kelly Trust.
Contact: Janis Isom, Secy.
Financial data (yr. ended 12/31/11): Assets, $19,893,782 (M); gifts received, $1,865,895; expenditures, $970,115; qualifying distributions, $910,450; giving activities include $242,000 for 33 grants (high: $50,000; low: $500) and $668,000 for 240 grants to individuals (high: $7,500; low: $500).
Purpose and activities: The foundation supports botanical gardens and organizations involved with education, health, housing development, human services, and other areas and awards college scholarships to undergraduate students.
Fields of interest: Education; Botanical gardens; Hospitals (general); Health care; Housing/shelter, development; Children, services; Human services; General charitable giving.
Type of support: Employee-related scholarships; General/operating support; Scholarship funds; Scholarships—to individuals.
Geographic limitations: Giving primarily in areas of company operations in FL.
Application information: Applications accepted. Generally, unsolicited requests for general operating support are not accepted. Application form required. Scholarship applications should include transcripts, letters of recommendation, and an essay.
Initial approach: Contact foundation for application form
Deadline(s): None for scholarships
Officers and Directors: Loyd G. Kelly, Chair. and Pres.; Nicholas D. Kelly, Vice.-Chair.; Janis Isom, Secy.; Barbara Kelly; Eileen Kelly; Loyd Patrick Kelly; Luisa Kelly; Robert W. Kelly, Jr.; Alden M. Wyse.
EIN: 596153269
Selected grants: The following grants are a representative sample of this grantmaker's funding activity:
$250,000 to University of Miami, Coral Gables, FL, 2010. For general support.
$50,000 to Immokalee Foundation, Naples, FL, 2010. For general support.
$10,000 to Habitat for Humanity of Greater Miami, Miami, FL, 2010. For general support.
$5,000 to New Hope Charities, West Palm Beach, FL, 2010. For general support.
$5,000 to Newark Museum, Newark, NJ, 2010. For general support.
$5,000 to Rollins College, Winter Park, FL, 2010. For general support.
$2,500 to Garden Conservancy, Cold Spring, NY, 2010. For general support.
$1,000 to Fishers Island Conservancy, Fishers Island, NY, 2010. For general support.
$1,000 to Northwest Missouri State University, Maryville, MO, 2010. For general support.

2123
Kemp, Klein, Umphrey, Endelman & May P.C.

201 W. Big Beaver Rd., Ste. 600
Troy, MI 48084-4136 (248) 528-1111

Company URL: http://www.kkue.com
Establishment information: Established in 1971.
Company type: Private company
Business activities: Provides legal services.
Business type (SIC): Legal services
Corporate officers: Ralph A. Castelli, Jr., Chair. and C.E.O.; Jean Russell, C.I.O.; Thomas C. Rauch, V.P. and Secy.; Pam Mackley, Cont.; John B. Kemp, Chair. Emeritus
Board of directors: Ralph A. Castelli, Jr., Chair.; William B. Acker; James P. Davey; Mark R. Filipp; John B. Kemp
Giving statement: Giving through the Kemp, Klein, Umphrey, Endelman & May Foundation.

Kemp, Klein, Umphrey, Endelman & May Foundation

(formerly Kemp Klein Foundation)
201 W. Big Beaver Rd., Ste. 600
Troy, MI 48084-4161 (248) 528-1111
URL: http://www.kkue.com/kemp-klein-charitable-foundation.php

Establishment information: Established in 1994 in MI.
Donors: Kemp, Klein, Umphrey, Endelman & May, PC; Turner & Turner, P.C.
Contact: Ralph A. Castelli, Jr., Pres.
Financial data (yr. ended 12/31/11): Assets, $11,842 (M); gifts received, $15,071; expenditures, $15,475; qualifying distributions,

$15,475; giving activities include $15,475 for 31 grants (high: $10,000; low: $25).
Purpose and activities: The foundation supports food banks and organizations involved with education, animal welfare, health, legal aid, human services, and voluntarism promotion.
Fields of interest: Higher education; Law school/education; Education, reading; Education; Animal welfare; Animals/wildlife, special services; Health care; Legal services; Food banks; Children/youth, services; Residential/custodial care, hospices; Human services; Voluntarism promotion.
Type of support: Curriculum development; General/operating support; Program development.
Geographic limitations: Giving primarily in MI.
Support limitations: No grants to individuals.
Application information: Applications accepted. Application form required.
Initial approach: Letter
Deadline(s): None
Officers: Ralph A. Castelli, Jr., Pres. and Treas.; Thomas J. O'Connor, Secy.
Directors: Gloria M. Chon; Cynthia A. Frobes; Faith M. Gaudean; Brian H. Rolfe; Diane Szalkiewicz; Thomas Trainer; Kathy Verlinde; Diane Vigliotti.
EIN: 383169464

2124
Kemper Sports Management, Inc.

500 Skokie Blvd., Ste. 444
Northbrook, IL 60062-2844 (847) 850-1818

Company URL: http://www.kempersports.com
Establishment information: Established in 1978.
Company type: Private company
Business activities: Provides golf course management services; provides golf course design services.
Business type (SIC): Management and public relations services; landscape and horticultural services
Corporate officers: Steven H. Lesnik, Chair.; Steven K. Skinner, C.E.O.; John W. Lesnik, Pres.; Brain Milligan, C.F.O.; James R. Seeley, Exec. V.P., Opers.; Tom Saathoff, V.P., Opers.; John C. Clarke, V.P. and Corp. Cont.
Board of director: Steven H. Lesnik, Chair.
Giving statement: Giving through the Lesnik Charitable Foundation.

Lesnik Charitable Foundation

c/o Steven H. Lesnik
500 Skokie Blvd., Ste. 444
Northbrook, IL 60062-2867

Establishment information: Established in 1999 in IL.
Donors: Kemper Sports Management, Inc.; KemperLesnik Integrated Comms.; Royal Melbourne.
Financial data (yr. ended 12/31/11): Assets, $39,853 (M); gifts received, $101,550; expenditures, $102,315; qualifying distributions, $102,315; giving activities include $74,375 for 22 grants (high: $25,000; low: $250).
Purpose and activities: The foundation supports museums and organizations involved with ballet, education, golf, and human services.
Fields of interest: Arts; Youth development; Religion.
Type of support: General/operating support; Scholarship funds.
Geographic limitations: Giving primarily in IL.
Support limitations: No grants to individuals.
Application information: Applications not accepted. Unsolicited requests for funds not accepted.
Trustees: Madeline S. Lesnik; Steven H. Lesnik.
EIN: 367293339

2125
Kennametal Inc.

1600 Technology Way
P.O. Box 231
Latrobe, PA 15650-0231 (724) 539-5000
FAX: (724) 539-5701

Company URL: http://www.kennametal.com/
Establishment information: Established in 1938.
Company type: Public company
Company ticker symbol and exchange: KMT/NYSE
Business activities: Manufactures, markets, and distributes metalworking, coal mining, and highway construction tools.
Business type (SIC): Machinery/metalworking; steel mill products; metal refining/primary nonferrous; metal products/primary; machinery/construction, mining, and materials handling; electrical industrial apparatus
Financial profile for 2012: Number of employees, 12,900; assets, $3,034,190,000; sales volume, $2,736,250,000; pre-tax net income, $389,970,000; expenses, $2,319,840,000; liabilities, $1,390,340,000
Fortune 1000 ranking: 2012—761st in revenues, 461st in profits, and 746th in assets
Corporate officers: Carlos M. Cardoso, Chair., Pres., and C.E.O.; Frank P. Simpkins, V.P. and C.F.O.; Steven R. Hanna, V.P. and C.I.O.; Kevin G. Nowe, V.P., Genl. Counsel, and Secy.; Brian E. Kelly, V.P. and Treas.; Martha A. Bailey, V.P., Finance, and Corp. Cont.
Board of directors: Carlos M. Cardoso, Chair.; Cindy L. Davis; Ronald M. DeFeo; Philip A. Dur; William J. Harvey; Timothy R. McLevish; William R. Newlin; Lawrence W. Stranghoener; Steven H. Wunning; Larry D. Yost
Subsidiary: J & L America, Inc., Detroit, MI
Plants: Fallon, NV; Henderson, Roanoke Rapids, NC; Orwell, Solon, OH; Bedford, Latrobe, PA; Johnson City, TN; New Market, VA
International operations: Australia; Cayman Islands; China; Germany; India; Italy; Japan; Luxembourg; Malaysia; Panama; Singapore; South Africa; South Korea; Taiwan; Thailand; United Kingdom
Giving statement: Giving through the Kennametal Inc. Corporate Giving Program and the Kennametal Foundation.
Company EIN: 250900168

Kennametal Inc. Corporate Giving Program

1600 Technology Way
Latrobe, PA 15650-4647 (724) 539-5000
URL: http://www.kennametal.com/kennametal/en/about-us/in-the-community.html

Purpose and activities: As a complement to its foundation, Kennametal also makes charitable contributions to the United Way. Support is given primarily in areas of company operations.
Fields of interest: United Ways and Federated Giving Programs.
Type of support: General/operating support.
Geographic limitations: Giving primarily in areas of company operations.
Application information: Applications not accepted. Contributes to the United Way only.

Kennametal Foundation

P.O. Box 231
Latrobe, PA 15650-0231 (724) 539-5000
Application address: 1600 Technology Way, Latrobe, PA 15650; URL: http://www.kennametal.com/kennametal/en/about-us/in-the-community.html

Establishment information: Established in 1955 in PA.
Donor: Kennametal Inc.
Contact: Erica Clayton Wright, Mgr., Public Affairs
Financial data (yr. ended 06/30/12): Assets, $79,201 (M); gifts received, $555,000; expenditures, $497,531; qualifying distributions, $479,936; giving activities include $479,936 for grants.
Purpose and activities: The foundation supports organizations involved with education and science.
Fields of interest: Secondary school/education; Higher education; Science, formal/general education; Engineering/technology; Science.
Programs:
Kennametal in the Community: The foundation supports partnerships with community organizations with which Kennametal employees volunteer their time.
TechEdNet: The foundation supports secondary and post secondary education, with emphasis on studies in areas of technical engineering, machine skill training and materials, and environmental sciences.
Type of support: Building/renovation; Continuing support; Employee volunteer services; Equipment; General/operating support; Scholarship funds.
Geographic limitations: Giving on a global basis in areas of company operations, with some emphasis on PA.
Support limitations: No support for sectarian or religious organizations, political organizations, private foundations, or trust funds. No grants to individuals, or for endowments, development campaigns, debt reduction, or operating reserves, fundraising events or sponsorships, trips, conferences, seminars, festivals, or one-day events, documentaries, videos, research projects/programs, or indirect or overhead costs.
Publications: Application guidelines.
Application information: Applications accepted. Application form required. Applicants should submit the following:
1) name, address and phone number of organization
2) detailed description of project and amount of funding requested
Initial approach: Complete online application form
Board meeting date(s): Annually
Deadline(s): Last Fri. in May
Trustees: Carlos M. Cardoso; Joy Chandler; David W. Greenfield; Frank P. Simpkins; Cathy Smith; Phil Wehl.
EIN: 256036009
Selected grants: The following grants are a representative sample of this grantmaker's funding activity:
$75,000 to Saint Vincent College, Latrobe, PA, 2011. For general purpose.
$25,000 to American Heart Association, Greensburg, PA, 2011. For general purpose.
$25,000 to New Century Careers, Pittsburgh, PA, 2011. For general purpose.
$15,000 to Childrens Institute of Pittsburgh, Pittsburgh, PA, 2011. For general purpose.
$12,000 to Tianjin University, Tianjin, China, 2011. For general purpose.
$8,250 to Seton Hill University, Greensburg, PA, 2011. For general purpose.

$7,500 to World Affairs Council of Pittsburgh, Pittsburgh, PA, 2011. For general purpose.
$5,000 to Milwaukee School of Engineering, Milwaukee, WI, 2011. For general purpose.
$5,000 to Pittsburgh Cancer Institute, Pittsburgh, PA, 2011. For general purpose.
$3,400 to Cabbage Patch Settlement House, Louisville, KY, 2011. For general purpose.

2126
Kennebunk Savings Bank

104 Main St.
P.O. Box 28
Kennebunk, ME 04043-7023
(207) 985-4903

Company URL: http://www.kennebunksavings.com
Establishment information: Established in 1871.
Company type: Private company
Business activities: Operates savings bank; sells casualty and automobile insurance.
Business type (SIC): Savings institutions; insurance/fire, marine, and casualty
Corporate officers: Brad Paige, Pres. and C.E.O.; Fred Scott, C.O.O.; Amanda Batson, Sr. V.P. and C.I.O.
Offices: Berwick, Eliot, Kittery, North Berwick, Ogunquit, Sanford, Wells, York, ME
Giving statement: Giving through the Kennebunk Savings Bank Foundation.

Kennebunk Savings Bank Foundation

104 Main St.
P.O. Box 28
Kennebunk, ME 04043-0028 (800) 339-6573
URL: http://www.kennebunksavings.com/community.html

Establishment information: Established in 2001 in ME.
Donors: Kennebunk Savings Bank; Autumn Health Svcs. of Kennebunk.
Financial data (yr. ended 12/31/11): Assets, $3,619,356 (M); gifts received, $92,556; expenditures, $227,889; qualifying distributions, $208,490; giving activities include $208,490 for grants.
Purpose and activities: The foundation supports organizations involved with arts and culture, education, conservation, wildlife, human services, community development, civic affairs, and senior citizens.
Fields of interest: Arts; Education; Environment, natural resources; Animals/wildlife, sanctuaries; Human services; Economic development; Community/economic development; Public affairs Aging.
Programs:

Arts: The foundation supports programs designed to preserve and enhance the cultural opportunities and infrastructure of the community.

Civic Initiatives: The foundation supports programs designed to promote economic development; improve quality of life for local citizens; and strengthen the basic foundation of the community.

Education: The foundation supports programs designed to enhance academic achievement and aspirations of all citizens in the community.

Environmental Programs: The foundation supports programs designed to protect and preserve unique landscapes and wildlife habitats.

Human Services: The foundation supports programs designed to enhance quality of life for citizens in the community, especially those most in need.

Huntington Common Charitable Fund for Seniors: The foundation supports programs designed to help York County seniors ages 65 or older lead more complete and fulfilled lives.

Type of support: General/operating support.
Geographic limitations: Giving limited to areas of company operations in ME.
Support limitations: No support for religious or political organizations. No grants to individuals.
Publications: Application guidelines; Program policy statement.
Application information: Applications accepted. Application form required. Applicants should submit the following:
1) population served
2) name, address and phone number of organization
3) copy of IRS Determination Letter
4) copy of most recent annual report/audited financial statement/990
5) listing of board of directors, trustees, officers and other key people and their affiliations
6) detailed description of project and amount of funding requested
7) contact person
8) copy of current year's organizational budget and/or project budget
9) listing of additional sources and amount of support

Initial approach: Complete online application form
Board meeting date(s): Monthly
Deadline(s): None

Officers and Directors:* Andrew T. Furlong, Jr.*, Chair.; Wayne F. Manchester*, Vice-Chair.; Bradford C. Paige*, Pres.; Dennis Byrd, Exec. V.P.; Stephen A. Morris*, Exec. V.P.; Stephen A. Soubble, Sr. V.P.; Robyn LeBuff, V.P.; Susan F. Hoctor, Secy. and Clerk; Pamela J. Drew*, Treas. and Mgr.; Richard V. Bibber; James J. Keating III; Raymond E. Mailhot; Geoffrey Titherington.
EIN: 010547392

2127
Kennecott Utah Copper Corporation

8362 W. 10200 S.
Bingham Canyon, UT 84006-1197
(801) 569-6000

Company URL: http://www.kennecott.com
Establishment information: Established in 1903.
Company type: Subsidiary of a foreign company
Business activities: Mines copper.
Business type (SIC): Mining/copper
Corporate officers: Kelly Sanders, Pres. and C.E.O.; Clayton Walker, C.O.O.; Patrick Keenan, C.F.O.; Nicky Firth, V.P., Human Resources
Giving statement: Giving through the Kennecott Utah Copper Corporation Contributions Program and the Kennecott Utah Copper Visitors Center Charitable Foundation.

Kennecott Utah Copper Corporation Contributions Program

P.O. Box 6001
Magna, UT 84044-6001
FAX: (801) 569-7434;
E-mail: chantae.lessard@kennecott.com;
URL: http://www.kennecott.com/?id=MjAwMDA5OQ==

Contact: Chantae Lessard, Community Rels. Advisor
Purpose and activities: As a complement to its foundation, Kennecott also makes charitable contributions to nonprofit organizations directly. Support is limited to Utah.
Fields of interest: Arts; Education; Environment; Youth development; Human services; Community/economic development.
Type of support: Donated equipment; Donated land; Employee matching gifts; General/operating support; In-kind gifts; Scholarship funds.
Geographic limitations: Giving limited to UT, with emphasis on Salt Lake County.
Publications: Corporate giving report.
Application information: Applications not accepted. Contributes only to pre-selected organizations. The Government and Public Affairs Department handles giving.
Administrators: Louis J. Cononelos, Dir., Govt. and Public Affairs; Chantae Lessard, Community Rels. Advisor.
Number of staff: 1 full-time professional.

Kennecott Utah Copper Visitors Center Charitable Foundation

4700 Daybreak Pkwy.
South Jordan, UT 84095-5120 (801) 204-2355
FAX: (801) 569-7434;
E-mail: brian.davis@riotinto.com; URL: http://www.kennecott.com/kennecott-foundation

Establishment information: Established in 1994 in UT.
Donors: Mrs. Herb Babcock; Kennecott Utah Copper Corp.
Contact: Brian Davis
Financial data (yr. ended 12/31/11): Assets, $740,616 (M); gifts received, $267,218; expenditures, $253,782; qualifying distributions, $253,601; giving activities include $253,601 for grants.
Purpose and activities: The foundation supports organizations involved with health, human services, senior citizens, disabled people, and homeless people.
Fields of interest: Health care; Children/youth, services; Human services Aging; Disabilities, people with; Homeless.
Type of support: Annual campaigns; Continuing support; General/operating support; Program development.
Geographic limitations: Giving primarily in areas of company operations in Salt Lake, UT.
Publications: Application guidelines.
Application information: Applications accepted. Application form required. Applicants should submit the following:
1) copy of IRS Determination Letter
2) detailed description of project and amount of funding requested

Initial approach: Download application form and mail proposal and application form to foundation
Copies of proposal: 1
Board meeting date(s): 2 to 3 times per year
Deadline(s): Oct. 15
Final notification: Dec.

Officers and Trustees:* Ted Himebaugh*, Pres.; Julie Cummings*, Secy.; Jack Welch*, Treas.; Rev. Patrick Carley; Gary Curtis; Norm Fitzgerald; Scott Whipple.
EIN: 870560044
Selected grants: The following grants are a representative sample of this grantmaker's funding activity:
$29,158 to Granite Education Foundation, Salt Lake City, UT, 2010.
$18,149 to Magna Fact, Magna, UT, 2010.

$18,134 to Utah Food Bank, Salt Lake City, UT, 2010.
$15,109 to Saint Vincent de Paul Center, Salt Lake City, UT, 2010.
$10,571 to Road Home, Salt Lake City, UT, 2010.
$6,000 to Regence Caring Foundation for Children, Salt Lake City, UT, 2010.
$4,000 to Crossroads Urban Center, Salt Lake City, UT, 2010.
$2,000 to Holy Cross Ministries, Salt Lake City, UT, 2010.
$1,500 to Salt Lake Sexual Assault Nurse Examiners, Salt Lake City, UT, 2010.
$1,158 to Salt Lake Education Foundation, Salt Lake City, UT, 2010. For general support.

2128
Kenneth Cole Productions, Inc.

603 W. 50th St.
New York, NY 10019 (212) 265-1500
FAX: (212) 315-8279

Company URL: http://www.kennethcole.com
Establishment information: Established in 1982.
Company type: Public company
Company ticker symbol and exchange: KCP/NYSE
Business activities: Designs, sources and markets fashion footwear, handbags and apparel and, through license agreements, designs and markets apparel and accessories.
Business type (SIC): Leather footwear
Financial profile for 2011: Number of employees, 1,600; assets, $249,820,000; sales volume, $478,940,000; pre-tax net income, -$2,010,000; expenses, $480,840,000; liabilities, $105,950,000
Corporate officers: Kenneth D. Cole, Chair.; Paul Blum, C.E.O.; David P. Edelman, C.F.O. and Treas.; Michael F. Colosi, Sr. V.P., Genl. Counsel, and Secy.
Board of directors: Kenneth D. Cole, Chair.; Michael J. Blitzer; Paul Blum; Robert C. Grayson; Denis F. Kelly; Philip R. Peller
International operations: Bahamas; China; Hong Kong; Netherlands
Giving statement: Giving through the Kenneth Cole Productions Foundation.
Company EIN: 133131650

Kenneth Cole Productions Foundation

400 Plaza Dr., 3rd Fl.
Secaucus, NJ 07094-3605
Application address: c/o Ms. C. Walker, 601 W. 50th St., New York, NY 10019, tel.: (212) 265-1500

Donor: Kenneth Cole Productions, Inc.
Financial data (yr. ended 12/31/11): Assets, $653,338 (M); gifts received, $38,274; expenditures, $641,466; qualifying distributions, $641,466; giving activities include $641,304 for 74 grants (high: $50,000; low: $80).
Purpose and activities: The foundation supports organizations involved with arts and culture, HIV/AIDS research, youth development, the fashion industry, and Judaism.
Fields of interest: Media, print publishing; Museums (art); Performing arts centers; Arts; AIDS; AIDS research; Legal services; Girl scouts; Business/industry; Jewish agencies & synagogues.
Type of support: General/operating support.
Geographic limitations: Giving primarily in New York, NY.
Application information: Applications accepted. Generally contributes only to pre-selected organizations. Application form not required. Applicants should submit the following:
1) detailed description of project and amount of funding requested
Initial approach: Proposal
Deadline(s): None
Directors: Kenneth D. Cole; Michael F. Colosi; David P. Edelman; Dieter C. Pasewaldt.
EIN: 562283049
Selected grants: The following grants are a representative sample of this grantmaker's funding activity:
$50,000 to Metropolitan Museum of Art, New York, NY, 2011.
$25,000 to Foundation for AIDS Research, New York, NY, 2011.
$25,000 to Two Ten Footwear Foundation, Waltham, MA, 2011.
$15,000 to Candies Foundation, New York, NY, 2011.
$15,000 to Figure Skating in Harlem, New York, NY, 2011.
$15,000 to YMA Fashion Scholarship Fund, New York, NY, 2011.
$10,000 to Phoenix House Foundation, New York, NY, 2011.
$5,904 to Community AIDS Resource, Miami, FL, 2011.
$5,000 to LitWorld International, New York, NY, 2011.
$3,333 to Oceana, Washington, DC, 2011.

2129
Kent Feeds, Inc.

1600 Oregon St.
P.O. Box 749
Muscatine, IA 52761 (563) 264-4211

Company URL: http://www.kentfeeds.com
Establishment information: Established in 1927.
Company type: Subsidiary of a private company
Business activities: Produces livestock feed.
Business type (SIC): Grain mill products, including pet food
Corporate officers: Gage A. Kent, Chair.; Richard M. Dwyer, Pres.; Dave Jones, Treas. and C.F.O.; J.S. Huff, Secy.; Tony Woods, V.P. and Cont.; Peter Simonsen, V.P., Opers.; Dan Paca, V.P., Sales; Janet R. Sichterman, V.P., Human Resources
Board of director: Gage A. Kent, Chair.
Giving statement: Giving through the Kent Feeds, Inc. Corporate Giving Program.

Kent Feeds, Inc. Corporate Giving Program

1600 Oregon St.
Muscatine, IA 52761-1404 (563) 264-4211

Contact: Jeff Bowling
Purpose and activities: Kent Feeds makes charitable contributions to nonprofit organizations involved with agriculture, youth development, and on a case by case basis. Support is given primarily in areas of company operations.
Fields of interest: Agriculture; Youth development; General charitable giving.
Type of support: Employee volunteer services; General/operating support; In-kind gifts; Sponsorships.
Geographic limitations: Giving primarily in areas of company operations.
Support limitations: No grants to individuals.
Application information: Applications accepted. A contributions committee reviews all requests. Application form not required.
Initial approach: Proposal to headquarters
Copies of proposal: 1
Deadline(s): None
Final notification: Following review

2130
Kentuckiana Roofing Co., Inc.

3816 Ethel Ave.
Louisville, KY 40218-2643 (502) 893-5149

Company URL: http://www.kyanaroof.com
Establishment information: Established in 1987.
Company type: Private company
Business activities: Provides general contract roofing services.
Business type (SIC): Contractors/roofing, siding, and sheet metal work
Corporate officer: David J. Brown, Pres.
Giving statement: Giving through the AEB Charities, Inc.

AEB Charities, Inc.

11316 Bodley Dr.
Louisville, KY 40223-1339 (502) 456-1067

Establishment information: Established in 1992 in KY.
Donor: Kentuckiana Roofing Co., Inc.
Contact: David J. Brown, Pres.
Financial data (yr. ended 09/30/11): Assets, $20,092 (M); expenditures, $5,200; qualifying distributions, $5,150; giving activities include $5,150 for 2 grants (high: $5,000; low: $150).
Purpose and activities: The foundation supports organizations involved with religion and other areas.
Fields of interest: Religion.
Type of support: General/operating support.
Geographic limitations: Giving primarily in Louisville, KY.
Application information: Applications accepted. Application form not required.
Initial approach: Proposal
Deadline(s): None
Officers: David J. Brown, Pres.; Amanda Brown, Secy.
Directors: Marie Bishop; Nicholas J. Bishop; John J. Sabbak.
EIN: 611258130

2131
Kenyon & Kenyon LLP

1 Broadway
New York, NY 10004-1007 (212) 908-6177

Company URL: http://www.kenyon.com
Establishment information: Established in 1879.
Company type: Private company
Business activities: Operates law firm.
Business type (SIC): Legal services
Offices: San Jose, CA; Washington, DC; New York, NY
Giving statement: Giving through the Kenyon & Kenyon LLP Pro Bono Program.

Kenyon & Kenyon LLP Pro Bono Program

1 Broadway
New York, NY 10004-1007 (212) 908-6117
E-mail: jtsavaris@kenyon.com; Contact for Pro Bono program: Dr. John Tsavaris, Dir. of Professional Devel., tel.: (212) 908-6117, fax: (212) 425-5288, e-mail: jtsavaris@kenyon.com; URL: http://www.kenyon.com/en/About/Community.aspx

Contact: Dr. John Tsavaris, Dir. of Professional Devel.
Fields of interest: Legal services.
Type of support: Pro bono services - legal.
Geographic limitations: Giving primarily in areas of company operations in San Jose, CA, Washington, DC, and New York, NY.
Application information: A Pro Bono Coordinator manages the pro bono program.

2132
Kepco, Inc.

131-38 Sanford Ave.
Flushing, NY 11355-4231 (718) 461-7000

Company URL: http://www.kepcopower.com
Establishment information: Established in 1946.
Company type: Private company
Business activities: Manufactures power supplies.
Business type (SIC): Electric transmission and distribution equipment
Corporate officers: Max L. Kupferberg, Chair.; Martin Kupferberg, C.E.O.; Charles Fay, C.O.O.
Board of director: Max L. Kupferberg, Chair.
Giving statement: Giving through the Kupferberg Foundation.

The Kupferberg Foundation

131-38 Sanford Ave.
Flushing, NY 11355-4231

Establishment information: Established in 1961 in NY.
Donors: Jesse Kupferberg; Max Kupferberg; Kepco, Inc.
Financial data (yr. ended 11/30/11): Assets, $11,614,457 (M); expenditures, $673,655; qualifying distributions, $576,021; giving activities include $576,021 for grants.
Purpose and activities: The foundation supports organizations involved with arts and culture, education, health, autism, eye disease research, human services, and Judaism.
Fields of interest: Museums (science/technology); Arts; Elementary school/education; Higher education; Education; Hospitals (general); Health care; Autism; Eye research; Children/youth, services; Human services; Jewish agencies & synagogues.
Type of support: General/operating support.
Geographic limitations: Giving primarily in New York and Queens, NY.
Support limitations: No grants to individuals.
Application information: Applications not accepted. Contributes only to pre-selected organizations.
Officer and Trustees: Max Kupferberg, Pres.; Martin Kupferberg; Saul Kupferberg.
EIN: 116008915
Selected grants: The following grants are a representative sample of this grantmaker's funding activity:
$20,000 to Autism Speaks, Port Chester, NY, 2011.
$12,000 to Queens Botanical Garden Society, Flushing, NY, 2011.
$12,000 to Ramapo for Children, Rhinebeck, NY, 2011.
$9,000 to MATAN: The Gift of Jewish Learning for Every Child, White Plains, NY, 2011.
$5,000 to Anti-Defamation League of Bnai Brith, New York, NY, 2011. For general support.
$5,000 to Saint Francis Hospital, Roslyn, NY, 2011.
$3,000 to Ackerman Institute for the Family, New York, NY, 2011. For general support.
$3,000 to Crohns and Colitis Foundation of America, Garden City, NY, 2011. For general support.
$3,000 to Queens Museum of Art, Flushing, NY, 2011. For general support.
$2,000 to International Rescue Committee, New York, NY, 2011. For general support.

2133
Kerzner International Resorts, Inc.

1000 S. Pine Island Rd., Ste. 800
Plantation, FL 33324-3907 (954) 809-2000
FAX: (954) 809-2337

Company URL: http://www.kerzner.com
Establishment information: Established in 1993.
Company type: Private company
Business activities: Operates luxury hotels and casino resorts.
Business type (SIC): Hotels and motels
Corporate officers: Solomon Kerzner, Chair.; Alan Leibman, C.E.O.; Bonnie Biumi, Pres. and C.F.O.; Monica Digilio, Exec. V.P., Human Resources, and Admin.
Board of director: Solomon Kerzner, Chair.
Giving statement: Giving through the Kerzner Marine Foundation, Inc.

Kerzner Marine Foundation, Inc.

1000 S. Pine Island Rd., Ste. 800
Plantation, FL 33324-3909
E-mail: info@kerznermarinefoundation.org; E-mail for Debra Erickson: debra.erickson@kerzner.com; URL: http://www.kerznermarinefoundation.org

Establishment information: Established in 2005 in FL.
Donor: Kerzner International Bahamas.
Contact: Debra Erickson, Exec. Dir.
Financial data (yr. ended 12/31/11): Assets, $489,936 (M); gifts received, $711,685; expenditures, $383,498; qualifying distributions, $328,000; giving activities include $328,000 for grants.
Purpose and activities: The foundation supports programs designed to preserve and enhance global marine ecosystems through scientific research, education, and community outreach. Special emphasis is directed toward marine protected areas, coral reef conservation, cetacean conservation, and research in the Caribbean, Middle East, and Southeast Asia.
Fields of interest: Environment, research; Environment, natural resources; Environment, water resources; Animals/wildlife, research; Animals/wildlife, endangered species; Animals/wildlife.
International interests: Asia; Caribbean; Middle East.
Type of support: Building/renovation; Continuing support; Management development/capacity building; Program development; Research.
Geographic limitations: Giving primarily in CA, FL, NY and in the Caribbean, Middle East, and Southeast Asia.
Support limitations: No support for political activism. No grants for litigation, or for fundraising, scholarships, endowments or overhead costs for universities.
Publications: Informational brochure.
Application information: Applications accepted. Proposals should include a cover page; 2 page abstract; a program or research description of up to 20 pages; an intuitional capacity description of up to 3 pages; a project team description with resumes; and past performance references. Applicants should submit the following:
1) timetable for implementation and evaluation of project
2) results expected from proposed grant
3) qualifications of key personnel
4) statement of problem project will address
5) copy of IRS Determination Letter
6) copy of most recent annual report/audited financial statement/990
7) how project's results will be evaluated or measured
8) detailed description of project and amount of funding requested
9) copy of current year's organizational budget and/or project budget

Initial approach: Proposal
Copies of proposal: 5
Deadline(s): Apr. 15 and Sept. 15

Officers and Directors:* George Markantonis*, Pres. and Managing Dir.; Paul K. Dayton*, V.P.; Tim Wise*, Treas.; Debra Erickson, Exec. Dir.; Steve Kaiser.
EIN: 342045752
Selected grants: The following grants are a representative sample of this grantmaker's funding activity:
$100,000 to Hubbs-SeaWorld Research Institute, San Diego, CA, 2009.
$43,100 to Perry Institute for Marine Science, Jupiter, FL, 2009.

2134
Key Container Corporation

21 Campbell St.
P.O. Box 2370
Pawtucket, RI 02861-2370 (401) 723-2000
FAX: (401) 725-5980

Company URL: http://www.keycontainercorp.com
Establishment information: Established in 1960.
Company type: Private company
Business activities: Manufactures corrugated products, foam polyethylene products, polyurethane components, and wood crating products.
Business type (SIC): Paperboard containers; wood containers; paper and paperboard/coated, converted, and laminated
Financial profile for 2009: Number of employees, 185
Corporate officers: David Strauss, Pres. and C.E.O.; Domenic Lapati, Sr. V.P., Finance
Board of director: David Strauss
Giving statement: Giving through the Sundel-Strauss Family Foundation.

Sundel-Strauss Family Foundation

(formerly Sundel Family Foundation)
P.O. Box 2370
Pawtucket, RI 02861-0370 (401) 723-2000

Establishment information: Established in 1969 in RI.
Donors: Jacob Sundel†; Claire Sundel†; Key Container Corp.
Contact: Sylvia S. Strauss, Tr.
Financial data (yr. ended 12/31/11): Assets, $528,757 (M); gifts received, $12,500; expenditures, $58,762; qualifying distributions, $52,302; giving activities include $52,302 for grants.
Purpose and activities: The foundation supports hospitals and organizations involved with higher education, human services, and Judaism.

Fields of interest: Education; Youth development; Religion.
Type of support: Scholarship funds.
Application information: Applications accepted. Application form not required.
Initial approach: Proposal
Deadline(s): None
Trustees: David Strauss; Sylvia Sundel Strauss; Debra Strauss-Levine.
Number of staff: None.
EIN: 237011406

2135
Key Food Stores Cooperative, Inc.

1200 S. Ave., Ste. 103
Staten Island, NY 10314 (718) 370-4200

Company URL: http://www.keyfood.com
Establishment information: Established in 1937.
Company type: Cooperative
Business activities: Operates supermarkets.
Business type (SIC): Groceries—retail
Corporate officers: Sheldon M. Geller, Chair.; Dean Janeway, C.E.O.; Lawrence Mandel, Pres.
Board of director: Sheldon M. Geller, Chair.
Subsidiaries: Dan's Supreme Supermarkets, Inc., Hempstead, NY; Man-Dell Food Stores, Inc., Bellerose, NY; Pick Quickfoods, Inc., Ozone Park, NJ
Giving statement: Giving through the Morris Levine Key Food Stores Foundation, Inc.

Morris Levine Key Food Stores Foundation, Inc.

(formerly Key Food Stores Foundation, Inc.)
1200 South Ave.
Staten Island, NY 10314-3413

Establishment information: Established in 1962 in NY.
Donors: Key Food Stores Cooperative, Inc.; Allen Newman; Man-Dell Food Stores, Inc.; Pick Quickfoods, Inc.; Dan's Supreme Supermarkets, Inc.; Frank & Roslyn Grobman Foundation; Donald & Linda Gross Foundation.
Financial data (yr. ended 08/31/11): Assets, $281,736 (M); gifts received, $58,500; expenditures, $374,001; qualifying distributions, $217,090; giving activities include $213,088 for 33 grants (high: $50,000; low: $250).
Purpose and activities: The foundation supports community centers and organizations involved with health, cystic fibrosis, cancer research, youth, homelessness, and Judaism.
Fields of interest: Education; Health care; Health organizations.
Type of support: General/operating support.
Geographic limitations: Giving primarily in NY.
Support limitations: No grants to individuals.
Application information: Applications not accepted. Unsolicited requests for funds not accepted.
Officers and Directors: Dean Janeway*, Pres.; Jerry Cesaro*, Secy.Treas.; Lawrence Mandel.
EIN: 116035538

2136
KeyBank N.A.

127 Public Sq., Ste. 5600
Cleveland, OH 44114-1226 (216) 689-3000

Company URL: http://www.keybank.com
Establishment information: Established in 1858.
Company type: Subsidiary of a public company
Business activities: Operates commercial bank.
Business type (SIC): Banks/commercial
Financial profile for 2010: Number of employees, 18,095; sales volume, $3,728,510,000
Corporate officers: Christopher M. Gorman, Chair. and C.E.O.; William R. Koehler, Pres.; Michael P. Barnum, Exec. V.P., Opers.
Board of directors: Christopher M. Gorman, Chair.; Michael P. Barnum; Paul N. Harris
Offices: Anchorage, AK; Denver, CO; Fort Myers, FL; Boise, ID; Indianapolis, South Bend, IN; Portland, ME; Ann Arbor, MI; Albany, Buffalo, Newburgh, Rochester, Syracuse, NY; Akron, Canton, Cincinnati, Columbus, Dayton, Toledo, OH; Portland, OR; Salt Lake City, UT; Burlington, VT; Bellevue, Bellingham, Tacoma, WA
Giving statement: Giving through the KeyBank N.A. Corporate Giving Program, the Evertrust Foundation, the Key Bank of Central Maine Foundation, and the KeyBank Foundation.

KeyBank N.A. Corporate Giving Program

c/o Civic Affairs, M.C. OH-01-27-0705
127 Public Sq., 7th Fl.
Cleveland, OH 44114-1306 (216) 689-5458
FAX: (216) 689-5444

Contact: Valerie Raines, V.P., Corp. Philanthropy
Financial data (yr. ended 12/31/07): Total giving, $5,973,000, including $5,973,000 for grants.
Purpose and activities: As a complement to its foundation, KeyBank also makes charitable contributions to nonprofit organizations directly. Support is given on a national basis.
Fields of interest: Arts; Education; Health care; Employment; Human services, financial counseling; Human services Economically disadvantaged.
Type of support: In-kind gifts; Sponsorships.
Geographic limitations: Giving on a national basis in areas of company operations.
Support limitations: No support for religious, international, or political organizations.
Publications: Application guidelines; Corporate giving report.
Application information: Application form not required.
Initial approach: Complete online application
Copies of proposal: 1
Deadline(s): None
Final notification: 1 month

Evertrust Foundation

(formerly Everett Mutual Savings Bank Foundation)
P.O. Box 1245
Everett, WA 98206-1245 (425) 339-1286
URL: http://www.evertrustfoundation.com/index.htm

Establishment information: Established in 1993.
Donor: Everett Mutual Savings Bank.
Contact: Mary B. Sievers, Secy. and Exec. Dir.
Financial data (yr. ended 12/31/11): Assets, $8,381,136 (M); expenditures, $569,380; qualifying distributions, $409,462; giving activities include $409,462 for grants.
Purpose and activities: The foundation supports programs designed to improve family services through food, shelter, clothing, healthcare, and educational initiatives that promote self-sufficiency.
Fields of interest: Higher education; Education; Health care; Employment, services; Food services; Food banks; Housing/shelter; Boys & girls clubs; Salvation Army; YM/YWCAs & YM/YWHAs; Youth, services; Family services; Human services; United Ways and Federated Giving Programs.
Type of support: Building/renovation; Capital campaigns; Continuing support; Equipment; General/operating support; Matching/challenge support; Program development; Scholarship funds; Sponsorships.
Geographic limitations: Giving limited to Snohomish County, WA.
Support limitations: No support for lobbying organizations. No grants to individuals, or for endowments, land acquisition, conferences or seminars, trips or tours, media productions, or religious activities that serve specific religious groups or denominations and are not of direct benefit to the entire community.
Publications: Application guidelines.
Application information: Applications accepted. A full proposal may be requested at a later date. Multi-year funding is not automatic. Organizations receiving support are asked to provide a final report. Application form not required. Applicants should submit the following:
1) detailed description of project and amount of funding requested
Initial approach: Letter of inquiry
Board meeting date(s): Feb., May, Aug. and Nov.
Deadline(s): 1 month before board meeting
Final notification: Following board meeting
Officers and Directors: Margaret Bavasi, Pres.; Tom Collins, V.P.; Mary B. Sievers*, Secy. and Exec. Dir.; Robert Baeur, Treas.; Michael Deller; Thomas J. Gaffney; Larry Hanson; Mike Kight; George Newland; Bill Rucker; Harry Stuchell.
EIN: 911510567
Selected grants: The following grants are a representative sample of this grantmaker's funding activity:
$35,000 to Housing Hope, Everett, WA, 2010.
$30,000 to Everett Community College Foundation, Everett, WA, 2010.
$25,000 to Housing Hope, Everett, WA, 2010.
$18,000 to Christmas House, Everett, WA, 2010.
$16,000 to Bethany of the Northwest Foundation, Everett, WA, 2010.
$15,000 to Christmas House, Everett, WA, 2010.
$15,000 to Medical Teams International, Redmond, WA, 2010.
$7,500 to Big Brothers Big Sisters of Snohomish County, Everett, WA, 2010.
$6,000 to Everett Public Schools Foundation, Everett, WA, 2010.
$5,000 to Bridgeways, Everett, WA, 2010.

Key Bank of Central Maine Foundation

c/o KeyBank N.A.
4900 Tiedeman Rd.
Brooklyn, OH 44144-2302

Establishment information: Established in 1954 in ME.
Donors: KeyBank of Maine; KeyBank N.A.
Financial data (yr. ended 11/30/11): Assets, $901,301 (M); expenditures, $66,099; qualifying distributions, $58,660; giving activities include $56,250 for 6 grants (high: $25,000; low: $5,000).
Purpose and activities: The foundation supports organizations involved with higher education, health, grief counseling, children and youth, and civic affairs.
Fields of interest: Education; Health care; Human services.

Type of support: General/operating support.
Geographic limitations: Giving primarily in ME.
Support limitations: No grants to individuals.
Application information: Applications not accepted. Unsolicited requests for funds not accepted.
Trustee: KeyBank, N.A.
EIN: 016017321

KeyBank Foundation

(formerly Key Foundation)
800 Superior Ave., 1st Fl.
M.C. OH-01-02-0126
Cleveland, OH 44114-2601 (216) 828-7349
FAX: (216) 828-7845;
E-mail: key_foundation@keybank.com; Additional tel.: (216) 828-7402, (212) 828-8539;
URL: https://www.key.com/about/community/key-foundation-philanthropy-banking.jsp

Establishment information: Established about 1969 in OH.
Donors: Society Corp.; Society Capital Corp.; KeyBank N.A.; KeyCorp.
Contact: Valerie Raines, Sr. Prog. Off.; Lorraine Vega, Sr. Prog. Off.
Financial data (yr. ended 12/31/11): Assets, $36,941,956 (M); gifts received, $12,000,000; expenditures, $12,704,363; qualifying distributions, $12,560,383; giving activities include $11,500,543 for 2,160 grants (high: $1,100,000; low: $100) and $1,059,840 for 2,502 employee matching gifts.
Purpose and activities: The foundation supports organizations involved with arts and culture, education, health, human services, and civic affairs. Special emphasis is directed toward programs designed to enhance economic self-sufficiency through financial education, workforce development, and diversity.
Fields of interest: Arts; Vocational education; Education; Health care; Employment, services; Employment, training; Employment; Human services, financial counseling; Human services; Civil/human rights, equal rights; Community development, small businesses; United Ways and Federated Giving Programs; Public affairs Physically disabled; Minorities; Economically disadvantaged; LGBTQ.
Programs:

Community Leadership Grant Program: The foundation awards annual $500 grants to nonprofit organizations with which employees of KeyBank volunteer.

Diversity: The foundation supports programs designed to foster an inclusive environment through systemic changes to improve the access for individuals of diverse backgrounds. Special emphasis is directed toward programs designed to provide vocational training and job placement for people with disabilities; and school-to-work readiness initiatives for underrepresented college students.

Financial Education: The foundation supports programs designed to promote effective financial management and understanding of financial services and tools to encourage the development of strong and productive populations. Special emphasis is directed toward programs that create systemic change and projects that can be replicated to serve other communities.

Matching Gift Program: The foundation provides a 1:1 match for qualifying donations made by employees up to $2,000 annually.

Workforce Development: The foundation supports programs designed to provide training and placement for people to access job opportunities. Special emphasis is directed toward programs designed to foster career exploration, training, and placement.

Type of support: Annual campaigns; Capital campaigns; Continuing support; Curriculum development; Employee matching gifts; Employee volunteer services; General/operating support; Matching/challenge support; Program development; Scholarship funds; Sponsorships.
Geographic limitations: Giving primarily in areas of company operations in AK, CO, ID, IN, KY, ME, MI, NY, OH, OR, UT, VT, and WA; giving also to national organizations.
Support limitations: No support for organizations outside geographic footprint, athletic teams, or fraternal organizations. No grants to individuals, or for memberships, lobbying or political activities, or advertising.
Publications: Application guidelines; Corporate report; Occasional report.
Application information: Applications accepted. Full proposals must include a proposal summary form. Visit website for nearest company district office. Organizations receiving support are asked to provide a final report 3 months after the completion of the project. Applicants should submit the following:
1) how project will be sustained once grantmaker support is completed
2) results expected from proposed grant
3) qualifications of key personnel
4) population served
5) name, address and phone number of organization
6) copy of IRS Determination Letter
7) brief history of organization and description of its mission
8) geographic area to be served
9) copy of most recent annual report/audited financial statement/990
10) how project's results will be evaluated or measured
11) what distinguishes project from others in its field
12) listing of board of directors, trustees, officers and other key people and their affiliations
13) detailed description of project and amount of funding requested
14) contact person
15) copy of current year's organizational budget and/or project budget
16) listing of additional sources and amount of support

Proposals should indicate the frequency of board meetings; the amounts and percentages of funds expended for fundraising, administrative costs, and programs for the past two years; and whether the organization is affiliated with the local chapter of any other organization.

Initial approach: Letter of inquiry, proposal summary form, or telephone for preliminary inquiries; full proposals to foundation for organizations located in northeast OH; full proposal to closest key district office for organizations located outside of northeast, OH
Copies of proposal: 1
Board meeting date(s): Quarterly
Deadline(s): None
Final notification: Within 3 months

Officers and Trustees:* Margot James Copeland*, Chair.; Christopher M. Gorman, Pres.; James Hoffman, V.P.; Paul N. Harris, Secy.; Mark Whitham, Treas.; Cindy P. Crotty; Bruce D. Murphy; Elizabeth J. Oliver.
Number of staff: 4 full-time professional.
EIN: 237036607
Selected grants: The following grants are a representative sample of this grantmaker's funding activity:
$50,000 to Cuyahoga Community College Foundation, Cleveland, OH, 2010. For scholarships.
$35,000 to Center for Disability Services, Albany, NY, 2010. For program support.
$20,000 to Indianapolis Symphony Orchestra Foundation, Indianapolis, IN, 2010. For program support.
$20,000 to New Avenues for Youth, Portland, OR, 2010. For program support.
$12,550 to Junior Achievement of Maine, Portland, ME, 2010. For program support.
$10,000 to Cincinnati Works, Cincinnati, OH, 2010. For program support.
$10,000 to Habitat for Humanity, Salt Lake Valley, Salt Lake City, UT, 2010. For program support.
$10,000 to Madison County Hospital Memorial Fund, London, OH, 2010. For operating support.
$10,000 to Rockland Family Shelter, New City, NY, 2010. For program support.
$5,000 to Culinary Skills Training Center, Boise, ID, 2010. For program support.
$5,000 to Locust Street Neighborhood Art Classes, Buffalo, NY, 2010. For program support.
$3,400 to Philanthropy Northwest, Seattle, WA, 2010. For program support.

2137
Keystone Foods LLC

(formerly Keystone Foods Corporation)
300 Barr Harbor Dr., Ste. 600
West Conshohocken, PA 19428-2998
(610) 667-6700
FAX: (610) 667-1460

Company URL: http://www.keystonefoods.com
Establishment information: Established in 1973.
Company type: Subsidiary of a public company
Business activities: Processes and distributes food products.
Business type (SIC): Groceries—wholesale; meat packing plants and prepared meats and poultry
Financial profile for 2012: Number of employees, 15,000
Corporate officers: Herbert Lotman, Chair.; Frank Ravndal, C.E.O.; Larry McWilliams, Pres.; Bill Andersen, Exec. V.P. and C.O.O.; John Coggins, Exec. V.P. and C.F.O.; William E. Hennessey, Sr. V.P. and Cont.; Charles D. Wallace, V.P. and C.I.O.; Jerry Gotro, V.P., Human Resources
Board of director: Herbert Lotman, Chair.
Giving statement: Giving through the Keystone Foods LLC Corporate Giving Program and the Stephen G. Calvert Memorial Merit Scholarship Foundation.

Stephen G. Calvert Memorial Merit Scholarship Foundation

5 Tower Bridge
300 Barr Harbor Dr., Ste. 600
West Conshohocken, PA 19428-2998

Establishment information: Established in 1996 in PA.
Donors: Keystone Foods Corp.; Keystone Foods LLC.
Financial data (yr. ended 10/31/11): Assets, $22,332 (M); gifts received, $220,000; expenditures, $218,852; qualifying distributions, $197,263; giving activities include $197,263 for 48 grants (high: $100,000; low: $863).
Purpose and activities: The foundation awards college scholarships to dependents of employees of Keystone Foods.
Fields of interest: Higher education.
Type of support: Employee-related scholarships.

Geographic limitations: Giving limited to areas of company operations.
Application information: Applications accepted. Application form required.
Initial approach: Letter
Deadline(s): None
Officers: John J. Coggins, Pres.; Donna Curtis, Secy.; D. Paul Macgarvie, Treas.
EIN: 232816413

2138
Keystone Group, L.P.

(formerly Robert M. Bass Group)
201 Main St., Ste. 3100
Fort Worth, TX 76102-3131 (817) 390-8400
FAX: (817) 338-2064

Establishment information: Established in 1985.
Company type: Private company
Business activities: Operates private investment company.
Business type (SIC): Investors/miscellaneous
Corporate officers: Robert Muse Bass, Pres.; J. Taylor Crandall, C.O.O.
Giving statement: Giving through the Keystone, Inc. Corporate Giving Program and the Bass Companies Employee Disaster Relief Fund.

Bass Companies Employee Disaster Relief Fund

201 Main St., Ste. 2300
Fort Worth, TX 76102-3137

Establishment information: Established in 2005 in TX.
Donors: BEPCO, LP; Stephen Neuse; Stewart L. Henry; Chester Carlock; W. Robert Cotham; Greg Kent; Qurumbli Foundation; Standard Tube Co.; Clive D. Bode; Darlene Clark; Joel Glenn; James Greve, Sr.; Frank Millett; Champions Pipe & Supply, Inc.; Fairweather Foundation.
Financial data (yr. ended 12/31/11): Assets, $12,152 (M); expenditures, $0; qualifying distributions, $0.
Type of support: Grants to individuals.
Application information: Applications not accepted. Unsolicited requests for funds not accepted.
Officers and Directors:* Stewart L. Henry*, Pres.; William O. Reimann IV, V.P.; Gary W. Reese, V.P.; Thomas W. White*, Secy.-Treas.
EIN: 203453930

2139
KFC Corporation

1441 Gardiner Ln.
Louisville, KY 40213 (502) 874-8300

Company URL: http://www.kfc.com
Establishment information: Established in 1952.
Company type: Subsidiary of a public company
Business activities: Operates restaurants.
Business type (SIC): Restaurants and drinking places
Corporate officers: Roger Eaton, Pres.; Jim Metevier, C.O.O.
Giving statement: Giving through the KFC Corporation Contributions Program and the Kentucky Fried Chicken Foundation, Inc.

Kentucky Fried Chicken Foundation, Inc.

(formerly Colonel's Kids, Inc.)
1900 Colonel Sanders Ln.
Louisville, KY 40213-5910 (502) 874-2075
E-mail: kfcscholars@act.org; URL: http://www.kfcscholars.org

Establishment information: Established in 1998 in KY.
Contact: Roger Eaton, Pres.
Financial data (yr. ended 12/31/10): Revenue, $1,670,771; assets, $8,587,773 (M); gifts received, $1,556,871; expenditures, $1,748,524; program services expenses, $1,618,508; giving activities include $1,194,734 for grants to individuals.
Purpose and activities: The foundation conducts a scholarship program which is intended to empower students to improve their lives with scholarship resources. The scholarship award is for $5,000 annually and is renewable for up to four years.
Fields of interest: Scholarships/financial aid.
Program:
Scholarships: The program provides scholarship awards of up to $5,000 annually for up to four years.
Type of support: Scholarships—to individuals.
Geographic limitations: Giving on a national basis.
Support limitations: No support for organizations lacking 501(c)(3) IRS status.
Publications: Application guidelines; Grants list.
Application information: Applications accepted.
Initial approach: Complete online application
Deadline(s): Feb. 15
Officers: Roger Eaton, Pres.; Darlene Pfeiffer, V.P.; Cindy Harbin, Secy.; Alan Forsythe, Treas.
Directors: Javier Benito; Tom Burress; John Cywinski; Laurie Schalow; David Sparks; Tom Slater; Peter Wasilevich.
Number of staff: 1
EIN: 611337601

2140
Kia Motors America, Inc

(also known as KMA)
111 Peters Canyon Rd.
Irvine, CA 92606-1790 (949) 468-4800
FAX: (949) 468-4905

Company URL: http://www.kia.com
Establishment information: Established in 1992.
Company type: Subsidiary of a foreign company
Business activities: Manufactures automobiles.
Business type (SIC): Motor vehicles and equipment
Corporate officers: Byung Mo Ahn, Pres. and C.E.O.; N.K. Kim, C.F.O.; John Yoon, V.P. and Genl. Counsel; Michael Sprague, V.P., Mktg. and Comms.; Tom Loveless, V.P., Sales
Giving statement: Giving through the Kia Motors America, Inc. Contributions Program.

Kia Motors America, Inc. Contributions Program

111 Peters Canyon Rd.
Irvine, CA 92606-1790 (949) 468-4800
URL: http://www.kia.com

2141
Kids II, Inc.

555 N. Point Ctr. E., Ste. 600
Alpharetta, GA 30022-8234
(770) 751-0442

Company URL: http://www.kidsii.com
Establishment information: Established in 1969.
Company type: Private company
Business activities: Operates developmental toys company.
Business type (SIC): Games, toys, and sporting and athletic goods
Corporate officers: Ryan Gunnigle, Pres. and C.E.O.; Grant Gunnigle, C.O.O. and C.I.O.; Karen Neblett, V.P., Sales; Miles Bohannan, V.P., Mktg.; Heather Crawford, V.P., Human Resources
International operations: Australia; Canada; China; Hong Kong; Mexico
Giving statement: Giving through the Kids II Foundation, Inc.

Kids II Foundation, Inc.

3333 Piedmont Rd.
Atlanta, GA 30305

Establishment information: Established in 2005 in GA.
Donors: Ryan T. Gunnigle; Kids II, Inc.; Kids II Employees; Kids II Vendors.
Financial data (yr. ended 12/31/11): Assets, $1,133 (M); gifts received, $122,588; expenditures, $172,830; qualifying distributions, $172,080; giving activities include $171,330 for 43 grants (high: $35,000; low: $200).
Fields of interest: Disasters, Hurricane Katrina; Children/youth, services.
Geographic limitations: Giving primarily in NJ.
Support limitations: No grants to individuals.
Application information: Applications not accepted. Contributes only to pre-selected organizations.
Officers: Ryan T. Gunnigle, Pres.; J. Dwaine Clarke, Secy.-Treas.; Carl J. Watry, V.P.
EIN: 203635565

2142
Peter Kiewit Sons', Inc.

Kiewit Plz.
3555 Farnam St.
Omaha, NE 68131 (402) 342-2052

Company URL: http://www.kiewit.com
Establishment information: Established in 1884.
Company type: Private company
Business activities: Provides general contract construction services; mines coal.
Business type (SIC): Heavy construction other than building construction contractors; coal mining
Financial profile for 2011: Number of employees, 24,700; assets, $5,171,000,000; sales volume, $9,938,000,000
Corporate officers: Kenneth E. Stinson, Chair.; Bruce E. Grewcock, Pres. and C.E.O.; Michael J. Piechoski, Sr. V.P., and C.F.O.
Board of director: Kenneth E. Stinson, Chair.
Subsidiaries: Bibb and Associates, Inc., Kansas City, KS; Mass. Electric Construction Co., Boston, MA
Offices: Anchorage, AK; Phoenix, Tucson, AZ; Little Rock, AR; Concord, San Diego, CA; Denver, CO; Washington, DC; Miami, Tampa, FL; Atlanta, Savannah, GA; Honolulu, HI; Boise, ID; Chicago, IL; Davenport, Des Moines, IA; New Orleans, LA; Minneapolis, MN; Las Vegas, NV; Albuquerque, NM;

New York, NY; Raleigh, NC; Austin, Corpus Christi, Dallas, Fort Worth, Houston, TX; Provo, UT; Tacoma, Vancouver, WA; Casper, WY
International operations: Australia; Canada
Giving statement: Giving through the Kiewit Companies Foundation.

Kiewit Companies Foundation

Kiewit Plz.
3555 Farnam St.
Omaha, NE 68131-3302 (402) 342-2052
FAX: (402) 943-1302;
E-mail: mike.faust@kiewit.com

Establishment information: Established in 1963 in NE.
Donors: Peter Kiewit Sons', Inc.; Wytana, Inc.; Big Horn Coal Co.; Kiewit Construction Group Inc.; Kiewit Diversified Group Inc.; Peter Kiewit & Sons Co.
Contact: Michael L. Faust, Fdn. Admin.
Financial data (yr. ended 12/31/11): Assets, $11,758,455 (M); gifts received, $6,000,000; expenditures, $3,531,726; qualifying distributions, $3,531,726; giving activities include $3,531,726 for grants.
Purpose and activities: The foundation supports organizations involved with arts and culture, higher education, youth development, human services, and community development. Special emphasis is directed toward nonprofits engaged in improving the quality of life in communities where there is a significant corporate presence.
Fields of interest: Arts; Higher education; Youth development; Human services; Community/economic development.
Type of support: Annual campaigns; Building/renovation; Capital campaigns; General/operating support; Scholarship funds.
Geographic limitations: Giving primarily in areas of company operations, with emphasis on Omaha, NE.
Support limitations: No support for elementary or secondary schools or individual churches or similar religious groups. No grants to individuals, or for endowments.
Publications: Annual report (including application guidelines).
Application information: Applications accepted. Application form not required.
Initial approach: Letter of inquiry
Copies of proposal: 1
Board meeting date(s): As needed
Deadline(s): None
Final notification: 1 to 3 months
Trustee: U.S. Bank, N.A.
Number of staff: None.
EIN: 476029996
Selected grants: The following grants are a representative sample of this grantmaker's funding activity:
$100,000 to Childrens Hospital and Medical Center, Omaha, NE, 2011. For Specialty Pediatric Center.
$100,000 to Omaha Community Playhouse, Omaha, NE, 2011. For information technology upgrade.
$50,000 to Durham Museum, Omaha, NE, 2011. For Abraham Lincoln exhibit.
$50,000 to Iowa State University Foundation, Ames, IA, 2011. For Student Services Center renovation project.
$50,000 to Joslyn Art Museum, Omaha, NE, 2011. For Treasury Joslyn Exhibit.
$50,000 to Omaha Symphony Association, Omaha, NE, 2011. For youth education program.
$20,000 to Arizona State University Foundation for a New American University, Tempe, AZ, 2011. For highway curriculum fund.
$10,000 to Brownell-Talbot School, Omaha, NE, 2011. For Discovery Summer Camp.
$10,000 to Skirball Cultural Center, Los Angeles, CA, 2011. For program support.
$5,000 to Prevent Cancer Foundation, Alexandria, VA, 2011. For cancer screening at state fair.

2143
Kifton Development, Inc.

1536 N.W. Skyline Heights Pkwy.
Portland, OR 97221 (503) 242-3898

Establishment information: Established in 1992.
Company type: Private company
Business activities: Operates general contracting company.
Business type (SIC): Operative builders
Corporate officers: Robert S. Morey, Pres.; Timothy Clark-Morey, Secy.
Giving statement: Giving through the Morey Family Foundation.

The Morey Family Foundation

1536 S.W. Highland Pkwy.
Portland, OR 97221-2630 (503) 242-3898

Establishment information: Established in 2005 in OR.
Donors: Kifton Development, Inc.; Timothy Clark-Morey; Robert Morey.
Financial data (yr. ended 08/31/11): Assets, $440,464 (M); gifts received, $3,000; expenditures, $3,605; qualifying distributions, $1,000; giving activities include $1,000 for 1 grant.
Purpose and activities: The foundation awards college sholarships to individuals based on academic performance and financial need.
Fields of interest: Higher education.
Type of support: Scholarship funds.
Application information: Applications accepted. Application form required.
Initial approach: Contact foundation for application form
Deadline(s): Spring
Officers: Timothy Clark-Morey, Pres.; Robert Morey, V.P.; Jeannine L. McGowan, Secy.
Board Member: Kiffi Harris.
EIN: 202033108

2144
Kikkoman Foods, Inc.

N1365 6 Corners Rd.
P.O. Box 420784
Walworth, WI 53184-5702 (262) 275-6181

Company URL: http://www.kikkoman.com/
Establishment information: Established in 1972.
Company type: Subsidiary of a foreign company
Business activities: Manufactures soy sauce and other sauces and spices and prepared foods.
Business type (SIC): Specialty foods/canned, frozen, and preserved
Financial profile for 2010: Number of employees, 160
Corporate officers: Kuniki Hatayama, Pres. and Treas.; Karl Keane, V.P., Finance; Milton E. Neshek, Secy.
Board of director: Kuniki Hatayama
Giving statement: Giving through the Kikkoman Foods Foundation, Inc.

Kikkoman Foods Foundation, Inc.

P.O. Box 69
Walworth, WI 53184-0069 (262) 275-6181

Establishment information: Established in 1993 in WI.
Donor: Kikkoman Foods, Inc.
Contact: Robert V. Conover, Dir.
Financial data (yr. ended 12/31/11): Assets, $9,764,182 (M); gifts received, $4,350; expenditures, $487,200; qualifying distributions, $482,060; giving activities include $482,060 for grants.
Purpose and activities: The foundation supports organizations involved with arts and culture, education, human services, and international exchange and economics.
Fields of interest: Performing arts; Arts; Secondary school/education; Higher education; Education; Disasters, preparedness/services; Youth, services; Developmentally disabled, centers & services; Human services; International exchange, students; International economics/trade policy.
Type of support: Annual campaigns; General/operating support; Scholarship funds; Sponsorships.
Geographic limitations: Giving primarily in WI.
Support limitations: No support for private organizations, political organizations, religious or sectarian organizations, or discriminatory organizations. No grants to individuals, or for raffle tickets or product purchases, non-food-related scientific or development research, travel or lodging, or promotional events.
Publications: Application guidelines.
Application information: Applications accepted. Application form not required. Applicants should submit the following:
1) role played by volunteers
2) results expected from proposed grant
3) population served
4) name, address and phone number of organization
5) copy of IRS Determination Letter
6) brief history of organization and description of its mission
7) geographic area to be served
8) detailed description of project and amount of funding requested
9) contact person
10) copy of current year's organizational budget and/or project budget
11) listing of additional sources and amount of support
Initial approach: Proposal
Board meeting date(s): Monthly
Deadline(s): None
Directors: Robert V. Conover; Noriaki Horikiri; Satoshi Kawamata; Karl N. Keane; Daniel P. Miller; Yuzaburo Mogi; Milton E. Neshek; Takashi Ozawa; Kazuo Shimizu; Mitsuo Someya; Ryohei Tsuji, Ph.D.
EIN: 391763633
Selected grants: The following grants are a representative sample of this grantmaker's funding activity:
$100,000 to University of Wisconsin Foundation, Madison, WI, 2010.
$49,170 to Youth for Understanding USA, Bethesda, MD, 2010. For scholarship program.
$20,000 to University of Wisconsin Foundation, Madison, WI, 2010.
$15,000 to Peter G. Peterson Institute for International Economics, Washington, DC, 2010.
$15,000 to Peter G. Peterson Institute for International Economics, Washington, DC, 2010. For annual contribution.
$15,000 to University of Wisconsin Foundation, Madison, WI, 2010.
$15,000 to VIP Services, Elkhorn, WI, 2010.

$10,000 to University of Wisconsin, Milwaukee, WI, 2010.
$10,000 to VIP Services, Elkhorn, WI, 2010.
$5,000 to University of Wisconsin Foundation, Madison, WI, 2010.

2145
Kilmartin Industries, Inc.

79 Walton St.
Attleboro, MA 02703-1412 (508) 226-3310

Establishment information: Established in 1926.
Company type: Private company
Business activities: Manufactures jewelry, tokens, and medallions.
Business type (SIC): Jewelry/precious metal; metal forgings and stampings
Financial profile for 2010: Number of employees, 65
Corporate officer: Peter A. Delekta, Pres.
Giving statement: Giving through the David & Betsey Kilmartin Charitable Foundation Inc.

David & Betsey Kilmartin Charitable Foundation Inc

(formerly Kilmartin Industries Charitable Foundation, Inc.)
247 Farnum Rd.
Glocester, RI 02814 (401) 949-1166

Establishment information: Established in 1986 in MA.
Donors: Kilmartin Industries; David F. Kilmartin.
Contact: David F. Kilmartin, Pres. and Dir.
Financial data (yr. ended 02/28/11): Assets, $615,534 (M); gifts received, $61,268; expenditures, $43,850; qualifying distributions, $32,000; giving activities include $32,000 for 22 grants (high: $4,000; low: $250).
Purpose and activities: The foundation supports zoological societies and hospitals and organizations involved with historic preservation, education, children's services, and military and veterans.
Fields of interest: Education; Animals/wildlife; Housing/shelter.
Type of support: General/operating support; Program development; Scholarship funds.
Support limitations: No grants to individuals.
Application information: Applications accepted. Application form required. Applicants should submit the following:
1) detailed description of project and amount of funding requested
Initial approach: Letter
Deadline(s): None
Officers and Directors:* David F. Kilmartin*, Pres.; Betsey Kilmartin*, Secy. and Clerk; Kim Nolan.
EIN: 222727613

2146
Kilpatrick Life Insurance Company

1818 Marshall St.
Shreveport, LA 71101-4109
(318) 222-0555
FAX: (318) 429-8010

Company URL: http://www.klic.com
Establishment information: Established in 1932.
Company type: Private company
Business activities: Sells life, fire, ambulance service, and hospital indemnity insurance; provides investment advisory services.
Business type (SIC): Insurance/life; security and commodity services; insurance/accident and health; insurance/fire, marine, and casualty
Corporate officers: Virginia K. Shehee, Chair.; John A. Hensarling, Pres. and C.E.O.; Dona Wilson, C.P.A., C.F.O.; Jackie Wine, Corp. Secy.
Board of directors: Virginia K. Shehee, Chair.; Veva M. Grant; Chris L. Martin; Harvey Rubin, Ph.D.; Andy Shehee; Margaret Shehee; Nell Shehee; Shane Shehee
Offices: Alexandria, Arcadia, Coushatta, Jena, Logansport, Mansfield, Marksville, Minden, Oakdale, Springhill, LA; Longview, TX
Giving statement: Giving through the Kilpatrick—Rose Neath Foundation, Inc.

Kilpatrick—Rose Neath Foundation, Inc.

1818 Marshall St.
Shreveport, LA 71101-4109 (318) 222-0555

Establishment information: Established in 2004 in LA.
Donor: Kilpatrick Life Insurance Co.
Contact: Nell E. Shehee, Dir.
Financial data (yr. ended 12/31/11): Assets, $468,652 (M); gifts received, $10,000; expenditures, $27,400; qualifying distributions, $25,000; giving activities include $25,000 for grants.
Purpose and activities: The foundation supports art museums and organizations involved with music, higher education, wildlife sanctuaries, and youth development.
Fields of interest: Arts; Education; Religion.
Type of support: General/operating support.
Geographic limitations: Giving primarily in Frierson and Shreveport, LA.
Support limitations: No grants to individuals.
Application information: Applications accepted. Application form required. Applicants should submit the following:
1) copy of IRS Determination Letter
Initial approach: Proposal
Deadline(s): None
Directors: Andrew M. Shehee; Ann Shane Shehee; Margaret S. Shehee; Nell E. Shehee; Virginia K. Shehee.
EIN: 201041965

2147
Kilpatrick Townsend & Stockton LLP

E. Whitney Deal, Ste. 2800
1100 Peachtree St
Atlanta, GA 30309-4528 (404) 815-6500

Company URL: http://www.kilpatricktownsend.com
Company type: Private company
Business activities: Operates law firm.
Business type (SIC): Legal services
Financial profile for 2010: Number of employees, 1,165
Corporate officers: William E. Dorris, Chair. and Partner; Diane L. Prucino, Co-Managing Partner; Maureen A. Sheehy, Co-Managing Partner
Giving statement: Giving through the Kilpatrick Townsend & Stockton LLP Corporate Giving Program and the Kilpatrick Townsend & Stockton LLP Pro Bono Program.

Kilpatrick Townsend & Stockton LLP Corporate Giving Program

E. Whitney Deal, Ste. 2800
1100 Peachtree St
Atlanta, GA 30309-4528 (404) 815-6651
E-mail: Wdeal@kilpatricktownsend.com; URL: http://www.kilpatricktownsend.com/en/About_Us/Social_Responsibility.aspx

Kilpatrick Townsend & Stockton LLP Pro Bono Program

1100 Peachtree St., Ste. 2800
Atlanta, GA 30309-4530 (404) 815-6167
E-mail: dsegal@kilpatricktownsend.com; Additional tel.: (404) 815-6500; URL: http://www.ktrecruits.com/#filter=.more

Contact: Debbie Segal, Pro Bono Partner
Fields of interest: Legal services.
Type of support: Pro bono services - legal.
Geographic limitations: Giving primarily in areas of company operations in Oakland, Palo Alto, San Diego, San Francisco, and Walnut Creek, CA, Denver, CO, Washington, DC, Atlanta and Augusta, GA, Charlotte, Raleigh, and Winston-Salem, NC, New York, NY, and Seattle, WA, and in Japan, Sweden, and the United Arab Emirates.
Application information: A Pro Bono Committee manages the pro-bono program.

2148
Miles Kimball Company

250 City Ctr.
Oshkosh, WI 54906-0100 (920) 231-3800

Company URL: http://www.mileskimball.com
Establishment information: Established in 1935.
Company type: Subsidiary of a public company
Business activities: Provides general merchandise catalog shopping services.
Business type (SIC): Nonstore retailers; greeting cards; paper and paper products—wholesale
Corporate officers: Stanley E. Krangel, Pres. and C.E.O.; Tim Little, V.P., Opers.; Ken Maher, V.P., Finance; Margie Harvey, V.P., Human Resources
Giving statement: Giving through the Miles Kimball Foundation Inc.

Miles Kimball Foundation Inc

250 City Center
Oshkosh, WI 54901

Establishment information: Established in 1951 in WI.
Donor: Miles Kimball Co.
Financial data (yr. ended 12/31/11): Assets, $1,054,671 (M); expenditures, $74,332; qualifying distributions, $60,469; giving activities include $60,469 for grants.
Purpose and activities: The foundation supports festivals and community foundations and organizations involved with leukemia, athletics, human services, and business promotion.
Fields of interest: Youth development; Human services; Community/economic development.
Type of support: General/operating support.
Support limitations: No grants to individuals.
Application information: Applications not accepted. Unsolicited requests for funds not accepted.
Officers: Margie Harvey, Pres.; Cam Ross, V.P.; Andrew Wojdula, Secy.

Directors: Stan Krangel; Tyler Schuessler; Robert Goergen, Jr.
EIN: 396075744

2149
Kimball International, Inc.

1600 Royal St.
Jasper, IN 47549-0001 (812) 482-1600
FAX: (812) 482-8804

Company URL: http://www.kimball.com
Establishment information: Established in 1950.
Company type: Public company
Company ticker symbol and exchange: KBALB/NASDAQ
Business activities: Manufactures office, health care, hospitality, and home furniture, television cabinets, electronic assemblies, and pianos.
Business type (SIC): Furniture/office; furniture/household; plastic products/miscellaneous; electronic components and accessories; musical instruments
Financial profile for 2012: Number of employees, 6,295; assets, $595,520,000; sales volume, $1,142,060,000; pre-tax net income, $17,700,000; expenses, $1,123,670,000; liabilities, $209,290,000
Corporate officers: Douglas A. Habig, Chair.; James C. Thyen, Pres. and C.E.O.; Robert F. Schneider, Exec. V.P. and C.F.O.; Gary W. Schwartz, Exec. V.P. and C.I.O.; John H. Kahle, Exec. V.P., Genl. Counsel, and Secy.; Michelle R. Schroeder, V.P. and C.A.O.; R. Gregory Kincer, V.P. and Treas.
Board of directors: Douglas A. Habig, Chair.; Harry W. Bowman; Geoffrey L. Stringer; James C. Thyen; Thomas J. Tischhauser; Christine M. Vujovich; Jack R. Wentworth
Subsidiary: Kimball Electronics, Inc., Jasper, IN
International operations: China; Mexico; Netherlands; Poland; Thailand; United Kingdom
Giving statement: Giving through the Kimball International—Habig Foundation Inc.
Company EIN: 350514506

The Kimball International—Habig Foundation Inc.

(formerly The Habig Foundation)
1600 Royal St.
Jasper, IN 47549-1022 (812) 482-8701
E-mail: HabigFoundation@Kimball.com; URL: http://www.kimball.com/foundation.aspx

Establishment information: Established in 1951 in IN.
Donor: Kimball International, Inc.
Financial data (yr. ended 06/30/12): Assets, $495,179 (M); gifts received, $30,000; expenditures, $111,467; qualifying distributions, $106,100; giving activities include $50,000 for 1 grant and $56,100 for 16 grants to individuals (high: $3,750; low: $1,800).
Purpose and activities: The foundation supports religious institutions and organizations involved with arts and culture, education, health, human services, and civic and community issues.
Fields of interest: Visual arts; Performing arts; Historic preservation/historical societies; Arts; Adult/continuing education; Libraries (public); Education, reading; Education; Environment, natural resources; Hospitals (general); Health care; Mental health, counseling/support groups; Disasters, fire prevention/control; Children/youth, services; Family services; Human services; Community development, service clubs; Community/economic development; Public affairs; Religion Children; Aging; Women.
Programs:

Arts & Culture: The foundation supports visual, written, and performing arts programs designed to enhance the human spirit; and provide exposure to the arts among youth, school systems, and communities at large. Special emphasis is directed toward programs designed to promote artistic exposure in community school systems; and provide for performances or exhibits in the local community.

Civic & Community Programs: The foundation supports programs designed to help communities become better places to live, work, and raise a family. Special emphasis is directed toward projects of local need or infrastructure improvements including those by fire departments and libraries; projects promoting local civic pride including revitalization and historic preservation; community celebrations and tourism events; and environmental protection and preservation.

Education: The foundation supports programs designed to improve education for children from pre-school through high school, and for adults through continuing education and development. Special emphasis is directed toward programs designed to foster critical thinking skills; reading and comprehension; and technology and business interests.

Health & Human Services: The foundation supports programs designed to improve the human condition and alleviate suffering by assisting local community organizations, charities, faith-based initiatives, and social services. Special emphasis is directed toward programs designed to promote care and protection for children and infants, women and families, and the elderly and infirmed; and provide healthcare, medical, and counseling services; and basic social and support services.

Kimball Scholarship Program: The foundation awards college scholarships to high school seniors who are children or dependents of full-time employees. Scholarships of $15,000 are awarded for four-year college programs and scholarships of $3,600 are awarded for two-year college programs. Recipients are chosen based on academic achievement and financial need.

Religious Institutions: The foundation supports faith-based projects and programs designed to alleviate suffering; improve the human condition; promote self-worth; and instill values regardless of denominational affiliation.

Type of support: Employee-related scholarships; General/operating support.
Geographic limitations: Giving limited to areas of company operations.
Publications: Application guidelines; Program policy statement.
Application information: Applications accepted. Telephone calls during the application process are not encouraged. Requests of $2,000 or more are reviewed and assessed on a quarterly basis. Standard requests under $2,000 are reviewed and approved monthly. Application form required.

Initial approach: Complete online application form
Board meeting date(s): Mar., June, Sept., and Dec.
Deadline(s): None

Officers: Douglas A. Habig, Chair.; James C. Thyen, Pres.; John H. Kahle, Secy.-Treas.
Number of staff: 2
EIN: 356022535

2150
Kimberly-Clark Corporation

P.O. Box 619100
Dallas, TX 75261-9100 (972) 281-1200
FAX: (972) 281-1435

Company URL: http://www.kimberly-clark.com
Establishment information: Established in 1872.
Company type: Public company
Company ticker symbol and exchange: KMB/NYSE
International Securities Identification Number: US4943681035
Business activities: Manufactures personal care and consumer tissue products.
Business type (SIC): Paper and paperboard/coated, converted, and laminated
Financial profile for 2012: Number of employees, 58,000; assets, $19,873,000,000; sales volume, $21,063,000,000; pre-tax net income, $2,420,000,000; expenses, $18,377,000,000; liabilities, $14,888,000,000
Fortune 1000 ranking: 2012—136th in revenues, 118th in profits, and 243rd in assets
Forbes 2000 ranking: 2012—444th in sales, 341st in profits, and 977th in assets
Corporate officers: Thomas J. Falk, Chair. and C.E.O.; Mark A. Buthman, Sr. V.P. and C.F.O.; Thomas J. Mielke, Sr. V.P., Genl. Counsel; Nancy Loewe, Treas.
Board of directors: Thomas J. Falk, Chair.; John R. Alm; John F. Bergstrom; Abelardo E. Bru; Robert W. Decherd; Fabian T. Garcia; Mae C. Jemison, M.D.; James M. Jenness; Nancy J. Karch; Ian C. Read; Linda Johnson Rice; Marc J. Shapiro
Subsidiaries: Avent, Inc., Tucson, AZ; Durafab, Inc., Cleburne, TX; Kimberly-Clark International Services Corp., Neenah, WI; Kimberly-Clark Puerto Rico, Inc., San Juan, PR
International operations: Bahrain; Bolivia; Chile; Colombia; Costa Rica; Israel; Luxembourg; Malta; Netherlands; Panama; Peru; Saudi Arabia; South Korea; Venezuela
Giving statement: Giving through the Kimberly-Clark Corporation Contributions Program and the Kimberly-Clark Foundation, Inc.
Company EIN: 390394230

Kimberly-Clark Corporation Contributions Program

351 Phelps Dr.
Irving, TX 75038-6507
URL: http://www.kimberly-clark.com/sustainability/people/communities.aspx

Purpose and activities: As a complement to its foundation, Kimberly-Clark also makes charitable contributions to nonprofit organizations directly. Support is given on a national and international basis in areas of company operations.
Fields of interest: Education; Health care; Disasters, preparedness/services; Boys & girls clubs; American Red Cross; Children/youth, services; Family services; International relief; United Ways and Federated Giving Programs.
Type of support: Continuing support; Donated products; Employee volunteer services; General/operating support; In-kind gifts; Sponsorships.
Geographic limitations: Giving on a national and international basis in areas of company operations.

Kimberly-Clark Foundation, Inc.

351 Phelps Dr.
Irving, TX 75038-6507 (972) 281-1200
Application address: P.O. Box 619100, Dallas, TX 75261-9100; URL: http://www.kimberly-clark.com/ourcompany/community/kc_foundation.aspx

Establishment information: Incorporated in 1952 in WI.
Donors: Kimberly-Clark Corp.; P.D. and Tracy Parsons Trust.
Financial data (yr. ended 12/31/11): Assets, $78,682 (M); gifts received, $4,086,258; expenditures, $4,231,544; qualifying distributions, $4,226,539; giving activities include $1,506,680 for grants, $1,385,000 for grants to individuals and $1,248,387 for employee matching gifts.
Purpose and activities: The foundation supports organizations involved with arts and culture, education, the environment, health, and human services. Special emphasis is directed toward programs designed to strengthen families around the world.
Fields of interest: Arts; Higher education; Education; Environment, natural resources; Environment; Hospitals (general); Health care; Disasters, preparedness/services; Salvation Army; Children/youth, services; Family services; Human services; United Ways and Federated Giving Programs.
Programs:
Bright Futures Scholarship Program: Through the Bright Futures Scholarship Program, the foundation awards college scholarships of up $20,000 to children of U.S. and Canadian employees of Kimberly-Clark.
Community Partners: Through the Community Partners program, the foundation awards $500 grants to nonprofit organizations with which employees and the spouses of employees of Kimberly-Clark volunteer at least 30 hours per year.
Matching Gifts Program: The foundation matches contributions made by employees of Kimberly-Clark to nonprofit organizations on a one-for-one basis, up to 10,000 per employee, per year.
Type of support: Capital campaigns; Continuing support; Curriculum development; Employee matching gifts; Employee volunteer services; Employee-related scholarships; General/operating support; Program development; Sponsorships.
Geographic limitations: Giving primarily in areas of company operations, with emphasis on CA and TX; giving also to national organizations.
Support limitations: No support for religious or political organizations. No grants to individuals (except for employee-related scholarships), or for non-disaster relief product donations, or sports or athletic activities; no loans.
Publications: Corporate giving report; Financial statement.
Application information: Applications accepted. Unsolicited requests from national or international organizations are not accepted. Application form not required.
Initial approach: Proposal to nearest K-C site manager
Deadline(s): None
Officers and Directors:* Anthony J. Palmer*, Pres.; Mark A. Buthman*, V.P.; Jennifer L. Lewis, V.P.; Steven E. Voskuil, V.P.; John W. Wesley, Secy.; Nancy S. Lowe, Treas.; Thomas J. Falk.
Number of staff: 1 full-time professional; 1 full-time support.
EIN: 396044304
Selected grants: The following grants are a representative sample of this grantmaker's funding activity:
$1,472,500 to Bright Futures Scholarship Program, Fort Worth, TX, 2010.
$796,000 to Community Partners, Houston, TX, 2010.
$170,104 to United Way of Metropolitan Dallas, Dallas, TX, 2010.
$10,000 to Family Gateway, Dallas, TX, 2010.

2151
Kimley-Horn and Associates, Inc.

(also known as The Kimley-Horn Group, Inc.)
3001 Weston Pkwy.
Cary, NC 27513-2301 (919) 677-2000

Company URL: http://www.kimley-horn.com
Establishment information: Established in 1967.
Company type: Private company
Business activities: Provides consulting services.
Business type (SIC): Management and public relations services
Corporate officers: Mark Wilson, Chair.; John C. Atz, Pres.; Nicholas Ellis, C.F.O.; Varner T. Olmsted, Cont.
Board of director: Mark Wilson, Chair.
Subsidiary: Kimley-Horn of Michigan, Inc., Detroit, MI
Offices: Phoenix, Tucson, AZ; Long Beach, Oakland, Orange, Pleasanton, Sacramento, San Diego, Tarzana, CA; Denver, CO; Fort Lauderdale, Fort Myers, Jacksonville, Miami, Miami Beach, Miami Lakes, North Port, Ocala, Orlando, Sarasota, Stuart, Tallahassee, Tampa, Vero Beach, West Palm Beach, FL; Atlanta, GA; Chicago, IL; Annapolis, MD; Bloomington, MN; Las Vegas, Reno, NV; Cary, Charlotte, Greensboro, NC; Knoxville, Memphis, TN; Austin, Dallas, Fort Worth, Frisco, Houston, TX; Chesapeake, Fairfax, Richmond, VA; Charleston, WV
Giving statement: Giving through the Kimley-Horn Foundation.

Kimley-Horn Foundation

c/o Branch Banking & Trust Co.
434 Fayetteville St., 14th Fl.
Raleigh, NC 27601-1701

Establishment information: Established in 2000 in NC.
Donor: Kimley-Horn and Associates, Inc.
Financial data (yr. ended 12/31/11): Assets, $1,333,754 (M); gifts received, $165,000; expenditures, $83,336; qualifying distributions, $65,800; giving activities include $65,800 for grants.
Purpose and activities: The foundation supports organizations involved with patient services, HIV/AIDS, hunger, housing, and human services.
Fields of interest: Youth development; Human services; Community/economic development.
Type of support: General/operating support; Program development.
Geographic limitations: Giving primarily in AZ, FL, and NC.
Support limitations: No grants to individuals.
Application information: Applications not accepted. Unsolicited requests for funds not accepted.
Officers: Mark S. Wilson, Chair.; Barry L. Barber, Secy.-Treas.
Board Members: Mark Bishop; Tom Fowler; J.P. Marchand; Beth Reed; Jonathan Thigpen; Jim West; Chuck Wright.
EIN: 562188912

2152
Kimmel & Associates, Inc.

(formerly Kimmel & Fredericks)
25 Page Ave.
Asheville, NC 28801 (828) 251-9900

Company URL: http://www.kimmel.com
Establishment information: Established in 1981 as Gulf Search, Ltd.
Company type: Private company
Business activities: Provides executive search services.
Business type (SIC): Personnel supply services
Corporate officers: Joseph W. Kimmel, Owner; Charlie Kimmel, Pres. and C.E.O.
Giving statement: Giving through the Kimmel & Associates, Inc. Corporate Giving Program.

Kimmel & Associates, Inc. Corporate Giving Program

25 Page Ave.
Asheville, NC 28801-2707 (828) 251-9900
URL: http://www.kimmel.com/index.cfm/do/construction.constructionScholarship

Purpose and activities: Kimmel awards college scholarships to college students studying construction or a field related to construction. Support is given on a national basis.
Fields of interest: Higher education; Scholarships/financial aid; Business/industry; Engineering/technology.
Program:
Kimmel & Associates Scholarship for Students in Construction: Kimmel annually awards up to 50 $1,000 college scholarships to college students studying construction or a field related to construction. Students must be currently enrolled in an accredited college or university and studying civil engineering, architectural engineering, construction management, construction technology, engineering technology, building construction, building science or another course of studies related to and leading to employment in construction. Preference is shown to students who are enrolled in the above coursework but who are also currently employed with a construction company while they attend school.
Type of support: Scholarships—to individuals.
Geographic limitations: Giving on a national basis.
Application information: Scholarship program is currently suspended until further notice.

2153
Kinder Morgan, Inc.

(formerly Knight Inc.)
1001 Louisiana St, Ste. 1000
Houston, TX 77002 (713) 369-9000
FAX: (713) 369-9394

Company URL: http://www.kindermorgan.com
Establishment information: Established in 1927.
Company type: Public company
Company ticker symbol and exchange: KMI/NYSE
Business activities: Transmits and distributes natural gas; operates petroleum products pipeline; generates electricity.
Business type (SIC): Gas production and distribution; pipelines (except natural gas/operation of); electric services
Financial profile for 2012: Number of employees, 10,685; assets, $68,185,000,000; sales volume, $9,973,000,000; pre-tax net income,

$1,343,000,000; expenses, $7,380,000,000; liabilities, $54,320,000,000
Fortune 1000 ranking: 2012—265th in revenues, 453rd in profits, and 85th in assets
Forbes 2000 ranking: 2012—932nd in sales, 1270th in profits, and 349th in assets
Corporate officers: Richard D. Kinder, Chair. and C.E.O.; Steven J. Kean, Pres. and C.O.O.; Kimberly Allen Dang, V.P. and C.F.O.; Henry W. Neumann, Jr., V.P. and C.I.O.; Anthony B. Ashley, V.P. and Treas.; Debra M. Witges, V.P. and Cont.; David R. DeVeau, V.P. and Genl. Counsel; James E. Street, V.P., Admin., and Human Resources; Larry S. Pierce, V.P., Corp. Comms. and Public Affairs
Board of directors: Richard D. Kinder, Chair.; Anthony W. Hall; Steven J. Kean; Deborah A. MacDonald; Michael Jaye Miller; Michael C. Morgan; Fayez Sarofim; Joel V. Staff; John Michael Stokes; C. Park Shaper; Robert F. Vagt
Subsidiaries: KN Gas Gathering, Inc., Lakewood, CO; MidCon Corp., Lombard, IL; Rocky Mountain Natural Gas Company, Glenwood Springs, CO
Giving statement: Giving through the Kinder Morgan Foundation.

Kinder Morgan Foundation

370 Van Gordon St.
Lakewood, CO 80228-1519 (303) 763-3471
FAX: (303) 984-3306;
E-mail: km_foundation@kindermorgan.com;
URL: http://www.kindermorgan.com/community/km_foundation.cfm

Establishment information: Established in 1990 in CO.
Donors: Knight Inc.; K N Energy, Inc.; Kinder Morgan, Inc.
Contact: Maureen Bulkley, Mgr.
Financial data (yr. ended 12/31/11): Assets, $14,181,517 (M); expenditures, $1,571,994; qualifying distributions, $1,558,917; giving activities include $1,558,917 for grants.
Purpose and activities: The foundation supports programs designed to promote the academic and artistic interests of youth. Special emphasis is directed toward academic programs including tutoring; arts education; and environmental education initiatives designed to work with local schools and meet curriculum standards.
Fields of interest: Arts education; Arts; Elementary/secondary education; Higher education; Libraries (public); Education, services; Education; Environmental education Youth.
Program:
Employee Matching Gift Program: The foundation matches contributions made by employees and directors of Kinder Morgan to college or university foundations, K-12 education foundations, and nonprofit organizations that supports arts and culture on a one-for-one basis up to $1,000 per contributor, per year.
Type of support: Continuing support; Curriculum development; Employee matching gifts; Program development.
Geographic limitations: Giving primarily in areas of company operations in the U.S. and in Canada.
Support limitations: No support for political candidates or lobbying organizations, service clubs, fraternal organizations, or organizations located outside the U.S. and Canada. No grants to individuals, or for scholarships, political causes, general operating support, capital projects (excluding libraries), religious projects, advertising, sponsorships, travel, conventions, conferences, or seminars, mentoring, leadership, or social development initiatives.
Publications: Application guidelines; Informational brochure (including application guidelines).
Application information: Applications accepted. Grants range between $1,000 and $5,000. Proposals should be no longer than 3 pages. CDs, DVDs, annual reports, and brochures are not accepted. Support is limited to 1 contribution per organization during any given year. Application form not required. Applicants should submit the following:
1) timetable for implementation and evaluation of project
2) how project will be sustained once grantmaker support is completed
3) results expected from proposed grant
4) statement of problem project will address
5) population served
6) name, address and phone number of organization
7) copy of IRS Determination Letter
8) brief history of organization and description of its mission
9) geographic area to be served
10) how project's results will be evaluated or measured
11) detailed description of project and amount of funding requested
12) plans for cooperation with other organizations, if any
13) contact person
14) copy of current year's organizational budget and/or project budget

Initial approach: E-mail or mail cover letter and proposal
Copies of proposal: 1
Deadline(s): Jan. 10, Mar. 10, May 10, July 10, Sept. 10, and Nov. 10
Final notification: 60 to 90 days

Directors: Jeffrey R. Armstrong; Larry S. Pierce; C. Park Shaper; James E. Street.
Number of staff: None.
EIN: 841148161

2154
Kindred Healthcare, Inc.

(formerly Vencor, Inc.)
680 S. 4th St.
Louisville, KY 40202-2407 (502) 596-7300

Company URL: http://www.kindredhealthcare.com
Establishment information: Established in 1998.
Company type: Public company
Company ticker symbol and exchange: KND/NYSE
Business activities: Operates hospitals.
Business type (SIC): Hospitals
Financial profile for 2011: Number of employees, 48,700; assets, $2,337,400,000; sales volume, $4,373,200,000
Fortune 1000 ranking: 2012—410th in revenues, 905th in profits, and 643rd in assets
Corporate officers: Edward L. Kuntz, Chair.; Paul J. Diaz, Pres. and C.E.O.; Benjamin A. Breier, C.O.O.; Richard A. Lechleither, Exec. V.P. and C.F.O.; Richard E. Chapman, Exec. V.P., C.A.O., and C.I.O.; Joseph L. Landenwich, Sr. V.P. and Corp. Secy.; M. Suzanne Riedman, Sr. V.P. and Genl. Counsel
Board of directors: Edward L. Kuntz, Chair.; Joel Ackerman; Ann C. Berzin; Jonathan D. Blum; Thomas P. Cooper, M.D.; Paul J. Diaz; Isaac Kaufman; Fred J. Kleisner; Eddy J. Rogers, Jr.; Phyllis R. Yale
International operations: Cayman Islands
Historic mergers: RehabCare Group, Inc. (June 1, 2011)
Giving statement: Giving through the Kindred Foundation, Inc. and the RehabCare Employee Disaster Fund.
Company EIN: 611323993

Kindred Foundation, Inc.

(formerly Vencor Foundation, Inc.)
c/o Kindred Healthcare, Inc.
680 S. 4th St.
Louisville, KY 40202-2412
FAX: (502) 596-4055; URL: http://www.kindredhealthcare.com/our-company/community-involvement/

Establishment information: Established in 1991 in KY.
Donors: Vencor, Inc.; Kindred Healthcare, Inc.; Ventas, Inc.; Kindred Healthcare Operating, Inc.; Kindred Hospice Charities, Inc.
Contact: Susan E. Moss, V.P.
Financial data (yr. ended 12/31/11): Assets, $397,764 (M); gifts received, $66,404; expenditures, $1,223,916; qualifying distributions, $1,209,247; giving activities include $1,209,247 for grants.
Purpose and activities: The foundation supports organizations involved with arts and culture, education, health, cancer, heart and lung diseases, Alzheimer's disease, diabetes, human services, and business promotion.
Fields of interest: Arts; Secondary school/education; Education; Nursing care; Health care; Cancer; Heart & circulatory diseases; Lung diseases; Alzheimer's disease; Diabetes; American Red Cross; Children/youth, services; Human services; Community development, business promotion; United Ways and Federated Giving Programs.
Type of support: General/operating support.
Geographic limitations: Giving primarily in areas of company operations, with emphasis on Louisville, KY.
Application information: Applications not accepted. Contributes only to pre-selected organizations.
Officers and Directors:* Richard E. Chapman*, Pres.; Joseph L. Landenwich*, V.P. and Secy.; John J. Lucchese, V.P.; Susan E. Moss*, V.P.; Hank Robinson, Treas.; Paul J. Diaz; William M. Altman.
EIN: 611204724
Selected grants: The following grants are a representative sample of this grantmaker's funding activity:
$271,450 to Alzheimers Association National Headquarters, Chicago, IL, 2010. For general support.
$120,269 to American Red Cross National Headquarters, Washington, DC, 2010. For general support.
$70,328 to American Heart Association, Louisville, KY, 2010. For general support.
$58,050 to American Lung Association of Kentucky, Louisville, KY, 2010. For general support.
$20,475 to American Diabetes Association, Louisville, KY, 2010. For general support.
$19,000 to Glass Slipper Society, Prospect, KY, 2010. For general support.
$16,750 to Saint Francis High School, Louisville, KY, 2010. For general support.
$16,020 to Health Enterprises Network, Louisville, KY, 2010. For general support.
$15,000 to American Nurses Credentialing Center, Silver Spring, MD, 2010. For general support.
$13,665 to Kentucky Country Day School, Louisville, KY, 2010. For general support.

RehabCare Employee Disaster Fund

680 S. Fourth St.
Louisville, KY 40202 (502) 596-7300

Establishment information: Established in 2005 in MO.
Donors: John Short; Ken R. Derrington; Shellee Essary; RehabCare Group, Inc.

Financial data (yr. ended 12/31/11): Assets, $251,945 (M); gifts received, $32,172; expenditures, $0; qualifying distributions, $0.
Purpose and activities: Giving for families of employees of RehabCare Group, Inc., and its related entities affected by natural or civil disaster.
Geographic limitations: Giving primarily in FL, LA, and MS.
Application information: Applications accepted. Application form required.
Initial approach: Proposal
Deadline(s): None
Directors: Jim Martin; Harry Rich; John Short*; Stephanie Warren.
EIN: 050627621

2155
KINeSYS Inc.

150 Bellam Blvd., Ste. 270
San Rafael, CA 94901-4849
(415) 453-0747
FAX: (415) 453-0780

Company URL: http://www.kinesys.com
Establishment information: Established in 1993.
Company type: Private company
Business type (SIC): Business services/ miscellaneous
Corporate officer: Jeff Kletter, Pres.
Giving statement: Giving through the KINeSYS Inc. Contributions Program.

KINeSYS Inc. Contributions Program

150 Bellam Blvd., Ste. 270
San Rafael, CA 94901-4849 (415) 453-0747
E-mail: contact@kinesys.com; URL: http://www.kinesys.com

Purpose and activities: KINeSYS is a certified B Corporation that donates a percentage of profits to charitable organizations.

2156
Kinetic Concepts, Inc.

8023 Vantage Dr.
P.O. Box 659508
San Antonio, TX 78230-4726
(210) 524-9000

Company URL: http://www.kci1.com
Establishment information: Established in 1976.
Company type: Private company
Business activities: Operates medical technology company that manufactures and markets high-technology therapies and products for the wound care, tissue regeneration and therapeutic support system markets.
Business type (SIC): Medical instruments and supplies
Financial profile for 2010: Number of employees, 6,900; assets, $3,076,000,000; sales volume, $2,017,750,000; pre-tax net income, $355,670,000; expenses, $1,571,380,000; liabilities, $1,592,920,000
Corporate officers: Joe F. Woody, Pres. and C.E.O.; Martin J. Landon, Exec. V.P. and C.F.O.; John T. Bibb, Exec. V.P. and Genl. Counsel; David Ball, Sr. V.P., Opers.; David Lillback, Sr. V.P., Human Resources
Board of directors: Lisa Colleran; Steven Dyson; Jim Fasano; William J. Gumina; Erik Levy; John F. Megrue, Jr.; Jim A. Pittman; Warren Roll; Joe Woody
Giving statement: Giving through the Kinetic Concepts, Inc. Corporate Giving Program.
Company EIN: 741891727

Kinetic Concepts, Inc. Corporate Giving Program

8023 Vantage Dr.
San Antonio, TX 78230-4726 (210) 524-9000
URL: http://www.kci1.com/KCI1/corporateresponsibility#

Purpose and activities: KCI makes charitable contributions to organizations involved with community development. Special emphasis is directed toward organizations involved with improving patient lives, especially those that provide holistic support to people who can benefit from the company's therapies, such as trauma victims and those with diabetes. Support is given primarily in areas of company operations; giving also to national organizations.
Fields of interest: Education; Holistic medicine; Health care; Heart & circulatory diseases; Diabetes; Housing/shelter.
Program:
Volunteer Program: Every employee at KCI is given 16 hours per year of paid time to participate in community or charitable projects. Recipient organizations include Communities in Schools, the American Heart Association, and Habitat for Humanity.
Type of support: Employee volunteer services; General/operating support.
Geographic limitations: Giving primarily in areas of company operations.

2157
King & Spalding

1180 Peachtree St., N.E.
Atlanta, GA 30309-3521 (404) 572-4600

Company URL: http://www.kslaw.com
Establishment information: Established in 1885.
Company type: Private company
Business activities: Operates law firm.
Business type (SIC): Legal services
Corporate officers: Patrick C. Glisson, C.O.O.; Gene R. Viscelli, C.I.O.
Offices: Redwood Shores, San Francisco, CA; Washington, DC; Atlanta, GA; New York, NY; Charlotte, NC; Austin, Houston, TX
International operations: France; Germany; Russia; Saudi Arabia; Singapore; Switzerland; United Arab Emirates; United Kingdom
Giving statement: Giving through the King & Spalding Pro Bono Program.

King & Spalding Pro Bono Program

1180 Peachtree St., N.E.
Atlanta, GA 30309-3521 (202) 737-8616
E-mail: jtoll@kslaw.com; Additional tel.: (404) 572-4600; URL: http://www.kslaw.com/About-Us/Public-Service/Pro-Bono-Matters

Contact: Joshua C. Toll, Pro Bono Counsel
Fields of interest: Legal services.
Type of support: Pro bono services - legal.
Application information: A Pro Bono Committee manages the pro bono program.

2158
King Arthur Flour Company, Inc.

135 U.S. Rte. 5 S.
Norwich, VT 05055 (802) 649-3361

Company URL: http://www.kingarthurflour.com
Establishment information: Established in 1790.
Company type: Private company
Business activities: Operates flour company.
Business type (SIC): Grain mill products, including pet food
Corporate officers: Frank E. Sands II, Chair.; Steve Voigt, Pres. and C.E.O.; Suzanne McDowell, V.P., Human Resources
Board of director: Frank E. Sands II, Chair.
Giving statement: Giving through the King Arthur Flour Company, Inc. Corporate Giving Program.

King Arthur Flour Company, Inc. Corporate Giving Program

c/o Donations
135 U.S. Rte. 5 S.
Norwich, VT 05055 (802) 649-3361
FAX: (802) 299-2256;
E-mail: donations@kingarthurflour.com;
URL: http://www.kingarthurflour.com/about/goodworks.html

Purpose and activities: King Arthur Flour Company is a certified B Corporation that donates a percentage of profits to nonprofit organizations. Special emphasis is directed toward organizations involved with nutrition education, hunger relief, and environmental sustainability. Support is limited to areas within a 100-mile radius of Norwich, Vermont.
Fields of interest: Environment, natural resources; Environment, energy; Environment; Food services; Food banks; Nutrition; Human services.
Program:
Employee Volunteer Program: King Arthur Flour provides 40 hours of paid volunteer time per year to full-time employees, and 20 hours to part-time employees.
Type of support: Donated products; Employee volunteer services; General/operating support.
Geographic limitations: Giving limited to areas within a 100-mile radius of Norwich, VT.
Support limitations: No support for political or discriminatory organizations, sports teams, or religious organizations that do not benefit a large segment of the community. No grants to individuals.
Publications: Application guidelines.
Application information: Applications accepted. Application form required. Applicants should submit the following:
1) population served
2) name, address and phone number of organization
3) copy of IRS Determination Letter
4) brief history of organization and description of its mission
5) contact person
6) plans for acknowledgement
Initial approach: Download application and e-mail completed form
Deadline(s): 145 days prior to event

2159
King Kullen Grocery Company, Inc.
185 Central Ave.
Bethpage, NY 11714 (516) 733-7100
FAX: (516) 827-6325

Company URL: http://www.kingkullen.com
Establishment information: Established in 1930.
Company type: Private company
Business activities: Operates supermarkets.
Business type (SIC): Groceries—retail
Financial profile for 2010: Number of employees, 4,500
Corporate officers: Ronald Conklin, Co-Chair.; Bernard D. Kennedy, Co-Chair. and C.E.O.; Brian C. Cullen, Co-Pres. and Co-C.O.O.; J. Donald Kennedy, Co-Pres. and Co-C.O.O.; Thomas Massaro, Sr. V.P., Opers.; James Flynn, Sr. V.P., Finance and Admin.; Joseph Brown, V.P., Sales; Dominick Fortugno, V.P., Human Resources
Board of directors: Ronald Conklin, Co-Chair.; Bernard D. Kennedy, Co-Chair.
Giving statement: Giving through the King Kullen Grocery Company, Inc. Corporate Giving Program.

King Kullen Grocery Company, Inc. Corporate Giving Program
185 Central Ave.
Bethpage, NY 11714-3927

Purpose and activities: King Kullen makes charitable contributions to nonprofit organizations involved with food services, and children and families services. Support is given primarily in Long Island, New York.
Fields of interest: Food services; Children, services; Family services.
Type of support: General/operating support; In-kind gifts.
Geographic limitations: Giving primarily in Long Island, NY.

2160
Kingsbury Corporation
(formerly Kingsbury Machine Tool Corporation)
80 Laurel St.
Keene, NH 03431-4278 (603) 352-5212
FAX: (603) 352-8789

Company URL: http://www.kingsburycorp.com
Establishment information: Established in 1890.
Company type: Subsidiary of a private company
Business activities: Manufactures machine tools.
Business type (SIC): Machinery/metalworking
Financial profile for 2009: Number of employees, 93
Corporate officer: Joseph Montisano, V.P., Opers.
Giving statement: Giving through the Kingsbury Fund.

Kingsbury Fund
P.O. Box 1802
Providence, RI 02901-1802

Establishment information: Trust established in 1952 in NH.
Donor: Kingsbury Corp.
Financial data (yr. ended 12/31/11): Assets, $3,107,016 (M); expenditures, $152,802; qualifying distributions, $132,843; giving activities include $117,078 for grants.
Purpose and activities: The foundation supports organizations involved with arts and culture, education, the environment, animal welfare, health, human services, and community economic development.
Fields of interest: Performing arts, music; Historic preservation/historical societies; Arts; Education, early childhood education; Elementary school/education; Higher education; Adult/continuing education; Education; Environment, natural resources; Environmental education; Environment; Animal welfare; Hospitals (general); Health care; American Red Cross; Children/youth, services; Family services; Aging, centers/services; Human services; Community development, business promotion; Community/economic development; United Ways and Federated Giving Programs.
Type of support: Annual campaigns; Capital campaigns; Employee matching gifts; Employee-related scholarships; Equipment; Matching/challenge support; Program development; Seed money; Sponsorships.
Geographic limitations: Giving limited to Cheshire County, Keene, and the Monadnock region of NH.
Support limitations: No support for religious or political organizations.
Application information: Applications accepted. Application form not required.
Initial approach: Proposal
Board meeting date(s): Spring and fall
Deadline(s): None
EIN: 026004465

2161
Kingston Technology Company, Inc.
17600 Newhope St.
Fountain Valley, CA 92708-4220
(714) 435-2600
FAX: (714) 435-2699

Company URL: http://www.kingston.com
Establishment information: Established in 1987.
Company type: Private company
Business activities: Manufactures computer memory, processor, networking, and storage products.
Business type (SIC): Computer and office equipment
Financial profile for 2011: Number of employees, 4,700; sales volume, $6,480,000,000
Corporate officers: John Tu, Pres.; David Sun, C.O.O.; Mike Sager, V.P., Sales and Mktg
Giving statement: Giving through the Kingston Technology Company, Inc. Corporate Giving Program.

Kingston Technology Company, Inc. Corporate Giving Program
c/o Charitable Contribs.
17600 Newhope St.
Fountain Valley, CA 92708-4220 (714) 435-2600
E-mail: donations@kingston.com; URL: http://www.kingston.com/company/charity.asp

Purpose and activities: Kingston makes charitable contributions to nonprofit organizations involved with arts and culture, education, community development, and science and technology. Support is given primarily in areas of company operations.
Fields of interest: Arts; Education; Human services; Community/economic development; Engineering/technology; Science.
Type of support: General/operating support.
Geographic limitations: Giving primarily in areas of company operations.
Support limitations: No support for veterans', labor, fraternal, or social organizations, or religious or political organizations. No grants to individuals, or for sponsorships, golf tournaments, or capital campaigns or endowments.
Application information: Applications accepted. Telephone calls and e-mails during the application process are not encouraged. Application form not required. Applicants should submit the following:
1) copy of IRS Determination Letter
2) brief history of organization and description of its mission
3) listing of board of directors, trustees, officers and other key people and their affiliations
4) detailed description of project and amount of funding requested
5) copy of current year's organizational budget and/or project budget

Initial approach: Mail proposal to headquarters
Copies of proposal: 1

2162
Kinney Drugs, Inc.
520 E. Main St.
Gouverneur, NY 13642-1561
(315) 287-3600

Company URL: http://www.kinneydrugs.com
Establishment information: Established in 1903.
Company type: Private company
Business activities: Operates drug stores.
Business type (SIC): Drug stores and proprietary stores
Corporate officers: Craig C. Painter, Chair and C.E.O.; Bridget-Ann Hart, Pres. and C.O.O.; Steve McCoy, Exec. V.P. and C.F.O.; Jeff Rorick, V.P. and C.I.O.; James Wuest, V.P., Mktg.; Richard McNulty, V.P., Human Resources
Board of directors: Craig Painter, Chair.; Mark Brackett; Richard Cognetti; John Dyer; Larry Greco; Bridget-Ann Hart; Steve McCoy; Dave McClure; Warren Wolfson
Giving statement: Giving through the Kinney Drugs Foundation, Inc.

Kinney Drugs Foundation, Inc.
29 E. Main St.
Gouverneur, NY 13642-1401
URL: http://www.kinneydrugsfoundation.com

Establishment information: Established as a company-sponsored operating foundation in 2002 in NY.
Donors: Kinney Drugs, Inc.; Mary Kinney Trust.
Financial data (yr. ended 12/31/10): Assets, $3,030,236 (M); gifts received, $623,050; expenditures, $784,640; qualifying distributions, $759,687; giving activities include $597,201 for 79 grants (high: $142,000; low: $100).
Purpose and activities: The foundation supports programs designed to help people live healthier lives within communities served by Kinney Drugs.
Fields of interest: Public health school/education; Hospitals (general); Health care, clinics/centers; Health care, EMS; Health care, home services; Health care; Cancer; Heart & circulatory diseases; Disasters, fire prevention/control; American Red Cross; Children/youth, services; Aging, centers/services; Developmentally disabled, centers & services; Human services.

Type of support: Annual campaigns; Building/renovation; Capital campaigns; Equipment; General/operating support; Sponsorships.
Geographic limitations: Giving limited to areas of company operations, primarily in central and northern NY and VT.
Support limitations: No grants to individuals.
Publications: Annual report; Application guidelines; Financial statement; Grants list; Informational brochure.
Application information: Applications accepted. Application form required. Applicants should submit the following:
1) name, address and phone number of organization
2) brief history of organization and description of its mission
3) geographic area to be served
4) detailed description of project and amount of funding requested
5) contact person
6) listing of additional sources and amount of support
7) plans for acknowledgement

Initial approach: Complete online application form
Board meeting date(s): 3rd Wed. of Feb., Mar., Apr., May, July, Aug., Oct., and Dec
Deadline(s): 1 month before board meeting

Officers and Directors:* Mark Brackett, R.Ph.*, Pres.; Rich McNulty*, V.P; Stephen McCoy*, Secy.-Treas.; Bernie Alden; Richard Cognetti; Fred Haggerty, R.Ph.; Owen Halloran, R.Ph.; Rebecca Horn; Timothy O'Connor, R.Ph.; Charles Owen, R.Ph.; James Spencer; Norton Taylor, R.Ph.; Daniel Villa, R.Ph.; Warren Wolfson.
EIN: 030406308
Selected grants: The following grants are a representative sample of this grantmaker's funding activity:
$100,000 to Samaritan Medical Center, Watertown, NY, 2010.
$50,000 to Albany College of Pharmacy, Albany, NY, 2010.
$25,092 to American Heart Association, Syracuse, NY, 2010.
$20,000 to Crouse Health Foundation, Syracuse, NY, 2010.
$15,000 to Northern Area Health Education Center, Canton, NY, 2010.
$10,000 to Carthage Area Hospital, Carthage, NY, 2010.
$10,000 to Disabled Persons Action Organization, Watertown, NY, 2010.
$6,862 to Canton-Potsdam Hospital Foundation, Potsdam, NY, 2010.
$5,000 to University of Connecticut Foundation, Storrs, CT, 2010. For scholarship.
$1,000 to Vermont Cares, Burlington, VT, 2010.

2163
The Kiplinger Washington Editors, Inc.

1729 H St., N.W.
Washington, DC 20006-3938
(202) 887-6491

Company URL: http://www.kiplinger.com
Establishment information: Established in 1920.
Company type: Private company
Business activities: Publishes newsletters and magazines.
Business type (SIC): Periodical publishing and/or printing; printing/commercial
Financial profile for 2010: Number of employees, 150
Corporate officers: Austin H. Kiplinger, Chair.; Knight A. Kiplinger, Pres.; Corbin M. Wilkes, Sr. V.P. and C.F.O.; Patricia J. Trudeau, V.P., Admin and Human Resources; Denise M. Elliott, V.P., Sales and Mktg.
Board of director: Austin H. Kiplinger, Chair.
Subsidiaries: Editors Press, Inc., Hyattsville, MD; Fairview Properties, Inc., Washington, DC; Fairview South, Stuart, FL; KCMS, Inc., Hyattsville, MD; Kiplinger Services, Inc., Washington, DC; Magazine Services Inc., New York, NY; Martin Gateway Center, LLC, Stuart, FL; Martin Gateway Estate, LLC, Stuart, FL; Outlook, Inc., Rehoboth Beach, DE; Sandstone, Inc., Lewes, DE; Shadow Lake Groves, Inc., Stuart, FL
Giving statement: Giving through the Kiplinger Washington Editors, Inc. Corporate Giving Program.

The Kiplinger Washington Editors, Inc. Corporate Giving Program

1729 H St., N.W.
Washington, DC 20006-3901

Contact: Patricia Trudeau; Courtenay Mullen
Purpose and activities: Kiplinger Washington Editors makes charitable contributions to nonprofit organizations on a case by case basis. Support is given primarily in the Washington, DC, area.
Fields of interest: General charitable giving.
Type of support: General/operating support.
Geographic limitations: Giving primarily in the Washington, DC, area.
Application information:
Committee meeting date(s): Quarterly

2164
Kirkland & Ellis LLP

(formerly Kirkland & Ellis)
300 N. LaSalle St.
Chicago, IL 60654 (312) 862-2000

Company URL: http://www.kirkland.com
Establishment information: Established in 1908.
Company type: Private company
Business activities: Provides legal services.
Business type (SIC): Legal services
Financial profile for 2010: Number of employees, 1,500
Corporate officers: Jeffrey C. Hammes, Chair.; Jay P. Lefkowitz, Pres.; Nicholas J. Willmott, C.F.O.
Board of director: Jeffrey C. Hammes, Chair.
Offices: Los Angeles, Palo Alto, San Francisco, CA; Washington, DC; Chicago, IL; New York, NY
International operations: China; Germany; Hong Kong; United Kingdom
Giving statement: Giving through the Kirkland & Ellis LLP Pro Bono Program and the Kirkland & Ellis Foundation.

Kirkland & Ellis LLP Pro Bono Program

300 N. LaSalle
Chicago, IL 60654-3406 (202) 879-5056
E-mail: thomas.yannucci@kirkland.com;
URL: http://www.kirkland.com/sitecontent.cfm?contentID=267

Contact: Thomas Yannucci, Firmwide Pro Bono Chair
Fields of interest: Legal services.
Type of support: Pro bono services - legal.
Geographic limitations: Giving primarily in areas of company operations in Los Angeles, Palo Alto, and San Francisco, CA, Washington, DC, Chicago, IL, and New York, NY, and in China, Germany, Hong Kong, and the United Kingdom.
Application information: A Pro Bono Committee manages the pro bono program.

Kirkland & Ellis Foundation

300 N. Lasalle Dr., Ste. 1018
Chicago, IL 60654-3413 (312) 862-2391
URL: http://www.kirkland.com/sitecontent.cfm?contentID=269

Establishment information: Established in 1981 in IL; status changed to a public charity in 1993.
Donors: Melvin S. Adess; Fred H. Bartlitt, Jr.; Francis J. Gerlits; Thomas A. Gottschalk; Glen E. Hess; William R. Jentes; John F. Kirkpatrick; Howard G. Krane; Jack S. Levin; James W. Rankin; Edward W. Warren; and others.
Financial data (yr. ended 12/31/11): Revenue, $6,662,526; assets, $4,289,959 (M); gifts received, $6,659,131; expenditures, $6,486,892; giving activities include $6,469,867 for grants.
Purpose and activities: The foundation provides financial support to charitable and law-related organizations that serve a wide range of initiatives.
Fields of interest: Community/economic development.
Type of support: Employee matching gifts.
Geographic limitations: Giving primarily to Mesa, AZ; Berkeley, Glendale, Los Angeles, and San Francisco, CA; Cos Cob and Norwalk, CT; Washington, DC; Naples, FL; Benton Harbor and Chicago, IL; Boston and Cambridge, MA; Columbia, MD; Manchester, NH; Newark and Princeton, NJ; Durham, NC; New York and White Plains, NY; Portland, OR; Newport, RI; and Dallas, TX.
Support limitations: No grants to individuals.
Application information: Applications not accepted. Contributes only to pre-selected organizations.
Officers and Directors:* Vicki V. Hood*, Pres.; Karen Walker*, Secy.-Treas.; Stephen Oetgen; Sally Smylie.
EIN: 363160355

2165
KLA-Tencor Corporation

1 Technology Dr.
Milpitas, CA 95035 (408) 875-3000
FAX: (408) 875-4144

Company URL: http://www.kla-tencor.com/
Establishment information: Established in 1976.
Company type: Public company
Company ticker symbol and exchange: KLAC/NASDAQ
Business activities: Supplies process control and yield management solutions for the semiconductor and related microelectronics industries.
Business type (SIC): Laboratory apparatus
Financial profile for 2012: Number of employees, 5,710; assets, $5,100,310,000; sales volume, $3,171,940,000; pre-tax net income, $974,090,000; expenses, $2,155,620,000; liabilities, $1,784,710,000
Fortune 1000 ranking: 2012—681st in revenues, 251st in profits, and 591st in assets
Forbes 2000 ranking: 2012—1608th in sales, 853rd in profits, and 1810th in assets
Corporate officers: Edward W. Barnholt, Chair.; Richard P. Wallace, Pres. and C.E.O.; Mark P. Dentinger, Exec. V.P. and C.F.O.; Brian M. Martin, Exec. V.P., Genl. Counsel, and Corp. Secy.; Virendra A. Kirloskar, Sr. V.P. and C.A.O.
Board of directors: Edward W. Barnholt, Chair.; Robert T. Bond; Robert M. Calderoni; John T.

Dickson; Emiko Higashi; Stephen P. Kaufman; Kevin J. Kennedy; Kiran M. Patel; Richard P. Wallace; David C. Wang
Giving statement: Giving through the KLA-Tencor Foundation.
Company EIN: 042564110

KLA-Tencor Foundation

1 Technology Dr.
Milpitas, CA 95035-7916
E-mail: foundation@kla-tencor.com; URL: http://www.kla-tencor.com/foundation/overview.html

Establishment information: Established in 2000 in CA.
Donor: KLA-Tencor Corporation.
Financial data (yr. ended 06/30/11): Assets, $6,194,253 (M); gifts received, $5,852,416; expenditures, $557,469; qualifying distributions, $527,502; giving activities include $527,502 for grants.
Purpose and activities: The foundation supports organizations involved with education, health and wellness, and social services. Special emphasis is directed toward science, technology, engineering, and math education.
Fields of interest: Higher education; Education; Health care; Human services; Community/economic development; Mathematics; Engineering/technology; Science.
Programs:
In-Kind Donations: The foundation, in partnership with KLA-Tencor, donates excess furniture and fixtures and spare computer and IT equipment to organizations around the world.
The KLA-Tencor Foundation Matching Gift Program: The foundation matches contributions made by employees of KLA-Tencor to charitable, cultural and civic programs that benefit their local communities up to $500 per employee, per year. The foundation also responds to regional and global disaster relief efforts by matching funds for employee donations to organizations providing relief services to affected areas.
Type of support: Donated equipment; Employee matching gifts; Employee volunteer services; General/operating support; In-kind gifts; Program development.
Geographic limitations: Giving primarily in areas of company operations in CA, FL, MA, NY, and VA, and in Hong Kong and Taiwan.
Support limitations: No support for individual schools, school organizations, clubs, radio or television stations, or Boy & Girl Scouts Troops, for-profit entities, discriminatory organizations, political candidates or organizations, professional associations, labor organizations, fraternal organizations, or social clubs, or religious organizations not of direct benefit to the entire community. No grants to individuals, or for scholarships, advertising journals or booklets, congresses, symposiums, or meetings, home-based child care or educational services, athletics, memorials, fundraising events or ticket purchases, travel, trips, tours, or cultural exchange programs, walk-a-thons, ride-a-thons, dance-a-thons, or bowl-a-thons.
Publications: Application guidelines.
Application information: Applications accepted. The foundation utilizes an invitation only process for its general grant program. The KLA-Tencor Foundation Committee establishes target organizations for grants and sends a Request for Consideration packet to those organizations. Multi-year funding is not automatic. Support is limited to 1 contribution per organization during any given year. Application form required.
Initial approach: E-mail foundation for application information and for in-kind gifts
Deadline(s): None
Directors: Brian M. Martin; John Van Camp; Rick Wallace.
EIN: 770557004
Selected grants: The following grants are a representative sample of this grantmaker's funding activity:
$100,000 to SEMI Foundation, San Jose, CA, 2011.
$25,000 to Teach for America, San Francisco, CA, 2011.
$20,000 to YMCA of Silicon Valley, San Jose, CA, 2011.
$12,500 to Glow Foundation, San Francisco, CA, 2011.
$10,000 to Family Giving Tree, Milpitas, CA, 2011.
$10,000 to Family Supportive Housing, San Jose, CA, 2011.
$5,000 to American Cancer Society, Oklahoma City, OK, 2011.
$3,000 to Save the Children Federation, Westport, CT, 2011.
$2,000 to American Cancer Society, Atlanta, GA, 2011.
$1,000 to UNICEF, New York, NY, 2011.

2166
Calvin Klein, Inc.

205 W. 39th St.
New York, NY 10018-3102 (866) 214-6694

Company URL: http://www.pvh.com/calvin_klein.aspx
Establishment information: Established in 1968.
Company type: Subsidiary of a public company
Business activities: Manufactures men's and women's apparel.
Business type (SIC): Apparel—men's and boys' outerwear; apparel—women's outerwear
Corporate officers: Barry K. Schwartz, Chair.; Paul Thomas Murry III, Pres. and C.E.O.; John Van Glahn, Exec. V.P., Finance, and Admin.
Board of director: Barry K. Schwartz, Chair.
Subsidiary: Calvin Klein Sport, New York, NY
Giving statement: Giving through the Calvin Klein Foundation.

The Calvin Klein Foundation

c/o Barry Schwartz
159 Mahopac Ave.
Granite Springs, NY 10527 (914) 248-5538

Establishment information: Established in 1981 in NY.
Donor: Calvin Klein, Inc.
Contact: Joel Semel, Mgr.
Financial data (yr. ended 06/30/11): Assets, $0 (M); expenditures, $0; qualifying distributions, $0.
Purpose and activities: The foundation supports organizations involved with arts and culture, health, cancer, HIV/AIDS, children and youth, and human services.
Fields of interest: Arts; Health care; Cancer; AIDS; Children/youth, services; Human services.
Type of support: General/operating support.
Geographic limitations: Giving primarily in NY.
Support limitations: No grants to individuals.
Application information: Applications accepted. Application form not required.
Initial approach: Proposal
Deadline(s): None
Officer: Joel I. Semel, Mgr.
Trustee: Robert Dipaola.
EIN: 133094765

2167
Julius Klein Diamonds Inc.

20 W. 47th St., 9th Fl.
New York, NY 10036-3303 (212) 981-0672

Company URL: http://www.juliusklein.com
Establishment information: Established in 1948.
Company type: Private company
Business activities: Cuts and polishes diamonds; sells diamonds wholesale.
Business type (SIC): Jewelry/precious metal; durable goods—wholesale
Corporate officer: Moshe Klein, Mgr.
Giving statement: Giving through the Sunrise Klein Foundation, Inc.

The Sunrise Klein Foundation, Inc.

307 S. Grandview Ave.
Monsey, NY 10952-3305 (845) 426-1214

Establishment information: Established in 2000.
Donors: Julius Klein Diamonds Inc.; Abraham Klein; Sunrise Venture LLC.
Contact: Abraham Klein, Tr.
Financial data (yr. ended 01/31/12): Assets, $490,496 (M); expenditures, $325,317; qualifying distributions, $324,560; giving activities include $324,560 for grants.
Purpose and activities: The foundation supports organizations involved with Judaism.
Fields of interest: Jewish agencies & synagogues.
Type of support: General/operating support.
Geographic limitations: Giving primarily in NY.
Application information: Applications accepted. Application form not required. Applicants should submit the following:
1) name, address and phone number of organization
2) detailed description of project and amount of funding requested
Initial approach: Proposal
Deadline(s): None
Officers: Abraham Klein, Pres.; Bella Klein, Secy.
EIN: 134097745

2168
Klein Tools, Inc.

450 Bond St.
P.O. Box 1418
Lincolnshire, IL 60069-1418
(847) 821-5500
FAX: (800) 553-4876

Company URL: http://www.kleintools.com/
Establishment information: Established in 1857.
Company type: Private company
Business activities: Manufactures hand tools, personal safety equipment, wire pulling tools, and accessories.
Business type (SIC): Cutlery, hand and edge tools, and hardware; fabricated textile products/miscellaneous; leather goods/miscellaneous; machinery/metalworking
Financial profile for 2010: Number of employees, 1,000
Corporate officers: Mathias A. Klein III, Chair.; Thomas R. Klein, Pres.; John McDevitt, Exec. V.P., Mktg. and Sales; Verne Tuite, C.F.O.; Bruce Beebe, V.P., Human Resources; Tom Condon, Corp. Cont.
Board of director: Mathias A. Klein III, Chair.
International operations: Mexico
Giving statement: Giving through the Klein Tools, Inc. Charitable Foundation.
Company EIN: 362474759

Klein Tools, Inc. Charitable Foundation

450 Bond St.
Lincolnshire, IL 60069-4225
FAX: (847) 478-0639

Establishment information: Established in 1985 in IL.
Donor: Klein Tools, Inc.
Contact: Thomas R. Klein, Secy.-Treas.
Financial data (yr. ended 11/30/11): Assets, $861,118 (M); expenditures, $41,358; qualifying distributions, $40,600; giving activities include $40,600 for 11 grants (high: $10,000; low: $100).
Purpose and activities: The foundation supports organizations involved with arts and culture, education, health, cancer, medical research, youth development, and human services.
Fields of interest: Arts; Education; Youth development.
Geographic limitations: Giving primarily in IL.
Support limitations: No grants to individuals, or for higher education.
Application information: Applications accepted. Application form not required. Applicants should submit the following:
1) copy of IRS Determination Letter
2) brief history of organization and description of its mission
3) copy of most recent annual report/audited financial statement/990
Initial approach: Proposal
Deadline(s): None
Officers and Directors:* Donna Grace Crusan*, Pres.; Mathias A. Klein III*, V.P.; Thomas R. Klein*, Secy.-Treas.; Sara J. Klein.
EIN: 363407613

2170
Klein-Kaufman Corp.

134 W. Hills Rd.
Huntington Station, NY 11746-3140
(631) 271-8055

Establishment information: Established in 1960.
Company type: Private company
Business activities: Operates restaurants.
Business type (SIC): Restaurants and drinking places
Financial profile for 2009: Number of employees, 900
Corporate officers: Irving Klein, C.E.O.; Jonah Kaufman, Pres.
Giving statement: Giving through the Klein-Kaufman Family Foundation.

The Klein-Kaufman Family Foundation

134 W. Hills Rd.
Huntington Station, NY 11746-3140

Establishment information: Established in 1993 in NY.
Donors: Klein-Kaufman Corp.; Kaufman Enterprises LLC.
Financial data (yr. ended 02/28/12): Assets, $11,401 (M); expenditures, $0; qualifying distributions, $0.
Purpose and activities: The foundation awards grants to individuals.
Geographic limitations: Giving primarily in Huntington, NY.
Application information: Applications not accepted. Unsolicited requests for funds not accepted.
Officer: Jonah Kaufman, Pres.
Directors: Melinda Kaufman; Irving Klein.
EIN: 113185247

2169
Klein's Super Markets, Inc.

(also known as Klein's Family Markets)
2101 Rockspring Rd.
Forest Hill, MD 21050-2617
(410) 420-8220

Company URL: http://www.kleinsonline.com
Establishment information: Established in 1925.
Company type: Subsidiary of a private company
Business activities: Operates grocery stores.
Business type (SIC): Groceries—retail
Financial profile for 2011: Number of employees, 1,000
Corporate officers: Andrew P. Klein, Pres.; Howard Klein, V.P. and Genl. Counsel; Patty Cones, C.A.O.
Giving statement: Giving through the Ralph and Shirley Klein Foundation, Inc.

The Ralph and Shirley Klein Foundation, Inc.

2101 Rockspring Rd.
Forest Hill, MD 21050-2617
FAX: (410) 838-5592

Establishment information: Established in 1991 in MD.
Donors: Klein's Super Markets, Inc.; Colgate Investments; Shirley S. Klein; Ralph Klein.
Contact: Shirley S. Klein, Secy.
Financial data (yr. ended 12/31/11): Assets, $2,802,325 (M); gifts received, $184,930; expenditures, $120,162; qualifying distributions, $96,837; giving activities include $96,837 for grants.
Purpose and activities: The foundation supports organizations involved with arts and culture, education, health, human services, and Judaism.
Fields of interest: Arts; Higher education, college (community/junior); Education; Medical care, in-patient care; Health care; Children/youth, services; Human services; United Ways and Federated Giving Programs; Jewish federated giving programs; Jewish agencies & synagogues.
Type of support: Annual campaigns; Capital campaigns; Continuing support; Curriculum development; Scholarship funds.
Geographic limitations: Giving primarily in MD, with emphasis on Hartford County.
Support limitations: No grants to individuals.
Application information: Applications accepted. Application form not required.
Initial approach: Proposal
Board meeting date(s): 1st of every month
Deadline(s): None
Final notification: 1 month
Officers: Ralph Klein, Pres.; Andrew P. Klein, V.P. and Treas.; Howard S. Klein, V.P.; Michael J. Klein, V.P.; Shirley S. Klein, Secy.
EIN: 521763518

2171
KLS Martin, L.P.

11201 St. Johns Industrial Pkwy. S.
P.O. Box 16369
Jacksonville, FL 32246-7652
(904) 641-7746

Company URL: http://www.klsmartinusa.com
Establishment information: Established in 1993.
Company type: Subsidiary of a foreign company
Business activities: Manufactures surgical instruments and products.
Business type (SIC): Medical instruments and supplies
Corporate officer: Warren Rodgers, Pres.
Board of directors: Jennifer Damato; Clay Hudgins; Tom Johnston
Giving statement: Giving through the Midwest Neuroscience Foundation.

Midwest Neuroscience Foundation

8005 Farnam Dr., Ste. 305
Omaha, NE 68114-4441 (402) 398-9243

Establishment information: Established in 2000 in NE.
Donors: KLS Martin, L.P.; Medtronic Neurological; Globus Medical, Inc.; Frank R. Krejci.
Contact: Lori Hill
Financial data (yr. ended 12/31/11): Assets, $98,448 (M); expenditures, $1,526; qualifying distributions, $0.
Purpose and activities: The foundation awards scholarships to students and individuals pursuing a career in neuroscience.
Type of support: Scholarships—to individuals.
Application information: Applications accepted. Application form required.
Initial approach: Letter
Deadline(s): None
Officers and Directors:* Leslie C. Hellbusch, M.D.*, Pres.; Douglas J. Long, M.D.*, V.P.; Stephen E. Doran, M.D.*, Secy.; John S. Treves, M.D.*, Treas.
EIN: 470825001

2172
Kmart Corporation

3333 Beverly Rd.
Hoffman Estates, IL 60179 (847) 286-2500

Company URL: http://www.kmartcorp.com
Establishment information: Established in 1962.
Company type: Subsidiary of a public company
Ultimate parent company: Sears Holdings Corporation
Business activities: Operates general merchandise stores.
Business type (SIC): Variety stores; merchandise stores/general
Financial profile for 2011: Number of employees, 800; sales volume, $15,590,000,000
Corporate officers: Louis J. D'Ambrosio, Pres. and C.E.O.; William K. Phelan, Sr. V.P., Finance
Division: Kmart Stores Div., Troy, MI
Giving statement: Giving through the Kmart Corporation Contributions Program.

Kmart Corporation Contributions Program

3333 Beverly Rd.
Hoffman Estates, IL 60179-0001
URL: http://www.kmartcorp.com/communityrelations/kmart/
Additional URL: http://www.searsholdings.com/communityrelations/kmart/

Purpose and activities: K-mart makes charitable contributions to nonprofit organizations involved with health, military, homes, and education. Support is given primarily in areas of company operations; giving also to national organizations.
Fields of interest: Education; Hospitals (specialty); Health care, infants; Health care; Diabetes; Children/youth, services; Human services, gift distribution; Military/veterans' organizations.
Type of support: Annual campaigns; Donated products; Employee volunteer services; Equipment; General/operating support; In-kind gifts.
Geographic limitations: Giving primarily in areas of company operations; giving also to national organizations.
Support limitations: No support for political organizations, or religious groups serving a single denomination. No grants to individuals, or for third party requests on behalf of an organization, family or individual emergency relief, individual or team fundraising, conferences, seminars, or travel, travel or academic research, parties, ceremonies, memorials, or courtesy advertising (programs, yearbooks, etc.).
Publications: Application guidelines.
Application information: Applications accepted. Printed material, faxes, or e-mailed donation requests will not be reviewed. Application form required. Applicants should submit the following:
1) copy of IRS Determination Letter
Applications should include a W-9 form.
Initial approach: Complete online application
Deadline(s): 30 days prior to event
Final notification: two weeks
Number of staff: 1 full-time professional.

2173
KMTSJ, Inc.

2503 N. Hillcrest Pkwy., Ste. 1
P.O. Box 3217
Altoona, WI 54720-2569 (715) 552-4300
FAX: (715) 552-3500

Establishment information: Established in 1982.
Company type: Private company
Business activities: Sells health insurance.
Business type (SIC): Insurance/accident and health
Corporate officers: Claire Johnson, Pres.; Peter Farrow, C.E.O.; Heidi Liedle, C.F.O.; John Brunstead, C.I.O.; Bob Hallowin, Secy.; David Sanford, Treas.
Giving statement: Giving through the KMTSJ Foundation, Inc.

KMTSJ Foundation, Inc.

P.O. Box 3217
Eau Claire, WI 54702-3217

Establishment information: Established in 1993 in WI.
Donors: KMTSJ, Inc.; Group Health Cooperative of Eau Claire.
Financial data (yr. ended 12/31/11): Assets, $5,235 (M); gifts received, $6,000; expenditures, $5,582; qualifying distributions, $5,000; giving activities include $5,000 for grants.
Purpose and activities: The foundation awards college scholarships to children of employees of KMTSJ, Inc. and Group Health Cooperative of Eau Claire.
Type of support: Employee-related scholarships.
Geographic limitations: Giving primarily in Eau Claire, WI.
Application information: Applications not accepted. Unsolicited requests for funds not accepted.
Officers: Peter Farrow, Pres.; Lon Blaser, V.P.; Heidi Liedl, Secy.-Treas.
Director: Carroll Carlson.
EIN: 391673898

2174
Knitcraft, Inc.

215 N. Main St.
Independence, MO 64050-2804
(816) 461-1248

Company URL: http://www.knitcraft.com/knitcraft/index.php
Establishment information: Established in 1972.
Company type: Private company
Business activities: Produces pile fabric and circular knit.
Business type (SIC): Hosiery and knitted fabrics
Corporate officer: Robert E. Bandlow, Pres.
Giving statement: Giving through the Howe Foundation, Inc.

The Howe Foundation, Inc.

P.O. Box 227
Belmont, NC 28012-0227 (704) 825-5372
Application address: P.O. Box 749, Belmont, NC 28012

Establishment information: Established in 1966 in NC.
Donors: Knitcraft, Inc.; Beltax Corp.
Contact: Henry Howe
Financial data (yr. ended 10/31/11): Assets, $2,455,909 (M); expenditures, $163,211; qualifying distributions, $141,800; giving activities include $141,800 for 44 grants (high: $58,000; low: $1,000).
Purpose and activities: The foundation supports organizations involved with arts and culture, education, human services, Christianity, and people with mental disabilities.
Fields of interest: Arts; Elementary/secondary education; Higher education; Education; Human services; Christian agencies & churches Mentally disabled.
Type of support: General/operating support.
Geographic limitations: Giving limited to the Belmont, NC, area.
Support limitations: No grants to individuals.
Application information: Applications accepted. Application form required.
Initial approach: Letter
Deadline(s): None
Officer: H.T. Howe, Treas.
Directors: Dave Hall; Dave Howe; G.M. Howe; H.R. Howe.
EIN: 566070727
Selected grants: The following grants are a representative sample of this grantmaker's funding activity:
$58,000 to First Presbyterian Church Belmont, Belmont, NC, 2011.
$2,000 to Belmont Abbey College, Belmont, NC, 2011.
$1,000 to House of Mercy, Belmont, NC, 2011.

2175
Knitcraft Corporation

4020 W. 6th St.
Winona, MN 55987-1660 (507) 454-1163

Company URL: http://www.stcroixknits.com
Establishment information: Established in 1960.
Company type: Private company
Business activities: Manufactures knitted apparel.
Business type (SIC): Hosiery and knitted fabrics
Corporate officer: Bernhard J. Brenner, Pres. and C.E.O.
Giving statement: Giving through the Knitcraft-St. Croix Foundation.

Knitcraft-St. Croix Foundation

4020 W. 6th St.
Winona, MN 55987-1532 (507) 454-1163

Establishment information: Established as a company-sponsored operating foundation in 1994 in MN; status changed to company-sponsored foundation in 2001.
Donors: Brenco L.P.; Knitcraft Corp.
Contact: Mary J. Bergin, V.P.
Financial data (yr. ended 06/30/12): Assets, $162,080 (M); gifts received, $16,945; expenditures, $8,852; qualifying distributions, $7,450.
Purpose and activities: The foundation supports organizations involved with education, health, children and youth, human services, and disabled people.
Fields of interest: Education; Human services.
Type of support: General/operating support.
Geographic limitations: Giving primarily in MN.
Support limitations: No grants to individuals.
Application information: Applications accepted. Application form required.
Initial approach: Contact foundation for application form
Deadline(s): None
Officers: Brenner Bernhard, Pres.; Mary Bergin, V.P.
Directors: Colleen Brenner; Dennis Meyer.
EIN: 411794859

2176
Knoll, Inc.

1235 Water St.
East Greenville, PA 18041 (215) 679-7991
FAX: (302) 655-5049

Company URL: http://www.knoll.com
Establishment information: Established in 1938.
Company type: Public company
Company ticker symbol and exchange: KNL/NYSE
Business activities: Designs, manufactures, and distributes office furniture products and accessories.
Business type (SIC): Furniture and fixtures/miscellaneous
Financial profile for 2012: Number of employees, 3,211; assets, $695,050,000; sales volume, $887,500,000; pre-tax net income, $78,340,000; expenses, $799,600,000; liabilities, $506,950,000
Corporate officers: Burton B. Staniar, Chair.; Andrew B. Cogan, C.E.O.; Barry L. McCabe, Exec. V.P. and C.F.O.; Michael A. Pollner, V.P., Genl. Counsel, and Secy.

Board of directors: Burton B. Staniar, Chair.; Kathleen G. Bradley; Andrew B. Cogan; Stephen F. Fisher; Jeffrey A. Harris; Sidney Lapidus; John F. Maypole; Sarah E. Nash
Giving statement: Giving through the Knoll, Inc. Corporate Giving Program and the Knoll Charitable Foundation.

The Knoll Charitable Foundation

P.O. Box 157
1235 Water Street
East Greenville, PA 18041-0157 (507) 931-1682

Establishment information: Established in 1999 in PA.
Donors: Knoll, Inc.; Warburg Pincus Foundation.
Financial data (yr. ended 12/31/11): Assets, $4,318,840 (M); expenditures, $224,416; qualifying distributions, $206,499; giving activities include $185,000 for 30 grants to individuals (high: $8,000; low: $3,500).
Purpose and activities: The foundation awards college scholarships to children of full-time employees of Knoll, Inc. The program is administered by Scholarship America.
Fields of interest: Higher education.
Type of support: Employee-related scholarships.
Geographic limitations: Giving limited to areas of company operations in MI and PA.
Application information: Applications accepted. Application form required.
Initial approach: Letter
Deadline(s): Mar. 15
Officers and Directors:* Marcia A. Thompson*, Pres.; Barry L. McCabe*, V.P. and Treas.; James Monzo, V.P.; Lynn Utter*, V.P.; Michael Pollner, Secy.
EIN: 232939762

2177
Knowledge Universe Education

(formerly Knowledge Learning Corporation)
650 N.E. Holladay St., Ste. 1400
Portland, OR 97232-2096 (503) 872-1300

Company URL: http://www.knowledgelearning.com
Establishment information: Established in 1983.
Company type: Private company
Business activities: Provides child care services.
Business type (SIC): Day care services/child
Financial profile for 2009: Number of employees, 36,000
Corporate officers: Tom Wyatt, C.E.O.; Mike Ensing, Exec. V.P. and C.F.O.; Elizabeth Large, Exec. V.P. and Genl. Counsel; Wei-Li Chong, Exec. V.P., Human Resources
Subsidiary: KinderCare Learning Centers, Inc., Portland, OR
Giving statement: Giving through the Knowledge Learning Corporation Contributions Program.

Knowledge Learning Corporation Contributions Program

650 N.E. Holladay St., Ste. 1400
Portland, OR 97232-2096 (503) 872-1519
E-mail: jeiland@klcorp.com

Contact: Jill Eiland, V.P., Corp. Comms.
Purpose and activities: Knowledge Learning makes charitable contributions to nonprofit organizations involved with at-risk youth. Support is given primarily in areas of company operations.
Fields of interest: Youth development.
Type of support: Employee volunteer services; General/operating support.
Geographic limitations: Giving primarily in areas of company operations.
Application information: Applications accepted. The Corporate Communications Department handles giving. A contributions committee reviews all requests. Application form not required. Applicants should submit the following:
1) population served
2) detailed description of project and amount of funding requested
Initial approach: Proposal to headquarters
Copies of proposal: 1
Deadline(s): None
Final notification: 1 month
Number of staff: 1 full-time professional; 1 part-time professional; 1 part-time support.

2178
KOA Speer Electronics, Inc.

199 Bolivar Dr.
Bradford, PA 16701 (814) 362-5536
FAX: (814) 362-8883

Company URL: http://www.koaspeer.com
Establishment information: Established in 1980.
Company type: Subsidiary of a public company
Business activities: Manufactures electronic components.
Business type (SIC): Electronic components and accessories
Corporate officers: Scott Rice, Pres.; Lance Eastman, C.F.O.; Jeffrey C. Rice, V.P., Sales and Mktg.
Giving statement: Giving through the Mukaiyama-Rice Foundation.

The Mukaiyama-Rice Foundation

c/o Lance Eastman
199 Bolivar Dr.
Bradford, PA 16701-1538

Establishment information: Established in 1998 in PA.
Donors: KOA Speer Electronics, Inc.; Katsuhiko Kichiji.
Financial data (yr. ended 12/31/11): Assets, $3,481,584 (M); gifts received, $18,225; expenditures, $147,990; qualifying distributions, $141,462; giving activities include $139,687 for 30 grants (high: $10,500; low: $100).
Purpose and activities: The foundation supports performing arts centers and organizations involved with education, health, and housing development.
Fields of interest: Performing arts centers; Higher education; Libraries (public); Education; Hospitals (general); Health care; Housing/shelter, development; YM/YWCAs & YM/YWHAs; United Ways and Federated Giving Programs.
Type of support: General/operating support; Scholarship funds.
Geographic limitations: Giving limited to Bradford, PA.
Support limitations: No grants to individuals.
Application information: Applications not accepted. Contributes only to pre-selected organizations.
Officers and Board Members:* Lance E. Eastman*, Pres.; Jeffrey C. Rice*, Secy.-Treas.; Tom Conklin; Lester Rice*; Scott Rice; Timothy D. Rice.
EIN: 232949160

2179
Koch Enterprises, Inc.

14 S. 11th Ave.
Evansville, IN 47712-5020 (812) 465-9800
FAX: (812) 465-9613

Company URL: http://www.kochenterprises.com
Establishment information: Established in 1873.
Company type: Private company
Business activities: Manufactures motor vehicle parts.
Business type (SIC): Motor vehicles and equipment
Corporate officers: Robert L. Koch II, Chair. and C.E.O.; James H. Muehlbauer, Vice-Chair.; Kevin R. Koch, Pres.; Susan E. Parsons, C.F.O. and Secy.-Treas.
Board of directors: Robert L. Koch II, Chair.; James H. Muehlbauer, Vice-Chair.; Jeffrey A. Bosse; Alan W. Braun; Steven A. Church; David M. Koch; Kevin R. Koch; Lawrence J. Kremer; P. Daniel Miller; Brad J. Muehlbauer; Susan E. Parsons; Ronald D. Romain
Subsidiaries: Audubon Metals LLC, Henderson, KY; Brake Supply Co., Inc., Evansville, IN; Comfort Financial Services, LLC, Evansville, IN; Gibbs Die Casting Corp., Henderson, KY; Koch Air LLC, Evansville, IN; George Koch Sons, LLC, Evansville, IN; South Western Communications, Inc., Newburgh, IN; Uniseal, Inc., Evansville, IN
Giving statement: Giving through the Koch Foundation, Inc.

Koch Foundation, Inc.

(formerly George Koch Sons Foundation, Inc.)
10 S. 11th Ave.
Evansville, IN 47744-0001
URL: http://www.kochenterprises.com/corporate/foundation.htm

Establishment information: Incorporated in 1945 in IN.
Donors: George Koch Sons, Inc.; George Koch Sons, LLC; Gibbs Die Casting Corp.; Koch Enterprises, Inc.
Contact: Jennifer K. Slade, Secy.
Financial data (yr. ended 12/31/11): Assets, $20,930,949 (M); gifts received, $780,000; expenditures, $1,157,525; qualifying distributions, $1,102,877; giving activities include $1,102,877 for grants.
Purpose and activities: The foundation supports organizations involved with arts and culture, education, health, human services, civic affairs, and religion. Special emphasis is directed toward organizations with which employees of Koch Enterprises are involved.
Fields of interest: Arts; Education; Health care; Human services; Public affairs; Religion.
Programs:
Mary L. Koch and Robert L. Koch Scholarship Awards: The foundation annually awards two four-year $2,500 college scholarships to children, stepchildren, and adopted children of full-time employees of Koch Enterprises and its subsidiaries.
Matching Gift Program: The foundation matches contributions made by full-time employees and retirees of Koch Enterprises and its subsidiaries to educational institutions and hospitals on a one-for-one basis from $25 to $2,500 per contributor, per year.
Type of support: Annual campaigns; Building/renovation; Capital campaigns; Employee matching gifts; Employee volunteer services; Employee-related scholarships; Matching/challenge support; Program development; Research; Sponsorships.
Geographic limitations: Giving limited to IN, KY, MO, Elko, NV, Schertz, TX, Beckley, WV, and Casper, WY,

with emphasis on the Evansville and the Vanderburgh County, IN, area.
Support limitations: No grants to individuals (except for employee-related scholarships).
Publications: Application guidelines.
Application information: Applications accepted. Application form not required. Applicants should submit the following:
1) copy of IRS Determination Letter
2) list of company employees involved with the organization
3) detailed description of project and amount of funding requested
Initial approach: Proposal
Copies of proposal: 1
Board meeting date(s): Fe., June, Sept. and Dec.
Deadline(s): None
Final notification: 3 months
Officers and Directors:* Robert L. Koch II*, Pres.; James H. Muehlbauer*, V.P.; Jennifer K. Slade, Secy.; Susan E. Parsons, Treas.; Steve A. Church; David M. Koch; Kevin R. Koch; Brad J. Muehlbauer.
Number of staff: 2 part-time support.
EIN: 356023372

2180
Koch Industries, Inc.

4111 E. 37th St. N.
P.O. Box 2256
Wichita, KS 67220-3203 (316) 828-5500

Company URL: http://www.kochind.com
Establishment information: Established in 1940.
Company type: Private company
Business activities: Refines petroleum; trades commodities; manufactures asphalt; produces natural gas liquids; produces minerals and fertilizer; produces cattle; manufactures chemical technology products; provides loans; operates pipelines; operates venture capital company.
Business type (SIC): Petroleum refining; farms/livestock; extraction/natural gas liquids; fertilizers and agricultural chemicals; asphalt and roofing materials; pipelines (except natural gas/operation of); non-depository credit institutions
Financial profile for 2011: Number of employees, 67,000; sales volume, $100,000,000,000
Corporate officers: Charles G. Koch, Chair. and C.E.O.; Joseph W. Moeller, Vice-Chair.; David L. Robertson, Pres. and C.O.O.; Steven J. Feilmeier, Exec. V.P. and C.F.O.
Board of directors: Charles G. Koch, Chair.; David L. Robertson, Vice-Chair.; Steven J. Feilmeier
Subsidiaries: Flint Hills Resources, LP, Wichita, KS; Georgia-Pacific Corporation, Atlanta, GA; Koch Oil Co., Sebring, FL
Divisions: Koch Materials Div., St. Louis, MO; Koch Minerals Div., Chicago, IL; Koch Nitrogen Div., Sterlington, LA
Plant: Akron, OH
International operations: Canada; United Kingdom
Giving statement: Giving through the Koch Industries, Inc. Corporate Giving Program.
Company EIN: 480484227

Koch Industries, Inc. Corporate Giving Program

c/o Community Affairs
P.O. Box 2256
Wichita, KS 67201-2256
E-mail: info@kochind.com; URL: http://www.kochind.com/Community/default.aspx

Purpose and activities: Koch Industries makes charitable contributions to nonprofit organizations involved with education, environmental stewardship, at-risk youth, and human services. Giving primarily in areas of company operations.
Fields of interest: Education; Environment, natural resources; Health care; Human services; Youth, services; Public affairs.
Type of support: Employee volunteer services; General/operating support; In-kind gifts; Sponsorships.
Geographic limitations: Giving primarily in areas of company operations.
Support limitations: No support for for-profit organizations. No grants to individuals, or for health-related causes, fundraising events, endowments, team or trip sponsorships, capital campaigns, contests, or advertising.
Publications: Application guidelines.
Application information: Applications accepted. Application form not required. Applicants should submit the following:
1) name, address and phone number of organization
2) detailed description of project and amount of funding requested
3) contact person
Proposals should include the amount requested, grant category, and type of support requested.
Initial approach: Complete online application
Number of staff: 1 full-time professional.

2182
Kohler Co.

444 Highland Dr.
Kohler, WI 53044-1515 (920) 457-4441

Company URL: http://www.kohler.com
Establishment information: Established in 1873.
Company type: Private company
Business activities: Manufactures plumbing and power systems products, furniture and accessories, cabinetry and tile, and engines and generators; operates resorts; develops real estate.
Business type (SIC): Pottery; furniture and fixtures; furniture/household; clay structural products; engines and turbines; real estate subdividers and developers; hotels and motels
Financial profile for 2011: Number of employees, 30,000; sales volume, $4,680,000,000
Corporate officers: Herbert V. Kohler, Jr., Chair. and C.E.O.; K. David Kohler, Pres. and C.O.O.; Jeffrey P. Cheney, Sr. V.P., Finance and C.F.O.; Natalie A. Black, Sr. V.P., Genl. Counsel, and Corp. Secy.; Laura Kohler, Sr. V.P., Human Resources; Herb Kohler, Mgr.
Board of director: Herbert V. Kohler, Jr., Chair.
Plants: Huntsville, AL; Sheridan, AR; Hattiesburg, MS; High Point, Hildebran, NC; Spartanburg, SC; Union City, TN; Brownwood, TX
International operations: China; France; India; Indonesia; Italy; Japan; Mexico; Singapore; Spain; Thailand; United Kingdom
Giving statement: Giving through the Kohler Co. Contributions Program.

Kohler Co. Contributions Program

444 Highland Dr.
Kohler, WI 53044-1515
FAX: (920) 459-1889;
E-mail: kohlergiving@kohler.com

Contact: Katie Jansen, Comms. Specialist
Purpose and activities: Kohler makes charitable contributions to nonprofit organizations involved with arts and culture, education, the environment, disease, medical research, housing, youth citizenship, human services, community development, people with disabilities, women, and homeless people. Support is given primarily in areas of company operations.
Fields of interest: Visual arts; Performing arts; Humanities; History/archaeology; Historic preservation/historical societies; Arts; Education, fund raising/fund distribution; Child development, education; Higher education; Adult education—literacy, basic skills & GED; Education, reading; Education; Environment, natural resources; Environment; Cancer; Organ diseases; Heart & circulatory diseases; AIDS; Health organizations; Cancer research; Heart & circulatory research; AIDS research; Medical research; Housing/shelter; Youth development, citizenship; Children/youth, services; Child development, services; Human services; Community/economic development Disabilities, people with; Women; Homeless.
Type of support: Annual campaigns; Building/renovation; Capital campaigns; Donated equipment; Donated products; Employee-related scholarships; Endowments; Equipment; General/operating support; In-kind gifts.
Geographic limitations: Giving primarily in areas of company operations, with emphasis on the Spartanburg, SC, Brownwood, TX, and Kohler, WI, areas.
Support limitations: No grants to individuals.
Publications: Informational brochure.
Application information: Applications accepted. The Communications Department handles giving. Application form not required. Applicants should submit the following:
1) results expected from proposed grant
2) statement of problem project will address
3) copy of IRS Determination Letter
4) copy of most recent annual report/audited financial statement/990
5) explanation of why grantmaker is considered an appropriate donor for project
6) listing of board of directors, trustees, officers and other key people and their affiliations
7) detailed description of project and amount of funding requested
8) copy of current year's organizational budget and/or project budget
9) listing of additional sources and amount of support
Initial approach: Mail proposal to nearest company facility
Copies of proposal: 1
Committee meeting date(s): Quarterly
Deadline(s): 2 months prior to need
Final notification: Before Dec. 31
Number of staff: 1 part-time support.

2181
Kohl's Corporation

N56 W17000 Ridgewood Dr.
Menomonee Falls, WI 53051
(262) 703-7000
FAX: (262) 703-6143

Company URL: http://www.kohls.com
Establishment information: Established in 1962.
Company type: Public company
Company ticker symbol and exchange: KSS/NYSE
International Securities Identification Number: US5002551043
Business activities: Operates department stores.
Business type (SIC): Department stores
Financial profile for 2013: Number of employees, 135,000; assets, $13,905,000,000; sales

volume, $19,279,000,000; pre-tax net income, $1,561,000,000; expenses, $17,389,000,000; liabilities, $7,857,000,000
Fortune 1000 ranking: 2012—148th in revenues, 201st in profits, and 314th in assets
Forbes 2000 ranking: 2012—482nd in sales, 624th in profits, and 1234th in assets
Corporate officers: Kevin B. Mansell, Chair., Pres., and C.E.O.; Wesley S. McDonald, Exec. V.P. and C.F.O.; John M. Worthington, C.A.O.
Board of directors: Kevin B. Mansell, Chair.; Steven A. Burd; Peter Boneparth; John F. Herma; Dale E. Jones; John E. Schlifske; Frank V. Sica; Peter M. Sommerhauser; Stephanie A. Streeter; Nina G. Vaca; Stephen E. Watson
Giving statement: Giving through the Kohl's Corporation Contributions Program.
Company EIN: 391630919

Kohl's Corporation Contributions Program

c/o Community Rels. Dept.
N56 W17000 Ridgewood Dr.
Menomonee Falls, WI 53051-5660 (262) 703-7000
FAX: (262) 703-7115;
E-mail: community.relations@kohls.com;
Application address for sponsorships: c/o Sponsorships and Promotions, N56 W17000 Ridgewood Dr., Menomonee Falls, WI 53051, e-mail: promotions@kohls.com; E-mail for youth soccer sponsorships: usyouthsoccer@kohls.com; URL: http://www.kohlscorporation.com/communityrelations/community01.htm

Purpose and activities: Kohl's makes charitable contributions to nonprofit organizations involved with children's education and health and youth soccer and awards college scholarships to kids ages six to 18 who volunteer in their communities. Support is given on a national basis in areas of company operations.
Fields of interest: Elementary/secondary education; Health care; Breast cancer; Athletics/sports, soccer; Children/youth, services Children; Youth.
Programs:
Associate Volunteers: Kohl's awards $500 grants to nonprofit organizations with which teams of five or more employees volunteer at least three hours. Participating organizations must enrich the lives of children.
Back-To-School Contest: Kohl's, in recognition of its 10th anniversary, awards $10 million to 20 K-12 schools to inspire students and school supporters to dream big about what their school could do with a half a million dollars. The contest is administered via Facebook where fans vote for schools and submit their ideas about how the money should be spent. The top 20 vote-getting schools receive $500,000 each.
Kohl's Kids Who Care: Through the Kohl's Kids Who Care program, Kohl's awards $50 gift cards to kids who volunteer in their communities. Regional winners receive $1,000 college scholarships. National winners receive $5,000 college scholarships. Additionally, Kohl's awards $1,000 grants to nonprofit organizations chosen by each national winner. Kids must be nominated by adults who are at least 21 years of age. Employees of Kohl's and their dependants are not eligible for nomination.
Type of support: Cause-related marketing; Donated products; Employee volunteer services; General/operating support; Scholarships—to individuals; Sponsorships.
Geographic limitations: Giving on a national basis in areas of company operations.
Publications: Application guidelines.
Application information: Applications accepted. A nomination form is required for Kohl's Kids Who Care. An application form is required for employee volunteer services. The Community Relations Department handles giving.
Requests for employee volunteer services should include the organization's IRS determination letter.
Initial approach: Download form and deliver or mail to nearest company store for Kohl's Kids Who Care and employee volunteer services; mail proposal to application address for sponsorships; E-mail proposal to headquarters for youth soccer sponsorships; vote online for Back-to-School-Contest
Deadline(s): Mar. 15 for Kohl's Kids Who Care; Sept. 3 for Back-to-School Contest
Final notification: July for Kohl's Kids Who Care; late Sept. for Back-to-School Contest

2183
The Howard Sloan Koller Group, Inc.

(also known as HSK)
(formerly Howard-Sloan Associates)
300 E. 42nd St., 15th Fl.
New York, NY 10017 (212) 661-5250

Company URL: http://www.hsksearch.com/our-history
Establishment information: Established in 1947.
Company type: Private company
Business activities: Provides executive placing services.
Business type (SIC): Personnel supply services
Corporate officers: Edward Koller, Co.-Pres. and C.E.O.; Alan Fleschner, Co.-Pres.
Board of directors: Carmela Cipriano; Collette Richardson; Rob Sullivan
Giving statement: Giving through the Koller Family Foundation, Inc.

Koller Family Foundation, Inc.

300 E. 42nd St., 15th Fl.
New York, NY 10017-5925

Donor: Howard Sloan Koller Group, Inc.
Financial data (yr. ended 11/15/11): Assets, $0 (M); expenditures, $1,262; qualifying distributions, $0.
Purpose and activities: The foundation supports health centers and organizations involved with cancer, diabetes, cancer research, human services, and Catholicism.
Fields of interest: Health care, clinics/centers; Cancer; Diabetes; Cancer research; Human services; Catholic agencies & churches.
Type of support: General/operating support.
Geographic limitations: Giving primarily in NY.
Support limitations: No grants to individuals.
Application information: Applications not accepted. Unsolicited requests for funds not accepted.
Directors: Michael J. Deutsch; Edward R. Koller, Jr.; Edward R. Koller III; Ross Koller.
EIN: 134091674

2184
Koniag, Inc.

4300 B St., Ste. 407
Anchorage, AK 99503-5946
(907) 561-2668
FAX: (907) 562-5258

Company URL: http://www.koniag.com
Establishment information: Established in 1972.
Company type: Native corporation
Business activities: Operates native corporation.
Business type (SIC): Nonclassifiable establishments
Corporate officers: Ron Unger, Chair.; Chris A. Johnson, Vice-Chair.; Will Anderson, Pres. and C.E.O.; Jim Erickson, Exec. V.P. and C.F.O.; Sandy Beital, V.P., Human Resources; M. Brent Parsons, Secy.; Mike Pestrikoff, Treas.
Board of directors: Margie Bezona; April Laktonen Counceller; Ronald Unger, Chair.; Chris A. Johnson, Vice-Chair.; Perry Eaton; Lois Fields; Richard Frost; M. Brent Parsons; Michael Pestrikoff; Conrad Peterson
Office: Kodiak, AK
Giving statement: Giving through the Koniag Education Foundation.

Koniag Education Foundation

4241 B. Street, Suite 303B
Anchorage, AK 99503-5920 (907) 562-9093
FAX: (907) 562-9023;
E-mail: kef@koniageducation.org; Additional tel.: (888) 562-9093; URL: http://www.koniageducation.org

Establishment information: Established in 1993 in AK.
Donors: Koniag, Inc.; Exxon Mobile; Alyeska Pipeline Co.; Gary Sampson.
Contact: Tyan Hayes, Exec. Dir.
Financial data (yr. ended 03/31/12): Assets, $5,615,586 (M); gifts received, $431,049; expenditures, $743,346; qualifying distributions, $297,004; giving activities include $297,004 for grants.
Purpose and activities: The foundation awards college scholarships and career development grants to Alaska Native shareholders and descendants of shareholders of Koniag, Inc.
Fields of interest: Vocational education, post-secondary; Higher education; Education Native Americans/American Indians.
Programs:
Alyeska: The foundation, in partnership with Alyeska Pipeline Service Company, awards scholarships of up to $2,500 to college students who are Alaska Native shareholders or descendents of shareholders of Koniag, Inc. Applicants must have a GPA of 2.0. and pursue study in select fields: engineering, health, safety, environment, quality, inspection professionals, security, planner/schedulers/project controls, project manager, information technology professionals, business planning, or technical positions.
Career Development Grants: The foundation awards grants of up to $1,000 to Alaska Native shareholders and descendents of shareholders of Koniag, Inc. who have chosen to further their education through a specific short-term class, seminar, or workshop lasting up to six weeks.
ExxonMobil: The foundation, in partnership with ExxonMobil, awards one $10,000 college scholarship to a student who is an Alaska Native shareholder or a descendent of shareholders of Koniag, Inc. Applicants must have a GPA of 3.0 and

must pursue study in a field directly related to the oil and gas industry.

Glenn Godfrey Memorial Scholarship: The foundation awards one $5,000 college scholarship to a college sophomore, junior, or senior who is an Alaska Native shareholder or descendent of a shareholder of Koniag, Inc. Applicants must have a GPA of 2.5 or higher and must demonstrate continued community service or civic duty. The scholarship was created to help Alutiiq people pursue self-improvement and positive leadership roles.

KEF General Scholarship: The foundation awards college scholarships of up to $2,500 to high school seniors with a GPA of 2.0 are higher who are Alaska Native shareholders or descendents of shareholders of Koniag, Inc.

Koniag Angayuk Scholarship & Internship: The foundation awards renewable college scholarships of up to $10,000 to high school seniors who are Alaska Native shareholders or descendents of shareholders of Koniag, Inc. Applicants must have a GPA of 3.0 and agree to intern at any one of Koniag's subsidiaries during the summer months. Students will receive a salary during the internship, travel, and lodging.

Larry Matfay Scholarship: The foundation awards one $1,000 college scholarship to an Alaska Native shareholder or descendent of a shareholder of Koniag, Inc. studying healthcare, anthropology, history, Alaska Native or American Indian studies, or other disciplines involving research and learning about Alutiiq culture.

Magnel Larsen Drabek: The foundation awards one $2,000 college scholarship to a college sophomore, junior, or senior who is an Alaska Native shareholder or descendent of a shareholder of Koniag, Inc. Applicants must have a GPA of 2.0 and must major in education, arts, or cultural studies.

Type of support: Grants to individuals; Internship funds; Scholarships—to individuals.
Geographic limitations: Giving primarily in AK and the Pacific Northwest, with emphasis on Kodiak Island, AK.
Publications: Application guidelines; Financial statement; Grants list; Informational brochure; Newsletter.
Application information: Applications accepted. Multi-year funding is not automatic. Application form required.
Requests should include a Koniag, Inc. shareholder enrollment number; a 300- to 600-word essay describing personal and family history, schooling, and educational and life goals; high school or college transcripts; 2 letters of recommendation; proof of acceptance to an institution of higher education; a recent photo; a resume; and a Koniag, Inc. descendent database form. Essays for Glenn Godfrey Scholarships should indicate what the applicant expects to accomplish in the next 10 years, how the scholarship will help the applicant achieve that goal, and how the applicant plans to give back to the community.

Initial approach: Complete online application or download application form and mail to foundation
Board meeting date(s): Quarterly
Deadline(s): Jan. 15 for Angayuk Scholarship & Internship; Mar. 15 for KEF General summer term; June 1 for KEF General fall term; Aug. 10 for Alyeksa, Drabek, ExxonMobil, Godfrey, and Matfay; None for Career Development Grants

Officers and Directors: Edward Ward, Pres.; Jon Panamaroff, V.P.; James Carmichael, Secy.-Treas.; Tyan Hayes, Exec. Dir.; William Anderson, Jr.; Peter Boskofsky; Laurie Fagnani; Uwe Gross; Janissa Johnson; Jacqueline Madsen; Stephen Parsons; Lorena Skonberg.
Number of staff: 1 full-time professional; 1 part-time professional; 1 part-time support.
EIN: 920145017

2185
Konica Minolta Danka Imaging Company

(formerly Danka Office Imaging Company)
11101 Roosevelt Blvd. N.
Saint Petersburg, FL 33716 (727) 622-2100

Company URL: http://www.danka.com
Establishment information: Established in 1997.
Company type: Subsidiary of a private company
Business activities: Sells and provides office imaging equipment, solutions, and related services and supplies wholesale.
Business type (SIC): Professional and commercial equipment—wholesale
Corporate officers: Ikuo Nakagawa, Chair. and C.E.O.; William Troxil, Pres. and C.O.O.
Board of director: Ikouo Nakagawa, Chair.
Giving statement: Giving through the Gregory T. Spagnoletti Memorial Foundation.

Gregory T. Spagnoletti Memorial Foundation

62 Wolff St.
Waterbury, CT 06708-1028

Establishment information: Established in 2000 in CT.
Donors: Danka Office Imaging Co.; Michael Petrucelli; Ron Zarella.
Financial data (yr. ended 12/31/11): Assets, $226,651 (M); gifts received, $10,686; expenditures, $103,121; qualifying distributions, $50,250; giving activities include $50,250 for 2 grants (high: $50,000; low: $250).
Purpose and activities: The foundation supports organizations involved with secondary education and housing.
Fields of interest: Secondary school/education; Housing/shelter.
Type of support: General/operating support.
Geographic limitations: Giving primarily in Waterbury, CT.
Support limitations: No grants to individuals.
Application information: Applications not accepted. Unsolicited requests for funds not accepted.
Trustees: Christopher Spagnoletti; Joseph Spagnoletti; Maria Spagnoletti; Mark Spagnoletti; Paul Spagnoletti; Richard Spagnoletti.
EIN: 061633779

2186
Michael Kors (USA)

11 West 42nd St.
New York, NY 10036 (212) 201-8100

Company URL: http://www.michaelkors.com/
Establishment information: Established in 1981.
Company type: Subsidiary of a foreign company
Business activities: Operates branded apparel company.
Business type (SIC): Apparel—women's outerwear
Corporate officers: Michael Kors, Chair.; John D. Idol, C.E.O.; Joseph B. Parsons, Exec. V.P. and C.F.O.
Giving statement: Giving through the Michael Kors (USA) Corporate Giving Program.

Michael Kors (USA) Corporate Giving Program

11 West 42nd St.
New York, NY 10036 (212) 201-8100
URL: http://www.michaelkors.com/

2187
Korum Automotive Group, Inc.

100 River Rd.
Puyallup, WA 98371 (253) 845-6600
FAX: (253) 841-7615

Company URL: http://www.korum.com/
Establishment information: Established in 1956.
Company type: Private company
Business activities: Operates car dealership.
Business type (SIC): Motor vehicles—retail
Financial profile for 2009: Number of employees, 475
Corporate officers: Jerome M. Korum, Pres.; Carol Skinner, C.F.O.
Giving statement: Giving through the Korum for Kids Foundation.

Korum for Kids Foundation

P.O. Box 538
Puyallup, WA 98371 (253) 927-0966

Establishment information: Established in 1994 in WA.
Donors: Korum Automotive Group, Inc.; Jerry Korum Investments; Jerome Korum; Korum Family Limited Partnership.
Contact: Sophia Hall, Tr.
Financial data (yr. ended 12/31/11): Assets, $5,696,697 (M); gifts received, $375,293; expenditures, $441,550; qualifying distributions, $334,675; giving activities include $334,675 for grants.
Purpose and activities: The foundation supports programs designed to promote and improve the health, welfare, and future of young people.
Fields of interest: Arts; Education; Health care; Recreation; Human services Children/youth.
Type of support: Building/renovation; Capital campaigns; Equipment; General/operating support; Matching/challenge support; Program development; Scholarship funds; Sponsorships.
Support limitations: No grants to individuals.
Application information: Applications accepted. Application form required.

Initial approach: Contact foundation for application form
Copies of proposal: 3
Deadline(s): None

Officer and Trustees:* Sophia Hall*, Mgr.; Germaine R. Korum; Jerry Korum.
EIN: 916528752
Selected grants: The following grants are a representative sample of this grantmaker's funding activity:
$35,250 to Good Samaritan Community Healthcare, Puyallup, WA, 2010.
$27,000 to Puyallup Fair Foundation, Puyallup, WA, 2010.
$15,000 to Mary Bridge Childrens Foundation, Tacoma, WA, 2010.
$10,000 to Point Defiance Zoological Society, Tacoma, WA, 2010.
$5,828 to Leukemia & Lymphoma Society, Seattle, WA, 2010.
$5,000 to Helping Hand House, Puyallup, WA, 2010.
$5,000 to Museum of Glass, Tacoma, WA, 2010.

$5,000 to TEARS Foundation, Puyallup, WA, 2010.
$5,000 to Young Life, Colorado Springs, CO, 2010.
$2,500 to HopeSparks, Tacoma, WA, 2010.

2188
Koss Corporation

4129 N. Port Washington Ave.
Milwaukee, WI 53212 (414) 964-5000

Company URL: http://www.koss.com
Establishment information: Established in 1953.
Company type: Public company
Company ticker symbol and exchange: KOSS/NASDAQ
Business activities: Manufactures stereo headphones and accessories and electrostatic and dynamic loudspeakers.
Business type (SIC): Audio and video equipment/household; electronic components and accessories
Financial profile for 2012: Number of employees, 60; assets, $28,750,000; sales volume, $37,870,000; pre-tax net income, $4,040,000; expenses, $33,980,000; liabilities, $11,650,000
Corporate officers: John C. Koss, Sr., Chair.; Michael J. Koss, Vice-Chair., Pres., C.E.O., and C.O.O.; David Donnan Smith, Exec. V.P. and C.F.O.; Lenore E. Lillie, V.P., Opers.; John C. Koss, Jr., V.P., Sales; Cheryl Mike, V.P., Human Resources
Board of directors: John C. Koss, Sr., Chair.; Michael J. Koss, Vice-Chair.; Thomas L. Doerr; Lawrence S. Mattson; Theodore H. Nixon; John J. Stollenwerk
Subsidiary: Koss Classics Ltd., Milwaukee, WI
International operations: Switzerland
Giving statement: Giving through the Koss Foundation, Inc.
Company EIN: 391168275

Koss Foundation, Inc.

(formerly John C. Koss Family Foundation, Inc.)
4129 N. Port Washington Rd.
Milwaukee, WI 53212-1029 (414) 964-5000

Establishment information: Established in 1968 in WI.
Donor: Koss Corp.
Contact: Michael J. Koss, Secy.-Treas.
Financial data (yr. ended 12/31/11): Assets, $1,511,960 (M); gifts received, $31,585; expenditures, $137,715; qualifying distributions, $135,755; giving activities include $135,755 for grants.
Purpose and activities: The foundation supports organizations involved with arts and culture, education, health, Crohn's disease, youth development, and Christianity.
Fields of interest: Education; Youth development; Religion.
Type of support: Annual campaigns; Capital campaigns; Continuing support; Matching/challenge support.
Geographic limitations: Giving primarily in the Milwaukee, WI, area.
Support limitations: No grants to individuals.
Application information: Applications accepted. Application form not required. Applicants should submit the following:
1) copy of IRS Determination Letter
Initial approach: Proposal
Deadline(s): None
Officers and Directors:* John C. Koss*, Pres.; Michael J. Koss, Secy.-Treas.; Nancy L. Koss.
Number of staff: 1 part-time support.
EIN: 391098935

2189
Kowalski Sausage Co., Inc.

2240-2300 Holbrook Ave.
Detroit, MI 48212 (313) 873-8200

Company URL: http://www.kowality.com/
Establishment information: Established in 1920.
Company type: Subsidiary of a private company
Business activities: Produces sausage and other meat products; sells meats wholesale.
Business type (SIC): Meat packing plants and prepared meats and poultry; groceries—wholesale
Corporate officers: Michael Kowalski, Co-Pres.; Stephen Z. Kowalski, Co-Pres.; Ronald J. Kowalski, Secy.-Treas.; Linda Jacob, Corp. Secy.
Giving statement: Giving through the Kowalski Sausage Company Charitable Trust.

Kowalski Sausage Company Charitable Trust

c/o JPMorgan Chase Bank, N.A.
P.O. Box 3038
Milwaukee, WI 53201-3038 (414) 977-1210
Application address: JPMorgan Chase Bank, N.A., 200 Ross Ave., FL 5, Dallas, TX 78201, tel.: (214) 965-2231

Establishment information: Established in 1951 in MI.
Donor: Kowalski Sausage Co.
Financial data (yr. ended 12/31/11): Assets, $993,492 (M); expenditures, $8,165; qualifying distributions, $0.
Purpose and activities: The trust supports organizations involved with education.
Fields of interest: Education, early childhood education; Higher education; Education.
Type of support: Program development.
Geographic limitations: Giving primarily in FL and MI.
Support limitations: No grants to individuals.
Application information: Applications accepted. Application form required. Applicants should submit the following:
1) statement of problem project will address
2) copy of IRS Determination Letter
3) detailed description of project and amount of funding requested
4) copy of current year's organizational budget and/or project budget
Initial approach: Contact foundation for application form
Copies of proposal: 1
Board meeting date(s): Varies
Deadline(s): None
Officers and Trustees:* Stephen Kowalski*, Chair.; Donald Kowalski, Pres.; Agnes Kowalski; Kenneth Kowalski; JPMorgan Chase Bank, N.A.
EIN: 386046508

2190
KPMG LLP

(formerly KPMG Peat Marwick LLP)
345 Park Ave.
New York, NY 10154-0102 (212) 758-9700

Company URL: http://www.us.kpmg.com
Establishment information: Established in 1897.
Company type: Private company
Business activities: Provides auditing, risk advisory, and tax services.
Business type (SIC): Accounting, auditing, and bookkeeping services; management and public relations services
Corporate officers: John B. Veihmeyer, Chair. and C.E.O.; Richard Anderson, C.I.O.; Henry Keizer, C.O.O.
Board of director: John B. Veihmeyer, Chair.
Giving statement: Giving through the KPMG Foundation, the KPMG (Stamford) Foundation, Inc., and the KPMG Disaster Relief Fund.

The KPMG Foundation

(formerly The KPMG Peat Marwick Foundation)
3 Chestnut Ridge Rd.
Montvale, NJ 07645-0435 (201) 307-7932
FAX: (201) 624-7763;
E-mail: us-kpmgfoundation@kpmg.com; E-mail for Tara Perino: tperino@kpmg.com; URL: http://www.kpmgfoundation.org
Application address for Minority Accounting Doctoral Scholarships: KPMG Foundation, Doctoral Scholarship Prog., c/o Joanne Berry

Establishment information: Trust established in 1968 in NY.
Donor: KPMG LLP.
Contact: Tara Perino, Dir.
Financial data (yr. ended 06/30/12): Assets, $4,892,000 (L); gifts received, $8,753,946; expenditures, $8,935,597; qualifying distributions, $8,900,662; giving activities include $3,364,564 for grants and $4,848,292 for 3,500 employee matching gifts.
Purpose and activities: The foundation supports organizations involved with business education and volunteerism and awards graduate scholarships to minority doctoral accounting students.
Fields of interest: Secondary school/education; Higher education; Business school/education; Education, reading; Human services, financial counseling; Business/industry; Community development, business promotion; Philanthropy/voluntarism Minorities; African Americans/Blacks; Hispanics/Latinos; Native Americans/American Indians.
Programs:
Matching Gifts Program: The KPMG Foundation matches employee/partner contributions to 4-year colleges and universities from which the donor graduated.
Minority Accounting Doctoral Scholarships: The foundation awards five-year $10,000 graduate scholarships to minority doctoral accounting students. The program is designed to increase the completion rate among African-American, Hispanic-American, and Native American doctoral students. The scholarship is eligible for annual renewal. Cumulative total scholarship amount may not exceed $50,000.
Type of support: Conferences/seminars; Continuing support; Curriculum development; Employee matching gifts; Professorships; Program development; Scholarship funds; Scholarships—to individuals; Sponsorships.
Geographic limitations: Giving primarily in CA, Washington, DC, FL, NJ, NY, and RI.
Publications: Annual report; Application guidelines; Grants list.
Application information: Applications accepted. Unsolicited applications for general grants not accepted. Application form required. Scholarship applications should include a cover letter, resume, transcripts, and proof of matriculation status.
Initial approach: Download application form and mail to foundation for scholarships
Board meeting date(s): May
Deadline(s): May 1 for scholarships

Officers and Trustees:* Jose R. Rodriguez*, Chair.; Bernard J. Milano*, Pres.; Theresa Ahlstrom; Kelly Brooks; Robert Fisher; Timothy H. Gillis; Laurel Hammer; Kathy H. Hannan; Laura Hay; Tammy Hunter; William P. Lovallo; Milford McGuirt; Bruce N. Pfau; Reginald C. Reed; Stacy M. Sturgeon; Michiko Yano.
Number of staff: 3 full-time professional; 6 full-time support.
EIN: 136262199
Selected grants: The following grants are a representative sample of this grantmaker's funding activity:
$275,000 to PhD Project, Montvale, NJ, 2012.

KPMG Disaster Relief Fund

3 Chestnut Ridge Rd.
Montvale, NJ 07645-1842
URL: http://www.kpmgcampus.com/whykpmg/ci_disaster.shtml

Financial data (yr. ended 06/30/11): Revenue, $1,372,706; assets, $1,390,159 (M); gifts received, $1,372,706; expenditures, $1,663,513; giving activities include $51,984 for grants.
Purpose and activities: The fund seeks to assist KPMG employees who have an immediate financial need and/or permanent financial loss resulting from a natural disaster.
Fields of interest: Safety/disasters.
Type of support: Emergency funds; Grants to individuals.
Officers: Bernard J. Milano, Pres.; Gregory R. Frazier, V.P. and Treas.; David Messer, Secy.
Directors: Larry R. Laughman; Bruce N. Pfau; Jeanne Sasek.
EIN: 223263347

2191
Kramer Levin Naftalis & Frankel LLP

1177 Avenue of the Americas
New York, NY 10036-2714 (212) 715-9100

Company URL: http://www.kramerlevin.com
Establishment information: Established in 1968.
Company type: Private company
Business activities: Operates law firm.
Business type (SIC): Legal services
Office: New York, NY
International operations: France
Giving statement: Giving through the Kramer Levin Naftalis & Frankel LLP Pro Bono Program.

Kramer Levin Naftalis & Frankel LLP Pro Bono Program

1177 Avenue of the Americas
New York, NY 10036-2714 (212) 715-7616
E-mail: jgrayer@kramerlevin.com; Additional tel.: (212) 715-9100; URL: http://www.kramerlevin.com/probono/overview/

Contact: James Grayer, Partner
Fields of interest: Legal services.
Type of support: Pro bono services - legal.
Geographic limitations: Giving primarily in areas of company operations in Menlo Park, CA, and New York, NY, and in France.
Application information: A Pro Bono Committee manages the pro bono program.

2192
Krasdale Foods, Inc.

65 W. Red Oak Ln.
400 Food Center Dr.
White Plains, NY 10604 (914) 694-6400

Company URL: http://www.krasdalefoods.com
Establishment information: Established in 1908.
Company type: Private company
Business activities: Operates grocery wholesaling company.
Business type (SIC): Groceries—wholesale
Corporate officers: Charles Krasne, C.E.O.; Steven Silver, Sr. V.P. and C.F.O.; Steven Laskowitz, Sr. V.P. and C.I.O.; Howard Jacobs, V.P. and Genl. Counsel
Giving statement: Giving through the Abraham Krasne Foundation, Inc.

Abraham Krasne Foundation, Inc.

65 W. Red Oak Ln.
White Plains, NY 10604-3616

Establishment information: Established around 1989 in NY.
Donors: Krasdale Foods, Inc.; Alpha I Marketing Corp; Beta II Marketing; Consolidated Supermarket Supply.
Financial data (yr. ended 12/31/11): Assets, $2,829,887 (M); gifts received, $300,000; expenditures, $403,973; qualifying distributions, $401,000; giving activities include $401,000 for grants.
Purpose and activities: Giving primarily for Jewish federated giving programs, health and medical services, and higher education.
Fields of interest: Higher education; Business school/education; Medical school/education; Health care; Jewish federated giving programs.
Geographic limitations: Giving primarily in CT and NY.
Support limitations: No grants to individuals.
Application information: Applications not accepted. Contributes only to pre-selected organizations.
Officers: Charles A. Krasne, Pres. and Secy.; Kenneth Krasne, V.P. and Secy.; Thatcher Krasne, Treas.
Directors: Kim Krasne Bacon; Steven Loeb, Esq.
EIN: 136112855
Selected grants: The following grants are a representative sample of this grantmaker's funding activity:
$28,000 to National Committee for the Furtherance of Jewish Education, Brooklyn, NY, 2010.
$25,000 to University of Hartford, West Hartford, CT, 2010.
$25,000 to Yale Alumni Fund, New Haven, CT, 2010.
$3,000 to United Way of Rye, Rye, NY, 2010.
$1,000 to Simon Wiesenthal Center, Los Angeles, CA, 2010.

2193
Kreindler & Kreindler LLP

750 3rd Ave.
New York, NY 10017 (212) 687-8181

Company URL: http://www.kreindler.com
Establishment information: Established in 1950.
Company type: Private company
Business activities: Provides legal services.
Business type (SIC): Legal services
Corporate officer: Paul S. Edelman, Partner
Offices: Los Angeles, CA; Boston, MA; Franklin Lakes, NJ
Giving statement: Giving through the Lee S. Kreindler Foundation, Inc.

Lee S. Kreindler Foundation, Inc.

750 3rd Ave., 32 Fl.
New York, NY 10017-5590
E-mail: jkreindler@kreindler.com

Establishment information: Established in 2004 in NY.
Donor: Kreindler & Kreindler LLP.
Financial data (yr. ended 12/31/11): Assets, $2,502,835 (M); gifts received, $2,191,309; expenditures, $78,477; qualifying distributions, $77,500; giving activities include $77,500 for grants.
Purpose and activities: The foundation supports hospitals and organizations involved with higher education, cancer, and philanthropy.
Type of support: General/operating support; Scholarship funds.
Application information: Applications not accepted. Unsolicited requests for funds not accepted.
Officers: Ruth Kreindler, Pres.; James Kreindler, V.P.; Steve Pounion, Secy.
Trustees: Michel Baumeister; Frank H. Granito III; Frank H. Granito, Jr.
EIN: 300259779

2194
Kroenke Sports Enterprises, L.L.C.

(also known as Colorado Rapids)
1000 Chopper Cir.
Denver, CO 80204 (303) 405-1100

Company URL: http://www.coloradorapids.com
Establishment information: Established in 1999.
Company type: Private company
Business activities: Operates professional soccer club.
Business type (SIC): Commercial sports
Corporate officers: E. Stanley Kroenke, Chair.; Jim Martin, Pres. and C.E.O.; Bruce Glazer, Exec. V.P. and C.F.O.; Charlie Wright, V.P., Finance; Mike Kurowski, V.P., Corp. Sales
Board of director: E. Stanley Kroenke, Chair.
Giving statement: Giving through the Colorado Rapids Corporate Giving Program.

Colorado Rapids Corporate Giving Program

c/o Community Rels. Dept.
6000 Victory Way
Commerce City, CO 80022-4203 (303) 727-3572
FAX: (303) 727-3536; URL: http://www.coloradorapids.com/community

Purpose and activities: The Colorado Rapids make charitable contributions of memorabilia and game tickets to nonprofit organizations involved with improving the lives of children, and on a case by case basis. Support is given primarily in Colorado.
Fields of interest: General charitable giving Children.
Type of support: In-kind gifts; Loaned talent.
Geographic limitations: Giving primarily in CO.
Application information: Applications accepted. Proposals should be submitted using organization letterhead. Application form not required. Applicants should submit the following:
1) name, address and phone number of organization

2) copy of IRS Determination Letter
3) brief history of organization and description of its mission
4) contact person
Proposals should indicate the date, time, and location of the event, and the intended use of the donated item.
Initial approach: Mail or fax proposal to headquarters
Copies of proposal: 1
Deadline(s): None
Final notification: Following review

2195
The Kroger Co.

1014 Vine St.
Cincinnati, OH 45202-1100 (513) 762-4000
FAX: (513) 762-1575

Company URL: http://www.kroger.com
Establishment information: Established in 1883.
Company type: Public company
Company ticker symbol and exchange: KR/NYSE
Business activities: Operates grocery stores; produces and processes food.
Business type (SIC): Groceries—retail; food and kindred products
Financial profile for 2013: Number of employees, 343,000; assets, $24,652,000,000; sales volume, $96,751,000,000; pre-tax net income, $2,302,000,000; expenses, $93,987,000,000; liabilities, $20,445,000,000
Fortune 1000 ranking: 2012—23rd in revenues, 141st in profits, and 210th in assets
Forbes 2000 ranking: 2012—66th in sales, 417th in profits, and 858th in assets
Corporate officers: David B. Dillon, Chair. and C.E.O.; W. Rodney McMullen, Pres. and C.O.O.; Paul W. Heldman, Exec. V.P., Genl. Counsel, and Secy.; J. Michael Schlotman, Sr. V.P. and C.F.O.; Christopher T. Hjelm, Sr. V.P. and C.I.O.; Kathleen S. Barclay, Sr. V.P., Human Resources; M. Marnette Perry, Sr. V.P., Opers.
Board of directors: David B. Dillon, Chair.; Reuben V. Anderson; Robert D. Beyer; Susan J. Kropf; John T. LaMacchia; David B. Lewis; W. Rodney McMullen; Jorge P. Montoya; Clyde R. Moore; Susan M. Phillips; Steven R. Rogel; James A. Runde; Ronald L. Sargent; Bobby S. Shackouls
Subsidiaries: Dillon Companies, Inc., Hutchinson, KS; Fred Meyer, Inc., Portland, OR; Fred Meyer Stores, Inc., Portland, OR; Ralphs Grocery Company, Compton, CA
Plants: Wichita, KS; Dayton, OH; Dallas, TX
International operations: Hong Kong
Giving statement: Giving through the Kroger Co. Contributions Program and the Kroger Co. Foundation.
Company EIN: 310345740

The Kroger Co. Contributions Program

c/o Community Rels. Dept.
1014 Vine St.
Cincinnati, OH 45202-1100 (513) 762-4000
URL: http://www.thekrogerco.com/community

Purpose and activities: As a complement to its foundation, Kroger also makes charitable contributions to nonprofit organizations directly. Special emphasis is directed towards programs designed to promote the advancement of women and minorities. Support is limited to areas of company operations in Alabama, Arizona, Arkansas, California, Colorado, Georgia, Illinois, Indiana, Kansas, Kentucky, Michigan, Mississippi, Nevada, North Carolina, Ohio, Oregon, Tennessee, Texas, Utah, Virginia, and Washington.
Fields of interest: Elementary/secondary education; Health care; Breast cancer research; Food services; Disasters, preparedness/services; Human services; American Red Cross; Salvation Army Minorities; Women.
Type of support: Donated products; Employee volunteer services; General/operating support.
Geographic limitations: Giving limited to areas of company operations in AL, AR, AZ, CA, CO, GA, IL, IN, KS, KY, MI, MS, NC, NV, OH, OR, TN, TX, UT, VA, and WA.
Application information: Applications accepted.
Initial approach: Contact Community Relations Department at nearest company retail division for application information

The Kroger Co. Foundation

1014 Vine St.
Cincinnati, OH 45202-1148
FAX: (513) 762-1295; Additional tel.: (513) 452-4441; URL: http://www.thekrogerco.com/community/kroger-foundation

Establishment information: Established in 1987 in OH.
Donor: The Kroger Co.
Contact: Lynn Marmer, Pres.
Financial data (yr. ended 01/31/12): Assets, $36,818,758 (M); gifts received, $4,772,699; expenditures, $8,360,484; qualifying distributions, $8,243,478; giving activities include $8,243,478 for 1,494 grants (high: $267,572; low: $15).
Purpose and activities: The foundation supports organizations involved with education, women's health, breast cancer, hunger, minorities, and women.
Fields of interest: Elementary/secondary education; Education; Health care; Breast cancer; Food services; Food banks; United Ways and Federated Giving Programs Minorities; Women.
Program:
Dollars for Doers: The foundation awards grants to nonprofit with which employees of Kroger volunteer.
Type of support: Capital campaigns; Employee volunteer services; Program development; Seed money.
Geographic limitations: Giving primarily in areas of company operations in AL, AR, AZ, CA, CO, GA, IL, IN, KS, KY, MI, MS, NV, OH, OR, TN, TX, UT, VA, WA, and WV.
Support limitations: No support for national or international organizations, non-educational foundations, medical research organizations, or religious organizations or institutions not of direct benefit to the entire community. No grants to individuals, or for conventions or conferences, dinners or luncheons, endowments, general operating support, sports event sponsorships, program advertisements, or membership dues.
Publications: Application guidelines.
Application information: Applications accepted. Visit Web site for company division addresses. Application form not required. Applicants should submit the following:
1) copy of IRS Determination Letter
2) detailed description of project and amount of funding requested
Initial approach: Proposal to nearest company division
Deadline(s): None
Officers and Trustees: Lynn Marmer, Pres.; Paul W. Heldman, Secy.; Scott M. Henderson, Treas.; David B. Dillon; Dennis Hackett; Marnette Perry; Pete Williams.
Number of staff: 1 part-time professional.
EIN: 311192929
Selected grants: The following grants are a representative sample of this grantmaker's funding activity:
$267,572 to USO World Headquarters, Arlington, VA, 2012.
$250,000 to Ozarks Food Harvest, Springfield, MO, 2012.
$125,000 to United Way of Greater Cincinnati, Cincinnati, OH, 2012.
$86,631 to Camp Fire USA, Portland, OR, 2012.
$74,940 to Susan G. Komen for the Cure, Los Angeles, CA, 2012.
$74,666 to Scholarship America, Saint Peter, MN, 2012.
$51,016 to Primary Childrens Medical Center, Salt Lake City, UT, 2012.
$7,036 to Northwest School of the Arts, Humanities and Environment, Seattle, WA, 2012.
$6,545 to Roadrunner Food Bank, Albuquerque, NM, 2012.
$5,000 to American Red Cross, Chicago, IL, 2012.

2196
Krueger International, Inc.

(also known as KI)
1330 Bellevue St.
Green Bay, WI 54308-8100 (920) 468-8100

Company URL: http://www.ki-inc.com
Establishment information: Established in 1941.
Company type: Private company
Business activities: Manufactures office, commercial, institutional, and educational furniture.
Business type (SIC): Furniture/office; furniture/public building
Corporate officer: Richard J. Resch, Pres. and C.E.O.
Plants: Los Angeles, CA; Madisonville, KY; Pontotoc, Tupelo, Winona, MS; High Point, NC; Bonduel, Fort Atkinson, Manitowoc, WI
Giving statement: Giving through the KI Corporate Giving Program.

KI Corporate Giving Program

1330 Bellevue St.
Green Bay, WI 54302-2119 (920) 468-8100
URL: http://www.ki.com/green/personalizing/social-responsibility.aspx

Purpose and activities: KI makes charitable contributions to nonprofit organizations involved with the environment, and on a case by case basis. Support is given primarily in areas of company operations, with emphasis on Green Bay, Wisconsin.
Fields of interest: Environment; General charitable giving.
Type of support: Employee volunteer services; General/operating support.
Geographic limitations: Giving primarily in areas of company operations, with emphasis on Green Bay, WI.

2082
K-Swiss Inc.
31248 Oak Crest Dr.
Westlake Village, CA 91361
(818) 706-5100

Company URL: http://www.kswiss.com/
Establishment information: Established in 1966.
Company type: Public company
Company ticker symbol and exchange: KSWS/NASDAQ
Business activities: Designs, develops, and markets athletic footwear.
Business type (SIC): Leather footwear
Financial profile for 2012: Number of employees, 542; assets, $176,720,000; sales volume, $222,850,000; pre-tax net income, -$31,580,000; expenses, $253,620,000; liabilities, $45,110,000
Corporate officers: Steven Nichols, Chair., Pres., and C.E.O.; Edward Flora, C.O.O.; George Powlick, V.P., Finance, C.A.O., C.F.O., and Secy.; Kimberly Scully, Corp. Cont.
Board of directors: Steven Nichols, Chair.; Lawrence Feldman; Stephen A. Fine; Mark Louie; George Powlick
Giving statement: Giving through the 324 Foundation.
Company EIN: 954265988

324 Foundation
(formerly The K-Swiss Foundation)
31248 Oak Crest Dr.
Westlake Village, CA 91361-4643

Establishment information: Established in 1994 in CA.
Donor: K-Swiss Inc.
Financial data (yr. ended 12/31/11): Assets, $422,492 (M); expenditures, $325,510; qualifying distributions, $325,500; giving activities include $325,500 for grants.
Purpose and activities: The foundation supports health centers and organizations involved with higher education, medical education, multiple sclerosis, business, and the footwear industry.
Fields of interest: Higher education; Medical school/education; Health care, clinics/centers; Multiple sclerosis; Business/industry.
Type of support: General/operating support.
Geographic limitations: Giving primarily in Los Angeles, CA, Waltham, MA, and New York, NY.
Support limitations: No grants to individuals.
Application information: Applications not accepted. Contributes only to pre-selected organizations.
Officers and Directors:* Steven Nichols*, Chair. and Pres.; George Powlick*, Secy.-Treas. and C.F.O.; David Nichols.
EIN: 954422206
Selected grants: The following grants are a representative sample of this grantmaker's funding activity:
$246,000 to Cedars-Sinai Medical Center, Los Angeles, CA, 2010. For general support.
$10,000 to University of Southern California, Los Angeles, CA, 2010.
$10,000 to Workshop in Business Opportunities, New York, NY, 2010. For general support.
$5,000 to Two Ten Footwear Foundation, Waltham, MA, 2010.

2197
Kuhns Investment Company
3131 S. Dixie Dr., Ste. 103
Dayton, OH 45439-2223 (937) 294-3933

Establishment information: Established in 1974.
Company type: Private company
Business activities: Operates holding company.
Business type (SIC): Security and commodity services
Corporate officer: Kristin Alexandre, Pres.
Giving statement: Giving through the Kuhns Brothers Company Foundation.

Kuhns Brothers Company Foundation
872-C E Franklin St.
Dayton, OH 45459

Donor: Kuhns Investment Co.
Financial data (yr. ended 12/31/11): Assets, $996,537 (M); expenditures, $63,995; qualifying distributions, $63,795; giving activities include $54,000 for 23 grants (high: $8,230; low: $110).
Purpose and activities: The foundation supports organizations involved with television, higher education, cancer, heart disease, muscular dystrophy, multiple sclerosis, and human services.
Fields of interest: Media, television; Higher education; Cancer; Heart & circulatory diseases; Muscular dystrophy; Multiple sclerosis; Boy scouts; American Red Cross; Salvation Army; YM/YWCAs & YM/YWHAs; Human services.
Type of support: General/operating support.
Geographic limitations: Giving limited to Cincinnati, Columbus, and Dayton, OH.
Support limitations: No grants to individuals.
Application information: Applications not accepted. Unsolicited requests for funds not accepted.
Trustees: Jana M. Johnson; Celeste L. Scheibert; Julie A. Stanton.
EIN: 316023926

2198
Kukui Gardens Corporation
1103 Liliha St., Apt. 102
Honolulu, HI 96817-4632 (808) 532-0033
FAX: (808) 532-0038

Establishment information: Established in 1967.
Company type: Private company
Business activities: Operates apartment building.
Business type (SIC): Real estate operators and lessors
Corporate officer: Lawrence S.L. Ching, Pres.
Giving statement: Giving through the Clarence T. C. Ching Foundation.

The Clarence T. C. Ching Foundation
1001 Bishop St., Ste. 770
Honolulu, HI 96813-3406 (808) 521-0344
E-mail: admin@chingfoundation.org; URL: http://www.clarencetcchingfoundation.org/

Establishment information: Established in 1967.
Donors: Loyalty Development Co., Ltd.; Kukui Gardens Corporation.
Contact: R. Stevens Gilley, Pres.
Financial data (yr. ended 12/31/11): Assets, $101,019,463 (M); expenditures, $5,994,374; qualifying distributions, $5,259,096; giving activities include $4,760,560 for 17 grants (high: $1,000,000; low: $15,000).
Purpose and activities: The foundation supports organizations involved with arts and culture, education, health care, and science. Special emphasis is directed toward programs designed to serve the needy, sick, or aged.
Fields of interest: Performing arts, music; Literature; Arts; Higher education; Education; Hospitals (general); Health care; YM/YWCAs & YM/YWHAs; Science Economically disadvantaged.
Type of support: Building/renovation; Capital campaigns; General/operating support; Matching/challenge support; Program development; Research; Scholarship funds.
Geographic limitations: Giving primarily in Honolulu, HI.
Support limitations: No support for political organizations or candidates. No grants to individuals, or for government services, publications, films, or videos, commercial or business development, conferences or seminars, benefit events, annual campaigns, or endowments.
Publications: Application guidelines.
Application information: Applications accepted. Faxed and e-mailed submissions are not accepted. Letters of inquiry should be two to three pages. Organizations receiving support are asked to submit an interim report and a final report. Applicants should submit the following:
1) brief history of organization and description of its mission
2) timetable for implementation and evaluation of project
3) copy of current year's organizational budget and/or project budget
4) detailed description of project and amount of funding requested
5) copy of IRS Determination Letter

Initial approach: Letter of inquiry
Board meeting date(s): Mar. and Sept.
Deadline(s): Mar. 1 and July 15

Officers and Trustees:* John K. Tsui*, Chair.; Raymond J. Tam, Vice-Chair. and Secy.; R. Stevens Gilley, Pres.; Peter P.J. Ng*, Treas.; Catherine H.Q. Ching; Kenneth T. Okamoto.
EIN: 996014634
Selected grants: The following grants are a representative sample of this grantmaker's funding activity:
$1,000,000 to Saint Louis School, Honolulu, HI, 2011. For capital improvement.
$714,285 to Chaminade University of Honolulu, Honolulu, HI, 2011. For capital improvement.
$600,000 to Maryknoll Schools, Honolulu, HI, 2011. For capital improvement.
$500,000 to Catholic Charities Hawaii, Honolulu, HI, 2011. For capital improvement.
$500,000 to Punahou School, Honolulu, HI, 2011. For program support.
$400,000 to Palolo Chinese Home, Honolulu, HI, 2011. For capital improvement.
$300,000 to Saint John the Baptist Catholic School, Honolulu, HI, 2011. For capital improvement.
$250,000 to Hanahauoli School, Honolulu, HI, 2011. For program support.
$100,000 to Saint Louis School, Honolulu, HI, 2011. For program support.

2199
Kum & Go, L.C.
6400 Westown Pkwy.
West Des Moines, IA 50266
(515) 226-0128
FAX: (515) 226-1595

Company URL: http://www.kumandgo.com
Establishment information: Established in 1959.
Company type: Private company
Business activities: Operates convenie stores and truck stops.
Business type (SIC): Merchandise stores/general
Financial profile for 2011: Number of employees, 4,000; sales volume, $2,100,000,000
Corporate officers: W. A. Krause, Chair.; Kyle J. Krause, Pres. and C.E.O.; Mark Hasting, C.O.O.; Craig A. Bergstrom, C.F.O.; David Miller, Sr. V.P., Mktg.; Charley Campbell, Genl. Counsel and Corp. Secy.
Board of director: W. A. Krause, Chair.
Giving statement: Giving through the Kum & Go, L.C. Contributions Program.

Kum & Go, L.C. Contributions Program
6400 Westown Pkwy.
West Des Moines, IA 50266-7709 (515) 226-0128
URL: http://www.kumandgo.com/philanthropy.cfm

2200
The Kuskokwim Corporation
4300 B St., Ste. 207
P.O. Box 227
Anchorage, AK 99503-5951
(907) 243-2944

Company URL: http://www.kuskokwim.com
Establishment information: Established in 1977.
Company type: Native corporation
Business activities: Operates native corporation.
Business type (SIC): Nonclassifiable establishments
Corporate officers: Dunia Morgan, Chair.; Marce Simeon, Vice-Chair.; Maver Carey, Pres. and C.E.O.; Rachel Klein, C.O.O.; Del Clark, C.F.O.; Angela Morgan, Secy.-Treas.; Nichola Ruedy, Human Resources
Board of directors: Kathleen Hoffman, Chair.; Marce Simeon, Vice-Chair.; Lorraine Egnaty; David Gregory; Wassilie Kameroff; Angela Morgan; Herman Morgan; Mona Morrow; Jeff Nelson; Jaylene Peterson-Nyren; Marcia Sherer
Office: Aniak, AK
Giving statement: Giving through the Kuskokwim Educational Foundation.

Kuskokwim Educational Foundation
4300 B St., Ste. 207
Anchorage, AK 99503-5951 (907) 675-4275
FAX: (907) 243-2984; E-mail: dg@kuskokwim.com; Additional tel.: P.O. Box 227, Aniak, AK 99557 (907) 675-4275; URL: http://www.kuskokwim.com/content/educational-foundation

Establishment information: Established in 1983.
Donor: The Kuskokwim Corp.
Contact: Sally Hoffman
Financial data (yr. ended 05/31/12): Assets, $39,759 (M); gifts received, $42,565; expenditures, $43,090; qualifying distributions, $32,000; giving activities include $32,000 for 48 grants to individuals (high: $1,250; low: $500).
Purpose and activities: The foundation awards college scholarships to shareholders and children of shareholders of Kuskokwim Corp. and other Alaska native corporations.
Fields of interest: Vocational education; Higher education; Business school/education; Medical school/education; Adult/continuing education; Education; Health care; Business/industry Native Americans/American Indians.
Programs:
General Scholarships: The foundation awards scholarships to shareholders and children of shareholders of Kuskokwim Corp. for college and university courses, vocational and continuing education, student exchange programs, and other educational opportunities as determined by the KEF board of directors. Awards range from $100 to $1,500.
Mary Morgan-Wolf Memorial Scholarships: The foundation annually awards a two- or four-year scholarship to a Native student from the middle Kuskokwim region who is entering a health-related field. Applicant must attend a college or vocational institution with a GPA of 2.0 and must be returning to the Kuskokwim area after the degree is received. Award amounts range from $1,500 for the first year to $2,000 or more for the following years.
Nick Mellick Memorial Scholarship Fund: The foundation annually awards scholarships to TKC Region shareholders and descendents to pursue a degree in business or a related field. Applicants must attend a college or vocational institution with a GPA of 3.25 and must be returning to the Kuskokwim area after the degree is received. Award amounts range from $2,500 for the first year to $3,500 or more for the following years.
Suulutaaq Construction Scholarship: The foundation, in partnership with Nugget Construction and TKC, awards scholarships to students interested in heavy equipment, electrical work, carpentry, or a related field.
Type of support: Scholarships—to individuals.
Geographic limitations: Giving limited to areas from the Lower Kalskag to the Stony River area, AK.
Publications: Application guidelines; Corporate report; Informational brochure; Newsletter.
Application information: Applications accepted. Application form required.
Applications should include a personal essay, 2 letters of recommendation, official transcripts, and a recent photograph.
Initial approach: Download application form and mail to foundation
Board meeting date(s): Apr., Sept., Nov., and Feb.
Deadline(s): Jun. 15 for fall semester; Nov. 15 for spring semester
Final notification: July 1 for fall semester; Dec. 1 for spring semester
Officers: Samantha John, Chair.; Jayleen Peterson-Nyren, Vice-Chair.; Rachel Klein, Secy.-Treas.
Board Members: Lucy Brown; Clara Morgan.
EIN: 920081529

2201
Kyanite Mining Corporation
30 Willis Mountains Plant Ln.
Dillwyn, VA 23936 (434) 983-2085
FAX: (434) 983-5178

Company URL: http://www.kyanite.com/
Establishment information: Established in 1948.
Company type: Private company
Business activities: Operates mining company.
Business type (SIC): Mining/clay, ceramic, and refractory mineral
Corporate officers: Gene Dixon, Jr., Pres. and C.E.O.; Barry Jones, V.P., Opers.; Hank Jamerson, V.P., Sales and Mktg.
Giving statement: Giving through the Terrell H. Dunnavant Scholarship Fund, Inc.

Terrell H. Dunnavant Scholarship Fund, Inc.
30 Willis Mountain Plant Ln.
Dillwyn, VA 23936

Establishment information: Established in 2002 in VA.
Donor: Kyanite Mining Corp.
Contact: Lakshmi Bertram, Dir.
Financial data (yr. ended 12/31/11): Assets, $2,771 (M); gifts received, $10,000; expenditures, $8,025; qualifying distributions, $8,025; giving activities include $8,000 for 4 grants to individuals (high: $2,000; low: $2,000).
Purpose and activities: The foundation awards scholarships to graduates of high schools in Buckingham and Prince Edward counties, Virginia.
Fields of interest: Higher education.
Type of support: Scholarships—to individuals.
Geographic limitations: Giving Primarily in VA.
Application information: Applications accepted. Application form required.
Applications should include letters of recommendation, college board scores, and an essay.
Initial approach: Letter and essay
Deadline(s): Apr. 15 of the applicant's senior year of high school
Directors: Lakshmi A. Bertram; Guy B. Dixon; Ron D. Hudgins.
EIN: 611417298

2202
L&L Franchise, Inc.
931 University Ave., Ste. 202
Honolulu, HI 96826-3241 (808) 951-9888

Company URL: http://www.hawaiianbarbecue.com/
Establishment information: Established in 1976.
Company type: Private company
Business activities: Operates franchised restaurants.
Business type (SIC): Restaurants and drinking places
Corporate officers: Johnson Kam, Chair.; Eddie Flores, Jr., Pres. and C.E.O.
Board of director: Johnson Kam, Chair.
Giving statement: Giving through the L & L Franchise Foundation, Inc.

L & L Franchise Foundation, Inc.
931 University Ave., Ste 202
Honolulu, HI 96826-3241

Establishment information: Established in 2007 in HI.
Donors: L&L Franchise, Inc.; Eddie Flores, Jr.
Financial data (yr. ended 12/31/11): Assets, $2,314 (M); expenditures, $6,419; qualifying distributions, $6,419; giving activities include $6,413 for 8 grants (high: $2,250; low: $240).
Purpose and activities: The foundation supports organizations involved with higher education, the restaurant industry, and Christianity.

Fields of interest: Higher education; YM/YWCAs & YM/YWHAs; Business/industry; Christian agencies & churches.
Type of support: General/operating support.
Geographic limitations: Giving primarily in Honolulu, HI.
Support limitations: No grants to individuals.
Application information: Applications not accepted. Unsolicited requests for funds not accepted.
Officers and Directors:* Eddie Flores, Jr.*, Pres.; Kwock Yum Kam*, V.P.; Bryan Andaya*, Secy.-Treas.
EIN: 208107538

2204
La Mariage, Inc.

4662 Aukai Ave., Ste. 1220
Honolulu, HI 96816-5205 (808) 924-2201

Establishment information: Established in 2003.
Company type: Private company
Business activities: Operates bridal shop.
Business type (SIC): Women's apparel stores
Corporate officers: Yasutomi Tsugo, Chair.; Yasushi Tsugo, Co-Pres.; Mari Bereday, Co-Pres.
Board of director: Yasutomi Tsugo, Chair.
Giving statement: Giving through the Keehi Memorial Organization.

Keehi Memorial Organization

P.O. Box 993
Honolulu, HI 96808 (808) 281-9082
Application address: 872 Paniolo Pl., Makawao, HI 96768, tel.: (808) 281-9082

Donor: La Mariage, Inc.
Contact: Archie Brito, Pres. and Dir.
Financial data (yr. ended 09/30/11): Assets, $647,260 (M); gifts received, $229,420; expenditures, $483,527; qualifying distributions, $0.
Purpose and activities: The foundation supports health centers and organizations involved with education, land conservation, and military and veterans.
Fields of interest: Human services.
Type of support: Building/renovation; General/operating support.
Geographic limitations: Giving limited to Honolulu, HI.
Support limitations: No grants to individuals.
Application information: Applications accepted. Application form required. Applicants should submit the following:
1) detailed description of project and amount of funding requested
Initial approach: Proposal
Deadline(s): None
Officers and Directors:* Archie Brito*, Pres.; Joseph O. McCloskey*, V.P.; Beverly Robinson*, Secy.; Gilbert Tam*, Treas.
EIN: 990300914

2206
LAC Basketball Club, Inc.

(also known as Los Angeles Clippers)
Staples Ctr., 1111 S. Figueroa St., Ste. 1100
Los Angeles, CA 90015 (213) 742-7500

Company URL: http://www.nba.com/clippers
Establishment information: Established in 1970.
Company type: Private company
Business activities: Operates professional basketball club.
Business type (SIC): Commercial sports
Corporate officers: Donald T. Sterling, Chair.; Andy Roeser, Pres.; Ed Lamb, C.F.O.; Carl Lahr, Sr. V.P., Mktg. and Sales; Joe Safety, V.P., Comms.; Bob Platt - Manatt, Genl. Counsel
Board of director: Donald T. Sterling, Chair.
Giving statement: Giving through the Los Angeles Clippers Foundation.

Los Angeles Clippers Foundation

1111 S. Figueroa St., Ste. 1100
Los Angeles, CA 90015-1345 (213) 742-7500
URL: http://www.nba.com/clippers/community/lacf.html

Establishment information: Established in 1994 in CA.
Contact: Denise Booth, Dir., Community Rels.
Financial data (yr. ended 06/30/11): Revenue, $354,102; assets, $1,105,428 (M); gifts received, $260,008; expenditures, $335,310; program services expenses, $159,401; giving activities include $80,334 for 2 grants (high: $15,000; low: $5,500) and $20,250 for grants to individuals.
Purpose and activities: As the philanthropic arm of the Los Angeles Clippers, the foundation aims to foster and support community outreach programs and activities with positive educational, civic, environmental, and humanitarian values that benefit and enhance the quality of life primarily for children in greater Los Angeles.
Fields of interest: Disasters, preparedness/services; Human services Children.
Program:
Scholarships: The foundation assists college-bound students by providing four scholarships of $2,500 annually to seniors planning to attend a four-year college. Scholarships will be made to students residing in the greater Los Angeles area.
Geographic limitations: Giving primarily in the greater Los Angeles, CA area.
Support limitations: No support for government agencies, religious organizations, legal aid societies, political lobbying, or advocacy groups. No grants to individuals.
Officers: Richard A. Roeser, Exec. V.P.; Christian Howard, V.P., Mktg.; Donna Johnson, V.P., Finance; Carl Lahr, V.P., Sales; Joseph Safety, V.P., Pub. Rels.; Patrick Lamb*, Treas.
EIN: 954493310

2207
Laclede Gas Company

720 Olive St., Ste. 1200
St. Louis, MO 63101-2389 (314) 342-0500

Company URL: http://www.lacledegas.com
Establishment information: Established in 1857.
Company type: Subsidiary of a public company
Business activities: Transmits and distributes natural gas.
Business type (SIC): Gas production and distribution
Corporate officers: Douglas H. Yaeger, Chair., Pres., and C.E.O.; Mark D. Waltermire, Sr. V.P. and C.F.O.; Mark C. Darrell, Sr. V.P. and Genl. Counsel; Michael R. Spotanski, Sr. V.P., Opers. and Mktg.; Richard A. Skau, Sr. V.P., Human Resources; Steven P. Rasche, V.P., Finance; Mary C. Kullman, Corp. Secy.; James A. Fallert, Cont.
Board of director: Douglas H. Yaeger, Chair.
Giving statement: Giving through the Laclede Gas Charitable Trust.
Company EIN: 430368139

Laclede Gas Charitable Trust

720 Olive St., Rm. 1517
St. Louis, MO 63101-2338
URL: http://staging.lacledegas.com/service/trust.php

Establishment information: Established in 1966 in MO.
Donor: Laclede Gas Co.
Contact: Mary C. Kullman, Secy.
Financial data (yr. ended 09/30/11): Assets, $4,107,786 (M); gifts received, $1,000,000; expenditures, $700,921; qualifying distributions, $697,765; giving activities include $697,765 for grants.
Purpose and activities: The foundation supports organizations involved with arts and culture, education, health, human services, community development, and civic affairs.
Fields of interest: Arts; Secondary school/education; Higher education; Education; Health care; Children/youth, services; Human services; Community/economic development; United Ways and Federated Giving Programs; Public affairs.
Program:
Matching Gift Program: The foundation matches contributions made by employees of Laclede Gas to secondary educational institutions.
Type of support: Annual campaigns; Building/renovation; Capital campaigns; Continuing support; Employee matching gifts; Equipment; General/operating support; Program development.
Geographic limitations: Giving primarily in areas of company operations in St. Louis, MO.
Support limitations: No support for political, labor, fraternal, or religious organizations, civic clubs, K-8 schools, or school-affiliated clubs. No grants to individuals, or for family services, advertising, school-affiliated events, sports, athletic events, or athletic programs, travel related events, student trips or tours, development or production of books, films, videos, or television programs, endowments, or memorial campaigns.
Publications: Application guidelines.
Application information: Applications accepted. Application form required. Applicants should submit the following:
1) timetable for implementation and evaluation of project
2) name, address and phone number of organization
3) copy of IRS Determination Letter
4) brief history of organization and description of its mission
5) copy of most recent annual report/audited financial statement/990
6) listing of board of directors, trustees, officers and other key people and their affiliations
7) detailed description of project and amount of funding requested
8) contact person
9) copy of current year's organizational budget and/or project budget
10) listing of additional sources and amount of support
Initial approach: Download application form and mail to foundation
Copies of proposal: 1
Board meeting date(s): Semi-annually
Deadline(s): None
Officers and Trustees:* Douglas H. Yaeger*, Chair.; Mary C. Kullman*, Secy.; L.D. Rawlings, Treas.; Micheal R. Spotanski.
EIN: 436068197

Selected grants: The following grants are a representative sample of this grantmaker's funding activity:
$45,000 to Saint Louis Science Center, Saint Louis, MO, 2011.
$40,000 to Saint Louis Zoo, Saint Louis, MO, 2011.
$20,000 to Barnes-Jewish Hospital Foundation, Saint Louis, MO, 2011.
$20,000 to Magic House, Saint Louis, MO, 2011.
$20,000 to Teach for America, Saint Louis, MO, 2011.
$20,000 to YMCA of Greater Saint Louis, Saint Louis, MO, 2011.
$15,000 to Webster University, Saint Louis, MO, 2011.
$10,000 to Boy Scouts of America, Saint Louis, MO, 2011.
$10,000 to Characterplus, Saint Louis, MO, 2011.
$10,000 to Ranken Technical College, Saint Louis, MO, 2011.

2208
The Laclede Group, Inc.
720 Olive St., Rm. 1517
St. Louis, MO 63101 (314) 342-0873
FAX: (314) 421-1979

Company URL: http://www.thelacledegroup.com
Establishment information: Established in 1857.
Company type: Public company
Company ticker symbol and exchange: LG/NYSE
Business activities: Operates natural gas company.
Business type (SIC): Gas production and distribution
Financial profile for 2012: Number of employees, 1,641; assets, $1,880,260,000; sales volume, $1,125,470,000; pre-tax net income, $88,930,000; expenses, $1,014,870,000; liabilities, $1,278,650,000
Corporate officers: William E. Nasser, Chair.; Suzanne Sitherwood, Pres. and C.E.O.; Steven L. Lindsey, Exec. V.P. and C.O.O.; Mark D. Waltermire, Exec. V.P. and C.F.O.; Mary Caola Kullman, Sr. V.P., C.A.O., and Corp. Secy.; Michael R. Spotanski, Sr. V.P. and C.I.O.; Mark C. Darrell, Sr. V.P. and Genl. Counsel; Steven P. Rasche, Sr. V.P., Finance; Lynn D. Rawlings, V.P. and Treas.; Sondra Brown, V.P. and Cont.
Board of directors: William E. Nasser, Chair.; Arnold W. Donald; Edward L. Glotzbach; Anthony V. Leness; W. Stephen Maritz; Brenda D. Newberry; Suzanne Sitherwood; John P. Stupp, Jr.; Mary Ann Van Lokeren
Giving statement: Giving through the Laclede Group, Inc., Contributions Program.
Company EIN: 742976504

The Laclede Group, Inc., Contributions Program
720 Olive St.
St. Louis, MO 63101 (314) 342-0500
URL: http://www.lacledegas.com/service/

2209
Ladies Professional Golf Association
100 International Golf Dr.
Daytona Beach, FL 32124-1092
(386) 274-6200

Company URL: http://www.lpga.com
Establishment information: Established in 1950.
Company type: Business league
Business activities: Operates governing body for ladies professional golf.
Business type (SIC): Business association; commercial sports; amusement and recreation services/miscellaneous
Corporate officers: William F. Susetka, Chair.; Christopher Higgs, Sr. V.P. and C.O.O.
Board of directors: William F. (Bill) Susetka, Chair.; Peter Carfagna; Leslie Greis; Dawn Hudson; Tony Ponturo; Dana Rader; Mike Trager; Mike Whan
Giving statement: Giving through the LPGA Foundation.

The LPGA Foundation
100 International Golf Dr.
Daytona Beach, FL 32124-1092 (386) 274-6200
FAX: (386) 274-1099; URL: http://www.lpgafoundation.org/

Establishment information: Established in 1991; supporting organization of the Ladies Professional Golf Association.
Financial data (yr. ended 12/31/11): Revenue, $3,677,165; assets, $3,971,654 (M); gifts received, $961,742; expenditures, $3,384,553; giving activities include $490,089 for grants and $12,300 for grants to individuals.
Fields of interest: Higher education; Athletics/sports, golf Minorities; Women.
Programs:
Dinah Shore Scholarship: The scholarship is granted annually to a female high school senior who played golf during high school and is pursuing a college education in the U.S., but will not be playing on a competitive collegiate golf team. One scholarship in the amount of $5,000 is awarded.
Dolores Hope LPGA Financial Assistance Initiative: The initiative assists the members of the LPGA and others within the golf industry who need financial assistance because of serious illness, injury, loss of income or other significant hardship.
Marilynn Smith Scholarship: The objective of the scholarship is to provide scholarship(s) to female high school seniors who have played golf in high school or in organized junior golf programs, and are planning to play competitive golf at an accredited college or university in the U.S. Seven scholarships are awarded in the amount of $5,000 each.
Phyllis G. Meekins Scholarship: The objective is to provide a need-based scholarship to a female high school senior from a recognized minority background who played golf during high school and is planning to play competitive golf at an accredited college or university in the U.S. One scholarship in the amount of $1,250 is awarded.
Type of support: Scholarships—to individuals.
Publications: Application guidelines.
Application information: Applications accepted. Application form required.
Initial approach: Download application form
Deadline(s): May 15 for scholarships
Officers: Leslie Greis, Chair.; Vicki Goetze-Ackerman, Pres.; Kim Hall, V.P.
Directors: Laura Diaz; Allison Fouch Duncan; Katie Futcher; Karin Sjodin; Karrie Webb.
EIN: 593085528

2210
Lafarge North America, Inc.
(formerly Lafarge Corporation)
12950 Worldgate Dr., Ste. 500
Herndon, VA 20170 (703) 480-3600

Company URL: http://www.lafargenorthamerica.com
Establishment information: Established in 1983.
Company type: Subsidiary of a foreign company
Business activities: Operates holding company; produces and sells construction materials; provides waste management services.
Business type (SIC): Concrete, gypsum, and plaster products; cement/hydraulic; sanitary services; lumber and construction materials—wholesale; holding company
Financial profile for 2011: Number of employees, 16,400
Corporate officers: Bruno Lafont, Chair. and C.E.O.; Eric C. Olsen, Exec. V.P. and C.F.O.
Board of director: Bruno Lafont, Chair.
Subsidiaries: Great Lakes Cement Region, Southfield, MI; Northeastern Cement Region, Whitehall, PA; Standard Slag, Youngstown, OH; Systech Environmental Corp., Xenia, OH
Plants: Port Manatee, Tampa, FL; Joppa, IL; Davenport, IA; Fredonia, KS; New Orleans, LA; Alpena, Detroit, MI; Kansas City, St. Louis, Sugar Creek, MO; Canfield, Marblehead, Paulding, OH; Vancouver, OR; West Mifflin, Whitehall, PA; Dallas, Houston, TX; Seattle, WA; Milwaukee, WI
International operations: Canada
Giving statement: Giving through the Lafarge North America Inc. Corporate Giving Program.
Company EIN: 581290226

Lafarge North America Inc. Corporate Giving Program
(formerly Lafarge Corporation Contributions Program)
12018 Sunrise Valley Dr., Ste. 500
Reston, VA 20191
URL: http://www.lafargenorthamerica.com/wps/portal/na/en/6-Sustainability

Purpose and activities: Lafarge makes charitable contributions to nonprofit organizations on a case by case basis.
Fields of interest: Environment, energy; Environment; Housing/shelter; Engineering.
Type of support: Donated products; General/operating support.
Geographic limitations: Giving on a national and international basis in areas of company operations, including Canada.

2211
Laird Norton Company LLC
801 2nd Ave., Ste. 1300
Seattle, WA 98104-1517 (206) 464-5245
FAX: (206) 464-5277

Company URL: http://www.lairdnorton.com
Establishment information: Established in 1855.
Company type: Private company

Business activities: Provides investment advisory services; operates real estate investment trust; operates nonresidential buildings; conducts investment activities.
Business type (SIC): Security and commodity services; real estate operators and lessors; investors/miscellaneous
Corporate officers: Deborah S. Brown, Chair.; Jeffery S. Vincent, Pres. and C.E.O.; Nick Pavelich, Sr. V.P. and C.F.O.
Board of director: Deborah S. Brown, Chair.
Giving statement: Giving through the Laird Norton Family Foundation.

Laird Norton Family Foundation

(formerly Laird Norton Foundation)
801 2nd Ave., 13th Fl.
Seattle, WA 98104-1576 (206) 501-4510
FAX: (206) 501-4511;
E-mail: kbriggs@lairdnorton.org; URL: http://www.lairdnorton.org

Establishment information: Incorporated in 1940 in Winona, MN, as the Briarcombe Fund.
Donors: Laird Norton Co. LLC; MDCCP; Mary Lee Clapp Irrevocable Trust; Matthew G. Norton Co.; Lanoga Corp.
Contact: Katie Briggs, Managing Dir.
Financial data (yr. ended 12/31/12): Assets, $34,713,738 (M); gifts received, $191,788; expenditures, $1,691,641; qualifying distributions, $1,301,091; giving activities include $1,301,091 for grants and $200,000 for 2 loans/ program-related investments.
Purpose and activities: The foundation supports programs that honor, support, and reflect the philanthropic values of the Laird Norton family. Special emphasis is directed toward programs designed to promote arts in education; climate change; global fundamentals; and watershed stewardship.
Fields of interest: Arts education; Environment, water resources; Public health, clean water supply; Public health, sanitation.
Programs:

Arts in Education: The foundation supports programs designed to increase arts education and improve K-12 student learning through the arts. Special emphasis is directed toward programs designed to provide arts education and arts-infused curricula in public school classrooms; organizations working to change the state of arts education; and out-of-school programs that collaborate with K-12 public schools.

Climate Change: The foundation supports programs designed to address the consequences of climate change and create a healthy and productive environment for current and future generations. Special emphasis is directed toward programs designed to promote energy policy; energy efficiency projects; and reduced greenhouse gas emissions.

Global Fundamentals: The foundation supports programs designed to improve quality of life in developing countries. Special emphasis is directed toward programs designed to develop water and sanitation resources including wells and springs; promote point-of-use technology including filters; and educate people on the impacts of government policy and policy proposals, enforcing laws, and increasing awareness of water and sanitation.

Sixth Sense: Through Sixth Sense, the foundation awards grants on behalf of young Laird Norton family members ages 14-21 to support organizations designed to serve youth, with emphasis on the environment and education. The program is designed to engage the younger generation in grantmaking, the nonprofit sector, and family philanthropy and includes fundraising by Sixth Sense committee members.

Watershed Stewardship: The foundation supports programs designed to improve the ecosystems of watersheds. Special emphasis is directed toward programs designed to promote ecological significance; foster partnerships between on-the-ground organizations; promote community engagement and support; provide supportive regulations or watershed improvement plans; endorse ongoing scientific monitoring; and promote the presence of other funders.

Type of support: General/operating support; Management development/capacity building; Program development; Program-related investments/loans; Research.
Geographic limitations: Giving primarily in the Pacific; giving also to U.S.-based organizations with international projects in Africa, Asia, and Central America.
Support limitations: No support for religious organizations, for-profit organizations, or unincorporated associations or groups. No grants to individuals, or for scholarships, endowments, capital campaigns, publications, documentary films, or television productions.
Application information: Applications not accepted. The foundation does not accept unsolicited applications for grants. Phone calls, e-mails, and mailed applications that have not been requested will not be accepted. Due to the high volume of inquiries, the foundation will only respond if work is well-aligned with their priorities. The foundation utilizes family advisory committees for its grantmaking and each committee has a slightly different invitation-only process for accepting applications.
Officer: Bruce Reed, Pres.
Number of staff: 1 full-time professional; 1 part-time professional.
EIN: 916339917
Selected grants: The following grants are a representative sample of this grantmaker's funding activity:
$45,000 to Water First International, Seattle, WA, 2010. For $30,000 to help launch the Accountability Forum, effort to move the clean water sector toward sustainability through utilization of third-party assessments of success of projects and $15,000 general operating support.
$40,000 to Arts Corps, Seattle, WA, 2010. For general operating support.
$40,000 to Puget Sound Educational Service District, PSESD Fife Office, Renton, WA, 2010. For general operating support.
$35,000 to Shorebank Enterprise Cascadia, Ilwaco, WA, 2010. To support efforts to develop a secondary market for SBEC's energy efficiency retrofit loan product.
$33,000 to A Childs Right, Tacoma, WA, 2010. For $10,000 for recruitment and hiring process for three key staff positions; $23,000 for pre-treatment equipment for 13 project sites in Nepal facing high risk of seasonal spikes in iron contamination.
$25,000 to Deschutes Land Trust, Bend, OR, 2010. For permanent protection of remaining stream habitats through targeted land conservation to support efforts to reintroduce salmon and steelhead to the upper Deschutes River. Funding supports increased staff capacity to carry out restoration and stewardship work, in cooperation with organizations like Deschutes River Conservancy and Upper Deschutes Watershed Council.
$25,000 to Pacific Forest Trust, San Francisco, CA, 2010. For general operating support.
$20,000 to Coos Watershed Association, Charleston, OR, 2010. For general operating support.
$15,000 to Adams Elementary School, Seattle, WA, 2010. For arts integration efforts.
$10,000 to Pratt Fine Arts Center, Seattle, WA, 2010. For program support for Kid and Youth Art Works (KYAW). KYAW offers youth in-depth, challenging visual arts training and skill building in glass art (fusing, flameworking, glassblowing), painting and drawing, book binding, printmaking and more.

2212
Lake Champlain Chocolates

(doing business as Lake Champlain Chocolates)
750 Pine St.
Burlington, VT 05401-4923 (802) 864-1808

Company URL: http://www.lakechamplainchocolates.com
Establishment information: Established in 1983.
Company type: Private company
Business activities: Manufactures and sells chocolate products.
Business type (SIC): Sugar, candy, and salted/ roasted nut production
Corporate officers: James S. Lampman, Pres. and C.E.O.; Allyson Brown, C.I.O.; Chris Meddings, V.P., Mktg.; Charles Shea, Secy.
Giving statement: Giving through the Lake Champlain Chocolates Corporate Giving Program.

Lake Champlain Chocolates Corporate Giving Program

750 Pine St.
Burlington, VT 05401-4923
E-mail: info@lakechamplainchocolates.com;
Applications for sponsorships or advertising should be sent to headquarters, with: ATTN: Sponsorships & Advertising, or by e-mail to: sales@lakechamplainchocolates.com. Applications for cash donations should be sent to headquarters, with: ATTN: Cash Donations.; URL: http://www.lakechamplainchocolates.com/CommunityService.Aspx

Purpose and activities: Lake Champlain Chocolates supports nonprofit organizations involved with the arts, education, and sustainable agriculture. The company contributes 10 percent of its pre-tax profits annually to non-profit organizations and programs. Giving is primarily in areas of company operations in Vermont.
Fields of interest: Performing arts; Arts; Education; Environment; Agriculture, sustainable programs; Community/economic development; United Ways and Federated Giving Programs.
Type of support: Donated products; General/ operating support; In-kind gifts; Sponsorships.
Geographic limitations: Giving primarily in areas of company operations in VT.
Support limitations: No support for religious organizations. No grants to individuals.
Publications: Application guidelines.
Application information: Applications accepted. Telephone calls are not accepted. Proposals should be submitted using organization letterhead. Preference is given to organizations submitting their first application. Application form required.
Applicants should submit the following:
1) copy of IRS Determination Letter
2) contact person
3) name, address and phone number of organization
Applications should include the date, location, and type of event, desired pick-up date for donations, and the type and quantity of product being requested.

Initial approach: Complete online application for cash donations; mail or e-mail proposal for sponsorships and advertising
Copies of proposal: 1
Committee meeting date(s): Annually for cash donations; twice per year for sponsorships and advertising
Deadline(s): Mar. 15 for cash donations; Mar. 1 and Aug. 1 for sponsorships and advertising
Final notification: Up to 7 weeks for cash donations

2213
Lake Region Electric Cooperative

P.O. Box 643
Pelican Rapids, MN 56572-4723
(218) 863-1171

Company URL: http://www.lrec.coop
Establishment information: Established in 1937.
Company type: Cooperative
Business activities: Distributes electricity.
Business type (SIC): Electric services
Corporate officers: Charles Kvare, Chair.; Denny Tollefson, Vice-Chair.; Tim Thompson, C.E.O.; Dave Weaklend, Pres.; Joyce Valley, Secy.; Robert Shaw, Treas.
Board of directors: Charles Kvare, Chair.; Denny Tollefson, Vice-Chair.; Ken Hendrickx; Thomas Jennen; Dennis Mathiason; Earl Rydell; Robert Shaw; Tim Thompson; Joyce Valley; Sid Wisness
Giving statement: Giving through the Lake Region Electric Cooperative Scholarship Fund.

Lake Region Electric Cooperative Scholarship Fund

P.O. Box 643
Pelican Rapids, MN 56572-4723
URL: http://www.lrec.coop/aboutUs/scholarships.aspx

Establishment information: Established in 2002 in MN.
Donor: Lake Region Electric Cooperative.
Financial data (yr. ended 08/05/11): Assets, $0 (M); expenditures, $37,568; qualifying distributions, $37,568; giving activities include $37,517 for 5 grants (high: $7,504; low: $7,503).
Purpose and activities: The foundation awards college scholarships to spouses and children of members of Lake Region Electric Cooperative.
Fields of interest: Education.
Type of support: Employee-related scholarships.
Geographic limitations: Giving primarily in MN.
Application information: Applications not accepted. Unsolicited requests for funds not accepted.
Officers: Joyce Valley, Pres.; Maggie Driscoll, V.P.; Stan Overgaard, Secy.; Daniel Husted, Treas.
Director: Tim Thompson.
EIN: 010575063

2214
Lam Research Corporation

4650 Cushing Pkwy.
P.O. Box 5010
Fremont, CA 94538 (510) 572-0200

Company URL: http://www.lamrc.com
Establishment information: Established in 1980.
Company type: Public company
Company ticker symbol and exchange: LRCX/NASDAQ
Business activities: Supplier of wafer fabrication equipment and services to the worldwide semiconductor industry.
Business type (SIC): Machinery/special industry
Financial profile for 2012: Number of employees, 6,600; assets, $8,004,650,000; sales volume, $2,665,190,000; pre-tax net income, $204,420,000; expenses, $2,427,460,000; liabilities, $2,872,870,000
Fortune 1000 ranking: 2012—775th in revenues, 622nd in profits, and 454th in assets
Corporate officers: Stephen G. Newberry, Chair.; Martin Anstice, Pres. and C.E.O.; Timothy M. Archer, Exec. V.P. and C.O.O.; Doug Bettinger, Exec. V.P. and C.F.O.
Board of directors: Stephen G. Newberry, Chair.; Martin B. Anstice; Eric K. Brandt; Michael R. Cannon; Youseff A. El-Mansy, Ph.D.; Christine A. Heckart; Grant M. Inman; Catherine P. Lego; Krishna C. Saraswat, Ph.D.; William R. Spivey; Abhjiti Y. Talwalkar
Historic mergers: Novellus Systems, Inc. (June 1, 2012)
Giving statement: Giving through the Lam Research Corporation Contributions Program.
Company EIN: 942634797

Lam Research Corporation Contributions Program

(also known as Lam Research Corporation Community Outreach Program)
c/o Community Rels.
4650 Cushing Pkwy.
Fremont, CA 94538-6401 (510) 572-0200
E-mail: communityrelations@lamresearch.com;
URL: http://www.lamrc.com/company_3.cfm

Purpose and activities: Lam Research makes charitable contributions to nonprofit organizations involved with education. Special emphasis is directed toward sustainable programs that focus on math and science. Support is given primarily in areas of company operations on a local, national, and international basis, with emphasis on Arizona, California, Idaho, New York, Ohio, Oregon, Texas, and Washington, and Asia and Europe.
Fields of interest: Secondary school/education; Higher education; Higher education, university; Engineering school/education; Health care, blood supply; Food banks; Disasters, preparedness/services; Human services, gift distribution; Homeless, human services; Mathematics; Engineering/technology; Science.
International interests: Asia; Europe.
Programs:

Core Values Scholarships: Lam Research awards Core Values Scholarships to graduating high school students who demonstrate the company's Core Values. In Fremont, California, where Lam Research has its corporate headquarters, a scholarship of $10,000 is typically given to one student from each of the six local high schools. The scholarships support the students while they are enrolled in a college of their choice.

Employee Gift Match Program: Lam Research matches monetary contributions dollar for dollar. Volunteer time is matched at the rate of $10 per hour. Lam Research will match up to $600 per calendar year for contributions made by each regular, full-time Lam Research employee. Nonprofit organizations and institutions that hold a tax-exempt status granted by the Internal Revenue Service are eligible for Lam Research's matching funds.

Type of support: Employee matching gifts; Employee volunteer services; Scholarships—to individuals; Sponsorships.
Geographic limitations: Giving primarily in areas of company operations on a local, national, and international basis, with emphasis on AZ, CA, ID, OH, OR, NY, TX, and WA, and Asia and Europe.
Application information: Lam Research has suspended its open grant application program and will not be reviewing unsolicited requests. The company will continue to provide targeted grants to help teachers bring interactive math and science programs to students.

2215
Lamont Limited

1530 N. Bluff Rd.
P.O. Box 399
Burlington, IA 52601-4758 (319) 753-5131

Company URL: http://www.lamontlimited.com
Establishment information: Established in 1972.
Company type: Private company
Business activities: Manufactures wicker furniture.
Business type (SIC): Furniture/household
Corporate officers: Stephen A. Fausel, Chair. and C.E.O.; Shelley A. Sapsin, Pres.; Tony L. Matteson, Secy.; Keith D. Garwood, Treas.
Board of director: Stephen A. Fausel, Chair.
Giving statement: Giving through the Fausel Foundation.

The Fausel Foundation

P.O. Box 399
Burlington, IA 52601-0399
URL: http://www.fauselco.com/foundation/index.php

Establishment information: Established in 1980 in IA.
Donors: Stephen A. Fausel; Lamont International, Inc.; Lamont Ltd.; Columbine Cody Corp.
Financial data (yr. ended 12/31/11): Assets, $450,214 (M); gifts received, $3,000; expenditures, $115,499; qualifying distributions, $105,000; giving activities include $105,000 for 3 grants (high: $50,000; low: $5,000).
Purpose and activities: The foundation supports organizations involved with ecosystems, wildlife, medical research, children, disability services, and public policy.
Fields of interest: Environment, natural resources; Environment, land resources; Animals/wildlife; Medical research; Children, services; Developmentally disabled, centers & services; International affairs, foreign policy.
Type of support: General/operating support.
Geographic limitations: Giving primarily in Ignacio and Pine, CO, Washington, DC, Burlington, IA, and Chicago, IL.
Support limitations: No grants to individuals.
Application information: Applications not accepted. Unsolicited requests for funds not accepted.
Director: Stephen A. Fausel.
EIN: 421141805

2216
Lancaster Colony Corporation

37 W. Broad St.
Columbus, OH 43215 (614) 224-7141
FAX: (614) 469-8219

Company URL: http://www.lancastercolony.com
Establishment information: Established in 1961.
Company type: Public company
Company ticker symbol and exchange: LANC/ NASDAQ
Business activities: Manufactures, produces, and markets specialty foods, glassware, candles, and automotive accessories.
Business type (SIC): Specialty foods/canned, frozen, and preserved; glass/pressed or blown; motor vehicles and equipment; manufacturing/ miscellaneous
Financial profile for 2012: Number of employees, 3,100; assets, $682,630,000; sales volume, $1,131,360,000; pre-tax net income, $146,030,000; expenses, $988,070,000; liabilities, $118,370,000
Corporate officers: John B. Gerlach, Jr., Chair., Pres., and C.E.O.; John L. Boylan, V.P., C.F.O., and Treas.; Matthew R. Shurte, Genl. Counsel and Secy.
Board of directors: John B. Gerlach, Jr., Chair.; James B. Bachmann; Neeli Bendapudi; John L. Boylan; Kenneth L. Cooke; Robert L. Fox; Alan F. Harris; Edward H. Jennings; Zuheir Sofia
Subsidiaries: Colony Printing & Labeling, Inc., Eaton, IN; Dee Zee, Inc., Des Moines, IA; Indiana Glass Co., Cincinnati, OH; Koneta, Inc., Wapakoneta, OH; LaGrange Molded Products, Inc., LaGrange, GA; New York Frozen Foods, Inc., Bedford Heights, OH; Waycross Molded Products, Inc., Waycross, GA
Plants: Milpitas, CA; Atlanta, GA; Wilson, NY
Giving statement: Giving through the Lancaster Colony Corporation Contributions Program.
Company EIN: 131955943

Lancaster Colony Corporation Contributions Program

37 W. Broad St., 5th Fl.
Columbus, OH 43215-4177 (614) 224-7141

Contact: John B. Gerlach, Pres. and C.E.O.
Purpose and activities: Lancaster Colony makes charitable contributions to nonprofit organizations on a case by case basis. Support is given primarily in the Columbus, Ohio, area.
Fields of interest: General charitable giving.
Type of support: Donated products; General/ operating support.
Geographic limitations: Giving primarily in the Columbus, OH, area.
Application information: Applications accepted. Telephone calls are not encouraged. Application form not required. Applicants should submit the following:
1) detailed description of project and amount of funding requested

Initial approach: Proposal to headquarters

2217
Land O'Lakes, Inc.

4001 Lexington Ave. N.
Arden Hills, MN 55126-2934
(651) 375-2222

Company URL: http://www.landolakesinc.com
Establishment information: Established in 1921.
Company type: Cooperative
Business activities: Sells dairy-based foods and agricultural products wholesale.
Business type (SIC): Groceries—wholesale; non-durable goods—wholesale
Financial profile for 2011: Number of employees, 9,000; assets, $3,842,091,000; sales volume, $12,849,000,000; pre-tax net income, $181,000,000; expenses, $12,684,581,000; liabilities, $3,023,699,000
Fortune 1000 ranking: 2012—194th in revenues, 533rd in profits, and 523rd in assets
Corporate officers: Peter Kappelman, Chair.; Ronnie Mohr, Co-Vice-Chair.; Christopher J. Policinski, Pres. and C.E.O.; Dan Knutson, Sr. V.P. and C.F.O.; Peter Janzen, Sr. V.P. and Genl. Counsel; Barry Wolfish, Sr. V.P., Corp. Mktg., and Comms.; Jim Fife, Sr. V.P., Public Affairs; Karen Grabow, Sr. V.P., Human Resources
Board of directors: Peter Kappelman, Chair.; Ronnie Mohr, Co-Vice-Chair.; Larry Kulp, Co-Vice-Chair.
Division: Croplan Genetics Div., Shoreview, MN
Giving statement: Giving through the Land O'Lakes Foundation.

Land O'Lakes Foundation

P.O. Box 64150
St. Paul, MN 55164-0150
E-mail: mlatkins-sakry@landolakes.com; Contact for California Regions Grant Prog. and Mid-Atlantic Grants Prog.: Martha Atkins-Sakry, Exec. Asst., tel.: (651) 375-2470, e-mail: mlatkins-sakry@landolakes.com; URL: http:// www.foundation.landolakes.com

Establishment information: Established in 1996 in MN.
Donor: Land O'Lakes, Inc.
Contact: Lydia Botham, Exec. Dir.
Financial data (yr. ended 12/31/11): Assets, $9,500,389 (M); gifts received, $2,417,428; expenditures, $2,478,556; qualifying distributions, $2,478,556; giving activities include $1,985,640 for 1,400 grants (high: $400,000; low: $25), $50,000 for 2 grants to individuals, $67,126 for 221 employee matching gifts and $220,850 for 3 foundation-administered programs.
Purpose and activities: The foundation supports organizations involved with arts and culture, education, human services, civic improvements, and youth and awards graduate scholarships to graduate students studying the dairy sciences. Special emphasis is directed toward programs designed to alleviate rural hunger.
Fields of interest: Media, film/video; Media, television; Visual arts; Performing arts; Literature; Arts; Elementary/secondary education; Higher education; Libraries (public); Education; Environment, water resources; Environment, land resources; Environment, plant conservation; Hospitals (general); Agriculture, sustainable programs; Food services; Food banks; Nutrition; Agriculture/food; Disasters, fire prevention/control; Recreation, parks/playgrounds; Youth development, agriculture; Youth development; Human services; Rural development; Community/ economic development; United Ways and Federated Giving Programs; Leadership development; Public affairs Youth; Native Americans/American Indians.
Programs:

Answer Plot Community Gardens: The foundation, in partnership with local co-ops, FFA chapters, and WinField Solutions agronomists, helps alleviates hunger in rural communities through community gardens. The program is designed to work with multiple groups to grow, harvest, and donate 14,000 servings of fresh produce to local shelves. Participant's plant and harvest produce in a section of their Answer Plot and donate to a food pantry in their community to help local families in need. This program currently operates in seventeen sites.

California Regions Grant Program: Through the California Regions Grant Program, the foundation awards grants to projects and charitable organizations recommended by California dairy-member leaders. Special emphasis is directed toward programs designed to address hunger relief; youth and education; civic improvements; and arts and culture. Support is limited to the Ontario, Orland, and Tulare/Kings/Bakersfield, California, areas. Grants range from $500 to $5,000.

Community Grants Program: Through the Community Grants Program, the foundation supports programs designed to alleviate hunger; build knowledge and leadership skills of rural youth; address and solve community problems; and promote artistic endeavors, especially in underserved rural areas and touring and outreach programs. Special emphasis is directed toward arts and education; human services, including hospitals and the United Way, and civic affairs, and hunger.

Dollars for Doers: The foundation awards grants to nonprofit organizations with which employees and retirees of Land O'Lakes volunteer or serve on nonprofit boards. The foundation awards $100 for 16 hours of service, $250 for 50 hours of service; and $500 for 100 hours of service.

Feeding Our Communities: Through the Feeding Our Communities initiative, Land O'Lakes and the Land O'Lakes foundation supports local and national efforts to reduce hunger in rural communities through grants, matching gifts of member cooperatives, and product donations to food banks.

John Brandt Memorial Scholarships: The foundation awards $25,000 scholarships to graduate students pursuing a program of study leading to a master's or doctorate degree in dairy cattle nutrition, genetics, physiology or management, or the manufacturing, processing or marketing of milk and dairy products. Students must be enrolled at and accepted into one of the four required universities, Iowa State University, South Dakota State University, the University of Minnesota, Twin Cities, or the University of Wisconsin, Madison.

Matching Gifts to Education Program: The foundation matches contributions made by employees, directors, and Leadership Council members of Land O'Lakes to educational institutions and public broadcasting stations on a one-for-one basis from $25 to $1,000 per contributor, per year.

Member Co-op Match Program: The foundation matches dollar-for-dollar cash donations made by member cooperatives. The program is designed to double the funds available for hometown projects and help rural communities prosper.

Mid-Atlantic Grants Program: Through the Mid-Atlantic Grants Program, the foundation awards grants to projects and charitable organization recommended by Mid-Atlantic dairy-member leaders. Special emphasis is directed toward programs designed to address hunger relief; youth and education; rural leadership; civic improvements; soil and water preservation; and arts and culture. Support is limited to Land O'Lakes dairy communities in Maryland, New Jersey, New York, Pennsylvania, and Virginia. Grants range from $500 to $5,000.

Purina Expert Dealer Match Hunger Program: The foundation matches dollar-for-dollar cash donations made by Purina Certified Expert Dealers to local organizations working to alleviate hunger within their community. This is a 2012 pilot program.

Type of support: Building/renovation; Capital campaigns; Employee matching gifts; Employee volunteer services; Equipment; General/operating support; Matching/challenge support; Scholarships—to individuals; Seed money.
Geographic limitations: Giving on a national basis in areas of company operations in AR, CA, IA, ID, IN, KS, MI, MN, MS, MO, ND, NE, OH, OR, PA, SD, TX, WA, and WI; giving also to statewide, regional, and national organizations.
Support limitations: No support for lobbying or political organizations, religious organizations not of direct benefit to the entire community, or veterans', fraternal, or labor organizations. No grants to individuals (except for scholarships), or for fundraising events, dinners, or benefits, advertising, higher education capital campaigns or endowments, travel, racing or sports sponsorships, or disease or medical research or treatment.
Publications: Annual report; Application guidelines; Grants list; Informational brochure (including application guidelines); IRS Form 990 or 990-PF printed copy available upon request.
Application information: Applications accepted. Application form required. Applicants should submit the following:
1) results expected from proposed grant
2) statement of problem project will address
3) copy of IRS Determination Letter
4) brief history of organization and description of its mission
5) detailed description of project and amount of funding requested

Applications for the John Memorial Scholarship should include a personal history; transcripts; a plan of study and research for the advanced degree; and faculty recommendations.
Initial approach: Complete online application for Community Grants Program; contact a Land O'Lakes dairy farmer or unit delegate for application form for California Regions Grants and Mid-Atlantic Grants; download application and mail for John Memorial Scholarships
Copies of proposal: 1
Board meeting date(s): Feb., June, Aug., and Dec.
Deadline(s): None for Community Grants Program requests under $25,000; Apr. 1 for Arts and Education, July 1 for Human Services and Civic, and Oct. 1 for Hunger for Community Grants Program requests of more than $25,000; none for California Regions Grants and Mid-Atlantic Grants; May 5 for John Brandt Memorial Scholarships
Final notification: 2 to 4 weeks for California Regions Grants and Mid-Atlantic Grants
Officers and Directors:* Jim Hager*, Chair.; James Netto*, Vice-Chair.; Nancy Breyfogle, Treas.; Lydia Botham*, Exec. Dir.; Tanya Dowda; John Ellenberger; Jim Fife; Pete Janzen; Ronnie Mohr; Tom Wakefield; Stephen Mancebo.
Number of staff: 1 full-time professional; 1 full-time support.
EIN: 411864977

2218
Landmark Media Enterprises, LLC

(formerly Landmark Communications, Inc.)
150 Granby St.
Norfolk, VA 23510-2075

Company URL: http://
Establishment information: Established in 1905.
Company type: Private company
Business activities: Publishes newspapers; broadcasts television; provides cable television, Internet information, and wireless communications services.
Business type (SIC): Newspaper publishing and/or printing; telephone communications; radio and television broadcasting; cable and other pay television services; advertising; computer services; education services
Corporate officers: Frank Batten, Jr., Chair. and C.E.O.; Jack J. Ross, Pres. and C.O.O.; Teresa F. Blevins, Exec. V.P. and C.F.O.
Board of director: Frank Batten, Jr., Chair.
Subsidiaries: Greensboro News Co., Greensboro, NC; KLAS-TV, Las Vegas, NV; Landmark Community Newspapers, Shelbyville, KY; Times-World Corp., Roanoke, VA; The Virginian-Pilot, Norfolk, VA; WTVF-News Channel 5 Network, Nashville, TN
International operations: United Kingdom
Giving statement: Giving through the Landmark Foundation.

The Landmark Foundation

(formerly Landmark Communications Foundation)
150 Granby St., 19th FL
Norfolk, VA 23510-1604

Establishment information: Incorporated in 1953 in VA.
Donors: Landmark Communications, Inc.; The Virginian-Pilot; Greensboro News Co.; Times-World Corp.; KLAS-TV; WTVF-News Channel 5 Network; Capital Gazette Communications, Inc.; Landmark Media Enterprises.
Contact: Tina Wright
Financial data (yr. ended 12/31/11): Assets, $68,668,100 (M); expenditures, $5,235,491; qualifying distributions, $4,842,137; giving activities include $4,816,614 for 131 grants (high: $1,210,000; low: $250).
Purpose and activities: The foundation supports organizations involved with secondary education, arts and culture, leadership development, and the environment.
Fields of interest: Museums; Arts; Higher education; Education; Environmental education; Environment; Food banks; Homeless, human services; United Ways and Federated Giving Programs; Leadership development Economically disadvantaged.
Type of support: Annual campaigns; Building/renovation; Capital campaigns; Continuing support; Curriculum development; Emergency funds; Equipment; Matching/challenge support; Program development; Scholarship funds; Seed money; Technical assistance.
Geographic limitations: Giving primarily in areas of company operations in Greensboro, NC, Las Vegas, NV, Nashville, TN, and Norfolk and Roanoke, VA.
Support limitations: No support for religious organizations not of direct benefit to the entire community, health-related organizations, or organizations whose primary purpose is economic development. No grants to individuals, or for debt reduction, special events, dinners, festivals, medical education or research, fundraising, political or political related purposes, or historic preservation.
Publications: Application guidelines.
Application information: Applications accepted. Letters of inquiry should be no longer than 1 page. Additional information may be requested at a later date. Application form not required. Applicants should submit the following:
1) timetable for implementation and evaluation of project
2) copy of IRS Determination Letter
3) detailed description of project and amount of funding requested
4) copy of current year's organizational budget and/or project budget
5) listing of additional sources and amount of support

Initial approach: Letter of inquiry to nearest company facility
Copies of proposal: 1
Board meeting date(s): As required
Deadline(s): None
Final notification: Within 3 months
Officers and Directors:* Frank Batten, Jr.*, Pres.; Richard F. Barry III*, V.P.; Teresa F. Blevins, Treas.; Jack Ross.
Number of staff: 1 part-time support.
EIN: 546038902

2219
Landry's Restaurants, Inc.

(formerly Landry's Seafood Restaurants, Inc.)
1510 W. Loop S. Fwy.
Houston, TX 77027-9505 (713) 850-1010

Company URL: http://www.landrysinc.com
Establishment information: Established in 1980.
Company type: Subsidiary of a private company
Business activities: Operates restaurants.
Business type (SIC): Restaurants and drinking places
Financial profile for 2011: Number of employees, 35,000; sales volume, $2,000,000,000
Corporate officers: Tilman J. Fertitta, Chair., Pres., and C.E.O.; Richard H. Liem, Exec. V.P. and C.F.O.
Board of director: Tilman J. Fertitta, Chair.
Subsidiary: Rainforest Cafe, Inc., Houston, TX
Giving statement: Giving through the Tilman & Paige Fertitta Family Foundation.
Company EIN: 760405386

Tilman & Paige Fertitta Family Foundation

1510 W. Loop South
Houston, TX 77027-9505

Establishment information: Established in 2000 in TX.
Donors: Landry's Seafood Restaurants, Inc.; Landry's Restaurants, Inc.
Financial data (yr. ended 12/31/11): Assets, $1,587,123 (M); gifts received, $300,000; expenditures, $205,098; qualifying distributions, $200,700; giving activities include $200,700 for grants.
Purpose and activities: The foundation supports police agencies and organizations involved with education, heart disease, and children.
Fields of interest: Secondary school/education; Higher education; Education; Heart & circulatory diseases; Crime/law enforcement, police agencies; Children, services.
Type of support: Capital campaigns; General/operating support; Scholarship funds.
Geographic limitations: Giving limited to Houston, TX.
Support limitations: No grants to individuals.
Application information: Applications not accepted. Unsolicited requests for funds not accepted.
Officers: Tilman J. Fertitta, Pres.; Paige Fertitta, V.P.; Steve L. Scheinthal, Secy.
EIN: 760626357

2220
Lands' End, Inc.
1 Lands' End Ln.
Dodgeville, WI 53595 (608) 935-9341

Company URL: http://www.landsend.com
Establishment information: Established in 1963.
Company type: Subsidiary of a public company
Business activities: Provides catalog shopping services; operates men's, women's, and children's clothing stores.
Business type (SIC): Nonstore retailers; men's and boys' apparel and accessory stores; women's apparel stores; women's specialty and accessory stores; children's apparel and accessory stores; shoe stores
Financial profile for 2010: Number of employees, 34
Corporate officers: Edgar O. Huber, Pres. and C.E.O.; Tim Martin, Sr. V.P. and C.F.O.; Frank Giannantonio, Sr. V.P. and C.I.O.
International operations: Germany; Japan; United Kingdom
Giving statement: Giving through the Lands' End, Inc. Corporate Giving Program.

Lands' End, Inc. Corporate Giving Program
5 Lands' End Ln.
Dodgeville, WI 53595-0001 (608) 935-9341
E-mail: donate@landsend.com; URL: http://www.landsend.com/aboutus/social/index.html

Purpose and activities: Lands' End makes charitable contributions to nonprofit organizations involved with education, the environment, healthcare, human services, and community development. Support is given primarily in areas of company operations, with emphasis on Wisconsin.
Fields of interest: Education; Environment; Health care; Human services; Community/economic development.
Type of support: Donated products; Employee matching gifts; Employee volunteer services; General/operating support; In-kind gifts; Program development.
Geographic limitations: Giving primarily in areas of company operations, with emphasis on WI.
Application information:
Initial approach: E-mail headquarters for application information
Number of staff: 1 full-time professional; 2 full-time support; 1 part-time support.

2221
Lane Powell PC
1420 5th Ave., Ste. 4100
Seattle, WA 98101-2338 (206) 223-7746

Company URL: http://www.lanepowell.com
Establishment information: Established in 1900.
Company type: Private company
Business activities: Operates law firm.
Business type (SIC): Legal services
Offices: Anchorage, AK; Portland, OR; Olympia, Seattle, Tacoma, WA
International operations: United Kingdom
Giving statement: Giving through the Lane Powell PC Pro Bono Program.

Lane Powell PC Pro Bono Program
1420 5th Ave., Ste. 4100
Seattle, WA 98101-2338 (206) 223-7000
E-mail: paytong@lanepowell.com; Additional tel.: (206) 223-7000; URL: http://www.lanepowell.com/226/pro-bono/

Contact: Gwendolyn C. Payton, Hiring Partner
Fields of interest: Legal services.
Type of support: Pro bono services - legal.
Application information: A Pro Bono Committee manages the pro bono program.

2222
Lanier Ford Shaver & Payne P.C.
P.O. Box 2087
Huntsville, AL 35804-2087 (256) 535-1100

Company URL: http://www.lanierford.com/
Establishment information: Established in 1988.
Company type: Private company
Business activities: Operates law firm.
Business type (SIC): Legal services
Giving statement: Giving through the Lanier Ford Shaver & Payne P.C. Pro Bono Program.

Lanier Ford Shaver & Payne P.C. Pro Bono Program
P.O. Box 2087
Huntsville, AL 35804-2087 (256) 535-1100
URL: http://www.lanierford.com

Fields of interest: Legal services.
Type of support: Pro bono services - legal.
Geographic limitations: Giving primarily in areas of company operations in Huntsville, AL.
Application information: Attorneys generate pro bono cases.

2223
Lapham-Hickey Steel Corporation
5500 W. 73rd St.
Chicago, IL 60638-6506 (708) 496-6111

Company URL: http://www.lapham-hickey.com
Establishment information: Established in 1926.
Company type: Private company
Business activities: Manufactures steel.
Business type (SIC): Steel mill products
Corporate officers: William M. Hickey, Jr., Pres. and C.E.O.; Robert Piland, C.F.O.; Jeff Hobson, V.P., Corp. Opers.
Giving statement: Giving through the Christiana Foundation, Inc.

Christiana Foundation, Inc.
222 N. LaSalle St., Ste. 300
Chicago, IL 60601-1013

Establishment information: Incorporated in 1957 in IL.
Donors: Lapham-Hickey Steel Corp.; Jerome A. Frazel, Jr.
Financial data (yr. ended 04/30/12): Assets, $45,056 (M); expenditures, $192,463; qualifying distributions, $182,000; giving activities include $182,000 for 3 grants (high: $109,000; low: $30,000).
Purpose and activities: The foundation supports food banks and organizations involved with education, reproductive health, patient services, housing development, human services, and religion.
Fields of interest: Higher education; Education; Reproductive health; Health care, patient services; Health care; Food banks; Housing/shelter, development; Children/youth, services; Residential/custodial care, hospices; Human services; Christian agencies & churches; Catholic agencies & churches; Religion.
Type of support: General/operating support.
Geographic limitations: Giving primarily in IL and WA.
Support limitations: No grants to individuals.
Application information: Applications not accepted. Contributes only to pre-selected organizations.
Directors: Jerome A. Frazel, Jr.; Francis J. Frazel; Jerome V. Frazel; Joanne K. Frazel; Mark J. Frazel.
EIN: 366065745
Selected grants: The following grants are a representative sample of this grantmaker's funding activity:
$8,000 to Catholic Charities of the Archdiocese of Chicago, Chicago, IL, 2010.
$3,000 to Glenmary Home Missioners, Cincinnati, OH, 2010.
$2,500 to United Negro College Fund, Fairfax, VA, 2010.

2224
Larkin, Hoffman, Daly & Lindgren, Ltd.
7900 Xerxes Ave. S., Ste. 1500
Minneapolis, MN 55431-1106
(952) 835-3800

Company URL: http://www.larkinhoffman.com/
Establishment information: Established in 1958.
Company type: Private company
Business activities: Provides legal services.
Business type (SIC): Legal services
Corporate officer: Richard A. Knutson, C.O.O
Giving statement: Giving through the Larkin, Hoffman, Daly & Lindgren, Ltd. Foundation.

Larkin, Hoffman, Daly & Lindgren, Ltd. Foundation
7900 Xerxes Ave. S., Ste. 1500
Minneapolis, MN 55431-1194 (952) 835-3800

Establishment information: Established in 1986 in MN.
Donors: Larkin, Hoffman, Daly & Lindgren, Ltd.; Gerald H. Friedell; Bruce J. Douglas.
Contact: Richard A. Knutson
Financial data (yr. ended 05/31/12): Assets, $5,120 (M); gifts received, $20,000; expenditures, $18,600; qualifying distributions, $18,600; giving activities include $18,600 for 68 grants (high: $2,000; low: $50).
Purpose and activities: The foundation supports organizations involved with education, health, legal aid, human services, and Judaism.
Fields of interest: Education; Human services; Religion.
Type of support: Annual campaigns; Capital campaigns; General/operating support; Matching/challenge support; Scholarship funds.
Geographic limitations: Giving primarily in MN.
Support limitations: No grants to individuals.
Application information: Applications accepted. Application form not required.

Initial approach: Proposal
Deadline(s): None
Officers: Jon Swierzewski, Pres.; John D. Fullmer, V.P.; Michael Smith, Secy.-Treas.
Director: Gerald Seck.
EIN: 363463116

2225
Las Vegas Sands Corp.
3355 Las Vegas Blvd. S., Rm. 1A
Las Vegas, NV 89109 (702) 414-1000

Company URL: http://www.lasvegassands.com
Establishment information: Established in 1988.
Company type: Public company
Company ticker symbol and exchange: LVS/NYSE
Business activities: Operates casino hotels; operates convention center.
Business type (SIC): Hotels and motels; real estate operators and lessors
Financial profile for 2012: Number of employees, 46,000; assets, $22,163,650,000; sales volume, $11,131,130,000; pre-tax net income, $2,062,580,000; expenses, $8,838,980,000; liabilities, $15,101,810,000
Fortune 1000 ranking: 2012—244th in revenues, 140th in profits, and 224th in assets
Forbes 2000 ranking: 2012—863rd in sales, 405th in profits, and 915th in assets
Corporate officers: Sheldon G. Adelson, Chair. and C.E.O.; Michael A. Leven, Pres. and C.O.O.; Kenneth J. Kay, Exec. V.P. and C.F.O.; Chris J. Cahill, Exec. V.P., Opers.; Ira H. Raphaelson, Exec. V.P. and Genl. Counsel.
Board of directors: Sheldon G. Adelson, Chair.; Jason N. Ader; Irwin Chafetz; Victor Chaltiel; Charles D. Forman; George P. Koo; Charles A. Koppelman; Michael A. Leven; Jeffrey H. Schwartz; Irwin A. Siegel
International operations: Cayman Islands; China; Hong Kong; India; Macau; Mauritius; Singapore; South Korea; Taiwan; Thailand; United Kingdom
Giving statement: Giving through the Sands Foundation.
Company EIN: 270099920

Sands Foundation
(formerly Venetian Foundation)
3355 Las Vegas Blvd. S.
Las Vegas, NV 89109-8941 (702) 607-4574
E-mail: foundation@venetian.com; URL: http://sands.com/sands-foundation/

Establishment information: Established in 2000 in NV.
Financial data (yr. ended 12/31/10): Revenue, $312,525; assets, $18,054 (M); gifts received, $312,525; expenditures, $401,416; giving activities include $397,786 for 21 grants (high: $72,500; low: $5,000) and $3,630 for grants to individuals.
Purpose and activities: Through this foundation, the Venetian Resort Hotel Casino seeks to participate with its team members, their spouses, children, and extended families, as well as the communities of Las Vegas and southern Nevada in programs and causes that motivate, educate, and enrich the lives of youth; the foundation will also support causes that provide empowerment to minority communities, promote health, and improve inner cities.
Fields of interest: Health care; Youth development Minorities; Economically disadvantaged.
Program:
Crisis Fund: Any member of the Las Vegas community facing a crisis is eligible to receive assistance from the fund. Crisis may consist of immediate family disasters such as fire, accident, sudden illness, personal tragedy, or other life-altering events in which the individual suffers severe financial hardship. Requests for assistance are considered on a case-by-case basis. Applicants must have first exhausted all other sources of financial assistance. The cost of mortgage/rent, utilities, and needs for living expenses are funded only in the case of an emergency. All assistance through the foundation will be paid directly to the source providing the service needed.
Geographic limitations: Giving primarily in Las Vegas and southern NV.
Application information: Applications accepted. Applicants should submit the following:
1) brief history of organization and description of its mission
2) listing of board of directors, trustees, officers and other key people and their affiliations
3) detailed description of project and amount of funding requested
Initial approach: Proposal submitted via regular mail or fax
Deadline(s): Eight weeks prior to the date when the donation is needed
Directors: Andy Abboud; Leslie Klinger; Ron Reese; Carol Wetzel.
EIN: 880494738

2226
Lassus Brothers Oil Company
1800 Magnavox Way
Fort Wayne, IN 46804-1540
(260) 436-1415

Company URL: http://www.lassus.com
Establishment information: Established in 1925.
Company type: Private company
Business activities: Operates gasoline service stations and grocery stores.
Business type (SIC): Gasoline service stations; groceries—retail
Corporate officers: Jon F. Lassus, C.E.O.; Todd J. Lassus, Pres.; Michael Bates, C.O.O.; David Fledderjohann, C.F.O.
Giving statement: Giving through the Lassus Bros. Oil, Inc. Foundation.

Lassus Bros. Oil, Inc. Foundation
1800 Magnavox Way
Fort Wayne, IN 46804-1540

Establishment information: Established in 1986 in IN.
Donors: Lassus Brothers Oil Co.; Lasco Leasing, Inc.
Financial data (yr. ended 09/30/11): Assets, $7,508 (M); gifts received, $45,000; expenditures, $42,410; qualifying distributions, $41,900; giving activities include $41,900 for 18 grants (high: $30,000; low: $100).
Purpose and activities: The foundation awards grants to various nonprofit organizations.
Fields of interest: General charitable giving.
Type of support: Employee-related scholarships; General/operating support.
Application information: Applications not accepted. Unsolicited requests for funds not accepted.
Trustees: David Fledderjohann; Greg L. Lassus; Jon F. Lassus; Jon R. Lassus; Todd J. Lassus.
EIN: 311190500

2227
Lateral Line, Inc.
8673 Commerce Dr., Ste. 4
Easton, MD 21601-3810 (443) 926-8016

Company URL: http://www.laterallineco.com
Establishment information: Established in 2005.
Company type: Private company
Business activities: Operates a fishing clothing company serving Striped Bass anglers.
Business type (SIC): Games, toys, and sporting and athletic goods
Corporate officers: Brandon White, C.E.O.; Spencer White, Pres.
Giving statement: Giving through the Lateral Line, Inc. Corporate Giving Program.

Lateral Line, Inc. Corporate Giving Program
(also known as 2 % for the Fish Foundation)
620 South St.
Easton, MD 21601-3810 (443) 926-8016
E-mail: 2forfish@LateralLineCo.com; URL: http://www.laterallineco.com/lateral_line_foundation_2percentforfish.html

Purpose and activities: Lateral Line is a certified B Corporation that donates 2 percent of gross sales to programs that improve fish populations and/or the ecosystems in which they live.
Fields of interest: Animals/wildlife, fisheries.
Type of support: General/operating support.
Publications: Application guidelines.
Application information: Applications accepted. Proposals should be no longer than 1 page. Application form not required. Applicants should submit the following:
1) timetable for implementation and evaluation of project
2) statement of problem project will address
3) name, address and phone number of organization
4) how project's results will be evaluated or measured
5) contact person
Initial approach: Proposal
Deadline(s): None

2228
Latham & Watkins LLP
885 3rd Ave., Ste. 1000
New York, NY 10022-4834 (212) 906-1200

Company URL: http://www.lw.com
Establishment information: Established in 1934.
Company type: Private company
Business activities: Operates law firm.
Business type (SIC): Legal services
Corporate officers: Robert M. Dell, Chair. and Managaing Partner; David A. Gordon, Vice-Chair and Chief Operating Partner
Offices: Costa Mesa, Los Angeles, Menlo Park, San Diego, San Francisco, CA; Washington, DC; Chicago, IL; Boston, MA; Newark, NJ; New York, NY; Houston, TX
International operations: Belgium; China; Germany; Hong Kong; Italy; Japan; Qatar; Russia; Saudi Arabia; Singapore; Spain; United Arab Emirates; United Kingdom
Giving statement: Giving through the Latham & Watkins LLP Pro Bono Program.

Latham & Watkins LLP Pro Bono Program

885 3rd Ave., Ste. 1000
New York, NY 10022-4834 (202) 637-2200
E-mail: wendy.atrokhov@lw.com; Additional tel.: (212) 906-1200, fax: (212) 751-4864; URL: http://www.lw.com/AboutLatham.aspx?page=ProBono

Contact: Wendy Atrokhov, Public Svc. Counsel
Fields of interest: Legal services.
Type of support: Pro bono services - legal.
Geographic limitations: Giving primarily in areas of company operations in Costa Mesa, Los Angeles, Menlo Park, San Diego, and San Francisco, CA, Washington, DC, Chicago, IL, Newark, NJ, Houston, TX, and in China, France, Germany, Hong Kong, Japan, Italy, Russia, Saudi Arabia, Singapore, Spain, Qatar, United Arab Emirates, and United Kingdom.
Application information: A Pro Bono Committee manages the pro bono program.

2229
Latham Entertainment Inc.

3200 Northline Ave., Ste. 132
Greensboro, NC 27408-7600
(336) 315-1440

Company URL: http://www.lathamentertainment.com
Establishment information: Established in 1993.
Company type: Private company
Business activities: Provides theatrical services.
Business type (SIC): Bands, orchestras, and entertainers
Corporate officers: Walter Latham, Co-Pres.; Bob Soljacich, Co-Pres.
Giving statement: Giving through the Walter Latham Foundation, Inc.

Walter Latham Foundation, Inc.

c/o Walter Lathman
P.O. Box 41023
Greensboro, NC 27404-1023 (336) 545-8062

Establishment information: Established in 2007 in NC.
Donors: Walter Latham; Latham Entertainment, Inc.
Contact: Yulonda Smith, Secy.-Treas.
Financial data (yr. ended 12/31/11): Assets, $1 (M); gifts received, $19,500; expenditures, $29,339; qualifying distributions, $15,965; giving activities include $15,965 for grants.
Purpose and activities: Scholarship awards to residents of Greensboro, North Carolina.
Fields of interest: Recreation; Youth development; Human services.
Type of support: Grants to individuals; Scholarships —to individuals.
Geographic limitations: Giving primarily in Greensboro, NC.
Application information: Applications accepted. Application form required.
Initial approach: Letter
Deadline(s): Mar. 15
Officers and Directors:* Walter Latham*, Pres.; Yulonda Smith, Secy.-Treas.; Steven H. Bouldin; Jay Harris; William M. Young; Irish Spencer; Rhonda Outlaw; Ralph Huey; Lori Middleton.
EIN: 208573363

2230
The Estee Lauder Companies Inc.

767 5th Ave.
New York, NY 10153 (212) 572-4200
FAX: (212) 893-7782

Company URL: http://www.elcompanies.com
Establishment information: Established in 1946.
Company type: Public company
Company ticker symbol and exchange: EL/NYSE
Business activities: Manufactures and markets skin care, makeup, fragrance, and hair care products.
Business type (SIC): Soaps, cleaners, and toiletries
Financial profile for 2012: Number of employees, 38,500; assets, $6,593,000,000; sales volume, $9,713,600,000; pre-tax net income, $1,261,100,000; expenses, $8,401,900,000; liabilities, $3,859,800,000
Fortune 1000 ranking: 2012—279th in revenues, 227th in profits, and 506th in assets
Forbes 2000 ranking: 2012—935th in sales, 634th in profits, and 1651st in assets
Corporate officers: William P. Lauder, Chair.; Fabrizio Freda, Pres. and C.E.O.; Tracey T. Travis, Exec. V.P. and C.F.O.; Sara E. Moss, Exec. V.P. and Genl. Counsel; Alexandra C. Trower, Exec. V.P., Comms.; Amy DiGeso, Exec. V.P., Human Resources; Leonard A. Lauder, Chair. Emeritus
Board of directors: William P. Lauder, Chair.; Charlene Barshefsky; Rose Marie Bravo; Wei Sun Christianson; Lynn Forester de Rothschild; Fabrizio Freda; Paul J. Fribourg; Mellody L. Hobson; Irvine O. Hockaday, Jr.; Aerin Lauder; Leonard A. Lauder; Jane Lauder; Richard D. Parsons; Barry S. Sternlicht; Richard F. Zannino
International operations: Canada; Portugal; United Kingdom
Giving statement: Giving through the Estee Lauder Companies Inc. Corporate Giving Program.
Company EIN: 112408943

The Estee Lauder Companies Inc. Corporate Giving Program

767 5th Ave.
New York, NY 10153-0023
URL: http://www.elcompanies.com/Pages/Corporate-Responsibility.aspx

Purpose and activities: Estee Lauder makes charitable contributions to nonprofit organizations involved with arts and culture, education, the environment, and health and human services. Support is given in areas of company operations.
Fields of interest: Arts; Education, reading; Education; Environment; Health care; Breast cancer; AIDS; Boy scouts; American Red Cross; Salvation Army; Children/youth, services; Human services Economically disadvantaged.
Type of support: Donated products; Employee volunteer services; General/operating support; In-kind gifts; Sponsorships.
Geographic limitations: Giving on a national and international basis in areas of company operations, with emphasis on New York, NY.
Application information: Applications not accepted. Contributes only to pre-selected organizations.

2231
Laureate Education, Inc.

(formerly Sylvan Learning Systems, Inc.)
650 S. Exeter St.
Baltimore, MD 21202-4382
(410) 843-6100

Company URL: http://www.laureate.net
Establishment information: Established in 1998.
Company type: Private company
Business activities: Operates adult career education services company.
Business type (SIC): Education services; computer services; colleges, universities, and professional schools
Corporate officers: Douglas L. Becker, Chair. and C.E.O.; William Dennis, Vice-Chair.; Eilif Serck-Hanssen, Exec. V.P. and C.F.O.; Daniel M. Nickel, Exec. V.P., Corp. Opers.; Robert W. Zentz, Sr. V.P. and Genl. Counsel
Board of directors: Douglas L. Becker, Chair.; William Dennis, Vice-Chair.
Giving statement: Giving through the Sylvan/Laureate Foundation, Inc.
Company EIN: 521492296

Sylvan/Laureate Foundation, Inc.

(formerly The Sylvan Learning Foundation, Inc.)
c/o Foundation Source
501 Silverside Rd., Ste. 123
Wilmington, DE 19809-1377
E-mail: SLFinfo@laureate.net; URL: http://www.laureate.net/HereforGood/TheSylvanLaureateFoundation

Establishment information: Established in 1997 in MD.
Donors: Sylvan Learning Systems, Inc.; Laureate Education, Inc.; Leadform Est. LTD.
Contact: Carol Maivelett, Admin.
Financial data (yr. ended 12/31/11): Assets, $9,412,717 (M); gifts received, $2,000,000; expenditures, $2,153,537; qualifying distributions, $1,910,353; giving activities include $1,910,353 for grants.
Purpose and activities: The foundation supports organizations involved with arts and culture, health, children and youth, youth development, international development, public policy research. Special emphasis is directed toward programs designed to promote best practices in education.
Fields of interest: Museums; Performing arts, theater; Performing arts, orchestras; Arts; Elementary/secondary education; Higher education; Teacher school/education; Education; Health care; Youth development, citizenship; Youth development; Children/youth, services; International development; Business/industry; United Ways and Federated Giving Programs; Public policy, research; Leadership development.
Type of support: Annual campaigns; Capital campaigns; General/operating support; Program development; Sponsorships.
Geographic limitations: Giving primarily in Baltimore, MD.
Support limitations: No support for religious organizations or political or lobbying organizations. No grants to individuals.
Application information: Applications not accepted. Contributes only to pre-selected organizations.
Board meeting date(s): Apr., July, Oct., and Jan.
Officers and Trustees:* Douglas L. Becker*, Pres.; R. Christopher Hoehn-Saric*, 1st V.P.; Robert W. Zentz, 2nd V.P. and Secy.; Eilif Serck-Hanssen, Treas.; B. Lee McGee.
EIN: 522044008

Selected grants: The following grants are a representative sample of this grantmaker's funding activity:
$520,365 to International Youth Foundation, Baltimore, MD, 2010.
$96,275 to International Youth Foundation, Baltimore, MD, 2010.
$50,000 to Baltimore Childrens Museum, Baltimore, MD, 2010.
$50,000 to Johns Hopkins University, Baltimore, MD, 2010.
$25,000 to Advocates for Children and Youth, Baltimore, MD, 2010.
$25,000 to Union Memorial Hospital, Baltimore, MD, 2010.
$20,000 to New Leaders for New Schools, New York, NY, 2010.
$20,000 to Volunteer Central, Baltimore, MD, 2010.
$15,000 to Family Tree, Baltimore, MD, 2010. For charitable event.
$10,000 to Performance Workshop, Baltimore, MD, 2010.

2232
Lauth Property Group, Inc.

111 Congressional
Carmel, IN 46032 (317) 848-6500
FAX: (317) 848-6511

Company URL: http://www.lauth.net
Establishment information: Established in 1977.
Company type: Private company
Business activities: Develops commercial real estate; provides nonresidential general contract construction services; owns and manages commercial real estate.
Business type (SIC): Real estate subdividers and developers; contractors/general nonresidential building; real estate operators and lessors; real estate agents and managers
Financial profile for 2010: Number of employees, 425
Corporate officers: Robert L. Lauth, Chair. and C.E.O.; Michael J. Jones, Pres.; Vernon C. Back, Exec. V.P. and Genl. Counsel; Michael J. Garvey, C.I.O.; Jonathon L. Goodburn, C.F.O.
Board of director: Robert L. Lauth, Chair.
Offices: Phoenix, AZ; Denver, CO; Orlando, FL; Charlotte, NC; Dallas, TX
Giving statement: Giving through the Lauth Group Foundation, Inc.

Lauth Group Foundation, Inc.

P.O. Box 1129
Carmel, IN 46032
E-mail: kivcevich@lauth.net; URL: http://www.lauth.net

Establishment information: Established in 2004 in IN.
Donors: Lauth Property Group, Inc.; Town Lake Partners, LLC.
Financial data (yr. ended 12/31/11): Assets, $783,947 (M); expenditures, $75,745; qualifying distributions, $70,311; giving activities include $66,588 for 9 grants (high: $35,578; low: $50).
Purpose and activities: The foundation supports programs designed to assist children by improving quality of life and enhancing learning; and ensure that those in need have access to the resources necessary to achieve and maintain self-sufficiency. Special emphasis is directed toward programs designed to address academics, health and physical well-being, leadership and citizenship, and parental involvement for low-income youth.
Fields of interest: Elementary/secondary education; Health care; Youth development, services; Youth development, citizenship; Children, services Youth; Economically disadvantaged.
Type of support: General/operating support.
Application information: Applications not accepted. Unsolicited requests for funds not accepted.
Officers: Robert L. Lauth, Jr., Pres.; Vernon C. Back, V.P.; Stephen G. Eppink, V.P.; Michael J. Garvey, V.P.; Michael J. Jones, V.P.; Jonathan Goodburn, Treas.
EIN: 200637680

2233
The Law Company, Inc.

345 Riverview
P.O. Box 1139
Wichita, KS 67203 (316) 268-0200

Company URL: http://www.law-co.com
Establishment information: Established in 1959.
Company type: Private company
Business activities: Provides general contract construction services.
Business type (SIC): Contractors/general nonresidential building; contractors/general residential building
Financial profile for 2010: Number of employees, 200
Corporate officers: Richard Kerschen, Pres.; Marc Porter, Sr. V.P. and Secy.; Larry Will, Treas.
Board of director: Richard Kerschen
Giving statement: Giving through the Law Company, Inc. Corporate Giving Program.

The Law Company, Inc. Corporate Giving Program

345 Riverview
Wichita, KS 67203-4200 (316) 268-0200
FAX: (316) 268-0210; URL: http://www.law-co.com/communityservice.html

Purpose and activities: Law makes charitable contributions to nonprofit organizations in the areas of food services, fundraising, disability services, blood drives, and recreation. Support is given primarily in areas of company operations in Kansas, and to national organizations.
Fields of interest: Health care, blood supply; Food services; Recreation, fund raising/fund distribution; Athletics/sports, baseball; Independent living, disability.
Type of support: Donated products; Employee matching gifts; Employee volunteer services; Loaned talent.
Geographic limitations: Giving primarily in areas of company operations in KS, and to national organizations.

2205
La-Z-Boy Incorporated

(formerly La-Z-Boy Chair Company)
1284 N. Telegraph Rd.
Monroe, MI 48162-3390 (734) 242-1444
FAX: (734) 457-2005

Company URL: http://www.la-z-boy.com
Establishment information: Established in 1927.
Company type: Public company
Company ticker symbol and exchange: LZB/NYSE
Business activities: Manufactures furniture.
Business type (SIC): Furniture/household
Financial profile for 2012: Number of employees, 8,160; assets, $685,740,000; sales volume, $1,231,680,000; pre-tax net income, $66,860,000; expenses, $1,182,050,000; liabilities, $243,840,000
Corporate officers: Kurt L. Darrow, Chair., Pres., and C.E.O.; Louis M. Riccio, Jr., Sr. V.P. and C.F.O.; Daniel F. Deland, C.I.O.; Greg A. Brinks, V.P. and Treas.; Margaret L. Mueller, V.P. and Corp. Cont.; R. Rand Tucker, V.P. and Genl. Counsel; Steven P. Rindskopf, V.P. and Human Resources; James P. Klarr, Secy.
Board of directors: Kurt L. Darrow, Chair.; John H. Foss; Richard Marcel Gabrys; Janet L. Gurwitch; David K. Hehl; Edwin J. Holman; Janet E. Kerr; H. George Levy, M.D.; W. Alan McCollough; Nido R. Qubein
Subsidiaries: England, Inc., New Tazewell, TN; Kincaid Furniture Co., Inc., Hudson, NC
Plants: Siloam Springs, AR; Redlands, CA; Newton, Saltillo, MS; Neosho, MO; Lenoir, Taylorsville, NC; Dayton, TN
Office: High Point, NC
International operations: Canada; Cayman Islands; Germany; Mexico; Netherlands; Thailand; United Kingdom
Giving statement: Giving through the La-Z-Boy Foundation.
Company EIN: 380751137

La-Z-Boy Foundation

(formerly La-Z-Boy Chair Foundation)
1284 N. Telegraph Rd.
Monroe, MI 48162-3390 (734) 242-1444

Establishment information: Incorporated in 1953 in MI.
Donors: La-Z-Boy Chair Co.; La-Z-Boy Inc.; E. M. Knabusch‡; Edwin J. Shoemaker‡; H. F. Gertz‡.
Contact: Donald E. Blohm, Admin.
Financial data (yr. ended 12/31/11): Assets, $18,671,462 (M); expenditures, $1,356,776; qualifying distributions, $1,196,500; giving activities include $1,196,500 for grants.
Purpose and activities: The foundation supports organizations involved with education, health, human services, and government and public administration. Support is given primarily in areas of company operations.
Fields of interest: Education; Health care; Human services; United Ways and Federated Giving Programs; Government/public administration.
Type of support: Building/renovation; General/operating support.
Geographic limitations: Giving primarily in areas of company operations in Siloam Springs, AR, Redlands, CA, Monroe, MI, Neosho, MO, Newton and Saltillo, MS, Hudson, Lenoir, and Taylorsville, NC, Dayton and New Tazewell, TN.
Support limitations: No support for religious or political organizations. No grants to individuals, or for travel or conferences, or start-up needs; no loans.
Publications: Annual report (including application guidelines); Application guidelines.
Application information: Applications accepted. Proposals should be brief. Additional information may be requested at a later date. Application form not required. Applicants should submit the following:
1) timetable for implementation and evaluation of project
2) results expected from proposed grant
3) copy of IRS Determination Letter
4) copy of most recent annual report/audited financial statement/990

5) listing of board of directors, trustees, officers and other key people and their affiliations
6) detailed description of project and amount of funding requested
7) copy of current year's organizational budget and/or project budget
Initial approach: Proposal
Copies of proposal: 1
Board meeting date(s): Mar., June, Sept., and Dec.
Deadline(s): Mar. 1, June 1, Sept. 1, and Dec. 1
Final notification: 3 months

Officer and Trustees:* June E. Knabush-Taylor*, Pres.; Marvin J. Bauman*, Secy.; Donald E. Blohm*, Treas.; Kurt L. Darrow; Greg A. Brinks; James P. Klarr; Louis Riccio, Jr.; Rand Tucker.
Number of staff: 1 part-time support.
EIN: 386087673
Selected grants: The following grants are a representative sample of this grantmaker's funding activity:
$50,000 to United Way, Rhea County, Dayton, TN, 2012.
$45,000 to American Red Cross, Monroe, MI, 2012.
$45,000 to United Way of Monroe County, Monroe, MI, 2012.
$35,000 to Neosho United Fund, Neosho, MO, 2012.
$30,000 to Salvation Army of Monroe, Monroe, MI, 2012.
$25,000 to Newton United Givers Fund, Newton, MS, 2012.
$25,000 to United Way of Northeast Mississippi, Tupelo, MS, 2012.

2234
Lazy Days RV Center, Inc.

6130 Lazy Days Blvd.
Seffner, FL 33584-2968 (813) 246-4999

Company URL: http://www.lazydays.com
Establishment information: Established in 1976.
Company type: Private company
Business activities: Operates recreational vehicle dealership; sells recreational vehicles wholesale.
Business type (SIC): Recreational vehicles—retail; motor vehicles, parts, and supplies—wholesale
Corporate officers: William P. Murnane, Chair.; John Horton, C.E.O.; Randall R. Lay, C.F.O.
Board of directors: William P. Murrane, Chair.; John Horton
Giving statement: Giving through the Lazydays Partners' Foundation, Inc.

Lazydays Partners' Foundation, Inc.

6130 Lazy Days Blvd.
Seffner, FL 33584-2968 (813) 342-4239
URL: http://www.lazydaysemployeefoundation.org/

Contact: Lay Randy, Pres.
Financial data (yr. ended 12/31/11): Revenue, $227,245; assets, $221,829 (M); gifts received, $231,563; expenditures, $188,680; program services expenses, $162,431; giving activities include $162,431 for 8 grants (high: $45,000; low: $5,371).
Purpose and activities: The foundation strives to measurably change the lives of children by instilling hope, inspiring dreams, and empowering them with education.
Fields of interest: Elementary/secondary education; Higher education Children.
Geographic limitations: Giving primarily in Tampa Bay, FL.
Officers and Board Members:* Lay Randy*, Pres.; Steve Ratcliff*, V.P.; Rainey Kathy*, V.P.; Andrea Neeper*, Secy.; Livingstpn Jean*, Treas.; Dube Debbie; Allan Karp; Tammy Lull; Chiodi Janet; Cohen Jason; and 14 additional Board Members.
EIN: 203032464

2235
Lea County Electric Cooperative, Inc.

(formerly Lea County Electric Corporation)
1300 W. Ave. D
Lovington, NM 88260-3806 (575) 396-3631

Company URL: http://www.lcecnet.com
Establishment information: Established in 1946.
Company type: Cooperative
Business activities: Transmits and distributes electricity.
Business type (SIC): Electric services
Corporate officers: John Ingle, Pres.; Dan Hardin, Secy.-Treas.
Board of directors: Esten Alexander; Robert Caudle; Terry Davis; Thurman Duncan; Dan Hardin; John Ingle; Dean Kinsolving; Billy Royce Medlin; William V. Palmer; Wade Roberts
Giving statement: Giving through the Lea County Electric Education Foundation.

Lea County Electric Education Foundation

P.O. Box 1447
Lovington, NM 88260-1447 (575) 396-3631
URL: http://www.lcecnet.com/

Establishment information: Established in 1986 in NM.
Donor: Lea County Electric Cooperative, Inc.
Financial data (yr. ended 12/31/11): Assets, $1,002,404 (M); gifts received, $186,539; expenditures, $155,888; qualifying distributions, $128,122; giving activities include $126,375 for 82 grants to individuals (high: $3,000; low: $250).
Purpose and activities: The foundation awards college scholarships to active members and children of active members of Lea County Electric Cooperative who are attending institutions of higher education in New Mexico or Texas.
Program:
Scholarship Program: The foundation annually awards 65 scholarships to active members and dependents of Lea County Electric Cooperative. The foundation awards $1,000 per semester up to a maximum of eight semesters. Recipients must reside in the Lea County Electric territory, maintain a 2.50 GPA, and attend an accredited school in New Mexico or Texas.
Type of support: Employee-related scholarships.
Geographic limitations: Giving limited to NM and TX.
Publications: Application guidelines.
Application information: Applications accepted. Application form required.
Requests should include most recent transcripts and 2 letters of recommendation.
Initial approach: Complete online application form or download application and mail
Deadline(s): Second Fri. in Jan.
Final notification: May 1
Officers: John Ingle, Pres.; Dean Kinsolving, V.P.; Dan Hardin, Secy.-Treas.
Trustees: Robert Caudle; Terry Davis; John Graham; Ray Hilburn; Will Palmer; Wade Roberts.
EIN: 850351147

2236
Leaco Rural Telephone Cooperative, Inc.

220 W. Broadway St.
Hobbs, NM 88240-6038 (505) 398-5352
FAX: (505) 734-3326

Company URL: http://www.leaco.net
Establishment information: Established in 1985.
Company type: Cooperative
Business activities: Provides cellular telephone communications services; provides Internet access services; provides paging services; provides cable television services.
Business type (SIC): Telephone communications; cable and other pay television services
Corporate officers: Laura Angell, C.E.O.; Wanda Munson, Pres.; Leon Hemann, Secy.-Treas.
Board of directors: Robert Garnett; Joel Klein; Glenn Thompson; Jimmy Wilbanks
Offices: Hobbs, Tatum, NM
Giving statement: Giving through the Leaco Rural Telephone Education Foundation.

Leaco Rural Telephone Education Foundation

220 West Broadway
Hobbs, NM 88240-6004 (505) 370-5010

Establishment information: Established in 1999 in NM.
Financial data (yr. ended 12/31/11): Assets, $36,091 (M); gifts received, $7,318; expenditures, $3,300; qualifying distributions, $3,300; giving activities include $3,300 for 7 grants to individuals (high: $500; low: $300).
Purpose and activities: The foundation awards college scholarships to active members and the immediate family members of active members of Leaco Rural Telephone Cooperative.
Fields of interest: Higher education.
Type of support: Scholarships—to individuals.
Geographic limitations: Giving limited to NM.
Publications: Application guidelines.
Application information: Applications accepted. Application form required.
Application must include official transcripts, ACT/SAT scores, 2 letters of reference, and a essay explaining why the foundation should invest in the applicant's education.
Initial approach: Letter
Copies of proposal: 1
Deadline(s): Mar. 15
Officers: Wanda Munson, Pres.; Luann Pearson, V.P.; Leon Hemann, Secy.-Treas.
EIN: 856120669

2237
Lear Corporation

(formerly Lear Seating Corporation)
21557 Telegraph Rd.
Southfield, MI 48033 (248) 447-1500
FAX: (302) 655-5049

Company URL: http://www.lear.com
Establishment information: Established in 1917.
Company type: Public company
Company ticker symbol and exchange: LEA/NYSE
Business activities: Manufactures automobile and truck seating and specialty seat products.
Business type (SIC): Furniture/public building; metal forgings and stampings; metal products/fabricated

Financial profile for 2012: Number of employees, 113,400; assets, $8,194,100,000; sales volume, $14,567,000,000; pre-tax net income, $648,900,000; expenses, $13,918,100,000; liabilities, $4,707,000,000
Fortune 1000 ranking: 2012—187th in revenues, 157th in profits, and 449th in assets
Forbes 2000 ranking: 2012—649th in sales, 474th in profits, and 1603rd in assets
Corporate officers: Henry D.G. Wallace, Chair.; Matthew J. Simoncini, Pres. and C.E.O.; Terrence B. Larkin, Exec. V.P. and Genl. Counsel; Jeffrey H. Vanneste, Sr. V.P. and C.F.O.
Board of directors: Henry D.G. Wallace, Chair.; Thomas P. Capo; Jonathan F. Foster; Kathleen Ligocki; Conrad L. Mallet, Jr.; Donald L. Runkle; Matthew J. Simoncini; Gregory C. Smith
International operations: Mexico; South Korea; Sweden
Giving statement: Giving through the Lear Corporation Contributions Program and the Lear Corporation Charitable Foundation.
Company EIN: 133386776

Lear Corporation Charitable Foundation

21557 Telegraph Rd.
Southfield, MI 48033-4248

Establishment information: Established in 2003 in MI.
Donor: Lear Corp.
Financial data (yr. ended 12/31/10): Assets, $0 (M); gifts received, $6,500,000; expenditures, $1,014,754; qualifying distributions, $1,005,958; giving activities include $1,005,958 for grants.
Purpose and activities: The foundation supports the United Way and organizations involved with hunger and mentoring offenders and ex-offenders.
Fields of interest: Food services; Youth development, adult & child programs; United Ways and Federated Giving Programs Offenders/ ex-offenders.
Type of support: General/operating support; Program development.
Geographic limitations: Giving primarily in MI, with emphasis on Detroit.
Application information: Applications not accepted. Contributes only to pre-selected organizations.
Officers: Mathew J. Smoncini, Pres.; William P. McLaughlin, V.P.; Dave Mullin, V.P.; Mel Stephens, V.P.; Terrence B. Larkin, Secy.; Shari L. Burgess, Treas.
EIN: 200302085
Selected grants: The following grants are a representative sample of this grantmaker's funding activity:
$73,528 to Motor City Blight Busters, Detroit, MI, 2010. For operating support.
$50,000 to American Red Cross, Detroit, MI, 2010.
$25,000 to Boy Scouts of America, Detroit, MI, 2010.
$10,000 to College for Creative Studies, Detroit, MI, 2010.
$5,000 to Arts League of Michigan, Detroit, MI, 2010.
$2,500 to City Mission, Detroit, MI, 2010.
$2,500 to HAVEN, Pontiac, MI, 2010.
$2,500 to Vista Maria, Dearborn Heights, MI, 2010.

2238
Lebanon Valley Insurance Company

(formerly Lebanon Mutual Insurance Company)
137 W. Penn Ave.
P.O. Box 2005
Cleona, PA 17042-3275 (717) 272-6655

Company URL: http://www.lebins.com
Establishment information: Established in 1856.
Company type: Mutual company
Business activities: Sells property and casualty insurance.
Business type (SIC): Insurance/fire, marine, and casualty
Corporate officer: Jay Chadwick, Pres. and C.E.O.
Giving statement: Giving through the Lebanon Mutual Foundation.

Lebanon Mutual Foundation

137 W. Penn Ave.
Cleona, PA 17042-3228 (717) 272-6655

Donor: Lebanon Mutual Insurance Co.
Contact: Kieth A. Ulsh, Secy.-Treas.
Financial data (yr. ended 12/31/11): Assets, $505,522 (M); expenditures, $31,874; qualifying distributions, $26,050; giving activities include $26,050 for grants.
Purpose and activities: The foundation supports hospitals and organizations involved with higher and business education, land conservation, cancer, and human services.
Fields of interest: Education; Housing/shelter; Human services.
Type of support: Annual campaigns; Building/ renovation; Capital campaigns; Endowments; General/operating support.
Geographic limitations: Giving limited to the Lebanon, PA, area.
Support limitations: No grants to individuals.
Application information: Applications accepted. Application form required. Applicants should submit the following:
1) detailed description of project and amount of funding requested
Initial approach: Letter
Deadline(s): None
Officers: Rollin Rissinger, Jr., Pres.; Milton Garrison, V.P.; Keith A. Ulsh, Secy.-Treas.
Directors: Mark J. Keyser; S. Bruce Kurtz; Joseph Lauck; Warren Lewis.
EIN: 222521649

2239
LeClaire Manufacturing Company

3225 Zimmerman Dr.
P.O. Box 1344
Bettendorf, IA 52722 (563) 332-6550

Company URL: http://www.leclairemfg.com
Establishment information: Established in 1966.
Company type: Private company
Business activities: Manufactures aluminum castings.
Business type (SIC): Metal foundries/nonferrous
Corporate officers: Ralph L. Zimmerman, Co-Pres.; Robert L. Zimmerman, Co-Pres.
Giving statement: Giving through the Robert L. Zimmerman Charitable Foundation.

Robert L. Zimmerman Charitable Foundation

P.O. Box 1344
Bettendorf, IA 52722-1344 (563) 332-6550
Application address: 3225 Zimmerman Dr., Bettendorf, IA 52722

Establishment information: Established in 1996 in IA.
Donor: LeClaire Manufacturing Co.
Contact: Margaret Agnew, Secy.
Financial data (yr. ended 12/31/11): Assets, $127,364 (M); gifts received, $13,000; expenditures, $4,961; qualifying distributions, $4,100; giving activities include $4,100 for 2 grants (high: $3,600; low: $500).
Purpose and activities: The foundation supports camps and organizations involved with higher education, hunger, and Christianity.
Fields of interest: Health organizations.
Type of support: General/operating support.
Geographic limitations: Giving primarily in Ames and Bettendorf, IA.
Support limitations: No grants to individuals.
Application information: Applications accepted. Application form required.
Initial approach: Letter
Deadline(s): None
Officers: Nancy Sue Mappin, V.P.; Elizabeth A. Moore, V.P.; Robert L. Zimmerman, Jr., V.P.; Margaret Agnew, Secy.; Ralph James Zimmerman, Treas.
EIN: 421461940

2240
Lee Beverage of Wisconsin, LLC

(formerly Sheboygan Beverage, Inc.)
2850 S. Oakwood Rd.
Oshkosh, WI 54904-6378 (920) 235-1140

Company URL: http://www.leebeverage.com
Establishment information: Established in 1963.
Company type: Private company
Business activities: Sells beer wholesale.
Business type (SIC): Beer, wine, and distilled beverages—wholesale
Corporate officer: Jeff Lindemann, Pres.
Giving statement: Giving through the John E. Kuenzl Foundation, Inc.

The John E. Kuenzl Foundation, Inc.

P.O. Box 2886
Oshkosh, WI 54903-2886 (920) 231-5890

Establishment information: Established in 2000 in WI.
Donors: Sheboygan Beverage, Inc.; Gambrinus Enterprises; John E. Kuenzl†.
Contact: Gerald J. Stadtmueller, Dir.
Financial data (yr. ended 12/31/11): Assets, $21,087,780 (M); expenditures, $1,231,262; qualifying distributions, $1,125,400; giving activities include $1,125,400 for grants.
Purpose and activities: The foundation supports museums, fire departments, and community foundations and organizations involved with performing arts, hunger, housing development, and human services.
Fields of interest: Museums; Performing arts, orchestras; Performing arts, opera; Food services; Housing/shelter, development; Disasters, fire prevention/control; Boys & girls clubs; Salvation Army; YM/YWCAs & YM/YWHAs; Children, services; Family services, domestic violence;

Developmentally disabled, centers & services; Human services; Foundations (community); United Ways and Federated Giving Programs.
Type of support: General/operating support.
Geographic limitations: Giving primarily in WI.
Support limitations: No grants to individuals.
Application information: Applications accepted. Application form not required. Applicants should submit the following:
1) name, address and phone number of organization
2) detailed description of project and amount of funding requested
Initial approach: Proposal
Deadline(s): Dec. 1
Directors: Norma Kuenzl; Gerald Stadtmueller; James J. Williamson.
EIN: 391998578
Selected grants: The following grants are a representative sample of this grantmaker's funding activity:
$400,000 to Oshkosh Area Community Foundation, Oshkosh, WI, 2010. For general purpose.
$100,000 to United Way, Oshkosh Area, Oshkosh, WI, 2010. For general purpose.
$55,000 to YMCA, Oshkosh Community, Oshkosh, WI, 2010. For general purpose.
$25,000 to Boys and Girls Club of Oshkosh, Oshkosh, WI, 2010. For general purpose.
$25,000 to Oshkosh Symphony Orchestra, Oshkosh, WI, 2010. For general purpose.
$15,000 to American Heart Association, Dallas, TX, 2010. For general purpose.
$10,000 to Humane Society, Oshkosh Area, Oshkosh, WI, 2010. For general purpose.
$5,000 to American Cancer Society, De Pere, WI, 2010. For general purpose.
$5,000 to Wisconsin Public Radio, Madison, WI, 2010. For general purpose.
$1,000 to Oshkosh Christian School, Oshkosh, WI, 2010. For general purpose.

2241
Lee Enterprises, Incorporated

201 N. Harrison St.
Davenport, IA 52801-1939 (563) 383-2100
FAX: (302) 636-5454

Company URL: http://www.lee.net
Establishment information: Established in 1890.
Company type: Public company
Company ticker symbol and exchange: LEE/NYSE
Business activities: Publishes newspapers and weekly, classified, and specialty publications; provides Internet information services.
Business type (SIC): Newspaper publishing and/or printing; periodical publishing and/or printing; computer services
Financial profile for 2012: Number of employees, 6,100; assets, $1,061,140,000; sales volume, $710,490,000; pre-tax net income, -$23,140,000; expenses, $645,430,000; liabilities, $1,175,770,000
Corporate officers: Mary E. Junck, Chair., Pres., and C.E.O.; Carl G. Schmidt, V.P., C.F.O., and Treas.; Kevin D. Mowbray, V.P. and C.O.O.; Michele White, V.P. and C.I.O.; Michael R. Gulledge, V.P., Sales and Mktg.; Daniel K. Hayes, V.P., Corp. Comms.; Vytenis P. Kuraitis, V.P., Human Resources
Board of directors: Mary E. Junck, Chair.; Richard R. Cole; Nancy S. Donovan; Leonard J. Elmore; Brent Magid; William E. Mayer; Herbert W. Moloney III; Andrew E. Newman; Gregory P. Schermer; Mark B. Vittert
Subsidiaries: Journal-Star Printing Co., Lincoln, NE; Pulitzer Inc., St. Louis, MO
Joint Venture: Madison Newspapers, Inc., Madison, WI
Giving statement: Giving through the Lee Enterprises, Incorporated Corporate Giving Program and the Lee Foundation.
Company EIN: 420823980

Lee Enterprises, Incorporated Corporate Giving Program

201 N. Harrison St.
Davenport, IA 52801-1918

Purpose and activities: As a complement to its foundation, Lee Enterprises also makes charitable contributions to nonprofit organizations directly. Support is given primarily in areas of company operations.
Fields of interest: General charitable giving.
Type of support: Building/renovation; Capital campaigns; Employee volunteer services; General/operating support; In-kind gifts; Professorships.
Geographic limitations: Giving primarily in areas of company operations.
Application information: Applications accepted. Application form not required.
Initial approach: Proposal to nearest company newspaper

Lee Foundation

201 N. Harrison St., Ste. 600
Davenport, IA 52801-1918

Establishment information: Incorporated in 1962 in IA.
Donor: Lee Enterprises, Inc.
Contact: Carl G. Schmidt, Treas.
Financial data (yr. ended 09/30/11): Assets, $4,612,585 (M); expenditures, $411,877; qualifying distributions, $400,325; giving activities include $400,325 for grants.
Purpose and activities: The foundation supports organizations involved with arts and culture, education, and business and industry.
Fields of interest: Media, print publishing; Museums (art); Performing arts; Performing arts, music; Arts; Higher education; Education; YM/YWCAs & YM/YWHAs; Business/industry; United Ways and Federated Giving Programs.
Type of support: Building/renovation; Capital campaigns; Endowments.
Geographic limitations: Giving primarily in areas of company operations in CA, ID, IA, IL, IN, KY, MN, MT, ND, NE, NV, NY, OR, PA, SC, SD, WA, WI, and WY.
Support limitations: No grants to individuals.
Application information: Applications accepted. Application form not required. Applicants should submit the following:
1) detailed description of project and amount of funding requested
2) copy of IRS Determination Letter
Initial approach: Letter of inquiry to nearest company newspaper publisher
Copies of proposal: 5
Deadline(s): None
Final notification: Within 4 months
Officers and Directors:* Mary E. Junck*, Pres.; Carl G. Schmidt*, Secy.; Daniel K. Hayes; Gregory P. Schermer; Greg Veon.
Number of staff: 1 part-time support.
EIN: 426057173
Selected grants: The following grants are a representative sample of this grantmaker's funding activity:
$80,000 to DavenportOne, Davenport, IA, 2009.
$20,000 to Madison Community Foundation, Madison, WI, 2009.
$10,000 to Montana Meth Project, Missoula, MT, 2009.
$10,000 to Montana State University, Bozeman, MT, 2009.
$5,000 to Aspen Institute, Washington, DC, 2009.
$5,000 to Aspen Institute, Washington, DC, 2009.
$5,000 to College of Southern Idaho, Twin Falls, ID, 2009.
$5,000 to Georgetown University, Washington, DC, 2009.
$5,000 to Lower Columbia College, Longview, WA, 2009.
$3,500 to University of Iowa Foundation, Iowa City, IA, 2009.

2242
Lee Industries, Inc.

402 W. 25th St.
Newton, NC 28658-3755 (828) 464-8318

Company URL: http://www.leeindustries.com
Establishment information: Established in 1969.
Company type: Private company
Business activities: Manufactures furniture.
Business type (SIC): Furniture/household
Corporate officers: Bill G. Coley, C.E.O.; Norman Coley, Pres.; Bill McKinney, C.F.O.; Dottie Coley, V.P., Sales and Mktg.; Mark Seavers, Cont.
Giving statement: Giving through the Lee Industries Educational Foundation, Inc.

Lee Industries Educational Foundation, Inc.

402 W. 25th St.
Newton, NC 28658-3755 (828) 464-8318

Establishment information: Established in 1997.
Donor: Lee Industries, Inc.
Financial data (yr. ended 12/31/11): Assets, $96,906 (M); gifts received, $42,365; expenditures, $31,317; qualifying distributions, $31,150; giving activities include $10,000 for 3 grants (high: $4,000; low: $3,000) and $21,150 for 31 grants to individuals (high: $1,800; low: $300).
Purpose and activities: The foundation awards college scholarships to residents of Catawba and adjacent counties, North Carolina.
Fields of interest: Youth development; Human services.
Type of support: Scholarships—to individuals.
Geographic limitations: Giving limited to Catawba and adjacent counties, NC.
Application information: Applications not accepted. Unsolicited requests for funds not accepted.
Officers: Norman Coley, Pres.; William C. McKinney, Secy.-Treas.
EIN: 562046037

2243
R.W. Leet Electric, Inc.

3225 E. Kilgore Rd.
Kalamazoo, MI 49001-5511
(616) 381-9030

Establishment information: Established in 2010.
Company type: Private company
Business activities: Provides general contract electrical services.
Business type (SIC): Contractors/electrical work
Corporate officers: Franklin D. Russell, C.E.O.; Timothy Russell, Pres.

Giving statement: Giving through the R. W. Leet Electric Foundation.

R. W. Leet Electric Foundation

31 Airport Rd.
Natchez, MS 39120-8914 (601) 442-6629

Establishment information: Established in 1997 in MI.
Donor: R.W. Leet Electric, Inc.
Contact: Richard Leet, Pres.
Financial data (yr. ended 12/31/11): Assets, $846 (M); expenditures, $26,261; qualifying distributions, $26,250; giving activities include $26,250 for 6 grants (high: $7,560; low: $910).
Purpose and activities: The foundation supports hospitals and organizations involved with education and Catholicism.
Fields of interest: Secondary school/education; Education; Hospitals (general); Catholic agencies & churches.
International interests: Mexico.
Type of support: General/operating support.
Geographic limitations: Giving primarily in Natchez, MS and in Mexico.
Application information: Applications accepted. Application form required.
Initial approach: Contact foundation for application form
Deadline(s): Jan. 1 to Mar. 31
Officer: Richard Leet, Pres.
Director: John Gardise.
EIN: 383325851

2244
Al Paul Lefton Company, Inc.

100 S. Independence Mall W.
Philadelphia, PA 19106-2399
(215) 923-9600

Company URL: http://www.lefton.com
Establishment information: Established in 1928.
Company type: Private company
Business activities: Provides advertising services.
Business type (SIC): Advertising
Corporate officers: Al Paul Lefton, Jr., Pres. and C.E.O.; Raymond D. Scanlon, V.P and C.F.O.
Giving statement: Giving through the Al Paul Lefton Company Foundation.

Al Paul Lefton Company Foundation

100 Independence Mall W.
Philadelphia, PA 19106-1521 (215) 923-9600

Donor: Al Paul Lefton Co., Inc.
Contact: Al Paul Lefton, Jr., Tr.
Financial data (yr. ended 12/31/10): Assets, $1 (M); expenditures, $714; qualifying distributions, $600; giving activities include $600 for grants.
Purpose and activities: The foundation supports libraries and organizations involved with arts and culture and higher education.
Fields of interest: Visual arts; Museums (art); Historic preservation/historical societies; Arts; Higher education; Libraries (public); Cancer.
Type of support: Annual campaigns; General/operating support.
Geographic limitations: Giving primarily in Siasconset and Nantucket, MA and Philadelphia, PA.
Support limitations: No grants to individuals.
Application information: Applications accepted. Application form not required.
Initial approach: Letter of inquiry
Deadline(s): None
Trustee: Al Paul Lefton, Jr.
EIN: 236298693

2245
Legg Mason, Inc.

100 International Dr.
Baltimore, MD 21202-1099
(410) 539-0000
FAX: (410) 528-3999

Company URL: http://www.leggmason.com
Establishment information: Established in 1899.
Company type: Public company
Company ticker symbol and exchange: LM/NYSE
International Securities Identification Number: US5249011058
Business activities: Operates holding company; provides investment advisory services; provides securities brokerage services; operates investment bank.
Business type (SIC): Brokers and dealers/security; security and commodity services; holding company
Financial profile for 2013: Number of employees, 2,975; assets, $7,269,660,000; sales volume, $2,612,650,000; pre-tax net income, -$510,610,000; expenses, $3,047,150,000; liabilities, $2,451,310,000
Fortune 1000 ranking: 2012—777th in revenues, 550th in profits, and 440th in assets
Corporate officers: W. Allen Reed, Chair.; Joseph A. Sullivan, Pres. and C.E.O.; Peter H. Nachtwey, C.F.O.; Jennifer Murphy, C.A.O.; Thomas P. Lemke, Genl. Counsel and Corp. Secy.
Board of directors: W. Allen Reed, Chair.; Harold L. Adams; Robert E. Angelica; Dennis R. Beresford; John T. Cahill; Barry W. Huff; Dennis M. Kass; John E. Koerner III; Cheryl Gordon Krongard; John V. Murphy; John H. Myers; Nelson Peltz; Margaret Milner Richardson; Kurt L. Schmoke; Nicholas J. St. George; Joseph A. Sullivan
Subsidiary: Western Asset Management Company, Pasadena, CA
International operations: Luxembourg
Giving statement: Giving through the Legg & Company Foundation, Inc. and the Legg Mason Charitable Foundation, Inc.
Company EIN: 521200960

Legg & Company Foundation, Inc.

2330 W. Joppa Rd., Ste. 107-A
Lutherville, MD 21093

Donors: Kenneth S. Battye†; Standish McCleary; Philip C. Rogers; Joseph W. Sener; Legg Mason, Inc.
Financial data (yr. ended 12/31/11): Assets, $33,526 (M); expenditures, $1,518; qualifying distributions, $600; giving activities include $600 for 4 grants (high: $250; low: $100).
Purpose and activities: The foundation supports organizations involved with performing arts, human services, and Christianity.
Fields of interest: Museums (art); Performing arts, orchestras; Higher education; Christian agencies & churches.
Type of support: General/operating support.
Geographic limitations: Giving limited to Baltimore, MD.
Support limitations: No grants to individuals.
Application information: Applications not accepted. Unsolicited requests for funds not accepted.
Officers: Charlotte B. Floyd, Secy.; Audrey B. Drossner, Treas.
Directors: R.S. Fisher; L.M. Greenebaum; C.R. Rahm.
EIN: 526054502

Legg Mason Charitable Foundation, Inc.

100 International Dr.
Baltimore, MD 21202-4673 (410) 454-4416
URL: http://www.leggmason.com/about/citizenship/overview.aspx

Donor: Legg Mason, Inc.
Contact: Kelly Spilman, Mgr., Corp. Citizenship
Financial data (yr. ended 03/31/12): Assets, $8,125,504 (M); gifts received, $1,504,000; expenditures, $1,409,197; qualifying distributions, $1,403,787; giving activities include $1,403,787 for grants.
Purpose and activities: The foundation supports organizations involved with arts and culture, the environment, health, human services, and community development. Special emphasis is directed toward programs designed to promote education.
Fields of interest: Arts education; Performing arts, orchestras; Arts; Higher education; Education; Environment, water resources; Environment; Health care, clinics/centers; Health care; Athletics/sports, baseball; Human services; Community/economic development; Foundations (community); United Ways and Federated Giving Programs.
Type of support: General/operating support; Program development.
Geographic limitations: Giving primarily in areas of company operations in Baltimore, MD.
Publications: Application guidelines.
Application information: Applications accepted. Application form not required.
Initial approach: Telephone
Deadline(s): None
Officers: Joseph A. Sullivan, Pres.; Charles J. Daley, Jr., V.P. and Co-Treas.; Peter H. Nachtwey, V.P. and Co-Treas.; Michael McCalister, V.P.; Thomas C. Merchant, Secy.
EIN: 311738146
Selected grants: The following grants are a representative sample of this grantmaker's funding activity:
$130,000 to Baltimore City Foundation, Baltimore, MD, 2009.
$120,000 to United Way of Central Maryland, Baltimore, MD, 2009.
$50,000 to Baltimore Symphony Orchestra, Baltimore, MD, 2009.
$25,000 to Baltimore School for the Arts, Baltimore, MD, 2009.
$25,000 to Living Classrooms Foundation, Baltimore, MD, 2009.
$10,000 to Big Brothers Big Sisters of Southwestern Connecticut, Bridgeport, CT, 2009.
$6,913 to Baltimore Curriculum Project, Baltimore, MD, 2009.
$6,000 to Business Volunteers Unlimited Maryland, Baltimore, MD, 2009.
$5,000 to Baltimore Community Foundation, Baltimore, MD, 2009.
$5,000 to Baltimore Festival of the Arts, Baltimore, MD, 2009.

2246
Leggett & Platt, Inc.

1 Leggett Rd.
P.O. Box 757
Carthage, MO 64836-9649 (417) 358-8131
FAX: (417) 358-8449

Company URL: http://www.leggett.com
Establishment information: Established in 1883.
Company type: Public company
Company ticker symbol and exchange: LEG/NYSE
Business activities: Manufactures and sells household furniture components and finished furniture and steel wire, rolled steel, aluminum, plastic, foam, and textile products.
Business type (SIC): Furniture/household; fixtures/office and store
Financial profile for 2012: Number of employees, 18,300; assets, $3,254,900,000; sales volume, $3,720,000,000; pre-tax net income, $304,400,000; expenses, $3,379,500,000; liabilities, $1,820,400,000
Fortune 1000 ranking: 2012—619th in revenues, 525th in profits, and 729th in assets
Corporate officers: Richard T. Fisher, Chair.; David S. Haffner, C.E.O.; Karl G. Glassman, Pres. and C.O.O.; Matthew C. Flanigan, Exec. V.P. and C.F.O.; John G. Moore, Sr. V.P. and Secy.; Scott S. Douglas, Sr. V.P. and Genl. Counsel; William S. Weil, V.P., C.A.O., and Corp. Cont.
Board of directors: Richard T. Fisher, Chair.; Robert E. Brunner; Ralph W. Clark; Robert Ted Enloe III; Matthew C. Flanigan; Karl G. Glassman; David S. Haffner; Joseph W. McClanathan; Judy C. Odom; Maurice E. Purnell, Jr.; Phoebe A. Wood
Subsidiaries: Buffalo Batt & Felt, L.L.C., Carthage, MO; Crest-Foam Corp., Edison, NJ; Dresher, Inc., Carthage, MO; Duro Metal Manufacturing, Inc., Dallas, TX; Flex-O-Lators, Inc., Carthage, MO; Fremont Wire Co., Fremont, IN; Gamber-Johnson, L.L.C., Stevens Point, WI; Hanes Companies, Inc., Winston Salem, NC; Hanes Companies, Inc., Winston-Salem, NC; Hanes Companies - New Jersey, L.L.C., Carlstadt, NJ; Hanes Companies Foundation, Salem, NC; Japenamelac Corp., Chelmsford, MA; L&P Financial Services Co., Lebanon, MO; L&P International Holdings Co., Carthage, MO; L&P Materials Manufacturing, Inc., Jacksonville, FL; L&P Transportation, L.L.C., Carthage, MO; Leaving Taos, Inc., Ontario, CA; Leggett & Platt International Service Corp., Carthage, MO; Leggett & Platt Office Components, L.L.C., High Point, NC; Malvern Property Holdings, L.L.C., Little Rock, AR; Metrock Steel & Wire Company, Inc., Montevallo, AL; MPI (A Leggett & Platt Company), Inc., Coldwater, MS; MPI, Inc., Houston, MS; Nagle Industries, Inc., White House, TN; Nestaway, L.L.C., Mc Kenzie, TN; Parthenon Metal Works, Inc., La Vergne, TN; Solon Specialty Wire Co., Cleveland, OH; Southwest Carpet Pad, Inc., Carson, CA; Sponge-Cushion, Inc., Morris, IL; Sterling Steel Company, L.L.C., Sterling, IL; Storage Products Group, L.L.C., Freeport, IL; Suncoast Lots 579, L.L.C., Carthage, MO; Vantage Industries, Inc., Atlanta, GA
Divisions: Foothills Manufacturing Co., Forest City, NC; Leggett & Platt Commercial Vehicle Products, Inc., Atlanta, GA
Plant: High Point, NC
Offices: Verona, MS; Clearfield, UT
International operations: Australia; Austria; Barbados; Belgium; Brazil; Canada; China; Croatia; Denmark; France; Germany; Greece; Hong Kong; Hungary; India; Italy; Japan; Luxembourg; Mauritius; Mexico; Netherlands; Russia; Singapore; South Africa; South Korea; Spain; Switzerland; United Kingdom; Uruguay
Giving statement: Giving through the Leggett & Platt, Incorporated Corporate Giving Program and the Leggett & Platt Scholarship Foundation.
Company EIN: 440324630

Leggett & Platt Scholarship Foundation

1 Leggett Rd.
Carthage, MO 64836-9649 (507) 931-0453

Establishment information: Established in 1996.
Donor: Leggett & Platt, Inc.
Financial data (yr. ended 12/31/11): Assets, $1,087,032 (M); gifts received, $68,501; expenditures, $157,327; qualifying distributions, $144,067; giving activities include $138,000 for 1 grant.
Purpose and activities: The foundation awards college scholarships to children of employees of Leggett & Platt and its subsidiaries. The program is administered by Scholarship America, Inc.
Fields of interest: Higher education.
Type of support: Employee-related scholarships.
Geographic limitations: Giving limited to the Carthage, MO, area.
Support limitations: No grants to individuals (except for employee-related scholarships).
Application information: Applications accepted. Application form required.
Initial approach: Contact Foundation for application form
Board meeting date(s): 4 times per year
Deadline(s): Contact Foundation for deadline
Officers: Tammy Trent, Pres.; Brian Davison, Secy.Treas.
Board Members: Travis Almandinger; Lance Beshore; Peter Connelly; Jim Walter; Kiley Williams.
EIN: 431752318

2247
Lego Systems, Inc.

555 Taylor Rd.
Enfield, CT 06082-2372 (860) 749-2291

Company URL: http://www.lego.com
Establishment information: Established in 1932.
Company type: Subsidiary of a foreign company
Business activities: Manufactures toys and games.
Business type (SIC): Games, toys, and sporting and athletic goods
Financial profile for 2009: Number of employees, 1,450
Corporate officers: Jorge Vig Knudstorp, C.E.O.; Stig Toftgaard, C.O.O.; Hal Yarbrough, C.I.O.
Board of director: Jorge Vig Knudstorp
Giving statement: Giving through the Lego Systems, Inc. Corporate Giving Program and the Lego Children's Fund, Inc.

Lego Systems, Inc. Corporate Giving Program

555 Taylor Rd.
P.O. Box 1138
Enfield, CT 06083-1138
FAX: (888) 329-5346; URL: http://aboutus.lego.com/en-us/sustainability/

Purpose and activities: As a complement to its foundation, Lego Systems also makes product donations directly to organizations.
Fields of interest: Education, early childhood education Children; Economically disadvantaged.
Type of support: Donated products.
Publications: Corporate report.

Lego Children's Fund, Inc.

555 Taylor Rd.
Enfield, CT 06082-2372 (860) 763-6670
E-mail: legochildrensfund@lego.com; Application address: c/o Grant Administrator, P.O. Box 916 Enfield, CT 06083-0916; URL: http://www.legochildrensfund.org/

Establishment information: Established in 2006 in CT.
Donor: Lego Systems, Inc.
Financial data (yr. ended 12/31/11): Assets, $4,455,069 (M); gifts received, $2,001,550; expenditures, $605,520; qualifying distributions, $605,470; giving activities include $605,470 for grants.
Purpose and activities: The foundation supports programs designed to help children develop their creativity and learning skills through constructive play. Special emphasis is directed toward programs designed to promote early childhood education and development that is directly related to creativity; and technology and communication projects that advance learning opportunities.
Fields of interest: Child development, education; Engineering/technology Children; Economically disadvantaged.
Type of support: Employee matching gifts; Employee volunteer services; Matching/challenge support; Program development.
Geographic limitations: Giving primarily in areas of company operations, with emphasis on CT and western MA.
Support limitations: No support for political or religious organizations. No grants to individuals, or for capital campaigns, direct humanitarian or disaster relief, debt retirement, ongoing operating costs, general or annual fundraising drives, institutional benefits, honorary functions, endowments, annual appeals, or similar appeals, overhead costs, operating budgets, staff salaries, capital projects including buildings, furniture, or renovation projects, deficit financing, operating budgets, efforts routinely supported by government agencies or the general public, or expansion or continuation funding of existing programs.
Publications: Application guidelines; Grants list.
Application information: Applications accepted. Preference is given to organizations and groups that support disadvantaged children and are supported by LEGO employee volunteers. Grants range from $500 to $5,000. Support is limited to 1 contribution per organization during any given year. Application form required. Applicants should submit the following:
1) copy of IRS Determination Letter
2) copy of most recent annual report/audited financial statement/990
3) listing of board of directors, trustees, officers and other key people and their affiliations
4) copy of current year's organizational budget and/or project budget
5) population served
6) how project's results will be evaluated or measured

Initial approach: Complete online eligibility quiz and application
Board meeting date(s): Quarterly
Deadline(s): Dec. 28, Mar. 28, July 12, and Sept. 28 for eligibility quiz; Jan. 15, Apr. 15, July 29, and Oct. 15 for application
Final notification: Mar., June, Sept., and Dec.
Officers and Directors:* Soren Torp Laursen*, Pres. and Treas.; Brian Specht*, V.P.; Peter Arakas; Michael McNally; Mary Sutton.
EIN: 205960904

Selected grants: The following grants are a representative sample of this grantmaker's funding activity:
$5,800 to Creative Spirit Center, Midland, MI, 2010.
$5,011 to Jefferson City Public Schools Foundation, Jefferson City, MO, 2010.
$5,000 to Abilis, Greenwich, CT, 2010.
$5,000 to BayKids, San Francisco, CA, 2010.
$5,000 to Camp Courant, Hartford, CT, 2010.
$5,000 to Center for Women and Families, Louisville, KY, 2010.
$5,000 to Connecticut River Museum, Essex, CT, 2010.
$5,000 to Friends of the Future, Kamuela, HI, 2010.
$4,984 to Brooklyn Free School, Brooklyn, NY, 2010.
$4,000 to Science City at Union Station, Kansas City, MO, 2010.

2248
Leibowitz Photography, Inc.

5482 Wilshire Blvd., Ste. 1510
Los Angeles, CA 90036-4218
(323) 933-1013

Company URL: http://www.leibowitzpictures.com
Establishment information: Established in 2003.
Company type: Private company
Business type (SIC): Business services/ miscellaneous
Financial profile for 2011: Number of employees, 3
Corporate officer: Mark Leibowitz, Owner
Giving statement: Giving through the Leibowitz Photography, Inc. Contributions Program.

Leibowitz Photography, Inc. Contributions Program

5482 Wilshire Blvd., Ste. 1510
Los Angeles, CA 90036-4218 (323) 933-1013
E-mail: mark@leibowitzpictures.com; URL: http://www.leibowitzpictures.com

Purpose and activities: Leibowitz Photography is a certified B Corporation that donates a percentage of net profits to charitable organizations.
Fields of interest: Environment; Human services; International development; International human rights.
Type of support: Continuing support; General/operating support.

2249
Lemieux Group LP

(also known as Pittsburgh Penguins)
1 Chatham Ctr., Ste. 400
Pittsburgh, PA 15219-3447 (412) 642-1300

Company URL: http://www.pittsburghpenguins.com
Establishment information: Established in 1967.
Company type: Private company
Business activities: Operates professional ice hockey club.
Business type (SIC): Commercial sports
Corporate officers: Mario Lemieux, Chair.; David Morehouse, Pres. and C.E.O.; Travis Williams, C.O.O.
Board of director: Mario Lemieux, Chair.
Giving statement: Giving through the Pittsburgh Penguins Corporate Giving Program.

Pittsburgh Penguins Corporate Giving Program

CONSOL Energy Ctr.
1001 Fifth Ave.
Pittsburgh, PA 15219-6201
URL: http://penguins.nhl.com/club/page.htm?id=57568

Purpose and activities: The Pittsburgh Penguins make charitable contributions of memorabilia to nonprofit organizations involved with education, health and wellness, and shelters. Special emphasis is directed towards programs designed to educate youth and support the underprivileged. Support is limited to the Pittsburgh, Pennsylvania tri-state area.
Fields of interest: Education; Public health; Youth development; Human services Economically disadvantaged.
Type of support: In-kind gifts.
Geographic limitations: Giving limited to the Pittsburgh, PA, tri-state area.
Publications: Application guidelines.
Application information: Applications accepted. Support is limited to one contribution per organization during any given year. Application form required. Applicants should submit the following:
1) name, address and phone number of organization
2) contact person
Applications should include the Tax ID Number of the organization; the organization's web site address; the name, date, site, expected attendance, and a description of the event; how many consecutive years the event has been held; the amount raised the previous year; and how the donation will be used.
Initial approach: Complete online eligibility quiz and application form
Deadline(s): 3 to 4 weeks prior to need
Final notification: 2 weeks

2250
Lennar Corporation

700 N.W. 107th Ave.
Miami, FL 33172-3139 (305) 559-4000
FAX: (302) 655-5049

Company URL: http://www.lennar.com
Establishment information: Established in 1954.
Company type: Public company
Company ticker symbol and exchange: LEN/NYSE
Business activities: Builds houses; provides mortgages; sells title insurance; provides Internet access services; provide cable television services.
Business type (SIC): Operative builders; cable and other pay television services; brokers and bankers/ mortgage; insurance/title
Financial profile for 2012: Number of employees, 4,062; assets, $10,362,210,000; sales volume, $4,104,710,000; pre-tax net income, $222,110,000; expenses, $38,825,590,000; liabilities, $6,947,440,000
Fortune 1000 ranking: 2012—573rd in revenues, 270th in profits, and 377th in assets
Corporate officers: Stuart A. Miller, C.E.O.; Rick Beckwitt, Pres.; John R. Nygard III, C.I.O.; Jonathan M. Jaffe, V.P. and C.O.O.; Bruce E. Gross, V.P. and C.F.O.; Diane J. Bessette, V.P. and Treas.; Mark Sustana, Secy. and Genl. Counsel; David Collins, Cont.
Board of directors: Irving Bolotin; Steven L. Gerard; Theron I. Gilliam, Jr.; Sherrill W. Hudson; R. Kirk Landon; Sidney Lapidus; Stuart A. Miller; Jeffrey Sonnenfeld
Subsidiaries: 360 Developers, L.L.C., Miami, FL; American Southwest Financial Group, L.L.C., Phoenix, AZ; Bay River Colony Development Limited, Houston, TX; BB Investment Holdings, L.L.C., Reno, NV; BCI Properties, L.L.C., Tacoma, WA; Blackstone CC, L.L.C., Aurora, CO; C & C Ranch, L.L.C., Mount Pleasant, TX; Camelot Ventures, L.L.C., Livonia, MI; Colonial Heritage, L.L.C., Miami, FL; Colony Escrow, Inc., Kirkland, WA; Concord at Cornerstone Lakes, L.L.C., Chicago, IL; Eagle Home Mortgage, L.L.C., Kirkland, WA; Eagle Home Mortgage of California, Inc., RENO, NV; Equity Home Mortgage, L.L.C., Portland, OR; F&R QVI Home Investments USA, L.L.C., Miami, FL; Fidelity Guaranty and Acceptance Corp., Miami, FL; Fortress Mortgage, Inc., Herndon, VA; Greystone Construction, Inc., Tempe, AZ; Greystone Homes, Inc., Tempe, AZ; Greystone Homes of Nevada, Inc., Mission Viejo, CA; Greystone Nevada, L.L.C., Las Vegas, NV; Homeward Development Corp., Clearwater, FL; HTC Golf Club, L.L.C., Thornton, CO; Lakelands at Easton, L.L.C., Waldorf, MD; Landmark Homes, Inc., Raleigh, NC; Legends Club, L.L.C., Prior Lake, MN; Len-Verandahs, L.L.P., Tampa, FL; Lennar Financial Services, L.L.C., Miami, FL; Lennar Homes of Arizona, Inc., Phoenix, AZ; Universal American Mortgage Co., L.L.C., Miami, FL
Division: U.S. Home Corp., Tucson, AZ
Plants: Phoenix, AZ; Fort Myers, Orlando, Sunrise, FL; Dallas, Houston, TX
Giving statement: Giving through the Lennar Foundation, Inc. and the Lennar Charitable Housing Foundation.
Company EIN: 954337490

The Lennar Foundation, Inc.

c/o Lennar Corp.
700 N.W. 107th Ave., Ste. 400
Miami, FL 33172-3139 (305) 229-6400
FAX: (305) 228-8383;
E-mail: marshall.ames@lennar.com; URL: http://www.lennar.com/about/community/foundation.aspx

Establishment information: Established in 1989 in FL.
Donor: Lennar Corp.
Contact: Marshall Ames, Pres.
Financial data (yr. ended 11/30/11): Assets, $39,610,718 (M); expenditures, $2,498,666; qualifying distributions, $1,523,034; giving activities include $1,523,034 for grants.
Purpose and activities: The foundation supports organizations involved with education, water resources, cancer, housing, disaster relief, children and youth, residential care, and homelessness. Special emphasis is directed toward programs designed to assist people who are less fortunate.
Fields of interest: Middle schools/education; Education; Environment, water resources; Cancer; Housing/shelter; Disasters, preparedness/ services; Children/youth, services; Residential/ custodial care; Homeless, human services; United Ways and Federated Giving Programs Economically disadvantaged.
Type of support: General/operating support.
Geographic limitations: Giving primarily in CA, Miami, FL, Las Vegas, NV, SC, and TX.
Support limitations: No grants to individuals.
Application information: Applications accepted. Application form not required. Applicants should submit the following:
1) copy of IRS Determination Letter
Initial approach: Proposal
Deadline(s): None
Officers and Directors:* Marshall Ames*, Pres.; Samantha Fels*, Secy.; Jim Carr; Ezra Katz;

Waynewright Malcolm; Stuart A. Miller; Allan J. Pekor; Shelley Rubin.
EIN: 650171539

Lennar Charitable Housing Foundation

25 Enterprise
Aliso Viejo, CA 92656-2601
FAX: (949) 349-0864; E-mail: lchf-info@lennar.com; Toll-free tel.: (866) 858-4673; URL: http://www.lchf.org

Establishment information: Established in 2002 in CA; supporting organization of Alternatives to Domestic Violence, Bakersfield Homeless Center, Casa de Amparo, Catholic Charities, The Coalition for Urban Renewal Excellence, Community Resource Center, East Bay Habitat for Humanity Inc., Families Forward, Habitat for Humanity of San Joaquin County Inc., Homeaid America Inc., Homeaid Inland Empire, Homeaid Sacramento, House of Ruth Inc., Human Options Inc., Interfaith Community Services, Mt. Diablo Habitat for Humanity, Operation Safehouse Inc., Orange County Rescue Mission Inc., Poverello House, Rancho Damacitas, South Bay Community Services, Sacramento Habitat for Humanity, and YWCA of San Diego County.
Financial data (yr. ended 12/31/11): Revenue, $346,235; assets, $2,642,852 (M); gifts received, $334,771; expenditures, $664,393; giving activities include $500,000 for grants.
Fields of interest: Housing/shelter, temporary shelter; Housing/shelter, homeless; Housing/shelter Homeless.
Geographic limitations: Giving limited to CA.
Publications: Financial statement.
Officers and Directors:* Jon Jaffe*, Pres.; Jeff Roos*, Secy.; Trudie Wilson, Asst. Secy.; Mike White*, C.F.O.; Lucy Dunn; Bob Gilmore; Scott Jackson; Michael Lennon; Jim LeSieur.
EIN: 912157016

2251
LensCrafters, Inc.

(doing business as Luxottica Retail North America, Inc.)
4000 Luxottica Pl.
Mason, OH 45040-8502 (513) 765-6000

Company URL: http://www.lenscrafters.com
Establishment information: Established in 1983.
Company type: Subsidiary of a foreign company
Business activities: Operates optical goods stores.
Business type (SIC): Retail stores/miscellaneous
Corporate officers: Pierson Dave, Pres.; Kerry Bradley, C.O.O.; Jack S. Dennis, C.F.O. and C.A.O.; Gar Gunter, C.I.O.
Giving statement: Giving through the Give the Gift of Sight Foundation.

Give the Gift of Sight Foundation

(formerly LensCrafters Foundation)
4000 Luxottica Pl.
Mason, OH 45040-8114 (513) 765-3123
FAX: (513) 492-6248;
E-mail: gos_info@luxotticaretail.com; E-mail for Susan Knobler: sknobler@luxotticaretail.com; additional tel.: (513) 765-6000; URL: http://www.givethegiftofsight.org

Establishment information: Established in 1993 in OH.
Donor: LensCrafters, Inc.
Contact: Greg Hare, Exec. Dir.
Financial data (yr. ended 12/31/11): Revenue, $10,341,510; assets, $12,845,039 (M); gifts received, $10,278,767; expenditures, $8,549,126.
Purpose and activities: The foundation sponsors missions in developing countries, where LensCrafters associates and doctors deliver eye exams and recycled glasses to the needy. The foundation also sponsors two vision vans that traverse across North America, delivering eye exams and new glasses to children.
Fields of interest: Optometry/vision screening; Eye diseases.
International interests: Developing countries.
Type of support: In-kind gifts.
Geographic limitations: Giving on a national and international basis.
Support limitations: No cash grants.
Application information:
Board meeting date(s): Quarterly
Officers and Directors:* Frank Baynham*, Chair.; Jeanine McHugh*, Secy.; Brian Haigis*, Treas.; Greg Hare*, Exec. Dir.; Jacqueline Culp; Mark Jacquot; Wallace W. Lovejoy; Robin Wilson; and 4 additioanl directors.
EIN: 311385607

2252
Leonard, Street & Deinard PC

150 S. 5th St., Ste. 2300
Minneapolis, MN 55402-4223
(612) 335-1954

Company URL: http://www.leonard.com
Establishment information: Established in 1922.
Company type: Private company
Business activities: Operates law firm.
Business type (SIC): Legal services
Offices: Washington, DC; Mankato, Minneapolis, St. Cloud, MN; Bismarck, ND
Giving statement: Giving through the Leonard, Street & Deinard PC Pro Bono Program.

Leonard, Street & Deinard PC Pro Bono Program

150 S. 5th St., Ste. 2300
Minneapolis, MN 55402-4223 (612) 335-1954
E-mail: theresa.hughes@leonard.com; Additional tel.: (612) 335-1500; URL: http://www.leonard.com/pro-bono

Contact: Theresa Hughes, Pro Bono Dir.
Fields of interest: Legal services.
Type of support: Pro bono services - legal.
Geographic limitations: Giving primarily in areas of company operations in Washington, DC, Mankato, Minneapolis, and St. Cloud, MN, and Bismarck, ND.
Application information: A Pro Bono Committee manages the pro bono program.

2253
Let Water Be Water, LLC

(doing business as WAT-AAH!)
133 W. 25th St., Ste. 9W
New York, NY 10001 (212) 627-2630

Company URL: http://www.wat-aah.com
Establishment information: Established in 2008.
Company type: Private company
Business activities: Operates bottled water company.
Business type (SIC): Nonstore retailers
Corporate officer: Rose Cameron, C.E.O.
Giving statement: Giving through the WAT-AAH! Corporate Giving Program.

WAT-AAH! Corporate Giving Program

133 W. 25th St., Ste. 9W
New York, NY 10001 (212) 627-2630
URL: http://www.wat-aah.com

Purpose and activities: WAT-AAH! makes charitable contributions to organizations on a case by case basis.
Fields of interest: Disasters, preparedness/services Children.
Type of support: Donated products.

2254
Levi, Ray & Shoup, Inc.

2401 W. Monroe St.
Springfield, IL 62704-1439 (217) 793-3800

Company URL: http://www.lrs.com
Establishment information: Established in 1979.
Company type: Private company
Business activities: Provides information technology solutions.
Business type (SIC): Computer services
Corporate officers: Richard H. Levi, Chair., Pres. and C.E.O.; A. Edward Hohenstein, Exec. V.P. and C.O.O.; A. E. Hohenstein, V.P. and C.F.O.
Board of director: Richard H. Levi, Chair.
Offices: Atlanta, GA; Bloomington, Peoria, IL; Indianapolis, IN; Kansas City, KS; St. Louis, MO
Giving statement: Giving through the Levi, Ray & Shoup Foundation.

Levi, Ray & Shoup Foundation

2401 W. Monroe St.
Springfield, IL 62704-1439

Establishment information: Established in 2001 in IL.
Donor: Levi, Ray & Shoup, Inc.
Financial data (yr. ended 07/31/11): Assets, $1 (M); gifts received, $1,000,000; expenditures, $514,993; qualifying distributions, $501,600; giving activities include $501,600 for grants.
Purpose and activities: The foundation supports health centers and camps and organizations involved with historic preservation, education, human services, and Christianity.
Fields of interest: Historic preservation/historical societies; Secondary school/education; Higher education; Education; Health care, clinics/centers; Recreation, camps; Salvation Army; Children/youth, services; Family services, domestic violence; Human services, gift distribution; Aging, centers/services; Human services; United Ways and Federated Giving Programs; Christian agencies & churches.
Type of support: Building/renovation; Equipment; General/operating support; Sponsorships.
Geographic limitations: Giving primarily in Springfield, IL.
Support limitations: No grants to individuals.
Application information: Applications not accepted. Contributes only to pre-selected organizations.
Trustees: Agnes E. Levi; Richard H. Levi; Ryan M. Levi; Lindsay M. Matthews.
EIN: 326007063
Selected grants: The following grants are a representative sample of this grantmaker's funding activity:

$51,500 to Eastern Illinois University Foundation, Charleston, IL, 2011.
$25,000 to Sparc, Springfield, IL, 2011.
$11,000 to Memorial Medical Center Foundation, Springfield, IL, 2011.
$11,000 to Springfield College in Illinois, Springfield, IL, 2011.
$10,000 to Lincoln Land Community College Foundation, Springfield, IL, 2011.
$1,000 to Central Illinois Foodbank, Springfield, IL, 2011.
$1,000 to Childrens Miracle Network, Springfield, IL, 2011.
$1,000 to Leukemia & Lymphoma Society, White Plains, NY, 2011.
$1,000 to Ricky King Foundation, Naples, FL, 2011.
$1,000 to Saint Johns Hospital, Springfield, IL, 2011.

2255
Leviton Manufacturing Company, Inc.

201 N. Service Rd.
Melville, NY 11747 (631) 812-6000

Company URL: http://www.leviton.com
Establishment information: Established in 1906.
Company type: Private company
Business activities: Manufactures electrical wiring devices and transistors.
Business type (SIC): Lighting and wiring equipment/electric; metal rolling and drawing/nonferrous; electric transmission and distribution equipment; electronic components and accessories
Corporate officers: Stephen B. Sokolow, Chair.; Donald J. Hendler, Pres. and C.E.O.; Daryoush Larizadeh, C.O.O.; William W. Marshall, Sr. V.P., Mktg. and Sales
Board of directors: Stephen B. Sokolov, Chair.; Ian Hendler
International operations: Canada; Mexico
Giving statement: Giving through the Leviton Foundation, Inc.—New York.

The Leviton Foundation, Inc.—New York

201 N. Service Rd.
Melville, NY 11747

Establishment information: Incorporated in 1952 in NY.
Donors: Leviton Manufacturing Co., Inc.; American Insulated Wire Corp.; Joel A. Shapiro; Alan R. Finkelstein.
Financial data (yr. ended 12/31/10): Assets, $254,387 (M); gifts received, $20,000; expenditures, $48,985; qualifying distributions, $48,985; giving activities include $48,750 for 7 grants (high: $20,000; low: $2,500).
Purpose and activities: The foundation supports organizations involved with health, human services, and Judaism.
Fields of interest: Education; Medical research; Human services.
Application information: Applications not accepted. Unsolicited requests for funds not accepted.
Officers: Donald Hendler, Pres.; Stephen Sokolow, V.P.; Mark Daybarian, Secy.; Shirley Leviton, Treas.
EIN: 116006368

2256
Lewis & Roca LLP

40 N. Central Ave., Ste. 1900
Phoenix, AZ 85004-4429 (602) 262-5311

Company URL: http://www.lrlaw.com
Company type: Private company
Business activities: Operates law firm.
Business type (SIC): Legal services
Offices: Phoenix, Tucson, AZ; Mountain View, CA; Las Vegas, Reno, NV; Albuquerque, NM
Giving statement: Giving through the Lewis & Roca LLP Pro Bono Program.

Lewis & Roca LLP Pro Bono Program

40 N. Central Ave., Ste. 1900
Phoenix, AZ 85004-4429 (702) 474-2638
E-mail: DWaite@LRLaw.com; Additional tel.: (602) 262-5311; URL: http://www.lrlaw.com/aboutus/xprGeneralContent2.aspx?xpST=AboutUsOverview

Contact: Dan R. Waite, Pro Bono Comm. Chair
Fields of interest: Legal services.
Type of support: Pro bono services - legal.
Application information: A Pro Bono Committee manages the pro bono program.

2257
Lexington Furniture Industries, Inc.

(also known as Lexington Home Brands)
(formerly Dixie Furniture Company)
1300 National Hwy.
Thomasville, NC 27360-2318
(336) 474-5300

Company URL: http://www.lexington.com
Establishment information: Established in 1901.
Company type: Private company
Business activities: Manufactures wood household furniture.
Business type (SIC): Furniture/household
Corporate officers: Philip D. Haney, Pres. and C.E.O.; Craig Spooner, C.F.O.; Robert A. Sitler, Jr., Sr. V.P., Opers.; Robert Stamper, Sr. V.P., Mktg.; Doug Hartzog, V.P., Sales
Giving statement: Giving through the Dixie Foundation, Inc.

Dixie Foundation, Inc.

1300 National Hwy.
Thomasville, NC 27360-2318 (336) 474-5300

Establishment information: Established in 1958.
Donor: Lexington Furniture Industries, Inc.
Financial data (yr. ended 09/30/12): Assets, $249 (M); gifts received, $18,200; expenditures, $18,226; qualifying distributions, $18,200; giving activities include $18,200 for 7 grants (high: $5,200; low: $1,000).
Purpose and activities: The foundation awards college scholarships to children of employees of Lexington Home Brands.
Fields of interest: Education.
Type of support: Employee-related scholarships.
Geographic limitations: Giving primarily in areas of company operations in NC.
Application information: Applications accepted. Application form required.
Initial approach: Proposal
Deadline(s): None
Officer: Craig Spooner, C.F.O.
EIN: 566042530

2258
Lexmark International, Inc.

(formerly Lexmark International Group, Inc.)
740 W. New Circle Rd.
Lexington, KY 40550 (859) 232-2000
FAX: (302) 655-5049

Company URL: http://www1.lexmark.com
Establishment information: Established in 1991.
Company type: Public company
Company ticker symbol and exchange: LXK/NYSE
International Securities Identification Number: US5297711070
Business activities: Develops, manufactures, and provides printing products and solutions; develops, manufactures, and markets office imaging products.
Business type (SIC): Computer and office equipment
Financial profile for 2011: Number of employees, 12,200; assets, $3,637,000,000; sales volume, $4,173,000,000; pre-tax net income, $413,600,000; expenses, $3,730,100,000; liabilities, $2,245,300,000
Fortune 1000 ranking: 2012—609th in revenues, 726th in profits, and 701st in assets
Corporate officers: Paul Rooke, Chair. and C.E.O.; John W. Gamble, Jr., Exec. V.P. and C.F.O.; Robert J. Patton, V.P., Genl. Counsel, and Secy.; Jeri L. Isbell, V.P., Human Resources
Board of directors: Paul Rooke, Chair.; Jared L. Cohon; J. Edward Coleman; W. Roy Dunbar; William R. Fields; Ralph E. Gomory; Stephen R. Hardis; Sandra L. Helton; Robert Holland, Jr.; Michael J. Maples; Jean-Paul L. Montupet; Kathi P. Seifert
Plant: Boulder, CO
International operations: Algeria; Australia; Austria; Belgium; Bosnia-Herzegovina; Brazil; Bulgaria; Canada; Chile; China; Croatia; Czech Republic; Egypt; France; Germany; Hungary; India; Ireland; Japan; Jersey; Malaysia; Mexico; Morocco and the Western Sahara; Netherlands; Peru; Philippines; Poland; Portugal; Romania; Serbia; Spain; Switzerland; United Arab Emirates; United Kingdom; Uruguay
Giving statement: Giving through the Lexmark International, Inc. Corporate Giving Program.
Company EIN: 061308215

Lexmark International, Inc. Corporate Giving Program

(formerly Lexmark International Group, Inc. Corporate Giving Program)
740 W. New Circle Rd.
Lexington, KY 40550-0001
E-mail: citizenship@lexmark.com; URL: http://www1.lexmark.com/en_US/about-us/corporate-responsibility/index.shtml
Scholarship contact: recruiting@lexmark.com

Contact: Juli Gaworski, Community Rels. Specialist
Financial data (yr. ended 12/31/11): Total giving, $1,750,000, including $1,750,000 for grants.
Purpose and activities: Lexmark makes charitable contributions to nonprofit organizations involved with education, with emphasis on science, technology, engineering, and mathematics; and on a case by case basis. Support is given on a national and international basis.
Fields of interest: Higher education; Teacher school/education; Education; Youth development, business; United Ways and Federated Giving

Programs; Mathematics; Engineering/technology; Science; General charitable giving Children/youth.

Program:

Volunteer of the Year Award: Lexmark International honors an employee for outstanding volunteer service to the community. The recipient is honored at an internal event and Lexmark donates $2,500 to an eligible nonprofit organization or school of the winner's choice.

Type of support: Donated equipment; Donated products; Employee volunteer services; Employee-related scholarships; General/operating support; In-kind gifts; Sponsorships; Use of facilities.

Geographic limitations: Giving on a national and international basis in areas of company operations, with emphasis on Boulder, CO, and Lexington, KY.

Support limitations: No support for political or religious organizations.

Publications: Corporate giving report; Informational brochure (including application guidelines); Program policy statement.

Application information: Applications accepted. The Corporate Citizenship Department handles giving. The company has a staff that only handles contributions. Application form not required. Applicants should submit the following:

1) copy of IRS Determination Letter
2) detailed description of project and amount of funding requested

Initial approach: E-mail proposal
Copies of proposal: 1
Final notification: 3 days

Administrators: Juli Gaworski, Community Rels. Specialist.

Number of staff: 1 full-time professional.

2259
Leyman Manufacturing Corporation

10900 Kenwood Rd.
Cincinnati, OH 45242-2814 (513) 891-6210

Company URL: http://www.leymanlift.com
Establishment information: Established in 1940.
Company type: Private company
Business activities: Manufactures hydraulic lift gates.
Business type (SIC): Machinery/construction, mining, and materials handling
Corporate officer: John McHenry, Pres.
Giving statement: Giving through the Leyman Foundation.

Leyman Foundation

10900 Kenwood Rd.
Cincinnati, OH 45242-2814

Donor: Leyman Manufacturing Corp.
Contact: Bill Margroum
Financial data (yr. ended 05/31/11): Assets, $419,952 (M); gifts received, $656; expenditures, $11,086; qualifying distributions, $6,100; giving activities include $6,000 for 6 grants (high: $1,500; low: $500).
Purpose and activities: The foundation supports hospitals and hospices and organizations involved with education.
Fields of interest: Education; Hospitals (general); Residential/custodial care, hospices.
Type of support: General/operating support.
Geographic limitations: Giving primarily in Cincinnati, OH.
Support limitations: No grants to individuals.
Application information: Applications accepted. Application form not required. Applicants should submit the following:

1) detailed description of project and amount of funding requested

Initial approach: Letter
Deadline(s): None

Trustees: Ray B. Leyman; Margaret L. McHenry.
EIN: 310568237

2260
LG&E and KU Energy, LLC

(formerly E.ON U.S. LLC)
220 W. Main St.
Louisville, KY 40202-1377 (502) 627-2000

Company URL: http://www.lge-ku.com/
Establishment information: Established in 1838.
Company type: Subsidiary of a public company
Business activities: Operates holding company; generates, transmits, and distributes electricity; transmits and distributes natural gas.
Business type (SIC): Combination utility services; holding company
Financial profile for 2009: Number of employees, 3,500
Corporate officers: Victor A. Staffieri, Chair., Pres., and C.E.O.; Kent Blake, C.F.O.; Eric Slavinsky, C.I.O.; Brad Rives, C.A.O.; Paula H. Pottinger, Sr. V.P., Human Resources; Gerald Reynolds, Genl. Counsel and Corp. Secy.; Daniel K. Arbough, Treas.; Valerie Scott, Cont.
Board of director: Victor A. Staffieri, Chair.
Giving statement: Giving through the LG&E and KU Energy LLC Corporate Giving Program and the LG&E and KU Foundation Inc.
Company EIN: 611174555

LG&E and KU Energy LLC Corporate Giving Program

(formerly E.ON U.S. LLC Corporate Giving Program)
c/o Corp. Responsibility and Community Affairs
220 W. Main St., 11th FL
Louisville, KY 40202-5301 (502) 627-3225
URL: http://www.lge-ku.com/community/default.asp

Purpose and activities: As a complement to its foundation, LG&E and KU also makes charitable contributions to nonprofit organizations directly. Support is given primarily in areas of company operations in Kentucky, Tennessee, and Virginia.
Fields of interest: Education; Environment; Civil/human rights, equal rights; Community/economic development Minorities; Economically disadvantaged.
Type of support: Employee volunteer services; General/operating support; Program development; Sponsorships.
Geographic limitations: Giving primarily in areas of company operations in KY, TN, and VA.
Application information: Applications accepted. Application form required. Applicants should submit the following:

1) how project will be sustained once grantmaker support is completed
2) name, address and phone number of organization
3) list of company employees involved with the organization
4) listing of board of directors, trustees, officers and other key people and their affiliations
5) detailed description of project and amount of funding requested
6) contact person
7) copy of current year's organizational budget and/or project budget
8) listing of additional sources and amount of support

Applications should include the Tax ID Number of the organization and the number of paid staff.

Initial approach: Download application form and mail to headquarters
Deadline(s): Nov. 28 to Dec. 21

LG&E and KU Foundation Inc.

(formerly E.ON U.S. Foundation Inc.)
220 W. Main St.
Louisville, KY 40202-1395 (502) 627-3337
FAX: (502) 627-3629; Application address: P.O. Box 32030, Louisville, KY 40232; URL: http://www.lge-ku.com/foundation/default.asp

Establishment information: Established in 1994 in KY.
Donors: LG&E Energy Corp.; LG&E Energy LLC; E.ON U.S. LLC.
Contact: Elaine Ashcraft, Grants Admin.
Financial data (yr. ended 12/31/11): Assets, $11,407,844 (M); expenditures, $718,344; qualifying distributions, $678,550; giving activities include $158,100 for 13 grants (high: $50,000; low: $25,000) and $520,450 for employee matching gifts.
Purpose and activities: The foundation supports programs designed to promote education, the environment, health, human services, and diversity.
Fields of interest: Arts, cultural/ethnic awareness; Arts; Education; Environment; Health care; Human services; Civil/human rights, equal rights; Civil rights, race/intergroup relations; United Ways and Federated Giving Programs; Science, formal/general education; Mathematics.

Programs:

Diversity: The foundation supports programs designed to promote diversity; and embrace and encourage the inclusion of diverse backgrounds, experiences, and perspectives.

Education: The foundation supports educational programs within public elementary, middle, and secondary schools and public and private post-secondary schools. Special emphasis is directed toward programs designed to promote math, science, and technology.

Environment: The foundation supports programs designed to promote environmental excellence and economic growth.

Health and Human Services: The foundation supports programs designed to better the health and welfare of society. Support is limited to the United Way.

LG&E and KU Foundation Scholarship Program: The foundation annually awards $1,500 college scholarships to high school seniors in Kentucky and Virginia who are children of employees of E.ON U.S. The program is administered by Scholarship America.

Type of support: Annual campaigns; Building/renovation; Employee matching gifts; Employee-related scholarships; General/operating support; Matching/challenge support; Program development; Scholarship funds.
Geographic limitations: Giving primarily in areas of company operations in KY.
Support limitations: No support for political, fraternal, labor, or religious organizations or United Way or Fund for the Arts agencies. No grants to individuals, or for pageants or travel expenses, capital campaigns, medical research or disease campaigns/walks, or athletic sponsorships.
Publications: Application guidelines; Program policy statement.

Application information: Applications accepted. Support is limited to 1 contribution per organization during any given year. Application form required.
Applicants should submit the following:
1) copy of IRS Determination Letter
2) listing of board of directors, trustees, officers and other key people and their affiliations
3) copy of current year's organizational budget and/ or project budget
Initial approach: Download application and mail to foundation
Copies of proposal: 1
Board meeting date(s): Annually
Deadline(s): Nov. 15
Officers and Directors:* Victor A. Staffieri*, Pres.; John R. McCall*, V.P. and Secy.; Laura M. Douglas, V.P.; S. Bradford Rives*, V.P.; Daniel K. Arbough, Treas.; Rudolph W. Keeling.
Number of staff: 1 full-time professional.
EIN: 611257368

2262
Liberty Bank

315 Main St.
Middletown, CT 06457-1359
(860) 638-2922
FAX: (860) 638-2969

Company URL: http://www.liberty-bank.com
Establishment information: Established in 1825.
Company type: Private company
Business activities: Operates full-service financial institution offering consumer and commercial banking, residential and commercial mortgages, insurance, and investment services.
Business type (SIC): Savings institutions
Financial profile for 2011: Assets, $3,382,983,000; liabilities, $2,908,445,000
Corporate officers: Mark R. Gingras, Chair.; Chandler J. Howard, Pres. and C.E.O.; Thomas J. Pastorello, Exec. V.P. and C.F.O.; Barry J. Abramowitz, Sr. V.P. and C.I.O.
Board of directors: Mark R. Gingras, Chair.; William T. Christopher; Jean M. D'Aquila; David Director; Winona S. Goings; Gary Gomola; Steve J. Gorss; Michael Helfgott; Chandler J. Howard; Lawrence D. McHugh; Timothy Ryan; Grace Sawyer-Jones; Richard W. Tomc
Subsidiary: Liberty Cash-A-Check Inc., Middletown, CT
Giving statement: Giving through the Liberty Bank Foundation, Inc.

Liberty Bank Foundation, Inc.

55 High St.
P.O. Box 1212
Middletown, CT 06457-1212 (860) 638-2961
E-mail: smurphy@liberty-bank.com; Tel. for Susan Murphy: (860) 638-2959; Additional contacts: Betty Sugerman Weintraub, Assoc. Dir. for Grantmaking and Community Initiatives, tel.: (860) 704-2181, e-mail: bweintraub@liberty-bank.com; Toral Maher, Grants Coord., e-mail: tmaher@liberty-bank.com; URL: https://www.liberty-bank.com/ your-community/liberty-foundation
Application e-mail: Toral Maher, Grants Coord., tmaher@liberty-bank.com

Establishment information: Established in 1997 in CT.
Donor: Liberty Bank.
Contact: Susan Murphy, V.P., Secy., and Exec. Dir.
Financial data (yr. ended 12/31/11): Assets, $8,815,570 (M); expenditures, $950,394; qualifying distributions, $863,865; giving activities include $564,464 for 75 grants (high: $72,424; low: $500).
Purpose and activities: The foundation supports preventative programs for children and families; affordable housing; building the capacity of nonprofits to address community needs; and basic human services for those most in need; and awards scholarships to high school seniors in areas of Liberty Bank operations.
Fields of interest: Education, early childhood education; Higher education; Higher education, college (community/junior); Adult/continuing education; Education, services; Education; Health care, infants; Public health; Health care; Employment, training; Employment; Food services; Food banks; Housing/shelter, development; Housing/shelter, temporary shelter; Housing/ shelter, home owners; Housing/shelter; Youth development, adult & child programs; Children/ youth, services; Children, day care; Family services; Family services, parent education; Family services, domestic violence; Human services, financial counseling; Homeless, human services; Human services; Community/economic development; United Ways and Federated Giving Programs; Engineering/technology; Utilities Economically disadvantaged.
Programs:
Academic Grant Program: The foundation awards grants of up to $2,000 to K-12 schools located in Liberty Bank service areas for remediation programs for students who are at risk of failing or performing poorly in school. Special emphasis is directed toward programs that can be replicated in other school systems; and programs that address systemic issues the school may be facing, including below average CMT scores or reading/math levels, the No Child Left Behind Act, and lack of females and minorities involved in math and science classes.
Adult Education Scholarships: The foundation annually awards $2,000 in scholarship funding to eight adult education agencies in Liberty's service area that offer an adult high school credit diploma program. Agencies select up to four students of low or moderate income to receive scholarship support. Participating agencies include Hamden Adult Education, Meriden Adult Education, Middletown Adult Education, New London Adult Education, Norwich Adult Education, Plainville Adult Education, Wallingford Adult Education, and Windham Adult Education.
Affordable Housing: The foundation supports programs designed to support families most affected by the current economic crisis. Special emphasis is directed toward development of low/ moderate-income housing with supportive services; public education and outreach to build support for affordable housing development; and foreclosure prevention and homeowner counseling programs.
Basic Human Needs in Hard Times: Through the "Good Neighbor Fund" the foundation supports programs that provide emergency services and address basic human needs. Special emphasis is directed toward food pantries and soup kitchens; emergency shelters for homeless individuals; programs designed to prevent homelessness and foster self-sufficiency; emergency assistance programs; and case management and informational services designed to help people gain access to safety net programs.
Building the Capacity of Nonprofits: The foundation awards grants to nonprofit organizations to address needs generated by the current economy; and assists in making organizations more effective, efficient, flexible, and productive. The foundation provides technical support, fosters collaboration, and serves as a convener.
Community College Scholarship Program: The foundation annually awards $5,000 in scholarship funds to four state-operated community colleges within Liberty Bank's market area. The program is designed to promote affordable ways to begin higher education and each college selects one or more students to receive scholarships. Middlesex, Quinebaug Valley, Three Rivers, and Gateway Community Colleges are current recipients of the program.
Donald B. Wilbur Scholarships: The foundation awards $1,000 college scholarships to high school seniors living in areas of Liberty operations who plan to pursue a career in engineering or technology-related field. Recipients are selected based on financial need, academic achievement, and extracurricular and community activities.
Liberty Bank Foundation Scholarship Program: The foundation annually awards college scholarships to high school seniors living in areas of Liberty Bank operations. The award consists of $2,000 for the first year, and $1,000 for the three years thereafter at an accredited college or university. Applicants are nominated by their guidance counselor, teacher, or administrator of a participating secondary school. Recipients are selected based on financial need, academic achievement, and extracurricular activities.
Liberty Bank/Rotary Club Thanksgiving Dinner Drive: The foundation annually matches contributions made by Rotary Clubs in 27 towns and funds collected at Liberty Bank offices to provide Thanksgiving dinners for local needy families.
Prevention for Children and Families: The foundation supports programs designed to prevent problems from occurring and becoming a crisis; strengthen children, families, and communities; and build capacity of people to address their own needs. Special emphasis is directed toward parenting skills training; maternal and infant health; early childhood education and services; after-school programs; mentoring and tutoring programs; adult basic education; job preparation and training; promoting social and emotional health, identity, self-esteem, positive character, basic life skills, and conflict resolution skills; and educating the public and policymakers on strengthening children and families.
Willard M. McRae Community Diversity Award: The foundation honors an individual who has made an outstanding contribution to the cause of promoting and celebrating diversity. Applicants must have exemplary involvement in one or more community organizations; extraordinary participation over an extended period of time in community activities that promote and celebrate diversity; demonstrated leadership in enhancing quality of life in their community; and significant impact on the building of positive relationships between people. Honorees receive $500 to be directed to the nonprofit organization of his or her choice.
Type of support: Building/renovation; Capital campaigns; Equipment; General/operating support; Management development/capacity building; Matching/challenge support; Program development; Scholarship funds; Scholarships—to individuals; Technical assistance.
Geographic limitations: Giving limited to areas of company operations in towns of Berlin, Cheshire, Clinton, Colchester, Cromwell, Deep River, Durham, East Haddam, East Hampton, East Lyme, Essex, Glastonbury, Groton, Haddam, Madison, Mansfield, Marlborough, Meriden, Middlefield, Montville, Mystic, North Haven, Norwich, Old Saybrook, Plainville, Portland, Stonington, Wallingford, Waterford, West Hartford, Wethersfield, and Windham, and Middlesex and New London counties, CT.

Support limitations: No support for political, religious, or fraternal organizations not of direct benefit to the entire community, or other grantmaking foundations. No grants to individuals (except for scholarships), or for multi-year capital campaigns, annual fund drives or campaigns (other than United Way), trips, tours, or conferences, sponsorships of events, scientific or medical research, single-disease research, deficit spending or debt liquidation, or endowments.
Publications: Application guidelines; Grants list; Program policy statement.
Application information: Applications accepted. Grants range from $2,000 to $5,000. Applications are not accepted via fax or e-mail. The Connecticut Council for Philanthropy Common Application Form is accepted. Support is limited to 1 contribution per organization during any given year. After three consecutive years of funding, an organization must refrain from re-applying until a waiting period of one calendar year has elapsed. Application form required. Applicants should submit the following:
1) results expected from proposed grant
2) qualifications of key personnel
3) population served
4) copy of IRS Determination Letter
5) brief history of organization and description of its mission
6) geographic area to be served
7) copy of most recent annual report/audited financial statement/990
8) listing of board of directors, trustees, officers and other key people and their affiliations
9) copy of current year's organizational budget and/ or project budget
10) listing of additional sources and amount of support

Applications for Liberty Bank Foundation Scholarships and the Donald B. Wilbur Scholarship should include transcripts; a complete Student Aid Report (SAR); a letter of recommendation; and a 500-1,000 word essay.
Initial approach: Telephone for preliminary discussion; download application form and mail for Academic Grant Program and Donald B. Wilbur Scholarships; download nomination form and mail for William M. McCrae Community Diversity Award; contact participating schools for nomination forms for Liberty Bank Foundation Scholarships
Copies of proposal: 1
Board meeting date(s): Mar., June, Sept., and Dec.
Deadline(s): Mar. 31, June 30, Sept. 30, and Dec. 31; Late Feb. for Academic Grant Program; Mar. 29 for Liberty Bank Foundation Scholarships; Early May for Donald B. Wilbur Scholarships; Aug. 20 for William M. McCrae Community Diversity Award
Final notification: Within 3 months; June 3 for Liberty Foundation Scholarships
Officers and Trustees:* Michael Helfgott*, Chair.; Chandler J. Howard*, Pres. and C.E.O.; Susan Murphy*, V.P, Secy., and Exec. Dir.; Kathleen Doucette, Treas.; Catalina Caban-Owen; Mark R. Gingras; Willard McRae; Mary G. Murphy; Wilfredo Nieves; Thomas J. Pastorello; Calvin K. Price; Richard W. Tomc.
Number of staff: 1 full-time professional; 1 part-time professional.
EIN: 061479957
Selected grants: The following grants are a representative sample of this grantmaker's funding activity:
$45,000 to United Way, Middlesex, Middletown, CT, 2010.
$25,000 to FRESH New London, New London, CT, 2010.
$20,000 to Backus Foundation, Norwich, CT, 2010.
$10,000 to Natchaug Hospital, Mansfield Center, CT, 2010.
$5,900 to Business Industry Foundation of Middlesex County, Middletown, CT, 2010.
$5,000 to Gateway Community College Foundation, New Haven, CT, 2010. For student scholarships.
$5,000 to Martin House, Norwich, CT, 2010. For general operating expenses.
$5,000 to New London Community Meal Center, New London, CT, 2010.
$5,000 to Norwich Community Care Team, Norwich, CT, 2010.
$3,500 to United Way of Meriden and Wallingford, Meriden, CT, 2010.

2263
Liberty Global, Inc.

12300 Liberty Blvd.
Englewood, CO 80112 (303) 220-6600
FAX: (303) 220-6601

Company URL: http://www.lgi.com/
Establishment information: Established in 2005.
Company type: Public company
Company ticker symbol and exchange: LBTYA/ NASDAQ
Business activities: Operates cable communications company.
Business type (SIC): Cable and other pay television services
Financial profile for 2012: Number of employees, 22,000; assets, $38,307,700,000; sales volume, $10,310,800,000; pre-tax net income, -$483,300,000; expenses, $8,491,000,000; liabilities, $36,097,700,000
Forbes 2000 ranking: 2012—910th in sales, 1498th in profits, and 596th in assets
Corporate officers: John C. Malone, Chair.; Michael T. Fries, Pres. and C.E.O.; Charles H.R. Bracken, Exec. V.P. and Co-C.F.O.; Bernard G. Dvorak, Exec. V.P. and Co-C.F.O.; Bryan H. Hall, Exec. V.P., Genl. Counsel, and Secy.; Rick Westerman, Sr. V.P., Corp. Comms.
Board of directors: John C. Malone, Chair.; John P. Cole, Jr.; Miranda Curtis; John W. Dick; Michael T. Fries; Richard R. Green; Paul A. Gould; David E. Rapley; Larry E. Romrell; J.C. Sparkman; J. David Wargo
International operations: Austria; Belgium; Chile; Czech Republic; Germany; Hungary; Ireland; Netherlands; Poland; Romania; Slovakia; Switzerland
Giving statement: Giving through the Chello Foundation (U.S.), Inc.
Company EIN: 202197030

The Chello Foundation (U.S.), Inc.

12300 Liberty Blvd.
Englewood, CO 80112-7009

Establishment information: Established in 2008.
Donor: John Malone.
Financial data (yr. ended 12/31/11): Assets, $247,494 (M); gifts received, $137,588; expenditures, $2,490; qualifying distributions, $0.
Application information: Applications not accepted. Unsolicited requests for funds not accepted.
Officer and Trustees:* Michelle Keist, Secy.; Amy M. Blair; Michael T. Fries.
EIN: 300521471

2264
Liberty Interactive Corporation

(formerly Liberty Media Corporation)
12300 Liberty Blvd.
Englewood, CO 80112 (720) 875-5300
FAX: (720) 875-5382

Company URL: http://www.libertyinteractive.com
Establishment information: Established in 1991.
Company type: Public company
Company ticker symbol and exchange: LINTA/ NASDAQ
Business activities: Operates electronic retailing, media, communications and entertainment company.
Business type (SIC): Cable and other pay television services
Financial profile for 2012: Number of employees, 22,000; assets, $15,115,000,000; sales volume, $10,018,000,000; pre-tax net income, $881,000,000; expenses, $8,894,000,000; liabilities, $8,104,000,000
Fortune 1000 ranking: 2012—270th in revenues, 138th in profits, and 209th in assets
Forbes 2000 ranking: 2012—925th in sales, 407th in profits, and 823rd in assets
Corporate officers: John C. Malone, Chair.; Gregory B. Maffei, Pres. and C.E.O.; Christopher W. Shean, Sr. V.P. and C.F.O.; Richard N. Baer, Sr. V.P. and Genl. Counsel
Board of directors: John C. Malone, Chair.; Michael A. George; Malcolm Lan Grant Gilchrist; Gregory B. Maffei; Evan D. Malone; David E. Rapley; M. LaVoy Robison; Larry E. Romrell; Andrea L. Wong
Giving statement: Giving through the Libertygives Foundation.
Company EIN: 841288730

Libertygives Foundation

12300 Liberty Blvd.
Englewood, CO 80112-7009 (720) 875-5400
E-mail: LibertyGives@libertymedia.com; URL: http://www.libertymedia.com/liberty-gives.aspx

Establishment information: Established in 2007 in CO.
Donor: Liberty Media Corporation.
Financial data (yr. ended 12/31/11): Assets, $0 (M); gifts received, $537,314; expenditures, $566,730; qualifying distributions, $561,277; giving activities include $561,277 for grants.
Purpose and activities: The foundation supports programs designed to serve underprivileged and at-risk youth, with a focus on proactive and preventative services.
Fields of interest: Higher education; Education; Girls clubs; Boys & girls clubs; Big Brothers/Big Sisters; Children/youth, services; Family services; Human services Youth; Economically disadvantaged.
Type of support: General/operating support; Program development.
Geographic limitations: Giving primarily in CO.
Publications: Application guidelines.
Application information: Applications accepted. Grants range from $1,000 to $150,000. Application form required.
Initial approach: Complete online application
Deadline(s): Varies
Officers and Directors:* Gregory B. Maffei*, Pres.; Charles Y. Tanabe*, Secy.; Christopher W. Shean*, Treas.
EIN: 208004437
Selected grants: The following grants are a representative sample of this grantmaker's funding activity:

$50,000 to Teach for America, New York, NY, 2010. For general purposes.
$10,000 to Adoption Exchange, Aurora, CO, 2010. For general purposes.
$2,500 to Mercy Housing, Denver, CO, 2010. For general purposes.
$2,425 to Parent Project Muscular Dystrophy, Middletown, OH, 2010. For general purposes.
$2,000 to Adoption Exchange, Aurora, CO, 2010. For general purposes.
$1,500 to Indiana University Foundation, Bloomington, IN, 2010. For general purposes.
$1,500 to University of Illinois Foundation, Urbana, IL, 2010. For general purposes.
$1,000 to University of Oklahoma Foundation, Norman, OK, 2010. For general purposes.

2265
Liberty Mutual Insurance Company

(also known as Liberty Mutual Group)
175 Berkeley St.
Boston, MA 02116-5066 (617) 357-9500

Company URL: http://www.libertymutual.com
Establishment information: Established in 1912.
Company type: Subsidiary of a mutual company
Business activities: Sells fire and casualty insurance.
Business type (SIC): Insurance/fire, marine, and casualty
Financial profile for 2011: Number of employees, 45,000; assets, $112,350,000,000; sales volume, $33,193,000,000
Corporate officers: Edmund F. Kelly, Chair.; David H. Long, Pres. and C.E.O.; A. Alexander Fontanes, Exec. V.P. and C.I.O.; Dennis J. Langwell, Sr. V.P. and C.F.O.; James M. McGlennon, Sr. V.P. and C.I.O.; Christopher C. Mansfield, Sr. V.P. and Genl. Counsel; Paul G. Alexander, Sr. V.P., Comms.; Helen E.R. Sayles, Sr. V.P., Human Resources, and Admin.; Dexter R. Legg, V.P. and Secy.; Laurance H.S. Yahia, V.P. and Treas.; John D. Doyle, V.P. and Compt.
Board of directors: Edmund F. Kelly, Chair.; Michael J. Babcock; Charles I. Clough, Jr.; Gary L. Countryman; Nicholas M. Donofrio; Francis A. Doyle III; John P. Hamill; Marian L. Heard; David H. Long; John P. Manning; Thomas J. May; Stephen F. Page; Ellen A. Rudnick; Martin P. Slark; William C. Van Faasen; Annette M. Verschuren
Subsidiaries: Employers Insurance Company of Wausau, Wausau, WI; The Netherlands Insurance Company, Keene, NH; Peerless Insurance, Co., Keene, NH; Safeco Insurance Company of America, Seattle, WA
Offices: Phoenix, AZ; Pleasanton, CA; Wilmington, DE; Tampa, FL; Atlanta, GA; Itasca, IL; Weston, MA; Dover, Portsmouth, NH; New York, NY; Berwyn, Pittsburgh, PA; Irving, TX
International operations: Canada
Giving statement: Giving through the Liberty Mutual Group Corporate Giving Program, the Liberty Mutual Foundation, Inc., and the Liberty Mutual Scholarship Foundation.

Liberty Mutual Group Corporate Giving Program

175 Berkeley St.
Boston, MA 02116-5066 (617) 357-9500
URL: http://www.libertymutualgroup.com/omapps/ContentServer?pagename=LMGroup/Views/LMG&ft=3&fid=1138356728819&ln=en

Purpose and activities: As a complement to its foundation, Liberty Mutual also makes charitable contributions to nonprofit organizations directly. Support is given primarily in areas of company operations.
Fields of interest: Education; Disasters, preparedness/services; Youth development; Children, services Economically disadvantaged.
Programs:
Employee Matching Gifts: Liberty matches contributions made by its employees to nonprofit organizations on a one-for-two basis.
Liberty Mutual Responsible Scholars: The company awards scholarships to five undergraduate students who initiate a service or volunteer program that impacts or engages their campus community. Students must be current freshmen, sophomore, or juniors attending a full time, undergraduate four-year degree program at an accredited college or university in the U.S. Applicant must have a cumulative GPA of 3.0 or better on a 4.0 scale. In addition to awarding scholarships, Liberty Mutual hosts a trip to Boston where the students meet with Liberty Mutual executives, learn about career opportunities, and tour the city.
Type of support: Employee matching gifts; General/operating support; In-kind gifts; Scholarships—to individuals; Sponsorships.
Geographic limitations: Giving primarily in areas of company operations.
Application information:
Initial approach: Complete online application form for Liberty Mutual Responsible Scholars program
Deadline(s): Visit website for deadlines for Liberty Mutual Responsible Scholars program

The Liberty Mutual Foundation, Inc.

175 Berkeley St.
Boston, MA 02116-5066
E-mail: foundation@LibertyMutual.com; URL: http://www.libertymutualfoundation.org

Establishment information: Established in 2003 in MA.
Donor: Liberty Mutual Insurance Co.
Financial data (yr. ended 12/31/11): Assets, $23,617,914 (M); gifts received, $8,500,000; expenditures, $8,665,043; qualifying distributions, $8,500,500; giving activities include $5,035,675 for 217 grants (high: $250,000; low: $1,000) and $3,464,325 for 4,830 employee matching gifts.
Purpose and activities: The foundation supports organizations involved with arts and culture, education, health, human services, community development, and civic affairs. Special emphasis is directed toward programs designed to serve youth, low-income families and individuals, and people with disabilities.
Fields of interest: Museums; Performing arts, orchestras; Arts; Elementary/secondary education; Elementary school/education; Higher education; Education, services; Education; Health care; Food banks; Safety/disasters; Recreation, camps; Boys & girls clubs; Youth development, adult & child programs; American Red Cross; Salvation Army; Family services; Developmentally disabled, centers & services; Homeless, human services; Human services; Community/economic development; Assistive technology; Public affairs Youth; Disabilities, people with; Economically disadvantaged.
Programs:
Chairman's Community Service Award: The foundation honors up to three employees of Liberty Mutual who have made "significant and sustained volunteer contributions" to charitable organizations in their communities. The award includes a $10,000 grant to the nonprofit organization where he or she serves.
Disability Inclusion RFP: The foundation supports programs designed to expand opportunities for people of all abilities to learn, love, work, and play together. Special emphasis is directed toward programs designed to promote the participation of people with disabilities in all aspects of life.
Education: The foundation supports programs designed to encourage disadvantaged youth to excel academically and create opportunities for life-long success through learning.
Give with Liberty: The foundation matches contributions made by employees of Liberty Mutual to health and human service organizations, $0.50 on the dollar through online pledging and payroll deductions.
Health and Human Services: The foundation supports programs designed to improve quality of life in communities where Liberty Mutual operates.
Type of support: Capital campaigns; Continuing support; Curriculum development; Employee matching gifts; Employee volunteer services; General/operating support; Program development; Scholarship funds.
Geographic limitations: Giving primarily in areas of company operations in Boston, Lawrence, and Springfield, MA.
Support limitations: No support for grantmaking foundations, religious organizations not of direct benefit to the entire community, or fraternal, social, or political organizations. No grants to individuals, or for trips, tours, or transportation, debt reduction, conferences, forums, or special events.
Publications: Application guidelines.
Application information: Applications accepted. Support is limited to 1 contribution per organization during any given year. Application form required. Applicants should submit the following:
1) population served
2) geographic area to be served
3) copy of most recent annual report/audited financial statement/990
4) how project's results will be evaluated or measured
5) listing of board of directors, trustees, officers and other key people and their affiliations
6) detailed description of project and amount of funding requested
7) copy of current year's organizational budget and/or project budget
8) listing of additional sources and amount of support

Initial approach: Complete online application form
Board meeting date(s): Monthly
Deadline(s): None; Nov. 30 for Disability Inclusion RFP
Final notification: 6 to 8 weeks

Officers and Directors:* David H. Long*, Chair. and C.E.O.; Dexter R. Legg*, V.P. and Secy.; Dennis J. Langwell*, V.P., C.F.O., and Treas.; Christopher C. Mansfield*, V.P. and Genl. Counsel; A. Alexander Fontanes*, V.P. and C.I.O; Melissa M. Macdonnell, V.P.; Gary J. Ostrow, V.P.
EIN: 141893520
Selected grants: The following grants are a representative sample of this grantmaker's funding activity:
$250,000 to American Red Cross of Massachusetts Bay, Cambridge, MA, 2010. For program support.
$250,000 to Camp Harbor View Foundation, Boston, MA, 2010. For capital funding.
$200,000 to Fund for Catholic Schools, Braintree, MA, 2010. For program support.
$200,000 to Museum of Science, Boston, MA, 2010. For program support.

$125,000 to Boys and Girls Clubs of Boston, Boston, MA, 2010. For program support.
$100,000 to Boston Health Care for the Homeless Program, Boston, MA, 2010. For capital funding.
$15,000 to Friends of the Children - Boston, Jamaica Plain, MA, 2010. For program support.
$15,000 to MATCH School Foundation, Boston, MA, 2010. For program support.
$12,000 to Community Day Care of Lawrence, Lawrence, MA, 2010. For program support.

Liberty Mutual Scholarship Foundation

P.O. Box 55122
Boston, MA 02205-8670
FAX: (617) 574-5616

Establishment information: Established in 2001 in MA.
Donor: Liberty Mutual Insurance Co.
Financial data (yr. ended 12/31/11): Assets, $3,249,139 (M); expenditures, $181,111; qualifying distributions, $160,210; giving activities include $148,126 for 1 grant.
Purpose and activities: The foundation awards college scholarships to children of employees of Liberty Mutual Insurance Co. The program is administered by National Merit Scholarship Corporation.
Fields of interest: Higher education.
Type of support: Employee-related scholarships.
Geographic limitations: Giving limited to areas of company operations.
Application information: Applications not accepted. Contributes only through employee-related scholarships.
Trustee: Bank of America, N.A.
EIN: 043548586

2261
Li-Cor, Inc.

4647 Superior St.
Lincoln, NE 68504-1357 (402) 467-3576
FAX: (402) 467-2819

Company URL: http://www.licor.com
Establishment information: Established in 1971.
Company type: Private company
Business activities: Designs, manufactures, and markets laboratory systems.
Business type (SIC): Laboratory apparatus
Corporate officers: William W. Biggs, Chair., Pres., and C.E.O.; Craig A. Jessen, C.F.O.; Daniel Hile, Exec. V.P., Corp. Opers.; Greg Biggs, V.P., Opers.; Elaine K. Biggs, Secy.
Board of director: William E. Biggs, Chair.
Giving statement: Giving through the Biggs Family Foundation.

Biggs Family Foundation

6531 Teton Dr.
Lincoln, NE 68510-4123

Establishment information: Established in 2006 in NE.
Donors: William W. Biggs; Elaine K. Biggs; Li-Cor of Lincoln; Li-Cor, Inc.
Financial data (yr. ended 12/31/11): Assets, $127,786 (M); gifts received, $97,635; expenditures, $215,857; qualifying distributions, $215,000; giving activities include $215,000 for grants.
Purpose and activities: The foundation supports organizations involved with education, human services, and Christianity.
Fields of interest: Elementary/secondary education; Education; Salvation Army; Homeless, human services; Human services; Christian agencies & churches.
Type of support: General/operating support.
Geographic limitations: Giving primarily in Lincoln, NE; some funding nationally.
Support limitations: No grants to individuals.
Application information: Applications not accepted. Contributes only to pre-selected organizations.
Officers: William W. Biggs, Pres.; Elaine K. Biggs, Secy.-Treas.
EIN: 205186196
Selected grants: The following grants are a representative sample of this grantmaker's funding activity:
$30,000 to City Impact, Lincoln, NE, 2011.
$12,000 to Life Action Ministries, Buchanan, MI, 2011.
$10,000 to Peoples City Mission, Lincoln, NE, 2011.
$3,000 to Grace University, Omaha, NE, 2011.
$3,000 to Interface Ministries, Atlanta, GA, 2011.
$2,000 to Samaritans Purse, Boone, NC, 2011.

2266
Lieberman Companies, Inc.

9549 Penn Ave. S.
Bloomington, MN 55431-2564
(952) 887-5299

Company URL: http://www.liebermancompanies.com
Establishment information: Established in 1907.
Company type: Private company
Business activities: Sells coin-operated amusement and vending machines wholesale.
Business type (SIC): Professional and commercial equipment—wholesale; durable goods—wholesale
Corporate officers: Stephen E. Lieberman, Chair.; Harold I. Lederman, Pres.
Board of director: Stephen E. Lieberman, Chair.
Giving statement: Giving through the Lieberman-Okinow Foundation.

The Lieberman-Okinow Foundation

9549 Penn Ave. S.
Minneapolis, MN 55431-2563

Establishment information: Incorporated in 1961 in MN.
Donors: Lieberman Music Co.; Carousel Snack Bars of Minnesota, Inc.; Melody Music City; Lieberman Cos., Inc.; Stephen E. Lieberman; Sheila Lieberman; Harold Okinow; Sandra Okinow; David Lieberman; Sara Lieberman.
Financial data (yr. ended 09/30/11): Assets, $2,830 (M); gifts received, $10,600; expenditures, $11,029; qualifying distributions, $10,950; giving activities include $10,950 for grants.
Purpose and activities: The foundation supports organizations involved with arts and culture, education, human services, and Judaism.
Fields of interest: Performing arts, theater; Performing arts, orchestras; Arts; Higher education; Education; Developmentally disabled, centers & services; Human services; United Ways and Federated Giving Programs; Jewish agencies & synagogues.
Type of support: General/operating support.
Geographic limitations: Giving primarily in MN.
Support limitations: No grants to individuals.
Application information: Applications not accepted. Unsolicited requests for funds not accepted.
Officers: Stephen E. Lieberman, Co-Pres.; Sheila Lieberman, Co-Pres.; David Lieberman, V.P.; Sara Lieberman, V.P.; Sandra Okinow*, Secy.; Daniel Lieberman*, Treas.
Trustee: Susan Lieberman.
EIN: 416036200

2267
Life Care Centers of America, Inc

3570 Keith St. N.W., Ste. 100
P.O. Box 3480
Cleveland, TN 37320-3480 (423) 472-9585

Company URL: http://www.lcca.com/
Establishment information: Established in 1976.
Company type: Private company
Business activities: Operates retirement communities, assisted living facilities, and nursing centers.
Business type (SIC): Real estate operators and lessors; nursing and personal care facilities
Financial profile for 2011: Number of employees, 38,000; sales volume, $2,650,000,000
Corporate officers: Forrest L. Preston, Chair.; Tony E. Oglesby, C.E.O.; Beecher Hunter, Pres.; Cathy Murray, C.O.O.
Board of director: Forrest L. Preston, Chair.
Giving statement: Giving through the Life Care Foundation for Education Research.

Life Care Foundation for Education Research

3570 Keith St., NW
Cleveland, TN 37312-4309 (423) 473-5854
Application address: P.O. Box 3480, Cleveland, TN 37320

Establishment information: Established in 1995.
Donors: Life Care Centers of America Inc.; Forrest L. Preston; Credit Suisse First Boston; Ethel Preston‡.
Contact: Jennie McClaren, Secy.
Financial data (yr. ended 12/31/11): Assets, $43,948 (M); expenditures, $720; qualifying distributions, $0.
Purpose and activities: The foundation supports organizations involved with financial aid for students studying long-term healthcare; and supports programs designed to improve the quality of life for the elderly.
Type of support: General/operating support; Scholarship funds.
Geographic limitations: Giving primarily in AZ, CO, FL, MA, and TX.
Support limitations: No grants to individuals.
Application information: Applications accepted. Application form not required. Applicants should submit the following:
1) copy of IRS Determination Letter
2) detailed description of project and amount of funding requested

Initial approach: Proposal
Deadline(s): None

Officers and Directors:* Beecher Hunter*, Chair.; Jennie McClaren*, Secy.; Steve Ziegler*, Treas.; Cathy Murray; Forrest L. Preston; Aaron Webb.
EIN: 621582584

2268
Life Technologies Corporation

(formerly Invitrogen Corporation)
5791 Van Allen Way
P.O. Box 6482
Carlsbad, CA 92008 (760) 603-7200
FAX: (302) 636-5454

Company URL: http://www.lifetechnologies.com/
Establishment information: Established in 1987.
Company type: Public company
Company ticker symbol and exchange: LIFE/NASDAQ
International Securities Identification Number: US53217V1098
Business activities: Develops, manufactures, and markets life sciences research and genetic engineering products.
Business type (SIC): Drugs
Financial profile for 2012: Number of employees, 10,000; assets, $8,638,070,000; sales volume, $3,798,510,000; pre-tax net income, $531,830,000; expenses, $3,133,270,000; liabilities, $3,985,380,000
Fortune 1000 ranking: 2012—607th in revenues, 369th in profits, and 435th in assets
Forbes 2000 ranking: 2012—1530th in sales, 1259th in profits, and 1573rd in assets
Corporate officers: Gregory T. Lucier, Chair. and C.E.O.; Mark P. Stevenson, Pres. and C.O.O.; David F. Hoffmeister, Sr. V.P. and C.F.O.; Joe Beery, Sr. V.P. and C.I.O.; Carol Cox, Sr. V.P., Corp. Comms.; Peter M. Leddy, Ph.D., Sr. V.P., Human Resources
Board of directors: Gregory T. Lucier, Chair.; George F. Adam, Jr.; Raymond V. Dittamore; Donald W. Grimm; Balakrishnan S. Iyer; Arnie Levine; Bradley Lorimier; Ronald A. Matricaria; Ora H. Pescovitz, M.D.; Per A. Peterson, Ph.D.; David C. U'Prichard, Ph.D.
Subsidiary: Applied Biosystems Inc., Norwalk, CT
International operations: Australia; Canada; Germany; Hong Kong; Israel; Japan; Netherlands; New Zealand; Singapore; Taiwan; United Kingdom
Historic mergers: Dexter Corporation (September 14, 2000)
Giving statement: Giving through the Life Technologies Corporation Contributions Program and the Life Technologies Charitable Foundation.
Company EIN: 330373077

Life Technologies Corporation Contributions Program

(formerly Invitrogen Corporation Contributions Program)
5781 Van Allen Way
Carlsbad, CA 92008-7313 (760) 746-7204
E-mail: Heather.Virdo@lifetech.com; URL: http://www.lifetechnologies.com/us/en/home/communities-social.html

Contact: Heather Virdo, Mgr., Community Rels. & Corp. Comms.
Purpose and activities: As a complement to its foundation, Life Technologies makes charitable contributions to nonprofit organizations directly. Support is given on a national and international basis.
Fields of interest: Education; Environment; Disasters, preparedness/services; Human services, gift distribution; Human services; Community/economic development; Science, formal/general education; Science.
Program:
Biotechnology Institute Genzyme-Life Technologies Biotech Educator Award: Life Technologies, in partnership with Genzyme Corporation, honors high school educators who are bringing technology into the classroom and encouraging fellow science teachers to do the same. The company awards $10,000 to the first place winner, $5,000 to the second place winner, and $2,500 to the third place winner. Finalists are chosen and nominated among teachers-leaders who participated in the Biotechnology Institute's National Biotechnology Teacher-Leader Program. The award program is administered by the Biotechnology Institute.
Type of support: Donated products; Employee volunteer services; Grants to individuals; Sponsorships.
Geographic limitations: Giving in areas of company operations on a national and international basis.
Publications: Corporate giving report.

Life Technologies Charitable Foundation

(formerly The Applera Charitable Foundation)
5791 Van Allen Way
Carlsbad, CA 92008-7321
E-mail: Heather.Virdo@lifetech.com

Establishment information: Established in 1999 in CT and DE.
Donors: PE Corp.; Applera Corp.; Life Technologies Inc.
Contact: Heather Vido, Pres. and Exec. Dir.
Financial data (yr. ended 06/30/12): Assets, $489,508 (M); gifts received, $90; expenditures, $114,753; qualifying distributions, $66,942; giving activities include $66,942 for 2 grants.
Purpose and activities: The foundation supports programs designed to advance science education and key scientific discoveries that use the application of biology to address societal needs. Special emphasis is directed toward programs designed to accelerate the adoption and understanding of genomics in healthcare; promote global exhibitions and science festivals; and advance life science education among educators and youth through K-12 initiatives.
Fields of interest: Museums (science/technology); Elementary/secondary education; Education; Health care; Biomedicine; Recreation, fairs/festivals; Science, public policy; Engineering/technology; Biology/life sciences; Science.
Type of support: Conferences/seminars; Continuing support; Curriculum development; Program development; Publication; Research; Sponsorships.
Geographic limitations: Giving primarily in areas of company operations, with emphasis on CA.
Support limitations: No support for political organizations, fraternal, labor, veterans', or religious organizations, or discriminatory organizations. No grants to individuals, or for political campaigns, fundraising, capital or building campaigns, legislative or lobbying efforts, endowments, contingency funds, memorials, general operating support, or debt reduction.
Application information: Applications not accepted. Unsolicited applications are currently not accepted.
Board meeting date(s): Quarterly
Officers and Directors: Gregory T. Lucier, C.E.O.; Mark P. Stevenson, C.O.O.; Heather Vido, Pres. and Exec. Dir.; Josephine Secondine, Secy.; Amanda Clardy, Treas.; Ben Hwang; Siddhartha Kadia; Janet Lambert.
EIN: 061553291

2269
Life Time Fitness, Inc.

2902 Corporate Pl.
Chanhassen, MN 55317 (952) 947-0000
FAX: (952) 947-9137

Company URL: http://investor.lifetimefitness.com
Establishment information: Established in 1992.
Company type: Public company
Company ticker symbol and exchange: LTM/NYSE
Business activities: Operates exercise and recreation centers.
Business type (SIC): Amusement and recreation services/miscellaneous
Financial profile for 2012: Number of employees, 21,700; assets, $2,072,170,000; sales volume, $1,126,950,000; pre-tax net income, $184,240,000; expenses, $918,720,000; liabilities, $999,260,000
Corporate officers: Bahram Akradi, Chair., Pres., and C.E.O.; Michael R. Robinson, Exec. V.P. and C.F.O.
Board of directors: Bahram Akradi, Chair.; Giles H. Bateman; Jack W. Eugster; Guy C. Jackson; John K. Lloyd; Martha A. Morfitt; John B. Richards; Joseph S. Vassalluzzo
Giving statement: Giving through the Life Time Fitness Foundation.
Company EIN: 411689746

Life Time Fitness Foundation

2902 Corporate Pl.
Chanhassen, MN 55317-4560 (952) 229-7226
FAX: (952) 947-0099;
E-mail: foundation@lifetimefitness.com;
URL: http://lifetimefitness.mylt.com/community/ltf-foundation

Establishment information: Established in 2005 in MN.
Financial data (yr. ended 12/31/11): Assets, $660,718 (M); gifts received, $562,031; expenditures, $67,189; qualifying distributions, $62,826; giving activities include $39,255 for 16 grants (high: $18,965; low: $1).
Purpose and activities: The foundation supports programs designed to improve children's nutrition through school lunch initiatives.
Fields of interest: Elementary school/education; Education; Health care, clinics/centers; Health care; Food services; Nutrition; Athletics/sports, school programs Children.
Type of support: General/operating support; Program development.
Geographic limitations: Giving limited to areas of company operations, with emphasis on Phoenix, AZ, Chicago, IL, Minneapolis and St. Paul, MN, and Dallas, TX.
Support limitations: No support for religious organizations, political or lobbying organizations, or for industry, trade or professional organizations. No grants to individuals, or for fundraising, endowments, or capital campaigns; generally no loans or investments.
Publications: Application guidelines.
Application information: Applications accepted. Application form required.
Initial approach: Download application form and e-mail or mail to foundation
Deadline(s): None
Officers and Directors:* Eric Buss, Chair and Pres.; Jason Thunstrom, Secy.; Michael Robinson, C.F.O and Treas.
EIN: 030533192
Selected grants: The following grants are a representative sample of this grantmaker's funding activity:

$2,000 to Mental Health America, Alexandria, VA, 2009.
$1,680 to Dream Foundation, Santa Barbara, CA, 2009.
$1,500 to Childrens Tumor Foundation, New York, NY, 2009.

2270
LifePoint Hospitals, Inc.

103 Powell Ct., Ste. 200
Brentwood, TN 37027 (615) 372-8500
FAX: (615) 372-8575

Company URL: http://www.lifepointhospitals.com
Establishment information: Established in 1997.
Company type: Public company
Company ticker symbol and exchange: LPNT/NASDAQ
Business activities: Operates hospitals.
Business type (SIC): Hospitals
Financial profile for 2012: Number of employees, 28,000; assets, $4,722,200,000; sales volume, $3,391,800,000; pre-tax net income, $244,100,000; expenses, $3,147,700,000; liabilities, $2,671,700,000
Fortune 1000 ranking: 2012—586th in revenues, 644th in profits, and 609th in assets
Corporate officers: William F. Carpenter III, Chair. and C.E.O.; David M. Dill, Pres. and C.O.O.; Jeffrey W. Sherman, Exec. V.P. and C.F.O.; John P. Bumpus, Exec. V.P. and C.A.O.
Board of directors: William F. Carpenter III, Chair.; Gregory T. Bier; Richard H. Evans; DeWitt Ezell, Jr.; Michael P. Haley; Marguerite W. Kondracke; John E. Maupin, Jr.; Owen G. Shell, Jr.
Subsidiaries: Lake Cumberland Regional Hospital, LLC, Somerset, KY; Livingston Regional Hospital, LLC, Livingston, TN; Riverton Memorial Hospital, LLC, Riverton, WY
Giving statement: Giving through the LifePoint Community Foundation.
Company EIN: 201538254

The LifePoint Community Foundation

103 Powell Ct., Ste. 200
Brentwood, TN 37027-5079
URL: http://www.lifepointhospitals.com/about-lifepoint/giving-back/

Establishment information: Established in 1999 in DE and TN.
Donors: LifePoint Hospitals, Inc.; Lifepoint Corporate Services Group; St. Jude Children's Research Hospital; Hillside Hospital.
Financial data (yr. ended 12/31/11): Assets, $410,551 (M); expenditures, $86,964; qualifying distributions, $86,964; giving activities include $86,964 for 10 grants (high: $25,000; low: $100).
Purpose and activities: The foundation supports community foundations and organizations involved with K-12 and higher education, health, genetic diseases, breast cancer, and human services.
Fields of interest: Elementary/secondary education; Higher education; Higher education, college (community/junior); Nursing school/education; Hospitals (general); Medical care, outpatient care; Health care, clinics/centers; Health care; Genetic diseases and disorders; Breast cancer; YM/YWCAs & YM/YWHAs; Homeless, human services; Human services; Foundations (community).
Type of support: Capital campaigns; Equipment; General/operating support; Program development; Scholarship funds.
Geographic limitations: Giving primarily in VA; giving also in FL, KS, KY, LA, TN, TX, and WY.
Support limitations: No grants to individuals.
Application information: Applications not accepted. Unsolicited requests for funds not accepted.
Officers: William F. Carpenter III, Pres. and C.E.O.; Christopher J. Monte, V.P.; Christy S. Green, Secy.; Michael S. Coggin, Treas.
EIN: 621794442
Selected grants: The following grants are a representative sample of this grantmaker's funding activity:
$3,000 to Tennessee Wesleyan College, Athens, TN, 2010.
$2,000 to Community Foundation of Southwest Kansas, Dodge City, KS, 2010.
$1,666 to Grambling State University, Grambling, LA, 2010.
$1,000 to Eastern Kentucky University, Richmond, KY, 2010.
$1,000 to Fort Morgan Community Hospital Association, Fort Morgan, CO, 2010.
$1,000 to Giles County Board of Education, Pulaski, TN, 2010.
$1,000 to Rockdale Cares, Conyers, GA, 2010.
$1,000 to United Way of Southern West Virginia, Beckley, WV, 2010.
$1,000 to United Way of the Bluegrass, Lexington, KY, 2010.
$1,000 to YMCA, Paris-Bourbon County, Paris, KY, 2010.

2271
LifeScan, Inc.

1000 Gibraltar Dr.
Milpitas, CA 95035-6301 (408) 263-9789
FAX: (408) 946-6070

Company URL: http://www.lifescan.com
Establishment information: Established in 1981.
Company type: Subsidiary of a public company
Business activities: Manufactures blood glucose monitoring systems.
Business type (SIC): Drugs
Financial profile for 2009: Number of employees, 1,500
Corporate officers: Eric Milledge, Chair.; Valerie Asbury, Pres.
Board of director: Eric Milledge, Chair.
International operations: Canada
Giving statement: Giving through the LifeScan, Inc. Corporate Giving Program.

LifeScan, Inc. Corporate Giving Program

1000 Gibraltar Dr.
Milpitas, CA 95035-6301
URL: http://www.lifescan.com/responsibility/giving

Purpose and activities: LifeScan makes charitable contributions to nonprofit organizations involved with diabetes and on a case by case basis. Special emphasis is directed toward programs designed to increase awareness of diabetes as a serious illness; educate people with diabetes and their families; and promote awareness that diabetes complications can be reduced with proper diabetes management. Support is given to national and international organizations.
Fields of interest: Health care, association; Health care, public policy; Health care, fund raising/fund distribution; Health care, formal/general education; Public health; Health care, insurance; Diabetes; Diabetes research; Recreation, camps; General charitable giving.
Programs:
Legislative Advocacy: LifeScan supports programs designed to help pass laws that increase insurance coverage and medical rights for people with diabetes.
Professional Associations: LifeScan supports programs designed to educate health care professionals in diabetes-related fields in order to provide the highest quality of care for people with diabetes.
Type of support: Advocacy; Donated products; Employee volunteer services; General/operating support; Program development.
Geographic limitations: Giving to national and international organizations; giving also in Silicon Valley, CA.

2272
Lifeway Foods, Inc.

6431 W. Oakton St.
Morton Grove, IL 60053-2727
(847) 967-1010
FAX: (847) 967-6558

Company URL: http://lifeway.net
Establishment information: Established in 1986.
Company type: Public company
Company ticker symbol and exchange: LWAY/NASDAQ
Business activities: Manufactures dairy products.
Business type (SIC): Groceries—wholesale
Financial profile for 2012: Number of employees, 330; assets, $53,510,000; sales volume, $81,350,000; pre-tax net income, $8,820,000; expenses, $72,510,000; liabilities, $14,190,000
Corporate officers: Ludmila Smolyansky, Chair.; Julie Smolyansky, Pres. and C.E.O.; Edward P. Smolyansky, Cont. and C.F.O.
Board of directors: Ludmila Smolyansky, Chair.; Renzo Bernardi; Julie Oberweis; Julie Smolyansky; Pol Sikar; Gustavo Valle
Giving statement: Giving through the Lifeway Foods, Inc. Contributions Program.
Company EIN: 363442829

Lifeway Foods, Inc. Contributions Program

6431 West Oakton
Morton Grove, IL 60053-2727 (847) 967-1010
URL: http://www.lifeway.net/LifewayWorld/CorporateSocialResponsibility.aspx

2273
Lighting & Supplies, Inc.

744 Clinton St., Ste. 1
Brooklyn, NY 11231-2101 (718) 768-7000
FAX: (718) 768-0970

Company URL: http://www.sunshinelighting.com
Establishment information: Established in 1980.
Company type: Private company
Business activities: Supplies bulbs to the wholesale lighting industry.
Business type (SIC): Electrical goods—wholesale
Corporate officers: Morty Kohn, C.E.O.; Mordechai Kohn, Pres.
Giving statement: Giving through the Mordechai & Sarah Kohn Charitable Foundation Trust.

Mordechai & Sarah Kohn Charitable Foundation Trust

744 Clinton St.
Brooklyn, NY 11231-2101

Establishment information: Established in NY.
Donors: Mordechai Kohn; Lighting and Supplies, Inc.
Financial data (yr. ended 12/31/10): Assets, $5,422 (M); gifts received, $36,000; expenditures, $35,528; qualifying distributions, $35,528; giving activities include $35,528 for 3+ grants (high: $18,000).
Purpose and activities: The trust supports organizations involved with Judaism and other areas.
Fields of interest: Jewish agencies & synagogues; General charitable giving.
Type of support: General/operating support.
Geographic limitations: Giving primarily in Brooklyn, NY and Fort Lauderdale, FL.
Application information: Applications not accepted. Contributes only to pre-selected organizations.
Trustees: Mordechai Kohn; Sarah Kohn.
EIN: 306067293

2274
Eli Lilly and Company

Lilly Corp. Ctr.
Indianapolis, IN 46285 (317) 276-2000
FAX: (317) 276-3492

Company URL: http://www.lilly.com
Establishment information: Established in 1876.
Company type: Public company
Company ticker symbol and exchange: LLY/NYSE
International Securities Identification Number: US5324571083
Business activities: Discovers, develops, manufactures, and sells pharmaceutical products.
Business type (SIC): Drugs
Financial profile for 2012: Number of employees, 38,350; assets, $34,398,900,000; sales volume, $22,603,400,000; pre-tax net income, $5,408,200,000; expenses, $17,195,200,000; liabilities, $19,633,700,000
Fortune 1000 ranking: 2012—130th in revenues, 47th in profits, and 163rd in assets
Forbes 2000 ranking: 2012—416th in sales, 135th in profits, and 659th in assets
Corporate officers: John C. Lechleiter, Ph.D., Chair., Pres., and C.E.O.; Derica W. Rice, Exec. V.P. and C.F.O.; Michael J. Harrington, Sr. V.P. and Genl. Counsel; Bart Peterson, Sr. V.P., Comms.; Stephen F. Fry, Sr. V.P., Human Resources
Board of directors: John C. Lechleiter, Ph.D., Chair.; Ralph Alvarez; Katherine Baicker, Ph.D.; Winfried F. W. Bischoff; Michael L. Eskew; J. Erik Fyrwald; Alfred G. Gilman, M.D., Ph.D.; R. David Hoover; Karen N. Horn, Ph.D.; William G. Kaelin, M.D.; Ellen R. Marram; Douglas R. Oberhelman; Franklyn G. Prendergast, M.D., Ph.D.; Kathi P. Seifert
Plants: Clinton, Greenfield, Lafayette, IN
International operations: Australia; British Virgin Islands; Dominican Republic; Guatemala; Hong Kong; Mexico; Singapore; Spain; Switzerland; United Kingdom
Giving statement: Giving through the Eli Lilly and Company Contributions Program, the Eli Lilly and Company Foundation, and the Lilly Cares Foundation, Inc.
Company EIN: 923470950

Eli Lilly and Company Contributions Program

Lilly Corporate Ctr.
Indianapolis, IN 46285-0001 (877) 545-5946
E-mail: grantinfo@lillygrantoffice.com; Additional tel. for international applicants: (269) 226-2738; URL: http://www.lillygrantoffice.com/pages/index.aspx
Contact for Welcome Back Awards: WBA Committee, P.O. Box 536, New York, NY 10008-0536, tel.: (212) 884-0650, fax: (614) 839-7395; Contact for Journey Awards: Lilly Diabetes Journey Awards Admin., 1427 W. 86th St., No. 218, Indianapolis, IN 46260, tel.: (888) 545-5115; Contact for Lilly Oncology on Canvas: c/o TogoRun, 220 E. 42nd St., 12th Fl., New York, NY 10017, tel.: (866) 991-5662, e-mail: artdirector@mylooc.com; Contact for Reintegration Scholarships: Lilly Secretariat, PMB 327, 310 Busse Hwy., Park Ridge, IL 60068-3251, tel.: (800) 809-8202, e-mail: lillyscholarships@reintegration.com

Purpose and activities: As a complement to its foundation, Eli Lilly also makes charitable contributions to nonprofit organizations directly. Support is given on a national and international basis.
Fields of interest: Medical school/education; Education; Medicine/medical care, public education; Medical care, community health systems; Hospitals (general); Public health; Public health, communicable diseases; Health care, patient services; Health care; Mental health, disorders; Mental health, depression; Mental health, schizophrenia; Mental health/crisis services; Cancer; Heart & circulatory diseases; Nerve, muscle & bone diseases; Diabetes; Neuroscience; Health organizations; YM/YWCAs & YM/YWHAs; Human services; Mathematics; Science.
Programs:
Journey Awards: Through the Lilly Diabetes Journey Awards, Eli Lilly honors diabetes patients who have managed their disease with the help of insulin for 25, 50, or 75 years or more. Recipients receive an engraved bronze 25-year medal, silver 50-year medal, or gold 75-year medal.
Lilly Oncology on Canvas: Eli Lilly, in partnership with the National Coalition for Cancer Survivorship, sponsors a biennial art competition for people who have been affected by cancer. The competition is open to artwork that best portrays an inspiring cancer journey and narratives that illustrate the journey. Prizes consist of monetary awards of up to $10,000 donated directly to the cancer charity of the winners' choice.
Lilly Reintegration Awards: Lilly awards to grants to recognize outstanding achievement in the work of reintegration. Special emphasis is directed toward treatment teams, programs, and services that support people living with severe mental illness; local and national efforts to improve services and decrease the stigma of mental illness; and achievements of people living with severe mental illness who give hope to others facing similar challenges.
Lilly Reintegration Scholarship: Eli Lilly awards scholarships to individuals with bipolar disorder, schizophrenia and/or related schizophrenia-spectrum disorders to help them acquire educational or vocational skills to reintegrate into society. Educational opportunities include high school equivalency programs, trade or vocational schools, or associate, bachelor, or graduate degrees. Applicants must currently receive medical treatment and be actively involved in rehabilitative or reintegrative efforts.
Welcome Back Awards: Eli Lilly annually awards grants in recognition of outstanding achievements in the mental health community. The program is designed to fight the stigma associated with depression and to help the public understand depression is treatable. Winners share a total of $55,000 to be donated to the not-for-profit organizations of their choice. An independent panel of national mental health experts selects honorees in five categories: Lifetime Achievement (award level: $15,000); Destigmatization (award level: $10,000); Community Service (award level: $10,000); Primary Care (award level: $10,000); and Psychiatry (award level: $10,000). Each award recipient and one guest will receive complimentary airfare and accommodations to attend a ceremony in San Francisco in May.
Type of support: Conferences/seminars; Donated products; Employee volunteer services; Grants to individuals; In-kind gifts; Program development; Scholarships—to individuals; Sponsorships.
Geographic limitations: Giving on a national and international basis in areas of company operations, with emphasis on IN, Austria, Belgium, Czech Republic, Denmark, Estonia, France, Germany, Hungary, Ireland, Italy, Netherlands, Norway, Portugal, Spain, Sweden, Switzerland, and the United Kingdom.
Support limitations: No grants to individuals (except for awards and scholarships), or for clinical grants (including Investigator Initiated Trials), travel, capital campaigns or building funds, website development not associated with an accredited educational program, service contracts, religious programs, entertainment (including class reunions and retirement dinners), general operating expenses, textbooks or journal subscriptions, advertising, exhibit, or display fees, mass media productions not associated with educational content, or personal development (including leadership training).
Publications: Application guidelines; Grants list; Informational brochure.
Application information: Applications accepted. Multi-year funding is not automatic. The Lilly Grant Office handles domestic giving and the Lilly Research Laboratories Grant Office handles international giving. Application form required. Applicants should submit the following:
1) copy of IRS Determination Letter
2) detailed description of project and amount of funding requested
3) copy of current year's organizational budget and/or project budget
Nominations for Welcome Back Awards should include a biography, a one page personal statement, and examples of nominee's accomplishments.
Initial approach: Complete online application at the Lilly Grant Office website; download nomination form and mail for Welcome Back Awards; download application form and mail for Journey Awards; varies for scholarships
Deadline(s): Jan. to Nov. for the current calendar year; Oct. to Dec. for the next calendar year; Jan. 1 Welcome Back Awards; None for Journey Awards; Varies for scholarships
Final notification: 45 days; Spring for Welcome Back Awards

Eli Lilly and Company Foundation

(also known as Lilly Foundation)
Lilly Corporate Ctr., D.C. 1627
Indianapolis, IN 46285-0001 (317) 276-2000
FAX: (371) 277-6719; URL: http://www.lillyfoundation.org

Establishment information: Incorporated in 1968 in IN.
Donors: Eli Lilly and Co.; Edmund A Cyrol Trust.

Contact: Robert Lee Smith, Pres.
Financial data (yr. ended 12/31/11): Assets, $65,823,787 (M); expenditures, $27,618,655; qualifying distributions, $26,984,147; giving activities include $15,199,845 for 224 grants (high: $2,900,000; low: $250) and $11,784,302 for 2,021 employee matching gifts.
Purpose and activities: The foundation supports programs designed to improve the lives of people who lack the resources to obtain quality healthcare, with a focus on low and middle-income countries; and strengthen public education, with an emphasis on science and math education.
Fields of interest: Arts; Elementary/secondary education; Higher education; Public health; Public health, communicable diseases; Health care; Mental health, depression; Mental health, schizophrenia; Mental health/crisis services; Cancer; Nerve, muscle & bone diseases; Diabetes; Disasters, preparedness/services; Youth development; American Red Cross; Community/economic development; United Ways and Federated Giving Programs; Mathematics; Engineering/technology; Science; Public policy, research Economically disadvantaged.
Programs:
Employee Matching Gifts Program: The foundation matches contributions made by employees and retirees of Eli Lilly to nonprofit organizations involved with arts and culture, education, and health on a one-for-one basis; and to human service organizations through the United Way.
Lilly Global Giving Program: The foundation, in partnership with the GlobalGiving Foundation, matches contributions made by Lilly employees to grassroots programs around the world. The program gives each employee the opportunity to direct a $50 toward a project of his or her choosing.
Volunteer Recognition Program: The foundation awards $250 grants to nonprofit organizations with which employees of Eli Lilly volunteer.
Type of support: Annual campaigns; Capital campaigns; Continuing support; Curriculum development; Donated products; Employee matching gifts; Employee volunteer services; Equipment; General/operating support; Matching/challenge support; Scholarship funds.
Geographic limitations: Giving on a national and international basis, with emphasis on areas of company operations, including Indianapolis, IN.
Support limitations: No support for religious or sectarian organizations not of direct benefit to the entire community, fraternal, labor, athletic, or veterans' organizations, political organizations or candidates, legislative organizations, or discriminatory organizations. No grants to individuals, or for scholarships or travel, endowments or capital campaigns (exceptions made by invitation only), debt reduction, medical missions, beauty or talent contests, fundraising activities related to individual sponsorship, conferences or media production, or memorials; no loans.
Publications: Corporate giving report.
Application information: Applications not accepted. Unsolicited requests are currently not accepted. The foundation develops and initiates partnerships in specific areas of interest.
Board meeting date(s): 1st quarter and 3rd quarter
Officer and Directors:* Robert Lee Smith*, Pres.; Robert A. Armitage; Enrique A. Contero; Maria Crowe; Stephen F. Frye; John C. Lechleiter, Ph.D.; Jan Lundberg; Susan Mahony; Anne Nobles; Bart Peterson; Derica W. Rice; David A. Ricks; Jeffrey N. Simmons; Jacques Tapiero; Fionnuala Walsh.
Number of staff: 1 full-time professional; 3 full-time support.
EIN: 356202479
Selected grants: The following grants are a representative sample of this grantmaker's funding activity:
$4,371,721 to American Academy of Family Physicians Foundation, Leawood, KS, 2010. For Peers for Progress, global diabetes peer support program complementing collaborative efforts of primary care physicians, patients, and diabetes educators, emphasizing peer-to-peer interactions, mentoring, and role-modeling toward sustaining individual behavioral changes improving long-term diabetes - Cyrol Gift.
$2,900,000 to American Academy of Family Physicians Foundation, Leawood, KS, 2011. For Peers for Progress.
$1,500,000 to Indiana University Foundation, Bloomington, IN, 2010. To recruit top research talent for the School of Medicine.
$1,100,000 to Purdue Foundation, West Lafayette, IN, 2010. For I-STEM Resource Network/Indiana Science Initiative.
$1,000,000 to Brigham and Womens Hospital, Boston, MA, 2010. For Partners in Health.
$1,000,000 to Joslin Diabetes Center, Boston, MA, 2010. For research project, The Role of Adipose Tissue in Obesity and Diabetes.
$1,000,000 to Juvenile Diabetes Research Foundation International, New York, NY, 2010. For Innovative and Academic R and D Grants in Type 1 Diabetes Biomarkers.
$1,000,000 to Mind Trust, Indianapolis, IN, 2011. For Grow What Works Campaign.
$1,000,000 to YMCA of Greater Indianapolis, Indianapolis, IN, 2011. For North of South YMCA.
$725,000 to Partners HealthCare System, Boston, MA, 2011. For Partners in Health.
$300,000 to Childrens Museum of Indianapolis, Indianapolis, IN, 2010. For Global Perspectives Exhibit.
$250,000 to Life Sciences Foundation, San Francisco, CA, 2011. For general operating support.
$200,000 to National Academy of Sciences, Washington, DC, 2011. For Improving Access to Second-Line MDR-TB Medications.
$100,000 to Central Indiana Community Foundation, Indianapolis, IN, 2011. For CICF Summer Youth Program Fund.
$50,000 to Indiana University Foundation, Indianapolis, IN, 2011. For Transfer of Hope Walk for Indy's Super Cure.
$25,000 to Leukemia & Lymphoma Society, White Plains, NY, 2010. For Leukemia Ball.
$25,000 to Mercy Corps, Portland, OR, 2010. For Pakistan Flood Relief.
$25,000 to National Black MBA Association, Indianapolis, IN, 2010. For National Meeting.
$25,000 to National Black MBA Association, Indianapolis, IN, 2011. For National Meeting.

Lilly Cares Foundation, Inc.
c/o Eli Lilly and Co.
Lilly Corp. Ctr.
Indianapolis, IN 46285-0001 (800) 545-6962
Application address: P.O. Box 230999, Centerville, VA 20120, fax: (703) 310-2534; URL: http://www.lilly.com/Responsibility/patients/Pages/PatientAssistance.aspx

Establishment information: Established as a company-sponsored operating foundation in 1996 in IN.
Donor: Eli Lilly and Co.
Financial data (yr. ended 12/31/11): Assets, $0; gifts received, $504,948,121; expenditures, $504,948,121; qualifying distributions, $504,948,121; giving activities include $504,938,121 for grants to individuals.
Purpose and activities: The foundation distributes pharmaceuticals to ill and economically disadvantaged people - including infants - who are below the federal poverty level and who are not eligible for any third-party medication payment assistance.
Fields of interest: Economically disadvantaged.
Type of support: Donated products; Grants to individuals.
Geographic limitations: Giving on a national basis.
Publications: Application guidelines.
Application information: Applications accepted. Application form required.
Applications must be filled out by a doctor and should include proof of the applicant's income.
Initial approach: Telephone foundation for application form or download application form and fax or mail to application address
Deadline(s): None
Final notification: 4 weeks
Officers and Directors:* Steven Stapleton*, Chair. and Pres.; David Garza, V.P.; Bronwen Mantlo, Secy.; Thomas W. Grein, Treas.; Michael J. Harrington; Jack Harris; Terrence M. Lyons.
EIN: 352027985

2275
Lim, Ruger, And Kim LLP
1055 W. 7th St., Ste. 2800
Los Angeles, CA 90017-2554
(213) 955-9500

Company URL: http://www.lrklawyers.com/
Establishment information: Established in 1984.
Company type: Private company
Business activities: Provides legal services.
Business type (SIC): Legal services
Financial profile for 2010: Number of employees, 16
Corporate officer: Richard Ruger, Partner
Giving statement: Giving through the Lim Ruger Foundation.

Lim Ruger Foundation
(formerly LRK Foundation)
1055 W. 7th St., Ste. 2800
Los Angeles, CA 90017-2554
E-mail: info@limruger.com; URL: http://www.limruger.com/foundation.html

Establishment information: Established in 2006 in CA.
Donor: Lim, Ruger & Kim, LLP.
Financial data (yr. ended 06/30/12): Assets, $10,888 (M); gifts received, $1,000; expenditures, $28,180; qualifying distributions, $26,500; giving activities include $26,500 for 8 grants (high: $10,000; low: $2,000).
Fields of interest: Education; Civil/human rights.
Type of support: Scholarships—to individuals.
Geographic limitations: Giving primarily in CA and WA.
Application information: Applications not accepted. Unsolicited requests for funds not accepted.
Officers: John S.C. Lim, C.E.O.; Bryan King Sheldon, C.F.O.; Richard M. Ruger, Secy.
EIN: 870776905

2276
Lime Rock Springs Co.

(also known as Pepsi-Cola Bottling Company of Dubuque)
10537 Rte. 52 N.
Dubuque, IA 52001-8857 (563) 556-2921

Company URL: http://www.pepsidbq.com
Establishment information: Established in 1917.
Company type: Private company
Business activities: Sells carbonated and other beverages wholesale.
Business type (SIC): Groceries—wholesale
Corporate officers: James P. Gantz, Pres.; Rosemary Gantz, Secy.; Eric J. Gantz, Cont.
Giving statement: Giving through the Gantz Foundation Charitable Trust.

Gantz Foundation Charitable Trust

10537 Rte. 52 N.
Dubuque, IA 52001-6874

Establishment information: Established in 1992 in IA.
Donor: Lime Rock Springs Co.
Financial data (yr. ended 03/31/12): Assets, $238,690 (M); gifts received, $45,000; expenditures, $83,738; qualifying distributions, $81,305; giving activities include $81,305 for 16 grants (high: $20,000; low: $205).
Purpose and activities: The foundation supports organizations involved with performing arts, higher education, and athletics.
Fields of interest: Performing arts; Performing arts, opera; Higher education; Higher education, college (community/junior); Athletics/sports, Special Olympics.
Type of support: General/operating support.
Geographic limitations: Giving limited to Dubuque, IA.
Support limitations: No grants to individuals.
Application information: Applications not accepted. Contributes only to pre-selected organizations.
Trustees: Charles Gantz; James P. Gantz.
EIN: 426487703

2277
Limited Brands, Inc.

(formerly The Limited, Inc.)
3 Limited Pkwy.
P.O. Box 16000
Columbus, OH 43230-1600
(614) 415-7000

Company URL: http://www.limitedbrands.com
Establishment information: Established in 1963.
Company type: Public company
Company ticker symbol and exchange: LTD/NYSE
International Securities Identification Number: US5327161072
Business activities: Operates women's intimate apparel, personal care products, and women's and men's apparel stores; provides catalog shopping services; provides Internet shopping services.
Business type (SIC): Women's apparel stores; men's and boys' apparel and accessory stores; women's specialty and accessory stores; drug stores and proprietary stores; nonstore retailers
Financial profile for 2013: Number of employees, 99,400; assets, $6,019,000,000; sales volume, $10,459,000,000; pre-tax net income, $1,281,000,000; expenses, $8,886,000,000; liabilities, $7,034,000,000
Fortune 1000 ranking: 2012—258th in revenues, 253rd in profits, and 540th in assets
Corporate officers: Leslie H. Wexner, Chair. and C.E.O.; Charles C. McGuigan, C.O.O.; Stuart Burgdoerfer, Exec. V.P. and C.F.O.; Martyn R. Redgrave, Exec. V.P. and C.A.O.; Jane L. Ramsey, Exec. V.P., Human Resources
Board of directors: Leslie H. Wexner, Chair.; E. Gordon Gee; Dennis S. Hersch; Donna Anita James; David T. Kollat; William R. Loomis, Jr.; Jeffrey H. Miro; Michael G. Morris; Allan R. Tessler; Abigail S. Wexner; Raymond Zimmerman
Subsidiary: Intimate Brands, Inc., Columbus, OH
International operations: Canada; Cayman Islands; Hong Kong
Giving statement: Giving through the Limited Brands, Inc. Corporate Giving Program and the Limited Brands Foundation.
Company EIN: 311029810

Limited Brands, Inc. Corporate Giving Program

(formerly The Limited, Inc. Corporate Giving Program)
3 Limited Pkwy.
Columbus, OH 43230-1467 (614) 415-6400
FAX: (614) 415-7786;
E-mail: MakeADifference@LimitedBrands.com;
URL: http://www.limitedbrands.com/responsibility/community/community_overview.aspx

Purpose and activities: As a complement to its foundation, Limited Brands also makes charitable contributions to nonprofit organizations directly. Special emphasis is directed towards programs designed to address women and children's health, welfare, and education. Support is given primarily in areas of company operations in Rio Rancho, New Mexico, New York, New York, Columbus and Kettering, Ohio, and Montreal, Canada.
Fields of interest: Arts; Education; Health care; Cancer research; Children, services; Women, centers/services; United Ways and Federated Giving Programs.
International interests: Canada.
Type of support: Donated products; Employee volunteer services; General/operating support; In-kind gifts; Program development.
Geographic limitations: Giving primarily in areas of company operations in Rio Rancho, NM, New York, NY, Columbus and Kettering, OH, and Montreal, Canada; giving also to national organizations.
Support limitations: No support for fraternal, labor, social, or veterans' organizations, religious organizations not of direct benefit to the entire community, discriminatory organizations, individual K-12 schools (unless the Limited Brand has a business partnership with the school), organizations with overhead and fundraising expenses exceeding 20 percent of the total operating budget, or public service agencies. No grants to individuals, or for non-academic educational activities, staff positions for governmental agencies, fundraising events, athletes, teams, sporting events, or tournaments, fashion shows, beauty pageants, or contestants, publications, audio or video productions (although exceptions may be made if they serve as supporting materials to a project within Limited Brand's focus), or travel.
Publications: Application guidelines; Grants list.
Application information: Applications accepted. Telephone calls during the application process are not encouraged. Support is limited to 1 contribution per organization during any given year. Application form required.
Initial approach: Complete online application form
Committee meeting date(s): Dec. 30, Apr. 30, and Aug. 30 for grant requests
Deadline(s): Nov. 1, Mar. 1, and July 1 for grant requests; 1 month prior to need for product donations
Final notification: 30 days for grant requests

Limited Brands Foundation

(formerly The Limited, Inc./Intimate Brands, Inc. Foundation)
c/o The Columbus Fdn.
1234 E. Broad St.
Columbus, OH 43205-1453 (614) 251-4000
FAX: (614) 251-4009; URL: http://columbusfoundation.org/giving/foundations/limited-brands/

Establishment information: Established in 1993 in OH; supporting organization of the Columbus Foundation.
Contact: Tami Durrence
Financial data (yr. ended 12/31/11): Revenue, $150,882,323; assets, $140,215,925 (M); gifts received, $163,435,754; expenditures, $14,101,810; giving activities include $14,046,671 for grants.
Purpose and activities: The foundation supports organizations whose major purpose is empowering women, mentoring and nurturing children, and improving education.
Fields of interest: Arts; Higher education; Education; Crime/violence prevention, domestic violence; Crime/violence prevention, child abuse; Children/youth, services; Women, centers/services Women.
Program:
Grants: The foundation provides monetary and in-kind support to 501(c)(3) public charities that support its mission. Eligible applicants must: serve Limited Brands' home office communities (Columbus and Kettering, Ohio; New York City; Rio Rancho, New Mexico, and Montreal, Canada); have a Limited Brands associate involved as a board member, committee member, long-time volunteer, or active partner; exhibit strong fiscal management and board commitment; encourage and explore community partnerships and leverage additional support; and provide volunteer opportunities for possible involvement of Limited Brands associates.
Type of support: Building/renovation; Capital campaigns; General/operating support; In-kind gifts; Program development.
Geographic limitations: Giving primarily to Columbus and Kettering, OH; Rio Rancho, NM; New York City; and Montreal, Canada.
Support limitations: No support for organizations lacking 501(c)(3) status, fraternal, labor, social, or veterans' organizations, sports teams, churches or religious or sectarian organizations (unless engaged in a significant project benefiting the entire community), bands or choirs, individual K-12 schools, or public service agencies such as police and fire departments. No grants to individuals, or for travel, publications, audio or video productions, sporting events or tournaments, or non-academic educational activities such as proms, after-proms, graduations, etc.
Publications: Application guidelines.
Application information: Applications accepted. See foundation website to link to online submission tool. Application form required.
Initial approach: Complete an online contribution request at foundation website
Deadline(s): Mar. 1, July 1, and Nov. 1
Final notification: 30 to 90 days after application submission
Officers: Abigail Wexner*, Chair.; Mary Beth, Vice-Chair.; Jameson Crane*, Vice-Chair.; Nancy

Kramer, Vice-Chair.; Doug Williams*, Vice-Chair.; Alex Shumate*, Pres.; Timothy J. Faber, Secy.-Treas.
Number of staff: 1 full-time professional.
EIN: 311387703

2278
Lincoln Benefit Life Company
2940 S. 84th St.
Lincoln, NE 68506-4142 (402) 475-4061

Company URL: https://www.understandlifeinsurance.com
Establishment information: Established in 1938.
Company type: Subsidiary of a public company
Ultimate parent company: The Allstate Corporation
Business activities: Sells life insurance and annuities.
Business type (SIC): Insurance/life; security and commodity services
Corporate officer: Lawrence W. Dahl, Pres. and C.O.O.
Giving statement: Giving through the Lincoln Benefit Life Company Contributions Program.

Lincoln Benefit Life Company Contributions Program
2940 South 84th St.
Lincoln, NE 68506-4142
FAX: (402) 328-6125;
E-mail: teresa.ingram@allstate.com

Contact: Teresa Ingram, Mgr., Corp. Comms.
Financial data (yr. ended 12/31/12): Total giving, $225,000, including $225,000 for grants.
Purpose and activities: Lincoln Benefit Life makes charitable contributions to nonprofit organizations involved with tolerance, inclusion, and diversity, economic empowerment, and safe and vital communities. Support is given primarily in Nebraska.
Fields of interest: Safety, education; Family services, domestic violence; Human services, financial counseling; Civil/human rights, equal rights; Civil rights, race/intergroup relations; Community/economic development.
Type of support: Continuing support; General/operating support; Program development.
Geographic limitations: Giving primarily in NE, with emphasis on Lincoln.
Support limitations: No support for athletic teams, bands, or choirs, religious organizations not of direct benefit to the entire community, pass-through organizations, scouting groups, or private secondary schools. No grants to individuals, or for fundraising or sponsorships, capital campaigns or endowments, equipment (except as part of a community outreach program), athletic events, memorials, travel, or audio, film, or video production.
Publications: Application guidelines.
Application information: Applications accepted. Multi-year funding is not automatic. The Corporate Communications Department handles giving. A contributions committee reviews all requests. Application form not required. Applicants should submit the following:
1) timetable for implementation and evaluation of project
2) qualifications of key personnel
3) population served
4) name, address and phone number of organization
5) copy of IRS Determination Letter
6) brief history of organization and description of its mission
7) geographic area to be served
8) copy of most recent annual report/audited financial statement/990
9) explanation of why grantmaker is considered an appropriate donor for project
10) listing of board of directors, trustees, officers and other key people and their affiliations
11) detailed description of project and amount of funding requested
12) contact person
13) copy of current year's organizational budget and/or project budget
14) listing of additional sources and amount of support

Initial approach: Proposal to headquarters
Copies of proposal: 1
Committee meeting date(s): Monthly
Deadline(s): Sept. 1 for grants over $5,000
Final notification: 2 to 3 months

Administrators: Teresa Ingram, Mgr., Corp. Comms.; Barbara Raymond, V.P.
Number of staff: 2 full-time professional.
Selected grants: The following grants are a representative sample of this grantmaker's funding activity:
$14,000 to Junior Achievement of Lincoln, Lincoln, NE, 2012. For Morley JA Program and After-School Company Program.
$13,465 to Center for People in Need, Lincoln, NE, 2012. For warehouse coordinator salary and job training program support.
$12,000 to American Red Cross, Lincoln, NE, 2012. For basic aid training progam.
$10,000 to Boys and Girls Clubs of Lincoln/Lancaster County, Lincoln, NE, 2012. For program support.
$10,000 to Salvation Army of Lincoln, Lincoln, NE, 2012. To expand community center.
$10,000 to TeamMates Mentoring Program, Lincoln, NE, 2012. For mentoring program.
$10,000 to Updowntowners, Inc., Lincoln, NE, 2012. For 2012 Celebrate Lincoln International Festival.
$7,500 to Friendship Home of Lincoln, Lincoln, NE, 2012. For Safe Quarters fundraising and emergency shelter.
$5,000 to Nebraska Council on Economic Education, Lincoln, NE, 2012. To train Nebraska teachers on teaching economics to kids in grades K-12.
$5,000 to Voices of Hope, Lincoln, NE, 2012. For crisis and intervention services.

2279
The Lincoln Electric Company
22801 St. Clair Ave.
Cleveland, OH 44117-2524 (216) 481-8100

Company URL: http://www.lincolnelectric.com
Establishment information: Established in 1895.
Company type: Subsidiary of a public company
Business activities: Manufactures arc welding products and industrial electric motors.
Business type (SIC): Machinery/metalworking; electrical industrial apparatus
Corporate officers: John M. Stropki, Jr., Chair.; Christopher L. Mapes, Pres. and C.E.O.; Vincent K. Petrella, Sr. V.P., C.F.O., and Treas.; Frederick G. Stueber, Sr. V.P., Genl. Counsel, and Secy.; Gretchen A. Farrell, Sr. V.P., Human Resources; Gabriel Bruno, V.P. and C.I.O.; Doug Lance, V.P., Opers.
Board of director: John M. Stropki, Jr., Chair.
Subsidiary: Harris Calorific Co., Gainesville, GA
Giving statement: Giving through the James F. Lincoln Arc Welding Foundation and the Lincoln Electric Foundation.

James F. Lincoln Arc Welding Foundation
22801 St. Clair Ave.
Cleveland, OH 44117-1199 (216) 481-4300
Application address: P.O. Box 17188, Cleveland, OH 44117-9949; URL: http://www.jflf.org

Establishment information: Established around 1936 in OH as a company-sponsored operating foundation.
Donor: The Lincoln Electric Co.
Financial data (yr. ended 12/31/11): Assets, $727,881 (M); gifts received, $11,321; expenditures, $215,778; qualifying distributions, $132,864; giving activities include $82,914 for 5 grants (high: $30,593; low: $10,000).
Purpose and activities: The foundation awards cash and welding equipment for student reports of arc welded shop projects or problems involving the use of welding.
Fields of interest: Arts; Education.
Programs:
Ag Proficiency Award: The foundation, in collaboration with the National Future Farmers of America, awards one $1,000 grant to the individual who demonstrates outstanding achievement in agribusiness gained through the establishment of new business, working for an existing company, or other hands-on-career experience.
Arc Welding Awards: The foundation makes awards of cash and welding equipment to students at various educational levels for projects or papers relating to design or uses of arc welding. Division I awards are for high school students age 18 and under. Division II awards are for career students ages 19 and over. Division III awards are for Skills U.S.A. students competing in statewide or national contests. Division IV awards are for four year engineering students and their reports on design, engineering, or fabrication problems relating to any type of building, bridge, or other generally stationary structure. Division X awards are for international career students ages 17 and over. The foundation is also introducing a new division dedicated to Associate degree programs or an equivalent that wish to enter a welding or manufacturing paper.
Type of support: Equipment; Grants to individuals.
Geographic limitations: Giving on a national basis.
Publications: Application guidelines; Informational brochure (including application guidelines).
Application information: Applications accepted. Application form required.
Initial approach: Download application form
Deadline(s): June 30 for Division I and Division II awards; Sept. 30 for Division III awards; and June 30 for Division IV awards
Officers and Trustees:* David F. Manning*, Chair.; Roy L. Morrow, Pres.; Lori Hurley, Secy.; Carl Peters, Exec. Dir.; Duane K. Miller.
Board Member: Lou Mendoza.
EIN: 346553433

The Lincoln Electric Foundation
22801 St. Clair Ave.
Cleveland, OH 44117-2524 (216) 481-8100
Application address: Key Bank, 127 Public Sq., Cleveland, OH 44114, tel.: (216) 689-0416

Establishment information: Trust established in 1952 in OH.
Donor: The Lincoln Electric Co.
Contact: Agnes Marountas

Financial data (yr. ended 12/31/11): Assets, $3,072,074 (M); expenditures, $1,011,374; qualifying distributions, $1,002,500; giving activities include $1,002,500 for grants.
Purpose and activities: The foundation supports charter schools and hospitals and organizations involved with arts and culture, higher education, lung diseases, human services, the welding industry, and community development.
Fields of interest: Media, television; Arts; Charter schools; Higher education; Hospitals (general); Lung diseases; Human services; Business/industry; Community/economic development; United Ways and Federated Giving Programs.
Type of support: General/operating support; Program development; Scholarship funds.
Geographic limitations: Giving primarily in areas of company operations, with emphasis on Cleveland, OH.
Support limitations: No loans or program-related investments.
Application information: Applications accepted. Application form not required. Applicants should submit the following:
1) copy of most recent annual report/audited financial statement/990
2) detailed description of project and amount of funding requested

Initial approach: Proposal
Board meeting date(s): Nov.
Deadline(s): Sept. 20

Trustee: KeyBank N.A.
Number of staff: 1
EIN: 346518355
Selected grants: The following grants are a representative sample of this grantmaker's funding activity:
$45,000 to United Way of Lake County, Mentor, OH, 2010.
$40,000 to Mentor Public Schools, Mentor, OH, 2010.
$25,000 to Cleveland Clinic Foundation, Cleveland, OH, 2010.
$25,000 to Manufacturing Advocacy and Growth Network, Cleveland, OH, 2010.
$20,000 to Lake Hospital Foundation, Painesville, OH, 2010.
$15,000 to JumpStart, Cleveland, OH, 2010.
$12,500 to Cleveland Museum of Natural History, Cleveland, OH, 2010.
$10,000 to Hospice of the Western Reserve, Cleveland, OH, 2010.
$8,000 to Case Western Reserve University, Cleveland, OH, 2010.
$5,000 to Westside Industrial Retention and Expansion Network, Cleveland, OH, 2010.

2280
Lincoln Hockey LLC

(also known as Washington Capitals)
401 9th St. N.W., Ste. 750
Washington, DC 20004-2132
(202) 266-2200

Company URL: http://capitals.nhl.com/
Establishment information: Established in 1974.
Company type: Subsidiary of a private company
Business activities: Operates professional ice hockey club.
Business type (SIC): Commercial sports
Corporate officers: Ted Leonsis, Chair.; Dick Patrick, Co-Vice-Chair., Pres., and C.O.O.; Raul Fernandez, Co-Vice-Chair.; Sheila C. Johnson, Co-Vice-Chair.; Keith Burrows, Sr. V.P., Finance; Michelle Trostle, V.P., Admin.
Board of directors: Ted Leonsis, Chair.; Raul Fernandez, Co-Vice-Chair.; Sheila C. Johnson, Co-Vice-Chair.; Dick Patrick, Co-Vice-Chair.
Giving statement: Giving through the Washington Capitals Corporate Giving Program and the Washington Capitals Charities.

Washington Capitals Corporate Giving Program

c/o Community Rels.
627 N. Glebe Rd., Ste. 850
Arlington, VA 22203-2144
FAX: (202) 266-2330;
E-mail: ewodatch@washcaps.com; URL: http://capitals.nhl.com/club/page.htm?id=64917

Contact: Elizabeth Wodatch, Dir., Community Rels.
Purpose and activities: The Washington Capitals make charitable contributions of memorabilia to nonprofit organizations involved with education, youth hockey, and youth development. Support is limited to Washington, D.C., Maryland, and Virginia.
Fields of interest: Education; Athletics/sports, winter sports; Youth development; General charitable giving.
Type of support: In-kind gifts.
Geographic limitations: Giving limited to Washington, DC, MD, and VA.
Application information: Applications accepted. The Community Relations Department handles giving. Donation requests are not accepted via fax, e-mail, or telephone. Support is limited to 1 contribution per organization during any given year. Telephone calls are not encouraged. Application form required. Applicants should submit the following:
1) name, address and phone number of organization
2) listing of additional sources and amount of support
3) contact person

Applications should include the organization's Tax ID Number; the name, date, location, expected attendance, and a description of the event; and the type of fundraiser.

Initial approach: Complete online application form
Deadline(s): 6 weeks prior to need

Washington Capitals Charities

627 N. Glebe Rd., Ste. 850
Arlington, VA 22203-2144
E-mail: ewodatch@washcaps.com; URL: http://capitals.nhl.com/club/page.htm?id=42563

Establishment information: Established in 2000 in VA.
Financial data (yr. ended 12/31/11): Revenue, $732,614; assets, $950,881 (M); gifts received, $718,886; expenditures, $437,195; giving activities include $395,395 for grants.
Purpose and activities: The organization provides grants to charitable organizations and governmental entities providing educational or charitable services.
Fields of interest: Education; Cancer; Alzheimer's disease; Autism; Food banks; American Red Cross; Children, services.
Geographic limitations: Giving on a national basis.
Officers and Directors:* Theodore Leonsis*, Chair.; Richard Patrick*, Pres.; Keith Burrows*, Secy.-Treas.; Raul Fernandez; George Stamas.
EIN: 522215790

2281
Lincoln National Corporation

(doing business as Lincoln Financial Group)
(formerly The Lincoln National Life Insurance Company)
150 N. Radnor Chester Rd., Ste. A305
Radnor, PA 19087 (484) 583-1400

Company URL: https://www.lfg.com
Establishment information: Established in 1904.
Company type: Public company
Company ticker symbol and exchange: LNC/NYSE
Business activities: Diversified financial services company.
Business type (SIC): Insurance/life
Financial profile for 2012: Number of employees, 8,700; assets, $218,869,000,000; sales volume, $11,532,000,000; pre-tax net income, $1,568,000,000; expenses, $9,964,000,000; liabilities, $203,896,000,000
Fortune 1000 ranking: 2012—235th in revenues, 153rd in profits, and 26th in assets
Forbes 2000 ranking: 2012—837th in sales, 475th in profits, and 126th in assets
Corporate officers: William H. Cunningham, Ph.D., Chair.; Dennis R. Glass, Pres. and C.E.O.; Randal J. Freitag, C.F.O.; Ellen Cooper, C.I.O.; Adam G. Ciongoli, Genl. Counsel
Board of directors: William H. Cunningham, Ph.D., Chair.; William J. Avery; Dennis R. Glass; George W. Henderson III; Eric G. Johnson; Gary C. Kelly; M. Leanne Lachman; Michael F. Mee; William Porter Payne; Patrick S. Pittard; Isaiah Tidwell
Subsidiaries: Delaware Investment Management, Philadelphia, PA; HMG, Schaumburg, IL; Lincoln Life & Annuity Co. of New York, Syracuse, NY
Giving statement: Giving through the Lincoln Financial Group Corporate Giving Program and the Lincoln Financial Foundation.
Company EIN: 350472300

Lincoln Financial Group Corporate Giving Program

(formerly The Lincoln National Life Insurance Company Contributions Program)
1300 S. Clinton St., P.O. Box 7863
Fort Wayne, IN 46801-7863
FAX: (260) 455-4004; E-mail: patti.grimm@lfg.com

Contact: Patti Grimm, Prog. Admin.
Financial data (yr. ended 12/31/08): Total giving, $637,538.
Purpose and activities: As a complement to its foundation, Lincoln Financial also makes charitable contributions to nonprofit organizations directly. Support is given primarily in Hartford, Connecticut, Chicago, Illinois, Fort Wayne, Indiana, Omaha, Nebraska, Greensboro, North Carolina, Cincinnati, Ohio, and Philadelphia, Pennsylvania.
Fields of interest: Arts; Higher education; Education; Employment, training; Youth development; Human services.
Type of support: Donated equipment; General/operating support; Sponsorships.
Geographic limitations: Giving primarily in Hartford, CT, Chicago, IL, Fort Wayne, IN, Omaha, NE, Greensboro, NC, Cincinnati, OH, and Philadelphia, PA.
Support limitations: No support for public or private K-12 schools, hospitals, hospital foundations, hospital programs, nursing homes, veterans' posts or organizations, service organizations, fraternal organizations, religious causes, political causes, sporting events or tournaments. No grants to individuals.
Publications: Application guidelines.

Application information: Applications accepted. The company has a staff that only handles contributions. A contributions committee reviews all requests. Application form required.

Initial approach: Complete online application
Copies of proposal: 1
Committee meeting date(s): Varies
Deadline(s): Visit website for deadlines
Final notification: Following review

Administrators: Byron Champlin, Prog. Off., Hartford, CT and Concord, NH; Patti Grimm, Corp. Public Involvement Prog. Admin.; Sandi Kemmish, Dir., Fort Wayne, IN; Susan Segal, Prog. Off., Philadelphia, PA; Jean Vrabel, Prog. Off., Fort Wayne, IN.
Number of staff: 1 full-time professional; 5 part-time professional; 1 full-time support.

Lincoln Financial Foundation

(formerly Lincoln Financial Group Foundation)
1300 S. Clinton St.
P.O. Box 7863
Fort Wayne, IN 46801-7863
FAX: (260) 455-4004;
E-mail: sandi.kemmish@lfg.com; Additional contact: Jean Vrabel, Prog. Off., tel.: (260) 455-3868, e-mail: Jean.Vrabel@LFG.com; URL: http://www.lincolnfinancial.com/LincolnPageServer?LFGPage=/lfg/lfgclient/abt/fingrp/index.html

Establishment information: Established in 1962 in IN as a company-sponsored operating foundation.
Donors: Lincoln National Corp.; The Lincoln National Life Insurance Co.
Contact: Sandi Kemmish, Dir.
Financial data (yr. ended 12/31/11): Assets, $6,771,727 (M); gifts received, $9,415,100; expenditures, $9,709,635; qualifying distributions, $9,705,766; giving activities include $9,693,953 for 1,418 grants (high: $270,000; low: $500).
Purpose and activities: The foundation supports programs designed to promote arts and culture; education; human services; and workforce and economic development.
Fields of interest: Arts education; Performing arts, music; Arts; Elementary/secondary education; Education, early childhood education; Adult/continuing education; Adult education—literacy, basic skills & GED; Education, ESL programs; Education, services; Education, drop-out prevention; Education, reading; Education; Employment, training; Employment; Food services; Food banks; Independent housing for people with disabilities; Housing/shelter, temporary shelter; Housing/shelter; Family services, domestic violence; Human services, financial counseling; Homeless, human services; Independent living, disability; Human services; Economic development; Business/industry; United Ways and Federated Giving Programs; Leadership development Children; Aging; Disabilities, people with; Economically disadvantaged.
Programs:

Arts: The foundation supports programs designed to promote arts education and economic development through increased access to the arts and cultural activities for individuals of all ages, economic strata, varying abilities, and ethnicities.

Education: The foundation supports programs designed to promote life-long learning, financial literacy, and improved student achievement. Special emphasis is directed toward increasing high school graduation rates.

Human Services: The foundation supports programs designed to address basic needs and independent living for individuals with special needs. Special emphasis is directed toward basic needs for food, housing, and independent living.

Lincoln Matching Gift Program: The foundation matches contributions made by full-time employees, retirees, and financial planners of Lincoln Financial Group to institutions of higher education and nonprofit organizations.

LIVE: Through LIVE (Lincoln Invests in Volunteer Experience), the foundation awards $500 grants to nonprofit organizations with which employees of Lincoln Financial Group volunteer at least 50 hours.

Workforce and Economic Development: The foundation supports programs designed to enhance the workforce with the intent of economic development for the area. Special emphasis is directed toward adult education and job skills training.

Type of support: Building/renovation; Employee matching gifts; Employee volunteer services; Equipment; Matching/challenge support; Program development; Scholarship funds; Sponsorships.
Geographic limitations: Giving limited to areas of company operations, with emphasis on Hartford, CT, Fort Wayne, IN, Greensboro, NC, Omaha, NE, Concord, NH, and Philadelphia, PA.
Support limitations: No support for religious organizations, public or private elementary or secondary schools or school foundations, hospitals, hospital foundations, fraternal, political, veterans', or sports organizations. No grants to individuals, or for endowments, continuing support, general operating support, capital campaigns, debt reduction, marketing programs, sporting events or tournaments, fundraising for national organizations, or national walks; generally, no grants for tickets, corporate tables, or testimonial events.
Publications: Application guidelines; Grants list.
Application information: Applications accepted. Visit website for nearest application address. Support is limited to 1 contribution per organization during any given year. Application form required. Applicants should submit the following:
1) copy of IRS Determination Letter
2) copy of most recent annual report/audited financial statement/990
3) listing of board of directors, trustees, officers and other key people and their affiliations
4) copy of current year's organizational budget and/or project budget

Initial approach: Complete online application form for specified cities
Copies of proposal: 1
Board meeting date(s): Quarterly
Deadline(s): Mar. 14 for Education; June 20 for Human Services; and Sept. 19 for Workforce and Economic Development; Dec. 5 for Arts;
Final notification: 3 to 4 months

Officers and Directors:* Dennis R. Glass*, Pres.; Sharon M. Jeffers, Secy.; Anant Bhalla, Treas.; Lisa M. Buckingham; Frederick J. Crawford; Charles C. Cornelio*; Sandra Kemmish; Mark E. Konen.
Number of staff: 1 full-time professional; 5 part-time professional; 1 full-time support.
EIN: 356042099
Selected grants: The following grants are a representative sample of this grantmaker's funding activity:
$500,000 to Action Greensboro, Greensboro, NC, 2011. For Greensboro Downtown Greenway, payable over 3.00 years.
$300,000 to Action Greensboro, Greensboro, NC, 2011. For Businesses for Excellence in Education, payable over 3.00 years.
$270,000 to United Way of Allen County, Fort Wayne, IN, 2011. For Community Campaign, Inclusiveness and Learn United.
$150,000 to Bell House, Greensboro, NC, 2011. For You Are Able Life Enrichment Partnership, payable over 2.00 years.
$140,000 to Arts United of Greater Fort Wayne, Fort Wayne, IN, 2011. For Annual Arts United Fund Drive and Nonprofit Arts Internship Initiative (NAII).
$100,000 to Eagles Charitable Foundation, Eagles Youth Partnership, Philadelphia, PA, 2011. For Eagles Eye Mobile and Eagles Book Mobile.
$7,500 to Artlink, Fort Wayne, IN, 2011. For 32nd Annual National Print Exhibition.
$5,000 to Brush Up Nebraska, Omaha, NE, 2011. For Paint-A-Thon.
$5,000 to Women Against Abuse, Philadelphia, PA, 2011. For Emergency Residential Services for Victims of Domestic Violence.
$2,500 to University of Mississippi Foundation, University, MS, 2011.

2282
Lincoln Savings Bank

(also known as LSB)
508 Main St.
Reinbeck, IA 50669-1052 (319) 788-6441

Company URL: http://www.mylsb.com/
Establishment information: Established in 1902.
Company type: Private company
Business activities: Operates savings bank.
Business type (SIC): Savings institutions
Corporate officers: Cordell Q. Peterson, Chair.; Steve Tscherter, Pres. and C.E.O.; Emily Girsch, Exec. V.P. and C.F.O.; Jeff Becker, C.I.O.; James Schneider, Secy.
Board of director: Cordell Q. Peterson, Chair.
Offices: Allison, Aplington, Cedar Falls, Garwin, Greene, Hudson, Lincoln, Nashua, Tama, Waterloo, IA
Giving statement: Giving through the Lincoln Savings Bank Corporate Giving Program and the LSB Foundation.

Lincoln Savings Bank Corporate Giving Program

242 Tower Park Dr.
Waterloo, IA 50701-9002
FAX: (319) 232-6526; URL: http://www.mylsb.com/corporate-info/careers-community/community.aspx

Contact: Jennifer Wilson
Purpose and activities: As a complement to its foundation, Lincoln Savings Bank also makes charitable contributions to nonprofit organization directly. Support is given primarily in areas of company operations in Iowa.
Fields of interest: Arts; Education; Health care; Recreation; Human services; Economic development, visitors/convention bureau/tourism promotion Economically disadvantaged.
Type of support: Employee volunteer services; General/operating support; In-kind gifts; Sponsorships.
Geographic limitations: Giving primarily in areas of company operations in IA.
Publications: Application guidelines.
Application information: Applications accepted. Grants generally do not exceed $250. Application form required. Applicants should submit the following:
1) plans for acknowledgement
2) contact person
3) detailed description of project and amount of funding requested
4) copy of IRS Determination Letter
5) name, address and phone number of organization
6) population served
7) results expected from proposed grant

Applications should include a description of past support by Lincoln Savings Bank with the organization; and indicate any current account relationship with Lincoln Savings Bank.

Initial approach: Download online application form and mail or fax to headquarters

Deadline(s): None

LSB Foundation

242 Tower Park Dr.
Waterloo, IA 50701-9002 (319) 233-1900
URL: http://www.mylsb.com/corporate-info/careers-community/community.aspx

Establishment information: Established in 2004 in IA.
Donors: Lincoln Savings Bank; Ray Rannfeldt.
Contact: James E. Thielen, Tr.
Financial data (yr. ended 07/31/12): Assets, $100,107 (M); gifts received, $109,598; expenditures, $102,269; qualifying distributions, $100,727; giving activities include $99,185 for 73 grants (high: $9,391; low: $120).
Purpose and activities: The foundation supports organizations involved with arts and culture, education, health, disaster relief, human services, and community development.
Fields of interest: Arts; Elementary/secondary education; Higher education; Education; Health care; Disasters, preparedness/services; Youth, services; Human services; Community/economic development; United Ways and Federated Giving Programs.
Type of support: Emergency funds; General/operating support; Grants to individuals; Program development.
Geographic limitations: Giving primarily in areas of company operations in IA.
Publications: Application guidelines.
Application information: Applications accepted. Application form required. Applicants should submit the following:

1) results expected from proposed grant
2) brief history of organization and description of its mission
3) how project's results will be evaluated or measured
4) listing of board of directors, trustees, officers and other key people and their affiliations
5) detailed description of project and amount of funding requested
6) copy of current year's organizational budget and/or project budget
7) listing of additional sources and amount of support

Initial approach: Contact Foundation for application form

Board meeting date(s): Quarterly

Deadline(s): Varies

Trustees: Steve Brouwer; Milt Dakovich; Jeffrey Dralle; Clem Havlik; Cordell Peterson; Dick Rickert; Jim Schneider; James E. Thielen; Steve Tscherter.
EIN: 201653464
Selected grants: The following grants are a representative sample of this grantmaker's funding activity:
$3,390 to Junior Achievement of Eastern Iowa, Waterloo, IA, 2010.
$3,000 to Iowa State University, Ames, IA, 2010.
$2,740 to Humane Society, Cedar Bend, Waterloo, IA, 2010.
$2,500 to Greater Poweshiek Community Foundation, Grinnell, IA, 2010.
$2,480 to YWCA of Black Hawk County, Waterloo, IA, 2010.
$2,250 to American Red Cross, Waterloo, IA, 2010.
$2,000 to Grinnell College, Grinnell, IA, 2010.
$1,500 to Iowa College Foundation, Des Moines, IA, 2010.
$1,500 to Northeast Iowa Food Bank, Waterloo, IA, 2010.
$1,100 to Exceptional Persons, Waterloo, IA, 2010.

2283
Linklaters LLP

1345 Avenue of the Americas
New York, NY 10105-0302 (212) 903-9000

Company URL: http://www.linklaters.com
Company type: Private company
Business activities: Operates law firm.
Business type (SIC): Legal services
Corporate officers: David Cheyne, Senior Partner; Simon Davies, Managing Partner
Office: New York, NY
International operations: Africa; Belgium; Brazil; China; France; Hong Kong; Italy; Japan; Kazakhstan; Luxembourg; Netherlands; Poland; Portugal; Russia; Singapore; Spain; Sweden; Thailand; Turkey; Ukraine; United Arab Emirates; United Kingdom
Giving statement: Giving through the Linklaters LLP Pro Bono Program.

Linklaters LLP Pro Bono Program

1345 Avenue of the Americas
New York, NY 10105-0302 (212) 830-9519
E-mail: karen.carbonell@linklaters.com;
URL: http://www.linklaters.com/Responsibility/community/Pages/index.aspx

Contact: Karen Carbonell, Pro Bono Mgr.
Fields of interest: Legal services.
Type of support: Pro bono services - legal.

2284
Liquid Combustion Technology, LLC

(also known as LCT)
100 Roe Rd.
Travelers Rest, SC 29690-1855
(877) 274-2214
FAX: (864) 834-4393

Company URL: http://www.lctllc.com
Establishment information: Established in 2002.
Company type: Private company
Business activities: Manufactures engines.
Business type (SIC): Motor vehicles and equipment
Corporate officers: Keith B. Giddens, C.E.O.; Gregg Giddens, V.P., Sales
Giving statement: Giving through the Liquid Combustion Technology, LLC Contributions Program.

Liquid Combustion Technology, LLC Contributions Program

100 Roe Rd.
Travelers Rest, SC 29690-1855 (877) 274-2214
URL: http://www.lctusa.com

2285
Liskow & Lewis

701 Poydras St., Ste. 5000
New Orleans, LA 70139-7758
(504) 581-7979

Company URL: http://www.liskow.com
Company type: Private company
Business activities: Operates law firm.
Business type (SIC): Legal services
Offices: Lafayette, New Orleans, LA; Houston, TX
Giving statement: Giving through the Liskow & Lewis Pro Bono Program.

Liskow & Lewis Pro Bono Program

701 Poydras St., Ste. 5000
New Orleans, LA 70139-7758 (504) 581-7979
URL: http://www.liskow.com/offices.aspx?id=26&page=Pro+Bono

Contact: Don Haycraft
Fields of interest: Legal services.
Type of support: Pro bono services - legal.
Geographic limitations: Giving primarily in areas of company operations in Lafayette and New Orleans, LA, and Houston, TX.
Application information: An attorney coordinates pro bono projects.

2286
Lisle Corp.

(formerly Lisle Corp.)
807 E. Main St.
P.O. Box 89
Clarinda, IA 51632 (712) 542-5101

Company URL: http://www.lislecorp.com
Establishment information: Established in 1903.
Company type: Private company
Business activities: Manufactures motor vehicle parts and accessories and hand tools.
Business type (SIC): Motor vehicles and equipment; cutlery, hand and edge tools, and hardware
Corporate officers: John C. Lisle, Chair. and C.E.O.; Fred Lisle, Pres.; Marty Williams, C.F.O.; Jon Bielfeldt, V.P., Sales and Mktg.
Board of director: John C. Lisle, Chair.
Giving statement: Giving through the Lisle Foundation.

Lisle Foundation

P.O. Box 89
Clarinda, IA 51632-0089 (712) 542-5101

Donor: Lisle Corp.
Contact: John C. Lisle, Tr.
Financial data (yr. ended 11/30/12): Assets, $164,973 (M); expenditures, $17,585; qualifying distributions, $17,400; giving activities include $17,400 for 9 grants (high: $10,000; low: $50).
Purpose and activities: The foundation supports organizations involved with arts education, performing arts, higher education, cancer, and community development.
Fields of interest: Education; Health organizations; Safety/disasters.
Type of support: General/operating support.
Geographic limitations: Giving primarily in Clarinda and Des Moines, IA.
Support limitations: No grants to individuals.
Application information: Applications accepted. Application form required.

Initial approach: Letter
Deadline(s): None
Trustees: Fredrick Lisle; John C. Lisle; William C. Lisle.
EIN: 426056080

2287
Lithia Motors, Inc.

(formerly Chrysler-Plymouth-Dodge Dealership)
150 N. Bartlett St.
Medford, OR 97501 (541) 776-6401
FAX: (541) 774-7617

Company URL: http://www.lithia.com
Establishment information: Established in 1946.
Company type: Public company
Company ticker symbol and exchange: LAD/NYSE
Business activities: Operates automotive franchises; sells new and used vehicles and provides financing and repair services.
Business type (SIC): Automotive dealers and gasoline service stations; motor vehicles—retail
Financial profile for 2012: Number of employees, 5,043; assets, $1,492,700,000; sales volume, $3,316,490,000; pre-tax net income, $128,460,000; expenses, $3,168,120,000; liabilities, $1,064,600,000
Fortune 1000 ranking: 2012—653rd in revenues, 774th in profits, and 922nd in assets
Corporate officers: Sidney B. DeBoer, Chair.; M.L. Heimann, Vice-Chair.; Bryan B. DeBoer, Pres. and C.E.O.; Chris Holzshu, Sr. V.P. and C.F.O.; Scott Hillier, Sr. V.P., Opers.; Mark Smith, V.P. and C.I.O.; John North, V.P., Finance and Corp. Cont.
Board of directors: Sidney B. DeBoer, Chair.; M.L. Heimann, Vice-Chair.; Thomas Becker; Susan O. Cain; Bryan B. DeBoer; Kenneth E. Roberts; William J. Young
Giving statement: Giving through the Lithia Motors, Inc. Corporate Giving Program.
Company EIN: 930572810

Lithia Motors, Inc. Corporate Giving Program

360 E. Jackson St.
Medford, OR 97501-5825
E-mail: CommunityContributions@lithia.com; URL: http://www.lithia.com/index.cfm?action=dealerlink&Link=1358125&linkname=Contribution%20Request

Purpose and activities: Lithia Motors makes charitable contributions to nonprofit organizations involved with education, community health, and child welfare. Support is given primarily in areas of company operations in Alaska, California, Idaho, Iowa, Montana, Nevada, New Mexico, North Dakota, Oregon, Texas, and Washington.
Fields of interest: Education; Public health; Health care; Children, services.
Type of support: Donated products; Employee volunteer services; General/operating support; In-kind gifts; Sponsorships.
Geographic limitations: Giving primarily in areas of company operations in AK, CA, CO, IA, ID, MT, ND, NE, NM, NV, OR, TX, and WA.
Support limitations: No support for political or religious organizations. No grants to individuals.
Publications: Application guidelines.
Application information: Applications accepted. A contributions committee reviews all requests. Application form required. Applicants should submit the following:
1) population served
2) name, address and phone number of organization
3) how company employees can become involved with the organization
4) list of company employees involved with the organization
5) contact person
6) copy of current year's organizational budget and/ or project budget
Initial approach: Complete online application form
Committee meeting date(s): Twice a month
Deadline(s): None

2288
Little Pickle Press LLC

P.O. Box 983
Belvedere, CA 94920 (877) 415-4488

Company URL: http://www.littlepicklepress.com
Establishment information: Established in 2009.
Company type: Private company
Business type (SIC): Business services/ miscellaneous
Financial profile for 2012: Number of employees, 10
Corporate officers: Rick DeGolia, Chair.; Rana DiOrio, C.E.O.; Tony Ritzie, C.O.O.
Board of director: Rick DeGolia, Chair.
Giving statement: Giving through the Little Pickle Press LLC Contributions Program.

Little Pickle Press LLC Contributions Program

PO Box 983
Belvedere, CA 94920-0983 (877) 415-4488
E-mail: info@littlepicklepress.com; URL: http://www.littlepicklepress.com

Purpose and activities: Little Pickle Press is a certified B Corporation that donates a percentage of profits to charitable organizations. Support is given primarily in California.
Fields of interest: Health care, patient services Children.
Type of support: Continuing support; General/ operating support.
Geographic limitations: Giving primarily in CA; giving also to national and international organizations.

2289
Littler Mendelson

650 California St.
San Francisco, CA 94108-2693
(415) 433-1940

Company URL: http://www.littler.com
Establishment information: Established in 1942.
Company type: Private company
Business activities: Operates law firm.
Business type (SIC): Legal services
Offices: Birmingham, Mobile, AL; Anchorage, AK; Phoenix, AZ; Fayetteville, AR; Fresno, Irvine, Los Angeles, Sacramento, San Diego, San Francisco, San Jose, Santa Maria, Walnut Creek, CA; Denver, CO; New Haven, CT; Washington, DC; Miami, Orlando, FL; Atlanta, GA; Chicago, IL; Indianapolis, IN; Kansas City, Overland Park, KS; Lexington, KY; Boston, MA; Detroit, MI; Minneapolis, MN; St. Louis, MO; Las Vegas, Reno, NV; Newark, NJ; Albuquerque, NM; Melville, New York, Rochester, NY; Charlotte, NC; Cleveland, Columbus, OH; Portland, OR; Philadelphia, Pittsburgh, PA; Providence, RI; Columbia, SC; Nashville, TN; Dallas, Houston, TX; Tysons Corner, VA; Seattle, WA; Milwaukee, WI
International operations: Venezuela
Giving statement: Giving through the Littler Mendelson Pro Bono Program.

Littler Mendelson Pro Bono Program

650 California St.
San Francisco, CA 94108-2693 (312) 372-5520
E-mail: DHaase@littler.com; URL: http://www.littler.com

Contact: David Haase, Shareholder
Fields of interest: Legal services.
Type of support: Pro bono services - legal.
Geographic limitations: Giving primarily in areas of company operations in Anchorage, AK, Birmingham, Mobile, AL, Fayetteville, AR, Phoenix, AZ, Fresno, Irvine, Los Angeles, Sacramento, San Diego, San Francisco, San Jose, Santa Maria, and Walnut Creek, CA, Denver, CO, New Haven, CT, Washington, DC, Miami and Orlando, FL, Atlanta, GA, Overland Park, KS, Boston, MA, Chicago, IL, Indianapolis, IN, Lexington, KY, Detroit, MI, Minneapolis, MN, Kansas City and St. Louis, MO, Charlotte, NC, Newark, NJ, Albuquerque, NM, Las Vegas and Reno, NV, Melville, New York and Rochester, NY, Cleveland and Columbus, OH, Portland, OR, Philadelphia and Pittsburgh, PA, Providence, RI, Columbia, SC, Dallas and Nashville, TN, Houston, TX, Tysons Corner, VA, Seattle, WA, and Milwaukee, WI.
Application information: A Pro Bono Committee manages the pro bono program.

2290
LivingSocial

(doing business as Hungry Machine, Inc.)
829 7th St., Ste. 301
Washington, DC 20001-3846
(202) 289-0693

Company URL: http://livingsocial.com
Establishment information: Established in 2007.
Company type: Private company
Business activities: Provides advertising, marketing and promotional services.
Business type (SIC): Advertising
Corporate officers: Tim O'Shaughnessy, C.E.O.; Eric Eichman, Co-Pres. and C.O.O.; Edward Frederick, Co-Pres.; John Bax, C.F.O.; Val Aleksenko, C.I.O.; Mandy Cole, Sr. V.P., Sales; Jennifer Trzepacz, V.P., Human Resources; Jim Bramson, Genl. Counsel
Giving statement: Giving through the LivingSocial Corporate Giving Program.

LivingSocial Corporate Giving Program

829 7th St., Ste. 301
Washington, DC 20001 (888) 808-6676
E-mail: maire.griffin@livingsocial.com; URL: http://livingsocial.com/about

2291
LJA Insurance Company

500 E. Olive Ave., Ste. 670
Burbank, CA 91501-2197 (818) 260-0544
FAX: (818) 260-0543

Establishment information: Established in 1994.
Company type: Private company

Business activities: Provides insurance brokerage services.
Business type (SIC): Insurance agents, brokers, and services
Corporate officer: Louis E. Jones, Owner
Giving statement: Giving through the Louis and Donna Jones Family Foundation.

Louis and Donna Jones Family Foundation

500 E. Olive Ave., Ste. 670
Burbank, CA 91501-2197 (818) 260-0544

Establishment information: Established in 1998 in CA.
Donors: LJA Insurance Co.; Donna D. Jones; Louis E. Jones.
Contact: Louis E. Jones, Dir.
Financial data (yr. ended 12/31/12): Assets, $2,152,937 (M); gifts received, $191,100; expenditures, $94,776; qualifying distributions, $96,000; giving activities include $96,000 for 11 grants (high: $15,000; low: $1,000).
Purpose and activities: The foundation supports organizations involved with education, health, and human services.
Fields of interest: Arts; Education; Human services.
Type of support: General/operating support.
Geographic limitations: Giving primarily in CA.
Support limitations: No grants to individuals.
Application information: Applications accepted. Application form not required.
Initial approach: Proposal
Deadline(s): None
Directors: Daniel E. Jones; Donna D. Jones*; Louis E. Jones*; Judi E. Shupper.
EIN: 954716272

2292
Lockheed Martin Corporation

6801 Rockledge Dr.
Bethesda, MD 20817-1877 (301) 897-6000
FAX: (301) 897-6919

Company URL: http://www.lockheedmartin.com
Establishment information: Established in 1995 from the merger of Lockheed Corp. with Martin Marietta Corp.
Company type: Public company
Company ticker symbol and exchange: LMT/NYSE
International Securities Identification Number: US5398301094
Business activities: Researches, designs, develops, manufactures, and integrates advanced technology products and services.
Business type (SIC): Guided missiles and space vehicles
Financial profile for 2012: Number of employees, 120,000; assets, $38,657,000,000; sales volume, $47,182,000,000; pre-tax net income, $4,072,000,000; expenses, $42,748,000,000; liabilities, $38,618,000,000
Fortune 1000 ranking: 2012—59th in revenues, 71st in profits, and 145th in assets
Forbes 2000 ranking: 2012—189th in sales, 217th in profits, and 590th in assets
Corporate officers: Robert J. Stevens, Chair.; Marilyn A. Hewson, Pres. and C.E.O.; Bruce L. Tanner, Exec. V.P. and C.F.O.
Board of directors: Robert J. Stevens, Chair.; Nolan D. Archibald; Rosalind G. Brewer; David B. Burritt; James O. Ellis, Jr.; Thomas J. Falk; Marilyn A. Hewson; Gwendolyn S. King; James M. Loy; Douglas H. McCorkindale; Joseph W. Ralston; Anne Stevens
Subsidiaries: KAPL, Inc., Schenectady, NY; Sandia Corp., Albuquerque, NM
Joint Venture: United Space Alliance, LLC, Houston, TX
Giving statement: Giving through the Lockheed Martin Corporation Contributions Program, the Lockheed Martin Corporation Foundation, and the Lockheed Martin Vought Systems Employee Charity Fund.
Company EIN: 521893632

Lockheed Martin Corporation Contributions Program

(formerly Lockheed Corporation Contributions Program)
6801 Rockledge Dr.
Bethesda, MD 20817-1803 (301) 897-6000
E-mail: community.relations@lmco.com;
URL: http://www.lockheedmartin.com/us/who-we-are/community.html

Purpose and activities: As a complement to its foundation, Lockheed Martin also makes charitable contributions to nonprofit organizations directly. Support is given on a national basis in areas of company operations.
Fields of interest: Arts; Elementary/secondary education; Environment; Health care; Human services; Community/economic development; Science, formal/general education; Mathematics; Engineering/technology; Military/veterans' organizations; Public affairs.
Type of support: Employee volunteer services; Program development; Sponsorships.
Geographic limitations: Giving on a national basis in areas of company operations.
Support limitations: No support for discriminatory organizations, religious organizations, K-12 educational institutions, professional associations, labor organizations, fraternal organizations or social clubs, athletic groups, or clubs or teams. No grants to individuals, or for home-based child care/educational services, or advertising in souvenir booklets, yearbooks, or journals unrelated to Lockheed Martin's business interests.
Publications: Application guidelines.
Application information: Applications accepted. Application form required.
Initial approach: Complete online eligibility quiz and application form
Committee meeting date(s): Quarterly
Deadline(s): None
Number of staff: 1 full-time professional; 1 part-time professional; 1 part-time support.

Lockheed Martin Corporation Foundation

(formerly Martin Marietta Corporation Foundation)
c/o Global Community Outreach
6801 Rockledge Dr.
Bethesda, MD 20817-1836 (301) 897-6866
E-mail: community.relations@lmco.com;
URL: http://www.lockheedmartin.com/us/who-we-are/community/philanthropy.html
Contact for Lockheed Martin Intl. Scholarships: Ms. Carol Jones, Lockheed Martin Intl. Scholarship Prog., 809 United Nations Plaza, New York, NY 10017-3580, tel.: (212) 984-5386, e-mail: cjones@iie.org

Establishment information: Established in 1955 in MD.
Donors: Martin Marietta Corp.; Lockheed Martin Corp.
Financial data (yr. ended 12/31/11): Assets, $3,389,837 (M); gifts received, $7,000,000; expenditures, $6,984,720; qualifying distributions, $6,986,230; giving activities include $4,568,473 for 121 grants (high: $1,029,000; low: $350) and $2,323,290 for employee matching gifts.
Purpose and activities: The foundation supports programs designed to promote education, including K-16 science, technology, engineering, and math (STEM) education; causes that are important to Lockheed Martin customers and constituents, the U.S. military, and government agencies; and community relations, including partnerships between Lockheed Martin employee volunteers and other civic, cultural, environmental, health, and human services initiatives in the community.
Fields of interest: Arts; Elementary/secondary education; Education; Environment; Health care; Human services; Community/economic development; Mathematics; Engineering/technology; Science; Military/veterans' organizations; Public affairs.
Programs:
Lockheed Martin International Scholarship Program: The foundation awards three $3,000 four-year college scholarships to children of non-US citizen employees of Lockheed Martin. The program is administered by the Institute of International Education.
Lockheed Martin Merit Scholarship Program: The foundation awards $3,000 four-year college scholarships to National Merit Finalists who are children of employees of Lockheed Martin. The program is administered by the National Merit Scholarship Corp.
Matching Gift Program for Colleges and Universities: The foundation matches contributions made by employees and directors of Lockheed Martin to institutions of higher education on a one-for-one basis from $25 to $10,000 per contributor, per year.
Type of support: Employee matching gifts; Employee volunteer services; Employee-related scholarships; General/operating support; Program development; Scholarship funds.
Geographic limitations: Giving primarily in areas of company operations, with emphasis on CA, CO, GA, IN, MD, MI, NY, TX, and VA.
Support limitations: No support for discriminatory organizations, religious organizations not of direct benefit to the entire community, professional associations, labor or fraternal organizations, social clubs, athletic groups, or private K-12 schools. No grants to individuals (except for employee-related scholarships), or for booklet, yearbook, or journal advertising or home-based child care or educational services.
Publications: Application guidelines.
Application information: Applications accepted. Contributions to national initiatives and organizations are made from corporate headquarters and contributions to local programs are made by local sites close to the program. Support is limited to 1 contribution per organization during any given year. Application form required.
Initial approach: Complete online eligibility quiz and application
Board meeting date(s): Quarterly
Deadline(s): Rolling
Officer and Trustees:* Emily D. Simone, Secy.; Patrick M. Dewar; Chris Gregoire; John T. Lucas; Ronald T. Rand.
Number of staff: 1 full-time professional; 1 full-time support.
EIN: 136161566
Selected grants: The following grants are a representative sample of this grantmaker's funding activity:
$2,000,000 to Scholarship Foundation, Cherry Hill, NJ, 2011.

$1,029,000 to National Merit Scholarship Corporation, Evanston, IL, 2011. For scholarships.
$500,000 to National Geographic Society, Washington, DC, 2011. For general support.
$285,000 to W G B H Educational Foundation, Boston, MA, 2011. For general support.
$256,690 to Scholarship Foundation, Cherry Hill, NJ, 2011.
$238,500 to National Geographic Society, Washington, DC, 2011. For general support.
$175,000 to American Friends of the Royal Naval Museum, New York, NY, 2011. For general support.
$92,000 to University of California, Los Angeles, CA, 2011. For general support.
$38,500 to Scholarship Foundation, Cherry Hill, NJ, 2011.
$15,000 to University of California, Los Angeles, CA, 2011. For general support.

Lockheed Martin Vought Systems Employee Charity Fund

P.O. Box 650003, PT 42
Dallas, TX 75265-0003 (972) 603-0587

Establishment information: Established in 1994 in TX.
Donors: Lockheed Martin Corp.; Lockheed Martin Vought Systems.
Contact: Hannah Stone, V.P.
Financial data (yr. ended 12/31/11): Assets, $267,750 (M); gifts received, $543,539; expenditures, $925,240; qualifying distributions, $925,223; giving activities include $925,223 for 97 grants (high: $100,000; low: $150).
Purpose and activities: The fund supports hospitals and organizations involved with patient services, cancer, hunger, children and youth, human services, and military and veterans and awards emergency grants to employees of Lockheed Martin Missiles and Fire Control for accidents, illness, or other catastrophes.
Fields of interest: Hospitals (general); Health care, patient services; Cancer; Food banks; Food distribution, meals on wheels; American Red Cross; Children/youth, services; Family services, domestic violence; Human services, gift distribution; Homeless, human services; Human services; United Ways and Federated Giving Programs; Military/veterans' organizations.
Type of support: Annual campaigns; Continuing support; Emergency funds; General/operating support; Grants to individuals; Research.
Geographic limitations: Giving primarily in Camden, AR and Arlington, Dallas, Fort Worth, and Lufkin, TX.
Application information: Applications accepted. Application form not required. Applicants should submit the following:
1) detailed description of project and amount of funding requested
Initial approach: Proposal
Copies of proposal: 1
Deadline(s): None
Officers and Directors:* James F. Berry*, Pres.; Hannah Stone*, V.P.; Donald Remenapp*, Secy.; Julia Novikoff; Craig Van Bebber.
EIN: 752528901
Selected grants: The following grants are a representative sample of this grantmaker's funding activity:
$100,000 to North Texas Food Bank, Dallas, TX, 2009.
$29,621 to United Fund of Ouachita Area, Camden, AR, 2009.
$29,500 to Grand Prairie United Charities, Grand Prairie, TX, 2009.
$29,000 to Brighter Tomorrows, Grand Prairie, TX, 2009.
$20,000 to A Wish with Wings, Arlington, TX, 2009.
$20,000 to Arlington Life Shelter, Arlington, TX, 2009.
$18,500 to American Cancer Society, Dallas, TX, 2009.
$10,000 to Fisher House Foundation, Rockville, MD, 2009.
$7,210 to American Red Cross, Fort Worth, TX, 2009.
$5,000 to Leukemia & Lymphoma Society, Dallas, TX, 2009.

2293
Lockwood International, Inc.

10203 Wallisville Rd.
P.O. Box 53466
Houston, TX 77013-4115 (713) 675-8186

Company URL: http://www.lockwoodint.com
Establishment information: Established in 1977.
Company type: Private company
Business activities: Supplies industrial valves.
Business type (SIC): Industrial machinery and equipment—wholesale
Corporate officers: Michael F. Lockwood, Pres. and C.E.O.; Mark Lindsey, C.F.O.; Betty Allen, C.A.O; Tim Alexander, C.I.O
Board of directors: Mike Lockwood; Tom Lockwood
Giving statement: Giving through the Lockwood Family Foundation.

Lockwood Family Foundation

10203 Wallisville Rd.
Houston, TX 77013

Establishment information: Established in 2008 in TX.
Donor: Lockwood International, Inc.
Financial data (yr. ended 01/31/12): Assets, $225,068 (M); expenditures, $82,110; qualifying distributions, $79,994; giving activities include $79,994 for grants.
Fields of interest: Education; Health care; Recreation.
Application information: Applications not accepted. Unsolicited requests for funds not accepted.
Officers and Directors:* Michael Lockwood*, Pres.; Thomas Lockwood*, V.P.; Gail Lockwood*, Secy.
EIN: 261879651

2294
Lodz Properties, L.P.

680 5th Ave., Lobby A
New York, NY 10019-5429 (212) 265-4120

Establishment information: Established in 1995.
Company type: Private company
Business activities: Operates real estate agency.
Business type (SIC): Real estate agents and managers
Corporate officer: Ted Haft, Partner
Giving statement: Giving through the Josef Buchmann Charitable Foundation.

The Josef Buchmann Charitable Foundation

c/o T. Haft
680 5th Ave., 26th Fl.
New York, NY 10019

Establishment information: Established in 2001 in NY.
Donors: Lodz Properties, L.P.; JB 680 5th Avenue Associates LP.
Financial data (yr. ended 12/31/11): Assets, $517,350 (M); expenditures, $402,590; qualifying distributions, $400,000; giving activities include $400,000 for grants.
Purpose and activities: The foundation supports organizations involved with higher education, biomedical research, human services, and Judaism.
International interests: Germany.
Type of support: General/operating support.
Application information: Applications not accepted. Unsolicited requests for funds not accepted.
Trustees: Josef Buchmann; Ted Haft.
EIN: 116569821

2295
Loeb & Loeb LLP

10100 Santa Monica Blvd., Ste. 2200
Los Angeles, CA 90067-4120
(310) 282-2000

Company URL: http://www.loeb.com
Establishment information: Established in 1909.
Company type: Private company
Business activities: Operates law firm.
Business type (SIC): Legal services
Corporate officers: Alan B. Cutler, C.O.O.; Ron Yano, C.F.O.; Judi Flournoy, C.I.O.
Offices: Los Angeles, CA; Washington, DC; Chicago, IL; New York, NY; Nashville, TN
International operations: China
Giving statement: Giving through the Loeb & Loeb LLP Pro Bono Program.

Loeb & Loeb LLP Pro Bono Program

10100 Santa Monica Blvd., Ste. 2200
Los Angeles, CA 90067-4120 (310) 282-2000
URL: http://www.loeb.com/firm/community/

Contact: Richard Nardi, Esq., Partner
Fields of interest: Legal services.
Type of support: Pro bono services - legal.
Geographic limitations: Giving primarily in areas of company operations in Los Angeles, CA, Washington, DC, Chicago, IL, New York, NY, and Nashville, TN, and in China.
Application information: A Pro Bono Coordinator manages the pro bono program.

2296
Loews Corporation

667 Madison Ave.
New York, NY 10065-8087 (212) 521-2000
FAX: (21) 545-2525

Company URL: http://www.loews.com
Establishment information: Established in 1959.
Company type: Public company
Company ticker symbol and exchange: L/NYSE
Business activities: Operates holding company; sells property, casualty, and life insurance; produces and sells cigarettes; operates hotels; operates offshore oil and gas drilling rigs; distributes and sells watches and clocks.
Business type (SIC): Holding company; extraction/oil and gas; tobacco products—cigarettes; shopping goods stores/miscellaneous; insurance/life; insurance/fire, marine, and casualty; hotels and motels
Financial profile for 2012: Number of employees, 18,300; assets, $80,021,000,000; sales volume,

$14,552,000,000; pre-tax net income, $1,399,000,000; expenses, $13,153,000,000; liabilities, $60,562,000,000
Fortune 1000 ranking: 2012—188th in revenues, 305th in profits, and 75th in assets
Forbes 2000 ranking: 2012—652nd in sales, 908th in profits, and 308th in assets
Corporate officers: Andrew H. Tisch, Co-Chair.; Jonathan M. Tisch, Co-Chair.; James S. Tisch, Pres. and C.E.O.; Peter W. Keegan, Sr. V.P. and C.F.O.; Richard W. Scott, Sr. V.P. and C.I.O.; Gary W. Garson, Sr. V.P., Genl. Counsel, and Secy.; Robert D. Fields, V.P. and C.I.O.; Alan Momeyer, V.P., Human Resources; Edmund Unneland, Treas.; Mark S. Schwartz, Cont.
Board of directors: Andrew H. Tisch, Co-Chair.; Jonathan M. Tisch, Co-Chair.; Lawrence S. Bacow; Ann E. Berman; Joseph L. Bower; Charles M. Diker; Jacob A. Frenkel; Paul J. Fribourg; Walter L. Harris; Philip A. Laskawy; Ken Miller; Gloria R. Scott; James S. Tisch
Subsidiaries: CNA Financial Corporation, Chicago, IL; Diamond Offshore Drilling, Inc., Houston, TX; Loews Hotels, New York, NY; Lorillard, Inc., New York, NY
Plant: Danville, VA
Giving statement: Giving through the Loews Hotels Corporate Giving Program and the Loews Foundation.
Company EIN: 132646102

Loews Hotels Corporate Giving Program

(also known as Loews Good Neighbor Policy)
c/o Loews Hotels Corp. Office
667 Madison Ave.
New York, NY 10065 (212) 521-2000
URL: http://www.loewshotels.com/en/AboutUs/Neighbor.aspx#1

Purpose and activities: Loews Hotels makes charitable contributions to nonprofit organizations involved with hunger relief and literacy, and to shelters. Support is given in areas of company operations.
Fields of interest: Arts; Education, reading; Education; Food services; Food banks; Housing/shelter, services.
Type of support: Employee volunteer services; General/operating support; In-kind gifts; Use of facilities.
Geographic limitations: Giving in areas of company operations.

Loews Foundation

655 Madison Ave.
New York, NY 10021-8043 (212) 521-2650
FAX: (212) 521-2634

Establishment information: Trust established in 1957 in NY.
Donors: Loews Corp.; Loews Hotel Holding Corp.
Contact: John J. Kenny, Tr.
Financial data (yr. ended 12/31/11): Assets, $240,130 (M); gifts received, $250,000; expenditures, $463,533; qualifying distributions, $462,209; giving activities include $462,209 for grants.
Purpose and activities: The foundation supports police agencies and parks and organizations involved with arts and culture, education, children and youth, business, and voluntarism promotion.
Fields of interest: Museums (art); Museums (history); Performing arts, theater; Arts; Higher education; Education; Crime/law enforcement, police agencies; Recreation, parks/playgrounds; American Red Cross; Children/youth, services; Business/industry; Voluntarism promotion; United Ways and Federated Giving Programs.
Programs:
Employee Matching Gifts: The foundation matches contributions made by full-time employees of Loews to institutions of higher education and nonprofit organizations on a one-for-one basis up to $2,500 per employee, per year.
Loews Corporate Children's Scholarship Program: The foundation awards up to four $3,000 college scholarships to children of employees of Loews and its wholly-owned subsidiaries. The program is administered by the National Merit Scholarship Corp.
Type of support: Annual campaigns; Employee matching gifts; Employee-related scholarships; Program development; Scholarship funds.
Geographic limitations: Giving primarily in NY.
Support limitations: No grants to individuals (except for employee-related scholarships).
Application information: Applications accepted. Application form not required.
Initial approach: Telephone or proposal
Board meeting date(s): As required
Deadline(s): None
Trustees: Peter W. Keegan; John J. Kenny; Andrew H. Tisch.
EIN: 136082817
Selected grants: The following grants are a representative sample of this grantmaker's funding activity:
$22,165 to United Way of New York City, New York, NY, 2011.
$15,000 to New York Cares, New York, NY, 2011.
$12,000 to Dress for Success New Orleans, New Orleans, LA, 2011.
$10,000 to American Friends of the Hebrew University, New York, NY, 2011.
$10,000 to Yeshiva University, New York, NY, 2011.
$5,000 to New York City Police Foundation, New York, NY, 2011.
$1,000 to United Negro College Fund, Fairfax, VA, 2011.

2297
Johnny Londoff Chevrolet

1375 Dunn Rd.
Florissant, MO 63031-8199
(314) 837-1800
FAX: (314) 837-8264

Company URL: http://www.londoff.com
Establishment information: Established in 1958.
Company type: Private company
Business activities: Operates car dealership.
Business type (SIC): Motor vehicles—retail
Corporate officers: John Londoff, Jr., Pres.; Sean Stayton, C.F.O.
Giving statement: Giving through the Johnny Londoff Foundation.

Johnny Londoff Foundation

c/o Johnny Londoff Chevrolet
1375 Dunn Rd.
Florissant, MO 63031-8117 (314) 837-1800

Establishment information: Established in 1958.
Donors: Johnny Londoff Chevrolet; John H. Londoff.
Contact: Sean Stayton
Financial data (yr. ended 12/31/11): Assets, $906 (M); gifts received, $6,000; expenditures, $7,119; qualifying distributions, $7,119; giving activities include $6,300 for 13 grants to individuals.
Purpose and activities: The foundation awards college scholarships to children of employees of Johnny Londoff Chevrolet.
Type of support: Employee-related scholarships.
Geographic limitations: Giving limited to MO, KS, and TN.
Application information: Applications accepted. Application form required.
Initial approach: Proposal
Deadline(s): May 15
Director: John H. Londoff, Jr.
EIN: 436054089

2298
Phil Long Automotive Group, Inc.

(also known as Phil Long Dealerships)
1212 A Motor City Dr.
Colorado Springs, CO 80906
(719) 575-7000

Company URL: http://www.phillong.com
Establishment information: Established in 1945.
Company type: Private company
Business activities: Operates car dealership.
Business type (SIC): Motor vehicles—retail
Corporate officers: Jay Cimino, Chair., Pres., and C.E.O.; Raymond Turner, C.F.O.; Bob Fenton, V.P., Opers.
Board of directors: Jay Cimino, Chair.; Scott Arnold
Subsidiaries: Academy Ford, Colorado Springs, CO; European Imports, Colorado Springs, CO; Phil Long Ford, LLC, Colorado Springs, CO; Phil Long Mitsubishi, Colorado Springs, CO; Phil Long Nissan, Colorado Springs, CO; Saturn of Colorado Springs, Colorado Springs, CO; Saturn of Denver, Denver, CO
Giving statement: Giving through the Phil Long Community Fund.

Phil Long Community Fund

1212 Motor City Dr.
Colorado Springs, CO 80906-1392 (719) 575-7093
E-mail: mnarone@phillong.com

Establishment information: Established in 1991 in CO.
Donors: Phil Long Automotive Group, Inc.; Phil Long Ford of Denver, LLC; Saturn of Denver, LLC; Phil Long Ford, LLC; Academy Ford, Inc.; Saturn of Colorado Springs, LLC; Phil Long Mitsubishi, LLC; Phil Long Nissan, LLC; Phil Long West, LLC; European Imports, LLC; Phil Long Ford Colorado Springs.
Contact: Michelle Hill, Secy.
Financial data (yr. ended 12/31/10): Assets, $15,963 (M); expenditures, $50; qualifying distributions, $50.
Purpose and activities: The foundation supports organizations involved with arts and culture, education, recreation, youth development, and human services.
Fields of interest: Arts; Education; Recreation, camps; Athletics/sports, amateur leagues; Athletics/sports, professional leagues; Recreation; Youth development; Children/youth, services; Human services.
Type of support: Curriculum development; Equipment; Internship funds; Program development; Scholarship funds.
Geographic limitations: Giving limited to the Colorado Springs and Denver, CO, metropolitan areas.

Publications: Annual report (including application guidelines); Financial statement; Informational brochure (including application guidelines); Program policy statement.
Application information: Applications accepted. Application form required.
Initial approach: Contact foundation for application form
Copies of proposal: 1
Board meeting date(s): Quarterly
Deadline(s): 1st Fri. of Mar., June, Sept., and Dec.
Officers: Randy Gradishar, Pres.; Scott Arnold, V.P.; Michelle Hill, Secy.; Greg Nelson, Treas.
Directors: Mike Cimino; Gary Fentiman; Kenn Patton; Cathi Trippe.
Number of staff: 8 full-time professional; 1 full-time support.
EIN: 841195814

2299
The Longaberger Company

1 Market Sq.
1500 E. Main St.
Newark, OH 43055-8847 (740) 322-5588

Company URL: http://www.longaberger.com
Establishment information: Established in 1973.
Company type: Private company
Business activities: Manufactures baskets and home and lifestyle products.
Business type (SIC): Wood products/ miscellaneous; food and kindred products; fabricated textile products/miscellaneous; furniture/household; pottery
Financial profile for 2010: Number of employees, 350
Corporate officers: Tami Longaberger, Chair. and C.E.O.; Robert Esson, V.P., Opers.; Tom Coles, V.P., Human Resources
Board of director: Tami Longaberger, Chair.
Giving statement: Giving through the Longaberger Company Contributions Program and the Longaberger Foundation.

The Longaberger Company Contributions Program

1500 E. Main St.
Newark, OH 43055-8847 (740) 322-5588
URL: http://www.longaberger.com/longabergerFoundation.aspx

Purpose and activities: As a complement to its foundation, Longaberger also makes charitable contributions to nonprofit organizations directly. Support is given primarily in Ohio.
Fields of interest: Breast cancer research Military/ veterans.
Type of support: Employee volunteer services; General/operating support.
Geographic limitations: Giving primarily in OH; giving also to national organizations.

The Longaberger Foundation

1500 E. Main St.
P.O. Box 3400
Newark, OH 43055-3400 (740) 322-5141
FAX: (740) 322-5616; URL: http://www.longaberger.com/longabergerFoundation.aspx

Establishment information: Established in 1997 in OH.
Donor: The Longaberger Co.
Contact: Michael Bennett
Financial data (yr. ended 12/31/11): Assets, $2,940,942 (M); gifts received, $2,122; expenditures, $161,181; qualifying distributions, $151,920; giving activities include $150,085 for 22 grants (high: $25,000; low: $250).
Purpose and activities: The foundation supports programs designed to stimulate a better quality of life through philanthropy. Special emphasis is directed toward programs designed to serve children and families; preserve American history; promote entrepreneurship; and address regional quality of life needs.
Fields of interest: Higher education; Environment, natural resources; Environment, forests; Environment; Animals/wildlife, sanctuaries; Health care; Food services; Disasters, preparedness/ services; Children/youth, services; Family services; Human services; Civil/human rights, women; Community/economic development; United Ways and Federated Giving Programs Women.
Type of support: Annual campaigns; General/ operating support; Program development; Scholarship funds; Sponsorships.
Geographic limitations: Giving primarily in areas of company operations in OH.
Support limitations: No grants to individuals.
Application information: Applications accepted. Application form not required. Applicants should submit the following:
1) population served
2) copy of IRS Determination Letter
3) brief history of organization and description of its mission
4) detailed description of project and amount of funding requested
5) listing of additional sources and amount of support
Initial approach: Brief letter of inquiry
Deadline(s): None
Officer: Tamala Longaberger, Pres.
EIN: 311575931
Selected grants: The following grants are a representative sample of this grantmaker's funding activity:
$50,000 to Columbus Partnership, Columbus, OH, 2010. For program support.
$25,000 to Marburn Academy, Columbus, OH, 2010. For scholarship support.
$10,000 to International Republican Institute, Washington, DC, 2010.
$5,000 to Direct Selling Education Foundation, Washington, DC, 2010.
$5,000 to GroundWork Group, Columbus, OH, 2010.
$3,000 to Muskingum County Community Foundation, Zanesville, OH, 2010.
$1,000 to Woodrow Wilson International Center for Scholars, Washington, DC, 2010.

2300
Longview Capital Corporation

116 S. Broadway
P.O. Box 377
Newman, IL 61942 (217) 837-2012
FAX: (217) 837-2431

Company URL: http://longviewcap.com/a_about.htm
Establishment information: Established in 1977.
Company type: Private company
Business activities: Operates bank holding company; operates commercial bank.
Business type (SIC): Banks/commercial; holding company
Financial profile for 2009: Number of employees, 70
Corporate officers: John S. Albin, Pres.; Stuart L. Schultz, C.O.O.; Perry S. Albin, V.P. and Secy.; Marjorie A. Albin, V.P. and Treas.
Board of director: Bill Glaze
Giving statement: Giving through the Longview Foundation.

The Longview Foundation

P.O. Box 377
Newman, IL 61942-9615

Establishment information: Established in 2000 in IL.
Donor: Longview Capital Corp.
Financial data (yr. ended 12/31/11): Assets, $1,790 (M); expenditures, $36,024; qualifying distributions, $35,924; giving activities include $35,924 for grants.
Fields of interest: Education.
Type of support: Equipment; General/operating support.
Application information: Applications not accepted. Unsolicited requests for funds not accepted.
Officers and Directors:* John S. Albin*, Pres.; Marjorie A. Albin*, V.P.; William A. Coolley*, Secy.-Treas.; David A. Albin; Perry S. Albin.
EIN: 371402686

2301
Loomis, Sayles and Co., L.P.

1 Financial Ctr.
Boston, MA 02111 (617) 482-2450

Company URL: http://www.loomissayles.com
Establishment information: Established in 1926.
Company type: Subsidiary of a foreign company
Business activities: Provides investment advisory services.
Business type (SIC): Security and commodity services
Corporate officers: Robert James Blanding, Chair. and C.E.O.; Daniel Joseph Fuss, Vice-Chair.; John E. Pelletier, C.O.O; Kevin Patrick Charleston, C.F.O.; Jaehoon Park, C.I.O.
Board of directors: Robert James Blanding, Chair.; Daniel J. Fuss, Vice-Chair.
Giving statement: Giving through the Loomis, Sayles and Co., L.P. Corporate Giving Program.

Loomis, Sayles and Co., L.P. Corporate Giving Program

1 Financial Ctr., 36th Fl.
Boston, MA 02111-2641 (617) 482-2450
URL: http://www.loomissayles.com/Internet/Internet.nsf/Charitable_Giving

Purpose and activities: Loomis, Sayles and Co. makes charitable contributions to nonprofit organizations involved with arts and culture, education, health, housing, and social services. Special emphasis is directed toward programs designed to improve the education and health of children and families. Support is given primarily in areas of company operations.
Fields of interest: Performing arts, ballet; Arts; Secondary school/education; Education; Health care, clinics/centers; Health care; Boys & girls clubs; Children, services; Family services; Human services.
Type of support: Donated equipment; Employee matching gifts; Employee volunteer services;

General/operating support; In-kind gifts; Program development; Sponsorships.
Geographic limitations: Giving primarily in areas of company operations, with emphasis on MA.

2302
Lord & Taylor, LLC

424 5th Ave.
New York, NY 10018 (212) 391-3344
FAX: (212) 391-3162

Company URL: http://www.lordandtaylor.com
Establishment information: Established in 1826.
Company type: Subsidiary of a private company
Business activities: Operates department store chain.
Business type (SIC): Department stores
Financial profile for 2010: Number of employees, 9,000
Corporate officers: Richard A. Baker, Chair.; Michael Culhane, Exec. V.P. and C.F.O.
Board of director: Richard A. Baker, Chair.
Giving statement: Giving through the Lord & Taylor Foundation.

The Lord & Taylor Foundation

250 Highland Park Blvd.
Wilkes Barre, PA 18702

Establishment information: Established in 2006 in PA.
Donor: Lord and Taylor, LLC.
Financial data (yr. ended 01/31/10): Assets, $0 (M); gifts received, $34,407; expenditures, $34,407; qualifying distributions, $34,407; giving activities include $27,611 for 7 grants (high: $18,400; low: $21) and $6,796 for 28 employee matching gifts.
Fields of interest: Education; Health care; Civil/human rights.
Support limitations: No grants to individuals.
Application information: Applications accepted. Application form required.
Initial approach: Proposal
Deadline(s): None
Officers: Christopher Sim, Pres.; Patti Betzendorfer, V.P.; John Manos, Secy.-Treas.
EIN: 208063883

2303
Lord, Abbett & Co., LLC

90 Hudson St.
Jersey City, NJ 07302-3900
(201) 827-2000

Company URL: http://www.lordabbett.com
Establishment information: Established in 1929.
Company type: Private company
Business activities: Investment company.
Business type (SIC): Investment offices
Corporate officers: Robert Stanley Dow, Chair. and C.E.O.; Daria L. Foster, Pres.; Joan Anne Binstock, C.O.O.; Lynn Marie Gargano, C.F.O.; Stacy P. Allen, C.A.O.; Robert I. Gerber, C.I.O.; Michael L. Radziemski, C.I.O.; Lawrence H. Kaplan, Genl. Counsel
Board of directors: Robert Stanley Dow, Ph.D., Chair.; Thayer Bigelow; Robert B. Calhoun, Jr.; Daria L. Foster; Evelyn E. Guernsey; Julie A. Hill; Franklin W. Hobbs; Thomas J. Neff; James L.L. Tullis
Giving statement: Giving through the Lord, Abbett & Co. Contributions Program.

Lord, Abbett & Co. Contributions Program

90 Hudson St.
Jersey City, NJ 07302-3900 (201) 827-2000
E-mail: dtornejal@lordabbett.com; URL: http://www.lordabbett.com/us/la2/about?key=inTheCommunity

Contact: Diane R. Tornejal, Partner, Dir., Human Resources
Purpose and activities: Lord Abbett makes charitable contributions to nonprofit organizations involved with cultural affairs, education, people with special needs, health, vocational services, children's services, and civic affairs. Support is given primarily in areas of company operations in New Jersey.
Fields of interest: Arts; Education; Health care; Employment, vocational rehabilitation; Children, services; Human services; Public affairs Disabilities, people with.
Type of support: Donated equipment; General/operating support; Sponsorships.
Geographic limitations: Giving primarily in areas of company operations in NJ.

2203
L'Oreal USA, Inc.

(formerly Cosmair, Inc.)
575 5th Ave., Fl. 23
New York, NY 10017-2430 (212) 818-1500

Company URL: http://www.lorealusa.com
Establishment information: Established in 1909.
Company type: Subsidiary of a foreign company
Business activities: Develops and manufactures hair care, hair color, and skin care products, color cosmetics, and fragrances.
Business type (SIC): Soaps, cleaners, and toiletries
Financial profile for 2010: Number of employees, 140; sales volume, $5,690,000,000; pre-tax net income, $364,700,000
Corporate officers: Frederic Roze, Pres. and C.E.O.; Arnaud Legain, C.F.O.; Barry Gilmore, Sr. V.P. and C.I.O.; Vincent Serpico, Sr. V.P., Opers.; Sarah Hibberson, Sr. V.P., Human Resources
Subsidiary: Maybelline, Inc., Memphis, TN
Division: Ralph Lauren Fragrance Div., New York, NY
International operations: Canada
Giving statement: Giving through the L'Oreal USA, Inc. Corporate Giving Program.

L'Oreal USA, Inc. Corporate Giving Program

(formerly Cosmair, Inc. Corporate Giving Program)
575 5th Ave.
New York, NY 10017-2422 (212) 984-4894
FAX: (212) 984-4564; Application address for Fellowships: c/o AAS, Attn: Yolanda George, Education and Human Resources, 120 New York Ave., NW, Washington, DC 20005; URL: http://www.lorealusa.com/_en/_us/html/our-company/as-a-corporate-citizen.aspx?

Contact: Rebecca Caruso, Exec. V.P., Corp. Comms.
Purpose and activities: L'Oreal USA makes charitable contributions to nonprofit organizations involved with arts and culture, health, cancer, medical research, science, and women and on a case by case basis. Support is given primarily on a national basis in areas of company operations.
Fields of interest: Arts; Education; Health care; Cancer; Medical research; Physical/earth sciences; Chemistry; Mathematics; Computer science; Engineering; Biology/life sciences; Science; General charitable giving Women.
Programs:
L'Oreal Fellowships for Women In Science: Through the L'Oreal Fellowships for Women in Science program, the company annually awards grants to U.S.-based postdoctoral associates involved with life and physical/material sciences, engineering, technology, computer science, mathematics, immunology, chemistry, earth science, and medical research. The company also awards grants to 15 international postdoctoral associates whose projects have been accepted by a reputable institution outside their home county. The program is designed to raise awareness of the contribution of women to the sciences; and identify exceptional female researchers to serve as role models for younger generations.
Women of Worth: L'Oreal Paris, a division of L'Oreal USA, annually honors 10 women who are making a difference in their communities through volunteerism. The company awards $5,000 to each honorees charity of choice; a $5,000 matching donation is made in their name to the Ovarian Cancer Research Fund; and one national nominee selected by online public vote will also receive an additional $25,000 for their cause. The program is administered by Points of Light Institute.
Type of support: Conferences/seminars; Fellowships; General/operating support; Research; Sponsorships.
Geographic limitations: Giving primarily on a national basis in areas of company operations; giving also to national organizations.
Publications: Application guidelines.
Application information: Applications accepted. The Communications and External Affairs Department handles giving. Application form required. Women in Science applications must include official transcripts, 3 letters of recommendation, a budget, a research plan, and a candidate's statement.
Initial approach: Contact company for partnerships and sponsorships; download application and mail for Women in Science; complete online nomination form for Women of Worth
Deadline(s): Dec. 13 for U.S. Women in Science; June 30 for international Women in Science; June 30 for Women of Worth
Final notification: Oct. for Women of Worth

2304
Lorillard Tobacco Company

714 Green Valley Rd.
P.O. Box 21688
Greensboro, NC 27408-7018
(336) 335-7000

Company URL: http://www.lorillard.com
Establishment information: Established in 1760.
Company type: Subsidiary of a public company
Business activities: Produces cigarettes.
Business type (SIC): Tobacco products—cigarettes
Financial profile for 2012: Assets, $3,400,000,000; sales volume, $4,600,000,000
Fortune 1000 ranking: 2012—516th in revenues, 185th in profits, and 712th in assets
Forbes 2000 ranking: 2012—1437th in sales, 544th in profits, and 1912th in assets
Corporate officers: Murray S. Kessler, Chair., Pres., and C.E.O.; David H. Taylor, Exec. V.P., Finance, and C.F.O.; Ronald S. Milstein, Exec. V.P., Genl. Counsel, and Secy.; Charles E. Hennighausen, Exec.

V.P., Opers.; Randy B. Spell, Exec. V.P., Mktg. and Sales; Anthony B. Petit, V.P., Cont., and C.A.O.
Board of directors: Murray S. Kessler, Chair.; Robert C. Almon; Virgis W. Colbert; David E.R. Dangoor; Kit D. Dietz; Murray S. Kessler; Richard W. Roedel; Nigel Travis
Giving statement: Giving through the Lorillard Tobacco Company Contributions Program.

Lorillard Tobacco Company Contributions Program

c/o Ext. Affairs
P.O. Box 10529
Greensboro, NC 27404-0529
E-mail: externalaffairs@lortobco.com; URL: http://www.lorillard.com/index.php?id=5

Purpose and activities: Lorillard supports programs designed to promote youth smoking prevention.
Fields of interest: Mental health, smoking; Youth development, information services.
Type of support: Film/video/radio; General/operating support.
Publications: Program policy statement.

2305
Los Angeles Dodgers, Inc.

1000 Elysian Park Ave.
Los Angeles, CA 90012-1199
(323) 224-1500
FAX: (323) 224-1269

Company URL: http://losangeles.dodgers.mlb.com
Establishment information: Established in 1884.
Company type: Private company
Business activities: Operates professional baseball club.
Business type (SIC): Commercial sports
Financial profile for 2010: Number of employees, 400
Corporate officers: Mark Walter, Chair.; Jeff Ingram, Vice-Chair.; Dennis Mannion, Pres.; Geoffrey P. Wharton, C.O.O.; Tucker Kain, C.F.O.; Sam Fernandez, Sr. V.P. and Genl. Counsel; Howard Sunkin, Sr. V.P., Public Affairs; Josh Rawitch, V.P., Comms.; Eric Hernandez, Cont.
Board of directors: Mark Walter, Jr., Chair.; Jeff Ingram, Vice-Chair.
Giving statement: Giving through the Los Angeles Dodgers, Inc. Corporate Giving Program and the Dodgers Dream Foundation, Inc.

Los Angeles Dodgers, Inc. Corporate Giving Program

c/o Community Rels. Dept.
1000 Elysian Park Ave.
Los Angeles, CA 90012-1112
URL: http://losangeles.dodgers.mlb.com/la/community/index.jsp

Purpose and activities: The Los Angeles Dodgers make charitable contributions of memorabilia to nonprofit organizations on a case by case basis. Support is limited to California, with emphasis in southern California.
Fields of interest: General charitable giving.
Type of support: In-kind gifts.
Geographic limitations: Giving limited to CA, with emphasis on southern CA.
Publications: Application guidelines.
Application information: Applications accepted. Proposals should be submitted using organization letterhead. Application form not required. Applicants should submit the following:
1) name, address and phone number of organization
2) copy of IRS Determination Letter
3) brief history of organization and description of its mission
4) contact person

Proposals should indicate the date of the event.
Initial approach: Proposal to headquarters
Copies of proposal: 1
Deadline(s): 6 weeks prior to need
Final notification: 2 weeks

The Dodgers Dream Foundation, Inc.

1000 Elysian Park Ave.
Los Angeles, CA 90012-1112 (323) 224-1413
URL: http://mlb.mlb.com/la/community/dream_foundation.jsp

Establishment information: Established in 1998 in CA.
Contact: Frank H. McCourt, Jr., Pres.
Financial data (yr. ended 12/31/11): Revenue, $1,466,040; assets, $996,184 (M); gifts received, $939,138; expenditures, $1,163,791; giving activities include $507,906 for grants.
Purpose and activities: The foundation provides educational, athletic, and recreational opportunities for the youth of the community.
Fields of interest: Education; Recreation; Human services.
Geographic limitations: Giving limited to CA.
Officers: Frank H. McCourt, Jr.*, Pres.; Jaime McCourt*, V.P.; Santiago Fernandez*, Secy.; Peter Wilhelm*, Treas.
EIN: 954623022

2306
The Los Angeles Kings Hockey Club, LP

1111 S. Figueroa St., Ste. 3100
Los Angeles, CA 90015 (213) 742-7100

Company URL: http://www.lakings.com
Establishment information: Established in 1967.
Company type: Private company
Ultimate parent company: The Anschutz Corporation
Business activities: Operates professional ice hockey club.
Business type (SIC): Commercial sports
Corporate officers: Dean Lombardi, Pres.; Kelly Cheeseman, C.O.O; Dan Beckerman, C.F.O.; Peter Mazur, V.P., Finance; Jonathan Lowe, V.P., Mktg.; Matt Rosenfeld, V.P., Sales; Michael Altieri, V.P., Comms.
Giving statement: Giving through the Los Angeles Kings Hockey Club, LP Corporate Giving Program and the Kings Care Foundation.

The Los Angeles Kings Hockey Club, LP Corporate Giving Program

1111 S. Figueroa St.
Los Angeles, CA 90015-1306

Purpose and activities: The Los Angeles Kings make charitable contributions of memorabilia to nonprofit organizations involved with children's recreation. Support is given primarily in the Los Angeles, California, area.
Fields of interest: Recreation Children.
Type of support: In-kind gifts.
Geographic limitations: Giving primarily in the Los Angeles, CA, area.

Kings Care Foundation

555 N. Nash St.
El Segundo, CA 90245-2818 (310) 535-4490

Establishment information: Established in 1996 in CA.
Financial data (yr. ended 06/30/11): Revenue, $466,693; assets, $338,427 (M); gifts received, $251,746; expenditures, $293,846; giving activities include $217,503 for grants.
Purpose and activities: The foundation provides children in the greater Los Angeles, California, area with educational and recreational opportunities.
Fields of interest: Education; Recreation; Youth development.
Officers and Directors:* James Cefaly, Pres.; Jennifer Pope, V.P.; Danielle Prado, Secy.; Yvonne Luong, Treas.; Mike Altieri; Kelly Cheeseman; Jim Fox; Peter Mazur; Chris McGowan; Luc Robitaille.
EIN: 954443065

2307
The Los Angeles Lakers, Inc.

555 N. Nash St.
El Segundo, CA 90245 (310) 426-6000

Company URL: http://www.nba.com/lakers
Establishment information: Established in 1946.
Company type: Private company
Business activities: Operates professional basketball clubs.
Business type (SIC): Commercial sports
Corporate officers: Frank Mariani, C.E.O.; Jeanie Buss, Exec. V.P., Opers.; Joe McCormack, Sr. V.P. Finance and C.F.O.
Division: Los Angeles Sparks, El Segundo, CA
Giving statement: Giving through the Los Angeles Lakers, Inc. Contributions Program and the Los Angeles Lakers Youth Foundation.

The Los Angeles Lakers, Inc. Contributions Program

555 N. Nash St.
El Segundo, CA 90245 (310) 426-6000
URL: http://www.nba.com/lakers/community/donation_request.html

Los Angeles Lakers Youth Foundation

555 N. Nash St.
El Segundo, CA 90245-2818 (310) 426-6000
URL: http://www.nba.com/lakers/community/foundation.html

Establishment information: Established in 1992 in CA.
Contact: Janie Drexel, Pres. and C.E.O.
Financial data (yr. ended 07/31/11): Revenue, $1,004,929; assets, $2,061,891 (M); gifts received, $939,450; expenditures, $623,811; giving activities include $480,778 for grants.
Purpose and activities: The organization provides charitable assistance to the homeless in the Los Angeles, California, area. In addition, the foundation provides support to the community, particularly charitable organizations that provide service to aid underprivileged youth.
Fields of interest: Disasters, preparedness/services; Recreation; Youth development; Children/youth, services; Youth, services Homeless.
Program:
Grants Program: Funding is available for Los Angeles-area youth organizations to aid in the foundation's mission to use sports to promote

education, teamwork, and self-esteem among Los Angeles area youth. Eligible organizations must have 501(c)(3) status and provide their tax ID number with their application.
Geographic limitations: Giving limited to the Los Angeles, CA area.
Application information: Applications accepted. Application form required.
Initial approach: Submit proposal
Deadline(s): Mar. 15, June 15, Sept. 15, and Dec. 15
Officers and Directors: Janie Drexel*, Pres. and C.E.O.; James L. Perzik*, Secy.; Susan Matson, C.F.O.; Jerry H. Buss; Linda Rambis.
EIN: 954372410

2308
Los Angeles Soccer Partners, L.P.

(also known as Los Angeles Galaxy)
18400 Avalon Blvd., Ste. 200
Carson, CA 90746-2172 (310) 630-2200

Company URL: http://www.lagalaxy.com
Establishment information: Established in 1996.
Company type: Subsidiary of a private company
Ultimate parent company: The Anschutz Corporation
Business activities: Operates professional soccer club.
Business type (SIC): Commercial sports
Corporate officer: Chris McGowan, Pres.
Giving statement: Giving through the Los Angeles Galaxy Corporate Giving Program and the Los Angeles Galaxy Foundation.

Los Angeles Galaxy Corporate Giving Program

c/o Community Devel. Dept., Donations
18400 Avalon Blvd., Ste. 200
Carson, CA 90746-2181 (310) 630-2200
URL: http://www.lagalaxy.com/community-development

Purpose and activities: The Los Angeles Galaxy makes charitable contributions to nonprofit organizations designed to assist disadvantaged children. Support is given primarily in the greater Los Angeles, California, area.
Fields of interest: Elementary school/education; Education; Athletics/sports, soccer; Youth development Children; Youth; Economically disadvantaged.
Program:
Star Student Program: The Los Angeles Galaxy rewards 2 middle school students who demonstrate hard work, exemplary academic efforts, citizenship, and school attendance. The selected students are recognized on the field; receive a LA Galaxy Star Student t-shirt, certificate, and gift package by a LA Galaxy player; and receive 2 game tickets and the opportunity to serve as a Ball Kid. The middle school with the most nominations receives an LA Galaxy visit.
Type of support: Donated products; In-kind gifts; Income development; Loaned talent.
Geographic limitations: Giving primarily in areas of company operations in the greater Los Angeles, CA, area.
Publications: Application guidelines.
Application information: Applications accepted. Proposals should be submitted using organization letterhead. Support is limited to 1 contribution per organization during any given year. The Community Development Department handles giving. Application form required. Applicants should submit the following:
1) name, address and phone number of organization
2) copy of IRS Determination Letter
3) detailed description of project and amount of funding requested
4) contact person
Proposals should indicate the date and location of the event and the type of fundraiser.
Initial approach: Download application form and mail proposal and application form to headquarters for memorabilia and player/coach appearances; download nomination form and mail to headquarters for Star Student Program
Copies of proposal: 1
Deadline(s): 6 weeks prior to need for memorabilia and player/coach appearances; None for Star Student Program
Final notification: 1 to 2 weeks prior to need; 2 to 4 weeks for player/coach appearances

Los Angeles Galaxy Foundation

18400 Avalon Blvd., Ste. 200
Carson, CA 90746-2181 (310) 630-2153
FAX: (310) 630-2250; E-mail: nmann@lagalaxy.com; Toll-free tel.: (877) 342-5299; URL: http://www.lagalaxy.com/galaxy-foundation

Establishment information: Established in CA.
Financial data (yr. ended 12/31/11): Revenue, $85,546; assets, $211,073 (M); gifts received, $107,942; expenditures, $70,353; program services expenses, $50,232; giving activities include $66,424 for grants.
Purpose and activities: The foundation supports educational and recreational programs for children and other charitable activities for youth in the southern California area.
Fields of interest: Education; Youth development.
Geographic limitations: Giving primarily in southern CA.
Officers and Directors:* Alexi Lalas*, Pres.; Gloria King*, Secy.; Dan Beckerman*, Treas.; Timothy J. Leiweke; Frank Moore; Thomas Payne.
EIN: 954770699

2309
Louisiana Health Service & Indemnity Company, Inc.

(doing business as Blue Cross and Blue Shield of Louisiana)
5525 Reitz Ave.
P.O. Box 98029
Baton Rouge, LA 70809-3802
(225) 295-3307

Company URL: http://www.bcbsla.com
Establishment information: Established in 1934.
Company type: Mutual company
Business activities: Operates medical service plan.
Business type (SIC): Insurance/accident and health
Financial profile for 2009: Number of employees, 1,500; assets, $1,210,000,000; sales volume, $2,230,000,000
Corporate officers: Thad Minaldi, Chair.; Dan Borne, Vice-Chair.; Mike Reitz, Pres. and C.E.O.; Peggy B. Scott, Exec. V.P. and C.O.O.; Ob Soonthornsima, Sr. V.P. and C.I.O.; Michele Calandro, Sr. V.P. and Genl. Counsel; Todd Schexnayder, Sr. V.P., Human Resources; Adam Short, V.P., Finance and Cont.; Gregory Cross, V.P., Sales
Board of directors: Thad Minaldi, Chair.; Dan Borne, Vice-Chair.; C. Richard Atkins; Michael B. Bruno; Frances T. Henry; Ann H. Knapp; Carl Luikart; Kevin McCotter; Charles Brent McCoy; Mike Reitz; Virgil Robinson, Jr.
Subsidiaries: HMO Louisiana, Inc., Baton Rouge, LA; Southern National Life Insurance Co., Baton Rouge, LA
Giving statement: Giving through the Blue Cross and Blue Shield of Louisiana Corporate Giving Program and the Blue Cross and Blue Shield of Louisiana Foundation.

Blue Cross and Blue Shield of Louisiana Corporate Giving Program

c/o Community Rels.
5525 Reitz Ave.
Baton Rouge, LA 70809-3802 (225) 298-7979
FAX: (225) 298-3175; E-mail: ComRel@bcbsla.com; Application address: Corp. Sponsorships, Community Rels., Blue Cross and Blue Shield of Louisiana, P.O. Box 98029, Baton Rouge, LA 70898; URL: http://www.bcbsla.com/AboutBlue/Company/Community/Pages/CommunityRelations.aspx

Purpose and activities: As a complement to its foundation, Blue Cross and Blue Shield of Louisiana also makes charitable contributions to nonprofit organizations directly. Support is limited to areas of company operations in Louisiana.
Fields of interest: Education; Public health; Health care; Human services, fund raising/fund distribution; United Ways and Federated Giving Programs.
Program:
Matching Gifts Program: Full-time employees, retirees and board members of Blue Cross and Blue Shield of Louisiana can increase the value of their donations to charitable and other organizations through a matching gift from the company. The program provides dollar-for-dollar matching contributions for a minimum gift of $100 up to a maximum $1,500.
Type of support: Donated products; Employee matching gifts; Employee volunteer services; In-kind gifts; Sponsorships.
Geographic limitations: Giving limited to areas of company operations in LA.
Support limitations: No support for non-accredited educational institutions or programs; fraternal, labor, athletic, veterans, band, discriminatory, or religious programs. No grants to individuals, or for capital projects, including building, renovations, or remodeling, religious purposes, political purposes, voter registration drives, memorials, or events that occur before the grant maker's notification date.
Publications: Application guidelines.
Application information: Applications accepted. All requests will receive an acknowledgement letter. Organizations that do not receive an acknowledgement within two weeks of submission should contact the grantmaker's offices. Sponsorships range from $500 to $7,500. Applications are not accepted via fax or e-mail. Application form required. Applicants should submit the following:
1) name, address and phone number of organization
2) copy of IRS Determination Letter
3) brief history of organization and description of its mission
4) detailed description of project and amount of funding requested
5) contact person

6) copy of current year's organizational budget and/ or project budget
7) plans for acknowledgement

Proposals for sponsorships should contain an income and expense budget from the previous year as well as a proposed budget for the current project; event name and date; e-mail addresses for the executive director and chief executive officer; target audience and expected revenue; and company affiliations, if applicable. Proposals for volunteering should include the number of volunteers needed, start time, and skills and materials needed.

Initial approach: Download application form and send completed form with requested attachments to application address

Deadline(s): Jan. 15, Apr. 15, July 15, and Oct. 15 for sponsorship requests; 6 weeks prior to event for Team Blue volunteer requests

Final notification: Apr., July, Oct., and Jan for sponsorships; 2 weeks prior to event for Team Blue volunteer requests

Blue Cross and Blue Shield of Louisiana Foundation

(formerly Louisiana Child Caring Foundation, Inc.)
P.O. Box 98029
Baton Rouge, LA 70898-9022 (225) 298-7051
FAX: (225) 298-3175;
E-mail: Christy.Reeves@bcbsla.com; Additional tel. and e-mail: (225) 298-7979, foundation@bcbsla.com; Tel. and e-mail for The Angel Award: (888) 219-2583, angel.award@bcbsla.com; Contact for Challenge for a Healthier Louisiana: Elizabeth Gollub, tel.: (225) 763-0945, e-mail: BCBSChallenge@pbrc.edu;
URL: http://www.bcbsla.com/web/reddotcm/html/64_205.asp

Donor: Blue Cross Blue Shield of Louisiana.
Contact: Christy Oliver Reeves, Exec. Dir.
Financial data (yr. ended 12/31/10): Assets, $19,644,854 (M); gifts received, $20,401,988; expenditures, $1,317,183; qualifying distributions, $1,308,710; giving activities include $1,240,006 for 87 grants (high: $76,022; low: $1,000).
Purpose and activities: The foundation supports programs designed to improve health and education in Louisiana.
Fields of interest: Elementary/secondary education; Education, early childhood education; Education; Medicine/medical care, public education; Hospitals (general); Health care, clinics/centers; Public health; Public health, obesity; Public health, physical fitness; Health care; Nutrition Children/youth; Aging; Economically disadvantaged.
Programs:

Challenge for a Healthier Louisiana Grant Program: The foundation, in partnership with the Pennington Biomedical Research Center, challenges communities to reshape their environments to support healthy living and prevent obesity. The foundation supports projects designed to encourage healthy lifestyles; promote physical activity; promote fitness and nutrition education; support parental involvement in their children's lives; provide access to safe facilities and neighborhoods for physical activity; and support adequate and healthy nutrition. Special emphasis is directed toward projects that target underserved or high risk populations. Challenge grants range from $250,000 to $1,00,000 for a one- to three-year period and grants must be matched dollar-for-dollar by either cash or in-kind resources identified by the applicant.

Impact Grants - Education: The foundation supports programs designed to help people learn ways to stay healthy and make wise decisions about healthcare. Special emphasis is directed toward programs designed to promote health literacy; train medical professionals; and serve young people age pre-kindergarten through college. Grants range from $5,000 to $20,000.

Impact Grants - Health: The foundation supports programs designed to improve public health; reduce barriers to care for the uninsured; and conduct research to prevent or cure disease. Special emphasis is directed toward programs designed to serve rural areas, children, seniors, and people who are at-risk and underserved. Grants range from $5,000 to $20,000.

Smart Bodies: Through Smart Bodies, the foundation and the LSU AgCenter provides an interactive school-based program designed to teach children in grades K-5 about nutrition and fitness. The program is designed to prevent childhood obesity and integrates classroom activities with hands-on learning.

The Angel Award: The foundation annually honors eight outstanding volunteers in Louisiana who work to improve the quality of life for children. The award includes a $20,000 grant to the honorees' charities and the honorees are celebrated at a special ceremony.
Type of support: Faculty/staff development; General/operating support; Management development/capacity building; Matching/challenge support; Program development; Program evaluation; Research; Sponsorships.
Geographic limitations: Giving primarily in areas of company operations in LA.
Support limitations: No support for political candidates or organizations, athletes or athletic teams, labor, fraternal, or veterans' organizations, parent-teacher organizations, or religious organizations. No grants to individuals, or for beauty pageants, students raising funds for travel, capital projects or campaigns, or memorials.
Publications: Application guidelines; Informational brochure.
Application information: Applications accepted. Proposals for Impact Grants should be no longer than 5 pages. Application form required. Applicants should submit the following:
1) timetable for implementation and evaluation of project
2) how project will be sustained once grantmaker support is completed
3) population served
4) name, address and phone number of organization
5) copy of IRS Determination Letter
6) brief history of organization and description of its mission
7) geographic area to be served
8) copy of most recent annual report/audited financial statement/990
9) how project's results will be evaluated or measured
10) listing of board of directors, trustees, officers and other key people and their affiliations
11) detailed description of project and amount of funding requested
12) plans for cooperation with other organizations, if any
13) contact person
14) copy of current year's organizational budget and/or project budget

Initial approach: Download application form and mail proposal and form for Impact Grants; e-mail letter of intent for Challenge Grant; complete online nomination form for The Angel Award

Deadline(s): Jan. 15 and July 15 for Impact Grants; Jan. 13 for letter of intent and Apr. 30 for full application for Challenge Grant; May 4 for The Angel Award

Final notification: Apr. and Oct. for Impact Grants

Officers and Directors :* Peggy B. Scott*, Chair. and Pres.; Christy Oliver Reed, Exec. Dir.; C. Richard Atkins, D.D.S.; Dan Borne; Frances T. Henry; Kevin McCotter; Sybil H. Morial; Todd Schexnayder.
EIN: 721232379
Selected grants: The following grants are a representative sample of this grantmaker's funding activity:
$76,022 to Louisiana State University and A & M College, Baton Rouge, LA, 2010.
$39,200 to Eyes Have It, New Orleans, LA, 2010.
$30,000 to American Cancer Society, Baton Rouge, LA, 2010.
$30,000 to Pennington Biomedical Research Foundation, Baton Rouge, LA, 2010.
$25,000 to Food Bank of Central Louisiana, Alexandria, LA, 2010.
$25,000 to Jefferson Performing Arts Society, Metairie, LA, 2010.
$25,000 to Special Olympics Louisiana, Hammond, LA, 2010.
$25,000 to United Way of Acadiana, Lafayette, LA, 2010.
$20,000 to Junior League of Baton Rouge, Baton Rouge, LA, 2010.
$10,000 to Baton Rouge Area Alcohol and Drug Center, Baton Rouge, LA, 2010.
$10,000 to Family and Youth Counseling Agency, Lake Charles, LA, 2010.

2310
Louisiana-Pacific Corporation

(also known as LP)
414 Union St., Ste. 2000
Nashville, TN 37219-1711 (615) 986-5600
FAX: (615) 986-5666

Company URL: http://www.lpcorp.com
Establishment information: Established in 1973.
Company type: Public company
Company ticker symbol and exchange: LPX/NYSE
Business activities: Manufactures building products.
Business type (SIC): Forest products; lumber and wood products (except furniture); lumber and wood products; wood millwork; wood products/miscellaneous; pulp mills
Financial profile for 2012: Number of employees, 3,900; assets, $2,331,000,000; sales volume, $1,715,800,000; pre-tax net income, $38,000,000; expenses, $1,640,600,000; liabilities, $1,297,200,000
Corporate officers: E. Gary Cook, Ph.D., Chair.; Curtis M. Stevens, C.E.O.; Sallie B. Bailey, Exec. V.P. and C.F.O.; Mark Fuchs, V.P., Genl. Counsel, and Corp. Secy.; Ann Harris, V.P., Human Resources
Board of directors: E. Gary Cook, Ph.D., Chair.; Archie W. Dunham; Daniel K. Frierson; Lizanne C. Gottung; Kurt M. Landgraf; Dustan E. McCoy; Curtis M. Stevens; Colin D. Watson; John W. Weaver
Giving statement: Giving through the Louisiana-Pacific Corporation Contributions Program and the Louisiana-Pacific Foundation.
Company EIN: 930609074

Louisiana-Pacific Corporation Contributions Program

414 Union Sq., Ste. 2000
Nashville, TN 37219-1711 (615) 986-5600
URL: http://www.lpcorp.com/sustainability/social_responsibility/

Purpose and activities: As a complement to its foundation, Louisiana-Pacific also makes charitable contributions to nonprofit organizations directly. Support is given primarily in areas of company operations.
Fields of interest: Education; Housing/shelter; Community/economic development; General charitable giving.
Type of support: Donated products; Employee volunteer services; General/operating support; In-kind gifts; Sponsorships.
Geographic limitations: Giving primarily in areas of company operations.

Louisiana-Pacific Foundation

414 Union Street, Ste. 2000
Nashville, TN 37219-1711 (615) 986-5886
E-mail: lpfoundation@lpcorp.com; URL: http://www.lpcorp.com/sustainability/contributions_and_foundation/

Establishment information: Established in 1973 in OR.
Donor: Louisiana-Pacific Corp.
Contact: Mary Louise Cohen, Chair. and Pres.
Financial data (yr. ended 12/31/10): Assets, $541,377 (M); expenditures, $296,367; qualifying distributions, $294,741; giving activities include $294,741 for 41 grants (high: $50,000; low: $200).
Purpose and activities: The foundation supports programs designed to promote shelter; public education; the environment; and social services.
Fields of interest: Elementary/secondary education; Education; Environment; Food banks; Housing/shelter, development; Housing/shelter; Human services.
Programs:
Community Relief Program: The foundation awards grants of $1,500 to $4,000 per community to support schools and nonprofit organizations providing relief services.
Employee Matching Grant Program: The foundation matches contributions made by employees of Louisiana-Pacific to workplace giving campaigns, company approved charities, United Way, and other nonprofit organizations on a one-for-one basis, up to $5,000 per employee per year. The foundation also matches funds raised by employee race teams for approved causes.
Type of support: Employee matching gifts; General/operating support; Program development; Sponsorships.
Geographic limitations: Giving primarily in areas of company operations, with emphasis on Hanceville, AL, Red Bluff, CA, Athens, GA, MN, Wilmington, NC, Nashville, TN, Carthage, TX, WI, and Canada.
Publications: Grants list; Informational brochure; IRS Form 990 or 990-PF printed copy available upon request.
Application information: Applications not accepted. Unsolicited applications are currently not accepted.
Board meeting date(s): Quarterly
Officers and Trustees:* Mary Louise Cohn*, Chair. and Pres.; Ashley Koch, Secy.; Robert Hopkins, Treas.; Russell L. Carroll; Tamara Lester; Laura Proctor; William B. Southern.
EIN: 237268660
Selected grants: The following grants are a representative sample of this grantmaker's funding activity:
$50,000 to Friends of Warner Park, Nashville, TN, 2010. For general support.
$31,000 to PENCIL Foundation, Nashville, TN, 2010. For general support.
$21,747 to American Heart Association, Nashville, TN, 2010. For employee match.
$10,000 to Oasis Center, Nashville, TN, 2010. For general support.
$5,000 to Cystic Fibrosis Foundation, Nashville, TN, 2010. For general support.
$3,750 to Boy Scouts of America, Nashville, TN, 2010. For general support.
$2,175 to American Cancer Society, Portland, OR, 2010.
$1,500 to Schoolhouse Supplies, Portland, OR, 2010. For general support.

2311
Love's Travel Stops & Country Stores, Inc.

10601 N. Pennsylvania Ave.
Oklahoma City, OK 73120 (405) 751-9000

Company URL: http://www.loves.com
Establishment information: Established in 1964.
Company type: Private company
Business activities: Operates chain of travel stops.
Business type (SIC): Gasoline service stations
Financial profile for 2011: Number of employees, 8,000; sales volume, $24,400,000,000
Corporate officers: Tom Love, Chair. and C.E.O.; Frank Love, Pres.; Doug Stussi, Exec. V.P. and C.F.O.; Jim Xenos, V.P. and C.I.O.; Kevin Asbury, V.P., Opers.
Board of director: Tom Love, Chair.
Giving statement: Giving through the Love's Travel Stops & Country Stores, Inc. Contributions Program.

Love's Travel Stops & Country Stores, Inc. Contributions Program

10601 N. Pennsylvania Ave.
Oklahoma City, OK 73120-4108 (405) 751-9000
E-mail: donations@loves.com; URL: http://www.loves.com/AboutUs/Community.aspx

Financial data (yr. ended 12/31/10): Total giving, $2,000,000, including $2,000,000 for grants.
Geographic limitations: Giving primarily in areas of company operations, with emphasis on OK.

2312
Lowe's Companies, Inc.

1000 Lowe's Blvd.
Mooresville, NC 28117 (704) 758-1000
FAX: (704) 757-0611

Company URL: http://www.lowes.com
Establishment information: Established in 1952.
Company type: Public company
Company ticker symbol and exchange: LOW/NYSE
International Securities Identification Number: US5486611073
Business activities: Operates home improvement and consumer electronics stores.
Business type (SIC): Hardware, plumbing, and heating equipment—wholesale; lumber and construction materials—wholesale; lumber and other building materials—retail; appliance stores/household; consumer electronics and music stores
Financial profile for 2013: Number of employees, 245,000; assets, $32,666,000,000; sales volume, $50,521,000,000; pre-tax net income, $3,137,000,000; expenses, $47,384,000,000; liabilities, $18,809,000,000
Fortune 1000 ranking: 2012—56th in revenues, 106th in profits, and 171st in assets
Forbes 2000 ranking: 2012—174th in sales, 310th in profits, and 686th in assets
Corporate officers: Robert A. Niblock, Chair., Pres., and C.E.O.; Rick D. Damron, C.O.O.; Robert F. Hull, Jr., Exec. V.P. and C.F.O.; Robert Ihrie, Sr. V.P., Human Resources; Matthew V. Hollifield, Sr. V.P. and C.A.O.; Kevin V. Summers, C.I.O.; Gaither M. Keener, Jr., Secy.
Board of directors: Robert A. Niblock, Chair.; Raul Alvarez; David W. Bernauer; Leonard L. Berry, Ph.D.; Peter C. Browning; Richard W. Dreiling; Dawn E. Hudson; Robert L. Johnson; Marshall O. Larsen; Richard K. Lochridge; Eric C. Wiseman
Giving statement: Giving through the Lowe's Companies, Inc. Corporate Giving Program, the Lowe's Charitable and Educational Foundation, and the Lowe's Employee Relief Fund.
Company EIN: 560578072

Lowe's Companies, Inc. Corporate Giving Program

1000 Lowe's Blvd.
Mooresville, NC 28117-8520 (704) 758-1000
URL: http://www.lowes.com/lowes/lkn?action=pg&p=AboutLowes/Community

Purpose and activities: As a complement to its foundation, Lowe's also makes charitable contributions to nonprofit organizations directly. Support is given on a national basis.
Fields of interest: Vocational education; Education; Environment; Housing/shelter; Youth development; American Red Cross; Community/economic development.
Programs:
Carl Buchan Scholarship: Lowe's Companies awards scholarships to employees and dependents of employees. The program is administered by Scholarship Program Administers.
Lowe's Community Pride Program: Lowe's Companies awards $250 grants to nonprofit organizations with which employees volunteer at least 25 hours.
The Lowe's Scholarship: Lowe's Companies awards college scholarships to high school seniors planning to attend a 2-year or 4-year college or university in the U.S. The company awards three hundred fifty-two $1,000 scholarships, twenty-two $5,000 regional scholarships to the most outstanding applicant from each Lowe's US region, and one $15,000 national grand prize scholarship to the best overall applicant. Scholarship recipients are selected based on leadership qualities, community involvement, and academic performance. The program is administered by Scholarship Program Administrators.
Type of support: Building/renovation; Employee volunteer services; Employee-related scholarships; General/operating support; Program development; Scholarships—to individuals; Sponsorships.
Geographic limitations: Giving on a national basis.
Publications: Application guidelines.
Application information: Applications accepted. Application form required.
Initial approach: Complete online application form for scholarships and sponsorships
Deadline(s): Visit website for scholarship deadlines; none for sponsorships

Lowe's Charitable and Educational Foundation

c/o Community Rels.
1000 Lowe's Blvd., NB3TA
Mooresville, NC 28117-8520 (704) 758-2831
FAX: (704) 757-4766;
E-mail: cindy.l.williams@lowes.com; Additional address: P.O. Box 1000, Mooresville, NC 28115; Application address for Outdoor Classroom Grant

Prog.: Outdoor Classroom Grant Prog., P.O. Box 3292, Memphis, TN 38173-0292; Tel. for Lowe's Toolbox for Education: (800) 644-3561, ext. 208; E-mail for Lowe's Toolbox for Education: info@toolboxforeducation.com; URL: http://www.lowes.com/community

Establishment information: Established in 1957.
Donors: Lowe's Cos., Inc.; The Valspar Corp.
Contact: Cindy Williams
Financial data (yr. ended 01/31/12): Revenue, $21,174,219; assets, $24,014,821 (M); gifts received, $21,171,863; expenditures, $19,357,368; program services expenses, $19,357,368; giving activities include $19,132,086 for grants.
Purpose and activities: The foundation supports parks and playgrounds and organizations involved with K-12 education, environmental beautification, environmental education, home safety, and community development.
Fields of interest: Elementary/secondary education; Vocational education; Education, PTA groups; Environment, beautification programs; Environmental education; Housing/shelter; Safety, education; Recreation, parks/playgrounds; Community/economic development; Science.
Programs:

Community Improvement: The foundation supports programs designed to beautify and enhance parks and neighborhoods; repair and renovate buildings and enhance landscaping of facilities serving the community; create community gardens, parks, and playgrounds; initiate community clean-up programs; and establish outdoor learning environments such as educational gardening programs.

K-12 Public School Initiative: The foundation supports programs designed to provide construction- and trade-related education; initiate clean-up, landscaping, and painting projects; enhance playgrounds; and make minor repairs and renovations of public school buildings.

Lowe's Toolbox for Education: Through the Lowe's Toolbox for Education program, in partnership with PTO Today, the foundation annually awards up to 1,000 grants from $2,000 to $5,000 to K-12 schools and parent teacher groups for school improvement projects initiated by parents. Special emphasis is directed toward programs designed to encourage parent involvement and build stronger community spirit.

Outdoor Classroom Grant Program: Through the Outdoor Classroom Grant Program, in partnership with International Paper Company and National Geographic Explorer! classroom magazine, the foundation annually awards at least 100 grants of up to $20,000 to K-12 schools with programs designed to engage students in outdoor hands-on natural science experiences leading to enrichment opportunities across the core curriculum.

Type of support: Employee volunteer services; General/operating support.
Geographic limitations: Giving on a national basis in areas of company operations; giving on a national basis for the Outdoor Classroom Grant Program and Lowe's Toolbox for Education.
Support limitations: No support for national health organizations or their local affiliates, religious organizations, political, labor, veterans', or fraternal organizations, civic clubs, or candidates, sports teams, animal rescue and support organizations, organizations not of direct benefit to the entire community, private schools, or local affiliates or chapters of Habitat for Humanity, the American Red Cross, the United Way, or the Home Safety Council; no support for schools established less than two years ago for Lowe's Toolbox for Education. No grants to individuals or families, or for academic or medical research, religious programs or events, special events, sponsorship of fundraising events, advertising or marketing, athletic events or athletic programs, arts-based programs, travel-related events, book, film, video, or television program development or production, capital campaigns, endowments, or endowed chairs, continuing education for teachers and staff, institutional overhead and/or indirect costs, memorial campaigns, continuing support, international programs, or tickets to events; no grants for stipends, salaries, scholarships, or third party funding for Lowe's Toolbox for Education.
Publications: Application guidelines; Grants list.
Application information: Applications accepted. Support is limited to 1 contribution per organization during any given year. The foundation reviews the first 1,500 applications only for Lowe's Toolbox for Education. Application form required.
Proposals for the Outdoor Classroom Grant Program should include an outdoor classroom plan, including illustrations, CD or DVD video footage, and photos, if applicable; the teacher's name and telephone number; and a letter of support from the school's principal or superintendent, including budget requirements.

Initial approach: Complete online application form; download application form and mail proposal and application form to application address for Outdoor Classroom Grant Program; complete online application form for Lowe's Toolbox for Education
Copies of proposal: 1
Deadline(s): None; postmarked by Dec. 31, Apr. 30, and Aug. 31 for the Outdoor Classroom Grant Program; Oct. 15 and Feb. 15 for Lowe's Toolbox for Education
Final notification: Mid-Jan., mid-May, and mid-Sept. for the Outdoor Classroom Grant Program; Dec. 15 and Apr. 15 for Lowe's Toolbox for Education

Officers and Trustees:* Larry D. Stone, Chair. and Pres.; Gregory M. Bridgeford*, V.P.; Gaither M. Keener, Secy.; David R. Green, Treas.; Maureen K. Ausura; Charles W. "Nick" Canter; Marshall A. Croom; William R. Johnson; N. Brian Peace.
EIN: 566061689
Selected grants: The following grants are a representative sample of this grantmaker's funding activity:
$1,500,000 to Bowling Green High School, Bowling Green, OH, 2011.
$1,250,000 to National Trust for Historic Preservation, Washington, DC, 2011.
$1,000,000 to Boys and Girls Clubs of Sarasota County, Sarasota, FL, 2011.
$1,000,000 to Rebuilding Together Madison County, Madison, IL, 2011.
$321,420 to YMCA of Greater Charlotte, Charlotte, NC, 2011.
$100,000 to Arts Council, Winston-Salem, NC, 2011.
$56,649 to Collin County Care Center, McKinney, TX, 2011.
$50,000 to Seaborn Lee Elementary School, College Park, GA, 2011.
$41,600 to Boys and Girls Clubs of Metropolitan Richmond, Richmond, VA, 2011.
$36,820 to Charlotte Center for Urban Ministry, Charlotte, NC, 2011.

Lowe's Employee Relief Fund

1000 Lowes Blvd., Ste. 2ETA
Mooresville, NC 28117-8520 (704) 758-2009

Establishment information: Established in 1999 in NC.
Financial data (yr. ended 09/30/11): Revenue, $2,427,530; assets, $4,470,718 (M); gifts received, $2,448,301; expenditures, $2,352,647; program services expenses, $2,352,647; giving activities include $2,281,300 for grants to individuals.
Purpose and activities: The organization provides Lowe's employees with relief from financial hardships due to disasters or emergency.
Fields of interest: Safety/disasters; Human services, emergency aid.
Type of support: Grants to individuals.
Officers: Andy Mottesheard*, Pres.; Will D. Spears*, V.P.; Matt Holden*, Secy.; David Green*, Treas.
EIN: 562160955

2313
Lowndes, Drosdick, Doster, Kantor & Reed PA

215 N. Eola Dr.
Orlando, FL 32801-2028 (407) 843-4600

Company URL: http://lowndes-law.com
Establishment information: Established in 1969.
Company type: Private company
Business activities: Operates law firm.
Business type (SIC): Legal services
Corporate officer: William T. Dymond, Jr., Pres., C.E.O. and Managing Partner
Office: Orlando, FL
Giving statement: Giving through the Lowndes, Drosdick, Doster, Kantor & Reed PA Pro Bono Program.

Lowndes, Drosdick, Doster, Kantor & Reed PA Pro Bono Program

215 N. Eola Dr.
Orlando, FL 32801-2028
E-mail: matt.brenner@lowndes-law.com;
URL: http://www.lowndes-law.com/our-firm/pro-bono

Contact: Matt Brenner, Partner & Chair. of Pro Bono Comm.
Fields of interest: Legal services.
Type of support: Pro bono services - legal.
Application information: A Pro Bono Committee manages the pro bono program.

2314
LSI Corporation

(doing business as LSI Logic)
1320 Ridder Park Dr.
San Jose, CA 95131 (800) 372-2447
FAX: (302) 636-5454

Company URL: http://www.lsi.com/
Establishment information: Established in 1980.
Company type: Public company
Company ticker symbol and exchange: LSI/NYSE
International Securities Identification Number: US5021611026
Business activities: Designs, develops, and markets semiconductors and storage systems.
Business type (SIC): Electronic components and accessories
Financial profile for 2012: Number of employees, 5,080; assets, $2,356,160,000; sales volume, $2,506,090,000; pre-tax net income,

$175,270,000; expenses, $2,368,530,000; liabilities, $1,196,540,000
Fortune 1000 ranking: 2012—808th in revenues, 581st in profits, and 816th in assets
Corporate officers: Gregorio Reyes, Chair.; Abhi Y. Talwalkar, Pres. and C.E.O.; Jeff Richardson, Exec. V.P. and C.O.O.; Bryon Look, Exec. V.P., C.F.O., and C.A.O.; Jean F. Rankin, Exec. V.P., Genl. Counsel, and Secy.; Gautam Srivastava, Sr. V.P., Mktg. and Human Resources
Board of directors: Gregorio Reyes, Chair.; Charles A. Haggerty; Richard S. Hill; John H.F. Miner; Arun N. Netravali; Charles C. Pope; Michael G. Strachan; Abhi Y. Talwalkar; Susan M. Whitney
International operations: Bermuda; Canada; Cayman Islands; China; France; Germany; Hong Kong; Hungary; India; Ireland; Italy; Japan; Malta; Netherlands; Singapore; South Korea; Sweden; Taiwan; United Arab Emirates; United Kingdom
Giving statement: Giving through the LSI Corporation Contributions Program.
Company EIN: 942712976

LSI Corporation Contributions Program

1621 Barber Ln.
Milpitas, CA 95035-7455 (800) 372-2447
URL: http://www.lsi.com/about/globalcitizen/Pages/ehs.aspx

Purpose and activities: LSI Logic makes charitable contributions to programs involved with K-12 math and science. Support is given primarily in areas of company operations in California, Colorado, Georgia, Kansas, Massachusetts, Minnesota, Oregon, Pennsylvania, and Texas.
Fields of interest: Elementary/secondary education; Science; Mathematics.
Type of support: Employee volunteer services; General/operating support; In-kind gifts; Program development.
Geographic limitations: Giving primarily in areas of company operations in CA, CO, GA, KS, MA, MN, OR, PA, and TX, and on an international basis in areas of company operations.
Application information:
Administrator: Tara Yingst, Mgr., Corp. Comms.

2315
The Lubrizol Corporation

29400 Lakeland Blvd.
Wickliffe, OH 44092-2298 (440) 943-4200

Company URL: http://www.lubrizol.com
Establishment information: Established in 1928.
Company type: Subsidiary of a public company
Parent company: Berkshire Hathaway Inc.
Business activities: Manufactures specialty chemical additives, ingredients, resins, and compounds.
Business type (SIC): Chemicals/industrial organic
Financial profile for 2011: Number of employees, 6,896; assets, $4,967,000,000; sales volume, $5,417,800,000
Corporate officers: James L. Hambrick, Chair., Pres., and C.E.O.; Brian A. Valentine, Corp. V.P., C.F.O., and Treas.; Suzanne F. Day, Corp. V.P. and Genl. Counsel; Larry D. Norwood, Corp. V.P., Opers.; Gregory D. Taylor, Corp. V.P., Comms.; Andrew B. Panega, Corp. V.P., Human Resources
Board of director: James L. Hambrick, Chair.
Plants: Paso Robles, CA; Countryside, IL; Calvert City, Louisville, KY; Wilmington, MA; Midland, MI; Pedricktown, NJ; Gastonia, NC; Avon Lake, Bowling Green, Brecksville, Painesville, OH; Spartanburg, SC; Bayport, Deer Park, Houston, TX
International operations: Belgium; Brazil; Canada; Cayman Islands; France; Germany; Gibraltar; Hong Kong; India; Japan; Luxembourg; Netherlands; Singapore; United Kingdom
Giving statement: Giving through the Lubrizol Corporation Contributions Program and the Lubrizol Foundation.
Company EIN: 340367600

The Lubrizol Foundation

29400 Lakeland Blvd.
Wickliffe, OH 44092-2298 (440) 347-1797
FAX: (440) 347-1858;
E-mail: karen.lerchbacher@lubrizol.com;
URL: http://www.lubrizol.com/CorporateResponsibility/Lubrizol-Foundation.html

Establishment information: Incorporated in 1952 in OH.
Donor: The Lubrizol Corp.
Contact: Karen A. Lerchbacher, Grants Mgr.
Financial data (yr. ended 12/31/12): Assets, $22,330,894 (M); gifts received, $5,000,000; expenditures, $2,646,768; qualifying distributions, $2,646,768; giving activities include $1,902,455 for 188 grants (high: $192,500; low: $703) and $744,313 for 1,530 employee matching gifts.
Purpose and activities: The foundation makes grants in support of education, health care, human services, civic, cultural, youth development and environmental activities. Strong emphasis on STEM (Science, Technology, Engineering and Mathematics) education.
Fields of interest: Museums; Charter schools; Higher education; Education; Environmental education; Environment; Youth development; Human services; Chemistry; Engineering Youth.
Programs:
Civic & Cultural: The foundation supports performing arts, public broadcasting stations, and special interest groups designed to enhance local communities.
Community Connection: The foundation awards $500 grants to nonprofit organizations with which employees of Lubrizol volunteer at least 40 hours per year.
Education: The foundation supports elementary, secondary, and higher education, educational programs, and combined educational funds.
Education Scholarships, Fellowships, and Awards: The foundation supports programs designed to promote higher education and provides scholarship funds to select colleges and universities. Special emphasis is directed toward the study of chemistry, chemical engineering, and mechanical engineering.
Environmental: The foundation supports parks, nature centers, conservancies, and environmental education efforts.
Health and Human Services: The foundation supports programs designed to promote health and human services. Special emphasis is directed toward hospitals, specialized health care providers, and organizations providing basic human services including clothing, rehabilitation, and hospice care for those in need.
Matching Gift Program: The foundation matches contributions made by employees of Lubrizol to educational institutions and nonprofit organizations on a one-for-one basis from $100 to $5,000 per employee, per year.
Youth Activities: The foundation supports programs designed to promote youth activity. Special emphasis is directed toward programs designed to provide training in leadership skills and responsible citizenship.
Type of support: Annual campaigns; Building/renovation; Capital campaigns; Continuing support; Employee matching gifts; Employee volunteer services; Equipment; Fellowships; General/operating support; Scholarship funds.
Geographic limitations: Giving primarily in areas of major company operations, with emphasis on the greater Cleveland, OH and Houston, TX, areas.
Support limitations: No support for religious or political organizations. No grants to individuals, or for start-up needs, debt reduction, demonstration projects, publications, or conferences; generally, no grants for endowments; no loans.
Publications: Annual report (including application guidelines); Application guidelines; Financial statement; Grants list; IRS Form 990 or 990-PF printed copy available upon request.
Application information: Applications accepted. Additional information may be requested at a later date. A site visit may be requested. Application form not required. Applicants should submit the following:
1) listing of additional sources and amount of support
2) detailed description of project and amount of funding requested
3) descriptive literature about organization
4) copy of most recent annual report/audited financial statement/990
5) copy of IRS Determination Letter
6) copy of current year's organizational budget and/or project budget
7) contact person
8) name, address and phone number of organization
9) additional materials/documentation

Initial approach: Proposal
Copies of proposal: 1
Board meeting date(s): As required, usually 4 times per year
Deadline(s): None
Final notification: 2 weeks following board meetings

Officers and Trustees:* James L. Hambrick*, Chair.; David J. Enzerra*, Pres.; Karen A. Lerchbacher*, Secy. and Grants Mgr.; Brian A. Valentine*, Treas.; Robert T. Graf; K. L. Jethrow.
Number of staff: 1 part-time professional; 1 full-time support.
EIN: 346500595
Selected grants: The following grants are a representative sample of this grantmaker's funding activity:
$192,500 to United Way of Greater Cleveland, Cleveland, OH, 2012.
$64,000 to Ohio State University, Columbus, OH, 2012. For scholarships.
$50,000 to American Red Cross, Greater Cleveland Chapter, Cleveland, OH, 2012. For Hurricane Sandy Disaster Relief Fund.
$50,000 to Cleveland Museum of Natural History, Cleveland, OH, 2012. For exhibit.
$30,000 to Cleveland Orchestra, Cleveland, OH, 2012. For general operating support.
$30,000 to Cleveland State University, Cleveland, OH, 2012. Toward purchase of laboratory equipment.

2316
Lucasfilm Ltd.

5858 Lucas Valley Rd.
P.O. Box 2009
Nicasio, CA 94946-9703 (415) 662-1800

Company URL: http://www.lucasfilm.com
Establishment information: Established in 1971.
Company type: Private company

Business activities: Produces motion pictures and television programming; provides motion picture visual effect and sound services; develops video games; licenses entertainment properties; provides Internet entertainment services.
Business type (SIC): Motion pictures/production and services allied to; investors/miscellaneous; computer services
Corporate officers: George W. Lucas, Jr., Chair.; Micheline Chau, Pres. and C.O.O.; Jan van der Voort, C.A.O.; Steve Condiotti, V.P., Finance, and C.A.O.; Colum Slevin, V.P., Opers.; Doug Yates, V.P., Mktg.
Board of director: George W. Lucas, Jr., Chair.
Subsidiaries: Lucas Digital Ltd., San Rafael, CA; Lucas Learning Ltd., San Rafael, CA; Lucas Licensing Ltd., San Rafael, CA; LucasArts Entertainment Co., San Rafael, CA
Giving statement: Giving through the George Lucas Educational Foundation and the Lucasfilm Foundation.

The George Lucas Educational Foundation

P.O. Box 3494
San Rafael, CA 94912-3494
FAX: (415) 662-1532; E-mail: info@edutopia.org; URL: http://www.edutopia.org/

Establishment information: Established as a company-sponsored operating foundation in 1993 in CA.
Donors: Lucasfilm Ltd.; Lucasfilm Foundation; George W. Lucas, Jr.
Financial data (yr. ended 12/31/11): Assets, $1,663,614 (M); gifts received, $4,449,687; expenditures, $4,661,629; qualifying distributions, $3,912,451; giving activities include $722,930 for 4 grants (high: $541,000; low: $30,000).
Purpose and activities: The foundation promotes the K-12 learning process through diverse and innovative media to connect and inspire positive change in all areas of education.
Fields of interest: Elementary/secondary education; Elementary/secondary school reform; Education.

Program:

Edutopia: Through Edutopia, the foundation promotes a website, newsletter, video, and magazine dedicated to practical, hands-on advice for educators and parents in all areas of education. The program is designed to highlight updated best practices from integrated studies, project learning, social and emotional learning, technology integration, teacher development, and comprehensive assessment.
Type of support: Program development.
Application information: Applications not accepted. Unsolicited requests for funds not accepted.
Officers: George W. Lucas, Jr., Chair.; Stephen D. Arnold, Vice-Chair. and C.F.O.; Cynthia Johanson Irish, Secy.
Directors: Micheline Chau; Kim Meredith; Kate Nyegaard; Marshall Turner.
EIN: 680065687
Selected grants: The following grants are a representative sample of this grantmaker's funding activity:
$155,044 to Bellevue Schools Foundation, Bellevue, WA, 2010.
$100,000 to University of Washington, Seattle, WA, 2010.
$29,925 to Envision Schools, Oakland, CA, 2010.

Lucasfilm Foundation

One Letterman Dr., Bldg B
San Francisco, CA 94129-1495
Application address: P.O. Box 2009, San Rafael, CA 94912; URL: http://www.lucasfilm.com/inside/faq/

Establishment information: Established in 2005 in CA.
Donors: George W. Lucas, Jr.; Lucasfilm Ltd.
Contact: Anne Merrifield
Financial data (yr. ended 12/31/11): Assets, $90,498,167 (M); gifts received, $55,000,000; expenditures, $35,060,225; qualifying distributions, $34,984,313; giving activities include $34,770,779 for grants.
Purpose and activities: The foundation supports organizations involved with arts and culture, education, and human services. Special emphasis is directed toward programs designed to benefit children.
Fields of interest: Media, film/video; Museums; Arts; Higher education; Education; Environment, land resources; American Red Cross; Children, services; Human services Children.
Type of support: Annual campaigns; Building/renovation; Continuing support; Endowments; General/operating support; Program development; Scholarship funds.
Geographic limitations: Giving primarily in the San Francisco Bay Area, CA.
Support limitations: No grants to individuals.
Publications: Application guidelines.
Application information: Applications accepted. Letters of inquiry should be submitted on organization letterhead. Support is limited to 1 contribution per organization during any given year. Application form not required.
Initial approach: Letter of inquiry
Deadline(s): None
Officers: George W. Lucas, Jr., C.E.O.; Micheline Chau, Secy.; Steve Condioti, C.F.O.
EIN: 203940983
Selected grants: The following grants are a representative sample of this grantmaker's funding activity:
$29,837,742 to University of Southern California, School of Cinema-Television (CNTV), Los Angeles, CA, 2010. For USC Cinematic Arts Building.
$4,250,000 to George Lucas Educational Foundation, San Rafael, CA, 2010.
$500,000 to Film Foundation, Los Angeles, CA, 2010. For general support.
$65,000 to Film Foundation, Los Angeles, CA, 2010. For preservation grants.
$25,000 to Thomas Downey High School Educational Foundation, Modesto, CA, 2010. For general support.
$10,000 to University of Nevada Reno Foundation, Reno, NV, 2010. For general support.

2317
Luck Stone Corp.

P.O. Box 29682
Richmond, VA 23242 (804) 784-6300

Company URL: http://www.luckstone.com
Establishment information: Established in 1923.
Company type: Private company
Business activities: Produces crushed stone, sand, and gravel; manufactures clay tennis court surfaces and tennis court accessories; develops real estate.
Business type (SIC): Mining/crushed and broken stone; mining/sand and gravel; clay structural products; real estate subdividers and developers
Corporate officers: Charles S. Luck III, Chair.; Charles S. Luck IV, Pres. and C.E.O.
Board of director: Charles S. Luck III, Chair.
Giving statement: Giving through the Luck Companies Foundation, Inc.

Luck Companies Foundation, Inc.

(formerly Luck Stone Foundation, Inc.)
P.O. Box 29682
Richmond, VA 23242-0682 (804) 784-6300
FAX: (804) 784-6390;
E-mail: Foundation@LuckCompanies.com

Establishment information: Established in 1966 in VA.
Donor: Luck Stone Corp.
Financial data (yr. ended 10/31/11): Assets, $12,003,778 (M); expenditures, $522,297; qualifying distributions, $465,199; giving activities include $156,783 for 22 grants (high: $83,333; low: $250) and $308,416 for 145 employee matching gifts.
Purpose and activities: The foundation supports programs designed to promote youth development and education; and environmental stewardship.
Fields of interest: Visual arts; Elementary/secondary education; Higher education; Education; Environment, natural resources; Environment; Youth development, citizenship; Youth development; YM/YWCAs & YM/YWHAs; Leadership development.

Programs:

Environmental Stewardship: The foundation supports programs designed to create a positive outcome for natural, built, and work environments. Special emphasis is directed toward programs with a multi-generational positive impact on the environment; environmental stewardship programs that are above and beyond what is required; and programs designed to return natural and built systems to an environmental condition that is as good as or better than before.

Youth Development & Education: The foundation supports programs designed to help youth build character and leadership though ethical decision-making, moral character, and fostering the ability to help others; encourage excellence in academics in the pursuit of a career, leadership opportunity, and/or higher education; and embrace citizenship through activities that positively impacts the lives of others and teach the value of being a good citizen.
Type of support: General/operating support; Program development.
Geographic limitations: Giving primarily in VA.
Support limitations: No support for religious organizations, for-profit organizations, or discriminatory organizations. No grants to individuals, or for national disease-related fundraising, event sponsorships, or political campaigns.
Publications: Application guidelines.
Application information: Applications accepted. A formal "request for funding" application may be requested at a later date. Organizations receiving support are asked to submit an annual report on long-term impact and project effectiveness post-grant. Application form required. Applicants should submit the following:
1) timetable for implementation and evaluation of project
2) statement of problem project will address
3) population served
4) name, address and phone number of organization
5) copy of IRS Determination Letter
6) brief history of organization and description of its mission
7) detailed description of project and amount of funding requested

Initial approach: Letter
Copies of proposal: 1
Board meeting date(s): Feb., Apr., July, and Oct.
Deadline(s): None
Final notification: 2 weeks following board meetings

Officers: Charles S. Luck III, Chair.; Charles S. Luck IV, V.P.; Linda Tissiere, Secy.; Wanda S. Ortwine, Treas.
EIN: 546064982
Selected grants: The following grants are a representative sample of this grantmaker's funding activity:
$100,000 to Visual Arts Center of Richmond, Richmond, VA, 2010.
$25,000 to Elijah House Academy, Richmond, VA, 2010.
$12,500 to Elizabeth River Project, Portsmouth, VA, 2010.
$10,000 to Newton Marasco Foundation, McLean, VA, 2010.
$5,000 to Audubon Naturalist Society, Leesburg, VA, 2010.
$5,000 to Capital Region Land Conservancy, Richmond, VA, 2010.
$3,000 to Virginia Historical Society, Richmond, VA, 2010.
$2,500 to VCU Massey Cancer Center, Richmond, VA, 2010.
$1,500 to YMCA of Greater Richmond, Richmond, VA, 2010.

2318
Luster Products, Inc.

1104 W. 43rd St.
Chicago, IL 60609-3342 (773) 579-1800

Company URL: http://www.lusterproducts.com
Establishment information: Established in 1957.
Company type: Private company
Business activities: Manufactures personal care products.
Business type (SIC): Soaps, cleaners, and toiletries
Corporate officer: Jory Luster, Sr., Pres.
Giving statement: Giving through the Luster Products Black Heritage Performance Foundation.

Luster Products Black Heritage Performance Foundation

(formerly S-Curl Black Heritage Performance Foundation)
1104 W. 43rd St.
Chicago, IL 60609-3342 (773) 579-1800
URL: http://www.lusterproducts.com/foundation.htm

Establishment information: Established in 1989 by Fred Luster, Sr.
Financial data (yr. ended 12/31/11): Revenue, $93,857; assets, $204,240 (M); gifts received, $105,271; expenditures, $74,012; giving activities include $70,725 for grants.
Purpose and activities: The foundation supports community-based organizations that promote positive values, community service, and aspirational role models for the African American community.
Fields of interest: African Americans/Blacks.
Officers: Jory Luster, Pres.; Sonja Luster-Munis, Secy.; Freddie Luster, Jr., Treas.
EIN: 363679513

2319
Luxottica Retail

4000 Luxottica Pl.
Mason, OH 45040 (513) 765-6000

Company URL: http://www.luxottica.com
Establishment information: Established in 1961.
Company type: Subsidiary of a foreign company
Business activities: Operates and franchises optical stores.
Business type (SIC): Retail stores/miscellaneous; investors/miscellaneous
Corporate officers: Leonardo Del Vecchio, Chair.; Luigi Francavilla, Vice-Chair.; Andrea Guerra, C.E.O.; Enrico Cavatorta, C.F.O.; L. Pela, Human Resources
Board of directors: Leonardo Del Vecchio, Chair.; Luigi Francavilla, Vice-Chair.; Roger Abravanel; Mario Cattaneo; Enrico Cavatorta; Claudio Costamagna; Claudio Del Vecchio; Sergio Erede; Andrea Guerra; Elisabetta Magistretti; Marco Mangiagalli; Anna Puccio; Marco Reboa
Giving statement: Giving through the OneSight Research Foundation.

OneSight Research Foundation

(formerly Pearle Vision Foundation, Inc.)
2465 Joe Field Rd.
Dallas, TX 75229-3402 (972) 277-6191
FAX: (972) 277-6422;
E-mail: tparasil@onesight.org; URL: http://www.onesight.org

Establishment information: Established as a company-sponsored operating foundation in 1986 in CA.
Donors: Pearle Vision, Inc.; Cole National Foundation; Luxottica Retail; Lenscrafters, Inc.
Contact: Trina Parasiliti, Secy.
Financial data (yr. ended 12/31/11): Assets, $1,323,370 (M); gifts received, $282,762; expenditures, $404,272; qualifying distributions, $395,471; giving activities include $297,200 for 9 + grants (high: $100,000) and $40,000 for 20 grants to individuals (high: $2,000; low: $2,000).
Purpose and activities: The foundation supports research projects designed to find better treatments and cures for vision threatening diseases and disorders with a focus on diabetic and pediatric eye diseases; and awards scholarships to optometry students through the Dr. Stanley Pearle Scholarship Fund.
Fields of interest: Medical school/education; Eye diseases; Eye research; Diabetes research.
Programs:

Block Grants - See the Cure: Through the See the Cure program, the foundation supports programs designed to conduct research and provide treatment for diabetic eye diseases; and to help find a cure for diabetic retinopathy, the number one cause of adult blindness in the U.S. Grants range from $5,000 to $50,000.

Dr. Stanley Pearle Scholarship Fund: Through the Dr. Stanley Pearle Scholarship Fund, The OneSight Research Foundation awards 20 scholarships in the amount of $2,000 each. Invitation to apply is extended to second and third year full-time students starting in the fall who are pursuing graduate studies leading to a Doctor of Optometry degree. Scholarships will be awarded on a competitive basis, based on scholastic performance, potential, and evidence of a commitment to a career in the optometric profession and to community service.

Type of support: Research; Scholarships—to individuals.
Geographic limitations: Giving on a national basis.
Support limitations: No grants for endowments or general operating support.
Publications: Application guidelines; Grants list.
Application information: Applications accepted. Only 2nd, 3rd, and 4th year students are eligible for Optometry Scholarships (application available online at www.onesight.org). Application form required. Applicants should submit the following:
1) results expected from proposed grant
2) qualifications of key personnel
3) name, address and phone number of organization
4) copy of IRS Determination Letter
5) brief history of organization and description of its mission
6) copy of most recent annual report/audited financial statement/990
7) explanation of why grantmaker is considered an appropriate donor for project
8) listing of board of directors, trustees, officers and other key people and their affiliations
9) detailed description of project and amount of funding requested
10) copy of current year's organizational budget and/or project budget
11) listing of additional sources and amount of support

Scholarship applications should include official transcripts, 2 letters of recommendation, and a list and description of leadership responsibilities undertaken by the applicant.
Initial approach: Download application form and mail to foundation
Copies of proposal: 1
Board meeting date(s): Feb. and Aug.
Deadline(s): Postmarked by Dec. 31 and June 30 for Block grants; Apr. 15 for Dr. Stanley Pearle Scholarship Fund
Final notification: Mid-Mar. and mid-Sept.; June 15 for Dr. Stanley Pearle Scholarship Fund

Officers and Directors:* Greg Hare*, Chair. and Exec. Dir.; Mark Jacquot, OD*, V.P.; Trina Parasiliti, Secy. and Admin.; Kevin Boyle, Treas.; Tami Hannaman, OD; Denver Kramer; Seth McLaughlin; Seth McLaughlin.
Number of staff: 1 part-time professional.
EIN: 752173714

2320
Lynden, Inc.

18000 International Blvd., Ste. 800
P.O. Box 3757
Seattle, WA 98188-4255 (206) 241-8778

Company URL: http://www.lynden.com
Establishment information: Established in 1977.
Company type: Subsidiary of a private company
Business activities: Provides air transportation services; provides trucking services; provides water transportation services.
Business type (SIC): Transportation by air; trucking and courier services, except by air; water transportation
Corporate officers: James H. Jansen, Pres. and C.E.O.; Alex McKallor, Exec. V.P. and C.O.O.; Richard A. Korpela, Exec. V.P. and Secy.-Treas.; Kitty Samuel, V.P. and Cont.
Subsidiaries: AJ Associates Inc., Seattle, WA; Alaska Marine Lines, Inc., Seattle, WA; Alaska West Express, Inc., Anchorage, AK; Alaskan Marine Lines, Inc., Seattle, WA; Bering Marine Corp., Seattle, WA; Bowhead Equipment Co., Seattle, WA; Douglas Management Co., Seattle, WA; Knik Construction Co., Inc., Seattle, WA; LTI, Inc., Lynden, WA; Lynden Air Cargo, LLC, Anchorage, AK; Lynden Air Freight, Inc., Seattle, WA; Lynden Logistics, Inc., Seattle,

WA; Lynden Services, Inc., Seattle, WA; Lynden Transport, Inc., Kent, WA
Giving statement: Giving through the Lynden Memorial Scholarship Fund.

Lynden Memorial Scholarship Fund
P.O. Box 3757
Seattle, WA 98124-3757

Establishment information: Established as a company-sponsored operating foundation in 1995 in WA.
Donors: Lynden, Inc.; Jill Jansen; Eleanor and Henry Jansen Foundation.
Financial data (yr. ended 12/31/11): Assets, $36,134 (M); gifts received, $6,000; expenditures, $9,424; qualifying distributions, $9,424; giving activities include $8,000 for 8 grants to individuals (high: $1,000; low: $1,000).
Purpose and activities: The fund awards college scholarships to dependents of full-time employees of Lynden, Inc. and its subsidiaries.
Fields of interest: Higher education.
Type of support: Employee-related scholarships.
Geographic limitations: Giving primarily in areas of company operations, with emphasis on WA.
Application information: Applications not accepted. Contributes only through employee-related scholarships.
Officers: Dianne E. Bauer, Pres.; Patricia J.W. Gaillard, V.P.; Mary Sutherland, V.P.; Everett H. Billingslea, Secy.; Brad McKeown, Treas.
EIN: 911684708

2321
Lyon & Healy Harps, Inc.
168 N. Ogden Ave.
Chicago, IL 60607-1465 (312) 786-1881
FAX: (312) 226-1502

Company URL: http://www.lyonhealy.com
Establishment information: Established in 1889.
Company type: Private company
Business activities: Manufactures harps.
Business type (SIC): Musical instruments
Financial profile for 2009: Number of employees, 140
Corporate officers: Antonio Forero, Pres. and C.E.O.; Ronald Koltz, C.F.O.
Plant: Salt Lake City, UT
Giving statement: Giving through the Victor Salvi Foundation.

Victor Salvi Foundation
168 N. Ogden Ave.
Chicago, IL 60607-1412
URL: http://www.victorsalvifoundation.com/

Establishment information: Established in 2000 in IL.
Donors: Lyon & Healy Harps, Inc.; Victor Salvi; Fundacion Salvi Columbia; Carlos Andres Cran Uribe; Julia Salvi; Posen Foundation; Jimmy Mayer; Mayra Esquenazi; Nsm Spa; Wartsila Peru Sac.
Contact: Ron Koltz, Secy.-Treas. and Dir.
Financial data (yr. ended 12/31/11): Assets, $75,412 (M); gifts received, $697,449; expenditures, $805,670; qualifying distributions, $0.
Purpose and activities: The foundation supports programs designed to promote harp music.
Fields of interest: Performing arts, music.
Type of support: General/operating support.
Application information: Applications accepted. Application form required.
Initial approach: Letter
Deadline(s): None
Officers and Directors:* Julia Salvi*, Pres.; Ron Koltz*, Secy.-Treas.; Carolyn Clarke.
EIN: 364360186

2322
LyondellBasell North America, Inc
(formerly Lyondell Chemical Company)
LyondellBasell Twr.
1221 McKinney St., Ste. 700
Houston, TX 77010 (713) 309-7200

Company URL: http://www.lyondell.com/Lyondell/
Company type: Private company
Business activities: Manufactures chemicals.
Business type (SIC): Petroleum refining; chemicals and allied products
Financial profile for 2009: Number of employees, 7,340; sales volume, $27,674,000,000
Corporate officers: James L. Gallogly, C.E.O.; Karyn Ovelmen, Exec. V.P. and C.F.O.; Waldemar Oldenburger, V.P., Corp. Comms.
Subsidiaries: Equistar Chemicals, LP, Houston, TX; LYONDELL-CITGO Refining LP, Houston, TX
Plants: Anaheim, CA; Morris, IL; Clinton, IA; Lake Charles, LA; Newark, NJ; Cincinnati, OH; Newtown Square, PA; Alvin, Bay City, Beaumont, Channelview, Corpus Christi, La Porte, Pasadena, Port Arthur, Victoria, TX; South Charleston, WV
Giving statement: Giving through the LyondellBasell North America Inc. Corporate Giving Program.

LyondellBasell North America Inc. Corporate Giving Program
(formerly Lyondell Chemical Company Contributions Program)
c/o Corp. Comms.
1221 McKinney St., Ste. 700
Houston, TX 77010-2045
URL: http://www.lyondellbasell.com/communityinvolvement/

Purpose and activities: LyondellBasell makes charitable contributions to educational institutions and nonprofit organizations involved with pre-K-12 education, the environment, and sustainable community development. Support is limited to company operations in Illinois, Iowa, Louisiana, Michigan, New Jersey, Ohio, Pennsylvania, Tennessee, and Texas.
Fields of interest: Elementary/secondary education; Environment; Community/economic development; Mathematics; Science.
Programs:
Community Sustainability: Lyondell supports programs designed to further solutions to community problems. Special emphasis is directed toward programs designed to address housing and hunger.
Environmental Quality: Lyondell supports programs designed to promote conservation, environmental education, and sustainable development.
Lyondell Environmental Awards for Educators: Through the Lyondell Environmental Awards for Educators program, Lyondell awards fellowships to school teachers and educators to participate in scientific field research projects organized by Earthwatch Institute.
Matching Gifts: Lyondell matches contributions made by its full-time employees and the full-time employees of Equistar Chemicals and Millennium Chemicals to nonprofit organizations on a one-for-one basis.
Pre-College Education: Lyondell supports programs designed to sustain improvements in learning readiness; and promote excellence in math and science education.
Volunteer Grants: Lyondell makes charitable contributions of $250 to $500 to nonprofit organizations with which its full-time employees and the full-time employees of Equistar Chemicals and Millennium Chemicals volunteer.
Type of support: Curriculum development; Employee volunteer services; Faculty/staff development; General/operating support.
Geographic limitations: Giving limited to company operations in IA, IL, LA, MI, NJ, OH, PA, TN, and TX.
Support limitations: No support for discriminatory organizations, or political, religious, labor, or fraternal organizations. No grants to individuals, or for travel.
Application information: Applications accepted. Application form not required. Applicants should submit the following:
1) copy of IRS Determination Letter
2) detailed description of project and amount of funding requested
Initial approach: Proposal to headquarters

2323
M&T Bank Corporation
1 M&T Plz.
Buffalo, NY 14203 (716) 842-5445

Company URL: https://www.mtb.com
Establishment information: Established in 1856.
Company type: Public company
Company ticker symbol and exchange: MTB/NYSE
Business activities: Operates state commercial bank.
Business type (SIC): Banks/commercial
Financial profile for 2012: Number of employees, 14,943; assets, $83,008,800,000; pre-tax net income, $1,552,530,000; liabilities, $72,806,210,000
Fortune 1000 ranking: 2012—521st in revenues, 193rd in profits, and 73rd in assets
Forbes 2000 ranking: 2012—1447th in sales, 570th in profits, and 293rd in assets
Corporate officers: Robert G. Wilmers, Chair. and C.E.O.; Jorge G. Pereira, Vice-Chair.; Michael P. Pinto, Vice-Chair.; Mark J. Czarnecki, Pres.; Rene F. Jones, Exec. V.P. and C.F.O.; Michele D. Trolli, Exec. V.P. and C.I.O.; D. Scott N. Warman, Exec. V.P. and Treas.; Drew J. Pfirrman, Sr. V.P. and Genl. Counsel; Michael R. Spychala, Sr. V.P. and Cont.
Board of directors: Robert G. Wilmers, Chair.; Jorge G. Pereira, Co-Vice-Chair.; Michael P. Pinto, Co-Vice-Chair.; Brent D. Baird; C. Angela Bontempo; Robert T. Brady; T. Jefferson Cunningham III; Mark J. Czarnecki; Gary N. Geisel; Patrick W.E. Hodgson; Richard G. King; Melinda R. Rich; Robert E. Sadler, Jr.; Herbert L. Washington; John D. Hawke, Jr.
Giving statement: Giving through the M & T Bank Corporate Giving Program, the Allfirst Foundation, Inc., the M & T Charitable Foundation, and the Provident Bank/Skip Johnson Charitable Foundation, Inc.
Company EIN: 160968385

Allfirst Foundation, Inc.

(formerly First Maryland Foundation, Inc.)
1 M&T Plz., 3rd Fl.
Buffalo, NY 14240 (716) 842-5110

Establishment information: Incorporated in 1967 in MD.
Donors: The First National Bank of Maryland; FMB Trust Co., N.A.; Allfirst Bank.
Contact: John A. Loewer
Financial data (yr. ended 12/31/10): Assets, $0 (M); expenditures, $113,941; qualifying distributions, $113,941; giving activities include $113,941 for 1 grant.
Purpose and activities: The foundation supports hospitals and organizations involved with music, higher education, and children and youth.
Fields of interest: Performing arts, music; Higher education; Hospitals (general); Children/youth, services; United Ways and Federated Giving Programs.
Program:
Employee Matching Gifts: The foundation matches contributions made by full-time and permanent part-time employees and retirees of Allfirst Bank to educational institutions on a one-for-one basis from $25 to $2,500 per contributor, per institution, per year.
Type of support: Annual campaigns; Employee matching gifts; General/operating support; Scholarship funds.
Application information: Applications accepted. Application form required. Applicants should submit the following:
1) detailed description of project and amount of funding requested
Initial approach: Letter
Copies of proposal: 1
Deadline(s): None
Officers: Shelley C. Drake, Pres.; Marie King, Secy.; Darlene A. Spychala, Treas.
Trustees: Atwood Collins III; J. Michael Riley; Eugene J. Sheehy.
EIN: 526077253

The M & T Charitable Foundation

1 M&T Plaza, 3rd Fl.
Buffalo, NY 14203-2309 (716) 848-7804
FAX: (716) 848-7318; E-mail: sdrake@mtb.com; URL: https://www.mtb.com/aboutus/community/Pages/TheMTCharitableFoundation.aspx

Establishment information: Established in 1993 in NY.
Donors: Manufacturers and Traders Trust Co.; M&T Bank; New York State Extended Day Grant.
Contact: Debbie Pringle, Charitable Contribs. Coord.; Shelly C. Drake, Pres.
Financial data (yr. ended 12/31/11): Assets, $29,620,650 (M); gifts received, $40,000,000; expenditures, $14,310,425; qualifying distributions, $14,310,425; giving activities include $14,310,425 for 2,691 grants (high: $359,000; low: $10).
Purpose and activities: The foundation supports organizations involved with arts and culture, education, health, human services, and civic affairs.
Fields of interest: Museums (art); Performing arts; Arts; Secondary school/education; Higher education; Education; Health care; American Red Cross; Youth, services; Human services; United Ways and Federated Giving Programs; Public policy, research; Public affairs.
Type of support: Annual campaigns; Building/renovation; Capital campaigns; Curriculum development; Employee volunteer services; Equipment; Film/video/radio; General/operating support; Income development; Management development/capacity building; Matching/challenge support; Program development; Publication; Research; Scholarship funds; Sponsorships.
Geographic limitations: Giving primarily in areas of company operations in Washington, DC, DE, MD, Albany, Buffalo, Fishkill, New York, Rochester, Southern Tier, Syracuse, and Tarrytown, NY, Altoona, Harrisburg, Hanover, Lancaster, Philadelphia, Pottsville, Reading, Wilkes-Barre, Williamsport, and York , PA, VA, and Toronto, Ontario Canada.
Support limitations: No support for political organizations, candidates, or lobbying organizations, fraternal or veterans' organizations, sports teams, national or international organizations (unless their programs have significant local impact), or religious organizations not of direct benefit to the entire community. No grants to individuals.
Publications: Application guidelines.
Application information: Applications accepted. Visit website for application addresses. Proposals from organizations located in Buffalo, NY must be submitted through an M&T Bank sponsor. Proposals from Rochester, NY must include a Logic Model form. Proposals should be no longer than 1 to 2 pages. A Supplemental Questionnaire is required for requests of $10,000 or more. Application form required. Applicants should submit the following:
1) copy of IRS Determination Letter
2) brief history of organization and description of its mission
3) copy of most recent annual report/audited financial statement/990
4) list of company employees involved with the organization
5) descriptive literature about organization
6) listing of board of directors, trustees, officers and other key people and their affiliations
7) copy of current year's organizational budget and/or project budget
8) listing of additional sources and amount of support
Initial approach: Download application form and mail proposal and application form to nearest application address
Copies of proposal: 1
Board meeting date(s): Monthly
Deadline(s): Contact nearest application address for deadlines
Final notification: Varies depending on amount requested
Officers and Directors:* Shelley C. Drake*, Chair. and Pres.; Keith M. Belanger, V.P.; Beth Beshaw, V.P.; Nancy E. Brock, V.P. and Prog. Dir.; Daniel J. Burns, V.P.; Sara A. Cardillo, V.P.; August J. Chiasera, V.P.; Atwood Collins III, V.P.; R. Joe Crosswhite, V.P.; Mark J. Czarnecki*, V.P.; James J. Donavan, V.P.; Ralph W. Emerson, Jr., V.P.; Steven I. Flax, V.P.; Stephen A. Foreman, V.P.; Brian E. Hickey, V.P.; Philip H. Johnson, V.P.; Michael T. Keegan, V.P.; Frederick M. Krajacic, V.P.; Nicholas P. Lambrow, V.P.; William C. Long, V.P.; Paula Mandell, V.P.; Gino A. Martocci, V.P.; Michael S. Murchie, V.P.; Thomas J. Murphy, V.P.; Allen J. Naples, V.P.; Peter G. Newman, V.P.; Robert H. Newman, Jr., V.P.; Kevin J. Pearson, V.P.; J. Michael Riley, V.P.; Gerald R. Siuda, V.P.; Glenn R. Small, V.P.; Darlene R. Spychala, V.P.; Alissa M. Viti, V.P.; Jeffrey A. Wellington, V.P.; Marie King, Secy.; Michael P. Pinto*, Treas.; John A. Carmichael; Drew J. Pfirrman; Robert G. Wilmers.
EIN: 161448017
Selected grants: The following grants are a representative sample of this grantmaker's funding activity:
$347,500 to Banking Partnership for Community Development, New York, NY, 2010.
$218,776 to Buffalo Philharmonic Orchestra, Buffalo, NY, 2010.
$175,000 to United Way of Buffalo and Erie County, Buffalo, NY, 2010.
$110,000 to American Red Cross, Buffalo, NY, 2010.
$108,049 to Canisius College, Buffalo, NY, 2010.
$107,000 to Roswell Park Alliance Foundation, Buffalo, NY, 2010.
$5,000 to Montgomery County Business Roundtable for Education, Rockville, MD, 2010.
$5,000 to Onondaga Historical Association, Syracuse, NY, 2010.
$5,000 to Washington Area Community Investment Fund, Washington, DC, 2010.
$3,400 to Make-A-Wish Foundation of America, Phoenix, AZ, 2010.

Provident Bank/Skip Johnson Charitable Foundation, Inc.

1 M&T Plaza, 3rd Fl.
Buffalo, NY 14203-2309

Establishment information: Established in 1995 in MD.
Donors: Provident Bank of Maryland; The Provident Bank.
Financial data (yr. ended 12/31/11): Assets, $0 (M); expenditures, $0; qualifying distributions, $0.
Purpose and activities: The foundation supports organizations involved with arts and culture, education, health, human services, and economic development.
Fields of interest: Arts; Education; Health organizations, association; Human services; Economic development.
Type of support: Annual campaigns; Building/renovation; Capital campaigns; Continuing support; Curriculum development; Emergency funds; Equipment; General/operating support; In-kind gifts; Program development; Research; Scholarship funds.
Geographic limitations: Giving primarily in the greater Washington, DC, area and the greater Baltimore, MD, area.
Support limitations: No support for churches not of direct benefit to the entire community. No grants to individuals, or for start-up needs.
Application information: Applications not accepted. Contributes only to pre-selected organizations.
Officers: Shelly C. Drake, Pres.; Mark K. Czarnecki, V.P.; Marie King, Secy.; Michael P. Pinto, Treas.
EIN: 521954579
Selected grants: The following grants are a representative sample of this grantmaker's funding activity:
$60,000 to United Way of Central Maryland, Baltimore, MD, 2007.
$60,000 to United Way of Central Maryland, Baltimore, MD, 2007.
$20,000 to Baltimore School for the Arts, Baltimore, MD, 2007.
$5,000 to Independent College Fund of Maryland, Baltimore, MD, 2007.
$5,000 to Teach for America, Baltimore, MD, 2007.
$1,000 to Frostburg State University, Frostburg, MD, 2007.
$1,000 to Johns Hopkins University, Baltimore, MD, 2007.

2324
M.D.C. Holdings, Inc.

(also known as Richmond American Holdings)
4350 S. Monaco St., Ste. 500
Denver, CO 80237 (303) 773-1100
FAX: (303) 771-3461

Company URL: http://www.richmondamerican.com
Establishment information: Established in 1972.
Company type: Public company
Company ticker symbol and exchange: MDC/NYSE
Business activities: Develops real estate.
Business type (SIC): Real estate subdividers and developers; contractors/general residential building; brokers and bankers/mortgage; real estate agents and managers
Financial profile for 2012: Number of employees, 920; assets, $1,945,440,000; sales volume, $1,203,020,000; pre-tax net income, $61,120,000; expenses, $1,141,910,000; liabilities, $1,064,540,000
Corporate officers: Larry A. Mizel, Chair. and C.E.O.; David D. Mandarich, Pres. and C.O.O.; John M. Stephens, Sr. V.P. and C.F.O.; John J. Heaney, Sr. V.P. and Treas.; Michael Touff, Sr. V.P. and Genl. Counsel; Robert N. Martin, V.P., Finance and Corp. Cont.; Karen Gard, V.P., Human Resources; Joseph H. Fretz, Secy.
Board of directors: Larry A. Mizel, Chair.; Raymond T. Baker; Michael A. Berman; David E. Blackford; Herbert T. Buchwald; David D. Mandarich; David Seigel
Subsidiaries: Financial Asset Management Corp., Denver, CO; HomeAmerican Mortgage Co., Denver, CO; Richmond American Homes, Inc., Phoenix, AZ; Richmond American Homes, Inc., Tucson, AZ; Richmond American Homes of California, Inc., Irvine, CA; Richmond American Homes of Nevada, Inc., Las Vegas, NV; Richmond American Homes of Northern California, Inc., Rancho Cordova, CA; Richmond American Homes of Virginia, Inc., Fairfax, VA; Richmond Homes, Inc. I, Denver, CO; Richmond Homes, Inc. II, Colorado Springs, CO
Giving statement: Giving through the M.D.C. Holdings, Inc. Corporate Giving Program and the M.D.C./Richmond American Homes Foundation.
Company EIN: 840622967

M.D.C./Richmond American Homes Foundation

(formerly M.D.C. Holdings, Inc. Charitable Foundation)
4350 S. Monaco St.
Denver, CO 80237-3400 (720) 977-3431
E-mail: communications@mdch.com; URL: http://www.mdcrahfoundation.org/

Establishment information: Established in 1999 in CO.
Donor: M.D.C. Holdings, Inc.
Contact: Michael Touff, V.P.
Financial data (yr. ended 12/31/11): Assets, $24,581,803 (M); expenditures, $1,270,651; qualifying distributions, $1,249,636; giving activities include $1,249,636 for grants.
Purpose and activities: The foundation supports organizations involved with performing arts, education, health, Down syndrome, cancer, child welfare, disaster relief, sports, human services, philanthropy, and Judaism.
Fields of interest: Performing arts; Higher education; Education; Health care; Down syndrome; Cancer; Cancer, leukemia; Crime/violence prevention, child abuse; Disasters, preparedness/services; Athletics/sports, amateur leagues; Children, services; Homeless, human services; Human services; Philanthropy/voluntarism; Jewish agencies & synagogues.
Type of support: Emergency funds; Endowments; General/operating support; Program development; Scholarship funds.
Geographic limitations: Giving primarily in Denver, CO.
Application information: Applications accepted. Application form not required.
Initial approach: Proposal
Deadline(s): None
Officers and Trustees:* Larry A. Mizel*, Chair. and C.E.O; David D. Mandanch*, Pres.; John J. Heaney, V.P. and Treas.; Michael Touff, V.P.; Joseph H. Fretz, Secy.; Steven J. Borick; Gilbert Godstein.
EIN: 841561013
Selected grants: The following grants are a representative sample of this grantmaker's funding activity:
$100,000 to Civic Center Conservancy, Denver, CO, 2011.
$30,000 to Manhattan Charter School, New York, NY, 2011.
$25,000 to Global Down Syndrome Foundation, Denver, CO, 2011.
$15,000 to Council on Foreign Relations, New York, NY, 2011.
$10,000 to American Transplant Foundation, Denver, CO, 2011.
$10,000 to Mental Health America of Colorado, Denver, CO, 2011.
$5,086 to Families First, Denver, CO, 2011.
$5,000 to Cherry Creek Arts Festival, Denver, CO, 2011.
$5,000 to Junior Achievement Rocky Mountain, Denver, CO, 2011.
$5,000 to Project PAVE, Denver, CO, 2011.

2325
M/I Homes, Inc.

(formerly M/I Schottenstein Homes, Inc.)
3 Easton Oval, Ste. 500
Columbus, OH 43219 (614) 418-8000
FAX: (614) 418-8080

Company URL: http://www.mihomes.com
Establishment information: Established in 1976.
Company type: Public company
Company ticker symbol and exchange: MHO/NYSE
Business activities: Builds single-family houses.
Business type (SIC): Operative builders
Financial profile for 2012: Number of employees, 651; assets, $831,300,000; sales volume, $761,900,000; pre-tax net income, $12,760,000; expenses, $749,150,000; liabilities, $495,870,000
Corporate officers: Robert H. Schottenstein, Chair., Pres., and C.E.O.; Phillip G. Creek, Exec. V.P. and C.F.O.; J. Thomas Mason, Exec. V.P., Genl. Counsel, and Secy.
Board of directors: Robert H. Schottenstein, Chair.; Joseph Anthony Alutto; Friedrich K. M. Bohm; William H. Carter; Phillip G. Creek; Michael P. Glimcher; Thomas D. Igoe; J. Thomas Mason; Norman L. Traeger; Sharen Jester Turney
Giving statement: Giving through the M/I Homes Foundation.
Company EIN: 311210837

M/I Homes Foundation

(formerly M/I Schottenstein Homes Foundation)
3 Easton Oval, Ste. 500
Columbus, OH 43219-6011
FAX: (614) 418-8030

Establishment information: Established in 1989 in OH.
Donors: M/I Homes, Inc.; M/I Schottenstein Homes, Inc.
Contact: Robert H. Schottenstein, Pres.
Financial data (yr. ended 12/31/11): Assets, $702,533 (M); expenditures, $643,830; qualifying distributions, $641,033; giving activities include $641,033 for grants.
Purpose and activities: The foundation supports community foundations and organizations involved with arts and culture, education, health, housing, human services, and community development.
Fields of interest: Arts; Higher education; Law school/education; Education; Health care; Housing/shelter; Children/youth, services; Human services; Community/economic development; Foundations (community).
Type of support: Annual campaigns; Building/renovation; Capital campaigns; Endowments; General/operating support; Program development; Scholarship funds.
Geographic limitations: Giving primarily in Columbus, OH.
Application information: Applications accepted. Application form not required.
Initial approach: Proposal
Copies of proposal: 1
Board meeting date(s): Semi-annually
Deadline(s): None
Final notification: Varies
Officers and Trustees:* Robert H. Schottenstein*, Pres.; Phillip G. Creek*, V.P.; J. Thomas Mason*, Secy.; Charlotte Stout, Treas.
Number of staff: None.
EIN: 311254013
Selected grants: The following grants are a representative sample of this grantmaker's funding activity:
$200,000 to National Housing Endowment, Washington, DC, 2009. For endowment fund.
$150,000 to New Albany Community Foundation, New Albany, OH, 2009. For capital campaign for performing arts center.
$117,500 to Central Ohio Diabetes Association, Columbus, OH, 2009. For operating support.
$50,000 to Susan G. Komen for the Cure, Westerville, OH, 2009. For 2009 sponsorship.
$40,000 to Ohio Dominican University, Columbus, OH, 2009. For endowment fund.
$25,000 to Columbus Coalition Against Family Violence, Columbus, OH, 2009. For operating support.
$20,000 to Wexner Center for the Arts, Columbus, OH, 2009. For operating support.

2326
Maali Enterprises, Inc.

7582 W. Sand Lake Rd., Ste. 300
Orlando, FL 32819-7263 (407) 352-9012

Establishment information: Established in 1989.
Company type: Private company
Business activities: Operates restaurants.
Business type (SIC): Restaurants and drinking places
Corporate officers: Bassel J. Maali, Pres.; Manar J. Maali, Secy.-Treas.
Board of directors: Bassel J. Maali; Jihad Maali; Manar J. Maali; Randa Maali
Giving statement: Giving through the Jesse Maali House of Mercy Foundation, Inc.

The Jesse Maali House of Mercy Foundation, Inc.

7932 W. Sand Lake Rd., Ste. 300
Orlando, FL 32819-7263

Establishment information: Established in 2005 in FL.
Donor: Maali Enterprises, Inc.
Financial data (yr. ended 12/31/11): Assets, $89 (M); gifts received, $4,250; expenditures, $5,346; qualifying distributions, $3,000; giving activities include $3,000 for 1 grant.
Purpose and activities: The foundation supports organizations involved with education and ALS.
Type of support: General/operating support; Scholarship funds.
Geographic limitations: Giving primarily in Orlando and Tampa, FL.
Support limitations: No grants to individuals.
Application information: Applications not accepted. Unsolicited requests for funds not accepted.
Officer and Directors: Bassel Maali*, Pres.; Samir Itani; AJ Maali; Bassel Maali; Ahmad Mubarak.
EIN: 202281095

2327
MAC Construction & Excavating, Inc.

1908 Unruh Ct.
New Albany, IN 47150-6948
(812) 941-7895
FAX: (812) 941-0699

Company URL: http://www.macconstruction.com
Establishment information: Established in 1980.
Company type: Private company
Business activities: Provides general contract construction services.
Business type (SIC): Heavy construction other than building construction contractors
Financial profile for 2011: Number of employees, 200
Corporate officers: Jeannie M. Unruh, Chair.; Chad Unruh, C.E.O.; Travis Unruh, Pres.; Bryan Wickens, V.P., Admin. and Genl. Counsel
Board of directors: Jeannie M. Unruh, Chair.; Victor Unruh
Giving statement: Giving through the Unruh Charitable Foundation, Inc.

Unruh Charitable Foundation, Inc.

2600 Old Hill Rd.
Floyds Knobs, IN 47119-9745

Establishment information: Established in 2001 in IN.
Donors: MAC Construction & Excavating, Inc.; Victor Unruh; Jeannie Unruh.
Contact: Jean M. Unruh
Financial data (yr. ended 12/31/11): Assets, $281,256 (M); expenditures, $61,850; qualifying distributions, $61,000; giving activities include $61,000 for grants.
Purpose and activities: The foundation supports organizations involved with medical education and medical transport services.
Fields of interest: Arts; Education; Health organizations.
Type of support: General/operating support.
Geographic limitations: Giving primarily in IN, MO, and TX.
Application information: Applications accepted. Application form required. Applicants should submit the following:
1) detailed description of project and amount of funding requested
Initial approach: Letter
Deadline(s): None
Officers: Jeannie M. Unruh; Victor O. Unruh.
EIN: 352149131

2328
Mac Swed, Inc.

20 W. 36th St., Ste.5
New York, NY 10018-8005 (212) 684-7730

Establishment information: Established in 1961.
Company type: Private company
Business activities: Manufactures electronic novelties.
Business type (SIC): Games, toys, and sporting and athletic goods
Financial profile for 2011: Number of employees, 8
Corporate officers: Natham Shams, Chair.; Marc Shams, C.F.O.
Board of director: Natham Shams, Chair.
Giving statement: Giving through the MSI Foundation.

MSI Foundation

20 W. 36th St.
New York, NY 10018-8005

Establishment information: Established in 2003 in NY.
Donors: Mac Swed, Inc.; Bag Arts, LLC.
Financial data (yr. ended 12/31/11): Assets, $5,912 (M); gifts received, $85,000; expenditures, $80,912; qualifying distributions, $80,687; giving activities include $80,687 for grants.
Purpose and activities: The foundation supports organizations involved with Judaism.
Fields of interest: Jewish agencies & synagogues.
Geographic limitations: Giving primarily in NY.
Application information: Applications not accepted. Contributes only to pre-selected organizations.
EIN: 836056412

2329
MAC Valves, Inc.

30569 Beck Rd.
Wixom, MI 48393-2842 (248) 624-7700

Company URL: http://www.macvalves.com
Establishment information: Established in 1948.
Company type: Private company
Business activities: Manufactures air valves and associated products.
Business type (SIC): Metal products/fabricated
Corporate officers: Robert H. Neff, Pres. and C.E.O.; Jay Diehl, V.P., Opers.; Kenneth J. Sorensen, Secy.
Plant: Dundee, MI
International operations: Belgium; New Zealand
Giving statement: Giving through the MAC Valves Foundation.

MAC Valves Foundation

P.O. Box 111
Wixom, MI 48393-0679 (248) 624-7770

Contact: Martha Welch, Secy.-Treas.
Financial data (yr. ended 11/30/12): Assets, $1,150,469 (M); expenditures, $80,556; qualifying distributions, $78,045; giving activities include $77,250 for 8 grants (high: $30,000; low: $750).
Purpose and activities: The foundation supports organizations involved with education, sleep disorders, and children's services.
Fields of interest: Education; Housing/shelter; Human services.
Type of support: General/operating support.
Geographic limitations: Giving primarily in Detroit, MI.
Application information: Applications accepted. Application form required. Applicants should submit the following:
1) detailed description of project and amount of funding requested
Initial approach: Letter
Deadline(s): None
Officers and Directors: Robert Neff*, Pres.; Martha Welch*, Secy.-Treas.; Ken Sorensen.
EIN: 382440953

2330
Macayo Restaurants, L.L.C.

3117 N. 16th St.
Phoenix, AZ 85016-7609 (602) 264-1831

Company URL: http://www.macayo.com
Establishment information: Established in 1946.
Company type: Private company
Business activities: Operates restaurants.
Business type (SIC): Restaurants and drinking places
Corporate officers: Stephen C. Johnson, Pres. and C.E.O.; Robert Meyers, C.F.O.; Lee Schnoor, C.I.O.; Sharisse Johnson, V.P., Corp. Comms.; Robert Bentz, Cont.
Giving statement: Giving through the Macayo Restaurants-Johnson Family Foundation.

Macayo Restaurants-Johnson Family Foundation

1480 E. Bethany Home Rd., Ste. 130
Phoenix, AZ 85014-2003

Establishment information: Established in 2005 in AZ.
Donor: Macayo Restaurants LLC.
Financial data (yr. ended 12/31/11): Assets, $1,526 (M); gifts received, $1,189; expenditures, $1,199; qualifying distributions, $1,189; giving activities include $1,189 for grants.
Fields of interest: Human services.
Geographic limitations: Giving primarily in Phoenix, AZ.
Support limitations: No grants to individuals.
Application information: Applications not accepted. Unsolicited requests for funds not accepted.
Officers and Directors:* Sharisse L. Johnson*, Pres. and Treas.; Stephen C. Johnson*, V.P. and Secy.; Gary M. Johnson, V.P.; Victoria R. Johnson.
EIN: 203281478

2331
Macfarlane-Chang DC Soccer, LLC

(doing business as DC United)
2400 E. Capitol St., S.E., Ste. 1
Washington, DC 20003-1734
(202) 587-5472

Establishment information: Established in 1996.
Company type: Private company
Business activities: Operates a professional soccer club.
Business type (SIC): Commercial sports
Corporate officers: Kevin Payne, Pres. and C.E.O.; Michael Williamson, C.O.O. and C.F.O.; Doug Hicks, Sr. V.P., Comms.
Giving statement: Giving through the DC United Corporate Giving Program.

DC United Corporate Giving Program

c/o Community Rels.
RFK Stadium
2400 E. Capitol St., S.E.
Washington, DC 20003 (202) 587-5000
FAX: (202) 587-5400; URL: http://www.dcunited.com/community

Contact: Aprile Pritchet
Purpose and activities: The DC United makes charitable contributions of team memorabilia and merchandise to nonprofit organizations for purposes of fundraising. Support is limited to the Washington, DC, area.
Fields of interest: General charitable giving Children/youth; Children.
Type of support: Donated products; In-kind gifts; Income development.
Geographic limitations: Giving primarily limited to Washington, DC, area.
Support limitations: No support for religious organizations not of direct benefit to the entire community.
Publications: Application guidelines.
Application information: Applications accepted. Proposals should be submitted using organization letterhead. No telephone calls or email requests will be accepted. Support may be limited to 1 contribution per organization during any given year. The Community Relations Department handles giving. Application form not required. Applicants should submit the following:
1) name, address and phone number of organization
2) contact person
Proposals should include organization's non-profit tax ID number; address to which to send the donation response; nature of the event; day, date, time and location of event; number in attendance; how funds raised will be used; and publication deadline/item "need by" date (if applicable).
Initial approach: Mail proposal to headquarters
Copies of proposal: 1
Deadline(s): 6 weeks prior to event
Final notification: 3 weeks

2332
Machias Savings Bank

4 Center St.
P.O. Box 318
Machias, ME 04654-1110 (207) 255-3347
FAX: (207) 255-3170

Company URL: http://www.machiassavings.com
Establishment information: Established in 1869.
Company type: Private company
Business activities: Operates savings bank.
Business type (SIC): Savings institutions
Financial profile for 2011: Assets, $933,475,000; liabilities, $933,475,000
Corporate officers: Edward L. Hennessey, Jr., Chair.; Lawrence Barker, Pres. and C.E.O.
Board of director: Edward L. Hennessey, Jr., Chair.
Offices: Baileyville, Bar Harbor, Calais, Columbia Falls, Danforth, Ellsworth, Houlton, Lincoln, Princeton, ME
Giving statement: Giving through the Machias Savings Bank Community Development Foundation.

Machias Savings Bank Community Development Foundation

P.O. Box 318
Machias, ME 04654-0318 (207) 255-3347

Establishment information: Established in 1997 in ME.
Donor: Machias Savings Bank.
Contact: Edward L. Hennessey, Jr., Pres.
Financial data (yr. ended 12/31/11): Assets, $1,004,467 (M); expenditures, $74,240; qualifying distributions, $74,000; giving activities include $74,000 for grants.
Purpose and activities: The foundation supports hospitals and organizations involved with economic development.
Fields of interest: Education; Health care; Community/economic development.
Type of support: Capital campaigns; General/operating support; Program development; Seed money.
Geographic limitations: Giving primarily in eastern ME.
Application information: Applications accepted. Application form required. Applicants should submit the following:
1) detailed description of project and amount of funding requested
Initial approach: Proposal
Copies of proposal: 1
Deadline(s): None
Officers and Directors:* Edward L. Hennessey, Jr.*, Pres.; J. Scott Whitney*, Secy.; Donald E. Reynolds*, Treas.; Gregory R. Coffin; William A. Estey; Donald A. Foster; Robert W. Foster; Patrick C. Jordan; Thomas A. Michaud; Thomas E. Thornton, Jr.; Wayne W. Wright.
EIN: 010514175

2333
Macy's, Inc.

(formerly Federated Department Stores, Inc.)
7 W. 7th St.
Cincinnati, OH 45202 (513) 579-7000

Company URL: http://www.macysinc.com/
Establishment information: Established in 1929.
Company type: Public company
Company ticker symbol and exchange: M/NYSE
International Securities Identification Number: US55616P1049
Business activities: Operates department stores.
Business type (SIC): Department stores
Financial profile for 2012: Number of employees, 171,000; assets, $22,095,000,000; sales volume, $26,405,000,000; pre-tax net income, $1,968,000,000; expenses, $23,994,000,000; liabilities, $16,162,000,000
Fortune 1000 ranking: 2012—109th in revenues, 150th in profits, and 233rd in assets
Forbes 2000 ranking: 2012—341st in sales, 470th in profits, and 949th in assets
Corporate officers: Terry J. Lundgren, Chair., Pres., and C.E.O.; Joel A. Belsky, Exec. V.P. and Cont.; Dennis J. Broderick, Exec. V.P., Genl. Counsel, and Secy.; Karen M. Hoguet, C.F.O.; Thomas L. Cole, C.A.O.
Board of directors: Terry J. Lundgren, Chair.; Stephen F. Bollenbach; Deirdre P. Connelly; Meyer Feldberg; Sara Levinson; Joseph Neubauer; Joseph A. Pichler; Joyce M. Roche; Craig E. Weatherup; Marna C. Whittington
Subsidiaries: Bloomingdale's, Inc., New York, NY; The Bon, Inc., Seattle, WA; Broadway Stores, Inc., Los Angeles, CA; Burdines, Inc., Miami, FL; Federated Retail Holdings, Inc., Cincinnati, OH; Fingerhut Companies, Inc., Minnetonka, MN; Macy's East, Inc., New York, NY; Macy's West, Inc., Los Angeles, CA; Rich's Department Stores, Inc., Atlanta, GA; Stern's Department Stores, Inc., Paramus, NJ
Historic mergers: The May Department Stores Company (August 30, 2005)
Giving statement: Giving through the Macy's, Inc. Corporate Giving Program and the Macy's Foundation.
Company EIN: 133324058

Macy's, Inc. Corporate Giving Program

(formerly Federated Department Stores, Inc. Corporate Giving Program)
7 W. 7th St.
Cincinnati, OH 45202 (513) 579-7000
E-mail: dbarker@fds.com; Additional contacts: San Francisco, CA: Louis Meunier, tel.: (415) 954-6406, Miami, FL: Ann Ruppert, tel.: (305) 577-2250, Atlanta, GA: Joe Vella, tel.: (770) 913-4489, Paramus, NJ: Tom Zapf, tel.: (212) 494-5669, New York, NY: Ed Goldberg, tel.: (212) 494-5568, Anne Keating, tel.: (212) 705-2434, Seattle, WA: Ed Cooney, tel.: (206) 344-7125; fax: (513) 579-7185; URL: http://www.federated-fds.com/community

Contact: Dixie Barker, Mgr., Corp. Contribs.
Purpose and activities: As a complement to its foundation, Macy's also makes charitable contributions to nonprofit organizations directly. Emphasis is given to organizations involved with arts and culture, education, the environment, HIV/AIDS, and women's issues. Support is given primarily in areas of company operations.
Fields of interest: Arts; Education; Environment; Health care; AIDS; AIDS research; Human services, fund raising/fund distribution Women.
Type of support: Annual campaigns; Cause-related marketing; Conferences/seminars; Emergency funds; Employee volunteer services; General/operating support; Program development; Seed money; Sponsorships.
Geographic limitations: Giving primarily in areas of company operations.
Support limitations: No support for religious organizations. No grants to individuals.
Publications: Application guidelines.
Application information: Application form not required. Applicants should submit the following:
1) copy of IRS Determination Letter
Initial approach: Complete online eligibility quiz and application
Copies of proposal: 1
Administrators: Dixie Barker, Mgr., Corp. Contribs.; Ed Cooney; Ed Goldberg; Anne Keating; Louis Meunier; Ann Ruppert; Joe Vella; Tom Zapf.

Macy's Foundation

(formerly Federated Department Stores Foundation)
c/o Macy's Corp. Svcs., Inc.
7 W. 7th St.
Cincinnati, OH 45202-2424 (513) 579-7000
FAX: (513) 579-7185;
E-mail: foundationapps@macys.com; Additional e-mail:
bloomingdalescontributions@bloomingdales.com;
URL: http://www.federated-fds.com/community/

Establishment information: Established in 1995 in OH.
Donors: Federated Department Stores, Inc.; The May Department Stores Foundation.
Financial data (yr. ended 01/28/12): Assets, $3,937,987 (M); gifts received, $13,800,000; expenditures, $13,722,515; qualifying distributions, $13,708,500; giving activities include $13,467,367 for 6,951 grants (high: $1,000,000; low: $25).
Purpose and activities: The foundation supports programs designed to promote arts and culture, education, the environment, HIV/AIDS, and women issues and programs designed to assist minorities.
Fields of interest: Arts; Education; Environment; AIDS; AIDS research; Food services; Food banks; Youth development, intergenerational programs; Aging, centers/services; United Ways and Federated Giving Programs Minorities; Women.
Programs:
Earning for Learning: The foundation awards $250 grants to K-12 schools with which employees, retirees, and family members of employees of Macy's volunteer.
Matching Gifts Program: The foundation matches contributions made by employees of Macy's to nonprofit organizations on a one-for-one basis.
Scholarship Program: The foundation awards 54 $1,000 college scholarships to high school seniors who are employees of Macy's or children of employees of Macy's. The program is administered by National Merit Scholarship Corp.
Type of support: Annual campaigns; Capital campaigns; Continuing support; Employee matching gifts; Employee volunteer services; Employee-related scholarships; General/operating support; Matching/challenge support; Program development; Scholarship funds; Seed money.
Geographic limitations: Giving on a national basis in areas of company operations, with emphasis on CA, FL, GA, MO, NY, and OH.
Support limitations: No support for private foundations, fraternal organizations, political or advocacy groups, religious organizations not of direct benefit to the entire community, charities whose focus and operations are primarily international, or fiscal agents or other umbrella organizations providing funding to nonprofit organizations. No grants to individuals, or for event or program sponsorships, or salaries for nonprofit staffing.
Publications: Application guidelines; Program policy statement.
Application information: Applications accepted. The foundation utilizes an invitation only process for applications. E-mailed letters of inquiry are reviewed by the foundation and applicants receive an invitation to formally apply, or notification that their request does not match the strategic focus of the foundation. Application form not required.
Applicants should submit the following:
1) name, address and phone number of organization
2) brief history of organization and description of its mission
3) detailed description of project and amount of funding requested

Initial approach: E-mail letter of inquiry to foundation
Copies of proposal: 1
Board meeting date(s): Quarterly
Deadline(s): None
Final notification: 4 weeks or more

Officers and Trustees:* Jim Sluzewski*, Pres.; Ann Munson Steines, Secy.; Matt Stautberg, Treas.; David W. Clark; Julie Greiner; Karen M. Hoguet; Ron Klein.
EIN: 311427325
Selected grants: The following grants are a representative sample of this grantmaker's funding activity:
$1,500,000 to OASIS Institute, Saint Louis, MO, 2011.
$1,116,426 to United Way of Metropolitan Atlanta, Atlanta, GA, 2011.
$450,000 to United Way of Greater Cincinnati, Cincinnati, OH, 2011.
$439,503 to ArtsWave, Cincinnati, OH, 2011. For Campaign Gift.
$391,300 to ArtsWave, Cincinnati, OH, 2011.
$370,580 to National Merit Scholarship Corporation, Evanston, IL, 2011. For Stipends for programs.
$17,265 to United Way, Valley of the Sun, Phoenix, AZ, 2011.
$10,000 to Portland Opera Association, Portland, OR, 2011. For Hansel and Gretel.
$10,000 to Saint Benedict Day Nursery, New York, NY, 2011. For Literacy Program.
$5,000 to New York Foundling Hospital, New York, NY, 2011. For Mott Haven Girls Leadership Program.

2334
Madison Gas and Electric Company

(also known as MGE)
133 S. Blair St.
P.O. Box 1231
Madison, WI 53703 (608) 252-7000

Company URL: http://www.mge.com
Establishment information: Established in 1896.
Company type: Subsidiary of a public company
Business activities: Generates, transmits, and distributes electricity; transmits and distributes natural gas.
Business type (SIC): Combination utility services
Corporate officers: Gary J. Wolter, Chair., Pres., and C.E.O.; Jeffrey C. Newman, V.P., C.F.O., and Secy.-Treas.; Peter J. Waldron, V.P. and C.I.O.; Kristine A. Euclide, V.P. and Genl. Counsel
Board of director: Gary J. Wolter, Chair.
Giving statement: Giving through the Madison Gas and Electric Foundation, Inc.
Company EIN: 392040501

Madison Gas and Electric Foundation, Inc.

P.O. Box 1231
Madison, WI 53701-1231 (608) 252-7279

Establishment information: Established in 1966 in WI.
Donor: Madison Gas and Electric Co.
Contact: Bonnie Juul
Financial data (yr. ended 12/31/11): Assets, $13,841,647 (M); expenditures, $830,093; qualifying distributions, $754,663; giving activities include $754,663 for grants.
Purpose and activities: The foundation supports organizations involved arts and culture, education, health, heart disease, rowing, human services, and civic affairs.
Fields of interest: Performing arts, orchestras; Arts; Higher education; Education; Hospitals (general); Health care; Heart & circulatory diseases; Athletics/sports, water sports; YM/YWCAs & YM/YWHAs; Independent living, disability; Human services; United Ways and Federated Giving Programs; Public affairs.
Program:
Employee-Related Scholarships: The foundation awards college scholarships to children of employees of Madison Gas and Electric to attend the University of Wisconsin-Madison.
Type of support: General/operating support; Program development.
Geographic limitations: Giving primarily in areas of company operations WI.
Application information: Applications accepted. Application form not required. Applicants should submit the following:
1) how project will be sustained once grantmaker support is completed
2) results expected from proposed grant
3) name, address and phone number of organization
4) copy of IRS Determination Letter
5) copy of most recent annual report/audited financial statement/990
6) how project's results will be evaluated or measured
7) detailed description of project and amount of funding requested
8) contact person
9) copy of current year's organizational budget and/or project budget
10) listing of additional sources and amount of support
11) additional materials/documentation

Initial approach: Proposal
Copies of proposal: 1
Deadline(s): None

Officers: Gary J. Wolter, Pres.; Kristine A. Euclide, V.P.; Lynn K. Hobbie, V.P.; Scott A. Neitzel, V.P.; Jeff. C. Newman, Secy.-Treas.
EIN: 396098118
Selected grants: The following grants are a representative sample of this grantmaker's funding activity:
$5,000 to American Cancer Society, Atlanta, GA, 2010. For program support.
$3,000 to American Heart Association, Dallas, TX, 2010. For program support.
$3,000 to World Vision, Federal Way, WA, 2010. For program support.
$2,500 to Multiple Sclerosis Society, National, New York, NY, 2010. For program support.
$2,000 to NAACP, Baltimore, MD, 2010. For program support.
$1,000 to Links Foundation, Washington, DC, 2010. For program support.

2335
Madison National Bank

538 Broadhollow Rd., Ste. 301
Melville, NY 11747 (631) 348-6999

Company URL: http://madisonnational.com
Establishment information: Established in 2007.
Company type: Private company
Business activities: Operates commercial bank.
Business type (SIC): Banks/commercial
Corporate officers: Paul B. Guenther, Chair.; John F. Stewart, C.E.O.; Stella M. Mendes, Pres.; William P. Mackey, Exec. V.P. and C.F.O.; Maureen P. Kiedaisch, 1st Sr. V.P. and Corp. Secy.

Board of directors: Paul B. Guenther, Chair.; John F. Stewart; Stella M. Mendes; Judith I. Byrd; Robert B. Catell; Michael J. Del Giudice; Bradford B. Kopp; Ronald S. Krolick; David M. Ledy; Howard S. Maier; Joseph L. Mancino; Lisa Rosenblum
Giving statement: Giving through the Madison National Foundation.

Madison National Foundation
888 Veterans Memorial Hwy., Ste. 400
Hauppauge, NY 11788 (631) 297-5936

Establishment information: Established in 2007 in NY.
Donor: Madison National Bank.
Contact: Sharon Grosser, Dir.
Financial data (yr. ended 12/31/11): Assets, $737,045 (M); expenditures, $54,190; qualifying distributions, $39,925; giving activities include $39,925 for grants.
Purpose and activities: The foundation supports organizations involved with higher education, cerebral palsy, heart disease, arthritis, hunger, and human services.
Fields of interest: Health care; Housing/shelter; Human services.
Type of support: General/operating support.
Support limitations: No grants to individuals.
Application information: Applications accepted. Application form not required. Applicants should submit the following:
1) copy of IRS Determination Letter
2) geographic area to be served
3) detailed description of project and amount of funding requested

Initial approach: Proposal
Deadline(s): None

Officers and Directors:* Daniel L. Murphy*, Chair.; Michael P. Puorro*, Pres.; Bonnie Seider, Secy. and Treas.; Richard Berman; John F. Coffey; Thomas Gilmartin; Sharon Grosser; Gerald J. Kaiser; William P. Mackey; Robert R. McMillan; Estela M. Mendes; John Sorrenti.
EIN: 020789057

2336
Madison Square Garden Company
2 Pennsylvania Plz.
New York, NY 10121-0091 (212) 465-6000
FAX: (212) 631-5422

Company URL: http://www.themadisonsquaregardencompany.com/
Establishment information: Established in 1879.
Company type: Public company
Company ticker symbol and exchange: MSG/NASDAQ
Business activities: Provides cable television services; operates concert hall; operates arenas; operates professional ice hockey clubs; operates professional basketball clubs.
Business type (SIC): Cable and other pay television services; bands, orchestras, and entertainers; commercial sports
Financial profile for 2012: Number of employees, 8,518; assets, $2,524,680,000; sales volume, $1,284,020,000; pre-tax net income, $179,850,000; expenses, $1,106,490,000; liabilities, $1,204,670,000
Corporate officers: James L. Dolan, Chair.; Hank J. Ratner, Pres. and C.E.O.; Robert M. Pollichino, Exec. V.P. and C.F.O.; Lawrence Burian, Exec. V.P., Genl. Counsel, and Secy.; Barry Watkins, Exec. V.P., Comms.
Board of directors: James L. Dolan, Chair.; Charles F. Dolan; Charles P. Dolan; Kristin A. Dolan; Thomas C. Dolan; Deborah A. Dolan-Sweeney; Wilt Hildenbrand; Richard D. Parsons; Alan D. Schwartz; Brian G. Sweeney; Vincent S. Tese; Marianne Dolan Weber
Divisions: New York Knicks, New York, NY; New York Rangers, New York, NY
Giving statement: Giving through the New York Knicks Corporate Giving Program and the Garden of Dreams Foundation.
Company EIN: 270624498

Madison Square Garden Company Contributions Program
2 Pennsylvania Plz.
New York, NY 10121-0091 (212) 465-6000
URL: http://www.themadisonsquaregardencompany.com

Garden of Dreams Foundation
(formerly Madison Square Garden Cheering for Children Foundation)
2 Penn Plz., 14th Fl.
New York, NY 10121-0091 (212) 465-4170
E-mail: gardenofdreamsfoundation@thegarden.com; URL: http://www.gardenofdreamsfoundation.org

Establishment information: Established in 1997 in NY; changed to current name in 2006.
Financial data (yr. ended 08/31/11): Revenue, $2,510,776; assets, $2,296,861 (M); gifts received, $2,329,378; expenditures, $2,321,307; program services expenses, $1,878,150; giving activities include $1,215,045 for 28 grants (high: $446,932; low: $5,144).
Purpose and activities: The foundation is dedicated to helping children in crisis in the New York/New Jersey/Connecticut tri-state area, whether they are suffering from devastating illness, homelessness, abuse, hunger, extreme poverty, or tragedy.
Fields of interest: Children.
Type of support: In-kind gifts.
Geographic limitations: Giving limited to CT, NJ, and NY.
Officer and Directors:* Hank Ratner*, Chair.; Michael Bair; Gary Fuhrman; Darryl McDaniels; Matthew Modine; Drew Nieporent; Melissa Ormond; Robert Pollichino; Barry Watkins; and 3 additional directors.
EIN: 133979726

2337
MAG Giddings & Lewis, LLC
(formerly Giddings & Lewis, Inc.)
142 Doty St.
P.O. Box 590
Fond du Lac, WI 54935 (920) 921-9400

Company URL: http://www.mag-ias.com
Establishment information: Established in 1859.
Company type: Subsidiary of a foreign company
Business activities: Produces flexible automation solutions; supplies industrial automation products.
Business type (SIC): Machinery/metalworking
Financial profile for 2010: Number of employees, 393
Corporate officer: Terry Groth, Cont.
Subsidiary: Cross and Trecker Corporation, Bloomfield Hills, MI
Giving statement: Giving through the Giddings & Lewis Foundation, Inc.

Giddings & Lewis Foundation, Inc.
P.O. Box 590
Fond Du Lac, WI 54936-0590 (920) 906-9400
Application address: 142 Doty St., Fond Du Lac, WI 549350590

Establishment information: Incorporated in 1952 in WI.
Donors: Giddings & Lewis, Inc.; Giddings & Lewis, LLC.
Contact: Terri L. Groth, V.P.
Financial data (yr. ended 12/31/10): Assets, $1,650,188 (M); expenditures, $67,281; qualifying distributions, $55,730; giving activities include $1,825 for 4 grants (high: $800; low: $25), $16,000 for 12 grants to individuals (high: $2,000; low: $1,000) and $18,860 for 43 employee matching gifts.
Purpose and activities: The foundation matches contributions made by employees of Giddings & Lewis and awards college scholarships to the family members of employees.
Fields of interest: Higher education; United Ways and Federated Giving Programs.
Type of support: Employee matching gifts; Employee-related scholarships.
Geographic limitations: Giving primarily in CA, MI, OH, and WI.
Support limitations: No grants to individuals (except for employee-related scholarships).
Application information: Applications accepted. Application form required.

Initial approach: Letter
Deadline(s): None

Officers: Paul A. Stelter, Pres.; Terri L. Groth, V.P.
EIN: 396061306

2338
MAGE SOLAR Projects, Inc.
(also known as MAGE SOLAR USA)
720 Industrial Blvd.
Dublin, GA 31021 (478) 609-6640

Company URL: http://www.magesolar.com/
Establishment information: Established in 2007.
Company type: Subsidiary of a foreign company
Business activities: Operates solar energy equipment company.
Business type (SIC): Electronic components and accessories
Financial profile for 2011: Number of employees, 180
Corporate officers: Norbert Philipp, C.E.O.; Catherine Brumfield, C.F.O.
Board of directors: Joe Thomas; Norbert Philipp
Giving statement: Giving through the MAGE Solar USA Corporate Giving Program.

MAGE Solar USA Corporate Giving Program
c/o Communications
720 Industrial Blvd.
Dublin, GA 31021 (478) 609-6640
E-mail: susanne.fischer-quinn@magesolar.com; URL: http://www.magesolar.com/

Contact: Sylvia Minton, Sr. V.P., Corp. Affairs

2339
Magline, Inc.
1205 W. Cedar St.
Standish, MI 48658-9535 (989) 879-2411

Company URL: http://www.magliner.com
Establishment information: Established in 1947.
Company type: Private company
Business activities: Manufactures hand trucks.
Business type (SIC): Machinery/construction, mining, and materials handling
Corporate officers: D. Brian Law, Chair. and C.E.O.; Bruce W. Law, Vice-Chair. and Secy.; Koke Veljasevic, C.I.O.
Board of directors: D. Brian Law, Chair.; Bruce W. Law, Vice-Chair.
Giving statement: Giving through the Magline Inc. Charitable Trust.

Magline Inc. Charitable Trust
1205 W. Cedar St.
Standish, MI 48658

Donor: Magline, Inc.
Financial data (yr. ended 12/31/12): Assets, $222,364 (M); gifts received, $100,000; expenditures, $9,392; qualifying distributions, $9,202; giving activities include $8,450 for 6 grants (high: $6,000; low: $100).
Purpose and activities: The trust supports organizations involved with housing development and economic development.
Type of support: General/operating support.
Geographic limitations: Giving limited to Bay City, MI.
Support limitations: No grants to individuals.
Application information: Applications not accepted. Unsolicited requests for funds not accepted.
Trustee: D. Brian Law.
EIN: 386082038

2340
Magnolia Plantation Corporation
3550 Ashley River Rd.
Charleston, SC 29414-7109
(843) 571-1266

Company URL: http://www.magnoliaplantation.com
Establishment information: Established in 1676.
Company type: Private company
Business activities: Operates tourist attraction.
Business type (SIC): Amusement and recreation services/miscellaneous
Corporate officer: Taylor Drayton Nealson, Pres.
Giving statement: Giving through the Magnolia Plantation Foundation.

Magnolia Plantation Foundation
3550 Ashley River Rd.
Charleston, SC 29414 (843) 571-1266

Establishment information: Established in 1999.
Donors: The Annenberg Foundation Grant; Magnolia Plantation Corp.; The Residuary Trust.
Contact: Taylor Nelson, Mgr.
Financial data (yr. ended 12/31/11): Assets, $1,728,437 (M); gifts received, $55,604; expenditures, $89,883; qualifying distributions, $72,650; giving activities include $72,650 for grants.
Purpose and activities: The foundation supports organizations involved with secondary education, historical activities, conservation, horticulture, environmental education, animal welfare, and human services.
Fields of interest: Historical activities; Historic preservation/historical societies; Secondary school/education; Environment, natural resources; Botanical gardens; Horticulture/garden clubs; Environmental education; Animal welfare; Animal population control; Children, services; Residential/custodial care, hospices; Human services.
Type of support: General/operating support.
Geographic limitations: Giving primarily in SC.
Application information: Applications accepted. Application form required.
Initial approach: Proposal
Deadline(s): None
Trustees: Fenanda Hastie; Eleanor Mertson.
EIN: 570789797

2341
Magyar Bancorp, Inc.
400 Somerset St.
New Brunswick, NJ 08901 (732) 342-7600
FAX: (302) 636-5454

Company URL: https://www.magbank.com
Establishment information: Established in 1922.
Company type: Public company
Company ticker symbol and exchange: MGYR/NASDAQ
Business activities: Operates bank holding company.
Business type (SIC): Savings institutions
Financial profile for 2012: Number of employees, 95; assets, $508,850,000; pre-tax net income, $630,000; liabilities, $463,840,000
Corporate officers: Joseph J. Lukacs, Jr., Chair.; Thomas Lankey, Vice-Chair.; John S. Fitzgerald, Pres. and C.E.O.; Jon R. Ansari, Sr. V.P. and C.F.O.
Board of directors: Joseph J. Lukacs, Jr., Chair.; Thomas Lankey, Vice-Chair.; John S. Fitzgerald; Andrew G. Hodulik, C.P.A.; Martin A. Lukacs; Salvatore J. Romano, Ph.D.; Edward C. Stokes III; Joseph A. Yelencsics
Giving statement: Giving through the Magyarbank Charitable Foundation.
Company EIN: 204154978

Magyarbank Charitable Foundation
400 Somerset St.
New Brunswick, NJ 08903-3265

Establishment information: Established in 2006 in DE.
Donor: Magyar Bancorp, Inc.
Contact: Jay Castillo
Financial data (yr. ended 09/30/11): Assets, $487,042 (M); expenditures, $49,516; qualifying distributions, $38,500; giving activities include $31,000 for 17 grants (high: $5,000; low: $500).
Purpose and activities: The foundation supports nonprofit organizations involved with education, health, affordable housing, youth, and human services. Special emphasis is directed toward programs designed to improve quality of life for residents of central Jersey.
Fields of interest: Education; Health care; Housing/shelter.
Type of support: General/operating support.
Geographic limitations: Giving primarily in areas of company operations in central NJ.
Application information: Applications accepted. Application form required.
Initial approach: Proposal
Deadline(s): None
Officers: Jay E. Castillo, Pres.; Jon Ansari, V.P. and Treas.; Robin E. Suydam, Secy.
Board Members: Elizabeth E. Hance; Joseph J. Luckacs, Jr.; Deborah L. Morgan; Salvatore J. Romano.
EIN: 204154914

2342
Main Line Health
(also known as Bryn Mawr Hospital)
130 S. Bryn Mawr Ave.
Bryn Mawr, PA 19010 (484) 337-3000

Company URL: http://www.mainlinehealth.org
Establishment information: Established in 1985.
Company type: Subsidiary of a private company
Business activities: Operates health care, recovery, and rehabilitation facilities.
Business type (SIC): Hospitals
Corporate officers: Frank P. Slattery, Jr., Esq., Chair.; John J. Lynch III, Pres. and C.E.O.; Michael J. Buongiorno, Exec. V.P. and C.F.O.
Board of director: Frank P. Slattery, Jr., Chair.
Giving statement: Giving through the Riddle HealthCare Foundation.

The Riddle HealthCare Foundation
1068 W. Baltimore Pike
Media, PA 19063-5104 (484) 227-3651
E-mail: derbys@mlhs.org; URL: http://www.mainlinehealth.org/oth/Page.asp?PageID=OTH001641

Establishment information: Established in 2001 in PA; supporting organization of Riddle Memorial Hospital.
Contact: Steven R. Derby, V.P. for Devel.
Financial data (yr. ended 06/30/11): Revenue, $2,666,958; assets, $24,459,730 (M); gifts received, $1,218,223; expenditures, $1,225,052; giving activities include $494,147 for grants.
Purpose and activities: The foundation seeks philanthropic support of the Riddle Memorial Hospital's programs and services that provide healthcare to members of its community. Grants for scholarships are only offered to employees of Riddle Memorial Hospital.
Fields of interest: Hospitals (general).
Type of support: Annual campaigns; Building/renovation; Capital campaigns; Continuing support; Employee-related scholarships; Endowments; Equipment; General/operating support; In-kind gifts; Program development; Scholarships—to individuals.
Geographic limitations: Giving limited to Delaware and Chester counties, PA.
Officers and Directors:* Thomas A. Bruder, Jr.*, Chair.; Catherine D. Granger, Vice-Chair.; Steven R. Derby, V.P., Devel.; Toni Cavanagh, Secy.; Donald S. Guthrie, Treas.; Robert F. Fischer; Thomas A. Goldsmith, Jr.; Jon D. Helms; Hassan C. Vakil, M.D.; James J. Walsh; and 15 additional directors.
EIN: 043601189

2343
Majestic Realty Co.
13191 Crossroads Pkwy. N., 6th Fl.
City of Industry, CA 91746-3497
(562) 692-9581

Company URL: http://www.majesticrealty.com
Establishment information: Established in 1948.
Company type: Private company
Business activities: Operates nonresidential buildings.
Business type (SIC): Real estate operators and lessors
Financial profile for 2010: Number of employees, 150
Corporate officers: Edward P. Roski, Jr., Chair. and Pres.; Jay Bradford, Exec. V.P. and C.F.O.; Gail Kiralla, Human Resources
Board of directors: Edward P. Roski, Jr., Chair.; Jakob Ackermann; Jay H. Bradford; John R. Burroughs; R. Stan Conway; Randall C. Hertel; Gail Kiralla; Kevin D. McCarthy; Patricia Reon Roski; Kent R. Valley
Offices: Aurora, CO; Atlanta, GA; Las Vegas, NV
Giving statement: Giving through the Majestic Realty Foundation.

Majestic Realty Foundation
13191 Crossroads Pkwy. N., 6th Fl.
City of Industry, CA 91746-3497 (562) 654-2725
FAX: (562) 692-4131;
E-mail: majesticfoundation@majesticrealty.com; Additional tel.: (562) 948-4375; URL: http://www.majesticfoundation.org

Establishment information: Established in 2002 in CA.
Donors: Majestic Realty Co.; David A. Wheeler; Edward P. Roski, Jr.; Commerce Construction; Curci-Turner Company LLC.
Contact: Frances L. Inman, Pres.
Financial data (yr. ended 12/31/11): Assets, $152,884 (M); gifts received, $357,301; expenditures, $281,595; qualifying distributions, $277,048; giving activities include $277,048 for grants.
Purpose and activities: The foundation supports organizations involved with education, health, violence prevention, youth, and families.
Fields of interest: Higher education; Education; Health care; Crime/violence prevention; YM/YWCAs & YM/YWHAs; Youth, services; Family services.
Program:
Employee Matching Funds: The foundation matches contributions made by employees of Majestic Realty and its related entities to nonprofit organizations up to $5,000 per employee, per year.
Type of support: Capital campaigns; Continuing support; Employee matching gifts; Employee volunteer services; General/operating support; Matching/challenge support; Program development.
Geographic limitations: Giving primarily in areas of company operations in Inland Empire, greater Los Angeles and San Gabriel Valley, CA, Aurora and Denver, CO, Atlanta, GA, Las Vegas, NV, Dallas and Fort Worth, TX.
Support limitations: No support for federated funds or pass-through organizations, religious or other organizations not of direct benefit to the entire community, or lobbying organizations. No grants to individuals, or for start-up needs.
Publications: Annual report (including application guidelines); Application guidelines.
Application information: Applications accepted. Additional information may be requested at a later date. A site visit may be requested. Application form not required. Applicants should submit the following:
1) timetable for implementation and evaluation of project
2) name, address and phone number of organization
3) copy of IRS Determination Letter
4) brief history of organization and description of its mission
5) descriptive literature about organization
6) listing of board of directors, trustees, officers and other key people and their affiliations
7) detailed description of project and amount of funding requested
8) copy of current year's organizational budget and/or project budget
9) listing of additional sources and amount of support

Initial approach: Letter of inquiry
Copies of proposal: 1
Deadline(s): None

Officers and Directors:* Frances L. Inman*, Pres.; Gail Kiralla*, Secy.; David A. Wheeler*, Treas.
EIN: 043722125
Selected grants: The following grants are a representative sample of this grantmaker's funding activity:
$19,683 to Mount San Antonio College Foundation, Walnut, CA, 2009.
$18,474 to Mount San Antonio College Foundation, Walnut, CA, 2009.
$18,452 to East Valley Community Health Center, West Covina, CA, 2009.
$16,656 to THINK Together, Santa Ana, CA, 2009.
$10,000 to Childrens Hospital Foundation, Aurora, CO, 2009.
$10,000 to YMCA of Southern Nevada, Las Vegas, NV, 2009.
$5,000 to THINK Together, Santa Ana, CA, 2009.
$4,000 to Boys and Girls Club of Redlands, Redlands, CA, 2009.
$2,300 to American Red Cross, Pomona, CA, 2009.
$2,000 to Boy Scouts of America, Long Beach Area Council, Long Beach, CA, 2009.

2344
The Majestic Star Casino, LLC
301 Freemont St., 12th Fl.
Las Vegas, NV 89101 (702) 388-2224
FAX: (702) 382-5562

Company URL: http://www.majesticstar.com/
Establishment information: Established in 1993.
Company type: Subsidiary of a private company
Business activities: Owns and operates casinos.
Business type (SIC): Amusement and recreation services/miscellaneous
Corporate officers: Don H. Barden, Chair., Pres., and C.E.O.; Michael L. Darley, Exec. V.P. and C.O.O.; Jon S. Bennett, Sr. V.P., C.F.O., and Treas.; Larry Wheeler, Sr. V.P. and Genl. Counsel
Board of director: Don H. Barden, Chair.
Giving statement: Giving through the Barden Gary Foundation.

Barden Gary Foundation
c/o Majestic Star Casinos & Hotel
1 Buffington Harbor Dr.
Gary, IN 46406-3000

Establishment information: Established in 2006 in IN.
Donors: Majestic Star Casinos & Hotel; Smokey Robinson Golf Classic.
Financial data (yr. ended 12/31/11): Assets, $126,741 (M); gifts received, $123,065; expenditures, $118,922; qualifying distributions, $116,630; giving activities include $85,745 for 19 + grants (high: $17,895).
Fields of interest: Education; Health care; Human services.
Type of support: Scholarship funds.
Support limitations: No grants to individuals.
Application information: Applications not accepted. Unsolicited requests for funds not accepted.
Officers: Chareice White, Pres.; Abuhassanali Young, V.P.; Regina Biddings Muro, Secy.; Danielle Ryan O'Reilly, Treas.
Directors: Speros A. Batistatos; Rochelle Brock; Myrtle Campbell; Dale S. Clapp; Renee Connelly; Cindy Hall; J. Allen Johnson; Caren Jones; Kevin Jones; Delta F. Jones-Walker; Bill Masterson, Jr.; Regina Biddings Muro.
EIN: 204223628

2345
Major League Baseball
(doing business as MLB)
245 Park Ave., 31st Fl.
New York, NY 10167 (212) 931-7800

Company URL: http://mlb.mlb.com
Establishment information: Established in 1903.
Company type: Business league
Business activities: Operates professional sports league.
Business type (SIC): Business association; commercial sports
Financial profile for 2010: Number of employees, 300; sales volume, $7,000,000,000
Corporate officers: Robert A. DuPuy, Pres. and C.O.O.; Jonathan D. Mariner, Exec. V.P. and C.F.O.; John McHale, Jr., Exec. V.P., Admin. and C.I.O.; Joe Torre, Exec. V.P., Opers.; Ethan Orlinsky, Sr. V.P. and Genl. Counsel
Giving statement: Giving through the Major League Baseball Corporate Giving Program, the Baseball Assistance Team, the Baseball Tomorrow Fund, and the Major League Baseball Charity, Inc.

Major League Baseball Corporate Giving Program
245 Park Ave., 31st Fl.
New York, NY 10167 (212) 931-7800
URL: http://mlb.mlb.com/mlb/official_info/community/programs.jsp

Purpose and activities: Major League Baseball makes charitable contributions to nonprofit organizations involved with youth development.
Fields of interest: Cancer research; Athletics/sports, baseball; Youth development; Philanthropy/voluntarism Economically disadvantaged.
Type of support: Continuing support; General/operating support; Program development.

Baseball Assistance Team
245 Park Ave., 34th Fl.
New York, NY 10167-0002 (212) 931-7800
FAX: (212) 949-5433; E-mail: BAT@mlb.com; Toll-free tel.: (866) 605-4594; URL: http://www.baseballassistanceteam.com

Establishment information: Established in 1986 in NY.
Financial data (yr. ended 12/31/10): Revenue, $2,488,826; assets, $12,554,371 (M); gifts received, $2,091,417; expenditures, $2,060,997; program services expenses, $1,857,023; giving activities include $1,515,973 for 382 grants to

individuals and $141,600 for foundation-administered programs.
Purpose and activities: The organization assists members of the baseball family who fall on hard times and are in need of financial or medical assistance.
Fields of interest: Athletics/sports, baseball Economically disadvantaged.
Type of support: Grants to individuals.
Publications: Informational brochure; Newsletter.
Application information: Applications accepted. Applicant must be a member of the baseball family. Application form required.
Initial approach: Download application form
Copies of proposal: 1
Board meeting date(s): Jan. and Sept.
Deadline(s): Every month
Final notification: Within 30 days
Officers: Mark Letendre, V.P.; Thomas Ostertag*, Secy.; Scott Stamp*, Treas.
Number of staff: 3
EIN: 133355155

Major League Baseball Charity, Inc.

245 Park Ave.
New York, NY 10167-0001 (212) 931-7800

Establishment information: Established in 1986 in NY.
Contact: Thomas C. Brasuell, Pres.
Financial data (yr. ended 12/31/10): Revenue, $4,784,877; assets, $8,662,935 (M); gifts received, $4,448,367; expenditures, $4,576,162; program services expenses, $4,525,096; giving activities include $2,860,612 for 49 grants (high: $597,000; low: $5,000) and $147,500 for grants to individuals.
Purpose and activities: The organization supports charitable organizations on a national basis. While most of its funds are committed to the Boys' and Girls' Clubs of America, it is open to receiving proposals from organizations with missions and projects which are in line with the priorities of the board of directors.
Fields of interest: Boys & girls clubs.
Type of support: Conferences/seminars; Continuing support; Curriculum development; Equipment; In-kind gifts; Program development; Research; Scholarship funds.
Geographic limitations: Giving on a national basis.
Publications: Annual report; Application guidelines.
Application information: Applications accepted. Application form not required. Applicants should submit the following:
1) brief history of organization and description of its mission
2) detailed description of project and amount of funding requested
3) additional materials/documentation
Initial approach: Proposal or letter
Copies of proposal: 1
Deadline(s): None
Officers: Thomas C. Brasuell*, Pres.; Thomas Ostertag*, Secy.; Scott Stamp*, Treas.
EIN: 133348589

2346
Major League Baseball Players Association

12 E. 49th St., 24th Fl.
New York, NY 10017 (212) 826-0808

Company URL: http://mlbplayers.mlb.com
Establishment information: Established in 1968.
Company type: Labor union
Business activities: Operates labor union.
Business type (SIC): Labor organization; commercial sports
Corporate officers: Marietta DiCamillo, C.F.O.; Martha Child, C.A.O.; Victor Lugo, Clerk
Giving statement: Giving through the Major League Baseball Players Trust.

Major League Baseball Players Trust

12 E. 49th St.
New York, NY 10017-1028 (212) 826-0808
URL: http://www.mlb.com/pa/trust

Establishment information: Established in 1996 in NY.
Financial data (yr. ended 12/31/11): Revenue, $1,977,122; assets, $5,844,093 (M); gifts received, $2,064,404; expenditures, $1,823,786; giving activities include $1,353,554 for grants and $43,500 for grants to individuals.
Purpose and activities: The organization operates exclusively for charitable, scientific, literary, and educational purposes, as well as for the prevention of cruelty to children and animals.
Fields of interest: Education; Animal welfare; Crime/violence prevention, child abuse; Athletics/sports, baseball; Volunteers of America; Children, services; Human services.
Geographic limitations: Giving on a national basis.
Trustees: Tony Clark; Craig Counsell; Curtis Granderson; Mark Loretta; Michael Weiner.
EIN: 133843389

2347
Major League Soccer, L.L.C.

(doing business as MLS)
4200 5th Ave., 7th Fl.
New York, NY 10018 (212) 450-1200

Company URL: http://web.mlsnet.com
Establishment information: Established in 1993.
Company type: Business league
Business activities: Operates professional sports league.
Business type (SIC): Business association; commercial sports
Corporate officers: Mark Abbott, Pres.; Sean Prendegast, C.F.O.; JoAnne Neale, Sr. V.P. and Genl. Counsel; Dan Courtemanche, Sr. V.P., Mktg. and Comms.; Nelson Rodriguez, Sr. V.P., Opers.; Russell Klein, V.P., Finance
Giving statement: Giving through the Major League Soccer, L.L.C., Corporate Giving Program.

Major League Soccer, L.L.C., Corporate Giving Program

(also known as MLS W.O.R.K.S.)
420 5th Ave.
New York, NY 10018 (212) 450-1200
URL: http://www.mlssoccer.com/community

Purpose and activities: Major League Soccer, through the MLS W.O.R.K.S. program, supports organizations involved with health and wellness, youth soccer, education, the environment, and civic initiatives. Special emphasis is directed toward programs for school-aged children. Support is given primarily in areas of company operations, and on a national and international basis.
Fields of interest: Education; Environment; Hospitals (specialty); Public health, communicable diseases; Public health, physical fitness; Health care; Cancer; Safety/disasters; Recreation, fund raising/fund distribution; Athletics/sports, soccer; Youth development; Youth, services; Human services; Civil/human rights; Public affairs Children.
Type of support: Annual campaigns; Donated products; Employee volunteer services; General/operating support; In-kind gifts.
Geographic limitations: Giving primarily in areas of company operations; giving also to national and international organizations.
Application information: Applications accepted. Organizations are limited to one request per calendar year. Application form required. Applicants should submit the following:
1) name, address and phone number of organization
2) contact person
Applications must include a Tax I.D. number, event name and date, expected number of attendees, and amount raised last year. Application form is available here: http://www.mlssoccer.com/mlsworks/donation-request-form.
Initial approach: Complete online application
Deadline(s): 6 weeks prior to event

2348
Makino, Inc.

(formerly LeBlond Makino Machine Tool Company)
7680 Innovation Way
Mason, OH 45040-9695 (513) 573-7200

Company URL: http://www.makino.com
Establishment information: Established in 1922.
Company type: Subsidiary of a foreign company
Business activities: Manufactures machine tools.
Business type (SIC): Machinery/metalworking
Corporate officers: Jiro Makino, Chair.; Donald D. Lane, Pres. and C.E.O.; Ronald D Brown, C.F.O.; Fumiyoshi Matsubara, Secy.
Board of director: Jiro Makino, Chair.
Giving statement: Giving through the LeBlond Foundation of Makino.

The LeBlond Foundation of Makino

(formerly LeBlond Foundation)
7680 Innovation Way
Mason, OH 45040-9695 (513) 573-7350

Establishment information: Established in 1952 in OH.
Donors: LeBlond Makino Machine Tool Co.; Makino, Inc.; Donald D. Lane.
Financial data (yr. ended 12/31/11): Assets, $452,323 (M); gifts received, $56,998; expenditures, $62,831; qualifying distributions, $55,400; giving activities include $55,400 for 30 grants (high: $5,000; low: $500).
Purpose and activities: The foundation supports art museums and organizations involved with education.
Fields of interest: Museums (art); Education, special; Higher education; Education.
Type of support: General/operating support.
Geographic limitations: Giving primarily in the greater Cincinnati, OH, area.
Support limitations: No grants to individuals.
Application information: Applications accepted. Application form required.
Initial approach: Letter
Deadline(s): None
Officers: Daniel W. LeBlond, Chair.; Donald D. Lane, Vice-Chair.; Thomas F. Clark, Secy.
EIN: 316036274

2349
Mal Warwick & Associates, Inc.
2550 9th St., Ste. 103
Berkeley, CA 94710 (510) 843-8888

Company URL: http://www.malwarwick.com
Establishment information: Established in 1979.
Company type: Private company
Business activities: Operates a fundraising consulting company serving nonprofit organizations.
Business type (SIC): Business services/ miscellaneous
Corporate officers: Mal Warwick, Chair.; Dan Doyle, Pres. and C.E.O.; Christina Chavez, V.P., Finance and Admin.
Board of directors: Mal Warwick, Chair.; Berit Ashla; Dan Doyle; Paul Hammond; Sherri Q. Pittman
Office: Washington, DC
Giving statement: Giving through the Mal Warwick Associates, Inc. Corporate Giving Program.

Mal Warwick Associates, Inc. Corporate Giving Program
2550 Ninth St., Ste. 103
Berkeley, CA 94710-2551 (510) 843-8888
FAX: (510) 843-0142;
E-mail: inquiry@malwarwick.com; URL: http://www.malwarwick.com/meet-our-team/socially-responsible-business.html

Purpose and activities: Mal Warwick Associates is a certified B Corporation that donates 10 percent of its pre-tax profits to nonprofit organizations. Support is given primarily in California, with some emphasis on Berkeley; giving also to national and international organizations.
Fields of interest: Higher education; Health care; Food banks; Community/economic development.
Program:
Matching Gifts Program: Mal Warwick Associates matches employee gifts to nonprofit organizations by 2:1.
Type of support: Employee matching gifts; General/ operating support.
Geographic limitations: Giving primarily in CA, with some emphasis on Berkeley; giving also to national and international organizations.

2350
Malco Industries, Inc.
1717 2nd St., Ste. A
Sarasota, FL 34236-8552 (941) 951-2511

Establishment information: Established in 1946.
Company type: Private company
Business activities: Sells mobile homes and recreational vehicles.
Business type (SIC): Mobile homes—retail; camps/ recreational
Corporate officers: Neil N. Malamud, Pres.; Sheldon Silverstein, Cont.
Giving statement: Giving through the Malco Charitable Foundation, Inc.

The Malco Charitable Foundation, Inc.
(formerly The Malco Charitable Foundation)
1717 2nd St.
Sarasota, FL 34236-8552

Establishment information: Established in 1980 as a company-sponsored operating foundation.
Donors: Malco Industries, Inc.; Neil Malamud.
Financial data (yr. ended 12/31/11): Assets, $430,894 (M); expenditures, $61,942; qualifying distributions, $61,692; giving activities include $61,442 for 49 grants (high: $10,000; low: $75).
Purpose and activities: The foundation supports organizations involved with arts and culture, K-12 and higher education, cancer, and Judaism.
Fields of interest: Performing arts, ballet; Arts; Elementary/secondary education; Higher education; Cancer; Girls clubs; Jewish agencies & synagogues.
Type of support: General/operating support.
Geographic limitations: Giving primarily in Sarasota, FL.
Support limitations: No grants to individuals.
Application information: Applications not accepted. Unsolicited requests for funds not accepted.
Officers: Neil Malamud, Pres. and Treas.; Lisa B. Cicero, V.P.; Heidi Pepper Lein, V.P.; Sandra Malamud, Secy.
EIN: 341307450

2351
Malt-O-Meal Company
80 S. 8th St., Ste. 2700
Minneapolis, MN 55402-2297
(612) 338-8551
FAX: (612) 339-5710

Company URL: http://www.malt-o-meal.com
Establishment information: Established in 1919.
Company type: Private company
Business activities: Produces hot wheat cereal and ready-to-eat cereal.
Business type (SIC): Grain mill products, including pet food
Financial profile for 2010: Number of employees, 1,400
Corporate officers: Chris Neugent, C.E.O.; John A. Gappa, C.F.O.; Gene Pagel, C.I.O.
Giving statement: Giving through the M-O-M Cares Employee Foundation.

M-O-M Cares Employee Foundation
20802 Kensington Blvd.
Lakeville, MN 55044-1655 (952) 322-8000

Financial data (yr. ended 12/31/11): Revenue, $167,378; assets, $80,106 (M); gifts received, $82,060; expenditures, $157,408; giving activities include $154,935 for grants.
Purpose and activities: The foundation provides grants to help in hardships.
Fields of interest: Human services.
Geographic limitations: Giving primarily in MN.
Officers: Brian Evenson, Pres.; Tina Fulgham, Secy.; Carol Howard, Treas.
EIN: 411843367

2352
Mamiye Brothers, Inc.
112 W. 34th St., Ste. 1000
New York, NY 10120-1000 (212) 279-4150

Company URL: http://www.mamiye.com/
Establishment information: Established in 1947.
Company type: Private company
Business activities: Manufactures children's clothing.
Business type (SIC): Apparel—girls' and children's outerwear
Corporate officers: Charles D. Mamiye, Pres. and C.E.O.; Hymie Mamiye, C.O.O. and C.F.O.
Giving statement: Giving through the Mamiye Foundation, Inc.

The Mamiye Foundation, Inc.
180 Raritan Center Pkwy., Ste. 11
Edison, NJ 08837-3646

Establishment information: Incorporated in 1982 in NJ.
Donors: Mamiye Brothers, Inc.; MB Kids Clothes LLC; Hyman M. Mamiye.
Contact: Charles M. Mamiye, Tr.
Financial data (yr. ended 12/31/11): Assets, $104,726 (M); gifts received, $175,140; expenditures, $209,351; qualifying distributions, $209,246; giving activities include $209,246 for grants.
Purpose and activities: The foundation supports hospitals and organizations involved with education, children and youth, disability services, and Judaism.
Fields of interest: Elementary/secondary education; Education; Hospitals (general); Children/ youth, services; Developmentally disabled, centers & services; Jewish federated giving programs; Jewish agencies & synagogues.
Type of support: Annual campaigns; Building/ renovation; Program development; Scholarship funds; Sponsorships.
Geographic limitations: Giving primarily in Deal and Ocean, NJ and Brooklyn and New York, NY.
Support limitations: No grants to individuals.
Application information: Applications accepted. Application form not required. Applicants should submit the following:
1) name, address and phone number of organization
2) copy of IRS Determination Letter
3) detailed description of project and amount of funding requested
Initial approach: Proposal
Deadline(s): None
Trustees: Abraham Mamiye; Charles D. Mamiye; Charles M. Mamiye; Hyman M. Mamiye.
EIN: 222471712
Selected grants: The following grants are a representative sample of this grantmaker's funding activity:
$26,000 to Yeshiva of Flatbush, Brooklyn, NY, 2010.
$18,000 to Sephardic Bikur Holim, Brooklyn, NY, 2010.
$18,000 to Sephardic Bikur Holim, Brooklyn, NY, 2010.
$17,000 to Hillel Yeshiva, Ocean, NJ, 2010.
$17,000 to Hillel Yeshiva, Ocean, NJ, 2010.
$10,000 to Sephardic Institute, Brooklyn, NY, 2010.
$10,000 to Yeshiva of Flatbush, Brooklyn, NY, 2010.
$8,000 to UJA-Federation of New York, New York, NY, 2010. For Annual Fund.
$2,500 to Sephardic Bikur Holim, Brooklyn, NY, 2010.
$1,200 to Mesivta Yeshiva Rabbi Chaim Berlin, Brooklyn, NY, 2010.

2353
Mamma Chia LLC
1209 Clos Duval
Bonsall, CA 92003-6114 (760) 624-8883
FAX: (760) 539-8881

Company URL: http://MammaChia.com
Establishment information: Established in 2009.
Company type: Private company

Business type (SIC): Business services/ miscellaneous
Corporate officers: Janie Hoffman, C.E.O.; Matt Buckley, Exec. V.P., Sales & Mktg.
Giving statement: Giving through the Mamma Chia LLC Contributions Program.

Mamma Chia LLC Contributions Program

1209 Clos Duval
Bonsall, CA 92003-6114 (760) 624-8883
URL: http://www.bcorporation.net/mammachia

Purpose and activities: Mamma Chia is a certified B Corporation that donates a percentage of profits to charitable organizations.
Fields of interest: Agriculture, sustainable programs.
Type of support: General/operating support.

2354
Manhattan Beer Distributors, Inc.

400 Walnut Ave.
Bronx, NY 10454-2018 (718) 292-9300
FAX: (718) 292-6348

Company URL: http://www.manhattanbeer.com/
Establishment information: Established in 1978.
Company type: Private company
Business activities: Produces and distributes beer, wine, and soft drinks.
Business type (SIC): Beer, wine, and distilled beverages—wholesale
Financial profile for 2010: Number of employees, 1,400
Corporate officers: Simon Bergson, Pres. and C.E.O.; Bill Bessette, C.O.O.; George Wertheimer, C.F.O.; Mike McCarthy, Sr. V.P., Opers.; Bill Deluca, Sr. V.P., Sales and Mktg.; Al Greco, V.P., Mktg.
Giving statement: Giving through the Saramar Charitable Fund.

The Saramar Charitable Fund

951 Frazier Rd.
Rydal, PA 19046-2407
Application address: 8275 N. Route 130, Pennsauken, NJ 08110-1435

Establishment information: Established in 2003 in PA.
Donors: Manhattan Beer Distributors, LLC; Marjorie Honickman.
Contact: Marjorie Honickman, Tr.
Financial data (yr. ended 12/31/11): Assets, $3,358,329 (M); gifts received, $250,000; expenditures, $165,763; qualifying distributions, $161,636; giving activities include $161,636 for grants.
Purpose and activities: The foundation supports organizations involved with arts and culture, education, cancer, human services, and Judaism.
Fields of interest: Museums (art); Performing arts; Arts; Elementary school/education; Secondary school/education; Higher education; Education; Hospitals (general); Health care; Cancer; Aging, centers/services; Human services; Jewish federated giving programs; Jewish agencies & synagogues.
Type of support: General/operating support; Program development; Scholarship funds.
Geographic limitations: Giving primarily in Philadelphia, PA.
Support limitations: No grants to individuals.
Application information: Applications accepted. Application form not required.
Initial approach: Proposal
Deadline(s): None
Trustees: Jeffrey A. Honickman; Marjorie Honickman.
EIN: 256839698
Selected grants: The following grants are a representative sample of this grantmaker's funding activity:
$2,550 to Jewish Family and Childrens Service, Waltham, MA, 2011.
$2,500 to George Washington University, Washington, DC, 2011.
$1,000 to American Cancer Society, Atlanta, GA, 2011.
$1,000 to Wilderness Society, Washington, DC, 2011.

2355
The Manitowoc Company, Inc.

2400 S. 44th St.
P.O. Box 66
Manitowoc, WI 54221-0066
(920) 684-4410
FAX: (920) 652-9778

Company URL: http://www.manitowoc.com
Establishment information: Established in 1902.
Company type: Public company
Company ticker symbol and exchange: MTW/NYSE
Business activities: Manufactures cranes and related products; manufactures foodservice equipment; provides marine vessel construction, repair, and maintenance services.
Business type (SIC): Machinery/construction, mining, and materials handling; machinery/ refrigeration and service industry; ship and boat building and repair
Financial profile for 2011: Number of employees, 13,500; assets, $4,057,300,000; sales volume, $3,927,000,000; pre-tax net income, $130,300,000; expenses, $3,651,500,000; liabilities, $3,457,000,000
Fortune 1000 ranking: 2012—591st in revenues, 737th in profits, and 659th in assets
Corporate officers: Glen E. Tellock, Chair., Pres., and C.E.O.; Carl J. Laurino, Sr. V.P. and C.F.O.; Maurice D. Jones, Sr. V.P., Genl. Counsel, and Secy.; Thomas G. Musial, Sr. V.P., Human Resources and Admin.; Dean J. Nolden, V.P., Finance and Treas.
Board of directors: Glen E. Tellock, Chair.; Roy V. Armes; Donald Marion Condon, Jr.; Cynthia M. Egnotovich; Kenneth W. Krueger; Keith D. Nosbusch; James L. Packard; Robert C. Stift
Subsidiaries: Grove U.S. LLC, Shady Grove, PA; Manitowoc Cranes, Inc., Manitowoc, WI; Manitowoc Equipment Works, Inc., Manitowoc, WI; Manitowoc Ice, Inc., Manitowoc, WI; Manitowoc Marine Group, LLC, Marinette, WI; Manitowoc Re-Manufacturing, Inc., Bauxite, AR; Marinette Marine Corp., Marinette, WI; National Crane Corp., Shady Grove, PA; North Central Crane & Excavator Sales Corp., Mokena, IL
International operations: Australia; Barbados; Bermuda; Brazil; British Virgin Islands; Cayman Islands; China; Czech Republic; France; Germany; Hungary; India; Ireland; Isle of Man; Italy; Luxembourg; Malaysia; Mauritius; Mexico; Netherlands; Philippines; Poland; Portugal; Russia; Singapore; Slovakia; South Korea; Spain; United Arab Emirates; United Kingdom
Giving statement: Giving through the Manitowoc Company, Inc. Corporate Giving Program.
Company EIN: 390448110

The Manitowoc Company, Inc. Corporate Giving Program

2400 S. 44th St.
Manitowoc, WI 54220-5846 (920) 684-4410
URL: http://www.manitowoc.com/EN/Our-Company/Pages/Corporate_Citizenship.aspx

Purpose and activities: Manitowoc makes charitable contributions to nonprofit organizations involved with children, human services, and community development. Support is given primarily in the Manitowoc, Wisconsin, area.
Fields of interest: Cancer research; Food banks; Athletics/sports, school programs; Human services; Community/economic development; United Ways and Federated Giving Programs; Public affairs; General charitable giving Children/youth.
Type of support: Employee-related scholarships; General/operating support; Sponsorships.
Geographic limitations: Giving primarily in the Manitowoc, WI, area; giving also to national organizations.

2356
Manitowoc Foodservice Companies, Inc.

(formerly Enodis Corporation)
2227 Welbilt Blvd.
New Port Richey, FL 34655-5130
(727) 375-7010

Company URL: http://www.manitowocfoodservice.com
Establishment information: Established in 1955.
Company type: Subsidiary of a foreign company
Business activities: Manufactures foodservice equipment.
Business type (SIC): Machinery/refrigeration and service industry
Corporate officers: Glen E. Tellock, Chair., Pres., and C.E.O.; Michael J. Kachmer, Pres.; Craig Reuther, Sr. V.P., Finance; Dean Landeche, Sr. V.P., Mktg.
Board of director: Glen E. Tellock, Chair.
Subsidiaries: Clevelend Range, L.L.C., Cleveland, OH; Frymaster L.L.C., Shreveport, LA; Garland Commercial Industries L.L.C., Freeland, PA; Jackson MSC L.L.C., Barbourville, KY; Kysor Industrial Corporation, Cadillac, MI; Lincoln Foodservice Products L.L.C., Fort Wayne, IN; Merco/Savory, Inc., Fort Wayne, IN; Mile High Equipment L.L.C., Denver, CO
Giving statement: Giving through the Manitowoc Company Foundation.

The Manitowoc Company Foundation

(formerly Welbilt Corporation Foundation)
2400 S. 44th St.
Manitowoc, WI 54220-5846

Establishment information: Established in 1972 in MI.
Donors: Kysor Industrial Corp.; Manitowoc Company.
Contact: S. Powers
Financial data (yr. ended 05/31/12): Assets, $1,880,972 (M); gifts received, $158,525; expenditures, $163,310; qualifying distributions, $156,322; giving activities include $151,525 for 40 grants (high: $75,000; low: $100).

Purpose and activities: The foundation supports organizations involved with education, health, cancer, and human services.
Fields of interest: Higher education; Libraries (public); Education; Health care, patient services; Health care; Cancer; Boys & girls clubs; Big Brothers/Big Sisters; American Red Cross; YM/YWCAs & YM/YWHAs; Children/youth, services; Human services; United Ways and Federated Giving Programs.
Type of support: Building/renovation; Capital campaigns; Continuing support; General/operating support; Publication; Research.
Geographic limitations: Giving primarily in areas of company operations in CO, GA, LA, MD, PA, and TX; giving also to national organizations.
Support limitations: No support for political organizations, religious organizations not of direct benefit to the entire community, or national or international organizations. No grants to individuals or for political campaigns.
Application information: Applications not accepted. Contributes only to pre-selected organizations.
Officers: Michael J. Kachner, Pres.; Carl J. Laurino, V.P. and Treas.; Maurice D. Jones, V.P. and Secy.; John G. Oros*, V.P. and Treas.; W. David Wrench*, V.P.; Irwin M. Shur*, Secy.
EIN: 237199469
Selected grants: The following grants are a representative sample of this grantmaker's funding activity:
$6,000 to Conservation International, Arlington, VA, 2009.
$5,000 to Johnson and Wales University, Providence, RI, 2009.
$4,373 to American Cancer Society, Atlanta, GA, 2009.
$1,000 to American Heart Association, Dallas, TX, 2009.

2357
Manocherian Brothers

150 E. 58th St., Ste. 2801
New York, NY 10155-2899 (212) 355-4900

Establishment information: Established in 1987.
Company type: Private company
Business activities: Operates real estate agencies.
Business type (SIC): Real estate agents and managers
Corporate officer: Amir Manocherian, Partner
Giving statement: Giving through the Amir and Rosita Manocherian Family Foundation.

Amir and Rosita Manocherian Family Foundation

150 E. 58th St.
New York, NY 10155-0001

Establishment information: Established in 2002.
Donors: Amir Manocherian; Rosita Manocherian; Robert Manocherian; Mireille Manocherian; Fameco, LLC; Jed Manocherian.
Financial data (yr. ended 12/31/11): Assets, $1,888,353 (M); gifts received, $1,064,500; expenditures, $335,134; qualifying distributions, $329,100; giving activities include $329,100 for grants.
Purpose and activities: The foundation supports organizations involved with education, cancer, multiple sclerosis, diabetes, medical research, and Judaism.
Fields of interest: Elementary/secondary education; Education; Cancer; Multiple sclerosis; Diabetes; Medical research, institute; Medical research; Food services; Jewish agencies & synagogues.
Type of support: General/operating support; Program development.
Geographic limitations: Giving primarily in NY.
Support limitations: No grants to individuals.
Application information: Applications not accepted. Unsolicited requests for funds not accepted.
Trustees: Amir Manocherian; Rosita Manocherian.
EIN: 137335693

2358
Manpower Inc.

(doing business as ManpowerGroup)
100 Manpower Pl.
Milwaukee, WI 53212 (414) 961-1000
FAX: (414) 961-7081

Company URL: http://www.manpower.com
Establishment information: Established in 1948.
Company type: Public company
Company ticker symbol and exchange: MAN/NYSE
Business activities: Provides temporary help services.
Business type (SIC): Personnel supply services
Financial profile for 2012: Number of employees, 28,000; assets, $7,012,600,000; sales volume, $20,678,000,000; pre-tax net income, $368,400,000; expenses, $20,266,300,000; liabilities, $4,511,800,000
Fortune 1000 ranking: 2012—140th in revenues, 579th in profits, and 491st in assets
Forbes 2000 ranking: 2012—456th in sales, 1568th in profits, and 1674th in assets
Corporate officers: Jeffrey A. Joerres, Chair., C.E.O., and Pres.; Darryl Green, Co-Pres.; Jonas Prising, Co-Pres.; Michael J. Van Handel, Exec. V.P. and C.F.O.; Denis Edwards, Sr. V.P. and C.I.O.; Richard Buchband, Sr. V.P., Genl. Counsel., and Secy.
Board of directors: Jeffrey A. Joerres, Chair.; Marc J. Bolland; Gina R. Boswell; Cari Dominguez; William Downe; Jack M. Greenberg; Patricia A. Hemingway Hall; Terry A. Hueneke; Roberto G. Mendoza; Ulice Payne, Jr.; Elizabeth P. Sartain; John R. Walter; Edward J. Zore
Subsidiaries: CareerHarmony, Inc., New York, NY; Complete Business Services of Illinois, Inc., Vernon Hills, IL; HR Staffing, L.L.C., Tyler, TX; Huntsville Service Contractors, Inc., Milwaukee, WI; Jefferson Wells International, Inc., Philadelphia, PA; Manpower Franchises, L.L.C., Milwaukee, WI; Manpower Incorporated of New York, Stamford, CT; Manpower International, Inc., Milwaukee, WI; Manpower Nominees, Inc., Milwaukee, WI; Manpower Professional Services, Inc., Milwaukee, WI; Resource Consulting Group, Inc., Orlando, FL; Right Management Consultants of Illinois, Chicago, IL; Signature Graphics Of Milwaukee, Inc., Milwaukee, WI; Topeka Services, Inc., Ottawa, KS; Transpersonnel, Inc., Milwaukee, WI; USCaden Corporation, PERU, IA; Wichita Services, Inc., Wichita, KS
International operations: Argentina; Australia; Austria; Bahrain; Belarus; Belgium; Brazil; British Virgin Islands; Bulgaria; Canada; China; Colombia; Costa Rica; Croatia; Czech Republic; Denmark; Dominican Republic; El Salvador; Estonia; Finland; France; Germany; Greece; Guatemala; Honduras; Hong Kong; Hungary; India; Ireland; Israel; Italy; Japan; Jordan; Kazakhstan; Kuwait; Latvia; Lithuania; Luxembourg; Macau; Malaysia; Martinique; Mexico; Monaco; Morocco and the Western Sahara; Netherlands; New Caledonia; New Zealand; Nicaragua; Norway; Panama; Paraguay; Peru; Philippines; Poland; Portugal; Qatar; Romania; Russia; Serbia; Singapore; Slovakia; Slovenia; South Africa; South Korea; Spain; Sweden; Switzerland; Taiwan; Thailand; Tunisia; Turkey; Ukraine; United Arab Emirates; United Kingdom; Uruguay; Venezuela; Vietnam
Giving statement: Giving through the Manpower Foundation, Inc.
Company EIN: 391672779

Manpower Foundation, Inc.

100 Manpower Pl.
Milwaukee, WI 53212-4030
URL: http://us.manpower.com/us/en/social-responsibility/philanthropy/default.jsp

Establishment information: Established in 1953 in WI.
Donor: Manpower Inc.
Financial data (yr. ended 12/31/11): Assets, $536,052 (M); gifts received, $655,000; expenditures, $663,119; qualifying distributions, $663,094; giving activities include $663,000 for 28 grants (high: $225,000; low: $1,000).
Purpose and activities: The foundation supports programs designed to promote youth development and bridges to employment.
Fields of interest: Education; Employment, training; Employment; Youth development; United Ways and Federated Giving Programs.
Type of support: Employee-related scholarships; General/operating support; Scholarship funds.
Geographic limitations: Giving primarily in areas of company operations in Milwaukee, WI.
Application information: Applications not accepted. Contributes only to pre-selected organizations and through employee-related scholarships.
Officers and Directors:* Jeffrey A. Joerres*, Pres.; Julie Krey, V.P.; Michael J. Van Handel*, Secy.-Treas.
EIN: 396052810
Selected grants: The following grants are a representative sample of this grantmaker's funding activity:
$225,000 to Junior Achievement Worldwide, Colorado Springs, CO, 2010.
$209,000 to United Way of Greater Milwaukee, Milwaukee, WI, 2010.
$15,000 to YMCA of Metropolitan Milwaukee, Milwaukee, WI, 2010.
$5,000 to United Negro College Fund, Fairfax, VA, 2010.
$2,500 to Hispanic Professionals of Greater Milwaukee, Milwaukee, WI, 2010.
$2,500 to Milwaukee Center for Independence, Milwaukee, WI, 2010.
$1,000 to University of Wisconsin, Milwaukee, WI, 2010.

2359
Manti Operating Company

800 N. Shoreline Blvd., Ste. 900 S.
Corpus Christi, TX 78401-3700
(361) 888-7708
FAX: (361) 880-5709

Company URL: http://www.mantires.com
Establishment information: Established in 1995.
Company type: Private company
Business activities: Produces crude petroleum and natural gas.
Business type (SIC): Extraction/oil and gas
Corporate officers: Lee Barberito, Pres.; Barry Clark, C.O.O.; Robert Hill, C.F.O.; Ben McCrackin, V.P., Opers.

Board of director: Lee Barberito
Giving statement: Giving through the Futureus Foundation.

Futureus Foundation
P.O. Box 2907
Corpus Christi, TX 78403-2907 (361) 888-7708
FAX: (361) 888-4418; E-mail: donna@mantires.com

Donor: Manti Operating Co., Inc.
Contact: Harold L. Simmons, Jr.
Financial data (yr. ended 10/31/11): Assets, $77,267 (M); expenditures, $11,834; qualifying distributions, $10,000; giving activities include $10,000 for 4 grants (high: $5,000; low: $500).
Purpose and activities: The foundation supports organizations involved with education, youth development, and human services and awards scholarships and financial relief to individuals in Texas.
Fields of interest: Education; Human services; Religion.
Type of support: Annual campaigns; Equipment; General/operating support; Grants to individuals; Scholarship funds; Scholarships—to individuals; Sponsorships.
Geographic limitations: Giving primarily in Corpus Christi, TX.
Application information: Applications accepted. Application form required.
Scholarship applications should include high school or college transcripts and a letter of recommendation from a current teacher, former teacher, or community leader.
Initial approach: Proposal
Deadline(s): None
Trustees: Lee Barberito; Kenton McDonald.
EIN: 270004671

2360
Mapes Industries, Inc.
2929 Cornhusker Hwy.
P.O. Box 80069
Lincoln, NE 68504-1519 (402) 466-1985
FAX: (402) 466-2790

Company URL: http://www.mapes.com
Establishment information: Established in 1952.
Company type: Private company
Business activities: Manufactures architectural laminated metal panels.
Business type (SIC): Metal products/structural
Corporate officers: William R. Cintani, Owner; Jay Marshall, Pres.
Giving statement: Giving through the Cintani Family Foundation.

Cintani Family Foundation
2929 Cornhusker Hwy.
Lincoln, NE 68504-1519

Establishment information: Established in 1998 in NE.
Donors: Mapes Industries Inc.; William R. Cintani.
Contact: William R. Cintani, Pres. and Treas.
Financial data (yr. ended 11/30/11): Assets, $780,286 (M); gifts received, $65,042; expenditures, $32,520; qualifying distributions, $32,500; giving activities include $32,500 for 23 grants (high: $5,000; low: $250).
Purpose and activities: The foundation supports hospitals and organizations involved with K-12 education, rehabilitation, youth development, and children and youth.
Fields of interest: Elementary/secondary education; Hospitals (general); Medical care, rehabilitation; Youth development, business; YM/YWCAs & YM/YWHAs; Children/youth, services.
Type of support: General/operating support.
Geographic limitations: Giving primarily in Lincoln, NE.
Support limitations: No grants to individuals.
Application information: Applications accepted. Application form required.
Initial approach: Letter
Deadline(s): None
Officers: William R. Cintani, Pres. and Treas.; Rich Bailey, V.P.; Marilyn Cintani, Secy.
EIN: 470811992

2361
Maquoketa State Bank
203 N. Main St.
P.O. Box 1210
Maquoketa, IA 52060-2204
(563) 652-2491

Company URL: http://www.maquoketasb.com
Establishment information: Established in 1958.
Company type: Subsidiary of a private company
Business activities: Operates state commercial bank.
Business type (SIC): Banks/commercial
Corporate officer: M.A. Dalchow, Pres.
Board of directors: Lynn Battles; Earl Boyer; M.A. Dalchow; Tom Myatt; M.J. Pooler; Darrell Reichling
Giving statement: Giving through the Ohnward Foundation.

Ohnward Foundation
107 E. Quarry St.
P.O. Box 968
Maquoketa, IA 52060-0968 (563) 652-2491

Establishment information: Established in 2005 in IA.
Donors: Maquoketa State Bank; Fagerland-Tubbs Trust; First Central State Bank.
Contact: Kendra Beck, Dir.
Financial data (yr. ended 12/31/11): Assets, $905,920 (M); gifts received, $45,836; expenditures, $60,314; qualifying distributions, $52,936; giving activities include $52,936 for 5 grants (high: $37,000; low: $2,500).
Purpose and activities: The foundation supports health centers and organizations involved with arts and culture, conservation, and school athletics.
Fields of interest: Arts; Environment, natural resources; Health care, clinics/centers; Athletics/sports, school programs.
Type of support: Building/renovation; General/operating support.
Geographic limitations: Giving primarily in IA.
Application information: Applications accepted. Application form not required.
Initial approach: Proposal
Deadline(s): None
Directors: Glenn Bartelt; Kendra Beck; Alan R. Tubbs; David Updegraff.
EIN: 201895465

2362
Marathon Ashland Petroleum, LLC
539 S. Main St.
Findlay, OH 45840 (419) 422-2121

Company URL: http://www.mapllc.com
Establishment information: Established in 1998.
Company type: Joint venture
Ultimate parent company: Marathon Oil Corporation
Business activities: Refines and markets petroleum; operates petroleum pipelines.
Business type (SIC): Petroleum refining; pipelines (except natural gas/operation of)
Financial profile for 2009: Number of employees, 25,000
Corporate officers: Gary R. Heminger, Pres. and C.E.O.; Donald C. Templin, Sr. V.P. and C.F.O.; Rodney P. Nichols, Sr. V.P., Human Resources and Admin.; Thomas M. Kelley, Sr. V.P., Mktg.; Donald W. Wehrly, V.P. and C.I.O.; J. Michael Wilder, V.P., Genl. Counsel and Secy.; Timothy T. Griffith, V.P., Finance and Treas.; Michael G. Braddock, V.P. and Cont.; Pamela K. Beall, V.P., Public Affairs
Subsidiaries: Marathon Ashland Pipe Line LLC, Findlay, OH; Speedway SuperAmerica LLC, Springfield, OH
Plants: Indianapolis, IN; Louisville, KY; Garyville, LA; Detroit, MI; St. Paul Park, MN; Oregon, OH; Texas City, TX
International operations: Canada
Giving statement: Giving through the Marathon Ashland Petroleum LLC Corporate Giving Program.

Marathon Ashland Petroleum LLC Corporate Giving Program
539 Main St.
Findlay, OH 45840
URL: http://www.marathonpetroleum.com/Corporate_Citizenship/

Purpose and activities: Marathon Petroleum Corporation makes charitable contributions to nonprofit organizations involved with human services and health. Support is given primarily in areas of company operations in Illinois, Indiana, Kentucky, Louisiana, Michigan, Canton, Enon, and Findlay, Ohio, Texas, and West Virginia.
Fields of interest: Education; Human services; United Ways and Federated Giving Programs Economically disadvantaged.
Type of support: Employee volunteer services; General/operating support; Scholarships—to individuals.
Geographic limitations: Giving primarily in areas of company operations in IL, IN, Kentucky, LA, MI, Canton, Enon, and Findlay, OH, TX, and WV.

2363
Marathon Oil Company
5555 San Felipe St.
Houston, TX 77056-2723 (713) 629-6600

Company URL: http://www.marathon.com
Establishment information: Established in 1887.
Company type: Subsidiary of a public company
Business activities: Conducts crude oil and natural gas exploration and production activities; refines, markets, and transports crude oil and petroleum products; markets and transports natural gas and natural gas products.

Business type (SIC): Petroleum refining; extraction/oil and gas; pipelines (except natural gas/operation of); gas production and distribution
Financial profile for 2011: Assets, $31,371,000,000; sales volume, $14,663,000,000; liabilities, $14,212,000,000
Corporate officers: Clarence P. Cazalot, Jr., Chair., Pres., and C.E.O.; Janet F. Clark, Exec. V.P. and C.F.O.
Board of director: Clarence P. Cazalot, Jr., Chair.
Subsidiaries: Delhi Gas Pipeline Corp., Dallas, TX; FWA Drilling Co., Inc., Wichita Falls, TX; Marathon Ashland Petroleum, LLC, Findlay, OH
Giving statement: Giving through the Rock Island Refining Foundation.

Rock Island Refining Foundation
c/o Edgar S. Joseph
P.O. Box 90114
Indianapolis, IN 46290-0114

Establishment information: Established in 1973 in IN.
Donor: Rock Island Refining Co.
Financial data (yr. ended 12/31/11): Assets, $1,864,125 (M); expenditures, $85,077; qualifying distributions, $70,000; giving activities include $70,000 for grants.
Purpose and activities: The foundation supports health centers and organizations involved with film, performing arts, secondary and higher education, family planning, and human services.
Fields of interest: Education; Youth development; Human services.
Type of support: General/operating support.
Application information: Applications not accepted. Unsolicited requests for funds not accepted.
Trustees: Edgar S. Joseph; Mella Thompson; Norma Winkler.
EIN: 356264479

2364
Marathon Oil Corporation
(formerly USX Corporation)
5555 San Felipe St.
Houston, TX 77056-2723 (713) 629-6600
FAX: (713) 296-2952

Company URL: http://www.marathonoil.com
Establishment information: Established in 1887.
Company type: Public company
Company ticker symbol and exchange: MRO/NYSE
International Securities Identification Number: US5658491064
Business activities: Conducts crude petroleum and natural gas exploration and production activities; refines petroleum; operates pipelines; operates gasoline service stations.
Business type (SIC): Extraction/oil and gas; petroleum refining; pipelines (except natural gas/operation of); gasoline service stations
Financial profile for 2012: Assets, $35,300,000,000; sales volume, $15,600,000,000
Fortune 1000 ranking: 2012—174th in revenues, 132nd in profits, and 161st in assets
Forbes 2000 ranking: 2012—603rd in sales, 396th in profits, and 639th in assets
Corporate officers: Clarence P. Cazalot, Jr., Chair., Pres., and C.E.O.; David E. Roberts, Jr., Exec. V.P. and C.O.O.; Janet F. Clark, Exec. V.P. and C.F.O.; Sylvia J. Kerrigan, Exec. V.P., Genl. Counsel, and Secy.; Thomas K. Sneed, V.P. and C.I.O.; Michael K. Stewart, V.P., Finance, Cont. and Treas.; Howard J. Thill, V.P., Public Affairs; Robert L. Sovine, V.P., Human Resources; Linda A. Capuano, V.P., Tech.
Board of directors: Clarence P. Cazalot, Jr., Chair.; Gregory H. Boyce; Pierre Brondeau; Linda Zarda Cook; Shirley Ann Jackson; Philip Lader; Michael E. J. Phelps; Dennis H. Reilley
Subsidiaries: Marathon Ashland Petroleum, LLC, Findlay, OH; Marathon Oil Company, Houston, TX
Giving statement: Giving through the Marathon Oil Corporation Contributions Program.
Company EIN: 250996816

Marathon Oil Corporation Contributions Program
c/o Charitable Contribs.
P.O. Box 3128
Houston, TX 77253
E-mail: philanthropy@marathonoil.com; URL: http://www.marathonoil.com/Social_Responsibility/SocioEconomic/Social_Investments/

2365
Marathon Petroleum Corporation
539 S. Main St.
Findlay, OH 45840-3229 (419) 422-2121
FAX: (302) 655-5049

Company URL: http://www.marathonpetroleum.com/
Establishment information: Established in 1887.
Company type: Public company
Company ticker symbol and exchange: MPC/NYSE
Business activities: Operates oil refining company.
Business type (SIC): Petroleum refining
Financial profile for 2012: Number of employees, 25,985; assets, $27,223,000,000; sales volume, $82,492,000,000; pre-tax net income, $5,238,000,000; expenses, $77,145,000,000; liabilities, $15,529,000,000
Fortune 1000 ranking: 2012—33rd in revenues, 56th in profits, and 201st in assets
Forbes 2000 ranking: 2012—93rd in sales, 165th in profits, and 794th in assets
Corporate officers: Thomas J. Usher, Chair.; Gary R. Heminger, Pres. and C.E.O.; Donald C. Templin, Sr. V.P. and C.F.O.; Thomas M. Kelley, Sr. V.P., Mktg.; Rodney P. Nichols, Sr. V.P., Human Resources; Donald W. Wehrly, V.P. and C.I.O.; J. Michael Wilder, V.P., Genl. Counsel, and Secy.; Michael G. Braddock, V.P. and Cont.; Timothy T. Griffith, V.P., Finance, and Treas.; Pamela K.M. Beall, V.P., Public Affairs
Board of directors: Thomas J. Usher, Chair.; Evan Bayh; David A. Daberko; William L. Davis; Gary R. Heminger; Donna A. James; Charles R. Lee; Seth E. Schofield; John W. Snow; John P. Surma
Giving statement: Giving through the Marathon Petroleum Corporation Contributions Program.
Company EIN: 271284632

Marathon Petroleum Corporation Contributions Program
539 S. Main St.
Findlay, OH 45840-3229 (419) 422-2121
E-mail: whconlisk@marathonpetroleum.com; Additional e-mail: lawhetstone@marathonpetroleum.com; E-mail addresses for Local Charitable Giving Committees: Findlay, OH: lawhetstone@marathonpetroleum.com; Canton, OH: kffarmer@marathonpetroleum.com; Enron, OH: bamayer@speedway.com; Illinois/Indiana: mjleland@marathonpetroleum.com; Louisiana: jjdelacruz@marathonpetroleum.com; Michigan: bsneumeister@marathonpetroleum.com; Texas: labradbury@marathonpetroleum.com; and tri-state KY, OH, and WV: gjjackson@marathonpetroleum.com;; URL: http://www.marathonpetroleum.com/Corporate_Citizenship/

Contact: Bill Conlisk
Purpose and activities: Marathon Petroleum Corp. makes charitable contributions to nonprofit organizations involved with education, civic and community causes, health and human services, and the environment. Special emphasis is directed toward programs that empower the socially or economically disadvantaged and provide opportunities for students to reach their full potential. Giving primarily in areas of company operations, and to national organizations.
Fields of interest: Arts; Scholarships/financial aid; Education; Environment; Health care; Children, services; Human services; Community/economic development; United Ways and Federated Giving Programs; Public affairs.
Program:
Matching Program: The company provides a cash donation to qualified charitable organizations for which an employee volunteers at least 24 hours during a calendar year. The company will also match employee donations to educational institutions and the United Way during its campaigns.
Type of support: Annual campaigns; Cause-related marketing; Employee matching gifts; General/operating support; In-kind gifts; Scholarships—to individuals.
Geographic limitations: Giving primarily in areas of company operations in IL, IN, KY, LA, MI, OH, TX, and WV. Giving also to national organizations.
Publications: Corporate giving report.
Application information: Applications accepted. The company has Local Charitable Giving Committees at each of its major locations.
Initial approach: E-mail nearest location

2366
Marathon Savings Bank
500 Scott St.
P.O. Box 1666
Wausau, WI 54403-4866 (715) 845-7331

Company URL: http://www.marathonsavingsbank.com/
Establishment information: Established in 1902.
Company type: Private company
Business activities: Operates savings bank.
Business type (SIC): Savings institutions
Corporate officer: Robert Brooks, Pres.
Board of director: Douglas Gjertson
Giving statement: Giving through the Marathon Savings Foundation, Inc.

Marathon Savings Foundation, Inc.
P.O. Box 1666
Wausau, WI 54402-1666 (715) 845-7331

Establishment information: Established in 1994 in WI.
Donor: Marathon Savings Bank.
Contact: Tom Terwilliger, Pres.
Financial data (yr. ended 06/30/12): Assets, $90,787 (M); gifts received, $30,000; expenditures, $27,382; qualifying distributions, $27,350; giving activities include $27,350 for grants.

Purpose and activities: The foundation supports community foundations and organizations involved with performing arts, animal welfare, abuse prevention, housing development, and human services.
Fields of interest: Arts; Youth development; Human services.
Type of support: General/operating support; Scholarship funds.
Geographic limitations: Giving primarily in areas of company operations in Wausau, WI.
Support limitations: No grants to individuals.
Application information: Applications accepted. Application form required. Applicants should submit the following:
1) copy of IRS Determination Letter
2) detailed description of project and amount of funding requested
Initial approach: Letter
Deadline(s): None
Officers: Tom Terwilliger, Pres.; Paul Shore, V.P.; Wanda Lyon, Secy.-Treas.
EIN: 391803453

2367
Tony March Buick, Inc.

77-149 Liebert Rd.
Hartford, CT 06120-1618 (860) 249-1301

Establishment information: Established in 1985.
Company type: Private company
Business activities: Operates car dealership.
Business type (SIC): Motor vehicles—retail
Corporate officer: Antony March, Pres.
Giving statement: Giving through the Tony March Foundation, Inc.

Tony March Foundation, Inc.

15438 N. Florida Ave.
Tampa, FL 33613 (813) 960-4717

Establishment information: Established in 1999 in CT.
Donor: Tony March Buick, Inc.
Contact: Anthony March, Pres.
Financial data (yr. ended 12/31/11): Assets, $73,691 (M); expenditures, $51; qualifying distributions, $0.
Purpose and activities: The foundation supports the Connecticut Center for Science and Exploration in Hartford, Connecticut.
Type of support: General/operating support.
Geographic limitations: Giving primarily in areas of company operations in Hartford, CT.
Support limitations: No grants to individuals.
Application information: Applications accepted. Application form required. Applicants should submit the following:
1) statement of problem project will address
2) detailed description of project and amount of funding requested
Initial approach: Proposal
Deadline(s): None
Officers: Anthony March, Pres.; Gail March, Treas.
EIN: 061443058

2368
Marcho Farms, Inc.

176 Orchard Ln.
Harleysville, PA 19438-1664
(215) 721-7131

Establishment information: Established in 1968.
Company type: Private company
Business activities: Operates meat packing plant.
Business type (SIC): Meat packing plants and prepared meats and poultry
Corporate officers: Wayne Marcho, Pres. and Treas.; Bryan Friesman, Cont.
Giving statement: Giving through the Marcho Family Foundation Inc.

Marcho Family Foundation Inc.

176 Orchard Ln.
Harleysville, PA 19438-1664 (215) 721-7131

Establishment information: Established in 2006 in PA.
Donors: Marcho Farms, Inc.; W. and M. Marco Family Limited Partnership.
Contact: Rachelle Bergey, Pres.
Financial data (yr. ended 12/31/11): Assets, $65,761 (M); expenditures, $97,527; qualifying distributions, $97,427; giving activities include $96,710 for 4 grants (high: $72,710; low: $5,000).
Fields of interest: Education.
Geographic limitations: Giving primarily in PA.
Application information: Applications accepted. Application form required. Applicants should submit the following:
1) detailed description of project and amount of funding requested
Initial approach: Letter
Deadline(s): None
Officers: Wayne A. Marcho, Chair.; Rachelle Bergey, Pres.; Julie Yoder, Secy.-Treas.
EIN: 205073454

2369
Marchon Eyewear, Inc.

35 Hub Dr.
Melville, NY 11747 (631) 755-2020
FAX: (631) 755-2045

Company URL: http://www.marchon.com
Establishment information: Established in 1983.
Company type: Subsidiary of a private company
Business activities: Manufactures and distributes eyewear and sunwear.
Business type (SIC): Ophthalmic goods
Financial profile for 2009: Number of employees, 1,055
Corporate officers: Al Berg, Pres. and C.E.O.; Marty Fox, C.O.O.; Len LaSalandra, Sr. V.P., Finance and C.F.O.
Giving statement: Giving through the Christopher Zider Scholarship Fund.

The Christopher Zider Scholarship Fund

1900 Embarcadero Rd., Ste. 100
Palo Alto, CA 94303-3310 (650) 233-8700
FAX: (650) 322-3546;
E-mail: info@chrisziderscholarship.org; URL: http://chrisziderscholarship.org/

Establishment information: Established in 1993 in CA.
Donors: Marchon Eyewear, Inc.; Robert Zider; Cheryl F. Zider.
Financial data (yr. ended 12/31/11): Assets, $195,794 (M); gifts received, $10,000; expenditures, $55,815; qualifying distributions, $44,604; giving activities include $44,604 for grants to individuals.
Purpose and activities: The foundation awards college scholarships to two high school sophomores residing in Atherton, East Palo Alto, Menlo Park, Palo Alto, Portola Valley, Stanford, and Woodside, California and/or attending Menlo School or Woodside High School.
Fields of interest: Higher education.
Type of support: Scholarships—to individuals.
Geographic limitations: Giving primarily in Atherton, East Palo Alto, Menlo Park, Palo Alto, Portola Valley, and Woodside, CA.
Publications: Application guidelines.
Application information: Applications accepted. Application form required.
Initial approach: Download application form and mail to foundation
Deadline(s): Mar. 26 for preliminary application and May 14 for the full application
Officer and Directors:* Robert Newell IV*, C.F.O.; Sandy Bondan; Gary Petersmeyer; Jeff Wiley; Cheryl F. Zider.
EIN: 946655102

2370
The Marcus & Millichap Company

2626 Hanover St.
Palo Alto, CA 94304-1102 (650) 391-1700

Company URL: http://www.marcusmillichap.com/
Establishment information: Established in 1971.
Company type: Private company
Business activities: Provides real estate brokerage services; develops real estate.
Business type (SIC): Real estate agents and managers; real estate subdividers and developers
Corporate officers: George M. Marcus, Co-Chair.; William A. Millichap, Co-Chair.; John J. Kerin, Pres. and C.E.O.; Richard H. Peltz, Sr. V.P. and C.I.O.
Board of directors: George M. Marcus, Co-Chair.; William A. Millichap, Co-Chair.
Giving statement: Giving through the Marcus & Millichap Company Foundation.

The Marcus & Millichap Company Foundation

777 California Ave.
Palo Alto, CA 94304-1102

Establishment information: Established in 1998 in CA.
Donor: The Marcus & Millichap Co.
Financial data (yr. ended 12/31/11): Assets, $6,337,975 (M); expenditures, $102,715; qualifying distributions, $91,000; giving activities include $91,000 for 19 grants (high: $15,000; low: $1,000).
Purpose and activities: The foundation supports food banks and organizations involved with ballet, higher and business education, land conservation, heart disease, human services, community development, and Judaism.
Fields of interest: Performing arts, ballet; Higher education; Business school/education; Environment, land resources; Heart & circulatory diseases; Food banks; YM/YWCAs & YM/YWHAs; Children/youth, services; Human services;

Community/economic development; Jewish federated giving programs; Jewish agencies & synagogues.
Type of support: General/operating support; Program development; Sponsorships.
Geographic limitations: Giving primarily in CA.
Support limitations: No grants to individuals.
Application information: Applications not accepted. Unsolicited requests for funds not accepted.
Officers and Directors: George M. Marcus*, C.E.O. and Pres.; Marianne Empedocles*, Secy.; Alex Yarmolinsky, Treas.; Robert H. Kennis.
EIN: 770480868
Selected grants: The following grants are a representative sample of this grantmaker's funding activity:
$13,500 to City of Hope, Los Angeles, CA, 2010.
$6,000 to Housing Industry Foundation, Milpitas, CA, 2010. For annual pledge.
$5,000 to Aim High for High School, San Francisco, CA, 2010.
$5,000 to Community Gatepath, Burlingame, CA, 2010.
$5,000 to Jewish Federation of Greater Philadelphia, Philadelphia, PA, 2010.
$2,500 to American Heart Association, San Francisco, CA, 2010.
$2,500 to Lambs Farm, Libertyville, IL, 2010.
$2,500 to Second Harvest Food Bank, San Carlos, CA, 2010.

2371
The Marcus Corporation

100 E. Wisconsin Ave., Ste. 1900
Milwaukee, WI 53202-4125
(414) 905-1000
FAX: (414) 905-2879

Company URL: http://www.marcuscorp.com/
Establishment information: Established in 1935.
Company type: Public company
Company ticker symbol and exchange: MCS/NYSE
Business activities: Operates restaurants, hotels and motels, and motion picture theaters.
Business type (SIC): Restaurants and drinking places; hotels and motels; motion picture theaters
Financial profile for 2012: Number of employees, 6,200; assets, $733,010,000; sales volume, $413,900,000; pre-tax net income, $37,440,000; expenses, $367,380,000; liabilities, $389,220,000
Corporate officers: Stephen H. Marcus, Chair.; Gregory S. Marcus, Pres. and C.E.O.; Thomas F. Kissinger, V.P., Genl. Counsel, and Secy.; Douglas A. Neis, Treas. and C.F.O.
Board of directors: Stephen H. Marcus, Chair.; James D. Ericson; Diane Marcus Gershowitz; Bronson J. Haase; Timothy E. Hoeksema; Gregory S. Marcus; Daniel F. McKeithan, Jr.; Philip L. Milstein; Bruce J. Olson; Allan H. Selig; Brian Jay Stark
Subsidiaries: Marcus Hotel Corp., Milwaukee, WI; Marcus Restaurants, Milwaukee, WI; Marcus Theatres Corp., Milwaukee, WI
Giving statement: Giving through the Marcus Corporation Contributions Program and the Marcus Corporation Foundation, Inc.
Company EIN: 391139844

Marcus Corporation Foundation, Inc.

100 E. Wisconsin Ave., Ste. 1900
Milwaukee, WI 53202-4125

Establishment information: Established in 1961 in WI.
Donor: The Marcus Corp.
Contact: Stephen H. Marcus, Pres. and Treas.
Financial data (yr. ended 12/31/11): Assets, $2,696,719 (M); gifts received, $226,775; expenditures, $877,033; qualifying distributions, $829,038; giving activities include $829,038 for grants.
Purpose and activities: The foundation supports organizations involved with arts and culture, education, cancer, heart disease, human services, and community development.
Fields of interest: Visual arts, architecture; Performing arts centers; Performing arts, orchestras; Arts; Higher education; Business school/education; Medical school/education; Education; Cancer; Heart & circulatory diseases; Boys & girls clubs; Youth development, business; Children/youth, services; Human services; Community/economic development; United Ways and Federated Giving Programs.
Type of support: General/operating support; Program development.
Geographic limitations: Giving limited to Milwaukee, WI.
Support limitations: No grants to individuals.
Application information: Applications accepted. Application form not required. Applicants should submit the following:
1) name, address and phone number of organization
2) detailed description of project and amount of funding requested
3) copy of IRS Determination Letter
Initial approach: Proposal
Board meeting date(s): Dec.
Deadline(s): None
Officers and Directors:* Stephen H. Marcus*, Pres. and Treas.; Thomas F. Kissinger*, Secy.; Gregory S. Marcus.
EIN: 396046268
Selected grants: The following grants are a representative sample of this grantmaker's funding activity:
$100,500 to United Way of Greater Milwaukee, Milwaukee, WI, 2011.
$75,000 to Milwaukee Symphony Orchestra, Milwaukee, WI, 2011.
$15,000 to Milwaukee Center for Independence, Milwaukee, WI, 2011.
$12,500 to Congress for the New Urbanism, Chicago, IL, 2011.
$10,000 to Milwaukee Art Museum, Milwaukee, WI, 2011.
$5,000 to Milwaukee Film, Milwaukee, WI, 2011.
$4,500 to Local Initiatives Support Corporation, New York, NY, 2011.
$4,375 to Boy Scouts of America, Milwaukee, WI, 2011.
$3,750 to American Heart Association, Dallas, TX, 2011.
$2,000 to Milwaukee Public Schools Foundation, Milwaukee, WI, 2011.

2372
Marena Group, Inc.

650 Progress Industrial Blvd.
Lawrenceville, GA 30043-4866
(770) 822-6925

Company URL: http://www.marenagroup.com
Establishment information: Established in 1994.
Company type: Private company
Business activities: Manufactures surgical garments.
Business type (SIC): Medical instruments and supplies
Corporate officers: Vera Watkins, Pres. and C.E.O.; James P. McCluskey, Co-C.F.O.; Angela Smith, Co-C.F.O.
Giving statement: Giving through the Marena Foundation, Inc.

The Marena Foundation, Inc.

650 Progress Industrial Blvd.
Lawrenceville, GA 30043-4800 (888) 462-7362
URL: http://marenagroup.com/About/Thefoundation/tabid/123/Default.aspx

Establishment information: Established in 1998 in GA.
Donor: Marena Group, Inc.
Financial data (yr. ended 12/31/11): Assets, $5,721 (M); gifts received, $160,244; expenditures, $167,861; qualifying distributions, $166,328; giving activities include $52,663 for 7 grants (high: $14,739; low: $1,000) and $113,665 for 41 grants to individuals (high: $28,395; low: $300).
Purpose and activities: The foundation supports organizations involved with education, recreation, single moms, and Christianity and awards grants to disadvantaged individuals.
Fields of interest: Education; Athletics/sports, school programs; Athletics/sports, amateur leagues; Recreation; Family services, single parents; Christian agencies & churches Economically disadvantaged.
Type of support: Employee volunteer services; General/operating support; Grants to individuals.
Geographic limitations: Giving limited to GA and NY.
Application information: Applications not accepted. Contributes only to pre-selected organizations and individuals.
Officers and Directors:* Vera Watkins*, Pres.; William Watkins*, Secy.
EIN: 582379368
Selected grants: The following grants are a representative sample of this grantmaker's funding activity:
$5,000 to West Point Fund, West Point, NY, 2009.

2373
Mariah Media Inc.

400 Market St.
Santa Fe, NM 87501-7300 (505) 989-7100
FAX: (505) 989-4700

Company URL: http://www.outsideonline.com
Establishment information: Established in 1977.
Company type: Private company
Business activities: Publishes magazine; provides Internet information services.
Business type (SIC): Periodical publishing and/or printing
Financial profile for 2010: Number of employees, 90
Corporate officer: Lawrence J. Burke II, Chair. and Pres.
Board of director: Lawrence J. Burke II, Chair.
Giving statement: Giving through the Mariah Foundation.

Mariah Foundation

(formerly Outside Evergreen Foundation)
400 Market St.
Santa Fe, NM 87501

Establishment information: Established in 1997 in NM.
Donor: Mariah Media Inc.

Financial data (yr. ended 06/30/12): Assets, $100 (M); expenditures, $0; qualifying distributions, $0.
Support limitations: No grants to individuals.
Application information: Applications not accepted. Unsolicited requests for funds not accepted.
Officers and Directors:* Lawrence J. Burke*, Pres.; Angelo Gaziano*, Secy.-Treas.; Christine Burke.
EIN: 850449264

2374
Mariani Nut Company, Inc.
709 Dutton St.
P.O. Box 809
Winters, CA 95694-1748 (530) 662-3311

Company URL: http://www.marianinut.com
Establishment information: Established in 1972.
Company type: Private company
Business activities: Produces walnuts and almonds; sells walnuts and almonds wholesale.
Business type (SIC): Farms/fruit and nut; farm-product raw materials—wholesale
Corporate officers: Jack N. Mariani, Pres.; Dennis Mariani, Founder
Giving statement: Giving through the Mariani Nut Company Foundation, Inc.

Mariani Nut Company Foundation, Inc.
709 Dutton St.
P.O. Box 808
Winters, CA 95694-1748

Establishment information: Established as a company-sponsored operating foundation in 1986 in CA.
Donor: Mariani Nut Co., Inc.
Contact: Martin Mariani, Dir.
Financial data (yr. ended 08/31/11): Assets, $1,259,222 (M); expenditures, $89,480; qualifying distributions, $76,337; giving activities include $76,337 for 45 grants (high: $41,000; low: $90).
Purpose and activities: The foundation supports organizations involved with education, health, cancer, food and agriculture, sports, youth, and financial services and awards scholarships to residents of Winter, CA.
Fields of interest: Secondary school/education; Higher education; Education; Hospitals (general); Health care; Cancer; Agriculture/food; Athletics/sports, amateur leagues; Athletics/sports, baseball; Athletics/sports, golf; Youth, services; Financial services.
Type of support: General/operating support; Scholarship funds; Scholarships—to individuals.
Geographic limitations: Giving primarily in CA.
Application information: Applications accepted. Application form not required.
Initial approach: Proposal
Deadline(s): None
Directors: Jack Dennis Mariani; Martin Mariani; John C. Wallace.
EIN: 680143635

2375
Marinello Schools of Beauty
(doing business as B&H Education, Inc.)
12449 Putnam St.
Whittier, CA 90602-1023 (800) 648-3413

Company URL: http://www.marinello.com
Establishment information: Established in 1905.
Company type: Subsidiary of a private company
Business activities: Operates beauty schools.
Business type (SIC): Vocational schools
Corporate officers: Nagui Elyas, Pres. and C.O.O.; Buzz Wolf, V.P., Human Resources
Giving statement: Giving through the Marinello Schools of Beauty Corporate Giving Program.

Marinello Schools of Beauty Corporate Giving Program
12449 Putnam St.
Whittier, CA 90602-1023 (800) 648-3413
E-mail: info@marinello.com; URL: http://www.marinello.com/def/scholarship/Marinello-HS-ScholarShip.aspx

2376
Maritz Holdings, Inc.
1375 N. Highway Dr.
Fenton, MO 63099 (636) 827-4000

Company URL: http://www.maritz.com
Establishment information: Established in 1894.
Company type: Private company
Business activities: Provides performance improvement, incentive travel, and consumer market research services.
Business type (SIC): Management and public relations services; travel and tour arrangers; research, development, and testing services
Corporate officers: W. Stephen Maritz, Chair. and C.E.O.; Dennis Hummel, Pres. and C.O.O.; Rick Ramos, C.F.O.; Gilbert Hoffman, C.I.O.
Board of directors: W. Stephen Maritz, Chair.; Jim Messina
Subsidiaries: American Express Incentive Services, LLC, Fenton, MO; Maritz Marketing Research, Inc., Fenton, MO; Maritz Performance Improvement Co., Fenton, MO; Maritz Travel Co., Fenton, MO
International operations: Canada; France; Germany; Spain; United Kingdom
Giving statement: Giving through the Maritz Holdings, Inc. Contributions Program.

Maritz Holdings, Inc. Contributions Program
1375 N. Highway Dr.
Fenton, MO 63099-1929 (636) 827-4000
E-mail: debbie.schirmer@maritz.com; Debbie Schirmer, Community Affairs Mgr.: tel.: (636) 827-1573; e-mail: debbie.schirmer@maritz.com; URL: http://www.maritz.com/About-Maritz/Company-Overview/Corporate-Responsibility.aspx

Contact: Debbie Schirmer, Community Affairs Mgr.
Purpose and activities: Maritz makes charitable contributions to nonprofit organizations involved with education, the environment, children and youth, disability services, recreation, and health. Support is given primarily in areas of company operations in the greater St. Louis, Missouri area. Giving also on a national basis.
Fields of interest: Elementary/secondary education; Education; Environment; Health care, fund raising/fund distribution; Health care; Breast cancer; Heart & circulatory diseases; ALS; Disasters, preparedness/services; Recreation, fairs/festivals; Children/youth, services; Self-advocacy services, disability; United Ways and Federated Giving Programs; Military/veterans' organizations.
Type of support: Annual campaigns; Cause-related marketing; Employee volunteer services; General/operating support; In-kind gifts.
Geographic limitations: Giving primarily in areas of company operations in the greater St. Louis, MO area. Giving also on a national basis.
Support limitations: No support for political, labor, or fraternal organizations, or religious organizations (i.e., churches or organizations directly tied to a place of worship). No grants to individuals or families, or for fundraising events such as golf, luncheons, dinners, or galas, capital campaigns, or multi-year pledges; sponsorship of local groups or individuals to participate in regional, national, or international competitions, conferences or events; or for-profit publications or organizations seeking advertisements or promotional support.
Publications: Application guidelines.
Application information: Applications accepted. The Maritz Corporate Giving Council reviews all requests over $10,000. Funding is limited to organizations that are fiscally sound with strong management practices and accountability. Maritz prefers programs that provide direct service to people and communities in need rather than event sponsorships. Specific projects with measurable results are preferred over general operating support and capital campaigns. Multi-year pledge requests are not encouraged. Grantees are encouraged to re-apply for funding annually. Generally, only one monetary donation will be given in a fiscal year to any organization. Grant applications should demonstrate a strategic link with education. Application form required. Applicants should submit the following:
1) listing of additional sources and amount of support
2) copy of current year's organizational budget and/or project budget
3) contact person
4) plans for cooperation with other organizations, if any
5) detailed description of project and amount of funding requested
6) listing of board of directors, trustees, officers and other key people and their affiliations
7) copy of most recent annual report/audited financial statement/990
8) geographic area to be served
9) brief history of organization and description of its mission
10) copy of IRS Determination Letter
11) name, address and phone number of organization
12) population served
13) statement of problem project will address
14) results expected from proposed grant
15) how project will be sustained once grantmaker support is completed
16) role played by volunteers

Proposals should be limited to 5 single-spaced pages and contain: an outline of current programs and activities, organizational accomplishments, staff and volunteer qualifications, and letters of agreement from the collaborating agencies, if applicable. Binders, videos, and books are not accepted.
Initial approach: Complete online application and submit proposal via email
Copies of proposal: 1
Deadline(s): Mar. 15 for requests of $30,000 or more; June 15 for requests of $20,001 - $29,999; Sept, 15 for requests of $10,000 - $20,000
Final notification: End of April for requests of $30,000 or more; end of July for requests of $20,001 - $29,999; end of Oct. for requests of $10,000 - $20,000

2377
Mark IV Industries, Inc.
(formerly Mark IV Homes, Inc.)
501 John James Audubon Pkwy.
P.O. Box 810
Amherst, NY 14226-0810 (716) 689-4972
FAX: (716) 689-6098

Company URL: http://www.mark-iv.com
Establishment information: Established in 1969.
Company type: Private company
Business activities: Manufactures mechanical and fluid power transmission, fluid transfer, and power systems and components.
Business type (SIC): Industrial and commercial machinery and computer equipment
Financial profile for 2011: Number of employees, 3,200; sales volume, $928,000,000
Corporate officers: James C. Orchard, Co-C.E.O.; Mark G. Barberio, Co-C.E.O.; Jim Currie, C.F.O.; Paul Manuel, V.P., Sales and Mktg.; Rick Gegenheimer, V.P., Opers.
Subsidiaries: Dayco Products, LLC, Tulsa, OK; Luminator Holding, LP, Plano, TX; Mark IV Automotive, LLC, Rochester Hills, MI; NRD LLC, Grand Island, NY
International operations: Australia; Belgium; Canada; Denmark; France; Germany; Italy; Spain; Sweden
Giving statement: Giving through the Mark IV Industries Foundation, Inc.
Company EIN: 231733979

Mark IV Industries Foundation, Inc.
P.O. Box 810, Tax Dept.
Amherst, NY 14226-0810 (716) 689-4972

Establishment information: Established in 1976 in NY.
Donor: Mark IV Industries, Inc.
Financial data (yr. ended 04/30/12): Assets, $278,967 (M); expenditures, $62,621; qualifying distributions, $62,621; giving activities include $62,603 for 16 grants (high: $25,000; low: $100).
Purpose and activities: The foundation supports hospitals and festivals and organizations involved with education, cancer, human services, and Catholicism.
Fields of interest: Environment; Health care; Religion.
Type of support: General/operating support.
Geographic limitations: Giving primarily in Buffalo, NY.
Application information: Applications accepted. Application form required. Applicants should submit the following:
1) copy of most recent annual report/audited financial statement/990
2) detailed description of project and amount of funding requested
Initial approach: Letter
Copies of proposal: 1
Board meeting date(s): Apr.
Deadline(s): None
Final notification: Varies
Officers: Mark G. Barberio, Co-C.E.O. and C.F.O.; Edward R. Steele, V.P. and Secy.-Treas.
EIN: 161082605

2378
Market Day Corporation
555 W. Pierce Rd., Ste. 200
Itasca, IL 60143-3155 (630) 285-1470
FAX: (630) 285-3340

Company URL: http://www.marketday.com
Establishment information: Established in 1978.
Company type: Private company
Business activities: Provides fundraising services.
Business type (SIC): Business services/miscellaneous
Corporate officers: Jeffrey E. Boies, Chair. and C.E.O.; Michael D. Wiedower, Pres. and C.O.O.
Board of director: Jeffrey E. Boies, Chair.
Giving statement: Giving through the William F. Temple Memorial Foundation.

William F. Temple Memorial Foundation
555 W. Pierce Rd., Ste. 200
Itasca, IL 60143-2647

Establishment information: Established in 1998 in IL.
Donor: Market Day Corpoaration.
Financial data (yr. ended 12/31/11): Assets, $50 (M); gifts received, $22,050; expenditures, $22,500; qualifying distributions, $22,500; giving activities include $22,500 for grants.
Purpose and activities: The foundation awards college scholarship to children of employees of Market Day Corp.
Type of support: Employee-related scholarships.
Geographic limitations: Giving limited to areas of company operations.
Application information: Applications not accepted. Unsolicited requests for funds not accepted.
Officers and Directors:* Kristine Holtz*, Pres.; William S. Sivak, Jr., Secy.-Treas.; Mary Beth Larson.
EIN: 364222360

2379
MarkleBank
180 E. Morse St.
P.O. Box 595
Markle, IN 46770-5441 (260) 758-3111

Company URL: http://www.marklebank.com
Establishment information: Established in 1947.
Company type: Subsidiary of a public company
Business activities: Operates commercial bank.
Business type (SIC): Banks/commercial
Corporate officers: Greg Myers, Chair.; Bobby Caley, Vice-Chair.; Gregory Smitley, Pres. and C.E.O.; Ann McPherren, Secy.
Board of directors: Greg Myers, Chair.; Bobby Caley, Vice-Chair.; Jeffery K. Espich; Rudy Frauhiger; Don Hoopingarner; Douglas LeMaster, Jr.; Michael C. Marhenke; Ann McPherren; Greg Smitley
Giving statement: Giving through the Markle Financial Charitable Foundation, Inc. and the MarkleBank Foundation, Inc.

Markle Financial Charitable Foundation, Inc.
314 Eagle Ct.
Ossian, IN 46777 (260) 402-7866

Establishment information: Established in 2003 in IN.
Donors: Jolloff Investments, Inc.; Timothy C. Jolloff; Independent Alliance Finacial Group, Inc.
Contact: Timothy Jolloff Markle, Pres.
Financial data (yr. ended 12/31/10): Assets, $114 (M); expenditures, $29; qualifying distributions, $29.
Purpose and activities: The foundation supports organizations involved with health, human services, and Christianity.
Fields of interest: Health care; Children/youth, services; Human services; United Ways and Federated Giving Programs; Christian agencies & churches.
Type of support: Annual campaigns; General/operating support; Grants to individuals.
Application information: Applications accepted. Application form required. Applicants should submit the following:
1) detailed description of project and amount of funding requested
2) copy of current year's organizational budget and/or project budget
Initial approach: Proposal
Deadline(s): None
Officers: Timothy Jolloff Markle, Pres.; Beverly Jolloff Markle, Secy.
EIN: 300172974

2380
Marlborough Country Club
200 Concord Rd.
Marlborough, MA 01752-5631
(508) 485-1660

Company URL: http://www.marlboroughcountryclub.com
Establishment information: Established in 1922.
Company type: Private company
Business activities: Operates country club.
Business type (SIC): Amusement and recreation services/miscellaneous
Corporate officers: Ralph Guertin, Pres.; Joseph Grimaldo, Treas.
Giving statement: Giving through the Marlborough Foundation, Inc.

The Marlborough Foundation, Inc.
c/o Robert Erconlani
170 Spoonhill Ave.
Marlborough, MA 01752-2537

Establishment information: Established in 1991 in MA.
Donor: Marlborough Country Club.
Financial data (yr. ended 12/31/11): Assets, $160,610 (M); gifts received, $11,500; expenditures, $13,500; qualifying distributions, $7,085; giving activities include $7,085 for grants.
Purpose and activities: The foundation supports food pantries and organizations involved with senior citizens.
Fields of interest: Education; Agriculture/food; Housing/shelter.
Type of support: Employee-related scholarships; General/operating support.
Geographic limitations: Giving limited to Hudson and Marlborough, MA.
Application information: Applications not accepted. Unsolicited requests for funds not accepted.
Officers and Directors:* Robert M. Ercolani*, Pres.; Enio Cipriano*, V.P.; Theresa Ercolani*, Clerk; Joseph Grimaldo*, Treas.; Robert Carver; Nicholas Dibuono, Jr.; Thomas Kamataris; Michael H. Ossing.
EIN: 223006211

2381
Marnier-Lapostolle Inc.

717 5th Ave., 22nd Fl.
New York, NY 10022-8106 (212) 207-4350

Company URL: http://www.grand-marnier.com
Establishment information: Established in 1880.
Company type: Subsidiary of a foreign company
Business activities: Operates wine and spirits company.
Business type (SIC): Beer, wine, and distilled beverages—wholesale
Corporate officer: R. Scott Green, Sr. V.P., Mktg. and Sales
Giving statement: Giving through the Grand Marnier Foundation.

The Grand Marnier Foundation

c/o Marnier-Lapostolle, Inc.
717 Fifth Ave., 22nd Fl.
New York, NY 10022-4328 (212) 207-4350

Establishment information: Established in 1985 in NY.
Donor: Carillon Importers, Ltd.
Contact: Elise Aubespin-Seignolle
Financial data (yr. ended 12/31/11): Assets, $4,900,973 (M); expenditures, $339,025; qualifying distributions, $250,000; giving activities include $250,000 for grants.
Purpose and activities: The foundation supports organizations involved with arts and culture, French culture, and education and awards fellowships to students at select schools to study French civilization and culture.
Fields of interest: Arts, cultural/ethnic awareness; Media, film/video; Museums; Performing arts, dance; Performing arts, music; Arts; Elementary/secondary education; Higher education; Education.
Type of support: Building/renovation; Fellowships; General/operating support; Program development; Scholarship funds; Sponsorships.
Geographic limitations: Giving primarily in New York, NY.
Application information: Applications accepted. Application form not required. Applicants should submit the following:
1) copy of IRS Determination Letter
2) detailed description of project and amount of funding requested
3) listing of additional sources and amount of support

Initial approach: Proposal
Deadline(s): None

Officers and Directors: Scott Green*, Pres.; ` Hattie K. Jutagir*, Secy.; Francois Letaconnoux*, Treas.; Francois De Gasperis.
EIN: 133258414
Selected grants: The following grants are a representative sample of this grantmaker's funding activity:
$25,000 to Episcopal Diocese of Connecticut, Hartford, CT, 2011.
$25,000 to Keep Memory Alive, Las Vegas, NV, 2011.
$25,000 to Lincoln Center for the Performing Arts, New York, NY, 2011.
$25,000 to Pierpont Morgan Library, New York, NY, 2011.
$20,000 to Frick Collection, New York, NY, 2011.
$15,000 to Chamber Music Society of Lincoln Center, New York, NY, 2011.
$15,000 to Columbia University, New York, NY, 2011.
$15,000 to Film Society of Lincoln Center, New York, NY, 2011.
$15,000 to French American Cultural Exchange, New York, NY, 2011.
$15,000 to New York City Center, New York, NY, 2011.

2382
Marr Equipment Corporation

1 D St.
Boston, MA 02127-2401 (617) 269-7200

Company URL: http://www.marrcompanies.com
Establishment information: Established in 1942.
Company type: Private company
Business activities: Operates heavy construction equipment rental company.
Business type (SIC): Equipment rental and leasing/miscellaneous
Corporate officers: Robert L. Marr, Chair. and C.E.O.; Paul S. Tilley, V.P. and Cont.
Board of director: Robert L. Marr, Chair.
Giving statement: Giving through the Marr Charitable Foundation.

Marr Charitable Foundation

25-27 D St.
South Boston, MA 02127-2466 (617) 269-7200

Establishment information: Established in 1984 in MA.
Donors: Marr Scaffolding Co.; Isaac Blair & Co., Inc.; Marr Equipment Corp.
Contact: Robert L. Marr, Tr.
Financial data (yr. ended 11/30/11): Assets, $639,926 (M); expenditures, $56,228; qualifying distributions, $55,575; giving activities include $55,575 for 29 grants (high: $20,000; low: $100).
Purpose and activities: The foundation supports medical centers and organizations involved with education, health, human services, and Catholicism.
Fields of interest: Health care; Health organizations; Human services.
Type of support: General/operating support; Program development; Scholarship funds.
Support limitations: No grants to individuals.
Application information: Applications accepted. Application form required. Applicants should submit the following:
1) brief history of organization and description of its mission
2) detailed description of project and amount of funding requested

Initial approach: Letter
Deadline(s): None

Trustees: Daniel F. Marr, III; Robert L. Marr.
EIN: 222699881

2383
Marriott International, Inc.

(formerly New Marriott MI, Inc.)
10400 Fernwood Rd.
Bethesda, MD 20817 (301) 380-3000
FAX: (301) 380-3967

Company URL: http://www.marriott.com
Establishment information: Established in 1927.
Company type: Public company
Company ticker symbol and exchange: MAR/NYSE
International Securities Identification Number: US5719032022
Business activities: Operates and franchises hotels and related lodging facilities; operates senior living communities.
Business type (SIC): Hotels and motels; residential care
Financial profile for 2012: Number of employees, 127,000; assets, $6,342,000,000; sales volume, $11,814,000,000; pre-tax net income, $849,000,000; expenses, $10,874,000,000; liabilities, $7,627,000,000
Fortune 1000 ranking: 2012—230th in revenues, 303rd in profits, and 525th in assets
Forbes 2000 ranking: 2012—817th in sales, 912th in profits, and 1733rd in assets
Corporate officers: John W. Marriott, Jr., Chair.; John W. Marriott III, Vice-Chair.; Arne M. Sorenson, Pres. and C.E.O.; Robert J. McCarthy, C.O.O.; Carl T. Berquist, Exec. V.P. and C.F.O.; Carolyn B. Handlon, Exec. V.P., Finance, and Treas.; Edward A. Ryan, Exec. V.P. and Genl. Counsel; Kathleen Matthews, Exec. V.P., Comms., and Public Affairs; Kevin M. Kimball, Exec. V.P., Finance; Bancroft S. Gordon, V.P. and Corp. Secy.
Board of directors: John W. Marriott, Jr., Chair.; John W. Marriott III, Vice-Chair.; Mary K. Bush; Frederick A. Henderson; Lawrence W. Kellner; Debra L. Lee; George Munoz; Harry J. Pearce; Steven S. Reinemund; W. Mitt Romney; Lawrence M. Small; Arne M. Sorenson
Subsidiaries: Marriott Distribution Services, Inc., Washington, DC; Marriott Ownership Resorts, Inc., Washington, DC; Marriott Senior Living Services, Inc., Washington, DC; Residence Inn by Marriott, Inc., Washington, DC; The Ritz-Carlton Hotel Co., LLC, Atlanta, GA
International operations: Anguilla; Antigua & Barbuda; Argentina; Armenia; Aruba; Australia; Austria; Bahamas; Bahrain; Belgium; Bermuda; Brazil; Canada; Cayman Islands; Chile; China; Czech Republic; Denmark; Dominican Republic; Ecuador; Egypt; El Salvador; France; Germany; Greece; Guatemala; Honduras; Hong Kong; India; Indonesia; Ireland; Israel; Italy; Jamaica; Japan; Jordan; Kazakhstan; Kuwait; Lebanon; Liberia; Luxembourg; Macau; Malaysia; Malta; Mexico; Netherlands; Netherlands Antilles; New Zealand; Panama; Peru; Philippines; Poland; Portugal; Romania; Russia; Saint Kitts-Nevis; Singapore; South Korea; Spain; Switzerland; Thailand; Trinidad & Tobago; Tunisia; Turkey; Turks & Caicos Islands; United Arab Emirates; United Kingdom; Venezuela
Giving statement: Giving through the Marriott International, Inc. Corporate Giving Program.
Company EIN: 522055918

Marriott International, Inc. Corporate Giving Program

c/o Social Responsibility and Community Engagement
10400 Fernwood Rd.
Bethesda, MD 20817-1102 (301) 380-3000
E-mail: community.engagement@marriott.com;
URL: http://www.marriott.com/corporateinfo/social-responsibility/default.mi

Financial data (yr. ended 12/31/11): Total giving, $23,100,000, including $7,500,000 for grants and $15,600,000 for in-kind gifts.
Purpose and activities: Marriott makes charitable contributions to nonprofit organizations involved with: 1) Food and shelter; 2) Environmental stewardship; 3) Readiness for hotel careers; 4) Children - almost exclusively through a partnership with Children's Miracle Network, and 5) Organizations that embrace diversity and disabilities.
Fields of interest: Environment; Employment, training; Agriculture/food; Housing/shelter; Civil/

human rights, minorities; Civil/human rights, disabled Children.
Type of support: Donated products; General/operating support.
Geographic limitations: Giving primarily in areas of company operations, with emphasis on supporting global and national organizations.
Application information: Applications accepted. Only proposals submitted via e-mail will be accepted. Telephone calls are not encouraged. Application form not required. Applicants should submit the following:
1) brief history of organization and description of its mission
2) copy of most recent annual report/audited financial statement/990
3) detailed description of project and amount of funding requested
4) copy of current year's organizational budget and/or project budget
5) listing of additional sources and amount of support

Initial approach: E-mail proposal to headquarters for general operating support; e-mail proposal to nearest company hotel for lodging and food and beverage donations
Copies of proposal: 1
Deadline(s): 6 weeks prior to need
Final notification: 1 month

2384
Mars, Incorporated

6885 Elm St.
McLean, VA 22101 (703) 821-4900

Company URL: http://www.mars.com
Establishment information: Established in 1911.
Company type: Private company
Business activities: Produces food and pet care products; vends beverages; manufactures electronic automated payment systems.
Business type (SIC): Food and kindred products; grain mill products, including pet food; machinery/refrigeration and service industry; nonstore retailers
Financial profile for 2011: Number of employees, 65,000; sales volume, $30,000,000,000
Corporate officers: Paul S. Michaels, Pres.; Reuben Gamoran, V.P. and C.F.O.; Alberto Mora, V.P., Secy., and Genl. Counsel
Board of directors: Reuben Gamoran; David Kamenetzky; Frank Mars; Paul S. Michaels; Alberto Mora; Martin Radvan; Grant Reid; Aileen Richards; Richard Ware; Poul Weihrauch
Subsidiaries: Ethel M. Chocolates, Inc., Las Vegas, NV; Wm. Wrigley Jr. Company, Chicago, IL
Division: Mars Chocolates Div., Hackettstown, NJ
International operations: Belgium; Canada; Finland; France; Germany; Ireland; Sweden; United Kingdom
Giving statement: Giving through the Mars, Incorporated, Contributions Program and the Mars Foundation.

Mars, Incorporated, Contributions Program

(formerly M & M/MARS Inc. Corporate Giving Program)
6885 Elm St.
McLean, VA 22101-6031 (703) 821-4900
URL: http://www.mars.com/global/commitments/corporate-responsibility.aspx

Purpose and activities: Mars makes charitable contributions to nonprofit organizations involved with the environment, animal welfare, and hunger relief. Support is given on a national and international basis in areas of company operations.
Fields of interest: Environment; Animal welfare; Food services.
Type of support: Donated products; Employee volunteer services; General/operating support; In-kind gifts.
Geographic limitations: Giving on a national and international basis in areas of company operations.

The Mars Foundation

6885 Elm St.
McLean, VA 22101-3810 (703) 821-4900
FAX: (703) 448-9678

Establishment information: Incorporated in 1956 in IL.
Donor: Mars, Inc.
Contact: Susan Martin, Asst. Secy.
Financial data (yr. ended 12/31/11): Assets, $12,407,343 (M); gifts received, $1,000,000; expenditures, $629,038; qualifying distributions, $557,000; giving activities include $557,000 for grants.
Purpose and activities: The foundation supports organizations involved with arts and culture, education, natural resources, animal welfare, health, and human services.
Fields of interest: Historic preservation/historical societies; Arts; Education; Environment, natural resources; Animals/wildlife, preservation/protection; Health care; Children/youth, services; Human services.
Type of support: Annual campaigns; Building/renovation; Continuing support; Endowments; Equipment; Matching/challenge support; Research.
Geographic limitations: Giving primarily in Washington, DC, MD, and VA.
Support limitations: No grants to individuals, or for scholarships, fundraising, or recognition dinners; no loans.
Publications: Application guidelines.
Application information: Applications accepted. Application form required.

Initial approach: Contact foundation for application form
Copies of proposal: 1
Board meeting date(s): Oct.
Deadline(s): Aug. 1
Final notification: Jan.

Officers: Jacqueline B. Mars, Pres.; Forrest E. Mars, Jr., V.P.; John F. Mars, V.P.; Otis O. Otih, Secy.-Treas.
EIN: 546037592

2385
Marsh & McLennan Companies, Inc.

1166 Ave. of the Americas
New York, NY 10036-2774 (212) 345-5000
FAX: (212) 345-4838

Company URL: http://www.mmc.com/
Establishment information: Established in 1871.
Company type: Public company
Company ticker symbol and exchange: MMC/NYSE
International Securities Identification Number: US5717481023
Business activities: Provides risk management consulting services; provides insurance and reinsurance brokerage services; provides human resource, management, and economic consulting services; provides investment advisory services.
Business type (SIC): Insurance agents, brokers, and services; security and commodity services; management and public relations services
Financial profile for 2012: Number of employees, 54,000; assets, $16,288,000,000; sales volume, $11,924,000,000; pre-tax net income, $1,696,000,000; expenses, $10,095,000,000; liabilities, $9,746,000,000
Fortune 1000 ranking: 2012—228th in revenues, 172nd in profits, and 280th in assets
Forbes 2000 ranking: 2012—810th in sales, 498th in profits, and 1107th in assets
Corporate officers: Ian Lang, Chair.; David A. Nadler, Vice-Chair.; Brian Duperreault, Pres. and C.E.O.; Daniel S. Glaser, C.O.O.; Peter J. Beshar, Exec. V.P. and Genl. Counsel; Benjamin F. Allen, Sr. V.P. and C.I.O.; Laurie Ledford, Sr. V.P., Human Resources; J. Michael Bischoff, V.P., Corp. Finance and C.F.O.
Board of directors: Ian Lang, Chair.; David A. Nadler, Vice-Chair.; Zachary W. Carter; Brian Duperreault; Oscar Fanjul; H. Edward Hanway; Elaine La Roche; Steven A. Mills; Lang Monkton; Bruce P. Nolop; Marc D. Oken; Morton O. Schapiro; Adele Simmons; Lloyd M. Yates; R. David Yost
Subsidiaries: Guy Carpenter & Co., Inc., New York, NY; J&H Marsh & McLennan, Inc., New York, NY; Marsh & McLennan Group Associates, Inc., New York, NY; National Economic Research Associates (NERA), White Plains, NY; Stone Point Capital LLC, Greenwich, CT; William M. Mercer, Inc., New York, NY
International operations: Bermuda; Canada; Cayman Islands
Historic mergers: Johnson & Higgins (March 27, 1997)
Giving statement: Giving through the Marsh & McLennan Companies, Inc. Corporate Giving Program.
Company EIN: 362668272

Marsh & McLennan Companies, Inc. Corporate Giving Program

c/o Grant Requests
1166 Ave. of the Americas
New York, NY 10036-2774
E-mail: corporatecitizenship@mmc.com;
URL: http://www.mmc.com/CorporateSocialResponsibility/

Financial data (yr. ended 12/31/10): Total giving, $5,700,000, including $5,700,000 for 1,400 grants.
Purpose and activities: Marsh & McLennan makes charitable contributions to nonprofit organizations involved with education, the environment, and health. Special emphasis is directed toward programs that support people and communities at risk. Support is given primarily in areas of company operations.
Fields of interest: Education; Environment; Health care; Community/economic development Economically disadvantaged.
Type of support: Emergency funds; Employee matching gifts; Employee volunteer services; General/operating support; In-kind gifts; Pro bono services - legal; Scholarship funds.
Geographic limitations: Giving primarily in areas of company operations.
Support limitations: No support for political or religious organizations, fraternal or professional organizations, tax-supported organizations, or United Way- or united fund-supported organizations. No grants to individuals.

2386
Marsh Associates, Inc.

2448 Park Rd.
P.O. Box 35329
Charlotte, NC 28203 (704) 376-0281
FAX: (704) 347-5754

Company URL: http://www.marshassociates.com/
Establishment information: Established in 1978.
Company type: Private company
Business activities: Provides mortgages; provides real estate services.
Business type (SIC): Brokers and bankers/ mortgage; investors/miscellaneous
Corporate officers: Gretchen Johnston, Chair.; James McLawhorn, Pres.; Roberta B. Vollick, Treas. and Cont.
Board of director: Gretchen Johnston, Chair.
Giving statement: Giving through the Marsh Foundation, Inc.

Marsh Foundation, Inc.

c/o Bank of America, N.A.
P.O. Box 26262
Greensboro, NC 27402-6262 (336) 272-5100
Application address: P.O. Box 35329, Charlotte, NC 28235

Establishment information: Established in 1954.
Donors: Marsh Assocs.; Marsh Realty Co.; Marsh Mortgage Co.
Contact: Gretchen M. Johnston, Pres.
Financial data (yr. ended 12/31/11): Assets, $2,679,345 (M); gifts received, $108,958; expenditures, $385,440; qualifying distributions, $28,050; giving activities include $28,050 for grants.
Purpose and activities: The foundation supports museums and organizations involved with K-12 education, health, human services, and Christianity.
Fields of interest: Arts; Health care; Religion.
Type of support: General/operating support; Scholarship funds.
Geographic limitations: Giving primarily in NC.
Support limitations: No support for political organizations. No grants to individuals.
Application information: Applications accepted. Application form required.
Initial approach: Letter
Deadline(s): None
Officers: Gretchen M. Johnston, Pres.; G. Alex Marsh III, V.P.; Hunter Johnston McLawhorn, V.P.; James H. McLawhorn, Secy.
EIN: 566056515
Selected grants: The following grants are a representative sample of this grantmaker's funding activity:
$40,000 to Carolinas HealthCare Foundation, Charlotte, NC, 2009.
$33,000 to Charlotte Country Day School, Charlotte, NC, 2009.
$23,500 to Levine Museum of the New South, Charlotte, NC, 2009.
$20,000 to Myers Park Presbyterian Church, Charlotte, NC, 2009.
$10,000 to Brookstone School, Columbus, GA, 2009.
$10,000 to Charlotte Housing Authority Scholarship Fund, Charlotte, NC, 2009.
$3,000 to Foundation for the Carolinas, Charlotte, NC, 2009.
$3,000 to YMCA of Greater Charlotte, Charlotte, NC, 2009.
$2,000 to Davidson College, Davidson, NC, 2009.
$1,500 to Boca Raton Historical Society, Boca Raton, FL, 2009.

2387
Marsh Supermarkets, Inc.

9800 Crosspoint Blvd.
Indianapolis, IN 46256 (317) 594-2100

Company URL: http://www.marsh.net
Establishment information: Established in 1931.
Company type: Private company
Business activities: Operates supermarkets; operates convenience stores; sells food wholesale; provides food services; operates florists.
Business type (SIC): Groceries—retail; groceries—wholesale; restaurants and drinking places; retail stores/miscellaneous
Financial profile for 2010: Number of employees, 9,000; sales volume, $1,200,000,000
Corporate officers: Tom O'Boyle, Chair., Pres. and C.E.O.; Bill Holsworth, C.O.O.; Michele B. Pascoe, C.F.O.; Bill Erickson, V.P., Opers.; Laura Gretencord, Genl. Counsel
Board of director: Tom O'Boyle, Chair.
Subsidiaries: Convenience Store Distributing Co., Richmond, IN; Crystal Food Services, LLC, Indianapolis, IN; Village Pantry, LLC, Indianapolis, IN
Giving statement: Giving through the Marsh Supermarkets, Inc. Corporate Giving Program.

Marsh Supermarkets, Inc. Corporate Giving Program

c/o Community Rels. Dept.
333 South Franklin Rd.
Indianapolis, IN 46219-7721 (800) 845-7686
URL: http://www.marsh.net/about/community/

Purpose and activities: Marsh makes charitable contributions to nonprofit organizations involved with arts and culture, education, health, hunger, youth development, and human services. Support is given primarily in areas of company operations in Indiana.
Fields of interest: Museums; Performing arts, orchestras; Arts; Education; Health care, patient services; Health care; Food services; Food banks; Boy scouts; Girl scouts; Children/youth, services; Human services; United Ways and Federated Giving Programs.
Type of support: Continuing support; Donated products; Employee volunteer services; General/ operating support; In-kind gifts; Income development; Sponsorships.
Geographic limitations: Giving primarily in areas of company operations in IN.
Publications: Application guidelines.
Application information: Applications accepted. Telephone requests are not accepted. Multi-year funding is not automatic. Application form required. Applicants should submit the following:
1) detailed description of project and amount of funding requested
Initial approach: Complete online application form
Deadline(s): 6 weeks prior to need for requests under $1,000; 6 months prior to need for requests over $1,000
Final notification: 4 to 6 weeks

2388
Marshall Motor Company, Inc.

3550 S. 9th St.
I-135 Waterwell Rd.
Salina, KS 67401-7882 (785) 827-9641

Company URL: http:///www.marshallmotor.com
Establishment information: Established in 1928.
Company type: Private company
Business activities: Operates car dealership.
Business type (SIC): Motor vehicles—retail
Corporate officers: Larry L. Marshall, Pres.; Barbara Marshall, Secy.-Treas.
Giving statement: Giving through the Marshall Family Foundation, Inc.

Marshall Family Foundation, Inc.

1714 Upper Mill Terr.
Salina, KS 67401-3374 (785) 823-2374

Establishment information: Established in 1997 in KS.
Donors: Marshall Motor Co., Inc.; Larry L. Marshall.
Contact: Larry L. Marshall, Pres.
Financial data (yr. ended 12/31/11): Assets, $558,502 (M); gifts received, $23,682; expenditures, $28,550; qualifying distributions, $28,450; giving activities include $26,450 for 23 grants (high: $3,500; low: $100).
Purpose and activities: The foundation supports museums and organizations involved with orchestras, higher education, disability services, and Christianity.
Fields of interest: Education; Human services; Religion.
Type of support: General/operating support.
Geographic limitations: Giving primarily in Salina, KS.
Support limitations: No grants to individuals.
Application information: Applications accepted. Application form required.
Initial approach: Letter
Deadline(s): None
Officers: Larry L. Marshall, Pres.; Barbara C. Marshall, Secy.-Treas.
Directors: Stacie A. Coder; Stephen W. Marshall.
EIN: 742832446

2389
Marshall, Gerstein & Borun LLP

233 S. Wacker Dr., 6300 Willis Twr.
Chicago, IL 60606-6357 (312) 474-6300

Company URL: http://www.marshallip.com
Establishment information: Established in 1955.
Company type: Private company
Business activities: Operates law firm.
Business type (SIC): Legal services
Corporate officer: Jeffrey S. Sharp, Managing Partner
Giving statement: Giving through the Marshall, Gerstein & Borun LLP Pro Bono Program.

Marshall, Gerstein & Borun LLP Pro Bono Program

233 S. Wacker Dr., 6300 Willis Twr.
Chicago, IL 60606-6357 (312) 474-6300
E-mail: pstephens@marshallip.com; URL: http://www.marshallip.com/about/3/pro-bono

Contact: Paul B. Stephens, Partner
Fields of interest: Legal services.
Type of support: Pro bono services - legal.
Geographic limitations: Giving primarily in areas of company operations in Chicago, IL.
Application information: A Pro Bono Committee manages the pro bono program.

2390
C. F. Martin & Co., Inc.
510 Sycamore St.
P.O. Box 329
Nazareth, PA 18064-1000 (610) 759-2837

Company URL: http://www.mguitar.com
Establishment information: Established in 1833.
Company type: Private company
Business activities: Manufactures guitars and guitar strings.
Business type (SIC): Musical instruments
Financial profile for 2010: Number of employees, 500
Corporate officers: Christian Frederick Martin IV, Chair. and C.E.O.; Keith H. Lombardi, Pres. and C.O.O.
Board of directors: Christian F. Martin IV, Chair.; Amani Duncan; Dick Boak
Giving statement: Giving through the Martin Guitar Charitable Foundation.

Martin Guitar Charitable Foundation
510 Sycamore St.
Nazareth, PA 18064-1000

Establishment information: Established in 1996 in PA.
Donors: C.F. Martin & Co., Inc.; C.F. Martin Guitar Co.
Financial data (yr. ended 12/31/11): Assets, $3,364,018 (M); gifts received, $202,687; expenditures, $163,038; qualifying distributions, $140,500; giving activities include $140,500 for grants.
Purpose and activities: The foundation supports hospitals and organizations involved with arts and culture, higher education, and human services.
Fields of interest: Arts; Education; Human services.
Type of support: General/operating support.
Geographic limitations: Giving primarily in PA.
Support limitations: No grants to individuals.
Application information: Applications not accepted. Unsolicited requests for funds not accepted.
Officers: Christian F. Martin IV, Pres.; Diane S. Martin, V.P.; Theresa Rothrock, Secy.; John A. Messer, Treas.
EIN: 311483218

2391
Martin Marietta Materials, Inc.
2710 Wycliff Rd.
Raleigh, NC 27607-3033 (919) 781-4550
FAX: (919) 783-4535

Company URL: http://www.martinmarietta.com
Establishment information: Established in 1993.
Company type: Public company
Company ticker symbol and exchange: MLM/NYSE
Business activities: Produces crushed stone, sand, and gravel.
Business type (SIC): Mining/crushed and broken stone; mining and quarrying of nonmetallic minerals (except fuels); mining/sand and gravel; abrasive, asbestos, and nonmetallic mineral products
Financial profile for 2012: Number of employees, 4,993; assets, $3,160,930,000; sales volume, $2,037,670,000; pre-tax net income, $102,910,000; expenses, $1,882,710,000; liabilities, $1,750,380,000
Fortune 1000 ranking: 2012—936th in revenues, 766th in profits, and 737th in assets
Corporate officers: Stephen P. Zelnak, Jr., Chair.; C. Howard Nye, Pres. and C.E.O.; Anne H. Lloyd, C.P.A., Exec. V.P., C.F.O., and Treas.; Dana F. Guzzo, Sr. V.P., C.A.O., and C.I.O.; Roselyn R. Bar, Sr. V.P., Genl. Counsel, and Corp. Secy.; Donald A. McCunniff, Sr. V.P., Human Resources
Board of directors: Stephen P. Zelnak, Jr., Chair.; Sue W. Cole; David G. Maffucci; William E. McDonald; Frank H. Menaker, Jr.; C. Howard Nye; Laree E. Perez; Michael J. Quillen; Dennis L. Rediker; Richard A. Vinroot
Subsidiary: American Aggregates Corporation, Greenville, OH
Plants: Augusta, Leesburg, GA; Carmel, Kokomo, IN; Cummings, Des Moines, IA; Tecumseh, Topeka, KS; Williamsport, MD; Mercer, Savannah, MO; Weeping Water, NE; Bessemer City, Charlotte, Concord, Denver, Greensboro, Kannapolis, Kings Mountain, Matthews, Monroe, Salisbury, NC; Culpeper, Rockville, VA
International operations: Bahamas
Giving statement: Giving through the Martin Marietta Materials, Inc. Corporate Giving Program.
Company EIN: 561848578

Martin Marietta Materials, Inc. Corporate Giving Program
2710 Wycliff Rd.
Raleigh, NC 27607-3033 (919) 781-4550
URL: http://www.martinmarietta.com/Corporate/communities.asp

Purpose and activities: Martin Marietta Materials makes charitable contributions to nonprofit organizations on a case by case basis. Support is given primarily in areas of divisional offices.
Fields of interest: Performing arts, dance; Performing arts, music; Arts; Secondary school/education; Education; Environment, natural resources; Food banks; Human services, gift distribution; General charitable giving.
Type of support: Employee volunteer services; General/operating support; In-kind gifts; Program development; Sponsorships.
Geographic limitations: Giving primarily in areas of divisional offices, with emphasis on GA, IA, KY, MN, NC, and TX.

2392
Mary Kay Inc.
16251 Dallas Pkwy.
Addison, TX 75001 (972) 687-6300

Company URL: http://www.marykay.com
Establishment information: Established in 1963.
Company type: Private company
Business activities: Manufactures skin care and cosmetics products; operates direct selling company.
Business type (SIC): Soaps, cleaners, and toiletries; nonstore retailers
Financial profile for 2011: Number of employees, 5,000; sales volume, $2,500,000,000
Corporate officers: Richard R. Rogers, Chair.; David B. Holl, Pres. and C.E.O.; Terry Smith, C.F.O; Kregg Jodie, C.I.O.; Nathan Moore, Secy.
Board of director: Richard R. Rogers, Chair.
Plants: Cypress, CA; Suwanee, GA; Hoffman Estates, IL; Somerset, NJ; Carrollton, TX
Giving statement: Giving through the Mary Kay Cosmetics Corporate Contributions Program, the Mary Kay Family Foundation, and the Mary Kay Foundation.

Mary Kay Cosmetics Corporate Contributions Program
16251 Dallas Pkwy.
Addison, TX 75001-6801 (800) 627-9529
URL: http://www.marykay.com/en-US/About-Mary-Kay/SocialResponsibility

Purpose and activities: As a complement to its foundation, Mary Kay Cosmetics also makes charitable contributions to nonprofit organizations directly. Support is given on a national basis.
Fields of interest: Environment; Crime/violence prevention, domestic violence; Family services, domestic violence Women; Girls.
Type of support: Advocacy; Building/renovation; Cause-related marketing; Donated products; In-kind gifts; Sponsorships.
Geographic limitations: Giving on a national basis.

The Mary Kay Family Foundation
(formerly Mary Kay Foundation)
16251 Dallas Pkwy.
Addison, TX 75001-6801 (972) 687-5734

Establishment information: Incorporated in 1969 in TX.
Donor: Mary Kay Ash†.
Contact: Michael Lunceford, Tr.
Financial data (yr. ended 06/30/10): Assets, $2,334,923 (M); expenditures, $135,334; qualifying distributions, $127,000; giving activities include $127,000 for 13 grants (high: $50,000; low: $1,000).
Purpose and activities: The foundation supports organizations involved with education, health, recreation, and human services.
Fields of interest: Elementary/secondary education; Higher education; Education; Health care; Athletics/sports, equestrianism; Recreation; YM/YWCAs & YM/YWHAs; Children/youth, services; Developmentally disabled, centers & services; Human services.
Type of support: Annual campaigns; Capital campaigns; General/operating support; Program development.
Geographic limitations: Giving primarily in TX, with emphasis on Dallas.
Application information: Applications not accepted. Unsolicited requests for funds not accepted.
Trustees: Kris Johnson; Michael Lunceford; Ryan Rogers.
EIN: 756081602

Mary Kay Foundation
(formerly Mary Kay Ash Charitable Foundation)
P.O. Box 799044
Dallas, TX 75379-9044 (972) 687-6300
E-mail: mkcares@marykayfoundation.org; Application address: P.O. Box 799044, Dallas, TX 75379-9044; toll-free tel.: (877) 652-2737; URL: http://www.mkacf.org

Establishment information: Established in 1996 in TX.
Donors: Mary Kay Ash†; Mary Kay Inc.
Contact: Michael Lunceford, Pres.
Financial data (yr. ended 12/31/11): Revenue, $7,558,248; assets, $14,990,850 (M); gifts received, $6,879,527; expenditures, $4,967,314; giving activities include $4,857,562 for grants.
Purpose and activities: The foundation provides support to other charitable organizations involved in education, medical research, cancer research, women's health issues, or raising awareness of the epidemic problem of violence against women.

Fields of interest: Cancer research; Medical research; Crime/violence prevention, abuse prevention Women.

Programs:

Break the Silence Against Violence Shelter Grants: The foundation provides grants of $20,000 each to worthwhile organizations that aid the victims of domestic violence. Funds awarded by the foundation may be used for the operating budget of the shelter, with the exception of staff travel.

Cancer Research Grants: Grants of up to $100,000 each are available towards translational research in ovarian, uterine, breast, or cervical cancer. Grants are for two years. Applications must be submitted by one principal investigator, selected by the institution. Only one grant application will be accepted from each accredited medical school and schools of public health in the United States.

Domestic Violence Shelter Grants: These grants are awarded to organizations in the United States that assist survivors of domestic violence by operating emergency shelters. The grants are announced each October in observance of National Domestic Violence Awareness Month. Funds awarded by the foundation may be used for operating expenses, with the exception of staff travel. The foundation will award a grant to at least one domestic violence shelter in every state. Any remaining funds will be distributed based on state population. In 2012, the foundation awarded grants of $20,000 each to more than a hundred and fifty women's domestic violence shelters across the nation.

Nature Explore Classroom Program: This program brings a unique tool to women's shelters: outdoor learning spaces that are designed to include nature in the daily lives and learning of children. Research shows that nature can help soften the impact of life stress on children and help them deal with adversity. It also helps reduce or eliminate anti-social behavior which can occur in children who have experienced or witnessed abuse. However, children who are currently residing at a domestic violence shelter with their mothers rarely have access to these locations because of the precarious nature of protecting a mother and a child from a potential abuser. Classrooms are traditionally constructed in areas such as schools, parks, and child care centers; along with the outdoor area, each classroom includes a curriculum with details on how to fully maximize the educational opportunities and healing effects of the outdoor environment.

Type of support: Research.
Geographic limitations: Giving on a national basis.
Publications: Application guidelines.
Application information: Applications accepted. Applicants should submit the following:

1) copy of IRS Determination Letter
2) descriptive literature about organization
3) listing of board of directors, trustees, officers and other key people and their affiliations
4) detailed description of project and amount of funding requested
5) copy of current year's organizational budget and/or project budget

Initial approach: Download application
Copies of proposal: 10
Board meeting date(s): Monthly
Deadline(s): Feb. 15 for Cancer Research Grants; Apr. 30 for Domestic Violence Shelter Grants; June 30 for Break the Silence Against Violence Shelter Grants; Aug 1 for Nature Explore Classrooms Program
Final notification: May 1 for Cancer Research Grants

Officers and Directors:* Michael Lunceford*, Pres.; Karen Rogers*, V.P.; Ryan Rogers, V.P.; Kris Johnsons*, Secy.-Treas.; Jennifer Cook; Anne Crews; Peggy Davidson; Yvette Franco; Nancy Thomason.
EIN: 752653742

2393
Masco Corporation

21001 Van Born Rd.
Taylor, MI 48180-1340 (313) 274-7400
FAX: (313) 792-4177

Company URL: http://www.masco.com
Establishment information: Established in 1929.
Company type: Public company
Company ticker symbol and exchange: MAS/NYSE
International Securities Identification Number: US5745991068
Business activities: Manufactures, sells, and installs home improvement and building products.
Business type (SIC): Wood millwork
Financial profile for 2012: Number of employees, 30,000; assets, $6,875,000,000; sales volume, $7,745,000,000; pre-tax net income, $42,000,000; expenses, $7,476,000,000; liabilities, $6,553,000,000
Fortune 1000 ranking: 2012—336th in revenues, 928th in profits, and 493rd in assets
Corporate officers: Verne G. Istock, Chair.; Timothy J. Wadhams, Pres. and C.E.O.; John G. Sznewajs, V.P., C.F.O., and Treas.; Timothy J. Monteith, V.P. and C.I.O.; John P. Lindow, V.P. and Cont.; Gregory D. Wittrock, V.P., Genl. Counsel, and Secy.; Karen R. Mendelsohn, V.P., Sales and Mktg.; Maria C. Duey, V.P., Comms.; Charles F. Greenwood, V.P., Human Resources
Board of directors: Verna G. Istock, Chair.; Dennis W. Archer; Thomas G. Denomme; Verne G. Istock; J. Michael Losh; Lisa A. Payne; John C. Plant; Mary Ann Van Lokeren; Timothy Wadhams
Subsidiaries: Alsons Corp., Hillsdale, MI; American Shower & Bath Corp., Moorestown, NJ; Aqua Glass Corp., Adamsville, TN; Arrow Fastener Co., Inc., Saddle Brook, NJ; Brass-Craft Manufacturing Co., Novi, MI; Brasstech, Inc., Santa Ana, CA; Chatsworth Bathrooms, Inc., Warwick, RI; The Faucet-Queens Inc., Vernon Hills, IL; Gamco Products Co., Henderson, KY; KraftMaid Cabinetry, Inc., Middlefield, OH; Liberty Hardware Mfg. Corp., Winston-Salem, NC; Masco Retail Sales Support, Inc., Mooresville, NC; Merillat Industries, LLC, Adrian, MI; Milgard Manufacturing Inc., Tacoma, WA; Mill's Pride, Inc., Columbus, OH; Vapor Technologies, Inc., Boulder, CO; Watkins Manufacturing Corp., Vista, CA
International operations: Argentina; Austria; Bahamas; Belgium; British Virgin Islands; Canada; China; Croatia; Cyprus; Czech Republic; Denmark; France; Germany; Hungary; Italy; Japan; Luxembourg; Mexico; Netherlands; New Zealand; Poland; Serbia; Singapore; South Korea; Spain; Sweden; Switzerland; Taiwan; Thailand; Turkey; United Kingdom
Giving statement: Giving through the Masco Corporation Contributions Program and the Masco Corporation Foundation.
Company EIN: 381794485

Masco Corporation Contributions Program

21001 Van Born Rd.
Taylor, MI 48180-1340 (313) 274-7400
FAX: (313) 792-6262;
E-mail: fran_sabo@mascohq.com; URL: http://www.masco.com/corporate_information/citizenship/index.html

Contact: Melonie B. Colaianne, Pres.; Cheryl L.M. Phillips, V.P.
Financial data (yr. ended 12/31/10): Total giving, $4,287,652, including $2,963,290 for grants, $238,502 for employee matching gifts and $1,085,860 for in-kind gifts.
Purpose and activities: As a complement to its foundation, Masco also makes charitable contributions to nonprofit organizations directly. Special emphasis is directed toward programs designed to provide affordable housing for low-income families. Support is given primarily in areas of company operations.
Fields of interest: Arts; Environment; Housing/shelter; Human services Military/veterans; Economically disadvantaged.
Type of support: Donated products; Employee matching gifts; Employee volunteer services; General/operating support; In-kind gifts.
Geographic limitations: Giving primarily in areas of company operations.
Support limitations: No support for discriminatory, political, or lobbying organizations, or religious organizations not of direct benefit to the entire community, or organizations benefiting few people, or candidates or athletic clubs. No grants for to individuals, or for debt reduction, conferences, travel, seminars, or film or video projects; no loans.
Application information: Applications accepted. Application form not required. Applicants should submit the following:

1) role played by volunteers
2) timetable for implementation and evaluation of project
3) how project will be sustained once grantmaker support is completed
4) site description
5) signature and title of chief executive officer
6) results expected from proposed grant
7) statement of problem project will address
8) population served
9) name, address and phone number of organization
10) copy of IRS Determination Letter
11) how company employees can become involved with the organization
12) brief history of organization and description of its mission
13) geographic area to be served
14) how project's results will be evaluated or measured
15) list of company employees involved with the organization
16) listing of board of directors, trustees, officers and other key people and their affiliations
17) detailed description of project and amount of funding requested
18) plans for cooperation with other organizations, if any
19) contact person
20) copy of current year's organizational budget and/or project budget
21) listing of additional sources and amount of support
22) plans for acknowledgement

Initial approach: Letter or phone call
Copies of proposal: 1
Deadline(s): None
Final notification: 6 weeks

Contributions Committee: Sharon Rothwell, Chair.; Melonie B. Colaianne, Pres.; Eugene A. Gargaro, Jr., Secy.; Richard A. Manoogian; Timothy J. Wadhams.
Number of staff: 2 part-time professional; 2 part-time support.

Masco Corporation Foundation

(formerly Masco Corporation Charitable Trust)
c/o Corp. Affairs
21001 Van Born Rd.
Taylor, MI 48180-1340 (313) 274-7400
FAX: (313) 792-6262; URL: http://www.masco.com/corporate_information/citizenship/foundation/index.html

Establishment information: Trust established in 1952 in MI.
Donor: Masco Corp.
Contact: Melonie B. Colaianne, Pres.
Financial data (yr. ended 12/31/11): Assets, $11,611,731 (M); gifts received, $3,000,000; expenditures, $4,357,608; qualifying distributions, $4,262,918; giving activities include $4,099,065 for 95 grants (high: $1,363,532; low: $300).
Purpose and activities: The foundation supports organizations involved with arts and culture, the environment, affordable housing, human services, civic affairs, economically disadvantaged, and military and veteran's.
Fields of interest: Performing arts; Arts; Environment; Food services; Housing/shelter, development; Housing/shelter; Homeless, human services; Human services; Military/veterans' organizations; Public affairs Economically disadvantaged.
Type of support: Annual campaigns; Building/renovation; Capital campaigns; Employee matching gifts; General/operating support.
Geographic limitations: Giving primarily in areas of company operations, with emphasis on the greater Detroit, MI, area.
Support limitations: No support for discriminatory organizations, political organizations or candidates, lobbying organizations, athletic clubs, religious organizations not of direct benefit to the entire community, or organizations benefiting few people. No grants to individuals, or for debt reduction, endowments, sports programs or events or school extracurricular activities, or conferences, travel, seminars, or film or video projects; no loans.
Publications: Application guidelines; Occasional report.
Application information: Applications accepted. A full proposal may be requested after inquiry. The Council of Michigan Foundations Common Grant Application form is also accepted. Application form not required. Applicants should submit the following:
1) copy of IRS Determination Letter
2) brief history of organization and description of its mission
3) copy of most recent annual report/audited financial statement/990
4) how project's results will be evaluated or measured
5) listing of board of directors, trustees, officers and other key people and their affiliations
6) detailed description of project and amount of funding requested
7) listing of additional sources and amount of support

Initial approach: Letter of inquiry or telephone
Copies of proposal: 1
Board meeting date(s): Spring and fall
Deadline(s): None
Final notification: Within 6 weeks following receipt of proposal

Officers and Directors: Sharon Rothwell*, Chair.; Melonie B. Colaianne, Pres.; Eugene A. Gargaro, Jr., Secy.; Richard A. Manoogian; Timothy J. Wadhams.
Trustee: Comerica Bank.
Number of staff: 2 part-time professional; 2 part-time support.
EIN: 386043605

2394
Mascoma Savings Bank

67 N. Park St.
P.O. Box 4399
Lebanon, NH 03766-1317 (603) 448-3650

Company URL: http://www.mascomabank.com
Establishment information: Established in 1899.
Company type: Mutual company
Business activities: Operates savings bank.
Business type (SIC): Banks/commercial
Financial profile for 2010: Assets, $998,469,311; pre-tax net income, $8,741,486; liabilities, $903,115,329
Corporate officers: Kathleen C. Hoyt, Chair.; Robert E. Bowers, Jr., Vice-Chair.; Stephen F. Christy, Pres. and C.E.O.; Barry E. McCabe, Exec. V.P. and C.O.O.; Donald N. Thompson, Sr. V.P., C.F.O., and Treas.; Carol A. Cone, Sr. V.P., Opers.; Samantha L. Pause, Sr. V.P., Mktg. and Sales.; Sally A. McEwen, Sr. V.P., Human Resources; Catherine A. Ells, Cont.
Board of directors: Kathleen C. Hoyt, Chair.; Robert E. Bowers, Jr., Vice-Chair.; Clayton R. Adams; Richard S. Bridgman, Jr.; Gretchen Cherington; Stephen F. Christy; Paul B. Gardent; Daniel P. Jantzen; Edward T. Kerrigan; Sara L. Kobylenski; Frank J. Leibly III; Barry E. McCabe; Margaret N. Mitchell; Scott W. Putney; Robert G. Rosenblum
Offices: Canaan, Enfield, Hanover, Lyme, West Lebanon, NH; Bethel, Chelsea, Hartland, Norwich, Strafford, White River Junction, VT
Giving statement: Giving through the Mascoma Savings Bank Foundation.

Mascoma Savings Bank Foundation

67 N. Park St.
Lebanon, NH 03766-0435 (603) 443-8639
E-mail: Anne.Daveni@mascomabank.com; Additional address: Kimberly Robinson, P.O. Box 435, Lebanon, NH 03766 tel.: (603) 448-3650; URL: http://www.mascomabank.com/foundation

Establishment information: Established in 1988 in NH.
Donor: Mascoma Savings Bank.
Contact: Anne D'Aveni
Financial data (yr. ended 12/31/11): Assets, $4,245,502 (M); gifts received, $299,527; expenditures, $223,519; qualifying distributions, $188,407; giving activities include $188,407 for grants.
Purpose and activities: The foundation supports organizations involved with arts and culture, education, health, mental health, legal aid, hunger, sports, and human services.
Fields of interest: Museums; Performing arts; Performing arts, ballet; Arts; Secondary school/education; Law school/education; Education; Hospitals (general); Dental care; Health care; Substance abuse, services; Mental health/crisis services; Legal services; Food services; Food banks; Athletics/sports, amateur leagues; Boys & girls clubs; Youth, services; Developmentally disabled, centers & services; Human services.
Type of support: Annual campaigns; Building/renovation; Continuing support; Equipment; General/operating support; Program development; Publication.
Geographic limitations: Giving primarily in areas of company operations in central western NH and central eastern VT.
Support limitations: No support for religious organizations not of direct benefit to the entire community. No grants to individuals or for major capital campaigns.
Publications: Application guidelines; Grants list.
Application information: Applications accepted. The foundation considers requests for up to $7,500. Application form not required. Applicants should submit the following:
1) name, address and phone number of organization
2) copy of IRS Determination Letter
3) copy of most recent annual report/audited financial statement/990
4) detailed description of project and amount of funding requested
5) contact person
6) listing of additional sources and amount of support

Initial approach: Proposal
Deadline(s): Apr. 1 and Oct. 1
Final notification: 10 weeks

Officer and Trustees:* Gretchen S. Taylor*, Chair.; Gretchen Cherington; Kathleen C. Hoyt; Nancy J. Reardon; Thomas F. Terry; Robert Resenblum.
EIN: 222816632
Selected grants: The following grants are a representative sample of this grantmaker's funding activity:
$7,500 to Have Justice Will Travel, Vershire, VT, 2011.
$5,250 to Clara Martin Center, Randolph, VT, 2011.
$5,000 to Health Connections of the Upper Valley, North Pomfret, VT, 2011.
$5,000 to Second Growth, West Lebanon, NH, 2011.
$5,000 to Vermont Institute of Natural Science, Quechee, VT, 2011.
$5,000 to Vermont Law School, South Royalton, VT, 2011.
$5,000 to Vital Communities, White River Junction, VT, 2011.
$4,835 to United Church of South Royalton, South Royalton, VT, 2011.
$4,000 to Upper Valley Educators Institute, Lebanon, NH, 2011.
$3,750 to Enfield Shaker Museum, Enfield, NH, 2011.

2395
Maslon Edelman Borman & Brand, LLP

3300 Wells Fargo Ctr.
90 South Seventh St
Minneapolis, MN 55402-4140
(612) 672-8379

Company URL: http://www.maslon.com
Establishment information: Established in 1948.
Company type: Private company
Business activities: Operates law firm.
Business type (SIC): Legal services
Corporate officers: Cooper Ashley, Chair.; Sarah Taylor, C.F.O.
Giving statement: Giving through the Maslon Edelman Borman & Brand, LLP Pro Bono Program.

Maslon Edelman Borman & Brand, LLP Pro Bono Program

3300 Wells Fargo Ctr.
90 South Seventh St.
Minneapolis, MN 55402-4140 (612) 672-8379
FAX: (612) 642-8379;
E-mail: astrid.eglitis@maslon.com; Additional tel.: (612) 672-8200; URL: http://www.maslon.com/CM/AboutUs/AboutUs197.asp

Contact: Astrid Eglitis, Dir., Recruiting & Prof. Dev
Fields of interest: Legal services.
Type of support: Pro bono services - legal.

Geographic limitations: Giving primarily in areas of company operations in Minneapolis, MN.

2396
Mason State Bank
322 S. Jefferson St.
P.O. Box 130
Mason, MI 48854-1652 (517) 676-0500

Company URL: http://www.masonstate.com/
Establishment information: Established in 1886.
Company type: Private company
Business activities: Operates commercial bank.
Business type (SIC): Banks/commercial
Corporate officers: Tim Gaylord, Pres. and C.E.O.; Tim Otto, Cont.
Giving statement: Giving through the Mason State Bank Centennial Fund.

Mason State Bank Centennial Fund
344 S. Jefferson
Mason, MI 48854-1652 (517) 676-4253

Donor: Mason State Bank.
Contact: Daniel Schlattman, Secy.-Treas.
Financial data (yr. ended 12/31/11): Assets, $0 (M); expenditures, $3,065; qualifying distributions, $3,065; giving activities include $3,000 for 1 grant.
Purpose and activities: The foundation supports organizations involved with education and community development.
Fields of interest: Elementary/secondary education; Education; Community/economic development.
Type of support: Equipment.
Geographic limitations: Giving limited to Alaiedon, Aurelius, Ingham, and Vevay townships and Mason, MI.
Support limitations: No grants to individuals.
Application information: Applications accepted. Application form required. Applicants should submit the following:
1) detailed description of project and amount of funding requested
Initial approach: Letter
Deadline(s): None
Officers: Larry Silsby, Pres.; Daniel Schlattman, Secy.-Treas.
Directors: Martin Colburn; Sandra Russell.
EIN: 382772901

2397
Massachusetts Mutual Life Insurance Company
(also known as MassMutual Financial Group)
1295 State St.
Springfield, MA 01111 (413) 744-1000

Company URL: http://www.massmutual.com
Establishment information: Established in 1851.
Company type: Mutual company
Business activities: Provides investment advisory services; sells life, disability, and long-term care insurance.
Business type (SIC): Security and commodity services; insurance/life; insurance/accident and health
Financial profile for 2011: Number of employees, 10,000; assets, $188,449,000,000; sales volume, $25,647,100,000
Corporate officers: Stuart H. Reese, Chair.; Roger W. Crandall, Pres. and C.E.O.; Michael T. Rollings, Exec. V.P. and C.F.O.; Robert J. Casale, Exec. V.P. and C.I.O.; Mark D. Roellig, Exec. V.P. and Genl. Counsel
Board of directors: Stuart H. Reese, Chair.; Thomas C. Barry; Kathleen A. Corbet; Roger W. Crandall; James H. DeGraffenreidt, Jr.; Patricia Diaz Dennis; William B. Ellis; Robert A. Essner; Robert M. Furek; Raymond W. LeBoeuf; Marc Racicot; William T. Spitz
Subsidiaries: Antares Capital Corp., Chicago, IL; David L. Babson & Co. Inc., Cambridge, MA; C.M. Life Insurance Co., Hartford, CT; Cornerstone Real Estate Advisers, Inc., Hartford, CT; MassMutual International, Inc., Springfield, MA; The MassMutual Trust Co., FSB, Hartford, CT; MML Bay State Life Insurance Co., Hartford, CT; MML Investors Services, Inc., Springfield, MA; OppenheimerFunds, Inc., New York, NY
Giving statement: Giving through the MassMutual Financial Group Corporate Giving Program.

MassMutual Financial Group Corporate Giving Program
1295 State St.
Springfield, MA 01111-0001 (413) 744-2389
E-mail: cyadams@massmutual.com; Additional tel.: (413) 744-2051; Additional e-mail: CommunityResponsibility@massmutual.com; for in-kind donations, contact Rhonda Augustus, Prog. Mgr., e-mail: raugustus@massmutual.com; tel.: 413-744-3653.; URL: http://www.massmutual.com/aboutmassmutual/corporateresponsibility/community

Contact: Cynthia Adams, Prog. Mgr.
Financial data (yr. ended 12/31/11): Total giving, $7,486,432, including $6,500,007 for grants, $946,238 for employee matching gifts and $40,187 for in-kind gifts.
Purpose and activities: MassMutual makes charitable contributions to nonprofit organizations involved with promoting academic achievement and the exploration of career pathways in grades 6-12, community vitality, and community development. Support is given primarily in Springfield, Massachusetts and Enfield, Connecticut.
Fields of interest: Arts; Education; Breast cancer; Community/economic development; United Ways and Federated Giving Programs Disabilities, people with.
Type of support: Annual campaigns; Capital campaigns; Employee matching gifts; Employee volunteer services; In-kind gifts; Program development; Scholarship funds.
Geographic limitations: Giving primarily in Springfield, MA and Enfield, CT; giving also to national organizations.
Publications: Application guidelines; Corporate giving report.
Application information: Applications accepted. A contributions committee reviews all requests. Organizations receiving support are asked to provide a final report. Application form required.
Initial approach: Complete online application form
Committee meeting date(s): Feb. 22, May 23, Aug. 22, and Nov. 14
Deadline(s): Jan. 2, Apr. 2, July 3, and Sept. 25
Final notification: 3 weeks following the review committee meeting
Number of staff: 7 full-time professional; 1 full-time support.

2398
Massey Knakal Realty Services
275 Madison Ave., 3rd Fl.
New York, NY 10016 (212) 696-2500

Company URL: http://www.masseyknakal.com
Establishment information: Established in 1988.
Company type: Private company
Business activities: Operates real estate sales company.
Business type (SIC): Real estate
Corporate officers: Robert A. Knakal, Chair.; John F. Ciraulo, Vice-Chair.; Paul J. Massey, Jr., C.E.O.; Neil Heilberg, C.O.O.; Michael Wlody, C.F.O.; Gia LaMarca, V.P., Human Resources
Board of directors: Robert Knakal, Chair.; John Ciraulo, Vice-Chair.
Giving statement: Giving through the Massey Knakal Charitable Foundation.

Massey Knakal Charitable Foundation
275 Madison Ave., 3rd Fl.
New York, NY 10016-1101 (212) 696-2500
E-mail: MK-Foundation@MasseyKnakai.com; Email for Jonathan Hagerman: jhageman@masseyknakal.com; URL: http://www.masseyknakal.com/about/charity.aspx

Establishment information: Established in 2005 in NY.
Donors: Massey Knakal Realty Services; Greater Miami Jewish Federation; Paul Massey; Robert Knakal.
Contact: Jonathan Hageman, Pres.
Financial data (yr. ended 12/31/11): Assets, $154,743 (M); gifts received, $29,893; expenditures, $26,823; qualifying distributions, $26,750; giving activities include $26,750 for grants.
Purpose and activities: The foundation supports nonprofit organizations involved with arts, child, family, and human services, education, homelessness, and hunger. Special emphasis is directed toward programs that target economically disadvantaged populations and underserved communities.
Fields of interest: Arts; Human services; Religion.
Type of support: General/operating support.
Geographic limitations: Giving in the Tri-State area, primarily in New York, NY.
Application information: Applications accepted. New York/New Jersey Area Common Application Form required. Application form required.
Initial approach: Letter
Deadline(s): Quarterly on Mar. 31, June 30, Sept. 30, and Dec. 31
Officers and Directors:* Jonathan Hageman*, Pres.; Gia LaMarca*, Secy.; Michael Wlody, Treas.; Nalini Chugh; Marin Nelson; Karl Brumback; J. Guthrie Garvin; Brock Emmetsberger.
EIN: 202541349

2399
MasterCard Incorporated
(also known as MasterCard Worldwide)
2000 Purchase St.
Purchase, NY 10577 (914) 249-2000
FAX: (302) 655-5049

Company URL: http://www.mastercard.com
Establishment information: Established in 1966.
Company type: Public company
Company ticker symbol and exchange: MA/NYSE
Business activities: Provides payment solutions.

Business type (SIC): Business services/ miscellaneous
Financial profile for 2012: Number of employees, 7,500; assets, $12,462,000,000; sales volume, $7,391,000,000; pre-tax net income, $3,932,000,000; expenses, $3,454,000,000; liabilities, $5,545,000,000
Fortune 1000 ranking: 2012—348th in revenues, 70th in profits, and 341st in assets
Forbes 2000 ranking: 2012—1149th in sales, 207th in profits, and 1310th in assets
Corporate officers: Richard N. Haythornthwaite, Chair.; Walt M. Macnee, Vice-Chair.; Ajay Banga, Pres. and C.E.O.; Martina Hund-Mejean, C.F.O.; Noah J. Hanft, Genl. Counsel and Corp. Secy.
Board of directors: Richard Haythornthwaite, Chair.; Walter M. Macnee, Vice-Chair.; Ajay Banga; Silvio Barzi; David R. Carlucci; Steven J. Freiberg; Nancy J. Karch; Marc Olivie; Rima Qureshi; Jose Octavio Reyes Lagunes; Mark Schwartz; Jackson P. Tai; Edward Suning Tian
Subsidiary: MasterCard International Inc., Purchase, NY
International operations: Argentina; Australia; Barbados; Belgium; Brazil; Chile; China; England; France; Hong Kong; Ireland; Japan; Mauritius; Mexico; Netherlands; New Zealand; North Korea; Panama; Singapore; United Kingdom; Uruguay
Giving statement: Giving through the MasterCard Incorporated Corporate Giving Program.
Company EIN: 134172551

MasterCard Incorporated Corporate Giving Program

2000 Purchase St.
Purchase, NY 10577-2405
URL: http://www.mastercard.com/corporate/responsibility/corporate-philanthropy.html

Purpose and activities: MasterCard makes charitable contributions to programs designed to help youth access education, understand and utilize technology, and develop skills to enter and succeed in a global workforce. Support is given primarily in areas of company operations.
Fields of interest: Arts; Elementary/secondary education; Scholarships/financial aid; Education, reading; Education; Youth development, adult & child programs; Youth development, business; Youth, services; Human services, financial counseling; Civil/human rights, equal rights; Economic development; Engineering/technology; General charitable giving Women.
Programs:
MasterCard Scholars Program: MasterCard, in partnership with the United Negro College Fund, awards $4,500 scholarships to college juniors and seniors to attend and graduate from a UNCF institution. Special preference is given to students living in NY and St. Louis metropolitan region and majoring in business, finance, accounting, marketing, or information control. The program is administered by the UNCF.
MasterCard Scholarship Program: MasterCard awards $5,000 college scholarships to 10 children of employees of the company. The program is designed to encourage academic excellence and to help employees of MasterCard meet the cost of their children's undergraduate college education.
MasterCard Volunteer Incentive Program: MasterCard makes charitable contributions to nonprofit organizations with which employees volunteer.
MasterCard Youth Education and Technology Fund: MasterCard annually awards 20 $10,000 grants to nonprofit organizations with programs designed to help underserved K-12 students achieve success in school, prepare for the transition from school to career, and understand and utilize technology to further their opportunities in life and in the global economy. Support is limited to Fairfield County, Connecticut, and Westchester County, New York.
Matching Gift Program: MasterCard matches contributions made by its employees and retirees to nonprofit organizations on a one-for-one basis up to $5,000 per contributor, per year.
Project Math: MasterCard makes charitable contributions to programs designed to advance excellence in the teaching of math. Special emphasis is directed toward engaging national and international expertise; deepening involvement with local districts; developing regional partnerships; sharing intellectual resources; and providing technology donations. Support is limited to the metropolitan St. Louis, Missouri, area.
Type of support: Building/renovation; Cause-related marketing; Continuing support; Donated equipment; Employee matching gifts; Employee volunteer services; Employee-related scholarships; General/operating support; In-kind gifts; Scholarship funds; Sponsorships.
Geographic limitations: Giving primarily in areas of company operations, with emphasis on Fairfield, CT, the metropolitan St. Louis, MO, and New York and Westchester, NY areas.
Support limitations: No grants to individuals (except for employee-related scholarships), or for seminars, conferences, or trips, goodwill advertising, endowments or capital campaigns, memorials, fundraising, basic or applied research, athletic or social programs or activities, debt reduction, or special events; no loans or multi-year pledges.
Publications: Application guidelines; Informational brochure.
Application information: Applications accepted. Support is limited to 1 contribution per organization during any given year. Support is limited to 3 years in length for the MasterCard Youth Education and Technology Fund. Multi-year funding is not automatic. A contributions committee reviews all requests for the MasterCard Youth Education and Technology Fund. Application form required.
Applicants should submit the following:
1) brief history of organization and description of its mission
2) detailed description of project and amount of funding requested
3) copy of current year's organizational budget and/or project budget
Initial approach: Complete online eligibility quiz and application form
Committee meeting date(s): Monthly
Deadline(s): Varies for MasterCard Youth Education and Technology Fund; None for Project Math
Final notification: 6 to 8 weeks

2400
The Masterson Company, Inc.

4023 W. National Ave.
Milwaukee, WI 53215-1000
(414) 647-1132

Company URL: http://www.mastersoncompany.com
Establishment information: Established in 1848.
Company type: Private company
Business activities: Produces dessert toppings and ingredients.
Business type (SIC): Sugar, candy, and salted/roasted nut production
Corporate officers: Joe A. Masterson, Chair. and C.E.O.; Nancy J. Masterson, Secy.
Board of director: Joe A. Masterson, Chair.
Giving statement: Giving through the Masterson Foundation, Inc.

The Masterson Foundation, Inc.

4023 W. National Ave.
Milwaukee, WI 53215-0691

Establishment information: Established in 1993 in WI.
Donor: The Masterson Co., Inc.
Financial data (yr. ended 09/30/11): Assets, $0 (M); expenditures, $24,091; qualifying distributions, $24,091; giving activities include $22,800 for 7 grants (high: $5,000; low: $2,000).
Purpose and activities: The foundation supports organizations involved with arts and culture, education, and Christianity.
Fields of interest: Arts; Education; Recreation.
Type of support: General/operating support.
Geographic limitations: Giving primarily in IL and Milwaukee, WI.
Support limitations: No grants to individuals.
Application information: Applications not accepted. Unsolicited requests for funds not accepted.
Officers: Nancy J. Masterson, Pres.; Joe A. Masterson, V.P.; Martin B. Masterson, V.P.; Melinda Masterson Kelly, Secy.; Michael Masterson, Treas.
EIN: 391758210

2401
The Material Handling Industry Of America

8720 Red Oak Blvd., Ste. 201
Charlotte, NC 28217-3996 (704) 676-1190

Company URL: http://www.mhia.org
Establishment information: Established in 1945.
Company type: Business league
Business activities: Operates a business association.
Business type (SIC): Business association
Corporate officers: Larry E. Strayhorn, Chair.; Dave Young, Vice-Chair.; George W. Prest, C.E.O.; Michael Laurent, V.P., Finance; Carol Miller, V.P., Mktg. and Comms.
Board of directors: Larry E. Strayhorn, Chair.; Dave Young, Vice-Chair.; Steve Ackerman; Ken Beckerman; Jim Bowes; Steve Buccella; Bryan Carey; William Casey; Brian Cohen; Ralph Deger; Paul Evanko; Don Frazier; Gregg E. Goodner; Kevin Gue; Craig Guttmann; Willard P. Heddles; John Hill; Dave Koch; Rick Lee; Dave Lippert; Brian McNamara; Benoit Montreuil; Brian Neuwirth; John Paxton; George Prest; David Reh; Janes Robertson; Joe Robillard; Markus Schmidt; Pat Sedlak; Clark Skeen; Arthur H. Stroyd, Jr.; Colin Wilson; Brett Wood; Ron Young
Giving statement: Giving through the Material Handling Educational Foundation, Inc.

Material Handling Educational Foundation, Inc.

8720 Red Oak Blvd., Ste. 201
Charlotte, NC 28217-3996 (704) 676-1190
FAX: (704) 676-1199; E-mail: vwheeler@mhia.org; URL: http://www.mhia.org/about/mhefi/scholarship
For scholarships: Donna Varner, dvarner@mhi.org

Establishment information: Established in 1976 in PA.
Financial data (yr. ended 12/31/11): Revenue, $247,319; assets, $699,789 (M); gifts received, $219,065; expenditures, $140,292; program services expenses, $115,700; giving activities include $99,300 for grants to individuals.
Purpose and activities: The organization is dedicated to encouraging and supporting material handling education.
Fields of interest: Vocational education.
Program:
Scholarship Program: The program promotes the study of material handling and seeks to expose as many students as possible to the material handling industry. Students must have completed at least two years of study. Students from two-year postsecondary schools are eligible if they have completed two years of study and have been accepted as transfer students at MHEFI prequalified institutions. All applicants must have a "B" equivalent GPA in postsecondary studies.
Application information: Applications accepted.
Initial approach: Online application
Deadline(s): Mar. 1
Officers: Will Heddles, Pres.; Gregg Meyer*, V.P.; Michael J. Laurent, Treas.; Victoria Wheeler, Exec. Dir.
Directors: Sprague Ackley; Kevin Gue; John Hill; David Lippert; Brian Mcnamara; John Nofsinger; and 9 additional Directors.
EIN: 251303313

2402
Material Service Corporation
181 W. Madison St., Ste. 1800
Chicago, IL 60602-4693 (312) 372-3600

Company URL: http://
Establishment information: Established in 1919.
Company type: Subsidiary of a foreign company
Ultimate parent company: General Dynamics Corporation
Business activities: Mines and sells aggregates.
Business type (SIC): Mining/crushed and broken stone; mining/sand and gravel
Corporate officers: Lester Crown, Chair.; Michael E. Stanczak, Pres.; Walter Serwa, V.P., Finance, and C.F.O.; Karen Townsend, Secy.
Board of directors: Lester Crown, Chair.; Michael E. Stanczak
Giving statement: Giving through the Material Service Foundation.

Material Service Foundation
181 W. Madison, St., Ste. 1800
Chicago, IL 60602-4693

Establishment information: Established about 1952 in IL; incorporated in 1960 in IL.
Donor: Material Service Corp.
Financial data (yr. ended 12/31/11): Assets, $0 (M); expenditures, $4,765; qualifying distributions, $4,765; giving activities include $4,750 for 10 grants (high: $2,000; low: $100).
Purpose and activities: The foundation supports hospices and organizations involved with historic preservation, cancer, children services, and military and veteran's.
Fields of interest: Housing/shelter; Recreation; Religion.
Type of support: Annual campaigns; Building/renovation; Capital campaigns; Continuing support; General/operating support; Program development.
Geographic limitations: Giving limited to Chicago, IL and northwest IN.
Support limitations: No grants to individuals.
Publications: Financial statement; Grants list.
Application information: Applications accepted. Application form required.
Initial approach: Letter
Copies of proposal: 1
Board meeting date(s): As required
Deadline(s): None
Final notification: Within 1 month
Officers and Directors:* James K. Kitzmiller*, Pres.; Michael H. Hyer*, V.P. and Secy.; Michael E. Stanczak*, V.P.
EIN: 366062106

2403
Matrix Development Group, Inc.
Forsgate Dr., CN 4000
Cranbury, NJ 08512 (732) 521-2900
FAX: (609) 395-8289

Company URL: http://www.matrixcompanies.com
Establishment information: Established in 1979.
Company type: Private company
Business activities: Operates real estate investment development firm.
Business type (SIC): Real estate subdividers and developers
Corporate officers: Joseph S. Taylor, Pres. and C.E.O.; Alexander B. Taylor, C.O.O.; Donald M. Epstein, V.P., Secy., and C.F.O.
Giving statement: Giving through the Matrix Foundation, Inc.

Matrix Foundation, Inc.
400 Forsgate Dr., CN4000
Cranbury, NJ 08512-3506

Establishment information: Established in 1994 in NJ.
Donors: Matrix Special Events; Matrix Realty; Joseph S. Taylor; MAT Construction Service.
Financial data (yr. ended 12/31/11): Assets, $55,882 (M); expenditures, $43,021; qualifying distributions, $38,500; giving activities include $38,500 for grants.
Fields of interest: Education; Housing/shelter; Religion.
Geographic limitations: Giving primarily in NJ.
Support limitations: No grants to individuals.
Application information: Applications not accepted. Unsolicited requests for funds not accepted.
Trustees: Donald M. Epstein; Gerald W. Hull, Jr.; Joseph S. Taylor; Robert J. Twomey.
EIN: 223231774

2404
Matson, Inc.
1411 Sand Island Pkwy.
Honolulu, HI 96819 (510) 628-4534

Company URL: http://www.matson.com
Establishment information: Established in 1882.
Company type: Public company
Company ticker symbol and exchange: MATX/NYSE
Business activities: Operates shipping company.
Business type (SIC): Water transportation
Corporate officers: Walter A. Dods, Jr., Chair.; Matthew J. Cox, Pres. and C.E.O.; Joel M. Wine, Sr. V.P. and C.F.O.; Kevin C. O'Rourke, Sr. V.P. and Genl. Counsel
Board of directors: Walter A. Dods, Jr., Chair.; W. Blake Baird; Michael J. Chun; Matthew J. Cox.; ADM. Thomas B. Fargo; Constance H. Lau; Jeffrey N. Watanabe

Matson Foundation
1411 Sand Island Pkwy.
Honolulu, HI 96819 (808) 848-1238
E-mail: Giving@matson.com; For mainland charities, contact Paul Merwin, tel.: (707) 421-8121, e-mail: plmifm@aol.com; URL: http://www.matson.com/foundation/index.html

Contact: Linda Howe
Purpose and activities: The Matson Foundation makes charitable donations to nonprofit organizations involved with maritime environment and ocean resource conservation, education, human services, culture and arts, and civic and community programs. Emphasis is given to organizations that involve company employees, are cost-effective and likely to be sustainable, have plans for measurable results, and enhance business interests. Support is given primarily in areas of company operations in Arizona, California, Georgia, Guam, Hawaii, Illinois, Oregon, and Washington.
Fields of interest: Arts, cultural/ethnic awareness; Arts; Elementary/secondary education; Higher education, university; Education; Environment, natural resources; Environment, water resources; Environment, energy; Employment, training; Human services; Community/economic development; United Ways and Federated Giving Programs; Engineering/technology; Science; Transportation; Public affairs.
Type of support: Donated products; Employee matching gifts; Employee volunteer services; General/operating support; In-kind gifts; Sponsorships.
Geographic limitations: Giving primarily in areas of company operations in AZ, CA, GA, GU, HI, IL, OR, and WA.
Support limitations: No support for political organizations. No grants to individuals, or for endowments (with some exceptions).
Publications: Application guidelines.
Application information: Contributions are generally limited to one donation per organization in any given year. Sponsorships are limited to events in which a minimum of 70 percent of gross proceeds are donated to a designated cause. Applicants should submit the following:
1) timetable for implementation and evaluation of project
2) name, address and phone number of organization
3) brief history of organization and description of its mission
4) geographic area to be served
5) how project's results will be evaluated or measured
6) explanation of why grantmaker is considered an appropriate donor for project
7) detailed description of project and amount of funding requested
8) contact person
9) copy of current year's organizational budget and/or project budget
10) plans for acknowledgement
Donation proposals should include EIN/ Federal Tax ID number, and website, a list of current sources of support that exceed 10 percent of the organization's budget. Sponsorship proposals should include expected attendance and use of proceeds, event

honorees (if applicable), and the fundraising goal and amount of funds raised for a previous event.

Initial approach: Complete online application

Officer: Matthew Cox, Pres.

2405
Mattel, Inc.

333 Continental Blvd.
El Segundo, CA 90245-5012
(310) 252-2000
FAX: (310) 655-5049

Company URL: http://www.mattel.com
Establishment information: Established in 1945.
Company type: Public company
Company ticker symbol and exchange: MAT/ NASDAQ
Business activities: Designs, manufactures, and markets children's products.
Business type (SIC): Games, toys, and sporting and athletic goods
Financial profile for 2012: Number of employees, 28,000; assets, $6,526,780,000; sales volume, $6,420,880,000; pre-tax net income, $945,040,000; expenses, $5,399,870,000; liabilities, $3,459,740,000
Fortune 1000 ranking: 2012—395th in revenues, 246th in profits, and 511th in assets
Forbes 2000 ranking: 2012—1230th in sales, 710th in profits, and 1711th in assets
Corporate officers: Bryan G. Stockton, Chair. and C.E.O.; Robert Normile, Exec. V.P. and Secy.; Thomas A. Debrowski, Exec. V.P., Opers.; Kevin M. Farr, C.P.A., C.F.O.; Mandana Sadigh, Sr. V.P. and Corp. Treas.; H. Scott Topham, Sr. V.P., Corp. Cont.
Board of directors: Bryan G. Stockton, Chair.; Michael J. Dolan; Trevor Edwards; Frances D. Fergusson; Kathy Brittain White Loyd; Dominic Ng; Vasant M. Prabhu; Andrea L. Rich; Dean A. Scarborough; Christopher A. Sinclair; Dirk Van de Put
Subsidiaries: Fisher-Price, Inc., East Aurora, NY; Pleasant Co., Middleton, WI
International operations: Bermuda; Hong Kong; Netherlands; Singapore; Venezuela
Historic mergers: The Learning Company, Inc. (May 13, 1999)
Giving statement: Giving through the Mattel, Inc. Corporate Giving Program, the SOFTBANK MOBILE Corp. Contributions Program, and the Mattel Children's Foundation.
Company EIN: 951567322

Mattel, Inc. Corporate Giving Program

333 Continental Blvd.
El Segundo, CA 90245-5032
URL: http://corporate.mattel.com/about-us/philanthropy/default.aspx

Purpose and activities: As a complement to its foundation, Mattel also makes charitable contributions to nonprofit organizations directly. Support is given on a national basis, with emphasis on areas of company operations in California, Florida, Illinois, New York, Texas, and Wisconsin.
Fields of interest: Education, early childhood education; Education, reading; Pediatrics; Children, services.
Type of support: Donated products; Employee volunteer services; In-kind gifts; Sponsorships.
Geographic limitations: Giving on a national basis, with emphasis on areas of company operations in CA, FL, IL, NY, TX, and WI.
Publications: Corporate report.
Application information: Applications not accepted. Contributes only to pre-selected organizations. The Corporate Communications Department handles giving.

Mattel Children's Foundation

(formerly Mattel Foundation)
333 Continental Blvd., M.S. M1-1418
El Segundo, CA 90245-5032 (310) 252-6552
E-mail: foundation@mattel.com; Additional e-mail for Deidre Lind: deidre.lind@mattel.com; Additional tel.: (310) 252-3630; URL: http://corporate.mattel.com/about-us/philanthropy/

Establishment information: Established in 1978 in CA.
Donor: Mattel, Inc.
Contact: Deidre Lind, Exec. Dir.
Financial data (yr. ended 12/31/11): Assets, $583,946 (M); gifts received, $4,402,703; expenditures, $4,079,848; qualifying distributions, $4,079,848; giving activities include $4,010,369 for 242 grants (high: $635,825; low: $25).
Purpose and activities: The foundation supports organizations involved with arts and culture, education, health, AIDS, athletics, youth development, human services, and girls. Special emphasis is directed toward programs designed to improve the lives of children in need.
Fields of interest: Arts; Education, reading; Education; Hospitals (general); Public health, physical fitness; Health care; AIDS; Disasters, preparedness/services; Athletics/sports, amateur leagues; Athletics/sports, Special Olympics; Youth development; Human services Children; Girls.

Programs:

Employee Matching Gifts: The foundation matches contributions made by employees of Mattel to educational institutions and nonprofit organizations involved with children up to $5,000 per employee, per year.

Girl Empowerment: The foundation supports programs designed to promote self-esteem in young girls up to age 12.

Health: The foundation supports programs designed to promote physical health and well-being of children. Special emphasis is directed toward programs designed to promote healthy, active lifestyles.

Learning: The foundation supports programs designed to increase access to education. Special emphasis is directed toward programs designed to address of issue of literacy.

Type of support: Employee matching gifts; Employee volunteer services; Employee-related scholarships; Equipment; General/operating support; In-kind gifts; Program development; Scholarship funds; Sponsorships; Technical assistance.
Geographic limitations: Giving primarily in CA, CT, Washington, DC, and NY, and in Argentina, Australia, Brazil, Canada, Chile, China, France, Germany, Hong Kong, Hungary, India, Indonesia, Italy, Japan, Malaysia, Mexico, Poland, Spain, Thailand, and the United Kingdom.
Support limitations: No support for political parties, candidates or partisan political organizations, labor or fraternal organizations, athletic or social clubs, sectarian or denominational religious organizations not of direct benefit to the entire community, or schools or school districts. No grants to individuals (except for employee-related scholarships), or for capital campaigns for physical property purchases, renovations, or developments, fundraising events, advertising, sponsorships, or research.
Publications: Annual report; Grants list; Program policy statement.
Application information: Applications not accepted. Unsolicited applications for funding are currently not accepted.
Officers: Kevin Farr, Chair.; Deidre Lind, Exec. Dir.
Number of staff: 2 full-time professional; 1 full-time support.
EIN: 953263647

2406
Matthews International Corporation

2 Northshore Ctr.
Pittsburgh, PA 15212-5851 (412) 442-8200
FAX: (412) 442-8298

Company URL: http://www.matw.com/
Establishment information: Established in 1850.
Company type: Public company
Company ticker symbol and exchange: MATW/ NASDAQ
Business activities: Designs, manufactures, markets, and provides bronze memorials and memorialization products, caskets, cremation equipment, graphics imaging products and services, merchandising solutions, and marking products.
Business type (SIC): Metal foundries/nonferrous; printing/commercial; printing trade services; machinery/general industry; computer and office equipment; electronic components and accessories; manufacturing/miscellaneous
Financial profile for 2012: Number of employees, 5,400; assets, $1,128,040,000; sales volume, $900,320,000; pre-tax net income, $83,920,000; expenses, $806,740,000; liabilities, $650,220,000
Corporate officers: John D. Turner, Chair.; Joseph C. Bartolacci, Pres. and C.E.O.; Steven F. Nicola, Secy.-Treas. and C.F.O.; David F. Beck, V.P. and Cont.; Brian D. Walters, V.P. and Genl. Counsel; Jennifer A. Ciccone, V.P., Human Resources
Board of directors: John D. Turner, Chair.; Gregory S. Babe; Joseph C. Bartolacci; Katherine Elizabeth Dietze; Alvaro Garcia-Tunon; Robert G. Neubert; Morgan K. O'Brien; John P. O'Leary, Jr.; Jerry R. Whitaker
International operations: Austria; Germany; Italy; Sweden; United Kingdom
Giving statement: Giving through the James H. Matthews & Company Educational and Charitable Trust.
Company EIN: 250644320

James H. Matthews & Company Educational and Charitable Trust

2 Northshore Ctr.
Pittsburgh, PA 15212-5838

Establishment information: Established in 1940.
Donor: Matthews International Corp.
Financial data (yr. ended 09/30/11): Assets, $1,498,889 (M); expenditures, $49,436; qualifying distributions, $48,451; giving activities include $48,451 for 28 grants (high: $30,471; low: $250).
Purpose and activities: The foundation supports organizations involved with arts and culture, education, substance abuse services, birth defects, heart disease, and human services.
Fields of interest: Health organizations; Human services.
Type of support: General/operating support.
Support limitations: No grants to individuals.
Application information: Applications not accepted. Contributes only to pre-selected organizations.
Officer: J. C. Bartolacci, Pres.

Trustees: J. A. Ciccone; S. F. Nicola.
EIN: 256028582

2407
Mattress Holding Corp.

5815 Gulf Fwy.
Houston, TX 77023-5341 (713) 923-1009

Company URL: http://www.mattressfirm.com/
Establishment information: Established in 1986.
Company type: Subsidiary of a private company
Business activities: Manufactures and distributes mattresses and bedding products.
Business type (SIC): Furniture and home furnishing stores
Corporate officers: William E. Watts, Chair.; R. Stephen Stagner, Pres. and C.E.O.; Mike Marrie, C.I.O.; James R. Black, C.P.A., Exec. V.P. and C.F.O.; Kenneth E. Murphy III, Exec. V.P., Sales and Opers.; R. Stephen Stagner, Sr. V.P. and C.O.O.; Christine Brinkley, V.P., Human Resources; Mark Henderson, Cont.
Board of director: William E. Watts, Chair.
Giving statement: Giving through the Mattress Firm Foundation Inc.

Mattress Firm Foundation Inc.

5815 Gulf Fwy.
Houston, TX 77023-5341

Establishment information: Established in TX.
Donor: Mattress Firm, Inc.
Financial data (yr. ended 01/31/11): Assets, $84 (M); gifts received, $500; expenditures, $500; qualifying distributions, $500; giving activities include $500 for 1 grant.
Fields of interest: Education.
Support limitations: No grants to individuals.
Application information: Applications not accepted. Unsolicited requests for funds not accepted.
Officers: Steve Stagner, Pres.; Karrie Forbes, V.P.; Steve Fendrich, V.P.; Christine Brinkley, V.P. and Secy.; Jim Black, V.P. and Treas.
EIN: 204330312

2408
Mautz Paint Company, Inc.

2030 S. Stoughton Rd.
Madison, WI 53716-2850 (608) 221-3772

Company URL: http://www.mautzpaint.com
Establishment information: Established in 1922.
Company type: Subsidiary of a public company
Business activities: Manufactures varnishes, stains, enamels, and paints.
Business type (SIC): Paints and allied products; furniture and home furnishings—wholesale; non-durable goods—wholesale; paint, glass, and wallpaper stores
Corporate officer: Joel Martinek, Mgr.
Giving statement: Giving through the Mautz Family Foundation, Inc.

Mautz Family Foundation, Inc.

(formerly Mautz Paint Foundation)
10 Oakman Branch Rd.
Hilton Head Island, SC 29928-3345
Application address: W10897 Corning St., Poynette, WI 53955 tel.: (608) 635-4487

Establishment information: Established about 1973 in WI.
Donor: Mautz Paint Co., Inc.
Contact: Dianna McCauley
Financial data (yr. ended 12/31/11): Assets, $402,715 (M); expenditures, $20,576; qualifying distributions, $12,210; giving activities include $12,210 for grants.
Purpose and activities: The foundation supports community foundations and organizations involved with arts and culture, education, and human services.
Fields of interest: Health care; Human services; Community/economic development.
Type of support: Endowments; General/operating support; Program development.
Geographic limitations: Giving limited to areas of company operations in Charleston and Hilton Head, SC.
Application information: Applications accepted. Application form required.
Initial approach: Letter
Deadline(s): None
Officers: Bernhard F. Mautz, Jr., Pres.; Elsa M.S. Mautz, V.P.; Allison J. Mautz, Secy.; Bernhard F. Mautz IV, Treas.
EIN: 396040508

2409
Maverick Capital, Ltd.

300 Crescent Ct., Ste. 1850
Dallas, TX 75201-7858 (214) 880-4000

Company URL: http://
Establishment information: Established in 1990.
Company type: Private company
Business activities: Operates private investment company.
Business type (SIC): Investors/miscellaneous
Corporate officers: Evan Acton Wyly, Pres.; Sharyl M. Robertson, C.F.O.; Lee S. Ainslie III, C.I.O.; Joseph Manogue, Treas.; Natalie Miller, Cont.
Giving statement: Giving through the Maverick Capital Foundation.

Maverick Capital Foundation

300 Crescent Ct., 18th Fl.
Dallas, TX 75201-1836

Establishment information: Established in 2002 in TX.
Donors: Brian L. Zied; Erika Long; Carter Creech; Glenn Engel; Keith Hennington; Winston Holt; Andrew Homan; Steven H. Kapp; Katherine Neufeld; Gunnar Overstrom; Michelle Perrin; Alex Rafal; Elena Ridloff; Vinay Saqi; Natalie Shea; David Singer; Sean Walsh; Christy Wyskiel; Pedro Zevallos; Maverick Capital Charities, Ltd.; Cohasset Ltd.; Marmalade, Inc.; Lee S. Ainslie III.
Financial data (yr. ended 12/31/11): Assets, $9,502,435 (M); gifts received, $1,866,676; expenditures, $2,699,173; qualifying distributions, $2,688,940; giving activities include $2,688,940 for grants.
Purpose and activities: The foundation supports organizations involved with education, health, medical research, child welfare, legal aid, hunger, youth development, human services, and economically disadvantaged people.
Fields of interest: Elementary school/education; Secondary school/education; Charter schools; Higher education; Education, services; Education; Health care, clinics/centers; Public health, obesity; Health care; Medical research; Crime/violence prevention, child abuse; Legal services; Food services; Food banks; Youth development; Children/youth, services; Family services; Human services Economically disadvantaged.
Type of support: General/operating support; Program development; Scholarship funds.
Geographic limitations: Giving in the U.S., with emphasis on NY and TX.
Support limitations: No grants to individuals.
Application information: Applications not accepted. Contributes only to pre-selected organizations.
Trustees: Lee S. Ainslie III; Carter Creech; Bates Brown; Donald Devine; Steve Galbraith; William Goodell; Keith Hennigton; Winston Holt IV; Steven H. Kapp; John McCafferty; Gunnar Overstrom; Michael A. Pausic; Alex Rafal; David Singer; Andrew Warford; Evan A. Wyly; Brian L. Zied.
EIN: 710917626
Selected grants: The following grants are a representative sample of this grantmaker's funding activity:
$210,000 to Robin Hood Foundation, New York, NY, 2010.
$130,000 to KIPP New York, New York, NY, 2010.
$55,000 to Good Shepherd Services, New York, NY, 2010.
$30,000 to City Squash, Bronx, NY, 2010.
$20,000 to Cystic Fibrosis Foundation, Bethesda, MD, 2010.
$15,000 to Boys and Girls Clubs of Greater Dallas, Dallas, TX, 2010.
$15,000 to Court Appointed Special Advocates, Piedmont, Charlottesville, VA, 2010.
$15,000 to North Texas Food Bank, Dallas, TX, 2010.
$11,250 to Partners in Health, Boston, MA, 2010.
$7,500 to Education Through Music Bay Area, San Francisco, CA, 2010.

2410
MAXIMUS, Inc.

11419 Sunset Hills Rd.
Reston, VA 20190-5207 (703) 251-8500
FAX: (703) 251-8240

Company URL: http://www.maximus.com
Establishment information: Established in 1975.
Company type: Public company
Company ticker symbol and exchange: MMS/NYSE
Business activities: Provides health and human services program management and consulting services and systems solutions.
Business type (SIC): Management and public relations services
Financial profile for 2012: Number of employees, 8,657; assets, $695,290,000; sales volume, $1,050,140,000; pre-tax net income, $131,750,000; expenses, $922,570,000; liabilities, $244,190,000
Corporate officers: Peter B. Pond, Chair.; Raymond B. Ruddy, Vice-Chair.; Richard A. Montoni, Pres. and C.E.O.; David N. Walker, C.F.O.; David R. Francis, Genl. Counsel and Secy.
Board of directors: Peter B. Pond, Chair.; Raymond B. Ruddy, Vice-Chair.; Russell A. Beliveau; John J. Haley; Paul R. Lederer; Richard A. Montoni; Marilyn R. Seymann; James R. Thompson, Jr.; Wellington E. Webb
Subsidiary: UNISON MAXIMUS, Inc., Chicago, IL
Giving statement: Giving through the MAXIMUS Foundation.
Company EIN: 541000588

MAXIMUS Foundation

11419 Sunset Hills Rd.
Reston, VA 20190-5207 (800) 629-4687
FAX: (703) 251-8245;
E-mail: maximuscharitablefoundation@maximus.com; URL: http://www.maximus.com/corporate-citizenship/charitable-foundation

Establishment information: Established in 2000 in VA.
Donor: MAXIMUS, Inc.
Contact: John F. Boyer, Chair. and Pres.
Financial data (yr. ended 09/30/11): Assets, $167,190 (M); gifts received, $203,795; expenditures, $231,358; qualifying distributions, $231,051; giving activities include $231,051 for 84 grants (high: $25,000; low: $500).
Purpose and activities: The foundation supports programs designed to help people who are economically disadvantaged to achieve self-sufficiency and personal growth. Special emphasis is directed toward programs designed to serve children and young adults.
Fields of interest: Arts; Housing/shelter; Family services; Human services Children; Youth; Economically disadvantaged.
Type of support: General/operating support; Program development.
Geographic limitations: Giving primarily in CA, Washington, DC, GA, IL, MA, NY, TN, TX, and VA.
Support limitations: No support for political candidates. No grants to individuals, or for advertising, ticket events, or dinners, political causes, endowments, or capital campaigns.
Publications: Annual report; Application guidelines; Grants list; Informational brochure (including application guidelines).
Application information: Applications accepted. Grants range from $1,000 to $5,000. Additional information may be requested at a later date. Support is limited to 1 contribution per organization during any given year. Application form required.
Applicants should submit the following:
1) copy of IRS Determination Letter
2) copy of most recent annual report/audited financial statement/990
3) descriptive literature about organization
4) listing of board of directors, trustees, officers and other key people and their affiliations
5) detailed description of project and amount of funding requested
   Initial approach: Download application form and mail to foundation
   Board meeting date(s): biannually
   Deadline(s): Jan. 31 and Aug. 31
   Final notification: Apr. and Oct.

Officers and Directors:* John F. Boyer*, Chair. and Pres.; David R. Francis, Secy.; Christa Ballew; Ilene Baylinson; David Casey; Katie Conrad; Kevin Dorney; Mark Elvin; Brenda Rivera; Deborah Sorden.
EIN: 541993677
Selected grants: The following grants are a representative sample of this grantmaker's funding activity:
$25,000 to Austin Recovery, Austin, TX, 2011. For general operating expenditure.
$5,000 to Monarch School Project, San Diego, CA, 2011. For general operating expenditure.
$3,280 to Hugh OBrian Youth Leadership, Westlake Village, CA, 2011. For general operating expenditure.
$3,034 to Project HOPE - The People-to-People Health Foundation, Millwood, VA, 2011. For general operating expenditure.
$2,500 to Breathe California of Los Angeles County, Los Angeles, CA, 2011. For general operating expenditure.
$2,500 to Chesapeake Service Systems, Chesapeake, VA, 2011. For general operating expenditure.
$2,500 to Child Advocates, Houston, TX, 2011. For general operating expenditure.
$2,500 to Friends of Housing Corporation, Milwaukee, WI, 2011. For general operating expenditure.
$2,500 to Volunteer Mid-South, Memphis, TN, 2011. For general operating expenditure.
$2,000 to RAW Art Works, Lynn, MA, 2011.

2411
Mayer Brown LLP

71 S. Wacker Dr.
Chicago, IL 60606-4637 (312) 782-0600

Company URL: http://www.mayerbrown.com
Establishment information: Established in 1863.
Company type: Private company
Business activities: Operates law firm.
Business type (SIC): Legal services
Corporate officers: Herbert W. Krueger, Chair.; Kenneth S. Geller, Managing Partner
Offices: Los Angeles, Palo Alto, CA; Washington, DC; Chicago, IL; New York, NY; Charlotte, NC; Houston, TX
International operations: Belgium; China; France; Germany; Hong Kong; Thailand; United Kingdom; Vietnam
Giving statement: Giving through the Mayer Brown LLP Pro Bono Program.

Mayer Brown LLP Pro Bono Program

71 S. Wacker Dr.
Chicago, IL 60606-4637 (312) 701-8747
E-mail: mkadish@mayerbrown.com; Additional tel.: (312) 782-0600, fax: (312) 701-7711; URL: http://www.mayerbrown.com/probono/commitment/index.asp

Contact: Marc R. Kadish, Dir. of Pro Bono Activities and Litigation Training
Fields of interest: Legal services.
Type of support: Pro bono services - legal.
Application information: A Pro Bono Committee manages the pro bono program.

2412
Mayer Electric Supply Company, Inc.

3405 4th Ave. S.
Birmingham, AL 35222-2300
(205) 583-3500

Company URL: http://www.mayerelectric.com/
Establishment information: Established in 1930.
Company type: Private company
Business activities: Wholesale-distributor of electrical equipment and supplies.
Business type (SIC): Electrical goods—wholesale
Corporate officers: Nancy Collat Goedecke, Chair. and C.E.O.; Jim Summerlin, Vice-Chair.; Wes Smith, Pres.; Charles A. Collat, Jr., Exec. V.P. and C.O.O.; Glenn Goedecke, Exec. V.P., Sales and Mktg.; David L. Morgan, C.F.O.; Karen Smith, Cont.; Charles A. Collat, Sr., Chair. Emeritus
Board of directors: Nancy Collat Goedecke, Chair.; Jim Summerlin, Vice-Chair.
Giving statement: Giving through the Mayer Electric Supply Foundation, Inc.

Mayer Electric Supply Foundation, Inc.

P.O. Box 1328
Birmingham, AL 35201-1328

Establishment information: Established about 1966.
Donors: Charles A. Collat; Mayer Electric Supply Co., Inc.
Financial data (yr. ended 11/30/11): Assets, $8,411,313 (M); gifts received, $589,304; expenditures, $910,237; qualifying distributions, $839,071; giving activities include $839,071 for grants.
Purpose and activities: The foundation supports hospitals and community foundations and organizations involved with higher education, neurology, children's services, and Judaism.
Fields of interest: Higher education; Hospitals (general); Neuroscience; Children, services; Foundations (community); Jewish agencies & synagogues.
Type of support: General/operating support.
Geographic limitations: Giving primarily in Birmingham, AL.
Support limitations: No grants to individuals.
Application information: Applications accepted. Application form not required. Applicants should submit the following:
1) detailed description of project and amount of funding requested
   Initial approach: Proposal
   Deadline(s): None

Officers and Directors:* Charles A. Collat*, Pres.; Nancy Collat Goedecke*, V.P.; Wes Smith*, V.P.; Charles A. Collat, Jr., Secy.-Treas.
EIN: 630505982

2413
Maynard, Cooper & Gale, P.C.

1901 Sixth Ave. N.
2400 Regions Harbert Plz.
Birmingham, AL 35203 (205) 254-1000

Company URL: http://www.mcglaw.com
Establishment information: Established in 1984.
Company type: Private company
Business activities: Provides legal services.
Business type (SIC): Legal services
Corporate officers: Booth Gale, Pres.; Ray Bullock, C.O.O.; Deborah H. Stern, Cont.
Offices: Huntsville, Mobile, Montgomery, AL
Giving statement: Giving through the Maynard, Cooper & Gale, P.C. Contributions Program.

Maynard, Cooper & Gale, P.C. Contributions Program

2400 Regions Harbert Plz.
1901 Sixth Ave. N.
Birmingham, AL 35203 (205) 254-1000
E-mail: sconnor@maynardcooper.com; URL: http://www.maynardcooper.com/community_service.aspx

2414
Mazda North American Operations

7755 Irvine Center Dr.
Irvine, CA 92618-2922 (949) 727-1990

Company URL: http://www.mazdausa.com
Establishment information: Established in 1988.
Company type: Subsidiary of a foreign company
Business activities: Manufactures motor vehicles.
Business type (SIC): Motor vehicles and equipment
Financial profile for 2010: Number of employees, 400; sales volume, $5,000,000,000
Corporate officers: James O'Sullivan, Pres. and C.E.O.; Keishi Egawa, Exec. V.P. and C.O.O.; Jim Lievois, Sr. V.P., Finance, Admin., and C.F.O.; Robert T. Davis, Sr. V.P., Opers.
Plant: Flat Rock, MI
Offices: Washington, DC; Jacksonville, FL; Somerset, NJ; Sugar Land, TX
Giving statement: Giving through the Mazda North American Operations Corporate Giving Program and the Mazda Foundation (USA), Inc.

Mazda North American Operations Corporate Giving Program

7755 Irvine Center Dr.
Irvine, CA 92618-2922 (949) 727-1990
URL: http://www.mazdausa.com

The Mazda Foundation (USA), Inc.

1025 Connecticut Ave. N.W., Ste. 910
Washington, DC 20036-5418 (202) 467-5097
FAX: (202) 223-6490;
E-mail: MazdaFoundationApplications@gmail.com;
URL: http://www.mazdafoundation.org

Establishment information: Established in 1990 in MI.
Donors: Mazda North American Opers.; Mazda Motor of America; Mazda Research & Development of North America.
Contact: Barbara Nocera, Prog. Dir.
Financial data (yr. ended 09/30/11): Assets, $7,523,815 (M); expenditures, $559,698; qualifying distributions, $507,005; giving activities include $505,700 for 16 grants (high: $150,000; low: $5,000).
Purpose and activities: The foundation supports programs designed to promote education and literacy; environmental conservation; cross-cultural understanding; social welfare; and scientific research.
Fields of interest: Arts, cultural/ethnic awareness; Historic preservation/historical societies; Education, reading; Education; Environment, natural resources; Hospitals (general); Medical research; Food banks; Human services; Civil rights, race/intergroup relations; Science, research Youth; Minorities.
Type of support: Curriculum development; Exchange programs; Fellowships; General/operating support; Program development; Research; Scholarship funds.
Geographic limitations: Giving to national organizations located in CA, Washington, DC, LA, NH, NC, and TX.
Support limitations: No support for political or religious organizations. No grants to individuals, or for fundraising dinners or events, capital campaigns, endowments, or debt reduction.
Publications: Annual report; Application guidelines.
Application information: Applications accepted. A full proposal may be requested at a later date. Organizations receiving support are asked to submit progress reports. Application form required.
Applicants should submit the following:
1) timetable for implementation and evaluation of project
2) copy of IRS Determination Letter
3) brief history of organization and description of its mission
4) copy of most recent annual report/audited financial statement/990
5) how project's results will be evaluated or measured
6) listing of board of directors, trustees, officers and other key people and their affiliations
7) detailed description of project and amount of funding requested
8) copy of current year's organizational budget and/or project budget
9) listing of additional sources and amount of support

Initial approach: Download application form and mail or fax to foundation
Copies of proposal: 1
Board meeting date(s): Oct.
Deadline(s): Between May 1 and July 1
Final notification: Early Nov.

Officers and Trustees:* James J. O'Sullivan*, Chair.; Jay Amestoy*, Pres.; Renee Lewis, Secy.; Robert T. Davis*, Treas.
EIN: 382952236

2415
MB Financial Bank, N.A.

800 W. Madison St.
Chicago, IL 60607-2630 (312) 633-0310

Company URL: http://www.mbfinancial.com/
Establishment information: Established in 1911.
Company type: Subsidiary of a public company
Business activities: Operates commercial bank.
Business type (SIC): Banks/commercial
Corporate officers: Thomas H. Harvey, Chair.; James N. Hallene, Vice-Chair.; Mitchell Feiger, Pres. and C.E.O.; Rosemarie Bouman, Exec. V.P., Admin.; Larry J. Kallembach, Exec. V.P., Tech. and Opers.; Jill E. York, V.P. and C.F.O.
Board of directors: Thomas H. Harvey, Chair.; James N. Hallene, Vice-Chair.; David P. Bolger; Robert S. Engelman, Jr.; Mitchell Feiger; Charles J. Gries; Richard J. Holmstrom; Karen J. May; Ronald D. Santo; Renee Togher
Giving statement: Giving through the MB Financial Charitable Foundation.

MB Financial Charitable Foundation

800 W. Madison St.
Chicago, IL 60607-2630
URL: http://www.mbfinancial.com/AboutMBFinancialBank/MBinYourCommunity/MBFinancialCharitableFoundation/tabid/171/Default.aspx

Establishment information: Established in 2006 in IL.
Donor: MB Financial Bank, N.A.
Contact: Vicky Arroyo, Pres.
Financial data (yr. ended 12/31/11): Assets, $2,349,810 (M); gifts received, $3,815; expenditures, $574,704; qualifying distributions, $546,782; giving activities include $546,782 for grants.
Purpose and activities: The foundation supports organizations involved with preservation, health, mental health, housing, human services, community economic development, and civic affairs. Special emphasis is directed toward programs designed to serve low- and moderate-income communities and households.
Fields of interest: Historic preservation/historical societies; Health care; Mental health/crisis services; Housing/shelter, development; Housing/shelter, rehabilitation; Housing/shelter; Family services; Human services, financial counseling; Human services; Community development, neighborhood development; Community development, business promotion; Community development, small businesses; Community/economic development; Public affairs Economically disadvantaged.
Programs:
Civic and Community: The foundation supports civic organizations designed to address neighborhood development, preservation, and local social issues.
Education: The foundation supports programs designed to enhance financial security of households; promote small business entrepreneurship skill development; and promote educational initiatives that benefit low- and moderate-income households.
Health and Human Services: The foundation supports programs designed to serve at-risk children and families; and promote medical and mental health treatment and research.
Housing and Economic Development: The foundation supports programs designed to rehabilitate or construct affordable housing; and community-based efforts designed to stimulate business activity and growth.
Type of support: General/operating support; Program development.
Geographic limitations: Giving primarily in the areas of company operations, with emphasis on the greater Chicagoland area, IL.
Support limitations: No support for religious or fraternal organizations (unless for a secular project of benefit to the entire community). No grants to individuals, or for dinner or galas tickets, golf fees, membership dues, publicity or advertising.
Application information: Applications accepted. Application form not required. Applicants should submit the following:
1) copy of IRS Determination Letter
2) copy of most recent annual report/audited financial statement/990
3) listing of board of directors, trustees, officers and other key people and their affiliations
4) detailed description of project and amount of funding requested
5) copy of current year's organizational budget and/or project budget
6) listing of additional sources and amount of support

Initial approach: Proposal
Deadline(s): None

Officers: Vicky Arroyo, Pres.; Lesly Flores, Secy.; Patricia Basan, Treas.
EIN: 203216854
Selected grants: The following grants are a representative sample of this grantmaker's funding activity:
$10,900 to ACCION Chicago, Chicago, IL, 2010.
$5,910 to Chicago Family Health Center, Chicago, IL, 2010.
$5,000 to DePaul University, Chicago, IL, 2010.
$5,000 to Local Initiatives Support Corporation, New York, NY, 2010.
$4,500 to Young Life, Colorado Springs, CO, 2010.
$2,500 to Chicago Center for Torah and Chesed, Chicago, IL, 2010.
$1,500 to Crohns and Colitis Foundation of America, New York, NY, 2010.
$1,000 to 100 Black Men of Chicago, Chicago, IL, 2010.

$1,000 to Chicago Anti-Hunger Federation, Chicago, IL, 2010.
$1,000 to Ronald McDonald House Charities, Oak Brook, IL, 2010.

2416
MBIA Insurance Corporation

113 King St., Ste. 13
Armonk, NY 10504-1611 (914) 273-4545

Company URL: http://www.mbia.com
Establishment information: Established in 1967.
Company type: Subsidiary of a public company
Business activities: Sells financial guarantee insurance.
Business type (SIC): Insurance/surety
Financial profile for 2011: Number of employees, 382; assets, $26,873,000,000; sales volume, $1,557,000,000; liabilities, $9,883,000,000
Corporate officers: Daniel P. Kaerney, Chair.; Clifford D. Corso, Co-C.E.O. and C.I.O.; Jay Brown, Co-C.E.O.; C. Edward Chaplin, Co-Pres., C.A.O., and C.F.O.; William C. Fallon, Co-Pres. and C.O.O.
Board of directors: Daniel P. Kearney, Chair.; Jay Brown; Maryann Bruce; David A. Coulter; Steven J. Gilbert; Kewsong Lee; Theodore Shasta; Richard C. Vaughan
Giving statement: Giving through the MBIA Foundation, Inc.

MBIA Foundation, Inc.

113 King St.
Armonk, NY 10504-1611 (914) 765-3834
E-mail: Jean.McGovern@mbia.com; Additional tel.: (914) 273-4545; URL: http://www.mbia.com/about/about_foundation.html

Establishment information: Established in 2001 in NY.
Donors: Optinuity Alliance Resources Corporation; MBIA Insurance Corp.; John Caouette; Francie Heller; Kathleen Okenica; Kevin D. Silva; Kutak Rock LLP; Richard L. Weil; Moody's Corp.
Contact: Jean McGovern, Secy.
Financial data (yr. ended 12/31/11): Assets, $8,913,621 (M); gifts received, $2,814,628; expenditures, $2,187,050; qualifying distributions, $2,118,416; giving activities include $2,118,416 for grants.
Purpose and activities: The foundation supports programs designed to serve children and families through education; health services; and human services.
Fields of interest: Museums; Arts; Elementary school/education; Higher education; Law school/education; Education; Health care; Diabetes; Medical research; Food banks; Family services; Family services, parent education; Human services; Community/economic development; Christian agencies & churches; Religion Children.
Programs:

Education: The foundation supports programs designed to serve children and their developmental needs; provide materials and transportation; encourage parent involvement; help children stay in school; promote children's education beyond the classroom; and foster life-long learning.

Health Services: The foundation supports programs designed to promote research, education, and awareness of particular diseases or health related risks. The foundation also supports programs designed to enhance the care and quality of life of the sick, disabled, and their caregivers.

Human Services: The foundation supports programs designed to provide food and shelter to benefit entire families.

Type of support: Building/renovation; Continuing support; Employee matching gifts; Employee volunteer services; Program development; Sponsorships.
Geographic limitations: Giving primarily in areas of company operations, with emphasis on CT, NJ, NY, and PA.
Support limitations: No support for discriminatory organizations, political or lobbying organizations, religious, fraternal, athletic, social, or veterans' organizations not of direct benefit to the entire community, or umbrella agencies such as the United Way. No grants to individuals, or for general operating support, fundraising activities related to individual sponsorship, capital campaigns, endowments, or fundraising events.
Publications: Application guidelines.
Application information: Applications accepted. A site visit may be requested. Organizations receiving support are asked to submit a post grant evaluation report. Application form required. Applicants should submit the following:
1) timetable for implementation and evaluation of project
2) qualifications of key personnel
3) statement of problem project will address
4) population served
5) copy of IRS Determination Letter
6) brief history of organization and description of its mission
7) copy of most recent annual report/audited financial statement/990
8) how project's results will be evaluated or measured
9) listing of board of directors, trustees, officers and other key people and their affiliations
10) detailed description of project and amount of funding requested
11) copy of current year's organizational budget and/or project budget
12) listing of additional sources and amount of support

Initial approach: Contact foundation for application form
Deadline(s): Nov. 26

Officers and Directors:* Chuck Chaplin*, Chair.; Williard Hill*, Pres.; Jean McGovern*, Secy.; Joseph Buonadonna*, Treas.; Cliff Corso; Bill Fallon; Gail Makode; Rich McKay; Mitchell Sonkin; Susan A. Voltz.
EIN: 134163899
Selected grants: The following grants are a representative sample of this grantmaker's funding activity:
$40,000 to Christian Brothers Conference, Washington, DC, 2010.
$40,000 to CPA Endowment Fund of Illinois, Chicago, IL, 2010.
$40,000 to DePaul University, Chicago, IL, 2010.
$36,000 to Syracuse University, College of Law, Syracuse, NY, 2010.
$14,000 to ETA Creative Arts Foundation, Chicago, IL, 2010.
$10,000 to Chicago Childrens Museum, Chicago, IL, 2010.
$10,000 to Scarsdale Synagogue, Scarsdale, NY, 2010.
$6,180 to Church of the Epiphany, New York, NY, 2010.
$5,000 to Hubbard Street Dance Chicago, Chicago, IL, 2010.
$4,000 to Nebraska Wesleyan University, Lincoln, NE, 2010.

2417
McAfee, Inc.

(formerly Networks Associates, Inc.)
2821 Mission College Blvd.
Santa Clara, CA 95054 (972) 963-8000

Company URL: http://www.nai.com
Establishment information: Established in 1989.
Company type: Subsidiary of a public company
Business activities: Develops, markets, distributes, and supports computer security solutions.
Business type (SIC): Computer services
Financial profile for 2010: Number of employees, 6,300; assets, $4,232,400,000; sales volume, $2,064,800,000
Corporate officers: Renee J. James, Chair.; David G. DeWalt, Pres. and C.E.O.; Jonathan Chadwick, Exec. V.P. and C.F.O.; Mark Cochran, Exec. V.P. and Genl. Counsel; Bryan Reed Barney, Exec. V.P., Opers.; Michael DeCesare, Exec. V.P., Sales; Joseph Gabbert, Exec. V.P., Human Resources; Keith Krzeminski, Sr. V.P., Finance, and C.A.O.
Board of directors: Renne J. James, Chair.; Carl Bass; Thomas Darcy; Leslie G. Denend; David DeWalt; Jeffrey A. Miller; Lorrie M. Norrington; Denis J. O'Leary; Robert Pangia; Anthony Zingale
Plants: Birmingham, AL; Phoenix, AZ; San Diego, Santa Clara, CA; Englewood, CO; Miami, FL; Atlanta, GA; Oakbrook Terrace, IL; Overland Park, KS; Edgewood, KY; Wakefield, MA; Minnetonka, MN; Chesterfield, MO; Hazlet, NJ; Rockville Centre, NY; Davidson, NC; Dayton, OH; Portland, OR; Carrollton, Houston, TX; Alexandria, VA; Bellevue, WA
Giving statement: Giving through the McAfee, Inc. Corporate Giving Program.
Company EIN: 770316593

McAfee, Inc. Corporate Giving Program

(formerly Networks Associates, Inc. Corporate Giving Program)
2821 Mission College Blvd.
Santa Clara, CA 95054-1838
Application address for Initiative to Fight Cybercrime: Silicon Valley Community Foundation, 2440 West El Camino Real, Ste. 300, Mountain View, CA 94040, tel.: (650) 450-5400; URL: http://www.mcafee.com/us/about/corporate-citizenship/index.aspx

Purpose and activities: McAfee makes charitable contributions to nonprofit organizations involved with fighting cybercrime. Support is given on a national and international basis.
Fields of interest: Crime/violence prevention; Crime/law enforcement; Computer science.
Program:

Initiative to Fight Cybercrime Grants Program: Through the Initiative to Fight Cybercrime Grants Program, McAfee awards grants from $20,000 to $40,000 to nonprofit organizations involved with fighting, researching, or educating about cybercrime or similar issues.

Type of support: Donated products; Employee matching gifts; Employee volunteer services; General/operating support; Program development.
Geographic limitations: Giving on a national and international basis.
Application information: Applications accepted. Contributions are limited to 1 contribution per organization during any given year. Application form required. Applicants should submit the following:
1) timetable for implementation and evaluation of project
2) results expected from proposed grant
3) qualifications of key personnel

4) statement of problem project will address
5) population served
6) name, address and phone number of organization
7) copy of IRS Determination Letter
8) brief history of organization and description of its mission
9) geographic area to be served
10) how project's results will be evaluated or measured
11) detailed description of project and amount of funding requested
12) contact person
13) copy of current year's organizational budget and/or project budget
Initial approach: Download application form and mail to Silicon Valley Community Foundation
Committee meeting date(s): Quarterly
Final notification: 6 weeks

2418
McBride & Son Homes, Inc.

(also known as McBride & Son Enterprises, Inc.)
1 McBride & Son Dr., Ste. 1
Chesterfield, MO 63005-1425
(636) 537-2000

Company URL: http://www.mcbridehomes.com
Establishment information: Established in 1946.
Company type: Private company
Business activities: Operates holding company; provides construction services.
Business type (SIC): Holding company; contractors/general residential building; contractors/general nonresidential building
Financial profile for 2010: Number of employees, 5
Corporate officers: John F. Eilermann, Jr., Co-Pres.; Ted Dettmer, Co-Pres.; John Eilermann, C.E.O.; David Marxkors, C.O.O.; Michael Arri, C.F.O.
Giving statement: Giving through the Joseph & Elsie McBride Charitable Foundation, Inc.

Joseph & Elsie McBride Charitable Foundation, Inc.

16091 Swingley Ridge Rd., Ste. 300
Chesterfield, MO 63017 (636) 537-2000

Establishment information: Established in 1984 in MO.
Donors: McBride & Son; Richard McBride.
Financial data (yr. ended 04/30/12): Assets, $25,999 (M); gifts received, $7,830; expenditures, $29,487; qualifying distributions, $29,487; giving activities include $24,806 for 3 grants (high: $16,530; low: $1,743).
Purpose and activities: The foundation supports organizations involved with education, health, food, human services, and Christianity.
Fields of interest: Housing/shelter; Human services; Religion.
Type of support: Equipment; General/operating support; Scholarship funds.
Application information: Applications accepted. Application form required.
Initial approach: Proposal
Deadline(s): None
Officers: Mary Hutchison, Pres.; Ben Ford, V.P.; Patricia Kiehl, Secy.; Denise Higgins, Treas.
Board Members: Michael Arri; John F. Eilermann, Jr.
Number of staff: 1 full-time support.
EIN: 431353387

2419
Mccar Development Corporation

(doing business as MDC Homes)
11525 Parks Woods Cir.
Alpharetta, GA 30005 (770) 206-9100

Establishment information: Established in 1956.
Company type: Private company
Business activities: Operates residential construction company.
Business type (SIC): Contractors/general residential building
Corporate officer: Keith McSwain, Pres. and C.E.O.
Giving statement: Giving through the Tennessee Walking Horse National Foundation, Inc.

Tennessee Walking Horse National Foundation, Inc.

(formerly Tennessee Walking Horse Foundation, Inc.)
P.O. Box 1010
Shelbyville, TN 37162-1010 (931) 684-5915
Application Address: c/o 1110 Evans St., Shelbyville, TN 37160

Establishment information: Established in 1999 in TN; 2005 became an independent foundation.
Donors: McCar Development Corp.; Robert Pollack; John Harmon Family Foundation.
Contact: Doyle Meadows, C.E.O.
Financial data (yr. ended 12/31/11): Assets, $35,815 (M); gifts received, $74,000; expenditures, $70,537; qualifying distributions, $70,500; giving activities include $70,500 for grants.
Purpose and activities: The foundation supports the activities of the Tennessee Walking Horse Museum and Hall of Fame.
Fields of interest: Museums (sports/hobby).
Type of support: General/operating support.
Geographic limitations: Giving primarily in TN.
Support limitations: No grants to individuals.
Application information: Applications accepted. Application form required. Applicants should submit the following:
1) detailed description of project and amount of funding requested
2) name, address and phone number of organization
Initial approach: Letter
Deadline(s): None
Officers: Charles McDonald, Chair.; D.B. Nelson, Jr., Vice-Chair.; Doyle Meadows, C.E.O.; Pat Marsh, Secy.; Henry Hulan, Treas.
Directors: James Allison; John T. Bobo; David L. Howard.
EIN: 581463835

2420
Mccar Homes-Raleigh, LLC

(doing business as McCar Realty, Inc.)
4125 Old Milton Pkwy.
Alpharetta, GA 30005-4443
(770) 206-9100
FAX: (770) 225-2967

Establishment information: Established in 2007.
Company type: Private company
Business activities: Constructs single family homes.
Business type (SIC): Contractors/general residential building
Corporate officers: Keith McSwain, Pres. and C.E.O.; Steve Roberts, C.F.O.; Kathy Ellis, V.P., Human Resources
Giving statement: Giving through the MDC Today Family Foundation.

The MDC Today Family Foundation

4125 Old Milton Pkwy.
Alpharetta, GA 30005-4443

Establishment information: Established in 2006 in GA.
Donor: McCar Homes, Inc.
Financial data (yr. ended 12/31/09): Assets, $172,382 (M); gifts received, $235,934; expenditures, $90,787; qualifying distributions, $79,650; giving activities include $79,650 for 3 grants (high: $55,000; low: $9,650).
Fields of interest: Education; Human services.
Type of support: General/operating support.
Geographic limitations: Giving primarily in GA.
Support limitations: No grants to individuals.
Application information: Applications not accepted. Unsolicited requests for funds not accepted.
Trustee: D. Jay McSwain; Keith McSwain.
EIN: 204009968

2421
McCarthy Bush Corporation

5401 Victoria Ave., Ste. 1
Davenport, IA 52807-2991 (563) 359-0500

Company URL: http://www.mccarthybushcorp.com/
Establishment information: Established in 1995.
Company type: Private company
Business activities: Provides general contract highway and street construction services.
Business type (SIC): Construction/highway and street (except elevated)
Financial profile for 2010: Number of employees, 450
Corporate officers: Jack Bush, Co-Chair.; John L. Bush, Co-Chair.; Gregory J. Bush, C.E.O.; Frank McCarthy, C.F.O.
Board of directors: Jack Bush, Co-Chair.; John L. Bush, Co-Chair.
Subsidiaries: Linwood Mining & Minerals Corp., Davenport, IA; McCarthy Improvement Co., Davenport, IA; McCarthy-Bush Inc., Davenport, IA; Tri-State Transport Inc., Davenport, IA
Giving statement: Giving through the McCarthy/Bush Foundation.

McCarthy/Bush Foundation

5401 Victoria Ave.
Davenport, IA 52807-3932

Establishment information: Established in 1989 in IA.
Donors: McCarthy Bush Corp.; John L. Bush; McCarthy Improvement Co.; Linwood Mining & Minerals Corp.
Financial data (yr. ended 12/31/11): Assets, $795 (M); gifts received, $223,000; expenditures, $219,121; qualifying distributions, $200,620; giving activities include $200,620 for grants.
Purpose and activities: The foundation supports organizations involved with arts and culture, education, school athletics, human services, and religion.
Fields of interest: Museums; Performing arts; Performing arts, music; Arts; Secondary school/education; Higher education; Education; Athletics/

sports, school programs; YM/YWCAs & YM/YWHAs; Family services; Human services; United Ways and Federated Giving Programs; Christian agencies & churches; Catholic agencies & churches; Religion.
Type of support: General/operating support.
Geographic limitations: Giving primarily in Davenport, IA.
Support limitations: No grants to individuals.
Application information: Applications not accepted. Contributes only to pre-selected organizations.
Officer: Patricia M. Bush, Pres.
Trustees: Barbara J. Johnson; Mary Walsh.
EIN: 421322400

2422
The McClatchy Company

2100 "Q" St.
Sacramento, CA 95816 (916) 321-1846
FAX: (302) 655-5049

Company URL: http://www.mcclatchy.com
Establishment information: Established in 1857.
Company type: Public company
Company ticker symbol and exchange: MNI/NYSE
Business activities: Publishes newspapers.
Business type (SIC): Newspaper publishing and/or printing
Financial profile for 2012: Number of employees, 7,400; assets, $3,005,130,000; sales volume, $1,230,720,000; pre-tax net income, -$21,530,000; expenses, $1,133,020,000; liabilities, $2,962,630,000
Corporate officers: Gary B. Pruitt, Chair.; Elaine Lintecum, V.P., Finace and C.F.O.; Patrick J. Talamantes, Pres. and C.E.O.; Karole Morgan-Prager, V.P., Genl. Counsel, and Secy.; Robert J. Weil, V.P., Opers.; Mark Zeiman, V.P., Opers.; Heather L. Fagundes, V.P., Human Resources
Board of directors: Kevin McClatchy, Chair.; Elizabeth A. Ballantine; Leroy Barnes, Jr.; Molly Maloney Evangelisti; Kathleen Foley Feldstein; Brown McClatchy Maloney; Theodore R. Mitchell; William B. McClatchy; S. Donley Ritchey; Frederick R. Ruiz; Patrick J. Talamantes
Subsidiaries: McClatchy Newspapers, Inc., Sacramento, CA; The Star Tribune Company, Minneapolis, MN; Tacoma News, Inc., Tacoma, WA
Historic mergers: Knight-Ridder, Inc. (June 27, 2006)
Giving statement: Giving through the McClatchy Company Foundation.
Company EIN: 522080478

McClatchy Company Foundation

(formerly Star Tribune Foundation)
2100 "Q" St.
Sacramento, CA 95816-6816 (916) 321-1844

Establishment information: Incorporated in 1945 in MN.
Donors: Cowles Media Co.; The Star Tribune Co.; The McClatchy Co.
Contact: Karole Morgan-Prager, Dir.
Financial data (yr. ended 12/31/11): Assets, $6,749,876 (M); expenditures, $401,139; qualifying distributions, $386,905; giving activities include $386,905 for grants.
Purpose and activities: The foundation supports hospitals and organizations involved with arts and culture, education, mental health, children's services, the first amendment, and Judaism.
Fields of interest: Media, print publishing; Visual arts; Museums (art); Arts; Higher education; Education; Hospitals (general); Mental health/crisis services; Children, services; Civil liberties, first amendment; United Ways and Federated Giving Programs; Jewish agencies & synagogues.
Type of support: Annual campaigns; Capital campaigns; Conferences/seminars; Continuing support; Employee matching gifts; Employee volunteer services; Endowments; General/operating support; Matching/challenge support; Program development; Scholarship funds.
Geographic limitations: Giving primarily in CA; giving also to national organizations.
Application information: Applications accepted. Application form required.
Initial approach: Contact foundation for application form
Board meeting date(s): Quarterly
Deadline(s): None
Officer and Directors:* Patrick J. Talamantes*, Treas.; Heather L. Fagundes; Karole Morgan-Prager; Gary B. Pruitt; Howard Weaver; Robert J. Weil.
Number of staff: 1 full-time professional; 1 part-time support.
EIN: 416031373
Selected grants: The following grants are a representative sample of this grantmaker's funding activity:
$100,000 to Stanford University, Stanford, CA, 2009.
$10,000 to American Jewish Committee, New York, NY, 2009.
$2,000 to Native American Journalists Association, Norman, OK, 2009.

2423
McCormick & Company, Inc.

18 Loveton Cir.
P.O. Box 6000
Sparks, MD 21152-9202 (410) 771-7301

Company URL: http://www.mccormickcorporation.com
Establishment information: Established in 1889.
Company type: Public company
Company ticker symbol and exchange: MKC/NYSE
Business activities: Produces, markets, and distributes spices, herbs, seasonings, and other food flavors.
Financial profile for 2012: Assets, $4,200,000,000; sales volume, $4,000,000,000
Fortune 1000 ranking: 2012—588th in revenues, 391st in profits, and 649th in assets
Forbes 2000 ranking: 2012—1515th in sales, 1190th in profits, and 1866th in assets
Corporate officers: Alan D. Wilson, Chair., Pres., and C.E.O.; Gordon M. Stetz, Exec. V.P. and C.F.O.; Kenneth A. Kelly, Jr., Sr. V.P. and Cont.; W. Geoffrey Carpenter, V.P., Genl. Counsel, and Secy.
Board of directors: Alan D. Wilson, Chair.; John P. Bilbrey; James T. Brady; J. Michael Fitzpatrick; Freeman A. Hrabowski III; Patricia Little; Michael D. Mangan; Margaret Mary V. Preston; George A. Roche; Gordon M. Stetz; William E. Stevens
Divisions: Food Service Div., Hunt Valley, MD; Frito Worldwide Div., Hunt Valley, MD; Global Restaurant Div., Hunt Valley, MD; McCormick Flavor Div., Hunt Valley, MD; U.S. Consumer Products Div., Hunt Valley, MD
Joint Ventures: McCormick Fresh Herbs, LLC, Commerce, CA; Signature Brands, LLC, Ocala, FL; SupHerb Farms, Turlock, CA
International operations: Australia; Canada; Cayman Islands; China; Cyprus; El Salvador; England; France; Mexico; Scotland; Singapore; South Africa; Switzerland
Giving statement: Giving through the McCormick & Company, Inc. Corporate Giving Program.
Company EIN: 520408290

McCormick & Company, Inc. Corporate Giving Program

c/o The Charitable Donations Comm.
18 Loveton Cir.
Sparks, MD 21152-6000 (410) 771-7301
URL: http://www.mccormickcorporation.com/Community-Involvement.aspx

Purpose and activities: McCormick makes charitable contributions to nonprofit organizations involved with education, health, human services, food banks, and civic projects. Emphasis is given to organizations with McCormick representation on their boards of directors. Support is given primarily in areas of company operations, and to national organizations.
Fields of interest: Museums; Higher education, college; Education; Hospitals (general); Health care; Food banks; Children, services; Human services; Community/economic development; Public affairs.
Programs:
Community Service Award: In 2004, the company created the McCormick Community Service Award. To recognize those employees who best exemplify McCormick's commitment to communities, employees are nominated from around the world. Annually a grand prize winner is awarded $25,000 to give to his or her charity of choice. Four runners-up are awarded $5,000 each for their charity of choice.
Unsung Heroes Award Program: The McCormick Unsung Heroes Award program honors Baltimore-area high school seniors who have been Unsung Heroes of their school sports teams. They are honored for demonstrating high character and sportsmanship and are held up as role models for their peers. Two top Unsung Heroes are selected each year to receive a college scholarship valued at $36,000 each over four years. Over the years, the program has honored thousands of young men and women and given out approximately $1.5 million in college scholarships.
Type of support: Building/renovation; Capital campaigns; Employee matching gifts; Employee volunteer services; General/operating support; In-kind gifts; Scholarship funds.
Geographic limitations: Giving primarily in areas of company operations, and to national organizations.
Support limitations: No support for fraternal, veterans', labor, religious, sectarian, political, or lobbying organizations, elementary or secondary schools, or organizations that might pose a conflict with the company's goals, products, or employees. No grants to individuals, or for travel, or promotional activities.
Publications: Application guidelines.
Application information: Applications accepted. The Charitable Donations Committee handles giving. Proposals are limited to one request per organization in any given year. Proposals should be limited to one page. A personal or phone interview may be required for consideration. Application form not required. Applicants should submit the following:
1) name, address and phone number of organization
2) copy of IRS Determination Letter
3) brief history of organization and description of its mission
4) copy of most recent annual report/audited financial statement/990
5) explanation of why grantmaker is considered an appropriate donor for project
6) listing of board of directors, trustees, officers and other key people and their affiliations

7) detailed description of project and amount of funding requested
8) contact person
9) copy of current year's organizational budget and/ or project budget

Proposals should be addressed to the Chairman of the Charitable Donations Committee. They should include key deadline dates, program or project needs, goals, and objectives.
Initial approach: Proposal to headquarters
Copies of proposal: 1

2424
McDermott Incorporated

777 N. Eldridge Pkwy.
Houston, TX 77079 (281) 870-5000

Company URL: http://www.mcdermott.com
Establishment information: Established in 1946.
Company type: Subsidiary of a foreign company
Company ticker symbol and exchange: MDR/NYSE
Business activities: Provides marine construction services; manufactures nuclear components; mines uranium; provides management consulting services; manufactures power generation systems.
Business type (SIC): Metal products/structural; mining/uranium, radium, vanadium, and other miscellaneous metal; oil and gas field services; engines and turbines; ship and boat building and repair; management and public relations services
Corporate officers: Bruce W. Wilkinson, Chair. and C.E.O.; Bob Deason, Pres. and C.O.O.; Francis S. Kalman, Exec. V.P. and C.F.O.; Louis J. Sannino, Exec. V.P., Human Resources
Board of director: Bruce W. Wilkinson, Chair.
International operations: Azerbaijan; Canada; China; Denmark; Indonesia; Mexico; Singapore; United Arab Emirates
Giving statement: Giving through the McDermott Incorporated Corporate Giving Program.

McDermott Incorporated Corporate Giving Program

777 N. Eldridge Pkwy.
Houston, TX 77079

Contact: Louis J. Sannino, Exec. V.P., Human Resources
Financial data (yr. ended 12/31/07): Total giving, $465,600, including $465,600 for grants.
Purpose and activities: McDermott makes charitable contributions to nonprofit organizations involved with arts and culture, education, the environment, human services, and civic affairs. Support is given primarily in areas of company operations.
Fields of interest: Arts; Education; Environment; Human services; Public affairs.
Type of support: Annual campaigns; Capital campaigns; Employee volunteer services; Employee-related scholarships; General/operating support; Loaned talent; Program development; Research; Scholarship funds; Scholarships—to individuals.
Geographic limitations: Giving primarily in areas of company operations, with emphasis on Morgan City and New Orleans, LA, West Point, MS, Akron, Alliance, Barberton, Copley, and Lancaster, OH, Houston and Paris, TX, and Lynchburg, VA.
Support limitations: No support for political or religious organizations, secondary schools, or United Way-supported organizations. No grants for advertising.
Publications: Program policy statement.
Application information: Applications accepted. The Human Resources Department handles giving. Application form not required. Applicants should submit the following:
1) detailed description of project and amount of funding requested
Initial approach: Proposal to headquarters
Copies of proposal: 1
Final notification: Following review

Contributions Committee: Kevin A. Blasini, Dir., Human Resources; Louis J. Sannino, Exec. V.P., Human Resources; Bruce Wilkinson, Chair. and C.E.O.; Tom Henzler, V.P., Corp. Compliance Off.
Number of staff: 3 full-time professional.

2425
McDermott, Will & Emery

227 W. Monroe St., Ste. 400
Chicago, IL 60606-5096 (312) 984-7755

Company URL: http://www.mwe.com
Establishment information: Established in 1934.
Company type: Private company
Business activities: Operates law firm.
Business type (SIC): Legal services
Offices: Irvine, Los Angeles, Menlo Park, CA; Washington, DC; Miami, FL; Chicago, IL; Boston, MA; New York, NY; Houston, TX
International operations: Belgium; China; France; Germany; Italy; United Kingdom
Giving statement: Giving through the McDermott, Will & Emery Pro Bono Program.

McDermott, Will & Emery Pro Bono Program

227 W. Monroe St., Ste. 400
Chicago, IL 60606-5096 (312) 984-7755
E-mail: lhkeith@mwe.com; Additional tel.: (312) 372-2000; URL: http://www.mwe.com/info/probono/services.html

Contact: Latonia Haney Keith, Pro Bono & Comm. Svc. Counsel
Fields of interest: Legal services.
Type of support: Pro bono services - legal.
Geographic limitations: Giving primarily in areas of company operations in Irvine, Los Angeles, and Menlo Park, CA, Washington, DC, Miami, FL, Chicago, IL, Boston, MA, New York, NY, Houston, TX, and in Belgium, China, France, Germany, Italy, and United Kingdom.
Application information: A Pro Bono Committee manages the pro bono program.

2426
A. Y. McDonald Industries, Inc.

4800 Chavenelle Rd.
P.O. Box 508
Dubuque, IA 52002-2631 (563) 583-7311

Company URL: http://www.aymcdonald.com
Establishment information: Established in 1856.
Company type: Private company
Business activities: Manufactures brass plumbing equipment, plumbing valves, pumps and water systems, and high pressure gas valves and meter bars.
Business type (SIC): Metal plumbing fixtures and heating equipment/nonelectric; metal products/fabricated; machinery/industrial and commercial
Financial profile for 2010: Number of employees, 364
Corporate officers: Roy Sherman, Chair.; Rob McDonald, Pres. and C.E.O.
Board of directors: Roy Sherman, Chair.; Rob McDonald
Giving statement: Giving through the A. Y. McDonald Manufacturing Company Charitable Foundation.

A. Y. McDonald Manufacturing Company Charitable Foundation

P.O. Box 508
Dubuque, IA 52004-0508

Establishment information: Established in 1967 in IA.
Donor: A.Y. McDonald Industries, Inc.
Financial data (yr. ended 12/31/11): Assets, $3,769,879 (M); gifts received, $325,000; expenditures, $367,125; qualifying distributions, $363,094; giving activities include $363,094 for 71 grants (high: $37,000; low: $100).
Purpose and activities: The foundation supports orchestras and recreation centers and organizations involved with education, health, medical research, and human services.
Fields of interest: Performing arts, orchestras; Higher education; Libraries (public); Education; Health care, clinics/centers; Health care, patient services; Health care; Medical research; Recreation, centers; Boys & girls clubs; Youth development, business; Children/youth, services; Human services; United Ways and Federated Giving Programs.
Type of support: Capital campaigns; General/operating support; Program development.
Geographic limitations: Giving primarily in eastern IA, with emphasis on Dubuque.
Support limitations: No grants to individuals.
Application information: Applications not accepted. Contributes only to pre-selected organizations.
Officers: Mike McDonald, Pres.; Scott Knapp, V.P.; J. M. McDonald III, V.P.; R. D. McDonald II, V.P.; L. J. Sherman, V.P.; Sarah Hasken, Secy.
EIN: 426119514
Selected grants: The following grants are a representative sample of this grantmaker's funding activity:
$1,000 to American Cancer Society, Atlanta, GA, 2010.

2427
McDonald's Corporation

(doing business as McDonald's)
1 McDonald's Plz.
Oak Brook, IL 60523 (630) 623-3000
FAX: (302) 636-5454

Company URL: http://www.mcdonalds.com
Establishment information: Established in 1940.
Company type: Public company
Company ticker symbol and exchange: MCD/NYSE
Business activities: Develops, operates, and franchises quick-service restaurants.
Business type (SIC): Restaurants and drinking places; investors/miscellaneous
Financial profile for 2012: Number of employees, 440,000; assets, $35,386,500,000; sales volume, $27,567,000,000; pre-tax net income, $8,079,000,000; expenses, $18,962,400,000; liabilities, $20,092,900,000
Fortune 1000 ranking: 2012—111th in revenues, 37th in profits, and 159th in assets

Forbes 2000 ranking: 2012—342nd in sales, 106th in profits, and 635th in assets
Corporate officers: Andrew J. McKenna, Chair.; Don Thompson, Pres. and C.E.O.; Tim Fenton, C.O.O.; Peter J. Bensen, Exec. V.P. and C.F.O.; Gloria Santona, Exec. V.P., Genl. Counsel, and Secy.
Board of directors: Andrew J. McKenna, Chair.; Susan E. Arnold; Robert A. Eckert; Enrique Hernandez, Jr.; Jeanne P. Jackson; Richard H. Lenny; Walter E. Massey; Cary D. McMillan; Sheila A. Penrose; John W. Rogers, Jr.; Roger W. Stone; Donald Thompson; Miles D. White
Subsidiary: Boston Market Corp., Golden, CO
International operations: Australia; Austria; Brazil; Canada; China; Denmark; France; Germany; Hong Kong; Mexico; Netherlands; New Zealand; Poland; Portugal; Russia; Spain; Sweden; Switzerland; Taiwan; United Kingdom
Giving statement: Giving through the McDonald's Corporation Contributions Program, the McDonald's Family Charity, Inc., and the Ronald McDonald House Charities.
Company EIN: 362361282

McDonald's Corporation Contributions Program

2111 McDonald's Dr.
Oak Brook, IL 60523-5500
URL: http://www.aboutmcdonalds.com/mcd/csr/about/community.html

Purpose and activities: As a complement to its foundation, McDonald's also makes charitable contributions to nonprofit organizations directly. Support is given on a national and international basis in areas of company operations.
Fields of interest: Disasters, preparedness/services; Athletics/sports, amateur leagues.
Type of support: Employee volunteer services; General/operating support; In-kind gifts.
Geographic limitations: Giving on a national and international basis in areas of company operations.

McDonald's Family Charity, Inc.

1 Kroc Dr.
Oak Brook, IL 60523-2275 (630) 623-1584

Establishment information: Established in 2000 in IL.
Contact: Martin J. Coyne, Jr., Pres.
Financial data (yr. ended 12/31/11): Revenue, $295,769; assets, $243,744 (M); gifts received, $295,769; expenditures, $244,090; program services expenses, $234,378; giving activities include $152,475 for 224 grants to individuals.
Purpose and activities: The charity provides individual assistance to persons who have been personally impacted by major natural disasters worldwide; individuals eligible for the assistance include employees working at any McDonald's and subsidiaries' restaurants and offices worldwide, as well as employees of McDonald's suppliers.
Fields of interest: Safety/disasters; Human services, emergency aid.
Type of support: Grants to individuals.
Officers and Trustees:* Martin J. Coyne, Jr.*, Pres.; Donald Horwitz*, V.P. and Secy.; Joseph P. Tylutki*, V.P. and Treas.; G. Lowell Dixon; Kenneth Norgan; Theodore Perlman.
EIN: 364381203

Ronald McDonald House Charities

(formerly Ronald McDonald Children's Charities)
1 Kroc Dr.
Oak Brook, IL 60523-2275 (630) 623-7048
FAX: (630) 623-7488; URL: http://www.rmhc.org
Scholarship address: RMHC U.S. Scholarship Program, International Scholarship and Tuition Services, Inc., P.O. Box 22376, Nashville, TN 37202-2376

Establishment information: Established in 1984 in IL in memory of Ray A. Kroc, founder of McDonald's Corp.
Contact: Jennifer Smith, Dir., Comms.
Financial data (yr. ended 12/31/11): Revenue, $37,743,256; assets, $122,101,567 (M); gifts received, $32,422,531; expenditures, $28,895,758; giving activities include $17,801,303 for grants and $375,000 for grants to individuals.
Purpose and activities: The organization creates, finds, and supports programs that directly improve the health and well being of children and their families around the world.
Fields of interest: Education; Health care; Health organizations; Medical research, institute; Children/youth, services; Youth, services; Child development, services Children/youth; Children.
Programs:
Awards of Excellence: These awards recognize individual efforts that have improved children's lives. The achievements of a physician who has made an outstanding contribution in the field of health care, and those of an individual who has done the same for the general well-being of children, are honored with a $100,000 grant to be given to the nonprofit children's organization identified by the recipient.
Global Grants: Grants are available to nonprofit, tax-exempt organizations whose national or global programs help improve the health and well-being of children. Eligible organizations should have a specific program that addresses a significant funding gap or critical opportunity, has long-term impact in terms of replication or reach, and produces measurable results. Priority is given to organizations whose project methodology uses a comprehensive ethnographic approach toward research, program development, program implementation, and/or evaluation. Projects must also include a sustainable train-the-trainer approach to their methodology and demonstrate quantifiable outcomes as they increase access to care for children.
Ronald McDonald Care Mobile Program: The program maintains a fleet of state-of-the-art vehicles that deliver cost-effective medical, dental, and education services directly to underserved children in their own neighborhoods. The vehicles are equipped with telemedicine capabilities that can transmit images and provide remote consultations, video conferencing, and medical/surgical follow-up. The vehicle accommodates two patient examination rooms, a laboratory, and a pharmacy. The mobile provides a number of medical and dental services, including primary care, specialty care, blood collection, diagnosis, treatment, referral, follow-up for serious medical conditions, health education, and federally-assisted health insurance program enrollment.
Ronald McDonald Family Room Program: These rooms provide a haven within the hospital for the families of children undergoing treatment. The family room serves as a place of respite for family members to step away from the stressful hospital environment. Designed to reflect a comfortable environment, many families use the family room to rest and reflect.
Ronald McDonald House Program: This program provides a 'home away from home' for families of seriously ill children receiving treatment at nearby hospitals. The house provides a comfortable, supportive lodging alternative for these families. It serves as a temporary residence near the medical facility where family members can sleep, eat, relax and find support from other families in similar situations. In return, families are asked to make a donation ranging on average from $5 to $20 per day, but if that isn't possible, their stay is free.
Scholarships: Scholarships to high school seniors who have demonstrated academic achievement, leadership, and community involvement. Eligible applicants must: live in an area where there is a participating local organization chapter; be younger than 21 years old; be eligible to attend a two- or four-year college or university with a full course of study; and be a legal U.S. resident. Scholarships are available through one of four channels: RMHC Scholars, RMHC/ASIA (Asian Students Increasing Achievement), RMHC/African-American Future Achievers, and RMHC/HACER.
Type of support: Building/renovation; Capital campaigns; Curriculum development; Emergency funds; Equipment; Program development; Publication; Research; Scholarship funds; Seed money.
Geographic limitations: Giving on a national and international basis.
Support limitations: No grants to individuals, or for advertising, fundraising drives, partisan/political/denominational programs, ongoing general and administrative costs (including salaries, travel, and overhead), intermediary funding agencies, endowment campaigns, or medical research.
Publications: Annual report; Application guidelines; Informational brochure.
Application information: Applications accepted. Only those organizations with successful letters of inquiry will be invited to submit full proposals. Grant requests for programs or projects that focus on one specific community or geographic area should be sent to a local organization chapter for consideration. Application form required. Applicants should submit the following:
1) how project will be sustained once grantmaker support is completed
2) statement of problem project will address
3) population served
4) brief history of organization and description of its mission
5) how project's results will be evaluated or measured

Initial approach: Letter of inquiry
Copies of proposal: 2
Board meeting date(s): Mar., Aug., and Dec.
Deadline(s): Jan. 28 for Scholarships; Aug. 23 for Global Grants; varies for all others
Final notification: Within three weeks of board meetings

Officers and Trustees:* Linda Dunham*, Chair.; Martin J. Coyne, Jr.*, Pres. and C.E.O.; Donald G. Lubin*, V.P.; James D. Watkins*, V.P.; Adele Jamieson*, Secy.; Michael D. Irgang*, Treas.; Aggie Dentice; Wai-Ling Eng; John M. Falletta, M.D.; Alan A. Harris, M.D.; Fred Huebner; Donna Hyland; Jonah Kaufman; Muhtar Kent; Jeff Kindler; and 17 additional trustees.
Number of staff: None.
EIN: 362934689

2428
McDonnell Boehen Hulbert & Berghoff LLP

300 S. Wacker Dr., Ste. 3100
Chicago, IL 60606-6705 (312) 913-0001

Company URL: http://www.mbhb.com
Company type: Private company
Business activities: Operates law firm.
Business type (SIC): Legal services
Offices: Chicago, IL; Port Townsend, WA
Giving statement: Giving through the McDonnell Boehen Hulbert & Berghoff LLP Pro Bono Program.

McDonnell Boehen Hulbert & Berghoff LLP Pro Bono Program

300 S. Wacker Dr., Ste. 3100
Chicago, IL 60606-6705 (312) 913-0001
E-mail: info@mbhb.com; URL: http://www.mbhb.com

Contact: Kimberly Yagelski, Legal Recruiting & Devel. Dir.
Fields of interest: Legal services.
Type of support: Pro bono services - legal.
Geographic limitations: Giving primarily in areas of company operations in Chicago, IL, and Port Townsend, WA.

2429
McGraw Hill Financial, Inc.

(formerly The McGraw Hill Companies, Inc.)
1221 Ave. of the Americas
New York, NY 10020-1095 (212) 512-2000
FAX: (212) 512-3840

Company URL: http://www.mhfi.com
Establishment information: Established in 1888.
Company type: Public company
Company ticker symbol and exchange: MHFI/NYSE
International Securities Identification Number: US5806451093
Business activities: Publishes books, magazines, and newsletters; provides Internet information services; broadcasts television.
Business type (SIC): Book publishing and/or printing; periodical publishing and/or printing; publishing/miscellaneous; radio and television broadcasting; computer services
Financial profile for 2012: Number of employees, 21,687; assets, $7,052,000,000; sales volume, $4,450,000,000; pre-tax net income, $1,130,000,000; expenses, $3,239,000,000; liabilities, $6,285,000,000
Fortune 1000 ranking: 2012—390th in revenues, 364th in profits, and 490th in assets
Forbes 2000 ranking: 2012—1476th in sales, 1346th in profits, and 1662nd in assets
Corporate officers: Harold W. McGraw III, Chair., Pres., and C.E.O.; Jack F. Callahan, Jr., Exec. V.P. and C.F.O.; Kenneth M. Vitor, Exec. V.P. and Genl. Counsel; John Berisford, Exec. V.P., Human Resources
Board of directors: Harold W. McGraw III, Chair.; Pedro Aspe; Sir Winfried F. W. Bischoff; William D. Green; Charles E. Haldeman, Jr.; Linda Koch Lorimer; Robert P. McGraw; Hilda Ochoa-Brillembourg; Sir Michael Rake; Edward B. Rust, Jr.; Kurt L. Schmoke; Sidney Taurel; Richard E. Thornburgh
Subsidiaries: KERO-TV, Bakersfield, CA; KGTV, San Diego, CA; KMGH-TV, Denver, CO; WRTV, Indianapolis, IN
Plants: Monterey, CA; Centennial, Colorado Springs, CO; Dubuque, IA; Lexington, MA; Hightstown, NJ; Blacklick, Westerville, OH; DeSoto, TX
International operations: Australia; Canada; Cayman Islands; Chile; Colombia; Hong Kong; India; Israel; Mexico; New Zealand; Panama; Portugal; United Kingdom; Venezuela
Giving statement: Giving through the McGraw Hill Financial, Inc. Corporate Giving Program and the McGraw-Hill Research Foundation.
Company EIN: 131026995

McGraw Hill Financial, Inc. Corporate Giving Program

(formerly The McGraw-Hill Companies, Inc. Corporate Giving Program)
1221 Ave. of the Americas, 47th Fl.
New York, NY 10020-1095 (212) 512-6480
FAX: (212) 512-3611; E-mail: crs@mhfi.com; For Volunteer Progs.: Amita Nagaraja, Dir., Strategic Giving and Community Engagement, tel.: (212) 512-3643, e-mail: amita_nagaraja@mcgraw-hill.com; For Sustainability: Jaclyn BouchardProg. Mgr., Corp. Responsibility and Sustainability, tel.: (212) 512-3244; e-mail: jaclyn.bouchard@mhfi.com; URL: http://www.mhfi.com/corporate-responsibility

Contact: Susan A. Wallman, Mgr., Corp. Contribs.
Purpose and activities: McGraw Hill Financial makes charitable contributions to nonprofit organizations involved with financial literacy, health and human services, education, arts and culture, and sustainability and the environment. Support is given primarily in areas of company operations.
Fields of interest: Arts; Elementary school/education; Environment; Health care; Safety/disasters; Human services, financial counseling; Human services; Microfinance/microlending; Community/economic development; Military/veterans' organizations.
Programs:
Employee Volunteer Grant program: Employees dedicating more than 50 hours a year are eligible to apply for employee volunteer grants on behalf of their favorite nonprofit group. Employees who volunteer in teams may apply for a $1,000 grant. In 2012, more than 400 volunteers dedicated approximately 11,300 hours through the Employee Volunteer Grant Program. In addition, the Corporation awarded grants close to $150,000 to nonprofits.
Matching Gift Program: The company matches employee donatations to eligible nonprofits on a one-for-one basis. The year-round program supports adult literacy, arts and culture, financial literacy, and higher education organizations. The Corporation's annual Employee Giving Programs match employee contributions to health and human service nonprofits. In 2012, close to $830,000 in employee and matching donations was donated to about 400 nonprofits. Additionally, the company's disaster relief matching gift program matches employee contributions to support disaster relief efforts. In 2012, employees from around the world raised more than $150,000 (including McGraw-Hill's matching contribution) for devastating disasters like Hurricane Sandy, Hurricane Isaac, and the Midwest tornadoes.
Type of support: Employee matching gifts; Employee volunteer services; In-kind gifts; Program development.
Geographic limitations: Giving primarily in areas of company operations; giving also to national organizations.
Support limitations: No support for libraries, or K-12 schools, institutes of higher learning, political, or religious organizations, member-based organizations such as fraternities, labor, or veterans' organizations, athletic organizations, or social clubs. No grants to individuals, or for endowments; no loans.
Publications: Application guidelines; Corporate report.
Application information: Applications accepted. Grant recipients are required to provide twice-yearly progress reports detailing the measurable results achieved. Multi-year funding is not automatic. Proposals should be limited to 3 pages. Application form not required. Applicants should submit the following:
1) role played by volunteers
2) timetable for implementation and evaluation of project
3) results expected from proposed grant
4) qualifications of key personnel
5) population served
6) name, address and phone number of organization
7) copy of IRS Determination Letter
8) brief history of organization and description of its mission
9) copy of most recent annual report/audited financial statement/990
10) how project's results will be evaluated or measured
11) listing of board of directors, trustees, officers and other key people and their affiliations
12) detailed description of project and amount of funding requested
13) copy of current year's organizational budget and/or project budget
14) listing of additional sources and amount of support
15) additional materials/documentation

Initial approach: Proposal to headquarters
Copies of proposal: 1
Committee meeting date(s): Quarterly
Deadline(s): None

Administrators: Eileen Gabriele, V.P., Corp. Affairs; Louise R. Raymond, Sr. Dir., Global Corp. Social Responsibility; Susan A. Wallman, Mgr., Corp. Contribs.; Amita Nagaraja, Sr. Prog. Officer, Global Employee Progs.
Number of staff: 5 full-time professional; 2 part-time professional; 1 full-time support.

The McGraw-Hill Research Foundation

1221 Ave. of the Americas, 47th Fl.
New York, NY 10020
URL: http://www.mcgraw-hillresearchfoundation.org/

Donor: The McGraw-Hill Companies Inc.
Financial data (yr. ended 12/31/10): Assets, $0 (M); gifts received, $83,498; expenditures, $83,498; qualifying distributions, $83,498.
Application information: Applications not accepted. Unsolicited requests for funds not accepted.
Officers and Directors:* James H. McGraw IV, Pres.; Deborah Flanagan, V.P.; Mary Eileen Gabriele*, V.P.; Elizabeth O' Melia, V.P.; Linda Poon, Secy.; Louise R. Raymond*, V.P.; Peter Scheschuk, V.P.; Thomas Selby, Treas.; D. Edward I. Smyth.
EIN: 273655593

2430
McGuireWoods LLP

901 E. Cary St.
Richmond, VA 23219-4030 (804) 775-1000

Company URL: http://www.mcguirewoods.com
Establishment information: Established in 1834.

Company type: Private company
Business activities: Operates law firm.
Business type (SIC): Legal services
Corporate officers: Richard Cullen, Chair.; Thomas E. Cabaniss, Managing Partner; Peter J. Covington, Vice-Chair.
Offices: Los Angeles, CA; Washington, DC; Jacksonville, FL; Atlanta, GA; Chicago, IL; Baltimore, MD; New York, NY; Charlotte, Raleigh, Wilmington, NC; Pittsburgh, PA; Austin, Houston, TX; Charlottesville, Norfolk, Richmond, Tysons Corner, VA
International operations: Belgium; United Kingdom
Giving statement: Giving through the McGuireWoods LLP Pro Bono Program.

McGuireWoods LLP Pro Bono Program

901 E. Cary St.
Richmond, VA 23219-4030 (804) 775-4743
E-mail: soostdyk@mcguirewoods.com; Additional tel.: (804) 775-1000, fax:(804) 775-1061;
URL: http://www.mcguirewoods.com/our_firm/pro_bono/community.asp

Contact: Scott Oostdyk, Partner in Charge of Pro Bono
Fields of interest: Legal services.
Type of support: Pro bono services - legal.
Application information: A Pro Bono Committee manages the pro bono program.

2431
McJunkin Red Man Corporation

(also known as MRC)
8023 E. 63rd Pl.
Tulsa, OK 74133 (918) 250-8541

Company URL: http://www.mcjunkinredman.com
Establishment information: Established in 1921.
Company type: Subsidiary of a private company
Business activities: Distributes steel pipe, valves, and fittings.
Business type (SIC): Metals and minerals, except petroleum—wholesale
Financial profile for 2011: Number of employees, 3,885; assets, $2,990,000,000; sales volume, $3,850,000,000
Corporate officers: Andrew R. Lane, Chair., Pres., and C.E.O.; James F. Underhill, Exec. V.P. and C.O.O.; James E. Braun, Exec. V.P. and C.F.O.; Daniel J. Churay, Exec. V.P.,Genl. Counsel and Corp. Secy.; Elton Bond, Sr. V.P. and C.A.O.; Nasser Farshchian, Sr. V.P. and C.I.O.; Theresa Dudding, Sr. V.P. and Cont.; John Durbin, Sr. V.P., Finance and Treas.; Diana Morris, Sr. V.P., Human Resources
Board of director: Andrew R. Lane, Chair.
Giving statement: Giving through the Ketchum Charitable Foundation Inc.

Ketchum Charitable Foundation Inc.

5100 E. Skelly Dr., Ste. 1040
Tulsa, OK 74135 (918) 491-4036
Application address: 31 Hallbrook Way Spring, TX 77389

Donors: Betts, LLC; McJunkin Red Man Corp.; Red Man Charitable Trust; Ketchum Charitable Lead Annuity Trust.
Contact: Kent B. Ketchum, Pres.
Financial data (yr. ended 12/31/11): Assets, $9,669,722 (M); gifts received, $2,600,000; expenditures, $180,862; qualifying distributions, $138,896; giving activities include $138,896 for 6 grants (high: $75,000; low: $6,656).
Purpose and activities: The foundation supports organizations involved with higher education and school athletics.
Fields of interest: Higher education; Athletics/sports, school programs; United Ways and Federated Giving Programs.
Type of support: General/operating support; Management development/capacity building; Program development.
Geographic limitations: Giving primarily in MO, OK, and TX.
Application information: Applications accepted. Application form required. Applicants should submit the following:
1) name, address and phone number of organization
2) detailed description of project and amount of funding requested
3) contact person
Initial approach: Letter
Copies of proposal: 1
Deadline(s): None
Officers: Lewis Craig Ketchum, Chair.; Kevin B. Ketchum, Pres.; Brian C. Ketchum, V.P.
Director: Kent H. Ketchum.
EIN: 262189909
Selected grants: The following grants are a representative sample of this grantmaker's funding activity:
$15,000 to Missouri State University, Springfield, MO, 2010.
$8,000 to University of Tulsa, Tulsa, OK, 2010.

2432
McKee Foods Corporation

10260 McKee Rd.
P.O. Box 750
Collegedale, TN 37315-0750
(423) 238-7111
FAX: (423) 238-7517

Company URL: http://www.mckeefoods.com
Establishment information: Established in 1934.
Company type: Private company
Business activities: Produces snack cakes.
Business type (SIC): Bakery products
Corporate officers: R. Ellsworth McKee, Chair. and C.A.O.; Michael K. McKee, Pres. and C.E.O.; Barry S. Patterson, V.P. and C.F.O.; Ed Hannah, V.P., Sales
Board of director: R. Ellsworth McKee, Chair.
Giving statement: Giving through the McKee Foods Corporation Contributions Program.

McKee Foods Corporation Contributions Program

P.O. Box 750
Collegedale, TN 37315-0750

Contact: Bonnie Carlton, Asst. to the Chair. of the Bd.
Purpose and activities: McKee Foods makes charitable contributions to nonprofit organizations involved with education, the environment, and community development. Support is given on a case by case basis in areas of company operations.
Fields of interest: Education; Environment; Community/economic development; General charitable giving.
Type of support: Employee matching gifts; General/operating support; In-kind gifts; Sponsorships.
Geographic limitations: Giving in areas of company operations in Kingman, AZ, Benton County, AR, Hamilton County, TN, and Augusta County, VA; giving also to national organizations.
Support limitations: No grants to individuals, or for fundraising, or travel expenses.
Application information: Applications accepted. Proposals should be no longer than 2 pages. Telephone calls are not encouraged. The office of the Chairman of the Board handles giving. A contributions committee reviews all requests. Application form not required. Applicants should submit the following:
1) name, address and phone number of organization
2) copy of IRS Determination Letter
3) brief history of organization and description of its mission
4) copy of most recent annual report/audited financial statement/990
5) listing of board of directors, trustees, officers and other key people and their affiliations
6) detailed description of project and amount of funding requested
7) contact person
8) listing of additional sources and amount of support
Initial approach: Proposal to headquarters
Copies of proposal: 1
Deadline(s): None
Final notification: Following review

2433
McKenna Long & Aldridge LLP

1900 K St., N.W.
Washington, DC 20006-1108
(202) 496-7500

Company URL: http://www.mckennalong.com
Establishment information: Established in 1939.
Company type: Private company
Business activities: Operates law firm.
Business type (SIC): Legal services
Corporate officers: Jeffrey K. Haidet, Chair.; T. Mark Flanagan, Jr., Managing Partner; S. Dan Anderson, C.O.O.; Roger Rushing, C.F.O.
Offices: Los Angeles, San Diego, San Francisco, CA; Denver, CO; Washington, DC; Atlanta, GA; Albany, New York, NY; Devon, PA
International operations: Belgium
Historic mergers: Luce, Forward, Hamilton & Scripps LLP (March 6, 2012)
Giving statement: Giving through the McKenna Long & Aldridge LLP Pro Bono Program.

McKenna Long & Aldridge LLP Pro Bono Program

1900 K St., N.W.
Washington, DC 20006-1108 (202) 496-7500
E-mail: jabrahams@mckennalong.com; URL: http://www.mckennalong.com/about-probono.html

Contact: Jessica Abrahams, Partner, Pro Bono Comm.
Fields of interest: Legal services.
Type of support: Pro bono services - legal.
Geographic limitations: Giving primarily in areas of company operations in Los Angeles, San Diego, and San Francisco, CA, Denver, CO, Washington, DC, Atlanta, GA, Albany and New York, NY, Devon, PA, and in Belgium.
Application information: A Pro Bono Committee manages the pro-bono program.

2434
McKesson Corporation

(formerly McKesson HBOC, Inc.)
McKesson Plz.
1 Post St.
San Francisco, CA 94104 (415) 983-8300
FAX: (415) 983-8464

Company URL: http://www.mckesson.com
Establishment information: Established in 1833.
Company type: Public company
Company ticker symbol and exchange: MCK/NYSE
Business activities: Provides health care supply and information management solutions.
Business type (SIC): Drugs, proprietaries, and sundries—wholesale
Financial profile for 2013: Number of employees, 43,500; assets, $34,786,000,000; sales volume, $122,455,000,000; pre-tax net income, $1,919,000,000; expenses, $120,331,000,000; liabilities, $27,716,000,000
Fortune 1000 ranking: 2012—14th in revenues, 146th in profits, and 168th in assets
Forbes 2000 ranking: 2012—37th in sales, 394th in profits, and 677th in assets
Corporate officers: John H. Hammergren, Chair., Pres., and C.E.O.; Jeffrey C. Campbell, Exec. V.P. and C.F.O.; Randall N. Spratt, Exec. V.P. and C.I.O.; Laureen E. Seeger, Exec. V.P. and Genl. Counsel; Jorge L. Figueredo, Exec. V.P., Human Resources
Board of directors: John H. Hammergren, Chair.; Andy D. Bryant; Wayne A. Budd; Alton F. Irby III; M. Christine Jacobs; Marie L. Knowles; David M. Lawrence, M.D.; Edward A. Mueller; Jane E. Shaw, Ph.D.
International operations: Ireland
Giving statement: Giving through the McKesson Corporation Contributions Program and the McKesson Foundation, Inc.
Company EIN: 943207296

McKesson Corporation Contributions Program

(formerly McKesson HBOC, Inc. Corporate Giving Program)
1 Post St.
San Francisco, CA 94104-5201
E-mail: carrie.varoquiers@mckesson.com;
URL: http://www.mckesson.com/community.html

Contact: Carrie Varoquiers, V.P., Corp. Citizenship
Purpose and activities: As a complement to its foundation, McKesson also makes charitable contributions to nonprofit organizations directly. Support is given primarily in the San Francisco Bay Area, California.
Fields of interest: General charitable giving.
Type of support: In-kind gifts; Sponsorships.
Geographic limitations: Giving primarily in the San Francisco Bay Area, CA.
Support limitations: No support for religious or political organizations.
Application information: Applications not accepted. Contributes only to pre-selected organizations. The Community Relations Department handles giving. The company has a staff that only handles contributions. A contributions committee reviews all requests.

McKesson Foundation, Inc.

(formerly McKesson HBOC Foundation, Inc.)
1 Post St.
San Francisco, CA 94104-5201 (415) 983-9325
FAX: (415) 983-7590;
E-mail: mckessonfoundation@mckesson.com;
Contact for Mobilizing Health: tel.: (415) 983-9478, e-mail: mhealth@mckesson.com; URL: http://www.mckesson.com/about-mckesson/corporate-citizenship/mckesson-foundation/

Establishment information: Incorporated in 1943 in FL.
Donors: McKesson Corp.; McKesson HBOC, Inc.
Financial data (yr. ended 03/31/12): Assets, $17,196,422 (M); gifts received, $10,000,757; expenditures, $5,527,024; qualifying distributions, $5,428,955; giving activities include $5,095,257 for 1,698 grants (high: $286,775; low: $10).
Purpose and activities: The foundation supports programs designed to improve the health of patients through access to quality healthcare; personal health management; and lower healthcare costs. Special emphasis is directed toward non-medical direct services to low-income cancer patients.
Fields of interest: Higher education; Medical school/education; Nursing school/education; Education; Health care, equal rights; Health care, clinics/centers; Public health; Health care, patient services; Cancer; Diabetes; United Ways and Federated Giving Programs Children; Youth; Economically disadvantaged.
Programs:

Employee-Related Scholarships: The foundation annually awards $1,000 four-year college scholarships to children of employees of McKesson. The program is administered by the National Merit Scholarship Corporation and Scholarship America, Inc.

Giving Comfort: The foundation, in partnership with the American Cancer Society, major hospitals, and grassroots NGOs, provides low-income cancer patients with items of comfort and relief during chemotherapy treatment. Items of comfort include a soft blanket, warm socks, soothing tea, moisturizer, lip balm, a sleeping cap, etc. Visit URL http://www.givingcomfort.org/ for more information.

McKesson's Matching Gift Program: The foundation matches contributions made by employees and retirees of McKesson to nonprofit organizations on a one-for-one basis from $10 to $2,500 per employee, per year.

Mobilizing for Health: The foundation supports pilot research projects and studies designed to promote mobile-based interventions for low-income patients with chronic diseases, with priority interest in cancer management. Proposals are evaluated on intellectual rigor; significance of the problem and anticipated results; feasibility; team qualifications; and study population. Grants of up to $250,000 are awarded.

President's Volunteer Service Award (PVSA): The foundation, in partnership with the President's Council on Service and Civic Participation, recognizes McKesson employees who demonstrate outstanding volunteer service and civic participation. Recipients log more than 100 hours of volunteer service and the award is given on behalf of the President of the United States.

Scholarships for Healthcare Education: The foundation, in partnership with the National Student Nurses Association (FNSNA), annually awards twenty-five undergraduate $1,000 scholarships to low-income nursing students to address the urgent need for nurses. The program is administered by the National Student Nurses Association. The foundation also awards 50 $1,000 scholarships to pharmacy school students nominated by McKesson independent, chain, and hospital pharmacy customers. The program is administered by Scholarship America, Inc.

Volunteer of the Year Award: The foundation recognizes five McKesson volunteers for outstanding service to a nonprofit organization. Grants of up to $5,000 are awarded to the nonprofit organization of the employee's choice. Winners are selected by a panel of Regional Volunteer Chairpersons from around the country.

Type of support: Continuing support; Employee matching gifts; Employee volunteer services; Employee-related scholarships; Equipment; General/operating support; Program development; Research; Scholarship funds.
Geographic limitations: Giving on a national basis in areas of company operations.
Support limitations: No support for religious organizations not of direct benefit to the entire community or disease-specific organizations. No grants to individuals (except for scholarships), or for endowments, political causes or campaigns, advertising, or research.
Publications: Application guidelines; Corporate giving report.
Application information: Applications accepted. Letters of inquiry should be no longer than 1 page. However, unsolicited grant proposals are generally not accepted. Applicants may be invited to submit a full proposal at a later date. Support is limited to 1 contribution per organization during any given year. Applicants should submit the following:
1) detailed description of project and amount of funding requested

Initial approach: E-mail letter of inquiry; complete online letter of intent for Mobilizing for Health
Board meeting date(s): Dec.
Deadline(s): None; Mar. 10 for Mobilizing for Health

Officers and Directors:* John H. Hammergren*, Chair.; Carrie J. Varoquiers*, Pres.; Jeffrey C. Campbell*, V.P.; Michele Lau, Secy.; Nicholas A. Loiacono*, Treas.; Patrick Blake; Jorge L. Figueredo; Paul C. Julian; Nigel A. Rees.
Number of staff: 1 full-time professional; 1 part-time professional; 1 full-time support.
EIN: 943140036

2435
McKinstry Company, LLC

5005 3rd Ave. S.
Seattle, WA 98134-2423 (206) 762-3311
FAX: (206) 762-2624

Company URL: http://www.mckinstry.com
Establishment information: Established in 1960.
Company type: Private company
Business activities: Provides contract mechanical services.
Business type (SIC): Contractors/plumbing, heating, and air-conditioning
Financial profile for 2009: Number of employees, 705
Corporate officers: Dean C. Allen, C.E.O.; Doug Moore, Pres.; Bill Teplicky, C.P.A., C.F.O.; Jamie Pedersen, V.P. and Genl. Counsel; Ned Gebert, V.P., Opers.; Tony Stewart, V.P., Mktg.
Giving statement: Giving through the McKinstry Company Charitable Foundation.

McKinstry Company Charitable Foundation

P.O. Box 24567
Seattle, WA 98124-0567
URL: http://www.mckinstry.com/about/giving

Establishment information: Established in 1998 in WA.
Donors: McKinstry Co.; Dean Allen; Earl Davie; Anita Davie; George Allen.

Contact: J. William Teplicky, Tr.
Financial data (yr. ended 09/30/11): Assets, $77,516 (M); gifts received, $707,700; expenditures, $642,765; qualifying distributions, $642,765; giving activities include $642,765 for grants.
Purpose and activities: The foundation supports arts museums and organizations involved with education, global health, medical research, human services, international development, and microfinance.
Fields of interest: Museums (art); Higher education; Education; Hospitals (general); Health care, clinics/centers; Health care; Diabetes research; Biomedicine research; Medical research; Boys & girls clubs; Boy scouts; YM/YWCAs & YM/YWHAs; Children/youth, services; Developmentally disabled, centers & services; Human services; International development; Microfinance/microlending Economically disadvantaged.
Type of support: Annual campaigns; General/operating support; Program development; Scholarship funds.
Geographic limitations: Giving primarily in Seattle, WA.
Support limitations: No grants to individuals.
Application information: Applications not accepted. Contributes only to pre-selected organizations.
Trustees: Dean C. Allen; Vicki Allen; J. William Teplicky, Jr.
EIN: 911942024
Selected grants: The following grants are a representative sample of this grantmaker's funding activity:
$100,250 to PATH, Seattle, WA, 2010.
$60,000 to Global Partnerships, Seattle, WA, 2010.
$30,250 to Boys and Girls Clubs of King County, Seattle, WA, 2010.
$26,000 to Childrens Museum, Seattle, WA, 2010.
$11,500 to YMCA of Greater Seattle, Seattle, WA, 2010.
$5,500 to Seattle University, Seattle, WA, 2010.
$5,000 to Seattle Parks Foundation, Seattle, WA, 2010.
$3,500 to Leukemia & Lymphoma Society, White Plains, NY, 2010.
$3,500 to Oregon Food Bank, Portland, OR, 2010.
$2,250 to Humane Society for Seattle-King County, Bellevue, WA, 2010.

2436
McLaughlin Body Company

2430 River Dr.
Moline, IL 61265-1564 (309) 762-7755

Company URL: http://www.mclbody.com
Establishment information: Established in 1902.
Company type: Private company
Business activities: Manufactures automotive cabs, weldments, and assemblies.
Business type (SIC): Motor vehicles and equipment
Corporate officers: Raymond L. McLaughlin, Chair.; Everett F. Pierce, C.E.O.; William R. Storm, C.F.O.; Curt Loewen, C.I.O.; Jerry Vonderhaar, V.P., Human Resources
Board of director: Raymond L. Mclaughlin, Chair.
Giving statement: Giving through the McLaughlin Family Foundation.

McLaughlin Family Foundation

2430 River Dr.
Moline, IL 61265-1564 (309) 736-6005

Establishment information: Established in 1997 in IL.
Donors: McLaughlin Body Company; Raymond L. McLaughlin; Peter J. McLaughlin.
Contact: William R. Storm, Tr.
Financial data (yr. ended 12/31/11): Assets, $2,996,133 (M); gifts received, $300,000; expenditures, $182,939; qualifying distributions, $164,003; giving activities include $163,438 for 16 grants (high: $95,437; low: $1,000).
Purpose and activities: The foundation supports community foundations and organizations involved with secondary and higher education, human services, community development, and Catholicism.
Fields of interest: Secondary school/education; Higher education; American Red Cross; Human services; Community/economic development; Foundations (community); Catholic agencies & churches.
Type of support: Capital campaigns; General/operating support.
Geographic limitations: Giving primarily in the Moline, IL, area.
Support limitations: No grants to individuals.
Application information: Applications accepted. Application form not required.
Initial approach: Proposal
Deadline(s): None
Trustees: Peter J. McLaughlin; Raymond L. McLaughlin; William R. Storm.
EIN: 364158320

2437
Rand McNally & Company

9855 Woods Dr.
Skokie, IL 60077-1074 (847) 329-8100

Company URL: http://www.randmcnally.com
Establishment information: Established in 1856.
Company type: Subsidiary of a private company
Business activities: Provides print, electronic, online, and handheld media navigation information.
Business type (SIC): Publishing/miscellaneous; computer services
Corporate officers: Dave Muscatel, Pres. and C.E.O.; Robert S. Apatoff, Pres. and C.E.O.; Norman Smagley, Sr. V.P. and C.F.O.; Lawrence A. Gyenes, Sr. V.P. and Treas.
Giving statement: Giving through the Rand McNally Foundation.

The Rand McNally Foundation

9855 Woods Dr.
Skokie, IL 60077-1074

Establishment information: Established in 1987.
Donor: Rand McNally & Co.
Financial data (yr. ended 12/31/11): Assets, $187,395 (M); expenditures, $1,042; qualifying distributions, $850; giving activities include $850 for grants.
Purpose and activities: The foundation supports organizations involved with arts and culture, higher education, health, and human services.
Fields of interest: Arts; Education.
Type of support: Employee matching gifts; General/operating support.
Geographic limitations: Giving primarily in Skokie, IL.
Support limitations: No grants to individuals.
Application information: Applications not accepted. Unsolicited requests for funds not accepted.
Officer and Directors:* David Muscatel*, Pres.; Emil Giliotti; Paul Leib.
EIN: 363514596

2438
McNamee, Lochner, Titus & Williams, P.C.

677 Broadway
P.O. Box 459
Albany, NY 12201-0459 (518) 447-3200

Company URL: http://www.mltw.com
Establishment information: Established in 1863.
Company type: Private company
Business activities: Operates law firm.
Business type (SIC): Legal services
Offices: Albany, Clifton Park, NY
Giving statement: Giving through the McNamee, Lochner, Titus & Williams, P.C. Pro Bono Program.

McNamee, Lochner, Titus & Williams, P.C. Pro Bono Program

677 Broadway
P.O. Box 459
Albany, NY 12201-0459 (518) 447-3200
FAX: (518) 426-4260; URL: http://www.mltw.com/lawyer-attorney-1362719.html

Contact: Vincent L. Valenza, Managing Principal
Fields of interest: Legal services.
Type of support: Pro bono services - legal.
Geographic limitations: Giving primarily in areas of company operations in Albany and Clifton Park, NY.

2439
McShane Construction Company

(formerly McShane Builders, Inc.)
9550 W. Higgins Rd., Ste. 200
Rosemont, IL 60018 (847) 292-4300
FAX: (847) 292-4310

Company URL: http://www.mcshane-construction.com
Establishment information: Established in 1984.
Company type: Subsidiary of a private company
Business activities: Provides architectural services.
Business type (SIC): Engineering, architectural, and surveying services; contractors/general nonresidential building
Corporate officers: James A. McShane, C.E.O.; Jeffrey A. Raday, Pres.; Ellen Hilgendorf, C.P.A., V.P., Finance
Board of directors: James A. McShane, Chair.; John S. Bakalar; Derek R. McClain; Daniel P. McShane, Esq.; Melvin D. Meyer; J. Stanley Pepper; Jeffrey A. Raday
Giving statement: Giving through the McShane Foundation.

The McShane Foundation

9550 W. Higgins Rd., Ste. 200
Rosemont, IL 60018-4906 (847) 292-4300

Establishment information: Established in 1988 in IL.
Donors: McShane Builders, Inc.; James A. McShane.
Contact: James A. McShane, Pres. and Secy.
Financial data (yr. ended 12/31/11): Assets, $779,785 (M); gifts received, $100,000; expenditures, $136,755; qualifying distributions, $130,278; giving activities include $129,000 for 10 grants (high: $42,500; low: $1,000).
Purpose and activities: The foundation supports organizations involved with education, youth

development, human services, international relief, and Christianity.
Fields of interest: Education; Youth development; Human services; International relief; Christian agencies & churches.
Type of support: General/operating support.
Geographic limitations: Giving primarily in IL.
Application information: Applications accepted. Application form required. Applicants should submit the following:
1) detailed description of project and amount of funding requested
Initial approach: Letter
Deadline(s): None
Officer and Directors:* James A. McShane*, Pres. and Secy.; Pat Glascow; Mary G. McShane.
EIN: 363627198
Selected grants: The following grants are a representative sample of this grantmaker's funding activity:
$42,500 to Concern Worldwide U.S., Chicago, IL, 2011.
$27,500 to Marquette University, Milwaukee, WI, 2011.
$7,500 to Broader Urban Involvement and Leadership Development, Chicago, IL, 2011.
$6,000 to Catholic Charities of the Archdiocese of Chicago, Chicago, IL, 2011.
$6,000 to Loyola Academy, Wilmette, IL, 2011.
$1,000 to Rainbows for All Children, Itasca, IL, 2011.

2440
McWane, Inc.

2900 Hwy. 280, Ste. 300
P.O. Box 43327
Birmingham, AL 35223-2469
(205) 414-3100
FAX: (205) 414-3170

Company URL: http://www.mcwane.com/
Establishment information: Established in 1921.
Company type: Private company
Business activities: Manufactures pipe and fittings.
Business type (SIC): Steel mill products; iron and steel foundries; insurance/life; insurance/accident and health; insurance/fire, marine, and casualty
Corporate officers: C. Phillip McWane, Chair.; G. Ruffner Page, Jr., Pres.; Charles F. Nowlin, Sr. V.P. and C.F.O.; James M. Proctor II, Sr. V.P. and Genl. Counsel; Jitendra Radia, Sr. V.P., Human Resources
Board of director: C. Phillip McWane, Chair.
Subsidiary: McWane Cast Iron Pipe Co., Birmingham, AL
International operations: Canada
Giving statement: Giving through the McWane Foundation.

McWane Foundation

P.O. Box 43327
Birmingham, AL 35243-0327 (205) 414-3100
URL: http://www.mcwane.com/community/charitable-giving-guidelines/

Establishment information: Established in 1961.
Donor: McWane, Inc.
Contact: C. Phillip McWane, Tr.
Financial data (yr. ended 12/31/11): Assets, $682,908 (M); gifts received, $1,602,365; expenditures, $1,637,938; qualifying distributions, $1,631,443; giving activities include $1,631,443 for 53 grants (high: $1,053,000; low: $300).
Purpose and activities: The foundation supports programs designed to promote arts and culture; education; environmental stewardship; heath and safety; and children.
Fields of interest: Museums (science/technology); Arts; Higher education; Education; Health care; Safety/disasters; YM/YWCAs & YM/YWHAs; Children, services.
Type of support: Capital campaigns; General/operating support.
Geographic limitations: Giving primarily in areas of company operations, with emphasis on Birmingham, AL.
Support limitations: No support for discriminatory organizations, political organizations, or athletic teams, fraternal orders, sectarian religious or veterans' organizations, or labor associations. No grants to individuals, or for telephone or mass mail appeals.
Publications: Application guidelines.
Application information: Applications accepted. Application form not required. Applicants should submit the following:
1) detailed description of project and amount of funding requested
2) timetable for implementation and evaluation of project
3) how project's results will be evaluated or measured
4) copy of IRS Determination Letter
5) listing of board of directors, trustees, officers and other key people and their affiliations
6) copy of current year's organizational budget and/or project budget
Initial approach: Proposal to the nearest company facility
Copies of proposal: 1
Board meeting date(s): Quarterly
Deadline(s): Mar. 15, June 15, Sept. 14, and. Dec. 15
Trustees: John McMahon; C. Phillip McWane.
EIN: 636044384
Selected grants: The following grants are a representative sample of this grantmaker's funding activity:
$1,000,000 to Childrens Hospital of Alabama, Birmingham, AL, 2009.
$1,000,000 to McWane Science Center, Discovery 2000, Birmingham, AL, 2009.
$319,000 to Community Foundation of Greater Birmingham, Birmingham, AL, 2009.
$30,000 to Alabama Symphonic Association, Birmingham, AL, 2009.
$21,250 to Birmingham Civil Rights Institute, Birmingham, AL, 2009.
$10,000 to Franklin and Eleanor Roosevelt Institute, New York, NY, 2009.

2441
MDU Resources Group, Inc.

1200 W. Century Ave.
P.O. Box 5650
Bismarck, ND 58506-5650 (701) 530-1000

Company URL: http://www.mdu.com
Establishment information: Established in 1924.
Company type: Public company
Company ticker symbol and exchange: MDU/NYSE
Business activities: Operates diversified natural resource company.
Business type (SIC): Combination utility services
Financial profile for 2012: Number of employees, 8,629; assets, $6,682,490,000; sales volume, $4,075,430,000; pre-tax net income, $45,470,000; expenses, $4,056,220,000; liabilities, $4,034,240,000
Fortune 1000 ranking: 2012—578th in revenues, 884th in profits, and 503rd in assets
Corporate officers: Harry J. Pearce, Chair.; James Wells, Vice-Chair.; David L. Goodin, Pres. and C.E.O.; Doran N. Schwartz, V.P. and C.F.O.; Nicole A. Kivisto, V.P., Cont., and C.A.O.; Cynthia J. Norland, V.P., Admin.; Mark A. Del Vecchio, V.P., Human Resources; Paul K. Sandness, Genl. Counsel and Secy.; Douglass A. Mahowald, Treas.
Board of directors: Harry J. Pearce, Chair.; James Wells, Vice-Chair.; Thomas Everist; Karen B. Fagg; David L. Goodin; A. Bart Holaday; Dennis W. Johnson; Thomas C. Knudson; Patricia L. Moss; John K. Wilson
Divisions: FIDELITY EXPLORATION & PRODUCTION CO., Denver, CO; Knife River Corp., Bismarck, ND; MDU CONSTRUCTION SERVICES, Bismark, ND; WBI ENERGY, Bismark, ND
Historic mergers: Fred Carlson Company, Inc. (February 6, 2004)
Giving statement: Giving through the PMC Production Co., Ltd. Contributions Program and the MDU Resources Foundation.
Company EIN: 410423660

MDU Resources Foundation

P.O. Box 5650
Bismarck, ND 58506-5650
FAX: (701) 530-1737;
E-mail: rita.o'neill@MDUResources.com;
URL: http://www.mdu.com/CorporateResponsibility/Foundation/Pages/Qualified.aspx

Establishment information: Established in 1983 in ND.
Donors: MDU Resources Group, Inc.; WBI Energy, Inc.; Knife River Corp.; Montana Dakota Utilities Co.; WBI Energy Transmission, Inc.; MDU Construction Services Grp.; Fidelity Exploration & Production Co.; Great Plains Natural Gas Co.; Cascade Natural Gas Corp.; Intermountain Gas Co.; WBI Energy Midstream, LLC.
Contact: Rita O'Neill, Fdn. Mgr.
Financial data (yr. ended 12/31/12): Assets, $4,245,085 (M); gifts received, $1,849,518; expenditures, $1,482,260; qualifying distributions, $1,480,040; giving activities include $1,480,040 for 550 grants (high: $50,000; low: $250).
Purpose and activities: The foundation supports organizations involved with arts and culture, education, the environment, health, human services, community development, civic affairs, and senior citizens.
Fields of interest: Arts councils; Museums; Performing arts, theater; Arts; Secondary school/education; Higher education; Business school/education; Libraries (public); Education; Environment, natural resources; Environment; Hospitals (general); Health care; Youth, services; Human services; Community/economic development Aging.
Programs:
Civic and Community Activities: The foundation supports programs designed to create opportunities and meet the needs of communities across the country.
Culture and Arts: The foundation supports programs designed to promote positive youth development through art funds and councils, museums, theaters, libraries, and cultural centers.
Education: The foundation supports private secondary and higher education institutions, education development foundations, and economic education programs and scholarships.
Employee Matching Gift Program: The foundation matches contributions made by employees of MDU to educational institutions on a 1 for 1 basis from

$50 to $500 per employee, per year and on a 1 for 2 basis for contributions over $500.

Employee Matching Program for Volunteerism: The foundation awards grants to nonprofit organizations with which employees volunteer.

Environment: The foundation supports programs designed to promote the wise use of resources without compromising the ability of future generations to meet their needs.

Health and Human Services: The foundation supports federated dives, national and local health and human service agencies, hospitals, youth agencies, and organizations involved with senior citizens.

Type of support: Annual campaigns; Building/renovation; Capital campaigns; Continuing support; Employee matching gifts; Employee volunteer services; Employee-related scholarships; Equipment; General/operating support; Program development; Scholarship funds.
Geographic limitations: Giving primarily in areas of company operations.
Support limitations: No support for athletic, labor, fraternal, political, lobbying, organizations or regional or national organizations without local affiliation. No grants to individuals (except for employee-related scholarships), or for endowments or economic development; no loans.
Publications: Annual report; Application guidelines; Program policy statement.
Application information: Applications accepted. Application form required. Applicants should submit the following:
1) timetable for implementation and evaluation of project
2) name, address and phone number of organization
3) copy of IRS Determination Letter
4) brief history of organization and description of its mission
5) geographic area to be served
6) listing of board of directors, trustees, officers and other key people and their affiliations
7) detailed description of project and amount of funding requested
8) copy of current year's organizational budget and/or project budget
9) additional materials/documentation

Initial approach: Download application form and mail to local MDU Resources office
Copies of proposal: 1
Board meeting date(s): Jan,
Deadline(s): Oct. 1

Officers and Directors:* Cynthia Norland*, Pres.; Paul K. Sandness, V.P.; Rita R. O'Neill, Secy. and Mgr.; Douglas A. Mahowald, Treas.; Steven L. Bietz; Nancy K. Christenson; David L. Goodin; Thomas D. Nosbusch; J. Kent Wells.
Number of staff: 1 full-time professional.
EIN: 450378937
Selected grants: The following grants are a representative sample of this grantmaker's funding activity:
$55,000 to Western Iowa Tech Community College Foundation, Sioux City, IA, 2011.
$45,000 to Scholarship America, Saint Peter, MN, 2011.
$40,000 to Theodore Roosevelt Medora Foundation, Bismarck, ND, 2011.
$25,000 to Wray, City of, Wray, CO, 2011.
$24,000 to United Way, Missouri Slope Areawide, Bismarck, ND, 2011.
$20,000 to Sheridan Heritage Center, Sheridan, WY, 2011.
$15,000 to Boise State University Foundation, Boise, ID, 2011.
$15,000 to CentraCare Foundation, Saint Cloud, MN, 2011.
$12,000 to Saint Josephs Hospital Foundation, Dickinson, ND, 2011.
$10,000 to Salvation Army, Coeur d Alene, ID, 2011.

2443
Mead Johnson Nutrition Company

2701 Patriot Blvd., 4th Fl.
Glenview, IL 60026 (847) 832-2420

Company URL: http://www.meadjohnson.com
Establishment information: Established in 1905.
Company type: Public company
Company ticker symbol and exchange: MJN/NYSE
International Securities Identification Number: US5828391061
Business activities: Operates a pediatric nutrition company.
Business type (SIC): Drugs
Financial profile for 2012: Number of employees, 6,800; assets, $3,258,200,000; sales volume, $3,901,300,000; pre-tax net income, $805,000,000; expenses, $3,096,300,000; liabilities, $3,239,500,000
Fortune 1000 ranking: 2012—600th in revenues, 293rd in profits, and 728th in assets
Forbes 2000 ranking: 2012—1524th in sales, 948th in profits, and 1920th in assets
Corporate officers: James M. Cornelius, Chair.; Peter Kasper Jakobsen, Pres. and C.E.O.; Peter G. Leemputte, Exec. V.P. and C.F.O.; William C. P'Pool, Sr. V.P., Genl. Counsel, and Secy.; Tom De Weerdt, V.P. and Corp. Cont.
Board of directors: James M. Cornelius, Chair.; Steven M. Altschuler, M.D.; Howard B. Bernick; Kimberly A. Casiano; Anna C. Catalano; Celeste A. Clark, Ph.D.; Stephen W. Golsby; Peter Kasper Jakobsen; Peter G. Ratcliffe; Elliott Sigal, M.D., Ph.D.; Robert S. Singer
Subsidiary: Ninety Commerce Road, Inc., Stamford, CT
Divisions: Bristol-Meyers International Group, New York, NY; Science and Technology Group, New York, NY; Westwood Pharmaceuticals Inc., Buffalo, NY
Giving statement: Giving through the Mead Johnson Nutrition Company Contributions Program.
Company EIN: 800318351

Mead Johnson Nutrition Company Contributions Program

2701 Patriot Blvd.
Glenview, IL 60026-8039 (847) 832-2420
URL: http://www.meadjohnson.com/CorporateCitizenship/Pages/Nurturing-Communities.aspx

Purpose and activities: Mead Johnson Nutrition Company makes charitable contributions to nonprofit organizations involved with nutritional care for vulnerable children and nutrition information for their caregivers. Support is given primarily in areas of company operations worldwide.
Fields of interest: Reproductive health, prenatal care; Nutrition; Children, services; Child development, services Children.
International interests: Asia; Europe; Latin America.
Type of support: Curriculum development; Donated products; Employee volunteer services; General/operating support; In-kind gifts.
Geographic limitations: Giving on an international basis in areas of company operations.

2444
W. R. Meadows, Inc.

300 Industrial Dr.
P.O. Box 338
Hampshire, IL 60140-0338 (847) 214-2100

Company URL: http://www.wrmeadows.com/
Establishment information: Established in 1926.
Company type: Private company
Business activities: Designs, manufactures, and markets products for the construction industry.
Business type (SIC): Industrial machinery and equipment—wholesale
Corporate officers: H.G. Meadows, Chair.; Jim F. Dwyer, C.E.O.; Matt L. Price, Pres.; Jeffrey Murrin, C.F.O.
Board of director: H.G. Meadows, Chair.
Giving statement: Giving through the W. R. Meadows Foundation.

W. R. Meadows Foundation

P.O. Box 338
Hampshire, IL 60140-0338

Establishment information: Established in 1987 in IL.
Donor: W.R. Meadows, Inc.
Financial data (yr. ended 12/31/11): Assets, $282,278 (M); gifts received, $55,000; expenditures, $55,518; qualifying distributions, $55,500; giving activities include $55,500 for 6 grants (high: $30,000; low: $2,000).
Fields of interest: Education; Religion.
Geographic limitations: Giving primarily in CA, IL, and MT.
Support limitations: No grants to individuals.
Application information: Applications not accepted. Contributes only to pre-selected organizations.
Trustees: Ann Dwyer; H. Meadows; R. Meadows.
EIN: 363468997

2445
MeadWestvaco Corporation

501 S. 5th St.
Richmond, VA 23219-0501 (804) 444-1000
FAX: (302) 655-5049

Company URL: http://www.mwv.com
Establishment information: Established in 1888.
Company type: Public company
Company ticker symbol and exchange: MWV/NYSE
International Securities Identification Number: US5833341077
Business activities: Manufactures packaging products, coated and specialty papers, consumer and office products, and specialty chemicals.
Business type (SIC): Paper mills; paperboard containers; paper and paperboard/coated, converted, and laminated; chemicals and allied products
Financial profile for 2012: Number of employees, 16,000; assets, $8,908,000,000; sales volume, $5,459,000,000; pre-tax net income, $306,000,000; expenses, $5,153,000,000; liabilities, $5,548,000,000
Fortune 1000 ranking: 2012—448th in revenues, 573rd in profits, and 429th in assets
Forbes 2000 ranking: 2012—1336th in sales, 1649th in profits, and 1551st in assets
Corporate officers: John A. Luke, Jr., Chair. and C.E.O.; James A. Buzzard, Pres.; E. Mark Rajkowski, Sr. V.P. and C.F.O.; Wendell L. Willkie II, Sr. V.P., Genl. Counsel, and Secy.; Robert E. Birkenholz, V.P.

and Treas.; Brent Harwood, V.P. and Cont.; Donna Owens Cox, V.P., Comms.
Board of directors: John A. Luke, Jr., Chair.; Michael E. Campbell; James G. Kaiser; Richard B. Kelson; James M. Kilts; Susan J. Kropf; Douglas S. Luke; Gracia C. Martore; Timothy H. Powers; Jane L. Warner; Alan D. Wilson
Subsidiaries: The Mead Corporation, Dayton, OH; Westvaco Corporation, Charleston, SC
International operations: Brazil
Giving statement: Giving through the MeadWestvaco Corporation Contributions Program and the MeadWestvaco Foundation.
Company EIN: 311797999

MeadWestvaco Corporation Contributions Program

(formerly The Mead Corporation Contributions Program)
1 High Ridge Park
Stamford, CT 06905-1322

Purpose and activities: As a complement to its foundation, MeadWestvaco also makes charitable contributions to nonprofit organizations directly. Support is given primarily in areas of company operations.
Fields of interest: Education; Environment; Community/economic development; Public policy, research.
Type of support: Donated products.
Geographic limitations: Giving primarily in areas of company operations.
Support limitations: No grants to individuals, or for endowments.
Publications: Informational brochure.
Application information: Application form not required.
Initial approach: Proposal to nearest company facility

The MeadWestvaco Foundation

501 South 5th St.
Richmond, VA 23219-0501 (804) 327-6402
FAX: (804) 444-1971;
E-mail: foundation@mwv.com; Additional contacts: Christine W. Hale, Sr. Mgr., tel.: (804) 444-2531; Jennifer C. Venable, Employee Progs. Mgr., tel.: (804) 444-5216; URL: http://www.mwvfoundation.org

Establishment information: Established in 2003 in DE.
Contact: Kathryn A. Strawn, V.P. and Exec. Dir.
Financial data (yr. ended 12/31/11): Assets, $31,113,277 (M); expenditures, $5,151,141; qualifying distributions, $4,976,697; giving activities include $4,828,555 for 458 grants (high: $550,000; low: $100) and $145,550 for 216 foundation-administered programs.
Purpose and activities: The foundation supports programs designed to promote sustainable communities; education; and environmental stewardship.
Fields of interest: Museums; Arts; Education; Environment, forests; Environment; Youth, services; Family services; Human services; Economic development; Urban/community development; Community/economic development; Public policy, research; Public affairs.
Programs:
Grants for Volunteers: The foundation awards $250 grants to nonprofit organizations with which employees and the spouses of employees of MeadWestvaco volunteer at least 25 hours per year.
Matching Gifts for Volunteer Leaders: The foundation matches contributions made by employees, directors, and the spouses of employees of MeadWestvaco to nonprofit organizations with which they serve on a governing body on a one-for-one basis from $25 to $2,500 per contributor household, per year.
Matching Gifts to Education: The foundation matches contributions made by employees, directors, and the spouses of employees of MeadWestvaco to educational institutions on a one-for-one basis from $25 to $2,500 per contributor household, per year.
Type of support: Employee matching gifts; Employee volunteer services; General/operating support; Program development.
Geographic limitations: Giving on a national basis in areas of company operations, with emphasis on Washington, DC, OH, MA, SC, and VA.
Support limitations: No support for lobbying or political organizations, religious organizations not of direct benefit to the entire community, fraternal organizations, sports teams, or student teams. No grants to individuals, or for academic fellowships or research, advertising, concert, dance, or theatrical tours, conferences, endowments, film, radio, or video productions, fundraising events, scholarships, sports events, or student trips or competitions.
Publications: Application guidelines; Program policy statement.
Application information: Applications accepted. Application form required. Applicants should submit the following:
1) results expected from proposed grant
2) statement of problem project will address
3) name, address and phone number of organization
4) copy of IRS Determination Letter
5) brief history of organization and description of its mission
6) copy of most recent annual report/audited financial statement/990
7) how project's results will be evaluated or measured
8) descriptive literature about organization
9) listing of board of directors, trustees, officers and other key people and their affiliations
10) detailed description of project and amount of funding requested
11) copy of current year's organizational budget and/or project budget
12) listing of additional sources and amount of support
Initial approach: Complete online application
Board meeting date(s): 4 times per year
Deadline(s): None
Officers and Directors:* Wendell L. Willkie II*, Chair.; Stephen R. Scherger*, Vice-Chair.; Kathryn A. Strawn, V.P. and Exec. Dir.; Patricia C. Norris, Secy.; Robert E. Birkenholz, Treas.; Donna O. Cox; Robert A. Feeser; Ned W. Massee; Neil A. McLachlan; Linda V. Schreiner.
Trustee: Mellon Trust of New England.
EIN: 061652243
Selected grants: The following grants are a representative sample of this grantmaker's funding activity:
$1,500,000 to American Enterprise Institute for Public Policy Research, Washington, DC, 2010.
$1,200,000 to CenterStage Foundation, Richmond, VA, 2010.
$1,000,000 to Duke University, Durham, NC, 2010.
$200,000 to Virginia Museum of Fine Arts, Richmond, VA, 2010.
$80,000 to Troy University Foundation, Troy, AL, 2010.
$50,000 to Juniata Valley Educational Trust, Alexandria, PA, 2010.
$40,000 to Chattahoochee Valley Community College, Phenix City, AL, 2010.
$40,000 to Columbus Technical College Foundation, Columbus, GA, 2010.
$14,000 to Sparks State Technical College Foundation, Eufaula, AL, 2010.

2446
The Mechanics Bank

3170 Hilltop Mall Rd.
P.O. Box 1786
Richmond, CA 94806 (510) 741-7656

Company URL: http://www.mechbank.com
Establishment information: Established in 1905.
Company type: Private company
Business activities: Operates commercial bank.
Business type (SIC): Banks/commercial
Corporate officers: Dianne Daiss Felton, Chair.; E. Michael Downer, Vice-Chair.; Steven K. Buster, Pres. and C.E.O.; Steven I. Barlow, Exec. V.P. and C.O.O.; Clinton Chew, Exec. V.P. and C.F.O.; Edward M. Downer III, Chair. Emeritus
Board of directors: Dianne Daiss Felton, Chair.; E. Michael Downer, Vice-Chair.; Daniel W. Albert; Patricia Cochran; Daniel M. Daiss; Edward M. Downer III; Martin B. McNair; J. David Powell; Mark F. Wilson
Giving statement: Giving through the Mechanics Bank Corporate Giving Program.

The Mechanics Bank Corporate Giving Program

725 Alfred Nobel Dr.
Hercules, CA 94547-1806 (510) 741-7656
FAX: (510) 741-3595;
E-mail: fernanda_rodrigues@mechbank.com;
URL: https://www.mechanicsbank.com/mechbank/MBwebsite.nsf/about/communityindex

Contact: Fernanda Rodrigues, V.P., Community Affairs Off.
Purpose and activities: Mechanics Bank makes charitable contributions to nonprofit organizations involved with arts and culture, K-12 education, health, youth development, human services, community development, and civic affairs. Support is given primarily in areas of company operations in northern California.
Fields of interest: Arts; Elementary/secondary education; Health care; Youth development; Human services; Community/economic development; Public affairs; General charitable giving.
Type of support: Employee volunteer services; Program development; Sponsorships.
Geographic limitations: Giving primarily in areas of company operations in northern CA.
Support limitations: No grants for general operating support.
Application information: Applications accepted. Proposals should be submitted using organization letterhead. Application form not required. Applicants should submit the following:
1) results expected from proposed grant
2) population served
3) copy of IRS Determination Letter
4) brief history of organization and description of its mission
5) geographic area to be served
6) copy of most recent annual report/audited financial statement/990
7) how project's results will be evaluated or measured
8) explanation of why grantmaker is considered an appropriate donor for project
9) listing of board of directors, trustees, officers and other key people and their affiliations

10) detailed description of project and amount of funding requested
11) listing of additional sources and amount of support

Proposals should indicate any banking relationships with Mechanics and whether any Mechanics shareholder endorses the request.

Initial approach: Telephone headquarters or mail proposal to headquarters
Copies of proposal: 1
Deadline(s): None

2447
Medeanalytics, Inc.

5858 Horton St., Ste. 475
Emeryville, CA 94608-2072 (510) 379-3300

Company URL: http://www.medeanalytics.com/
Establishment information: Established in 1994.
Company type: Private company
Business activities: Provides healthcare management performance solutions.
Business type (SIC): Management and public relations services
Corporate officers: Michael E. Gallagher, Chair. and C.E.O.; Sal DeTrane, C.A.O.; John Lee, C.I.O.; Marc Taxay, Sr. V.P. and Genl. Counsel; Ken Perez, Sr. V.P., Mktg.
Board of directors: Michael E. Gallagher, Chair.; William Binch; Jeff Crisan; Richard M. Mastaler; Edward P. Schneider
Giving statement: Giving through the Stevie & Wyatt Priceless Foundation.

Stevie & Wyatt Priceless Foundation

P.O. Box 4780
Jackson, WY 83001

Establishment information: Established in 2006 in WY.
Donor: Medefinance, Inc.
Financial data (yr. ended 11/30/10): Assets, $16,064 (M); expenditures, $3,335; qualifying distributions, $2,050; giving activities include $2,050 for 4 grants (high: $550; low: $500).
Purpose and activities: The foundation supports the Community Foundation of Jackson Hole in Jackson, Wyoming.
Fields of interest: Health care; Recreation; Human services.
Type of support: Matching/challenge support.
Application information: Applications not accepted. Unsolicited requests for funds not accepted.
Trustees: Derek Goodson; Lisa K. Price; Stephen Price.
EIN: 207196690

2448
Medical Mutual of Ohio, Inc.

2060 E. 9th St.
Cleveland, OH 44115 (216) 687-7000

Company URL: http://www.medmutual.com
Establishment information: Established in 1934.
Company type: Mutual company
Business activities: Sells health insurance.
Business type (SIC): Insurance/accident and health
Financial profile for 2011: Number of employees, 1,906; assets, $1,495,700,000; sales volume, $2,374,600,000
Fortune 1000 ranking: 2012—782nd in revenues, 830th in profits, and 905th in assets
Corporate officers: Rick Chiricosta, Pres. and C.E.O.; Dennis Jancsy, Exec. V.P. and C.F.O.; Kenneth Sidon, Exec. V.P. and C.I.O.; Ray Mueller, V.P., Finance and Cont.; Michael P. Walker, V.P., Sales; Thomas E. Greene, V.P., Human Resources
Giving statement: Giving through the Medical Mutual of Ohio Charitable Foundation.

The Medical Mutual of Ohio Charitable Foundation

1422 Euclid Ave., Ste. 1300
Cleveland, OH 44115-2015 (216) 861-3810

Establishment information: Established in 1997 in OH; supporting organization of the Cleveland Foundation.
Financial data (yr. ended 12/31/10): Revenue, $44,870; assets, $1,831,912 (M); expenditures, $156,970; giving activities include $143,070 for grants.
Fields of interest: Medical care, community health systems; Health care, clinics/centers; Public health; Health care.
Geographic limitations: Giving limited to the greater Cleveland, OH, area.
Officers and Trustees:* Susan Tyler*, Pres.; Arthur Lavin, M.D.*, V.P.; Pamela F. Jaffe, Secy.; Linda L. Fousek*, Treas.; Ruth Ann Carlos; Inajo Davis Chappell; Margo Roth.
EIN: 341879613

2449
Medieval Times Management Inc.

(doing business as Medieval Times Dinner Tournament)
7662 Beach Blvd.
Buena Park, CA 90620-1838
(714) 521-4740

Company URL: http://www.medievaltimes.com
Establishment information: Established in 1973.
Company type: Subsidiary of a private company
Business activities: Operates dinner theaters.
Business type (SIC): Restaurants and drinking places
Financial profile for 2009: Number of employees, 250
Corporate officers: Pedro Montaner, Chair.; Kenneth Kim, Pres.; Eric Chiusolo, V.P. and Secy.-Treas.
Board of director: Pedro Montaner, Chair.
Giving statement: Giving through the Medieval Times Foundation.

Medieval Times Foundation

7662 Beach Blvd.
Buena Park, CA 90620-1838

Establishment information: Established in 2004 in CA.
Donors: Medieval Times Management, Inc.; The Meadowlands Castle; Medieval Castle, Inc.; Medieval Dinner & Tourmanent, Inc.; Medieval Show; Medieval Times Maryland, Inc.; Medieval Times Myrtle Beach, Inc.; Schaumburg Castle, Inc.
Financial data (yr. ended 09/30/11): Assets, $45,861 (M); gifts received, $11; expenditures, $5,010; qualifying distributions, $0.
Fields of interest: Education; Human services.
Support limitations: No grants to individuals.
Application information: Applications not accepted. Unsolicited requests for funds not accepted.
Officer: Kenneth H, Kim, Chair.
Directors: Pedro De Montaner; Celeste Lanuza.
EIN: 201842259

2450
MedImmune, Inc.

1 MedImmune Way
Gaithersburg, MD 20878 (301) 398-0000

Company URL: http://www.medimmune.com
Establishment information: Established in 1988.
Company type: Subsidiary of a foreign company
Business activities: Manufactures pharmaceutical products.
Business type (SIC): Drugs
Corporate officers: Peter S. Greenleaf, Pres.; Tim Gray, C.F.O.; William C. Bertrand, Jr., Exec. V.P. and Genl. Counsel; Andrew D. Skibo, Exec. V.P., Opers.; Max Donley, Exec. V.P., Human Resources
Board of director: Lawrence Hoff
Subsidiary: MedImmune Oncology, Inc., Conshohocken, PA
International operations: Netherlands
Giving statement: Giving through the MedImmune, Inc. Corporate Giving Program.
Company EIN: 521555759

MedImmune, Inc. Corporate Giving Program

One MedImmune Way
Gaithersburg, MD 20878-2204 (301) 398-0000
E-mail: corporatefunding@medimmune.com; Contact for Independent Medical Education Grants: e-mail: MedEdGrants@MedImmune.com; tel.: (866) 396-6235; URL: http://www.medimmune.com/culture_giving.aspx

Purpose and activities: MedImmune makes charitable contributions to nonprofit organizations and independent medical education programs that promote health and science education and provide health care to infants and children. Support is given primarily in areas of company operations; giving also to national organizations, and in the Netherlands and United Kingdom.
Fields of interest: Elementary/secondary education; Higher education, university; Education; Environment; Health care, infants; Public health, communicable diseases; End of life care; Palliative care; Health care; Cancer; Pediatrics; Immunology; Pediatrics research; Family services; Science Children.
Type of support: Employee matching gifts; Employee volunteer services; Exchange programs; Fellowships; General/operating support; Program development; Sponsorships.
Geographic limitations: Giving primarily in areas of company operations; giving also to national organizations, and in the Netherlands and United Kingdom.
Support limitations: No support for hospital foundations. No support for corporate foundations for Independent Medical Education Grants. No grants for endowments, capital campaigns, building appeals, printing services or advertising, staffing or salaries, product purchase, entertainment events such as fundraising galas or golf tournaments, or programs that promote a particular medicine. No grants to individuals, or for operating expenses, textbooks, conference exhibitions or display booths, education programs at luxury resorts or hotels with spas or golf courses, or retroactive support for Indepdendent Medical Education Grants.

Publications: Application guidelines.
Application information: Applications accepted. Application form not required.
Initial approach: Complete online application
Deadline(s): 6 weeks prior to need
Final notification: 8 weeks for charitable grants; 6 weeks for Independent Medical Education Grants

2451
Medline Industries, Inc.
1 Medline Pl.
Mundelein, IL 60060 (847) 949-5500
FAX: (847) 643-3295

Company URL: http://www.medline.com
Establishment information: Established in 1966.
Company type: Private company
Business activities: Manufactures health care products.
Business type (SIC): Medical instruments and supplies
Financial profile for 2010: Number of employees, 8,000; sales volume, $4,010,000,000
Corporate officers: Charles N. Mills, C.E.O.; Andrew Mills, Pres.; Jim Abrams, C.O.O.; Lesly Marban, V.P., Mktg.; Timothy Jacobson, V.P., Corp. Sales
Divisions: Accucare Div., Mundelein, IL; Dermal Management Systems Div., Mundelein, IL; Dynacor Div., Mundelein, IL; Medcrest Div., Mundelein, IL
Giving statement: Giving through the Medline Foundation.

The Medline Foundation
1 Medline Pl.
Mundelein, IL 60060-4486 (847) 949-2291

Establishment information: Established in 2002 in IL.
Donors: Medline Industries, Inc.; James Abrams.
Financial data (yr. ended 12/31/11): Assets, $3,348,628 (M); gifts received, $33,336; expenditures, $1,026,309; qualifying distributions, $952,079; giving activities include $952,079 for grants.
Purpose and activities: The foundation supports general charitable giving and awards disaster relief grants, welfare grants, and scholarships to employees and children of employees of Medline.
Fields of interest: Higher education; Disasters, preparedness/services; General charitable giving.
Type of support: Employee-related scholarships; General/operating support; Scholarships—to individuals.
Geographic limitations: Giving primarily in areas of company operations.
Application information: Applications accepted.
Initial approach: Proposal
Copies of proposal: 1
Deadline(s): None
Officers and Directors: Andrew J. Mills, Pres.; Ann Ford, V.P.; Alex Liberman, V.P.; Laura Knudson, Secy.-Treas.; James D. Abrams.
EIN: 421563666
Selected grants: The following grants are a representative sample of this grantmaker's funding activity:
$100,000 to National Breast Cancer Foundation, Frisco, TX, 2009.
$90,000 to Chicago Cares, Chicago, IL, 2009.
$50,000 to Golden Rule Foundation, Maitland, FL, 2009.
$50,000 to Golden Rule Foundation, Maitland, FL, 2009.
$40,000 to Los Angeles Jewish Home for the Aging, Reseda, CA, 2009.
$15,000 to American Heart Association, Indianapolis, IN, 2009.
$10,000 to Beth Abraham Foundation, Bronx, NY, 2009.
$10,000 to Mount Sinai Hospital, New York, NY, 2009.
$2,000 to Jamaica Hospital, Jamaica, NY, 2009.
$1,500 to Capital Hospice, Falls Church, VA, 2009.

2452
MEDRAD, Inc.
100 Global View Dr.
Warrendale, PA 15086 (724) 940-6800

Company URL: http://www.medrad.com
Establishment information: Established in 1964.
Company type: Subsidiary of a foreign company
Business activities: Manufactures medical imaging products.
Business type (SIC): Medical instruments and supplies
Corporate officers: Samuel M. Liang, Pres. and C.E.O.; Gary W. Bucciarelli III, Sr. V.P. and C.A.O.; Jeff Owoc, Sr. V.P., Opers.; Wyman Lee, V.P., Human Resources; Julie Coletti, Corp. Secy.
Giving statement: Giving through the MEDRAD, Inc. Corporate Giving Program.

MEDRAD, Inc. Corporate Giving Program
c/o Corp. Giving Comm.
100 Global View Dr.
Warrendale, PA 15086-7601 (724) 940-6800
FAX: (412) 767-4120; URL: http://www.medrad.com/en-us/aboutmedrad/Pages/CorporateGiving.aspx

Purpose and activities: MEDRAD makes charitable contributions to nonprofit organizations involved with arts and culture, education, healthcare, and community development. Support is given primarily in southwestern Pennsylvania.
Fields of interest: Arts; Education; Health care; Human services; Community/economic development.
Type of support: Continuing support; Employee matching gifts; Employee volunteer services; General/operating support.
Geographic limitations: Giving primarily in southwestern PA.
Support limitations: No support for political, religious, or discriminatory organizations, or fraternal or labor organizations. No grants to individuals, or for endowments, debt reduction, capital campaigns, political candidates, fundraising activities related to individual sponsorships, or travel.
Publications: Application guidelines.
Application information: Applications accepted. A contributions committee reviews all requests. Application form not required. Applicants should submit the following:
1) name, address and phone number of organization
2) copy of IRS Determination Letter
3) detailed description of project and amount of funding requested
4) contact person

Initial approach: Proposal to headquarters
Copies of proposal: 1
Committee meeting date(s): Quarterly, in Mar., June, Sept., and Dec.
Deadline(s): None
Final notification: Following review

2453
Medtronic, Inc.
710 Medtronic Pkwy.
Minneapolis, MN 55432-5604
(763) 514-4000
FAX: (763) 514-4879

Company URL: http://www.medtronic.com
Establishment information: Established in 1949.
Company type: Public company
Company ticker symbol and exchange: MDT/NYSE
International Securities Identification Number: US5850551061
Business activities: Operates medical technology company.
Business type (SIC): Medical instruments and supplies
Financial profile for 2013: Number of employees, 45,000; assets, $34,794,000,000; sales volume, $16,590,000,000; pre-tax net income, $4,251,000,000; expenses, $12,339,000,000; liabilities, $16,123,000,000
Fortune 1000 ranking: 2012—172nd in revenues, 52nd in profits, and 169th in assets
Forbes 2000 ranking: 2012—573rd in sales, 158th in profits, and 651st in assets
Corporate officers: Omar Ishrak, Chair. and C.E.O.; Gary L. Ellis, Sr. V.P. and C.F.O.; D. Cameron Findlay, Sr. V.P., Genl. Counsel, and Secy.; H. James Dallas, Sr. V.P., Opers.; Caroline Stockdale, Sr. V.P., Human Resources
Board of directors: Omar Ishrak, Chair.; Richard H. Anderson; Victor J. Dzau, M.D.; Shirley Ann Jackson, Ph.D.; Michael O. Leavitt; James T. Lenehan; Denise M. O'Leary; Kendall J. Powell; Robert C. Pozen; Preetha Reddy, M.D.; Jack W. Schuler
International operations: Argentina; Australia; Austria; Belgium; Brazil; Canada; Cayman Islands; China; Czech Republic; Denmark; Finland; France; Germany; Greece; Hungary; India; Ireland; Israel; Italy; Japan; Lebanon; Luxembourg; Mauritius; Mexico; Netherlands; New Zealand; Norway; Poland; Portugal; Russia; Singapore; South Africa; South Korea; Spain; Sweden; Switzerland; Taiwan; Thailand; Turkey
Giving statement: Giving through the Medtronic, Inc. Corporate Giving Program and the Medtronic Foundation.
Company EIN: 410793183

Medtronic, Inc. Corporate Giving Program
710 Medtronic Pkwy.
Minneapolis, MN 55432-5604 (763) 514-4000
FAX: (763) 514-4879; URL: http://www.medtronic.com/about-medtronic/corporate-citizenship/index.htm

Financial data (yr. ended 12/31/11): Total giving, $32,553,053, including $32,553,053 for grants.
Purpose and activities: As a complement to its foundation, Medtronic also makes charitable contributions to nonprofit organizations directly. Support is given on a national and international basis in areas of company operations.
Fields of interest: Health care; Medical research; Disasters, preparedness/services; United Ways and Federated Giving Programs; General charitable giving.
Type of support: Conferences/seminars; Donated products; Employee volunteer services; General/operating support; In-kind gifts; Program development; Research; Sponsorships.
Geographic limitations: Giving on a national and international basis in areas of company operations.
Publications: Corporate giving report.

Application information: Applications accepted. Application form required.
Initial approach: Complete online application form

The Medtronic Foundation

710 Medtronic Pkwy., LC110
Minneapolis, MN 55432-5604 (763) 505-2639
FAX: (763) 505-2648;
E-mail: medtronicfoundation@medtronic.com; Additional tel.: (800) 328-2518; Contact for PatientLink and Strengthening Health Systems in Africa, Europe, Middle East, and South America: Luc Girad, Medtronic Fdn., Medtronic Europe, Route du Molliau 31, Case postale, CH-1131 Tolochenaz, Switzerland, tel.: +41 21 802 7574, e-mail: foundation.emea@medtronic.com; E-mail for Global Heroes: mtcm.globalheroes@medtronic.com; URL: http://www.medtronic.com/foundation

Establishment information: Established in 1979 in MN.
Donor: Medtronic, Inc.
Contact: Deb Anderson, Grants Admin.
Financial data (yr. ended 04/30/12): Assets, $22,335,281 (M); gifts received, $356,428; expenditures, $32,725,938; qualifying distributions, $32,462,960; giving activities include $29,241,817 for grants.
Purpose and activities: The foundation supports programs designed to promote health, with a focus on heath systems in developing countries, chronic disease, patient advocacy and support, and sudden cardiac arrest; education, including primary and secondary science, math, and engineering initiatives and education reform; and community, through local human services and arts initiatives and disaster relief efforts providing short- and long-term help.
Fields of interest: Arts, cultural/ethnic awareness; Media, radio; Museums (science/technology); Arts; Education, reform; Elementary/secondary education; Elementary school/education; Higher education; Teacher school/education; Education; Medical care, community health systems; Hospitals (general); Health care, emergency transport services; Health care, EMS; Public health; Health care, patient services; Health care; Cancer; Heart & circulatory diseases; Lung diseases; Diabetes; Disasters, preparedness/services; Human services; United Ways and Federated Giving Programs; Science, formal/general education; Mathematics; Engineering/technology; Science; Public affairs Youth; Minorities; Women; Economically disadvantaged.
International interests: Australia; Austria; Belgium; Brazil; Canada; China; Czech Republic; Denmark; France; Germany; India; Ireland; Italy; Japan; Mexico; Netherlands; Poland; Portugal; Russia; South Africa; Spain; Sweden; Switzerland; United Kingdom.
Programs:
CommunityLink: Through CommunityLink grants, the foundation responds to community needs with emphasis on: A) Health - The foundation supports programs designed to help people develop and maintain healthy lifestyles. Special emphasis is directed toward programs designed to reduce disparities in healthcare B) Education - The foundation supports STEM education programs designed to promote public understanding of health and medical technology, and stimulate interest among young people. Special emphasis is directed toward education projects at schools, science museums, and community centers; and programs designed to improve educational and career opportunities of underserved people and C) Arts, Civic, and Human Services - The foundation supports arts, civic, and human services programs designed to reach out to the widest possible audiences.
Education Reform: The foundation supports programs designed to improve educational systems and close the gap between underserved and affluent school districts through education reform. Special emphasis is directed toward programs designed to improve administration and teacher quality in grades K-12.
Global Heroes: The foundation, in partnership with Twin Cities in Motion, annually honors runners diagnosed with medical conditions who benefit from medical technology as Global Heroes. The foundation selects individual runners from around the world running with medical devices such as a pacemaker, spinal device, neurological device, insulin pump, or heart valve to run in the Medtronic Twin Cities Marathon or Medtronic TC 10 Mile Race. The award includes a travel package, lodging and meals, and events such as the Medtronic Twin Cities Marathon Global Heroes reception. Visit URL: http://www.medtronic.com/2012globalheroes/index.html for more information.
HeartRescue: Working with select premier partners, the foundation is leading an effort to increase overall Sudden Cardiac Arrest (SCA) survival rates in the United States. The foundation supports regional and state-wide initiatives designed to develop and expand SCA response through coordinating measurement, education, training, and the application of evidence-based, best practices among the general public, first responders, emergency medical services (EMS) and hospitals. Grants range from $250,000 to $500,000. Invitations to become a HeartRescue Partner are announced periodically. Visit URL http://www.medtronic.com/heartrescueproject/index.html for more information.
Matching Gifts to Education: The foundation matches contributions made by employees of Medtronic to educational institutions up to $15,000 per employee, per year.
Medtronic Fellows: The foundation partners with pre-selected universities and national diversity organizations to support college and university scholars and fellows in science, engineering, and health-related fields. This program is by invitation only.
PatientLink - Empowering Patient Communities: The foundation helps to improve the lives of people with chronic diseases and conditions by partnering with patient associations that educate, support, and advocate on behalf of patients. The partnerships promote awareness of chronic disease, prevalence, risks, and resources; education of patients and families to be informed and active in managing their condition; and advocacy of personal health and patient representation on the boards of patient organizations. The program is by invitation only in the U.S. Organizations in Canada, Europe, and Japan are welcome to apply.
PatientLink Leadership Development Awards: The foundation provides professional development and training opportunities for executive-level leaders of participating PatientLink organizations. Awards are given to leadership development programs that promote collaboration, including leadership training and development of core team members across collaborating groups; mergers, including strategic planning and development of implementation plans; and succession, including planning for future leader transitions and management realignment. Grants range from $1,000 to $20,000.
STEM Education: The foundation supports programs designed to encourage students' curiosity in science and technology and develop innovators through science and engineering scholarships and fellowships at selected post-secondary institutions. Special emphasis is directed toward programs designed to provide access to quality STEM (science, technology, engineering, and math) education for under-represented students in primary (five years old) through post-secondary institutions.
Strengthening Heath Systems - The Global Burden of NCDs: The foundation awards grants to non-governmental organizations, public institutions, and chronic disease centers to strengthen health systems and to integrate non-communicable diseases (NCDs) including cardiovascular disease, cancer, and chronic respiratory disease into primary care. Special emphasis is directed toward programs designed to increase awareness and prioritization of NCDs in national and global development agendas; strengthen health systems in developing countries by integrating NCDs; and improve global understanding of best practices in cardiovascular disease and diabetes. Grants range from $50,000 to $250,000. This program is limited to Africa, Brazil, Central and Eastern Europe, China, India, and Russia.
Volunteer Grants: The foundation awards $500 grants to nonprofit organizations with which employees of Medtronic volunteer at least 25 hours per year.
Type of support: Annual campaigns; Conferences/seminars; Continuing support; Curriculum development; Donated products; Employee matching gifts; Employee volunteer services; Fellowships; Management development/capacity building; Program development; Publication; Scholarship funds; Seed money; Sponsorships.
Geographic limitations: Giving primarily in areas of company operations, with emphasis on Maricopa County and Tempe, AZ, Santa Clarita, San Fernando, and Simi Valley regions, western Los Angeles, and Orange, Santa Barbara, Sonoma, Sunnyvale, and Ventura counties, CA, Denver metro area and Louisville, CO, Jacksonville, FL, Kosciusko County, IN, Beverly, Danvers, Middleton, North Shore, Peabody, and Salem, MA, Minneapolis, St. Paul, and Twin Cities-Seven County metro, MN, area, Humacao, Juncos, and Villalba, PR, Memphis, TN, Fort Worth and San Antonio, TX, and King and Snohomish County, WA, and in Africa, Australia, Austria, Belgium, Brazil, Canada, Czech Republic, Shanghai, China, Denmark, Europe, France, Germany, Hungary, India, Ireland, Italy, Japan, Mexico, Netherlands, Poland, Russia, South Africa, Spain, Switzerland, and the United Kingdom.
Support limitations: No support for lobbying, political, or fraternal organizations, fiscal agents, religious groups not of direct benefit to the entire community, or private foundations. No grants individuals, or for scholarships, Continuing Medical Education (CME) grants, capital campaigns, fundraising events or activities, social events, goodwill advertising, general operating support, general support for educational institutions, long-term counseling or personal development, endowments, automatic external defibrillators (AEDs) purchases, or research.
Publications: Corporate giving report; Financial statement; Grants list; Program policy statement.
Application information: Applications not accepted. The foundation currently has an invitation only process for giving.
Board meeting date(s): Quarterly
Officers and Directors:* Gary L. Ellis*, Chair.; H. James Dallas, Vice-Chair.; Jacob A. Gayle, Ph.D., V.P. and Exec. Dir.; Kristin L. Gorsuch; Stephen N. Oesterle, M.D.; Chris J. O'Connell; Herb F. Riband; Tony B. Semedo; David M. Steinhaus, M.D.; Caroline Stockdale; Tom M. Tefft.

Number of staff: 3 full-time professional; 2 part-time professional; 1 full-time support; 1 part-time support.
EIN: 411306950
Selected grants: The following grants are a representative sample of this grantmaker's funding activity:
$2,239,222 to United Way, Greater Twin Cities, Minneapolis, MN, 2011. For matching grant for employee campaign.
$800,000 to Teach for America, New York, NY, 2011. For Teach for America Math And Science Initiative, Teach for America, Twin Cities, Teach For America, Memphis, Teach For America-Jacksonville.
$517,588 to Scholarship America, Saint Peter, MN, 2011. For Medtronic Family Scholarships.
$500,000 to University of Washington, Harborview Medical Center, CPEC, Seattle, WA, 2011. For HeartRescue Flagship Premier Partner Program.
$333,334 to Partners in Health, Boston, MA, 2011. For construction of Mirebalais Hospital in Haiti.
$39,264 to Italian Multiple Sclerosis Society, Genoa, Italy, 2011. For Living Beyond MS, A Project Dedicated to Young People.
$27,431 to United Way, Foothills, Lafayette, CO, 2011. For matching grant for Employee Campaign.
$20,000 to Deer Valley Unified School District No. 97, Phoenix, AZ, 2011. To link Science, Technology, Engineering and Mathematics (STEM) students from elementary through middle to high school and beyond in Step it Up program.
$15,000 to Volunteers in Medicine Jacksonville, Jacksonville, FL, 2011. To support free health care clinic for the low-income working uninsured.

2454
Meecorp Capital Markets, LLC
2115 Linwood Ave., Ste. 301
Fort Lee, NJ 07024-5022 (201) 944-9330

Company URL: http://www.meecorp.com
Establishment information: Established in 1994.
Company type: Private company
Business activities: Operates a commercial real estate lending company.
Business type (SIC): Credit institutions/business
Corporate officer: Michael Edrei, Chair.
Board of directors: Michael Edrei, Chair.; Daniel Edrei
Giving statement: Giving through the New Course Charity Foundation Inc.

New Course Charity Foundation Inc.
c/o Michael Edrei
2115 Linwood Ave., Ste. 301
Fort Lee, NJ 07024-3240
URL: http://www.newcoursefoundation.org

Establishment information: Established in 2007 in NJ.
Donors: Mee Corp. Group, LLC; Mee Corp. Capital Markets LLC.
Financial data (yr. ended 12/31/11): Assets, $624 (M); gifts received, $74,150; expenditures, $73,558; qualifying distributions, $72,320; giving activities include $59,820 for 2 grants (high: $36,975; low: $22,845).
Fields of interest: Philanthropy/voluntarism.
Geographic limitations: Giving primarily in Tel Aviv, Israel.
Support limitations: No grants to individuals.
Application information: Applications not accepted. Unsolicited requests for funds not accepted.
Trustees: Daniel Edrei; Mary Edrei; Michael Edrei; Sharon Edrei.
EIN: 260334496

2455
MEEMIC Insurance Co.
(formerly Michigan Educational Employees Mutual Insurance Company)
1685 N. Opdyke Rd.
P.O. Box 217019
Auburn Hills, MI 48326 (248) 373-5700

Company URL: http://www.meemic.com
Establishment information: Established in 1950.
Company type: Subsidiary of a public company
Business activities: Sells automobile, property, boat, and umbrella insurance.
Business type (SIC): Insurance/fire, marine, and casualty
Corporate officers: Victor T. Adamo, Esq., Chair.; Steven D. Monahan, Pres. and C.E.O.; Christine Schmitt, C.F.O.
Board of director: Victor T. Adamo, Esq., Chair.
Giving statement: Giving through the MEEMIC Foundation for the Future of Education.

MEEMIC Foundation for the Future of Education
1685 N. Opdyke Rd.
Auburn Hills, MI 48326-2656
FAX: (248) 377-1459;
E-mail: foundation@meemic.com; URL: http://www.meemic.com/foundation/

Establishment information: Established in 1992 in MI.
Donors: Michigan Educational Employees Mutual Insurance Co.; MEEMIC Insurance Co.
Financial data (yr. ended 12/31/11): Assets, $1,704,706 (M); gifts received, $25,000; expenditures, $98,538; qualifying distributions, $85,549; giving activities include $84,995 for grants.
Purpose and activities: The foundation awards grants to educators at public, private, charter, and parochial schools in Michigan for programs designed to incorporate technology, science, literacy, mentoring, and the arts.
Fields of interest: Arts education; Education, reading; Education; Science.
Type of support: Grants to individuals.
Geographic limitations: Giving limited to MI.
Support limitations: No grants for school supplies or equipment.
Publications: Application guidelines; Grants list.
Application information: Applications accepted. Application form required.
Initial approach: Complete online application
Deadline(s): June 30
Final notification: July
Officers: Steve Monahan, Chair. and C.E.O.; Donald Weatherspoon, Vice-Chair. and Pres.; Sean Maloney, Sr. V.P.; Tim Bannon, V.P., Mktg.
Board Members: James Ballard; Terry Ann Boguth; Pam Harlin; Daniel Pappas; Dan Stafford.
Number of staff: 1 full-time professional; 1 part-time professional.
EIN: 383048526

2456
Meijer, Inc.
2929 Walker Ave. N.W.
Grand Rapids, MI 49544 (616) 453-6711

Company URL: http://www.meijer.com/
Establishment information: Established in 1934.
Company type: Private company
Business activities: Operates department stores.
Business type (SIC): Department stores
Financial profile for 2011: Number of employees, 74,000; sales volume, $14,630,000,000
Corporate officers: Hendrik G. Meijer, Co-Chair. and Co.-C.E.O.; Doug Meijer, Co-Chair.; Paul Boyer, Vice-Chair. and Co.-C.E.O.; Mark A. Murray, Pres.; Jim Walsh, C.F.O.
Board of directors: Doug Meijer, Co-Chair.; Hendrick G. Meijer, Co-Chair.; Paul Boyer, Vice-Chair.; Mark A. Murray
Plant: Lansing, MI
Giving statement: Giving through the Meijer, Inc. Corporate Giving Program.

Meijer, Inc. Corporate Giving Program
2929 Walker Ave. N.W.
Grand Rapids, MI 49544-6402
URL: http://www.meijer.com/content/content.jsp?pageName=meijer_75th_anniversary_community

Purpose and activities: Meijer makes charitable contributions to nonprofit organizations involved with food services. Support is given primarily in areas of company operations in Illinois, Indiana, Kentucky, Michigan, and Ohio.
Fields of interest: Food banks; General charitable giving.
Type of support: Donated products; General/operating support; In-kind gifts.
Geographic limitations: Giving primarily in areas of company operations in IL, IN, KY, MI, and OH.

2457
Melaleuca, Inc.
3910 S. Yellowstone Hwy.
Idaho Falls, ID 83402 (208) 522-0700
FAX: (208) 535-2362

Company URL: http://www.melaleuca.com/
Establishment information: Established in 1985.
Company type: Private company
Business activities: Sells tree oil, personal care products, cosmetics, household cleaning supplies, and vitamins directly to consumers.
Business type (SIC): Nonstore retailers
Financial profile for 2009: Number of employees, 1,200
Corporate officers: Frank L. VanderSloot, Pres. and C.E.O.; Thomas K. Knutson, C.F.O. and Treas.; Jan Nielson, C.A.O.; Noel Jenkins, V.P., Opers.
Giving statement: Giving through the Melaleuca Foundation.

Melaleuca Foundation
3910 S. Yellowstone Hwy.
Idaho Falls, ID 83402-4342
E-mail: info@melaleucafoundation.org; URL: http://www.melaleuca.org/

Establishment information: Established in 2003 in ID.
Donor: Melaleuca, Inc.
Financial data (yr. ended 12/31/11): Assets, $330,037 (M); gifts received, $231,620;

expenditures, $273,919; qualifying distributions, $266,891; giving activities include $266,891 for grants.
Purpose and activities: The foundation supports organizations involved with education and the Saint Lucia Children's Home in Quito, Ecuador.
Fields of interest: Education; Children/youth, services; Residential/custodial care.
Type of support: General/operating support; Scholarship funds.
Geographic limitations: Giving primarily in ID and Quito, Ecuador.
Support limitations: No grants to individuals.
Application information: Applications not accepted. Contributes only to pre-selected organizations.
Officers: Frank L. VanderSloot, Pres.; Thomas K. Knutson, Treas.
EIN: 200513976

2458
Melissa Joy Manning, Inc.
2500 Market St.
Oakland, CA 94607-3438 (510) 465-2269

Company URL: http://www.melissajoymanning.com
Establishment information: Established in 1997.
Company type: Private company
Business activities: Designs and manufactures jewelry.
Business type (SIC): Jewelry/precious metal
Corporate officer: Melissa Joy Manning, Pres. and C.E.O.
Office: New York, NY
Giving statement: Giving through the Melissa Joy Manning, Inc. Corporate Giving Program.

Melissa Joy Manning, Inc. Corporate Giving Program
2500 Market St., Unit A
Oakland, CA 94607-3438 (510) 465-4413
E-mail: info@mjmmetal.com; URL: http://www.melissajoymanning.com/mm5/merchant.mvc?Screen=PHIL

Purpose and activities: Melissa Joy Manning, Inc. donates a percentage of profits to nonprofit organizations involved with the arts, community and economic development, education, entrepreneurship, and the environment. Support is given primarily in California.
Fields of interest: Arts; Education; Environment; Social entrepreneurship; Community/economic development Children; Women; Girls; Economically disadvantaged.
Type of support: Donated products; General/operating support.
Geographic limitations: Giving primarily in CA; giving also to national organizations.

2459
MEMC Electronic Materials, Inc.
501 Pearl Dr.
P.O. Box 8
St. Peters, MO 63376 (636) 474-5000
FAX: (314) 279-5158

Company URL: http://www.memc.com/
Establishment information: Established in 1959.
Company type: Public company
Company ticker symbol and exchange: WFR/NYSE
Business activities: Manufactures silicon wafers.
Business type (SIC): Electronic components and accessories
Financial profile for 2012: Number of employees, 5,630; assets, $4,701,600,000; sales volume, $2,529,900,000; pre-tax net income, -$81,500,000; expenses, $2,472,700,000; liabilities, $4,126,300,000
Fortune 1000 ranking: 2012—803rd in revenues, 936th in profits, and 610th in assets
Corporate officers: Emmanuel T. Hernandez, Chair.; Ahmad R. Chatila, Pres. and C.E.O.; Brian Wuebbels, Exec. V.P. and C.F.O.; Bradley Kohn, Sr. V.P., Genl. Counsel and Corp. Secy.; David Ranhoff, Sr. V.P., Sales and Mktg.
Board of directors: Emmanuel T. Hernandez, Chair.; Antonio Alvarez; Peter Blackmore; Ahmad R. Chatila; Jeffry Quinn; William E. Stevens; Steven Tesoriere; Marshall C. Turner; James B. Williams
Giving statement: Giving through the MEMC Foundation.
Company EIN: 561505767

MEMC Foundation
501 Pearl Dr.
P.O. Box 8
St. Peters, MO 63376-0090

Establishment information: Established in 2007 in MO.
Donor: MEMC Electronic Materials, Inc.
Financial data (yr. ended 12/31/11): Assets, $4,410,161 (M); gifts received, $21,000; expenditures, $263,976; qualifying distributions, $263,223; giving activities include $263,223 for 8 grants (high: $143,173; low: $1,500).
Purpose and activities: The foundation supports science museums and organizations involved with cancer, multiple sclerosis, disaster relief, children and youth, and residential care.
Fields of interest: Museums (science/technology); Cancer; Cancer, leukemia; Multiple sclerosis; Disasters, preparedness/services; Children/youth, services; Residential/custodial care.
Type of support: General/operating support; Sponsorships.
Geographic limitations: Giving primarily in St. Louis, MO; giving also to national organizations.
Support limitations: No grants to individuals.
Application information: Applications not accepted. Unsolicited requests for funds not accepted.
Officers: Steve Edens, Chair. and Pres.; Bradley Kohn, Secy.; Kenneth Hannah, Treas.
EIN: 208722904

2461
MenashaCorporation
1645 Bergstrom Rd.
Neenah, WI 54956-9701 (920) 751-1000
FAX: (920) 751-1236

Company URL: http://www.menasha.com
Establishment information: Established in 1849.
Company type: Private company
Business activities: Manufactures corrugated packaging, paperboard, and printed products, plastic material handling products, engineered plastics, and promotional products; manufactures pharmaceutical labels, identification tags, specialty screen printed products, injection molded plastics, and food service supplies.
Business type (SIC): Paperboard containers; paper and paperboard/coated, converted, and laminated; printing/commercial; rubber and miscellaneous plastics products; plastic products/miscellaneous
Financial profile for 2010: Number of employees, 3,800; sales volume, $1,000,000,000
Corporate officers: Donald C. Shepard III, Chair.; James M. Kotek, Pres. and C.E.O.; Thomas M. Rettler, Sr. V.P. and C.F.O.; Lea Ann Hammen, V.P. and Treas.; Mark P. Fogarty, V.P., Genl. Counsel, and Corp. Secy.; Rick J. Fantini, V.P., Human Resources
Board of directors: Donald C. Shepard III, Chair.; Robert G. Bohn; Rhonda L. Brooks; James C. Janning; James M. Kotek; Richard A. Meeusen; Bruce W. Schnitzer; Donald C. Shepard; Charles E. Shepard; Onnie Leach Smith
Plants: Nevada City, CA; St. Petersburg, FL; Bogart, GA; Fort Wayne, IN; Manchester, Monticello, IA; Monson, MA; Coloma, Otsego, MI; Hopkins, Lakeville, MN; Olive Branch, MS; Farmingdale, South Brunswick, NJ; Columbus, Urbana, OH; North Bend, OR; Delmont, Scranton, Yukon, PA; Mount Pleasant, TN; Danville, VA; Olympia, WA; Dane, Green Lake, Hartford, Menasha, Watertown, WI
Giving statement: Giving through the Menasha Corporation Foundation.

Menasha Corporation Foundation
P.O. Box 367
Neenah, WI 54957-0367 (920) 751-2036
E-mail: foundation@menasha.com; Additional tel.: (800) 558-5073; URL: http://www.menasha.com/Foundation

Establishment information: Established in 1953 in WI.
Donor: Menasha Corp.
Contact: Kevin Schuh, Treas.
Financial data (yr. ended 12/31/11): Assets, $1,413,923 (M); gifts received, $741,000; expenditures, $791,886; qualifying distributions, $791,886; giving activities include $780,100 for 468 grants (high: $100,000; low: $25).
Purpose and activities: The foundation supports programs designed to promote safe and healthy citizens; an educated society; community betterment; and environmental sustainability.
Fields of interest: Arts; Elementary/secondary education; Higher education; Education; Environment, natural resources; Environment; Health care; Safety/disasters; Children/youth, services; Human services; Community/economic development; United Ways and Federated Giving Programs.

Programs:

An Educated Society: The foundation supports programs designed to create and expand learning experiences and opportunities to both children and adults.

Community Betterment: The foundation supports community improvement programs and arts and cultural activities that enrich quality of life.

Dollars for Doers: The foundation awards $250 to any elementary or secondary school with which employees of Manesha volunteer a least 20 hours during the school year. Participating schools are also entered in a $2,500 drawing.

Environmental Sustainability: The foundation supports programs designed to encourage the understanding, protections, and sustainability of our natural resources.

Matching Gifts: The foundation matches contributions made by shareholders, employees, and retirees to educational institutions on a one-for-one basis from $25 to $1,000 per contributor, per year.

Safe and Healthy Citizens: The foundation supports programs designed to meet basic needs for safe living, food, and health care; and programs that raise awareness of social needs and work to facilitate change.

Scholarships: The foundation annually awards $3,000 college scholarships to children of employees of Manesha.

Type of support: Annual campaigns; Building/renovation; Capital campaigns; Continuing support; Employee matching gifts; Employee volunteer services; Employee-related scholarships; Equipment; General/operating support; Program development; Scholarship funds; Sponsorships.
Geographic limitations: Giving primarily in areas of company operations in Neenah, WI.
Support limitations: No grants to individuals (except for employee-related scholarships).
Publications: Application guidelines.
Application information: Applications accepted. Proposals should be no longer than 4 pages. Application form not required. Applicants should submit the following:
1) population served
2) copy of IRS Determination Letter
3) brief history of organization and description of its mission
4) detailed description of project and amount of funding requested
5) copy of current year's organizational budget and/or project budget
6) listing of additional sources and amount of support
7) copy of most recent annual report/audited financial statement/990
8) how project's results will be evaluated or measured
9) list of company employees involved with the organization
10) additional materials/documentation

Initial approach: Proposal
Copies of proposal: 1
Board meeting date(s): Mar., June, Sept. and Dec.
Deadline(s): Feb. 1, May 1, Aug., 1, and Nov. 1

Officers and Directors:* Arthur W. Huge*, Chair.; Ralph L. Evans*, Pres.; James J. Sarosiek*, V.P.; Angie Burns, Secy.; Kevin Schuh, Treas.; Katherine Gansner; James M. Kotek; Timothy C. Shepard; Michael K. Waite; Margie Weiss, Ph.D.
EIN: 396047384
Selected grants: The following grants are a representative sample of this grantmaker's funding activity:
$3,000 to City of Hope, Duarte, CA, 2010.
$2,500 to Susan G. Komen for the Cure, Dallas, TX, 2010.
$1,500 to American Cancer Society, Atlanta, GA, 2010.
$1,500 to City of Hope, Duarte, CA, 2010.
$1,500 to Cystic Fibrosis Foundation, Bethesda, MD, 2010.
$1,500 to Huntingtons Disease Society of America, New York, NY, 2010.
$1,500 to Indiana University, Bloomington, IN, 2010.
$1,500 to University of Michigan, Ann Arbor, MI, 2010.
$1,500 to University of Minnesota, Minneapolis, MN, 2010.
$1,500 to University of Saint Thomas, Saint Paul, MN, 2010.

2460
The Men's Wearhouse, Inc.

6380 Rogerdale Rd.
Houston, TX 77072-1624 (281) 776-7000

Company URL: http://www.menswearhouse.com
Establishment information: Established in 1973.
Company type: Public company
Company ticker symbol and exchange: MW/NYSE
Business activities: Operates men's apparel stores.
Business type (SIC): Apparel and accessory stores; men's and boys' apparel and accessory stores
Financial profile for 2013: Number of employees, 17,500; assets, $1,496,350,000; sales volume, $2,488,280,000; pre-tax net income, $197,670,000; expenses, $2,289,710,000; liabilities, $400,090,000
Fortune 1000 ranking: 2012—813th in revenues, 680th in profits, and 920th in assets
Corporate officers: George Zimmer, Chair.; David H. Edwab, Vice-Chair.; Douglas S. Ewert, Pres. and C.E.O.; Diana M. Wilson, Exec. V.P., Finance; Charles Bresler, Ph.D., Exec. V.P., Mktg. and Human Resources
Board of directors: George Zimmer, Chair.; David H. Edwab, Vice-Chair.; Rinaldo S. Brutoco; Deepak Chopra, M.D.; Douglas S. Ewert; Larry Katzen; Grace Nichols; Michael L. Ray, Ph.D.; William B. Sechrest; Sheldon I. Stein
Office: Fremont, CA
International operations: Canada
Giving statement: Giving through the Men's Wearhouse, Inc. Corporate Giving Program.
Company EIN: 741790172

The Men's Wearhouse, Inc. Corporate Giving Program

c/o Store Mgr.
6380 Rogerdale Rd.
Houston, TX 77072 (800) 851-6744
URL: http://www.menswearhouse.com

Purpose and activities: The Men's Wearhouse makes charitable contributions of gift cards, merchandise, and tuxedo rentals to nonprofit organizations providing wardrobing services, career development, and/or job placement to specific male populations. Support is given on a national basis.
Fields of interest: Substance abuse, services; Offenders/ex-offenders, services; Employment, services; Employment, training; Youth, services; Developmentally disabled, centers & services; Homeless, human services; Military/veterans' organizations Economically disadvantaged.
Type of support: Annual campaigns; Donated products; Employee volunteer services; General/operating support; In-kind gifts.
Geographic limitations: Giving on a national basis in areas of company operations.
Support limitations: No grants to organizations requiring clients to attend religious services in order to benefit from receiving donated merchandise.
Publications: Application guidelines.
Application information: Application form required.

Initial approach: Download application form and mail with letter of inquiry to nearest company store
Copies of proposal: 1

Number of staff: 1 full-time professional.

2462
Mentor Graphics Corporation

8005 S.W. Boeckman Rd.
Wilsonville, OR 97070-9733
(503) 685-7000
FAX: (503) 685-1204

Company URL: http://www.mentor.com
Establishment information: Established in 1981.
Company type: Public company
Company ticker symbol and exchange: MENT/NASDAQ
Business activities: Develops, manufactures, markets, sells, and supports electronic design automation products and services.
Business type (SIC): Computer services
Financial profile for 2013: Number of employees, 5,029; assets, $1,745,280,000; sales volume, $1,088,730,000; pre-tax net income, $141,340,000; expenses, $927,090,000; liabilities, $711,800,000
Corporate officers: Walden C. Rhines, Chair. and C.E.O.; Gregory K. Hinckley, C.P.A., Pres. and C.F.O.; Richard Trebing, Corp. Cont. and C.A.O.; Ananthan Thandri, V.P. and C.I.O.; Dean MacLean Freed, V.P., Genl. Counsel, and Secy.; Michael Vishny, V.P., Human Resources; Brian Derrick, V.P., Corp. Mktg.; Marc Corbacho, V.P., Sales; Ethan Manuel, Corp. Treas.
Board of directors: Walden C. Rhines, Chair.; Keith L. Barnes; Peter Bonfield; Gregory K. Hinckley; Daniel J. McCranie; Kevin C. McDonough; Patrick B. McManus; David Schechter
Subsidiary: Ikos Systems, Inc., Cupertino, CA
Plants: Huntsville, AL; San Jose, CA; Longmont, CO
International operations: Armenia; Australia; Canada; China; Denmark; England; Finland; France; Germany; Hungary; India; Israel; Italy; Japan; Netherlands; Pakistan; Poland; Russia; Singapore; South Korea; Spain; Sweden; Switzerland; Taiwan; United Kingdom
Giving statement: Giving through the Mentor Graphics Foundation.
Company EIN: 930786033

Mentor Graphics Foundation

8005 S.W. Boeckman Rd.
Wilsonville, OR 97070-7777
E-mail: mentorgraphics_foundation@mentor.com; URL: http://www.mentor.com/company/foundation/index.cfm

Establishment information: Established in 1981 in OR.
Donor: Mentor Graphics Corp.
Contact: Twiaa Bennett, Admin.
Financial data (yr. ended 12/31/11): Assets, $97,814 (M); gifts received, $302,550; expenditures, $289,509; qualifying distributions, $286,749; giving activities include $286,749 for grants.
Purpose and activities: The foundation supports organizations involved with arts and culture, education, health, disaster relief, and human services.
Fields of interest: Visual arts; Museums; Performing arts; Arts; Education; Health care; Disasters, preparedness/services; Human services; Science, formal/general education; Mathematics; Engineering/technology.
Programs:

Culture and the Arts: The foundation supports programs designed to promote the full spectrum of artistic expression, including visual and performing arts, museums, and organizations that broaden cultural experience.

Education: The foundation supports programs designed to enable students to participate in scientific projects and engage in intellectual dialogue with current scientific theories. Special emphasis is directed toward programs (usually after-school) designed to promote science, math, and engineering for K-12 students.

Health and Human Services: The foundation supports organizations involved with health, disaster relief, and human services.

Type of support: Employee matching gifts; General/operating support; Program development.
Geographic limitations: Giving primarily in areas of major company operations, with emphasis on OR.
Support limitations: No support for religious, political, or gender-based organizations, or for animal rights organizations. No grants to individuals, or for environmental causes, capital campaigns, building, political campaigns or ballots, sponsorships of dinners or social events, or fundraisers.
Publications: Application guidelines; Program policy statement.
Application information: Applications accepted. Grants limited to $25,000; no grants less than $1,000; grants cannot represent more than 5% of organization's annual budget. Application form required. Applicants should submit the following:
1) copy of IRS Determination Letter
2) listing of board of directors, trustees, officers and other key people and their affiliations
3) detailed description of project and amount of funding requested
4) copy of current year's organizational budget and/or project budget
5) listing of additional sources and amount of support

Initial approach: Download application form and mail or e-mail to foundation
Copies of proposal: 1
Board meeting date(s): Mar.
Deadline(s): Feb. 28
Final notification: 2 weeks following board meeting

Officers and Directors:* Alan Friedman, Pres.; Dean Freed, Secy.; Twila Bennett*, Admin.; Michael Buehler; Diane Cain-Pozzo; John Issac; John Stedman.
Number of staff: None.
EIN: 930870309
Selected grants: The following grants are a representative sample of this grantmaker's funding activity:
$25,000 to FIRST Regional Tournament, 2009.
$25,000 to Institute for Science Engineering and Public Policy, 2009.
$25,000 to Oregon Museum of Science and Industry, Portland, OR, 2009. For Space: A Journey to Our Future exhibit.
$15,000 to Oregon Ballet Theater, Portland, OR, 2009. For Nutcracker, single performance.
$10,000 to Portland Opera, Portland, OR, 2009. For Barber of Seville, single performance.
$5,000 to Lake Oswego Robotics Team, 2009.
$5,000 to Oregon City Robotics Team, 2009.
$5,000 to San Jose Museum of Art Association, San Jose, CA, 2009.
$2,500 to First Robotics, Manchester, NH, 2009.

2463
Mercedes-Benz USA, L.L.C.

(also known as MBUSA)
1 Mercedes Dr.
P.O. Box 350
Montvale, NJ 07645-1815 (201) 573-0600

Company URL: http://www.mbusa.com/mercedes/#/companyInfo/
Establishment information: Established in 1965.
Company type: Subsidiary of a foreign company
Business activities: Manufactures automobiles.
Business type (SIC): Motor vehicles and equipment; motor vehicles, parts, and supplies—wholesale
Financial profile for 2009: Number of employees, 1,400
Corporate officers: Stephen Cannon, Pres. and C.E.O.; Norbert H. Litzkow, C.F.O.
Subsidiaries: Mercedes-Benz Hollywood, Inc., Hollywood, CA; Mercedes-Benz Manhattan, Inc., New York, NY
Giving statement: Giving through the Mercedes-Benz USA, LLC Corporate Giving Program.

Mercedes-Benz USA, LLC Corporate Giving Program

c/o Corp. Comms. Dept.
1 Mercedes Dr.
Montvale, NJ 07645-1815 (201) 573-0600
URL: http://www.mbusa.com/mercedes/about_us/companyinfo

Contact: Joe Johnson
Purpose and activities: Mercedes-Benz USA makes charitable contributions to nonprofit organizations involved with education, health, youth development, human services, community development, women, and on a case by case basis. Support is given on a national basis.
Fields of interest: Education; Health care; Youth development; Children, services; Human services; Community/economic development; General charitable giving Women.
Type of support: Employee matching gifts; General/operating support; Scholarship funds; Sponsorships.
Geographic limitations: Giving on a national basis in areas of company operations.
Support limitations: No support for religious, labor, or political organizations or fraternal or social clubs. No grants to individuals; no loans.
Application information: Faxes are not encouraged. Application form not required.

Initial approach: Proposal to nearest company facility
Copies of proposal: 1
Deadline(s): None
Final notification: 6 weeks

2464
Merchant & Gould

3200 IDS Ctr.
80 S. 8th St.
Minneapolis, MN 55402-2215
(612) 336-4673

Company URL: http://www.merchantgould.com
Establishment information: Established in 1954.
Company type: Private company
Business activities: Operates law firm.
Business type (SIC): Legal services
Offices: Denver, CO; Washington, DC; Atlanta, GA; Minneapolis, MN; New York, NY; Knoxville, TN; Seattle, WA; Madison, WI
Giving statement: Giving through the Merchant & Gould Pro Bono Program.

Merchant & Gould Pro Bono Program

3200 IDS Ctr.
80 S. 8th St.
Minneapolis, MN 55402-2215 (612) 336-4673
FAX: (612) 332-9081;
E-mail: jrandolph@merchantgould.com; Additional tel.: (612) 332-5300; URL: http://www.merchantgould.com/OurFirm_Pro_Bono.aspx

Contact: Jennie Randolph, Pro Bono Coord.
Fields of interest: Legal services.
Type of support: Pro bono services - legal.
Geographic limitations: Giving primarily in areas of company operations in Denver, CO, Atlanta, GA, Minneapolis, MN, New York, NY, Alcoa, TN, Alexandria, VA, Seattle, WA, and Madison, WI.

2465
Merchants Trust Company, Inc.

275 Kennedy Dr., Ste. 100
South Burlington, VT 05403-6700
(802) 865-1635

Company URL: https://www.mbvt.com
Establishment information: Established in 1870.
Company type: Subsidiary of a public company
Business activities: Operates nondeposit trust facilities.
Business type (SIC): Depository banking/functions related to
Corporate officers: Molly Dillon, Pres.; Sheldon Prentice, Sr. V.P. and Genl. Counsel; Arabella Hubbert, Secy.
Giving statement: Giving through the Merchants Bank Foundation, Inc.

Merchants Bank Foundation, Inc.

275 Kennedy Dr.
South Burlington, VT 05403-6785 (802) 865-1627

Establishment information: Established in 1967 in VT.
Donors: Merchants Bancshares, Inc.; Merchants Bank.
Contact: Stephanie Macaskill, Secy.
Financial data (yr. ended 08/31/12): Assets, $1,341,750 (M); gifts received, $100,000; expenditures, $190,896; qualifying distributions, $179,287; giving activities include $179,287 for 120 grants (high: $30,000; low: $50).
Purpose and activities: The Foundation provides funding to organizations for programs and services that support general education, human services, or community enrichment for all Vermonters for purposes of advancing education, household self-sufficiency, sustainable independence, and viable community development.
Fields of interest: Arts; Education; Hospitals (general); Human services; Family services.
Type of support: Building/renovation; Capital campaigns; Curriculum development; Equipment; Program development; Scholarship funds.
Geographic limitations: Giving primarily in VT.
Support limitations: No grants to individuals.
Publications: Application guidelines.
Application information: Applications accepted. Contact local MB branch; the foundation aims to

support causes that are important to the communities served and that are highly recommended by branch managers. Application form required. Applicants should submit the following:
1) population served
2) copy of IRS Determination Letter
3) copy of most recent annual report/audited financial statement/990
4) listing of board of directors, trustees, officers and other key people and their affiliations
5) copy of current year's organizational budget and/ or project budget
6) additional materials/documentation

Initial approach: Contact nearest company bank for application form
Copies of proposal: 1
Board meeting date(s): Feb., May, Aug., and Nov.
Deadline(s): Feb. 1, May 1, Aug. 1, and Nov. 1
Final notification: 2 months

Officers: Martha Davis, Chair. and Pres.; Pamela Matweecha, V.P.; Erinn Perry, Secy.; Stephanie Macaskill, Treas.
Trustees: Kevin Farley; Diane Gagnon; Sean Houghton; Kathryn Leech; Jessica Rohde.
EIN: 036016628

2466
Merck & Co., Inc.

1 Merck Dr.
P.O. Box 100
Whitehouse Station, NJ 08889-0100
(908) 423-1000
FAX: (908) 423-1987

Company URL: http://www.merck.com
Establishment information: Established in 1891.
Company type: Public company
Company ticker symbol and exchange: MRK/NYSE
International Securities Identification Number: US58933Y1055
Business activities: Discovers, develops, manufactures, and markets human and animal health products.
Business type (SIC): Drugs
Financial profile for 2012: Number of employees, 83,000; assets, $106,132,000,000; sales volume, $47,267,000,000; pre-tax net income, $8,739,000,000; expenses, $38,528,000,000; liabilities, $53,112,000,000
Fortune 1000 ranking: 2012—58th in revenues, 29th in profits, and 62nd in assets
Forbes 2000 ranking: 2012—188th in sales, 82nd in profits, and 239th in assets
Corporate officers: Kenneth C. Frazier, Chair., Pres., and C.E.O.; Peter N. Kellogg, Exec. V.P. and C.F.O.; Clark Golestani, Exec. V.P. and C.I.O.; Bruce N. Kuhlik, Exec. V.P. and Genl. Counsel; Mirian M. Graddick-Weir, Exec. V.P., Human Resources
Board of directors: Kenneth C. Frazier, Chair.; Leslie A. Brun; Thomas R. Cech, Ph.D.; Thomas H. Glocer; William B. Harrison, Jr.; C. Robert Kidder; Rochelle B. Lazarus; Carlos E. Represas; Patricia F. Russo; Craig B. Thompson, M.D.; Wendell P. Weeks; Peter C. Wendell
Subsidiary: Medco Containment Services, Montvale, NJ
Plants: Rahway, NJ; Wilson, NC; West Point, PA; Caguas, PR; Elkton, VA
Joint Venture: Johnson & Johnson-Merck Consumer Pharmaceuticals Co., Fort Washington, PA
International operations: Argentina; Australia; Austria; Barbados; Belgium; Bermuda; Bolivia; Bosnia-Herzegovina; Brazil; Bulgaria; Canada; Chile; China; Colombia; Costa Rica; Croatia; Cyprus; Czech Republic; Ecuador; Egypt; Estonia; Finland; France; Germany; Greece; Hong Kong; Hungary; Iceland; India; Indonesia; Ireland; Israel; Italy; Japan; Latvia; Lebanon; Lithuania; Luxembourg; Malaysia; Mexico; Morocco and the Western Sahara; Netherlands; Norway; Pakistan; Panama; Paraguay; Peru; Philippines; Poland; Portugal; Romania; Russia; Singapore; Slovenia; South Africa; Spain; Sweden; Switzerland; Taiwan; Thailand; Tunisia; Turkey; United Kingdom; Uruguay; Venezuela
Historic mergers: Schering-Plough Corporation (November 3, 2009)
Giving statement: Giving through the Merck & Co., Inc. Corporate Giving Program, the Merck Company Foundation, the Merck Genome Research Institute, Inc., the Merck Institute for Science Education, Inc., and the Merck Patient Assistance Program, Inc.
Company EIN: 221918501

Merck & Co., Inc. Corporate Giving Program

1 Merck Dr.
P.O. Box 100
Whitehouse Station, NJ 08889-3497 (908) 423-1000
URL: http://www.merckresponsibility.com/giving-at-merck/home.html?WT.svl=mainnav

Purpose and activities: As a complement to its foundation, Merck also makes charitable contributions to nonprofit organizations directly. Support is given on a national and international basis in areas of company operations.
Fields of interest: Health care, public policy; Pharmacy/prescriptions; Health care; AIDS; Diabetes; Heart & circulatory research; Asthma research; Food services; Nutrition; Disasters, preparedness/services.
Type of support: Donated products; Employee volunteer services; General/operating support; Program development; Sponsorships.
Geographic limitations: Giving on a national and international basis in areas of company operations.
Publications: Corporate giving report.
Application information: Applications not accepted. Contributes only to pre-selected organizations. The Office of Corporate Contributions handles giving. The company has a staff that only handles contributions.
Contributions Staff: Brenda D. Colatrella, Sr. Dir., Office of Corp. Contribs.; Christine Funk, Assoc. Mgr., Corp. Contribs.; Ken Gustavsen, Mgr., Global Product Donations; Leslie M. Hardy, Dir., Corp. Contribs.
Number of staff: 8 full-time professional; 3 full-time support.

The Merck Company Foundation

1 Merck Dr.
P.O. Box 100
Whitehouse Station, NJ 08889-3400 (908) 423-2042
FAX: (908) 423-1987;
E-mail: OCP_TMCFSupport@Merck.com; Additional tel.: (908) 423-1000; Contact for Neighbor of Choice Program in New Jersey: Doreen Robert, e-mail: doreen_robert@merck.com; URL: http://www.merckresponsibility.com/giving-at-merck/home.html

Establishment information: Incorporated in 1957 in NJ.
Donor: Merck & Co., Inc.
Contact: Ellen Lambert, Exec. V.P.
Financial data (yr. ended 12/31/11): Assets, $244,058,282 (M); expenditures, $54,039,379; qualifying distributions, $53,793,890; giving activities include $53,306,196 for grants.
Purpose and activities: The foundation supports programs designed to promote health, education, and community. Special emphasis is directed toward programs designed to improve healthcare quality and capacity; increase access to care for underserved populations; alleviate barriers to good health through strategic collaborations and investments; foster educational opportunity and academic success through initiatives that eliminate achievement gaps among disadvantaged people; expand quality education in science; and programs that include financial support, Merck innovation, and Merck employee expertise to address critical health and social issues in communities where Merck has a presence.
Fields of interest: Arts; Higher education; Education, services; Education; Environment; Animal welfare; Health care, public policy; Health care, equal rights; Medical care, community health systems; Health care, clinics/centers; Public health; Health care; Asthma; AIDS; Diabetes; Biomedicine; Pediatrics; Health organizations; Medical research; Food services; Food banks; Food distribution, meals on wheels; Nutrition; Disasters, preparedness/services; American Red Cross; Children, services; Family services; Aging, centers/services; Human services; Community/economic development; Science, formal/general education; Mathematics; Engineering/technology; Science African Americans/Blacks; Hispanics/Latinos; Economically disadvantaged.

Programs:

African Comprehensive HIV/AIDS Partnerships (ACHAP): The foundation, in partnership the Bill & Melinda Gates Foundation, promotes the improvement of HIV/AIDS prevention, care, and treatment in Botswana. The initiative includes Merck medications for the Botswana's national antiretroviral (ARV) treatment program; and HIV prevention efforts focusing on safe male circumcision, intervention for young women and girls, HIV counseling and testing services, and integration for HIV and TB services.

Alliance to Reduce Disparities in Diabetes: The foundation supports programs designed to decrease diabetes disparities and enhance the quality of healthcare by improving prevention and management services, with emphasis on low-income and underserved populations with a high prevalence of type 2 diabetes. The program is limited to Chicago, Illinois, Camden, New Jersey, Memphis, Tennessee, Dallas, Texas, and Fort Washakie, Wyoming. Visit URL: http://ardd.sph.umich.edu/ for more information.

China-MSD HIV/AIDS Partnership: The foundation, in partnership with China's Ministry of Health, supports HIV/AIDS prevention, patient care, and treatment in China. The initiative is designed to raise awareness and reduce discrimination among target populations; reduce HIV transmission through integrated risk-reduction; provide consecutive treatment and care to people living with HIV/AIDS through an established service network; provide support to orphans and families affected by HIV; build capacity of healthcare works and organizations; and strengthen HIV surveillance, monitoring, and evaluation systems and data management to track program implementation, access, and outcomes.

Merck Childhood Asthma Network, Inc. (MCAN): The foundation created MCAN, a 501(c)(3) organization, to support and advance evidence-based programs that improve the quality of life for children with asthma and their families. The organization supports programs designed to tailor asthma case management and reduce environmental risk factors and triggers in the home; the American Academy of Pediatrics to support education for pediatricians to implement asthma diagnosis and implementation; the National Education Association to train educators to recognize asthma symptoms and manage acute episodes; and various partnership organizations to advocate support for science-based asthma care.

Merck Institute for Science Education (MISE): The foundation created the MISE to improve science education for K-12 students and to influence educational policy. Special emphasis is directed toward STEM, science, technology, engineering, and mathematics. Visit URL: http://www.mise.org/secure/index.html for more information.

Merck Vaccine Network - Africa (MVN-A): Through MVN-A, the foundation develops training centers in Africa to help increase the capacity of immunization programs to effectively deliver vaccines. The MVN-A training programs provide mid- to high-level immunization program managers in Kenya, Mali, Uganda and Zambia with customized, hands-on training in vaccine management and immunization services.

Neighbor of Choice Program: Through the Neighbor of Choice program, the foundation addresses community and quality of life issues in communities where Merck has a major presence. The program is designed to listen and identify the community's essential needs, issues and concerns; respond appropriately to those needs, issues and concerns: and establish and grow relationships of trust with community organizations and individuals.

Partnership for Giving/Touched by an Agency: The foundation matches contributions made by U.S. and Puerto-Rico based employees and retirees of Merck to organizations involved with arts and culture, education, the environment, animal welfare, health, and human services. The foundation also awards a $1,000 "Thank You Grant" to nominated nonprofit organizations that have made a difference in the lives of Merck employees.

Rx for Hunger: Through Rx to Fight Hunger initiative, the foundation supports hunger-related local and regional partnerships to develop, implement, and share approaches for treating and preventing hunger and malnutrition in children, seniors, and families. Current partnerships include Sesame Workshop's "Food for Thought: Eating Well on a Budget" bilingual education outreach program, and the Drexel School of Public Health to develop approaches to treating child hunger and access to healthy food for low-income families in impoverished urban communities.

The Alliance/Merck Ciencia (Science) Hispanic Scholars Program: The foundation, in partnership with the National Alliance for Hispanic Health, annually provides college scholarships, a 10-week summer internship, and a stipend each summer to Hispanic high school seniors to pursue a degree in a STEM field. The program is limited to Los Angeles, California, Elizabeth, New Jersey, and Brownsville, Texas. The program is administered by the National Alliance for Health. Visit URL: http://www.alliancescholars.org/ for more information.

UNCF/Merck Science Initiative: The foundation, in partnership with the United Negro College Fund, awards scholarships and fellowships to African-American biomedical students pursuing studies and careers in the biological and chemical sciences. The initiative is designed to expand the pool of world-class African-American biomedical scientists. The program is administered by the United Negro College Fund. Visit URL: http://umsi.uncf.org/ for more information.

Type of support: Building/renovation; Conferences/seminars; Continuing support; Curriculum development; Employee matching gifts; Employee volunteer services; Fellowships; Internship funds; Management development/capacity building; Program development; Research; Scholarship funds; Seed money.

Geographic limitations: Giving on a national and international basis in areas of company operations, with emphasis on CA, Washington, DC, IL, MA, MD, NJ, NY, PA, TN, TX, VA, and WY, and in Africa, China, and Puerto Rico.

Support limitations: No support for political organizations, fraternal, labor, or veterans' organizations, religious organizations not of direct benefit to the entire community, or discriminatory organizations. No grants to individuals, or for capital campaigns, endowments, basic or clinical research projects including epidemiological studies, clinical trials, or other pharmaceutical studies, direct medical care including medical screening or testing, or the purchase of medicines, vaccines, or devices, meetings, conferences, symposia or workshops that do not have or are not associated with long-term program objectives, unrestricted general operating support, or fundraising events including concerts, sporting events, annual appeals, membership drives, benefit dinners, or galas unrelated the strategic priorities of the Merck Company Foundation.

Publications: Application guidelines; Corporate giving report; Grants list; Program policy statement.

Application information: Applications accepted. Merck typically initiates specific requests for charitable contributions and donations. Support is limited to 1 contribution per organization during any given year. A site visit may be requested for the Neighbor of Choice Program in New Jersey. Organizations receiving support may be asked to submit a final report. Application form not required. Applicants should submit the following:

1) timetable for implementation and evaluation of project
2) copy of IRS Determination Letter
3) brief history of organization and description of its mission
4) copy of most recent annual report/audited financial statement/990
5) how project's results will be evaluated or measured
6) listing of board of directors, trustees, officers and other key people and their affiliations
7) detailed description of project and amount of funding requested
8) copy of current year's organizational budget and/or project budget
9) listing of additional sources and amount of support

Initial approach: Complete online application
Board meeting date(s): Semiannually and as required
Deadline(s): 45 days prior to need; Sept. 1 to 30 for Neighbor of Choice Program in New Jersey
Final notification: 4 to 6 weeks; up to 10 weeks for Neighbor of Choice Program in New Jersey

Officers and Trustees:* Richard T. Clark*, Chair.; Geralyn S. Ritter*, Pres.; Ellen Lambert, Exec. V.P.; Leslie M. Hardy, V.P.; Celia A. Colbert, Secy.; Mark E. McDonough, Treas.

EIN: 226028476

Selected grants: The following grants are a representative sample of this grantmaker's funding activity:

$6,950,000 to China-Merck Sharp and Dohme HIV-AIDS Partnership, China, 2010. For partnership with China's Ministry of Health to strengthen HIV/AIDS prevention, patient care, treatment, and support programs.

$6,000,000 to African Comprehensive HIV/AIDS Partnerships, White House Station, NJ, 2010. For improvement of HIV/AIDS prevention, care, and treatment in Botswana.

$5,920,801 to Merck Institute for Science Education, Rahway, NJ, 2010. For general support to improve teaching of science in selected areas of New Jersey and Pennsylvania.

$1,500,000 to Childrens Inn at NIH, Bethesda, MD, 2010. For new transitional housing program at The Children's Inn.

$400,000 to Cooper Foundation, Camden, NJ, 2010. For comprehensive diabetes program through Camden Coalition of Healthcare Providers, as part of Merck Alliance to Reduce Disparities in Diabetes.

$62,000 to Dollars for Doers, Philadelphia, PA, 2010.

$50,000 to Boys and Girls Clubs of Union County, Union, NJ, 2010. For two programs to make a difference in youth obesity and other health problems.

$40,000 to Temple University, Philadelphia, PA, 2010. For fellowship in biostatistics as part of Merck Quantitative Sciences Fellowship Program.

The Merck Genome Research Institute, Inc.

c/o Merck & Co., Inc.
1 Merck Dr., WS2F-96
Whitehouse Station, NJ 08889-3400

Establishment information: Established in 1996 in NJ.

Donor: Merck & Co., Inc.

Financial data (yr. ended 12/31/11): Assets, $0 (M); expenditures, $0; qualifying distributions, $0.

Purpose and activities: The institute supports projects at academic and research centers designed to enable scientists to write essays and develop methodologies to be applied broadly across genomic research with the objective of improving the accuracy and speed in which functional associations can be made with sequence of genetic information.

Fields of interest: Higher education; Medical research, institute; Science, research; Biology/life sciences; Science.

Type of support: Conferences/seminars; Research.

Geographic limitations: Giving primarily in MA.

Application information: Applications not accepted. Unsolicited requests for funds not accepted.

Officers: Anthony W. Ford-Hutchinson, Pres.

EIN: 223431383

Selected grants: The following grants are a representative sample of this grantmaker's funding activity:

$1,800,000 to Massachusetts Institute of Technology, Cambridge, MA, 2006.

$600,000 to Massachusetts Institute of Technology, Cambridge, MA, 2006.

Merck Institute for Science Education, Inc.

P.O. Box 100, WS2F-96
Whitehouse Station, NJ 08889-0100
E-mail: contactus@mise.org; Additional address: P.O. Box 2000 RY60-215, Rahway, NJ 07065, tel.: (732) 594-3443; fax: (732) 594-3977; URL: http://www.mise.org

Establishment information: Established in 1992 in NJ.

Donor: Merck & Co., Inc.

Contact: Carlo Parravano, Exec. Dir.

Financial data (yr. ended 12/31/10): Assets, $0; gifts received, $6,926,186; expenditures, $6,926,186; qualifying distributions, $6,926,186; giving activities include $1,995,235 for 21 grants and $1,313,111 for 37 grants to individuals (high: $70,000; low: $1,420).

Purpose and activities: The institute supports programs designed to improve science education; raise levels of science performance in students grades K-12; and provide professional development for teachers and administrators to enhance their knowledge and skills.
Fields of interest: Education, fund raising/fund distribution; Elementary/secondary education; Higher education; Teacher school/education; Science, formal/general education; Mathematics; Engineering/technology; Science.
Programs:
The Alliance/Merck Ciencia Hispanic Scholars Program: The institute, in partnership with the National Alliance for Hispanic Health, annually awards scholarships to improve access to higher education in the pursuit of undergraduate degrees in science, technology, engineering, and mathematics (STEM) related fields. The program awards 25 scholarships of up to $2,000 to college STEM majors and 10 scholarships of up to $5,000 to high school seniors in selected districts who have committed to major in a STEM field. The program includes paid internships and an annual seminar program. The program is administered by the National Alliance for Hispanic Health.
The Merck/AAAS Undergraduate Science Research Program (USRP): The institute awards grants of up to $60,000 paid over a three year period to biology and chemistry departments to enhance undergraduate science education in the life sciences and chemistry. The funding also supports research stipends for undergraduate students and ancillary programs that foster interactions between biology and chemistry departments.
The UNCF/Merck Science Initiative (UMSI): The institute, in partnership with the United Negro College Fund, provides scholarships, fellowships, and mentoring to outstanding African-American students pursuing studies and careers in the field of biological and chemical sciences. Awards are made at the undergraduate, graduate, and post-doctoral levels and ranges from $25,000 up to $92,000.
Type of support: Conferences/seminars; Curriculum development; Fellowships; General/operating support; Internship funds; Management development/capacity building; Program development; Publication; Research; Scholarships—to individuals.
Geographic limitations: Giving limited to NJ and PA.
Publications: Grants list.
Application information: Unsolicited grant requests are not accepted. Applicants for the UNCF/Merck Science Initiative should contact the United Negro College Fund.
Officers and Directors:* Carlo Parravano, Exec. V.P. and Exec. Dir.; Celia A. Colbert*, Secy.; Mark E. McDonough, Treas.
EIN: 223208944
Selected grants: The following grants are a representative sample of this grantmaker's funding activity:
$800,000 to National Alliance for Hispanic Health, Washington, DC, 2010. For Hispanic students.
$150,000 to Washington and Jefferson College, Washington, PA, 2010. For undergraduate student research stipends.
$100,000 to United Negro College Fund, UNCF Stem Initiative, Fairfax, VA, 2010. To increase minority student interest and access to careers in science, technology, engineering and mathematics.
$30,000 to Barnard College, New York, NY, 2010. For student stipends and research support.
$28,275 to New Jersey Science Teachers Association, Hightstown, NJ, 2010. For administration of state-wide science competition.
$20,000 to Ashland University, Ashland, OH, 2010. For supplies and programs for students and faculty.
$20,000 to Bowdoin College, Brunswick, ME, 2010. For supplies and programs for students and faculty.
$20,000 to Colorado College, Colorado Springs, CO, 2010. For supplies and programs for students and faculty.
$20,000 to Furman University, Greenville, SC, 2010. For supplies and programs for students and faculty.
$20,000 to Lebanon Valley College, Annville, PA, 2010. For supplies and programs for students and faculty.

Merck Patient Assistance Program, Inc.

1 Merck Dr.
P.O. Box 100, Ste. WSF-96
Whitehouse Station, NJ 08889-0100 (800) 727-5400
Application address: P.O. Box 690, Horsham, PA 19044-9979; URL: http://www.merckresponsibility.com/focus-areas/access-to-health/community-investment/patient-assistance-program/home.html

Establishment information: Established as a company-sponsored operating foundation in 2001 in New Jersey.
Donors: Merck & Co., Inc.; Merck Sharp & Dohme Corp.
Financial data (yr. ended 12/31/11): Assets, $10,234,569 (M); gifts received, $441,424,919; expenditures, $441,424,919; qualifying distributions, $441,424,919; giving activities include $441,424,919 for grants to individuals.
Purpose and activities: The foundation provides Merck medication to economically disadvantaged individuals lacking prescription drug coverage when a physician has determined that a Merck product may be appropriate.
Fields of interest: Economically disadvantaged.
Type of support: Donated products; Grants to individuals.
Geographic limitations: Giving on a national basis and in Guam, Puerto Rico, the U.S. Virgin Islands, and U.S. Territories.
Application information: Applications not accepted.
Officers: Patrick Magri, Pres.; Patrick Davish, Exec. V.P.; Scott Brevic, Secy.; Susan L. Reindel, Treas.
EIN: 010575520

2467
Merck Millipore

(formerly Millipore Corporation)
290 Concord Rd.
Billerica, MA 01821 (978) 715-4321

Company URL: http://www.millipore.com
Establishment information: Established in 1954.
Company type: Subsidiary of a foreign company
Business activities: Provides products and services for bioscience research and biopharmaceutical manufacturing.
Business type (SIC): Laboratory apparatus
Financial profile for 2009: Number of employees, 6,100; assets, $2,810,790,000; sales volume, $1,654,410,000; pre-tax net income, $219,590,000; expenses, $1,377,220,000; liabilities, $1,307,760,000
Corporate officers: David Hutchinson, Pres., Genl. Counsel, and Secy.; Bruce J. Bonnevier, V.P., Global Human Resources
Plants: Temecula, CA; Kankakee, IL; Bedford, Burlington, Danvers, MA; St. Charles, MO; Jaffrey, NH; Cidra, PR
International operations: Australia; Austria; Belgium; China; Denmark; Finland; France; Germany; Ireland; Japan; Mexico; Netherlands; South Korea; Spain; Sweden; Switzerland; United Kingdom
Giving statement: Giving through the Millipore Corporate Giving Program.
Company EIN: 042170233

Millipore Corporate Giving Program

290 Concord Rd.
Billerica, MA 01821-3405 (978) 715-4321
E-mail: tara.duplaga@merckgroup.com; URL: http://www.millipore.com/corporategiving/mf3/corporate_giving

Contact: Tara Duplaga
Purpose and activities: Millipore Corporation makes charitable contributions to nonprofit organizations involved with science, education, and the environment. Support is given primarily in areas of company operations.
Fields of interest: Education; Environment; Housing/shelter; Safety/disasters; Human services; Community/economic development; Science, formal/general education; Biology/life sciences; Science.
Programs:
Matching Gift Program: Millipore Corporation offers a dollar-for-dollar match for contributions made by its employees to nonprofit organizations in the areas of education, social services, culture, health care, and the environment up to $1,000 per employee per year.
Millipore Scholarship Program: Millipore Corporation annually awards two $5,000 college scholarships to the children of Millipore employees renewable for an additional three years for a total award of $20,000.
Voluntary Service Grant Program: Through the Voluntary Service Grant Program, employees who devote significant volunteer time to non-profits in their communities may request program support from Millipore to assist these organizations.
Type of support: Employee matching gifts; Employee volunteer services; Employee-related scholarships; Fellowships; General/operating support; Matching/challenge support; Program development; Sponsorships.
Geographic limitations: Giving primarily in areas of company operations in Temecula, CA, Kankakee, IL, Bedford, Billerica, greater Boston, Burlington, Danvers, Lawrence, and Lowell, MA, Jaffrey, NH, and St. Charles, MO.
Publications: Application guidelines; Grants list.
Application information: Applications accepted. Contributions are handled by a central office, but Millipore site managers around the country are encouraged to submit funding proposals that address the specific needs of their local communities. Letters of inquiry should be limited to 2 pages. Current grantees seeking renewed funding are asked to submit a report on the previous year's grant before requesting renewed funding. Application form required. Applicants should submit the following:
1) copy of IRS Determination Letter
2) descriptive literature about organization
3) detailed description of project and amount of funding requested

Initial approach: Mail or e-mail letter of inquiry. Full proposals are accepted by invitation only
Copies of proposal: 1
Committee meeting date(s): Every 8 to 10 weeks

2468
Mercury Aircraft, Inc.
17 Wheeler Ave.
Hammondsport, NY 14840-9566
(607) 569-4200

Company URL: http://www.mercurycorp.com
Establishment information: Established in 1920.
Company type: Private company
Business activities: Produces sheet metal, commercial cooking and food warming equipment, and other metal products.
Business type (SIC): Metal forgings and stampings; machinery/refrigeration and service industry
Corporate officers: Joseph F. Meade III, Pres.; Marc Mason, V.P., Sales; Gregory Hintz, Sr. V.P., Opers. and C.I.O.
Giving statement: Giving through the Mercury Aircraft Foundation.

Mercury Aircraft Foundation
c/o Mercury Aircraft, Inc.
17 Wheeler Ave.
Hammondsport, NY 14840-9566

Establishment information: Established in 1952 in NY.
Donors: Mercury Aircraft, Inc.; Mercury Minnesota, Inc.
Financial data (yr. ended 12/31/11): Assets, $2,894,960 (M); expenditures, $131,455; qualifying distributions, $130,850; giving activities include $130,600 for 47 grants (high: $22,250; low: $200).
Purpose and activities: The foundation supports fire departments and organizations involved with arts and culture, education, health, and religion.
Fields of interest: Museums; Arts; Higher education; Libraries (public); Education; Hospitals (general); Health care, EMS; Health care; Disasters, fire prevention/control; United Ways and Federated Giving Programs; Christian agencies & churches; Catholic agencies & churches; Religion.
Type of support: Building/renovation; General/operating support.
Geographic limitations: Giving primarily in western NY.
Application information: Applications accepted. Application form not required.
Initial approach: Proposal
Deadline(s): None
Officers: Joseph F. Meade III, Pres.; David C. Meade, V.P.; Marcia M. Coon, Secy.; Gregory J. Hintz, Treas.
EIN: 166028162

2469
Mercury Computer Systems, Inc.
201 Riverneck Rd.
Chelmsford, MA 01824-2820
(978) 256-1300
FAX: (978) 256-3599

Company URL: http://www.mc.com
Establishment information: Established in 1981.
Company type: Public company
Company ticker symbol and exchange: MRCY/NASDAQ
Business activities: Designs, manufactures, and markets digital signal and image processing computer systems.
Business type (SIC): Electronic components and accessories; computer and office equipment
Financial profile for 2012: Number of employees, 713; assets, $385,610,000; sales volume, $244,930,000; pre-tax net income, $31,770,000; expenses, $214,820,000; liabilities, $52,500,000
Corporate officers: Vincent Vitto, Chair.; Mark Aslett, Pres. and C.E.O.; Kevin M. Bisson, Sr. V.P., C.F.O., and Treas.; Charles A. Speicher, V.P., Cont., and C.A.O.
Board of directors: Vincent Vitto, Chair.; Mark Aslett; James K. Bass; George W. Chamillard; Michael A. Daniels; George K. Muellner; William K. O'Brien; Lee C. Steele
Offices: Campbell, Escondido, Hermosa Beach, CA; New Fairfield, CT; Orlando, FL; Chanhassen, MN; Point Pleasant, NJ; Warwick, NY; Dallas, TX; Vienna, VA; Madison, WI
International operations: France; Japan; United Kingdom
Giving statement: Giving through the Mercury Computer Systems, Inc. Corporate Giving Program.
Company EIN: 042741391

Mercury Computer Systems, Inc. Corporate Giving Program
199 Riverneck Rd.
Chelmsford, MA 01824-2820 (866) 627-6951
URL: http://www.mc.com/careers/work-culture/

Purpose and activities: Mercury Computer Systems makes charitable contributions to nonprofit organizations involved with education, and on a case by case basis. Special emphasis is directed toward programs designed to promote STEM (science, technology, engineering, and mathematics) education in high schools. Support is given primarily in areas of company operations in Alabama, Massachusetts, New Hampshire, Texas, and Virginia.
Fields of interest: Secondary school/education; Health care, blood supply; United Ways and Federated Giving Programs; Science; Mathematics; Engineering/technology; General charitable giving.
Type of support: Employee volunteer services; General/operating support; Sponsorships.
Geographic limitations: Giving primarily in Support is given primarily in areas of company operations in AL, MA, NH, TX, and VA.

2470
Mercury Wire Products, Inc.
1 Mercury Dr.
Spencer, MA 01562-1916 (508) 885-6363

Company URL: http://www.mercurywire.com/index.html
Establishment information: Established in 1967.
Company type: Private company
Business activities: Manufactures insulated wire and cable.
Business type (SIC): Metal rolling and drawing/nonferrous
Corporate officers: Kenneth G. Yard, Chair.; Robert Yard, Pres.; Chris Yard, C.O.O.; Perry Harrison, C.F.O.; Beverly Yard, Treas.
Board of director: Kenneth G. Yard, Chair.
Giving statement: Giving through the Mercury Wire Products Charitable Foundation.

Mercury Wire Products Charitable Foundation
Mercury Dr.
Spencer, MA 01562-1999

Donor: Mercury Wire Products, Inc.
Financial data (yr. ended 09/30/12): Assets, $341,864 (M); expenditures, $9,384; qualifying distributions, $6,545; giving activities include $6,545 for 12 grants (high: $1,500; low: $200).
Purpose and activities: The foundation supports police agencies and organizations involved with secondary and higher education, leukemia, and safety.
Fields of interest: Education; Health care; Health organizations.
Type of support: General/operating support.
Geographic limitations: Giving primarily in Spencer, MA.
Support limitations: No grants to individuals.
Application information: Applications not accepted. Unsolicited requests for funds not accepted.
Trustees: Christopher Yard; Robert Yard.
EIN: 042785455

2471
Meredith Corporation
1716 Locust St.
Des Moines, IA 50309-3023
(515) 284-3000
FAX: (515) 284-2700

Company URL: http://www.meredith.com
Establishment information: Established in 1902.
Company type: Public company
Company ticker symbol and exchange: MDP/NYSE
Business activities: Publishes magazines and books; broadcasts television; provides marketing services; provides Internet information services.
Business type (SIC): Periodical publishing and/or printing; book publishing and/or printing; radio and television broadcasting; computer services
Financial profile for 2012: Number of employees, 3,410; assets, $2,016,300,000; sales volume, $1,376,690,000; pre-tax net income, $172,880,000; expenses, $1,190,920,000; liabilities, $1,218,850,000
Corporate officers: Stephen M. Lacy, Chair., Pres., and C.E.O.; D. Mell Meredith Frazier, Vice-Chair.; Joseph H. Ceryanec, V.P. and C.F.O.; John S. Zieser, Genl. Counsel; Steven M. Cappaert, Corp. Cont.
Board of directors: Stephen M. Lacy, Chair.; D. Mell Meredith Frazier, Vice-Chair.; Donald C. Berg; Mary Sue Coleman, Ph.D.; James R. Craigie; Frederick B. Henry; Joel W. Johnson; Philip A. Marineau; Elizabeth E. Tallett
Subsidiaries: KCTV, Kansas City, MO; KPHO-TV, Phoenix, AZ; KVVU Broadcasting Corp., Henderson, NV; WFSB-TV, Rocky Hill, CT; WGCL-TV, Atlanta, GA; WHNS-TV, Greenville, SC; WNEM-TV, Flint, MI; WSMV-TV, Nashville, TN
Giving statement: Giving through the Meredith Corporation Foundation.
Company EIN: 420410230

Meredith Corporation Foundation
1716 Locust St.
Des Moines, IA 50309-3023
FAX: (515) 284-2620;
E-mail: cheri.cipperley@meredith.com; URL: http://www.meredith.com/meredith_corporate/meredith_foundation.html

Establishment information: Established around 1994 in IA.
Donor: Meredith Corp.
Contact: Cheri Cipperley
Financial data (yr. ended 06/30/11): Assets, $15,607,049 (M); expenditures, $1,443,501; qualifying distributions, $1,442,467; giving activities include $1,441,217 for 841 grants (high: $130,000; low: $25).
Purpose and activities: The foundation supports organizations involved with arts and culture, education, and human services.
Fields of interest: Media, print publishing; Media, journalism; Visual arts; Performing arts; Arts; Higher education; Journalism school/education; Education; Children/youth, services; Family services; Human services; United Ways and Federated Giving Programs Children; Aging; Disabilities, people with; Economically disadvantaged.
Programs:
Arts and Culture: The foundation supports programs designed to ensure that the arts are accessible to all residents, including children, the elderly, the disabled, and the disadvantaged. Grants are limited to Des Moines, IA.
Education: The foundation supports programs designed to provide journalism, graphic design, and advertising education. Special emphasis is directed toward programs designed to provide magazine journalism education.
Employee Matching Gifts: The foundation matches contributions made by employees of Meredith Corporation to nonprofit organizations involved with arts and culture, human services, and educational institutions on a one-for-one basis from $25 to $5,000 per employee, per year.
Human Services: The foundation supports organizations involved with human services. Grants are limited to the Des Moines, IA community.
Volunteer Grant Program: The foundation awards $200 grants to nonprofit organizations with which employees of Meredith Corporation volunteer from 20 to 29 hours; $300 for 30-39 hours; $400 for 40-49 hours; and $500 for 50 hours or more.
Type of support: Annual campaigns; Capital campaigns; Employee matching gifts; Employee volunteer services; General/operating support; Program development.
Geographic limitations: Giving primarily in the metropolitan Des Moines, IA, area.
Support limitations: No support for religious or political organizations. No grants to individuals, or for fundraising events or sports or health-related programs.
Publications: Application guidelines.
Application information: Applications accepted. Telephone requests are not accepted. Applicants should submit the following:
1) name, address and phone number of organization
2) contact person
3) copy of IRS Determination Letter
4) detailed description of project and amount of funding requested
5) copy of current year's organizational budget and/or project budget
6) listing of board of directors, trustees, officers and other key people and their affiliations
7) results expected from proposed grant
8) how project's results will be evaluated or measured

Initial approach: Proposal
Board meeting date(s): Apr. and Oct.
Deadline(s): Jan. 15 to Mar. 15 and July 15 to Sept. 15

Officers and Directors:* Mell Meredith Frazier*, Chair.; Stephen M. Lacy*, Pres.; John S. Zieser*, Secy.; Kevin Wagner, Treas.; Joseph H. Ceryanec.
EIN: 421426258

2472
N. Merfish Supply Company

(also known as Merfish Pipe & Supply, LP)
1211 Kress St.
P.O. Box 15879
Houston, TX 77020-5879 (713) 869-5731

Company URL: http://www.merfish.com
Establishment information: Established in 1920.
Company type: Private company
Business activities: Sells pipes and pipe fittings wholesale.
Business type (SIC): Hardware, plumbing, and heating equipment—wholesale
Corporate officer: Gerrie Richards, Cont.
Giving statement: Giving through the Merfish-Jacobson Foundation.

Merfish-Jacobson Foundation

P.O. Box 15879
Houston, TX 77220-5879 (713) 869-5731

Establishment information: Established in 1988 in TX.
Donors: Merfish Pipe & Supply; Abe Merfish; Ida K. Merfish; Gerald Merfish.
Contact: Rochelle M. Jacobson, Tr.
Financial data (yr. ended 12/31/11): Assets, $2,455,350 (M); gifts received, $118,600; expenditures, $271,255; qualifying distributions, $265,800; giving activities include $265,800 for grants.
Purpose and activities: The foundation supports organizations involved with higher education, family planning, patient services, children and youth, and Judaism.
Fields of interest: Higher education; Medical care, in-patient care; Reproductive health, family planning; Health care, patient services; Children/youth, services; United Ways and Federated Giving Programs; Jewish federated giving programs; Jewish agencies & synagogues.
Type of support: Endowments; General/operating support; Program development; Scholarship funds.
Geographic limitations: Giving primarily in Houston, TX.
Support limitations: No grants to individuals.
Application information: Applications accepted. Application form not required.
Initial approach: Proposal
Deadline(s): None
Trustees: Rochelle M. Jacobson; Gerald Merfish; Ida K. Merfish.
EIN: 760239810
Selected grants: The following grants are a representative sample of this grantmaker's funding activity:
$80,500 to Jewish Federation of Greater Houston, Houston, TX, 2010.
$31,650 to Congregation Beth Israel, Houston, TX, 2010.
$23,250 to Seven Acres Jewish Senior Care Services, Houston, TX, 2010.
$20,000 to Houston Area Womens Center, Houston, TX, 2010.
$5,540 to Jewish Family Service, Houston, TX, 2010.
$5,000 to Cystic Fibrosis Foundation, Houston, TX, 2010.
$5,000 to Houston Food Bank, Houston, TX, 2010.
$5,000 to UNICEF, New York, NY, 2010.
$3,000 to Congregation Beth Yeshurun, Houston, TX, 2010.
$2,000 to River Performing and Visual Arts Center, Houston, TX, 2010.

2473
Meritor, Inc.

(formerly ArvinMeritor, Inc.)
2135 W. Maple Rd.
Troy, MI 48084-7186 (248) 435-1000
FAX: (248) 435-1393

Company URL: http://www.meritor.com
Establishment information: Established in 1909.
Company type: Public company
Company ticker symbol and exchange: MTOR/NYSE
Business activities: Manufactures light vehicle, commercial truck, and trailer systems, modules, and components; provides coil coating services.
Business type (SIC): Motor vehicles and equipment; metal coating and plating
Financial profile for 2011: Number of employees, 9,300; assets, $2,501,000,000; sales volume, $4,418,000,000; pre-tax net income, $137,000,000; expenses, $4,245,000,000; liabilities, $3,524,000,000
Fortune 1000 ranking: 2012—536th in revenues, 818th in profits, and 803rd in assets
Corporate officers: Ivor J. Evans, Jr., Chair., Pres., and C.E.O.; Jeffrey A. Craig, Sr. V.P. and C.F.O.; Vernon G. Baker II, Sr. V.P. and Genl. Counsel; Larry E. Ott, Sr. V.P., Human Resources and Comms.; Barbara Griffin Novak, V.P. and Corp. Secy.
Board of directors: Ivor J. Evans, Chair.; Joseph B. Anderson, Jr.; Rhonda L. Brooks; David W. Devonshire; Victoria Bridges Jackson; James E. Marley; William R. Newlin
Subsidiaries: Arvin International Holdings, Inc., Wilmington, DE; Arvin Technologies, Inc., Bingham Farms, MI; Maremont Corp., Wilmington, DE; Meritor Heavy Vehicle Systems, LLC, Troy, MI; Meritor Holdings, LLC, Wilmington, DE; Meritor Light Vehicle Systems, Inc., Wilmington, DE; Purolator Products Co., Wilmington, DE; Roll Coater, Inc., Indianapolis, IN
Division: Light Vehicle Aftermarket Div., Brentwood, TN
Plant: Columbus, IN
International operations: Australia; Barbados; Belgium; Canada; Cayman Islands; China; Czech Republic; England; France; Germany; India; Ireland; Italy; Japan; Mexico; Netherlands; North Korea; Panama; Poland; South Africa; Spain; Sweden; Switzerland; Turkey; Venezuela; Wales
Giving statement: Giving through the Meritor, Inc. Trust.
Company EIN: 383354643

Meritor, Inc. Trust

(formerly ArvinMeritor, Inc. Trust)
2135 W. Maple Rd.
Troy, MI 48084-7186
FAX: (248) 435-1031;
E-mail: jerry.rush@meritor.com; URL: http://www.meritor.com/ourcompany/communities/responsibility/default.aspx

Establishment information: Established in 1997 in MI.
Donors: Meritor Automotive, Inc.; ArvinMeritor, Inc.
Contact: Jerry Rush
Financial data (yr. ended 02/10/11): Assets, $258,158 (M); gifts received, $289,229;

expenditures, $281,229; qualifying distributions, $281,229; giving activities include $281,229 for 103 grants (high: $63,514; low: -$1,000).
Purpose and activities: The foundation supports organizations involved with arts and culture, education, health, human services, community development, and civic affairs. Special emphasis is directed toward engineering, science, and technology education.
Fields of interest: Performing arts, orchestras; Performing arts, opera; Arts; Secondary school/education; Higher education; Education; Health care; Boys & girls clubs; Youth development, business; Human services; Business/industry; Community/economic development; United Ways and Federated Giving Programs; Engineering/technology; Science; Public affairs.
Type of support: Employee matching gifts; Employee volunteer services; Program development.
Geographic limitations: Giving primarily in areas of company operations, with emphasis on MI.
Support limitations: No support for discriminatory organizations, religious or sectarian organizations not of direct benefit to the entire community, labor, political, or veterans' organizations, or fraternal, athletic, or social clubs. No grants to individuals, or for general operating support for local United Way agencies, sponsorship of fundraising activities for individuals, debt reduction, or seminars, conferences, trips, or tours; no loans.
Publications: Application guidelines.
Application information: Applications accepted. Application form required. Applicants should submit the following:
1) timetable for implementation and evaluation of project
2) how project will be sustained once grantmaker support is completed
3) results expected from proposed grant
4) qualifications of key personnel
5) statement of problem project will address
6) population served
7) copy of IRS Determination Letter
8) brief history of organization and description of its mission
9) copy of most recent annual report/audited financial statement/990
10) how project's results will be evaluated or measured
11) explanation of why grantmaker is considered an appropriate donor for project
12) descriptive literature about organization
13) listing of board of directors, trustees, officers and other key people and their affiliations
14) copy of current year's organizational budget and/or project budget
15) listing of additional sources and amount of support

Initial approach: Proposal
Deadline(s): Aug.

Officers: Charles G. "Chip" McClure, Chair., Pres., and C.E.O.; Jeffrey A. Craig, Sr. V.P. and C.F.O.; Vernon G. Baker II, Sr. V.P. and Genl. Counsel; Larry Ott, Sr. V.P., Human Resources; Barbara Griffin Novak, V.P. and Secy.; Pedro Ferro, V.P.; Joseph Mejaly, V.P.
EIN: 522089611
Selected grants: The following grants are a representative sample of this grantmaker's funding activity:
$5,000 to Detroit Institute of Arts, Detroit, MI, 2010.
$5,000 to Detroit Symphony Orchestra, Detroit, MI, 2010.
$1,200 to ArtsWave, Cincinnati, OH, 2010.
$1,200 to Urban League of Greater Cincinnati, Cincinnati, OH, 2010.

2474
Merrimack County Savings Bank

89 N. Main St.
P.O. Box 2826
Concord, NH 03302-2826 (603) 225-2793

Company URL: http://www.mcsbnh.com
Establishment information: Established in 1867.
Company type: Private company
Business activities: Operates savings bank.
Business type (SIC): Savings institutions
Corporate officers: Paul C. Rizzi, Jr., Pres. and C.E.O.; Philip B. Emma, Exec. V.P.and C.O.O.; Richard E. Wyman, Exec. V.P. and C.F.O.; Nicole Blaise, V.P. and Cont.; Nancy Swenson, V.P., Opers.; Kim McDonald, V.P., Human Resources
Giving statement: Giving through the Merrimack County Savings Bank Foundation.

Merrimack County Savings Bank Foundation

89 N. Main St.
Concord, NH 03301 (603) 223-2793
Application address: P.O. Box 2826, Concord, NH 03302; URL: http://www.mcsbnh.com/about/mcsbFoundation.php

Establishment information: Established in 1997.
Donor: Merrimack County Savings Bank.
Contact: Christine Scheiner
Financial data (yr. ended 12/31/11): Assets, $947,431 (M); expenditures, $57,696; qualifying distributions, $45,348; giving activities include $44,800 for 19 grants (high: $4,000; low: $500).
Purpose and activities: The foundation supports organizations involved with arts and culture, education, health, affordable housing, human services, and economic development.
Fields of interest: Arts; Education; Health care; Housing/shelter; Children/youth, services; Family services; Human services, financial counseling; Human services; Economic development.
Type of support: General/operating support; Program development.
Geographic limitations: Giving primarily in areas of company operations in Allenstown, Andover, Boscawen, Bow, Bradford, Canterbury, Chichester, Concord, Danbury, Dunbarton, Epsom, Franklin, Henniker, Hill, Hollis, Hooksett, Hopkinton, Hudson, Loudon, Merrimack, Nashua, New London, Newbury, Northfield, Pembroke, Pittsfield, Salisbury, Sutton, Warner, Weare, Webster, and Wilmot, NH.
Support limitations: No support for political, religious, labor, or fraternal organizations, pass-through organizations, municipalities, or private schools. No grants to individuals, or for endowments; no multi-year support.
Publications: Application guidelines.
Application information: Applications accepted. Organizations receiving support are asked to submit a final report on the usage of funds. Application form required. Applicants should submit the following:
1) copy of IRS Determination Letter
2) brief history of organization and description of its mission
3) copy of most recent annual report/audited financial statement/990
4) listing of board of directors, trustees, officers and other key people and their affiliations
5) detailed description of project and amount of funding requested
6) contact person
7) copy of current year's organizational budget and/or project budget
8) listing of additional sources and amount of support

Initial approach: Download application form and mail application form and proposal to foundation
Copies of proposal: 5
Board meeting date(s): Apr. and Oct.
Deadline(s): Oct. 1

Officer: Paul C. Rizzi, Secy.-Treas.
Directors: William H. Dunlap; Allison Dunn; William H. Dunlap; Eillen Slepper.
EIN: 043370159

2475
Merrimack Valley Distributing Company, Inc.

50 Prince St.
P.O. Box 417
Danvers, MA 01923-1438 (978) 777-2213
FAX: (978) 774-7487

Establishment information: Established in 1935.
Company type: Private company
Business activities: Operates a beer distribution company.
Business type (SIC): Beer, wine, and distilled beverages—wholesale
Corporate officers: Richard Tatelman, Pres. and Treas.; Thomas R. Decoff, Cont. and V.P., Finance
Giving statement: Giving through the L. Dexter Woodman Scholarship, Inc.

L. Dexter Woodman Scholarship, Inc.

127R Main St.
Essex, MA 01929-0002 (978) 768-3636
URL: http://www.woodmans.com/scholarship/

Establishment information: Established in 1988 in MA.
Donors: Merrimack Valley Distributing Co.; Woodman's, Inc.
Financial data (yr. ended 06/30/11): Assets, $466,893 (M); gifts received, $20,080; expenditures, $63,143; qualifying distributions, $30,000; giving activities include $4,500 for 2 grants (high: $2,500; low: $2,000) and $25,500 for 10 grants to individuals (high: $6,250; low: $500).
Purpose and activities: The foundation awards scholarships to graduates of Essex Elementary and Middle School, and Hamilton-Wenham Regional High School.
Fields of interest: Education.
Type of support: Scholarships—to individuals.
Geographic limitations: Giving limited to residents of Essex County, MA.
Application information: Applications accepted. Application form required.

Initial approach: Letter
Deadline(s): Apr. 3

Officers: Donald Burnham, Pres.; Edward Lafferty, V.P.; Suzanne Lynch, Clerk.
Directors: Karen Bernier; Julia Burroughs; Betsy DeVries; Katrina Haskell; Timothy Lane; Marnie Lawler; Richard Merullo; Jenna Roy; Carolyn Walfield.
EIN: 222925975

2476
Merritt & Merritt & Moulton
60 Lake St., 2nd Fl.
P.O. Box 5839
Burlington, VT 05402 (802) 658-7830
FAX: (802) 658-0978

Company URL: http://www.merritt-merritt.com
Establishment information: Established in 1989.
Company type: Private company
Business type (SIC): Business services/ miscellaneous
Corporate officers: Sharon J. Merritt, Partner; H. Kenneth Merritt, Jr., Partner; R.W. Eli Moulton III, Partner
Giving statement: Giving through the Merritt & Merritt & Moulton Corporate Giving Program.

Merritt & Merritt & Moulton Corporate Giving Program
60 Lake St., 2nd Fl.
P.O. Box 5839
Burlington, VT 05402-5839 (802) 658-7830
E-mail: info@merritt-merritt.com; URL: http://www.merritt-merritt.com

Purpose and activities: Merritt & Merritt & Moulton is a certified B Corporation that donates a percentage of profits to charitable organizations.

2477
Messer Construction Co.
5158 Fishwick Dr.
Cincinnati, OH 45216-2216 (513) 242-1541
FAX: (513) 242-6467

Company URL: http://www.messer.com
Establishment information: Established in 1932.
Company type: Private company
Business activities: Provides general contract construction services.
Business type (SIC): Building construction general contractors and operative builders
Corporate officers: Thomas M. Keckeis, Pres. and C.E.O.; E. Paul Hitter, Sr. V.P. and C.F.O.; Richard A. Hensley, V.P. and C.I.O.
Giving statement: Giving through the Messer Construction Foundation.

Messer Construction Foundation
5158 Fishwick Dr.
Cincinnati, OH 45216-2216
E-mail: kspangler@messer.com; URL: http://www.messer.com/who_we_are/corporate_citizenship.aspx

Establishment information: Established in 2003 in OH.
Donor: Messer Construction Co.
Contact: Kim Spangler
Financial data (yr. ended 09/30/11): Assets, $129,787 (M); gifts received, $200,000; expenditures, $224,157; qualifying distributions, $218,500; giving activities include $218,500 for grants.
Purpose and activities: The foundation supports programs designed to promote economic inclusion, education, and workforce development.
Fields of interest: Education; Employment, training; Employment; Boys & girls clubs; Civil/human rights, equal rights; Economic development Economically disadvantaged.
Programs:
Economic Inclusion: The foundation supports programs designed to create a more effective workforce; provide practical approaches to supporting diversity; and promote cost-effective methods for economic inclusion.
Education: The foundation supports programs designed to promote elementary and secondary education to prepare students for performance and life-long learning; and higher education to prepare future leaders of construction.
Workforce Development: The foundation supports programs designed to promote training and essential skills necessary for workers to succeed in today's workforce.
Type of support: General/operating support.
Geographic limitations: Giving primarily in areas of company operations in Indianapolis, IN, Knoxville, Lexington, and Louisville, KY, Cincinnati, Columbus, and Dayton, OH, and Nashville, TN.
Support limitations: No grants to individuals.
Publications: Application guidelines; Grants list; Program policy statement.
Application information: Applications accepted. Requests must be endorsed by a Messer Construction employee. Proposals should be no longer than 3 pages. Additional information may be requested at a later date. Application form required.
Applicants should submit the following:
1) timetable for implementation and evaluation of project
2) results expected from proposed grant
3) statement of problem project will address
4) copy of IRS Determination Letter
5) brief history of organization and description of its mission
6) geographic area to be served
7) copy of most recent annual report/audited financial statement/990
8) list of company employees involved with the organization
9) explanation of why grantmaker is considered an appropriate donor for project
10) listing of board of directors, trustees, officers and other key people and their affiliations
11) detailed description of project and amount of funding requested

Initial approach: Download application form and mail proposal and application form to foundation
Copies of proposal: 12
Deadline(s): Postmarked by Mar. 28
Final notification: June 30

Officers and Directors:* Kathleen C. Daly*, Pres.; J. Stephen Eder, Secy.; David Miller, Treas.
EIN: 200262239
Selected grants: The following grants are a representative sample of this grantmaker's funding activity:
$50,000 to Norton Healthcare Foundation, Louisville, KY, 2011. For general support.
$25,000 to Childrens Hospital Medical Center, Cincinnati, OH, 2011. For general support.
$25,000 to City Gospel Mission, Cincinnati, OH, 2011. For general support.
$25,000 to Emerald Youth Foundation, Knoxville, TN, 2011. For general support.
$25,000 to Greater Cincinnati Workforce Network, Cincinnati, OH, 2011. For general support.
$11,000 to University of Louisville, Louisville, KY, 2011. For general support.
$2,500 to Partnership Initiatives Fund, Knoxville, TN, 2011. For general support.

2478
Metal Industries, Inc.
(also known as METALAIRE)
1985 Carroll St.
Clearwater, FL 33765 (727) 441-2651

Company URL: http://www.metalindustriesinc.com
Establishment information: Established in 1947.
Company type: Subsidiary of a private company
Business activities: Manufactures air distribution products.
Business type (SIC): Machinery/refrigeration and service industry
Corporate officers: Peter Desoto, Co-Pres. and C.E.O.; Damian Macaluso, Co-Pres.; Dan Frankiewicz, Cont.
Giving statement: Giving through the Metal Industries Foundation, Inc.

Metal Industries Foundation, Inc.
861 N. Hercules Ave.
Clearwater, FL 33765-2025

Establishment information: Established in 1971.
Donors: Metal Industries, Inc.; Metal Industries of California Foundation, Inc.
Contact: Sarah Walker Guthrie, Tr.
Financial data (yr. ended 10/31/11): Assets, $3,130,114 (M); expenditures, $23,951; qualifying distributions, $11,738; giving activities include $11,738 for grants.
Purpose and activities: The foundation supports organizations involved with education, health, human services, and community development and awards student loans to individuals.
Type of support: Capital campaigns; General/operating support; Student loans—to individuals.
Geographic limitations: Giving primarily in FL.
Application information: Applications accepted. Application form required.
Initial approach: Letter
Deadline(s): None
Trustees: Pete DeSoto; Sarah Walker Guthrie; Jay K. Poppleton.
EIN: 237098483

2442
Me-Tex Oil & Gas, Inc.
119 E. Bender Blvd.
P.O. Box 2070
Hobbs, NM 88240-6053 (575) 397-7750

Company URL: http://www.me-tex.com
Establishment information: Established in 1988.
Company type: Private company
Business activities: Produces crude petroleum and natural gas.
Business type (SIC): Extraction/oil and gas
Corporate officers: Mark Veteto, Pres.; Ash Roan, V.P., Finance; Rodena Hiser, Secy.-Treas.
Giving statement: Giving through the Veteto Foundation.

The Veteto Foundation
119 E. Bender
Hobbs, NM 88240 (575) 397-7750
Application address: 401 W. Taylor, Hobbs, NM 88240; URL: http://www.vetetofoundation.com/

Establishment information: Established in 2006 in NM.
Donors: Me-Tex Oil & Gas, Inc.; Mark Veteto; Vondal Veteto.

Financial data (yr. ended 06/30/11): Assets, $84,514 (M); gifts received, $120,000; expenditures, $39,629; qualifying distributions, $36,000; giving activities include $11,000 for 4 grants (high: $5,000; low: $500) and $25,000 for 5 grants to individuals (high: $5,000; low: $5,000).
Purpose and activities: Grant awards to full-time teachers in the Hobbs Municipal School District, New Mexico.
Fields of interest: Arts; Recreation; Human services.
Type of support: Grants to individuals.
Geographic limitations: Giving limited to residents of Hobbs, NM.
Application information: Applications accepted. Application form required.
Initial approach: Proposal
Deadline(s): None
Officers and Directors:* Mark Veteto, Pres. and Secy.-Treas.; Scotty Holloman; Janey Roan; Kali Veteto; Patti Veteto.
EIN: 205181651

2479
Metro-Goldwyn-Mayer Inc.

(also known as MGM)
10250 Constellation Blvd.
Los Angeles, CA 90067-6421
(310) 449-3000

Company URL: http://www.mgm.com
Establishment information: Established in 1924.
Company type: Private company
Business activities: Develops, produces, and distributes motion pictures and television programs.
Business type (SIC): Motion pictures/production and services allied to
Financial profile for 2012: Assets, $2,616,151,000; liabilities, $1,148,588,000
Corporate officers: Gary Barber, Co-Chair. and Co-C.E.O.; Roger Birnbaum, Co-Chair. and Co-C.E.O.; Ken Schapiro, C.O.O.
Board of directors: Gary Barber, Co-Chair.; Roger Birnbaum, Co-Chair.
Subsidiaries: Metro-Goldwyn-Mayer Distribution Co., Santa Monica, CA; Metro-Goldwyn-Mayer Pictures Inc., Santa Monica, CA; Orion Pictures Corp., Santa Monica, CA; United Artists Pictures Inc., Santa Monica, CA
Giving statement: Giving through the MGM Corporate Giving Program.

MGM Corporate Giving Program

c/o Corp. Contribs.
10250 Constellation Blvd.
Los Angeles, CA 90067-6200 (310) 449-3798
FAX: (310) 586-8750; E-mail: jlake@mgm.com

Contact: Jayme Lake, Exec. Asst.
Purpose and activities: MGM makes charitable contributions to nonprofit organizations on a case by case basis. Support is given on a national basis.
Fields of interest: General charitable giving.
Type of support: Donated products; Employee volunteer services; General/operating support; Sponsorships.
Geographic limitations: Giving in areas of company operations on a national basis, with emphasis on CA.
Application information: Applications accepted. Application form not required.
Initial approach: Proposal to headquarters
Copies of proposal: 1
Deadline(s): None
Final notification: 2 weeks

2480
The Metropolitan Auto Dealers Association

(doing business as METROPO)
(also known as MADA)
1120 N.W. 63rd St., Ste. 109
Oklahoma City, OK 73116-6500
(405) 607-0400

Company URL: http://www.okcautoshow.org
Establishment information: Established in 1917.
Company type: Business league
Business activities: Operates auto dealership business association.
Business type (SIC): Business association
Corporate officer: Peter L. Hodges, Pres.
Giving statement: Giving through the Car Dealers Care Foundation.

Car Dealers Care Foundation

1710 N. Broadway Ave.
Oklahoma City, OK 73103 (405) 607-0400

Establishment information: Established in OK.
Donor: Metropolitan Oklahoma City Motor Car Dealers and Association.
Contact: Peter L. Hodges, Pres.
Financial data (yr. ended 12/31/11): Assets, $40,152 (M); gifts received, $18,680; expenditures, $15,617; qualifying distributions, $14,500; giving activities include $14,500 for 10 grants to individuals (high: $2,000; low: $500).
Purpose and activities: The foundation provides educational or medical assistance to needy individuals and families.
Fields of interest: Education; Health care; Family services.
Type of support: Grants to individuals.
Geographic limitations: Giving primarily in OK.
Application information: Applications accepted. Application form not required.
Initial approach: Proposal
Deadline(s): None
Officers: Jeff Robinson, Chair.; Tom Davis, Vice-Chair.; Peter L. Hodges, Pres.; John Holt, Treas.
Directors: Greg Cable; Mike Fowler; Marc Heitz; Bob Nouri.
EIN: 721536899

2481
Metropolitan Life Insurance Company

(also known as MetLife)
200 Park Ave., Fl. 1200
New York, NY 10166-1299 (212) 578-2211

Company URL: http://www.metlife.com
Establishment information: Established in 1868.
Company type: Subsidiary of a public company
International Securities Identification Number: US59156R1086
Business activities: Sells life insurance; provides investment advisory services.
Business type (SIC): Insurance/life; security and commodity services
Corporate officers: Steven A. Kandarian, Chair., Pres., and C.E.O.; William J. Wheeler, Pres.; Steven J. Goulart, Exec. V.P. and C.I.O.; Ricardo Anzaldua, Exec. V.P. and Genl. Counsel; Frans Hij Koop, Exec. V.P., Human Resources
Board of directors: Steven A. Kandarian, Chair.; Sylvia Mathews Burwell; Cheryl W. Grise; R. Glenn Hubbard; John M. Keane; Alfred F. Kelly, Jr.; James M. Kilts; Catherine R. Kinney; Hugh B. Price; David Satcher; Kenton J. Sicchitano; Lulu C. Wang
Subsidiaries: Farmers National Co., Omaha, NE; General American Life Insurance Co., St. Louis, MO; Hyatt Legal Plans, Inc., Cleveland, OH; MetLife Funding, Inc., New York, NY; MetLife Securities, Inc., New York, NY; Metropolitan Property and Casualty Insurance Co., Warwick, RI; New England Life Insurance Company, Boston, MA; Security First Life Insurance Co., Los Angeles, CA; SSR Realty Advisors, Inc., White Plains, NY
Giving statement: Giving through the MetLife Corporate Giving Program and the MetLife Foundation.

MetLife Corporate Giving Program

200 Park Ave.
New York, NY 10166-0005
URL: http://www.metlife.org

Purpose and activities: As a complement to its foundation, MetLife also makes charitable contributions to nonprofit organizations directly. Support is given on a national basis in areas of company operations.
Fields of interest: Arts, equal rights; Arts; Education, continuing education; Education; Health care; Alzheimer's disease; Youth development; Aging, centers/services; Human services; Public affairs.
Type of support: Employee volunteer services; General/operating support.
Geographic limitations: Giving on a national basis in areas of company operations.
Publications: Corporate giving report.
Selected grants: The following grants are a representative sample of this grantmaker's funding activity:
$1,206,096 to Lincoln Center for the Performing Arts, Live From Lincoln Center in collaboration with Thirteen/WNET, New York, NY, 2009. For Public Broadcasting.
$125,000 to National Association of Secondary School Principals, Reston, VA, 2009. For Teacher Effectiveness.
$100,000 to Boy Scouts of America, Greater New York Councils, New York, NY, 2009. For Community Betterment.
$35,000 to Parents, Families and Friends of Lesbians and Gays, Washington, DC, 2009. For Youth Development.
$30,000 to Museum of Fine Arts, Boston, MA, 2009. For Lifelong Learning.
$25,000 to Museum of Modern Art, New York, NY, 2009. For Lifelong Learning.
$25,000 to Special Olympics Rhode Island, Smithfield, RI, 2009. For Youth Development.
$23,500 to Inroads, Saint Louis, MO, 2009. For College Access and Success.
$15,000 to National Corporate Theater Fund, New York, NY, 2009. For Reaching Global Audiences.
$15,000 to Take Our Daughters and Sons to Work Foundation, Elizabeth City, NC, 2009. For Youth Development.

MetLife Foundation

1095 Ave. of the Americas
New York, NY 10036-6797 (212) 578-6272
FAX: (212) 578-0617;
E-mail: metlifefoundation@metlife.com;
URL: http://www.metlife.org

Establishment information: Incorporated in 1976 in NY.
Donor: Metropolitan Life Insurance Co.
Contact: A. Dennis White, C.E.O. and Pres.

Financial data (yr. ended 12/31/12): Assets, $166,318,974 (M); expenditures, $41,195,014; qualifying distributions, $41,195,014; giving activities include $41,107,662 for grants (high: $1,000,000; low: $250) and $87,352 for 1,364 employee matching gifts.
Purpose and activities: The foundation supports food banks and organizations involved with arts and culture, education, health, Alzheimer's disease, housing, human services, community development, voluntarism promotion, civic affairs, senior citizens, and economically disadvantaged people. Special emphasis is directed toward programs designed to strengthen communities; promote good health; and improve education.
Fields of interest: Arts education; Museums (art); Arts; Higher education; Higher education, college (community/junior); Education, services; Education; Public health; Health care; Alzheimer's disease; Alzheimer's disease research; Food banks; Housing/shelter; Youth development, adult & child programs; Youth development, business; Children/youth, services; Human services, financial counseling; Human services; Urban/community development; Community/economic development; Voluntarism promotion; Leadership development; Public affairs Infants/toddlers; Children; Youth; Adults; Aging; Young adults; Disabilities, people with; Physically disabled; Minorities; Asians/Pacific Islanders; African Americans/Blacks; Hispanics/Latinos; Native Americans/American Indians; Women; Infants/toddlers, female; Girls; Adults, women; Young adults, female; Men; Infants/toddlers, male; Boys; Adults, men; Young adults, male; Military/veterans; Economically disadvantaged; Homeless; LGBTQ.
International interests: Japan; Mexico; South Korea.

Programs:

Civic Affairs: The foundation supports programs designed to promote revitalization of urban neighborhoods, with emphasis on affordable housing and economic development; financial literacy; after-school initiatives and mentoring; and volunteerism and civic engagement.

Culture: The foundation supports initiatives designed to promote innovative arts education for people of all ages; and accessible and inclusive programming.

Education: The foundation supports programs designed to promote teachers and principal leadership; school community connections; and access to higher education, with emphasis on community colleges.

Employee Matching Gifts: The foundation matches contributions made by full-time employees, directors, retirees, and spouses of employees of MetLife to institutions of higher education on a one-for-one basis from $25 to $5,000 per contributor, per year.

Employee Volunteer Programs: Through Volunteer Ventures and the MetLife Volunteer Service Awards, the foundation provides grants to nonprofit organizations with which employees of MetLife volunteer.

Employee-Related Scholarships: The foundation awards college scholarships to children of associates of MetLife. The program is administered by the National Merit Scholarship Corp. and Scholarship America.

Health: The foundation supports programs designed to promote Alzheimer's disease research, public awareness and understanding; issues related to healthy aging and caregiving; and health education and information.

Social Investment Program: The foundation provides loans and equity investments to organizations that do not meet customary investment criteria of private and institutional investors. Investments are made to projects designed to improve the quality of life for individuals and communities. Special emphasis is directed toward programs designed to promote community revitalization; economic development; and health.
Type of support: Continuing support; Employee matching gifts; Employee volunteer services; Employee-related scholarships; General/operating support; In-kind gifts; Program development; Program evaluation; Program-related investments/loans; Publication; Research; Scholarship funds.
Geographic limitations: Giving on a national and international basis, with emphasis in CA, CT, DC, FL, IL, MA, NJ, NY, PA, and TX.
Support limitations: No support for private foundations, religious, fraternal, athletic, political, or social organizations, hospitals, local chapters of national organizations, disease-specific organizations, labor groups, organizations primarily engaged in patient care or direct treatment, drug treatment centers, community health clinics, or elementary or secondary schools. No grants to individuals (except for Medical Research Awards and employee-related scholarships), or for endowments, courtesy advertising, or festival participation.
Publications: Annual report (including application guidelines); Corporate giving report (including application guidelines); Financial statement; Grants list.
Application information: Applications accepted. Additional information may be requested at a later date. Application form required. Applicants should submit the following:
1) name, address and phone number of organization
2) brief history of organization and description of its mission
3) copy of most recent annual report/audited financial statement/990
4) listing of board of directors, trustees, officers and other key people and their affiliations
5) detailed description of project and amount of funding requested
6) contact person
7) copy of current year's organizational budget and/or project budget
8) additional materials/documentation

Initial approach: Complete online application
Copies of proposal: 1
Deadline(s): None
Final notification: 1 month

Officers and Directors:* Christopher B. Smith*, Chair.; A. Dennis White*, C.E.O. and Pres.; Phyllis Zanghi, Counsel and Secy.; Jonathan Rosenthal*, Treas.; Robert C. Tarnok, Cont.; Frans Hijkoop; Michel Khalaf; Maria Morris; Oscar Schmidt.
Number of staff: None.
EIN: 132878224
Selected grants: The following grants are a representative sample of this grantmaker's funding activity:
$1,000,000 to American Council on Education, Washington, DC, 2012. For D79 Accelerated Learning Pilot Project.
$600,000 to Trust for Public Land, San Francisco, CA, 2012. For More Parks for More People.
$500,000 to Urban League, National, New York, NY, 2012. For MetLife Healthy Communities Fund.
$410,000 to National Association of Secondary School Principals, Reston, VA, 2012. For NASSP Breakthrough Schools Program.
$300,000 to Alzheimers Association National Headquarters, Chicago, IL, 2012. For early stage program and outreach campaign.
$250,000 to Childrens Health Fund, New York, NY, 2012. For Healthy Kids, Healthy Smiles Initiative.
$250,000 to Generations United, Washington, DC, 2012. For Stronger Together: Developing Youth Intergenerational Entrepreneurs and Recognizing Excellence in Intergenerational Communities.
$200,000 to Partners for Livable Communities, Washington, DC, 2012. For MetLife Foundation City Leaders Institute for Aging in Place.
$200,000 to Reach Out and Read, Boston, MA, 2012. For Supporting Military Families.
$125,000 to Smithsonian Institution, Washington, DC, 2012. For Smithsonian Community Grant Program.
$100,000 to Smithsonian Institution, Washington, DC, 2012. For Black Wings: American Dreams of Flight.
$50,000 to Partners for Livable Communities, Washington, DC, 2012. For Institutions as Fulcrums of Change: Creative Re-imagining of Community Assets to Meet the Challenges of the Next Decade.

2482
Metropolitan Regional Information Systems, Inc.

9707 Key W. Ave., Ste. 200
Rockville, MD 20850 (301) 838-7200
FAX: (301) 838-7171

Company URL: http://www.mris.com
Establishment information: Established in 2001.
Company type: Private company
Business activities: Provides real estate services.
Business type (SIC): Real estate agents and managers
Corporate officers: David Howell, Chair.; David Charron, Pres. and C.E.O.; Michael Belak, C.I.O.; Brian Donnellan, Sr. V.P., Opers. and C.F.O.; Monica Goodwyn, V.P., Admin. and Human Resources; Leslie Oleynik, Cont.; Erik M. Feig, Esq., Genl. Counsel
Board of directors: David Howell, Chair.; Cindy Ariosa; James E. Barb; Barbara Baumier; James Boss; Boyd Campbell; Thomas Carruthers III; David Charron; Jon Coile; Thomas G. Donegan; Brain Donnellan; Paul W. Foster; Greg Hangemanole; Joseph Himali; Alexander Karavasilis; Scott Lederer; Gilbert D. Marsiglia; Terrence McDermott; Michael Moran; Vinh Ngugen; Tom Quattlebaum; Patricia Savani; Steve Spray; Paul C. Valentino; Katie Wethman
Giving statement: Giving through the Metropolitan Regional Information Systems, Inc. Contributions Program.

Metropolitan Regional Information Systems, Inc. Contributions Program

9707 Key West Ave., Ste. 200
Baltimore, MD 21297-3093 (301) 838-7100
URL: http://www.mris.com

2483
Metropolitan Theatres Corporation

8727 W. 3rd St., 3rd Fl.
Los Angeles, CA 90048 (310) 858-2800

Company URL: http://www.metrotheatres.com
Establishment information: Established in 1923.
Company type: Private company
Business activities: Operates movie theaters.
Business type (SIC): Motion picture theaters
Corporate officers: Bruce C. Corwin, Chair. and C.E.O.; David Corwin, Pres.; Phillip Hermann, C.F.O.;

Dale Davison, Sr. V.P., Opers.; Tim Spain, V.P., Opers.; Victoria Uy, V.P., Finance and Human Resources
Board of director: Bruce C. Corwin, Chair.
Giving statement: Giving through the Metropolitan Theatres Foundation.

Metropolitan Theatres Foundation

8727 W. 3rd St., Ste. 301
Los Angeles, CA 90048-3865

Establishment information: Established in 1980 in CA.
Donors: Metropolitan Theatres Corp.; Bruce C. Corwin.
Financial data (yr. ended 04/30/12): Assets, $1 (M); gifts received, $2,510; expenditures, $2,510; qualifying distributions, $2,500; giving activities include $2,500 for 2 grants (high: $1,500; low: $1,000).
Purpose and activities: The foundation supports organizations involved with arts and culture, education, youth development, children's services, and Judaism.
Fields of interest: Performing arts; Arts; Higher education; Education; Youth development; Children, services; Human services; Jewish federated giving programs; Jewish agencies & synagogues; General charitable giving.
Type of support: General/operating support; Scholarship funds.
Geographic limitations: Giving primarily in CA.
Support limitations: No grants to individuals.
Application information: Applications not accepted. Unsolicited requests for funds not accepted.
Officers: Bruce C. Corwin, Pres. and C.E.O.; Jill Cowan, Secy.
EIN: 953520828

2484
Metropolitan Water District of Southern California

700 N. Alameda St.
P.O. Box 54153
Los Angeles, CA 90054-0153
(213) 217-6000

Company URL: http://www.mwdh2o.com
Establishment information: Established in 1928.
Company type: Cooperative
Business activities: Distributes water.
Business type (SIC): Water suppliers
Corporate officers: John V. Foley, Chair.; David D. De Jesus, Vice-Chair.; Gloria Gray, Vice-Chair.; Randy A. Record, Vice-Chair.; John W. Murray, Jr., Vice-Chair.; Jeffrey Kightlinger, C.E.O.; Debra C. Man, C.O.O.; Gary Breaux, C.F.O.; Gilbert F. Ivey, C.A.O.; John T. Morris, Secy.; Karen Tachiki, Genl. Counsel
Board of directors: John V. Foley, Chair.; Randy A. Record, Vice-Chair.; Gloria Gray, Vice-Chair.; John W. Murray, Jr., Vice-Chair.; David D. De Jesus, Vice-Chair.; John T. Morris
Giving statement: Giving through the Metropolitan Water District of Southern California Community Partnering Program.

Metropolitan Water District of Southern California Community Partnering Program

c/o Community Partnering Prog.
P.O. Box 54153
Los Angeles, CA 90054-0153
FAX: (213) 217-6500;
E-mail: ymartinez@mwdh2o.com; Kevin McLaughlin: tel.: (213) 217-6619; email: kmclaughlin@mwdh2o.com; Maria Murray: tel.: (213) 217-7262; e-mail: mmurray@mwdh2o.com; URL: http://www.mwdh2o.com/mwdh2o/pages/yourwater/cpp/cpp.html

Contact: Yvette Martinez, Conservation & Community Svc(s). Mgr.
Purpose and activities: Metropolitan makes charitable contributions to nonprofit organizations, professional associations, educational institutions, and public agencies. Emphasis is given to programs that promote discussion and educational activities for regional water conservation and water-use efficiency issues, community water awareness programs, water-related education outreach programs, public policy water conferences, and programs with member agency involvement. Support is given primarily in the six-county Los Angeles, California, area.
Fields of interest: Environment, water resources; Botanical/horticulture/landscape services; Environmental education; Youth development, services; Public utilities, water.
Type of support: Continuing support; Program development; Public relations services; Sponsorships.
Geographic limitations: Giving primarily in Support is given primarily in the six-county Los Angeles, CA, area.
Support limitations: No grants for labor expenses, leasing or rental expenses, legal, lobbying, or consultant fees, meals or refreshments, travel or transportation, film festivals, office space, or utility expenses such as gas, electric, internet, or water, scholarships, internships, stipends, honorariums, or teacher release time, or equipment or devices that are eligible for rebates.
Publications: Application guidelines.
Application information: Applications accepted. Requests should be limited to a maximum of $2,000, and one proposal per year. Multi-year funding is not automatic. Application form required. Applicants should submit the following:
1) copy of IRS Determination Letter
2) additional materials/documentation
Proposals should include a signed W-9 Federal Tax Form, Liability Waiver, and Conflict of Interest Waiver.
Initial approach: Complete online application form and mail or fax supplemental documents to the Community Partnering Program
Deadline(s): 30 days prior to need
Number of staff: 3 full-time professional.

2485
Fred Meyer Stores, Inc.

3800 S.E. 22nd Ave.
Portland, OR 97202 (503) 232-8844

Company URL: http://www.fredmeyerstores.com
Establishment information: Established in 1922.
Company type: Subsidiary of a public company
Ultimate parent company: The Kroger Co.
Business activities: Operates general merchandise stores.
Business type (SIC): Merchandise stores/general
Financial profile for 2010: Number of employees, 1,313; sales volume, $5,050,000,000
Corporate officers: Lynn Gust, Pres.; David Deatherage, Sr. V.P. and C.F.O.
Giving statement: Giving through the Fred Meyer Stores, Inc. Corporate Giving Program.

Fred Meyer Stores, Inc. Corporate Giving Program

P.O. Box 42121
Portland, OR 97242-0121 (503) 797-3830
E-mail: fmsponsorship@fredmeyer.com; Address for sponsorship proposals: Attn: Sponsorship Comm. 34N, P.O. Box 42121, Portland, OR 97242; URL: http://www.fredmeyer.com/company_information/FM_Community/Pages/donations.aspx

Purpose and activities: As a complement to its foundation, Fred Meyer Store also makes charitable contributions to nonprofit organizations. Support is limited to organizations involved with youth development, hunger relief, and community services in Alaska, Idaho, Oregon, and Washington.
Fields of interest: Food services; Food banks; Food distribution, meals on wheels; Nutrition; Youth development; Community/economic development.
Type of support: Donated products; Employee volunteer services; General/operating support; In-kind gifts; Sponsorships.
Geographic limitations: Giving limited to AK, ID, OR, and WA.
Support limitations: No support for sectarian or religious organizations not of direct benefit to the entire community, discriminatory organizations, or pass-through organizations. No grants to individuals, or for capital campaigns, or travel.
Publications: Application guidelines.
Application information: Applications accepted. Proposals for sponsorships should be limited to 5 pages and should include in-kind donation requests. Application form required. Applicants should submit the following:
1) population served
Sponsorship proposals should include audience size, varying sponsorship levels, list of promotional apps, and benefits of the sponsorship.
Initial approach: Contact the customer service desk at local company store for donations; E-mail or mail proposal for sponsorships
Deadline(s): Aug. 31 for funding in the next fiscal year starting Feb. 1; or 3 months prior to event
Administrators: Glynda Brockhoff, Coord., Philanthropy; Melinda Merrill, Dir., Public Affairs.
Number of staff: 1 full-time professional; 1 part-time professional.

2486
MFA, Inc.

201 Ray Young Dr.
Columbia, MO 65201-3599 (573) 874-5111

Company URL: http://www.mfaincorporated.com
Establishment information: Established in 1914.
Company type: Cooperative
Business activities: Sells agronomy and livestock products wholesale.
Business type (SIC): Non-durable goods—wholesale
Financial profile for 2011: Assets, $408,330,452; liabilities, $346,637,764
Corporate officers: Don Mills, Chair.; John Moffitt, Vice-Chair.; Bill Streeter, Pres. and C.E.O.; Janice Schuerman, Sr. V.P. and Corp. Secy.; J. Brian Griffith, Sr. V.P., Corp. Opers.; Ernie Verslues, V.P.

and C.F.O.; John Akridge, Treas.; John Ruth, Genl. Counsel
Board of directors: Don Mills, Chair.; John Moffitt, Vice-Chair.; David Callis; Glen Cope; Tom Dent; Tim Engemann; Barry Kagay; Kendall Kircher; Tim Lichte; Randy Ludwig; Wayne Nichols; Jimmie Reading; Carlton Spencer; Harry Thompson
Giving statement: Giving through the MFA Foundation.

MFA Foundation

201 Ray Young Dr.
Columbia, MO 65201-3568
URL: http://www.mfafoundation.com/

Establishment information: Established in 1958 in MO.
Donors: Robert O. Wurmb; MFA Inc.; MFA Oil Co.
Contact: Larna Lavelle, Secy.-Treas.
Financial data (yr. ended 06/30/11): Assets, $14,423,361 (M); gifts received, $575,903; expenditures, $817,733; qualifying distributions, $739,721; giving activities include $739,721 for grants.
Purpose and activities: The foundation supports programs designed to provide educational opportunity for youth and awards college scholarships to high school seniors.
Fields of interest: Higher education; Education; Agriculture; Youth development, agriculture; Youth development.
Program:
Scholarships: The foundation awards college scholarships of $2,000 to high school seniors located in areas of MFA agency operations planning to study agriculture or other fields of study that benefit rural life. Recipients are selected based on applicant's participation and leadership in school, church, and community; the applicants reputation for good citizenship and moral character; applicant's financial need, sources of income, and willingness to work; and the applicant's academic progress.
Type of support: General/operating support; Scholarship funds; Scholarships—to individuals.
Geographic limitations: Giving primarily in areas of company operations, with emphasis on MO.
Publications: Application guidelines; Informational brochure.
Application information: Unsolicited requests for grants are not accepted.
Initial approach: Contact high school guidance counselor for application form for scholarships
Board meeting date(s): June and Nov.
Deadline(s): Mar. 15 for scholarships
Officers and Trustees:* Jerry Taylor*, Pres.; Bill Streeter*, V.P.; Larna Lavelle, Secy.-Treas.; Don Copenhaver; Ken Caspall; Bill Coen; Larry Fick; J. Brian Griffith; John Percival; Phil Perkins; Janice Schuerman; Ernie Verslues.
EIN: 436026877
Selected grants: The following grants are a representative sample of this grantmaker's funding activity:
$5,000 to Columbia College, Columbia, MO, 2011.
$5,000 to Drury University, Springfield, MO, 2011.
$5,000 to Four-H Foundation, Missouri, Columbia, MO, 2011.
$5,000 to Missouri Young Farmers Association, Jefferson City, MO, 2011.
$4,000 to Job Point, Columbia, MO, 2011.
$2,500 to College of the Ozarks, Point Lookout, MO, 2011.
$1,500 to Boys and Girls Town of Missouri, Saint James, MO, 2011.
$1,500 to Missouri Girls Town Foundation, Kingdom City, MO, 2011.
$1,000 to Alzheimers Association, Columbia, MO, 2011.
$1,000 to Missouri Lions Eye Research Foundation, Columbia, MO, 2011.

2487
MFA Oil Company

1 Ray Young Dr.
P.O. Box 519
Columbia, MO 65205 (573) 442-0171

Company URL: http://www.mfaoil.com
Establishment information: Established in 1929.
Company type: Private company
Business activities: Refines petroleum; sells tires wholesale; operates tire stores; operates automobile service stations; operates convenience stores; operates gasoline service stations; distributes propane.
Business type (SIC): Petroleum refining and related industries; gas production and distribution; motor vehicles, parts, and supplies—wholesale; groceries—retail; auto and home supplies—retail; gasoline service stations
Corporate officers: Benny Farrell, Chair.; Ralph Schallert, Vice-Chair.; Jerry Taylor, Pres.
Board of directors: Benny Farrell, Chair.; Ralph Schallert, Vice-Chair.; Floyd Buckman; Kevin Buckstead; Ronald Felten; Marion Kertz; Joey Massey; Rusty Wayman
Giving statement: Giving through the MFA Oil Foundation.

MFA Oil Foundation

P.O. Box 519
Columbia, MO 65205-0519
E-mail: lflick@mfaoil.com; URL: http://www.mfaoil.com/index.cfm?show=10&mid=11&pid=7

Establishment information: Established in 1998.
Donor: MFA Oil Co.
Financial data (yr. ended 08/31/11): Assets, $21,385 (M); gifts received, $250,000; expenditures, $132,895; qualifying distributions, $112,100; giving activities include $112,100 for 51 grants (high: $20,000; low: $500).
Purpose and activities: The foundation supports organizations involved with education, human services, civic affairs, and youth. Special emphasis is directed toward programs designed to build knowledge and leadership skills of rural youth; promote agricultural and cooperative education; and address and solve community problems and improve quality of life.
Fields of interest: Education; Human services; Public affairs Youth.
Program:
Dale H. Creach Scholarship: The foundation awards a college scholarship to children of employees of MFA Oil and MFA Petroleum.
Type of support: Building/renovation; Employee-related scholarships; Equipment; Program development.
Geographic limitations: Giving primarily in MO.
Support limitations: No support for lobbying, political, or religious organizations, national organizations, or veterans', fraternal, or labor organizations. No grants to individuals, or for operating expenses, fundraising events, dinners, benefits, advertising, travel expenses, or sports sponsorships.
Publications: Application guidelines.
Application information: Applications accepted. Grants are awarded in amounts not to exceed $2,000. Support is limited to 1 contribution per organization during any given year. Application form required. Applicants should submit the following:
1) results expected from proposed grant
2) statement of problem project will address
3) copy of IRS Determination Letter
4) brief history of organization and description of its mission
5) copy of most recent annual report/audited financial statement/990
6) copy of current year's organizational budget and/or project budget
Initial approach: Download application form and mail to foundation
Deadline(s): None
Officers: Ken Caspall, Chair.; Tom May, Vice Chair.; Beverly Twellman, Secy.-Treas.
Board Members: Joe Case; Ronnie Felten; Keith Forbes; Ralph Schallert; Jerry Taylor.
EIN: 431831800

2488
MGIC Investment Corporation

MGIC Plz., 250 E. Kilbourn Ave.
P.O. Box 488
Milwaukee, WI 53202 (414) 347-6480
FAX: (414) 347-6959

Company URL: http://www.mgic.com
Establishment information: Established in 1957.
Company type: Public company
Company ticker symbol and exchange: MTG/NYSE
Business activities: Operates holding company; sells mortgage guaranty insurance.
Business type (SIC): Insurance/surety; holding company
Financial profile for 2012: Number of employees, 877; assets, $5,574,320,000; sales volume, $1,378,360,000; pre-tax net income, -$928,640,000; expenses, $2,307,010,000; liabilities, $5,377,380,000
Corporate officers: Curt S. Culver, Chair. and C.E.O.; Patrick Sinks, Pres. and C.O.O.; Jon Michael Lauer, Exec. V.P. and C.F.O.; Jeffrey H. Lane, Exec. V.P., Genl. Counsel, and Secy.
Board of directors: Curt S. Culver, Chair.; James A. Abbott; Thomas M. Hagerty; Timothy A. Holt; Kenneth M. Jastrow II; Daniel P. Kearney; Michael E. Lehman; William A. McIntosh; Leslie M. Muma; Donald T. Nicolaisen; Mark Zandi, Ph.D.
Subsidiary: Mortgage Guaranty Insurance Corporation, Milwaukee, WI
International operations: Australia; Denmark
Giving statement: Giving through the MGIC Investment Corporation Contributions Program.
Company EIN: 391486475

MGIC Investment Corporation Contributions Program

c/o Corporate Contributions Committee
250 E. Kilbourn Ave.
Milwaukee, WI 53202-3102
URL: http://mtg.mgic.com/company/citizenship.html

Purpose and activities: MGIC makes charitable contributions to nonprofit organizations involved with arts and culture, education, human services, civic affairs, health, housing and economic development, social services, and on a case by case basis. Support is given primarily in the Milwaukee, Wisconsin, area.
Fields of interest: Arts; Education; Health care; Housing/shelter; Human services; Community/

economic development; Public affairs; General charitable giving.

Program:

Matching Gifts to Learning Institutions: MGIC matches, dollar-for-dollar, co-worker contributions to colleges or universities and high schools, up to $1,000 per school, $2,000 maximum annually.

Type of support: Annual campaigns; Capital campaigns; Continuing support; Employee matching gifts; Employee-related scholarships; General/operating support.

Geographic limitations: Giving primarily in the Milwaukee, WI, area.

Application information: Applications accepted.

Initial approach: Proposal

2489
MGM Resorts International

(formerly MGM Mirage)
3600 Las Vegas Blvd. S.
Las Vegas, NV 89109-4303
(702) 693-7120
FAX: (702) 693-8626

Company URL: http://www.mgmmirage.com
Establishment information: Established in 1986.
Company type: Public company
Company ticker symbol and exchange: MGM/NYSE
Business activities: Operates casino resorts.
Business type (SIC): Amusement and recreation services/miscellaneous; hotels and motels
Financial profile for 2012: Number of employees, 61,000; assets, $26,284,740,000; sales volume, $9,160,840,000; pre-tax net income, -$1,734,210,000; expenses, $9,080,320,000; liabilities, $21,919,190,000
Fortune 1000 ranking: 2012—292nd in revenues, 992nd in profits, and 208th in assets
Forbes 2000 ranking: 2012—991st in sales, 1954th in profits, and 823rd in assets
Corporate officers: James Joseph Murren, Chair. and C.E.O.; William J. Hornbuckle, Pres.; Corey Ian Sanders, C.O.O.; Daniel J. D'Arrigo, Exec. V.P., C.F.O., and Treas.; Robert C. Selwood, Exec. V.P. and C.A.O.; John M. McManus, Exec. V.P., Genl. Counsel, and Secy.; Christopher Nordling, Exec. V.P., Opers.
Board of directors: James Joseph Murren, Chair.; Robert H. Baldwin; William A. Bible; Burton M. Cohen; Willie D. Davis; William Grounds; Alexis M. Herman; Roland A. Hernandez; Anthony L. Mandekic; Rose McKinney-James; Daniel J. Taylor; Gregory Taylor
Subsidiary: Mirage Resorts, Incorporated, Las Vegas, NV
Giving statement: Giving through the MGM Resorts International Corporate Giving Program and the MGM Mirage Voice Foundation.
Company EIN: 000000000

MGM Resorts International Corporate Giving Program

(formerly MGM Mirage Corporate Giving Program)
3600 Las Vegas Blvd. S.
Las Vegas, NV 89109-4303 (702) 693-7120
E-mail: philanthropy@mgmresorts.com; URL: http://www.mgmmiragevoice.com/pages/cg_giving.asp

Purpose and activities: MGM Resorts International makes charitable contributions to nonprofit organizations involved with childhood development, community development, diversity, and education. Special emphasis is directed towards programs designed to focus on at-risk youth and early childhood development. Support is limited to areas of company operations in Detroit, Michigan, Mississippi, and Nevada.

Fields of interest: Education, public education; Education; Child development, services; Civil/human rights, equal rights Economically disadvantaged.

Program:

Dollars for Doers Program: Through the Dollars for Doers Program, MGM Mirage will consider a $250 grant to eligible organizations at the request of an employee who has volunteered 25 - 50 hours per calendar year. A $500 grant will be considered for 51 + volunteer hours. Each organization may receive up to $2,000, per calendar year. To be considered for a grant, employees must complete an on-line request form, which is available through the MGM MIRAGE Voice Web site.

Type of support: Employee volunteer services; General/operating support.

Geographic limitations: Giving limited to organizations that benefit communities in areas of company operations in the Detroit, MI area, MS, and NV.

Support limitations: No support for discriminatory organizations. No grants to individuals, or for athletic sponsorships of individuals and/or teams, or for new or used gaming-casino items for children.

Publications: Application guidelines.

Application information: Applications accepted. Application form not required. Applicants should submit the following:

1) results expected from proposed grant
2) statement of problem project will address
3) population served
4) name, address and phone number of organization
5) detailed description of project and amount of funding requested
6) contact person
7) copy of current year's organizational budget and/or project budget

Applications should include the Tax ID number of the organization; and a description of past support by MGM Resorts International with the organization.

Initial approach: E-mail proposal to headquarters
Copies of proposal: 1
Deadline(s): Sept. 1

MGM Mirage Voice Foundation

3260 Industrial Rd.
Las Vegas, NV 89109-1132 (702) 650-7469
FAX: (702) 650-7401; Application address for southern MS: c/o Sara Miller, P.O. Box 7777, Biloxi, MS 39540-7777; Toll-free tel.: (800) 477-5110; URL: http://www.mgmmiragevoice.com/pages/eg_foundation.asp

Establishment information: Established in 2002 in NV.
Donor: MGM Mirage.
Contact: Christina Roth, Dir., Corp. Philanthropy
Financial data (yr. ended 04/30/11): Revenue, $4,793,666; assets, $3,721,696 (M); gifts received, $4,793,648; expenditures, $3,795,993; program services expenses, $3,772,225; giving activities include $3,623,600 for 104 grants (high: $131,847; low: $5,170) and $148,625 for grants to individuals.

Purpose and activities: The foundation supports charitable organizations in the communities where MGM Mirage employees live, work, and care for their families.

Fields of interest: Education; Safety/disasters; Human services; Community/economic development; Foundations (community).

Program:

Grants Program: The foundation directs funding to programs that best address the needs and problems of communities through three initiatives: strengthening neighborhoods (promoting self-sufficiency and the revitalization of communities through providing affordable housing, utility assistance, vocational training, programs that address high-risk neighborhoods, and programs that increase health, safety, and collaboration among residents), strengthening children (advocating for early childhood development, success in school, and prevention/intervention programs that empower children to be successful), and strength in difficult times (providing recovery and counseling services, placing an emphasis on families, children, parents, and individuals touched by addictive behaviors, mental health problems, abuse, or special life circumstances). Eligible organizations must provide human services within the regions where MGM Mirage employees live, work, and care for their families (Nevada, Mississippi, and the greater Detroit, Michigan area).

Geographic limitations: Giving limited to Detroit, MI; southern MS; and southern NV.

Support limitations: No support for individual public or private schools or governmental entities. No grants for sponsorship of fundraising events, capital campaigns, or endowments.

Application information: Applications accepted. For Nevada or the Detroit, Michigan area, submit original application plus 10 copies; for Mississippi, submit original application plus 8 copies. Application form required.

Initial approach: Complete application form
Deadline(s): May 5

Officers and Directors:* Merlinda Gallegos*, Pres.; Jeanette Renard*, Secy.; Keri King; Punam Mathur.
EIN: 010640027

2490
MH Equipment Company

(also known as MH Logistics)
2001 E. Hartman Rd.
Chillicothe, IL 61523 (309) 579-2080

Company URL: http://www.mhequipment.com
Establishment information: Established in 1952.
Company type: Private company
Business activities: Operates material handling equipment dealerships.
Business type (SIC): Industrial machinery and equipment—wholesale
Corporate officers: John S. Wieland, Chair. and Co-Pres.; Coit Edison, Co.-Pres.; Brad Barrow, C.F.O
Board of director: John Weiland, Chair.
Giving statement: Giving through the His First Foundation.

His First Foundation

P.O. Box 50
Mossville, IL 61552-0050 (309) 686-4048
E-mail: jwieland@mheupment.com; URL: http://www.mhequipment.com/custompage.asp?pg=Community

Establishment information: Established in 2001.
Donors: MH Logistics; MH Equipment Co.
Contact: John S. Wieland, Dir.
Financial data (yr. ended 12/31/11): Assets, $1,302,645 (M); gifts received, $756,665; expenditures, $208,692; qualifying distributions, $199,148; giving activities include $199,148 for grants.

Purpose and activities: The foundation supports programs designed to promote areas of faith, secular good works, and acts of kindness.
Fields of interest: Education; Health care; Children/youth, services; Homeless, human services; Human services; Christian agencies & churches.
Type of support: General/operating support.
Geographic limitations: Giving primarily in Peoria, IL.
Support limitations: No grants to individuals.
Application information: Applications not accepted. Contributes only to pre-selected organizations nominated by employees.
Directors: Clyde Wieland; John S. Wieland; Julie Wieland.
EIN: 371414330
Selected grants: The following grants are a representative sample of this grantmaker's funding activity:
$25,000 to Peoria Christian School, Peoria, IL, 2010.
$15,000 to Lifesong for Orphans, Gridley, IL, 2010.
$15,000 to Samaritans Purse, Boone, NC, 2010.
$10,000 to Citivision, New York, NY, 2010.
$10,000 to North American Indian Mission, Point Roberts, WA, 2010.
$5,000 to Crescent Project, Indianapolis, IN, 2010.
$3,000 to Central Asia Institute, Bozeman, MT, 2010.
$1,000 to Smile Train, New York, NY, 2010.

2491
The Miami Marlins, L.P.

Marlins Park
501 Marlins Way
Miami, FL 33125 (305) 480-1442

Company URL: http://miami.marlins.mlb.com/
Establishment information: Established in 1993.
Company type: Private company
Business activities: Operates professional baseball club.
Business type (SIC): Commercial sports
Corporate officers: Jeffrey H. Loria, Chair. and C.E.O.; Joel A. Mael, Vice-Chair.; David P. Samson, Pres.; Michel Bussiere, Exec. V.P. and C.F.O.; Claude Delorme, Exec. V.P., Opers.; Susan Jaison, Sr. V.P., Finance; Andy Silverman, Sr. V.P., Sales; Sean Flynn, Sr. V.P., Mktg.; Derek Jackson, V.P. and Genl. Counsel
Board of directors: Jeffrey H. Loria, Chair.; Joel A. Mael, Vice-Chair.
Giving statement: Giving through the Marlins Foundation and the Florida Marlins Community Foundation.

The Marlins Foundation

501 Marlins Way
Miami, FL 33125 (305) 480-1442
E-mail: Foundation@marlins.com; URL: http://mlb.mlb.com/mia/community/foundation_programs.jsp

Contact: Alfredo Mesa, Exec. Dir.
Purpose and activities: The Florida Marlins make charitable contributions of memorabilia to nonprofit organizations on a case by case basis. Support is limited to Florida, with emphasis on southern Florida.
Fields of interest: General charitable giving.
Type of support: In-kind gifts.
Geographic limitations: Giving limited to FL, with emphasis on southern FL.
Application information: Applications accepted. Proposals should be submitted using organization letterhead. Application form required. Applicants should submit the following:
1) name, address and phone number of organization
2) contact person
Proposals should indicate the type and date of the event.
Initial approach: Download application form and mail with proposal to headquarters
Copies of proposal: 1
Deadline(s): 4 weeks prior to need
Officers: David Samson, Chair.; Joel Mael, Vice-Chair.; P.J. Loyello, Secy.-Treas.; Alfredo Mesa, Exec. Dir.

Florida Marlins Community Foundation

2267 Dan Marino Blvd.
Miami, FL 33056-2600 (305) 626-7253
FAX: (305) 626-7481;
E-mail: community@marlins.mlb.com; Additional email: FMCF@flamarlins.com; additional URL: http://www.cornerstonesforkids.com; URL: http://florida.marlins.mlb.com/fla/community/foundation.jsp

Establishment information: Established in 1999 in FL.
Contact: Alfredo Mesa, Exec. Dir.
Financial data (yr. ended 12/31/10): Revenue, $788,076; assets, $431,203 (M); gifts received, $355,123; expenditures, $681,220; program services expenses, $413,182; giving activities include $413,182 for 21 grants (high: $67,515; low: $5,000).
Purpose and activities: The foundation promotes educational, athletic, health, art, social, and community service programs with a particular focus on south Florida's youth.
Fields of interest: Arts; Education; Athletics/sports, baseball; Youth development Children/youth; Children; Youth; Girls; Boys.
Type of support: Continuing support; Curriculum development; Donated equipment; Employee matching gifts; Employee volunteer services; Equipment; General/operating support; In-kind gifts; Program development; Scholarship funds.
Geographic limitations: Giving primarily in southern FL.
Support limitations: No support for political organizations. No grants for capital campaigns.
Publications: Annual report; Application guidelines; Grants list; Informational brochure; Newsletter.
Application information: Applications accepted. Applicants must also provide evidence of registration with the State of Florida Solicitation of Contributions Act. Application form required. Applicants should submit the following:
1) copy of IRS Determination Letter
Initial approach: Download application form
Copies of proposal: 1
Board meeting date(s): Apr. 1 and Nov. 1
Deadline(s): Jan. 31, Apr. 30, July 31, and Oct. 31
Final notification: 1 month following deadlines
Officers and Directors:* David Samson*, Pres.; Alfredo Mesa, Exec. Dir.; Joel A. Mael; Peter J. Loyello.
Number of staff: 1 full-time professional; 2 full-time support; 1 part-time support.
EIN: 650912375

2492
Michael Best & Friedrich LLP

100 E. Wisconsin Ave., Ste. 3300
Milwaukee, WI 53202-4108
(414) 271-6560

Company URL: http://ww.michaelbest.com
Establishment information: Established in 1848.
Company type: Private company
Business activities: Operates law firm.
Business type (SIC): Legal services
Corporate officers: David A. Krutz, Managing Partner; L. David Lentz, C.O.O.; Alan W. Ciochon, C.I.O.; Brian J. Ammerman, Cont.
Offices: Chicago, IL; Madison, Manitowoc, Milwaukee, Waukesha, WI
Giving statement: Giving through the Michael Best & Friedrich LLP Pro Bono Program.

Michael Best & Friedrich LLP Pro Bono Program

100 E. Wisconsin Ave., Ste. 3300
Milwaukee, WI 53202-4108 (414) 271-6560
FAX: (414) 277-0656;
E-mail: iapitz@michaelbest.com; URL: http://www.michaelbest.com/community-outreach/

Contact: Ian A. Pitz, Partner
Fields of interest: Legal services.
Type of support: Pro bono services - legal.

2493
Michael Foods, Inc.

301 Carson Pkwy., Ste. 400
Minnetonka, MN 55305 (952) 258-4000

Company URL: http://www.michaelfoods.com
Establishment information: Established in 1908.
Company type: Private company
Business activities: Produces and distributes food products in the areas of egg products, cheese and other dairy case products, and potato products in North America and internationally.
Business type (SIC): Food and kindred products
Financial profile for 2009: Number of employees, 3,762; assets, $1,310,000,000; sales volume, $1,542,780,000
Corporate officers: Gregg A. Ostrander, Chair.; John D. Reedy, Vice-Chair.; James E. Dwyer, Jr., Pres. and C.E.O.; Mark D. Witmer, Secy.-Treas.
Board of directors: Gregg A. Ostrander, Chair.; John D. Reedy, Vice-Chair.; James E. Dwyer, Jr.
Giving statement: Giving through the Michael Foods, Inc. Corporate Giving Program.

Michael Foods, Inc. Corporate Giving Program

301 Carson Pkwy. Ste. 400
Minnetonka, MN 55305 (952) 258-4000
URL: http://www.michaelfoods.com/company/community.cfm

Purpose and activities: Michael Foods makes charitable contributions to nonprofit organizations in areas of company operations; giving also to national organizations.
Fields of interest: Education; Health care; Food services; Athletics/sports, Special Olympics; United Ways and Federated Giving Programs; General charitable giving.
Type of support: Annual campaigns; Donated products; Employee matching gifts; Employee

volunteer services; General/operating support; In-kind gifts; Sponsorships.
Geographic limitations: Giving primarily in areas of company operations; giving also to national organizations.

2494
Michaels Stores, Inc.

8000 Bent Branch Dr.
Irving, TX 75063 (972) 409-1300

Company URL: http://www.michaels.com
Establishment information: Established in 1984.
Company type: Subsidiary of a public company
Business activities: Operates arts and crafts specialty stores.
Business type (SIC): Shopping goods stores/ miscellaneous
Financial profile for 2011: Number of employees, 45,300; assets, $1,770,000,000; sales volume, $4,031,000,000
Corporate officers: John B. Menzer, C.E.O.; Charles M. Sonsteby, C.F.O. and C.A.O.; Michael J. Veitenheimer, Sr. V.P., Genl. Counsel, and Secy.; Shawn E. Hearn, Sr. V.P., Human Resources
Giving statement: Giving through the Michaels Stores, Inc. Corporate Giving Program.
Company EIN: 751943604

Michaels Stores, Inc. Corporate Giving Program

8000 Bent Branch Dr.
Irving, TX 75063-6023 (800) 642-4235
URL: http://www.michaels.com/art/online/displayArticle?articleNum=as0167

Purpose and activities: Michaels Stores makes charitable contributions to national organizations.
Fields of interest: General charitable giving.
Type of support: Employee volunteer services; General/operating support.
Geographic limitations: Giving to national organizations.
Support limitations: No support for fraternal or veterans' groups, professional associations, membership groups, or international organizations, or private, corporate, or government foundations. No grants to individuals, or for individual or group participation in events or fundraisers, religious fundraisers, books, research papers, or articles in professional journals.
Application information: Applications not accepted. Contributes only to pre-selected organizations.

2495
Michelin North America, Inc.

1 Parkway S.
P.O. Box 19001
Greenville, SC 29615 (864) 458-5000

Company URL: http://www.michelin-us.com
Establishment information: Established in 1950.
Company type: Subsidiary of a foreign company
Business activities: Manufactures tires, inner tubes, wire, and wheels; publishes tourist maps and guides.
Business type (SIC): Tires and inner tubes; publishing/miscellaneous; steel mill products
Financial profile for 2012: Number of employees, 22,270
Corporate officers: Pete Selleck, Chair. and Pres.; Dick Wilkerson, C.E.O.; Eric Le Corre, C.F.O.; Mark Williams, V.P., Genl. Counsel, and Secy.
Board of director: Pete Selleck, Chair.
Giving statement: Giving through the Michelin North America, Inc. Corporate Giving Program.

Michelin North America, Inc. Corporate Giving Program

c/o Community Rels.
P.O. Box 19001
Greenville, SC 29602-9001

Purpose and activities: Michelin makes charitable contributions to nonprofit organizations involved with STEM (science, technology, engineering, and math) education, the environment, and automotive safety. Support is given on a national basis in areas of company operations in Alabama, Indiana, Kentucky, North Carolina, Oklahoma, and South Carolina, and in Canada.
Fields of interest: Arts; Education; Environment; Health care; Safety, automotive safety; Human services; Science; Mathematics; Engineering/ technology.
International interests: Canada.
Programs:
Community Enhancement: Michelin makes charitable contributions to nonprofit organizations involved with arts and culture, health, and human services.
Education: Michelin supports programs designed to challenge students and teachers to be innovative in the areas of science, math, technology, and engineering.
Environment and Safety: Michelin supports programs designed to encourage awareness for sustaining the environment; and demonstrate the importance of vehicle, tire, and driving safety.
Type of support: Employee volunteer services; In-kind gifts; Program development; Sponsorships.
Geographic limitations: Giving primarily in areas of company operations in AL, IN, KY, NC, OK, SC, and in Canada.
Support limitations: No support for religious organizations not of direct benefit to the entire community, political candidates or lobbying organizations, fraternal, labor, veterans', or similar organizations with a limited constituency, or anti-business organizations. No grants to individuals, or for travel, national conferences, sports events, or other one-time, short-term events, advertising, or team sponsorships or athletic scholarships.
Application information: Applications accepted. Application form required. Applicants should submit the following:
1) copy of IRS Determination Letter
2) contact person
3) detailed description of project and amount of funding requested
4) name, address and phone number of organization
5) population served
Applications should include the organization's Tax ID Number, a description of past support by Michelin with the organization, and any applicable deadlines.
Initial approach: Download application form and upload completed application form to web site
Deadline(s): None

2496
Michigan Automotive Compressor, Inc.

(also known as MACI)
2400 N. Dearing Rd.
Parma, MI 49269-9415 (517) 622-7000

Company URL: http://www.michauto.com
Establishment information: Established in 1989.
Company type: Subsidiary of a private company
Business activities: Manufactures motor vehicle equipment.
Business type (SIC): Motor vehicles and equipment
Corporate officers: Hiroyo Kono, Co-Pres.; Yuji Ishizaki, Co-Pres.; Ladonna Alcenius, C.F.O.
Giving statement: Giving through the Michigan Automotive Compressor, Inc. Corporate Giving Program.

Michigan Automotive Compressor, Inc. Corporate Giving Program

2400 N. Dearing Rd.
Parma, MI 49269-9415
URL: http://www.michauto.com/MACI/community_page.htm

Purpose and activities: Michigan Automotive compressor makes charitable contributions to nonprofit organizations involved with education and the environment. Support is given primarily in Jackson County, Michigan.
Fields of interest: Education; Environmental education; Environment; United Ways and Federated Giving Programs.
Type of support: Employee-related scholarships; General/operating support; In-kind gifts; Scholarship funds.
Geographic limitations: Giving primarily in Jackson County, MI.
Support limitations: No grants to individuals.

2497
Michigan CardioVascular Institute

1015 S. Washington Ave.
Saginaw, MI 48601 (989) 754-3000

Company URL: http://www.mcvi.com/
Establishment information: Established in 1970.
Company type: Private company
Business activities: Cardiovascular service provider.
Business type (SIC): Offices and clinics/doctors'
Corporate officer: Patrick Tagget, C.E.O.
Giving statement: Giving through the Michigan CardioVascular Institute Foundation.

Michigan CardioVascular Institute Foundation

(also known as MCVI Foundation)
1015 S. Washington Ave.
Saginaw, MI 48601-2556 (989) 754-7283
FAX: (989) 754-3365; E-mail: dfong@mcvi.com; URL: http://www.mcvifoundation.org/

Establishment information: Established in MI.
Donor: Michigan Cardiovascular Institute PC.
Financial data (yr. ended 12/31/11): Assets, $669,377 (M); gifts received, $152,834; expenditures, $202,864; qualifying distributions,

$125,755; giving activities include $12,240 for 4 grants (high: $10,000; low: $130).
Purpose and activities: The foundation supports programs designed to empower people of all ages to live and lead healthy lives. Special emphasis is directed toward education, prevention, and treatment of cardiac-related diseases.
Fields of interest: Education; Health care.
Program:
AED Grants: The foundation, in partnership with Jiri Fischer's Healthy Hope Foundation and the Mobile Medical Response provides automated external defibrillators (AED) in area ice arenas, schools, and nonprofit organization with which people gather.
Type of support: Donated products; General/operating support; Scholarship funds.
Application information: Applications not accepted. Unsolicited requests for funds not accepted.
Officers: Peter Fatal, M.D., Pres.; John F. Collins, M.D., V.P.; Clarence M. Rivette, Secy.-Treas.; Diane M. Fong, Exec. Dir.
Directors: Christopher M. Genco, M.D.; Rao Gudipati, M.D.; Sharon Miller; James VanTiflin.
EIN: 383146518

2498
Micro Analog, Inc.

1773 Wright St.
La Verne, CA 91750-5841 (909) 392-8277

Company URL: http://www.micro-analog.com
Establishment information: Established in 1991.
Company type: Private company
Business activities: Manufactures printed circuit board and custom cable assemblies.
Business type (SIC): Electronic components and accessories
Corporate officers: Hung Ta, Pres. and C.E.O.; Khanh V. Nguyen, C.F.O.
Giving statement: Giving through the Hung & Kv Family Foundation, Inc.

The Hung & Kv Family Foundation, Inc.

1773 Wright Ave.
La Verne, CA 91750

Establishment information: Established in 2001 in CA.
Donor: Micro Analog, Inc.
Financial data (yr. ended 12/31/11): Assets, $2,052,813 (M); expenditures, $227,749; qualifying distributions, $222,200; giving activities include $222,200 for grants.
Fields of interest: Education; Youth development; Human services.
International interests: Vietnam.
Geographic limitations: Giving primarily in CA.
Support limitations: No grants to individuals.
Application information: Applications not accepted. Unsolicited requests for funds not accepted.
Officers: Hung Ta Nguyen, Pres.; Anne Kim Nguyen, Secy.; Khanh-Van T. Nguyen, Treas.
EIN: 680484099

2499
Microchip Technology Incorporated

2355 W. Chandler Blvd.
Chandler, AZ 85224-6199 (480) 792-7200
FAX: (480) 899-9210

Company URL: http://www.microchip.com
Establishment information: Established in 1989.
Company type: Public company
Company ticker symbol and exchange: MCHP/NASDAQ
International Securities Identification Number: US5950171042
Business activities: Develops and manufactures specialized semiconductor products.
Business type (SIC): Electronic components and accessories
Financial profile for 2013: Number of employees, 8,003; assets, $3,925,240,000; sales volume, $1,581,620,000; pre-tax net income, $152,180,000; expenses, $1,403,070,000; liabilities, $1,991,770,000
Corporate officers: Steve Sanghi, Chair., Pres., and C.E.O.; Ganesh Moorthy, Exec. V.P. and C.O.O.; J. Eric Bjornholt, V.P. and C.F.O.; Mitchell R. Little, V.P., Sales; Lauren A. Carr, V.P., Human Resources; Kimberly van Herk, Corp. Secy.
Board of directors: Steve Sanghi, Chair.; Matthew W. Chapman; L.B. Day; Albert J. Hugo-Martinez; Wade F. Meyercord
International operations: Australia; Austria; Canada; Cayman Islands; China; Denmark; England; France; Germany; Hong Kong; Hungary; India; Ireland; Italy; Japan; Malaysia; Mexico; Philippines; Romania; Singapore; Spain; Sweden; Switzerland; Taiwan; Thailand
Giving statement: Giving through the Microchip Technology Incorporated Corporate Giving Program.
Company EIN: 860629024

Microchip Technology Incorporated Corporate Giving Program

2355 W. Chandler Blvd.
Chandler, AZ 85224-6199 (480) 792-7200
FAX: (480) 899-9210; URL: http://www.microchip.com/

Purpose and activities: Microchip Technology makes charitable contributions to nonprofit organizations involved with science, technology, engineering, and mathematics (STEM) education, and on a case by case basis. Support is given primarily in Arizona.
Fields of interest: United Ways and Federated Giving Programs; Science; Mathematics; Engineering/technology; General charitable giving.
Type of support: Employee matching gifts; General/operating support; Sponsorships.
Geographic limitations: Giving primarily in AZ.

2500
Micron Technology, Inc.

8000 S. Federal Way
P.O. Box 6
Boise, ID 83707-0006 (208) 368-4000
FAX: (208) 368-4435

Company URL: http://www.micron.com
Establishment information: Established in 1978.
Company type: Public company
Company ticker symbol and exchange: MU/NASDAQ
International Securities Identification Number: US5951121038
Business activities: Designs, develops, manufactures, and markets semiconductor memory products.
Business type (SIC): Lighting and wiring equipment/electric; electronic components and accessories
Financial profile for 2012: Number of employees, 27,400; assets, $14,328,000,000; sales volume, $8,234,000,000; pre-tax net income, -$754,000,000; expenses, $8,852,000,000; liabilities, $6,628,000,000
Fortune 1000 ranking: 2012—318th in revenues, 982nd in profits, and 305th in assets
Forbes 2000 ranking: 2012—1095th in sales, 1933rd in profits, and 1234th in assets
Corporate officers: Robert E. Switz, Chair.; Mark D. Duncan, C.E.O.; Mark W. Adams, Pres.; Ronald C. Foster, V.P., Finance and C.F.O.; Roderick W. Lewis, V.P., Genl. Counsel, and Corp. Secy.; Steven L. Thorsen, Jr., V.P., Sales and Mktg.; Patrick T. Otte, V.P., Human Resources; Brian J. Shields, V.P., Opers.
Board of directors: Robert E. Switz, Chair.; Robert L. Bailey; Richard M. Beyer; Patrick J. Byrne; D. Mark Durcan; Mercedes Johnson; Lawrence N. Mondry
International operations: China; Germany; Italy; Japan; Singapore; United Kingdom
Giving statement: Giving through the Micron Technology, Inc. Corporate Giving Program and the Micron Technology Foundation, Inc.
Company EIN: 751618004

Micron Technology, Inc. Corporate Giving Program

8000 S. Federal Way
P.O. Box 6
Boise, ID 83716-9632
URL: http://www.micron.com/about/communities/

Purpose and activities: As a complement to its foundation, Micron Technology also makes charitable contributions to nonprofit organizations directly. Support is given primarily in areas of company operations in California, Colorado, Idaho, Minnesota, Texas, Utah, and Virginia, and in China, India, Israel, Italy, Japan, Malaysia, the Philippines, Puerto Rico, Singapore, South Korea, Switzerland, Taiwan, and the United Kingdom.
Fields of interest: Education; Disasters, preparedness/services; Science; Engineering/technology.
International interests: China; India; Israel; Italy; Japan; Malaysia; Philippines; Singapore; South Korea; Switzerland; Taiwan; United Kingdom.
Type of support: Employee volunteer services; General/operating support.
Geographic limitations: Giving primarily in areas of company operations in CA, CO, ID, MN, TX, UT, and VA, and in China, India, Israel, Italy, Japan, Malaysia, the Philippines, Puerto Rico, Singapore, South Korea, Switzerland, Taiwan, and the United Kingdom.
Application information:
Number of staff: 3 full-time professional; 1 full-time support.

Micron Technology Foundation, Inc.

8000 S. Federal Way, MS 1-407
P.O. Box 6
Boise, ID 83707-0006
E-mail: mtf@micron.com; Contact for applications: Kami Faylor, Community Rels. Mgr.; URL: http://www.micron.com/foundation

Establishment information: Established in 1999 in ID.
Donors: Micron Technology, Inc.; Micron Semiconductor Products, Inc.; Blue Cross of Idaho Health Service, Inc.
Contact: Dee K. Mooney, Exec. Dir.
Financial data (yr. ended 12/31/11): Assets, $79,860,532 (M); gifts received, $150; expenditures, $5,556,782; qualifying distributions, $4,937,330; giving activities include $4,157,141 for grants.
Purpose and activities: The foundation supports organizations involved with K-12 and higher education. Special emphasis is directed toward programs designed to promote education in the areas of engineering, science, chemistry, mathematics, and computer science.
Fields of interest: Education, research; Elementary/secondary education; Secondary school/education; Higher education; Teacher school/education; Engineering school/education; Science, formal/general education; Chemistry; Mathematics; Engineering/technology; Computer science.
International interests: Italy; Singapore.
Programs:
Chip Camp: The foundation annually hosts Chip Camp, a free day of activities for students completing 7th or 8th grade in Boise, Idaho. The camp is lead by Micron engineers and professionals and includes competitive challenges; problem solving; engineering simulations; electronics; chemistry; robotics; and emerging technologies. The program is designed to teach students what engineers and scientists do every day.
Community and K-12 Grants: The foundation supports programs designed to drive advancements in education, with emphasis on science, math, and engineering. Special emphasis is directed toward programs designed to provide opportunities for hands-on experiences; improve teaching content and teacher knowledge; support extracurricular science and math opportunities; provide advanced learning opportunities; and address the priorities and concerns of Micron site communities.
University Partnerships: The foundation supports research opportunities at select universities; improves engineering education through hands-on opportunities and state-of-the-art equipment; funds laboratories; and furthers the advancement of semiconductor materials, devices, and processes.
Type of support: Continuing support; Curriculum development; Employee matching gifts; Employee volunteer services; Fellowships; Professorships; Program development; Research; Scholarship funds; Scholarships—to individuals; Sponsorships.
Geographic limitations: Giving limited to areas of company operations in Boise, ID, Manassas, VA, Avezzano, Italy, and Singapore.
Support limitations: No support for religious, fraternal, veterans', or political organizations, discriminatory organizations, pass-through organizations, or private foundations. No grants to individuals (except for scholarships), or for general operating support, luncheons, dinners, auctions, or events, travel or related expenses, courtesy advertisements, endowments, annual campaigns, or lobbying activities.
Publications: Application guidelines.
Application information: Applications accepted. University participation in the University Partnerships program is by invitation only. Applications for Chip Camp require a teacher recommendation. Application form required.
Applicants should submit the following:
1) timetable for implementation and evaluation of project
2) statement of problem project will address
3) principal source of support for project in the past
4) copy of IRS Determination Letter
5) copy of most recent annual report/audited financial statement/990
6) how project's results will be evaluated or measured
7) listing of board of directors, trustees, officers and other key people and their affiliations
8) copy of current year's organizational budget and/or project budget
9) listing of additional sources and amount of support

Initial approach: Download application form and mail proposal and application form to foundation for Community and K-12 Grants; visit website for Chip Camp
Deadline(s): None; Apr. 15 for Chip Camp
Final notification: Monthly

Officers and Directors:* Mark D. Duncan*, Chair.; Kipp A. Bedard*, Pres.; Roderick W. Lewis*, Secy.; Tom L. Laws, Treas.; Dee K. Mooney, Exec. Dir.; Jay L. Hawkins.
Number of staff: 8 full-time professional; 2 part-time professional.
EIN: 820516178
Selected grants: The following grants are a representative sample of this grantmaker's funding activity:
$10,811,345 to Boise State University, Boise, ID, 2010.
$1,276,644 to University of Utah, Salt Lake City, UT, 2011.
$256,600 to Utah State University, Logan, UT, 2011.
$203,450 to Utah State University, Logan, UT, 2010.
$158,880 to Boise State University, Boise, ID, 2011.
$151,456 to National University of Singapore, Singapore, Singapore, 2011.
$142,452 to National University of Singapore, Singapore, Singapore, 2010.
$126,050 to University of Idaho Foundation, Moscow, ID, 2010.
$122,500 to George Mason University, Fairfax, VA, 2011.
$100,000 to Library Square Foundation for Arts, Culture, and Science, Salt Lake City, UT, 2011.
$83,400 to Brigham Young University, Provo, UT, 2010.
$75,000 to Iowa State University, Ames, IA, 2010.
$75,000 to University of Illinois at Urbana-Champaign, Urbana, IL, 2010.
$63,816 to Universita degli Studi dell'Aquila, Coppito, Italy, 2010.
$50,000 to University of Bristol, Bristol, England, 2010.
$26,200 to Idaho Shakespeare Festival, Boise, ID, 2011.
$25,000 to Idaho Governors Challenge Cup for Education, Boise, ID, 2011.
$16,700 to Discovery Center of Idaho, Boise, ID, 2011.
$15,445 to Associazione Culturale Harmonia Novissima, Avezzano, Italy, 2011.
$10,000 to Concordia University School of Law, Boise, ID, 2010.

2501
Microsoft Corporation

1 Microsoft Way
Redmond, WA 98052-6399 (425) 882-8080

Company URL: http://www.microsoft.com
Establishment information: Established in 1975.
Company type: Public company
Company ticker symbol and exchange: MSFT/NASDAQ
International Securities Identification Number: US5949181045
Business activities: Develops, manufactures, licenses, and supports computer software products; provides consulting services; develops and sells video game consoles, games, and peripherals; provides Internet information services.
Business type (SIC): Electrical goods—wholesale; computer services; management and public relations services
Financial profile for 2012: Number of employees, 94,000; assets, $121,271,000,000; sales volume, $73,723,000,000; pre-tax net income, $22,267,000,000; expenses, $51,662,000,000; liabilities, $54,908,000,000
Fortune 1000 ranking: 2012—35th in revenues, 8th in profits, and 54th in assets
Forbes 2000 ranking: 2012—105th in sales, 18th in profits, and 202nd in assets
Corporate officers: William H. Gates III, Chair.; Steven A. Ballmer, C.E.O.; B. Kevin Turner, C.O.O.; Amy Hood, C.F.O.; Bradford L. Smith, Exec. V.P. and Genl. Counsel
Board of directors: William H. Gates III, Chair.; Steve Ballmer; Dina Dublon; Maria M. Klawe; Stephen J. Luczo; David F. Marquardt; Charles H. Noski; Helmut Panke; John W. Thompson
International operations: Ireland; Singapore
Giving statement: Giving through the Microsoft Corporation Contributions Program, the Internet Safety Foundation, and the Microsoft Charitable Trust.
Company EIN: 911144442

Microsoft Corporation Contributions Program

c/o Community Affairs
1 Microsoft Way
Redmond, WA 98052-8300
E-mail: cause@microsoft.com; URL: http://www.microsoft.com/about/corporatecitizenship/en-us/default.aspx

Financial data (yr. ended 12/31/11): Total giving, $949,000,000, including $105,000,000 for grants, $19,395,791 for employee matching gifts and $824,604,209 for in-kind gifts.
Purpose and activities: As a complement to its foundation, Microsoft also makes charitable contributions to nonprofit organizations directly. Support is given on a national and international basis in areas of company operations, with emphasis on the Puget Sound, Washington, area.
Fields of interest: Arts; Elementary/secondary education; Employment; Human services; Mathematics; Engineering/technology; Science; Public affairs Economically disadvantaged.
Programs:
Employee Matching Gifts: Microsoft matches contributions made by its employees to nonprofit organizations on a one-for-one basis up to $12,000 per employee, per year.
Employee Volunteer Program: Microsoft donates $17 per hour to eligible nonprofit organizations with which employees volunteer.
Microsoft Unlimited Potential Program: Through the Microsoft Unlimited Potential Program, Microsoft supports workforce development and IT skills training programs in underserved communities. Microsoft provides cash grants, software, and specialized curriculum to nonprofit community technology centers (CTCs) around the world.

Type of support: Donated products; Employee matching gifts; Employee volunteer services; General/operating support.
Geographic limitations: Giving on a national and international basis in areas of company operations, with emphasis on the Puget Sound, WA, area.
Support limitations: No support for political, religious, or fraternal organizations, or hospitals or medical clinics (except those designated as Community Health Center Programs by the U.S. Department of Health). No grants to individuals, or for sports groups, teams, or events, conferences or symposia, or endowments.
Application information: Applications accepted. Unsolicited applications for grants are rarely supported. Applications for Puget Sound grants are currently not accepted.
Initial approach: E-mail local Community Affairs Manager for monetary contributions; visit TechSoup website for Microsoft software donations
Administrators: Bruce M. Brooks, Dir., Community Affairs; Rodney Hines, Prog. Mgr.; Cathy MacCaul, Prog. Mgr.; Jane Meseck, Prog. Mgr.; Sarah Meyer, Sr. Prog. Mgr.; Heidi Salstrom, Prog. Mgr.; Linda Testa, Prog. Mgr.

Internet Safety Foundation
1201 3rd Ave., Ste. 4800
Seattle, WA 98101-3266

Establishment information: Established in 2005 in WA.
Donor: Microsoft Corp.
Financial data (yr. ended 12/31/11): Assets, $119,221 (M); expenditures, $8,424; qualifying distributions, $0.
Purpose and activities: Giving primarily for the safety of children on the internet.
Support limitations: No grants to individuals.
Application information: Applications not accepted. Contributes only to pre-selected organizations.
Officers and Directors:* Lorri Anne Dunsmore*, Pres. and Treas.; Elizabeth L. McDougall*, V.P. and Secy.
EIN: 202889376

Microsoft Charitable Trust
c/o Wells Fargo Bank, N.A.
101N Independence Mall E. Macy 1372-062
Philadelphia, PA 19106-2112

Establishment information: Established in 1994 in WA.
Donors: Microsoft Corp.; US Agency for International Development.
Financial data (yr. ended 06/30/12): Assets, $2,609,609 (M); gifts received, $60,230; expenditures, $160,884; qualifying distributions, $134,087; giving activities include $125,000 for 2 grants (high: $100,000; low: $25,000).
Purpose and activities: The foundation supports organizations involved with arts and culture.
Fields of interest: Performing arts centers; Arts.
Type of support: General/operating support.
Geographic limitations: Giving limited to Bellevue and Seattle, WA.
Support limitations: No grants to individuals.
Application information: Applications not accepted. Unsolicited requests for funds not accepted.
Trustee: Wells Fargo Bank, N.A.
EIN: 916374992
Selected grants: The following grants are a representative sample of this grantmaker's funding activity:
$250,000 to United Way of King County, Seattle, WA, 2010.

2504
MidAmerican Energy Company
666 Grand Ave.
P.O. Box 657
Des Moines, IA 50303-0657

Company URL: http://www.midamericanenergy.com
Establishment information: Established in 1995 from the merger of Iowa-Illinois Gas and Electric Co. with Midwest Resources Inc.
Company type: Subsidiary of a public company
Ultimate parent company: Berkshire Hathaway Inc.
Business activities: Generates, transmits, and distributes electricity.
Business type (SIC): Electric services
Financial profile for 2005: Number of employees, 3,704; assets, $5,864,137,000; sales volume, $3,160,337,000
Corporate officers: Gregory E. Abel, Chair., Pres., and C.E.O.; Patrick J. Goodman, Exec. V.P. and C.F.O.; Douglas L. Anderson, Exec. V.P., Genl. Counsel, and Corp. Secy.; Maureen E. Sammon, Sr. V.P. and C.A.O.; Brian K. Hankel, V.P. and Treas.; Thomas B. Specketer, V.P. and Cont.
Board of director: Gregory E. Abel, Chair.
Giving statement: Giving through the MidAmerican Energy Company Contributions Program and the MidAmerican Energy Foundation.

MidAmerican Energy Company Contributions Program
(formerly Midwest Resources Inc. Corporate Giving Program)
666 Grand Ave., Ste. 500
Des Moines, IA 50309-2511
URL: http://www.midamericanenergy.com/careers6.aspx

Purpose and activities: MidAmerican makes charitable contributions to nonprofit organizations involved with the environment, education, disaster relief, and on a case by case basis. Support is given primarily in areas of company operations in Iowa, Illinois, Nebraska, and South Dakota.
Fields of interest: Education; Environment; Disasters, preparedness/services; General charitable giving.
Type of support: Employee volunteer services; General/operating support.
Geographic limitations: Giving primarily in areas of company operations in IA, IL, NE, and SD.
Application information: Applications not accepted.

MidAmerican Energy Foundation
(formerly Midwest Foundation)
P.O. Box 657, DMR8
Des Moines, IA 50306-0657
E-mail: kmkunert@midamerican.com

Establishment information: Established as a company-sponsored foundation in 1990 in IA; status changed to public charity; status changed to company-sponsored foundation in 2004.
Donors: Midamerican Energy Holdings Co.; MHC Investment Co.
Financial data (yr. ended 12/31/11): Assets, $12,934,741 (M); expenditures, $461,730; qualifying distributions, $455,030; giving activities include $454,868 for 450 grants (high: $100,000; low: $25).
Purpose and activities: The foundation supports fairs and civic centers and organizations involved with arts and culture, higher education, cancer, baseball, and human services.
Fields of interest: Museums (children's); Performing arts; Performing arts, ballet; Arts; Higher education; Cancer; Recreation, fairs/festivals; Athletics/sports, baseball; Boy scouts; Children, services; Women, centers/services; Homeless, human services; Human services; Community development, civic centers; United Ways and Federated Giving Programs.
Type of support: Annual campaigns; Building/renovation; Capital campaigns; Employee matching gifts; Scholarship funds; Sponsorships.
Geographic limitations: Giving primarily in IA.
Application information: Applications accepted. Additional information may be requested at a later date. Application form required. Applicants should submit the following:
1) brief history of organization and description of its mission
2) detailed description of project and amount of funding requested
Initial approach: Letter
Copies of proposal: 1
Board meeting date(s): Quarterly
Deadline(s): None
Officers and Directors:* Gregory E. Abel*, Pres.; Sara Schillinger, V.P. and Secy.; Calvin D. Haack, Treas.; David L. Sokol.
EIN: 421338550
Selected grants: The following grants are a representative sample of this grantmaker's funding activity:
$10,000 to Civic Center of Greater Des Moines, Des Moines, IA, 2009.
$3,000 to Cystic Fibrosis Foundation, Bethesda, MD, 2009.

2502
Mid-Atlantic Packaging, Inc.
P.O. Box 445
436 Stump Rd.
Montgomeryville, PA 18936-0445
(215) 362-5100

Company URL: http://www.mid-atlanticpkg.com
Establishment information: Established in 1961.
Company type: Private company
Business activities: Provides customized corrugated packaging.
Business type (SIC): Paperboard containers
Corporate officers: Allen Kanter, Chair. and C.E.O.; Andrew Pierson, Pres.; John Burke, C.F.O.
Board of director: Allen Kanter, Chair.
Giving statement: Giving through the Kanter Foundation.

The Kanter Foundation
436 Stump Rd.
Montgomeryville, PA 18936-0445

Establishment information: Established in 1999 in PA.
Donors: Mid-Atlantic Packaging, Inc.; Allen L. Kanter.
Financial data (yr. ended 12/31/11): Assets, $129,126 (M); gifts received, $100,000; expenditures, $40,000; qualifying distributions, $40,000; giving activities include $40,000 for 2 grants (high: $20,000; low: $20,000).
Fields of interest: Health care.
Support limitations: No grants to individuals.
Application information: Applications not accepted. Unsolicited requests for funds not accepted.
Officers: Allen L. Kanter, Pres. and Treas.; Michael P. Haney, Secy.
Director: William Levy.
EIN: 232972888

2505
Midcontinent Media, Inc.

3600 Minnesota Dr., Ste. 700
Minneapolis, MN 55435-7918
(952) 844-2600
FAX: (952) 844-2660

Company URL: http://www.mmi.net
Establishment information: Established in 1933.
Company type: Private company
Business activities: Provides cable television services; provides telephone communications services; provides paging services; broadcasts radio; provides advertising services; develops computer software.
Business type (SIC): Cable and other pay television services; telephone communications; radio and television broadcasting; advertising; computer services
Corporate officers: N. Larry Bentson, Chair.; Joseph H. Floyd, Vice-Chair.; Patrick McAdaragh, Pres. and C.E.O.; Dick Busch, C.O.O.; Steven E. Grosser, C.F.O.; Debbie Stang, V.P. Human Resources
Board of directors: N. Larry Bentson, Chair.; Joseph H. Floyd, Vice-Chair.
Giving statement: Giving through the Midcontinent Media Foundation.

Midcontinent Media Foundation

(formerly Midcontinent Foundation)
3600 Minnesota Dr., Ste. 700
Minneapolis, MN 55435-7979
URL: http://www.midcocomm.com/aboutmidcontinent/midcontinentmediafoundation

Establishment information: Established in 1987.
Donors: Midcontinent Media, Inc.; Midcontinent Communications.
Contact: Steven E. Grosser, Exec. Dir.
Financial data (yr. ended 12/31/11): Assets, $64,337 (M); gifts received, $179,996; expenditures, $161,509; qualifying distributions, $161,509; giving activities include $156,549 for 153 grants (high: $5,000; low: $25).
Purpose and activities: The foundation supports zoos and organizations involved with arts and culture, education, health, diabetes, crime and violence prevention, housing development, recreation, human services, and community economic development.
Fields of interest: Arts; Elementary school/education; Higher education; Education; Zoos/zoological societies; Nursing home/convalescent facility; Health care; Diabetes; Crime/violence prevention; Crime/violence prevention, domestic violence; Housing/shelter, development; Disasters, fire prevention/control; Recreation, centers; Recreation; Youth development, business; American Red Cross; YM/YWCAs & YM/YWHAs; Children, services; Human services; Community/economic development; United Ways and Federated Giving Programs.
Type of support: Building/renovation; Emergency funds; Employee matching gifts; Equipment; Program development; Seed money.
Geographic limitations: Giving primarily in areas of company operations in MN, ND, and SD.
Support limitations: No support for organizations not endorsed by a Midcontinent Media employee.
Publications: Application guidelines.
Application information: Applications accepted. The foundation gives priority to organizations endorsed by a Midcontinent Communications employee. Application form required. Applicants should submit the following:
1) population served
2) name, address and phone number of organization
3) copy of IRS Determination Letter
4) detailed description of project and amount of funding requested
5) contact person

Initial approach: Letter
Copies of proposal: 1
Board meeting date(s): Mar. and Sept.
Deadline(s): None

Officers: Judy Johnson, Secy.; Tom Simmons, Exec. Dir.
Directors: Steve Mattern; Pat McAdaragh; Brad Schoenfelder; Debbie Stang.
EIN: 363556764

2506
Middlesex Savings Bank

6 Main St.
Natick, MA 01760-4535 (508) 653-0300

Company URL: http://www.middlesexbank.com/default.asp
Establishment information: Established in 1835.
Company type: Private company
Business activities: Operates savings bank.
Business type (SIC): Savings institutions
Financial profile for 2011: Assets, $4,011,257,000; liabilities, $3,577,419,000
Corporate officers: John R. Heerwagen, Chair., Pres., and C.E.O.; Brian D. Lanigan, Exec. V.P. and C.O.O.; Paul M. Totino, Exec. V.P. and Co.-C.F.O.; Brian D. Stewart, Exec. V.P. and Co.-C.F.O.; Carole H. Bernstein, Sr. V.P. and Cont.
Board of directors: John R. Heerwagen, Chair.; Peter M. Burke; Robert E. Carr; Arthur J. Chaves; Robert G. Ciccarelli; Betty C. Courtemanche; Joan M. Craig; Arthur B. Fair III; George F. Fiske, Jr.; Carolyn Hatch Flood; Paul J. Gerry, Jr.; Anisia R. Gifford-Lundberg; Janice P. Guy; Donald A. Hoyt; William W. Jackson; A. James Lavoie; Jean H. Lynch; Richard J. Massarelli; Joann C. McKenna; Richard J. Napoli; Raymond L. Page; Richard M. Presti; Lauren Stiller Rikleen; Carl W. Schnapp; William G. Wilkinson
Giving statement: Giving through the Middlesex Savings Charitable Foundation, Inc.

Middlesex Savings Charitable Foundation, Inc.

P.O. Box 358
6 Main St.
Natick, MA 01760-4506 (508) 315-5360
E-mail: dneshe@middlesexbank.com; Additional tel.: (508) 315-5361; URL: http://www.middlesexbank.com/community/charitablefoundation/
Application address: Michael Kuza, 36 Summer Street, SS2-1, Natick, MA 07160, tel.: (508) 315-5361, e-mail: mkuza@middlesexbank.com

Establishment information: Established in 2000 in MA.
Donor: Middlesex Savings Bank.
Contact: Dana M. Neshe, Pres.
Financial data (yr. ended 12/31/11): Assets, $6,640,871 (M); gifts received, $1,000,000; expenditures, $366,894; qualifying distributions, $320,750; giving activities include $320,750 for grants.
Purpose and activities: The foundation supports organizations involved with arts and culture, health and wellness, employment training, youth development, human services, and economically disadvantaged people. Special emphasis is directed toward programs designed to promote education; capacity building; and community development.
Fields of interest: Arts; Vocational education; Adult/continuing education; Education, ESL programs; Education; Employment, training; Youth development; Human services, financial counseling; Human services; Community/economic development Economically disadvantaged.
Programs:

A. James Lavoie Essay Contest Scholarship: The foundation awards a $5,000 scholarship to a graduating senior from one of 24 area public or vocational schools with plans to attend a four-year college program. Applicants must submit a 2-3 page essay describing a developed skill through hard work and perseverance and plans to use that skill to improve the community. Essay topics may change yearly. Applicants must also present evidence of good academic standing, exhibit active involvement in the community, and demonstrate financial need.

Capacity Building Program: The foundation awards grants of up to $15,000 to initiatives designed to strengthen and increase the impact of nonprofits by improving their organizational capacity. Desired outcomes includes improved governance and leadership; improved staff skills; improved management systems and practices; completed strategic plans; improved, expanded, or additional services; and expanded strategic assets, including financial and human resources.

Community Development Program: The foundation awards grants of up to $15,000 to programs designed to improve the lives of low-and moderate-income families and individuals.

Educational Opportunities Program: The foundation awards grants of up to $15,000 to programs designed to provide educational opportunities for youth and adults. Special emphasis is directed toward job training and job readiness; adult education; ESL programs; credit education and home buying seminars; and youth enrichment programs.

Type of support: Equipment; General/operating support; Income development; Management development/capacity building; Program development; Scholarships—to individuals; Technical assistance.
Geographic limitations: Giving primarily in areas of company operations in Acton, Ashland, Ayer, Bedford, Bellingham, Berlin, Bolton, Boxborough, Carlisle, Chelmsford, Concord, Dover, Dunstable, Framingham, Franklin, Groton, Harvard, Holliston, Hopedale, Hopkinton, Hudson, Lexington, Lincoln, Littleton, Marlborough, Maynard, Medfield, Medway, Milford, Millis, Natick, Needham, Newton, Norfolk, Northborough, Pepperell, Sherborn, Shirley, Southborough, Stow, Sudbury, Townsend, Tyngsborough, Upton, Walpole, Waltham, Wayland, Wellesley, Westborough, Westford, and Weston, MA.
Support limitations: No support for religious, political, or discriminatory organizations. No grants for sponsorships, trips, or conferences; no in-kind donations.
Publications: Application guidelines; Grants list; Program policy statement.
Application information: Applications accepted. Due to current economic challenges in the community, the foundation will give preference to grant submissions from organizations providing basic human services like food and shelter. Support is limited to 1 contribution per organization during any given year. Application form required. Applicants should submit the following:
1) timetable for implementation and evaluation of project
2) statement of problem project will address
3) population served
4) copy of IRS Determination Letter

5) brief history of organization and description of its mission
6) geographic area to be served
7) copy of most recent annual report/audited financial statement/990
8) how project's results will be evaluated or measured
9) listing of board of directors, trustees, officers and other key people and their affiliations
10) detailed description of project and amount of funding requested
11) copy of current year's organizational budget and/or project budget

Scholarship applications should include official transcripts, FAFSA's assessments, a personal statement, and a 2 to 3 page essay.

Initial approach: Complete online application; download application form and mail to application address for A. James Lovie Essay Contest Scholarship
Copies of proposal: 1
Board meeting date(s): Semi-annually
Deadline(s): Postmarked by Mar. 1 and Aug. 1; Mar. for A. James Lavoie Essay Contest Scholarship
Final notification: 1 to 2 months; May for A. James Lavoie Essay Contest Scholarship

Officers: Dana M. Neshe, Pres.; John R. Heerwagen, V.P.; Paul M. Totino, Clerk and Treas.
Directors: George F. Fiske, Jr.; Carrie Hatch Flood; Rudman J. Ham; Brian D. Lanigan; Raymond Page; Arnold I. Zaltas.
Number of staff: 1 full-time support.
EIN: 043521246
Selected grants: The following grants are a representative sample of this grantmaker's funding activity:
$36,000 to Greater Worcester Community Foundation, Worcester, MA, 2010.
$5,000 to Framingham State University Foundation, Framingham, MA, 2010.
$5,000 to Programs for People, Framingham, MA, 2010.
$1,000 to Natick Service Council, Natick, MA, 2010.

2507
Midmark Corporation

60 Vista Dr.
P.O. Box 286
Versailles, OH 45380-0286 (937) 526-3662
FAX: (937) 526-5542

Company URL: http://www.midmark.com
Establishment information: Established in 1915.
Company type: Private company
Business activities: Manufactures medical goods and metal castings.
Business type (SIC): Medical instruments and supplies; fixtures/office and store; machinery/industrial and commercial
Financial profile for 2010: Number of employees, 1,400
Corporate officers: Anne Eiting-Klamar, M.D., Pres. and C.E.O.; R. Gregoire Blackmore, C.O.O.; Robert Morris, C.F.O.; Sharyl S. Gardner, C.A.O. and Secy.; Joe Rothstein, V.P., Mktg. and Sales
Giving statement: Giving through the Midmark Foundation.

Midmark Foundation

P.O. Box 286
Versailles, OH 45380-0286 (937) 526-3662

Establishment information: Established in 1969 in OH.
Donor: Midmark Corp.
Financial data (yr. ended 12/31/11): Assets, $955,148 (M); gifts received, $50,000; expenditures, $43,046; qualifying distributions, $22,417; giving activities include $22,417 for grants.
Purpose and activities: The foundation supports organizations involved with arts and culture, education, employment, and human services.
Fields of interest: Historic preservation/historical societies; Arts; Higher education; Libraries (public); Education; Employment, training; Employment; Athletics/sports, Special Olympics; Boy scouts; YM/YWCAs & YM/YWHAs; Human services.
Program:
Employee-Related Scholarships: The foundation awards college scholarships to children of full-time employees of Midmark.
Type of support: Employee-related scholarships; General/operating support; Program development; Scholarship funds; Sponsorships.
Geographic limitations: Giving primarily in OH.
Officers: Mitchell Eiting, Pres.; James E. Eiting, V.P.; Polly Grow, Secy.-Treas.
EIN: 237068805

2503
Mid-States Aluminum, Corp.

132 Trowbridge Dr.
P.O. Box 1107
Fond du Lac, WI 54936-1107
(920) 922-7207

Company URL: http://www.midstal.com/company.html
Establishment information: Established in 1964.
Company type: Private company
Business activities: Manufactures aluminum extrusions.
Business type (SIC): Metal rolling and drawing/nonferrous
Corporate officers: Joseph P. Colwin, Chair.; Stephen M. Peterson, Pres. and C.E.O.; Robert Sippel, C.F.O.
Board of director: Joseph P. Colwin, Chair.
Giving statement: Giving through the Mid-States Aluminum Foundation, Inc.

Mid-States Aluminum Foundation, Inc.

132 Trowbridge Dr.
Fond du Lac, WI 54937-9177

Establishment information: Established in 2001 in WI.
Donor: Mid-States Aluminum, Inc.
Financial data (yr. ended 12/31/11): Assets, $398,544 (M); gifts received, $361,238; expenditures, $341,912; qualifying distributions, $336,015; giving activities include $336,015 for grants.
Purpose and activities: The foundation supports public libraries and organizations involved with arts and culture, K-12 education, human services, and Christianity.
Fields of interest: Arts; Elementary/secondary education; Libraries (public); Human services; Christian agencies & churches.
Type of support: Building/renovation; General/operating support.
Geographic limitations: Giving primarily in Fond du Lac, WI.
Application information: Applications not accepted. Unsolicited requests for funds not accepted.
Directors: Dawn Colwin; Betty Koenigs.
EIN: 392014920
Selected grants: The following grants are a representative sample of this grantmaker's funding activity:
$4,165 to American Cancer Society, De Pere, WI, 2010.
$2,000 to United Way, Fond du Lac Area, Fond du Lac, WI, 2010. For general expenses.
$1,250 to American Red Cross, Fond du Lac, WI, 2010.

2508
Midwestone Bank

(formerly Iowa State Bank & Trust Company)
102 S. Clinton St., Ste. 100
Iowa City, IA 52240-4024 (319) 356-5800

Company URL: http://midwestone.com/index2.php
Establishment information: Established in 1934.
Company type: Subsidiary of a public company
Business activities: Operates commercial bank.
Business type (SIC): Banks/commercial
Corporate officers: Charles N. Funk, C.E.O.; Susan R. Evans, C.O.O.; Gary J. Ortale, Exec. V.P. and C.F.O.
Offices: Coralville, North Liberty, IA
Giving statement: Giving through the Midwestone Bank Foundation.

Midwestone Bank Foundation

(formerly Iowa State Bank & Trust Company Foundation)
c/o Nick Pfeiffer
P.O. Box 1700
Iowa City, IA 52244-1700

Establishment information: Established in 2001 in IA.
Donors: Iowa State Bank & Trust Co.; Midwestone Bank.
Financial data (yr. ended 12/31/11): Assets, $1,242,574 (M); gifts received, $75,000; expenditures, $70,002; qualifying distributions, $68,083; giving activities include $68,083 for grants.
Purpose and activities: The foundation supports libraries and community foundations and organizations involved with higher education, cancer, and human services.
Fields of interest: Higher education; Libraries (public); Cancer; Family services, domestic violence; Developmentally disabled, centers & services; Foundations (community).
Type of support: Building/renovation; General/operating support; Program development.
Geographic limitations: Giving primarily in Iowa City, IA.
Support limitations: No grants to individuals.
Application information: Applications not accepted. Unsolicited requests for funds not accepted.
Officers: W. Richard Summerwill, Pres.; Suzanne Summerwill, Secy.; Nicholas D. Pfeiffer, Treas.
Directors: Charles N. Funk; Charles S. Howard; John P. Pothoven.
EIN: 753023674

2509
Mike's Train House, Inc.
(also known as MTH Electric Trains)
7020 Columbia Gateway Dr.
Columbia, MD 21046-1532 (410) 381-2580

Company URL: http://www.mthtrains.com
Establishment information: Established in 1980.
Company type: Private company
Business activities: Manufactures model trains.
Business type (SIC): Games, toys, and sporting and athletic goods
Corporate officer: Mike Wolf, Pres.
Giving statement: Giving through the MTH Electric Trains Foundation, Inc.

MTH Electric Trains Foundation, Inc.
7020 Columbia Gateway Dr.
Columbia, MD 21046-2119

Establishment information: Established in 1998 in MD.
Donors: Michael P. Wolf; Mike's Train House, Inc.
Financial data (yr. ended 12/31/11): Assets, $202,436 (M); gifts received, $1,000; expenditures, $8,895; qualifying distributions, $7,945; giving activities include $7,945 for grants.
Purpose and activities: The foundation supports Young Life of Howard County in Columbia, Maryland.
Fields of interest: Youth development; Religion.
Type of support: General/operating support.
Geographic limitations: Giving primarily in Columbia, MD.
Support limitations: No grants to individuals.
Application information: Applications not accepted. Unsolicited requests for funds not accepted.
Officers and Directors:* Michael P. Wolf*, Pres.; Rasamee Wolf*, V.P.
EIN: 522127275

2510
Mikimoto (America) & Company, Ltd.
680 5th Ave., 4th Fl.
New York, NY 10019 (212) 457-4500

Company URL: http://www.mikimotoamerica.com
Establishment information: Established in 1899.
Company type: Subsidiary of a foreign company
Business activities: Designs and sells pearl jewelry.
Business type (SIC): Jewelry/precious metal
Corporate officers: Mitsuhiro Mitsui, C.E.O.; Kikuichiro Ishii, Pres.; Meyer Hoffman, C.O.O.
Giving statement: Giving through the Mikimoto (America) & Co., Ltd. Corporate Giving Program.

Mikimoto (America) & Co., Ltd. Corporate Giving Program
680 5th Ave., Fl. 6
New York, NY 10019-5429 (212) 457-4500
FAX: (212) 457-4635

Purpose and activities: Mikimoto makes charitable contributions to nonprofit organizations involved with breast cancer, and on a case by case basis. Support is given on a national basis.
Fields of interest: Breast cancer; General charitable giving.
Type of support: General/operating support.
Geographic limitations: Giving on a national basis.
Application information:

2511
Milbank, Tweed, Hadley & McCloy LLP
1 Chase Manhattan Plz.
New York, NY 10005-1401 (212) 530-5532

Company URL: http://www.milbank.com
Establishment information: Established in 1866.
Company type: Private company
Business activities: Operates law firm.
Business type (SIC): Legal services
Offices: Los Angeles, CA; Washington, DC; New York, NY
International operations: Brazil; China; Germany; Hong Kong; Japan; Singapore; United Kingdom
Giving statement: Giving through the Milbank, Tweed, Hadley & McCloy LLP Pro Bono Program.

Milbank, Tweed, Hadley & McCloy LLP Pro Bono Program
1 Chase Manhattan Plz.
New York, NY 10005-1401 (212) 530-5532
FAX: (212) 822-5532;
E-mail: jgenova@milbank.com; Additional tel.: (212) 530-5000, fax: (212) 530-5219; URL: http://www.milbank.com/about-us/pro-bono.html

Contact: Joseph Genova, Partner
Fields of interest: Legal services.
Type of support: Pro bono services - legal.
Geographic limitations: Giving primarily in areas of company operations in Los Angeles, CA, Washington, DC, and New York, NY, and in Brazil, China, Germany, Hong Kong, Japan, Singapore, Sweden, and United Kingdom.

2512
Miles & Stockbridge, P.C.
10 Light St.
Baltimore, MD 21202-1435
(410) 727-3626

Company URL: http://www.milesstockbridge.com
Establishment information: Established in 1932.
Company type: Private company
Business activities: Operates law firm.
Business type (SIC): Legal services
Corporate officers: John B. Frisch, Chair.; John H. Murray, Pres.; Kenneth E. Adams, C.I.O.; Charles E. Johnson, Jr., Cont.
Offices: Baltimore, Cambridge, Columbia, Easton, Frederick, Rockville, Towson, MD; Tysons Corner, VA
Giving statement: Giving through the Miles & Stockbridge, P.C. Pro Bono Program and the Miles & Stockbridge Foundation Inc.

Miles & Stockbridge, P.C. Pro Bono Program
10 Light St.
Baltimore, MD 21202-1435 (410) 385-3626
E-mail: dbillian@milesstockbridge.com; URL: http://www.milesstockbridge.com/ourfirm/givingback/default.aspx

Contact: Dina R. Billian, Recruitment Mgr. & Pro Bono Coord.
Fields of interest: Legal services.
Type of support: Pro bono services - legal.
Application information: A Pro Bono Coordinator manages the pro bono program.

Miles & Stockbridge Foundation Inc.
10 Light St.
Baltimore, MD 21202-1435
URL: http://www.milesstockbridge.com/careers/whymands/givingback.aspx

Financial data (yr. ended 12/31/11): Revenue, $181,573; assets, $101,796 (M); gifts received, $181,573; expenditures, $173,999; program services expenses, $173,999; giving activities include $173,999 for 5 grants (high: $105,506; low: $8,500).
Purpose and activities: The foundation provides funds for charitable, educational, scientific, and religious endeavors.
Fields of interest: Legal services; General charitable giving Economically disadvantaged.
Program:
Pro Bono Advocate Program: The foundation provides pro bono advocacy services to individuals and organizations in need of legal services. The firm works closely with prominent public interest organizations that provide legal services to the disadvantaged in communities throughout Maryland and Virginia (specifically in communities where the firm has an offer: Baltimore, Cambridge, Columbia, Easton, Frederick, Rockville, and Towson, Maryland; and Tysons Corner, Virginia). Firm members also provide pro bono services on behalf of victims of domestic violence, primarily women and children of color, as well as on behalf of missing and abducted children and their families.
Type of support: Pro bono services; Pro bono services - advocacy; Pro bono services - legal.
Geographic limitations: Giving limited to MD and VA.
Officers and Directors:* Shaun Carrick, Pres.; J. W. Thomas Webb, V.P.; Bradford Bernstein; Michele L. Cohen; John B. Frisch; Demetrois G. Kaouris; Jeffery S. Poretz; John A. Stalfort; James M. Timmerman; Angela N. Whitaker-Pion; G. Randall Whittenberger.
EIN: 521946155

2513
The Milford Bank
33 Broad St.
Milford, CT 06460-3349 (203) 783-5700

Company URL: http://www.milfordbank.com
Establishment information: Established in 1872.
Company type: Private company
Business activities: Operates commercial bank.
Business type (SIC): Banks/commercial
Financial profile for 2011: Assets, $371,844,000; liabilities, $332,603,000
Corporate officers: Leo P. Carroll, Chair.; Robert V. Macklin, Pres. and C.E.O.; Susan L. Shields, Exec. V.P., Treas., and C.F.O.; Ann Marie C. Lenart, Sr. V.P., Human Resources and Corp. Secy.
Board of directors: Leo P. Carroll, Chair.; James R. Beard; Samuel S. Bergami, Jr.; Josephine R. Culmone; Louis J. D'Amato; Raymond A. Macaluso; Robert V. Macklin; Carol A. McInnis; Joseph Pelaccia; David B. Rubin; DeForest W. Smith
Offices: Devon, Woodmont, CT
Giving statement: Giving through the Milford Bank Corporate Giving Program and the Milford Bank Foundation, Inc.

The Milford Bank Corporate Giving Program
33 Broad St.
Milford, CT 06460-3319 (203) 783-5700
E-mail: jsantiago@milfordbank.com; Toll-free tel. in Connecticut: (800)-340-4862; tel. for Jorge Santiago: (203) 783-5700; for promotional item requests: Lynn Viesti Berube, tel.: (203) 783-5700; e-mail: lviesti@milfordbank.com; URL: http://www.milfordbank.com/inside-the-bank/community-events-relations/

Contact: Jorge Santiago
Purpose and activities: As a complement to its foundation, Milford Bank also makes charitable contributions to nonprofit organizations directly. Support is given primarily in areas of company operations in Connecticut.
Fields of interest: General charitable giving.
Type of support: General/operating support; Sponsorships.
Geographic limitations: Giving primarily in areas of company operations in CT.
Publications: Application guidelines.
Application information: Applications accepted. Application form required. Applicants should submit the following:
1) name, address and phone number of organization
Proposals for promotional item and banner requests should include the event name, date, and location, items and quantity requested, and the date when the items are needed by.
Initial approach: Complete online application for promotional item and banner requests
Deadline(s): 3 weeks prior to need for promotional item and banner requests

The Milford Bank Foundation, Inc.
33 Broad St.
Milford, CT 06460-3319

Establishment information: Established in 2001 in CT.
Donor: The Milford Bank.
Financial data (yr. ended 12/31/11): Assets, $240,730 (M); gifts received, $1,000; expenditures, $13,774; qualifying distributions, $12,750; giving activities include $12,750 for grants.
Purpose and activities: The foundation supports organizations involved with nursing care, ALS, law enforcement, and day care services.
Fields of interest: Arts; Housing/shelter; Human services.
Type of support: General/operating support.
Geographic limitations: Giving primarily in Milford, CT.
Support limitations: No grants to individuals.
Application information: Applications not accepted. Unsolicited requests for funds not accepted.
Officers and Directors:* Robert V. Macklin*, Pres.; Ann Marie C. Lenhart, Secy.; Susan L. Shields, Treas.; James Beard; Leo P. Carroll; Josephine R. Culmone; Raymond Macaluso; DeForest W. Smith.
EIN: 020600478

2514
The Milford National Bank and Trust Company
300 E. Main St., Ste. 100
P.O. Box 228
Milford, MA 01757-2806 (508) 634-4100

Company URL: http://www.milfordnationalonline.com
Establishment information: Established in 1849.
Company type: Subsidiary of a private company
Business activities: Operates commercial bank.
Business type (SIC): Banks/commercial
Corporate officers: Henry C. Papuga, Chair.; Robert J. Lewis, Pres. and C.E.O.; Anne M. Dygon, Sr. V.P. and C.F.O.
Board of director: Henry C. Papuga, Chair.
Giving statement: Giving through the Milford National Charitable Foundation, Inc.

The Milford National Charitable Foundation, Inc.
300 E. Main St.
Milford, MA 01757-0228 (508) 634-4100
URL: http://www.milfordnational.com/

Establishment information: Established in 1999 in MA.
Donor: The Milford National Bank and Trust Co.
Contact: Kristin T. Carvalho, Pres.
Financial data (yr. ended 12/31/11): Assets, $16,761 (M); gifts received, $31,325; expenditures, $23,234; qualifying distributions, $21,909; giving activities include $21,909 for grants.
Purpose and activities: The foundation supports public libraries and organizations involved with human services and senior citizens.
Fields of interest: Youth development; Human services; Religion.
Type of support: Continuing support; Donated equipment; Equipment; General/operating support; Program development; Sponsorships.
Geographic limitations: Giving primarily in Milford, MA.
Publications: Application guidelines.
Application information: Applications accepted. Application form required.
Initial approach: Proposal
Deadline(s): None
Officers and Directors:* Kristin T. Carvalho*, Pres.; William J. Vitalini, Treas.; George R. Marino*, Clerk; Fatima Alfonso; Maria Morte; Abram Rosenfeld; Thomas C. Sawyer, Sr.; Bernard Stock.
EIN: 043479749

2516
Millennia Media, Inc.
(doing business as Millennia Music & Media Systems)
4600 Missouri Flat Rd.
Placerville, CA 95667 (530) 647-0750

Company URL: http://www.mil-media.com
Establishment information: Established in 1989.
Company type: Private company
Business activities: Operates audio recording electronics and software company.
Business type (SIC): Professional and commercial equipment—wholesale; audio and video equipment/household
Corporate officer: John La Grou, Pres.
Giving statement: Giving through the Millennia Foundation.

The Millennia Foundation
(also known as Millennia Media, Inc. Corporate Giving Program)
4600 Missouri Flat Rd.
Placerville, CA 95667 (530) 647-0750
E-mail: cynth@compathos.com; URL: http://www.millenniamediagroup.com/foundation/index.php

Purpose and activities: Millennia Media is a certified B Corporation that makes charitable contributions to nonprofit organizations involved with cultural renewal, humanitarian service, global sustainability, and education.
Fields of interest: Arts; Education; Environment; Human services.
Type of support: Donated products; General/operating support; Scholarships—to individuals.
Publications: Application guidelines.
Application information: Applications accepted. E-mail should be no longer than 500 words. Application form not required. Applicants should submit the following:
1) brief history of organization and description of its mission
Initial approach: E-mail proposal
Deadline(s): None

2517
Herman Miller, Inc.
855 E. Main Ave.
P.O. Box 302
Zeeland, MI 49464-0302 (616) 654-3000
FAX: (616) 654-3632

Company URL: http://www.hermanmiller.com
Establishment information: Established in 1905.
Company type: Public company
Company ticker symbol and exchange: MLHR/NASDAQ
Business activities: Designs, manufactures, provides, and sells office furniture systems, products, and related services.
Business type (SIC): Furniture/office; furniture and fixtures/miscellaneous
Financial profile for 2012: Number of employees, 5,652; assets, $837,400,000; sales volume, $1,724,100,000; pre-tax net income, $119,500,000; expenses, $1,586,500,000; liabilities, $589,100,000
Corporate officers: Michael A. Volkema, Chair.; Brian C. Walker, Pres. and C.E.O.; Gregory J. Bylsma, Exec. V.P. and C.F.O.; Kenneth L. Goodson, Jr., Exec. V.P., Opers.; Jeffrey M. Stutz, V.P. and Treas.; James Christenson, Sr. V.P. and Secy.; Jeffrey Stutz, C.A.O. and Treas.
Board of directors: Michael A. Volkema, Chair.; Mary Vermeer Andringa; David Brandon; Douglas D. French; J. Barry Griswell; John R. Hoke III; James R. Kackley; Lisa Kro; Dorothy A. Terrell; David O. Ulrich; Brian C. Walker
Subsidiaries: Brandrud Furniture, Inc., Auburn, WA; Convia, Inc., Buffalo Grove, IL; Coro Acquisition Corporation-California, La Mirada, CA; Geiger International, Inc., Atlanta, GA; Integrated Metal Technologies, Inc., Spring Lake, MI; Meridian Inc., Spring Lake, MI; Office Pavilion South Florida, Inc., Jacksonville, FL; OP Corporate Furnishings, Inc., Autin, TX; OP Spectrum, L.L.P., King of Prussia, PA; OP Ventures, Inc., Denver, CO; OP Ventures of Texas, Inc., Carrollton, TX

International operations: Australia; Barbados; Canada; China; England; Italy; Japan; Mexico
Giving statement: Giving through the Herman Miller, Inc. Corporate Giving Program and the Jubilee Foundation.
Company EIN: 380837640

Herman Miller, Inc. Corporate Giving Program

855 E. Main Ave.
P.O. Box 302
Zeeland, MI 49464-0302
URL: http://www.hermanmiller.com/about-us/our-values-in-action/a-better-world-report.html

Purpose and activities: Herman Miller makes charitable contributions to nonprofit organizations on a case by case basis. Support is given on a national and international basis in areas of company operations.
Fields of interest: General charitable giving.
Type of support: Employee volunteer services.
Geographic limitations: Giving on a national and international basis in areas of company operations.

The Jubilee Foundation

(formerly Herman Miller Design Foundation)
c/o Comerica Bank
P.O. Box 75000, M.C. 3462
Detroit, MI 48275-3462

Establishment information: Established in 1994 in MI.
Donor: Herman Miller, Inc.
Financial data (yr. ended 05/31/12): Assets, $4,925,265 (M); gifts received, $1,483,580; expenditures, $2,021,281; qualifying distributions, $2,014,627; giving activities include $2,014,627 for grants.
Purpose and activities: The foundation supports community foundations and organizations involved with arts and culture, education, the environment, hunger, human services, international affairs, Christianity, neighborhood development, and economically disadvantaged people.
Fields of interest: Arts; Elementary/secondary education; Higher education; Theological school/education; Education; Environment, natural resources; Environment, water resources; Environment; Health care; Food services; Developmentally disabled, centers & services; Human services; International relief; International affairs; Community development, neighborhood development; Foundations (community); Christian agencies & churches Economically disadvantaged.
Type of support: General/operating support; Scholarship funds.
Geographic limitations: Giving primarily in CA, GA, and VA, with emphasis on MI.
Support limitations: No grants to individuals.
Application information: Applications not accepted. Contributes only to pre-selected organizations.
Officers: Michael A. Volkema, Pres.; James E. Christenson, Secy.; Gregory J Bylsma, Treas.
EIN: 383003821

2518
Miller Automobile Corporation

1335 Post Rd.
Darien, CT 06820-5417 (203) 655-7451

Establishment information: Established in 1930.
Company type: Private company
Business activities: Operates car dealership.
Business type (SIC): Motor vehicles—retail
Financial profile for 2010: Number of employees, 50
Corporate officers: Frank A. Miller, Chair.; William Steinmetz, Pres.; Darline Reynolds, Secy.
Board of director: Frank A. Miller, Chair.
Giving statement: Giving through the Frank A. Miller Family Foundation, Inc.

Frank A. Miller Family Foundation, Inc.

1335 Post Rd.
Darien, CT 06820-5417

Establishment information: Established in 1984 in CT.
Donor: Miller Automobile Corp.
Financial data (yr. ended 12/31/11): Assets, $496,904 (M); expenditures, $24,544; qualifying distributions, $21,250; giving activities include $21,250 for 30 grants (high: $5,000; low: $50).
Purpose and activities: The foundation supports hospices and organizations involved with arts and culture, education, animal welfare, health, mental health, and civic affairs.
Fields of interest: Historic preservation/historical societies; Arts; Libraries (public); Education; Animals/wildlife, preservation/protection; Hospitals (general); Health care; Mental health/crisis services; Residential/custodial care, hospices; Public affairs.
Type of support: General/operating support; Scholarship funds.
Geographic limitations: Giving primarily in CT and FL.
Support limitations: No grants to individuals.
Application information: Applications not accepted. Unsolicited requests for funds not accepted.
Officers: Frank A. Miller, Pres.; John S. Miller, V.P.; Elizabeth Miller, Secy.-Treas.
EIN: 222540718

2519
Miller Canfield P.L.C.

150 West Jefferson, Ste. 2500
Detroit, MI 48226 (313) 963-6420

Company URL: http://www.millercanfield.com
Establishment information: Established in 1852.
Company type: Private company
Business activities: Operates law firm.
Business type (SIC): Legal services
Corporate officers: Joseph M. Fazio, Chair.; Michael W. Hartmann, C.E.O.; David A. Robson, C.O.O.; Thomas W. Linn, Chair. Emeritus
Board of director: Joseph M. Fazio, Chair.
International operations: Canada; China; Mexico; Poland
Giving statement: Giving through the Miller Canfield P.L.C. Pro Bono Program.

Miller Canfield P.L.C. Pro Bono Program

150 West Jefferson, Ste. 2500
Detroit, MI 48226 (313) 496-7511
E-mail: linn@millercanfield.com; URL: http://www.millercanfield.com/firm-probono.html

Contact: Thomas W. Linn, Pro Bono Chair.
Fields of interest: Legal services.
Type of support: Pro bono services - legal.

2520
Miller Johnson

250 Monroe Ave., N.W., Ste. 800
Grand Rapids, MI 49503-2283
(616) 831-1700

Company URL: http://www.millerjohnson.com
Establishment information: Established in 1959.
Company type: Private company
Business activities: Operates law firm.
Business type (SIC): Legal services
Corporate officers: Betsy Raymond, C.O.O.; Erik Goltzer, C.I.O.; Andrea Myers, Cont.
Offices: Grand Rapids, Kalamazoo, MI
Giving statement: Giving through the Miller Johnson Pro Bono Program.

Miller Johnson Pro Bono Program

250 Monroe Ave., N.W., Ste. 800
Grand Rapids, MI 49503-2283 (616) 831-1700
URL: http://www.millerjohnson.com/aboutus/xprCallOut.aspx?xpST=AboutUsGeneral&key=d219dcb6-3962-4f70-9470-ed0e2c041dca

Contact: J. Michael Smith, Member
Fields of interest: Legal services.
Type of support: Pro bono services - legal.
Application information: A Department Chair manages the pro-bono program.

2521
Miller Nash LLP

3400 U.S. Bancorp Twr.
111 S.W. 5th Ave.
Portland, OR 97204-3699 (503) 224-5858

Company URL: http://www.millernash.com
Establishment information: Established in 1873.
Company type: Private company
Business activities: Operates law firm.
Business type (SIC): Legal services
Corporate officers: Donald A. Burns, Managing Partner; Erica Daley, C.F.O.
Offices: Bend, Portland, Prineville, OR; Seattle, WA
International operations: Canada
Giving statement: Giving through the Miller Nash LLP Pro Bono Program.

Miller Nash LLP Pro Bono Program

3400 U.S. Bancorp Twr.
111 S.W. 5th Ave.
Portland, OR 97204-3699 (503) 224-5858
E-mail: justin.sawyer@millernash.com; URL: http://www.millernash.com/community/xpqGC.aspx?xpST=ProBono

Contact: Justin Sawyer, Pro Bono Partner
Fields of interest: Legal services.
Type of support: Pro bono services - legal.
Application information: A Pro Bono Committee manages the pro bono program.

2523
MillerCoors LLC

(formerly Miller Brewing Company)
250 S. Wacker, Ste. 250
Chicago, IL 60606-5888 (312) 496-2700

Company URL: http://www.millercoors.com
Establishment information: Established in 1855.
Company type: Private company
Business activities: Operates brewing company.
Business type (SIC): Beverages
Financial profile for 2009: Number of employees, 4,500
Corporate officers: Peter H. Coors, Chair.; Graham Mackay, Vice-Chair.; Tom Long, Pres. and C.E.O.; Dennis Puffer, Exec. V.P. and C.O.O.; Tracey Joubert, C.F.O.; Karen Alber, C.I.O.
Board of directors: Peter H. Coors, Chair.; Graham Mackay, Vice-Chair.; Alan Clark; Nick Fell; Stewart Glendinning; Gavin Hattersley; Peter Swinburn; Tony van Kralingen; Samuel Walker; James Wilson
Subsidiaries: The Jacob Leinenkugel Brewing Co., Chippewa Falls, WI; Miller International, Milwaukee, WI; Molson Brewery U.S.A., Inc., Reston, VA
Plants: Irwindale, Los Angeles, CA; Albany, GA; Eden, Reidsville, NC; Hamilton, Trenton, OH; Oklahoma City, Tulsa, OK; Fort Worth, TX; Chippewa Falls, Milwaukee, WI
Historic mergers: Coors Brewing Company (July 1, 2008)
Giving statement: Giving through the MillerCoors LLC Corporate Giving Program and the Renaissance Performing Arts Co.

MillerCoors LLC Corporate Giving Program

(formerly Miller Brewing Company Contributions Program)
250 S. Wacker Dr.
Chicago, IL 60606-5888 (312) 496-2700
URL: http://www.greatbeergreatresponsibility.com/People-and-Communities.aspx

Purpose and activities: As a complement to its foundation, MillerCoors also makes charitable contributions to nonprofit organizations directly. Support is given to organizations involved with higher education, economic empowerment, human services, water stewardship, domestic violence, business development, and diversity. Support is given primarily in areas of company operations.
Fields of interest: Higher education; Education; Environment, water resources; Environment; Crime/violence prevention, child abuse; Food services; Food banks; Boys clubs; Girls clubs; Family services; Family services, domestic violence; Human services, gift distribution; Homeless, human services; Civil/human rights, equal rights; Civil/human rights, LGBTQ; Community development, business promotion; Community/economic development; United Ways and Federated Giving Programs; Military/veterans' organizations.
Type of support: Annual campaigns; Donated equipment; Donated products; Employee matching gifts; Employee volunteer services; Equipment; General/operating support; In-kind gifts; Scholarships—to individuals.
Geographic limitations: Giving primarily in areas of company operations.

Renaissance Performing Arts Co.

11056 Renaissance Dr., #103
Davidson, NC 28036-7797 (520) 463-2600
Application address: 12601 E. Hwy. 60, Apache Junction, AZ 85118

Establishment information: Established in 1994.
Donors: Miller Brewing Co.; Guiness Bass Import Co.; I.H. Caffey Distributing Co., Inc.; Carolina Beer and Beverage, LLC; Mutual Distributing Co.; Carolina Renaissance LP; I.H. Caffey Distributors; Foothills Brewing Co.; Carolina Premium.
Contact: Jeff Siegel, Tr.
Financial data (yr. ended 12/31/11): Assets, $1,958 (M); gifts received, $43,456; expenditures, $44,001; qualifying distributions, $44,001; giving activities include $41,988 for 24 grants (high: $7,200; low: $175).
Purpose and activities: The foundation supports organizations involved with and individuals performing at the Carolina Renaissance Festival in Charlotte, North Carolina.
Fields of interest: Performing arts; Recreation, fairs/festivals.
Type of support: General/operating support; Grants to individuals.
Application information: Applications accepted. Application form not required.
Initial approach: Proposal
Deadline(s): None
Trustees: Robert Levine; Jeff Siegel.
EIN: 411794770

2522
Miller-Davis Co.

1029 Portage St.
Kalamazoo, MI 49001-3007
(269) 345-3561

Company URL: http://www.miller-davis.com/index.php
Establishment information: Established in 1936.
Company type: Private company
Business activities: Provides general contract construction services.
Business type (SIC): Building construction general contractors and operative builders
Corporate officers: Rex Bell, Pres.; Thomas Georgoff, C.F.O.
Subsidiary: D.S.I. Inc., Kalamazoo, MI
Giving statement: Giving through the Miller-Davis Foundation.

The Miller-Davis Foundation

1029 Portage St.
Kalamazoo, MI 49001-3007

Establishment information: Established in 2001 in MI.
Donor: Miller-Davis Co.
Financial data (yr. ended 12/31/11): Assets, $381,478 (M); expenditures, $20,500; qualifying distributions, $20,500; giving activities include $20,500 for grants.
Purpose and activities: The foundation supports organizations involved with arts and culture, education, the environment, recreation, and economically disadvantaged people.
Fields of interest: Arts; Education; Agriculture/food.
Type of support: General/operating support; Scholarship funds.
Geographic limitations: Giving limited to areas of company operations in southwestern MI, with emphasis on Kalamazoo.
Support limitations: No grants to individuals.
Application information: Applications not accepted. Unsolicited requests for funds not accepted.
Officers: Rex L. Bell, Chair. and Pres.; Thomas Georgoff, Secy.-Treas.
EIN: 383607242

2524
Millhiser-Smith Agency, Inc.

3100 Oakland Rd., N.E.
P.O. Box 3100
Cedar Rapids, IA 52406-3100
(319) 365-8611

Company URL: http://www.millhisersmith.com/
Establishment information: Established in 1928.
Company type: Private company
Business activities: Operates insurance and brokerage agency.
Business type (SIC): Insurance agents, brokers, and services
Corporate officers: Tom King, Chair. and C.E.O.; Tim Gassmann, Pres.; Lynne DeVore, C.O.O. and Treas.; Patrick C. Scheetz, Sr. V.P., and Secy.
Board of director: Tom King, Chair.
Giving statement: Giving through the Millhiser Smith Foundation.

Millhiser Smith Foundation

3100 Oakland Rd., N.E.
Cedar Rapids, IA 52402

Establishment information: Established in 2007 in IA.
Donor: Millhiser Smith Agency, Inc.
Financial data (yr. ended 12/31/11): Assets, $73,484 (M); gifts received, $17,179; expenditures, $12,357; qualifying distributions, $10,486; giving activities include $10,486 for grants.
Purpose and activities: The foundation supports health centers and organizations involved with higher education, diabetes, cancer research, athletics, children services, community development, and Christianity.
Fields of interest: Education; Recreation; Human services.
Type of support: Annual campaigns; Capital campaigns; Continuing support; Equipment; General/operating support; Sponsorships.
Application information: Applications not accepted. Unsolicited requests for funds not accepted.
Officers: Jennifer Preymark, Pres.; Jessica Rhatigan, Secy.; Lynne DeVore, Treas.
EIN: 208359918

2525
Milliken and Company

920 Milliken Rd.
P.O. Box 1926
Spartanburg, SC 29304 (864) 503-2020

Company URL: http://www.milliken.com
Establishment information: Established in 1865.
Company type: Private company
Business activities: Manufactures textiles.
Business type (SIC): Fabrics/broadwoven natural cotton; fabrics/broadwoven synthetic and silk; yarn and thread mills
Corporate officers: Joe Sally, Pres. and C.E.O.; Jim McNulty, C.F.O.; Dennis Blanks, Cont.
Subsidiary: Kingstree Manufacturing Co., Kingstree, SC
Divisions: Apparel Fabrics Div., Spartanburg, SC; Enterprises Div., Marietta, SC
Giving statement: Giving through the Milliken Foundation.

Milliken Foundation

c/o Citibank, N.A.
666 5th Ave., 12 FL
New York, NY 10103-0001

Establishment information: Trust established in 1945 in NY.
Donor: Milliken and Co.
Financial data (yr. ended 12/31/11): Assets, $6,471,457 (M); expenditures, $6,779,332; qualifying distributions, $6,759,568; giving activities include $6,744,579 for 41 grants (high: $1,125,000; low: $100).
Purpose and activities: The foundation supports organizations involved with arts and culture, education, health, cancer research, food distribution, and human services.
Fields of interest: Media/communications; Arts; Elementary/secondary education; Higher education; Education; Health care; Cancer research; Food distribution, meals on wheels; YM/YWCAs & YM/YWHAs; Children/youth, services; Homeless, human services; Human services; United Ways and Federated Giving Programs.
Type of support: General/operating support.
Geographic limitations: Giving in areas of company operations, with emphasis on SC.
Support limitations: No grants to individuals.
Application information: Applications not accepted. Contributes only to pre-selected organizations.
Trustee: Citibank, N.A.
Advisory Committee: G. Ashley Allen; J. L. Hamrick; Gerrish H. Milliken; Justine V.R. Russell.
EIN: 136055062
Selected grants: The following grants are a representative sample of this grantmaker's funding activity:
$1,125,000 to Wofford College, Spartanburg, SC, 2011. For general support.
$1,000,000 to Furman University, Greenville, SC, 2011. For general support.
$1,000,000 to South Eastern Efforts Developing Sustainable Spaces, Durham, NC, 2011. For general support.
$500,000 to Middlebury College, Middlebury, VT, 2011. For general support.
$400,000 to H. Lee Moffitt Cancer Center and Research Institute, Tampa, FL, 2011. For general support.
$400,000 to Lake Forest Ranch, Macon, MS, 2011. For general support.
$373,950 to University of South Carolina Business Partnership Foundation, Columbia, SC, 2011. For general support.
$300,000 to Mississippi State University, Mississippi State, MS, 2011. For general support.
$250,000 to Hotchkiss School, Lakeville, CT, 2011. For general support.
$250,000 to Yale University, New Haven, CT, 2011. For general support.

2515
The Mill-Rose Company

7995 Tyler Blvd.
Mentor, OH 44060 (440) 255-9171

Company URL: http://www.millrose.com
Establishment information: Established in 1919.
Company type: Private company
Business activities: Manufactures industrial brushes.
Business type (SIC): Manufacturing/miscellaneous
Financial profile for 2010: Number of employees, 160
Corporate officers: Victor F. Miller, C.E.O.; Paul M. Miller, Co-Pres.; Paul Staats, Co-Pres.
Giving statement: Giving through the Mill-Rose Foundation.

Mill-Rose Foundation

7995 Tyler Blvd.
Mentor, OH 44060-4805

Establishment information: Established in 1980.
Donor: Mill-Rose Company.
Financial data (yr. ended 06/30/12): Assets, $16,262 (M); gifts received, $15,000; expenditures, $10,775; qualifying distributions, $9,800; giving activities include $9,800 for grants.
Purpose and activities: The foundation supports museums and organizations involved with education, cancer research, human services, and Christianity.
Fields of interest: Education; Housing/shelter; Human services.
Type of support: Endowments; General/operating support.
Support limitations: No grants to individuals.
Application information: Applications not accepted. Unsolicited requests for funds not accepted.
Trustees: Lawrence W. Miller; Paul M. Miller; Richard M. Miller.
EIN: 341345012

2526
Mills Meyers Swartling

1000 2nd Ave., 30th Fl.
Seattle, WA 98104-1094 (206) 382-1000

Company URL: http://www.mms-seattle.com
Company type: Private company
Business activities: Operates law firm.
Business type (SIC): Legal services
Giving statement: Giving through the Mills Meyers Swartling Pro Bono Program.

Mills Meyers Swartling Pro Bono Program

1000 2nd Ave., 30th Fl.
Seattle, WA 98104-1094 (206) 382-1000
E-mail: alyter@millsmeyers.com; URL: http://www.mms-seattle.com/

Contact: Anita Lyter, Exec. Dir.
Fields of interest: Legal services.
Type of support: Pro bono services - legal.
Geographic limitations: Giving primarily in areas of company operations in Seattle, WA.
Application information: A Pro Bono Committee manages the pro bono program.

2527
Milwaukee Brewers Baseball Club, L.P.

1 Brewers Way
Miller Park
Milwaukee, WI 53214-3652
(414) 902-4452
FAX: (414) 902-4053

Company URL: http://milwaukee.brewers.mlb.com
Establishment information: Established in 2001.
Company type: Private company
Business activities: Operates professional baseball club.
Business type (SIC): Commercial sports
Corporate officers: Mark Attanasio, Chair.; Rick Schlesinger, C.O.O.; Bob Quinn, Exec. V.P., Finance, and Admin.; Marti Wronski, V.P. and Genl. Counsel; Joe Zidanic, V.P., Cont.; Tom Hecht, V.P., Corp. Mktg.; Tyler Barnes, V.P., Comms.; Sally Andrist, V.P, Human Resources; Nick Watson, V.P., Tech. and Inf. Systems
Board of director: Mark Attanasio, Chair.
Giving statement: Giving through the Milwaukee Brewers Baseball Club, L.P. Corporate Giving Program and the Brewers Community Foundation, Inc.

Milwaukee Brewers Baseball Club, L.P. Corporate Giving Program

c/o Community Rels.
1 Brewer Way
Milwaukee, WI 53214-3651 (414) 902-4800
FAX: (414) 902-4058; Contact for Community Achievers: Erica Bowring, e-mail: Erica.Bowring@brewers.com; URL: http://milwaukee.brewers.mlb.com/NASApp/mlb/mil/community/index.jsp

Contact: Katina Shaw, Dir., Community Rels.
Purpose and activities: The Milwaukee Brewers make charitable contributions to nonprofit organizations on a case by case basis. Support is given primarily in Wisconsin.
Fields of interest: Education; Athletics/sports, baseball; Recreation; Youth, services; General charitable giving.
Programs:

Brewers Pep Rally Contest: Through the Bowers Pep Rally Contest, elementary and middle school students submit a one-page essay about what their school is doing to make the community a better place. The winning school receives a visit from a Brewers player and personnel, Brewers apparel, game tickets, and transportation to and from Miller Park.

Community Achievers Award: The Milwaukee Brewers honors volunteers, philanthropists, and other heroes who have helped their community in extraordinary ways. Community Achievers are nominated by fans monthly and winners receive 4 game tickets, on-field recognition, the opportunity to throw out the first pitch prior to the game, a Community Achiever certificate, and a gift bag of Brewers memorabilia.

Speaker Bureau: Through the Speakers Bureau program, Milwaukee Brewers players and staff visit local schools, organizations, and youth groups.

Type of support: Donated products; In-kind gifts; Income development; Loaned talent.
Geographic limitations: Giving primarily in areas of company operations in WI, with emphasis on Milwaukee.
Publications: Application guidelines; Newsletter.
Application information: Applications accepted. Proposals should be submitted using organization letterhead. The Community Relations Department handles giving. Applicants should submit the following:
1) name, address and phone number of organization
2) copy of IRS Determination Letter
3) detailed description of project and amount of funding requested
4) contact person

Initial approach: Proposal to headquarters for promotional items and autographed memorabilia; download application form and mail to headquarters for Speakers Bureau; complete online nomination form for

Community Achievers; essay to headquarters for Brewers Pep Rally Contest

Deadline(s): 45 days prior to need for promotional items and memorabilia; 60 days prior to need for Speakers Bureau; None for Community Achievers; Apr. 23 for Brewers Pep Rally Contest

Brewers Community Foundation, Inc.

(formerly Brewers Charities, Inc.)
Miller Park
1 Brewers Way
Milwaukee, WI 53214-3651 (414) 902-4611
URL: http://milwaukee.brewers.mlb.com/mil/community/bcf.jsp

Establishment information: Established in 2000 in WI.
Contact: Lynn Sprangers, Pres.
Financial data (yr. ended 12/31/11): Revenue, $2,215,613; assets, $1,560,755 (M); gifts received, $1,193,290; expenditures, $2,274,775; giving activities include $2,089,219 for grants.
Purpose and activities: The foundation supports organizations in Wisconsin that specialize in activities for children, particularly in recreational activities that help promote interest in baseball and for specific educational programs that are directed toward children.
Fields of interest: Athletics/sports, baseball; Youth development.
Program:
Brewers Community Foundation Grants: The foundation provides support between $1,000 and $10,000 for organizations that provide quality programming in the areas of health, education, recreation, and basic needs that focus on low-income and disadvantaged youth and their families.
Type of support: Scholarship funds.
Geographic limitations: Giving limited to WI.
Support limitations: No grants to individuals (except for scholarships), or for debt retirement, operating deficits, endowments, general operating costs, sponsorships, annual membership or affiliation campaigns, dinners, special events, conferences, symposiums, workshops, or group trips.
Publications: Application guidelines.
Application information: Applications accepted. Applicants should submit the following:
1) name, address and phone number of organization
2) copy of IRS Determination Letter
3) copy of most recent annual report/audited financial statement/990
4) listing of board of directors, trustees, officers and other key people and their affiliations
5) detailed description of project and amount of funding requested
6) listing of additional sources and amount of support

Initial approach: Proposal (no more than two pages) for Brewers Community Foundation Grants
Deadline(s): None
Final notification: Nov. 1

Officers and Directors:* Wendy Selig-Prieb*, Chair.; Lynn Sprangers*, Pres.; Robert Quinn, Treas.; Cecelia Gore, Exec. Dir.; Tyler Barnes.
EIN: 391970152

2528
Milwaukee Bucks, Inc.

Bradley Ctr., 1001 N. 4th St.
Milwaukee, WI 53203-1314
(414) 227-0500
FAX: (414) 227-0543

Company URL: http://www.nba.com/bucks
Establishment information: Established in 1968.
Company type: Private company
Business activities: Operates professional basketball club.
Business type (SIC): Commercial sports
Corporate officers: Herb Kohl, Pres.; Michael Burr, Exec. V.P. and C.F.O.; Rita Huber, Secy.; Jim Woloszyk, V.P., Finance.; David Snyder, V.P., Sales; Dustin Godsey, V.P., Mktg.
Giving statement: Giving through the Milwaukee Bucks, Inc. Corporate Giving Program.

Milwaukee Bucks, Inc. Corporate Giving Program

c/o Community Rels.
1001 N. 4th St.
Milwaukee, WI 53203-1314 (414) 227-0983
E-mail: dlogan@bucks.com; URL: http://www.nba.com/bucks/community/contact_community.html

Contact: Deb Logan
Purpose and activities: The Milwaukee Bucks make charitable contributions to nonprofit organizations involved with children and youth and on a case by case basis. Support is given primarily in Wisconsin.
Fields of interest: Education, reading; Education; Hospitals (general); Athletics/sports, basketball; Athletics/sports, Special Olympics; Boy scouts; Girl scouts; Salvation Army; YM/YWCAs & YM/YWHAs; Children/youth, services; Human services, gift distribution; General charitable giving.
Programs:
Home Court Heroes: The Milwaukee Bucks, in partnership with Kapco Inc., honors individuals who have made exceptional and lasting contributions to the community. The honorees receive 4 game tickets, a special Home Court Heroes recognition plaque, and in-game recognition.
Kapco Community Corners: The Milwaukee Bucks, in partnership with Kapco, provides game tickets to area children's organizations and charities.
Type of support: Donated products; In-kind gifts; Income development; Loaned talent.
Geographic limitations: Giving primarily in areas of company operations in WI.
Publications: Application guidelines.
Application information: Applications accepted. Proposals should be submitted using organization letterhead. The Community Relations Department handles giving. Applicants should submit the following:
1) name, address and phone number of organization
2) descriptive literature about organization
3) detailed description of project and amount of funding requested
4) contact person

Initial approach: Proposal to headquarters for donations, player appearances, and player tickets; complete online nomination form for Home Court Heroes; contact headquarters for Kapco Community Corners
Copies of proposal: 1
Deadline(s): 4 to 6 weeks prior to need for donations; 2 months prior to need for player appearances; None for player tickets, Home Court Heroes, and Kapco Community Corners

2529
Mine Safety Appliances Company

1000 Cranberry Woods Dr.
P.O. Box 426
Cranberry Township, PA 16066-5207
(727) 776-8600
FAX: (412) 967-3326

Company URL: http://www.msasafety.com/
Establishment information: Established in 1914.
Company type: Public company
Company ticker symbol and exchange: MSA/NYSE
Business activities: Manufactures and sells safety equipment and process control instruments.
Business type (SIC): Laboratory apparatus; medical instruments and supplies
Financial profile for 2011: Number of employees, 5,300; assets, $1,111,750,000; sales volume, $1,179,890,000; pre-tax net income, $134,290,000; expenses, $1,045,610,000; liabilities, $648,790,000
Corporate officers: John T. Ryan III, Chair.; William M. Lambert, Pres. and C.E.O.; Dennis L. Zeitler, Sr. V.P., C.F.O., and Treas.; Markus Weber, V.P. and C.I.O.; Douglas K. McClaine, V.P., Secy., and Genl. Counsel; Paul R. Uhler, V.P., Human Resources
Board of directors: John T. Ryan III, Chair.; Robert A. Bruggeworth, Jr.; James A. Cederna; Thomas B. Hotopp; William M. Lambert; Diane M. Pearse; L. Edward Shaw, Jr.; John C. Unkovic; Thomas H. Witmer
Subsidiaries: Callery Chemical Co., Pittsburgh, PA; MSA International, Pittsburgh, PA
International operations: Argentina; Australia; Belgium; Brazil; Canada; Chile; China; France; Germany; Hungary; Italy; Japan; Mexico; Netherlands; Peru; Poland; Russia; Singapore; South Africa; Spain; Sweden; Switzerland; United Kingdom; Zimbabwe
Giving statement: Giving through the Mine Safety Appliances Company Charitable Foundation.
Company EIN: 250668780

Mine Safety Appliances Company Charitable Foundation

1000 Cranberry Woods Dr.
Cranberry Township, PA 16066-5207 (724) 776-8231
URL: http://us.msasafety.com/corporateGiving

Establishment information: Established in 1991 in PA as successor to the Mine Safety Appliances Company Charitable Trust.
Donor: Mine Safety Appliances Co.
Contact: Dennis L. Zeitler, V.P.
Financial data (yr. ended 12/31/11): Assets, $18,907 (M); gifts received, $850,025; expenditures, $898,248; qualifying distributions, $898,135; giving activities include $898,135 for grants.
Purpose and activities: The foundation supports botanical gardens and fire fighters and organizations involved with arts and culture, education, health, children, residential care, foreign policy, and engineering.
Fields of interest: Museums; Performing arts, ballet; Performing arts, orchestras; Arts; Higher education; Libraries (public); Scholarships/financial aid; Education; Botanical gardens; Hospitals (general); Health care; Disasters, fire prevention/control; Youth development, business; Children, services; Residential/custodial care, senior continuing care; International affairs, foreign policy; United Ways and Federated Giving Programs; Engineering.

Type of support: Annual campaigns; Continuing support; General/operating support; Program development; Scholarship funds.
Geographic limitations: Giving primarily in Pittsburgh, PA.
Support limitations: No grants to individuals.
Application information: Applications accepted. Application form not required. Applicants should submit the following:
1) brief history of organization and description of its mission
2) detailed description of project and amount of funding requested
Initial approach: Letter of inquiry
Deadline(s): None
Officer: Dennis L. Zeitler, V.P. and Secy.
EIN: 256023104
Selected grants: The following grants are a representative sample of this grantmaker's funding activity:
$150,000 to United Way of Allegheny County, Pittsburgh, PA, 2010. For unrestricted grant.
$27,500 to Pittsburgh Symphony, Pittsburgh, PA, 2010. For unrestricted grant.
$20,000 to Carnegie Library of Pittsburgh, Pittsburgh, PA, 2010. For unrestricted grant.
$10,000 to Phipps Conservatory and Botanical Gardens, Pittsburgh, PA, 2010. For unrestricted grant.
$10,000 to World Affairs Council of Pittsburgh, Pittsburgh, PA, 2010. For unrestricted grant.
$7,500 to Boy Scouts of America, Pittsburgh, PA, 2010. For unrestricted grant.
$7,112 to United Way, Mile High, Denver, CO, 2010. For unrestricted grant.
$5,000 to Family Guidance, Sewickley, PA, 2010. For unrestricted grant.
$5,000 to Frick Art and Historical Center, Pittsburgh, PA, 2010. For unrestricted grant.
$5,000 to National Kidney Foundation, New York, NY, 2010. For unrestricted grant.

2530
Minnesota Vikings Football Club, LLC

9520 Viking Dr.
Eden Prairie, MN 55344-3825
(952) 828-6500

Company URL: http://www.vikings.com
Establishment information: Established in 1961.
Company type: Private company
Business activities: Operates professional football club.
Business type (SIC): Commercial sports
Financial profile for 2010: Number of employees, 300
Corporate officers: Zygi Wilf, Chair.; Leonard Wilf, Vice-Chair.; Mark Will, Pres.; Kevin Warren, V.P. and C.A.O.; Steve Poppen, V.P., Finance and C.F.O.; Rob Brzezinski, V.P., Opers.; Steve LaCroix, V.P., Sales and Mktg.; Lester Bagley, V.P., Public Affairs; Carl Miklas, Cont.
Board of directors: Zygi Wilf, Chair.; Leonard Wilf, Vice-Chair.
Giving statement: Giving through the Minnesota Vikings Football Club, LLC Corporate Giving Program and the Vikings Children's Fund, Inc.

Minnesota Vikings Football Club, LLC Corporate Giving Program

9520 Viking Dr.
Eden Prairie, MN 55344-3825 (952) 828-6527
FAX: (952) 828-6540; URL: http://www.vikings.com/outreach/index.html

Contact: Brad Madson
Purpose and activities: The Minnesota Vikings makes charitable contributions to nonprofit organizations on a case by case basis. Support is given primarily in Minnesota.
Fields of interest: Education; Athletics/sports, football; Athletics/sports, Special Olympics; Youth, services; General charitable giving.
Type of support: Building/renovation; Donated products; In-kind gifts; Loaned talent.
Geographic limitations: Giving primarily in areas of company operations in MN.
Publications: Application guidelines.
Application information: Applications accepted. The Community Relations Department handles giving. Application form not required.
Proposals should indicate the date of the event.
Initial approach: Mail or fax proposal to headquarters for donations and player appearances
Copies of proposal: 1
Deadline(s): 1 month prior to need for donations and player appearances

Vikings Children's Fund, Inc.

(formerly Minnesota Vikings Children's Fund)
9520 Viking Dr.
Eden Prairie, MN 55344-3825 (952) 828-6500
URL: http://www.vikings.com/outreach/vikings-childrens-fund.html

Establishment information: Established in 1978 in MN.
Financial data (yr. ended 01/31/11): Revenue, $623,066; assets, $531,820 (M); gifts received, $666,794; expenditures, $665,021; giving activities include $619,293 for grants.
Purpose and activities: The fund is a means for the Viking players, coaches, staff and their families to focus their community support by supporting child-related nonprofit organizations in the upper Midwest. Half of the funds are awarded to the University of Minnesota Department of Pediatrics for research.
Fields of interest: Pediatrics research; Children, services.
Program:
Grants: The fund makes available grants ranging from $500 to $5,000 to support organizations that focus on pediatric research, child-related health and wellness programs, education (including drug and alcohol abuse treatment/rehabilitation and education, child abuse education, and at-risk youth and mentor programs), and family services (including family support, family rehabilitation, child protection, shelters for homeless with children, and shelters during intervention for family crises).
Type of support: Research.
Geographic limitations: Giving limited to the upper Midwest.
Publications: Application guidelines.
Application information: Applications accepted. Application form required. Applicants should submit the following:
1) copy of IRS Determination Letter
2) copy of most recent annual report/audited financial statement/990
3) listing of board of directors, trustees, officers and other key people and their affiliations
4) detailed description of project and amount of funding requested
5) copy of current year's organizational budget and/or project budget
6) listing of additional sources and amount of support
Initial approach: Download application form
Deadline(s): Mar. 13
Final notification: Fall
Officers and Directors:* Dave Mona*, Pres.; Lester Bagley*, Secy.; Steve LaCroix*, Treas.; Beth Bennett; Brad Childress; Debbie Estes; Mike Fiterman; Aaron Friedman; Brad Madson; Alfred Michael; Stacy Rubsam.
EIN: 411337790

2531
Minnesota Wild Hockey Club, LP

317 Washington St.
St. Paul, MN 55102-1609 (651) 602-6000

Company URL: http://www.wild.com
Establishment information: Established in 1997.
Company type: Private company
Business activities: Operates professional ice hockey club.
Business type (SIC): Commercial sports
Corporate officers: Matt Majka, C.O.O.; Pamela Wheelock, Exec. V.P. and Co-C.F.O.; Jeff Pellegrom, Co-C.F.O.; Steven Weinreich, V.P. and Genl. Counsel; John Maher, V.P., Mktg. and Comms.
Board of directors: Mark Falcone; Philip Falcone; Craig Leipold; Quinn Martin; Mark Pacchini; Jac Sperling
Giving statement: Giving through the Minnesota Wild Hockey Club, LP Corporate Giving Program.

Minnesota Wild Hockey Club, LP Corporate Giving Program

317 Washington St.
St. Paul, MN 55102-1609
URL: http://wild.nhl.com/club/page.htm?id=51760

Purpose and activities: As a complement to its foundation, the Minnesota Wild also makes charitable contributions of memorabilia to nonprofit organizations directly. Special emphasis is directed towards programs designed to benefit youth hockey, disadvantaged youth, medical-related causes, and educational initiatives. Support is limited to Minnesota.
Fields of interest: Elementary/secondary education; Health care; Athletics/sports, winter sports; Youth development Economically disadvantaged.
Type of support: In-kind gifts.
Geographic limitations: Giving limited to MN.
Support limitations: No support for veterans', fraternal, labor, or political groups. No grants for individuals, or for general operating support, operating expenses, or third-party requests.
Publications: Application guidelines.
Application information: Applications accepted. Support is limited to 1 contribution per organization during any given year. Application form required. Applicants should submit the following:
1) name, address and phone number of organization
2) contact person
Applications should include the organization's Tax ID Number and website; the name, location, expected attendance, and a brief description of the event; how many years the event has been held; and

the season ticket holder account number, and referral name, if applicable.
Initial approach: Complete online application form
Deadline(s): 6 weeks prior to need
Final notification: 2 weeks prior to need

2532
The Minster Machine Company
240 W. 5th St.
P.O. Box 120
Minster, OH 45865-0120 (419) 628-2331

Company URL: http://www.minster.com/
Establishment information: Established in 1901.
Company type: Private company
Business activities: Produces mechanical presses.
Business type (SIC): Machinery/general industry; machinery/metalworking
Corporate officers: John J. Winch, Pres.; David C. Winch, Exec. V.P., Sales and Mktg.; Stephen Kill, V.P., Human Resources
Subsidiary: Minster Automation Inc., Beaufort, SC
Giving statement: Giving through the Minster Machine Company Foundation.

The Minster Machine Company Foundation
240 W. 5th St.
Minster, OH 45865-1027 (419) 628-2331

Donor: Minster Machine Co.
Contact: John Winch
Financial data (yr. ended 11/30/11): Assets, $782,169 (M); expenditures, $15,312; qualifying distributions, $14,116; giving activities include $14,116 for 20 grants (high: $2,000; low: $100).
Purpose and activities: The foundation supports hospitals and fire departments and organizations involved with secondary and higher education, safety, children, and the fabric industry.
Fields of interest: Education; Youth development.
Type of support: General/operating support; Scholarship funds.
Geographic limitations: Giving primarily in OH.
Support limitations: No grants to individuals.
Application information: Applications accepted. Application form required.
Initial approach: Proposal
Deadline(s): None
Officers: Nancy E. Winch, Pres.; John J. Winch*, V.P.; David C. Winch, Secy.-Treas.
EIN: 346559271

2533
Minto Communities, Inc
4400 W. Sample Rd., Ste. 200
Coconut Creek, FL 33073-3450
(954) 973-4490

Company URL: http://www.minto.com
Establishment information: Established in 1955.
Company type: Private company
Business activities: Develops residential communities.
Business type (SIC): Operative builders
Financial profile for 2011: Number of employees, 80
Corporate officers: Roger Greenberg, Chair.; Michael J. Belmont, Pres.
Board of director: Roger Greenberg, Chair.
Giving statement: Giving through the Minto Foundation, Inc.

Minto Foundation, Inc.
c/o Minto Holdings, Inc.
4400 W. Sample Rd., Ste. 200
Coconut Creek, FL 33073-3473 (954) 973-4490
E-mail: communications@minto.com; URL: http://www.minto.com/corporate_citizenship.html

Establishment information: Established in 1996 in FL.
Donors: Minto Communities, Inc.; Kenneth Greenberg; Michael Greenberg.
Contact: Lilliam Costello
Financial data (yr. ended 04/30/11): Assets, $4,419,253 (M); expenditures, $268,628; qualifying distributions, $264,385; giving activities include $263,500 for 36 grants (high: $50,000; low: $500).
Purpose and activities: The foundation supports public charities and community foundations and organizations involved with education, heath care, human services, and the arts.
Fields of interest: Elementary/secondary education; Education; Cancer; Multiple sclerosis; Health organizations; Children, services; Aging, centers/services; Developmentally disabled, centers & services; Human services; Foundations (public); Foundations (community); Jewish agencies & synagogues.
Type of support: Employee volunteer services; General/operating support.
Geographic limitations: Giving primarily in FL, MA, and NC.
Support limitations: No grants to individuals.
Application information: Applications not accepted. Contributes only to pre-selected organizations.
Directors: Daniel Greenberg; Michael Greenberg; Roger Greenberg.
EIN: 650655805
Selected grants: The following grants are a representative sample of this grantmaker's funding activity:
$7,500 to Cystic Fibrosis Foundation, Bethesda, MD, 2011.
$2,500 to Alzheimers Association, Chicago, IL, 2011.
$2,500 to American Cancer Society, Atlanta, GA, 2011.
$2,500 to Cystic Fibrosis Foundation, Bethesda, MD, 2011.
$2,500 to Leukemia & Lymphoma Society, White Plains, NY, 2011.
$2,500 to Multiple Sclerosis Society, National, New York, NY, 2011.

2534
Mintz, Levin, Cohn, Ferris, Glovsky & Popeo, P.C.
1 Financial Ctr.
Boston, MA 02111-2621 (617) 542-6000

Company URL: http://www.mintz.com
Establishment information: Established in 1933.
Company type: Private company
Business activities: Operates law firm.
Business type (SIC): Legal services
Offices: Los Angeles, Palo Alto, San Diego, CA; Stamford, CT; Washington, DC; Boston, MA; New York, NY
International operations: Israel; United Kingdom
Giving statement: Giving through the Mintz, Levin, Cohn, Ferris, Glovsky & Popeo, P.C. Pro Bono Program.

Mintz, Levin, Cohn, Ferris, Glovsky & Popeo, P.C. Pro Bono Program
1 Financial Ctr.
Boston, MA 02111-2621 (617) 542-6000
E-mail: SMFinegan@mintz.com; URL: http://www.mintz.com/aboutus/8/Community_Service

Contact: Susan Finegan, Pro Bono Comm. Chair/Pro Bono Partner
Fields of interest: Legal services.
Type of support: Pro bono services - legal.
Application information: A Pro Bono Committee manages the pro bono program.

2535
Miracle-Ear, Inc.
5000 Cheshire Pkwy. N., Ste. 1
Minneapolis, MN 55446-3729
(763) 268-4000

Company URL: http://www.miracle-ear.com
Establishment information: Established in 1948.
Company type: Subsidiary of a foreign company
Business activities: Manufactures hearing aids and related products.
Business type (SIC): Medical instruments and supplies
Giving statement: Giving through the Miracle-Ear Children's Foundation.

Miracle-Ear Children's Foundation
5000 Cheshire Pkwy. N.
Plymouth, MN 55446-4103 (763) 268-4000
FAX: (763) 268-4295; URL: http://www.miracle-ear.com/childrenrequest.aspx

Establishment information: Established in 1990 in MN.
Donors: Dahlberg, Inc.; Miracle Ear Inc.; Ken and Betty Dahlberg Foundation.
Contact: Kitty Curran, Dir.
Financial data (yr. ended 12/31/11): Assets, $65,918 (M); gifts received, $11,267; expenditures, $66,178; qualifying distributions, $66,178; giving activities include $66,153 for 1 grant.
Purpose and activities: The foundation provides Miracle-Ear hearing aids to needy hearing-impaired children, aged 16 or younger.
Type of support: Donated products; Grants to individuals.
Application information: Applications accepted. Application form required.
Initial approach: Proposal
Deadline(s): None
Officers: Heinz Ruch, Pres.; Paul D'Amico, V.P.
EIN: 411677967

2536
Mississippi Power Company
2992 W. Beach Blvd.
Gulfport, MS 39501-1907 (228) 864-1211

Company URL: http://www.mississippipower.com/
Establishment information: Established in 1924.
Company type: Subsidiary of a public company

Business activities: Generates, transmits, and distributes electricity.
Business type (SIC): Electric services
Corporate officers: Edward Day VI, Pres. and C.E.O.; Moses H. Feagin, V.P., C.F.O., and Treas.; Michelle Kinsey, C.A.O.
Giving statement: Giving through the Mississippi Power Education Foundation, Inc. and the Mississippi Power Foundation, Inc.
Company EIN: 640205820

Mississippi Power Education Foundation, Inc.

P.O. Box 4079
Gulfport, MS 39502-4079 (228) 865-5925
URL: http://www.mississippipower.com/education/home.asp

Establishment information: Established in 1984 in MS; supporting organization of the Gulf Coast Community Foundation.
Donor: Mississippi Power Co.
Contact: Domenica L. Plitt, Exec. Dir.
Financial data (yr. ended 12/31/10): Assets, $11,524,106 (M); expenditures, $468,552; qualifying distributions, $337,951; giving activities include $278,247 for 82 grants (high: $25,000; low: $7).
Purpose and activities: The foundation is dedicated to supporting, promoting, and providing opportunities for excellence in education to the citizens of Mississippi.
Fields of interest: Elementary school/education; Education.
Program:
The Alan R. Barton Excellence in Teaching Awards: The foundation annually honors six outstanding teachers in grades K-12 from schools in the Mississippi Power Company service area. The award includes $3,000 for the teacher, and $3,000 to be used at the teacher's discretion for supplies, equipment, and/or professional development.
Type of support: Conferences/seminars; Curriculum development; Equipment; Program development; Scholarship funds.
Geographic limitations: Giving limited to areas of company operations in MS.
Support limitations: No support for legislative or lobbying organizations. No grants to individuals, or for electric appliances purchases, athletic field lighting installations, or any activity that would produce a tangible economic benefit to Mississippi Power Company.
Application information: Applications not accepted. The foundation is in the process of merging with the Mississippi Power Foundation.
Officers and Directors: David Mauffray, Pres.; Raymos McMillion, V.P.; Gene Lentz, Secy.; Vickie Pierce, Treas.; Rebecca Montgomery, Exec. Dir.; David Buckner; Moses Feagin; Valerie Wade.
Number of staff: 1 full-time professional; 1 full-time support.
EIN: 640707536
Selected grants: The following grants are a representative sample of this grantmaker's funding activity:
$333,333 to University of Mississippi, University, MS, 2009.
$25,000 to Lynn Meadows Discovery Center, Gulfport, MS, 2009.
$20,562 to Mississippi Gulf Coast Community College Foundation, Perkinston, MS, 2009.
$6,000 to Magnolia Park Elementary School, Ocean Springs, MS, 2009.
$5,000 to Lynn Meadows Discovery Center, Gulfport, MS, 2009.
$5,000 to Public Education Forum of Mississippi, Jackson, MS, 2009.
$5,000 to William Carey College, Hattiesburg, MS, 2009.
$2,500 to Mississippi State University Foundation, Mississippi State, MS, 2009.
$2,000 to Mississippi Gulf Coast Community College Foundation, Perkinston, MS, 2009.
$2,000 to Petal School District Education Foundation Trust, Petal, MS, 2009.

Mississippi Power Foundation, Inc.

P.O. Box 4079
Gulfport, MS 39502-4079 (228) 865-5925
FAX: (228) 865-5616; Additional tel.: (228) 865-5904

Establishment information: Established in 1997 in MS.
Donor: Mississippi Power Co.
Contact: Rebecca Montgomery, Pres.
Financial data (yr. ended 12/31/11): Assets, $17,554,274 (M); gifts received, $8,993,136; expenditures, $1,038,669; qualifying distributions, $884,030; giving activities include $884,030 for grants.
Purpose and activities: The foundation supports organizations involved with arts and culture, education, the environment, health, cancer, heart disease, housing, youth development, human services, and community development.
Fields of interest: Museums; Museums (art); Arts; Higher education; Education; Environment, natural resources; Environment, water resources; Environment, beautification programs; Environment; Health care; Cancer; Heart & circulatory diseases; Housing/shelter, repairs; Housing/shelter; Youth development, centers/clubs; American Red Cross; Children/youth, services; Human services; Nonprofit management; Community/economic development; United Ways and Federated Giving Programs.
Type of support: Annual campaigns; Building/renovation; Capital campaigns; Continuing support; Employee matching gifts; General/operating support; Program development; Scholarship funds.
Geographic limitations: Giving primarily in MS.
Support limitations: No support for lobbying or legislative organizations. No grants to individuals, or for voter registration drives, electric appliance purchases, athletic field lighting installation, or any activity that provides a tangible economic benefit to Mississippi Power Company.
Application information: Applications accepted. Application form required. Applicants should submit the following:
1) copy of IRS Determination Letter
2) listing of board of directors, trustees, officers and other key people and their affiliations
3) detailed description of project and amount of funding requested
4) copy of current year's organizational budget and/or project budget
5) listing of additional sources and amount of support

Initial approach: Contact foundation for application form
Deadline(s): None

Officers and Directors:* John Atherton*, Chair.; Rebecca Montgomery, Pres.; Moses Feagin, Secy.; Vicki L. Pierce, Treas.; Michael G. Collins; Cindy Webb.
EIN: 721370746
Selected grants: The following grants are a representative sample of this grantmaker's funding activity:
$50,262 to Mississippi State University Foundation, Mississippi State, MS, 2009. For matching grant.
$37,544 to Mississippi Power Community Connection, Gulfport, MS, 2009. For matching grant to support Salvation Army Angel Tree program.
$35,000 to Keep Mississippi Beautiful, Jackson, MS, 2009. For community clean up within MPC territory.
$30,000 to Tougaloo College, Tougaloo, MS, 2009.
$28,161 to University of Southern Mississippi Foundation, Hattiesburg, MS, 2009. For matching grant.
$24,327 to United Way of South Mississippi, Gulfport, MS, 2009. For matching grant.
$24,327 to United Way of Southeast Mississippi, Hattiesburg, MS, 2009. For matching grant.
$20,000 to Four-H Club Foundation of Mississippi, Mississippi State, MS, 2009. For United State Congressional Awards Program.
$18,688 to American Heart Association, Gulfport, MS, 2009.
$11,800 to Area Development Partnership, Hattiesburg, MS, 2009.

2537
Mitchell Industries Inc.

820 Shades Creek Pkwy., Ste. 1200
Birmingham, AL 35209-4532
(205) 802-2226
FAX: (205) 802-2227

Company URL: http://www.mitchell-industries.com/
Establishment information: Established in 2006.
Company type: Private company
Business activities: Provides temporary help services.
Business type (SIC): Personnel supply services
Corporate officers: Guy K. Mitchell, Jr., Chair. and C.E.O.; Guy K. Mitchell III, Pres. and C.O.O.; James T. Ivey, C.P.A., V.P. and C.F.O.
Board of director: Guy K. Mitchell, Jr., Chair.
Giving statement: Giving through the Mitchell Industries Foundation.

Mitchell Industries Foundation

820 Shades Creek Pkwy., Ste. 1200
Birmingham, AL 35209-4500

Establishment information: Established in 1998 in AL.
Donors: Mitchell Industries; Guy K. Mitchell, Jr.
Financial data (yr. ended 12/31/11): Assets, $13,160 (M); gifts received, $117,500; expenditures, $152,110; qualifying distributions, $150,750; giving activities include $150,750 for 27 grants (high: $50,000; low: $500).
Purpose and activities: The foundation supports organizations involved with arts and culture, education, human services, and Christianity.
Fields of interest: Museums (art); Performing arts; Performing arts, ballet; Arts; Higher education; Athletics/sports, school programs; Human services; Christian agencies & churches.
Type of support: General/operating support.
Geographic limitations: Giving primarily in AL.
Support limitations: No grants to individuals.
Application information: Applications not accepted. Contributes only to pre-selected organizations.
Officers: Guy K. Mitchell, Jr., Pres.; Katherine J. Mitchell, V.P.
Directors: Dorothy L. Mitchell; Guy K. Mitchell III; Malvina M. Whatley.
EIN: 631190038
Selected grants: The following grants are a representative sample of this grantmaker's funding activity:

$10,000 to University of Alabama, Tuscaloosa, AL, 2011.
$5,000 to Samaritans Purse, Boone, NC, 2011.

2538
Mitsubishi Electric & Electronics USA, Inc.

5900-A Katella Ave.
Cypress, CA 90630-5023 (714) 220-2500

Company URL: http://www.mitsubishielectric-usa.com
Establishment information: Established in 1973.
Company type: Subsidiary of a foreign company
Business activities: Researches, engineers, manufactures, markets, and sells electrical and electronic equipment.
Business type (SIC): Electronic and other electrical equipment and components
Financial profile for 2011: Sales volume, $3,645,331,000
Corporate officers: Akira Tasaki, Pres. and C.E.O.; Bruce Brenizer, Sr. V.P., Human Resources; Cayce Blanchard, Sr. V.P., Comms.; Ittetsu Mori, V.P. and Treas.
Giving statement: Giving through the Mitsubishi Electric America Foundation and the RTA-NC Funds, Inc.

Mitsubishi Electric America Foundation

1560 Wilson Blvd., Ste. 1150
Arlington, VA 22209-2463 (703) 276-8240
FAX: (714) 220-4855;
E-mail: kevin.webb@meus.mea.com; URL: http://www.meaf.org/index.php

Establishment information: Established in 1991 in DC.
Donor: Mitsubishi Electric Corp.
Contact: Kevin R. Webb, Exec. Dir.
Financial data (yr. ended 12/31/11): Assets, $17,809,495 (M); expenditures, $817,379; qualifying distributions, $445,558; giving activities include $445,558 for grants.
Purpose and activities: The foundation supports programs designed to advance the independence, productivity, and community of young people with disabilities. Special emphasis is directed toward programs designed to promote inclusion.
Fields of interest: Education, equal rights; Education; Employment, services; Independent living, disability; Leadership development Children; Youth; Disabilities, people with; Physically disabled.
Programs:
Inclusion: The foundation supports programs designed to enable young people with disabilities to have full access to educational, vocational, and recreational opportunities and to participate alongside their non-disabled peers.
M.O.V.E. Award: The foundation annually honors the most outstanding volunteer project organized by employees of a Mitsubishi Electric company in the U.S. The award includes a crystal trophy and a $1,000 donation to the benefiting charity.
Matching Grants: The foundation matches contributions made by employees of Mitsubishi Electric to nonprofit organizations on a two-for-one basis and awards grants of $10 per hour to nonprofit organizations with which employees volunteer.
National Grants: Through the National Grant program, the foundation supports full inclusion projects for disabled youth that are national in scope and impact or projects that are replicable at multiple sites.
Starfish Matching Gifts: The foundation matches contributions made by employees of Mitsubishi Electric to nonprofit organizations involved with disabled youth on a one-for-one basis from $25 to $500 per employee, per year.
Type of support: Curriculum development; Employee matching gifts; Employee volunteer services; General/operating support; Program development; Seed money.
Geographic limitations: Giving on a national basis, with emphasis on areas of company operations, with emphasis on CA, Washington, DC, GA, IL, KY, MA, MI, OH, PA, TN, and VA; giving also to national organizations.
Support limitations: No support for religious organizations not of direct benefit to the entire community, intermediary organizations, fraternal, labor, political, or lobbying organizations, discriminatory organizations, or individual schools or school districts. No grants to individuals, or for endowments, capital campaigns, equipment or devices for individual users, fundraising events, controversial social or political issues, or local activities without national impact; no loans or product donations.
Publications: Application guidelines; Grants list; Informational brochure (including application guidelines); Multi-year report.
Application information: Applications accepted. The foundation is in the process of revising its grant giving priorities and guidelines. Visit website for updated information. Telephone calls during the application process are not encouraged. Application form required.
Initial approach: Concept paper
Board meeting date(s): Fall
Deadline(s): June 1 for concept paper; July 1 for full proposal
Final notification: 1 month
Officers and Directors:* Katsuya Takamiya*, Pres.; Helaine Lobman, Esq., Secy.; Ittetsu Mori, Treas.; Kevin R. Webb, Exec. Dir.; Cayce Blanchard; Bruce Brenizer; Mike DeLano; Jack Greaf; Nobushi Moro-oka; Perry Pappous; David Rebmann; Susan Renda; Veronica Vasilik; Richard C. Waters; Jeff Whitelaw; Kenichiro Yamanishi.
Number of staff: 2 full-time professional.
EIN: 521700855
Selected grants: The following grants are a representative sample of this grantmaker's funding activity:
$210,000 to University of California, Tarjan Center, Los Angeles, CA, 2012. For Include Students in Entrepreneurial Leadership Programs for youth with disabilities.
$165,000 to American Association of People with Disabilities, Washington, DC, 2012. For AAPD Summer Internship Program.
$150,000 to Girl Scouts of the U.S.A., Council of the Nation's Capital, Washington, DC, 2012. For Include All Girls Initiative to develop inclusion tools and identify best practices from other Councils, disseminating those tools and practices to Councils throughout the Unites States.
$60,000 to Partners for Youth with Disabilities, Boston, MA, 2012. To develop Mentoring for All project to help Big Brothers Big Sisters develop strategies to ensure youth with disabilities have mentoring opportunities and professional role models.
$55,470 to University of New Hampshire, Durham, NH, 2012. To create Autistic Campus Leadership Academy for autistic college students.
$35,000 to American Association of People with Disabilities, Washington, DC, 2012. To expand Disability Mentoring Day into Piplines of Talent Project.
$25,000 to National Inclusion Project, Research Triangle Park, NC, 2012. For I am Norm: Redefining Normal, Promoting Inclusion national campaign.

RTA-NC Funds, Inc.

(formerly Mitsubishi Semiconductor America, Inc. Funds)
7412 Lakefall Dr.
Wake Forest, NC 27587-5777 (919) 948-4111
Application address: 1708 Wallace St., Durham, NC 27707

Establishment information: Established in 1988 in NC.
Donor: Mitsubishi Semiconductor America, Inc.
Contact: Pat Hefferan, Pres. and Secy.
Financial data (yr. ended 12/31/10): Assets, $1,404,255 (M); expenditures, $137,009; qualifying distributions, $120,000; giving activities include $120,000 for 8 grants (high: $50,000; low: $5,000).
Purpose and activities: The foundation supports organizations involved with education, patient services, children and youth, and disability services.
Fields of interest: Higher education; Engineering school/education; Education, reading; Education; Health care, patient services; Children/youth, services; Developmentally disabled, centers & services.
Type of support: Continuing support; General/operating support; Program development; Scholarship funds.
Geographic limitations: Giving primarily in Durham and Raleigh, NC.
Support limitations: No grants to individuals.
Application information: Applications accepted. Application form required.
Initial approach: Contact foundation for application form
Copies of proposal: 1
Deadline(s): May 1
Officers: Pat Hefferan, Pres. and Secy.; Kim Evans, Treas.
Director: Gary Edge.
EIN: 561637250

2539
Mitsubishi International Corporation

(also known as MIC)
655 3rd Ave., Fl. 4
New York, NY 10017 (212) 605-2000

Company URL: http://www.mitsubishicorp.com
Establishment information: Established in 1954.
Company type: Subsidiary of a foreign company
Business activities: Operates holding company; operates trading company.
Business type (SIC): Investors/miscellaneous; holding company
Financial profile for 2010: Number of employees, 328; sales volume, $2,370,000,000
Corporate officers: Yasuyuki Sugiura, Pres., and C.E.O.; Katsuhiro Ito, Sr. V.P., C.F.O., and C.I.O.; Yuzo Nouchi, V.P., Treas. and Cont.; Jason Stevens, V.P. and Secy.
Board of directors: Yasuyuki Sugiura; Hideto Nakahara; Masaru Oda; Osamu Sasaki
Giving statement: Giving through the Mitsubishi International Corporation Contributions Program and the Mitsubishi Corporation Foundation for the Americas.

Mitsubishi International Corporation Contributions Program

655 3rd Ave.
New York, NY 10017-5617 (212) 605-2000
URL: http://www.mitsubishicorp.com/us/en/csr/

Purpose and activities: As a complement to its foundation, Mitsubishi International also makes charitable contributions to nonprofit organizations directly. Special emphasis is directed towards programs designed to promote Japanese arts and culture. Support is given primarily in areas of company operations, with emphasis on New York, New York.
Fields of interest: Arts, cultural/ethnic awareness; Arts; General charitable giving.
Program:
Employee Matching Gifts: Mitsubishi International matches charitable contributions made by its employees to nonprofit organizations on a two-for-one basis up to $1,000 per employee, per year.
Type of support: Employee matching gifts; Employee volunteer services; General/operating support; Program development; Sponsorships.
Geographic limitations: Giving primarily in areas of company operations, with emphasis on New York, NY.
Application information:
Number of staff: 3 part-time professional; 1 part-time support.

Mitsubishi Corporation Foundation for the Americas

(also known as MC Foundation for the Americas)
(formerly Mitsubishi International Corporation Foundation)
c/o Mitsubishi International Corp.
655 3rd Ave.
New York, NY 10017-5617
FAX: (212) 605-1856;
E-mail: mic.foundation@org.mitsubishicorp.com;
E-mail for Tracy Austin:
tracy.austin@mitsubishicorp.com; Additional contact: Joseph Reganato, Secy. and Prog. Off, e-mail: joseph.reganato@mitsubishicorp.com;
URL: http://www.mitsubishicorp.com/us/en/csr/foundation.html

Establishment information: Established in 1992 in NY.
Donors: Mitsubishi Corp.; Mitsubishi International Corp.
Contact: Tracy Austin, Exec. Dir.
Financial data (yr. ended 12/31/11): Assets, $4,081,361 (M); expenditures, $69,365; qualifying distributions, $43,025; giving activities include $27,350 for 1 grant.
Purpose and activities: The foundation supports programs designed to promote the physical and social environments in which we live. Special emphasis is directed toward biodiversity conservation; sustainable development; environmental justice; and environmental education.
Fields of interest: Environment, natural resources; Environment, water resources; Environment, land resources; Environment, forests; Botanical gardens; Environmental education; Environment; Civil/human rights.
International interests: Latin America.
Type of support: Conferences/seminars; Continuing support; Employee volunteer services; General/operating support; Land acquisition; Mission-related investments/loans; Program development; Program-related investments/loans; Research; Sponsorships.
Geographic limitations: Giving primarily in the Americas, with emphasis on areas of company operations; giving also in Latin America.
Support limitations: No support for religious, political, or lobbying organizations, or discriminatory organizations. No grants to individuals.
Publications: Application guidelines; Grants list.
Application information: Applications accepted. Letters of inquiry should be brief. The foundation gives preference to programs where Mitsubishi has a strong presence or where there is an opportunity for employee volunteerism. Application form not required. Applicants should submit the following:
1) name, address and phone number of organization
2) copy of IRS Determination Letter
3) how project's results will be evaluated or measured
4) descriptive literature about organization
5) detailed description of project and amount of funding requested
6) contact person
7) copy of current year's organizational budget and/or project budget
8) listing of additional sources and amount of support

Letters of inquiry should include the fax number and e-mail address of the contact person.
Initial approach: Letter of inquiry
Copies of proposal: 1
Board meeting date(s): Fall
Deadline(s): None
Final notification: Summer
Officers and Directors:* Koichi Komatsu*, Chair.; Seiei Ono*, Pres.; Joseph Reganato, Secy. and Prog. Off.; Yuzo Nouchi, Treas.; Tracy L. Austin*, Exec. Dir.; Minoru Akita; Katsuhiro Ito; Seiji Shiraki; Yasuyuki Sugiura; Tetsuro Terada.
Number of staff: 3 part-time professional; 1 part-time support.
EIN: 133676166

2540
Mitsubishi Motors North America, Inc.

(formerly Mitsubishi Motor Sales of America, Inc.)
6400 Katella Ave.
P.O. Box 6014
Cypress, CA 90630-0064 (714) 372-6000

Company URL: http://www.mitsubishicars.com
Establishment information: Established in 1981.
Company type: Subsidiary of a foreign company
Business activities: Manufactures, markets, and distributes automobiles; provides automobile financing services.
Business type (SIC): Motor vehicles and equipment; credit institutions/personal
Corporate officers: Yoichi Yokozawa, Pres. and C.E.O.; Dan Booth, Exec. V.P. and C.F.O.; John Koenig, Exec. V.P., Opers.; Akinobu Saito, Exec. V.P.and Treas.
Subsidiary: Mitusubishi Motors Credit of America, Inc., Cypress, CA
Giving statement: Giving through the Mitsubishi Motors North America, Inc. Corporate Giving Program and the Mitsubishi Motors USA Foundation.

Mitsubishi Motors USA Foundation

6400 Katella Ave.
Cypress, CA 90630-5208

Establishment information: Established in 1997 in DE and MI.
Donor: Mitsubishi Motors America, Inc.
Financial data (yr. ended 12/31/11): Assets, $1,429,688 (M); expenditures, $127,355; qualifying distributions, $127,000; giving activities include $127,000 for grants.
Purpose and activities: The foundation supports programs designed to promote workplace diversity and provide workplace diversity education and information; provide workplace advocacy for women and minorities; and recognize women and minorities who have demonstrated outstanding leadership in their communities.
Fields of interest: Human services; Civil/human rights.
Type of support: General/operating support.
Support limitations: No grants to individuals.
Application information: Applications not accepted. Unsolicited requests for funds not accepted.
Officers and Directors: Shinichi Kurihara*, Chair.; Dan Irvin*, Pres.; Kazuki Sato*, V.P.; John McElroy, Secy.; Dan Booth*, Treas.; Dan Irvin.
EIN: 330773994

2541
Mitsui & Co. (U.S.A.), Inc.

200 Park Ave., Fl. 35
New York, NY 10166-3599 (212) 878-4000

Company URL: http://www.mitsui.com
Establishment information: Established in 1966.
Company type: Subsidiary of a foreign company
Business activities: Operates trading company.
Business type (SIC): Investors/miscellaneous
Financial profile for 2010: Sales volume, $10,742,690,000
Corporate officers: Mitsuhiko Kawai, Pres. and C.E.O.; Toshio Mukai, Sr. V.P. and C.F.O.; Annette Caudiano, Mgr.
Plants: Los Angeles, San Francisco, CA; Washington, DC; Miami, FL; Atlanta, GA; Chicago, IL; Lafayette, IN; Lexington, KY; Southfield, MI; Cleveland, OH; Portland, OR; Nashville, TN; Houston, Irving, TX; Seattle, WA
Giving statement: Giving through the Mitsui U.S.A. Foundation.

The Mitsui U.S.A. Foundation

200 Park Ave.
New York, NY 10166-0001
URL: http://www.mitsui.com/us/en/index.html

Establishment information: Established in 1987 in NY.
Donors: Mitsui & Co. (U.S.A.), Inc.; Intercontinental Terminals Co. LCC.
Financial data (yr. ended 03/31/12): Assets, $15,931,330 (M); gifts received, $39,250; expenditures, $790,767; qualifying distributions, $653,115; giving activities include $653,115 for grants.
Purpose and activities: The foundation supports programs designed to promote education; community welfare and disabled individuals welfare; and arts and culture. Special emphasis is directed toward programs designed to promote international understanding and deepen U.S.-Japan relations.
Fields of interest: Arts education; Arts; Education; Human services; International exchange, students; International affairs; Community/economic development Disabilities, people with.
Programs:
Employee Matching Gift Program: The foundation matches contributions made by full-time employees of Mitsui & Co. (U.S.A.) to nonprofit organizations from $25 to $1,000 per employee, per year.

Mitsui USA Scholars of CUNY: The foundation annually awards two $5,000 scholarships to students in the Business and Liberal Arts Program (BALA) undergoing undergraduate studies at Queens College, and the Weissman Center for International Business undergoing MBA studies at Baruch College. The scholarships are administered by Queens College and Baruch College.

Mitsui USA Sons and Daughters Scholarship: The foundation awards up to 10 $5,000 college scholarships to children of employees of Mitsui & Co. (U.S.A.).

YFU/Mitsui SA "Student Ambassador" to Japan: The foundation, in collaboration with Youth for Understanding (YFU), sponsors and awards scholarships to children of employees of Mitsui & Co. (U.S.A.) and local community students located in areas where Mitsui USA does business, for summer visits to host-families in Japan for complete immersion into day-to-day life, or all aspects of family and social life.

Type of support: Conferences/seminars; Employee matching gifts; Employee volunteer services; Employee-related scholarships; Exchange programs; Fellowships; Scholarship funds; Scholarships—to individuals; Sponsorships.
Geographic limitations: Giving primarily in areas of company operations in Los Angeles, CA, Chicago, IL, and New York, NY.
Support limitations: No support for discriminatory organizations, religious, fraternal, veterans', or athletic organizations, or political and lobbying groups. No grants to individuals (except for scholarships), or for endowments, building campaigns, advertisements, film or television productions, social events, galas, or dinner tables or tickets; no in-kind or non-monetary support.
Publications: Informational brochure.
Application information: Applications not accepted. Contributes only to pre-selected organizations.
Officers and Directors:* Shinichi Hirabayashi*, C.E.O. and Pres.; Eric Campbell, V.P.; Glenn Clarke; Yoshiyuki Kawashima.
EIN: 133415220
Selected grants: The following grants are a representative sample of this grantmaker's funding activity:
$100,000 to Council on Foreign Relations, New York, NY, 2011.
$76,250 to Scholarship America, Saint Peter, MN, 2011.
$38,750 to Scholarship America, Saint Peter, MN, 2011.
$30,000 to New York City Partnership Foundation, New York, NY, 2011.
$10,000 to Columbia University, New York, NY, 2011.
$5,000 to University of Utah, Salt Lake City, UT, 2011.

2542
Mizuho Corporate Bank (USA)

(formerly The Industrial Bank of Japan Trust Company)
1251 Ave. of the Americas
New York, NY 10020 (212) 282-3030

Company URL: http://www.mizuhocbk.com/americas/index.html
Establishment information: Established in 1974.
Company type: Subsidiary of a foreign company
Business activities: Operates foreign bank.
Business type (SIC): Banks/foreign
Corporate officers: Shinya Wako, Chair.; Hideki Shirato, Pres. and C.E.O.
Board of director: Shinya Wako, Chair.
Giving statement: Giving through the Mizuho USA Foundation, Inc.

Mizuho USA Foundation, Inc.

(formerly The IBJ Foundation, Inc.)
1251 Ave. of the Americas, 31st Fl.
New York, NY 10020-1104 (212) 282-4192
FAX: (212) 282-4250;
E-mail: mizuho.usa.foundation@mizuhocbus.com;
URL: http://www.mizuhocbk.com/americas/community/foundation/index.html

Establishment information: Established in 1989 in NY.
Donors: The Industrial Bank of Japan Trust Co.; Mizuho Corporate Bank (USA); The Industrial Bank of Japan, Ltd.; Mizuho Securities USA Inc.; DKB Foundation.
Contact: Lesley Palmer, Exec. Dir.
Financial data (yr. ended 12/31/12): Assets, $13,600,504 (M); gifts received, $82,203; expenditures, $810,534; qualifying distributions, $735,104; giving activities include $564,110 for grants and $113,665 for employee matching gifts.
Purpose and activities: The foundation supports organizations involved with workforce development, affordable housing, and economic development. Special emphasis is directed toward programs designed to promote the development of urban neighborhoods.
Fields of interest: Employment, training; Employment; Housing/shelter, home owners; Housing/shelter; Human services, financial counseling; Homeless, human services; Community/economic development, management/technical assistance; Community development, neighborhood development; Economic development; Community development, small businesses; Community/economic development Economically disadvantaged.
Programs:

Fostering Economic Self-Sufficiency: The foundation supports programs designed to promote workforce development through technical assistance and/or training; and programs designed to assist low- and moderate-income individuals in the development of skills essential to self-sufficiency, with emphasis on work-entry programs, employment retention, career advancement, and personal financial education.

Mizuho Community Involvement Grants Program: The foundation awards grants to nonprofit organizations with which employees of Mizuho volunteer.

Mizuho Matching Gift Program: The foundation matches contributions made by Mizuho employees on a one-for-one basis to nonprofit organizations.

Promoting Economic Development: The foundation supports programs designed to promote economic and commercial revitalization through business development, entrepreneurship, job creation, and job retention. The foundation is particularly interested in capacity-building efforts that improve the ability of organizations to provide needed services to organizations and individuals.

Strengthening Affordable Housing: The foundation supports programs designed to facilitate access to affordable housing for low- and moderate-income individuals and families. Special emphasis is directed toward preservation and first-time homeownership, including educational and training programs in homeownership counseling, home maintenance, and foreclosure prevention. The foundation also supports initiatives to advance "green" affordable housing.

Type of support: Continuing support; Employee matching gifts; Employee volunteer services; Management development/capacity building; Program development; Seed money; Technical assistance.
Geographic limitations: Giving limited to New York, NY.
Support limitations: No support for discriminatory, religious or sectarian, fraternal, veterans', labor, athletic, or political organizations. No grants to individuals, or for building or construction, capital campaigns, general operating support, endowments, capital campaigns, fundraising, dinners, benefits, sporting events, journal advertising, or tickets.
Publications: Application guidelines; Grants list; Informational brochure (including application guidelines).
Application information: Applications accepted. Concept paper should be no longer than 3 pages and may be submitted using the NY/NJ Common Area Application Form. A full proposal may be requested at a later date. Multi-year funding is not automatic. Application form not required. Applicants should submit the following:

1) timetable for implementation and evaluation of project
2) population served
3) copy of IRS Determination Letter
4) brief history of organization and description of its mission
5) geographic area to be served
6) how project's results will be evaluated or measured
7) detailed description of project and amount of funding requested
8) copy of current year's organizational budget and/or project budget

Initial approach: Mail concept paper
Copies of proposal: 1
Board meeting date(s): Nov.
Deadline(s): 1st weekday in July
Final notification: Within 8 weeks following deadlines

Officers and Directors:* Merlin E. Nelson*, Chair.; Hideki Shirato*, Pres.; Koji Nishiwaki*, Secy.; Paul Dankers, Treas.; Lesley Palmer, Exec. Dir.; Leah Markham, Prog. Off.; John H. Higgs; Shinya Wako.
Number of staff: None.
EIN: 133550008
Selected grants: The following grants are a representative sample of this grantmaker's funding activity:
$100,000 to Nonprofit Finance Fund, New York, NY, 2012. For New York City Community Resilience Fund.
$76,000 to Financial Clinic, New York, NY, 2012. For New Ground: A Foundation to Build Wealth Pilot Program.
$75,000 to Center for New York City Neighborhoods, New York, NY, 2012. For Housing Mobility Pilot Program.
$75,000 to Womens Housing and Economic Development Corporation, Bronx, NY, 2012. For Childcare Improvement Project.
$50,000 to New York City Workforce Development Fund, New York, NY, 2012. For New York Alliance for Careers in Healthcare.
$50,000 to Trust for Public Land, New York, NY, 2012. For New York City Playgrounds Program.
$40,000 to Pratt Center for Community Development, Brooklyn, NY, 2012. For Retrofit Block by Block: Standardizing Retrofits in NYC's Small Homes.
$35,000 to ACCION USA, New York, NY, 2012. For Certified Credit Counselor Pilot Program.

2543
MN Airlines, LLC
(doing business as Sun Country Airlines)
1300 Mendota Heights Rd.
Mendota Heights, MN 55120
(651) 681-3900

Company URL: http://www.suncountry.com
Establishment information: Established in 1982.
Company type: Subsidiary of a private company
Business activities: Operates airline.
Business type (SIC): Transportation/scheduled air
Financial profile for 2009: Number of employees, 750
Corporate officers: Stanley J. Gadek, Chair., Pres., and C.E.O.; Deb Bauman, C.I.O.
Board of director: Stanley J. Gadek, Chair.
Giving statement: Giving through the Sun Country Airlines Foundation.

Sun Country Airlines Foundation
1300 Mendota Hts. Rd.
Mendota Heights, MN 55120-1128

Establishment information: Established in 2004 in MN.
Donors: Raymond Lipkin; M.N. Airlines, LLC.
Financial data (yr. ended 12/31/11): Assets, $3,135 (M); gifts received, $35,652; expenditures, $35,465; qualifying distributions, $35,100; giving activities include $35,100 for grants.
Type of support: Employee-related scholarships.
Geographic limitations: Giving primarily in MN.
Application information: Applications not accepted. Unsolicited requests for funds not accepted.
Officers: John Fredericksen; Stanley Gadek; Thomas Hay.
EIN: 470943188

2544
Modine Manufacturing Company
1500 DeKoven Ave.
Racine, WI 53403-2552 (262) 636-1200
FAX: (262) 636-1424

Company URL: http://www.modine.com
Establishment information: Established in 1916.
Company type: Public company
Company ticker symbol and exchange: MOD/NYSE
Business activities: Develops, manufactures, and markets thermal management products, components, and systems.
Business type (SIC): Motor vehicles and equipment
Financial profile for 2012: Number of employees, 6,500; assets, $893,460,000; sales volume, $1,577,150,000; pre-tax net income, $47,910,000; expenses, $1,509,630,000; liabilities, $568,550,000
Corporate officers: Gary L. Neale, Chair.; Thomas A. Burke, Pres. and C.E.O.; Thomas F. Marry, Exec. V.P. and C.O.O.; Michael B. Lucareli, V.P., Finance and C.F.O.; Margaret C. Kelsey, V.P., Genl. Counsel, and Secy.; Kathleen T. Powers, V.P. and Treas.
Board of directors: Gary L. Neale, Chair.; David J. Anderson; Thomas A. Burke; Charles P. Cooley; Suresh V. Garimella; Larry O. Moore; Christopher W. Patterson; Mary L. Petrovich; Marsha C. Williams
Plants: McHenry, IL; Logansport, IN; Washington, IA; Harrodsburg, KY; Jackson, MS; Camdenton, Jefferson City, Joplin, Trenton, MO; Pemberville, OH; West Kingston, RI; Lawrenceburg, TN; Buena Vista, VA
International operations: Australia; Austria; Barbados; Brazil; China; Germany; Hong Kong; Hungary; India; Italy; Japan; Mexico; Netherlands; South Africa; Taiwan; United Kingdom
Giving statement: Giving through the Modine Manufacturing Company Foundation, Inc.
Company EIN: 390482000

Modine Manufacturing Company Foundation, Inc.
1500 DeKoven Ave.
Racine, WI 53403-2540 (262) 636-1200
URL: http://www.modine.com/v2portal/page/portal/modine/modineAboutModineDefault/modine_com/about/level_2_content_036.htm

Establishment information: Established in 1995 in WI.
Donor: Modine Manufacturing Co.
Contact: Valerie Madala
Financial data (yr. ended 03/31/12): Assets, $5,930 (M); gifts received, $219,512; expenditures, $219,894; qualifying distributions, $219,894; giving activities include $219,698 for 13 grants (high: $50,904; low: $1,924).
Purpose and activities: The foundation supports organizations involved with arts and culture, education, health, human services, community development, and civic affairs.
Fields of interest: Performing arts; Historic preservation/historical societies; Arts; Elementary/secondary education; Higher education; Education; Health care; Human services; Business/industry; Community/economic development; United Ways and Federated Giving Programs; Mathematics; Engineering/technology; Science; Public affairs Economically disadvantaged.
Program:
Modine Scholars Program: The foundation awards college scholarships of $1,000 to $2,500 to children of employees of Modine Manufacturing or Modine Manufacturing subsidiaries. The program is administered by the National Merit Scholarship Corp.
Type of support: Building/renovation; Capital campaigns; Continuing support; Employee volunteer services; Employee-related scholarships; Matching/challenge support; Program development; Scholarship funds; Sponsorships.
Geographic limitations: Giving limited to areas of company operations, with emphasis on Racine, WI.
Support limitations: No support for religious or political organizations, organizations lacking a business plan, political parties or candidates, or discriminatory organizations. No grants for travel or debt reduction.
Publications: Application guidelines.
Application information: Applications accepted. Support is limited to 1 contribution per organization during any given year. Multi-year finding is not automatic. Multi-year grants are limited to 5 years in length. Application form required. Applicants should submit the following:
1) copy of IRS Determination Letter
Initial approach: Contact foundation website www.modline.com for application form
Copies of proposal: 1
Board meeting date(s): Quarterly
Deadline(s): Quaterly on May 31, Jun. 31, Sept. 30, and Dec. 31
Final notification: 1 to 2 months
Officers and Directors:* Thomas A. Burke*, Pres.; Margaret C. Kelsey*, V.P. and Secy.; Michael B. Lucareli*, V.P. and Treas.
EIN: 391818362

Selected grants: The following grants are a representative sample of this grantmaker's funding activity:
$42,637 to United Way of Racine County, Racine, WI, 2011.
$40,000 to United Way of Racine County, Racine, WI, 2011.
$40,000 to United Way of Racine County, Racine, WI, 2011.
$40,000 to United Way of Racine County, Racine, WI, 2011.
$40,000 to United Way of Racine County, Racine, WI, 2011.
$21,650 to United Way of Central Missouri, Jefferson City, MO, 2011.
$5,000 to Medical College of Wisconsin, Milwaukee, WI, 2011.
$5,000 to United Way of Racine County, Racine, WI, 2011.
$3,901 to United Way of Rockbridge, Lexington, VA, 2011.
$2,000 to Racine Unified School District, Racine, WI, 2011.

2545
Mohawk Industries, Inc.
160 S. Industrial Blvd.
P.O. Box 12069
Calhoun, GA 30701 (706) 629-7721
FAX: (302) 655-5049

Company URL: http://www.mohawkind.com
Establishment information: Established in 1988.
Company type: Public company
Company ticker symbol and exchange: MHK/NYSE
Business activities: Manufactures commercial and residential carpets, rugs, and other floor coverings.
Business type (SIC): Carpets and rugs
Financial profile for 2012: Number of employees, 25,100; assets, $6,303,680,000; sales volume, $5,787,980,000; pre-tax net income, $304,490,000; expenses, $5,408,470,000; liabilities, $2,584,070,000
Fortune 1000 ranking: 2012—442nd in revenues, 523rd in profits, and 528th in assets
Forbes 2000 ranking: 2012—1309th in sales, 1468th in profits, and 1733rd in assets
Corporate officers: Jeffrey S. Lorberbaum, Chair. and C.E.O.; W. Christopher Wellborn, Pres. and C.O.O.; Frank A. Boykin, C.F.O.; James F. Brunk, C.A.O. and Corp. Cont.; James T. Lucke, V.P., Genl. Counsel and Secy.
Board of directors: Jeffrey S. Lorberbaum, Chair.; Bruce C. Bruckmann; Frans G. De Cock; John F. Fiedler; Joseph A. Onorato; C. Richard III; Karen A. Smith-Bogart; Christopher Wellborn
Giving statement: Giving through the Mohawk Carpet Foundation, Inc.
Company EIN: 521604305

Mohawk Carpet Foundation, Inc.
P.O. Box 1448
Dalton, GA 30722-1448
FAX: (706) 272-4996;
E-mail: mowhawkfoundation@mohawkind.com

Establishment information: Established in 1991 in GA.
Donor: Mohawk Industries, Inc.
Contact: Robert Webb, Pres.
Financial data (yr. ended 12/31/11): Assets, $407,465 (M); gifts received, $1,250,000; expenditures, $1,301,231; qualifying distributions, $1,295,540; giving activities include $1,295,540 for grants.

Purpose and activities: The foundation improves the quality of life for Mohawk employees and their families through partnerships with nonprofit service providers.
Fields of interest: Arts; Higher education; Health care; Youth development; Community/economic development.
Type of support: Annual campaigns; Building/renovation; Emergency funds; Employee matching gifts; General/operating support; Matching/challenge support.
Geographic limitations: Giving primarily in AL, GA, NC, SC, and VA in communities where the company operates manufacturing facilities.
Support limitations: No support for houses of worship, individual schools or political organizations. No grants, loans, or scholarships to individuals, or for professorships, fellowships, internship funds, or land acquisition.
Application information: Applications accepted. Application form required. Applicants should submit the following:
1) brief history of organization and description of its mission
2) copy of IRS Determination Letter
3) detailed description of project and amount of funding requested
Initial approach: Application
Copies of proposal: 1
Deadline(s): Dec. 1
Final notification: By Jan. 4 of following year
Officers: Robert Webb, Pres.; Frank Boykin, V.P.; Suzanne Alcocer, Secy.; Scott Veldman, Treas.
EIN: 581902607
Selected grants: The following grants are a representative sample of this grantmaker's funding activity:
$130,000 to United Way of Northwest Georgia, Dalton, GA, 2010.
$117,500 to Creative Arts Guild, Dalton, GA, 2010.
$90,000 to Creative Arts Guild, Dalton, GA, 2010.
$75,000 to Creative Arts Guild, Dalton, GA, 2010.
$50,000 to Northwest Georgia Healthcare Partnership, Dalton, GA, 2010.
$25,000 to United Way of Gordon County, Calhoun, GA, 2010.
$11,000 to United Way of the Piedmont, Spartanburg, SC, 2010.
$10,000 to Robert W. Woodruff Arts Center, Atlanta, GA, 2010.
$10,000 to United Way of Marlboro County, Bennettsville, SC, 2010.
$3,000 to John W. Looper Jr. Speech and Hearing Center, Dalton, GA, 2010.

2546
Mohegan Basketball Club, LLC

(also known as Connecticut Sun)
1 Mohegan Sun Blvd.
Uncasville, CT 06382-1355 (860) 862-4000

Company URL: http://www.wnba.com/sun
Establishment information: Established in 2003.
Company type: Subsidiary of a private company
Business activities: Operates professional basketball club.
Business type (SIC): Commercial sports
Corporate officers: Mitchell Etess, C.E.O.; Jeffrey E. Hartman, Exec. V.P., Mktg. and C.F.O.
Giving statement: Giving through the Connecticut Sun Corporate Giving Program.

Connecticut Sun Corporate Giving Program

c/o Community Appearance Requests
1 Mohegan Sun Blvd.
Uncasville, CT 06382-1355
FAX: (860) 862-4010; URL: http://www.wnba.com/sun/community

Purpose and activities: The Connecticut Sun makes charitable contributions to nonprofit organizations. Support is given primarily in southern New England.
Fields of interest: Education; Athletics/sports, basketball; Recreation; Youth, services; Family services.
Type of support: Donated products; Employee volunteer services; In-kind gifts.
Geographic limitations: Giving primarily in southern New England.
Support limitations: No grants for operating expenses, or donated autographed merchandise for prizes, volunteer recognition gifts, or giveaways.
Publications: Application guidelines.
Application information: Applications accepted. Proposals should be submitted using organization letterhead. Support is limited to 1 contribution per organization during any given year. The Community Relations Department handles giving for events and requests. Phone calls are discouraged. Application form required. Applicants should submit the following:
1) copy of IRS Determination Letter
2) detailed description of project and amount of funding requested
3) geographic area to be served
4) name, address and phone number of organization
Proposals should include the date, name, and location of the event, estimated attendance, confirmed speakers, plans for promotion, video technology to be used, the representatives(s) requested, and the time frame they are requested to attend. Requests for autographed memorabilia are limited to auction and/or raffle prizes.
Initial approach: Download application and mail or fax completed proposal to headquarters
Copies of proposal: 1
Deadline(s): 60 days prior to need
Final notification: 5 days after the application is received and reviewed, and 21 days prior to the event
Number of staff: 1 full-time professional.

2547
Moka Joe Coffee

2118 James St.
Bellingham, WA 98225 (360) 714-1953

Company URL: http://www.mokajoe.com
Company type: Private company
Business activities: Operates wholesale coffee roasting company.
Business type (SIC): Miscellaneous prepared foods
Corporate officer: Trudy Scherting, Pres.
Giving statement: Giving through the Moka Joe Coffee Corporate Giving Program.

Moka Joe Coffee Corporate Giving Program

2118 James St.
Bellingham, WA 98225-4140 (360) 714-1953
E-mail: mokajoe@comcast.net; Application address: 1050 Larrabee Ave., Ste. 104, PMB 721, Bellingham WA 98225; URL: http://www.mokajoe.com/about.html

Purpose and activities: Moka Joe Coffee is a certified B Corporation that donates a percentage of sales to benefit the Clean Water Foundation.
Fields of interest: Environment, water resources.
Type of support: General/operating support.
Application information: Applications not accepted. Contributes only to pre-selected organizations.

2548
Molly Maid, Inc.

3948 Ranchero Dr.
Ann Arbor, MI 48108 (734) 822-6800
FAX: (734) 822-6888

Company URL: http://www.mollymaid.com
Establishment information: Established in 1979.
Company type: Subsidiary of a private company
Business activities: Provides maid services.
Business type (SIC): Services to dwellings
Corporate officers: David G. McKinnon, Chair. and C.E.O.; Meg Roberts, Pres.
Board of director: David G. McKinnon, Chair.
Giving statement: Giving through the Ms. Molly Foundation.

Ms. Molly Foundation

c/o Molly Maid, Inc.
3948 Ranchero Dr.
Ann Arbor, MI 48108-2775 (800) 886-6559
FAX: (734) 822-6888; URL: http://www.mollymaid.com/MainMsMollyFoundation.aspx

Establishment information: Established in 1996 in MI.
Financial data (yr. ended 06/30/11): Revenue, $202,434; assets, $42,111 (M); gifts received, $142,470; expenditures, $188,827; giving activities include $178,160 for grants.
Purpose and activities: The foundation is dedicated to assisting victims and families affected by domestic violence through its support of hundreds of local shelters and safe houses across America providing refuge and personal care items to victims of domestic violence.
Fields of interest: Crime/violence prevention, domestic violence; Family services, domestic violence; Residential/custodial care.
Geographic limitations: Giving on a national basis.
Officers: Danessa Itaya, Pres.; David Dickinson, V.P.; Michelle Mikosz, Secy.; Ted Kennedy, Treas.; Shelley Blaszak, Dir. and C.F.O.; Mary Dickinson; Bill Foley; Donna Reilly; David Taccolini.
EIN: 383290026

2549
Molson Coors Brewing Company

(formerly Adolph Coors Company)
1225 17th St., Ste. 3200
Denver, CO 80202 (303) 927-2337
FAX: (302) 655-5049

Company URL: http://www.coors.com
Establishment information: Established in 1873.
Company type: Public company
Company ticker symbol and exchange: TAP/NYSE
International Securities Identification Number: US60871R2094
Business activities: Operates brewing company.
Business type (SIC): Beverages

Financial profile for 2012: Number of employees, 18,700; assets, $16,212,200,000; sales volume, $3,916,500,000; pre-tax net income, $592,100,000; expenses, $3,049,100,000; liabilities, $8,245,300,000
Fortune 1000 ranking: 2012—598th in revenues, 363rd in profits, and 282nd in assets
Forbes 2000 ranking: 2012—1521st in sales, 1297th in profits, and 1114th in assets
Corporate officers: Andrew T. Molson, Chair.; Peter H. Coors, Vice-Chair.; Peter Swinburn, Pres. and C.E.O.; Gavin Hattersley, C.F.O.
Board of directors: Andrew T. Molson, Chair.; Peter H. Coors, Vice-Chair.; Francesco Bellini; Christein Coors-Ficeli; Roger G. Eaton; Brian Goldner; Charles M. Herington; Franklin W. Hobbs; Geoff Molson; Iain Napier; H. Sanford Riley; Peter Swinburn; Doug Tough; Louis Vachon
Giving statement: Giving through the Molson Coors Brewing Company Contributions Program.
Company EIN: 840178360

Molson Coors Brewing Company Contributions Program

1225 17th St.
Denver, CO 80202 (303) 279-6565
URL: http://molsoncoors.com/responsibility

2550
Molycorp, Inc.

5619 Denver Tech Ctr. Pkwy., Ste. 1000
Greenwood Village, CO 80111
(303) 843-8040
FAX: (303) 843-8082

Company URL: http://www.molycorp.com
Establishment information: Established in 1950.
Company type: Public company
Company ticker symbol and exchange: MCP/NYSE
Business activities: Operates mining company.
Business type (SIC): Mining/uranium, radium, vanadium, and other miscellaneous metal
Financial profile for 2012: Number of employees, 2,700; assets, $2,994,710,000; sales volume, $528,910,000; pre-tax net income, -$494,310,000; expenses, $965,180,000; liabilities, $1,757,640,000
Corporate officers: Ross Randolph Bhappu, Ph.D., Chair.; Mark A. Smith, Pres. and C.E.O.; John F. Ashburn, Jr., Exec. V.P. and Genl. Counsel; James S. Allen, C.F.O. and Treas.; John K. Bassett, Sr. V.P. Opers.; Ksenia A. Adams, Corp. Cont.
Board of directors: Ross Randolph Bhappu, Ph.D., Chair.; Russell D. Ball; Brian T. Dolan; Charles R. Henry; Constantine Karayannopoulos; Mark S. Kristoff; Alec Machiels; John Graell Moore; Mark Alan Smith; Jack E. Thompson, Ph.D.
Giving statement: Giving through the Molycorp, Inc. Corporate Giving Program.
Company EIN: 272301797

Molycorp, Inc. Corporate Giving Program

5619 DTC Pkwy., Ste. 1000
Greenwood Village, CO 80111-3075 (303) 843-8040
E-mail: info@molycorp.com; URL: http://www.molycorp.com

2551
Monadnock Paper Mills, Inc.

117 Antrim Rd.
Bennington, NH 03442 (603) 588-3311

Company URL: http://www.mpm.com
Establishment information: Established in 1819.
Company type: Private company
Business activities: Manufactures technical and industrial paper products.
Business type (SIC): Paper and paperboard/coated, converted, and laminated; paper mills
Corporate officers: Richard G. Verney, Chair. and C.E.O.; Terry M. Plummer, Pres. and C.O.O.; Andrew Manns, C.F.O. and Treas.; T. J. Tryon, C.I.O.; David Lunati, V.P., Mktg.; Joe Fletcher, V.P., Human Resources; Gregory H. Smith, Secy.
Board of director: Richard G. Verney, Chair.
Giving statement: Giving through the Gilbert Verney Foundation.

Gilbert Verney Foundation

117 Antrim Rd.
Bennington, NH 03442-4205 (603) 588-3311

Establishment information: Established in 1947 in MA.
Donor: Monadnock Paper Mills, Inc.
Contact: Richard G. Verney, Pres.
Financial data (yr. ended 12/31/11): Assets, $2,447,579 (M); gifts received, $150,000; expenditures, $212,778; qualifying distributions, $178,583; giving activities include $167,595 for grants.
Purpose and activities: The foundation supports hospitals and organizations involved with arts and culture, secondary education, conservation, human services, and Christianity.
Fields of interest: Museums; Museums (art); Performing arts, theater; Arts; Secondary school/education; Environment, natural resources; Environment, land resources; Hospitals (general); Children/youth, services; Family services; Developmentally disabled, centers & services; Human services; Christian agencies & churches.
Type of support: Annual campaigns; Building/renovation; Capital campaigns; Continuing support; General/operating support; Program development.
Geographic limitations: Giving primarily in NH and MA.
Support limitations: No support for religious organizations or lobbying organizations. No grants to individuals.
Application information: Applications accepted. Application form not required.
Initial approach: Proposal
Deadline(s): None
Officer: Richard G. Verney, Pres.
Trustees: Lumina V. Greenway; E. Geoffrey Verney.
EIN: 026007363

2552
Monarch Beverage Company, Inc.

9347 E. Pendleton Pike
Indianapolis, IN 46236 (317) 612-1310

Company URL: http://www.monarch-beverage.com
Establishment information: Established in 1947.
Company type: Private company
Business activities: Sells beer and wine wholesale.
Business type (SIC): Beer, wine, and distilled beverages—wholesale
Financial profile for 2009: Number of employees, 600
Corporate officers: Phillip A. Terry, V.P. and C.E.O.; Alfred Dufour, Sr. V.P., Opers.; Scott Shipley, V.P., Sales; Natalie Roberts, V.P., Human Resources
Board of directors: Ben Francis; Dave Rogers
Giving statement: Giving through the Monarch Beverage Charitable Foundation, Inc.

Monarch Beverage Charitable Foundation, Inc.

9347 E. Pendleton Pike
Indianapolis, IN 46236-2768

Establishment information: Established in 2000 in IN.
Donor: Monarch Beverage Co., Inc.
Financial data (yr. ended 12/31/11): Assets, $19,805 (M); gifts received, $44,249; expenditures, $50,396; qualifying distributions, $44,810; giving activities include $44,810 for grants.
Purpose and activities: The foundation supports organizations involved with arts and culture, health, recreation, and youth development.
Fields of interest: Arts; Recreation; Youth development.
Type of support: General/operating support.
Geographic limitations: Giving primarily in IN.
Support limitations: No grants to individuals.
Application information: Applications not accepted. Unsolicited requests for funds not accepted.
Officer: Lloyd Brown, Treas.
Board Members: Brett Glaze; Bill Wade; Todd Welch.
EIN: 352099555

2553
The Monarch Cement Company

(formerly Monarch Cement Co.)
449 1200 St.
P.O. Box 1000
Humboldt, KS 66748-0900 (620) 473-2222
FAX: (620) 473-2447

Company URL: http://www.monarchcement.com
Establishment information: Established in 1908.
Company type: Public company
Company ticker symbol and exchange: MCEM/OTC
Business activities: Manufactures specialty cements.
Business type (SIC): Cement/hydraulic; asphalt and roofing materials
Financial profile for 2012: Number of employees, 700; assets, $181,290,000; sales volume, $151,770,000; pre-tax net income, $4,390,000; expenses, $151,770,000; liabilities, $78,930,000
Corporate officers: Walter H. Wulf, Jr., Chair. and Pres.; Byron K. Radcliff, Vice-Chair. and Secy.-Treas.; Debra P. Roe, C.P.A., C.F.O.; Norma Joan Perez, V.P., Sales
Board of directors: Walter H. Wulf, Jr., Chair.; Byron K. Radcliff, Vice-Chair.; Jack R. Callahan; Ronald E. Callaway; David L. Deffner; Robert M. Kissick; Gayle C. McMillen; Michael R. Wachter; Walter H. Wulf
Subsidiary: Concrete Materials, Inc., Kansas City, KS
Giving statement: Giving through the Monarch Cement Company Academic Achievement Award.
Company EIN: 480340590

The Monarch Cement Company Academic Achievement Award

(formerly Monarch Cement Co. Academic Achievement Award)
P.O. Box 1000
Humboldt, KS 66748-0900 (620) 473-2251
Application address: Counselor Humboldt High School, 1011 Bridge St., Humboldt, KS 66748, tel.: (620) 473-2251

Establishment information: Established in 1988 in KS.
Donor: Monarch Cement Co.
Financial data (yr. ended 12/31/11): Assets, $108,171 (M); gifts received, $4,200; expenditures, $8,637; qualifying distributions, $7,265; giving activities include $7,265 for 3 grants to individuals (high: $4,507; low: $552).
Purpose and activities: The foundation awards college scholarships to graduating seniors of Humboldt High School in Humboldt, Kansas.
Fields of interest: Education.
Type of support: Scholarships—to individuals.
Geographic limitations: Giving limited to the Humboldt, KS, area.
Application information: Applications accepted. Scholarships are limited to members of Humboldt High School's graduating senior class with a GPA in the top 10 percent. Application form required. Essays should include a description of school and civic activities, financial need, leadership qualities, citizenship, and attitude.
Initial approach: Letter
Deadline(s): Prior to graduation
Trustees: Curt Mueller; KB Criss.
EIN: 481055534

2554
Monarch Corp.

(also known as Monarch, LLC)
7050 N. 76th St.
Milwaukee, WI 53223-5090
(414) 353-8820

Company URL: http://www.monarchcorp.com
Establishment information: Established in 1933.
Company type: Private company
Business activities: Produces steel; manufactures general machinery.
Business type (SIC): Iron and steel foundries; machinery/metalworking; machinery/special industry; machinery/general industry
Corporate officer: David M. Mitchell, Pres. and C.O.O.
Giving statement: Giving through the Gebhardt Foundation, Inc.

Gebhardt Foundation, Inc.

(formerly Monarch Foundation, Inc.)
7123 W. Calumet Rd.
Milwaukee, WI 53223-4007

Establishment information: Established in 1986 in WI.
Donors: Monarch Corp.; Uihlein Electric Co., Inc.; Ritus Rubber Corp.; Kenny Electric Svcs.
Financial data (yr. ended 12/31/11): Assets, $1,262,399 (M); gifts received, $55,000; expenditures, $65,796; qualifying distributions, $57,700; giving activities include $57,700 for grants.
Purpose and activities: The foundation supports hospitals and organizations involved with arts and culture, education, and breast cancer.
Fields of interest: Arts; Health care; Human services.
Type of support: General/operating support.
Geographic limitations: Giving limited to Milwaukee, WI.
Support limitations: No grants to individuals.
Application information: Applications not accepted. Unsolicited requests for funds not accepted.
Directors: Susan G. Gebhardt; William Gebhardt.
EIN: 391574609

2555
Monavie LLC

10855 S. River Front Pkwy., Ste. 100
South Jordan, UT 84095-5763
(801) 748-3100
FAX: (801) 748-3200

Company URL: http://www.monavie.com
Establishment information: Established in 2005.
Company type: Private company
Business activities: Provides health care services.
Business type (SIC): Miscellaneous health services
Corporate officers: Dallin A. Larsen, Chair. and C.E.O.; Randy Larsen, Co-Vice-Chair.; Henry Marsh, Co-Vice-Chair.; Mauricio Bellora, Pres. and C.E.O.; Walter Nott, C.O.O.; James Marsh, C.F.O.
Board of directors: Dallin A. Larsen, Chair.; Randy Larsen, Co-Vice-Chair.; Henry Marsh, Co-Vice-Chair.
Giving statement: Giving through the Monavie LLC Contributions Program.

Monavie LLC Contributions Program

10855 S. River Front Pkwy., Ste. 100
South Jordan, UT 84095-5763 (801) 748-3100
URL: http://www.monavie.com/company/the-more-project

2556
Mondelez International, Inc.

(formerly Kraft Foods Inc.)
3 Pkwy. N.
Deerfield, IL 60015 (847) 943-4000
FAX: (847) 646-6005

Company URL: http://www.mondelezinternational.com
Establishment information: Established in 1903.
Company type: Public company
Company ticker symbol and exchange: MDLZ/NASDAQ
Business activities: Produces and sells foods and beverages.
Business type (SIC): Food and kindred products; beverages
Financial profile for 2012: Number of employees, 110,000; assets, $75,478,000,000; sales volume, $35,015,000,000; pre-tax net income, $1,774,000,000; expenses, $31,987,000,000; liabilities, $43,263,000,000
Fortune 1000 ranking: 2012—88th in revenues, 60th in profits, and 78th in assets
Forbes 2000 ranking: 2012—271st in sales, 384th in profits, and 327th in assets
Corporate officers: Irene B. Rosenfeld, Chair. and C.E.O.; David Brearton, Exec. V.P. and C.F.O.; Gerhard Pleuhs, Exec. V.P. and Genl. Counsel; Karen May, Exec. V.P., Human Resources
Board of directors: Irene B. Rosenfeld, Chair.; Stephen F. Bollenbach; Lewis W.K. Booth; Lois D. Juliber; Mark D. Ketchum; Jorge S. Mesquita; Fredric G. Reynolds; Patrick T. Siewert; Ruth J. Simmons; Jean-Francois M.L. Van Boxmeer
Subsidiary: Balance Bar Company, Rye Brook, NY
International operations: Algeria; Argentina; Australia; Austria; Bahamas; Bahrain; Belgium; Bolivia; Brazil; British Virgin Islands; Bulgaria; Canada; Chile; China; Colombia; Costa Rica; Croatia; Czech Republic; Denmark; Dominican Republic; Ecuador; Egypt; El Salvador; Estonia; Finland; France; Germany; Greece; Guatemala; Honduras; Hong Kong; Hungary; India; Indonesia; Ireland; Italy; Jamaica; Japan; Kazakhstan; Latvia; Lithuania; Luxembourg; Malaysia; Mexico; Morocco and the Western Sahara; Netherlands; New Zealand; Nicaragua; Norway; Pakistan; Panama; Peru; Philippines; Poland; Portugal; Romania; Russia; Saudi Arabia; Serbia; Singapore; Slovakia; South Africa; Spain; Sweden; Switzerland; Taiwan; Thailand; Trinidad & Tobago; Tunisia; Turkey; Ukraine; United Arab Emirates; United Kingdom; Uruguay; Venezuela
Giving statement: Giving through the Mondelez International, Inc. Contributions Program, the Mondelez International Foundation, and the Planters Educational Foundation.
Company EIN: 522284372

Mondelez International, Inc. Contributions Program

(formerly Mondelez International Corporate Giving Program)
3 Pkwy. N.
Deerfield, IL 60015 (847) 643-4000
URL: http://www.mondelezinternational.com/About/community-involvement/community-involvement.aspx

Purpose and activities: As a complement to its foundation, Mondelez International also makes charitable contributions to nonprofit organizations directly. Support is given on a national and international basis in areas of company operations.
Fields of interest: Food services; Nutrition.
Type of support: Advocacy; Employee volunteer services; Program development.
Geographic limitations: Giving primarily in areas of company operations; giving also to national organizations.
Application information: Applications not accepted. Contributes only to pre-selected organizations. The Corporate Community Involvement Department handles giving. The company has a staff that only handles contributions.
Number of staff: 7 full-time professional; 1 full-time support.

The Mondelez International Foundation

(formerly The Kraft Foods Foundation)
3 Lakes Dr., NF-132
Northfield, IL 60093-2753
URL: http://www.mondelezinternational.com/About/community-involvement/community-involvement.aspx

Establishment information: Established in 2005 in IL.
Donor: Kraft Foods Global, Inc.
Financial data (yr. ended 12/31/11): Assets, $33,041,934 (M); gifts received, $18,000,385; expenditures, $15,915,320; qualifying distributions, $15,915,101; giving activities include $15,915,101 for grants.
Purpose and activities: The foundation supports programs designed to address hunger; promote healthy lifestyles; and provide humanitarian aid.

Fields of interest: Public health, obesity; Public health, physical fitness; Health care; Agriculture; Food services; Food banks; Nutrition; Disasters, preparedness/services; American Red Cross; Salvation Army; YM/YWCAs & YM/YWHAs; Human services; Community/economic development Children; African Americans/Blacks; Hispanics/Latinos.

Programs:

Dollars for Doers: The foundation awards $500 grants to nonprofit organizations with which employees of Kraft volunteer 25 hours during a calendar year.

Kraft Foods Matching Gifts Program: The foundation matches contributions made by Kraft employees to nonprofit organizations on a one-for-one basis from $25 to $15,000 per donor, per year.

Kraft Foods Mobile Pantry Program: The foundation, in partnership with Kraft Foods and Feeding America, operates mobile pantry vehicles in low-income areas to serve those affected by food insecurity. The trucks provide fresh fruit, vegetables, protein, and dairy products to neighborhood pantries, churches, and school parking lots. The program is geared toward African-American and Latino populations in Concord, California, Greeley, Colorado, Columbus and Valdosta, Georgia, Newark, NJ, Elmsford, NY, Corpus Christi, Houston, and San Antonio, Texas, and Milwaukee, Wisconsin.

Type of support: Donated products; Employee matching gifts; Employee volunteer services; General/operating support; In-kind gifts; Program development; Sponsorships.

Geographic limitations: Giving on a national and international basis in areas of company operations, with emphasis on CA, CO, Washington, DC, FL, GA, IA, IL, MN, MO, NJ, NY, PA, TX, VA, WI, Argentina, Australia, Brazil, Canada, France, Germany, Indonesia, Italy, Mexico, Philippines, Spain, Russia, and the United Kingdom.

Application information: Applications not accepted. Contributes only to pre-selected organizations.

Officers and Directors:* Cynthia P. Yeatman*, Pres.; Nancy Daigle, V.P. and Secy.; Carol J. Ward, V.P. and Secy.; Marc S. Firestone*, V.P.; Nicole R. Robinson*, V.P.; Joseph Klauke, Counsel; James Portnoy, Counsel.

EIN: 203881590

Selected grants: The following grants are a representative sample of this grantmaker's funding activity:

$1,000,000 to Kaboom, Washington, DC, 2010.
$800,000 to Food Trust, Philadelphia, PA, 2010.
$800,000 to YMCA of the U.S.A., Chicago, IL, 2010.
$400,000 to Kids Against Hunger, New Hope, MN, 2010.
$360,000 to Chicago Public Library Foundation, Chicago, IL, 2010.
$275,000 to Kaboom, Washington, DC, 2010.
$100,000 to International Federation of Red Cross and Red Crescent Societies at the United Nations, New York, NY, 2010.
$25,000 to International Federation of Red Cross and Red Crescent Societies, Geneva, Switzerland, 2010.
$5,000 to Catholic Charities of the Diocese of Saint Cloud, Saint Cloud, MN, 2010.
$5,000 to Mid-Ohio Foodbank, Grove City, OH, 2010.

Planters Educational Foundation

245 Culloden St.
Suffolk, VA 23434-4608 (757) 925-3000

Establishment information: Established in 1986 as a company-sponsored operating foundation.

Donor: Planters LifeSavers Co.

Contact: Ginny Tuttle, Secy.

Financial data (yr. ended 12/31/10): Assets, $117,435 (M); expenditures, $6,262; qualifying distributions, $5,074; giving activities include $4,000 for 4 grants to individuals (high: $1,000; low: $1,000).

Purpose and activities: The foundation awards college scholarships to children of current and former (living or deceased) employees and retirees of the Planters LifeSavers Company Suffolk, Virginia, plant and division.

Type of support: Employee-related scholarships.

Geographic limitations: Giving limited to areas of company operations in VA.

Application information: Applications accepted. Application form required.

Initial approach: Proposal
Deadline(s): None

Officers: Lynn Charles, Pres.; Ginny Tuttle, Secy.; Amelia Seiling, Treas.

EIN: 541178802

2557
Moneta Group, LLC

100 S. Brentwood Blvd., Ste. 500
Clayton, MO 63105-1649 (314) 726-2300

Company URL: http://www.monetagroup.com
Establishment information: Established in 1869.
Company type: Private company
Business activities: Provides investment advisory services.
Business type (SIC): Security and commodity services
Corporate officers: Donald T. Kukla, Chair.; Gene Michael Diederich, C.P.A., C.E.O.; Christopher W. Whiting, C.O.O.; William Allen Hornbarger, C.I.O; Steven Robert Frontczak, Genl. Counsel; Peter Gregory Schick, Chair. Emeritus
Board of director: Donald T. Kukla, Chair.
Giving statement: Giving through the Moneta Group Charitable Foundation.

Moneta Group Charitable Foundation

100 S. Brentwood Blvd., Ste. 500
Saint Louis, MO 63105 (314) 726-2300
URL: http://www.monetagroup.com

Establishment information: Established in 2000 in MO.

Donors: Peter G. Schick; Joe Sheehan; Donald T. Kula; Chandler Taylor; Daniel West; Joseph Sheehan; Dave Sadler; Don Kukla; Jim Blair; Linda Pietroburgo; Michael Johnson; Steve Finerty; Tim Halls; Tom O' Meara.

Contact: Janet Bandera, Tr.

Financial data (yr. ended 12/31/11): Assets, $1,261,422 (M); gifts received, $159,157; expenditures, $201,346; qualifying distributions, $194,668; giving activities include $194,668 for 38 grants (high: $37,500; low: $500).

Purpose and activities: The foundation supports organizations involved with education, housing, human services, community development, senior citizens, economically disadvantaged people, and other areas.

Fields of interest: Education; Housing/shelter; Children/youth, services; Human services; Community/economic development Aging; Economically disadvantaged.

Geographic limitations: Giving limited to St. Louis, MO, including the Metro East area.

Support limitations: No support for churches or religious organizations not of direct benefit to the entire community, national organizations (except for local branches), or controversial organizations. No grants to individuals, or for fundraising events, endowments, debt reduction, general operating support for private or parochial schools, or start-up needs.

Publications: Annual report (including application guidelines); Application guidelines; Informational brochure (including application guidelines).

Application information: Applications accepted. Application must be accompanied by an employee recommendation. Application form required.

Initial approach: Request application form
Board meeting date(s): Feb., May, and Oct.
Deadline(s): None

Officers: Chandler Taylor, Chair.; Daniel West, Treas.

Trustees: Janet Bandera; Katie Kearins; Donald T. Kukla; Doug Weber.

EIN: 431871586

Selected grants: The following grants are a representative sample of this grantmaker's funding activity:

$5,000 to Barnes-Jewish Hospital Foundation, Saint Louis, MO, 2010. For general operating funds.
$5,000 to Boys and Girls Town of Missouri, Saint Louis, MO, 2010. For general operating funds.
$5,000 to Center of Creative Arts, Saint Louis, MO, 2010. For general operating funds.
$5,000 to Forest Park Forever, Saint Louis, MO, 2010. For general operating funds.
$5,000 to Hope Happens, Saint Louis, MO, 2010. For general operating funds.
$5,000 to Pedal the Cause, Saint Louis, MO, 2010. For general operating funds.
$4,727 to Saint Louis Crisis Nursery, Saint Louis, MO, 2010. For general operating funds.
$3,500 to Southern Illinois University Foundation, Carbondale, IL, 2010. For general operating funds.
$2,500 to Friends of Kids With Cancer, Saint Louis, MO, 2010. For general operating funds.
$1,500 to Kingdom House, Saint Louis, MO, 2010. For general operating funds.

2558
MoneyGram International, Inc.

1550 Utica Ave. S., Ste. 100
Minneapolis, MN 55416 (952) 591-3000
FAX: (302) 636-5454

Company URL: http://www.moneygram.com
Establishment information: Established in 1940.
Company type: Public company
Company ticker symbol and exchange: MGI/NYSE
Business activities: Provides payment services.
Business type (SIC): Business services/miscellaneous
Financial profile for 2012: Number of employees, 1,610; assets, $5,115,740,000; sales volume, $1,166,650,000; pre-tax net income, $39,770,000; expenses, $1,007,920,000; liabilities, $5,058,860,000
Corporate officers: Pamela H. Patsley, Chair. and C.E.O.; W. Alexander Holmes, Exec. V.P. and C.F.O.; F. Aaron Henry, Exec. V.P., Genl. Counsel, and Corp. Secy.; J. Lucas Wimer, Exec. V.P., Opers.; Steven Piano, Exec. V.P., Human Resources
Board of directors: Pamela H. Patsley, Chair.; J. Coley Clark; Victor W. Dahir; Antonio O. Garza; Thomas M. Hagerty; Seth W. Lawry; Ganesh Rao; W. Bruce Turner
International operations: Canada; Italy; South Africa; United Kingdom
Giving statement: Giving through the MoneyGram International Corporate Giving Program.
Company EIN: 161690064

MoneyGram International Corporate Giving Program

(formerly Travelers Express Company, Inc. Corporate Giving Program)
1550 Utica Ave. S., Ste. 100
Minneapolis, MN 55416-5301 (952) 591-3839
FAX: (952) 591-3865;
E-mail: jhinkle@moneygram.com; URL: http://moneygram.com/MGICorp/CompanyInformation/CommunityGiving/index.htm

Contact: Jodi Hinkle, Admin., Global Giving
Financial data (yr. ended 12/31/11): Total giving, $500,000, including $500,000 for grants.
Purpose and activities: MoneyGram makes charitable contributions to nonprofit organizations involved with education, entrepreneurship, and microfinance. Support is given primarily outside the United States.
Fields of interest: Education; Economic development; Business/industry; Community development, business promotion.
Programs:
Employee Matching Gifts: MoneyGram matches contributions made by its employees to nonprofit organizations up to $1,000 per employee, per year.
MoneyGram Global Giving Grants: MoneyGram considers grant applications for up to $10,000 for the focus areas of education, entrepreneurship and microfinance programs providing support in areas of company operations.
Type of support: Continuing support; Employee matching gifts; General/operating support; Program development.
Geographic limitations: Giving primarily for international programs in areas of company operations.
Support limitations: No support for political organizations, religious organizations, unions, labor or veterans' organizations, private foundations, or fraternal organizations. No grants to individuals, or for public broadcasting or recreation or athletic events.
Publications: Application guidelines; Newsletter (including application guidelines).
Application information: Applications accepted. The Corporate Communications Department handles giving. A contributions committee reviews all requests. Application form required. Applicants should submit the following:
1) copy of IRS Determination Letter
2) copy of most recent annual report/audited financial statement/990
Initial approach: Download application form and mail or fax to headquarters
Deadline(s): Mar. 15, July 15, and Nov. 15
Final notification: Within 3 weeks of deadlines
Number of staff: 1 full-time professional.

2559
Monsanto Company

800 N. Lindbergh Blvd.
St. Louis, MO 63167 (314) 694-1000

Company URL: http://www.monsanto.com
Establishment information: Established in 1901.
Company type: Public company
Company ticker symbol and exchange: MON/NYSE
International Securities Identification Number: US61166W1018
Business activities: Provides agricultural solutions.
Business type (SIC): Fertilizers and agricultural chemicals
Financial profile for 2012: Number of employees, 21,500; assets, $20,224,000,000; sales volume, $13,504,000,000; pre-tax net income, $2,988,000,000; expenses, $10,356,000,000; liabilities, $8,391,000,000
Fortune 1000 ranking: 2012—206th in revenues, 97th in profits, and 238th in assets
Forbes 2000 ranking: 2012—689th in sales, 245th in profits, and 910th in assets
Corporate officers: Hugh M. Grant, Chair. and C.E.O.; Brett D. Begemann, Pres.; David F. Snively, Exec. V.P., Secy., and Genl. Counsel; Steven C. Mizell, Exec. V.P., Human Resources; Pierre Courduroux, Sr. V.P. and C.F.O.; Thomas D. Hartley, V.P. and Treas.; Nicole M. Ringenberg, V.P. and Cont.
Board of directors: Hugh Grant, Chair.; David L. Chicoine; Janice L. Fields; Arthur H. Harper; Laura K. Ipsen; Gwendolyn S. King; C. Steven McMillan; Jon R. Moeller; William U. Parfet; George H. Poste; Robert J. Stevens
Subsidiary: DEKALB Genetics Corporation, St. Louis, MO
International operations: Argentina; Australia; Belgium; Brazil; Canada; Chile; Colombia; France; India; Italy; Luxembourg; Malaysia; Mauritius; Mexico; Netherlands; Panama; Philippines; Romania; Singapore; South Africa; South Korea; Spain; Turkey
Giving statement: Giving through the Monsanto Company Contributions Program and the Monsanto Fund.
Company EIN: 431878297

Monsanto Company Contributions Program

800 N. Lindbergh Blvd.
St. Louis, MO 63167-0001 (314) 694-1000
URL: http://www.monsanto.com/whoweare/Pages/corporate-giving.aspx

Purpose and activities: As a complement to its foundation, Monsanto also makes charitable contributions to nonprofit organizations directly. Special emphasis is directed toward programs that promote the sustainability and growth of the agricultural industry. Support is given on a national basis.
Fields of interest: Education; Environment; Agriculture; Youth development; Community/economic development; Science.
Program:
Monsanto Commitment to Agriculture Scholarship: Through the Monsanto Commitment to Agriculture Scholarship program, Monsanto annually awards 100 $1,500 college scholarships to high school seniors from a farm family with an above-average academic record, and plans to enroll as a full-time student in an agriculture-related academic major at an accredited school.
Type of support: Curriculum development; Donated products; General/operating support; In-kind gifts; Scholarship funds; Sponsorships.
Geographic limitations: Giving on a national basis; giving also to national and international organizations.
Publications: Application guidelines.
Application information: Applications accepted.
Initial approach: Complete online application forms
Deadline(s): Feb. 15 for Agriculture Scholarships
Number of staff: 2 full-time professional; 1 part-time professional; 1 full-time support; 1 part-time support.

Monsanto Fund

800 N. Lindbergh Blvd.
St. Louis, MO 63167-7843 (314) 694-4391
FAX: (314) 694-7658;
E-mail: monsanto.fund@monsanto.com; Additional tel.: (314) 694-1000, fax: (314) 694-1001; Contact for America's Farmers Grow Communities and America's Farmers Grow Rural Education: Eileen Jensen, 914 Spruce St., St. Louis, MO 63102, tel.: (877) 267-3332; URL: http://www.monsantofund.org/

Establishment information: Incorporated in 1964 in MO as successor to the Monsanto Charitable Trust.
Donor: Monsanto Co.
Contact: Deborah J. Patterson, Pres.
Financial data (yr. ended 12/31/12): Assets, $22,204,719 (M); gifts received, $23,400,000; expenditures, $18,070,828; qualifying distributions, $18,048,164; giving activities include $16,231,494 for grants and $1,394,727 for 5,710 employee matching gifts.
Purpose and activities: The fund supports programs designed to strengthen farming communities and the communities where Monsanto employees live and work. Special emphasis is directed toward programs designed to improve education in farming communities, including schools, libraries, science centers, farmer training, and academic initiatives that enrich school programming; and meet critical needs in communities through food security, sanitation, access to clean water, public safety, and various other local needs.
Fields of interest: Arts education; Visual arts; Performing arts; Literature; Arts; Elementary/secondary education; Libraries (public); Education; Environment, pollution control; Environment, water pollution; Botanical/horticulture/landscape services; Environment; Public health, clean water supply; Public health, sanitation; Agriculture/food, research; Agriculture/food, public education; Agriculture; Agriculture, farmlands; Agriculture, farm bureaus/granges; Food services; Nutrition; Disasters, fire prevention/control; Safety, education; Safety/disasters; Youth development, agriculture; Human services; Science, formal/general education; Mathematics; Science; Public affairs Children; Youth; Economically disadvantaged.
Programs:
Access to the Arts: The fund supports programs designed to broaden opportunities for underserved children and adults in the performing, visual, or literary arts; identify real or perceived barriers that keep underserved groups from participating in the arts; and engage the underserved in arts education experiences. The program is limited to St. Louis, MO.
America's Farmers: Grow Communities: Through America's Farmers Grow Communities program, local farmers register to win $2,500 for their favorite community nonprofit organizations including FFA, 4-H, schools, fire departments, and other civic groups; and one winner is selected from each county in 39 states. An additional $2,500 donation is available to assist counties that have been declared disaster areas by the USDA due to drought. Visit URL http://www.americasfarmers.com/growcommunities/ for more information.
America's Farmers: Grow Rural Education: Through Americas Farmers Grow Rural Education Program, farmers nominate their public school district to compete for a merit-based grant of up to $25,000 to enhance education in the areas of math and science. Visit URL http://www.americasfarmers.com/growruraleducation/ for more information.

Kids Garden Fresh Program: The fund, in partnership with Gateway Greening, supports youth-center gardens in schools, licensed child care facilities, and youth-focused nonprofits serving ages 5-21. Awardees receive assistance with project planning, coordination, and installation; plant materials, seeds, seedling, plant beds, soil, compost, mulch, garden tools, and season extension items; curricula to use with young people/students; technical assistance including training for staff, volunteers, and education; access to Gateway Greening's education library, garden visits, and workshops; and additional volunteers if needed. The program is limited to St. Louis, MO.

Matching Gifts Program: The fund matches contributions made by employees and directors of Monsanto to nonprofit organizations on a one-for-one basis from $25 to $5,000 per contributor, per year.

Math and Science Education K-12: The fund supports programs designed to nurture students' interest science and/or math; promote innovative approaches to teaching or learning in math and science; and foster student achievement in science and/or math. Special emphasis is directed toward programs using evidenced-based methodology. This program is limited to St. Louis, MO.

US Site Grants: The fund awards grants to communities in which Monsanto employees live and work. Special emphasis is directed toward K-12 education and critical needs in communities. Visit website to request an invitation code in order to apply.

Type of support: Conferences/seminars; Continuing support; Curriculum development; Employee matching gifts; Equipment; General/operating support; Matching/challenge support; Program development; Program evaluation; Research; Seed money.

Geographic limitations: Giving on a national and international basis primarily in areas of company operations in GA, IA, ID, IL, and LA, with emphasis on the greater St. Louis, MO, area. Giving outside the U.S. in Canada, Mexico, the United Kingdom, and Africa, including Malawi, Burkina Faso, Kenya, South Africa, and Uganda, Asia, including China, India, Indonesia, Philippines, and Thailand, and South America including Argentina, Brazil, Chile, Columbia, Guatemala, Honduras, Paraguay, and Uruguay.

Support limitations: No support for start-up organizations, fraternal, labor, or veterans' organizations not of direct benefit to the entire community, religious, politically partisan, or similar organizations, or discriminatory organizations. No grants to individuals, or for debt reduction, benefits, dinners, or advertisements, endowments, marketing, or projects in which Monsanto Company has a financial interest or could derive a financial benefit through cash or rights to intellectual property; no donations of printers, computer software, copiers, scanners, or computers.

Publications: Annual report; Application guidelines; Grants list; Program policy statement.

Application information: Applications accepted. Support is limited to 1 contribution per organization during any given year. Organizations receiving support are asked to submit a mid-year report and a final report. A site visit may be requested for Kids Garden Fresh Program. All applicants are welcome to attend a grant information session at Monsanto headquarters. Session dates are available on Monsanto's website. Applicants should submit the following:

1) timetable for implementation and evaluation of project
2) population served
3) name, address and phone number of organization
4) copy of IRS Determination Letter
5) brief history of organization and description of its mission
6) copy of most recent annual report/audited financial statement/990
7) how project's results will be evaluated or measured
8) list of company employees involved with the organization
9) explanation of why grantmaker is considered an appropriate donor for project
10) detailed description of project and amount of funding requested
11) contact person
12) copy of current year's organizational budget and/or project budget
13) plans for acknowledgement

Initial approach: Complete online application; complete online nomination for America's Farmers: Grow Rural Education
Board meeting date(s): Twice per year
Deadline(s): Feb. 28 and Aug. 31 for Math & Science Education K-12 and Access to Arts; Feb. 28 for US Site Grants; Feb. 28 and Aug. 31 for international organizations; Apr. 15 for America's Farmers: Grow Rural Education; June 1 for Kids Garden Fresh Program; and Nov. 30 for America's Farmers: Grow Communities
Final notification: July for Kids Garden Fresh Program

Officers and Directors:* Brett D. Begemann*, Chair.; Deborah J. Patterson*, Pres.; Sonya Meyers Davis, Secy.; Thomas D. Hartley, Treas.; Janet M. Holloway; Consuelo E. Madere; Jesus Madrazo; Kerry J. Preete; Derek K. Rapp; Gerald A. Steiner.

Number of staff: 1 full-time professional; 1 part-time professional; 2 full-time support.

EIN: 436044736

Selected grants: The following grants are a representative sample of this grantmaker's funding activity:
$800,716 to United Way of Greater Saint Louis, Saint Louis, MO, 2011.
$500,000 to Washington University, Saint Louis, MO, 2011.
$500,000 to Washington University, Saint Louis, MO, 2011.
$225,000 to INICIA Emprender para el Futuro, Buenos Aires, Argentina, 2011.
$115,500 to Food, Health and Hope Foundation, 2011.
$56,265 to Professional Assistance for Development Action, New Delhi, India, 2011.
$30,000 to Western Growers Charitable Foundation, Irvine, CA, 2011.
$13,082 to North County Joint Union School District, Hollister, CA, 2011.
$2,400 to United Fund of Grinnell Iowa, Grinnell, IA, 2011.

2560
Monster Worldwide, Inc.

(formerly TMP Worldwide Inc.)
622 3rd Ave., 39th Fl.
New York, NY 10017 (212) 351-7000
FAX: (646) 658-0540

Company URL: http://www.monsterworldwide.com
Establishment information: Established in 1994.
Company type: Public company
Company ticker symbol and exchange: MWW/NYSE
Business activities: Provides Internet information services; provides employee recruitment advertising services; provides executive search services; provides direct marketing services.
Business type (SIC): Advertising; computer services; management and public relations services
Financial profile for 2012: Number of employees, 5,000; assets, $1,684,870,000; sales volume, $890,390,000; pre-tax net income, $26,270,000; expenses, $858,240,000; liabilities, $804,830,000
Corporate officers: Salvatore Iannuzzi, Chair., Pres., and C.E.O.; James M. Langrock, Exec. V.P. and C.F.O.; Lise Poulos, Exec. V.P. and C.A.O.
Board of directors: Salvatore Iannuzzi, Chair.; John Gaulding; Cynthia P. McCague; Jeffrey F. Rayport; Roberto Tunioli; Timothy T. Yates
Giving statement: Giving through the Monster Worldwide, Inc. Corporate Giving Program.
Company EIN: 133906555

Monster Worldwide, Inc. Corporate Giving Program

622 3rd Ave.
New York, NY 10017-6711 (212) 351-7000
E-mail: philanthropy@monster.com; URL: http://www.about-monster.com/content/our-worldwide-community

Purpose and activities: Monster makes charitable contributions to nonprofit organizations involved with education and career development/training.
Fields of interest: Education; Employment, training Economically disadvantaged.
Type of support: Employee volunteer services; In-kind gifts; Program development.
Geographic limitations: Giving primarily in areas of company operations; giving also to regional, national, and international organizations.
Application information: Applications not accepted.

2561
Monumental Life Insurance Company

100 Light St., Fl. B1
Baltimore, MD 21202-1098
(410) 685-2900

Company URL: http://www.monlife.com
Establishment information: Established in 1858.
Company type: Subsidiary of a foreign company
Business activities: Sells life insurance.
Business type (SIC): Insurance/life
Corporate officers: H. Stacey Boyer, V.P., Genl. Counsel, and Secy.; Susan Reier, V.P. and C.A.O.; Duane Davies, V.P., Sales
Giving statement: Giving through the Monumental Life Charitable Foundation.

Monumental Life Charitable Foundation

c/o Karana Chol
100 Light St. B1
Mail 3132
Baltimore, MD 21202-2559

Donors: Monumental Life Insurance Co.; United Way of Central Maryland.
Financial data (yr. ended 12/31/11): Assets, $37,585 (M); expenditures, $1,012; qualifying distributions, $938; giving activities include $938 for 10 grants (high: $100; low: $38).
Purpose and activities: The foundation matches contributions made by employees or retirees of Monumental Life to institutions of higher education.

Fields of interest: Higher education.
Type of support: Employee matching gifts.
Application information: Applications not accepted. Contributes only through employee matching gifts.
Officers: Shawn C. Davis, Pres.; Eric Lippert, V.P.; Stacey H. Boyer, Secy.; Martha Hershman, Treas.
EIN: 364389109

2562
The Moody Company

600 Jefferson St., Ste. 1500
Lafayette, LA 70501-6953 (337) 266-2100

Establishment information: Established in 1982.
Company type: Private company
Business activities: Operates holding company.
Business type (SIC): Holding company
Corporate officers: Richard K. Moody, Co-Pres.; Kevin Moody, Co-Pres.; Paulette Benvel, Secy.
Giving statement: Giving through the Moody Company Foundation.

The Moody Company Foundation

600 Jefferson St., Ste. 1500
Lafayette, LA 70501-6942

Establishment information: Established in 1994 in LA.
Donors: The Moody Co.; BIM3 Investments; Braxton I. Moody III; Thelma H. Moody; Rosalind Moody Robertson; Valerie Moody Hensgens; Beverly Moody Lagroue; Katherine Moody Hundley; Kevin Moody; Charlotte Moody Leonards; Stephen Moody; Elizabeth Moody Gielen.
Financial data (yr. ended 12/31/11): Assets, $120,760 (M); expenditures, $65,009; qualifying distributions, $65,000; giving activities include $65,000 for 8 grants (high: $25,000; low: $500).
Purpose and activities: The foundation supports organizations involved with performing arts, elementary education, child abuse prevention, and Christianity.
Fields of interest: Education; Religion.
Geographic limitations: Giving primarily in Lafayette, LA.
Support limitations: No grants to individuals.
Application information: Applications not accepted. Unsolicited requests for funds not accepted.
Officers and Directors:* Beverly Moody Lagroue*, Pres.; Katherine Moody Hundley*, V.P.; Rosalind Moody Robertson*, Secy.; Charlotte Moody Leonards*, Treas.; Kevin Moody, Mgr.; Elizabeth Moody Gielen; Valerie Moody Hensgens; Braxton I. Moody III; Stephen Moody; Thelma H. Moody.
EIN: 721259852

2563
Moody's Corporation

7 World Trade Ctr.
250 Greenwich St.
New York, NY 10007-2707 (212) 553-0300

Company URL: http://www.moodys.com/
Establishment information: Established in 1900.
Company type: Public company
Company ticker symbol and exchange: MCO/NYSE
International Securities Identification Number: US6153691059
Business activities: Provides business information and credit risk management software.
Business type (SIC): Credit reporting and collection agencies; book publishing and/or printing; publishing/miscellaneous; advertising; mailing, reproduction, commercial art, photography, and stenographic service; computer services; research, development, and testing services
Financial profile for 2012: Number of employees, 6,800; assets, $3,960,900,000; sales volume, $2,730,300,000; pre-tax net income, $1,024,000,000; expenses, $1,652,900,000; liabilities, $3,575,700,000
Fortune 1000 ranking: 2012—765th in revenues, 265th in profits, and 668th in assets
Forbes 2000 ranking: 2012—1657th in sales, 861st in profits, and 1878th in assets
Corporate officers: Henry A. McKinnell, Jr, Chair.; Raymond W. McDaniel, Jr., Pres. and C.E.O.; Linda S. Huber, Exec. V.P. and C.F.O.; John J. Goggins, Exec. V.P. and Genl. Counsel; Tony Stupas, Sr. V.P. and C.I.O.; Joseph McCabe, Sr. V.P. and Corp. Cont.; Anthony G. Mirenda, V.P., Comms.; Jane B. Clark, Corp. Secy.
Board of directors: Henry A. McKinnell, Jr., Ph.D., Chair.; Basil L. Anderson; Jorge A. Bermudez; Darrell Duffie, Ph.D.; Robert R. Glauber; Kathryn M. Hill; Ewald Kist; Raymond W. McDaniel, Jr.; John K. Wulff
Subsidiary: Moody's Investors Service, Inc., New York, NY
International operations: Australia; Brazil; Canada; China; Cyprus; France; Germany; Singapore; Spain; United Kingdom
Giving statement: Giving through the Moody's Foundation.
Company EIN: 133998945

The Moody's Foundation

c/o Mgr., Philanthropy Progs.
7 World Trade Ctr.
250 Greenwhich St., 14th Fl.
New York, NY 10007-2140 (212) 553-3667
E-mail: philanthropy@moodys.com; URL: http://www.moodys.com/Pages/itc003.aspx

Establishment information: Established in 2002 in NY.
Donor: Moody's Investors Service, Inc.
Financial data (yr. ended 12/31/11): Assets, $10,963,392 (M); gifts received, $5,000,000; expenditures, $4,597,321; qualifying distributions, $4,597,321; giving activities include $4,165,192 for 78 grants (high: $742,208; low: $862).
Purpose and activities: The foundation supports organizations involved with arts and culture, education, health, workforce development, hunger, housing, human services, economic development, microfinance, mathematics, economics, civic affairs, minorities, and women.
Fields of interest: Arts; Elementary/secondary education; Secondary school/education; Higher education; Business school/education; Education; Hospitals (general); Health care; Employment, services; Food services; Housing/shelter; Disasters, preparedness/services; Human services; Economic development; Microfinance/microlending; Mathematics; Economics; Public affairs Minorities; Women.
Programs:
Arts, Culture, and Civic: The foundation supports organizations involved with arts and culture and civic affairs. Special emphasis is directed towards programs designed to enrich quality of life in communities where Moody employees live and work.
Dollars for Doers: The foundation awards $500 grants to nonprofit organizations with which employees of Moody's volunteer at least 40 hours a year.
Economic Development: The foundation supports programs designed to promote microfinance and workforce development to enable people to become financially independent.
Education: The foundation supports programs designed to improve mathematics and economics K-12 education; increase basic understanding of financial markets for students in grades 9 through 12; and encourage women and minorities to study finance and economics at institutions of higher education and seek employment in the financial sector.
Employee Matching Gifts: The foundation matches contributions made by employees of Moody's to nonprofit organizations on a one-for-one basis up to $5,000 per employee, per year.
Health and Human Services: The foundation supports programs designed to promote intellectual health in adults and children. Limited grants are awarded in this area.
Moody's Mega Math Challenge: The foundation supports an internet-based applied mathematics competition for high school students designed to increase students' enthusiasm for mathematics and to encourage their interest in pursuing math-related studies and careers. The day-long competition asks contestants to solve a challenging modeling problem based on real-world issues. The foundation awards up to $60,000 in scholarships to the top six teams. The competition is administered by the Society for Industrial and Applied Mathematics (SIAM). Visit URL http://m3challenge.siam.org/ for more information.
Moody's National Merit Scholars: The foundation awards two four-year college scholarships to children of employees of Moody's. The program is administered by the National Merit Scholarship Corp.
The College Fed Challenge: The foundation, in partnership with the Federal Reserve Bank of New York, supports an academic competition in which teams of college students participate in a mock Federal Open Market Committee meeting. The foundation annually awards up to $100,000 in scholarships to the winners.
The Euro Challenge: Through the Euro Challenge, the Delegation of the European Commission to the United States tests U.S. high school students' knowledge of the European economy and the Euro. The foundation awards college scholarships to the top teams, and sponsors a trip to Washington, D.C. for the winners to meet with officials from the Delegation of the European Commission to the United States and the Federal Reserve Bank. Visit URL http://www.euro-challenge.org/wordpress/ for more information.
Type of support: Annual campaigns; Continuing support; Employee matching gifts; Employee volunteer services; Employee-related scholarships; Equipment; Fellowships; General/operating support; Management development/capacity building; Program development; Research; Scholarship funds.
Geographic limitations: Giving primarily in areas of company operations in San Francisco, CA, New York, NY, and London, England.
Support limitations: No support for political candidates or lobbying organizations, fraternal, labor, religious, or similar organizations not of direct benefit to the entire community, or anti-business groups. No grants to individuals, or for travel, national conferences, sponsorships or advertising, team sponsorships, or athletic scholarships; generally, no support for general operating costs or capital campaigns.
Publications: Application guidelines; Corporate giving report; Grants list; Newsletter; Program policy statement.
Application information: Applications accepted. Letters of inquiry should be no longer than 1 page. Telephone calls during the application process are not encouraged. A full proposal may be requested at

a later date. Multi-year funding is not automatic. Application form not required. Applicants should submit the following:
1) results expected from proposed grant
2) population served
3) brief history of organization and description of its mission
4) detailed description of project and amount of funding requested
5) copy of current year's organizational budget and/or project budget
6) listing of additional sources and amount of support

Initial approach: Mail or e-mail letter of inquiry
Board meeting date(s): Quarterly
Deadline(s): None
Final notification: Within 8 weeks

Officers and Directors:* Frances G. Laserson*, Pres.; Elizabeth M. McCarroll, V.P.; Jane B. Clark, Secy.; Jeffrey R. Hare, Treas.; Mark E. Almeda; Robert Fauber; John J. Goggins; Linda S. Huber; Michel F. Madelain; Lisa Simone Westlake.
EIN: 134200757

2564
Moody's Investors Service, Inc.

7 World Trade Ctr.
250 Greenwich St.
New York, NY 10007-2140 (212) 553-0300
FAX: (212) 553-4047

Company URL: http://www.moodys.com
Establishment information: Established in 1914.
Company type: Subsidiary of a public company
Business activities: Provides commercial credit reporting and investment research services.
Business type (SIC): Credit reporting and collection agencies
Corporate officer: Michel Madelain, Pres. and C.O.O.
Giving statement: Giving through the Moody's Credit Markets Research Fund.

Moody's Credit Markets Research Fund

c/o Mgr., Philanthropy Progs.
7 World Trade Ctr.
New York, NY 10007-2140 (212) 553-3667
E-mail: cmrf@moodys.com; URL: http://philanthropy.moodys.com/page.asp?template=cmr&context=cmr§ion=hglts

Purpose and activities: Through the Moody's Credit Markets Research Fund, a direct corporate giving program, Moody's supports programs at academic institutions designed to study and conduct research on credit markets and credit-related topics. Support is given on a national and international basis.
Fields of interest: Higher education.
Type of support: Continuing support; Research.
Geographic limitations: Giving on a national and international basis.
Support limitations: No support for non-accredited academic institutions. No grants to individuals, or for conferences or sponsorships or advertising.
Publications: Application guidelines.
Application information: Applications accepted. Proposals should be no longer than 5 pages. Multi-year funding is not automatic. Contributions generally do not exceed $25,000. A contributions committee reviews all requests. Application form required. Applicants should submit the following:
1) timetable for implementation and evaluation of project
2) results expected from proposed grant
3) qualifications of key personnel
4) name, address and phone number of organization
5) brief history of organization and description of its mission
6) how project's results will be evaluated or measured
7) descriptive literature about organization
8) detailed description of project and amount of funding requested
9) contact person
10) copy of current year's organizational budget and/or project budget

Proposals should include the name and contact information of the principal researcher and the person responsible for administering funds if different from the contact person, and the resumes of the researchers involved; proposals should also indicate any affiliation or relationship between Moody's and the institution and any potential conflict of interest if the request is approved.

Initial approach: Download grant agreement form and mail with proposal to headquarters
Copies of proposal: 1
Committee meeting date(s): Semiannually
Deadline(s): None

Administrators and Directors: Frances G. Laserson, V.P., Corp. Comms.; Richard Cantor, Team Managing Dir.; Jerome Fons, Team Managing Dir.; Roger Stein, Team Managing Dir.; Jing Zhang, Managing Dir., Research.
Number of staff: 1 full-time professional; 1 part-time support.

2565
Benjamin Moore & Co.

5101 Paragon Dr.
Montvale, NJ 07645 (201) 573-9600

Company URL: http://www.benjaminmoore.com
Establishment information: Established in 1883.
Company type: Subsidiary of a public company
Business activities: Manufactures oil-based, alkyd, automobile, and water-based paints, enamels, wax and oil-based stains, and varnishes.
Business type (SIC): Paints and allied products
Corporate officers: Denis S. Abrams, Pres. and C.E.O.; Michael A. Bonner, V.P., Tech.; Joann Glaccum, Co-Secy.; John T. Rafferty, Co-Secy. and Genl. Counsel.; James E. Henderson, Treas.; Nancy Bauer, Cont.
International operations: Canada
Giving statement: Giving through the Benjamin Moore & Co. Contributions Program and the Benjamin Moore Educational Foundation, Inc.

Benjamin Moore & Co. Contributions Program

101 Paragon Dr.
Montvale, NJ 07645-1727
URL: http://www.benjaminmoore.com

Purpose and activities: Benjamin Moore makes charitable contributions to programs designed to promote historic preservation, color and design education, housing, wildlife conservation, pediatrics, and diversity. Support is given on a national basis.
Fields of interest: Visual arts, design; Historic preservation/historical societies; Education; Environment; Animals/wildlife, preservation/protection; Health care; Pediatrics; Housing/shelter; Disasters, preparedness/services; Children/youth, services; Civil/human rights, equal rights Minorities.
Type of support: Donated products; Employee matching gifts; General/operating support; In-kind gifts; Program development.
Geographic limitations: Giving on a national basis.

Benjamin Moore Educational Foundation, Inc.

101 Paragon Dr.
Montvale, NJ 07645-1727

Establishment information: Established in 1985 in NJ.
Donors: Benjamin Moore & Co.; Marie Haller Charitable Remander Trust.
Financial data (yr. ended 12/31/09): Assets, $0 (M); gifts received, $4,984; expenditures, $47,951; qualifying distributions, $47,951.
Purpose and activities: The foundation awards college scholarships to children of employees of Benjamin Moore & Co.
Fields of interest: Higher education.
Type of support: Employee-related scholarships.
Geographic limitations: Giving limited to areas of company operations.
Application information: Applications not accepted. Contributes only through employee-related scholarships.
Officers and Trustees:* James L. Megin, Pres.; JoAnn Glaccum, Secy.; Barton S. Finegan*, Treas.
EIN: 222637513

2566
Moore & Van Allen PLLC

Bank of America Corp. Ctr.
100 N. Tryon St., Ste. 4700
Charlotte, NC 28202-4003 (704) 331-1000

Company URL: http://www.mvalaw.com/
Establishment information: Established in 1949.
Company type: Private company
Business activities: Provides legal services.
Business type (SIC): Legal services
Offices: Charlotte, Research Triangle Park, NC; Charleston, SC
Giving statement: Giving through the Moore & Van Allen PLLC Pro Bono Program and the Moore & Van Allen Foundation, Inc.

Moore & Van Allen PLLC Pro Bono Program

Bank of America Corp. Ctr.
100 N. Tryon St., Ste. 4700
Charlotte, NC 28202-4003 (704) 331-2380
E-mail: stephaniegryder@mvalaw.com; Additional fax: (704) 409-5605; URL: http://www.mvalaw.com/firm-community.html

Contact: Stephanie M. Gryder, Mgr. of Diversity & Community Initiatives
Fields of interest: Legal services.
Type of support: Pro bono services - legal.
Geographic limitations: Giving primarily in areas of company operations in Charlotte, and Research Triangle Park, NC, and in Charleston, SC.
Application information: A Pro Bono Committee manages the pro bono program.

Moore & Van Allen Foundation, Inc.

100 N. Tryon St., Fl. 47
Charlotte, NC 28202-4003

Establishment information: Established in 1991 in NC.

Donor: Moore & Van Allen PLLC.
Financial data (yr. ended 12/31/11): Assets, $9,542 (M); gifts received, $16,914; expenditures, $11,534; qualifying distributions, $9,485; giving activities include $9,485 for grants.
Purpose and activities: The foundation supports organizations involved with education, health, and human services.
Fields of interest: Elementary school/education; Education; Health care; Disasters, preparedness/services; Family services; Human services.
Type of support: General/operating support.
Geographic limitations: Giving primarily in NC.
Support limitations: No grants to individuals.
Application information: Applications not accepted. Unsolicited requests for funds not accepted.
Officer and Directors:* W.B. Hawfield, Jr.*, Chair. and Pres.; James W. Hovis; Reich L. Welborn.
EIN: 581940952

2567
The Moore Company

36 Beach St.
P.O. Box 538
Westerly, RI 02891 (401) 596-2816

Company URL: http://www.themooreco.com
Establishment information: Established in 1909.
Company type: Private company
Business activities: Operates holding company; manufactures textiles, rubber products, and wood products.
Business type (SIC): Textile mill products; wood products/miscellaneous; rubber products/fabricated; holding company
Corporate officers: Peter F. Moore, Chair.; Dena Barlow, Pres.
Board of director: Peter F. Moore, Chair.
Giving statement: Giving through the TMC Foundation.

TMC Foundation

(formerly The Moore Company Foundation)
c/o Alexandra Moore Barber
P.O. Box 538
Westerly, RI 02891-0538

Establishment information: Established in 1998.
Donor: The Moore Co.
Financial data (yr. ended 12/31/11): Assets, $121,538 (M); expenditures, $57,181; qualifying distributions, $53,500; giving activities include $53,500 for grants.
Purpose and activities: The foundation supports organizations involved with choral music, higher education, and Catholicism.
Fields of interest: Arts; Education; Human services.
Type of support: General/operating support.
Geographic limitations: Giving limited to CT, NY, and RI.
Application information: Applications not accepted. Unsolicited requests for funds not accepted.
Trustees: Alexandra Moore; Dorothea B. Moore; George C. Moore, Jr.; Peter F. Moore.
EIN: 050499128

2568
Morgan Construction Company

15 Belmont St., Ste. 1
Worcester, MA 01605-2650
(508) 755-6111

Company URL: http://
Establishment information: Established in 1888.
Company type: Subsidiary of a foreign company
Business activities: Designs and installs rod, bar, and billet mills.
Business type (SIC): Machinery/metalworking
Corporate officer: Philip R. Morgan, Pres. and C.E.O.
International operations: Brazil; China; France; India; Japan; Taiwan; United Kingdom
Giving statement: Giving through the Morgan-Worcester, Inc.
Company EIN: 041635140

Morgan-Worcester, Inc.

15 Belmont St.
Worcester, MA 01605-2665

Establishment information: Incorporated in 1953 in MA.
Donor: Morgan Construction Co.
Contact: Gail M. Morgan, Pres.
Financial data (yr. ended 09/30/11): Assets, $2,216,316 (M); expenditures, $726,367; qualifying distributions, $689,580; giving activities include $689,580 for grants.
Purpose and activities: The foundation supports organizations involved with arts and culture, education, and human services.
Fields of interest: Museums; Arts; Education; Human services; United Ways and Federated Giving Programs.
Type of support: Annual campaigns; Building/renovation; Capital campaigns; Continuing support; Emergency funds; Employee matching gifts; Equipment; General/operating support; Land acquisition; Program development; Seed money.
Geographic limitations: Giving limited to Worcester County, MA.
Support limitations: No support for religious organizations. No grants to individuals, or for endowments, special projects, research, publications, conferences, scholarships, or fellowships; no loans.
Publications: Annual report; Program policy statement.
Application information: Applications accepted. Application form not required.
Initial approach: Proposal
Copies of proposal: 1
Board meeting date(s): Quarterly
Deadline(s): None
Officers and Directors:* Gail M. Morgan*, Pres. and Treas.; Philip R. Morgan*, V.P. and Secy.; John W. Bergan; Barrett Morgan; Daniel M. Morgan; Paul S. Morgan; Russell H. Vanderbaan.
EIN: 046111693

2569
Morgan Services, Inc.

323 N. Michigan Ave.
Chicago, IL 60601-3701 (312) 346-3181

Company URL: http://www.morganservices.com
Establishment information: Established in 1887.
Company type: Private company
Business activities: Provides linen and uniform rental services.
Business type (SIC): Laundry, cleaning, and garment services
Financial profile for 2010: Number of employees, 20
Corporate officer: Richard J.L. Senior, Chair. and C.E.O.
Board of director: Richard J.L. Senior, Chair.
Giving statement: Giving through the Morgan-Senior Foundation.

Morgan-Senior Foundation

323 N. Michigan Ave.
Chicago, IL 60601-3716

Establishment information: Established in 1985 in IL.
Donor: Morgan Services, Inc.
Financial data (yr. ended 11/30/11): Assets, $232,998 (M); expenditures, $39,956; qualifying distributions, $39,610; giving activities include $39,585 for 29 grants (high: $9,240; low: $30).
Purpose and activities: The foundation supports zoos and organizations involved with arts and culture, higher education, health, and crime and violence prevention.
Fields of interest: Arts; Education; Youth development.
Type of support: General/operating support.
Geographic limitations: Giving primarily in Chicago, IL.
Support limitations: No grants to individuals.
Application information: Applications not accepted. Unsolicited requests for funds not accepted.
Officers and Directors:* Richard J.L. Senior*, Pres.; Diana M. Senior*, Secy.; Allen L. Senior*, Treas.
EIN: 363420644

2570
Morgan Stanley

(formerly Morgan Stanley Dean Witter & Co.)
1585 Broadway
New York, NY 10036 (212) 761-4000
FAX: (212) 761-0086

Company URL: http://www.morganstanley.com
Establishment information: Established in 1935.
Company type: Public company
Company ticker symbol and exchange: MS/NYSE
International Securities Identification Number: US6174464486
Business activities: Operates bank holding company.
Business type (SIC): Holding company; credit institutions/personal; brokers and dealers/security; security and commodity services
Financial profile for 2012: Number of employees, 57,061; assets, $780,960,000,000; sales volume, $32,036,000,000; pre-tax net income, $515,000,000; expenses, $31,521,000,000; liabilities, $718,851,000,000
Fortune 1000 ranking: 2012—96th in revenues, 787th in profits, and 9th in assets
Forbes 2000 ranking: 2012—298th in sales, 1739th in profits, and 39th in assets
Corporate officers: James P. Gorman, Chair. and C.E.O.; Thomas Nides, Vice-Chair.; Ruth Porat, Exec. V.P. and C.F.O.; James A. Rosenthal, Exec. V.P. and C.O.O.
Board of directors: James P. Gorman, Chair.; Erskine B. Bowles; Howard J. Davies; Thomas H. Glocer; Robert H. Herz; C. Robert Kidder; Klaus Kleinfeld; Donald T. Nicolaisen; Hutham S. Olayan; James W. Owens, Jr.; O. Griffith Sexton; Ryosuke Tamakoshi; Masaaki Tanaka; Laura D. Tyson
Subsidiary: Morgan Stanley DW Inc., New York, NY

International operations: Bermuda; Canada; Cayman Islands; Germany; Luxembourg; Netherlands; United Kingdom
Historic mergers: Morgan Stanley Group Inc. (May 31, 1997); Crescent Real Estate Equities Company (August 1, 2007)
Giving statement: Giving through the Morgan Stanley Corporate Giving Program, the Crescent Scholarship Foundation, and the Morgan Stanley Foundation, Inc.
Company EIN: 363145972

Morgan Stanley Corporate Giving Program

(formerly Morgan Stanley Dean Witter & Co. Contributions Program)
c/o Community Affairs Dept.
1585 Broadway
New York, NY 10036 (212) 537-1400
FAX: (646) 519-5460;
E-mail: whatadifference@morganstanley.com;
URL: http://www.morganstanley.com/globalcitizen/index.html

Contact: Joan E. Steinberg, Exec. Dir., Morgan Stanley Fdn.
Purpose and activities: As a complement to its foundation, Morgan Stanley also makes charitable contributions to nonprofit organizations directly. Support is given to organizations involved with the environment, social finance, community development, and pediatric care. Support is given on a national and international basis.
Fields of interest: Museums; Arts; Environment; Human services, financial counseling; Civil/human rights, equal rights; Community/economic development.

Program:

Matching Gifts: Morgan Stanley matches contributions made by its employees to educational institutions on a one-for-one basis up to $2,000 per employee, per year.
Type of support: Employee matching gifts; Employee volunteer services; Program development; Sponsorships.
Geographic limitations: Giving on a national and international basis in areas of company operations, with emphasis on the Phoenix, AZ, Los Angeles and San Francisco, CA, Wilmington, DE, Chicago, IL, New York, NY, Columbus and Dayton, OH, Philadelphia, PA, Houston, TX, and Salt Lake City, UT, metropolitan areas, as well as Sao Paulo, Brazil, Hong Kong, Mumbai, India, Tokyo, Japan, Seoul, Singapore, South Korea, and London, United Kingdom; giving also to national and international organizations.
Support limitations: No support for political candidates or lobbying organizations, religious, fraternal, or professional sports organizations, or individual performing arts organizations. No grants to individuals (except for scholarships), or for capital campaigns or endowments, construction or renovation, political causes or campaigns, or documentaries or productions.
Application information: Applications not accepted. Unsolicited letters of inquiry are not accepted. The Community Affairs Department handles giving.
Community Affairs Staff: Anna Farber, Prog. Asst.; Lina Klebanov, Prog. Analyst; Debra Maniaci, Prog. Analyst; Suzane Rhee, Prog. Analyst; Mynesha Rogers, Prog. Asst.; Joan E. Steinberg, Exec. Dir., Morgan Stanley Fdn.
Number of staff: 4 full-time professional; 2 full-time support.

Crescent Scholarship Foundation

777 Main St., Ste. 2100
Fort Worth, TX 76102-5366 (817) 321-1000

Establishment information: Established in 2002 in TX.
Donors: Crescent Stock Match Fund; Crescent Operating, Inc.
Contact: Melissa Matlock, Secy.
Financial data (yr. ended 12/31/11): Assets, $504,473 (M); gifts received, $7,405; expenditures, $53,752; qualifying distributions, $50,500; giving activities include $50,500 for grants.
Purpose and activities: The foundation awards college scholarships to children of non-officer employees of Crescent Real Estate Equities.
Type of support: Employee-related scholarships.
Geographic limitations: Giving primarily in TX.
Application information: Applications accepted. Application form not required.

Deadline(s): Feb. 28

Officers: Jason Anderson, Pres.; Suzanne M. Stevens, V.P. and Treas.; Melissa Matlock, Secy.
Directors: Cris Briad; Jason T. Phinney.
EIN: 752993151

Morgan Stanley Foundation, Inc.

(formerly Morgan Stanley Foundation)
c/o Community Affairs
1633 Broadway, 25th Fl.
New York, NY 10019-6708 (212) 537-1555
FAX: (646) 519-5460;
E-mail: whatadifference@morganstanley.com;
E-mail for Richard B. Fisher Scholarship Program: richardbfisherprogram@morganstanley.com;
URL: http://www.morganstanley.com/globalcitizen/ms_foundation.html

Establishment information: Trust established in 1961 in NY.
Donors: Morgan Stanley Group Inc.; Morgan Stanley & Co. Inc.; Morgan Stanley, Dean Witter, Discover & Co.; Morgan Stanley Dean Witter & Co.; Morgan Stanley.
Financial data (yr. ended 12/31/11): Assets, $54,728,581 (M); expenditures, $10,572,268; qualifying distributions, $10,572,268; giving activities include $10,572,268 for 764 grants (high: $2,500,000; low: $1,500).
Purpose and activities: The foundation supports programs designed to promote children's health, diversity education, and employee community involvement.
Fields of interest: Elementary/secondary education; Secondary school/education; Higher education; Education; Hospitals (general); Health care, clinics/centers; Health care; Pediatrics; Food services; Food banks; Nutrition; Disasters, preparedness/services; American Red Cross; Human services; Civil/human rights, equal rights Children; Disabilities, people with; Minorities; Economically disadvantaged.

Programs:

Global Alliance for Children's Health: The foundation, in partnership with Morgan Stanley, promotes pediatric care, so that more children can get the healthy start they need for consistent and meaningful achievement in life. Special emphasis is directed toward preventable death and disease in young children; supporting leading centers of pediatric excellence and other children's outreach groups; and creating centers of excellence, thought leadership, and direct care for underserved children.

Morgan Stanley Scholarship Initiatives: The foundation supports students and faculty in minority and underserved communities through scholarships, fellowships, and internships at the undergraduate and graduate level. Through the Richard B. Fisher Scholars Program, the foundation awards $7,500 scholarships to underrepresented undergraduate minority students for academic achievement and a paid summer internship at Morgan Stanley in Global Wealth Management or National Sales. Applicants must be in their junior year of college, have a 3.2 GPA, and have desire to build a career in the financial services industry.

Volunteer Incentive Program (VIP): The foundation awards grants to nonprofit organizations involved with health and human services with which employees of Morgan Stanley are involved. Grants range from $500 to $2,000.
Type of support: Continuing support; Employee volunteer services; Fellowships; General/operating support; Internship funds; Program development; Scholarship funds; Scholarships—to individuals.
Geographic limitations: Giving primarily in areas of company operations, with emphasis on the Phoenix, AZ, Los Angeles and San Francisco, CA, Wilmington, DE, Chicago, IL, MA, New York, NY, Columbus, OH, Philadelphia, PA, Dallas and Houston, TX, and Salt Lake City, UT, metropolitan areas; giving also to national organizations.
Support limitations: No support for local organizations with which Morgan Stanley employees are not involved, political candidates or lobbying organizations, religious, fraternal, or professional sports organizations, or individual performing arts organizations. No grants to individuals (except for Morgan Stanley Scholarship Initiatives), or for capital campaigns or endowments, dinners, walks or runs, golf events, political causes or campaigns, or documentaries or productions.
Publications: Application guidelines; Corporate giving report.
Application information: Applications accepted. Letters of inquiry should be no longer than 1 to 2 pages. Morgan Stanley initiates the majority of grants. Priority is given to national initiatives and those serving multiple cities across the U.S. Support for local organizations serving only one metropolitan area or state is limited to organizations with which Morgan Stanley employees volunteer and is coordinated through the Volunteer Incentive Program. Application form not required. Applicants should submit the following:

1) population served
2) brief history of organization and description of its mission
3) geographic area to be served
4) how project's results will be evaluated or measured
5) detailed description of project and amount of funding requested

Initial approach: Letter of inquiry for Global Alliance for Children's Health or Richard B. Scholars Program
Board meeting date(s): Mar., June, Sept., and Dec.
Deadline(s): Varies for Richard B. Scholars Program

Officers and Trustees:* Carla Harris*, Chair.; Joan E. Steinberg*, Pres.; Matt Berke; Marilyn Booker; Charlie Chasin; Jeff Brodsky; Audrey Choi; Josh Connor; Gordon Dean; Jeanmarie McFadden; Kathleen McCabe; Bill McMahon; Shelley O'Connor; Mary Lou Peters; James A. Rosenthal.
EIN: 261226280
Selected grants: The following grants are a representative sample of this grantmaker's funding activity:
$3,500,000 to Great Ormond Street Hospital for Children, London, England, 2009.

2571
Morgan, Lewis & Bockius LLP
1701 Market St.
Philadelphia, PA 19103-2921
(215) 963-5000

Company URL: http://www.morganlewis.com
Establishment information: Established in 1873.
Company type: Private company
Business activities: Operates law firm.
Business type (SIC): Legal services
Corporate officer: Francis M. Milone, Chair.
Offices: Irvine, Los Angeles, Palo Alto, San Francisco, CA; Wilmington, DE; Washington, DC; Miami, FL; Chicago, IL; Boston, MA; Princeton, NJ; New York, NY; Harrisburg, Philadelphia, PA; Dallas, Houston, TX
International operations: Belgium; China; France; Germany; Japan; United Kingdom
Giving statement: Giving through the Morgan, Lewis & Bockius LLP Pro Bono Program.

Morgan, Lewis & Bockius LLP Pro Bono Program
1701 Market St.
Philadelphia, PA 19103-2921 (212) 309-7130
E-mail: adsmith@morganlewis.com; Additional tel.: (212) 963-5000, fax: (212) 432-9652; URL: http://www.morganlewis.com/index.cfm/fuseaction/probono.page/nodeID/505c4640-7a67-4b10-8a41-922df4b0ab9e/

Contact: Amanda D. Smith, Pro Bono Partner
Fields of interest: Legal services.
Type of support: Pro bono services - legal.
Application information: A Pro Bono Committee manages the pro bono program.

2572
Morley Group, Inc.
3330 Ocean Park Blvd.
Santa Monica, CA 90405-3240
(310) 399-1600

Company URL: http://www.morleybuilders.com
Establishment information: Established in 1984.
Company type: Private company
Business activities: Provides concrete, condominium, and commercial and office building construction services.
Business type (SIC): Contractors/concrete work; contractors/general residential building; contractors/general nonresidential building
Corporate officers: Mark Benjamin, Pres. and C.E.O.; Frank Lee, Cont.
Subsidiary: Morley Construction Co., Inc., Santa Monica, CA
Giving statement: Giving through the Mark Benjamin Foundation and the Morley Group Foundation.

Mark Benjamin Foundation
(formerly Mark & Cynthia Benjamin Foundation)
30362 Morning View Dr.
Malibu, CA 90265

Establishment information: Established in 1986 in CA.
Donor: Morley Group, Inc.
Financial data (yr. ended 03/31/12): Assets, $615,560 (M); expenditures, $167,000; qualifying distributions, $167,000; giving activities include $167,000 for 9 grants (high: $102,500; low: $25,000).
Purpose and activities: The foundation supports organizations involved with secondary education, the environment, health, youth, and families.
Fields of interest: Secondary school/education; Environment, natural resources; Environment, land resources; Environment; Health care; Youth, services; Family services.
Type of support: General/operating support; Scholarship funds.
Application information: Applications not accepted. Unsolicited requests for funds not accepted.
Officers: Mark Benjamin, Pres.; Lucas Benjamin, Secy.; Matthew Benjamin, Treas.
EIN: 954039919

Morley Group Foundation
2901 28th St., Ste. 100
Santa Monica, CA 90405-2975

Establishment information: Established in 1989 in CA.
Donor: Morley Group, Inc.
Financial data (yr. ended 09/30/12): Assets, $284,522 (M); gifts received, $20,000; expenditures, $128,809; qualifying distributions, $127,343; giving activities include $127,343 for grants.
Purpose and activities: The foundation supports health clinics and organizations involved with arts and culture, education, hunger, housing, and human services.
Fields of interest: Education; Recreation; Youth development.
Type of support: General/operating support.
Geographic limitations: Giving primarily in CA.
Support limitations: No grants to individuals.
Application information: Applications not accepted. Unsolicited requests for funds not accepted.
Officers: Mark Benjamin, Pres.; Bert Lewitt, Secy.
EIN: 954281717

2573
Morris Communications Company, LLC
(formerly Morris Communications Corporation)
725 Broad St.
Augusta, GA 30901 (706) 724-0851

Company URL: http://www.morris.com
Establishment information: Established in 1945.
Company type: Subsidiary of a private company
Business activities: Publishes newspapers; provides advertising services.
Business type (SIC): Newspaper publishing and/or printing; advertising
Corporate officers: William S. Morris III, Chair. and C.E.O.; Williams S. Morris IV, Pres.; Craig S. Mitchell, Sr. V.P., Finance, and Secy.-Treas.; Steve K. Stone, Sr. V.P. and C.F.O.; Tony Bernados, V.P., Sales; Martha Jean McHaney, V.P., Human Resources; Darrel K. Fry, Cont.
Board of director: William S. Morris III, Chair.
Giving statement: Giving through the Morris Communications Company, LLC Corporate Giving Program, the Morris Communications Foundation, Inc., and the Morris Museum of Art.

Morris Communications Foundation, Inc.
(formerly Stauffer Communications Foundation)
P.O. Box 936
Augusta, GA 30903-0936

Establishment information: Established in 1976 in KS.
Donors: Stauffer Communications, Inc.; Morris Communications Corp.; Morris Communications Co., LLC.
Contact: William S. Morris IV, Tr.
Financial data (yr. ended 12/31/11): Assets, $293,726 (M); gifts received, $35,000; expenditures, $7,800; qualifying distributions, $0.
Purpose and activities: The foundation supports organizations involved with performing arts, education, animals and wildlife, human services, and religion.
Fields of interest: Performing arts; Elementary school/education; Secondary school/education; Higher education; Theological school/education; Education; Animals/wildlife; YM/YWCAs & YM/YWHAs; Human services; Christian agencies & churches; Religion.
Type of support: Building/renovation; Capital campaigns; General/operating support.
Geographic limitations: Giving primarily in AL, CA, Washington, DC, FL, GA, and TX.
Support limitations: Generally no grants to individuals.
Application information: Applications not accepted. Contributes only to pre-selected organizations.
Board meeting date(s): 3rd week of Mar., June, Sept., and Dec.
Trustees: Craig S. Mitchell; William S. Morris IV; Steve K. Stone.
EIN: 486212412
Selected grants: The following grants are a representative sample of this grantmaker's funding activity:
$50,000 to Columbia Theological Seminary, Decatur, GA, 2010. For general support.
$12,500 to FreshMinistries, Jacksonville, FL, 2010. For general support.
$10,000 to Rachel Longstreet Foundation, Augusta, GA, 2010.
$10,000 to United Way of the Central Savannah River Area, Augusta, GA, 2010. For general support.
$3,000 to Heritage Foundation, Washington, DC, 2010. For general support.
$1,000 to Cato Institute, Washington, DC, 2010. For general support.
$1,000 to Longleaf Alliance, Andalusia, AL, 2010. For general support.

Morris Museum of Art
1 Tenth St., Ste. 320
Augusta, GA 30901-1139
URL: http://www.themorris.org

Establishment information: Established as a company-sponsored operating foundation in 1987 in GA.
Donors: Morris Communications Corp.; Morris Communications Co., LLC; Southeastern Newspapers Corp.; J. Timothy Shelnut; William S. Morris III; First Union National Bank; Four Seasons Securities, Inc.; Georgia Council for The Arts; SunTrust Bank; Wachovia Bank; J. Carlisle Overstreet; Augusta Convention & Visitors Bureau; Julia J. Norrell; A.B. Beverage Co., Inc.; Augusta Convention & Visitors Bureau; Georgia Council for the arts; Hull Storey Gibson Retail Group; Julia J. Norrell; Robert P. Kirby; Nola Maddox Falcone Charitable Foundation; SRP Federal Credit Union; Greater Augusta Arts Council; Augusta Westobou

Festival; Porter Fleming Foundation; MCG Health; Trustees of the Academy of Richmond County; University Health Care System; Wells Fargo Bank; Augusta First Bank & Trust; Fletcher Family Foundation; Gordon Chevrolet; James C. Currow; Osbon Associates; Creel-Harrison Foundation; Christian Stracke.
Financial data (yr. ended 12/31/11): Assets, $40,404,573 (M); gifts received, $411,679; expenditures, $1,664,988; qualifying distributions, $1,620,762.
Purpose and activities: The foundation operates the Morris Museum of Art.
Fields of interest: Museums (art).
Type of support: Loans—to individuals.
Application information: Applications not accepted. Unsolicited requests for funds not accepted.
Officer: Kevin Grogan, Exec. Dir.
Trustees: Lee Baker; W. Hale Barrett; David E. Hudson; J. Tyler Morris; William S. Morris III; William S. Morris IV; Paul S. Simon.
Advisory Directors: Christopher Bannochie; Lowell Barnhart; Barbara Coleman; Ann Megan Douglass; Patricia Elam; Richard Fairey; Kevin Glass; Susan Hunnicutt; Brad Means; Julia Norrell.
EIN: 586189260

2574
Philip Morris USA, Inc.

6601 W. Broad St.
Richmond, VA 23230 (804) 274-2000

Company URL: http://www.philipmorrisusa.com
Establishment information: Established in 1968.
Company type: Subsidiary of a public company
Business activities: Produces cigarettes.
Business type (SIC): Tobacco products—cigarettes
Corporate officers: William F. Gifford, Jr., Pres. and C.E.O.; Gary R. Ruth, Sr. V.P., Opers.
Board of director: Gary R. Ruth
Giving statement: Giving through the Philip Morris USA Inc. Corporate Giving Program.

Philip Morris USA Inc. Corporate Giving Program

P.O. Box 18583
Pittsburgh, PA 15236
Application address: Attn.: Specialist, Contribs. Progs., Philip Morris USA, Ext. Affairs, HQ, 2nd Fl., 615 Maury St., Richmond, VA 23224; URL: http://www.philipmorrisusa.com/en/cms/Responsibility/Investing_in_Our_Communities/default.aspx?src=top_nav

Purpose and activities: Philip Morris USA makes charitable contributions to nonprofit organizations involved with arts and culture, education, environment, and positive youth development. Support is given on a national basis.
Fields of interest: Arts; Education; Environment; Youth development.
Type of support: Employee matching gifts; Employee volunteer services; General/operating support; In-kind gifts; Scholarship funds; Sponsorships.
Geographic limitations: Giving on a national basis in areas of company operations, with some emphasis on Cabarrus County, NC, including Charlotte, and Richmond, VA.
Application information: Applications not accepted.

2575
Morris, Nichols, Arsht & Tunnell LLP

1201 N. Market St., 18th Fl.
P.O. Box 1347
Wilmington, DE 19801-1347
(302) 351-9357

Company URL: http://www.mnat.com
Establishment information: Established in 1930.
Company type: Private company
Business activities: Operates law firm.
Business type (SIC): Legal services
Corporate officers: Robert Watson, C.O.O.; Gina Kammann, Cont.
Giving statement: Giving through the Morris, Nichols, Arsht & Tunnell LLP Pro Bono Program.

Morris, Nichols, Arsht & Tunnell LLP Pro Bono Program

1201 N. Market St., 18th Fl.
P.O. Box 1347
Wilmington, DE 19801-1347 (302) 351-9357
E-mail: dabbott@mnat.com; Additional tel.: (302) 658-9200, fax: (302) 658-3989; URL: http://www.mnat.com/firm-service.html

Contact: Derek Abbott, Pro Bono Chair
Fields of interest: Legal services.
Type of support: Pro bono services - legal.
Geographic limitations: Giving primarily in areas of company operations in Wilmington, DE.
Application information: A Pro Bono Committee manages the pro bono program.

2576
Morrison & Foerster LLP

425 Market St.
San Francisco, CA 94105-2482
(415) 268-6370

Company URL: http://www.mofo.com
Company type: Private company
Business activities: Operates law firm.
Business type (SIC): Legal services
Offices: Los Angeles, Palo Alto, Sacramento, San Diego, San Francisco, CA; Denver, CO; Washington, DC; New York, NY; McLean, VA
International operations: Belgium; China; Hong Kong; Japan; United Kingdom
Giving statement: Giving through the Morrison & Foerster LLP Pro Bono Program.

Morrison & Foerster LLP Pro Bono Program

425 Market St.
San Francisco, CA 94105-2482 (212) 336-4094
E-mail: jbrown@mofo.com; Additional tel.: (415) 268-7000, fax: (415) 268-7522; URL: http://www.mofo.com/community/pro-bono/

Contact: Jennifer Brown, Pro Bono Counsel
Fields of interest: Legal services.
Type of support: Pro bono services - legal.
Geographic limitations: Giving primarily in areas of company operations in Los Angeles, Palo Alto, Sacramento, San Diego, and San Francisco, CA, Denver, CO, Washington, DC, New York, NY, and McLean, VA, and in Belgium, China, Hong Kong, Japan, and United Kingdom.
Application information: A Pro Bono Committee manages the pro bono program.

2577
M. A. Mortenson Company

700 Meadow Ln. N.
P.O. Box 1333
Minneapolis, MN 55422 (763) 522-2100
FAX: (763) 287-5430

Company URL: http://www.mortenson.com
Establishment information: Established in 1954.
Company type: Private company
Business activities: Provides non-residential general contract construction services.
Business type (SIC): Contractors/general nonresidential building
Financial profile for 2011: Number of employees, 2,175; sales volume, $2,460,000,000
Corporate officers: Maurice A. Mortenson, Jr., Chair.; Thomas F. Gunkel, C.E.O.; David Mortenson, Pres.; Dan Johnson, C.O.O.; Sandy Sponem, Sr. V.P. and C.F.O.; Paul V. Campbell, Sr. V.P., Admin.; Bradley C. Funk, Sr. V.P., Opers.; Mark Mortenson, Corp. Secy.
Board of director: Maurice A. Mortenson, Jr., Chair.
Offices: Tempe, AZ; Denver, CO; Elk Grove Village, IL; Overland Park, KS; Charlotte, NC; Addison, TX; Bellevue, WA; Brookfield, WI
Giving statement: Giving through the Mortenson Family Foundation.

The Mortenson Family Foundation

700 Meadow Lane North
Minneapolis, MN 55422-5351 (763) 287-5388
E-mail: donna.dalton@mortenson.com

Establishment information: Established in 1999 in MN.
Donors: M.A. Mortenson Co.; Alice D. Mortenson; Maurice Mortenson, Jr.
Contact: Donna Dalton
Financial data (yr. ended 12/31/11): Assets, $34,409,507 (M); gifts received, $5,701,425; expenditures, $1,179,009; qualifying distributions, $955,028; giving activities include $800,000 for 45 grants (high: $170,000; low: $1,000).
Purpose and activities: The foundation supports organizations involved with education, hunger, youth development, human services, religion, and economically disadvantaged people.
Fields of interest: Education; Environment; Youth development; Children/youth, services; Human services Economically disadvantaged.
International interests: Bangladesh; Cambodia; Ghana; Guatemala; Honduras; Laos; Liberia; Malawi; Mozambique; Nicaragua; Senegal; Sierra Leone; Tanzania, Zanzibar and Pemba; Zambia.
Type of support: General/operating support; Program development.
Geographic limitations: Giving primarily in MN, and in Bangladesh, Cambodia, Ghana, Guatemala, Honduras, Laos, Liberia, Malawi, Mozambique, Nicaragua, Senegal, Sierra Leone, Tanzania, and Zambia.
Support limitations: No support for political, religious, or proselytizing organizations. No grants to individuals, or for sponsorships or events.
Application information: Applications not accepted. Contributes only to pre-selected organizations.
Officers and Directors:* Alice D. Mortenson*, Chair. and Pres.; Mauritz A. Mortenson, Jr., V.P. and Treas.; Mark A. Mortenson, Secy.; Donna Dalton, Exec. Dir.; Christopher D. Mortenson; David C. Mortenson; Mathias H. Mortenson.
Number of staff: 1 full-time professional.
EIN: 411958621

2578
Mortgage Funding Corporation
14 Plaza Dr.
P.O. Box 15637
Hattiesburg, MS 39402-1312
(601) 264-3805
FAX: (601) 264-5805

Establishment information: Established in 1978.
Company type: Private company
Business activities: Provides securities brokerage services.
Business type (SIC): Brokers and dealers/security
Corporate officers: Edward J. Langton, Pres.; Howell Rucker, Exec. V.P. and C.O.O.; Lynda M. Langton, Secy.
Giving statement: Giving through the If I Corporation.

If I Corporation
P.O. Drawer 15637
Hattiesburg, MS 39402-5637

Establishment information: Established in 1988 in MS.
Donors: Mortgage Funding Corp.; Grand Bank for Savings, FSB; Edward Langton; Lynda Langton.
Financial data (yr. ended 12/31/11): Assets, $0 (M); expenditures, $83,812; qualifying distributions, $83,542; giving activities include $83,542 for 36 grants (high: $40,100; low: $100).
Purpose and activities: The foundation supports community foundations and organizations involved with education, athletics, youth development, Christianity, and Judaism.
Fields of interest: Higher education; Education; Athletics/sports, amateur leagues; Athletics/sports, baseball; Boy scouts; Youth, services; Foundations (community); Christian agencies & churches; Jewish agencies & synagogues.
Type of support: General/operating support; Program development; Scholarship funds.
Geographic limitations: Giving limited to Hattiesburg, MS.
Application information: Applications accepted. Application form not required. Applicants should submit the following:
1) detailed description of project and amount of funding requested
Initial approach: Proposal
Deadline(s): None
Officers: Edward J. Langton, Pres.; Lynda M. Langton, V.P.; Rucker W. Howell, Secy.-Treas.
EIN: 570898151

2579
Morton International, Inc.
(doing business as Morton Salt)
123 N. Wacker Dr.
Chicago, IL 60606-1743 (800) 725-8847

Company URL: http://www.mortonsalt.com
Establishment information: Established in 1848.
Company type: Subsidiary of a public company
Business activities: Produces organic and inorganic chemicals, dyestuffs, adhesives, packaging chemicals, and salt.
Business type (SIC): Chemicals/industrial inorganic; plastics and synthetics; soaps, cleaners, and toiletries; paints and allied products
Financial profile for 2010: Number of employees, 250
Corporate officers: Mark Roberts, C.E.O.; Walter W. Becky II, Pres.; Thomas F. McDevitt, V.P., Finance and C.F.O.; Raymond P. Buschmann, V.P., Secy., and Genl. Counsel
Plants: Newark, Tustin, CA; Elk Grove Village, Lansing, Ringwood, Woodstock, IL; Hutchinson, KS; New Iberia, LA; Danvers, Woburn, MA; Manistee, MI; Paterson, NJ; Silver Springs, NY; Cincinnati, Painesville, Rittman, OH; Reading, PA; Greenville, SC; Grand Saline, TX; Brigham City, Salt Lake City, UT
Giving statement: Giving through the Morton International, Inc. Corporate Giving Program.

Morton International, Inc. Corporate Giving Program
123 N. Wacker Dr.
Chicago, IL 60606-1743 (800) 725-8847
URL: http://www.mortonsalt.com/our-company/sustainability

Purpose and activities: Morton makes charitable contributions to nonprofit organizations on a case-by-case basis. Support is given primarily in areas of company operations.
Fields of interest: Animal welfare; Public health.
Type of support: Employee volunteer services; General/operating support; In-kind gifts.
Geographic limitations: Giving primarily in areas of company operations.
Number of staff: 1 part-time professional; 1 part-time support.

2580
The Mosaic Company
3033 Campus Dr., Ste. E490
Plymouth, MN 55441 (763) 577-2700
FAX: (763) 559-2860

Company URL: http://www.mosaicco.com
Establishment information: Established in 2004.
Company type: Public company
Company ticker symbol and exchange: MOS/NYSE
Business activities: Manufactures, markets, and distributes fertilizer.
Business type (SIC): Fertilizers and agricultural chemicals
Financial profile for 2012: Number of employees, 8,000; assets, $16,690,400,000; sales volume, $11,107,800,000; pre-tax net income, $2,628,900,000; expenses, $8,496,700,000; liabilities, $4,707,300,000
Fortune 1000 ranking: 2012—246th in revenues, 109th in profits, and 273rd in assets
Forbes 2000 ranking: 2012—926th in sales, 320th in profits, and 1064th in assets
Corporate officers: Robert L. Lumpkins, Chair.; James T. Prokopanko, Pres. and C.E.O.; Lawrence W. Stranghoener, Exec. V.P. and C.F.O.; Richard L. Mack, Esq., Exec. V.P., Genl. Counsel, and Corp. Secy.; James C. O'Rourke, Exec. V.P., Opers. and C.O.O.; Mark E. Kaplan, V.P., Public Affairs; Corrine D. Ricard, V.P., Human Resources
Board of directors: Robert L. Lumpkins, Chair.; Phyllis E. Cochran; Nancy E. Cooper; William R. Graber; Emery N. Koenig; Gregory L. Ebel; Harold H. MacKay; William T. Monahan; James L. Popowich; James T. Prokopanko; David T. Seaton; Steven M. Seibert
Subsidiaries: Cargill Fertilizer Inc., Bradley, FL; Mosaic Global Holdings Inc., Lake Forest, IL
Plants: Bartow, Fort Meade, Riverview, FL
Giving statement: Giving through the Mosaic Company Contributions Program and the Mosaic Company Foundation.
Company EIN: 201026454

The Mosaic Company Contributions Program
Atria Corporate Ctr., Ste. E490
3033 Campus Dr.
Plymouth, MN 55441
E-mail: community@mosaicco.com; URL: http://www.mosaicco.com/community.htm

Purpose and activities: As a complement to its foundation, The Mosaic Company supports organizations involved with global food security, agricultural research and education, water conservation, watershed preservation and restoration, community investments, and disaster relief. Local support is limited to areas of company operations; giving also to national and international organizations.
Fields of interest: Environment, water resources; Public health, clean water supply; Agriculture/food, research; Agriculture/food, formal/general education; Agriculture, farmlands; Food services; Agriculture/food; Safety/disasters; Community/economic development.
Type of support: Donated products; Employee volunteer services; General/operating support; In-kind gifts.
Geographic limitations: Giving is limited to areas of company operations for local support. Giving also to national and international organizations, including those in Argentina, Brazil, Canada, China, and India.
Support limitations: No support for granting organizations, or political, faith-based, or private membership organizations not of direct benefit to the entire community. No grants to individuals, or for residential recycling programs, energy development, including dams and renewable energy, or sewage improvement projects in developing countries; or for public policy, grassroots organizing, advocacy, electoral, or endowment campaigns.
Publications: Application guidelines.
Application information: Applications accepted. Requests should not exceed 10 percent of an organization's annual operating budget or 50 percent of the program's annual budget.
Initial approach: Complete online application
Deadline(s): 1st of each month for requests up to $20,000; Jul. 31, Sept. 30, and Dec. 31, 2012 and June 29, 2013 for requests over $20,000
Final notification: 1st of the month following application for requests up to $20,000; within 120 days of application deadline for requests over $20,000

Mosaic Company Foundation
3033 Campus Dr., Rm. E490
Plymouth, MN 55441-2655 (763) 577-2700
FAX: (763) 559-2860; Toll free tel.: (800) 918-8270; URL: http://www.mosaicco.com

Establishment information: Established in 2009 in MN.
Donor: The Mosaic Company.
Financial data (yr. ended 05/31/11): Assets, $5,796,391 (M); expenditures, $3,942,583; qualifying distributions, $3,942,583; giving activities include $3,942,421 for 19 grants (high: $1,000,000; low: $11,079).
Purpose and activities: The foundation supports programs designed to address food; water; and local community investments.
Fields of interest: Education; Human services; Community/economic development.

Programs:

Food Program: The foundation supports programs designed to help the world grow the food it needs. Special emphasis is directed toward hunger, food insecurity, and food system development in local communities where Mosaic operates; global food security through development initiatives focused on smallholder farmers in developing nations; and agricultural research, education, and extension programs focused on soil health, balanced nutrition, and increasing the capacity of farmers to grow more food sustainably.

Local Community Investments: The foundation supports programs designed to protect and enhance long-term quality of life for communities, families, and neighbors. Special emphasis is directed towards philanthropic and civic partnerships that enrich the long-term health of Mosaic communities; and organizations with which Mosaic employees volunteer their time.

Water Program: The foundation supports programs designed to address water preservation through resource conservation and encouraging stewardship of the environment, biodiversity, and habitat protection; nutrient stewardship and ecosystem management initiatives that promote sustainable agriculture and best management practices in key watersheds where Mosaic has sales and customer relationships; and watershed protection and restoration in regions where Mosaic has facilities and offices.

Type of support: Capital campaigns; Continuing support; Donated products; Employee volunteer services; General/operating support; In-kind gifts; Program development; Sponsorships.
Geographic limitations: Giving primarily in areas of company operations in FL, LA, MN, Argentina, Brazil, Canada, Chile, China, and India; giving also to national organizations.
Support limitations: No support for political, private membership, or faith-based organizations not of direct benefit of the entire community. No grants to individuals, or for endowments, public policy, grassroots organizing, advocacy, or electoral campaigns, residential recycling, energy development including dams or renewable energy, or sewage improvement projects in developed countries.
Application information: Applications not accepted. Unsolicited requests for funds not accepted.
Officers: James T. Prokopanko, Chair.; Mark E. Kaplan, Secy.; Richard L. Mack, Treas.; Christopher Lambe, Exec. Dir.
Directors: Richard McLellan; Lawrence W. Stranghoener.
EIN: 270304734

2581
Moss Adams LLP

999 3rd Ave., Ste. 3300
Seattle, WA 98104-4019 (206) 302-6800
FAX: (206) 652-2098

Company URL: http://www.mossadams.com/
Establishment information: Established in 1913.
Company type: Private company
Business activities: Operates accounting and financial consultation firm.
Business type (SIC): Accounting, auditing, and bookkeeping services
Financial profile for 2013: Number of employees, 2,000; sales volume, $344,000,000
Corporate officers: Chris Schmidt, Chair. and C.E.O.; Dick Fohn, Pres. and C.O.O.; Tom Bourne, C.F.O.; Scott Kallander, Legal Counsel
Giving statement: Giving through the Moss Adams Foundation.

Moss Adams Foundation

999 Third Ave., Ste. 300
Seattle, WA 98104-4019
FAX: (206) 447-0734;
E-mail: christopher.myers@mossadams.com

Establishment information: Established in 1994 in WA.
Donors: Moss Adams, LLP; Robert Bunting; Roger Peterson; Arthur Miles; Chris Schmidt; Rick Anderson; Joe Karas; Tony Maki; Russ Wilson.
Contact: Christopher Myers, Treasury Mgr.
Financial data (yr. ended 12/31/11): Assets, $309,054 (M); gifts received, $436,194; expenditures, $461,555; qualifying distributions, $460,252; giving activities include $460,252 for grants.
Purpose and activities: Giving to support accounting programs at institutions of higher learning located in the western states.
Fields of interest: Business school/education; Human services.
Type of support: General/operating support.
Geographic limitations: Giving primarily in the Western U.S.
Support limitations: No grants to individuals.
Application information: Applications not accepted. Contributes only to pre-selected organizations.
Officers: Russ Wilson, Pres.; Randy Fenich, Secy.; Gary Grimstad, Treas.
Directors: Corinne Baughman; Tina Caratan; Robert Ryker; Chris Schmidt; Trace Skopil; Jim Thompson.
EIN: 911496816

2582
The Motley Fool, Inc.

2000 Duke St., 4th Fl.
Alexandria, VA 22314-3128 (703) 838-3665

Company URL: http://www.fool.com
Establishment information: Established in 1993.
Company type: Private company
Business activities: Provides Internet information services.
Business type (SIC): Computer services
Corporate officers: Tom Gardner, Co-Chair. and C.E.O.; David Gardner, Co-Chair.; Scott Schedler, Pres.; Ollen Douglass, C.F.O.; Andy Cross, C.I.O.
Board of directors: David Garner, Co-Chair.; Tom Garner, Co-Chair.; Putnam Coes; Steve Kerr; Kerra McDonough; John B. McKinnon; Lloyd Sams
Giving statement: Giving through the Motley Fool, Inc. Foolanthropy Program.

The Motley Fool, Inc. Foolanthropy Program

c/o Foolanthropy Prog.
2000 Duke St., 4th Fl.
Alexandria, VA 22314-6101
URL: http://www.foolanthropy.com

Purpose and activities: During the annual Foolanthropy charity drive, visitors to the Motley Fool Web site are invited to contribute to financial literacy and education-related causes. For every post made to a Motley Fool message board during the drive, the company contributes ten cents to an educational institution or nonprofit organization. Support is given primarily in the Washington, DC, area.
Fields of interest: Secondary school/education; Youth development, business; Human services, financial counseling; Financial services; General charitable giving.
Type of support: Cause-related marketing; Employee volunteer services; General/operating support; Program development.
Geographic limitations: Giving primarily in the Washington, DC, area.
Application information:

2583
Motor Castings Company, Inc.

1323 S. 65th St.
Milwaukee, WI 53214-3251
(414) 476-1434
FAX: (414) 476-2845

Company URL: http://www.motorcastings.com
Establishment information: Established in 1919.
Company type: Private company
Business activities: Manufactures motor castings.
Business type (SIC): Iron and steel foundries
Financial profile for 2009: Number of employees, 200
Corporate officers: James J. O'Sullivan, Chair.; Joseph Kemfton, Pres. and C.F.O.
Board of director: James J. O'Sullivan, Chair.
Giving statement: Giving through the Motor Castings Foundation, Inc.

Motor Castings Foundation, Inc.

1323 S. 65th St.
West Allis, WI 53214-3251 (414) 476-1434

Establishment information: Established in 1965 in WI.
Donor: Motor Castings Co.
Contact: Joseph Kempen
Financial data (yr. ended 09/30/12): Assets, $443,881 (M); expenditures, $61,669; qualifying distributions, $61,520; giving activities include $61,520 for 24 grants (high: $25,000; low: $250).
Purpose and activities: The foundation supports centennials and organizations involved with higher education, employment training, school athletics, and civic affairs.
Fields of interest: Education; Health care; Human services.
Type of support: General/operating support.
Geographic limitations: Giving primarily in Milwaukee County, WI.
Support limitations: No grants to individuals.
Application information: Applications accepted. Application form not required.
Initial approach: Proposal
Deadline(s): None
Officer: Peter Sommerhauser, Pres.
EIN: 396086724

2584
Motorists Mutual Insurance Company

(also known as The Motorists Insurance Group)
471 E. Broad St., Ste. 200
Columbus, OH 43215 (614) 225-8211

Company URL: http://www.motoristsmutual.com
Establishment information: Established in 1928.
Company type: Private company
Business activities: Sells automobile and casualty insurance.

Business type (SIC): Insurance/fire, marine, and casualty
Corporate officers: John J. Bishop, Chair., Pres., and C.E.O.; Michael L. Wiseman, C.F.O. and Treas.; Charles Wickert, Sr. V.P. and C.O.O.; David L. Kaufman, Sr. V.P. and C.I.O.; Susan E. Haack, Secy.
Board of directors: John J. Bishop, Chair.; Susan E. Haack; Michael L. Wiseman; Thomas C. Ogg; Archie M. Griffin; Thomas C. Ogg; Michael L. Wiseman
Subsidiaries: American Hardware Mutual Insurance Co., Columbus, OH; MICO Insurance Co., Columbus, OH; Motorists Life Insurance Co., Columbus, OH
Giving statement: Giving through the Motorists Insurance Group Foundation.

The Motorists Insurance Group Foundation

471 E. Broad St.
Columbus, OH 43215-3861 (614) 255-3861

Establishment information: Established in 2000 in OH.
Donor: Motorists Mutual Insurance Co.
Contact: John J. Bishop, Tr.
Financial data (yr. ended 12/31/11): Assets, $122,781 (M); gifts received, $182; expenditures, $493,557; qualifying distributions, $486,724; giving activities include $486,724 for grants.
Purpose and activities: The foundation supports organizations involved with arts and culture, education, health, cancer, law enforcement, youth development, and the insurance industry.
Fields of interest: Arts councils; Museums (art); Arts; Higher education; Education; Health care; Cancer; Crime/law enforcement; Youth development, adult & child programs; Youth development; Business/industry; United Ways and Federated Giving Programs.
Type of support: Annual campaigns; Building/renovation; Capital campaigns; General/operating support.
Geographic limitations: Giving primarily in OH, with emphasis on Columbus.
Support limitations: No grants to individuals.
Application information: Applications accepted. Application form not required. Applicants should submit the following:
1) detailed description of project and amount of funding requested
2) contact person
3) name, address and phone number of organization

Initial approach: Proposal
Deadline(s): None

Trustees: John J. Bishop; Susan E. Haack; Michael L. Wiseman.
EIN: 311712343
Selected grants: The following grants are a representative sample of this grantmaker's funding activity:
$150,000 to Ohio State University, Columbus, OH, 2011.
$125,000 to United Way of Central Ohio, Columbus, OH, 2011.
$40,000 to Columbus Museum of Art, Columbus, OH, 2011.
$30,000 to Buckeye Ranch Foundation, Grove City, OH, 2011.
$25,000 to Columbus Downtown Development Corporation, Columbus, OH, 2011.
$15,000 to Griffith Foundation for Insurance Education, Worthington, OH, 2011.
$10,000 to Cystic Fibrosis Foundation, Worthington, OH, 2011.
$10,000 to Law Enforcement Foundation, Dublin, OH, 2011.
$10,000 to YMCA Camp Coniston, Grantham, NH, 2011.
$1,744 to United Way, Greater Twin Cities, Minneapolis, MN, 2011.

2585
Motorola Mobility Holdings, Inc.

600 N. U.S. Hwy. 45
Libertyville, IL 60048 (847) 523-5000
FAX: (302) 655-5049

Company URL: http://www.motorola.com
Establishment information: Established in 2011.
Company type: Subsidiary of a public company
International Securities Identification Number: US6200971058
Business activities: Operates mobile communications technology company.
Business type (SIC): Communications equipment
Financial profile for 2011: Number of employees, 20,500; assets, $9,730,000,000; sales volume, $13,064,000,000; pre-tax net income, -$148,000,000; expenses, $13,209,000,000; liabilities, $4,642,000,000
Corporate officers: Dennis Woodside, C.E.O.; Daniel M. Moloney, Pres.; Vanessa Wittman, Sr. V.P. and C.F.O.; David Scott Offer, Sr. V.P. and Genl. Counsel; Bill Morgan, Sr. V.P. and Mktg.
Giving statement: Giving through the Motorola Mobility Foundation.
Company EIN: 272780868

Motorola Mobility Foundation

(formerly Motorola Foundation)
600 N. U.S. Hwy. 45
Libertyville, IL 60048-1286 (847) 523-3597
E-mail: giving@motorola.com; URL: http://responsibility.motorola.com/index.php/community/motofoundation/

Donor: Motorola Solutions Foundation.
Contact: Eileen Sweeney, V.P.
Financial data (yr. ended 12/31/11): Assets, $11,467,561 (M); gifts received, $14,227,609; expenditures, $2,762,984; qualifying distributions, $2,762,984; giving activities include $2,547,188 for 799 grants (high: $100,000; low: $50).
Purpose and activities: The foundation supports programs designed to promote education, community, health and wellness, and disaster response.
Fields of interest: Arts; Elementary/secondary education; Higher education; Education; Environmental education; Environment; Health care; Disasters, preparedness/services; Human services; United Ways and Federated Giving Programs; Science, formal/general education; Engineering/technology; Science Youth.
Programs:
Empowerment Grants: The foundation supports programs designed to leverage technology to build stronger communities and close the digital divide. Special emphasis is directed toward programs designed to use innovative approaches with digital, social, or mobile technology to address community issues. Organizations must collaborate with a least one other nonprofit, social enterprise, or community group; and must support education, health and wellness, community, or arts and culture.
Get Mobile! Grants: The foundation awards $200 grants to non-profit groups to help Motorola employees with fundraising goals, including walks, runs, and other "a-thons" that benefit charity.
Matching Gifts: The foundation matches contributions made by employees of Motorola to nonprofit organizations on a one-to-one basis, up to $10,000 per employee.
Volunteer Grants: The foundation awards $300 grants to nonprofit organizations with which Motorola employees volunteers 40 or more hours within a year.
Type of support: Curriculum development; Employee matching gifts; Employee volunteer services; Equipment; General/operating support; Program development.
Geographic limitations: Giving primarily on a national and international basis in areas of company operations, with emphasis on CA, Washington, DC, FL, GA, IL, MA, MD, NJ, NY, OR, PA, TX, Afghanistan, Argentina, Brazil, China, England, and Mexico.
Support limitations: No support for political or lobbying organizations, political candidates, trade schools, or private foundations. No grants to individuals or for political campaigns, endowments, sports sponsorships, fundraising events, conferences, benefits, sponsorships, dinners, tickets, courtesy advertising, capital campaigns, or media projects; no product or equipment donations (except for disaster relief situations).
Publications: Application guidelines; Grants list.
Application information: Applications accepted. Application form required.

Initial approach: Complete online application for Empowerment Grants
Board meeting date(s): Monthly and as required
Deadline(s): Mar. 23 for Empowerment Grants
Final notification: May for Empowerment Grants

Officers: Sanjay Jha, Pres.; Carol Forsyte, V.P. and Secy.; Marc Rothman, V.P. and Treas.; Marshall Brown, V.P.; Jennifer Weyrauch Erickson, V.P.; Daniel M. Moloney, V.P.; Eileen Sweeney, V.P.
EIN: 272451177

2586
Motorola Solutions, Inc.

(formerly Motorola, Inc.)
1303 E. Algonquin Rd.
Schaumburg, IL 60196-4041
(847) 576-5000
FAX: (847) 576-5372

Company URL: http://www.motorolasolutions.com
Establishment information: Established in 1928.
Company type: Public company
Company ticker symbol and exchange: MSI/NYSE
International Securities Identification Number: US6200763075
Business activities: Operates a data communications and telecommunications equipment company.
Business type (SIC): Communications equipment; electronic components and accessories; electrical equipment and supplies
Financial profile for 2012: Number of employees, 22,000; assets, $12,679,000,000; sales volume, $8,698,000,000; pre-tax net income, $1,215,000,000; expenses, $7,456,000,000; liabilities, $9,414,000,000
Fortune 1000 ranking: 2012—304th in revenues, 222nd in profits, and 334th in assets
Forbes 2000 ranking: 2012—1026th in sales, 629th in profits, and 1293rd in assets
Corporate officers: Gregory Q. Brown, Chair. and C.E.O.; Edward J. Fitzpatrick, Exec. V.P. and C.F.O.; Lewis Steverson, Sr. V.P. and Genl. Counsel; Michele Aguilar Carlin, Sr. V.P., Human Resources
Board of directors: Gregory Q. Brown, Chair.; William J. Bratton; Kenneth C. Dahlberg; David W. Dorman; Michael V. Hayden; Judy C. Lewent; Anne

R. Pramaggiore; Samuel C. Scott III; Bradley E. Singer; John A. White
Subsidiary: General Instrument Corporation, Chicago, IL
Plants: Chandler, Mesa, Scottsdale, AZ; Boynton Beach, Plantation, FL; Arlington Heights, Harvard, Libertyville, Northbrook, IL; Mount Pleasant, IA; Elma, NY; Austin, Dallas, Fort Worth, Seguin, TX
International operations: Australia; Austria; Brazil; Canada; China; Denmark; France; Germany; Hong Kong; India; Israel; Japan; Malaysia; Mexico; Saudi Arabia; Singapore; Sweden; Taiwan; Turkey; United Kingdom
Historic mergers: Symbol Technologies, Inc. (January 9, 2007)
Giving statement: Giving through the Motorola Solutions Foundation.
Company EIN: 361115800

Motorola Solutions Foundation

(formerly Motorola Foundation)
1303 East Algonquin Rd.
Schaumburg, IL 60196-4041 (847) 538-7639
FAX: (847) 538-1456;
E-mail: foundation@motorolasolutions.com;
URL: http://www.motorolasolutions.com/giving

Establishment information: Established in 1953 in IL.
Donors: Motorola, Inc.; Motorola Solutions, Inc.
Contact: Matt Blakely, Dir.
Financial data (yr. ended 12/31/11): Assets, $72,852,482 (M); gifts received, $32,000; expenditures, $15,259,102; qualifying distributions, $15,109,507; giving activities include $15,003,084 for grants.
Purpose and activities: The Motorola Solutions Foundation focuses its funding on education, especially science, technology, engineering, and math programming.
Fields of interest: Education, formal/general education; Elementary/secondary education; Education; Disasters, preparedness/services; Disasters, fire prevention/control; Safety/disasters; Human services; Mathematics; Engineering/technology; Science Youth; Minorities; Girls.
Programs:
CEO Award for Volunteerism: The foundation annually awards $5,000 grants to employees or teams of employees of Motorola to contribute to the nonprofit organization with which they volunteer. The award is given in recognition of the individual or teams community involvement. The individual award honors long-term commitment, while team awards recognize exceptional group projects or programs.
Employee Matching Gifts: The foundation matches contributions made by employees and directors of Motorola Solutions, Inc. to nonprofit organizations on a one-for-one basis from $50 to $10,000 per contributor, per year.
Innovation Generation Grants: The foundation supports programs designed to inspire young people to embrace science, technology, engineering, and math. Special emphasis is directed toward programs designed to serve communities in San Jose, CA, Plantation, FL, Schaumburg, IL, Columbia, MD, Long Island, NY, and McAllen, TX; focus on girls and minorities; promote STEM and innovative thinking and creative problem-solving skills; provide opportunities for Motorola Solutions, Inc. employee volunteerism; facilitate measurable change in STEM awareness, skills, or education through evaluation systems and measurement tools; collaborate with other STEM education providers or institutions; and move students through the pipeline to advanced STEM education or careers. The foundation provides local impact grants of $15,000 to $60,000 for elementary through university students and teachers, and national impact grants of $50,000 to $250,000 for large-scale and multi-regional STEM programs that impact at least 150 primary participants.
Motorola Solutions Foundation Service Corps Program: Through the Service Corps Program, the foundation collaborates with customers and employees to support communities with which Motorola Solutions, Inc. has a presence through volunteer projects. Through the Motorola Solutions Service Corps, Motorola Solutions employees can bring purpose to those in the community who need a helping hand. Employees will have the opportunity to volunteer in their communities at projects organized by Service Corps Volunteer Coordinators in their regions. In many cases, employees will volunteer alongside customers to help strengthen their community commitment programs.
Motorola Solutions Public Safety and Security Institute: Through the Institute, the foundation addresses issues that affect the safety and security of local and global communities. The institute utilizes Motorola Solutions technology and foundation funding to protect communities, secure borders, and respond effectively to natural and man-made disasters.
Type of support: Curriculum development; Employee volunteer services; Equipment; General/operating support; Program development.
Geographic limitations: Giving primarily on a national and international basis in areas of company operations, with emphasis on CA, Washington, DC, FL, GA, IL, MA, MD, NJ, NY, TX, Argentina, Belgium, Brazil, China, England, France, Mexico, Poland, and Singapore.
Support limitations: No support for political or lobbying organizations, political candidates, religious organizations, or private foundations described under the U.S. IRS Code Section 509(a). No grants to individuals, or for endowments, sports sponsorships, or capital campaigns; no Motorola Solutions product or equipment donations.
Publications: Application guidelines; Grants list; Program policy statement.
Application information: Applications accepted. Application form required.
Initial approach: Complete online eligibility quiz and application
Board meeting date(s): Monthly and as required
Deadline(s): None; Mar. 23 for Innovation Generation Grants
Director: Matt Blakely, Dir.
Number of staff: 1 full-time professional; 3 part-time professional; 1 full-time support.
EIN: 366109323
Selected grants: The following grants are a representative sample of this grantmaker's funding activity:
$600,000 to Police Executive Research Forum, Washington, DC, 2010.
$500,700 to Girl Scouts of the U.S.A. National Headquarters, New York, NY, 2010. For Innovation Generation-Collaborative Grant.
$300,200 to Field Museum of Natural History, Chicago, IL, 2010. For Innovation Generation-Collaborative Grant.
$250,700 to Cornell University, Ithaca, NY, 2010. For Innovation Generation-Collaborative Grant.
$250,000 to National Academy Foundation, New York, NY, 2010.
$250,000 to Parikrma USA, New York, NY, 2010.
$50,200 to Perspectives Charter School, Chicago, IL, 2010. For Innovation Generation Grant.
$50,000 to Chicago Police Memorial Foundation, Chicago, IL, 2010.
$25,000 to Victory Gardens Theater, Chicago, IL, 2010.
$15,000 to Chicago Public Library Foundation, Chicago, IL, 2010.

2587
Mound Cotton Wollan & Greengrass

1 Battery Park Plz., Fl. 9
New York, NY 10004-1405 (212) 804-4200

Company URL: http://www.moundcotton.com
Establishment information: Established in 1933.
Company type: Private company
Business activities: Operates law firm.
Business type (SIC): Legal services
Offices: San Francisco, CA; Fort Lauderdale, FL; Newark, NJ; Garden City, New York, NY
Giving statement: Giving through the Mound Cotton Wollan & Greengrass Pro Bono Program.

Mound Cotton Wollan & Greengrass Pro Bono Program

1 Battery Park Plz., Fl. 9
New York, NY 10004-1405 (212) 804-4573
E-mail: Akallal@moundcotton.com; URL: http://www.moundcotton.com/careers/pro-bono-program

Contact: Amy Kallal, Partner
Fields of interest: Legal services.
Type of support: Pro bono services - legal.
Geographic limitations: Giving primarily in areas of company operations in San Francisco, CA, Fort Lauderdale, FL, Newark, NJ, and Garden City, and New York, NY.
Application information: An attorney coordinates pro bono projects as an ancillary duty to other work.

2588
Mount Wheeler Power, Inc.

1600 Great Basin Blvd.
P.O. Box 151000
Ely, NV 89315 (775) 289-8981

Company URL: http://www.mwpower.net
Establishment information: Established in 1963.
Company type: Private company
Business activities: Generates, transmits, and distributes electricity.
Business type (SIC): Electric services
Corporate officers: Jerald Anderson, Co-Pres.; Gary Perea, Co-Pres.; Wilma Sanford, Secy.; Sandra L. Green, Treas.
Board of directors: Jerald Anderson; Sandra L. Green; Rick Hendrix; Frank Leon; Ron Miller; Jerry T. Morrill; Don Phillips; Wilma Sanford; Bob Swetich
Giving statement: Giving through the Mount Wheeler C.A.R.E. Program.

Mount Wheeler C.A.R.E. Program

P.O. Box 151000
Ely, NV 89315-1000 (775) 289-3271
Application address: c/o White Pine County Welfare Office, 995 Campton St., Ely, NV 89301, tel.: (775) 289-3271; URL: http://www.mwpower.net/content/member-services-rates

Donor: Mount Wheeler Power, Inc.
Financial data (yr. ended 12/31/11): Assets, $21,796 (M); gifts received, $11,256; expenditures, $7,807; qualifying distributions,

$7,807; giving activities include $7,807 for 3 grants (high: $5,142; low: $400).
Purpose and activities: The foundation provides assistance to economically disadvantaged households for energy service.
Fields of interest: Utilities Economically disadvantaged.
Geographic limitations: Giving limited to White Pine County, NV.
Support limitations: No grants to individuals.
Publications: Application guidelines; Informational brochure (including application guidelines).
Application information: Applications accepted. Application form required.
Initial approach: Contact the White Pine County Welfare Office for application form
Deadline(s): None
Officers: Kevin Robison, Pres.; Desiree Robinson, Secy.; Wilma Sanford, Treas.
Director: Bunny Hill.
EIN: 880195091

2589
Mountain Sky Guest Ranch, LLC

480 Big Creek Rd.
P.O. Box 1219
Emigrant, MT 59027 (406) 333-4911

Company URL: http://www.mtnsky.com
Establishment information: Established in 1929.
Company type: Private company
Business activities: Operates guest ranch resort.
Business type (SIC): Camps/recreational
Corporate officers: Arthur M. Blank, Owner; Alan Brutge, C.E.O.
Giving statement: Giving through the Mountain Sky Guest Ranch, LLC Corporate Giving Program.

Mountain Sky Guest Ranch, LLC Corporate Giving Program

(also known as Mountain Sky Guest Ranch Fund)
P.O. Box 1219
Emigrant, MT 59027-1219 (406) 333-4911
E-mail: tawnyar@mtnsky.com; URL: http://www.mtnsky.com/philanthropy.aspx

Contact: Tawnya Rupe
Purpose and activities: Mountain Sky Guest Ranch makes charitable contributions to nonprofit organizations involved with youth development and family services. Special emphasis is directed toward programs that empower youth through the challenges of physical activity and outdoor adventure, including innovations that make use of the natural resources in Paradise Valley. Support is limited to areas of company operations in Park and Gallatin counties, Montana.
Fields of interest: Youth development; Family services Youth.
Type of support: General/operating support.
Geographic limitations: Giving limited to areas of company operations in Park and Gallatin counties, MT.
Support limitations: No support for religious or discriminatory organizations, or government agencies, municipalities, or parochial/private schools. No grants to individuals, or for events or therapeutic programs.
Publications: Application guidelines.
Application information: Applications accepted. Organizations may apply once per calendar year. Double-sided pages are strongly encouraged. Application form required. Applicants should submit the following:
1) copy of IRS Determination Letter
2) brief history of organization and description of its mission
3) copy of most recent annual report/audited financial statement/990
4) how project's results will be evaluated or measured
5) listing of board of directors, trustees, officers and other key people and their affiliations
6) copy of current year's organizational budget and/or project budget
7) listing of additional sources and amount of support

Initial approach: Complete online application; mail or e-mail 1 copy of required attachments
Copies of proposal: 2
Deadline(s): Mar. 19

2590
Mountaire Corporation

204 E. 4th St.
North Little Rock, AR 72114-5402
(501) 372-6524
FAX: (501) 372-3972

Company URL: http://www.mountaire.com
Establishment information: Established in 1964.
Company type: Private company
Business activities: Produces poultry.
Business type (SIC): Farms/poultry and egg
Financial profile for 2010: Number of employees, 6,000
Corporate officers: Ronald M. Cameron, Chair. and C.E.O.; David L. Pogge, Pres. and C.O.O; Alan H. Duncan, Secy. and C.F.O.; Michael W. Lofton, V.P., Finance
Board of director: Ronald M. Cameron, Chair.
Giving statement: Giving through the Jesus Fund.

The Jesus Fund

1901 Napa Valley Dr.
Little Rock, AR 72212-3913

Establishment information: Established in 2004 in AR.
Donors: Mountaire Corp.; Ronald M. Cameron.
Financial data (yr. ended 12/31/11): Assets, $35,009,636 (M); gifts received, $1,000,000; expenditures, $5,273,145; qualifying distributions, $4,910,417; giving activities include $4,910,417 for grants.
Purpose and activities: The foundation supports various public charities.
Fields of interest: General charitable giving.
Support limitations: No grants to individuals.
Application information: Applications not accepted. Contributes only to pre-selected organizations.
Trustees: Ronald M. Cameron; Genevieve R. Couch.
EIN: 861108441

2591
MPB Corporation

7 Optical Ave.
Keene, NH 03431-4382 (603) 352-0310

Company URL: http://www.timken.com/en-us/Pages/Home.aspx
Establishment information: Established in 1941.
Company type: Subsidiary of a public company
Business activities: Manufactures ball bearings.
Business type (SIC): Machinery/general industry
Giving statement: Giving through the Timken Company Charitable Trust of New Hampshire.

Timken Company Charitable Trust of New Hampshire

(formerly MPB Corporation Fund)
P.O. Box 547
Keene, NH 03431-0547 (603) 355-4531

Donor: MPB Corp.
Contact: Kevin Beck
Financial data (yr. ended 12/31/11): Assets, $182,071 (M); expenditures, $503; qualifying distributions, $503; giving activities include $500 for 1 grant.
Purpose and activities: The foundation supports festivals and organizations involved with arts and culture, athletics, and human services.
Fields of interest: Arts; Human services.
Type of support: General/operating support; Program development; Sponsorships.
Geographic limitations: Giving primarily in Keene, NH.
Application information: Applications accepted. Application form required. Applicants should submit the following:
1) detailed description of project and amount of funding requested

Initial approach: Letter
Deadline(s): None
Trustees: Robert J. Bauman; James R. Menning; Erick A. Paulhardt.
EIN: 026012774

2592
Mrs. Fields' Original Cookies, Inc.

2855 Cottonwood Pkwy., Ste. 400
Salt Lake City, UT 84121-1050
(801) 736-5600

Company URL: http://www.mrsfields.com
Establishment information: Established in 1977.
Company type: Subsidiary of a private company
Business activities: Operates, develops, and franchises bakery stores and cafes; operates frozen yogurt and ice cream shops.
Business type (SIC): Restaurants and drinking places
Corporate officers: Timothy Casey, Pres. and C.E.O.; Michael Ward, Exec. V.P. and Secy.; Gregory Barber, C.F.O.; Ron Curtis, V.P., Opers.
Subsidiary: Fairfield Foods, Inc., Fairfield, NJ
Giving statement: Giving through the Children's Health Foundation.

The Children's Health Foundation

3160 Pinebrook Rd.
Park City, UT 84098-5380 (435) 649-2221

Establishment information: Established in 1986 in UT.
Donors: Randall K. Fields; Debra J. Fields; Mrs. Fields' Original Cookies, Inc.; Vallarta Cuatro Ltd.
Financial data (yr. ended 12/31/11): Assets, $37,820 (M); expenditures, $2,965; qualifying distributions, $2,200; giving activities include $2,200 for grants.
Purpose and activities: The foundation supports organizations involved with health, disaster relief, and children and youth.

Fields of interest: Health care; Safety/disasters, fund raising/fund distribution; Children/youth, services.
Support limitations: No grants to individuals.
Application information: Applications not accepted. Unsolicited requests for funds not accepted.
Officers: Debra J. Fields Rose*, Chair.; Randall K. Fields, Pres.
EIN: 742450465

2593
MSC Industrial Direct Co., Inc.

75 Maxess Rd.
Melville, NY 11747-3151 (516) 812-2000
FAX: (516) 349-7096

Company URL: http://www1.mscdirect.com
Establishment information: Established in 1941.
Company type: Public company
Company ticker symbol and exchange: MSM/NYSE
Business activities: Direct marketer of industrial products to industrial customers.
Business type (SIC): Industrial machinery and equipment—wholesale
Financial profile for 2012: Number of employees, 4,982; assets, $1,444,880,000; sales volume, $2,355,920,000; pre-tax net income, $412,140,000; expenses, $1,943,700,000; liabilities, $257,760,000
Fortune 1000 ranking: 2012—846th in revenues, 514th in profits, and 926th in assets
Corporate officers: Mitchell Jacobson, Chair.; David Sandler, Vice-Chair.; Erik Gershwind, Pres. and C.E.O.; Jeffrey Kaczka, Exec. V.P. and C.F.O.; Thomas Cox, Exec. V.P., Sales; Eileen McGuire, Exec. V.P., Human Resources; Charles Bonomo, Sr. V.P. and C.I.O.; Steve Armstrong, Sr. V.P., Genl. Counsel., and Corp. Secy.; Christopher Davanzo, V.P., Finance, Cont.; John Chironna, Treas.
Board of directors: Mitchell Jacobson, Chair.; Jonathan L.S. Byrnes; Roger Fradin; Erik Gershwind; Louise K. Goeser; Denis Kelly; Philip Peller; David Sandler
Giving statement: Giving through the MSC Industrial Direct Co., Inc. Contributions Program.
Company EIN: 113289165

MSC Industrial Direct Co., Inc. Contributions Program

(also known as MSC Community Action Team)
c/o Community Rels.
75 Maxess Rd.
Melville, NY 11747-3151 (516) 812-2000
E-mail: communityrelations@mscdirect.com;
URL: http://www1.mscdirect.com/content/aboutmsc/comm_rel.html

Purpose and activities: MSC Industrial Direct makes charitable contributions to nonprofit organizations in areas of company operations; giving also to national organizations. Special emphasis is directed toward organizations and programs involved with children, disaster relief, health care, veterans, and food services.
Fields of interest: Health care; Food services; Safety/disasters; Children, services; United Ways and Federated Giving Programs; Military/veterans' organizations.
Type of support: Annual campaigns; Employee volunteer services; General/operating support; In-kind gifts; Sponsorships.
Geographic limitations: Giving primarily in areas of company operations; giving also to national organizations.
Support limitations: No support for religious or sectarian organizations, organizations whose programs do not benefit the entire community, or organizations whose chief purpose is to influence legislation, and/or participate or intervene in political campaigns on behalf of or against any candidate for public office. No grants to individuals (except for participation in company-sponsored events), or for sports teams or sports-related activities (except those that qualify under the Community Relations Charter); donations of, or discounts on, products and services as precluded by supplier and customer agreements that would constitute a conflict of interest; or donations that are focused only on profit for an organization.
Publications: Application guidelines.
Application information: Applications accepted. The Community Relations department handles giving in conjunction with Regional Community Outreach Teams at the company's Customer Fulfillment Centers. Application form required. Applicants should submit the following:
1) name, address and phone number of organization
2) brief history of organization and description of its mission
3) copy of most recent annual report/audited financial statement/990
4) descriptive literature about organization
Proposals should include potential sponsorship options, proposed conditions of sponsorship, the type of donation requested, how the group will continue development with MSC Industrial Supply's support, and the names of any company associates involved with the group.
Initial approach: Download application form and mail to headquarters with sponsorship request letter
Copies of proposal: 1

2594
Mt. Olive Pickle Company, Inc.

1 Cucumber Blvd.
P.O. Box 609
Mount Olive, NC 28365 (919) 658-2535
FAX: (919) 658-6296

Company URL: http://www.mtolivepickles.com
Establishment information: Established in 1926.
Company type: Private company
Business activities: Produces pickles.
Business type (SIC): Specialty foods/canned, frozen, and preserved
Corporate officers: William H. Bryan, Pres. and Treas.; Dan Bowen, C.F.O.; Doug Brock, V.P., Opers.
Giving statement: Giving through the Mt. Olive Pickle Company, Inc. Contributions Program and the Mount Olive Pickle Company Foundation.

Mt. Olive Pickle Company, Inc. Contributions Program

1 Cucumber Blvd.
P.O. Box 609
Mount Olive, NC 28365 (800) 672-5041
URL: http://www.mtolivepickles.com/mtolive101/our-giving/

Purpose and activities: As a complement to its foundation, Mt. Olive Pickle Company also makes charitable contributions to local nonprofit organizations directly; also giving to national organizations that operate in Wayne County, North Carolina.
Fields of interest: Elementary/secondary education; Higher education, college; Recreation; Human services, fund raising/fund distribution; Community/economic development; United Ways and Federated Giving Programs.
Type of support: Donated products; Employee volunteer services; General/operating support; Matching/challenge support.
Geographic limitations: Giving primarily in areas of company operations, with emphasis on Wayne County, NC.

Mount Olive Pickle Company Foundation

812 N. Chestnut St.
Mount Olive, NC 28365-1218

Establishment information: Established in 1994 in NC.
Donor: Mount Olive Pickle Co., Inc.
Financial data (yr. ended 04/30/12): Assets, $2,134,529 (M); gifts received, $400,000; expenditures, $206,849; qualifying distributions, $205,000; giving activities include $205,000 for grants.
Purpose and activities: The foundation supports organizations involved with theater, education, housing development, youth development, and community development.
Fields of interest: Arts; Education; Community/economic development.
Type of support: Capital campaigns; General/operating support.
Geographic limitations: Giving primarily in Mount Olive and Wayne County, NC.
Support limitations: No grants to individuals.
Application information: Applications not accepted. Unsolicited requests for funds not accepted.
Officers: Malcolm T. Murray, Jr., Pres.; William H. Bryan, Secy.
Directors: Margaret Ann P. Parvin; Emmett Judson Pope III.
EIN: 561888088

2595
MTD Products, Inc.

5903 Grafton Rd.
Valley City, OH 44280 (330) 225-2600

Company URL: http://www.mtdproducts.com
Establishment information: Established in 1932.
Company type: Subsidiary of a private company
Business activities: Manufactures outdoor power equipment.
Business type (SIC): Machinery/farm and garden; metal forgings and stampings; machinery/metalworking
Financial profile for 2010: Number of employees, 500
Corporate officers: Theodore S. Moll, Chair.; Hartmut Kaesgen, Vice-Chair.; Robert T. Moll, C.E.O.; Jean H. Hlay, Pres. and C.O.O.; Roy G. Pullum, Exec. V.P., Opers.; David Duckhouse, C.F.O.; John Bondi, C.I.O.; Randy Parish, V.P., Opers.; David J. Hessler, Secy.
Board of directors: Theodore S. Moll, Chair.; Hartmut Kaesgen, Vice-Chair.
Giving statement: Giving through the Jochum-Moll Foundation.

The Jochum-Moll Foundation

P.O. Box 368022
Cleveland, OH 44136-9722

Establishment information: Incorporated in 1961 in OH.

Donors: MTD Products, Inc.; A.F. Holding Co.
Financial data (yr. ended 07/31/11): Assets, $33,384,212 (M); gifts received, $500,000; expenditures, $1,112,922; qualifying distributions, $782,300; giving activities include $782,300 for grants.
Purpose and activities: The foundation supports food banks and organizations involved with education, health, employment, agriculture, human services, business and industry, and Christianity.
Fields of interest: Secondary school/education; Higher education; Theological school/education; Hospitals (general); Health care; Goodwill Industries; Agriculture; Food banks; Salvation Army; YM/YWCAs & YM/YWHAs; Children, services; Residential/custodial care, hospices; Human services; Business/industry; United Ways and Federated Giving Programs; Christian agencies & churches.
Type of support: Annual campaigns; Building/renovation; Capital campaigns; Equipment; General/operating support; Program development.
Geographic limitations: Giving primarily in OH.
Support limitations: No grants to individuals.
Application information: Applications not accepted. Contributes only to pre-selected organizations.
Officers and Trustees:* Carol M. Manning*, Pres.; Theodore S. Moll*, V.P.; David J. Hessler*, Secy.; Curtis E. Moll*, Treas.; Emma E. Jochum; Darrell Moll.
EIN: 346538304
Selected grants: The following grants are a representative sample of this grantmaker's funding activity:
$46,400 to National Inventors Hall of Fame, Akron, OH, 2010.
$25,000 to Cleveland Foodbank, Cleveland, OH, 2010. For operations.
$25,000 to Manufacturing Advocacy and Growth Network, Cleveland, OH, 2010.
$25,000 to Rust College, Holly Springs, MS, 2010.
$25,000 to Sanctuary Hospice House, Tupelo, MS, 2010.
$20,000 to Lutheran Chaplaincy Service, Cleveland, OH, 2010.
$15,000 to Ohio Roundtable, Strongsville, OH, 2010.
$12,000 to Youth Challenge, Westlake, OH, 2010.
$10,000 to Building Hope in the City, Cleveland, OH, 2010.
$7,500 to Boy Scouts of America, Tupelo, MS, 2010.

2596
MTV Networks Company

1515 Broadway
New York, NY 10036 (212) 258-8000

Company URL: http://www.mtv.com
Company type: Subsidiary of a public company
Business activities: Operates cable television networks; provides Internet entertainment services.
Business type (SIC): Cable and other pay television services; computer services
Financial profile for 2009: Number of employees, 329
Corporate officers: Judy McGrath, Chair. and C.E.O.; William Roedy, Vice-Chair.; Rich Eigendorff, C.O.O.; Jacques Tortoli, Exec. V.P. and C.F.O.; David Kline, C.I.O.
Board of directors: Judy McGrath, Chair.; William Roedy, Vice-Chair.
Divisions: Nickelodeon, New York, NY; VH1, New York, NY
Giving statement: Giving through the Nickelodeon Corporate Giving Program and the VH1 Save The Music Foundation.

Nickelodeon Corporate Giving Program

1515 Broadway, 39th Fl.
New York, NY 10036-8901 (212) 258-6000
E-mail: publicaffairs@nick.com; Application address: Nickelodeon's "Let's Just Play" Giveaway, P.O. Box 10850, Rochester, NY 14610

Purpose and activities: Nickelodeon makes charitable contributions to K-9 schools and after-school organizations to encourage children's play.
Fields of interest: Elementary/secondary education; Youth development; Children, day care.
Program:
Nickelodeon's Let's Just Play Giveaway Grants: Through Nickelodeon's Let's Just Play Giveaway Grants program, Nickelodeon annually awards 200 $5,000 grants to K-9 schools and after-school organizations to encourage children's play.
Type of support: Program development.
Publications: Grants list.
Application information: Applications accepted. Contributes only to organizations nominated by children between the ages of 6 and 15. Postcards should be hand-printed. Applicants should submit the following:
1) signature and title of chief executive officer
2) name, address and phone number of organization
3) contact person
Postcards should include the child's name, address, daytime telephone number, and age and three reasons why play is important to them.
Initial approach: Download application form and mail to application address or mail 3X5 postcard to application address
Copies of proposal: 1
Deadline(s): None

VH1 Save The Music Foundation

(formerly Viacom Foundation)
1515 Broadway, 20th Fl.
New York, NY 10036-8901 (212) 846-7882
FAX: (212) 846-1827; URL: http://www.vh1savethemusic.com

Establishment information: Incorporated as a company-sponsored foundation in 1997 in NY; status changed to public charity in 2005.
Donors: New York State Music Fund, Inc.; The Baltimore Community Foundation; MTV Networks; Rockefeller Philanthropy Advisors; The Paul Singer Family Foundation; VH1.
Contact: Jessica Ecker, Dir., Devel.
Financial data (yr. ended 09/30/11): Revenue, $3,272,925; assets, $1,130,591 (M); gifts received, $3,271,463; expenditures, $3,612,303; program services expenses, $2,232,742; giving activities include $1,669,590 for 39 grants.
Purpose and activities: The foundation restores instrumental music programs in public schools across the U.S.
Fields of interest: Performing arts, music; Elementary/secondary education Children/youth.
Program:
Grants: Grants of up to $30,000 are available to public elementary and middle schools in the U.S. to help develop long-term, sustainable instrumental music programs that provide children with equal access to music education, regardless of their financial situation. Recipients will be provided with new musical instruments (band, string, keyboard lab, guitar lab, or mariachi instruments) to jump start a beginning instrumental music program. Eligible applicants must not currently have an instrumental music program, but plans to add one to the regular school curriculum, offering no less than weekly, in-school instrumental music classes for all interested students (though general music and recorder classes can and should be currently available at the school). Schools must also provide for at least one certified instrumental music teacher's salary within its budget for a new program, and must have adequate and secure storage space for instruments and equipment.
Type of support: Donated equipment.
Geographic limitations: Giving on a national basis.
Support limitations: No grants to individuals, or for annual campaigns, start-up needs, emergency needs, debt reduction, equipment, land acquisition, renovation, endowments, research, demonstration projects, publications, or conferences; no loans.
Publications: Annual report; Application guidelines; Financial statement; Informational brochure; Newsletter; Program policy statement.
Application information: Applications accepted. The grant application process opens on Mar. 1 of each year; applications are accessible only after an initial consultation with foundation staff. Application form required.
Initial approach: Email foundation for application form
Copies of proposal: 1
Board meeting date(s): Three times per year
Deadline(s): June 1
Officer and Directors:* Paul Cothran*, Exec. Dir.; Tom Calderone; Larry Cohen; Wynton Marsalis; David Nathan; Christina Norman; Scott H. Rauch; Morris L. Reid; Gordon Singer; John Sykes; John Varvatos; Dirk Ziff; and 4 additional Directors.
Number of staff: 9 full-time professional.
EIN: 136089816

2597
Mueller and Company, Inc.

641 5th St.
Lakewood, NJ 08701-2702 (732) 364-0286

Establishment information: Established in 1996.
Company type: Private company
Business activities: Provides securities brokerage services.
Business type (SIC): Brokers and dealers/security
Corporate officer: Mark Mueller, Pres.
Giving statement: Giving through the M & S Family Foundation.

M & S Family Foundation

242 4th St.
Lakewood, NJ 08701-3227

Establishment information: Established in 2000 in NJ.
Donors: Mueller and Co., Inc.; Moshe Mueller; Merit Consulting LLC; Harry Adler; Cashmere Capital; Shlansky Free Loan Fund of BMG; Valcent Products Inc.; Global Green Solutions.
Financial data (yr. ended 05/31/11): Assets, $1,498,796 (M); gifts received, $190,887; expenditures, $925,347; qualifying distributions, $912,216; giving activities include $912,216 for grants.
Purpose and activities: The foundation supports organizations involved with education and Judaism.
Fields of interest: Education; Jewish agencies & synagogues.
Type of support: General/operating support.
Geographic limitations: Giving primarily in NJ.

Support limitations: No grants to individuals.
Application information: Applications not accepted. Contributes only to pre-selected organizations.
Trustee: Shoshana Englander.
EIN: 316642915

2598
Munger, Tolles & Olson LLP

355 S. Grand Ave., 35th Fl.
Los Angeles, CA 90071-1560
(213) 683-9225

Company URL: http://www.mto.com
Establishment information: Established in 1962.
Company type: Private company
Business activities: Operates law firm.
Business type (SIC): Legal services
Corporate officer: Sandra Seville-Jones, Managing Partner
Offices: Los Angeles, San Francisco, CA
Giving statement: Giving through the Munger, Tolles & Olson LLP Pro Bono Program.

Munger, Tolles & Olson LLP Pro Bono Program

355 S. Grand Ave., 35th Fl.
Los Angeles, CA 90071-1560 (213) 683-9225
Additional tel.: (213) 683-9100; alternate pro bono contact: David H. Fry, Co-Chair, Pro Bono Comm., tel.: (415) 512-4082, e-mail: david.fry@mto.com; URL: http://www.mto.com/pro-bono

Contact: Grant Davis-Denny, Co-Chair, Pro Bono Comm.
Fields of interest: Legal services.
Type of support: Pro bono services - legal.
Geographic limitations: Giving primarily in areas of company operations in Los Angeles and San Francisco, CA.
Application information: A Pro Bono Committee manages the pro bono program.

2599
Murphy Brothers, Inc.

3812 E. Broadway Ave.
Spokane, WA 99202 (509) 535-1591

Establishment information: Established in 1937.
Company type: Private company
Business activities: Operates heavy construction company specializing in asphalt paving and other municipal projects.
Business type (SIC): Construction/highway and street (except elevated)
Corporate officers: William O. Murphy, Pres.; T. Chuck Murphy, Secy.
Giving statement: Giving through the William O. Murphy Foundation.

William O. Murphy Foundation

P.O. Box 8317
Spokane, WA 99203

Establishment information: Established in WA.
Donors: William O. Murphy; Murphy Brothers, Inc.; Shamrock Paving; Carol Murphy Ellis; Willam T. Murphy.
Financial data (yr. ended 12/31/11): Assets, $1,335,350 (M); gifts received, $125,000; expenditures, $64,487; qualifying distributions, $62,495; giving activities include $62,470 for 17 grants (high: $6,000; low: $1,500).
Fields of interest: Human services; Christian agencies & churches.
Type of support: General/operating support.
Geographic limitations: Giving limited to Spokane, WA.
Support limitations: No grants to individuals.
Application information: Applications not accepted. Unsolicited requests for funds not accepted.
Trustees: Carol Murphy Ellis; William O. Murphy; William T. Murphy.
EIN: 911531342

2600
Murphy Oil Corporation

200 Peach St.
P.O. Box 7000
El Dorado, AR 71731-7000 (870) 862-6411
FAX: (302) 655-5049

Company URL: http://www.murphyoilcorp.com
Establishment information: Established in 1950.
Company type: Public company
Company ticker symbol and exchange: MUR/NYSE
Business activities: Produces, refines, and markets crude oil and natural gas.
Business type (SIC): Extraction/oil and gas
Financial profile for 2012: Number of employees, 9,185; assets, $17,522,640,000; sales volume, $28,626,050,000; pre-tax net income, $1,622,980,000; expenses, $27,003,060,000; liabilities, $8,580,610,000
Fortune 1000 ranking: 2012—104th in revenues, 203rd in profits, and 261st in assets
Forbes 2000 ranking: 2012—330th in sales, 610th in profits, and 1055th in assets
Corporate officers: Claiborne P. Deming, Chair.; Steven A. Cosse, Pres. and C.E.O.; Kevin G. Fitzgerald, Exec. V.P. and C.F.O.; Walter K. Compton, Sr. V.P. and Genl. Counsel; Mindy K. West, V.P. and Treas.; John W. Eckart, V.P. and Cont.; Kelli M. Hammock, V.P., Admin.; John Moore, Corp. Secy.
Board of directors: Claiborne P. Deming, Chair.; Frank W. Blue; Steven A. Cosse; Robert A. Hermes; James V. Kelley; Roger Jenkins; Walentin Mirosh; Robert Madison Murphy; Jeffrey W. Nolan; Neal E. Schmale; David J.H. Smith; Caroline G. Theus
Subsidiaries: El Dorado Engineering, Inc., Salt Lake City, UT; Marine Land Co., El Dorado, AR; Murphy Eastern Oil Co., El Dorado, CA; Murphy Exploration & Production Co., Houston, TX; Murphy Oil USA, Inc., El Dorado, AR; Murphy Ventures Corp., Wilmington, DE
International operations: Canada; Italy; United Kingdom
Giving statement: Giving through the Murphy Oil Corporation Contributions Program, the El Dorado Promise, Inc., the Fondation BNP Paribas, and the Murphy Education Program, Inc.
Company EIN: 710361522

Murphy Oil Corporation Contributions Program

200 Peach St.
P.O. Box 7000
El Dorado, AR 71731-7000 (870) 881-6866
E-mail: sandiks@murphyoilcorp.com; URL: http://www.murphyoilcorp.com/responsibility/community.aspx
Application address for El Dorado Promise: 200 W. Oak, El Dorado, AR 71730, tel.: (870) 864-5046

Contact: Katie Sandifer, Community Rels. Mgr.
Purpose and activities: Murphy Oil makes charitable contributions to nonprofit organizations involved with education, the environment, and on a case by case basis. Support is given on a national and international basis in areas of company operations.
Fields of interest: Secondary school/education; Higher education; Adult/continuing education; Education; Environment, natural resources; Environment; United Ways and Federated Giving Programs.
Programs:
Community Spirit Award: Through the Community Spirit Award program, Murphy Oil annually awards a $5,000 grant to a nonprofit organization chosen by a resident of the St. Bernard Parish, Louisiana, community or an employee at the company's Meraux refinery recognized for volunteerism.
Employee Educational Assistance Program: Through the Employee Educational Assistance Program, Murphy Oil supports the ongoing needs of its employees. The company reimburses the costs of tuition, textbooks and some required fees that employees incur at accredited colleges, universities, or trade schools. The program is designed to encourage employees to extend their knowledge and capability through outside study.
Type of support: Employee volunteer services; Employee-related scholarships; General/operating support; Grants to individuals; Program development; Scholarship funds.
Geographic limitations: Giving on a national and international basis in areas of company operations including AR, LA, and Canada.

El Dorado Promise, Inc.

200 Peach St.
El Dorado, AR 71730-5836 (870) 864-5046
URL: http://www.eldoradopromise.com/
Application address: 2000 Wildcat Dr., El Dorado, AR 71730

Establishment information: Established in 2007 in AR.
Donor: Murphy Oil Corp.
Financial data (yr. ended 12/31/11): Assets, $19,600,796 (M); gifts received, $5,000,000; expenditures, $2,672,501; qualifying distributions, $2,546,316; giving activities include $2,546,316 for grants to individuals.
Purpose and activities: The foundation awards college scholarships to graduates of El Dorado High Schools in El Dorado, Arkansas.
Fields of interest: Scholarships/financial aid; Education.
Type of support: Scholarships—to individuals.
Geographic limitations: Giving primarily in El Dorado, AR.
Publications: Application guidelines.
Application information: Applications accepted. Application form required.
Initial approach: Download application form and mail to application address or participating high school counseling office
Deadline(s): Student's senior year of high school
Officers: David M. Wood, Pres.; Kelli Hammock, V.P.; Mindy K. West, Treas.
EIN: 208303418

Murphy Education Program, Inc.

200 Peach St.
P.O. Box 7000
El Dorado, AR 71731-7000
URL: http://www.murphyoilcorp.com/responsibility/community.aspx

Establishment information: Established in 1998 in AR.
Donor: Murphy Oil Corp.
Financial data (yr. ended 12/31/11): Assets, $231,287 (M); gifts received, $191,748; expenditures, $184,449; qualifying distributions, $183,151; giving activities include $183,151 for grants to individuals.
Purpose and activities: The foundation awards grants to El Dorado, Arkansas, public school students in grades 1 through 12 who score high on standardized tests, and to teachers.
Fields of interest: Elementary/secondary education.
Type of support: Grants to individuals.
Geographic limitations: Giving limited to El Dorado, AR.
Application information: Applications not accepted. Contributes only to pre-selected individuals.
Officers and Directors:* David Wood*, Pres.; Walter K. Compton, V.P.; J. A. Moore, Secy.; Mindy K. West, Treas.
EIN: 710814094

2601
Murray Guard, Inc.

58 Murray Guard Dr.
Jackson, TN 38305-3609 (731) 668-3121
FAX: (731) 664-1343

Company URL: http://www.murrayguard.com
Establishment information: Established in 1967.
Company type: Private company
Business activities: Provides security guard services.
Business type (SIC): Business services/ miscellaneous
Corporate officers: Gerald P. Ferguson, Jr., Pres.; David M. Harris, V.P. and Cont.; Bruce K. Burch, V.P., Sales and Mktg.; Claude H. Kelly, Jr., V.P., Human Resources
Giving statement: Giving through the Murray Foundation, Inc.

The Murray Foundation, Inc.

58 Murray Guard Dr.
Jackson, TN 38305-3609

Establishment information: Established in 2002 in TN.
Donors: Roger Murray; Muarry Guard, Inc.
Financial data (yr. ended 12/31/11): Assets, $175,661 (M); expenditures, $9,577; qualifying distributions, $9,000; giving activities include $9,000 for 9 grants (high: $2,000; low: $250).
Purpose and activities: The foundation supports organizations involved with higher education.
Fields of interest: Education; Youth development; Human services.
Support limitations: No grants to individuals.
Application information: Applications not accepted. Unsolicited requests for funds not accepted.
Officers and Directors:* Roger Murray*, Pres.; Gerald Ferguson*, Secy.; Judith Murray; Luanne Story.
EIN: 760708303

2602
Murtha Cullina LLP

CityPlace I
185 Asylum St., 29th Fl.
Hartford, CT 06103-3469 (860) 240-6000

Company URL: http://www.murthalaw.com
Company type: Private company
Business activities: Operates law firm.
Business type (SIC): Legal services
Offices: Hartford, Madison, New Haven, Stamford, CT; Boston, Woburn, MA
Giving statement: Giving through the Murtha Cullina LLP Corporate Giving Program.

Murtha Cullina LLP Corporate Giving Program

CityPlace I
185 Asylum St., 29th Fl.
Hartford, CT 06103-3469
Contact for pro bono program: Lissa Paris, Partner, Pro Bono Comm., tel.: (860) 240-6032, e-mail: lparis@murthalaw.com; URL: http://www.murthalaw.com/about_us/community-involvement

Contact: Lissa Paris, Partner
Fields of interest: Legal services.
Type of support: Pro bono services - legal.

2603
Mutual Bank

(formerly Mutual Federal Savings Bank)
110 E. Charles St.
Muncie, IN 47305 (765) 747-2800

Company URL: http://www.bankwithmutual.com/
Establishment information: Established in 1889.
Company type: Subsidiary of a public company
Business activities: Operates savings bank.
Business type (SIC): Savings institutions
Corporate officers: Wilbur R. Davis, Chair; David W. Heeter, Pres. and C.E.O.; Christopher D. Cook, Sr. V.P., Treas., and C.F.O.
Board of director: Wilbur R. Davis, Chair.
Giving statement: Giving through the Mutual Charitable Foundation, Inc.

Mutual Charitable Foundation, Inc.

110 E. Charles St.
P.O. Box 551
Muncie, IN 47308-0551

Establishment information: Established in 1998 in IN.
Donor: Mutual Financial, Inc.
Financial data (yr. ended 06/30/12): Assets, $3,672,211 (M); gifts received, $25,000; expenditures, $182,606; qualifying distributions, $181,250; giving activities include $171,350 for 43 grants (high: $35,000; low: $500).
Purpose and activities: The foundation supports food banks and organizations involved with education, housing development, human services, and economic development.
Fields of interest: Performing arts, theater; Higher education; Higher education, college (community/junior); Education; Food banks; Housing/shelter, development; YM/YWCAs & YM/YWHAs; Homeless, human services; Human services; Economic development; United Ways and Federated Giving Programs.
Type of support: Continuing support; Equipment; General/operating support; Program development; Scholarship funds; Sponsorships.
Geographic limitations: Giving primarily in Indianapolis, Marion, Muncie, and Warsaw, IN.
Support limitations: No grants to individuals.
Publications: Annual report.
Application information: Applications not accepted. Contributes only to pre-selected organizations.
Board meeting date(s): Quarterly
Officers: Chris Caldwell, Secy.; David Heeter, V.P.; Chris Cook, Treas.
Directors: Sam Abram; Patrick C. Botts; Linn A. Crull; R. Donn Roberts; Earl R. Williams.
EIN: 352064221
Selected grants: The following grants are a representative sample of this grantmaker's funding activity:
$35,000 to United Way of Delaware County, Muncie, IN, 2011.
$21,000 to Ball State University, Muncie, IN, 2011.
$7,000 to United Way of Saint Joseph County, South Bend, IN, 2011.
$6,000 to United Way of Kosciusko County, Warsaw, IN, 2011.
$5,000 to Muncie Childrens Museum, Muncie, IN, 2011.
$3,778 to Big Brothers Big Sisters of East Central Indiana, Muncie, IN, 2011.
$3,000 to Ball Memorial Hospital Foundation, Muncie, IN, 2011.
$3,000 to Energize-ECI, Muncie, IN, 2011.
$2,500 to Syracuse-Wawasee Park Foundation, Syracuse, IN, 2011.
$1,800 to Project Leadership, Marion, IN, 2011.

2604
The Mutual Fire Marine & Inland Insurance Co.

120 E. Uwchlan Ave., Ste. 101
Exton, PA 19341-1275 (610) 524-4700

Establishment information: Established in 1902.
Company type: Mutual company
Business activities: Provides fire and casualty insurance.
Business type (SIC): Insurance/fire, marine, and casualty
Corporate officers: Alexander Bratic, C.E.O.; G. Alan Bailey, Secy.; Michael J. Petrelia, Treas.
Giving statement: Giving through the Mutual Fire Foundation, Inc.

Mutual Fire Foundation, Inc.

120 E. Uwchlan Ave., Ste. 101
Exton, PA 19341-1275

Establishment information: Established in 2004 in PA.
Donors: The Mutual Fire Marine and Inland Insurance Co.; FHA Holding Company; Franklin Homeowners Assurance Company.
Financial data (yr. ended 12/31/11): Assets, $2,206,009 (M); gifts received, $241,000; expenditures, $312,289; qualifying distributions, $287,500; giving activities include $287,500 for grants.
Fields of interest: Higher education.
Type of support: Scholarship funds.
Support limitations: No grants to individuals.
Application information: Applications not accepted. Unsolicited requests for funds not accepted.
Officers: Michael J. Petrelia, Chair.; James McGuigan, Secy.-Treas.

Directors: Caroline Bratic; Walter Bratic.
EIN: 383704483
Selected grants: The following grants are a representative sample of this grantmaker's funding activity:
$20,000 to Elizabethtown College, Elizabethtown, PA, 2010. For scholarship.
$17,000 to Widener University, School of Law, Wilmington, DE, 2010. For general fund.
$15,000 to International Orthodox Christian Charities, Baltimore, MD, 2010. For general fund.
$15,000 to Widener University, School of Law, Wilmington, DE, 2010. For scholarship.
$10,000 to Haverford School, Haverford, PA, 2010. For scholarship.
$10,000 to Hill Top Preparatory School, Rosemont, PA, 2010. For scholarship.
$10,000 to Malvern Preparatory School, Malvern, PA, 2010. For scholarship.
$8,000 to ARC of Dauphin and Lebanon Counties, Harrisburg, PA, 2010. For scholarship.
$8,000 to Benchmark School, Media, PA, 2010. For scholarship.
$1,500 to Sunday Breakfast Association Corporation, Philadelphia, PA, 2010.

2605
Mutual of America Life Insurance Company

320 Park Ave.
New York, NY 10022-6839 (212) 224-1600

Company URL: http://www.mutualofamerica.com
Establishment information: Established in 1945.
Company type: Mutual company
Business activities: Provides investment advisory services; sells life and disability insurance.
Business type (SIC): Security and commodity services; insurance/life; insurance/accident and health
Financial profile for 2011: Number of employees, 1,123; assets, $13,661,800,000; sales volume, $2,111,100,000
Corporate officers: Thomas J. Moran, Chair., Pres., and C.E.O.; William S. Conway, Sr. Exec. V.P. and C.O.O.; John R. Greed, Sr. Exec. V.P. and C.F.O.; George L. Medlin, Exec. V.P. and Treas.; James J. Roth, Exec. V.P. and Genl. Counsel; Diane Marie Aramony, Exec. V.P. and Corp. Secy.
Board of directors: Thomas J. Moran, Chair.; Clifford L. Alexander, Jr.; Patrick A. Burns; Kimberly A. Casiano; Roselyn P. Epps, M.D.; Earle H. Harbison, Jr.; Maureen A. Haver; Frances R. Hesselbein; Connie Mack; Robert J. McGuire, Esq.; Roger B. Porter, Ph.D.; Peter J. Powers; Dennis J. Reimer; Elie Wiesel
Giving statement: Giving through the Mutual of America Foundation.

Mutual of America Foundation

320 Park Ave.
New York, NY 10022-6839 (212) 224-1147
FAX: (212) 207-3001;
E-mail: thomas.gilliam@mutualofamerica.com;
URL: http://www.mutualofamerica.com/about/CommunityBuilding.asp

Establishment information: Established in 1989.
Donor: Mutual of America Life Insurance Co.
Contact: Thomas Gilliam, Chair. and C.E.O.; Theodore Herman, Vice-Chair.
Financial data (yr. ended 12/31/11): Assets, $348,759 (M); gifts received, $2,947,227; expenditures, $2,947,227; qualifying distributions, $2,947,227; giving activities include $2,406,402 for grants.
Purpose and activities: The foundation supports organizations involved with education, and health and human services.
Fields of interest: Secondary school/education; Higher education; Education; Health care, patient services; Health care; Disasters, preparedness/services; Girl scouts; Children/youth, services; Homeless, human services; Human services; United Ways and Federated Giving Programs.
Program:
Community Partnership Award: Through the Community Partnership Award program, the foundation awards grants of up to $25,000 to organizations with programs designed to partner with public, private, and social sector organizations devoted to the public good to build a cohesive community that serves as a model for collaborating with others for the greater good. A video of the award-winner's project will also be produced and used as a tool to education, inform, and provide a model of coordinated action for others to emulate.
Type of support: General/operating support.
Geographic limitations: Giving primarily in CA, Washington, DC, GA, IL, NV, TN, TX, and WI.
Publications: Annual report; Application guidelines; Informational brochure (including application guidelines).
Application information: Applications accepted. Proposals should be no longer than 3 pages. Application form required. Applicants should submit the following:
1) name, address and phone number of organization
2) copy of most recent annual report/audited financial statement/990
3) listing of board of directors, trustees, officers and other key people and their affiliations
4) contact person
5) detailed description of project and amount of funding requested

Proposals should include a description of the partnership and indicate the role of each partner; how the partnership was started; the duration of the partnership to date; how the partnership has made a difference; the ability of the partnership to be replicated and stimulate new ideas in addressing social issues; and the partnership's commitment to advancing the mission and principles of the organization.
Initial approach: Download application form and mail proposal and application form to foundation for Community Partnership Award
Copies of proposal: 1
Board meeting date(s): Mar., May, June, Sept., and Nov.
Deadline(s): Apr. 1 for Community Partnership Award
Officers and Directors:* Thomas Gilliam*, Chair. and C.E.O.; Theodore L. Herman*, Vice-Chair.; Manfred Altstadt*, C.O.O.; Patrick A. Burns*, Exec. V.P., Secy., and Genl. Counsel; John R. Greed, Exec. V.P. and C.F.O.; George L. Medlin, Exec. V.P. and Treas.; James J. Roth.
EIN: 133443360

2606
Mutual of Omaha Bank

3333 Farnam St., Ste. 10
Omaha, NE 68131-3406 (866) 351-5646

Company URL: http://mutualofomahabank.com/
Establishment information: Established in 1927.
Company type: Subsidiary of a mutual company
Business activities: Operates commercial bank.
Business type (SIC): Banks/commercial
Financial profile for 2011: Assets, $5,556,624,000; liabilities, $4,927,864,000
Corporate officers: Jeffrey Schmid, Chair. and C.E.O.; Lynn Crane, Exec. V.P., Opers.; Marjorie Heller, C.F.O.; Michael Huss, Genl. Counsel
Board of directors: Jeffrey Schmid, Chair.; Tod Ellis; Michael Fosdick; Marjorie Heller; Michael Homa; Edward Keller; Terry Kroeger; George Little; Barry Major; John Nahas
Historic mergers: First National Bank Holding Company (July 25, 2008)
Giving statement: Giving through the First National Bank Charitable Foundation.

First National Bank Charitable Foundation

17550 N Perimeter Dr., Ste. 370
Scottsdale, AZ 85255-5440

Establishment information: Established in 2002 in AZ and NV.
Donors: First National Bank Holding Co.; First National Bank of Arizona.
Financial data (yr. ended 12/31/11): Assets, $1,221,747 (M); expenditures, $14,008; qualifying distributions, $0.
Purpose and activities: The foundation supports organizations involved with health, cancer research, housing development, human services, community and economic development, and voluntarism.
Fields of interest: Health care, patient services; Health care; Cancer research; Housing/shelter, development; Boys & girls clubs; Youth development, business; Children/youth, services; Residential/custodial care, hospices; Human services; Community/economic development; Voluntarism promotion.
Type of support: General/operating support.
Geographic limitations: Giving primarily in AZ.
Application information: Applications not accepted. Unsolicited requests for funds not accepted.
Directors: Gary A. Dorris; M. Christopher Evans; Philip A. Lamb; Raymond A. Lamb.
EIN: 510423211

2607
Mutual of Omaha Insurance Company

Mutual of Omaha Plz.
Omaha, NE 68175 (402) 342-7600

Company URL: http://www.mutualofomaha.com
Establishment information: Established in 1909.
Company type: Mutual company
Business activities: Operates insurance company.
Business type (SIC): Insurance carriers
Financial profile for 2011: Number of employees, 1,123; assets, $13,661,800,000; sales volume, $2,111,100,000
Fortune 1000 ranking: 2012—394th in revenues, 488th in profits, and 180th in assets
Corporate officers: Daniel P. Neary, Chair. and C.E.O.; David A. Diamond, Exec. V.P., C.F.O., and Treas.; Richard A. Witt, Exec. V.P. and C.I.O.; Richard C. Anderl, Exec. V.P. and Genl. Counsel
Board of directors: Daniel P. Neary, Chair.; Robert L. Clarke; W. Gary Gates; Jeffrey M. Heller; Derek R. McClain; James G. McFarlane; Paula R. Meyer; Admiral Richard W. Mies; Anthony J. Principi
Subsidiaries: Companion Life Insurance Co., Lynbrook, NY; Exclusive Healthcare, Inc., Omaha, NE; Kirkpatrick Pettis Smith Polian, Inc., Omaha, NE; Mutual of Omaha Investor Services, Inc., Omaha,

NE; Omaha Property and Casualty Insurance Co., Omaha, NE; United of Omaha Life Insurance Co., Omaha, NE; United World Life Insurance Co., Omaha, NE
Giving statement: Giving through the Mutual of Omaha Insurance Company Contributions Program and the Mutual of Omaha Foundation.

Mutual of Omaha Insurance Company Contributions Program

(formerly Mutual of Omaha Companies Contributions Program)
Mutual of Omaha Plz.
Omaha, NE 68175-0001 (402) 351-5263
E-mail: community.affairs@mutualofomaha.com; URL: http://www.mutualofomaha.com/about/corporate_support/index.html

Purpose and activities: As a complement to its foundation, Mutual of Omaha also makes charitable contributions to nonprofit organizations directly. Special emphasis is directed towards programs working with residents to improve their neighborhood. Support is given primarily in the Omaha-Council Bluffs metropolitan area, Nebraska.
Fields of interest: Public health; Crime/violence prevention; Recreation, parks/playgrounds; Recreation; Community development, neighborhood development; Community development, neighborhood associations.
Type of support: Employee volunteer services; Program development.
Geographic limitations: Giving primarily in the Omaha-Council Bluffs metropolitan area, NE.
Application information: Applications accepted. Grants generally do not exceed $2,500. Application form required.
Initial approach: E-mail or telephone headquarters for application information
Committee meeting date(s): May
Deadline(s): Apr. 1 to Apr. 30
Final notification: June
Number of staff: 3 full-time professional.

Mutual of Omaha Foundation

Mutual of Omaha Plz.
Omaha, NE 68175-0002 (866) 663-5665
E-mail: mutualofomaha.foundation@mutualofomaha.com; Additional tel.: (866) 663-8665; URL: http://www.mutualofomahafoundation.org

Establishment information: Established in 2005.
Donor: Mutual of Omaha Insurance Co.
Contact: Christine D. Johnson, Pres. and Secy.
Financial data (yr. ended 12/31/11): Assets, $34,380,000 (M); gifts received, $350,000; expenditures, $3,073,159; qualifying distributions, $2,887,364; giving activities include $2,887,364 for grants.
Purpose and activities: The foundation supports programs designed to empower families to overcome obstacles and work toward positive change. Special emphasis is directed toward programs designed to address behavioral health; youth violence; domestic abuse; early childhood education; preparedness of graduation; literacy and language; financial literacy; and food and shelter.
Fields of interest: Education, early childhood education; Secondary school/education; Adult education—literacy, basic skills & GED; Education, drop-out prevention; Education; Substance abuse, services; Mental health/crisis services; Crime/violence prevention, youth; Food services; Children, services; Family services; Family services, domestic violence; Human services, financial counseling; Homeless, human services; Human services.
Programs:
Behavioral Health: The foundation supports programs designed to directly assist individuals with behavioral issues and mental illness; and programs that work to prevent substance abuse.
Domestic Violence: The foundation supports programs designed to prevent domestic abuse and come to the aid of those who have been victims of domestic violence.
Early Childhood Education: The foundation supports programs designed to provide early childhood education to children from underserved populations.
Financial Literacy: The foundation supports programs designed to education families about fundamentals financial matters like budgeting, saving, understanding credit, and purchasing a home.
Food: The foundation supports programs designed to address the problem of hunger in the community; and organizations that work to provide food for those in need.
Literacy/Language: The foundation supports programs designed to help individuals suffering from illiteracy and language deficiencies.
Preparedness for Graduation: The foundation supports programs designed to provide services to at-risk youth with the goal of helping them stay in school.
Shelter: The foundation supports programs designed to provide homeless prevention, emergency shelter, or services within a shelter.
Voluntary Aid to Education (Matching Gifts): The foundation matches contributions made by employees of Mutual of Omaha to high schools, colleges, and universities up to $1,000 per employee, per year.
Youth Violence: The foundation supports programs designed to help prevent and address the growing problem of youth violence.
Type of support: Building/renovation; Capital campaigns; Emergency funds; Employee matching gifts; Employee volunteer services; General/operating support; In-kind gifts; Matching/challenge support; Program development.
Geographic limitations: Giving primarily in areas of company operations in Council Bluffs, IA and Omaha, NE.
Support limitations: No support for religious or sectarian organizations, social clubs, fraternal organizations, or political organizations or candidates. No grants to individuals, or for tickets and tables, endowment funds, travel, team sponsorships or athletic scholarships, civic or commemorative advertising, festivals, monuments or memorials.
Publications: Application guidelines; Grants list; Informational brochure.
Application information: Applications accepted. Support is limited to 1 contribution per organization during any given year. Organizations receiving support are asked to submit a final report. Application form required. Applicants should submit the following:
1) results expected from proposed grant
2) statement of problem project will address
3) population served
4) name, address and phone number of organization
5) copy of IRS Determination Letter
6) brief history of organization and description of its mission
7) how project's results will be evaluated or measured
8) listing of board of directors, trustees, officers and other key people and their affiliations
9) detailed description of project and amount of funding requested
10) plans for cooperation with other organizations, if any
11) contact person
12) copy of current year's organizational budget and/or project budget
13) listing of additional sources and amount of support
Initial approach: Complete online application
Board meeting date(s): Quarterly
Deadline(s): Feb. 15, May 15. Aug. 15. and Nov. 15
Final notification: Within 2 months
Officers and Directors:* Christine D. Johnson*, Pres. and Secy.; Richard A. Witt*, V.P.; Michael J. Jareske, Treas.; Daniel P. Martin; Jeffrey R. Schmid; Stacy A. Scholtz; Michael C. Weekly.
EIN: 202176636
Selected grants: The following grants are a representative sample of this grantmaker's funding activity:
$700,000 to Heritage Services, Omaha, NE, 2010.
$345,000 to United Way of the Midlands, Omaha, NE, 2010.
$300,000 to Creighton University, Omaha, NE, 2010.
$100,000 to Heritage Services, Omaha, NE, 2010.
$100,000 to Project Harmony, Omaha, NE, 2010.
$50,000 to Durham Museum, Omaha, NE, 2010.
$50,000 to Literacy Center for the Midlands, Omaha, NE, 2010.
$40,000 to Boy Scouts of America National Council, Irving, TX, 2010.
$25,000 to Partnership for Our Kids, Omaha, NE, 2010.
$20,000 to Youth Emergency Services, Omaha, NE, 2010.

2608
MWH Global, Inc.

370 Interlocken Blvd., Ste. 300
Broomfield, CO 80021 (303) 410 4000
FAX: (303) 410 4100

Company URL: http://www.mwhglobal.com
Establishment information: Established in 1844.
Company type: Private company
Business activities: Provides engineering services.
Business type (SIC): Engineering, architectural, and surveying services
Financial profile for 2009: Number of employees, 7,000; sales volume, $1,188,200,000
Corporate officers: Robert B. Uhler, Chair.; Don Smith, Vice-Chair.; Alan J. Krause, Pres. and C.E.O.; David G. Barnes, C.F.O.; Meg Vanderlaan, V.P., Corp. Comms.
Board of directors: Robert B. Uhler, Chair.; Don Smith, Vice-Chair.; Joseph D. Adams; David G. Barnes; Paul F. Boulos; Janet Linden Cooper; Wim Drossaert; Alan J. Fohrer; Charles L. Henry; Bruce K. Howard; Alan J. Krause; Blair Lavoie; Daniel McConville; John Vereker
Giving statement: Giving through the MWH Caring Foundation, Inc.

MWH Caring Foundation, Inc.

380 Interlocken Crescent, Ste. 200
Broomfield, CO 80021-8026

Establishment information: Established in 2002 in CO and DE.
Donors: MWH Americas, Inc.; MWH Global, Inc.
Financial data (yr. ended 12/31/11): Assets, $117,752 (M); expenditures, $99,662; qualifying distributions, $99,662; giving activities include

$99,575 for 2 grants (high: $50,000; low: $49,575).
Purpose and activities: The foundation supports parks and organizations involved with secondary and higher education, and disaster relief.
Fields of interest: Secondary school/education; Higher education; Disasters, preparedness/services; Recreation, parks/playgrounds.
Type of support: Building/renovation; Emergency funds; Scholarship funds.
Application information: Applications not accepted. Unsolicited requests for funds not accepted.
Officers and Directors:* Robert B. Uhler*, Pres.; Garry J. Sanderson*, V.P.; Angela R. Shirrell, Secy.; Chad C. Scherer, Treas.; James G. Kuiken.
EIN: 010643285

2609
D. Myers and Sons, Inc.

4311 Erdman Ave.
Baltimore, MD 21213 (410) 522-7500

Company URL: http://www.dmyers.com/
Company type: Private company
Business activities: Sells footwear wholesale.
Business type (SIC): Apparel, piece goods, and notions—wholesale
Corporate officers: E. Carey Ries, Chair.; Ann Ries, Secy.; Mark McLean, Cont. and Treas.
Board of director: E. Carey Ries, Chair.
Giving statement: Giving through the D. Myers and Sons Foundation, Inc.

D. Myers and Sons Foundation, Inc.

2423 Still Forest Rd.
Baltimore, MD 21208

Establishment information: Established in 1943 in MD.
Donor: D. Myers and Sons, Inc.
Contact: E. Carey Ries, Pres.
Financial data (yr. ended 12/31/09): Assets, $0 (M); expenditures, $10,374; qualifying distributions, $10,370; giving activities include $50 for 1 grant.
Purpose and activities: The foundation supports organizations involved with arts and culture, youth, and Judaism.
Fields of interest: Performing arts; Arts; Youth, services; United Ways and Federated Giving Programs; Jewish federated giving programs; Jewish agencies & synagogues.
Type of support: Annual campaigns.
Geographic limitations: Giving primarily in Baltimore, MD.
Support limitations: No grants to individuals.
Application information: Applications accepted.
Initial approach: Contact foundation for application information
Deadline(s): None
Officers: E. Carey Ries, Pres.; Ann W. Ries, V.P. and Secy.; James M. Ries, V.P.
EIN: 526034755

2610
Mylan Inc.

(formerly Mylan Laboratories Inc.)
1500 Corporate Dr.
Canonsburg, PA 15317 (724) 514-1800
FAX: (724) 514-1870

Company URL: http://www.mylan.com
Establishment information: Established in 1961.
Company type: Public company
Company ticker symbol and exchange: MYL/NASDAQ
Business activities: Develops, licenses, manufactures, markets, and distributes pharmaceutical products.
Business type (SIC): Drugs
Financial profile for 2012: Number of employees, 18,000; assets, $11,931,900,000; sales volume, $6,796,110,000; pre-tax net income, $804,080,000; expenses, $5,686,060,000; liabilities, $8,591,180,000
Fortune 1000 ranking: 2012—374th in revenues, 277th in profits, and 352nd in assets
Corporate officers: Robert J. Coury, Chair.; Rodney L. Piatt, C.P.A., Vice-Chair.; Heather Bresch, C.E.O.; Rajiv Malik, Pres.; Harry A. Korman, C.O.O.; John D. Sheehan, Exec. V.P. and C.F.O.
Board of directors: Robert J. Coury, Chair.; Rodney L. Piatt, Vice-Chair.; Heather Bresch; Wendy Cameron; Robert J. Cindrich; Neil F. Dimick; Melina Higgins; Douglas J. Leech; Rajiv Malik; Joseph C. Maroon, M.D.; Mark W. Parrish; Clarence B. Todd; Randall L. Vanderveen, Ph.D.
Subsidiaries: Mylan Technologies Inc., St. Albans, VT; UDL Laboratories, Inc., Rockford, IL
Plant: Morgantown, WV
International operations: Australia; Austria; Belgium; Bermuda; Canada; China; Congo; Czech Republic; Denmark; Finland; France; Germany; Gibraltar; Greece; Hungary; India; Ireland; Italy; Japan; Luxembourg; Mauritius; Morocco and the Western Sahara; Netherlands; New Zealand; Norway; Portugal; Singapore; Slovakia; Slovenia; South Africa; Spain; Sweden; Switzerland; United Kingdom
Giving statement: Giving through the Mylan Charitable Foundation.
Company EIN: 251211621

The Mylan Charitable Foundation

1500 Corporate Dr., Ste. 400
Canonsburg, PA 15317-8580
E-mail: christina.matluck@mylanfoundation.org

Establishment information: Established in 2002 in PA and WV.
Donors: Mylan Laboratories Inc.; Mylan Pharmaceuticals.
Contact: Christina Matluck, Exec. Admin.
Financial data (yr. ended 12/31/11): Assets, $11,168,261 (M); expenditures, $679,457; qualifying distributions, $595,000; giving activities include $595,000 for grants.
Purpose and activities: The foundation supports organizations involved with education, health, human services, and community development.
Fields of interest: Education; Health care; Athletics/sports, school programs; Family services; Human services; Community/economic development; United Ways and Federated Giving Programs.
Type of support: Building/renovation; General/operating support.
Geographic limitations: Giving primarily in PA and WV as well as Rockford, IL, Sugar Land, TX, and St. Albans, VT.
Support limitations: No grants to individuals.
Publications: Application guidelines.
Application information: Applications accepted. Application form required.
Initial approach: Letter of inquiry
Copies of proposal: 1
Final notification: Varies
Officers and Directors: Rodney L. Piatt, Chair.; C. B. Todd, Secy.; Brian Byala, Treas.; Heather Bresch; Robert J. Coury.
Number of staff: 1 full-time professional.
EIN: 431954390

2611
N.E.W. Customer Service Companies, LLC

22660 Executive Dr., Ste. 122
Sterling, VA 20166-9535 (703) 375-8100

Company URL: http://www.newcorp.com
Establishment information: Established in 1983.
Company type: Private company
Business activities: Provides warranty, product protection, and risk-avoidance services.
Business type (SIC): Personal services/miscellaneous
Corporate officers: Frederick Schaufeld, Chair.; Anthony Nader, Pres. and C.E.O.; David Bosserman, Sr. V.P., C.O.O., and C.F.O.; Steven Voss, Sr. V.P., Finance and Treas.; Terri Feely, Sr. V.P., Human Resources; Christina DeRosa, Sr. V.P., Mktg.
Board of director: Fred Schaufeld, Chair.
Giving statement: Giving through the N.E.W. Charitable Foundation.

N.E.W. Charitable Foundation

(formerly The N.E.W. Relief Fund, Inc.)
22660 Executive Dr., Ste. 122
Sterling, VA 20166-9535
URL: https://www.newcorp.com/index.php/about_us/corporate_giving/

Establishment information: Established in 2001.
Donors: N.E.W. Customer Service Cos., Inc.; AIG Warranty Guard; National Electronics Warranty Corp.
Financial data (yr. ended 03/31/12): Assets, $213,252 (M); expenditures, $132,025; qualifying distributions, $132,025; giving activities include $132,025 for 58 grants (high: $20,000; low: $250).
Purpose and activities: The foundation supports community foundations and organizations involved with performing arts, health, cancer, disaster relief, youth development, and human services.
Fields of interest: Performing arts; Hospitals (general); Health care; Cancer; Disasters, preparedness/services; Athletics/sports, Special Olympics; Boys & girls clubs; Youth development; American Red Cross; Human services; Foundations (community); United Ways and Federated Giving Programs.
Type of support: General/operating support.
Geographic limitations: Giving primarily in FL, MT, and VA.
Support limitations: No grants to individuals.
Application information: Applications not accepted. Contributes only to pre-selected organizations.
Officers and Board Member: Frederick Schaufeld*, Chair. and Pres.; Anthony Nader*, V.P.; Terri Feely, Secy.-Treas.
EIN: 542055525
Selected grants: The following grants are a representative sample of this grantmaker's funding activity:
$32,500 to Loudoun Cares, Leesburg, VA, 2010. For unrestricted gift.

$12,500 to Wolf Trap Foundation for the Performing Arts, Vienna, VA, 2010. For unrestricted gift.
$5,500 to United Way of Cascade County, Great Falls, MT, 2010. For unrestricted gift.
$3,000 to State Games of Mississippi, Meridian, MS, 2010. For unrestricted gift.
$1,525 to Special Olympics Virginia, Richmond, VA, 2010. For unrestricted gift.
$1,525 to Special Olympics Virginia, Richmond, VA, 2010. For unrestricted gift.
$1,500 to United Way, River Valley, Russellville, AR, 2010. For unrestricted gift.
$1,000 to Covenant Hospice, Pensacola, FL, 2010. For unrestricted gift.
$1,000 to State Games of Mississippi, Meridian, MS, 2010. For unrestricted gift.
$1,000 to United Way, River Valley, Russellville, AR, 2010. For unrestricted gift.

2612
Nackard Bottling Company

(doing business as Pepsi-Cola Bottling Co.)
4980 E. Railhead Ave.
Flagstaff, AZ 86004-2420 (928) 526-0653
FAX: (928) 527-3165

Establishment information: Established in 1984.
Company type: Private company
Business activities: Operates soft drink bottling company.
Business type (SIC): Beverages
Corporate officers: Patrick M. Nackard, Pres.; Todd Rovelstad, C.O.O.; James Bushnell, C.F.O.
Giving statement: Giving through the Monica Heaney Nackard Foundation.

The Monica Heaney Nackard Foundation

c/o Patrick M. Nackard
4880 E. Railhead Ave.
Flagstaff, AZ 86004-2419

Establishment information: Established in AZ.
Donors: Fred Nackard Land Co.; Nackard Bottling Co.; Jewel Trucking Co.
Financial data (yr. ended 12/31/11): Assets, $619,892 (M); gifts received, $58,500; expenditures, $66,412; qualifying distributions, $61,500; giving activities include $61,500 for grants.
Fields of interest: Arts; Education; Religion.
Support limitations: No grants to individuals.
Application information: Applications not accepted. Unsolicited requests for funds not accepted.
Trustees: P. Jewel Nackard; Patrick M. Nackard.
EIN: 866302338

2613
Nalco Company

(formerly Ondeo Nalco Company)
1601 W. Diehl Rd.
Naperville, IL 60563-1198 (630) 305-1000
FAX: (630) 305-2900

Company URL: http://www.nalco.com
Establishment information: Established in 1928.
Company type: Subsidiary of a public company
Parent company: Ecolab Inc.
Business activities: Manufactures specialty chemicals; produces and refines petroleum; manufactures paper.
Business type (SIC): Chemicals/industrial inorganic; extraction/oil and gas; chemicals/industrial organic; petroleum refining
Financial profile for 2009: Number of employees, 10,500
Corporate officers: J. Erik Frywald, Chair., Pres., and C.E.O.; Abbe Kaye, C.I.O.
Board of director: J. Erik Frywald, Chair.
Plants: Carson, CA; Chicago, IL; Garyville, LA; Paulsboro, NJ; Ellwood City, PA; Freeport, Sugar Land, TX
International operations: Argentina; Australia; Brazil; Canada; China; India; Japan; Saudi Arabia; Singapore; South Africa; South Korea; Thailand
Giving statement: Giving through the Nalco Foundation.
Company EIN: 361520480

The Nalco Foundation

Nalco Ctr.
1601 W. Diehl Rd.
Naperville, IL 60563-1198 (630) 305-1566
FAX: (630) 305-2896;
E-mail: foundation@nalco.com

Establishment information: Incorporated in 1953 in IL.
Donors: Nalco Chemical Co.; Ondeo Nalco Co.; Nalco Co.
Contact: Laurie Marsh, Pres.
Financial data (yr. ended 12/31/11): Assets, $1,147,888 (M); gifts received, $384,488; expenditures, $1,096,370; qualifying distributions, $1,092,000; giving activities include $1,092,000 for grants.
Purpose and activities: The foundation supports organizations involved with clean water.
Fields of interest: Environment, water pollution; Environment, water resources.
Type of support: General/operating support.
Geographic limitations: Giving primarily in areas of major company operations, with emphasis on CO and IL.
Support limitations: No support for public colleges or universities, secondary or elementary schools, or churches. No grants to individuals, or for endowments, capital campaigns, advertising, tickets, religious education, or political or lobbying activities; no loans; no matching gifts.
Application information: Applications not accepted. Unsolicited applications are currently not accepted.
Board meeting date(s): Mar., June, Sept., and Dec.
Officers and Directors:* Laurie Marsh, Pres.; Mary Jane Anderson, Secy.; Charles Pechman, Treas.; Michael Bushman; Bryan Sill.
Number of staff: 1 full-time professional; 1 full-time support.
EIN: 366065864

2614
Namaste Solar

4571 Broadway St.
Boulder, CO 80304-0585 (303) 447-0300
FAX: (303) 443-8855

Company URL: http://www.namastesolar.com
Establishment information: Established in 2005.
Company type: Private company
Business type (SIC): Business services/miscellaneous
Corporate officers: Amanda Bybee, Owner; Alex Garland, Owner
Giving statement: Giving through the Namaste Solar Corporate Giving Program.

Namaste Solar Corporate Giving Program

4571 Broadway St.
Boulder, CO 80304-0585 (303) 447-0300
E-mail: outreach2@namastesolar.com; URL: http://www.namastesolar.com

Purpose and activities: Namaste Solar is a certified B Corporation that donates a percentage of its profits to charitable organizations. Support is given primarily in the greater Denver/Boulder area, Colorado.
Fields of interest: Education; Health care; Homeless, human services.
Type of support: In-kind gifts; Sponsorships.
Geographic limitations: Giving primarily in the greater Denver/Boulder area, CO.

2615
NANA Regional Corporation, Inc.

P.O. Box 49
Kotzebue, AK 99752 (907) 442-3301

Company URL: http://www.nana.com
Establishment information: Established in 1971.
Company type: Native corporation
Business activities: Operates native corporation.
Business type (SIC): Nonclassifiable establishments
Financial profile for 2009: Number of employees, 3,600
Corporate officers: Donald G. Sheldon, Chair.; Harvey B. Vestal, 1st Vice-Chair.; Henry Igitaanuluk Horner, Sr., 2nd Vice-Chair.; Marie N. Greene, Pres. and C.E.O.; Kevin Thomas, C.F.O.; Gladys E. Pungowiyi, V.P. and C.O.O.; Red Seeberger, V.P., Admin.; Jacquelyn Luke, Genl. Counsel
Board of directors: Donald Sheldon, Chair.; Harvey B. Vestal, 1st Vice-Chair.; Henry Horner, 2nd Vice-Chair.; Frank Adams, Sr.; Levi Cleveland; Charlie Curtis; Pearl Gomez; Gladys Jones; Tony Jones, Jr.; Linda Lee; Joseph T. Luther; Alice Moore, Sr.; Emerson Moto; Ronald Moto, Sr.; Diana Ramoth; Mary Sage; Luke Sampson; Robert Sampson; Nellie Sheldon; Lowell Sage, Jr.; Frederick Sun; Allen Ticket, Sr.; Michael Tickett; Janice Westlake-Reich
Subsidiary: NANA Development Corp., Kotzebue, AK
Giving statement: Giving through the Robert "Aqqaluk" Newlin, Sr. Memorial Trust.

Robert "Aqqaluk" Newlin, Sr. Memorial Trust

333 Shore Ave., Ste. 241
P.O. Box 509
Kotzebue, AK 99752-0509 (907) 442-1607
FAX: (907) 442-2289;
E-mail: erica.nelson@nana.com; Toll-free tel.: (866) 442-1607; URL: http://aqqaluktrust.com

Establishment information: Established in 1990 in AK; status changed to a public charity in 2002.
Contact: Erica Nelson, Pres.
Financial data (yr. ended 12/31/10): Revenue, $3,331,526; assets, $14,756,846 (M); gifts received, $2,253,211; expenditures, $2,336,345; program services expenses, $1,847,599; giving activities include $820,862 for grants to individuals.
Purpose and activities: The trust awards scholarships to NANA shareholders, their descendents and dependents who are interested in pursuing college and post-graduate degrees, and post-secondary education.

Fields of interest: Indigenous peoples.
Program:
Scholarships: Awards up to $2,000 for full-time students, or up to $1,000 for part-time students, are available to NANA shareholders, descendants of NANA shareholders, or dependents of NANA shareholders or their descendents.
Type of support: Scholarships—to individuals.
Geographic limitations: Giving limited to the Northwest Arctic Borough of AK.
Publications: Application guidelines; Informational brochure (including application guidelines).
Application information: Applications accepted. Application form required.
Initial approach: Download application form
Officers and Trustees:* Dood Lincoln*, Chair.; Linda Lee*, Vice-Chair.; Charlie Curtis*, Pres.; Levi Cleveland; Cheryl Edenshaw; Raymond Hawley; Lester Hadley; Diana Ramoth; Helvi Sandvik.
EIN: 943116762

2616
Nansemond Insurance Agency, Inc

(formerly Nansemond Insurance Services)
453 W. Washington St.
P.O. Box 1569
Suffolk, VA 23434-1569 (757) 539-3421

Company URL: http://nansemondins.com
Establishment information: Established in 1957.
Company type: Private company
Business activities: Sells insurance.
Business type (SIC): Insurance agents, brokers, and services
Corporate officers: Jack W. Webb, Chair.; Joseph Webb, Pres.
Board of director: Jack W. Webb, Chair.
Giving statement: Giving through the Nansemond Charitable Foundation, Inc.

Nansemond Charitable Foundation, Inc.

453 W. Washington St.
Suffolk, VA 23434-5344 (757) 539-3421

Donor: Nansemond Insurance Svcs.
Contact: Jack W. Webb, Jr., V.P.
Financial data (yr. ended 08/31/11): Assets, $149,092 (M); gifts received, $2,000; expenditures, $11,020; qualifying distributions, $7,500; giving activities include $7,500 for 4 grants to individuals (high: $6,000; low: $500).
Purpose and activities: The foundation supports organizations involved with arts and culture, higher education, health, human services, and Christianity and awards college scholarships to individuals.
Type of support: General/operating support; Scholarships—to individuals.
Geographic limitations: Giving primarily in Suffolk, VA.
Application information: Applications accepted. Application form required.
Attach a copy an application form is required for scholarships.
Initial approach: Letter of inquiry; contact foundation for application form for scholarships
Deadline(s): May 15 for scholarships
Directors: Jack W. Webb, Jr.; Joseph N. Webb; Melinda Webb; Jarrett Webb; Jamie V. Weaver.
Officer: Jay A. Dorschel, Chair.
EIN: 541291449

2617
The NASDAQ OMX Group, Inc.

(formerly The NASDAQ Stock Market, Inc.)
1 Liberty Plz.
165 Broadway
New York, NY 10006 (212) 401-8700
FAX: (302) 655-5049

Company URL: http://www.nasdaqomx.com/
Establishment information: Established in 1976.
Company type: Public company
Company ticker symbol and exchange: NDAQ/NASDAQ
Business activities: Operates electronic equity securities market.
Business type (SIC): Security and commodity exchange
Financial profile for 2012: Number of employees, 2,506; assets, $9,132,000,000; sales volume, $3,119,000,000; pre-tax net income, $548,000,000; expenses, $2,469,000,000; liabilities, $3,924,000,000
Fortune 1000 ranking: 2012—690th in revenues, 432nd in profits, and 418th in assets
Corporate officers: H. Furlong Baldwin, Chair.; Meyer Frucher, Vice-Chair.; Robert Greifeld, C.E.O.; Lee Shavel, Exec. V.P., C.F.O., and Corp. Secy.; Brad Peterson, Exec. V.P. and C.I.O.; Edward S. Knight, Exec. V.P. and Genl. Counsel
Board of directors: H. Furlong Baldwin, Chair.; Meyer Frucher, Vice-Chair.; Steven D. Black; Borje Ekholm; Robert Greifeld; Glenn H. Hutchins; Essa Kazim; John D. Markese; Ellyn A. McColgan; Thomas F. O'Neill; James S. Riepe; Michael R. Splinter; Lars Wedenborn
International operations: Australia; Canada; China; Denmark; Estonia; Finland; Iceland; Ireland; Italy; Latvia; Lithuania; Luxembourg; Norway; Singapore; Sweden; Switzerland; United Kingdom
Giving statement: Giving through the NASDAQ OMX Group Educational Foundation, Inc.
Company EIN: 521165937

NASDAQ OMX Group Educational Foundation, Inc.

(formerly The Nasdaq Stock Marked Educational Foundation, Inc.)
9600 Blackwell Rd.
Rockville, MD 20850-3655 (800) 842-0356
E-mail: foundation@nasdaqomx.com; URL: http://www.nasdaqomx.com/services/initiatives/educationalfoundation

Establishment information: Established in 1993 in MD and DE.
Donor: The Nasdaq Stock Market, Inc.
Financial data (yr. ended 12/31/11): Assets, $28,622,081 (M); expenditures, $2,955,080; qualifying distributions, $2,624,597; giving activities include $2,624,597 for grants.
Purpose and activities: The foundation supports programs designed to promote capital formation, financial markets, and entrepreneurship through education and awards fellowships to individuals for the purpose of conducting independent academic study or research on financial markets.
Fields of interest: Elementary/secondary education; Higher education; Education; Disasters, preparedness/services; Human services, financial counseling; Community/economic development; Economics.
Type of support: Continuing support; Curriculum development; Fellowships; Program development; Research.
Geographic limitations: Giving primarily in CA, CT, Washington, DC, IN, MD, MN, NY, NC, and TX.
Support limitations: No support for discriminatory organizations.
Publications: Application guidelines; Grants list.
Application information: Applications accepted. Letters of inquiry should be no longer than one page. Grant seekers may be invited to submit a full proposal at a later date. Ph.D. dissertation fellowships are granted in a set amount of $15,000. Application form not required. Applicants should submit the following:
1) name, address and phone number of organization
2) brief history of organization and description of its mission
3) detailed description of project and amount of funding requested
4) contact person

Initial approach: E-mail or mail letter of inquiry
Deadline(s): Feb. 1 and Aug. 1
Final notification: Mar. 1 and Sept. 1
Officers and Directors:* Robert Greifeld*, Chair.; Joan C. Conley, Secy.; Peter Strandell, Treas.; Bruce E. Aust; H. Furlong Baldwin; Marc Baum; John J. Lucchese; Eric W. Noll.
EIN: 521864429

2618
Nasdaq OMX PHLX

(also known as The PHLX)
(formerly Philadelphia Stock Exchange)
1900 Market St., Ste. 616
Philadelphia, PA 19103-3584
(215) 496-5000

Company URL: http://www.nasdaqomx.com
Establishment information: Established in 1790.
Company type: Subsidiary of a public company
Business activities: Operates securities and commodities exchange.
Business type (SIC): Security and commodity exchange; security and commodity services; management and public relations services
Corporate officers: Merit E. Janow, Chair.; Eric W. Noll, C.E.O.; Thomas A. Wittman, Pres.; Joan C. Conley, Sr. V.P. and Corp. Secy.; Thomas Kelly, V.P. and Treas.
Board of director: Merit E. Janow, Chair.
Subsidiaries: Center for Currency Options, Philadelphia, PA; Financial Automation Corp., Philadelphia, PA; Philadelphia Board of Trade, Inc., Philadelphia, PA; Philadelphia Depository Trust Co., Philadelphia, PA; Stock Clearing Corp. of Philadelphia, Philadelphia, PA
Giving statement: Giving through the Philadelphia Stock Exchange Foundation.

Philadelphia Stock Exchange Foundation

119 Sharptown-Auburn Rd.
Pilesgrove, NJ 08098-2634

Establishment information: Established in 1982 in PA.
Donors: Philadelphia Stock Exchange; NASDAQ OMX PHLX, Inc.
Financial data (yr. ended 12/31/11): Assets, $927,735 (M); expenditures, $253,252; qualifying distributions, $136,902; giving activities include $126,315 for 19 grants (high: $12,500; low: $15).
Purpose and activities: The foundation supports orchestras and organizations involved with education, arthritis, Crohn's and Colitis research, and children and youth.
Fields of interest: Performing arts, orchestras; Secondary school/education; Education, special;

Education; Arthritis; Medical research; Children/youth, services.
Type of support: General/operating support; Program development; Scholarship funds.
Support limitations: No grants to individuals.
Application information: Applications not accepted. Unsolicited requests for funds not accepted.
Board meeting date(s): Varies
Officers and Directors:* Sandy Frucher*, Pres.; Scott Donnini*, V.P. and Secy.; Chris Concannon; John F. Wallace*.
EIN: 222437173

2619
Nash Finch Company

7600 France Ave. S.
P.O. Box 355
Minneapolis, MN 55440-0355
(952) 832-0534

Company URL: http://www.nashfinch.com
Establishment information: Established in 1885.
Company type: Public company
Company ticker symbol and exchange: NAFC/NASDAQ
Business activities: Sells food wholesale; operates supermarkets.
Business type (SIC): Groceries—wholesale; groceries—retail
Financial profile for 2012: Number of employees, 8,134; assets, $1,003,620,000; sales volume, $4,820,800,000; pre-tax net income, -$121,690,000; expenses, $4,942,490,000; liabilities, $707,230,000
Fortune 1000 ranking: 2012—500th in revenues, 923rd in profits, and 969th in assets
Corporate officers: William R. Voss, Chair.; Alec C. Covington, Pres. and C.E.O.; Robert B. Dimond, Exec. V.P., C.F.O., and Treas.; Calvin S. Sihilling, Exec V.P. and C.I.O.; Kathleen M. Mahoney, Exec V.P., Genl. Counsel, and Secy.; Michael W. Rotelle III, Sr. V.P., Human Resources
Board of directors: William R. Voss, Chair.; Christopher W. Bodine; Alec C. Covington; Mickey P. Foret; Douglas A. Hacker; Hawthorne L. Proctor
Subsidiaries: Gillette Dairy of the Black Hills, Inc., Rapid City, SD; GTL Truck Lines, Inc., Norfolk, NE; T.J. Morris Co., Statesboro, GA; Nash De-Camp Co., Visalia, CA; Nash Finch Funding Corp., Edina, MN; Nebraska Dairies, Inc., Norfolk, NE; Piggly Wiggly Northland Corp., Edina, MN; Super Food Services, Inc., Dayton, OH
Plants: Denver, CO; Cedar Rapids, IA; Liberal, KS; Baltimore, MD; St. Cloud, MN; Grand Island, NE; Lumberton, Rocky Mount, NC; Fargo, Minot, ND; Sioux Falls, SD; Bluefield, Norfolk, VA; Appleton, WI
Giving statement: Giving through the Nash Finch Company Contributions Program and the NFC Foundation.
Company EIN: 410431960

Nash Finch Company Contributions Program

c/o Labels for Learning
7600 France Ave. S., P.O. Box 355
Minneapolis, MN 55440-0355 (952) 832-0534
URL: http://www.nashfinch.com/about_lflprogram.html

Purpose and activities: Nash Finch makes charitable contributions to nonprofit organizations involved with education. Support is limited to areas of store operations.
Fields of interest: Elementary/secondary education; Education; Religion.
Program:
Labels for Learning: Nash Finch awards grants to K-12 schools in exchange for UPC barcodes from Nash Finch "Our Family" products brought in by customers participating in the program. The company awards $25 to schools for every 500 "Our Family" UPC barcodes, and the grants can be used for athletic equipment, band uniforms, new text books, teaching aids, etc.
Type of support: General/operating support.
Geographic limitations: Giving limited to areas of store operations in CO, GA, IA, IL, IN, KS, KY, MD, MI, MN, MO, MT, NC, ND, NE, OH, PA, SC, VI, WI, WV, and WY.
Publications: Application guidelines.
Application information: Applications accepted. Application form required.
Initial approach: Download registration form for Labels for Learning Program and mail to headquarters
Deadline(s): July, 2014

NFC Foundation

c/o Nash Finch Co.
7600 France Ave. S.
Edina, MN 55435-5924 (952) 844-1201
E-mail: NFCFoundation@NashFinch.com;
URL: http://www.nfcfoundation.org/

Establishment information: Established in 1997 in MN.
Donors: Nash Finch Co.; General Mills, Inc.
Contact: Brian Numanville, Chair.
Financial data (yr. ended 12/31/11): Assets, $1,085,481 (M); gifts received, $902,594; expenditures, $542,231; qualifying distributions, $469,094; giving activities include $469,094 for grants.
Purpose and activities: The foundation supports programs designed to address hunger and shelter.
Fields of interest: Education, reading; Food services; Food banks; Nutrition; Housing/shelter, homeless; Athletics/sports, Special Olympics; Children/youth, services; Family services; Family services, domestic violence; Homeless, human services Economically disadvantaged.
Program:
Feeding Imagination: The foundation, in partnership with nonprofit organizations and schools, donates books to children in grades K-6 who have limited access to reading books at school or at home. Special emphasis is directed toward children in areas of low poverty and need.
Type of support: Donated products; Employee volunteer services; General/operating support; Program development; Scholarship funds.
Geographic limitations: Giving primarily in areas of company operations in MN.
Support limitations: No grants to individuals.
Publications: Application guidelines; Grants list.
Application information: Applications accepted. Application form required. Applicants should submit the following:
1) copy of IRS Determination Letter
2) explanation of why grantmaker is considered an appropriate donor for project
3) detailed description of project and amount of funding requested
4) listing of additional sources and amount of support
Initial approach: Download application form and mail to foundation
Deadline(s): None
Officers and Directors:* Brian Numanville*, Chair.; Michael Campbell*, Secy.; Robert B. Dimond*, Treas.; Alec C. Covington; Paula Docken; Kathleen M. Mahoney*; Gary Spinazzo.
EIN: 411878919
Selected grants: The following grants are a representative sample of this grantmaker's funding activity:
$25,000 to Loaves and Fishes Too, Minneapolis, MN, 2010.
$16,000 to Neighborhood House, Saint Paul, MN, 2010.
$15,000 to Casa de Esperanza, Saint Paul, MN, 2010.
$15,000 to Catholic Charities of the Archdiocese of Saint Paul and Minneapolis, Minneapolis, MN, 2010.
$15,000 to Dakota Woodlands, Eagan, MN, 2010.
$15,000 to Families Moving Forward, Minneapolis, MN, 2010.
$15,000 to Neighbors, Inc., South Saint Paul, MN, 2010.
$15,000 to Theresa Living Center, Saint Paul, MN, 2010.
$5,000 to Food Bank for the Heartland, Omaha, NE, 2010.
$5,000 to Great Plains Food Bank, Fargo, ND, 2010.

2620
Nashville Hockey Club L.P.

(also known as Nashville Predators)
Bridgestone Arena
501 Broadway
Nashville, TN 37203-3980 (615) 770-2300

Company URL: http://www.nashvillepredators.com
Establishment information: Established in 1998.
Company type: Private company
Business activities: Operates professional ice hockey club.
Business type (SIC): Commercial sports
Corporate officers: Thomas Cigarran, Chair.; Jeff Cogen, C.E.O.; Sean Henry, Pres. and C.O.O.; Michelle Kennedy, Exec. V.P., Genl. Counsel, and C.F.O.; Beth Snider, Sr. V.P., Finance; Bruce Wagner, V.P., Opers.; Allison Simms, V.P., Human Resources; Jane Avinger, Cont.
Board of director: Thomas Cigarran, Chair.
Giving statement: Giving through the Nashville Predators Corporate Giving Program and the Nashville Predators Foundation.

Nashville Predators Corporate Giving Program

c/o Community Rels.
501 Broadway
Nashville, TN 37203-3932 (615) 770-2188
FAX: (615) 770-2309;
E-mail: ewilhelm@nashvillepredators.com;
Additional tel.: (615) 770-2331; URL: http://predators.nhl.com/club/page.htm?id=36951

Contact: Alexis Herbster
Purpose and activities: The Nashville Predators make charitable contributions of memorabilia to nonprofit organization involved with education, youth hockey, and disadvantaged youth. Support is given primarily in the Nashville, Tennessee, area.
Fields of interest: Elementary school/education; Education, reading; Education; Athletics/sports, winter sports; Youth development Youth.
Programs:
Predators Teacher of the Month: Through Predators Teachers of the Month, the Nashville Predators recognizes teachers in the greater Nashville area who has impacted students, school

faculty, and others around. Selected teachers receive a visit from the Predators mascot GNASH, a certificate, game tickets, a Predators gift basket, and a feature on the Predators website.

Speakers Bureau: Through the Speaker Bureau, Nashville Predators television and radio broadcasters visit professional associations, civic groups, corporate events, colleges, and universities and delivers a high energy 40 minute presentation.

Stick to Reading = Succeeding Program: The Nashville Predators rewards elementary school children with prizes for reading books to promote literacy. Participating students receive a registration from to keep track of their books and are awarded bookmarks, backpacks, and game tickets depending on the number of books they read. The program also includes Predators mascot GNASH and Predators player or broadcaster monthly visits to participating schools.

Youth Player and Volunteer of the Month: The Nashville Predators honors a youth hockey player and a youth hockey volunteer in the Nashville area who demonstrates character skills that make youth hockey a better experience for all involved. Honorees receive 4 game tickets, in-game recognition, and a feature on the Predators website.

Type of support: Donated products; In-kind gifts; Income development; Loaned talent.

Geographic limitations: Giving primarily in areas of company operations in the Nashville, TN, area.

Support limitations: No support for religious, fraternal, political, labor, social, or veterans' organizations. No grants for conferences, newsletters, or magazines.

Publications: Application guidelines.

Application information: Applications accepted. Proposals should be submitted using organization letterhead. Support is limited to 1 contribution per organization during any given year. The Community Relations Department handles giving. Application form required. Applicants should submit the following:

1) name, address and phone number of organization
2) copy of IRS Determination Letter
3) brief history of organization and description of its mission
4) descriptive literature about organization
5) listing of board of directors, trustees, officers and other key people and their affiliations
6) detailed description of project and amount of funding requested
7) contact person

Proposals should indicate the date, time, and location of the event and the type of fundraiser.

Initial approach: Proposal to headquarters for donations and player appearances; fax proposal to headquarters for Speakers Bureau; complete online nomination form for Youth Player and Volunteer of the Month

Copies of proposal: 1

Deadline(s): 6 weeks prior to need for donations and player appearances; None for Speaker Bureau and Youth Player and Volunteer of the Month

Nashville Predators Foundation

501 Broadway
Nashville, TN 37203-3932 (615) 770-2303
FAX: (615) 770-2309;
E-mail: ewilhelm@nashvillepredators.com;
URL: http://predators.nhl.com/club/page.htm?id=37108

Establishment information: Established in 1998 in TN.

Contact: Gerry Helper, Pres.

Financial data (yr. ended 06/30/11): Revenue, $960,732; assets, $628,510 (M); gifts received, $542,155; expenditures, $748,999; giving activities include $627,436 for grants and $10,000 for grants to individuals.

Purpose and activities: The foundation strives to meet the educational, social, health and cultural needs of local communities by offering unique resources and financial support to local youth-oriented organizations.

Fields of interest: Education; Youth development, centers/clubs.

Type of support: Scholarships—to individuals.

Geographic limitations: Giving primarily in Nashville and the central TN area.

Support limitations: No support for religious, fraternal, political, labor, social or veterans groups. No grants for operational expenses or staff funding.

Publications: Application guidelines; Grants list.

Application information: Applications accepted. Application form required. Applicants should submit the following:

1) population served
2) name, address and phone number of organization
3) copy of IRS Determination Letter
4) brief history of organization and description of its mission
5) geographic area to be served
6) descriptive literature about organization
7) listing of board of directors, trustees, officers and other key people and their affiliations
8) detailed description of project and amount of funding requested
9) contact person
10) copy of current year's organizational budget and/or project budget
11) listing of additional sources and amount of support
12) additional materials/documentation

Initial approach: Download application form

Copies of proposal: 2

Deadline(s): Feb. 2

Final notification: Mar. 19

Officers and Directors:* Jack Diller*, Chair.; Gerry Helper*, Pres.; Ed Lang, V.P.; Mike Kaplan*, Secy.; Beth Snider*, Treas.; Sharon Bell; Laura Currie; Willie Diehl; Jim Fyke; and 10 additional directors.

EIN: 621751832

2621
National Association for Stock Car Auto Racing, Inc.

(doing business as NASCAR)
1801 W. Intl. Speedway Blvd.
Daytona Beach, FL 32114 (386) 253-0611
FAX: (386) 252-8804

Company URL: http://www.nascar.com

Establishment information: Established in 1948.

Company type: Private company

Business activities: Operates national stock car racing circuit.

Business type (SIC): Commercial sports

Corporate officers: Brian Z. France, Chair. and C.E.O.; James C. France, Vice-Chair.; Mike Helton, Pres.; R. Todd Wilson, C.F.O.; W. Garrett Crotty, Genl. Counsel and Secy.; James Hunter, V.P., Comms

Board of directors: Brian Z. France, Chair.; James C. France, Vice-Chair.

Giving statement: Giving through the NASCAR Foundation.

The NASCAR Foundation

(also known as NASCAR Corporate Giving Program)
1801 W. International Speedway Blvd.
Daytona Beach, FL 32114-1215 (704) 348-9681
E-mail: foundation@nascarfoundation.com;
URL: http://foundation.nascar.com/NetCommunity

2622
National Association of Chain Drug Stores, Inc.

(also known as NACDS)
413 North Lee St.
P.O. Box 1417-D49
Alexandria, VA 22313-1480 (703) 549-3001

Company URL: http://www.nacds.org

Establishment information: Established in 1933.

Company type: Business league

Business activities: Operates business association.

Business type (SIC): Business association

Corporate officers: Gregory D. Wasson, Chair.; Bob Narveson, Vice-Chair.; Steven C. Anderson, Pres. and C.E.O.; John Standley, Treas.

Board of directors: Gregory D. Wasson, Chair.; Robert J. Narveso, Vice-Chair.; John Agwunobi, M.D.; Steven C. Anderson; Jose Barra; George D. Bartell; Paul E. Beahm; Anthony N. Civello; Jerry D. Cline; Joe Courtright; Kermit R. Crawford; Chris T. Dimos; Lynne Fruth; Andrew A. Giancamilli; Mark E. Griffin; Richard J. Hartig; Paul C. Julian; Michael C. Kaufmann; Robert D. Loeffler; Larry J. Merlo; Craig C. Painter; Mary F. Sammons; John Standley; Sharon Sternheim

Giving statement: Giving through the National Association of Chain Drug Stores Foundation.

National Association of Chain Drug Stores Foundation

(also known as NACDS Foundation)
413 N. Lee St.
Alexandria, VA 22314-2301 (703) 837-4276
FAX: (703) 683-3587;
E-mail: foundation@nacds.org; E-mail for Kathleen Jaeger: kjaeger@nacds.org; URL: http://www.nacdsfoundation.org/

Establishment information: Established in 1973 in VA; supporting organization of National Association of Chain Drug Stores.

Donors: The Coca-Cola Company/Coca-Cola Enterprises; National Association of Chain Drug Stores, Inc.; Colgate-Palmolive Co. Consumer Products Division; GENPHARM, L.P.; GlaxoSmithKline; Hallmark Cards, Inc.; L'Oreal USA; The Novartis Corp.; Barr Laboratories, Inc.; NACDS Charitable Foundation.

Contact: Kathleen Jaeger, Pres.

Financial data (yr. ended 12/31/11): Revenue, $2,461,778; assets, $8,721,961 (M); gifts received, $2,098,555; expenditures, $2,846,099; giving activities include $1,728,418 for grants and $214,000 for grants to individuals.

Purpose and activities: The foundation provides scholarships for pharmacy students and supports pharmacy education programs that address the needs of community pharmacy practice; additionally, the foundation supports research efforts documenting community pharmacy's role and value in America's healthcare system, as well as addressing effective and safe use of medicines.

Fields of interest: Scholarships/financial aid; Pharmacy/prescriptions; Public affairs, fund raising/fund distribution.

Programs:

Charitable Grants: Grant awards, generally ranging from $1,000 to $25,000, are available to support activities of beneficiary organizations that benefit the public at-large. The program gives priority to charitable endeavors that promote the health and welfare of the nation's families and youth; support research, health care, and health management services to treat disease states where patients are most likely to benefit from pharmacy care; and enhance the role of community pharmacy as an essential health care provider in the communities in which they serve. Grants are generally awarded for one year.

Mission Advancing Projects: Grants of up to $20,000 are awarded to research projects that seek to enhance the role and value of community pharmacies as a healthcare provider, and supports education programs in pharmacy schools that help advance a community pharmacy's ability to more effectively serve the public.

Pharmacy Student Scholarship Program: A minimum of forty-five scholarships will be awarded annually to support the development of future leaders in chain community pharmacy and to recognize pharmacy students who have a strong interest in pursuing a career in chain community pharmacy. Scholarships will generally be awarded in amounts of $2,000 each; select recipients of named scholarships will receive $2,500. Student applicants must have completed at least one professional year of pharmacy school to apply.

Research Funding: The program seeks to improve medication use outcomes for patients served by community pharmacies in the U.S. Grant awards generally range from $20,000 to $50,000 to support in whole, or in part, an overall project budget.

Type of support: Program development; Research; Scholarship funds; Scholarships—to individuals.
Geographic limitations: Giving on a national basis.
Support limitations: No support for religious programs; political candidates, committees, or organizations; or organizations that act as fundraisers for other agencies. No grants to individuals (except for scholarships) or for conferences, endowments, capital campaigns, travel, building, or renovation purposes.
Publications: Annual report; Application guidelines.
Application information: Applications accepted. Applicants must submit three proposal copies for scholarships, and five for formal research grant proposals. Application form required.

Initial approach: Download application for Pharmacy Student Scholarship; submit letter of inquiry for Research Funding and Mission Advancing Projects

Board meeting date(s): Apr. and Dec.

Officers and Directors:* Steven C. Anderson, I.O.M., C.A.E.*, Chair.; Kathleen Jaeger*, Pres.; Nicki Robins*, Secy.; R. James Huber*, Treas.; Robert Belknap, Jr.; Charles Vance Burnett, J.D., B.S.; James Caro; Anthony N. Civello; Teri Coward; Jack W. Fragie; Mark E. Griffin; Theresa Parker, R.Ph.; Bryan K. Stuke; David A. Waldock; and 15 additional directors.
EIN: 510144922

2623
National Basketball Association, Inc.

(doing business as NBA)
Olympic Tower
645 5th Ave.
New York, NY 10022 (212) 407-8000

Company URL: http://www.nba.com
Establishment information: Established in 1946.
Company type: Business league
Business activities: Operates professional sports league.
Business type (SIC): Business association; commercial sports
Corporate officers: Joel M. Litvin, Esq., Pres.; Adam Silver, C.O.O.; Carol Sawdye, Exec. V.P. and C.F.O.; Richard Buchanan, Exec. V.P. and Genl. Counsel; Stephen M. Hellmuth, Exec. V.P., Opers.; Kerry D. Chandler, Exec. V.P., Human Resources; Michael Bass, Exec. V.P., Comms.; Michael S. Gliedman, Sr. V.P. and C.I.O.
Giving statement: Giving through the National Basketball Association Corporate Giving Program.

National Basketball Association Corporate Giving Program

(also known as NBA Cares)
645 5th Ave.
New York, NY 10022 (212) 407-8000
URL: http://www.nba.com/caravan/

Purpose and activities: The National Basketball Association supports organizations involved with education, youth, the environment, family development, and healthcare. Giving primarily in areas of company operations.
Fields of interest: Education; Hospitals (specialty); Public health, physical fitness; Health care; Cancer; Diabetes; Food services; Recreation, parks/playgrounds; Athletics/sports, basketball; Boys clubs; Girls clubs; Youth development; Family services; Family resources and services, disability Children.
Type of support: Employee volunteer services; General/operating support.
Geographic limitations: Giving on a national basis primarily in areas of company operations.

2624
National Basketball Players Association

310 Lenox Ave.
New York, NY 10027 (212) 655-0880

Company URL: http://www.nbpa.com
Establishment information: Established in 1954.
Company type: Labor union
Business activities: Operates labor union.
Business type (SIC): Labor organization; commercial sports
Corporate officers: Derek Fisher, Pres.; James Jones, Secy.-Treas.
Giving statement: Giving through the National Basketball Players Association Foundation.

National Basketball Players Association Foundation

310 Lenox Ave.
New York, NY 10027-4405 (212) 655-0880
FAX: (212) 655-0881

Establishment information: Established in NY.
Financial data (yr. ended 06/30/11): Revenue, $3,484,540; assets, $24,443,514 (M); gifts received, $2,159,986; expenditures, $674,465; giving activities include $594,055 for grants.
Fields of interest: Arts; Education; Recreation; Human services.
Officers and Directors:* Derek Fisher, Pres.; Adonal Foyle, 1st V.P.; G. William Hunter.
EIN: 133894132

2625
National Cable Satellite Corporation

(also known as C-SPAN)
400 N. Capitol St. N.W., Ste. 650
Washington, DC 20001 (202) 737-3220
FAX: (202) 737-6226

Company URL: http://www.c-span.org
Establishment information: Established in 1979.
Company type: Private company
Business activities: Operates public access cable television company.
Business type (SIC): Cable and other pay television services
Corporate officers: Brian Lamb, Chair. and C.E.O.; Rob Kennedy, Pres. and Co-C.O.O.; Susan Swain, Pres. and Co-C.O.O.; Angelo Seldon, Sr. V.P., Human Resources; Bob Everett, Cont.
Board of directors: Brian Lamb, Chair.; Colleen Abdoulah; Alan Block; Rocco Commisso; Pat Esser; Amos Hostetter; David J. Keefe; John Evans; Rich Fickle; Jerry Kent; Brian Lamb; Pat McAdaragh; Thomas O. Might; Robert Miron; Steve Miron; Bob Rosencrans; Neil Smit; Amy Tykeson
Giving statement: Giving through the C-SPAN Education Foundation.

C-SPAN Education Foundation

400 N. Capital St., N.W., Ste. 650
Washington, DC 20001-1511 (202) 737-3220

Establishment information: Established in 1993 in DC; supporting organization of the National Cable Satellite Corporation.
Financial data (yr. ended 03/31/11): Revenue, $123,262; assets, $3,231,565 (M); gifts received, $118,519; expenditures, $164,062; program services expenses, $160,775; giving activities include $25,000 for grants.
Fields of interest: Media/communications; Secondary school/education.

Program:

Middle & High school Teacher Fellowship Program: In conjunction with the cable industry, this program awards fellowships to educators for research and training in the general area of using the electronic media in education with an emphasis on programming produced by C-SPAN.

Application information: Applications accepted. Application form required.
Officers and Trustees:* Brain Lamb*, Pres.; Robert Kennedy*, Secy.-Treas.; Bruce Collins; John Evans; Amos Hostetter; Susan Swain; Amy Tykeson.
EIN: 521867105

2626
National Football League
280 Park Ave., 15th Fl.
New York, NY 10017 (212) 450-2000

Company URL: http://www.nfl.com
Establishment information: Established in 1920.
Company type: Business league
Business activities: Operates professional sports league.
Business type (SIC): Business association; commercial sports
Corporate officers: Steve Bornstein, Pres. and C.E.O.; Jeff Pash, Exec. V.P. and Genl. Counsel; Joe Browne, Exec. V.P., Comms. and Public Affairs
Giving statement: Giving through the National Football League Disaster Relief Fund and the NFL Charities.

National Football League Disaster Relief Fund
345 Park Ave.
New York, NY 10154-0004 (212) 450-2000
URL: http://www.jointheteam.com/programs/program.asp?p=7&c=6

Establishment information: Established in 2001 in DC.
Financial data (yr. ended 03/31/11): Revenue, $2,468; assets, $1,545,068 (M); gifts received, $24; expenditures, $203,729; program services expenses, $200,652; giving activities include $200,652 for grants.
Purpose and activities: The fund supports organizations involved with disaster relief and education.
Fields of interest: Education; Disasters, preparedness/services; Safety/disasters.
Program:
Pro Bowl Grants: In connection with the NFL All-Star Game, grants totaling $100,000 are available to nonprofit organizations in the state of Hawaii that focus on youth and emphasize the following: motivation to learn, to stay in school, to complete one's education, and to continue studying toward college or other post-secondary pursuits, and the promotion of good health and participation in athletics and physical fitness. No grants to individuals.
Type of support: General/operating support.
Geographic limitations: Giving on a national basis.
Application information: Applications accepted. Application form required.
Initial approach: Complete online application
Deadline(s): Jan. 8
Trustees: Trace Armstrong; Joe Brown; Roger Goodell; Darrell Green; Harold Henderson; Troy Vincent; DeMaunce Smith; Paul Tagilabue.
EIN: 300046025

NFL Charities
345 Park Ave.
New York, NY 10154-0004 (212) 450-2000
URL: http://www.jointheteam.com/programs/programs.asp?c=6

Establishment information: Established in 1972 in DC.
Contact: Roger Goodell, Pres.
Financial data (yr. ended 03/31/11): Revenue, $11,478,524; assets, $9,619,613 (M); gifts received, $11,336,649; expenditures, $9,929,383; giving activities include $9,724,637 for grants.
Purpose and activities: The foundation supports programs and initiatives that deliver education and youth services; designates funds to assist the foundations of current and former players working in local communities; and awards sports-related medical research grants that advance the body of knowledge of sports medicine for professional and recreational athletes.
Fields of interest: Health care; Medical research; Recreation; Youth development; Human services.
Programs:
Medical Research Grants: Annual medical research grants are provided that target sports injury prevention, injury treatment, and other related research that affects the health and performance of athletes. Funding is available for nonprofit educational and research institutions only. For-profit enterprises are not eligible to apply. Maximum funding is $125,000 per application.
Player Foundation Grants: These grants seek to support the charitable and community service activities of both current and former National Football League players. The recipient organization must be defined as tax-exempt under section 501(c)(3) or Section 509 of the IRS Code. Grants will not be made to memorial foundations on behalf of deceased former players.
Pro Bowl Grants: In connection with the Pro Bowl, the NFL's All-Star Game, the foundation awards grants to nonprofit organizations located in the state of Hawaii. The foundation will only support organizations that are defined as tax-exempt under section 501(c)(3) of the IRS Code. No grants will be made to individuals.
Type of support: General/operating support; Management development/capacity building; Program development; Research.
Geographic limitations: Giving on a national basis.
Publications: Application guidelines.
Application information: Applications accepted. Application form required.
Initial approach: Online application
Deadline(s): May 6 for Medical Research Grants
Officers: Roger Goodell, Pres.; Dolores Weaver, Secy.; Michael Bidwell, Treas.
Directors: Charlotte Jones Anderson; Mary Owen; Justice Alan Page; Paul Tagliabue.
EIN: 237315236

2627
National Football League Players Association
1133 20th St., N.W.
Washington, DC 20036 (202) 756-9100

Company URL: http://www.nflplayers.com
Establishment information: Established in 1956.
Company type: Labor union
Business activities: Operates labor union.
Business type (SIC): Labor organization; commercial sports
Corporate officer: Domonique Foxworth, Pres.
Board of director: DeMaurice Smith
Giving statement: Giving through the National Football League Players Association.

National Football League Players Association
1133 20th St., N.W.
Washington, DC 20036-3408 (202) 756-9100
Toll-free tel.: (202) 463-2200; URL: https://www.nflplayers.com/About-us/Community-Partners/

Establishment information: Established in 1956 in VA.
Contact: Kevin Mawae, Pres.
Financial data (yr. ended 02/28/11): Revenue, $92,763,194; assets, $252,916,460 (M); expenditures, $113,601,238.
Purpose and activities: The association seeks to promote and advance all NFL players and the sport of professional football; the association also works to improve the economic and other working conditions of players.
Fields of interest: Athletics/sports, football.
Officers: Kevin Mawae*, Pres.; Charlie Batch*, V.P.; Drew Bress*, V.P.; Brian Dawkins*, V.P.; Domonique Foxworth*, V.P.; Scott Fujita*, V.P.; Sean Morey*, V.P.; Tony Richardson*, V.P.; Jeff Saturday*, V.P.; Eugene Upshaw, Exec. Dir.
EIN: 521169809

2628
National Fuel Gas Company
6363 Main St.
Williamsville, NY 14221-5855
(716) 857-7000
FAX: (716) 857-7439

Establishment information: Established in 1902.
Company type: Public company
Company ticker symbol and exchange: NFG/NYSE
Business activities: Operates holding company; transmits and distributes natural gas; conducts natural gas and crude petroleum exploration and production activities; operates timber tracts; conducts logging activities.
Business type (SIC): Gas production and distribution; forestry—timber tracts; extraction/oil and gas; logging; pipelines (except natural gas/operation of); holding company
Financial profile for 2012: Number of employees, 1,874; assets, $5,935,140,000; sales volume, $1,626,850,000; pre-tax net income, $370,630,000; expenses, $1,178,800,000; liabilities, $3,975,050,000
Corporate officers: David F. Smith, Chair.; Ronald J. Tanski, Pres. and C.E.O.; David P. Bauer, Treas.; Karen M. Camiolo, Cont.; Paula M. Ciprich, Genl. Counsel and Secy.
Board of directors: David F. Smith, Chair.; Phillip C. Ackerman; Robert T. Brady; David C. Carroll; R. Don Cash; Stephen E. Ewing; Rolland E. Kidder; Craig G. Matthews; Frederic V. Salerno
Subsidiaries: Data-Track Account Services, Inc., Buffalo, NY; Highland Forest Resources, Inc., Buffalo, NY; Horizon Energy Development, Inc., Buffalo, NY; National Fuel Gas Distribution Corp., Buffalo, NY; National Fuel Gas Supply Corp., Erie, PA; National Fuel Resources, Inc., Buffalo, NY; Seneca Resources Corp., Houston, TX
International operations: Netherlands
Giving statement: Giving through the National Fuel Gas Company Contributions Program and the National Fuel Gas Company Foundation.
Company EIN: 131086010

National Fuel Gas Company Contributions Program
c/o Corp. Comms. Dept.
6363 Main St.
Williamsville, NY 14221-5887
FAX: (716) 857-7439

Contact: Emily L. Ciraolo, Corp. Comms. Assoc.
Purpose and activities: National Fuel Gas makes charitable contributions to nonprofit organizations involved with veteran services, education, community vitality and economic development,

energy efficiency, and the environment. Support is given primarily in areas of company operations in New York and Pennsylvania.
Fields of interest: Education; Environment, energy; Environment; Community/economic development Military/veterans.
Type of support: Annual campaigns; Building/renovation; Capital campaigns; Employee-related scholarships; In-kind gifts; Scholarship funds; Sponsorships.
Geographic limitations: Giving limited to areas of company operations in western NY, with emphasis on Buffalo, and northwestern PA.
Support limitations: No support for religious or political organizations. No grants to individuals (except for employee-related scholarships).
Application information: Applications not accepted. Contributes only to pre-selected organizations. The Corporate Communications Department handles giving. A contributions committee reviews all requests.
Committee meeting date(s): Monthly
Administrators: Julie Coppola Cox, Sr. Mgr.; Brenda L. Spillman, Supvr., Corp. Comms.
Number of staff: 2 full-time professional; 1 full-time support.

National Fuel Gas Company Foundation

6363 Main St.
Williamsville, NY 14221-5855 (716) 857-7861
FAX: (716) 857-7439; E-mail: ciraoloe@natfuel.com

Establishment information: Established in NY.
Donor: National Fuel Gas Company.
Contact: Emily L. Ciraolo, Corp. Comms. Assoc.
Financial data (yr. ended 09/30/11): Assets, $674,970 (M); gifts received, $500,000; expenditures, $551,593; qualifying distributions, $551,485; giving activities include $551,485 for grants.
Purpose and activities: The foundation matches contributions made by its employees to nonprofit organizations; also a small number of grants on a case by case basis. Special emphasis is directed toward programs that promote community development. Support is limited to areas of company operations in western New York and northwestern Pennsylvania.
Fields of interest: Community/economic development.
Type of support: Annual campaigns; Capital campaigns; Scholarship funds.
Geographic limitations: Giving limited to areas of company operations in western NY and northwestern PA.
Support limitations: No support for political organizations or candidates, sports teams, or religious or sectarian organizations. No grants to individuals or for lobbying efforts.
Application information: Applications accepted. Proposals should be no longer than 1 to 2 pages. Application form required. Applicants should submit the following:
1) results expected from proposed grant
2) principal source of support for project in the past
3) copy of IRS Determination Letter
4) brief history of organization and description of its mission
5) copy of most recent annual report/audited financial statement/990
6) descriptive literature about organization
7) listing of board of directors, trustees, officers and other key people and their affiliations
8) detailed description of project and amount of funding requested
9) plans for cooperation with other organizations, if any
10) listing of additional sources and amount of support

Proposals should include a description of past accomplishments.
Initial approach: Contact foundation for application form and mail proposal and application form to foundation
Copies of proposal: 1
Board meeting date(s): Quarterly
Deadline(s): None
Officers and Directors:* David F. Smith*, Pres.; Paula M. Ciprich*, V.P. and Secy.; D.L. DeCarolis*, V.P. and Treas.; A.M. Cellino*, V.P.; Ronald J. Tanski*, V.P.
EIN: 201860605
Selected grants: The following grants are a representative sample of this grantmaker's funding activity:
$25,000 to Kaleida Health Foundation, Buffalo, NY, 2011.
$25,000 to Urban League of Buffalo, Buffalo, NY, 2011.
$6,000 to Boys and Girls Club of Erie, Erie, PA, 2011.
$5,000 to American Cancer Society, Atlanta, GA, 2011.
$5,000 to Elk Regional Health System, Saint Marys, PA, 2011.
$5,000 to Erie Art Museum, Erie, PA, 2011.
$5,000 to Gannon University, Erie, PA, 2011.
$4,904 to United Way of Erie County, Erie, PA, 2011.
$4,627 to Catholic Charities of Buffalo, Buffalo, NY, 2011.
$2,081 to PXE International, Washington, DC, 2011.

2629
National Grange Mutual Insurance Company

(also known as Main Street America Group)
55 West St.
Keene, NH 03431 (603) 352-4000

Company URL: http://www.msagroup.com
Establishment information: Established in 1923.
Company type: Mutual company
Business activities: Sells casualty and property insurance.
Business type (SIC): Insurance/fire, marine, and casualty; insurance/surety
Financial profile for 2011: Assets, $2,009,005,000; liabilities, $1,233,664,000
Corporate officers: Thomas M. Van Berkel, Chair., Pres., and C.E.O.; Steve Peeters, Exec. V.P. and C.O.O.; Edward J. Kuhl, Exec. V.P., and C.F.O.; Toni Porterfield, Sr. V.P., Human Resources; Joel Gelb, C.I.O.; Bruce Fox, Genl. Counsel
Board of directors: Thomas M. Van Berkel, Chair.; Terry L. Baxter; Cotton M. Cleveland; John A. Delaney; Chris Doerr; Albert H. Elfner III; David Freeman; William D. Gunter, Jr.; Idalene Kesner; Philip D. Koerner; James E. Morley, Jr.
Giving statement: Giving through the National Grange Mutual Charitable Foundation, Inc.

National Grange Mutual Charitable Foundation, Inc.

55 West St.
Keene, NH 03431-3348
URL: http://www.msagroup.com/aboutmsa/community.cfm

Establishment information: Established in 1972.
Donor: National Grange Mutual Insurance Company.
Contact: Antonia Porterfield, Tr.
Financial data (yr. ended 12/31/11): Assets, $1,782,962 (M); gifts received, $10,000; expenditures, $127,657; qualifying distributions, $126,326; giving activities include $126,326 for 172 grants (high: $17,912; low: $25).
Purpose and activities: The foundation supports museums and organizations involved with performing arts, education, health, cancer, heart disease, and human services.
Fields of interest: Museums; Museums (art); Performing arts; Performing arts centers; Performing arts, theater; Performing arts, orchestras; Secondary school/education; Higher education; Education; Health care; Cancer; Heart & circulatory diseases; Salvation Army; YM/YWCAs & YM/YWHAs; Human services; United Ways and Federated Giving Programs.
Type of support: Employee matching gifts; General/operating support.
Geographic limitations: Giving primarily in areas of company operations in FL, MI, and NH.
Application information: Applications accepted. Application form required. Applicants should submit the following:
1) detailed description of project and amount of funding requested

Initial approach: Proposal
Deadline(s): None
Trustees: Edward J. Kuhl; Steven Peeters; Antonia Porterfield; Thomas M. Van Berkel.
Number of staff: 1 part-time support.
EIN: 237228264
Selected grants: The following grants are a representative sample of this grantmaker's funding activity:
$5,000 to American Heart Association, Dallas, TX, 2010.
$1,750 to American Heart Association, Dallas, TX, 2010.

2630
National Grid USA

(formerly New England Electric System)
40 Sylvan Rd.
Waltham, MA 02451-1120 (781) 907-1000

Company URL: http://www.nationalgridus.com
Establishment information: Established in 1926.
Company type: Subsidiary of a foreign company
Business activities: Generates, transmits, and distributes electricity.
Business type (SIC): Electric services
Corporate officers: Peter Gershon, Chair.; Steven John Holliday, C.E.O.; Thomas B. King, Pres.; John J. Donleavy, Exec. V.P. and C.O.O.; Helen Mahy, Secy. and Genl. Counsel
Board of director: Peter Gershon, Chair.
Subsidiaries: Granite State Electric Co., Lebanon, NH; KeySpan Corporation, Brooklyn, NY; Massachusetts Electric Co., Westborough, MA; The Narragansett Electric Co., Providence, RI; Narragansett Energy Resources Co., Providence, RI; New England Electric Resources, Inc., Westborough, MA; New England Electric Transmission Corp., Concord, NH; New England Energy Inc., Westborough, MA; New England Hydro-Transmission Corp., Lebanon, NH; New England Hydro-Transmission Electric Co., Inc., Westborough, MA; New England Power Co., Westborough, MA; New England Power Service Co., Westborough, MA
Giving statement: Giving through the National Grid USA Corporate Giving Program and the National Grid Foundation.

National Grid USA Corporate Giving Program

(formerly NEES Corporate Giving Program)
40 Sylvan Road
Waltham, MA 02451-1120 (508) 309-2000
URL: http://www2.nationalgridus.com/corpinfo/community/sponsorships_all_all.jsp
Contact for the Samuel Huntington Public Service Award: Amy Stacy, National Grid, tel.: (781) 901-3358, fax: (781) 907-5717; e-mail: amy.stacy@us.ngrid.com

Purpose and activities: As a complement to its foundation, National Grid USA also makes charitable contributions to nonprofit organizations directly. Support is given primarily in areas of company operations.
Fields of interest: Higher education; Education; Environment, climate change/global warming; Environment, energy; Environmental education; Environment; Safety/disasters; Community/economic development; United Ways and Federated Giving Programs; Engineering.
Programs:
Community Investment: National Grid supports programs designed to address safety, inclusion, and diversity; and programs that support the company's employees and their initiatives in the community.
Education and Skills: National Grid supports programs designed to promote engineering, research, and development skills that are central to the company's business activities.
Energy and Environment: National Grid supports programs designed to reduce the causes and impact of climate change; promote local environments around National Grids operations sites; and support the delivery of energy efficiency and alleviating fuel poverty.
Samuel Huntington Public Service Award: National Grid awards a $10,000 stipend to a graduating college senior to pursue one year of public service anywhere in the world. The award is designed to allow recipients to engage in a public service before proceeding on to graduate school or a career. Recipients are selected based on the quality of proposal, academic record, and personal achievements. $5,000 is awarded at the beginning of the project, and the remaining $5,000 is awarded upon receipt of a six-month progress report.
Type of support: Employee volunteer services; Employee-related scholarships; General/operating support; Program development; Research; Seed money; Sponsorships.
Geographic limitations: Giving primarily in areas of company operations, with emphasis on Westborough, MA.
Support limitations: No support for political, religious, fraternal, lobbying, veterans', or discriminatory organizations, or organizations that spend more than 25% of their budget on overhead and fundraising, or agencies already receiving company support through the United Way. No grants to individuals (except for the Samuel Huntington Public Service Award), or for capital campaigns, travel, or conferences.
Publications: Application guidelines.
Application information: Applications accepted. Application form required. Applicants should submit the following:
1) copy of IRS Determination Letter
2) detailed description of project and amount of funding requested

Applications for the Samuel Huntington Public Service Award should include a budget, letters of recommendation, a transcript, and a resume.
Initial approach: Complete online eligibility quiz and application; download application form and mail proposal and form for the Samuel Huntington Public Service Award
Copies of proposal: 1
Deadline(s): None; Feb. 15 for the Samuel Huntington Public Service Award
Final notification: Following review; Mid-Apr. for the Samuel Huntington Public Service Award

The National Grid Foundation

(formerly The KeySpan Foundation)
175 E. Old Country Rd.
Hicksville, NY 11801-4257 (516) 545-5147
FAX: (516) 545-6094; URL: http://www2.nationalgridus.com/corpinfo/community/foundation_all.jsp

Establishment information: Established in 1998 in NY.
Donors: MarketSpan Corp.; KeySpan Corp.
Contact: Robert G. Keller, Exec. Dir.
Financial data (yr. ended 12/31/10): Assets, $26,160,746 (M); expenditures, $1,161,380; qualifying distributions, $807,000; giving activities include $807,000 for grants.
Purpose and activities: The foundation supports organizations involved with education and the environment.
Fields of interest: Elementary/secondary education; Higher education; Scholarships/financial aid; Education; Environment, natural resources; Environment, beautification programs; Environment; United Ways and Federated Giving Programs.
Programs:
Education: The foundation supports programs designed to promote classroom-based education for K-12 students; provide innovative scholarships and encourage university partnerships that support and advance underserved communities; and provide skills training that helps people of all ages lead more productive lives.
Environment: The foundation supports programs designed to promote the sustainability of natural resources; inspire and educate young people about their connection to and responsibility for the preservation of the environment; and preserve open spaces for future generations.
Type of support: Program development; Scholarship funds.
Geographic limitations: Giving primarily in areas of company operations in MA and Brooklyn, Long Island, Nassau, Queens, and Staten Island, NY.
Support limitations: No support for religious, political, or fraternal organizations. No grants to individuals, or for capital campaigns or endowments, advertisements, or tables or tickets at dinners or other functions.
Publications: Annual report; Application guidelines.
Application information: Applications accepted. Support is limited to 1 contribution per organization during any given year. Application form required. Applicants should submit the following:
1) population served
2) copy of IRS Determination Letter
3) brief history of organization and description of its mission
4) geographic area to be served
5) copy of most recent annual report/audited financial statement/990
6) descriptive literature about organization
7) listing of board of directors, trustees, officers and other key people and their affiliations
8) detailed description of project and amount of funding requested
9) copy of current year's organizational budget and/or project budget
10) listing of additional sources and amount of support

Initial approach: Complete online eligibility quiz and application
Copies of proposal: 1
Board meeting date(s): Quarterly
Deadline(s): Oct. 31
Final notification: 60 to 90 days
Officers and Directors:* Basil A. Paterson*, Chair.; Donald H. Elliot*, Vice-Chair.; Albert Wiltshire, Vice-Chair.; Robert G. Keller, Pres.; Jean T. Tesoriero, Secy.; Michael J. Taunton*, Treas.; Stephen W. McCaffrey, Chief Counsel; Robert B. Catell; Eileen R. Cohen; Susan M. Crossett; Carmen Fields; George Mayhew; Rev. Gary V. Simpson.
Number of staff: 1 full-time professional; 1 full-time support.
EIN: 113466416

2631
National Hockey League

(doing business as NHL)
1185 Ave. of the Americas, 12th Fl.
New York, NY 10036 (212) 789-2000

Company URL: http://www.nhl.com
Establishment information: Established in 1917.
Company type: Business league
Business activities: Operates professional sports league.
Business type (SIC): Business association; commercial sports
Corporate officers: Chris Zimmerman, Pres. and C.E.O.; John Collins, C.O.O.; Craig C. Harnett, Sr. Exec. V.P, C.F.O., and Treas.; David Zimmerman, Exec. V.P. and Genl. Counsel; Joseph Desousa, Exec. V.P., Finance; Brian Jennings, Exec. V.P., Mktg.; Bob Murray, Sr. V.P., Opers.; Kim Kutcher, V.P., Human Resources; Phil Legault, V.P., Comms.
Giving statement: Giving through the National Hockey League Foundation.

National Hockey League Foundation

c/o National Hockey League
1185 Ave. of the Americas, 14th Fl.
New York, NY 10036-2601

Establishment information: Established in 1991 in NY.
Donors: National Hockey League; Athletic Sport Fund of America; Norwalk Police Union Show Fund; Richmond Hockey Fights Cancer.
Financial data (yr. ended 06/30/11): Assets, $1,752,410 (M); gifts received, $193,380; expenditures, $1,243,415; qualifying distributions, $1,134,447; giving activities include $1,134,447 for grants.
Purpose and activities: The foundation supports museums and organizations involved with education, health, cancer, sports, and children and youth.
Fields of interest: Museums; Education; Hospitals (general); Health care, clinics/centers; Health care, patient services; Health care; Cancer; Athletics/sports, amateur leagues; Athletics/sports, winter sports; Boy scouts; Children/youth, services; Jewish federated giving programs.
Type of support: Equipment; General/operating support; Program development; Scholarship funds; Sponsorships.
Geographic limitations: Giving primarily in CA, CO, MA, MI, NC, and NY.
Support limitations: No grants to individuals.
Application information: Applications not accepted. Contributes only to pre-selected organizations.
Officers: William Daly, Pres.; Bernadette Mansur, V.P. and Secy.; Craig C. Harnett, Treas.

Directors: Joseph DeSousa; David Zimmerman.
EIN: 133498589
Selected grants: The following grants are a representative sample of this grantmaker's funding activity:
$205,000 to Companions in Courage Foundation, Huntington, NY, 2011.
$100,000 to Leukemia & Lymphoma Society, White Plains, NY, 2011.
$40,000 to Autism Speaks, New York, NY, 2011. For fundraiser.
$15,000 to Childrens Hospital of Pittsburgh Foundation, Pittsburgh, PA, 2011.
$10,000 to Friends of Independent Schools and Better Education, Tacoma, WA, 2011.
$10,000 to Kevin Guest House, Buffalo, NY, 2011.
$10,000 to UJA-Federation of New York, New York, NY, 2011.
$10,000 to USA Hockey Foundation, Colorado Springs, CO, 2011. For sponsorship.
$7,500 to Boys Club of New York, New York, NY, 2011. For fundraiser.
$5,000 to Friends of Kids With Cancer, Saint Louis, MO, 2011.

2632
National Instruments Corporation

11500 N. MoPac Expwy.
Austin, TX 78759-3504 (512) 338-9119
FAX: (302) 655-5049

Company URL: http://www.ni.com
Establishment information: Established in 1976.
Company type: Public company
Company ticker symbol and exchange: NATI/NASDAQ
Business activities: Manufactures measurement and automation products.
Business type (SIC): Laboratory apparatus; computer services
Financial profile for 2012: Number of employees, 6,869; assets, $1,284,770,000; sales volume, $1,143,690,000; pre-tax net income, $114,840,000; expenses, $1,026,760,000; liabilities, $345,640,000
Corporate officers: James J. Truchard, Ph.D., Chair., Pres., and C.E.O.; Alexander M. Davern, Exec. V.P., C.O.O., and C.F.O.; Peter Zogas, Sr. V.P., Sales; David Hugley, V.P., Genl. Counsel, and Secy.; John Roiko, V.P., Finance; Mark A. Finger, V.P., Human Resources
Board of directors: James J. Truchard, Ph.D., Chair.; John M. Berra; Donald M. Carlton, Ph.D.; Jeffrey L. Kodosky; Duy-Loan T. Le; John K. Medica; Charles J. Roesslein
Giving statement: Giving through the National Instruments Foundation.
Company EIN: 741871327

National Instruments Foundation

11500 N. Mopac Expwy., Bldg. A
Austin, TX 78759 (512) 683-8500

Establishment information: Established in 2002 in TX.
Donor: National Instruments Corp.
Contact: Ray Almgren, V.P. and Treas.
Financial data (yr. ended 12/31/11): Assets, $14,197 (M); expenditures, $0; qualifying distributions, $0.
Purpose and activities: The foundation supports organizations involved with higher education and science.
Fields of interest: Higher education; Engineering school/education; Health care, clinics/centers; Engineering/technology; Computer science; Science.
Type of support: Continuing support; General/operating support; Matching/challenge support; Program development; Sponsorships.
Geographic limitations: Giving primarily in CA, MA, and TX.
Support limitations: No support for religious organizations. No grants to individuals, or for employee-related scholarships, or non-engineering or science research.
Application information: Applications accepted. Application form not required. Applicants should submit the following:
1) detailed description of project and amount of funding requested
Initial approach: Proposal
Copies of proposal: 1
Deadline(s): None
Officers and Directors:* James J. Truchard*, Pres.; Raymond Almgren*, V.P. and Treas.; Jan Kubicek, Secy.; Howard Neal; Melodie Zamora Summersett.
EIN: 383667781
Selected grants: The following grants are a representative sample of this grantmaker's funding activity:
$6,250 to Institute of Electrical and Electronics Engineers Foundation, Piscataway, NJ, 2009.
$5,000 to Skillpoint Alliance, Austin, TX, 2009.

2633
National Life Insurance Company

(also known as National Life Group)
1 National Life Dr.
Montpelier, VT 05604 (802) 229-3333

Company URL: http://www.nationallife.com
Establishment information: Established in 1848.
Company type: Mutual company
Business activities: Sells life, disability, and accident insurance.
Business type (SIC): Insurance/life; insurance/accident and health; insurance/fire, marine, and casualty
Financial profile for 2011: Number of employees, 901; assets, $17,821,800,000; sales volume, $3,009,300,000
Corporate officers: Thomas H. MacLeay, Chair.; Mehran Assadi, Pres. and C.E.O.; Bob Cotton, Sr. V.P. and C.F.O.; Thomas H. Brownell, Sr. V.P. and C.I.O.; Gregory D. Woodworth, Sr. V.P. and Genl. Counsel; Christopher Graff, V.P. and Comms.
Board of directors: Thomas H. MacLeay, Chair.; Mehran Assadi; David R. Coates; James H. Douglas; Deborah G. Ellinger; Bruce M. Lisman; V. Louise McCarren; Roger B. Porter; E. Miles Prentice; Harris H. Simmons
Subsidiaries: Equity Services, Inc., Montpelier, VT; National Life Investment Management Co., Inc., Montpelier, VT
Giving statement: Giving through the National Life Group Charitable Foundation Inc.

National Life Group Charitable Foundation Inc.

1 National Life Drive
Montpelier, VT 05604-3377
E-mail: mtrombleyoakes@nationallife.com;
URL: http://www.nlgcf.com

Establishment information: Established in 2007 in VT.
Donor: National Life Insurance Company.
Contact: Martha Trombley-Oakes, Pres.
Financial data (yr. ended 12/31/11): Assets, $1,074,929 (M); gifts received, $953,665; expenditures, $454,837; qualifying distributions, $445,067; giving activities include $445,067 for grants.
Purpose and activities: The foundation supports organizations involved with arts and culture, the environment, health, housing, and human services.
Fields of interest: Arts; Environment; Health care; Housing/shelter; Children/youth, services; Family services; Human services.

Program:
Employee Matching Education Grants: The foundation matches contributions made by employees and directors of National Life Group to institutes of higher education on a one-for-one basis, up to 500 per contributor, per year.
Type of support: Employee matching gifts; Employee volunteer services; General/operating support; Program development; Public relations services.
Geographic limitations: Giving primarily in areas of company operations in VT, with emphasis on central VT.
Support limitations: No support for veterans', labor, religious, political, fraternal, or athletic organizations, organizations currently receiving Employee Action Grants, higher educational institutions (except for employee matching gifts), daycare facilities, or discriminatory organizations. No grants to individuals, or for endowments, debt reduction, or school trips.
Publications: Application guidelines.
Application information: Applications accepted. Telephone calls during the application process are not encouraged. Application form required. Applicants should submit the following:
1) results expected from proposed grant
2) statement of problem project will address
3) copy of IRS Determination Letter
4) copy of most recent annual report/audited financial statement/990
5) how project's results will be evaluated or measured
6) detailed description of project and amount of funding requested
7) copy of current year's organizational budget and/or project budget
Initial approach: Complete online eligibility quiz and application
Copies of proposal: 1
Deadline(s): Dec. 31 for grant requests under $5,000; Mar. 31 and Sept. 30 for grant requests over $5000
Final notification: 4 to 6 weeks for grant request under $5,000; 6 weeks for grant requests over $5,000
Officers and Directors:* Thomas H. MacLeay*, Chair.; Martha Trombley-Oakes*, C.E.O. and Pres.; James McQueston, Secy.; Robert Cotton, Treas.; Thomas Bronwell, C.I.O.; Jeffrey M. Kemp, Tax Off.; David Soccodato, Tax Off.; Mehran Assadi; Christopher Graff.
EIN: 204818866
Selected grants: The following grants are a representative sample of this grantmaker's funding activity:
$50,000 to Central Vermont Medical Center, Barre, VT, 2010.
$36,581 to United Way, Green Mountain, Montpelier, VT, 2010.
$25,000 to Kellogg-Hubbard Library, Montpelier, VT, 2010.
$25,000 to Vermont Symphony Orchestra, Burlington, VT, 2010.

$20,000 to Vermont Historical Society, Barre, VT, 2010.
$10,000 to Central Vermont Community Action Council, Barre, VT, 2010.
$10,000 to Chandler Center for the Arts, Randolph, VT, 2010.
$10,000 to Lund Family Center, Burlington, VT, 2010.
$10,000 to Richard A. Snelling Center for Government, Burlington, VT, 2010.
$10,000 to Veterans Place, Northfield, VT, 2010.

2634
National Machinery LLC

(formerly National Machinery Company)
161 Greenfield St.
Tiffin, OH 44883-2471 (419) 447-5211
FAX: (419) 443-2379

Company URL: http://www.nationalmachinery.com
Establishment information: Established in 1874.
Company type: Subsidiary of a private company
Business activities: Manufactures metal forming industrial machinery.
Business type (SIC): Machinery/metalworking
Corporate officers: Andrew H. Kalnow, C.E.O.; John H. Bolte, Exec. V.P., Opers. and Human Resources; Patrick Bowers, Cont.
Giving statement: Giving through the National Machinery Foundation, Inc.

National Machinery Foundation, Inc.

161 Greenfield St.
P.O. Box 747
Tiffin, OH 44883-0747
FAX: (419) 443-2184;
E-mail: lfbaker@nationalmachinery.com

Establishment information: Incorporated in 1948 in OH.
Donors: National Machinery Co.; National Machinery LLC.
Contact: Larry F. Baker, Treas.
Financial data (yr. ended 12/31/11): Assets, $13,815,873 (M); expenditures, $773,890; qualifying distributions, $707,107; giving activities include $596,557 for 100 grants (high: $100,000; low: $160) and $85,590 for 230 grants to individuals (high: $1,000; low: $25).
Purpose and activities: The foundation supports organizations involved with theater, education, health, child welfare, housing development, animal welfare, human services, and community development; and awards grants for good citizenship to high school students and relief assistance to needy individuals in Seneca County, OH.
Fields of interest: Performing arts, theater; Elementary/secondary education; Higher education; Education; Animal welfare; Hospitals (general); Health care; Crime/violence prevention, child abuse; Housing/shelter, development; Salvation Army; YM/YWCAs & YM/YWHAs; Youth, services; Human services; Community/economic development; United Ways and Federated Giving Programs.
Program:
National Machinery Citizenship Awards: The foundation annually honors high school students for citizenship, conduct, character, and moral outlook in Seneca, OH. Honorees receive certificates as citizenship award recipients, a pin, and monetary awards ranging from $50 to $300.
Type of support: Annual campaigns; Capital campaigns; Emergency funds; Employee-related scholarships; Equipment; General/operating support; Grants to individuals; Program development; Scholarship funds; Scholarships—to individuals; Sponsorships.
Geographic limitations: Giving limited to the Seneca County, OH, area.
Application information: Applications accepted. Application form not required. Applicants should submit the following:
1) detailed description of project and amount of funding requested
Initial approach: Proposal
Board meeting date(s): Semi-annually
Deadline(s): None
Final notification: Up to 6 months
Officer: Larry F. Baker*, Treas.
Number of staff: 1 part-time professional.
EIN: 346520191
Selected grants: The following grants are a representative sample of this grantmaker's funding activity:
$50,000 to Heidelberg University, Tiffin, OH, 2010.
$37,500 to United Way, Tiffin-Seneca, Tiffin, OH, 2010.
$25,000 to Ritz Theater, Tiffin, OH, 2010.
$25,000 to Salvation Army, Tiffin, OH, 2010.
$25,000 to United Way, Tiffin-Seneca, Tiffin, OH, 2010.
$15,000 to Ritz Theater, Tiffin, OH, 2010.
$10,000 to Tiffin-Seneca Teen Center, Tiffin, OH, 2010.
$5,333 to Ohio State University, Columbus, OH, 2010. For scholarship.
$2,500 to Salvation Army, Tiffin, OH, 2010.
$1,000 to Ohio State University, Columbus, OH, 2010. For scholarship.

2635
National Penn Bancshares, Inc.

Philadelphia and Reading Aves.
P.O. Box 547
Boyertown, PA 19512 (610) 705-9101
FAX: (610) 369-6118

Company URL: http://www.natpennbank.com
Establishment information: Established in 1982.
Company type: Public company
Company ticker symbol and exchange: NPBC/NASDAQ
Business activities: Operates commercial bank.
Business type (SIC): Banks/commercial
Financial profile for 2012: Number of employees, 1,772; assets, $8,529,520,000; pre-tax net income, $131,660,000; liabilities, $7,368,230,000
Corporate officers: Thomas A. Beaver, C.P.A., Chair.; Jeffrey Feather, Vice-Chair.; Wayne R. Weidner, Vice-Chair.; Scott V. Fainor, Pres. and C.E.O.; Michael J. Hughes, Sr. Exec. V.P. and C.F.O.; H. Anderson Ellsworth, Esq., Corp. Secy.
Board of directors: Thomas A. Beaver, C.P.A., Chair.; Jeffrey P. Feather, Vice-Chair.; Wayne R. Weidner, Vice-Chair.; Scott V. Fainor; Donna D. Holton; Thomas L. Kennedy, Esq.; Patricia L. Langiotti; Christian F. Martin IV; Micheal E. Martin; R. Chadwick Paul, Jr.; Natalye Paquin, Esq.; C. Robert Roth
Giving statement: Giving through the Keystone Nazareth Charitable Foundation.
Company EIN: 232215075

Keystone Nazareth Charitable Foundation

90 Highland Ave.
Bethlehem, PA 18017-9408 (610) 861-5002
E-mail: michele.linsky@knbt.com

Establishment information: Established in 2004.
Donor: Keystone Nazareth Bank & Trust Co.
Contact: Michele Linsky, Secy.
Financial data (yr. ended 12/31/11): Assets, $12,459,011 (M); expenditures, $628,549; qualifying distributions, $563,350; giving activities include $563,350 for grants.
Purpose and activities: The foundation supports organizations involved with arts and culture, education, the environment, health, housing, human services, neighborhood development, leadership development, youth, senior citizens, and the disabled.
Fields of interest: Visual arts; Museums; Performing arts; Arts; Elementary/secondary education; Higher education; Libraries (public); Education, drop-out prevention; Education; Environment, natural resources; Environment; Hospitals (general); Health care; Housing/shelter; Human services; Community development, neighborhood development; Leadership development Youth; Aging; Disabilities, people with.
Programs:
Civic and Community Development: The foundation supports programs designed to promote leadership development and environmental protection and conservation.
Culture and Arts: The foundation supports public libraries, museums, cultural centers and organizations involved with visual and performing arts.
Economic Development: The foundation supports programs designed to promote revitalization of neighborhoods and affordable housing.
Education: The foundation supports libraries and programs designed to promote public and secondary schools, drop out prevention, and higher education.
Health and Human Services: The foundation support hospitals and medical centers and programs designed to provide services for youth, the disabled, elderly, and local affiliates of health and human service organizations.
Type of support: Building/renovation; Capital campaigns; Equipment; General/operating support; Matching/challenge support; Program development; Scholarship funds; Sponsorships.
Geographic limitations: Giving limited to areas of company operations in Lehigh, Northampton, and Southern Carbon counties, PA.
Support limitations: No grants to individuals, or for golf tournaments, dinners, lunches, auction, or other similar events, endowments, or debt reduction.
Publications: Application guidelines; Program policy statement.
Application information: Applications accepted. Grant requests less than $25,000 are reviewed quarterly. Grant requests of $25,000 or more are reviewed once a year. E-mailed applications are not accepted. Support is limited to 1 contribution per organization during any given year. Organizations receiving support are asked to submit a report within 6 months of receiving funds. Application form required. Applicants should submit the following:
1) timetable for implementation and evaluation of project
2) how project will be sustained once grantmaker support is completed
3) results expected from proposed grant
4) statement of problem project will address
5) population served
6) principal source of support for project in the past

7) copy of IRS Determination Letter
8) geographic area to be served
9) copy of most recent annual report/audited financial statement/990
10) descriptive literature about organization
11) listing of board of directors, trustees, officers and other key people and their affiliations
12) detailed description of project and amount of funding requested
13) copy of current year's organizational budget and/or project budget
14) listing of additional sources and amount of support

Initial approach: Download application form and mail to foundation
Copies of proposal: 1
Board meeting date(s): Mar., June, Sept. and Dec.
Deadline(s): Feb. 15, May 15, Aug. 15, and Nov. 15; Aug 15. for grant requests of $25,000 or more

Officers and Directors:* Jeffrey P. Feather*, Chair., Pres., and Treas.; Michele A. Linsky, Secy.; Scott V. Fainor; Daniel G. Gambet; R. Charles Stehy.
EIN: 421607170

2636
National Presto Industries, Inc.

3925 N. Hastings Way
Eau Claire, WI 54703-3703 (715) 839-2121
FAX: (715) 839-2148

Company URL: http://www.gopresto.com/
Establishment information: Established in 1905.
Company type: Public company
Company ticker symbol and exchange: NPK/NYSE
Business activities: Manufactures firearms, household appliances, and fabricated metal products.
Business type (SIC): Industrial machinery and equipment—wholesale; appliances/household
Financial profile for 2012: Number of employees, 1,006; assets, $353,910,000; sales volume, $472,490,000; pre-tax net income, $60,420,000; expenses, $412,770,000; liabilities, $63,340,000
Corporate officers: Maryjo R. Cohen, Chair., Pres., and C.E.O.; Randy F. Lieble, V.P., Treas., and C.F.O.; Donald E. Hoeschen, V.P., Sales; Douglas J. Frederick, Corp. Secy. and Genl. Counsel
Board of directors: Maryjo R. Cohen, Chair.; Richard N. Cardozo; Randy F. Lieble; Patrick J. Quinn; Joseph G. Stienessen, C.P.A.
Subsidiaries: National Defense Corp., Eau Claire, WI; National Holding Investment Co., Wilmington, DE
Giving statement: Giving through the Singapore Exchange Ltd. Corporate Giving Program and the Presto Foundation.
Company EIN: 390494170

The Presto Foundation

1011 Centre Rd., Ste. 310
Wilmington, DE 19805-1267
Application address: 3925 N. Hastings Way, Eau Claire, WI 54703, tel.: (715) 839-2119

Establishment information: Incorporated in 1952 in WI.
Donor: National Presto Industries, Inc.
Contact: Norma Jaenke
Financial data (yr. ended 05/31/12): Assets, $20,390,465 (M); expenditures, $848,059; qualifying distributions, $799,564; giving activities include $793,371 for 111 grants (high: $135,500; low: -$200).
Purpose and activities: The foundation supports organizations involved with arts and culture, education, conservation, animals and wildlife, health, employment, recreation, human services, and religion.
Fields of interest: Arts; Higher education; Libraries (public); Education; Environment, natural resources; Animals/wildlife, preservation/protection; Hospitals (general); Health care, clinics/centers; Health care; Employment; Recreation; Boys & girls clubs; YM/YWCAs & YM/YWHAs; Youth, services; Human services; United Ways and Federated Giving Programs; Religion.
Type of support: Employee-related scholarships; General/operating support.
Geographic limitations: Giving primarily in northwestern WI, with emphasis on Chippewa Falls and Eau Claire counties.
Application information: Applications accepted. Application form not required. Applicants should submit the following:
1) copy of current year's organizational budget and/or project budget

Initial approach: Letter of inquiry
Deadline(s): None

Officers and Trustees:* Maryjo R. Cohen*, Pres.; Lawrence J. Tienor*, V.P. and Treas.; Arthur Petzold*, V.P.; Libby Stupak*, Secy.; Eileen Phillips Cohen; Vernon B. Haas; Richard Myhers.
EIN: 396045769
Selected grants: The following grants are a representative sample of this grantmaker's funding activity:
$215,000 to Mayo Foundation, Rochester, MN, 2011.
$102,000 to University of Wisconsin, Eau Claire, WI, 2011.
$15,100 to United Way of the Greater Chippewa Valley, Eau Claire, WI, 2011.
$11,000 to Saint Johns University, Collegeville, MN, 2011.
$11,000 to Tulane University, New Orleans, LA, 2011.
$11,000 to University of Phoenix, Phoenix, AZ, 2011.
$11,000 to Vanderbilt University, Nashville, TN, 2011.
$10,450 to YMCA of Eau Claire, Eau Claire, WI, 2011.
$5,000 to Boys and Girls Club of Langlade County, Antigo, WI, 2011.
$3,500 to Long Island Head Injury Association, Commack, NY, 2011.

2637
National Resources, Inc.

12425 Rivers Edge Dr.
Potomac, MD 20854-1071 (301) 670-0410

Establishment information: Established in 1991.
Company type: Private company
Business activities: Provides child care services.
Business type (SIC): Day care services/child
Corporate officer: Barry R. Meil, Pres.
Giving statement: Giving through the Meil Family Foundation, Inc.

The Meil Family Foundation, Inc.

(formerly The Winwood Children's Foundation, Inc.)
12425 Rivers Edge Dr.
Potomac, MD 20854

Establishment information: Established in 2003 in MD.
Donors: National Resources, Inc.; Leslie A. Meil Revocable Trust.
Financial data (yr. ended 12/31/11): Assets, $186,443 (M); gifts received, $20,000; expenditures, $39,364; qualifying distributions, $36,770; giving activities include $36,770 for grants.
Purpose and activities: The foundation supports organizations involved with education, health, heart disease, autism, human services, and children.
Fields of interest: Education; Health care; Human services.
Type of support: General/operating support.
Geographic limitations: Giving primarily in MD, PA, and VA.
Support limitations: No grants to individuals.
Application information: Applications not accepted. Unsolicited requests for funds not accepted.
Officers and Directors:* Barry R. Meil*, Pres.; Wendy E. Meil*, Treas.
EIN: 200230903

2638
National Restaurant Association

(also known as NRA)
2055 L St. N.W., Ste. 700
Washington, DC 20036-3016
(202) 331-5900

Company URL: http://www.restaurant.org/
Establishment information: Established in 1919.
Company type: Business league
Business activities: Operates restaurant industry association.
Business type (SIC): Business association
Corporate officers: Phil Hickey, Chair.; Ken Conrad, Vice-Chair.; Dawn Sweeney, Pres. and C.E.O.; Marvin Irby, C.F.O. and C.A.O.; Ed Beck, C.I.O.; Dawn Cacciotti, Sr. V.P., Human Resources; Sue Hensley, Sr. V.P., Public Affairs and Comms.; Jack Crawford, Treas.
Board of directors: Phil Hickey, Chair.; Ken Conrad, Vice-Chair.; Dawn Sweeney
Giving statement: Giving through the National Restaurant Association Corporate Giving Program and the National Restaurant Association Educational Foundation.

National Restaurant Association Corporate Giving Program

2055 L St. N.W., Ste. 700
Washington, DC 20036-4985 (202) 331-5900
FAX: (202) 331-2429;
E-mail: aprince@restaurant.org; URL: http://www.restaurant.org/Industry-Impact/Giving-Back

Purpose and activities: As a complement to its foundation, the National Restaurant Association works with members and other food service companies to facilitate charitable donations of leftover food to social service agencies that provide feeding programs for people at risk of hunger. Support is given primarily in areas of member company operations.
Fields of interest: Agriculture/food, fund raising/fund distribution; Food services; Safety/disasters; Military/veterans' organizations.
Programs:
Dine for America: When disaster strikes, restaurants become part of emergency relief efforts, whether offering food and beverages to first responders or offering cash donations to help those affected. Nationally, the NRA created Dine for America, a national fundraising campaign that

supported the efforts of the American Red Cross in the wake of 9/11 and Hurricane Katrina.

Restaurant Neighbor Award: Through the Restaurant Neighbor Award program, the National Restaurant Association annually awards $5,000 each to four restaurateurs who go above and beyond in giving back to their communities. They are honored with a gala in Washington, DC.

Type of support: Annual campaigns; Donated products; Employee volunteer services; In-kind gifts.

Geographic limitations: Giving primarily in areas of member company operations.

National Restaurant Association Educational Foundation

(formerly National Institute for the Food Service Industry)
175 W. Jackson Blvd., Ste. 1500
Chicago, IL 60604-2814 (312) 715-1010
FAX: (312) 715-0807; E-mail: scholars@nraef.org; Toll-free tel.: (800) 765-2122; URL: http://www.nraef.org

Establishment information: Established in 1971 in IL; supporting organization of the National Restaurant Association.

Contact: Ellen Nash

Financial data (yr. ended 12/31/11): Revenue, $9,004,220; assets, $21,627,798 (M); gifts received, $3,730,412; expenditures, $8,405,628; giving activities include $770,000 for grants and $1,102,519 for grants to individuals.

Fields of interest: Vocational education, post-secondary; Business school/education; Education; Food services Minorities.

Programs:

Al Schuman Ecolab Undergraduate Entrepreneurial Scholarship: Scholarships, ranging from $3,000 to $5,500, are awarded to current undergraduate students who are committed to their education and careers in the restaurant and foodservice industry while demonstrating a strong entrepreneurial spirit. Applicants must be citizens or permanent residents of the U.S., be enrolled full-time or substantial part-time (minimum of nine credit hours) at a selected U.S.-accredited culinary school, college, or university in a food service-related program (California State Polytechnic University - Pomona, Cornell University, Culinary Institute of America, DePaul University, Johnson and Wales University, Kendall College, Lynn University, Michigan State University, New York University, Pennsylvania State University, Purdue University, University of Denver, University of Houston, University of Nevada - Las Vegas, and University of Massachusetts - Amherst); and have a minimum GPA of at least 3.0 (on a 4.0 scale).

GRI/Giacomo Bologna Scholarship: Awarded in conjunction with Gruppo Ristoratori Italiani (GRI), this program will award up to six students with an all-expense-paid trip from New York City to Italy, and enable them to participate in various culinary and restaurant industry-related classes and tours. During this program, students will be offered a first-hand experience in Italian winemaking and cooking. Applicants must be citizens or permanent residents of the U.S., be undergraduate students who are currently enrolled full-time in a U.S.-accredited culinary school, college, or university, demonstrate a commitment to Italian viticulture, and have at least two years of culinary experience and/or viticulture training, working directly with a chef in the preparation of food or with a sommelier.

High School/GED Graduate/ProStart Students Scholarships: Awards of $2,500 each are available to students who will be first-time freshmen, including graduating high school seniors, GED graduates, and high school graduates enrolling in college for the first time. Applicant must be a citizen or permanent resident of the U.S., be a first-time freshman (including a graduating high-school senior, a GED graduate enrolling in college for the first time, or a high school graduate enrolling in college for the first time), be accepted and plan to enroll in a U.S.-accredited culinary school, college, or university, and plan to major in culinary arts, restaurant management, or another foodservice-related major.

Professional Development Scholarships for Educators: This program offers scholarships of $1,750 each to restaurant/foodservice educators to attend the foundation's annual Summer Institute, or to participate in its annual 'Hands On' Industry Work Experience Program, with the goal of providing educators the opportunity to enhance their teaching skills by providing practical, industry-related experience that can be brought back to the classroom. Applicant must be a citizen or permanent resident of the U.S., and be an educator in a restaurant/foodservice-related program at a secondary or post-secondary school.

Undergraduate Student/ProStart Alumni/Manage First Students: Scholarships of $2,500 each are available to current undergraduate students enrolled in a foodservice-related program. Applicant must be a citizen or permanent resident of the U.S., be a college student currently enrolled full-time or substantially part-time (with a minimum of nine credit hours) in a foodservice-related program at a U.S.-accredited culinary school, college, or university, and have completed at least one grading term of his/her college or postsecondary program.

Type of support: Annual campaigns; Capital campaigns; Grants to individuals; In-kind gifts; Matching/challenge support; Scholarships—to individuals.

Geographic limitations: Giving on a national basis.

Publications: Annual report; Application guidelines; Newsletter.

Application information: Applications accepted. Application form required.

Initial approach: Submit application
Board meeting date(s): May, Sept., and Jan.
Deadline(s): Feb. 8 for Professional Development Scholarships for Educators; Feb. 22 for GRI/Giacomo Bologna Scholarship; Mar. 14 for Al Schuman Ecolab Undergraduate Entrepreneurial Scholarship and Undergraduate Student/ProStart Alumni/Manage First Students; July 25 for High School/GED Graduate/ProStart Students Scholarships

Officers and Trustees:* Xavier Teixido*, Chair.; Denise Fugo*, Vice-Chair.; Dawn Sweeney, Pres. and C.E.O.; Lynnette McKee*, Exec. Dir.; Mike Gibbons*, Treas.; William C. Anton, F.M.P.; William Barry; Marilyn Benson; Mary Ann Cricchio, F.M.P.; Jeffrey W. Davis; Sam J. Facchini, F.M.P.; Julie A. Flik, F.M.P.; Ted M. Fowler, Jr., F.M.P.; Philip Friedman; Michael Gibbons; and 19 additional trustees.

Number of staff: 10 full-time professional; 98 full-time support; 12 part-time support.

EIN: 366103388

2639
Nationwide Mutual Insurance Company

1 Nationwide Plz.
Columbus, OH 43215-2220
(614) 249-7111

Company URL: http://www.nationwide.com

Establishment information: Established in 1925.

Company type: Mutual company

Business activities: Sells insurance; provides investment advisory services.

Business type (SIC): Insurance carriers; security and commodity services

Financial profile for 2011: Number of employees, 32,711; assets, $148,702,000,000; sales volume, $20,265,000,000

Corporate officers: Stephen S. Rasmussen, C.E.O.; Mark A. Pizzi, Pres. and C.O.O.; Michael Keller, Exec. V.P. and C.I.O.

Board of directors: Lewis J. Alphin; James B. Bachmann; A.I. Bell; Timothy J. Corcoran; Yvonne M. Curl; Kenneth D. Davis; Keith W. Eckel; Fred C. Finney; Daniel T. Kelley; M. Diane Koken; Lydia M. Marshall; Terry W. McClure; Barry J. Nalebuff; Brent R. Porteus; Stephen S. Rasmussen; Jeffrey W. Zellers

Subsidiaries: Allied Group, Inc., Des Moines, IA; Nationwide Agribusiness Insurance Co., Des Moines, IA; Nationwide Life Insurance Company of America, Berwyn, PA; Western Heritage Insurance Co., Scottsdale, AZ

Giving statement: Giving through the Nationwide Mutual Insurance Company Contributions Program and the Nationwide Insurance Foundation.

Nationwide Mutual Insurance Company Contributions Program

(formerly Nationwide Insurance Enterprise Corporate Giving Program)
1 Nationwide Plz., M.C. 1-12-16
Columbus, OH 43215-2239 (614) 249-4310
FAX: (866) 212-7960;
E-mail: corpcit@nationwide.com; URL: http://www.nationwide.com/nw/about-us/community-involvement/index.htm?WT.svl=2

Contact: Karen Blickley, Sr. Dir., Nationwide Fdn.

Financial data (yr. ended 12/31/12): Total giving, $4,721,635, including $4,721,635 for grants.

Purpose and activities: As a complement to its foundation, Nationwide also makes charitable contributions to nonprofit organizations directly. Support is given on a national basis in areas of company operations.

Fields of interest: Arts; Health care; Human services; Community/economic development; Public affairs.

Type of support: General/operating support; In-kind gifts; Sponsorships.

Geographic limitations: Giving on a national basis in areas of company operations, with emphasis on central OH.

Publications: Application guidelines.

Application information: Applications accepted. The Office of Corporate Citizenship handles giving. The company has a staff that only handles contributions. Application form required.

Initial approach: Complete online application
Copies of proposal: 1
Deadline(s): None
Final notification: Following review

Number of staff: 3 full-time professional.

Nationwide Insurance Foundation

(formerly Nationwide Foundation)
1 West Nationwide Blvd., 1-2-16
Columbus, OH 43215-2220 (614) 249-4310
FAX: (866) 212-7960;
E-mail: corpcit@nationwide.com; URL: http://www.nationwide.com/about-us/corporate-philanthropy.jsp

Establishment information: Incorporated in 1959 in OH.
Donors: Nationwide Mutual Insurance Co.; Nationwide Corp.; Nationwide Life Insurance Co. of America.
Contact: Karen Blickley, Sr. Dir.
Financial data (yr. ended 12/31/11): Assets, $88,792,349 (M); gifts received, $13,171,000; expenditures, $26,938,184; qualifying distributions, $26,780,821; giving activities include $25,530,938 for 634 grants (high: $7,522,687; low: $100) and $983,087 for 435 employee matching gifts.
Purpose and activities: The foundation supports programs designed to address emergency and basic needs; crisis stabilization; personal and family empowerment; and community enrichment.
Fields of interest: Hospitals (general); Health care; Substance abuse, services; Food services; Food banks; Housing/shelter, temporary shelter; Housing/shelter; Disasters, preparedness/services; Boys & girls clubs; Big Brothers/Big Sisters; American Red Cross; Youth, services; Family services; Homeless, human services; Human services; Community/economic development Economically disadvantaged.
Programs:
Community Enrichment: The foundation supports community enrichment through partnerships with organizations that contribute to the overall quality of life of the community.
Crisis Stabilization: The foundation supports programs designed to provide resources to prevent crisis or help pick up the pieces after one occurs.
Emergency and Basic Needs: The foundation supports the community in times of emergency through partnerships with organizations that provide life's basis necessities.
Employee Matching Gifts: The foundation matches contributions made by employees, directors, retirees, and insurance agents of Nationwide to the United Way campaign and to institutions of higher education on a one-for-one basis.
On Your Side Volunteer Network Grants Program: The foundation awards grants to nonprofit organizations with which employees and agents of Nationwide volunteer at least 25 hours.
Personal and Family Empowerment: The foundation supports at-risk youth and families in poverty situations who need tools and resources to advance their lives through partnerships with organizations that assist individuals in becoming productive members of society.
Type of support: Annual campaigns; Capital campaigns; Continuing support; Emergency funds; Employee matching gifts; Employee volunteer services; General/operating support; Matching/challenge support; Program development; Seed money.
Geographic limitations: Giving primarily in areas of company operations in Sacramento, CA, Denver, CO, Gainesville, FL, Atlanta, GA, Baltimore, MD, Lincoln, NE, Durham and Raleigh, NC, Syracuse, NY, Canton and Cleveland, OH, Harrisburg and Philadelphia, PA, Nashville, TN, Richardson and San Antonio, TX, and Lynchburg and Richmond, VA, with emphasis on Scottsdale, AZ, Des Moines, IA, and Columbus, OH.
Support limitations: No support for athletic teams, public or private primary or secondary schools, pass-through organizations (except United Way), veterans', labor, religious, or fraternal organizations not of direct benefit to the entire community, lobbying or political organizations, or bands or choirs; generally, no support for hospitals, hospital foundations, or national organizations (except local branches or chapters). No grants to individuals, or for fundraising events, sponsorships, athletic events, debt reduction, retirement campaigns, research, travel, or endowments.
Publications: Application guidelines.
Application information: Applications accepted. Videos, albums, and binder submissions are not accepted. Application form required. Applicants should submit the following:
1) timetable for implementation and evaluation of project
2) how project will be sustained once grantmaker support is completed
3) population served
4) copy of IRS Determination Letter
5) brief history of organization and description of its mission
6) geographic area to be served
7) copy of most recent annual report/audited financial statement/990
8) how project's results will be evaluated or measured
9) explanation of why grantmaker is considered an appropriate donor for project
10) what distinguishes project from others in its field
11) listing of board of directors, trustees, officers and other key people and their affiliations
12) detailed description of project and amount of funding requested
13) copy of current year's organizational budget and/or project budget
14) listing of additional sources and amount of support
15) additional materials/documentation
Initial approach: Complete online application
Board meeting date(s): Feb., May, and Nov.
Deadline(s): Sept. 1
Final notification: Mar. 31
Officers and Trustees:* Stephen S. Rasmussen, Chair. and C.E.O.; Chad A. Jester, Pres.; Mark R. Thresher, Exec. V.P. and C.F.O.; Harry H. Hollowell, Sr. V.P.; Pamela A. Biesecker, Sr. V.P., Taxation; Robert W. Horner III, V.P. and Secy.; Carol L. Dove, V.P. and Treas.; James B. Bachman; Timothy J. Corcoran; Daniel T. Kelley; M. Diane Koken; Lydia M. Marshall.
Number of staff: 1 part-time professional; 1 full-time support.
EIN: 316022301
Selected grants: The following grants are a representative sample of this grantmaker's funding activity:
$7,378,089 to United Way, Oakland, CA, 2010.
$5,000,000 to Nationwide Childrens Hospital Foundation, Columbus, OH, 2010.
$1,830,000 to American Red Cross National Headquarters, Washington, DC, 2010.
$700,000 to Columbus Museum of Art, Columbus, OH, 2010.
$600,000 to Feeding America, Chicago, IL, 2010.
$500,000 to Columbus Metropolitan Library, Columbus, OH, 2010.
$50,000 to Community Arts Project, Columbus, OH, 2010.
$20,000 to South County Community Clinic, Conroe, TX, 2010.
$15,000 to Clackamas Womens Services, Oregon City, OR, 2010.
$1,400 to United Way of Central Iowa, Des Moines, IA, 2010.

2640
The Natori Company

180 Madison Ave., 18th Fl.
New York, NY 10016 (212) 532-7796

Company URL: http://www.natori.com
Establishment information: Established in 1977.
Company type: Private company
Business activities: Manufactures lingerie.
Business type (SIC): Apparel—women's, girls', and children's undergarments
Financial profile for 2010: Number of employees, 40
Corporate officers: Josie C. Natori, Co-Chair. and C.E.O.; Ken Natori, Co-Chair.
Board of directors: Josie C. Natori, Co-Chair.; Ken Natori, Co-Chair.
Giving statement: Giving through the Natori Foundation.

The Natori Foundation

c/o The Natori Co.
180 Madison Ave., 18th Fl.
New York, NY 10016-5267

Establishment information: Established in 2001 in NY.
Donors: The Natori Co.; Josie C. Natori; Kenneth Natori.
Financial data (yr. ended 12/31/11): Assets, $101,802 (M); gifts received, $25,000; expenditures, $126,550; qualifying distributions, $126,500; giving activities include $126,500 for grants.
Purpose and activities: The foundation supports organizations involved with arts and culture, secondary education, Parkinson's disease research, golf, human services, and the fashion industry.
Fields of interest: Arts; Human services; Religion.
Type of support: General/operating support.
Geographic limitations: Giving primarily in NY.
Support limitations: No grants to individuals.
Application information: Applications not accepted. Unsolicited requests for funds not accepted.
Directors: Aida Chinloy; Josie C. Natori; Kenneth Natori.
EIN: 134168478

2641
Natural Gas Partners

125 E. John Carpenter Fwy., Ste. 600
Irving, TX 75062-2324 (972) 432-1440

Company URL: http://www.naturalgaspartners.com/
Establishment information: Established in 1988.
Company type: Private company
Business activities: Operates private equity investment firm.
Business type (SIC): Investors/miscellaneous
Corporate officer: Kenneth A. Hersh, C.E.O.
Giving statement: Giving through the Natural Gas Partners Foundation.

Natural Gas Partners Foundation

125 E.J. Carpenter Freeway, Ste. 600
Irving, TX 75062-2318

Establishment information: Established in 2004 in TX.
Donors: Petne Parkman & Co., Inc.; Mark Doenng; Rising Starr Energy, LLC; Action Energy, Inc.; Bravo

Natural Resources; Fleet; NGP Energy Capital Management, LLC; and 24 additional donors.
Financial data (yr. ended 12/31/11): Assets, $31,148 (M); gifts received, $500; expenditures, $4,000,000; qualifying distributions, $4,000,000; giving activities include $4,000,000 for 1 grant.
Purpose and activities: The foundation supports museums and organizations involved with higher education, children services, and economically disadvantaged people.
Fields of interest: Museums; Higher education, college; Children, services Economically disadvantaged.
Type of support: General/operating support.
Geographic limitations: Giving primarily in CT, NM, TX, and WA.
Support limitations: No grants to individuals.
Application information: Applications not accepted. Contributes only to pre-selected organizations.
Officers: Kenneth A. Hersh*, Pres.; David R. Albin*, V.P.; Christopher Ray, Secy.; Stacie Moore, Treas.
EIN: 770620172

2642
Natural Investments LLC

P.O. Box 390595
Keauhou, HI 96739-0595 (808) 331-0910

Company URL: http://www.naturalinvesting.com
Establishment information: Established in 1985.
Company type: Private company
Business type (SIC): Business services/ miscellaneous
Financial profile for 2012: Number of employees, 10
Corporate officer: Michael Kramer, Owner
Giving statement: Giving through the Natural Investments LLC Contributions Program.

Natural Investments LLC Contributions Program

P.O. Box 390595
Keauhou, HI 96739-0595 (808) 331-0910
URL: http://www.naturalinvesting.com

Purpose and activities: Natural Investments is a certified B Corporation that donates a percentage of net profits to charitable organizations.
Fields of interest: Environment.
Type of support: General/operating support.

2643
Natural Stone Bridge and Caves, Inc.

535 Stone Bridge Rd.
Pottersville, NY 12860-1713
(518) 494-2283
FAX: (518) 494-2283

Company URL: http:// www.stonebridgeandcaves.com
Establishment information: Established in 1970.
Company type: Private company
Business activities: Operates natural cave attraction.
Business type (SIC): Amusement and recreation services/miscellaneous
Corporate officers: Gregory S. Beckler, Chair. and C.E.O.; Edward Beckler, Pres. and Treas.; Janet Beckler, V.P. and Secy.
Board of director: Gregory S. Beckler, Chair.
Giving statement: Giving through the Edward and Janet Beckler Foundation.

The Edward and Janet Beckler Foundation

330 Stone Bridge Rd.
Pottersville, NY 12860-1708

Establishment information: Established in 2000 in TX.
Donor: Natural Stone Bridge and Caves, Inc.
Financial data (yr. ended 12/31/11): Assets, $31,418 (M); gifts received, $956; expenditures, $8,390; qualifying distributions, $7,100; giving activities include $7,100 for 15 grants (high: $3,000; low: $100).
Purpose and activities: The foundation supports libraries and organizations involved with hunger and children.
Fields of interest: Agriculture/food; Safety/ disasters; Religion.
Type of support: Capital campaigns; General/ operating support.
Geographic limitations: Giving limited to New York, NY.
Support limitations: No grants to individuals.
Application information: Applications not accepted. Contributes only to pre-selected organizations.
Directors: Edward Beckler; Janet J. Beckler; Philip A. Beckler.
EIN: 760581103

2644
Naturescapes

451 Darby Paoli Rd.
Paoli, PA 19301-2005 (610) 640-0164

Company URL: http://www.naturescapes-pa.com
Establishment information: Established in 1988.
Company type: Private company
Business type (SIC): Business services/ miscellaneous
Corporate officer: John Fridy, Owner
Giving statement: Giving through the Naturescapes Corporate Giving Program.

Naturescapes Corporate Giving Program

451 Darby Paoli Rd.
Paoli, PA 19301-2005 (610) 640-0164
E-mail: info@naturescapes-pa.com; URL: http:// www.naturescapes-pa.com

Purpose and activities: Naturescapes is a certified B Corporation that donates a percentage of net profits to charitable organizations.

2645
Naugatuck Savings Bank

727 Rubber Ave., Ste. 31
Naugatuck, CT 06770-3642
(203) 720-3129

Company URL: http:// www.naugatucksavingsbank.com
Establishment information: Established in 1870.
Company type: Private company
Business activities: Operates savings bank.
Business type (SIC): Savings institutions
Financial profile for 2009: Number of employees, 11; assets, $941,975,000; liabilities, $858,968,000
Corporate officers: Mark C. Yanarella, Chair.; Charles J. Boulier III, Pres. and C.E.O.; Kathleen McPadden, V.P., Human Resources
Board of directors: Mark C. Yanarella, Chair.; Charles J. Boulier III; Anna Merriam Feinberg; Richard H. Gesseck; Lucille Janatka; David W. Nurnberger; Francis R. Powell; John H. Tobin; Stephen C Widman
Offices: Cheshire, Middlebury, Oxford, Prospect, Southbury, Watertown, Woodbury, CT
Giving statement: Giving through the Naugatuck Savings Bank Foundation, Inc.

Naugatuck Savings Bank Foundation, Inc.

251 Church St.
P.O. Box 370
Naugatuck, CT 06770-4121 (203) 729-4442
FAX: (203) 720-5329;
E-mail: caren.bouchard@nutmegfinancial.com; Toll free: (877) 729-4442; Additional contact: Josh Carey, tel.: (203) 753-1315, e-mail: josh@conncf.org; URL: http:// www.naugatucksavingsbank.com/about-us/ our-foundation.aspx

Donor: Naugatuck Savings Bank.
Contact: Caren G. Bouchard, Secy.
Financial data (yr. ended 12/31/11): Assets, $6,474,411 (M); gifts received, $300,226; expenditures, $464,342; qualifying distributions, $436,579; giving activities include $436,579 for grants.
Purpose and activities: The foundation supports organizations involved with arts and culture, education, health, human services, and community economic development. Special emphasis is directed toward programs designed to promote education and homeownership.
Fields of interest: Museums; Performing arts, theater; Arts; Education; Hospitals (general); Health care; Housing/shelter, development; Housing/ shelter; YM/YWCAs & YM/YWHAs; Family services, domestic violence; Human services; Business/ industry; Community/economic development; United Ways and Federated Giving Programs.
Type of support: Annual campaigns; Capital campaigns; Continuing support; Equipment; Program development; Sponsorships.
Geographic limitations: Giving primarily in areas of company operations in Ansonia, Cheshire, Meridan, Middlebury, Naugatuck, Oxford, Prospect, Southbury, Waterbury, Watertown, and Woodbury, CT.
Support limitations: No support for political or lobbying organizations, or religious organizations not of direct benefit to the entire community. No grants to individuals.
Publications: Application guidelines.
Application information: Applications accepted. Support is limited to 1 contribution per organization during any given year. Application form not required. Applicants should submit the following:
1) timetable for implementation and evaluation of project
2) how project will be sustained once grantmaker support is completed
3) results expected from proposed grant
4) statement of problem project will address
5) copy of IRS Determination Letter
6) brief history of organization and description of its mission
7) copy of most recent annual report/audited financial statement/990

8) how project's results will be evaluated or measured
9) listing of board of directors, trustees, officers and other key people and their affiliations
10) copy of current year's organizational budget and/or project budget

Initial approach: Download application form and mail proposal and application form to foundation
Copies of proposal: 2
Deadline(s): Feb. 19, May 14, Sept. 10, and Nov. 12

Officer and Directors:* Mark C. Yanarella*, Pres.; Caren Bouchard, Secy.; Charles J. Boulier III, Treas; John D. Arresta; Harry X. Cashin III; Ann Merriam Feinberg; Richard H. Gesseck; Lucille Janatka; Francis R. Powell; John H. Tobin.
EIN: 061513293
Selected grants: The following grants are a representative sample of this grantmaker's funding activity:
$49,000 to United Way of Naugatuck and Beacon Falls, Naugatuck, CT, 2010.
$15,000 to Neighborhood Housing Services of Waterbury, Waterbury, CT, 2010.
$11,000 to United Way of the Central Naugatuck Valley, Waterbury, CT, 2010.
$10,000 to American Cancer Society, Meriden, CT, 2010.
$10,000 to Saint Marys Hospital Foundation, Waterbury, CT, 2010.
$7,000 to Greater Waterbury Interfaith Ministries, Waterbury, CT, 2010. For annual contribution.
$5,000 to Saint Marys Hospital, Waterbury, CT, 2010. For annual contribution.
$3,000 to Operation Fuel, Bloomfield, CT, 2010. For annual contribution.
$3,000 to United Way of Meriden and Wallingford, Meriden, CT, 2010.
$2,500 to Multiple Sclerosis Society, National, Newington, CT, 2010.

2646
Naugatuck Valley Financial Corporation

333 Church St.
Naugatuck, CT 06770 (203) 720-5000
FAX: (203) 720-5016

Company URL: http://www.nvsl.com
Establishment information: Established in 1922.
Company type: Subsidiary of a private company
Company ticker symbol and exchange: NVSLD/NASDAQ
Business activities: Operates bank holding company; operates savings bank.
Business type (SIC): Savings institutions; holding company
Financial profile for 2011: Number of employees, 146; assets, $568,250,000; pre-tax net income, $2,280,000; liabilities, $515,990,000
Corporate officers: Carlos S. Batista, Chair.; William C. Calderara, Pres. and C.E.O.; James Cotter, Exec. V.P. and C.O.O.; James Hastings, Exec. V.P. and C.F.O.; Bernadette A. Mole, Secy.
Board of directors: Carlos S. Batista, Chair.; Orvile Aarons; William C. Calderara; Frederick A. Dlugokecki; Richard M. Famiglietti; Kevin A. Kennedy; James A. Mengacci; Jane H. Walsh
Subsidiary: Naugatuck Valley Savings and Loan, Naugatuck, CT
Giving statement: Giving through the Naugatuck Valley Savings and Loan Foundation.
Company EIN: 651233977

Naugatuck Valley Savings and Loan Foundation

333 Church St.
Naugatuck, CT 06770-2806 (203) 720-5000
URL: http://www.nvsl.com

Establishment information: Established in 2004 in CT.
Donor: Naugatuck Valley Financial Corp.
Contact: Bernadette A. Mole, Secy.
Financial data (yr. ended 12/31/11): Assets, $884,375 (M); expenditures, $13,557; qualifying distributions, $8,654; giving activities include $8,654 for grants.
Purpose and activities: The foundation supports organizations involved with arts and culture, cancer, sexual abuse prevention, youth development, economic development, and business.
Fields of interest: Crime/law enforcement; Youth development; Human services.
Type of support: Annual campaigns; Building/renovation; Conferences/seminars; Equipment; General/operating support; Program development; Scholarship funds.
Geographic limitations: Giving primarily in western CT.
Application information: Applications accepted. Application form required.
Initial approach: Letter
Deadline(s): None
Officers: John C. Roman, Pres.; Bernadette A. Mole, Secy.; Lee R. Schlesinger, Treas.
EIN: 201730743

2647
Navistar International Corporation

2701 Navistar Dr.
Lisle, IL 60532 (331) 332-5000
FAX: (331) 332-2573

Company URL: http://www.navistar.com
Establishment information: Established in 1902.
Company type: Public company
Company ticker symbol and exchange: NAV/NYSE
Business activities: Manufactures commercial and military trucks, diesel engines, and school and commercial buses.
Business type (SIC): Motor vehicles and equipment; engines and turbines
Financial profile for 2012: Number of employees, 16,900; assets, $9,102,000,000; sales volume, $12,948,000,000; pre-tax net income, -$1,182,000,000; expenses, $14,101,000,000; liabilities, $12,407,000,000
Fortune 1000 ranking: 2012—216th in revenues, 995th in profits, and 421st in assets
Forbes 2000 ranking: 2012—774th in sales, 1974th in profits, and 1580th in assets
Corporate officers: James H. Keyes, Chair.; Troy Clarke, Pres. and C.E.O.; Jack Allen, Ex. V.P. and C.O.O.; Andrew J. Cederoth, Exec. V.P. and C.F.O.; Steven K. Covey, Sr. V.P. and Genl. Counsel; Gregory W. Elliott, Sr. V.P., Human Resources and Admin.; James M. Moran, V.P. and Treas.; Richard C. Tarapchak, V.P. and Cont.; Curt A. Kramer, Corp. Secy.
Board of directors: James H. Keyes, Chair.; Troy Clarke; John D. Correnti; Michael N. Hammes; Vincent J. Intrieri; Stanley A. McChrystal; Samuel Merksamer; John C. Pope; Mark H. Rachesky; Dennis D. Williams
Subsidiary: Navistar, Inc., Warrenville, IL
Plants: Richmond, San Ramon, CA; Miami, FL; Atlanta, GA; Melrose Park, Rolling Meadows, West Chicago, Westchester, IL; Fort Wayne, IN; Overland Park, KS; Baltimore, MD; Mount Laurel, NJ; Columbus, Springfield, OH; Dallas, Plano, TX; Waukesha, WI
International operations: Brazil; Canada
Giving statement: Giving through the Navistar, Inc. and the Navistar Foundation.
Company EIN: 363359573

Navistar Foundation

4201 Winfield Rd.
Warrenville, IL 60555-4025 (630) 753-5000

Establishment information: Incorporated in 1944 in IL.
Donors: International Harvester Co.; Navistar International Corp.; Navistar International Transportation Corp.; International Truck and Engine Corp.
Contact: Greg W. Elliott, Pres.
Financial data (yr. ended 10/31/11): Assets, $56,572 (L); gifts received, $1,546; expenditures, $7,599; qualifying distributions, $6,000; giving activities include $6,000 for 2 grants to individuals (high: $3,500; low: $2,500).
Purpose and activities: The foundation supports organizations involved with education and human services.
Fields of interest: Education, association; Scholarships/financial aid; Education; Human services; United Ways and Federated Giving Programs.
Application information: Applications accepted. Application form required. Applicants should submit the following:
1) copy of IRS Determination Letter
2) detailed description of project and amount of funding requested

Initial approach: Letter
Copies of proposal: 1
Deadline(s): None

Officers: Greg W. Elliot, Pres.; Debra D. Boens, Secy.; Lisa Hartenberger, Treas.
EIN: 366058875

2648
NAVTEQ Corporation

425 W. Randolph St.
Chicago, IL 60606 (312) 894-7000

Company URL: http://www.navteq.com/
Establishment information: Established in 1985.
Company type: Subsidiary of a private company
Business activities: Produces digital map data and content.
Business type (SIC): Computer services
Corporate officers: Judson C. Green, Vice-Chair.; Lawrence M. Kaplan, Pres. and C.E.O.; Steve Collins, Exec. V.P. and C.F.O.; Jeffrey L. Mize, Exec. V.P., Sales; Jason S. Rice, Sr. V.P. and Genl. Counsel; Christine C. Moore, Sr. V.P., Human Resources
Board of director: Judson C. Green, Vice-Chair.
Giving statement: Giving through the NAVTEQ Foundation.

NAVTEQ Foundation

425 W. Randolph St.
Chicago, IL 60606

Establishment information: Established in 2006 in IL.

Donors: Navteq Corporation; Navteq North America, LLC.
Financial data (yr. ended 12/31/11): Assets, $25,967 (M); expenditures, $297,500; qualifying distributions, $297,499; giving activities include $285,000 for 7 grants (high: $100,000; low: $5,000).
Fields of interest: Environment; Human services; Civil/human rights.
Support limitations: No grants to individuals.
Application information: Applications not accepted. Unsolicited requests for funds not accepted.
Officers and Directors:* Lawrence M. Kaplan*, Pres.; Jason Rice, Secy.; Steve Collins*, Co-Treas.; Kelly Smith*, Co-Treas.; Christine C. Moore.
EIN: 208064861

2649
NBC Universal, Inc.

(formerly National Broadcasting Company, Inc.)
30 Rockefeller Plz.
New York, NY 10112 (212) 644-4444

Company URL: http://www.nbcuni.com
Establishment information: Established in 1926.
Company type: Subsidiary of a public company
Business activities: Broadcasts television; produces motion pictures; provides cable television services; provides satellite television services; operates theme parks; provides Internet information services.
Business type (SIC): Radio and television broadcasting; cable and other pay television services; computer services; motion pictures/ production and services allied to; amusement and recreation services/miscellaneous
Financial profile for 2011: Sales volume, $21,100,000,000
Corporate officers: Patricia Fili-Krushel, Co-Chair.; Ted Harbert, Co-Chair.; Stephen B. Burke, C.E.O.; Ron Meyer, Pres. and C.O.O; Richard Cotton, Exec. V.P. and Genl. Counsel; Richard Licata, Exec. V.P., Comms.; Stuart J. Epstein, Exec. V.P and C.F.O.; David Angehrn, Sr. V.P., Mktg.
Board of directors: Patricia Fili-Krushel, Co-Chair.; Ted Harbert, Co-Chair.; Michael Angelakis; Jeffrey Immelt; Brian Roberts; Keith Sherin
Subsidiaries: iVillage Inc., New York, NY; Universal Studios, Inc., Universal City, CA
Giving statement: Giving through the NBC Universal, Inc. Corporate Giving Program and the NBC Universal Foundation.
Company EIN: 141682529

NBC Universal, Inc. Corporate Giving Program

30 Rockefeller Plz.
New York, NY 10112-0015 (212) 664-4444
URL: http://www.nbcuni.com/corporate/initiatives

Purpose and activities: As a complement to its foundation, NBC Universal also makes contributions to nonprofit organizations directly. Support is given primarily in areas of company operations.
Fields of interest: Education; Environment; Health care; Safety/disasters; Children/youth, services; Community/economic development; General charitable giving.
Program:
The More You Know: NBC Universal promotes awareness about important societal issues through a national public service campaign and an interactive website. The public service campaign features NBC stars and is designed to educate viewers. The campaign focuses on health, safety, and education, with emphasis on diversity/ anti-prejudice, drinking and driving, the environment, internet safety, monitoring kids' TV viewing, nutrition and physical activity, reading, smoking, and violence prevention.
Type of support: Advocacy; Employee volunteer services; General/operating support.
Geographic limitations: Giving primarily in areas of company operations.

NBC Universal Foundation

(formerly Universal Studios Foundation, Ltd.)
c/o NBC Universal
30 Rockefeller Plz.
New York, NY 10012-0015
URL: http://www.nbcuni.com/corporate/ initiatives/nbc-universal-foundation

Establishment information: Incorporated in 1956 in CA.
Donors: Universal Studios, Inc.; NBC Universal, Inc.
Contact: Jennifer Fitzgerald
Financial data (yr. ended 12/31/11): Assets, $11,003,897 (M); gifts received, $3,000,000; expenditures, $1,015,727; qualifying distributions, $1,013,477; giving activities include $960,000 for 31 grants (high: $100,000; low: $15,000).
Purpose and activities: The foundation supports organizations involved with arts and culture, education, the environment, employment, community and economic development, and civic affairs.
Fields of interest: Arts; Secondary school/ education; Education; Environment; Employment; Economic development; Community/economic development; Engineering/technology; Public affairs.
Program:
21st Century Solutions: Through 21st Century Solutions, the foundation in partnership with NBC Owned Televisions, enables nonprofit organizations in select cities to compete for funding to help communities identify and implement opportunities for positive change. Special emphasis is directed toward programs designed to promote arts and media, civic engagement, community development, education, environment, jobs and economic empowerment, and technology and innovation. The initiative is limited to NBC Stations in the Bay Area, Chicago, Connecticut, Dallas and Fort Worth, Los Angeles, Miami, New York, Philadelphia, San Diego, and Washington, DC.
Type of support: General/operating support; Program development.
Geographic limitations: Giving primarily in Los Angeles, CA, Washington, DC, Miami, FL, Chicago, IL, New York, NY, and Dallas, TX.
Support limitations: No support for private foundations or organizations with overhead expenses exceeding 15 percent of the total project budget. No grants for endowments or major equipment purchases, capital campaigns, annual fundraising events or fund drives, partisan lobbying or political campaigns or activities, individual film or television projects, sponsorship of special events, debt reduction, or religious or sectarian purposes.
Application information: Applications are only accepted for the 21st Century Solutions Initiative in August. Visit website for details.
Officers and Directors:* Ron Meyer*, Pres.; Maren Christensen*, Exec. V.P. and Secy.; Christa Shibata*, Exec. V.P. and Treas.; Kenneth L. Kahrs, Sr. V.P.; Bridget Baker; Bob Corcoran; Patricia Fili-Krushel; Cindy Gardner; Susan Haspel; Charisse Lillie; Adam Miller; Valari Staab; Lauren Zalaznick.
Number of staff: 2 full-time professional.
EIN: 136096061

Selected grants: The following grants are a representative sample of this grantmaker's funding activity:
$100,000 to Motion Picture and Television Fund, Woodland Hills, CA, 2011.
$50,000 to Sponsors for Educational Opportunity, New York, NY, 2011.
$45,000 to Committee for Hispanic Children and Families, New York, NY, 2011.
$37,500 to City Year, Boston, MA, 2011.
$35,000 to Lawrence Hall Youth Services, Chicago, IL, 2011.
$35,000 to Urban Arts Partnership, New York, NY, 2011.
$25,000 to Aspire of Illinois, Westchester, IL, 2011.
$20,000 to Camp Fire USA, Fort Worth, TX, 2011.
$20,000 to Hispanic Unity of Florida, Hollywood, FL, 2011.
$20,000 to STRIVE DC, Washington, DC, 2011.

2650
NCR Corporation

(also known as National Cash Register Company)
3097 Satellite Blvd.
Building 700
Duluth, GA 30096 (937) 445-5000

Company URL: http://www.ncr.com
Establishment information: Established in 1884.
Company type: Public company
Company ticker symbol and exchange: NCR/NYSE
Business activities: Provides information solutions.
Business type (SIC): Business services/ miscellaneous; computer and office equipment
Financial profile for 2012: Number of employees, 25,700; assets, $6,371,000,000; sales volume, $5,730,000,000; pre-tax net income, $182,000,000; expenses, $5,498,000,000; liabilities, $5,124,000,000
Fortune 1000 ranking: 2012—441st in revenues, 657th in profits, and 521st in assets
Corporate officers: William R. Nuti, Chair., Pres., and C.E.O.; Robert Fishman, Sr. V.P., C.F.O., and C.A.O.; Jennifer Daniels, Sr. V.P., Genl. Counsel, and Corp. Secy.
Board of directors: William R. Nuti, Chair.; Edward P. (Pete) Boykin; Richard L. Clemmer; Gary J. Daichendt; Robert P. DeRodes; Kurt P. Kuehn; Linda Fayne Levinson; Deanna W. Oppenheimer
Subsidiaries: Compris Technologies, Inc., Duluth, GA; First Level Technology LLC, Austin, TX; Research Computer Services, Inc., Dayton, OH
International operations: Argentina; Australia; Austria; Bahrain; Belgium; Bermuda; Brazil; Canada; Chile; China; Colombia; Cyprus; Czech Republic; Denmark; Dominican Republic; Finland; France; Germany; Ghana; Greece; Hong Kong; Hungary; India; Indonesia; Ireland; Italy; Japan; Kenya; Macau; Malaysia; Mexico; Netherlands; New Zealand; Nigeria; Norway; Panama; Peru; Philippines; Poland; Portugal; Russia; Singapore; South Africa; South Korea; Spain; Switzerland; Taiwan; Thailand; Turkey; Ukraine; United Kingdom; Zimbabwe
Giving statement: Giving through the NCR Corporation Contributions Program, the NCR Foundation, and the NCR Scholarship Foundation.
Company EIN: 310387920

NCR Corporation Contributions Program

1700 S. Patterson Blvd.
Dayton, OH 45479-0001
FAX: (937) 445-5541

Contact: Janet J. Brewer, V.P., Corp. Comms.
Financial data (yr. ended 12/31/07): Total giving, $235,000, including $235,000 for 54 grants.
Purpose and activities: As a complement to its foundation, NCR also makes charitable contributions to nonprofit organizations directly. Support is given on a national and international basis in areas of company operations.
Fields of interest: Arts; Education; Health care; Human services; Public affairs.
Type of support: Annual campaigns; Employee volunteer services; General/operating support; Sponsorships.
Geographic limitations: Giving on a national and international basis in areas of company operations, with emphasis on San Diego, CA, Atlanta, GA, Dayton, OH, and Columbia, SC.
Support limitations: No support for athletic organizations or religious or political organizations. No grants to individuals, or for athletics.
Application information: Applications accepted. The Corporate Communications and Community Relations departments handle giving. Application form not required.
Initial approach: Proposal to headquarters
Copies of proposal: 1
Deadline(s): None
Final notification: 2 months
Administrators: Janet J. Brewer, V.P., Corp. Comms.; Nancy Oney, Asst.
Number of staff: 1 full-time professional; 1 full-time support.

The NCR Foundation
3095 Satellite Blvd. Bldg. 800, 3rd Fl.
Duluth, GA 30096-5814

Establishment information: Incorporated in 1953 in OH.
Donor: NCR Corp.
Contact: Andrea Ledford, Tr.
Financial data (yr. ended 12/31/11): Assets, $7,898,465 (M); expenditures, $374,877; qualifying distributions, $360,497; giving activities include $360,497 for grants.
Purpose and activities: The foundation supports organizations involved with arts and culture, education, health, human services, and civic affairs.
Fields of interest: Historic preservation/historical societies; Arts; Education; Health care; American Red Cross; Salvation Army; Human services; United Ways and Federated Giving Programs; Public affairs.
Program:
Employee Matching Gifts: The foundation matches contributions made by full-time U.S. employees and the spouses of full-time U.S. employees of NCR to institutions of higher education, arts and culture organizations, and public television and radio stations on a one-for-one basis from $50 to $3,000 per contributor, per year.
Type of support: Employee matching gifts; General/operating support.
Geographic limitations: Giving primarily in areas of company operations, with emphasis on Dayton, OH.
Support limitations: No support for religious or political organizations. No grants to individuals, or loans, or for athletic programs.
Application information: Applications accepted. Application form not required. Applicants should submit the following:
1) population served
2) copy of IRS Determination Letter
3) geographic area to be served
4) copy of most recent annual report/audited financial statement/990
5) list of company employees involved with the organization
6) listing of board of directors, trustees, officers and other key people and their affiliations
7) copy of current year's organizational budget and/or project budget
8) listing of additional sources and amount of support
Initial approach: Proposal
Copies of proposal: 1
Board meeting date(s): July and Dec.
Deadline(s): None
Officer and Trustees: Bo Sawyer, Treas.; Janet J. Brewer; Peter Dorsman; Robert Fishman; Elise Kirban; Andrea Ledford.
Number of staff: 1 part-time professional; 1 part-time support.
EIN: 316030860

NCR Scholarship Foundation
3095 Satellite Blvd., Bldg. 800, 3rd Fl.
Duluth, GA 30096-5814 (770) 623-7479
E-mail: ncr.scholarship@ncr.com; Additional tel.: (800) 225-5627

Establishment information: Established around 1975.
Donor: NCR Corp.
Contact: William Ryan
Financial data (yr. ended 12/31/11): Assets, $282,622 (M); expenditures, $25,444; qualifying distributions, $20,000; giving activities include $20,000 for 18 grants to individuals (high: $2,000; low: $200).
Purpose and activities: The foundation awards college scholarships to children of employees and retirees of NCR.
Fields of interest: Higher education.
Type of support: Employee-related scholarships.
Geographic limitations: Giving primarily in areas of company operations in CO, FL, OH, Canada, Italy, and Pakistan.
Application information: Applications accepted. Application form required.
Completed application, required essay, copy of official transcript, current resume.
Initial approach: Proposal
Deadline(s): May 31
Officer and Trustees: B. Sawyer*, Treas.; Q.J. Coburn.
EIN: 237431180

2651
Neace Lukens, Inc.
2305 River Rd.
Louisville, KY 40206-1010 (502) 894-2100
FAX: (502) 894-8602

Company URL: http://www.neacelukens.com/
Establishment information: Established in 1991.
Company type: Private company
Business activities: Provides property and casualty insurance brokerage services.
Business type (SIC): Insurance agents, brokers, and services
Financial profile for 2010: Number of employees, 427
Corporate officers: John F. Neace, Chair. and C.E.O.; Joseph T. Lukens, Pres.; David Prisco, C.O.O.; Gerald Budde, C.F.O.; Charles Biernetzky, Treas.; Will Dierking, Corp. Cont.
Board of director: John F. Neace, Chair.
Giving statement: Giving through the Neace Lukens Charitable Foundation.

Neace Lukens Charitable Foundation
895 Central Ave., Ste. 1100
Cincinnati, OH 45202-5757

Establishment information: Established in 1999 in OH.
Donors: Neace Lukens Holding Co.; Joseph Lukens.
Financial data (yr. ended 12/31/11): Assets, $1,691,524 (M); gifts received, $1,934,652; expenditures, $386,284; qualifying distributions, $367,946; giving activities include $367,946 for 96 grants (high: $50,000; low: $100).
Purpose and activities: The foundation supports organizations involved with education, health, grief counseling, sports, children services, and religion.
Fields of interest: Elementary school/education; Secondary school/education; Education; Health care; Mental health, grief/bereavement counseling; Athletics/sports, amateur leagues; Children, services; Catholic agencies & churches; Jewish agencies & synagogues; Religion.
Type of support: General/operating support.
Geographic limitations: Giving primarily in IN, KY, and OH.
Support limitations: No grants to individuals.
Application information: Applications not accepted. Contributes only to pre-selected organizations.
Trustees: Robert Ernst; Joseph T. Lukens; John F. Neace.
EIN: 311642444

2652
Neal, Gerber & Eisenberg LLP
2 N. LaSalle St., Ste. 1700
Chicago, IL 60602-4000 (312) 269-8038

Company URL: http://www.ngelaw.com
Company type: Private company
Business activities: Operates law firm.
Business type (SIC): Legal services
Corporate officer: Jerry H. Biederman, Managing Partner
Giving statement: Giving through the Neal, Gerber & Eisenberg LLP Pro Bono Program.

Neal, Gerber & Eisenberg LLP Pro Bono Program
2 N. LaSalle St., Ste. 1700
Chicago, IL 60602-4000 (312) 269-5226
E-mail: mminor@ngelaw.com; Additional tel.: (312) 269-8000; URL: http://www.ngelaw.com/about/about.aspx?ID=5104

Contact: Maria J. Minor, Professional Devel. and Pro Bono Mgr.
Fields of interest: Legal services.
Type of support: Pro bono services - legal.
Geographic limitations: Giving primarily in areas of company operations in Chicago, IL.
Application information: A Pro Bono Committee manages the pro bono program.

2653
NEBCO, Inc.
1815 Y St.
P.O. Box 80268
Lincoln, NE 68501-1233 (402) 434-1212

Company URL: http://www.nebcoinc.com
Establishment information: Established in 1908.
Company type: Private company

Business activities: Manufactures concrete and construction materials; mines limestone and aggregates; provides general contract highway and street construction services; sells surety insurance; develops real estate; produces corn, soybeans, and alfalfa; provides railroad transportation services; operates professional baseball club; operates golf course; provides warehousing services.
Business type (SIC): Concrete, gypsum, and plaster products; farms/miscellaneous cash grain; farms, except cash grains/field crop; mining/crushed and broken stone; mining/sand and gravel; construction/highway and street (except elevated); transportation/railroad; warehousing and storage; insurance/surety; real estate subdividers and developers; commercial sports; amusement and recreation services/miscellaneous
Financial profile for 2010: Number of employees, 300
Corporate officers: James P. Abel, Chair., Pres., and C.E.O.; Shawn Paskevic, C.I.O.; Nancy Kahler, Cont.
Board of director: James P. Abel, Chair.
Subsidiary: Constructors, Inc., Lincoln, NE
Giving statement: Giving through the Abel Foundation.

Abel Foundation

1815 Y. St.
P.O. Box 80268
Lincoln, NE 68501-0268
FAX: (402) 434-1799;
E-mail: rossm@nebcoinc.com; Additional e-mail: nebcoinfo@nebconic.com; URL: http://www.abelfoundation.org/

Establishment information: Trust established in 1951.
Donors: Constructors, Inc.; NEBCO, Inc.; Alice V. Abel.
Contact: J. Ross McCown, V.P. and Secy.
Financial data (yr. ended 12/31/11): Assets, $8,108,891 (M); gifts received, $212,400; expenditures, $553,244; qualifying distributions, $547,000; giving activities include $547,000 for 64 grants (high: $225,000; low: $100).
Purpose and activities: The foundation supports organizations involved with arts and culture, education, the environment, endangered species, human services, and community development.
Fields of interest: Performing arts; Humanities; Arts; Higher education; Education; Environment, natural resources; Environment; Animals/wildlife, endangered species; YM/YWCAs & YM/YWHAs; Human services; Community/economic development; United Ways and Federated Giving Programs.
Type of support: Building/renovation; Capital campaigns; General/operating support; Program development.
Geographic limitations: Giving limited to areas of company operations in NE, with emphasis on Lincoln and Lancaster County.
Support limitations: No support for businesses, private foundations, or religious organizations. No grants to individuals, or for endowments, travel, or membership fees.
Publications: Application guidelines; Grants list.
Application information: Applications accepted. The Lincoln/Lancaster County Grantmakers Common Application Form is accepted. Application form required. Applicants should submit the following:
1) signature and title of chief executive officer
2) qualifications of key personnel
3) statement of problem project will address
4) population served
5) name, address and phone number of organization
6) copy of IRS Determination Letter
7) brief history of organization and description of its mission
8) how project's results will be evaluated or measured
9) listing of board of directors, trustees, officers and other key people and their affiliations
10) detailed description of project and amount of funding requested
11) plans for cooperation with other organizations, if any
12) contact person
13) copy of current year's organizational budget and/or project budget
14) listing of additional sources and amount of support

Initial approach: Download application form and mail to foundation
Copies of proposal: 1
Board meeting date(s): Apr., Aug., and Dec.
Deadline(s): Mar. 15, July 15, and Oct. 31
Final notification: Mid-May, mid-Sept., and mid-Jan

Officers and Directors: James P. Abel, Pres.; J. Ross McCown, V.P. and Secy.; Shannon Doering, V.P. and Treas.; Elizabeth N. Abel; John C. Abel; Mary C. Abel.
Number of staff: None.
EIN: 476041771
Selected grants: The following grants are a representative sample of this grantmaker's funding activity:
$3,000 to Cystic Fibrosis Foundation, Bethesda, MD, 2010.
$1,000 to Alzheimers Association, Chicago, IL, 2010.
$1,000 to Christian Record Services, Lincoln, NE, 2010.

2654
NEC Corporation of America

(formerly NEC USA, Inc.)
6535 N. State Hwy. 161., Ste. 150
Irving, TX 75039-2402 (214) 262-2000

Company URL: http://www.necam.com
Establishment information: Established in 1977.
Company type: Subsidiary of a foreign company
Business activities: Manufactures computers, communications equipment, and semiconductors.
Business type (SIC): Computer and office equipment; communications equipment; electronic components and accessories
Financial profile for 2010: Number of employees, 200
Corporate officers: Takayuki Okada, Pres. and C.E.O.; Hiroyuki Matsukura, Sr. V.P., C.F.O., and Treas.; Gerald Kenney, Sr. V.P., Genl. Counsel, and Secy.
Subsidiaries: HNSX Supercomputers Inc., Littleton, MA; NEC America, Inc., Melville, NY; NEC Business Communication Systems (East), Inc., Dallas, TX; NEC Electronics Inc., Santa Clara, CA; NEC Industries Inc., New York, NY; NEC Research Institute, Inc., Princeton, NJ; NEC Systems Laboratory, Inc., Princeton, NJ; NEC Technologies, Inc., Itasca, IL; NMI Corp., Dallas, TX
Plants: Roseville, San Jose, CA; Atlanta, GA; Irving, TX; Herndon, VA
Giving statement: Giving through the NEC Foundation of Americas.

NEC Foundation of Americas

6555 N. State Hwy., Ste. 161
Irving, TX 75039-2402 (212) 262-2238
E-mail: foundation@necfoundation.org; URL: http://www.necam.com/About/doc.cfm?t=NECFoundation

Establishment information: Established in 1991 in NY.
Donors: NEC Corp.; NEC USA, Inc.
Contact: Lourdes Cogswell—Wojtecki, V.P.
Financial data (yr. ended 03/31/12): Assets, $8,894,889 (M); expenditures, $123,875; qualifying distributions, $57,050; giving activities include $50,000 for 1 grant.
Purpose and activities: The foundation supports programs designed to have national reach and impact in areas of assistive technology for people with disabilities.
Fields of interest: Secondary school/education; Science, formal/general education; Engineering/technology Youth; Disabilities, people with.
Programs:

Innovation: The foundation supports nonprofit groups who lead society in accessible design. Special emphasis is directed toward programs designed to promote the exchange of information among technology developers; new application of existing technology; and programs designed to encourage social entrepreneurs by believing in their ideas and in their talent for engaging key partners from public and private sectors.

Instructional Technology: The foundation supports programs designed to promote instructional technology to improve teaching and learning. Special emphasis is directed toward initiatives designed to make use of materials that already exist and that avoid "recreating the wheel;" impart knowledge that is transferable and not dependent on a single piece of curriculum; and initiatives that include practical and focused efforts to deliver outcomes to an audience that will expand the circle of those engaged in accessible instructional technology.

Raising Awareness: The foundation supports programs designed to improve understanding of technology for people with disabilities. Special emphasis is directed toward initiatives designed to promote marketing efforts which include new 'partners' from new domains who will, in turn, carry the message to their own constituents.

Science and Technology Education: The foundation supports programs designed to address the intersection of science and technology, for people with and without disabilities, and assistive technology. Special emphasis is directed toward programs that introduce science and engineering students to the field of assistive technology, universal design, and related topics; and programs that promote science and technology education, particularly at the secondary level.

Universal Design: The foundation supports programs designed to utilize universal design, including environments, products, and information that can be used by the greatest number of people, regardless of age or physical ability, and without the need for adaptation or specialized design. Universal design applies to educational software and internet content and navigation for people with cognitive disabilities.

Type of support: Conferences/seminars; Curriculum development; General/operating support; Program development; Publication; Research; Technical assistance.
Geographic limitations: Giving primarily in Washington, DC, GA, HI, MA, MD, NC, NJ, and NY.
Support limitations: No support for individual elementary or secondary schools, school districts,

or regional consortia, local chapters of national organizations, sports teams, or organizations located outside of the U.S. No grants to individuals, or for capital campaigns or building funds, endowments, athletic competitions, fundraising events or advertising, sectarian or religious activities, or political campaigns or causes; no product donations.
Application information: Applications accepted. Application form required. Applicants should submit the following:
1) copy of most recent annual report/audited financial statement/990
2) detailed description of project and amount of funding requested

Initial approach: Proposal
Board meeting date(s): Quarterly
Deadline(s): None

Officers and Directors:* Takayuki Okada*, Pres.; Lourdes Cogswell-Wojtecki, V.P.; Deon Retemeyer, Secy.; Hiroyuki Matsukura, Treas.; Masaki Fukui.
Number of staff: 1 full-time professional; 1 full-time support.
EIN: 113059554
Selected grants: The following grants are a representative sample of this grantmaker's funding activity:
$45,000 to Straight Ahead Pictures, Conway, MA, 2009.
$42,250 to Illinois State University, Special Education Assistive Technology (seat) Center, Normal, IL, 2009.
$40,000 to American Association of People with Disabilities, Washington, DC, 2009.
$32,000 to New Jersey Institute of Technology, Rehabilitation Engineering Research Center on Technology for Children with Orthopedic Disabilities (rerc), Department of Biomedical Engineering, Newark, NJ, 2009.
$25,000 to Academy for Educational Development, Educational Equity Center at Aed, New York, NY, 2009.
$25,000 to Art Education for the Blind, New York, NY, 2009.
$10,000 to Disability Funders Network, Midlothian, VA, 2009.
$10,000 to Neighborhood Studios of Fairfield County, National Resource Center for Blind Musicians, Bridgeport, CT, 2009.

2655
Needham & Company, Inc.
445 Park Ave.
New York, NY 10022-2606 (212) 371-8300

Company URL: http://www.needhamco.com
Establishment information: Established in 1985.
Company type: Private company
Business activities: Operates investment bank; provides investment advisory services.
Business type (SIC): Brokers and dealers/security; security and commodity services
Corporate officers: George A. Needham, Co-Chair. and Co-C.E.O.; Andrew J. Malik, Co-Chair.; John J. Prior, Jr., Pres. and Co-C.E.O.
Board of directors: George A. Needham, Co-Chair.; Andrew J. Malik, Co-Chair.
Offices: Menlo Park, San Francisco, CA; Boston, MA
Giving statement: Giving through the Needham September 11th Scholarship Fund.

Needham September 11th Scholarship Fund
c/o Needham & Company, LLC
445 Park Ave.
New York, NY 10022-2606 (212) 705-0314

Establishment information: Established in 2001 in NY.
Donors: Needham & Company, LLC; John Michaelson; Warren Foss; The Strauch Family Foundation.
Contact: Joseph J. Turano, Secy.-Treas.
Financial data (yr. ended 12/31/11): Assets, $1,143,549 (M); expenditures, $70,330; qualifying distributions, $68,000; giving activities include $68,000 for grants to individuals.
Purpose and activities: The foundation awards college scholarships to the children of the victims who lost their lives in the World Trade Center and Pentagon tragedies on September 11, 2001.
Type of support: Scholarships—to individuals.
Application information: Applications accepted. Application form required. Applicants should submit the following:
1) copy of IRS Determination Letter
2) detailed description of project and amount of funding requested
3) copy of most recent annual report/audited financial statement/990

Initial approach: Proposal
Deadline(s): None

Officers and Directors:* George A. Needham*, Chair.; John J. Prior, Jr.*, Pres.; Glen W. Albanese*, V.P.; Joseph J. Turano*, Secy.-Treas.; Charles S. Strauch.
EIN: 134196881

2656
Neenah Foundry Company
2121 Brooks Ave.
Neenah, WI 54956-4756 (920) 725-7000
FAX: (920) 729-3661

Company URL: http://www.nfco.com
Establishment information: Established in 1872.
Company type: Subsidiary of a private company
Business activities: Designs, manufactures, and markets metal castings and forgings.
Business type (SIC): Iron and steel foundries; steel mill products
Corporate officers: Joseph V. Lash, Chair.; Thomas J. Riordan, Pres. and C.E.O.; Jeffrey S. Jenkins, C.F.O.; Frank C. Headington, V.P., Tech.
Board of directors: Joseph V. Lash, Chair.; Peter Alderman; Timothy J. Bernlohr; James N. Champman; John H. Forsgren; Walter A. Jones; Ted S. Lodge; Mark Richards; Thomas J. Riordan
Subsidiaries: Hartley Controls, Inc., Neenah, WI; Neenah Transport, Inc., Neenah, WI
Giving statement: Giving through the Aylward Family Foundation.
Company EIN: 391580331

Aylward Family Foundation
(formerly Neenah Foundry Foundation, Inc.)
P.O. Box 409
Neenah, WI 54957-0409

Establishment information: Incorporated in 1953 in WI.
Donor: Neenah Foundry Co.
Contact: E.W. Alyward, Pres.
Financial data (yr. ended 12/31/11): Assets, $3,791,474 (M); expenditures, $176,972; qualifying distributions, $170,662; giving activities include $166,000 for 18 grants (high: $25,000; low: $1,000).
Purpose and activities: The foundation supports organizations involved with television, secondary and higher education, substance abuse treatment, human services, and Christianity.
Fields of interest: Media, television; Secondary school/education; Higher education; Substance abuse, treatment; ALS; Youth development, business; Salvation Army; Children/youth, services; Human services; United Ways and Federated Giving Programs; Christian agencies & churches.
Type of support: Building/renovation; Endowments; General/operating support; Program development.
Geographic limitations: Giving primarily in Appleton, Menasha, Neenah, and New London, WI.
Support limitations: No grants to individuals.
Application information: Applications accepted. Application form required.

Initial approach: Letter
Board meeting date(s): May and as required
Deadline(s): Oct. 31

Officers: E.W. Aylward, Sr., Pres.; A.A. Aylward, Jr., V.P.; R.J. Aylward, Secy.-Treas.
EIN: 396042143
Selected grants: The following grants are a representative sample of this grantmaker's funding activity:
$35,000 to Saint Thomas Episcopal Church, Menasha, WI, 2010. For general program support.
$30,000 to Saint Thomas Episcopal Church, Menasha, WI, 2010. For general program support.
$15,000 to Lawrence University, Appleton, WI, 2010. For general program support.
$15,000 to Ripon College, Ripon, WI, 2010. For general program support.
$10,000 to Amyotrophic Lateral Sclerosis Association, Woodland Hills, CA, 2010. For general program support.
$10,000 to United Way Fox Cities, Menasha, WI, 2010. For general program support.
$10,000 to Wayland Academy, Beaver Dam, WI, 2010. For general program support.
$5,000 to Boys and Girls Brigade, Neenah, WI, 2010. For general program support.
$2,000 to International Crane Foundation, Baraboo, WI, 2010. For general program support.
$1,000 to EAA Aviation Foundation, Oshkosh, WI, 2010. For general program support.

2657
The Neiman Marcus Group, Inc.
(also known as Neiman Marcus, Inc.)
1618 Main St.
Dallas, TX 75201-4748 (214) 741-6911

Company URL: http://www.neimanmarcus.com
Establishment information: Established in 1908.
Company type: Subsidiary of a private company
Business activities: Operates fashion apparel and accessories stores.
Business type (SIC): Department stores
Financial profile for 2011: Number of employees, 14,400; assets, $5,532,300,000; sales volume, $3,692,800,000
Corporate officers: Karen W. Katz, Pres. and C.E.O.; James E. Skinner, Exec. V.P., C.O.O., and C.F.O.
Division: Neiman Marcus Stores Div., Dallas, TX
Giving statement: Giving through the Neiman Marcus Group, Inc. Corporate Giving Program.
Company EIN: 303509435

The Neiman Marcus Group, Inc. Corporate Giving Program

1618 Main St.
Dallas, TX 75201-4720 (214) 741-6911
URL: http://www.neimanmarcus.com/store/service/company_overview.jhtml

Purpose and activities: Neiman Marcus makes charitable contributions to nonprofit organizations on a case by case basis.

2658
Nektar Therapeutics

455 Mission Bay Blvd. S.
San Francisco, CA 94158 (415) 482-5300
FAX: (415) 339-5300

Company URL: http://www.nektar.com/
Establishment information: Established in 1990.
Company type: Public company
Company ticker symbol and exchange: NKTR/NASDAQ
Business activities: Operates clinical-stage biopharmaceutical company.
Business type (SIC): Drugs
Financial profile for 2012: Number of employees, 433; assets, $497,790,000; sales volume, $81,190,000; pre-tax net income, -$171,450,000; expenses, $222,390,000; liabilities, $450,770,000
Corporate officers: Robert B. Chess, Chair.; Howard W. Robin, Pres. and C.E.O.; John Nicholson, Sr. V.P. and C.F.O.; Gil M. Labrucherie, Sr. V.P., Genl. Counsel, and Secy.; Jillian B. Thomsen, Sr. V.P., Finance and C.A.O.; Dorian Hirth, Sr. V.P., Human Resources
Board of directors: Robert B. Chess, Chair.; R. Scott Greer; Joseph J. Krivulka; Christopher A. Kuebler; Lutz Lingnau; Howard W. Robin; Susan S. Wang; Roy A. Whitfield; Dennis Winger
Giving statement: Giving through the Nektar Employees Foundation.
Company EIN: 943134940

Nektar Employees Foundation

201 Industrial Rd.
San Carlos, CA 94070

Establishment information: Established in CA.
Financial data (yr. ended 12/31/09): Assets, $3,262 (M); gifts received, $7,388; expenditures, $62,785; qualifying distributions, $58,650; giving activities include $58,650 for 28 grants (high: $7,150; low: $50).
Purpose and activities: The foundation supports food banks and organizations involved with education, animal services, cancer, multiple sclerosis, housing development, youth development, and foster care.
Fields of interest: Education; Health care; Agriculture/food.
Type of support: Employee matching gifts; General/operating support; Program development.
Support limitations: No grants to individuals.
Application information: Applications not accepted. Contributes only to pre-selected organizations.
Officers: Mike Quattro, Pres.; Ginger Monroy, Secy.; Tracy Winton, Treas.
EIN: 912169113

2659
Nellie Mae Corporation

50 Braintree Hill Pk., Ste. 300
Braintree, MA 02184-8724 (781) 849-1325

Company URL: http://www.nelliemae.com
Establishment information: Established in 1982.
Company type: Subsidiary of a public company
Business activities: Operates student loan company.
Business type (SIC): Credit institutions/personal
Financial profile for 2010: Number of employees, 80
Corporate officers: Albert L. Lord, Vice-Chair. and C.E.O; John F. Remondi, Pres. and C.O.O; Jonathan Clark, Exec. V.P. and C.F.O.; Laurent C. Lutz, Exec. V.P., Genl. Counsel
Board of director: Albert L. Lord, Vice-Chair.
Giving statement: Giving through the Nellie Mae Education Foundation.

Nellie Mae Education Foundation

(formerly Nellie Mae Foundation, Inc.)
1250 Hancock St., Ste. 205N
Quincy, MA 02169-4331 (781) 348-4200
FAX: (781) 348-4299; E-mail: info@nmefdn.org; Toll-free tel.: (877) 635-5436; URL: http://www.nmefdn.org/

Establishment information: Established in 1999 in MA; Supporting Organization of the Nellie Mae Education Foundation.
Financial data (yr. ended 12/31/11): Revenue, $6,219,061; assets, $452,722,307 (M); gifts received, $359,575; expenditures, $21,260,618; giving activities include $14,662,357 for grants.
Purpose and activities: The foundation promotes accessibility, quality, and effectiveness of education, especially for under-served populations in New England.
Fields of interest: Adult education—literacy, basic skills & GED; Education, ESL programs; Education; Youth development, public education; Youth development, formal/general education.
Programs:
Adult Literacy Initiative: This initiative focuses on increasing the number of non-traditional, adult basic education students who transition from New England adult literacy programs into college.
College Prep Initiative: This initiative supports efforts to increase the percentage of New England's low-income, minority, and immigrant middle- and high-school students who are prepared for, enter, and succeed in college through academic enrichment and support.
District Level Systems Change Grants: The foundation believes that achieving educational system change requires a systematic approach at the district level, and that collaboration between school and community plays a critical role in this approach. This program will analyze the readiness of interested New England districts and their communities to work in collaboration using model development, policy change, and public understanding and demand to plan, implement, and support a transition to student-centered models of learning. Programs should primarily focus on students at the high-school level, especially those who are underserved. Proposals should also represent a partnership of education entities, individuals (both parents and community members), and organizations most closely connected to the public school system. Grants of up to $200,000 each will initially be awarded to up to ten applicants; following a 12- to 15-month planning period, four to eight districts will be invited to move forward, with multi-year grants ranging from $800,000 to $1,500,000.
Minority High Achievement Initiative: This initiative seeks to close the minority achievement gap by increasing the number of New England students from underrepresented minority groups who achieve the highest levels of academic achievement.
Opportunity Fund Grants: Grants will be made available to organizations that work to: build the capacity of, test, or evaluate innovative and scaleable student-centered learning approaches in such areas as model, tool, and curriculum development; focus on bold strategies to achieve systemic change by removing significant, entrenched, and persistent barriers at the policy level (sate accountability systems for district schools; Carnegie unit requirements, etc.); and/or that galvanize a wide variety of community members, including parents and students, to demand an active and authentic role in reforming education systems to meet the 21st-century needs of all youth. Eligible applicants must: have demonstrated experience working with or supporting middle and/or high school students in New England; have 501(c)(3), 509(a)(1), or 509(a)(2) status, or be part of a public entity (public school, etc.); and be education-focused, as evidenced in their articles of incorporation.
Out of School Matters: This program is designed to improve the academic preparedness and achievement of underserved middle school students in New England by expanding and strengthening out-of-school programs.
Type of support: Conferences/seminars; Continuing support; Employee matching gifts; General/operating support; Matching/challenge support; Program development; Program evaluation; Research; Seed money; Technical assistance.
Geographic limitations: Giving primarily in New England.
Support limitations: No grants to individuals, or for capital campaigns, endowments, scholarships, fellowships, debt reduction, building construction, or certain indirect costs at agencies and higher education institutions.
Publications: Application guidelines; Financial statement; Grants list; Informational brochure.
Application information: Applications accepted. Applicants should submit the following:
1) statement of problem project will address
2) additional materials/documentation
Initial approach: Proposal
Board meeting date(s): Quarterly
Deadline(s): Varies
Officers and Directors:* Dudley Williams*, Chair.; Nicholas C. Donohue*, Pres. and C.E.O.; Henry Bourgeois*, Vice-Chair.; James P. Comer; Karen Hammond; James W. MacAllen; Janet Phlegar; David S. Wolk; and 7 additional directors.
Number of staff: 20 full-time professional; 4 full-time support.
EIN: 042755323

2660
Nelnet, Inc.

(also known as National Education Loan Network)
(formerly UNIPAC Service Corporation)
121 S. 13th St., Ste. 201
Lincoln, NE 68508-1911 (402) 458-2370
FAX: (402) 458-2344

Company URL: http://www.nelnet.com/
Establishment information: Established in 1978.
Company type: Public company

Company ticker symbol and exchange: NNI/NYSE
Business activities: Provides student loan products and services.
Business type (SIC): Credit institutions/personal
Financial profile for 2012: Number of employees, 2,500; assets, $26,607,900,000; sales volume, $613,850,000; pre-tax net income, $274,500,000; expenses, $339,350,000; liabilities, $25,442,690,000
Forbes 2000 ranking: 2012—1915th in sales, 1611th in profits, and 811th in assets
Corporate officers: Michael S. Dunlap, Chair. and C.E.O.; Stephen F. Butterfield, Vice-Chair.; Jeffrey R. Noordhoek, Pres.; Terry J. Heimes, C.F.O.; William J. Munn, Genl. Counsel and Secy.
Board of directors: Michael S. Dunlap, Chair.; Stephen F. Butterfield, Vice-Chair.; James P. Abel; William R. Cintani; Kathleen A. Farrell, Ph.D.; Thomas E. Henning; Kimberly Rath; Michael D. Reardon
Giving statement: Giving through the Nelnet Foundation.
Company EIN: 840748903

Nelnet Foundation

121 S. 13th St., Ste. 201
Lincoln, NE 68508-1911
E-mail: nelnetfoundation@nelnet.net; URL: http://www.nelnet.com/overview.aspx?id=1052&path=nel.cor.nap.cm#corp

Establishment information: Established in 2005 in NE.
Donor: Nelnet, Inc.
Financial data (yr. ended 12/31/11): Assets, $4,821,085 (M); gifts received, $3,500,000; expenditures, $1,191,454; qualifying distributions, $1,181,434; giving activities include $1,181,434 for grants.
Purpose and activities: The foundation supports programs designed to expand educational possibilities for youth and adults and awards college scholarships to high school seniors.
Fields of interest: Secondary school/education; Higher education; Scholarships/financial aid; Education; Youth development, business; American Red Cross; United Ways and Federated Giving Programs Youth.
Programs:
Big Mama Nelnet Scholarship Fund: The foundation provides scholarship funds to "kids" raised by "Big Mama" Essie Reed of Fort Lauderdale, Florida who helps raise less fortunate children through meals, housing, and counseling. ABC's Extreme Makeover selected Big Mama's house for a makeover after Hurricane Katrina, and the foundation created the fund to provide higher education opportunities for Big Mama's children.
Matching Gifts: The foundation matches contributions made by employees of Nelnet to civic organizations on a one-for-one basis and to secondary and higher education institutions on a three-for-one basis.
Nelnet Scholars: The foundation awards two $5,000 and ten $1,000 college scholarships to children of employees of Nelnet. The program is administered by Scholarship America.
Seed Scholarships: The foundation awards seed scholarships based on need and merit to high school seniors and to individuals who have passed the GED within the last 6 months.
Type of support: Annual campaigns; Employee matching gifts; Employee-related scholarships; General/operating support; Scholarship funds; Scholarships—to individuals.
Geographic limitations: Giving on a national basis in areas of company operations, with emphasis on NE.
Publications: Application guidelines.
Application information: Applications accepted. Application form required. Applicants should submit the following:
1) timetable for implementation and evaluation of project
2) signature and title of chief executive officer
3) population served
4) copy of IRS Determination Letter
5) brief history of organization and description of its mission
6) geographic area to be served
7) copy of most recent annual report/audited financial statement/990
8) listing of board of directors, trustees, officers and other key people and their affiliations
9) detailed description of project and amount of funding requested
10) copy of current year's organizational budget and/or project budget

Requests for seed scholarships should include transcripts, letter of acceptance to an educational institution, and a copy of ACT/SAT scores.
Initial approach: Contact foundation for application form
Copies of proposal: 2
Deadline(s): None; Mar. 31 for Seed Scholarships
Officers and Directors: Richard Pierce, Pres.; Ben Kiser, V.P.; Edward P. Martinez, Secy.; Jeff Noordhoek, Treas.; James P. Abel; Steve Butterfield; Michael S. Dunlap; Kathy Farrell; Terry J. Heimes; Thomas E. Henning; Brian J. O'Connor; Kimberly Rath; Michael D. Reardon.
EIN: 202202134
Selected grants: The following grants are a representative sample of this grantmaker's funding activity:
$79,000 to Scholarship America, Saint Peter, MN, 2010.
$50,000 to Lincoln Childrens Museum, Lincoln, NE, 2010.
$25,000 to Imagine America Foundation, Washington, DC, 2010.
$21,600 to Pius X High School, Lincoln, NE, 2010.
$11,200 to Pius X High School, Lincoln, NE, 2010.
$10,000 to ThanksUSA, McLean, VA, 2010.
$3,900 to Randolph College, Lynchburg, VA, 2010.
$3,750 to University School of Nashville, Nashville, TN, 2010.
$3,000 to Creighton University, Omaha, NE, 2010.
$1,000 to Lincoln Childrens Museum, Lincoln, NE, 2010.

2661
Nelson Mullins Riley & Scarborough LLP

Glenlake 1, Ste. 200
4140 Parklake Ave.
Raleigh, NC 27612-3731 (803) 255-9546

Company URL: http://www.nelsonmullins.com
Company type: Private company
Business activities: Operates law firm.
Business type (SIC): Legal services
Corporate officers: Douglas M. Webb, C.F.O.; David N. Worth, C.I.O.
Offices: Washington, DC; Tallahassee, FL; Atlanta, GA; Boston, MA; Raleigh, Winston-Salem, NC; Charleston, Columbia, Greenville, Myrtle Beach, SC; Huntington, WV
Giving statement: Giving through the Nelson Mullins Riley & Scarborough LLP Pro Bono Program.

Nelson Mullins Riley & Scarborough LLP Pro Bono Program

Glenlake 1, Ste. 200
4140 Parklake Ave.
Raleigh, NC 27612-3731 (803) 255-9546
E-mail: norah.rogers@nelsonmullins.com; Additional tel.: (919) 329-3857; URL: http://www.nelsonmullins.com/overview/pro-bono

Contact: Norah Rogers, Pro Bono Coord.
Fields of interest: Legal services.
Type of support: Pro bono services - legal.
Geographic limitations: Giving primarily in areas of company operations in Washington, DC, Tallahassee, FL, Atlanta, GA, Boston, MA, Charlotte, Raleigh, and Winston-Salem, NC, Charleston, Columbia, Greenville, and Myrtle Beach, SC, and Huntington, WV.
Application information: A Pro Bono Committee manages the pro bono program.

2662
Nestle Purina PetCare Company

(formerly Ralston Purina Company)
Checkerboard Sq.
St. Louis, MO 63164-0001 (314) 982-1000

Company URL: http://www.purina.com
Establishment information: Established in 1894.
Company type: Subsidiary of a foreign company
Business activities: Produces dog and cat foods, cereals, and bakery products; operates ski resort; manufactures batteries and lighting products.
Business type (SIC): Grain mill products, including pet food; miscellaneous prepared foods; electrical equipment and supplies; hotels and motels
Corporate officers: W. Patrick McGinnis, Pres. and C.E.O.; Rock Foster, C.F.O.; Steve Crimmins, V.P., Mktg.
Subsidiaries: Benco Pet Foods, Inc., Zanesville, OH; Eveready Battery Co., Inc., St. Louis, MO; Protein Technologies International, St. Louis, MO; Purina Grocery Products Group, St. Louis, MO
Plants: Sparks, NV; Urbana, Westlake, OH
Giving statement: Giving through the Nestle Purina PetCare Company Contributions Program and the Nestle Purina PetCare Trust Fund.

Nestle Purina PetCare Company Contributions Program

(formerly Ralston Purina Company Contributions Program)
c/o Community Affairs
Checkerboard Sq., 1C
St. Louis, MO 63164-0001 (314) 982-1607
URL: http://www.purina.com/animal-welfare/animalwelfare.aspx

Purpose and activities: As a complement to its foundation, Nestle Purina PetCare also makes charitable contributions to nonprofit organizations directly. Special emphasis is directed toward organizations involved with animal welfare. Support is given primarily in areas of company operations.
Fields of interest: Animal welfare Economically disadvantaged.
Type of support: Donated products; General/operating support; In-kind gifts; Sponsorships.
Geographic limitations: Giving in areas of company operations in Flagstaff, AZ, Maricopa, CA, Denver, CO, Atlanta, GA, Davenport and Fort Dodge, IA, Bloomfield, Cape Girardeau, St. Joseph, St. Louis, and Springfield, MO, Clinton, NE, Dunkirk, NY,

Zanesville, OH, Oklahoma City, OK, Allentown and Mechanicsburg, PA, Hager City and Jefferson, WI, Weirton, WV, and King William, VA; giving also to national organizations.
Support limitations: No support for sports teams, churches, or veterans' or fraternal organizations not of direct benefit to the entire community. No grants to individuals, or for religious or politically partisan purposes or investment funds; no loans; no funding directed to an entity located outside the U.S. or its possessions.
Publications: Application guidelines.
Application information: Applications accepted. Application form not required. Applicants should submit the following:
1) brief history of organization and description of its mission
2) explanation of why grantmaker is considered an appropriate donor for project
3) detailed description of project and amount of funding requested

Proposals should specifically note the nature of the request being made. Requests for sponsorships should indicate the expected attendance and date of the event, if applicable.
Initial approach: Proposal to headquarters for organizations located in the greater St. Louis, MO, area; proposal to nearest company facility for organizations located outside the greater St. Louis, MO, area
Copies of proposal: 1
Deadline(s): None
Final notification: Up to 2 to 3 months

Nestle Purina PetCare Trust Fund

(formerly Ralston Purina Trust Fund)
c/o Nestle Purina PetCare Community Affairs
Checkerboard Sq., 1C
St. Louis, MO 63164-0001
E-mail: CommunityAffairs@purina.nestle.com;
URL: http://www.nestlepurina.com/CommunityInv_Index.aspx

Establishment information: Trust established in 1951 in MO.
Donors: Ralston Purina Co.; Nestle Purina PetCare Co.
Contact: Kasey Bergh, Mgr., Community Affairs
Financial data (yr. ended 12/31/11): Assets, $15,246,168 (M); expenditures, $826,970; qualifying distributions, $729,245; giving activities include $729,245 for 11 grants (high: $560,000; low: $2,500).
Purpose and activities: The foundation supports organizations involved with animal welfare and the education and wellbeing of disadvantaged youth.
Fields of interest: Education, services; Education; Animal welfare; Animals/wildlife, preservation/protection; Animals/wildlife, special services; Animals/wildlife, training; Disasters, preparedness/services; Boys & girls clubs; Youth development; United Ways and Federated Giving Programs Youth; Economically disadvantaged.
Type of support: Annual campaigns; Building/renovation; Capital campaigns; Continuing support; Equipment; General/operating support; Program development; Sponsorships.
Geographic limitations: Giving primarily in manufacturing operations in Flagstaff, AZ, Maricopa, CA, Denver, CO, Atlanta, GA, Clinton, Davenport, and Fort Dodge, IA, Bloomfield, Cape Girardeau, Springfield, and St. Joseph, MO, Crete, NE, Dunkirk, NY, Zanesville, OH, Oklahoma City, OK, Allentown and Mechanicsburg, PA, King William, VA, Hager City and Jefferson, WI, and Weirton, WV, with emphasis on the greater St. Louis area.
Support limitations: No support for veterans' or fraternal organizations not of direct benefit to the entire community. No grants to individuals, or for religious or politically partisan purposes, investment funds, tickets for dinners, benefits, exhibits, conferences, sports events, or other short-term activities, advertisements, debt reduction, or post-event support; no loans.
Publications: Application guidelines.
Application information: Applications accepted. Application form required. Applicants should submit the following:
1) copy of IRS Determination Letter
2) explanation of why grantmaker is considered an appropriate donor for project
3) detailed description of project and amount of funding requested
4) copy of current year's organizational budget and/or project budget
5) contact person

Initial approach: Complete online application
Board meeting date(s): Quarterly
Deadline(s): None
Final notification: 60 to 90 days
Trustees: Stephen Degnan; Susan Denigan; Rock A. Foster.
Number of staff: 1 part-time professional; 1 part-time support.
EIN: 431209652
Selected grants: The following grants are a representative sample of this grantmaker's funding activity:
$25,000 to American Red Cross, Saint Louis, MO, 2010. For general support.
$15,000 to Kingdom House, Saint Louis, MO, 2010. For general support.
$10,000 to Coconino Humane Association, Flagstaff, AZ, 2010. For general support.

2663
Nestle USA, Inc.

800 N. Brand Blvd., Fl. 5
Glendale, CA 91203-4281 (818) 549-6000

Company URL: http://www.nestleusa.com
Establishment information: Established in 1899.
Company type: Subsidiary of a foreign company
Business activities: Produces foods and beverages.
Business type (SIC): Food and kindred products; beverages
Corporate officers: Paul Grimwood, Chair. and C.E.O.; Dan Stroud, C.F.O.
Board of director: Paul Grimwood, Chair.
Subsidiaries: Nestle Beverage Co., San Francisco, CA; Nestle Brand Food Service Co., Glendale, CA; Nestle Enterprises, Solon, OH; Nestle Ice Cream Co., Solon, OH; Nestle Puerto Rico, Inc., San Juan, PR; Nestle Purina PetCare Company, St. Louis, MO; Nestle Refrigerated Food Co., Glendale, CA; PowerBar Inc., Glendale, CA; The Stouffer Corporation, Solon, OH; Sunmark Inc., St. Louis, MO; Wine World Estates, St. Helena, CA
Giving statement: Giving through the Nestle USA, Inc. Corporate Giving Program, the Nestle Scholarship Foundation, and the Nestle USA Foundation.

Nestle USA, Inc. Corporate Giving Program

800 N. Brand Ave.
Glendale, CA 91203-1245 (818) 549-6000
URL: http://www.nestleusa.com/creating-shared-value/community
Contact for Nestle Very Best In Youth: Cristina Bastida, Exec. Dir., tel.: (818) 549-6677, e-mail: NestleVeryBestInYouth@us.nestle.com
Contact: Kenneth Bentley, V.P., Community Affairs
Purpose and activities: As a complement to its foundation, Nestle USA also makes charitable contributions to nonprofit organizations directly. Support is given primarily in areas of company operations.
Fields of interest: Elementary school/education; Education, reading; Education; Public health, obesity; Health care; Food services; Food banks; Nutrition; Disasters, preparedness/services; Youth development; American Red Cross; Children, services; Human services; Community development, neighborhood development Children/youth.

Programs:

Nestle's Adopt-A-School Program: Through Adopt-A-School Program, Nestle employees volunteer at local elementary schools. The program includes tutoring, where volunteers help children in English, math, science, and computers; pen friends, where volunteers and students exchange hand-written letters to help students excel in composition, grammar, and penmanship; speakers and readers bureau, where volunteers visit classrooms to share their knowledge of a subject; and mentoring, where volunteers become role models through tutoring and self-esteem building exercises.

Nestle's Share the Joy of Reading Program: Through the Share the Joy of Reading Program, a child receives a new book when customers buy select Nestle's candy. Nestle donates $0.10 to Reading Is Fundamental when customers enter promotion codes on the program website. Nestle donates a book in the form of $2 if a customer is an instant winner. Customers are also able to win prizes in the form of a $10 book certificate and are entered in a monthly drawing for $5,000.

Nestle's Very Best In Youth Program: Nestle USA annually honors young people ages 13 to 18 who have excelled in youth leadership and have contributed to their community. Applicants are selected based on academic records, special contributions to their school, church, or community, good citizenship, and personal obstacles the youth has overcome. Honorees have their story published in the Nestle Very Best in Youth publication and is awarded a trip with his/her parent or legal guardian to Los Angeles for the Nestle Very Best In Youth awards ceremony. The trip includes round-trip air travel, hotel accommodations for three nights, and $500 spending money. Nestle USA also donates $1,000 in the name of each winner to the charity of his or her choice.

Type of support: Donated products; Employee volunteer services; General/operating support; In-kind gifts; Sponsorships.
Geographic limitations: Giving on a national basis in areas of company operations.
Publications: Application guidelines.
Application information: Applications accepted. The Community Affairs Department handles giving. Applications for Nestle's Very Best In Youth Program should include an essay, transcripts, letters of reference, and a signed consent form from a parent or legal guardian.
Initial approach: Complete online application for Nestle's Very Best In Youth Program
Deadline(s): Varies for Nestle's Very Best In Youth Program

Nestle Scholarship Foundation

(formerly Carnation Company Scholarship Foundation)
c/o Bank of America, N.A.
P.O. Box 831041
Dallas, TX 75283-1041

Establishment information: Established in 1952 in CA.
Donors: Carnation Co.; Nestle USA, Inc.
Financial data (yr. ended 12/31/11): Assets, $10,337,232 (M); expenditures, $656,073; qualifying distributions, $558,300; giving activities include $558,300 for grants.
Purpose and activities: The foundation awards college scholarships to children of employees of Nestle USA. The program is administered by Scholarship America, Inc.
Fields of interest: Higher education.
Type of support: Employee-related scholarships.
Geographic limitations: Giving primarily in areas of company operations.
Application information: Applications not accepted. Contributes only through employee-related scholarships.
Trustee Bank: Bank of America, N.A.
Advisory Committee: Bradley A. Alford; Judy Cascepara; Don Stroud.
EIN: 956118622

Nestle USA Foundation

(formerly Carnation Company Foundation)
800 N. Brand Blvd.
Glendale, CA 91203-1289 (818) 549-6000

Establishment information: Incorporated in 1952 in CA.
Donor: Nestle USA, Inc.
Financial data (yr. ended 12/31/11): Assets, $21,906,544 (M); expenditures, $1,498,925; qualifying distributions, $1,369,922; giving activities include $1,369,922 for grants.
Purpose and activities: The foundation supports programs designed to address the health and wellness of children and youth; and promote education and literacy.
Fields of interest: Museums; Elementary/secondary education; Higher education; Libraries (public); Education, reading; Education; Hospitals (general); Health care, patient services; Health care; Food services; Boys & girls clubs; American Red Cross; Human services; United Ways and Federated Giving Programs Children; Youth.
Type of support: General/operating support; Program development.
Geographic limitations: Giving primarily in CA, Washington, DC, FL, and OH.
Support limitations: No grants to individuals.
Application information: Applications accepted. Application form not required. Applicants should submit the following:
1) copy of IRS Determination Letter
2) copy of most recent annual report/audited financial statement/990

Initial approach: Proposal
Deadline(s): None

Officers: Bradley A. Alford, Pres.; Dan Stroud, V.P. and C.F.O.; Judy Cascepara, V.P.; Jonathan Jackman, Secy.; Don W. Gosline, Treas.
EIN: 956027479

2664
Network Management Group, Inc.

901 Corporate Center Dr., Ste. 524
Monterey Park, CA 91754-7630
(323) 263-2632

Company URL: http://www.networkm.com
Establishment information: Established in 1996.
Company type: Private company
Business activities: Provides management and management consulting services.
Business type (SIC): Management and public relations services
Corporate officers: John Park, Pres. and C.E.O.; Tom Chan, Cont.
Giving statement: Giving through the Pacific Scholarship Foundation.

Pacific Scholarship Foundation

1100 South Flower St., Suite 3100
Los Angeles, CA 90015-2127 (323) 263-2632
E-mail: rshindle@fortiss.net; Additional tel.: (323) 263-2632
Application address: Pacific Scholarship Foundation, 901 Corporate Center Dr., Ste. 524, Monterey Park, CA 91754

Establishment information: Established in 2006 in CA and NV.
Donor: Network Management Group, Inc.
Financial data (yr. ended 12/31/10): Assets, $49 (M); gifts received, $24,000; expenditures, $28,101; qualifying distributions, $28,101; giving activities include $22,500 for 2 grants to individuals (high: $17,500; low: $5,000).
Purpose and activities: The foundation awards scholarships to graduating seniors from a private or public high school located in California and Nevada and to foreign students with (F1) VISA's to pursue higher education.
Fields of interest: Education.
Type of support: Scholarships—to individuals.
Geographic limitations: Giving primarily in CA and NV.
Application information: Applications not accepted. Unsolicted requests for funds not accepted.
Officers and Director: John Park, Pres.; Roy Choi, Secy.-Treas.; Jeffrey Hiebert.
EIN: 204727428

2665
Neurology Clinic of South Arkansas

(doing business as Neurol)
425 Thompson Ave.
El Dorado, AR 71730-4553 (870) 863-4186

Company type: Private company
Business activities: Operates neurology clinic.
Business type (SIC): Offices and clinics/doctors'
Corporate officer: Ghulam Khaleel, Pres.
Giving statement: Giving through the G. M. Khaleel Charitable and Educational Foundation.

G. M. Khaleel Charitable and Educational Foundation

137 Grizzly Bear Dr.
White Hall, AR 71602-4782

Establishment information: Established in 2006 in IL.
Donors: Neurology Clinic of South Arkansas; Ghulam Khaleel.
Financial data (yr. ended 12/31/11): Assets, $135 (M); gifts received, $40,200; expenditures, $40,235; qualifying distributions, $40,235; giving activities include $31,123 for 1 grant and $900 for 3 grants to individuals (high: $600; low: $100).
Purpose and activities: The foundation supports the Dr. G. M. Khaleel Educational and Charitable Trust in India.
Fields of interest: Education.
Type of support: General/operating support.
Geographic limitations: Giving primarily in India.
Application information: Applications accepted. Application form not required.

Initial approach: Proposal
Deadline(s): None

Officers: Ghulam Khaleel, Pres. and Secy.; Mohammed Khaleel, Treas.
Directors: Adeeb Khaleel; Maria C. Morales; Mir Abul Qasim; Amanda Reynolds.
EIN: 204982776

2666
Neuwirth Motors, Inc.

219 S. College Rd.
P.O. Box 4107//28406
Wilmington, NC 28403-1609
(910) 799-1815
FAX: (910) 791-6475

Company URL: http://www.neuwirthmotors.com
Establishment information: Established in 1958.
Company type: Private company
Business activities: Operates car dealership.
Business type (SIC): Motor vehicles—retail
Corporate officer: John Gillian, Pres.
Giving statement: Giving through the Way Foundation.

The Way Foundation

P.O. Box 4107
Wilmington, NC 28406-1107 (910) 799-1815

Establishment information: Established in 2007 in NC.
Donor: Neuwirth Motors, Inc.
Contact: John S. Gillilan, Jr., Chair.
Financial data (yr. ended 12/31/11): Assets, $22,454 (M); gifts received, $157,854; expenditures, $179,347; qualifying distributions, $179,272; giving activities include $179,272 for grants.
Fields of interest: Human services; Religion.
Geographic limitations: Giving primarily in NC and TN.
Support limitations: No grants to individuals.
Application information: Applications accepted. Application form required.

Initial approach: Proposal
Deadline(s): None

Officers: John S. Gillilan, Jr., Chair.; John C. Martin, Jr., Vice-Chair.; Armied A. Godwin III, Pres.; Jackie Martin, Secy.; Cindy P. Godwin, Treas.
EIN: 450572015

2667
Neville Chemical Company

2800 Neville Rd.
Pittsburgh, PA 15225-1496 (412) 331-4200
FAX: (412) 771-0226

Company URL: http://www.nevchem.com
Establishment information: Established in 1925.
Company type: Private company
Business activities: Manufactures synthetic hydrocarbon resins and coumarone-indene resins.
Business type (SIC): Plastics and synthetics
Financial profile for 2010: Number of employees, 240
Corporate officers: L. Van V. Dauler, Jr., Chair.; Thomas F. McKnight, Pres., Treas. and C.E.O.;

Denise J. Butler, C.F.O.; William J. Pesce, Genl. Counsel and Secy.
Board of director: L. Van V. Dauler, Jr., Chair.
Plant: Anaheim, CA
Giving statement: Giving through the Neville Chemical Company Contributions Program.

Neville Chemical Company Contributions Program

2800 Neville Rd.
Pittsburgh, PA 15225-1496 (412) 331-4200
URL: http://www.nevchem.com/index.asp?pid=01_05

Purpose and activities: Neville makes charitable contributions to nonprofit organizations on a case by case basis. Support is given primarily in Pittsburgh, Pennsylvania.
Fields of interest: Environment, water pollution; Health care, blood supply; Food services; Human services, gift distribution; United Ways and Federated Giving Programs.
Type of support: Annual campaigns; Employee volunteer services; General/operating support; Sponsorships.
Geographic limitations: Giving primarily in Pittsburgh, PA.

2668
New Balance Athletic Shoe, Inc.

Brighton Landing
20 Guest St.
Boston, MA 02135-2088 (617) 783-4000
FAX: (617) 787-9355

Company URL: http://www.newbalance.com
Establishment information: Established in 1906.
Company type: Private company
Business activities: Manufactures athletics shoes and sportswear.
Business type (SIC): Leather footwear; apparel—men's and boys' outerwear
Corporate officers: James S. Davis, Chair.; Anne M. Davis, Vice-Chair., Exec. V.P., and Admin.; Robert DeMartini, Pres. and C.E.O.; Dennis Langlais, C.O.O.; Elaine Ritchie, C.I.O.; John Withee, Exec. V.P. and C.F.O.; Alan Rosen, V.P. and Treas.; Bill Hayden, V.P., Finance; Courtney English, V.P., Admin.; Georianna Wright, V.P., Sales; Carol O'Donnell, V.P., Corp. Human Resources
Board of directors: James S. Davis, Chair.; Anne Davis, Vice-Chair.
Plants: Norridgewock, Skowhegan, ME; Lawrence, Norway, MA
International operations: Canada
Giving statement: Giving through the New Balance Athletic Shoe, Inc. Corporate Giving Program and the New Balance Foundation.

New Balance Athletic Shoe, Inc. Corporate Giving Program

c/o Corp. Comms.
20 Guest St.
Brighton, MA 02135-2088
FAX: (617) 787-9355; URL: http://www.newbalance.com/Responsible-Leadership/about_responsible_leadership,default,pg.html

Purpose and activities: As a complement to its foundation, New Balance also makes charitable contributions to nonprofit organizations directly. Support is given primarily in areas of company operations in Norridgewock, Norway, and Skowhegan, Maine, and Boston and Lawrence, Massachusetts, and in Canada and England; giving also to national organizations.
Fields of interest: Humanities; Arts; Education; Public health, physical fitness; Health care; Recreation, community; Athletics/sports, school programs; Athletics/sports, amateur leagues; Youth development; Homeless, human services; Science.
Type of support: Cause-related marketing; Donated products; Employee matching gifts; Employee volunteer services; In-kind gifts; Sponsorships.
Geographic limitations: Giving primarily in areas of company operations, with emphasis on Boston and Lawrence, MA, and Norridgewock, Norway, and Skowhegan, ME, and in Canada and England; giving also to national organizations.
Support limitations: No support for political or discriminatory organizations. No grants to individuals. Gift certificates are limited to raffles, door prizes, awards, and auctions.
Publications: Application guidelines.
Application information: Applications accepted. Application form not required.
Initial approach: Mail, fax, or e-mail proposal to headquarters for product donations
Copies of proposal: 1
Administrators: Megan L. Davidson, Prog. Mgr., Charitable Giving; Molly Santry, Prog. Mgr., Charitable Giving; Andrea Henry, Community Outreach Assoc.
Number of staff: 3 full-time professional.

New Balance Foundation

20 Guest St.
Boston, MA 02135-2040 (617) 783-4000
E-mail: newbalancefoundation@newbalance.com; URL: http://www.newbalancefoundation.org/

Establishment information: Established in 1981 in MA.
Donor: New Balance Athletic Shoe, Inc.
Contact: Anne M. Davis, Managing Tr.
Financial data (yr. ended 11/30/12): Assets, $115,984,852 (M); expenditures, $6,400,000; qualifying distributions, $6,281,911; giving activities include $6,281,411 for 106 grants (high: $900,000; low: $100).
Purpose and activities: The foundation supports organizations involved with education, the environment, health, nutrition, disaster relief, school athletics, and human services. Special emphasis is directed toward programs designed to promote healthy lifestyles and prevent childhood obesity.
Fields of interest: Education; Environment; Hospitals (general); Public health, obesity; Public health, physical fitness; Health care; Nutrition; Disasters, preparedness/services; Athletics/sports, academies; Family services; Human services; United Ways and Federated Giving Programs Children; Economically disadvantaged.
Programs:
Arts & Culture: The foundation supports cultural programs designed to reach out to underserved communities and blend fun with related educational programming.
Childhood Obesity: The foundation supports programs designed to prevent childhood obesity. Special emphasis is directed toward programs designed to address childhood obesity through a holistic approach that engages children and those whose impact their lives, including caregivers, educators, medical professionals, after-school providers, and the community; and through nutrition, fitness, and educational perspective.
Education & Athletics: The foundation supports academic and fitness programs designed to encourage learning, integrate curricula, and promote fitness as a fundamental link in a balanced, healthy lifestyle. Special emphasis is directed toward programs designed to provide opportunities to children who most need it.
Environment: The foundation supports programs designed to improve overall quality of life; and provide innovative and sustainable solutions to key community issues involving the environment.
Health & Human Services: The foundation supports organizations involved with health and human services; and programs designed to assist individuals and families who would otherwise be unable to afford care.
Type of support: Continuing support; General/operating support; Matching/challenge support; Research; Scholarship funds.
Geographic limitations: Giving primarily in Boston and Lawrence, MA and Norridgewock, Norway, and Skowhegan, ME.
Support limitations: No support for political parities or discriminatory organizations. No grants to individuals, or for capital campaigns, fundraising dinners or galas, team sponsorships, sporting events, or film or television underwriting.
Publications: Application guidelines; Financial statement; Grants list; Program policy statement.
Application information: Applications accepted. Concept papers should be no longer than 1 page. Proposals should be no longer than 3 pages. Support is limited to 1 contribution per organization during any given year. Organizations receiving support are asked to submit interim reports and a final report. Application form not required.
Applicants should submit the following:
1) how project will be sustained once grantmaker support is completed
2) statement of problem project will address
3) population served
4) name, address and phone number of organization
5) copy of IRS Determination Letter
6) brief history of organization and description of its mission
7) geographic area to be served
8) how project's results will be evaluated or measured
9) explanation of why grantmaker is considered an appropriate donor for project
10) listing of board of directors, trustees, officers and other key people and their affiliations
11) detailed description of project and amount of funding requested
12) contact person
13) copy of current year's organizational budget and/or project budget
14) listing of additional sources and amount of support
Initial approach: Concept paper for new grant seekers; proposal for existing grant partners
Copies of proposal: 1
Deadline(s): Mar. 1 for new grant seekers; Feb. 1 for existing grant partners
Final notification: Apr. 1 for new grant seekers
Trustees: Anne M. Davis; James S. Davis; Paul R. Gauron.
EIN: 046470644
Selected grants: The following grants are a representative sample of this grantmaker's funding activity:
$1,500,000 to Childrens Hospital Corporation, Boston, MA, 2010. For general support.
$500,000 to Tufts University, Freidman School of Nutrition Science and Policy, Medford, MA, 2010. For general support.
$250,000 to MetroLacrosse, Boston, MA, 2010. For general support.
$150,000 to Boys and Girls Club of Lawrence, Lawrence, MA, 2010. For general support.

$125,000 to Two Ten Footwear Foundation, Waltham, MA, 2010. For general support.
$100,000 to Partners in Health, Boston, MA, 2010. For general support.
$100,000 to Tenacity, Boston, MA, 2010. For general support.
$50,000 to Camp Sunshine, 2010. For general support.
$25,000 to CLASS, Lawrence, MA, 2010. For general support.
$25,000 to North Elementary School, North, SC, 2010. For general support.

2669
New Champions Golf & Country Club Inc.

(doing business as Pinnacle Country Club)
3 Clubhouse Dr.
Rogers, AR 72758-9563 (479) 273-0500

Company URL: http://www.pinnaclecc.com
Establishment information: Established in 1988.
Company type: Private company
Business activities: Operates country club.
Business type (SIC): Amusement and recreation services/miscellaneous
Financial profile for 2012: Sales volume, $236,355; expenses, $133,100
Corporate officers: Michael Hudson, Pres.; Kelly Sudduth, Cont.
Giving statement: Giving through the Pinnacle Scholarship Foundation.

Pinnacle Scholarship Foundation

3 Clubhouse Dr.
Rogers, AR 72758 (479) 273-0500

Establishment information: Established in 2002 in AR.
Donor: Pinnacle Country Club.
Contact: Michael T. Hudson, Dir.
Financial data (yr. ended 12/31/11): Assets, $39,593 (M); gifts received, $5,400; expenditures, $10,047; qualifying distributions, $7,762; giving activities include $7,762 for 5 grants (high: $2,000; low: $662).
Purpose and activities: The foundation awards college scholarships to employees of Pinnacle Country Club.
Type of support: Employee-related scholarships.
Geographic limitations: Giving limited to AR.
Application information: Applications accepted. Application form required.
Application should be submitted with a photograph.
Initial approach: Proposal
Deadline(s): End of Aug.
Directors: Michael T. Hudson; Charles Jurgensmeyer.
EIN: 010648135

2670
New England Biolabs, Inc.

(also known as NEB)
240 County Rd.
Ipswich, MA 01938-2723 (978) 927-5054

Company URL: http://www.neb.com
Establishment information: Established in 1970.
Company type: Private company
Business activities: Produces life science reagent products.
Business type (SIC): Drugs
Corporate officer: James V. Ellard, C.E.O.
Giving statement: Giving through the NEB Corporate Giving Program and the New England Biolabs Foundation.

NEB Corporate Giving Program

240 County Rd.
Ipswich, MA 01938-2723 (978) 927-5054
URL: https://www.neb.com/about-neb/environmental-commitment

Purpose and activities: As a complement to its foundation, NEB also makes charitable contributions to nonprofit organizations directly. Support is given primarily in areas of company operations.
Fields of interest: General charitable giving.
Geographic limitations: Giving primarily in areas of company operations.
Application information: A contributions committee reviews all requests.

New England Biolabs Foundation

240 County Rd.
Ipswich, MA 01938-2723 (978) 998-7990
FAX: (978) 356-3250; E-mail: fosters@nebf.org; URL: http://www.nebf.org

Establishment information: Established in 1982 in MA.
Donors: New England Biolabs, Inc.; Donald G. Combs; Martine Kellett.
Contact: Jessica Brown, Exec. Dir.; Susan Foster, Asst. Dir.
Financial data (yr. ended 12/31/11): Assets, $6,813,572 (M); gifts received, $195,531; expenditures, $562,899; qualifying distributions, $330,704; giving activities include $330,704 for grants.
Purpose and activities: The foundation supports programs designed to promote conservation of biological diversity including terrestrial and marine; sustain cultural diversity including linguistic diversity and traditional knowledge systems and practices; maintain ecosystem services with emphasis on water, soil, and carbon sequestration; promote food security and economic vitality of local communities; and sustain healthy reefs and fisheries. The foundation also awards limited grants to individuals for small environmental research projects.
Fields of interest: Arts; Elementary school/education; Environment, research; Environment, water resources; Environmental education; Animals/wildlife, preservation/protection; Animals/wildlife, fisheries; Agriculture, sustainable programs; Food services; Economic development; Biology/life sciences.
International interests: Belize; Bolivia; Cameroon; Central America; Developing countries; Ecuador; El Salvador; Ghana; Guatemala; Honduras; Madagascar; Nicaragua; Papua New Guinea; Peru; South America; Tanzania, Zanzibar and Pemba.
Type of support: Curriculum development; Grants to individuals; Matching/challenge support; Program development; Research; Seed money.
Geographic limitations: Giving primarily in New England, with emphasis on the Boston, MA, area, particularly the North Shore region; giving also in Belize, Bolivia, Cameroon, Central America, Ecuador, El Salvador, Ghana, Guatemala, Honduras, Madagascar, Nicaragua, Papua New Guinea, Peru, South America, and Tanzania.
Support limitations: No support for organizations located in Argentina, Belize, Brazil, Chile, Columbia, Costa Rica, French Guiana, Mexico, Panama, the Philippines, Suriname, Uruguay, Venezuela, or Vietnam or private schools. No grants to individuals (except for environmental research), or for non-marine issues in the Caribbean or Madagascar, non-environmental education projects in Guatemala, non-environmental projects in Ghana, educational or community projects of U.S. organizations not located in the Boston, MA, area, art projects located outside the immediate community, capital campaigns, renovations or building funds, conferences, workshops, or travel, production of videos, movies, or books, religious activities, general operating support, scholarships, fellowships, or internships, scientific research eligible for funding by major agencies, services for senior citizens, economically disadvantaged people, or disabled people, or species-specific projects.
Publications: Application guidelines; Grants list; Informational brochure (including application guidelines).
Application information: Applications accepted. Letters of inquiry should be no longer than 1 page. A full proposal may be requested at a later date. Grants generally do not exceed $8,000. Priority is given to organizations that have received prior funding. Organizations receiving support are asked to provide a final report. Application form not required. Applicants should submit the following:
1) detailed description of project and amount of funding requested
Initial approach: E-mail or mail letter of inquiry to foundation
Copies of proposal: 1
Board meeting date(s): May and Dec.
Deadline(s): None for letter of inquiry; Mar. 1 and Aug. 29 for proposal
Final notification: 2 months following board meetings
Officer: Jessica Brown, Exec. Dir.
Trustees: David Comb; Heidi Ellard; Henry P. Paulus, Ph.D.
Number of staff: 2 part-time professional.
EIN: 042776213

2671
New England Federal Credit Union

P.O. Box 527
Williston, VT 05495 (802) 879-8790

Company URL: https://www.nefcu.com
Establishment information: Established in 1968.
Company type: Federal credit union
Business activities: Operates federal credit union.
Business type (SIC): Credit unions
Financial profile for 2011: Assets, $858,755,782; liabilities, $757,579,771
Corporate officers: Charles T. DesLauriers, Chair.; William F. Meyer, 1st Vice-Chair.; Frank G. Harris III, 2nd Vice-Chair.; John J. Dwyer, Jr., Pres. and C.E.O.; Susan E. Leonard, Sr. V.P. and C.F.O.; Grace T. Gilbert-Davis, Secy.; Ronald D. Mussen, Co-Treas.; Michael E. Nix, Co-Treas.; Margaret H. O'Donnell, Co-Treas.; Jeff A. Wasserman, Co-Treas.; Arthur G. Woolf, Co-Treas.; Martin J. Mara, Chair. Emritus; William F. Meyer, Chair. Emritus
Board of directors: Charles T. DesLauriers, Chair.; William F. Meyer, 1st. Vice-Chair; Frank G. Harris III, 2nd. Vice-Chair; Grace T. Gilbert-Davis; Ronald D. Mussen; Michael E. Nix; Jeff A. Wasserman
Giving statement: Giving through the New England Federal Credit Union Contributions Program.

New England Federal Credit Union Contributions Program

c/o Marketing Dept.
P.O. Box 527
Williston, VT 05495-0527 (800) 400-8790
URL: http://www.nefcu.com/about_nefcu.html

Purpose and activities: As a complement to its foundation, New England Federal Credit Union makes charitable contributions to nonprofit organizations directly. Special emphasis is directed toward programs that are designed to improve the financial well-being of individuals and communities, and community-based programs focusing on projects and events that improve the quality of life, or benefit the social and cultural health of a community. Support is limited to Addison, Chittenden, Franklin, Grand Isle, Lamoille, and Washington counties, Vermont.
Fields of interest: Nursing school/education; Human services, financial counseling; Community/economic development; Mathematics; Science Children.
Type of support: General/operating support; Scholarships—to individuals; Sponsorships.
Geographic limitations: Giving is limited to Addison, Chittenden, Franklin, Grand Isle, Lamoille, and Washington counties, VT.
Support limitations: No support for religious, political, or discriminatory organizations, or organizations or projects that are considered to be in direct competition with NEFCU. No grants to individuals (except for scholarships).
Publications: Application guidelines.
Application information: Applications accepted. To ensure complete fairness and objectivity in giving policies, qualifying applications for charitable giving that meet the criteria outlined above will be entered into a blind drawing four times per year. Each quarter, NEFCU will grant a maximum of four awards, depending on the number of qualifying applications received, in amounts not to exceed $625 per request. Requests for support may come from members, individual Credit Union management and staff, and the general public. Application form not required. Applicants should submit the following:
1) population served
2) copy of IRS Determination Letter
3) detailed description of project and amount of funding requested

Initial approach: Proposal
Committee meeting date(s): Quarterly
Deadline(s): Dec. 31, Mar. 31, June 30 and Sept. 30
Final notification: 4 to 6 weeks

2672
New England Patriots LP

1 Patriot Pl.
Foxborough, MA 02035-1388
(508) 543-8200

Company URL: http://www.patriots.com
Establishment information: Established in 1960.
Company type: Private company
Business activities: Operates professional football club.
Business type (SIC): Commercial sports
Corporate officers: Robert K. Kraft, Chair. and C.E.O.; Jonathan A. Kraft, Pres. and C.O.O.; Jim Hausmann, Exec. V.P., Finance
Board of director: Robert K. Kraft, Chair.
Giving statement: Giving through the New England Patriots Charitable Foundation, Inc.

The New England Patriots Charitable Foundation, Inc.

c/o Donation Requests
1 Patriot Pl.
Foxboro, MA 02035-1388
FAX: (508) 698-0122;
E-mail: CharitableEvents@patriots.com;
URL: http://www.patriots.com/community/volunteerism.html

Establishment information: Established in 1994 in MA.
Donors: New England Patriots LP; Communication Technology Services, LLC; Fidelity Capital; Fidelity Investments.
Financial data (yr. ended 12/31/11): Assets, $2,550,784 (M); gifts received, $1,698,341; expenditures, $1,189,729; qualifying distributions, $1,064,893; giving activities include $1,064,893 for grants.
Purpose and activities: The foundation supports programs designed to foster cultural diversity, education, family services, and health. Special emphasis is directed toward programs designed to serve youth through education, creativity, and development of character.
Fields of interest: Education; Health care; Boys & girls clubs; Youth development; Family services; Civil/human rights, equal rights; Foundations (community); United Ways and Federated Giving Programs Youth.
Programs:
Community MVP Awards: The foundation honors members of the New England community for their leadership, dedication, commitment, and service to nonprofit organizations. The award includes a donation of up to $10,000 in their name to the nonprofit organization with which they volunteer.
Write On Scholarship Program: The foundation, in partnership with Fidelity Investments, awards college scholarships to local students. Students are required to write a 500-750 word essay on the most recent Patriot game. Following a 4-game stretch, first place winners will be awarded a $5,000 scholarship, two second place winners will receive $2,500, and six third place winners will receive $1,000. At the end of the season, winners are eligible to win a $15,000 grand prize.
Type of support: Building/renovation; Continuing support; Employee volunteer services; Equipment; General/operating support; In-kind gifts; Program development; Scholarship funds.
Geographic limitations: Giving limited to New England, with some emphasis on MA.
Support limitations: No support for religious organizations or for start-up organizations seeking first-time cash grant support. No grants to individuals, or for game tickets or online auctions.
Publications: Application guidelines.
Application information: Applications accepted. Proposals should be submitted using organization letterhead. Applicants should submit the following:
1) brief history of organization and description of its mission
2) descriptive literature about organization
3) detailed description of project and amount of funding requested
4) contact person

Proposals should include the organization's URL address, if available.
Initial approach: Proposal; download application form and mail to foundation for Write On Scholarship; download nomination form and mail to foundation for Community MVP Awards
Deadline(s): 8 weeks prior to need; Mar. 31 for Write On Scholarship and Community MVP Awards

Officers and Directors:* Robert K. Kraft*, Chair.; Joshua M. Kraft, Treas.; Daniel A. Kraft; David H. Kraft; Jonathan A. Kraft.
EIN: 043244069
Selected grants: The following grants are a representative sample of this grantmaker's funding activity:
$25,000 to American Ireland Fund, Boston, MA, 2011.
$20,000 to University of Massachusetts, Boston, MA, 2011.
$10,000 to City of Hope, Duarte, CA, 2011.
$5,625 to Scholarship America, Saint Peter, MN, 2011.
$5,000 to University of Notre Dame, Notre Dame, IN, 2011. For scholarship.
$4,000 to Harvard University, Cambridge, MA, 2011. For scholarship.
$3,000 to University of Massachusetts, Boston, MA, 2011.
$3,000 to University of Massachusetts, Amherst, MA, 2011. For scholarship.
$2,500 to Cystic Fibrosis Foundation, Bethesda, MD, 2011.
$2,500 to University of New Hampshire, Durham, NH, 2011. For scholarship.

2673
New Era Cap Co., Inc.

160 Delaware Ave.
Buffalo, NY 14202 (716) 604-9000
FAX: (716) 604-9299

Company URL: http://shop.neweracap.com
Establishment information: Established in 1920.
Company type: Private company
Business activities: Operates headwear and apparel company.
Business type (SIC): Apparel—hats, caps, and millinery
Corporate officers: Christopher H. Koch, C.E.O.; Peter Augustine, Pres.; Raymond Barry, C.F.O.; James Scott Patterson, Sr. V.P. and C.O.O.; Rusty Hurst, V.P., Opers.; Roni Brown, V.P., Human Resources
International operations: Canada; Europe; Hong Kong; Japan
Giving statement: Giving through the New Era Cap Company Contributions Program.

New Era Cap Company Contributions Program

160 Delaware Ave.
Buffalo, NY 14202-2404 (716) 604-9000
URL: http://www.neweracap.com/en_US/SocialResponsibility.aspx

2674
New Hampshire Ball Bearings, Inc.

175 Jaffrey Rd.
Peterborough, NH 03458 (603) 924-4100

Company URL: http://www.nhbb.com/
Establishment information: Established in 1946.
Company type: Subsidiary of a foreign company
Business activities: Manufactures precision miniature instruments, metric ball bearings, steel balls, spherical bearings, and rod-end assemblies and sub-assemblies.

Business type (SIC): Machinery/general industry; metal products/primary; metal products/fabricated
Financial profile for 2009: Number of employees, 500
Corporate officers: Gary C. Yomantas, Pres.; Dan Lemieux, V.P., Mktg.; Jim Geary, V.P., Sales
Subsidiary: Precision Products Group, Chatsworth, CA
Plant: Laconia, NH
Giving statement: Giving through the New Hampshire Ball Bearings Foundation.

New Hampshire Ball Bearings Foundation

9700 Independence Ave.
Chatsworth, CA 91311-4323

Establishment information: Established in 1960 in NH.
Donor: New Hampshire Ball Bearings, Inc.
Contact: Richard H. Conner, Jr., Secy.
Financial data (yr. ended 12/31/11): Assets, $116,686 (M); gifts received, $24,000; expenditures, $25,079; qualifying distributions, $25,000; giving activities include $25,000 for 22 grants (high: $3,000; low: $250).
Purpose and activities: The foundation supports youth centers and organizations involved with higher education, housing, and athletics. Support is given primarily in areas of company operations.
Fields of interest: Higher education; Housing/shelter; Athletics/sports, school programs; Athletics/sports, amateur leagues; Youth development, centers/clubs; Boys & girls clubs.
Type of support: General/operating support; Scholarship funds.
Geographic limitations: Giving primarily in areas of company operations in Chatsworth, CA, and Jaffrey, Laconia, and Peterborough, NH.
Application information: Applications accepted. Application form required. Applicants should submit the following:
1) copy of most recent annual report/audited financial statement/990
2) detailed description of project and amount of funding requested

Initial approach: Letter
Board meeting date(s): Quarterly
Deadline(s): None

Officers: Gary C. Yomantas, Pres.; Richard H. Conner, Jr., Secy.; James B. Peterson, Treas.
Trustees: Gary Groleau; Jack Langridge.
EIN: 026005861

2675
New Hotel Monteleone, LLC

214 Royal St.
New Orleans, LA 70130-2201
(504) 523-3341
FAX: (504) 528-1019

Company URL: http://www.hotelmonteleone.com
Establishment information: Established in 1886.
Company type: Private company
Business activities: Operates hotel.
Business type (SIC): Hotels and motels
Corporate officers: William A. Monteleone, Jr., Pres.; Edward Thieman, C.O.O.; Stephen Guerra, Cont.
Giving statement: Giving through the Monteleone Family Foundation.

Monteleone Family Foundation

214 Royal St.
New Orleans, LA 70130-2201

Establishment information: Established in 2002 in LA.
Donor: New Hotel Monteleone, LLC.
Financial data (yr. ended 12/31/10): Assets, $3,495,809 (M); expenditures, $631,901; qualifying distributions, $631,000; giving activities include $631,000 for 5 grants (high: $500,000; low: $1,000).
Purpose and activities: The foundation supports organizations involved with education, cancer, and crime and law enforcement.
Fields of interest: Higher education; Education; Cancer; Crime/law enforcement; United Ways and Federated Giving Programs.
Type of support: General/operating support.
Geographic limitations: Giving limited to New Orleans, LA and Houston, TX.
Support limitations: No grants to individuals.
Application information: Applications not accepted. Contributes only to pre-selected organizations.
Officers and Directors: William A. Monteleone, Jr., Pres.; Ronald Pincus, V.P.; Charles Lacinak, Jr., Secy.-Treas.; Anna Monteleone Burr; David G. Monteleone.
EIN: 820569393
Selected grants: The following grants are a representative sample of this grantmaker's funding activity:
$100,000 to Project GRAD USA, Houston, TX, 2010. For general support.

2676
New Jersey Devils, LLC

165 Mulberry St.
Newark, NJ 07102 (973) 757-6100
FAX: (973) 757-6399

Company URL: http://devils.nhl.com/
Establishment information: Established in 1974.
Company type: Private company
Business activities: Operates professional ice hockey club.
Business type (SIC): Commercial sports
Financial profile for 2010: Number of employees, 99
Corporate officers: Jeffrey Vanderbeek, Chair.; Louis A. LaMoriello, Pres. and C.E.O.; Chris Modrzynski, Sr. Exec. V.P. and C.O.O.; Scott Struble, Exec. V.P. and C.F.O.; Gordon Lavalette, Exec. V.P., Admin.; Mike Levine, Sr. V.P., Comms.; Joseph C. Benedetti, V.P. and Genl. Counsel; Jason Siegel, V.P., Sales and Mktg.
Board of director: Jeffrey Vanderbeek, Chair.
Giving statement: Giving through the New Jersey Devils LLC Corporate Giving Program.

New Jersey Devils LLC Corporate Giving Program

c/o Comms. Dept.
Prudential Center
165 Mulberry St.
Newark, NJ 07102-3607
Contact for Speakers Bureau: Heather Hall, tel.: (973) 757-6141,
e-mail: speakers@newjerseydevils.com;
URL: http://devils.nhl.com/club/page.htm?id=42011

Purpose and activities: The New Jersey Devils make charitable contributions to nonprofit organizations on a case by case basis. Support is given primarily in the New York, New York, metropolitan area.
Fields of interest: Education, reading; Education; Food services; Athletics/sports, winter sports; Children/youth, services; Human services, gift distribution; General charitable giving.
Programs:

Dr. John J. McMullen Service to New Jersey Hockey Award: The Devils honors an individual or individuals who have served the sport of ice hockey throughout the state of New Jersey. The award is named after the club's late founder, Dr. John J. McMullen.

HS Player of the Month: Through the HS Player of the Month program, the Devil honors six-student athletes, one from each of the six different conferences, each month from December through February. The athletes are nominated by varsity ice hockey coaches throughout the state and voted on by local media. Winners receive tickets to a Devil's game, a plaque presented by a Devil's player, and dinner compliments of the Devils. An overall HS Player of the Year is also chosen.

PSE&G Power Play Kids: The Devils, in partnership with PSE&G, rewards youth groups like Boys & Girls Club, P.A.L.'s., YMCA's, schools and charitable organizations for their positive contribution to the community. Recipients receive t-shirts and tickets to selected home games.

School Assembly Program: Through the School Assembly program, Devils Alumni Association conducts free assemblies at local schools to promote determination, goal setting, and commitment to excellence to succeed in life. The assembly includes an introductory video, a verbal presentation from a New Jersey Devils representative, and a follow-up question and answer session.

Speakers Bureau: Through Speakers Bureau, Devils Alumni and staff visit and provide presentations to community groups, businesses, and social clubs.

Type of support: Donated products; In-kind gifts; Income development; Loaned talent.
Geographic limitations: Giving primarily in the New York, NY, metropolitan area.
Publications: Application guidelines.
Application information: Applications accepted. Proposals should be submitted using organization letterhead. The Communications Department handles giving. Application form not required. Applicants should submit the following:
1) name, address and phone number of organization
2) detailed description of project and amount of funding requested
3) contact person

Proposals should indicate the date of the event.
Initial approach: Proposal to headquarters for memorabilia and Speakers Bureau; complete online application for School Assembly program
Copies of proposal: 1
Deadline(s): 6 to 8 weeks prior to need for memorabilia; None for Speakers Bureau and School Assembly program
Final notification: 1 month prior to need

2677
New Living

6111 Kirby Dr.
Houston, TX 77005-3140 (713) 797-2935
FAX: (713) 880-3202

Company URL: http://www.newliving.net
Establishment information: Established in 2007.
Company type: Private company

Business type (SIC): Business services/ miscellaneous
Corporate officers: Jeff Kaplan, Owner; Lewis Cauffman, Owner; Adam Brackman, Owner
Giving statement: Giving through the New Living Corporate Giving Program.

New Living Corporate Giving Program

6111 Kirby Dr.
Houston, TX 77005-3140 (713) 521-1921
E-mail: getgreen@newliving.net; URL: http://www.newliving.net/about-us-shop-sustainable-materials/our-mission/

Purpose and activities: New Living is a certified B Corporation that donates a percentage of profits to charitable organizations.

2678
New Orleans Hornets NBA L.P.

1250 Poydras St., Fl. 19
New Orleans, LA 70113-1804
(504) 593-4700

Company URL: http://www.nba.com/hornets
Establishment information: Established in 1988.
Company type: Subsidiary of a private company
Business activities: Operates professional basketball club.
Business type (SIC): Commercial sports
Corporate officers: Hugh Weber, Pres. and C.O.O.; Brice Collier, C.F.O.; Sam Russo, Exec. V.P., Opers. and Genl. Counsel; Greg King, Cont.
Giving statement: Giving through the New Orleans Hornets NBA L.P. Corporate Giving Program and the George Shinn Foundation, Inc.

George Shinn Foundation, Inc.

P.O. Box 56989
New Orleans, LA 70156-6989 (504) 593-4882
Application address: 1250 Poydras St., 19th Fl., New Orleans, LA 70112-1804

Establishment information: Established in 1973 in NC.
Donors: The Charlotte Hornets; George Shinn; George Shinn & Assocs., Inc.
Contact: George Shinn, Pres.
Financial data (yr. ended 12/31/10): Assets, $1,024,610 (M); gifts received, $400,012; expenditures, $505,235; qualifying distributions, $487,648; giving activities include $487,648 for grants.
Fields of interest: Education; Crime/law enforcement; Youth, services; Community/ economic development; United Ways and Federated Giving Programs; Christian agencies & churches.
Type of support: General/operating support; Scholarship funds.
Geographic limitations: Giving primarily in Charlotte, NC.
Application information: Applicants should submit the following:
1) detailed description of project and amount of funding requested
Initial approach: Letter
Board meeting date(s): Varies
Deadline(s): None
Officers and Directors:* George Shinn, Pres.; Hugh Weber*, Secy.; Harold Bouillion, Treas.; Chris Shinn; Chad Shinn.
EIN: 561083525

Selected grants: The following grants are a representative sample of this grantmaker's funding activity:
$10,000 to Ochsner Clinic Foundation, New Orleans, LA, 2010.
$2,010 to American Red Cross, New Orleans, LA, 2010.

2679
New Orleans Louisiana Saints, L.P.

(also known as New Orleans Saints)
5800 Airline Dr.
Metairie, LA 70003-3876 (504) 733-0255

Company URL: http://www.neworleanssaints.com
Establishment information: Established in 1966.
Company type: Private company
Business activities: Operates professional football club.
Business type (SIC): Commercial sports
Corporate officers: Tom Benson, Chair.; Rita Benson LeBlanc, Vice-Chair.; Dennis Lauscha, Pres.; Vicky Neumeyer, Sr. V.P. and Genl. Counsel; Ben Hales, Sr. V.P., Mktg.; Greg Bensel, Sr. V.P., Comms.; Charleen Sharpe, Compt.
Board of directors: Tom Benson, Chair.; Rita Benson LeBlanc, Vice-Chair.
Giving statement: Giving through the New Orleans Saints Corporate Giving Program and the New Orleans Saints Hurricane Katrina Relief Fund.

New Orleans Saints Corporate Giving Program

c/o Community Affairs Dept.
5800 Airline Dr.
Metairie, LA 70003-3876 (504) 733-0255
URL: http://www.neworleanssaints.com/community/index.html

Purpose and activities: As a complement to its foundation, the New Orleans Saints also makes in-kind donations to organizations directly. Support is given primarily in Louisiana and throughout the Gulf South region.
Fields of interest: Safety/disasters, information services; Youth, services; General charitable giving.
Type of support: Donated products; In-kind gifts.
Geographic limitations: Giving primarily in LA and the Gulf South region.
Publications: Application guidelines.
Application information: Applications accepted. Proposals should be submitted on organization letterhead. The Saints do not accept fan merchandise for the purpose of autographing and will return any merchandise received. Application form not required. Applicants should submit the following:
1) name, address and phone number of organization
2) contact person
Proposals should include the type of event or program, as well as the date, time, length, and location.
Initial approach: Proposal
Deadline(s): 4 to 6 weeks prior to event

The New Orleans Saints Hurricane Katrina Relief Fund

755 E. Mulberry, Ste. 200
San Antonio, TX 78212-4285 (504) 733-0255

Establishment information: Established in 2005 in TX.
Donor: Bank of America Corp.
Contact: Tom Benson, Chair.
Financial data (yr. ended 12/31/11): Assets, $347 (M); expenditures, $20,000; program services expenses, $20,000; giving activities include $20,000 for grants.
Purpose and activities: The fund provides aid and assistance to the people of New Orleans, Louisiana and the Gulf Coast region affected by Hurricane Katrina.
Fields of interest: Disasters, Hurricane Katrina.
Geographic limitations: Giving primarily in AL; New Orleans, LA; and MS.
Officers and Directors:* Tom Benson*, Chair.; Stanley Rosenberg*, Secy.-Treas.; Rene Benson; Dennis Lauscha; Rita Benson Leblanc; Ryan Leblanc; Mickey Loomis; R. Tom Roddy.
EIN: 203423114

2680
New Penn Motor Express, Inc.

625 S. 5th Ave.
Lebanon, PA 17042-7715 (717) 274-2521

Company URL: http://www.newpenn.com/
Establishment information: Established in 1931.
Company type: Subsidiary of a public company
Ultimate parent company: YRC Worldwide Inc.
Business activities: Provides trucking services.
Business type (SIC): Trucking and courier services, except by air
Financial profile for 2010: Number of employees, 2,300
Corporate officers: Steven D. Gast, Pres. and C.E.O.; Anthony S. Nicosia, V.P., Sales and Mktg.; Joe Schappell, Cont.
Giving statement: Giving through the New Penn Motor Express Scholarship Foundation.

New Penn Motor Express Scholarship Foundation

(formerly Arnold Industries Scholarship Foundation)
1525 W. W.T. Harris Blvd., D1114-044
Charlotte, NC 28288-1161 (717) 274-2521

Establishment information: Established in 1985 in PA.
Donors: Arnold Industries, Inc.; New Penn Motor Express, Inc.
Financial data (yr. ended 12/31/10): Assets, $0 (M); expenditures, $25,584; qualifying distributions, $25,330; giving activities include $25,246 for 15 grants to individuals (high: $3,000; low: $750).
Purpose and activities: The foundation awards college scholarships to dependents of full-time employees of New Penn Motor Express and its subsidiaries.
Fields of interest: Education.
Type of support: Employee-related scholarships.
Application information: Applications not accepted. Contributes only through employee-related scholarships.
Trustee: Wells Fargo Bank, N.A.
EIN: 232386384

2681
New York Business Development Corporation

(also known as NYBDC)
50 Beaver St., Ste. 600
Albany, NY 12207 (518) 463-2268

Company URL: http://www.nybdc.com
Establishment information: Established in 1955.
Company type: Private company
Business activities: Provides commercial loans.
Business type (SIC): Credit institutions/business
Financial profile for 2012: Assets, $184,990,115; expenses, $12,650,370; liabilities, $160,207,323
Corporate officers: James J. Byrnes, Chair.; Bruce W. Boyea, Vice-Chair.; Patrick J. MacKrell, Pres. and C.E.O.; Nancy A. Reinhart, Exec. V.P. and C.A.O.; Owen F. Burns, Sr. V.P. and C.F.O.; Leesa Naimo-Fredette, V.P. and Genl. Counsel; Kathleen M. Russom, Secy.
Board of directors: James J. Byrnes, Chair.; Bruce W. Boyea, Vice-Chair.; Ronald M. Bentley; G. Gary Berner; Mary C. Bintz; Mark C. Boyce; Dale A. Burnett; Robert L. Como; Robert M. Curley; F. Edward Devitt; Hugh J. Donlon; Daryl R. Forsythe; Thomas F. Goldrick, Jr.; Linda Dickerson Hartsock; Hugh A. Johnson; Robert C. Jussen; Robert W. Lazar; Patrick J. MacKrell; Brian T. McMahon; Carl E. Meyer; Dennis M. Mullen; Allen J. Naples; John Rhea; Marjorie Rovereto; Michael P. Smith; George Strayton; Mark E. Tryniski; Maryann M. Winters; Lewis Yevoli
Giving statement: Giving through the NYBDC Charitable Foundation, Inc.

NYBDC Charitable Foundation, Inc.

50 Beaver Street
Albany, NY 12207-1511

Establishment information: Established in 2000 in NY.
Donors: New York Business Development Corp.; Empire State Certified Development Corporation.
Financial data (yr. ended 09/30/11): Assets, $933,353 (M); gifts received, $178,833; expenditures, $126,005; qualifying distributions, $85,964; giving activities include $85,964 for 81 grants (high: $2,500; low: $100).
Purpose and activities: The foundation supports fire departments and organizations involved with secondary and higher education and community economic development.
Type of support: Continuing support; General/operating support.
Application information: Applications not accepted. Contributes only to pre-selected organizations.
Officer: Patrick J. Mackrell, Pres.
Directors: James J. Byrnes; Herbert G. Chorbajian; Thomas F. Goldrick, Jr.; Robert W. Lazar; Christopher J. Taylor.
EIN: 141834499

2682
New York Community Bancorp, Inc.

615 Merrick Ave.
Westbury, NY 11590 (516) 683-4100
FAX: (516) 683-8385

Company URL: http://www.mynycb.com
Establishment information: Established in 1859.
Company type: Public company
Company ticker symbol and exchange: NYB/NYSE
Business activities: Operates bank holding company.
Business type (SIC): Holding company
Financial profile for 2012: Number of employees, 3,458; assets, $44,145,100,000; pre-tax net income, $780,910,000; liabilities, $38,488,840,000
Forbes 2000 ranking: 2012—1748th in sales, 1057th in profits, and 522nd in assets
Corporate officers: Dominick Ciampa, Chair.; Joseph R. Ficalora, Pres. and C.E.O.; Robert Wann, Sr. Exec. V.P. and C.O.O.; Thomas R. Cangemi, Sr. Exec. V.P. and C.F.O.; John J. Pinto, C.P.A., Sr. Exec. V.P. and C.A.O.; R. Patrick Quinn, Exec. V.P. and Secy.
Board of directors: Dominick Ciampa, Chair.; Maureen E. Clancy; Hanif W. Dahya; Joseph R. Ficalora; William C. Frederick, M.D.; Max L. Kupferberg; Michael J. Levine, C.P.A.; Guy V. Molinari; James J. O'Donovan; Ronald A. Rosenfeld; John M. Tsimbinos, Jr.; Spiros J. Voutsinas; Robert Wann
Subsidiary: New York Community Bank, Westbury, NY
Giving statement: Giving through the New York Community Bancorp, Inc. Contributions Program.
Company EIN: 061377322

New York Community Bancorp, Inc. Contributions Program

615 Merrick Ave.
Westbury, NY 11590 (516) 683-4100
URL: https://www.mynycb.com/Community/Pages/Giving-Back.aspxdivID=9§ionID=other&subsectionID=about

2683
New York Community Bank

615 Merrick Ave.
Westbury, NY 11590-6644 (516) 683-4100

Company URL: http://www.mynycb.com
Establishment information: Established in 1859.
Company type: Subsidiary of a public company
Business activities: Operates savings bank.
Business type (SIC): Savings institutions
Corporate officers: Dominick Ciampa, Chair.; Joseph R. Ficalora, Pres. and C.E.O.; Robert Wann, Sr. Exec. V.P. and C.O.O.; Thomas R. Cangemi, C.P.A., Sr. Exec. V.P. and C.F.O.; John J. Pinto, C.P.A., Exec. V.P. and C.A.O.; R. Patrick Quinn, Exec. V.P. and Corp. Secy.
Board of directors: Dominick Ciampa, Chair.; Maureen E. Clancy; Hanif "wally" Dahya; Joseph R. Ficalora; William C. Frederick, M.D.; Max L. Kupferberg; Michael J. Levine, C.P.A.; Guy V. Molinari; James J. O'Donovan; Ronald A. Rosenfeld; John M. Tsimbinos, Jr.; Spiros J. Voutsinas; Robert Wann
Divisions: CFS Bank, Baldwin, NY; Queens County Savings Bank, Westbury, NY; Richmond County Savings Bank, Staten Island, NY
Giving statement: Giving through the New York Community Bank Foundation and the Richmond County Savings Foundation.

The New York Community Bank Foundation

(formerly The Roslyn Savings Foundation)
c/o New York Community Bank
1400 Old Northern Blvd.
Roslyn, NY 11576-2127 (516) 484-1344
FAX: (516) 484-1599;
E-mail: mconway@roslynsavingsfoundation.org; Additional contact: Cindy Krezel, Prog. Off, ckkrezel@roslynsavinigsfoundation.org;
URL: http://www.roslynsavingsfoundation.org

Establishment information: Established in 1997 in NY.
Donor: Roslyn Bancorp, Inc.
Contact: Marian Conway, Exec. Dir.
Financial data (yr. ended 12/31/11): Assets, $18,256,218 (M); expenditures, $2,408,136; qualifying distributions, $2,262,402; giving activities include $2,262,402 for grants.
Purpose and activities: The foundation supports organizations involved with arts and culture, education, health, hunger, and human services. Special emphasis is directed toward programs designed to promote community development; expand home ownership opportunities; and provide access to affordable housing.
Fields of interest: Museums; Arts; Higher education; Libraries (public); Education; Hospitals (general); Health care, clinics/centers; Health care; Food services; Housing/shelter, home owners; Housing/shelter; Family services; Human services; Community/economic development.
Type of support: Capital campaigns; Continuing support; Endowments; Equipment; General/operating support; Program development; Scholarship funds; Sponsorships.
Geographic limitations: Giving primarily in Long Island and Queens, NY.
Support limitations: No support for religious, political, or fraternal organizations. No grants to individuals.
Publications: Application guidelines; Grants list.
Application information: Applications accepted. Letters of inquiry should be no longer than 1 to 2 pages. Letters of inquiry should list any grants or contributions received from the banks in the New York Community Bank family. Multi-year funding is not automatic. Organizations receiving support are asked to submit periodic progress reports. A site visit may be requested. Application form not required. Applicants should submit the following:
1) copy of IRS Determination Letter
2) copy of most recent annual report/audited financial statement/990
3) listing of board of directors, trustees, officers and other key people and their affiliations
4) listing of additional sources and amount of support
5) detailed description of project and amount of funding requested
6) geographic area to be served

Initial approach: Letter of inquiry
Copies of proposal: 1
Board meeting date(s): Quarterly
Deadline(s): None
Final notification: Within 3 months

Officers and Directors:* John R. Bransfield, Jr.*, Chair.; Maureen E. Clancy*, Pres.; R. Patrick Quinn, Secy.; Thomas Calabrese*, Treas.; Marian Conway, Exec. Dir.; Thomas Calabrese; Dominick Ciampa; Joseph R. Ficalora; Michael J. Levine; James O'Donavan; John M. Tsimbinos; Gerry Voutsinas.
Number of staff: 2 full-time professional.
EIN: 113354472

Richmond County Savings Foundation

900 South Ave., Exec. Ste. 17
Staten Island, NY 10314-7869 (718) 568-3516
FAX: (718) 568-3551; E-mail: Staff@rcsf.org; Additional tels.: (718) 568-3517 and (718) 568-3631; URL: http://www.rcsf.org

Establishment information: Established in 1998 in DE.
Donors: Richmond County Financial Corp.; New York Community Bancorp., Inc.
Contact: Cesar J. Claro, Exec. Dir.
Financial data (yr. ended 12/31/11): Assets, $59,099,368 (M); expenditures, $3,783,254; qualifying distributions, $4,047,421; giving activities include $3,428,575 for 191 grants (high: $1,000,000; low: $95).
Purpose and activities: The foundation supports programs designed to advance educational opportunity; enrich cultural development; and strengthen health and human services.
Fields of interest: Museums; Arts; Higher education; Education; Hospitals (general); Food services; Housing/shelter; Human services; Community development, neighborhood development; Community/economic development.
Programs:
Capital Initiatives: The foundation awards grants of up to $75,000 to support construction, renovation, and enhancements for "bricks and mortar" type projects. Organizations must have the following to apply: 75% of funding requirements already committed; architectural plans, designs, and permits secured by the organization; the request must be made within 12 months in which the project is scheduled to commence; and organizations must agree to set aides up to 1% for RCSF grant funds to hire an inspector to draft a conditional grant agreement and/or benchmarks.
Programmatic Funding: The foundation awards program grants of up to $40,000 to organizations involved with human services, public benefits, health, education, the environment, and arts and culture.
Signature Projects: The foundation supports general charitable giving at the discretion of the Executive Director. Grant requests are by invitation only.
Type of support: Annual campaigns; Building/renovation; Capital campaigns; Conferences/seminars; Endowments; Equipment; General/operating support; Management development/capacity building; Matching/challenge support; Program development; Publication; Research; Sponsorships; Technical assistance.
Geographic limitations: Giving primarily in areas of company operations in Staten Island, NY.
Support limitations: No support for political organizations or private non-operating foundations. No grants to individuals.
Publications: Annual report; Application guidelines; Informational brochure.
Application information: Applications accepted. The foundation awards general grants of up to $5,000 and board grants for requests over $5,000. Organizations requesting a grant over $10,000 are required to submit a summary of their proposed request on organization letterhead. Additional information, a grantee interview, or a site visit may be requested. Organizations receiving grants of more than $10,000 will be required to file a final report. Application form required. Applicants should submit the following:
1) copy of IRS Determination Letter
2) copy of most recent annual report/audited financial statement/990
3) listing of board of directors, trustees, officers and other key people and their affiliations
4) copy of current year's organizational budget and/or project budget

Groups receiving two consecutive year grants of more than $25,000 will be prohibited from applying for funding in the third year, but may reapply in the fourth year, commencing a new cycle. Continual funding will be considered by invitation only.
Initial approach: Complete online application form or download application form and mail completed application to foundation; organizations submitting online are required to confirm, by phone, the receipt of the submission with foundation staff
Copies of proposal: 1
Board meeting date(s): Quarterly
Deadline(s): None
Officers and Directors:* Michael F. Manzulli*, Chair. and Pres.; Kim Seggio, Secy. and Sr. Prog. Off.; Thomas R. Cangemi*, Treas.; Cesar J. Claro, Exec. Dir.; Godfrey H. Carstens, Jr.; Edward Cruz; Alfred B. Curtis, Jr.; Robert S. Farrell; Joseph R. Ficalora; William C. Frederick; Caroline Diamond Harrison; James L. Kelley; Patrick F.X. Nilan.
Number of staff: 4 full-time support.
EIN: 061503051

2684
New York Football Giants, Inc.

(also known as New York Giants)
1925 Giants Dr.
East Rutherford, NJ 07073 (201) 935-8111

Company URL: http://www.giants.com
Establishment information: Established in 1925.
Company type: Private company
Business activities: Operates professional football club.
Business type (SIC): Amusement and recreation services/miscellaneous
Corporate officers: Steve Tisch, Chair.; John K. Marac, Esq., Pres. and C.E.O.; Christine Procops, Sr. V.P. and C.F.O.; William J. Heller, Esq., Sr. V.P. and Genl. Counsel; Pat Hanlon, Sr. V.P., Comms.; Kevin Frattura, V.P., Sales and Mktg.; E. Peter John-Baptiste, V.P., Comms.; Steve Hamrahi, V.P., Finance; Rusty Hawley, V.P., Mktg.; Jonathan Tisch, Treas.
Board of director: Steve Tisch, Chair.
Giving statement: Giving through the New York Giants Corporate Giving Program and the Giants Foundation, Inc.

New York Giants Corporate Giving Program

c/o Community Rels. Dept.
Giants Stadium
East Rutherford, NJ 07073
URL: http://www.giants.com/community.asp

Purpose and activities: The New York Giants make charitable contributions to nonprofit organizations on a case by case basis. Support is given primarily in the Connecticut, New Jersey, and the New York tri-state area.
Fields of interest: Education, reading; Education; Public health, physical fitness; Health care, patient services; Food banks; Athletics/sports, Special Olympics; Children/youth, services; Human services, gift distribution; United Ways and Federated Giving Programs; General charitable giving Youth.
Program:
What Moves You: The Giants, in partnership with the American Heart Association and the New Jersey Education Association, promotes physical fitness for area middle schools. The program is designed to encourage kids to play actively every day through public service announcements, school visits, and school materials from Giant players and the program spokesperson Eli Manning.
Type of support: Building/renovation; Donated products; In-kind gifts; Income development.
Geographic limitations: Giving primarily in areas of company operations in the CT, NJ, and NY tri-state area.
Publications: Application guidelines.
Application information: Applications accepted. Proposals should be submitted using organization letterhead. Support is limited to 1 contribution per organization during any given year. The Community Relations Department handles giving. Application form not required. Applicants should submit the following:
1) name, address and phone number of organization
2) detailed description of project and amount of funding requested
3) contact person

Proposals should indicate the date of the event.
Initial approach: Mail proposal to headquarters for memorabilia donations
Copies of proposal: 1
Deadline(s): 8 weeks prior to need for memorabilia donations
Final notification: 1 month prior to need for memorabilia donations

The Giants Foundation, Inc.

Giants Stadium
50 Rte. 120
East Rutherford, NJ 07073-2131 (201) 935-8111
E-mail: Stangeby@giants.nfl.net; For GameOn! Grant Program: c/o Allison Stangeby, Community Rels. Dept., tel.: (201) 939-1673; URL: http://www.giants.com/Community.asp

Establishment information: Established in 1992 in NJ.
Donors: New York Football Giants, Inc.; The National Football League; The Quaker Oats Co.; Nelson Ferreira; New Jersey Sports & Exposition Authority; Christie Family Foundation; Paul Queally; Dan Ward; Craig Martone; Tim Shinn; JPMorgan Chase; Anheuser Busch; Michael Brennan; McLane Securities.
Contact: Allison Stangeby, Exec. Dir.
Financial data (yr. ended 12/31/11): Assets, $372,711 (M); gifts received, $357,692; expenditures, $570,095; qualifying distributions, $555,500; giving activities include $555,500 for grants.
Purpose and activities: The foundation supports organizations involved with education, health, youth, and civic affairs. Special emphasis is directed toward programs designed to support disadvantaged youth and their families.
Fields of interest: Education; Health care; Athletics/sports, football; Youth, services; Family services; Family services, domestic violence; Public affairs Economically disadvantaged.
Program:
GameOn! Grant Program: The foundation awards grants of up to $2,500 to recreational and high school football coaches on behalf of local youth football teams. Grants may be used for football equipment purchases, football uniforms, insurance costs, and transportation to games for children.
Type of support: Annual campaigns; Equipment; General/operating support; Program development; Scholarship funds.
Geographic limitations: Giving primarily in the metropolitan New York, NY, area, including NJ.

Publications: Annual report; Application guidelines.
Application information: Applications accepted. Proposals for GameOn! Grant Program should include coaching and high school histories. Visit website for detailed proposal requirements. Application form not required. Applicants should submit the following:
1) copy of IRS Determination Letter
2) descriptive literature about organization
3) detailed description of project and amount of funding requested
4) copy of current year's organizational budget and/or project budget
5) listing of additional sources and amount of support
Initial approach: Proposal
Copies of proposal: 1
Board meeting date(s): Feb.
Deadline(s): Oct. 1 to Dec. 31
Final notification: Following board review; Mar. for GameOn! Grant Program
Officers: Laurie Tisch*, Chair.; John K. Mara, Pres.; Jonathan Tisch, V.P.; Francis X. Mara, Secy.-Treas.; Alison Stangeby, Exec. Dir.
EIN: 223183916
Selected grants: The following grants are a representative sample of this grantmaker's funding activity:
$25,000 to AmeriCares, Stamford, CT, 2010. For general purposes.
$25,000 to Save the Children Federation, Westport, CT, 2010. For general purposes.
$20,000 to Hudson Cradle, Jersey City, NJ, 2010. For general purposes.
$15,000 to My Sisters Place, White Plains, NY, 2010. For general purposes.
$15,000 to Pet Rescue, Larchmont, NY, 2010. For general purposes.
$15,000 to Susan G. Komen for the Cure, Summit, NJ, 2010. For general purposes.
$15,000 to Trinitas Hospital, Elizabeth, NJ, 2010. For general purposes.
$7,500 to Town School, New York, NY, 2010. For general purposes.
$7,500 to Tuesdays Children, Manhasset, NY, 2010. For general purposes.
$5,000 to American Heart Association, Robbinsville, NJ, 2010. For general purposes.

2685
New York Health and Racquet Club

18 E. 50th St., Fl. 4
New York, NY 10022-9116 (212) 797-1500

Company URL: http://www.nyhrc.com
Establishment information: Established in 1972.
Company type: Private company
Business activities: Operates physical fitness facilities.
Business type (SIC): Amusement and recreation services/miscellaneous
Corporate officers: Fraydun Manocherian, Chair.; Jeff Bodner, Pres.; Howard Brodsky, Pres. and C.E.O.; Sean Bremman, C.O.O.; Carla Rodriguez, Corp. Cont.
Board of director: Fraydun Manocherian, Chair.
Giving statement: Giving through the New York Health and Racquet Club Foundation.

New York Health and Racquet Club Foundation

c/o Pan Am Equities Inc.
18 E. 50th St.
New York, NY 10022-6817

Establishment information: Established around 1985 in NY.
Donors: New York Health and Racquet Club; Pamela Equities Inc.
Financial data (yr. ended 04/30/12): Assets, $1,547,662 (M); expenditures, $82,399; qualifying distributions, $79,975; giving activities include $75,000 for 2 grants (high: $49,000; low: $26,000).
Purpose and activities: The foundation supports hospitals and ranches and organizations involved with patient services, automotive safety, and children and youth.
Fields of interest: Education; Safety/disasters; Religion.
Type of support: General/operating support.
Geographic limitations: Giving limited to New York, NY.
Application information: Applications not accepted. Unsolicited requests for funds not accepted.
Directors: Fraydun Manocherian; John Manocherian; Kimberly Manocherian.
EIN: 133165187

2686
New York Islanders Hockey Club, L.P.

1255 Hempstead Tpke.
Nassau Veterans Memorial Coliseum
Uniondale, NY 11553-1260 (516) 501-6700

Company URL: http://www.newyorkislanders.com
Establishment information: Established in 1972.
Company type: Private company
Business activities: Operates professional ice hockey club.
Business type (SIC): Commercial sports
Corporate officers: Paul Lancey, Sr. V.P., Mktg. and Sales; Tim Beach, V.P., Opers.; Frank Romano, Cont.
Giving statement: Giving through the New York Islanders Hockey Club, LP Corporate Giving Program.

New York Islanders Hockey Club, LP Corporate Giving Program

c/o Community Rels.
1255 Hempstead Tpke.
Uniondale, NY 11553-1260 (516) 501-6700
Additional tel.: (800) 992-ISLES, ext. 4; Contact for We're All Islanders School Assembly: Ann Rina, tel.: (516) 501-6870; Contact for Rexcorp Islanders Inspire: islandersinspire@newyorkislanders.com; URL: http://islanders.nhl.com/club/page.htm?id=43123

Purpose and activities: The New York Islanders make charitable contributions of game tickets and memorabilia to nonprofit organizations involved with education, health, youth hockey, and families. Support is given primarily on Long Island, New York.
Fields of interest: Elementary school/education; Education, reading; Education; Health care; Cancer; Athletics/sports, winter sports; Youth development; Family services; Human services, gift distribution.
Programs:
New York Islanders Hockey With A Heart: Through Hockey With A Heart, the Islanders partner with nonprofit organizations to hold fundraising campaigns. Selected organizations receive fundraising dollars through ticket sales, receive in game recognition, and are invited to be onsite for select Islanders home games.
Rexcorp Islanders Inspire: The Islanders, in partnership with Rexcop, provides donated game tickets and bus transportation to children who otherwise would not be able to attend a game.
We're All Islanders School Assembly Program: The Islanders visit local schools and conducts assemblies to stress the importance of teamwork in life and to draw comparisons between hockey teams and schools. The Islanders, in partnership with Paton Publishing, also promotes Islanders@school, a web-based curriculum resource for grades 3,4,5, and 6, which includes hockey themed lesson plans covering reading, writing, math, physical education, and health studies.
Type of support: Curriculum development; Donated products; In-kind gifts; Income development.
Geographic limitations: Giving primarily in areas of company operations in Long Island, NY.
Publications: Application guidelines.
Application information: Applications accepted. Proposals should be submitted using organization letterhead. Support is limited to 1 contribution per organization during any given year. The Community Relations Department handles giving. Application form not required. Applicants should submit the following:
1) name, address and phone number of organization
2) detailed description of project and amount of funding requested
3) contact person
Requests for memorabilia donations should indicate the date of the event.
Initial approach: Proposal to headquarters for memorabilia donations; contact headquarters to enroll in We're All Islanders School Assembly Program and Rexcorp Islanders Inspire
Copies of proposal: 1
Deadline(s): 4 weeks prior to need for memorabilia donations; Oct. 1 to Mar. 5 for We're All Islanders School Assembly Program

2687
New York Jets Football Club, Inc.

1000 Fulton Ave.
Hempstead, NY 11550-1030
(516) 560-8100

Company URL: http://www.newyorkjets.com
Establishment information: Established in 1963.
Company type: Private company
Business activities: Operates professional football club.
Business type (SIC): Commercial sports; amusement and recreation services/miscellaneous
Corporate officers: Robert Wood Johnson IV, Chair.; Michael Tannenbaum, C.E.O.; L. Jay Cross, Pres.; Michael Gerstle, C.F.O.; Clay Hampton, C.O.O.
Board of director: Robert Wood Johnson IV, Chair.
Giving statement: Giving through the New York Jets Corporate Giving Program and the New York Jets Foundation, Inc.

New York Jets Corporate Giving Program

c/o Community Rels. Donations
1 Jets Dr.
Florham Park, NJ 07932-1215
URL: http://www.newyorkjets.com/community/index.html

Purpose and activities: As a complement to its foundation, the New York Jets also make charitable contributions of team memorabilia for use in charitable fundraising events and to nonprofit organizations such as schools. Support is given primarily in in the tri-state area of Connecticut, New Jersey, and New York.
Fields of interest: Lupus; United Ways and Federated Giving Programs; General charitable giving.
Type of support: Cause-related marketing; Donated products; General/operating support.
Geographic limitations: Giving primarily in the Tri-state area of NY, NJ, and CT.
Publications: Application guidelines.
Application information: Applications accepted. Letters should be submitted on organization letterhead. No game ticket donations are made. Items are not accepted to be autographed. Support is limited to 1 contribution per organization during any given year. Requests are not accepted via fax, e-mail, or mail. Inquiries into the status of a request are not encouraged unless no response has been received one week prior to the event. Application form required. Applicants should submit the following:
1) brief history of organization and description of its mission
2) contact person
Letters must include the event name and date.
Initial approach: Complete online application
Deadline(s): 8 weeks prior to event

New York Jets Foundation, Inc.

1 Jets Dr.
Florham Park, NJ 07932-1215 (973) 549-4800
URL: http://www.newyorkjets.com/community/be-lean-and-green/new-york-jets-foundation.html

Establishment information: Established in 1969.
Donors: Bett Wold Johnson, Inc.; NFL Charities; New York Mercantile Exchange, Inc.; NFL Youth Football Fund; Kraft Total.
Contact: Brian Friedman, Treas.
Financial data (yr. ended 12/31/11): Assets, $4,029,553 (M); gifts received, $1,240,867; expenditures, $437,598; qualifying distributions, $307,049; giving activities include $260,832 for 72 grants (high: $50,000; low: $741).
Purpose and activities: The foundation supports programs designed to promote youth education, fitness, and health with an emphasis on disadvantaged communities.
Fields of interest: Secondary school/education; Education; Public health, obesity; Public health, physical fitness; Health care; Athletics/sports, football Youth; Economically disadvantaged.
Type of support: General/operating support; Program development; Scholarship funds.
Geographic limitations: Giving primarily in Chicago, IL, NJ, and NY.
Application information: Applications accepted. Application form not required.
Initial approach: Proposal
Deadline(s): None
Officers and Trustees:* Robert Wood Johnson IV*, Chair.; Neil J. Burmeister*, V.P.; Brian Friedman*, Treas.
EIN: 237108291

Selected grants: The following grants are a representative sample of this grantmaker's funding activity:
$50,000 to New York City Department of Education, New York, NY, 2009.
$50,000 to New York City Department of Education, New York, NY, 2009.
$25,189 to United Way of Northern New Jersey, Morris County, Cedar Knolls, NJ, 2009.
$12,900 to United Way of Northern New Jersey, Morris County, Cedar Knolls, NJ, 2009.
$10,000 to United Way of Northern New Jersey, Morris County, Cedar Knolls, NJ, 2009.
$1,257 to Automotive High School, Brooklyn, NY, 2009.

2688
New York Life Insurance Company

51 Madison Ave.
New York, NY 10010 (212) 576-7000

Company URL: http://www.newyorklife.com
Establishment information: Established in 1845.
Company type: Mutual company
Business activities: Sells life insurance.
Business type (SIC): Insurance/life
Financial profile for 2011: Number of employees, 16,068; assets, $199,645,700,000; sales volume, $34,947,200,000
Corporate officers: Theodore A. Mathas, Chair., Pres., and C.E.O.; Gary E. Wendlandt, Vice-Chair.; Michael E. Sproule, Exec. V.P. and C.F.O.; Frank M. Boccio, Exec. V.P. and C.A.O.; Sheila K. Davidson, Exec. V.P. and Genl. Counsel; Eileen T. Slevin, Sr. V.P. and C.I.O.; Susan A. Thrope, Sr. V.P. and Corp. Secy.
Board of directors: Theodore A. Mathas, Chair.; Gary E. Wendlandt, Vice-Chair.; Betty C. Alewine; Robert M. Baylis; Ralph de la Vega; Mark L. Feidler; Kent B. Foster; Christina A. Gold; Conrad A. Harper; S. Thomas Moser; Joseph W. Prueher; Thomas C. Schievelbein; William G. Walter
Subsidiaries: Institutional Capital Corp., Chicago, IL; MacKay-Shields Financial Corp., New York, NY; Madison Capital Funding, Chicago, IL; New York Life Insurance and Annuity Corporation, New York, NY; New York Life International, Inc., New York, NY; New York Life Investment, Parsippany, NJ; NYLIFE Insurance Co. of Arizona, Scottsdale, AZ
International operations: Argentina; China; Hong Kong; India; Mexico; South Korea; Taiwan; Thailand
Giving statement: Giving through the New York Life Insurance Company Contributions Program and the New York Life Foundation.
Company EIN: 135582869

New York Life Insurance Company Contributions Program

51 Madison Ave.
New York, NY 10010-1603 (212) 576-7000
URL: http://www.newyorklife.com/

Purpose and activities: As a complement to its foundation, New York Life also makes charitable contributions to nonprofit organizations directly.
Fields of interest: Mental health, grief/bereavement counseling; Safety/disasters, volunteer services; Recreation, camps; Athletics/sports, amateur leagues; Athletics/sports, baseball; Children/youth, services; Human services, financial counseling.
Type of support: Advocacy; Donated equipment; Employee volunteer services; Sponsorships.
Geographic limitations: Giving primarily in areas of company operations.
Number of staff: 5 full-time professional; 1 full-time support.

New York Life Foundation

51 Madison Ave.
New York, NY 10010-1655 (212) 576-7341
E-mail: NYLFoundation@newyorklife.com; Additional tel.: (212) 576-3466; URL: http://www.newyorklife.com/foundation

Establishment information: Established in 1979 in NY.
Donor: New York Life Insurance Co.
Contact: Christine Park, Pres.
Financial data (yr. ended 12/31/11): Assets, $81,583,648 (M); gifts received, $113,000; expenditures, $12,756,640; qualifying distributions, $12,724,855; giving activities include $11,535,843 for 279 grants (high: $34,500; low: $500) and $1,179,766 for 2,171 employee matching gifts.
Purpose and activities: The foundation supports organizations and programs that benefit young people, particularly in the areas of mentoring, safe places to learn and grow, educational enhancement opportunities, and childhood bereavement.
Fields of interest: Elementary/secondary education; Child development, education; Education, reading; Education; Mental health, grief/bereavement counseling; Recreation, camps; Boys & girls clubs; Youth development, adult & child programs; Youth development, citizenship; Youth development Children/youth; Children; Economically disadvantaged.
International interests: Mexico.
Programs:
Community Impact Grants: The foundation awards grants to nonprofit organizations that have a personal involvement with a New York Life employee; address the needs of the local community; and demonstrate New York Life's commitment to being the company of the community. Preference is given to organizations involved with childhood bereavement. Grants range from $5,000 to $25,000.
Educational Matching Gifts: The foundation matches contributions made by employees, agents, and retirees of New York Life to educational institutions on a two-for-one basis from $25 to $100 for the first $100 per donor per institution. All other gifts are matched on a one-for-one basis up to $3,000 per individual donor, per year, and up to $5,000 per council agent or senior level executive, per year.
Family Scholars Program—National Merit Finalists: The foundation awards four-year $2,000 college scholarships to children of employees and agents of New York Life who qualify as National Merit finalists. The program is administered by the National Merit Scholarship Corp.
Family Scholars Program—Scholarship America: The foundation awards four-year college scholarships from $1,000 to $3,000 to children of employees and agents of New York Life. The program is administered by Scholarship America, Inc.
Nurturing the Children—Childhood Bereavement: Through the Childhood Bereavement program, the foundation promotes increased awareness, education, and services to youth, their families and communities affected by loss.
Nurturing the Children—Educational Enhancement: The foundation supports programs designed to enhance and augment classroom instruction during the critical out-of-school hours; and prepare young people for higher education and

the workplace and equip them to be responsible citizens.

Volunteers for Life - Individual Grant Program: The foundation awards grants of up to $500 to local organizations with which employees of New York Life volunteer at least 60 hours within a year, and grants of up to $1,000 to organizations designed to serve children.

Volunteers for Life - Team Grant Program: The foundation awards grants of $500 to $10,000 to nonprofit organizations with which teams of at least five employees, agents, and/or retirees of New York Life volunteer at least 40 hours. Preference is given to organizations serving children.

Type of support: Continuing support; Curriculum development; Employee matching gifts; Employee volunteer services; Employee-related scholarships; General/operating support; Program development.

Geographic limitations: Giving primarily in New York and Westchester County, NY; giving also to national organizations serving two or more of the following cities and regions: Phoenix, AZ, Los Angeles, Sacramento, San Francisco, and San Ramon, CA, Denver, CO, Washington, DC, Fort Lauderdale, Miami, and Tampa, FL, Atlanta, GA, Chicago, IL, Kansas City, KS, Boston and Westwood, MA, Detroit, MI, Minneapolis, MN, Clinton, Hunterdon, and Morris counties, and Edison, and Parsippany, NJ, Cleveland, OH, Philadelphia, PA, Austin, Dallas, and Houston, TX, Salt Lake City, UT, Richmond, VA, Seattle, WA, and Mexico.

Support limitations: No support for religious or sectarian organizations not of direct benefit to the entire community, or fraternal, social, professional, veterans', athletic, or discriminatory organizations. No grants to individuals (except for employee-related scholarships), or for seminars, conferences, or trips, endowments, memorials, or capital campaigns, fundraising events, telethons, races, or other benefits, goodwill advertising, or basic or applied research.

Publications: Annual report; Application guidelines; Grants list.

Application information: Applications accepted. Community Impact Grants must be initiated by a New York Life employee. A full proposal may be requested at a later date. Interviews and site visits may be requested. Organizations receiving support are asked to submit progress reports. Application form required.

Initial approach: Complete online application form
Board meeting date(s): Apr. and Nov.
Deadline(s): None
Final notification: 2 to 3 months for regular grants

Officers and Directors:* Theodore A. Mathas*, Chair.; Christine M. Park*, Pres.; Jefferson C. Boyce, Sr. V.P., Investments; Michael J. Oliviero, 1st V.P., Tax; Richard Witterschein, 1st V.P., Investments; Catherine A. Marrion, V.P. and Secy.; Nidhi Incantalupo, V.P., Investments; Kenneth Roman, Corp. V.P. and Cont.; Frank Boccio; Cynthia Bolker; Sheila K. Davidson; Lance Laverne.

Number of staff: 5 full-time professional; 1 full-time support.

EIN: 132989476

Selected grants: The following grants are a representative sample of this grantmaker's funding activity:
$810,000 to Developmental Studies Center, Oakland, CA, 2011.
$417,000 to United Ways of the Greater New York, New Jersey and Connecticut Tri-State Area, New York, NY, 2011.
$260,000 to Boys and Girls Clubs of America, Atlanta, GA, 2011.
$250,000 to American Museum of Natural History, New York, NY, 2011.
$250,000 to Tragedy Assistance Program for Survivors, Washington, DC, 2011.
$150,000 to Childrens Aid Society, New York, NY, 2011.
$100,000 to Classroom, Inc., New York, NY, 2011.
$5,000 to Robertas House, Baltimore, MD, 2011.
$3,000 to United Way of Northeast Florida, Jacksonville, FL, 2011.
$2,000 to Boy Scouts of America, Northern Star Council, Saint Paul, MN, 2011. For volunteer grant.

2689
New York Road Runners, Inc.
9 E. 89th St.
New York, NY 10128-0602 (212) 860-4455

Company URL: http://www.nyrr.org
Establishment information: Established in 1958.
Company type: Membership organization
Business activities: Operates membership organization.
Business type (SIC): Membership organization/miscellaneous
Corporate officers: George Hirsch, Chair.; Mary Wittenberg, Pres. and C.E.O.
Board of directors: George Hirsch, Chair.; Grant Behrman; Richard Byrne; Raul Damas; David Dittmann; Doug Feltman; Norman Goluskin; Nina Brody; Michael Gross; Juanne Renee Harris; Tom Labrecque, Jr.; John Legere; Claudia Malley; Adam Manus; Bryant McBride; James Milne; Martin Oppenheimer; Steve Pamon; Lucia Rodriguez; Steve Roth; Anne Beane Rudman; Norbert Sander; Eric A. Seiff; Allan Steinfeld; Toby Tanser; Mary Wittenberg
Giving statement: Giving through the New York Road Runners, Inc.

New York Road Runners, Inc.
9 E. 89th St.
New York, NY 10128-0602 (212) 860-4455
E-mail: customerservice@nyrr.org; URL: http://www.nyrr.org

Establishment information: Established in 1979 in NY.
Contact: Mary Wittenberg, Pres. and C.E.O.
Financial data (yr. ended 03/31/11): Revenue, $53,988,543; assets, $41,217,749 (M); gifts received, $16,416,685; expenditures, $52,226,065; program services expenses, $47,106,791; giving activities include $474,500 for grants (high: $208,340), $5,000 for grants to individuals and $46,588,908 for foundation-administered programs.
Purpose and activities: The organization's mission is to be the premier community running organization as evidenced by our economic, community, and charitable impact in the markets we serve.
Fields of interest: Public health, physical fitness; Recreation, community; Athletics/sports, training.
Geographic limitations: Giving on a national and international basis.
Officers and Directors:* George Hirsch, Chair.; Mary Wittenberg, Pres. and C.E.O.; Michael Capiraso, Exec. V.P., Opers., Admin., and Strategy; Peter Ciaccia, Exec. V.P., Event Devel. and Broadcast Production; Linda A. Franken, V.P., Finance and Admin.; Kerin Hempel, V.P., Strategy and Planning; Bob Laufer, V.P., Legal; Maria Note, V.P., Human Resources; Cliff Sperber, V.P., Youth and Community Svcs.; Ronnie Tucker, V.P., Mktg. and Digital; Michael Frankfurt, Secy.; Grant Behrman; Nina Brody; Richard Byrne; Raul Damas; David Dittmann; Doug Feltman; Norman Goluskin; Michael Gross; Juanne Renee Harris; and 15 additional directors.
EIN: 132949483

2690
The New York Times Company
620 8th Ave.
New York, NY 10018 (212) 556-1234
FAX: (212) 556-7389

Company URL: http://www.nytco.com
Establishment information: Established in 1896.
Company type: Public company
Company ticker symbol and exchange: NYT/NYSE
Business activities: Operates media company; creates, collects, and distributes news, information, and entertainment; publishes newspaper.
Business type (SIC): Newspaper publishing and/or printing; paper mills; radio and television broadcasting; computer services
Financial profile for 2012: Number of employees, 5,363; assets, $2,806,340,000; sales volume, $1,990,080,000; pre-tax net income, $263,300,000; expenses, $1,887,240,000; liabilities, $2,173,840,000
Fortune 1000 ranking: 2012—923rd in revenues, 678th in profits, and 770th in assets
Corporate officers: Arthur O. Sulzberger, Jr., Chair.; Michael Golden, Vice-Chair.; Mark Thompson, Pres. and C.E.O.; James M. Follo, Exec. V.P. and C.F.O.; Kenneth A. Richieri, Exec. V.P. and Genl. Counsel
Board of directors: Arthur O. Sulzberger, Jr., Chair.; Michael Golden, Vice-Chair.; Raul E. Cesan; Robert E. Denham; Steven B. Green; Carolyn D. Greenspon; Joichi Ito; James A. Kohlberg; David E. Liddle; Ellen R. Marram; Brian P. McAndrews; Thomas Middelhoff; Mark Thompson; Doreen A. Toben
Subsidiary: About, Inc., New York, NY
Divisions: About Group, New York, NY; The New York Times Media Group, Memphis, TN; Regional Media Group, New York, NY
International operations: Brazil; Italy; United Kingdom
Giving statement: Giving through the New York Times Company Foundation Inc. and the New York Times Neediest Cases Fund, Inc.
Company EIN: 131102020

The New York Times Company Foundation Inc.
620 Eighth Ave., 17th Fl.
New York, NY 10018-1618
FAX: (212) 556-1979; URL: http://www.nytco.com/foundation
Additional URL: http://www.nytimes.com/scholarship

Establishment information: Incorporated in 1955 in NY.
Donor: The New York Times Co.
Financial data (yr. ended 12/31/11): Assets, $252,090 (M); gifts received, $735,000; expenditures, $419,253; qualifying distributions, $419,253; giving activities include $68,640 for 1 grant.
Purpose and activities: The foundation manages The New York Times Neediest Cases Fund and awards college scholarships to high school seniors located in New York, City through The New York Times College Scholarship Program.
Fields of interest: Higher education; Human services.

Program:
New York Times College Scholarship Program: The foundation annually awards four-year college scholarships of up to $7,500 to six New York City public high school students who have overcome exceptional hardship including financial, racial, ethnic, language, or other obstacles to achieve excellence. Preference is given to students whose parents did not graduate from a four-year college or university. The award includes a summer internship at the New York Times, educational and job counseling, mentoring, cultural and civic activities, and a laptop computer.
Type of support: Continuing support; Scholarship funds; Scholarships—to individuals.
Geographic limitations: Giving primarily in areas of company operations, with emphasis on the New York, NY, metropolitan area.
Support limitations: No support for religious organizations not of direct benefit to the entire community. No grants to individuals (except for New York Times College Scholars), or for capital campaigns, or health, drug, or alcohol therapy purposes; no loans.
Application information: Applications not accepted. Unsolicited requests for funds not accepted.
Officers and Directors:* Janet L. Robinson*, Chair.; Michael Golden*, Pres.; James M Follo*, Sr. V.P., Finance; R. Anthony Benten, Sr. V.P.; Laurena L. Emhoff, V.P. and Treas.; Desiree Dancy, V.P.; Kenneth A. Richieri, Secy.
Number of staff: 2 full-time support.
EIN: 136066955
Selected grants: The following grants are a representative sample of this grantmaker's funding activity:
$75,000 to American Museum of Natural History, New York, NY, 2009. For general operating support.
$29,877 to National Merit Scholarship Corporation, Evanston, IL, 2009. For Achievement Scholarships for minority high school graduates and four-year college Merit Scholarship for employee children.
$20,000 to Committee to Protect Journalists, New York, NY, 2009. To create permanent endowment to cover core expenses.

The New York Times Neediest Cases Fund, Inc.

620 8th Ave.
New York, NY 10018-1618 (212) 556-1137
FAX: (212) 730-0927; Toll-free tel.: (800) 381-0075; URL: http://www.nytimes.com/neediest

Establishment information: Established in 1941 in NY.
Donors: The New York Times Co.; and readers of the New York Times.
Contact: Michael Golden, Pres.
Financial data (yr. ended 02/28/11): Revenue, $8,210,058; assets, $51,204,662 (M); gifts received, $5,543,976; expenditures, $9,433,961; program services expenses, $9,433,961; giving activities include $9,060,073 for 13 grants (high: $1,539,588; low: $83,333), $359,305 for 134 grants to individuals and $14,583 for foundation-administered programs.
Purpose and activities: The fund seeks to give direct assistance to troubled children, families, and elders in the New York City metropolitan area.
Fields of interest: Philanthropy/voluntarism, single organization support.
Type of support: Annual campaigns; Emergency funds; Grants to individuals; In-kind gifts.
Geographic limitations: Giving limited to the New York, NY metropolitan area.
Application information: Applications not accepted. Contributes only to pre-selected organizations.
Officers: Janet Robinson*, Chair.; Michael Golden*, Pres.; R. Anthony Benten*, Sr. V.P.; James M. Folio*, Sr. V.P.; Kenneth A. Richieri*, Sr. V.P. and Secy.; Desiree Dancy*, V.P.; Laurena L. Emhoff*, V.P. and Treas.
Number of staff: 1 full-time professional; 4 full-time support; 2 part-time support.
EIN: 136066063

2691
New York Yankees Partnership

Yankee Stadium, 1 E. 161st St.
Bronx, NY 10451-2128 (718) 293-4300
FAX: (718) 293-8431

Company URL: http://newyork.yankees.mlb.com
Establishment information: Established in 1903.
Company type: Private company
Business activities: Operates professional baseball club.
Business type (SIC): Commercial sports
Corporate officers: Harold Steinbrenner, Co-Chair.; Henry G. Steinbrenner, Co-Chair.; Jennifer Steinbrenner Swindal, Co.-Vice-Chair.; Jessica Steinbrenner, Co.-Vice-Chair.; Joan Steinbrenner, Co.-Vice-Chair.; Randy Levine, Esq., Pres.; Lonn A. Trost, Esq., C.O.O.; Robert Brown, V.P. and C.F.O.; Deborah A. Tymon, Sr. V.P., Mktg.; Michael J. Tusiani, Sr. V.P., Corp. Sales; Derrick Baio, Cont.
Board of directors: Harold Steinbrenner, Co-Chair.; Henry Steinbrenner, Co-Chair.; Jessica Steinbrenner, Co. Vice-Chair.; Joan Steinbrenner, Co. Vice-Chair.; Jennifer Steinbrenner Swindal, Co. Vice-Chair.
Giving statement: Giving through the New York Yankees Corporate Giving Program, the New York Yankees Foundation, Inc., and the New York Yankees Tampa Foundation, Inc.

The New York Yankees Corporate Giving Program

Yankee Stadium
E. 161st St. and River Ave.
Bronx, NY 10451-2128 (718) 293-4300
URL: http://newyork.yankees.mlb.com/nyy/community/yankees_in_the_community.jsp

Purpose and activities: The New York Yankees makes charitable contributions to nonprofit organizations involved with at-risk youth. Support is given primarily in the New York, New York, metropolitan area.
Fields of interest: Elementary/secondary education; Health care, blood supply; Health care, patient services; Food services; Disasters, preparedness/services; Youth development; Children/youth, services.
Type of support: General/operating support; In-kind gifts; Loaned talent.
Geographic limitations: Giving primarily in the New York, NY, metropolitan area; giving also to national organizations.

New York Yankees Foundation, Inc.

1 E. 161st St.
Bronx, NY 10451-2100 (212) 579-4491

Contact: Jennifer Steinbrenner Swindal, Pres.
Financial data (yr. ended 04/30/11): Revenue, $2,140,924; assets, $5,740,650 (M); gifts received, $38,091; expenditures, $2,725,858; program services expenses, $2,607,265; giving activities include $2,417,397 for 95 grants (high: $150,000; low: $6,000) and $60,000 for grants to individuals.
Purpose and activities: The organization promotes, arranges, and holds amateur athletic contests, exhibitions, and competitions as well as contributes toward and provides for the promotion and encouragement of public interest in amateur sports, particularly baseball.
Fields of interest: Athletics/sports, baseball.
Type of support: Grants to individuals.
Officers and Directors:* Jennifer Steinbrenner Swindal*, Pres.; Lonn Trost*, V.P. and Secy.; Robert Brown*, Treas.; Derrick Baio; Anthony Bruno; Randy Levine; Brian Smith; Harold Z. Steinbrenner; Henry G. Steinbrenner.
EIN: 136089577

New York Yankees Tampa Foundation, Inc.

1 Steinbrenner Dr.
Tampa, FL 33614-7064 (813) 875-7753

Establishment information: Established in FL.
Contact: Jennifer Steinbrenner Swindal, Pres.
Financial data (yr. ended 04/30/11): Revenue, $1,107,199; assets, $2,342,391 (M); gifts received, $20,057; expenditures, $1,028,610; program services expenses, $1,003,225; giving activities include $398,643 for 16 grants (high: $38,372; low: $6,000).
Purpose and activities: The foundation promotes, arranges, and holds amateur athletic contests, exhibitions, and competitions and contributes towards and provides for the promotion of and encouragement of public interest in amateur sports, particularly baseball.
Fields of interest: Athletics/sports, baseball.
Type of support: Grants to individuals.
Geographic limitations: Giving primarily to Tampa, FL.
Officers and Directors:* Jennifer Steinbrenner Swindal*, Pres.; Harold Z. Steinbrenner*, V.P.; Henry G. Steinbrenner*, V.P.; Norm Stallings*, Secy.; Derrick Baio*, Treas.; Anthony Bruno; Monsignor L. Higgins; Malio Lavarone; George Levy; Philip A. McNiff; Hon. Manuel Menedez; Jessica Steinbrenner; James W. Warren III.
EIN: 593205804

2692
Neways, Inc.

2089 W. Neways Dr.
Springville, UT 84663 (801) 418-2000
FAX: (801) 418-2195

Company URL: http://www.neways.com
Establishment information: Established in 1992.
Company type: Private company
Business activities: Operates personal care products company.
Business type (SIC): Soaps, cleaners, and toiletries
Financial profile for 2011: Number of employees, 1,100
Corporate officers: Robert Conlee, Chair. and C.E.O.; Scott St. Clair, C.E.O.; Kevin Givan, C.I.O.; Will Burgess, V.P., Opers.; Will Burgess, V.P., Finance; Chris Crump, Genl. Counsel and C.A.O.
Board of director: Robert Conlee, Chair.
Giving statement: Giving through the Neways, Inc. Contributions Program.

Neways, Inc. Contributions Program

2089 Neways Dr.
Springville, UT 84663 (801) 418-2000
URL: http://neways.com

2693
The Newburyport Five Cents Savings Bank

63 State St.
Newburyport, MA 01950-6615
(978) 462-3136

Company URL: http://www.newburyportbank.com
Establishment information: Established in 1854.
Company type: Mutual company
Business activities: Operates savings bank.
Business type (SIC): Savings institutions
Corporate officers: Richard A. Eaton, Chair.; Janice C. Morse, Pres. and C.E.O.; Timothy L. Felter, V.P. and C.F.O.; Sandra Licciardo, V.P. and Cont.; Lynne A. Carter, Clerk
Board of director: Richard A. Eaton, Chair.
Giving statement: Giving through the Newburyport Five Cents Savings Charitable Foundation Inc.

Newburyport Five Cents Savings Charitable Foundation Inc.

63 State St.
Newburyport, MA 01950-6615 (978) 462-3136
E-mail: jmorse@newburyportbank.com; URL: http://www.newburyportbank.com/home/about-us/charitable-foundation

Establishment information: Established in 2003 in MA.
Donor: Newburyport Five Cents Savings Bank.
Contact: Janice C. Morse, Treas.
Financial data (yr. ended 12/31/11): Assets, $3,492,361 (M); expenditures, $174,064; qualifying distributions, $174,064; giving activities include $172,494 for 19 grants (high: $25,000; low: $2,000).
Purpose and activities: The foundation supports arts associations and organizations involved with education, water conservation, and human services.
Fields of interest: Arts, association; Education, reading; Education; Environment, water resources; YM/YWCAs & YM/YWHAs; Youth, services; Residential/custodial care, hospices; Aging, centers/services; Human services.
Type of support: Building/renovation; Capital campaigns; Employee matching gifts; Equipment; Program development.
Geographic limitations: Giving limited to areas of company operations in the greater Newburyport, MA, area.
Application information: Applications accepted. Application form not required. Applicants should submit the following:
1) copy of IRS Determination Letter
2) brief history of organization and description of its mission
3) geographic area to be served
4) listing of board of directors, trustees, officers and other key people and their affiliations
5) detailed description of project and amount of funding requested
6) copy of current year's organizational budget and/or project budget
7) listing of additional sources and amount of support

Initial approach: Proposal
Deadline(s): None

Officers and Directors:* Janice C. Morse*, Pres.; Lynne A. Carter, Clerk; Timothy L. Felter, Treas.; James Brian Butler; Charles W. Morse III; Edward Shephard; Michael Webber.
EIN: 200318941
Selected grants: The following grants are a representative sample of this grantmaker's funding activity:
$25,000 to Greater Newburyport Opportunities, Newburyport, MA, 2010.
$15,000 to Newburyport Education Foundation, Newburyport, MA, 2010.
$8,200 to Jumpstart Youth Connection, Amesbury, MA, 2010.
$5,000 to Salvation Army of Newburyport, Newburyport, MA, 2010.

2694
Newell Rubbermaid Inc.

(formerly Newell Co.)
3 Glenlake Pkwy.
Atlanta, GA 30328 (770) 418-7000
FAX: (770) 677-8662

Company URL: http://www.newellrubbermaid.com
Establishment information: Established in 1903.
Company type: Public company
Company ticker symbol and exchange: NWL/NYSE
Business activities: Manufactures and markets household products, hardware and home furnishings, and office products.
Business type (SIC): Glass/pressed or blown; furniture and fixtures/miscellaneous; rubber and miscellaneous plastics products; cutlery, hand and edge tools, and hardware; pens, pencils, and art supplies
Financial profile for 2012: Number of employees, 18,300; assets, $6,222,000,000; sales volume, $5,902,700,000; pre-tax net income, $565,900,000; expenses, $5,261,700,000; liabilities, $4,225,300,000
Fortune 1000 ranking: 2012—433rd in revenues, 395th in profits, and 532nd in assets
Forbes 2000 ranking: 2012—1300th in sales, 1287th in profits, and 1745th in assets
Corporate officers: Michael T. Cowhig, Chair.; Michael B. Polk, Pres. and C.E.O.; Douglas L. Martin, C.F.O.; William A. Burke III, C.O.O.; Gordon C. Steele, Sr. V.P. and C.I.O.; John Sitpancich, Corp. Secy.
Board of directors: Michael T. Cowhig, Chair.; Thomas E. Clarke, Ph.D.; Kevin Conroy; Scott S. Cowen; Elizabeth Cuthbert-Millett; Domenico De Sole; Ignacio Perez Lizaur; Cynthia A. Montgomery; Michael B. Polk; Steven J. Strobel; Michael A. Todman; Raymond G. Viault
Subsidiaries: Intercraft Co., Taylor, TX; Newell Operating Co., Freeport, IL; Rubbermaid Incorporated, Wooster, OH; Sanford, L.P., Bellwood, IL
Plants: Peachtree City, GA; Rockford, IL; Fenton, MI; Medina, NY; High Point, NC; Hudson, Lancaster, Toledo, OH; Elverson, Monaca, PA; Lewisburg, Memphis, TN; Winchester, VA; Madison, Manitowoc, Milwaukee, WI
International operations: Australia; Barbados; Belgium; Brazil; Canada; Cayman Islands; Colombia; Denmark; France; Germany; Italy; Japan; Luxembourg; Mauritius; Mexico; Netherlands; Scotland; United Kingdom; Venezuela
Giving statement: Giving through the Newell Rubbermaid Inc. Corporate Giving Program.
Company EIN: 363514169

Newell Rubbermaid Inc. Corporate Giving Program

(formerly Newell Co. Contributions Program)
3 Glenlake Pkwy.
Atlanta, GA 30328
E-mail: community@newellco.com; URL: http://www.newellrubbermaid.com/public/Corporate-Responsibility.aspx

Purpose and activities: Newell Rubbermaid makes charitable contributions to nonprofit organizations involved with childhood education and job training, with emphasis on women, seniors, and people with disabilities, and disaster relief. Support is given primarily in areas of company operations in Bentonville, Arkansas, Weston, Florida, Atlanta, Georgia, Oakbrook and Freeport, Illinois, East Longmeadow, Massachusetts, and Huntersville, North Carolina; and in Argentina, Australia, Austria, Brazil, Canada, Chile, Colombia, Denmark, France, Germany, Hong Kong, India, Ireland, Italy, Japan, Malaysia, Mexico, New Zealand, Poland, Puerto Rico, South Korea, Switzerland, Taiwan, Thailand, Turkey, United Arab Emirates, United Kingdom, and Venezuela.
Fields of interest: Elementary/secondary education; Education, early childhood education; Child development, education; Vocational education; Employment; Safety/disasters Aging; Disabilities, people with; Women.
Programs:

Getting Ahead: Newell Rubbermaid supports programs designed to promote education and advancement of the professionals who use Rubbermaid products. Special emphasis is directed toward trade, technical, and vocational schools focused on cosmetology, culinary arts, hotel and restaurant management, carpentry, electrical, HVAC, and interior design; child development programs; and women, seniors, and disable-to-work programs.

Giving Back: Newell Rubbermaid supports programs designed to enrich the lives of its employees and consumers through activism and awareness. Special emphasis is directed toward cause-marketing initiatives designed to promote education and women's health; and the connections between consumers, employees, and their communities through national charity walks and runs.

Growing Up: Newell Rubbermaid supports programs designed to provide infants and children with the tools they need to succeed to adulthood. Special emphasis is directed toward child development and pre-school education; and K-12 in-classroom programs.

Type of support: Cause-related marketing; Employee volunteer services; In-kind gifts; Loaned talent.
Geographic limitations: Giving primarily in areas of company operations in Bentonville, AR, Weston, FL, Atlanta, GA, Oakbrook, and Freeport, IL, East Longmeadow, MA, Huntersville, NC, and PR, and in Argentina, Australia, Austria, Brazil, Canada, Chile, Colombia, Denmark, France, Germany, Hong Kong, India, Ireland, Italy, Japan, Malaysia, Mexico, New Zealand, Poland, South Korea, Switzerland, Taiwan, Thailand, Turkey, United Arab Emirates, United Kingdom, and Venezuela.
Application information: Applications not accepted. Applications process is currently closed and will resume at a future date.

2695
Newfield Exploration Company
4 Waterway Sq. Pl., Ste. 100
The Woodlands, TX 77380 (281) 210-5100
FAX: (281) 210-5101

Company URL: http://www.newfld.com/
Establishment information: Established in 1989.
Company type: Public company
Company ticker symbol and exchange: NFX/NYSE
Business activities: Conducts crude oil and natural gas exploration, development, and acquisition activities.
Business type (SIC): Extraction/oil and gas
Financial profile for 2012: Number of employees, 1,643; assets, $7,912,000,000; sales volume, $2,567,000,000; pre-tax net income, -$988,000,000; expenses, $3,534,000,000; liabilities, $5,132,000,000
Fortune 1000 ranking: 2012—798th in revenues, 986th in profits, and 455th in assets
Corporate officers: Lee K. Boothby, Chair., Pres., and C.E.O.; Gary D. Packer, Exec. V.P. and C.O.O.; Terry W. Rathert, Exec. V.P. and C.F.O.; Deanna L. Jones, V.P., Human Resources; Susan G. Riggs, Treas.; John D. Marziotti, Genl. Counsel and Secy.
Board of directors: Lee K. Boothby, Chair.; Pamela J. Gardner; John Randolph Kemp III; Joseph H. Netherland; Howard H. Newman; Thomas G. Ricks; Juanita F. Romans; Charles E. Shultz; Richard K. Stoneburner; J. Terry Strange
Subsidiaries: Newfield Exploration Mid-Continent Inc., Tulsa, OK; Newfield Gulf Coast Inc., Houston, TX
Giving statement: Giving through the Newfield Foundation.
Company EIN: 721133047

Newfield Foundation
363 N. Sam Houston Pkwy. E., Ste. 2020
Houston, TX 77060-2424 (281) 847-6000
URL: http://www.newfld.com/foundation.aspx

Establishment information: Established in 2001 in TX.
Donor: Newfield Exploration Co.
Contact: Coral Morozoff
Financial data (yr. ended 12/31/11): Assets, $15,470,321 (M); gifts received, $1,200,000; expenditures, $777,348; qualifying distributions, $639,000; giving activities include $639,000 for grants.
Purpose and activities: The foundation supports programs designed to promote the environment, medical, cultural arts, and community services.
Fields of interest: Museums; Arts; Education; Environment; Health care; Big Brothers/Big Sisters; Human services.
Type of support: Annual campaigns; Capital campaigns; General/operating support; Program development.
Geographic limitations: Giving primarily in areas of company operations in Tulsa, OK and Houston, TX.
Support limitations: No grants to individuals.
Publications: Application guidelines.
Application information: Applications accepted. Applicants should submit the following:
1) copy of IRS Determination Letter
2) listing of board of directors, trustees, officers and other key people and their affiliations
3) detailed description of project and amount of funding requested
4) copy of current year's organizational budget and/ or project budget

Initial approach: Telephone or submit an online application request
Deadline(s): Sept. 30
Final notification: Jan.

Officers and Directors:* Lee K. Boothby*, Pres.; Susan G. Riggs, V.P. and Treas.; Terry W. Rathert*, V.P.; Coral Morozoff, Secy.; Dolores Vasquez, Exec. Dir.; George Dunn; David A. Trice.
EIN: 760663978
Selected grants: The following grants are a representative sample of this grantmaker's funding activity:
$25,000 to Big Brothers Big Sisters of Greater Houston, Houston, TX, 2009.
$20,000 to Denver Rescue Mission, Denver, CO, 2009.
$10,000 to Houston Food Bank, Houston, TX, 2009.
$5,000 to Houston Area Womens Center, Houston, TX, 2009.
$5,000 to Houston Zoo, Houston, TX, 2009.
$2,500 to Houston Museum of Natural Science, Houston, TX, 2009.

2696
J. C. Newman Cigar Company
2701 N. 16th St.
P.O. Box 76246
Tampa, FL 33605-2616 (813) 248-2124

Company URL: http://www.jcnewmanonline.com
Establishment information: Established in 1895.
Company type: Private company
Business activities: Produces cigars.
Business type (SIC): Tobacco products—cigars
Financial profile for 2010: Number of employees, 100
Corporate officers: Stanford J. Newman, Chair.; Eric Newman, Pres.; Herzog Karl, V.P., Opers.
Board of director: Stanford J. Newman, Chair.
Giving statement: Giving through the Newman Foundation, Inc.

Newman Foundation, Inc.
P.O. Box 2030
Tampa, FL 33601-2030

Establishment information: Established in 1963.
Donors: J.C. Newman Cigar Co.; M&N Cigar Manufacturers, Inc.; Tampa Products Co.
Financial data (yr. ended 09/30/11): Assets, $302,257 (M); gifts received, $150,000; expenditures, $73,181; qualifying distributions, $73,108; giving activities include $73,047 for 21 grants (high: $18,790; low: $100).
Purpose and activities: The foundation supports organizations involved with arts and culture, education, health, and human services.
Fields of interest: Education; Animals/wildlife; Human services.
Type of support: General/operating support; Scholarship funds.
Geographic limitations: Giving primarily in Tampa, FL.
Support limitations: No grants to individuals.
Application information: Applications not accepted. Unsolicited requests for funds not accepted.
Officers: Shira D. Martin, Treas.; Eric Newman, Mgr.
EIN: 596150341

2697
Newman's Own, Inc.
246 Post Rd. E.
Westport, CT 06880 (203) 222-0136

Company URL: http://www.newmansown.com
Establishment information: Established in 1982.
Company type: Private company
Business activities: Produces salad dressings, pasta sauces, salsas, popcorn, lemonade, and steak sauce.
Business type (SIC): Specialty foods/canned, frozen, and preserved; beverages; miscellaneous prepared foods
Corporate officers: Thomas Indoe, Pres. and C.O.O.; Eric Fuller, V.P. and Treas.; Jeff Smith, V.P., Opers.; David Best, V.P., Mktg.
Subsidiary: Newman's Own Organics, Inc., Aptos, CA
Giving statement: Giving through the Newman's Own, Inc. Corporate Giving Program and the Newman's Own Foundation.

Newman's Own Foundation
790 Farmington Ave., No. 4B
Farmington, CT 06032-2300
E-mail: info@newmansownfoundation.org;
URL: http://www.newmansownfoundation.org/

Establishment information: Established in 2004 in DE and CT.
Donors: Paul L. Newman†; Newman's Own.
Financial data (yr. ended 12/31/11): Assets, $222,281,733 (M); expenditures, $30,435,598; qualifying distributions, $30,050,627; giving activities include $27,350,169 for 667 grants (high: $1,381,227; low: $1,000).
Purpose and activities: Newman's Own Foundation funds a broad geographic range of 501(c) 3 nonprofits that fit within its focus areas (listed under Program Areas). In addition, the Foundation supports grantees that: Demonstrate potential for significant impact or growth; Present innovative and effective model programs with potential for replication; Encourage philanthropy by leveraging Foundation resources to stimulate giving from other sources; Possess existing or potential for strong organizational leadership/governance; Demonstrate fiscal responsibility.
Fields of interest: Agriculture/food, alliance/ advocacy; Nutrition; Disasters, preparedness/ services; Children/youth, services; Civil/human rights; Community/economic development; Voluntarism promotion; Philanthropy/voluntarism; Public affairs, equal rights; Military/veterans' organizations; Leadership development Children; Military/veterans; Economically disadvantaged.
Programs:
Campus Community Service Challenge (NOF Challenge): The foundation, in partnership with American East Conference, invites nine service-focused student groups who are affiliated with a nonprofit organization to apply for a Campus Community Service Challenge grant. Awardees are selected based on the student group's involvement with the nonprofit; the degree in which that involvement reflects Paul Newman's philanthropic spirit; and the mission and programs of the nonprofit, the populations and purposes it serves, and the impact the foundation's grant will have. Grants range from $5,000 to $25,000. Visit URL http://newmansownfoundation.org/challenge/ for more information.
Children with Life-Limiting Conditions: The foundation supports programs designed to enhance the quality of life for children with life-limiting

medical conditions and for children for whom the experience of childhood has been disrupted by circumstances beyond their control.

Community Partners Program: The foundation awards grants to nonprofit organizations recommended by a group of advisors. This program was created by Paul Newman who annually invited grant recommendations from people he knew and trusted.

Empowerment: The foundation supports programs designed to empower people to overcome extraordinary circumstances; provide equal access to human rights; and contribute to the development of a civil society.

Encouraging Philanthropy: The foundation supports programs designed to promote the practice of philanthropy and/or rely on philanthropic support to fulfill their missions.

Nutrition: The foundation supports programs designed to implement model solutions to issues of hunger and nutrition for underserved communities.

Type of support: Fellowships; General/operating support; Management development/capacity building; Matching/challenge support; Program development.
Geographic limitations: Giving on a national and international basis.
Support limitations: No support for No funding goes to: organizations that discriminate on any basis; private foundations, Type III supporting organizations, or other organizations that require expenditure responsibility by the Foundation; direct grants to individuals. No funding goes to: specific religious activities or beliefs; lobbying or political activities; major research projects; any commercial business purpose; any litigation that is underway, contemplated, or completed; endowments, building campaigns, special events, or annual funds.
Application information: Applications not accepted. Grant process is by invitation only.
Officers and Directors:* Joanne Woodward Newman*, Chair.; Robert H. Forrester*, C.E.O. and Pres.; Brian Murphy*, V.P. and Treas.; Clea Newman Soderlund*, V.P.; Jamie Gerard, Esq.*, Secy.; Robert Patricelli*.
EIN: 061606588
Selected grants: The following grants are a representative sample of this grantmaker's funding activity:
$2,000,000 to Rockefeller Philanthropy Advisors, Philanthropic Collaborative, New York, NY, 2011. For NOF Donor Advised Fund.
$1,600,000 to Association of Hole in the Wall Camps, Westport, CT, 2011. For program services.
$700,000 to Connecticut Public Broadcasting, Hartford, CT, 2011. For Individual Grants to the Following: Chan. 13, WTTW, TPT, KCET, WETA, KCTS.
$625,000 to Safe Water Network, Westport, CT, 2011. For Strategic Initiative and Program.
$430,000 to Shining Hope for Communities, Middletown, CT, 2011. For program services.
$250,000 to Food Research and Action Center, Washington, DC, 2011. For Breakfast in the Classroom Initiative.
$50,000 to Greater Hartford Community Foundation, Hartford, CT, 2011. For CT Philanthropy Day the Travelers Championships.
$30,000 to Central Vermont Community Action Council, Barre, VT, 2011. For Vermont Irene Flood Relief Fund.
$25,000 to Applied Behavioral Rehabilitation and Research Institute, Bridgeport, CT, 2011. For Female Soldiers Forgotten Heroes.
$20,000 to Happiness is Camping, Bronx, NY, 2011. For 10 camperships.

2698
Newmont Mining Corporation

6363 S. Fiddlers Green Cir., Ste. 800
Greenwood Village, CO 80111
(303) 863-7414
FAX: (303) 837-5837

Company URL: http://www.newmont.com
Establishment information: Established in 1921.
Company type: Public company
Company ticker symbol and exchange: NEM/NYSE
International Securities Identification Number: US6516391066
Business activities: Conducts gold exploration and production activities; conducts copper production activities.
Business type (SIC): Mining/gold and silver; mining/copper
Financial profile for 2012: Number of employees, 16,400; assets, $29,650,000,000; sales volume, $9,868,000,000; pre-tax net income, $3,114,000,000; expenses, $6,830,000,000; liabilities, $15,877,000,000
Fortune 1000 ranking: 2012—274th in revenues, 115th in profits, and 188th in assets
Forbes 2000 ranking: 2012—937th in sales, 344th in profits, and 745th in assets
Corporate officers: Vincent A. Calarco, Chair.; Gary J. Goldberg, Pres. and C.E.O.; Bill MacGowan, Exec. V.P., Human Resources and Comms.; Stephen P. Gottesfeld, Exec. V.P., Genl. Counsel, and Corp. Secy.; Chris Robison, Exec., Opers.; Gerald Gluscic, V.P. and C.I.O.; Thomas P. Mahoney, V.P. and Treas.; Christopher S. Howson, V.P. and Cont.
Board of directors: Vincent A. Calarco, Chair.; Bruce R. Brook; J. Kofi Bucknor; Joseph Carrabba; Noreen Doyle; Gary J. Goldberg; Veronica Hagen; Jane Nelson; Donald C. Roth; Simon R. Thompson
Subsidiaries: Battle Mountain Gold Company, Houston, TX; Newmont Exploration, Ltd., Tucson, AZ; Newmont Exploration, Ltd., Danbury, CT; Newmont Oil Co., Houston, TX; Resurrection Mining Co., New York, NY
International operations: Australia; Bermuda; Canada; Cyprus; France; Ghana; Malaysia; Netherlands; New Zealand; Romania; Singapore; United Kingdom
Giving statement: Giving through the Newmont Mining Corporation Contributions Program.
Company EIN: 841611629

Newmont Mining Corporation Contributions Program

6363 South Fiddler's Green Cir., Ste. 800
Greenwood Village, CO 80111-5011 (303) 863-7414
FAX: (303) 837-5837; URL: http://www.newmont.com/about/corporate-contributions

Purpose and activities: Newmont makes charitable contributions to nonprofit organizations involved with education, arts and sciences, welfare and human services, and environmental stewardship. Support is given primarily in areas of company operations in Colorado.
Fields of interest: Arts; Education; Environment; Health care; Youth, services; Human services; Science.
Type of support: Employee volunteer services; General/operating support.
Geographic limitations: Giving primarily in areas of company operations in CO.
Application information: Applications accepted.
Initial approach: Complete online application

2699
Newport Bancorp, Inc.

100 Bellevue Ave.
P.O. Box 210
Newport, RI 02840-3231 (401) 847-5500
FAX: (401) 847-5370

Company URL: http://www.newportfederal.com/
Establishment information: Established in 1888.
Company type: Public company
Company ticker symbol and exchange: NFSB/NASDAQ
Business activities: Operates federal savings bank.
Business type (SIC): Savings institutions
Financial profile for 2012: Number of employees, 83; assets, $449,410,000; pre-tax net income, $2,240,000; liabilities, $396,260,000
Corporate officers: Kevin M. McCarthy, Pres. and C.E.O.; Nino Moscardi, Exec. V.P. and C.O.O.; Bruce A. Walsh, Sr. V.P. and C.F.O.
Board of directors: Peter T. Crowley; William R. Harvey; Michael J. Hayes; Donald N. Kaull; Arthur H. Lathrop; Robert S. Lazar; Arthur P. MacAuley; Kevin M. McCarthy; Nino Moscardi; Kathleen A. Nealon; Alicia S. Quirk; Barbara Saccucci-Radebach
Giving statement: Giving through the Newportfed Charitable Foundation.
Company EIN: 204465271

Newportfed Charitable Foundation

100 Belleuve Ave.
Newport, RI 02840-3231 (401) 847-5500
FAX: (401) 849-2393;
E-mail: info@newportfederal.com; URL: http://www.newportfederal.com/community.html

Establishment information: Established in 2006 in RI.
Donor: Newport Bancorp, Inc.
Contact: Susan Oulette
Financial data (yr. ended 12/31/11): Assets, $3,430,316 (M); expenditures, $211,046; qualifying distributions, $200,550; giving activities include $200,550 for 195 grants (high: $10,000; low: $25).
Purpose and activities: The foundation supports bird preserves, festivals, and service clubs and organizations involved with education, health, crime and violence prevention, sports, and human services.
Fields of interest: Higher education; Education; Animals/wildlife, bird preserves; Health care; Crime/violence prevention; Athletics/sports, school programs; Recreation, fairs/festivals; Athletics/sports, amateur leagues; Athletics/sports, racquet sports; American Red Cross; YM/YWCAs & YM/YWHAs; Human services; Community development, service clubs.
Type of support: Annual campaigns; General/operating support; Scholarship funds; Sponsorships.
Geographic limitations: Giving primarily in RI.
Application information: Applications accepted. Application form not required. Applicants should submit the following:
1) name, address and phone number of organization
2) geographic area to be served
3) detailed description of project and amount of funding requested
4) contact person
5) listing of additional sources and amount of support

Initial approach: Letter
Deadline(s): None

Officers and Directors:* Kevin M. McCarthy*, Pres.; Judy Tucker*, Secy.; Bruce A. Walsh*, Treas.; Ray

Gilmore; Kelly Lee; Nino Moscardi; Carol Silven; Mark Stenning.
EIN: 205140473

2700
News Corporation

1211 Ave. of the Americas
New York, NY 10036 (212) 852-7017
FAX: (212) 852-7145

Company URL: http://www.newscorp.com
Establishment information: Established in 1922.
Company type: Public company
Company ticker symbol and exchange: NWS/NASDAQ
International Securities Identification Number: US65248E1047
Business activities: Operates global media conglomerate.
Business type (SIC): Newspaper publishing and/or printing
Financial profile for 2012: Number of employees, 48,000; assets, $5,663,000,000; sales volume, $33,706,000,000; pre-tax net income, $2,212,000,000; expenses, $31,494,000,000; liabilities, $31,979,000,000
Forbes 2000 ranking: 2012—276th in sales, 140th in profits, and 375th in assets
Corporate officers: Keith Rupert Murdoch, Chair. and C.E.O.; Chase Carey, Pres. and C.O.O.; David F. DeVoe, Sr. Exec. V.P. and C.F.O.; Gerson Zweifach, Sr. Exec. V.P. and Genl. Counsel
Board of directors: Keith Rupert Murdoch, Chair.; Jose Maria Aznar; Natalie Bancroft; Peter L. Barnes; James W. Breyer; Chase Carey; Elaine L. Chao; David F. DeVoe; Viet D. Dinh; Roderick I. Eddington; Joel I. Klein; James R. Murdoch; Lachlan K. Murdoch; Stanley S. Shuman; Arthur M. Siskind; Alvaro Uribe
Giving statement: Giving through the News Corporation Contributions Program.
Company EIN: 260075658

News Corporation Contributions Program

1211 Ave. of the Americas
New York, NY 10036

2701
News World Communications, Inc.

(also known as The Washington Times)
3600 New York Ave., N.E.
Washington, DC 20002-1949
(202) 636-3000

Company URL: http://www.washingtontimes.com
Establishment information: Established in 1976.
Company type: Subsidiary of a nonprofit
Business activities: Publishes newspapers.
Business type (SIC): Newspaper publishing and/or printing
Corporate officers: Chung Hwan Kwak, Chair. and Pres.; Keith Cooperrider, V.P. and C.F.O.
Board of director: Chung Hwan Kwak, Chair.
Subsidiary: United Press International, Inc., Washington, DC
Giving statement: Giving through the Washington Times Foundation, Inc.

The Washington Times Foundation, Inc.

3600 New York Ave., N.E.
Washington, DC 20002-4288

Establishment information: Established in 2002.
Donors: International Peace Foundation; News World Media Development; United Vision Foundation; Washington Times Aviation, Inc.
Financial data (yr. ended 03/31/11): Assets, $142,177 (M); gifts received, $37,010; expenditures, $201,179; qualifying distributions, $201,179; giving activities include $21,000 for grants.
Purpose and activities: The foundation supports organizations involved with journalism, volunteerism, and civic affairs.
Fields of interest: Media, print publishing; Boy scouts; Voluntarism promotion; Public affairs.
Type of support: Conferences/seminars; General/operating support.
Geographic limitations: Giving primarily in Washington, DC.
Support limitations: No grants to individuals.
Application information: Applications not accepted. Contributes only to pre-selected organizations.
Officers: Hyun-Jin Moon, Chair.; Douglas Joo, Pres.; Larry Moffitt, V.P.; Thomas McDevitt, Secy.; Keith Cooperrider, Treas.
EIN: 521832151
Selected grants: The following grants are a representative sample of this grantmaker's funding activity:
$125,000 to Points of Light Institute, Washington, DC, 2010.
$30,000 to Wounded Warrior Project, Jacksonville, FL, 2010.

2702
Newspapers of New England, Inc.

1 Monitor Dr.
Concord, NH 03301-1834 (603) 224-5301

Establishment information: Established in 1978.
Company type: Private company
Business activities: Publishes newspapers.
Business type (SIC): Newspaper publishing and/or printing
Corporate officers: Tom Brown, Pres. and C.E.O.; Daniel D. McClory, C.F.O.; Scott H. Graff, Treas.
Giving statement: Giving through the Newspaper Foundation.

The Newspaper Foundation

P.O. Box 1177
Concord, NH 03302-1177

Establishment information: Established in 2000 in NH.
Donor: Newspapers of New England, Inc.
Contact: James Foudy, Tr.
Financial data (yr. ended 12/31/11): Assets, $343,146 (M); expenditures, $21,468; qualifying distributions, $19,500; giving activities include $19,500 for 8 grants (high: $4,500; low: $1,000).
Purpose and activities: The foundation supports libraries and organizations involved with conservation.
Fields of interest: Libraries (public); Environment, natural resources; Environment, plant conservation; YM/YWCAs & YM/YWHAs.
Type of support: General/operating support.
Geographic limitations: Giving primarily in NH and MA.
Application information: Applications accepted. Application form not required.
Initial approach: Proposal
Deadline(s): None
Officers and Trustees:* Aaron D. Julien*, Pres.; John W. Miller*, Secy.; Daniel D. McClory*, Treas.; James Foudy; Heather McKernan; Dennis Skogland; Mark Travis.
EIN: 020522262

2703
The Newsweek/Daily Beast Company LLC

(formerly Newsweek, Inc.)
7 Hanover Sq.
New York, NY 10004 (212) 445-4600

Company URL: http://www.newsweek.com
Establishment information: Established in 1933.
Company type: Joint venture
Business activities: Operates print magazine and online content company.
Business type (SIC): Periodical publishing and/or printing
Corporate officers: Richard M. Smith, Chair.; Stephen Colvin, Pres.; Thomas Ascheim, C.E.O.; Gary Starr, C.F.O.; Randy Shapiro, V.P. and Genl. Counsel; Jeanne Sakas, V.P., Human Resources
Board of director: Richard Smith, Chair.
Giving statement: Giving through the Newsweek/Daily Beast Company LLC Contributions Program.

The Newsweek/Daily Beast Company LLC Contributions Program

(formerly Newsweek, Inc. Corporate Giving Program)
7 Hanover Sq.
New York, NY 10004

Contact: Tricia Luh, Sr. V.P. and C.F.O.
Purpose and activities: Newsweek makes charitable contributions to nonprofit organizations involved with publishing, and education, and to museums. Support is given primarily in areas of company operations.
Fields of interest: Media, print publishing; Museums; Education.
Type of support: Employee matching gifts; Employee volunteer services; General/operating support; In-kind gifts; Scholarship funds; Sponsorships.
Geographic limitations: Giving primarily in areas of company operations, with emphasis on Los Angeles and San Francisco, CA, Chicago, IL, Boston, MA, Detroit, MI, New York, NY, Dallas, TX, and in FL.
Application information: Applications accepted. Application form not required. Applicants should submit the following:
1) listing of board of directors, trustees, officers and other key people and their affiliations
2) detailed description of project and amount of funding requested
Initial approach: Proposal to headquarters
Deadline(s): None
Final notification: Following review

2704
Newtown Savings Bank

39 Main St.
Newtown, CT 06470-2139 (203) 426-2563
FAX: (203) 364-2995

Company URL: http://www.nsbonline.com
Establishment information: Established in 1855.
Company type: Private company
Business activities: Operates savings bank.
Business type (SIC): Savings institutions
Financial profile for 2010: Number of employees, 202; assets, $942,692,000; liabilities, $942,692,000
Corporate officers: John J. Martocci, Chair.; John F. Trentacosta, Pres. and C.E.O.; William J. McCarthy, Sr. V.P. and C.F.O.; Dan Long, Sr. V.P., Mktg.; Duane H. Giannini, Sr. V.P., Human Resources
Board of directors: John J. Martocci, Chair.; Alan J. Clavette; James C. Driscoll III; Joseph R. Humeston; John S. Madzula; Carol L. Mahoney; James T. Morley, Jr.; K. Michael Snyder; John F. Trentacosta; Brian C. White
Offices: Bethel, Brookfield, Danbury, Monroe, Newtown, Shelton, Southbury, Trumbull, Woodbury, CT
Giving statement: Giving through the Newtown Savings Bank Foundation Inc.

Newtown Savings Bank Foundation Inc.

c/o Newtown Savings Bank
39 Main St.
Newtown, CT 06470-2134 (203) 426-4440

Establishment information: Established in 1997 in CT.
Donor: Newtown Savings Bank.
Contact: John F. Trentacosta, Pres. and C.E.O.
Financial data (yr. ended 09/30/11): Assets, $923,182 (M); gifts received, $83,229; expenditures, $57,501; qualifying distributions, $45,500; giving activities include $45,500 for 25 grants (high: $5,000; low: $1,000).
Purpose and activities: The foundation supports organizations involved with education, health, and housing.
Fields of interest: Higher education; Scholarships/financial aid; Education; Hospitals (general); Health care; Housing/shelter, development.
Type of support: General/operating support; Scholarship funds.
Geographic limitations: Giving limited to the Newtown, CT, area.
Support limitations: No grants to individuals.
Application information: Applications accepted. Application form required.
Initial approach: Letter
Deadline(s): None
Officers: John J. Martocci, Chair.; John F. Trentacosta, Pres. and C.E.O.; Duane Giannini, Sr. V.P.; Tanya Wulff Traux, Secy.
Trustees: Alan C. Clavette; James C. Driscoll III; John S. Madzula; Carol L. Mahoney; John J. Martocci; James T. Morley, Jr.; K. Michael Snyder; Brian C. White.
EIN: 061514980

2705
Nexion Health, Inc.

6937 Warfield Ave.
Sykesville, MD 21784 (410) 552-4800

Company URL: http://www.nexion-health.com/
Establishment information: Established in 2000.
Company type: Private company
Business activities: Operates skilled nursing facilities.
Business type (SIC): Nursing and personal care facilities
Corporate officers: Francis P. Kirley, Pres. and C.E.O.; Bretton J. Bolt, Exec. V.P. and C.F.O.; Meera Riner, V.P., Opers.; Keith Mutschler, Treas.; Marguerite Jenkins, Cont.; Brian Lee, Genl. Counsel
Giving statement: Giving through the Nexion Health Foundation.

Nexion Health Foundation

6937 Warfield Ave.
Sykesville, MD 21784-7454 (410) 552-4800
URL: http://www.nexion-health.com/about-us/

Establishment information: Established in 2004 in DE.
Donor: Nexion Health Management, Inc.
Financial data (yr. ended 12/31/11): Assets, $67,673 (M); gifts received, $30,400; expenditures, $21,514; qualifying distributions, $21,195; giving activities include $21,195 for 22 grants to individuals (high: $1,195; low: $250).
Purpose and activities: The foundation supports programs designed to address the health and well-being of the elderly and the disabled.
Fields of interest: Health care; Aging, centers/services; Developmentally disabled, centers & services; Human services Aging; Disabilities, people with.
Programs:
Emergency Relief: The foundation provides financial assistance to Nexion Associates and their dependents who suffer loss as a result of widespread natural disasters or other major, unforeseeable life circumstances. The Emergency Relief Program provides funds for shelter, medical attention, clothing, food and other basic needs.
Excellence Through Education Scholarship: The foundation awards $1,000 scholarships to eligible Associates, or the children of Associates, who attend an accredited college or vocational school. Primary consideration will be given to applicants pursuing careers related to health and/or elder care.
One 4 One Giving: The foundation matches donations made by eligible Nexion Associates to one qualified local, regional, or national charitable organization per year through the One 4 One Giving Program. Annual contributions to any one organization may be limited.
Volunteer Plus: The foundation provides financial assistance to eligible charitable organizations for which Nexion Associates volunteer their time and talent. Annual contributions to any one organization shall not exceed $250 and will be limited to two (2) organizations per employee per year. Qualified associates must submit evidence of at least 25 hours of unpaid service to a qualified organization that serves their community and supports the health, well-being and futures of the elderly and disabled, their families and caregivers.
Type of support: Employee volunteer services; Employee-related scholarships; Sponsorships.
Geographic limitations: Giving primarily in communities served by Nexion Health affiliate facilities in CO, LA, and TX.
Application information: Applications accepted. Application form required.
Initial approach: See website for application form
Deadline(s): See website for deadline
Officers and Director:* Francis P. Kirley*, Pres. and C.E.O.
EIN: 412129020

2706
NexTier Bank

(formerly Citizens National Bank of Evans City)
101 E. Diamond St., Ste. 100
P.O. Box 1232
Butler, PA 16001-5946 (724) 287-3791
FAX: (724) 940-5401

Company URL: http://www.thebank.com
Establishment information: Established in 1878.
Company type: Private company
Business activities: Operates commercial bank.
Business type (SIC): Banks/commercial
Corporate officers: S.J. Irvine III, Chair.; Donald Shamey, C.E.O.; Margaret Irvine Weir, Pres.
Board of director: S.J. Irvine III, Chair.
Giving statement: Giving through the Nextier Bank Foundation.

Nextier Bank Foundation

(formerly Citizens Bank Foundation)
P.O. Box 1550
Butler, PA 16003-1550

Establishment information: Established in 1998 in PA.
Donors: Nextier Bank; Citizens National Bank of Evans City, PA.
Financial data (yr. ended 12/31/11): Assets, $751 (M); expenditures, $5,500; qualifying distributions, $5,500; giving activities include $5,500 for grants.
Purpose and activities: The foundation supports organizations involved with k-12 education, health, housing, human services, and community development.
Fields of interest: Education; Human services.
Type of support: Annual campaigns; Building/renovation; Capital campaigns; Continuing support; Employee-related scholarships; General/operating support; Scholarship funds; Sponsorships.
Application information: Applications not accepted. Unsolicited requests for funds not accepted.
Trustee: Nextier Bank.
EIN: 311631195

2707
NIBCO, Inc.

1516 Middlebury St.
P.O. Box 1167
Elkhart, IN 46516-4740 (574) 295-3000
FAX: (574) 295-3307

Company URL: http://www.nibco.com
Establishment information: Established in 1904.
Company type: Private company
Business activities: Manufactures flow control products.
Business type (SIC): Metal plumbing fixtures and heating equipment/nonelectric
Corporate officers: Rex Martin, Chair. and C.E.O.; Alice A. Martin, Vice-Chair.; Steven E. Malm, Pres. and C.O.O.; Thomas L. Eisele, Sr. V.P. and Secy.; Christopher Wynne, V.P., Finance, C.F.O., and Treas.; Mark Hamilton, V.P., Sales and Mktg.

Board of directors: Rex Martin, Chair.; Alice A. Martin, Vice-Chair.
Plants: Blytheville, AR; Greensboro, GA; Charlestown, Goshen, IN; South Glens Falls, NY; Denmark, SC; Nacogdoches, TX; Stuarts Draft, VA
Offices: Los Angeles, CA; Atlanta, GA; Columbus, OH
Giving statement: Giving through the NIBCO Inc. Corporate Giving Program.

NIBCO Inc. Corporate Giving Program

1516 Middlebury St.
Elkhart, IN 46516-4740
URL: http://www.nibco.com/cms.do?id=29

Purpose and activities: NIBCO makes charitable contributions to nonprofit organizations involved with education, community development, and on a case by case basis. Support is given primarily in areas of company operations in Arkansas, California, Georgia, Indiana, Ohio, Texas, and Virginia, and in Mexico and Poland.
Fields of interest: Education; Environment, water resources; Housing/shelter; Recreation, parks/playgrounds; Recreation; American Red Cross; Community/economic development; United Ways and Federated Giving Programs; General charitable giving.
International interests: Mexico; Poland.
Type of support: Building/renovation; Donated products; Employee volunteer services; Employee-related scholarships; General/operating support; In-kind gifts.
Geographic limitations: Giving primarily in areas of company operations in AR, CA, GA, IN, OH, TX, and VA, and in Mexico and Poland; giving also to national organizations.

2708
Niemann Foods, Inc.

1501 N. 12th St.
Quincy, IL 62301 (217) 221-5600

Establishment information: Established in 1917.
Company type: Private company
Business activities: Operates supermarkets and convenience stores.
Business type (SIC): Groceries—retail
Corporate officers: Richard Niemann, Sr., Chair.; Richard Niemann, Jr., Pres., C.E.O., and C.O.O.; Christopher Niemann, Exec. V.P. and C.F.O.; Chuck Lynch, Sr. V.P., Opers.
Board of director: Richard Niemann, Sr., Chair.
Giving statement: Giving through the Niemann Foods Foundation.

Niemann Foods Foundation

P.O. Box C847
Quincy, IL 62306-0847 (217) 221-5600
Application address: 1501 N. 12th St., Quincy, IL 62301-1916

Establishment information: Established in 2005 in IL.
Donor: Niemann Foods, Inc.
Contact: Richard H. Niemann, Dir.
Financial data (yr. ended 12/31/11): Assets, $393,796 (M); gifts received, $37,171; expenditures, $68,719; qualifying distributions, $23,496; giving activities include $22,500 for 9 grants (high: $5,000; low: $1,000).
Purpose and activities: The foundation supports organizations involved with television, education, and human services.
Fields of interest: Media, television; Secondary school/education; Higher education; Libraries (public); Education; American Red Cross; YM/YWCAs & YM/YWHAs.
Type of support: Endowments; Equipment; General/operating support; Program development; Sponsorships.
Geographic limitations: Giving primarily in Quincy, IL.
Support limitations: No grants to individuals.
Application information: Applications accepted. Application form required.
Initial approach: Proposal
Deadline(s): None
Directors: Christopher J. Niemann; Richard H. Niemann, Sr.; Richard H. Niemann, Jr.
EIN: 203675996

2709
NII Holdings, Inc.

1875 Explorer St., Ste. 1000
Reston, VA 20190 (703) 390-5100

Company URL: http://www.nii.com
Establishment information: Established in 1995.
Company type: Public company
Company ticker symbol and exchange: NIHD/NASDAQ
Business activities: Provides digital wireless communication services through operating companies located in selected Latin American markets.
Business type (SIC): Telephone communications; holding company
Financial profile for 2012: Number of employees, 16,100; assets, $9,223,080,000; sales volume, $6,086,460,000; pre-tax net income, -$543,140,000; expenses, $6,209,720,000; liabilities, $6,906,630,000
Fortune 1000 ranking: 2012—421st in revenues, 973rd in profits, and 414th in assets
Corporate officers: Steven M. Shindler, Chair. and C.E.O.; Gokul V. Hemmady, C.O.O.; Juan R. Figuereo, Exec. V.P. and C.F.O.; Dave Truzinski, Exec. V.P. and C.I.O.; Gary Begeman, Exec. V.P. and Genl. Counsel; Alfonso Martinez, Exec. V.P., Human Resources; Daniel E. Freiman, V.P. and Treas.
Board of directors: Steven M. Shindler, Chair.; Paulino do Rego Barros, Jr.; Kevin L. Beebe; Donald Guthrie; Charles M. Herington; Carolyn F. Katz; Rosendo G. Parra; John W. Risner
International operations: Argentina; Brazil; Chile; Mexico
Giving statement: Giving through the NII Holdings, Inc. Corporate Giving Program.
Company EIN: 911671412

NII Holdings, Inc. Corporate Giving Program

c/o Social Responsibility Committee
1875 Explorer St., Ste. 100
Reston, VA 20190 (703) 390-5100
URL: http://www.nii.com/socialresponsibility.html

Purpose and activities: NII Holdings makes charitable contributions to nonprofit organizations that benefit families and children in Reston, Virginia, the greater Washington, DC metropolitan area, and areas where local subsidiaries are located; giving also to national organizations.
Fields of interest: Education; Health care, blood supply; Breast cancer; Food services; Housing/shelter, volunteer services; American Red Cross; Children, services; Family services; Homeless, human services.
Type of support: Employee volunteer services; General/operating support; Sponsorships.
Geographic limitations: Giving primarily in areas of company operations in Reston, VA, the greater metropolitan Washington, DC area, and areas where local subsidiaries are located; giving also to national organizations.
Support limitations: No support for political, or religious organizations.

2710
NIKE, Inc.

1 Bowerman Dr.
Beaverton, OR 97005-6453
(503) 671-6453
FAX: (503) 671-6300

Company URL: http://www.nike.com
Establishment information: Established in 1964.
Company type: Public company
Company ticker symbol and exchange: NKE/NYSE
International Securities Identification Number: US6541061031
Business activities: Designs, develops, and markets footwear, apparel, athletic equipment, and related accessories.
Business type (SIC): Footwear/rubber and plastic; apparel and other finished products made from fabrics and similar materials; games, toys, and sporting and athletic goods
Financial profile for 2012: Number of employees, 44,000; assets, $15,600,000,000; sales volume, $25,300,000,000; pre-tax net income, $2,983,000,000; expenses, $21,145,000,000; liabilities, $5,084,000,000
Fortune 1000 ranking: 2012—126th in revenues, 90th in profits, and 291st in assets
Forbes 2000 ranking: 2012—369th in sales, 235th in profits, and 1149th in assets
Corporate officers: Philip H. Knight, Chair.; Mark G. Parker, Pres. and C.E.O.; Donald W. Blair, Exec. V.P. and C.F.O.; Hans van Alebeek, Exec. V.P., Opers . and Tech.; David Ayre, Exec. V.P., Human Resources; Bernie Pliska, V.P. and Corp. Cont.; Tom Peddie, V.P., Sales; Nigel Powell, V.P., Comms.; John F. Coburn III, Corp. Secy.
Board of directors: Philip H. Knight, Chair.; Elizabeth J. Comstock; John G. Connors; Timothy D. Cook; Alan B. Graf, Jr.; Douglas G. Houser; John C. Lechleiter, Ph.D.; Mark G. Parker; Johnathan A. Rodgers; Orin C. Smith; John R. Thompson, Jr.; Phyllis M. Wise, Ph.D.
Subsidiaries: Bauer NIKE Hockey Inc., Greenland, NH; Cole Haan Holdings, Inc., Yarmouth, ME; Converse Inc., North Andover, MA; Hurley International LLC, Costa Mesa, CA
Offices: Wilsonville, OR; Memphis, TN
International operations: Austria; Canada; China; Denmark; France; Germany; Italy; Japan; Netherlands; Norway; Spain; Sweden; United Kingdom
Giving statement: Giving through the NIKE, Inc. Corporate Giving Program, the NIKE Foundation, and the NIKE Employee Disaster Relief Foundation.
Company EIN: 930584541

NIKE, Inc. Corporate Giving Program

c/o Global Community Affairs Dept.
1 Bowerman Dr.
Beaverton, OR 97005-0979
Nonprofit organizations outside of the U.S. or the Netherlands should send requests to: Consumer.Services@nike.com.; URL: http://

www.nikebiz.com/responsibility/community_programs/

Purpose and activities: As a complement to its foundation, NIKE also makes charitable contributions to nonprofit organizations directly. Emphasis is given to organizations dedicated to creating social change through sport and disaster relief efforts. Support is given on a national and international basis.
Fields of interest: Safety/disasters; Athletics/sports, school programs; Recreation; Youth development Economically disadvantaged.
Type of support: Donated equipment; Donated products; Employee matching gifts; Employee volunteer services; General/operating support; In-kind gifts; Sponsorships.
Geographic limitations: Giving on a national and international basis in areas of company operations, with emphasis on Beaverton, Portland, and Wilsonville, OR, and Memphis, TN.
Support limitations: No support for fraternal, religious, discriminatory, lobbying, or political organizations. No grants to individuals, or for capital campaigns, endowments, memorials, individual sports team sponsorships, individual study, research, or travel, awards that require Nike and/or its employees to raise monies on behalf of an organization bestowing the award, or unsolicited auction products or table sponsorships.
Publications: Application guidelines; Corporate report.
Application information: Nike only supports product donation requests and will not accept unsolicited cash proposals. Hard copy applications are not accepted in the U.S. or the Netherlands. Applicants should submit the following:
1) copy of IRS Determination Letter
2) copy of most recent annual report/audited financial statement/990
3) listing of board of directors, trustees, officers and other key people and their affiliations

Application guidelines are available here: http://nikeinc.com/pages/giving-guidelines.
Initial approach: Complete online application for product donations
Deadline(s): None
Number of staff: 9 full-time professional; 3 full-time support.

NIKE Foundation

(formerly NIKE P.L.A.Y. Foundation)
1 Bowerman Dr.
Beaverton, OR 97005-6453 (888) 448-6453
E-mail: nike.foundation@nike.com; URL: http://nikeinc.com/pages/the-nike-foundation

Establishment information: Established in 1994 in OR.
Donors: NIKE, Inc.; NoVo Foundation.
Financial data (yr. ended 05/31/12): Assets, $39,698,757 (M); gifts received, $26,362,725; expenditures, $27,334,957; qualifying distributions, $27,331,905; giving activities include $13,840,324 for 47 grants (high: $2,000,000; low: $5,010) and $434,542 for 1 foundation-administered program.
Purpose and activities: The foundation supports programs designed to empower adolescent girls in the developing world. Special emphasis is directed toward ending early marriage and delaying first birth; ensuring health and safety; secondary school completion and transitions to employment; and expanding direct access to economic assets.
Fields of interest: Secondary school/education; Education; Health care; Employment; Safety/disasters; Youth development, adult & child programs; Human services, financial counseling; Economic development; Social entrepreneurship; Microfinance/microlending Girls; Economically disadvantaged.
International interests: Africa; Brazil; Developing countries; India.
Program:
The Girl Effect: The foundation, in partnership with the NoVo Foundation, United Nations Foundation, and the Coalition for Adolescent Girls, empowers girls and women to create social and economic change in developing countries. The initiative includes financial support from the foundation, celebrity partnerships, fundraising via The Girl Effect website, social media, videos, and conferences designed to advocate for girls in communities, schools, businesses, organizations, and governments. Visit URL: http://www.girleffect.org/question for more information.
Type of support: General/operating support; Management development/capacity building; Program development.
Geographic limitations: Giving primarily in CA, Washington, DC, NY; giving on an international basis in Africa, Bangladesh, Brazil, India, Kenya, Nigeria, Paraguay, Tanzania, Uganda, and Zambia.
Support limitations: No support for discriminatory organizations. No grants to individuals, or for general operating support for established programs, research or travel, films, television, or radio programs that are not an integral part of a project, religious programs, endowments or fundraising campaigns, lobbying or political activities, or depreciation or debt reduction.
Application information: Applications not accepted. Contributes only to pre-selected organizations. The foundation utilizes an invitation only Request for Proposal (RFP) process.
Officers and Directors:* Maria S. Eitel*, C.E.O. and Pres.; Howard Taylor, V.P. and Managing Dir.; Donald W. Blair; Jennifer Buffett; Peter Buffett; Charlie D. Denson; Gary DeStefano; Trevor Edwards; Hannah Jones; Hilary Krane*; Mark Parker.
EIN: 931159948
Selected grants: The following grants are a representative sample of this grantmaker's funding activity:
$1,003,312 to Academia para o Desenvolvimento da Educacao-Brasil, Recife, Brazil, 2011. For training and employment skills program in slums of Recife.
$845,716 to TechnoServe, Washington, DC, 2011. For safe income generation opportunities for girls in harsh urban slums.
$747,998 to Cardno Emerging Markets USA, Ltd., Arlington, VA, 2011. To increase girls' participation in high-return value chains.
$700,069 to CARE USA, Atlanta, GA, 2011. For savings, loans and financial literacy for rural and urban girls.
$540,000 to Grameen Healthcare Trust, Dhaka, Bangladesh, 2011. For girls nursing institute at the center of health care transformation in Bangladesh.
$475,000 to Population Services International, Washington, DC, 2011. To establish a New Normal for girls' health In Rwanda.
$459,800 to International Rescue Committee, New York, NY, 2011. For Urban Microfinancing for girls.
$182,850 to Population Services International, Washington, DC, 2011. To build girl expertise capacity within PSI.
$64,355 to Tostan, Washington, DC, 2011. For community led education to advance girls' life prospects in Senegal.
$47,276 to Association for the Support of Contemporary Living, Istanbul, Turkey, 2011. For transition of girls to secondary school and to keep them there through a conditional cash grant directly to girls.

NIKE Employee Disaster Relief Foundation

1 Bowerman Dr.
Beaverton, OR 97005-6453

Financial data (yr. ended 05/31/10): .
Purpose and activities: The foundation provides disaster relief for NIKE employees who were victims of Hurricane Katrina.
Fields of interest: Disasters, Hurricane Katrina.
Type of support: Grants to individuals.
Officers and Directors:* Wes Colman*, Pres.; John Coburn*, Secy.; Bob Woodruff*, Treas.; Hannah Jones; Mark Parker.
EIN: 203470884

2711
Nikon Inc.

1300 Walt Whitman Rd.
Melville, NY 11747-3064 (631) 547-4200

Company URL: http://www.nikonusa.com
Establishment information: Established in 1917.
Company type: Subsidiary of a foreign company
Business activities: Manufactures optical products.
Business type (SIC): Photographic equipment and supplies; laboratory apparatus
Corporate officers: Nobuyoshi Gokyu, Co-C.E.O.; Toshiyuki Masai, Co-C.E.O.; Lorie Buckingham, C.I.O.; Jay Vannatter, Sr. V.P., Sales; Joseph J. Carfora, V.P., Sales; Jerry Grossman, V.P., Mktg.; John P. Browne, Secy.
Giving statement: Giving through the W. Eugene Smith Memorial Fund, Inc.

W. Eugene Smith Memorial Fund, Inc.

11 Hanover Sq., 26th Fl.
New York, NY 10005
Application address: International Center of Photography, 1114 Avenue of the Americas, New York, NY 10036; URL: http://smithfund.org/

Establishment information: Established in 1980 in NY.
Donors: Nikon Inc.; New World Foundation; John Harris; Open Society Institute; Getty Images.
Financial data (yr. ended 02/29/12): Assets, $10,997 (M); gifts received, $47,660; expenditures, $58,620; qualifying distributions, $58,620; giving activities include $40,000 for 3 grants to individuals (high: $30,000; low: $5,000).
Purpose and activities: The foundation awards grants to photojournalists whose work is based on a humanistic theme.
Fields of interest: Visual arts, photography.
Programs:
Howard Chapnick Grant: The foundation awards $5,000 grants to individuals to promote leadership in photojournalism fields, such as editing, research, education, and management. Special emphasis is directed toward projects designed to promote social change and/or serve significant concerns of photojournalism.
W. Eugene Smith Grant in Humanistic Photography: The foundation awards grants to photographers whose past work and proposed project follow in the tradition of W. Eugene Smith.
Type of support: Grants to individuals.
Geographic limitations: Giving on a national and international basis.
Publications: Application guidelines; Grants list.
Application information: Applications accepted. Application form required.

Initial approach: Download application form and mail proposal and application form to foundation
Deadline(s): June 8
Officers and Trustees:* Marcel Saba*, Pres.; W. M. Hunt*, V.P.; Aaron Schindler*, Secy.; Robert Stevens*, Treas.; Stuart Alexander; Rich Clarkson; Donna Ferrato; David Friend; Helen Marcus; John G. Morris; Robert Pledge; Rick Smolan; Brian Storm; Aidan Sullivan; Lauren Wendle.
EIN: 133060631

2712
Nintendo of America, Inc.

4820 150th Ave., N.E.
Redmond, WA 98052-5111 (425) 882-2040

Company URL: http://www.nintendo.com
Establishment information: Established in 1981.
Company type: Subsidiary of a foreign company
Business activities: Manufactures electronic games, home video equipment, and watches.
Business type (SIC): Games, toys, and sporting and athletic goods; watches, clocks, and parts; electrical goods—wholesale; durable goods—wholesale
Financial profile for 2011: Number of employees, 855; sales volume, $4,800,000,000
Corporate officers: Tatsumi Kimishima, Chair. and C.E.O.; Reginald Fils-Aime, Pres. and C.O.O.; Jim Cannataro, C.A.O.; Don James, Exec. V.P., Opers.; Scott Moffitt, Exec. V.P., Sales and Mktg.; Richard Flamm, Sr. V.P. and Genl. Counsel
Board of director: Tatsumi Kimishima, Chair.
Division: Consumer Products Div., Redmond, WA
Giving statement: Giving through the Nintendo of America Inc. Corporate Giving Program.

Nintendo of America Inc. Corporate Giving Program

4820 150th Ave. NE
Redmond, WA 98052-5111
URL: http://www.nintendo.com/corp/csr/index.jsp

Purpose and activities: Nintendo of America makes charitable contributions to nonprofit organizations involved with children and food services. Support is given primarily in areas of company operations.
Fields of interest: Health care, patient services; Food services; Boys & girls clubs; Family services Children.
Program:
Employee Matching Gifts: Nintendo of America matches contributions made by its employees to nonprofit organizations on a one-for-one basis.
Type of support: Donated products; Employee matching gifts; Employee volunteer services; General/operating support.
Geographic limitations: Giving primarily in areas of company operations; giving also to national organizations.

2713
Nippon Express U.S.A., Inc.

590 Madison Ave.
New York, NY 10022 (212) 758-6100

Company URL: http://www.nipponexpressusa.com
Establishment information: Established in 1962.
Company type: Subsidiary of a foreign company
Business activities: Provides transportation and forwarding services.
Business type (SIC): Transportation/deep sea domestic freight; transportation/scheduled air; transportation services/freight
Financial profile for 2011: Assets, $1,201,801; liabilities, $705,918
Corporate officers: Masanori Kawa, Co-Pres. and C.E.O.; Kenryo Senda, Co-Pres.; Tadaaki Hashimoto, Co-Pres.; Kazuhiro Ono, V.P. and Treas.; Eiji Iaano, C.A.O.; Yoshiyuki Fukadome, C.I.O
Subsidiaries: Nippon Express Travel USA Inc., San Francisco, CA; Nippon Express USA (Illinois), Inc., Wood Dale, IL; Nittsu New York, New York, NY
Giving statement: Giving through the Nippon Express Foundation, Inc.

Nippon Express Foundation, Inc.

590 Madison Ave., 24th Fl.
New York, NY 10022-8555 (212) 758-6100
FAX: (212) 750-9353

Establishment information: Established in 1992 in NY.
Donor: Nippon Express U.S.A., Inc.
Contact: Tsutomu Nagatani, Secy.
Financial data (yr. ended 12/31/11): Assets, $1,476,094 (M); gifts received, $525,980; expenditures, $164,233; qualifying distributions, $163,861; giving activities include $163,861 for grants.
Purpose and activities: The foundation supports organizations involved with Japanese arts and culture, education, and business promotion.
Fields of interest: Arts; Education; Human services.
Type of support: General/operating support; Program development.
Geographic limitations: Giving primarily in New York, NY.
Support limitations: No grants to individuals.
Application information: Applications accepted. Application form required. Applicants should submit the following:
1) copy of IRS Determination Letter
2) detailed description of project and amount of funding requested
Initial approach: Proposal
Deadline(s): None
Officers: Kenryo Senda, Pres.; Tsutomu Nagatani, Secy.; Tomoyuki Nakano, Treas.
EIN: 133693444

2714
Nishnabotna Valley Rural Electric Cooperative

1317 Chatburn Ave.
P. O. Box 714
Harlan, IA 51537-2012 (712) 755-2166

Company URL: http://www.nvrec.com
Establishment information: Established in 1936.
Company type: Cooperative
Business activities: Distributes electricity.
Business type (SIC): Electric services
Corporate officer: John Euchner, C.E.O.
Board of directors: Don Applegate; Dale Christiansen; Galen Grabill; Bryan Greve; Gene Kenkel; Wayne Paulsen; Darrell Stamp
Giving statement: Giving through the Nishnabotna Valley Foundation.

Nishnabotna Valley Foundation

P.O. Box 714
Harlan, IA 51537-0714
E-mail: mjohnson@nvrec.com; URL: http://www.nvrec.com/aspx/general/clientpage.aspx?pageid=794&n=1363&n1=1465&n2=1496

Establishment information: Established as a company-sponsored operating foundation in 1998.
Donors: Western Ventures, Inc.; NIPCO Student Loan Fund.
Contact: Janell Cheek
Financial data (yr. ended 12/31/11): Assets, $14,849 (M); gifts received, $3,312; expenditures, $2,009; qualifying distributions, $2,000; giving activities include $2,000 for 4 grants (high: $500; low: $500).
Purpose and activities: The foundation awards college scholarships to residents of counties served by Nishnabotna Valley Rural Electric Cooperative.
Fields of interest: Higher education.
Type of support: Scholarships—to individuals.
Geographic limitations: Giving limited to Audubon, Cass, Crawford, Harrison, Pottawatternie, and Shelby counties, IA.
Publications: Application guidelines.
Application information: Applications accepted. Application form required.
Applications should include recent academic transcripts, ACT and/or SAT scores, an essay, and 1 letter of recommendation.
Initial approach: Contact foundation for application form
Deadline(s): Mar. 1
Officers: John Euchner, Pres.; Carmen P. Hosack, V.P.
EIN: 421467824

2715
NiSource Inc.

(formerly NIPSCO Industries, Inc.)
801 E. 86th Ave.
Merrillville, IN 46410-6271 (877) 647-5990
FAX: (302) 636-5454

Company URL: http://www.nisource.com/
Establishment information: Established in 1912.
Company type: Public company
Company ticker symbol and exchange: NI/NYSE
Business activities: Generates, transmits, and distributes electricity; transmits and distributes natural gas.
Business type (SIC): Combination utility services
Financial profile for 2012: Number of employees, 8,286; assets, $21,844,700,000; sales volume, $5,061,200,000; pre-tax net income, $626,100,000; expenses, $4,050,700,000; liabilities, $16,290,400,000
Fortune 1000 ranking: 2012—480th in revenues, 387th in profits, and 227th in assets
Forbes 2000 ranking: 2012—1373rd in sales, 1325th in profits, and 928th in assets
Corporate officers: Ian M. Rolland, Chair.; Robert C. Skaggs, Jr., Pres. and C.E.O.; Stephen P. Smith, Exec. V.P. and C.F.O.; Violet G. Sistovaris, Sr. V.P. and C.I.O.; Robert D. Campbell, Sr. V.P., Human Resources; Jon D. Veurink, C.P.A., V.P., C.A.O., and Cont.; David J. Vajda, V.P. and Treas.; Robert E. Smith, V.P. and Corp. Secy.
Board of directors: Ian M. Rolland, Chair.; Richard A. Abdoo; Aristides S. Candris; Sigmund L. Cornelius; Michael E. Jesanis; Marty R. Kittrell; Wallace Lee Nutter; Deborah S. Parker; Robert C. Skaggs, Jr.; Teresa A. Taylor; Richard L. Thompson; Carolyn Y. Woo

Subsidiaries: Columbia Energy Group, Merrillville, IN; Columbia Gas of Kentucky, Inc., Lexington, KY; Columbia Gas of Maryland, Inc., Canonsburg, PA; Columbia Gas of Massachusetts, Westborough, MA; Columbia Gas of Ohio, Inc., Columbus, OH; Columbia Gas of Pennsylvania, Inc., Canonsburg, PA; Columbia Gas of Virginia, Inc., Chester, VA; Columbia Gas Transmission Corporation, Charleston, WV; Northern Indiana Public Service Company, Merrillville, IN; Northern Utilities, Inc., Portsmouth, NH
Giving statement: Giving through the NiSource Charitable Foundation.
Company EIN: 352108964

NiSource Charitable Foundation

(formerly Columbia Gas Foundation)
200 Civic Center Dr.
Columbus, OH 43215-4138
E-mail: jmoench@nisource.com; Tel. for Jennifer L. Moench: (219) 647-6209; Additional address: NiSource Corp. Citizenship, 801 E. 86th Ave., Merrillville, IN 46410-6271; URL: http://www.nisource.com/en/sustainability/communities/corporate-giving.aspx

Establishment information: Established in 1990 in DE.
Donors: The Columbia Gas System, Inc.; Columbia Energy Group; Columbia Gas of Ohio, Inc.; NiSource Corporate Services Co.
Contact: Jennifer L. Moench, Exec. Dir.
Financial data (yr. ended 12/31/11): Assets, $11,181,753 (M); expenditures, $1,361,409; qualifying distributions, $1,305,788; giving activities include $1,305,788 for grants.
Purpose and activities: The foundation supports programs designed to promote community vitality and development; environmental and energy sustainability; learning and science education; and public safety and human services.
Fields of interest: Education; Environment, energy; Environment; Safety/disasters; Salvation Army; Human services; Community/economic development; United Ways and Federated Giving Programs; Science, formal/general education; Science.
Type of support: Annual campaigns; Building/renovation; Continuing support; Program development.
Geographic limitations: Giving on a national basis in areas of company operations, with some emphasis on IN and OH.
Support limitations: No support for religious organizations, political candidates or organizations, or discriminatory organizations. No grants to individuals, or for sports sponsorships, goodwill advertising, fundraising benefits, or program books.
Publications: Application guidelines.
Application information: Applications accepted. Application form required. Applicants should submit the following:
1) results expected from proposed grant
2) statement of problem project will address
3) population served
4) copy of IRS Determination Letter
5) brief history of organization and description of its mission
6) geographic area to be served
7) copy of most recent annual report/audited financial statement/990
8) how project's results will be evaluated or measured
9) listing of board of directors, trustees, officers and other key people and their affiliations
10) detailed description of project and amount of funding requested
11) copy of current year's organizational budget and/or project budget
12) listing of additional sources and amount of support

Initial approach: Contact foundation for application form
Copies of proposal: 1
Board meeting date(s): May and Oct.
Deadline(s): Varies

Officers and Trustees: Gary W. Pottorff, Secy.; David J. Vadja, Treas.; Susanne M. Taylor, Cont.; Jennifer L. Moench, Exec. Dir.; Robert D. Campbell; Christopher A. Helms; Carrie J. Hightman; Glen L. Kettering; Kathleen O'Leary; Robert C. Skaggs, Jr.; Jimmy D. Staton.
EIN: 510324200

2716
Nissan North America, Inc.

1670 W. Redondo Beach Blvd.
Gardena, CA 90248-4504 (310) 532-1600

Company URL: http://www.nissanusa.com
Establishment information: Established in 1960.
Company type: Subsidiary of a foreign company
Business activities: Manufactures and distributes automobiles, buses, and trucks.
Business type (SIC): Motor vehicles and equipment; motor vehicles, parts, and supplies—wholesale
Corporate officers: Norio Matsumura, Pres. and C.E.O.; Simon Sproule, V.P., Corp. Comms.
Subsidiaries: Nissan Motor Acceptance Corp., Torrance, CA; Nissan Motor Manufacturing Corp., U.S.A., Smyrna, TN; Nissan North America, Inc., Torrance, CA; Nissan Research and Development Corp., Ann Arbor, MI
Giving statement: Giving through the Nissan North America, Inc. Corporate Giving Program and the Nissan Foundation.

Nissan North America, Inc. Corporate Giving Program

c/o Nissan Neighbors
1 Nissan Way
Franklin, TN 37067-6367
URL: http://www.nissanusa.com/about/corporate-info/community-relations.html

Purpose and activities: As a complement to its foundation, Nissan also makes charitable contributions to nonprofit organizations directly. Support is given primarily in areas of company operations in southern California, metropolitan Detroit, Michigan, south central Mississippi, middle Tennessee, and Dallas and Fort Worth, Texas.
Fields of interest: Education; Environment; Human services; International relief.
Programs:

Education: Nissan supports programs designed to promote education tied to Nissan's core interests, including manufacturing, engineering, design, safety, sales and marketing, finance, and diversity.

Environment: Nissan supports programs designed to promote fuel efficiencies; decrease emissions; and beautify and preserve parks and neighborhoods.

Type of support: General/operating support; In-kind gifts; Scholarships—to individuals.
Geographic limitations: Giving primarily in southern CA, metropolitan Detroit, MI, south central MS, middle TN, and Dallas and Fort Worth, TX.
Application information: Applications accepted.
Initial approach: Complete online application form
Deadline(s): None

The Nissan Foundation

P.O. Box 685001, M.S. B5B
Franklin, TN 37068-5001 (615) 725-1501
E-mail: nissanfoundation@nissan-usa.com; URL: http://www.nissanusa.com/about/corporate-info/community-relations.html

Establishment information: Established in 1993 in CA.
Donors: Nissan Motor Corp. U.S.A.; Nissan North America, Inc.
Financial data (yr. ended 06/30/12): Assets, $12,432,539 (M); expenditures, $672,899; qualifying distributions, $655,000; giving activities include $655,000 for grants.
Purpose and activities: The foundation supports educational programs designed to promote diverse cultural heritage.
Fields of interest: Arts, cultural/ethnic awareness; Museums; Performing arts; Education.
Program:

Building Community Through Valuing Cultural Diversity: The foundation supports programs designed to promote learning about diverse cultural origins, beliefs, and traditions as an integral aspect of education. Grants range from $10,000 to $50,000.

Type of support: General/operating support; Program development.
Geographic limitations: Giving limited to areas of company operations in southern CA, the Atlanta, GA, metropolitan area, Detroit, MI, south central MS, the New York, NY, metropolitan area, middle TN, and Dallas and Forth Worth, TX.
Support limitations: No support for disease advocacy, research, or religious organizations. No grants to individuals, or for fundraising events, sponsorships, or political activities or capital campaigns.
Publications: Application guidelines; Informational brochure (including application guidelines).
Application information: Applications accepted. Grants range from $10,000 to $50,000. A full proposal may be requested at a later date. Support is limited to 1 contribution per organization during any given year. Application form not required. Applicants should submit the following:
1) results expected from proposed grant
2) population served
3) name, address and phone number of organization
4) copy of IRS Determination Letter
5) brief history of organization and description of its mission
6) copy of most recent annual report/audited financial statement/990
7) how project's results will be evaluated or measured
8) listing of board of directors, trustees, officers and other key people and their affiliations
9) detailed description of project and amount of funding requested
10) plans for cooperation with other organizations, if any
11) contact person
12) copy of current year's organizational budget and/or project budget
13) listing of additional sources and amount of support
14) plans for acknowledgement

Initial approach: Complete online letter of intent
Deadline(s): Nov.
Final notification: June

Officers and Directors:* Scott Becker, Pres.; David Reuter, V.P.; John M. Dab, Secy.; William H. Scott, Jr., Treas.; Alfonso Albaisa; Holly Braco; Bryan

Dumas; Gary Frigo; Felicia Johnson; Rich Latek; Tony Lucente; Mark Perry; Bradley D. Thacker; George Vazquez; Jeffrey Webster; Paula Wells.
EIN: 954413799
Selected grants: The following grants are a representative sample of this grantmaker's funding activity:
$60,000 to Nashville Public Television, Nashville, TN, 2011.
$50,000 to Oasis Center, Nashville, TN, 2011.
$30,000 to 100 Black Men of Jackson, Jackson, MS, 2011.
$30,000 to Brooklyn Childrens Museum, Brooklyn, NY, 2011.
$30,000 to International Museum of Muslim Cultures, Jackson, MS, 2011.
$30,000 to Jobs for Mississippi Graduates, Jackson, MS, 2011.
$25,000 to Global Education Center, Nashville, TN, 2011.
$20,000 to National Black Arts Festival, Atlanta, GA, 2011.
$15,000 to Bayside Community Center, San Diego, CA, 2011.
$10,000 to New York University, New York, NY, 2011.

2717
Niu Pia Land Company

900 Fort Street Mall, Ste. 1640
Honolulu, HI 96813-3719 (808) 585-8900

Company type: Private company
Business activities: Operates commercial real estate company.
Business type (SIC): Real estate agents and managers
Corporate officer: Samuel W. Pratt, Pres.
Giving statement: Giving through the E.H.W. Broadbent Foundation.

E.H.W. Broadbent Foundation

900 Fort Street Mall, Ste. 1640
Honolulu, HI 96813-3719

Establishment information: Established in 2005 in HI.
Donor: Niu Pia Land Company Ltd.
Financial data (yr. ended 12/31/11): Assets, $905,256 (M); gifts received, $76,000; expenditures, $44,842; qualifying distributions, $42,000; giving activities include $42,000 for grants.
Fields of interest: Arts; Environment; Human services.
Support limitations: No grants to individuals.
Application information: Applications not accepted. Unsolicited requests for funds not accepted.
Officers and Directors:* Melinda P. Walker*, Pres.; Ann B. Leighton*, Secy.; Samuel W. Pratt*, Treas.
EIN: 161737197

2718
Nolan Painting Inc.

181 W. Hillcrest Ave.
Havertown, PA 19083 (610) 789-3156
FAX: (610) 449-7796

Company URL: http://www.Nolanpainting.com
Establishment information: Established in 1979.
Company type: Private company
Business type (SIC): Business services/ miscellaneous
Corporate officers: Kevin Nolan, Pres.; Steve Nafranowicz, C.F.O.; Jon P. Meyer, V.P., Sales; Colin McGroary, V.P., Opers.
Giving statement: Giving through the Nolan Painting Inc. Contributions Program.

Nolan Painting Inc. Contributions Program

181 West Hillcrest Ave.
Havertown, PA 19083 (610) 789-3156
E-mail: info@nolanpainting.com; URL: http://www.Nolanpainting.com

Purpose and activities: Nolan Painting is a certified B Corporation that donates a percentage of profits to charitable organizations.

2719
Noland Company

80 29th St.
Newport News, VA 23607 (757) 928-9000

Company URL: http://www.noland.com/
Establishment information: Established in 1915.
Company type: Subsidiary of a private company
Business activities: Sells mechanical equipment wholesale.
Business type (SIC): Hardware, plumbing, and heating equipment—wholesale
Financial profile for 2010: Number of employees, 600
Corporate officers: Richard W. Schwartz, Chair. and C.E.O.; Jack W. Johnston, Pres.; John W. Simmons, C.O.O.; Jeffrey M. Dice, C.F.O.
Board of director: Richard W. Schwartz, Chair.
Giving statement: Giving through the Noland Foundation.
Company EIN: 540320170

Noland Foundation

(formerly Noland Company Foundation)
11832 Rock Landing Dr., Ste. 106
Newport News, VA 23606 (757) 240-5650

Establishment information: Established in 1962 in VA.
Donor: Noland Co.
Financial data (yr. ended 12/31/11): Assets, $1,026,609 (M); expenditures, $50,940; qualifying distributions, $41,781; giving activities include $41,781 for grants.
Purpose and activities: The foundation supports organizations involved with arts and culture, education, health, and children and youth services.
Fields of interest: Arts; Education; Recreation.
Type of support: Annual campaigns; Capital campaigns; General/operating support.
Geographic limitations: Giving primarily in VA.
Support limitations: No grants to individuals.
Application information: Applications accepted. Application form required. Applicants should submit the following:
1) copy of most recent annual report/audited financial statement/990
Initial approach: Proposal
Deadline(s): None
Trustees: Lawrence O. Myers; Lloyd U. Noland III; Benjamin A. Williams III.
EIN: 540754191

2720
Nomura Holding America Inc.

2 World Financial Ctr., Bldg. B
New York, NY 10281-1198 (212) 667-9000

Company URL: http://www.nomura.com/americas/
Establishment information: Established in 1989.
Company type: Subsidiary of a foreign company
Business activities: Provides securities brokerage services; provides investment advisory services; operates investment bank.
Business type (SIC): Brokers and dealers/security; security and commodity services
Corporate officers: Masahiro Muroi, Chair.; Hideyuki Takahashi, Pres. and C.E.O.; Takeo Sumino, C.O.O.; Nathen Gorin, C.F.O.; Drew Vaden, C.I.O.
Board of director: Masahiro Muroi, Chair.
Giving statement: Giving through the Nomura America Foundation.

Nomura America Foundation

2 World Financial Ctr., Bldg. B
New York, NY 10281-1198 (212) 667-9505

Establishment information: Established in 1994 in NY.
Donors: Nomura Holding America Inc.; Nomura Securities International, Inc.
Contact: Penny Tehrani-Littrell, Exec. Dir.
Financial data (yr. ended 12/31/11): Assets, $2,792,800 (M); expenditures, $186,808; qualifying distributions, $163,796; giving activities include $163,796 for 90 grants (high: $50,000; low: $100).
Purpose and activities: The foundation supports organizations involved with arts and culture, education, disaster relief, children and youth, international relief, and science.
Fields of interest: Arts, cultural/ethnic awareness; Performing arts, music; Arts; Higher education; Education; Disasters, preparedness/services; Children/youth, services; International relief; Science.
Type of support: Program development.
Geographic limitations: Giving primarily in NY.
Application information: Applications accepted. Application form not required.
Initial approach: Proposal
Deadline(s): None
Officers and Directors:* David Moser, C.F.O.; Faron Webb, Secy.; Penny Tehrani-Littrell, Exec. Dir.; David Findlay*.
EIN: 133772961
Selected grants: The following grants are a representative sample of this grantmaker's funding activity:
$50,000 to Japan Society, New York, NY, 2010. For program services.
$7,681 to Save the Children Federation, Westport, CT, 2010. For program services.
$5,711 to Oxfam America, Boston, MA, 2010. For program services.
$5,586 to CARE USA, Atlanta, GA, 2010. For program services.
$5,000 to Museum of the City of New York, New York, NY, 2010. For program services.
$4,536 to International Rescue Committee, New York, NY, 2010. For program services.
$1,300 to Hackley School, Tarrytown, NY, 2010. For program services.
$1,000 to Cathedral School of Saint John the Divine, New York, NY, 2010. For program services.
$1,000 to Saint Bernards School, New York, NY, 2010. For program services.

$1,000 to University of Nebraska Foundation, Lincoln, NE, 2010. For program services.

2721
Nord Capital Group, Inc.

9226 Teddy Ln., Ste. 125
Lonetree, CO 80124-6727 (303) 705-8020

Company URL: http://www.nordcapital.com
Establishment information: Established in 1992.
Company type: Private company
Business activities: Provides business consulting services.
Business type (SIC): Management and public relations services
Corporate officers: Erck R.C. Rickmers, Chair.; Felix Von Buchwaldt, Co.-C.E.O; Florian Maack, Co.-C.E.O.; Arlen D. Nordhagen, Pres.
Board of director: Erck R.C. Rickmers, Chair.
Giving statement: Giving through the Nord Foundation.

The Nord Foundation

9226 Teddy Ln., Rm. 125
Lone Tree, CO 80124-6725
FAX: (303) 705-8021

Establishment information: Established in 1997 in CO.
Donors: Nord Capital Group, Inc.; Arlen D. Nordhagen; Wendy P. Nordhagen.
Financial data (yr. ended 11/30/11): Assets, $5,837,123 (M); expenditures, $183,228; qualifying distributions, $170,864; giving activities include $160,619 for 13 grants (high: $58,500; low: $700).
Purpose and activities: The foundation supports organizations involved with Christianity.
Fields of interest: Christian agencies & churches.
Type of support: Continuing support; Emergency funds; General/operating support; Loans—to individuals; Seed money.
Geographic limitations: Giving on a national and international basis, with some emphasis on Denver and Littleton, CO.
Support limitations: No support for secular organizations. No grants to individuals.
Publications: Financial statement.
Application information: Applications not accepted. Unsolicited requests for funds not accepted.
Board meeting date(s): June 1st and Oct. 10th
Officers and Directors:* Arlen D. Nordhagen*, Pres. and Treas.; Wendy P. Nordhagen*, V.P. and Secy.; Fred V. Lian; Ken J. Timboe.
Number of staff: None.
EIN: 841409115
Selected grants: The following grants are a representative sample of this grantmaker's funding activity:
$16,280 to Christian World Outreach, Littleton, CO, 2010.
$10,000 to Alternatives Pregnancy Center, Denver, CO, 2010.
$10,000 to Denver Rescue Mission, Denver, CO, 2010.
$10,000 to FoodWorks Colorado, Denver, CO, 2010.
$5,000 to Young Life, Colorado Springs, CO, 2010.

2722
Nordic Group of Companies, Ltd.

715 Lynn Ave., Ste. 100
Baraboo, WI 53913-2744 (608) 356-0136
FAX: (608) 356-5773

Company URL: http://www.nordicgroup.com
Establishment information: Established in 1947.
Company type: Private company
Business activities: Manufactures multi-use, low-speed vehicles; manufactures vehicle seating; manufactures injection and blow molded thermoplastic products; manufactures service vehicle racking and shelving; manufactures steel wall panels and trusses; leases vehicles and office equipment; manufactures data storage networking solutions; operates ski resort.
Business type (SIC): Transportation equipment/miscellaneous; plastic products/miscellaneous; metal products/structural; metal products/fabricated; computer and office equipment; motor vehicles and equipment; hotels and motels; equipment rental and leasing/miscellaneous; motor vehicle rentals and leasing
Corporate officer: William R. Sauey, Chair.
Board of director: William R. Sauey, Chair.
Subsidiaries: Columbia ParCar Corp., Reedsburg, WI; Flambeau, Inc., Baraboo, WI; Seats Inc., Reedsburg, WI
Giving statement: Giving through the W. R. and Floy A. Sauey Family Foundation.

W. R. and Floy A. Sauey Family Foundation

715 Lynn Ave.
Baraboo, WI 53913-2488 (608) 356-0136
FAX: (608) 356-5773;
E-mail: info@nordicgroup.com; Additional tel.: (608) 356-2130; URL: http://www.saueyfamily.org/

Establishment information: Established in 1998 in WI.
Donors: Flambeau, Inc.; Seats Inc.; Nordic Group of Cos., Ltd.
Contact: Alison Martin, Pres.
Financial data (yr. ended 12/31/11): Assets, $1,118,084 (M); gifts received, $40,615; expenditures, $176,009; qualifying distributions, $153,235; giving activities include $153,235 for 13 grants (high: $115,750; low: $500).
Purpose and activities: The foundation supports programs designed to promote education; preserve and increase participation in the free market system; and promote quality of life in local communities with emphasis on child and family issues.
Fields of interest: Higher education; Education, reading; Education; Children/youth, services; Family services; Family services, domestic violence; Homeless, human services; Human services; Community/economic development.
Type of support: Annual campaigns; Employee-related scholarships; General/operating support.
Geographic limitations: Giving primarily in areas of company operations, with emphasis on MN and WI.
Publications: Informational brochure.
Application information: Applications accepted. Application form required.
Initial approach: Proposal
Deadline(s): None
Officers: Alison Martin, Pres.; Floy A. Sauey, Secy.; William Hans, Treas.
Directors: Charles Frank; Todd L. Sauey; William R. Sauey.
EIN: 391934775
Selected grants: The following grants are a representative sample of this grantmaker's funding activity:
$347,250 to Tentmakers, Hopkins, MN, 2010.
$2,000 to Carroll University, Waukesha, WI, 2010. For scholarship.
$2,000 to Edgewood College, Madison, WI, 2010. For scholarship.
$2,000 to Hampton University, Hampton, VA, 2010. For scholarship.
$2,000 to Northland College, Ashland, WI, 2010. For scholarship.

2723
Nordson Corporation

28601 Clemens Rd.
Westlake, OH 44145-1148 (440) 892-1580
FAX: (440) 892-9507

Company URL: http://www.nordson.com
Establishment information: Established in 1954.
Company type: Public company
Company ticker symbol and exchange: NDSN/NASDAQ
Business activities: Designs, manufactures, and markets adhesive, sealant, and coating application systems.
Business type (SIC): Machinery/general industry; machinery/special industry
Financial profile for 2012: Number of employees, 5,361; assets, $1,829,520,000; sales volume, $1,409,580,000; pre-tax net income, $326,250,000; expenses, $1,074,100,000; liabilities, $1,159,740,000
Corporate officers: Joseph P. Keithley, Chair.; Michael F. Hilton, Pres. and C.E.O.; Gregory A. Thaxton, Sr. V.P. and C.F.O.; Shelly M. Peet, V.P., Human Resources and C.I.O.; Robert E. Veillette, V.P., Genl. Counsel, and Secy.
Board of directors: Joseph P. Keithley, Chair.; Lee C. Banks; Randolph W. Carson; Arthur L. George, Jr.; Michael F. Hilton; Frank M. Jaehnert; Michael J. Merriman, Jr.; Mary G. Puma; Victor L. Richey, Jr.; William L. Robinson
Subsidiaries: Asymptotic Technologies, Inc., Carlsbad, CA; Electrostatic Technology, Inc., Branford, CT
Plants: Duluth, Norcross, GA; Amherst, OH
International operations: Australia; Austria; Brazil; Canada; China; Colombia; Czech Republic; Finland; France; Germany; India; Italy; Japan; Malaysia; Mexico; Netherlands; Poland; Portugal; Russia; Singapore; South Korea; Spain; Sweden; Switzerland; Venezuela
Giving statement: Giving through the Nordson Corporation Contributions Program and the Nordson Corporation Foundation.
Company EIN: 340590250

Nordson Corporation Contributions Program

28601 Clemens Rd.
Westlake, OH 44145-4551 (440) 892-1580
FAX: (440) 414-5751; For employee matching gifts: (440) 414-5656; URL: http://www.nordson.com/EN-US/ABOUT-NORDSON/COMMUNITY/Pages/NordsonInTheCommunity.aspx

Purpose and activities: As a complement to its foundation, Nordson also makes charitable contributions to nonprofit organizations and

educational institutions directly. Support is given primarily in areas of company operations, with emphasis on San Diego County, California, Gwinnett County, Dawson County, and Emanuel County, Georgia, southeastern Massachusetts, Mercer County, New Jersey, Lorain County, Ohio, and Rhode Island.
Fields of interest: Arts; Education; Human services; United Ways and Federated Giving Programs; Public affairs; General charitable giving.
Program:
Matching Gifts Program: Nordson matches contributions made by its employees and retirees to nonprofit organizations and educational institutions on a one-for-one basis up to $6,000 per employee, per year.
Type of support: Donated equipment; Employee matching gifts; General/operating support; In-kind gifts; Program development; Sponsorships; Technical assistance; Use of facilities.
Geographic limitations: Giving primarily in areas of company operations, with emphasis on San Diego County, CA, Gwinnett County, Dawson County, and Emanuel County, GA, southeastern MA, Mercer County, NJ, Lorain County, OH, and RI.
Support limitations: No support for No matching gifts for religious organizations not of benefit to the entire community, organizations or institutions located outside the United States, or to the United Way. No matching gifts for tuition, bequests, value of personal services, dues payable to alumni groups, insurance premiums, or other similar indirect payments; subscription fees for publications, membership or admission fees, or payments for goods and services.
Application information: Applications accepted. Application form not required. Applicants should submit the following:
1) copy of IRS Determination Letter
Initial approach: Letter
Copies of proposal: 1
Deadline(s): None

The Nordson Corporation Foundation

28601 Clemens Rd.
Westlake, OH 44145-1119
E-mail: crender@nordson.com; Additional application addresses: GA: Maggie McElhannon, Mgr., Community Rels. Nordson Corp., 11475 Lakefield Dr., Duluth, GA 30097, tel.: (770) 497-3672, e-mail: mmcelhannon@nordson.com, San Diego County, CA: Ray McHenry, Mgr., Human Resource, Asymtek, 2762 Loker Ave. W., Carlsbad, CA 92008-6603, tel.: (760) 930-7258, e-mail: rmchenry@asymtek.com, southeastern MA and RI: Elizabeth Cabral, Dir., Human Resources, EFD, Inc., 40 Catamore Blvd., East Providence, RI 02914-1378, tel.: (401) 431-7105, e-mail: ecabral@efd-inc.com, NJ: Jennifer Kuhn, TAH Industries, 8 Applegate Dr., Robbinsville, NJ 08691, tel.: (609) 259-9222, e-mail: jkuhn@tah.com; URL: http://www.nordson.com/en-us/about-nordson/community/Pages/NordsonCorporationFoundationWelcomePage1.aspx

Establishment information: Established in 1988 in OH as successor to the Nordson Foundation, established in 1952.
Donor: Nordson Corp.
Contact: Cecilia H. Render, Exec. Dir.
Financial data (yr. ended 10/31/12): Assets, $14,019,925 (M); gifts received, $4,099,881; expenditures, $3,023,578; qualifying distributions, $2,967,020; giving activities include $2,967,020 for 185 grants (high: $275,000; low: $1,000).
Purpose and activities: The foundation supports organizations involved with education. Special emphasis is directed toward programs that cultivate educational curriculum and experiences that foster self-sufficiency, job readiness, and goals to aspire to higher education.
Fields of interest: Arts, cultural/ethnic awareness; Visual arts; Performing arts; Historic preservation/historical societies; Arts; Education, reform; Elementary/secondary education; Education, reading; Education; Environment; Employment, training; Housing/shelter; Human services, alliance/advocacy; Human services, reform; Children/youth, services; Family services; Human services, personal services; Human services; Economic development; Voluntarism promotion; Science, formal/general education; Mathematics; Public affairs, citizen participation; Accessibility/universal design; Public affairs Youth; Economically disadvantaged; Homeless.
Programs:
Arts and Culture: The foundation supports programs designed to broaden audience bases in Nordson communities; promote the visual and performing arts; provide educational enrichment for students; motivate at-risk youth; provide access to the arts for special needs audiences; and promote greater understanding among people via the arts.
Civic: The foundation supports programs designed to improve the physical or economic environment; promote cultural or historical preservation; and inform citizens and increase their participation in community improvement.
Education: The foundation supports programs designed to promote early childhood care and education; maximize student success; provide access to quality educational opportunities; promote innovation; facilitate partnerships/collaborations with school districts; fill gaps not covered by public monies; augment core curriculum; expand on traditional education; promote workforce preparation; retrain for new job markets; and strengthen communities.
Human Welfare: The foundation supports programs designed to promote prevention and lifestyle maintenance; crisis intervention; life transition opportunities; and systemic and/or policy change.
Type of support: Annual campaigns; Building/renovation; Capital campaigns; Continuing support; Emergency funds; Employee volunteer services; Equipment; Scholarship funds; Seed money; Technical assistance.
Geographic limitations: Giving primarily in areas of company operations, with emphasis on San Diego County, CA, Dawson County, Gwinnett County, and Emanuel County, GA, Lorain County, OH, southeastern, MA, Mercer County, NJ, and East Providence, RI.
Support limitations: No support for political organizations or candidates or discriminatory organizations. No grants to individuals, or for loans, endowments, membership drives, or travel.
Publications: Annual report; Application guidelines; Grants list; Program policy statement.
Application information: Applications accepted. Organizations receiving support are asked to provide a final report. Application form required. Applicants should submit the following:
1) copy of IRS Determination Letter
2) copy of most recent annual report/audited financial statement/990
3) listing of board of directors, trustees, officers and other key people and their affiliations
Initial approach: Complete online application
Copies of proposal: 1
Board meeting date(s): Feb., Apr., July, and Oct.
Deadline(s): Feb.15, May 15, Aug.15, and Oct.15 (All areas do not accept applications for all deadlines; check the website for your area)
Final notification: Within 3 months of application
Officers and Directors:* Michael F. Hilton, Pres. and C.E.O.; Doug Bloomfield, V.P.; John J. Keane, V.P.; Peter Lambert, V.P.; Shelly Peet, V.P.; Beverly J. Coen*, Secy.-Treas.; Greg Thaxton, C.F.O.; Cecilia H. Render, Exec. Dir.; James DeVries.
Number of staff: 3 full-time professional; 1 full-time support.
EIN: 341596194
Selected grants: The following grants are a representative sample of this grantmaker's funding activity:
$250,000 to Cleveland Play House, Cleveland, OH, 2011. For general support.
$101,000 to Case Western Reserve University, Cleveland, OH, 2011. For general support.
$50,000 to Cleveland Museum of Art, Cleveland, OH, 2011. For general support.
$25,000 to Case Western Reserve University, Cleveland, OH, 2011. For general support.
$15,000 to Family Promise of Greater Cleveland, Cleveland, OH, 2011. For general support.
$10,000 to City Club of Cleveland, Cleveland, OH, 2011. For general support.
$6,000 to Cleveland Museum of Natural History, Cleveland, OH, 2011. For general support.
$6,000 to Junior Achievement of Greater Cleveland, Cleveland, OH, 2011. For general support.
$5,000 to Cleveland Council on World Affairs, Cleveland, OH, 2011. For general support.
$5,000 to Cleveland Play House, Cleveland, OH, 2011. For general support.

2724
Nordstrom, Inc.

1617 6th Ave., 6th Fl.
P.O. Box 2737
Seattle, WA 98101-1742 (206) 628-2111
FAX: (206) 628-1795

Company URL: http://shop.nordstrom.com/
Establishment information: Established in 1901.
Company type: Public company
Company ticker symbol and exchange: JWN/NYSE
Business activities: Operates women's, men's, and children's apparel, shoes, and accessories stores.
Business type (SIC): Family apparel and accessory stores
Financial profile for 2013: Number of employees, 61,000; assets, $8,089,000,000; sales volume, $12,148,000,000; pre-tax net income, $1,185,000,000; expenses, $10,803,000,000; liabilities, $6,176,000,000
Fortune 1000 ranking: 2012—227th in revenues, 260th in profits, and 452nd in assets
Forbes 2000 ranking: 2012—801st in sales, 804th in profits, and 1608th in assets
Corporate officers: Enrique Hernandez, Jr., Chair.; Blake W. Nordstrom, Pres.; Michael G. Koppel, Exec. V.P. and C.F.O.; Daniel F. Little, Exec. V.P. and C.A.O.; R. Michael Richardson, Exec. V.P. and C.I.O.; Robert B. Sari, Exec. V.P., Genl. Counsel, and Secy.; Delena M. Sunday, Exec. V.P., Human Resources; James A. Howell, V.P., Finance
Board of directors: Enrique Hernandez, Jr., Chair.; Phyllis J. Campbell; Michelle M. Ebanks; Robert G. Miller; Blake W. Nordstrom; Erik B. Nordstrom; Peter E. Nordstrom; Philip G. Satre; B. Kevin Turner; Robert D. Walter; Alison A. Winter
Subsidiary: Nordstrom Credit, Inc., Englewood, CO
Giving statement: Giving through the Nordstrom, Inc. Corporate Giving Program.

Company EIN: 910515058

Nordstrom, Inc. Corporate Giving Program

1617 6th Ave.
Seattle, WA 98101-1742 (206) 373-4015
Nordstrom Scholarship Program: Ellen Greene, Nordstrom Scholarship Program Manager, tel.: (206) 373-4550;
e-mail: nordscholar@nordstrom.com; Corporate contributions outside Washington and Alaska: Claudia Gonzalez, Contrib. Coord., Nordstrom, 701 Harger Rd., Oak Brook, IL 60523; tel.: (630) 218-7913; URL: http://shop.nordstrom.com/c/nordstrom-cares?origin=footer

Contact: Anne Nordstrom Gittinger, Dir., Corp. Contribs.
Purpose and activities: Nordstrom makes charitable contributions to nonprofit organizations involved with arts and culture, education, health, community development, and the environment, with diversity also playing a key role. Support is limited to areas of company operations.
Fields of interest: Arts, cultural/ethnic awareness; Education; Environment; Health care; Human services; Community/economic development.
Program:
Nordstrom Scholarship Program: Nordstrom awards $10,000 scholarships to 80 outstanding high school students and help them achieve their dreams of going to college. The Nordstrom Scholarship recognizes students across the country for their exceptional scholastic achievement and community involvement. The program is open to high school juniors who live and attend school in one of the participating 30 states where Nordstrom currently has a full-line store; have at least a 2.7 GPA (based on a 4.0 scale) throughout high school; volunteer or participate in community services or extracurricular activities; plan on attending an accredited four-year college or university during the four years over which the scholarship is distributed; and plan to apply for financial assistance in order to attend college.
Type of support: Annual campaigns; Employee volunteer services; General/operating support; Scholarship funds.
Geographic limitations: Giving is limited to areas of company operations.
Support limitations: No support for individual primary or secondary schools or religious organizations not of direct benefit to the entire community. No grants to individuals, or for general operating support, political projects, individual scholarships, pageants or talent competitions, special occasion, goodwill, or program advertising, table purchases for fundraising events, loans or investments, auctions, raffles, or opportunity drawings, team sponsorships or fundraising competitions, production of films, videotapes, recordings, publications or displays, merchandise promotions, conferences or conventions, or event underwriting.
Publications: Application guidelines.
Application information: Applications accepted. A contributions committee reviews all requests. Application form not required. Applicants should submit the following:
1) copy of IRS Determination Letter
2) brief history of organization and description of its mission
3) copy of most recent annual report/audited financial statement/990
4) listing of board of directors, trustees, officers and other key people and their affiliations
5) detailed description of project and amount of funding requested

Organizations must demonstrate sound and responsible financial policies and management, and must show that the requested funds will support a project that provides a service not readily available elsewhere.
Initial approach: Proposal to headquarters
Committee meeting date(s): Annually
Deadline(s): Oct. 1
Final notification: January

2725
Norfolk Southern Corporation

3 Commercial Pl.
Norfolk, VA 23510-2191 (757) 629-2680

Company URL: http://www.nscorp.com
Establishment information: Established in 1982.
Company type: Public company
Company ticker symbol and exchange: NSC/NYSE
International Securities Identification Number: US6558441084
Business activities: Provides railroad transportation services.
Business type (SIC): Transportation/railroad
Financial profile for 2012: Number of employees, 30,943; assets, $30,342,000,000; sales volume, $11,040,000,000; pre-tax net income, $2,758,000,000; expenses, $7,922,000,000; liabilities, $20,582,000,000
Fortune 1000 ranking: 2012—247th in revenues, 119th in profits, and 185th in assets
Forbes 2000 ranking: 2012—871st in sales, 356th in profits, and 735th in assets
Corporate officers: Charles W. Moorman IV, Chair., Pres., and C.E.O.; Mark D. Manion, Exec. V.P. and C.O.O.; John P. Rathbone, Exec. V.P., Finance and C.F.O.; Deborah H. Butler, Exec. V.P. and C.I.O.; James A. Squires, Exec. V.P., Admin.; Marta R. Stewart, V.P. and Treas.; Clyde H. Allison, Jr., V.P. and Cont.; Cindy C. Earhart, V.P., Human Resources; Howard D. McFadden, Corp. Secy.
Board of directors: Charles W. Moorman IV, Chair.; Thomas D. Bell, Jr.; Erskine B. Bowles; Robert A. Bradway; Wesley G. Bush; Daniel A. Carp; Karen N. Horn, Ph.D.; Burton M. Joyce; Steven F. Leer; Michael D. Lockhart; Martin H. Nesbitt; John R. Thompson
Subsidiary: Conrail Inc., Philadelphia, PA
Offices: Atlanta, GA; Roanoke, VA
International operations: Bermuda
Giving statement: Giving through the Norfolk Southern Corporation Contributions Program and the Norfolk Southern Foundation.
Company EIN: 521188014

Norfolk Southern Corporation Contributions Program

P.O. Box 3040
Norfolk, VA 23514-3040 (757) 629-2881
E-mail: deborah.wyld@nscorp.com; E-mail: dhwyld@nscorp.com

Contact: Deborah H. Wyld, Exec. Dir., Norfolk Southern Fdn.
Financial data (yr. ended 12/31/08): Total giving, $36,864,252, including $3,158,445 for grants and $33,705,807 for in-kind gifts.
Purpose and activities: As a complement to its foundation, Norfolk Southern also makes charitable contributions to nonprofit organizations on a case by case basis. Support is given in areas of company operations.
Fields of interest: Arts; Higher education; Environment; Human services; Economic development.
Type of support: Conferences/seminars; Donated equipment; Donated land; Donated products; Equipment; Sponsorships.
Geographic limitations: Giving in areas of company operations east of the Mississippi River.
Support limitations: No support for athletic, disease-specific, or animal-related organizations.
Application information: Applications accepted. Application form not required.
Initial approach: Proposal to headquarters
Copies of proposal: 1
Committee meeting date(s): As needed
Deadline(s): None

Norfolk Southern Foundation

P.O. Box 3040
Norfolk, VA 23514-3040 (757) 629-2881
E-mail: katie.fletcher@nscorp.com; URL: http://www.nscorp.com/nscportal/nscorp/Community/NS%20Foundation/

Establishment information: Established in 1983 in VA.
Donors: Norfolk Southern Corp.; The Cincinnati, New Orleans and Texas Pacific Railway Co.; Rail Investment Co.
Contact: Katheryn Fletcher, Exec. Dir.
Financial data (yr. ended 12/31/11): Assets, $3,878,238 (M); gifts received, $5,996,779; expenditures, $6,251,234; qualifying distributions, $6,221,896; giving activities include $4,477,210 for 391 grants (high: $225,000; low: $400) and $1,713,835 for 1,675 employee matching gifts.
Purpose and activities: The foundation supports programs designed to promote education with emphasis on the post-secondary level; community enrichment with emphasis on cultural and artistic organizations; and health and human services.
Fields of interest: Museums; Performing arts; Arts; Education, early childhood education; Higher education; Education; Environment, natural resources; Environment; Health care, clinics/centers; Health care; Food banks; Homeless, human services; Human services; Business/industry; Community/economic development; United Ways and Federated Giving Programs; Mathematics; Engineering/technology; Science.
Programs:
Local Discretionary Grant Program: The foundation awards grants on behalf of each operating division of Northern Southern Railway Company. This program allows employees to have a direct impact on local communities. Each division is allowed to make recommendations for up to $12,000 of contributions annually.
Matching Gifts Program: The foundation matches contributions made by employees, retirees, and directors of Norfolk Southern to educational institutions and nonprofit organizations involved with arts and culture and the environment on a one-for-one basis from $50 to $35,000 per employee, per year, and from $50 to $25,000 per retiree, per year.
Type of support: Annual campaigns; Building/renovation; Capital campaigns; Continuing support; Employee matching gifts; Employee-related scholarships; Endowments; Equipment; General/operating support; Matching/challenge support; Program development; Scholarship funds; Sponsorships.
Geographic limitations: Giving primarily in areas of company operations, with emphasis on Atlanta, GA and Hampton Roads, Norfolk, and Roanoke, VA.
Support limitations: No support for religious, fraternal, social, or veterans' organizations, political

or lobbying organizations, public or private elementary or secondary schools, sports or athletic organizations, community or private foundations or pass-through organizations, or disease-related organizations, hospitals, or social services organizations. No grants to individuals (except for employee-related scholarships), or for fundraising events, telethons, races, or benefits, or sports or athletic activities.
Publications: Annual report; Application guidelines; Program policy statement.
Application information: Applications accepted. Additional information may be requested at a later date. Application form not required. Applicants should submit the following:
1) copy of IRS Determination Letter
2) brief history of organization and description of its mission
3) copy of most recent annual report/audited financial statement/990
4) listing of board of directors, trustees, officers and other key people and their affiliations
5) detailed description of project and amount of funding requested
6) listing of additional sources and amount of support
Initial approach: Proposal
Copies of proposal: 1
Board meeting date(s): As needed
Deadline(s): From July 15 to Sept. 30
Final notification: Dec. 31
Officers: Charles W. Moorman IV*, Chair., C.E.O., and Pres.; Deborah H. Butler, V.P.; James A. Hixon, V.P.; Mark D. Manion, V.P.; John P. Rathbone, V.P.; Donald W. Seale, V.P.; James A. Squires, V.P.; Howard D. McFadden, Secy.; Colin M. Barton, Treas.; Katheryn Fletcher, Exec. Dir.
Number of staff: 1 full-time professional.
EIN: 521328375
Selected grants: The following grants are a representative sample of this grantmaker's funding activity:
$217,800 to United Way of South Hampton Roads, Norfolk, VA, 2010. For general operating support.
$171,600 to United Way of Roanoke Valley, Roanoke, VA, 2010. For general operating support.
$138,600 to United Way of Metropolitan Atlanta, Atlanta, GA, 2010. For general operating support.
$95,000 to Chrysler Museum of Art, Norfolk, VA, 2010. For operating support.
$77,620 to National Merit Scholarship Corporation, Evanston, IL, 2010. For National Merit and Norfolk Southern Special Scholarship.
$69,300 to Virginia Opera, Norfolk, VA, 2010. For general operating support.
$50,000 to Virginia Foundation for Independent Colleges, Richmond, VA, 2010. To endow Norfolk Southern Scholars program.
$10,000 to North Carolina A & T State University, Greensboro, NC, 2010. For general operating support for College Partnership Program.
$10,000 to Robert R. Moton Museum, Farmville, VA, 2010. For general operating support.
$7,260 to United Way of Miami County, Peru, IN, 2010. For general operating support.

2726
Noritz America Corporation

11160 Grace Ave.
Fountain Valley, CA 92708-5436
(714) 433-2905
FAX: (714) 241-1196

Company URL: http://www.noritz.com
Establishment information: Established in 2002.
Company type: Subsidiary of a foreign company
Business activities: Operates tankless water heater company.
Business type (SIC): Hardware, plumbing, and heating equipment—wholesale
Corporate officers: Masaaki Tokunou, Pres.; Kapsusha Okamura, V.P.
Giving statement: Giving through the Noritz America Corporation Contributions Program.

Noritz America Corporation Contributions Program

11160 Grace Ave.
Fountain Valley, CA 92708-5436 (714) 433-2905
URL: http://www.noritz.com

2727
Nortex Corporation

1415 Louisiana St., Ste. 3100
Houston, TX 77002 (713) 658-1142

Company URL: http://www.nortexcorp.com/
Establishment information: Established in 1957.
Company type: Private company
Business activities: Conducts crude oil and natural gas exploration, development, and production activities.
Business type (SIC): Extraction/oil and gas
Corporate officers: Albert W. Dugan, Chair., Pres., and C.E.O.; Patrick W. Dugan, V.P. and Genl. Counsel
Board of director: Albert W. Dugan, Chair.
Giving statement: Giving through the Dugan Foundation.

The Dugan Foundation

1415 Louisiana St., Ste. 3100
Houston, TX 77002-7353

Establishment information: Established in 2000.
Donors: Nortex Corp.; A.W. Dugan; Lydia P. Dugan.
Financial data (yr. ended 12/31/11): Assets, $1,668,012 (M); gifts received, $300,000; expenditures, $87,150; qualifying distributions, $87,150; giving activities include $87,150 for grants.
Purpose and activities: The foundation supports organizations involved with performing arts, health, human services, and Christianity.
Fields of interest: Performing arts; Performing arts, dance; Performing arts, music; Health care, patient services; Health care; Human services, gift distribution; Human services, mind/body enrichment; Human services; Christian agencies & churches.
Type of support: General/operating support.
Geographic limitations: Giving primarily in Houston, TX.
Support limitations: No grants to individuals.
Application information: Applications not accepted. Unsolicited requests for funds not accepted.
Officers and Directors:* Lydia P. Dugan*, Pres.; Albert W. Dugan*, V.P.; Patrick W. Dugan*, Secy.-Treas.
EIN: 760649328

2728
North American Rescue Products

35 Tedwall Ct.
Greer, SC 29650-4791 (864) 675-9800

Company URL: http://www.narescue.com
Establishment information: Established in 1995.
Company type: Private company
Business activities: Operates equipment lease and rental company.
Business type (SIC): Equipment rental and leasing/miscellaneous
Corporate officers: Robert Castellani, Vice-Chair.; Matt Westra, V.P., Sales
Board of director: Robert Castellani, Vice-Chair.
Giving statement: Giving through the North American Rescue Products Foundation Inc.

North American Rescue Products Foundation Inc.

481 Garlington Rd., Ste A
Greenville, SC 29615-4619 (864) 271-0966

Establishment information: Established in 2005 in SC.
Donors: North American Rescue Products, Inc.; Robert A. Castellani.
Contact: Robert Castellani, Pres.
Financial data (yr. ended 12/31/11): Assets, $20,230 (M); gifts received, $49,600; expenditures, $43,380; qualifying distributions, $33,982; giving activities include $33,982 for grants.
Purpose and activities: The foundation supports organizations involved with education, health, autism, human services, and Christianity. Special emphasis is directed toward programs designed to serve military personnel.
Fields of interest: Secondary school/education; Education; Hospitals (general); Health care; Autism; Children/youth, services; Human services; Military/veterans' organizations; Christian agencies & churches Military/veterans.
Type of support: General/operating support; Program development.
Geographic limitations: Giving primarily in Greenville and Simpsonville, SC; giving also to national organizations.
Application information: Applications not accepted. Unsolicited requests for funds not accepted.
Officers: Robert A. Castellani, Pres.; Curtis W. Stodghill, Secy.-Treas.
EIN: 203128585
Selected grants: The following grants are a representative sample of this grantmaker's funding activity:
$25,000 to Operation Comfort, San Antonio, TX, 2010.
$10,000 to Step Up for Soldiers, Kure Beach, NC, 2010.
$2,500 to Saint Josephs Catholic School, Greenville, SC, 2010.

2729
North Carolina Electric Membership Corporation

3400 Sumner Blvd.
Raleigh, NC 27616-2950 (919) 872-0800

Company URL: http://www.ncemc.com
Establishment information: Established in 1949.

Company type: Cooperative
Business activities: Generates, transmits, and distributes electricity.
Business type (SIC): Electric services
Corporate officers: David Eggers, Pres.; Joe Brannan, Exec. V.P. and C.E.O.; Mike Burnette, Sr. V.P. and C.O.O.; Tony E. Herrin, Secy.-Treas.
Giving statement: Giving through the Touchstone Energy Bright Ideas Grant Program.

Touchstone Energy Bright Ideas Grant Program

P.O. Box 27306
Raleigh, NC 27611-7306
E-mail: lindsey.listrom@ncemcs.com; URL: http://www.ncbrightideas.com

Contact: Lindsey Listrom
Purpose and activities: Through the Touchstone Energy Bright Ideas Grant Program, North Carolina Electric Membership Corporation awards grants to K-12 teachers for innovative, classroom-based projects. Support is limited to North Carolina.
Fields of interest: Elementary/secondary education.
Program:
Bright Ideas Education Grant Program: North Carolina Electric Cooperatives awards grants of up to $2,000 to K-12 teachers for innovative classroom-based projects. Winning projects must involve students directly, achieve clearly defined goals and learning objectives, use innovative and creative teaching methods, provide ongoing benefits to students, and feature measurable results that can be evaluated upon completion. This program is administered by individual cooperatives and award amounts may vary.
Type of support: Grants to individuals.
Geographic limitations: Giving limited to NC.
Support limitations: No grants for salaries or professional development.
Publications: Application guidelines.
Application information: Applications accepted. Teachers who submit applications for the early-bird deadline will be entered to win a $500 Visa gift card. Support is limited to 1 contribution per teacher during any given year. Application form required.
Initial approach: Complete online application form
Copies of proposal: 1
Deadline(s): Aug. 15 for early-birds; Sept. 23
Final notification: Nov. and Dec.

2730
North Carolina Foam Industries, Inc.

1515 Carter St.
P.O. Box 1528
Mount Airy, NC 27030-5721
(336) 789-9161

Company URL: http://www.ncfi.com
Establishment information: Established in 1964.
Company type: Subsidiary of a private company
Business activities: Manufactures foam and plastic products.
Business type (SIC): Plastic products/miscellaneous
Corporate officers: Robert R. Ferris, Co-Pres. and C.E.O.; Swanson Snow, Co-Pres.; Steve Riddle, Co-Pres.; Kenny Moles, C.F.O.
Board of director: Mitch Clifton
Giving statement: Giving through the North Carolina Foam Industries Foundation.

North Carolina Foam Industries Foundation

(formerly North Carolina Foam Foundation)
P.O. Box 34276
Charlotte, NC 28234-4276

Establishment information: Established in 1965.
Donors: North Carolina Foam Industries, Inc.; Thomas Barnhardt; NCFI Banhardt Foundation.
Contact: Robert H. Perkins, Dir.
Financial data (yr. ended 12/31/11): Assets, $6,047,700 (M); expenditures, $379,610; qualifying distributions, $347,300; giving activities include $347,300 for grants.
Purpose and activities: The foundation supports arts councils and organizations involved with education, health, and human services.
Fields of interest: Arts councils; Higher education; Medical school/education; Education; Hospitals (general); Palliative care; Health care; Boy scouts; American Red Cross; Salvation Army; Children/youth, services; Family services, domestic violence; Residential/custodial care, hospices; Human services; United Ways and Federated Giving Programs.
Type of support: Capital campaigns; General/operating support; Program development.
Geographic limitations: Giving primarily in Charlotte, NC.
Support limitations: No grants to individuals.
Application information: Applications not accepted. Contributes only to pre-selected organizations.
Trustee: Ralph Falero.
EIN: 566068247
Selected grants: The following grants are a representative sample of this grantmaker's funding activity:
$20,000 to United Way of Central Carolinas, Charlotte, NC, 2011. For general support.
$17,500 to Boy Scouts of America, Winston-Salem, NC, 2011. For general support.
$10,000 to Safe Alliance, Charlotte, NC, 2011. For general support.
$10,000 to Surry Arts Council, Mount Airy, NC, 2011. For general support.
$6,000 to Surry Community College, Dobson, NC, 2011. For general support.
$5,000 to United Way of Catawba County, Hickory, NC, 2011. For general support.
$4,000 to Crisis Assistance Ministry, Charlotte, NC, 2011. For general support.
$4,000 to Friendship Trays, Charlotte, NC, 2011. For general support.
$2,500 to Catawba Lands Conservancy, Charlotte, NC, 2011. For general support.
$1,000 to Alexander Youth Network, Charlotte, NC, 2011. For general support.

2731
North Community Bank

3639 N. Broadway St.
Chicago, IL 60613-4489 (773) 244-7000
FAX: (773) 244-7075

Company URL: http://www.northcommunitybank.com
Establishment information: Established in 1972.
Company type: Private company
Business activities: Operates commercial bank.
Business type (SIC): Banks/commercial
Corporate officers: Peter A. Fasseas, Chair. and C.E.O.; Daniel J. Healy, Pres.; Tariq Altaf, V.P., Opers.
Board of director: Peter A. Fasseas, Chair.
Giving statement: Giving through the Peter & Paula Fasseas Foundation.

Peter & Paula Fasseas Foundation

c/o Peter Fasseas
1110 W. 35th St.
Chicago, IL 60609-1442

Establishment information: Established in 1995 in IL.
Donors: Alpha Bancorp; Metropolitan Bancorp; Plaza Bancorp; Metropolitan Bank Group; North Community Bank.
Financial data (yr. ended 12/31/11): Assets, $28,006,051 (M); expenditures, $1,477,749; qualifying distributions, $1,346,829; giving activities include $1,318,350 for 27 grants (high: $1,000,000; low: $300).
Purpose and activities: The foundation supports hospitals and organizations involved with education, animal welfare, and cancer.
Fields of interest: Secondary school/education; Higher education; Law school/education; Education; Animal welfare; Animals/wildlife, preservation/protection; Cancer; Boys & girls clubs.
Type of support: General/operating support.
Geographic limitations: Giving limited to Chicago, IL.
Support limitations: No grants to individuals.
Application information: Applications not accepted. Contributes only to pre-selected organizations.
Officer and Directors: Peter A. Fasseas, Pres.; Alexis Fasseas; Drew Fasseas; Paula Fasseas.
EIN: 364010374
Selected grants: The following grants are a representative sample of this grantmaker's funding activity:
$450,000 to Dana-Farber Cancer Institute, Boston, MA, 2009.
$13,100 to PAWS Chicago, Chicago, IL, 2009.
$10,000 to Pacific Marine Mammal Center, Laguna Beach, CA, 2009.
$5,000 to Ann and Robert H. Lurie Children's Hospital of Chicago, Chicago, IL, 2009.
$5,000 to Boys and Girls Clubs of Chicago, Chicago, IL, 2009.
$1,000 to Rehabilitation Institute of Chicago, Chicago, IL, 2009.

2732
North Group Consultants, Inc.

(formerly North & Schanz Consulting Group, Inc.)
617 W. Chestnut St.
Lancaster, PA 17603 (717) 299-9800
FAX: (717) 299-9300

Company URL: http://northgroupconsultants.com/
Establishment information: Established in 1997.
Company type: Private company
Business activities: Provides management consulting services.
Business type (SIC): Management and public relations services
Corporate officers: Dennis Clemmer, Partner; Daryl Leisey, Partner; Roger S. North, Partner
Giving statement: Giving through the North Foundation, Inc.

North Foundation, Inc.

(formerly North & Schanz Charitable Foundation, Inc.)
617 W. Chestnut St.
Lancaster, PA 17603-3410 (717) 299-9800
E-mail: foundation@northgroupconsultants.com;
URL: http://northgroupconsultants.com/who-we-are/

Establishment information: Established in 2001 in PA.
Donors: North & Schanz Consulting Group, Inc.; North Group Consultants, Inc.
Contact: Roger S. North, Pres.
Financial data (yr. ended 12/31/11): Assets, $1,023 (M); gifts received, $25,653; expenditures, $25,160; qualifying distributions, $24,500; giving activities include $24,500 for grants.
Purpose and activities: The foundation supports organizations involved with Christianity.
Fields of interest: Youth development; Human services; Religion.
Geographic limitations: Giving limited to a 75-mile radius of Lancaster, PA.
Support limitations: No grants to individuals.
Application information: Applications not accepted. Unsolicited requests for funds not accepted.
Board meeting date(s): Dec.
Officer and Directors:* Roger S. North*, Pres.; Virginia Badger; Dennis M. Clemmer; Ronald Ford; Daryl L. Leisey; Scott R. Scheffey; Mary Ann Stoltzfus.
Number of staff: None.
EIN: 311795470

2733
North Jersey Media Group, Inc.

(formerly The Evening Record)
1 Garret Mountain Plz.
P.O. Box 471
Woodland Park, NJ 07424-0471
(201) 646-4000

Company URL: http://www.northjersey.com
Establishment information: Established in 1895.
Company type: Private company
Business activities: Publishes newspapers; publishes magazines; provides Internet information services; provides commercial printing services.
Business type (SIC): Newspaper publishing and/or printing; periodical publishing and/or printing; printing/commercial; computer services
Corporate officers: Malcolm A. Borg, Chair.; Stephen A. Borg, Pres.; Thomas G. Heffernan, C.F.O.; Charles W. Gibney, Exec. V.P., Treas., and C.F.O.; Jennifer A. Borg, V.P., Genl. Counsel, and Secy.; Christopher P. Krasas, V.P., Finance; Susan Beard, V.P., Human Resources; Kristen A. Von Hassel, V.P., Mktg.
Board of director: Malcolm A. Borg, Chair.
Giving statement: Giving through the North Jersey Media Group Foundation, Inc.

North Jersey Media Group Foundation, Inc.

P.O. Box 75
Hackensack, NJ 07602-9192 (973) 569-7681
FAX: (973) 569-7268

Establishment information: Established in 2002 in NJ.
Donor: North Jersey Media Group Inc.
Contact: Jenifer A. Borg, Pres.
Financial data (yr. ended 12/31/11): Revenue, $457,234; assets, $672,849 (M); gifts received, $409,687; expenditures, $484,216; program services expenses, $449,609; giving activities include $449,609 for 10 grants (high: $25,000; low: $5,000).
Purpose and activities: The foundation's mission is to provide charitable funding and services in order to make a significant difference in the lives of its North Jersey neighbors.
Fields of interest: Disasters, 9/11/01; Community/economic development.
Programs:
Compassion Fund: The fund assists individuals or families in northern New Jersey who are impacted by an immediate personal crisis. The fund's purpose is to provide short-term assistance to those who have suffered losses due to natural causes (e.g. fire, flood, hurricane), medical illness or injury, or personal reasons. In order to qualify for donations from the fund, an individual must currently reside in Bergen, Essex, Hudson, Morris, Passaic, Sussex, or Union counties in New Jersey.
Disaster Relief Fund: The fund assists the victims and families of the September 11, 2001 tragedy. The fund's purpose is to provide help in the areas of food, clothing, shelter, medical needs, property damage or loss, as well as therapeutic and educational benefits. In order to qualify for donations from the fund, the individual victim and/or the victim's family must currently reside in Bergen, Essex, Hudson, Morris, Passaic, Sussex, or Union counties in New Jersey. In addition, nonprofit agencies representing victims and/or the families of victims may also be eligible to apply for funds.
General Fund: The fund was established so that the foundation could support programs managed by other nonprofits that improve the quality of life for residents of North Jersey. It was designed to fund innovative projects that can have measurable impact and create meaningful change.
Geographic limitations: Giving primarily in Bergen, Essex, Hudson, Morris, Passaic, Sussex, and Union counties, NJ.
Publications: Application guidelines.
Application information: Applications accepted. Application form required.
Initial approach: Download application form
Deadline(s): Jan. 1, Apr. 1, Aug. 1, and Oct. 1
Officers: Sandra A. Borg*, Chair.; Jennifer A. Borg*, Pres.; Stephen A. Borg*, V.P.; Janine Harlop*, Secy.; Thomas Haffernman*, Treas.
EIN: 352165636

2734
North Middlesex Savings Bank Inc.

7 Main St.
Ayer, MA 01432-1325 (978) 772-3306

Company URL: https://www.nmsb.com
Establishment information: Established in 1885.
Company type: Private company
Business activities: Operates savings bank.
Business type (SIC): Savings institutions
Corporate officers: Paul D. Bresnahan, Chair.; William P. Marshall, Pres. and C.E.O.; John J. Spinello, V.P. and Cont.; Nancy M. Partridge, V.P., Opers.; Patricia A. Thorpe, V.P., Mktg.; Paula F. Carmichael, V.P., Human Resources
Board of directors: Paul D. Bresnahan, Chair.; David B. Alexander; Murray W. Clark; David J. Eliades; Richard Everett III; Paul J. Farley; Stephen L. Gervais; Robert H. Hughes; William P. Marshall; Warren M. McFague; Stephen M. Slarsky; Peter E. Warren
Giving statement: Giving through the North Middlesex Charitable Foundation Inc.

North Middlesex Charitable Foundation Inc.

7 Main St.
Ayer, MA 01432-1325 (978) 772-3306

Establishment information: Established in 2004 in MA.
Donor: North Middlesex Savings Bank.
Contact: Warren W. Chase, Jr., Treas.
Financial data (yr. ended 10/31/11): Assets, $134,560 (M); expenditures, $8,165; qualifying distributions, $8,065; giving activities include $8,000 for 2 grants (high: $5,000; low: $3,000).
Purpose and activities: Giving primarily to organizations located in the greater northern Middlesex County, Massachusetts.
Fields of interest: Arts; Education; Safety/disasters.
Geographic limitations: Giving primarily in northern Middlesex County, MA.
Support limitations: No grants to individuals.
Application information: Applications accepted. Application form required.
Initial approach: Proposal
Deadline(s): None
Officers and Directors:* William P. Marshall*, Pres.; David J. Eliades*, Clerk; Warren W. Chase, Jr., Treas.; Paul D. Bresnahan; Stephen M. Slarsky.
EIN: 201834861

2735
North Shore Gas

130 E. Randolph St.
Chicago, IL 60601-6222 (312) 240-4000
FAX: (312) 240-4350

Company URL: http://www.northshoregasdelivery.com
Establishment information: Established in 1850.
Company type: Subsidiary of a public company
Business activities: Operates natural gas distribution company.
Business type (SIC): Gas production and distribution
Corporate officers: Lawrence T. Borgard, Vice-Chair. and C.E.O.; Willard S. Evans, Jr., Pres.; Joseph P. O'Leary, Sr., Sr. V.P., and C.F.O.; William E. Morrow, Exec. V.P., Opers.; Douglas M. Ruschau, V.P. and Treas.; Diane L. Ford, V.P. and Cont.
Board of directors: Willard S. Evans, Jr.; Joseph P. O'Leary, Sr.
Giving statement: Giving through the North Shore Gas Corporate Giving Program.

North Shore Gas Corporate Giving Program

130 E. Randolph St.
Chicago, IL 60601-6222 (312) 240-4000
FAX: (312) 240-4389;
E-mail: contributions@integrysgroup.com;
URL: http://northshoregasdelivery.com/company/guidelines.aspx

Contact: Richard Turner, Mgr., Corp. Contribs.
Purpose and activities: North Shore Gas makes charitable contributions to nonprofit organizations involved with arts and culture, education, community and economic development, the environment, human services, and wellness. Support is limited to

areas of company operations in the northern suburbs of Chicago, Illinois; giving also to national organizations whose funds are used locally.
Fields of interest: Arts; Education; Environment; Health care; Youth development; Human services; Community/economic development Minorities; Women; Economically disadvantaged.
Type of support: General/operating support.
Geographic limitations: Giving limited to areas of company operations in northern suburbs of Chicago, IL.
Support limitations: No support for religious, political, or discriminatory organizations, or public or private K-12 schools. No grants to individuals, or for post-secondary scholarships other than those provided through the company's scholarship program, or free natural gas or electric service, moving of poles, or utility-related construction.
Application information: Applications accepted. Application form required.
Initial approach: Complete online application

2736
North Shore-Long Island Jewish Health System

145 Community Dr.
Great Neck, NY 11021 (516) 465-8100

Company URL: http://www.northshorelij.com
Company type: Private company
Business activities: Operates healthcare network.
Business type (SIC): Hospitals
Corporate officers: Michael J. Dowling, Pres. and C.E.O.; Mark J. Solazzo, Exec. V.P. and C.O.O.; Robert S. Shapiro, Exec. V.P. and C.F.O.; Keith Thompson, Sr. V.P. and Gen. Counsel
Giving statement: Giving through the North Shore-Long Island Jewish Health System Corporate Giving Program.

North Shore-Long Island Jewish Health System Corporate Giving Program

145 Community Dr.
Great Neck, NY 11021 (516) 465-8100
URL: http://www.northshorelij.com

2737
Northeast Utilities

(formerly Northeast Utilities System)
1 Federal St., Bldg. 111-4
Springfield, MA 01105 (413) 785-5871

Company URL: http://www.nu.com
Establishment information: Established in 1966.
Company type: Public company
Company ticker symbol and exchange: NU/NYSE
International Securities Identification Number: US6643971061
Business activities: Generates, transmits, and distributes electricity.
Business type (SIC): Electric services
Financial profile for 2012: Number of employees, 8,842; assets, $28,302,820,000; sales volume, $66,273,790,000; pre-tax net income, $808,000,000; expenses, $5,155,580,000; liabilities, $18,910,210,000
Fortune 1000 ranking: 2012—402nd in revenues, 323rd in profits, and 193rd in assets
Forbes 2000 ranking: 2012—1250th in sales, 1064th in profits, and 766th in assets
Corporate officers: Charles W. Shivery, Chair.; Thomas J. May, Pres. and C.E.O.; Leon J. Olivier, Exec. V.P. and C.O.O.; James J. Judge, Exec. V.P. and C.F.O.; David R. McHale, Exec. V.P. and C.A.O.; Gregory B. Butler, Sr. V.P., Genl. Counsel, and Secy.; Jay S. Buth, V.P., C.A.O., and Cont.; Philip J. Lembo, V.P. and Treas.
Board of directors: Charles W. Shivery, Chair.; Richard H. Booth; Paul A. La Camera; John S. Clarkeson; Cotton M. Cleveland; Sanford Cloud, Jr.; James S. DiStasio; Francis A. Doyle; William C. Van Faasen; Charles K. Gifford; Kenneth R. Leibler; Thomas J. May; Frederica M. Williams; Dennis R. Wraase
Subsidiaries: The Connecticut Light and Power Company, Berlin, CT; Holyoke Water Power Co., Holyoke, MA; North Atlantic Energy Corp., Manchester, NH; Public Service Company of New Hampshire, Manchester, NH; Western Massachusetts Electric Co., West Springfield, MA
Giving statement: Giving through the Northeast Utilities System Corporate Giving Program and the Northeast Utilities Foundation, Inc.
Company EIN: 042147929

Northeast Utilities Foundation, Inc.

P.O. Box 270
Hartford, CT 06141-0270 (860) 665-2333
FAX: (860) 728-4594; E-mail: paynesm@nu.com; Additional tel. and e-mail: (888) 682-4639, nufoundation@nu.com; Contact in CT: Lindsay Parke, Comm. Rels., tel.: (860) 665-3306, e-mail: parkelw@nu.com; Contact in Western MA: Edgar Alejandro, Economic and Community Devel., Western Massachusetts Electric Co., P.O. Box 2010, West Springfield, MA 01090-2010, tel.: (413) 785-5871, fax: (413) 787-9289, ext. 2289, e-mail: alejae@nu.com; Contact in NH: Paulette Faggiano, Comms. and Public Affairs, Public Service Co. of New Hampshire, P.O. Box 330, Manchester, NH 03105, tel.: (603) 634-3386, fax: (603) 634-2367, e-mail: faggips@nu.com; URL: http://www.northeastutilitiesfoundation.org
Additional URL: http://www.cl-p.com/community/partners/grants/nufoundation.asp

Establishment information: Established in 1998 in CT.
Donors: The Connecticut Light and Power Co.; Northeast Nuclear Energy Co.; Northeast Utilities; Public Service Co. of New Hampshire; Western Massachusetts Electric Co.; Select Energy, Inc.; Yankee Gas Services Company.
Contact: Shirley M. Payne, Pres. and Exec. Dir.
Financial data (yr. ended 12/31/11): Assets, $20,372,619 (M); expenditures, $1,772,303; qualifying distributions, $1,741,988; giving activities include $1,741,988 for grants.
Purpose and activities: The foundation supports programs designed to promote economic and community development, workforce development, and environmental stewardship.
Fields of interest: Museums (science/technology); Education; Environment, water resources; Environment, land resources; Environment, energy; Environment; Employment, training; Employment; Salvation Army; Economic development; Community development, small businesses; Community/economic development.
Programs:
Community Investment Program: The foundation provides small grants to nonprofit organizations within Northeast Utilities Connecticut, western Massachusetts, and New Hampshire service territories. The program is administered by local Northeast Utilities State Community Investment Councils.
Economic and Community Development: The foundation supports programs designed to promote economic and community development. Special emphasis is directed toward programs designed to promote job creation; small business development; and smart growth.
Education Matching Gift Program: The foundation matches contributions made by employees, retirees, and outside directors and trustees of Northeast Utilities System to institutions of higher education from $25 to $1,000 per contributor, per year.
Environmental Leadership & Stewardship: The foundation supports programs designed to promote environmental leadership and stewardship. Special emphasis is directed toward programs designed to protect, preserve, and improve the environment, natural habitats, and biological diversity; promote renewable energy; and foster energy efficiency.
Sons & Daughters Scholarship Program: The foundation awards $2,500 four-year college scholarships to high school seniors who are children of employees of Northeast Utilities System. Ten scholarship recipients will be selected from Connecticut, Massachusetts, and New Hampshire. The program is administered by Scholarship Management Services.
Workforce Development: The foundation supports programs designed to promote workforce development. Special emphasis is directed toward programs designed to promote training and education.
Type of support: Continuing support; Employee matching gifts; Employee-related scholarships; General/operating support; Program development; Sponsorships.
Geographic limitations: Giving primarily in areas of company operations, with emphasis on CT, western MA, and NH.
Support limitations: No support for private foundations, religious, political, or fraternal organizations, or organizations not of direct benefit to the entire community. No grants to individuals (except for employee-related scholarships), or for endowments, debt reduction, or athletic trips.
Publications: Application guidelines; Grants list.
Application information: Applications accepted. The foundation supports large regional projects through select partners and through requests for proposals that address a specific issue or focus areas. Inquiries and proposals for small grant requests should be directed toward local state representatives. Application form not required.
Initial approach: Proposal to local state representative in Connecticut, Massachusetts, and New Hampshire
Board meeting date(s): Feb., May, Aug., and Nov.
Deadline(s): None
Officers and Directors:* Charles W. Shivery*, Chair.; Shirley M. Payne, Pres., Secy., and Exec. Dir.; David R. McHale, Treas.; Gregory B. Butler; Jeffrey D. Butler; Peter J. Clarke; Jean M. LaVecchia; Gary A. Long; Leon J. Oliver; Rodney O. Powell; Marie T. Van Luling.
EIN: 061527290

2738
Northern Arkansas Telephone Company

(also known as NATCO)
301 E. Main St.
P.O. Box 209
Flippin, AR 72634 (870) 453-8800

Company URL: http://www.natconet.com
Establishment information: Established in 1951.
Company type: Private company
Business activities: Provides telephone communications services; provides data telephone communications services.
Business type (SIC): Telephone communications
Corporate officers: Steven Sanders, Chair. and C.E.O.; Steven G. Sanders, Jr., Pres.; Deanna Sullivan, Secy-Treas.; David White, Cont.
Board of director: Steven Sanders, Chair.
Giving statement: Giving through the South Shore Foundation.

South Shore Foundation

P.O. Box 209
Flippin, AR 72634-0209 (870) 453-8811
E-mail: dlatting@southshore.com; URL: http://www.southshore.com/foundation/

Establishment information: Established in 1995 in AR.
Donor: Northern Arkansas Telephone Co.
Contact: Deanna Sullivan, Tr.
Financial data (yr. ended 12/31/11): Assets, $31,356 (M); expenditures, $40,973; qualifying distributions, $38,949; giving activities include $38,949 for grants.
Purpose and activities: The foundation supports organizations involved with education, the environment, and community development.
Fields of interest: Education; Youth development; Community/economic development.
Program:
Scholarships: The foundation awards college scholarships to academic achievers in areas of company operations.
Type of support: Building/renovation; Equipment; Scholarships—to individuals.
Geographic limitations: Giving to government agencies limited to the South Shore area of north central AR and south central MO; all other potential grantees must reside in the United States.
Support limitations: No grants to individuals (except for scholarships).
Application information: Applications accepted. Application form required.
Initial approach: Proposal
Deadline(s): None
Trustees: Roger Bates; Fred Berry; Curt Bryant; Bobby Gray; Carol Gresham; Hank Hudson; Steve Smith; Phyllis Speer; Deanna Sullivan.
EIN: 621666363

2739
Northern Indiana Public Service Company

(also known as NIPSCO)
(formerly Northern Indiana Fuel and Light Company, Inc.)
801 E. 86th Ave.
Merrillville, IN 46410 (877) 647-5990

Company URL: http://www.nipsco.com
Establishment information: Established in 1912.
Company type: Subsidiary of a public company
Business activities: Transmits and distributes natural gas.
Business type (SIC): Gas production and distribution
Corporate officers: Jimmy D. Staton, C.E.O.; Kathleen O'Leary, Pres.; Peter T. Disser, C.F.O.
Giving statement: Giving through the Northern Indiana Fuel and Light Company Scholarship Fund.

Northern Indiana Fuel and Light Company Scholarship Fund

c/o PNC Bank, N.A
P.O. Box 94651
Cleveland, OH 44101 (260) 461-6218

Donor: Northern Indiana Fuel and Light Co., Inc.
Contact: Margaret A. Sturm
Financial data (yr. ended 12/31/11): Assets, $292,068 (M); expenditures, $31,149; qualifying distributions, $29,078; giving activities include $5,000 for 5 grants to individuals (high: $1,000; low: $1,000).
Purpose and activities: The foundation awards college scholarships to children of employees of Northern Indiana Fuel and Light.
Type of support: Employee-related scholarships.
Geographic limitations: Giving primarily in areas of company operations.
Application information: Applications accepted. Application form required.
Initial approach: Proposal
Deadline(s): June 1
Trustee: PNC Bank, N.A.
EIN: 311030243

2740
Northern Trust Corporation

50 S. LaSalle St.
Chicago, IL 60603 (312) 630-6000
FAX: (312) 444-5244

Company URL: http://www.northerntrust.com
Establishment information: Established in 1889.
Company type: Public company
Company ticker symbol and exchange: NTRS/NASDAQ
International Securities Identification Number: US6658591044
Business activities: Operates a financial holding company that is a provider of investment management, asset and fund administration, fiduciary, and banking solutions for corporations, institutions, and affluent individuals.
Business type (SIC): Banks/commercial; security and commodity services
Financial profile for 2012: Assets, $97,500,000,000; sales volume, $4,200,000,000
Fortune 1000 ranking: 2012—561st in revenues, 267th in profits, and 64th in assets
Forbes 2000 ranking: 2012—1488th in sales, 840th in profits, and 259th in assets
Corporate officers: Frederick H. Waddell, Chair. and C.E.O.; William L. Morrison, Pres. and C.O.O.; Michael G. O'Grady, Exec. V.P. and C.F.O.; Timothy P. Moen, Exec. V.P. and C.A.O.; Kelly R. Welsh, Exec. V.P. and Genl. Counsel; Richard D. Kukla, Sr. V.P. and Cont.
Board of directors: Frederick H. Waddell, Chair.; John R. H. Bond; Linda Walker Bynoe; Nicholas D. Chabraja; Susan M. Crown; Dipak C. Jain; Robert W. Lane; Edward J. Mooney; Jose Luis Prado; John W. Rowe; Martin P. Slark; David H. B. Smith, Jr.; Charles A. Tribbett III
Subsidiary: The Northern Trust Company, Chicago, IL
International operations: England; Japan
Giving statement: Giving through the Northern Trust Corporation Contributions Program, the Northern Trust Company Charitable Trust, and the Northern Trust/Lake Forest Foundation.
Company EIN: 362723087

Northern Trust Corporation Contributions Program

50 South LaSalle St.
Chicago, IL 60603 (312) 444-3578
URL: http://www.northerntrust.com/pws/jsp/display2.jsp?XML=pages/nt/0706/1180976037316_272.xml&TYPE=interior

Contact: Connie Lindsey, Exec. V.P., Corp. Social Responsibility

The Northern Trust Company Charitable Trust

50 S. LaSalle St., L7
Chicago, IL 60675-0001 (312) 630-1762
E-mail: northern_trust_charitable_trust@ntrs.com; URL: http://www.northerntrust.com/pws/jsp/display2.jsp?XML=pages/nt/0601/1137700254265_667.xml

Establishment information: Trust established in 1966 in IL.
Donor: The Northern Trust Co.
Contact: Chastity Davis, Community Affairs
Financial data (yr. ended 12/31/11): Assets, $3,287,885 (M); gifts received, $4,681,333; expenditures, $4,302,788; qualifying distributions, $4,302,608; giving activities include $4,302,593 for grants.
Purpose and activities: The trust supports organizations involved with arts and culture, education, and social welfare. Special emphasis is directed toward programs designed to advance the well being of disadvantaged women and children and people with disabilities.
Fields of interest: Arts education; Arts; Teacher school/education; Education; Environment; Health care; Employment, training; Food services; Housing/shelter; Family services; Human services; Community/economic development Children; Disabilities, people with; Women; Economically disadvantaged.
Programs:
Employee Matching Gifts: The trust matches contributions made by employees, directors, and retirees of Northern Trust to nonprofit organizations involved with arts and culture, education, health, and social welfare on a one-for-one basis from $25 to $2,000 per contributor, per year.
Employee Volunteer Grants: The trust awards grants to nonprofit organizations with which employees of Northern Trust volunteer.
Enriching Neighborhoods: The trust supports programs designed to improve the quality of life in communities. Special emphasis is directed toward

programs designed to provide affordable and supportive housing for families and people with disabilities; quality accessible healthcare; and basic human needs.

Impacting Education: The trust supports educational programs designed to strengthen academic achievement and leadership development. Special emphasis is directed toward programs designed to improve student achievement through innovative programming; develop the talent of teachers and principals; and prepare students to compete globally.

Preserving the Environment: The trust supports programs designed to preserve the environment. Special emphasis is directed toward programs designed to incorporate elements of green construction into affordable housing initiatives; and create green job training initiatives for disadvantaged women and people with disabilities.

Sharing the Arts: The trust supports programs designed to create forums for social interaction that celebrates diversity, heritage, and healthy communities. Special emphasis is directed programs designed to create open access to the city's cultural life; and integrate the arts into education and other community outreach initiatives.

Type of support: Annual campaigns; Building/renovation; Capital campaigns; Continuing support; Employee matching gifts; Employee volunteer services; Endowments; General/operating support; Program development.

Geographic limitations: Giving limited to Cook County, IL, primarily in the Chicago neighborhoods of Chatham, Englewood, Humboldt Park, Logan Square, Loop, Washington Park, and West Town.

Support limitations: No support for United Way-supported organizations (over 5 percent of budget), national health organizations or the local affiliates of national health organizations or research or disease advocacy organizations, political, labor, or fraternal organizations or civic clubs, religious organizations not of direct benefit to the entire community, individual pre-K-12 schools, or organizations established less than 2 years ago. No grants to individuals, or for scholarships or fellowships, fundraising events, advertising or marketing, sports, athletic events, or athletic programs, travel-related events, book, film, video, or television development or production, memorial campaigns, or multi-year general operating support.

Publications: Annual report (including application guidelines); Application guidelines; Corporate giving report (including application guidelines).

Application information: Applications accepted. A full application may be requested at a later date. Support is limited to 3 consecutive years, with 1 year off before an organization is eligible to apply again. Multi-year funding is not automatic. A site visit may be requested. Application form required. Applicants should submit the following:

1) qualifications of key personnel
2) copy of IRS Determination Letter
3) copy of most recent annual report/audited financial statement/990
4) listing of board of directors, trustees, officers and other key people and their affiliations
5) copy of current year's organizational budget and/or project budget
6) listing of additional sources and amount of support

Initial approach: Complete online questionnaire and letter of inquiry form for new applicants; complete online application form for previous grantees

Board meeting date(s): Late Mar., July, and Oct.

Deadline(s): Nov. 15 and June 20 for Social Welfare; Mar. 2 for Arts and Culture and Education; Jan. 3 and Aug. 1 for Social Welfare for previous grantees; May 1 for Arts and Culture and Education for previous grantees

Final notification: Following review

Officers and Directors:* Timothy P. Moen*, Chair.; Deborah Liverett, Secy.; Gregg D. Behrens; William A. Osborn; Alison Winter.

Trustee: The Northern Trust Co.

Number of staff: 2 full-time professional; 1 part-time professional; 1 full-time support; 1 part-time support.

EIN: 366147253

Northern Trust/Lake Forest Foundation

(formerly First National of Lake Forest Foundation)
265 E. Deerpath Rd.
Lake Forest, IL 60045-1938 (847) 234-5100

Donor: The Northern Trust Co.

Contact: Karen S. Crider, Secy.-Treas.

Financial data (yr. ended 12/31/11): Assets, $6,075 (M); expenditures, $1,000; qualifying distributions, $1,000; giving activities include $1,000 for 2 grants.

Purpose and activities: The foundation supports libraries and organizations involved with arts and culture and secondary education.

Fields of interest: Arts; Secondary school/education; Libraries (public).

Type of support: General/operating support; Scholarship funds.

Geographic limitations: Giving primarily in Lake County, IL.

Support limitations: No grants to individuals.

Publications: Application guidelines.

Application information: Applications accepted. Application form required. Applicants should submit the following:

1) copy of IRS Determination Letter
2) copy of most recent annual report/audited financial statement/990
3) listing of board of directors, trustees, officers and other key people and their affiliations
4) detailed description of project and amount of funding requested
5) copy of current year's organizational budget and/or project budget

Initial approach: Letter

Board meeting date(s): Feb.

Deadline(s): None

Officers and Directors:* Arthur M. Wood, Jr.*, Pres.; Martha R. Hinchman*, V.P.; Karen S. Crider, Secy.-Treas.; Brayton B. Alley; Stephen H. Butzlaff.

EIN: 237015827

2741
Northfield Bancorp, Inc.

1410 St. Georges Ave.
Avenel, NJ 07001 (732) 499-7200
FAX: (732) 499-8083

Company URL: http://www.enorthfield.com

Establishment information: Established in 1887.

Company type: Private company

Business activities: Operates savings bank.

Business type (SIC): Savings institutions; holding company

Financial profile for 2011: Number of employees, 292; assets, $2,376,920,000; pre-tax net income, $23,320,000; liabilities, $1,994,270,000

Corporate officers: John W. Alexander, Chair., Pres., and C.E.O.; Steven M. Klein, Exec. V.P., C.F.O., and C.O.O.; Michael J. Widmer, Exec. V.P., Opers.

Board of directors: John W. Alexander, Chair.; John R. Bowen; Annette Catino; Gil Chapman; John P. Connors, Jr.; John J. DePierro; Susan Lamberti; Albert J. Regen; Patrick E. Scura, Jr.

Giving statement: Giving through the Northfield Bank Foundation.

Company EIN: 421572539

Northfield Bank Foundation

1731 Victory Blvd.
Staten Island, NY 10314-3511 (718) 303-4265
FAX: (718) 448-5035;
E-mail: info@northfieldbankfoundation.org;
Additional tel.: (732) 587-2225; URL: http://www.northfieldbankfoundation.org

Establishment information: Established in 2007 in NY.

Contact: Diane Senerchia, Exec. Dir.

Financial data (yr. ended 12/31/11): Assets, $13,924,868 (M); expenditures, $668,475; qualifying distributions, $659,644; giving activities include $579,405 for 56+ grants (high: $50,000).

Purpose and activities: The foundation supports organizations involved with education, health, human services, community development, civic affairs, and projects designed to improve quality of life.

Fields of interest: Performing arts; Performing arts centers; Higher education; Education; Hospitals (general); Health care, clinics/centers; Health care; Children/youth, services; Human services; Community/economic development; Public affairs.

Type of support: Building/renovation; Equipment; General/operating support; Program development; Scholarship funds; Sponsorships.

Geographic limitations: Giving in areas of company operations, specifically in Brooklyn and Staten Island, NY, and in Central NJ.

Support limitations: No support for political organizations.

Publications: Annual report; Application guidelines.

Application information: Applications accepted. A formal grant application package may be requested a later date. Organizations receiving support are asked to submit a final report. Application form required. Applicants should submit the following:

1) qualifications of key personnel
2) statement of problem project will address
3) population served
4) copy of IRS Determination Letter
5) brief history of organization and description of its mission
6) copy of most recent annual report/audited financial statement/990
7) how project's results will be evaluated or measured
8) descriptive literature about organization
9) listing of board of directors, trustees, officers and other key people and their affiliations
10) detailed description of project and amount of funding requested
11) copy of current year's organizational budget and/or project budget
12) listing of additional sources and amount of support
13) additional materials/documentation

Initial approach: Download application form and mail application form and preliminary proposal summary to foundation

Board meeting date(s): Quarterly

Deadline(s): None

Officers and Directors:* Susan Lamberti*, Chair.; John W. Alexader*, Pres.; Steven M. Klein, C.F.O.; Diane Senerchia, Exec. Dir.; Stanley A. Applebaum; John R. Bowen; Lucille Chazanoff; John P. Connors, Jr.; John DePierro; Albert J. Regen.

EIN: 261317178

2742
Northfield Savings Bank

33 S. Main St.
P.O. Box 347
Northfield, VT 05663-6703 (802) 485-5871

Company URL: http://www.nsbvt.com
Establishment information: Established in 1867.
Company type: Mutual company
Business activities: Operates savings bank.
Business type (SIC): Savings institutions
Financial profile for 2011: Assets, $685,140,000; liabilities, $598,179,000
Corporate officers: Charles E. Haynes, Chair.; Thomas N. Pelletier, Pres. and C.E.O.; Timothy M. Ross, Sr. V.P. and Treas.; Cheryl A. LaFrance, Sr. V.P., Mktg.; Carol A. Seaver, Corp. Secy.; Edward T. Sulva, Cont.
Board of directors: Charles E. Haynes, Chair.; J. Timothy Burke; Brain C. Eagan; Anne L. Gould; Brain C. Harwood; Jonathan M. Jamieson; John W. Lyon; Mary Alice McKenzie; Robin C. Nicholson; Nancy F. Pope; Lauren D. Wobby
Offices: Barre, Bethel, Burlington, Essex, Essex Junction, Montpelier, Randolph, South Burlington, Waitsfield, Waterbury, Williston, VT
Giving statement: Giving through the Northfield Savings Bank Corporate Giving Program and the NSB Foundation Inc.

Northfield Savings Bank Corporate Giving Program

c/o Donations
33 S. Main St.
P.O. Box 347
Northfield, VT 05663-0347 (800) 672-2274
Contact for scholarships: Kristin Fontaine, Norwich University, tel.: (802) 485-2282; contact for the Seaver Fund: Carol A. Seaver; URL: https://www.nsbvt.com/learn/community-support/

Purpose and activities: Northfield Savings Bank makes charitable contributions to nonprofit organizations involved with performing arts, education, the environment, health, housing, and human services. Special emphasis is directed toward programs designed to support job development and serve at-risk or low to moderate income individuals and families. Support is given primarily in Chittenden County and central Vermont.
Fields of interest: Performing arts; Education; Environment, natural resources; Environment; Health care; Employment; Housing/shelter; Youth development; Family services; Human services; United Ways and Federated Giving Programs Economically disadvantaged.
Programs:
Employee Matching Program: The company matches contributions made its employees to nonprofit organizations on a one-for-one basis up to $1,000 per employee, per year.
NSB Founders Award: The company awards a scholarship to a Vermont high school senior entering Norwich University as a Freshman.
NSB/NU Scholarship: The company, in partnership with Norwich University, awards scholarships to two students who live in the service area of the Northfield Savings Bank.
Seaver Fund: Through the Seaver Fund, the company supports artistic, cultural, educational, and scientific events within the Northfield community.
Type of support: Donated equipment; Employee matching gifts; Employee volunteer services; In-kind gifts; Program development; Scholarships—to individuals; Sponsorships.
Geographic limitations: Giving primarily in areas of company operations in Chittenden County and central VT.
Support limitations: No support for national charities or their local affiliates, private schools, or political, labor, religious, fraternal, veterans', or lobbying organizations. No grants for multi-year facility or endowment campaigns.
Publications: Application guidelines; Corporate giving report (including application guidelines).
Application information: Applications accepted. Contributions do not exceed $3,000. Support is limited to 1 contribution per organization during any given year. The Marketing Department handles giving. Application form required. Applicants should submit the following:
1) statement of problem project will address
2) population served
3) copy of IRS Determination Letter
4) brief history of organization and description of its mission
5) geographic area to be served
6) copy of most recent annual report/audited financial statement/990
7) how project's results will be evaluated or measured
8) listing of board of directors, trustees, officers and other key people and their affiliations
9) detailed description of project and amount of funding requested
10) copy of current year's organizational budget and/or project budget
11) listing of additional sources and amount of support
12) plans for acknowledgement
Initial approach: Download application form and mail to headquarters; contact branch manager at nearest company bank for requests less than $250; contact Norwich University for scholarships
Copies of proposal: 1
Committee meeting date(s): Jan. 15, Apr. 15, July 15, and Oct. 15
Deadline(s): Mar. 31, June 30, Sept. 30, and Dec. 31
Final notification: Jan. 31, Apr. 30, July 31, and Oct. 31
Administrators: Tom Pelletier, Pres. and C.E.O.

NSB Foundation Inc.

c/o Northfield Savings Bank
33 S. Main St.
Northfield, VT 05663-6703
URL: https://www.nsbvt.com/learn/community-support/donations

Establishment information: Established in 2000 in VT.
Donor: Northfield Savings Bank.
Financial data (yr. ended 12/31/11): Assets, $1,311,831 (M); gifts received, $150,000; expenditures, $171,671; qualifying distributions, $170,003; giving activities include $165,000 for 2 grants (high: $150,000; low: $15,000).
Purpose and activities: The foundation supports Hunger Free Vermont to expand access to healthy meals in Central Vermont and Chittenden County.
Fields of interest: Food services.
Type of support: Continuing support; General/operating support.
Geographic limitations: Giving limited to central VT.
Support limitations: No grants to individuals.
Application information: Applications not accepted. Contributes only to a pre-selected organization.
Board meeting date(s): Feb., June, and Oct.
Officers and Directors:* J. Timothy Burke, Chair. and Pres.; Carol Seaver Holt, V.P. and Secy.; Edward T. Sulva, Treas.; Laura Carlsmith; Samuel FitzPatrick; Anne L. Gould*; James MacIntyre III; Sandra Rousse*; Nancy Wasseman; Nancy Zom.
EIN: 311713065

2743
Northrim Bank

3111 C St., Ste. 400
Anchorage, AK 99503-3925
(907) 562-0062

Company URL: http://www.northrim.com
Establishment information: Established in 1990.
Company type: Subsidiary of a public company
Business activities: Operates a commercial bank.
Business type (SIC): Banks/commercial
Corporate officers: Marc Langland, Chair.; Joseph Beedle, Pres. and C.E.O.; Chris Knudson, Exec. V.P. and C.O.O.; Joe Schierhorn, Exec. V.P. and C.F.O.; Dennis Bingham, Sr. V.P., Admin.; Audrey Amundson, Sr. V.P. and Cont.
Board of directors: Marc Langland, Chair.; Larry S. Cash; Mark G. Copeland; Ronald A. Davis; Anthony Drabek; Chris Knudson; Richard L. Lowell; Irene Sparks Rowan; John C. Swalling; David G. Wight
Giving statement: Giving through the Northrim Bank Corporate Giving Program.

Northrim Bank Corporate Giving Program

c/o Blythe Campbell, Sr. V.P., Mktg. & Comms.
3111 C. St.
Anchorage, AK 99503 (907) 562-0062
E-mail: marketing@nrim.com; Blythe Campbell, Sr. V.P., Mktg. & Comms. tel.: (907) 261-3302; URL: http://www.northrim.com/home/about/contribution

Contact: Blythe Campbell, Sr. V.P., Mktg. and Comms.
Purpose and activities: Northrim Bank makes charitable contributions to nonprofit organizations involved with community and economic development, family services, and higher education. Support is limited to areas of company operations in Alaska.
Fields of interest: Higher education; Family services; Community/economic development Economically disadvantaged.
Type of support: Continuing support; Employee volunteer services; General/operating support; In-kind gifts; Sponsorships.
Geographic limitations: Giving primarily in areas of company operations in AK.
Support limitations: No support for religious organizations, the arts, or individual schools. No grants to individuals, including pledges, or for religious activities, health-related programs, sports teams, programs or events, travel, or underwriting or sponsorship of fundraising events.
Publications: Application guidelines.
Application information: Applications accepted. Grants for higher education given only to pre-selected universities. Most contributions are approved in the first quarter of the year. The organization's Senior Vice President, Marketing & Communications Manager coordinates all contributions. Form letters and telephone solicitations are not accepted. Application form not required.
Initial approach: Mail proposal to application address
Copies of proposal: 1
Deadline(s): Oct. 31

Number of staff: 1 part-time professional; 1 part-time support.

2744
Northrop Grumman Corporation

(formerly NNG, Inc.)
2980 Fairview Park Dr.
Falls Church, VA 22042 (703) 280-2900

Company URL: http://www.northropgrumman.com
Establishment information: Established in 1939.
Company type: Public company
Company ticker symbol and exchange: NOC/NYSE
Business activities: Designs, develops, and manufactures advanced weaponry, space products, aircraft, electronic guidance and navigational systems, and defense electronics.
Financial profile for 2012: Assets, $26,500,000,000; sales volume, $25,200,000,000
Fortune 1000 ranking: 2012—120th in revenues, 103rd in profits, and 205th in assets
Forbes 2000 ranking: 2012—371st in sales, 296th in profits, and 813th in assets
Corporate officers: Wesley Bush, Chair., Pres., and C.E.O.; James F. Palmer, Corp. V.P. and C.F.O.; Kenneth L. Bedingfield, Corp. V.P., Cont., and C.A.O.; Sheila C. Cheston, Corp. V.P. and Genl. Counsel; Jennifer C. McGarey, Corp. V.P. and Secy.; Mark A. Caylor, Corp. V.P. and Treas.; Darryl M. Fraser, Corp. V.P., Comms.
Board of directors: Wesley Bush, Chair.; Lewis Coleman; Victor H. Fazio; Donald E. Felsinger; Stephen E. Frank; Bruce S. Gordon; Madeleine Kleiner; Karl J. Krapek; Richard B. Myers; Aulana L. Peters; Kevin W. Sharer; Thomas M. Schoewe
Subsidiary: Northrop Grumman Space & Mission Systems Corp., Cleveland, OH
Divisions: B-Z Div., Pico Rivera, CA; Data Systems & Services Div., Bethpage, NY; Electronics & Systems Integration Div., Bethpage, NY; Military Aircraft Div., Hawthorne, CA
Plants: Washington, DC; Fairborn, OH; Arlington, VA
Historic mergers: Newport News Shipbuilding Inc. (January 1, 2001); Integic Corporation (March 21, 2005)
Giving statement: Giving through the Northrop Grumman Corporation Contributions Program, the Square Enix Group Corporate Giving Program, and the Northrop Grumman Foundation.
Company EIN: 954840775

Northrop Grumman Corporation Contributions Program

(formerly Northrop Corporation Contributions Program)
c/o Corp. Citizenship
2980 Fairview Park Dr.
Falls Church, VA 22042 (703) 280-2900
E-mail: chery.horn@ngc.com; URL: http://www.northropgrumman.com/corporateresponsibility/Pages/default.aspx

Contact: Cheryl Horn
Purpose and activities: As a complement to its foundation, Northrop Grumman also makes charitable contributions to nonprofit organizations directly. Emphasis is given to organizations that work to improve education, health and human services, and the environment, promote cultural awareness and diversity, and support troops and veterans. Support is given primarily in areas of company operations.
Fields of interest: Arts, cultural/ethnic awareness; Arts; Elementary/secondary education; Education; Environment; Health care; Disasters, preparedness/services; Human services; Civil/human rights, equal rights; Community/economic development; Mathematics; Engineering/technology; Science; Military/veterans' organizations.
Type of support: Continuing support; Employee volunteer services; General/operating support; Program development.
Geographic limitations: Giving primarily in areas of company operations, with emphasis on southern CA; giving also to national organizations.
Support limitations: No support for religious organizations, political groups, fraternal organizations, athletic groups, charter schools, bands or choirs, organizations providing services to animals, discriminatory organizations, or international organizations. No grants to individuals, or for athletic activities, endowments, or capital campaigns.
Publications: Application guidelines; Corporate giving report.
Application information: Applications accepted. The office of Corporate Citizenship handles giving. Application form required. Applicants should submit the following:
1) statement of problem project will address
2) name, address and phone number of organization
3) copy of IRS Determination Letter
4) brief history of organization and description of its mission
5) geographic area to be served
6) copy of most recent annual report/audited financial statement/990
7) descriptive literature about organization
8) listing of board of directors, trustees, officers and other key people and their affiliations
9) detailed description of project and amount of funding requested
10) contact person
11) copy of current year's organizational budget and/or project budget
12) listing of additional sources and amount of support

Initial approach: Complete online application

The Northrop Grumman Foundation

(formerly Foundation of the Litton Industries)
2980 Fairview Park Dr.
Falls Church, VA 22042
E-mail: ngfoundation@ngc.com.; URL: http://www.northropgrumman.com/CorporateResponsibility/CorporateCitizenship/Philanthropy/Pages/Foundation.aspx

Establishment information: Incorporated in 1954 in CA.
Donors: Litton Industries, Inc.; Northrop Grumman Corp.
Contact: Carlene Beste, Secy. and Mgr.
Financial data (yr. ended 12/31/11): Assets, $26,971,837 (M); gifts received, $10,000,000; expenditures, $8,113,089; qualifying distributions, $7,929,075; giving activities include $6,378,438 for 91 grants (high: $1,750,000; low: $1,000), $830,377 for 2,138 employee matching gifts and $720,000 for 1 foundation-administered program.
Purpose and activities: The foundation supports programs designed to provide educational opportunities for youth and educators. Special emphasis is directed toward programs designed to promote science, technology, engineering and mathematics (STEM) for students and teachers.
Fields of interest: Elementary/secondary education; Higher education; Education, reading; Education; Mathematics; Engineering/technology; Science Youth.
Program:
Educational Matching Gifts Program: The foundation matches contributions made by employees and directors of Northrop Grumman to educational institutions from $50 to $1,000 per employee, per year.
Type of support: Employee matching gifts; Program development; Scholarship funds.
Geographic limitations: Giving on a national basis for STEM programming.
Support limitations: No support for campus student organizations, fraternities, sororities, honor societies, religious schools or colleges with a primary focus on religious beliefs, athletic teams or athletic support organizations, or choirs, bands, or drill teams. No grants to individuals (except for employee-related scholarships), or for fundraising events, advertising or underwriting expenses, capital campaigns, endowments, or tuition.
Publications: Annual report; Application guidelines; Grants list; Program policy statement.
Application information: Applications accepted. Support is limited to 1 contribution per organization during any given year. Application form required. Applicants should submit the following:
1) population served
2) name, address and phone number of organization
3) brief history of organization and description of its mission
4) geographic area to be served
5) listing of board of directors, trustees, officers and other key people and their affiliations
6) detailed description of project and amount of funding requested
7) contact person
8) copy of current year's organizational budget and/or project budget
9) listing of additional sources and amount of support

Initial approach: Complete online application
Board meeting date(s): Annually
Deadline(s): Fall
Final notification: Jan.-Feb.

Officers and Directors:* Sandra Evers-Manly*, Pres.; Carleen Beste, Secy. and Mgr.; Silva Thomas*, Treas.; Shelia Cheston; Frank Flores; Darryl M. Fraser; Denise Peppard.
EIN: 956095343

2745
NorthSide Community Bank

5103 Washington St.
Gurnee, IL 60031-5912 (847) 244-5100
FAX: (847) 244-5175

Company URL: http://www.nscombank.com
Establishment information: Established in 1997.
Company type: Private company
Business activities: Operates commercial bank.
Business type (SIC): Banks/commercial
Corporate officers: James S. Randall, Chair.; Patricia A. Clausen, Pres. and C.E.O.; Nick Phillips, V.P. and C.O.O.; Ron Marrs, Cont.
Board of director: James S. Randall, Chair.
Offices: Chicago, Mundelein, Niles, Riverwoods, IL
Giving statement: Giving through the NorthSide Community Bank Charitable Foundation.

The NorthSide Community Bank Charitable Foundation

5103 Washington St.
Gurnee, IL 60031-5912 (847) 244-5100

Establishment information: Established in 2004 in IL.
Donor: NorthSide Community Bank.
Contact: James S. Randall, Pres.
Financial data (yr. ended 12/31/11): Assets, $88,481 (M); expenditures, $14,521; qualifying distributions, $14,472; giving activities include $14,472 for grants.
Purpose and activities: The foundation supports organizations involved with health, hunger, housing, and human services.
Fields of interest: Education; Recreation; Human services.
Geographic limitations: Giving limited to northern IL.
Application information: Applications accepted. Application form required. Applicants should submit the following:
1) name, address and phone number of organization
2) brief history of organization and description of its mission
3) detailed description of project and amount of funding requested

Initial approach: Letter
Copies of proposal: 1
Board meeting date(s): Quarterly
Deadline(s): None

Officers: James S. Randall, Pres.; Patricia A. Clausen, V.P. and Secy.-Treas.
Number of staff: None.
EIN: 200752173

2746
Northwest Bancorp, MHC

100 Liberty St.
P.O. Box 128
Warren, PA 16365-2411 (814) 726-2140

Company URL: http://www.northwestsavingsbank.com
Establishment information: Established in 1896.
Company type: Subsidiary of a public company
Business activities: Operates bank holding company; operates savings bank.
Business type (SIC): Savings institutions; holding company
Corporate officers: William J. Wagner, Chair., Pres., and C.E.O.; William W. Harvey, Jr., Exec. V.P., Finance and C.F.O.; Andrew C. Young, Sr. V.P. and C.I.O.; Gerald J. Ritzert, Sr. V.P. and Cont.
Board of director: William J. Wagner, Chair.
Subsidiary: Northwest Bancorp, Inc., Warren, PA
Giving statement: Giving through the Northwest Bancorp, Inc. Charitable Foundation.

Northwest Bancorp, Inc. Charitable Foundation

Liberty at 2nd Ave.
Warren, PA 16365 (814) 728-7261

Establishment information: Established in 1998 in PA.
Donors: Corry Savings Bank; Northwest Bancorp, MHC.
Contact: Vicki Stec, Secy.
Financial data (yr. ended 06/30/12): Assets, $1,755,856 (M); gifts received, $350; expenditures, $105,888; qualifying distributions, $87,382; giving activities include $87,382 for grants.
Purpose and activities: The foundation supports art councils and hospitals and organizations involved with higher education and human services.
Fields of interest: Arts councils; Higher education; Hospitals (general); YM/YWCAs & YM/YWHAs; Residential/custodial care, hospices; Human services.
Type of support: Employee-related scholarships; General/operating support.
Geographic limitations: Giving primarily in Corry and Elgin, PA.
Support limitations: No grants to individuals (except for employee-related scholarships).
Application information: Applications accepted. Application form required.

Initial approach: Contact foundation for application information
Deadline(s): None

Officers: William J. Wagner, Pres.; Vicki Stec, Secy.; William W. Harvey, Treas.
EIN: 251819537

2747
Northwest Natural Gas Company

220 N.W. 2nd Ave.
Portland, OR 97209-3943 (503) 226-4211
FAX: (503) 273-4824

Company URL: http://www.nwnatural.com
Establishment information: Established in 1859.
Company type: Public company
Company ticker symbol and exchange: NWN/NYSE
Business activities: Transmits and distributes natural gas.
Business type (SIC): Gas production and distribution
Financial profile for 2011: Number of employees, 623; assets, $2,818,750,000; sales volume, $730,610,000; pre-tax net income, $103,960,000; expenses, $588,430,000; liabilities, $2,085,720,000
Corporate officers: Tod R. Hamachek, Chair.; Gregg S. Kantor, Pres. and C.E.O.; Steve Feltz, Co-Sr. V.P. and Co-C.F.O.; David Hugo Anderson, Co-Sr. V.P. and Co-C.F.O.; Lea Anne Doolittle, Sr. V.P., Human Resources; Margaret D. Kirkpatrick, V.P. and Genl. Counsel; Grant M. Yoshihara, V.P., Opers.; C. Alex Miller, V.P., Finance; Mardilyn Saathoff, Corp. Secy.
Board of directors: Tod R. Hamachek, Chair.; Timothy P. Boyle; Martha L. Byorum; John D. Carter; Mark S. Dodson; Charles Scott Gibson; Gregg S. Kantor; Jane L. Peverett; George Joseph Puentes; Kenneth Thrasher
Subsidiaries: NNG Energy Systems, Inc., Portland, OR; Oregon Natural Gas Development Corp., Portland, OR; Pacific Square Corp., Portland, OR
Giving statement: Giving through the Northwest Natural Gas Company Contributions Program.
Company EIN: 930256722

Northwest Natural Gas Company Contributions Program

c/o Contributions Committee
220 N.W. 2nd Ave.
Portland, OR 97209-3942 (503) 226-4211
URL: https://www.nwnatural.com/AboutNWNatural/Community

Purpose and activities: NW Natural makes charitable contributions to nonprofit organizations involved with at-risk children, and families. Support is limited to areas of company operations in western Oregon and southwest Washington.
Fields of interest: Environment, natural resources; Environment, energy; Environment; Human services, fund raising/fund distribution; Children/youth, services; Family services Economically disadvantaged.
Type of support: Continuing support; Donated equipment; Donated products; Employee volunteer services; General/operating support; In-kind gifts; Sponsorships.
Geographic limitations: Giving limited to areas of company operations in western OR and southwest WA.
Support limitations: Generally no support for discriminatory organizations, individual schools, sports teams, umbrella agencies that represent numerous nonprofit organizations, religious organizations that are solely denominational or sectarian, political organizations, campaigns for public office, or organizations whose primary purpose is to influence legislation. Generally no grants for school projects that are not curriculum related, school events, religious events, when purely denominational or sectarian in purpose, contests, trips, tours, capital funds, fundraising events such as auctions, benefit dinners, awards banquets, or golf tournaments, weddings, graduations, reunions, anniversaries, or birthdays, events or programs for political organizations, campaigns for public office or organizations whose primary purpose is to influence legislation.
Publications: Application guidelines.
Application information: Applications accepted. Proposal should be no longer than 2 pages. The Public Affairs Department handles giving. Application form required. Applicants should submit the following:
1) statement of problem project will address
2) population served
3) brief history of organization and description of its mission
4) explanation of why grantmaker is considered an appropriate donor for project
5) detailed description of project and amount of funding requested
6) contact person

Sponsorship requests must include event date, event name, e-mail address, and anticipated audience.

Initial approach: Proposal to headquarters for grant applications; Complete online application form for sponsorship requests
Deadline(s): 90 days prior to event for sponsorships
Final notification: 30 work days

Number of staff: 0.75 part-time professional; 0.5 part-time support.

2748
NorthWestern Corporation

(doing business as NorthWestern Energy)
3010 W. 69th St.
Sioux Falls, SD 57108 (605) 978-2900
FAX: (302) 655-5049

Company URL: http://www.northwesternenergy.com
Establishment information: Established in 1923.
Company type: Public company
Company ticker symbol and exchange: NWE/NYSE
Business activities: Generates, transmits, and distributes electricity; transmits and distributes natural gas.
Business type (SIC): Combination utility services
Financial profile for 2012: Number of employees, 1,430; assets, $3,485,530,000; sales volume, $1,070,340,000; pre-tax net income, $116,500,000; expenses, $893,160,000; liabilities, $2,551,500,000

Corporate officers: E. Linn Draper, Jr., Chair.; Robert C. Rowe, Pres. and C.E.O.; Brian B. Bird, V.P. and C.F.O.; Kendall G. Kliewer, V.P. and Cont.; Heather H. Grahame, V.P. and Genl. Counsel; Bobbi L. Schroeppel, V.P., Comms., and Human Resources; Timothy P. Olson, Corp. Secy.; Daniel L. Rausch, Treas.
Board of directors: E. Linn Draper, Jr., Chair.; Stephen P. Adik; Dorothy M. Bradley; Dana J. Dykhouse; Julia L. Johnson; Philip L. Maslowe; D. Louis Peoples; Robert C. Rowe
Subsidiaries: Blue Dot Services, Inc., Sunrise, FL; Cornerstone Propane GP, Inc., Watsonville, CA; Expanets, Inc., Englewood, CO; Grant, Inc., Huron, SD; Nekota Resources, Inc., Huron, SD; NorthWestern Energy Corp., Huron, SD; NorthWestern Growth Corp., Sioux Falls, SD
Giving statement: Giving through the NorthWestern Energy Corporate Giving Program.
Company EIN: 460172280

NorthWestern Energy Corporate Giving Program

c/o Charitable Giving Prog.
3010 W. 69th St.
Sioux Falls, SD 57108-5613 (605) 978-2900
Application address in MT: Charitable Giving Prog., 40 E. Broadway, Butte, MT 59701-9350; NE and SD: Charitable Giving Prog., 3010 W. 69th St., Sioux Falls, SD 57108-5613; URL: http://www.northwesternenergy.com/display.aspx?Page=Charitable_Giving&Item=89

Financial data (yr. ended 12/31/11): Total giving, $618,740, including $618,740 for grants.
Purpose and activities: NorthWestern Energy makes charitable contributions to nonprofit organizations involved with education, health and human services, civic and community improvements, arts and culture, and resource conservation. Support is given primarily in areas of company operations in Montana, Nebraska, and South Dakota.
Fields of interest: Museums; Performing arts; Arts; Secondary school/education; Higher education, college; Higher education, university; Libraries/library science; Education; Animals/wildlife, preservation/protection; Safety/disasters; Athletics/sports, Special Olympics; Youth development; Human services; Youth, services; Aging, centers/services; United Ways and Federated Giving Programs; Science, public education; Mathematics.
Type of support: Building/renovation; Capital campaigns; Employee matching gifts; Employee volunteer services; Equipment; General/operating support; In-kind gifts; Scholarship funds.
Geographic limitations: Giving primarily in areas of company operations in MT, NE, and SD.
Support limitations: No support for national organizations except local affiliates, or for political, religious, or national health organizations. Generally no support for fraternal, service, veterans', or social organizations. No grants to individuals, or for economic and commercial development projects, medical equipment, or research. Generally no grants for sporting events. Individual United Way agency requests are generally not considered except for capital projects.
Publications: Application guidelines.
Application information: Applications accepted. A contributions committee reviews all requests. Multi-year funding is not automatic. Requests for physical improvements and equipment purchases are generally favored over operating funds except for social service organizations. Donations are generally monetary; in limited instances, non-monetary gifts may be considered. Application form not required. Applicants should submit the following:
1) copy of IRS Determination Letter
Initial approach: Download application form and mail to headquarters
Deadline(s): None
Final notification: 12 weeks

2749
The Northwestern Mutual Life Insurance Company

720 E. Wisconsin Ave.
Milwaukee, WI 53202-4797
(414) 271-1444

Company URL: http://www.northwesternmutual.com/
Establishment information: Established in 1857.
Company type: Mutual company
Business activities: Sells life, disability, and long-term care insurance; provides investment advisory services.
Business type (SIC): Insurance/life; security and commodity services; insurance/accident and health
Financial profile for 2011: Number of employees, 4,781; assets, $180,037,900,000; sales volume, $23,384,300,000
Corporate officers: John E. Schlifske, Chair. and C.E.O.; Gary A. Poliner, Pres.; Marcia Rimai, Exec. V.P. and C.A.O.; Mark G. Doll, Exec. V.P. and C.I.O.
Board of directors: John E. Schlifske, Chair.; Facundo L. Bacardi; John N. Balboni; David J. Drury; Connie K. Duckworth; David A. Erne; James P. Hackett; P. Russell Hardin; Hans Helmerich; Dale E. Jones; Margery Kraus; David J. Lubar; Ulice Payne, Jr.; Gary A. Poliner; Peter M. Sommerhauser; Mary Ellen Stanek; Timothy W. Sullivan; S. Scott Voynich; Ralph A. Weber; Barry L. Williams; Benjamin F. Wilson; Edward J. Zore
Subsidiaries: Northwestern Long Term Care Insurance Co., Milwaukee, WI; Northwestern Mutual Investment Services, LLC, Milwaukee, WI; Frank Russell Co., Tacoma, WA
Office: Franklin, WI
Giving statement: Giving through the Northwestern Mutual Foundation, Inc.
Company EIN: 390509570

Northwestern Mutual Foundation, Inc.

(formerly Northwestern Mutual Foundation)
720 E. Wisconsin Ave.
Milwaukee, WI 53202-4703 (414) 665-2200
FAX: (414) 665-2199;
E-mail: foundationonline@northwesternmutual.com;
URL: http://www.nmfn.com/tn/aboutus—fd_intro

Establishment information: Established in 1992 in WI.
Donors: The Northwestern Mutual Life Insurance Co.; Lydell Inc.
Contact: John Kordsmeier, Pres.
Financial data (yr. ended 06/30/12): Assets, $97,688,105 (M); gifts received, $13,953,653; expenditures, $15,984,094; qualifying distributions, $15,744,772; giving activities include $10,932,873 for 497+ grants (high: $1,595,000) and $3,816,127 for employee matching gifts.
Purpose and activities: The foundation supports organizations involved with arts and culture, education, health, childhood cancer, disaster relief, human services, and community economic development.
Fields of interest: Arts education; Museums; Performing arts; Arts; Elementary/secondary education; Education, early childhood education; Higher education; Education, reading; Education; Health care; Cancer; Disasters, preparedness/services; Boys & girls clubs; Youth development, adult & child programs; American Red Cross; Family services; Human services; Community development, neighborhood development; Economic development, visitors/convention bureau/tourism promotion; Community/economic development; United Ways and Federated Giving Programs Economically disadvantaged.
Programs:
Academic Success: The foundation supports programs designed to improve the academic success of underserved children in Milwaukee and promote academic results and student inspiration. Special emphasis is directed toward early children education; literacy programs; higher education; arts education and mentoring.
Childhood Cancer Program: The foundation supports programs designed to accelerate the search for a cure to childhood cancer and provide support to families facing the disease. The foundation currently partners with Alex's Lemonade Stand Foundation and Starlight Children's Foundation.
Community Impact Awards: Through the Community Impact Awards, the foundation recognizes Northwestern Mutual employees for philanthropic and volunteer commitments. The award includes a $50,000 grant to each of four network offices' nonprofit partners.
Community Service Award Program: The foundation annually awards grants to nonprofit organizations with which financial representatives of Northwestern Mutual contribute volunteer service. The award is given to recognize representatives whose outstanding dedication to local organizations has significantly improved the community. In addition, a $25,000 grant is awarded to a nonprofit organization on behalf of the financial representative recognized as the Most Exceptional Volunteer.
Days of Caring: Through Days of Sharing, the foundation awards grants totaling $100,000 to 25 nonprofit organizations nominated by employees. Grants are given in the name of the employee winners.
Matching Gifts Program: The foundation matches contributions made by employees of Northwestern Mutual to educational institutions on a one-for-one basis.
Supporting Our Community: The foundation supports programs designed to make Milwaukee a destination place, including cultural attractions and annual events; and build neighborhood capacity, including holistic solutions on behalf of children and families, and welcoming, safe, and healthy environments with access to quality education in the following neighborhoods: Metcalfe Park, Muskego Way, and Amani.
Volunteer Support Program: The foundation awards $500 grants to nonprofit organizations with which employees or retirees of Northwestern Mutual volunteer 40 hours per year.
Type of support: Annual campaigns; Building/renovation; Capital campaigns; Continuing support; Curriculum development; Emergency funds; Employee matching gifts; Employee volunteer services; General/operating support; Matching/challenge support; Program development; Research; Scholarship funds; Sponsorships.
Geographic limitations: Giving primarily in Milwaukee, WI; giving also to national organizations.
Support limitations: No support for organizations with an operating budget under $300,000, groups or organizations that re-grant to other organizations or individuals, school teams, bands, or choirs, or

labor, religious, or fraternal groups. No grants to individuals, or for debt reduction, capital, or endowment campaigns unless approved by the foundation in advance; conferences, conventions, golf outings, school trips, concerts, or performances, athletic events, equipment, uniforms, travel or any in-kind support of special events, or lobbying activities.
Publications: Application guidelines; Corporate giving report.
Application information: Applications accepted. Applications are accepted up to 30 days in advance of deadlines. There are no open national deadlines for Northwestern Mutual's Childhood Cancer Program. Support is limited to 1 contribution per organization during any given year. Applicants should submit the following:
1) copy of IRS Determination Letter
2) copy of most recent annual report/audited financial statement/990
3) explanation of why grantmaker is considered an appropriate donor for project
4) listing of board of directors, trustees, officers and other key people and their affiliations
5) detailed description of project and amount of funding requested
6) copy of current year's organizational budget and/or project budget
7) listing of additional sources and amount of support

Requests for sponsorships should include a listing of all sponsorship and benefit levels, and an electronic version of the event invitation or save-the-date card, if available.
Initial approach: Complete online application
Board meeting date(s): Bimonthly
Deadline(s): 60 days prior to need for table or event sponsorships; Sept. 15 for Higher Education; Oct. 15 for Early Childhood Education and Literacy; Mar. 15 for Arts Education and Mentoring; Feb. 15 for Building Neighborhood Capacity
Final notification: 90 days
Officers and Directors:* John E. Schlifske*, C.E.O.; John Kordsmeier*, Pres.; Scott J. Morns, Secy.; Karen A. Molloy, Treas.; Kimberley Goode; Jean M. Maier; Gregory C. Oberland; Gary A. Poliner.
Number of staff: 3 full-time professional; 1 full-time support.
EIN: 391728908
Selected grants: The following grants are a representative sample of this grantmaker's funding activity:
$1,500,000 to United Way of Greater Milwaukee, Milwaukee, WI, 2011.
$680,000 to United Performing Arts Fund, Milwaukee, WI, 2011.
$425,000 to American Red Cross National Headquarters, Washington, DC, 2011.
$425,000 to Boys and Girls Clubs of Greater Milwaukee, Milwaukee, WI, 2011.
$220,575 to Scholarship America, Saint Peter, MN, 2011.
$150,000 to Aurora Health Care, Milwaukee, WI, 2011.
$10,000 to American Red Cross, Louisville Area Chapter, Louisville, KY, 2011.
$7,500 to Sharon Lynne Wilson Center for the Arts, Brookfield, WI, 2011.
$6,280 to United Way of the National Capital Area, Vienna, VA, 2011.
$2,500 to Lander University, Greenwood, SC, 2011.

2750
Northwestern National Casualty Company

2640 S. 162nd St.
New Berlin, WI 53151-2810
(262) 792-0414

Establishment information: Established in 1995.
Company type: Private company
Business activities: Sells insurance.
Business type (SIC): Insurance/life; insurance/accident and health; insurance/fire, marine, and casualty
Giving statement: Giving through the Vik Brothers Foundation.

The Vik Brothers Foundation

(formerly Northwestern National Insurance Foundation)
10 Ashton Dr.
Greenwich, CT 06831-3762

Establishment information: Established in 1967 in WI.
Donors: Armco Insurance Group, Inc.; Sebastian Holdings, Inc.
Financial data (yr. ended 12/31/10): Assets, $0 (M); gifts received, $5,000; expenditures, $23,220; qualifying distributions, $20,457; giving activities include $17,695 for 9 grants (high: $15,370; low: $25).
Purpose and activities: The foundation supports organizations involved with performing arts, K-12 and higher education, and land conservation.
Fields of interest: Arts; Education; Human services.
Type of support: Capital campaigns; General/operating support; Scholarship funds.
Support limitations: No grants to individuals.
Application information: Applications not accepted. Unsolicited requests for funds not accepted.
Trustees: Alexander M. Vik; G.M. Vik.
EIN: 396102416

2751
Norwood Cooperative Bank

11 Central St.
Norwood, MA 02062-3505 (781) 762-1800

Company URL: http://norwoodbank.com
Establishment information: Established in 1889.
Company type: Private company
Business activities: Operates cooperative bank.
Business type (SIC): Credit institutions/federal and federally-sponsored
Corporate officers: Edward Donovan, Chair.; Christopher B. Dixon, Pres. and C.E.O.; Richard Brenner, C.F.O.
Board of directors: Edward Donovan, Chair.; Paul G. Keady; William P. O'Donnell
Giving statement: Giving through the Norwood Charitable Foundation, Inc.

The Norwood Charitable Foundation, Inc.

11 Central St.
Norwood, MA 02062-3505

Establishment information: Established in 1999 in MA.
Donor: Norwood Cooperative Bank.
Financial data (yr. ended 12/31/11): Assets, $1,462,124 (M); expenditures, $91,654; qualifying distributions, $91,619; giving activities include $91,619 for 96 grants (high: $5,000; low: $40).
Fields of interest: Education; Human services.
Support limitations: No grants to individuals.
Application information: Applications not accepted. Unsolicited requests for funds not accepted.
Officers: Christopher B. Dixon, Pres.; Ronald G. McElman, Secy. and Clerk; Karen Goggin, Treas.
Directors: Joseph F. Curran; Robert J. Donahue; Robert M. Thornton.
Trustee: Norwood Cooperative Bank.
EIN: 043469424

2752
Novartis Corporation

(formerly Ciba-Geigy Corporation)
230 Park Ave., 21st Fl.
New York, NY 10169 (212) 307-1122

Company URL: http://www.us.novartis.com
Establishment information: Established in 1996.
Company type: Subsidiary of a foreign company
Business activities: Researches, manufactures, provides, and sells health care products and services.
Business type (SIC): Drugs
Financial profile for 2010: Number of employees, 30; sales volume, $5,060,000,000
Corporate officers: Robert E. Pelzer, Pres.; Helen Boudreau, C.F.O.; Brandi Robinson, V.P., Comms.; Jim Elkin, V.P., Public Affairs; Frank Maness, V.P., Human Resources
Subsidiaries: Gerber Products Co., Fremont, MI; Master Builders, Inc., Cleveland, OH; Northrup King Co., Golden Valley, MN; Novartis Pharmaceuticals Corporation, East Hanover, NJ; Rogers Seed Co., Boise, ID; Sandoz Agro, Inc., Des Plaines, IL; Sandoz Nutrition Corp., Minneapolis, MN; Sandoz Pharmaceuticals Corp., East Hanover, NJ
Historic mergers: Chiron Corporation (April 19, 2006)
Giving statement: Giving through the Novartis US Foundation.

Novartis US Foundation

(formerly Sandoz Foundation of America)
230 Park Ave., 21st FL
New York, NY 10169-2403
URL: http://www.corporatecitizenship.novartis.com/people-communities/foundations.shtml

Establishment information: Incorporated in 1965 in DE; adopted current name in 1997 following a merger with the Ciba Educational Foundation, Inc.
Donors: Sandoz Corp.; Novartis Inc.
Financial data (yr. ended 12/31/11): Assets, $21,196,172 (M); gifts received, $1,030,463; expenditures, $1,791,060; qualifying distributions, $1,512,166; giving activities include $1,512,166 for grants.
Purpose and activities: The foundation matches contributions made by its employees to nonprofit organizations.
Fields of interest: Education; Public affairs.
Type of support: Employee matching gifts.
Geographic limitations: Giving on a national basis, with emphasis on areas of company operations.
Support limitations: No support for religious organizations or social, labor, veterans', fraternal, athletic, or alumni organizations.
Application information: Applications not accepted. Contributes only to pre-selected organizations and through employee matching gifts.
Board meeting date(s): As required

Officer and Trustee:* Robert E. Pelzer*, Chair.; Brenda Blanchard; James Elkin; Brandi Robinson; Meryl Zausner.
EIN: 136193034

2753
Novartis Pharmaceuticals Corporation

1 Health Plz.
East Hanover, NJ 07936-1080
(862) 778-8300

Company URL: http://www.pharma.us.novartis.com
Establishment information: Established in 1996.
Company type: Subsidiary of a foreign company
Parent company: Novartis Corporation
Business activities: Operates pharmaceuticals company.
Business type (SIC): Drugs
Financial profile for 2009: Number of employees, 7,000; sales volume, $9,540,000,000
Corporate officers: Andre Wyss, Pres.; Kaul Kaul, V.P., C.F.O., and C.A.O.; Thomas N. Kendris, V.P. and Genl. Counsel; Steven Baert, V.P., Human Resources
Giving statement: Giving through the Novartis Patient Assistance Foundation, Inc.

Novartis Patient Assistance Foundation, Inc.

1 Health Plz.
USEH 701-441
East Hanover, NJ 07936-1080 (800) 277-2254
Application address: P.O. Box 66531, St. Louis, MO 63166-6556; fax: (866) 470-1750; URL: http://www.pharma.us.novartis.com/about-us/our-patient-caregiver-resources/index.shtml

Establishment information: Established in 2008 in NJ.
Donor: Novartis Pharmaceuticals Corp.
Financial data (yr. ended 12/31/11): Assets, $23,278,108 (M); gifts received, $345,394,640; expenditures, $338,808,892; qualifying distributions, $338,808,892; giving activities include $331,911,548 for grants to individuals.
Purpose and activities: The foundation provides medication assistance to patients experiencing financial hardship who have no third party insurance coverage.
Fields of interest: Economically disadvantaged.
Type of support: Donated products; In-kind gifts.
Geographic limitations: Giving on a national basis.
Publications: Application guidelines.
Application information: Applications accepted. Faxed applications must be sent from a physician's office. Application address varies per medication requested. Application form required.
Application should include a copy of the applicant's most recent federal tax return.
Initial approach: Telephone, complete online application, or download application form and fax or mail to application address
Copies of proposal: 1
Deadline(s): None
Officers and Directors:* Kevin Rigby*, Pres.; Joe Visaggio*, V.P.; Rhonda Crichlow, Secy.; Marc Lewis, Treas.; Alissa Jaffenagler; Brandi Robinson; Barry Rosenfeld.
EIN: 262502555

2754
Novell, Inc.

1800 South Novell Pl.
Provo, UT 84606 (801) 861-4272

Company URL: http://www.novell.com
Company type: Subsidiary of a private company
Business activities: Develops computer network services.
Business type (SIC): Computer services
Corporate officers: Bob Flynn, Pres. and Mgr.; Katherine Tate, V.P., Sales
Subsidiary: Novonyx, Inc., Orem, UT
Plants: Phoenix, AZ; Irvine, Los Angeles, Sacramento, San Diego, San Francisco, San Jose, CA; Englewood, CO; Glastonbury, CT; Fort Lauderdale, Tampa, FL; Atlanta, GA; Rolling Meadows, IL; Wellesley, MA; Southfield, MI; Bloomington, MN; Kansas City, St. Louis, MO; Berkeley Heights, NJ; New York, Pittsford, NY; Charlotte, NC; Cincinnati, Cleveland, Columbus, Independence, OH; Portland, OR; Berwyn, Pittsburgh, PA; Memphis, TN; Austin, Dallas, Houston, TX; Salt Lake City, UT; Herndon, VA; Kirkland, WA
International operations: Argentina; Australia; Austria; Belgium; Brazil; Canada; Chile; China; Colombia; Czech Republic; Denmark; Finland; France; Germany; Hungary; India; Ireland; Israel; Italy; Japan; Malaysia; Mexico; Netherlands; New Zealand; Norway; Poland; Portugal; Russia; Singapore; South Africa; South Korea; Spain; Sweden; Switzerland; Taiwan; Thailand; United Arab Emirates; United Kingdom; Uruguay; Venezuela
Historic mergers: WordPerfect Corporation (June 24, 1994)
Giving statement: Giving through the Novell, Inc. Corporate Giving Program.
Company EIN: 870393339

Novell, Inc. Corporate Giving Program

c/o Community Rels.
1800 South Novell Pl.
Provo, UT 84606-6101 (801) 861-4272
Application address for software donations: Good360, 1330 Braddock Pl., Ste. 600, Alexandria, VA 22314, tel.: (703) 836-2121; URL: http://www.novell.com/company/cr/corporate_giving.html

Purpose and activities: Novell makes charitable contributions to nonprofit organizations involved with education, the homeless and hungry, and arts and culture. Support is given primarily in areas of company operations Georgia, Massachusetts, Michigan, Utah, and Virginia.
Fields of interest: Arts; Education; Food services Homeless.
Type of support: Donated products; Employee volunteer services; General/operating support; Scholarship funds.
Geographic limitations: Giving primarily in areas of company operations in GA, MA, MI, UT, and VA; giving on a national basis for software donations.
Support limitations: No support for discriminatory organizations, national health organizations, political or religious organizations, political or religious organizations, fraternal organizations, or organizations with overhead expenses exceeding 20 percent of total operating budget. No grants to individuals, or for parties, conferences, or sports or entertainment marketing.
Application information:
Initial approach: Visit Good360 website for application information for software donations

2755
Novetta Solutions

(formerly FGM Inc.)
7921 Jones Branch Dr.
McLean, VA 22102 (571) 282-3000

Company URL: http://www.fgm.com
Establishment information: Established in 1987.
Company type: Private company
Business activities: Develops computer software and systems.
Business type (SIC): Computer services
Corporate officers: Peter B. LaMontagne, C.E.O.; Scott Gessay, Pres.; Rich Sawchak, C.F.O.; Chas Sumser, V.P., Human Resources
Giving statement: Giving through the Novetta Solutions Corporate Giving Program.

Novetta Solutions Corporate Giving Program

(formerly FGM Inc. Corporate Giving Program)
7921 Jones Branch Dr.
McLean, VA 22102
URL: http://www.novetta.com/community-relations.html

Purpose and activities: FGM makes charitable contributions to nonprofit organizations involved with multiple sclerosis research, family services, science, engineering, and youth education. Support is given primarily in areas of company operations in California, Colorado, Hawaii, Maryland, and Nebraska, with some emphasis on northern Virginia.
Fields of interest: Secondary school/education; Multiple sclerosis research; Boys & girls clubs; Family services; Engineering.
Type of support: Employee volunteer services; General/operating support; In-kind gifts; Sponsorships.
Geographic limitations: Giving primarily in areas of company operations in CA, CO, HI, MD, and NE, with some emphasis on northern VA.

2756
NRG Energy, Inc.

211 Carnegie Ctr.
Princeton, NJ 08540-6213 (609) 524-4500
FAX: (609) 524-4501

Company URL: http://www.nrgenergy.com
Establishment information: Established in 1989.
Company type: Public company
Company ticker symbol and exchange: NRG/NYSE
International Securities Identification Number: US6293775085
Business activities: Operates power generation facilities.
Business type (SIC): Electric services
Financial profile for 2012: Assets, $35,100,000,000; sales volume, $8,400,000,000
Fortune 1000 ranking: 2012—314th in revenues, 310th in profits, and 162nd in assets
Forbes 2000 ranking: 2012—1054th in sales, 924th in profits, and 645th in assets
Corporate officers: Howard E. Cosgrove, Chair.; David W. Crane, Pres. and C.E.O.; Mauricio Gutierrez, Exec. V.P. and C.O.O.; Kirkland B. Andrews, Exec. V.P. and C.F.O.; David Hill, Exec. V.P. and Genl. Counsel; Patti Helfer, Sr. V.P. and C.A.O.; G. Gary Garcia, Sr. V.P. and Treas.; Tanuja Dehne, Sr. V.P., Human Resources; Ron Stark, V.P. and C.A.O.

Board of directors: Howard E. Cosgrove, Chair.; E. Spencer Abraham; Kirbyjon H. Caldwell; John F. Chlebowski, Jr.; Lawrence S. Coben; David W. Crane; Terry G. Dallas; William E. Hantke; Paul W. Hobby; Gerald Luterman; Kathleen A. McGinty; Edward R. Muller; Anne C. Schaumburg; Evan J. Silverstein; Thomas H. Weidemeyer; Walter R. Young, Jr.
Subsidiaries: NRG Engine Services, Harrisburg, PA; NRG Thermal LLC, Minneapolis, MN; Nuclear Innovation North America LLC, New York, NY; Reliant Energy, Houston, TX
International operations: Australia; Bermuda; Germany; Netherlands
Giving statement: Giving through the NRG Energy, Inc. Corporate Giving Program.
Company EIN: 411724239

NRG Energy, Inc. Corporate Giving Program

(also known as NRG Global Giving Program)
211 Carnegie Ctr.
Princeton, NJ 08540-6213 (609) 524-4500
URL: http://www.nrgenergy.com/responsibility/global-giving.html

Contact: Jennifer Brunelle, Mgr., Special Events & Philanthropy
Purpose and activities: NRG Energy makes charitable contributions to nonprofit organizations involved with community development, education, human welfare, and the environment. Special emphasis is directed toward programs that reach underserved populations. Support is given primarily in areas of company operations.
Fields of interest: Higher education; Education; Environment; Food services; Food banks; Disasters, preparedness/services; Youth development; Homeless, human services; Human services; Community/economic development Economically disadvantaged.
Programs:
Dollars for Hours Program: To supplement employee volunteerism at qualifying organizations, NRG contributes $2 for every hour of volunteer service, up to 50 hours annually.
Matching Gifts Program: NRG matches each employee's donations to qualifying organizations dollar-for-dollar, up to $1,400 annually.
TEAMNRG Program: NRG makes a $2,000 grant to any qualifying organization for which an employee team of six or more participates in a fundraising event.
Type of support: Employee matching gifts; Employee volunteer services; General/operating support.
Geographic limitations: Giving primarily in areas of company operations; giving also to national organizations.

2757
NRT Arizona Success, Inc.

(also known as Coldwell Banker Residential Brokerage Arizona)
10446 N. 74th St., Ste. 100
Scottsdale, AZ 85258-1046
(480) 481-8400

Company URL: http://www.nrtinc.com
Establishment information: Established in 1906.
Company type: Subsidiary of a private company
Business activities: Operates real estate agency.
Business type (SIC): Real estate agents and managers
Corporate officers: Malcolm MacEwen, Pres. and C.O.O.; John Joyner Becker, V.P., Finance; Dan Barnett, Sr. V.P., Mktg.
Giving statement: Giving through the McCord Family Foundation.

McCord Family Foundation

(formerly Success Charitable Foundation)
10446 N. 74th St., Ste. 170
Scottsdale, AZ 85258

Establishment information: Established in 1998 in AZ.
Donors: NRT Arizona Success, Inc.; Robert McCord.
Financial data (yr. ended 12/31/11): Assets, $1,427 (M); expenditures, $675; qualifying distributions, $0.
Purpose and activities: The foundation supports food banks and organizations involved with education, child abuse prevention, housing development, and human services.
Fields of interest: Education; Crime/violence prevention, child abuse; Food banks; Housing/shelter, development; Children/youth, services; Homeless, human services; Human services.
Type of support: General/operating support.
Application information: Applications not accepted. Unsolicited requests for funds not accepted.
Officers: Sharon DuPont McCord, Pres.; Kevin Dupont, V.P.; Denise Von Derlinn, Secy.
EIN: 860750666

2758
NTELOS Holdings Corp.

(formerly CFW Communications Company)
1154 Shenandoah Village Dr.
P.O. Box 1990
Waynesboro, VA 22980-4547
(540) 946-3500

Company URL: http://www.ntelos.com
Establishment information: Established in 1897.
Company type: Private company
Business activities: Provides wireless telephone communications services.
Business type (SIC): Telephone communications
Corporate officers: Michael Huber, Chair.; James S. Hyde, Pres. and C.E.O.; Conrad J. Hunter, Exec. V.P. and C.O.O.; Stebbins B. Chandor, Jr., Exec. V.P., C.F.O., and Treas.; Brian J. O'Neil, Exec. V.P., Genl. Counsel, and Secy.; Robert L. McAvoy, Jr., Sr. V.P., Opers.; S. Craig Highland, Sr. V.P., Finance
Board of directors: Michael Huber, Chair.; Timothy G. Biltz; Rodney D. Dir; Jerry V. Elliott; Steven G. Felsher; Daniel J. Heneghan; James A. Hyde; Ellen O'Connor Vos
Giving statement: Giving through the NTELOS Foundation.
Company EIN: 364573125

NTELOS Foundation

(formerly CFW Communications Foundation)
P.O. Box 1990
Waynesboro, VA 22980-7990 (540) 146-3511

Establishment information: Established in 1990 in VA.
Donors: CFW Communications Co.; Clifton Forge-Waynesboro Telephone Co.; NTELOS Inc.
Contact: Michael B. Moneymaker, Pres.
Financial data (yr. ended 12/31/11): Assets, $2,561,929 (M); expenditures, $97,628; qualifying distributions, $76,686; giving activities include $76,686 for grants.
Purpose and activities: The foundation supports organizations involved with arts and culture, education, health, and human services.
Fields of interest: Museums; Arts; Higher education; Education; Hospitals (general); Health care; YM/YWCAs & YM/YWHAs; United Ways and Federated Giving Programs.
Type of support: General/operating support.
Geographic limitations: Giving primarily in VA and WV.
Support limitations: No support for religious organizations. No grants to individuals.
Application information: Applications accepted. Application form required. Applicants should submit the following:
1) statement of problem project will address
2) brief history of organization and description of its mission
3) detailed description of project and amount of funding requested

Initial approach: Proposal
Deadline(s): None

Officers: James A. Hyde, Chair. and C.E.O.; Michael B. Moneymaker, Pres., C.F.O., and Secy.-Treas.; Frank L. Berry, Exec. V.P.; C. J. Hunger, Exec. V.P.
EIN: 541552737
Selected grants: The following grants are a representative sample of this grantmaker's funding activity:
$9,040 to United Way of Greater Augusta, Staunton, VA, 2010. For general operations.
$5,000 to YMCA, Alleghany Highlands, Covington, VA, 2010. For general operations.
$1,000 to Averett University, Danville, VA, 2010. For general operations.
$1,000 to Hollins University, Roanoke, VA, 2010. For general operations.

2759
Nu Skin Enterprises, Inc.

75 W. Center St.
Provo, UT 84601 (801) 345-1000
FAX: (801) 345-5999

Company URL: http://www.nuskin.com
Establishment information: Established in 1984.
Company type: Public company
Company ticker symbol and exchange: NUS/NYSE
Business activities: Develops personal care products, nutritional supplements, and home care products; operates direct selling company.
Business type (SIC): Nonstore retailers
Financial profile for 2012: Number of employees, 3,733; assets, $1,152,910,000; sales volume, $2,169,660,000; pre-tax net income, $345,240,000; expenses, $1,828,820,000; liabilities, $562,290,000
Fortune 1000 ranking: 2012—891st in revenues, 548th in profits, and 956th in assets
Corporate officers: Steven J. Lund, Chair.; M. Truman Hunt, Pres. and C.E.O.; Ritch N. Wood, C.F.O.; D. Matthew Dorny, V.P., Genl. Counsel, and Secy.
Board of directors: Steven J. Lund, Chair.; Nevin N. Andersen; Daniel W. Campbell; M. Truman Hunt; Andrew D. Lipman; Patricia A. Negron; Neil H. Offen; Thomas R. Pisano
International operations: Australia; Belgium; Brazil; Canada; China; Denmark; France; Germany; Guatemala; Hong Kong; Italy; Japan; Malaysia; Mexico; Netherlands; New Zealand; Philippines; Poland; Singapore; South Korea; Taiwan; Thailand; United Kingdom

Giving statement: Giving through the Nu Skin Enterprises, Inc. Corporate Giving Program and the Nu Skin Force for Good Foundation.
Company EIN: 870565309

Nu Skin Enterprises, Inc. Corporate Giving Program

75 W. Center St.
Provo, UT 84601-4432 (801) 345-0100
URL: http://www.nuskin.com/us/en/culture/social_responsibility/sponsorships.html

Purpose and activities: As a complement to its foundation, Nu Skin Enterprises also makes charitable contributions to organizations directly. Support is given primarily in Provo, Utah.
Fields of interest: Performing arts, dance; Performing arts, music; Recreation, fairs/festivals; Athletics/sports, football.
Type of support: Sponsorships.
Geographic limitations: Giving primarily in Provo, UT.

The Nu Skin Force for Good Foundation

(formerly The Force for Good Foundation)
c/o Nu Skin Enterprises, Inc.
75 W. Center St.
Provo, UT 84601-4432 (801) 345-2187
E-mail: forceforgood@nuskin.com; Additional contact: Kara Schneck, tel.: (801) 345-2116, e-mail: kschneck@nuskin.com; E-mail for Jordan Karpowitz: jkarpowi@nuskin.com; URL: http://www.forceforgood.org

Establishment information: Established in 1998 in UT.
Donors: Diamond Technology Partners Inc.; Nu Skin Enterprises, Inc.; Blake M. Roney.
Contact: Jordan Karpowitz
Financial data (yr. ended 12/31/11): Assets, $1,538,731 (M); gifts received, $2,781,144; expenditures, $1,768,440; qualifying distributions, $1,631,118; giving activities include $1,631,118 for 18 grants (high: $129,811; low: $500).
Purpose and activities: The foundation supports programs designed to improve the lives of children by offering hope for a life free for disease, illiteracy, and poverty.
Fields of interest: Elementary/secondary education; Education, reading; Education; Health care; Heart & circulatory diseases; Skin disorders research; Medical research; Agriculture; Disasters, preparedness/services; Children, services; Human services; Economic development Economically disadvantaged.
Type of support: Building/renovation; Continuing support; Equipment; General/operating support; Research.
Geographic limitations: Giving primarily in CA, UT, China, Ethiopia, Kenya, Malawi, and Uganda; giving also to national and international organizations.
Support limitations: No support for fraternal organizations, religious organizations, or political lobbyists. No grants to individuals, or for administrative costs, capital campaigns, seed money, advertising, or travel.
Application information: Applications not accepted. Contributes only to pre-selected organizations.
Officers and Trustees:* Blake M. Roney*, Chair. and Pres.; Gary Garrett, V.P.; M. Truman Hunt*, V.P.; Sandra N. Tillotson*, V.P.; Steven J. Lund*, Secy.; B.G. Hunt, Cont.; Brooke Roney.
EIN: 870577244
Selected grants: The following grants are a representative sample of this grantmaker's funding activity:
$554,194 to China Foundation for Poverty Alleviation, Beijing, China, 2009.
$245,450 to Support Africa Empowerment Foundation International, Aurora, CO, 2009.
$150,000 to Mayo Clinic, Rochester, MN, 2009.
$130,000 to Epidermolysis Bullosa Medical Research Foundation, Beverly Hills, CA, 2009.
$127,496 to Seacology, Berkeley, CA, 2009.
$100,000 to After-School All-Stars, Los Angeles, CA, 2009.
$70,000 to Educate the Children, Long Beach, CA, 2009.
$15,000 to American Chamber Foundation Philippines, Hilton Head Island, SC, 2009.
$15,000 to Child Foundation, Portland, OR, 2009.
$13,250 to China Youth Development Foundation, China Hope Project, Beijing, China, 2009. For Nu Hope Schools in China.

2760
Nucor Corporation

1915 Rexford Rd.
Charlotte, NC 28211 (704) 366-7000
FAX: (704) 362-4208

Company URL: http://www.nucor.com
Establishment information: Established in 1905.
Company type: Public company
Company ticker symbol and exchange: NUE/NYSE
Business activities: Manufactures and sells steel and steel products.
Business type (SIC): Steel mill products
Financial profile for 2012: Number of employees, 22,200; assets, $14,152,060,000; sales volume, $19,429,270,000; pre-tax net income, $852,940,000; expenses, $18,576,330,000; liabilities, $6,510,490,000
Fortune 1000 ranking: 2012—146th in revenues, 332nd in profits, and 308th in assets
Forbes 2000 ranking: 2012—481st in sales, 1074th in profits, and 1221st in assets
Corporate officers: Daniel R. Dimicco, Chair. and C.E.O.; John J. Ferriola, Pres. and C.O.O.; James D. Frias, Exec. V.P., C.F.O., and Treas.
Board of directors: Daniel R. Dimicco, Chair.; Peter C. Browning; Clayton C. Daley, Jr.; John J. Ferriola; Harvey B. Gantt; Victoria F. Haynes, Ph.D.; James D. Hlavacek; Bernard L.M. Kasriel; Christopher J. Kearney; John H. Walker
Subsidiaries: Ambassador Steel Corporation, Auburn, IN; The David J. Joseph Company, Cincinnati, OH; Harris Steel, Inc., Belleville, MI; Magnatrax Corporation, Alpharetta, GA; Nucor Steel Auburn, Inc., Auburn, NY; Nucor Steel Birmingham, Inc., Birmingham, AL; Nucor Steel Decatur, L.L.C., Trinity, AL; Nucor Steel Jackson, Inc., Flowood, MS; Nucor Steel Kankakee, Inc., Bourbonnais, IL; Nucor Steel Marion, Inc., Marion, OH; Nucor Steel Memphis, Inc., Memphis, TN; Nucor Steel Seattle, Inc., Seattle, WA; Nucor Steel Tuscaloosa, Inc., Tuscaloosa, AL; Nucor-Yamato Steel Company, Blytheville, AR; Nustrip Arkansas, L.L.C., Armorel, AR
Plants: Grapeland, Jewett, TX; Brigham City, Plymouth, UT
International operations: Barbados; Canada; Italy
Giving statement: Giving through the Nucor Corporation Contributions Program and the Nucor Foundation.
Company EIN: 831860817

Nucor Corporation Contributions Program

1915 Rexford Rd.
Charlotte, NC 28211-3888 (704) 366-7000
FAX: (704) 362-4208; URL: http://www.nucor.com/responsibility/

Purpose and activities: Nucor makes charitable contributions to K-12 schools and nonprofit organizations involved with science, technology, engineering, and mathematics (STEM) education and the environment. Support is given primarily in areas of company operations in Alabama, Arizona, Arkansas, California, Connecticut, Illinois, Indiana, Louisiana, Mississippi, Missouri, Nebraska, Nevada, New York, North Carolina, Ohio, Pennsylvania, South Carolina, Tennessee, Texas, Utah, Virginia, Washington, and Wisconsin.
Fields of interest: Elementary/secondary education; Environment; Science; Mathematics; Engineering/technology; General charitable giving.
Type of support: Employee volunteer services; General/operating support; In-kind gifts.
Geographic limitations: Giving primarily in areas of company operations in AL, AR, AZ, CA, CT, IL, IN, LA, MO, MS, NC, NE, NV, NY, OH, PA, SC, TN, TX, UT, VA, WA, and WI.

Nucor Foundation

1915 Rexford Rd.
Charlotte, NC 28211-3465 (704) 366-7000

Establishment information: Established in 1973 in NC.
Donor: Nucor Corp.
Contact: Donovan Marks
Financial data (yr. ended 12/31/11): Assets, $315,856 (M); gifts received, $1,800,000; expenditures, $1,673,244; qualifying distributions, $1,672,041; giving activities include $1,672,041 for grants.
Purpose and activities: The foundation awards undergraduate and vocational education scholarships to children and stepchildren of employees of Nucor Corporation and scholarships to students pursuing degrees in engineering and metallurgy form communities where Nucor operates.
Fields of interest: Vocational education; Higher education; Engineering school/education.
Programs:
Community Scholarships: The foundation awards four-year $3,000 college scholarships to students from areas of Nucor operations to pursue a degree in engineering or metallurgy. Recipients are selected based on personal background, academic abilities, leadership traits, character, and financial need.
Employee-Related Scholarships: The foundation awards $3,000 undergraduate and vocational education scholarships to children and stepchildren of current or deceased employees of Nucor Corporation. Recipients are selected based on personal background, academic abilities, leadership traits, character, and financial need.
Type of support: Employee-related scholarships; Scholarships—to individuals.
Geographic limitations: Giving primarily in areas of company operations.
Application information: Applications accepted. Application form required.
Applications should include transcripts, class rank, test scores, and a letter of recommendation.
Initial approach: Contact foundation for application form
Deadline(s): Mar. 1 for Community Scholarships
Directors: Daniel R. Dimicco; James D. Frias; Daniel W. Krug.
EIN: 237318064

2761
Nucor-Yamato Steel Co.
5929 E. State Hwy. 18
Blytheville, AR 72316-1228 (870) 762-5500
FAX: (870) 763-9107

Company URL: http://www.nucoryamato.com/
Establishment information: Established in 1987.
Company type: Subsidiary of a foreign company
Business activities: Operates structural steel mill.
Business type (SIC): Steel mill products
Corporate officers: John Cross, V.P., Mktg.; Keith Prevost, Cont.
Giving statement: Giving through the Nucor-Yamato Steel Co. Contributions Program.

Nucor-Yamato Steel Co. Contributions Program
P.O. Box 1228
Blytheville, AR 72316-1228 (870) 762-5500
URL: http://www.nucoryamato.com

2762
Nursery Equipment Supply Co.
13430 Hobson Simmons Rd.
Lithia, FL 33547 (813) 689-3601

Establishment information: Established in 1984.
Company type: Private company
Business activities: Operates nursery equipment company.
Business type (SIC): Garden supplies—retail
Corporate officers: Douglas A. Holmberg, Chair. and Pres.; Gregory J. Holmberg, V.P. and Secy.-Treas.
Board of director: Douglas A. Holmberg, Chair.
Giving statement: Giving through the Freedom 2000 Foundation, Inc.

Freedom 2000 Foundation, Inc.
13430 Hobson Simmons Rd.
Lithia, FL 33547-1912

Establishment information: Established in FL.
Donors: Ben Holt; Don Freiling; Nursery Equipment Supply Co., Inc.; Douglas A. Holmberg.
Contact: Douglas A. Holmberg, Pres.
Financial data (yr. ended 12/31/11): Assets, $66,666 (L); gifts received, $9,000; expenditures, $23,114; qualifying distributions, $23,106; giving activities include $23,106 for 3 grants (high: $15,706; low: $1,400).
Purpose and activities: Giving for the development and production of workbooks and manuals that promote Bible study and enhance religious education; some scholarship awards to students desiring to study the Bible along with other liberal arts courses.
Fields of interest: Christian agencies & churches.
Application information: Applications accepted. Application form required. Applicants should submit the following:
1) brief history of organization and description of its mission
2) detailed description of project and amount of funding requested
Initial approach: Letter
Deadline(s): Apr. 30
Officers and Directors:* Douglas A. Holmberg*, Pres.; Greg Holberg*, Secy.-Treas.; Keith Graig; Tim Morris.
EIN: 593135348

2763
NuStar Energy L.P.
19003 IH-10 West
San Antonio, TX 78257 (210) 918-2000

Company URL: http://www.nustarenergy.com/
Establishment information: Established in 2001.
Company type: Public company
Company ticker symbol and exchange: NS/NYSE
Business activities: Operates petroleum products company.
Business type (SIC): Pipelines (except natural gas/ operation of)
Financial profile for 2012: Number of employees, 1,478; assets, $5,613,090,000; sales volume, $5,955,680,000; pre-tax net income, -$155,640,000; expenses, $6,009,560,000; liabilities, $3,040,700,000
Fortune 1000 ranking: 2012—389th in revenues, 943rd in profits, and 560th in assets
Corporate officers: Bill Greehey, Chair.; Curtis V. Anastasio, Pres. and C.E.O.; Douglas W. Comeau, Exec. V.P. and C.O.O.; Steven A. Blank, Exec. V.P., C.F.O., and Treas.; Bradley C. Barron, Exec. V.P. and Genl. Counsel; Amy Perry, V.P. and Corp. Secy.; Robert Grimes, V.P., Human Resources
Board of directors: William E. Greehey, Chair.; Curtis V. Anastasio; Jesse Dan Bates; Dan J. Hill; Stan L. McLelland; Rodman D. Patton; W. Grady Rosier
Giving statement: Giving through the NuStar Foundation.
Company EIN: 742956831

NuStar Foundation
19003 IH-10 W., Attn.: Tax Dept.
San Antonio, TX 78257-9518
Application address: c/o Cynthia Pena, P.O. Box 781609, San Antonio, TX 78269, tel.: (210) 918-2000

Donor: NuStar Logistics, L.P.
Financial data (yr. ended 12/31/11): Assets, $16,855 (M); gifts received, $4,935,392; expenditures, $5,152,817; qualifying distributions, $4,791,470; giving activities include $4,791,470 for 567 grants (high: $650,000; low: $20).
Fields of interest: Education; Health organizations, association; Youth development; Human services.
Geographic limitations: Giving in the U.S., primarily in TX; with some emphasis on San Antonio.
Application information: Applications accepted. Application form required.
Initial approach: Proposal
Deadline(s): None
Directors: Curtis V. Anastasio; Mary Rose Brown; William E. Greehey.
EIN: 260629473

2764
Nutter, McClennen & Fish, LLP
Seaport W.
155 Seaport Blvd.
Boston, MA 02210-2604 (617) 439-2000

Company URL: http://www.nutter.com
Establishment information: Established in 1879.
Company type: Private company
Business activities: Operates law firm.
Business type (SIC): Legal services
Offices: Boston, Hyannis, MA
Giving statement: Giving through the Nutter, McClennen & Fish, LLP Pro Bono Program.

Nutter, McClennen & Fish, LLP Pro Bono Program
Seaport W.
155 Seaport Blvd.
Boston, MA 02210-2604 (617) 439-2852
E-mail: tgarner@nutter.com; URL: http://www.nutter.com/Pro-Bono/

Contact: Tammie C. Garner, Dir. of Professional Devel.
Fields of interest: Legal services.
Type of support: Pro bono services - legal.
Geographic limitations: Giving primarily in areas of company operations in Boston, and Hyannis, MA.
Application information: A Pro Bono Committee manages the pro bono program.

2765
NV Energy, Inc.
(formerly Sierra Pacific Resources)
6100 Neil Rd.
6226 W. Sahara Ave.
Las Vegas, NV 89146 (702) 402-5000
FAX: (775) 834-3815

Company URL: http://www.nvenergy.com
Establishment information: Established in 1984.
Company type: Public company
Company ticker symbol and exchange: NVE/NYSE
Business activities: Generates, transmits, and distributes electricity; transmits and distributes natural gas. At press time, the company is in the process of merging with MidAmerican Energy Holdings Company.
Business type (SIC): Combination utility services
Financial profile for 2012: Number of employees, 2,699; assets, $11,984,140,000; sales volume, $2,979,180,000; pre-tax net income, $488,540,000; expenses, $2,194,110,000; liabilities, $8,426,760,000
Fortune 1000 ranking: 2012—718th in revenues, 447th in profits, and 350th in assets
Corporate officers: Philip G. Satre, Chair.; Michael W. Yackira, Pres. and C.E.O.; Dilek Samil, Exec. V.P. and C.O.O.; Jonathan S. Halkyard, Exec. V.P. and C.F.O.; Paul J. Kaleta, Exec. V.P., Genl. Counsel, and Corp. Secy.; Alice A. Cobb, Sr. V.P., Human Resources; E. Kevin Bethel, V.P., C.A.O., and Cont.; Kevin Judice, V.P. and C.I.O.
Board of directors: Philip G. Satre, Chair.; Joseph B. Anderson, Jr.; Glenn C. Christenson; Susan F. Clark; Stephen E. Frank; Brian J. Kennedy; Maureen T. Mullarkey; John F. O'Reilly; Donald D. Snyder; Michael W. Yackira
Subsidiaries: Lands of Sierra, Reno, NV; Sierra Pacific Power Company, Reno, NV; Tuscarora Gas Pipeline Co., Reno, NV
Giving statement: Giving through the NV Energy, Inc. Corporate Giving Program and the NV Energy Charitable Foundation.
Company EIN: 880198358

NV Energy, Inc. Corporate Giving Program
c/o Community Rels.
6226 West Sahara Ave.
Las Vegas, NV 89146-3060 (702) 402-5000
E-mail: SMccaffrey@nvenergy.com; For application information about in-kind donations in northern Nevada, contact: Stefanie McCaffrey, Sr. Corp. Comms. Specialist, e-mail: SMccaffrey@nvenergy.com; tel.: (775) 834-3615; in southern Nevada, contact: Jennifer Vargas, Corp. Comms. Coord., e-mail: JVargas@nvenergy.com;

tel.: (702) 402-2202. Application addresses for sponsorship requests: in northern Nevada, contact: Community Rels. Mgr., NV Energy, P.O. Box 10100, Reno, NV 89520; in southern Nevada, contact: Community Rels. Mgr., NV Energy, P.O. Box 98910, Las Vegas, NV 89151.; URL: http://www.nvenergy.com/community/

Contact: Stefanie McCaffrey, Sr. Corp. Comms. Specialist
Financial data (yr. ended 12/31/10): Total giving, $1,100,000, including $1,100,000 for grants.
Purpose and activities: As a complement to its foundation, NV Energy also makes charitable contributions to nonprofit organizations directly. Donations are made in the form of used items, printing services, and event sponsorships. Emphasis is given to organizations that are involved with education, the environment, diversity, health and human services, and youth development. Support is limited to areas of company operations in Nevada.
Fields of interest: Education; Environment; Health care; Youth development; Human services; Civil/human rights, equal rights; Community/economic development; Financial services Economically disadvantaged.
Type of support: Donated products; In-kind gifts; Sponsorships.
Geographic limitations: Giving limited to areas of company operations in NV.
Application information: Applications accepted. Applicants should submit the following:
1) population served
2) detailed description of project and amount of funding requested
3) plans for acknowledgement

Initial approach: Call or e-mail for application information about in-kind donations; Mail proposal to application address for sponsorship requests

NV Energy Charitable Foundation

(formerly NV Energy Foundation)
P.O. Box 10100
Reno, NV 89520-3150 (775) 834-5642
Application address for Northern Nevada: Admin., NV Energy Fdn., P.O. Box 10100, Reno, NV 89520-3150, tel.: (775) 834-5741,
e-mail: Communitynorth@nvenergy.com; application address for Southern Nevada: Admin., NV Energy Fdn., P.O. Box 98910, Las Vegas, NV 89151-0001, tel.: (702) 402-5741,
e-mail: Communitysouth@nvenergy.com;
URL: http://www.nvenergy.com/community/funding/sprfoundation/
Application address for Southern Nevada: NV Energy, Powerful Partnership Scholarship - M/S 15, P.O. Box 98910, Las Vegas, NV 89151; Northern Nevada: NV Energy, Powerful Partnership Scholarship, Community Foundation of Western Nevada, 1885 South Arlington Ave., Ste. 103, Reno, NV 89509

Establishment information: Established in 1987 in NV.
Donors: Sierra Pacific Resources; NV Energy, Inc.
Contact: Mary Simmons, Secy.
Financial data (yr. ended 12/31/11): Assets, $7,903,117 (M); gifts received, $3,000,000; expenditures, $4,145,554; qualifying distributions, $4,145,500; giving activities include $4,145,500 for 170 grants (high: $500,000; low: $100).
Purpose and activities: The foundation supports programs designed to promote arts and culture; education; the environment; youth; and health and human services.
Fields of interest: Arts, cultural/ethnic awareness; Arts; Higher education; Education; Environment, recycling; Environment, natural resources; Environment, energy; Environment; Animals/wildlife; Health care; Recreation, parks/playgrounds; Youth development; Youth, services; Human services; United Ways and Federated Giving Programs.
Programs:
Arts and Multicultural: The foundation supports programs designed to expand access to public participation in the arts, with emphasis on bringing arts and cultural opportunities to under-served populations in both urban centers and rural towns.
Education: The foundation supports educational institutions and nonprofit organizations involved with education with a demonstrated history of delivering effective programs that produce measurable results.
Environment: The foundation supports programs designed to foster a safe and sustainable environment; and address environmental concerns such as renewable resources, energy conservation, air, land, and water quality, wildlife habitat, open space, parks and trails, and waste recycling.
Health and Human Services: The foundation supports programs designed to concentrate on improving quality of life health indicators.
Powerful Partnerships High School Scholarship: The foundation annually awards $1,000 scholarships to high school seniors attending school or homeschooled in NV Energy's northern and southern service territory. The scholarship is based on demonstrated leadership, academic achievement, financial need, and 20 hours of community service. In southern Nevada application forms are available through Clark County School District. In northern Nevada application forms are available through the Community Foundation of Western Nevada.
Youth: The foundation supports programs designed to focus on strong prevention and/or intervention activities; and empower young people to gain self-confidence, personal independence, and personal growth.
Type of support: Annual campaigns; Capital campaigns; Continuing support; Employee matching gifts; Employee volunteer services; General/operating support; Matching/challenge support; Program development; Scholarship funds; Scholarships—to individuals; Sponsorships.
Geographic limitations: Giving limited to areas of company operations in northeastern CA and northeastern NV.
Support limitations: No support for religious organizations, foundations, political or partisan organizations, or sports leagues. No grants to individuals (except for scholarships), or for tickets for contests, raffles, or other activities with prizes; film, television, or video productions, advertising, debt reduction, sporting events or tournaments, trips or tours, talent or beauty contests, or conferences.
Publications: Application guidelines; Informational brochure (including application guidelines); Program policy statement.
Application information: Applications accepted. Multi-year funding is not automatic. An application form is required for scholarships. Applications are not accepted by e-mail, fax, or telephone. Applicants should submit the following:
1) statement of problem project will address
2) population served
3) name, address and phone number of organization
4) copy of IRS Determination Letter
5) brief history of organization and description of its mission
6) how project's results will be evaluated or measured
7) list of company employees involved with the organization
8) listing of board of directors, trustees, officers and other key people and their affiliations
9) detailed description of project and amount of funding requested
10) contact person
11) copy of current year's organizational budget and/or project budget
12) plans for acknowledgement

Scholarship applications should include official high school transcripts; evidence of enrollment at an institution of higher education; a personal statement outlining career goals and aspirations; a 100 to 300-word essay explaining why community service is important; a letter of recommendation from a school official; and one to three letters of recommendation from an agency or organization where the student has volunteered.
Initial approach: Proposal; download application form and mail to application address for scholarships
Copies of proposal: 1
Board meeting date(s): Bi-monthly
Deadline(s): None; Mar. 1 for Powerful Partnerships High School Scholarships
Final notification: 2 months; Apr. 30 for Powerful Partnerships High School Scholarships
Officers and Directors:* Michael W. Yackira*, Pres.; Mary Simmons, Secy.; Dimek Samil*, Treas.; Jeff Ceccarelli; Tony Sanchez.
Number of staff: 1 part-time professional; 1 part-time support.
EIN: 880244735

2766
NVF Company

1166 Yorklyn Rd.
P.O. Box 68
Yorklyn, DE 19763 (302) 239-5281

Company URL: http://www.nvf.com
Establishment information: Established in 1875.
Company type: Private company
Business activities: Manufactures vulcanized fibers, laminated plastics and thermoplastics, fine papers, and other industrial products.
Business type (SIC): Steel mill products; paper mills; metal products/structural
Corporate officers: Brenda Nester, Pres. and C.E.O.; Edward T. McGann, C.F.O.; Marco B. Loffredo, V.P. and Secy.
Subsidiaries: Brainard Strapping, Warren, OH; Continental Mine, Yorklyn, DE; Damascus Tubular Products, Greenville, PA; Industrial Laminated Plastics, Yorklyn, DE; NVF Company Parsons Paper, Holyoke, MA; Sharon Steel Co., Sharon, PA
Plant: Kennett Square, PA
Giving statement: Giving through the NVF Corporate Giving Program, the Siemens AG Corporate Giving Program, and the National Vulcanized Fibre Company Community Services Trust Fund.

National Vulcanized Fibre Company Community Services Trust Fund

3310 Lake Ridge Ln.
Weston, FL 33332

Establishment information: Trust established in 1956 in DE.
Donors: National Vulcanized Fibre Co.; NVF Co.
Financial data (yr. ended 12/31/11): Assets, $118 (M); expenditures, $290; qualifying distributions, $200; giving activities include $200 for grants.

Purpose and activities: The foundation supports organizations involved with arts and culture, education, child welfare, and Christianity.
Fields of interest: Education; Human services; Religion.
Type of support: General/operating support.
Geographic limitations: Giving primarily in Coral Gables, Miami, and Palm Beach, FL.
Support limitations: No grants to individuals.
Application information: Applications not accepted. Unsolicited requests for funds not accepted.
Officers: Brenda Nestor, Pres.; Blanche Launer, Secy.-Treas.
EIN: 516021550

2767
NVIDIA Corporation

2701 San Tomas Expwy.
Santa Clara, CA 95050 (408) 486-2000
FAX: (408) 486-2200

Company URL: http://www.nvidia.com
Establishment information: Established in 1993.
Company type: Public company
Company ticker symbol and exchange: NVDA/NASDAQ
International Securities Identification Number: US67066G1040
Business activities: Operates semiconductor company.
Business type (SIC): Electronic components and accessories
Financial profile for 2013: Number of employees, 5,783; assets, $6,412,240,000; sales volume, $4,280,160,000; pre-tax net income, $662,040,000; expenses, $3,631,920,000; liabilities, $1,584,540,000
Fortune 1000 ranking: 2012—553rd in revenues, 307th in profits, and 514th in assets
Corporate officers: Jen-Hsun Huang, Pres. and C.E.O.; David M. Shannon, Exec. V.P., Genl. Counsel, and Secy.; Debora Shoquist, Exec. V.P., Opers.; Jay Puri, Exec. V.P., Sales; Karen Burns, C.F.O.; Bob Worrall, Sr. V.P. and C.I.O.
Board of directors: Robert K. Burgess; Tench Coxe; James C. Gaither; Jen-Hsun Huang; Harvey C. Jones; William J. Miller; Mark L. Perry; A. Brooke Seawell; Mark A. Stevens
Giving statement: Giving through the NVIDIA Foundation.
Company EIN: 943177549

NVIDIA Foundation

2701 San Tomas Expwy.
Santa Clara, CA 95050-2519 (408) 486-2000
E-mail: corporategrants@siliconvalleycf.org; E-mail for Tonie Hansen: thansen@nvidia.com;
URL: http://www.nvidia.com/object/gcr-community.html

Contact: Tonie Hansen, Dir., NVIDIA Foundation
Purpose and activities: NVIDIA makes charitable contributions to nonprofit organizations involved with education, the environment, healthcare, medical research, youth development, and human services. Support is given primarily in areas of company operations in Alabama, California, Colorado, Florida, Massachusetts, Missouri, North Carolina, Oregon, Texas, Utah, Virginia, and Washington, and in China, Finland, France, Germany, Hong Kong, Japan, Russia, Singapore, Switzerland, Taiwan, and the United Kingdom.
Fields of interest: Disasters, preparedness/services; General charitable giving.
International interests: China; Finland; France; Germany; Hong Kong; Japan; Russia; Singapore; Switzerland; Taiwan; United Kingdom.
Type of support: Continuing support; Employee matching gifts; Employee volunteer services; General/operating support.
Geographic limitations: Giving primarily in areas of company operations in AL, CA, CO, FL, MA, MO, NC, OR, TX, UT, VA, and WA, and in China, Finland, France, Germany, Hong Kong, Japan, Russia, Singapore, Switzerland, Taiwan, and the United Kingdom.
Application information: Applications must have an employee sponsor and be submitted by the employee. Support is limited to 1 contribution per organization during any given year. Application form required. Applicants should submit the following:
1) how project will be sustained once grantmaker support is completed
2) results expected from proposed grant
3) qualifications of key personnel
4) statement of problem project will address
5) copy of IRS Determination Letter
6) brief history of organization and description of its mission
7) geographic area to be served
8) copy of most recent annual report/audited financial statement/990
9) listing of board of directors, trustees, officers and other key people and their affiliations
10) detailed description of project and amount of funding requested
11) copy of current year's organizational budget and/or project budget
12) listing of additional sources and amount of support

Initial approach: Download application form and e-mail with proposal to Silicon Valley Foundation
Deadline(s): Apr. 22
Final notification: July

2768
NYK Line (North America) Inc.

300 Lighting Way
Secaucus, NJ 07094-3647 (201) 330-3000

Company URL: http://www.nykline.com
Establishment information: Established in 1988.
Company type: Subsidiary of a foreign company
Business activities: Provides deep sea freight transportation services.
Business type (SIC): Transportation/deep sea foreign freight
Corporate officers: Hiroyuki Shimizu, Chair. and C.E.O.; Tomoo Kitayama, Pres.; William Payne, Exec. V.P. and C.O.O.; Paula Nitto, C.F.O.; Joey Fajarito, C.A.O.; Eric Nichols, C.I.O.; Bill Niemann, Sr. V.P., Sales; Richard Breffeilh, V.P., Opers.
Board of directors: Hiroyuki Shimizu, Chair.; Paula Nitto
Plants: Long Beach, CA; Atlanta, GA; Lombard, IL
Giving statement: Giving through the NYK Line (North America) Inc. Corporate Giving Program.

NYK Line (North America) Inc. Corporate Giving Program

300 Lighting Way, 5th Fl.
Secaucus, NJ 07094-3647 (201) 330-3000
URL: http://www.nyk.com/english/csr/

Purpose and activities: NYK Line makes charitable contributions to nonprofit organizations involved with the environment, health, and human services. Support is given primarily in areas of company operations.
Fields of interest: Environment; Health organizations; Human services.
Type of support: Employee matching gifts; Employee volunteer services; General/operating support.
Geographic limitations: Giving primarily in areas of company operations.

2769
NYSE Euronext, Inc.

(formerly NYSE Group, Inc.)
11 Wall St.
New York, NY 10005 (212) 656-3000
FAX: (212) 656-5549

Company URL: http://www.nyse.com
Establishment information: Established in 1792.
Company type: Public company
Company ticker symbol and exchange: NYX/NYSE
International Securities Identification Number: US6294911010
Business activities: Operates holding company; operates securities exchanges.
Business type (SIC): Security and commodity exchange
Financial profile for 2012: Assets, $12,600,000,000; sales volume, $3,700,000,000
Fortune 1000 ranking: 2012—616th in revenues, 435th in profits, and 338th in assets
Forbes 2000 ranking: 2012—1539th in sales, 1522nd in profits, and 1300th in assets
Corporate officers: Jan-Michiel Hessels, Chair.; Duncan L. Niederauer, C.E.O.; Dominique Cerutti, Pres.; Lawrence Leibowitz, C.O.O.; Michael S. Geltzeiler, C.F.O.; John K. Halvey, Genl. Counsel
Board of directors: Jan-Michiel Hessels, Chair.; Andre Bergen; Ellyn L. Brown; Marshall N. Carter; Dominique Cerutti; George Cox; Luis Maria Viana Palha da Silva; Sylvain Hefes; Lawrence Leibowitz; Duncan M. McFarland; James J. McNulty; Duncan L. Niederauer; Robert G. Scott; Jackson Peter Tai; Rijnhard Van Tets; Brian Williamson
Subsidiaries: Archipelago Holdings, Inc., Chicago, IL; New York Stock Exchange, L.L.C., New York, NY
Giving statement: Giving through the NYSE Euronext Corporate Giving Program, the New York Stock Exchange Fallen Heroes Fund, and the NYSE Euronext Foundation, Inc.
Company EIN: 205110848

NYSE Euronext Corporate Giving Program

(formerly New York Stock Exchange, L.L.C. Corporate Giving Program)
11 Wall St.
New York, NY 10005-1916 (212) 656-3000
URL: http://www.nyse.com/corpcitizenship/1091792165924.html#charity

Contact: Steve Wheeler
Purpose and activities: As a complement to its foundation, the New York Stock Exchange also makes charitable contributions to nonprofit organizations directly. Support is given primarily in the greater New York, New York, area.
Fields of interest: Arts; Higher education; Scholarships/financial aid; Education; Health care; Medical research; Employment, training; Food services; Safety/disasters; Youth development; Human services, financial counseling; Human services; Civil/human rights, equal rights; Community development, small businesses;

Community/economic development Disabilities, people with; Homeless.
Type of support: Employee volunteer services; General/operating support; Scholarship funds.
Geographic limitations: Giving primarily in the greater New York, NY, area.
Application information: A contributions committee reviews all requests.
Contributions Committee: Michael S. Geltzeiler; Catherine R. Kinney; Duncan L. Niederauer.

New York Stock Exchange Fallen Heroes Fund

11 Wall St.
New York, NY 10005-1916
URL: http://corporate.nyx.com/en/who-we-are/corporate-responsibility/our-community/philanthropy

Establishment information: Incorporated in 1999 in DE.
Donors: New York Stock Exchange, Inc.; New York Stock Exchange LLC.
Contact: Steve Wheeler
Financial data (yr. ended 12/31/11): Assets, $2,620,375 (M); expenditures, $194,000; qualifying distributions, $194,000; giving activities include $194,000 for grants.
Purpose and activities: The fund provides assistance to the families of police officers, firefighters, and other employees of the New York police and fire departments who were killed in the line of duty. As a result of the events of September 11, 2001, assistance is also provided to families of the police officers of the Port Authority of New York and New Jersey.
Fields of interest: Crime/law enforcement, police agencies; Disasters, fire prevention/control; Disasters, 9/11/01; Safety/disasters.
Type of support: General/operating support; Grants to individuals.
Geographic limitations: Giving limited to NJ and NY.
Publications: IRS Form 990 or 990-PF printed copy available upon request.
Application information: Applications accepted. Application form not required.
Initial approach: Letter of inquiry for application information
Deadline(s): Varies
Officers and Directors:* Arthur D. Cashin, Jr.*, Chair. and Pres.; John K. Halvey, Secy.; Patrick Boyle, Treas.; Michael S. Geltzeiler, Cont.; Robert M. Murphy; Richard A. Rosenblatt.
EIN: 134048148

NYSE Euronext Foundation, Inc.

(formerly New York Stock Exchange Foundation, Inc.)
c/o Tax Dept.
11 Wall St.
New York, NY 10005-1916
FAX: (212) 656-5629;
E-mail: foundation@nyse.com; URL: http://www.nyse.com/corpcitizenship/1091792165924.html

Establishment information: Incorporated in 1983 in NY.
Donors: Charity Folks, Inc., Inc.; New York Stock Exchange LLC; Merrill Lynch, Pierce, Fenner & Smith Inc.
Contact: Steven Wheeler, Asst. Secy.
Financial data (yr. ended 12/31/11): Assets, $10,646,928 (M); gifts received, $2,148,099; expenditures, $3,076,385; qualifying distributions, $3,004,647; giving activities include $2,962,320 for grants.
Purpose and activities: The foundation supports organizations involved with financial counseling, economic opportunity, and entrepreneurship. Support is given primarily in areas of company operations.
Fields of interest: Youth development; Human services, financial counseling; Business/industry; Community/economic development; Economics Minorities; Economically disadvantaged.
Programs:
Matching Gifts Program: The foundation matches contributions made by employees of New York Stock Exchange to educational institutions and nonprofit organizations whose missions and activities are within program areas supported by the foundation up to $5,000 per employee, per year.
Volunteer Incentive Program (VIP): The foundation awards $1,000 grants to nonprofit organizations with which employees of NYSE volunteer at least 50 hours.
Type of support: Annual campaigns; Capital campaigns; Employee matching gifts; Employee volunteer services; General/operating support; Program development; Research; Scholarship funds; Sponsorships.
Geographic limitations: Giving primarily in areas of company operations in New York, NY.
Support limitations: No support for businesses, political, fraternal, or religious organizations, discriminatory organizations, donor advised funds, or private foundations. No grants to individuals, or for tickets to dinners, receptions, or other fundraising events.
Publications: Annual report (including application guidelines); Application guidelines.
Application information: Applications accepted. Proposals should be no longer than 3 to 6 pages in length. Application form not required. Applicants should submit the following:
1) population served
2) copy of IRS Determination Letter
3) brief history of organization and description of its mission
4) geographic area to be served
5) copy of most recent annual report/audited financial statement/990
6) listing of board of directors, trustees, officers and other key people and their affiliations
7) detailed description of project and amount of funding requested
8) copy of current year's organizational budget and/or project budget
Initial approach: Proposal
Copies of proposal: 1
Board meeting date(s): Rolling
Deadline(s): None
Final notification: Varies
Officers and Directors:* Duncan L. Niederauer*, Chair.; Janet M. Kissane, Secy.; Michael S. Geltzeiler, Treas.; Stephane P. Biehler, Cont.; Michelle D. Greene, Exec. Dir.; Andrew T. Brandman; Arthur D. Cashin, Jr.; Dominique Cerruti; Charles P. Dolan; Richard A. Genna; Lawrence E. Leibowitz; Jeffrey S. Reymann; Marisa Ricciardi; Richard A. Rosenblatt; Daniel W. Tandy.
EIN: 133203195

2772
The Oakland Raiders, L.P.

1220 Harbor Bay Pkwy.
Alameda, CA 94502-6501 (510) 864-5000

Company URL: http://www.raiders.com
Establishment information: Established in 1960.
Company type: Private company
Business activities: Operates professional football club.
Business type (SIC): Commercial sports
Corporate officer: Amy Jeanne Trask, C.E.O.
Giving statement: Giving through the Oakland Raiders, L.P. Corporate Giving Program.

The Oakland Raiders, L.P. Corporate Giving Program

1220 Harbor Bay Pkwy.
Alameda, CA 94502-6501 (510) 864-5000
URL: http://www.raiders.com/news/community-news.html

Contact: Scott Fink
Purpose and activities: The Oakland Raiders make charitable contributions to nonprofit organizations on a case by case basis. Support is given primarily in California.
Fields of interest: Education; Recreation, fairs/festivals; Athletics/sports, football; Youth development; General charitable giving.
Program:
Back to Football Friday: Through the Back to Football contest and NFL Play 60 initiative, schools compete to show their NFL team pride and submit 3 essays. 34 winning schools are named NFL Play 60 Super Schools and receive a visit from a NFL player and a $10,000 NFL Play 60 health and wellness grant.
Type of support: Donated products; In-kind gifts; Income development; Loaned talent; Sponsorships.
Geographic limitations: Giving primarily in areas of company operations in CA.

2773
Oaklandish, LLC

3421 Hollis St., Ste. M
Emeryville, CA 94608 (510) 652-7490

Company URL: http://www.oaklandish.com
Establishment information: Established in 2000.
Company type: Private company
Business activities: Sells women's and children's clothing apparel.
Business type (SIC): Apparel, piece goods, and notions—wholesale
Corporate officer: Henry Aasand, Principal
Giving statement: Giving through the Oaklandish, LLP Corporate Giving Program.

Oaklandish, LLP Corporate Giving Program

(also known as Oakland Innovators Awards Fund)
3421 Hollis St., Ste. M
Oakland, CA 94608-4109 (510) 652-7490
E-mail: grants@oaklandish.com; URL: http://www.oaklandish.com/community

Contact: Natalie Nadimi, Community Outreach
Financial data (yr. ended 12/31/10): Total giving, $30,000, including $30,000 for grants to individuals.
Purpose and activities: Oklandish supports organizations and individuals who exemplify the values of innovation in all areas of civic life, including the arts, education, technology, and business. Support is limited to Oakland, California.
Fields of interest: Arts; Education; Community/economic development.
Program:
Arts in Action Grant Program: Through the Arts in Action Grant program Oaklandish aims to provoke

public discourse and inspire creative activity throughout the urban landscape. The annual grant award of $5,000 goes to an artist for an approved project that is located in public space, or is readily accessible to the public; addresses or reflects the identity, culture, or history of Oakland; and is sponsored by a 501c3 non-profit organization.
Type of support: General/operating support; Grants to individuals; Program development.
Geographic limitations: Giving limited to Oakland, CA.
Publications: Application guidelines.
Application information: Applications accepted. Organizations may receive only one grant per calendar year. Individual artists must work under a fiscal sponsor in order to be funded. Application form required. Applicants should submit the following:
1) timetable for implementation and evaluation of project
2) copy of IRS Determination Letter
3) listing of board of directors, trustees, officers and other key people and their affiliations
4) detailed description of project and amount of funding requested
5) copy of current year's organizational budget and/or project budget

Project description should not exceed 2 pages; history and mission statement of the project or organization should not exceed 2 paragraphs. Work samples can be submitted as a DVD, CD, print, etc. Proposal should include proof of Oakland residency.
Initial approach: Download online application and mail to headquarters
Copies of proposal: 1
Deadline(s): Dec. 1 for Oakland Innovators Award
Final notification: Jan. 31 for Oakland Innovators Award

2774
Oakley Industries, Inc.

3211 W. Bear Creek Dr.
Englewood, CO 80110-3210
(303) 761-1835

Company URL: http://www.oakleyindustries.com
Establishment information: Established in 1948.
Company type: Private company
Business activities: Manufactures industrial machinery, instant heat terminal pins, and stainless steel tubes.
Business type (SIC): Industrial and commercial machinery and computer equipment; steel mill products; machinery/general industry
Financial profile for 2010: Number of employees, 60
Corporate officers: Gary A. Oakley, Chair.; David Scott Olivet, C.E.O.; Michael Oakley, Pres.; Donald Hester, C.O.O.
Board of director: Gary A. Oakley, Chair.
Giving statement: Giving through the Oakley Foundation.

Oakley Foundation

3211 W. Bear Creek Dr.
Englewood, CO 80110

Establishment information: Established in 1994 in CO.
Donors: Oakley Industries, Inc.; Goa Industries, Inc.; Gary Joann Oakley.
Financial data (yr. ended 12/31/11): Assets, $288,230 (M); expenditures, $6,132; qualifying distributions, $0.
Purpose and activities: The foundation supports art museums and organizations involved with K-12 education, children and youth, and Christianity.
Fields of interest: Museums (art); Elementary/secondary education; Children/youth, services; Christian agencies & churches.
Type of support: General/operating support.
Geographic limitations: Giving limited to CO.
Support limitations: No grants to individuals.
Application information: Applications not accepted. Unsolicited requests for funds not accepted.
Officers: Gary A. Oakley, Pres.; David Oakley, V.P.; Nancy Dufficy, Secy.
EIN: 841290669

2775
Oatey Supply Chain Services, Inc.

4700 W. 160th St.
Cleveland, OH 44135-2632 (216) 267-7100

Company URL: http://www.oatey.com
Establishment information: Established in 1916.
Company type: Private company
Business activities: Manufactures plumbing products.
Business type (SIC): Metal plumbing fixtures and heating equipment/nonelectric
Corporate officers: Gary Oatey, Chair.; John H. McMillan, Pres. and C.E.O.; Neal Restivo, V.P. and C.F.O.; Darren Hilliard, V.P. and Corp. Cont.; Lennon Taylor, Co-Cont.
Board of director: Gary Oatey, Chair.
Giving statement: Giving through the Oatey Foundation.

Oatey Foundation

4700 W. 160th St.
Cleveland, OH 44135-2632

Establishment information: Established in 2001 in OH.
Donor: Oatey Supply Chain Services, Inc.
Financial data (yr. ended 12/31/11): Assets, $1,488,346 (M); gifts received, $10,000; expenditures, $64,823; qualifying distributions, $48,000; giving activities include $48,000 for grants.
Purpose and activities: The foundation supports libraries and organizations involved with performing arts, health, youth, and the disabled.
Fields of interest: Arts; Education; Science.
Type of support: General/operating support.
Support limitations: No grants to individuals.
Application information: Applications not accepted. Unsolicited requests for funds not accepted.
Officers and Trustees:* William Oatey*, Pres.; Nancy McMillan*, Secy.; Karen Oatey*, Treas.; Gary Oatey.
EIN: 866314738

2776
Obagi Medical Products, Inc.

3760 Kilroy Airport Way, Ste. 500
Long Beach, CA 90806-2485
(562) 628-1007
FAX: (562) 628-1008

Company URL: http://www.obagi.com
Establishment information: Established in 1988.
Company type: Public company
Company ticker symbol and exchange: OMPI/NASDAQ
Business activities: Operates specialty pharmaceutical company.
Business type (SIC): Drugs
Financial profile for 2012: Number of employees, 203; assets, $82,110,000; sales volume, $120,680,000; pre-tax net income, $27,410,000; expenses, $93,250,000; liabilities, $20,250,000
Corporate officers: Albert J. Fitzgibbons III, Chair.; Albert F. Hummel, Pres. and C.E.O.; Preston S. Romm, Exec. V.P., Finance, Admin, and Opers., and C.F.O.; David S. Goldstein, Exec V.P., Sales; Laura B. Hunter, V.P., Genl. Counsel, and Secy.
Board of directors: Albert J. Fitzgibbons III, Chair.; Ronald P. Badie; John A. Bartholdson; John H. Duerden; Edward A. Grant; Albert F. Hummel; Kristina M. Leslie
Giving statement: Giving through the Obagi Medical Products, Inc. Contributions Program.
Company EIN: 223904668

Obagi Medical Products, Inc. Contributions Program

3760 Kilroy Airport Way, Ste. 500
Long Beach, CA 90806-2485 (562) 628-1007
URL: http://www.obagi.com

2777
Ober, Kaler, Grimes & Shriver, A.P.C.

100 Light St.
Baltimore, MD 21202-1036
(410) 685-1120

Company URL: http://www.ober.com
Establishment information: Established in 1903.
Company type: Private company
Business activities: Operates law firm.
Business type (SIC): Legal services
Corporate officers: John Anthony Wolf, Chair.; S. Craig Holden, Pres. and C.O.O.
Offices: Washington, DC; Baltimore, Towson, MD; Falls Church, VA
Giving statement: Giving through the Ober, Kaler, Grimes & Shriver, A.P.C. Corporate Giving Program.

Ober, Kaler, Grimes & Shriver, A.P.C. Corporate Giving Program

100 Light St.
Baltimore, MD 21202-1036
E-mail: oberkalergrants@ober.com; Contact for pro bono program: Paul S. Sugar, Esq., Shareholder, tel.: (410) 347-7318, e-mail: pssugar@ober.com; URL: http://www.ober.com/our_firm/community-grants

Fields of interest: Legal services.
Type of support: Pro bono services - legal.

2778
Objectwin Technology, Inc.

14800 St. Mary's Ln., Ste. 107
Houston, TX 77079 (713) 782-8200

Company URL: http://www.objectwin.com/
Establishment information: Established in 1997.
Company type: Private company
Business activities: Operates computer software company.

Business type (SIC): Computer services
Corporate officers: Shawn S. Karande, C.E.O.; Santosh S. Karande, Pres. and Secy.-Treas.; Karen Nerwani, C.F.O.; Soumitra Panda, V.P., Opers.
Giving statement: Giving through the ObjectWin Foundation.

ObjectWin Foundation

2815 Pinebend Dr.
Pearland, TX 77584-9107 (713) 302-6172

Establishment information: Established in TX.
Donors: Objectwin Technology, Inc.; Santosh S. Karande; Seema V. Karande.
Financial data (yr. ended 12/31/11): Assets, $688,563 (M); gifts received, $50,000; expenditures, $30,873; qualifying distributions, $30,000; giving activities include $30,000 for grants.
Fields of interest: Education; Health organizations; Human services.
Application information: Applications accepted. Application form required. Applicants should submit the following:
1) detailed description of project and amount of funding requested
Initial approach: Proposal
Deadline(s): None
Directors: Santosh S. Karande; Seema V. Karande; Vijay B. Vad.
EIN: 203811786

2779
Oblon, Spivak, McClelland, Maier & Neustadt, L.L.P.

1940 Duke St.
Alexandria, VA 22314-3451 (703) 413-3000

Company URL: http://www.oblon.com
Establishment information: Established in 1968.
Company type: Private company
Business activities: Operates law firm.
Business type (SIC): Legal services
Office: Alexandria, VA
International operations: Japan
Giving statement: Giving through the Oblon, Spivak, McClelland, Maier & Neustadt, L.L.P. Pro Bono Program.

Oblon, Spivak, McClelland, Maier & Neustadt, L.L.P. Pro Bono Program

1940 Duke St.
Alexandria, VA 22314-3451 (703) 413-3000
E-mail: rmattson@oblon.com; URL: http://www.oblon.com/pro-bono

Contact: Robert Mattson, Partner
Fields of interest: Legal services.
Type of support: Pro bono services - legal.
Geographic limitations: Giving primarily in areas of company operations in Alexandria, VA, and in Japan.
Application information: An attorney coordinates pro bono projects as an ancillary duty to other work.

2780
Occidental Petroleum Corporation

10889 Wilshire Blvd.
Los Angeles, CA 90024-4201
(310) 208-8800
FAX: (302) 655-5049

Company URL: http://www.oxy.com
Establishment information: Established in 1920.
Company type: Public company
Company ticker symbol and exchange: OXY/NYSE
International Securities Identification Number: US6745991058
Business activities: Produces and markets natural gas, oil, and chemicals.
Business type (SIC): Extraction/oil and gas; extraction/natural gas liquids; oil and gas field services; chemicals/industrial inorganic; chemicals/industrial organic; fertilizers and agricultural chemicals; plastic products/miscellaneous
Financial profile for 2012: Number of employees, 12,300; assets, $64,210,000,000; sales volume, $24,253,000,000; pre-tax net income, $7,390,000,000; expenses, $16,863,000,000; liabilities, $24,194,000,000
Fortune 1000 ranking: 2012—125th in revenues, 39th in profits, and 90th in assets
Forbes 2000 ranking: 2012—390th in sales, 117th in profits, and 369th in assets
Corporate officers: Edward P. DjerejianIrani, Chair.; Stephen I. Chazen, Pres. and C.E.O.; James M. Lienert, Exec. V.P. and C.F.O.; Donald P. de Brier, Exec. V.P., Genl. Counsel, and Secy.; Martin A. Cozyn, Exec. V.P., Human Resources; Donald L. Moore, Jr., V.P. and C.I.O.; Robert J. Williams, Jr., V.P. and Treas.; Roy Pineci, V.P. and Cont.
Board of directors: Amb. Edward P. Djerejian, Chair.; Spencer Abraham; Howard I. Atkins; Stephen I. Chazen; John E. Feick; Margaret M. Foran; Carlos M. Gutierrez; Avedick B. Poladian
Subsidiaries: Centurion Pipeline, L.P., Houston, TX; Centurion Pipeline LP, Inc., Houston, TX; D. S. Ventures, Inc., Brooklyn, NY; Glenn Springs Holdings, Inc., Ducktown, TN; INDSPEC Chemical Corp., Pittsburgh, PA; INDSPEC Holding Corp., Pittsburgh, PA; INDSPEC Technologies Limited, Pittsburgh, PA; Ingleside Cogeneration, L.P., Ingleside, TX; Laguna Petroleum Corp., Midland, TX; Occidental Chemical Corp., Dallas, TX; Occidental Chemical Corp., Dallas, TX; Occidental Chemical Holding Corp., Dallas, TX; Occidental Crude Sales, Inc., Houston, TX; Occidental Energy Marketing, Inc., Houston, TX; Occidental Energy Ventures Corp., Long Beach, CA; Occidental International Exploration and Production Co., Bakersfield, CA; Occidental of Elk Hills, Inc., Tupman, CA; Occidental Permian Limited, Los Angeles, CA; Occidental Petroleum Investment Co., Los Angeles, CA; Occidental Power Services, Inc., Houston, TX; Oxy Energy Services, Inc., Houston, TX; OXY Long Beach, Inc., Long Beach, CA; OXY USA Inc., Ulysses, KS; OXY USA WTP, L.P., Houston, TX; Oxy Vinyls, L.P., Dallas, TX; Oxy Westwood Corp., Los Angeles, CA; OXYMAR, Ingleside, TX; Plains AAP, L.P., Houston, TX; PXP CV Pipeline, L.L.C., Houston, TX; Stockdale Oil and Gas, Inc., Bakersfield, CA; Vintage Petroleum International, Inc., Tulsa, OK; Vintage Production California, L.L.C., Bakersfield, CA
International operations: Bermuda; Brazil; Canada; Cayman Islands; Chile; Colombia
Giving statement: Giving through the Occidental Petroleum Corporation Contributions Program.
Company EIN: 954035997

Occidental Petroleum Corporation Contributions Program

10889 Wilshire Blvd.
Los Angeles, CA 90024-4200 (310) 208-8800

Purpose and activities: Occidental makes charitable contributions to nonprofit organizations involved with arts and culture, education, the environment, and community development. Support is given primarily in areas of company operations.
Fields of interest: Arts; Education; Environment; Community/economic development.
Type of support: Employee matching gifts; General/operating support.
Geographic limitations: Giving primarily in areas of company operations.
Application information: Applications not accepted. Contributes only to pre-selected organizations.

2781
Ocean City Home Bank

1001 Asbury Ave.
Ocean City, NJ 08226-3329
(609) 927-7722
FAX: (609) 398-6670

Company URL: http://www.ochome.com
Establishment information: Established in 1887.
Company type: Subsidiary of a public company
Business activities: Operates savings bank.
Business type (SIC): Savings institutions
Financial profile for 2011: Assets, $994,926,000
Corporate officers: Roy Gillian, Chair.; Steven E. Brady, Pres. and C.E.O.; Donald F. Morgenweck, Sr. V.P. and C.F.O.; Francine Crudo, V.P. and C.I.O.; Tricia Ciliberto, V.P., Mktg.; Dave Krause, Cont.
Board of director: Roy Gillian, Chair.
Giving statement: Giving through the Ocean City Home Charitable Foundation.

Ocean City Home Charitable Foundation

1001 Asbury Ave.
Ocean City, NJ 08226-3329
E-mail: jjacobson@ochome.com; URL: http://www.ochome.com/home/about/charity/grant

Establishment information: Established in 2004 in DE.
Donors: Ocean City Holding Company; Ocean City Home Bank.
Financial data (yr. ended 12/31/11): Assets, $1,246,564 (M); expenditures, $100,534; qualifying distributions, $100,000; giving activities include $100,000 for 14 grants (high: $3,000; low: $1,000).
Fields of interest: Arts; Community/economic development.
Geographic limitations: Giving primarily in NJ.
Application information: Applications not accepted. Unsolicited requests for funds not accepted.
Officers: Jean Jacobsen, Pres.; Kathleen Rubba, V.P.; Tricia Ciliberto, Secy.; Donald Morgenweck, Treas.
Board Members: Sylvia A. Bertini; Keith Dawn; Chris Ford; Fred Miller; John L. Van Duyne.
EIN: 202097333

2782
OceanFirst Financial Corp., Inc.

(formerly Ocean Financial Corp.)
975 Hooper Ave.
Toms River, NJ 08753 (732) 240-4500
FAX: (732)349-5070

Company URL: http://www.oceanfirst.com
Establishment information: Established in 1902.
Company type: Public company
Company ticker symbol and exchange: OCFC/NASDAQ
Business activities: Operates bank holding company; operates savings bank.
Business type (SIC): Savings institutions; holding company
Financial profile for 2011: Number of employees, 401; assets, $2,303,710,000; pre-tax net income, $30,950,000; liabilities, $2,084,160,000
Corporate officers: John R. Garbarino, Chair. and C.E.O.; Michael J. Fitzpatrick, Exec. V.P. and C.F.O.; Joseph R. Iantosca, Sr. V.P. and C.A.O.; Steven J. Tsimbinos, Sr. V.P., Genl. Counsel, and Corp. Secy.; Christopher D. Maher, Pres. and C.O.O.
Board of directors: John R. Garbarino, Chair.; Joseph J. Burke; Angelo Catania; John W. Chadwick; Donald E. McLaughlin; Diane F. Rhine; Mark G. Solow; John E. Walsh
Subsidiary: OceanFirst Bank, Toms River, NJ
Giving statement: Giving through the OceanFirst Foundation.
Company EIN: 223412577

OceanFirst Foundation

(formerly Ocean Federal Foundation)
1415 Hooper Ave., Ste. 304
Toms River, NJ 08753-2800 (732) 341-4676
FAX: (732) 473-9641;
E-mail: kdurante@oceanfirstfdn.org; Additional e-mail: info@oceanfirstfdn.org; URL: http://www.oceanfirstfdn.org

Establishment information: Established in 1996 in NJ.
Donors: Ocean Financial Corp.; OceanFirst Financial Corp.; Ocean Federal Savings Bank; OceanFirst Bank.
Contact: Katherine B. Durante, Secy. and Exec. Dir.
Financial data (yr. ended 12/31/11): Assets, $17,311,807 (M); expenditures, $1,080,208; qualifying distributions, $1,074,936; giving activities include $798,705 for 248 grants (high: $50,000; low: $8).
Purpose and activities: The foundation supports programs designed to promote health and wellness, housing, quality of life, and youth development and education.
Fields of interest: Museums; Performing arts, theater; Performing arts, music; Arts; Libraries (school); Education; Environment, water resources; Environment; Health care, equal rights; Health care; Mental health, counseling/support groups; Mental health/crisis services; Employment, training; Food banks; Housing/shelter, homeless; Housing/shelter; Youth development, adult & child programs; Youth development; Children/youth, services; Family services, domestic violence; Aging, centers/services; Homeless, human services; Human services Children/youth; Disabilities, people with; Economically disadvantaged.
Programs:

Arts & Cultural Grants: The foundation awards grants to organizations that are positive catalysts for bringing people and neighborhoods together while providing enriching arts and cultural opportunities.

Good Neighbor Grants: The foundation awards grants of up to $5,000 for community and volunteer driven projects with a broad benefit and up to $3,500 for special event sponsorship. Grants are awarded to nonprofits, service organizations, and education foundations.

Health and Wellness: The foundation supports medical facilities with programs designed to provide essential services; and improve access to services, especially for vulnerable populations and the underserved.

Home Runs for Heroes Grants: The foundation, in partnership with Lakewood BlueClaws, provides grants to nine military-based charities that meet the emergency needs of local servicemen and servicewomen and their families. The foundation awards $1,000 for each home run hit at FirstEnergy Park during the season by the Lakewood BlueClaws.

Housing: The foundation supports programs designed to create affordable housing; meet the housing needs of special populations, including the disabled; provide support to emergency shelters that assist youth who have been abused, neglected, or abandoned and domestic violence victims; and provide transitional housing and support services that prevent homelessness and increase self-sufficiency.

Improving Quality of Life: The foundation supports programs designed to preserve and improve quality of life. Special emphasis is directed toward programs designed to meet basic needs including food banks, senior services, and behavioral health counseling; arts and cultural programs including live theater, music, and museums; and programs that preserve and protect the coastal environment.

Model Classroom Grants: The foundation awards grants to public and private K-12 schools to develop innovative and model classrooms for learning. The program is designed to promote academic excellence, enhance classroom instruction, and support schools that embrace new technology, tools, and training to add value to the learning experience. Schools must be located in an OceanFirst market area.

Youth Development and Education: The foundation supports programs designed to enrich and improve life options through education, work skills, and mentoring; provide safe, supportive places to grow; and improve the health and well being of children.

Type of support: Annual campaigns; Building/renovation; Capital campaigns; Continuing support; Emergency funds; Employee matching gifts; Equipment; General/operating support; Matching/challenge support; Program development; Scholarship funds; Sponsorships.
Geographic limitations: Giving primarily in areas of company operations in Monroe Township, southern and western Monmouth County, and Ocean County, NJ.
Support limitations: No support for religious congregations, political candidates or organizations, lobbying organizations or sports teams. No grants to individuals, or for research or political causes or campaigns, or personnel expenses.
Publications: Application guidelines; IRS Form 990 or 990-PF printed copy available upon request; Program policy statement.
Application information: Applications accepted. Major Grants are grants greater than $5,000 and applicants must address an OceanFirst Foundation priority area. Organizations receiving Major Grants are asked to provide a final report. Application form required. Applicants should submit the following:
1) copy of IRS Determination Letter
2) descriptive literature about organization
3) listing of board of directors, trustees, officers and other key people and their affiliations
4) detailed description of project and amount of funding requested
5) copy of current year's organizational budget and/or project budget

Initial approach: Telephone foundation and complete online application form for Arts & Cultural Grants, Good Neighbor Grants, Home Runs for Heroes Grants, and Major Grants
Copies of proposal: 1
Board meeting date(s): Quarterly
Deadline(s): Varies; 2 months prior to need for Good Neighbor Grants

Officers and Directors:* John R. Garbarino*, Chair. and Pres.; Katherine B. Durante*, Secy. and Exec. Dir.; Michael J. Fitzpatrick, Treas.; Joseph J. Burke; Angelo Catania; John W. Chadwick; Anthony J. DiCroce; Anita M. Kneeley; Msgr. Casimir H. Ladzinski; Amy W. Lotano; Donald E. McLaughlin; Samuel T. Melillo; Diane F. Rhine; James T. Snyder; Mark G. Solow; John E. Walsh; David C. Wintrode; David W. Wolfe.
Number of staff: 1 full-time professional; 1 part-time support.
EIN: 223465454

2783
Ochoco Lumber Company

200 S.E. Coombs Flat Rd.
P.O. Box 668
Prineville, OR 97754-2549 (541) 447-6296

Company URL: http://www.ochocolumber.com
Establishment information: Established in 1938.
Company type: Private company
Business activities: Manufactures lumber.
Business type (SIC): Lumber and wood products
Corporate officer: Bruce Daucsavage, Pres.
Subsidiary: Malheur Lumber Co., John Day, OR
Giving statement: Giving through the Ochoco Charitable Fund.

Ochoco Charitable Fund

(formerly Ochoco Scholarship Fund)
P.O. Box 668
Prineville, OR 97754-0668 (541) 416-6900

Donors: Ochoco Lumber Co.; Malheur Lumber Co.
Financial data (yr. ended 12/31/11): Assets, $404,609 (M); gifts received, $868; expenditures, $31,756; qualifying distributions, $31,756; giving activities include $30,800 for 43 grants to individuals (high: $1,200; low: $100).
Purpose and activities: The foundation awards college scholarships to graduating high school students in Crook and Grant counties, Oregon.
Fields of interest: Higher education.
Type of support: Scholarships—to individuals.
Geographic limitations: Giving primarily in the Prineville, OR, area.
Application information: Applications accepted. Application form required.
Application should include GPA, name of college attended, and credit hours.

Initial approach: Contact foundation for application form
Deadline(s): None

Officer: Stuart J. Shelk, Jr., Pres.
Trustee: Steve Markell.
EIN: 936024017

2770
O'Connor Company, Inc.
14851 W. 99th St.
Lenexa, KS 66215 (913) 894-8788

Company URL: http://www.oconnor-hvac.com
Establishment information: Established in 1920.
Company type: Private company
Business activities: Sells heating and air conditioning equipment, controls, parts, and accessories wholesale.
Business type (SIC): Hardware, plumbing, and heating equipment—wholesale
Corporate officers: Lynn J. Piller, Pres.; Karen Osborn, Secy.
Giving statement: Giving through the O'Connor Company—Piller Foundation.

O'Connor Company—Piller Foundation
14851 W. 99th St.
Lenexa, KS 66215-1110 (913) 894-8788

Donors: O'Connor Co., Inc.; J.M. O'Connor, Inc.
Contact: Lynn J. Piller, Tr.
Financial data (yr. ended 12/31/11): Assets, $86,047 (M); gifts received, $46,000; expenditures, $31,850; qualifying distributions, $31,850; giving activities include $31,850 for 14 grants (high: $7,500; low: $500).
Purpose and activities: The foundation supports organizations involved with arts and culture, education, and homelessness.
Fields of interest: Museums (art); Performing arts, orchestras; Arts; Higher education; Education; Homeless, human services; United Ways and Federated Giving Programs.
Type of support: Endowments; General/operating support; Research; Sponsorships.
Geographic limitations: Giving primarily in Lawrence and Wichita, KS.
Support limitations: No grants to individuals.
Application information: Applications accepted. Application form required. Applicants should submit the following:
1) name, address and phone number of organization
2) copy of IRS Determination Letter
3) brief history of organization and description of its mission
4) detailed description of project and amount of funding requested
Initial approach: Proposal
Deadline(s): None
Trustee: Lynn J. Piller.
EIN: 480932998

2784
Odyssey Investment Partners, LLC
280 Park Ave., 38th Fl., W. Tower
New York, NY 10017 (212) 351-7900

Company URL: http://www.odysseyinvestment.com
Establishment information: Established in 1997.
Company type: Private company
Business activities: Operates department stores and supermarkets.
Business type (SIC): Department stores; fabrics/broadwoven natural wool; plastic products/miscellaneous; groceries—retail; real estate operators and lessors; holding company; investors/miscellaneous
Financial profile for 2010: Number of employees, 23
Corporate officers: Stephen Berger, Chair.; William F. Hopkins, Co-Pres.; Brian Kwait, Co-Pres.; Teresa Paggi, Cont.
Board of director: Stephen Berger, Chair.
Giving statement: Giving through the Odyssey Partners Foundation, Inc.

Odyssey Partners Foundation, Inc.
1 Rockefeller Plz., 20th Fl.
New York, NY 10020

Establishment information: Established in 1965 in NY.
Donor: Odyssey Investment Partners, LLC.
Financial data (yr. ended 01/31/12): Assets, $260,071 (M); expenditures, $161,505; qualifying distributions, $159,505; giving activities include $157,280 for 6 grants (high: $150,000; low: $1,000).
Purpose and activities: The foundation supports organizations involved with arts and culture, education, health, and human services.
Fields of interest: Arts; Secondary school/education; Higher education; Education; Hospitals (general); Health care; Human services; Jewish federated giving programs.
Type of support: General/operating support.
Geographic limitations: Giving primarily in New York, NY.
Support limitations: No grants to individuals.
Application information: Applications not accepted. Unsolicited requests for funds not accepted.
Officer: Joshua Nash, Pres.
Trustee: Morris Rosenthal.
EIN: 136186566

2785
Office Depot, Inc.
6600 N. Military Trail
Boca Raton, FL 33496 (561) 438-4800
FAX: (561) 438-4400

Company URL: http://www.officedepot.com
Establishment information: Established in 1986.
Company type: Public company
Company ticker symbol and exchange: ODP/NYSE
Business activities: Operates office products stores; provides business services.
Business type (SIC): Shopping goods stores/miscellaneous; business services
Financial profile for 2012: Number of employees, 38,000; assets, $4,010,780,000; sales volume, $10,695,650,000; pre-tax net income, -$75,420,000; expenses, $10,738,600,000; liabilities, $2,962,940,000
Fortune 1000 ranking: 2012—253rd in revenues, 919th in profits, and 663rd in assets
Corporate officers: Neil R. Austrian, Chair. and C.E.O.; Mike Newman, Exec. V.P. and C.F.O.; Elisa D. Garcia C., Exec. V.P., Genl Counsel, and Corp. Secy.; Michael Allison, Jr., Exec. V.P., Human Resources; Kim Moehler, Sr. V.P. and Cont.
Board of directors: Neil R. Austrian, Chair.; Justin Bateman; Thomas J. Colligan; Eugene V. Fife; Brenda J. Gaines; W. Scott Hedrick; Marsha Johnson Evans; Kathleen Mason; Raymond Svider; Nigel Travis
Plants: Concord, CA; Detroit, MI
International operations: Bermuda; Canada; France; Japan; Luxembourg; Netherlands; United Kingdom
Giving statement: Giving through the Office Depot, Inc. Corporate Giving Program and the Office Depot Foundation.
Company EIN: 592663954

Office Depot, Inc. Corporate Giving Program
6600 N. Military Trail
Boca Raton, FL 33496-2434 (561) 438-4800
URL: http://www.officedepotcitizenship.com/

Purpose and activities: As a complement to its foundation, Office Depot also makes charitable contributions to nonprofit organizations. Support is given on a national and international basis in areas of company operations.
Fields of interest: Elementary/secondary education; Children, services; General charitable giving.
Type of support: In-kind gifts; Program development; Sponsorships.
Geographic limitations: Giving on a national basis and in areas of company operations.

Office Depot Foundation
6600 N. Military Tr.
Boca Raton, FL 33496-2434 (561) 438-8439
E-mail: communityrelations@officedepot.com;
URL: http://www.officedepotfoundation.org/

Establishment information: Established in 1994 in IL.
Contact: Mary Wong, Pres.
Financial data (yr. ended 06/30/12): Revenue, $1,145,567; assets, $3,742,521 (M); gifts received, $1,068,990; expenditures, $1,320,536; program services expenses, $1,149,355; giving activities include $866,299 for grants.
Purpose and activities: The foundation assists Office Depot employees, outside nonprofit organizations, and local communities during times of extreme hardship, such as fire, flood, hurricane, or tornado.
Fields of interest: Safety/disasters.
Program:
Grants: The foundation makes grants to 501(c)(3) nonprofit organizations in three focus areas: making a difference in children's lives (to support activities that serve, teach, and inspire children, youth, and families); building communities (to support civic organizations and activities that serve the needs of the communities Office Depot serves); and disaster relief (to support disaster relief efforts of recognized national, regional, and local agencies, and to provide disaster relief to Office Depot associates who have experienced catastrophic loss). Grants range from $50 to $3,000, with the average grant amount being $1,000.
Type of support: Grants to individuals; In-kind gifts.
Geographic limitations: Giving on a national and international basis.
Support limitations: No grants for event sponsorship, product donations, or deficit financing,.
Publications: Application guidelines.
Application information: Applicants should submit the following:
1) name, address and phone number of organization
2) contact person
3) copy of IRS Determination Letter
4) detailed description of project and amount of funding requested
5) copy of current year's organizational budget and/or project budget
6) how project will be sustained once grantmaker support is completed

7) listing of board of directors, trustees, officers and other key people and their affiliations
8) copy of most recent annual report/audited financial statement/990
9) additional materials/documentation
Initial approach: Submit proposal
Deadline(s): None
Final notification: Within one month of proposal receipt

Officer and Directors:* Mary Wong*, Pres.; Casey Ahlbum; Jay Hein; Richard Leland; Louis Pokriefka; Henry Sauls; Kathy Schroeder; Brian Turcotte; Glenn Ubertino; and 4 additional directors.
EIN: 650596803

2786
OfficeMax Incorporated

263 Shuman Blvd.
Naperville, IL 60563 (630) 438-7800

Company URL: http://www.officemax.com
Establishment information: Established in 1913.
Company type: Public company
Company ticker symbol and exchange: OMX/NYSE
Business activities: Operates office supplies company. At press time, the company is in the process of merging with Office Depot Inc.
Business type (SIC): Paper and paper products—wholesale
Financial profile for 2012: Assets, $3,800,000,000; sales volume, $6,900,000,000
Fortune 1000 ranking: 2012—367th in revenues, 384th in profits, and 681st in assets
Forbes 2000 ranking: 2012—1189th in sales, 1197th in profits, and 1888th in assets
Corporate officers: Rakesh Gangwal, Chair.; Ravi K. Saligram, Pres. and C.E.O.; Bruce Besanko, Exec. V.P., C.F.O., and C.A.O.; Randy G. Burdick, Exec. V.P. and C.I.O.; Matt Broad, Exec. V.P. and Genl. Counsel
Board of directors: Rakesh Gangwal, Chair.; Warren Bryant; Joseph DePinto; William Montgoris; V. James Marino; Francesca Ruiz de Luzuriaga; Ravi K. Saligram; David M. Szymanski
Giving statement: Giving through the OfficeMax Incorporated Contributions Program and the OfficeMax Charitable Foundation.
Company EIN: 820100960

OfficeMax Incorporated Contributions Program

263 Shuman Blvd.
Naperville, IL 60563-5502 (630) 438-7800
URL: http://about.officemax.com/html/officemax_giving_back.shtml

OfficeMax Charitable Foundation

263 Shuman Blvd.
Naperville, IL 60563-8147
E-mail: goodworks@officemax.com; URL: http://about.officemax.com/html/officemax_goodworks_foundation.shtml

Establishment information: Established in 2000 in OH.
Financial data (yr. ended 12/31/11): Revenue, $1,048,505; assets, $1,784,507 (M); gifts received, $1,048,505; expenditures, $1,910,484; program services expenses, $633,333; giving activities include $1,666,848 for 22 grants (high: $333,333; low: $6,000) and $18,185 for 19 grants to individuals.
Purpose and activities: The foundation supports 501(c)(3) organizations that promote education, and provides emergency disaster relief to OfficeMax employees.
Fields of interest: Education; Human services.
Type of support: Emergency funds; General/operating support.
Geographic limitations: Giving limited to the U.S., including PR.
Officers and Trustees:* Carolyn Brooks*, Pres.; Susan Wagner-Fleming, V.P. and Secy.; Tony Giuliano, V.P. and Treas.; Richard Haas, V.P.; Brad Seigfreid, V.P.; Matthew R. Broad.
EIN: 341925320

2787
Ogden Publications, Inc.

1503 S.W. 42nd St.
Topeka, KS 66609-1265 (785) 274-4300
FAX: (785) 274-4305

Company URL: http://www.ogdenpubs.com/
Establishment information: Established in 1996.
Company type: Private company
Business type (SIC): Business services/miscellaneous
Corporate officers: Bryan Welch, Pres.; Bill Uhler, Genl. Mgr.
Giving statement: Giving through the Ogden Publications, Inc. Contributions Program.

Ogden Publications, Inc. Contributions Program

1503 SW 42nd St.
Topeka, KS 66609-1265 (785) 274-4300
URL: http://www.ogdenpubs.com/

Purpose and activities: Ogden Publications is a certified B Corporation that donates a percentage of profits to charitable organizations.

2788
Ogilvy & Mather Worldwide, Inc.

The Chocolate Factory
636 11th Ave.
New York, NY 10036 (212) 237-4000
FAX: (212) 237-5123

Company URL: http://www.ogilvy.com
Establishment information: Established in 1948.
Company type: Subsidiary of a foreign company
Business activities: Provides advertising services.
Business type (SIC): Advertising
Corporate officers: Miles Young, Chair. and C.E.O.; Steve Goldstein, C.F.O.; Shelly Lazarus, Chair. Emeritus
Board of directors: Miles Young, Chair.; Steve Goldstein
International operations: Angola; Argentina; Australia; Austria; Bahrain; Barbados; Belgium; Bolivia; Botswana; Brazil; Bulgaria; Canada; Chile; China; Colombia; Costa Rica; Croatia; Cyprus; Czech Republic; Denmark; Dominican Republic; Ecuador; Egypt; El Salvador; Estonia; Ethiopia; Finland; France; Germany; Greece; Guatemala; Guinea; Guyana; Hungary; India; Indonesia; Ireland; Israel; Italy; Ivory Coast; Jamaica; Japan; Kazakhstan; Kenya; Kuwait; Latvia; Lebanon; Lithuania; Malaysia; Mauritius; Mexico; Morocco and the Western Sahara; Mozambique; Namibia; Netherlands; New Zealand; Nicaragua; Nigeria; Norway; Pakistan; Panama; Peru; Philippines; Poland; Portugal; Romania; Russia; Saudi Arabia; Senegal; Serbia; Singapore; Slovakia; South Africa; South Korea; Spain; Sri Lanka; Sweden; Switzerland; Taiwan; Thailand; Togo; Trinidad & Tobago; Tunisia; Turkey; Ukraine; United Arab Emirates; United Kingdom; Uruguay; Venezuela; Vietnam; Zimbabwe
Giving statement: Giving through the Ogilvy & Mather Worldwide Corporate Giving Program and the Ogilvy Foundation, Inc.

Ogilvy & Mather Worldwide Corporate Giving Program

c/o The Chocolate Factory
636 11th Ave.
New York, NY 10036-2005 (212) 237-4000
URL: http://www.ogilvy.com/company/csr/main.html

Purpose and activities: As a complement to its foundation, Ogilvy & Mather also makes charitable contributions to nonprofit organizations directly. Support is given on a national and international basis in areas of company operations.
Fields of interest: General charitable giving.
Type of support: Employee volunteer services; General/operating support; Loaned talent; Pro bono services - communications/public relations; Program development.
Geographic limitations: Giving on a national and international basis in areas of company operations.

Ogilvy Foundation, Inc.

c/o WPP Group USA, Inc.
125 Park Ave., 4th Fl.
New York, NY 10017-5599 (212) 632-2200
Application address: 636 11th Ave., New York, NY 10036

Establishment information: Established in 1984 in NY.
Donor: Ogilvy & Mather Worldwide, Inc.
Contact: Stacey Ryan-Cornelius, Treas.
Financial data (yr. ended 06/30/11): Assets, $1,213,887 (M); gifts received, $364,294; expenditures, $414,178; qualifying distributions, $151,533; giving activities include $140,149 for 5 grants (high: $81,170; low: $10,000).
Purpose and activities: The foundation supports organizations involved with higher and business education, cancer, and disaster relief.
Fields of interest: Higher education; Business school/education; Cancer; Disasters, preparedness/services.
Type of support: Continuing support; General/operating support; Program development; Scholarship funds.
Geographic limitations: Giving primarily in NY and the United Kingdom; giving also to national organizations.
Application information: Applications accepted. Application form required. Applicants should submit the following:
1) copy of IRS Determination Letter
2) detailed description of project and amount of funding requested
Initial approach: Letter
Deadline(s): None

Officers: S. Lazarus*, Chair.; P. Young, C.E.O.; E. Mascheroni, Secy.; Stacey Ryan-Cornelius, Treas.
Directors: Steve Goldstein; W. Phillips.
EIN: 133230406
Selected grants: The following grants are a representative sample of this grantmaker's funding activity:
$81,170 to Cancer Care, New York, NY, 2011.

2789
Ohio Casualty Corporation

9450 Seward Rd.
Fairfield, OH 45014-5412 (513) 603-2400

Company URL: http://www.ohiocasualty-ins.com
Establishment information: Established in 1969.
Company type: Subsidiary of a mutual company
Business activities: Sells property and casualty insurance.
Business type (SIC): Insurance/fire, marine, and casualty
Corporate officers: Michael Winner, C.P.A., Pres. and Co-C.E.O.; Dan R. Carmichael, Co-C.E.O.; Deborah Pooley, V.P., Finance
Subsidiary: The Ohio Casualty Insurance Co., Fairfield, OH
Giving statement: Giving through the Ohio Casualty Foundation, Inc.
Company EIN: 310783294

Ohio Casualty Foundation, Inc.

9450 Seward Rd.
Fairfield, OH 45014-5412
FAX: (513) 881-1327; URL: http://www.ohiocasualty-ins.com/omapps/ContentServer?pagename=OhioCasualty/Views/OhioCasualty&ft=3&fid=2237826814890&ln=en

Establishment information: Established in 1992 in OH.
Donor: Liberty Mutual Insurance Company.
Contact: Connie Ewald
Financial data (yr. ended 12/31/11): Assets, $5,375,290 (M); gifts received, $750,000; expenditures, $523,098; qualifying distributions, $500,000; giving activities include $500,000 for grants.
Purpose and activities: The foundation supports organizations involved with arts and culture, education, health, human services, community development, civic affairs, and economically disadvantaged people.
Fields of interest: Arts; Education; Health care; Youth development, adult & child programs; Human services; Community/economic development; United Ways and Federated Giving Programs; Public affairs Children/youth; Disabilities, people with; Economically disadvantaged.
Programs:
Education: The foundation supports programs designed to encourage disadvantaged youth to excel academically and create opportunities for life-long success through learning.
Health and Safety: The foundation supports programs designed to improve quality of life and safety in communities where Ohio Casualty operates.
Type of support: Annual campaigns; Building/renovation; Capital campaigns; Continuing support; Curriculum development; Equipment; General/operating support; Program development.
Geographic limitations: Giving limited to areas of company operations in Washington, DC, DE, KY, MD, OH, PA, VA, and WV.
Support limitations: No support for religious organizations not of direct benefit to the entire community, fraternal, social, labor, or political organizations. No grants to individuals, or for trips, tours, or transportation, debt reduction or liquidation, or conferences, forums, or special events.
Publications: Application guidelines; Program policy statement.
Application information: Applications accepted. Support is limited to 1 contribution per organization during any given year. A site visit may be requested. Organizations receiving support may be asked to submit periodic progress reports and a final report. Application form required. Applicants should submit the following:
1) detailed description of project and amount of funding requested
2) brief history of organization and description of its mission
3) listing of board of directors, trustees, officers and other key people and their affiliations
4) copy of current year's organizational budget and/or project budget
5) copy of most recent annual report/audited financial statement/990
6) copy of IRS Determination Letter
7) listing of additional sources and amount of support

Initial approach: Complete online application
Copies of proposal: 1
Board meeting date(s): Sept.
Deadline(s): Sept. 1
Final notification: End of Nov.

Officers and Trustees:* Michael A. Winner*, Pres.; Richard P. Quinlan*, Secy.; Gary J. Ostrow*, Treas.; John S. Busby; Melissa MacDonnell; Matt L. Wayre.
EIN: 311357883
Selected grants: The following grants are a representative sample of this grantmaker's funding activity:
$30,000 to Insuring the Children of Southern Ohio, Cincinnati, OH, 2010. For program support.
$30,000 to Marvin Lewis Community Fund, Cincinnati, OH, 2010. For program support.
$15,000 to Boy Scouts of America, Dan Beard Council, Cincinnati, OH, 2010. For operating support.
$10,000 to Boys and Girls Club of Hamilton, Hamilton, OH, 2010. For operating support.
$10,000 to Our Daily Bread, Cincinnati, OH, 2010. For operating support.
$6,300 to Fishing School, Washington, DC, 2010. For operating support.
$5,000 to Community Kitchen, Columbus, OH, 2010. For operating support.
$4,750 to United Way of Greater Cincinnati, Cincinnati, OH, 2010.
$3,531 to American Cancer Society, Pittsburgh, PA, 2010.
$1,485 to American Cancer Society, Washington, DC, 2010.

2790
The Ohio National Life Insurance Company

1 Financial Way, Ste. 100
Cincinnati, OH 45242-5852 (513) 794-6100

Company URL: http://www.ohionatl.com
Establishment information: Established in 1959.
Company type: Subsidiary of a private company
Business activities: Sells life insurance.
Business type (SIC): Insurance/life
Financial profile for 2011: Assets, $30,600,000,000
Corporate officers: David B. O'Maley, Co-Chair.; Gary T. Huffman, Co-Chair., Pres., and C.E.O.; Ronald J. Dolan, Vice-Chair.; Howard C. Becker, Exec. V.P. and C.A.O.; Christopher A. Carlson, Exec. V.P. and C.I.O.; Arthur J. Roberts, Sr. V.P. and C.F.O.; Diane S. Hagenbuch, Sr. V.P., Comms.; Anthony G. Esposito, Sr. V.P., Human Resources and Admin.; Michael F. Haverkamp, Secy.
Board of directors: David B. O'Maley, Co-Chair.; Gary T. Huffman, Co-Chair.; Ronald J. Dolan, Vice-Chair.; Thomas A. Barefield; Howard C. Becker; Jack E. Brown; Joseph A. Campanella; Christopher A. Carlson; Thomas G. Cody; Victoria Buyniski Gluckman; John W. Hayden; James F. Orr; John R. Phillips; J. Michael Schlotman
Giving statement: Giving through the Ohio National Foundation.

The Ohio National Foundation

1 Financial Way
Cincinnati, OH 45242-5851 (513) 794-6493

Establishment information: Established in 1987 in OH.
Donors: The Ohio National Life Insurance Co.; Ohio National Financial Svcs.
Contact: Anthony G. Esposito, Tr.
Financial data (yr. ended 12/31/11): Assets, $1,847,092 (M); gifts received, $400; expenditures, $1,319,724; qualifying distributions, $1,313,919; giving activities include $1,313,919 for grants.
Purpose and activities: The foundation supports hospitals and organizations involved with arts and culture, education, housing development, and human services.
Fields of interest: Arts, association; Museums; Museums (art); Performing arts, orchestras; Performing arts, opera; Arts; Education, early childhood education; Higher education; Libraries (public); Education; Hospitals (general); Housing/shelter, development; Boy scouts; American Red Cross; Children/youth, services; Residential/custodial care; Aging, centers/services; Developmentally disabled, centers & services; Human services; United Ways and Federated Giving Programs.
Type of support: Annual campaigns; Building/renovation; Capital campaigns; Employee matching gifts; General/operating support; Sponsorships.
Geographic limitations: Giving primarily in Cincinnati, OH.
Support limitations: No grants to individuals.
Application information: Applications accepted. Application form not required. Applicants should submit the following:
1) detailed description of project and amount of funding requested
2) copy of IRS Determination Letter

Initial approach: Proposal
Deadline(s): None

Trustees: Howard C. Becker; Joseph Campanella; Christopher A. Carlson; Ronald J. Dolan; Anthony G. Esposito; Diane S. Hagenbuch; Gary T. Huffman; David B. O'Maley.
EIN: 311230164
Selected grants: The following grants are a representative sample of this grantmaker's funding activity:
$52,200 to Childrens Home of Cincinnati, Cincinnati, OH, 2010. For sponsorship.
$25,653 to ArtsWave, Cincinnati, OH, 2010. For annual campaign.
$20,000 to Boy Scouts of America, Dan Beard Council, Cincinnati, OH, 2010. For sponsorship.
$15,000 to Crayons to Computers, Cincinnati, OH, 2010. For annual campaign.
$10,000 to UJA-Federation of New York, New York, NY, 2010. For event sponsorship.
$9,250 to Bethesda Foundation, Cincinnati, OH, 2010. For sponsorship.
$7,000 to BRIDGES for a Just Community, Cincinnati, OH, 2010. For sponsorship.
$6,050 to American Heart Association, Cincinnati, OH, 2010. For sponsorship.
$5,000 to Keep Cincinnati Beautiful, Cincinnati, OH, 2010. For capital campaign.

$5,000 to Montgomery, City of, Montgomery, OH, 2010. For sponsorship.

2791
Ohio Savings Bank

(formerly AmTrust Bank)
1801 E. 9th St., Ste. 200
Cleveland, OH 44114-3103 (216) 588-4100

Company URL: https://www.amtrust.com/
Establishment information: Established in 1889.
Company type: Subsidiary of a public company
Business activities: Operates savings bank.
Business type (SIC): Savings institutions
Corporate officers: David Goldberg, Co-Chair.; Jerald Goldberg, Co-Chair.; Robert J. Goldberg, Pres. and C.E.O.
Board of directors: David Goldberg, Co-Chair.; Jerald Goldberg, Co-Chair.
Giving statement: Giving through the Ohio Savings Charitable Foundation.

Ohio Savings Charitable Foundation

25700 Science Park Dr., Rm. 365
Beachwood, OH 44122-7312

Establishment information: Established around 1970.
Donors: Ohio Savings Bank; AmTrust Financial Corp.
Financial data (yr. ended 11/30/11): Assets, $97,431 (M); expenditures, $75; qualifying distributions, $0.
Purpose and activities: The foundation supports art museums and organizations involved with education, health, breast cancer, children and youth, family services, international relief, and Judaism.
Fields of interest: Museums (art); Elementary school/education; Higher education; Education; Health care, clinics/centers; Health care; Breast cancer; Children/youth, services; Family services; International relief; Jewish federated giving programs; Jewish agencies & synagogues.
Type of support: General/operating support; Program development; Scholarship funds.
Geographic limitations: Giving primarily in Cleveland, OH; giving also to national organizations.
Support limitations: No grants to individuals.
Application information: Applications not accepted. Contributes only to pre-selected organizations.
Officers: Robert Goldberg, Pres.; David Goldberg, Secy.
EIN: 237055858

2792
Ohio Wholesale, Inc.

5180 Greenwich Rd.
Seville, OH 44273-9530 (330) 769-5050

Company URL: http://www.ohiowholesale.com
Establishment information: Established in 1977.
Company type: Private company
Business activities: Sells giftware wholesale.
Business type (SIC): Furniture and home furnishings—wholesale
Corporate officer: Tony Williams, C.I.O.
Giving statement: Giving through the Nick and Terry's Foundation.

Nick and Terry's Foundation

5180 Greenwich Rd.
Seville, OH 44273

Establishment information: Established in 2001 in OH.
Donor: Ohio Wholesale, Inc.
Financial data (yr. ended 12/31/11): Assets, $76,074 (M); expenditures, $1,737; qualifying distributions, $650; giving activities include $650 for grants.
Purpose and activities: The foundation supports hospitals and organizations involved with education, children, and international relief.
Fields of interest: Education; Health care.
Type of support: General/operating support.
Application information: Applications not accepted. Unsolicited requests for funds not accepted.
Officers: Mark N. Harbarger, C.E.O.; Jeffrey Koncz, Pres.; Terry E. Harbarger, Secy.-Treas.
Trustees: Dave Carlisle; Jim Eckelberry.
EIN: 912139815

2793
The Oilgear Company

2300 S. 51st St.
Milwaukee, WI 53219 (414) 327-1700
FAX: (414) 327-0532

Company URL: http://www.oilgear.com
Establishment information: Established in 1921.
Company type: Private company
Business activities: Manufactures hydraulic power transmission machinery.
Business type (SIC): Engines and turbines
Financial profile for 2010: Number of employees, 750
Corporate officers: Richard Armbrust, Pres. and C.E.O.; Roland J. Parker, C.F.O.; Dale C. Boyke, V.P., Mktg. and Sales
Plant: Fremont, NE
International operations: Australia; France; Germany; Italy; Mexico; Spain; United Kingdom
Giving statement: Giving through the Oilgear Ferris Foundation.
Company EIN: 390514580

Oilgear Ferris Foundation

P.O. Box 2977
Milwaukee, WI 53201-2977 (414) 287-8481
Application Address: 111 E Kilbourn Ave., Milwaukee, WI 53202; tel.:(414) 287-8481

Establishment information: Established in 1958 in WI.
Donor: The Oilgear Co.
Contact: Deirdre Snyder
Financial data (yr. ended 12/31/11): Assets, $804,138 (M); expenditures, $60,046; qualifying distributions, $48,720; giving activities include $47,500 for 11 grants (high: $5,000; low: $1,000).
Purpose and activities: The foundation supports museums and organizations involved with higher education, cancer, housing development, and human services.
Fields of interest: Human services.
Type of support: Employee-related scholarships; General/operating support.
Geographic limitations: Giving primarily in areas of company operations, with some emphasis on Milwaukee, WI.
Application information: Applications accepted. Application form required.
Initial approach: Letter
Deadline(s): Quarterly
Officers: David Zuege, Pres.; Thomas J. Price, Secy.-Treas.
Director: Richard Armbrust.
EIN: 396050126

2794
Oklahoma Gas and Electric Company

(also known as OG&E)
321 N. Harvey
P.O. Box 321
Oklahoma City, OK 73102 (405) 533-3000

Company URL: http://www.oge.com
Company type: Subsidiary of a public company
Business activities: Generates, transmits, and distributes electricity.
Business type (SIC): Electric services
Financial profile for 2010: Number of employees, 2,146; sales volume, $2,110,000,000
Corporate officers: Peter B. Delaney, Chair., Pres., and C.E.O.; Danny P. Harris, Sr. V.P. and C.O.O.; H. Scott Forbes, C.A.O. and Cont.; Reid V. Nuttall, C.I.O.; R. Sean Trauschke, V.P. and C.F.O.; Paul L. Renfrow, V.P., Human Resources; Max J. Myers, Treas.
Board of director: Peter B. Delaney, Chair.
Giving statement: Giving through the OG&E Corporate Giving Program and the Oklahoma Gas and Electric Company Foundation, Inc.
Company EIN: 730382390

OG&E Corporate Giving Program

P.O. Box 321
Oklahoma City, OK 73101-0321 (405) 553-3642
E-mail: ogecommunityrelationsteam@oge.com; Application address for Teacher Grant Program: OGE Energy Corp. Community Rels. Dept., P.O. Box 321 M/C 1200, Oklahoma City, OK 73101-0321; URL: http://www.oge.com/community/CommunityPrograms/Pages/CommunityPrograms.aspx

Purpose and activities: As a complement to its foundation, OG&E also makes charitable contributions to nonprofit organizations directly. Support is given primarily in areas of company operations in western Arkansas and Oklahoma.
Fields of interest: Museums; Museums (science/technology); Elementary/secondary education; Libraries (school); Education; Safety/disasters; Recreation, fairs/festivals; Recreation; Youth development; Salvation Army; Utilities.
Program:
Teacher Grant Program: OG&E annually awards grants of up $1,000 to K-12 teachers in public schools for projects that assist students with math, reading, and science skills.
Type of support: Donated products; Employee volunteer services; General/operating support; Program development; Sponsorships.
Geographic limitations: Giving primarily in areas of company operations in western AR and OK.
Support limitations: No grants for seminars, workshops, teacher or staff salaries, trips for teachers or staff, camps, competitions, field trips, reducing or eliminating debt, purchase or maintenance of computer hardware, honoraria, capital improvement projects, or advertising.
Publications: Application guidelines.
Application information: Applications accepted. The Community Relations Department handles giving. Only one proposal may be submitted per teacher for

Teacher Grant Program. Project applicant must be a teacher in grades pre-K-12 in a public school district within the OG&E or Enogex service territory. Applicants should submit the following:
1) how project's results will be evaluated or measured
2) copy of current year's organizational budget and/or project budget
Teacher Grant Program proposals must include an explanation of goals and need, along with evidence of advancement of skills for knowledge in science, math or reading, how the project will enrich and augment the curriculum rather than take the place of a district funded project, and the number of students who will benefit.
Initial approach: Submit proposal for the Teacher Grant Program via e-mail, mail, or hand delivery
Deadline(s): June 1 for Teacher Grant Program

Oklahoma Gas and Electric Company Foundation, Inc.

(also known as OGE Energy Corp. Foundation)
P.O. Box 321, M.C. 1100
Oklahoma City, OK 73101-0321 (405) 553-3203
Additional tel.: (405) 553-3397; URL: http://www.oge.com/community/OGEFoundation/Pages/OGEFoundation.aspx

Establishment information: Incorporated in 1957 in OK.
Donor: Oklahoma Gas and Electric Co.
Contact: Peter B. Delaney, Pres.
Financial data (yr. ended 12/31/11): Assets, $11,933,580 (M); gifts received, $6,000,000; expenditures, $2,003,362; qualifying distributions, $2,076,636; giving activities include $1,970,910 for grants.
Purpose and activities: The foundation supports organizations involved with arts and culture, human services, and community development. Special emphasis is directed toward early education, primarily math and science.
Fields of interest: Arts; Education, early childhood education; Human services; Community/economic development; Mathematics; Science.
Type of support: Annual campaigns; Building/renovation; Continuing support; Employee matching gifts; Equipment; General/operating support; Professorships; Program development; Scholarship funds; Sponsorships.
Geographic limitations: Giving limited to areas of company operations in OK.
Support limitations: No support for religious or faith-based organizations not of direct benefit to the entire community or political parties or candidates. No grants to individuals or families, or for sporting events, golf tournaments, dinners, luncheons, or other forms of indirect support, or capital campaigns; no loans.
Publications: Application guidelines.
Application information: Applications accepted. Grants range from $500 to $5,000. Organizations receiving support are asked to submit a final report. Application form not required. Applicants should submit the following:
1) statement of problem project will address
2) population served
3) principal source of support for project in the past
4) copy of IRS Determination Letter
5) brief history of organization and description of its mission
6) how project's results will be evaluated or measured
7) list of company employees involved with the organization
8) detailed description of project and amount of funding requested
9) contact person
10) listing of additional sources and amount of support
11) plans for acknowledgement
Initial approach: Proposal
Copies of proposal: 1
Board meeting date(s): Mar., June, Sept., and Dec.
Deadline(s): Mar. 15, June 15, Sept. 15, and Dec. 15
Final notification: 30 days
Officers and Directors:* Peter B. Delaney*, Pres.; Danny P. Harris*, V.P.; Susie White, Secy.-Treas.; Paul Renfrow.
EIN: 736093572
Selected grants: The following grants are a representative sample of this grantmaker's funding activity:
$145,000 to Oklahoma City Museum of Art, Oklahoma City, OK, 2009.
$75,000 to Allied Arts Foundation, Oklahoma City, OK, 2009.
$60,000 to National Cowboy and Western Heritage Museum, Oklahoma City, OK, 2009.
$60,000 to Oklahoma City Educare, Oklahoma City, OK, 2009.
$50,000 to Boy Scouts of America, Oklahoma City, OK, 2009.
$40,000 to Oklahoma Heritage Association, Oklahoma City, OK, 2009.
$30,000 to Oklahoma City National Memorial Foundation, Oklahoma City, OK, 2009.
$25,000 to Oklahoma Centennial Commemoration Fund, Oklahoma City, OK, 2009.
$15,000 to Junior Achievement of Greater Oklahoma City, Oklahoma City, OK, 2009.
$10,000 to Oklahoma City Public Schools Foundation, Oklahoma City, OK, 2009.

2795
The Oklahoma Publishing Company

9000 N. Broadway
Oklahoma City, OK 73114-3708
(405) 475-3311

Company URL: http://www.opubco.com/
Establishment information: Established in 1903.
Company type: Private company
Business activities: Publishes newspapers.
Business type (SIC): Newspaper publishing and/or printing
Financial profile for 2010: Number of employees, 300
Corporate officers: Christopher P. Reen, Pres.; Dan Barth, C.I.O.; Scott Briggs, V.P., Admin.; Pat Dennis, V.P., Opers.; Patrice S. Hannan, V.P., Sales and Mktg.
Subsidiary: The Daily and Sunday Oklahoman, Oklahoma City, OK
Giving statement: Giving through the Oklahoma Publishing Company Contributions Program and the Oklahoman Foundation.

The Oklahoman Foundation

P.O. Box 25125
Oklahoma City, OK 73125-0125

Establishment information: Established in 1990 in OK.
Donor: The Oklahoma Publishing Co.
Financial data (yr. ended 12/31/11): Assets, $12,321,315 (M); expenditures, $120,305; qualifying distributions, $110,000; giving activities include $110,000 for grants.
Purpose and activities: The foundation supports organizations involved with arts and culture, education, patient services, legal aid, children and youth, community development, and Christianity.
Fields of interest: Arts; Higher education; Education; Health care, patient services; Legal services; YM/YWCAs & YM/YWHAs; Children/youth, services; Community development, service clubs; Community/economic development; United Ways and Federated Giving Programs.
Type of support: Building/renovation; General/operating support; Program development.
Geographic limitations: Giving limited to Oklahoma City, OK.
Support limitations: No grants to individuals.
Application information: Applications not accepted. Contributes only to pre-selected organizations.
Trustees: Louise Gaylord Bennett; Christine Gaylord Everest; David O. Hogan; Mary Gaylord McClean.
EIN: 731363152
Selected grants: The following grants are a representative sample of this grantmaker's funding activity:
$181,695 to United Way of Central Oklahoma, Oklahoma City, OK, 2010. For general operations.
$30,000 to Make-A-Wish Foundation of Oklahoma, Oklahoma City, OK, 2010. For general operations.
$25,000 to Creative Oklahoma, Oklahoma City, OK, 2010. For general operations.
$10,000 to Citizens Caring for Children, Oklahoma City, OK, 2010. For general operations.
$7,500 to Legal Aid Services of Oklahoma, Oklahoma City, OK, 2010. For general operations.
$6,620 to University of Central Oklahoma Foundation, Edmond, OK, 2010. For general operations.
$5,000 to Possibilities, Inc., Oklahoma City, OK, 2010. For general operations.
$2,500 to Myriad Gardens Foundation, Oklahoma City, OK, 2010. For general operations.
$1,000 to YWCA of Tulsa, Tulsa, OK, 2010. For general operations.

2796
The Old Dominion Box Company

271 Mitchell Bell Rd.
Madison Heights, VA 24572-2579
(434) 929-4002

Establishment information: Established in 2003.
Company type: Private company
Business activities: Manufactures boxes.
Business type (SIC): Paperboard containers; paperboard mills; machinery/special industry
Corporate officers: Michael O. Buhler, Pres.; Tom Scott, V.P. and Genl. Mgr.
Giving statement: Giving through the Old Dominion Box Company Foundation, Inc.

Old Dominion Box Company Foundation, Inc.

P.O. Box 680
Lynchburg, VA 24505

Establishment information: Established in 1951.
Donors: Old Dominion Box Co.; Dillard Investment Corp.; Little Rock Packaging Co., Inc.; Hall Town Paperboard Co.; Palmetto Box Co.
Financial data (yr. ended 11/30/11): Assets, $414,576 (M); expenditures, $27,418; qualifying distributions, $15,584; giving activities include $14,600 for 20 grants (high: $5,000; low: $100).

Purpose and activities: The foundation supports museums and organizations involved with fine arts, hunger, human services, and Christianity.
Fields of interest: Visual arts; Museums; Higher education; Food distribution, meals on wheels; YM/YWCAs & YM/YWHAs; Aging, centers/services; Human services; Christian agencies & churches.
Type of support: Continuing support; General/operating support; Program development.
Geographic limitations: Giving primarily in Lynchburg, VA.
Support limitations: No grants to individuals.
Application information: Applications not accepted. Contributes only to pre-selected organizations.
Officer: Michael O. Buhler, Admin.
EIN: 546036792

2797
Old Harbor Native Corporation

2702 Denali St., Ste. 100
Anchorage, AK 99503-2747
(907) 278-6100

Company URL: http://www.oldharbornativecorp.com/
Establishment information: Established in 1971.
Company type: Native corporation
Business activities: Operates native corporation.
Business type (SIC): Nonclassifiable establishments
Corporate officers: Carl H. Marrs, C.E.O.; Emil Christiansen, Sr., Pres.; Freddie Christiansen, Secy.; Lily O'Brien, Treas.
Board of directors: Tony Azuyak, Sr.; Emil Christiansen, Sr.; Freddy Christiansen; Al Cratty, Jr.; Doug Inga; Tanya Inga; Lily O'Brien; Jeffery Peterson; Alex Shugak, Sr.
Giving statement: Giving through the Old Harbor Scholarship Foundation.

Old Harbor Scholarship Foundation

2702 Denali St., Ste. 100
Anchorage, AK 99503-0071 (907) 286-2286

Establishment information: Established in 1994 in AK.
Donor: Old Harbor Native Corp.
Contact: Kim Fraser
Financial data (yr. ended 12/31/11): Assets, $146,386 (M); gifts received, $20,809; expenditures, $100,814; qualifying distributions, $25,500; giving activities include $25,500 for grants to individuals.
Purpose and activities: The foundation awards college scholarships to shareholders and dependents and lineal descendants of shareholders of Old Harbor Native Corporation.
Type of support: Scholarships—to individuals.
Geographic limitations: Giving limited to AK.
Application information: Applications accepted. Application form required.
Requests should include transcripts, an acceptance letter, and a letter of recommendation.
Initial approach: Contact foundation for application form
Deadline(s): None
Officers: Tanya Inga, Pres.; Freddie Christiansen, V.P.; Zora Inga, Secy.; Miranda Christjansen, Treas.
Directors: Ron Bernsten, Sr.; Mitch Chya; Coyte Cooper; Laverna Demientieff; Zora Inga.
EIN: 920154160

2798
Old National Bancorp

1 Main St.
Evansville, IN 47708-1464 (812) 464-1294

Company URL: http://www.oldnational.com
Establishment information: Established in 1982.
Company type: Public company
Company ticker symbol and exchange: ONB/NYSE
Business activities: Operates bank holding company; operates commercial bank.
Business type (SIC): Holding company; banks/commercial
Financial profile for 2011: Number of employees, 2,551; assets, $8,609,680,000; pre-tax net income, $99,760,000; liabilities, $7,576,130,000
Corporate officers: Larry E. Dunigan, Chair.; Robert G. Jones, Pres. and C.E.O.; Christopher A. Wolking, Sr. Exec. V.P. and C.F.O.; John R. Kamin, Exec. V.P. and C.I.O.; Kendra L. Vanzo, Exec. V.P., Human Resources
Board of directors: Larry E. Dunigan, Chair.; Alan W. Braun; Neil C. Ellerbrook; Andrew E. Goebel; Robert G. Jones; Phelps L. Lambert; Arthur H. McElwee, Jr.; James T. Morris; Randall T. Shepard; Kelly N. Stanley; Linda E. White
Subsidiary: Old National Bank, Evansville, IN
Giving statement: Giving through the Old National Bancorp Contributions Program and the Old National Bank Foundation, Inc.
Company EIN: 351539838

Old National Bancorp Contributions Program

1 Main St.
Evansville, IN 47708 (800) 731-2265
E-mail: grants&sponsorships@oldnational.com;
URL: https://www.oldnational.com/about-us/community-partnership/index.asp

Purpose and activities: As a complement to its foundation, Old National Bancorp also makes charitable contributions to nonprofit organizations directly. Support is given primarily in areas of company operations.
Fields of interest: General charitable giving.
Type of support: Employee volunteer services; General/operating support; Sponsorships.
Geographic limitations: Giving primarily in areas of company operations.
Publications: Application guidelines.
Application information: Applications accepted. Application form required. Applicants should submit the following:
1) name, address and phone number of organization
2) copy of IRS Determination Letter
3) brief history of organization and description of its mission
4) geographic area to be served
5) detailed description of project and amount of funding requested
6) listing of additional sources and amount of support
7) plans for acknowledgement

Sponsorships are typically provided in exchange for advertising and/or publicity that directly benefits Old National. Proposals should include the event name, date, and time, number of expected attendees, and a list of past funding received from the company.
Initial approach: Complete online application
Deadline(s): 30 days prior to event
Final notification: 30 days

Old National Bank Foundation, Inc.

1 Main St.
Evansville, IN 47708 (812) 465-7277
E-mail: grants&sponsorships@oldnational.com;
URL: https://www.oldnational.com/about-us/community-partnership/foundation-grants/index.asp

Establishment information: Established in 2006.
Donor: Old National Bank.
Contact: Danyelle Granger, Prog. Off.; Janet Heldt Baas, Pres.
Financial data (yr. ended 12/31/11): Assets, $1,167,417 (M); expenditures, $1,143,799; qualifying distributions, $1,139,517; giving activities include $1,102,994 for 224 grants (high: $50,000; low: $25).
Purpose and activities: The foundation supports organizations involved with arts and culture, health, and human services. Special emphasis is directed toward programs designed to promote community and economic development and education.
Fields of interest: Arts, cultural/ethnic awareness; Arts; Education, early childhood education; Higher education; Education, services; Education, reading; Education; Health care; Employment, training; Employment; Housing/shelter, rehabilitation; Housing/shelter, home owners; Children/youth, services; Human services, financial counseling; Human services; Community/economic development; Mathematics Economically disadvantaged.

Programs:
Community & Economic Development: The foundation supports programs designed to promote job training and workplace skills; youth and adult literacy and entrepreneurship; rehabilitation and construction of affordable housing that assists low-and moderate-income individuals and families; and homeownership education.
Education: The foundation supports programs designed to promote youth and adult literacy/reading; early childhood development focusing on math and reading; cultural education and diversity awareness; and tutoring and mentoring initiatives focusing on academic achievement.
Type of support: Building/renovation; Capital campaigns; Curriculum development; Program development; Scholarship funds.
Geographic limitations: Giving limited to areas of company operations in IL, IN, KY.
Support limitations: No support for school clubs/organizations, including bands, athletic or academic teams, booster clubs, or PTO/PTA, summer camps, political, labor, military, veterans', international, or fraternal organizations, discriminatory organizations, or religious organizations not of direct benefit to the entire community. No grants to individuals, or for endowments, salaries or general operating support, meals, tickets, dues, memberships, fees, travel, tuition, subscriptions, or other tangible benefits, childcare fees/subsidies or K-12 tuition, meetings, conferences, or workshops, debt retirement, contests, competitions, athletic events, beauty pageants, or talent contests, operating costs or capital campaigns for faith-based organizations, sponsorships, fundraisers, races, telethons, marathons, benefits, banquets, galas, golf tournaments, festivals or other events, or scholarly or medical research, feasibility studies, project research or development phases, including the cost of hiring consultants or planners.
Publications: Application guidelines; Corporate giving report; Program policy statement.
Application information: Applications accepted. A full proposal may be required at a later date. Support is limited to 1 contribution per organization during

any given year. Applicants should submit the following:
1) how project will be sustained once grantmaker support is completed
2) results expected from proposed grant
3) statement of problem project will address
4) copy of IRS Determination Letter
5) how project's results will be evaluated or measured
6) explanation of why grantmaker is considered an appropriate donor for project
7) what distinguishes project from others in its field
8) listing of additional sources and amount of support

Initial approach: Complete online application
Copies of proposal: 1
Board meeting date(s): Spring and Fall
Deadline(s): Feb. 1 and May 31
Final notification: 4 weeks following deadlines

Officers: Janet Heldt Baas, Pres.; Doug Gregurich, V.P.; Danyelle Granger, Secy.; Jackie Russell, Treas.
EIN: 260130059
Selected grants: The following grants are a representative sample of this grantmaker's funding activity:
$10,000 to University of Notre Dame, Notre Dame, IN, 2010.
$7,500 to Boys and Girls Clubs of Indianapolis, Indianapolis, IN, 2010.
$7,500 to Habitat for Humanity International, Americus, GA, 2010.
$7,500 to Local Initiatives Support Corporation, New York, NY, 2010.
$5,000 to Keep Indianapolis Beautiful, Indianapolis, IN, 2010.

2799
Old Westbury Golf & Country Club

270 Wheatley Rd.
Old Westbury, NY 11568 (516) 626-1810
FAX: (516) 621-7740

Company URL: http://www.owgolf.com/
Establishment information: Established in 1960.
Company type: Private company
Business activities: Operates country club.
Business type (SIC): Amusement and recreation services/miscellaneous
Corporate officers: Jeffrey J. Sands, Pres.; Herbert Selzer, Secy.; Alex Chernoff, Treas.; Judith Moran, Cont.
Giving statement: Giving through the Old Westbury Golf & Country Club Foundation, Inc.

Old Westbury Golf & Country Club Foundation, Inc.

270 Wheatley Rd.
Old Westbury, NY 11568-1000 (516) 626-1810

Establishment information: Established in NY.
Donor: Old Westbury Golf & Country Club.
Financial data (yr. ended 12/31/10): Revenue, $89,155; assets, $6,669 (M); gifts received, $89,155; expenditures, $89,163; program services expenses, $89,155; giving activities include $89,155 for grants.
Purpose and activities: The foundation raises funds for local charities.
Fields of interest: Human services.
Geographic limitations: Giving primarily in NY.
Support limitations: No grants to individuals.
Directors: Charles Miller; Jeffrey Sands; Herbert M. Selzer.
EIN: 113523001

2800
Ole South Properties, Inc.

201 E. Main St., Ste. 300
Murfreesboro, TN 37130 (615) 896-0019
FAX: (615) 896-9380

Company URL: http://www.olesouth.com
Establishment information: Established in 1986.
Company type: Private company
Business activities: Builds single-family houses.
Business type (SIC): Operative builders
Corporate officers: John D. Floyd, Pres.; Gary Bowman, C.O.O.; Tim Hensley, C.F.O.
Giving statement: Giving through the John D. Floyd Charitable Foundation, Inc.

John D. Floyd Charitable Foundation, Inc.

201 E. Main, 3rd Fl.
Murfreesboro, TN 37130 (615) 896-0019

Establishment information: Established in 2002 in TN.
Donors: Ole South Properties, Inc.; John D. Floyd.
Contact: Trudy Wells, Dir.
Financial data (yr. ended 06/30/11): Assets, $11,053 (M); expenditures, $10,800; qualifying distributions, $9,450; giving activities include $8,000 for 2 grants (high: $5,000; low: $3,000).
Purpose and activities: The foundation supports organizations involved with education, health, heart disease, children's services, and business promotion.
Fields of interest: Education; Health care, clinics/centers; Health care; Heart & circulatory diseases; Boys & girls clubs; Children, services; Community development, business promotion; United Ways and Federated Giving Programs.
Type of support: General/operating support; Program development; Sponsorships.
Geographic limitations: Giving primarily in TN.
Support limitations: No grants to individuals.
Application information: Applications accepted. Application form required. Applicants should submit the following:
1) copy of IRS Determination Letter
2) detailed description of project and amount of funding requested

Initial approach: Letter
Deadline(s): None

Officers and Director: John D. Floyd, Pres.; Angela Floyd, V.P.; Pat Kennedy, Secy.-Treas.; Trudy Wells.
EIN: 680510961

2801
Olin Corporation

190 Carondelet Plz., Ste. 1530
Clayton, MO 63105-3443 (314) 480-1400
FAX: (314) 480-1487

Company URL: http://www.olin.com
Establishment information: Established in 1892.
Company type: Public company
Company ticker symbol and exchange: OLN/NYSE
Business activities: Manufactures chlor alkali products, metals, and ammunition.
Business type (SIC): Chemicals and allied products; primary metal industries; ammunition, ordinance, and accessories
Financial profile for 2012: Number of employees, 4,100; assets, $2,777,700,000; sales volume, $2,184,700,000; pre-tax net income, $225,200,000; expenses, $1,925,800,000; liabilities, $1,779,300,000
Fortune 1000 ranking: 2012—884th in revenues, 652nd in profits, and 775th in assets
Corporate officers: Joseph D. Rupp, Chair., Pres., and C.E.O.; John E. Fischer, Sr. V.P. and C.F.O.; George H. Pain, Sr. V.P., Genl. Counsel, and Secy.; John L. McIntosh, Sr. V.P., Opers.; Stephen C. Curley, V.P. and Treas.; Todd A. Slater, V.P., Finance and Cont.; Dolores J. Ennico, V.P., Human Resources
Board of directors: Joseph D. Rupp, Chair.; Gray G. Benoist; Donald W. Bogus; C. Robert Bunch; Randall W. Larrimore; John M. B. O'Connor; Richard M. Rompala; Philip J. Schulz; Vince J. Smith
Plants: McIntosh, AL; Waterbury, CT; Augusta, GA; East Alton, IL; Indianapolis, IN; Cuba, Independence, MO; Niagara Falls, NY; Bryan, OH; Charleston, Cleveland, TN; Baraboo, WI
International operations: Australia; Bermuda; Brazil; Canada; Italy; United Kingdom
Giving statement: Giving through the Olin Corporation Charitable Trust.
Company EIN: 131872319

Olin Corporation Charitable Trust

1525 W. WT Harris Blvd.
Charlotte, NC 28288-5709 (618) 258-2961
FAX: (618) 258-2028;
E-mail: olincharitableinfo@olin.com; Application address: 427 N. Shamrock St., East Alton, IL 62024, tel.: (618) 258-2961

Establishment information: Established in 1945 in MO.
Donor: Olin Corp.
Contact: Susan Dona
Financial data (yr. ended 06/30/12): Assets, $957,707 (M); gifts received, $500,000; expenditures, $487,218; qualifying distributions, $479,365; giving activities include $470,380 for 72 + grants (high: $63,000).
Purpose and activities: The foundation supports fire departments and organizations involved with arts and culture, education, health, youth development, human services, business promotion, and mining.
Fields of interest: Arts; Elementary school/education; Higher education; Education; Health care, patient services; Health care; Disasters, fire prevention/control; Youth development, business; Salvation Army; Children/youth, services; Human services; Community development, business promotion; United Ways and Federated Giving Programs; Geology.
Type of support: Annual campaigns; Building/renovation; Capital campaigns; Continuing support; Curriculum development; Employee matching gifts; Equipment; General/operating support; Program development; Research; Scholarship funds.
Geographic limitations: Giving primarily in areas of company operations in AL, IL, MO, SC, TN, and WA.
Support limitations: No grants to individuals or for endowments; no loans.
Application information: Applications accepted. Application form not required.

Initial approach: Proposal
Copies of proposal: 1
Board meeting date(s): Dec.
Deadline(s): None
Final notification: 2 to 3 months

Officers and Trustees:* Brenda M. Pantalone, Secy.; Thomas J. Fitgerald, Admin.; Dennis R. MGough; George H. Pain; Wachovia Bank, N.A.
Number of staff: 1 full-time professional; 1 part-time support.
EIN: 436022750
Selected grants: The following grants are a representative sample of this grantmaker's funding activity:
$2,500 to Purdue University, West Lafayette, IN, 2010.
$2,500 to University of Iowa, Iowa City, IA, 2010.
$1,500 to Junior Achievement of Greater Saint Louis, Chesterfield, MO, 2010.

2802
Olivetti Office USA, Inc.
22255 Greenfield Rd.
Southfield, MI 48075-3710 (248) 569-1933

Company type: Private company
Business activities: Manufactures computers, calculators, typewriters, and other office equipment.
Business type (SIC): Computer and office equipment
Giving statement: Giving through the Dino Olivetti Foundation, Inc.

Dino Olivetti Foundation, Inc.
(formerly Olivetti Foundation, Inc.)
c/o Foundation Source
501 Silverside Rd., Ste. 123
Wilmington, DE 19809-1377

Establishment information: Incorporated in 1957 in NY.
Donors: Olivetti Office USA; Dino Olivetti†.
Financial data (yr. ended 12/31/11): Assets, $1,500,420 (M); expenditures, $107,611; qualifying distributions, $63,000; giving activities include $63,000 for grants.
Purpose and activities: The foundation supports organizations involved with higher education and cancer.
Fields of interest: Higher education; Cancer; Cancer research.
International interests: Italy.
Type of support: General/operating support; Program development; Research; Scholarship funds.
Support limitations: No grants to individuals.
Application information: Applications not accepted. Unsolicited requests for funds not accepted.
Officers and Directors:* Alfred C. Olivetti*, Chair. and Secy.; Philip Olivetti, Pres.; Marc Olivetti*, Treas.; Jaffray K. Olivetti McMorrow; Peter Olivetti; Christina Spencer.
Number of staff: 1 part-time professional.
EIN: 046043143

2803
Olshan Grundman Frome Rosenzweig & Wolosky LLP
Park Ave. Twr.
65 E. 55th St.
New York, NY 10022-3219 (212) 451-2300

Company URL: http://www.olshanlaw.com
Company type: Private company
Business activities: Operates law firm.
Business type (SIC): Legal services
Offices: Newark, NJ; New York, NY
Giving statement: Giving through the Olshan Grundman Frome Rosenzweig & Wolosky LLP Pro Bono Program.

Olshan Grundman Frome Rosenzweig & Wolosky LLP Pro Bono Program
Park Ave. Twr.
65 E. 55th St.
New York, NY 10022-3219 (212) 451-2300
E-mail: eholloman@olshanlaw.com; URL: http://www.olshanlaw.com/

Contact: Ellen Holloman, Partner
Fields of interest: Legal services.
Type of support: Pro bono services - legal.
Geographic limitations: Giving primarily in areas of company operations in Newark, NJ, and New York, NY.
Application information: A Pro Bono Committee manages the pro bono program.

2804
Olympus Corporation of the Americas
3500 Corporate Pkwy.
Center Valley, PA 18034-0610
(484) 896-5000

Company URL: http://www.olympusamerica.com
Establishment information: Established in 1977.
Company type: Subsidiary of a foreign company
Business activities: Operates photo imaging company.
Business type (SIC): Photographic equipment and supplies
Corporate officers: Michael C. Woodford, Chair. and C.E.O.; Karl Watanabe, Pres.
Board of director: Michael C. Woodford, Chair.
Giving statement: Giving through the Olympus Medical Charitable Foundation.

Olympus Medical Charitable Foundation
3500 Corporate Pkwy.
Center Valley, PA 18034-0610

Establishment information: Established in 2007 in PA.
Donor: Olympus America, Inc.
Financial data (yr. ended 03/31/11): Assets, $16,631 (M); gifts received, $100,000; expenditures, $103,518; qualifying distributions, $100,000; giving activities include $100,000 for 1 grant.
Purpose and activities: The foundation supports programs designed to advance science, research, general health care education and health care technology, particularly in the fields of endoscopic diagnosis and therapy.
Fields of interest: Medical school/education; Hospitals (general); Health care, clinics/centers; Digestive diseases; Medical research.
Type of support: General/operating support; Program development; Research.
Geographic limitations: Giving primarily in CA.
Application information: Applications not accepted. Unsolicited requests for funds not accepted.
Officer: Hiroshi Ichikawa, Chair.
Advisory Committee: Dr. Peter Cotton; Dr. Charles Lightdale; Dr. Michael Sivak, Jr.
EIN: 260375840

2805
Omaha Steaks International, Inc.
11030 O St.
P.O. Box 2575
Omaha, NE 68137 (402) 597-8106
FAX: (402) 597-8222

Company URL: http://www.omahasteaks.com
Establishment information: Established in 1917.
Company type: Private company
Business activities: Manufactures, markets and distributes boneless sirloin, filet mignon, and other specialty meats.
Business type (SIC): Groceries—wholesale
Financial profile for 2009: Number of employees, 600
Corporate officers: Alan D. Simon, Chair. and C.E.O.; Bruce A. Simon, Pres. and C.O.O.; David Hershiser, V.P. and C.F.O.; James Bohan, V.P., Human Resources
Board of director: Alan D. Simon, Chair.
Giving statement: Giving through the Todd and Betiana Simon Foundation.

The Todd and Betiana Simon Foundation
11030 O St.
Omaha, NE 68137-2346

Establishment information: Established in 2004 in NE.
Donor: Omaha Steaks International, Inc.
Financial data (yr. ended 12/31/11): Assets, $2,712,579 (M); expenditures, $783,117; qualifying distributions, $764,166; giving activities include $764,166 for grants.
Purpose and activities: The foundation supports organizations involved with arts and culture, education, family planning, and youth services.
Fields of interest: Media, film/video; Visual arts; Museums; Historic preservation/historical societies; Arts; Higher education; Education; Reproductive health, family planning; Big Brothers/Big Sisters; Youth, services; United Ways and Federated Giving Programs.
Type of support: General/operating support; Program development; Scholarship funds.
Geographic limitations: Giving primarily in Omaha, NE; some giving in CA and NY.
Support limitations: No grants to individuals.
Application information: Applications not accepted. Contributes only to pre-selected organizations.
Officers: Todd D. Simon, Pres. and Treas.; Joanna Simon, V.P.; Barbara Goldstein, Secy.
EIN: 470820673
Selected grants: The following grants are a representative sample of this grantmaker's funding activity:
$70,000 to Bemis Center for Contemporary Arts, Omaha, NE, 2010.
$50,000 to United States Artists, Los Angeles, CA, 2010.
$26,000 to Film Streams, Omaha, NE, 2010.
$25,000 to Center for Independent Documentary, Sharon, MA, 2010.
$25,000 to United Way of the Midlands, Omaha, NE, 2010.
$25,000 to Uta Halee Girls Village, Omaha, NE, 2010.
$20,000 to Project Harmony, Omaha, NE, 2010.
$8,350 to Partnership for Our Kids, Omaha, NE, 2010.
$5,000 to Youth Frontiers, Minneapolis, MN, 2010.
$2,000 to Joslyn Art Museum, Omaha, NE, 2010.

2806
Omaha World-Herald Company
1314 Douglas St., Ste. 1500
Omaha, NE 68102-1138 (402) 444-1000
FAX: (402) 444-1211

Company URL: http://www.omaha.com
Establishment information: Established in 1885.
Company type: Private company
Business activities: Publishes newspapers.
Business type (SIC): Newspaper publishing and/or printing
Corporate officers: John Gottschalk, Chair.; Terry Kroeger, Pres.; Duane Polodna, Sr. V.P. and C.F.O.; Scott Searl, V.P. and Genl. Counsel; Doug Hiemstra, V.P., Opers.
Board of director: John Gottschalk, Chair.
Giving statement: Giving through the Omaha World-Herald Foundation Trust.

The Omaha World-Herald Foundation Trust
c/o Wells Fargo Bank, NA
1919 Douglas St., 2nd FL, MACN8000-027
Omaha, NE 68102 (402) 444-1000

Establishment information: Trust established in 1968 in NE.
Donors: Omaha World-Herald Co.; Omaha World Herald Branching Out.
Financial data (yr. ended 12/31/11): Assets, $1 (M); gifts received, $245,500; expenditures, $337,985; qualifying distributions, $335,000; giving activities include $335,000 for grants.
Purpose and activities: The foundation supports organizations involved with higher education, health, and children's services.
Fields of interest: Higher education; Hospitals (general); Health care; Boy scouts; Children, services; United Ways and Federated Giving Programs.
Type of support: Capital campaigns; Continuing support; General/operating support; Program development; Scholarship funds; Sponsorships.
Geographic limitations: Giving primarily in the western Omaha, NE area.
Support limitations: No grants to individuals, or for endowments, research, seminars, or dinners.
Application information: Applications not accepted. Contributes only to pre-selected organizations.
Board meeting date(s): As required
Trustee: Wells Fargo Bank Nebraska, N.A.
EIN: 476058691
Selected grants: The following grants are a representative sample of this grantmaker's funding activity:
$160,000 to Creighton University, Omaha, NE, 2009.
$150,000 to United Way of the Midlands, Omaha, NE, 2009.
$90,000 to Heritage Services, Omaha, NE, 2009.
$50,000 to Childrens Hospital and Medical Center Foundation, Omaha, NE, 2009.
$40,000 to College of Saint Mary, Omaha, NE, 2009.
$10,000 to College World Series of Omaha, Omaha, NE, 2009.
$10,000 to Live Well Omaha, Omaha, NE, 2009.
$5,000 to Omaha Schools Foundation, Omaha, NE, 2009.
$3,310 to University of Nebraska Foundation, Omaha, NE, 2009.

2807
Omnicare, Inc.
900 Omnicare Ctr.
201 East Fourth St.
Cincinnati, OH 45202 (513) 719-2600

Company URL: http://www.omnicare.com/
Establishment information: Established in 1981.
Company type: Public company
Company ticker symbol and exchange: OCR/NYSE
Business activities: Provides health care services.
Business type (SIC): Miscellaneous health services; drug stores and proprietary stores
Financial profile for 2012: Number of employees, 14,400; assets, $6,989,260,000; sales volume, $6,160,390,000; pre-tax net income, $312,070,000; expenses, $5,713,210,000; liabilities, $3,483,550,000
Fortune 1000 ranking: 2012—416th in revenues, 587th in profits, and 492nd in assets
Corporate officers: James D. Shelton, Chair.; John L. Workman, C.P.A, C.E.O.; Nitin Sahney, Pres. and C.O.O.; Rocky Craft, C.F.O.; Kirsten Marriner, Sr. V.P., Human Resources; Alexander M. Kayne, Sr. V.P., Genl. Counsel, and Secy.
Board of directors: James D. Shelton, Chair.; John L. Bernbach; Mark A. Emmert, Ph.D.; Steven J. Heyer; Samuel R. Leno; Andrea R. Lindell, Ph.D.; Barry P. Schochet; Amy Wallman; John L. Workman, C.P.A.
Subsidiary: United Group, Oklahoma City, OK
International operations: Australia; Belgium; Canada; Czech Republic; Denmark; Finland; France; India; Netherlands; Singapore; South Africa; Sweden; Switzerland; United Kingdom
Giving statement: Giving through the Omnicare Foundation.
Company EIN: 311001351

Omnicare Foundation
c/o Omnicare, Inc.
201 East Fourth St.
Cincinnati, OH 45202 (513) 719-2600

Establishment information: Established in 1993 in KY.
Donors: Omnicare, Inc.; Thomas R. Isgrig.
Contact: Regis T. Robbins, Treas.
Financial data (yr. ended 12/31/11): Assets, $6,931 (M); gifts received, $380,000; expenditures, $416,482; qualifying distributions, $416,121; giving activities include $402,300 for 22 grants (high: $200,000; low: $1,000).
Purpose and activities: The foundation supports organizations involved with education, health, children and youth, and Judaism. Special emphasis directed toward programs designed to benefit the geriatric population.
Fields of interest: Elementary school/education; Higher education; Theological school/education; Education; Health care; Geriatrics; Children/youth, services; Jewish federated giving programs; Jewish agencies & synagogues Aging.
Type of support: Capital campaigns; General/operating support; Program development; Research; Sponsorships.
Geographic limitations: Giving primarily in IL, NY, and OH, and in Israel.
Support limitations: No grants to individuals.
Application information: Applications accepted. Application form not required. Applicants should submit the following:
1) brief history of organization and description of its mission
2) copy of IRS Determination Letter
3) detailed description of project and amount of funding requested

Initial approach: Letter of inquiry
Deadline(s): None
Officers and Directors :* Andrea R. Lindell*, Chair.; Erin Ascher*, Vice-Chair.; Alexander Kayne, Secy.; Regis T. Robbins, Treas.; Nitin Sahney; Jeffrey M. Stamps; John L. Workman.
EIN: 311389112

2808
Omnicom Group Inc.
437 Madison Ave.
New York, NY 10022-7001 (212) 415-3600
FAX: (212) 415-3530

Company URL: http://www.omnicomgroup.com
Establishment information: Established in 1986.
Company type: Public company
Company ticker symbol and exchange: OMC/NYSE
International Securities Identification Number: US6819191064
Business activities: Operates holding company; provides advertising services.
Business type (SIC): Holding company; advertising
Financial profile for 2012: Number of employees, 71,100; assets, $22,151,900,000; sales volume, $14,219,400,000; pre-tax net income, $1,659,600,000; expenses, $12,415,200,000; liabilities, $18,691,100,000
Fortune 1000 ranking: 2012—191st in revenues, 199th in profits, and 225th in assets
Forbes 2000 ranking: 2012—676th in sales, 606th in profits, and 915th in assets
Corporate officers: Bruce Crawford, Chair.; Peter Mead, Vice-Chair.; John D. Wren, Pres. and C.E.O.; Randall J. Weisenburger, Exec. V.P. and C.F.O.; Michael J. O'Brien, Sr. V.P., Genl. Counsel, and Secy.; Philip J. Angelastro, Sr. V.P., Finance and Cont.; Dennis E. Hewitt, Treas.
Board of directors: Bruce Crawford, Chair.; Peter Mead, Vice-Chair.; Alan R. Batkin; Mary C. Choksi; Robert Charles Clark; Leonard S. Coleman, Jr.; Errol M. Cook; Susan S. Denison; Michael A. Henning; John R. Murphy; John R. Purcell; Linda Johnson Rice; Gary L. Roubos; John D. Wren
Subsidiaries: BBDO Worldwide Inc., New York, NY; DDB Worldwide Communications Group, Inc., New York, NY; Ketchum Communications Inc., Pittsburgh, PA; Tracy-Locke, Inc., Dallas, TX
International operations: United Kingdom
Giving statement: Giving through the Omnicom Group Inc. Corporate Giving Program.
Company EIN: 131514814

Omnicom Group Inc. Corporate Giving Program
437 Madison Ave., 9th Fl.
New York, NY 10022-7000 (212) 415-3600
FAX: (212) 415-3530; URL: http://www.omnicomgroup.com/aboutomnicomgroup/csr

Purpose and activities: Omnicom Group Inc. makes charitable contributions to nonprofit organizations involved with education, the environment, human services, international relief, and children. Support is given primarily in areas of company operations.
Fields of interest: Education; Environment; Health organizations; Human services; Children/youth, services; International relief; International human rights.
Type of support: Employee volunteer services; General/operating support; Pro bono services - communications/public relations; Pro bono services - marketing/branding; Sponsorships.

Geographic limitations: Giving primarily in areas of company operations.

2809
OMNOVA Solutions Inc.

175 Ghent Rd.
Fairlawn, OH 44333-3330 (330) 869-4200
FAX: (330) 869-4211

Company URL: http://www.omnova.com
Establishment information: Established in 1999.
Company type: Public company
Company ticker symbol and exchange: OMN/NYSE
Business activities: Designs, manufactures, and markets decorative and functional building products; manufactures emulsion polymers and specialty chemicals.
Business type (SIC): Chemical preparations/ miscellaneous; wood millwork; chemicals and allied products; plastics and synthetics
Financial profile for 2012: Number of employees, 2,390; assets, $873,700,000; sales volume, $1,125,500,000; pre-tax net income, $36,900,000; expenses, $1,088,600,000; liabilities, $743,500,000
Corporate officers: Kevin M. McMullen, Chair., Pres., and C.E.O.; Michael E. Hicks, Sr. V.P. and C.F.O.; Douglas E. Wenger, Sr. V.P. and C.I.O.; James C. LeMay, Sr. V.P. and Genl. Counsel; Chester W. Fox, V.P. and Treas.; Kristine C. Syrvalin, V.P., Human Resources and Secy.
Board of directors: Kevin McMullen, Chair.; David J. D'Antoni; Michael J. Merriman; Steven W. Percy; Larry B. Porcellato; Allan R. Rothwell; William .R. Seelbach; Robert A. Stefanko
Divisions: Decorative Products Div., Fairlawn, OH; Performance Chemicals Div., Fairlawn, OH
International operations: China; Thailand; United Kingdom
Giving statement: Giving through the OMNOVA Solutions Foundation Inc.
Company EIN: 341897652

OMNOVA Solutions Foundation Inc.

175 Ghent Rd.
Fairlawn, OH 44333-3300 (330) 869-4289
FAX: (330) 869-4345;
E-mail: theresa.carter@omnova.com; URL: http://www.omnova.com/about/community/community.aspx

Establishment information: Established in 1999 in OH.
Donor: GenCorp Foundation Inc.
Contact: Theresa Carter, Pres.
Financial data (yr. ended 11/30/11): Assets, $21,421,303 (M); expenditures, $1,917,265; qualifying distributions, $1,841,615; giving activities include $1,590,035 for 551 grants and $94,465 for 118 employee matching gifts.
Purpose and activities: The foundation supports programs designed to create educational opportunities; connect people to health and social services; energize civic pride; and create access to the arts. Special emphasis is directed toward programs designed to help motivate future leaders and workers to gain the desire, knowledge, and work readiness skills required for companies to succeed and maintain a competitive edge.
Fields of interest: Arts councils; Museums; Performing arts; Arts; Elementary/secondary education; Higher education; Education; Hospitals (general); Health care, patient services; Health care; Employment, services; Food services; Food banks; Disasters, preparedness/services; Disasters, fire prevention/control; Safety/disasters; Boys & girls clubs; Children/youth, services; Residential/ custodial care, hospices; Homeless, human services; Human services; Community/economic development; Science, formal/general education; Mathematics; Engineering/technology; Science; Public affairs, public education; Public affairs.
International interests: Canada; China; France; India; Thailand.
Program:
Employee Community Leadership Award: The foundation awards grants to nonprofit organizations with which employees of OMNOVA volunteer.
Type of support: Annual campaigns; Building/ renovation; Capital campaigns; Continuing support; Employee matching gifts; Employee volunteer services; Employee-related scholarships; Endowments; General/operating support; In-kind gifts; Program development; Scholarship funds.
Geographic limitations: Giving primarily in areas of company operations in GA, MA, MS, NC, OH, PA, SC, WI, and in Canada, China, France, India, and Thailand; giving also to national organizations.
Support limitations: No support for private foundations, fraternal, social, labor, or veterans' organizations, discriminatory organizations, organizations not of direct benefit to the entire community, political parties or candidates, organizations posing a conflict of interest with OMNOVA, or churches or religious organizations. No grants to individuals (except for employee-related scholarships), or for lobbying activities, local athletic or sports programs or sports equipment, travel, advertising, benefits, raffles, or similar fundraising events, or research or conferences.
Publications: Annual report; Application guidelines.
Application information: Applications accepted. Organizations receiving support are asked to provide periodic progress reports. Multi-year funding is not automatic. Proposals should be brief. Application form not required. Applicants should submit the following:
1) timetable for implementation and evaluation of project
2) results expected from proposed grant
3) statement of problem project will address
4) copy of IRS Determination Letter
5) brief history of organization and description of its mission
6) copy of most recent annual report/audited financial statement/990
7) how project's results will be evaluated or measured
8) list of company employees involved with the organization
9) descriptive literature about organization
10) listing of board of directors, trustees, officers and other key people and their affiliations
11) detailed description of project and amount of funding requested
12) copy of current year's organizational budget and/or project budget
13) plans for acknowledgement

Initial approach: Mail proposal to foundation
Copies of proposal: 1
Board meeting date(s): As required
Deadline(s): None
Final notification: 4 to 6 weeks

Officers and Trustees:* Michael E. Hicks*, Chair.; Theresa Carter, Pres.; Kristine C. Syrvalin*, Secy.; Frank P. Robers*, Treas.; Robin McCann; Nick Triantafillopoulos.
Number of staff: 1 full-time professional; 1 part-time support.
EIN: 341909350
Selected grants: The following grants are a representative sample of this grantmaker's funding activity:
$118,000 to United Way, 2011.
$111,860 to Akron Public Schools, Akron, OH, 2011.
$110,000 to University of Akron, Akron, OH, 2011.
$45,000 to Western Michigan University, Kalamazoo, MI, 2011.
$20,000 to Case Western Reserve University, Cleveland, OH, 2011.
$17,500 to Habitat for Humanity of Summit County, Akron, OH, 2011.
$17,300 to Mogadore Local School District, Mogadore, OH, 2011.
$15,000 to Akron-Canton Regional Foodbank, Akron, OH, 2011.
$15,000 to Greater Akron Chamber, Akron, OH, 2011.
$5,500 to Mogadore Fire Department, Mogadore, OH, 2011.
$5,000 to YWCA Chester County, West Chester, PA, 2011.
$3,000 to Tuesday Musical Association, Akron, OH, 2011.

2810
Omron Electronics LLC

(formerly Omron Electronics Inc.)
1 E. Commerce Dr.
Schaumburg, IL 60173-5302
(847) 843-7900

Company URL: http://www.omron247.com
Establishment information: Established in 1977.
Company type: Subsidiary of a foreign company
Business activities: Manufactures industrial automation sensor and controls technologies.
Business type (SIC): Industrial and commercial machinery and computer equipment
Corporate officers: Hisao Sakuta, Chair.; Fumio Tateishi, Vice Chair.; Gregg Holst, Pres. and C.O.O.; Jeff Nowling, Principal; Allan Vail, V.P., Sales
Board of directors: Hisao Sakuta, Chair.; Fumio Tateishi, Vice Chair.
Subsidiary: Omron IDM Controls Inc., Houston, TX
Giving statement: Giving through the Omron Foundation, Inc.

Omron Foundation, Inc.

c/o Omron Managment Center of America
55 Commerce Drive
Schaumburg, IL 60173-5302 (224) 520-7654
URL: http://www.components.omron.com/components/web/webfiles.nsf/philanthropy.html

Establishment information: Established in 1989 in IL.
Donors: Omron Electronics Inc.; Omron Electronics LLC; Omron Healthcare, Inc.; Omron Electronics Components, LLC.
Contact: James P. Eberhart, Treas.
Financial data (yr. ended 03/31/12): Assets, $750,964 (M); gifts received, $242,217; expenditures, $459,445; qualifying distributions, $459,342; giving activities include $459,342 for grants.
Purpose and activities: The foundation supports food banks and organizations involved with arts and culture, education, health, breast cancer, heart disease, housing development, disaster relief, human services, the disabled, and the elderly.
Fields of interest: Arts, cultural/ethnic awareness; Arts; Secondary school/education; Higher education; Engineering school/education; Education; Health care; Breast cancer; Heart & circulatory diseases; Food banks; Housing/shelter, development; Disasters, preparedness/services;

American Red Cross; Aging, centers/services; Developmentally disabled, centers & services; Human services; United Ways and Federated Giving Programs Disabilities, people with.
Type of support: Building/renovation; Continuing support; Employee matching gifts; Employee-related scholarships; Endowments; General/operating support; Program development; Scholarship funds.
Geographic limitations: Giving primarily in CA, IL, NY, and TX.
Support limitations: No support for political, fraternal, veterans', athletic, or lobbying organizations, or religious organizations not of direct benefit to the entire community. No grants to individuals (except for employee-related scholarships).
Application information: Applications accepted. No phone or fax requests will be accepted. No multi-year funding. Application form not required.
Applicants should submit the following:
1) copy of IRS Determination Letter
2) brief history of organization and description of its mission
3) copy of most recent annual report/audited financial statement/990
4) listing of board of directors, trustees, officers and other key people and their affiliations
5) detailed description of project and amount of funding requested
Initial approach: Proposal
Board meeting date(s): Quarterly
Deadline(s): None
Officers: Takuji Yamamoto, Pres. and V.P.; K. Blake Thatcher, Secy.; James P. Eberhart, Treas.
EIN: 363644055
Selected grants: The following grants are a representative sample of this grantmaker's funding activity:
$75,700 to Little City Foundation, Palatine, IL, 2011.
$57,000 to Illinois State University, Normal, IL, 2011.
$50,000 to Northern Illinois University, DeKalb, IL, 2011.
$41,980 to American Red Cross, Des Moines, IA, 2011.
$36,899 to Northern Illinois Food Bank, Geneva, IL, 2011.
$16,000 to North Central College, Naperville, IL, 2011.
$15,000 to Safe Alternatives to Violent Environments, Fremont, CA, 2011.
$12,400 to Narconon International, Los Angeles, CA, 2011.
$10,810 to Houston Food Bank, Houston, TX, 2011.
$10,000 to Gleaners Community Food Bank, Detroit, MI, 2011.

2811
One Village Coffee
18 Cassel Rd.
Souderton, PA 18964 (215) 721-4818

Company URL: http://www.onevillagecoffee.com
Establishment information: Established in 2007.
Company type: Private company
Business activities: Operates a regional coffee roasting company.
Business type (SIC): Miscellaneous prepared foods
Corporate officer: Steve Hackman, Pres.
Giving statement: Giving through the One Village Coffee Corporate Giving Program.

One Village Coffee Corporate Giving Program
18 Cassel Rd.
Souderton, PA 18964-2603 (215) 721-4818
URL: http://www.onevillagecoffee.com

Purpose and activities: One Village Coffee is a certified B Corporation that donates a percentage of revenues of designated products to nonprofit organizations. Special emphasis is directed toward international organizations and programs that help to alleviate poverty.
Fields of interest: Education; Environment, water resources; International economic development; Community/economic development.
Type of support: General/operating support.
Geographic limitations: Giving in Egypt, Honduras, Indonesia, and Kenya.

2812
One World Futbol Project Foundation
1303 Jefferson St., Ste 100B
Napa, CA 94559-2442 (888) 993-8826

Company URL: http://oneworldfutbol.com/
Establishment information: Established in 2006.
Company type: Private company
Business type (SIC): Business services/ miscellaneous
Corporate officers: Lisa Tarver, C.O.O.; Timothy Jahnigen, C.I.O.
Giving statement: Giving through the One World Futbol Project Foundation.

One World Futbol Project Foundation
1303 Jefferson St., Ste 100B
Napa, CA 94559-2442 (888) 993-8826
E-mail: lisa@oneworldfutbolproject.org; URL: http://oneworldfutbol.com/

Purpose and activities: The One World Futbol Project is a certified B Corporation that donates a percentage of profits to charitable organizations.
Fields of interest: Athletics/sports, soccer; Youth development Economically disadvantaged.
Type of support: Cause-related marketing; In-kind gifts.

2771
O'Neal Steel, Inc.
(also known as O'Neal Steel International, LLC)
744 41st St. N.
P.O. Box 2623
Birmingham, AL 35222-1124
(205) 599-8000

Company URL: http://www.onealsteel.com
Establishment information: Established in 1921.
Company type: Private company
Business activities: Manufactures metal products.
Business type (SIC): Steel mill products
Financial profile for 2010: Number of employees, 200
Corporate officers: Craft O'Neal, Chair.; Bill Jones, Vice-Chair.; Holman Head, Pres. and C.E.O.; Mary Valenta, Exec. V.P. and C.F.O.; Michael Gooldrup, C.I.O.; Mark Woolnough, V.P. and Treas.; Suzanne Lane, V.P. and Cont.; Jay Satterfield, V.P., Opers.
Board of directors: Craft O'Neal, Chair.; Bill Jones, Vice-Chair.
Subsidiaries: Aerodyne Alloys, LLC, South Windsor, CT; Denman & Davis, Clifton, NJ; Leeco Steel, LLC, Ambridge, PA; Metalwest LLC, Brighton, CO; Supply Dynamics, LLC, Loveland, OH; Tad Metals, Inc., Monroe Township, NJ; TW Metals, Inc., Exton, PA; United Performance Metals, Hamilton, OH
Giving statement: Giving through the O'Neal Steel, Inc. Corporate Giving Program.

O'Neal Steel, Inc. Corporate Giving Program
c/o Corp. Contribs.
P.O. Box 2623
Birmingham, AL 35202
URL: http://www.onealsteel.com

Purpose and activities: O'Neal makes charitable contributions to nonprofit organizations on a case by case basis. Support is given primarily in areas of company operations.
Fields of interest: General charitable giving Children; Youth; Economically disadvantaged.
Type of support: Capital campaigns; Continuing support; General/operating support; Research.
Geographic limitations: Giving primarily in areas of company operations.
Support limitations: No grants to individuals.
Application information: Applications not accepted. Contributes only to pre-selected organizations.
Administrators: Henry Craft O'Neal, Chair.; Charles W. Jones, Vice-Chair.; R. Holman Head, Exec. V.P.; Shirley Fagan, Comms./Mktg.; Cindy Persall, Exec. Asst.

2813
OneBeacon Insurance Group, L.L.C.
1 Beacon Ln.
Canton, MA 02021-1030 (617) 725-6000

Company URL: http://www.onebeacon.com
Establishment information: Established in 1831.
Company type: Subsidiary of a foreign company
Business activities: Sells property and casualty insurance.
Business type (SIC): Insurance/fire, marine, and casualty
Financial profile for 2012: Assets, $5,800,000,000
Corporate officers: Lowndes A. Smith, Chair.; Paul F. Romano, Pres.; T. Michael Miller, Pres. and C.E.O.; Paul H. McDonough, Sr. V.P. and C.F.O.; Ann Marie Andrews, C.A.O.; Bradford W. Rich, Sr. V.P. and Genl. Counsel
Board of directors: Lowndes A. Smith, Chair.; Raymond Barrette; Reid T. Campbell; Morgan W. Davis; David T. Foy; Lois W. Grady; Richard P. Howard; Ira H. Malis; T. Michael Miller; Kent D. Urness
Subsidiaries: CGU/North Pacific Insurance Co., Portland, OR; Hawkeye Security Insurance Co., Des Moines, IA; Oregon Automobile Insurance Co., Portland, OR
Giving statement: Giving through the OneBeacon Charitable Trust.

OneBeacon Charitable Trust
(formerly CGU Charitable Trust)
1 Beacon Ln.
Canton, MA 02021-1030 (781) 332-7101

Establishment information: Established in 1987 in PA.
Donor: General Accident Insurance Co. of America.

Financial data (yr. ended 12/31/11): Assets, $2,166,863 (M); expenditures, $295,279; qualifying distributions, $284,318; giving activities include $284,318 for grants.
Purpose and activities: The foundation supports food banks and organizations involved with arts and culture, education, health, cancer research, human services, community development, and other areas.
Fields of interest: Arts; Higher education; Cancer research; Food banks; American Red Cross; Children/youth, services; Developmentally disabled, centers & services; Human services; Community/economic development; United Ways and Federated Giving Programs; General charitable giving.
Program:
Scholarship Program: The foundation annually awards $1,500 college scholarships to children of employees of OneBeacon and children of OneBeacon independent agents. The program is administered by Scholarship America.
Type of support: Employee matching gifts; Employee-related scholarships; General/operating support; Sponsorships.
Geographic limitations: Giving primarily in areas of company operations, with emphasis on Boston, MA.
Support limitations: No grants to individuals (except for employee-related scholarships).
Application information: Applications not accepted. Contributes only to pre-selected organizations and through employee-related scholarships.
Trustees: Drew Carnarse; Paul H. McDonough; Thomas N. Schmitt.
EIN: 232441567

2814
Oneida Financial Corp.

182 Main St.
Oneida, NY 13421-1676 (315) 363-2000
FAX: (315) 361-5080

Company URL: http://www.oneidabank.com
Establishment information: Established in 1866.
Company type: Public company
Company ticker symbol and exchange: ONFC/NASDAQ
Business activities: Operates holding company; operates savings bank.
Business type (SIC): Savings institutions; holding company
Financial profile for 2012: Number of employees, 319; assets, $661,580,000; pre-tax net income, $7,860,000; liabilities, $578,220,000
Corporate officers: Richard B. Myers, Chair.; Michael R. Kallet, Pres. and C.E.O.; Eric E. Stickels, Exec. V.P., Secy., and C.F.O.
Board of directors: Richard B. Myers, Chair.; Robert J. Benson; Thomas S. Bielicki; Patricia D. Caprio; Thomas H. Dixon; John E. Haskell; Michael R. Kallet; Michael T. Keville; Rodney D. Kent; Michael W. Milmoe; Nancy E. Ryan; Eric E. Stickels; Ralph L. Stevens, M.D.; Gerald N. Volk; Frank O. White, Jr.; John A. Wight, M.D.
Subsidiary: The Oneida Savings Bank, Oneida, NY
Giving statement: Giving through the Oneida Savings Bank Charitable Foundation.
Company EIN: 161561678

Oneida Savings Bank Charitable Foundation

P.O. Box 240
Oneida, NY 13421-1607 (315) 363-2000

Establishment information: Established in 1998.
Donor: Oneida Financial Corp.
Contact: Eric E. Stickels, Dir.
Financial data (yr. ended 12/31/11): Assets, $1,420,844 (M); expenditures, $35,983; qualifying distributions, $33,500; giving activities include $33,500 for grants.
Purpose and activities: The foundation supports organizations involved with education, recreation, children, and disability services.
Fields of interest: Education; Recreation.
Program:
Scholarships: The foundation awards college scholarships. The program is administered by Scholarship America, Inc.
Type of support: General/operating support; Scholarship funds.
Geographic limitations: Giving primarily in areas of company operations in NY.
Application information: Applications accepted. Application form required.
Initial approach: Proposal
Deadline(s): None
Directors: Thomas H. Dixon; Michael R. Kallet; Ann K. Pierz; Eric E. Stickles.
EIN: 161561680

2815
ONEOK, Inc.

100 W. 5th St., 10K Plz.
P.O. Box 871
Tulsa, OK 74103-4240 (918) 588-7000
FAX: (918) 588-7273

Company URL: http://www.oneok.com
Establishment information: Established in 1906.
Company type: Public company
Company ticker symbol and exchange: OKE/NYSE
Business activities: Transmits and distributes natural gas; conducts crude petroleum, natural gas, and natural gas liquid exploration and production activities; sells electricity wholesale.
Business type (SIC): Gas production and distribution; extraction/oil and gas; extraction/natural gas liquids; electric services
Financial profile for 2012: Number of employees, 4,859; assets, $15,855,270,000; sales volume, $12,632,560,000; pre-tax net income, $944,450,000; expenses, $11,530,060,000; liabilities, $13,725,670,000
Fortune 1000 ranking: 2012—219th in revenues, 427th in profits, and 286th in assets
Corporate officers: John W. Gibson, Chair. and C.E.O.; Terry K. Spencer, Pres.; Pierce H. Norton II, Exec. V.P. and C.O.O.; Robert F. Martinovich, Exec. V.P., Opers.; Brien Brown, C.I.O.; Derek S. Reiners, Sr. V.P., C.F.O., and Treas.; Stephen W. Lake, Sr. V.P. and Genl. Counsel; Mike Miers, V.P. and C.A.O.; Eric Grimshaw, V.P. and Corp. Secy.
Board of directors: John W. Gibson, Chair.; James C. Day; Julie H. Edwards; William L. Ford; Bert H. Mackie; Steve J. Malcolm; Jim W. Mogg; Pattye L. Moore; Gary D. Parker; Eduardo A. Rodriguez
Subsidiaries: Energy Cos. of ONEOK, Tulsa, OK; Kansas Gas Service Co., Overland Park, KS; Oklahoma Natural Gas Co., Tulsa, OK; ONEOK Gas Marketing Co., Tulsa, OK; ONEOK Leasing Co., Tulsa, OK; ONEOK Products Co., Tulsa, OK; ONEOK Resources Co., Tulsa, OK; ONEOK Sayre Storage Co., Tulsa, OK; ONEOK Technology Co., Tulsa, OK; ONG Transmission Co., Tulsa, OK
International operations: Canada
Giving statement: Giving through the ONEOK, Inc. Corporate Giving Program and the ONEOK Foundation, Inc.
Company EIN: 731520922

ONEOK, Inc. Corporate Giving Program

c/o Community Investment Program
P.O. Box 871
Tulsa, OK 74102-0871
URL: http://www.oneok.com/en/CorporateResponsibility.aspx

Purpose and activities: As a complement to its foundation, ONEOK also makes charitable contributions to nonprofit organizations directly. Special emphasis is directed toward programs that promote skills for self-sufficiency. Support is given primarily in areas of company operations in Kansas, Oklahoma, and Texas.
Fields of interest: Arts; Education; Health care; Human services; Community/economic development.
Type of support: Employee matching gifts; Employee volunteer services; General/operating support.
Geographic limitations: Giving primarily in areas of company operations in KS, OK, and TX.
Support limitations: No support for religious organizations or churches not of direct benefit to the entire community, individual college preparatory schools or their foundations, or tax-supported organizations. No grants to individuals.
Publications: Application guidelines.
Application information: Applicants should submit the following:
1) role played by volunteers
2) results expected from proposed grant
3) population served
4) copy of IRS Determination Letter
5) brief history of organization and description of its mission
6) list of company employees involved with the organization
7) listing of board of directors, trustees, officers and other key people and their affiliations
8) detailed description of project and amount of funding requested
9) copy of current year's organizational budget and/or project budget
10) listing of additional sources and amount of support

Proposals should include the number of people who will be served by the program, a history of ONEOK's contributions to the organization, and a copy of the organization's W-9 form.
Initial approach: Complete online application
Deadline(s): None

ONEOK Foundation, Inc.

P.O. Box 871
Tulsa, OK 74102-0871 (918) 588-7000
FAX: (918) 588-7490;
E-mail: CommunityInvestments@oneok.com;
URL: http://www.oneok.com/CorporateResponsibility/CommunityInvestments/ONEOKFoundation.aspx

Establishment information: Established in 1997 in OK.
Donor: ONEOK, Inc.
Contact: Terri A. Pirtle, Exec. Dir.
Financial data (yr. ended 12/31/11): Assets, $32,999,169 (M); expenditures, $2,511,850; qualifying distributions, $2,438,677; giving activities include $2,438,677 for 46+ grants (high: $628,000).
Purpose and activities: The foundation supports organizations involved with arts and culture, education, health, human services, and community development. Special emphasis is directed toward programs designed to help people gain skills for self-sufficiency.

Fields of interest: Performing arts, theater; Historic preservation/historical societies; Arts; Elementary/secondary education; Higher education; Education; Hospitals (general); Health care; Children/youth, services; Family services; Human services; Community/economic development; Foundations (community); United Ways and Federated Giving Programs; Utilities Economically disadvantaged.
Programs:
Matching Grants Program: The foundation matches contributions made by employees and directors of ONEOK to nonprofit organizations on a one-for-one basis from $25 to $5,000 per contributor, per year.
Public School Foundation Grants: The foundation awards grants to K-12 public schools to improve the educational experience and provide opportunities to cultivate relationships with community leaders while improving public education. Special emphasis is directed toward classroom enrichment projects and instructional technology; assistance for disadvantaged students; curriculum-based materials and equipment; and programs designed to help improve student performance.
Share the Warmth: Through Share the Warmth program, customers, employees, and businesses donate funds while paying their natural gas bills to help families facing financial emergencies. The foundation annually matches 15 percent of donations raised.
Volunteers with Energy - One Good Deed: The foundation honors employees who volunteer in their communities outside of Volunteers With Energy projects. Selected employees are featured on the company's intranet site and is awarded a $100 grant to the nonprofit organization with which they volunteer.
Type of support: Building/renovation; Capital campaigns; Curriculum development; Employee matching gifts; Employee volunteer services; Equipment; General/operating support; Matching/challenge support.
Geographic limitations: Giving primarily in areas of company operations in KS, OK, and TX.
Support limitations: No support for churches or religious organizations not of direct benefit to the entire community, private foundations, tax-supported organizations, disease-specific organizations, or college preparatory schools or their foundations. No grants to individuals or for fundraising walks or runs.
Publications: Application guidelines.
Application information: Applications accepted. Requests for capital campaigns generally should not exceed one percent of the total capital campaign goal. Application form required. Applicants should submit the following:
1) name, address and phone number of organization
2) copy of IRS Determination Letter
3) brief history of organization and description of its mission
4) list of company employees involved with the organization
5) listing of board of directors, trustees, officers and other key people and their affiliations
6) detailed description of project and amount of funding requested
7) copy of current year's organizational budget and/or project budget
8) listing of additional sources and amount of support

Applications should also include a copy of the organization's W-9 form.
Initial approach: Complete online application
Copies of proposal: 1
Board meeting date(s): Feb., May, Aug., and Nov.
Deadline(s): None for grant requests of $5,000 or less; 4 weeks prior to quarterly board meetings for grant requests over $5,000
Final notification: 1 month
Officers and Directors:* John W. Gibson, Chair. and Pres.; Curtis L. Dinan, Sr. V.P., C.F.O., and Treas.; Stephen W. Lake, Sr. V.P. and Genl. Counsel; Eric Grimshaw, Secy.; Terri A. Pirtle, Exec. Dir.; Caron A. Lawhorn; Robert F. Marinovich; Pierce H. Norton II; David E. Roth; Terry K. Spencer.
EIN: 731503823
Selected grants: The following grants are a representative sample of this grantmaker's funding activity:
$2,075,000 to Tulsa Community Foundation, Tulsa, OK, 2010. For Tulsa Stadium Trust Fund.
$378,000 to University of Tulsa, Tulsa, OK, 2010. For H. A. Chapman Stadium.
$250,000 to University of Oklahoma, College of Earth and Energy, Norman, OK, 2010. For endowment.
$100,000 to Oklahoma Heritage Association, Oklahoma City, OK, 2010.
$100,000 to Tulsa Ballet Theater, Tulsa, OK, 2010.
$50,000 to Oklahoma Centennial Commemoration Fund, Oklahoma City, OK, 2010.
$26,500 to Arts and Humanities Council of Tulsa, Tulsa, OK, 2010.
$25,000 to Lyric Theater of Oklahoma, Oklahoma City, OK, 2010.
$20,000 to Oklahoma City Public Schools Foundation, Oklahoma City, OK, 2010.
$10,000 to Sapulpa Park Friends Foundation, Sapulpa, OK, 2010.

2816
ONSPOT of North America, Inc.

1075 Rodgers Park Dr.
P.O. Box 1077
North Vernon, IN 47265-6428
(812) 346-1719

Company URL: http://www.onspot.com
Establishment information: Established in 1988.
Company type: Private company
Business activities: Manufactures and markets automatic tire chain systems.
Business type (SIC): Metal products/fabricated
Financial profile for 2010: Number of employees, 22
Corporate officers: Patrick D. Freyer, Pres.; Doris Short, Mgr.
Giving statement: Giving through the ONSPOT Foundation, Inc.

ONSPOT Foundation, Inc.

P.O. Box 1077
North Vernon, IN 47265 (812) 346-1719

Establishment information: Established in 1997 in IN.
Donors: ONSPOT of North America, Inc.; Jennings Co.
Contact: Irvin French, Pres. and Dir.
Financial data (yr. ended 12/31/11): Assets, $127,426 (M); gifts received, $50,000; expenditures, $28,950; qualifying distributions, $28,000; giving activities include $28,000 for grants.
Purpose and activities: The foundation supports organizations involved with animal welfare, cancer, Christianity, and other areas.
Type of support: General/operating support.
Support limitations: No grants to individuals.
Application information: Applications accepted. Application form required. Applicants should submit the following:
1) brief history of organization and description of its mission
2) detailed description of project and amount of funding requested

Initial approach: Letter
Deadline(s): None
Officers and Directors: Irvin French, Pres.; Patrick Freyer, V.P.; Joe Meloa, Secy.-Treas.
Director: Patrick Freyer.
EIN: 352004081

2817
Oppenheimer Wolff & Donnelly LLP

Plaza VII
45 S. 7th St., Ste. 3300
Minneapolis, MN 55402-1650
(612) 607-7000

Company URL: http://www.oppenheimer.com
Establishment information: Established in 1886.
Company type: Private company
Business activities: Operates law firm.
Business type (SIC): Legal services
Giving statement: Giving through the Oppenheimer Wolff & Donnelly LLP Pro Bono Program.

Oppenheimer Wolff & Donnelly LLP Pro Bono Program

Plaza VII
45 S. 7th St., Ste. 3300
Minneapolis, MN 55402-1650 (612) 607-7418
E-mail: mschneebeck@oppenheimer.com; Additional tel.: (612) 607-7000; URL: http://www.oppenheimer.com/Community/Default.aspx?id=72

Contact: Mark Schneebeck, Partner
Fields of interest: Legal services.
Type of support: Pro bono services - legal.
Application information: A Pro Bono Committee manages the pro bono program.

2818
OppenheimerFunds, Inc.

2 World Financial Ctr.
225 Liberty St.
New York, NY 10281-1008 (212) 323-0200

Company URL: http://www.oppenheimerfunds.com
Establishment information: Established in 1960.
Company type: Subsidiary of a mutual company
Business activities: Provides investment advisory services.
Business type (SIC): Security and commodity services
Corporate officers: William F. Glavin, Jr., Chair., Pres., and C.E.O.; Michael Baldwin, Exec. V.P. and C.O.O.; David Matthew Pfeffer, Sr. V.P. and C.F.O.; Arthur P. Steinmetz, C.I.O
Board of director: William F. Glavin, Jr., Chair.
Giving statement: Giving through the OppenheimerFunds, Inc. Corporate Giving Program.

OppenheimerFunds, Inc. Corporate Giving Program

(also known as OppenheimerFunds, Inc. Community Investment Program)
2 World Financial Center, 11th Fl.
225 Liberty St.
New York, NY 10281 (212) 323-5224
FAX: (212) 912-6710;
E-mail: jstevens@oppenheimerfunds.com

Contact: Jennifer Stevens, V.P., Dir. of Corp. Comms.
Purpose and activities: OppenheimerFunds makes charitable contributions to nonprofit organizations involved with youth entrepreneurship and business education. Support is given to local community initiatives in Denver, Colorado, and New York, New York.
Fields of interest: Youth development, business; Community/economic development.
Program:
Future Enterprisers program: The Future Enterprisers program provides students kindergarten through college with access to a continuum of proven entrepreneurship education programming designed to equip and inspire students to succeed in school, work and life. Types of support includes employee volunteerism and corporate matches of employee donations.
Type of support: Employee matching gifts; Employee volunteer services; General/operating support; In-kind gifts; Sponsorships.
Geographic limitations: Giving in Denver, CO, and New York, NY.
Support limitations: No support for political, religious, social, labor, veterans', alumni, or fraternal organizations serving a limited constituency. No grants to individuals, or for research, mass appeal solicitations, events, sponsorships, or publication of books, articles, newsletters, videos, or electronic media.
Publications: Corporate giving report.
Application information: The company has a staff that only handles contributions. Application form not required. Applicants should submit the following:
1) detailed description of project and amount of funding requested
Initial approach: Proposal to headquarters
Copies of proposal: 1
Final notification: Following review
Number of staff: 1 full-time professional; 1 part-time professional.

2819
Optima Fund Management LP

10 E. 53rd St., 29th Fl.
New York, NY 10022 (212) 484-3000

Company URL: http://www.optima.com
Establishment information: Established in 1988.
Company type: Private company
Business activities: Operates investment company.
Business type (SIC): Investment offices
Financial profile for 2011: Number of employees, 50
Corporate officers: D. Dixon Boardman, Chair., C.E.O. and C.I.O.; Robert Rans, Pres.; Geoffrey M. Lewis, C.F.O.; Robert A. Picard, C.I.O.
Board of director: D. Dixon Boardman, Chair.
Giving statement: Giving through the Optima Charitable Foundation.

The Optima Charitable Foundation

c/o Optima Fund Management
10 E. 53rd St.
New York, NY 10022-5244

Establishment information: Established in 2008 in NY.
Donors: Optima Fund Management, Ltd.; Optima Group Holdings, LLC.
Financial data (yr. ended 06/30/12): Assets, $261,150 (M); expenditures, $103,520; qualifying distributions, $100,100; giving activities include $100,100 for grants.
Purpose and activities: The foundation supports hospitals and organizations involved with education, animal welfare, optometry, muscular dystrophy, and religion.
Fields of interest: Education; Health care; Recreation.
Type of support: General/operating support; Scholarship funds.
Geographic limitations: Giving primarily in NY.
Support limitations: No grants to individuals.
Application information: Applications not accepted. Unsolicited requests for funds not accepted.
Officers: D. Dixon Boardman, Pres.; Nancy Littman, V.P.; Christine Rivera, Secy.; Frank Rocchio, Treas.
EIN: 261266975
Selected grants: The following grants are a representative sample of this grantmaker's funding activity:
$100,000 to Stowe School, Stowe, England, 2009.
$25,000 to Episcopal Diocese of Long Island, Garden City, NY, 2009.
$25,000 to Saint Johns of Lattingtown, Locust Valley, NY, 2009.
$12,500 to American Society for the Prevention of Cruelty to Animals, New York, NY, 2009.
$10,000 to Bascom Palmer Eye Institute, Miami, FL, 2009.
$10,000 to Muscular Dystrophy Association, New York, NY, 2009.
$10,000 to New York-Presbyterian Hospital, New York, NY, 2009.
$5,000 to American Society for the Prevention of Cruelty to Animals, New York, NY, 2009. For Equine Fund.
$5,000 to Environmental Defense Fund, New York, NY, 2009.
$5,000 to Juvenile Diabetes Research Foundation International, New York, NY, 2009.
$5,000 to National Center for Learning Disabilities, New York, NY, 2009.
$5,000 to North Shore University Hospital at Glen Cove, Glen Cove, NY, 2009.
$5,000 to Remote Area Medical Foundation, Knoxville, TN, 2009.
$1,000 to Greener Pastures Equine Sanctuary, Warwick, MD, 2009.

2820
Opus Corporation

(formerly Opus, Corp.)
10350 Bren Rd. W.
Minnetonka, MN 55343-9014
(952) 656-4444

Company URL: http://www.opus-group.com
Establishment information: Established in 1953.
Company type: Private company
Business activities: Develops real estate; provides architectural and engineering services; provides nonresidential general contract construction services; manages real estate; provides investment advisory services.
Business type (SIC): Real estate subdividers and developers; contractors/general nonresidential building; security and commodity services; real estate agents and managers; engineering, architectural, and surveying services
Corporate officers: Mark H. Rauenhorst, Chair. and C.E.O.; John Greer, Pres. and C.E.O.
Board of director: Mark H Rauenhorst, Chair.
Subsidiaries: Opus East, L.L.C., Rockville, MD; Opus National, L.L.P., Minnetonka, MN; Opus North Corp., Rosemont, IL; Opus Northwest, L.L.C., Minnetonka, MN; Opus South Corp., Alpharetta, GA; Opus West Corp., Phoenix, AZ
Offices: Irvine, Los Angeles, Pleasanton, Sacramento, San Jose, CA; Denver, CO; Maitland, Pensacola, Sunrise, Tampa, FL; Indianapolis, IN; Overland Park, KS; Novi, MI; St. Louis, MO; Westerville, OH; Portland, OR; Allentown, Plymouth Meeting, PA; Addison, Houston, Round Rock, TX; Bellevue, WA; Milwaukee, WI
Giving statement: Giving through the Enkel Foundation and the Opus Foundation.

Enkel Foundation

c/o Adler Management LLC
10350 Bren Rd. W.
Minnetonka, MN 55343

Establishment information: Established in 2004 in MN.
Donor: Arbeit Investment, LP.
Financial data (yr. ended 12/31/11): Assets, $1,039,537 (M); expenditures, $48,526; qualifying distributions, $32,070; giving activities include $32,070 for grants.
Fields of interest: Education; Safety/disasters; Human services.
Geographic limitations: Giving primarily in MN.
Support limitations: No grants to individuals.
Application information: Applications not accepted. Unsolicited requests for funds not accepted.
Officers and Directors:* Sarah Rauenhorst*, Chair. and Pres.; Sophie Kelley, V.P.; Charles Mahoney, V.P.; Peter Mahoney, V.P.; Mary Pickard, V.P.; Anne Mahoney*, Secy.; Joseph Mahoney*, Treas.
EIN: 202040284

Opus Foundation

10350 Bren Rd. W., Tax Dept.
Minnetonka, MN 55343-9014
URL: http://www.opus-group.com/AboutUs/Community

Establishment information: Established in 2000 in MN.
Donors: Opus Corp.; Opus, LLC; North Star Ventures.
Financial data (yr. ended 12/31/11): Assets, $66,989,041 (M); expenditures, $3,097,355; qualifying distributions, $3,097,355; giving activities include $2,428,412 for 79 grants (high: $1,000,000; low: $50).
Purpose and activities: The foundation supports programs designed to foster human and community development. Special emphasis is directed toward programs designed to promote early childhood education; youth development; workforce and employment training; and community revitalization.
Fields of interest: Education, early childhood education; Higher education; Theological school/education; Education; Employment, training; Employment; Boys & girls clubs; Youth development; Human services; Community development, neighborhood development; Community/economic development.
Type of support: Annual campaigns; Building/renovation; Capital campaigns; Endowments;

General/operating support; Program development; Scholarship funds; Sponsorships.
Geographic limitations: Giving limited to AZ, FL, and MN.
Support limitations: No grants to individuals.
Application information: Applications not accepted. Contributes only to pre-selected organizations.
Officers and Directors:* Mark H. Rauenhorst*, Pres.; Steven Polacek, V.P. and Secy.-Treas.; Margaret Bozesky, Tax Off.; John Albers; Mark Murphy; Joe Rauenhorst.
EIN: 411983284
Selected grants: The following grants are a representative sample of this grantmaker's funding activity:
$1,000,000 to Marquette University, Milwaukee, WI, 2010.
$40,000 to Habitat for Humanity, Twin Cities, Minneapolis, MN, 2010.
$40,000 to United Way, Greater Twin Cities, Minneapolis, MN, 2010.
$35,000 to Opportunities Industrialization Center, Summit Academy, Minneapolis, MN, 2010.
$35,000 to YMCA of Metropolitan Milwaukee, Milwaukee, WI, 2010.
$25,257 to Girl Scouts of the U.S.A., Milwaukee, WI, 2010.
$25,000 to Minnesota Architectural Foundation, Minneapolis, MN, 2010.
$20,000 to Mattie Rhodes Center, Kansas City, MO, 2010.
$15,000 to Saint Marcus Lutheran School, Milwaukee, WI, 2010.
$5,000 to Catholic Charities of the Archdiocese of Chicago, Chicago, IL, 2010.

2821
Oracle Corporation

(formerly Ozark Holding Inc.)
500 Oracle Pkwy.
Redwood City, CA 94065-1675
(650) 506-7000

Company URL: http://www.oracle.com
Establishment information: Established in 1977.
Company type: Public company
Company ticker symbol and exchange: ORCL/NASDAQ
Business activities: Develops, manufactures, markets, distributes, and services database and middleware software and applications software.
Business type (SIC): Computer services
Financial profile for 2012: Number of employees, 115,000; assets, $78,327,000,000; sales volume, $37,121,000,000; pre-tax net income, $12,962,000,000; expenses, $23,415,000,000; liabilities, $34,639,000,000
Fortune 1000 ranking: 2012—80th in revenues, 18th in profits, and 77th in assets
Forbes 2000 ranking: 2012—259th in sales, 40th in profits, and 310th in assets
Corporate officers: Jeffrey O. Henley, Chair.; Lawrence J. Ellison, C.E.O.; Safra A. Catz, Co-Pres. and C.F.O.; Mark V. Hurd, Co-Pres.; Mark Sunday, Sr. V.P. and C.I.O.; Dorian E. Daley, Sr. V.P., Genl. Counsel, and Secy.; Cindy Reese, Sr. V.P., Opers.
Board of directors: Jeffrey O. Henley, Chair.; Jeffrey S. Berg; H. Raymond Bingham; Michael J. Boskin; Safra A. Catz; Bruce R. Chizen; George H. Conrades; Lawrence J. Ellison; Hector Garcia-Molina; Mark V. Hurd; Naomi O. Seligman
Subsidiaries: Delphi Asset Management Corp., Reno, NV; Oracle Caribbean, Inc., Hato Rey, PR; Siebel Systems, Inc., San Mateo, CA
Office: Pleasanton, CA
International operations: Argentina; Australia; Austria; Barbados; Belgium; Bermuda; Bosnia-Herzegovina; Brazil; British Virgin Islands; Canada; Cayman Islands; Chile; China; Colombia; Costa Rica; Croatia; Cyprus; Czech Republic; Denmark; Egypt; Finland; France; Germany; Greece; Hong Kong; Hungary; India; Indonesia; Ireland; Israel; Italy; Japan; Jersey; Kazakhstan; Luxembourg; Malaysia; Mauritius; Mexico; Netherlands; Netherlands Antilles; New Zealand; Nigeria; Norway; Pakistan; Peru; Philippines; Poland; Portugal; Romania; Saudi Arabia; Serbia; Singapore; Slovakia; Slovenia; South Africa; South Korea; Spain; Sweden; Switzerland; Taiwan; Thailand; Turkey; United Arab Emirates; United Kingdom; Venezuela; Vietnam
Historic mergers: PeopleSoft, Inc. (January 7, 2005); Sun Microsystems, Inc. (January 27, 2010)
Giving statement: Giving through the Oracle Corporation Contributions Program and the Oracle Education Foundation.
Company EIN: 542185193

Oracle Corporation Contributions Program

500 Oracle Pkwy.
Redwood City, CA 94065 (650) 506-7000
URL: http://www.oracle.com/us/corporate/citizenship/index.html

Contact: Rosalie Gann, Dir. of Global Citizenship
Purpose and activities: As a complement to its foundation, Oracle makes charitable contributions to nonprofit organizations. Emphasis is given to organizations involved with science, technology, engineering, and math (STEM) education. Support is given on a national and international basis.
Fields of interest: Elementary/secondary education; Engineering school/education; Health care; Food banks; Safety/disasters; Boys clubs; Girls clubs; Mathematics; Engineering/technology; Science.
Program:
Matching Gift Program: When a disaster occurs, Oracle matches employee contributions to disaster relief dollar-for-dollar. To make a significant impact and speed aid to those in need, the company typically selects one or two nonprofit organizations working in the disaster zone as recipients of funds.
Type of support: Continuing support; Employee matching gifts; Employee volunteer services; General/operating support; In-kind gifts; Use of facilities.
Geographic limitations: Giving on a national and international basis in areas of company operations.
Application information: Applications not accepted.

2822
Orange and Rockland Utilities, Inc.

1 Blue Hill Plz.
Pearl River, NY 10965 (845) 352-6000

Company URL: http://www.oru.com
Establishment information: Established in 1899.
Company type: Subsidiary of a public company
Business activities: Generates, transmits, and distributes electricity; transmits and distributes natural gas.
Business type (SIC): Combination utility services
Financial profile for 2012: Number of employees, 1,070
Corporate officers: John McAvoy, Pres. and C.E.O.; Louis M. Bevilacqua, C.F.O. and Cont.; Yoram Bronicki, C.O.O.; Francis W. Peverly, V.P., Opers.; Nancy Jakobs, V.P., Human Resources
Subsidiaries: Pike County Light & Power Co., Milford, PA; Rockland Electric Co., Saddle River, NJ
Giving statement: Giving through the Orange and Rockland Utilities, Inc. Corporate Giving Program.

Orange and Rockland Utilities, Inc. Corporate Giving Program

c/o Community Investment Prog.
1 Blue Hill Plz.
Pearl River, NY 10965 (845) 577-2545
Application contact: Lisa Culhane; URL: http://www.oru.com/aboutoru/communitysupport/index.html

Contact: Lisa Feger
Purpose and activities: Orange and Rockland makes charitable contributions to nonprofit organizations involved with education, the environment, and cultural and public safety programs. Support is limited to areas of company operations in northern New Jersey, New York, and the northeastern corner of Pennsylvania.
Fields of interest: Arts, cultural/ethnic awareness; Education; Environment; Safety/disasters.
Programs:
NJ Shares: NJ SHARES provides financial assistance to Rockland Electric Company customers who find themselves unable to pay their home-heating bills because of emergency conditions. These grants are funded by contributions from thousands of other Rockland Electric Company customers. The shareholders of Consolidated Edison, Inc., Orange & Rockland's parent company, also make a contribution to the fund. Rockland Electric Company is a wholly owned subsidiary of Orange and Rockland Utilities, Inc.
The Neighbor Fund: Orange and Rockland awards financial assistance grants to Orange & Rockland and Pike County Light & Power customers who find themselves temporarily unable to pay their home-heating bills because of emergency conditions such as medical or financial challenges, a household breakup or layoff, or a tragic accident. The grants are funded by O&R and PCL&P customers and are matched by Consolidated Edison, Inc., O&R's parent company. The program is administered by local human service agencies in the community.
Type of support: Employee matching gifts; Employee volunteer services; General/operating support.
Geographic limitations: Giving limited to areas of company operations in northern NJ, NY, and the northeastern corner of PA.
Support limitations: No support for government or United Way-funded organizations, private grantmaking foundations, school districts or municipalities with taxing authority. No grants to individuals, or for advertising, administrative salaries, general operating expenses, large capital construction projects, beauty or talent contests, athletic scholarships, recreational activities such as leagues or teams, parties, banquets, or golf outings, electric or gas service donations, in-kind gifts, or events that have passed or will happen within 5 to 6 weeks of the application.
Publications: Application guidelines; Grants list.
Application information: Applications accepted. Request for less than $500 will not be considered. Support per project is limited to 1 contribution during any given year. A contributions committee reviews all requests. Application form required. Applicants should submit the following:
1) statement of problem project will address
2) population served
3) copy of IRS Determination Letter

4) brief history of organization and description of its mission
5) geographic area to be served
6) how project's results will be evaluated or measured
7) detailed description of project and amount of funding requested
8) name, address and phone number of organization
9) copy of current year's organizational budget and/or project budget

Local chapters of national organizations must include with application their local chapter letter. Monies are to be used within a 12-month period. Organizations must have an active governing board and officers to apply.

Initial approach: Download application form and mail proposal and application form to headquarters
Copies of proposal: 1
Committee meeting date(s): Monthly
Deadline(s): None
Final notification: 5 weeks

2823
OrePac Building Products, Inc.

30170 S.W. OrePac Ave.
Wilsonville, OR 97070-9794
(503) 685-5499

Company URL: http://www.orepac.com
Establishment information: Established in 1977.
Company type: Private company
Business activities: Sells building materials wholesale.
Business type (SIC): Lumber and construction materials—wholesale
Financial profile for 2009: Number of employees, 125
Corporate officers: Glenn Hart, Chair. and C.E.O.; Bradley Hart, Pres. and C.O.O.; Alan Kirk, C.F.O.
Board of director: Glenn Hart, Chair.
Giving statement: Giving through the Hart Family/OrePac Foundation.

The Hart Family/OrePac Foundation

c/o Foundation Source
501 Silverside Rd., Ste. 123
Wilmington, DE 19809-1377

Establishment information: Established in 2004 in OR.
Donors: OrePac Building Products, Inc.; Glenn Hart; Marilyn Hart.
Financial data (yr. ended 12/31/11): Assets, $2,334,927 (M); expenditures, $153,027; qualifying distributions, $105,500; giving activities include $105,500 for grants.
Purpose and activities: The foundation supports organizations involved with higher education, health, and human services.
Fields of interest: Health care; Human services; Community/economic development.
Type of support: General/operating support; Sponsorships.
Geographic limitations: Giving primarily in CA, ID, Portland, OR and WA.
Support limitations: No grants to individuals.
Application information: Applications not accepted. Unsolicited requests for funds not accepted.
Officers and Directors:* Glenn Hart*, Pres.; Marilyn Hart*, Secy.; Alan Kirk*, Treas.
EIN: 562445438

2824
Orlando Magic, Ltd.

8701 Maitland Summit Blvd.
Orlando, FL 32810-5915 (407) 916-2400

Company URL: http://www.nba.com/magic
Establishment information: Established in 1989.
Company type: Private company
Business activities: Operates professional basketball club.
Business type (SIC): Commercial sports
Corporate officers: Dan DeVos, Co-Chair.; Rich DeVos, Sr., Co-Chair.; Alex Martins, C.E.O.; Jim Fritz, C.F.O.; Chris D'Orso, V.P., Sales; Joel Glass, V.P., Comms.
Board of directors: Dan DeVos, Co-Chair.; Richard M. DeVos, Co-Chair.
Giving statement: Giving through the Orlando Magic, Ltd. Corporate Giving Program and the Orlando Magic Foundation, Inc.

Orlando Magic, Ltd. Corporate Giving Program

8701 Maitland Summit Blvd.
Orlando, FL 32810-5915 (407) 916-2400
E-mail: community@orlandomagic.com; Application e-mail address for the Community Ambassador Program: CommunityAmbassadors@OrlandoMagic.com; URL: http://www.nba.com/magic/community/community-index

Purpose and activities: As a complement to its foundation, the Orlando Magic makes charitable contributions of game tickets and memorabilia to nonprofit organizations directly. Support is given primarily in central Florida.
Fields of interest: Arts, services; Education, reading; Education, computer literacy/technology training; Education; Public health; Food services; Recreation, parks/playgrounds; Children, services; Family services; Human services, gift distribution; Military/veterans' organizations.
Type of support: Donated products; Employee volunteer services; General/operating support; In-kind gifts; Scholarship funds; Sponsorships.
Geographic limitations: Giving primarily in central FL.
Support limitations: No support for private schools, PTA's, or discriminatory organizations or organizations with values or philosophies contradictory to those of the Orlando Magic.
Publications: Application guidelines.
Application information: Applications accepted. An application form is required for game ticket donation requests. Applicants should submit the following:
1) name, address and phone number of organization
2) copy of IRS Determination Letter
3) detailed description of project and amount of funding requested

Community Ambassador Program requests should include the date, time, and details about the event and appearance. Donation proposals should include organization type, website, event date, type, and location, number of guests, and event sponsor/underwriter.

Initial approach: Complete online application form for donation requests. Email the Community Ambassador Program for appearance requests

Orlando Magic Foundation, Inc.

(also known as Orlando Magic Youth Foundation)
(formerly Orlando Magic Youth Fund)
8701 Maitland Summit Blvd.
Orlando, FL 32810-5915 (407) 916-2490
E-mail: omyf@orlandomagic.com; URL: http://www.nba.com/magic/photos/Philanthropy.pdf

Establishment information: Established in 1988 in FL.
Donor: Orlando Magic, Ltd.
Contact: Kari Conley, Exec. Dir.
Financial data (yr. ended 06/30/11): Revenue, $943,433; assets, $737,398 (M); gifts received, $852,855; expenditures, $390,000; giving activities include $390,000 for grants.
Purpose and activities: The foundation is committed to helping every child in central Florida realize their full potential, especially those most at risk, by supporting programs and partnerships that empower families and change lives.
Fields of interest: Education; Food services; Housing/shelter, homeless; Youth development, services; Youth development; Human services, mind/body enrichment; Human services Children.
Programs:
Grants: The foundation awards grants, ranging from $5,000 to $50,000, to organizations focusing on education, health and wellness, art, childhood hunger, and homelessness. Programs for which funds are being sought must administer services to low-income, at-risk children or families.
Valencia and Seminole State Magic Scholarship: The program provides three, two-year scholarships, respectively, at $3,000 per year given to students attending Valencia College and Seminole State College. A total of six high school seniors are awarded scholarships. Applicants must have a weighted cumulative GPA of 2.5 on a 4.0 scale, a minimum 880 SAT or 18 ACT score, be a graduating high school senior from Seminole, Orange, or Osceola counties, and demonstrate financial need.
Type of support: Program development; Program evaluation.
Geographic limitations: Giving limited to central FL, particularly in Orange, Seminole and Osceola counties.
Support limitations: No support for programs that have any religious components, legal aid societies, political, lobbying, or advocacy groups. No grants for operating expenses, fundraising, salary expenses, or capital requests for building and/or major improvements.
Publications: Application guidelines; Grants list; Newsletter; Program policy statement (including application guidelines).
Application information: Only organizations with letters of intent of interest to the foundation will be asked to submit proposals; unsolicited requests outside of the foundation's scholarship program otherwise not considered or acknowledged.

Initial approach: Submit letter of intent via email
Deadline(s): Apr. 1 for Grants; varies for scholarships

Officers and Directors:* Pam Devos*, Chair.; Linda Landman Gonzalez, Pres.; Kari Conley*, Secy.; Jeff Bissey*, Treas.; Otis Smith.
EIN: 592940230

2825
Orleans Realty LLC
100 W. 80th St.
New York, NY 10024-6343 (212) 362-5087

Establishment information: Established in 1978.
Company type: Private company
Business activities: Operates apartment buildings.
Business type (SIC): Real estate operators and lessors
Corporate officer: David Sterling, Partner
Giving statement: Giving through the Lavori Sterling Foundation, Inc.

Lavori Sterling Foundation, Inc.
100 W. 80th St.
New York, NY 10024-6343

Establishment information: Established as a company-sponsored operating foundation in 1999 in NY.
Donor: Orleans Realty LLC.
Financial data (yr. ended 12/31/11): Assets, $699,078 (M); gifts received, $30,133; expenditures, $72,489; qualifying distributions, $62,730; giving activities include $60,380 for 27 grants (high: $26,500; low: $120).
Purpose and activities: The foundation supports organizations involved with arts and culture, education, and civic affairs.
Fields of interest: Museums (art); Museums (natural history); Arts; Higher education; Law school/education; Education; Public affairs.
Type of support: Capital campaigns; General/operating support.
Support limitations: No grants to individuals.
Application information: Applications not accepted. Unsolicited requests for funds not accepted.
Officers: Nora Lavori, Pres.; David Bennett Sterling, V.P. and Treas.; Alexander Sterling, V.P.; Liana Sterling, Secy.
EIN: 134067505

2826
Orrick, Herrington & Sutcliffe LLP
405 Howard St.
San Francisco, CA 94105 (415) 773-5700

Company URL: http://www.orrick.com/
Establishment information: Established in 1863.
Company type: Private company
Business activities: Operates law firm.
Business type (SIC): Legal services
Financial profile for 2011: Number of employees, 1,100
Corporate officers: Ralph H. Baxter, Jr., Chair. and C.E.O.; P. Douglas Benson, C.O.O.; Patrick Tisdale, C.I.O.
Board of director: Ralph H. Baxter, Jr., Chair.
Offices: Los Angeles, Sacramento, CA; Washington, DC; New York, NY
Giving statement: Giving through the Orrick, Herrington & Sutcliffe LLP Pro Bono Program and the Orrick, Herrington & Sutcliffe Foundation.

Orrick, Herrington & Sutcliffe LLP Pro Bono Program
The Orrick Bldg.
405 Howard St.
San Francisco, CA 94105-2669 (212) 506-5100
E-mail: rkathawala@orrick.com; Additional tel.: (415) 773-5700, fax: (415) 773-5759; URL: http://www.orrick.com/about/probono/index.asp

Contact: Rene Kathawala, Pro Bono Counsel
Fields of interest: Legal services.
Type of support: Pro bono services - legal.
Application information: A Pro Bono Committee manages the pro bono program.

Orrick, Herrington & Sutcliffe Foundation
2121 Main St.
Wheeling, WV 26003-2809 (304) 231-2766

Establishment information: Established in 1999 in CA.
Financial data (yr. ended 12/31/10): Revenue, $2,121; assets, $118,990 (M); gifts received, $2,068; expenditures, $1,450,198; giving activities include $1,450,198 for 95 grants (high: $78,000; low: $300).
Fields of interest: Crime/law enforcement; Human services.
Officers and Directors:* Ralph H. Baxter, Jr.*, C.E.O.; Douglas P. Benson, C.O.O.; Mark R. Levie*, Secy.; Alan G. Benjamin; J. Peter Coll; Carl F. Lyon.
EIN: 943372036

2827
Orscheln Group
1177 N. Morley St.
P.O. Box 280
Moberly, MO 65270-2736 (660) 263-4377

Company URL: http://www.orscheln.com/
Establishment information: Established in 1960.
Company type: Subsidiary of a private company
Business activities: Manufactures automotive and industrial brakes.
Business type (SIC): Motor vehicles and equipment
Corporate officers: Barry L. Orscheln, C.E.O.; William L. Orschein, Pres.
Giving statement: Giving through the Orscheln Industries Foundation, Inc.

Orscheln Industries Foundation, Inc.
P.O. Box 280
Moberly, MO 65270-0280 (660) 263-4377
Application address: c/o Scholarship Committee, P.O. Box 266, Moberly, MO, 65270

Establishment information: Established in 1968 in MO.
Donors: ADEO, LLC; AGAO, LLC; Orscheln Co.
Contact: R. Brent Bradshaw
Financial data (yr. ended 09/30/11): Assets, $17,278,757 (M); expenditures, $1,120,689; qualifying distributions, $1,024,156; giving activities include $1,024,156 for grants.
Purpose and activities: The foundation supports organizations involved with performing arts, theater, education, health, Alzheimer's disease, human services, and Catholicism and awards college scholarships.
Fields of interest: Performing arts; Performing arts, theater; Secondary school/education; Higher education; Education; Health care; Alzheimer's disease; YM/YWCAs & YM/YWHAs; Children/youth, services; Developmentally disabled, centers & services; Homeless, human services; Human services; United Ways and Federated Giving Programs; Catholic agencies & churches.
Program:
Orscheln Industries Foundation Scholarships: The foundation awards college scholarships to graduating seniors from Cairo, Higbee, Madison, Moberly, and Western High Schools in Randolph County, MO. Applicants must have of a GPA of 3.5 and excel in academic achievement and leadership ability. The award consists of $500 per semester to assist the student in meeting educational expenses. A limited number of college scholarships are also awarded to dependent children of full-time employees of Orscheln and affiliated companies.
Type of support: Annual campaigns; Building/renovation; Continuing support; Employee-related scholarships; General/operating support; Scholarship funds; Scholarships—to individuals.
Geographic limitations: Giving primarily in MO.
Publications: Application guidelines.
Application information: Applications accepted. A personal interview may be required for scholarships. Application form required.
Initial approach: Contact foundation for application form
Deadline(s): Apr. 1 for scholarships
Officers and Directors:* W. L. Orscheln*, Chair., Exec. V.P., and Treas.; D. W. Orscheln*, Pres.; James L. O'Loughlin*, Sr. V.P., Secy., Genl. Counsel, and Exec. Dir.; Phillip A. Orscheln*, Exec. V.P.; R. J. Orscheln, Exec. V.P.; W. C. Orscheln.
EIN: 237115623
Selected grants: The following grants are a representative sample of this grantmaker's funding activity:
$200,000 to YMCA, Randolph Area, Moberly, MO, 2011.
$114,640 to Diocese of Jefferson City, Jefferson City, MO, 2011.
$46,026 to United Way of Randolph County, Moberly, MO, 2011.
$37,500 to Moberly Area Community College, Moberly, MO, 2011. For scholarships.
$15,000 to Carroll College, Helena, MT, 2011.
$13,640 to Alzheimers Association, Columbia, MO, 2011.
$12,500 to Arrow Rock Lyceum Theater, Arrow Rock, MO, 2011.
$10,000 to Safe Passage, Moberly, MO, 2011.
$5,000 to Avila University, Kansas City, MO, 2011.
$5,000 to Saint Louis Roman Catholic Theological Seminary, Saint Louis, MO, 2011.

2828
Ortec International, Inc.
505 Gentry Memorial Hwy
P.O. Box 1469
Easley, SC 29640 (864) 859-1471

Company URL: http://www.ortecinc.com
Establishment information: Established in 1980.
Company type: Private company
Business activities: Operates polymer technology company.
Business type (SIC): Chemicals and allied products
Corporate officers: Costa Papastephanou, C.E.O.; Freda Lark, Mgr.
Giving statement: Giving through the Ortec, Inc. Contributions Program and the Brotherton Foundation.

Ortec, Inc. Contributions Program

505 Gentry Memorial Hwy.
Easley, SC 29640-1165 (864) 859-1471
URL: http://www.ortecinc.com/citizenship.php

Purpose and activities: As a complement to its foundation, Ortec makes charitable contributions to nonprofit organizations directly. Support is given primarily in areas of company operations.
Fields of interest: Arts; Education; Food services; Human services.
Type of support: Employee volunteer services; General/operating support.
Geographic limitations: Giving primarily in areas of company operations.

The Brotherton Foundation

524 Sheffield Rd.
Easley, SC 29642-3405

Establishment information: Established in 2006.
Donor: Ortec, Inc.
Financial data (yr. ended 12/31/11): Assets, $1,618,922 (M); gifts received, $100,000; expenditures, $79,162; qualifying distributions, $66,250; giving activities include $66,250 for grants.
Fields of interest: Education; Health organizations; Human services.
Application information: Applications not accepted.
Trustees: Carmen K. Brotherton; David L. Brotherton.
EIN: 205623767

2829
The Orthopaedic Center

(also known as TOC)
Franklin Medical Tower
927 Franklin St.
Huntsville, AL 35801-4305 (256) 539-2728

Company URL: http://www.visittoc.com/
Establishment information: Established in 1982.
Company type: Private company
Business activities: Operates medical practice.
Business type (SIC): Offices and clinics/doctors'
Corporate officer: Jeff Hamilton, Mgr.
Giving statement: Giving through the TOC Foundation.

TOC Foundation

927 Franklin St.
Huntsville, AL 35801-4306
E-mail: blauderdale@visittoc.com; URL: http://www.tocfoundation.com/

Establishment information: Established in 2005 in AL.
Donors: The Orthopaedic Center; Apatech, Inc.
Financial data (yr. ended 12/31/11): Assets, $5,502 (M); gifts received, $100; expenditures, $5,381; qualifying distributions, $3,750; giving activities include $3,750 for 2 grants (high: $2,900; low: $850).
Purpose and activities: The foundation supports the advancement and development of orthopaedic science and technology through research, training, and education.
Fields of interest: Medical school/education; Orthopedics research.
Type of support: Grants to individuals; Research; Sponsorships.
Geographic limitations: Giving primarily in Huntsville, AL.
Application information: Applications not accepted. Unsolicited requests for funds not accepted.
Trustees: T. Joe Akin, Jr.; Barney Heyward; Mark A. Leberte, M.D.; Oscar N. Maxwell; Howard G. Miller, M.D.
EIN: 202821421

2830
The Orvis Company, Inc.

178 Conservation Way
Sunderland, VT 05250-4465
(802) 362-3622

Company URL: http://www.orvis.com/
Establishment information: Established in 1856.
Company type: Private company
Business activities: Manufactures and distributes fishing rods.
Business type (SIC): Games, toys, and sporting and athletic goods; nonstore retailers
Corporate officers: Leigh H. Perkins, Sr., Chair.; Leigh H. Perkins, Jr., Co-C.E.O.; Perk Perkins, Co-C.E.O.; Brian Gowen, V.P., C.O.O., and C.F.O.; William Wood, V.P., Corp. Cont.; Jim Evans, V.P., Human Resources
Board of director: Leigh H. Perkins, Sr., Chair.
Subsidiary: The Orvis Company, Roanoke, VA
Giving statement: Giving through the Orvis-Perkins Foundation.

The Orvis-Perkins Foundation

(formerly The Leigh H. Perkins Foundation)
1030 Hanna Bldg.
1422 Euclid Ave.
Cleveland, OH 44115-2001 (216) 621-0465

Establishment information: Established in 1985 in OH.
Donor: The Orvis Co., Inc.
Contact: Marilyn Best, Secy.-Treas.
Financial data (yr. ended 12/31/11): Assets, $2,300,744 (M); expenditures, $348,115; qualifying distributions, $337,942; giving activities include $337,942 for grants.
Purpose and activities: The foundation supports museums and historical societies and organizations involved with the environment and animals and wildlife.
Fields of interest: Museums (natural history); Museums (specialized); Historic preservation/historical societies; Higher education; Environment, natural resources; Environment, water resources; Environment; Animals/wildlife, preservation/protection.
Type of support: General/operating support.
Geographic limitations: Giving primarily in Washington, DC, FL, and OH.
Application information: Applications accepted. Application form not required.
Initial approach: Proposal
Deadline(s): None
Officers and Directors: Leigh H. Perkins, Sr., Pres.; Romi M. Perkins, V.P.; Marilyn Best, Secy.-Treas.; David D. Perkins; Leigh H. Perkins, Jr.; Mary B. Perkins; Melissa M. Perkins.
EIN: 341496755
Selected grants: The following grants are a representative sample of this grantmaker's funding activity:
$30,000 to National Fish and Wildlife Foundation, Washington, DC, 2011.
$20,000 to Theodore Roosevelt Conservation Partnership, Washington, DC, 2011.
$20,000 to Trout Unlimited, Arlington, VA, 2011.
$10,942 to Cleveland Museum of Natural History, Cleveland, OH, 2011.

2831
Osborn Maledon, PA

The Phoenix Plz.
2929 N. Central Ave., 21st Fl.
Phoenix, AZ 85012-2793 (602) 640-9000

Company URL: http://www.omlaw.com
Company type: Private company
Business activities: Operates law firm.
Business type (SIC): Legal services
Giving statement: Giving through the Osborn Maledon, PA Pro Bono Program.

Osborn Maledon, PA Pro Bono Program

The Phoenix Plz.
2929 N. Central Ave., 21st Fl.
Phoenix, AZ 85012-2793 (602) 640-9391
E-mail: tlowe@omlaw.com; Additional tel.: (602) 640-9000; URL: http://www.omlaw.com/about-community.html

Contact: Thayne Lowe, Chair, Pro Bono Comm.
Fields of interest: Legal services.
Type of support: Pro bono services - legal.
Geographic limitations: Giving primarily in areas of company operations in Phoenix, AZ.
Application information: A Pro Bono Committee manages the pro bono program.

2832
OSCO Industries, Inc.

734 11th Chillicothe St.
Portsmouth, OH 45662 (740) 354-3183

Company URL: http://www.oscoind.com
Establishment information: Established in 1872.
Company type: Private company
Business activities: Manufactures gray iron castings.
Business type (SIC): Iron and steel foundries
Corporate officers: John Burke, C.E.O.; John M. Burke, Pres.; Philip L. Vetter, V.P., Finance
Giving statement: Giving through the OSCO Industries Foundation.

OSCO Industries Foundation

P.O. Box 1388
Portsmouth, OH 45662-1388

Establishment information: Established in 1961 in OH.
Donor: OSCO Industries, Inc.
Contact: John M. Burke, Chair.
Financial data (yr. ended 12/31/11): Assets, $75,593 (M); gifts received, $61,000; expenditures, $63,080; qualifying distributions, $63,000; giving activities include $63,000 for 7 grants (high: $25,000; low: $1,000).
Purpose and activities: The foundation supports organizations involved with higher education, the environment, and wildlife.
Fields of interest: Higher education; Environment, natural resources; Environment, forests; Animals/wildlife; United Ways and Federated Giving Programs.
Type of support: Equipment; General/operating support.

Support limitations: No grants to individuals.
Application information: Applications accepted. Application form not required.
Initial approach: Proposal
Deadline(s): None
Officer: John M. Burke, Chair.
Trustees: Jeffrey A. Burke; Philip L. Vetter.
EIN: 316025158

2833
Oshkosh Corporation

(formerly Oshkosh Truck Corporation)
2307 Oregon St.
P.O. Box 2566
Oshkosh, WI 54903-2566 (920) 235-9150
FAX: (920) 233-9251

Company URL: http://www.oshkoshcorporation.com
Establishment information: Established in 1917.
Company type: Public company
Company ticker symbol and exchange: OSK/NYSE
Business activities: Manufactures specialized heavy duty trucks and transportation equipment.
Business type (SIC): Motor vehicles and equipment; machinery/construction, mining, and materials handling
Financial profile for 2012: Number of employees, 13,200; assets, $4,947,800,000; sales volume, $8,180,900,000; pre-tax net income, $286,700,000; expenses, $7,814,900,000; liabilities, $3,094,300,000
Fortune 1000 ranking: 2012—322nd in revenues, 545th in profits, and 599th in assets
Corporate officers: Richard M. Donnelly, Chair.; Charles L. Szews, C.E.O.; Wilson R. Jones, Pres. and C.O.O.; David M. Sagehorn, Exec. V.P. and C.F.O.; Michael K. Rohrkaste, Exec. V.P. and C.A.O.; Bryan J. Blankfield, Exec. V.P., Genl. Counsel, and Secy.; Gary W. Schmiedel, Exec. V.P., Tech.; Thomas J. Polnaszek, Sr. V.P., Finance and Cont.; Scott R. Grennier, Sr. V.P. and Treas.; Dave Schecklman, V.P. and C.I.O.; J. Chris Freeders, V.P., Finance; John Daggett, V.P., Comms.
Board of directors: Richard M. Donnelly, Chair.; Michael W. Grebe; Peter B. Hamilton; Kathleen J. Hempel; Leslie F. Kenne; J. Peter Mosling, Jr.; Stephen D. Newlin; Craig P. Omtvedt; Duncan J. Palmer; John S. Shiely; Richard G. Sim; Charles L. Szews; William Scott Wallace
Subsidiaries: Kewaunee Fabrications, L.L.C., Kewaunee, WI; McNeilus Companies, Inc., Dodge Center, MN; Oshkosh Logistics Corp., Oshkosh, WI; Pierce Manufacturing Inc., Bradenton, FL; Summit Performance Systems, Inc., Oshkosh, WI; Total Mixer Technologies, L.L.C., Oshkosh, WI
International operations: Belgium; Mauritius; United Arab Emirates; United Kingdom
Giving statement: Giving through the Oshkosh Corporation Foundation, Inc.
Company EIN: 390520270

Oshkosh Corporation Foundation, Inc.

(formerly Oshkosh Truck Foundation, Inc.)
2307 Oregon St.
Oshkosh, WI 54902-2566
Application address: P.O. Box 2566, Oshkosh, WI 54903-2566, tel.: (920) 235-9151 ext. 22206

Establishment information: Incorporated in 1960 in WI.
Donors: Oshkosh Corp.; Oshkosh Truck Corp.
Contact: Jana Heft
Financial data (yr. ended 09/30/11): Assets, $2,451,426 (M); gifts received, $1,000,000; expenditures, $628,766; qualifying distributions, $624,625; giving activities include $624,625 for grants.
Purpose and activities: The foundation supports community foundations and firefighters and organizations involved with education, health, hunger, housing development, youth development, and human services. Special emphasis is directed toward programs designed to address basic needs and cultural development.
Fields of interest: Performing arts centers; Arts; Education; Health care, clinics/centers; Health care; Food services; Food banks; Housing/shelter, development; Disasters, fire prevention/control; Boys & girls clubs; Big Brothers/Big Sisters; Boy scouts; Youth development; American Red Cross; YM/YWCAs & YM/YWHAs; Family services, domestic violence; Human services; Foundations (community); United Ways and Federated Giving Programs.
Type of support: Annual campaigns; Continuing support; General/operating support; Program development.
Geographic limitations: Giving primarily in areas of company operations in Oshkosh and the Winnebago County, WI, area.
Support limitations: No grants for start-up needs, debt reduction, land acquisition, special projects, research, publications, conferences, or endowments; no loans; no matching gifts.
Application information: Applications accepted. Application form not required. Applicants should submit the following:
1) detailed description of project and amount of funding requested
2) brief history of organization and description of its mission
3) copy of IRS Determination Letter
Initial approach: Proposal
Copies of proposal: 1
Board meeting date(s): Mar., June, Sept., and Dec.
Deadline(s): None
Officers and Trustees:* Robert G. Bohn*, Pres.; Connie S. Stellmacher, V.P. and Secy.; David M. Sagehorn*, V.P. and Treas.; Bryan J. Blankfield*, V.P.; Mathew K. Rohrkaste, V.P.; Charles L. Szews*, V.P.
EIN: 396062129

2834
Osram Sylvania Inc.

100 Endicott St.
Danvers, MA 01923-3623 (978) 777-1900

Company URL: http://www.sylvania.com
Establishment information: Established in 1901.
Company type: Subsidiary of a foreign company
Business activities: Manufactures lighting products.
Business type (SIC): Lighting and wiring equipment/electric
Financial profile for 2010: Number of employees, 600
Corporate officers: Rick Leaman, Pres. and C.E.O.; Jean-Paul Michel, Exec. V.P. and C.F.O.; Francis M. Piscitelli, Sr. V.P., Sales and Mktg.
Board of director: Rick Leaman
Plants: Watertown, CT; Seymour, IN; Versailles, Winchester, KY; Bangor, Waldoboro, ME; Exeter, Hillsboro, Manchester, NH; Maybrook, NY; St. Marys, Towanda, Warren, Wellsboro, York, PA; Central Falls, RI
Giving statement: Giving through the Osram Sylvania Inc. Corporate Giving Program.

Osram Sylvania Inc. Corporate Giving Program

100 Endicott St.
Danvers, MA 01923-3782 (978) 777-1900
FAX: (978) 750-2152; URL: http://www.sylvania.com/Sustainability/SocialResponsibility/

Purpose and activities: Osram Sylvania makes charitable contributions to nonprofit organizations involved with historic preservation, education, breast cancer, disaster relief, and human services. Support is given in areas of company operations.
Fields of interest: Historic preservation/historical societies; Education; Breast cancer; Disasters, preparedness/services; Disasters, fire prevention/control; Big Brothers/Big Sisters; Homeless, human services; Human services; United Ways and Federated Giving Programs.
Programs:
Employee Matching Gifts: Osram Sylvania matches contributions made by its employees to educational institutions.
Employee Volunteer Grants: Osram Sylvania awards grants to organizations with which its employees volunteer.
Type of support: Employee matching gifts; Employee volunteer services; Employee-related scholarships; General/operating support; Matching/challenge support; Scholarship funds; Sponsorships.
Geographic limitations: Giving primarily in areas of company operations.

2835
Otis Elevator Company

10 Farm Springs Rd.
Farmington, CT 06032-2577
(860) 676-6000

Company URL: http://www.otis.com
Establishment information: Established in 1853.
Company type: Subsidiary of a public company
Business activities: Manufactures elevators, escalators, and moving walkways.
Business type (SIC): Machinery/construction, mining, and materials handling
Financial profile for 2006: Number of employees, 61,103; sales volume, $10,300,000,000
Corporate officers: Pedro Baranda, Pres.; Angelo Messina, V.P. and C.F.O.; Johan Bill, V.P., Genl. Counsel, and Secy.; Vincent Della Val, V.P., Opers.; Maureen Waterston, V.P., Human Resources
Subsidiaries: ACM Elevator Co., Des Plaines, IL; Delta Elevator Service Corp., Boston, MA; North American Elevator Services Co., Farmington, CT; Vertical Transportation Svcs., Seattle, WA
Giving statement: Giving through the Otis Elevator Company Contributions Program.

Otis Elevator Company Contributions Program

10 Farm Springs Rd.
Farmington, CT 06032-2577
URL: http://www.otisworldwide.com/d40-community.html

Purpose and activities: Otis makes charitable contributions to nonprofit organizations involved with arts and culture, education, health and human services, and public policy. Special emphasis is directed toward programs designed to provide engineering, science, and technology education. Support is given on a national and international basis.

Fields of interest: Arts; Education, reading; Education; Health care; Food services; Housing/shelter, development; Athletics/sports, Special Olympics; Youth development, business; Child development, services; Human services, gift distribution; Developmentally disabled, centers & services; Human services; United Ways and Federated Giving Programs; Public policy, research.
Programs:
President's Award: The company honors employees or teams of employees who have made outstanding contributions in process improvement, safety, customer service, and innovation. The award includes a $5,000 grant to be donated to their charities of choice.
Volunteer Grant Program: The company awards $250 grants to nonprofit organization with which employees of Otis volunteer.
Type of support: Employee volunteer services; General/operating support.
Geographic limitations: Giving on a national basis in areas of company operations; giving also to international programs.
Support limitations: No support for partisan political organizations or religious organizations not of direct benefit to the entire community. No grants to individuals, or for controversial social causes on which there are strong differences of opinion or endowments.
Publications: Application guidelines.
Application information: Applications accepted. Additional information may be requested at a later date. Telephone calls are not encouraged. Application form required.
Initial approach: Complete online application form
Deadline(s): Between Mar. 1 and June 1
Final notification: 1st quarter

2836
Otter Tail Corporation

(formerly Otter Tail Power Company)
215 S. Cascade St.
P.O. Box 496
Fergus Falls, MN 56538-0496
(866) 410-8780
FAX: (218) 998-3165

Company URL: http://www.ottertail.com
Establishment information: Established in 1907.
Company type: Public company
Company ticker symbol and exchange: OTTR/NASDAQ
Business activities: Generates, transmits, and distributes electricity; manufactures polyvinyl chloride and polyethylene pipe; manufactures waterfront equipment, wind towers, material and handling trays and horticultural containers, and stamped and fabricated metal parts; sells diagnostic medical equipment, patient monitoring equipment, and related supplies and accessories wholesale; produces dehydrated potato products.
Business type (SIC): Electric services; specialty foods/canned, frozen, and preserved; plastic products/miscellaneous; metal forgings and stampings; industrial and commercial machinery and computer equipment; engines and turbines; professional and commercial equipment—wholesale
Financial profile for 2012: Number of employees, 1,960; assets, $1,602,340,000; sales volume, $859,240,000; pre-tax net income, $41,100,000; expenses, $790,320,000; liabilities, $1,064,860,000
Corporate officers: Nathan I. Partain, Chair.; Edward J. McIntyre, Pres. and C.E.O.; Kevin G. Moug, Sr. V.P. and C.F.O.; George A. Koeck, Sr. V.P., Genl. Counsel, and Secy.; Michael J. Olsen, Sr. V.P., Corp. Comms. and Public Affairs; Paul Knutson, V.P., Human Resources
Board of directors: Nathan I. Partain, Chair.; Karen M. Bohn; John D. Erickson; Kathryn O. Johnson; Edward J. McIntyre; Mark Olson; Joyce Nelson Schuette; Gary J. Spies; James B. Stake
Subsidiaries: Aevenia, Inc., Moorhead, MN; BTD Manufacturing, Detroit Lakes, MN; DMI Industries, Fargo, ND; DMS Health Group, Fargo, ND; E.W. Wylie, West Fargo, ND; Foley Company, Kansas City, MO; Idaho Pacific, Ririe, ID; Northern Pipe Products, Fargo, ND; Shore Master, Fergus Falls, MN; T.O. Plastics, Clearwater, MN; Vinyltech, Phoenix, AZ
Division: Otter Tail Power Co., Fergus Falls, MN
Giving statement: Giving through the Otter Tail Power Company Contributions Program.
Company EIN: 270383995

Otter Tail Power Company Contributions Program

215 S. Cascade St.
Fergus Falls, MN 56537-2801
FAX: (218) 739-8218; E-mail: ckling@otpco.com; Tel. for Becky Luhning: (218) 739-8206; e-mail: bluhning@otpco.com; URL: https://www.otpco.com/AboutCompany/DonationsGrantsCommConnect/Pages/DonationsGrantsCommConnectMain.aspx

Contact: Cris Kling, Dir., Public Rels.; Becky Luhning
Financial data (yr. ended 12/31/10): Total giving, $400,000, including $400,000 for grants.
Purpose and activities: Otter Tail makes charitable contributions to nonprofit organizations involved with arts and culture, education, environmental research, environmental conservation, environmental education, health, human services, and community development. Special emphasis is directed toward scholarships designed to promote future workforce needs. Support is given primarily in areas of company operations.
Fields of interest: Arts; Elementary/secondary education; Education; Environment, research; Environment, natural resources; Environmental education; Health care; Children, services; Family services; Human services; Community/economic development.
Type of support: Annual campaigns; Building/renovation; Capital campaigns; Conferences/seminars; Continuing support; Donated equipment; Employee matching gifts; Employee volunteer services; Endowments; Equipment; General/operating support; In-kind gifts; Matching/challenge support; Program development; Research; Scholarship funds; Sponsorships; Use of facilities.
Geographic limitations: Giving primarily in areas of company operations, with emphasis on MN, ND, and SD.
Application information: Applications accepted. The Public Relations Department handles giving. A contributions committee reviews all requests. Application form required.
Initial approach: Complete online application form or download application form and mail to headquarters
Copies of proposal: 1
Committee meeting date(s): 2nd week of Mar., June, Sept., and Dec.
Deadline(s): 2 weeks prior to committee meetings
Final notification: 1 week to 3 months
Administrators: Cris King, Dir., Public Rels.; Nancy Heck, Financial Analyst; Mark Helland, V.P., Customer Svc.; Becky Luhning, Exec. Asst.; Mike Van Voorhis, Mgr., Customer Svc.
Number of staff: 1 part-time professional; 1 part-time support.
Selected grants: The following grants are a representative sample of this grantmaker's funding activity:
$32,000 to Bismarck State College, Bismarck, ND, 2010.
$18,000 to Lake Area Technical Institute, Watertown, SD, 2010.
$15,000 to Lakeland Hospice and Home Care, Fergus Falls, MN, 2010.
$14,000 to Mitchell Technical Institute Foundation, Mitchell, SD, 2010.
$12,500 to Lake Region Hospital Foundation, Fergus Falls, MN, 2010.
$12,000 to Minnesota State Community and Technical College, Moorhead, MN, 2010.
$10,710 to Scholarship America, Bloomington, MN, 2010.
$10,000 to Jamestown College, Jamestown, ND, 2010.
$10,000 to Minnesota State University, Moorhead, MN, 2010. For Minnesota Small Business Development Center.
$8,500 to University of North Dakota, Grand Forks, ND, 2010.

2837
Ounalashka Corporation

400 Salmon Way
P.O. Box 149
Unalaska, AK 99685 (907) 581-1276

Company URL: http://www.ounalashka.com
Establishment information: Established in 1973.
Company type: Native corporation
Business activities: Operates native corporation.
Business type (SIC): Nonclassifiable establishments
Corporate officers: Vincent M. Tutiakoff, Sr., Chair.; Richard A. Miller, C.E.O.; Denise M. Rankin, Pres. and V.P., Mktg.; Margaret A. Lekanoff, Secy.-Treas.; Chris Salts, Cont.
Board of directors: Vincent M. Tutiakoff, Sr., Chair.; Lois A. Burrece; Margaret A. Lekanoff; Nicholai E. Lekanoff; Sandra Moller; A. Barbara Rankin; Brenda A. Tellman; Janis L. Krukoff; Caroline Sue Williams
Giving statement: Giving through the Edna P. McCurdy Scholarship Foundation.

Edna P. McCurdy Scholarship Foundation

c/o Ounalashka Corp.
P.O. Box 149
Unalaska, AK 99685-0149 (907) 581-1276
E-mail: scholarships@ounalashka.com; URL: http://www.ounalashka.com/Edna%20P.%20McCurdy%20Scholarship%20Foundation.htm

Establishment information: Established in 1995 in AK.
Donor: Ounalashka Corp.
Contact: Chris Salts
Financial data (yr. ended 12/31/11): Assets, $638,088 (M); gifts received, $100,000; expenditures, $75,446; qualifying distributions, $72,798; giving activities include $70,734 for 12 grants to individuals (high: $10,000; low: $2,000).
Purpose and activities: The foundation awards college scholarships to shareholders and the descendants of shareholders of Ounalashka Corporation.
Fields of interest: Higher education.
Program:
Scholarships: The foundation awards scholarships of up to $5,000 to shareholders of

Ounalashka Corp. and their descendents. Scholarships are available for trade and career schools, Bachelor programs lasting five years, Masters programs lasting two years, and Ph.D. programs lasting one year. Funding for tuition, room, and board are only offered to full-time students living on campus. Students must meet certain criteria including a base GPA.
Type of support: Scholarships—to individuals.
Geographic limitations: Giving primarily in Unalaska, AK.
Publications: Application guidelines.
Application information: Applications accepted. Application form not required.
Applications should include transcripts; written evidence of acceptance from a school; estimation of school expenses; an essay; and 2 letters of recommendation.
Initial approach: Proposal
Deadline(s): None
Officer: Margaret A. Lekanoff, Pres.
Trustees: Teri Legrand; A. Barbara Rankin.
EIN: 920157058

2838
Our 365, Inc.

(formerly Growing Family, Inc.)
3613 Mueller Rd.
St. Charles, MO 63301 (639) 946-5115

Company URL: http://www.our365.com
Establishment information: Established in 1947.
Company type: Private company
Business activities: Provides photographic services; provides Internet shopping services; provides Internet information services.
Business type (SIC): Photographic portrait studios; computer services
Financial profile for 2009: Number of employees, 45
Giving statement: Giving through the Growing Family Foundation, Inc.

Growing Family Foundation, Inc.

3613 Mueller Rd.
Saint Charles, MO 63301-8003 (636) 946-5115
FAX: (866) 295-7540

Establishment information: Established in 2000 in MO.
Donor: Growing Family, Inc.
Contact: Janet Keith, Secy.
Financial data (yr. ended 12/31/11): Assets, $92,700 (M); gifts received, $15,488; expenditures, $20,143; qualifying distributions, $19,850; giving activities include $19,850 for grants.
Purpose and activities: The foundation awards grants to families in North America who have a child under the age of one.
Fields of interest: Family services.
International interests: Canada; Mexico.
Type of support: Grants to individuals.
Geographic limitations: Giving on a national basis.
Publications: Application guidelines.
Application information: Applications accepted. Application form required.
Initial approach: Proposal
Board meeting date(s): Monthly
Deadline(s): None
Officers: Thomas Schaefer, Pres.; Janet Keith, Secy.; Rose Buchholz, Treas.
EIN: 431877493

2839
Outokumpu American Brass, Inc.

70 Sayre St.
P.O. Box 981
Buffalo, NY 14207 (716) 879-6700

Company URL: http://www.outokumpu.com
Establishment information: Established in 1920.
Company type: Subsidiary of a foreign company
Business activities: Manufactures copper products.
Business type (SIC): Metal rolling and drawing/nonferrous
Corporate officers: Jyrki Juusela, Chair.; Warren E. Bartel, Pres.; Martin Degerth, Sr. V.P., Mktg.
Board of director: Jyrki Juusela, Chair.
Giving statement: Giving through the Outokumpu American Brass, Inc. Corporate Giving Program.

Outokumpu American Brass, Inc. Corporate Giving Program

70 Sayre St.
P.O. Box 981
Buffalo, NY 14240-0981 (716) 879-6700

Purpose and activities: Outokumpu American Brass makes charitable contributions to nonprofit organizations involved with education. Support is given primarily in Buffalo, New York.
Fields of interest: Education.
Type of support: Employee matching gifts; Employee volunteer services; General/operating support; Sponsorships.
Geographic limitations: Giving primarily in Buffalo, NY.

2840
Owen Industries, Inc.

501 Ave. H
Carter Lake, IA 51510-1513
(712) 347-5500

Company URL: http://www.owenind.com
Establishment information: Established in 1885.
Company type: Private company
Business activities: Manufactures and distributes fabricated structural metals.
Business type (SIC): Metal products/structural; metals and minerals, except petroleum—wholesale
Corporate officers: Robert E. Owen, Chair.; John Sunderman, Pres.; Keith Siebels, Sr. V.P., Sales; Edward Korbel, V.P., Finance and C.F.O.; Craig Bence, V.P. and C.I.O.
Board of director: Robert E. Owen, Chair.
Subsidiaries: Lincoln Steel, Lincoln, NE; Paxton & Vierling, Omaha, NE
Giving statement: Giving through the Owen Foundation.

The Owen Foundation

P.O. Box 1085
Omaha, NE 68101-1085 (712) 347-5500

Establishment information: Incorporated in 1959 in NE.
Donors: Owen Industries, Inc.; Paxton & Vierling Steel Co.; Missouri Valley Steel Co.; Northern Plains Steel Co.
Contact: Robert E. Owen, Pres.
Financial data (yr. ended 11/30/12): Assets, $487,844 (M); gifts received, $250,000; expenditures, $179,540; qualifying distributions, $174,550; giving activities include $174,550 for 16 grants (high: $100,750; low: $200).
Purpose and activities: The foundation supports art museums and organizations involved with opera, patient services, heart disease, equestrianism, youth, and Christianity.
Fields of interest: Arts; Recreation; Youth development.
Type of support: General/operating support.
Geographic limitations: Giving primarily in NE.
Support limitations: No grants to individuals.
Application information: Applications accepted. Application form not required.
Initial approach: Proposal
Deadline(s): None
Officers and Trustees:* Robert E. Owen*, Co-Pres.; Tyler R. Owen*, Co-Pres.; James Pfeffer*, Secy.
EIN: 476025298

2841
Owens & Minor, Inc.

9120 Lockwood Blvd.
Mechanicsville, VA 23116 (804) 723-7000
FAX: (804) 723-7100

Company URL: http://www.owens-minor.com
Establishment information: Established in 1882.
Company type: Public company
Company ticker symbol and exchange: OMI/NYSE
Business activities: Sells medical and surgical supplies wholesale.
Business type (SIC): Professional and commercial equipment—wholesale
Financial profile for 2012: Number of employees, 4,800; assets, $2,207,700,000; sales volume, $8,909,150,000; pre-tax net income, $183,360,000; expenses, $8,711,390,000; liabilities, $1,235,170,000
Fortune 1000 ranking: 2012—297th in revenues, 719th in profits, and 831st in assets
Corporate officers: Craig R. Smith, Chair., Pres., and C.E.O.; James L. Bierman, Exec. V.P. and C.O.O.; Richard W. Mears, Sr. V.P. and C.I.O.; Richard A. Meier, V.P. and C.F.O.; Grace R. Den Hartog, Sr. V.P., Genl. Counsel, and Corp. Secy.; Charles C. Colpo, Sr. V.P., Opers.; Erika T. Davis, Sr. V.P., Human Resources
Board of directors: Craig R. Smith, Chair.; Richard E. Fogg; John W. Gerdelman; Lemuel E. Lewis; Eddie N. Moore, Jr.; James E. Rogers; Robert C. Sledd; Craig R. Smith; Anne Marie Whittemore
Plants: Birmingham, Pelham, AL; Phoenix, AZ; Los Angeles, San Francisco, CA; Denver, CO; Fort Lauderdale, Jacksonville, Orlando, FL; Atlanta, Augusta, GA; Honolulu, HI; Hanover Park, IL; Indianapolis, IN; Des Moines, IA; Hebron, KY; New Orleans, LA; Hanover, MD; Boston, MA; Belleville, MI; Minneapolis, MN; Jackson, MS; St. Louis, MO; Omaha, NE; Bridgeton, NJ; Albuerque, NM; Kings Mountain, Raleigh, NC; Cincinnati, Glenwillow, OH; Oklahoma City, OK; Portland, OR; Allentown, Greensburg, PA; Knoxville, Memphis, TN; Dallas, Harlingen, Houston, TX; Salt Lake City, UT; Seattle, WA
International operations: British Virgin Islands
Giving statement: Giving through the Owens & Minor, Inc. Corporate Giving Program.
Company EIN: 541701843

Owens & Minor, Inc. Corporate Giving Program

c/o Donations Comm.
P.O. Box 27626
Richmond, VA 23261-7626

Contact: Hugh F. Gouldthorpe, Jr., Sr. V.P., Comms.
Purpose and activities: Owens & Minor makes charitable contributions to nonprofit organizations involved with healthcare and children. Support is given primarily in the Richmond, Virginia, area.
Fields of interest: Health care; Children, services.
Type of support: Employee volunteer services; General/operating support; Sponsorships.
Geographic limitations: Giving primarily in the Richmond, VA, area.
Support limitations: No support for political or religious organizations, golf tournaments, high school functions, or celebrity-related events.
Application information: Applications accepted. A contributions committee reviews all requests. Application form not required. Applicants should submit the following:
1) detailed description of project and amount of funding requested
Initial approach: Proposal to headquarters
Copies of proposal: 1
Committee meeting date(s): Every 6 to 8 weeks
Final notification: Following review

2842
Owens Corning

1 Owens Corning Pkwy.
Toledo, OH 43659-0001 (419) 248-8000
FAX: (419) 248-8445

Company URL: http://www.owenscorning.com
Establishment information: Established in 1938.
Company type: Public company
Company ticker symbol and exchange: OC/NYSE
Business activities: Manufactures building materials systems and composites systems.
Business type (SIC): Abrasive, asbestos, and nonmetallic mineral products
Financial profile for 2012: Number of employees, 15,000; assets, $7,568,000,000; sales volume, $5,172,000,000; expenses, $5,098,000,000; liabilities, $4,030,000,000
Fortune 1000 ranking: 2012—476th in revenues, 894th in profits, and 465th in assets
Corporate officers: Michael H. Thaman, Chair., Pres., and C.E.O.; Michael C. McMurray, Sr. V.P. and C.F.O.; John William Christy, Sr. V.P., Genl. Counsel, and Secy.; Daniel T. Smith, Sr. V.P., Human Resources; Kelly J. Schmidt, V.P. and Cont.
Board of directors: Michael H. Thaman, Chair.; Norman P. Blake, Jr.; J. Brian Ferguson; Ralph F. Hake; F. Philip Handy; Ann Iverson; James J. McMonagle; W. Howard Morris; Joseph F. Neely; Suzanne P. Nimocks; John D. Williams
Subsidiary: Fibreboard Corporation, Dallas, TX
Plants: Phenix City, AL; Fort Smith, AR; Compton, Santa Clara, CA; Denver, CO; Jacksonville, FL; Atlanta, Fairburn, Savannah, GA; Brookville, IN; Jessup, MD; Minneapolis, MN; Kansas City, MO; Kearny, Parsippany, NJ; Delmar, NY; Morehead City, NC; Granville, Medina, Mount Vernon, Newark, Tallmadge, OH; Oklahoma City, OK; Portland, OR; Hazleton, Huntingdon, PA; Aiken, Anderson, SC; Jackson, Memphis, TN; Amarillo, Houston, Irving, Waxahachie, TX; Salt Lake City, UT; Charleston, WV
International operations: Argentina; Australia; Belgium; Brazil; Canada; Cayman Islands; China; Cyprus; France; Germany; India; Italy; Japan; Mexico; Netherlands; Norway; Romania; Russia; Singapore; South Korea; Spain; Sweden; Switzerland; Thailand; United Kingdom; Uruguay
Giving statement: Giving through the Owens Corning Corporate Giving Program and the Owens Corning Foundation.
Company EIN: 432109021

Owens Corning Foundation

c/o Owens Corning World Headquarters
1 Owens Corning Pkwy., 2E
Toledo, OH 43659-1000 (419) 248-8000
FAX: (419) 325-3031;
E-mail: OCFoundation@owenscorning.com;
URL: http://sustainability.owenscorning.com/contents/Community-Alliances/OC-Foundation/

Establishment information: Established around 1960.
Donor: Owens Corning.
Contact: Simone Hayes, Pres.
Financial data (yr. ended 12/31/11): Assets, $10,411,709 (M); gifts received, $258,279; expenditures, $541,858; qualifying distributions, $498,535; giving activities include $498,535 for grants.
Purpose and activities: The foundation supports programs designed to provide access to education and affordable housing for those most in need, and organizations involved with arts and culture and civic betterment. Special emphasis is directed toward projects and organizations that promote diversity and social welfare; serve a broad sector of the community; and have a proven record of success.
Fields of interest: Arts; Elementary/secondary education; Education; Housing/shelter, development; Housing/shelter; Human services; Civil/human rights, equal rights; Community/economic development; United Ways and Federated Giving Programs; Public affairs.
Programs:
Matching Gift Program: The foundation matches contributions made employees and directors of Owens Corning to secondary and higher education institutions up to $2,500 per contributor, per year.
Scholarships: The foundation provides scholarship opportunities to children of employees of Owens Corning, including the National Merit and Canadian Scholarship program that awards scholarships for academic achievement.
Type of support: Employee matching gifts; Employee-related scholarships; In-kind gifts; Program development; Scholarship funds.
Geographic limitations: Giving on a national basis in areas of company operations, with emphasis on OH.
Support limitations: No support for religious, political, or discriminatory organizations or United Way supported agencies. No grants for travel, capital campaigns, general operating support, or special events, conferences, or sports competitions.
Publications: Program policy statement.
Application information: Applications not accepted. Unsolicited requests for funds not accepted.
Board meeting date(s): Quarterly
Officers and Directors:* Steve Krull*, Chair.; Simone Hayes*, Pres.; Rodney Nowland, Secy.; Mathew Fortunak, Treas.; Michael McMurray; Gary Niemen; Steven Vermeulen.
Number of staff: 1 part-time professional; 1 part-time support.
EIN: 341270856
Selected grants: The following grants are a representative sample of this grantmaker's funding activity:
$40,000 to United Way of Greater Toledo, Toledo, OH, 2010.
$27,500 to Toledo Symphony, Toledo, OH, 2010.
$20,000 to Toledo Community Foundation, Toledo, OH, 2010.
$7,000 to United Way, Licking County, Newark, OH, 2010.
$3,500 to United Way of Anderson County, Anderson, SC, 2010.
$2,500 to Darlington School, Rome, GA, 2010.
$2,500 to Episcopal High School, Alexandria, VA, 2010.
$2,000 to Habitat for Humanity International, Americus, GA, 2010.
$1,500 to Habitat for Humanity International, Americus, GA, 2010.
$1,250 to Dartmouth College, Hanover, NH, 2010.

2843
The Owens Group Inc.

(also known as OG)
619 Palisade Ave.
Englewood Cliffs, NJ 07632-1834
(201) 568-2300

Company URL: http://www.owensgroup.com
Establishment information: Established in 1957.
Company type: Private company
Business activities: Operates insurance and brokerage agency.
Business type (SIC): Insurance agents, brokers, and services
Corporate officers: Herbert Owens, Chair.; Robert Owens, Pres.
Board of director: Herbert Owens, Chair.
Giving statement: Giving through the Owens Group Foundation, Inc.

Owens Group Foundation, Inc.

619 Palisade Ave.
Englewood Cliffs, NJ 07632-1812 (201) 568-2300

Establishment information: Established in 1991 in NJ.
Donor: Owens Group Ltd.
Contact: Robert O. Owens, Pres. and Treas.
Financial data (yr. ended 12/31/11): Assets, $3,021 (M); gifts received, $17,296; expenditures, $18,700; qualifying distributions, $18,700; giving activities include $18,700 for 41 grants (high: $1,544; low: $25).
Fields of interest: Arts; Education; Human services.
Geographic limitations: Giving primarily in NJ and NY.
Support limitations: No grants to individuals.
Application information: Applications accepted. Application form required.
Initial approach: Letter
Deadline(s): None
Officers: Robert Owens, Pres. and Treas.; Margaret Bartolotto, Secy.
EIN: 223096419

2844
Owens-Illinois, Inc.

1 Michael Owens Way
Perrysburg, OH 43551-2999
(567) 336-5000

Company URL: http://www.o-i.com
Establishment information: Established in 1903.
Company type: Public company
Company ticker symbol and exchange: OI/NYSE
International Securities Identification Number: US6907684038
Business activities: Manufactures glass containers and plastic products.
Business type (SIC): Glass/pressed or blown; plastic products/miscellaneous
Financial profile for 2012: Number of employees, 22,500; assets, $8,598,000,000; sales volume,

$7,000,000,000; pre-tax net income, $328,000,000; expenses, $6,672,000,000; liabilities, $7,717,000,000
Fortune 1000 ranking: 2012—364th in revenues, 604th in profits, and 438th in assets
Corporate officers: Albert P.L. Stroucken, Chair., Pres., and C.E.O.; Stephen P. Bramlage, Jr., Sr. V.P. and C.F.O.; Paul Arthur Jarrell, Sr. V.P. and C.A.O.; James W. Baehren, Sr. V.P. and Genl. Counsel
Board of directors: Albert P.L. Stroucken, Chair.; Gary F. Colter; Jay L. Geldmacher; Peter S. Hellman; Anastasia D. Kelly; John J. McMackin, Jr.; Corbin A. McNeill, Jr.; Hugh H. Roberts; Helge H. Wehmeier; Dennis K. Williams; Thomas L. Young
International operations: Brazil; Colombia; Finland; France; Germany; Italy; Mauritius; Netherlands; Peru; Russia; Switzerland; United Kingdom; Venezuela
Giving statement: Giving through the Owens-Illinois, Inc. Corporate Giving Program, the Charities Foundation, and the Fifty Men and Women of Toledo, Inc.
Company EIN: 222781933

Charities Foundation

1 Michael Owens Way
Plaza 1, 3rd Fl.
Perrysburg, OH 43551-2999 (419) 247-2929
Additional tel.: (419) 247-1386

Establishment information: Established in 1937 in OH.
Donors: Owens-Illinois, Inc.; William E. Levis†; Harold Boeschenstein†.
Contact: Cher Johnson, Contribs. Admin.
Financial data (yr. ended 12/31/11): Assets, $301,676 (M); gifts received, $1,650,675; expenditures, $1,705,051; qualifying distributions, $1,697,163; giving activities include $1,697,163 for grants.
Purpose and activities: The foundation supports organizations involved with arts and culture, education, the environment, health, and human services.
Fields of interest: Visual arts; Museums (art); Performing arts, orchestras; Arts; Secondary school/education; Higher education; Scholarships/financial aid; Education, reading; Education; Environment, natural resources; Environment, beautification programs; Health care, clinics/centers; Health care; Children/youth, services; Homeless, human services; Human services; United Ways and Federated Giving Programs.
Type of support: Employee matching gifts; General/operating support; Matching/challenge support; Scholarship funds.
Geographic limitations: Giving primarily in OH, with emphasis on Toledo.
Support limitations: No grants to individuals, or for scholarships.
Application information: Applications not accepted. Contributes only to pre-selected organizations.
Officer and Trustees: Catherine Neel, Treas.; Jim Baehren; Stephen Bramlage.
Number of staff: 1 part-time support.
EIN: 346554560
Selected grants: The following grants are a representative sample of this grantmaker's funding activity:
$25,000 to Keep America Beautiful, Stamford, CT, 2010.
$21,000 to University of Notre Dame, Notre Dame, IN, 2010. For matching gifts.
$10,320 to Multiple Sclerosis Society, National, New York, NY, 2010. For matching gifts.
$10,000 to Ocean Conservancy, Washington, DC, 2010.
$4,220 to Michigan State University, East Lansing, MI, 2010. For matching gifts.
$3,100 to Case Western Reserve University, Cleveland, OH, 2010. For matching gifts.
$2,700 to Pennsylvania State University, University Park, PA, 2010. For matching gifts.
$2,000 to Harvard University, Cambridge, MA, 2010. For matching gifts.
$1,290 to Clemson University, Clemson, SC, 2010. For matching gifts.
$1,145 to American Cancer Society, Atlanta, GA, 2010. For matching gifts.

2845
Owner Revolution Incorporated

1000 Flag Rd.
Adair, IA 50002-8110 (877) 742-5084

Company URL: http://www.ownerrevolution.com
Establishment information: Established in 1986.
Company type: Private company
Business activities: Manufactures lottery ticket dispensers and other lottery products.
Business type (SIC): Amusement and recreation services/miscellaneous
Corporate officers: Don Hudak, Pres. and Co-C.E.O.; J. Michael Downey, Co-C.E.O.; Diane Robert, V.P., Finance
Giving statement: Giving through the Owner Revolution Foundation.

Owner Revolution Foundation

1000 Flag Rd.
Adair, IA 50002-0338

Establishment information: Established in 2006 in IA.
Donor: Owner Revolution, Inc.
Financial data (yr. ended 12/31/11): Assets, $111,345 (M); gifts received, $10,000; expenditures, $7,844; qualifying distributions, $7,825; giving activities include $7,825 for grants.
Purpose and activities: The foundation supports organizations involved with education, health, and human services.
Fields of interest: Education; Youth development; Human services.
Type of support: General/operating support.
Geographic limitations: Giving primarily in IA.
Support limitations: No grants to individuals.
Application information: Applications not accepted. Unsolicited requests for funds not accepted.
Trustee: Diane Roberts.
EIN: 205791476

2846
Ox Bodies, Inc.

719 Columbus St. E.
P.O. Box 886
Fayette, AL 35555-2623 (205) 932-5720
FAX: (205) 932-5794

Company URL: http://www.oxbodies.com
Establishment information: Established in 1972.
Company type: Subsidiary of a private company
Business activities: Operates truck bodies and related equipment company.
Business type (SIC): Motor vehicles and equipment
Corporate officers: Robert Fines, Co-Pres.; Lehman Pendley, Co-Pres.; Johny Baker, Secy.
Giving statement: Giving through the Ox Bodies, Inc. Contributions Program.

Ox Bodies, Inc. Contributions Program

719 Columbus St. E.
P.O. Box 886
Fayette, AL 35555-2623 (205) 932-5720
E-mail: tfowler@tbei.com; URL: http://www.oxbodies.com

2847
Oxford Industries, Inc.

999 Peachtree St. N.E., Ste. 688
Atlanta, GA 30309 (404) 659-2424
FAX: (404) 653-1545

Company URL: http://www.oxfordinc.com/
Establishment information: Established in 1942.
Company type: Public company
Company ticker symbol and exchange: OXM/NYSE
Business activities: Manufactures clothing.
Business type (SIC): Apparel—men's and boys' outerwear; apparel—women's outerwear; apparel—girls' and children's outerwear
Financial profile for 2013: Number of employees, 4,800; assets, $556,070,000; sales volume, $855,540,000; pre-tax net income, $50,890,000; expenses, $795,710,000; liabilities, $326,230,000
Corporate officers: J. Hicks Lanier, Chair.; Thomas C. Chubb III, Pres. and C.E.O.; K. Scott Grassmyer, Jr., Sr. V.P., Finance, C.F.O., and Cont.; Thomas E. Campbell, Sr. V.P., Admin., Genl. Counsel, and Secy.; Christine B. Cole, Sr. V.P., Human Resources; Anne M. Shoemaker, Jr., V.P. and Treas.; Mark B. Kirby, V.P., Opers.
Board of directors: J. Hicks Lanier, Chair.; Thomas C. Chubb III; George C. Guynn; John R. Holder; J. Reese Lanier, Sr.; Dennis M. Love; Clarence H. Smith; Clyde C. Tuggle; Helen Ballard Weeks; E. Jenner Wood III
Subsidiary: Oxford Slacks, Monroe, GA
Plants: Lyons, GA; New York, NY; Dallas, TX
International operations: Australia; Costa Rica; Guatemala; Honduras; Hong Kong; Mexico; Philippines; Singapore; United Kingdom
Giving statement: Giving through the Oxford Industries Foundation, Inc.
Company EIN: 580831862

Oxford Industries Foundation, Inc.

222 Piedmont Ave., N.E.
Atlanta, GA 30308-3391 (404) 653-1419
E-mail: sbennett@oxfordinc.com; URL: http://investor.oxfordinc.com/community.cfm

Establishment information: Established in 1975 in GA.
Donor: Oxford Industries, Inc.
Contact: Ginger Moff
Financial data (yr. ended 12/31/11): Assets, $785,328 (M); gifts received, $750,000; expenditures, $170,121; qualifying distributions, $156,643; giving activities include $156,643 for 17 grants (high: $78,000; low: $200).
Purpose and activities: The foundation supports organizations involved with arts and culture, education, health, human services, and civic affairs.
Fields of interest: Humanities; Arts; Education; Health care; Human services; United Ways and Federated Giving Programs; Public affairs.
Type of support: Annual campaigns; Capital campaigns; Continuing support; Employee matching gifts; General/operating support.
Geographic limitations: Giving limited to Pasadena, CA, Atlanta, Lyons, Toccoa, and Vidalia, GA, New York, NY, Lebanon, TN, and Seattle, WA.

Support limitations: No grants to individuals.
Publications: Program policy statement.
Application information: Applications accepted. Application form not required. Applicants should submit the following:
1) copy of IRS Determination Letter
2) copy of current year's organizational budget and/or project budget
3) detailed description of project and amount of funding requested
Initial approach: Proposal
Deadline(s): None
Trustees: Thomas C. Chubb III; K. Scott Grassmyer; J. Hicks Lanier.
EIN: 581209452
Selected grants: The following grants are a representative sample of this grantmaker's funding activity:
$10,000 to Atlanta Speech School, Atlanta, GA, 2011.

2848
Oxford Travel Inc.

(also known as Travel of America)
668 Arrow Grand Cir.
Covina, CA 91722-2145 (626) 814-6350

Company URL: http://www.travelofamerica.com
Establishment information: Established in 1994.
Company type: Private company
Business activities: Operates travel agency.
Business type (SIC): Travel and tour arrangers
Corporate officers: Richard Molander, Pres. and C.E.O.; Jim Petzel, V.P., Mktg.

The Molander Foundation, Inc.

668 Arrow Grand Cir.
Covina, CA 91722-5115

Establishment information: Established as a company-sponsored operating foundation in 2001 in CA.
Donor: Oxford Travel Inc.
Financial data (yr. ended 10/31/11): Assets, $107,800 (M); expenditures, $61; qualifying distributions, $61.
Purpose and activities: The foundation seeks to expose young American students, who have recently graduated or are about to graduate from secondary school, to people, languages, opinions, cultures, and ways of life as they exist in other parts of the world.
Application information: Applications not accepted. Unsolicited requests for funds not accepted.
Officer: Richard Molander, Pres.
EIN: 912171812

2849
P.E.L, Inc.

(also known as Wine Discount Center)
1350 Old Skokie Rd., Ste. 203
Highland Park, IL 60035-3058
(847) 831-1049

Company URL: http://www.winediscountcenter.com
Establishment information: Established in 1984.
Company type: Private company
Business activities: Operates liquor stores.
Business type (SIC): Liquor stores
Corporate officers: Howard Schwarzbach, Pres.; Diane Schwarzbach, Secy.
Giving statement: Giving through the Schwarzbach Family Foundation.

Schwarzbach Family Foundation

718 Sheridan Rd.
Glencoe, IL 60022-1339

Establishment information: Established in 2002 in IL.
Donor: P.E.L., Inc.
Financial data (yr. ended 12/31/11): Assets, $418,919 (M); expenditures, $65,136; qualifying distributions, $62,586; giving activities include $62,586 for grants.
Purpose and activities: The foundation supports botanical gardens and festivals and organizations involved with education, health, human services, and Judaism.
Fields of interest: Middle schools/education; Secondary school/education; Education; Botanical gardens; Health care; Recreation, fairs/festivals; Youth, services; Family services; Human services; Jewish federated giving programs; Jewish agencies & synagogues.
Type of support: General/operating support.
Geographic limitations: Giving primarily in Chicago, IL.
Application information: Applications not accepted. Unsolicited requests for funds not accepted.
Officers and Directors:* Howard Schwarzbach*, Pres.; Diane Schwarzbach*, Secy.; Ellen Schwarzbach; Laura Schwarbach; Peter Schwarzbach.
EIN: 383661200

2850
PACCAR Inc

777 106th Ave., N.E.
Bellevue, WA 98004-5027 (425) 468-7400
FAX: (425) 468-8216

Company URL: http://www.paccar.com
Establishment information: Established in 1905.
Company type: Public company
Company ticker symbol and exchange: PCAR/NASDAQ
Business activities: Manufactures light, medium, and heavy-duty trucks; provides financial services, information technology, and truck parts related to its principal business.
Business type (SIC): Motor vehicles and equipment; machinery/construction, mining, and materials handling
Financial profile for 2012: Number of employees, 21,800; assets, $18,627,800,000; sales volume, $17,050,500,000; pre-tax net income, $1,628,900,000; expenses, $15,454,700,000; liabilities, $12,780,900,000
Fortune 1000 ranking: 2012—168th in revenues, 184th in profits, and 254th in assets
Corporate officers: Mark C. Pigott, Chair. and C.E.O.; Ronald E. Armstrong, Pres.; Robert J. Christensen, Exec. V.P. and C.F.O.; Thomas Kyle Quinn, V.P. and C.I.O.; Michael T. Barkley, V.P. and Cont.; David C. Anderson, V.P. and Genl. Counsel; Jack K. LeVier, V.P., Human Resources; Janice M. D'Amato, Secy.; Robin E. Easton, Treas.
Board of directors: Mark C. Pigott, Chair.; Alison J. Carnwath; John M. Fluke, Jr.; Kirk S. Hachigian; Luiz Kaufmann; Roderick C. McGeary; John M. Pigott; Mark A. Schulz; Gregory M.E. Spierkel; Warren R. Staley; Charles R. Williamson
International operations: Australia; Belgium; Brazil; Canada; China; India; Mexico; Netherlands; United Kingdom
Giving statement: Giving through the PACCAR Foundation.
Company EIN: 910351110

PACCAR Foundation

c/o PACCAR Inc
P.O. Box 1518
Bellevue, WA 98009-1518
E-mail for Ken Hastings: ken.hastings@paccar.com; URL: http://www.paccar.com/company/foundation.asp

Establishment information: Incorporated in 1951 in WA.
Donor: PACCAR Inc.
Contact: Ken Hastings
Financial data (yr. ended 12/31/11): Assets, $2,600,000 (M); gifts received, $6,000,000; expenditures, $5,800,000; qualifying distributions, $5,800,000; giving activities include $5,700,000 for 182 grants and $100,000 for employee matching gifts.
Purpose and activities: The foundation supports hospitals and organizations involved with arts and culture, higher education, and economic education.
Fields of interest: Arts; Higher education; Hospitals (general); Human services, financial counseling; United Ways and Federated Giving Programs.
Program:
Employee Matching Gifts: The foundation matches contributions made by employees of PACCAR to institutions of secondary and higher education from $100 to $5,000 per employee, per year.
Type of support: Annual campaigns; Building/renovation; Capital campaigns; Continuing support; Employee matching gifts; Scholarship funds.
Geographic limitations: Giving primarily in areas of company operations, with emphasis on King County, WA.
Support limitations: No support for churches for the purpose of religious activity. No grants to individuals, or for scholarships or fellowships, program development, general operating support, fundraising events, sponsorships, dinners, or event tickets, or advertising space for charitable causes in yearbooks, programs, or publications.
Publications: Application guidelines.
Application information: Applications accepted. Support is limited to 1 contribution per organization during any given year. Multi-year funding is not automatic. Application form not required. Applicants should submit the following:
1) qualifications of key personnel
2) name, address and phone number of organization
3) copy of IRS Determination Letter
4) brief history of organization and description of its mission
5) copy of most recent annual report/audited financial statement/990
6) listing of board of directors, trustees, officers and other key people and their affiliations
7) detailed description of project and amount of funding requested
8) contact person
9) copy of current year's organizational budget and/or project budget
10) listing of additional sources and amount of support
Initial approach: Proposal
Copies of proposal: 1
Board meeting date(s): Semi-annual; dates vary
Deadline(s): None
Final notification: 6 months
Officers and Directors:* Mark C. Pigott*, Pres.; Ken Hastings, V.P. and Genl. Mgr.; Ron Armstrong, V.P.; David C. Anderson, Secy.; Robin J. Easton, Treas.; Dan Sobic.

Number of staff: None.
EIN: 916030638

2851
PACE Incorporated

9030 Junction Dr.
Annapolis Junction, MD 20701-1166
(301) 490-9860

Company URL: http://www.paceworldwide.com
Establishment information: Established in 1958.
Company type: Private company
Business activities: Manufactures electronic assembly development, production, and repair systems.
Business type (SIC): Cutlery, hand and edge tools, and hardware
Financial profile for 2010: Number of employees, 40
Corporate officers: William J. Siegel, Chair.; Paul Dunham, Pres.; Mike Prasch, C.F.O.
Board of director: William J. Siegel, Chair.
International operations: United Kingdom
Giving statement: Giving through the William J. and Sally R. Siegel Foundation Ltd.

William J. and Sally R. Siegel Foundation Ltd.

14209 Woodcrest Dr.
Rockville, MD 20853-2332

Establishment information: Established in 1990 in MD.
Donor: PACE Inc.
Financial data (yr. ended 12/31/11): Assets, $1,057,476 (M); expenditures, $62,949; qualifying distributions, $48,000; giving activities include $48,000 for grants.
Purpose and activities: The foundation supports organizations involved with arts and culture, higher education, reproductive health, legal aid, civil liberties advocacy, and Judaism.
Fields of interest: Media/communications; Museums; Arts; Higher education; Reproductive health, family planning; Legal services; Civil liberties, advocacy; Jewish agencies & synagogues.
Type of support: General/operating support.
Geographic limitations: Giving limited to AL, CA, Washington, DC, FL, MD, and NY.
Support limitations: No grants to individuals.
Application information: Applications not accepted. Unsolicited requests for funds not accepted.
Officers: William J. Siegel, Pres. and Treas.; Sally R. Siegel, V.P. and Secy.
Director: Jeffrey E. Sabot.
EIN: 521708205

2852
Pacers Basketball Corporation

(doing business as Pacers Sports & Entertainment)
(also known as Indiana Pacers)
125 S. Pennsylvania St.
Indianapolis, IN 46204-3610
(317) 917-2500

Company URL: http://www.pacers.com
Establishment information: Established in 1976.
Company type: Private company
Business activities: Operates professional basketball club.
Business type (SIC): Commercial sports
Corporate officers: Herbert Simon, Chair. and C.E.O.; Jim Morris, Pres.; Rick Fuson, C.O.O.; Kevin Bower, Exec. V.P. and C.F.O.; Todd Taylor, Sr. V.P., Mktg.; Matt Albrecht, V.P., Finance and Cont.; Harry James, V.P., Admin.; Tom Rutledge, V.P., Opers.; Quinn Buckner, V.P., Comms.; Greg Schenkel, V.P., Public Rels.; Donna Wilkinson, V.P., Human Resources
Board of director: Herbert Simon, Chair.
Giving statement: Giving through the Indiana Pacers Corporate Giving Program and the Pacers Foundation, Inc.

Indiana Pacers Corporate Giving Program

c/o Community Rels.
125 S. Pennsylvania St.
Indianapolis, IN 46204-3610 (317) 917-2500
URL: http://www.nba.com/pacers/community/

Contact: Richard Smith, Coord.
Purpose and activities: As a complement to its foundation, the Indiana Pacers also make charitable donations of team memorabilia to nonprofit organizations directly. Support is given primarily in the greater Indianapolis, Indiana, area.
Fields of interest: General charitable giving.
Type of support: In-kind gifts.
Geographic limitations: Giving primarily in the greater Indianapolis, IN, area.
Application information: Applications accepted. Support is limited to 1 contribution per organization during any given year. Application form required. Applicants should submit the following:
1) name, address and phone number of organization
2) contact person
Applications should include the Tax ID Number of the organization; the name and date of the event; and the type of fundraiser.
Initial approach: Complete online application form
Deadline(s): 6 weeks prior to event

Pacers Foundation, Inc.

(formerly Pacers Basketball Corporation Foundation, Inc.)
125 S. Pennsylvania St.
Indianapolis, IN 46204-2603 (317) 917-2864
FAX: (317) 917-2599;
E-mail: foundation@pacers.com; URL: http://www.pacersfoundation.org/

Establishment information: Established in 1993 in IN.
Contact: Dan Gaines
Financial data (yr. ended 06/30/11): Revenue, $471,642; assets, $1,399,309 (M); gifts received, $358,180; expenditures, $798,149; giving activities include $587,450 for grants.
Purpose and activities: The foundation aims to build collaborative initiatives to encourage Indiana's youth to make winning life choices.
Fields of interest: Education; Public health, obesity; Public health, physical fitness; Health care; Substance abuse, prevention; Recreation; Children/youth, services.
Program:
Linda Craig Memorial Scholarship Foundation: Two awards of $2,000 are made each year for use at any accredited four-year Indiana college or university or two-year junior or community college to students who are enrolling in, or plan to enroll in, medicine, sports medicine, physical therapy, and/or related disciplines. Eligible applicants must be enrolled in good standing in an undergraduate college program, must have at least four semesters completed, must have a minimum GPA of 3.0 (on a 4.0 scale), and must be a U.S. citizen.
Type of support: Program development; Scholarships—to individuals.
Geographic limitations: Giving limited to IN.
Support limitations: No support for political candidates or parties, or corporate memberships. No grants to individuals (except for scholarships), or for emergency funds, or fundraisers.
Publications: Annual report; Application guidelines; Grants list; Informational brochure (including application guidelines).
Application information: Applications accepted. Application form required. Applicants should submit the following:
1) copy of IRS Determination Letter
2) copy of most recent annual report/audited financial statement/990
3) listing of board of directors, trustees, officers and other key people and their affiliations
4) copy of current year's organizational budget and/or project budget
5) listing of additional sources and amount of support
Board meeting date(s): Feb., May, Aug., and Nov.
Deadline(s): July 1 for Linda Craig Memorial Scholarship Foundation
Officers: Rick Fuson, Chair.; Cindy Simon Skjodt, Vice-Chair.; Quinn Buckner, Secy.; Kevin Bower, Treas.; Greg Schenkel, Exec. Dir.
EIN: 351908365

2853
Pacific Gas and Electric Company

(also known as PG&E)
77 Beale St., Ste. 100
P.O. Box 770000
San Francisco, CA 94105 (415) 973-7000

Company URL: http://www.pge.com
Establishment information: Established in 1905.
Company type: Subsidiary of a public company
Business activities: Generates, transmits, and distributes electricity; transmits and distributes natural gas.
Business type (SIC): Electric services; gas production and distribution; combination utility services
Financial profile for 2012: Assets, $52,400,000,000; sales volume, $15,000,000,000
Forbes 2000 ranking: 2012—635th in sales, 692nd in profits, and 439th in assets
Corporate officers: Peter A. Darbee, Chair. and C.E.O.; Christopher P. Johns, Pres.; Karen Austin, Sr. V.P. and C.I.O.; John R. Simon, Sr. V.P., Human Resources; Dinyar B. Mistry, V.P., C.F.O., and Cont.; Linda Y.H. Cheng, V.P. and Corp. Secy.; Nicholas M. Bijur, V.P. and Treas.; Jason P. Wells, V.P., Finance; Andrew K. Williams, V.P., Human Resources
Board of directors: Peter A. Darbee, Chair.; Christopher P. Johns
Giving statement: Giving through the Pacific Gas & Electric Company Contributions Program and the Pacific Forest & Watershed Lands Stewardship Council.

Pacific Gas & Electric Company Contributions Program

77 Beale St.
P.O. Box 770000
San Francisco, CA 94177-0001 (415) 973-0898
FAX: (415) 973-8239; E-mail: ljg8@pge.com;
URL: http://www.pge.com/giving/

Contact: Larry J. Goldzband, Mgr., Charitable Contribs.
Financial data (yr. ended 12/31/09): Total giving, $8,277,741, including $8,249,232 for 1,092 grants (high: $333,000; low: $50) and $28,509 for 10 in-kind gifts.
Purpose and activities: Pacific Gas & Electric Company makes charitable contributions to nonprofit organizations involved with environmental and energy sustainability, emergency preparedness, education, and emergency energy assistance. Special emphasis is directed toward programs that benefit underserved populations and communities. Support is given primarily in areas of company operations.
Fields of interest: Education; Environment, energy; Environment; Disasters, preparedness/services; Economic development.
Program:
Matching Gifts Program: The company matches contributions made by employees of Pacific Gas & Electric Company to schools, institutions of higher education, and environmental organizations on a one-for-one basis from $25 to $2,500 per employee, per year.
Type of support: Donated equipment; Donated land; Emergency funds; Employee matching gifts; Employee volunteer services; Equipment; General/operating support; In-kind gifts; Matching/challenge support; Program development; Use of facilities.
Geographic limitations: Giving primarily in areas of company operations in central and northern CA.
Support limitations: No support for religious organizations not of direct benefit to the entire community, fraternal organizations, political or partisan organizations, or hospitals or medical organizations. No grants to individuals, or for debt reduction, endowments, films or videos, tickets, continuing support, sports tournaments, trips or tours, talent or beauty contests, fellowships, or conferences.
Publications: Application guidelines; Corporate report; Grants list.
Application information: Applications accepted. Grants range from $1,000 to $25,000, with most under $15,000. Online application for grants only. Visit company Web site for details. The Community Relations Department handles giving. The company has a staff that only handles contributions. Application form required. Applicants should submit the following:
1) role played by volunteers
2) population served
3) name, address and phone number of organization
4) brief history of organization and description of its mission
5) geographic area to be served
6) how project's results will be evaluated or measured
7) listing of board of directors, trustees, officers and other key people and their affiliations
8) detailed description of project and amount of funding requested
9) contact person

Initial approach: Complete online application
Copies of proposal: 1
Deadline(s): Sept. 4
Final notification: 3 months or less

Administrators: Karalee Browne, Prog. Mgr.; Leah Casey, Prog. Mgr.; Doug Carrillo, Database Mgr.; Larry Goldzband, Mgr., Charitable Contribs.; Andrea Gooden, Prog. Mgr.
Number of staff: 4 full-time professional; 1 full-time support; 0.5 part-time support.

Pacific Forest & Watershed Lands Stewardship Council

15 N. Ellsworth, Ste. 100
San Mateo, CA 94401-2831 (650) 344-9072
FAX: (650) 401-2140;
E-mail: info@stewardshipcouncil.org; Additional tel.: (866) 791-5150; E-mail for questions regarding grants for youth:
youthgrants@stewardshipcouncil.org; E-mail for Allene Zanger, Exec. Dir.:
azanger@stewardshipcouncil.org; URL: http://www.stewardshipcouncil.org

Establishment information: Established in 2004 in CA.
Donor: Pacific Gas and Electric Co.
Financial data (yr. ended 12/31/11): Assets, $75,882,668 (M); gifts received, $893,299; expenditures, $4,761,651; qualifying distributions, $4,653,458; giving activities include $1,533,222 for 50 grants (high: $250,000; low: $7,500) and $5,345,930 for 2 foundation-administered programs.
Purpose and activities: The foundation supports watershed land conservation and invests in programs designed to improve the lives of Californian youth through connections with the outdoors.
Fields of interest: Environment, public education; Environment, land resources; Environmental education; Environment; Recreation, parks/playgrounds; Recreation; Boys & girls clubs; Youth development; Children/youth, services Youth; Economically disadvantaged.
Programs:
Land Conservation Program: The council overseas acres of watershed lands in California to promote outdoor recreation; sustainable forestry; agriculture; habitat protection; open space preservation; and protection of cultural and historic resources.
Youth Investment Program: The council invests in organizations that seek to improve the lives of underserved youth through greater access to outdoor experiences. Special emphasis is directed toward existing community parks, youth development programs, and new programs in underserved communities. The council has also established the Foundation for Youth Investment (FYI) to continue the mission of connecting kids to the great outdoors. FYI will administer youth investment grants on behalf of the council, including Catalyst Funds aimed at reducing barriers for youth engagement in outdoor activities, Impact Funds which supports day-to-day operations of promising programs and high-impact organizations, Collaboration Funds which supports collaborative venture, and Infrastructure Funds aimed at the infrastructure of community parks and urban open spaces.
Type of support: Capital campaigns; Continuing support; General/operating support; Management development/capacity building; Program development.
Geographic limitations: Giving primarily in CA, with emphasis on the metropolitan Bay Area, urban areas of the Central Valley, and rural areas with high rates of poverty.
Support limitations: No grants to individuals; no multi-year grants.
Publications: Application guidelines.
Application information: Applications accepted. The Youth Investment Program is administered by the Foundation for Youth Investment. Application form required. Applicants should submit the following:
1) detailed description of project and amount of funding requested
2) copy of current year's organizational budget and/or project budget

Initial approach: Complete online eligibility quiz and application for Youth Investment Program
Board meeting date(s): Jan. 19, Mar. 7, May 2, June 27, Sept. 5, and Nov. 14
Deadline(s): Generally Mar., June., and Aug. but varies for Youth Investment Program Catalyst Fund, Impact Fund, and Infrastructure Fund. Visit website for specific deadlines
Final notification: Apr., June, Aug., and Nov. for Youth Investment Program

Officers and Directors:* Art Baggett, Jr.*, Pres.; Truman Burns*, V.P.; Soapy Mulholland*, V.P.; Lee Adams, Treas.; Allene Zanger, Exec. Dir.; David A. Bischel; Truman Burns; Cherie Chan; Paul Clanon; Noelle Cremers; Todd Ferrara; Kathy Hardy; John Laird; Steve Larson; Randy Livingston; Robert A. Meacher; Karen Mills*; Larry Myers; Chris Nota; Mark Rentz; Richard Roos-Collins; Nancy Ryan; Mike Schonherr; Dave Sutton.
EIN: 201358125
Selected grants: The following grants are a representative sample of this grantmaker's funding activity:
$100,000 to Hunters Point Affordable Housing, San Francisco, CA, 2010.
$65,000 to Bay Area Open Space Council, San Francisco, CA, 2010.
$47,500 to California State Parks Foundation, San Francisco, CA, 2010.
$47,000 to City Slicker Farms, Oakland, CA, 2010.
$45,000 to Seven Tepees Youth Program, San Francisco, CA, 2010.
$30,000 to East Oakland Boxing Association, Oakland, CA, 2010.
$30,000 to Environmental Traveling Companions, San Francisco, CA, 2010.
$30,000 to University of California, Berkeley, CA, 2010.
$20,000 to Youth Enrichment Strategies, Richmond, CA, 2010.
$12,000 to Wilderness Arts and Literacy Collaborative, San Francisco, CA, 2010.

2854
Pacific Giant, Inc.

4625 District Blvd.
Vernon, CA 90058 (323) 587-5000
FAX: (323) 587-5050

Company URL: http://www.pacificgiant.com
Establishment information: Established in 1983.
Company type: Private company
Business activities: Seafood products.
Business type (SIC): Fishing/commercial
Corporate officer: Chang Yun Lim, Pres.
Board of director: Chul Park
Giving statement: Giving through the PGI Foundation.

PGI Foundation

4625 District Blvd.
Vernon, CA 90058-2731 (323) 582-2880

Establishment information: Established as a company-sponsored operating foundation in 1998.
Donor: Pacific Giant, Inc.
Contact: Chang Yun Lim, C.E.O.

Financial data (yr. ended 12/31/11): Assets, $10,783 (M); expenditures, $35; qualifying distributions, $0.
Purpose and activities: The foundation awards college scholarships to full-time students with a GPA of 3.0 or above.
Type of support: Scholarships—to individuals.
Geographic limitations: Giving primarily in CA.
Application information: Applications accepted. Application form required.
Letters of inquiry should include a photograph of the applicant, tax returns of the applicant's parent or guardian, and college transcripts.
Initial approach: Letter of inquiry
Deadline(s): None
Officers: Chang Yun Lim, C.E.O.; Jacob Seong, C.F.O.; Jong Hoon Bae, Secy.
Director: Anthony Bachman.
EIN: 954694835

2855
Pacific Life Insurance Company

700 Newport Center Dr.
P.O. Box 9000
Newport Beach, CA 92660-6397
(949) 219-3011

Company URL: http://www.pacificlife.com
Establishment information: Established in 1868.
Company type: Subsidiary of a mutual company
Business activities: Sells life and health insurance; provides investment advisory services.
Business type (SIC): Insurance/life; security and commodity services; insurance/accident and health
Financial profile for 2011: Number of employees, 2,659; assets, $115,992,000,000; sales volume, $5,603,000,000
Corporate officers: James T. Morris, Chair., Pres., and C.E.O.; Khanh T. Tran, Exec. V.P. and C.F.O.; Sharon A. Cheever, Sr. V.P. and Genl. Counsel; Carol R. Sudbeck, Sr. V.P., Human Resources
Board of director: James T. Morris, Chair.
Subsidiaries: Associated Securities Corp., Los Angeles, CA; Aviation Capital Group Holding Corp., Newport Beach, CA; College Savings Bank, Princeton, NJ; Mutual Service Corp., West Palm Beach, FL; Pacific Asset Funding, Newport Beach, CA; Pacific Investment Management Co., Newport Beach, CA; Pacific Life & Annuity Co., Irvine, CA; Pacific Select Distributors, Inc., Newport Beach, CA; M.L. Stern & Co., LLC, Beverly Hills, CA; United Planners' Financial Services of America, Scottsdale, AZ; Waterstone Financial Group, Inc., Itasca, IL
Giving statement: Giving through the Pacific Life Insurance Company Contributions Program, the Volkswagen AG Corporate Giving Program, and the Pacific Life Foundation.
Company EIN: 951079000

Pacific Life Insurance Company Contributions Program

700 Newport Center Dr.
Newport Beach, CA 92660-6397 (949) 219-3787

Contact: Robert G. Haskell, Sr. V.P., Public Affairs
Financial data (yr. ended 12/31/09): Total giving, $154,390, including $154,390 for 105 employee matching gifts.
Purpose and activities: As a complement to its foundation, Pacific Life also makes charitable contributions to nonprofit organizations directly. Support is given primarily in areas of company operations.
Fields of interest: Arts; Education; Environment; Health care; Human services; Community/economic development; Public affairs.
Type of support: Donated equipment; Employee matching gifts; In-kind gifts; Sponsorships; Use of facilities.
Geographic limitations: Giving primarily in areas of company operations.
Publications: Corporate report.
Application information: Applications not accepted. Contributes only to pre-selected organizations. The Public Affairs Department handles giving. The company has a staff that only handles contributions.
Administrator: Michele Townsend, Dir., Community Rels.
Number of staff: 2 full-time professional; 1 part-time support.

Pacific Life Foundation

(formerly Pacific Mutual Charitable Foundation)
700 Newport Center Dr.
Newport Beach, CA 92660-6397 (949) 219-3214
FAX: (949) 719-7614;
E-mail: PLFoundation@PacificLife.com; URL: http://www.pacificlife.com/PL/FoundationCommunity/Overview/Corp_PLF_Home.htm

Establishment information: Established in 1984 in CA.
Donors: Pacific Life Insurance Co.; Pacific Mutual Holding Co.
Contact: Robert G. Haskell, Pres.
Financial data (yr. ended 12/31/11): Assets, $69,499,558 (M); gifts received, $6,215,251; expenditures, $5,550,808; qualifying distributions, $5,450,587; giving activities include $3,567,600 for 373 grants (high: $1,000,000; low: $50).
Purpose and activities: The foundation supports organizations involved with arts and culture, education, the environment, marine life and fisheries, health, human services, mathematics, civic affairs, the disabled, homeless, and economically disadvantaged people.
Fields of interest: Performing arts, dance; Performing arts, theater; Performing arts, music; Arts; Elementary/secondary education; Education, reading; Education; Environment, natural resources; Environment, water resources; Environment, land resources; Environmental education; Environment; Animals/wildlife, fisheries; Health care; Youth development, adult & child programs; Children, services; Family services, domestic violence; Human services, financial counseling; Human services; Mathematics; Leadership development; Public affairs Disabilities, people with; Economically disadvantaged; Homeless.
Programs:
3T's of Education Program: The foundation awards grants of $1,500 to $10,000 to K-12 schools to enhance student achievement and promote and provide for teacher training, textbooks, and technology.
Arts and Culture: The foundation supports programs designed to provide the public with a broad spectrum of arts and cultural initiatives including workshops and performances, to help build the public's appreciation and participation in dance, music, and theater.
Civic, Community, and Environment: The foundation supports programs designed to protect and preserve the environment on land and in the ocean; and promote leadership training, civic responsibility, and diversity.
Economic Impact Grants: The foundation awards one-time grants to health and human service nonprofit agencies whose services and/or staff have been or will be reduced or eliminated as a result of the State of California or County of Orange budget reductions. Grants range from $25,000 to $75,000.
Education: The foundation supports programs designed to provide quality education for youth and adults, including after-school tutoring, K-12 science and math enrichment, and literacy education.
Focus Program Funding: The foundation awards grants to programs designed to impact critical community issues. Target areas of focus for this program changes yearly, and may include collaborative nonprofit capacity-building, economic literacy, enhancing autism resources, homeless families, industry education, mandatory reporters of child abuse, middle and high school leadership development, nonprofit internship experience, Orange County math initiative, protection of marine mammals, and sustainable fisheries.
Health and Human Services: The foundation supports programs designed improve the quality of life for those in need including the homeless, senior citizens, youth, working poor, victims of domestic violence, and individuals with chronic disease or specific unmet health needs.
Matching Gifts Program: The foundation matches contributions made by employees, directors, and life insurance providers of Pacific Life to institutions of higher education, up to $2,000 per contributor, and up to $500 to other eligible nonprofits.
Type of support: Capital campaigns; Conferences/seminars; Continuing support; Employee matching gifts; Equipment; General/operating support; Management development/capacity building; Program development; Research.
Geographic limitations: Giving primarily in areas of company operations in the greater Orange County, CA, area and Omaha, NE; giving also to statewide and national organizations.
Support limitations: No support for political parties or candidates or partisan political organizations, labor or fraternal organizations, athletic or social clubs, K-12 schools, school districts, or school foundations (except for 3T's of Education), sectarian or denominational religious organizations not of direct benefit to the entire community, or sports leagues or teams. No grants to individuals, or for fundraising events or advertising sponsorships; no in-kind donations.
Publications: Annual report (including application guidelines); Application guidelines; Grants list.
Application information: Applications accepted. Support is limited to 1 contribution per organization during any given year for three years in length. Organizations must reapply each year. Multi-year funding is not automatic. Audio and video submissions are not accepted. Unsolicited applications for Focus Program Funding and 3T's of Education Program are not accepted. General grants range from $5,000 to $10,000 and are given to support programs, operating expenses, and collaborative programs with other agencies. Capital grants range from $10,000 to $100,000 and are given to an agency with an organized campaign already under way. Application form required.
Applicants should submit the following:
1) principal source of support for project in the past
2) copy of IRS Determination Letter
3) copy of most recent annual report/audited financial statement/990
4) descriptive literature about organization
5) listing of board of directors, trustees, officers and other key people and their affiliations
6) detailed description of project and amount of funding requested
7) copy of current year's organizational budget and/or project budget
8) listing of additional sources and amount of support

Initial approach: Download application form and mail proposal and application form to foundation
Copies of proposal: 1
Board meeting date(s): Oct. or Nov.
Deadline(s): July 15 to Aug. 15
Final notification: Nov.
Officers and Directors:* James T. Morris*, Chair.; Robert G. Haskell*, Pres.; Michele A. Townsend*, V.P.; Tennyson S. Oyler*, V.P.; Jane M. Guon, Secy.; Joseph L. Tortorelli, Genl. Counsel; Edward R. Byrd, C.F.O.; Jennifer S. Annala; Sharon A. Cheever; Alyssa C. Dowding; R. Stephen Hannahs; Robert G. Haskell; John C. Mulvihill; Cathy L. Schwartz; Alice P. Terlecky; Christine A. Tucker.
Number of staff: 2 full-time professional; 1 part-time professional; 1 full-time support.
EIN: 953433806
Selected grants: The following grants are a representative sample of this grantmaker's funding activity:
$10,000 to University of California, Irvine, CA, 2010. For COSMOS Program.
$10,000 to University of Nebraska-Omaha, Omaha, NE, 2010. For Inside Art Program.

2856
Pacific Office Automation, Inc.
14747 N.W. Greenbrier Pkwy
Beaverton, OR 97006 (503) 601-2228
FAX: (503) 601-2293

Company URL: http://www.pacificoffice.com
Establishment information: Established in 1976.
Company type: Private company
Business activities: Provides document imaging catalog shopping services.
Business type (SIC): Nonstore retailers; consumer electronics and music stores
Corporate officers: Terry E. Newsom, C.E.O.; Doug Pitassi, Pres.; Gerry N. Romjue, C.F.O.
Giving statement: Giving through the Pacific Office Automation Charitable Foundation.

Pacific Office Automation Charitable Foundation
14747 N.W. Greenbrier Pkwy.
Beaverton, OR 97006-5601

Establishment information: Established in 2000 in OR.
Donor: Pacific Office Automation, Inc.
Financial data (yr. ended 12/31/11): Assets, $1 (M); gifts received, $22,120; expenditures, $22,120; qualifying distributions, $22,110; giving activities include $22,110 for grants.
Purpose and activities: The foundation awards college scholarships to individuals.
Type of support: Scholarships—to individuals.
Geographic limitations: Giving primarily in OR.
Application information: Applications not accepted. Unsolicited requests for funds not accepted.
Board Members: Connie Holt; Karen C. Newsom; Terry E. Newsom.
EIN: 931283813

2857
Pacific Software Publishing, Inc.
1404 140th Pl. N.E.
Bellevue, WA 98007 (425) 957-0808

Company URL: http://www.carelloweb.com
Establishment information: Established in 1987.
Company type: Private company
Business activities: Operates e-commerce site service company.
Business type (SIC): Telephone communications
Corporate officers: Ken Uchikura, Chair.; Mayumi Nakamura, Pres. and C.E.O.
Board of director: Ken Uchikura, Chair.
Giving statement: Giving through the Pacific Software Publishing, Inc. Corporate Giving Program.

Pacific Software Publishing, Inc. Corporate Giving Program
1404 140th Pl. NE
Bellevue, WA 98007-3915 (425) 957-0808
E-mail: info@pspinc.com; URL: http://www.pspinc.com/japanrelief

Fields of interest: Asians/Pacific Islanders.
Type of support: Donated products; General/operating support.

2858
Pacific World Corporation
25800 Commercentre Dr.
Lake Forest, CA 92630 (949) 598-2400

Company URL: http://www.pacificworldcorp.com
Establishment information: Established in 1973.
Company type: Private company
Business activities: Manufactures natural and artificial fingernail products.
Business type (SIC): Soaps, cleaners, and toiletries
Corporate officers: Robert A. Leathers, Chair.; Joseph Fracassi, Pres. and C.E.O.; Joseph Jaeger, C.O.O and C.F.O.; Joel Carden, Exec. V.P., Sales and Mktg.; V. Craig Finney, Exec. V.P., Opers.; Marwan Zreik, Sr. V.P., Mktg.; Mike Matulis, Sr. V.P., Sales
Board of director: Robert A. Leathers, Chair.
Giving statement: Giving through the Leathers Family Foundation.

Leathers Family Foundation
P.O. Box 1186
Ross, CA 94957-1186

Establishment information: Established in 1993 as a company-sponsored operating foundation.
Donors: Pacific World Corp.; Robert A. Leathers.
Financial data (yr. ended 12/31/10): Assets, $1,978,532 (L); expenditures, $153,034; qualifying distributions, $143,820; giving activities include $143,820 for 17 grants (high: $89,300; low: $100).
Purpose and activities: The foundation supports libraries and organizations involved with arts and culture, secondary, human services, and religion.
Fields of interest: Media/communications; Museums (art); Performing arts, theater; Arts; Secondary school/education; Libraries (public); Homeless, human services; Human services; Religion.
Type of support: General/operating support.
Geographic limitations: Giving limited to CA.
Support limitations: No grants to individuals.
Application information: Applications not accepted. Contributes only to pre-selected organizations.
Officers: Robert A. Leathers, Pres.; Betty Jane Leathers, V.P.; Jennifer Leathers, Secy.
EIN: 931135081
Selected grants: The following grants are a representative sample of this grantmaker's funding activity:
$88,875 to Marin Academy, San Rafael, CA, 2009.
$3,215 to Ross School Foundation, Ross, CA, 2009.
$1,000 to K Q E D, San Francisco, CA, 2009.

2859
Pacifico Airport Valet Service
6715 Essington Ave.
Philadelphia, PA 19153 (215) 492-0990
FAX: (215) 492-1488

Company URL: http://www.pacificovalet.com
Establishment information: Established in 1923.
Company type: Private company
Business activities: Provides valet parking services.
Business type (SIC): Personal services/miscellaneous
Corporate officers: Joe D. Pacifico, Partner; Kerry T. Pacifico, Partner
Giving statement: Giving through the Pacifico Family Foundation.

Pacifico Family Foundation
6701 Essington Ave.
Philadelphia, PA 19153-3407

Establishment information: Established in 1988 in PA.
Donors: Pacifico Airport Valet Svc.; Joseph R. Pacifico; Pacifico Ford; Kerry Pacifico; Pacifico Hyundai, Inc.
Financial data (yr. ended 12/31/11): Assets, $1,405,857 (M); gifts received, $30,000; expenditures, $38,916; qualifying distributions, $37,350; giving activities include $37,350 for grants.
Purpose and activities: The foundation supports organizations involved with education, health, and Catholicism.
Fields of interest: Arts; Education; Health care.
Type of support: General/operating support; Program development; Scholarship funds.
Geographic limitations: Giving primarily in Philadelphia, PA.
Support limitations: No grants to individuals.
Application information: Applications not accepted. Unsolicited requests for funds not accepted.
Directors: Joseph R. Pacifico; Kerry T. Pacifico; Maria Shore.
EIN: 222782890

2860
PacifiCorp
(also known as Pacific Power/Rocky Mountain Power)
825 N.E. Multnomah St.
Portland, OR 97232 (503) 813-5000

Company URL: http://www.pacificorp.com
Establishment information: Established in 1910.
Company type: Subsidiary of a public company
Ultimate parent company: Berkshire Hathaway Inc.
Business activities: Generates, transmits, and distributes electricity.

Business type (SIC): Electric services
Financial profile for 2010: Number of employees, 100; sales volume, $4,460,000,000
Corporate officers: Gregory E. Abel, Chair. and C.E.O.; Douglas K. Stuver, Sr. V.P. and C.F.O.; Mark C. Moench, Sr. V.P. and Genl. Counsel
Board of directors: Gregory E. Abel, Chair.; Douglas L. Anderson; Micheal G. Dunn; Brent E. Gale; Patrick J. Goodman; Natalie L. Hocken; Mark C. Moench; R. Patrick Reiten; A. Richard Walje
Giving statement: Giving through the PacifiCorp Contributions Program and the PacifiCorp Foundation.
Company EIN: 930246090

PacifiCorp Contributions Program

825 N.E. Multnomah St.
Portland, OR 97232 (503) 813-5000
URL: http://www.pacificorp.com/about/itc.html

Purpose and activities: As a complement to its foundation, PacifiCorp also makes charitable contributions to nonprofit organizations directly. Emphasis is given to organizations that target health and welfare of disadvantaged people, and environmental education. Support is limited to areas of company operations in California, Idaho, Oregon, Utah, Washington, and Wyoming.
Fields of interest: Arts; Environment, formal/general education; Environment, energy; Health care; Housing/shelter, volunteer services; Housing/shelter, rehabilitation; Youth development, fund raising/fund distribution; Children, services; Family services, domestic violence; Aging, centers/services; Developmentally disabled, centers & services; Independent living, disability; Human services; United Ways and Federated Giving Programs Economically disadvantaged.

Program:

The Community Energy Project: The Community Energy Project offers free home weatherization services for low-income senior citizens and people with disabilities who live in Portland. PacifiCorp employee volunteers and others install energy-saving materials.

Type of support: Annual campaigns; Employee volunteer services; General/operating support; Program development.
Geographic limitations: Giving limited to areas of company operations in CA, ID, OR, UT, WA, and WY.

PacifiCorp Foundation

(doing business as Pacific Power/Rocky Mountain Power Foundation)
(also known as PacifiCorp Foundation For Learning)
825 N.E. Multnomah St., Ste. 2000
Portland, OR 97232-4116 (503) 813-7257
FAX: (503) 813-7249;
E-mail: pacificorpfoundation@pacificorp.com;
URL: http://www.pacificorpfoundation.org

Establishment information: Established in 1988 in OR.
Donor: PacifiCorp.
Contact: Lilisa Hall, Exec. Dir.
Financial data (yr. ended 12/31/11): Assets, $36,646,598 (M); expenditures, $2,398,228; qualifying distributions, $2,094,588; giving activities include $1,870,200 for grants.
Purpose and activities: The foundation supports programs designed to promote education; civic and community betterment; culture and arts; and health, welfare, and social services.
Fields of interest: Arts, cultural/ethnic awareness; Arts councils; Visual arts; Museums; Performing arts; Historic preservation/historical societies; Arts; Elementary/secondary education; Education, early childhood education; Higher education; Education, reading; Education; Environment; Health care; Substance abuse, services; Courts/judicial administration; Crime/law enforcement; Children/youth, services; Family services, domestic violence; Aging, centers/services; Human services; Urban/community development; Community/economic development; United Ways and Federated Giving Programs; Public affairs.

Programs:

Civic and Community: The foundation supports environmental and ecological groups, justice and law, housing and urban renewal, neighborhood and community based groups, and state and local government agencies.

Culture and Arts: The foundation supports theaters, dance groups, orchestras, operas, museums, arts councils, cultural centers, halls of fame, heritage foundations, and nonacademic libraries.

Education: The foundation supports organizations involved with K-12 and higher education, literacy, and scholarship funds through intermediary organizations.

Health, Welfare, and Social Service: The foundation supports national health and human service agencies, hospitals, agencies for youth, and the United Way.

Type of support: Annual campaigns; Building/renovation; Continuing support; Curriculum development; Emergency funds; Employee matching gifts; General/operating support; Matching/challenge support; Program development; Scholarship funds.
Geographic limitations: Giving primarily in areas of company operations in northern CA, southeastern, ID, OR, UT, central and southeastern WA, and WY.
Support limitations: No support for religious organizations not of direct benefit to the entire community, political organizations or candidates for public office, discriminatory organizations, veterans' or fraternal organizations, or memberships in chambers of commerce, service clubs, or taxpayer associations. No grants to individuals, or for ballot measuring campaigns, endowments, debt reduction, capital campaigns, computers, software, or related items, maintenance of existing facilities, or conferences, conventions, or events.
Publications: Application guidelines; Grants list.
Application information: Applications accepted. Organizations receiving support are asked to provide a final report. Application form required. Applicants should submit the following:
1) signature and title of chief executive officer
2) qualifications of key personnel
3) statement of problem project will address
4) population served
5) name, address and phone number of organization
6) copy of IRS Determination Letter
7) brief history of organization and description of its mission
8) geographic area to be served
9) how project's results will be evaluated or measured
10) detailed description of project and amount of funding requested
11) contact person
12) copy of current year's organizational budget and/or project budget
13) listing of additional sources and amount of support
14) plans for acknowledgement

Proposals should include a description of past involvement by the foundation with the organization and a one page business letter formally requesting foundation assistance from the organization's C.E.O. or the chair of its board of directors.

Initial approach: Complete online application form and mail proposal and application form to foundation
Copies of proposal: 1
Board meeting date(s): Mar., June, Sept., and Dec.
Deadline(s): Mar. 15 for Education, June 15 for Civic and Community, Sept. 15 for Culture and Arts, and Dec. 15 for Health, Welfare, and Social Service
Final notification: 3 months following deadlines

Officers and Directors:* A. Richard Walje*, Chair.; Mark C. Moench, Secy.; Bruce Williams, Treas.; Karen Gilmore; Lilisa Hall, Exec. Dir.; Pat Reiten; Sara Schillinger.
Number of staff: 1 full-time professional; 2 part-time support.
EIN: 943089826
Selected grants: The following grants are a representative sample of this grantmaker's funding activity:
$250,000 to Institute for Energy Research, Washington, DC, 2009. For education and research.
$143,750 to Horatio Alger Association of Distinguished Americans, Alexandria, VA, 2009. For Horatio Alger Wyoming Scholarship Program.
$50,000 to Building the Wyoming We Want, Casper, WY, 2009. For project.
$50,000 to Horatio Alger Association of Distinguished Americans, Alexandria, VA, 2009. In honor of Mike Morris, Chairman and Chief Executive Office, American Electric Power Company.
$30,000 to University of Utah, David Eccles School of Business, Salt Lake City, UT, 2009. For Opportunity Scholars Program.
$15,000 to Portland Rose Festival Charitable Foundation, Portland, OR, 2009. For intern positions.
$10,000 to American Red Cross, Greater Salt Lake Area Chapter, Salt Lake City, UT, 2009. For disaster and emergency services programs.
$10,000 to Emanuel Medical Center Foundation, Portland, OR, 2009. For Oregon Burn Center's Burn Education and Prevention program providing support for full-time burn center education coordinator, part-time burn educator, educational materials, posters and other burn educational information.

2861
Packaging Corporation of America

1955 W. Field Ct.
Lake Forest, IL 60045-4824
(847) 482-3000
FAX: (302) 655-5049

Company URL: http://www.packagingcorp.com
Establishment information: Established in 1867.
Company type: Public company
Company ticker symbol and exchange: PKG/NYSE
Business activities: Manufactures container board and corrugated products.
Business type (SIC): Paperboard containers; paperboard mills
Financial profile for 2012: Number of employees, 86,300; assets, $2,453,770,000; sales volume, $2,843,880,000; pre-tax net income, $380,560,000; expenses, $2,400,420,000; liabilities, $1,484,310,000
Fortune 1000 ranking: 2012—740th in revenues, 628th in profits, and 807th in assets
Corporate officers: Paul T. Stecko, Chair.; Mark W. Kowlzan, C.E.O.; Richard B. West, Sr. V.P. and C.F.O.; Thomas W. H. Walton, Sr. V.P., Sales and Mktg.; Kent A. Pflederer, V.P., Secy., and Genl.

Counsel; Stephen T. Calhoun, V.P., Human Resources
Board of directors: Paul T. Stecko, Chair.; Cheryl K. Beebe; Hasan Jameel; Mark W. Kowlzan; Robert C. Lyons; Samuel M. Mencoff; Roger B. Porter; Thomas S. Souleles; James D. Woodrum
Plants: Winter Haven, FL; Gas City, IN; Marshalltown, IA; Lancaster, PA; Counce, TN
International operations: Hong Kong
Giving statement: Giving through the Packaging Corporation of America Corporate Giving Program.
Company EIN: 364277050

Packaging Corporation of America Corporate Giving Program

1900 West Field Ct.
Lake Forest, IL 60045-4828
URL: http://www.packagingcorp.com/pages/community_outreach/18.php

Purpose and activities: Packaging Corporation of America makes charitable contributions to nonprofit organizations involved with education and on a case by case basis. Support is given in areas of company operations in Alabama, Arizona, Arkansas, California, Colorado, Florida, Georgia, Illinois, Indiana, Iowa, Maryland, Massachusetts, Michigan, Minnesota, Mississippi, Missouri, Nebraska, Nevada, New Jersey, New York, North Carolina, Ohio, Oklahoma, Pennsylvania, South Carolina, Tennessee, Texas, Utah, Virginia, and Wisconsin.
Fields of interest: Education, reading; Education; General charitable giving Military/veterans.
Type of support: Donated equipment; Donated products; Employee volunteer services; General/operating support; Sponsorships.
Geographic limitations: Giving in areas of company operations in AL, AR, AZ, CA, CO, FL, GA, IA, IL, IN, MD, MI, MN, MO, MS, NC, NE, NJ, NV, NY, OH, OK, PA, SC, TN, TX, UT, VA, and WI.
Application information: Applications not accepted. Contributes only to pre-selected organizations.

2862
Packard, Packard & Johnson

4 Main St., Ste. 200
Los Altos, CA 94022-2904 (650) 947-7300

Company URL: http://www.packard.com
Establishment information: Established in 1979.
Company type: Private company
Business activities: Provides legal services.
Business type (SIC): Legal services
Corporate officers: Ron Packard, Pres.; Von G. Packard, Secy.; Craig H. Johnson, Treas.
Offices: Beaumont, TX; Salt Lake City, UT
Giving statement: Giving through the Packard, Packard & Johnson Foundation.

Packard, Packard & Johnson Foundation

4 Main St., Ste. 200
Los Altos, CA 94022-2904

Establishment information: Established as a company-sponsored operating foundation in 2000 in CA.
Donors: Ann Packard; Crystal Packard; Debra Packard; Dennis Packard; Lon D. Packard; Packard, Packard & Johnson; Ron Packard; Seth Packard; Von G. Packard; Jay Packard; Flo Packard; Steve Anderson; Patricia Anderson; Deseret Trust Company.
Financial data (yr. ended 12/31/11): Assets, $228,960 (M); gifts received, $16,328; expenditures, $132,804; qualifying distributions, $132,804; giving activities include $78,302 for 29 grants (high: $3,784; low: $20).
Purpose and activities: The foundation supports organizations involved with education and human services and awards grants for individual and family needs.
Fields of interest: Historical activities, genealogy; Education, ESL programs; Scholarships/financial aid; Education; Family services; Human services Economically disadvantaged.
Type of support: General/operating support; Grants to individuals; Publication; Research; Scholarship funds; Scholarships—to individuals.
Support limitations: No support for institutions or other foundations.
Application information: Applications accepted. Application form not required.
Initial approach: Proposal
Deadline(s): None
Officers and Directors:* Craig H. Johnson*, Pres.; Von G. Packard*, V.P. and Secy.; Lon D. Packard*, V.P.; Ronald D. Packard*, C.F.O.
EIN: 770549749

2863
Pactiv Corporation

(formerly Tenneco Packaging Inc.)
1900 W. Field Ct.
Lake Forest, IL 60045-4828
(847) 482-2000

Company URL: http://www.pactiv.com
Establishment information: Established in 1965.
Company type: Subsidiary of a foreign company
Business activities: Manufactures packaging, paper products, and consumer products.
Business type (SIC): Paper and paperboard/coated, converted, and laminated; forestry—timber tracts; paperboard mills; paperboard containers; metal products/fabricated; machinery/construction, mining, and materials handling
Financial profile for 2009: Number of employees, 12,000; assets, $3,574,000,000; sales volume, $3,360,000,000; pre-tax net income, $486,000,000; expenses, $2,781,000,000; liabilities, $2,589,000,000
Corporate officers: Donald King, Corp. Cont. and C.A.O.; Edward T. Walters, V.P. and Cont.; Joseph E. Doyle, V.P., Genl. Counsel, and Secy.; Dan Cummins, V.P., Finance and Opers.
Subsidiary: Hexacomb, Inc., Lincolnshire, IL
Plants: Phoenix, AZ; Malvern, AR; Los Angeles, CA; Denver, CO; North Haven, CT; Jacksonville, FL; Smyrna, GA; Wanatah, IN; Marshalltown, IA; Shelbyville, KY; South Portland, ME; Baltimore, MD; Northampton, MA; Filer City, MI; Minneapolis, MN; Fulton, MS; St. Louis, MO; Omaha, NE; North Brunswick, NJ; Buffalo, NY; Morganton, NC; Columbus, OH; Lancaster, PA; Jackson, TN; Salt Lake City, UT; Winchester, VA; Yakima, WA; Tomahawk, WI
Offices: Evanston, IL; Dallas, TX
International operations: Canada; Germany; Mexico; Netherlands; Singapore; United Kingdom
Giving statement: Giving through the Pactiv Corporation Contributions Program.
Company EIN: 362552989

Pactiv Corporation Contributions Program

(formerly Tenneco Packaging Inc. Corporate Giving Program)
c/o Corp. Contribs.
1900 West Field Ct.
Lake Forest, IL 60045-4828 (847) 482-2000
URL: http://www.pactiv.com/Career/diversity2.aspx

Purpose and activities: Pactiv makes charitable contributions to nonprofit organizations that promote the development and advancement of women and minorities in the workforce. Support is given in areas of company operations.
Fields of interest: Employment; Community/economic development Minorities; Women.
Type of support: General/operating support.
Geographic limitations: Giving primarily in areas of company operations.

2864
Padilla Speer Beardsley Inc.

1101 W. River Pkwy., Ste. 400
Minneapolis, MN 55415-1256
(612) 455-1700
FAX: (612) 455-1060

Company URL: http://www.psbpr.com
Establishment information: Established in 1961.
Company type: Private company
Business activities: Provides public relations services.
Business type (SIC): Management and public relations services
Financial profile for 2010: Number of employees, 99
Corporate officer: Lynn Casey, Chair. and C.E.O.
Board of directors: Lynn Casey, Chair.; Bob Brin
Giving statement: Giving through the Padilla Speer Beardsley Inc. Corporate Giving Program.

Padilla Speer Beardsley Inc. Corporate Giving Program

1101 West River Pkwy., Ste. 400
Minneapolis, MN 55415-1241 (612) 455-1700
URL: http://www.psbpr.com/content/about-us/community-spirit.aspx

Purpose and activities: As a complement to its foundation, Padilla Speer Beardsley also makes charitable contributions to nonprofit organizations directly. Support is given primarily in areas of company operations in Minneapolis, Minnesota, and New York, New York.
Fields of interest: Arts; Education; Youth development; Children/youth, services; Family services.
Type of support: Consulting services; Employee volunteer services; Loaned talent; Public relations services; Sponsorships.
Geographic limitations: Giving primarily in areas of company operations in Minneapolis, MN, and New York, NY.

2865
Pagnol et Cie, Inc.

(also known as Chez Panisse Restaurant and Cafe)
1517 Shattuck Ave.
Berkeley, CA 94709-1516 (510) 548-5049

Company URL: http://www.chezpanisse.com/
Establishment information: Established in 1971.
Company type: Private company
Business activities: Operates restaurant and cafe.
Business type (SIC): Restaurants and drinking places
Corporate officers: Alice Waters, Chair. and Pres.; Charles Shere, Secy.
Board of director: Alice Waters, Chair.
Giving statement: Giving through the Edible Schoolyard Project.

The Edible Schoolyard Project

(formerly Chez Panisse Foundation)
1517 Shattuck Ave.
Berkeley, CA 94709-1516 (510) 843-3811
FAX: (510) 843-3880; URL: http://edibleschoolyard.org/

Establishment information: Established in 1996 in CA.
Contact: Carina Wong, Exec. Dir.
Financial data (yr. ended 06/30/12): Revenue, $1,907,065; assets, $3,425,092 (M); gifts received, $1,353,889; expenditures, $1,703,480; program services expenses, $1,046,991; giving activities include $61,338 for 4 grants (high: $40,000; low: $10,939).
Purpose and activities: The foundation is committed to transforming public education by using food traditions and rituals to teach, nurture, and empower young people.
Fields of interest: Agriculture/food, public education; Nutrition.
Geographic limitations: Giving primarily in CA.
Publications: Annual report.
Application information: Applications not accepted. Contributes only to pre-selected organizations.
Officers and Directors:* Mark Buell*, Chair.; Katrina Heron*, Vice-Chair.; Alice Waters*, Pres.; Susan Andrews*, Secy.; Martin Krasney*, Treas.; Francesca Vietor, Exec. Dir.; Sherry Hirota; Christina Kim; Peggy Knickerbocker; John Lyons; Sally Willcox.
Number of staff: 10 full-time professional.
EIN: 943248671

2866
Palace Sports & Entertainment, Inc.

(also known as Detroit Pistons/Detroit Shock)
4 Championship Dr.
Auburn Hills, MI 48326 (248) 377-0100

Company URL: http://www.palacenet.com
Establishment information: Established in 1988.
Company type: Private company
Business activities: Operates arena; operates theaters; operates professional basketball clubs; operates professional ice hockey club.
Business type (SIC): Commercial sports; real estate operators and lessors
Corporate officers: Alan Ostfield, Pres. and C.E.O.; Robert E. Feller, Exec. V.P. and C.F.O.; Marilyn Hauser, Exec. V.P., Corp. Mktg.; John Ciszewski, Exec. V.P., Corp. Sales
Subsidiaries: Center Ice, LLC, Tampa, FL; Detroit Pistons Basketball Company, Auburn Hills, MI
Division: Detroit Shock, Auburn Hills, MI
Giving statement: Giving through the Tulsa Shock Corporate Giving Program.

Tulsa Shock Corporate Giving Program

(formerly Detroit Shock)
c/o Community Rels.
1 W. 3rd St., Ste. 1100
Tulsa, OK 74103-3515
FAX: (918) 599-7729; URL: http://www.wnba.com/shock/community

Purpose and activities: The Tulsa Shock makes charitable contributions of game tickets and memorabilia to nonprofit organizations involved with education, health, fitness in both youth and adults, women, and youth. Support is given primarily in Tulsa.
Fields of interest: Education; Environment; Public health, physical fitness; Health care; Breast cancer; Nutrition; Youth, services; General charitable giving Women.
Type of support: Donated products; In-kind gifts; Income development; Loaned talent.
Geographic limitations: Giving primarily in areas of company operations in Tulsa, OK.
Support limitations: No support for political organizations or candidates. No grants to individuals, or for general operating support, political campaigns, trips or tours, or seminars; no game ticket or memorabilia donations for prizes, volunteer recognition gifts, or giveaways.
Publications: Application guidelines.
Application information: Applications accepted. Telephones calls regarding ticket requests are not encouraged. Support is limited to 1 contribution per organization during any given year. The Community Relations Department handles giving. Application form not required. Applicants should submit the following:
1) name, address and phone number of organization
2) copy of IRS Determination Letter
3) detailed description of project and amount of funding requested
4) contact person

Initial approach: Complete online application for ticket donations; download application form and mail to headquarters for player appearances
Copies of proposal: 1
Deadline(s): 4 weeks prior to need
Final notification: 2 weeks

2867
Palm Bay International, Inc.

301 Yamato Rd., Ste. 1150
Boca Raton, FL 33431-4919
(561) 362-9642
FAX: (561) 362-7296

Company URL: http://www.palmbayimports.com
Establishment information: Established in 1975.
Company type: Private company
Business activities: Sells wine and spirits wholesale.
Business type (SIC): Beer, wine, and distilled beverages—wholesale
Corporate officers: Marc D. Taub, Pres. and C.O.O.; Harish Parekh, Sr. V.P., Finance and C.F.O.
Giving statement: Giving through the Taub Family Foundation, Inc.

Taub Family Foundation, Inc.

48 Harbor Park Dr.
Port Washington, NY 11050-4653

Establishment information: Established in 2000 in FL.
Donors: Palm Bay Imports, Inc.; Linda Taub; Richard Taub; David S. Taub.
Contact: David S. Taub, Pres.
Financial data (yr. ended 12/31/11): Assets, $5,090 (M); gifts received, $12,500; expenditures, $12,561; qualifying distributions, $12,500; giving activities include $12,500 for grants.
Purpose and activities: The foundation supports camps and organizations involved with K-12 education, health, and medical research.
Fields of interest: Elementary/secondary education; Hospitals (specialty); Health care; Brain research; Medical research; Recreation, camps.
Type of support: General/operating support.
Geographic limitations: Giving primarily in MN and NY.
Support limitations: No grants to individuals.
Application information: Applications not accepted.
Officers: David S. Taub, Pres.; Richard Taub, Secy.
Director: Linda Taub.
EIN: 651052540

2868
Pan-American Life Insurance Company

601 Poydras St.
New Orleans, LA 70130-6029
(504) 566-1300
FAX: (506) 2288-0931

Company URL: http://www.panamericanlife.com
Establishment information: Established in 1911.
Company type: Private company
Business activities: Sells life insurance; sells disability insurance; provides investment advisory services.
Business type (SIC): Insurance/life; security and commodity services; insurance/accident and health
Corporate officers: Jose S. Suquet, Chair., Pres., and C.E.O.; Carlos F. Mickan, Exec. V.P. and C.F.O.; Rodolfo J. Revuelta, Sr. V.P. and C.I.O.; Patrick Fraizer, Sr. V.P., Human Resources, and Genl. Counsel; Scott Reitan, Sr. V.P., Admin.; Marta Reeves, V.P., Corp. Mktg.
Board of director: Jose S. Suquet, Chair.
Offices: Fair Oaks, Orange, Pleasanton, Sacramento, Vista, CA; Tampa, FL; Alpharetta, GA; Naperville, IL; Metairie, LA; Ann Arbor, MI; Greensboro, NC; Cleveland, OH; San Juan, PR; Memphis, Nashville, TN; Dallas, The Woodlands, TX
Giving statement: Giving through the Pan-American Life Insurance Company Contributions Program.

Pan-American Life Insurance Company Contributions Program

601 Poydras St.
New Orleans, LA 70130-6029 (877) 939-4550
URL: http://www.palig.com/about/corporate_giving.aspx

Purpose and activities: Pan-American makes charitable contributions to nonprofit organizations involved with arts and culture, zoos, health, law enforcement, community development, and Hispanics/Latinos. Support is given primarily in areas of company operations in New Orleans, Louisiana.

Fields of interest: Museums (art); Performing arts, orchestras; Arts; Zoos/zoological societies; Health care; Crime/law enforcement; YM/YWCAs & YM/YWHAs; Community/economic development; United Ways and Federated Giving Programs Hispanics/Latinos.
Type of support: Continuing support; Employee volunteer services; General/operating support; Sponsorships.
Geographic limitations: Giving on a national and international basis primarily in areas of company operations in New Orleans, LA.

2869
Panasonic Corporation of North America

(formerly Matsushita Electric Corporation of America)
1 Panasonic Way
Panazip 2F-10
Secaucus, NJ 07094-2917 (201) 348-7000

Company URL: http://www.panasonic.com
Establishment information: Established in 1959.
Company type: Subsidiary of a foreign company
Business activities: Manufactures home, office, industrial, and systems electronics.
Business type (SIC): Electronic and other electrical equipment and components
Financial profile for 2010: Number of employees, 2,000
Corporate officers: Joseph M. Taylor, Chair. and C.E.O.; Robert Marin, V.P. and Genl. Counsel; Megan Lee, V.P., Human Resources; Michael Riccio, V.P., Treas., and Cont.; Sandra Karriem, Secy.
Board of directors: Joseph Taylor, Chair.; Robert Marin
Subsidiaries: America Kotobuki Electronics Industries, Inc., Vancouver, WA; Solbourne Computers, Inc., Longmont, CO
Plants: Chula Vista, Cypress, Irvine, San Diego, CA; Columbus, Norcross, Peachtree City, GA; Aiea, HI; Elgin, Franklin Park, IL; Danville, KY; Burlington, NJ; Mooresville, NC; Troy, OH; Caguas, Carolina, PR; Knoxville, Vonore, TN; Brownsville, Fort Worth, TX; Bothell, Kent, WA
Giving statement: Giving through the Panasonic Corporation of North America Corporate Giving Program and the Panasonic Foundation, Inc.

Panasonic Corporation of North America Corporate Giving Program

1 Panasonic Way
Secaucus, NJ 07094-2999
URL: http://www.panasonic.com/community/default.asp

Purpose and activities: As a complement to its foundation, Panasonic Corporation of North America also makes charitable contributions to nonprofit organizations directly. Support is given primarily in areas of company operations, with some emphasis on New Jersey.
Fields of interest: Elementary/secondary education; Environmental education; General charitable giving Children/youth.
Type of support: Donated products; Employee volunteer services; General/operating support; Scholarship funds; Sponsorships; Use of facilities.
Geographic limitations: Giving primarily in areas of company operations, with some emphasis on NJ; giving also to national organizations.
Application information: Applications accepted. Application form not required.
Initial approach: Proposal to headquarters
Final notification: 10 to 15 days

Panasonic Foundation, Inc.

(formerly Matsushita Foundation)
3 Panasonic Way, Ste. 21-1
Secaucus, NJ 07094-2917
E-mail: info@foundation.us.panasonic.com;
URL: http://www.panasonictoolkit.org/foundation/Site.nsf/ID/home

Establishment information: Established in 1984 in DE.
Donors: Matsushita Electric Corp. of America; Panasonic Corp. of North America; Robert S. Ingersoll.
Contact: Larry Leverett, Exec. Dir.
Financial data (yr. ended 12/31/11): Assets, $14,303,872 (M); expenditures, $1,942,926; qualifying distributions, $9,341; giving activities include $9,341 for grants.
Purpose and activities: The foundation supports programs designed to improve public education.
Fields of interest: Education, reform; Education, public education; Elementary/secondary education; Education.
Program:
Panasonic Partnership Program: Through the Panasonic Partnership Program, the foundation forms long-term partnerships with public school districts in Stamford, CT, Atlanta, GA, Santa Fe, NM, Columbus, OH, Norristown, PA, Norfolk, VA, Highline, WA, and Racine, WI to help restructure education systems. The partnership includes evaluations using ESSPAR Protocol, a system to assess systematic education reform, and seminars, consultations, and workshops led by teams of Panasonic Foundation consultants.
Type of support: Conferences/seminars; Consulting services; Management development/capacity building; Technical assistance.
Geographic limitations: Giving primarily in Washington, DC, NJ, NY, OR, and VA.
Support limitations: No grants to individuals, or for annual campaigns, emergency needs, debt reduction, building, land acquisition, endowments, publications, exhibitions, regular conferences of professional organizations, or cultural performances; generally, no grants for general operating support or renovation projects; no loans; no employee matching gifts.
Application information: Applications accepted. Application form required.
Initial approach: Proposal
Deadline(s): None
Officer: Larry Leverett, Exec. Dir.
Directors: C. Kent McGuire; Deborah Meier; Robert M. Orr; Ira Perlman; Sophie Sa.
Number of staff: 2 full-time professional; 2 full-time support.
EIN: 222548639

2870
Panasonic Electronic Devices Corporation of America

(formerly Matsushita Electric Components Corporation of America)
5105 S. National Dr.
Knoxville, TN 37914-6518 (865) 673-0700
FAX: (865) 673-0309

Company URL: http://panasonic.net/corporate
Establishment information: Established in 1982.
Company type: Subsidiary of a foreign company
Business activities: Manufactures electronic components.
Business type (SIC): Electronic components and accessories
Financial profile for 2009: Number of employees, 2,800
Corporate officers: Fumio Ohtsubo, Chair.; Masayuki Matsushita, Vice-Chair.; Ronald J. Green, Pres.; Hideo Nakano, C.F.O.
Board of directors: Fumio Ohtsubo, Chair.; Masayuki Matsushita, Vice-Chair.
Giving statement: Giving through the Panasonic Rio Grande Valley Educational Foundation.

Panasonic Rio Grande Valley Educational Foundation

(formerly Panasonic Tennessee-Japan Cultural Exchange Foundation)
2223 South 10th St.
McAllen, TX 78503

Establishment information: Established in 1994 in TN.
Donors: Matsushita Electronic Components Corp. of America; Panasonic Electronic Devices Corp. of America.
Financial data (yr. ended 02/28/12): Assets, $404,075 (M); expenditures, $0; qualifying distributions, $0.
Purpose and activities: The foundation awards grants to high school students located in Knox County, Tennessee, traveling to Japan for studies.
Fields of interest: International exchange; International studies.
Type of support: Grants to individuals.
Geographic limitations: Giving limited to Knoxville, TN.
Application information: Applications not accepted. Contributes only to pre-selected individuals.
Officers and Directors:* Ronald J. Green*, Pres.; Stephen C. Weingarton, Secy.; David A. Klinkerman*, Treas.; Elva P. Arroyo; Teresa Hernandez.
EIN: 621558047

2871
Panda Restaurant Group, Inc.

1683 Walnut Grove Ave.
P.O. Box 1159
Rosemead, CA 91770-3711
(626) 799-9898

Company URL: http://www.pandarg.com
Establishment information: Established in 1973.
Company type: Private company
Business activities: Operates restaurants.
Business type (SIC): Restaurants and drinking places
Corporate officers: Andrew Cherng, Co-Chair. and Co-C.E.O.; Peggy T. Cherng, Co-Chair. and Co-C.E.O.; Al Chaib, C.O.O.; Leonard Yip, Sr. V.P. and C.I.O.
Board of directors: Andrew Cherng, Co-Chair.; Peggy T. Cherng, Co-Chair.
Subsidiary: Panda Express Inc., Rosemead, CA
Giving statement: Giving through the Panda Cares and the Panda Charitable Foundation.

Panda Cares

c/o Panda Cares Dept.
P.O. Box 1159
Rosemead, CA 91770-3711
URL: http://www.pandacares.org/

Purpose and activities: Panda Cares makes charitable donations of food and gift cards to nonprofit organizations, educational institutions, and hospitals. Special emphasis is directed towards programs designed to assist disadvantaged K-12 children and youth in the areas of education and health. Support is given primarily in areas of company operations, with emphasis on California.
Fields of interest: Elementary/secondary education; Vocational education; Hospitals (specialty); Health care Children/youth.
Type of support: Donated products; Employee volunteer services; In-kind gifts.
Geographic limitations: Giving primarily in areas of company operations, with emphasis on CA.
Support limitations: No support for religious or political organizations. No grants to individuals.
Application information: Applications accepted. Application form required. Applicants should submit the following:
1) brief history of organization and description of its mission
2) geographic area to be served
3) detailed description of project and amount of funding requested
4) contact person

Applications should include the organization's Tax ID Number; and the date, time, address, and expected attendance of the event. Food donation requests should indicate the number of children that will be present.
Initial approach: Complete online application form
Deadline(s): 4 weeks prior to need
Final notification: 1 to 2 weeks

The Panda Charitable Foundation
1683 Walnut Grove Ave.
Rosemead, CA 91770-3711 (626) 799-9898

Establishment information: Changed status to a company-sponsored operating foundation in 1999.
Donors: Panda Management Co., Inc.; Panda Restaurant Group, Inc.
Contact: Winnie Chan, Mgr.
Financial data (yr. ended 12/31/10): Assets, $2,330,261 (M); gifts received, $1,771,760; expenditures, $1,374,257; qualifying distributions, $1,265,399; giving activities include $1,265,399 for 27 grants (high: $266,184; low: $100).
Purpose and activities: The foundation supports organizations involved with Asian culture, cancer, legal aid, disaster relief, international development, leadership development, and Buddhism. Special emphasis is directed toward the educational and medical assistance of children.
Fields of interest: Arts, cultural/ethnic awareness; Higher education; Education; Hospitals (general); Health care; Cancer; Legal services; Disasters, preparedness/services; Children, services; International development; Leadership development; Buddhism Children; Asians/Pacific Islanders.
Type of support: General/operating support; Program development.
Geographic limitations: Giving primarily in CA.
Application information: Applications accepted. Application form not required. Applicants should submit the following:
1) detailed description of project and amount of funding requested

Initial approach: Letter of inquiry
Deadline(s): None
Trustee: Andrew Cherng.
EIN: 954142346
Selected grants: The following grants are a representative sample of this grantmaker's funding activity:
$220,000 to Methodist Hospital Foundation, Arcadia, CA, 2009.
$100,000 to City of Hope, Los Angeles, CA, 2009.
$56,191 to Childrens Miracle Network, Salt Lake City, UT, 2009.
$50,000 to Muscular Dystrophy Association, Orange, CA, 2009.
$20,000 to Cal Poly Pomona Foundation, Pomona, CA, 2009.
$5,000 to Discover a Star Foundation, Universal City, CA, 2009.

2872
Panduit Corp.
18900 Panduit Dr.
Tinley Park, IL 60477-3093 (708) 532-1800

Company URL: http://www.panduit.com/
Establishment information: Established in 1955.
Company type: Private company
Business activities: Provides integrated services and complete product systems to address needs across information technology, manufacturing operations, and facilities management.
Business type (SIC): Electronic components and accessories
Corporate officers: John E. Caveney, Chair. and C.E.O.; Thomas C. Donovan, Pres.; Ron Partridge, V.P., Sales and Mktg.; Gerald W. Caveney, Genl. Counsel and Secy.; Stanley L. Szudrowlcz, Treas.
Board of director: John E. Caveney, Chair.
Giving statement: Giving through the Caveney Family Foundation.

Caveney Family Foundation
18900 Panduit Dr.
Tinley Park, IL 60487

Establishment information: Established in 2007 in IL.
Donor: Caveney Family Enterprises, LP.
Financial data (yr. ended 12/31/11): Assets, $2,830,775 (M); expenditures, $5,695; qualifying distributions, $0.
Fields of interest: Cancer; Human services; Catholic agencies & churches.
Application information: Applications not accepted. Unsolicited requests for funds not accepted.
Trustee: Jack E. Caveney.
EIN: 261333690

2873
Panera Bread Company
3630 S. Geyer Rd., Ste. 100
St. Louis, MO 63127 (314) 984-1000
FAX: (314) 909-3300

Company URL: http://www.panerabread.com
Establishment information: Established in 1981.
Company type: Public company
Company ticker symbol and exchange: PNRA/NASDAQ
Business activities: Operates bakery cafes.
Business type (SIC): Restaurants and drinking places
Financial profile for 2012: Number of employees, 20,800; assets, $1,268,160,000; sales volume, $2,130,060,000; pre-tax net income, $283,000,000; expenses, $1,847,190,000; liabilities, $446,240,000
Fortune 1000 ranking: 2012—907th in revenues, 615th in profits, and 940th in assets
Corporate officers: Ronald M. Shaich, Chair. and Co-C.E.O.; William W. Moreton, Pres. and Co-C.E.O.; Charles J. Chapman III, Exec. V.P. and C.O.O.; Roger Matthews, Exec. V.P. and Co-C.F.O.; William H. Simpson, Sr. V.P. and Co-C.F.O.; Thomas C. Kish, Sr. V.P. and C.I.O.; Scott G. Blair, Sr. V.P. and Genl. Counsel
Board of directors: Ronald M. Shaich, Chair.; Domenic Colasacco; Fred K. Foulkes; Larry J. Franklin; Diane Hessan; Thomas E. Lynch; William W. Moreton
Giving statement: Giving through the Panera Bread Company Contributions Program and the Panera Bread Foundation, Inc.
Company EIN: 042723701

Panera Bread Company Contributions Program
3630 S. Geyer Rd., Ste. 100
St. Louis, MO 63127 (314) 984-1000
FAX: (314) 909-3350; URL: http://www.panerabread.com/about/community/

Financial data (yr. ended 12/31/10): Total giving, $100,000,000, including $100,000,000 for in-kind gifts.
Purpose and activities: As a complement to its foundation, Panera Bread Company also makes charitable contributions to nonprofit organizations directly.
Fields of interest: Human services; Community/economic development.
Type of support: Donated products; Employee matching gifts; General/operating support; In-kind gifts.
Geographic limitations: Giving on a national basis in areas of company operations, and in Canada.
Support limitations: No grants to individuals.
Application information: Applications accepted.
Initial approach: Complete online application

Panera Bread Foundation, Inc.
(formerly Au Bon Pain Foundation, Inc.)
6710 Clayton Rd.
Richmond Heights, MO 63117-1604 (314) 633-7100
URL: http://www.panerabread.com/about/community/

Establishment information: Established in 2002 in MO reincorporated in 1998 in MO.
Donors: Au Bon Pain Co., Inc.; Panera Bread Co.
Contact: Ronald M. Shaich, Chair.
Financial data (yr. ended 12/31/11): Revenue, $7,162,416; assets, $5,218,863 (M); gifts received, $7,162,361; expenditures, $6,445,946; program services expenses, $6,445,946; giving activities include $3,937,818 for grants.
Purpose and activities: The foundation supports various charitable organizations, with an emphasis on food banks.
Fields of interest: Food banks.
Geographic limitations: Giving on a national basis.
Officers: Ronald M. Shaich*, Pres.; John M. Maguire*, V.P.; Scott G. Blair*, Secy.; Jeffrey W. Kip*, Treas.
EIN: 431950869

2874
Panosian Enterprises Inc.
(doing business as Allcom Commercial Brokerage)
111 N. Main St., Ste. 9
Elmira, NY 14901-2921 (607) 737-5280

Establishment information: Established in 1985.
Company type: Private company
Business activities: Provides management services.
Business type (SIC): Management and public relations services
Corporate officers: Daniel P. Panosian, Pres.; Susan Frisbie, Secy.
Giving statement: Giving through the Panosian Family Foundation, Inc.

Panosian Family Foundation, Inc.
111 N. Main St.
Elmira, NY 14901-2921

Establishment information: Established in 1995 in NY.
Donor: Panosian Enterprises, Inc.
Financial data (yr. ended 12/31/11): Assets, $351,154 (M); gifts received, $30,000; expenditures, $21,543; qualifying distributions, $21,300; giving activities include $21,300 for 31 grants (high: $3,000; low: $200).
Purpose and activities: The foundation supports Christian agencies and churches and organizations involved with education and human services.
Fields of interest: Education; Human services; Religion.
Type of support: General/operating support.
Geographic limitations: Giving limited to CA, CO, FL, NJ, NY, and PA, with emphasis on Elmira, NY.
Support limitations: No grants to individuals.
Application information: Applications not accepted. Unsolicited requests for funds not accepted.
Officers: Lucille A. Panosian, Pres.; Manual N. Panosian, V.P.; Daniel P. Panosian, Secy.-Treas.
Directors: Susan P. Frisbie; David M. Panosian; Ronald N. Panosian.
EIN: 161487436

2875
The Pantry, Inc.
305 Gregson Dr.
P.O. Box 8019
Cary, NC 27511 (919) 774-6700
FAX: (302) 636-5454

Company URL: http://www.thepantry.com
Establishment information: Established in 1967.
Company type: Public company
Company ticker symbol and exchange: PTRY/NASDAQ
Business activities: Operates convenience stores.
Business type (SIC): Automotive dealers and gasoline service stations; groceries—retail
Financial profile for 2012: Number of employees, 13,709; assets, $1,799,540,000; sales volume, $8,253,240,000; pre-tax net income, -$5,550,000; expenses, $8,174,580,000; liabilities, $1,474,990,000
Fortune 1000 ranking: 2012—347th in revenues, 886th in profits, and 878th in assets
Corporate officers: Edwin J. Holman, Chair.; Dennis G. Hatchell, Pres. and C.E.O.; Thomas Carney, Sr. V.P., Genl. Counsel, and Secy.; Keith A. Oreson, Sr. V.P., Human Resources; Clyde Preslar, Sr. V.P. and C.F.O.; Joe Venezia, Sr. V.P., Opers.
Board of directors: Edwin J. Holman, Chair.; Robert F. Bernstock; Paul L. Brunswick; Wilfred A. Finnegan; Dennis G. Hatchell; Terry L. McElroy; Mark D. Miles; Bryan E. Monkhouse; Thomas M. Murnane
Giving statement: Giving through the Kangaroo Express Foundation.
Company EIN: 561574463

Kangaroo Express Foundation
(formerly The Pantry Hurricane Relief Fund)
305 Gregson Dr.
Cary, NC 27511 (919) 774-6700

Establishment information: Established in 2005 in NC.
Donors: The Pantry, Inc.; The McLane Co., Inc.
Contact: Keith Oreson
Financial data (yr. ended 09/30/11): Assets, $73,582 (M); gifts received, $17,200; expenditures, $46,000; qualifying distributions, $46,000; giving activities include $46,000 for 27 grants to individuals (high: $2,500; low: $500).
Purpose and activities: The foundation supports the Mississippi Hurricane Katrina School Relief Fund.
Type of support: General/operating support.
Geographic limitations: Giving primarily in LA and MS.
Support limitations: No grants to individuals.
Application information: Applications accepted. Application form required.
Initial approach: Proposal
Deadline(s): None
Officers and Directors:* Paul Moody*, Pres.; Thomas Sheehan*, Secy.; Mark R. Bierley*, Treas.
EIN: 203516326

2876
Papa John's International, Inc.
2002 Papa John's Blvd.
Louisville, KY 40299-2334 (502) 261-7272
FAX: (502) 266-2925

Company URL: http://www.papajohns.com
Establishment information: Established in 1984.
Company type: Public company
Company ticker symbol and exchange: PZZA/NASDAQ
Business activities: Operates and franchises restaurants.
Business type (SIC): Restaurants and drinking places; investors/miscellaneous
Financial profile for 2012: Number of employees, 18,800; assets, $438,410,000; sales volume, $1,342,650,000; pre-tax net income, $98,390,000; expenses, $1,242,850,000; liabilities, $256,890,000
Corporate officers: John H. Schnatter, Chair. and C.E.O.; Lance F. Tucker, Sr. V.P., Treas., C.F.O., and C.A.O.
Board of directors: John H. Schnatter, Chair.; Norborne P. Cole, Jr.; Philip Guarascio; Olivia F. Kirtley; Mark S. Shapiro; William M. Street; W. Kent Taylor
International operations: United Kingdom
Giving statement: Giving through the Papa John's International, Inc. Corporate Giving Program and the Papa John's Team Member Emergency Relief Fund, Inc.
Company EIN: 611203323

Papa John's International, Inc. Corporate Giving Program
2002 Papa Johns Blvd.
Louisville, KY 40299-2334
Address for Papa John's Scholars: Scholarly Pursuits, c/o Scholarship Admin., 4005 Briar Ridge Rd., LaGrange, KY 40031; E-mail for "The Works" Scholarship: pjtws@aol.com; URL: http://www.papajohns.com/about/community.shtm

Purpose and activities: Papa John's makes charitable contributions to nonprofit organizations involved with higher education and on a case by case basis. The company also awards college scholarships to high school seniors.
Fields of interest: Higher education; Health care, patient services; Boys & girls clubs; Youth development, business; Children/youth, services.
Program:
Papa John's Pizza Scholars Program: Papa John's awards college scholarships of up to $1,000 to high school seniors located in immediate delivery areas of participating Papa John's restaurants. Recipients are selected based on academic achievement, demonstrated leadership, community involvement, athletic achievement, and obstacles overcome.
Type of support: Building/renovation; Employee-related scholarships; General/operating support; Scholarships—to individuals; Sponsorships.
Geographic limitations: Giving primarily in areas of company operations, with emphasis on Louisville, KY; giving also to national organizations.
Support limitations: No grants for scholarships for students attending high schools not sponsored by a local Papa John's restaurant for Papa John's Scholars.
Application information: Applications accepted.
Initial approach: Proposal to nearest company restaurant; contact participating restaurants or high school guidance counselor for scholarships
Deadline(s): None; varies for scholarships

Papa John's Team Member Emergency Relief Fund, Inc.
P.O. Box 99900
Louisville, KY 40269-0900 (502) 261-4227

Financial data (yr. ended 12/31/11): Revenue, $86,606; assets, $96,664 (M); gifts received, $51,199; expenditures, $65,951; giving activities include $64,700 for grants.
Purpose and activities: The fund provides financial assistance to individual employees of Papa John's, Inc. who are in need.
Fields of interest: Human services, emergency aid.
Type of support: Grants to individuals.
Officers: Caroline Oyler*, Pres.; Robin Kennedy*, Secy.; Robin Cecil*, Treas.
EIN: 201892180

2877
Paper City Savings Association
4200 8th St., S.
P.O. Box 339
Wisconsin Rapids, WI 54494
(715) 423-8100

Company URL: http://www.papercitysavings.com
Establishment information: Established in 1923.
Company type: Private company
Business activities: Operates savings bank.
Business type (SIC): Credit institutions/personal

Corporate officers: Pamela Ross, Chair.; Lawrence A. Turba, Pres. and C.E.O.; Deborah Edwards, Exec. V.P. and Secy.; Tamera Jepson, Treas.
Board of director: Pamela Ross, Chair.
Giving statement: Giving through the Paper City Savings Charitable Foundation, Inc.

Paper City Savings Charitable Foundation, Inc.

P.O. Box 339
Wisconsin Rapids, WI 54495-0339 (715) 423-8100
Application address: 4200 8th St. S, Wisconsin Rapids WI 54494

Establishment information: Established in 2005 in WI.
Donor: Paper City Savings Association.
Contact: Lawrence A. Turba, Pres.
Financial data (yr. ended 12/31/11): Assets, $180,110 (M); gifts received, $18,000; expenditures, $20,036; qualifying distributions, $19,975; giving activities include $19,975 for grants.
Fields of interest: Education; Human services; Community/economic development.
Geographic limitations: Giving primarily in WI.
Support limitations: No grants to individuals.
Application information: Applications accepted. Application form required. Applicants should submit the following:
1) copy of most recent annual report/audited financial statement/990
Initial approach: Letter
Deadline(s): None
Officers: Lawrence A. Turba, Pres.; Tamera Jepson, Treas.
EIN: 203333369

2878
Parametric Technology Corporation

(also known as PTC)
140 Kendrick St.
Needham, MA 02494-2714 (781) 370-5000
FAX: (781) 370-6000

Company URL: http://www.ptc.com
Establishment information: Established in 1985.
Company type: Public company
Company ticker symbol and exchange: PMTC/NASDAQ
Business activities: Develops, markets, and supports collaborative product commerce software solutions.
Business type (SIC): Computer services
Financial profile for 2012: Number of employees, 5,897; assets, $1,791,630,000; sales volume, $1,255,680,000; pre-tax net income, $120,740,000; expenses, $1,127,580,000; liabilities, $994,380,000
Corporate officers: Donald K. Grierson, Chair.; James E. Heppelmann, Pres. and C.E.O.; Jeffrey D. Glidden, Exec. V.P. and C.F.O.; Robert C. Gremley, Exec. V.P., Corp. Mktg.; Tom Kearns, Sr. V.P. and C.I.O.; Aaron C. Von Staats, V.P. and Genl. Counsel
Board of directors: Donald K. Grierson, Chair.; Thomas Bogan; James E. Heppelmann; Paul A. Lacy; Michael E. Porter; Robert P. Schechter; Renato Zambonini
International operations: Austria; Brazil; Canada; France; Germany; Hong Kong; Netherlands; Switzerland; United Kingdom
Giving statement: Giving through the PTC Corporate Giving Program.
Company EIN: 042866152

PTC Corporate Giving Program

140 Kendrick St.
Needham, MA 02494-2739 (781) 370-5000
FAX: (781) 370-5647; E-mail: schools@ptc.com; URL: http://www.ptc.com/company/community-relations.htm

Purpose and activities: PTC makes charitable contributions to secondary schools and secondary school teachers and on a case by case basis. Support is given in areas of company operations.
Fields of interest: Secondary school/education; Higher education; Education; Cancer; Voluntarism promotion; Science, formal/general education; Mathematics; Engineering/technology; Science.
International interests: Africa; Asia; China; Europe; Middle East.
Program:
PTC DesignQuest Schools Program: Through the PTC Design & Technology in Schools Program, PTC provides donated or low cost software and a learning program to teachers to bring 3D design to the classroom. The program includes teacher training, classroom materials, discussion groups, and web-based resources for design collaboration between schools.
Type of support: Conferences/seminars; Curriculum development; Donated equipment; Donated products; Employee volunteer services; Grants to individuals; In-kind gifts; Sponsorships.
Geographic limitations: Giving in areas of company operations, with emphasis on MA, Africa, Asia, China, Europe, and the Middle East.
Publications: Application guidelines.
Application information: Applications accepted. Teachers receiving software donations are expected to attend training classes. The Partners Department handles giving. The company has a staff that only handles contributions. A contributions committee reviews all requests.
E-mail messages for the PTC Design & Technology in Schools Program should include the teacher's name, address, telephone number, fax number, and e-mail address; the name of the teacher's school; the name of the school's principal; and the school's address, telephone number, and fax number; and indicate the teacher's subject and grade level; the number of years the teacher has taught; and the nearest major city.
Initial approach: E-mail headquarters for PTC DesignQuest Schools Program
Committee meeting date(s): Bimonthly
Deadline(s): None for PTC DesignQuest Schools Program
Final notification: Following review
Number of staff: 12 full-time professional; 3 part-time professional.

2879
Park Bank

330 E. Kilbourn Ave.
Milwaukee, WI 53202 (414) 466-8000

Company URL: http://www.parkbankonline.com
Establishment information: Established in 1915.
Company type: Subsidiary of a private company
Business activities: Operates commercial bank.
Business type (SIC): Banks/commercial
Corporate officers: P. Michael Mahoney, Chair. and C.E.O.; David P. Werner, Pres.; Robert J. Makowski, Jr., Exec. V.P. and C.F.O.; Cheryl L. Sorgi, 1st V.P., Human Resources; Robert A. Mihm, V.P. and Cont.; Elizabeth S. Borst, V.P., Mktg.
Board of directors: Michael P. Mahoney, Chair.; William J. Abraham, Jr.; Helmut M. Adam; Thomas L. Ducrest; Kevin P. Egan; Michael J. Kelly; James H. Schloemer; K. Terrence Wakefield; Michael H. White
Giving statement: Giving through the Park Bank Foundation, Inc.

Park Bank Foundation, Inc.

330 E. Kilbourn Ave., Ste. 150
Milwaukee, WI 53202-6619

Establishment information: Established in 1980 in WI.
Donor: Park Bank.
Contact: Susan Baudo, Secy.
Financial data (yr. ended 12/31/11): Assets, $617,952 (M); gifts received, $200,000; expenditures, $222,336; qualifying distributions, $206,185; giving activities include $206,185 for grants.
Purpose and activities: The foundation supports hospitals and organizations involved with arts and culture, education, hunger, human services, and community development.
Fields of interest: Arts; Higher education; Education; Hospitals (general); Food services; YM/YWCAs & YM/YWHAs; Family services; Human services; Community/economic development; United Ways and Federated Giving Programs.
Type of support: Annual campaigns; Capital campaigns; Continuing support; General/operating support.
Geographic limitations: Giving limited to the greater Milwaukee, WI, area.
Support limitations: No grants to individuals.
Application information: Applications accepted. Letters of inquiry should be submitted using organization letterhead. Application form not required. Applicants should submit the following:
1) copy of IRS Determination Letter
2) copy of most recent annual report/audited financial statement/990
Initial approach: Letter of inquiry
Copies of proposal: 1
Board meeting date(s): Apr., Aug., and Dec.
Deadline(s): Apr 1, Aug. 1, and Dec. 1
Officers and Directors:* P. Michael Mahoney*, Pres.; Michael J. Kelly*, V.P.; Lorraine A. Kelly*, V.P.; Susan Baudo, Secy.; James W. Wright*, Treas.
EIN: 391365837

2880
Park Corporation

6200 Riverside Dr.
Cleveland, OH 44135 (216) 267-4870
FAX: (216) 267-7876

Company URL: http://www.parkcorp.com
Establishment information: Established in 1948.
Company type: Private company
Business activities: Manufactures machinery and components for the steel and energy industries.
Business type (SIC): Machinery/metalworking
Financial profile for 2010: Number of employees, 2,260
Corporate officers: Raymond P. Park, Chair.; Daniel K. Park, Pres. and Co-C.E.O.; Rich Schuitz, C.I.O.; Joseph J. Adams, V.P. and C.F.O.; Shelva J. Davis, V.P. and Secy.; Robert J. Peterson, V.P. and Genl. Counsel
Board of director: Raymond P. Park, Chair.

Giving statement: Giving through the Park Foundation.

The Park Foundation

6200 Riverside Dr.
Cleveland, OH 44135-3132

Establishment information: Established in 2004 in OH.
Donors: Georgia Financial, LLC; Park Corp.; Piper A. Park; Raymond P. Park.
Financial data (yr. ended 12/31/11): Assets, $53,191,507 (M); expenditures, $2,546,869; qualifying distributions, $2,457,250; giving activities include $2,457,250 for grants.
Purpose and activities: The foundation supports community foundations and organizations involved with education, health, cancer, learning disorders, human services, Christianity, and economically disadvantaged people.
Fields of interest: Education, special; Education; Health care, clinics/centers; Health care; Cancer; Learning disorders; Disasters, fire prevention/control; Children, services; Human services; Foundations (community); Christian agencies & churches Economically disadvantaged.
Type of support: Capital campaigns; General/operating support; Program development; Scholarship funds.
Geographic limitations: Giving primarily in CA, FL, NV, OH, OR, PA, TX, and WV.
Support limitations: No grants to individuals.
Application information: Applications not accepted. Contributes only to pre-selected organizations.
Officers: Raymond P. Park, Pres.; Kelly C. Park, V.P. and Treas.; Dan K. Park, V.P.; Patrick M. Park, V.P.; Piper A. Park, V.P.; Ricky L. Bertram, Secy.
EIN: 200791170
Selected grants: The following grants are a representative sample of this grantmaker's funding activity:
$332,500 to University of Texas M.D. Anderson Cancer Center, Houston, TX, 2011.
$250,000 to Scripps Translational Science Institute, La Jolla, CA, 2011.
$125,000 to American Heart Association, West Palm Beach, FL, 2011.
$50,000 to HopeKids, Phoenix, AZ, 2011.
$50,000 to Preservation Foundation of Palm Beach, Palm Beach, FL, 2011.
$50,000 to Providence Saint Vincent Medical Foundation, Portland, OR, 2011.
$35,000 to Nathan Adelson Hospice Foundation, Las Vegas, NV, 2011.
$25,000 to Shared Hope International, Vancouver, WA, 2011.
$20,000 to International Society of Palm Beach, Palm Beach, FL, 2011.
$15,000 to NAACP, Cleveland, OH, 2011.

2881
Park National Corporation

50 N. 3rd St.
P.O. Box 3500
Newark, OH 43058-3500 (740) 349-8451

Company URL: http://www.parknationalcorp.com
Establishment information: Established in 1908.
Company type: Public company
Company ticker symbol and exchange: PRK/AMEX
Business activities: Operates bank holding company; operates commercial bank.
Business type (SIC): Banks/commercial
Financial profile for 2012: Number of employees, 1,826; assets, $6,642,800,000; pre-tax net income, $104,330,000; liabilities, $5,992,440,000
Corporate officers: Charles Daniel DeLawder, Chair. and C.E.O.; Harry O. Egger, Vice-Chair.; David L. Trautman, Pres. and Secy.; Brady T. Burt, C.F.O.
Board of directors: Charles Daniel DeLawder, Chair.; Harry O. Egger, Vice-Chair.; Maureen Buchwald; F. William Englefield IV; Stephen J. Kambeitz; Timothy S. McLain; William T. McConnell; John J. O'Neill; David L. Trautman; Rick R. Taylor; Sarah Reese Wallace; Leon Zazworsky
Subsidiaries: Century National Bank, Zanesville, OH; The First-Knox National Bank of Mount Vernon, Mount Vernon, OH; Park National Bank, Newark, OH; The Richland Trust Co., Mansfield, OH; Second National Bank, Greenville, OH; United Bank, N.A., Bucyrus, OH
Giving statement: Giving through the Park National Corporation Foundation.
Company EIN: 311179518

The Park National Corporation Foundation

(formerly The Park National Bank Foundation)
P.O. Box 3500
Newark, OH 43058-3500

Establishment information: Established in 1983 in OH.
Donors: The Park National Bank; Fairfield National Bank; The Richland Trust Co.; Park National Corp.
Financial data (yr. ended 12/31/11): Assets, $9,637,770 (M); gifts received, $500; expenditures, $1,379,433; qualifying distributions, $1,373,801; giving activities include $1,373,801 for grants.
Purpose and activities: The foundation supports community foundations and organizations involved with arts and culture, education, health, and human services.
Fields of interest: Arts councils; Performing arts; Arts; Elementary/secondary education; Higher education; Education; Hospitals (general); Health care; Salvation Army; YM/YWCAs & YM/YWHAs; Human services; Foundations (community); United Ways and Federated Giving Programs.
Type of support: General/operating support; Scholarship funds.
Geographic limitations: Giving primarily in OH, with emphasis on Columbus, Newark, and Springfield.
Support limitations: No grants to individuals.
Application information: Applications not accepted. Contributes only to pre-selected organizations.
Officers and Trustees: C. Daniel DeLawder*, Chair.; David L. Trautman, Pres.; Cheryl L. Snyder, Secy.-Treas.; John W. Kozak; Laura B. Lewis.
EIN: 316249406
Selected grants: The following grants are a representative sample of this grantmaker's funding activity:
$50,000 to Denison University, Granville, OH, 2010.
$46,150 to United Way of Knox County, Mount Vernon, OH, 2010.
$20,000 to Knox Community Hospital, Mount Vernon, OH, 2010.
$16,500 to YMCA of Mount Vernon, Mount Vernon, OH, 2010.
$12,000 to Lancaster Festival, Lancaster, OH, 2010.
$5,130 to United Way of Central Ohio, Columbus, OH, 2010.
$5,000 to Lehman Foundation, Sidney, OH, 2010.
$5,000 to Piqua Arts Council, Piqua, OH, 2010.
$3,750 to Licking Memorial Hospital Foundation, Newark, OH, 2010.
$2,000 to Fairhope Hospice and Palliative Care, Lancaster, OH, 2010.

2882
Park Place Corporation

6801 Augusta Rd.
Greenville, SC 29605-5124 (864) 422-8118

Company URL: http://www.parkplacecorp.com
Establishment information: Established in 1931.
Company type: Private company
Business activities: Manufactures mattresses; manufactures furniture.
Business type (SIC): Furniture/household
Financial profile for 2010: Number of employees, 210
Corporate officers: Jimmy Orders, Pres. and C.E.O.; David Orders, C.O.O.; Jason Kelly, C.F.O.; Lynn Mancino, Cont.
Giving statement: Giving through the Orders Foundation.

Orders Foundation

P.O. Box 8127
Greenville, SC 29604-8127
Application address: 6801 Augusta Rd., Greenville, SC 29605, tel.: (864) 422-8118

Donors: Orderest, Inc.; Park Place Corporation.
Contact: Kay Williams
Financial data (yr. ended 12/31/11): Assets, $0 (M); expenditures, $0; qualifying distributions, $0.
Purpose and activities: The foundation supports organizations involved with higher education, health, and Christianity.
Type of support: Employee-related scholarships; General/operating support.
Geographic limitations: Giving limited to areas of company operations.
Application information: Applications accepted. Application form required.
Initial approach: No Public Application Accepted
Deadline(s): None
Trustee: David E. Karr.
EIN: 576021152

2883
Park Region Mutual Telephone Co.

100 Main St. N.
P.O. Box 277
Underwood, MN 56586 (218) 826-6161

Company URL: http://www.prtel.com
Establishment information: Established in 1906.
Company type: Private company
Business activities: Provides local telephone communications services.
Business type (SIC): Telephone communications
Corporate officers: Dave Bickett, C.E.O.; Bonnie Denzel, Secy.; Mary Jo Biegler, Cont.
Board of directors: Dan Barry; Paul Beckman; Dennis Delzer; Bonnie Denzel; Norbert Evavold; Eugene Ouren; Richard Rossum; Keith Sellner; Glen Thomas
Subsidiary: Otter Tail Telecom, LLC, Fergus Falls, MN
Giving statement: Giving through the Park Region Telephone Charitable Trust, Inc.

Park Region Telephone Charitable Trust, Inc.

100 Main St.
P.O. Box 277
Underwood, MN 56586-0277

Establishment information: Established in 1993.
Donor: Park Region Mutual Telephone Co.
Financial data (yr. ended 12/31/11): Assets, $7,394 (M); gifts received, $292; expenditures, $500; qualifying distributions, $500; giving activities include $500 for grants.
Purpose and activities: The trust supports historical societies and organizations involved with recreation and community development.
Fields of interest: Human services; Community/economic development.
Type of support: General/operating support.
Geographic limitations: Giving primarily in MN.
Support limitations: No grants to individuals.
Application information: Applications not accepted. Unsolicited requests for funds not accepted.
Directors: Dan Barry; Paul Beckman; Dennis Delzer; Eugene Ouren; Larry Peasley; Richard Rossum; Glenn Thomas.
Officers: Norbert Evavold, Pres.; Keith Sellner, V.P.; Bonnie Denzel, Secy.
EIN: 411746244

2884
Parker Development Company

4525 Serrano Pkwy.
El Dorado Hills, CA 95762 (916) 939-4060

Company URL: http://www.parkerdevco.com
Establishment information: Established in 1956.
Company type: Private company
Business activities: Operates real estate development company.
Business type (SIC): Real estate subdividers and developers
Corporate officers: Bill Parker, Pres.; Timothy Parker, C.O.O.; Clark Winn, C.F.O.; Florence Tanner, Corp. Secy.; Patty Peck, Cont.
Giving statement: Giving through the Parker Development Company Contributions Program and the Parker Family Foundation.

Parker Development Company Contributions Program

4525 Serrano Pkwy.
El Dorado Hills, CA 95762-7510 (916) 939-4060
URL: http://www.parkerdevco.com/community.html

Purpose and activities: As a complement to its foundation, Parker Development Company makes charitable contributions to nonprofit organizations directly. Support is given primarily in areas of company operations in El Dorado Hills, California.
Fields of interest: Crime/violence prevention, sexual abuse; Boys & girls clubs; Family services, domestic violence.
Type of support: General/operating support; Sponsorships.
Geographic limitations: Giving primarily in areas of company operations in El Dorado County, CA.

Parker Family Foundation

4525 Serrano Pkwy.
El Dorado Hills, CA 95762-7510 (916) 939-4060
E-mail: ftanner@parkerdevco.com

Establishment information: Established in 2006 in CA.
Donor: Parker Development Co.
Financial data (yr. ended 09/30/11): Assets, $891,214 (M); expenditures, $50,587; qualifying distributions, $49,759; giving activities include $47,965 for 12 grants (high: $10,600; low: $100).
Fields of interest: YM/YWCAs & YM/YWHAs.
Geographic limitations: Giving primarily in CA.
Support limitations: No grants to individuals.
Application information: Applications accepted. Application form required.
Initial approach: Mail proposal
Deadline(s): None
Officers and Directors:* William R. Parker*, Pres.; L. Clark Winn, C.F.O.; Susan D. Parker*, V.P.; Florence Tanner*, Secy.; Jennifer Parker Dodson; James E. Parker; Lauren Parker.
EIN: 208106323

2885
Parker Poe Adams & Bernstein LLP

3 Wachovia Ctr.
401 S. Tryon St., Ste. 3000
Charlotte, NC 28202-1935 (704) 372-9000

Company URL: http://www.parkerpoe.com
Establishment information: Established in 1884.
Company type: Private company
Business activities: Operates law firm.
Business type (SIC): Legal services
Corporate officers: William P. Farthing, Jr., Managing Partner; Dale E. Hower, C.F.O.; Steve M. Fletcher, C.I.O.
Offices: Washington, DC; Charlotte, Raleigh, NC; Charleston, Columbia, Myrtle Beach, Spartanburg, SC
Giving statement: Giving through the Parker Poe Adams & Bernstein LLP Pro Bono Program.

Parker Poe Adams & Bernstein LLP Pro Bono Program

3 Wachovia Ctr.
401 S. Tryon St., Ste. 3000
Charlotte, NC 28202-1935 (704) 372-9000
E-mail: jaybutler@parkerpoe.com; URL: http://www.parkerpoe.com/about-us/pro-bono/

Contact: Jay Butler, Partner
Fields of interest: Legal services.
Type of support: Pro bono services - legal.
Geographic limitations: Giving primarily in areas of company operations in Washington, DC, Charlotte, and Raleigh, NC, Charleston, Columbia, Myrtle Beach, and Spartanburg, SC.
Application information: A Pro Bono Committee manages the pro bono program.

2886
Parker-Hannifin Corporation

6035 Parkland Blvd.
Cleveland, OH 44124-4141 (216) 896-3000
FAX: (216) 896-4000

Company URL: http://www.parker.com
Establishment information: Established in 1918.
Company type: Public company
Company ticker symbol and exchange: PH/NYSE
International Securities Identification Number: US7010941042
Business activities: Produces motion control and fluid system components.
Business type (SIC): Machinery/industrial and commercial; metal products/fabricated; machinery/refrigeration and service industry; aircraft and parts
Financial profile for 2012: Number of employees, 59,300; assets, $11,170,280,000; sales volume, $13,145,940,000; pre-tax net income, $1,576,700,000; expenses, $11,569,240,000; liabilities, $6,273,770,000
Fortune 1000 ranking: 2012—211th in revenues, 178th in profits, and 361st in assets
Forbes 2000 ranking: 2012—745th in sales, 579th in profits, and 1380th in assets
Corporate officers: Donald E. Washkewicz, Chair., Pres., and C.E.O.; Jon P. Marten, Exec. V.P., Finance, Admin, and C.F.O.; Daniel S. Serbin, Exec. V.P., Human Resources; William G. Eline, V.P. and C.I.O.; Thomas A. Piraino, V.P., Genl. Counsel, and Secy.; Pamela J. Huggins, V.P. and Treas.; Catherine A. Suever, V.P. and Corp. Cont.; M. Craig Maxwell, V.P., Tech.
Board of directors: Donald E. Washkewicz, Chair.; Robert G. Bohn; Linda S. Harty; William E. Kassling; Robert J. Kohlhepp; Klaus-Peter Mueller; Candy M. Obourn; Joseph M. Scaminace; Wolfgang R. Schmitt; Ake Svensson; James L. Wainscott
Subsidiary: SAES-Parker UHP Components Corp., San Luis Obispo, CA
Divisions: Automotive & Refrigeration Group, Cleveland, OH; Parker Bertea Aerospace Group, Irvine, CA
Plants: Macedonia, OH; Ogden, UT
International operations: Argentina; Australia; Austria; Belgium; Bermuda; Brazil; Canada; Chile; China; Czech Republic; Denmark; Finland; France; Germany; Gibraltar; Hong Kong; Hungary; India; Ireland; Italy; Japan; Luxembourg; Malaysia; Malta; Mexico; Namibia; Netherlands; New Zealand; Norway; Poland; Portugal; Russia; Scotland; Singapore; South Africa; South Korea; Spain; Sweden; Switzerland; Taiwan; Thailand; Turkey; United Arab Emirates; United Kingdom; Venezuela
Historic mergers: Commercial Intertech Corp. (April 11, 2000)
Giving statement: Giving through the Parker-Hannifin Foundation and the Precision Rubber Products Foundation, Inc.
Company EIN: 340451060

The Parker-Hannifin Foundation

6035 Parkland Blvd.
Cleveland, OH 44124-4186
URL: http://www.parker.com/

Establishment information: Incorporated in 1953 in OH.
Donor: Parker-Hannifin Corp.
Financial data (yr. ended 06/30/12): Assets, $2,267,130 (M); gifts received, $1,277,711; expenditures, $4,930,223; qualifying distributions, $4,930,223; giving activities include $4,544,759 for 719 grants (high: $364,350; low: $25) and $361,051 for 411 employee matching gifts.
Purpose and activities: The foundation supports organizations involved with arts and culture, education, health, sports, human services, community economic development, and civic affairs.
Fields of interest: Performing arts, theater; Performing arts, orchestras; Arts; Secondary school/education; Higher education; Libraries (public); Education; Hospitals (general); Health care, clinics/centers; Health care; Athletics/sports, amateur leagues; Boy scouts; Girl scouts; Youth development, business; Salvation Army; YM/YWCAs & YM/YWHAs; Children/youth, services; Residential/custodial care, hospices; Aging, centers/services; Human services; Community/economic development; United Ways and Federated Giving Programs; Public affairs.
Program:
Employee Matching Gifts: The foundation matches contributions made by employees of

Parker-Hannifin to educational institutions on a one-for-one basis from $20 to $5,000 per employee, per institution, per year up to $10,000 per employee, per year.
Type of support: Annual campaigns; Building/renovation; Capital campaigns; Employee matching gifts; Endowments; General/operating support; Scholarship funds.
Geographic limitations: Giving primarily in areas of company operations, with emphasis on Cleveland, OH.
Support limitations: No support for fraternal or labor organizations.
Application information: Applications not accepted. Contributes only to pre-selected organizations.
Board meeting date(s): Jan. and July
Officers and Trustees:* Donald E. Washkewicz*, Pres.; Daniel S. Serbin, V.P.; Thomas A. Piraino*, Secy.
EIN: 346555686

Precision Rubber Products Foundation, Inc.

6 Hale Ct.
Lebanon, TN 37087-8401

Donor: Wynn's-Precision, Inc.
Financial data (yr. ended 06/30/12): Assets, $1,632,625 (M); expenditures, $75,119; qualifying distributions, $71,000; giving activities include $71,000 for grants.
Purpose and activities: The foundation supports organizations involved with higher education, health, cancer, and human services.
Fields of interest: Education; Health care; Religion.
Type of support: Employee-related scholarships; General/operating support.
Application information: Applications not accepted. Unsolicited requests for funds not accepted.
Officers and Board Members:* Anita Huddleston*, Pres.; Mary Mathis*, Secy.; Mark Clemmons; Howard Gillette; Jerry L. McFadden; Shirley Mitchell; Sherry Piercey.
EIN: 310503347

2887
Parsons Corporation

100 W. Walnut St.
Pasadena, CA 91124-0001 (626) 440-2000

Company URL: http://www.parsons.com
Establishment information: Established in 1944.
Company type: Private company
Business activities: Provides engineering services; provides general contract construction services.
Business type (SIC): Engineering, architectural, and surveying services; heavy construction other than building construction contractors
Financial profile for 2011: Number of employees, 10,574; sales volume, $2,710,000,000
Corporate officers: Charles L. Harrington, Chair. and C.E.O.; Curtis A. Bower, Vice-Chair.; George L. Ball, Exec. V.P., Treas., and C.F.O.; Clyde E. Ellis, Sr. V.P. and Genl. Counsel
Board of directors: Charles L. Harrington, Chair.; Curtis A. Bower, Vice-Chair.; C. Michael Armstrong; Molly Corbett Broad; Mark K. Holdsworth; Lawrence V. Jackson; William L. Kimsey; James S. Marlen; James F. McGovern; James F. McNulty; Adm. R.J. Zlatoper
Subsidiaries: Barton-Ashman Associates, Inc., Evanston, IL; Engineering-Science, Inc., Pasadena, CA; Chas. T. Main, Inc., Boston, MA; The Ralph M. Parsons Co., Pasadena, CA; Parsons Construction Services, Inc., Houston, TX; Parsons Constructors Inc., Pasadena, CA; Parsons Municipal Services, Inc., Pasadena, CA; S.I.P. Engineering, Inc., Houston, TX
International operations: United Kingdom
Giving statement: Giving through the Parsons Corporation Contributions Program and the Toyota Motor Corporation.

Parsons Corporation Contributions Program

100 W. Walnut St.
Pasadena, CA 91124-0001 (626) 440-2000
FAX: (626) 440-2630; URL: http://www.parsons.com/about-parsons/Pages/csr.aspx

Purpose and activities: Parsons makes charitable contributions to nonprofit organizations involved with education, culture, and civic affairs. Support is given on a national and international basis in areas of company operations.
Fields of interest: Arts; Higher education; Environment, pollution control; Environment; Health care, blood supply; Health care; Housing/shelter, volunteer services; Safety/disasters; Human services.
Type of support: Employee volunteer services; General/operating support; Scholarship funds; Sponsorships.
Geographic limitations: Giving on a national and international basis in areas of company operations.

2888
Parsons Public Relations

768 Garfield St.
Seattle, WA 98109 (206) 789-5668

Company URL: http://parsonspr.com
Establishment information: Established in 1992.
Company type: Private company
Business activities: Operates a full-service public relations company.
Business type (SIC): Management and public relations services
Corporate officer: Joanie Parsons, Pres.
Giving statement: Giving through the Parsons Public Relations Corporate Giving Program.

Parsons Public Relations Corporate Giving Program

768 Garfield St.
Seattle, WA 98109-3005 (206) 789-5668
E-mail: info@parsonspr.com; URL: http://parsonspr.com

Purpose and activities: Parsons Public Relations is a certified B Corporation that donates a percentage of revenues to nonprofit organizations. Support is given primarily in areas of company operations in Washington, with emphasis on Seattle; giving also to national and international organizations.
Fields of interest: General charitable giving.
Type of support: Employee volunteer services; General/operating support.
Geographic limitations: Giving primarily in areas of company operations in Washington, with emphasis on Seattle; giving also to national and international organizations.

2889
Parthenon Sportswear Limited, Inc.

95 Ethel Rd.
Edison, NJ 08817-2209 (732) 248-9440

Establishment information: Established in 2010.
Company type: Private company
Business activities: Sells men's, women's, and children's sportswear wholesale.
Business type (SIC): Apparel, piece goods, and notions—wholesale
Corporate officer: Alan Shamah, Principal
Giving statement: Giving through the Isadore Shamah & Sons Foundation, Inc.

Isadore Shamah & Sons Foundation, Inc.

(formerly Parthenon Sportswear Foundation, Inc.)
219 N. Broadway
Nyack, NY 10960-2908

Establishment information: Established in 1981.
Donors: Parthenon Sportswear Ltd., Inc.; Harold Shamah; Isaac Shamah; Isadore Shamah; Shamrani Realty.
Financial data (yr. ended 12/31/11): Assets, $574,529 (M); expenditures, $98,891; qualifying distributions, $85,531; giving activities include $76,069 for 68 grants (high: $12,000; low: $36).
Purpose and activities: The foundation supports organizations involved with education, cancer, and Judaism.
Fields of interest: Religion.
Type of support: General/operating support.
Geographic limitations: Giving limited to NY.
Support limitations: No grants to individuals.
Application information: Applications not accepted. Unsolicited requests for funds not accepted.
Officers: Isadore Shamah, Pres.; Harold Shamah, Secy.; Isaac Shamah, Treas.
EIN: 222366563

2890
Partnership Capital Growth Advisor

1 Embarcadero Ctr., Ste. 3810
San Francisco, CA 94111 (415) 705-8008

Company URL: http://www.pcg-advisors.com
Establishment information: Established in 2006.
Company type: Private company
Business activities: Operates investment company that facilitates capital relationships in the healthy, active, and sustainable living marketplace.
Business type (SIC): Investors/miscellaneous
Corporate officers: Zach Stout, C.F.O.; Kim Mueller, V.P., Finance and Admin.
Giving statement: Giving through the Partnership Capital Growth Advisor Corporate Giving Program.

Partnership Capital Growth Advisor Corporate Giving Program

1 Embarcadero Ctr., Ste. 3810
San Francisco, CA 94111-3726 (415) 705-8008
URL: http://www.pcg-advisors.com

Purpose and activities: Partnership Capital Growth Advisor is a certified B Corporation that donates a percentage of profits to nonprofit organizations that promote healthy, active, and sustainable living.
Fields of interest: Health care.

Type of support: General/operating support.

2891
The Pastime Amusement Company

211 King St., Ste. 300
Charleston, SC 29401-3190
(843) 722-3198

Establishment information: Established in 1908.
Company type: Private company
Business activities: Operates nonresidential buildings.
Business type (SIC): Real estate operators and lessors
Corporate officer: Joyce Darby, Mgr.
Giving statement: Giving through the Sottile Foundation.

Sottile Foundation

P.O. Box 242
Charleston, SC 29402-0242 (843) 722-2615

Establishment information: Established in SC.
Donor: Pastime Amusement Co.
Contact: Mike Macy, Accountant
Financial data (yr. ended 12/31/11): Assets, $384,298 (M); expenditures, $46,849; qualifying distributions, $46,000; giving activities include $46,000 for grants.
Purpose and activities: The foundation supports organizations involved with arts and culture, education, and Catholicism.
Fields of interest: Arts; Education; Human services.
Geographic limitations: Giving limited to the Charleston, SC, area.
Support limitations: No grants to individuals.
Application information: Applications accepted. Application form required.
Initial approach: Letter
Deadline(s): None
Trustees: Joyce L. Darby; Mary Ellen Way.
EIN: 576025623

2892
Patagonia, Inc.

259 W. Santa Clara St.
Ventura, CA 93001-2545 (805) 643-8616

Company URL: http://www.patagonia.com
Establishment information: Established in 1953.
Company type: Subsidiary of a private company
Business activities: Manufactures outdoor clothing and equipment.
Business type (SIC): Apparel and other finished products made from fabrics and similar materials
Financial profile for 2009: Number of employees, 300
Corporate officers: Casey Sheahan, Pres. and C.E.O.; Martha Groszewski, V.P., Finance and C.F.O.
Giving statement: Giving through the Patagonia Environmental Grants Program.

Patagonia Environmental Grants Program

8550 White Fir St.
P.O. Box 32050
Reno, NV 89523-2050
URL: http://www.patagonia.com/web/us/contribution/patagonia.go?assetid=2927

Purpose and activities: Patagonia makes charitable contributions to nonprofit organizations involved with the environment. Special emphasis is directed toward programs that build a strong base of citizen support. Support is given on a national basis, and to Argentina, Austria, Belgium, Canada, Chile, Denmark, France, Germany, Ireland, Italy, Japan, Luxembourg, the Netherlands, Norway, Spain, Sweden, Switzerland, and United Kingdom.
Fields of interest: Environment, natural resources; Environment, forests; Environment.
International interests: Argentina; Austria; Belgium; Canada; Chile; Denmark; Europe; France; Germany; Ireland; Italy; Japan; Luxembourg; Netherlands; Norway; Spain; Sweden; Switzerland; United Kingdom.
Type of support: General/operating support; In-kind gifts; Sponsorships.
Geographic limitations: Giving on a national basis, and in Argentina, Austria, Belgium, Canada, Chile, Denmark, France, Germany, Ireland, Italy, Japan, Luxembourg, the Netherlands, Norway, Spain, Sweden, Switzerland, and the United Kingdom.
Support limitations: No grants for land acquisition, land trusts, conservation easements, endowments, green building projects, political purposes, environmental conferences, research not in support of a developed plan for specific action to alleviate an environmental problem, political campaigns, or general environmental education efforts.
Publications: Application guidelines.
Application information: Applications accepted. Support is limited to 1 contribution per organization during any given year. Application form required. Applicants should submit the following:
1) results expected from proposed grant
2) how project's results will be evaluated or measured
Applications should specifically note the nature of the request being made; and include the name and date of the event.
Initial approach: Complete online eligibility quiz and application form
Copies of proposal: 1
Deadline(s): None if submitted to nearest local retail store; Apr. 30 and Aug. 31 if submitted to corporate headquarters
Final notification: Aug. for applications received by Apr. 30; Jan. for applications received by Aug. 31
Number of staff: 2 full-time professional.

2893
Paterson Mills Sales Agency, Inc.

(also known as Paterson Design)
1167 E. 26th St.
Brooklyn, NY 11210-4608 (718) 252-4300

Establishment information: Established in 1944.
Company type: Private company
Business activities: Operates interior design company.
Business type (SIC): Business services/miscellaneous
Corporate officer: Joseph Lieber, Chair., Pres., and C.E.O.
Board of director: Joseph Lieber, Chair.
Giving statement: Giving through the Joseph & Idii Lieber Foundation.

The Joseph & Idii Lieber Foundation

1167 E. 26th St.
Brooklyn, NY 11210

Establishment information: Established in 1996 in NY.
Donors: Joseph Lieber; Patterson Mills Sales.
Financial data (yr. ended 12/31/10): Assets, $1,718,782 (M); gifts received, $120,655; expenditures, $43,410; qualifying distributions, $36,669; giving activities include $35,807 for grants.
Fields of interest: Education; Human services; Religion.
Support limitations: No grants to individuals.
Application information: Applications not accepted. Unsolicited requests for funds not accepted.
Trustees: Idii Lieber; Joseph Lieber.
EIN: 113352010

2894
Pathmark Stores, Inc.

200 Milik St.
Carteret, NJ 07008 (732) 499-3000

Company URL: http://www.pathmark.com
Establishment information: Established in 1968.
Company type: Subsidiary of a public company
Business activities: Operates grocery stores.
Business type (SIC): Groceries—retail
Financial profile for 2006: Assets, $1,254,600,000; sales volume, $3,977,000,000; pre-tax net income, -$65,700,000; expenses, $3,978,000,000; liabilities, $1,083,300,000
Corporate officers: James L. Moody, Jr., Chair.; Chris Liberatore, Pres.; John T. Standley, C.E.O.; John Sheehan, Exec. V.P., Opers.; Robert Schoening, Sr. V.P. and C.I.O.; Marc Strassler, Sr. V.P. and Genl. Counsel; Bob Joyce, Sr. V.P., Admin.; Joseph W. Adelhardt, V.P. and Cont.; John Derderian, V.P., Sales and Mktg.
Board of directors: James Moody, Jr., Chair.; John T. Standley
Giving statement: Giving through the Pathmark Stores, Inc. Corporate Giving Program.

Pathmark Stores, Inc. Corporate Giving Program

2 Paragon Dr.
Montvale, NJ 07645-1718
URL: http://www.pathmark.com/community_helpingHands.asp

Purpose and activities: As a complement to its foundation, Pathmark also makes charitable contributions to nonprofit organizations involved with causes including food banks and community fundraising. Support is given primarily in areas of company operations in Delaware, New Jersey, New York, and Pennsylvania.
Fields of interest: Health care, research; Hospitals (general); Reproductive health, prenatal care; Breast cancer; Food banks; Children, services; Family services.
Type of support: Employee volunteer services; General/operating support; In-kind gifts; Sponsorships.
Geographic limitations: Giving primarily in areas of company operations in DE, NJ, NY, and PA.
Support limitations: No support for political or discriminatory organizations. No grants for journal ads of any kind.
Publications: Application guidelines.
Application information: Applications accepted. Proposals should be submitted using organization letterhead and include the date the donation is needed. Support is limited to 1 contribution per organization during any given year. Application form required. Applicants should submit the following:

1) statement of problem project will address
2) name, address and phone number of organization
3) copy of IRS Determination Letter
4) detailed description of project and amount of funding requested
5) contact person
6) plans for acknowledgement

Initial approach: Download application form and submit proposal and application form to nearest local store
Copies of proposal: 1
Deadline(s): 4 weeks prior to need
Final notification: 4 weeks

Number of staff: None.

2895
Patterson Belknap Webb & Tyler LLP

1133 Ave. of the Americas
New York, NY 10036-6710 (212) 336-2733

Company URL: http://www.pbwt.com
Establishment information: Established in 1919.
Company type: Private company
Business activities: Operates law firm.
Business type (SIC): Legal services
Giving statement: Giving through the Patterson Belknap Webb & Tyler LLP Pro Bono Program.

Patterson Belknap Webb & Tyler LLP Pro Bono Program

1133 Ave. of the Americas
New York, NY 10036-6710 (212) 336-2000
E-mail: lecleary@pbwt.com; Additional tel.: (212) 336-2000; URL: http://www.pbwt.com/probono/

Contact: Lisa Cleary, Chair, Pro Bono Comm.
Fields of interest: Legal services.
Type of support: Pro bono services - legal.
Geographic limitations: Giving primarily in areas of company operations in New York, NY.
Application information: A Pro Bono Committee manages the pro bono program.

2896
Robert Pattillo Properties, Inc.

2200 Century Pkwy., Ste. 100
Atlanta, GA 30345-3103 (678) 365-4702

Company URL: http://www.pattillo.com/
Company type: Private company
Business activities: Operates a real estate development and investment firm specializing in providing speculative buildings for regional and national distribution centers.
Business type (SIC): Real estate operators and lessors
Corporate officers: Robert A. Pattillo, Pres.; Danny Wald, C.F.O.; Clay Reese, Genl. Counsel and C.O.O.; Brenda Bracken, Cont.
Giving statement: Giving through the Gray Matters Capital Foundation, Inc. and the Gray Matters Charitable Foundation, Inc.

Gray Matters Capital Foundation, Inc.

2200 Century Pkwy., Ste. 100
Atlanta, GA 30345-3103

Establishment information: Established in 2006 in GA.
Donors: Robert A. Pattillo; Robert A. Pattillo Properties, Inc.; Pattillo-Markaz Industrial Partners, LLC.
Financial data (yr. ended 12/31/11): Assets, $18,202,774 (M); gifts received, $6,219,929; expenditures, $1,496,475; qualifying distributions, $1,448,731; giving activities include $99,167 for 36 grants to individuals (high: $3,045; low: $208).
Purpose and activities: The foundation researches and co-creates initiatives with local partners to build sustainable, replicable business models for the benefit of underserved populations. Special emphasis is directed toward programs that improve the quality and access to education for poor children in developing countries.
Fields of interest: Community development, small businesses Children; Economically disadvantaged.
Type of support: Mission-related investments/ loans; Program-related investments/loans; Seed money.
Support limitations: No grants to individuals.
Application information: Applications not accepted. Unsolicited requests for funds not accepted.
Officers and Director:* Robert A. Pattillo*, Pres., V.P., and Treas.; Clay Reese, Secy.
EIN: 205176973

Gray Matters Charitable Foundation, Inc.

(formerly The Rockdale Foundation, Inc.)
2200 Century Pkwy., Ste. 100
Atlanta, GA 30345-3103

Establishment information: Established in 1995 in GA.
Donors: Robert A. Patillo; Katy Patillo; Robert Pattillo Properties, Inc.
Financial data (yr. ended 12/31/11): Assets, $2,219,622 (M); expenditures, $315,801; qualifying distributions, $244,052; giving activities include $244,052 for grants.
Purpose and activities: The foundation supports organizations involved with education, international economic development, community development, and civic affairs.
Fields of interest: Education, reform; Higher education; Business school/education; Teacher school/education; Education; International economic development; Microfinance/ microlending; Community/economic development; Financial services; Public affairs.
International interests: Dominican Republic; Ghana; India.
Type of support: Conferences/seminars; Employee matching gifts; General/operating support; Matching/challenge support; Program development; Research; Sponsorships.
Geographic limitations: Giving primarily in the metropolitan Atlanta, GA area; giving also on an international basis in the Dominican Republic, Ghana, and India.
Support limitations: No grants to individuals.
Application information: Applications not accepted. Contributes only to pre-selected organizations.
Officers and Directors:* Robert A. Pattillo*, Pres.; Terry L. Galloway, Secy.; Eugenia Topple Cayce, Treas.; Ricardo Carvalho.
Number of staff: 2 full-time professional; 2 full-time support.
EIN: 582147850

2897
Pattishall, McAuliffe, Newbury, Hilliard & Geraldson LLP

311 S. Wacker Dr., Ste. 5000
Chicago, IL 60606-6631 (312) 554-8000

Company URL: http://www.pattishall.com
Establishment information: Established in 1898.
Company type: Private company
Business activities: Operates law firm.
Business type (SIC): Legal services
Giving statement: Giving through the Pattishall, McAuliffe, Newbury, Hilliard & Geraldson LLP Pro Bono Program.

Pattishall, McAuliffe, Newbury, Hilliard & Geraldson LLP Pro Bono Program

311 S. Wacker Dr., Ste. 5000
Chicago, IL 60606-6631 (312) 554-8000
E-mail: pbarengolts@pattishall.com; URL: http://www.pattishall.com/index.aspx

Contact: Phillip Barengolts, Pro Bono Chair
Fields of interest: Legal services.
Type of support: Pro bono services - legal.
Geographic limitations: Giving primarily in areas of company operations in Chicago, IL.
Application information: A Pro Bono Committee manages the pro bono program.

2898
Patton Boggs LLP

2550 M St., N.W.
Washington, DC 20037 (202) 457-6312

Company URL: http://www.pattonboggs.com/
Establishment information: Established in 1962.
Company type: Private company
Business activities: Operates law firm.
Business type (SIC): Legal services
Corporate officers: Thomas Hale Boggs, Jr., Chair.; Donald V. Moorehead, Vice-Chair.; Edward J. Newberry, Managing Partner
Offices: Anchorage, AK; Denver, CO; Washington, DC; Newark, NJ; New York, NY; Dallas, TX; McLean, VA
International operations: Qatar; United Arab Emirates
Giving statement: Giving through the Patton Boggs LLP Pro Bono Program and the Patton Boggs Foundation.

Patton Boggs LLP Pro Bono Program

2550 M St., N.W.
Washington, DC 20037 (214) 758-3540
E-mail: mforshey@pattonboggs.com; Additional tel.: (202) 457-6000; URL: http://www.pattonboggs.com/probono/

Contact: Michael Forshey
Fields of interest: Legal services.
Type of support: Pro bono services - legal.
Application information: A Pro Bono Committee manages the pro bono program.

Patton Boggs Foundation

2550 M St. NW
Washington, DC 20037-1350 (202) 457-6424
E-mail: joberdorfer@pattonboggs.com; URL: http://www.pattonboggs.com/about/PBFoundation/

Establishment information: Established in 2000.
Contact: John L. Oberdorfer, V.P. and Secy.-Treas.
Financial data (yr. ended 09/30/11): Revenue, $184,730; assets, $1,271,022 (M); gifts received, $121,537; expenditures, $81,940; giving activities include $70,000 for grants and $5,000 for grants to individuals.
Purpose and activities: The foundation's focus is to create new and valuable opportunities for exceptional law students interested in the field of public policy.
Fields of interest: Public affairs, formal/general education.
Type of support: Fellowships.
Officers and Directors:* James R. Patton, Jr., Chair. and Pres.; Thomas Hale Boggs, Jr., Vice-Chair.; John L. Oberdorfer, V.P. and Secy.-Treas; Timothy J. May, V.P.; Mary Patton.
EIN: 522284635

2899
Patton's Inc.

3201 South Blvd.
Charlotte, NC 28209-1950 (704) 523-4122

Company URL: http://www.pattonsinc.com
Establishment information: Established in 1945.
Company type: Private company
Business activities: Sells compressed air equipment wholesale.
Business type (SIC): Industrial machinery and equipment—wholesale
Corporate officer: John C. Patton, Pres.
Giving statement: Giving through the Patton Foundation, Inc.

Patton Foundation, Inc.

3201 South Blvd.
Charlotte, NC 28209-1950

Establishment information: Established in NC.
Donors: Patton's Inc.; John C. Patton.
Financial data (yr. ended 07/31/12): Assets, $559,733 (M); gifts received, $21,000; expenditures, $36,372; qualifying distributions, $26,500; giving activities include $26,500 for 8 grants (high: $8,000; low: $500).
Purpose and activities: The foundation supports organizations involved with education, mental health, multiple sclerosis, hunger, athletics, human services, and Christianity. Special emphasis is directed toward programs designed to serve children.
Fields of interest: Education; Mental health/crisis services; Multiple sclerosis; Food distribution, meals on wheels; Athletics/sports, Special Olympics; Youth development, business; Salvation Army; Homeless, human services; Human services; Christian agencies & churches Children.
Type of support: General/operating support.
Geographic limitations: Giving primarily in Charlotte, NC.
Support limitations: No grants to individuals.
Application information: Applications not accepted. Unsolicited requests for funds not accepted.
Officers: John C. Patton, Pres.; Michael S. Cranford, V.P.; Joe D. Pool, Secy.-Treas.
Trustee: First Citizens Bank, N.A.
EIN: 237026742

2900
Paul Hastings LLP

Paul Hastings Tower
515 S. Flower St., 25th Fl.
Los Angeles, CA 90071-2371
(213) 683-6000

Company URL: http://www.paulhastings.com/default.aspx
Establishment information: Established in 1951.
Company type: Private company
Business activities: Operates law firm.
Business type (SIC): Legal services
Corporate officers: Seth M. Zachary, Chair.; Greg Nitzkowski, Managing Partner
Offices: Costa Mesa, Los Angeles, Palo Alto, San Diego, San Francisco, CA; Washington, DC; Atlanta, GA; Chicago, IL; New York, NY
International operations: Belgium; China; France; Germany; Hong Kong; Italy; Japan; United Kingdom
Giving statement: Giving through the Paul Hastings LLP Pro Bono Program.

Paul Hastings LLP Pro Bono Program

Paul Hastings Tower
515 S. Flower St., 25th Fl.
Los Angeles, CA 90071-2371 (213) 683-6234
E-mail: jamiebroder@paulhastings.com; URL: http://www.paulhastings.com/community_involvement.aspx

Contact: Jamie Broder, Corporate Social Responsibility Partner
Fields of interest: Legal services.
Type of support: Pro bono services - legal.
Application information: A Pro Bono Committee manages the pro bono program.

2901
Paul, Weiss, Rifkind, Wharton & Garrison

1285 Avenue of the Americas
New York, NY 10019-6064 (212) 373-2277

Company URL: http://ww.paulweiss.com/
Company type: Private company
Business activities: Operates law firm.
Business type (SIC): Legal services
Offices: Wilmington, DE; Washington, DC; New York, NY
International operations: Canada; China; Hong Kong; Japan; United Kingdom
Giving statement: Giving through the Paul, Weiss, Rifkind, Wharton & Garrison LLP Pro Bono Program.

Paul, Weiss, Rifkind, Wharton & Garrison LLP Pro Bono Program

1285 Avenue of the Americas
New York, NY 10019-6064 (212) 373-2277
E-mail: rbehr@paulweiss.com; Additional tel.: (212) 373-3000; URL: http://www.paulweiss.com/practices/pro-bono.aspx

Contact: Rebecca Behr, Pro Bono Attorney
Fields of interest: Legal services.
Type of support: Pro bono services - legal.
Application information: A Pro Bono Committee manages the pro bono program.

2902
Pawtucket Credit Union

1200 Central Ave.
Pawtucket, RI 02861 (401) 722-2212

Company URL: https://www.pcu.org
Establishment information: Established in 1928.
Company type: State-chartered credit union
Business activities: Operates state credit union.
Business type (SIC): Credit unions
Financial profile for 2011: Assets, $1,311,991,742; liabilities, $1,311,991,742
Corporate officers: Ronald W. LeClair, Chair.; Lynn A.M. Weinstein, Vice-Chair.; Karl A. Kozak, Pres. and C.E.O.; Robert P. Andrade, Exec. V.P. and C.O.O.; George J. Charette III, Exec. V.P. and C.F.O.; Valerie Pimenta, V.P., Cont.; Laurie-Ann Flaxington, V.P., Opers.; Anne Lafleur, V.P., Human Resources; Paul F. Lefebvre, Secy.; John B. Richer, Jr., Treas.
Board of directors: Ronald W. LeClair, Chair.; Lynn A.M. Weinstein, Vice-Chair.; Frank P. Casarella; Richard H. Leclerc; Gerard J. Lupien; Paul F. Lefebvre; Linda C. Lyons; Lawrence J. Monastesse; John B. Richer, Jr.; Leo R. Mongeau; Kevin Tracey
Giving statement: Giving through the Pawtucket Credit Union Corporate Giving Program.

Pawtucket Credit Union Corporate Giving Program

1200 Central Ave.
Pawtucket, RI 02861-2200 (401) 722-2212
URL: https://www.pcu.org/community.html

Purpose and activities: Pawtucket Credit Union makes charitable donations to nonprofit organizations that promote the positive development and self-esteem of children, youth and teens; promote education, financial literacy and self-reliance for low- and moderate-income families; promote fair, affordable housing and home ownership opportunities in economically distressed areas; and provide support for the hungry and homeless. Special emphasis is directed toward programs that are multi-cultural and positively impact low- and moderate-income populations. Support is given primarily in areas of company operations in Cranston, East Providence, North Providence, Pawtucket, Smithfield, and Warwick, Rhode Island.
Fields of interest: Education; Food services; Housing/shelter, development; Housing/shelter, homeless; Housing/shelter, home owners; Youth development; Children/youth, services; Homeless, human services; Community/economic development Minorities; Economically disadvantaged.
Program:
Investing in Your Future Scholarship: Pawtucket Credit Union annually awards 4 $8,000 scholarships to graduating high school seniors that will be dispersed each year for four consecutive years of the recipient's college career. The scholarship recipient will have $2,000 each year of their four year college career.
Type of support: In-kind gifts; Program development; Scholarships—to individuals; Seed money; Sponsorships.
Geographic limitations: Giving primarily in areas of company operations in Cranston, East Providence, North Providence, Pawtucket, Smithfield, and Warwick, RI.
Support limitations: No support for fraternal or political organizations, colleges or universities (except capital campaigns), or local Chapters of national health organizations. No grants to individuals (except for scholarships), or for annual

operating support, endowments, operating deficits, scientific or medical research, trips, tours, transportation costs, seminars or conferences, or payment on loans (including loans from Pawtucket Credit Union).
Publications: Application guidelines.
Application information: Applications accepted. Requests for donations, advertising, sponsorships, or grants are limited to a consecutive three-year period for each organization. Proposals should be submitted in writing using organization letterhead; submissions via fax are not accepted. Grants are restricted to community-based organizations serving local residents. Application form required.
Applicants should submit the following:
1) population served
2) name, address and phone number of organization
3) copy of IRS Determination Letter
4) brief history of organization and description of its mission
5) geographic area to be served
6) listing of board of directors, trustees, officers and other key people and their affiliations
7) detailed description of project and amount of funding requested
8) contact person
Initial approach: Proposal
Copies of proposal: 1
Deadline(s): Apr. 24 for Investing in Your Future Scholarships
Final notification: 6 to 8 weeks; May 21 for Investing in Your Future Scholarships

2903
Pawtucket Red Sox Baseball Club, Inc.

1 Ben Mondor Way
P.O. Box 2365
Pawtucket, RI 02860 (401) 724-7300

Company URL: http://www.pawsox.com
Establishment information: Established in 1994.
Company type: Private company
Business activities: Operates professional baseball club.
Business type (SIC): Commercial sports
Corporate officers: Bernard G. Mondor, Chair.; Mike Tamburro, Pres.; Matt White, V.P. and C.F.O.; Bill Wanless, V.P., Public Rels.; Michael Gwynn, V.P., Sales and Mktg.; Jackie Dryer, Secy.
Board of director: Bernard G. Mondor, Chair.
Giving statement: Giving through the Pawtucket Red Sox Charitable Foundation.

Pawtucket Red Sox Charitable Foundation

P.O. Box 2365
Pawtucket, RI 02861-0365

Establishment information: Established in 1997 in RI.
Donor: Pawtucket Red Sox Baseball Club, Inc.
Financial data (yr. ended 12/31/12): Assets, $284,119 (M); gifts received, $73,224; expenditures, $52,245; qualifying distributions, $50,935; giving activities include $49,250 for 13 grants (high: $15,000; low: $500).
Purpose and activities: The foundation supports organizations involved with education, cancer, and human services.
Fields of interest: Education; Youth development; Human services.
Type of support: General/operating support.
Geographic limitations: Giving limited to RI.
Support limitations: No grants to individuals.
Application information: Applications not accepted. Unsolicited requests for funds not accepted.
Trustees: James F. McAleer; Daniel J. Ryan; Michael Tamburro; Matt White.
EIN: 061494102

2904
Paychex, Inc.

911 Panorama Trail S.
Rochester, NY 14625-0397 (585) 385-6666

Company URL: http://www.paychex.com
Establishment information: Established in 1971.
Company type: Public company
Company ticker symbol and exchange: PAYX/NASDAQ
Business activities: Provides payroll, human resource, and employee benefit outsourcing solutions.
Business type (SIC): Engineering, accounting, research, management, and related services; accounting, auditing, and bookkeeping services
Financial profile for 2012: Number of employees, 12,400; assets, $6,479,600,000; sales volume, $2,229,800,000; pre-tax net income, $860,300,000; expenses, $1,375,900,000; liabilities, $4,875,100,000
Fortune 1000 ranking: 2012—869th in revenues, 316th in profits, and 513th in assets
Forbes 2000 ranking: 2012—1728th in sales, 936th in profits, and 1630th in assets
Corporate officers: B. Thomas Golisano, Chair.; Martin Mucci, Pres. and C.E.O.; Efrain Rivera, Sr. V.P., C.F.O., and Treas.; Mark Bottini, Sr. V.P., Sales; Stephanie L. Schaeffer, V.P. and Secy.; Jennifer R. Vossler, C.P.A., V.P. and Cont.; Lauri L. Zaucha, V.P., Human Resources; Andrew Childs, V.P., Mktg.
Board of directors: B. Thomas Golisano, Chair.; Joseph D. Doody; David J.S. Flaschen; Phillip Horsley; Grant M. Inman; Pamela A. Joseph; Martin Mucci; Joseph M. Tucci; Joseph M. Velli
International operations: Germany
Giving statement: Giving through the Paychex, Inc. Corporate Giving Program.
Company EIN: 161124166

Paychex, Inc. Corporate Giving Program

c/o Michael Nesbitt
911 Panorama Trail S.
Rochester, NY 14625-2311 (585) 385-6666
URL: https://www.paychex.com/secure/contact/contributions.aspx

Contact: Michael Nesbitt
Purpose and activities: Paychex makes charitable contributions to nonprofit organizations involved with education, substance abuse, hunger, homelessness, human services, community economic development, and people with disabilities. Emphasis is given to initiatives that will improve the quality of life in the community. Support is given primarily in areas of company operations, with emphasis on Rochester, New York.
Fields of interest: Education, drop-out prevention; Education; Substance abuse, services; Food services; Children/youth, services; Family services; Developmentally disabled, centers & services; Homeless, human services; Human services; Community/economic development.
Type of support: General/operating support; Program development.
Geographic limitations: Giving primarily in areas of company operations, with emphasis on Rochester, NY.
Support limitations: No support for sports teams. No grants for fundraising events, or initiatives that benefit a single individual or a small group of individuals.
Publications: Application guidelines.
Application information: Applications accepted. Application form not required. Applicants should submit the following:
1) statement of problem project will address
2) population served
3) copy of most recent annual report/audited financial statement/990
4) how project's results will be evaluated or measured
5) detailed description of project and amount of funding requested
6) listing of additional sources and amount of support
Proposals should include the approximate number of people the program will serve, the process for identifying beneficiaries, the past success of the program, and a financial summary for the organization's most recent fiscal year for any request for $1,000 or more.
Initial approach: Proposal to headquarters
Copies of proposal: 1
Committee meeting date(s): Monthly
Deadline(s): None
Final notification: Following review

2905
PCI Paper Conversions, Inc.

(also known as PCI)
6761 Thompson Rd., N.
Syracuse, NY 13211-2119 (315) 437-1641

Company URL: http://www.padmaker.com
Establishment information: Established in 1973.
Company type: Private company
Business activities: Manufactures note pads.
Business type (SIC): Paper and paperboard/coated, converted, and laminated
Corporate officers: Lloyd M. Withers, Pres.; Raymond Ryan, C.F.O.
Giving statement: Giving through the PCI Foundation.

PCI Foundation

6761 Thompson Rd. N.
Syracuse, NY 13211-2119

Establishment information: Established as a company-sponsored operating foundation in 2000; status changed to company-sponsored foundation in 2002.
Donor: Paper Conversions Inc.
Financial data (yr. ended 12/31/11): Assets, $73,811 (M); expenditures, $8,518; qualifying distributions, $8,232; giving activities include $8,232 for grants.
Purpose and activities: The foundation supports food banks and hospices and organizations involved with secondary education.
Type of support: General/operating support; Scholarship funds.
Geographic limitations: Giving limited to Liverpool and Syracuse, NY.
Support limitations: No grants to individuals.
Application information: Applications not accepted. Unsolicited requests for funds not accepted.

Trustees: Laura McDermott; Marya Withers; Rochette Withers.
EIN: 161579435

2906
PDB Sports, Ltd.

(also known as Denver Broncos)
13655 Broncos Pkwy.
Englewood, CO 80112 (303) 649-9000

Company URL: http://www.denverbroncos.com
Establishment information: Established in 1959.
Company type: Private company
Business activities: Operates professional football club.
Business type (SIC): Commercial sports
Corporate officers: Pat Bowlen, Chair. and C.E.O.; Joe Ellis, Pres.; Rich Slivka, Exec. V.P. and Genl. Counsel; Chip Conway, V.P., Opers.; Justin Webster, V.P., Finance; Dennis Moore, V.P., Sales and Mktg.; Jim Saccomano, V.P., Comms.; Dianne Sehgal, Cont.
Board of directors: Pat Bowlen, Chair.; John Bowlen
Giving statement: Giving through the Denver Broncos Corporate Giving Program and the Denver Broncos Charities.

Denver Broncos Corporate Giving Program

c/o Community Development
1701 Bryant Street, Ste. 1400
Denver, CO 80204-1701 (720) 258-3000
URL: http://www.denverbroncos.com/page.php?id=1147

Contact: Cindy Kellog, V.P., Community Devel.
Purpose and activities: The Denver Broncos make charitable contributions to nonprofit organizations involved with health, hunger, youth development, and homeless relief. Support is given primarily in Colorado.
Fields of interest: Education, reading; Education; Health care, clinics/centers; Health care, blood supply; Public health, physical fitness; Health care; Breast cancer; Heart & circulatory diseases; Food services; Housing/shelter, homeless; Athletics/sports, football; Boys & girls clubs; Youth development; Homeless, human services; United Ways and Federated Giving Programs.
Programs:

Accelerated Reader Summer Reading Program: The Broncos, in partnership with The Carmel Hill Fund and Renaissance Learning's Accelerated Reader, provides an online reading program for student members of Boys and Girls Clubs of metro Denver to improve their literacy during the summer. The Broncos provides incentives throughout the program to reward achievements and milestones. This program is a part of the Read Like a Pro initiative.

NFL Play 60 Challenge: The Broncos and the American Heart Association partner with eight local Boys and Girls Clubs of Metro Denver to inspire kids to get the recommended 60 minutes of physical activity a day at school and at home. The top participants from each Club will be recognized on field at halftime during a Broncos Thanksgiving Day game.

Reading Like a Pro: Through Reading Like a Pro, the Broncos and U.S. Bank, supports literacy programs designed enhance reading abilities for kids of all ages.

Type of support: Donated products; Employee volunteer services; General/operating support; In-kind gifts; Loaned talent; Program development.
Geographic limitations: Giving primarily in areas of company operations in CO.
Publications: Application guidelines; Newsletter.
Application information: Applications accepted. Additional information may be requested at a later date. The Community Development Department handles giving. Application form required.

Initial approach: Complete online application form for donations, player appearances, and memorabilia

Deadline(s): None

Community Development Staff: Cindy Kellogg, V.P., Community Devel.; Billy Thompson, Dir., Community Outreach; Kelly Woodward, Dir., Community Devel.

Denver Broncos Charities

13655 Broncos Pkwy.
Englewood, CO 80112-4150 (303) 649-9000
FAX: (720) 258-3848;
E-mail: suggestions@broncos.nfl.net; URL: http://www.denverbroncos.com/community/index.html

Establishment information: Established in 1994 in CO.
Contact: Joe Ellis, Pres.
Financial data (yr. ended 03/31/12): Revenue, $154,431; assets, $81,956 (M); gifts received, $101,658; expenditures, $155,422; giving activities include $145,889 for grants.
Purpose and activities: The fund supports programs designed to impact young people in the areas of education and youth football with particular emphasis on programs aimed at disadvantaged and at-risk youth. Organizations that have programs devoted to health and hunger, including specific programs relating to the physically or mentally challenged, will be considered.
Fields of interest: Youth development, services; Youth, services.
Type of support: Program development.
Geographic limitations: Giving primarily in CO, with emphasis on the Denver metropolitan area.
Publications: Annual report.
Application information:

Board meeting date(s): Quarterly

Officers and Directors:* Pat Bowlen*, Chair.-C.E.O.; Josiah Ellis*, Pres.; John Bowlen; Bill Britton; Tim Guard; Jeff Harman; Fred Hemmings; Bob Masten.
Number of staff: 1 full-time professional; 1 part-time professional.
EIN: 841305294

2907
Peabody Energy Corporation

(doing business as Peabody Energy)
(formerly Peabody Holding Company)
701 Market St., Peabody Plz.
St. Louis, MO 63101-1826 (314) 342-3400
FAX: (302)0 636-5454

Company URL: http://www.peabodyenergy.com
Establishment information: Established in 1883.
Company type: Public company
Company ticker symbol and exchange: BTU/NYSE
Business activities: Operates holding company; mines coal.
Business type (SIC): Mining/coal and lignite surface; metals and minerals, except petroleum—wholesale
Financial profile for 2012: Number of employees, 8,200; assets, $15,809,000,000; sales volume, $8,077,500,000; pre-tax net income, -$208,600,000; expenses, $7,905,000,000; liabilities, $10,904,100,000
Fortune 1000 ranking: 2012—315th in revenues, 962nd in profits, and 288th in assets
Forbes 2000 ranking: 2012—1082nd in sales, 1904th in profits, and 1139th in assets
Corporate officers: Gregory H. Boyce, Chair. and C.E.O.; Michael C. Crews, Exec. V.P. and C.F.O.; Sharon D. Fiehler, Exec. V.P. and C.A.O.; Alexander C. Schoch, Exec. V.P. and Secy.
Board of directors: Gregory H. Boyce, Chair.; William A. Coley; William E. James; Robert B. Karn III; Henry E. Lentz, Jr.; Robert A. Malone; William C. Rusnack; John F. Turner; Sandra A. Van Trease; Alan H. Washkowitz
International operations: Australia; British Virgin Islands; England; Gibraltar; Luxembourg; Netherlands; Venezuela; Wales
Giving statement: Giving through the Peabody Energy Corporation Contributions Program.
Company EIN: 134004153

Peabody Energy Corporation Contributions Program

701 Market St.
St. Louis, MO 63101-1826 (314) 342-3400
URL: http://www.peabodyenergy.com/content/153/Community-Partnerships

Financial data (yr. ended 12/31/11): Total giving, $9,548,000, including $9,548,000 for grants.
Purpose and activities: Peabody Energy makes charitable contributions to nonprofit organizations involved with arts and culture, education, the environment, health, human services, diversity, community development, and civic affairs. Support is given in areas of company operations.
Fields of interest: Arts; Elementary/secondary education; Vocational education; Higher education; Education; Environment; Health care; Youth, services; Human services; Civil/human rights, equal rights; Community/economic development; United Ways and Federated Giving Programs; Public affairs.
Programs:

Dollars for Doers Program: Peabody Energy will donate $250 for every 10 hours that an employee volunteers with a qualifying organization, up to $1,000 per employee per year.

Employee Matching Gifts: Peabody Energy matches contributions made by its employees to nonprofit organizations on a one-for-one basis from $50 to $5,000 per employee, per year.

Type of support: Employee matching gifts; Employee volunteer services; General/operating support; Sponsorships.
Geographic limitations: Giving primarily in areas of company operations.

2908
Peachtree Planning Corporation

(also known as The Mathis Hill Robertson Agency)
5040 Roswell Rd., Ste. 200
Atlanta, GA 30342-2207 (404) 260-1600

Company URL: http://www.peachtreeplanning.com
Establishment information: Established in 1987.
Company type: Private company
Business activities: Provides investment advisory services.
Business type (SIC): Security and commodity services

Corporate officers: Robert E. Mathis, Chair. and C.E.O.; John J.D. Hill, Pres.
Board of director: Robert E. Mathis, Chair.
Giving statement: Giving through the Peachtree Planning Foundation, Inc.

Peachtree Planning Foundation, Inc.

5040 Roswell Rd., Ste. 100
Atlanta, GA 30342-2207

Establishment information: Established in 2002 in GA as a public charity; status changed to company-sponsored operating foundation in 2004.
Donors: Peachtree Planning Corp.; The Mathis Hill Robertson Agency.
Financial data (yr. ended 12/31/11): Assets, $26,259 (M); gifts received, $23,835; expenditures, $15,314; qualifying distributions, $14,225; giving activities include $14,225 for grants.
Purpose and activities: The foundation supports community endeavors and meets human needs through focused, funded initiatives; it also seeks to promote volunteerism at the local level.
Fields of interest: Human services; Religion.
Application information: Applications not accepted. Unsolicited requests for funds not accepted.
Directors: John Hill; Robert E. Mathis; Al Roberston.
EIN: 582543597

2909
Peapack-Gladstone Financial Corp.

500 Hills Dr., Ste. 300
P.O. Box 700
Bedminster, NJ 07921-1538
(908) 234-0700
FAX: (908) 234-0795

Company URL: http://www.pgbank.com
Establishment information: Established in 1921.
Company type: Public company
Company ticker symbol and exchange: PGC/NASDAQ
Business activities: Operates state chartered commercial bank.
Business type (SIC): Banks/commercial
Financial profile for 2012: Number of employees, 292; assets, $1,667,840,000; pre-tax net income, $16,100,000; liabilities, $1,545,780,000
Corporate officers: Frank A. Kissel, Chair.; Douglas L. Kennedy, C.E.O.; Jeffrey J. Carfora, Exec. V.P. and C.F.O.; Finn M.W. Caspersen, Jr., Sr. V.P. Genl. Counsel. and C.O.O.; Hubert P. Clarke, Sr. V.P. and C.I.O.
Board of directors: Frank A. Kissel, Chair.; Finn M. W. Caspersen, Jr.; Anthony J. Consi II; Edward A. Gramigna, Jr.; Douglas L. Kennedy; John D. Kissel; James R. Lamb; Edward A. Merton; F. Duffield Meyercord; John R. Mulcahy; Philip W. Smith III; Craig C. Spengeman; Beth Welsh
Giving statement: Giving through the Peapack-Gladstone Bank Corporate Giving Program.
Company EIN: 222491488

Peapack-Gladstone Bank Corporate Giving Program

500 Hills Dr., Ste. 300
P.O. Box 700
Bedminster, NJ 07921-1538 (908) 234-0700
URL: http://www.pgbank.com

2910
Pearce Land Company, LP

(also known as Holland Realty Company)
1943 Hoffmeyer Rd., Ste. A
Florence, SC 29501-3939 (843) 662-0401

Company URL: http://pearcelandcompany.com/index.html
Company type: Private company
Business activities: Operates real estate agency.
Business type (SIC): Real estate agents and managers
Corporate officers: Evans P. Holland, Mgr.; Chris Scott, Mgr.
Giving statement: Giving through the Evans P. & Mary Jane P. Holland Foundation, Inc.

Evans P. & Mary Jane P. Holland Foundation, Inc.

P.O. Box 5387
Florence, SC 29502-5387 (843) 662-0401

Establishment information: Established in 2002 in SC.
Donors: Evans P. Holland, Sr.; Mary Jane Holland.
Contact: Evans P. Holland Sr., Dir.
Financial data (yr. ended 12/31/11): Assets, $94,023 (M); gifts received, $17,633; expenditures, $39,782; qualifying distributions, $38,737; giving activities include $38,737 for grants.
Purpose and activities: The foundation supports service clubs and organizations involved with education, human services, and Christianity.
Fields of interest: Education; Youth development; Civil/human rights.
Type of support: Endowments; Equipment; General/operating support; Program development.
Geographic limitations: Giving primarily in Florence and Spartanburg, SC.
Support limitations: No grants to individuals.
Application information: Applications accepted. Application form not required.
Initial approach: Proposal
Deadline(s): None
Directors: Evans P. Holland, Sr.; Mary Jane P. Holland.
EIN: 431988607

2911
Pearson Education, Inc.

1 Lake St.
Upper Saddle River, NJ 07458-1813
(201) 236-7000

Company URL: http://www.pearsoned.com
Establishment information: Established in 1998.
Company type: Subsidiary of a foreign company
Business activities: Publishes educational books.
Business type (SIC): Book publishing and/or printing
Financial profile for 2009: Number of employees, 7,742
Corporate officers: William T. Ethridge, C.E.O.; Jeff Walsh, Exec. V.P. and C.F.O.; John LaVacca, Exec. V.P., Opers.
International operations: Canada; Mexico; Singapore
Giving statement: Giving through the Pearson Education Inc. Corporate Giving Program.

Pearson Education Inc. Corporate Giving Program

1 Lake St.
Upper Saddle River, NJ 07458-1813
E-mail for AP Book Donations: apworkshops@pearson.com; URL: http://www.pearsoned.com/community/index.htm

Purpose and activities: Pearson Education makes charitable contributions to nonprofit organizations involved with education. Support is given in areas of company operations.
Fields of interest: Higher education; Teacher school/education; Scholarships/financial aid; Education, services; Education, reading; Education; Youth, services; Mathematics; Science.
Programs:
Pearson Cite Awards of Excellence: The company awards $1,000 in scholarship funds to honor outstanding accomplishments in online higher education in using the Pearson LearningStudio Platform. The program is designed to encourage and support innovations that drive student success. The award is given to teachers for Excellence in Online Teaching and for Excellence in Online Administration.
Pearson Supporting the AP Community: The company supports the professional development of teachers through donations of textbooks and supplements to teachers attending College Board AP workshops. The company donates one book per participant per workshop and institute directors and leaders can choose books from Prentice Hall, Allyn & Bacon, Longman, Benjamin Cummings, and Addison Wesley.
Type of support: Conferences/seminars; Curriculum development; Donated products; Employee volunteer services; General/operating support; In-kind gifts; Program development; Scholarship funds; Sponsorships.
Geographic limitations: Giving primarily in areas of company operations.
Publications: Application guidelines.
Application information: Applications accepted.
Initial approach: E-mail for AP book donations
Deadline(s): 3 weeks prior to need for AP book donations

2912
Pearson Inc.

1330 Avenue of the Americas, Fl. 7
New York, NY 10019-5400 (212) 641-2400

Company URL: http://www.pearson.com/
Establishment information: Established in 1724.
Company type: Subsidiary of a foreign company
Business activities: Operates media company.
Business type (SIC): Book publishing and/or printing
Corporate officers: Glen Moreno, Chair.; Jeff Taylor, Pres.
Board of director: Glen Moreno, Chair.
Giving statement: Giving through the Pearson Charitable Foundation.

Pearson Charitable Foundation

1330 Avenue of the Americas, 7th Fl.
New York, NY 10019-5400 (212) 641-2400
E-mail: media@pearsonfoundation.org; URL: http://www.pearsonfoundation.org/

Establishment information: Established in 2004 in DE.
Contact: Shaheda Sayed, Secy.

Financial data (yr. ended 12/31/10): Revenue, $17,140,554; assets, $1,585,691 (M); gifts received, $15,782,636; expenditures, $18,442,348; giving activities include $6,003,839 for grants and $10,300 for grants to individuals.
Purpose and activities: The foundation works with leading nonprofit, civic, and business organizations to provide financial, organizational, and publishing assistance worldwide, and to promote literacy, learning, and great teaching.
Fields of interest: Scholarships/financial aid; Education, services; Education, reading; Education.
Programs:

Pearson Fellowship for Social Innovation: This fellowship supports exemplary young leaders around the globe who are using their ingenuity, passion, and energy to build better lives for themselves and their communities. Two International Fellows will be named and receive a $5,000 award to help launch their project, while 10 addition fellows will receive a $1,000 award; all fellows will also receive one-on-one mentoring from experienced social innovators who consult with them as they implement their project plans.

Pearson Prize for Higher Education: This prize celebrates students who are giving back to their college communities by providing cash awards to seventy students in recognition of their academic achievements and their commitment to their local communities. The prize recognizes students who have been attending a two- or four-year school, completed at least one year in college, and demonstrated leadership in community service. Twenty National Fellows will be named and awarded a two-year cash prize of $10,000; fifty Community Fellows will be chosen and receive a $500 award.

Type of support: Donated products; General/operating support; In-kind gifts; Program development.
Geographic limitations: Giving on a national and international basis.
Publications: Application guidelines.
Application information: Applications accepted. Application form required.
Initial approach: Submit application
Deadline(s): Mar. 18 for Pearson Prize for Higher Education
Officers and Directors:* David Bell*, Chair.; Mark Nieker*, Pres.; Shaheda Sayed*, Secy.; Philip Hoffman*, Treas.; Rabin Baliszewski; Michael Benjamin; Steven Dowling; David Shanks.
EIN: 113690722

2913
Pebble Beach Company

1700 17-Mile Dr.
Pebble Beach, CA 93953-2668
(831) 624-3811
FAX: (831) 625-8598

Company URL: http://www.pebblebeach.com
Establishment information: Established in 1919.
Company type: Private company
Business activities: Operates hotel resorts.
Business type (SIC): Hotels and motels
Financial profile for 2010: Number of employees, 1,700
Corporate officers: William Perocchi, C.E.O.; Cody Plott, Pres. and C.O.O.; David Heuck, Exec. V.P. and C.F.O.; Mark Stilwell, Exec. V.P. and Genl. Counsel; Susan Merfeld, Sr. V.P., Human Resources; Robert Lapso, V.P. and Cont.; Tim Ryan, V.P., Sales; Lisa Cotter, V.P., Mktg.
Giving statement: Giving through the Pebble Beach Company Foundation.

Pebble Beach Company Foundation

P.O. Box 1767
Pebble Beach, CA 93953-1767 (831) 625-8445
FAX: (831) 625-8441

Establishment information: Established in 1975 in CA.
Financial data (yr. ended 12/31/11): Revenue, $1,014,039; assets, $5,559,968 (M); gifts received, $778,983; expenditures, $513,400; program services expenses, $344,065; giving activities include $239,371 for 4 grants (high: $41,750; low: $6,621) and $100,600 for grants to individuals.
Purpose and activities: The foundation seeks to raise and distribute funds for charitable purposes through hosting events for the benefit of the community.
Fields of interest: Arts; Education; Recreation; Children/youth, services; Community/economic development.
Type of support: Grants to individuals.
Geographic limitations: Giving limited to CA.
Officers and Directors:* Susan Merfeld*, Pres.; Mark J. Verbonich*, V.P.; Nanci Perocchi*, Secy.; David W. Hoopingarner*, Treas.; Hubert Allen; Marggie Hardy; Jack Holt.
EIN: 510189888

2914
Pedernales Electric Cooperative, Inc.

302 S. Ave. F
P.O. Box 1
Johnson City, TX 78636-0001
(830) 868-7155

Company URL: http://www.pec.coop
Establishment information: Established in 1938.
Company type: Cooperative
Business activities: Distributes electricity.
Business type (SIC): Electric services
Corporate officers: Cristi Clement, Pres.; R.B. Sloan, C.E.O.; Frank A. Skube, C.F.O.
Board of directors: Cristi Clement; Patrick Cox, Ph.D.; Ross Fischer; Larry Landaker; Chris Perry; Kathryn Scanlon
Subsidiary: Envision Utility Software Corp., Santa Fe, NM
Giving statement: Giving through the Pedernales Electric Cooperative Scholarship Fund.

Pedernales Electric Cooperative Scholarship Fund

201 South Ave. F
Johnson City, TX 78636-4827 (830) 868-5112

Establishment information: Established in 1998.
Donors: Pedernales Electric Cooperative, Inc.; Escheated Funds; PEC Board of Directors.
Contact: Vicki Hiser, Treas.
Financial data (yr. ended 12/31/11): Assets, $111,550 (M); gifts received, $149,994; expenditures, $53,005; qualifying distributions, $53,000; giving activities include $53,000 for grants to individuals.
Purpose and activities: The foundation awards college scholarships to children of employees of Pedernales Electric Cooperative.
Type of support: Employee-related scholarships.
Geographic limitations: Giving limited to TX.
Application information: Applications not accepted. Unsolicited requests for funds not accepted.
Officers: Toni Reyes, Pres.; Steve Lucas, V.P.; Yolie Garcia, Secy.; Vicki Hiser, Treas.
EIN: 742897600

2915
Peerless Publications, Inc.

24 N. Hanover St.
P.O. Box 599
Pottstown, PA 19464-5410 (610) 323-3000

Company URL: http://www.journalregister.com
Establishment information: Established in 1902.
Company type: Subsidiary of a private company
Business activities: Publishes newspapers.
Business type (SIC): Newspaper publishing and/or printing
Corporate officers: Bob Gelmick, Pres.; Patti Mckelvey, Cont.
Giving statement: Giving through the Pottstown Mercury Foundation.

Pottstown Mercury Foundation

24 N. Hanover St.
Pottstown, PA 19464-5410

Establishment information: Established around 1969.
Donors: Pottstown Mercury; Peerless Publications, Inc.
Financial data (yr. ended 11/30/11): Assets, $34,815 (M); gifts received, $55,378; expenditures, $79,134; qualifying distributions, $77,415; giving activities include $77,415 for 1 grant.
Purpose and activities: The foundation supports organizations involved with economically disadvantaged people.
Fields of interest: Economically disadvantaged.
Type of support: Annual campaigns.
Geographic limitations: Giving limited to Pottstown, PA.
Support limitations: No grants to individuals.
Application information: Applications not accepted. Unsolicited requests for funds not accepted.
Trustees: Nancy March; Patricia McKelvey.
Director: Thomas Abbott.
EIN: 236256419

2916
Peet's Coffee & Tea, Inc.

1400 Park Ave.
Emeryville, CA 94608-3520 (510) 594-2100
FAX: (510) 594-2180

Company URL: http://www.peets.com
Establishment information: Established in 1966.
Company type: Public company
Company ticker symbol and exchange: PEET/NASDAQ
Business activities: Operates coffee shops.
Business type (SIC): Restaurants and drinking places
Financial profile for 2012: Number of employees, 3,642; assets, $215,270,000; sales volume, $371,920,000; pre-tax net income, $27,610,000; expenses, $344,310,000; liabilities, $37,310,000
Corporate officers: Jean-Michel Valette, Chair.; Patrick J. O'Dea, Pres. and C.E.O.; Thomas P. Cawley, V.P. and C.F.O.; Isobel A. Jones, V.P., Genl. Counsel, and Secy.; Kay L. Bogeajis, V.P., Opers.; Paul Yee, V.P., Finance; Laila J. Tarraf, V.P., Human Resources; Maria Latushkin, V.P., Tech.

Board of directors: Jean-Michel Valette, Chair.; Gerald Baldwin; Hilary Billings; David J. Deno; Ted W. Hall; Michael Linton; Patrick J. O'Dea; Elizabeth Sartain
Giving statement: Giving through the Peet's Coffee & Tea, Inc. Corporate Giving Program.
Company EIN: 910863396

Peet's Coffee & Tea, Inc. Corporate Giving Program

P.O. Box 12509
Berkeley, CA 94712-3509
E-mail: webmail@peets.com; Application address for large in-kind donation requests: Peet's Coffee & Tea, Attn: Special Events and Donations, P.O. Box 12509, Berkeley, CA 94712; URL: http://www.peets.com/community/community-local-commitment.html

Purpose and activities: Peet's Coffee & Tea makes charitable contributions to schools and nonprofit organizations involved with arts, education, community development, and housing. Support is given primarily in areas of company operations in California, Colorado, Illinois, Massachusetts, Oregon, and Washington.
Fields of interest: Performing arts centers; Arts; Education; Housing/shelter, volunteer services; Community/economic development.
Type of support: Donated products; Employee matching gifts; Employee volunteer services; In-kind gifts; Sponsorships.
Geographic limitations: Giving primarily in areas of company operations in CA, CO, IL, MA, OR, and WA.
Support limitations: No support for discriminatory organizations, or religious organizations not of benefit to the entire community.
Publications: Application guidelines.
Application information: Applications accepted. Application form not required. Applicants should submit the following:
1) name, address and phone number of organization
2) copy of IRS Determination Letter
3) brief history of organization and description of its mission
4) contact person

Proposals should include the date and name of the event, the number of attendees, the date when the donation is needed, and the type of donation requested, as well as demographic and investment information.
Initial approach: Submit letter to store manager for small donation requests; for event sponsorships or donation requests for events with more than 500 people, send proposal to Peet's Home Office
Deadline(s): 3-6 months prior to need for small donation requests; 6 months prior to need for large donation requests; one year prior to need for event sponsorship requests

2917
Pella Corporation

102 Main St.
Pella, IA 50219-2147 (641) 621-1000

Company URL: http://www.pella.com
Establishment information: Established in 1925.
Company type: Private company
Business activities: Manufactures aluminum-clad windows, glass sliding doors, and wood windows.
Business type (SIC): Metal products/structural; wood millwork; glass products/miscellaneous
Financial profile for 2010: Number of employees, 8,600
Corporate officers: Charles Farver, Chair.; Patrick J. Meyer, Pres. and C.E.O.; Steve Printz, C.I.O.; David Smart, Sr. V.P. and C.F.O.; Elaine Sagers, V.P., Mktg.; Karin Peterson, V.P., Human Resources
Board of directors: Charles Farver, Chair.; Pat Meyer
Giving statement: Giving through the Pella Rolscreen Foundation.

Pella Rolscreen Foundation

102 Main St.
Pella, IA 50219-2147
FAX: (641) 621-6950; E-mail: mavzante@pella.com; URL: http://www.pellarolscreen.com/

Establishment information: Trust established in 1952 in IA.
Donor: Pella Corp.
Contact: Mary A. Van Zante, Secy. and Exec. Dir.
Financial data (yr. ended 12/31/11): Assets, $11,190,242 (M); gifts received, $82,352; expenditures, $1,311,293; qualifying distributions, $1,131,708; giving activities include $1,131,708 for grants.
Purpose and activities: The foundation supports organizations involved with arts and culture, education, the environment, human services, and civic affairs.
Fields of interest: Arts; Higher education; Education; Environment; Human services; Public affairs.
Programs:
Employee Matching Gifts: The foundation matches contributions made by employees and retirees of Pella Corp. to approved charitable organizations on a one-for-one basis from $25 to $5,000 per contributor, per year.
Sons & Daughters Scholarship Program: The foundation annually awards $1,500 four-year college scholarships to children of employees of Pella Corp. The foundation also awards the Pella Engineering Innovation Scholarship to children of employees of Pella Corp.
Volunteer Recognition Program: The foundation awards $100 grants to nonprofit organizations with which employees of Pella volunteer at least 50 hours per year.
Type of support: Building/renovation; Capital campaigns; Employee matching gifts; Employee volunteer services; Employee-related scholarships; Program development; Scholarship funds.
Geographic limitations: Giving primarily in areas of company manufacturing operations in Carroll, Pella, Shenandoah, and Sioux Center, IA, Macomb, IL, Murray, KY, Portland, OR, Gettysburg, PA, and Wylie, TX.
Support limitations: No support for religious or political organizations or organizations with a narrow scope. No grants to individuals (except for employee-related scholarships); no loans.
Publications: Annual report; Application guidelines; Program policy statement.
Application information: Applications accepted. Application form required. Applicants should submit the following:
1) copy of IRS Determination Letter
2) copy of most recent annual report/audited financial statement/990
3) detailed description of project and amount of funding requested

Initial approach: Download application form and mail to foundation
Copies of proposal: 1
Board meeting date(s): Quarterly
Deadline(s): None
Final notification: 1 to 4 months

Officers and Directors:* Pat Meyer*, Chair. and Pres.; Mary A. Van Zante, Secy. and Exec. Dir.; Charles Farver*, Treas.; Joan Farver.
Number of staff: 2 part-time support.
EIN: 237043881
Selected grants: The following grants are a representative sample of this grantmaker's funding activity:
$10,674 to A Call to Serve Ministries of Iowa, Pella, IA, 2010.
$10,000 to University of Cincinnati Foundation, Cincinnati, OH, 2010.
$6,000 to Brown University, Providence, RI, 2010.
$3,000 to Knoxville Education Foundation, Knoxville, IA, 2010.
$2,500 to Santa Fe Chamber Music Festival, Santa Fe, NM, 2010.
$2,500 to Santa Fe Opera, Santa Fe, NM, 2010.
$2,365 to Civic Center of Greater Des Moines, Des Moines, IA, 2010.
$1,500 to American University, Washington, DC, 2010.
$1,500 to University of Illinois at Urbana-Champaign, Urbana, IL, 2010.
$1,300 to Portland Rescue Mission, Portland, OR, 2010.

2918
Pellitteri's Container Haul Away

7035 Raywood Rd.
P.O. Box 259426
Madison, WI 53725 (608) 257-4285

Company URL: http://www.pellitteri.com/default.jsp
Establishment information: Established in 2010.
Company type: Private company
Business activities: Provides recycling services.
Business type (SIC): Sanitary services
Corporate officer: Danielle Pellitteri, V.P., Sales
Giving statement: Giving through the Salt and Light Foundation, Inc.

Salt and Light Foundation, Inc.

P.O. Box 259426
Madison, WI 53725-9426 (608) 259-0845

Establishment information: Established in 1995 in WI.
Donors: Pellitteri's Container Haul Away; Pellitteri Waste Systems, Inc.
Contact: Thomas Pellitteri, Pres.
Financial data (yr. ended 12/31/11): Assets, $23,050 (M); gifts received, $24,100; expenditures, $18,656; qualifying distributions, $18,205; giving activities include $18,205 for grants.
Purpose and activities: The foundation supports student organizations and organizations involved with higher education, athletics, and Christianity.
Fields of interest: Arts; Religion.
Type of support: General/operating support.
Geographic limitations: Giving limited to Madison, WI.
Support limitations: No grants to individuals.
Application information: Applications accepted. Application form required. Applicants should submit the following:
1) descriptive literature about organization
2) name, address and phone number of organization

Initial approach: Proposal
Deadline(s): None

Officers: Thomas J. Pellitteri, Pres.; Michele J. Pellitteri, V.P.
EIN: 391810850

2919
PEMCO Mutual Insurance Company
325 Eastlake Ave. E.
P.O. Box 778
Seattle, WA 98109-5466 (206) 628-4000

Company URL: https://www.pemco.com
Establishment information: Established in 1949.
Company type: Mutual company
Business activities: Operates property damage and liability insurance company.
Business type (SIC): Insurance/fire, marine, and casualty
Corporate officer: Stanley William McNaughton, Chair. and C.E.O.
Board of director: Stanley William McNaughton, Chair.
Giving statement: Giving through the PEMCO Foundation.

PEMCO Foundation
325 Eastlake Ave. E.
Seattle, WA 98109-5407

Establishment information: Established in 1965 in WA.
Donors: Gladys McLaughlin†; PEMCO Corp.; Washington School Employees Credit Union; Evergreen Bank, N.A.; Evergreen Bancorp, Inc.; Teachers Foundation; PEMCO Technology Services, Inc.; School Employees Credit Union of Washington; PEMCO Mutual Insurance Co.; PCCS, Inc.
Contact: Stan W. McNaughton, Pres. and Treas.
Financial data (yr. ended 06/30/12): Assets, $2,615,373 (M); gifts received, $334,510; expenditures, $590,665; qualifying distributions, $589,685; giving activities include $476,087 for 131 grants (high: $94,625; low: -$500) and $112,150 for 80 grants to individuals (high: $3,000; low: $200).
Purpose and activities: The foundation supports organizations involved with television, education, crime and violence prevention, youth development, human services, and business and awards college scholarships to high school students located in Washington.
Fields of interest: Media, television; Secondary school/education; Higher education; Education; Crime/violence prevention; Boys & girls clubs; Camp Fire; Youth development, business; Youth development; American Red Cross; Children, services; Human services; Business/industry; United Ways and Federated Giving Programs.
Type of support: General/operating support; Program development; Scholarship funds; Scholarships—to individuals.
Geographic limitations: Giving primarily in WA, with emphasis on Seattle; giving limited to WA for scholarships.
Application information: Applications accepted. Application form not required.
Initial approach: Letter from school principal stating academic qualifications for scholarships
Deadline(s): None
Final notification: 2 months for scholarships
Officers and Trustees:* Stan W. McNaughton*, Pres. and Treas.; Sandra M. Kurack*, V.P.; Denice M. Town, Secy.; Gayle C. Grass; Brian R. McNaughton; Astrid I. Thompson.
EIN: 916072723
Selected grants: The following grants are a representative sample of this grantmaker's funding activity:
$55,000 to Independent Colleges of Washington, Seattle, WA, 2011.
$25,091 to United Way of King County, Seattle, WA, 2011.
$25,000 to Boys and Girls Clubs of King County, Seattle, WA, 2011.
$20,000 to Discovery Institute, Seattle, WA, 2011.
$10,000 to American Red Cross, Spokane, WA, 2011.
$10,000 to Association of Washington School Principals, Olympia, WA, 2011.
$10,000 to Camp Fire USA, Everett, WA, 2011.
$6,339 to United Way of Snohomish County, Everett, WA, 2011.
$5,500 to Northwest Burn Foundation, Seattle, WA, 2011.
$3,000 to Pacific Northwest Ballet, Seattle, WA, 2011.

2920
Penasco Valley Telephone Cooperative, Inc.
(doing business as Penasco Valley Telecommunications)
(also known as PVT)
4011 W. Main St.
Artesia, NM 88210-9566 (575) 748-1241

Company URL: http://www.pvt.com
Establishment information: Established in 1949.
Company type: Cooperative
Business activities: Provides telephone communications services.
Business type (SIC): Telephone communications
Corporate officers: Glenn Lovelace, C.E.O.; Mike G. Casabonne, Pres.; Dwight Menefee, Secy.
Board of directors: Joe Acosta; Mike G. Casabonne; Sam M. Elkins; Carol Gutierezz; Ronald Houghtaling; Marc E. Kincaid; Glenn Lovelace; Dwight Menefee; Roxann Sallee; Frank L. Sisneros
Subsidiary: PVT NetWorks, Inc., Artesia, NM
Giving statement: Giving through the Penasco Valley Telephone Education Foundation.

Penasco Valley Telephone Education Foundation
4011 W. Main St.
Artesia, NM 88210-9566 (575) 748-1241
E-mail: janiceb@pvt.com; URL: http://www.pvt.com/about/community/scholarships/

Establishment information: Established in 1995 in NM.
Donor: Penasco Valley Telephone Cooperative Inc.
Contact: Janice Southard Bark, Community Rels. Mgr.
Financial data (yr. ended 12/31/11): Assets, $616,948 (M); gifts received, $38,226; expenditures, $42,045; qualifying distributions, $40,500; giving activities include $40,500 for grants to individuals.
Purpose and activities: The foundation awards college scholarships to active members and the immediate family members of active members of Penasco Valley Telephone Cooperative Inc.
Fields of interest: Higher education.
Type of support: Scholarships—to individuals.
Geographic limitations: Giving limited to areas of company operations in NM.
Publications: Application guidelines.
Application information: Applications accepted. Application form required.
Applications should include official transcripts, a 100-word essay, 2 letters of recommendation, and a photograph.
Initial approach: Download application form and mail to foundation, or pick up an application at a PVT location
Deadline(s): Mar. 1
Officers: Mike Casabonne, Pres.; Sam Elkins, V.P.; Peggy Bell, Secy.; Elizabeth Mahill, Treas.
Directors: Carol Guiterrez; Marc Kincaid; Dwight Menefee; Roxann Sallee; Frank Sisneros; J.S. Waldrip.
EIN: 850422272

2921
Pendleton Construction Corporation
1200 W. Pine St.
Wytheville, VA 24382 (276) 228-8601

Company type: Private company
Business activities: Provides street and highway construction services.
Business type (SIC): Construction/highway and street (except elevated)
Giving statement: Giving through the Pendleton Construction Corporation Foundation.

Pendleton Construction Corporation Foundation
P.O. Box 549
Wytheville, VA 24382-0549 (276) 228-8601

Donor: Pendleton Construction Corp.
Contact: William N. Pendleton, Dir.
Financial data (yr. ended 12/31/11): Assets, $102,712 (M); expenditures, $1,374; qualifying distributions, $600; giving activities include $600 for grants.
Purpose and activities: The foundation supports hospices and organizations involved with education.
Fields of interest: Education; Agriculture/food; Civil/human rights.
Type of support: General/operating support.
Geographic limitations: Giving primarily in Wythe County, VA.
Application information: Applications not accepted. Unsolicited requests for funds not accepted.
Directors: Edmund Pendleton; William N. Pendleton.
EIN: 540846282

2922
Penguin Random House
(formerly Random House, Inc.)
1745 Broadway
New York, NY 10019 (212) 782-9000

Company URL: http://www.penguinrandomhouse.com
Establishment information: Established in 1927.
Company type: Subsidiary of a foreign company
Business activities: Publishes books.
Business type (SIC): Book publishing and/or printing
Financial profile for 2009: Number of employees, 5,432; sales volume, $2,469,400,000
Corporate officers: John Makinson, Chair.; Markus Dohle, C.E.O.; Madeline Mcintosh, Pres. and C.O.O.; Coram Williams, C.F.O.; Stuart Applebaum, Exec. V.P., Comms.; Frank Steinert, Chief Human Resources Off.

Board of director: John Makinson, Chair.
International operations: Canada
Giving statement: Giving through the Random House, Inc. Corporate Giving Program.

Random House, Inc. Corporate Giving Program

1745 Broadway, 4th Fl.
New York, NY 10019-4368 (212) 782-8319
FAX: (212) 940-7590; Application address for Creative Writing Competition: Random House, Inc. Creative Writing Competition, c/o Scholarship America, One Scholarship Way, P.O. Box 297, St. Peter, MN 56082; e-mail creativewriting@randomhouse.com; URL: http://careers.randomhouse.com/wms/bmhr/index.php?ci=3917pagesize=&pg=1

Contact: Melanie Fallon-Houska, Dir., Corp. Contrib.
Purpose and activities: Random House makes charitable contributions to nonprofit organizations on a case-by-case basis. Support is given primarily in areas of company operations.
Fields of interest: Education, public education; Education, reading; Disasters, Hurricane Katrina; American Red Cross.
Programs:
Creative Writing Competition: Random House annually awards college scholarships of $500 to $10,000 to New York City high school seniors who submit original compositions in fiction and drama, personal essay and memoir, poetry and spoken word, and graphic novel.
Employee Gift Matching: Random House matches contributions made by its employees to nonprofit organizations.
The World of Expression Scholarship Program: The World of Expression Scholarship Program is open to all New York City public high school seniors and offers a total of $135,000 in scholarship awards ranging from $1,000 to $10,000. Each year, forty-six students are recognized for their original compositions in either music or literature.
Type of support: Donated products; Employee matching gifts; Employee volunteer services; General/operating support; In-kind gifts; Scholarship funds.
Geographic limitations: Giving primarily in areas of company operations in Emeryville and Roseville, CA, Colorado Springs and Waterbrook, CO, Crawfordsville, IN, Westminster, MD, New York, NY, and Seattle, WA.
Publications: Application guidelines.
Application information: Applications accepted. Submissions for the Creative Writing Competition should be no longer than 10 pages. One entry is permitted per person. Application form required. Applicants for the Creative Writing Competition must be .
Initial approach: Mail proposal to headquarters for Creative Writing Competition
Copies of proposal: 1
Deadline(s): Feb. 15 for the Creative Writing Competition; Apr. 1 for graphic novel entries for the Creative Writing Competition

2923
Penn National Gaming, Inc.

825 Berkshire Blvd., Ste. 200
Wyomissing, PA 19610 (610) 373-2400
FAX: (610) 373-4966

Company URL: http://www.pngaming.com
Establishment information: Established in 1972.
Company type: Public company
Company ticker symbol and exchange: PENN/NASDAQ
Business activities: Owner and operator of gaming and pari-mutuel properties.
Business type (SIC): Amusement and recreation services/miscellaneous
Financial profile for 2012: Number of employees, 20,003; assets, $5,644,060,000; sales volume, $2,899,470,000; pre-tax net income, $364,530,000; expenses, $2,456,880,000; liabilities, $3,393,130,000
Fortune 1000 ranking: 2012—729th in revenues, 561st in profits, and 557th in assets
Corporate officers: Peter M. Carlino, Chair. and C.E.O.; Timothy J. Wilmott, Pres. and C.O.O.; William J. Clifford, Sr. V.P., Finance and C.F.O.; Jordan B. Savitch, Esq., Sr. V.P. and Genl. Counsel; D. Eric Schippers, Sr. V.P., Public Affairs; Gene Clark, Sr. V.P., Human Resources; Robert S. Ippolito, V.P. and Secy.-Treas.
Board of directors: Peter M. Carlino, Chair.; Harold Cramer, Esq.; Wesley Robert Edens; David A. Handler; John M. Jacquemin; Barbara Shattuck Kohn; Robert P. Levy; Saul Reibstein
Giving statement: Giving through the Penn National Gaming Foundation.
Company EIN: 232234473

Penn National Gaming Foundation

825 Berkshire Blvd., Ste. 200
Wyomissing, PA 19610-1247 (610) 378-8325
FAX: (610) 375-7632; URL: http://www.pngaming.com/Community

Establishment information: Established in 2005 in PA.
Donor: Penn National Gaming, Inc.
Contact: Amanda Garber, Exec. Dir.
Financial data (yr. ended 12/31/11): Assets, $59,592 (M); gifts received, $382,662; expenditures, $541,140; qualifying distributions, $535,430; giving activities include $534,005 for 47 grants (high: $200,000; low: $100).
Purpose and activities: The foundation supports organizations involved with cultural affairs and diversity, education, health, human services, and community development.
Fields of interest: Arts, cultural/ethnic awareness; Historic preservation/historical societies; Arts; Elementary/secondary education; Higher education; Education; Health care; Housing/shelter; Disasters, preparedness/services; Safety/disasters; Children/youth, services; Aging, centers/services; Human services; Civil/human rights, equal rights; Community/economic development; Leadership development; Public affairs Economically disadvantaged.
Programs:
Community Development: The foundation supports programs designed to promote community infrastructure improvement; public safety; economic development; housing; historic preservation; citizen involvement; and civic leadership.
Cultural Affairs & Diversity: The foundation supports programs designed to foster understanding and appreciation of different cultures; and encourage participation among individuals of different cultures and belief systems.
Education: The foundation supports programs designed to address pre-school, elementary and secondary education; post-secondary education; and special education initiatives.
Health: The foundation supports programs designed to address local health and medical-related initiatives.
Human Services: The foundation supports programs designed to address the needs of children and youth; senior citizens; and disadvantaged people.
Type of support: Emergency funds; General/operating support; Grants to individuals; Program development.
Geographic limitations: Giving primarily in areas of company operations in CO, FL, IL, IN, IA, LA, ME, MS, MO, NJ, NM, OH, PA, TX, and WV.
Publications: Application guidelines; Program policy statement.
Application information: Applications accepted. Application form required. Applicants should submit the following:
1) qualifications of key personnel
2) copy of IRS Determination Letter
3) copy of most recent annual report/audited financial statement/990
4) listing of board of directors, trustees, officers and other key people and their affiliations
5) detailed description of project and amount of funding requested
6) copy of current year's organizational budget and/or project budget

Initial approach: Download application form and mail to headquarters
Copies of proposal: 2
Board meeting date(s): Quarterly
Deadline(s): Jan. 1, Apr. 1, July 1, and Oct. 1
Final notification: 3 months

Officers and Directors:* D. Eric Schippers*, Chair.; Robert S. Ippolito*, Secy.-Treas.; Amanda Garber, Exec. Dir.; Thomas Burke; Eugene Clark; John Finamore; Jordan B. Savitch, Esq.; Timothy Wilmott.
EIN: 203477997
Selected grants: The following grants are a representative sample of this grantmaker's funding activity:
$100,000 to Toledo Classic, Toledo, OH, 2010.
$95,250 to Opportunity House, Reading, PA, 2010.
$41,000 to National Center for Responsible Gaming, Washington, DC, 2010.
$30,000 to NAACP, Columbus, OH, 2010.
$25,000 to Foundation for Ethnic Understanding, New York, NY, 2010.
$22,500 to Rush Philanthropic Arts Foundation, New York, NY, 2010.
$20,000 to Northside Center for Child Development, New York, NY, 2010.
$10,000 to National Council on Problem Gambling, Washington, DC, 2010.
$10,000 to Pennsylvania Regional Ballet, Enola, PA, 2010.
$3,500 to Philadelphia Theater Company, Philadelphia, PA, 2010.

2924
Penn Security Bank and Trust Company

150 N. Washington Ave.
Scranton, PA 18503-1843 (570) 346-7741
FAX: (570) 961-3768

Company URL: http://www.pennsecurity.com
Establishment information: Established in 1902.
Company type: Subsidiary of a public company
Business activities: Operates commercial bank.
Business type (SIC): Banks/commercial
Corporate officers: D. William Hume, Chair.; Craig W. Best, Pres. and C.E.O.; Patrick M. Scanlon, Sr. V.P., Treas., and Cont.; P. Frank Kozik, Secy.
Board of directors: D. William Hume, Chair.; Craig W. Best; Joseph G. Cesare, M.D.; Richard E. Grimm; James G. Keisling; P. Frank Kozik; Robert W. Naismith, Ph.D.; James B. Nicholas; Emily S. Perry; Sandra C. Phillips; Steven L. Weinberger

Giving statement: Giving through the Penn Security Charitable Foundation.

Penn Security Charitable Foundation

(formerly Penseco Foundation)
150 N. Washington Ave.
Scranton, PA 18503-1843 (570) 436-7741
E-mail: p.scanlon@pennsecurity.com

Establishment information: Established in 2000.
Donor: Penn Security Bank & Trust Co.
Contact: Patrick Scanlon, Tr.
Financial data (yr. ended 12/31/11): Assets, $83,203 (M); gifts received, $361,450; expenditures, $377,871; qualifying distributions, $377,500; giving activities include $377,500 for grants.
Purpose and activities: The foundation supports organizations involved with higher education.
Fields of interest: Higher education.
Type of support: Capital campaigns; Scholarship funds.
Geographic limitations: Giving primarily in Scranton, PA.
Application information: Applications not accepted. Contributes only to pre-selected organizations.
Trustees: Richard E. Grimm; Peter F. Moylan; Patrick Scanlon.
EIN: 251886434

2925
J. C. Penney Company, Inc.

6501 Legacy Dr.
Plano, TX 75024-3698 (972) 431-1000

Company URL: http://www.jcpenney.net
Establishment information: Established in 1902.
Company type: Public company
Company ticker symbol and exchange: JCP/NYSE
Business activities: Operates department stores; provides catalog shopping services; provides Internet shopping services.
Business type (SIC): Department stores; nonstore retailers; computer services
Financial profile for 2012: Number of employees, 159,000; assets, $11,424,000,000; sales volume, $17,260,000,000; pre-tax net income, -$229,000,000; expenses, $17,262,000,000; liabilities, $7,414,000,000
Fortune 1000 ranking: 2012—215th in revenues, 980th in profits, and 395th in assets
Forbes 2000 ranking: 2012—747th in sales, 1926th in profits, and 1488th in assets
Corporate officers: Thomas Engibous, Chair.; Myron E. Ullman III, C.E.O.; Mike Kramer, C.O.O.; Janet Dhillon, Exec. V.P., Genl. Counsel, and Secy.
Board of directors: Thomas Engibous, Chair.; William Ackman; Colleen C. Barrett; Kent Foster; Ronald Johnson; Geraldine B. Laybourne; Burl Osborne; Leonard Roberts; Steven Roth; Javier Teruel; R. Gerald Turner; Mary Beth West
Giving statement: Giving through the J. C. Penney Company, Inc. Corporate Giving Program, the J. C. Penney Company Fund, Inc., and the JCPenney Afterschool Fund.
Company EIN: 260037077

J. C. Penney Company, Inc. Corporate Giving Program

6501 Legacy Dr., MS 8211
Plano, TX 75024-3612
URL: http://www.jcpenney.net/about/social_resp/default.aspx

Purpose and activities: As a complement to its foundation, J.C. Penney also makes charitable contributions to nonprofit organizations directly. Support is given on a national basis.
Fields of interest: Education, fund raising/fund distribution; Vocational education; Education; American Red Cross; Salvation Army; Civil/human rights, minorities; Community development, business promotion; United Ways and Federated Giving Programs Children; Aging; Minorities; Military/veterans; Economically disadvantaged.
Type of support: Employee volunteer services; General/operating support; In-kind gifts.
Geographic limitations: Giving on a national basis.
Application information: Applications not accepted. Unsolicited applications are currently not accepted.

J. C. Penney Company Fund, Inc.

6501 Legacy Dr., MS 1205
Plano, TX 75024-3612 (972) 431-1431
FAX: (972) 431-1355; URL: http://www.jcpenney.net/Our-Company/Social-Responsibility.aspx

Establishment information: Established in 1984 in NY.
Donors: J.C. Penney Co., Inc.; J.C. Penney Corp., Inc.
Contact: Jodi Gibson, Pres. and Exec. Dir.
Financial data (yr. ended 01/28/12): Assets, $11,075,182 (M); gifts received, $3,478,942; expenditures, $7,747,897; qualifying distributions, $7,747,897; giving activities include $7,660,392 for 820 grants (high: $2,500,000; low: $50) and $85,150 for 136 grants to individuals (high: $1,250; low: $100).
Purpose and activities: The fund supports organizations involved with arts and culture, education, health and welfare, cancer, disaster relief, youth development, human services, the retail industry, and civic betterment.
Fields of interest: Arts; Elementary/secondary education; Higher education; Scholarships/financial aid; Education; Health care; Cancer; Disasters, preparedness/services; Youth development, business; Youth development; American Red Cross; Developmentally disabled, centers & services; Human services; Business/industry; United Ways and Federated Giving Programs; Public affairs.
Programs:
Associate Disaster Relief: The fund awards grants to active and retired J.C. Penney Associates who live in a county where a federally declared disaster has occurred and have encountered emergency financial hardship or loss of their principal residence and property.
James Cash Penney Award for Community Service: The fund awards grants to charitable organizations with which employees and retirees of J.C. Penney volunteer.
Type of support: Annual campaigns; Employee volunteer services; Equipment; General/operating support; Grants to individuals; Program development; Scholarship funds; Sponsorships.
Geographic limitations: Giving on a national basis in areas of company operations.
Support limitations: No support for individual K-12 schools lacking a community partnership with J.C. Penney, PTO's or PTA's, higher education institutions lacking a business or recruiting relationship with J.C. Penney, or membership, religious, political, labor, or fraternal organizations. No grants to individuals (except for disaster relief grants), or for door prizes, gift certificates, or other giveaways, fundraising or special events, proms or graduations, scholarships for colleges lacking a recruiting relationship with J.C. Penney, conferences or seminars, capital campaigns, multi-year or long-term support, or film or video projects or research projects; no merchandise donations; no employee matching gifts.
Publications: Application guidelines; Corporate giving report.
Application information: Applications accepted. Additional information may be requested at a later date. Telephone calls are not encouraged. Application form not required. Applicants should submit the following:
1) results expected from proposed grant
2) name, address and phone number of organization
3) brief history of organization and description of its mission
4) explanation of why grantmaker is considered an appropriate donor for project
5) detailed description of project and amount of funding requested
6) contact person
Initial approach: Letter of inquiry
Copies of proposal: 1
Deadline(s): None
Final notification: 6 to 8 weeks
Officers and Directors: Jodie Gibson, Pres. and Exec. Dir.; Darcie Brossart, V.P.; Charlotte Thacker, Secy.; Windon Chau, Treas. and Co.-Cont.; Roger Peterson, Co.-Cont.; Robert B. Cavanaugh; Thomas M. Nelson; Michael W. Texter; Michael T. Theilmann.
EIN: 133274961
Selected grants: The following grants are a representative sample of this grantmaker's funding activity:
$1,500,000 to J. C. Penney Afterschool Fund, Plano, TX, 2011. For program support.
$875,307 to United Way of Metropolitan Atlanta, Atlanta, GA, 2011. For program support.
$871,704 to United Way of Metropolitan Atlanta, Atlanta, GA, 2011. For program support.
$870,962 to United Way of Metropolitan Atlanta, Atlanta, GA, 2011. For program support.
$865,987 to United Way of Metropolitan Atlanta, Atlanta, GA, 2011. For program support.
$225,000 to United Way of Metropolitan Dallas, Dallas, TX, 2011. For program support.
$35,500 to United Way Worldwide, Alexandria, VA, 2011. For program support.
$25,000 to American Red Cross, Greater Ozarks Chapter, Springfield, MO, 2011. For program support.
$25,000 to USO World Headquarters, Arlington, VA, 2011. For program support.
$10,000 to American Red Cross, Greater Ozarks Chapter, Springfield, MO, 2011. For program support.

JCPenney Afterschool Fund

c/o Jodi M. Gibson
6501 Legacy Dr.
Plano, TX 75024-3612 (972) 431-1341
E-mail: afterschool@jcpenney.com; URL: http://www.jcpenneyafterschool.org

Establishment information: Established in 2001 in TX.
Financial data (yr. ended 12/31/11): Revenue, $12,447,980; assets, $3,433,203 (M); gifts received, $12,444,137; expenditures, $15,626,042; giving activities include $15,583,407 for grants.
Purpose and activities: The fund seeks to ensure that every child is safe and constructively engaged during the afternoon hours, and works to raise awareness of the benefits of afterschool programming and the importance of these programs to America's families.
Fields of interest: Boys & girls clubs; Children, day care; Children, services.
Geographic limitations: Giving on a national basis.

Application information: Applications not accepted. Contributes only to pre-selected organizations.
Officers and Directors:* Michael T. Thielmann*, Chair.; Jodi M. Gibson*, Pres.; Julie B. Berkhouse, V.P.; Darcie M. Brossart, V.P.; Kervin G. Hartman, V.P.; Gary Piper, V.P. and Treas.; Roger Petersen, V.P. and Cont.; Kristin L. Hays*, Secy.; Jeffrey J. Vawrinek*, Co-Secy.; Michael J. Boylson; Shawn Stelow Griffin; Michael W. Taxter.
EIN: 752966166

2926
Pentair, Inc.

5500 Wayzata Blvd., Ste. 800
Minneapolis, MN 55416-1259
(763) 545-1730

Company URL: http://www.pentair.com
Establishment information: Established in 1966.
Company type: Public company
Company ticker symbol and exchange: PNR/NYSE
Business activities: Manufactures water movement, treatment, and storage products and systems; designs and manufactures electronic and electrical component, thermal management product, and other enclosures.
Business type (SIC): Machinery/special industry; metal forgings and stampings; machinery/general industry
Financial profile for 2011: Number of employees, 15,300; assets, $4,586,310,000; sales volume, $3,456,690,000; pre-tax net income, $111,580,000; expenses, $3,288,170,000; liabilities, $2,652,980,000
Corporate officers: Randall J. Hogan, Chair. and C.E.O.; Michael V. Schrock, Pres. and C.O.O.; John L. Stauch, Exec. V.P. and C.F.O.; Angela D. Lageson, Sr. V.P., Genl. Counsel, and Secy.; Frederick S. Koury, Sr. V.P., Human Resources; Michael G. Meyer, V.P., Treas.; Mark C. Borin, Corp. Cont. and C.A.O.
Board of directors: Randall J. Hogan, Chair.; Leslie Abi-Karam; Glynis A. Bryan; Jerry W. Burris; T. Michael Glenn; Charles A. Haggerty; David H.Y. Ho; David A. Jones; Ronald L. Merriman; William T. Monahan
International operations: Argentina; Australia; Belgium; Brazil; Canada; Chile; China; Czech Republic; France; Germany; Hong Kong; Hungary; India; Ireland; Italy; Japan; Luxembourg; Mauritius; Mexico; New Zealand; Poland; Singapore; South Africa; Spain; Sweden; Taiwan; United Kingdom
Giving statement: Giving through the Pentair Foundation.
Company EIN: 410907434

The Pentair Foundation

5500 Wayzata Blvd., Ste. 800
Golden Valley, MN 55416-1261 (763) 545-1730
FAX: (763) 656-5404;
E-mail: susan.carter@pentair.com; URL: http://www.pentair.com/About_pentair_foundation.aspx

Establishment information: Established in 1998 in MN.
Donor: Pentair, Inc.
Contact: Susan Carter, Fdn. Mgr.
Financial data (yr. ended 12/31/11): Assets, $3,908,527 (M); gifts received, $4,400,004; expenditures, $4,451,236; qualifying distributions, $4,448,357; giving activities include $4,182,768 for 210 grants (high: $279,875; low: $836) and $152,564 for 127 employee matching gifts.
Purpose and activities: The foundation supports organizations involved with arts and culture, education, employment, housing, community development, and economically disadvantaged people. Special emphasis is directed toward programs that promote education, sustainability in water and energy, and workforce development.
Fields of interest: Arts, cultural/ethnic awareness; Arts education; Performing arts, music; Elementary/secondary education; Vocational education; Higher education; Education; Environment, water resources; Environment, energy; Public health, clean water supply; Employment, training; Employment; Housing/shelter; Youth, services; Family services; Community/economic development; United Ways and Federated Giving Programs; Mathematics; Science Economically disadvantaged.
Programs:

Community: The foundation supports programs designed to provide resources that strengthen and enhance the lives of individuals. Special emphasis is directed toward programs designed to promote water quality, education, and conservation; assist individuals in achieving self-sufficiency through job training, education assistance and resources, and affordable housing; promote entrepreneurial opportunities for and with economically disadvantaged individuals; provide opportunities for youth to gain life skills in an environment that encourages cross-cultural understanding and respect for individuals; and provide services for youth in crisis.

Education: The foundation supports programs designed to serve K-12 youth. Special emphasis is directed toward programs designed to enhance science and math education with a focus on applied skills including math and science for career development; provide school-to-work initiatives, including business concepts and their applications, work readiness, career development, and guidance on post-secondary education options; offer alternative education methods and instruction that provide opportunities for students to excel and advance, with emphasis placed on environments which recognize and support the individual needs and skill levels of students; and enhance arts education by introducing students to art concepts, processes, and applications including literature, music, and dramatic arts, highlighting the importance of cultural influences.

Project SafeWater - Colon: The foundation, in partnership with Water Missions International, creates sustainable and safe water access and sanitation in Colon, Honduras. The program is designed to create viable solutions to the global water crisis.

Type of support: Employee matching gifts; General/operating support; Program development; Scholarship funds.
Geographic limitations: Giving primarily in areas of company operations in Moorpark, CA, Hanover Park and North Aurora, IL, Kansas City, KS, Mt. Sterling, KY, Anoka, Minneapolis/St. Paul, and New Brighton, MN, Sanford, NC, Ashland and Chardon, OH, Warwick, RI, Radford, VA, Brookfield and Delavan, WI and Colon, Honduras.
Support limitations: No support for political, lobbying, or fraternal organizations, religious groups for religious purposes, athletic or sports-related organizations, or non 501 (c)(3) organizations or those operating under a fiscal agent. No grants to individuals, or for scholarships, medical research, fundraising events, sponsorships, or advertising, travel or tour expenses, conferences, seminars, workshops, or symposiums.
Publications: Application guidelines.
Application information: Applications accepted. Support is limited to 1 contribution per organization during any given year. Application form required. Applicants should submit the following:

1) timetable for implementation and evaluation of project
2) how project will be sustained once grantmaker support is completed
3) statement of problem project will address
4) copy of IRS Determination Letter
5) brief history of organization and description of its mission
6) copy of most recent annual report/audited financial statement/990
7) how project's results will be evaluated or measured
8) listing of board of directors, trustees, officers and other key people and their affiliations
9) detailed description of project and amount of funding requested
10) plans for cooperation with other organizations, if any
11) copy of current year's organizational budget and/or project budget
12) listing of additional sources and amount of support

Initial approach: Complete online eligibility quiz and application
Board meeting date(s): Feb. and Aug.
Deadline(s): Mar. 1, June 1, and Oct. 1
Final notification: May 31, Sept. 30, and Dec. 31

Officers and Directors:* Michael G. Meyer, Pres. and Treas.; Michael Conklin*, Secy.; Eric Dettmer; Randall J. Hogan; Pete Dyke; Frederick S. Koury; Michael V. Schrock.
Number of staff: 1 full-time professional.
EIN: 411890149

2927
PENTAX Imaging Company

633 17th St., Ste. 2600
Denver, CO 80202-3627 (800) 877-0155

Company URL: http://www.pentaximaging.com
Establishment information: Established in 1919.
Company type: Subsidiary of a foreign company
Business activities: Sells photographic and optical equipment.
Business type (SIC): Professional and commercial equipment—wholesale
Corporate officer: Bob Bender, Pres.
Giving statement: Giving through the PENTAX Imaging Company Contributions Program.

PENTAX Imaging Company Contributions Program

600 12th St., Ste. 300
Golden, CO 80401-6142 (800) 877-0155
URL: http://www.pentaximaging.com

2929
Peoples Bank, N.A.

138 Putnam St.
Marietta, OH 45750-2923 (740) 373-3155

Company URL: http://www.peoplesbancorp.com
Establishment information: Established in 1902.
Company type: Subsidiary of a public company
Business activities: Operates commercial bank.
Business type (SIC): Banks/commercial

Corporate officers: David L. Mead, Pres. and C.E.O.; Carol A. Schneeberger, Exec. V.P. and C.A.O.; Edward G. Sloane, Exec. V.P., C.F.O., and Treas.
Giving statement: Giving through the Peoples Bancorp Foundation Inc.

Peoples Bancorp Foundation Inc.
138 Putnam St.
P.O. Box 738
Marietta, OH 45750-2923 (740) 376-7128
E-mail: kclose@peoplesbancorp.com; Contact for Robert E. Evans Scholarship: Larry E. Holdren; URL: http://www.peoplesbancorp.com

Establishment information: Established in 2003 in OH.
Donor: Peoples Bank.
Contact: Kristi Close, Secy.
Financial data (yr. ended 12/31/11): Assets, $563,192 (M); gifts received, $308,500; expenditures, $129,990; qualifying distributions, $125,900; giving activities include $122,900 for 42 grants (high: $25,000; low: $500).
Purpose and activities: The foundation supports organizations involved with arts and culture, education, human services, youth, and community development. Special emphasis is directed toward programs designed to assist low- to moderate-income families.
Fields of interest: Visual arts; Performing arts; Humanities; Literature; Arts; Higher education; Education; Youth development; YM/YWCAs & YM/YWHAs; Children/youth, services; Human services; Community/economic development; United Ways and Federated Giving Programs; Science; Social sciences Economically disadvantaged.
Programs:
Festival of Learning Scholarship: The foundation awards scholarships to students competing for awards by displaying their skills in language arts, business, social science, science/math/health, fine and applied arts, foreign language and family consumer sciences. The scholarships range from $100 to $300. Each participant can compete in up to two categories and can win up to $600. Scholarships are awarded each year for youth in grades 9 through 12.
Robert E. Evans Scholarship: The foundation awards scholarships to high school seniors locations in market areas served by Peoples Bank to pursue a four-year degree in business, social sciences, fine art, literature, or the humanities at select universities. Awards will go to students attending Marietta College, Washington State Community College, Ohio Valley University, WVU-Parkersburg, and other college and universities located in market areas served by Peoples Bank. Applicants must have a GPA of 2.8 or higher. Awards are based on demonstration of financial need with preference given to those having a higher need.
Type of support: General/operating support; Program development; Scholarships—to individuals.
Geographic limitations: Giving primarily in areas of company operations in Athens, Belmont, Fairfield, Franklin, Gallia, Guernsey, Meigs, Morgan, Noble, and Washington counties, OH, Boyd and Greenup counties, KY, and Cabell, Mason, Wetzel, and Wood counties, WV.
Publications: Application guidelines.
Application information: Applications accepted. Application form required. Applicants should submit the following:
1) qualifications of key personnel
2) copy of IRS Determination Letter
3) descriptive literature about organization
4) listing of board of directors, trustees, officers and other key people and their affiliations
5) detailed description of project and amount of funding requested
6) copy of current year's organizational budget and/or project budget

Scholarship applications should include SAT/ACT scores, letters of recommendation, an essay, and a FAFSA.
Initial approach: Contact foundation for application form; download application and mail for Robert E. Evans Scholarship
Board meeting date(s): Quarterly
Deadline(s): None; Mar. 31 for Robert E. Evans Scholarship
Final notification: 60 to 90 days
Officers: Larry E. Holdren, Pres.; Kristi A. Close, Secy.; Beth A. Worthington, Treas.
Directors: David E. Brighitbill; George W. Broughton; Roger W. McCauley; Theodore Pat Sauber; Charles W. Sulerzyski.
EIN: 300222364
Selected grants: The following grants are a representative sample of this grantmaker's funding activity:
$25,000 to Marietta College, Marietta, OH, 2011.
$10,000 to Marietta Memorial Health Foundation, Marietta, OH, 2011.
$3,500 to Lancaster Festival, Lancaster, OH, 2011.
$3,000 to Main Street Point Pleasant, Point Pleasant, WV, 2011.
$2,500 to Artsbridge, Parkersburg, WV, 2011.
$2,500 to Friends of the Museum, Marietta, OH, 2011.
$2,000 to United Way of Kentucky, Louisville, KY, 2011.
$2,000 to Washington State Community College Foundation, Marietta, OH, 2011.
$1,000 to Eastside Community Ministry, Zanesville, OH, 2011.
$1,000 to United Way of the Upper Ohio Valley, Wheeling, WV, 2011.

2930
The Peoples Bank
209 S. Jefferson Ave.
P.O. Box 4250
Eatonton, GA 31024 (706) 854-8542

Company URL: https://www.tpbeatonton.com
Establishment information: Established in 1943.
Company type: Subsidiary of a private company
Business activities: Operates commercial bank.
Business type (SIC): Banks/commercial
Corporate officers: Amelia A. Wilson, Chair.; Charles Haley, Pres. and Co-C.E.O.; Harvey L. Wilson, Sr., Co-C.E.O.
Board of director: Amelia A. Wilson, Chair.
Giving statement: Giving through the Peoples Bank Foundation, Ltd.

The Peoples Bank Foundation, Ltd.
P.O. Box 4250
Eatonton, GA 31024-4250

Establishment information: Established in 1988 in GA.
Donor: The Peoples Bank.
Financial data (yr. ended 12/31/11): Assets, $125,971 (M); expenditures, $3,646; qualifying distributions, $3,600; giving activities include $3,600 for grants.
Purpose and activities: The foundation awards college scholarships to graduating seniors in Putnam County, Georgia, and Gatewood Schools, Inc.
Type of support: Scholarships—to individuals.
Geographic limitations: Giving limited to Putnam County, GA.
Application information: Applications accepted. Application form required.
Initial approach: proposal
Deadline(s): Mar. 1
Directors: Ann H. Copelan; William Kitchen III; Michael W. Rountree; Mark Sertich; Laura Thompson; Carol Williams.
Officers: Amelia A. Wilson, Pres.; Jesse Copelan, Secy.
EIN: 581811866

2931
Peoples Gas
130 E. Randolph St.
Chicago, IL 60601 (312) 240-4000

Company URL: http://www.peoplesgasdelivery.com/
Establishment information: Established in 1850.
Company type: Subsidiary of a public company
Business activities: Operates holding company; transmits and distributes natural gas.
Business type (SIC): Gas production and distribution; holding company
Corporate officers: Willard S. Evans, Jr., Co-Pres.; Thomas Patrick, Co-Pres. and C.E.O.
Giving statement: Giving through the Peoples Gas Corporate Giving Program.
Company EIN: 362642766

Peoples Gas Corporate Giving Program
(formerly Peoples Energy Corporation Contributions Program)
c/o Mgr., Corp. Contribs.
130 E. Randolph St.
Chicago, IL 60601-6207 (312) 240-7516
E-mail: rbturner@peoplesgasdelivery.com; URL: http://www.peoplesgasdelivery.com/company/community.aspx

Contact: Richard Turner, Mgr., Corp. Contribs.
Financial data (yr. ended 12/31/11): Total giving, $1,124,696, including $1,124,696 for grants.
Purpose and activities: Peoples Energy makes charitable contributions to nonprofit organizations involved with arts and culture, education, health, employment, housing, human services, community development, and leadership development. Support is limited to areas of company operations, with emphasis on the Chicagoland, Illinois, area.
Fields of interest: Visual arts; Museums; Performing arts; Historic preservation/historical societies; Arts; Elementary/secondary education; Libraries/library science; Education, reading; Education; Environment; Health care, equal rights; Public health; Health care; Employment, training; Employment; Housing/shelter; Children, services; Family services; Family services, domestic violence; Aging, centers/services; Homeless, human services; Human services; Economic development; Community/economic development; Leadership development Disabilities, people with; Economically disadvantaged.
Programs:
Culture: Peoples Energy supports historical societies, libraries, museums, and organizations involved with arts and culture and performing and visual arts.

Education: Peoples Energy supports programs designed to address systemic and system-wide education issues; provide basic literacy and school readiness; promote professional development of teachers and school personnel; encourage relationships between community residents and local schools; build partnerships and collaborative efforts with business and volunteers; assist economically disadvantaged students further their education; and initiate early intervention to prevent failing grades.

Health: Peoples Energy supports programs designed to provide neighborhood medical care; promote prevention efforts; and provide educational health programming. Special emphasis is directed toward programs designed to focus on the health of high-risk populations; provide access to quality health care for low-income families; and provide outreach to promote, develop, and maintain a healthy lifestyle.

Neighborhood Development: Peoples Energy supports programs designed to promote community and economic development efforts; provide housing; promote job development and job training; encourage community organizing; and promote leadership development. Special emphasis is directed toward programs designed to provide direct services to children and their families, the elderly, the homeless, victims of domestic abuse, and people with disabilities.

Type of support: Continuing support; Curriculum development; Employee matching gifts; Employee volunteer services; General/operating support; Program development; Sponsorships.
Geographic limitations: Giving limited to areas of company operations, with emphasis on the Chicagoland, IL, area.
Support limitations: No support for organizations that discriminate for any reason, including race, color, religion, creed, age, gender, national origin or sexual orientation; political organizations or campaigns; disease specific organizations or outreach or education programs of disease specific organizations; or individual elementary or secondary schools. No grants to individuals, or for trips or tours, or advertising.
Publications: Application guidelines; Corporate giving report; Grants list; Informational brochure (including application guidelines).
Application information: Applications accepted. A site visit may be requested. Proposals may be submitted using the Chicago Area Grant Application Form. Proposals should be no longer than 4 pages. The Corporate Contributions Department handles giving. The company has a staff that only handles contributions. Application form not required.
Applicants should submit the following:
1) timetable for implementation and evaluation of project
2) results expected from proposed grant
3) name, address and phone number of organization
4) copy of IRS Determination Letter
5) brief history of organization and description of its mission
6) copy of most recent annual report/audited financial statement/990
7) how project's results will be evaluated or measured
8) explanation of why grantmaker is considered an appropriate donor for project
9) listing of board of directors, trustees, officers and other key people and their affiliations
10) detailed description of project and amount of funding requested
11) contact person
12) copy of current year's organizational budget and/or project budget
13) listing of additional sources and amount of support

Initial approach: Proposal to headquarters
Copies of proposal: 1
Deadline(s): None
Final notification: 2 months

Number of staff: 2 full-time professional; 1 full-time support.

2932
Peoples Mutual Telephone Company

123 E. Watts St,
Gretna, VA 24557 (434) 656-2291

Company URL: http://
Establishment information: Established in 1978.
Company type: Private company
Business activities: Provides telephone communications services.
Business type (SIC): Telephone communications
Financial profile for 2010: Number of employees, 18
Corporate officer: Hart Ashworth, Mgr.
Giving statement: Giving through the Educational and Benevolent Foundation of Peoples Mutual.

Educational and Benevolent Foundation of Peoples Mutual

2828 Emerywood Pkwy.
Richmond, VA 23294

Establishment information: Established in 1995 in VA.
Donor: Peoples Mutual Telephone Co.
Financial data (yr. ended 12/31/11): Assets, $419,809 (M); expenditures, $84,060; qualifying distributions, $80,430; giving activities include $80,000 for 2 grants (high: $40,000; low: $40,000).
Purpose and activities: The foundation supports the First Baptist Church of Gretna in Gretna, Virginia.
Fields of interest: Christian agencies & churches.
Type of support: General/operating support.
Geographic limitations: Giving primarily in VA.
Support limitations: No grants to individuals.
Application information: Applications not accepted. Unsolicited requests for funds not accepted.
Trustee: Virginia Baptist Foundation.
EIN: 541779633

2928
People's United Bank

(formerly People's Bank)
850 Main St.
Bridgeport, CT 06604-4917 (203) 338-7001

Company URL: http://www.peoples.com
Establishment information: Established in 1842.
Company type: Subsidiary of a public company
Business activities: Operates commercial bank.
Business type (SIC): Savings institutions
Financial profile for 2012: Assets, $30,300,000,000; sales volume, $1,300,000,000
Forbes 2000 ranking: 2012—1884th in sales, 1599th in profits, and 735th in assets
Corporate officers: George P. Carter, Chair.; John P. Barnes, Pres. and C.E.O.; Kirk W. Walters, Sr. Exec. V.P. and C.F.O.; Lee Powlus, Sr. Exec. V.P. and C.A.O.; Robert E. Trautmann, Sr. Exec. V.P. and Genl. Counsel; David Norton, Sr. Exec. V.P., Human Resources; Jeffrey A. Hoyt, Sr. V.P. and Cont.
Board of directors: George P. Carter, Chair.; John P. Barnes; Collin P. Baron; Kevin T. Bottomley; John K. Dwight; Jerry Franklin; Janet M. Hansen; Richard M. Hoyt; Mark W. Richards; Krik W. Walter
Subsidiaries: Olson Moloeck & Assocs., Bridgeport, CT; People's Capital & Leasing, Bridgeport, CT; People's Securities Inc., Bridgeport, CT
Historic mergers: Danversbank (June 30, 2011)
Giving statement: Giving through the People's United Bank Corporate Giving Program, the Danversbank Charitable Foundation, Inc., and the People's United Community Foundation, Inc.

People's United Bank Corporate Giving Program

(formerly People's Bank Corporate Giving Program)
850 Main St.
Bridgeport, CT 06604 (203) 338-7171
E-mail: Carolyn.Caffrey@peoples.com; Tel. for Carolyn Caffrey, Customer Contact Progs. Mgr., People's United Bank Community Rels.: (203) 338-7252; URL: https://www.peoples.com/portal/site/peoples/

Contact: Carolyn Caffrey, Customer Contact Progs. Mgr.
Purpose and activities: As a complement to its foundation, People's United Bank makes charitable contributions to nonprofit organizations involved with food drives and distribution, economically disadvantaged families, book drives, and children's services. Support is given primarily in areas of company operations in Connecticut, Maine, Massachusetts, New Hampshire, New York, and Vermont.
Fields of interest: Education, reading; Food banks; Girls clubs; Big Brothers/Big Sisters; Youth development; Human services, fund raising/fund distribution; Children, services; Family services Economically disadvantaged.
Programs:

Masters Program: Through the Masters Program, People's United Bank promotes financial safety and awareness for senior citizens. The program trains law enforcement officers on senior citizen crime prevention and includes public seminars on safety at airports, keeping personal property secure, and learning how to use automated banking services.

Samuel W. Hawley Award: People's United Bank honors an employee who demonstrates qualities of community leadership exemplified by former President and C.E.O Samuel Hawley.

Type of support: Annual campaigns; Continuing support; Employee volunteer services; General/operating support; In-kind gifts; Loaned talent; Sponsorships.
Geographic limitations: Giving primarily in areas of company operations in CT, MA, ME, NH, NY, and VT.
Application information:
Initial approach: E-mail letter of inquiry

The Danversbank Charitable Foundation, Inc.

1 Conant St.
Danvers, MA 01923-2902 (978) 739-0253
FAX: (978) 739-4998;
E-mail: kevin.noyes@peoples.com; URL: https://www.peoples.com/peoples/Footer/About-People's-United/Community-Leadership/Charitable-Giving/Danversbank-Charitable-Foundation

Establishment information: Established in 2007 in MA.

Donor: Danversbank.
Contact: Kevin Noyes, Dir.
Financial data (yr. ended 12/31/11): Assets, $12,171,410 (M); expenditures, $538,588; qualifying distributions, $533,588; giving activities include $531,767 for 81 grants (high: $30,000; low: $1,000).
Purpose and activities: The foundation supports nonprofit organizations involved with arts and culture, education, health, affordable housing, human services, and low and moderate income individuals.
Fields of interest: Arts; Secondary school/education; Higher education; Libraries (public); Education, services; Education; Health care, clinics/centers; Speech/hearing centers; Health care; Housing/shelter; YM/YWCAs & YM/YWHAs; Youth, services; Developmentally disabled, centers & services; Human services Economically disadvantaged.
Programs:
Danversbank Grant Program: The foundation awards grants to nonprofit organizations that provide programs or service focused on social, health, and youth services, education, affordable housing, cultural events, or low and moderate income individuals. Grants of up to $50,000 will be awarded for annual gifts and grants of up to $100,000 will be awarded for multiyear grants.
Maiden Community Fund: The foundation awards grants of up to $10,000 to nonprofit organizations located in Maiden that provide programs or services focusing on social, health, and youth services, affordable housing, education, cultural events, or low and moderate income individuals. Grants can be used for capital needs or one-time special projects.
Neighborhood Fund: The foundation awards grants of up to $2,500 on a monthly basis to nonprofit organizations at the local level.
Type of support: Building/renovation; Capital campaigns; Continuing support; General/operating support; Program development; Scholarship funds.
Geographic limitations: Giving primarily in areas of company operations in Andover, Beverly, Boston, Boxford, Burlington, Chelsea, Danvers, Hamilton, Ipswich, Lynnfield, Malden, Middleton, Newbury, Newburyport, North Andover, North Reading, Peabody, Reading, Revere, Rowley, Salem, Saugus, Topsfield, Wakefield, Wenham, Wilmington and Woburn, MA.
Support limitations: No support for political, religious, labor, or discriminatory organizations, or foundations, or governmental agencies. No grants to individuals, or for operating deficits, conferences or seminars, trips or tours including transportation costs, foundations, or annual appeals.
Publications: Annual report; Application guidelines; IRS Form 990 or 990-PF printed copy available upon request.
Application information: Applications accepted. Proposals should be submitted using organization letterhead. Support is limited to 1 contribution per organization during any given year. Multi-year funding is not automatic. Application form required. Applicants should submit the following:
1) timetable for implementation and evaluation of project
2) how project will be sustained once grantmaker support is completed
3) results expected from proposed grant
4) statement of problem project will address
5) population served
6) copy of IRS Determination Letter
7) copy of most recent annual report/audited financial statement/990
8) listing of board of directors, trustees, officers and other key people and their affiliations
9) detailed description of project and amount of funding requested
10) copy of current year's organizational budget and/or project budget
11) listing of additional sources and amount of support
12) plans for acknowledgement

Initial approach: Download application form and e-mail, fax, or mail to foundation
Copies of proposal: 1
Board meeting date(s): Mar., June, Sept. and Dec.
Deadline(s): 1 month prior to need for Neighborhood Fund; Feb. 15rh, May 15th, Aug. 15th, and Nov. 15th for Danversbank Grant Program; Feb.1, May 1, Aug. 1, and Nov. 1 for the Malden Community Fund
Final notification: 60 days for Neighborhood Fund; 30 days after board meetings for Danversbank Grant Program and Malden Community Fund

Officers and Directors:* Kevin T. Bottomley*, Pres.; Thomas Ford*, Clerk; Anthony Petrazzuoli*, Treas.; Ralph Ardiff; Diane C. Brinkley; Timothy Crimmins; John T. Dawley; Matt Hegarty; Eleanor M. Hersey; J. Michael O'Brien; John J. O'Neil; John M. Pereira; Diane T. Stringer.
EIN: 260814452
Selected grants: The following grants are a representative sample of this grantmaker's funding activity:
$2,500 to Center for Women and Enterprise, Boston, MA, 2010.

The People's United Community Foundation, Inc.

850 Main St.
Bridgeport, CT 06604-4917
FAX: (203) 338-6116; E-mail: foundation@pucf.org; Tel. and e-mail for Tammy L. Torres: (203) 338-6112, tammy.torres@peoples.com; Additional contacts: Vincent E. Santilli, tel.: (203) 338-5157, e-mail: Vincent.Santilli@peoples.com, Karen Galbo, Mktg., Public & Community Rels. Dir., tel.: (203) 338-6113, e-mail: Karen.Galbo@peoples.com; URL: https://www.pucf.org/

Establishment information: Established in 2007 in CT.
Donor: People's United Bank.
Contact: Tammy L. Torres, Admin. and Agency Liaison Dir.
Financial data (yr. ended 12/31/11): Assets, $43,097,329 (M); gifts received, $381,941; expenditures, $2,897,074; qualifying distributions, $2,335,366; giving activities include $2,335,366 for 276 grants (high: $167,176; low: $2,500).
Purpose and activities: The foundation supports programs designed to promote affordable housing, youth development, and community development. Special emphasis is directed toward programs and services designed to advance economic self-sufficiency, education, and improved quality of life for low-income individuals and families, at-risk children and youth, and individuals with special needs.
Fields of interest: Education, early childhood education; Education, special; Charter schools; Higher education; Teacher school/education; Education, services; Education, reading; Education; Employment, services; Food banks; Housing/shelter, home owners; Housing/shelter, services; Housing/shelter; Youth development, adult & child programs; Youth development; Human services, financial counseling; Developmentally disabled, centers & services; Community development, neighborhood development; Business/industry; Community development, business promotion; Community development, small businesses; Community/economic development; United Ways and Federated Giving Programs; Mathematics; Engineering/technology; Science Children/youth; Youth; Disabilities, people with; Minorities; Women; Economically disadvantaged.
Programs:
Affordable Housing: The foundation supports programs designed to create affordable housing: and create or sustain safe, clean, and desirable neighborhoods in which People's United does business. Special emphasis is directed toward bricks and mortar projects; first-time homebuyer training; closing costs and assistance; homebuyer education; nonprofit organizations that develop affordable housing or assist developer programs that create affordable housing that revitalizes neighborhoods; community loan funds; and state and national programs that serve as developers of affordable housing.
Community Development: The foundation supports programs designed to enhance quality of life in areas served by People's United and promote economic development in low-income neighborhoods. Special emphasis is directed toward initiatives that transition people from assistance to independence; small business development programs; entrepreneurial programs; programs that encourage economic self-sufficiency; programs that promote fiscal education and responsibility; and job creation programs.
Youth Development: The foundation supports programs designed to serve the educational and developmental needs of children and youth, with a focus on school districts that serve low-income children and families. Special emphasis is directed toward improved classroom quality; literacy; teacher development and improvement; skill and confidence-building programs for low-income and low performance students in school and after-school programs; early-childhood development (Early Head Start) and school readiness (Head Start) programs; charter and magnet schools; college preparation (school-ready) programs that increase access for minorities and women to higher education; college programs that support special needs; and STEM programs.
Type of support: General/operating support; Management development/capacity building; Program development.
Geographic limitations: Giving primarily in areas of company operations in CT, MA, ME, NH, Long Island and Westchester County, NY, and VT.
Support limitations: No support for arts and culture organizations, childcare or daycare agencies, discriminatory organizations, disease-specific organizations, health organizations, historic preservation, organizations serving a limited constituency, municipal or government entities, nursery schools, political action committees (PAC's), political, labor, or fraternal, or health care organizations, private foundations, private schools or colleges, private pre-college schools, public school districts and their individual schools, religious organizations not of direct benefit to the entire community, assisted living for seniors, or pass-through organizations. No grants to individuals, or for activism, advertising, advocacy, animal causes, annual appeals or operational fundraising campaigns, beauty contests, capital campaigns, conferences, seminars, panel discussions, or trips, conservation or environmental causes, consultants, debt reduction, endowments, event sponsorships, fundraising activities or events, media including television, radio, film, video, or books, medical equipment or patient treatment funds, pilot programs or start-ups, research or feasibility studies, sports, athletic events, or recreational programs, sponsorships or projects where the Bank or its employees receive benefits,

student trips or tours, substance abuse programs, or theater, dance, or music programs.
Publications: Annual report; Application guidelines; Grants list; Newsletter; Program policy statement.
Application information: Applications accepted. The minimum grant request is $2,500. The average grant range is between $2,500 and $7,500. Support is limited to 1 contribution per organization during any 12-month period. Multi-year funding is not automatic. Telephone calls during the application process are not encouraged. Organizations receiving support are required to submit a final report. Application form required. Applicants should submit the following:
1) brief history of organization and description of its mission
2) copy of most recent annual report/audited financial statement/990
3) how project's results will be evaluated or measured
4) detailed description of project and amount of funding requested
5) copy of current year's organizational budget and/or project budget
6) listing of additional sources and amount of support

Applications should also include a completed and signed W9 Form.
Initial approach: Complete online eligibility quiz and application
Copies of proposal: 1
Board meeting date(s): Trimester funding cycle
Deadline(s): Feb. 1, June 1, and Oct. 1
Officers and Directors:* Jack P. Barnes, Chair.; Robert R. D'Amore*, Exec. V.P.; Michael J. Casparino, V.P.; Timothy P. Crimmins, Jr., V.P.; Armando F. Goncalves, V.P.; Kathleen E. Jones, V.P.; Samuel A. Ladd III, V.P.; William P. Lucy, V.P.; Dianne Mercer, V.P.; Michael L. Seaver, V.P.; Susan D. Stanley, Secy.; Jeremy Araujo, Treas.; Vincent E. Santilli, Exec. Dir.; George P. Carter; Arthur F. Casavant; Robert B. Dannies, Jr.; Eunice S. Groark.
Number of staff: 2 full-time professional; 1 part-time professional.
EIN: 208675365

2933
Pepco Holdings, Inc.

701 9th St., N.W.
Washington, DC 20068 (202) 872-2000

Company URL: http://www.pepcoholdings.com
Establishment information: Established in 2002 from the merger of Conectiv with Potomac Electric Power Co.
Company ticker symbol and exchange: POM/NYSE
International Securities Identification Number: US7132911022
Business activities: Operates holding company; generates, transmits, and distributes electricity; transmits and distributes natural gas.
Business type (SIC): Combination utility services
Financial profile for 2012: Assets, $15,800,000,000; sales volume, $5,100,000,000
Fortune 1000 ranking: 2012—483rd in revenues, 487th in profits, and 289th in assets
Forbes 2000 ranking: 2012—1380th in sales, 1407th in profits, and 1139th in assets
Corporate officer: Dennis R. Wraase, Chair., Pres., and C.E.O.
Subsidiaries: Conectiv, Wilmington, DE; Delmarva Power & Light Company, Wilmington, DE; Potomac Electric Power Company, Washington, DC

Pepco Holdings, Inc. Contributions Program

701 Ninth Street, N.W.
Washington, DC 20068 (202) 872-2000
URL: http://www.pepcoholdings.com/services/outreach/

2934
Pepper Hamilton LLP

3000 2 Logan Sq., 18th and Arch St.
Philadelphia, PA 19103-2799
(215) 981-4000

Company URL: http://www.pepperlaw.com/default.aspx
Establishment information: Established in 1890.
Company type: Private company
Business activities: Operates law firm.
Business type (SIC): Legal services
Corporate officer: John E. Pooler, Jr., C.A.O.
Offices: Irvine, CA; Wilmington, DE; Washington, DC; Boston, MA; Southfield, MI; Princeton, NJ; New York, NY; Berwyn, Harrisburg, Philadelphia, Pittsburgh, PA
Giving statement: Giving through the Pepper Hamilton LLP Pro Bono Program.

Pepper Hamilton LLP Pro Bono Program

3000 2 Logan Sq., 18th and Arch St.
Philadelphia, PA 19103-2799 (215) 981-4304
E-mail: sullivanja@pepperlaw.com; URL: http://www.pepperlaw.com/PracticeArea_preview.aspx?PracticeAreaKey=32

Contact: Joseph A. Sullivan, Special Counsel and Dir. of Pro Bono Progs.
Fields of interest: Legal services.
Type of support: Pro bono services - legal.
Application information: A Pro Bono Committee manages the pro bono program.

2935
PepsiCo, Inc.

700 Anderson Hill Rd.
Purchase, NY 10577-1444 (914) 253-2000
FAX: (914) 253-2070

Company URL: http://www.pepsico.com
Establishment information: Established in 1919.
Company type: Public company
Company ticker symbol and exchange: PEP/NYSE
International Securities Identification Number: US7134481081
Business activities: Produces, markets, and sells snacks, carbonated and non-carbonated beverages, and foods.
Business type (SIC): Beverages; food and kindred products; miscellaneous prepared foods
Financial profile for 2012: Number of employees, 278,000; assets, $74,638,000,000; sales volume, $65,492,000,000; pre-tax net income, $8,304,000,000; expenses, $56,380,000,000; liabilities, $52,344,000,000
Fortune 1000 ranking: 2012—43rd in revenues, 28th in profits, and 81st in assets
Forbes 2000 ranking: 2012—123rd in sales, 84th in profits, and 329th in assets
Corporate officers: Indra K. Nooyi, Chair. and C.E.O.; Zein Abdalla, Pres.; Hugh F. Johnston, Exec. V.P. and C.F.O.; Larry D. Thompson, Exec. V.P., Genl. Counsel, and Corp. Secy.; Cynthia M. Trudell, Exec. V.P., Human Resources; Jim Wilkinson, Exec. V.P., Comms.; Robert Dixon, Sr. V.P. and C.I.O.
Board of directors: Indra K. Nooyi, Chair.; Shona L. Brown; George W. Buckley; Ian M. Cook; Dina Dublon; Victor J. Dzau, M.D.; Ray L. Hunt; Alberto Ibarguen; Sharon Percy Rockefeller; James J. Schiro; Lloyd G. Trotter; Daniel L. Vasella; Alberto Weisser
Subsidiaries: Frito-Lay, Inc., Plano, TX; Golden Grain Company, Pleasanton, CA; Pepsi-Cola Co., Purchase, NY; Pepsi-Cola International Ltd. (U.S.A.), Somerset, NY; The Quaker Oats Company, Chicago, IL; Tropicana Products, Inc., Bradenton, FL
International operations: Argentina; Australia; Bahamas; Bangladesh; Barbados; Bermuda; Bosnia-Herzegovina; Bulgaria; Canada; Cayman Islands; Chile; China; Colombia; Croatia; Cyprus; Denmark; Dominican Republic; Ecuador; Egypt; El Salvador; Estonia; France; Germany; Greece; Guatemala; Honduras; Hong Kong; Hungary; India; Ireland; Jordan; Kazakhstan; Latvia; Liechtenstein; Lithuania; Luxembourg; Malaysia; Mexico; Morocco and the Western Sahara; Netherlands; Netherlands Antilles; New Zealand; Nicaragua; Nigeria; Pakistan; Panama; Peru; Philippines; Poland; Portugal; Romania; Russia; Saudi Arabia; Serbia; Singapore; South Africa; South Korea; Spain; Taiwan; Trinidad & Tobago; Turkey; Ukraine; United Arab Emirates; United Kingdom; Uruguay; Venezuela; Vietnam
Historic mergers: PepsiAmericas, Inc. (February 26, 2010); The Pepsi Bottling Group, Inc. (February 26, 2010)
Giving statement: Giving through the PepsiCo, Inc. Corporate Giving Program, the Pepsi Bottling Group Foundation, Inc., and the PepsiCo Foundation, Inc.
Company EIN: 131584302

PepsiCo, Inc. Corporate Giving Program

700 Anderson Hill Rd.
Purchase, NY 10577-1401 (914) 253-2000
URL: http://www.pepsico.com/Purpose/Corporate-Contributions.html

Financial data (yr. ended 12/31/11): Total giving, $62,400,000, including $14,800,000 for grants and $47,600,000 for in-kind gifts.
Purpose and activities: As a complement to its foundation, PepsiCo also makes charitable contributions to nonprofit organizations directly. Support is given primarily in areas of company operations.
Fields of interest: Education; Environment; Health care; Disasters, preparedness/services; YM/YWCAs & YM/YWHAs; Human services; Civil/human rights, equal rights; Leadership development; General charitable giving Economically disadvantaged.
Programs:
Pepsi Refresh Project: Through the Pepsi Refresh Project, Pepsi awards $1.3 million in grants every month to 32 ideas posted on the Pepsi refresh website with the most votes. The website is open to anyone in the public and Pepsi funds projects that make a difference in six categories: health, arts and culture, the planet, neighborhoods, and education.
QTG Scholarship Program: Through the QTG Scholarship Program, PepsiCo, Inc. annually awards ten $10,000 scholarships to current college freshman through junior (award may be renewed) who attend select East Coast universities and have a minimum 3.0 GPA, demonstrate leadership activities and community service, major in Business or Liberal Arts with an interest in a sales or marketing career, and demonstrate financial need. Recipients must also complete an essay on how

Quaker, Tropicana and Gatorade have adopted the values of quality, trust and growth.
Type of support: Donated products; Employee volunteer services; In-kind gifts; Sponsorships.
Geographic limitations: Giving primarily on a national and international basis in areas of company operations, including NY, Canada, Chile, China, India, Lebanon, Pakistan, Philippines, and the United Kingdom.
Publications: Application guidelines; Grants list.
Application information: Applications accepted. Unsolicited applications for sponsorships and in-kind gifts are currently not accepted. The company is undergoing a revision of its global grant investment strategy. Requests for direct monetary donations should be sent to the PepsiCo Foundation for consideration. The Community Affairs Department handles giving. Applicants should submit the following:
1) name, address and phone number of organization
2) brief history of organization and description of its mission
3) contact person

Initial approach: Submit ideas online for Pepsi Refresh

Deadline(s): 15th of every month for Pepsi Refresh

The Pepsi Bottling Group Foundation, Inc.

c/o The Pepsi Bottling Group, Inc.
1 Pepsi Way
Somers, NY 10589-2201 (914) 767-6000
E-mail: catherine.patterson@pepsi.com; Additional tel.: (914) 767-7897

Establishment information: Established in 1999 in NY.
Donors: The Pepsi Bottling Group, Inc.; Bottling Group, LLC.
Contact: Catherine Patterson, Sr. Mgr.
Financial data (yr. ended 12/31/11): Assets, $1,124 (M); expenditures, $465,061; qualifying distributions, $465,061; giving activities include $465,061 for 37 grants (high: $203,043; low: $85).
Purpose and activities: The foundation supports programs designed to promote strengthening families, youth development, diversity, and the environment. Special emphasis is directed towards organizations with which employees of Pepsi Bottling Group demonstrate their interest through charitable contributions or volunteer work.
Fields of interest: Environment; Disasters, preparedness/services; Youth development; Family services; Civil/human rights, equal rights; United Ways and Federated Giving Programs.
Programs:

Individual Volunteer Grants: The foundation awards grants of $250 or $500 to nonprofit organization with which employees of Pepsi Bottling Group volunteers 20 or 40 or more hours a year.

Matching Gifts: The foundation matches contribution made by employees, retirees, and directors of Pepsi Bottling Group to nonprofit organizations on a one-for-one basis from $25 to $10,000 per contributor, per year, and on a two-for-one basis for organizations with which employees serves as a Board Member up to $25,000 per contributor, per year.

Team Fundraising Grants: The foundation matches funds up to $1,000 raised by teams of three or more full-time employees or retirees for nonprofit organizations through a one-time activity, including walk-a-thons, bowl-a-thons, and bicycle rides.

Team Volunteer Project Grants: The foundation awards grants to nonprofit organizations with which employees complete a "hands-on" team volunteer project. A team for three to nine employees are eligible for a $500 grant, a team of ten or more employees eligible for a $1,000 grant, and a team of three or more employees who volunteer with an eligible organization on three or more separate occasions are eligible for a $2,500 grant.
Type of support: Donated products; Employee matching gifts; Employee volunteer services; General/operating support; Scholarship funds.
Geographic limitations: Giving primarily in areas of company operations, with emphasis on CT, GA, NJ, NY, and VA.
Support limitations: No support for political candidates, religious organizations, fraternal organizations, or family foundations. No grants to individuals, or for proposals that involve any PepsiCo brand, fundraising initiatives, sponsorships, dinners, or events, or political causes or campaigns.
Application information: Applications accepted. Application form not required.

Initial approach: Proposal

Deadline(s): None

Officers and Directors:* Eric J. Foss*, Chair.; John L. Bensford, Vice-Chair.; Paula Davis*, Vice-Chair.; Steven M. Rapp, Secy.; Alfred H. Drewes*, Treas.; Victor Crawford; Andrea Forster; Robert King.
EIN: 134090130
Selected grants: The following grants are a representative sample of this grantmaker's funding activity:
$62,625 to Drew University, Madison, NJ, 2006.
$51,304 to Charities Aid Foundation America, Alexandria, VA, 2006.
$42,303 to Junior Achievement, 2006.
$33,494 to American Cancer Society, 2006.
$11,174 to American Red Cross, 2006.
$2,500 to United Way, 2006.
$1,500 to Big Brothers Big Sisters, Nutmeg, Hartford, CT, 2006.
$775 to Arthritis Foundation, Atlanta, GA, 2006.
$500 to Angel House, Franklin, MI, 2006.
$325 to Sacred Heart University, Fairfield, CT, 2006.

The PepsiCo Foundation, Inc.

700 Anderson Hill Rd.
Purchase, NY 10577-1401
URL: http://www.pepsico.com/Purpose/PepsiCo-Foundation.aspx

Establishment information: Incorporated in 1962 in NY.
Donor: PepsiCo, Inc.
Financial data (yr. ended 12/31/11): Assets, $92,105,183 (M); expenditures, $29,941,448; qualifying distributions, $29,773,085; giving activities include $29,773,085 for 4,153 grants (high: $3,375,024; low: $25).
Purpose and activities: The foundation supports programs designed to promote education, the environment, and health in underserved regions. Special emphasis is directed toward nutrition and safety; safe water and water usage efficiencies; and education and empowerment.
Fields of interest: Higher education; Education; Environment, water pollution; Environment, water resources; Public health; Public health, physical fitness; Public health, clean water supply; Health care; Employment, training; Employment; Food services; Food banks; Nutrition; Agriculture/food; Disasters, preparedness/services; Safety/disasters; Children, services; Civil/human rights, equal rights; Economic development; United Ways and Federated Giving Programs Minorities; Women; Economically disadvantaged.
International interests: Africa; Asia; Bangladesh; Ghana; India.
Programs:

Diamond Scholars Program: The foundation annually awards four-year $2,500 college scholarships to urban youth in San Jose and Los Angeles, California, Miami, Florida, Detroit, Michigan, and Dallas, Texas who have demonstrated an ability to overcome adversity. The program is administered by Scholarship America, Inc.

Education: The foundation supports programs designed to promote diversity in education and workforce development to foster economic achievement and mobility for underserved and minority populations. Special emphasis is directed toward programs designed to promote access to education and training; and women's empowerment.

Employee Matching Gifts: The foundation matches contributions made by full-time associates of PepsiCo to nonprofit organizations in the environmental, educational, civic, arts, health, and the human service fields on a one-for-one basis. The foundation also provides a double match if the associate serves on the board of a nonprofit organization and volunteers 50 hours of personal time with that organization during the year.

Environment: The foundation supports programs designed to protect water sources and create better use for existing water to minimize the growing water crisis. Special emphasis is directed toward programs designed to promote water security; sustainable agriculture; and adaptive approaches to changing climate.

ExCel Awards: The foundation awards college scholarships to children of employees of PepsiCo. The program is administered by Scholarship America, Inc.

Health: The foundation supports programs designed to promote food security; improved and optimum nutrition; and energy balance activity models. Special emphasis is directed toward programs designed to promote and allow for change at the systems-level; and programs that serve underserved populations and communities.

PepsiCo Foundation National Merit Scholarship Program: The foundation awards college scholarships to children of employees of PepsiCo. The program is administered by the National Merit Scholarship Corporation.
Type of support: Continuing support; Employee matching gifts; Employee volunteer services; Employee-related scholarships; General/operating support; In-kind gifts; Management development/capacity building; Program development; Scholarships—to individuals.
Geographic limitations: Giving on a national and international basis, with emphasis on Washington, DC, FL, IL, MA, NY, TX, and VA, and in Africa, Asia, Bangladesh, Canada, China, Ghana, India, Mexico, and the United Kingdom.
Support limitations: No support for private charities or foundations, religious organizations, political candidates or organizations, discriminatory organizations, or legislative organizations, or for playgrounds, or sports fields. No grants to individuals (except for employee-related and Diamond scholarships), or for political causes or campaigns, endowments or capital campaigns, equipment, film, music, TV, video, or media productions, sports sponsorships, performing arts tours, or association memberships.
Publications: Grants list; Program policy statement.
Application information: Applications not accepted. Unsolicited letters of inquiry or proposals are currently not accepted. Foundation staff solicits proposals for all major grants over $100,000.
Officers and Directors:* Indra K. Nooyi*, Chair.; Sue Tsokris, V.P.; Christine Griff, Secy.; Tessa

Hilado, Treas.; Zein Abdalla; Saad Abdul-Latif; Rich Delaney; Hugh F. Johnston; Donald M. Kendall; Mehmood Khan; Cynthia M. Trudell.
Number of staff: 2 full-time professional; 2 full-time support.
EIN: 136163174
Selected grants: The following grants are a representative sample of this grantmaker's funding activity:
$3,375,024 to Scholarship America, Saint Peter, MN, 2011.
$2,000,000 to Give2Asia, San Francisco, CA, 2011.
$2,000,000 to Inter-American Development Bank, Washington, DC, 2011.
$733,993 to United Way of Westchester and Putnam, White Plains, NY, 2011. For corporate match.
$161,000 to Friends of the World Food Program, Washington, DC, 2011.
$45,537 to United Way of Peel Region, Mississauga, Canada, 2011.
$20,000 to Green Hill Therapy, Louisville, KY, 2011.
$12,200 to Immaculate High School, Danbury, CT, 2011.

2936
Perdue Farms, Inc.
31149 Old Ocean City Rd.
Salisbury, MD 21804-1806 (410) 543-3000
FAX: (410) 543-3532

Company URL: http://www.perdue.com
Establishment information: Established in 1920.
Company type: Private company
Business activities: Produces poultry.
Business type (SIC): Farms/poultry and egg
Financial profile for 2011: Number of employees, 20,500; sales volume, $4,600,000,000
Corporate officers: James A. Perdue, Chair. and C.E.O.; Robert Turley, Pres. and C.O.O.; Eileen F. Burza, Sr. V.P. and C.F.O.; Sandy Rasel, V.P. and C.I.O.; Clint Rivers, Sr. V.P., Opers.; Luis A. Luna, V.P., Corp. Comms.; Robert H. Heflin, V.P., Human Resources
Board of director: James A. Perdue, Chair.
Subsidiaries: Perdue Farms, Inc., Showell, MD; Perdue Transportation Inc., Salisbury, MD
Giving statement: Giving through the Perdue Farms Incorporated Corporate Giving Program.

Perdue Farms Incorporated Corporate Giving Program
31149 Old Ocean City Rd.
Salisbury, MD 21804-1806
URL: http://www.perdue.com/company/commitments/communities.html

Purpose and activities: Perdue makes charitable contributions to nonprofit organizations involved with education, the environment, agriculture, health and social services, public safety, and hunger and poverty. Support is limited to areas of company operations in Alabama, Delaware, Georgia, Indiana, Kentucky, Maryland, North Carolina, South Carolina, Tennessee, and Virginia.
Fields of interest: Education; Environment; Agriculture; Food services; Safety/disasters; Human services Economically disadvantaged.
Type of support: Donated products; General/operating support.
Geographic limitations: Giving limited to areas of company operations in AL, DE, GA, IN, KY, MD, NC, SC, TN, and VA.
Publications: Application guidelines.
Application information: Applications accepted. Application form required. Applicants should submit the following:
1) population served
2) copy of IRS Determination Letter
3) brief history of organization and description of its mission
4) geographic area to be served
5) list of company employees involved with the organization
6) detailed description of project and amount of funding requested
7) contact person
8) additional materials/documentation

Initial approach: Complete online application form
Committee meeting date(s): Quarterly
Deadline(s): None
Final notification: Following review

2937
Perforce Software, Inc.
2320 Blanding Ave.
Alameda, CA 94501-1403 (510) 864-7400

Company URL: http://www.perforce.com/
Establishment information: Established in 1995.
Company type: Private company
Business activities: Operates software company.
Business type (SIC): Computer services
Corporate officers: Christopher Seiwald, Pres.; Nigel Chanter, C.O.O.; Carrie Ewing, V.P., Opers.; Nick Telford, V.P., Finance; Robin Ryan, Cont.
Giving statement: Giving through the Perforce Foundation.

Perforce Foundation
2320 Blanding Ave.
Alameda, CA 94501-1403
URL: http://www.perforce.com/company/perforce-foundation

Establishment information: Established in 1999 in CA.
Donor: Perforce Software, Inc.
Financial data (yr. ended 03/31/12): Assets, $5,928,570 (M); gifts received, $1,871; expenditures, $1,139,992; qualifying distributions, $546,218; giving activities include $546,218 for grants.
Purpose and activities: The foundation supports food banks and organizations involved with arts and culture, education, animal welfare, health, breast cancer, soccer, human services, and science.
Fields of interest: Arts; Secondary school/education; Higher education; Education; Animal welfare; Health care, volunteer services; Hospitals (general); Health care; Breast cancer; Food banks; Athletics/sports, soccer; Boys & girls clubs; American Red Cross; Homeless, human services; Human services; Science.
Type of support: Building/renovation; General/operating support; Matching/challenge support.
Geographic limitations: Giving primarily in CA; giving also to national organizations.
Support limitations: No grants to individuals.
Application information: Applications not accepted. Unsolicited requests for funds not accepted. The foundation awards grants to nonprofit organizations recommended by Perforce employees.
Officers and Directors:* Christopher Seiwald*, Pres.; Trudi Seiwald*, Secy.-Treas.
EIN: 943327346
Selected grants: The following grants are a representative sample of this grantmaker's funding activity:
$1,500 to Multiple Sclerosis Society, National, New York, NY, 2011.

2938
Performance Food Group Company
(doing business as Vistar)
12500 W. Creek Pkwy.
Richmond, VA 23238 (804) 484-7700

Company URL: http://www.pfgc.com
Establishment information: Established in 1875.
Company type: Subsidiary of a private company
Business activities: Operates foodservice distribution businesses.
Business type (SIC): Groceries—wholesale
Financial profile for 2011: Number of employees, 10,000; sales volume, $10,600,000,000
Corporate officers: Doug Steenland, Chair.; George L. Holm, Pres. and C.E.O.; Bob Evans, Sr. V.P. and C.F.O.; Terry West, Sr. V.P. and C.I.O.; Mike Miller, Sr. V.P., Genl. Counsel; Jeff Fender, V.P. and Treas.; Doug Jobe, V.P., Finance and Cont.; Kevin Lester, V.P., Human Resources
Board of directors: Doug Steenland, Chair.; Martin Brand; William Dawson; George Holm; Bruce McEvoy; Prakash Melwani
Subsidiary: Roma of New Jersey, Piscataway, NJ
Giving statement: Giving through the Performance Food Group Company Contributions Program.

Performance Food Group Company Contributions Program
12500 West Creek Pkwy.
Richmond, VA 23238-1110 (804) 484-7700
URL: http://www.pfgc.com/About/Pages/Responsibility.aspx

Purpose and activities: Performance Food Group makes charitable contributions to nonprofit organizations involved with food services. Support is given primarily in areas of company operations.
Fields of interest: Food services; Food banks; General charitable giving.
Type of support: Donated products; Employee volunteer services; General/operating support; In-kind gifts.
Geographic limitations: Giving primarily in areas of company operations; giving also to national organizations.

2939
PerkinElmer, Inc.
(formerly EG&G, Inc.)
940 Winter St.
Waltham, MA 02451 (781) 663-6900
FAX: (781) 663-5985

Company URL: http://www.perkinelmer.com/
Establishment information: Established in 1947.
Company type: Public company
Company ticker symbol and exchange: PKI/NYSE
International Securities Identification Number: US7140461093
Business activities: Provides optoelectronic, mechanical, and electromechanical components and instruments and technical and managerial services.
Business type (SIC): Services/miscellaneous; laboratory apparatus; manufacturing/miscellaneous

Financial profile for 2012: Number of employees, 7,500; assets, $3,901,760,000; sales volume, $2,115,200,000; pre-tax net income, $50,590,000; expenses, $2,016,660,000; liabilities, $1,961,950,000
Fortune 1000 ranking: 2012—911th in revenues, 786th in profits, and 673rd in assets
Corporate officers: Robert F. Friel, Chair., Pres., and C.E.O.; Frank Anders Wilson, C.P.A., Sr. V.P. and C.F.O.; Joel S. Goldberg, Sr. V.P., Genl. Counsel, and Secy.; John R. Letcher, Sr. V.P., Human Resources; Andrew Okun, V.P. and C.A.O.
Board of directors: Robert F. Friel, Chair.; Peter Barrett; Nicholas A. Lopardo; Alexis P. Michas; James C. Mullen; Vicki L. Sato, Ph.D.; Kenton J. Sicchitano; Patrick J. Sullivan
Subsidiaries: Antarctic Support Associates, Englewood, CO; EG&G Astrophysics Research Corp., Long Beach, CA; EG&G Automotive Research, Inc., San Antonio, TX; EG&G Birtcher, Inc., El Monte, CA; EG&G Defense Materials, Inc., Tooele, UT; EG&G Dynatrend, Inc., Burlington, MA; EG&G Electronic Components, Salem, MA; EG&G Energy Measurements, Inc., Las Vegas, NV; EG&G Florida, Inc., Kennedy Space Center, FL; EG&G Flow Technology, Inc., Phoenix, AZ; EG&G Idaho, Inc., Idaho Falls, ID; EG&G Instruments, Inc./Princeton Applied Research, Trenton, NJ; EG&G Instruments/Gamma Scientific, Inc., San Diego, CA; EG&G Instruments/Process Measurements/Chandler Engineering Co., Broken Arrow, OK; EG&G KT AeroFab, El Cajon, CA; EG&G Management Services, Inc., Albuquerque, NM; EG&G Marine Instruments, Burlington, MA; EG&G Mound Applied Technologies, Inc., Miamisburg, OH; EG&G Ortec, Oak Ridge, TN; EG&G Power Systems, Covina, CA; EG&G Pressure Science, Inc., Beltsville, MD; EG&G Reynolds Electrical & Engineering Co., Inc., Las Vegas, NV; EG&G Rocky Flats, Inc., Golden, CO; EG&G Rotron, Inc., Woodstock, NY; EG&G Sealol, Inc., Cranston, RI; EG&G Special Projects, Inc., Las Vegas, NV; EG&G Structural Kinematics, Inc., Troy, MI; EG&G Washington Analytic Services Center, Inc., Rockville, MD; EG&G Washington Analytical Services Center, Morgantown, WV; EG&G Wright Components, Inc., Phelps, NY
Divisions: EG&G Optoelectronics/Electro Optics Div., Salem, MA; EG&G Optoelectronics/Judson, Montgomeryville, PA; EG&G Optoelectronics/Reticon, Sunnyvale, CA; EG&G Optoelectronics/Vactec, Inc., St. Louis, MO; EG&G Rotron Industrial Div., Saugerties, NY
Plants: National City, San Luis Obispo, CA; Cocoa, FL; Cataumet, Fall River, Natick, Wakefield, Watertown, Woburn, MA; Cincinnati, OH; Tulsa, OK; Warwick, RI; Alexandria, VA
International operations: Canada; Germany; Thailand
Giving statement: Giving through the PerkinElmer Foundation.
Company EIN: 042052042

PerkinElmer Foundation

(formerly EG&G Foundation)
c/o PerkinElmer, Inc.
940 Winter Street
Waltham, MA 02451-1457 (781) 663-6900
URL: http://www.perkinelmer.com/AboutUs/CorporateCitizenship/Community/default.xhtml

Establishment information: Established in 1979 in MA.
Donors: EG&G, Inc.; PerkinElmer, Inc.
Contact: Suzanne Hurley
Financial data (yr. ended 06/30/12): Assets, $7,020,323 (M); expenditures, $531,788; qualifying distributions, $461,845; giving activities include $461,845 for grants.
Purpose and activities: The foundation supports programs designed to address human and environmental health. Special emphasis is directed toward the accurate diagnosis of disease; and protecting the environment.
Fields of interest: Museums; Arts; Elementary/secondary education; Education; Aquariums; Health care, clinics/centers; Health care; Genetic diseases and disorders; Homeless, human services; Human services.
Type of support: Employee matching gifts; General/operating support.
Geographic limitations: Giving primarily in MA.
Support limitations: No grants to individuals.
Application information: Applications accepted. Application form not required. Applicants should submit the following:
1) copy of IRS Determination Letter
Initial approach: Letter of inquiry
Deadline(s): None
Trustees: Robert F. Friel; Joel S. Goldberg; John Letcher.
EIN: 042683042
Selected grants: The following grants are a representative sample of this grantmaker's funding activity:
$5,000 to Boy Scouts of America, Boston, MA, 2010.
$5,000 to Saint Jude Childrens Research Hospital, Memphis, TN, 2010.
$3,000 to Houston Ballet, Houston, TX, 2010.
$1,000 to Leukemia & Lymphoma Society, White Plains, NY, 2010.

2940
Perkins Coie, LLP

1201 3rd Ave., Ste. 4800
Seattle, WA 98101-3099 (206) 359-8000

Company URL: http://www.perkinscoie.com
Establishment information: Established in 1912.
Company type: Private company
Business activities: Provides legal services.
Business type (SIC): Legal services
Corporate officers: Craig E. Courter, C.O.O.; Rick L. Johnson, C.F.O.; Gavin Cullen, C.A.O.; Gavin Gray, C.I.O.
Offices: Anchorage, AK; Phoenix, AZ; Menlo Park, San Francisco, Santa Monica, CA; Denver, CO; Washington, DC; Boise, ID; Chicago, IL; Portland, OR; Bellevue, Olympia, WA
Giving statement: Giving through the Perkins Coie LLP Corporate Giving Program.

Perkins Coie LLP Corporate Giving Program

1201 3rd Ave., Ste. 4900
Seattle, WA 98101-3095 (206) 359-8000
E-mail: ralli@perkinscoie.com; URL: http://www.perkinscoie.com/Firm/Firm.aspx?Section=Community

Purpose and activities: Perkins Coie makes charitable contributions to nonprofit organizations on a case by case basis. Support is given primarily in areas of company operations.
Fields of interest: Children, day care; Aging, centers/services; Community development, neighborhood development; United Ways and Federated Giving Programs.
Type of support: Employee volunteer services; General/operating support; Sponsorships.
Geographic limitations: Giving primarily in areas of company operations in Anchorage, AK, Phoenix, AZ, Los Angeles, Palo Alto, Perkins Coie, San Diego, and San Francisco, CA, Denver, CO, Washington, DC, Boise, ID, Chicago, IL, New York, NY, Portland, OR, Dallas, TX, Bellevue, and Seattle, WA, and Madison, WI, and in China and Taiwan.

2941
Perkins Coie LLP

1201 3rd Ave., Ste. 4800
Seattle, WA 98101-3099 (206) 359-3985

Company URL: http://www.perkinscoie.com
Establishment information: Established in 1912.
Company type: Private company
Business activities: Operates law firm.
Business type (SIC): Legal services
Corporate officers: Robert Giles, Managing Partner; Rick Johnson, C.F.O.; Gavin Cullen, C.A.O.; Gavin Gray, C.I.O.
Offices: Anchorage, AK; Phoenix, AZ; Los Angeles, Palo Alto, San Diego, San Francisco, CA; Denver, CO; Washington, DC; Boise, ID; Chicago, IL; New York, NY; Portland, OR; Dallas, TX; Bellevue, Seattle, WA; Madison, WI
International operations: China
Giving statement: Giving through the Perkins Coie LLP Pro Bono Program.

Perkins Coie LLP Pro Bono Program

1201 3rd Ave., Ste. 4800
Seattle, WA 98101-3099 (206) 359-3985
E-mail: lmedway@perkinsocoie.com; Additional tel.: (206) 359-8000; URL: http://www.perkinscoie.com/Firm/Firm.aspx?Section=Probono

Contact: Leah Medway, Pro Bono Counsel
Fields of interest: Legal services.
Type of support: Pro bono services - legal.
Application information: A Pro Bono Committee manages the pro bono program.

2942
Pernod Ricard, USA

100 Manhattanville Rd.
Purchase, NY 10577 (914) 848-4800

Company URL: http://www.pernod-ricard-usa.com
Establishment information: Established in 1805.
Company type: Subsidiary of a foreign company
Business activities: Operates spirits and wine company.
Business type (SIC): Beverages
Corporate officers: Bryan Fry, Pres. and C.E.O.; John Nicodemo, C.F.O.; Thomas R. Lalla, Jr., Sr. V.P. and Genl. Counsel; Emmanuel Cargill, Sr. V.P., Human Resources
Giving statement: Giving through the Pernod Ricard, USA Corporate Giving Program.

Pernod Ricard, USA Corporate Giving Program

100 Manhattanville Rd.
Purchase, NY 10577 (914) 848-4800
URL: http://www.pernod-ricard-usa.com

2943
L. Perrigo Company
515 Eastern Ave.
Allegan, MI 49010-9070 (269) 673-8451

Company URL: http://www.perrigo.com
Establishment information: Established in 1981.
Company type: Subsidiary of a public company
Business activities: Manufactures over-the-counter pharmaceutical and nutritional products.
Business type (SIC): Drugs
Corporate officers: Joseph C. Papa, Chair., Pres., and C.E.O.; Judy L. Brown, Exec. V.P. and C.F.O.; Tom Farrington, Sr. V.P. and C.I.O.
Board of directors: Joseph C. Papa, Chair.; Laurie Brlas; Gray M. Cohen; David T. Gibbons; Ran Gottfried; Ellen R. Hoffing; Michael J. Jandernoa; Gary K. Kunkle, Jr.; Herman Morris, Jr.; Ben-Zion Zilberfarb
Giving statement: Giving through the Perrigo Company Charitable Foundation.

Perrigo Company Charitable Foundation
515 Eastern Ave.
Allegan, MI 49010-9070 (269) 673-8451

Establishment information: Established in 2000 in MI.
Donor: L. Perrigo Co.
Contact: Michael R. Stewart, Dir.
Financial data (yr. ended 06/30/12): Assets, $895,717 (M); gifts received, $1,870,166; expenditures, $847,502; qualifying distributions, $847,502; giving activities include $847,502 for 134 grants (high: $100,000; low: $100).
Purpose and activities: The foundation supports organizations involved with arts and culture, education, health, substance abuse prevention, cancer, and human services.
Fields of interest: Arts; Higher education; Education; Hospitals (general); Health care; Substance abuse, prevention; Cancer; Boy scouts; Girl scouts; American Red Cross; Developmentally disabled, centers & services; Homeless, human services; Human services; United Ways and Federated Giving Programs.
Type of support: Building/renovation; General/operating support; Program development; Scholarship funds.
Geographic limitations: Giving primarily in areas of company operations in MI.
Support limitations: No grants to individuals.
Application information: Applications accepted.
Initial approach: Proposal
Deadline(s): None
Officers and Director: Joseph C. Papa, Pres.; Judy L. Brown, Exec. V.P. and C.F.O.; John T. Hendrickson, Exec. V.P.; Todd W. Kingma, Secy.; Ronald L. Winowiecki, Treas.; Michael R. Stewart.
EIN: 383553518
Selected grants: The following grants are a representative sample of this grantmaker's funding activity:
$18,800 to Safeway Foundation, Pleasanton, CA, 2011. For charitable activities.
$15,000 to Borgess Foundation, Kalamazoo, MI, 2011. For charitable activities.
$15,000 to Center for Women in Transition, Holland, MI, 2011. For charitable activities.
$15,000 to Hope College, Holland, MI, 2011.
$15,000 to Kids Food Basket, Grand Rapids, MI, 2011. For charitable activities.
$10,000 to Business Leaders for Michigan, Detroit, MI, 2011. For charitable activities.
$10,000 to International Aid, Spring Lake, MI, 2011. For charitable activities.
$5,000 to American Cancer Society, Grand Rapids, MI, 2011. For charitable activities.
$5,000 to Bethany Christian Services, Grand Rapids, MI, 2011. For charitable activities.
$3,000 to Otsego Public Schools Foundation, Otsego, MI, 2011.

2944
Persis Corporation
900 Fort St. Mall, Ste. 1725
Honolulu, HI 96813-3702 (808) 599-8000

Company URL: http://www.persis.com
Establishment information: Established in 1967.
Company type: Private company
Business activities: Operates nonresidential buildings; conducts investment activities.
Business type (SIC): Real estate operators and lessors; investors/miscellaneous
Corporate officers: Thurston Twigg-Smith, Chair. and C.E.O.; Easton Manson, Pres.
Board of director: Thurston Twigg-Smith, Chair.
Giving statement: Giving through the Laniakea Foundation.

Laniakea Foundation
765 Kumukahi Pl.
Honolulu, HI 96825-1114

Establishment information: Established as a company-sponsored operating foundation in 2002 in HI.
Donors: Persis Corp.; Thurston Twigg-Smith; David Twigg-Smith; Benedict Twigg-Smith; Christian Twigg-Smith; Lisa Twigg-Smith.
Financial data (yr. ended 12/31/11): Assets, $1,971,051 (M); gifts received, $22,584; expenditures, $32,059; qualifying distributions, $0.
Purpose and activities: The foundation supports, restores, and operates Laniakea property in Hawaii.
Application information: Applications not accepted. Unsolicited requests for funds not accepted.
Officers: Patricia Godfrey, Pres.; Louisa Twigg-Smith, V.P.; Magdalena Twigg-Smith, Secy.-Treas.
Directors: Sarah Li; Michael Pfeffer.
EIN: 300107896

2945
PETCO Animal Supplies, Inc.
9125 Rehco Rd.
San Diego, CA 92121 (858) 453-7845

Company URL: http://www.petco.com
Establishment information: Established in 1965.
Company type: Private company
Business activities: Operates pet shops; provides Internet shopping services.
Business type (SIC): Retail stores/miscellaneous; computer services
Financial profile for 2011: Number of employees, 23,500; assets, $7,593,200; liabilities, $7,593,200
Corporate officers: Brian K. Devine, Chair.; James M. Myers, C.E.O.; Charlie Piscitello, Pres.; Michael Foss, Exec. V.P. and C.F.O.; Thomas A. Farello, Sr. V.P., Opers.; Patty Ward, V.P. and Cont.; Kevin Whalen, Secy.; Dave Carr, Treas.
Board of directors: Brian K. Devine, Chair.; Dave Carr; Elisabeth Charles; Bruce Hall; Peggy Hillier; Reg Holden; Paul Jolly; Duncan Mathison; Judith T. Munoz; Maggie Osburn; Charlie Piscitello; Michael Peterson; Kailas Rao; Lance Schwimmer; Richard M. Segal; Kevin Whalen
Giving statement: Giving through the PETCO Foundation.
Company EIN: 330479906

The PETCO Foundation
9125 Rehco Rd.
San Diego, CA 92121-2270
FAX: (626) 287-9704;
E-mail: petcofoundation@petco.com; URL: http://www.petco.com/Content/Content.aspx?PC=petcofoundationhome&Nav=11

Establishment information: Established in 1999 in CA.
Contact: Paul Jolly, V.P.
Financial data (yr. ended 04/30/12): Revenue, $16,807,063; assets, $8,765,963 (M); gifts received, $16,798,439; expenditures, $15,690,699; program services expenses, $14,327,344; giving activities include $14,300,650 for 516 grants (high: $841,277; low: $902).
Purpose and activities: The foundation supports community organizations and efforts that enhance the lives of companion animals while strengthening the bond between people and pets.
Fields of interest: Animal welfare.
Program:
Grants Program: Support is available for 501(c)(3) organizations based in the U.S. that work to better the lives of animal companions, while strengthening the relationships between people and their pets. Emphasis is given to the projects and groups that most closely conform to fulfilling the mission of the foundation.
Type of support: Building/renovation; Capital campaigns; Conferences/seminars; Continuing support; Emergency funds; Equipment; General/operating support; In-kind gifts; Program development; Research.
Geographic limitations: Giving on a national basis.
Support limitations: No grants for salaries or the purchase of animals.
Publications: Annual report; Application guidelines; Informational brochure.
Application information: Applications accepted. Application form required. Applicants should submit the following:
1) copy of IRS Determination Letter
Initial approach: Download application form
Copies of proposal: 1
Board meeting date(s): Quarterly
Deadline(s): None
Final notification: 8 to 12 weeks
Officers and Directors:* Bruce C. Hall*, Pres.; Janet D. Mitchell*, Sr. V.P. and Secy.; Therese Helmer, V.P.; Paul Jolly, V.P.; Donald Cowan*, Treas.; Duncan Mathison; Carol McAvoy.
Number of staff: 3 full-time professional; 1 full-time support; 1 part-time support.
EIN: 330845930

2946
Peterson Industries, Inc.
616 E. Hwy. 36
Smith Center, KS 66967-9592
(785) 282-6825
FAX: (785) 282-3810

Company URL: http://www.petersonind.com
Establishment information: Established in 1966.
Company type: Private company
Business activities: Manufactures recreational vehicles.
Business type (SIC): Motor vehicles and equipment
Corporate officers: Vaughn D. Peterson, Chair. and C.E.O.; Bryan E. Tillett, Pres.; Duana J. Peterson, Secy.-Treas.
Board of directors: Vaughn D. Peterson, Chair.; Curtis Peterson
Giving statement: Giving through the Peterson Industries Charitable Foundation.

Peterson Industries Charitable Foundation
136 S. Main
P.O. Box 307
Smith Center, KS 66967-0307 (785) 282-6825
Application address: Peterson Industries, Inc., 617 E. Hwy. 36 Smith Center, KS 66967, tel.: (785) 282-6825

Establishment information: Established in 1994 in KS.
Donor: Peterson Industries, Inc.
Financial data (yr. ended 03/31/12): Assets, $56,909 (M); expenditures, $1,273; qualifying distributions, $500; giving activities include $500 for grants.
Purpose and activities: The foundation awards college scholarships to children and spouses of employees of Peterson Industries.
Fields of interest: Education.
Type of support: Employee-related scholarships.
Geographic limitations: Giving limited to KS.
Application information: Applications accepted. Application form required.
Initial approach: Letter
Deadline(s): June 1
Trustee: The Peoples Bank.
EIN: 481158653

2947
Petroleum Products Corp.
900 S. Eisenhower Blvd.
Middletown, PA 17057 (717) 939-0466

Company URL: http://www.ppcterminals.com
Establishment information: Established in 1960.
Company type: Private company
Business activities: Wholesaler of oil, gasoline and kerosene.
Business type (SIC): Petroleum and petroleum products—wholesale
Corporate officers: John M. Arnold, Chair. and C.E.O.; Robert G. Bost, Pres.; Dennis M. Shaw, C.F.O.
Board of director: John M. Arnold, Chair.
Giving statement: Giving through the Arnold Family Foundation.

Arnold Family Foundation
c/o John M. Arnold
P.O. Box 2621
Harrisburg, PA 17105-2621
Application address: 160 N. Pointe Blvd., Ste. 200, Lancaster, PA 17601-4134, tel.: (717) 735-8000

Establishment information: Established in 2005 in PA.
Donor: Petroleum Products Corp.
Financial data (yr. ended 06/30/12): Assets, $734,262 (M); expenditures, $109,372; qualifying distributions, $105,000; giving activities include $105,000 for grants.
Fields of interest: Education; Human services.
Type of support: General/operating support.
Geographic limitations: Giving primarily in PA.
Support limitations: No grants to individuals.
Application information: Applications not accepted. Unsolicited requests for funds not accepted.
Directors: John H. Arnold; John M. Arnold; Kara Hanlon Arnold; Katharine G. Arnold; Robert M. Arnold.
EIN: 203724672

2948
PetSmart, Inc.
19601 N. 27th Ave.
Phoenix, AZ 85027 (623) 580-6100
FAX: (623) 395-6517

Company URL: http://www.petsmart.com
Establishment information: Established in 1994.
Company type: Public company
Company ticker symbol and exchange: PETM/NASDAQ
Business activities: Operates pet shops; provides Internet shopping services; provides catalog shopping services; provides pet grooming and training services; provides pet veterinary services.
Business type (SIC): Retail stores/miscellaneous; veterinary services; animal services, except veterinary; nonstore retailers; computer services
Financial profile for 2013: Number of employees, 52,000; assets, $2,536,980,000; sales volume, $6,758,240,000; pre-tax net income, $596,890,000; expenses, $6,107,020,000; liabilities, $1,413,390,000
Fortune 1000 ranking: 2012—377th in revenues, 406th in profits, and 799th in assets
Forbes 2000 ranking: 2012—1200th in sales, 1245th in profits, and 1961st in assets
Corporate officers: Robert F. Moran, Chair. and C.E.O.; David K. Lenhardt, Pres. and C.O.O.; Chip Molloy, Exec. V.P. and C.F.O.; Paulette Dodson, Sr. V.P., Secy., and Genl. Counsel; Donald Beaver, Sr. V.P. and C.I.O.; Mel Tucker, Sr. V.P., Finance; Erick Goldberg, Sr. V.P., Human Resources
Board of directors: Robert F. Moran, Chair.; Angel Cabrera, Ph.D.; Rita V. Foley; Philip L. Francis; Rakesh Gangwal; Joseph S. Hardin, Jr.; Gregory P. Josefowicz; Amin I. Khalifa; Richard K. Lochridge; Barbara A. Munder; Thomas G. Stemberg
Giving statement: Giving through the PetSmart Charities, Inc.
Company EIN: 943024325

PetSmart Charities, Inc.
19601 N. 27th Ave.
Phoenix, AZ 85027-4008 (623) 587-2832
FAX: (623) 580-6561;
E-mail: info@petsmartcharities.org; Toll-free tel.: (800) 423-7387; URL: http://www.petsmartcharities.org

Establishment information: Established in 1994 in AZ.
Donor: PetSmart, Inc.
Contact: Susana Della Maddalena, Sr. V.P. and Exec.Dir.
Financial data (yr. ended 01/31/12): Revenue, $43,763,199; assets, $40,823,533 (M); gifts received, $42,424,641; expenditures, $44,618,467; giving activities include $26,163,166 for grants.
Purpose and activities: The organization gives grants to help homeless pets and end euthanasia as a means to controlling the pet population.
Fields of interest: Animal welfare.
International interests: Canada.
Programs:
Emergency Relief Funding: Provides emergency relief aid to assist pets in times of hurricanes, fire, and other natural catastrophes. The program also provides much-needed support in times of man-made emergencies, including pet hoarders and puppy mill rescues and for animal victims of violence.
Free-roaming Cat Spay/Neuter Program: This grant is intended to provide funding and mentoring for high impact Trap-Neuter-Return (TNR) projects. The goal is to stabilize and ultimately reduce the free-roaming cat population within a specific geographic area. Target areas may include all or part of a county, city, township, ZIP code, census tract, neighborhood, mobile home park or other location. Your budget for the grant may include spay/neuter expenses, trapping equipment, transportation, marketing materials or other outreach expenses, certain personnel costs or other items directly related to your TNR project. Applications will be considered for requests up to $100,000 per year with the possibility of a two-year commitment. The maximum possible grant is thus for $200,000 for two years (at $100,000 per year). Mentorship for grantees is also available during the course of a funded project and ongoing communication with the organization's staff is highly recommended.
Targeted Spay/Neuter Program: This grant is intended to provide funding and mentoring for high impact spay/neuter projects that focus on owned pets in areas where there is a critical need. Target areas may include all or part of a county, city, township, ZIP code, census tract, neighborhood, mobile home park or other location. our budget for the grant may include spay/neuter expenses, transportation, marketing materials or other outreach expenses, and/or other items directly related to your project. Applications will be considered for requests up to $100,000 per year with the possibility of a two-year commitment. The maximum possible grant is $200,000 for two years (at $100,000 per year). Mentorship for grantees is also available during the course of a funded project and ongoing communication with PetSmart Charities staff is highly recommended.
Type of support: Conferences/seminars; Emergency funds; Equipment; Program development; Seed money.
Geographic limitations: Giving on a national basis, as well as in Canada and U.S. territories.
Support limitations: No support for wildlife or endangered species programs. No grants to individuals, or for building projects, endowments, or operating expenses.
Publications: Annual report; Application guidelines; Financial statement; Informational brochure; Newsletter.
Application information: Applications accepted. See web site for additional application information. Application form required.
Copies of proposal: 1
Board meeting date(s): Feb., June and Oct.

Deadline(s): Varies
Final notification: About 30 to 60 days after deadline; Day of receipt for emergency relief grants
Officers and Directors:* Philip L. Francis*, Chair.; Jaye Perricone, Vice-Chair.; Susana Della Maddalena*, V.P. and Exec. Dir.; Jeremiah Beitzel*, Secy.; Susan Gulig*, Treas.; Herb Baum; Donald Beaver; Dr. Philip A. Bushby; Donna Fleischer; and 5 additional directors.
Number of staff: 16 full-time professional; 7 full-time support.
EIN: 931140967

2949
Pfister & Vogel Tanning Company, Inc.

1531 N. Water St.
Milwaukee, WI 53202-3108

Company type: Private company
Business activities: Tans and finishes leather.
Business type (SIC): Leather tanning and finishing
Corporate officer: Charles P. Vogel, Chair.
Board of director: Charles P. Vogel, Chair.
Giving statement: Giving through the Pfister & Vogel Tanning Company Foundation.

Pfister & Vogel Tanning Company Foundation

P.O. Box 2043
Milwaukee, WI 53201-9668 (414) 765-6038
Application address: Pfister & Vogel Tanning Co., Inc., 1531 N. Water St., Milwaukee, WI 53202

Donor: Pfister & Vogel Tanning Co., Inc.
Financial data (yr. ended 05/31/12): Assets, $373,296 (M); expenditures, $27,505; qualifying distributions, $20,000; giving activities include $20,000 for grants.
Purpose and activities: The foundation supports cemeteries and organizations involved with elementary education, conservation, HIV/AIDS, and human services.
Fields of interest: Education; Environment; Human services.
Type of support: Employee-related scholarships; General/operating support.
Geographic limitations: Giving primarily in the Milwaukee County, WI, area.
Application information: Applications accepted. Application form required.
Initial approach: Proposal
Deadline(s): None
Committee Members: Dan Brierton; Dan Diedrich.
Trustee: U.S. Bank, N.A.
EIN: 396036556

2950
Pfizer Inc.

235 E. 42nd St.
New York, NY 10017-5755 (212) 733-2323

Company URL: http://www.pfizer.com
Establishment information: Established in 1849.
Company type: Public company
Company ticker symbol and exchange: PFE/NYSE
International Securities Identification Number: US7170811035
Business activities: Discovers, develops, manufactures, and markets human and animal pharmaceuticals and consumer products.
Business type (SIC): Drugs
Financial profile for 2012: Number of employees, 91,500; assets, $185,798,000,000; sales volume, $58,986,000,000; pre-tax net income, $12,080,000,000; expenses, $46,906,000,000; liabilities, $104,538,000,000
Fortune 1000 ranking: 2012—48th in revenues, 11th in profits, and 33rd in assets
Forbes 2000 ranking: 2012—137th in sales, 21st in profits, and 147th in assets
Corporate officers: Ian C. Read, Chair. and C.E.O.; Frank D'Amelio, Exec. V.P. and C.F.O.; Amy Schulman, Exec. V.P. and Genl. Counsel; Chuck Hill, Exec. V.P., Human Resources; Sally Susman, Exec. V.P., Comms.
Board of directors: Ian C. Read, Chair.; Dennis A. Ausiello, M.D.; M. Anthony Burns; W. Don Cornwell; Frances D. Fergusson, Ph.D.; William H. Gray III; Helen H. Hobbs, M.D.; Constance J. Horner; Suzanne Nora Johnson; James M. Kilts; George A. Lorch; Stephen W. Sanger; Marc Tessier-Lavigne, Ph.D.
Subsidiaries: Pharmacia & Upjohn LLC, Peapack, NJ; Pharmacia Corporation, Peapack, NJ
International operations: Algeria; Angola; Argentina; Australia; Austria; Bahamas; Barbados; Belgium; Bermuda; Bolivia; Bosnia-Herzegovina; Brazil; Canada; Cayman Islands; Chile; China; Colombia; Costa Rica; Croatia; Czech Republic; Denmark; Dominican Republic; Ecuador; Egypt; El Salvador; Finland; France; Germany; Ghana; Gibraltar; Greece; Guatemala; Guernsey; Honduras; Hong Kong; Hungary; India; Indonesia; Ireland; Israel; Italy; Jamaica; Japan; Kenya; Luxembourg; Malaysia; Mexico; Morocco and the Western Sahara; Mozambique; Namibia; Netherlands; Netherlands Antilles; New Zealand; Nigeria; Norway; Pakistan; Panama; Peru; Philippines; Poland; Portugal; Romania; Russia; Senegal; Serbia; Singapore; South Africa; South Korea; Spain; Sweden; Switzerland; Taiwan; Tanzania, Zanzibar and Pemba; Thailand; Tunisia; Turkey; Uganda; United Arab Emirates; United Kingdom; Uruguay; Venezuela; Zimbabwe
Historic mergers: Wyeth (October 15, 2009); King Pharmaceuticals, Inc. (February 28, 2011)
Giving statement: Giving through the Pfizer Inc. Corporate Giving Program, the Contraception Foundation, the Pfizer Foundation, Inc., and the Pfizer Patient Assistance Foundation, Inc.
Company EIN: 835315170

Pfizer Inc. Corporate Giving Program

235 E. 42nd St.
New York, NY 10017-5703 (212) 733-2323
Event sponsorships email: publicaffairssupport@pfizer.com; Medical & Academic Partnerships: tel.: (877) 254-6953; e-mail: MAPinfo@clinicalconnexion.com; Carmine Novembre, MPH, CPH, Dir., Ext. Medical Affairs, email: carmine.novembre@pfizer.com; URL: http://www.pfizer.com/pfizer/subsites/philanthropy/index.jsp

Purpose and activities: As a complement to its foundations, Pfizer also makes charitable contributions to nonprofit organizations directly. Support is given on a national and international basis.
Fields of interest: Medicine/medical care, public education; Health care, formal/general education; Hospitals (general); Public health; Health care, cost containment; Health care, patient services; AIDS; Biology/life sciences.
Type of support: Continuing support; Curriculum development; Fellowships; General/operating support; Program development; Scholarship funds; Sponsorships.
Geographic limitations: Giving on a national and international basis.
Support limitations: No grants to individuals, or for activities aimed at improperly influencing healthcare professionals, or government officials, or other entities aimed at improperly influencing prescribing, formulary positioning, or recommendation of Pfizer projects, that may result in off-label promotion of Pfizer products, or undermine the organization's independence, as quid pro quo for service or support; no support for capital costs, including building or start-up costs, for non-research grant proposals, or to individual healthcare professionals or group practices for programs that do not provide broad public benefit, primarily benefit patient care, or advance medical science, or activities that do not align with Pfizer's policy or business goals.
Publications: Application guidelines; Informational brochure.
Application information: Applications accepted. Proposals for event sponsorships should be submitted using organization letterhead. Each Medical & Academic Partnerships award area has an independent academic selection committee. Applicants should submit the following:
1) copy of IRS Determination Letter
2) detailed description of project and amount of funding requested
3) copy of current year's organizational budget and/or project budget
4) listing of additional sources and amount of support
5) plans for acknowledgement
6) additional materials/documentation

Requests for event sponsorships should include a proposal letter, location, date, whether the organization has received funding from Pfizer before, and, if applicable, an agenda, and flyer, brochure, or invitation. Fellowship applications should include an institution's W9, letter of support, CV, and project plan. The potential fellow's name must not be included in the application.
Initial approach: E-mail proposal for event sponsorships; complete online application for fellowships
Deadline(s): 60 days prior to need for event sponsorships; Feb. 24 for fellowships
Final notification: Apr. 1 for fellowships

The Pfizer Foundation, Inc.

235 E. 42nd St.
New York, NY 10017-5703
URL: http://www.pfizer.com/pfizer/subsites/philanthropy/index.jsp

Establishment information: Incorporated in 1953 in Brooklyn, NY.
Donor: Pfizer Inc.
Financial data (yr. ended 12/31/11): Assets, $205,048,166 (M); gifts received, $700,000; expenditures, $17,269,654; qualifying distributions, $16,894,276; giving activities include $16,218,488 for grants.
Purpose and activities: The foundation supports programs designed to promote access to quality healthcare; nurture innovation; and support the community involvement of Pfizer colleagues.
Fields of interest: Higher education; Education, services; Education; Health care, public policy; Medicine/medical care, public education; Medical care, community health systems; Health care, patient services; Health care; Cancer; Lung diseases; AIDS; Children, services; International development; Philanthropy/voluntarism; United

Ways and Federated Giving Programs; Science, formal/general education; Mathematics; Science Women.

Programs:

Faces of the Future Campaign: Through Faces of the Future, the foundation supports smoking prevention and cessation efforts that specifically targets women. The initiative supports smoking prevention and cessation activities in 10 nations through social media; educational materials; training of healthcare providers to pass information on to their female patients; and through local celebrities and student leaders who act as "messengers" to build awareness.

Global Health Partnerships: The foundation, in partnership with Pfizer, Inc., supports innovative public health partnerships designed to strengthen healthcare systems and infrastructure to support cancer and tobacco control efforts. Special emphasis is directed toward programs designed to address public education and policy and advocacy; change patient behavior; change attitudes toward smoking and smoking-related disease and prevention; increase the number of patients screened for cancer; and reduce cancer and smoking-related health problems.

Matching Gifts: The foundation matches contributions made by employees and board members of Pfizer to nonprofit organizations on a one-for-one basis from $25 to $15,000 per contributor, per year, and on a two-for-one basis from $25 to $5,000 per retiree, per year.

Pfizer Volunteer Program (PVP): The foundation awards $1,000 grants to nonprofit organizations with which employees and retirees of Pfizer volunteers at least 72 hours a year.

United Way Program: The foundation matches contributions made by employees, retirees, and board members of Pfizer to the United Way.

Type of support: Building/renovation; Continuing support; Curriculum development; Employee matching gifts; Employee volunteer services; General/operating support; Management development/capacity building; Program development; Program evaluation; Sponsorships; Technical assistance.

Geographic limitations: Giving on a national and international basis.

Support limitations: No support for political organizations. No grants to individuals, or for capital campaigns or scholarships; no loans to individuals.

Publications: Corporate giving report; Grants list; Program policy statement.

Application information: Applications not accepted. Contributes only to pre-selected organizations.

Board meeting date(s): As required

Officers and Directors:* William C. Steere, Jr.*, Chair.; Caroline Roan, Pres.; Dezarie Mayers, Secy; Richard Passov, Treas.; Anneka Norgren, Exec. Dir.; C. L. Clemente*; Frank D'Amelio; Jean-Michel Halfon; Kirsten Lund-Jurgensen; Gary Nicholson; Sally Susman.

EIN: 136083839

Selected grants: The following grants are a representative sample of this grantmaker's funding activity:

$1,310,165 to King Baudouin Foundation United States, New York, NY, 2010.
$1,026,000 to Give2Asia, San Francisco, CA, 2010.
$242,000 to Heart and Stroke Foundation of Canada, Ottawa, Canada, 2010.
$225,000 to Partnership for Prevention, Washington, DC, 2010.
$200,000 to George Washington University, Washington, DC, 2010.
$30,000 to Three Rivers Community College, Norwich, CT, 2010.
$1,000 to Les Passees, Memphis, TN, 2010.
$1,000 to Linda Creed Epstein Foundation, Philadelphia, PA, 2010.
$1,000 to Owen J. Roberts School District, Pottstown, PA, 2010.
$1,000 to Sower of Seeds International Ministries, Keller, TX, 2010.

Pfizer Patient Assistance Foundation, Inc.

235 E. 42nd St.
New York, NY 10017-5703 (866) 706-2400
Application address: Pfizer Connection to Care Prog., P.O. Box 66585, St. Louis, MO 63166; Pfizer MAINTAIN, P.O. Box 66549, St. Louis, MO 63166; Tel. for Sharing the Care Prog.: (800) 984-1500; Tel. for Pfizer Bridge Prog.: (800) 645-1280;
URL: http://www.pfizerhelpfulanswers.com/pages/misc/Default.aspx

Donor: Pfizer Inc.

Financial data (yr. ended 12/31/11): Assets, $19,176,178 (M); gifts received, $593,344,673; expenditures, $593,597,387; qualifying distributions, $593,191,046; giving activities include $247,646,911 for grants and $329,787,199 for grants to individuals.

Purpose and activities: The foundation provides Pfizer medicines to uninsured, underinsured, and economically disadvantaged patients in need through health centers, hospitals, and healthcare providers. Patient assistance is administered through Pfizer Helpful Answers, a joint program of Pfizer, Inc. and the Pfizer Patient Assistance Foundation.

Fields of interest: Hospitals (general); Health care, clinics/centers; Pharmacy/prescriptions Economically disadvantaged.

Programs:

Connection to Care: Through Connection to Care, the foundation provides free Pfizer medicines to individuals through healthcare providers. Applicants should have no prescription coverage or should qualify for hardship assistance. The program includes a 90-day supply of medicine that is shipped directly to healthcare provider's office.

First Resource: The foundation provides reimbursement support services and patient assistance to help patients gain access to select Pfizer medicines. The program also provides free medicine and co-payment assistance to patients with prescription coverage who are having financial difficulties.

Pfizer Bridge Program: Through the Pfizer Bridge Program, the foundation provides reimbursement support services and patient assistance for the Pfizer medications Genotropin and Somavert. Applicants must be uninsured or underinsured, have no prescription coverage, and meet the household income guidelines.

RSVP: Through Reimbursement Solutions, Verification, and Payment HELPline, the foundation offers reimbursement support services and patient assistance for select Pfizer medicines. The program also provides free medicine and co-payment assistance to patients with prescription coverage who are having financial difficulties.

Sharing the Care: Through Sharing the Care, the foundation partners with federally qualified health centers and Disproportionate Share hospitals to provide free medicine to eligible uninsured patients across the country.

Type of support: Donated products; In-kind gifts.

Geographic limitations: Giving on a national basis and in Puerto Rico, and the US Virgin Islands.

Publications: Application guidelines; Informational brochure.

Application information: Applications accepted. Application form required.
Applications should include proof of income and must be signed by a health physician.

Initial approach: Download application and mail to application address

Deadline(s): None

Officers and Directors:* Caroline Roane*, Chair.; Daniel Murphy, Secy.; Diane Krisko, Treas.; Gary Pelletier, Exec. Dir.; Elizabeth Barrett; William Kennally; Jim Sage; Amy Schmeltz.

EIN: 261437283

2951
PFS Bancorp, Inc.

2nd and Bridgeway Sts.
Aurora, IN 47001 (812) 926-0631

Establishment information: Established in 1887.

Company type: Private company

Business activities: Operates bank holding company; operates savings bank.

Business type (SIC): Savings institutions; holding company

Corporate officers: Robert L. Laker, Chair.; Gilbert L. Houze, Vice-Chair.; Mel E. Green, Pres. and C.E.O.; Stuart M. Suggs, V.P., C.O.O., C.F.O., and Treas.; Jack D. Tandy, Secy.

Board of directors: Robert L. Laker, Chair.; Gilbert L. Houze, Vice-Chair.; Jack D. Tandy

Subsidiary: Peoples Federal Savings Bank, Aurora, IN

Giving statement: Giving through the PFS Community Foundation.

PFS Community Foundation

6776 Cross Rd.
Aurora, IN 47001-1777 (859) 441-5182

Establishment information: Established in 2001 in DE and IN.

Donor: PFS Bancorp, Inc.

Financial data (yr. ended 12/31/11): Assets, $640,117 (M); expenditures, $34,668; qualifying distributions, $33,925; giving activities include $33,925 for grants.

Purpose and activities: The foundation supports organizations involved with youth development and community development and awards college scholarships to students in Dearborn County, Indiana.

Fields of interest: Arts; Education; Public affairs.

Type of support: Building/renovation; Equipment; General/operating support; Program development; Scholarships—to individuals.

Geographic limitations: Giving primarily in Dearborn County, IN.

Application information: Applications accepted. Application form required. Applicants should submit the following:

1) copy of IRS Determination Letter
2) detailed description of project and amount of funding requested
3) copy of current year's organizational budget and/or project budget

Initial approach: Letter of inquiry

Deadline(s): None

Officers: Robert L. Laker, Chair. and Pres.; Mel E. Green, Secy.; Stuart M. Suggs, Treas.

EIN: 352152955

2952
PG&E Corporation

77 Beale St.
P.O. Box 770
San Francisco, CA 94177 (415) 267-7000

Company URL: http://www.pgecorp.com
Establishment information: Established in 1905.
Company type: Public company
Company ticker symbol and exchange: PCG/NYSE
Business activities: Operates holding company; generates, transmits, and distributes electricity; transmits and distributes natural gas.
Financial profile for 2011: Number of employees, 19,274; assets, $49,750,000,000; sales volume, $14,956,000,000; pre-tax net income, $1,298,000,000; expenses, $13,014,000,000; liabilities, $37,649,000,000
Fortune 1000 ranking: 2012—183rd in revenues, 236th in profits, and 107th in assets
Corporate officers: Anthony F. Earley, Jr., Chair., Pres., and C.E.O.; Kent M. Harvey, Sr. V.P. and C.F.O; Hyun Park, Sr. V.P. and Genl. Counsel; John R. Simon, Sr. V.P., Human Resources; Linda Y.H. Cheng, V.P. and Corp. Secy.; Dinyar B. Mistry, V.P. and Cont.; Ezra Garrett, V.P. and Chief Sustainability Off.
Board of directors: Anthony F. Earley, Jr., Chair.; David R. Andrews; Lewis Chew; C. Lee Cox; Fred J. Fowler; Maryellen C. Herringer; Roger H. Kimmel; Richard A. Meserve; Forrest E. Miller; Rosendo G. Parra; Barbara L. Rambo; Barry Lawson Williams
Subsidiary: Pacific Gas and Electric Company, San Francisco, CA
Giving statement: Giving through the New Vision Santa Rosa Foundation and the PG&E Corporation Foundation.
Company EIN: 943234914

The PG&E Corporation Foundation

77 Beale St.
San Francisco, CA 94105-1814
E-mail: communityrelations@exchange.pge.com;
E-mail for Tiffany Fakava: TVF3@pge.com;
URL: http://pgecorporationfoundation.org/

Establishment information: Established in 2000 in CA.
Donors: PG&E Corporation; Pacific Gas and Electric Company; PG&E Gas Transmission, Texas Corp.
Contact: Tiffany Fakava
Financial data (yr. ended 12/31/11): Assets, $19,979,401 (M); gifts received, $19,057,926; expenditures, $16,259,664; qualifying distributions, $15,897,682; giving activities include $15,897,682 for 696 grants (high: $1,350,000; low: $250).
Purpose and activities: The foundation supports programs designed to promote education, environmental stewardship, and economic and community vitality. Special emphasis is directed toward underserved communities and populations.
Fields of interest: Secondary school/education; Education; Environment, natural resources; Environment, land resources; Environment, energy; Environment, plant conservation; Environmental education; Environment; Employment, services; Disasters, preparedness/services; Recreation, parks/playgrounds; American Red Cross; Family services; Human services; Utilities Disabilities, people with; Minorities; Women; Girls; Economically disadvantaged; LGBTQ.

Programs:

Economic and Community Vitality: The foundation supports programs designed to reduce utility bills for income-qualified families; and promote emergency preparedness and local economic-related workforce development initiatives.

Education: The foundation supports programs designed to give students and teachers opportunities to learn and prepare for their future.

Environmental Stewardship: The foundation supports programs designed to promote energy sustainability, environmental conservation, and stewardship of land and resources.

Type of support: Building/renovation; Continuing support; Employee matching gifts; General/operating support; Program development; Scholarship funds.
Geographic limitations: Giving primarily in areas of company operations in CA.
Support limitations: No support for religious organizations not of direct benefit to the entire community, political or partisan organizations, or discriminatory organizations. No grants to individuals, or for tickets for contests, raffles, or other activities with prizes; endowments, filmmaking, debt-reduction campaigns, or political or partisan events.
Publications: Application guidelines; Grants list; Program policy statement.
Application information: Applications accepted. Applications from organizations that do not make preliminary contact with PG&E Public Affairs staff are rarely funded. Grants range from $1,000 to $25,000. Multi-year funding is not automatic. Application form required. Applicants should submit the following:
1) copy of IRS Determination Letter
2) detailed description of project and amount of funding requested

Initial approach: Contact local PG&E Public Affairs representative to discuss grant proposal; complete online application
Deadline(s): Sept. 16
Final notification: 3 months

Officers and Directors:* Greg S. Pruett*, Chair.; Linda Y.H. Cheng, Secy.; Christopher P. Johns*, C.F.O.; Ezra Garrett, Exec. Dir.; Hyun Park; Dinyar B. Mistry.
EIN: 943358729
Selected grants: The following grants are a representative sample of this grantmaker's funding activity:
$1,750,000 to Salvation Army, Golden State Division, San Francisco, CA, 2010. For Reach Program.
$1,211,640 to Habitat for Humanity International, Operational Headquarters, Americus, GA, 2010. For Solar Panel Installation Program.
$728,500 to National Energy Education Development Project, Manassas, VA, 2010. For PG and E Solar Schools.
$727,857 to Foundation for Environmental Education, Columbus, OH, 2010. For Green Solar Schools.
$519,571 to JK Group, Plainsboro, NJ, 2010. For Education Includes Q2 2010 Mef, Q3 2010 Mef, Additional Q1 2010 Mef.
$179,292 to JK Group, Plainsboro, NJ, 2010. For Campaign One-Time Employee Funds Paid Thru Education.
$50,000 to Community Action Partnership of San Bernardino County, San Bernardino, CA, 2010. To Expand Food Bank and Emergency Assistance Programs in Barstow and Hinkley Regions of San Bernardino County.
$10,000 to Central Valley Opportunity Center, Winton, CA, 2010. For Mobile Energy Education Resource Center.
$5,000 to Bakersfield Association for Retarded Citizens, Bakersfield, CA, 2010. For Energy Efficient Barc Building.
$5,000 to United Way Silicon Valley, San Jose, CA, 2010. For Volunteer Assessment Study.

New Vision Santa Rosa Foundation

1260 N. Dutton Ave., Rm. 272
Santa Rosa, CA 95401-4673

Establishment information: Established in 1996 in CA.
Donors: PG&E Corp.; Santa Rosa Chamber of Commerce; NYT Capital Inc.; Sutter Medical Foundation North Bay.
Financial data (yr. ended 12/31/11): Revenue, $1,411,094; assets, $1,788,763 (M); gifts received, $1,411,094; expenditures, $336,500.
Purpose and activities: The foundation supports organizations involved with cycling, children's services, and business promotion.
Fields of interest: Recreation, adaptive sports; Children, services; Community development, business promotion.
Type of support: General/operating support.
Geographic limitations: Giving primarily in Santa Rosa, CA.
Support limitations: No grants to individuals.
Application information: Applications not accepted. Contributes only to pre-selected organizations.
Officers and Directors: Mari Featherstone, Chair.; Jonathan Coe, Pres.; Carl Campbell, V.P.; Sheridan Rapolla, Secy.-Treas.; Rolf Nelson; Bob Reynolds; Kevin Smith.
EIN: 680074807

2953
The PGA of America

100 Ave. of Champions
Palm Beach Gardens, FL 33418
(561) 624-8400

Company URL: http://www.pga.com
Establishment information: Established in 1916.
Company type: Business league
Business activities: Operates professional sports membership organization.
Business type (SIC): Business association; commercial sports; amusement and recreation services/miscellaneous
Corporate officers: Ted Bishop, Pres.; Darrell Crall, C.O.O.; Peter Bevacqua, C.E.O.; Paul Levy, Secy.
Giving statement: Giving through the PGA Foundation, Inc.

PGA Foundation, Inc.

(formerly PGA of America)
100 Ave. of the Champions
Palm Beach Gardens, FL 33418-3653 (888) 532-6662
Toll-free tel.: (888) 532-6662; URL: http://www.pgafoundation.com

Establishment information: Established in 1978 in FL.
Financial data (yr. ended 06/30/11): Revenue, $542,706; assets, $1,456,311 (M); gifts received, $398,660; expenditures, $448,980; program services expenses, $416,829; giving activities include $303,575 for 5 grants (high: $75,000; low: $10,000) and $13,000 for grants to individuals.
Purpose and activities: The organization is dedicated to providing resources and the professional expertise to make golf accessible to all segments of every community.
Fields of interest: Athletics/sports, golf.

Program:
Grants: Considers grant proposals that introduce golf to juniors, high school students (including all ethnic groups) and people with disabilities. Grant amounts vary widely based on the type of program being funded and that program's specific needs. The organization also accept proposals that support community golf developmental programs for juniors, high school students and the physically challenged. In these cases, the PGA of America will partner with a community-based organization and provide funding and resources to secure PGA Professionals to deliver golf instruction. This partnership with community organizations such as the Urban League, Boys and Girls Clubs, Special Olympics, Police Athletic League, YMCA, YWCA, Girl Scouts, Boy Scouts, elementary and secondary schools is an important component of expanding access to golf, while providing benefits to citizens within that community.
Type of support: In-kind gifts.
Support limitations: No support for athletic teams or events, religious organizations, or organizations that discriminate against a person or a group on the basis of age, political affiliation, race, national origin, ethnicity, gender, disability, sexual orientation or religious belief. No grants to individuals, or for salaries, stipends, general operating support, research projects, publications, audio visual or video projects endowment funds, annual fund drives, or construction of buildings.
Publications: Application guidelines.
Application information: Applications accepted. Preliminary application and cover letter will be reviewed and applicant will be notified within 30 days of receipt whether to proceed to the final grant process or whether they have been denied. There are four grant cycles per year, and grants are awarded every quarter. Grant applications submitted after one cycle has closed will be considered during the next cycle. Application form required.
Initial approach: Download preliminary application
Deadline(s): Feb. 1, May 1, Aug. 1, and Nov. 1 for final grant application
Final notification: Apr. 15, July 15, Oct. 15, and Jan. 15 for final grant application
Officers and Directors:* Mike McCallister*, Chair.; Ted Bishop*, Pres.; Derek Sprague*, V.P.; Peter Bevacqua*, C.E.O.; Paul Levy*, Secy.; Junior Bridgeman; Roger Nanney; David Seaton.
EIN: 591809626

2954
PGA TOUR, Inc.
100 PGA Tour Blvd.
Ponte Vedra Beach, FL 32082
(904) 285-3700

Company URL: http://www.pgatour.com
Establishment information: Established in 1968.
Company type: Business league
Business activities: Operates professional sports membership organization.
Business type (SIC): Business association; commercial sports
Corporate officers: Victor F. Ganzi, Chair.; Edward L. Moorhouse, Co-C.O.O.; Charles L. Zink, Co-C.O.O.
Board of director: Victor F. Ganzi, Chair.
Giving statement: Giving through the PGA Tour, Inc. and the PGA Tour Charities, Inc.

PGA Tour, Inc.
100 PGA Tour Blvd.
Ponte Vedra Beach, FL 32082-3046 (904) 285-3700
URL: http://together.pgatour.com/

Establishment information: Established in 1974 in MD.
Financial data (yr. ended 12/31/11): Revenue, $972,648,046; assets, $1,610,161,857 (M); expenditures, $950,992,200; giving activities include $40,223,200 for grants.
Purpose and activities: The organization seeks to promote the sport of professional golf by supporting education, health and human services, youth development, and community services.
Fields of interest: Education; Health care; Athletics/sports, golf; Youth development; Human services; Community/economic development.
Type of support: In-kind gifts.
Officers and Directors:* Victor F. Ganzi*, Chair. and Pres.; Davis Love, III*, Secy.; David W. Toms*, Treas.; Timothy W. Finchem, Commissioner; Brad Faxon; John B. McCoy; Hal Sutton; G. Kennedy Thompson; Edward E. Whitacre.
EIN: 520999206

PGA Tour Charities, Inc.
100 PGA Tour Blvd.
Ponte Vedra Beach, FL 32082-3046 (904) 285-3700
URL: http://together.pgatour.com/

Establishment information: Established in 1986 in FL.
Contact: Timothy W. Finchem, Pres.
Financial data (yr. ended 12/31/11): Revenue, $5,917,890; assets, $4,042,586 (M); gifts received, $6,042,143; expenditures, $4,772,199; giving activities include $4,544,285 for grants.
Purpose and activities: The organization supports various charitable and educational purposes, particularly those which help to develop an avid interest in golf.
Fields of interest: Athletics/sports, golf.
Geographic limitations: Giving on a national basis.
Officers and Directors:* Timothy W. Finchem*, Pres.; Richard D. Anderson*, V.P. and Secy.; Edward L. Moorhouse*, V.P.; Charles L. Zink*, V.P.; Ronald E. Price*, V.P. and Treas.; Victor F. Ganzi; Dais Love III; James R. Remy; David Toms; Allen Wronowski.
EIN: 592774423

2955
Pharmaceutical Innovations, Inc.
897 Frelinghuysen Ave.
Newark, NJ 07114-2195 (973) 242-2900
FAX: (973) 242-0578

Company URL: http://www.pharminnovations.com
Establishment information: Established in 1971.
Company type: Private company
Business activities: Manufactures ultrasound and electromedical conductive gels, sprays, lotions, and skin preparations.
Business type (SIC): Medical instruments and supplies
Corporate officer: Gilbert Buchalter, Pres.
Giving statement: Giving through the Samuel & Esther Buchalter Foundation, Inc.

The Samuel & Esther Buchalter Foundation, Inc.
897 Frelinghuysen Ave.
Newark, NJ 07114 (973) 242-2900

Establishment information: Established in 1995 in NJ.
Donor: Pharmaceutical Innovations, Inc.
Contact: Gilbert Buchalter, Tr.
Financial data (yr. ended 12/31/11): Assets, $221,856 (M); expenditures, $14,832; qualifying distributions, $11,050; giving activities include $275 for 1 grant and $10,775 for 13 grants to individuals (high: $3,000; low: $50).
Purpose and activities: The foundation supports organizations involved with cultural awareness, education, and Judaism and awards college scholarships to children and other relatives of employees of Pharmaceutical Innovations, Inc.
Fields of interest: Religion.
Type of support: Employee-related scholarships; General/operating support.
Geographic limitations: Giving primarily in NJ.
Application information: Applications accepted. Application form required.
Initial approach: Proposal
Deadline(s): None
Trustees: Gilbert Buchalter*; Frances Ruth Paduano*; Alan Serxner*.
EIN: 223269458

2956
Pharmacy Network National Corporation
4020 Wake Forest Rd., Ste. 102
Raleigh, NC 27609-6866 (919) 876-4642

Establishment information: Established in 2002.
Company type: Subsidiary of a public company
Business activities: Provides pharmacy benefit management services.
Business type (SIC): Insurance/accident and health
Corporate officer: J. Andrew Barrett, Pres.
Giving statement: Giving through the Pharmacy Network Foundation, Inc.

The Pharmacy Network Foundation, Inc.
P.O. Box 31603
Raleigh, NC 27622-1603 (919) 772-4371
Application address: 2015 Navan Ln., Garner, NC 27529

Donors: Pharmacy Network National Corp.; United Pharmacy Cooperative Inc.; Pharmacy Network National Corporation Trust.
Contact: Jimmy S. Jackson, Secy.-Treas.
Financial data (yr. ended 12/31/10): Assets, $18,184,802 (M); expenditures, $1,088,365; qualifying distributions, $715,000; giving activities include $715,000 for grants.
Purpose and activities: The foundation supports organizations involved with education and health and awards college scholarships to pharmacy students enrolled at the University of North Carolina at Chapel Hill and Campbell University.
Fields of interest: Education; Pharmacy/prescriptions; Health care.
Type of support: Building/renovation; Scholarships—to individuals.
Geographic limitations: Giving limited to NC and SC.
Application information: Applications accepted. Application form required.

Initial approach: Proposal
Copies of proposal: 1
Board meeting date(s): 4th Tue. of each month
Deadline(s): None

Officers and Directors: Mitchell W. Watts, Pres.; Lloyd M. Whaley, V.P.; Jimmy S. Jackson, Secy.-Treas.; J. Andrew Barrett; Jonathan A. Hill, Sr.; Julian E. Upchurch.
EIN: 561690027

2957
Philadelphia 76ers, L.P.

3601 S. Broad St., Ste. 4
Philadelphia, PA 19148-5287
(215) 339-7676

Company URL: http://www.nba.com/sixers
Establishment information: Established in 1937.
Company type: Subsidiary of a public company
Ultimate parent company: Comcast Corporation
Business activities: Operates professional basketball club.
Business type (SIC): Commercial sports
Corporate officers: Edward Snider, Chair.; Fred A. Shabel, Vice-Chair.; Adam Aron, C.E.O.; Rod Thorn, Pres.; Andy Speiser, Sr. V.P., Finance; Mark Gullett, V.P., Mktg.; Tina Szwak, Cont.
Board of directors: Edward Snider, Chair.; Fred Shabel, Vice-Chair.
Giving statement: Giving through the Philadelphia 76ers, L.P. Corporate Giving Program.

Philadelphia 76ers, L.P. Corporate Giving Program

c/o Community Rels.
3601 S. Broad St.
Philadelphia, PA 19148-5250
FAX: (215) 339-7615; URL: http://www.nba.com/sixers/community/guidelines.html

Purpose and activities: The Philadelphia 76ers make charitable contributions to nonprofit organizations involved with education, health, and at risk youth. Support is given primarily in Delaware, southern New Jersey, and southeastern Pennsylvania.
Fields of interest: Elementary school/education; Education, reading; Education; Public health, physical fitness; Health care; Nutrition; Youth development Youth.
Programs:
76's Community Assist Program: Through the Community Assist Program, 76ers players, coaches, season ticket holders, and local businesses donate game tickets to nonprofit organizations and to youth groups.
76ers Fit for Fun: Through Fit for Fun initiative, the 76ers encourages kids in grades 1-9 to live a healthier lifestyle through nutrition and staying active. The initiative includes a visit by sixers personalities and staff for a day filled with basketball, dance, condition, and aerobics. Participants receive a certificate and prizes.
Book Break Program: Through the Book Break Program, the 76ers challenge local elementary schools to read 760 pages between September and October. All winners receive a completion certificate and a game ticks to a 76ers home game.
Hometown Heroes: In the Spirit of Alex Scott: Through Hometown Heroes, the 76ers and Eastern University honors six individuals in the Delaware Valley that have made exceptional, overwhelming, and lasting contributions to the community. Recipients receive a $1,000 donation to the charity of their choice, an on-court award presentation, and a feature in a short video documenting their contribution to the community.
Read to Achieve: The 76ers, in partnership with Pepsi, encourages young people to develop a life-long love of reading through player appearances, school visits, book drives and the establishment of reading corners and learning centers.
Shoot for Success 3.0: The 76ers honors middle school students in grades 6 to 9 that can obtain and maintain a 3.0 grade point average or higher during one grading period. Honorees receive a completion certificate and a game tickets to a 76ers home game.
Type of support: Donated products; General/operating support; In-kind gifts; Income development.
Geographic limitations: Giving primarily in DE, southern NJ, and southeastern PA.
Publications: Application guidelines.
Application information: Applications accepted. Telephone calls during the application process are not encouraged. Support is limited to 1 contribution per organization during any given year. The Community Relations Department handles giving. Application form required. Applicants should submit the following:
1) population served
2) copy of IRS Determination Letter
3) brief history of organization and description of its mission
4) descriptive literature about organization
5) detailed description of project and amount of funding requested

Initial approach: Complete online application for memorabilia donations and Community Assist Program
Copies of proposal: 1
Deadline(s): 6 weeks prior to need for memorabilia donations; Sept. 1 to Dec. 31 for Community Assist Program; none for Fit for Fun
Final notification: 2 weeks prior to need for memorabilia donations

2958
Philadelphia Eagles LP

1 NovaCare Way
Philadelphia, PA 19145-5900
(215) 463-2500
FAX: (215) 339-5464

Company URL: http://www.philadelphiaeagles.com
Establishment information: Established in 1933.
Company type: Private company
Business activities: Operates professional football club.
Business type (SIC): Commercial sports
Corporate officers: Jeffrey Lurie, Chair. and C.E.O.; Donald Smolenski, Pres.; Frank Gumienny, C.F.O.; Anne Gordon, Sr. V.P., Comms.; Greg McDonald, Cont.; Aileen Daly, Genl. Counsel
Board of director: Jeffrey Lurie, Chair.
Giving statement: Giving through the Philadelphia Eagles LP Corporate Giving Program and the Eagles Charitable Foundation, Inc.

Philadelphia Eagles LP Corporate Giving Program

c/o Community Rels.
NovaCare Complex
1 NovaCare Way
Philadelphia, PA 19145-5900
FAX: (215) 339-5464; URL: http://www.philadelphiaeagles.com/community/

Purpose and activities: The Philadelphia Eagles make charitable contributions to nonprofit organizations on a case by case basis. Support is given primarily in Delaware, southern New Jersey, and southeastern Pennsylvania.
Fields of interest: Education, reading; Animal welfare; Animals/wildlife; Public health, physical fitness; Breast cancer; Athletics/sports, football; Human services, gift distribution; General charitable giving Youth.
Programs:
Coach of the Week: Through the Coach of the Week Program, the Eagles honors high school coaches who have made a difference in the lives of their players, communities, and schools. The honorees receive a $1,000 grant to his high school athletic department.
Community Quarterback Award: The Eagles, in partnership with Teva Pharmaceuticals, honors volunteers who exemplify leadership, dedication, and a commitment to improving their community. The honor includes grants to nonprofit organizations of the finalist and winners choice, a $4,000 grant for seven finalists, $11,000 grant for two runners-up, and a $50,000 grant for the overall winner.
Equipment Donation Program: The Eagles, in partnership with Good Sports, provides football equipment to increase the capacities of inner city youth football programs to serve more youth.
Philadelphia Eagles Treating Animals With Kindness (TAWK): Through the TAWK initiative, the Eagles promote public education and awareness to reduce animal abuse, promote responsible adoption, encourage spay and neutering, and to end dogfighting. The Eagles awards grants of up to $5,000 to local organizations that demonstrate a sustainable commitment to end dogfighting and/or promote the welfare of animals. The program is limited to the greater Philadelphia area.
Type of support: Donated products; Equipment; In-kind gifts; Income development.
Geographic limitations: Giving primarily in areas of company operations in DE, southern NJ, and southeastern PA.
Publications: Application guidelines.
Application information: Applications accepted. Proposals should be submitted using organization letterhead. Additional information may be requested at a later date. A phone interview or site visit may be requested for the Equipment Donation Program. Support is limited to 1 contribution per organization during any given year. The Community Relations Department handles giving. Applicants should submit the following:
1) name, address and phone number of organization
2) detailed description of project and amount of funding requested
3) contact person

Proposals should include the contact person's e-mail address, if available; and indicate the date and location of the event.
Initial approach: Mail or fax proposal to headquarters for memorabilia donations; complete online application form for Eagles TAWK; download application form and mail, fax, or e-mail to headquarters for Equipment Donation Program and Community Quarterback Award
Copies of proposal: 1
Deadline(s): 4 to 6 weeks prior to need for memorabilia donations; none for Eagles TAWK; 12 weeks prior to need for Equipment Donation Program; Apr. 1 for Community Quarterback Award
Final notification: 6 weeks for Eagles TAWK

The Eagles Charitable Foundation, Inc.

(doing business as Eagles Youth Partnership)
NovaCare Complex
1 Novacare Way
Philadelphia, PA 19145-5900 (215) 339-5478
FAX: (215) 339-5464;
E-mail: eyp@philadelphiaeagles.com; URL: http://www.philadelphiaeagles.com/partnership/

Establishment information: Established in 1995 in DE.
Contact: Sarah Martinez-Helfman, Exec. Dir.
Financial data (yr. ended 12/31/11): Revenue, $1,216,995; assets, $4,840,516 (M); gifts received, $935,877; expenditures, $2,302,611; giving activities include $1,109,571 for grants.
Purpose and activities: As the philanthropic arm of the Philadelphia Eagles, the organization aims to enhance opportunities and improve the quality of life for children and youth in the Philadelphia, Pennsylvania, region by enhancing opportunities through education.
Fields of interest: Arts; Education; Children/youth, services.
Geographic limitations: Giving limited to the Philadelphia, PA, region.
Officers and Directors:* Jeffrey Lurie*, Chair.; Christina Lurie*, Pres.; Don Smolenski*, Treas.; Sarah Martinez-Helfman, Exec. Dir.; David R. Binswanger; Patricia Coulter; Dennis P. Donovan; Christine James-Brown; Dan Kaplan; James Korman; Iliana Kloesmeyer Strauss; Kathleen Unger; and 3 additional directors.
EIN: 232794290

2959
Philadelphia Flyers, L.P.

3601 S. Broad St.
Wachovia Ctr.
Philadelphia, PA 19148 (215) 952-5763

Company URL: http://flyers.nhl.com/
Establishment information: Established in 1966.
Company type: Subsidiary of a public company
Ultimate parent company: Comcast Corporation
Business activities: Operates professional ice hockey club.
Business type (SIC): Commercial sports
Corporate officers: Edward Snider, Chair.; Angelo Cardone, C.F.O.; Shawn Tilger, Sr. V.P., Opers.; Jim Willits, V.P., Sales; Lindsey Masciangelo, V.P., Mktg.; Judy Zdunkiewicz, Cont.
Board of director: Edward Snider, Chair.
Giving statement: Giving through the Philadelphia Flyers, L.P. Corporate Giving Program.

Philadelphia Flyers, L.P. Corporate Giving Program

c/o Community Rels.
3601 S. Broad St.
Philadelphia, PA 19148-5250 (215) 952-5405
FAX: (215) 952-5210;
E-mail: flyerscommunity@comcast-spectacor.com; Contact for Face Off for Fitness: E-mail: jtempesta@comcast-spectacor.com, tel.: (215) 218-4334; URL: http://flyers.nhl.com/club/page.htm?id=36111

Purpose and activities: The Philadelphia Flyers make charitable contributions to nonprofit organizations involved with education, youth hockey, and disadvantaged youth. Support is given primarily in the Philadelphia, Pennsylvania, area.
Fields of interest: Education; Public health, physical fitness; Cancer; Nutrition; Athletics/sports, winter sports; Youth development; General charitable giving Youth.
Programs:

Community Teammate Program: The Philadelphia Flyers honors an individual or group for their positive contribution to the local community. The program awards 2 tickets to a Flyers home game and recognition on the Arenavision scoreboard at the game.

Face Off For Fitness: The Philadelphia Flyers, in partnership with the Phantoms, encourages kids in grades 1-5 to make positive nutritional and behavioral choices. The initiative includes a 45-minute program during a normal physical education class or after school period. Kids participate in physical activities, receive fitness and nutrition tips, and receive giveaways to take home.

Hat Tricks for Kids: Through Hat Tricks for Kids, the Philadelphia Flyers visits local oncology units of children battling cancer. The program includes a Flyers goodie bag with a hat and activity books, and each event includes an activity that the children can participate in.

Type of support: Donated products; In-kind gifts; Income development; Loaned talent.
Geographic limitations: Giving primarily in areas of company operations in the Philadelphia, PA, area.
Support limitations: No grants for general operating support or sponsorships.
Publications: Application guidelines.
Application information: Applications accepted. Proposals should be submitted using organization letterhead. The Community Relations Department handles giving. Applicants should submit the following:
1) name, address and phone number of organization
2) copy of IRS Determination Letter
3) brief history of organization and description of its mission
4) descriptive literature about organization
5) detailed description of project and amount of funding requested
6) contact person

Proposals should indicate the date, time, and location of the event and the type of fundraiser.
Initial approach: Mail proposal to headquarters for memorabilia; download nomination form and E-mail to headquarters for Community Teammate Program; complete online request form for Face Off For Fitness
Copies of proposal: 1
Deadline(s): 4 to 6 weeks prior to need for memorabilia; none for Community Teammate Program; Oct. 15 to June 15 for Face Off For Fitness

2960
Philadelphia Insurance Companies

231 Saint Asaph's Rd., Ste. 100
Bala Cynwyd, PA 19004 (610) 617-7900

Company URL: http://www.phly.com
Establishment information: Established in 1981.
Company type: Private company
Business activities: Operates commercial insurance company.
Business type (SIC): Insurance/fire, marine, and casualty
Corporate officers: James J. Maguire, Jr., Chair.; Robert D. O'Leary, Pres. and C.E.O.; Craig P. Keller, Exec. V.P., Secy.-Treas., and C.F.O
Board of director: James J. Maguire, Jr., Chair.
Giving statement: Giving through the Philadelphia Insurance Companies Contributions Program.

Philadelphia Insurance Companies Contributions Program

1 Bala Plaza, Ste. 100
Bala Cynwyd, PA 19004 (610) 617-7900
URL: http://www.phly.com/aboutphly/Community/Default.aspx

Purpose and activities: Philadelphia Insurance Companies make charitable contributions to nonprofit organizations involved with helping people with disabilities. Support is given primarily in Philadelphia, Pennsylvania.
Fields of interest: Education, special; Public health, physical fitness; Cancer research; Disasters, preparedness/services; Recreation, adaptive sports; Athletics/sports, Special Olympics; Children, services Disabilities, people with.
Type of support: Employee matching gifts; Employee volunteer services; General/operating support; Sponsorships.
Geographic limitations: Giving primarily in Philadelphia, PA.

2961
Philadelphia Newspapers, Inc.

400 N. Broad St.
Philadelphia, PA 19130-4015
(215) 854-2000

Company URL: http://www.pnionline.com
Establishment information: Established in 1829.
Company type: Subsidiary of a private company
Business activities: Publishes newspapers.
Business type (SIC): Newspaper publishing and/or printing
Financial profile for 2010: Number of employees, 2,000
Corporate officers: Robert J. Hall, Chair.; Frederick B. Mott, Pres.; Brian P. Tierny, C.E.O.; Mike Miller, C.F.O.; Nancy Burd, Sr. V.P., Finance; George Loesch, Sr. V.P., Sales; Astrid Garcia, V.P., Human Resources
Board of director: Robert J. Hall, Chair.
Giving statement: Giving through the Philadelphia Newspapers, Inc. Corporate Giving Program.

Philadelphia Newspapers, Inc. Corporate Giving Program

c/o Community Rels.
400 N. Broad St.
Philadelphia, PA 19101-4015
FAX: (215) 854-4216;
E-mail: rauslander@phillynews.com; URL: http://www.pnionline.com/publicaffairs

Contact: Ruth Auslander
Purpose and activities: Philadelphia Newspapers makes charitable contributions to nonprofit organizations involved with journalism, arts and culture, education, health, housing, youth development, human services, voter registration and education, community development, civic affairs, and disadvantaged people. Support is given primarily in areas of company operations, with emphasis on Pennsylvania.
Fields of interest: Media, print publishing; Arts; Education, reading; Education; Health care; Housing/shelter; Youth development; Children, services; Aging, centers/services; Homeless, human services; Human services; Civil rights, voter education; Economic development; Community/

economic development; Public affairs, citizen participation; Public affairs Economically disadvantaged.
Type of support: In-kind gifts; Sponsorships.
Geographic limitations: Giving primarily in areas of company operations, with emphasis on PA.
Support limitations: No support for political organizations or candidates, religious organizations not of direct benefit to the entire community, veterans', fraternal, or private or neighborhood organizations not of direct benefit to the entire community, national health organizations lacking a regional presence, or non-community foundation grantmaking organizations. No grants to individuals, or for trips or tours or dinners not directly connected to Philadelphia Newspapers' community role.
Publications: Application guidelines.
Application information: Applications accepted. Support is limited to 1 contribution per organization during any given year. Application form required.
Applicants should submit the following:
1) population served
2) name, address and phone number of organization
3) copy of IRS Determination Letter
4) detailed description of project and amount of funding requested
5) copy of current year's organizational budget and/or project budget

Initial approach: Download application form and mail to headquarters
Committee meeting date(s): Monthly
Deadline(s): 3 to 4 months prior to need

2962
Philip Morris International Inc.

120 Park Ave.
New York, NY 10017-5592 (917) 663-2000

Company URL: http://www.philipmorrisinternational.com
Establishment information: Established in 1987.
Company type: Public company
Company ticker symbol and exchange: PM/NYSE
International Securities Identification Number: US7181721090
Business activities: Manufactures and sells cigarettes and other tobacco products in markets outside of the United States.
Business type (SIC): Tobacco products—cigarettes
Financial profile for 2012: Number of employees, 87,100; assets, $37,670,000,000; sales volume, $77,393,000,000; pre-tax net income, $12,987,000,000; expenses, $63,547,000,000; liabilities, $41,146,000,000
Fortune 1000 ranking: 2012—99th in revenues, 20th in profits, and 150th in assets
Forbes 2000 ranking: 2012—301st in sales, 50th in profits, and 603rd in assets
Corporate officers: Louis C. Camilleri, Chair.; Andre Calantzopoulos, C.E.O.; Jacek Olczak, C.F.O.; Patrick Brunel, Sr. V.P. and C.I.O.; Marc S. Firestone, Sr. V.P. and Genl. Counsel; Martin King, Sr. V.P., Opers.; Frederic de Wilde, Sr. V.P., Mktg. and Sales; Kevin Click, Sr. V.P., Human Resources; Marco Kuepfer, V.P., Finance and Treas.; Joachim Psotta, V.P. and Cont.
Board of directors: Louis C. Camilleri, Chair.; Harold Brown; Mathis Cabiallavetta; Andre Calantzopoulos; J. Dudley Fishburn; Carlos Slim Helu; Jennifer Li; Graham Mackay; Sergio Marchionne; Kalpana Morparia; Lucio A. Noto; Robert B. Polet; Stephen M. Wolf
Giving statement: Giving through the Philip Morris International Inc. Corporate Giving Program.
Company EIN: 133435103

Philip Morris International Inc. Corporate Giving Program

120 Park Ave.
New York, NY 10017 (917) 663-2233
URL: http://www.philipmorrisinternational.com/PMINTL/pages/eng/community/Community.asp

Purpose and activities: Philip Morris International makes charitable contributions to nonprofit organizations and develops partnerships with non-governmental organizations involved with education, the conservation of natural resources, environmental sustainability, hunger and poverty, domestic violence, and quality of life in rural areas. Support is given primarily in areas of company operations, and where tobacco farms that supply the company are located.
Fields of interest: Education; Environment, natural resources; Public health, clean water supply; Health care; Employment, training; Agriculture, sustainable programs; Food services; Safety/disasters; Family services, domestic violence; Family resources and services, disability; Rural development; Microfinance/microlending Economically disadvantaged.
Type of support: Building/renovation; Continuing support; Donated products; Employee volunteer services; General/operating support; Loaned talent; Program development; Program-related investments/loans; Scholarship funds.
Geographic limitations: Giving primarily in areas of company operations, and where tobacco farms that supply the company are located. Giving on an international basis, with emphasis on Germany, Guatemala, Indonesia, Japan, Malawi, Mexico, Mozambique, Pakistan, Russia, Serbia, South Africa, Tanzania, and Thailand.
Support limitations: No grants.
Application information: A contributions department handles giving. Applicants should submit the following:
1) copy of current year's organizational budget and/or project budget

Proposals must include a line-by-line breakdown of a project's budget, the rationale for each project and how many people will benefit, as well as a sustainability plan for continuing the project beyond the grant.

2963
Philips Electronics North America Corporation

3000 Minuteman Rd.
Andover, MA 01810

Company URL: http://www.usa.philips.com
Company type: Subsidiary of a foreign company
Business activities: Manufactures electrical and electronic components and equipment, consumer products, and lighting fixtures.
Business type (SIC): Appliances/household; steel mill products; computer and office equipment; machinery/refrigeration and service industry; audio and video equipment/household; communications equipment; medical instruments and supplies
Corporate officers: Gregory M. Sebasky, Chair.; Scott M. Weisenhoff, C.E.O.; Dave Dripchak, C.F.O.; Donald Welsko, V.P., Human Resources; Raymond Fleming, V.P. and Cont.
Board of director: Gregory M. Sebasky, Chair.
Subsidiaries: Advance Transformer Co., Rosemont, IL; Airvision, Valencia, CA; American Color & Chemical Corp., New York, NY; Application Specific Products Group, Sunnyvale, CA; Chicago Magnet Wire Corp., Elk Grove Village, IL; CSD, Inc., Piscataway, NJ; Edax International, Inc., Prairie View, IL; N.A.P. Commercial Electronic Corp., Waltham, MA; Norelco Consumer Products Co., Stamford, CT; Optimage Interactive Services Co., Des Moines, IA; Philip Laser Magnetic Storage, Colorado Springs, CO; Philips & Dupont Optical Co., Wilmington, DE; Philips Broadband Networks, Manlius, NY; Philips Circuit Assemblies, Riviera Beach, FL; Philips Components, Jupiter, FL; Philips Consumer Electronics, Knoxville, TN; Philips Credit Corp., New York, NY; Philips Display Components, Ann Arbor, MI; Philips Electronics Instruments Co., Mahwah, NJ; Philips Information Systems, Dallas, TX; Philips Laboratories, Briarcliff Manor, NY; Philips Lighting, Somerset, NJ; Philips Medical Systems North America Co., Shelton, CT; Philips Semiconductors, Sunnyvale, CA; Philips Speech Processing, Atlanta, GA; Radiant Lamp, Somerset, NJ; Standard Procducts Group, Sunnyvale, CA; T H Agriculture & Nutrition Co. Inc., Kansas City, KS; V-L Service Lighting, Somerset, NJ
Divisions: Beauty Care Div., Stamford, CT; Coffeemaker Div., Stamford, CT; Health Care Div., Stamford, CT; Home Products Div., Stamford, CT; Linear Div., Sunnyvale, CA; Microprocessor & Microcontroller Div., Sunnyvale, CA; Military Products Div., Sunnyvale, CA; Musser Div., La Grange, IL; Philips Components-Discrete Products Div., Slatersville, RI; Razor Div., Stamford, CT; Semi-Custom Products Div., Sunnyvale, CA
Plants: Lewiston, ME; Ann Arbor, MI; Woodbury, NY
Giving statement: Giving through the Philips Electronics North American Foundation.

Philips Electronics North American Foundation

(formerly North American Philips Foundation)
c/o PENAC Scholarship Prog. Administrator
3000 Minuteman Rd.
Andover, MA 01810-1032

Establishment information: Established in 1979 in NY.
Donor: Philips Electronics North America Corp.
Financial data (yr. ended 12/31/11): Assets, $3,364 (M); gifts received, $328,250; expenditures, $324,886; qualifying distributions, $323,750; giving activities include $323,750 for grants.
Purpose and activities: The foundation awards college scholarships to children of employees of Philips Electronics North America Corporation.
Fields of interest: Higher education.
Type of support: Employee-related scholarships.
Geographic limitations: Giving primarily in IL, KS, KY, MA, NJ, NY, OH, PA, WA, and WI.
Application information: Applications not accepted. Contributes only through employee-related scholarships.
Officers: Pamela L. Dunlap, Pres.; Paul Cavanaugh, V.P.; Raymond C. Fleming, V.P.; Joseph E. Innamorati, Secy.
EIN: 132961300

2964
The Phillies

(also known as Philadelphia Phillies)
Citizens Bank Park
1 Citizens Bank Way
Philadelphia, PA 19148-5249
(215) 463-6000

Company URL: http://philadelphia.phillies.mlb.com
Establishment information: Established in 1883.

Company type: Private company
Business activities: Operates professional baseball club.
Business type (SIC): Commercial sports
Corporate officers: Bill Giles, Chair.; David Montgomery, Pres. and C.E.O.; Michael Stiles, Sr. V.P., Admin. and Opers.; David Buck, Sr. V.P., Mktg.; John Nickolas, V.P. and C.F.O.; Rick Strouse, V.P. and Genl. Counsel; John Weber, V.P., Sales; Bonnie Clark, V.P., Comms.; Kathy Killian, V.P., Human Resources; Bill Webb, Secy.; Mike Carson, Cont.
Board of director: Bill Giles, Chair.
Giving statement: Giving through the Phillies Charities, Inc.

Phillies Charities, Inc.

1 Citizens Bank Way
Philadelphia, PA 19148-5205

Establishment information: Established in 1994 in PA.
Financial data (yr. ended 12/31/11): Revenue, $962,728; assets, $905,182 (M); gifts received, $562,268; expenditures, $944,287; giving activities include $941,365 for grants.
Purpose and activities: The organization raises money for and distributes funds to other charitable organizations.
Fields of interest: Human services.
Officers: Carolyn S. Montgomery, Pres.; Sharon R. Clothier, Treas.
EIN: 231994699

2965
Phillips 66

P.O. Box 4428
Houston, TX 77210 (281) 293-6600

Company URL: http://www.phillips66.com
Establishment information: Established in 1875.
Company type: Public company
Company ticker symbol and exchange: PSX/NYSE
Business activities: Operates independent energy company.
Business type (SIC): Petroleum refining; extraction/oil and gas; extraction/natural gas liquids; oil and gas field services; plastics and synthetics; chemicals/industrial organic; pipelines (except natural gas/operation of)
Financial profile for 2012: Number of employees, 13,500; assets, $48,073,000,000; sales volume, $182,922,000,000; pre-tax net income, $6,631,000,000; expenses, $176,291,000,000; liabilities, $27,298,000,000
Fortune 1000 ranking: 2012—4th in revenues, 46th in profits, and 115th in assets
Forbes 2000 ranking: 2012—14th in sales, 139th in profits, and 476th in assets
Corporate officers: Greg C. Garland, Chair. and C.E.O.; Greg G. Maxwell, Exec. V.P., Finance, and C.F.O.; Paula Johnson, Sr. V.P., Genl. Counsel, and Corp. Secy.; C. Doug Johnson, V.P. and Cont.; Chantal Veevaete, V.P., Human Resources; Ann M. Oglesby, V.P., Comms. and Public Affairs
Board of directors: Greg. C. Garland, Chair.; J. Brian Ferguson; William R. Loomis, Jr.; John E. Lowe; Harold W. McGraw III; Glenn F. Tilton; Victoria J. Tschinkel; Marna C. Whittington
Giving statement: Giving through the Phillips 66 Corporate Giving Program.
Company EIN: 453779385

Phillips 66 Corporate Giving Program

P.O. Box 4428
Houston, TX 77210 (281) 293-6600
URL: http://www.phillips66.com/EN/susdev/communities/Pages/index.aspx

Purpose and activities: Phillips 66 makes charitable contributions to nonprofit organizations involved with education, health and safety, and the environment. The company provides assistance during the relief stage of major natural disasters, and provides support for community-based social services, the arts, and civic organizations.
Fields of interest: Arts; Elementary/secondary education; Higher education; Education; Environment, formal/general education; Environment, energy; Environment; Disasters, preparedness/services.
Type of support: Employee matching gifts; Employee volunteer services; General/operating support.
Geographic limitations: Giving primarily in areas of company operations.

2966
Phillips Plastics Corp.

1201 Hanley Rd.
Hudson, WI 54016-9372 (877) 508-0252

Company URL: http://www.phillipsplastics.com
Establishment information: Established in 1964.
Company type: Private company
Business activities: Manufactures custom injection molded plastic products.
Business type (SIC): Plastic products/miscellaneous
Corporate officers: Matthew J. Jennings, Pres. and C.E.O.; Tom Schinella, C.F.O.; Arnie DeWitt, C.I.O.; Daniel J. Kunst, V.P., Sales and Mktg.
Giving statement: Giving through the Phillips Plastics Corporation Contributions Program and the AnnMarie Foundation.

Phillips Plastics Corporation Contributions Program

7 Long Lake Dr.
Phillips, WI 54555-1528
URL: http://www.phillipsplastics.com/about-us/scholarship-programs

Purpose and activities: As a complement to its foundation, Phillips Plastics also awards a limited number of college scholarships to children of employees.
Fields of interest: Higher education; Scholarships/financial aid.
Programs:
Bob Farley, Jr. Scholarship Program: Philips Plastics award one $1,250 scholarship to students who have completed their first year in an accredited Associate, Baccalaureate, or Graduate degree program. The program is limited to children and dependents of employees of Phillips Plastics and is given in honor of Bob Farley, Jr. Applicants must have a GPA of 3.0, participation in academic and/or non-academic extracurricular activities, and have financial need.
Philips Plastics Corporation Scholarship Program: Phillips Plastics annually awards ten $1,250 college scholarships to students who have completed the first year of an Associate, Baccalaureate, or Graduate degree program. The program is limited to children and dependents of employees of Phillips Plastics. Applicants must have a GPA of 3.0, participation in academic and/or non-academic extracurricular activities, and have financial need.
Type of support: Employee-related scholarships.
Geographic limitations: Giving in areas of company operations.
Application information: Applications not accepted. Contributes only through employee-related scholarships.

AnnMarie Foundation

N4660 1165th St.
Prescott, WI 54021-7644
FAX: (715) 262-8080;
E-mail: AnnMarieFoundation@phillipsplastics.com;
E-mail for Lori Feiten:
lori.feiten@phillipsplastics.com; URL: http://www.phillipsplastics.com/about-us/community-giving

Establishment information: Established in 1973 in WI.
Donors: Phillips Plastics Corp.; Mike Litvinoff Memorial; Robert Cervenka; Debbie Cervenka.
Contact: Lori Feiten
Financial data (yr. ended 04/30/12): Assets, $6,264,667 (M); gifts received, $166,000; expenditures, $258,171; qualifying distributions, $218,282; giving activities include $218,282 for 141 grants (high: $5,200; low: $300).
Purpose and activities: The foundation supports organizations involved with arts and culture, education, recreation, youth development, and human services and awards college scholarships to high school seniors located in areas where Philip Plastics Corporation has a facility.
Fields of interest: Arts; Libraries (public); Education; Recreation; Youth development; Youth, services; Human services.
Program:
AnnMarie Scholarship Program: The foundation awards $1,500 college scholarships to high school seniors located in areas where Philips Plastics Corporation has a facility.
Type of support: General/operating support; Scholarships—to individuals.
Geographic limitations: Giving limited to areas of company operations in WI (not Milwaukee).
Support limitations: No support for cities, counties, or municipalities, foundations, or individual colleges. No grants to individuals (except for AnnMarie scholarships), or for political or religious purposes, discretionary funds, salaries, or state or national fundraising.
Publications: Application guidelines; Program policy statement.
Application information: Applications accepted. Support is limited to 1 contribution per organization during any given year. Telephone calls are not encouraged. Application form required.
Initial approach: Download application form and mail to foundation; contact participating schools' scholarship committee or guidance office for scholarships
Board meeting date(s): Quarterly
Deadline(s): Feb. 1., May 1, Aug. 1, and Nov. 1
Final notification: Following board meetings
Members: Duane Dingmann; Lynn Downing; Sue Hanson; Jeff Heinzen; Donnie Magadauce; Kaye Ommen; Tim Popp; Steve Russ.
EIN: 237301323

2967
Phoenix Pharmaceuticals, Inc.
330 Beach Rd.
Burlingame, CA 94010-2004
(650) 558-8898
FAX: (650) 9881205

Company URL: http://www.phoenixpeptide.com
Company type: Private company
Business activities: Sells pharmaceuticals wholesale.
Business type (SIC): Drugs, proprietaries, and sundries—wholesale
Corporate officers: Jaw-Kang Chang, Pres.; Eng Tau, C.O.O.
Giving statement: Giving through the Phoenix Scholarship Foundation Inc.

Phoenix Scholarship Foundation Inc.
3200 Crain Hwy., Ste. 100
Waldorf, MD 20603-4964 (301) 870-0001

Establishment information: Established in 1996 in MD.
Donor: Phoenix Pharmaceuticals, Inc.
Contact: Parran Foster, Dir.
Financial data (yr. ended 12/31/11): Assets, $0 (M); expenditures, $16,506; qualifying distributions, $11,000; giving activities include $11,000 for 1 grant.
Purpose and activities: The foundation awards college scholarships to individuals.
Fields of interest: Higher education; Scholarships/financial aid.
Type of support: Scholarship funds; Scholarships—to individuals.
Geographic limitations: Giving limited to areas of company operations.
Application information: Applications accepted. Application form required.
Initial approach: Proposal
Deadline(s): None
Director: Parran Foster.
Trustee: Charles Curry.
EIN: 311490141

2968
Phoenix Suns L.P.
(also known as Suns Legacy Partners, LLC)
201 E. Jefferson St.
Phoenix, AZ 85004-2412 (602) 379-7900

Company URL: http://www.nba.com/suns
Establishment information: Established in 1968.
Company type: Private company
Business activities: Operates professional basketball club.
Business type (SIC): Commercial sports
Corporate officers: Jerry Colangelo, Chair.; Sam Garvin, Vice-Chair.; Andrew Kohlberg, Vice-Chair.; Jahm Najafi, Vice-Chair.; Jason Rowley, Pres.; Jim Pitman, Exec. V.P., Finance and Admin.; Tanya Wheeless, Sr. V.P., Comms. and Public Affairs; Jon Phillips, V.P., Finance; Jeff Ianello, V.P., Sales; Aaron Jerz, Cont.
Board of directors: Jerry Colangelo, Chair.; Sam Garvin, Vice-Chair.; Andrew Kohlberg, Vice-Chair.; Jahm Najafi, Vice-Chair.
Giving statement: Giving through the Phoenix Suns L.P. Corporate Giving Program and the Phoenix Suns Charities, Inc.

Phoenix Suns L.P. Corporate Giving Program
P.O. Box 1369
Phoenix, AZ 85001-1369 (602) 379-7900
Application address for memorabilia donations: 201 E. Jefferson St., Phoenix, AZ 85004; Contact for Quest for Quality: Nicole Childers, tel.: (602) 379-79243; URL: http://www.nba.com/suns/community/community_index.html

Contact: Tom Ambrose
Purpose and activities: The Phoenix Suns make charitable contributions to nonprofit organizations involved with arts and culture, education, the environment, health and human services, athletics, children, and senior citizens. Support is given primarily in Arizona.
Fields of interest: Arts; Education, reading; Education; Environment; Health care; Recreation; Children, services; Human services Aging.
Programs:
Quest for Quality: Through Quest for Quality, the Suns, APS, and Phelps Dodge, donate game tickets to elementary schools in Arizona. A mailing list is provided by the Arizona Department of Education, the Suns invite schools to apply, and each school distributes tickets to students who they feel are most deserving. One student from each school has his/her picture taken with a Suns player on court during half-time, and every student receives a certificate of achievement.
Read to Achieve: The Suns encourages children to develop a life-long love of reading through free book distribution to students in low-income schools, donation of teaching materials for teachers in grades 4-6, and the creation of Reading and Learning Centers.
Sun Nite Hoops: The Sun promotes education, job advancement, and recreation for young at-risk adults through an organization basketball league two nights each week. The program includes educational workshops, case management, and job opportunities 45 minutes prior to each game.
Suns Alumni Summer Youth Basketball Camps: The Suns invitees kids ages 6-15 living in state-wide housing projects to attend a free camp. The camp includes basketball drills and games, special appearances, anti-tobacco presentations, and t-shirts and other gifts for each child.
Type of support: Donated products; General/operating support; In-kind gifts; Income development.
Geographic limitations: Giving primarily in areas of company operations in AZ.
Support limitations: No grants to individuals, or for team sponsorships, travel, or conferences or seminars; no game ticket donations for fundraising.
Publications: Application guidelines.
Application information: Applications accepted. Proposals should be submitted using organization letterhead. The Community Relations Department handles giving. A contributions committee reviews all requests for monetary contributions. Application form not required. Applicants should submit the following:
1) population served
2) name, address and phone number of organization
3) descriptive literature about organization
4) detailed description of project and amount of funding requested
5) contact person
Proposals should specifically note the nature of the request being made, indicate the date and location of the event, and must include a valid e-mail address for memorabilia donations.
Initial approach: Proposal to headquarters for monetary contributions and Gorilla appearances; proposal to application address for memorabilia donations and celebrity appearances
Copies of proposal: 1
Committee meeting date(s): Monthly
Deadline(s): None for monetary contributions; 5 weeks prior to need for memorabilia donations; 3 weeks prior to need for appearances
Final notification: Following committee meetings for monetary contributions

Phoenix Suns Charities, Inc.
P.O. Box 1369
Phoenix, AZ 85001-1369 (602) 379-7767
FAX: (602) 379-7922; E-mail: sburgus@suns.com; URL: http://www.nba.com/suns/news/charities_index.html

Establishment information: Established in 1987 in AZ.
Donor: Phoenix Suns L.P.
Contact: Thomas P. Ambrose, Exec. Dir.
Financial data (yr. ended 06/30/11): Revenue, $1,521,609; assets, $1,222,233 (M); gifts received, $1,416,892; expenditures, $1,478,246; giving activities include $1,305,313 for grants and $33,707 for grants to individuals.
Purpose and activities: The foundation contributes funds to charitable organizations that provide services that promote the positive growth and development of Arizona's children; in addition, the charity awards college scholarships.
Fields of interest: Children, services.
Programs:
Phoenix Suns Charities Playmaker Award: The organization offers one-time grants of $100,000, which can be used for capital or to operate programs, or a combination of both. The organization, for this grant, looks favorably on collaborative ideas and naming or branding opportunities.
Phoenix Suns Charities Program Grants: The organization offers grants ranging from $1,000 to $10,000 to Arizona non-profit organizations whose programs and activities focus on helping children and families maximize their potential.
Type of support: Scholarships—to individuals.
Geographic limitations: Giving primarily in AZ.
Publications: Application guidelines; Grants list.
Application information: Applications accepted. Application form required.
Initial approach: Download application form
Deadline(s): Apr. 15
Officers: Brad Gould, Chair.; Kelly Morton, Chair.-Elect; James R. Pitman*, Secy.-Treas.; Kathryn A. Pidgeon, Exec. Dir.
Board Members: Lynn Agnello; Susan Anable; Ray Artigue; Ken Barile; Rich Bauer; Rick Chafey; John R. Cook; Dominique Dady; Matt Dana; Joann Fitzsimmons; Kim Fricke; Debbie Gaby; Barbara Gallagher; Brad Gould; Rob Harris; Carrie Martz; and 21 additional board members.
EIN: 860633919

2969
Photronics, Inc.
(formerly Photronic Labs, Inc.)
15 Secor Rd.
Brookfield, CT 06804 (203) 775-9000
FAX: (203) 775-5601

Company URL: http://www.photronics.com
Establishment information: Established in 1969.
Company type: Public company

Company ticker symbol and exchange: PLAB/NASDAQ
Business activities: Manufactures photomasks.
Business type (SIC): Electronic components and accessories; photographic equipment and supplies
Financial profile for 2012: Number of employees, 1,300; assets, $849,230,000; sales volume, $450,440,000; pre-tax net income, $40,650,000; expenses, $406,020,000; liabilities, $297,850,000
Corporate officers: Constantine S. Macricostas, Chair., Pres., and C.E.O.; Sean T. Smith, Sr. V.P. and C.F.O.
Board of directors: Constantine S. Macricostas, Chair.; Walter M. Fiederowicz; Joseph A. Fiorita, Jr., C.P.A.; Liang-Choo Hsia; George C. Macricostas; Mitchell G. Tyson
International operations: China; Germany; Singapore; Switzerland; Taiwan; United Kingdom
Giving statement: Giving through the Macricostas Scholarship Trust, Inc.
Company EIN: 060854886

Macricostas Scholarship Trust, Inc.
(formerly Photronics Scholarship Foundation, Inc.)
15 Secor Rd.
Brookfield, CT 06804-3937 (203) 740-5283

Establishment information: Established in 1997 in CT.
Donor: Photronics, Inc.
Contact: Daniel Lipton
Financial data (yr. ended 10/31/12): Assets, $116,737 (M); gifts received, $100,000; expenditures, $42,000; qualifying distributions, $39,850; giving activities include $39,850 for 44 grants (high: $1,875; low: $250).
Purpose and activities: The foundation awards college scholarships to dependent and custodial children of employees of Photronics, Inc.
Type of support: Employee-related scholarships.
Application information: Applications accepted. Application form required. Applicants should submit the following:
1) copy of IRS Determination Letter
Initial approach: Letter
Deadline(s): Apr. 15
Officers and Director:* Constantine S. Macricostas*, Chair.; Sean Smith, C.F.O.; Pricilla J. Shurick, Secy.
EIN: 061462843

2970
Physicians Mutual Insurance Company
2600 Dodge St.
Omaha, NE 68131-2671 (402) 633-1604

Company URL: http://www.physiciansmutual.com
Establishment information: Established in 1902.
Company type: Private company
Business activities: Sells health and life insurance.
Business type (SIC): Insurance/accident and health; insurance/life
Corporate officers: William R. Hamsa, Chair.; Robert A. Reed, Sr., Pres. and C.E.O.; Roger J. Hermsen, Exec. V.P. and C.F.O.
Board of director: William R. Hamsa, Chair.
Subsidiary: Physicians Life Insurance Co., Omaha, NE
Giving statement: Giving through the Physicians Mutual Insurance Company Foundation.

Physicians Mutual Insurance Company Foundation
2600 Dodge St.
Omaha, NE 68102-2672 (402) 633-1000
FAX: (402) 633-1096

Establishment information: Established in 1985 in NE.
Donor: Physicians Mutual Insurance Co.
Contact: Debra L. Walton
Financial data (yr. ended 12/31/11): Assets, $799,128 (M); expenditures, $146,349; qualifying distributions, $142,934; giving activities include $142,934 for 17 grants (high: $65,000; low: $100).
Purpose and activities: The foundation supports museums and botanical gardens and organizations involved with higher education, youth development, human services, and business and industry.
Fields of interest: Museums; Higher education; Botanical gardens; Boy scouts; Youth development, business; YM/YWCAs & YM/YWHAs; Aging, centers/services; Human services; Business/industry; United Ways and Federated Giving Programs.
Type of support: Capital campaigns; Continuing support; General/operating support; Scholarship funds.
Geographic limitations: Giving primarily in Omaha, NE.
Support limitations: No grants to individuals.
Application information: Applications accepted. Application form not required. Applicants should submit the following:
1) descriptive literature about organization
2) detailed description of project and amount of funding requested
Initial approach: Proposal
Deadline(s): None
Officers and Directors:* Robert A. Reed*, Pres.; Robert A. Reed, Jr.*, Secy.-Treas.; William R. Hamsa.
EIN: 363424068
Selected grants: The following grants are a representative sample of this grantmaker's funding activity:
$68,000 to United Way of the Midlands, Omaha, NE, 2010.
$38,600 to Knights of Ak-Sar-Ben Foundation, Omaha, NE, 2010.
$15,000 to Omaha Botanical Center, Omaha, NE, 2010.
$10,000 to Omaha Symphony Association, Omaha, NE, 2010.
$1,000 to Omaha Community Service Foundation, Omaha, NE, 2010.

2971
Piedmont Natural Gas Company, Inc.
4720 Piedmont Row Dr.
P.O. Box 33068
Charlotte, NC 28210 (704) 364-3120
FAX: (704) 365-3849

Company URL: http://www.piedmontng.com
Establishment information: Established in 1950.
Company type: Public company
Company ticker symbol and exchange: PNY/NYSE
Business activities: Transmits and distributes natural gas and propane.
Business type (SIC): Gas production and distribution
Financial profile for 2012: Number of employees, 1,752; assets, $3,769,940,000; sales volume, $1,122,780,000; pre-tax net income, $188,950,000; expenses, $927,960,000; liabilities, $2,742,930,000
Corporate officers: Thomas E. Skains, Chair., Pres., and C.E.O.; Karl W. Newlin, Sr. V.P. and C.F.O.; Kevin M. O'Hara, Sr. V.P. and C.A.O.; Jane R. Lewis-Raymond, Sr. V.P., Genl. Counsel, and Corp. Secy.; Robert O. Pritchard, V.P. and Treas.; Jose M. Simon, C.P.A., V.P. and Cont.; Bill Williams, V.P., Sales
Board of directors: Thomas E. Skains, Chair.; Eric James Burton; Malcolm E. Everett III; John W. Harris; Aubrey B. Harwell, Jr.; Frank B. Holding, Jr.; Frankie T. Jones, Sr.; Vicki W. McElreath; Minor Mickel Shaw; Muriel W. Sheubrooks; David E. Shi; Phillip D. Wright
Subsidiaries: Piedmont Energy Co., Charlotte, NC; Piedmont Hardy Storage Co., Charlotte, NC; Piedmont Interstate Pipeline Co., Charlotte, NC; Piedmont Intrastate Pipeline Co., Charlotte, NC; Piedmont Propane Co., Charlotte, NC
Giving statement: Giving through the Piedmont Natural Gas Company, Inc. Corporate Giving Program and the Piedmont Natural Gas Foundation.
Company EIN: 560556998

Piedmont Natural Gas Company, Inc. Corporate Giving Program
4720 Piedmont Row Dr.
Charlotte, NC 28210-4269 (704) 731-4223
FAX: (704) 731-4086;
E-mail: barbara.davis@piedmontng.com;
URL: http://www.piedmontng.com/ourcommunity/communityoutreach.aspx

Contact: Barbara Davis, Coord., Legislative and Community Affairs; Additional contact: Marty Viser
Financial data (yr. ended 10/31/08): Total giving, $796,000, including $726,000 for 113 grants (high: $68,000; low: $25) and $70,000 for 221 employee matching gifts.
Purpose and activities: As a complement to its foundation, Piedmont also makes charitable contributions to nonprofit organizations directly. The company supports organizations involved with arts and culture, education, the environment, health, employment, housing, youth development, human services, community development, and civic affairs. Special emphasis is directed toward programs designed to produce significant results in environmental quality, including conservation, public policy, research and education, and environmental management; support community development and revitalization efforts; expand the availability of educational resources; improve the quality of education; help children and young people reach their full potential; and enable individuals to overcome barriers to self-sufficiency. Support is given primarily in North Carolina, South Carolina, and Tennessee.
Fields of interest: Media, television; Media, radio; Visual arts; Museums; Performing arts; Arts; Education, reform; Higher education; Libraries/library science; Education, drop-out prevention; Education; Environment, research; Environment, public policy; Environment, natural resources; Environmental education; Environment; Zoos/zoological societies; Medical care, in-patient care; Health care; Employment, training; Employment; Housing/shelter; Recreation, parks/playgrounds; Youth development; Aging, centers/services; Human services; Economic development; Community/economic development; Public policy, research; Public affairs Infants/toddlers; Children/youth; Children; Young adults; Minorities; African Americans/Blacks; Hispanics/Latinos; Women; Adults, women; Men; Boys; Adults, men; Economically disadvantaged; Homeless.

Program:
Piedmont Natural Gas Matching Gift Program: The company will match contributions made by full-time employees of Piedmont Natural Gas to nonprofit organizations involved with arts and culture, education, health, human services, community development, and civic affairs on a one-for-one basis from a minimum donation of $25 to a maximum of $2,500 per fiscal year, per employee.
Type of support: Capital campaigns; Employee matching gifts; Employee volunteer services; General/operating support; Program development.
Geographic limitations: Giving primarily in NC, SC, and TN.
Support limitations: No support for K-12 private schools, third-party professional fundraising organizations, fraternal or veterans' organizations or private clubs, religious organizations not of direct benefit to the entire community, or United Way- or united arts drive-supported organizations (except for capital campaigns). No grants to individuals, or for travel or conferences, controversial social causes, or athletic events or programs.
Publications: Corporate giving report; Corporate report; Financial statement.
Application information: Applications accepted. A formal contributions committee reviews all requests. Application form required.
Initial approach: Letter or telephone
Deadline(s): None
Final notification: 1 month
Administrator: Barbara Ashford, Coord., Community Affairs.

Piedmont Natural Gas Foundation

4720 Piedmont Row Dr.
Charlotte, NC 28210-4269 (704) 731-4223
FAX: (704) 731-4086;
E-mail: barbara.davis@piedmontng.org; URL: http://www.piedmontng.com/ourcommunity/ourfoundation.aspx

Establishment information: Established in 2004 in NC.
Donor: Piedmont Natural Gas Co., Inc.
Contact: Barbara Davis, Coord., Legislative & Community Affairs
Financial data (yr. ended 12/31/11): Assets, $7,126,651 (M); gifts received, $902,500; expenditures, $769,633; qualifying distributions, $699,869; giving activities include $699,869 for grants.
Purpose and activities: The foundation supports programs designed to promote environmental stewardship and sustainability; K-12 science, technology, engineering, and math education; workforce development; health and human services; and energy assistance.
Fields of interest: Elementary/secondary education; Vocational education; Higher education, college (community/junior); Education, services; Education, reading; Environment, research; Environment, public policy; Environment, pollution control; Environment, natural resources; Environment, energy; Environmental education; Environment; Dental care; Pharmacy/prescriptions; Health care, patient services; Health care; Substance abuse, services; Mental health/crisis services; Crime/violence prevention; Employment, training; Employment, retraining; Employment; Housing/shelter, temporary shelter; Youth development, adult & child programs; Youth development; Children/youth, services; Developmentally disabled, centers & services; Homeless, human services; Human services; Economic development; United Ways and Federated Giving Programs; Mathematics; Engineering/technology; Science; Leadership development Economically disadvantaged.
Programs:
Community Enrichment Initiative - Health and Human Services: The foundation supports programs designed to provide outreach services to community members with basic needs, including shelter, food, and clothing; address substance abuse and mental illness; promote youth engagement and mentoring, special needs and disability assistance, transitional housing and homelessness support, and gang violence prevention; provide emergency and disaster relief and preparedness; promote increased access to critical healthcare services and medical treatment, including preventative care, prescription medication, medical exams, screenings, immunizations, and dental care; and increased access to mental health services.
Community Enrichment Initiative - K-12 STEM Education: Through K-12 Science, Technology, Engineering, and Math (STEM) Education, the foundation supports programs designed to enhance student performance, grade level readiness, literacy, graduation rates, and overall success; develop high-quality leadership in schools and classrooms, with emphasis on recruitment and retention of teachers and principals; incorporate science, technology, math, and engineering skills critical to success in a global economy; promote positive behaviors and motivation to stay in school; and incorporate energy and environmental education in K-12 schools and curriculum.
Community Enrichment Initiative - Regional Rotating Grant Program: Through the Regional Rotating Grant Program, the foundation awards 1 to 2 rotating capacity building/collaboration/innovation grants to bolster regional dollars. Organizations are invited to apply through a Request for Proposals (RFP) process.
Community Enrichment Initiative - Workforce Development: The foundation supports programs designed to coordinate with economic development efforts to promote the region's availability of qualified workers; provide high-quality, affordable, and accessible training to those entering the workforce; promote training initiatives that serve to upgrade employee skills and wages; and encourage life-long learning and opportunities to engage in professional development. The foundation also supports programs designed to incorporate vocational and technical training through community colleges.
Environmental Stewardship & Energy Sustainability: The foundation annually awards grants to programs designed to provide increased access to interaction with nature and the environment; promote local accountability or actions to create cleaner cities, reduce emissions, and incorporate environmental decision-making in everyday life; foster energy and/or environmental education in K-12 schools and curriculum; promote awareness about environmental and energy-related issues for the public; and preserve or restore a natural resources of the community, including green/open spaces. Organizations are invited to apply through a Request for Proposals (RFP) process.
Share the Warmth: Through Share the Warmth Energy Assistance Program, customers allow Piedmont to round up their monthly Piedmont Natural Gas bill to the nearest dollar and donate the difference to an approved Share the Warmth organization.
Type of support: Annual campaigns; Continuing support; Curriculum development; Emergency funds; Employee volunteer services; Equipment; General/operating support; Management development/capacity building; Program development.
Geographic limitations: Giving primarily in areas of company operations in NC, SC, and TN.
Support limitations: No support for religious organizations not of direct benefit to the entire community, fraternal or political organizations, athletic organizations, private foundations, social or veterans' organizations, pre-college level private schools, third-party professional fundraising organizations, or private clubs. No grants to individuals, or for scholarships, travel or conferences, controversial social causes, athletic events or programs, or causes from which Piedmont Natural Gas will receive any benefit.
Publications: Application guidelines; Program policy statement.
Application information: Applications accepted. Only competitive grants have a defined deadline that is specified during the Request for Proposal (RFP) process. Additional information may be requested at a later date. An interview or site visit may be requested. Application form required.
Initial approach: Complete online application form
Copies of proposal: 1
Board meeting date(s): Mar., June, Sept., and Dec.
Deadline(s): 6 weeks prior to board meetings
Final notification: Within 30 days, unless board approval is required
Officers and Directors:* Kevin O'Hara, Chair.; George Baldwin, Pres.; Ranelle Q. Warfield, V.P.; Jane R. Lewis-Raymond, Secy.; Robert O. Pritchard, Treas.; David Trusty; Theresa VonCannon.
Trustee: Wachovia Bank, N.A.
EIN: 201786431

2972
Pieper Electric, Inc.

5070 N. 35th St.,
Milwaukee, WI 53209-5302
(414) 462-7700

Company URL: http://www.pieperpower.com
Establishment information: Established in 1947.
Company type: Private company
Business activities: Provides contract electrical, plumbing, heating, air conditioning, temperature control, and energy management services.
Business type (SIC): Contractors/electrical work; contractors/plumbing, heating, and air-conditioning
Corporate officers: Mike Michels, Pres.; Richard Pieper, C.E.O.; Ken Phelps, V.P., Corp. Comms.; Dan Melstrand, Cont.
Giving statement: Giving through the PPC Foundation, Inc.

PPC Foundation, Inc.

(formerly Pieperpower Foundation, Inc.)
5070 N. 35th St.
Milwaukee, WI 53209-5302 (414) 462-7700

Establishment information: Established in 1968.
Donors: MetroPower, Inc.; Pieper Electric, Inc.; PPC Partners, Inc.
Contact: Michelle Millard, Coord.
Financial data (yr. ended 12/31/11): Assets, $55,439 (L); gifts received, $485,300; expenditures, $465,629; qualifying distributions, $465,629.
Purpose and activities: The foundation supports organizations involved with arts and culture, education, health, human services, and government and public administration. Giving primarily in southeastern Wisconsin.

Fields of interest: Arts; Education; Health care; Children/youth, services; Human services; United Ways and Federated Giving Programs; Government/public administration.
Type of support: Employee matching gifts; General/operating support.
Geographic limitations: Giving primarily in southeastern WI.
Support limitations: No grants to individuals.
Application information: Applications accepted. Application form not required.
Initial approach: Proposal
Copies of proposal: 1
Board meeting date(s): Nov.
Deadline(s): Oct. 1
Final notification: Dec. 31 of proposal year
Officers and Directors: Ronnie Hinson, C.E.O.; Mike Michels, Pres. and C.O.O.; Richard Pieper, Sr., Secy.; Dan Melstrand, Treas.; Norman Doll.
Number of staff: 1 full-time professional.
EIN: 396124770

2973
Pier 1 Imports, Inc.

100 Pier 1 Pl.
Fort Worth, TX 76102-4106 (817) 252-8000
FAX: (817) 252-8174

Company URL: http://www.pier1.com
Establishment information: Established in 1962.
Company type: Public company
Company ticker symbol and exchange: PIR/NYSE
Business activities: Operates furniture, decorative home furnishings, dining and kitchen goods, and bath and bedding accessories stores.
Business type (SIC): Home furniture, furnishings, and equipment stores
Financial profile for 2013: Number of employees, 21,400; assets, $857,220,000; sales volume, $1,704,880,000; pre-tax net income, $201,000,000; expenses, $1,505,900,000; liabilities, $320,080,000
Corporate officers: Terry E. London, Chair.; Alexander W. Smith, Pres. and C.E.O.; Charles H. Turner, Sr. Exec. V.P. and C.F.O.; Gregory S. Humenesky, Exec. V.P., Human Resources; Michael A. Carter, Sr. V.P., Genl. Counsel, and Secy.; Donald L. Kinnison, Sr. V.P., Mktg.
Board of directors: Terry E. London, Chair.; Claire H. Babrowski; Cheryl A. Bachelder; John H. Burgoyne; Hamish A. Dodds; Brendan L. Hoffman; Alexander W. Smith; Cece Smith
International operations: Canada
Giving statement: Giving through the Pier 1 Imports, Inc. Corporate Giving Program.
Company EIN: 751729843

Pier 1 Imports, Inc. Corporate Giving Program

c/o Charitable Giving
P.O. Box 961020
Fort Worth, TX 76161-0020 (817) 252-8808
URL: http://www.pier1.com/SideMenu/Pressroom/GivingBack/tabid/66/Default.aspx

Purpose and activities: Pier 1 makes charitable contributions to nonprofit organizations involved with the arts, community services, and children's education. Support is given primarily in Fort Worth, Texas.
Fields of interest: Arts; Elementary/secondary education; Breast cancer research; Children, services; Human services; Community/economic development; United Ways and Federated Giving Programs.
Type of support: Donated products; Employee volunteer services; General/operating support; In-kind gifts.
Geographic limitations: Giving primarily in Fort Worth, TX.
Support limitations: No support for religious, political, or fraternal organizations, private schools, or sports organizations. No grants to individuals, or for school activities, advertising, beauty or talent contests, endowments, conferences or seminars, travel, or scholarships; no returned, damaged, or excess merchandise donations.
Publications: Application guidelines.
Application information: Applications accepted. An application form is required for contributions over $1,000. Applicants should submit the following:
1) population served
2) copy of IRS Determination Letter
3) brief history of organization and description of its mission
4) detailed description of project and amount of funding requested
5) copy of current year's organizational budget and/or project budget

Initial approach: Download application form and mail to application address for requests over $1,000; proposal to headquarters for requests under $1,000
Deadline(s): None
Final notification: 4 to 6 weeks

2974
Pierce Atwood LLP

1 Monument Sq., 7th Fl.
Portland, ME 04101 (207) 791-1186

Company URL: http://www.pierceatwood.com/
Company type: Private company
Business activities: Operates law firm.
Business type (SIC): Legal services
Corporate officers: Gloria Pinza, Managing Partner; Maggie Callicrate, C.O.O.
Offices: Washington, DC; Augusta, Portland, ME; Boston, MA; Portsmouth, NH; Providence, RI
International operations: Sweden
Giving statement: Giving through the Pierce Atwood LLP Pro Bono Program.

Pierce Atwood LLP Pro Bono Program

1 Monument Sq., 7th Fl.
Portland, ME 04101 (207) 791-1186
E-mail: cruprecht@pierceatwood.com; Additional tel.: (207) 791-1100; URL: http://www.pierceatwood.com/probono

Contact: Cliff Ruprecht, Partner
Fields of interest: Legal services.
Type of support: Pro bono services - legal.
Application information: An attorney coordinates pro bono projects as an ancillary duty to other work.

2975
Pillsbury Winthrop Shaw Pittman LLP

1540 Broadway
New York, NY 10036-4039 (415) 983-1920

Company URL: http://www.pillsburylaw.com/index.cfm?pageid=1
Company type: Private company
Business activities: Operates law firm.
Business type (SIC): Legal services
Offices: Costa Mesa, Los Angeles, Palo Alto, Sacramento, San Diego, San Francisco, CA; Washington, DC; New York, NY; Houston, TX; McLean, VA
International operations: China; Japan; United Arab Emirates; United Kingdom
Giving statement: Giving through the Pillsbury Winthrop Shaw Pittman LLP Pro Bono Program.

Pillsbury Winthrop Shaw Pittman LLP Pro Bono Program

1540 Broadway
New York, NY 10036-4039 (415) 983-1920
E-mail: tania.shah@pillsburylaw.com; Additional tel.: (212) 858-1000; URL: http://www.pillsburylaw.com/index.cfm?pageID=59

Contact: Tania Shah, Dir. of Corp. and Social Responsibility
Fields of interest: Legal services.
Type of support: Pro bono services - legal.
Application information: A Pro Bono Committee manages the pro bono program.

2976
Pine State Trading Co.

(formerly Pine State Tobacco & Candy Company, Inc.)
8 Ellis Ave.
Augusta, ME 04330 (207) 622-3741

Company URL: http://www.pinestatetrading.com/Home/tabid/36/Default.aspx
Establishment information: Established in 1941.
Company type: Private company
Business activities: Sells tobacco and alcoholic beverages wholesale.
Business type (SIC): Non-durable goods—wholesale; beer, wine, and distilled beverages—wholesale; candy stores
Corporate officers: Charles F. Canning, Jr., Chair. and C.E.O.; Paul Cottrell, Pres.; Gary Pelletier, C.F.O.
Board of director: Charles F. Canning, Jr., Chair.
Subsidiaries: Pine State Beverage Co., Augusta, ME; Pine State Vending Co., Augusta, ME
Giving statement: Giving through the Charles F. Canning, Sr. Foundation.

Charles F. Canning, Sr. Foundation

c/o Paul Cottrell
47 Market St.
Gardiner, ME 04345-7199

Establishment information: Established in 1990 in ME.
Donors: Pine State Tobacco & Candy Co., Inc.; Pine State Trading.
Financial data (yr. ended 09/30/12): Assets, $53,046 (M); gifts received, $250; expenditures, $10,500; qualifying distributions, $10,500; giving

activities include $10,500 for 16 grants to individuals (high: $1,000; low: $500).
Purpose and activities: The foundation awards college scholarships to children of employees of Pine State Tobacco & Candy Company.
Type of support: Employee-related scholarships.
Geographic limitations: Giving primarily in areas of company operations.
Application information: Applications accepted. Application form required.
Initial approach: Contact Foundation for Application Form
Deadline(s): May 31
Trustees: Larry Auger; Alan McPherson; John Miller.
EIN: 223147792

2977
Pinnacle Communities, Ltd.
363 Bloomfield Ave., Ste. 2A
Montclair, NJ 07042 (973) 379-1900
FAX: (973) 376-1886

Company URL: http://www.pinnaclecommunities.com
Establishment information: Established in 1984.
Company type: Private company
Business activities: Builds houses.
Business type (SIC): Operative builders
Corporate officers: Brian M. Stolar, Pres. and C.E.O.; Mary Boorman, Sr. V.P., Sales and Mktg.; Charles Applebaum, Genl. Counsel
Giving statement: Giving through the Pinnacle Foundation, Inc.

The Pinnacle Foundation, Inc.
363 Bloomfield Ave., Ste. 2A
Montclair, NJ 07042

Establishment information: Established as a company-sponsored operating foundation in 2000 in NJ.
Donors: Pinnacle Communities, Ltd.; Brian M. Stolar, Esq.; Pinnacle Realty.
Financial data (yr. ended 12/31/10): Assets, $25,852 (M); gifts received, $10,723; expenditures, $31,380; qualifying distributions, $31,381; giving activities include $19,110 for 7 grants (high: $16,445; low: $125).
Purpose and activities: The foundation supports museums and health centers and organizations involved with education, children, and Judaism.
Fields of interest: Museums; Theological school/education; Education; Health care, clinics/centers; Children, services; Jewish agencies & synagogues.
Type of support: General/operating support; Publication; Sponsorships.
Geographic limitations: Giving primarily in NJ.
Support limitations: No grants to individuals.
Application information: Applications not accepted. Unsolicited requests for funds not accepted.
Officers: Brian M. Stolar, Pres.; Michael Cantor, V.P.; Howard Irwin, V.P.
EIN: 223377688

2978
Pinnacle Entertainment, Inc.
8918 Spanish Ridge Ave.
Las Vegas, NV 89148 (702) 784-7777

Company URL: http://www.pnkinc.com/
Establishment information: Established in 1938.
Company type: Public company
Company ticker symbol and exchange: PNK/NYSE
Business activities: Operates hotels and casinos.
Business type (SIC): Amusement and recreation services/miscellaneous
Financial profile for 2012: Number of employees, 8,479; assets, $2,108,990,000; sales volume, $1,197,100,000; pre-tax net income, -$17,960,000; expenses, $1,090,600,000; liabilities, $1,661,880,000
Corporate officers: Richard J. Goeglein, Chair.; Anthony Sanfilippo, Pres. and C.E.O.; Carlos Ruisanchez, Exec. V.P. and C.F.O.; John A. Godfrey, Exec. V.P., Genl. Counsel, and Secy.; Daniel Boudreaux, Sr. V.P. and C.A.O.
Board of directors: Richard J. Goeglein, Chair.; James L. Martineau, Vice-Chair.; Stephen Comer; Bruce A. Leslie; Desiree Rogers; Anthony M. Sanfilippo; Jaynie Miller Studenmund
International operations: Argentina; Bahamas; Greece; Netherlands
Giving statement: Giving through the Pinnacle Entertainment Foundation.
Company EIN: 953667491

The Pinnacle Entertainment Foundation
8918 Spanish Ridge Ave.
Las Vegas, NV 89148 (702) 541-7777
URL: https://www.pnkinc.com/pinnacle-entertainment-foundation/pinnacle-entertainment-foundation/

Donor: Pinnacle Entertainment, Inc.
Contact: Shelly Peterson
Financial data (yr. ended 12/31/11): Assets, $25,575 (M); gifts received, $223,000; expenditures, $228,207; qualifying distributions, $216,444; giving activities include $216,444 for grants.
Fields of interest: Recreation.
Application information: Applications accepted. Application form required.
Initial approach: Complete online application
Deadline(s): None
Final notification: 90 days prior to event publicity deadline
Officers and Directors:* Anthony M. Sanfillipo*, Pres.; John A. Godfrey*, Secy.; Stephen H. Capp, Treas.
EIN: 272612545

2979
Pioneer Federal Savings and Loan Association
32 N. Washington St.
Dillon, MT 59725-2514 (406) 683-5191

Company URL: http://www.pioneerfed.com
Establishment information: Established in 1912.
Company type: Private company
Business activities: Operates savings bank.
Business type (SIC): Savings institutions
Financial profile for 2010: Number of employees, 13
Corporate officers: Spence Hegstad, Chair.; William Mosier, Jr., Vice-Chair.; Thomas G. Welch, Pres. and C.E.O.; Julie James, Treas.; Jamie Secor, Secy.
Board of directors: Spence Hegstad, Chair.; William Mosier, Jr., Vice-Chair.
Office: Deer Lodge, MT
Giving statement: Giving through the Pioneer Federal Community Foundation, Inc.

Pioneer Federal Community Foundation, Inc.
102 N. Washington St.
Dillon, MT 59725-1103

Establishment information: Established in 1998.
Donor: Pioneer Federal Savings and Loan.
Financial data (yr. ended 12/31/11): Assets, $572,924 (M); gifts received, $50,000; expenditures, $28,693; qualifying distributions, $23,100; giving activities include $23,100 for grants.
Purpose and activities: The foundation supports arts councils and organizations involved with journalism, education, and health.
Fields of interest: Arts; Health care; Agriculture/food.
Type of support: General/operating support; Program development; Scholarship funds.
Geographic limitations: Giving primarily in Deer Lodge and Dillon, MT.
Support limitations: No grants to individuals.
Application information: Applications not accepted. Unsolicited requests for funds not accepted.
Directors: Tom Beck; Spence Hegstad; Bill Mosier; Tedd Stanisich; Thomas G. Welch.
EIN: 810522327

2980
Pioneer Hi-Bred International, Inc.
7100 N.W. 62nd Ave.
P.O. Box 1000
Johnston, IA 50131-1050 (515) 270-3200

Company URL: http://www.pioneer.com
Establishment information: Established in 1926.
Company type: Subsidiary of a public company
Business activities: Produces seed corn, sorghum seed, alfalfa, forage, microbial cultures, and soybean and wheat seed.
Business type (SIC): Farms/miscellaneous cash grain; farms, except cash grains/field crop; drugs; fertilizers and agricultural chemicals; non-durable goods—wholesale; research, development, and testing services
Corporate officers: Paul E. Schickler, Pres.; Judith E. McKay, V.P. and Genl. Counsel; Laurie Conslato, V.P., Finance
International operations: Argentina; Australia; Brazil; Canada; Chile; France; India; Thailand
Giving statement: Giving through the Pioneer Hi-Bred International, Inc. Corporate Giving Program and the Pioneer Hi-Bred International, Inc. Foundation.

Pioneer Hi-Bred International, Inc. Corporate Giving Program
P.O. Box 1000
Johnston, IA 50131-0814 (515) 535-3200
FAX: (515) 535-4415; URL: http://www.pioneer.com/home/site/about/business/pioneer-giving/

Purpose and activities: As a complement to its foundation, Pioneer Hi-Bred also makes charitable contributions to nonprofit organizations directly. Support is given on a national and international basis.
Fields of interest: Education; Agriculture; Safety, education; General charitable giving.
Type of support: Conferences/seminars; Employee matching gifts; Employee volunteer services; General/operating support; Program development.

Geographic limitations: Giving on a national and international basis in areas of company operations.

Pioneer Hi-Bred International, Inc. Foundation

P.O. Box 1000
Johnston, IA 50131-1000 (515) 535-6677
FAX: (515) 248-4842;
E-mail: Community.GrantsProgram@pioneer.com; Additional tel.: (800) 247-6803 ext. 56867; E-mail for Michelle Gowdy: michelle.gowdy@pioneer.com; URL: http://www.pioneer.com/home/site/about/business/pioneer-giving/

Establishment information: Established in 1992.
Donor: Pioneer Hi-Bred International, Inc.
Contact: Michelle Gowdy, V.P.
Financial data (yr. ended 12/31/11): Assets, $1 (M); gifts received, $101,810; expenditures, $101,810; qualifying distributions, $101,810; giving activities include $101,810 for grants.
Purpose and activities: The foundation supports programs designed to promote science education; food security; and community betterment.
Fields of interest: Elementary/secondary education; Education; Health care; Agriculture; Agriculture, sustainable programs; Agriculture, farmlands; Food services; Nutrition; Community/economic development; Science, formal/general education; Science.
Programs:

Community Betterment: The foundation supports programs designed to address the needs of local communities.

Food Security: The foundation supports global programs designed to build agricultural capacity; teach sustainable farming techniques; increase crop yields; and improve the economics of local agriculture. The foundation also supports local food security programs designed to improve healthy food accessibility for at-risk populations; foster healthy food choices; provide nutritional education; and enable healthy food preparation.

International Scholarships: The foundation awards international scholarships to outstanding students working toward graduate level degrees in plant breeding. Scholarships are limited to the University of Buenos Aries, Federal University of Vicos, Federal University of Santa Maria, China Agricultural University, Henan Agricultural University, University of Qingdao Agriculture, Maharana Pratap University of Agriculture and Technology, Tamil Nadu Agricultural University, Gandhi Krishi Vignana Kendra, University of Ag Sciences, Punjab Agricultural University, Universidad Autonoma Agraria, and the University of Los Banos. Recipients are selected based on academic excellence, proposed study program/area, future professional plans, leadership, and other experiences.

Science Education Grants: The foundation supports programs designed to improve science literacy; enable science discovery; and grow future talent in the sciences. Special emphasis is directed toward K-12 science and agricultural programs.

Type of support: Conferences/seminars; Employee matching gifts; Equipment; Matching/challenge support; Program development; Research; Scholarship funds; Scholarships—to individuals.
Geographic limitations: Giving primarily in areas of company operations in the U.S and in Argentina, Brazil, Canada, Chile, China, India, Indonesia, Mexico, Philippines, and Turkey.
Support limitations: No support for religious or political organizations, discriminatory organizations, or athletic teams. No grants to individuals (except for scholarships), or for marketing or advertising, or athletic events.
Publications: Application guidelines.
Application information: Applications accepted. Application form required. Applicants should submit the following:
1) population served
2) copy of IRS Determination Letter
3) copy of most recent annual report/audited financial statement/990
4) listing of board of directors, trustees, officers and other key people and their affiliations
5) detailed description of project and amount of funding requested
6) copy of current year's organizational budget and/or project budget
7) listing of additional sources and amount of support

Initial approach: Complete online eligibility quiz and application
Board meeting date(s): Quarterly
Deadline(s): None
Final notification: Up to 3 months

Officers and Directors:* Jeffrey A. Austin*, Pres.; Michelle Gowdy, V.P.; Jeffrey D. Rowe, V.P.; Steve Schaaf*, V.P.; Paul E. Schickler*, V.P.; Judith E. McKay*, Secy.; Jeffrey L. Burnison, Treas.
EIN: 421388269
Selected grants: The following grants are a representative sample of this grantmaker's funding activity:
$10,000 to Bioversity International, Rome, Italy, 2011.

2981
Pioneer Natural Resources Company

5205 N. O'Connor Blvd., Ste. 200
Irving, TX 75039-3745 (972) 444-9001
FAX: (972) 402-7023

Company URL: http://www.pxd.com/
Establishment information: Established in 1997 from the merger of Mesa Inc. with Parker & Parsley Petroleum Co.
Company type: Public company
Company ticker symbol and exchange: PXD/NYSE
Business activities: Conducts crude oil and natural gas exploration and production activities.
Business type (SIC): Extraction/oil and gas
Financial profile for 2012: Number of employees, 3,667; assets, $13,069,030,000; sales volume, $3,228,310,000; pre-tax net income, $280,060,000; expenses, $2,948,250,000; liabilities, $7,379,680,000
Fortune 1000 ranking: 2012—667th in revenues, 590th in profits, and 326th in assets
Forbes 2000 ranking: 2012—1600th in sales, 1567th in profits, and 1274th in assets
Corporate officers: Scott D. Sheffield, Chair. and C.E.O.; Timothy L. Dove, Pres. and C.O.O.; Richard P. Dealy, Exec. V.P. and C.F.O.; Mark Stephen Berg, Exec. V.P. and Genl. Counsel; Frank W. Hall, V.P. and C.A.O.; Thomas C. Hatbouty, V.P. and C.I.O.; Mark H. Kleinman, V.P. and Corp. Secy.; Larry N. Paulsen, V.P., Admin.; John C. Distaso, V.P., Mktg.; Susan A. Spratlen, V.P., Comms.
Board of directors: Scott D. Sheffield, Chair.; Thomas D. Arthur; Edison C. Buchanan; Andrew F. Cates; R. Hartwell Gardner; Charles E. Ramsey; Frank A. Risch; J. Kenneth Thompson; Jim A. Watson
International operations: Argentina; Bahamas; Cayman Islands; England; Nigeria; South Africa
Giving statement: Giving through the Pioneer Natural Resources Company Contributions Program and the Pioneer Natural Resources Foundation.
Company EIN: 752702753

Pioneer Natural Resources Company Contributions Program

5205 N. O'Connor Blvd., Ste. 200
Irving, TX 75039 (972) 444-9001
URL: http://www.pxd.com/communities

Purpose and activities: As a complement to its foundation, Pioneer also makes charitable contributions to nonprofit organizations directly. Special emphasis is directed toward programs that promote education, especially engineering and geoscience. Support is limited to areas of company operations in Alaska and Texas.
Fields of interest: Elementary/secondary education; Higher education; Higher education, college (community/junior); Engineering school/education; Housing/shelter, volunteer services; Children, foster care; Human services, gift distribution; Homeless, human services; Science Economically disadvantaged.
Type of support: Employee matching gifts; Employee volunteer services; General/operating support.
Geographic limitations: Giving limited to areas of company operations in AK and TX.
Application information: Charitable Contribution Committees in Pioneer's corporate headquarters and key divisions handle giving.

Pioneer Natural Resources Foundation

(formerly Pioneer Natural Resources Scholarship Foundation)
5205 N. O'Connor Blvd., Ste. 200
Irving, TX 75039-3789
URL: http://www.pxd.com

Establishment information: Established in 1992 in TX.
Donors: Parker & Parsley Petroleum Co.; Norris Sucker Rods; Pioneer Natural Resources Co.; Pioneer Natural Resources USA, Inc.; Scott Sheffield; Michael Wortley; Charles Ramsey.
Contact: Larry N. Paulsen, V.P. and Treas.
Financial data (yr. ended 12/31/11): Assets, $72,803 (M); expenditures, $16,750; qualifying distributions, $16,750; giving activities include $16,750 for 23 grants to individuals (high: $1,000; low: $500).
Purpose and activities: The foundation awards college scholarships to children of full-time employees of Pioneer Natural Resources.
Type of support: Employee-related scholarships.
Geographic limitations: Giving primarily in TX.
Application information: Applications accepted.

Initial approach: Proposal
Deadline(s): Jun. 1st

Officers and Directors:* Timothy L. Dove*, Pres.; Mark S. Berg*, Exec. V.P.; Richard P. Dealy*, Exec. V.P.; Mark H. Kleinman, V.P. and Secy.; Larry N. Paulsen*, V.P. and Treas.; Susan A. Spratlen*, V.P.
EIN: 752443728

2982
Pioneer Trust Bank, N.A.

109 Commercial St., N.E.
P.O. Box 2305
Salem, OR 97301 (503) 363-3136
FAX: (503) 364-4669

Company URL: https://www.pioneertrustbank.com/
Establishment information: Established in 1968.
Company type: Subsidiary of a private company
Business activities: Operates commercial bank.

Business type (SIC): Banks/commercial
Corporate officers: William Meier, Chair.; Michael Compton, C.E.O.; Randy Compton, Pres.; John Willburn, C.F.O.
Board of director: William Meier, Chair.
Giving statement: Giving through the Pioneer Trust Bank, N.A. Foundation.

Pioneer Trust Bank, N.A. Foundation

P.O. Box 2305
Salem, OR 97308-2305

Establishment information: Established in 1984 in OR.
Donor: Pioneer Trust Bank, N.A.
Financial data (yr. ended 12/31/11): Assets, $893,518 (M); expenditures, $42,752; qualifying distributions, $41,900; giving activities include $41,900 for grants.
Purpose and activities: The foundation supports organizations involved with arts and culture, education, natural resources, health, human services, religion, and disabled people.
Fields of interest: Animals/wildlife; Human services; Religion.
Geographic limitations: Giving primarily in Salem, OR.
Application information: Applications accepted. Application form required. Applicants should submit the following:
1) copy of IRS Determination Letter
2) copy of most recent annual report/audited financial statement/990
3) detailed description of project and amount of funding requested

Initial approach: Letter
Copies of proposal: 1
Deadline(s): Aug. 15

Trustee: Pioneer Trust Bank, N.A.
EIN: 930881673

2983
Piper Jaffray Companies

(formerly Piper Jaffray & Co.)
800 Nicollet Mall, Ste. 800
Minneapolis, MN 55402-7020
(612) 303-6000
FAX: (302) 655-5049

Company URL: http://www.piperjaffray.com
Establishment information: Established in 1895.
Company type: Public company
Company ticker symbol and exchange: PJC/NYSE
Business activities: Provides securities brokerage services; provides investment advisory services.
Business type (SIC): Brokers and dealers/security; security and commodity services
Financial profile for 2012: Number of employees, 966; assets, $2,087,730,000; sales volume, $518,240,000; pre-tax net income, $69,010,000; expenses, $449,230,000; liabilities, $1,354,440,000
Corporate officers: Andrew S. Duff, Chair. and C.E.O.; Thomas P. Schnettler, Vice-Chair.; Debbra L. Schoneman, C.F.O.; Shawn Quant, C.I.O.; John W. Geelan, Genl. Counsel and Secy.
Board of directors: Andrew S. Duff, Chair.; Thomas P. Schnettler, Vice-Chair.; Michael R. Francis; B. Kristine Johnson; Addison L. Piper; Lisa Polsky; Frank L. Sims; Jean Taylor; Michele Volpi; Hope Woodhouse
Giving statement: Giving through the Piper Jaffray Companies Contributions Program and the Piper Jaffray Foundation.
Company EIN: 300168701

Piper Jaffray Companies Contributions Program

(formerly Piper Jaffray & Co. Contributions Program)
800 Nicollet Mall, Ste. 800
Minneapolis, MN 55402-7020
E-mail: communityrelations@pjc.com.; URL: http://www.piperjaffray.com/2col_largeright.aspx?id=427

Purpose and activities: As a complement to its foundation, Piper Jaffray also makes charitable contributions to nonprofit organizations directly. Support is limited to areas of company operations in Arizona, California, Colorado Connecticut, Florida, Iowa, Illinois, Indiana, Kansas, Massachusetts, Minnesota, Missouri, New York, North Carolina, Ohio, Oklahoma, Pennsylvania, Tennessee, Texas, Washington, Wisconsin, and in China, Switzerland, and the United Kingdom.
Fields of interest: Arts; Education; Environment; Health care; Children, services; Community development, small businesses; Community/economic development; United Ways and Federated Giving Programs; Mathematics; Engineering/technology; Science; Economics.
International interests: China; Switzerland; United Kingdom.
Type of support: Employee matching gifts; Employee volunteer services; General/operating support; Program development; Sponsorships.
Geographic limitations: Giving primarily in Support is limited to areas of company operations in AZ, CA, CO, CT, FL, IA, IL, IN, KS, MA, MN, MO, NC, NY, OH, OK, PA, TN, TX, WA, WI, and in China, Switzerland, and the United Kingdom.
Support limitations: No support for lobbying, political, or fraternal organizations, United Way-supported organizations (primary funding), or religious organizations not of direct benefit to the entire community. No grants to individuals (except for employee-related scholarships), or for research, planning, personal needs, or travel, public service or political campaigns, athletic or pageant scholarships, advertising, publications, or audio or video production.
Publications: Application guidelines.
Application information: Applications accepted. Unsolicited requests for capital campaign support are not accepted. Unsolicited requests from health organizations are not accepted. Support for arts and culture organizations are limited to sponsorships. The Community Relations Department handles giving. The company has a staff that only handles contributions. A contributions committee reviews all requests.

Initial approach: Complete online inquiry form
Deadline(s): Jan. 1 to Mar. 15
Final notification: Following review

Piper Jaffray Foundation

(formerly U.S. Bancorp Piper Jaffray Companies Foundation)
800 Nicollet Mall, J09SFA
Minneapolis, MN 55402-7000 (612) 303-8202
FAX: (612) 303-1309;
E-mail: communityrelations@pjc.com; URL: http://www.pjc.com/community

Establishment information: Established in 1993 in MN.
Donor: Piper Jaffray Cos. Inc.
Financial data (yr. ended 12/13/11): Assets, $996,675 (M); expenditures, $958,560; qualifying distributions, $937,255; giving activities include $935,270 for 91 grants (high: $110,000; low: $25).
Purpose and activities: The foundation supports organizations involved with arts and culture, economic education, community development, and civic engagement.
Fields of interest: Arts; Higher education; Engineering school/education; Health care; Youth development; Community development, small businesses; Community/economic development; Science, formal/general education; Mathematics; Economics; Public affairs, citizen participation Economically disadvantaged.
Type of support: Capital campaigns; Employee matching gifts; General/operating support; Program development.
Geographic limitations: Giving limited to areas of company operations in CA, Denver, CO, Chicago, IL, Kansas City, KS, Boston, MA, Minneapolis and St. Paul, MN, St. Louis, MO, New York, NY, Portland, OR, and Seattle, WA.
Support limitations: No support for religious, political, veterans', or fraternal groups, teams, organizations receiving primary funding from the United Way, or newly formed nonprofit organizations. No grants to individuals, or for groups seeking support for planning, personal needs, or travel, public service or political campaigns, athletic or pageant scholarships, publications, audio-visual pieces, or debt reduction.
Publications: Application guidelines.
Application information: Applications accepted. Multi-year support is limited to three years in length. Unsolicited requests for capital support are not accepted. Application form required. Applicants should submit the following:
1) copy of IRS Determination Letter
2) brief history of organization and description of its mission
3) copy of most recent annual report/audited financial statement/990
4) listing of board of directors, trustees, officers and other key people and their affiliations
5) copy of current year's organizational budget and/or project budget
6) listing of additional sources and amount of support

Initial approach: Complete online application
Copies of proposal: 1
Board meeting date(s): 2nd qtr.
Deadline(s): Jan. 5 to Mar. 15
Final notification: End of June

Officers and Directors:* R. Todd Firebaugh*, Pres.; Debra L. Schoneman*, C.F.O.; Connie McCuskey, V.P.; John W. Geelan, Secy.; Timothy L. Carter, Treas.
Number of staff: 2 full-time professional; 1 full-time support.
EIN: 411734808
Selected grants: The following grants are a representative sample of this grantmaker's funding activity:
$74,400 to United Way, Greater Twin Cities, Minneapolis, MN, 2010.

2984
Pitney Bowes Inc.

1 Elmcroft Rd.
Stamford, CT 06926-0700 (203) 356-5000
FAX: (302) 655-5049

Company URL: http://www.pb.com
Establishment information: Established in 1920.
Company type: Public company
Company ticker symbol and exchange: PBI/NYSE
International Securities Identification Number: US7244791007
Business activities: Manufactures and provides mail and document management solutions.

Business type (SIC): Computer and office equipment
Financial profile for 2012: Number of employees, 20,800; assets, $7,859,890,000; sales volume, $4,408,890,000; pre-tax net income, $60,461; expenses, $4,299,400,000; liabilities, $77,492,600,000
Fortune 1000 ranking: 2012—489th in revenues, 360th in profits, and 456th in assets
Corporate officers: Michael I. Roth, Chair.; Michael Monahan, Exec. V.P. and C.F.O.; Marc B. Lautenbach, Pres. and C.E.O.; Gregory E. Buonconti, Exec. V.P. and C.I.O.; Steven J. Green, V.P., Finance and C.A.O.; Helen Shan, V.P., Finance and Treas.
Board of directors: Michael I. Roth, Chair.; Linda G. Alvarado; Anne M. Busquet; Roger Fradin; Anne Sutherland Fuchs; Eduardo R. Menasce; David L. Shedlarz; David B. Snow, Jr.; Robert E. Weissman
Subsidiary: Pitney Bowes Credit Corp., Norwalk, CT
Divisions: Pitney Bowes Business Svcs., Stamford, CT; Pitney Bowes Intl., Stamford, CT; Pitney Bowes Office Systems, Trumbull, CT; U.S. Mailing Systems, Stamford, CT
International operations: Australia; Austria; Belgium; Brazil; Canada; China; Denmark; England; Finland; France; Germany; Hong Kong; India; Ireland; Italy; Japan; Luxembourg; Malaysia; Mexico; Netherlands; New Zealand; Norway; Panama; Portugal; Singapore; South Africa; South Korea; Spain; Sweden; Switzerland; Thailand; United Kingdom
Giving statement: Giving through the Pitney Bowes Inc. Corporate Giving Program, the Pitney Bowes Foundation, the Pitney Bowes Literacy and Education Fund, Inc., and the Pitney Bowes Relief Fund Charitable Trust.
Company EIN: 060495050

Pitney Bowes Inc. Corporate Giving Program

1 Elmcroft Rd.
Stamford, CT 06926-0700 (203) 351-6669
E-mail: community.investments@pb.com; Additional tel.: (203) 351-6377; URL: http://www.pb.com/cgi-bin/pb.dll/jsp/GenericEditorial.do?editorial_id=ed_CorporateGiving&rootCatOID=-18274&lang=en&country=US

Contact: Polly Mormon
Purpose and activities: As a complement to its foundation, Pitney Bowes also makes charitable contributions to nonprofit organizations directly. Support is given on a national basis in areas of company operations.
Fields of interest: Arts; Education; Health care; Community/economic development; Public affairs Children; Youth; Disabilities, people with; Minorities; Women; Economically disadvantaged.
Type of support: Continuing support; Employee volunteer services; Program development; Sponsorships.
Geographic limitations: Giving on a national basis in areas of company operations, including in Bridgeport, Danbury, Hartford, Shelton, and Stamford, CT, Washington, DC, Atlanta, GA, Spokane, WA, and Appleton, WI.
Support limitations: No support for religious organizations not of direct benefit to the entire community, political candidates or lobbying organizations, fraternal, labor, veterans', or similar organizations, disease-specific organizations, or anti-business organizations. No grants to individuals, or for general operating support, capital campaigns, travel, conferences, sporting events, auctions, or other one-time, short-term events, advertising or television programming, or team sponsorships or athletic scholarships; no product donations.
Publications: Application guidelines; Grants list.
Application information: Applications accepted. Support is limited to 1 contribution per organization during any given year. Multi-year funding is not automatic. Candidates will receive an e-mail notification verifying receipt of application. Telephone calls during the application process are not encouraged. The Corporate Philanthropy and Citizenship Department handles giving. A contributions committee reviews all requests. Application form required. Applicants should submit the following:
1) copy of IRS Determination Letter
2) copy of most recent annual report/audited financial statement/990
3) listing of board of directors, trustees, officers and other key people and their affiliations
4) copy of current year's organizational budget and/or project budget

Initial approach: Complete online application form
Copies of proposal: 1
Committee meeting date(s): Biannual
Deadline(s): None
Final notification: 6 to 8 weeks

Administrator: Polly O'Brien Morrow.

The Pitney Bowes Foundation

(formerly The Pitney Bowes Employees Involvement Fund, Inc.)
1 Elmcroft Rd., MSC 6101
Stamford, CT 06926-0700
FAX: (203) 460-5336;
E-mail: Kathleen.RyanMufson@pb.com;
URL: http://www.pb.com/Our-Company/Corporate-Responsibility/Community/index.shtml

Donor: Pitney Bowes Inc.
Contact: Kathleen Ryan Mufson, Pres.
Financial data (yr. ended 12/31/11): Assets, $11,264,894 (M); expenditures, $3,400,789; qualifying distributions, $3,400,789; giving activities include $3,352,159 for 180 grants (high: $1,294,500; low: $70).
Purpose and activities: The foundation supports programs designed to promote literacy and education.
Fields of interest: Education, early childhood education; Higher education; Adult/continuing education; Adult education—literacy, basic skills & GED; Education, continuing education; Education, services; Education, reading; Education; Employment, services; Employment, training; Employment; Youth development, adult & child programs; Engineering Disabilities, people with; Minorities; Women.
Programs:
Global Grants for Volunteerism: The foundation awards grants to nonprofit organizations with which employees and retirees of Pitney Bowes volunteer; $125 grants for 25 hours of service; $250 grants for 50 hours of service; and $500 grants for 100 hours of service.
Literacy and Education Program: The foundation supports literacy and education programs designed to promote workforce preparation; and give individuals the skills they need to succeed through partnerships with national and local nonprofit organizations. The foundation supports early childhood education, after-school initiatives, mentoring, literacy, and job training. Special emphasis is directed toward higher education at two- and four-year colleges; continuing education programs that focus on curriculum improvement and attracting minorities; and communication and engineering.
Local Community Grants: The foundation supports programs designed to close the academic achievement gap and prepare the future workforce; target diverse populations including women, minorities, and the disabled; and organizations with which Pitney Bowes employees are strongly involved.
Matching Gifts Program: The foundation matches contributions made by employees of Pitney Bowes on a one-for-one basis and retirees of Pitney Bowes on a two-for-one basis to nonprofit organizations up to $5,000 per contributor, per year. Through the Employment Involvement Campaign, the fund matches contributions made by employees of Pitney Bowes to Pitney Bowes Relief Fund, United Way, and public charities up to $50,000 per employee, per year.
Type of support: Curriculum development; Employee matching gifts; Employee volunteer services; General/operating support; Program development.
Geographic limitations: Giving primarily in areas of company operations in Bridgeport, Danbury, Hartford, Shelton, and Stamford, CT, Washington, DC, Atlanta, GA, Boston and Waltham, MA, Grand Rapids, MI, Albany and Troy, NY, Chesapeake, VA, Dallas, TX, Spokane, WA, and Appleton, WI; giving also to national organizations.
Support limitations: No support for religious organizations not of direct benefit to the entire community, political candidates or lobbying organizations, organizations with limited constituency including fraternal, labor, veterans' groups, or business associations, anti-business groups, discriminatory organizations, or single disease health organizations. No grants to individuals, or for conferences, sporting events, auctions, trade shows, or other one-time short term events, sponsorships, advertising or television programming, team sponsorships or athletic scholarships, fundraising, or indirect costs that exceeds 20% of program budget.
Publications: Application guidelines.
Application information: Applications accepted. Support is limited to 1 contribution per organization during any given year. Application form required. Applicants should submit the following:
1) qualifications of key personnel
2) copy of IRS Determination Letter
3) copy of most recent annual report/audited financial statement/990
4) how project's results will be evaluated or measured
5) listing of board of directors, trustees, officers and other key people and their affiliations
6) detailed description of project and amount of funding requested
7) copy of current year's organizational budget and/or project budget
8) listing of additional sources and amount of support
9) brief history of organization and description of its mission
10) statement of problem project will address
11) geographic area to be served
12) population served

Initial approach: Complete online application
Board meeting date(s): Quarterly
Deadline(s): Jan. 15 and June 1 for Literacy and Education; Feb. 15, May 15, Aug. 15, and Oct. 15 for Local Community Grants
Final notification: 4 to 6 months for Literacy and Education

Officers and Directors:* Kathleen Ryan Mufson*, Pres.; Russell Hochman, Secy.; Michael Monahan*, Treas.; Johnna G. Torsone; Juanita James; Murray D. Martin.
Number of staff: 1 full-time professional; 1 part-time professional.
EIN: 200523317

The Pitney Bowes Relief Fund Charitable Trust

1 Elmcroft Rd., MSC 6101
Stamford, CT 06926-0700 (203) 351-6669
URL: http://www.pb.com/communityinvestments

Donor: Pitney Bowes Inc.
Financial data (yr. ended 08/31/11): Revenue, $194,563; assets, $430,011 (M); gifts received, $194,563; expenditures, $157,660; giving activities include $82,920 for grants.
Purpose and activities: The trust meets the immediate needs of employees of Pitney Bowes and others who have sustained significant property damage or other losses as a result of personal tragedy or natural disasters.
Fields of interest: Safety/disasters.
Type of support: Grants to individuals.
Geographic limitations: Giving primarily in the U.S.
Publications: Annual report.
Trustees: Bruce Donatuti; Tom Gawlak; Eileen Springer.
EIN: 223198214

2985
The Pittsburgh Associates

(also known as Pittsburgh Pirates)
115 Federal St.
P.O. Box 7000
Pittsburgh, PA 15212-5707 (412) 323-5000

Company URL: http://pittsburgh.pirates.mlb.com
Establishment information: Established in 1891.
Company type: Private company
Business activities: Operates professional baseball club.
Business type (SIC): Commercial sports
Corporate officers: Bob Nutting, Chair.; Frank Coonelly, Pres.; Jim Plake, Exec. V.P. and C.F.O.; Bryan Stroh, V.P. and Genl. Counsel; Patricia Paytas, V.P., Public Affairs
Board of director: Bob Nutting, Chair.
Giving statement: Giving through the Pittsburgh Pirates Corporate Giving Program.

Pittsburgh Pirates Corporate Giving Program

c/o Community Rels.
115 Federal St.
Pittsburgh, PA 15212-5724 (412) 325-4992
FAX: (412) 325-4944; URL: http://pirates.com/community

Purpose and activities: The Pittsburgh Pirates make charitable contributions of memorabilia and game tickets to nonprofit organizations on a case by case basis. Support is limited to the greater Pittsburgh, Pennsylvania, area and the Ohio, Pennsylvania, and West Virginia tri-state area.
Fields of interest: General charitable giving.
Type of support: Donated products; In-kind gifts.
Geographic limitations: Giving limited to the greater Pittsburgh, PA, area and the OH, PA, and WV tri-state area.
Publications: Corporate giving report.
Application information: Applications accepted. The Community Relations Department handles giving. Telephone calls are not encouraged. Support is limited to 1 contribution per organization during any given year. Application form required. Applicants should submit the following:
1) name, address and phone number of organization
2) contact person

Applications should include the organization's Tax ID Number; and the name, date, and a description of the event; and indicate the type of fundraiser.
Initial approach: Complete online application form
Number of staff: 1 full-time professional; 1 full-time support.

2986
Pittsburgh Steelers Sports, Inc.

3400 S. Water St.
P.O. Box 6763
Pittsburgh, PA 15203 (412) 432-7800

Company URL: http://www.steelers.com
Establishment information: Established in 1933.
Company type: Private company
Business activities: Operates professional football club.
Business type (SIC): Commercial sports
Corporate officers: Daniel M. Rooney, Chair.; Arthur J. Rooney II, Pres.
Board of director: Daniel M. Rooney, Chair.
Giving statement: Giving through the Pittsburgh Steelers Sports, Inc. Corporate Giving Program.

Pittsburgh Steelers Sports, Inc. Corporate Giving Program

c/o Community Rels.
3400 S. Water St.
Pittsburgh, PA 15203-2349
Application address for mascot appearances: Steely McBeam Appearances, 100 Art Rooney Ave., Pittsburgh, PA 15212; URL: http://www.steelers.com/community/index.html

Purpose and activities: The Pittsburgh Steelers make charitable contributions to nonprofit organizations on a case by case basis. Support is given primarily in the western Pennsylvania tri-state area.
Fields of interest: Education; Hospitals (general); Public health, physical fitness; Health care, patient services; Cancer; Breast cancer; Athletics/sports, football; Boys & girls clubs; Salvation Army; Human services, gift distribution; General charitable giving Youth.
Programs:
High School Coach of the Week: The Steelers selects and honors a local high school coach weekly for their contribution to football. The honor includes game tickets and a ceremony during the two-minute warning at a Steelers home game. The High School Coach of the Year is also selected at the end of the football season.
NFL Play 60: The Steelers encourages kids to be physically active for 60 minutes each day to combat childhood obesity. The program demonstrates the importance of fitness and activity and includes the What Moves U campaign, a health and fitness program that incorporates classroom curriculum with physical activity for middle school students.
Type of support: Donated products; In-kind gifts; Income development; Loaned talent.
Geographic limitations: Giving primarily in areas of company operations in the western PA tri-state area.
Support limitations: No game ticket donations.
Publications: Application guidelines.
Application information: Applications accepted. Proposals should be submitted using organization letterhead. Support is limited to 1 contribution per organization during any given year. The Community Relations Department handles giving. Application form not required. Applicants should submit the following:
1) name, address and phone number of organization
2) descriptive literature about organization
3) detailed description of project and amount of funding requested

Proposals should indicate the date of the event and the type of fundraiser; and include return shipping labels and the e-mail address of the organization, if available.
Initial approach: Proposal to headquarters for memorabilia donations and player appearances; proposal to application address for mascot appearances
Copies of proposal: 1
Deadline(s): 6 weeks prior to need for memorabilia donations and player appearances; 30 days prior to need for mascot appearances

2987
Pivotal Production LLC

516 N. Ogden Ave., Ste. 139
Chicago, IL 60642-6421 (773) 983-6328

Company URL: http://www.pivotalchicago.com
Establishment information: Established in 2007.
Company type: Private company
Business type (SIC): Business services/miscellaneous
Corporate officer: Shannon Downey, Pres.
Giving statement: Giving through the Pivotal Production LLC Contributions Program.

Pivotal Production LLC Contributions Program

516 N. Ogden Ave., Ste. 139
Chicago, IL 60642-6421 (773) 983-6328
E-mail: events@pivotalchicago.com; URL: http://www.pivotalchicago.com

Purpose and activities: Pivotal Production is a certified B Corporation that donates a percentage of net profits to charitable organizations.

2988
Pizza Hut, Inc.

14841 Dallas Pkwy.
Dallas, TX 75254 (972) 338-7700

Company URL: http://www.pizzahut.com
Establishment information: Established in 1958.
Company type: Subsidiary of a public company
Business activities: Operates restaurants.
Business type (SIC): Restaurants and drinking places
Financial profile for 2010: Number of employees, 600; sales volume, $16,390,000,000
Corporate officers: Scott O. Bergren, Pres. and C.E.O.; Patrick C. Murtha, C.O.O.; David Gibbs, C.F.O.
Giving statement: Giving through the Pizza Hut, Inc. Corporate Giving Program.

Pizza Hut, Inc. Corporate Giving Program

c/o Community Rels.
14841 Dallas Pkwy.
Dallas, TX 75254-7685
For the BOOK IT! Program: P.O. Box 2999, Wichita, KS, 67201; For the BOOK IT! Program in Canada: Zerina Pai, YUM! Restaurants International

(Canada) LP, 101 Exchange Ave., Vaughan, Ontario L4K 5R6, tel.: (416) 664-5316, fax: (416) 739-6158, e-mail: Zerina.Pai@yum.com; For the BOOK IT! Program in Puerto Rico: Veronica Sanchez, Encanto Restaurants, Inc., Amelia Industrial Park, Diana St., Guaynabo, PR 00968, tel.: (787) 277-7765, fax: (787) 277-7783, e-mail: veronica.sanchez@encantopr.com; URL: http://www.pizzahut.com/ContactUs/CorporateContributionGuidelines.aspx
Additional URL: http://www.bookitprogram.com

Purpose and activities: Pizza Hut makes charitable contributions to nonprofit organizations involved with the arts, reading, and food services. Special emphasis is directed towards programs designed to encourage at-risk youth to express themselves through the arts. Support is given on a national basis, with emphasis on Dallas, Texas, and in Canada and Puerto Rico.
Fields of interest: Arts; Elementary/secondary education; Education, early childhood education; Education, reading; Education; Food services; Youth development Economically disadvantaged.
International interests: Canada.
Program:
BOOK IT! National Reading Incentive Program: Through the BOOK IT! National Reading Incentive Program, Pizza Hut makes charitable contributions of gift certificates to K-6 schools. Teachers award the gift certificates to students in return for attaining reading goals established by the teachers.
Type of support: General/operating support; In-kind gifts; Program development.
Geographic limitations: Giving on a national basis, with emphasis on Dallas, TX, and in Canada and Puerto Rico.
Support limitations: No support for religious or political organizations. No grants to individuals, or for athletic groups, activities, or fundraisers, endowments, capital campaigns, or memorials, religious organizations or programs, travel expenses for school groups or individuals, or medical care.
Application information: Applications accepted.
Initial approach: Contact nearest restaurant for application information; mail proposal to headquarters for funding requests for arts programs in the Dallas-Fort Worth, TX area; complete online application form for BOOK IT! Program
Deadline(s): June for BOOK IT! Program

2989
The Plain Dealer Publishing Company

1801 Superior Ave. E
Plain Dealer Plz.
Cleveland, OH 44114-2107 (216) 999-5000

Company URL: http://www.plaindealer.com/contact/index.php
Establishment information: Established in 1842.
Company type: Subsidiary of a private company
Business activities: Publishes newspapers.
Business type (SIC): Newspaper publishing and/or printing
Corporate officers: Terrance C.Z. Egger, Pres. and C.E.O; Virginia Wang, Sr. V.P. and C.F.O.; Andrea Hogben, Sr. V.P., Sales and Mktg.; William Calaiacovo, Sr. V.P., Human Resources
Offices: Columbus, Medina, Northfield, OH
Giving statement: Giving through the Plain Dealer Charities, Inc.

Plain Dealer Charities, Inc.

1801 Superior Ave.
Cleveland, OH 44114-2107 (216) 999-4461

Establishment information: Established in 1960 in OH.
Financial data (yr. ended 05/31/12): Revenue, $217,445; assets, $274,195 (M); gifts received, $211,648; expenditures, $227,200; giving activities include $227,000 for grants.
Purpose and activities: Support primarily to assist social service organizations in the greater Cleveland, Ohio, area; giving also for the arts, education, health, and youth.
Fields of interest: Museums; Performing arts; Higher education; Education; Public health; Youth development; Human services; American Red Cross; Community/economic development.
Geographic limitations: Giving primarily in the greater Cleveland, OH, area.
Officers: Shirley D. Stineman, Pres.; Terrance C.Z. Egger, V.P.; Virginia Wang, Secy.-Treas.
Trustees: Robert M. Long; Clara Roberts.
EIN: 340941992

2990
Playboy Enterprises, Inc.

680 N. Lake Shore Dr., Ste. 1500
Chicago, IL 60611 (312) 751-8000

Company URL: http://www.playboyenterprises.com
Establishment information: Established in 1953.
Company type: Private company
Business activities: Publishes magazines; produces television programming; produces DVDs; provides catalog shopping services; provides Internet entertainment services.
Business type (SIC): Periodical publishing and/or printing; nonstore retailers; computer services; motion pictures/production and services allied to
Corporate officers: Scott N. Flanders, Chair. and C.E.O.; Alex L. Vaickus, Pres.; Christopher M. Pachler, Exec. V.P. and C.F.O.; Rachel Sagan, Exec. V.P., and Genl. Counsel; Kendice K. Briggs, Sr. V.P., Human Resources; Theresa (Hennessey) Barcy, V.P., Public Rels.
Board of director: Scott N. Flanders, Chair.
Office: Chicago, IL
Giving statement: Giving through the Playboy Foundation.
Company EIN: 364249478

The Playboy Foundation

680 N. Lake Shore Dr.
Chicago, IL 60611-4455
FAX: (312) 266-8506;
E-mail: pbfoundation@playboy.com; E-mail for HMH First Amendment Awards: hmhfaa@playboy.com; URL: http://www.playboyenterprises.com/foundation

Contact: Matthew Pakula, Dir.
Purpose and activities: Through the Playboy Foundation, a direct corporate giving program, Playboy makes charitable contributions to nonprofit organizations that protect the rights of the individual in a free society. Special emphasis is directed toward programs that promote First Amendment Rights, support socially aware documentary filmmakers, and uphold civil rights and civil liberties. Support is given on a national basis.
Fields of interest: Media, film/video; Reproductive health, family planning; AIDS; Civil liberties, advocacy; Civil liberties, first amendment; Civil/human rights.
Programs:
Freedom of Expression Award: Through the Freedom of Expression Award, Playboy awards $25,000 to a nominee who has a project or program dedicated to defending, advocating, or supporting the First Amendment through their personal or professional pursuits. A successful nominee should demonstrate a promising future as a First Amendment advocate based on their history or accomplishment and the potential for the award to facilitate additional work. Preference is given to nominees who would benefit from having financing to relieve inhibitions or burdens of pursuing the First Amendment ideals of their program or project.
Hugh M. Hefner First Amendment Awards: Through the Hugh M. Hefner First Amendment Awards program, Playboy Enterprises honors individuals who have made significant contributions to the ongoing effort to protect and enhance First Amendment rights for all Americans, including high school students, lawyers, journalists and educators have been honored. Nominees traditionally come from the areas of journalism, arts and entertainment, education, publishing, law and government, and winners are selected by a panel of distinguished judges. The winners are given a cash award of $10,000 and a commemorative plaque.
Matching Gifts Program: Playboy Enterprises matches contributions made by its employees to nonprofit organizations on a one-for-one basis up to $1,000 per employee, per year.
Social Change Documentary Film Grant Program: Through the Social Change Documentary Film Grant Program, Playboy Enterprises supports film projects that have nationwide impact and scope. Grants range from $1,000 to $5,000 and are limited to projects in post-production and distribution.
Type of support: Cause-related marketing; Donated equipment; Donated products; Employee matching gifts; Employee volunteer services; Film/video/radio; General/operating support; Grants to individuals; In-kind gifts; Use of facilities.
Geographic limitations: Giving on a national basis, with emphasis on Los Angeles, CA, and Chicago, IL.
Support limitations: No support for religious organizations or international organizations. No grants for research or writing projects, scholarships, capital campaigns, endowments, debt reduction, conferences or symposia, or direct service programs.
Publications: Application guidelines.
Application information: Applications accepted. Proposals for Social Change Documentary Film Grant Program should include a copy of your film or rough-cut on DVD. The Corporate Communications Department handles giving. Application form not required. Applicants should submit the following:
1) qualifications of key personnel
2) copy of IRS Determination Letter
3) brief history of organization and description of its mission
4) copy of most recent annual report/audited financial statement/990
5) listing of board of directors, trustees, officers and other key people and their affiliations
6) detailed description of project and amount of funding requested
7) copy of current year's organizational budget and/or project budget

Freedom of Expression nomination forms should include a description of the candidate's contribution to First Amendment Rights, a resume, and a list of references.
Initial approach: Letter of inquiry; download nomination form for Freedom of Expression Award and mail; proposal for Social Change Documentary Film Grant Program

Copies of proposal: 1
Deadline(s): None; May 1 to June 30 for Social Change Documentary Film Grant Program
Number of staff: 1 full-time professional; 1 part-time professional.

2991
Plum Creek Timber Company, Inc.

(formerly Plum Creek Timber Company, L.P.)
999 3rd Ave., Ste. 4300
Seattle, WA 98104-4096 (206) 467-3600
FAX: (302) 655-5049

Company URL: http://www.plumcreek.com
Establishment information: Established in 1989.
Company type: Public company
Company ticker symbol and exchange: PCL/NYSE
International Securities Identification Number: US7292511083
Business activities: Operates timber tracts; operates real estate investment trust.
Business type (SIC): Investors/miscellaneous; forestry—timber tracts
Financial profile for 2012: Number of employees, 1,223; assets, $4,384,000,000; sales volume, $1,339,000,000; pre-tax net income, $200,000,000; expenses, $1,058,000,000; liabilities, $3,161,000,000
Corporate officers: John F. Morgan, Sr., Chair.; Thomas M. Lindquist, Pres. and C.O.O.; Rick R. Holley, C.E.O.; David W. Lambert, Sr. V.P. and C.F.O.; James A. Kraft, Sr. V.P., Genl. Counsel, and Secy.; David A. Brown, V.P. and C.A.O.; Mark A. Miller, V.P. and C.I.O.; Laura B. Smith, V.P. and Treas.; Joan K. Fitzmaurice, V.P., Corp. Comms.; Barbara L. Crowe, V.P., Human Resources
Board of directors: John F. Morgan, Sr., Chair.; Rick R. Holley; Robin Josephs; John G. McDonald; Robert B. McLeod; Marc F. Racicot; Lawrence A. Selzer; Stephen C. Tobias; Martin A. White
Subsidiary: Plum Creek Manufacturing, L.P., Spokane, WA
Giving statement: Giving through the Plum Creek Foundation.
Company EIN: 911912863

Plum Creek Foundation

999 3rd Ave., Ste. 4300
Seattle, WA 98104-4096 (206) 467-3664
FAX: (206) 467-3795;
E-mail: foundation@plumcreek.com; Contact for Montana Great Classroom Awards: Renee Erickson, tel.: (406) 892-6227, e-mail: renee.erickson@plumcreek.com; URL: http://www.plumcreek.com/CommunityInvolvement/tabid/69/Default.aspx

Establishment information: Established in 1993 in WA.
Donors: Plum Creek Timber Co., L.P.; Plum Creek Timber Co., Inc.
Contact: Kristen Smith, V.P.
Financial data (yr. ended 12/31/10): Assets, $65,728 (M); gifts received, $1,470,000; expenditures, $1,433,939; qualifying distributions, $1,433,666; giving activities include $1,200,865 for 298 grants (high: $50,000; low: $300), $63,450 for 21 grants to individuals (high: $6,461; low: $285) and $169,351 for 256 employee matching gifts.
Purpose and activities: The foundation supports organizations involved with arts and culture, education, the environment, health, youth development, human services, community development, and civic affairs. Special emphasis is directed toward programs designed to improve the quality of life and provide services that would not otherwise be available to residents in areas of company operations.
Fields of interest: Museums; Performing arts; Arts; Elementary/secondary education; Higher education; Libraries (public); Education; Environmental education; Environment; Hospitals (general); Health care; Food banks; Disasters, fire prevention/control; Girl scouts; Youth development; American Red Cross; Children/youth, services; Human services; Community/economic development; Public affairs.
Programs:
Arts: The foundation supports programs designed to creatively deliver quality arts and performance programs and events.
Community: The foundation supports programs designed to improve the quality of life and provide services that would not otherwise be available to residents in areas of company operations. Special emphasis is directed toward programs designed to target smaller, rural communities that do not have access to other funding.
Education: The foundation supports programs designed to enhance the learning experience for students of all ages; and help students become self sufficient and productive within their communities.
Employee Matching Gifts: The foundation matches contributions made by employees of Plum Creek to nonprofit organizations and educational institutions. The foundation matches employee donations of money and time.
Environment: The foundation supports programs designed to promote environmental stewardship and awareness; and teach environmental education.
Montana Great Classroom Awards Program: The foundation awards grants to public K-12 teachers to enhance the learning environment in the classroom and enrich educational experiences of students. The program is designed to promote teacher innovation, learning opportunities beyond the core curriculum, and opportunities to get youth excited about learning. The program is limited to Flathead, Granite, Lake, Lewis & Clark, Lincoln, Mineral, Missoula, Powell, Ravalli, and Sanders counties, MT. Grants range from $2,000 to $5,000.
Plum Creek Community Scholarship: The foundation awards $1,000 scholarships to high school seniors located in Plum Creek Operating areas to pursue education at a university or vocational school. The program is administered by Scholarship America.
Type of support: Building/renovation; Employee matching gifts; Employee volunteer services; Employee-related scholarships; Equipment; Grants to individuals; Program development.
Geographic limitations: Giving primarily in areas of company operations in AL, AR, FL, GA, LA, ME, MI, MS, MT, NH, OK, OR, SC, TX, VT, WA, WI, and WV.
Support limitations: No support for religious organizations not of direct benefit to the entire community, veterans' or fraternal organizations, national health organizations, Chambers of Commerce or taxpayer associations, or political organizations or candidates. No grants to individuals (except for the Plum Creek Scholarship Program and Montana Great Classroom awards), or for salaries, stipends, or other forms of compensation, endowments, fundraising events, tickets, dinners, or telethons, corporate memberships, general operating support for United Way agencies, or political campaigns; no loans or land donations.
Publications: Annual report; Application guidelines; Grants list; Program policy statement.
Application information: Applications accepted. Applications for Montana Great Classroom Awards must be approved by the school's principal or district administrator. Faxed or e-mailed applications are not accepted. Support is limited to 1 contribution per organization during any given year. Application form required. Applicants should submit the following:
1) timetable for implementation and evaluation of project
2) statement of problem project will address
3) copy of IRS Determination Letter
4) copy of most recent annual report/audited financial statement/990
5) how project's results will be evaluated or measured
6) listing of board of directors, trustees, officers and other key people and their affiliations
7) detailed description of project and amount of funding requested
8) copy of current year's organizational budget and/or project budget
9) listing of additional sources and amount of support

Initial approach: Download application form and mail to foundation
Copies of proposal: 1
Board meeting date(s): Mar., June, Sept., and Dec.
Deadline(s): Postmarked by Jan. 31, Apr. 30, July 30, and Oct. 31; June 1 and Dec. 1 for Montana Great Classroom Awards
Final notification: 2 weeks following board meeting; Feb. and Aug. for Montana Great Classroom Awards
Officers and Trustees:* James A. Kraft*, Chair.; Robert J. Jirsa*, Pres.; Kirsten D. Smith, V.P.; Julie Stewart, Secy.; Elizabeth J. Duxbury, Treas.; Jacey Barnaby; Charlie Becker; Christie Bennett; Charlie Cornish; Pete Coutu; Paul Davis; Bill Dempsey; Mark A. Doty; Ben Dow; Rose Fagler; Greg Galpin; Steve Hanley; Rebecca Hendrix; Scott D. Henker; Rob Hicks; Jenny Krueger; Dan Lemke; Luke Muzzy; Bill O'Brion; Todd Powell; Tricia Quinn; Tom Ray; Charlie Reece; Thomas M. Reed; Jim Rundorff; Mark Sherman; Jerry Sorensen; Richard Stitch; Jack Thomas; Arnulfo Zendejas.
EIN: 911621028
Selected grants: The following grants are a representative sample of this grantmaker's funding activity:
$50,000 to Nature Conservancy of Montana, Helena, MT, 2010.
$50,000 to University of Montana Foundation, Missoula, MT, 2010.
$10,000 to American Red Cross, Des Moines, IA, 2010.
$10,000 to East Gainesville Development Corporation, Gainesville, FL, 2010.
$10,000 to Food Bank of Northeast Georgia, Athens, GA, 2010.
$10,000 to Jobs for Maine's Graduates, Augusta, ME, 2010.
$10,000 to Rebuilding Together North Central Florida, Gainesville, FL, 2010.
$9,999 to Girl Scouts of the U.S.A., Gainesville, FL, 2010.
$7,500 to Long Live the Kings, Seattle, WA, 2010.
$7,500 to Northeast Louisiana Arts Council, West Monroe, LA, 2010.

2992
Plum Organics
391 Broadway, Ste. 3F
New York, NY 10013-3572 (978) 475-0358

Company URL: http://www.plumorganics.com
Establishment information: Established in 2005.
Company type: Private company
Business type (SIC): Business services/ miscellaneous
Corporate officers: Gigi Lee Chang, Pres.; Brian Banks, V.P., Sales
Giving statement: Giving through the Plum Organics Corporate Giving Program.

Plum Organics Corporate Giving Program
391 Broadway, Ste. 3F
New York, NY 10013-3572 (877) 914-7586
E-mail: info@plumorganics.com; URL: http:// www.plumorganics.com

Purpose and activities: Plum Organics is a certified B Corporation that donates a percentage of its profits to charitable organizations.
Fields of interest: Environment, toxics; Nutrition; Youth development, public education Children.
Type of support: Cause-related marketing; General/ operating support; Sponsorships.

2993
Plymouth Foam, Inc.
1800 Sunset Dr.
P.O. Box 407
Plymouth, WI 53073-3539 (920) 893-0535
FAX: (920) 892-4986

Company URL: http://www.plymouthfoam.com
Establishment information: Established in 1978.
Company type: Private company
Business activities: Manufactures plastic foam products.
Business type (SIC): Plastic products/ miscellaneous
Corporate officers: Thomas R. Testwuide, Sr., Chair.; Tec Roberts, Vice-Chair.; David Bolland, Pres., C.E.O., and C.O.O.; Jason P. Hassel, V.P. and C.F.O.; Thomas Groth, V.P., Sales and Mktg.; Karen Bouchard, Secy.
Board of director: Thomas R. Testwuide, Sr., Chair.
Plants: Becker, MN; Newcomerstown, OH; Plymouth, WI
Giving statement: Giving through the Plymouth Foam Foundation, Inc.

Plymouth Foam Foundation, Inc.
1800 Sunset Dr.
Plymouth, WI 53073-3539

Establishment information: Established in 2005 in WI.
Donors: Plymouth Foam, Inc.; Diana L. Roberts; Diana L. Shircel.
Financial data (yr. ended 12/31/11): Assets, $476,258 (M); gifts received, $147,724; expenditures, $58,127; qualifying distributions, $57,591; giving activities include $57,591 for grants.
Purpose and activities: The foundation supports organizations involved with arts and culture, secondary education, cystic fibrosis, and Christianity.
Fields of interest: Education; Housing/shelter; Religion.
Type of support: General/operating support.
Geographic limitations: Giving primarily in WI.
Support limitations: No grants to individuals.
Application information: Applications not accepted. Unsolicited requests for funds not accepted.
Officers and Directors:* David S. Bolland*, Pres. and Secy.; Karen Nytes*, V.P. and Treas.; Diana E. Roberts; Karen Rooker; Diana L. Shircel.
EIN: 203995483

2994
PMC Global Incorporated
12243 Branford St.
Sun Valley, CA 91352-1010
(818) 896-1101
FAX: (818) 897-0180

Company URL: http://www.pmcglobalinc.com
Establishment information: Established in 1964.
Company type: Private company
Business activities: Manufactures chemicals, equipment, and miscellaneous plastic products.
Business type (SIC): Chemicals/industrial inorganic; plastics and synthetics; chemicals/ industrial organic
Financial profile for 2010: Number of employees, 3,600
Corporate officers: Philip E. Kamins, Pres. and C.E.O.; Jeff Erickson, Exec. V.P., Sales and Mktg.; Thian C. Cheong, C.F.O.; Jim Bauer, Co-C.I.O.; Harout Samuelian, Co-C.I.O.; David Keller, Corp. Cont.
Giving statement: Giving through the PMC Foundation.

The PMC Foundation
12243 Branford St.
Sun Valley, CA 91352-1010

Establishment information: Established in 1988.
Donor: PMC Global Inc.
Financial data (yr. ended 10/31/11): Assets, $0 (M); gifts received, $61,949; expenditures, $61,949; qualifying distributions, $61,949; giving activities include $60,109 for 21 grants to individuals (high: $6,600; low: $1,444).
Purpose and activities: The foundation awards college scholarships to dependents and children of employees of Wilsonart International.
Fields of interest: Higher education.
Type of support: Employee-related scholarships.
Application information: Applications not accepted. Unsolicited requests for funds not accepted.
Officers and Directors:* Philip E. Kamins*, Chair. and Pres.; Thian C. Cheong*, Exec. V.P. and Secy.-Treas.
EIN: 954194948

2995
PMI Mortgage Insurance Co.
3003 Oak Rd.
Walnut Creek, CA 94597 (925) 658-7878
FAX: (925) 658-6944

Company URL: http://www.pmigroup.com/ index2.html
Establishment information: Established in 1993.
Company type: Subsidiary of a public company
Business activities: Sells mortgage insurance.
Business type (SIC): Insurance/surety
Corporate officers: L. Stephen Smith, C.E.O.; Andrew D. Cameron, Pres. and Genl. Counsel; Chris A. Hovey, C.O.O.; Thomas H. Jeter, Jr., C.F.O. and C.A.O.; Joe Lynch, Sr. V.P. and C.I.O.; Ray D. Chang, Sr. V.P. and Corp. Treas.; Leslie R. Marquart, Sr. V.P. and Corp. Cont.; Charles F. Broom, Sr. V.P., Human Resources
Board of director: L. Stephen Smith, Chair.
Giving statement: Giving through the PMI Foundation.

The PMI Foundation
3003 Oak Rd.
Walnut Creek, CA 94597-4541 (925) 658-6252
FAX: (925) 658-6944; Additional tel.: (800) 288-1970; URL: http://www.pmifoundation.org./

Establishment information: Established in 2000 in CA.
Donor: PMI Mortgage Insurance Co.
Contact: Laura Kinney, Mgr.
Financial data (yr. ended 12/31/11): Assets, $0 (M); gifts received, $375,010; expenditures, $245,760; qualifying distributions, $231,488; giving activities include $231,488 for grants.
Purpose and activities: The foundation supports organizations involved with arts and culture, education, the environment, health, law and justice, employment training, safety education, human services, and public policy. Special emphasis is directed toward programs designed to create housing opportunities; and revitalize neighborhoods in communities.
Fields of interest: Arts education; Media, television; Media, radio; Arts; Elementary/secondary education; Higher education; Graduate/ professional education; Education, reading; Education; Environment; Health care; Crime/law enforcement; Employment, training; Housing/ shelter, development; Housing/shelter; Safety, education; Children, day care; Youth, services; Aging, centers/services; Developmentally disabled, centers & services; Human services; Community development, neighborhood development; Community/economic development; Public policy, research Economically disadvantaged.
Programs:
Arts and Culture: The foundation supports cultural centers, museums, libraries, botanical gardens, and zoos; public radio and television; and arts education programs.
Civic and Community: The foundation supports housing and economic development organizations; neighborhood groups; environment and public policy organizations; government groups; law and justice organizations; and job training and skill development programs.
Education: The foundation supports day-care facilities; pre-collegiate (K-12 grades) education; community colleges, colleges, universities, graduate schools, and agencies promoting educational access; safety education; and literacy training.
Health and Human Services: The foundation supports organizations involved with health and human services and programs designed to provide aid to the disabled, youth groups, and senior citizens.
Type of support: Employee matching gifts; General/ operating support; Program development; Scholarship funds; Sponsorships.
Geographic limitations: Giving primarily in CA.
Support limitations: No support for fraternal, veterans', labor, athletic, or religious organizations not of direct benefit to the entire community, political or lobbying organizations, or political candidates. No grants to individuals, or for travel, films, videotapes, or audio productions.

Application information: Applications not accepted. Unsolicited applications are currently not accepted.
Officers: Charles Broom, Pres.; David Katkov, V.P.; Victoria Vazquez, Secy.; Jesse Gentry, C.F.O.; Ray Chang, Treas.
EIN: 943309069
Selected grants: The following grants are a representative sample of this grantmaker's funding activity:
$70,350 to Habitat for Humanity International, Americus, GA, 2010.
$60,000 to Social Compact, Washington, DC, 2010.
$15,000 to Habitat for Humanity International, Americus, GA, 2010.
$2,500 to American Cancer Society, Atlanta, GA, 2010.
$2,500 to Habitat for Humanity Greater San Francisco, San Francisco, CA, 2010.

2996
PNC Bank, N.A.

1 PNC Plz.
249 5th Ave.
Pittsburgh, PA 15222 (412) 762-2000

Company URL: http://www.pnc.com
Company type: Subsidiary of a public company
Ultimate parent company: The PNC Financial Services Group, Inc.
International Securities Identification Number: US6934751057
Business activities: Operates commercial bank.
Business type (SIC): Banks/commercial
Corporate officers: James E. Rohr, Chair. and C.E.O.; Thomas K. Whitford, Vice-Chair.; William S. Demchak, Pres.; Richard J. Johnson, C.F.O.; Gregory Kozich, C.I.O.; E. William Parsley III, Treas. and C.I.O; Robert F. Hoyt, Genl. Counsel
Board of directors: James E. Rohr, Chair.; Thomas K. Whitford, Vice-Chair.; Richard O. Berndt; Charles E. Bunch; Paul W. Chellgren; Kay Coles James; Richard B. Kelson; Bruce C. Lindsay; Anthony A. Massaro; Jane G. Pepper; Donald J. Shepard; Lorene K. Steffes; Dennis F. Strigl; Thomas J. Usher; George H. Walls, Jr.; Helge H. Wehmeier
Giving statement: Giving through the PNC Memorial Foundation.

PNC Memorial Foundation

(formerly PNC Bank Memorial Foundation)
c/o PNC Bank
620 Liberty Ave., 10th Fl.
Pittsburgh, PA 15222-2705 (412) 762-3502

Establishment information: Established in 1994 in PA.
Donor: PNC Bank, N.A.
Contact: R. Bruce Bickel
Financial data (yr. ended 12/31/11): Assets, $180,590 (M); expenditures, $9,543; qualifying distributions, $6,000; giving activities include $6,000 for grants.
Purpose and activities: The foundation awards college scholarships to children of current employees and children of deceased employees who died during their period of employment at PNC Bank.
Type of support: Employee-related scholarships.
Geographic limitations: Giving limited to areas of company operations.
Application information: Applications not accepted. Unsolicited requests for funds not accepted.
Trustee: PNC Bank, N.A.
EIN: 256487950

2997
The PNC Financial Services Group, Inc.

(formerly PNC Bank Corp.)
1 PNC Plz.
249 5th Ave.
Pittsburgh, PA 15222-2707 (412) 762-2000

Company URL: http://www.pnc.com
Establishment information: Established in 1983.
Company type: Public company
Company ticker symbol and exchange: PNC/NYSE
Business activities: Operates financial holding company; operates commercial bank.
Business type (SIC): Banks/commercial; holding company
Financial profile for 2012: Number of employees, 56,285; assets, $305,107,000,000; pre-tax net income, $3,943,000,000; liabilities, $266,104,000,000
Fortune 1000 ranking: 2012—170th in revenues, 62nd in profits, and 19th in assets
Forbes 2000 ranking: 2012—564th in sales, 186th in profits, and 96th in assets
Corporate officers: James E. Rohr, Chair.; Joseph C. Guyaux, Sr. Vice-Chair.; William S. Demchak, Pres. and C.E.O.; Richard J. Johnson, C.F.O.; E. William Parsley III, C.I.O. and Treas.; Anuj Dhanda, C.I.O.; George P. Long III, Corp. Secy.; Gregory Kozich, Cont.; Robert F. Hoyt, Genl. Counsel
Board of directors: James E. Rohr, Chair.; Richard O. Berndt; Charles E. Bunch; Paul W. Chellgren; Kay Coles James; Richard B. Kelson; Bruce C. Lindsay; Anthony A. Massaro; Jane G. Pepper; Donald J. Shepard; Lorene K. Steffes; Dennis F. Strigl; Thomas J. Usher; George H. Walls, Jr.; Helge H. Wehmeier
Subsidiary: PNC Bank, N.A., Pittsburgh, PA
Historic mergers: Midlantic Corporation (December 31, 1995); United National Bancorp (January 1, 2004); Riggs National Corporation (May 13, 2005); National City Corporation (December 31, 2008)
Giving statement: Giving through the EFS Foundation, the PNC Foundation, and the Sterling Financial Foundation.
Company EIN: 251435979

EFS Foundation

(formerly Elgin Financial Foundation)
1695 Larkin Ave.
Elgin, IL 60123-5944 (847) 289-0513
E-mail: efsfoundation@efsfoundation.org;
URL: http://www.efsfoundation.org/

Establishment information: Established in 1998 in DE and IL as the Elgin Financial Foundation; current name adopted in 2004.
Donors: Elgin Financial Savings Bank; EFC Bancorp, Inc.
Contact: Ursula Wilson, Exec. Dir.
Financial data (yr. ended 12/31/11): Assets, $11,272,074 (M); expenditures, $625,758; qualifying distributions, $492,406; giving activities include $492,406 for grants.
Purpose and activities: The foundation supports programs designed to promote community development; and support community organizations that contribute to the quality of life in Elgin and surrounding communities. Special emphasis is directed toward programs designed to promote housing for low or moderate-income individuals; benefit local performing art groups; promote educational initiatives that enhance and expand youth development; and provide scholarship funds to local, deserving students.
Fields of interest: Performing arts; Higher education; Education; Health care; Housing/shelter, home owners; Housing/shelter; Boys & girls clubs; Youth development; Human services; Community/economic development Economically disadvantaged.
Type of support: Continuing support; Program development; Scholarship funds.
Geographic limitations: Giving limited to Carpentersville, East Dundee, Elgin, Hampshire, Huntley, South Elgin, and West Dundee, IL.
Support limitations: No support for discriminatory organizations or religious organizations not of direct benefit to the entire community. No grants for budget deficits, operating expenses for established programs, fundraising events by an organization for the benefit of another organization.
Publications: Application guidelines.
Application information: Applications accepted. Letters of inquiry should be no longer than 2 pages. A full proposal may be requested at a later date. If submitting proposals via mail, six individual packets must be submitted. Multi-year funding is not automatic. Support is limited to 1 contribution per organization during any given year. Application form required. Applicants should submit the following:
1) results expected from proposed grant
2) statement of problem project will address
3) population served
4) how project's results will be evaluated or measured
5) detailed description of project and amount of funding requested
6) copy of current year's organizational budget and/or project budget

Initial approach: E-mail or mail letter of inquiry; full proposal if invited
Board meeting date(s): May, Aug., and Nov.
Deadline(s): Feb. 15. May 15, and Aug. 15 for letters of inquiry; Mar. 31, June 30, and Sept. 30 for proposals
Final notification: Mid-May, Mid-Aug., and Mid-Nov. for proposals

Officers and Directors:* Thomas I. Anderson*, Chair. and Pres.; Randolph W. Brittain, Vice-Chair.; Ursula Wilson, Secy. and Exec. Dir.; James J. Kovac, Treas.; James A. Alpeter; Leo M. Flanagan, Jr.; Ralph W. Helm; Larry Narum; Barrett J. O'Connor; Thomas S. Rakow; Jack Shales; Peter A. Traeger.
Number of staff: 1 part-time professional.
EIN: 364219647
Selected grants: The following grants are a representative sample of this grantmaker's funding activity:
$40,000 to Habitat for Humanity of Northern Fox Valley, Carpentersvle, IL, 2006.
$30,000 to Creative Assistance Development, Elgin, IL, 2006.
$29,075 to Boys and Girls Clubs of Elgin, Elgin, IL, 2006.
$28,300 to YMCA of Elgin, Elgin, IL, 2006.
$15,000 to Elgin Symphony Orchestra, Elgin, IL, 2006.
$15,000 to Judson University, Elgin, IL, 2006.
$12,840 to Ecker Center for Mental Health, Elgin, IL, 2006.
$11,500 to Larkin Center, Elgin, IL, 2006.
$7,500 to Boy Scouts of America, Saint Charles, IL, 2006.
$5,000 to Glenwood School, Glenwood, IL, 2006.

The PNC Foundation

(formerly PNC Bank Foundation)
1 PNC Plz.
249 5th Ave., 20th Fl.
Pittsburgh, PA 15222-1119 (412) 762-2748
FAX: (412) 705-3584; E-mail: eva.blum@pnc.com;
Additional contact: Michael Labriola, Secy., tel.:

(412) 762-2803, e-mail: michael.labriola@pnc.com; URL: https://www.pncsites.com/pncfoundation/foundation_overview.html

Establishment information: Established in 1970 in PA.
Donors: PNC Equity Partners, LP; PNC Bank, N.A.; The PNC Financial Services Group, Inc.
Contact: Eva Tansky Blum, Chair. and Pres.
Financial data (yr. ended 12/31/11): Assets, $75,908,103 (M); gifts received, $1,405,026; expenditures, $58,723,250; qualifying distributions, $58,588,768; giving activities include $49,508,535 for 2,062 grants (high: $500,000; low: $100), $4,713,374 for 3,918 employee matching gifts and $472,917 for loans/program-related investments.
Purpose and activities: The foundation supports programs designed to enhance educational opportunities for children, with emphasis on underserved pre-K children; and to promote the growth of targeted communities through economic development initiatives.
Fields of interest: Arts education; Arts; Elementary/secondary education; Education, early childhood education; Child development, education; Teacher school/education; Environment; Employment, training; Housing/shelter, temporary shelter; Housing/shelter, home owners; Housing/shelter; Human services, financial counseling; Human services; Community development, neighborhood development; Economic development; Business/industry; Community development, small businesses; Community/economic development; Mathematics; Science Children; Economically disadvantaged.
Programs:

Affordable Housing: The foundation supports programs designed to promote affordable housing for low-and moderate-income individuals; provide counseling and services to help individuals maintain housing stock; offer transitional housing units and initiatives; and provide credit counseling assistance to individuals to help them prepare for homeownership.

Arts and Culture: The foundation supports cultural enrichment programs designed to benefit the community.

Community Development: The foundation supports programs designed to provide technical assistance to, or loans for, small businesses located in low-and moderate-income areas; and supports small businesses that employ low-and moderate-income individuals.

Community Services: The foundation supports programs designed to provide social services; job training; essential services; early learning and educational enrichment; and construction of community facilities for low-and moderate-income individuals and families.

Economic Development: The foundation supports programs designed to enhance quality of life through neighborhood revitalization, cultural enrichment, and human services. Special emphasis is directed toward programs designed to promote growth of targeted low-and moderate-income communities and/or provide services to those communities.

Education: The foundation supports educational programs for children and youth, teachers, and families, with emphasis on early education initiatives for low-and moderate-income children. Special emphasis is directed toward programs designed to promote math, science, the arts, or financial education; provide direct services for children in their classroom or community; foster professional development for teachers; promote family engagement in the early education of children being served by grants; and include volunteer opportunities for PNC employees.

Matching Gift Program: The foundation matches contributions made by employees of PNC Financial Services Group and its subsidiaries to educational institutions and human service organizations on a one-for-one basis from $50 to $2,500 per employee, per year.

PNC Grow Up Great: Through the PNC Grow Up Great 10-year initiative, the foundation supports programs designed to improve school readiness of children from birth to age five through grants to nonprofit organizations and early education centers involved with math, science, the arts, and financial education for young children.

Revitalization and Stabilization of Low-and Moderate-Income Areas: The foundation supports programs designed to improve living and working conditions of low-and moderate-income communities; eliminate blight; and attract and retain businesses and residents to the community.
Type of support: Building/renovation; Capital campaigns; Continuing support; Curriculum development; Employee matching gifts; General/operating support; Matching/challenge support; Program development; Program-related investments/loans; Publication.
Geographic limitations: Giving primarily in areas of company operations in Washington, DC, DE, FL, IL, IN, KY, MD, MI, MO, NJ, OH, TN, VA, and WI, with emphasis on PA.
Support limitations: No support for discriminatory organizations, churches, religious organizations, advocacy groups, or private foundations. No grants to individuals, or for endowments, conferences, seminars, tickets, or goodwill advertising, or annual campaigns for hospitals, colleges, or universities; no loans (except for program-related investments).
Publications: Application guidelines; Corporate report.
Application information: Applications accepted. Visit Web site for representative address information. An interview may be requested. Proposals may be submitted using the Delaware Valley Grantmakers, Greater Cincinnati Foundation, or Grantmakers of Western Pennsylvania Common Grant Application formats. Application form not required. Applicants should submit the following:
1) timetable for implementation and evaluation of project
2) how project will be sustained once grantmaker support is completed
3) qualifications of key personnel
4) statement of problem project will address
5) population served
6) name, address and phone number of organization
7) copy of IRS Determination Letter
8) brief history of organization and description of its mission
9) copy of most recent annual report/audited financial statement/990
10) how project's results will be evaluated or measured
11) descriptive literature about organization
12) listing of board of directors, trustees, officers and other key people and their affiliations
13) detailed description of project and amount of funding requested
14) copy of current year's organizational budget and/or project budget
15) listing of additional sources and amount of support
16) additional materials/documentation

Proposals should include a description of how the organization plans to address a PNC foundation funding priority.

Initial approach: Proposal to nearest local representative
Copies of proposal: 1
Board meeting date(s): Quarterly
Deadline(s): None
Final notification: Approximately 6 weeks

Officers and Trustees:* Eva T. Blum*, Chair. and Pres.; Michael A. Labriola, Secy.; Thomas F. Garbe, Treas.; George P. Long III, Counsel; Joseph C. Guyaux; Joan L. Gulley; Peter K. Classen; Neil Hall; Roberta London; Donna C. Peterman; James E. Rohr; Shelley J. Seifert; PNC Bank, N.A.
EIN: 251202255
Selected grants: The following grants are a representative sample of this grantmaker's funding activity:
$3,250,000 to Sesame Workshop, New York, NY, 2011. For Math Is Everywhere.
$600,000 to United Way of Greater Cleveland, Cleveland, OH, 2011. For annual contribution to United Way of Cleveland to support social services, health, education and other community services.
$500,000 to Point Park University, Pittsburgh, PA, 2011. For architectural design phase of the Pittsburgh Playhouse Project.
$300,000 to Local Initiatives Support Corporation Greater Newark and Jersey City, Newark, NJ, 2011. To provide technical support and assistance to develop information-based action plans and projects that improve appearance and viability of commercial corridors, attract more customers and help businesses improve profitability.
$250,000 to YMCA of Greater Pittsburgh, Pittsburgh, PA, 2011. For the construction and operation of the new flagship Fifth Avenue facility and operation of the US Steel Tower Facility.
$215,000 to Detroit Public Schools Foundation, Detroit, MI, 2011. To facilitate a partnership with DPSF, The Detroit Science Center and Music Hall Center for the Performing Arts in a pilot program to use science and the arts to prepare 200 preschool children for school.
$50,000 to Franklin County Genealogical and Historical Society, Columbus, OH, 2011. To provide science programming to three Columbus Early Learning Centers and two South Side Learning and Development Centers during the school year.
$20,000 to Arts United of Greater Fort Wayne, Fort Wayne, IN, 2011. For Arts United member groups' partnership with Fort Wayne Community Schools' pre-K program serving low- to moderate-income families.
$12,500 to Kalamazoo Valley Community College Foundation, Kalamazoo, MI, 2011. To provide financial assistance to students furthering their education.
$10,000 to Michigan Community Action Agency Association, Okemos, MI, 2011. For financial education courses to low- and moderate-income individuals in the Mid-Michigan market.

2998
Poarch Band of Creek Indians

5811 Jack Springs Rd.
Atmore, AL 36502-5025 (251) 368-9136
FAX: (251) 368-1026

Company URL: http://www.poarchcreekindians.org
Company type: Tribal corporation
Business activities: Indian Tribe.
Business type (SIC): Executive and legislative offices combined
Corporate officers: Buford L. Rolin, Chair.; Stephanie Bryan, Vice-Chair.; Mike Wesaw, C.F.O.; David W. Gehman, Secy.
Board of directors: Buford L. Rolin, Chair.; Stephanie Bryan, Vice-Chair.

Giving statement: Giving through the Poarch Band of Creek Indians Contributions Program.

Poarch Band of Creek Indians Contributions Program

5811 Jack Springs Rd.
Atmore, AL 36502-5025
URL: http://www.poarchcreekindians.org

2999
Polaris Industries Inc.

(formerly Hetteen Hoist and Derrick)
2100 Hwy. 55
Medina, MN 55340-9770 (763) 542-0500
FAX: (763) 542-0599

Company URL: http://www.polarisindustries.com/
Establishment information: Established in 1954.
Company type: Public company
Company ticker symbol and exchange: PII/NYSE
Business activities: Manufactures snowmobiles, small water crafts, and allied clothing and accessories.
Business type (SIC): Durable goods—wholesale; transportation equipment/miscellaneous
Financial profile for 2012: Number of employees, 4,500; assets, $1,486,490,000; sales volume, $3,209,780,000; pre-tax net income, $479,840,000; expenses, $2,731,360,000; liabilities, $795,960,000
Fortune 1000 ranking: 2012—674th in revenues, 456th in profits, and 923rd in assets
Corporate officers: Scott W. Wine, Chair. and C.E.O.; Bennett J. Morgan, Pres. and C.O.O.; Michael W. Malone, V.P., Finance, and C.F.O.; William C. Fisher, V.P. and C.I.O.; Stacy L. Bogart, V.P., Genl. Counsel, and Corp. Secy.; Suresh Krishna, V.P., Opers.; James P. Williams, V.P., Human Resources
Board of directors: Scott W. Wine, Chair.; Annette K. Clayton; Brian Cornell; Gary Hendrickson; Bernd F. Kessler; Mark R. Schreck; William Grant Van Dyke; John P. Wiehoff
International operations: Australia; Austria; Canada; France; Germany; Norway; Spain; Sweden; Switzerland; United Kingdom
Giving statement: Giving through the Polaris Industries Inc. Contributions Program and the Polaris Foundation.
Company EIN: 411790959

Polaris Industries Inc. Contributions Program

2100 Highway 55
Medina, MN 55340-9770 (763) 542-0500
URL: http://www.polarisindustries.com

Purpose and activities: As a complement to its foundation, Polaris Industries makes charitable contributions to nonprofit organizations directly on a case by case basis.
Fields of interest: Disasters, preparedness/services.

The Polaris Foundation

2100 Hwy. 55
Medina, MN 55340-9770
URL: http://www.polaris.com/en-us/company/2012/polaris-foundation.aspx

Establishment information: Established in 1996 in MN.
Donor: Polaris Industries Inc.
Financial data (yr. ended 12/31/11): Assets, $83,746 (M); gifts received, $100,000; expenditures, $458,798; qualifying distributions, $457,798; giving activities include $457,439 for 17 grants (high: $256,919; low: $500).
Purpose and activities: The foundation supports programs designed to promote youth; the environment; and community development.
Fields of interest: Education; Environment, land resources; Environment; Recreation; Youth development; Human services; Community/economic development Youth.
Programs:
Community Development: The foundation supports programs designed to promote economic development, community development, and infrastructure.
Environment: The foundation supports programs designed to address trail system improvement and recreational area development.
Youth: The foundation supports programs designed to improve the quality and service gap in the systems already in place for youth services and agencies located in areas of company operations. Special emphasis is directed toward youth development and youth education.
Type of support: General/operating support; In-kind gifts; Program development.
Geographic limitations: Giving primarily in areas of company operations in Spirit Lake, IA, Roseau and Wyoming, MN, Vermillion, SD, Osceola, WI, and Winnipeg, Canada.
Support limitations: No support for public charities or foundations, political, fraternal, or veterans' organizations, for-profit organizations, state agencies, religious organizations not of direct benefit to the entire community, international or foreign based organizations, social service organizations, or discriminatory organizations. No grants to individuals, or for research projects, discretionary or emergency funds, capital campaigns, or courtesy advertising.
Publications: Application guidelines; Program policy statement.
Application information: Applications accepted. Paper applications are not accepted. Application form required. Applicants should submit the following:
1) name, address and phone number of organization
2) contact person
3) copy of current year's organizational budget and/or project budget
4) detailed description of project and amount of funding requested
5) how project's results will be evaluated or measured
6) listing of additional sources and amount of support
7) how project will be sustained once grantmaker support is completed
Initial approach: Complete online application
Deadline(s): Feb. 1, May 1, Aug. 1, and Nov. 1
Final notification: Apr. 1, July 1, Oct. 1, and Jan. 1
Officers: Stacy L. Bogart, Pres.; Paul Moe, V.P. and Treas.; Jennifer Carbert, Secy.
Directors: Michael W. Malone; Bennett J . Morgan; Scott W. Wine; James P. Williams.
EIN: 411828276
Selected grants: The following grants are a representative sample of this grantmaker's funding activity:
$100,000 to American Red Cross, Minneapolis, MN, 2011.
$5,000 to Family Hope Services, Edina, MN, 2011.
$5,000 to Minnesotans Military Appreciation Fund, Minneapolis, MN, 2011.
$2,500 to Kids Care Connection, Plymouth, MN, 2011.
$1,000 to Lakes Area Youth Service Bureau, Forest Lake, MN, 2011.

3000
R. L. Polk & Co.

26533 Evergreen Rd., Ste. 900
Southfield, MI 48076 (248) 728-7000

Company URL: http://www.polk.com
Establishment information: Established in 1870.
Company type: Private company
Business activities: Publishes directories.
Business type (SIC): Publishing/miscellaneous
Corporate officers: Stephen R. Polk, Chair., Co-Pres., and C.E.O.; Tim Rogers, Co-Pres.; Michelle L. Goff, Sr. V.P. and C.F.O.; Joe LaFeir, Sr. V.P. and C.I.O.; Patrick Barrett, Sr. V.P. and Genl. Counsel; Kendra Rawls, Sr. V.P., Sales, and Mktg.; Deborah Young, V.P., Human Resources; Christine Hammond, V.P. and Cont.
Board of director: Stephen R. Polk, Chair.
Division: Marketing Information Group, Southfield, MI
Giving statement: Giving through the R. L. Polk & Co. Contributions Program.

R. L. Polk & Co. Contributions Program

26533 Evergreen Rd., Ste. 900
Southfield, MI 48076-4249
URL: https://www.polk.com/company/commitment

Purpose and activities: R. L. Polk makes charitable contributions to nonprofit organizations on a case by case basis. Support is given primarily in areas of company operations, with emphasis on Michigan.
Fields of interest: General charitable giving.
Type of support: General/operating support; In-kind gifts; Sponsorships.
Geographic limitations: Giving primarily in areas of company operations, with emphasis on MI.

3001
Polsinelli Shughart PC

700 W. 47th St., Ste. 1000
Kansas City, MO 64112-1802
(816) 753-1000

Company URL: http://www.polsinelli.com/
Establishment information: Established in 1972.
Company type: Private company
Business activities: Operates law firm.
Business type (SIC): Legal services
Corporate officer: W. Russell Welsh, C.E.O.
Offices: Phoenix, AZ; Los Angeles, CA; Denver, CO; Wilmington, DE; Washington, DC; Chicago, Edwardsville, IL; Overland Park, Topeka, KS; Jefferson City, Kansas City, Springfield, St. Joseph, St. Louis, MO; New York, NY; Dallas, TX
Giving statement: Giving through the Polsinelli Shughart PC Pro Bono Program.

Polsinelli Shughart PC Pro Bono Program

700 W. 47th St., Ste. 1000
Kansas City, MO 64112-1802
E-mail: tfroderman@polsinelli.com; URL: http://www.polsinelli.com/probono/

Contact: Troy Froderman, Shareholder
Fields of interest: Legal services.
Type of support: Pro bono services - legal.
Application information: A Pro Bono Committee manages the pro bono program.

3002
Pony Sales, Inc.
1600 W. La Quinta Rd., Ste. B
Nogales, AZ 85621 (520) 281-4444

Company type: Private company
Business activities: Produces agricultural crops.
Business type (SIC): Agricultural production crops
Giving statement: Giving through the Panousopoulos Scholastic Charitable Foundation, Inc.

Panousopoulos Scholastic Charitable Foundation, Inc.
P.O. Box 1806
Nogales, AZ 85628-1806

Establishment information: Established in 1995 in AZ.
Donors: Pony Sales, Inc.; Yory Produce, LLC; Delta Fresh, LLC.
Financial data (yr. ended 12/31/11): Assets, $596,787 (M); gifts received, $3,000; expenditures, $39,454; qualifying distributions, $30,500; giving activities include $30,500 for grants.
Purpose and activities: The foundation supports service clubs and organizations involved with Greek culture, animal welfare, and Christianity.
Fields of interest: Housing/shelter; Youth development.
Geographic limitations: Giving primarily in AZ.
Application information: Applications not accepted. Unsolicited requests for funds not accepted.
Officers and Trustees: Constantine Panousopoulos*, Pres.; Nelida Panousopoulos, Secy.-Treas.
EIN: 860811044

3003
Popular, Inc.
Popular Ctr. Bldg., 209 Munoz Rivera Ave.
San Juan, PR 00918 (787) 765-9800

Company URL: http://www.popular.com
Establishment information: Established in 1893.
Company type: Public company
Company ticker symbol and exchange: BPOP/NASDAQ
Business activities: Operates bank holding company.
Business type (SIC): Banks/commercial; motor vehicle rentals and leasing
Financial profile for 2012: Number of employees, 8,072; assets, $36,507,540,000; pre-tax net income, $218,870,000; liabilities, $32,397,530,000
Fortune 1000 ranking: 2012—875th in revenues, 528th in profits, and 153rd in assets
Corporate officers: Richard L. Carrion, Chair., Pres., and C.E.O.; Carlos J. Vazquez, C.F.O.; Eduardo J. Negron, Exec. V.P., Admin.
Board of directors: Richard L. Carrion, Chair.; Alejandro M. Ballester; Maria Luisa Ferre; David Goel; Kim Goodwin; Manuel Morales, Jr.; William J. Teuber, Jr.; Carios A. Unanue; Jose R. Vizcarrondo
Giving statement: Giving through the Popular Community Bank Corporate Giving Program and the Banco Community Bank Foundation, Inc.
Company EIN: 660667416

Popular Community Bank Corporate Giving Program
Popular Ctr. Bldg.
209 Munoz Rivera Ave.
Hato Rey, PR 00918 (787) 765-9800
URL: https://www.popularcommunitybank.com/us/about-us/community

Banco Community Bank Foundation, Inc.
(formerly Banco Popular Foundation, Inc.)
9600 W. Bryn Mawr Ave.
Rosemont, IL 60018-5209
URL: https://www.mypopularbanking.com/us/about-us/community/banco-popular-foundation

Establishment information: Established in 2005 in IL.
Donors: Banco Popular North America; Richard C. Peterson; Michelle Imbasciani; Cesar Medina; Chris A. McFadden; Banco Popular Foundation, Inc.
Contact: Beatriz Polhamus, Exec. Dir.
Financial data (yr. ended 12/31/11): Assets, $1,896,483 (M); gifts received, $157,586; expenditures, $167,454; qualifying distributions, $133,115; giving activities include $133,115 for grants.
Purpose and activities: The foundation supports programs designed to strengthen the social and economic well-being of communities.
Fields of interest: Education; Housing/shelter, development; Housing/shelter; Youth development, business; Family services; Developmentally disabled, centers & services; Minorities/immigrants, centers/services; Human services; Business/industry; Community/economic development.
Type of support: Continuing support; General/operating support; Program development; Scholarship funds.
Geographic limitations: Giving primarily in CA, FL, IL, and NY.
Support limitations: No support for religious or political organizations. No grants to individuals, or for fundraising events, table purchases, event sponsorships, or capital campaigns.
Publications: Application guidelines.
Application information: Applications accepted. Priority is given to organizations that demonstrate ongoing sustainability. Multi-year funding is not automatic. Application form required.
Initial approach: Complete online application
Deadline(s): July 1 to Aug. 31
Officers and Directors:* Richard L. Carrion*, Chair.; Carlos J. Vasquez*, Vice-Chair.; Brian F. Doran, Secy.; Eduardo J. Negron*, Treas.; Beatriz Polhamus, Exec. Dir.
EIN: 753175825
Selected grants: The following grants are a representative sample of this grantmaker's funding activity:
$10,000 to Housing and Services, New York, NY, 2010.
$9,000 to Hope Center, Miami, FL, 2010.
$7,500 to International Institute of New Jersey, Jersey City, NJ, 2010.
$5,730 to ACCION USA-Miami, Miami, FL, 2010.
$4,000 to Aspire of Illinois, Westchester, IL, 2010.
$4,000 to Big Brothers Big Sisters of Central Florida, Winter Park, FL, 2010.
$3,940 to Publicolor, New York, NY, 2010.
$3,940 to Salvation Army of Perth Amboy, Perth Amboy, NJ, 2010.
$3,000 to Metropolitan Family Services, Chicago, IL, 2010.
$3,000 to YMCA, McCormick Tribune, Chicago, IL, 2010.

3004
Portcullis Partners, L.P.
4400 Post Oak Pkwy., Ste. 1450
Houston, TX 77027-3421 (713) 877-8031

Company type: Private company
Business activities: Conducts investment activities; provides investment advisory services.
Business type (SIC): Investors/miscellaneous; security and commodity services
Corporate officers: William V. Morgan, Chair.; Michael C. Morgan, Pres. and C.E.O.
Board of director: William V. Morgan, Chair.
Giving statement: Giving through the Morgan Foundation.

Morgan Foundation
11 Greenway Plz.
Houston, TX 77046

Establishment information: Established in 2002 in TX.
Donor: Portcullis Partners, L.P.
Contact: Sara S. Morgan, Secy.
Financial data (yr. ended 12/31/11): Assets, $19,957,949 (M); expenditures, $2,436,579; qualifying distributions, $2,150,000; giving activities include $2,150,000 for 5 grants (high: $1,600,000; low: $100,000).
Purpose and activities: The foundation supports hospitals and community foundations and organizations involved with folk arts, secondary education, cancer, and children and youth.
Fields of interest: Arts, folk arts; Secondary school/education; Hospitals (general); Cancer; Children/youth, services; Foundations (community).
Type of support: General/operating support; Program development.
Geographic limitations: Giving limited to Houston, TX.
Support limitations: No grants to individuals.
Application information: Applications not accepted. Contributes only to pre-selected organizations.
Board meeting date(s): As needed
Officers and Directors:* William V. Morgan*, Pres. and Treas.; Sara S. Morgan*, V.P. and Secy.; Catherine A. Morgan; Christine R. Morgan; Michael C. Morgan*.
Number of staff: None.
EIN: 223886549

3005
Porter & Porter, PC CPA
1370 Ramar Rd., Ste. B
Bullhead City, AZ 86442-7117
(928) 758-4106

Establishment information: Established in 1980.
Company type: Private company
Business activities: Provides accounting services.
Business type (SIC): Accounting, auditing, and bookkeeping services
Corporate officer: Ronald J. Porter, Pres.
Giving statement: Giving through the Hegner Foundation, Inc.

Hegner Foundation, Inc.
1660 Lakeside Dr., No. 321
Bullhead City, AZ 86442-6544

Establishment information: Established in 1994 in AZ.
Donors: Porter & Porter; Ronald J. Porter; Judith F. Porter.
Financial data (yr. ended 06/30/10): Assets, $0 (M); expenditures, $42,907; qualifying distributions, $36,034; giving activities include $36,034 for grants.
Fields of interest: Human services; Christian agencies & churches.
Geographic limitations: Giving primarily in AZ.
Support limitations: No grants to individuals.
Application information: Applications not accepted. Unsolicited requests for funds not accepted.
Officers: Judith F. Porter, Pres.; Ronald J. Porter, Secy.; Neil A. Porter, Treas.
EIN: 860740524

3006
Porter, Inc.
(also known as Thunderbird Products)
2200 W. Monroe St.
Decatur, IN 46733-3028 (800) 736-7685

Company URL: http://www.formulaboats.com/history.aspx
Establishment information: Established in 1956.
Company type: Private company
Business activities: Manufactures and repairs inboard and outboard motors.
Business type (SIC): Ship and boat building and repair
Giving statement: Giving through the Porter Family Foundation, Inc.

Porter Family Foundation, Inc.
2200 W. Monroe St.
Decatur, IN 46733-3028

Establishment information: Classified as a company-sponsored operating foundation in 1985 in IN.
Donor: Porter, Inc.
Financial data (yr. ended 05/31/12): Assets, $432,628 (M); expenditures, $99,125; qualifying distributions, $97,895; giving activities include $97,895 for 35 grants (high: $15,000; low: $20).
Purpose and activities: The foundation supports community foundations and organizations involved with higher education, human services, and Christianity.
Fields of interest: Youth development; Human services; Religion.
Type of support: Employee matching gifts; General/operating support; Scholarship funds.
Geographic limitations: Giving primarily in Decatur, IN.
Support limitations: No grants to individuals.
Application information: Applications not accepted. Contributes only to pre-selected organizations.
Officers: Scott Porter, Pres.; Grant Porter, Exec. V.P.
EIN: 311144513

3007
Porter Corporation
2603 S. Lafayette St.
Shelby, NC 28152-7584

Company type: Private company
Business activities: Operates holding company.
Business type (SIC): Holding company
Giving statement: Giving through the Paul and Margaret Porter Charitable Foundation.

The Paul and Margaret Porter Charitable Foundation
(formerly Porter Brothers Foundation)
105 Sycamore Ln.
Shelby, NC 28152-9603

Donors: Porter Corp.; Paul B. Porter.
Financial data (yr. ended 12/31/11): Assets, $893,138 (M); expenditures, $65,333; qualifying distributions, $43,000; giving activities include $43,000 for 10 grants (high: $25,000; low: $500).
Purpose and activities: The foundation supports libraries and organizations involved with arts and culture, K-12 and higher education, health, and human services.
Fields of interest: Arts; Human services; Religion.
Type of support: General/operating support; Program development; Scholarship funds.
Geographic limitations: Giving primarily in NC.
Support limitations: No grants to individuals.
Application information: Applications not accepted. Unsolicited requests for funds not accepted.
Officers: Ellen Porter Warlick, Pres.; Patricia Taylor Porter, V.P.; J. William Porter, Secy.; Scott Porter, Treas.
EIN: 591750571

3008
Porter Hedges LLP
1000 Main St., 36th Fl.
Houston, TX 77002-6336 (713) 226-6607

Company URL: http://www.porterhedges.com/Home
Establishment information: Established in 1981.
Company type: Private company
Business activities: Operates law firm.
Office: Houston, TX
Giving statement: Giving through the Porter Hedges LLP Pro Bono Program.

Porter Hedges LLP Pro Bono Program
1000 Main St., 36th Fl.
Houston, TX 77002-6336 (713) 226-6607
E-mail: cholub@porterhedges.com; Additional tel.: (713) 226-6000; URL: http://www.porterhedges.com/OurFirm/ProBono

Contact: Cynthia A. Holub, Partner
Fields of interest: Legal services.
Type of support: Pro bono services - legal.
Application information: A Pro Bono Committee manages the pro bono program.

3009
Porter Wright Morris & Arthur LLP
41 South High St., Ste. 2800
Columbus, OH 43215-6194
(614) 227-2045

Company URL: http://www.porterwright.com
Establishment information: Established in 1846.
Company type: Private company
Business activities: Operates law firm.
Business type (SIC): Legal services
Offices: Washington, DC; Naples, FL; Cincinnati, Cleveland, Columbus, Dayton, OH
Giving statement: Giving through the Porter Wright Morris & Arthur LLP Pro Bono Program.

Porter Wright Morris & Arthur LLP Pro Bono Program
41 South High St., Ste. 2800
Columbus, OH 43215-6194 (614) 227-2045
E-mail: dshouvlin@porterwright.com; Additional tel.: (614) 227-2000; URL: http://www.porterwright.com/probono/

Contact: David P. Shouvlin, Partner
Fields of interest: Legal services.
Type of support: Pro bono services - legal.
Application information: A Pro Bono Committee manages the pro bono program.

3010
Portland General Electric Company
(also known as PGE)
121 S.W. Salmon St.
P.O. Box 4438
Portland, OR 97204-2901 (503) 464-8000

Company URL: http://www.portlandgeneral.com
Establishment information: Established in 1889.
Company type: Public company
Company ticker symbol and exchange: POR/NYSE
Business activities: Generates, transmits, and distributes electricity.
Business type (SIC): Electric services
Financial profile for 2012: Number of employees, 2,603; assets, $5,670,000,000; sales volume, $1,805,000,000; pre-tax net income, $204,000,000; expenses, $1,503,000,000; liabilities, $3,942,000,000
Corporate officers: Corbin A. McNeill, Jr., Chair.; James J. Piro, Pres. and C.E.O.; Maria M. Pope, Sr. V.P., Finance, C.F.O., and Treas.; Cam Henderson, V.P. and C.I.O.; Jay Dudley, V.P. and Genl. Counsel; Arleen Barnett, V.P., Admin.
Board of directors: Corbin A. McNeill, Jr., Chair.; John W. Ballantine; Rodney L. Brown, Jr.; Jack E. Davis; David A. Dietzler; Kirby A. Dyess; Mark B. Ganz; Neil J. Nelson; M. Lee Pelton; Jim Piro; Robert T.F. Reid
Giving statement: Giving through the PGE Corporate Giving Program and the PGE Foundation.
Company EIN: 930256820

PGE Corporate Giving Program
121 S.W. Salmon St.
Portland, OR 97204 (503) 464-8000
URL: http://www.portlandgeneral.com/community_environment/default.aspx

Purpose and activities: As a complement to its foundation, PGE also makes charitable contributions to nonprofit organizations on a case by case basis. Support is limited to areas of company operations, with emphasis on Portland, Oregon.
Fields of interest: Education; Environment, energy; Environment; Employment, training; Safety/disasters; Community/economic development Economically disadvantaged.
Type of support: Advocacy; Curriculum development; Donated products; Employee volunteer services; General/operating support; In-kind gifts; Sponsorships.
Geographic limitations: Giving limited to areas of company operations, with emphasis on Portland, OR.
Support limitations: No support for religious organizations not of direct benefit to the entire community, or to political, fraternal, or discriminatory organizations, sports teams, or for-profit organizations. No grants to individuals for study, travel or personal events, or for capital campaigns, endowments, or memorials.
Application information: Applications accepted. Application form required. Applicants should submit the following:
1) name, address and phone number of organization
Requests for a presentation should include expected attendance and location of the event, date and time preference, audience age group, and the presentation topic.
Initial approach: Proposal

PGE Foundation

(formerly PGE-Enron Foundation)
One World Trade Center, 3rd Fl.
121 W. Salmon St.
Portland, OR 97204-2901 (503) 464-8818
FAX: (503) 464-2929;
E-mail: pgefoundation@pgn.com; Additional contact: Rachel DeRosia, Prog. Off., tel.: (503) 464-8599, e-mail: rachel.derosia@pgn.com; URL: http://www.pgefoundation.org/

Establishment information: Established in 1994 in OR.
Donor: Portland General Electric Co.
Contact: Melissa Sircy, Grant Admin.
Financial data (yr. ended 12/31/11): Assets, $21,112,546 (M); gifts received, $26,976; expenditures, $1,256,340; qualifying distributions, $1,043,366; giving activities include $1,043,366 for grants.
Purpose and activities: The foundation supports programs designed to promote education, healthy families, and arts and culture. Special emphasis is directed toward education programs and basic needs services.
Fields of interest: Arts education; Arts; Elementary/secondary education; Vocational education, post-secondary; Higher education; Education, reading; Education; Health care; Substance abuse, services; Mental health/crisis services; Food services; Children/youth, services; Children, foster care; Family services; Family services, parent education; Family services, domestic violence; Aging, centers/services; Developmentally disabled, centers & services; Homeless, human services; Human services; United Ways and Federated Giving Programs; Mathematics; Engineering/technology; Science.
Program:
Community 101: The foundation, in partnership with the Oregon Community Foundation, supports the community involvement of students through grantmaking and volunteerism. Through the service-learning program, philanthropy education is incorporated into the curriculum; and high school students volunteer and distribute foundation funds of up to $5,000 to the nonprofit organization of their choice. The program is administered by the Oregon Community Foundation.
Type of support: Continuing support; Curriculum development; General/operating support; Program development; Scholarship funds; Sponsorships.
Geographic limitations: Giving primarily in areas of company operations in OR.
Support limitations: No support for political entities or candidates for political office, discriminatory organizations, or fraternal, sectarian, or religious organizations not of direct benefit to the entire community. No grants to individuals, or for bridge grants, debt retirements, or operational deficits, endowments, general operating support, annual campaigns, ballot measure campaigns, travel, conferences, symposiums, festivals, events, team sponsorships, or user fees, or salaries of employees (unless costs relate directly to the funded project); generally no capital campaigns that include building improvements, equipment purchases, or anything considered an asset of the organization.
Publications: Annual report; Application guidelines.
Application information: Applications accepted. Grants range from $2,500 to $10,000. A full application may be requested at a later date. Support is limited to 1 contribution per organization during any given year. Organizations receiving support are asked to submit a final report. Application form not required. Applicants should submit the following:
1) population served
2) copy of IRS Determination Letter
3) geographic area to be served
4) detailed description of project and amount of funding requested
5) listing of additional sources and amount of support
Initial approach: Complete online letter of inquiry
Deadline(s): Jan. 13, Apr. 6, July 6, and Nov. 2
Final notification: 30 days
Officers and Directors:* Gwyneth Gamble-Booth*, Chair.; Carole E. Morse, Pres.; Rosalie Duron, Secy.; Maria M. Pope, Treas.; David K. Carboneau; Carol Dillin; Peggy Y. Fowler; Randolph L. Miller; James J. Piro; David Robertson; DeAngeloa Wells.
EIN: 931138806
Selected grants: The following grants are a representative sample of this grantmaker's funding activity:
$99,385 to Oregon Community Foundation, Portland, OR, 2010.
$25,000 to Oregon State University Foundation, Corvallis, OR, 2010.
$20,000 to Boys and Girls Clubs of Portland Metropolitan Area, Portland, OR, 2010.
$20,000 to Oregon Symphony Association, Portland, OR, 2010.
$17,500 to Childrens Center of Clackamas County, Oregon City, OR, 2010.
$15,000 to Dougy Center, Portland, OR, 2010.
$10,000 to Dental Foundation of Oregon, Wilsonville, OR, 2010.
$7,500 to Juvenile Rights Project, Portland, OR, 2010.
$7,500 to Loaves and Fishes Centers, Portland, OR, 2010.
$5,000 to Open Door Counseling Center, Hillsboro, OR, 2010.

3011
Portland Pirates, LLC

94 Free St.
Portland, ME 04101-3920 (207) 828-4665

Company URL: http://www.portlandpirates.com
Establishment information: Established in 2000.
Company type: Private company
Business activities: Operates professional ice hockey club.
Business type (SIC): Commercial sports
Corporate officers: Lyman G. Bullard, Jr., Chair.; Brian S. Petrovek, C.E.O.
Board of director: Lyman G. Bullard, Jr., Chair.
Giving statement: Giving through the Portland Pirates Foundation, Inc.

Portland Pirates Foundation, Inc.

94 Free St.
Portland, ME 04101-3306

Establishment information: Established in 2003 in ME.
Financial data (yr. ended 06/30/10): Revenue, $18,540; assets, $2,632 (M); gifts received, $375; expenditures, $16,788.
Purpose and activities: The foundation seeks to enrich the city of Portland and the state of Maine through educational, sports-based, community-building, and fundraising programs.
Fields of interest: Education; Community/economic development.
Geographic limitations: Giving primarily in Portland, ME.
Officers and Directors:* Brian S. Petrovek*, Pres.; Brian J. Williams*, Treas.; Lyman G. Bullard, Jr.*, Clerk; John Hart; Robert F. Higgins; Raymond Kelley, Jr.; Jane McKay Morrell; Rich Strabley; Robert T. Thompson; Steve Tsujiura; Tracy Weinrich.
EIN: 300191590

3012
Portrait, Inc.

(formerly Portrait Brokers of America, Inc.)
2801 6th Ave., S.
Birmingham, AL 35233 (205) 879-1222
FAX: (2050 879-6112

Company URL: http://www.portraitsinc.com/
Establishment information: Established in 1942.
Company type: Private company
Business activities: Provides portrait brokerage services.
Business type (SIC): Business services/miscellaneous
Corporate officers: Beverly McNeal, Owner; John A. McNeil, Jr., Pres. and C.O.O.
Giving statement: Giving through the Portraits, Inc. Scholarship Foundation.

Portraits, Inc. Scholarship Foundation

(formerly Portraits, Inc., Scholarship Foundation)
c/o Scholarship Selection Comm.
P.O. Box 131384
Birmingham, AL 35213-6384 (205) 879-1222

Establishment information: Established in 2001.
Donor: Portrait Brokers of America, Inc.
Financial data (yr. ended 12/31/11): Assets, $47 (M); gifts received, $8,018; expenditures, $8,200; qualifying distributions, $8,000; giving activities include $8,000 for 10 grants (high: $1,000; low: $500).

Purpose and activities: The foundation awards college scholarships to children and grandchildren of artists. Special emphasis is directed toward artists affiliated with Portrait Brokers of America.
Fields of interest: Higher education; Education.
Type of support: Scholarships—to individuals.
Geographic limitations: Giving primarily in AL, CA, CO, FL, MS, and PA.
Application information: Applications accepted. Application form required.
Applications should include transcripts, GPA, rank, SAT and ACT scores, and 2 letters of reference.
Initial approach: Contact foundation for application form
Deadline(s): Mar 15
Officers and Directors:* Beverly Blount McNeil*, Chair.; Margaret Hayes Brunstad, Pres.; Margie Sweet Walker, V.P.; Jane Rast Arendall; James Wade Brunstad.
EIN: 631241622

3013
Porzio, Bromberg & Newman, P.C.

100 Southgate Pkwy.
P.O Box 1997
Morristown, NJ 07962-1997
(973) 538-4006

Company URL: http://www.pbnlaw.com/index.php
Establishment information: Established in 1962.
Company type: Private company
Business activities: Operates law firm.
Business type (SIC): Legal services
Offices: Westborough, MA; Morristown, Princeton, NJ; New York, NY
Giving statement: Giving through the Porzio, Bromberg & Newman, P.C Pro Bono Program.

Porzio, Bromberg & Newman, P.C Pro Bono Program

100 Southgate Pkwy.
P.O Box 1997
Morristown, NJ 07962-1997 (973) 538-4006
E-mail: tlbarnes@pbnlaw.com; URL: http://www.pbnlaw.com/pages/about/about.php?page=probono

Contact: Timothy L. Barnes, Principal
Fields of interest: Legal services.
Type of support: Pro bono services - legal.
Application information: A Pro Bono Committee manages the pro bono program.

3014
Posillico Civil, Inc.

(formerly J D Posillico Incorporated)
1750 New Hwy.
Farmingdale, NY 11735-1562
(631) 249-1872

Company URL: http://www.jdposillico.com
Establishment information: Established in 1946.
Company type: Private company
Business activities: Operates engineering contracting company.
Business type (SIC): Construction/highway and street (except elevated)
Corporate officers: Mario A. Posillico, Chair.; Joseph K. Posillico, Pres. and C.E.O.; Fred Locher, C.O.O.; Paul F. Posillico, Sr. V.P., Secy.-Treas., Finance, and Admin.; Joseph D. Posillico III, Sr. V.P., Opers.; Thomas Spatafora, Sr. V.P., Sales and Mktg.
Board of directors: Mario A. Posillico, Chair.; Joseph D. Posillico III; Joseph K. Posillico; Michael J. Posillico; Paul F. Posillico
Giving statement: Giving through the Posillico Group Foundation, Inc.

The Posillico Group Foundation, Inc.

(formerly The Posillico Group Foundation, inc)
1750 New Hwy.
Farmingdale, NY 11735-1510

Establishment information: Established in 2004 in NY.
Donors: J.D. Posillico, Inc.; Blue Water Environmental; Posillico Materials, LLC; Posillico Civil, inc; Haiti Relief Donations.
Financial data (yr. ended 12/31/11): Assets, $59,479 (M); expenditures, $91,880; qualifying distributions, $91,830; giving activities include $91,830 for grants.
Purpose and activities: The foundation supports organizations involved with secondary and higher education, cancer, school athletics, human services, the construction industry, and Christianity.
Fields of interest: Education; Human services; Religion.
Type of support: General/operating support.
Geographic limitations: Giving primarily in NY.
Support limitations: No grants to individuals.
Application information: Applications not accepted. Contributes only to pre-selected organizations.
Officers: Mario Posillico, Chair.; Joseph K. Posillico, Pres.; Michael J. Posillico, V.P.; Joseph D. Posillico III, Secy.; Paul F. Posillico, Treas.
EIN: 202143917

3015
Post-Bulletin Company, LLC

18 1st Ave. S.E.
P.O. Box 6118
Rochester, MN 55904-3722
(507) 285-7600

Company URL: http://www.postbulletin.com
Establishment information: Established in 1977.
Company type: Subsidiary of a private company
Business activities: Publishes newspapers.
Business type (SIC): Newspaper publishing and/or printing
Corporate officers: Randy Chapman, C.A.O.; Mark Kelm, C.I.O.
Giving statement: Giving through the Rochester Post Bulletin Charities.

Rochester Post Bulletin Charities

18 1st Ave. S.E.
Rochester, MN 55904-3722

Donors: Post-Bulletin, Co.; AAA Minnesota/Iowa; Bursch Travel; Kiwanis; Voiture 327; American Legion.
Financial data (yr. ended 12/31/11): Assets, $57,225 (M); gifts received, $37,314; expenditures, $39,293; qualifying distributions, $38,345; giving activities include $38,345 for grants.
Purpose and activities: The foundation supports organizations involved with journalism, education, and community celebrations.
Type of support: General/operating support.
Geographic limitations: Giving limited to the Rochester, MN, area.
Application information: Applications not accepted. Unsolicited requests for funds not accepted.
Officers: Randolph Chapman, Chair.; Layne Retzlaff*, Vice-Chair. and Secy.; Christy Blade, Treas.
EIN: 363485241

3016
Post-Newsweek Media, Inc.

9030 Comprint Ct.
Gaithersburg, MD 20877-1307
(301) 670-2565

Company URL: http://www.gazette.net
Establishment information: Established in 1992.
Company type: Subsidiary of a public company
Business activities: Publishes newspapers; provides Internet information services; provides commercial printing services; publishes trade periodicals; produces trade shows and conferences.
Business type (SIC): Newspaper publishing and/or printing; periodical publishing and/or printing; printing/commercial; computer services; business services/miscellaneous
Corporate officer: Chuck Lyons, C.E.O.
Giving statement: Giving through the Maryland-Delaware-D.C. Press Foundation, Inc.

Maryland-Delaware-D.C. Press Foundation, Inc.

Capital Gazette Bldg.
2000 Capital Dr.
Annapolis, MD 21401-3151
FAX: (410) 721-4557;
E-mail: foundation@mddcpress.com; Contact Jen Thornberry: (855) 721-6332 x2, e-mail: jthornberry@mddcpress.com; URL: http://www.mddcpress.com/mc/page.do?sitePageId=72868&orgId=mdp

Establishment information: Established as a company-sponsored operating foundation in 1998.
Donors: Maryland-Delaware-D.C. Press Service, Inc.; Post-Newsweek Media, Inc.; Gazette Newspapers.
Financial data (yr. ended 12/31/11): Assets, $77,949 (M); gifts received, $18,497; expenditures, $21,955; qualifying distributions, $21,119; giving activities include $20,700 for 9 grants (high: $2,400; low: $1,500).
Purpose and activities: The foundation supports programs designed to protect the First Amendment freedoms of press and speech and the role of newspapers and journalism in a free society through educational programs, grants to high school journalism students, and paid internships.
Fields of interest: Media, print publishing; Secondary school/education; Journalism school/education; Civil liberties, first amendment.
Programs:
Michael S. Powell High School Journalist of the Year: The foundation awards a $1,500 scholarship to an outstanding senior staff member of a Delaware, District of Columbia, or Maryland high school newspaper. The winner is also honored at the MDDC Editorial Conference in the spring.
The Reese Cleghorn MDDC Internship Program: The foundation supports an eight week internship program at participating newspapers. The program is open to student journalists attending any four-year college in Delaware, District of Columbia, or Maryland or residents in the MDDC region who attend four-year colleges out of state. Each intern is provided a $2,400 stipend and internships are

available in news reporting, copy editing, and photojournalism.
Type of support: Internship funds; Program development; Scholarships—to individuals.
Geographic limitations: Giving limited to areas of company operations in Washington, DC, DE, and MD.
Publications: Application guidelines.
Application information: Applications accepted. Application form required.
Applications for the Michael S. Powell High School Journalist of the Year Award must include 5 samples of work mounted on unlined paper, an autobiographical review of the applicant's journalism background and experience, and a brief essay on the most important aspect of scholastic journalism.
Initial approach: Letter
Deadline(s): Dec. 1st
Officers: Carol Melamed, Pres.; John League, V.P.; Jack Murphy, Exec. Dir.
Trustees: Jim Donahue; Chris Eddings; Kevin Klose; Tom Linthicum; John McIntyre; Jack Murphy; John J. Oliver, Jr.; Myron Randall; Pat Richardson; Nathan Siegel.
EIN: 522135767

3017
Potlatch Corporation
601 W. 1st Ave., Ste. 1600
Spokane, WA 99201-0603 (509) 835-1500
FAX: (302) 655-5049

Company URL: http://www.potlatchcorp.com
Establishment information: Established in 1903.
Company type: Public company
Company ticker symbol and exchange: PCH/ NASDAQ
Business activities: Operates real estate investment trust; operates timber tracts; manufactures commodity wood products and bleached pulp products.
Business type (SIC): Investors/miscellaneous; forestry—timber tracts; lumber and wood products (except furniture); pulp mills
Financial profile for 2012: Number of employees, 875; assets, $718,900,000; sales volume, $525,130,000; pre-tax net income, $59,400,000; expenses, $440,190,000; liabilities, $580,250,000
Corporate officers: Michael J. Covey, Chair. and C.E.O.; Eric J. Cremers, Pres., C.O.O., and C.F.O.; Lorrie D. Scott, V.P., Genl. Counsel, and Corp. Secy.; Mark J. Benson, V.P., Public Affairs; Jane E. Crane, V.P., Human Resources
Board of directors: Michael J. Covey, Chair.; Boh A. Dickey; William L. Driscoll; Ruth Ann M. Gillis; Jerome C. Knoll; John S. Moody; Lawrence S. Peiros; Gregory L. Quesnel
Subsidiaries: The Prescott and Northwestern Railroad Co., Prescott, AR; St. Maries River Railroad Co., Lewiston, ID; Warren & Saline River Railroad Co., Warren, AR
Divisions: Consumer Products Div., Lewiston, ID; Land Sales & Development Div., Spokane, WA; Pulp and Paperboard Div., Lewiston, ID; Resource Div., Spokane, WA; Wood Products Div., Lewiston, ID
Giving statement: Giving through the Potlatch Foundation for Higher Education.
Company EIN: 820156045

Potlatch Foundation for Higher Education
601 W. First Ave., Ste. 1600
Spokane, WA 99201-0603 (509) 344-5922
E-mail: foundation@potlatchcorp.com

Establishment information: Incorporated in 1952 in DE.
Donors: Potlatch Corp.; Potlach Foundation II.
Contact: Sharon M. Pegau, Secy.
Financial data (yr. ended 12/31/11): Assets, $6,986 (M); gifts received, $55,000; expenditures, $52,664; qualifying distributions, $52,664; giving activities include $51,450 for 89 grants to individuals (high: $700; low: $700).
Purpose and activities: The foundation awards college scholarships to undergraduate students living in certain areas of company operations of Potlatch Corporation.
Fields of interest: Higher education.
Type of support: Scholarships—to individuals.
Geographic limitations: Giving limited to areas of company operations, with emphasis on AR, ID, and MN.
Support limitations: No grants for general operating support, building or endowments, or research; no loans; no employee matching gifts; no graduate school scholarships.
Publications: Informational brochure.
Application information: Applications not accepted. The foundation no longer awards new scholarships; it will honor those already granted.
Officers and Trustees:* Mark J. Benson*, Pres.; Sharon M. Pegau*, Secy.; Matt Van Vleet*, Treas.; A.L. Alford, Jr.; Jack A. Buell; John B. Frazer, Jr.; Jack Hogan; Sally J. Ihne.
EIN: 826005250

3018
Potomac Electric Power Company
(also known as Pepco)
701 9th St., N.W., Ste. 1100, 10th Fl.
Washington, DC 20001-4572
(202) 872-2000

Company URL: http://www.pepco.com
Establishment information: Established in 1896.
Company type: Subsidiary of a public company
Business activities: Generates, transmits, and distributes electricity.
Business type (SIC): Electric services
Financial profile for 2010: Number of employees, 1,375; sales volume, $2,288,000,000
Corporate officers: Dennis R. Wraase, Chair.; Joseph M. Rigby, Pres. and C.E.O.; Anthony J. Kamerick, Sr. V.P. and C.F.O.; Ronald K. Clark, V.P. and Cont.
Board of director: Dennis R. Wraase, Chair.
Subsidiary: Potomac Capital Investment Corp., Washington, DC
Giving statement: Giving through the Potomac Electric Power Company Contributions Program.

Potomac Electric Power Company Contributions Program
701 9th St., N.W.
Washington, DC 20068-0001 (202) 872-3488
URL: http://www.pepco.com/welcome/community

Contact: Pamela Holman, Coord., Contribs.
Purpose and activities: Potomac Electric Power makes charitable contributions to nonprofit organizations involved with arts and culture, education, the environment, health, business, and civic affairs. Support is given primarily in Washington, DC, and Montgomery and Prince George's counties, Maryland.
Fields of interest: Arts; Education; Environment; Health care; Youth development; Children/youth, services; Human services; Business/industry; Community/economic development; United Ways and Federated Giving Programs; Public affairs.
Type of support: Employee matching gifts; Employee volunteer services; General/operating support; In-kind gifts.
Geographic limitations: Giving primarily in Washington, DC, and Montgomery and Prince George's counties, MD.
Application information: Applications accepted.
Initial approach: Telephone headquarters for application information

3019
Potter Anderson & Corroon LLP
Hercules Plz., 1313 N. Market St.
P.O Box 951
Wilmington, DE 19801-6101
(302) 984-6000

Company URL: http://www.potteranderson.com/
Establishment information: Established in 1826.
Company type: Private company
Business activities: Operates law firm.
Business type (SIC): Legal services
Office: Wilmington, DE
Giving statement: Giving through the Potter Anderson & Corroon LLP Pro Bono Program.

Potter Anderson & Corroon LLP Pro Bono Program
Hercules Plz., 1313 N. Market St.
P.O Box 951
Wilmington, DE 19801-6101 (302) 984-6000
E-mail: jbrady@potteranderson.com; URL: http://www.potteranderson.com/about-involvement.html

Contact: Jennifer Gimler Brady, Pro Bono Coord.
Fields of interest: Legal services.
Type of support: Pro bono services - legal.
Application information: An attorney coordinates pro bono projects as an ancillary duty to other work.

3020
Power Equipment Distributors, Inc.
69250 Burke Dr.
Richmond, MI 48062-1550 (586) 727-2401
FAX: (586) 727-4362

Company URL: http://www.powereqp.com
Establishment information: Established in 1956.
Company type: Private company
Business activities: Wholesale distributor of lawn mower machinery, equipment, and parts.
Business type (SIC): Industrial machinery and equipment—wholesale
Corporate officers: Beverly Devriendt, Pres.; Edward Radtke, Secy.
Giving statement: Giving through the Weingartz Family Foundation.

Weingartz Family Foundation
P.O. Box 182008
Shelby Township, MI 48318-2008

Establishment information: Established in 2004 in MI.
Donors: Power Equipment Distributors, Inc.; Weingartz Supply Co.
Financial data (yr. ended 12/31/11): Assets, $2,525,927 (M); gifts received, $300,000; expenditures, $399,415; qualifying distributions, $399,415; giving activities include $399,415 for grants.
Purpose and activities: The foundation supports organizations involved with hunger, human services, international relief, and religion.
Fields of interest: Food services; Food banks; Homeless, human services; Human services; International relief; Christian agencies & churches; Catholic agencies & churches; Religion.
Type of support: General/operating support.
Geographic limitations: Giving primarily in Washington, DC, MI, and NY.
Support limitations: No grants to individuals.
Application information: Applications not accepted. Contributes only to pre-selected organizations.
Officers and Directors:* Raymond Weingartz*, Pres.; Marie Weingartz*, V.P.; Edward Radtke*, Secy.; Daniel Weingartz, Treas.; Beverly Devriendt; Angela Malburg; Donald Malburg; Catherine Radtke; Amy Weingartz; Debbie Weingartz; Kenneth Weingartz; Kris Weingartz; Peggy Weingartz; Ronald Weingartz; Thomas Weingartz.
EIN: 201516609

3021
Power Fuel & Transport, LLC
2822 Norborne Pl.
Oakton, VA 22124-5001 (703) 753-0151

Establishment information: Established in 2009.
Company type: Private company
Business activities: Provides transportation services.
Business type (SIC): Transportation services/ miscellaneous
Corporate officer: Wesley Dick, Principal
Giving statement: Giving through the Dick Foundation Inc.

Dick Foundation Inc.
602 Live Oak Rd.
Vero Beach, FL 32963

Establishment information: Established in 2005 in MD.
Donor: Power Fuel & Transport, LLC.
Financial data (yr. ended 12/31/11): Assets, $54,029 (M); expenditures, $2,850; qualifying distributions, $64,275.
Purpose and activities: The foundation provides grants to public charities for general funding.
Fields of interest: General charitable giving.
Application information: Applications not accepted. Unsolicited requests for funds not accepted.
Officer: Wesley Dick, Pres.
EIN: 203981164

3022
Power Service Products, Inc.
513 Peaster Hwy.
P.O. Box 1089
Weatherford, TX 76086-1089
(817) 599-9486

Company URL: http://www.powerservice.com
Establishment information: Established in 1956.
Company type: Private company
Business activities: Manufactures diesel fuel additives.
Business type (SIC): Chemicals/industrial inorganic
Corporate officers: Edward M. Kramer, Pres. and C.E.O.; Ruth Swain, C.F.O.; Jeffrey Kramer, V.P., Sales
Giving statement: Giving through the Kramer Family Foundation.

Kramer Family Foundation
(formerly Power Service Products Foundation)
513 Peaster Hwy.
Weatherford, TX 76086

Establishment information: Established in 1997 in TX.
Donor: Power Service Products, Inc.
Financial data (yr. ended 12/31/11): Assets, $547,723 (M); gifts received, $500,000; expenditures, $35,250; qualifying distributions, $35,250; giving activities include $35,250 for grants.
Purpose and activities: The foundation supports organizations involved with health, Alzheimer's disease, children, and gift distribution.
Fields of interest: Education; Mental health/crisis services; Human services.
Type of support: General/operating support; Research.
Geographic limitations: Giving primarily in north TX, with emphasis on Weatherford.
Support limitations: No grants to individuals.
Application information: Applications not accepted. Contributes only to pre-selected organizations.
Officers: Eddie M. Kramer, Pres. and Treas.; Patricia A. Kramer, V.P.
Directors: Amanda C. Kramer; Jeffrey J. Kramer; Ruth B. Swain.
EIN: 752693125

3023
Power Townsend Company
1387 E. Custer Ave.
Helena, MT 59601 (406) 442-2770

Company URL: http://www.powertownsend.com
Establishment information: Established in 1867.
Company type: Private company
Business activities: Operates home improvement store.
Business type (SIC): Hardware stores
Corporate officers: John A. Wall, Chair.; Mike Wall, Pres.
Board of director: John A. Wall, Chair.
Giving statement: Giving through the Wall Family—Power Townsend Foundation, Inc.

The Wall Family—Power Townsend Foundation, Inc.
1387 Custer Ave.
P.O. Box 4879
Helena, MT 59604-4879

Establishment information: Established in 2004 in MT.
Donors: JAW, LLC; Power Townsend Co.; Mike A. Wall; John Wall; Arlene Wall.
Financial data (yr. ended 12/31/11): Assets, $640,707 (M); gifts received, $10,000; expenditures, $19,037; qualifying distributions, $17,000; giving activities include $17,000 for grants.
Fields of interest: Education.
Support limitations: No grants to individuals.
Application information: Applications not accepted. Unsolicited requests for funds not accepted.
Officers: Mike Wall, Pres.; Kevin Wall, V.P. and Secy.-Treas.
EIN: 201980581

3024
Powers Steel & Wire Products, Inc.
4118 E. Elwood St.
Phoenix, AZ 85040-1922 (602) 437-1160

Company URL: http://www.powerssteel.com
Establishment information: Established in 1966.
Company type: Private company
Business activities: Manufactures steel and wire products.
Business type (SIC): Steel mill products
Corporate officers: John A. Powers, C.E.O.; Alice Powers, Pres. and C.F.O.; Dave Sauer, Cont.
Giving statement: Giving through the John & Alice Powers Foundation.

John & Alice Powers Foundation
5310 E. Wonderview Rd.
Phoenix, AZ 85018-1941

Establishment information: Established in 2007 in AZ.
Donor: Powers Steel & Wire Products, Inc.
Financial data (yr. ended 12/31/11): Assets, $331,568 (M); gifts received, $350,000; expenditures, $388,496; qualifying distributions, $384,866; giving activities include $384,866 for grants.
Purpose and activities: The foundation supports organizations involved with health, human services, and other areas.
Fields of interest: Health care, clinics/centers; Health care; Residential/custodial care, hospices; Human services; General charitable giving.
Type of support: General/operating support.
Geographic limitations: Giving primarily in AZ.
Support limitations: No grants to individuals.
Application information: Applications not accepted. Contributes only to pre-selected organizations.
EIN: 202735962
Selected grants: The following grants are a representative sample of this grantmaker's funding activity:
$24,715 to Valley of the Sun Hospice Association, Phoenix, AZ, 2010.

3025
PPG Industries, Inc.

1 PPG Pl.
Pittsburgh, PA 15272-0001 (412) 434-3131
FAX: (412) 434-2125

Company URL: http://www.ppg.com
Establishment information: Established in 1883.
Company type: Public company
Company ticker symbol and exchange: PPG/NYSE
International Securities Identification Number: US6935061076
Business activities: Manufactures industrial, aerospace, packaging, architectural, automotive, and refinish coatings, flat, automotive, and replacement glass and fiber glass, and chlor-alkali and specialty chemicals.
Business type (SIC): Paints and allied products; chemicals and allied products; glass/flat; glass/ pressed or blown
Financial profile for 2012: Number of employees, 39,200; assets, $15,878,000,000; sales volume, $15,200,000,000; pre-tax net income, $1,402,000,000; expenses, $13,798,000,000; liabilities, $11,815,000,000
Fortune 1000 ranking: 2012—182nd in revenues, 209th in profits, and 285th in assets
Forbes 2000 ranking: 2012—626th in sales, 676th in profits, and 1133rd in assets
Corporate officers: Charles E. Bunch, Chair. and C.E.O.; Frank S. Sklarsky, Exec. V.P., Finance; David B. Navikas, Sr. V.P., Finance and C.F.O.; Glenn E. Bost II, Sr. V.P. and Genl. Counsel; J. Craig Jordan, V.P., Human Resources; John C. Richter, V.P., Opers.; Eric Thiele, Treas.
Board of directors: Charles E. Bunch, Chair.; Stephen F. Angel; James G. Berges; John V. Faraci; Hugh Grant; Victoria F. Haynes; Michele J. Hooper; Robert Mehrabian; Martin H. Richenhagen; Robert Ripp; Thomas J. Usher; David R. Whitwam
Plants: Huntsville, AL; Fresno, CA; Dover, DE; East Point, GA; Mount Zion, IL; Evansville, IN; Berea, Louisville, KY; Lake Charles, LA; Detroit, Evart, MI; Greensboro, Lexington, Shelby, NC; Barberton, Chillicothe, Circleville, Cleveland, Crestline, Delaware, Euclid, Milford, OH; Carlisle, Creighton, Meadville, Springdale, Tipton, PA; Chester, SC; La Porte, Wichita Falls, TX; Batavia, WA; New Martinsville, WV; Oak Creek, WI
Offices: Harmarville, Monroeville, PA
International operations: Australia; Belgium; Bermuda; Brazil; Cameroon; Canada; Chile; China; Czech Republic; Denmark; England; France; Gabon; Germany; Hong Kong; Hungary; Indonesia; Ireland; Italy; Luxembourg; Malaysia; Mexico; Netherlands; Poland; Singapore; Slovakia; Slovenia; South Africa; South Korea; Spain; Suriname; Switzerland; Thailand; Turkey; United Kingdom; Uruguay
Giving statement: Giving through the PPG Industries Foundation.
Company EIN: 250730780

PPG Industries Foundation

1 PPG Pl., Ste. 7E
Pittsburgh, PA 15272-0001
E-mail: foundation@ppg.com; URL: http://www.ppg.com/en/ppgfoundation/Pages/default.aspx

Establishment information: Incorporated in 1951 in PA.
Donor: PPG Industries, Inc.
Contact: Sue Sloan, Exec. Dir.
Financial data (yr. ended 12/31/11): Assets, $9,225,433 (M); gifts received, $5,000,000; expenditures, $4,488,287; qualifying distributions, $4,488,297; giving activities include $4,018,287 for grants and $270,000 for employee matching gifts.
Purpose and activities: The foundation supports organizations that enhance the quality of life in communities where PPG has a presence. Special emphasis is directed toward programs designed to promote educational opportunities and access to community services.
Fields of interest: Arts, equal rights; Museums (science/technology); Performing arts; Arts; Elementary/secondary education; Higher education; Libraries (public); Scholarships/financial aid; Education; Environmental education; Zoos/ zoological societies; Aquariums; Disasters, preparedness/services; Youth development, adult & child programs; American Red Cross; YM/YWCAs & YM/YWHAs; Human services, financial counseling; Human services; Economic development; Community/economic development; United Ways and Federated Giving Programs; Science, formal/general education; Chemistry; Mathematics; Engineering/technology; Science; Public affairs Disabilities, people with; Minorities; African Americans/Blacks; Women.
Programs:

American Chemical Society PPG Scholarships Plus Program: Through the American Chemical Society PPG Scholarships Plus Program, the foundation awards four-year $2,500 college scholarships to under-represented minorities planning to study chemistry or chemical engineering. The award also includes mentoring by PPG employees and a summer internship at a PPG facility in the students' junior and senior year. The program is administered by the American Chemical Society.

Civic and Culture: The foundation supports programs designed to increase accessibility to arts activities and performances through intervention and outreach, computers and technology at libraries, and the country's public and natural resources. The foundation also supports civic programs designed to provide leadership in public affairs, with emphasis on environmental education, community and economic development, and promotion of an effective civic environment.

Disaster Relief: The foundation provides support to communities and employees affected by manmade and natural disasters through a matching gift program to the American Red Cross, cash contributions to major disaster relief agency or affiliate, product donations, and volunteerism.

Education: The foundation supports programs designed to promote academic excellence and prepare the next generation of leaders in business, science, and technology. Special emphasis is directed toward science, technology, engineering, and mathematics (STEM) initiatives designed to reflect PPG's global footprint and promote diversity and under-represented populations.

Employee-Child Scholarship Program: The foundation awards four-year $1,500 college scholarships to children of employees of PPG. The program is administered by the National Merit Scholarship Corporation.

Global Charitable Contributions Program: The foundation and PPG supports programs designed to enhance qualify of life in communities where PPG has a presence throughout the world. Special emphasis is directed toward education; human services; culture and arts; and civic and community. The program is administered by a Contribution Committee in each region and is limited to Asia/ Pacific and EMEA (Europe, Middle East, and Africa).

Grant Incentives for Volunteerism by PPG Employees (GIVE): The foundation awards $250 grants to nonprofit organizations with which employees of PPG volunteer.

Human Services: The foundation support programs designed to provides resources to people in need through the United Way in communities with concentrations of PPG employees; and awards capital support to upgrade facilities and expand access for person with special needs.

Matching Gifts Program: The foundation matches contributions made by employees and directors of PPG to nonprofit organizations involved with education, the United Negro College Fund, and the American Red Cross during a disaster on a one-for-one basis from $25 to $10,000 per contributor, per organization, per year.

National Achievement Scholarship Program: The foundation annually awards two four-year $1,500 college scholarships to outstanding African-American students. The program is administered by the National Merit Scholarship Corporation.

Plant Community Scholarship Program: Through the Plant Community Scholarship Program, the foundation awards four-year $1,500 college scholarships to outstanding students in areas of major PPG facilities. The program is administered by the National Merit Scholarship Corporation.

PPG Care Fund (Concern, Assistance, & Relief for Employees): The foundation provides assistance to PPG employees whose lives have been disrupted by disasters. The fund is established within The Pittsburgh Foundation and the PPG Foundation matches contributions made by employees to the fund.

Public Education Leadership Community Grants (PELC): Through PELC, the foundation awards grants of up to $1,000 to public schools with which employees of PPG are involved for projects that promote systemic change, cannot be paid for with tax dollars, directly benefit and engage students, demonstrate results that motivate students to learn, and have a total budget of less than $5,000.

Type of support: Annual campaigns; Building/ renovation; Capital campaigns; Continuing support; Emergency funds; Employee matching gifts; Employee volunteer services; Employee-related scholarships; Equipment; General/operating support; Program development; Scholarship funds.
Geographic limitations: Giving on a national basis in areas of company operations in AL, AR, CA, CT, DE, GA, KY, IA, IL, LA, MI, NC, NV, OH, SC, TX, WA, WI, and WV, with emphasis on Pittsburgh, PA; giving also to national organizations and in Africa, Asia, Europe, and the Middle East for the Global Charitable Contributions Program.
Support limitations: No support for lobbying organizations, political organizations, or religious organizations not of direct benefit to the entire community. No grants to individuals (except for scholarships), or for advertising or sponsorships, endowments, projects that would directly benefit PPG, special events or telephone solicitation, or general operating support for United Way-supported organizations.
Publications: Annual report (including application guidelines); Application guidelines; Financial statement.
Application information: Applications accepted. Additional information may be requested at a later date. Application form required. Applicants should submit the following:
1) timetable for implementation and evaluation of project
2) results expected from proposed grant
3) qualifications of key personnel
4) statement of problem project will address
5) population served
6) copy of IRS Determination Letter
7) brief history of organization and description of its mission

8) copy of most recent annual report/audited financial statement/990
9) how project's results will be evaluated or measured
10) listing of board of directors, trustees, officers and other key people and their affiliations
11) detailed description of project and amount of funding requested
12) copy of current year's organizational budget and/or project budget

Initial approach: Complete online application
Board meeting date(s): Usually in June and Dec.
Deadline(s): None
Final notification: Following board meetings

Officers and Directors:* Charles E. Bunch*, Chair. and Pres.; Lynn D. Schmidt, V.P.; Donna Lee Walker, V.P.; Daniel Fayock, Secy.; Aziz S. Giga, Treas. and Cont.; Sue Sloan, Exec. Dir.; Glenn E. Bost II; David Navikas; J. Craig Jordan.
Number of staff: 1 full-time professional; 1 part-time professional; 1 part-time support.
EIN: 256037790

3026
PPL Corporation

(formerly PP&L Resources, Inc.)
2 N. 9th St.
Allentown, PA 18101-1179 (610) 774-5151
FAX: (610) 774-5281

Company URL: http://www.pplweb.com
Establishment information: Established in 1920.
Company type: Public company
Company ticker symbol and exchange: PPL/NYSE
Business activities: Generates, transmits, and distributes electricity.
Business type (SIC): Electric services
Financial profile for 2012: Number of employees, 17,729; assets, $43,634,000,000; sales volume, $12,286,000,000; pre-tax net income, $2,082,000,000; expenses, $9,204,000,000; liabilities, $33,154,000,000
Fortune 1000 ranking: 2012—224th in revenues, 139th in profits, and 126th in assets
Corporate officers: William H. Spence, Chair., Pres., and C.E.O.; Paul A. Farr, Exec. V.P. and C.F.O.; Robert J. Grey, Sr. V.P., Genl. Counsel, and Secy.; Mark F. Wilten, V.P., Finance and Treas.; Vincent Sorgi, V.P. and Cont.
Board of directors: William H. Spence, Chair.; Frederick M. Bernthal; John W. Conway; Philip G. Cox; Steven G. Elliott; Louise K. Goeser; Stuart E. Graham; Stuart Heydt; Raja Rajamannar; Craig A. Rogerson; Natica Von Althann; Keith H. Williamson
Subsidiary: PPL Montana, Billings, MT
International operations: United Kingdom
Giving statement: Giving through the PPL Corporation Contributions Program.
Company EIN: 232758192

PPL Corporation Contributions Program

(formerly PP&L Resources, Inc. Corporate Giving Program)
2 N. 9th St.
Allentown, PA 18101-1139 (570) 542-2886
FAX: (570) 542-2890;
E-mail: aroberts@pplweb.com; URL: http://www.pplweb.com/citizenship/community.aspx

Contact: Alana Roberts, Community Affairs Specialist
Financial data (yr. ended 12/31/10): Total giving, $8,678,359, including $8,678,359 for grants.
Purpose and activities: PPL makes charitable contributions to nonprofit organizations involved with arts and culture, education, environmental education, renewable energy, wildlife preservation, healthcare, and human services. Support is given primarily in areas of company operations, with some emphasis on Pennsylvania.
Fields of interest: Arts; Education; Environment, energy; Environmental education; Environment; Animals/wildlife; Health care; Human services; United Ways and Federated Giving Programs; Public affairs.
Type of support: Curriculum development; Employee matching gifts; Employee volunteer services; General/operating support; Program development; Sponsorships.
Geographic limitations: Giving primarily in areas of company operations, with some emphasis on PA.

3027
PPL Montana

303 N. Broadway, Ste. 400
Billings, MT 59101-1255 (406) 237-6900

Company URL: http://www.pplmontana.com
Establishment information: Established in 1999.
Company type: Subsidiary of a public company
Business activities: Operates electric power company.
Business type (SIC): Electric services
Corporate officer: Pete Simonich, V.P. and C.O.O.
Giving statement: Giving through the PPL Montana Corporate Giving Program.

PPL Montana Corporate Giving Program

303 N. Broadway, Ste. 400
Billings, MT 59101-1255 (406) 237-6914
FAX: (406) 237-6901; E-mail: LRPerry@pplweb.com; URL: http://www.pplmontana.com/community/a+good+neighbor.htm

Purpose and activities: PPL Montana makes charitable contributions to nonprofit organizations involved with education, the environment, and economic development. Support is limited to areas of company operations in Montana.
Fields of interest: Education; Environment; Community/economic development.
Program:
PPL Montana Family Scholarship Program: Through the PPL Montana Family Scholarship Program, graduating high school sons and daughters of permanent PPL Montana employees, retirees or deceased employees can attend the college or university of their choice.
Type of support: Employee-related scholarships; General/operating support.
Geographic limitations: Giving limited to areas of company operations in MT.
Publications: Application guidelines.
Application information: Local Community Involvement program is for volunteer resources or funding requests under $1,000 and is intended to support programs and events that provide opportunities for PPL Montana employee involvement.
Initial approach: Complete online application for Community Fund; download application and e-mail completed form to PPL Montana Community Involvement Committee

3028
Pratt & Whitney Power Systems, Inc.

400 Main St.
East Hartford, CT 06118-0968
(860) 565-5776

Company URL: http://www.pratt-whitney.com
Establishment information: Established in 1925.
Company type: Subsidiary of a public company
Business activities: Manufactures aircraft engines; manufactures gas turbines.
Business type (SIC): Engines and turbines
Corporate officers: David P. Hess, Pres.; Paul Adams, C.O.O.; Bob Bailey, V.P. and C.F.O.; Larry Volz, V.P. and C.I.O.; Joe Santos, V.P. and Genl. Counsel; Rajeev Bhalla, V.P., Finance; Nadia Villeneuve, V.P., Human Resources
Subsidiary: Engine Services, Inc., Rocky Hill, CT
Giving statement: Giving through the Pratt & Whitney Power Systems, Inc. Corporate Giving Program.

Pratt & Whitney Power Systems, Inc. Corporate Giving Program

JFK Access Rd
Jamaica, NY 11430 (718) 917-8500
URL: http://www.pw.utc.com/Corporate_Citizenship

Purpose and activities: Pratt & Whitney makes charitable contributions to nonprofit organizations involved with developing the next generation of engineers, researchers and business professionals, promoting a clean and safe environment, and encouraging excellence through the arts. Support is given primarily in areas of company operations.
Fields of interest: Arts; Business school/education; Education; Environment; Employment, formal/general education; Human services; Engineering/technology.
Programs:
Community Power Grant Program: A team of Pratt & Whitney volunteers, consisting of 5 to 15 people, chooses a local educational institution or non-profit human services organization in need of support. The Pratt & Whitney team and the nonprofit partner then select a project that furthers the goals of the organization. Each team member must work on the project for a minimum of 15 hours over a two to six month period. Upon completion of the project, the partner organization receives a $2,500 grant from Pratt & Whitney.
Green Power Grant: A Pratt & Whitney volunteer team consisting of a minimum of three employees, partners with a nonprofit organization whose primary focus is on the environment. The team works on a project which will enhance, protect or preserve the environment or teach others the value of doing so. The Pratt & Whitney volunteers each work a minimum of three hours on the project. When the project is completed, the partner organization will receive a $500 to $5,000 grant from Pratt & Whitney.
UTC Matching Gifts: Pratt & Whitney's Matching Gift Program offers a way for employees to double their contributions to some of their favorite nonprofit educational, cultural, and environmental organizations. Since 1967, United Technologies Corporation has matched millions of dollars of employee donations to schools, colleges and universities, cultural institutions and environmental organizations.
Volunteer Grant Program: Regular, full-time employees may apply for a $250 grant for non-profit organizations to which they volunteer. To be eligible,

an employee must be actively involved with the organization for at least one year and volunteer a minimum of 60 hours per calendar year.
Type of support: Employee volunteer services; General/operating support.
Geographic limitations: Giving primarily in areas of company operations.
Publications: Application guidelines.
Application information: Applications accepted. Application form required.
Initial approach: Complete online application form through URL link to Pratt & Whitney's parent company, United Technologies
Copies of proposal: 1

3029
Praxair, Inc.

39 Old Ridgebury Rd.
Danbury, CT 06810-5113 (203) 837-2000
FAX: (302) 636-5454

Company URL: http://www.praxair.com
Establishment information: Established in 1907.
Company type: Public company
Company ticker symbol and exchange: PX/NYSE
International Securities Identification Number: US74005P1049
Business activities: Manufactures atmospheric and process gases; provides metallic and ceramic coatings and powders application services.
Business type (SIC): Metal coating and plating; chemicals/industrial inorganic
Financial profile for 2012: Number of employees, 26,539; assets, $18,090,000,000; sales volume, $11,224,000,000; pre-tax net income, $2,296,000,000; expenses, $8,787,000,000; liabilities, $12,026,000,000
Fortune 1000 ranking: 2012—241st in revenues, 124th in profits, and 256th in assets
Corporate officers: Stephen F. Angel, Chair., Pres., and C.E.O.; James S. Sawyer, Exec. V.P. and C.F.O.; James T. Breedlove, Sr. V.P., Genl. Counsel, and Secy.; Marc A. Franciosa, V.P. and C.I.O.; Elizabeth T. Hirsch, V.P. and Cont.; Sunil Mattoo, V.P., Mktg.; Susan M. Neumann, V.P., Corp. Comms. and Public Rels.; Sally A. Savoia, V.P., Human Resources
Board of directors: Stephen F. Angel, Chair.; Oscar Bernardes; Bret K. Clayton; Nance K. Dicciani; Edward G. Galante; Claire W. Gargalli; Ira D. Hall; Raymond W. Leboeuf; Larry D. McVay; Wayne T. Smith; Robert L. Wood
Subsidiaries: Amko Service Co., Dover, OH; Innovative Membrane Systems, Inc., Norwood, MA; Jasksonville Welding Supply, Inc., Jacksonville, FL; Praxair Puerto Rico, Inc., Gurabo, PR; Praxair Surface Technologies, Inc., Indianapolis, IN; UCISCO Inc., Houston, TX
Joint Ventures: HydroGEN Supply, Inc., Bellaire, TX; Niject Services Co., Tulsa, OK; Wellnite Svcs., Houston, TX
International operations: Argentina; Austria; Belgium; Bermuda; Bolivia; Brazil; British Virgin Islands; Canada; China; Czech Republic; France; Germany; Hungary; India; Ireland; Italy; Japan; Luxembourg; Malaysia; Mauritius; Mexico; Netherlands; Norway; Paraguay; Portugal; Russia; Singapore; Slovakia; South Korea; Spain; Sweden; Thailand; United Kingdom; Uruguay; Venezuela
Giving statement: Giving through the Praxair Foundation, Inc.
Company EIN: 061249050

Praxair Foundation, Inc.

39 Old Ridgebury Rd.-K2
Danbury, CT 06810-5113
FAX: (203) 837-2454;
E-mail: Praxair_Foundation@praxair.com;
URL: http://www.praxair.com/our-company/our-people/praxair-foundation

Establishment information: Established in 1994.
Donor: Praxair, Inc.
Contact: Susan M. Neuman, Pres.
Financial data (yr. ended 11/30/11): Assets, $502,875 (M); gifts received, $2,945,333; expenditures, $2,797,833; qualifying distributions, $2,797,833; giving activities include $2,797,833 for 205 grants (high: $300,000; low: $150).
Purpose and activities: The foundation supports public libraries and organizations involved with higher education, the environment, health, disaster relief, diversity, and community development.
Fields of interest: Higher education; Libraries (public); Environment; Hospitals (general); Health care; Disasters, preparedness/services; Civil rights, race/intergroup relations; Community/economic development; United Ways and Federated Giving Programs.
Programs:
Employee Volunteer Grants: The foundation awards grants to nonprofit organizations with which employees of Praxair volunteer.
Matching Gifts: The foundation matches contributions made by employees of Praxiar to U.S. colleges and universities and nonprofit organizations on a one-for-one basis from $100 to $15,000 per employee, per year.
Type of support: Building/renovation; Employee matching gifts; Employee volunteer services; Equipment; General/operating support; Program development; Scholarship funds.
Geographic limitations: Giving on a national and international basis in areas of company operations, with emphasis on CT, Asia, Brazil, India, and South America.
Support limitations: No support for religious organizations, fraternal or labor organizations, or discriminatory organizations. No grants to individuals or for sports programs.
Publications: Application guidelines.
Application information: Applications accepted. Organizations receiving support of $25,000 or more are required to submit a final report. Application form required. Applicants should submit the following:
1) detailed description of project and amount of funding requested
2) listing of additional sources and amount of support
3) name, address and phone number of organization
4) contact person
Initial approach: Complete online application form
Deadline(s): None
Officers: Susan M. Neumann, Pres.; Anthony M. Pepper, Secy.; Timothy S. Heenan, Treas.
EIN: 061413665

3030
Praxis Consulting Group, Inc.

9 A/B W. Highland Ave.
Philadelphia, PA 19118 (215) 753-0303
FAX: (215) 753-0305

Company URL: http://www.praxisCG.com
Establishment information: Established in 1988.
Company type: Private company
Business type (SIC): Business services/miscellaneous
Corporate officers: Virginia J. Vanderslice, Pres.; Karrie Imbrogno, Admin.
Giving statement: Giving through the Praxis Consulting Group, Inc. Contributions Program.

Praxis Consulting Group, Inc. Contributions Program

9 A/B W. Highland Ave.
Philadelphia, PA 19118 (215) 753-0303
URL: http://www.praxisCG.com

Purpose and activities: Praxis Consulting Group is a certified B Corporation that donates a percentage of net profits to charitable organizations.
Type of support: Employee volunteer services; General/operating support; Pro bono services - strategic management.

3031
Preferred Mutual Insurance Company

1 Preferred Way
New Berlin, NY 13411 (607) 847-6161

Company URL: http://www.pminsco.com
Establishment information: Established in 1896.
Company type: Mutual company
Business activities: Sells property and casualty insurance.
Business type (SIC): Insurance/fire, marine, and casualty
Financial profile for 2011: Number of employees, 259; assets, $430,243,000; liabilities, $275,111,000
Corporate officers: Robert A. Wadsworth, Chair.; Paul O. Stillman, Vice-Chair.; Christopher P. Taft, C.P.A., Pres. and C.E.O.; Aaron J. Valentine, Sr. V.P., Treas., and C.F.O.; Karlyn T. Myers, V.P. and Corp. Secy.
Board of directors: Robert A. Wadsworth, Chair.; Paul O. Stillman, Vice-Chair.; Matthew T. Conney, Jr.; William C. Craime; Martin A. Dietrick; David B. Emerson; Patrick J. Flanagam; Irad S. Ingraham; Mary Ellen Luker; John C. Mitchell; Geoffrey A. Smith; Christopher P. Taft, C.P.A.; William C. Westbrook
Giving statement: Giving through the Preferred Mutual Insurance Company Foundation.

Preferred Mutual Insurance Company Foundation

c/o NBT Bank, N.A.
52 S. Broad St.
Norwich, NY 13815-1646 (800) 333-7642
E-mail: info@pminsco.com; Application address: 1 Preferred Way, New Berlin, NY 13411-1800,tel.: (800) 333-7642

Establishment information: Established in 1985 in NY.
Donor: Preferred Mutual Insurance Co.
Contact: Kecia Burton
Financial data (yr. ended 12/31/11): Assets, $988,971 (M); gifts received, $106,348; expenditures, $34,788; qualifying distributions, $34,101; giving activities include $34,000 for 19 grants (high: $5,000; low: $500).
Purpose and activities: The foundation supports organizations involved with health and awards college scholarships to individuals located in

Chenango, Delaware, and Otsego counties, New York.
Fields of interest: Health care; Recreation.
Type of support: General/operating support; Scholarships—to individuals.
Geographic limitations: Giving limited to Chenango, Delaware, and Otsego counties, NY.
Application information: Applications accepted. Application form required.
Attach a Copy an interview is required for scholarships. Unsolicited requests for general operating support are not accepted.
Initial approach: Contact foundation for application form
Deadline(s): Apr. 12
Commitee Members: Marcia Cornelius; Eugene T. Heaney; Amy Law; Karlyn Myers; Christopher P. Taft.
Trustee: NBT Bank, N.A.
EIN: 226423721

3032
Preformed Line Products Company

660 Beta Dr.
Cleveland, OH 44143 (440) 461-5200

Company URL: http://www.preformed.com
Establishment information: Established in 1947.
Company type: Public company
Company ticker symbol and exchange: PLPC/NASDAQ
Business activities: Manufactures cable anchoring and control hardware and systems, overhead and underground splice cases, and fiber optic splicing and high speed cross-connect devices.
Business type (SIC): Lighting and wiring equipment/electric; communications equipment
Financial profile for 2012: Number of employees, 2,901; assets, $333,060,000; sales volume, $439,190,000; pre-tax net income, $44,830,000; expenses, $395,070,000; liabilities, $92,000,000
Corporate officers: Robert G. Ruhlman, Chair., Pres., and C.E.O.; Eric R. Graef, V.P., Finance, and C.F.O.; William H. Haag III, V.P., Opers.; Dennis F. McKenna, V.P., Mktg.; J. Cecil Curlee, Jr., V.P., Human Resources; Caroline S. Vaccariello, Genl. Counsel and Corp. Secy.
Board of directors: Robert G. Ruhlman, Chair.; Glenn E. Corlett; Richard R. Gascoigne; Michael E. Gibbons; R. Steven Kestner; Barbara P. Ruhlman; Randall M. Ruhlman
Subsidiary: Direct Power & Water, Albuquerque, NM
Plants: Rogers, AR; Albemarle, NC
International operations: Australia; Brazil; Canada; China; Mexico; South Africa; Spain; Thailand; United Kingdom
Giving statement: Giving through the Preformed Line Products Company Contributions Program.
Company EIN: 340676895

Preformed Line Products Company Contributions Program

P.O. Box 91129
Cleveland, OH 44101-3129
FAX: (440) 473-9162;
E-mail: jmooney@preformed.com

Contact: Jacqueline Mooney, Asst. to C.E.O.
Purpose and activities: Preformed Line Products makes charitable contributions to nonprofit organizations involved with higher education and on a case by case basis. Support is given primarily in areas of company operations.
Fields of interest: Higher education; General charitable giving.
Type of support: Employee matching gifts; General/operating support.
Geographic limitations: Giving primarily in areas of company operations.
Application information: Applications accepted. The Office of the Chairman handles giving. Application form not required.
Initial approach: Proposal to headquarters
Deadline(s): None
Final notification: Following review

3033
PREM Group

351 N.W., 12th Ave.
Portland, OR 97209-2905 (503) 224-1460

Company URL: http://www.premgrp.com
Establishment information: Established in 1993.
Company type: Private company
Business type (SIC): Business services/miscellaneous
Corporate officers: Jacob Johnson, C.E.O.; Doug Forst, C.O.O.; Lance Inouye, C.F.O.
Giving statement: Giving through the PREM Group Corporate Giving Program.

PREM Group Corporate Giving Program

351 NW 12th
Portland, OR 97209-2905 (503) 224-1460
URL: http://www.premgrp.com

Purpose and activities: PREM Group is a certified B Corporation that donates a percentage of net profits to charitable organizations.

3034
Premera Blue Cross

7001 - 220th St. S.W., Bldg. 1
Mountlake Terrace, WA 98043-2124
(800) 722-1471

Company URL: http://www.premera.com
Establishment information: Established in 1933.
Company type: Subsidiary of a private company
Business activities: Operates medical service plan.
Business type (SIC): Insurance/accident and health
Financial profile for 2010: Number of employees, 500
Corporate officers: H.R. Brereton Barlow, Pres. and C.E.O.; Kent S. Marquardt, Exec. V.P. and C.F.O.; Kirsten Simonitsch, Sr. V.P. and C.I.O.; John Pierce, Sr. V.P. and Genl. Counsel; Kristen Kemp, Sr. V.P., Opers.; Barbara Magusin, Sr. V.P., Human Resources
Board of directors: Robert Cremin; John Gollhofer, M.D.; Richard P. Fox; John Heath III; Rosalio Lopez, M.D.; Kathryn L. Munro; Carol K. Nelson; Maria M. Pope; Gary Pruitt; Robert Wallace
Subsidiaries: Blue Cross Blue Shield of Alaska, Anchorage, AK; LifeWise, Bend, OR; MSC/Premera Blue Cross, Spokane, WA
Giving statement: Giving through the Premera CARES Program.

Premera CARES Program

7001 220th St. S.W., Bldg. 1
Mountlake Terrace, WA 98043-2160
For Alaska: Johanna Raisch, tel.: (917) 677-2426; For eastern Washington: Stefanie Bruno, tel.: (509) 252-7431; For western Washington: tel.: (425) 918-5933; URL: https://www.premera.com/stellent/groups/public/documents/xcpproject/social_responsibility.asp

Purpose and activities: Premera makes charitable contributions to educational institutions, government agencies, and nonprofit organizations involved with health and wellness. Special emphasis is directed towards programs designed to encourage exercise and stress-management. Support is limited to areas of company operations in Alaska and Washington.
Fields of interest: Public health; Public health, physical fitness; Mental health, stress Economically disadvantaged.
Type of support: Employee volunteer services; General/operating support; In-kind gifts; Program development.
Geographic limitations: Giving limited to areas of company operations in AK and WA.
Support limitations: No support for religious organizations not of direct benefit to the entire community, discriminatory organizations, or arts organizations. No grants to individuals or for capital campaigns.
Publications: Application guidelines; Corporate giving report.
Application information: Applications accepted. Application form required. Applicants should submit the following:
1) timetable for implementation and evaluation of project
2) results expected from proposed grant
3) copy of IRS Determination Letter
4) brief history of organization and description of its mission
5) copy of most recent annual report/audited financial statement/990
6) how project's results will be evaluated or measured
7) listing of board of directors, trustees, officers and other key people and their affiliations
8) detailed description of project and amount of funding requested
9) copy of current year's organizational budget and/or project budget
10) listing of additional sources and amount of support
11) additional materials/documentation
Proposals should include information showing the effectiveness, reliability, and community credibility of the organization.
Initial approach: Complete online application form
Deadline(s): None
Final notification: 90 days

3035
Premier Communications

339 1st Ave., N.E.
Sioux Center, IA 51250 (712) 722-3451
FAX: (712) 722-1113

Company URL: http://www.mypremieronline.com/
Company type: Mutual company
Business activities: Provides telecommunications services.
Business type (SIC): Telephone communications
Corporate officer: Douglas A. Boone, C.E.O.

Giving statement: Giving through the Premier Communications Foundation.

Premier Communications Foundation

(formerly MTC Foundation, Inc.)
c/o Mutual Telephone Company
P.O. Box 200
Sioux Center, IA 51250-0200

Establishment information: Established in 1990 in IA.
Donor: Mutual Telephone Co.
Financial data (yr. ended 12/31/11): Assets, $3,653,619 (M); gifts received, $50,000; expenditures, $272,926; qualifying distributions, $233,750; giving activities include $233,750 for 45 grants (high: $30,000; low: $250).
Purpose and activities: The foundation supports fire departments and organizations involved with education, health, human services, and community development.
Fields of interest: Elementary/secondary education; Higher education; Education; Hospitals (general); Health care; Disasters, fire prevention/control; Family services; Human services; Community/economic development; Christian agencies & churches.
Type of support: General/operating support; Scholarship funds.
Geographic limitations: Giving primarily in IA.
Application information: Applications not accepted. Unsolicited requests for funds not accepted.
Officers: Howard Beernink, Pres.; Owen Dykshorn, V.P.; Glen Vermeer, Secy.; Douglas Boone, Treas.
Directors: Ted Hengeveld; John Koerselman; David Krahling; Michael D. McAlpine; Lauren Vos.
EIN: 421358494
Selected grants: The following grants are a representative sample of this grantmaker's funding activity:
$22,000 to Northwestern College, Orange City, IA, 2010. For scholarships.
$20,000 to Northwestern College, Orange City, IA, 2010. For general fund.
$5,000 to Hull Christian School, Hull, IA, 2010.

3036
Premier Dental Products Company

1710 Romano Dr.
Plymouth Meeting, PA 19462-2822
(610) 239-6000

Company URL: http://www.premusa.com/home/default.asp
Establishment information: Established in 1913.
Company type: Private company
Business activities: Sells dental supplies and instruments wholesale.
Business type (SIC): Professional and commercial equipment—wholesale
Corporate officers: Gary Charlestein, C.E.O.; Julie Charlestein, Pres.; Joseph V. Hosack, Jr., C.O.O.; Joe Simon, Sr. V.P., Mktg.; Alan Kegerise, V.P., Sales; Cindy Pugliese, Cont.; Morton L. Charlestein, Chair. Emeritus
Giving statement: Giving through the Julius and Ray Charlestein Foundation, Inc.

Julius and Ray Charlestein Foundation, Inc.

1710 Romano Dr.
Plymouth Meeting, PA 19462-2822 (610) 239-6004

Establishment information: Established in 1963 in PA.
Donors: Morton L. Charlestein; Premier Dental Products Co.; Premier Medical Co.
Contact: Ellyn Phillips, Exec. Dir.
Financial data (yr. ended 06/30/12): Assets, $2,938,440 (M); gifts received, $1,581,027; expenditures, $1,055,265; qualifying distributions, $1,006,444; giving activities include $1,006,444 for grants.
Purpose and activities: The foundation supports organizations involved with education, ALS, human services, and Judaism.
Fields of interest: Secondary school/education; Theological school/education; Education; ALS; Human services; United Ways and Federated Giving Programs; Jewish federated giving programs; Jewish agencies & synagogues.
Type of support: Annual campaigns; General/operating support; Program development; Scholarship funds.
Geographic limitations: Giving primarily in the Philadelphia, PA, area.
Support limitations: No grants to individuals.
Application information: Applications accepted. Application form not required.
Initial approach: Proposal
Deadline(s): None
Officers: Morton L. Charlestein, Pres.; Gary Charlestein, Secy.-Treas.; Ellyn Phillips, Exec. Dir.
EIN: 232310090
Selected grants: The following grants are a representative sample of this grantmaker's funding activity:
$72,500 to Jewish Federation of Greater Philadelphia, Philadelphia, PA, 2011.
$61,200 to Amyotrophic Lateral Sclerosis Association, Ambler, PA, 2011.
$16,125 to Camp Ramah in the Poconos, Jenkintown, PA, 2011.
$10,000 to Friends of Yemin Orde, Rockville, MD, 2011.
$10,000 to Jewish National Fund, New York, NY, 2011.
$5,000 to Jack M. Barrack Hebrew Academy, Bryn Mawr, PA, 2011.
$1,000 to Madlyn and Leonard Abramson Center for Jewish Life, North Wales, PA, 2011.

3037
Premix Inc.

3365 E. Center St.
P.O. Box 281
North Kingsville, OH 44068-0281
(440) 224-2181

Company URL: http://www.premix.com
Establishment information: Established in 1959.
Company type: Private company
Business activities: Manufactures plastic products and custom moldings.
Business type (SIC): Plastic products/miscellaneous
Financial profile for 2011: Number of employees, 430
Corporate officers: William Kennedy, C.E.O.; Dane Zoul, C.F.O.; Mae Zyjewski, V.P., Opers.
Board of directors: Jeff Cash; Mike Seibert
Giving statement: Giving through the Premix Foundation.

Premix Foundation

3365 E. Center St.
North Kingsville, OH 44068

Establishment information: Established in 1986 in OH.
Donor: Premix, Inc.
Contact: Dane T. Zoul, Pres.
Financial data (yr. ended 12/31/11): Assets, $42,417 (M); expenditures, $17,230; qualifying distributions, $16,798; giving activities include $16,048 for 32 grants (high: $6,000; low: $50).
Purpose and activities: The foundation supports organizations involved with arts and culture, education, health, community development, and civic affairs.
Fields of interest: Arts; Education; Health care; Economic development; Community/economic development; United Ways and Federated Giving Programs; Leadership development; Public affairs.
Type of support: Annual campaigns; Building/renovation; Capital campaigns; Continuing support; Equipment; General/operating support; Program development; Technical assistance.
Geographic limitations: Giving primarily in MI and OH.
Support limitations: No grants to individuals.
Application information: Applications accepted. Application form required. Applicants should submit the following:
1) copy of most recent annual report/audited financial statement/990
2) detailed description of project and amount of funding requested
Initial approach: Letter
Deadline(s): None
Officers: Dane T. Zoul, Pres.; Ken W. Lazo*, Secy.-Treas.
EIN: 341530598

3038
Elvis Presley Enterprises, Inc.

3734 Elvis Presley Blvd.
Memphis, TN 38116-0508 (901) 332-3322
FAX: (901) 344-3101

Company URL: http://www.elvis.com
Establishment information: Established in 1981.
Company type: Subsidiary of a private company
Business activities: Operates tourist attraction; licenses entertainment properties; provides Internet entertainment services; operates hotel; develops real estate.
Business type (SIC): Amusement and recreation services/miscellaneous; real estate subdividers and developers; investors/miscellaneous; hotels and motels; computer services
Financial profile for 2010: Number of employees, 250
Corporate officers: Jack R. Soden, Pres. and C.E.O.; Nancy Alyea, V.P. and C.F.O.; Regina Gambill, V.P., Opers.
Office: Los Angeles, CA
Giving statement: Giving through the Elvis Presley Charitable Foundation, Inc.

Elvis Presley Charitable Foundation, Inc.

(formerly Elvis Presley Memorial Foundation, Inc.)
3734 Elvis Presley Blvd.
Memphis, TN 38116 (901) 332-3322
E-mail: Graceland@Elvis.com; Additional tel.: (800) 238-2000; TTY: (901) 344-3146; URL: http://www.elvis.com/about-epe/giving.aspx

Establishment information: Established as a grantmaking public charity in 1984 in TN; status changed to company-sponsored foundation in 1990; classified as a company-sponsored operating foundation in 2002.
Donors: Elvis Presley Enterprises, Inc.; Easter Unlimited Inc.
Financial data (yr. ended 07/31/11): Assets, $19,396 (M); gifts received, $41,595; expenditures, $126,278; qualifying distributions, $125,175; giving activities include $125,175 for 22 grants (high: $62,500; low: $500).
Purpose and activities: The foundation supports organizations involved with arts and culture, cancer, diabetes, child welfare, human services, and business promotion and operates Presley Place, a facility offering housing and human services to homeless families.
Fields of interest: Museums; Performing arts, music; Arts; Cancer; Crime/violence prevention, child abuse; Housing/shelter; Children, services; Family services; Human services; Community development, business promotion; United Ways and Federated Giving Programs Homeless.
Type of support: Annual campaigns; Program development; Research; Scholarship funds; Sponsorships.
Geographic limitations: Giving limited to Memphis, TN.
Support limitations: No grants to individuals.
Application information: Applications not accepted. Contributes only to pre-selected organizations.
Officers and Trustees:* Lisa Marie Presley*, Pres.; Jack R. Soden*, V.P.; Gary Hovey.
EIN: 581632547
Selected grants: The following grants are a representative sample of this grantmaker's funding activity:
$102,500 to Metropolitan Inter-Faith Association, Memphis, TN, 2010.
$24,500 to National Civil Rights Museum, Memphis, TN, 2010.
$12,500 to American Cancer Society, Memphis, TN, 2010.
$12,000 to United Way of the Mid-South, Memphis, TN, 2010.
$10,500 to University of Memphis, Memphis, TN, 2010.
$10,000 to Memphis Symphony Orchestra, Memphis, TN, 2010.
$5,000 to American Heart Association, Memphis, TN, 2010.
$5,000 to Teach for America, Memphis, TN, 2010.
$3,000 to University of Memphis, Memphis, TN, 2010.
$2,238 to University of Memphis Foundation, Memphis, TN, 2010.

3039
Price Chopper Operating Co., Inc.

(also known as Price Chopper Supermarkets)
501 Duanesburg Rd.
Schenectady, NY 12306-1058
(518) 355-5000

Company URL: http://www.pricechopper.com
Establishment information: Established in 1937.
Company type: Subsidiary of a private company
Business activities: Operates supermarkets.
Business type (SIC): Groceries—retail
Corporate officers: Neil M. Golub, Chair. and C.E.O.; Jerel T. Golub, Pres. and C.O.O.; Richard Bauer, C.I.O.; John Endres, Sr. V.P. and C.F.O.; William J. Kenneally, Sr. V.P. and Corp. Secy.
Board of director: Neil M. Golub, Chair.
Giving statement: Giving through the Price Chopper Supermarkets Corporate Giving Program.

Price Chopper Supermarkets Corporate Giving Program

501 Duanesburg Rd.
Schenectady, NY 12306-1058
URL: http://www.pricechopper.com

Purpose and activities: Price Chopper makes charitable contributions to nonprofit organizations involved with historic preservation, arts and culture, historic preservation, education, health, and disaster relief. Support is given primarily in areas of company operations in Connecticut, Massachusetts, New Hampshire, New York, Pennsylvania, and Vermont.
Fields of interest: Historic preservation/historical societies; Arts; Education; Hospitals (general); Public health; Health care; Disasters, preparedness/services; Athletics/sports, amateur leagues; Community/economic development; United Ways and Federated Giving Programs.
Programs:
Price Chopper Annual Minority Achievement Scholarships: Price Chopper annually awards twelve $2,000 scholarships to minority young people to help them realize their educational potential and dreams.
Price Chopper Associate Scholarship Program: Through the Price Chopper Associate Scholarship Program, Price Chopper funds more than $1 million in scholarships for part-time Associates who are high school juniors at least 16 years old wishing to further their education at a degree-granting college or university.
Type of support: Cause-related marketing; Employee volunteer services; Employee-related scholarships; Scholarships—to individuals; Sponsorships.
Geographic limitations: Giving limited to areas of company operations in CT, MA, NH, NY, PA, and VT; giving also to national organizations.
Application information: Applications accepted. Application form not required.
Initial approach: Proposal to headquarters for sponsorships; contact nearest company store for product donations; visit website for application information for scholarships

3040
T. Rowe Price Group, Inc.

(formerly T. Rowe Price Associates, Inc.)
100 E. Pratt St.
Baltimore, MD 21202-1009
(410) 345-2000

Company URL: http://www.troweprice.com
Establishment information: Established in 1937.
Company type: Public company
Company ticker symbol and exchange: TROW/NASDAQ
Business activities: Operates financial services company.
Business type (SIC): Security and commodity services; security and commodity brokers, dealers, exchanges, and services
Financial profile for 2012: Number of employees, 5,372; assets, $4,202,800,000; sales volume, $3,022,500,000; pre-tax net income, $1,435,100,000; expenses, $1,658,200,000; liabilities, $356,700,000
Fortune 1000 ranking: 2012—709th in revenues, 221st in profits, and 645th in assets
Forbes 2000 ranking: 2012—1625th in sales, 658th in profits, and 1866th in assets
Corporate officers: Brian Rogers, Chair.; Edward Bennard, Vice-Chair.; James A. Kennedy, Pres. and C.E.O.; Kenneth V. Moreland, V.P., Treas., and C.F.O.
Board of directors: Brian Rogers, Chair.; Edward Bennard, Vice-Chair.; James T. Brady; J. Alfred Broaddus, Jr.; Mary K. Bush; Freeman A. Hrabowski III; Donald B. Hebb, Jr.; Robert F. MacLellan; Dr. Alfred Sommer; Dwight S. Taylor; Anne Marie Whittemore
Subsidiaries: T. Rowe Price Investment Services, Inc., Baltimore, MD; T. Rowe Price Services, Inc., Colorado Springs, CO
Offices: San Francisco, CA; Tampa, FL; Owings Mills, MD
Giving statement: Giving through the T. Rowe Price Foundation.
Company EIN: 522264646

T. Rowe Price Foundation

(formerly T. Rowe Associates Foundation, Inc.)
100 E. Pratt St.
Baltimore, MD 21202-1008 (410) 345-3603
FAX: (410) 345-2848;
E-mail: community_involvement@troweprice.com; Additional tel.: (410) 345-6673; URL: http://corporate.troweprice.com/ccw/home/responsibility/corporateSocialResponsibilityOverview.do

Establishment information: Established in 1981 in MD.
Donors: T. Rowe Price Associates, Inc.; T. Rowe Price Group, Inc.
Contact: Stacy Van Horn, Exec. Dir.
Financial data (yr. ended 12/31/11): Assets, $49,495,032 (M); gifts received, $15,018,823; expenditures, $5,316,934; qualifying distributions, $5,327,525; giving activities include $5,268,252 for 1,148 grants (high: $1,016,833; low: $25).
Purpose and activities: The foundation supports organizations involved with arts and culture, education, youth development, human services, and community development.
Fields of interest: Museums (art); Arts; Elementary school/education; Secondary school/education; Higher education; Libraries (public); Education; Youth development; Salvation Army; Human services; Community/economic development; United Ways and Federated Giving Programs.

Program:

Employee Matching Gifts: The foundation matches contributions made by employees of T. Rowe Price Associates and its subsidiaries to institutions of secondary and higher education and nonprofit organizations involved with arts and culture, human services, community development, and civic affairs on a one-for-one basis from $25 to $20,000 per employee, per year.

Type of support: Capital campaigns; Continuing support; Employee matching gifts; Employee volunteer services; General/operating support; Program development; Scholarship funds.

Geographic limitations: Giving primarily in areas of company operations in Baltimore, MD, area.

Support limitations: No support for religious or political organizations, hospitals, healthcare providers, recreational sports leagues, or private foundations. No grants to individuals, or for sports-related fundraisers.

Application information: Applications not accepted. The foundation generally practices an invitation only process for giving.

Officers and Trustees:* Ann Allston Boyce*, Pres.; Stephen W. Boesel*, V.P.; Barbara J. Burdett*, V.P.; Meredith C. Callahan*, V.P.; Hugh M. Evans III*, V.P.; Jacqueline C. Hrabowski*, V.P.; George A. Roche*, V.P.; William F. Wendler II*, V.P.; Vernon A. Reid, Jr.*, Secy.-Treas.; Stacy Van Horn, Exec. Dir.

Number of staff: 1 full-time professional; 1 full-time support.

EIN: 521231953

Selected grants: The following grants are a representative sample of this grantmaker's funding activity:

$1,000,907 to T. Rowe Price Program for Charitable Giving, Baltimore, MD, 2010.
$300,000 to United Way of Central Maryland, Baltimore, MD, 2010.
$136,350 to Baltimore Museum of Art, Baltimore, MD, 2010.
$90,250 to Teach for America, Baltimore, MD, 2010.
$68,000 to Center for Urban Families, Baltimore, MD, 2010.
$51,145 to Enoch Pratt Free Library of Baltimore City, Baltimore, MD, 2010.
$8,000 to United Way of the Bay Area, San Francisco, CA, 2010.
$5,000 to Baltimore Clayworks, Baltimore, MD, 2010.
$5,000 to Emily Krzyzewski Family Life Center, Durham, NC, 2010.
$5,000 to National Summer Learning Association, Baltimore, MD, 2010.

3041
Priceless Resource Inc.

63 Flushing Ave., Ste. 11A
P.O. Box 321
Brooklyn, NY 11205-1005 (718) 643-8951

Company URL: http://www.pricelessresource.com
Establishment information: Established in 1995.
Company type: Private company
Business activities: Electrical equipment and appliance wholesaler.
Business type (SIC): Electrical goods—wholesale
Corporate officers: Isaac Meisels, Pres. and C.E.O.; Joseph Bailey, Exec. V.P., Sales; Joel Meisels, V.P., Opers.
Giving statement: Giving through the IGW Charitable Foundation Trust.

IGW Charitable Foundation Trust

4211 16th Ave.
Brooklyn, NY 11204-1003

Establishment information: Established in 2002 in NY.
Donors: The Closing Network; Anthony Pinkesz; Isaac Meisels; Priceless Resource.
Financial data (yr. ended 12/31/11): Assets, $1,415,036 (M); gifts received, $37,000; expenditures, $92,141; qualifying distributions, $90,391; giving activities include $90,391 for grants.
Purpose and activities: The foundation supports organizations involved with Judaism.
Type of support: General/operating support.
Geographic limitations: Giving primarily in NY.
Support limitations: No grants to individuals.
Application information: Applications not accepted. Unsolicited requests for funds not accepted.
Trustees: Anthony Pinkesz; Sara Pinkesz.
EIN: 376392153

3042
PricewaterhouseCoopers, LLP

300 Madison Ave., 24th Fl.
New York, NY 10017 (646) 471-4000

Company URL: http://www.pwcglobal.com/us
Establishment information: Established in 1749.
Company type: Private company
Business activities: Provides auditing, accounting, and tax advisory services; provides management, information technology, and human resource consulting services; provides financial advisory services; provides legal advisory services.
Business type (SIC): Accounting, auditing, and bookkeeping services; security and commodity services; legal services; management and public relations services
Financial profile for 2011: Number of employees, 168,000; sales volume, $29,200,000,000
Corporate officers: Robert E. Moritz, Chair.; Mike Burwell, C.F.O.; John Carter, C.A.O.; Stuart W. Fulton, C.I.O.; Niloufar Molavi, Chief Diversity Off.
Board of director: Robert E. Moritz., Chair.
Giving statement: Giving through the PricewaterhouseCoopers LLP Corporate Giving Program and the PricewaterhouseCoopers Charitable Foundation, Inc.

PricewaterhouseCoopers LLP Corporate Giving Program

300 Madison Ave., 24th Fl.
New York, NY 10017-6232 (312) 298-6669
FAX: (813) 286-6000; Contacts for Impact Program: Charlotte Coker Gibson, Prog. Dir., tel.: (703) 918-3286, e-mail: charlotee.coker.gibson@us.pwc.com; Heather Tilis, Sr. Assoc., tel. (877) 934-6722, fax: (813) 281-6238, e-mail: heather.tilis@us.pwc.com; Additional e-mail: impact@us.pwc.com; Application address for Impact Program: Attn: Heather Tilis, Pricewaterhouse Coopers LLC, 1900 St. Antoine St., Detroit, MI, 48226; URL: http://www.pwc.com/us/en/about-us/corporate-responsibility/index.jhtml

Contact: Shannon Schuyler, U.S. Managing Dir., Corp. Responsibility
Purpose and activities: As a complement to its foundation, PricewaterhouseCoopers also makes charitable contributions to nonprofit organizations directly. Support is given primarily in areas of company operations, with emphasis on Washington, DC, Atlanta, Georgia, Boston, Massachusetts, New York, New York, Charlotte, North Carolina, and Philadelphia, Pennsylvania.
Fields of interest: Secondary school/education; Higher education; Education; Disasters, preparedness/services; Youth development, business; Youth, services; International affairs, U.N.; United Ways and Federated Giving Programs; General charitable giving African Americans/Blacks.

Program:

Impact Program: PricewaterhouseCoopers supports the Impact educational community initiative to benefit Black/African-American high school juniors. The program is designed to provide students with skills, tools, and strategies necessary to make educational and career choices, and enhance their understanding of career opportunities in the business word. Impact scholars will broaden their awareness of academic options; prepare for pursuing higher education; acquire tools for managing the necessary financial commitment; and gain exposure to leadership networks. The program includes monthly workshops and mentorship.

Type of support: Conferences/seminars; Employee matching gifts; Employee volunteer services; General/operating support; Program development.
Geographic limitations: Giving primarily in areas of company operations, with emphasis on Washington, DC, Atlanta, GA, Boston, MA, Charlotte, NC, New York, NY, and Philadelphia, PA.
Publications: Application guidelines.
Application information: Applications accepted. An interview may be requested for Impact Program. Application form required.
Applications for Impact Program should include PSAT/SAT/ACT scores, official transcripts, a personal essay, and a completed recommendation form.

Initial approach: Download application form and mail to application address for Impact Program
Deadline(s): Dec. 1 for Impact Program

PricewaterhouseCoopers Charitable Foundation, Inc.

(formerly Coopers & Lybrand Foundation)
300 Madison Ave.
New York, NY 10017-6232 (813) 348-7725
URL: http://www.pwc.com/us/en/about-us/corporate-responsibility/corporate-responsibility-report-2011/community/charitable-foundation.jhtml

Establishment information: Established in 1941 in NY.
Financial data (yr. ended 09/30/11): Revenue, $11,217,709; assets, $16,564,273 (M); gifts received, $10,760,148; expenditures, $2,661,257; program services expenses, $2,092,719; giving activities include $1,191,095 for 41 grants (high: $500,000; low: $7,000) and $432,124 for grants to individuals.
Purpose and activities: Giving primarily for higher education, including accounting and business education, as well as to victims of, and to organizations that assisted victims of, the September 11, 2001 terrorist attacks.
Fields of interest: Higher education; Business school/education; Education; Disasters, 9/11/01; United Ways and Federated Giving Programs.
Type of support: Employee matching gifts; Fellowships; General/operating support; Grants to individuals; Professorships; Research.
Officers and Directors:* Mary Ann Cloyd*, Co-Pres.; Joseph C. Simmons*, Pres.-Elect; W. Jeffrey Hoover*, Treas.; Shannon L. Schuyler*, Secy.; Joseph C. Atkinson; Mark Bruno; Ronald M. Cofield;

Thomas J. Craven; Ronald D. Haas; and 2 additional Director.
EIN: 136116238

3043
Primary Health Care Associates, P.C.

(doing business as CareNow)
645 E. State Hwy. 121
Coppell, TX 75019-7942 (972) 745-7500

Establishment information: Established in 1993.
Company type: Private company
Business activities: Operates medical doctors' office.
Business type (SIC): Offices and clinics/doctors'
Financial profile for 2009: Number of employees, 120
Corporate officers: David J. Walter, Pres.; Mike Mayden, C.F.O.
Giving statement: Giving through the PHM Foundation.

The PHM Foundation

P.O. Box 1333
Coppell, TX 75019-1333
URL: http://phmfoundation.org/

Establishment information: Established in 2006 in TX.
Donors: Care Now; Dura Medical Inc.; Primary Health Management, Ltd.; Primary Health, Inc.
Financial data (yr. ended 12/31/11): Assets, $5,259,116 (M); gifts received, $11,255,000; expenditures, $8,582,523; qualifying distributions, $8,574,373; giving activities include $8,574,373 for 19 grants (high: $3,738,500; low: $5,000).
Purpose and activities: The foundation supports religious ministries and organizations involved with print publishing, reproductive health, and youth. The foundation also operates an economic development program to promote entrepreneurship and development in developing countries.
Fields of interest: Media, print publishing; Reproductive health; Youth, services; International economic development; Social entrepreneurship; Christian agencies & churches; Jewish agencies & synagogues; Religion, interfaith issues; Religion.
International interests: Developing countries.
Type of support: General/operating support; Program-related investments/loans.
Geographic limitations: Giving primarily in CA, Washington, DC, FL, MO, NM, NV, and TX; giving also to developing countries through program-related investments.
Support limitations: No grants to individuals.
Application information: Applications not accepted. Unsolicited applications are not accepted. The foundation utilizes an invitation only process for giving.
Officers and Directors:* David Walter*, Pres.; Jennifer L. Walter*, Secy.; Daniel E. Walter*, Exec. Dir.
EIN: 204948182
Selected grants: The following grants are a representative sample of this grantmaker's funding activity:
$5,770,000 to International House of Prayer, Kansas City, MO, 2010.
$3,738,500 to International House of Prayer, Kansas City, MO, 2011.
$1,300,000 to International Justice Mission, Arlington, VA, 2011.
$1,220,000 to General Council of the Assemblies of God, Springfield, MO, 2011.
$680,000 to Global Network Ministries, Laguna Niguel, CA, 2011.
$450,000 to International Justice Mission, Arlington, VA, 2010.
$400,000 to Exodus Cry, Kansas City, MO, 2011.
$350,000 to Friends of India Christian Ministries, Dana Point, CA, 2010.
$325,000 to Hosanna, Albuquerque, NM, 2011.
$257,000 to Call, The, Kansas City, MO, 2011.
$170,000 to Metro Family Ministries, Garland, TX, 2011.
$151,500 to General Council of the Assemblies of God, Springfield, MO, 2010.
$100,000 to Love Mercy, Olathe, KS, 2011.
$75,000 to Hosanna, Albuquerque, NM, 2010.
$75,000 to Wycliffe Bible Translators, Orlando, FL, 2010.
$50,000 to Call, The, Kansas City, MO, 2010.
$50,000 to Messianic Jewish Bible Institute, Euless, TX, 2010.
$50,000 to Metro Family Ministries, Garland, TX, 2010.
$30,000 to Agape International Missions, Roseville, CA, 2011.
$30,000 to Youth With a Mission, Las Vegas, NV, 2010.

3044
Prime Packaging Corp.

1290 Metropolitan Ave.
Brooklyn, NY 11237-1104 (718) 417-1116

Company URL: http://primepackaging.com
Establishment information: Established in 1978.
Company type: Private company
Business activities: Sells wholesale nondurable goods and industrial service paper.
Business type (SIC): Non-durable goods—wholesale
Corporate officers: Arnold Kohn, Pres.; Solomon Wieder, Corp. Secy.
Giving statement: Giving through the Keren Yehuda Foundation.

Keren Yehuda Foundation

c/o A. Ringel
1750 44th St.
Brooklyn, NY 11204-1050

Establishment information: Established in 2006 in NY.
Donors: Yosef Gold; Yehuda Weber; Prime Packaging Corp.; Sophie Weber Trust; Very Very Good Brokers, Inc.; AEB Asset Trust; CEW Asset Trust; JHW Asset Trust; RW Asset Trust; YPW Asset Trust; Prime Packaging Corp.; Sophie Weber Trust; Samuel D. Friedman; Metro Park, LLC; Josef Kohn; 4514 Realty Trust; GSF Asset Trust; Sophie Weber Trust.
Financial data (yr. ended 06/30/12): Assets, $1,385,590 (M); gifts received, $97,000; expenditures, $69,572; qualifying distributions, $68,636; giving activities include $68,636 for grants.
Purpose and activities: The foundation supports organizations involved with education and Judaism.
Fields of interest: Elementary/secondary education; Education; Jewish agencies & synagogues.
Type of support: General/operating support.
Geographic limitations: Giving primarily in Brooklyn, NY.
Application information: Applications not accepted. Unsolicited requests for funds not accepted.
Trustees: Pearl Weber; Yehuda Weber.
EIN: 208045732

3045
Primerica, Inc.

3120 Breckinridge Blvd.
Duluth, GA 30099 (770) 381-1000
FAX: (770) 564-6216

Company URL: http://www.primerica.com
Establishment information: Established in 1977.
Company type: Public company
Company ticker symbol and exchange: PRI/NYSE
Business activities: Operates insurance and asset management services company.
Business type (SIC): Insurance/life
Financial profile for 2012: Number of employees, 1,971; assets, $10,337,880,000; sales volume, $1,190,710,000; pre-tax net income, $266,890,000; expenses, $923,830,000; liabilities, $9,062,460,000
Corporate officers: D. Richard Williams, Chair. and Co-C.E.O.; John A. Addison, Jr., Co-C.E.O.; Glenn J. Williams, Pres.; Gregory C. Pitts, Exec. V.P. and C.O.O.; Alison S. Rand, Exec. V.P. and C.F.O.; Peter W. Schneider, Exec. V.P., Genl. Counsel, Corp. Secy., and C.A.O.
Board of directors: D. Richard Williams, Chair.; John A. Addison, Jr.; Joel M. Babbit; P. George Benson; Michael E. Martin; Mark Mason; Robert F. McCullough; Barbara A. Yastine; Daniel A. Zilberman
Giving statement: Giving through the Primerica Foundation Inc.
Company EIN: 271204330

The Primerica Foundation Inc.

3120 Breckinridge Blvd.
Duluth, GA 30099
E-mail: PRIFoundation@primerica.com; URL: http://www.primerica.com/public/foundation/index.html

Establishment information: Established in GA.
Donor: Primerica Inc.
Financial data (yr. ended 12/31/11): Assets, $400,302 (M); gifts received, $1,005,200; expenditures, $604,960; qualifying distributions, $603,126; giving activities include $570,000 for 24 grants (high: $75,000; low: $10,000).
Purpose and activities: The foundation supports programs designed to promote self-sufficiency for low- to moderate-income families and individuals.
Fields of interest: Secondary school/education; Education, drop-out prevention; Education; Health care; Employment; Housing/shelter, expense aid; Housing/shelter; Children/youth, services; Family services; Human services, financial counseling; Human services Economically disadvantaged; Homeless.
Type of support: General/operating support; Management development/capacity building; Program development.
Geographic limitations: Giving primarily in GA.
Support limitations: No support for religious, political, veteran or fraternal organizations. No grants to individuals, or for advertising, special events, dinners, telethons, benefits, memorials, pass-through funding, or general fundraising activities.
Publications: Grants list.
Application information: Applications not accepted. The foundation practices an invitation only process of giving.

Officers: Karen Fine Saltiel, Chair. and Pres.; Anne Soutter, Vice-Chair. and V.P.; Margaret Halbert, Secy.; William J. Nemetz, Treas.
EIN: 274689647

3046
F. H. Prince & Company, Inc.

303 W. Madison St., Ste. 1900
Chicago, IL 60606-3394 (312) 419-9500

Establishment information: Established in 1957.
Company type: Private company
Business activities: Operates holding company; provides real estate investor services; provides warehousing services.
Business type (SIC): Holding company; warehousing and storage; investors/miscellaneous
Corporate officers: William Norman Wood Prince, C.E.O.; Frederick Henry Prince, Pres.; Randall Highley, V.P. and Treas.; James Neis, Secy.
Giving statement: Giving through the Prince Foundation.

Prince Foundation

c/o Trustees of Prince Charitable Trusts
303 W. Madison St., Ste. 1900
Chicago, IL 60606-3394 (312) 419-8700

Establishment information: Incorporated in 1955 in IL.
Donors: F.H. Prince & Co., Inc.; John D. and Catherine T. MacArthur Foundation.
Financial data (yr. ended 12/31/11): Assets, $2,361,044 (M); gifts received, $1,658,000; expenditures, $1,661,475; qualifying distributions, $1,494,700; giving activities include $1,494,700 for grants.
Purpose and activities: The foundation supports organizations involved with arts and culture and children and youth.
Fields of interest: Museums; Performing arts, dance; Performing arts, theater; Performing arts, orchestras; Performing arts, opera; Performing arts, music (choral); Arts; Elementary/secondary education; Children/youth, services.
Type of support: Employee matching gifts; General/operating support.
Geographic limitations: Giving primarily in IL.
Support limitations: No grants to individuals.
Application information: Applications not accepted. Contributes only to pre-selected organizations.
Officers and Trustees:* William Norman Wood Prince*, Pres.; Randall M. Highley*, V.P.; Frederick Henry Prince*, V.P.; Sarah A. Richardson*, Secy.-Treas.
EIN: 366116507
Selected grants: The following grants are a representative sample of this grantmaker's funding activity:
$35,000 to Black Ensemble Theater Corporation, Chicago, IL, 2010. For operating support.
$35,000 to Chicago Chamber Musicians, Chicago, IL, 2010. For operating support.
$35,000 to Chicago Public Art Group, Chicago, IL, 2010. For operating support.
$35,000 to Luna Negra Dance Theater, Chicago, IL, 2010. For operating support.
$35,000 to Remy Bumppo Theater Company, Chicago, IL, 2010. For operating support.
$30,000 to About Face Theater Collective, Chicago, IL, 2010. For operating support.
$30,000 to Art Institute of Chicago, Chicago, IL, 2010. For operating support.
$30,000 to Chicago Human Rhythm Project, Chicago, IL, 2010. For operating support.
$30,000 to Hyde Park Art Center, Chicago, IL, 2010. For operating support.
$25,000 to International Latino Cultural Center of Chicago, Chicago, IL, 2010. For operating support.

3047
Principal Life Insurance Company

711 High St.
Des Moines, IA 50392-0001
(515) 247-5111

Company URL: http://www.principal.com
Establishment information: Established in 1998.
Company type: Subsidiary of a public company
International Securities Identification Number: US74251V1026
Business activities: Sells life, health, dental, disability, and vision insurance; provides investment advisory services; provides mortgages; operates savings bank.
Business type (SIC): Insurance/life; savings institutions; brokers and bankers/mortgage; security and commodity services; insurance/accident and health; pension, health, and welfare funds
Financial profile for 2010: Number of employees, 13,627; assets, $145,631,100,000; sales volume, $9,158,600,000
Corporate officers: Larry D. Zimpleman, Chair., Pres., and C.E.O.; Karen E. Shaff, Exec. V.P. and Genl. Counsel; Terrance J. Lillis, Sr. V.P. and C.F.O.; Julia M. Lawler, Sr. V.P. and C.I.O.; Gary P. Scholten, Sr. V.P. and C.I.O.; Joyce N. Hoffman, Sr. V.P. and Corp. Secy.
Board of directors: Larry D. Zimpleman, Chair.; Betsy J. Bernard; Jocelyn E. Carter-Miller; Gary E. Costley, Ph.D.; Michael T. Dan; Dennis H. Ferro; C. Daniel Gelatt; Sandra L. Helton, Ph.D.; Richard L. Keyser; Luca Maestri; Elizabeth E. Tallett
Subsidiaries: The Admar Group, Inc., Santa Clara, CA; Principal Financial Advisors, Inc., Des Moines, IA; Principal International, Inc., Des Moines, IA; Principal Marketing Services, Inc., Des Moines, IA; Principal Residential Mortgage, Inc., Des Moines, IA; Princor Financial Services Corp., Des Moines, IA
Offices: Mason City, Waterloo, IA; Grand Island, NE; Spokane, WA
Giving statement: Giving through the Principal Life Insurance Company Contributions Program and the Principal Financial Group Foundation, Inc.

Principal Life Insurance Company Contributions Program

711 High St.
Des Moines, IA 50392-0150 (515) 247-7227
URL: http://www.principal.com/community

Purpose and activities: As a complement to its foundation, The Principal also makes charitable contributions to nonprofit organizations directly. Support is given primarily in areas of company operations.
Fields of interest: Arts, cultural/ethnic awareness; Education, computer literacy/technology training; Education; Environment; Medicine/medical care, public education; Public health; Health care; Substance abuse, prevention; Substance abuse, treatment; Youth development; Family services; Human services, financial counseling; Community/economic development.
Type of support: Capital campaigns; General/operating support; Sponsorships.
Geographic limitations: Giving primarily in areas of company operations, with emphasis on Wilmington, DE, Cedar Falls, Des Moines, Mason City, and Ottumwa, IA, Grand Island, NE, Spokane, WA, and Appleton, WI. Giving also to national organizations.
Support limitations: Generally no support for fraternal organizations such as police, fire associations, and Greek letter societies, individual K-12 schools, except those where the grantmaker is the official business partner, private foundations, retirement communities or nursing homes, social organizations, political parties, campaigns, or candidates, partisan political organizations, sectarian, religious and denominational organizations not of direct public benefit. Generally no grants to individuals, athletes or athletic organizations, capital fund drives for hospitals or healthcare facilities, conference or seminar attendance, courtesy or goodwill advertising in benefit publications, endowments or memorials, or fellowships.
Publications: Application guidelines.
Application information: Applications accepted. Capital support is considered mainly in Des Moines, IA. Requests for capital support are considered independent of annual support and require a separate application. Video tapes, CDs, and DVDs are not accepted. Application form required.
Applicants should submit the following:
1) role played by volunteers
2) results expected from proposed grant
3) statement of problem project will address
4) brief history of organization and description of its mission
5) geographic area to be served
6) copy of most recent annual report/audited financial statement/990
7) list of company employees involved with the organization
8) what distinguishes project from others in its field
9) listing of board of directors, trustees, officers and other key people and their affiliations
10) detailed description of project and amount of funding requested
11) plans for cooperation with other organizations, if any
12) contact person
13) copy of current year's organizational budget and/or project budget
14) listing of additional sources and amount of support

Proposals should include the number of employees, any significant changes at the organization since the last request, the other grantmakers the organization is seeking funding from and the amount requested, administrative expenses as a percentage of total budget, evaluation of any previous years' funding from the grantmaker, current IRS tax filing - Form 990, an annual report (if applicable), the total corporate fundraising goal, and type of funding requested. Organizations who have previously received funding must submit the grant evaluation form to be considered for future funding. Grant requests for $10,000 or more should include 11 copies.
Initial approach: Download application form and mail completed proposal to regional application address listed on website
Deadline(s): Mar. 1, June 1, Sept. 1, and Dec. 1
Final notification: 8 to 10 weeks
Number of staff: 1 full-time professional; 1 part-time professional; 1 part-time support.

Principal Financial Group Foundation, Inc.

711 High St.
Des Moines, IA 50392-0150 (515) 247-7227
FAX: (515) 246-5475;
E-mail: allen.andrew@principal.com; URL: http://www.principal.com/about/giving

Establishment information: Established in 1987 in IA.
Donor: Principal Life Insurance Co.
Contact: Andrew Allen, Community Rels.
Financial data (yr. ended 12/31/11): Assets, $66,246,190 (M); gifts received, $32,000,000; expenditures, $5,186,792; qualifying distributions, $5,070,940; giving activities include $3,502,000 for 117 grants (high: $975,000; low: $500) and $1,568,940 for 55 employee matching gifts.
Purpose and activities: The foundation supports organizations involved with arts and culture, education, the environment, health, substance abuse, diseases, employment training, nutrition, housing, recreation and tourism, youth development, human services, community development, civic affairs, babies, and senior citizens.
Fields of interest: Arts, equal rights; Arts, cultural/ethnic awareness; Arts; Education, equal rights; Child development, education; Higher education; Business school/education; Education; Environment; Health care, equal rights; Public health; Health care; Substance abuse, services; Health organizations, public education; Geriatrics; Employment, training; Nutrition; Housing/shelter; Recreation; Youth development, adult & child programs; Youth development; Family services; Human services, financial counseling; Human services; Economic development, visitors/convention bureau/tourism promotion; Community/economic development; Computer science; Public affairs Infants/toddlers; Aging.
Programs:
Arts and Culture: The foundation supports programs designed to promote the arts as a key component of viable communities. Special emphasis is directed toward programs designed to celebrate cultural diversity and make the arts more accessible to all audiences.
Civic, Community, and Environment: The foundation supports quality-of-life attractions and civic betterment programs designed to promote the vitality of communities; and programs designed to protect and enhance the environment.
Education: The foundation supports programs designed to provide access to higher education for diverse populations of students; promote areas of study important to the business objectives of Principal Financial Group, including actuarial science, business, information technology, accounting, and finance; and reward high performing students.
Employee Matching Gifts: The foundation matches contributions made by full-time employees, retirees, directors, and the spouses of full-time employees, retirees, and directors of Principal Financial Group to institutions of higher education on a one-for-one basis from $25 to $3,000 per contributor, per year.
Health and Human Services: The foundation supports programs designed to provide access to primary and preventative health services to medically underserved populations, giving special preference to programs targeting nutrition and care for the elderly; provide public health outreach; facilitate disease and disorder prevention/awareness and education; promote substance abuse prevention and treatment programs; strengthen families by building positive social networks; assist families in their efforts toward self-sufficiency and financial independence through financial literacy, affordable housing, and workforce preparedness programs; promote physical and social independence for older adults; and support youth development through mentoring programs, school readiness, and healthy baby initiatives.
Type of support: Annual campaigns; Building/renovation; Capital campaigns; Continuing support; Curriculum development; Employee matching gifts; General/operating support; Professorships; Program development; Program evaluation; Scholarship funds; Seed money.
Geographic limitations: Giving limited to Des Moines, IA, and areas of company operations in Wilmington, DE, Cedar Falls, Mason City, and Ottumwa, IA, Grand Island, NE, Spokane, WA, and Appleton, WI.
Support limitations: No support for athletes or athletic organizations, fraternal organizations, individual K-12 schools, libraries, pass-through organizations, partisan political organizations, private foundations, retirement communities or nursing homes, sectarian, religious, or denominational organizations, social organizations, tax-supported city, county, or state organizations, trade, industry, or professional associations, or veterans' organizations. No grants to individuals, or for conference or seminar attendance, courtesy or goodwill advertising in benefit publications, endowments or memorials, fellowships, festival participation, hospital or healthcare facility capital campaigns, or United Way-funded programs.
Publications: Application guidelines; Biennial report; Corporate giving report; Grants list; Program policy statement.
Application information: Applications accepted. Video submissions are not encouraged. Support is limited to 1 contribution per organization during any given year. Multi-year funding is not automatic. Organizations receiving support are asked to submit a grant evaluation form. Visit website for additional application addresses. Application form required.
Applicants should submit the following:
1) role played by volunteers
2) staff salaries
3) statement of problem project will address
4) copy of IRS Determination Letter
5) brief history of organization and description of its mission
6) geographic area to be served
7) copy of most recent annual report/audited financial statement/990
8) how project's results will be evaluated or measured
9) listing of board of directors, trustees, officers and other key people and their affiliations
10) detailed description of project and amount of funding requested
11) plans for cooperation with other organizations, if any
12) copy of current year's organizational budget and/or project budget
13) listing of additional sources and amount of support

Proposals should indicate the frequency of board meetings and include an evaluation of the foundation's prior year funding, if applicable.
Initial approach: Download application form and mail proposal and application form to nearest company facility; download application form and mail proposal and application form to foundation for organizations located in Des Moines, IA
Copies of proposal: 11
Board meeting date(s): Quarterly
Deadline(s): June 1 for organizations located outside of Des Moines, IA; Mar. 1 for Health and Human Services, June 1 for Education, Sept. 1 for Arts and Culture, and Dec. 1 for Civic, Community, and Environment for organizations located in Des Moines, IA
Final notification: 8 to 10 weeks
Officers and Directors:* Mary O'Keefe*, Chair. and Pres.; Andrew Allen, Secy.; Jed A. Fisk*, Treas.; Pat Barry; Nora Everett; Joyce Hoffman; Terrance J. Lillis; Renee Schaaf; Larry Zimpleman.
EIN: 421312301
Selected grants: The following grants are a representative sample of this grantmaker's funding activity:
$1,400,000 to Community Foundation of Greater Des Moines, Des Moines, IA, 2011. For line of credit for Principal Riverwalk, which features lighted, landscaped public spaces, public art and pedestrian bridges and pathways that connect 300 miles of Central Iowa trails.
$1,000,000 to Community Foundation of Greater Des Moines, Des Moines, IA, 2010. For Principal Charity Classic, fundraising golf tournament that benefits children's charities in Des Moines.
$975,000 to Community Foundation of Greater Des Moines, Des Moines, IA, 2011. For Principal Charity Classic, fundraising golf tournament that benefits children's charities in Des Moines.
$485,386 to Truist, Washington, DC, 2011. For matching gifts.
$473,964 to Truist, Washington, DC, 2011. For matching gifts.
$250,000 to Community Foundation of Greater Des Moines, Des Moines, IA, 2010. To support work of Downtown Maintenance Advisory Committee for Riverwalk: Operation Downtown. Riverwalk features lighted, landscaped public spaces, public art and pedestrian bridges and pathways that connect 300 miles of Central Iowa trails.
$250,000 to Community Foundation of Greater Des Moines, Des Moines, IA, 2011. To support work of Downtown Maintenance Advisory Committee for Riverwalk: Operation Downtown. Riverwalk features lighted, landscaped public spaces, public art and pedestrian bridges and pathways that connect 300 miles of Central Iowa trails.
$183,704 to United Way of Central Iowa, Des Moines, IA, 2011. For matching gifts.
$150,000 to Central Iowa Shelter and Services, Des Moines, IA, 2010. For new homeless shelter.
$150,000 to Community Foundation of Greater Des Moines, Des Moines, IA, 2010. For Sculpture Park.
$125,000 to World Food Prize Foundation, Des Moines, IA, 2010. For Dr. Norman E. Borlaug Hall of Laureates.
$110,000 to United Way of Northeast Florida, Jacksonville, FL, 2011. For matching gifts.
$50,000 to American Red Cross, Central Iowa Chapter, Des Moines, IA, 2010. For Haiti earthquake relief.
$40,551 to Truist, Washington, DC, 2011. For matching gifts.
$20,000 to Easter Seals Iowa, Des Moines, IA, 2010. For Camp Sunnyside Easter Seals.
$15,000 to University of Northern Iowa Foundation, Cedar Falls, IA, 2010. For Center for Real Estate Education (CREE).
$10,000 to Hope Harbor, Grand Island, NE, 2011. For Building Hope for Tomorrow Capital Campaign.
$10,000 to Youth Homes of Mid-America, Johnston, IA, 2010. For annual fund.
$5,000 to Iowa Public Television, Johnston, IA, 2010. For Raising Readers of Professional Development.
$5,000 to United Way of Broward County, Fort Lauderdale, FL, 2011. For matching gifts.

3048

Print Net Inc.

7728 Edgerton Ave.
Pittsburgh, PA 15221-3184 (412) 243-9060

Company URL: http://www.printnetinc.com
Establishment information: Established in 1997.
Company type: Private company
Business activities: Operates full service commercial printing company.
Business type (SIC): Mailing, reproduction, commercial art, photography, and stenographic service
Corporate officer: Jeffrey A. Shaw, C.E.O
Offices: San Diego, San Francisco, CA
Giving statement: Giving through the Print Net Inc. Corporate Giving Program.

Print Net Inc. Corporate Giving Program

7728 Edgerton Ave.
Pittsburgh, PA 15221-3184 (412) 243-9060

Purpose and activities: Print Net Inc. donates a percentage of profits to nonprofit organizations involved with the environment.
Fields of interest: Environment.
Type of support: General/operating support.

3049

Printpack Inc.

2800 Overlook Pkwy., N.E.
Atlanta, GA 30339 (404) 460-7000
FAX: (404) 699-7122

Company URL: http://www.printpack.com
Establishment information: Established in 1956.
Company type: Private company
Business activities: Manufactures flexible packaging products.
Business type (SIC): Paper and paperboard/ coated, converted, and laminated
Financial profile for 2010: Number of employees, 3,800
Corporate officers: Dennis M. Love, Chair., Pres., and C.E.O.; R. Michael Hembree, V.P., Finance and Admin., and C.F.O.
Board of director: Dennis M. Love, Chair.
Giving statement: Giving through the Gay and Erskine Love Foundation, Inc.

Gay and Erskine Love Foundation, Inc.

2800 Overlook Pkwy., NE
Atlanta, GA 30339-6240 (404) 691-5830
E-mail: Foundation@Printpack.com; Application address: P.O. Box 723608, Atlanta, GA 31139; URL: http://www.printpack.com/Who-We-Are/Community/The-Gay-and-Erskine-Love-Foundation.aspx

Establishment information: Established in 1976 in GA.
Donors: Printpack Inc.; Love Family Charitable Lead Trust.
Contact: Gay M. Love, Chair.
Financial data (yr. ended 12/31/11): Assets, $7,157,228 (M); gifts received, $1,262,819; expenditures, $3,708,658; qualifying distributions, $3,659,044; giving activities include $3,659,044 for 71 grants (high: $1,211,000; low: $500).
Purpose and activities: The foundation supports organizations involved with arts and culture, health, heart disease, youth development, human services, community development, civic affairs, and religion. Special emphasis is directed toward education.
Fields of interest: Performing arts; Arts; Elementary/secondary education; Higher education; Theological school/education; Education; Health care; Heart & circulatory diseases; Boy scouts; Youth development; Children, services; Human services; Community development, service clubs; Community/economic development; United Ways and Federated Giving Programs; Public affairs; Christian agencies & churches; Religion.
Type of support: General/operating support; Program development; Scholarship funds.
Geographic limitations: Giving primarily in areas of company operations, with emphasis on Atlanta, GA.
Support limitations: No grants to individuals.
Publications: Application guidelines.
Application information: Applications accepted. Application form not required. Applicants should submit the following:
1) detailed description of project and amount of funding requested
2) brief history of organization and description of its mission
3) listing of board of directors, trustees, officers and other key people and their affiliations
4) listing of additional sources and amount of support

Initial approach: Mail or e-mail proposal to foundation
Board meeting date(s): Quarterly
Deadline(s): None

Officers: Gay M. Love, Chair.; Dennis M. Love, Pres.; Dellmer B. Seitter III, Secy.
EIN: 510198585

3050

Private Asset Management, Inc.

(also known as PAM)
5348 Carroll Canyon Rd., Ste. 200
San Diego, CA 92121-1733
(858) 750-4200

Company URL: http://www.pamgmt.com
Establishment information: Established in 1993.
Company type: Private company
Business activities: Provides investment advisory services.
Business type (SIC): Security and commodity services
Corporate officers: Stephen J. Cohen, Pres.; Edward Z. Estrin, V.P. and C.F.O.; Eric Blase, Corp. V.P. and C.I.O.; Michael D. Berlin, V.P. and Genl. Counsel; Suzanne Cohen, V.P., Opers. and Corp. Secy.
Offices: Indian Wells, Pasadena, CA
Giving statement: Giving through the Private Asset Management, Inc. Foundation.

Private Asset Management, Inc. Foundation

5348 Carroll Canyon Rd., Ste. 200
San Diego, CA 92121
E-mail: michael@pamgmt.com

Establishment information: Established in 1997 in CA.
Donors: Private Asset Management, Inc.; Stephen J. Cohen.
Financial data (yr. ended 12/31/11): Assets, $53,981 (M); gifts received, $40,000; expenditures, $28,334; qualifying distributions, $28,250; giving activities include $28,250 for grants.
Purpose and activities: The foundation supports organizations involved with marine life, health, senior citizen services, homelessness, and Judaism.
Fields of interest: Arts; Community/economic development.
Type of support: Continuing support; General/ operating support; Research.
Geographic limitations: Giving limited to Encinitas, La Jolla, and San Diego, CA.
Support limitations: No grants to individuals.
Application information: Applications not accepted. Unsolicited requests for funds not accepted.
Officers: Stephen J. Cohen, Pres.; Edward Z. Estrin, C.F.O.; Michael D. Berlin, V.P.
Director: Suzanne Cohen.
EIN: 330766760

3051

Pro Brand International, Inc.

1900 W. Oak Cir.
Marietta, GA 30062-2251 (770) 423-7072

Company URL: http://www.pbigroup.com
Establishment information: Established in 1983.
Company type: Private company
Business activities: Manufactures satellite accessories and equipment.
Business type (SIC): Communications equipment
Corporate officers: Philip M. Shou, Chair. and C.E.O.; Cecilia Shou, Pres.; James Crownover, Exec. V.P. and C.O.O.
Board of director: Philip M. Shou, Chair.
Giving statement: Giving through the PBI Foundation, Inc.

PBI Foundation, Inc.

1900 W. Oak Cir.
Marietta, GA 30062-2248 (770) 423-7072

Establishment information: Established in 2002 in GA.
Donors: Pro Brand International, Inc.; Atlanta Chinese Christian Church.
Contact: Stanton J. Singleton, Jr., Secy.
Financial data (yr. ended 11/30/11): Assets, $779,083 (M); gifts received, $130,722; expenditures, $44,526; qualifying distributions, $44,526; giving activities include $44,526 for 8 grants (high: $21,050; low: $100).
Purpose and activities: The foundation supports organizations involved with music, human services, Christianity, the hearing impaired, and Chinese heritage.
Fields of interest: Health organizations; Human services; Religion.
International interests: China.
Type of support: Building/renovation; General/ operating support.
Geographic limitations: Giving primarily in GA; giving also in China.
Application information: Applications accepted. Application form not required. Applicants should submit the following:
1) timetable for implementation and evaluation of project
2) copy of IRS Determination Letter
3) brief history of organization and description of its mission
4) copy of most recent annual report/audited financial statement/990
5) how project's results will be evaluated or measured

6) listing of board of directors, trustees, officers and other key people and their affiliations
7) detailed description of project and amount of funding requested
8) copy of current year's organizational budget and/ or project budget

Initial approach: Proposal or contact foundation for application form

Deadline(s): None

Trustees: Gen Chu ("Celia") Shou; Philip M. Shou; Stanton J. Singleton, Jr.
EIN: 800005908

3052
Pro Legends, Inc.

3696 N. Federal Hwy., Ste. 202
Fort Lauderdale, FL 33308-6245
(800) 878-5437

Establishment information: Established in 1983.
Company type: Private company
Business activities: Provides marketing and promotional services for former National Football League players.
Business type (SIC): Management and public relations services; commercial sports
Corporate officer: Frank Leistner, Secy.-Treas.
Giving statement: Giving through the National Football League Alumni, Inc.

National Football League Alumni, Inc.

1 Washington Pk.
1 Washington St., 14th Fl.
Newark, NJ 07102-3140 (954) 630-2100
FAX: (862) 772-0277;
E-mail: katie.hilder@nflalumni.org; Toll-free tel.: (877) 258-6635; additional address (Ft. Lauderdale office): 3696 N. Federal Hwy., Ste. 202, Fort Lauderdale, FL 33308-6262, toll-free tel. (FL only): (800) 878-5437, fax: (862) 772-0277; URL: http://www.nflalumniplayers.com/about/foundation

Establishment information: Established in 1977 in DC.
Financial data (yr. ended 12/31/10): Revenue, $3,957,390; assets, $1,616,058 (M); gifts received, $3,899,708; expenditures, $3,788,700; giving activities include $1,560,904 for grants and $17,599 for grants to individuals.
Purpose and activities: The organization seeks to provide support to former professional football players experiencing financial or medical hardship.
Fields of interest: Athletics/sports, football Economically disadvantaged.
Program:

Financial Assistance: The organization provides monetary grants to qualified National Football League (NFL) alumni who are experiencing financial hardships, including grants to eligible players who need financial assistance in paying for the cost of Player Care Plan programs (such as joint replacement, spine treatment, or neurological care). Eligible applicants must be former NFL players, with at least two credited seasons of NFL play (both spouses and children are also eligible for care), and must meet financial qualifications. Preference will be given to first-time applicants.

Type of support: Emergency funds.
Geographic limitations: Giving on a national basis.
Publications: Application guidelines.
Application information:

Initial approach: Submit online application

Deadline(s): None

Officers: Lee A. Nystrom*, Chair.; Todd Kalis*, Vice-Chair.; Frank W. Krauser, Pres. and C.E.O.; William Chip*, Secy.; Don Fitzgerald*, Treas.
Directors: Raul Allegre; Larry Ball; Leroy Mitchell; Randy Minniear; Tim Sherwin; Brett Wiese.
EIN: 591782262

3053
PRO*ACT, LLC

24560 Silver Cloud Ct.
Monterey, CA 93940-6536 (831) 655-4250

Company URL: http://www.proactusa.com
Establishment information: Established in 1990.
Company type: Private company
Business activities: Operates fresh produce distribution company.
Business type (SIC): Groceries—wholesale
Corporate officers: Steve Grinstead, C.E.O.; Max Yeater, Pres.; Bob Kiehnle, C.F.O.; Mike Kissner, V.P., Human Resources; Kelly Jacob, V.P., Sales; Bonnie Kilgore, V.P., Finance; Cheryl Wong, Cont.
Giving statement: Giving through the PRO*ACT Foundation.

PRO*ACT Foundation

24560 Silver Cloud Ct.
Monterey, CA 93940-6536 (831) 655-4250
E-mail: info@proactusa.com; URL: http://www.proactusa.com

Purpose and activities: PRO*ACT makes charitable contributions to nonprofit organizations involved with disaster relief on a case by case basis.
Fields of interest: Disasters, preparedness/ services.
Type of support: General/operating support.

3055
The Procter & Gamble Company

(also known as P & G)
1 Procter & Gamble Plz.
Cincinnati, OH 45201 (513) 983-1100
FAX: (513) 983-4381

Company URL: http://www.pg.com
Establishment information: Established in 1837.
Company type: Public company
Company ticker symbol and exchange: PG/NYSE
Business activities: Manufactures and markets consumer products.
Business type (SIC): Soaps, cleaners, and toiletries
Financial profile for 2012: Number of employees, 126,000; assets, $132,244,000,000; sales volume, $83,680,000,000; pre-tax net income, $12,785,000,000; expenses, $70,388,000,000; liabilities, $68,805,000,000
Fortune 1000 ranking: 2012—28th in revenues, 16th in profits, and 47th in assets
Forbes 2000 ranking: 2012—82nd in sales, 25th in profits, and 184th in assets
Corporate officers: Alan G. Lafley, Chair., Pres., and C.E.O.; Jon R. Moeller, C.F.O.; Teri L. List-Stoll, Sr. V.P. and Treas.; Valarie L. Sheppard, Sr. V.P. and Compt.; Deborah Platt Majoras, Secy.
Board of directors: Alan G. Lafley, Chair.; Angela F. Braly; Kenneth I. Chenault; Scott D. Cook; Susan Desmond-Hellmann, M.D.; W. James McNerney, Jr.; Johnathan A. Rodgers; Margaret C. Whitman; Mary Agnes Wilderotter; Patricia A. Woertz; Ernesto Zedillo
Subsidiaries: The Folger Coffee Co., New Orleans, LA; The Iams Company, Dayton, OH; Noxell Corporation, Hunt Valley, MD
Plants: Phoenix, AZ; Russellville, AR; Anaheim, Modesto, Oxnard, Sacramento, CA; Dover, DE; Albany, Augusta, GA; Iowa City, IA; Kansas City, KS; Alexandria, LA; Auburn, ME; Cape Girardeau, Kansas City, St. Louis, MO; Aurora, NE; Avenel, South Brunswick, NJ; Greensboro, Henderson, NC; Leipsir, Lewisburg, Lima, OH; Mehoopany, PA; Cayey, PR; North Sioux, SD; Jackson, TN; Sherman, TX; Green Bay, WI
International operations: Albania; Algeria; Australia; Austria; Azerbaijan; Bangladesh; Belarus; Belgium; Bosnia-Herzegovina; Brazil; Bulgaria; Canada; Cayman Islands; China; Costa Rica; Cuba; Czech Republic; Ecuador; Egypt; El Salvador; Estonia; Finland; France; Germany; Greece; Guatemala; India; Indonesia; Ireland; Israel; Italy; Japan; Kazakhstan; Lebanon; Luxembourg; Macedonia; Malaysia; Mexico; Moldova; Morocco and the Western Sahara; Netherlands; New Zealand; Nigeria; Pakistan; Paraguay; Peru; Philippines; Poland; Portugal; Romania; Saudi Arabia; Serbia; Singapore; Slovenia; South Africa; South Korea; Spain; Sri Lanka; Sweden; Switzerland; Thailand; United Arab Emirates; United Kingdom; Venezuela; Vietnam
Historic mergers: The Gillette Company (October 1, 2005)
Giving statement: Giving through the Procter & Gamble Company Contributions Program.
Company EIN: 310411980

Procter & Gamble Company Contributions Program

1 Procter & Gamble Plz.
Cincinnati, OH 45202-3315 (513) 983-1100
URL: http://www.pg.com/en_US/sustainability/social_responsibility/index.shtml

Purpose and activities: Procter & Gamble makes charitable contributions to organizations involved with health and social service, companion animal programs, arts, culture and economic vitality, homelessness prevention, and science, technology, engineering, and mathematics in middle and high school. Special emphasis is directed towards children and youth in need. Support is given on a national and international basis in areas of company operations.
Fields of interest: Arts; Elementary/secondary education; Animal welfare; Public health; Disasters, preparedness/services; Human services; Children/ youth, services; Child development, services; Human services; Economic development; Science, formal/general education; Mathematics; Engineering/technology Homeless.
Program:

Higher Education Grant Program: Through the Higher Education Grant Program, Procter & Gamble awards up to $10,000 for college curriculum programs intended to better prepare students within the areas of study most pertinent to Procter & Gamble and other similar employers for success in business.

Type of support: Donated products; Employee volunteer services; General/operating support; In-kind gifts; Program development.
Geographic limitations: Giving on a national and international basis in areas of company operations.
Support limitations: No support for religious or political organizations. No grants for endowments, fundraisers, or conferences.
Publications: Application guidelines.
Application information: Applications accepted. Application form required.

Initial approach: Complete online eligibility quiz and application form
Deadline(s): July 1 to Sept. 30 and Dec. 1 to Feb. 28; July 1 to Sept. 1 for Higher Education Grant

3056
Professional Management Inc.

9095 S.W. 87th Ave., Ste. 777
Miami, FL 33176-2310 (305) 270-0870

Company type: Private company
Business activities: Develops real estate.
Business type (SIC): Real estate subdividers and developers
Financial profile for 2009: Number of employees, 250
Corporate officers: Joanne S. Mitchell, Pres.; Yolanda Lopez, Treas. and Cont.
Giving statement: Giving through the James and Joanne Mitchell Foundation Inc.

James and Joanne Mitchell Foundation Inc.

9095 S.W. 87th Ave., Ste. 777
Miami, FL 33176-2310

Establishment information: Established in 1999 in FL.
Donors: Professional Management Inc.; Professional Management for Condominium, Inc.; J&M Holdings, Inc.; James R. Mitchell; Joanne S. Mitchell.
Financial data (yr. ended 12/31/11): Assets, $2,137,062 (M); gifts received, $100,000; expenditures, $63,567; qualifying distributions, $51,725; giving activities include $51,725 for 32 grants (high: $9,000; low: $100).
Purpose and activities: The foundation supports hospitals and organizations involved with performing arts and religion.
Fields of interest: Performing arts; Hospitals (general); Religion.
Type of support: General/operating support.
Geographic limitations: Giving limited to the Miami, FL, area.
Support limitations: No grants to individuals.
Application information: Applications not accepted. Unsolicited requests for funds not accepted.
Directors: James R. Mitchell; Joanne S. Mitchell.
EIN: 650947655

3054
Pro-Football, Inc.

(also known as Washington Redskins)
21300 Redskin Park Dr.
Ashburn, VA 20147 (703) 726-7000

Company URL: http://www.redskins.com
Establishment information: Established in 1932.
Company type: Private company
Business activities: Operates professional football club.
Business type (SIC): Commercial sports
Corporate officers: Robert Rothman, Chair. and Co-C.E.O.; Dwight Schar, Chair.; Daniel M. Snyder, Co-C.E.O.; Dennis Greene, Pres.; Lon Rosenberg, Sr. V.P., Opers.
Board of directors: Robert Rothman, Chair.; Dwight Schar, Chair.
Giving statement: Giving through the Washington Redskins Corporate Giving Program and the Washington Redskins Charitable Foundation, Inc.

Washington Redskins Corporate Giving Program

c/o Community Rels. Dept.
21300 Redskin Park Dr.
Ashburn, VA 20147-6100
URL: http://www.redskins.com/community/index.html

Purpose and activities: As a complement to its foundation, the Washington Redskins also make charitable contributions of memorabilia to nonprofit organizations directly. Support is limited to Washington, DC, Montgomery County and Prince George's County, Maryland, Virginia, and West Virginia.
Fields of interest: General charitable giving.
Type of support: In-kind gifts.
Geographic limitations: Giving limited to Washington, DC, Montgomery County and Prince George's County, MD, VA, and WV.
Support limitations: No game ticket donations.
Application information: Applications accepted. Support is limited to 1 contribution per organization during any given year. The Community Relations Department handles giving. Telephone, fax, and e-mail requests will not be accepted. Application form required. Applicants should submit the following:
1) name, address and phone number of organization
2) detailed description of project and amount of funding requested
3) contact person
Applications should include the organization's Tax ID Number, and indicate the date, location, and expected attendance of the event, and the type of fundraiser.
Initial approach: Complete online application form
Number of staff: 1 part-time support.

The Washington Redskins Charitable Foundation, Inc.

(formerly The Washington Redskins Leadership Council)
21300 Redskin Park Dr.
Ashburn, VA 20147-6100 (703) 726-7255
URL: http://www.redskins.com/community/charitable-foundation.html

Establishment information: Established in 2000 in DE.
Financial data (yr. ended 03/31/11): Revenue, $1,289,368; assets, $1,779,685 (M); gifts received, $1,289,368; expenditures, $1,022,673; program services expenses, $863,822; giving activities include $236,489 for 8 grants (high: $65,000; low: $5,000).
Purpose and activities: The foundation provides services and community benefits to nonprofits in the Washington, DC area.
Fields of interest: Human services.
Geographic limitations: Giving limited to Washington, DC.
Officers: Mike Shanahan*, Chair.; Bruce Allen*, Pres.; Tony Wyllie*, Sr. V.P.; Jane Rodgers, Exec. Dir.; Matthew J. Lorusso, Cont.
EIN: 541982366

3057
The Progressive Corporation

6300 Wilson Mills Rd.
Mayfield Village, OH 44143 (440) 461-5000
FAX: (440) 446-7436

Company URL: http://www.progressive.com
Establishment information: Established in 1937.
Company type: Public company
Company ticker symbol and exchange: PGR/NYSE
Business activities: Holding company; life, casualty, and marine insurance; insurance premium financing.
Business type (SIC): Insurance/fire, marine, and casualty; insurance/life; insurance/accident and health; holding company
Financial profile for 2012: Number of employees, 25,889; assets, $22,694,700,000; sales volume, $17,083,900,000; pre-tax net income, $1,317,700,000; expenses, $15,766,200,000; liabilities, $16,687,700,000
Fortune 1000 ranking: 2012—166th in revenues, 217th in profits, and 222nd in assets
Forbes 2000 ranking: 2012—548th in sales, 633rd in profits, and 907th in assets
Corporate officers: Peter B. Lewis, Chair.; Glenn M. Renwick, Pres. and C.E.O.; Brian C. Domeck, C.F.O.; Ray Voelker, C.I.O.; William M. Cody, C.I.O.
Board of directors: Peter B. Lewis, Chair.; Stuart B. Burgdoerfer; Charles A. Davis; Roger N. Farah; Lawton Wehle Fitt; Stephen R. Hardis; Jeffrey D. Kelly; Heidi G. Miller; Patrick H. Nettles, Ph.D; Glenn M. Renwick; Bradley T. Sheares, Ph.D
Subsidiaries: Gold Key Insurance Agency, Mayfield Heights, OH; Greenberg Financial Insurance Services, Inc., Palm Desert, CA; Insurance Confirmation Services, Mayfield Heights, OH; Lakeside Insurance Agency, Inc., Mayfield Heights, OH; NCI Educational Services, Inc., Mayfield Heights, OH; Progressive American Insurance Co., Tampa, FL; Progressive Casualty Insurance Company, Cleveland, OH; Transportation Recoveries, Inc., Mayfield Heights, OH
Plant: Beachwood, OH
Giving statement: Giving through the Progressive Insurance Foundation.
Company EIN: 340963169

The Progressive Insurance Foundation

6300 Wilson Mills Rd.
Mayfield Village, OH 44143-2109
URL: http://www.progressive.com/progressive-insurance/foundation.aspx

Establishment information: Established in 2001 in OH.
Donors: Progressive Specialty Insurance Company; Progressive Casualty Insurance Co.
Financial data (yr. ended 12/31/11): Assets, $1,166,106 (M); gifts received, $5,409,482; expenditures, $5,270,955; qualifying distributions, $5,224,755; giving activities include $5,158,506 for 2,751 grants (high: $1,846,219; low: $15).
Purpose and activities: The foundation supports the Insurance Institute for Highway Safety to reduce human traumas and the economic cost of auto acccidents.
Fields of interest: Safety, automotive safety.
Program:
Matching Funds: The foundation matches contributions made by employees of Progress Corporation and its subsidiaries to nonprofit organizations from $20 to $2,500 per employee, per year.
Type of support: Annual campaigns; Employee matching gifts; General/operating support.

Geographic limitations: Giving primarily in areas of company operations, with emphasis on OH and VA.
Application information: Applications not accepted. Contributes only to a pre-selected organization and through employee-matching gifts.
Officers and Trustees:* Glenn M. Renwick, Pres.; Brian Domeck, V.P.; Charles E. Jarrett, Secy.; James Kusmer, Treas.; W. Thomas Forrester; R. Steven Kestner.
EIN: 300013138

3058
Progressive Foundry, Inc.

1518 1st Ave.
P.O. Box 338
Perry, IA 50220-0338 (515) 465-5697
FAX: (515) 465-3101

Company URL: http://www.progressivefoundry.com
Establishment information: Established in 1981.
Company type: Private company
Business activities: Manufactures gray iron castings.
Business type (SIC): Iron and steel foundries
Financial profile for 2009: Number of employees, 85
Corporate officers: Dallas Van Kirk, Pres.; Kirk Vankirk, V.P., Opers. and Sales; Darek Vankirk, V.P., Finance
Giving statement: Giving through the Progressive Foundry Foundation.

Progressive Foundry Foundation

P.O. Box 338
Perry, IA 50220-0338 (515) 465-5697

Donor: Progressive Foundry, Inc.
Contact: Darek Van Kirk, Secy.-Treas.
Financial data (yr. ended 04/30/12): Assets, $19,217 (M); gifts received, $10,000; expenditures, $1,230; qualifying distributions, $1,200; giving activities include $1,200 for grants to individuals.
Purpose and activities: The foundation supports hospitals and organizations involved with education and athletics.
Fields of interest: Education; Hospitals (general); Athletics/sports, amateur leagues.
Type of support: General/operating support; Scholarship funds.
Geographic limitations: Giving primarily in Perry, IA.
Application information: Applications accepted. Application form required. Applicants should submit the following:
1) detailed description of project and amount of funding requested
Initial approach: Letter
Deadline(s): None
Officers: Dallas Van Kirk, Pres.; Kirk Van Kirk, V.P.; Darek Van Kirk, Secy.-Treas.
EIN: 421367878

3059
Progressive Savings Bank

500 N. Main St.
Jamestown, TN 38556-3241
(931) 752-2265

Company URL: https://www.psbgroup.net/
Establishment information: Established in 1980.
Company type: Private company
Business activities: Operates federal savings institution.
Business type (SIC): Savings institutions
Corporate officers: Steven Rains, Pres. and C.E.O.; Gary Hicks, Cont.; Vanessa Herren, Exec. V.P., Mktg.
Giving statement: Giving through the Rains Foundation.

Rains Foundation

500 N. Main St.
Jamestown, TN 38556-3241 (931) 752-2112
URL: http://www.rainsfoundation.org/

Establishment information: Established in 2004 in TN.
Donors: Joann Rains; Progressive Savings Bank; John Davis; Kelly Davis.
Contact: Steven Rains, Pres.
Financial data (yr. ended 05/31/11): Assets, $6,326 (M); gifts received, $4,857; expenditures, $40,014; qualifying distributions, $15,760; giving activities include $15,760 for 20 grants (high: $2,000; low: $25).
Purpose and activities: The foundation supports organizations involved with education, recreation, youth development, and business promotion and awards scholarships to graduating students from each high school in Pickett, Fentress, Cumberland, and Morgan counties, Tennessee.
Fields of interest: Higher education; Education; Athletics/sports, school programs; Recreation; Boys & girls clubs; Community development, business promotion; United Ways and Federated Giving Programs.
Type of support: General/operating support; Scholarships—to individuals; Sponsorships.
Geographic limitations: Giving limited to Pickett, Fentress, Cumberland and Morgan counties, TN.
Application information: Applications accepted. Application form required.
Initial approach: Proposal
Deadline(s): May 1
Officers: Steven Rains, Pres.; Roy Stucker, Secy.
EIN: 201446832

3060
ProLogis, Inc.

(formerly AMB Property Corporation)
Pier 1, Bay 1
San Francisco, CA 94111 (415) 394-9000
FAX: (415) 394-9001

Company URL: http://www.prologis.com
Establishment information: Established in 1991.
Company type: Public company
Company ticker symbol and exchange: PLD/NYSE
International Securities Identification Number: US74340W1036
Business activities: Operates real estate investment trust.
Business type (SIC): Investors/miscellaneous
Financial profile for 2012: Number of employees, 1,445; assets, $27,310,150,000; sales volume, $2,005,960,000; pre-tax net income, -$89,620,000; expenses, $1,927,760,000; liabilities, $14,241,130,000
Fortune 1000 ranking: 2012—919th in revenues, 904th in profits, and 199th in assets
Forbes 2000 ranking: 2012—1771st in sales, 1781st in profits, and 790th in assets
Corporate officers: Hamid R. Moghadam, Chair. and Co-C.E.O.; Gary E. Anderson, Co-C.E.O.; Thomas S. Olinger, C.F.O.; Michael S. Curless, C.I.O.; Edward S. Nekritz, Genl. Counsel
Board of directors: Hamid R. Moghadam, Chair.; George L. Fotiades; Christine N. Garvey; Lydia H. Kennard; J. Michael Losh; Irving F. Lyons III; Jeffrey Skelton; D. Michael Steuert; Carl B. Webb; William D. Zollars
Giving statement: Giving through the ProLogis Foundation.

ProLogis Foundation

4545 Airport Way
Denver, CO 80239-5716 (303) 567-5000
URL: http://www.prologis.com/en/aboutus/CommunityInvolvement.aspx

Establishment information: Established in 2001 in CO.
Donors: Catellus Land & Development Corporation and Subsidiaries; Development Services Trust; ProLogis.
Contact: Edward S. Nekritz, Sr. V.P. and Secy.-Treas.
Financial data (yr. ended 12/31/11): Assets, $11,826,937 (M); gifts received, $511,965; expenditures, $597,436; qualifying distributions, $591,872; giving activities include $591,872 for grants.
Purpose and activities: The foundation supports museums and organizations involved with education, health, spine injuries, human services, and international relief.
Fields of interest: Museums; Elementary school/education; Higher education; Scholarships/financial aid; Education; Hospitals (general); Health care, patient services; Spine disorders; Boys & girls clubs; Youth development, adult & child programs; Boy scouts; Youth development, business; Children/youth, services; Human services; International relief.
Type of support: Employee matching gifts; General/operating support; Program development; Scholarship funds.
Geographic limitations: Giving primarily in areas of company operations, with emphasis on CO; giving also to national organizations.
Application information: Applications accepted. Application form not required.
Initial approach: Proposal
Deadline(s): None
Officers and Directors:* Walter C. Rakowich*, Pres.; Edward S. Nekritz*, Sr. V.P. and Secy.-Treas.; Lori Palazzolo, V.P.
EIN: 364439409
Selected grants: The following grants are a representative sample of this grantmaker's funding activity:
$60,000 to University of Colorado Foundation, Boulder, CO, 2010.
$30,782 to Mercy Corps, Portland, OR, 2010.
$1,250 to Vanderbilt University, Nashville, TN, 2010.
$1,000 to College of William and Mary, Williamsburg, VA, 2010.
$1,000 to Harvard University, Cambridge, MA, 2010.
$1,000 to University of Chicago, Chicago, IL, 2010.

3061
Promotional Management, Inc.

(also known as PMI Entertainment Group)
1901 S. Oneida St.
P.O. Box 10567
Green Bay, WI 54304-4537 (920) 497-5664

Company URL: http://www.pmiwi.com
Establishment information: Established in 1982.

Company type: Private company
Business activities: Provides promotions management services.
Business type (SIC): Management and public relations services
Corporate officers: Peter Mancuso, Chair.; Ken Wachter, Pres. and C.E.O.; Cora Haltaufderheid, C.O.O.; Kathie Mickle, V.P., Mktg. and Sales; Paula Kirchman, V.P., Admin.
Board of directors: Peter Mancuso, Chair.; Robert Atwell; Jere Dhein; Jeffrey Kanzelberger; Thomas Meinz; Thomas Olejniczak; Ron Weyers
Giving statement: Giving through the PMI Community Foundation, Inc.

PMI Community Foundation, Inc.

1901 S. Oneida St.
Green Bay, WI 54304 (920) 405-1155
Application address: P.O. Box 23200, Green Bay, WI 54305-3200

Establishment information: Established in 1997 in WI.
Donor: Promotional Management, Inc.
Contact: Thomas Olejniczak, Secy.
Financial data (yr. ended 12/31/11): Assets, $42,809 (M); expenditures, $1,075; qualifying distributions, $0.
Purpose and activities: The foundation supports community foundations and organizations involved with education and awards grants and college scholarships to individuals.
Fields of interest: Arts.
Type of support: General/operating support; Grants to individuals; Scholarships—to individuals.
Geographic limitations: Giving primarily in Brown County, WI.
Application information: Applications accepted. Application form required.
Initial approach: Letter
Deadline(s): None
Officers: Ronald Weyers, Pres.; Thomas Olejniczak, Secy.
Board Member: Peter Mancuso.
EIN: 391916843

3062
Property Management, Inc.

1300 Market St., Ste. 201
P.O. Box 622
Lemoyne, PA 17043-1420 (717) 730-4141

Company URL: http://www.rentpmi.com
Establishment information: Established in 1967.
Company type: Private company
Business activities: Manages real estate.
Business type (SIC): Real estate agents and managers
Corporate officers: Eric Kunkle, Pres. and C.O.O.; Mark Stephens, C.F.O.; David E. Dyson, Jr., Sr. V.P. and Cont.; Michael A. Campbell, Admin.
Subsidiary: Rhodes Development Group, Inc., Lemoyne, PA
Giving statement: Giving through the Property Management, Inc. Charitable Foundation.

Property Management, Inc. Charitable Foundation

1300 Market St.
P.O. Box 622
Lemoyne, PA 17043-0622 (717) 730-7055

Establishment information: Established in 1994 in PA.
Donors: Property Management, Inc.; Rhodes Development Group, Inc.
Contact: Lawrence M. Meams, Pres.
Financial data (yr. ended 12/31/11): Assets, $279,714 (M); gifts received, $25,000; expenditures, $30,087; qualifying distributions, $29,270; giving activities include $29,270 for 18 grants (high: $5,000; low: $175).
Purpose and activities: The foundation supports community foundations and organizations involved with human services. Support is limited to central Pennsylvania.
Fields of interest: Human services; Foundations (community).
Type of support: General/operating support.
Geographic limitations: Giving limited to central PA.
Support limitations: No grants to individuals.
Application information: Applications accepted. Application form required. Applicants should submit the following:
1) statement of problem project will address
2) copy of IRS Determination Letter
3) copy of most recent annual report/audited financial statement/990
4) listing of board of directors, trustees, officers and other key people and their affiliations
5) detailed description of project and amount of funding requested
6) copy of current year's organizational budget and/or project budget
Initial approach: Proposal
Deadline(s): Apr. 1 and Oct. 1
Officers: Lawrence M. Means, Pres.; John H. Rhodes, V.P.; Sandra J. Hauenstein, Secy.; Mark J. Stephens, Treas.; Bonnie F. Rhodes, Exec. Dir.
Directors: David E. Dyson; Eric S. Kunkle; Monica D. Rhodes; Carrie Traeger.
Number of staff: None.
EIN: 251721134

3063
The Prophet Corporation

(also known as Gopher Sport)
2525 Lemond St., S.W.
P.O. Box 998
Owatonna, MN 55060-0998
(507) 451-7470

Company URL: http://www.gophersport.com
Establishment information: Established in 1947.
Company type: Private company
Business activities: Sells physical education, athletic, recreation, and fitness products wholesale.
Business type (SIC): Durable goods—wholesale
Financial profile for 2010: Number of employees, 85
Corporate officers: Joel Jennings, Chair. and C.E.O.; Todd Jennings, Co-Pres.; Doug Nelson, Co-Pres.
Board of director: Joel Jennings, Chair.
Giving statement: Giving through the Jennings Family Foundation.

The Jennings Family Foundation

(formerly The Prophet Corporation Foundation)
P.O. Box 998
Owatonna, MN 55060-0998 (507) 444-1522

Donors: The Prophet Corp.; Joel Jennings; Mary Lee Jennings; Genesis Apparel, Inc.
Contact: Joel Jennings, Pres.
Financial data (yr. ended 12/31/11): Assets, $4,469,770 (M); gifts received, $340,318; expenditures, $476,944; qualifying distributions, $424,818; giving activities include $424,818 for grants.
Purpose and activities: The foundation supports hospitals and organizations involved with Alzheimer's disease, hunger, housing development, human services, Christianity, and economically disadvantaged people.
Fields of interest: Hospitals (general); Alzheimer's disease; Food services; Housing/shelter, development; Children/youth, services; Family services; Homeless, human services; Human services; Christian agencies & churches Economically disadvantaged.
Type of support: General/operating support.
Geographic limitations: Giving primarily in Minneapolis and Owatonna, MN.
Application information: Applications accepted. Application form not required. Applicants should submit the following:
1) detailed description of project and amount of funding requested
2) copy of IRS Determination Letter
Initial approach: Proposal
Deadline(s): None
Officer and Director: Joel Jennings, Pres.; Mary Lee Jennings.
EIN: 411765206
Selected grants: The following grants are a representative sample of this grantmaker's funding activity:
$27,700 to Fellowship of Christian Athletes, Kansas City, MO, 2010.
$15,000 to Kenya Childrens Fund, Hopkins, MN, 2010.
$10,000 to Steele County Food Shelf, Owatonna, MN, 2010.
$7,500 to Urban Ventures Leadership Foundation, Minneapolis, MN, 2010.
$7,000 to Pilgrim Center for Reconciliation, Edina, MN, 2010.
$5,000 to Search Ministries, Ellicott City, MD, 2010.
$4,500 to American Cancer Society, Mendota Heights, MN, 2010.
$4,000 to Special Olympics Minnesota, Minneapolis, MN, 2010.
$2,000 to Gillette Childrens Hospital Foundation, Saint Paul, MN, 2010.
$1,500 to Friendship Ventures, Annandale, MN, 2010.

3064
Proskauer Rose LLP

11 Times Sq.
New York, NY 10036-8299 (212) 969-3952

Company URL: http://www.proskauer.com/
Establishment information: Established in 1875.
Company type: Private company
Business activities: Operates law firm.
Business type (SIC): Legal services
Offices: Washington, DC; Boca Raton, FL; Chicago, IL; New Orleans, LA; Boston, MA; Newark, NJ; New York, NY
International operations: Brazil; France; Hong Kong; United Kingdom
Giving statement: Giving through the Proskauer Pro Bono Program.

Proskauer Pro Bono Program

11 Times Sq.
New York, NY 10036-8299 (212) 969-3952
E-mail: sfahey@proskauer.com; Additional tel.: (212) 969-3000; URL: http://www.proskauer.com/probono/

Contact: Stacey O'Haire Fahey, Firmwide Pro Bono Counsel
Fields of interest: Legal services.
Type of support: Pro bono services - legal.
Application information: A Pro Bono Committee manages the pro bono program.

3065
ProtechSoft, Inc.

303 W. Capitol, Ste. 330
Little Rock, AR 72201 (501) 687-2400

Company URL: http://www.protechsoft.com
Establishment information: Established in 1995.
Company type: Private company
Business activities: Provides computer integrated systems design services.
Business type (SIC): Computer services
Corporate officers: Nagaraj Garimalla, C.E.O.; Judy Jordan, Pres.; Shiva Duvvru, C.F.O.
Office: Edina, MN
Giving statement: Giving through the ProtechSoft Charitable Foundation, Inc.

ProtechSoft Charitable Foundation, Inc.

303 Capitol Ave., Ste. 330
Little Rock, AR 72201 (501) 687-2302

Establishment information: Established in 2001 in AR.
Donors: Protech Solutions, Inc.; ProtechSoft, Inc.
Contact: Shiva Duvvuru, Dir.
Financial data (yr. ended 10/31/11): Assets, $233,915 (M); expenditures, $12,324; qualifying distributions, $9,069; giving activities include $9,069 for grants.
Purpose and activities: The foundation supports organizations involved with athletics, human services, and Hinduism.
Fields of interest: Health care; Human services.
Type of support: General/operating support; Program development; Scholarship funds.
Geographic limitations: Giving primarily in Little Rock, AR and India.
Application information: Applications accepted. Application form required. Applicants should submit the following:
1) copy of IRS Determination Letter
2) detailed description of project and amount of funding requested
Initial approach: Proposal
Deadline(s): None
Directors: Shiva Duvvuru; Nagaraj Garimalla; Satish Garimalla.
EIN: 752972385

3066
Protective Life Insurance Company

2801 Hwy. 280 S.
Birmingham, AL 35223-2488
(205) 268-1000

Company URL: http://www.protectivelife.com
Establishment information: Established in 1906.
Company type: Subsidiary of a public company
Business activities: Sells life insurance.
Business type (SIC): Insurance/life
Financial profile for 2010: Number of employees, 1,840; sales volume, $2,940,000,000
Corporate officers: John D. Johns, Chair., Pres., and C.E.O.; Richard J. Bielen, Vice-Chair. and C.F.O.; Carolyn M. Johnson, Exec. V.P. and C.O.O.; Carl S. Thigpen, Exec. V.P. and C.I.O.; Steven G. Walker, Sr. V.P., C.A.O., and Cont.; Deborah J. Long, Exec. V.P., Genl. Counsel, and Secy.
Board of directors: John D. Johns, Chair.; Richard J. Bielen, Vice-Chair.; Robert O. Burton; Elaine L. Chao; Thomas L. Hamby; John D. Johns; Vanessa Leonard; Charles D. McCrary; John J. McMahon, Jr.; Hans H. Miller; Malcolm Portera; C. Dowd Ritter; Jesse J. Spikes; William A. Terry; W. Michael Warren, Jr.; Vanessa Wilson
Subsidiary: West Coast Life Insurance Co., San Francisco, CA
Giving statement: Giving through the Protective Life Insurance Company Contributions Program and the Protective Life Foundation.

Protective Life Insurance Company Contributions Program

2801 Hwy. 280 S.
Birmingham, AL 35223-2488
URL: http://www.protective.com/default.asp?id=4

Purpose and activities: As a complement to its foundation, Protective Life Insurance also makes charitable contributions to nonprofit organizations directly. Support is given primarily in areas of company operations in Alabama, California, Georgia, Illinois, Kansas, Minnesota, Missouri, Nebraska, North Carolina, Ohio, Tennessee, and Virginia, and in Canada.
Fields of interest: Arts; Education; Human services; Community/economic development.
International interests: Canada.
Type of support: Employee volunteer services; Sponsorships.
Geographic limitations: Giving primarily in areas of company operations in AL, CA, GA, IL, KS, MN, MO, NC, NE, OH, TN, and VA, and in Canada.
Application information:

Protective Life Foundation

P.O. Box 2606
Birmingham, AL 35202-2606 (205) 268-4434
FAX: (205) 268-5547;
E-mail: kate.cotton@protective.com; URL: http://www.protective.com/giving-back.aspx

Establishment information: Established in 1994 in AL.
Donor: Protective Life Insurance Co.
Contact: Kate H. Cotton, Exec. Dir.
Financial data (yr. ended 12/31/11): Assets, $98,517 (M); gifts received, $2,625,000; expenditures, $2,605,702; qualifying distributions, $2,501,148; giving activities include $2,433,569 for 154+ grants (high: $365,000) and $67,579 for 44 grants to individuals (high: $2,500).
Purpose and activities: The foundation supports organizations involved with arts and culture, education, health and health initiatives, human services, community development, civic affairs, and youth.
Fields of interest: Museums (art); Performing arts, orchestras; Arts; Elementary school/education; Higher education; Education; Hospitals (general); Health care; Food banks; YM/YWCAs & YM/YWHAs; Children/youth, services; Human services; Community/economic development; United Ways and Federated Giving Programs; Public affairs Youth.
Program:
Scholarship and Academic Award Program: The foundation awards college scholarships to children of employees of Protective Life who have excelled in academics and/or civic service.
Type of support: Annual campaigns; Capital campaigns; Continuing support; Employee matching gifts; Employee-related scholarships; General/operating support; Program development; Research; Scholarship funds; Sponsorships.
Geographic limitations: Giving primarily in areas of company operations in the metro Birmingham, AL, area.
Support limitations: Generally, no support for K-12 public or private schools, churches, public facilities, or state organizations, or other corporate or private foundations. Generally, no grants for animal-related causes, sporting events, walks, or runs, or start-up costs.
Publications: Annual report; Application guidelines.
Application information: Applications accepted. Proposals should be submitted using organization letterhead and should be no longer than 4 pages. Support is limited to 1 contribution per organization during any given year. Application form not required. Applicants should submit the following:
1) qualifications of key personnel
2) population served
3) name, address and phone number of organization
4) copy of IRS Determination Letter
5) brief history of organization and description of its mission
6) copy of most recent annual report/audited financial statement/990
7) how project's results will be evaluated or measured
8) what distinguishes project from others in its field
9) listing of board of directors, trustees, officers and other key people and their affiliations
10) detailed description of project and amount of funding requested
11) contact person
12) copy of current year's organizational budget and/or project budget
13) listing of additional sources and amount of support

Proposals should also include an Executive Director's brief bio and the number of full-time and part-rime staff members.
Initial approach: Proposal
Copies of proposal: 1
Board meeting date(s): Mar., June, Sept., and Dec.
Deadline(s): Feb. 19, May 21, Aug. 20, and Nov. 19
Final notification: Varies
Officers: John D. Johns*, Pres.; Kate H. Cotton*, Secy. and Exec. Dir.
Advisory Council: Robert L. Beeman; Rita E. Fulton; Ben W. Ingram; Ellen A. Michael; M. Kevin Sullivan; Sherri D. Swickard.
Number of staff: 1 full-time professional; 1 part-time professional.
EIN: 631129596
Selected grants: The following grants are a representative sample of this grantmaker's funding activity:
$347,288 to United Way of Central Alabama, Birmingham, AL, 2010. For corporate gift.
$70,000 to Cornerstone Schools of Alabama, Birmingham, AL, 2010. For operating support.
$50,000 to Park Project - Greening of the Community, Mobile, AL, 2010.
$40,000 to Alabama Symphonic Association, Birmingham, AL, 2010. For 2010 series sponsorship.
$35,000 to YWCA of Birmingham, Birmingham, AL, 2010. For capital campaign — Woodlawn revitalization.
$30,000 to Minor Elementary School, Birmingham, AL, 2010. For financial support.
$28,000 to United Way of Metropolitan Nashville, Nashville, TN, 2010. For corporate gift.

$25,000 to Birmingham Athletic Partnership, Birmingham, AL, 2010. For Business Partners Program.
$15,000 to Kings Ranch, Chelsea, AL, 2010. For operating support.
$10,000 to Alabama Heritage, Tuscaloosa, AL, 2010. For sponsorship.

3067
The Protector Group Insurance Agency, Inc.

100 Front St., Ste. 800
Worcester, MA 01608-1435
(508) 852-8500

Company URL: http://www.protectorgroup.com
Establishment information: Established in 1928.
Company type: Private company
Business activities: Operates insurance company.
Business type (SIC): Insurance agents, brokers, and services
Corporate officer: Robert J. Vaudreuil, Pres. and C.E.O.
Offices: Leominster, Millbury, Wellesley, MA
Giving statement: Giving through the Protector Group Charitable Foundation Inc.

The Protector Group Charitable Foundation Inc.

100 Front St., Ste. 800
Worcester, MA 01608-1435

Establishment information: Established in 1999 in MA.
Donor: The Protector Group Insurance Agency, Inc.
Financial data (yr. ended 12/31/11): Assets, $337,225 (M); expenditures, $23,685; qualifying distributions, $20,000; giving activities include $20,000 for 7 grants (high: $8,333; low: $167).
Purpose and activities: The foundation supports organizations involved with higher education, health, and human services.
Fields of interest: Higher education; Health care, insurance; Nursing care; Health care; Athletics/ sports, golf; YM/YWCAs & YM/YWHAs; Residential/ custodial care, hospices; Human services.
Type of support: General/operating support.
Geographic limitations: Giving primarily in Worcester, MA.
Support limitations: No grants to individuals.
Application information: Applications not accepted. Unsolicited requests for funds not accepted.
Officers and Directors:* Robert J. Vaudreuil*, Pres.; John J. Cahill*, Treas.; George W. Tetler III, Clerk; Patrick J. Cronin; Robert J. Vaudreuil.
EIN: 043431782

3068
The Providence Journal Co.

(also known as Providence Journal-Bulletin)
75 Fountain St.
Providence, RI 02902 (401) 277-7600

Company URL: http://www.projo.com
Establishment information: Established in 1829.
Company type: Subsidiary of a public company
Business activities: Publishes newspapers; broadcasts radio and television.
Business type (SIC): Newspaper publishing and/or printing; radio and television broadcasting; cable and other pay television services
Corporate officers: Howard G. Sutton II, Pres. and C.E.O.; Sandra J. Radcliffe, Exec. V.P., Finance and Admin., and C.F.O.; Scott Connolly, Sr. V.P., Sales and Mktg.
Giving statement: Giving through the Providence Journal Charitable Foundation.

Providence Journal Charitable Foundation

P.O. Box 224866
Dallas, TX 75222-4866
Application address: 75 Fountain St., Providence, RI 02902

Establishment information: Trust established in 1956 in RI.
Donor: The Providence Journal Co.
Financial data (yr. ended 12/31/11): Assets, $2,566 (M); expenditures, $65,812; qualifying distributions, $0.
Purpose and activities: The foundation supports zoological societies and hospitals and organizations involved with arts and culture, education, sexual abuse, and human services.
Fields of interest: Media, radio; Visual arts, design; Arts; Secondary school/education; Higher education; Libraries (public); Education; Zoos/ zoological societies; Hospitals (general); Crime/ violence prevention, sexual abuse; Children/youth, services; Developmentally disabled, centers & services; Human services; United Ways and Federated Giving Programs.
Type of support: Capital campaigns; General/ operating support.
Geographic limitations: Giving primarily in RI, with emphasis on Providence.
Support limitations: No grants to individuals.
Application information: Applications accepted. Application form required. Applicants should submit the following:
1) detailed description of project and amount of funding requested
   Initial approach: Letter
   Copies of proposal: 1
   Board meeting date(s): Quarterly
   Deadline(s): None

Trustees: Sandra J. Radcliffe; Howard G. Sutton; John W. Wall.
EIN: 056015372

3069
Provident Financial Services, Inc.

830 Bergen Ave.
Jersey City, NJ 07306-4599
(732) 590-9200
FAX: (302) 655-5049

Company URL: http://www.providentbanknj.com
Establishment information: Established in 1839.
Company type: Public company
Company ticker symbol and exchange: PFS/NYSE
Business activities: Operates bank holding company; operates savings bank.
Business type (SIC): Savings institutions; holding company
Financial profile for 2012: Number of employees, 941; assets, $7,283,690,000; pre-tax net income, $96,120,000; liabilities, $6,302,450,000
Corporate officers: Christopher P. Martin, Chair., Pres., and C.E.O.; Thomas M. Lyons, Exec. V.P. and C.F.O.; John F. Kuntz, Exec V.P., Genl. Counsel, and Corp. Secy.
Board of directors: Christopher Martin, Chair.; Laura L. Brooks; Thomas W. Berry, C.P.A.; Geoffrey M. Connor; Frank L. Fekete; Terence Gallagher; Carlos M. Hernandez; Thomas B. Hogan, Jr.; Katharine Laud; Edward O'Donnell; Jeffries Shein
Subsidiary: The Provident Bank, Jersey City, NJ
Giving statement: Giving through the Provident Bank Foundation.
Company EIN: 421547151

The Provident Bank Foundation

250 Madison Ave.
Morristown, NJ 07960-6168 (862) 260-3990
FAX: (866) 353-3172;
E-mail: Jane.Kurek@ProvidentNJ.com; Additional contact: Dariell Leak, Fdn. Asst., tel.: (862) 260-3990, e-mail: Foundation@providentnj.com; Application address: 830 Bergen Ave., 7th Fl., Jersey City, NJ 07306, tel.: (201) 915-5434; URL: http://www.providentnjfoundation.org

Establishment information: Established in 2003 in NJ.
Donor: Provident Financial Services, Inc.
Contact: Jane Kurek, Exec. Dir.
Financial data (yr. ended 12/31/11): Assets, $18,487,441 (M); expenditures, $1,725,171; qualifying distributions, $1,676,264; giving activities include $1,365,200 for 309 grants (high: $50,000; low: $500).
Purpose and activities: The foundation supports programs designed to promote family and youth services; community enrichment; education; and health and human services.
Fields of interest: Arts education; Museums; Arts; Elementary/secondary education; Adult/continuing education; Libraries (public); Education, services; Education; Hospitals (general); Health care; Mental health/crisis services; Employment, services; Food services; Food banks; Housing/shelter; Recreation; Youth development, centers/clubs; Youth development, adult & child programs; Youth, services; Human services, financial counseling; Residential/custodial care, hospices; Homeless, human services; Human services; Public affairs.
Program:
Sandy Relief and Recovery Grants: The foundation awards grants of up to $25,000 to support Sandy relief and recovery efforts in New Jersey. Special emphasis is directed towards proposals that focus on small businesses.
Type of support: Building/renovation; Capital campaigns; Continuing support; Curriculum development; Equipment; General/operating support; Management development/capacity building; Matching/challenge support; Program development; Research; Scholarship funds; Seed money.
Geographic limitations: Giving is limited to areas of company operations in NJ, with emphasis on Bergen, Essex, Hudson, Mercer, Middlesex, Monmouth, Morris, Ocean, Passaic, Somerset, and Union counties.
Support limitations: No support for political organizations or religious organizations not of direct benefit to the entire community, or for pass-through organizations.
Publications: Annual report; Application guidelines.
Application information: Applications accepted. The Mini-Grant Program is for requests of $3,500 or less. The Grant Program is for requests over $3,500 to a maximum of $15,000. Sponsorships are limited events that will be sponsored by and attended by foundation representatives. Support is limited to 1 contribution per organization during any given year. Application form required. Applicants should submit the following:
1) copy of IRS Determination Letter

2) brief history of organization and description of its mission
3) geographic area to be served
4) copy of most recent annual report/audited financial statement/990
5) descriptive literature about organization
6) listing of board of directors, trustees, officers and other key people and their affiliations
7) detailed description of project and amount of funding requested
8) copy of current year's organizational budget and/ or project budget
9) listing of additional sources and amount of support

Initial approach: Complete online application for Mini-Grants; download application form and mail or fax to foundation for the Grant Program; contact foundation for Sandy Relief and Recovery Grants
Copies of proposal: 1
Board meeting date(s): Jan., Apr., July, and Oct.
Deadline(s): None for Mini-Grants; Jan. 1, Apr. 1, July 1, and Oct. 1 for the Grant Program; None for Sandy Relief and Recovery Grants
Final notification: 60 to 90 days

Officers and Directors:* Carlos M. Hernandez*, Chair.; Christopher P. Martin*, Pres.; John F. Kuntz, Secy.; George Dailey, Jr., Treas.; Jane Kurek, Exec. Dir.; Katharine Laud; Karen McMullen.
Number of staff: 1 part-time professional.
EIN: 043739441
Selected grants: The following grants are a representative sample of this grantmaker's funding activity:
$350,000 to Christ Hospital Foundation, Jersey City, NJ, 2010.
$20,000 to New Jersey SEEDS, Newark, NJ, 2010.
$15,000 to Liberty Science Center, Jersey City, NJ, 2010.
$10,000 to Big Brothers Big Sisters of Monmouth County, Eatontown, NJ, 2010.
$10,000 to Center in Asbury Park, Asbury Park, NJ, 2010.
$10,000 to Collier Services, Wickatunk, NJ, 2010.
$10,000 to Grameen America, New York, NY, 2010.
$7,500 to Saint Clares Foundation, Denville, NJ, 2010.
$5,000 to House of Faith, Jersey City, NJ, 2010.
$5,000 to T.J. Martell Foundation, New York, NY, 2010.

3070
Provident New York Bancorp

400 Rella Blvd.
P.O. Box 600
Montebello, NY 10901-4243
(845) 369-8040
FAX: (302) 636-5454

Company URL: http://www.providentbanking.com
Establishment information: Established in 1888.
Company type: Public company
Company ticker symbol and exchange: PBNY/ NASDAQ
Business activities: Operates commercial bank.
Business type (SIC): Banks/commercial
Financial profile for 2012: Number of employees, 456; assets, $4,022,980,000; pre-tax net income, $26,050,000; liabilities, $3,531,860,000
Corporate officers: Willima F. Helmer, Chair.; Dennis L. Coyle, Vice-Chair.; Jack L. Kopnisky, Pres. and C.E.O.; Rodney C. Whitwell, Exec. V.P. and C.O.O.; Luis Massiani, Exec. V.P. and C.F.O.; Daniel G. Rothstein, Exec. V.P. and Genl. Counsel
Board of directors: William F. Helmer, Chair.; Dennis L. Coyle, Vice-Chair.; Navy E. Djonovic; James F. Deutsch; Thomas F. Jauntig, Jr.; Thomas Graham Kahn; R. Michael Kennedy; Jack L. Kopnisky; Victoria Kossover; Richard O'Toole; Carl J. Rosenstock; Burt B. Steinberg; George L. Strayton
Historic mergers: Warwick Community Bancorp, Inc. (October 1, 2004)
Giving statement: Giving through the Provident Bank Charitable Foundation and the Warwick Savings Foundation.
Company EIN: 800091851

Provident Bank Charitable Foundation

400 Rella Blvd.
Montebello, NY 10901-4241
URL: http://www.providentbanking.com/ foundation_Mission.cfm

Establishment information: Established in 2004 in NY as a company-sponsored operating foundation.
Donors: The Provident Bank; Barry Lewis.
Financial data (yr. ended 12/31/10): Assets, $3,600,486 (M); expenditures, $154,080; qualifying distributions, $153,685; giving activities include $140,491 for 10+ grants (high: $50,000) and $139,991 for 2 foundation-administered programs.
Purpose and activities: The foundation supports organizations involved with education, health, youth development, and human services.
Fields of interest: Education; Health care; Youth development; Youth, services; Human services.
Program:
Community Involvement Scholarship Program: The foundation awards $2,000 scholarships to local high seniors who demonstrate an outstanding commitment to community service.
Type of support: Continuing support; Program development; Scholarships—to individuals.
Geographic limitations: Giving limited to Bergen County, NJ, and Orange, Putnam, Rockland, Sullivan, Ulster counties, NY.
Support limitations: No support for labor organizations, religious organizations (except for health and human services or programs benefiting all students), or political, legislative, or lobbying organizations, private foundations, or municipalities with tax authority. No grants to individuals (except for scholarships), or for general operating support, administrative salaries, or advertising costs, beauty or talent contests, or athletic scholarships; no banking service donations.
Publications: Annual report; Application guidelines.
Application information: Applications accepted. Support is limited to 1 contribution per organization during any given year. Multi-year funding is not automatic. Scholarship applicants must have a minimal 2 years of community involvement over the past 4 years with at least 40 hours over the past two year period. Application form required. Applicants should submit the following:
1) timetable for implementation and evaluation of project
2) copy of IRS Determination Letter
3) brief history of organization and description of its mission
4) copy of most recent annual report/audited financial statement/990
5) descriptive literature about organization
6) listing of board of directors, trustees, officers and other key people and their affiliations
7) listing of additional sources and amount of support

Scholarship applications must include 3 letters of recommendation, an acceptance letter from a locally based college, and a short essay focusing on past community involvement.
Initial approach: Contact foundation for application form for grants; download application form and mail to foundation for Community Involvement Scholarship Program
Board meeting date(s): Quarterly
Deadline(s): Varies
Final notification: June for Community Involvement Scholarship Program

Officers and Directors: George Strayton, C.E.O. and Pres.; Paul A. Maisch, Exec. V.P. and C.F.O.; Katherine Brown, V.P. and Secy; Miranda Grimm, V.P. and Treas.; Stephanie Yaniga, V.P. and Exec. Dir.; Thomas A. Jauntig, Jr.; Donald T. McNelis.
EIN: 321013899
Selected grants: The following grants are a representative sample of this grantmaker's funding activity:
$50,000 to Saint Thomas Aquinas College, Sparkill, NY, 2010.
$20,000 to Orange Regional Medical Center Foundation, Goshen, NY, 2010.
$3,000 to Arts Alliance of Haverstraw, Haverstraw, NY, 2010.

The Warwick Savings Foundation

28 Railroad Ave.
Warwick, NY 10990-1525
Application address: 39 Washington, Rd., Monroe, NY 10950

Establishment information: Established in 1997 in NY.
Donor: Warwick Community Bancorp, Inc.
Contact: Louis Ulatowski, Secy.
Financial data (yr. ended 12/31/11): Assets, $4,539,615 (M); expenditures, $268,925; qualifying distributions, $250,310; giving activities include $250,310 for grants.
Purpose and activities: The foundation supports historical societies and organizations involved with education, health, housing development, therapeutic riding, and human services.
Fields of interest: Historic preservation/historical societies; Secondary school/education; Higher education; Education; Hospitals (general); Health care, clinics/centers; Health care; Housing/shelter, development; Athletics/sports, equestrianism; Children/youth, services; Residential/custodial care, hospices; Developmentally disabled, centers & services; Human services.
Type of support: General/operating support.
Geographic limitations: Giving limited to NY.
Support limitations: No grants to individuals.
Application information: Applications accepted. Application form not required.
Initial approach: Proposal
Deadline(s): Sept. 30

Officers and Directors:* John McDermott III*, Pres.; Lois E. Ulatowski, Secy.; R. Michael Kennedy*, Treas.; Frances M. Gorish; Sr. Ann Sakac; Mary Smith; Thomas Sullivan.
EIN: 061504632
Selected grants: The following grants are a representative sample of this grantmaker's funding activity:
$40,000 to Hospice of Orange and Sullivan Counties, Newburgh, NY, 2010.
$30,000 to Winslow Therapeutic Riding Unlimited, Warwick, NY, 2010.
$20,000 to Occupations, Inc., Middletown, NY, 2010.
$15,000 to Mount Saint Mary College, Newburgh, NY, 2010.
$10,000 to Orange Regional Medical Center Foundation, Goshen, NY, 2010.
$5,000 to Safe Harbors of the Hudson, Newburgh, NY, 2010.

$2,950 to Literacy Partners of Orange County New York, Middletown, NY, 2010.
$2,000 to Newburgh Day Nursery, Newburgh, NY, 2010.

3071
Provident Savings Bank, FSB

3756 Central Ave.
Riverside, CA 92506-2469 (951) 686-6060

Company URL: http://www.myprovident.com
Establishment information: Established in 1956.
Company type: Subsidiary of a public company
Business activities: Operates savings bank.
Business type (SIC): Savings institutions
Corporate officers: Craig G. Blunden, Chair. and C.E.O.; Donavon P. Ternes, Pres.; Lillian Brunner-Salter, Sr. V.P. and C.I.O.
Board of director: Craig G. Blunden, Chair.
Giving statement: Giving through the Provident Savings Bank Charitable Foundation, Inc.

Provident Savings Bank Charitable Foundation, Inc.

3756 Central Ave.
Riverside, CA 92506-2421 (951) 782-6160
Tel: (951) 782-6160

Establishment information: Established in 2006 in CA.
Donor: Provident Savings Bank.
Contact: Craig G. Blunden, C.E.O.
Financial data (yr. ended 05/31/12): Assets, $482,057 (M); gifts received, $43,240; expenditures, $98,665; qualifying distributions, $98,665; giving activities include $98,665 for 13 grants (high: $21,165; low: $1,000).
Purpose and activities: The foundation supports orchestras and organizations involved with education, animal welfare, housing, basketball, and children services.
Fields of interest: Education; Housing/shelter; Human services.
Type of support: Capital campaigns; General/operating support; Scholarship funds; Sponsorships.
Geographic limitations: Giving limited to Riverside, CA.
Application information: Applications accepted. Application form required. Applicants should submit the following:
1) copy of IRS Determination Letter
2) detailed description of project and amount of funding requested
Initial approach: Proposal
Deadline(s): None
Officers and Directors:* Craig G. Blunden*, C.E.O.; Deborah Hill*, V.P.; Debbie Guthrie*, Secy.; Debra Baker; Bruce Bennett; William O'Laverty.
EIN: 205664114

3072
Prudential Financial, Inc.

751 Broad St.
Newark, NJ 07102-3714 (973) 802-6000

Company URL: http://www.prudential.com
Establishment information: Established in 1875.
Company type: Public company
Company ticker symbol and exchange: PRU/NYSE
Business activities: Provides life insurance and other financial products and services.
Business type (SIC): Insurance/life; insurance/accident and health
Financial profile for 2012: Number of employees, 48,498; assets, $709,298,000,000; sales volume, $84,815,000,000; pre-tax net income, $676,000,000; expenses, $84,139,000,000; liabilities, $670,723,000,000
Fortune 1000 ranking: 2012—29th in revenues, 347th in profits, and 10th in assets
Forbes 2000 ranking: 2012—80th in sales, 1145th in profits, and 42nd in assets
Corporate officers: John R. Strangfeld, Chair. and C.E.O.; Mark B. Grier, Vice-Chair.; Charles F. Lowrey, Exec. V.P. and C.O.O.; Robert Falzon, Exec. V.P. and C.F.O.; Barbara G. Koster, Sr. V.P. and C.I.O.; Susan L. Blount, Sr. V.P. and Genl. Counsel; Sharon C. Taylor, Sr. V.P. and Human Resources
Board of directors: John R. Strangfeld, Chair.; Mark B. Grier, Vice-Chair.; Thomas J. Baltimore, Jr.; Gordon M. Bethune; Gaston Caperton; Gilbert F. Casellas; James G. Cullen; William H. Gray III; Constance J. Horner; Martina Hund-Mejean; Karl J. Krapek; Christine A. Poon; James A. Unruh
Giving statement: Giving through the Prudential Financial, Inc. Corporate Giving Program and the Prudential Foundation.
Company EIN: 223703799

Prudential Financial, Inc. Corporate Giving Program

c/o Prudential Financial, Inc., Comm. Resources
751 Broad St.
Newark, NJ 07102-3714
FAX: (973) 802-3345;
E-mail: scharron.little@prudential.com; URL: http://www.prudential.com/community
Application address for Spirit of Community Awards: Prudential Spirit of Community Awards, State-Level Judging Comm., One Scholarship Way, P.O. Box 297, St. Peter, MN 56082,
e-mail: spirit@prudential.com

Contact: Mary O'Malley, V.P., Local Initiatives; Scharron N. Little, Contribs. Mgr.
Purpose and activities: As a complement to its foundation, Prudential also makes charitable contributions to nonprofit organizations and awards grants to secondary school students directly. Support is given primarily in areas of company operations.
Fields of interest: Arts; Elementary/secondary education; Education, early childhood education; Employment, training; Children/youth, services; Youth, services; Family services; Economic development; Community/economic development; Leadership development.
Program:
Prudential Spirit of Community Awards: Through the Prudential Spirit of Community Awards program, Prudential annually awards two $1,000 grants to middle level and secondary school students in each state, Washington, DC, and Puerto Rico for outstanding volunteer service to their communities. Ten national winners receive an additional $5,000.
Type of support: Donated equipment; Employee volunteer services; General/operating support; Grants to individuals; In-kind gifts.
Geographic limitations: Giving primarily in Phoenix, AZ, Los Angeles, CA, Hartford, CT, Jacksonville, FL, Chicago, IL, New Orleans, LA, Boston, MA, Minneapolis, MN, Newark, NJ, New York, NY, Philadelphia, PA, and Dallas and Houston, TX; giving on a national basis for the Spirit of Community Awards.
Application information: Applications are accepted in other languages besides English, but are not encouraged. The company has a staff that only handles contributions. Application form required.
Initial approach: Proposal to headquarters; download application form and submit 2 copies to school principal or head of officially designated local organization for Spirit of Community Awards
Deadline(s): Last weekday in Oct. for Spirit of Community Awards
Final notification: Feb. for Spirit of Community Awards

The Prudential Foundation

751 Broad St., 15th Fl.
Prudential Plz.
Newark, NJ 07102-3777 (973) 802-4070
E-mail: community.resources@prudential.com; URL: http://www.prudential.com/view/page/public/12182

Establishment information: Incorporated in 1977 in NJ.
Donors: The Prudential Insurance Co. of America; Prudential Equity Group, LLC.
Contact: Lata Reddy, V.P., Corp. Social Responsibility
Financial data (yr. ended 12/31/11): Assets, $100,215,074 (M); gifts received, $32,934,838; expenditures, $29,919,178; qualifying distributions, $31,758,058; giving activities include $20,920,775 for 1,012 grants (high: $784,000; low: $250), $7,966,416 for employee matching gifts and $2,580,120 for 3 loans/program-related investments.
Purpose and activities: The foundation supports organizations involved with education; economic development; and arts and culture.
Fields of interest: Arts education; Arts; Education, reform; Education; Employment, services; Community development, neighborhood development; Economic development; Community development, small businesses; Leadership development Youth; Economically disadvantaged.
International interests: Brazil; India; Japan; Mexico; North Korea; South Korea; Taiwan.
Programs:
Arts and Culture: The foundation supports programs designed to contribute to the local economy and provide diverse opportunities for individuals to experience and participate in the arts.
Economic Development: The foundation supports programs designed to transform neighborhoods distressed by declining populations, property values, job loss, and poverty; provide low-income families with assets and workforce development; promote small business development to drive economic growth and job creation; and promote community assets like parks, schools, medical and cultural institutions, and transit networks to bring needed resources and services to the community.
Education: The foundation supports programs designed to transform the public education system to improve long-term social and economic outcomes for children; develop strong educational leaders to manage school systems, schools, and classrooms; improve academic achievement through motivation and engagement in the classroom; and promote public and parent participation to sustain education reform efforts.
Employee Matching Gifts: The foundation matches contributions made by full-time employees, retirees, agents, and directors of Prudential and its subsidiaries to nonprofit organizations on a two-for-one basis from $25 to $100 and on a one-for-one basis from $100 to $5,000 per employee, per year.
Prudential CARES Volunteer Grants: The foundation awards grants of up to $5,000 to

nonprofit organizations with which employees, retirees, and agents of Prudential volunteer at least 40 hours per year.
Type of support: Capital campaigns; Emergency funds; Employee matching gifts; General/operating support; Management development/capacity building; Mission-related investments/loans; Program development; Program-related investments/loans; Seed money; Technical assistance.
Geographic limitations: Giving primarily in areas of company operations, with emphasis on Phoenix, AZ, Los Angeles, CA, Hartford, CT, Jacksonville, FL, Dubuque, IA, Chicago, IL, New Orleans, LA, Minneapolis, MN, Newark, NJ, New York, NY, Philadelphia and Scranton, PA, and in Brazil, India, Japan, Korea, Mexico, and Taiwan; giving also to national organizations.
Support limitations: No support for discriminatory organizations or labor, religious, fraternal, or athletic organizations, or single-disease health groups. No grants to individuals or for goodwill advertising.
Publications: Annual report (including application guidelines); Application guidelines.
Application information: Applications accepted. The foundation accepts the New York/ New Jersey Area Common Application Form and the New York/ New Jersey Common Report Form. Additional information may be requested at a later date. Video submissions are not encouraged. Application form required. Applicants should submit the following:
1) results expected from proposed grant
2) population served
3) copy of IRS Determination Letter
4) geographic area to be served
5) how project's results will be evaluated or measured
6) detailed description of project and amount of funding requested
7) contact person
8) copy of current year's organizational budget and/ or project budget
9) listing of additional sources and amount of support

Initial approach: Complete online application
Board meeting date(s): Feb., June, and Oct.
Deadline(s): None
Final notification: Within 60 days

Officers and Trustees:* Sharon C. Taylor*, Chair.; Lata N. Reddy, Pres.; Shane Harris, V.P. and Secy.; James W. McCarthy, Treas.; Brian Cloonan, Cont.; Gilbert F. Casellas; Constance J. Horner; Barbara G. Koster; John R. Strangfeld, Jr.
Number of staff: 5 full-time professional; 4 full-time support.
EIN: 222175290
Selected grants: The following grants are a representative sample of this grantmaker's funding activity:
$650,000 to New Jersey Symphony Orchestra, Newark, NJ, 2010. For Artistic Operations and Endowment fund.
$200,000 to International Rescue Committee, New York, NY, 2010. To provide aid to victims of the worst flooding in Pakistan.
$100,000 to Clinton Bush Haiti Fund, Washington, DC, 2010. For disaster relief fund.
$35,000 to Support Center for Nonprofit Management, New York, NY, 2010. For the Support Center to provide comprehensive management consulting, transition management, and professional development services to Newark nonprofit organizations.
$25,000 to Capital Corridor Community Development Corporation, Trenton, NJ, 2010. For the CDF Freedom School, Summer Program providing 150 Trenton youth with academic enrichment focused on literacy, cultural heritage, and social action.
$15,000 to Independent School District No. 279, Maple Grove, MN, 2010. For the Prudential Arts Grants Program.
$1,000 to Cornucopia Society, Jamaica, NY, 2010. For PruCARES.

3073
Pryor Cashman LLP
850 Main St.
P.O Box 7006
Bridgeport, CT 06601-7006 (203) 330-2230

Company URL: http://www.pryorcashman.com/
Establishment information: Established in 1963.
Company type: Private company
Business activities: Operates law firm.
Business type (SIC): Legal services
Corporate officers: Gideon Cashman, Chair.; Ronald H. Shechtman, Managing Partner
Offices: Los Angeles, CA; New York, NY
Giving statement: Giving through the Pryor Cashman LLP Pro Bono Program.

Pryor Cashman LLP Pro Bono Program
7 Times Sq.
New York, NY 10036-6569 (212) 421-4100
E-mail: wcharron@pryorcashman.com

Contact: William L. Charron
Fields of interest: Legal services.
Type of support: Pro bono services - legal.
Application information: A Pro Bono Committee manages the pro bono program.

3074
PSS World Medical, Inc.
4345 Southpoint Blvd.
Jacksonville, FL 32216 (904) 332-3000

Company URL: http://ir.pssd.com/
Establishment information: Established in 1983.
Company type: Public company
Company ticker symbol and exchange: PSSI/ NASDAQ
Business activities: Markets and distributes medical products and services to caregivers.
Business type (SIC): Medical instruments and supplies; professional and commercial equipment —wholesale
Financial profile for 2012: Number of employees, 4,100; assets, $1,155,970,000; sales volume, $2,102,000,000; pre-tax net income, $115,470,000; expenses, $1,968,650,000; liabilities, $768,840,000
Corporate officers: Delores M. Kesler, Chair.; Gary A. Corless, Pres. and C.E.O.; David M. Bronson, Exec. V.P. and C.F.O.; Joshua H. DeRienzis, V.P., Genl. Counsel, and Corp. Secy.
Board of directors: Delores M. Kesler, Chair.; Charles E. Adair; Alvin R. Carpenter; Gary A. Corless; Jeffrey C. Crowe; A. Hugh Greene; Steven T. Halverson; Melvin L. Hecktman; Jenny Kobin; Stephen H. Rogers
Giving statement: Giving through the PSS/Gulf South Employee Relief Fund Inc. and the PSS/Gulf South Medical Supply Relief Fund Inc.
Company EIN: 592280364

PSS/Gulf South Employee Relief Fund Inc.
4345 Southpoint Blvd.
Jacksonville, FL 32216

Establishment information: Established in 2006 in FL.
Donor: PSS World Medical, Inc.
Financial data (yr. ended 04/01/11): Assets, $15,898 (M); gifts received, $615; expenditures, $1,423; qualifying distributions, $900; giving activities include $900 for 1 grant to an individual.
Fields of interest: Disasters, Hurricane Katrina.
Type of support: Grants to individuals.
Application information: Applications not accepted. Unsolicited requests for funds not accepted.
Directors: David Bronson; Gary Corless; David Klarner.
EIN: 203423329

PSS/Gulf South Medical Supply Relief Fund Inc.
4345 Southpoint Blvd.
Jacksonville, FL 32216

Establishment information: Established in 2006 in FL.
Donors: Little Rapids Corporation; Midmark; Cholestech Corporation; PSS World Medical, Inc.
Financial data (yr. ended 04/01/11): Assets, $12,628 (M); expenditures, $632; qualifying distributions, $0.
Fields of interest: Disasters, Hurricane Katrina; Human services.
Application information: Applications not accepted. Unsolicited requests for funds not accepted.
Directors: David Bronson; Gary Corless; David Klarner.
EIN: 203536883

3075
Public Service Company of New Hampshire
(also known as PSNH)
780 N. Commercial St.
Manchester, NH 03101-1134
(603) 669-4000

Company URL: http://www.psnh.com
Establishment information: Established in 1926.
Company type: Subsidiary of a public company
Business activities: Generates, transmits, and distributes electricity.
Business type (SIC): Electric services
Corporate officers: Charles W. Shivery, Chair.; Leon J. Olivier, C.E.O.; Gary A. Long, Pres. and C.O.O.; David R. McHale, Sr. V.P. and C.F.O.; Gregory B. Butler, Sr. V.P. and Genl. Counsel; Randall A. Shoop, V.P. and Treas.; Shirley M. Payne, V.P. and Cont.; Samuel K. Lee, Secy.
Board of director: Charles W. Shivery, Chair.
Giving statement: Giving through the PSNH Corporate Giving Program.

PSNH Corporate Giving Program
P.O. Box 330
Manchester, NH 03105-0330
URL: http://www.psnh.com/CommunityRelations/Community.aspx

Purpose and activities: PSNH makes charitable contributions to nonprofit organizations involved with environmental stewardship, human services,

and economic opportunity. Support is given primarily in New Hampshire.
Fields of interest: Education; Environment; Human services; Community/economic development; United Ways and Federated Giving Programs; Engineering; General charitable giving.
Type of support: Employee volunteer services; General/operating support; Program development; Scholarship funds; Sponsorships.
Geographic limitations: Giving primarily in areas of company operations in NH.

3076
Public Service Company of New Mexico

(also known as PNM)
Alvarado Sq.
414 Silver Ave., S.W.
Albuquerque, NM 87158-0001
(505) 241-2700

Company URL: http://www.pnm.com
Establishment information: Established in 1917.
Company type: Subsidiary of a public company
Business activities: Generates, transmits, and distributes electricity; transmits and distributes natural gas.
Business type (SIC): Combination utility services
Financial profile for 2010: Number of employees, 40; sales volume, $1,020,000,000
Corporate officers: Jeffry E. Sterba, Chair.; Pat Vincent-Collawn, Pres. and C.E.O.; Charles Eldred, Exec. V.P. and C.F.O.; Ron Talbot, Sr. V.P. and C.O.O.; Patrick T. Ortiz, Sr. V.P. and Genl. Counsel; Terry Horn, V.P. and Treas.; Tom G. Sategna, V.P. and Cont.
Board of director: Jeffry E. Sterba, Chair.
Subsidiaries: Meadows Resources, Inc., Albuquerque, NM; Paragon Resources, Inc., Albuquerque, NM; Sunbelt Mining Co., Inc., Albuquerque, NM
Giving statement: Giving through the PNM Resources Foundation, Inc.
Company EIN: 750204070

PNM Resources Foundation, Inc.

(formerly PNM Foundation, Inc.)
Alvarado Sq., M.S. 0410
Albuquerque, NM 87158-1410 (505) 241-2872
Contact for PNM Energy Exploration Grants and Reduce Your Use Grants: Jaci Bertand, tel.: (505) 241-2864,
e-mail: jaci.bertand@pnmresources.com;
URL: http://www.pnm.com/foundation/home.htm

Establishment information: Incorporated in 1983 in NM.
Donors: Public Service Co. of New Mexico; PNM Resources, Inc.
Contact: Diane Harrison Ogawa, Exec. Dir.
Financial data (yr. ended 12/31/11): Assets, $12,347,221 (M); expenditures, $756,277; qualifying distributions, $715,295; giving activities include $715,295 for grants.
Purpose and activities: The foundation supports programs designed to promote education, environmental awareness and education, and economic vitality.
Fields of interest: Arts; Elementary/secondary education; Middle schools/education; Charter schools; Education, services; Education, reading; Education; Environment, natural resources; Environment, energy; Environmental education; Environment; Food services; Food banks; Aging, centers/services; Human services; Economic development.
Programs:
Directors' Discretionary Grants: The foundation awards grants of up to $1,000 to nonprofit organizations chosen by directors of the foundation.
Employee Matching Gifts: The foundation matches contributions made by employees and retirees of PNM to nonprofit organizations in New Mexico and institutions of higher education on a one-for-one basis from $25 to $1,000 per contributor, per year.
Hunger Initiative Grants: The foundation supports programs designed to eliminate childhood hunger in New Mexico; provide adequate food for New Mexico seniors; improve access to food in rural and underserved communities; encourage participation in public food assistance initiatives; and create hunger awareness in New Mexico.
PNM Energy Exploration Grants: The foundation awards grants of up to $1,000 to teachers of grades K-12 with projects designed to creatively answer questions about energy. The program will not award grants in 2012.
PNM Reduce Your Use Grants: The foundation awards grants of up to $5,000 to nonprofit organizations to promote energy efficiency through energy-saving projects. Special emphasis is directed towards energy-saving building upgrades; energy-efficient equipment and appliances; environmental education that encourages and awareness; and projects that conserve valuable resources for public use and future generations.
Volunteer Grants: The foundation awards $100 grants to nonprofit organizations with which employees or retirees of PNM volunteer at least 12 hours per year; $200 grants to nonprofit organizations with which employees and retirees of PNM volunteer at least 25 hours per year; and $500 grants to nonprofit organizations with which employees and retirees of PNM volunteer at least 25 hours per year and serve on the board of directors.
Type of support: Building/renovation; Employee matching gifts; Employee volunteer services; Equipment; General/operating support; Program development.
Geographic limitations: Giving primarily in NM and TX.
Support limitations: No support for discriminatory organizations, sectarian or religious organizations, veterans', labor, or political organizations, fraternal, athletic, or social clubs, or municipalities. No grants to individuals, or for testimonial dinners, fundraising events, or advertising, debt reduction, special events, annual events, or one-time only events, endowments, capital campaigns, administrative or overhead costs, documentaries or film production, or programs or projects that duplicate existing services and/or programs.
Publications: Application guidelines; Grants list; Program policy statement.
Application information: Applications accepted. Support is limited to 1 contribution per organization during any given year. Organizations receiving support are asked to submit a final report. Application form required.
Initial approach: Complete online application form
Board meeting date(s): 3 times per year
Deadline(s): Apr. 23 for PNM Reduce Your Use Grants
Officers and Trustees: Shirley Ragin, Pres.; Maureen Gannon, V.P.; Jeff Mechenbier, Secy.-Treas.; Diane Harrison Ogawa, Exec. Dir.; Patrick Apodaca; Kevin Judice; Valerie Smith; Neal Walker; Sayuri Yamada.
Number of staff: 1 full-time professional; 1 full-time support.
EIN: 850309005
Selected grants: The following grants are a representative sample of this grantmaker's funding activity:
$50,000 to Adelante Development Center, Albuquerque, NM, 2010.
$40,000 to Albuquerque Community Foundation, Albuquerque, NM, 2010.
$8,345 to Leukemia & Lymphoma Society, Albuquerque, NM, 2010.
$6,471 to University of New Mexico Foundation, Albuquerque, NM, 2010.
$5,000 to Albuquerque Center for Peace and Justice, Albuquerque, NM, 2010.
$5,000 to Albuquerque Little Theater, Albuquerque, NM, 2010.
$5,000 to Roadrunner Food Bank, Albuquerque, NM, 2010.
$5,000 to Santa Fe Community Housing Trust, Santa Fe, NM, 2010.
$5,000 to Talking Talons Youth Leadership, Tijeras, NM, 2010.
$4,955 to New Mexico BioPark Society, Albuquerque, NM, 2010.

3077
Public Service Enterprise Group Incorporated

(also known as PSEG)
80 Park Plz.
P.O. Box 570
Newark, NJ 07101-1171 (973) 430-7000
FAX: (973) 430-5845

Company URL: http://www.pseg.com
Establishment information: Established in 1903.
Company type: Public company
Company ticker symbol and exchange: PEG/NYSE
Business activities: Generates, transmits, and distributes electricity; transmits and distributes natural gas.
Business type (SIC): Combination utility services
Financial profile for 2012: Number of employees, 10,000; assets, $31,725,000,000; sales volume, $9,800,000,000; pre-tax net income, $2,011,000,000; expenses, $7,536,000,000; liabilities, $20,945,000,000
Fortune 1000 ranking: 2012—276th in revenues, 158th in profits, and 175th in assets
Forbes 2000 ranking: 2012—946th in sales, 463rd in profits, and 707th in assets
Corporate officers: Ralph Izzo, Chair., Pres., and C.E.O.; Caroline D. Dorsa, Exec. V.P. and C.F.O.; J.A. Bouknight, Jr., Exec. V.P. and Genl. Counsel
Board of directors: Ralph Izzo, Chair.; Albert R. Gamper, Jr.; William V. Hickey; Shirley Ann Jackson; David Lilley; Thomas A. Renyi; Hak Cheol Shin; Richard J. Swift; Susan Tomasky; Alfred W. Zollar
Plants: Bridgeport, New Haven, CT; Bayonne, Burlington, Edison, Hamilton, Harrison, Hope Creek, Jersey City, Kearny, National Park, Ridgefield, Woodbridge, NJ; Albany, NY; Conemaush, Keystone, Peach Bottom, PA
Giving statement: Giving through the PSEG Corporate Giving Program and the PSEG Foundation, Inc.
Company EIN: 222625848

PSEG Corporate Giving Program

c/o Corp. Contribs.
80 Park Plz.
Newark, NJ 07102-4109 (973) 430-7842
URL: http://www.pseg.com/info/community/index.jsp

Contact: Marion C. O'Neill, Mgr., Corp. Contribs.
Financial data (yr. ended 12/31/12): Total giving, $2,280,000, including $2,280,000 for grants.
Purpose and activities: As a complement to its foundation, PSEG also makes charitable contributions to nonprofit organizations directly. Support is given primarily in areas of company operations.
Fields of interest: Education; Environment; Disasters, preparedness/services; Community/economic development; Mathematics; Engineering/technology; Science.
Type of support: General/operating support.
Geographic limitations: Giving primarily in areas of company operations.
Support limitations: No support for religious or political organizations. No grants to individuals.
Publications: Application guidelines; Corporate report; Newsletter (including application guidelines).
Application information: Applications accepted. Corporate grants are awarded primarily for events. The Corporate Social Responsibility Department handles giving. Application form required.
Initial approach: Complete online application
Committee meeting date(s): 3-4 times annually
Deadline(s): Oct. 31
Final notification: 6 months
Administrators: Ellen Lambert, Dir., Corp. Social responsibility; Marion C. O'Neil, Mgr., Corp. Contribs.
Number of staff: 3 full-time professional; 2 full-time support.
Selected grants: The following grants are a representative sample of this grantmaker's funding activity:
$189,874 to New Jersey SHARES, Ewing, NJ, 2012.
$63,149 to Community Foundation of New Jersey, Morristown, NJ, 2012.
$50,000 to New Jersey Performing Arts Center, Newark, NJ, 2012.
$50,000 to United Way of Bergen County, Paramus, NJ, 2012.
$41,000 to Newark Alliance, Newark, NJ, 2012.
$30,000 to Regional Youth Adult Social Action Partnership, Bridgeport, CT, 2012.
$28,000 to Liberty Science Center, Jersey City, NJ, 2012.
$25,000 to All Stars Project of New Jersey, Newark, NJ, 2012.
$25,000 to American Heart Association, North Brunswick, NJ, 2012.
$25,000 to National Center on Addiction and Substance Abuse at Columbia University, New York, NY, 2012.
$25,000 to Newark Museum, Newark, NJ, 2012.

PSEG Foundation, Inc.

(formerly Public Service Electric and Gas Company Foundation, Inc.)
80 Park Plz., 10C
Newark, NJ 07102-4109 (973) 430-7842
FAX: (973) 297-1480;
E-mail: marion.oneill@pseg.com; Additional tel.: (973) 430-5874; URL: http://pseg.com/info/community/nonprofit/foundation.jsp

Establishment information: Established in 1991 in NJ.
Donors: Public Service Electric and Gas Co.; Public Service Enterprise Group, Inc.
Contact: Marion C. O'Neill, Mgr., Corp. Contribs.
Financial data (yr. ended 12/31/12): Assets, $31,919,220 (M); gifts received, $8,000,000; expenditures, $6,500,893; qualifying distributions, $6,341,914; giving activities include $5,351,072 for grants and $990,842 for employee matching gifts.
Purpose and activities: The foundation supports organizations involved with the environment, STEM education, community and economic development, safety and disaster preparedness and response.
Fields of interest: Elementary/secondary education; Higher education; Environment, climate change/global warming; Environment, natural resources; Environment, energy; Environmental education; Disasters, preparedness/services; Economic development; Urban/community development; Community/economic development; Science, formal/general education; Mathematics; Engineering/technology; Science.
Programs:
Dollars for Doers: The foundation supports up to 100 hours of volunteer service per employee valued at $10 per hour, up to $1,000 per employee.
Education: The foundation supports workforce development for K-12 and higher education; math, science, technology, and engineering programs; and special youth programs providing education for underserved populations.
Environment: The foundation supports programs designed to promote the environment. Special emphasis is directed toward global warming and climate change; conservation; community greening; and environmental education.
Power of Giving: The foundation matches contributes made by employees, retirees, directors, and retired directors of PSEG to institutions of higher education on a one-for-one basis from $20 to $5,000 per contributor, per year, and up to $250 per year per contributor for all other 501(c)(3) charitable organizations.
Recognizing Excellence in Volunteerism: The foundation provides competitive grants of $1,000 to $10,000 to nonprofit organizations on behalf of exemplary PSEG volunteers. Employees and teams of employees must volunteer a minimum of 50 hours of service per year to an organization. The program includes awards of merit, awards of achievement, and awards of excellence.
Type of support: Continuing support; Employee matching gifts; Employee volunteer services; Program development; Use of facilities.
Geographic limitations: Giving primarily in areas where PSEG does business.
Support limitations: No support for religious or political organizations, discriminatory organizations, lobbying organizations, athletic, labor, or fraternal groups, or disease-specific organizations. No grants to individuals, or for political causes or campaigns, or endowments.
Publications: Application guidelines; Corporate report; Newsletter (including application guidelines).
Application information: Applications accepted. Multi-year funding is not automatic. Application form required. Applicants should submit the following:
1) population served
2) copy of IRS Determination Letter
3) brief history of organization and description of its mission
4) copy of most recent annual report/audited financial statement/990
5) how project's results will be evaluated or measured
6) explanation of why grantmaker is considered an appropriate donor for project
7) listing of board of directors, trustees, officers and other key people and their affiliations
8) plans for cooperation with other organizations, if any
9) copy of current year's organizational budget and/or project budget
10) listing of additional sources and amount of support
11) plans for acknowledgement
Initial approach: Complete online application form
Board meeting date(s): 3 times per year
Deadline(s): Jan to Oct. 31
Final notification: 6 months
Officers and Trustees:* Richard T. Thigpen*, Chair. and C.E.O.; Ellen Lambert*, Pres.; Courtney M. McCormick, Secy.; Derek M. DiRisio, Cont.; Caroline Dorsa; Ralph A. LaRossa; William Levis; Tamara L. Linde; Randall E. Mehrberg.
Number of staff: 7 full-time professional.
EIN: 223125880
Selected grants: The following grants are a representative sample of this grantmaker's funding activity:
$500,000 to Childrens Specialized Hospital, Mountainside, NJ, 2012.
$285,000 to Rutgers, The State University of New Jersey, Newark, NJ, 2012.
$275,000 to Sustainable Jersey, Trenton, NJ, 2012.
$200,000 to New Jersey Performing Arts Center, Newark, NJ, 2012.
$200,000 to Newark Museum, Newark, NJ, 2012.
$135,000 to Boys and Girls Clubs in New Jersey, Clifton, NJ, 2012.
$133,000 to Montclair State University, Sustainablility Institute, Montclair, NJ, 2012.
$100,000 to Cooper University Hospital, Camden, NJ, 2012.
$80,000 to Foundation for New Jersey Public Broadcasting, Trenton, NJ, 2012.
$60,000 to Saint Peters College, Jersey City, NJ, 2012.
$50,000 to Cooper's Ferry Partnership, Camden, NJ, 2012.

3078
Public Service Mutual Insurance Company

(also known as Magna Carta Companies)
1 Park Ave., Fl. 15
New York, NY 10016-5807 (212) 591-9500

Company URL: http://www.mcarta.com
Establishment information: Established in 1925.
Company type: Subsidiary of a mutual company
Business activities: Sells commercial casualty insurance.
Business type (SIC): Insurance/fire, marine, and casualty
Corporate officers: Andrew L. Furgatch, Chair. and C.E.O.; John T. Hill II, Pres. and C.O.O.; David A. Lawless, Sr. V.P. and C.A.O.; Lon Cagley, V.P., Opers.; Gary Stewart, V.P., Human Resources
Board of directors: Andrew L. Furgatch, Chair.; Charles L. Crouch III; John T. Hill II
Giving statement: Giving through the Magna Carta Foundation, Inc.

Magna Carta Foundation, Inc.

1 Park Ave.
New York, NY 10016-5801

Establishment information: Established in 2002 in NY.
Donor: Public Service Mutual Insurance Co.
Financial data (yr. ended 06/30/12): Assets, $1,863,105 (M); gifts received, $41,220; expenditures, $77,170; qualifying distributions,

$72,310; giving activities include $72,310 for grants.
Purpose and activities: The foundation supports organizations involved with education, substance abuse treatment, cancer, Parkinson's disease, housing development, and human services.
Fields of interest: Education; Health organizations; Human services.
Type of support: General/operating support.
Geographic limitations: Giving primarily in CA and NY.
Support limitations: No grants to individuals.
Application information: Applications not accepted. Unsolicited requests for funds not accepted.
Officers: Andrew L. Furgatch, Pres.; David A. Lawless, V.P.; John T. Hill II, Secy.-Treas.
EIN: 223875602

3079
Publix Super Markets, Inc.

3300 Publix Corporate Pkwy.
P.O. Box 32024
Lakeland, FL 33811 (863) 688-1188
FAX: (863) 616-5802

Company URL: http://www.publix.com
Establishment information: Established in 1930.
Company type: Public company
Company ticker symbol and exchange: PUSH/Pink Sheets
Business activities: Operates supermarkets.
Business type (SIC): Groceries—retail; meat and seafood markets; bakeries
Financial profile for 2012: Number of employees, 158,000; assets, $12,278,320,000; sales volume, $27,706,770,000; pre-tax net income, $2,302,590,000; expenses, $25,541,520,000; liabilities, $3,196,140,000
Corporate officers: Charles H. Jenkins, Jr., Chair.; Hoyt R. Barnett, Vice-Chair.; William E. Crenshaw, C.E.O.; Randall T. Jones, Sr., Pres.; David P. Phillips, C.F.O. and Treas.; Laurie Zeitlin Douglas, Sr. V.P. and C.I.O.; John A. Attaway, Jr., Sr. V.P., Genl. Counsel, and Secy.; G. Gino DiGrazia, V.P. and Co-Cont.; Sandra J. Estep, V.P. and Co-Cont.
Board of directors: Charles H. Jenkins, Jr., Chair.; Hoyt R. Barnett, Vice-Chair.; Carol Jenkins Barnett; William E. Crenshaw; Jane B. Finley; Sherrill W. Hudson; Howard M. Jenkins; E. Vane McClurg; Maria A. Sastre
Giving statement: Giving through the Publix Super Markets, Inc. Corporate Giving Program.

Publix Super Markets, Inc. Corporate Giving Program

c/o Corp. Office
P.O. Box 407
Lakeland, FL 33802-0407 (800) 242-1227
URL: http://sustainability.publix.com/what_we_are_doing/community.php

Purpose and activities: Publix makes charitable contributions to nonprofit organizations involved with education, housing, health care, the environment, and youth. Support is given primarily in areas of company operations; giving also to national organizations.
Fields of interest: Education; Environment; Health care; Food services; Housing/shelter, volunteer services; Youth, services; United Ways and Federated Giving Programs.
Type of support: Employee matching gifts; General/operating support; In-kind gifts; Program development; Sponsorships.
Geographic limitations: Giving primarily in areas of company operations; giving also to national organizations.

3080
Wolfgang Puck Worldwide, Inc.

100 N. Crescent Dr., Ste. 100
Beverly Hills, CA 90210 (310) 432-1500

Company URL: http://www.wolfgangpuck.com
Establishment information: Established in 1985.
Company type: Private company
Business activities: Operates cafes; operates and franchises quick service restaurants; licenses brand name.
Business type (SIC): Restaurants and drinking places; investors/miscellaneous
Corporate officers: Wolfgang Puck, Chair. and C.E.O.; Joe Essa, Pres.
Board of director: Wolfgang Puck, Chair.
Giving statement: Giving through the Puck-Lazaroff Charitable Foundation.

Puck-Lazaroff Charitable Foundation

11400 W. Olympic Blvd., Ste. 330
Los Angeles, CA 90064-1523 (310) 473-2773

Establishment information: Established in 1987 in CA.
Financial data (yr. ended 06/30/11): Revenue, $1,573,157; assets, $20,662 (M); gifts received, $37,893; expenditures, $1,579,842; program services expenses, $1,554,079; giving activities include $181,000 for 4 grants (high: $154,000; low: $6,000).
Purpose and activities: The foundation supports organizations helping the elderly, handicapped, and infirm.
Fields of interest: Food distribution, meals on wheels Aging; Disabilities, people with.
Geographic limitations: Giving primarily in CA.
Officers: Barbara Lazaroff, Secy.
Directors: Sister Alice Marie; Carl Schuster.
EIN: 954124876

3081
Puget Sound Energy

(also known as PSA)
(formerly Puget Sound Energy, Inc.)
10885 N.E. 4th St., Ste. 1200
P.O. Box 97034
Bellevue, WA 98004-5591 (425) 454-6363

Company URL: http://www.pse.com
Establishment information: Established in 1873.
Company type: Subsidiary of a private company
Business activities: Generates, transmits, and distributes electricity; transmits and distributes natural gas.
Business type (SIC): Electric services
Financial profile for 2011: Number of employees, 2,800; assets, $11,929,300,000; sales volume, $3,122,200,000
Corporate officers: William S. Ayer, Chair.; Kimberly J. Harris, Pres. and C.E.O.; Daniel A. Doyle, Sr. V.P. and C.F.O.; Marla D. Mellies, Sr. V.P. and C.A.O.; Susan McLain, Sr. V.P., Opers.; Rudiger H. Wolf, V.P. and C.I.O.; Steve R. Secrist, V.P. and Genl. Counsel; James W. Eldredge, V.P. and Cont.; Donald E. Gaines, V.P., Finance and Treas.
Board of directors: William S. Ayer, Chair.; Andrew Chapman; Melanie J. Dressel; Kimberly J. Harris; Benjamin Hawkins; Alan W. James; Alan Kadic; Christopher J. Leslie; Herbert B. Simon; Chris Trumpy; Mark Wiseman; Mary O. McWilliams
Subsidiaries: GP Acquisition Corp., Bellevue, WA; Hydro Energy Development Corp., Bellevue, WA; LP Acquisition Corp., Bellevue, WA; Puget Western, Inc., Bothell, WA; Rainier Receivables, Inc., Bellevue, WA; WNG CAP I, Inc., Bellevue, WA
Giving statement: Giving through the Puget Sound Energy, Inc. Corporate Giving Program and the Puget Sound Energy Foundation.
Company EIN: 910374630

Puget Sound Energy, Inc. Corporate Giving Program

(formerly Puget Sound Power & Light Company Contributions Program)
c/o Community Rels. Mgr.
P.O. Box 97034
Bellevue, WA 98009-9734 (425) 462-3799
For Island & Snohomish counties: Dom Amor, tel.: (425) 424-6795; For Jefferson & Kitsap counties: Linda Streissguth, tel.: (360) 394-6618; For Kittitas County & Eastern Washington: Brian Lenz, tel.: (206) 604-5314; For Auburn, Federal Way, Kent & Pierce County: Gary Nomensen, tel.: (253) 476-6403; For Seattle, Central & South King County: David Namura, tel.: (425) 462-3753; For Bellevue & Eastside communities: Jim Hutchinson, tel.: (425) 462-3786; For North King County: Jason Van Nort, tel.: (425) 462-3820; For Lewis & Thurston counties: Casey Cochrane, tel.: (360) 786-5987; For Skagit & Whatcom counties: Ray Trzynka, tel.: (360) 647-6524; URL: http://pse.com/aboutpse/GivingBack/Pages/default.aspx

Purpose and activities: As a complement to its foundation, Puget Sound Energy also makes charitable contributions to nonprofit organizations directly. Support is limited to areas of company operations in western Washington.
Fields of interest: Arts; Education; Environment, energy; Safety/disasters; Salvation Army; Human services; Community/economic development; United Ways and Federated Giving Programs.
Type of support: Continuing support; Employee volunteer services; General/operating support; Program development; Scholarship funds; Sponsorships.
Geographic limitations: Giving limited to areas of company operations in western WA.
Support limitations: No support for individual schools, youth groups, teams, choirs, bands, clubs, or similar organizations, or religious organizations. No grants to individuals.
Publications: Application guidelines; Corporate giving report.
Application information: Applications accepted. The Community Relations Department handles giving. Application form not required. Applicants should submit the following:
1) population served
2) name, address and phone number of organization
3) brief history of organization and description of its mission
4) geographic area to be served
5) explanation of why grantmaker is considered an appropriate donor for project
6) listing of board of directors, trustees, officers and other key people and their affiliations
7) detailed description of project and amount of funding requested
8) contact person
9) listing of additional sources and amount of support

Initial approach: E-mail proposal to nearest company Community Relations Manager
Copies of proposal: 1
Deadline(s): None
Number of staff: 9 full-time professional.

Puget Sound Energy Foundation

10885 N.E. 4th St., Ste. 1200
Bellevue, WA 98004-5591
E-mail: psefoundation@pse.com; URL: http://www.psefoundation.org/

Establishment information: Established in 2006 in WA.
Donor: Puget Energy.
Contact: Sandra M. Carson, Exec. Dir.
Financial data (yr. ended 12/31/10): Assets, $20,106,564 (M); expenditures, $741,637; qualifying distributions, $715,148; giving activities include $642,540 for 375 grants (high: $70,300; low: $13).
Purpose and activities: The foundation supports programs designed to promote public safety and emergency preparedness. Special emphasis is directed toward programs designed to respond to the needs of vulnerable communities; encourage energy conservation and environmental stewardship; and promote workforce development at universities and community and technical colleges.
Fields of interest: Education; Environment, natural resources; Environment, energy; Environment; Employment, services; Disasters, preparedness/services; Safety/disasters; Human services.
Program:
PSE Employee Matching Gift Program: The foundation matches contributions made by employees, board members, and retirees of Puget Sound Energy on a two-for-one basis from $25 to $300 per contributor per year; and matches 10 hours of volunteer time with $10 per hour, up to 30 hours per year.
Type of support: Capital campaigns; Employee matching gifts; Employee volunteer services; Program development; Scholarship funds.
Geographic limitations: Giving primarily in areas where Puget Sound Energy provides services or has operations: Chelan, Columbia, Cowlitz, Douglas, Island, Jefferson, King, Kitsap, Kittitas, Klickitat, Lewis, Pierce, Snohomish, Skagit, Thurston, and Whatcom counties, WA.
Support limitations: No support for individual K-12 schools, youth groups, clubs, teams, choirs, or bands, political or discriminatory organizations, or religious organizations of any kind, unless the program is open to the public such as a food bank, for tuition or membership dues made to service clubs, social or fraternal organizations. No grants to individuals, or for general operating expenses, fundraising events, or endowments.
Publications: Application guidelines; Grants list.
Application information: Applications accepted. Organizations that receive funding will be eligible to apply for another grant one year later. Application form required.
Initial approach: Complete online eligibility quiz and application
Copies of proposal: 1
Deadline(s): Apr. 1 and Oct. 1
Officers and Directors.: Andy Wappler*, Chair. and Pres.; Marla D. Mellies, V.P.; Paul Wiegand, Secy.; Donald E. Gaines, Treas.; Sandra M. Carson, Exec. Dir.; Daniel A. Doyle.
EIN: 204863534
Selected grants: The following grants are a representative sample of this grantmaker's funding activity:
$70,300 to United Way of King County, Seattle, WA, 2011.
$30,060 to ArtsFund, Seattle, WA, 2011.
$15,000 to Western Washington University Foundation, Bellingham, WA, 2011.
$10,000 to American Red Cross of King and Kitsap Counties, Seattle, WA, 2011.
$7,500 to Church of Mary Magdalene, Seattle, WA, 2011.
$7,500 to Plymouth Housing Group, Seattle, WA, 2011.
$5,000 to Arlington Community Food Bank, Arlington, WA, 2011.
$5,000 to Boys and Girls Clubs of South Puget Sound, Tacoma, WA, 2011.
$5,000 to Climate Solutions, Olympia, WA, 2011.
$5,000 to RMH Services, Bremerton, WA, 2011.

3082
Pukall Lumber Company

(formerly Pukall Lumber, Inc.)
10894 State Hwy. 70 E.
Arbor Vitae, WI 54568 (715) 356-3252
FAX: (715) 356-5222

Company URL: http://www.pukall-lumber.com
Establishment information: Established in 1937.
Company type: Private company
Business activities: Manufactures lumber and wood products.
Business type (SIC): Lumber and wood products
Corporate officer: Roger Pukall, Pres.
Giving statement: Giving through the Pukall Lumber Foundation, Inc.

Pukall Lumber Foundation, Inc.

AV 10894 Hwy., 70 E.
Woodruff, WI 54568 (715) 356-3252

Contact: Roger L. Pukall, Dir.
Financial data (yr. ended 06/30/12): Assets, $637,652 (M); expenditures, $36,598; qualifying distributions, $31,140; giving activities include $31,140 for grants.
Purpose and activities: The foundation supports fire departments and organizations involved with arts and culture, health, cancer, hunger, human services, international relief, and Christianity.
Fields of interest: Performing arts; Arts; Health care; Cancer; Food services; Disasters, fire prevention/control; American Red Cross; Salvation Army; Residential/custodial care, hospices; Aging, centers/services; International relief; Christian agencies & churches.
Type of support: Annual campaigns; Endowments; General/operating support; Program development.
Geographic limitations: Giving primarily in north central WI.
Application information: Applications accepted. Application form required. Applicants should submit the following:
1) copy of IRS Determination Letter
2) detailed description of project and amount of funding requested
Initial approach: Letter
Deadline(s): None
Directors: Debra J. Christensen; Mary E. Pukall; Roger L. Pukall; Susan C. Pukall.
EIN: 237396586

3083
Pulte Homes, Inc.

(formerly Pulte Corporation)
100 Bloomfield Hills Pkwy., Ste. 300
Bloomfield Hills, MI 48304 (248) 647-2750
FAX: (248) 433-4599

Company URL: http://www.pultegroupinc.com/
Establishment information: Established in 1950.
Company type: Public company
Company ticker symbol and exchange: PHM/NYSE
Business activities: Operates holding company; provides construction services.
Business type (SIC): Real estate subdividers and developers
Financial profile for 2012: Number of employees, 3,634; assets, $6,734,410,000; sales volume, $4,820,000,000; pre-tax net income, $183,550,000; expenses, $4,636,440,000; liabilities, $4,544,790,000
Fortune 1000 ranking: 2012—501st in revenues, 569th in profits, and 501st in assets
Corporate officers: Richard J. Dugas, Jr., Chair., Pres., and C.E.O.; Robert T. O'Shaughnessy, Exec. V.P. and C.F.O.; James R. Ellinghausen, Exec. V.P., Human Resources; Steven M. Cook, Sr. V.P., Genl. Counsel, and Secy.
Board of directors: Richard J. Dugas, Jr., Chair.; Brian P. Anderson; Bryce Blair; Thomas J. Folliard; Cheryl W. Grise; Debra J. Kelly-Ennis; David N. McCammon; Patrick J. O'Leary; James J. Postl
Subsidiary: Del Webb Corporation, Phoenix, AZ
Offices: Tempe, Tucson, AZ; Santa Clara, CA; Denver, CO; Wilmington, DE; Fort Lauderdale, Fort Myers, Sarasota, Tampa Bay, FL; Atlanta, GA; Hoffman Estates, IL; Indianapolis, IN; Baltimore, Potomac, MD; Kansas City, MO; Las Vegas, NV; Charlotte, Raleigh, NC; Cleveland, OH; Austin, Dallas, Fort Worth, Houston, San Antonio, TX
International operations: Canada; Cayman Islands; Chile; Mexico
Historic mergers: Centex Corporation (August 18, 2009)
Giving statement: Giving through the Pulte Homes, Inc. Corporate Giving Program.
Company EIN: 382766606

Pulte Homes, Inc. Corporate Giving Program

(formerly Pulte Corporation Contributions Program)
100 Bloomfield Hills Pkwy.
Bloomfield Hills, MI 48304-2950 (248) 647-2750
FAX: (248) 433-4598; URL: http://phx.corporate-ir.net/phoenix.zhtml?c=147717&p=irol-social

Purpose and activities: Pulte Homes makes charitable contributions to nonprofit organizations involved with higher education, the environment, health and human services, and housing. Support is given primarily in areas of company operations in Arizona, California, Colorado, Florida, Georgia, Illinois, Indiana, Minnesota, Missouri, Nevada, New Jersey, New Mexico, North Carolina, Ohio, South Carolina, Tennessee, Texas, Virginia, and Washington, with emphasis on Michigan.
Fields of interest: Education; Environment; Health care; Housing/shelter; Human services.
Type of support: Capital campaigns; Employee volunteer services; Program development; Scholarships—to individuals.
Geographic limitations: Giving primarily in areas of company operations in AZ, CA, CO, FL, GA, IL, IN, MN, MO, NC, NJ, NM, NV, OH, SC, TN, TX, VA, and WA, with emphasis on MI.

Support limitations: No support for discriminatory organizations, religious, fraternal, or veterans' organizations not of direct benefit to the entire community, or pass-through organizations. No grants to individuals (except for scholarships), or for general operating support.
Application information: Applications accepted. A contributions committee reviews all requests. Application form not required. Applicants should submit the following:
1) population served
2) name, address and phone number of organization
3) copy of IRS Determination Letter
4) brief history of organization and description of its mission
5) copy of most recent annual report/audited financial statement/990
6) how project's results will be evaluated or measured
7) detailed description of project and amount of funding requested

Initial approach: Proposal to headquarters for organizations located in southeastern MI; for programs outside southeastern MI, contact nearest market office
Copies of proposal: 1
Deadline(s): None

3084
Pura Vida Coffee
3517 Stone Way N.
Seattle, WA 98103 (206) 328-9606

Company URL: http://www.puravidacoffee.com
Establishment information: Established in 1998.
Company type: Private company
Business activities: Operates company that sells Fair Trade, organic, and shade-grown coffee.
Business type (SIC): Beverages
Giving statement: Giving through the Pura Vida Partners.

Pura Vida Partners
3517 Stone Way N.
Seattle, WA 98103-8923
E-mail: info@puravidacoffee.org

Establishment information: Established in 1998 in WA.
Donor: Stewardship Foundation.
Financial data (yr. ended 12/31/11): Revenue, $313,456; assets, $216,072 (M); gifts received, $313,456; expenditures, $275,793.
Purpose and activities: The organization is committed to creating good in the lives of poor people who live and work in coffee-growing communities around the world.
Fields of interest: Health care; Children/youth, services; International development; Community/economic development.
Geographic limitations: Giving primarily to Costa Rica, Ethiopia, Guatemala, Nicaragua, and Peru.
Support limitations: No grants to individuals.
Application information: Applications not accepted. Contributes only to pre-selected organizations.
Officers: John Sage*, Chair.; Ken Kierstead*, Secy.; Jeff Hussey*, Treas.; Samuel Snyder*, Exec. Dir.
EIN: 912032119

3085
Putnam, LLC
1 Post Office Sq.
P.O. Box 8383
Boston, MA 02109 (617) 292-1000

Company URL: http://www.putnam.com
Establishment information: Established in 1937.
Company type: Subsidiary of a foreign company
Business activities: Provides investment advisory services.
Business type (SIC): Investment offices
Financial profile for 2010: Number of employees, 1,321
Corporate officers: John A. Hill, Chair.; Robert L. Reynolds, Pres. and C.E.O.; Clare S. Richer, C.F.O.; Walter C. Donovan, C.I.O.; Robert T. Burns, Genl. Counsel
Board of director: John A. Hill, Chair.
Giving statement: Giving through the Putnam Investments Foundation.

The Putnam Investments Foundation
1 Post Office Sq., Ste. A-16-B
Boston, MA 02109-2106

Establishment information: Established in 1992 in MA.
Donor: Putnam Investments, Inc.
Contact: C. Nancy Fisher, Tr.
Financial data (yr. ended 12/31/11): Assets, $265,440 (M); gifts received, $716,287; expenditures, $513,210; qualifying distributions, $510,079; giving activities include $510,079 for grants.
Purpose and activities: The foundation supports hospitals and organizations involved with education, children and youth, and family services.
Fields of interest: Education; Hospitals (general); Children/youth, services; Family services.
Type of support: General/operating support; Program development; Scholarship funds.
Geographic limitations: Giving primarily in the greater metropolitan Boston, MA, area.
Support limitations: No grants to individuals.
Application information: Applications not accepted. Contributes only to pre-selected organizations.
Trustees: Jonathan M. Goldstein; Clare S. Richer.
EIN: 043175266
Selected grants: The following grants are a representative sample of this grantmaker's funding activity:
$15,000 to Rodman Ride for Kids, Foxboro, MA, 2009.
$2,500 to Boston Partners in Education, Boston, MA, 2009.

3086
Putnam Bank
(formerly Putnam Savings Bank)
40 Main St.
P.O. Box 151
Putnam, CT 06260-1953 (860) 928-6501

Company URL: http://www.putnamsavings.com
Establishment information: Established in 1862.
Company type: Subsidiary of a public company
Business activities: Operates savings bank.
Business type (SIC): Savings institutions
Corporate officers: Charles H. Puffer, Chair.; Thomas A. Borner, Vice-Chair., Pres., and C.E.O.; Robert J. Halloran, Jr., Exec. V.P., Treas., and C.F.O.; Sandra J. Maciag, V.P. and Cont.
Board of directors: Charles H. Puffer, Chair.; Thomas A. Borner, Vice-Chair.; Charles W. Bentley, Jr.; Robert J. Halloran, Jr.; Paul M. Kelly; Richard A. Loomis; John P. Miller; Jitendra Sinha
Giving statement: Giving through the Putnam Bank Foundation.

The Putnam Bank Foundation
(formerly The Putnam Savings Foundation)
40 Main St.
Putnam, CT 06260-1918
URL: http://www.putnambank.com/home/about/foundation

Establishment information: Established in 2005 in CT.
Donor: Putnam Savings Bank Holdings, Inc.
Contact: Thomas A. Borner, Pres.
Financial data (yr. ended 06/30/12): Assets, $521,677 (M); gifts received, $45,000; expenditures, $85,182; qualifying distributions, $0.
Purpose and activities: The foundation supports organizations involved with arts and culture, education, health, housing, and human services.
Fields of interest: Performing arts; Arts; Higher education; Education; Hospitals (general); Health care; Housing/shelter; Human services; Community/economic development.
Type of support: Annual campaigns; Building/renovation; Continuing support; Equipment; Program development; Scholarship funds; Sponsorships.
Geographic limitations: Giving in areas of company operations in CT.
Application information: Applications accepted. Application form required.

Initial approach: Letter
Copies of proposal: 1
Deadline(s): None

Officers: Thomas A. Borner, Chair. and Pres.; Robert J. Halloran, Jr.*, V.P. and Secy.-Treas.
Directors: Charles W. Bentley, Jr.; Paul M. Kelly; Richard A. Loomis; John P. Miller; Wilbur D. Neumann; Mary E. Patenaude; Charles H. Puffer; Jitendra Sinha.
EIN: 201716876

3087
Putnam-Greene Financial Corporation
100 S. Madison Ave.
Eatonton, GA 31024-1008 (706) 485-9941

Establishment information: Established in 1986.
Company type: Private company
Business activities: Operates bank holding company; operates commercial bank.
Business type (SIC): Banks/commercial; holding company
Corporate officers: Lurner O. Benton III, Pres. and C.E.O.; Don Mongin, C.F.O.; Jay Cox, C.I.O.; Joe P. Hudson, Secy.
Giving statement: Giving through the L. O. Benton Banking Foundation, Inc.

L. O. Benton Banking Foundation, Inc.
P.O. Box 4450
Eatonton, GA 31024-4450

Establishment information: Established as a company-sponsored operating foundation in 2000.
Donors: Putnam-Greene Financial Corp.; Farmers and Merchants Bank; First Bank of Coastal Georgia; The Farmers Bank.

Financial data (yr. ended 12/31/11): Assets, $10,176,316 (M); gifts received, $48,500; expenditures, $440,577; qualifying distributions, $397,500; giving activities include $397,500 for grants.
Purpose and activities: The foundation supports fire departments and organizations involved with theater and K-12 education.
Fields of interest: Education.
Type of support: Equipment; General/operating support; Scholarship funds.
Geographic limitations: Giving primarily in the Eatontown, Greensboro, Monticello, and Pembroke, GA, areas.
Support limitations: No grants to individuals.
Application information: Applications not accepted. Unsolicited requests for funds not accepted.
Officer: Lurner O. Benton III, Pres.
EIN: 582568248
Selected grants: The following grants are a representative sample of this grantmaker's funding activity:
$16,000 to Piedmont Academy, Monticello, GA, 2009.

3088
PVH Corp.

(formerly Phillips-Van Heusen Corporation)
200 Madison Ave.
New York, NY 10016-3903 (212) 381-3500
FAX: (212) 381-3950

Company URL: http://www.pvh.com
Establishment information: Established in 1881.
Company type: Public company
Company ticker symbol and exchange: PVH/NYSE
Business activities: Manufactures men's and women's apparel.
Business type (SIC): Apparel—men's and boys' outerwear; leather footwear; apparel, piece goods, and notions—wholesale
Financial profile for 2013: Number of employees, 11,800; assets, $7,781,550,000; sales volume, $6,043,000,000; pre-tax net income, $543,110,000; expenses, $5,382,640,000; liabilities, $4,528,980,000
Fortune 1000 ranking: 2012—422nd in revenues, 367th in profits, and 460th in assets
Corporate officers: Emanuel Chirico, Chair. and C.E.O.; Michael A. Shaffer, Exec. V.P., C.O.O., and C.F.O.; Dana Perlman, Sr. V.P. and Treas.; Bruce Goldstein, Sr. V.P. and Corp. Cont.; Mark D. Fischer, Sr. V.P., Genl. Counsel, and Secy.; David Kozel, Sr. V.P., Human Resources
Board of directors: Emanuel Chirico, Chair. and C.E.O; Mary Baglivo; Juan Figuereo; Joseph B. Fuller; Fred Gehring; Margaret L. Jenkins; Bruce Maggin; V. James Marino; Helen McCluskey; Henry Nasella; Rita M. Rodriguez; Craig Rydin
Subsidiaries: G.H. Bass Franchises Inc., Falmouth, ME; BassNet, Inc., New York, NY; The IZOD Corp., New York, NY; izod.com inc., New York, NY; Calvin Klein, Inc., New York, NY; PVH Retail Corp., New York, NY; The Warnaco Group, Inc., New York, NY
International operations: Canada; Guatemala; Honduras; Hong Kong; Italy; United Kingdom
Giving statement: Giving through the PVH Corp. Contributions Program and the Phillips-Van Heusen Foundation, Inc.
Company EIN: 131166910

PVH Corp. Contributions Program

200 Madison Ave.
New York, NY 10016 (212) 381-3500
URL: http://www.pvh.com/corporate_responsibility.aspx

Phillips-Van Heusen Foundation, Inc.

200 Madison Ave., 10th Fl.
New York, NY 10016-3903 (212) 381-3500
FAX: (212) 381-3960

Establishment information: Incorporated in 1969 in NY.
Donor: Phillips-Van Heusen Corp.
Contact: Emanuel Chirico, Chair.
Financial data (yr. ended 12/31/11): Assets, $3,994,369 (M); gifts received, $6,405,328; expenditures, $7,012,955; qualifying distributions, $7,006,900; giving activities include $7,006,900 for 365 grants (high: $625,000; low: $5).
Purpose and activities: The foundation supports organizations involved with arts and culture, education, health, cancer, domestic violence prevention, human services, the fashion industry, and economically disadvantaged women and children.
Fields of interest: Museums; Arts; Higher education; Education; Environment; Health care, clinics/centers; Health care, patient services; Health care; Cancer; Cancer, leukemia; Breast cancer; Crime/violence prevention, domestic violence; Disasters, preparedness/services; American Red Cross; Children/youth, services; Family services; Human services; Business/industry; Jewish federated giving programs; Jewish agencies & synagogues Children; Women; Economically disadvantaged.
Type of support: Annual campaigns; Continuing support; Emergency funds; General/operating support; Program development; Research; Scholarship funds.
Geographic limitations: Giving on national basis in areas of company operations, with emphasis on New York, NY; giving also to national organizations.
Support limitations: No grants to individuals.
Application information: Applications accepted. Application form not required.
Initial approach: Proposal
Copies of proposal: 1
Board meeting date(s): Sept.
Deadline(s): None
Officers: Emanuel Chirico, Chair.; Mark D. Fischer, V.P.; Pamela N. Hootkin, V.P.; Michael A. Shaffer, V.P.
EIN: 237104639

3089
Pyles, Haviland, Turner & Smith, LLP

408 Main St.
Logan, WV 25601-3908 (304) 752-6000

Establishment information: Established in 1982.
Company type: Private company
Business activities: Provides legal services.
Business type (SIC): Legal services
Corporate officer: William D. Turner, Partner
Giving statement: Giving through the Pyles & Turner Foundation, Inc.

Pyles & Turner Foundation, Inc.

(formerly Pyles, Haviland, Turner & Smith Foundation, Inc.)
408 Main St.
P.O. Box 596
Logan, WV 25601-3908 (304) 752-6000

Establishment information: Established in 1992 in WV.
Donors: Crandall, Pyles, Haviland, Turner & Smith, LLP; Crandall, Pyles, Haviland & Turner, LLP.
Contact: Brad Pyles, Pres.
Financial data (yr. ended 12/31/11): Assets, $231,141 (M); expenditures, $11,799; qualifying distributions, $10,500; giving activities include $10,500 for 15 grants (high: $1,000; low: $400).
Purpose and activities: The foundation supports organizations involved with education, water conservation, human services, community development, mining, and economically disadvantaged people.
Fields of interest: Law school/education; Education; Environment, water resources; Family services, domestic violence; Human services; Community/economic development; Geology Economically disadvantaged.
Type of support: Equipment; General/operating support; Program development; Scholarship funds.
Geographic limitations: Giving limited to WV.
Support limitations: No grants to individuals.
Application information: Applications accepted. Application form required. Applicants should submit the following:
1) name, address and phone number of organization
2) copy of IRS Determination Letter
3) brief history of organization and description of its mission
4) detailed description of project and amount of funding requested
Initial approach: Letter
Deadline(s): Usually late spring
Officers: Brad Pyles, Pres.; William Turner, V.P. and Secy.-Treas.
EIN: 550717420

3090
Quabaug Corporation

(doing business as QB Soling)
18 School St.
North Brookfield, MA 01535-1937
(800) 325-5022

Company URL: http://www.quabaug.com/
Establishment information: Established in 1916.
Company type: Private company
Business activities: Manufactures rubber shoe service products.
Business type (SIC): Rubber products/fabricated
Corporate officers: Kevin M. Donahue, Chair. and C.E.O.; Gary Ross, C.I.O.; Arthur Glispin, Cont.
Board of director: Kevin M. Donahue, Chair.
Giving statement: Giving through the Quabaug Corporation Charitable Foundation.

Quabaug Corporation Charitable Foundation

18 School St.
North Brookfield, MA 01535-1937 (508) 867-7731

Establishment information: Established about 1976.
Donor: Quabaug Corp.
Contact: Eric Rosen, Tr.

Financial data (yr. ended 12/31/11): Assets, $363,379 (M); expenditures, $59,144; qualifying distributions, $52,600; giving activities include $52,600 for grants.
Purpose and activities: The foundation supports organizations involved with education, school athletics, and civic affairs and awards college scholarships to students attending North Brookfield High School in Massachusetts.
Fields of interest: Arts; Education; Safety/disasters.
Type of support: General/operating support; Scholarship funds; Scholarships—to individuals.
Geographic limitations: Giving primarily in the Worcester, MA, area.
Application information: Applications accepted. Application form required. Applicants should submit the following:
1) copy of most recent annual report/audited financial statement/990
2) copy of IRS Determination Letter
Initial approach: Letter
Deadline(s): May 31
Trustees: James Barkoski; Kevin M. Donahue; Eric A. Rosen.
EIN: 510179366

3091
Quad/Graphics, Inc.
N61 W. 23044 Harry's Way
Sussex, WI 53089-3995 (414) 566-6000

Company URL: http://www.qg.com
Establishment information: Established in 1971.
Company type: Public company
Company ticker symbol and exchange: QUAD/NYSE
Business activities: Provides commercial printing services.
Business type (SIC): Printing/commercial
Financial profile for 2012: Number of employees, 21,400; assets, $4,098,900,000; sales volume, $4,094,000,000; pre-tax net income, $22,500,000; expenses, $3,987,500,000; liabilities, $2,863,500,000
Fortune 1000 ranking: 2012—567th in revenues, 764th in profits, and 656th in assets
Corporate officers: J. Joel Quadracci, Chair., Pres., and C.E.O.; John C. Fowler, Exec. V.P. and C.F.O.; Tom Frankowski, Exec. V.P., Opers.; Dave Blais, Exec. V.P., Sales; Andy Schiesl, V.P. and Genl. Counsel; Maura Packham, V.P., Mktg. and Comms.; Nancy Ott, V.P., Human Resources
Board of directors: J. Joel Quadracci, Chair.; William J. Abraham; Douglas P. Buth; Christopher B. Harned; Betty E. Quadracci; Thomas Ryder; John S. Shiely
Plants: Anaheim, San Francisco, CA; Wilton, CT; The Rock, GA; Braintree, MA; Minneapolis, MN; New York, Saratoga Springs, NY; Oklahoma City, OK; Addison, TX; Alexandria, VA; Martinsburg, WV; Hartford, Lomira, Pewaukee, West Allis, WI
Offices: Marina del Rey, CA; Louisville, CO; Atlanta, GA; Chicago, IL; Erlanger, KY; Troy, MI; Bellevue, WA
Giving statement: Giving through the Quad/Graphics, Inc. Corporate Giving Program, the Alco Gravure Education Fund, Inc., and the Windhover Foundation, Inc.

Quad/Graphics, Inc. Corporate Giving Program
N61 W23044 Harry's Way
Sussex, WI 53089-3995 (414) 566-6000
E-mail: qgraphics@qg.com; URL: http://www.qg.com/aboutus/community/community_involvement.asp

Purpose and activities: As a complement to its foundation, Quad/Graphics also makes charitable contributions to nonprofit organizations directly. Support is given on a national basis in areas of company operations, with some emphasis on Wisconsin.
Fields of interest: Education, reading; Education; Medical research; Disasters, preparedness/services; Human services; Christian agencies & churches; General charitable giving.
Type of support: Employee matching gifts; Matching/challenge support.
Geographic limitations: Giving on a national basis in areas of company operations, with emphasis on WI.

Alco Gravure Education Fund, Inc.
(formerly Quebecor World Education Fund, Inc.)
N63 W23075 State Hwy 74
Sussex, WI 53089

Donor: Alco Gravure Industries, Inc.
Financial data (yr. ended 12/31/10): Assets, $30,795 (M); expenditures, $33,057; qualifying distributions, $30,500; giving activities include $25,000 for 25 grants to individuals (high: $1,000; low: $1,000).
Purpose and activities: The foundation awards college scholarships to children of employees of Alco Gravure Industries, Inc. The program is administered by Scholarship America.
Fields of interest: Higher education.
Type of support: Employee-related scholarships.
Geographic limitations: Giving limited to areas of company operations.
Application information: Applications not accepted. Contributes only through employee-related scholarships.
Officers: David Mccarthy, Pres.; Debbie Sirot, V.P.
EIN: 222684634

Windhover Foundation, Inc.
W224 N3322 Duplainville Rd.
Sussex, WI 53072-4137
E-mail: WindhoverFoundation@qg.com; URL: http://www.qg.com/aboutus/community/windhover.asp

Establishment information: Established in 1983.
Donors: Quad/Graphics, Inc.; Harry V. Quadracci 1998 Trust.
Financial data (yr. ended 12/31/11): Assets, $71,989,428 (M); gifts received, $5,999,637; expenditures, $5,135,362; qualifying distributions, $4,788,391; giving activities include $4,414,911 for 1,825 grants (high: $200,000; low: $25) and $359,250 for 234 grants to individuals (high: $2,500; low: $1,000).
Purpose and activities: The foundation supports parks and playgrounds and organizations involved with arts and culture, education, the environment, health, hunger, sports, human services, and Christianity.
Fields of interest: Museums (art); Arts; Elementary/secondary education; Higher education; Libraries (public); Education; Environment, natural resources; Environment, land resources; Environment; Hospitals (general); Reproductive health, family planning; Health care; Food services; Food banks; Recreation, parks/playgrounds; Athletics/sports, amateur leagues; Youth development, business; American Red Cross; Children/youth, services; Residential/custodial care, hospices; Women, centers/services; Human services; United Ways and Federated Giving Programs; Christian agencies & churches.
Program:
Community Fund: Through the Community Fund, employees of QuadGraphics donate money and their donation is matched and disbursed to the nonprofit organization of his or her choice. If a specific nonprofit organization is not designated, the money is funneled into a general fund and is distributed on a people-to-people basis in neighboring communities.
Type of support: Annual campaigns; Continuing support; Employee matching gifts; Employee-related scholarships; General/operating support.
Geographic limitations: Giving primarily in areas of company operations in Milwaukee, WI.
Support limitations: No support for religious organizations or teams or leagues. No grants to individuals (except for employee-related scholarships), or for sponsorships, fundraising events, competitions, or contests.
Publications: Application guidelines.
Application information: Applications accepted. Application form not required. Applicants should submit the following:
1) brief history of organization and description of its mission
2) detailed description of project and amount of funding requested
3) contact person
4) name, address and phone number of organization
5) population served
Initial approach: Complete online application
Copies of proposal: 1
Deadline(s): None
Officers and Director: Elizabeth E. Quadracci, Pres.; Elizabeth Quadracci Harned, V.P.; John C. Fowler, Secy.-Treas.; J. Joel Quadracci.
EIN: 391482470

3092
Quadion Corporation
(doing business as Minnesota Rubber & Plastics)
1100 Xenium Ln. N.
Minneapolis, MN 55441-4440
(952) 927-1400

Company URL: http://www.quadion.com
Establishment information: Established in 1945.
Company type: Private company
Business activities: Manufactures rubber and plastic components and assemblies.
Business type (SIC): Rubber products/fabricated; plastic products/miscellaneous
Corporate officers: Robert W. Carlson, Jr., Chair.; James R. Lande, Pres. and C.E.O.; Bruce Richardson, C.F.O.; Pete Peterson, V.P., Human Resources
Board of director: Robert W. Carlson, Chair.
Subsidiaries: Minnesota Rubber, Plymouth, MN; QMR Plastics, Plymouth, MI
Giving statement: Giving through the Quadion Foundation.

Quadion Foundation
1100 Xenium Ln. N.
Plymouth, MN 55441-4445

Establishment information: Established in 1980 in MN.
Donors: Robert W. Carlson, Jr.; Quadion Corp.

Financial data (yr. ended 12/31/11): Assets, $439,454 (M); expenditures, $21,662; qualifying distributions, $15,722; giving activities include $15,722 for grants.
Purpose and activities: The foundation supports organizations involved with arts and culture, education, birth defects, children and youth, and disability services.
Fields of interest: Education; Youth development; Human services.
Type of support: General/operating support; Scholarship funds.
Geographic limitations: Giving primarily in MN.
Support limitations: No grants to individuals.
Application information: Applications not accepted. Unsolicited requests for funds not accepted.
Officers: Robert W. Carlson, Jr., Pres.; James R. Lande, V.P. and Secy.-Treas.
Director: Pete Peterson.
EIN: 411377918

3093
Quaker Chemical Corporation

1 Quaker Park
901 Hector St.
Conshohocken, PA 19428-0809
(610) 832-4000
FAX: (610) 832-4495

Company URL: http://www.quakerchem.com
Establishment information: Established in 1918.
Company type: Public company
Company ticker symbol and exchange: KWR/NYSE
Business activities: Develops, manufactures, and markets specialty chemical products; provides and markets chemical management services.
Business type (SIC): Petroleum and coal products/miscellaneous; chemicals/industrial inorganic
Financial profile for 2012: Number of employees, 1,711; assets, $536,630,000; sales volume, $708,230,000; pre-tax net income, $62,950,000; expenses, $645,000,000; liabilities, $255,530,000
Corporate officers: Michael F. Barry, Chair., Pres., and C.E.O.; Margaret M. Loebl, V.P., C.F.O., and Treas.; D. Jeffrey Benoliel, V.P. and Corp. Secy.; Ronald S. Ettinger, V.P., Human Resources
Board of directors: Michael F. Barry, Chair.; Joseph B. Andersen, Jr.; Patricia C. Barron; Donald R. Caldwell; Robert E. Chappell; William R. Cook; Mark A. Douglas; Jeffrey D. Frisby; Robert H. Rock
Plants: Detroit, MI; Middletown, OH
International operations: Argentina; Australia; Brazil; China; France; Hungary; India; Italy; Japan; Mexico; Netherlands; Russia; South Africa; Spain; United Kingdom; Venezuela
Giving statement: Giving through the Quaker Chemical Corporation Contributions Program and the Quaker Chemical Foundation.
Company EIN: 230993790

Quaker Chemical Corporation Contributions Program

1 Quaker Park
901 Hector St.
Conshohocken, PA 19428-2380 (610) 832-4000
E-mail: waldauej@quakerchem.com; URL: http://www.quakerchem.com/about_us/about_our_communities.html

Contact: Jan Waldauer, Mgr., Comms. and Community Rels.
Purpose and activities: As a complement to its foundation, Quaker Chemical makes charitable contributions to nonprofit organizations directly.
Fields of interest: Museums; Elementary school/education; Disasters, preparedness/services; Science.
Type of support: General/operating support.

The Quaker Chemical Foundation

1 Quaker Park
901 Hector St.
Conshohocken, PA 19428-2307 (610) 832-4301
URL: http://www.quakerchem.com/about_us/about_foundation.html

Establishment information: Established in 1959 in PA.
Donor: Quaker Chemical Corp.
Financial data (yr. ended 06/30/12): Assets, $29,058 (M); expenditures, $170,834; qualifying distributions, $167,998; giving activities include $167,998 for grants.
Purpose and activities: The foundation supports organizations involved with arts and culture, education, health, human services, community development, and civic affairs. Special emphasis is directed toward programs designed to provide chemistry and physical science education. Support is limited to areas of company operations in Pennsylvania.
Fields of interest: Arts; Education; Hospitals (general); Health care; Human services; Community/economic development; United Ways and Federated Giving Programs; Physical/earth sciences; Chemistry.
Type of support: Employee matching gifts; Employee-related scholarships; General/operating support; Matching/challenge support; Scholarship funds.
Geographic limitations: Giving limited to areas of company operations in PA.
Support limitations: Generally, no support for national organizations. No grants to individuals (except for employee-related scholarships), or for building or endowments; no loans.
Application information: Applications accepted. Application form required.
Initial approach: Proposal
Copies of proposal: 1
Deadline(s): Apr. 30
Trustees: Craig E. Bush; Katherine N. Coughenour; Irene M. Kisleiko; Christian Scholund; Jane L. Williams.
Number of staff: None.
EIN: 236245803

3094
The Quaker Oats Company

555 W. Monroe St.
P.O. Box 049003
Chicago, IL 60661-3605 (312) 821-1000

Company URL: http://www.quakeroats.com
Establishment information: Established in 1901.
Company type: Subsidiary of a public company
Business activities: Produces beverages, hot cereals, rice products, granola bars, pancake syrups and mixes, and cold cereals.
Business type (SIC): Beverages; grain mill products, including pet food; sugar, candy, and salted/roasted nut production; miscellaneous prepared foods
Corporate officers: Gary Rodkin, Pres.; Hugh F. Johnston, C.F.O.
Plants: Tolleson, AZ; Oakland, CA; Kissimmee, FL; Atlanta, GA; Bridgeview, Danville, IL; Indianapolis, IN; Cedar Rapids, IA; Columbia, MO; Mountain Top, PA; Dallas, TX
International operations: Brazil; Netherlands; United Kingdom
Giving statement: Giving through the Quaker Oats Company Contributions Program.

The Quaker Oats Company Contributions Program

P.O. Box 049003
Chicago, IL 60604-9003
URL: http://www.quakeroats.com/about-quaker-oats/content/quaker-faq.aspx

Purpose and activities: Quaker makes charitable contributions to nonprofit organizations involved with pre-school-12 education, youth volunteerism, and nutrition for mothers and infants. Special emphasis is directed toward programs that include tutoring, mentoring, and coaching. Support is given on a national basis in areas of company operations.
Fields of interest: Education, public education; Elementary/secondary education; Health care, infants; Food services; Nutrition; Human services; Women, centers/services Children; Economically disadvantaged.
Program:
Quaker Go Grants Program: Quaker Oats will award 20 grants of $500 to winning applicants who describe how they will develop community projects to help combat hunger. Winners will be selected each month from April through August 2009; 100 total winners will be selected. Visit www.quakeroats.com/gohumansgo for applications.
Type of support: Donated products; General/operating support; Sponsorships.
Geographic limitations: Giving on a national basis in areas of company operations.
Application information: Applications accepted. Application form required.
Copies of proposal: 1
Number of staff: 1 full-time professional; 1 part-time support.

3095
QUALCOMM Incorporated

5775 Morehouse Dr.
San Diego, CA 92121-1714
(858) 587-1121
FAX: (858) 458-9096

Company URL: http://www.qualcomm.com
Establishment information: Established in 1985.
Company type: Public company
Company ticker symbol and exchange: QCOM/NASDAQ
International Securities Identification Number: US7475251036
Business activities: Designs, develops, manufactures, and markets digital wireless communications products, technologies, and services.
Business type (SIC): Communications equipment
Financial profile for 2012: Number of employees, 26,600; assets, $43,012,000,000; sales volume, $19,121,000,000; pre-tax net income, $6,562,000,000; expenses, $13,522,000,000; liabilities, $9,489,000,000
Fortune 1000 ranking: 2012—149th in revenues, 30th in profits, and 130th in assets

Forbes 2000 ranking: 2012—459th in sales, 71st in profits, and 513th in assets
Corporate officers: Paul E. Jacobs, Chair. and C.E.O.; Steven R. Altman, Vice-Chair.; Steven M. Mollenkopf, Pres. and C.O.O.; George S. Davis, Exec. V.P. and C.F.O.; Donald J. Rosenberg, Exec. V.P., Genl. Counsel, and Corp. Secy.; Daniel L. Sullivan, Exec. V.P., Human Resources; Norm Fjeldheim, Sr. V.P. and C.I.O.
Board of directors: Paul E. Jacobs, Chair.; Steven R. Altman, Vice-Chair.; Barbara T. Alexander; Donald G. Cruickshank; Raymond V. Dittamore; Thomas W. Horton; Susan Hockfield; Sherry Lansing; Duane A. Nelles; Francisco Ros; Jonathan J. Rubinstein; Brent Scowcroft; Marc I. Stern
Division: Wireless Business Solutions Div., San Diego, CA
International operations: British Virgin Islands; Canada; China; Finland; Germany; India; Italy; Japan; Malaysia; Mauritius; Netherlands; Singapore; South Korea; Taiwan; United Kingdom
Giving statement: Giving through the QUALCOMM Incorporated Corporate Giving Program.
Company EIN: 953685934

QUALCOMM Incorporated Corporate Giving Program

c/o Community Involvement
5775 Morehouse Dr.
San Diego, CA 92121-1714 (858) 651-3200
FAX: (858) 651-3255;
E-mail: philanthropy@qualcomm.com; Tel. for Allison Kelly: (858) 651-4027, e-mail: allison@qualcomm.com; URL: http://www.qualcomm.com/about/citizenship/community

Contact: Allison Kelly, Sr. Mgr., Community Involvement
Purpose and activities: QUALCOMM makes charitable contributions to nonprofit organizations designed to promote educated communities; healthy sustainable communities; and culturally vibrant communities. Support is given primarily in areas of company operations.
Fields of interest: Arts education; Arts; Elementary/secondary education; Vocational education; Higher education; Adult/continuing education; Education; Health care, clinics/centers; Health care; Children, services; Homeless, human services; Human services; Mathematics; Engineering/technology; Science Economically disadvantaged.
Program:
Employee Scholarship Program: The company awards reimbursement scholarships of up to $5,250 per calendar year for the cost of tuition, books, and parking for courses toward continuing education, certification programs, and associate's or bachelor's degrees. Reimbursement is based on grade achieved and the program of study must be pre-approved and considered job-related. Employees become eligible on their date of hire.
Type of support: Annual campaigns; Conferences/seminars; Continuing support; Donated products; Employee matching gifts; Employee volunteer services; Employee-related scholarships; Equipment; General/operating support; In-kind gifts; Matching/challenge support; Program development; Research; Scholarship funds.
Geographic limitations: Giving primarily in areas of company operations in CA, CO, NC, NJ, NV, TX, Belgium, Canada, China, France, India, Germany, Ireland, Italy, Netherlands, Spain, and the United Kingdom.
Support limitations: No support for discriminatory organizations, or religious organizations or faith-based schools not of direct benefit to the entire community. No grants to individuals (except for employee-related scholarships), or for capital campaigns, non-charitable sporting events, fundraising, salaries, or political contributions.
Publications: Application guidelines; Corporate giving report (including application guidelines); Informational brochure (including application guidelines); Program policy statement.
Application information: Applications accepted. A full proposal may be requested at a later date. The Corporate Giving Department handles giving. The company has a staff that only handles contributions. A contributions committee reviews all requests. Application form not required. Applicants should submit the following:
1) brief history of organization and description of its mission
2) list of company employees involved with the organization
3) detailed description of project and amount of funding requested

Initial approach: Complete online letter of Inquiry form to be considered for funding
Committee meeting date(s): Monthly
Deadline(s): 1st day of the month to be considered for the following month
Final notification: 7 business days
Number of staff: 3 full-time professional.

3096
Quality Custom Cabinetry, Inc.

125 Peters Rd.
New Holland, PA 17557-0189
(717) 661-6900
FAX: (717) 661-6902

Company URL: http://www.qcc.com
Establishment information: Established in 1968.
Company type: Private company
Business activities: Manufactures wood cabinetry.
Business type (SIC): Wood millwork
Corporate officers: Martin H. Weaver, Chair.; Glenn L. Good, Pres. and C.E.O.; Jerle B. Weaver, Secy.-Treas.
Board of director: Martin H. Weaver, Chair.
Giving statement: Giving through the QCCI Foundation.

QCCI Foundation

(formerly The WG Foundation)
125 Peters Rd.
P.O. Box 189
New Holland, PA 17557-9205 (717) 661-6900

Establishment information: Established in 2004 in PA.
Donor: Quality Custom Cabinetry, Inc.
Contact: Jerle B. Weaver, Secy.-Treas.
Financial data (yr. ended 12/31/11): Assets, $196,914 (M); expenditures, $38,357; qualifying distributions, $34,725; giving activities include $33,000 for 2 grants (high: $23,000; low: $10,000).
Purpose and activities: The foundation supports organizations involved with human services, international development, Christianity, and economically disadvantaged people.
Fields of interest: American Red Cross; Children, services; Human services; International development; International relief; Christian agencies & churches Economically disadvantaged.
Type of support: Building/renovation; General/operating support; Sponsorships.
Support limitations: No grants to individuals.
Application information: Applications accepted. Application form not required.
Initial approach: Proposal
Deadline(s): None
Officers: Glenn L. Good, Pres.; Jerry Weaver, Secy.-Treas.
EIN: 412148371

3097
Quality Home Care Providers, Inc.

345 Grand Ave.
Leonia, NJ 07010-2238 (201) 585-9234
FAX: (201) 585-9633

Company URL: http://www.thehomecarecompany.com/quality/default.asp
Establishment information: Established in 1991.
Company type: Private company
Business activities: Provides home healthcare services.
Business type (SIC): Home healthcare services
Corporate officers: Munr Kazmir, Pres. and C.E.O.; Paula Kaplan, C.F.O.
Giving statement: Giving through the M. K. Foundation, Inc.

M. K. Foundation, Inc.

345 Grand Ave.
Leonia, NJ 07605-2238

Establishment information: Established in 2004 in NJ.
Donors: Quality Home Care Providers, Inc.; Ansar Batool; Munr Kazmir.
Financial data (yr. ended 12/31/11): Assets, -$5,000 (M); gifts received, $67,870; expenditures, $72,897; qualifying distributions, $67,965; giving activities include $67,965 for 11 grants (high: $18,000; low: $1,500).
Purpose and activities: The foundation supports organizations involved with financial aid, higher education, and Judaism.
Fields of interest: Higher education; Scholarships/financial aid; Jewish agencies & synagogues.
Type of support: General/operating support; Scholarship funds.
Geographic limitations: Giving primarily in AL, NY, NJ, PA, and RI.
Application information: Applications not accepted. Unsolicited requests for funds not accepted.
Trustees: Mendel Herson; Munr Kazmir; William Shulman.
EIN: 201534556

3098
Quality Metal Finishing Co.

421 N. Walnut St.
P.O. Box 922
Byron, IL 61010-0922 (815) 234-2711

Company URL: http://www.qmfco.com
Establishment information: Established in 1947.
Company type: Private company
Business activities: Manufactures plumbing hardware.
Business type (SIC): Metal plumbing fixtures and heating equipment/nonelectric
Corporate officers: Mario Bortoli, Chair.; Matt Bortoli, Pres. and C.E.O.; Jim Day, V.P., Opers.; Bill Wohrley, Cont.
Board of director: Mario Bortoli, Chair.

Giving statement: Giving through the Quality Metal Finishing Foundation Inc.

Quality Metal Finishing Foundation Inc.

4th Walnut St., S.
Byron, IL 61010

Establishment information: Established in 1964 in IL.
Donor: Quality Metal Finishing Co.
Financial data (yr. ended 09/30/12): Assets, $7,974 (M); expenditures, $1,549; qualifying distributions, $1,549; giving activities include $1,500 for 2 grants (high: $1,000; low: $500).
Purpose and activities: The foundation supports health centers and organizations involved with education.
Fields of interest: Education; Health care.
Type of support: General/operating support.
Geographic limitations: Giving primarily in Byron and Rockford, IL.
Support limitations: No grants to individuals.
Application information: Applications not accepted. Unsolicited requests for funds not accepted.
Officers: Mario Bortoli, Pres.; Marvin Webber, V.P.; R. Earl Pierson, Secy.-Treas.
Director: Matt Bortoli.
EIN: 362604285

3099
The Quandel Group, Inc.

3003 N. Front St., Ste. 201
Harrisburg, PA 17110-1224 (717) 657-0909

Company URL: http://www.quandel.com
Establishment information: Established in 1882.
Company type: Private company
Business activities: Provides nonresidential general contract construction services.
Business type (SIC): Contractors/general nonresidential building
Corporate officers: Noble C. "Bud" Quandel, Pres. and C.E.O.; Chris Bushey, C.F.O. and Treas.
Offices: Westerville, OH; Minersville, PA
Giving statement: Giving through the Quandel Foundation.

The Quandel Foundation

3003 North Front St., Ste. 201
Harrisburg, PA 17110-1224 (717) 657-0909

Establishment information: Established in 2003 in PA as a company-sponsored foundation. Changed status to company-sponsored foundation in 2004.
Donor: The Quandel Group, Inc.
Contact: Noble C. Quandel, Jr., Dir.
Financial data (yr. ended 12/31/11): Assets, $314,197 (M); gifts received, $202,000; expenditures, $49,430; qualifying distributions, $48,515; giving activities include $47,600 for 14 grants (high: $11,000; low: $500).
Purpose and activities: The foundation supports organizations involved with arts and culture, higher education, medical education, health, cancer, human services, and Christianity.
Fields of interest: Arts; Health care; Housing/shelter.
Type of support: General/operating support.
Geographic limitations: Giving primarily in PA.
Application information: Applications accepted. Application form required.
Initial approach: Letter
Deadline(s): None
Directors: Chris C. Bushey; Karen Chimahusky; Julia T. Quandel; Noble C. Quandel, Jr.
EIN: 200097749

3100
Quanex Building Products Corporation

(formerly Quanex Corporation)
1900 W. Loop S., Ste. 1500
Houston, TX 77027 (713) 961-4600
FAX: (302) 655-5049

Company URL: http://www.quanex.com
Establishment information: Established in 1927.
Company type: Public company
Company ticker symbol and exchange: NX/NYSE
Business activities: Manufactures steel bars, steel tubing, and fabricated metal products.
Business type (SIC): Steel mill products; metal refining/secondary nonferrous; metal products/primary
Financial profile for 2012: Number of employees, 2,228; assets, $589,540,000; sales volume, $828,980,000; pre-tax net income, -$25,180,000; expenses, $853,930,000; liabilities, $167,710,000
Corporate officers: David D. Petratis, Chair., Pres., and C.E.O.; Brent L. Korb, Sr. V.P., Finance and C.F.O.; Kevin P. Delaney, Sr. V.P., Genl. Counsel, and Secy.; Jairaj Chetnani, V.P. and Treas.; Deborah M. Gadin, V.P. and Cont.
Board of directors: David D. Petratis, Chair.; Robert R. Buck; Susan F. Davis; William C. Griffiths; LeRoy D. Nosbaum; Joseph D. Rupp; Curtis M. Stevens
Subsidiaries: AMSCO, Rice Lake, WI; Homeshield Fabricated Products, Chatsworth, IL; Homeshield Fabricated Products, Naperville, IL; La Salle Steel Co., Hammond, IN; MacSteel, Jackson, MI; Nichols Aluminum, Davenport, IL; Nichols Aluminum, Lincolnshire, IL; Nichols-Homeshield, Davenport, IL; Nichols-Homeshield Casting, Davenport, IA; Quanex Tube Group, Livonia, MI
Divisions: Arkansas Div., Fort Smith, AR; Fluid Power Div. of La Salle Steel Co., Griffith, IN; Gulf States Tube Div., Rosenberg, TX; Heat Treating Div., Huntington, IN; Michigan Div., Jackson, MI; Michigan Seamless Tube Div., South Lyon, MI
Giving statement: Giving through the Quanex Corporation Contributions Program and the Quanex Foundation.
Company EIN: 261561397

Quanex Foundation

1900 W. Loop S., Ste. 1500
Houston, TX 77027-3267

Establishment information: Incorporated in 1951 in IL.
Donors: Quanex Corp.; LaSalle Steel Co.
Financial data (yr. ended 12/31/11): Assets, $6,487,671 (M); expenditures, $280,432; qualifying distributions, $271,910; giving activities include $271,910 for grants.
Purpose and activities: The foundation supports organizations involved with education, health, Parkinson's disease research, rodeos, human services, and the forging industry.
Fields of interest: Elementary/secondary education; Education, reading; Education; Parkinson's disease research; Athletics/sports, equestrianism; Human services; Business/industry; United Ways and Federated Giving Programs.
Type of support: Employee matching gifts; General/operating support; Scholarship funds.
Support limitations: No support for organizations supporting dependent children. No grants to individuals.
Application information: Applications accepted. Application form not required.
Initial approach: Proposal
Copies of proposal: 1
Deadline(s): Oct. 31
Officers and Directors:* Kevin P. Delaney, Pres.; Brent L. Korb, V.P.
EIN: 366065490

3101
Quarles & Brady LLP

411 E. Wisconsin Ave., Ste. 2040
Milwaukee, WI 53202-4426
(414) 277-5000

Company URL: http://www.quarles.com/home.aspx
Company type: Private company
Business activities: Operates law firm.
Business type (SIC): Legal services
Corporate officers: Thomas Schoewe, C.F.O.; Todd D. Thorson, C.I.O.
Offices: Phoenix, Tucson, AZ; Washington, DC; Naples, Tampa, FL; Chicago, IL; Madison, Milwaukee, WI
International operations: China
Giving statement: Giving through the Quarles & Brady LLP Pro Bono Program.

Quarles & Brady LLP Pro Bono Program

411 E. Wisconsin Ave., Ste. 2040
Milwaukee, WI 53202-4426 (414) 277-5359
E-mail: michael.gonring@quarles.com; Additional tel.: (414) 277-5000; Chicago: Robert Gamrath, robert.gamrath@quarles.com; Madison: Grant Sovern, grant.sovern@quarles.com; Milwaukee: Michael Gonring, michael.gonring@quarles.com; Naples: Jennifer Nackley, jennifer.nackley@quarles.com; Phoenix: Dawn Valdivia, dawn.valdivia@quarles.com; Tampa: Philip Martino, philip.martino@quarles.com; Tucson: Luis Ochoa, luis.ochoa@quarles.com; URL: http://www.quarles.com/About/pro_bono/

Contact: Michael J. Gonring, Natl. Pro Bono Coord.
Fields of interest: Legal services.
Type of support: Pro bono services - legal.
Application information: A Pro Bono Coordinator manages the pro bono program.

3102
Queen Apparel NY, Inc.

246 W. 38th St., Fl. 5A
New York, NY 10018-9089 (212) 819-0401

Establishment information: Established in 1998.
Company type: Private company
Business activities: Operates wholesale clothing company.
Business type (SIC): Apparel, piece goods, and notions—wholesale
Corporate officers: Hank H. Choi, Pres. and C.E.O.; Benjamin Chen, C.F.O
Board of director: Simon Jung

Giving statement: Giving through the Hank & Hannah Choi Foundation, Inc.

Hank & Hannah Choi Foundation, Inc.

16 Academy Ln.
Demarest, NJ 07627-2700
URL: http://www.hhcfoundationusa.org

Establishment information: Established in 2004 in NJ.
Donors: Hyun Ho Choi; Queen Apparel NY, Inc.
Financial data (yr. ended 06/30/12): Assets, $517,650 (M); gifts received, $2,000; expenditures, $44,776; qualifying distributions, $44,776; giving activities include $36,500 for 5 grants (high: $27,500; low: $1,000).
Fields of interest: Education; Human services.
Type of support: Scholarships—to individuals.
Application information: Applications not accepted. Unsolicited requests for funds not accepted.
Officers: Hank H. Choi, Pres.; Hannah Choi, Secy.-Treas.
Trustee: Joe Y. Choi.
EIN: 201138494

3103
Quest Diagnostics Incorporated

3 Giralda Farms
Madison, NJ 07940 (201) 393-5000
FAX: (302) 655-5049

Company URL: http://www.QuestDiagnostics.com
Establishment information: Established in 1967.
Company type: Public company
Company ticker symbol and exchange: DGX/NYSE
Business activities: Provides laboratory diagnostic testing and information services.
Business type (SIC): Laboratories/medical and dental
Financial profile for 2012: Number of employees, 41,000; assets, $9,283,860,000; sales volume, $7,382,560,000; pre-tax net income, $1,068,390,000; expenses, $6,181,770,000; liabilities, $5,120,820,000
Fortune 1000 ranking: 2012—341st in revenues, 312th in profits, and 410th in assets
Forbes 2000 ranking: 2012—1150th in sales, 970th in profits, and 1525th in assets
Corporate officers: Dan C. Stanzione, Ph.D., Chair.; Stephen H. Rusckowski, Pres. and C.E.O.; Robert A. Hagemann, Sr. V.P. and C.F.O.; Michael E. Prevoznik, Sr. V.P. and Genl. Counsel; John B. Haydon, Sr. V.P., Opers.; Gary D. Samuels, V.P., Corp. Comms.
Board of directors: Dan C. Stanzione, Ph.D., Chair.; John C. Baldwin, M.D.; Jenne K. Britell, Ph.D.; William F. Buehler; Gary M. Pfeiffer; Timothy M. Ring; Stephen H. Rusckowski; Gail R. Wilensky, Ph.D.; John B. Ziegler
Subsidiaries: American Medical Laboratories, Inc., Chantilly, VA; MedPlus, Inc., Cincinnati, OH; Unilab Corp., Tarzana, CA
International operations: Australia; Brazil; Germany; Netherlands; Sweden; United Kingdom
Giving statement: Giving through the Quest Diagnostics Incorporated Contributions Program and the Quest Diagnostics Foundation, Inc.
Company EIN: 161387862

Quest Diagnostics Incorporated Contributions Program

3 Giralda Farms
Madison, NJ 07940-1027
URL: http://www.questdiagnostics.com/home/about/corporate-citizenship.html

Financial data (yr. ended 12/31/09): Total giving, $1,197,000, including $1,197,000 for grants.
Purpose and activities: As a complement to its foundation, Quest Diagnostics also makes charitable contributions to nonprofit organizations and individuals directly. Support is giving primarily in areas of company operations.
Fields of interest: Education; Hospitals (general); Health care; Cancer; Breast cancer; Diabetes; Medical research, fund raising/fund distribution Economically disadvantaged.
Type of support: Employee matching gifts; Employee volunteer services; General/operating support; Grants to individuals.
Geographic limitations: Giving primarily in areas of company operations.
Publications: Application guidelines.
Application information: Applications accepted. Giving only to pre-selected organizations; applications accepted for individual assistance. Eligibility for the Financial Assistance Program is based on the applicant's income and the U.S. Department of Health and Human Services poverty guidelines. Applicants should submit the following: 1) name, address and phone number of organization Applications for the Financial Assistance Program should include an invoice number, insurance information, lab code, personal and household income, and an explanation of extenuating circumstances, if applicable.
Initial approach: Download application form and mail completed form to headquarters, or call customer service, for the Financial Assistance Program
Deadline(s): Two weeks for the Financial Assistance Program

The Quest Diagnostics Foundation, Inc.

(formerly The MetPath Foundation, Inc.)
3 Giralda Farms
Madison, NJ 07940-1027 (973) 520-2045
URL: http://www.questdiagnostics.com/home/about/corporate-citizenship/community-giving/foundation.html

Establishment information: Established in 1991 in NJ.
Donors: MetPath Inc.; Quest Diagnostics Inc.
Contact: Barb Short, Exec. Dir.
Financial data (yr. ended 12/31/11): Assets, $5,207 (M); gifts received, $10,000; expenditures, $25,000; qualifying distributions, $20,000; giving activities include $20,000 for 5 grants (high: $5,000; low: $2,000).
Purpose and activities: The foundation supports programs designed to promote early detection and prevention of disease; and provide research for curing disease.
Fields of interest: Health care; AIDS; Cancer research; Autism research; Diabetes research; Pediatrics research; Medical research.
Type of support: General/operating support; Program development.
Geographic limitations: Giving primarily in CA, CO, FL, NY, TN, and TX.
Application information: Applications not accepted. Unsolicited requests for funds not accepted.
Officers: Laure E. Park, Chair. and Pres.; Deirdre Flannery, Secy.; Robert O'Keef, Treas.; Barb Short, Exec. Dir.
Trustees: Luis Diaz-Rosario, M.D.; Steve Ellsworth; Harvey Kaufman, M.D.; Michael A. Peat; Pat O'Brien.
Number of staff: 1 part-time professional.
EIN: 223093807

3104
Questar Corporation

333 S. State St.
P.O. Box 45433
Salt Lake City, UT 84145-0433
(801) 324-5000
FAX: (801) 324-5483

Company URL: http://www.questar.com
Establishment information: Established in 1922.
Company type: Public company
Company ticker symbol and exchange: STR/NYSE
Business activities: Conducts natural gas exploration and production activities; sells hydrocarbon liquids wholesale; transmits and distributes natural gas.
Business type (SIC): Gas production and distribution; extraction/oil and gas; petroleum and petroleum products—wholesale
Financial profile for 2012: Number of employees, 1,738; assets, $3,757,100,000; sales volume, $1,098,900,000; pre-tax net income, $328,500,000; expenses, $723,200,000; liabilities, $2,721,500,000
Corporate officers: Ronald W. Jibson, Chair., Pres., and C.E.O.; Thomas C. Jepperson, Exec. V.P., Genl. Counsel, and Corp. Secy.; Kevin W. Hadlock, Exec. V.P. and C.F.O.; David M. Curtis, V.P. and Cont.; Kelly B. Maxfield, V.P., Admin.; Anthony R. Ivins, Treas.
Board of directors: Ronald W. Jibson, Chair.; Teresa Beck; R. Don Cash; Laurence M. Downes; Gary G. Michael; Keith O. Rattie; Harris H. Simmons; Bruce A. Williamson
Subsidiaries: Questar Gas Co., Salt Lake City, UT; Questar Market Resources Co., Salt Lake City, UT; Questar Pipeline Co., Salt Lake City, UT
Giving statement: Giving through the Lawson Lundell LLP Pro Bono Program, the Questar Corporation Contributions Program, the Questar Corporation Arts Foundation, the Questar Corporation Educational Foundation, and the Questar Corporation Native American Scholarship Foundation.
Company EIN: 870407509

Questar Corporation Contributions Program

180 E. 1st South St.
P.O. Box 45433
Salt Lake City, UT 84145-0433
FAX: (801) 324-5483;
E-mail: debra.hoyt@questar.com; URL: http://www.questar.com/4EnvironmentCommunity/Community.php

Contact: Debra Hoyt, Govt. Rels. & Corp. Giving
Financial data (yr. ended 12/31/08): Total giving, $1,300,000, including $1,300,000 for grants.
Purpose and activities: Questar makes charitable contributions to nonprofit organizations involved with arts and culture, higher education, animal therapy, health, human services, community development, senior citizens, disabled people, and homeless people. Support is limited to areas of company operations.

Fields of interest: Museums; Arts; Higher education; Engineering school/education; Animal welfare; Health care; Children/youth, services; Family services; Human services; Community/economic development Aging; Disabilities, people with; Military/veterans; Economically disadvantaged; Homeless.
Type of support: Annual campaigns; Building/renovation; Continuing support; Donated equipment; Emergency funds; Employee matching gifts; Employee volunteer services; Equipment; In-kind gifts; Loaned talent; Program development; Scholarship funds; Sponsorships.
Geographic limitations: Giving limited to areas of company operations in CO, LA, ND, OK, UT, TX, and WY.
Support limitations: No support for religious or fraternal organizations, athletic teams, Boy Scout or Girl Scout troops, national health organizations, or largely government-supported organizations. No grants to individuals, or for trips, exhibitions, general operating support, athletic competitions, or advertising.
Publications: Corporate report.
Application information: Applications accepted. The Community Affairs Department handles giving. The company has a staff that only handles contributions. A contributions committee reviews all requests. Application form not required.
Initial approach: Proposal to nearest company facility
Copies of proposal: 1
Committee meeting date(s): Every 6 to 8 weeks
Deadline(s): None
Final notification: 8 to 10 weeks
Number of staff: 1 part-time professional; 1 part-time support.

Questar Corporation Arts Foundation

180 E. 1st South St.
P.O. Box 45433
Salt Lake City, UT 84145-0433
FAX: (801) 324-5483;
E-mail: debra.hoyt@questar.com; URL: http://www.questar.com/4EnvironmentCommunity/Community.php

Establishment information: Established in 1991 in UT.
Donor: Questar Corp.
Contact: Debra Hoyt, Govt. Rels. & Corp. Giving
Financial data (yr. ended 12/31/11): Assets, $3,111,423 (M); expenditures, $263,605; qualifying distributions, $262,396; giving activities include $262,396 for grants.
Purpose and activities: The foundation supports organizations involved with arts and culture.
Fields of interest: Performing arts; Performing arts, ballet; Performing arts, theater; Performing arts, opera; Arts.
Type of support: Building/renovation; Continuing support; Program-related investments/loans.
Geographic limitations: Giving limited to UT.
Support limitations: No grants to individuals.
Publications: Annual report.
Application information: Applications not accepted. Contributes only to pre-selected organizations.
Officers and Trustees:* Keith O. Rattie*, Chair. and Pres.; Ronald W. Jibson, V.P.; Abigail L. Jones, Secy.; Richard Doleshek.
EIN: 870489086

Questar Corporation Educational Foundation

180 E. 1st South St.
P.O. Box 45433
Salt Lake City, UT 84145-0433
FAX: (801) 324-5483;
E-mail: debra.hoyt@questar.com; URL: http://www.questar.com/4EnvironmentCommunity/Community.php

Establishment information: Established in 1988 in UT.
Donor: Questar Corp.
Contact: Debra Hoyt, Govt. Rels. & Corp. Giving
Financial data (yr. ended 12/31/11): Assets, $3,763,858 (M); gifts received, $25,500; expenditures, $303,257; qualifying distributions, $301,378; giving activities include $301,378 for grants.
Purpose and activities: The foundation supports institutions of higher education.
Fields of interest: Higher education.
Type of support: Building/renovation; Capital campaigns; Scholarships—to individuals.
Geographic limitations: Giving limited to areas of company operations in AZ, CO, OK, TX, UT, and WY.
Support limitations: No grants to individuals (except for scholarships).
Publications: Corporate report.
Application information: Applications not accepted. Contributes only to pre-selected organizations.
Trustees: Richard Doleshek; Abigail L. Jones; Keith O. Rattie.
EIN: 870461487

Questar Corporation Native American Scholarship Foundation

P.O. Box 45433
Salt Lake City, UT 84145-0433
E-mail: jan.bates@questar.com

Establishment information: Established in 1998 in UT.
Donor: Questar Corp.
Financial data (yr. ended 12/31/11): Assets, $92,217 (M); expenditures, $5,110; qualifying distributions, $5,000; giving activities include $5,000 for grants.
Purpose and activities: The foundation supports a scholarship fund for Native Americans attending Arizona State University.
Fields of interest: Education.
Type of support: Scholarships—to individuals.
Geographic limitations: Giving limited to Tempe, AZ.
Publications: Corporate giving report.
Application information: Applications not accepted. Unsolicited requests for funds not accepted.
Officers: Keith O. Rattie, Chair. and Pres.; Ronald W. Jibson, V.P.; Abigail L. Jones, Secy.; Richard J. Doleshek, Treas.
EIN: 870623588

3105
Questar Properties, Inc.

124 Slade Ave., Ste. 200
Baltimore, MD 21208-4991
(410) 486-1234

Company URL: http://questar.net/company.html`
Establishment information: Established in 1987.
Company type: Private company
Business activities: Provides building construction and management services.
Business type (SIC): Contractors/general residential building; contractors/general nonresidential building; services to dwellings
Corporate officers: Stephen Gorn, Chair., Pres., and C.E.O.; Mike Armacost, Co-C.F.O.; Joe Davies, Co-C.F.O.
Board of director: Stephen Gorn, Chair.
Giving statement: Giving through the Questar Foundation, Inc.

Questar Foundation, Inc.

124 Slade Ave., Ste. 200
Baltimore, MD 21208-4900 (410) 486-1234

Establishment information: Established in 1989 in MD.
Donors: Questar Properties & Management Builders, Inc.; Questar Builders, Inc.; Questar Homes, Inc.
Contact: Stephen M. Gorn, Pres. and Treas.
Financial data (yr. ended 12/31/11): Assets, $30,561 (M); expenditures, $200; qualifying distributions, $0.
Purpose and activities: The foundation supports hospices and organizations involved with suicide prevention, nutrition, and civil rights.
Fields of interest: Mental health/crisis services, suicide; Nutrition; Residential/custodial care, hospices; Civil/human rights; Jewish federated giving programs.
Type of support: General/operating support.
Geographic limitations: Giving primarily in MD.
Support limitations: No grants to individuals.
Application information: Applications accepted. Application form required.
Initial approach: Letter
Deadline(s): None
Officers: Stephen M. Gorn, Pres. and Treas.; John B. Colvin, V.P. and Secy.
EIN: 521665987

3106
Quicksilver Resources Inc.

801 Cherry St., Ste. 3700, Unit 19
Fort Worth, TX 76102 (817) 665-5000
FAX: (817) 665-5005

Company URL: http://www.qrinc.com
Establishment information: Established in 1963.
Company type: Public company
Company ticker symbol and exchange: KWK/NYSE
Business activities: Conducts natural gas, crude oil, and natural gas liquid acquisition, development, exploration, production, and marketing activities; gathers, processes, and transmits natural gas.
Business type (SIC): Extraction/oil and gas; extraction/natural gas liquids; gas production and distribution
Financial profile for 2012: Number of employees, 417; assets, $1,381,790,000; sales volume, $709,040,000; pre-tax net income, -$2,648,180,000; expenses, $3,174,800,000; liabilities, $2,514,590,000
Corporate officers: Thomas F. Darden, Ph.D., Chair.; Glenn M. Darden, Pres. and C.E.O.; John C. Cirone, Exec. V.P. and Genl. Counsel; John C. Regan, Sr. V.P. and C.F.O.; Vanessa Gomez LaGatta, V.P. and Treas.; Anne Darden Self, V.P., Human Resources
Board of directors: Thomas F. Darden, Chair.; Byron W. Dunn; Glenn F. Darden; Steven M. Morris; W. Yandell Rogers III; Anne Darden Self; Mark J. Warner
Giving statement: Giving through the Quicksilver Resources Inc. Corporate Giving Program.
Company EIN: 752756163

Quicksilver Resources Inc. Corporate Giving Program

801 Cherry St., Ste., 3700
Fort Worth, TX 76102-6883 (817) 665-5000
URL: http://www.qrinc.com/about/community_involvement/

Purpose and activities: Quicksilver makes charitable contributions to nonprofit organizations on a case by case basis. Support is given primarily in areas of company operations in north Texas, and the Rocky Mountain region of Colorado, Montana, and Wyoming.
Fields of interest: General charitable giving.
Type of support: Employee volunteer services; General/operating support; Sponsorships; Use of facilities.
Geographic limitations: Giving primarily in areas of company operations in northern TX, and the Rocky Mountain region of CO, MT, and WY.

3107
Quidel Corporation

10165 McKellar Ct.
San Diego, CA 92121 (858) 552-1100
FAX: (858) 453-4338

Company URL: http://www.quidel.com
Establishment information: Established in 1979.
Company type: Public company
Company ticker symbol and exchange: QDEL/NASDAQ
Business activities: Provides rapid diagnostic solutions for infectious diseases and reproductive health at the point of care.
Business type (SIC): Drugs
Financial profile for 2012: Number of employees, 514; assets, $242,100,000; sales volume, $155,740,000; pre-tax net income, $7,610,000; expenses, $146,900,000; liabilities, $42,320,000
Corporate officers: Mark A. Pulido, Chair.; Douglas C. Bryant, Pres. and C.E.O.; Randall J. Steward, C.F.O.; Robert Joseph Bujarski, Sr. V.P. and Genl. Counsel; Scot M. McLeod, Sr. V.P., Opers.
Board of directors: Mark A. Pulido, Chair.; Douglas C. Bryant; Thomas D. Brown; Kenneth F. Buechler, Ph.D.; Rod F. Dammeyer; Mary Lake Polan, Ph.D.; Jack W. Schuler
Giving statement: Giving through the Quidel Corporation Contributions Program.
Company EIN: 942573850

Quidel Corporation Contributions Program

10165 McKellar Ct.
San Diego, CA 92121
URL: http://www.quidel.com/about/charitable_giving.htm

Purpose and activities: Quidel Corporation makes charitable contributions to nonprofit organizations involved with health education.
Fields of interest: Health care, formal/general education.
Type of support: Employee matching gifts; Employee volunteer services; General/operating support.
Geographic limitations: Giving primarily in areas of company operations.
Support limitations: No support for political, religious, social, labor, veterans', alumni, or fraternal organizations serving a limited constituency, or athletic associations. No grants to individuals, or for research projects, endowments, travel, annual membership or affiliation campaigns, benefits, dinners, galas, and special fundraising events, sponsorship events or the purchase of corporate tables, or recreational/sporting events.
Application information: Applications not accepted. The company is not currently accepting unsolicited proposals.

3108
Quiksilver, Inc.

15202 Graham St.
Huntington Beach, CA 92649-1109
(714) 889-2200
FAX: (714) 889-3700

Company URL: http://www.quiksilverinc.com
Establishment information: Established in 1976.
Company type: Public company
Company ticker symbol and exchange: ZQK/NYSE
Business activities: Manufactures and distributes branded apparel, wintersports equipment, footwear, accessories and related products.
Business type (SIC): Apparel—men's and boys' outerwear
Financial profile for 2012: Number of employees, 7,000; assets, $1,718,240,000; sales volume, $2,013,240,000; pre-tax net income, -$2,190,000; expenses, $1,956,270,000; liabilities, $1,134,930,000
Fortune 1000 ranking: 2012—944th in revenues, 891st in profits, and 889th in assets
Corporate officers: Robert B. McKnight, Jr., Chair.; Andrew P. Mooney, Pres. and C.E.O.; Carol Scherman, Exec. V.P., Human Resources; Richard Shields, C.F.O.; Charles S. Exon, Secy., Genl. Counsel, and C.A.O.
Board of directors: Robert B. McKnight, Jr., Chair.; William M. Barnum, Jr.; Joseph F. Berardino; Michael A. Clarke; James Ellis; M. Steven Langman; Andrew P. Mooney; Robert Lewis Mettler; Andrew W. Sweet
International operations: Australia; Austria; Belgium; Brazil; Canada; China; Cyprus; Czech Republic; France; Germany; Hong Kong; Indonesia; Ireland; Italy; Japan; Luxembourg; Mexico; Netherlands; New Zealand; Poland; Portugal; Russia; Singapore; Slovakia; South Africa; Spain; Switzerland; Taiwan; Thailand; United Kingdom
Giving statement: Giving through the Quiksilver Foundation.
Company EIN: 330199426

Quiksilver Foundation

15202 Graham St.
Huntington Beach, CA 92649-1109 (714) 889-7132
E-mail: ryan.ashton@quiksilver.com; Additional contact: Kathie Armstrong, Dir., kathie.armstrong@quicksilver.com; E-mail for U.S., Canada, and Latin America inquiries: foundation@quicksilver.com; E-mail for South Pacific and Australia inquiries: quicksilver.foundation@quicksilver.com.au; URL: http://www.quiksilverfoundation.org/

Establishment information: Established in 2004 in CA.
Donor: Quiksilver, Inc.
Contact: Ryan Ashton, Dir.
Financial data (yr. ended 10/31/11): Assets, $169,915 (M); gifts received, $532,293; expenditures, $604,018; qualifying distributions, $568,893; giving activities include $568,893 for grants.
Purpose and activities: The foundation supports programs that benefit and enhance the quality of life for communities of boardriders across the world. Special emphasis is directed towards community-based organizations involved with education, oceans, the environment, health, science, children, and youth.
Fields of interest: Education; Environment, water resources; Environmental education; Environment; Health care; Community/economic development; Science Children; Youth.
International interests: Asia; Australia; Europe.
Type of support: Continuing support; Donated products; General/operating support; In-kind gifts; Program development; Research; Scholarship funds.
Geographic limitations: Giving primarily in areas of company operations, with emphasis on CA, Asia, Australia, and Europe.
Support limitations: No grants to individuals or for fundraising activities.
Publications: Grants list.
Application information: Applications not accepted. Unsolicited applications are currently not accepted. The foundation utilizes an invitation only process for giving at this time.
Officers and Directors:* Ryan Ashton, Mgr.; Fernando Aguerre; Kathie Armstrong; Maritxu Darrigrand; Scott Fullerton; Richard A. Gadbois III; Jeffrey Ishmael; Julia Ladgrove; Sean Pence; Jeff Wilson.
Number of staff: 1 full-time professional; 1 part-time professional.
EIN: 200986472
Selected grants: The following grants are a representative sample of this grantmaker's funding activity:
$50,000 to University of Southern California, Los Angeles, CA, 2010.
$50,000 to University of Southern California, Los Angeles, CA, 2010.
$50,000 to University of Southern California, Los Angeles, CA, 2010.
$30,000 to Tony Hawk Foundation, Vista, CA, 2010.
$28,000 to SurfAid International USA, Encinitas, CA, 2010.
$26,000 to Smithsonian Institution, Washington, DC, 2010.
$25,000 to SurfAid International USA, Encinitas, CA, 2010.
$7,500 to Stoked Mentoring, New York, NY, 2010.
$5,000 to Cystic Fibrosis Foundation, Anaheim, CA, 2010.
$5,000 to Miocean Foundation, Irvine, CA, 2010.

3109
QuikTrip Corporation

4777 S. 129th East Ave.
P.O. Box 3475
Tulsa, OK 74134 (918) 615-7900
FAX: (918) 615-7377

Company URL: http://www.quiktrip.com
Establishment information: Established in 1958.
Company type: Private company
Business activities: Operates gasoline service stations; operates convenience food stores.
Business type (SIC): Gasoline service stations; groceries—retail
Financial profile for 2011: Number of employees, 11,973; assets, $1,370,000,000; sales volume, $8,770,000,000
Corporate officers: Chester Cadieux III, Chair., Pres., and C.E.O.; Sandra J. Westbrook, V.P. and C.F.O.; Chris Truesdell, C.I.O.; Mike Stanford, Sr. V.P., Opers.; James Denny, V.P., Mktg.; Kimberly J. Owen, V.P., Human Resources

Board of director: Chester Cadieux III, Chair.
Subsidiary: Quik N Tasty Foods, Belton, MO
Giving statement: Giving through the QuikTrip Corporation Contributions Program.

QuikTrip Corporation Contributions Program
P.O. Box 3475
Tulsa, OK 74101-3475 (918) 615-7700
Application e-mail addresses by city: Tulsa
area: Dist-GrantApplication-Tulsa@QuikTrip.com;
Kansas City
area: Dist-GrantApplication-KC@QuikTrip.com;
Wichita
area: Dist-GrantApplication-Wichita@QuikTrip.com;
Iowa / Omaha
area: Dist-GrantApplication-Iowa@QuikTrip.com;
Phoenix / Tucson
area: Dist-GrantApplication-Phoenix@QuikTrip.com;
St. Louis
area: Dist-GrantApplication-StLouis@QuikTrip.com;
Atlanta
area: Dist-GrantApplication-Atlanta@QuikTrip.com
Dallas Area -
Dist-GrantApplication-Dallas@QuikTrip.com
Carolinas Area -
Dist-GrantApplication-Carolinas@QuikTrip.com;
URL: http://www.quiktrip.com/Who-is-QT/Community

Purpose and activities: QuikTrip supports programs designed to discourage negative behavior in young people, including alcohol, smoking, violence, and crime; focus on educational reform and change; and emphasize family support, education, and preventive healthcare for pre-schoolers.
Fields of interest: Education, early childhood education; Substance abuse, prevention; Mental health, smoking; Crime/violence prevention, youth; Food banks; Big Brothers/Big Sisters; Children, services; United Ways and Federated Giving Programs.
Type of support: Continuing support; Donated equipment; Donated products; Employee matching gifts; Employee volunteer services; General/operating support; In-kind gifts; Loaned talent.
Geographic limitations: Giving primarily in Phoenix and Tucson, AZ, Atlanta, GA, Des Moines, IA, Kansas City and Wichita, KS, Kansas City and St. Louis, MO, NC, Omaha, NE, Tulsa, OK, SC, and Dallas, TX.
Support limitations: No support for religious organizations or affiliations, or individual schools (private or public). No grants for personal assistance, general solicitations, loans or education funds for individuals, school-related band or sports events, sports teams, tournaments, races, or events, school-related activities or sports, national medical fundraising causes, or additional funding to United Way agencies.
Publications: Application guidelines.
Application information: Applications accepted. QuikTrip does not accept unsolicited applications for grants over $1,000. Application form not required. Applicants should submit the following:
1) contact person
Initial approach: E-mail proposal to appropriate local contact for requests under $1,000 or in-kind donations
Number of staff: 1 full-time professional; 1 full-time support.

3110
Quincy Broadcasting Company
513 Hampshire St.
P.O. Box 909
Quincy, IL 62301-2928 (217) 228-6600

Company URL: http://www.wgem.com
Establishment information: Established in 1954.
Company type: Subsidiary of a private company
Business activities: Broadcasts television; broadcasts radio; produces radio and television programming; provides Internet information services.
Business type (SIC): Radio and television broadcasting; motion pictures/production and services allied to
Corporate officer: Brady E. Dreasler, Mgr.
Giving statement: Giving through the Oakley-Lindsay Foundation of Quincy Newspapers and Quincy Broadcasting Company, Inc.

Oakley-Lindsay Foundation of Quincy Newspapers and Quincy Broadcasting Company, Inc.
1130 S. 5th St.
Quincy, IL 62301-3916 (217) 223-5100

Establishment information: Established in 1968 in IL.
Donors: Quincy Newspapers, Inc.; Quincy Broadcasting Co.; Quincy Herald-Whig LLC; KTVI Television, Inc.; KTTC Television, Inc.; WVVA Television, Inc.; The New Jersey Hearld; WSJV Television, Inc.
Contact: Ralph M. Oakley, Pres.
Financial data (yr. ended 12/31/11): Assets, $25,799 (M); expenditures, $57,728; qualifying distributions, $57,700; giving activities include $57,700 for grants.
Purpose and activities: The foundation supports community foundations and organizations involved with arts and culture, animal welfare, recreation, and community development.
Fields of interest: Arts; Education; Recreation.
Type of support: Annual campaigns; Building/renovation; Capital campaigns; Endowments; General/operating support; Scholarship funds; Sponsorships.
Geographic limitations: Giving primarily in Quincy, IL.
Application information: Applications accepted. Application form not required.
Initial approach: Proposal
Deadline(s): None
Officers: Ralph M. Oakley, Pres. and Treas.; Mary O. Winters, Secy.
Directors: Susan Oakley Day; Martin M. Lindsay; Lucy Lindsay Smith; Dennis Williams; Thomas A. Oakley; Harold B. Oakley.
EIN: 237025198

3111
Quinn Emanuel Urquhart & Sullivan LLP
865 S. Figueroa St., 10th Fl.
Los Angeles, CA 90017-5003
(213) 443-3000

Company URL: http://www.quinnemanuel.com/
Company type: Private company
Business activities: Operates law firm.
Business type (SIC): Legal services
Offices: Los Angeles, Redwood Shores, San Francisco, CA; Washington, DC; Chicago, IL; New York, NY
International operations: Germany; Japan; United Kingdom
Giving statement: Giving through the Quinn Emanuel Urquhart & Sullivan LLP Pro Bono Program.

Quinn Emanuel Urquhart & Sullivan LLP Pro Bono Program
865 S. Figueroa St., 10th Fl.
Los Angeles, CA 90017-5003 (213) 443-3000
FAX: (213) 443-3100; URL: http://www.quinnemanuel.com/work-at-quinn/the-firm/talent-mandatory-suit-optional/why-work-here.aspx

Contact: Alison Morgan, Coord., Pro Bono Prog.
Fields of interest: Legal services.
Type of support: Pro bono services - legal.

3112
QVC, Inc.
1200 Wilson Dr.
West Chester, PA 19380 (484) 701-1000

Company URL: http://www.qvc.com
Establishment information: Established in 1986.
Company type: Subsidiary of a public company
Business activities: Operates television home shopping company.
Business type (SIC): Furniture and home furnishing stores
Corporate officers: John Thomas, Chair. and Co-C.E.O.; Michael George, Pres. and Co-C.E.O.; Linda Dillman, Exec. V.P. and C.I.O.; Dan O'Connell, C.F.O.
Board of director: John Thomas, Chair.
Giving statement: Giving through the QVC, Inc. Contributions Program.

QVC, Inc. Contributions Program
1200 Wilson Dr.
West Chester, PA 19380 (484) 701-1000
URL: http://www.qvc.com

3113
R & B Plastics Machinery, LLC
(formerly R & B Machine Tool Company)
1605 E. Woodland Dr.
Saline, MI 48176-1638 (734) 429-9421

Company URL: http://www.rbplasticsmachinery.com/
Establishment information: Established in 1980.
Company type: Private company
Business activities: Manufactures specialized metal cutting machines and plastics machinery.
Business type (SIC): Machinery/metalworking; machinery/special industry
Corporate officers: Bob Laganke, Pres.; Paul Sieloff, C.F.O.; Tom Redies, V.P., Opers.; Geri Theobald, Cont.
Giving statement: Giving through the R & B Machine Tool Company Contributions Program and the Edward F. Redies Foundation, Inc.

Edward F. Redies Foundation, Inc.

P.O. Box 411
Saline, MI 48176-0411 (734) 429-9421
Application address: c/o R&B Machine Tool Co., 118 E. Michigan Ave., Saline, MI 48176

Establishment information: Incorporated in 1981 in MI.
Donor: R&B Machine Tool Co.
Financial data (yr. ended 12/31/11): Assets, $4,006,187 (M); expenditures, $248,696; qualifying distributions, $200,000; giving activities include $200,000 for grants.
Purpose and activities: The foundation supports hospitals and parks and organizations involved with education, child welfare, and human services.
Fields of interest: Higher education; Scholarships/financial aid; Education; Hospitals (general); Crime/violence prevention, child abuse; Recreation, parks/playgrounds; Youth, services; Residential/custodial care, hospices; Aging, centers/services; Human services.
Type of support: Annual campaigns; Building/renovation; Capital campaigns; Equipment; Scholarship funds.
Geographic limitations: Giving primarily in the greater Washtenaw County, MI, area.
Support limitations: No grants to individuals.
Publications: Application guidelines.
Application information: Applications accepted. Application form not required. Applicants should submit the following:
1) signature and title of chief executive officer
2) copy of IRS Determination Letter
3) copy of most recent annual report/audited financial statement/990
4) detailed description of project and amount of funding requested
5) listing of additional sources and amount of support
Initial approach: Proposal
Copies of proposal: 1
Deadline(s): Mar. 31
Officers and Directors: R. Edward Redies, Pres.; Robert D. Redies, V.P.; Karen Redies, Secy.-Treas.; Paul Bunten; Elizabeth J. Redies; Thomas D. Redies; William D. Redies; Milton Stemen; Dennis Valenti.
EIN: 382391326
Selected grants: The following grants are a representative sample of this grantmaker's funding activity:
$10,000 to Eastern Michigan University, Ypsilanti, Ypsilanti, MI, 2009.
$5,000 to Dawn Farm, Ypsilanti, MI, 2009.
$5,000 to Holy Cross Childrens Services, Clinton, MI, 2009.
$5,000 to Ozone House, Ann Arbor, MI, 2009.
$5,000 to Saint Louis Center, Chelsea, MI, 2009.
$5,000 to Young Adults Health Center, Ypsilanti, MI, 2009.
$1,000 to Hope Medical Clinic, Ypsilanti, MI, 2009.

3114
R & R Investors Inc.

(also known as R & R Realty Group)
1225 Jordan Creek Pkwy., Ste. 200
West Des Moines, IA 50266-2345
(515) 223-4500

Company URL: http://www.rrrealty.com/
Establishment information: Established in 1985.
Company type: Private company
Business activities: Develops real estate; operates real estate.
Business type (SIC): Real estate subdividers and developers; real estate operators and lessors
Corporate officers: Daniel P. Rupprecht, Chair.; Mark Rupprecht, Pres.; Steve K. Gaer, C.O.O. and Genl. Counsel; Tony Rogers, C.F.O.
Board of director: Daniel P. Rupprecht, Chair.
Giving statement: Giving through the R & R Realty Group Foundation.

R & R Realty Group Foundation

1225 Jordan Creek Pkwy., Ste. 200
West Des Moines, IA 50266-2346

Establishment information: Established in 1999 in IA.
Donors: R&R Investors Inc.; Daniel P. Rupprecht.
Financial data (yr. ended 06/30/12): Assets, $15,939 (M); gifts received, $294,000; expenditures, $280,985; qualifying distributions, $279,207; giving activities include $279,207 for grants.
Purpose and activities: The foundation supports organizations involved with education, health, athletics, human services, and Catholicism.
Fields of interest: Secondary school/education; Higher education; Education; Health care; Athletics/sports, amateur leagues; Athletics/sports, golf; United Ways and Federated Giving Programs; Catholic agencies & churches.
Type of support: General/operating support.
Geographic limitations: Giving primarily in Ames, Des Moines, Urbandale, and West Des Moines, IA.
Support limitations: No grants to individuals.
Application information: Applications not accepted. Contributes only to pre-selected organizations.
Trustees: Daniel P. Rupprecht; Phyllis M. Rupprecht.
EIN: 421494641
Selected grants: The following grants are a representative sample of this grantmaker's funding activity:
$33,279 to Iowa State University Foundation, Ames, IA, 2010.
$22,625 to United Way of Central Iowa, Des Moines, IA, 2010.
$10,000 to Fellowship of Christian Athletes, Des Moines, IA, 2010.
$9,600 to University of Nebraska Foundation, Lincoln, NE, 2010.
$5,000 to Drake University, Des Moines, IA, 2010.
$5,000 to Iowa Health Foundation, Des Moines, IA, 2010.
$2,000 to Civic Center of Greater Des Moines, Des Moines, IA, 2010.
$2,000 to Diocese of Des Moines, Des Moines, IA, 2010.
$1,000 to Science Center of Iowa, Des Moines, IA, 2010.

3115
Raabe Company, LLC

(formerly Raabe Corporation)
N92 W14701 Anthony Ave.
Menomonee Falls, WI 53051
(262) 255-9500

Company URL: http://www.raabecorp.com
Establishment information: Established in 1951.
Company type: Private company
Business activities: Manufactures touch-up paint and aerosol packaging products.
Business type (SIC): Paints and allied products; metal containers
Corporate officers: David Wacker, Pres.; Gerard A. Loftus, C.O.O.
Giving statement: Giving through the Raabe Foundation.

Raabe Foundation

1080 Hawthorne Ridge Dr.
Brookfield, WI 53045-4511 (262) 797-9476

Establishment information: Established in 1994 in WI.
Donors: Kent A. Raabe; Raabe Corp.
Contact: Kent A. Raabe, Tr.
Financial data (yr. ended 12/31/11): Assets, $766,857 (M); gifts received, $1,000; expenditures, $338,054; qualifying distributions, $325,000; giving activities include $325,000 for grants.
Purpose and activities: The foundation only supports organizations affiliated with the Wisconsin Evangelical Lutheran Synod.
Fields of interest: Secondary school/education; Higher education; Protestant agencies & churches.
Geographic limitations: Giving limited to WI.
Support limitations: No grants to individuals.
Application information: Applications accepted. Application form not required. Applicants should submit the following:
1) detailed description of project and amount of funding requested
Initial approach: Proposal
Deadline(s): None
Trustees: Daryl K. Raabe; Kent A. Raabe.
EIN: 396589876
Selected grants: The following grants are a representative sample of this grantmaker's funding activity:
$125,000 to Wisconsin Lutheran College, Milwaukee, WI, 2010.
$10,000 to Wisconsin Evangelical Lutheran Synod, Milwaukee, WI, 2010.

3116
Raccoon Valley Bank

(formerly Perry State Bank)
1202 2nd St.
P.O. Box 129
Perry, IA 50220-1584 (515) 465-3521
FAX: (515) 465-4346

Company URL: http://www.raccoonvalleybank.com
Establishment information: Established in 1927.
Company type: Private company
Business activities: Operates commercial bank.
Business type (SIC): Banks/commercial
Corporate officer: Terry Nielsen, Pres. and C.E.O.
Giving statement: Giving through the Raccoon Valley Bank Charitable Foundation.

Raccoon Valley Bank Charitable Foundation

(formerly Perry State Bank Charitable Foundation)
1202 2nd Ave.
Perry, IA 50220-1506 (515) 465-3521

Establishment information: Established in 1989 in IA.
Donors: Perry State Bank; Raccoon Valley State Bank Charitable Foundation; Raccoon Valley Bank.
Contact: Robert Baird, Pres.
Financial data (yr. ended 12/31/11): Assets, $56,317 (M); gifts received, $54,000; expenditures, $82,172; qualifying distributions, $81,872; giving activities include $81,872 for grants.

Purpose and activities: The foundation supports organizations involved with education and community development.
Fields of interest: Education; Environment; Human services.
Application information: Applications accepted. Application form required. Applicants should submit the following:
1) detailed description of project and amount of funding requested
Initial approach: Proposal
Deadline(s): None
Officers and Directors:* Robert Baird*, Pres.; Kendall Rathje, Secy.-Treas.; Elizabeth Garst; Sarah Garst; Sally Haerr; H.T. Holcomb; Doug McDermott; Jon Peters; Marvin Shirley; Joel Wright.
EIN: 421347634

3117
Rackspace Hosting, Inc.
5000 Walzem Rd.
San Antonio, TX 78218 (210) 312-4000
FAX: (210) 312-4848

Company URL: http://www.rackspace.com
Establishment information: Established in 1998.
Company type: Public company
Company ticker symbol and exchange: RAX/NYSE
Business activities: Operates enterprise-level data hosting services company.
Business type (SIC): Computer services
Financial profile for 2012: Number of employees, 4,852; assets, $1,295,550,000; sales volume, $1,309,240,000; pre-tax net income, $168,010,000; expenses, $1,136,500,000; liabilities, $451,900,000
Corporate officers: Graham Weston, Chair.; Lanham Napier, C.E.O.; Lew Moorman, Pres.; Mark Roenigk, C.O.O.; Karl Pichler, Sr. V.P., C.F.O., and Treas.; Alan Schoenbaum, Sr. V.P., Genl. Counsel; Henry Sauer, Sr. V.P., Human Resources
Board of directors: Graham Weston, Chair.; S. James Bishkin; Sam Gilliland; Mark P. Mellin; Palmer L. Moe; Lew Moorman; A. Lanham Napier; Fred Reichheld; George J. Still, Jr.
Giving statement: Giving through the Rack Gives Back and the Rackspace Foundation.
Company EIN: 743016523

Rack Gives Back
5000 Walzem Rd.
San Antonio, TX 78218 (210) 312-4000
E-mail: cara.nichols@rackspace.com; URL: http://www.rackspace.com/information/events/rackgivesback/

Contact: Cara Nichols, Community Affairs Dir.
Purpose and activities: As a complement to its foundation, Rackspace Hosting, Inc. also makes charitable contributions to nonprofit organizations directly. Support is limited to areas of company operations, with emphasis in San Antonio, Texas, and in San Francisco, California, Chicago, Illinois, Austin and Dallas/Ft. Worth, Texas, and Blacksburg, Virginia; giving also in Hong Kong and United Kingdom.
Fields of interest: Arts; Education; Food banks; Big Brothers/Big Sisters; Children, services; Philanthropy/voluntarism, information services; Mathematics; Engineering/technology; Science.
Type of support: Employee volunteer services; General/operating support.
Geographic limitations: Giving is limited to company operations, with emphasis on San Antonio, TX. Giving also in San Francisco, CA, Chicago, IL, Austin and Dallas/Ft. Worth, TX, and Blacksburg, VA, and in Hong Kong and United Kingdom.
Support limitations: No support for discriminatory, or religious organizations, or disease-specific groups. No grants to individuals, or for political purposes, organization-based walks, runs, tournaments, or skeet shoots, loans or investments, or merchandise or advertising promotions; generally no grants for hospital or city projects, banquets, parties, galas, or community festivals, except under special circumstances.
Publications: Application guidelines.
Application information: Applications accepted. Additional information such as relevant tax forms and budget documents may be requested at a later date. Applicants should submit the following:
1) timetable for implementation and evaluation of project
2) results expected from proposed grant
3) statement of problem project will address
4) name, address and phone number of organization
5) brief history of organization and description of its mission
6) how project's results will be evaluated or measured
7) explanation of why grantmaker is considered an appropriate donor for project
8) plans for cooperation with other organizations, if any
9) contact person
10) copy of current year's organizational budget and/or project budget
11) listing of additional sources and amount of support

Proposals should include the names and positions of those responsible for the expected outcomes, and confirmation of a Guidestar Exchange Membership (guidestar.org).
Initial approach: E-mail letter of inquiry
Committee meeting date(s): Quarterly
Deadline(s): Jan. 31, Apr. 30, July 31, and Oct. 31

The Rackspace Foundation
5000 Walzem Rd.
San Antonio, TX 78218-2117
URL: http://www.rackspacefoundation.com/

Establishment information: Established in 2008 in TX.
Contact: Alan Schoenbaum, Vice-Chair.
Financial data (yr. ended 12/31/11): Revenue, $128,844; assets, $135,618 (M); gifts received, $117,736; expenditures, $79,044; giving activities include $44,309 for grants.
Purpose and activities: The organization's mission is to extend the Rackspace "Culture of Service" to create a more vibrant, livable community.
Fields of interest: Education; Youth, services; Community/economic development, public education.
Geographic limitations: Giving primarily in the N.E. quadrant of San Antonio, TX.
Officers: Graham Weston, Chair.; Alan Schoenbaum, Vice-Chair.; Cara Nichols, Pres.; Kathy Kersten, Secy.; Anna Ziegler, Treas.
EIN: 263332818

3118
Rahr Malting Co.
800 1st Ave. W.
Shakopee, MN 55379-1148
(952) 445-1431

Company URL: http://www.rahr.com
Establishment information: Established in 1847.
Company type: Private company
Business activities: Produces malt.
Business type (SIC): Beverages
Corporate officers: Roger L. Headrick, Chair.; Gary Lee, Pres. and C.E.O.; Paul Kramer, C.I.O.
Board of director: Roger L. Headrick, Chair.
International operations: Canada
Giving statement: Giving through the Rahr Foundation.

Rahr Foundation
800 W. 1st Ave.
Shakopee, MN 55379-1148 (952) 496-7003
FAX: (952) 496-7055; E-mail: mtech@rahr.com

Establishment information: Incorporated in 1942 in WI.
Donor: Rahr Malting Co.
Contact: Frederick W. Rahr, Pres.
Financial data (yr. ended 12/31/11): Assets, $4,000,892 (M); gifts received, $27,000; expenditures, $275,490; qualifying distributions, $219,803; giving activities include $183,000 for 60 grants (high: $7,000; low: $1,000).
Purpose and activities: The foundation supports health centers and organizations involved with performing arts, education, conservation, animal welfare, and human services.
Fields of interest: Performing arts; Performing arts, opera; Higher education; Education; Environment, natural resources; Animal welfare; Animals/wildlife, preservation/protection; Health care, clinics/centers; Boys & girls clubs; Human services.
Type of support: Annual campaigns; Continuing support; Employee-related scholarships; Fellowships; General/operating support; Program development.
Geographic limitations: Giving primarily in MN.
Support limitations: No grants for endowments or research programs; no loans.
Application information: Applications accepted. Application form not required.
Initial approach: Proposal
Copies of proposal: 1
Board meeting date(s): June and Nov.
Deadline(s): Sept. 1
Final notification: 1 month following Nov. board meeting
Officers and Director: Frederick W. Rahr*, Pres.; William T. Rahr*, V.P.; Marilyn T. Tech, Secy.; George D. Gackle*, Treas.; Laurel Mallon.
Number of staff: 2 part-time support.
EIN: 396046046

3119
Railway Equipment Co.
(also known as RECO)
15400 Mediana Rd.
Plymouth, MN 55447-1473 (763) 972-2200

Company URL: http://www.rwy.com
Establishment information: Established in 1980.
Company type: Subsidiary of a private company
Business activities: Manufactures railroad gas hot air blowers, crossing gate arms, and battery chargers.
Business type (SIC): Metal plumbing fixtures and heating equipment/nonelectric; electrical industrial apparatus; electrical equipment and supplies
Giving statement: Giving through the Lakeland Group Foundation, Inc.

The Lakeland Group Foundation, Inc.
5735 Lindsay St.
Minneapolis, MN 55422-4655

Establishment information: Established in 1993 in MN.
Donors: Lakeland Engineering Equipment Co., Inc.; Control Assemblies Co.; Railway Equipment Co.; CACO Services Co.
Financial data (yr. ended 01/31/12): Assets, $291,344 (M); gifts received, $48,000; expenditures, $24,286; qualifying distributions, $21,500; giving activities include $17,500 for 3 grants (high: $8,000; low: $5,000) and $4,000 for 4 grants to individuals (high: $1,000; low: $1,000).
Purpose and activities: The foundation supports the Salvation Army in Roseville, Minnesota.
Fields of interest: Human services.
Type of support: Employee-related scholarships; General/operating support.
Support limitations: No grants to individuals (except for employee-related scholarships).
Application information: Applications not accepted. Unsolicited requests for funds not accepted.
Officers: Bill C. Fox, Pres.; John L. Tambornino, Secy.
Directors: David K. Fox; Margene B. Fox.
EIN: 411738234

3120
Rainforest Cafe, Inc.
1510 W. Loop S.
Houston, TX 77027-9505 (713) 850-1010

Company URL: http://www.rainforestcafe.com
Establishment information: Established in 1994.
Company type: Subsidiary of a public company
Business activities: Operates restaurants.
Business type (SIC): Restaurants and drinking places
Corporate officers: Tilman J. Fertitta, Chair., C.E.O. and Pres.; Richard H. Liem, Exec. V.P. and C.F.O.; Steven L. Scheinthal, Genl. Counsel
Board of director: Tilman J. Fertitta, Chair.
Giving statement: Giving through the Rainforest Cafe Friends of the Future Foundation.

Rainforest Cafe Friends of the Future Foundation
(doing business as Landry's Foundation)
1510 W. Loop S.
Houston, TX 77027-9505 (713) 386-8094

Establishment information: Established in 1998 in MN.
Financial data (yr. ended 12/31/10): Revenue, $132,045; assets, $765,968 (M); gifts received, $106,679; expenditures, $128,761; giving activities include $115,915 for grants.
Purpose and activities: The foundation supports environmental causes as well as causes that enrich the lives of children, their families, and the community in areas where Rainforest Cafe operates.
Fields of interest: Environment.
Support limitations: No support for organizations that are not 501(c)(3) or equivalent. No grants to individuals.
Application information: Applications accepted.
Initial approach: Mail proposal to foundation
Officers: Tilman Fertitta; Rick Liem; Steve Scheinthal.
EIN: 411909838

3121
Rainsville Technology , Inc.
189 RTI Dr.
Rainsville, AL 35986-4471 (256) 638-9760

Company URL: http://www.rainsvillealabama.com
Establishment information: Established in 2000.
Company type: Private company
Business activities: Manufactures plastic products; manufactures automotive parts.
Business type (SIC): Plastic products/miscellaneous; motor vehicles and equipment
Financial profile for 2012: Number of employees, 325
Corporate officers: Akio Moramoto, Pres.; Allen Tucker, C.F.O.; Perry Bellomy, V.P., Admin.
Giving statement: Giving through the Rtitaka Fund.

The Rtitaka Fund
(formerly The RTI/TAKA Fund)
189 RTI Dr.
Rainsville, AL 35986-4471

Establishment information: Established in 2003 in AL.
Donor: Rainsville Technology Inc.
Financial data (yr. ended 12/31/11): Assets, $57,452 (M); expenditures, $2,045; qualifying distributions, $2,000; giving activities include $2,000 for grants.
Purpose and activities: The foundation awards college scholarships to individuals.
Type of support: Scholarships—to individuals.
Application information: Applications not accepted. Unsolicited requests for funds not accepted.
Officers: Akio Morimoto, Pres.; Perry Bellomy, V.P.
EIN: 300118850

3122
Raley's Inc.
500 W. Capitol Ave.
West Sacramento, CA 95605-2624
(916) 373-3333

Company URL: http://www.raleys.com
Establishment information: Established in 1935.
Company type: Private company
Business activities: Operates supermarkets and drug stores.
Business type (SIC): Groceries—retail; merchandise stores/general; drug stores and proprietary stores; liquor stores
Financial profile for 2011: Number of employees, 13,400; sales volume, $3,000,000,000
Corporate officers: James E. Teel, Co-Chair.; Joyce N. Raley Teel, Co-Chair.; Michael J. Teel, Pres. and C.E.O.; Michael O'Dell, C.I.O.; David Palmer, V.P., Mktg.
Board of directors: James E. Teel, Co-Chair.; Joyce N. Raley Teel, Co-Chair.
Subsidiaries: Bel Air Markets, West Sacramento, CA; Warehouse Concepts, Inc., West Sacramento, CA
Giving statement: Giving through the Raley's Inc. Corporate Giving Program and the Thomas P. Raley Foundation.

Raley's Inc. Corporate Giving Program
500 W. Capitol Ave.
West Sacramento, CA 95605-2624 (916) 373-6590

Contact: Nancy McGagin, Mgr., Public Affairs
Purpose and activities: Raley's makes charitable contributions to nonprofit organizations involved with arts and culture, education, health, hunger, and human services. Support is given primarily in areas of company store operations.
Fields of interest: Arts; Education; Health care; Food services; Human services.
Type of support: Donated equipment; Donated products; Employee matching gifts; Employee volunteer services; General/operating support; In-kind gifts.
Geographic limitations: Giving primarily in areas of company store operations in CA and NV.
Support limitations: No support for political organizations.
Application information: Applications accepted. Telephone calls are not encouraged. Application form not required.
Initial approach: Proposal to headquarters

Thomas P. Raley Foundation
P.O. Box 15618
Sacramento, CA 95852-0618

Establishment information: Established in 1995 in CA.
Donor: Raley's.
Financial data (yr. ended 12/31/11): Assets, $5,479,030 (M); expenditures, $432,933; qualifying distributions, $350,000; giving activities include $350,000 for grants.
Purpose and activities: The foundation supports the Salvation Army and organizations involved with domestic violence.
Fields of interest: Crime/violence prevention, domestic violence; Salvation Army; Family services, domestic violence.
Type of support: General/operating support.
Geographic limitations: Giving primarily in Placerville and Sacramento, CA.
Support limitations: No grants to individuals.
Application information: Applications not accepted. Contributes only to pre-selected organizations.
Officers and Directors: Joyce N. Raley Teel, Chair.; James E. Teel, V.P.; Neil Doerhoff, Secy.-Treas.; Lisa Davidson; Claudia Doerhoff; Diane Perry; Laurie Struck; Michael J. Teel.
EIN: 680358149

3123
Ralph Lauren Corporation
(formerly Polo Ralph Lauren Corporation)
650 Madison Ave.
New York, NY 10022-1029 (212) 318-7000
FAX: (212) 318-7690

Company URL: http://www.ralphlauren.com
Establishment information: Established in 1967.
Company type: Public company
Company ticker symbol and exchange: RL/NYSE
Business activities: Designs, markets, and sells apparel.
Business type (SIC): Apparel—men's and boys' outerwear
Financial profile for 2013: Number of employees, 23,000; assets, $5,418,200,000; sales volume, $6,944,800,000; pre-tax net income, $1,089,300,000; expenses, $5,818,100,000; liabilities, $1,633,600,000
Fortune 1000 ranking: 2012—370th in revenues, 269th in profits, and 567th in assets
Forbes 2000 ranking: 2012—1191st in sales, 841st in profits, and 1783rd in assets
Corporate officers: Ralph Lauren, Chair. and C.E.O.; Roger N. Farah, Pres. and C.O.O.;

Christopher H. Peterson, Sr. V.P. and C.F.O.; Mitchell A. Kosh, Sr. V.P., Human Resources
Board of directors: Ralph Lauren, Chair.; John R. Alchin; Arnold H. Aronson; Frank A. Bennack, Jr.; Joyce F. Brown; Roger N. Farah; Joel L. Fleishman; Hubert Joly; Judith McHale; Steven P. Murphy; Jackwyn L. Nemerov; Robert C. Wright
Subsidiary: Fashions Outlet of America, Inc., Lyndhurst, NJ
Office: Lyndhurst, NJ
International operations: Argentina; Australia; Austria; Belgium; Canada; Denmark; France; Germany; Hong Kong; Ireland; Italy; Japan; Monaco; Netherlands; North Korea; Singapore; Spain; Sweden; Switzerland; United Kingdom
Giving statement: Giving through the Polo Ralph Lauren Corporation Contributions Program and the Polo Ralph Lauren Foundation.
Company EIN: 132622036

The Polo Ralph Lauren Foundation

c/o CBIZ MHM LLC.
1065 Ave. of the Americas
New York, NY 10018-1847
URL: http://global.ralphlauren.com/en-us/about/philanthropy/pages/default.aspx

Establishment information: Established in 2001 in NY.
Donors: Polo Ralph Lauren Corp.; Jones Apparel Group, Inc.; L'Oreal USA; New Times Group Holdings Ltd.; Ralph Lauren Media Polo.com; Winnitex Ltd.; Kuohwa Garment & Enamel Industry Co., Inc.; Yee Tung Garment Co., Ltd.; Timemax International, Ltd.; Mo Villa Productions, Inc.; Bathco (The Navy Yard); Beijing Industrial Development Co. Ltd.; Peter S. Goldstein.
Financial data (yr. ended 04/02/11): Assets, $15,824,605 (M); gifts received, $6,976,913; expenditures, $1,316,116; qualifying distributions, $1,187,601; giving activities include $1,187,601 for 27 grants (high: $360,570; low: $500).
Purpose and activities: The foundation supports programs designed to promote care; education; and service in underserved communities.
Fields of interest: Secondary school/education; Education; Hospitals (general); Cancer; Breast cancer; Housing/shelter, development; Recreation, parks/playgrounds; Children/youth, services; Community/economic development Economically disadvantaged.
Type of support: Employee volunteer services; General/operating support; Program development; Scholarship funds.
Geographic limitations: Giving primarily in CA, Washington, DC, MD, MN, NC, NJ, and NY, and in Switzerland.
Support limitations: No support for political campaigns. No grants to individuals.
Application information: Applications not accepted. Contributes only to pre-selected organizations.
Officers and Directors:* Ralph Lauren*, Chair.; David Lauren, Pres.; Paul Campbell, V.P.; Bette-Ann Gwathmey, V.P.; Avery Fischer, Secy.; Tracy Travis*, Treas.; Arthur Crispo, Exec. Dir.; Roger Farah; Mitchell Kosh.
EIN: 522316766

3124
Ramallah Trading Company, Inc.

255-47th St.
Brooklyn, NY 11220-1009 (718) 439-5555
FAX: (718)439-7878

Company URL: http://www.ramallahtrading.com
Establishment information: Established in 1916.
Company type: Private company
Business activities: Sells home textiles wholesale.
Business type (SIC): Furniture and home furnishings—wholesale
Corporate officers: James A. Bateh, Pres.; Robert Bateh, Treas.
Giving statement: Giving through the Ramallah Foundation, Inc.

Ramallah Foundation, Inc.

255 47th St.
Brooklyn, NY 11220-1009

Donors: Eissa A. Bateh & Brothers Foundation, Inc.; Victor Moses†; Hathihe Ramallah Magazine; American Ramallah Federation.
Financial data (yr. ended 06/30/11): Assets, $632,546 (M); gifts received, $15,000; expenditures, $17,179; qualifying distributions, $15,000; giving activities include $15,000 for 1 grant.
Purpose and activities: The foundation supports the American Federation of Ramallah Palestine Educational Foundation.
Fields of interest: Education.
Type of support: General/operating support.
Geographic limitations: Giving primarily in Westland, MI.
Support limitations: No grants to individuals.
Application information: Applications not accepted. Unsolicited requests for funds not accepted.
Officers: John Joubran, Pres.; George Salamy, V.P.; Robert A. Bateh, Secy.; James A. Bateh, Treas.
EIN: 136129479

3125
Ramerica International, Inc.

12 E. 49th St., Ste. 17
New York, NY 10117-8287 (212) 759-7216

Company URL: http://www.ramericainternational.com/
Establishment information: Established in 1981.
Company type: Subsidiary of a foreign company
Business activities: Operates general trading company.
Business type (SIC): Investors/miscellaneous
Corporate officer: Nur Emirgil, Mgr.
Giving statement: Giving through the Ramerica Foundation, Inc.

Ramerica Foundation, Inc.

12 E. 49th St., 17th Fl.
New York, NY 10017-1028

Establishment information: Established in 1987 in NY.
Donors: Triskel, S.A.; Commanditer Finance, Ltd.; Ramerica International Inc.; Kofisa Trading Co., S.A.; American Express Foundation.
Financial data (yr. ended 12/31/11): Assets, $1,858,340 (M); expenditures, $16,960; qualifying distributions, $13,305.
Purpose and activities: The foundation supports organizations involved with film and international relations with Turkey.
Fields of interest: Media, film/video; International development.
International interests: Turkey.
Type of support: General/operating support; Program development.
Geographic limitations: Giving primarily in New York, NY and Istanbul, Turkey.
Support limitations: No grants to individuals.
Application information: Applications not accepted. Unsolicited requests for funds not accepted.
Officers: Hasan Bengu, Pres.; Ali Y. Koc, V.P.; Yonca Sarigedik, Secy.-Treas.
Director: Erdal Yeldirim.
EIN: 133407012
Selected grants: The following grants are a representative sample of this grantmaker's funding activity:
$25,000 to Film Society of Lincoln Center, New York, NY, 2009.
$10,000 to American Turkish Society, New York, NY, 2009.

3126
Ramona's Mexican Food Products, Inc.

13633 S. Western Ave.
Gardena, CA 90249-2503 (310) 323-1950

Company URL: http://ramonas.com/
Establishment information: Established in 1947.
Company type: Private company
Business activities: Operates restaurants; produces prepared foods.
Business type (SIC): Restaurants and drinking places; miscellaneous prepared foods
Corporate officers: Martin Acosta Torres, Sr., Pres. and C.E.O.; Natalia Valdez, C.O.O.; Ramona Acosta Banuelos, C.F.O.
Giving statement: Giving through the Ramona's Mexican Food Products Scholarship Foundation.

Ramona's Mexican Food Products Scholarship Foundation

13633 S. Western Ave.
Gardena, CA 90249

Donor: Ramona's Mexican Food Products, Inc.
Financial data (yr. ended 09/30/11): Assets, $72,160 (M); gifts received, $91,296; expenditures, $8,835; qualifying distributions, $8,835; giving activities include $500 for 1 grant to an individual.
Purpose and activities: The foundation awards college scholarships to students of Mexican descent who are graduates of Garfield, Lincoln, or Roosevelt high schools in California.
Fields of interest: Hispanics/Latinos.
Type of support: Scholarships—to individuals.
Geographic limitations: Giving limited to CA.
Application information: Applications accepted. Application form required.
Initial approach: Proposal
Deadline(s): None
Officer and Director:* Ramona Banuelos, Pres.
EIN: 237425268

3127
Rapoca Energy Company, LLC
2700 Lee Hwy.
Bristol, VA 24202-5873 (276) 669-3400

Establishment information: Established in 1985.
Company type: Private company
Business activities: Mines, refines, and distributes bituminous coal.
Business type (SIC): Mining/coal and lignite surface
Corporate officer: Clyde Stacy, Mgr.
Giving statement: Giving through the Blankenship/Justice Scholarship Fund Trust.

Blankenship/Justice Scholarship Fund Trust
P.O. Box 1908
Orlando, FL 32802-1908
E-mail: Cheryl.godwin@suntrust.com
Application address: c/o SunTrust Bank, Trustee for the Blankenship/Justice Scholarship Fund, P.O. Box 1638, TN-Chatt-0310, Johnson City, TN 37401, tel.: (423) 757-3845, fax: (423) 757-3100

Establishment information: Established in 2003 in TN.
Donors: Rapoca Energy Co.; U.S. Dist. Court Roanoke VA.
Contact: Cheryl Godwin
Financial data (yr. ended 12/31/11): Assets, $1,441,944 (M); gifts received, $110,127; expenditures, $63,069; qualifying distributions, $49,260; giving activities include $35,750 for 53 grants (high: $1,000; low: $250).
Purpose and activities: The trust awards college scholarships to children or dependents of a coal miner; disabled coal miners seeking a degree; individuals seeking a degree in a field related to coal mine safety and health; and to individuals who are high school graduates or GED certified.
Scholarships are limited to residents of Buchanan, Dickenson, Lee, Russell, Scott, Smyth, Tazewell, Washington, and Wise counties, and Bristol and Norton, Virginia.
Fields of interest: Education.
Type of support: Scholarships—to individuals.
Geographic limitations: Giving primarily in Norton and Bristol and the following counties; Buchanan, Dickenson, Lee, Russell, Scott, Smith, Tazewell, Washington, and Wise, VA.
Application information: Applications accepted. Application form required.
Applications must include a Free Application for Federal Student Aid (FAFSA) and recent transcripts.
Initial approach: Contact foundation for application form
Deadline(s): Feb. 1 to Mar. 30
Trustee: SunTrust Bank.
EIN: 626398586

3128
C. A. Rasmussen, Inc.
28548 Livingston Ave.
Valencia, CA 91355-4171 (661) 367-9040

Company URL: http://www.carasmussen.com
Establishment information: Established in 1964.
Company type: Private company
Business activities: Operates general engineering contracting company.
Business type (SIC): Construction/miscellaneous heavy; construction/highway and street (except elevated)
Corporate officers: Charles A. Rasmussen, Pres.; Dick Greenburg, C.F.O.; Mike Medema, V.P., Opers.; Lisa Punches, Corp. Secy.
Giving statement: Giving through the Charles and Patricia Rasmussen Family Foundation and the Rasmussen Foundation.

Charles and Patricia Rasmussen Family Foundation
28548 Livingston Ave.
Valencia, CA 91355-4171

Establishment information: Established in 2005 in CA.
Donor: C.A. Rasmussen, Inc.
Financial data (yr. ended 12/31/11): Assets, $710,450 (M); expenditures, $78,110; qualifying distributions, $74,408; giving activities include $74,408 for 24 grants (high: $15,000; low: $40).
Purpose and activities: The foundation supports organizations involved with historical activities, ALS, youth development, and senior citizen services.
Fields of interest: Arts; Health organizations; Crime/law enforcement.
Type of support: General/operating support.
Geographic limitations: Giving primarily in CA and MS.
Support limitations: No grants to individuals.
Application information: Applications not accepted. Contributes only to pre-selected organizations.
Officers: Patricia Rasmussen, Pres.; Casey Rasmussen, V.P.; Richard Greenberg, Secy.-Treas.
Trustees: Adam Rasmussen; Charles A. Rasmussen; Stephen Rasmussen; Taylor Rasmussen.
EIN: 870753737

Rasmussen Foundation
2320 Shasta Way, Ste. F
Simi Valley, CA 93065-1800

Establishment information: Established in 1987 in CA.
Donor: C.A. Rasmussen, Inc.
Financial data (yr. ended 12/31/10): Assets, $1,341,007 (M); expenditures, $184,271; qualifying distributions, $179,190; giving activities include $179,190 for 12 grants (high: $100,000; low: $100).
Purpose and activities: The foundation supports museums and organizations involved with higher education, health, ALS, and youth development.
Fields of interest: Museums; Higher education; Health care; ALS; Boy scouts.
Type of support: General/operating support.
Support limitations: No grants to individuals.
Application information: Applications not accepted. Unsolicited requests for funds not accepted.
Officers: C. Dean Rasmussen, Pres.; Richard Greenberg, C.F.O.; James Rasmussen, Secy.
Director: Charles A. Rasmussen.
EIN: 770166925
Selected grants: The following grants are a representative sample of this grantmaker's funding activity:
$1,000 to American Cancer Society, Atlanta, GA, 2010.

3129
Ratio Architects, Inc.
107 S. Penn St.
Indianapolis, IN 46204-3684
(317) 633-4040

Company URL: http://www.ratioarchitects.com
Establishment information: Established in 1982.
Company type: Private company
Business activities: Operates an interdisciplinary design firm offering services in architecture, preservation, interior design, landscape architecture and urban planning.
Business type (SIC): Engineering, architectural, and surveying services
Corporate officers: Joseph Briggs, Esq., Chair.; William A. Browne, Jr., Pres.
Board of director: Joseph Briggs, Esq., Chair.
Giving statement: Giving through the Ratio Foundation, Inc.

Ratio Foundation, Inc.
107 S. Pennsylvania St., Ste. 100
Indianapolis, IN 46204-3681

Establishment information: Established in 2004 in IN.
Donor: Ratio Architects, Inc.
Financial data (yr. ended 12/31/11): Assets, $34 (M); gifts received, $73,714; expenditures, $74,652; qualifying distributions, $73,393; giving activities include $73,393 for 40 grants (high: $20,000; low: $40).
Purpose and activities: The foundation supports organizations involved with arts and culture, higher education, health, football, children, and industry and trade.
Fields of interest: Arts; Health care; Recreation.
Type of support: General/operating support.
Geographic limitations: Giving primarily in areas of company operations in Indianapolis, IN.
Support limitations: No grants to individuals.
Application information: Applications not accepted. Unsolicited requests for funds not accepted.
Officers: William A. Browne, Jr., Pres.; R. Timothy Barrick, Secy.-Treas.
EIN: 201436022

3130
Ratner Companies, L.C.
1577 Spring Hill Rd., Ste. 500
Vienna, VA 22182 (703) 269-5400
FAX: (703) 269-5409

Company URL: http://www.ratnerco.com
Establishment information: Established in 1974.
Company type: Private company
Business activities: Operates chain of hair salons.
Business type (SIC): Beauty shops
Financial profile for 2011: Number of employees, 12,000
Corporate officers: Dennis Ratner, C.E.O.; Susan Gustafson, Pres.; Ben Teicher, C.F.O.
Giving statement: Giving through the Ratner Family Foundation.

The Ratner Family Foundation
1577 Spring Hill Rd., Ste. 500
Vienna, VA 22182-2223

Establishment information: Established in 1990 in VA.

Donors: Creative Hairdressers, Inc.; and its subsidiaries.
Financial data (yr. ended 12/31/11): Assets, $175,370 (M); gifts received, $250,000; expenditures, $540,952; qualifying distributions, $535,110; giving activities include $535,110 for grants.
Purpose and activities: The foundation supports museums and camps and organizations involved with education, science, and Judaism.
Fields of interest: Museums; Education; Recreation, camps; Residential/custodial care, group home; Jewish federated giving programs; Science; Jewish agencies & synagogues.
Type of support: General/operating support; Program development.
Geographic limitations: Giving primarily in CO, Washington, DC, and MD, with emphasis on Bethesda, and Rockville.
Support limitations: No grants to individuals.
Application information: Applications not accepted. Contributes only to pre-selected organizations.
Officers: Dennis F. Ratner, Pres.; Warren A. Ratner, Secy.
EIN: 521099125
Selected grants: The following grants are a representative sample of this grantmaker's funding activity:
$2,500 to Georgetown Day School, Washington, DC, 2009.
$2,000 to Hebrew Home of Greater Washington, Rockville, MD, 2009.
$2,000 to Washington Hebrew Congregation, Washington, DC, 2009.
$1,500 to Buddy Program, Aspen, CO, 2009.
$1,000 to Coalition for Pulmonary Fibrosis, Culver City, CA, 2009.
$1,000 to Imagination Stage, Bethesda, MD, 2009.
$1,000 to Suburban Hospital Foundation, Bethesda, MD, 2009.

3131
Ray, Quinney & Nebeker Law Firm, P.C.

36 S. State St., Ste. 1400
P.O. Box 45385
Salt Lake City, UT 84111-1451
(801) 532-1500

Company URL: http://www.rqn.com/firmprofile/index.php
Establishment information: Established in 1940.
Company type: Private company
Business activities: Provides legal services.
Business type (SIC): Legal services
Corporate officers: Samuel C. Straight, Chair.; Eric Visser, C.O.O.
Board of director: Samuel C. Straight, Chair.
Giving statement: Giving through the Ray, Quinney & Nebeker Foundation.

Ray, Quinney & Nebeker Foundation

P.O. Box 45385
Salt Lake City, UT 84145-0385
URL: http://www.rqn.com/commitment-community

Donors: Ray, Quinney & Nebeker Law Firm, P.C.; Clark P. Giles; Herbert C. Livsey.
Financial data (yr. ended 12/31/11): Assets, $400,825 (M); expenditures, $22,449; qualifying distributions, $22,100; giving activities include $22,100 for grants.
Purpose and activities: The foundation supports museums and organizations involved with performing arts and higher education.
Fields of interest: Arts; Education; Health care.
Type of support: General/operating support.
Support limitations: No grants to individuals.
Application information: Applications not accepted. Contributes only to pre-selected organizations.
Trustees: Clark P. Giles; Herbert C. Livsey; Stephen B. Nebeker.
EIN: 870389313

3132
Ray-Carroll County Grain Growers, Inc.

(formerly Ray County Grain Growers, Inc.)
807 W. Main St.
P.O. Box 158
Richmond, MO 64085-1321
(816) 776-2291

Company URL: http://www.ray-carroll.com
Establishment information: Established in 1931.
Company type: Cooperative
Business activities: Sells agricultural products wholesale.
Business type (SIC): Farm-product raw materials—wholesale
Financial profile for 2009: Number of employees, 105
Corporate officers: David Minnick, Pres.; C. Douglas Courtney, Cont.
Giving statement: Giving through the Ray-Carroll Scholarship Fund.

Ray-Carroll Scholarship Fund

(formerly Ray-Carroll County Grain Growers Scholarship Fund, Inc.)
P.O. Box 158
Richmond, MO 64085-0158 (816) 776-2291

Donor: Ray-Carroll County Grain Growers, Inc.
Contact: Mike Nordwald
Financial data (yr. ended 09/30/11): Assets, $160,004 (M); gifts received, $9,000; expenditures, $15,748; qualifying distributions, $15,000; giving activities include $15,000 for 29 grants to individuals (high: $1,000; low: $250).
Purpose and activities: The foundation awards college scholarships to students living in areas of company operations of Ray-Carroll County Grain Growers to attend a college in Missouri.
Type of support: Scholarships—to individuals.
Geographic limitations: Giving limited to MO.
Application information: Applications accepted. Application form required.
Initial approach: Letter
Deadline(s): None
Officers: Terry Watts, Pres.; Judith Waters, Secy.-Treas.
EIN: 431244005

3133
The Raymond Corporation

22 S. Canal St.
Greene, NY 13778-0130 (607) 656-2311

Company URL: http://www.raymondcorp.com
Establishment information: Established in 1922.
Company type: Subsidiary of a foreign company
Business activities: Manufactures automated material handling systems and electric industrial lift trucks.
Business type (SIC): Machinery/construction, mining, and materials handling
Corporate officers: Michael G. Field, Chair.; Charles Pascarelli, Pres.; Edward J. Rompala, C.F.O.; John Everts, V.P., Finance; David M. Furman, V.P., Mktg.; Timothy Combs, V.P., Sales; Stephen E. VanNostrand, V.P., Human Resources
Board of director: Michael G. Fields, Chair.
Subsidiaries: Robert Abel & Co., Inc., Woburn, MA; Air-Mac Handling & Storage Techniques, Inc., Portland, OR; Air-Mac Handling & Storage Techniques, Inc., Kent, WA; Allied Handling Equip Co., Ltd., Peoria, IL; Andersen & Associates, Inc., Farmington, MI; Arbor Handling Services, Inc., Willow Grove, PA; Associated Mak Handling Industries, Inc., Elmhurst, IL; W.T. Billard, Inc., Santa Fe Springs, CA; Brauer Mat Handling System, Inc., Goodlettsville, TN; Carolina Handling, Inc., Charlotte, NC; Royce W. Day Co., Inc., Voorheesville, NY; Georgia-Alabama Handling, Lithonia, GA; Handling Systems, Inc., Phoenix, AZ; Hooper Handling, Inc., Hamburg, NY; ICM, Salt Lake City, UT; Pengate Handling Systems, Inc., York, PA; Raymond Carousel Corp., Greene, NY; Raymond Control Products Corp., Hollister, CA; Raymond Leasing Corp., Greene, NY; Raymond Production Systems, Hollister, CA; Raymond Sales Corp., Greene, NY; Raymond Transportation Corp., Greene, NY; Ring Lift, Jacksonville, FL; Storage Concepts, Inc., Cincinnati, OH; Werres Corp., Rockville, MD
International operations: Canada
Giving statement: Giving through the Raymond Foundation.

Raymond Foundation

c/o Raymond Corp.
P.O. Box 518
Greene, NY 13778-0518 (607) 656-2481

Establishment information: Trust established in 1964 in NY.
Donors: The Raymond Corp.; George G. Raymond‡; Madeline Young.
Contact: Terri Brant, Exec. Secy.
Financial data (yr. ended 12/31/11): Assets, $5,783,470 (M); gifts received, $88,179; expenditures, $153,195; qualifying distributions, $117,317; giving activities include $117,317 for 102 grants (high: $20,000; low: $25).
Purpose and activities: The foundation supports fire departments and organizations involved with theater, education, health, housing development, human services, and community economic development.
Fields of interest: Arts; Education; Environment.
Type of support: Annual campaigns; Building/renovation; Capital campaigns; Matching/challenge support; Program development; Scholarship funds; Sponsorships.
Geographic limitations: Giving primarily in areas of company operations in CA and NY.
Support limitations: No grants to individuals, or for endowments or general operating support; no loans.
Publications: Annual report; Application guidelines; Program policy statement.
Application information: Applications accepted. Application form required. Applicants should submit the following:
1) copy of IRS Determination Letter
2) detailed description of project and amount of funding requested
3) copy of current year's organizational budget and/or project budget
4) listing of additional sources and amount of support

Initial approach: Letter
Board meeting date(s): Mar., June, Sept., and Dec.
Deadline(s): None
Officers: James F. Barton, Chair.; Pete Raymond, Vice-Chair.; Terri Brant, Exec. Secy.; Patrick J. McManus, Treas.
Trustees: Richard Najarian; John Pilkington; Jean C. Raymond; Karen Raymond; Stephen S. Raymond; Steve VanNostrand; Jeanette L. Williamson.
EIN: 166047847
Selected grants: The following grants are a representative sample of this grantmaker's funding activity:
$1,500 to American Heart Association, Dallas, TX, 2009.
$1,000 to American Cancer Society, Atlanta, GA, 2009.

3134
Rayonier Inc.

(formerly ITT Rayonier Incorporated)
50 N. Laura St., Ste. 2300
1301 Riverplace Blvd.
Jacksonville, FL 32207 (904) 357-9100
FAX: (904) 357-9101

Company URL: http://www.rayonier.com
Establishment information: Established in 1926.
Company type: Public company
Company ticker symbol and exchange: RYN/NYSE
Business activities: Operates timber tracts; develops real estate; manufactures and sells performance cellulose fibers; manufactures lumber.
Business type (SIC): Forestry—timber tracts; lumber and wood products; plastics and synthetics; real estate subdividers and developers
Financial profile for 2012: Number of employees, 1,900; assets, $3,122,950,000; sales volume, $1,571,000,000; pre-tax net income, $367,080,000; expenses, $1,159,550,000; liabilities, $1,684,950,000
Corporate officers: Paul G. Boynton, Chair., Pres., and C.E.O.; Hanse E. Vanden Noort, Sr. V.P. and C.F.O.; W. Edwin Frazier III, Sr. V.P., C.A.O., and Corp. Secy.; Carl E. Kraus, Sr. V.P., Finance; Michael R. Herman, V.P. and Genl. Counsel; Charles H. Hood, V.P., Public Affairs and Comms.; James L. Posze, Jr., V.P., Human Resources
Board of directors: Paul G. Boynton, Chair.; C. David Brown II; John Ellis Bush; Mark E. Gaumond; Richard D. Kincaid; V. Larkin Martin; James H. Miller; Thomas I. Morgan; David W. Oskin; Ronald Townsend
Plants: Atlanta, GA; Seattle, WA
Giving statement: Giving through the Rayonier Foundation.
Company EIN: 132607329

The Rayonier Foundation

(formerly The ITT Rayonier Foundation)
1301 Riverplace Blvd., Ste. 2300
Jacksonville, FL 32207-9062 (904) 357-9100
Application address: 50 N. Laura Street, Ste. 1900, Jacksonville, FL 32202, tel.: (904) 357-9120

Establishment information: Incorporated in 1952 in NY.
Donors: ITT Rayonier Inc.; Rayonier Inc.
Contact: Charles H. Hood, Pres.
Financial data (yr. ended 12/31/11): Assets, $4,709,173 (M); expenditures, $407,068; qualifying distributions, $407,033; giving activities include $407,033 for 171 grants (high: $7,079; low: -$1,000).
Purpose and activities: The foundation supports organizations involved with arts and culture, education, the environment, health, human services, community economic development, civic affairs, and science and awards college scholarships to individuals.
Fields of interest: Museums; Performing arts; Arts; Elementary/secondary education; Higher education; Engineering school/education; Education, reading; Education; Environment, natural resources; Environment, forests; Environmental education; Environment; Hospitals (general); Health care; American Red Cross; Children/youth, services; Human services; Community/economic development; United Ways and Federated Giving Programs; Chemistry; Engineering/technology; Science; Public affairs.
Programs:
Community Scholarship: The foundation annually awards two $1,000 college scholarships to high school seniors to pursue an academic interest in forestry. The program is limited to the Pacific Northwest.
Engineering Scholarship: The foundation annually awards two $6,000 four-year college scholarships to high school seniors to pursue an academic interest in chemical, mechanical, paper, or science engineering. The program is limited to Nassau County, Florida, Wayne County, Georgia, and the Pacific Northwest.
Forestry Scholarship: The foundation annually awards a $6,000 four-year college scholarship to a high school senior to pursue an academic interest in forestry. The program is limited to Nassau County, Florida, Wayne County, Georgia, and the Pacific Northwest.
Rayonier College Scholarship Program: The foundation annually awards $2,500 four year college scholarships to children of employees of Rayonier.
Technical/Vocational Scholarship: The foundation annually awards three $2,000 two-year college scholarships to high school seniors to pursue an academic interest in manufacturing. The program is limited to Nassau County, Florida and Wayne County, Georgia.
Type of support: Annual campaigns; Capital campaigns; Conferences/seminars; Continuing support; Employee-related scholarships; Equipment; General/operating support; Matching/challenge support; Program development; Scholarship funds; Scholarships—to individuals.
Geographic limitations: Giving primarily in areas of company operations in Nassau County, FL, Wayne County, GA, and the Olympic Peninsula, WA, area.
Support limitations: No support for religious organizations, advocacy organizations, fraternal or political organizations, or discriminatory organizations. No grants for chairs or professorships, courtesy or goodwill advertising for festival participation, tickets, telethons, raffles, auction, or memberships.
Publications: Application guidelines.
Application information: Applications accepted. Grants range from $250 to $2,500. Application form not required. Applicants should submit the following:
1) timetable for implementation and evaluation of project
2) how project will be sustained once grantmaker support is completed
3) statement of problem project will address
4) copy of IRS Determination Letter
5) geographic area to be served
6) copy of most recent annual report/audited financial statement/990
7) explanation of why grantmaker is considered an appropriate donor for project
8) detailed description of project and amount of funding requested
9) listing of additional sources and amount of support

Initial approach: Contact foundation for application form; contact guidance counselor from participating schools for scholarships
Copies of proposal: 1
Board meeting date(s): Feb.
Deadline(s): Oct. 31; Nov. 13 for scholarships
Officers and Directors:* Lee M. Thomas*, Chair.; Charles H. Hood, Pres.; W. Edwin Frazier III*, Secy.; Macdonald Auguste, Treas.; Hans E. Vanden Noort, Cont.; Paul G. Boynton; Timothy H. Brannon; Charles Margiotta.
EIN: 136064462
Selected grants: The following grants are a representative sample of this grantmaker's funding activity:
$2,500 to Georgia Institute of Technology, Atlanta, GA, 2010.
$2,500 to Georgia Institute of Technology, Atlanta, GA, 2010.
$2,500 to Georgia Institute of Technology, Atlanta, GA, 2010.
$2,500 to Georgia Institute of Technology, Atlanta, GA, 2010.
$2,500 to Urban League of Jacksonville, Jacksonville, FL, 2010.
$1,500 to University of West Georgia, Carrollton, GA, 2010.
$1,000 to Dreams Come True of Jacksonville, Jacksonville, FL, 2010.
$1,000 to Habitat for Humanity of Jacksonville, Jacksonville, FL, 2010.
$1,000 to Jacksonville Symphony Association, Jacksonville, FL, 2010.
$1,000 to Urban League of Jacksonville, Jacksonville, FL, 2010.

3135
Raytheon Company

870 Winter St.
Waltham, MA 02451 (781) 522-3000
FAX: (781) 860-2172

Company URL: http://www.raytheon.com
Establishment information: Established in 1922.
Company type: Public company
Company ticker symbol and exchange: RTN/NYSE
International Securities Identification Number: US7551115071
Business activities: Manufactures missiles, radar systems, sensors and electro-optics, intelligence, surveillance, and reconnaissance systems, command, control, communication, and information systems, naval systems, air traffic control systems, and aircraft integration systems; manufactures aircraft.
Business type (SIC): Search and navigation equipment; aircraft and parts; guided missiles and space vehicles
Financial profile for 2012: Number of employees, 67,800; assets, $26,686,000,000; sales volume, $24,414,000,000; pre-tax net income, $2,779,000,000; expenses, $21,425,000,000; liabilities, $18,660,000,000
Fortune 1000 ranking: 2012—124th in revenues, 112th in profits, and 204th in assets
Forbes 2000 ranking: 2012—386th in sales, 317th in profits, and 808th in assets
Corporate officers: William H. Swanson, Chair. and C.E.O.; Thomas A. Kennedy, Exec. V.P. and C.O.O.; David C. Wajsgras, Sr. V.P. and C.F.O.; Jay B. Stephens, Sr. V.P., Genl. Counsel, and Secy.; Keith

J. Peden, Sr. V.P., Human Resources; Mike J. Wood, V.P., Cont., and C.A.O.; Rebecca R. Rhoads, V.P. and C.I.O.; Richard A. Goglia, V.P. and Treas.; Pamela A. Wickham, V.P., Comms.
Board of directors: William H. Swanson, Chair.; James E. Cartwright; Vernon E. Clark; John M. Deutch; Stephen Hadley; Frederic M. Poses; Michael C. Ruettgers; Ronald L. Skates; William R. Spivey, Ph.D.; Linda G. Stuntz
Subsidiary: Raytheon Aircraft Company, Wichita, KS
Plants: Huntsville, AL; Tucson, AZ; El Segundo, Goleta, CA; Washington, DC; St. Petersburg, FL; Fort Wayne, IN; Andover, Bedford, Burlington, Marlborough, Sudbury, Tewksbury, Waltham, MA; Nashua, NH; White Sands, NM; Portsmouth, RI; Dallas, El Paso, Fort Worth, Greenville, Sherman, Waco, TX
Giving statement: Giving through the Raytheon Company Contributions Program.
Company EIN: 951778500

Raytheon Company Contributions Program

Waltham Woods
870 Winter St.
Waltham, MA 02451-1449 (781) 522-5119
E-mail: corporatecontributions@raytheon.com; URL: http://www.raytheon.com/responsibility/community/local/giving/

Contact: Michael Greenberg, Community Rels. Opers. Mgr.
Purpose and activities: Raytheon makes charitable contributions to nonprofit organizations involved with math and science education, armed services, and local communities. Support is given in areas of company operations.
Fields of interest: Education, services; Education; Boys & girls clubs; Youth development, adult & child programs; Community/economic development; Mathematics; Science; Military/veterans' organizations.
Programs:
FIRST Robotics Scholarship Program: The company annually awards $1,000 scholarships to First Robotics team members and competitors who plan to pursue higher education as math, science, or technology majors. Scholarships are available for vocational and technical training and associate's and bachelor's degrees. The program is administered by Scholarship America.
Matching Gifts for Education Program: The company matches contributions made by employees of Raytheon to public and private elementary and secondary schools, community colleges, and universities on a one-for-one basis. The company also matches employee contributions made to the United Negro College Fund, the American Indian College Fund, and the Hispanic Association of Colleges and Universities.
MathMovesU: Through MathMovesU, the company engages middle school students in math by demonstrating the connection between math, their passions and interests, and "cool" careers to encourage more success in STEM. The program includes MathMovesU events at local schools; a Sum of all Thrills experience at Walt Disney Epcot; the "In the Numbers" game in partnership with the New England Patriots on display at the Hall at Patriot Place; a Mathcounts National Competition; a website; and scholarship and grant opportunities.
MathMovesU - Math Hero Award: The company awards grants to teachers who are currently teaching a mathematics curriculum at a middle or high school and volunteer working with an approved math-related nonprofit organization. Recipients are chosen based on their plans for using the grant to promote math and make learning fun in their schools. The company awards up to three $2,500 grants to recipients located in areas of Raytheon operations in AZ, CO, FL, IN, MA, RI, TX, and VA, and five awards of $2,500 to recipients located outside of Raytheon's operations. The company will also award a matching grant of $2,500 to the school where each recipient is employed or to another approved math-related nonprofit organization of the recipient's choice. The program is administered by Scholarship America.
MathMovesU Middle School Scholarship and Grant Program: The company honors 6th, 7th, and 8th grade students who submit a paper or multimedia response to "How does MATH put the action in your passion?" Honorees are awarded a STEM campership of up to $1, 000 or a traditional scholarship of $1,000 for post-secondary education. A matching grant of $1,000 is also awarded to the recipient's school to be used for math-related programs. The program is administered by Scholarship America.
Raytheon Employee Disaster Relief Fund: The company awards disaster relief grants of up to $2,500 to employees of Raytheon who have faced catastrophic events. Recipients must be working in a full or part-time capacity at the time of the disaster and must be nominated by a Raytheon Company Human Resources Manager.
Raytheon Scholars: The company awards $1,000 scholarships to children of employees of Raytheon for higher education, including vocational and technical training, and associate's and bachelor's degrees. The program is administered by Scholarship America.
The Fund in Support of Our Troops: The company, in partnership with Raytheon employees, supports a variety of initiatives that honor members of the armed services. Through the Fund, the company supports nine pre-selected organizations: Air Force Aid Society, American Red Cross Armed Forces Emergency Services, Army Emergency Relief Fund, Coast Guard Mutual Assistance Organization, Navy-Marine Corps Relief Society, Special Operations Warrior Foundation, USO, Veterans of Foreign Wars Foundation, and the Wounded Warrior Project.
Type of support: Building/renovation; Capital campaigns; Donated equipment; Emergency funds; Employee matching gifts; Employee volunteer services; Employee-related scholarships; Endowments; General/operating support; Grants to individuals; Program development; Sponsorships; Technical assistance.
Geographic limitations: Giving in areas of company operations, with emphasis on AZ, CO, FL, IN, MA, RI, TX, and VA.
Support limitations: No support for United Way-supported organizations, religious, fraternal, political, athletic, or veterans' organizations, health or disease-specific organizations, private foundations, private K-12 schools, clubs, or social groups. No grants to individuals (except for scholarships), or for basic research projects, sponsorships of athletic teams, golf tournaments, or band competitions, conferences, tournaments, or events.
Publications: Application guidelines.
Application information: Applications accepted. Telephone calls are not encouraged. The Corporate Contributions Department handles giving. The company has a staff that only handles contributions. Application form required.
Initial approach: Complete online eligibility quiz and application
Copies of proposal: 1
Deadline(s): None
Final notification: 2 months
Number of staff: 2 full-time professional; 1 part-time support.

3136
RBC Wealth Management

(formerly RBC Dain Rauscher Corp.)
60 S. 6th St.
Minneapolis, MN 55402-4422
(612) 371-2811

Company URL: http://www.rbcwm-usa.com
Establishment information: Established in 1909.
Company type: Subsidiary of a foreign company
Business activities: Provides investment advisory services.
Business type (SIC): Security and commodity services
Corporate officer: John Godfrey Taft, C.E.O.
Giving statement: Giving through the RBC Wealth Management Corporate Giving Program, the Ferris, Baker Watts Foundation, and the RBC Foundation USA.

RBC Wealth Management Corporate Giving Program

(formerly RBC Dain Rauscher Corp. Contributions Program)
RBC Plaza, MS P20
60 S. 6th St.
Minneapolis, MN 55402-4422 (612) 371-2811
E-mail: Shana.Deuel@rbc.com; Tel. for Shana Deuel, Sponsorship Mktg. Mgr.: (612) 371-2938; Contact for The Human Touch: Sheena Doman, Sponsorship Consultant, RBC Wealth Management, RBC Plaza, MS P20, 60 South 6th St., Minneapolis, MN 55402; tel.: (612) 371-7270; e-mail: sheena.doman@rbc.com. Application address for RBC Blue Water Project Leadership Grants: Senior Mgr., Corp Donations, RBC, RBC Centre, 155 Wellington Street West, 18th Fl., Toronto, Ontario, M5V 3K7; e-mail: bluewaterproject@rbc.com; URL: http://www.rbcwm-usa.com/DRP_1.0/Public_Site/Common_Pages/DRP_1.0VContentIndex/1,73373,4-3-0-0,00.html

Contact: Shana Deuel, Sponsorship Mktg. Mgr.
Purpose and activities: As a complement to its foundation, RBC Wealth Management also makes charitable contributions to nonprofit organizations directly. Special emphasis is directed toward organizations with which employees are involved. Support is given primarily in areas of company operations in the U.S., Canada, the Caribbean, and United Kingdom.
Fields of interest: Performing arts, theater; Performing arts, music; Arts; Elementary/secondary education; Education; Environment, water pollution; Environment, water resources; Public health, clean water supply; Athletics/sports, training; Human services, fund raising/fund distribution; Children, services; Family services; Human services.
Program:
RBC Blue Water Project: The RBC Blue Water Project is a wide-ranging, multi-year program to help foster a culture of water stewardship. The program will provide $50 million (CAD) in charitable grants to nonprofit organizations that protect watersheds and provide or ensure access to clean drinking water; promote responsible and sustainable water use with RBC employees and clients through education and awareness programs that create an understanding of the value and vulnerability of water resources, and reduce the intensity of RBC's water footprint; encourage the growth of North American businesses

that develop and commercialize innovative solutions to the water issues facing the world and increase RBC's ability to provide financial services to these companies; take a leadership role to encourage the involvement of other corporations and foster a spirit of collaboration among and between all sectors to help protect the world's fresh water resources.
Type of support: Employee volunteer services; General/operating support; Sponsorships.
Geographic limitations: Giving primarily in areas of company operations in the U.S., Canada, the Caribbean, and United Kingdom.
Support limitations: No support for political organizations or parties, organizations whose primary purpose is lobbying or political action, organizations that have religious or sectarian elements or outcomes, third parties raising funds for charity, private (fee-based) schools, or post-secondary schools that have received capital funding from RBC in the last 10 years, for RBC Blue Water Project Community Action Grants. No grants for fundraising events in which less than 80 percent of event proceeds are used to benefit a qualified charitable organization or effort; no grants that are solely for research or infrastructure, or are used to underwrite advertising, media production, or media buys for the RBC Blue Water Project; no grants to individuals, or for endowments, conferences or events, sports tournaments, or student trips, for RBC Blue Water Project Community Action Grants.
Publications: Application guidelines; Informational brochure.
Application information: Applications accepted. Application form required. Applicants should submit the following:
1) role played by volunteers
2) timetable for implementation and evaluation of project
3) results expected from proposed grant
4) statement of problem project will address
5) name, address and phone number of organization
6) brief history of organization and description of its mission
7) geographic area to be served
8) copy of most recent annual report/audited financial statement/990
9) how project's results will be evaluated or measured
10) list of company employees involved with the organization
11) listing of board of directors, trustees, officers and other key people and their affiliations
12) detailed description of project and amount of funding requested
13) plans for cooperation with other organizations, if any
14) contact person
15) copy of current year's organizational budget and/or project budget
16) plans for acknowledgement
17) additional materials/documentation

Proposals for the RBC Blue Water Project Leadership Grants should include the names and contact information for all partner organizations in a collaborative project, two letters of support, an explanation of the organization's two most significant accomplishments, a list of stakeholders.
Initial approach: Download application form and send completed proposal by e-mail, or mail to headquarters, for RBC Blue Water Projects Leadership Grants; Complete online application for RBC Blue Water Project Community Action Grants
Deadline(s): Feb. 3 for the RBC Blue Water Project Leadership Grants
Final notification: July 1 for RBC Blue Water Project Leadership Grants; 45 days for RBC Blue Water Project Community Action Grants

RBC Foundation USA

(formerly RBC Dain Rauscher Foundation)
60 S. 6th St., M.S. P20
Minneapolis, MN 55402-4422 (612) 371-2936
FAX: (612) 371-7933;
E-mail: fndapplications@rbc.com; Additional tel.: (612) 371-2765; E-mail for Sherry Koster, Mgr., sherry.koster@rbc.com; URL: http://www.rbcwealthmanagement.com/usa/community/cid-273369.html

Establishment information: Incorporated in 1960 in MN.
Donors: Dain Rauscher Inc.; RBC Dain Rauscher Corp.; RBC Capital Markets Corp.
Contact: Sherry Koster, Mgr.
Financial data (yr. ended 10/31/11): Assets, $952,355 (M); gifts received, $2,247,000; expenditures, $2,244,666; qualifying distributions, $2,244,666; giving activities include $2,244,666 for grants.
Purpose and activities: The foundation supports organizations involved with arts and culture, human services, and civic affairs. Special emphasis is directed toward programs designed to promote education and health.
Fields of interest: Arts, cultural/ethnic awareness; Visual arts; Performing arts, music; Arts; Elementary/secondary education; Adult education —literacy, basic skills & GED; Education, services; Education, reading; Education; Health care; Mental health/crisis services, public education; Mental health, treatment; Mental health, disorders; Mental health, depression; Mental health/crisis services; Employment, training; Food services; Youth development, adult & child programs; Youth development; Family services; Human services, financial counseling; Human services; Community/economic development; Public affairs, citizen participation; Public affairs Children; Youth; Economically disadvantaged.
Programs:
Arts and Culture: The foundation supports arts and culture programs designed to enrich the quality of life in the communities where RBC employees and clients live. Special emphasis is directed toward the RBC Emerging Artists Project; and programs designed to provide arts access for diverse populations.
Civic Programs: The foundation supports programs designed to promote economic growth and community diversity. Special emphasis is directed toward citizenship and support for newcomers; and community economic development.
Education: The foundation supports K-12 education programs designed to prepare students for future success. Special emphasis is directed toward programs designed to promote academic mentoring or college-preparatory activities; and youth financial literacy.
Employee Gift Matching Program: The foundation matches contributions made by employees and executives of RBC Wealth Management to nonprofit organizations.
Employee Volunteer Grant Program: The foundation awards $500 grants to nonprofit organizations with which employees of RBC Wealth Management volunteer at least 40 hours per year.
Health: The foundation supports the RBC Children's Mental Health Project designed to help children lead normal and productive lives and reduce the social and economic burden of mental illness through early intervention and public education. Health grants are exclusive to the RBC Children's Mental Health Project.
Human Services: The foundation supports programs designed to foster economic independence and promote self-sufficiency. Special emphasis is directed toward programs designed to provide emergency food, shelter, and basic needs; promote adult literacy and employment training; and programs designed to serve at-risk youth through advocacy or job skill or readiness training.
RBC After School Grants Project: The foundation supports programs designed to provide a range of structured activities for K-12 students after the school day ends. The program is designed to improve academic achievement of students; increase students' self-esteem through skill development, team-building and conflict resolution; promote mentoring, tutoring, literacy education, music and art lessons, computer instruction, and homework help; develop partnerships between home, schools, and the community; promote a financially accessible initiative with no or very low participation fees; provide a safe environment; and assist at-risk or underserved communities. Special emphasis is directed toward community-based organizations with multiple program partners and volunteers that have broad participant appeal within a community.
RBC Children's Mental Health Project - Early Intervention: The foundation supports mental illness early intervention programs designed to address prevalent childhood and adolescent mental illnesses, including anxiety, conduct disorders, and mood disorders; promote evidence-based programs validated by scientific data and scientifically sound studies that have demonstrated consistent positive outcomes; facilitate through a community-based organization or family resource center that collaborates with all levels of service providers to provide an integrated model of service delivery; and focus on children and youth between the ages of 0 to 18.
RBC Children's Mental Health Project - Public Education: The foundation supports mental health public education programs designed to teach parents, caregivers, teachers, and professionals to recognize the early signs of mental illness and to encourage the family to seek treatment from a health professional. Special emphasis is directed toward programs designed to educate parents on how to access appropriate services and effectively advocate for their children; educate teachers and healthcare professionals on how to identify the signs of mental health problems and learn how to take early action; educate the public, including adults, youth and children on the nature and prevalence of children's mental health issues and how to access help; and increase understanding and awareness and reduce the stigma attached to mental illness.
RBC Emerging Artists Project: The foundation awards grants and supports apprentice programs designed to bridge the gap from academic excellence to professional careers in all aspects of the arts. Special emphasis is directed toward programs designed to support artists at an early stage in their careers who have completed their basic educational training and have created a modest independent body of work; educate and raise awareness about the importance of arts in the community; and provide emerging artists the opportunity to demonstrate their talent publicly through performance or exhibition and/or to provide connections to professional contacts including agents, publishers, etc.
Type of support: Annual campaigns; Continuing support; Employee matching gifts; Employee volunteer services; General/operating support; Program development.
Geographic limitations: Giving on a national basis in areas of company operations, with emphasis on the Twin Cities, MN, metropolitan area.

Support limitations: No support for religious, political, fraternal, or veterans' organizations, athletic teams, or hospitals, nursing homes, hospices, or daycare facilities. No grants to individuals, or for sponsorships, fundraising events, athletic events or scholarships, travel, academic, medical, or scientific research, recreational or athletic programs, audio or video recording projects, literary or media art projects, artist enrichment programs, medical, health, mental health, or disease-specific or disease-related services, senior citizen programs, or developmental disabilities or disorders, including deafness and blindness, non-K-12 educational programs, environmental education programs, programs limited to special needs students, or childcare or day care programs.
Publications: Application guidelines.
Application information: Applications accepted. Letters of inquiry for organizations located in the Twin Cities, MN, area should be submitted if the applying organization did not receive funding from the RBC Foundation last year. Support is limited to 1 contribution per organization during any given year. Application form required. Applicants should submit the following:
1) statement of problem project will address
2) principal source of support for project in the past
3) name, address and phone number of organization
4) brief history of organization and description of its mission
5) copy of most recent annual report/audited financial statement/990
6) how project's results will be evaluated or measured
7) list of company employees involved with the organization
8) listing of board of directors, trustees, officers and other key people and their affiliations
9) detailed description of project and amount of funding requested
10) contact person
11) copy of current year's organizational budget and/or project budget
12) listing of additional sources and amount of support

Initial approach: Complete online letter of inquiry for new applicants located in Twin Cities, MN; complete online application form for returning grantees located in Twin Cities, MN; complete online application form for organizations located outside of the Twin Cities, MN metropolitan area
Board meeting date(s): Feb., Mar., Aug., and Sept.
Deadline(s): Jan. 15 and June 15 for new applicants located in Twin Cities, MN; Feb. 2 and June 29 for returning grantees located in Twin Cities, MN; generally Feb. 17, Mar. 15, July 13, and July 31 for organizations located outside of Twin Cities, MN, metropolitan area. Deadlines vary per state. Please check website
Final notification: Within 90 days

Directors: Martha Baumbach; Mike Kavanagh; John Taft; Mary Zimmer.
Number of staff: 1 full-time professional; 1 full-time support.
EIN: 416030639
Selected grants: The following grants are a representative sample of this grantmaker's funding activity:
$25,000 to Artspace, Minneapolis, MN, 2010.
$15,000 to Baltimore Community Foundation, Baltimore, MD, 2010.
$8,000 to YMCA of Metropolitan Minneapolis, Minneapolis, MN, 2010.
$7,500 to Boys and Girls Club of New Haven, New Haven, CT, 2010.
$5,000 to Achieve Minneapolis, Minneapolis, MN, 2010.
$5,000 to Trust for Public Land, San Francisco, CA, 2010.
$3,000 to Baltimore School for the Arts Foundation, Baltimore, MD, 2010.
$3,000 to Community Theater of Cedar Rapids, Cedar Rapids, IA, 2010.
$3,000 to Jewish Community Center of Houston, Houston, TX, 2010.
$3,000 to Legal Aid Society of Milwaukee, Milwaukee, WI, 2010.

3137
RBS Citizens, N.A.

1 Citizens Plz.
Providence, RI 02903-1344 (401) 456-7000

Company URL: http://www.citizensbank.com
Establishment information: Established in 1828.
Company type: Subsidiary of a private company
Business activities: Operates commercial bank.
Business type (SIC): Banks/commercial
Financial profile for 2011: Assets, $129,654,000,000; liabilities, $106,261,000,000
Corporate officers: Ellen Alemany, Chair. and C.E.O.; John Fawcett, Exec. V.P. and C.F.O.; Robert Nelson, C.A.O.
Board of director: Ellen Alemany, Chair.
Subsidiary: Citizens Mortgage Corp., Manchester, NH
Giving statement: Giving through the RBS Citizens, N.A. Corporate Giving Program and the Citizens Charitable Foundation.

RBS Citizens, N.A. Corporate Giving Program

1 Citizens Plz. #1
Providence, RI 02903-1345 (401) 456-7096
URL: http://www.citizensbank.com/community/corporate/sponsorships.aspx

Purpose and activities: As a complement to its foundation, Citizens Bank makes charitable contributions to organizations directly. Emphasis is given to organizations involved with affordable housing, serving basic human needs, community development, and economic self-sufficiency. Giving limited to areas of company operations.
Fields of interest: Housing/shelter, expense aid; Housing/shelter; Human services, financial counseling; Human services; Community/economic development Economically disadvantaged.
Type of support: General/operating support; Sponsorships.
Geographic limitations: Giving primarily in areas of company operations in CT, DE, MA, ME, NH, NJ, NY, PA, RI, and VT.
Support limitations: No support for political, religious, labor, fraternal, veterans', or discriminatory organizations, governmental or quasi-governmental public agencies or organizations, foundations, public or private educational institutions, or single disease/issue information or research organizations. No grants to individuals, or for annual appeals, operating deficits, underwriting of conferences or seminars, endowments, annual operating support, trips or tours, payment on bank loans (including loans from Citizens Bank), advertising or fundraising activities, or historic preservation.
Publications: Application guidelines.
Application information: Applications accepted. State Contributions Committees review all requests. A meeting and additional information may be required prior to a final determination. Citizens' charitable grants range widely in size. Multi-year grants are generally for a capital campaign and are paid over a three-year period. Application form required. Applicants should submit the following:
1) brief history of organization and description of its mission
2) listing of board of directors, trustees, officers and other key people and their affiliations
3) listing of additional sources and amount of support

Initial approach: Complete online eligibility quiz and application
Deadline(s): None
Final notification: 8 weeks

Citizens Charitable Foundation

770 Legacy Pl., MLP 120
Dedham, MA 02026
URL: http://www.citizensbank.com/community/corporate/grants.aspx

Establishment information: Established in 1967 in RI; reincorporated in 2005.
Donors: Citizens Savings Bank; Citizens Trust Co.; Citizens Bank of Rhode Island; Cambridgeport Bank; Charter One Bank; The Citizens Bank Mid-Atlantic Charitable Foundation; Citizens Charitable Foundation; RBS Citizens, N.A.
Financial data (yr. ended 12/31/11): Assets, $12,539,376 (M); gifts received, $8,857,298; expenditures, $12,861,599; qualifying distributions, $12,820,631; giving activities include $12,778,977 for 3,045 grants (high: $180,000; low: $10).
Purpose and activities: The foundation supports organizations involved with affordable housing, hunger programs, economic development activities, and financial education.
Fields of interest: Employment; Nutrition; Agriculture/food; Housing/shelter, development; Housing/shelter; Human services; Economic development; Community/economic development Economically disadvantaged.
Program:
Colleague Matching Gift Program: The foundation matches contributions made by employees of RBS Citizens Financial Group to nonprofit organizations on a one-for-one basis from $25 to $1,000 per employee, per year.
Type of support: Employee matching gifts; Employee volunteer services; General/operating support; Program development; Public relations services; Scholarship funds; Sponsorships.
Geographic limitations: Giving on a national basis in areas of company operations, with emphasis on CT, DE, IL, MA, MI, NH, NJ, NY, OH, PA, RI, and VT.
Support limitations: No support for discriminatory organizations, single disease/issue information or research organizations, religious organizations, labor, fraternal, or veterans' organizations, political organizations, governmental or quasi-governmental public agencies or organizations, grantmakers, or public or private educational institutions. No grants to individuals, or for annual campaigns, political projects, debt reduction, conferences or seminars, endowments, trips or tours, advertising or fundraising activities, or historic preservation; no loans.
Publications: Application guidelines; Informational brochure.
Application information: Applications accepted. Prospective applicants must take the charitable grant eligibility quiz on the foundation's website. A site visit and additional information may be requested at a later date. Application form not required. Applicants should submit the following:
1) principal source of support for project in the past
2) name, address and phone number of organization
3) copy of IRS Determination Letter

4) brief history of organization and description of its mission
5) copy of most recent annual report/audited financial statement/990
6) how project's results will be evaluated or measured
7) listing of board of directors, trustees, officers and other key people and their affiliations
8) detailed description of project and amount of funding requested
9) copy of current year's organizational budget and/or project budget

Proposals should include a copy of the organization's Affirmative Action/Equal Opportunity policy.

Initial approach: Complete online application or submit proposal to nearest Public Relations Department
Copies of proposal: 1
Board meeting date(s): Monthly
Deadline(s): None
Final notification: 8 weeks

Directors: Reza Aghamirzadeh; Heidi Brooks; Cindy Erikson; Bruce Figueroa; Denise Leyhe; Robert Matthews; Quincy Miller; Tony Moscrop; Kevin Walsh.
Trustee: RBS Citizens, N.A.
Number of staff: 4 full-time professional.
EIN: 202302039
Selected grants: The following grants are a representative sample of this grantmaker's funding activity:
$250,000 to United Way of Massachusetts Bay, Boston, MA, 2010. For general charitable purpose.
$180,000 to United Way of Rhode Island, Providence, RI, 2011. For general support.
$125,000 to Comprehensive Community Action Program, Cranston, RI, 2010. For general support.
$100,000 to Chamber of Commerce, Greater Philadelphia, Philadelphia, PA, 2010. For general charitable purpose.
$100,000 to Cradles to Crayons, Brighton, MA, 2011. For general support.
$100,000 to Greater Boston Interfaith Organization, Dorchester, MA, 2011. For general support.
$100,000 to Greater Chicago Food Depository, Chicago, IL, 2011. For general support.
$100,000 to Massachusetts Housing and Shelter Alliance, Boston, MA, 2010. For general charitable purpose.
$100,000 to Philadelphia Mural Arts Advocates, Philadelphia, PA, 2010. For general charitable purpose.
$100,000 to Rhode Island Community Food Bank Association, Providence, RI, 2010. For general charitable purpose.
$75,000 to HAP, Inc., Springfield, MA, 2011. For general support.
$40,000 to Brown University, Providence, RI, 2010. For general charitable purpose.
$33,334 to Roxbury Community College, Roxbury Crossing, MA, 2011. For general support.
$10,000 to Affordable Housing, Education and Development, Littleton, NH, 2011. For general support.
$10,000 to Lawrence CommunityWorks, Lawrence, MA, 2010. For general charitable purpose.
$10,000 to Mount Airy USA, Philadelphia, PA, 2011. For general support.
$10,000 to Rodman Ride for Kids, Foxboro, MA, 2010. For general charitable purpose.
$7,000 to Bucks County Opportunity Council, Doylestown, PA, 2011. For general support.
$7,000 to Jewish Family Services of Delaware, Wilmington, DE, 2010. For general charitable purpose.
$5,550 to Massachusetts Nonprofit Network, Boston, MA, 2011. For general support.

3138
RBS Securities Inc.

(doing business as RBS)
(formerly Greenwich Capital Markets, Inc.)
600 Steamboat Rd., Ste. 2
Stamford, CT 06901-7168 (866) 884-2071

Company URL: http://ci.rbs.com
Establishment information: Established in 1981.
Company type: Subsidiary of a foreign company
Business activities: Provides investment advisory services; provides securities brokerage services.
Business type (SIC): Security and commodity services; brokers and dealers/security
Financial profile for 2009: Number of employees, 563
Corporate officers: Ben Carpenter, Co-Pres. and Co-C.E.O.; Jay N. Levine, Co-Pres. and Co-C.E.O.
Offices: San Francisco, CA; Washington, DC; Atlanta, GA; Chicago, IL; Boston, MA
Giving statement: Giving through the RBS Foundation Inc.

RBS Foundation Inc.

(formerly Greenwich Capital Foundation)
600 Washington Blvd.
Stamford, CT 06901-3726

Establishment information: Established in 2002.
Donors: Benjamin Carpenter; Jay Levine; Greenwich Capital Markets, Inc.; Jeffrey Mullins.
Financial data (yr. ended 08/31/11): Assets, $529,357 (M); gifts received, $206; expenditures, $131,516; qualifying distributions, $131,516; giving activities include $131,000 for 13 grants (high: $25,000; low: $1,000).
Purpose and activities: The foundation supports camps and organizations involved with health, legal aid, human services, and small businesses.
Fields of interest: Health care; Legal services; Recreation, camps; Boys & girls clubs; Children, services; Developmentally disabled, centers & services; Human services; Community development, small businesses; United Ways and Federated Giving Programs.
Type of support: General/operating support; Program development.
Geographic limitations: Giving primarily in CT and NY.
Support limitations: No grants to individuals.
Application information: Applications not accepted. Contributes only to pre-selected organizations.
Officers and Directors:* Robert McKillip*, Chair. and Pres.; Carol P. Mathis*, C.F.O.; Jennifer Fitzgibbon*, Treas.; James Esposito*, Genl. Counsel.
EIN: 061630962
Selected grants: The following grants are a representative sample of this grantmaker's funding activity:
$15,000 to Faith Tabernacle Missionary Baptist Church, Stamford, CT, 2009.
$10,000 to My Sisters Place, White Plains, NY, 2009.
$10,000 to Philharmonic-Symphony Society of New York, New York, NY, 2009.
$5,000 to Pro Bono Partnership, White Plains, NY, 2009.
$3,700 to Multiple Sclerosis Society, National, New York, NY, 2009.
$2,500 to Good Shepherd Services, New York, NY, 2009.
$1,790 to Amyotrophic Lateral Sclerosis Association, Ambler, PA, 2009.
$1,000 to Bucknell University, Lewisburg, PA, 2009.
$1,000 to Lutheran South Academy, Houston, TX, 2009.
$1,000 to Picture House Regional Film Center, Pelham, NY, 2009.

3139
RCM Capital Management, LLC

(formerly Dresdner RCM Global Investors LLC)
555 Mission St., Ste. 1700
San Francisco, CA 94105-0924
(415) 954-5400

Company URL: http://www.rcm.com
Establishment information: Established in 1970.
Company type: Subsidiary of a foreign company
Business activities: Provides investment advisory services.
Business type (SIC): Security and commodity services
Corporate officers: Simon Fraser, Chair.; Udo Frank, C.E.O.; Andreas Utermann, C.I.O.
Board of director: Simon Fraser, Chair.
Giving statement: Giving through the RCM Capital Management LLC Corporate Giving Program.

RCM Capital Management LLC Corporate Giving Program

(formerly Dresdner RCM Global Investors LLC Corporate Giving Program)
555 Mission St., Ste. 1700
San Francisco, CA 94105-0924 (415) 954-5400
FAX: (415) 954-8200; URL: http://www.rcm.com/sanfran/about_charitable.php

Purpose and activities: RCM makes charitable contributions to nonprofit organizations involved with arts and culture, education, the environment, health, and human services. Support is given primarily in the San Francisco Bay area, California.
Fields of interest: Arts; Education; Environment; Health care; Human services.
Type of support: General/operating support.
Geographic limitations: Giving primarily in the San Francisco Bay area, CA.
Publications: Grants list.
Application information: Applications not accepted. Unsolicited requests are not accepted. All giving is handled through the Vanguard Charitable Endowment Program.
Number of staff: None.

3140
RE/MAX International, Inc.

(doing business as RE/MAX Equity Group, Inc.)
5075 S. Syracuse St.
P.O. Box 3907
Denver, CO 80237-2712 (303) 770-5531

Company URL: http://www.remax.com
Establishment information: Established in 1973.
Company type: Private company
Business activities: Operates network of franchisee owned and operated real estate offices.
Business type (SIC): Real estate agents and managers
Corporate officers: David Liniger, Chair.; Gail A. Liniger, Vice-Chair.; Margaret M. Kelly, C.E.O.; Vinnie Tracey, Pres.; David M. K. Metzger, Exec. V.P., C.O.O., and C.F.O.; Pat Lawrence, Sr. V.P., Human Resources; Kelly Hickey, V.P. and Cont.; Shaun White, V.P., Corp. Comms.
Board of directors: David Liniger, Chair.; Gail A. Liniger, Vice-Chair.; Gilbert Baird; Richard Covey;

Roger Dow; David L. Ferguson; Ronald Harrison; Daryl Jesperson; Margaret Kelly; Daniel Predovich; Vinnie Tracey
Giving statement: Giving through the Equity Group Foundation and the RE/MAX Relief Fund.

The Equity Group Foundation

P.O. Box 25308
Portland, OR 97298-0308 (503) 670-3000
FAX: (503) 670-8108; URL: http://aboutnwrealestate.com/foundation/

Establishment information: Established in 2000 in OR.
Donor: RE/MAX Equity Group, Inc.
Financial data (yr. ended 12/31/12): Assets, $12,420 (M); gifts received, $53,542; expenditures, $52,065; qualifying distributions, $50,915; giving activities include $50,915 for 21 grants (high: $5,694; low: $120).
Purpose and activities: The foundation supports organizations involved with health, cancer, recreation, and human services.
Fields of interest: Health care; Health organizations; Human services.
Type of support: Equipment; General/operating support; Program development; Scholarship funds; Sponsorships.
Geographic limitations: Giving primarily in areas of company operations in Portland, Salem, and Willamette, OR and Vancouver, WA.
Support limitations: No grants to individuals.
Publications: Application guidelines; Grants list.
Application information: Applications accepted. Application form required. Applicants should submit the following:
1) timetable for implementation and evaluation of project
2) results expected from proposed grant
3) statement of problem project will address
4) name, address and phone number of organization
5) copy of IRS Determination Letter
6) how project's results will be evaluated or measured
7) contact person
8) copy of current year's organizational budget and/or project budget
9) listing of additional sources and amount of support

Initial approach: Proposal
Copies of proposal: 2
Deadline(s): None
Final notification: 2 months

Officer and Directors:* Sharlene Giard*, Chair.; S. Joan Hamrick; James Homolka.
EIN: 931293204

RE/MAX Relief Fund

5075 S. Syracuse St.
Denver, CO 80237-2712 (303) 770-5531

Financial data (yr. ended 12/31/11): Revenue, $7,135; assets, $90,848 (M); gifts received, $6,810; expenditures, $18,321; giving activities include $10,250 for grants.
Purpose and activities: The fund provides assistance to current and future employees and independent affiliates of the RE/MAX franchise network, their families, and others that are victims of a natural or civil disaster.
Fields of interest: Safety/disasters.
Officers: Mike Reagan, Pres.; Kelly Hickey, V.P. and Treas.; Abby Lee, V.P.; Tamara Schulte, Secy.
Director: Terri Bohannon.
EIN: 203606368

3141
The Reader's Digest Association, Inc.

750 3rd Ave.
New York, NY 10017 (914) 238-1000
FAX: (914) 238-4559

Company URL: http://www.rda.com
Establishment information: Established in 1922.
Company type: Private company
Business activities: Publishes, markets, creates, and delivers printed and recorded products.
Business type (SIC): Periodical publishing and/or printing; book publishing and/or printing; audio and video equipment/household; motion picture and video tape distribution
Financial profile for 2011: Number of employees, 2,090; sales volume, $1,440,000,000
Corporate officers: Randall E. Curran, Chair.; Robert E. Guth, Pres. and C.E.O.; Paul R. Tomkins, Exec. V.P. and C.F.O.; Joe Held, Sr. V.P. and C.I.O.; Andrea Newborn, Sr. V.P., Genl. Counsel, and Secy.; Susan W. Cummiskey, Sr. V.P., Human Resources; Susan Fraysse Russ, V.P., Comms.
Board of directors: Randall Curran, Chair.; Robert E. Guth; Nick Cyprus; William Drewry; Keith Richman; Ryan Schaper; Doug Teitelbaum; Martin Wade
Subsidiaries: Ardee Music Publishing, Inc., Pleasantville, NY; QSP, Inc., Ridgefield, CT; R.D. Manufacturing Corp., Pleasantville, NY; RD Publications, Inc., Pleasantville, NY; Reader's Digest Entertainment, Inc., Pleasantville, NY; Reader's Digest Latinoamerica, S.A., Pleasantville, NY; Reader's Digest Sales and Services, Inc., New York, NY; SMDDMS, Inc., Pleasantville, NY; W.A. Publications, LLC, Pleasantville, NY
International operations: Australia; Austria; Belgium; Brazil; Canada; China; Colombia; Czech Republic; Finland; France; Germany; Hungary; Italy; Japan; Malaysia; Mexico; Netherlands; New Zealand; Norway; Philippines; Poland; Portugal; South Africa; Spain; Sweden; Switzerland; Thailand; United Kingdom
Giving statement: Giving through the Reader's Digest Association, Inc. Corporate Giving Program and the Reader's Digest Foundation.
Company EIN: 131726769

The Reader's Digest Association, Inc. Corporate Giving Program

Reader's Digest Rd.
Pleasantville, NY 10570-7001
URL: http://www.rda.com/our-company/philanthropy

Purpose and activities: As a complement to its foundation, Reader's Digest makes charitable contributions to nonprofit organizations directly. Support is given primarily in areas of company operations.
Fields of interest: Community/economic development; General charitable giving.
Program:
We Hear You America: Through the We Hear You America campaign, the company helps Americans and their hometowns with stimulus packages to stimulate tourism, civic works, job growth, and economic development. Individuals vote online and nominate their towns with photos and descriptions of what their town needs; and the company honors the towns with the most votes. Individuals will also be entered in a sweepstakes to win a family vacation anywhere in the U.S and a new car to take them there.
Type of support: General/operating support.
Geographic limitations: Giving primarily in areas of company operations.
Publications: Application guidelines.
Application information: Applications accepted.
Initial approach: Complete online nominations for We Hear You America
Deadline(s): Nov. 8 to Feb. 7 for We Hear You America
Final notification: Following review
Number of staff: None.

Reader's Digest Foundation

44 S. Broadway
White Plains, NY 10601-4425
URL: http://www.rda.com/our-company/philanthropy

Establishment information: Incorporated in 1938 in NY.
Donors: The Reader's Digest Association, Inc.; Wallace Preferred Stock Trust.
Contact: Elizabeth Longley
Financial data (yr. ended 06/30/11): Assets, $5,082,132 (M); expenditures, $576,500; qualifying distributions, $534,866; giving activities include $177,550 for 28 grants (high: $140,500; low: $500) and $97,250 for 308 employee matching gifts.
Purpose and activities: The foundation support organizations involved with arts and culture, education, health, hunger, and human services. Special emphasis is directed toward programs designed to create opportunities for Reader's Digest employees to make a difference in their local and global communities.
Fields of interest: Media, film/video; Media, print publishing; Arts; Health care; Food services; Food banks; Human services, gift distribution; Homeless, human services; Human services.
Programs:
Matching Gift Program: The foundation matches contributions made by employees of Reader's Digest Association to nonprofit organizations on a one-for-one basis from $25 to $25,000 per employee, per year.
Reader's Digest Foundation Scholarship Program: The foundation awards college scholarships of $1,000 up to $10,000 to children of employees of Reader's Digest Association. The program is administered by Scholarship America.
Volunteer Incentive Program: The foundation awards grants to local nonprofit organizations with which employees of Reader's Digest Association volunteer. The grants are available for ongoing volunteering and for volunteering at a one-time project.
Type of support: Employee matching gifts; Employee volunteer services; Employee-related scholarships; General/operating support; Scholarship funds.
Geographic limitations: Giving primarily in areas of company operations, with emphasis on Westchester County, NY; giving also to national organizations.
Support limitations: No support for religious, veterans', or fraternal organizations, private foundations, cultural organizations, environmental organizations, or local chapters of national organizations. No grants to individuals (except for employee-related scholarships), or for capital campaigns, endowments, annual campaigns, start-up needs, emergency needs, debt reduction, special projects, charitable dinners or fundraising events, television, film, or video productions, publications, workshops, conferences, seminars, religious endeavors, medical research, or health-related activities; no loans.
Application information: Applications not accepted. Unsolicited proposals are not accepted.

Officers and Directors:* Robert E. Guth, Chair.; Janis L. Braun, Secy.; William H. Magill, Treas.; Susan F. Russ*, Exec. Dir.; Mary Berner*, Chair.; Paul Gillow; Joanne Murray.
Number of staff: 3
EIN: 136120380
Selected grants: The following grants are a representative sample of this grantmaker's funding activity:
$500,000 to Boys and Girls Clubs of America, Atlanta, GA, 2010.
$131,000 to Scholarship America, Saint Peter, MN, 2010.
$10,000 to WestHab, Elmsford, NY, 2010. For general support.
$5,000 to Jacob Burns Film Center, Pleasantville, NY, 2010. For general support.

3142
Reading Blue Mountain & Northern Railroad Company

(formerly Blue Mountain & Reading Railroad)
P.O. Box 218
Port Clinton, PA 19549 (610) 562-2100

Company URL: http://www.readingnorthern.com
Establishment information: Established in 1983.
Company type: Private company
Business activities: Provides railroad transportation services.
Business type (SIC): Transportation/railroad
Corporate officers: Andy M. Muller, Jr., Chair. and C.E.O.; Wayne A. Michel, Pres.; Christina Muller-Levan, V.P., Admin; Tyler A. Glass, V.P., Opers.; Daniel R. Gilchrist, V.P., Sales and Mktg.; Andrea Coller, V.P., Sales
Board of directors: Andy M. Muller, Jr., Chair.; Beverly B. Hess; Laura Kennedy
Giving statement: Giving through the Reading Blue Mountain & Northern Railroad Scholarship Fund.

Reading Blue Mountain & Northern Railroad Scholarship Fund

P.O. Box 218
Port Clinton, PA 19549-0218

Establishment information: Classified as a company-sponsored operating fund in 1997.
Donor: Reading Blue Mountain & Northern Railroad Co.
Financial data (yr. ended 12/31/11): Assets, $1,408 (M); expenditures, $0; qualifying distributions, $0.
Purpose and activities: The foundation supports organizations involved with education.
Type of support: Scholarship funds.
Application information: Applications not accepted. Unsolicited requests for funds not accepted.
Officers: Christina J. Muller, Pres. and Secy.; Aaron P. Muller, V.P.; Philip Geschwindt, Treas.
EIN: 232971151

3143
Reagent Chemical & Research, Inc.

115 Rte. 202
Ringoes, NJ 08551-1908 (908) 284-2800

Company URL: http://www.reagentchemical.com
Establishment information: Established in 1959.
Company type: Private company
Business activities: Manufactures industrial inorganic chemicals; manufactures clay shooting targets.
Business type (SIC): Chemicals/industrial inorganic; games, toys, and sporting and athletic goods
Corporate officer: Jack Skeuse, Pres.
Subsidiaries: Cali'Co Foreign Sales Inc., Santa Rosa, CA; Cali'Co Hardwoods Inc., Santa Rosa, CA
Giving statement: Giving through the Thomas J. and Rita T. Skeuse Scholarship Fund, Inc.

The Thomas J. and Rita T. Skeuse Scholarship Fund, Inc.

115 Rte. 202-31 S.
Ringoes, NJ 08551

Establishment information: Established in 2000 in NJ.
Donor: Reagent Chemical & Research, Inc.
Financial data (yr. ended 12/31/11): Assets, $7,798 (M); gifts received, $16,100; expenditures, $11,250; qualifying distributions, $11,250; giving activities include $11,250 for grants to individuals.
Purpose and activities: The foundation awards college scholarships to employees of Reagent Chemical & Research, Inc.
Type of support: Employee-related scholarships.
Geographic limitations: Giving primarily in areas of company operations.
Application information: Applications not accepted. Unsolicited requests for funds not accepted.
Officer and Trustees:* John T. Skeuse*, Pres.; Elaine J. Finney; Nancy A. Maximuck; Brian Skeuse; Richard Skeuse; Thomas J. Skeuse, Jr.; Carol Skeuse-Hart.
EIN: 223741423

3144
RealNetworks, Inc.

2601 Elliott Ave.
P.O. Box 91123
Seattle, WA 98121-3306 (206) 674-2700
FAX: (206) 674-2696

Company URL: http://www.realnetworks.com
Establishment information: Established in 1994.
Company type: Public company
Company ticker symbol and exchange: RNWK/ NASDAQ
Business activities: Provides Internet media delivery and digital distribution solutions.
Business type (SIC): Computer services
Financial profile for 2012: Number of employees, 991; assets, $433,900,000; sales volume, $258,840,000; pre-tax net income, $57,360,000; expenses, $203,280,000; liabilities, $91,170,000
Corporate officers: Robert Glaser, Chair. and C.E.O.; Michael Parham, Sr. V.P. and Genl. Counsel.; Tim M. Wan, C.F.O. and Treas.
Board of directors: Robert Glaser, Chair.; John E. Cunningham IV; Michael T. Galgon; Kalpana Raina; Janice M. Roberts; Michael B. Slade; Dominique Trempont
International operations: France; Germany; Japan; United Kingdom
Giving statement: Giving through the RealNetworks, Inc. Corporate Giving Program and the RealNetworks Foundation.
Company EIN: 911628146

RealNetworks Foundation

c/o RealNetworks, Inc.
2601 Elliot Ave.
Seattle, WA 98121-1399 (866) 545-9205
E-mail: realgrants@easymatch.com; URL: http://www.realnetworks.com/realnetworks-foundation/

Establishment information: Established in 2000 in WA.
Donor: RealNetworks, Inc.
Financial data (yr. ended 12/31/11): Assets, $16,523,265 (M); expenditures, $1,537,554; qualifying distributions, $1,268,340; giving activities include $1,268,340 for grants.
Purpose and activities: The foundation supports programs designed to enhance the quality of life in areas of company operations; and enable alternative voices or foster the right of free speech throughout the world.
Fields of interest: Arts; Education; Environment, climate change/global warming; Environment; Employment, services; Employment, training; Employment; Human services; Civil liberties, first amendment; Civil/human rights; Community/ economic development; Public affairs Economically disadvantaged.
Programs:
Community Enhancements Grants: The foundation supports programs designed to address human services; education; arts and culture; and climate and the environment. Special emphasis is directed toward programs designed promote basic human services, including job creation, employment, and training. Grants of up to $10,000 are awarded. This program is limited to New York, NY, Reston, VA (Metro D.C.), and Seattle, WA (Puget Sound Region).
Employee Matching Gifts: The foundation matches contributions made by employees of RealNetworks to nonprofit organizations on a one-for-one basis from $25 to $10,000 per employee, per year.
Employee Volunteer Matching Program: The foundation awards grants to nonprofit organizations with which employees of RealNetworks volunteer. The foundation awards $15 per volunteer hour up to 60 hours, per employee, per year.
Five-Year Anniversary Benefit: The foundation honors an employee's five years of employment service with a $500 grant to the nonprofit organization or educational institution of the employee's choice.
Freedom of Expression & Independent Media Grants (FEIM): Through FEIM Grants, the foundation supports programs designed to promote and protect human rights and civil liberties. Special emphasis is directed toward freedom of speech and freedom of the press. This program is currently on hold.
Type of support: Continuing support; Employee matching gifts; Employee volunteer services; Program development.
Geographic limitations: Giving primarily in areas of company operations for Community Enhancement Grants, with emphasis on San Francisco, CA (Bay Area), New York, NY, Reston, VA (Metro D.C.), and Seattle, WA (Puget Sound Region).
Support limitations: No support for religious or membership-based organizations unless the program is open to the public without regard to affiliation; discriminatory organizations, organizations designated under Section 509 of the U.S. Internal Revenue Service code, K-12 schools, youth groups, clubs, teams, choirs, bands, or PTSA. No grants to individuals, or for capital campaigns, general operating funds, endowments, or event or conference sponsorships.
Publications: Application guidelines; Grants list.

Application information: Applications accepted. Support is limited to 1 contribution per organization during any given year. Applicants should submit the following:
1) statement of problem project will address
2) brief history of organization and description of its mission
3) copy of most recent annual report/audited financial statement/990
4) how project's results will be evaluated or measured
5) listing of board of directors, trustees, officers and other key people and their affiliations
6) detailed description of project and amount of funding requested
7) copy of current year's organizational budget and/ or project budget
8) listing of additional sources and amount of support

Initial approach: Complete online eligibility quiz and application
Deadline(s): Apr. 12 and Oct. 11 for Community Enhancement Grants
Final notification: Mid. Aug. and Mid. Feb. for Community Enhancement Grants

Officers: Robert Glaser, Pres.; Sid Ferrales, V.P.; Kelly Jo MacArthur, Secy.-Treas.
EIN: 912033075

3145
Realogy Corporation

1 Campus Dr.
Parsippany, NJ 07054 (973) 407-2000

Company URL: http://www.realogy.com
Establishment information: Established in 1997.
Company type: Subsidiary of a foreign company
Business activities: Operates real estate agency.
Business type (SIC): Real estate agents and managers
Corporate officers: Richard A. Smith, Chair., Pres., and C.E.O.; Anthony E. Hull, Exec. V.P., Treas., and C.F.O.; David J. Weaving, Exec. V.P. and Co-C.A.O.; Marilyn J. Wasser, Exec. V.P. and Genl. Counsel; Dea Benson, Sr. V.P., Cont., and Co-C.A.O.
Board of director: Richard A. Smith, Chair.
Giving statement: Giving through the Realogy Charitable Foundation.

Realogy Charitable Foundation

(formerly The NRT Foundation, Inc.)
1 Campus Dr.
Parsippany, NJ 07054-4407 (973) 407-5231
URL: http://www.realogyfoundation.org/

Establishment information: Established in 2004 in DE.
Contact: Steven Yaqozinski
Financial data (yr. ended 09/30/11): Revenue, $2,284,637; assets, $2,498,682 (M); gifts received, $1,581,715; expenditures, $2,059,805; program services expenses, $1,849,796; giving activities include $1,849,796 for 66 grants (high: $74,000; low: $5,375).
Purpose and activities: The foundation works to improve the quality of life in communities where NRT Inc. and its related parties have a presence.
Fields of interest: Housing/shelter; American Red Cross; Human services; Community/economic development.
Officers: Kevin Greene*, Pres.; Kenneth Hoffert*, V.P.; Patrick Treacy*, Treas.; Steven Yaqozinski, Exec. Dir.
EIN: 200755090

3146
Reckitt Benckiser (North America), Inc.

(formerly Reckitt & Colman, Inc.)
399 Interpace Pkwy., Ste. 101
P.O. Box 225
Parsippany, NJ 07054-0225
(973) 404-2600

Company URL: http://www.reckittprofessional.com
Establishment information: Established in 1889.
Company type: Subsidiary of a foreign company
Business activities: Manufactures, markets, and sells household cleaning products; produces mustard.
Business type (SIC): Soaps, cleaners, and toiletries; specialty foods/canned, frozen, and preserved
Financial profile for 2011: Number of employees, 20,000
Corporate officers: Stafford Dow, C.E.O.; Simon Nash, Sr. V.P., Human Resources
Giving statement: Giving through the Reckitt Benckiser (North America) Inc. Corporate Giving Program.

Reckitt Benckiser (North America) Inc. Corporate Giving Program

(formerly Reckitt & Colman, Inc. Corporate Giving Program)
Morris Corporate Ctr. IV
399 Interpace Pkwy.
Parsippany, NJ 07054-0225 (973) 404-2600
URL: http://www.rb.com/Our-responsibility

Purpose and activities: Reckitt Benckiser makes charitable contributions to nonprofit organizations involved with children, health, and economically disadvantaged people. Support is given on a national and international basis.
Fields of interest: Health care Children; Economically disadvantaged.
Type of support: Donated products; Employee matching gifts; Employee volunteer services; General/operating support; In-kind gifts.

3147
Reckitt Benckiser Pharmaceuticals, Inc.

The Fairfax Bldg.
10710 Midlothian Tpke., Ste.430
North Chesterfield, VA 23235-4722
(804) 379-1090

Company type: Subsidiary of a foreign company
Business activities: Operates pharmaceuticals comapny.
Business type (SIC): Drugs, proprietaries, and sundries—wholesale
Corporate officer: Shaun Thaxter, Pres.
Giving statement: Giving through the Reckitt Benckiser Pharmaceuticals Patient Help Foundation.

Reckitt Benckiser Pharmaceuticals Patient Help Foundation

10710 Midlothian Tpke., Ste. 430
Richmond, VA 23235-4759

Donor: Reckitt Benckiser Pharmaceuticals, Inc.
Financial data (yr. ended 12/31/11): Assets, $0 (M); gifts received, $33,447,139; expenditures, $33,447,139; qualifying distributions, $33,447,139; giving activities include $30,592,240 for grants to individuals.
Application information: Applications not accepted. Unsolicited requests for funds not accepted.
Officers and Trustees:* Dr. Rolley Johnson*, Pres.; Vicky Seeger, Secy.; Martyn Gibson*, Treas.; Shaun Thaxter.
EIN: 800723342

3148
RECO Constructors, Inc.

710 Hospital St.
P.O. Box 25189
Richmond, VA 23219 (804) 644-2611

Company URL: http://www.recoconstructors.com/
Establishment information: Established in 1914.
Company type: Private company
Business activities: Provides contract structural steel building construction services.
Business type (SIC): Contractors/miscellaneous special trade
Corporate officers: Robert C. Courain, Jr., Chair.; Jerry L. Dawson, Pres.; Leslie W. Dixon, V.P. and Secy.; John O. Moss, V.P., Sales
Board of director: Robert C. Courain, Jr., Chair.
Giving statement: Giving through the RECO Foundation.

The RECO Foundation

710 Hospital St.
P.O. Box 25189
Richmond, VA 23260-5189 (804) 644-2800

Donors: RECO Constructors, Inc.; RECO Industries, Inc.; Virginia American Industries, Inc.
Contact: Robert C. Courain, Jr., Pres.
Financial data (yr. ended 09/30/11): Assets, $4,722,691 (M); gifts received, $250,000; expenditures, $269,466; qualifying distributions, $232,900; giving activities include $232,900 for grants.
Purpose and activities: The foundation supports food banks and health clinics and organizations involved with historic preservation, education, cancer, temporary housing, youth, and family services.
Fields of interest: Historic preservation/historical societies; Elementary school/education; Higher education; Education, reading; Education; Health care, clinics/centers; Cancer; Food banks; Housing/shelter, temporary shelter; Boy scouts; Youth, services; Family services; United Ways and Federated Giving Programs.
Type of support: Annual campaigns; Capital campaigns; General/operating support; Program development; Research; Scholarship funds.
Geographic limitations: Giving primarily in Richmond, VA.
Support limitations: No grants to individuals.
Application information: Applications accepted. Application form not required.

Initial approach: Proposal
Deadline(s): None

Officers and Directors:* Robert C. Courain, Jr.*, Pres. and Treas.; Ruth D. Courain*, Secy.; Jennifer R. Courain; Robert C. Courain III; Allen C. Goolsby III; Frank G. Louthan, Jr.; Lauren C. Luke; William M. Richardson.
EIN: 546039609

Selected grants: The following grants are a representative sample of this grantmaker's funding activity:
$3,000 to American Red Cross, Richmond, VA, 2011.
$3,000 to VCU Massey Cancer Center, Richmond, VA, 2011.
$2,500 to John Marshall Foundation, Richmond, VA, 2011.
$2,000 to Virginia Military Institute Foundation, Lexington, VA, 2011.
$1,500 to Virginia Home, Richmond, VA, 2011.
$1,000 to Boaz and Ruth, Richmond, VA, 2011.
$1,000 to Carver Promise, Richmond, VA, 2011.
$1,000 to Comfort Zone Camp, Richmond, VA, 2011.
$1,000 to Freedom House, Washington, DC, 2011.
$1,000 to State Fair of Virginia, Doswell, VA, 2011.

3149
Record Journal Publishing Co.

11 Crown St.
Meriden, CT 06450-5713 (203) 235-1661

Company URL: http://www.myrecordjournal.com
Establishment information: Established in 1867.
Company type: Private company
Business activities: Publishes newspapers.
Business type (SIC): Newspaper publishing and/or printing
Financial profile for 2010: Number of employees, 325
Corporate officers: John Ausanka, Sr. V.P. and C.F.O.; Alison W. Muschinsky, Sr. V.P. and Secy.; Michael F. Killian, Sr. V.P., Sales and Mktg.
Giving statement: Giving through the Meriden Record Journal Foundation.

Meriden Record Journal Foundation

P.O. Box 1802
Providence, RI 02901-1802

Establishment information: Established in 1987 in CT.
Donor: Record Journal Publishing Co.
Contact: Elliott White
Financial data (yr. ended 12/31/11): Assets, $50,401 (M); gifts received, $15,000; expenditures, $21,515; qualifying distributions, $20,454; giving activities include $19,800 for 6+ grants (high: $8,000).
Purpose and activities: The foundation supports organizations involved with youth and awards college scholarships to children of employees of the Meriden Record Journal, to carrier employees, and to residents of the circulation area studying journalism or journalism-related subjects such as advertising.
Fields of interest: Education; Recreation; Human services.
Type of support: Employee-related scholarships; Scholarships—to individuals.
Geographic limitations: Giving primarily in the Meriden, CT, area.
Application information: Applications accepted. Application form required.
Initial approach: Contact foundation for application form
Deadline(s): Varies
Trustee: Bank of America.
EIN: 066074903

3150
Recreational Equipment, Inc.

(also known as REI)
6750 S. 228th St.
P.O. Box 1938
Kent, WA 98032 (253) 891-2500

Company URL: http://www.rei.com
Establishment information: Established in 1938.
Company type: Cooperative
Business activities: Operates outdoor gear stores; provides Internet shopping services; provides catalog shopping services.
Business type (SIC): Shopping goods stores/ miscellaneous; nonstore retailers; computer services
Financial profile for 2009: Number of employees, 10,000; assets, $919,910,000; sales volume, $1,460,000,000
Corporate officers: Anne V. Farrell, Chair.; John Hamlin, Vice-Chair.; Sally Jewell, Pres. and C.E.O.; Ivar Chhina, Exec. V.P. and C.F.O.; Catherine Walker, Sr. V.P., Genl. Counsel, and Corp. Secy.; Angela Owen, Sr. V.P., Mktg.; Michelle Clements, Sr. V.P., Human Resources; Michael Collins, V.P., Public Affairs
Board of directors: Anne Farrell, Chair.; John Hamlin, Vice-Chair.; Brenda Davis; Joanne Harrell; Sally Jewell; Charles Katz, Jr.; Jesse King; Stephen Lockhart; Jose Ignacio Lozano; Cheryl Scott; Michael Smith
Subsidiaries: MSR, Seattle, WA; Thaw & Edgeworks, Inc., Seattle, WA
Giving statement: Giving through the REI Corporate Giving Program and the REI Foundation.

REI Corporate Giving Program

6750 S. 228th St.
Kent, WA 98032-4803
URL: http://www.rei.com/aboutrei/gives02.html

Financial data (yr. ended 12/31/08): Total giving, $4,282,441, including $3,700,000 for 415 grants and $582,441 for 1,200 employee matching gifts.
Purpose and activities: As a complement to its foundation, REI also makes charitable contributions to nonprofit organizations directly. Support is given primarily in areas of company operations.
Fields of interest: Environment, legal rights; Environment, natural resources; Environment; Recreation.
Programs:
Grants Program: REI supports programs designed to protect and restore the environment; increase access to outdoor activities; and encourage involvement in responsible outdoor recreation.
Stewards for the Environment: Through the Stewards for the Environment program, REI makes charitable contributions of REI gift cards valued at $500 to individual volunteers dedicated to environmental stewardship. The organizations with which the individuals volunteer receive $20,000 grants.
Type of support: Donated products; Employee volunteer services; Grants to individuals; Program development; Sponsorships.
Geographic limitations: Giving primarily in areas of company operations.
Application information: Unsolicited requests are accepted from REI employees on behalf of nonprofit organizations only. Unsolicited requests for Stewardship for the Environment are not accepted.

The REI Foundation

P.O. Box 1938
Sumner, WA 98390-0800 (253) 395-5928
URL: http://www.rei.com/stewardship/report/community/rei-foundation.html

Establishment information: Established in 1993 in WA.
Donor: Recreational Equipment Inc.
Contact: David Jayo, Secy.
Financial data (yr. ended 12/31/11): Assets, $9,355,342 (M); gifts received, $511,060; expenditures, $553,799; qualifying distributions, $445,850; giving activities include $445,850 for grants.
Purpose and activities: The foundation supports programs designed to ensure that tomorrow's outdoor enthusiasts and conservation stewards reflect the diversity of America.
Fields of interest: Environment, natural resources; Environment, land resources; Recreation; American Red Cross; YM/YWCAs & YM/YWHAs; Youth, services.
Type of support: General/operating support.
Geographic limitations: Giving primarily in CA.
Application information: Applications not accepted. Contributes only to pre-selected organizations.
Officers and Directors: Michael Collins*, Pres.; David Jayo, V.P.; Catherine Walker, Secy.; Rick Palmer, Treas.; Sally Jewell; Tom Vogl.
EIN: 911577992
Selected grants: The following grants are a representative sample of this grantmaker's funding activity:
$20,000 to Ocean Discovery Institute, San Diego, CA, 2009.
$20,000 to Outdoor Outreach, San Diego, CA, 2009.
$20,000 to Wildcoast, Inc., Imperial Beach, CA, 2009.

3151
RecycleBank

95 Morton St., 7th Fl.
New York, NY 10014-3336 (212) 659-9900

Company URL: http://www.recyclebank.com
Establishment information: Established in 2004.
Company type: Private company
Business type (SIC): Business services/ miscellaneous
Corporate officers: Jonathan K. Hsu, C.E.O.; Kris Heinrichs, C.F.O.
Giving statement: Giving through the RecycleBank Corporate Giving Program.

RecycleBank Corporate Giving Program

95 Morton St., Ste. 7N
New York, NY 10014-3336 (212) 659-6486
URL: http://www.recyclebank.com

Purpose and activities: RecycleBank is a certified B Corporation that donates a percentage of net profits to charitable organizations.
Fields of interest: Environment.

3152
Red Bull North America, Inc.
1740 Stewart St.
Santa Monica, CA 90404-4022
(310) 393-4647

Company URL: http://www.redbullusa.com
Establishment information: Established in 1995.
Company type: Subsidiary of a foreign company
Business activities: Produces bottled and canned soft drinks.
Business type (SIC): Beverages
Financial profile for 2010: Number of employees, 100
Corporate officers: Stefan Kazok, C.E.O.; Amy Taylor, V.P., Mktg.
Giving statement: Giving through the Taurus World Stunt Awards (USA) Foundation.

Taurus World Stunt Awards (USA) Foundation
937 N. Citrus Ave.
Hollywood, CA 90038-2401
Application address: 3940 Laurel Canyon Blvd., No. 236, Studio City, CA 91604, tel.: (310) 586-7876; URL: http://www.worldstuntawards.com

Establishment information: Established in 2004 in CA.
Donor: Red Bull North America, Inc.
Financial data (yr. ended 12/31/11): Assets, $31,305 (M); gifts received, $5,450; expenditures, $20,441; qualifying distributions, $20,000; giving activities include $20,000 for grants.
Purpose and activities: Giving primarily to individuals within the stunt profession who are also members of the World Stunt Academy.
Application information: Applications accepted. Application form required. Applicants should submit the following:
1) copy of IRS Determination Letter
Initial approach: Proposal
Deadline(s): None
Officers and Directors:* Dietrich Mateschitz*, Pres.; Steve Katleman*, Secy.; Mitch Geller*, Treas.
EIN: 200839916

3153
Red Devil, Inc.
Boulder Towers
1437 S. Boulder Ave., Ste. 750
Tulsa, OK 74119-3609 (918) 585-8111

Company URL: http://www.reddevil.com
Establishment information: Established in 1872.
Company type: Private company
Business activities: Manufactures painting tools and supplies and wallpaper, ceramic, masonry, and glazing tools.
Business type (SIC): Chemical preparations/miscellaneous; cutlery, hand and edge tools, and hardware
Corporate officers: Jane Lee, Chair.; William S. Lee, Pres. and C.E.O.; Robert Duess, C.F.O.
Board of director: Jane Lee, Chair.
Plant: Pryor, OK
Giving statement: Giving through the Red Devil Foundation.

Red Devil Foundation
24 Sidney School Rd.
Annandale, NJ 08801-3509

Donor: Red Devil, Inc.
Financial data (yr. ended 11/30/12): Assets, $13,877 (M); gifts received, $2,500; expenditures, $1,127; qualifying distributions, $500; giving activities include $500 for grants.
Purpose and activities: The foundation supports organizations involved with arts and culture, higher education, recreation, and civic affairs.
Fields of interest: Arts; Higher education; Recreation; Government/public administration.
Type of support: Annual campaigns; Continuing support; Employee-related scholarships; General/operating support.
Geographic limitations: Giving primarily in areas of company operations.
Support limitations: No grants to individuals (except for employee-related scholarships).
Application information: Applications not accepted. Unsolicited requests for funds not accepted.
Trustees: Jane T. Lee; Mary T. Lee; Mary Todd Subourne.
EIN: 226063889

3154
Red Wing Shoe Company, Inc.
314 Main St.
Red Wing, MN 55066-2300 (651) 388-8211

Company URL: http://www.redwingshoes.com/
Establishment information: Established in 1905.
Company type: Private company
Business activities: Manufactures shoes.
Business type (SIC): Leather footwear
Corporate officers: William J. Sweasy, C.E.O.; David D. Murphy, Pres. and C.O.O.; Rick Bawek, Exec. V.P. and C.F.O.; Dave Baker, Exec. V.P., Genl. Counsel, and Secy.; Joe Topinka, C.I.O.; Carrie Heimer, V.P., Human Resources
Subsidiaries: Red Wing Hotel Corp., Red Wing, MN; S.B. Foot Tanning Co., Red Wing, MN
Divisions: Irish Setter Sport Bouts Div., Red Wing, MN; Vasque Outdoor Footwear Div., Red Wing, MN
Giving statement: Giving through the Red Wing Shoe Company Foundation.

Red Wing Shoe Company Foundation
314 Main St.
Red Wing, MN 55066-2300

Establishment information: Incorporated in 1955 in MN.
Donor: Red Wing Shoe Co., Inc.
Contact: Stacy Crownhart, Dir.
Financial data (yr. ended 12/31/11): Assets, $152,470 (M); gifts received, $600,000; expenditures, $710,051; qualifying distributions, $709,521; giving activities include $709,521 for grants.
Purpose and activities: The foundation supports organizations involved with arts and culture, education, environmental education, human services, and community development.
Fields of interest: Museums (science/technology); Performing arts, music; Performing arts, orchestras; Arts; Higher education; Education; Environmental education; Housing/shelter, development; American Red Cross; YM/YWCAs & YM/YWHAs; Human services; Community/economic development; United Ways and Federated Giving Programs.
Type of support: Capital campaigns; Continuing support; Employee matching gifts; General/operating support; Matching/challenge support; Program development; Scholarship funds; Sponsorships.
Geographic limitations: Giving primarily in the Danville, KY, Red Wing, MN, and Potosi, MO, areas.
Support limitations: No grants to individuals.
Publications: Annual report.
Application information: Applications accepted. Application form not required.
Initial approach: Proposal
Deadline(s): None
Officer and Directors: William J. Sweasy, C.E.O.; Suzanne Blue; Stacy Crownhart; Silas B. Foot III.
EIN: 416020177
Selected grants: The following grants are a representative sample of this grantmaker's funding activity:
$4,389 to American Cancer Society, Atlanta, GA, 2011.

3155
Redco Foods, Inc.
1 Hansen Island
P.O. Box 1027
Little Falls, NY 13365-1997
(315) 823-1300

Company URL: http://www.redcofoods.com/
Establishment information: Established in 1985.
Company type: Subsidiary of a foreign company
Business activities: Produces teas and desserts.
Business type (SIC): Miscellaneous prepared foods
Corporate officers: Rainer Verstgyn, Pres.; Debo Mukherjee, C.E.O.; Glenn Mucica, C.F.O.
Giving statement: Giving through the Redco Foods Inc. Corporate Giving Program.

Redco Foods Inc. Corporate Giving Program
100 Northfield Dr.
P.O. Box 589
Windsor, CT 06095-4701 (860) 688-2121

Contact: Mary Register, Coord., Consumer Rels.
Purpose and activities: Redco makes charitable contributions to nonprofit organizations involved with cancer. Support is given on a national basis.
Fields of interest: Cancer; Cancer, leukemia.
Type of support: General/operating support.
Support limitations: No support for political or religious organizations.
Application information: Applications accepted. Telephone calls are not encouraged. Application form not required. Applicants should submit the following:
1) detailed description of project and amount of funding requested
Initial approach: Letter of inquiry to headquarters

3156
Redlum, Ltd.
257 Norwood Dr.
Holland, MI 49424

Company type: Private company
Business activities: Develops real estate.
Business type (SIC): Real estate subdividers and developers

Giving statement: Giving through the Redlum Foundation.

The Redlum Foundation

201 W. Washington St.
Zeeland, MI 49464

Establishment information: Established in 1998 in MI.
Donors: Redlum, Ltd.; Karen Mulder; Jeffrey Mulder; Jeri Mulder; Michael Mulder; Kimberly Mulder.
Financial data (yr. ended 12/31/11): Assets, $3,564 (M); expenditures, $480; qualifying distributions, $0.
Purpose and activities: The foundation supports camps and organizations involved with human services.
Fields of interest: Human services.
Type of support: General/operating support; Program development.
Geographic limitations: Giving limited to Fremont, Grand Rapids, and Holland, MI.
Support limitations: No grants to individuals.
Application information: Applications not accepted. Unsolicited requests for funds not accepted.
Directors: Jeffrey Mesler; Jeffrey Mulder; Jeri Mulder; Karen Mulder; Kimberly Mulder; Michael Mulder.
EIN: 383443698

3157
Redner's Markets, Inc.

3 Quarry Rd.
Reading, PA 19605 (610) 926-3700

Company URL: http://www.rednersmarkets.com
Establishment information: Established in 1970.
Company type: Private company
Business activities: Operates grocery stores.
Business type (SIC): Groceries—retail
Corporate officers: Richard R. Redner, Chair., Pres., and C.E.O.; Ryan Redner, C.O.O.; Jason Hopp, V.P. and Genl. Counsel; Michael McNaney, V.P., Finance; Robert McDonough, V.P., Human Resources; Roger Pasquale, Cont.
Board of directors: Richard R. Redner, Chair.; Gary M. Redner; Ryan Redner
Giving statement: Giving through the Redner Foundation.

Redner Foundation

3 Quarry Rd.
Reading, PA 19605-9787

Establishment information: Established in 1989 in PA.
Donors: Redner's Markets, Inc.; Gordon B. Hoch.
Financial data (yr. ended 12/31/11): Assets, $32,981 (M); gifts received, $35,418; expenditures, $34,207; qualifying distributions, $33,907; giving activities include $33,907 for grants.
Purpose and activities: The foundation supports organizations involved with education, nerve disorders, arthritis, disaster relief, and athletics.
Fields of interest: Secondary school/education; Higher education; Education; Nerve, muscle & bone diseases; Arthritis; Disasters, preparedness/services; Athletics/sports, amateur leagues.
Type of support: General/operating support.
Geographic limitations: Giving limited to PA, with emphasis on Reading.
Support limitations: No grants to individuals.
Application information: Applications not accepted. Unsolicited requests for funds not accepted.
Officer: Roger Pasquale, Mgr.
Trustees: Earl W. Redner; Richard E. Redner.
EIN: 232527369

3158
The Redwoods Group

2801 Slater Rd., Ste. 220
Morrisville, NC 27560-8477
(919) 462-9730

Company URL: http://www.redwoodsgroup.com
Establishment information: Established in 1997.
Company type: Private company
Business activities: Operates a property and casualty insurance company.
Business type (SIC): Insurance/fire, marine, and casualty
Financial profile for 2012: Assets, $15,758,000
Corporate officers: Kevin A. Trapani, Pres. and C.E.O.; William C. Mecklenburg, Jr., Exec. V.P. and C.O.O.; Brian Keel, C.F.O.; James R. Fryling, Genl. Counsel
Board of directors: Jennifer A. Trapani; William C. Mecklenburg; Brain Keel
Giving statement: Giving through the Redwoods Group Corporate Giving Program and the Redwoods Group Foundation, Inc.

The Redwoods Group Corporate Giving Program

(also known as Serve Others)
2801 Slater Rd., Ste. 220
Morrisville, NC 27560 (919) 462-9730
E-mail: serveothers@redwoodsgroup.com;
URL: http://redwoodsgroup.com/giving

Purpose and activities: As a complement to its foundation, The Redwoods Group also makes charitable contributions to community organizations in areas of company operations in North Carolina; giving also national and international organizations.
Fields of interest: Housing/shelter; YM/YWCAs & YM/YWHAs; Community/economic development.
Type of support: Employee matching gifts; Employee volunteer services; Equipment; General/operating support; Use of facilities.
Geographic limitations: Giving primarily in areas of company operations in NC; giving also to national and international organizations.
Application information: The Redwoods Community Outreach (RCO) committee handles giving.

The Redwoods Group Foundation, Inc.

2801 Slater Rd., Ste. 220
Morrisville, NC 27560-8477 (919) 481-6440
FAX: (919) 481-6441;
E-mail: info@redwoodsgroupfoundation.org; Contact for Christina Holloway: tel.: (919) 462-9743, fax: (919) 481-6468, e-mail: cholloway@redwoodsgroup.com; URL: http://redwoodsgroup.com/foundation

Establishment information: Established in 2007 in NC.
Donor: The Redwoods Group, Inc.
Contact: Christina Holloway, Grants Facilitator
Financial data (yr. ended 12/31/11): Assets, $1,001,707 (M); gifts received, $2,000; expenditures, $561,858; qualifying distributions, $501,862; giving activities include $438,662 for grants, $75,792 for foundation-administered programs and $63,200 for loans/program-related investments.
Purpose and activities: The foundation supports nonprofit organizations that promote safe and adequate access to shelter, nutrition, health care, education, economic opportunity, and a sustainable environment.
Fields of interest: Education; Environment, natural resources; Environment, energy; Environment; Animals/wildlife; Health care; Mental health/crisis services; Nutrition; Housing/shelter; YM/YWCAs & YM/YWHAs; Civil/human rights, equal rights; Civil rights, race/intergroup relations; Community/economic development; Public policy, research.
Programs:
Economic Opportunity: The foundation supports programs designed to narrow the income gap by creating opportunities for the poor to develop skills to move out of poverty.
Education: The foundation supports programs designed to promote educational opportunities, employer-valued skills, and strong character for low-income and at-risk students; and programs designed to promote tolerance, diversity, and improved race relations.
Healthcare: The foundation supports programs designed to promote prevention, treatment, and management of illness; and the preservation of mental and physical well-being.
Nutrition: The foundation supports programs designed to prevent deficiencies, excesses, and imbalances in diet that harm health, reduce quality of life, and lead to disease or death.
Public Policy: The foundation supports public policy initiatives designed to encourage the public and private sectors to work together to support shelter, nutrition, healthcare, education, economic opportunity, and sustainable environment.
Shelter: The foundation supports programs designed to rebuild lives, livelihoods, families, and communities through shelter.
Sustainable Environment: The foundation supports programs deigned to protect and conserve natural resources, wildlife, and wildlife habitats; efforts related to biodiversity and a sustainable world; and the development of new sources of clean energy.
Type of support: Annual campaigns; Continuing support; Employee matching gifts; Employee volunteer services; General/operating support; Program-related investments/loans; Scholarship funds.
Geographic limitations: Giving in the U.S., with emphasis on central and rural NC.
Support limitations: No support for labor organizations, religious organizations for religious purposes or fraternal or social organizations. No grants to individuals, or for arts for the general public or aid to domestic animals.
Publications: Application guidelines; Program policy statement.
Application information: Applications accepted. New applicants should submit a short application and a letter of introduction. Applicants who have a relationship with Redwoods or the foundation should submit the long application. Applicants with requests over $1,000 should also submit the long application. Organizations receiving support are asked to submit an evaluation plan to report back on results of programs or services funded. Application form required. Applicants should submit the following:
1) signature and title of chief executive officer
2) population served
3) name, address and phone number of organization
4) brief history of organization and description of its mission
5) geographic area to be served

6) detailed description of project and amount of funding requested
7) contact person
Initial approach: Download application form and e-mail, fax, or mail to foundation
Deadline(s): Mar. 11, June 16, Sept. 2, and Dec. 2

Officers: Kevin A. Trapani, Pres.; Jennifer A. Trapani, V.P. and Secy.; William C. Mecklenburg, Jr., V.P.; Stephen B. Cook, Treas.
EIN: 770698917
Selected grants: The following grants are a representative sample of this grantmaker's funding activity:
$100,000 to Darkness to Light, Charleston, SC, 2010. For general support.
$14,000 to YMCA of the USA, Armed Services, Alexandria, VA, 2010.
$11,500 to YMCA of the Triangle Area, Raleigh, NC, 2010. For capital campaign.
$10,000 to Family Violence Prevention Center, Raleigh, NC, 2010.
$10,000 to Third Sector New England, Boston, MA, 2010. For general support.
$10,000 to YMCA, Cleveland County Family, Shelby, NC, 2010. For general support.
$7,500 to Jorge Posada Foundation, New York, NY, 2010. For general support.
$5,000 to Teach for America, Durham, NC, 2010. For general support.
$3,000 to North Carolina Sustainability Center, Raleigh, NC, 2010. For general support.
$1,500 to YMCA of Greater Oklahoma City, Oklahoma City, OK, 2010.

3159
Reebok International Ltd.

1895 J.W. Foster Blvd.
Canton, MA 02021-1099 (781) 401-5000
FAX: (781) 401-7402

Company URL: http://www.reebok.com
Establishment information: Established in 1979.
Company type: Subsidiary of a foreign company
Business activities: Designs and markets sports and fitness products and footwear and apparel.
Business type (SIC): Footwear/rubber and plastic; apparel and other finished products made from fabrics and similar materials; games, toys, and sporting and athletic goods
Financial profile for 2010: Number of employees, 9,102
Corporate officers: Ulrich Becker, Pres. and C.E.O.; John Warren, C.F.O.; John Lynch, V.P., Mktg.
Subsidiary: The Rockport Co., Inc., Canton, MA
International operations: Canada
Giving statement: Giving through the Reebok International Ltd. Corporate Giving Program and the Reebok Foundation.
Company EIN: 042678061

Reebok International Ltd. Corporate Giving Program

c/o Community Rels.
1895 JW Foster Blvd.
Canton, MA 02021-1099 (781) 401-5000
E-mail for Reebok Recognition Program: Recognition.Program@reebok.com; URL: http://www.adidas-group.com/en/sustainability/Community_involvement/default.aspx

Purpose and activities: As a complement to its foundation, Reebok also makes charitable contributions to nonprofit organizations directly. Support is given primarily in areas of company operations.
Fields of interest: Athletics/sports, amateur leagues; Youth development, volunteer services Youth; Economically disadvantaged.

Programs:
Reach: Reebok awards grants to its employees for nonprofit organizations, so that employees can "reach" beyond their own personal means to support a cause that is important to them or their family. The program is designed to encourage Reebok employees to get involved and make a positive difference in their communities.
Reebok Recognition Program: Through the Recognition Program, Reebok supports and recognizes individuals who make a positive difference in the lives of youth through their chosen profession or volunteer activities. Reebok invites select groups of individuals who work with youth to visit Reebok World Headquarters for one week to shop at the corporate store and enjoy a %50 discount. The program is limited to Massachusetts.
Sponsorship: Reebok supports sports and entertainment related organizations and events through sponsorship. Special emphasis is directed toward athletic grassroots events; competitive sporting events; and product placement in entertainment projects.
Type of support: Donated products; Employee volunteer services; In-kind gifts; Program development; Sponsorships.
Geographic limitations: Giving primarily in areas of company operations, with emphasis on MA.

The Reebok Foundation

1895 J.W. Foster Blvd.
Canton, MA 02021-1099 (781) 401-5000
FAX: (781) 401-4744;
E-mail: geri.noonan@reebok.com; URL: http://www.adidas-group.com/en/sustainability/Community_involvement/Reebok_programmes/default.aspx

Establishment information: Established in 1986 in MA.
Donor: Reebok International Ltd.
Financial data (yr. ended 12/31/11): Assets, $113,896 (M); gifts received, $1,717,056; expenditures, $1,689,761; qualifying distributions, $1,630,625; giving activities include $316,243 for 422 grants (high: $39,473; low: $25).
Purpose and activities: The foundation supports programs designed to serve inner-city youth and provide youth with the tools they need to lead healthy, happy, and active lives.
Fields of interest: Education; Youth, services; Human services Youth.

Program:
Matching Gift Program: The foundation matches contributions made by employees of Reebok on a one-for-one basis up to $1,500 per employee, per year.
Type of support: Employee matching gifts; General/operating support; Program development.
Geographic limitations: Giving primarily in areas of company operations, with emphasis on the greater Boston, MA area.
Support limitations: No grants to individuals, or for seminars or conferences, documentaries or media projects, publications, medical research or other research, or political projects; no product donations; no loans.
Publications: Application guidelines.
Application information: Applications accepted. Unsolicited requests from national organizations are not accepted. Associated Grant Makers Common Proposal Form accepted. Application form not required. Applicants should submit the following:
1) detailed description of project and amount of funding requested
Initial approach: Proposal
Copies of proposal: 1
Board meeting date(s): Biannually
Deadline(s): None
Final notification: 4 to 6 weeks

Officers: Ulrich Becker, Pres.; Eric Bodenhofer, V.P. and Secy.; William Holmes, V.P.; John Warren, Treas.; Megan Grimaldi, Exec. Dir.
Number of staff: 1 full-time professional.
EIN: 043073548

3160
Reed & Barton Corp.

144 W. Britannia St.
Taunton, MA 02780-1634 (508) 824-6611

Company URL: https://www.reedandbarton.com
Establishment information: Established in 1824.
Company type: Private company
Business activities: Manufactures and distributes silverware and jewelry.
Business type (SIC): Jewelry/precious metal; durable goods—wholesale; non-durable goods—wholesale; shopping goods stores/miscellaneous; nonstore retailers
Corporate officers: Timothy K. Riddle, Pres. and C.E.O.; Charles Daly, Co-C.F.O.; Joe D'Allessandro, Sr. V.P., Sales and Mktg.; Stephen Normandin, V.P., Finance, Treas., Cont., and Co-C.F.O.; Sara Carcieri, V.P., Mktg.; Karen Cataldo, V.P., Human Resources
Subsidiary: Eureka Manufacturing Co., Inc., Norton, MA
Divisions: Reed & Barton Housewares, Taunton, MA; Reed & Barton Silversmiths, Taunton, MA
Giving statement: Giving through the Reed & Barton Foundation, Inc.

Reed & Barton Foundation, Inc.

144 W. Britannia St.
Taunton, MA 02780-1634 (508) 824-6611

Establishment information: Established in 1953.
Donor: Reed & Barton Corp.
Contact: Charles Daly, Treas.
Financial data (yr. ended 12/31/11): Assets, $1,264,400 (M); expenditures, $61,601; qualifying distributions, $44,550; giving activities include $44,550 for grants.
Purpose and activities: The foundation supports organizations involved with arts and culture, education, the environment, health, youth development, and family services.
Fields of interest: Arts; Education; Human services.
Type of support: Annual campaigns; Building/renovation; Capital campaigns; Employee matching gifts; Scholarship funds.
Geographic limitations: Giving primarily in MA.
Support limitations: No grants to individuals.
Application information: Applications accepted. Application form required. Applicants should submit the following:
1) detailed description of project and amount of funding requested
Initial approach: Proposal
Deadline(s): None

Officer and Trustees:* Sinclair Weeks, Jr.*, Pres.; Charles Daly; William D. Weeks.
EIN: 046040591

3161
Reed Elsevier Inc.
125 Park Ave., 23rd Fl.
New York, NY 10017 (212) 309-8100

Company URL: http://www.reed-elsevier.com
Establishment information: Established in 1894.
Company type: Subsidiary of a foreign company
Business activities: Publishes books; provides database information retrieval services.
Business type (SIC): Book publishing and/or printing; computer services
Financial profile for 2012: Assets, $17,900,000,000; sales volume, $9,900,000,000
Forbes 2000 ranking: 2012—939th in sales, 358th in profits, and 1040th in assets
Corporate officers: Erik Engstrom, C.E.O.; Henry Z. Horbaczewski, Sr. V.P. and Genl. Counsel; Kenneth Fogarty, Treas.
Board of director: Erik Engstrom
Division: LexisNexis, Miamisburg, OH
Giving statement: Giving through the LexisNexis Corporate Giving Program, the Ronald G. Segel Memorial Scholarship Fund Inc., and the J. Allan Sheehan Scholarship Fund, Inc.

LexisNexis Corporate Giving Program
c/o LexisNexis Cares
9443 Springboro Pike
Miamisburg, OH 45342-4425 (937) 865-6800
E-mail: community.relations@lexisnexis.com; URL: http://www.lexisnexis.com/cares

Purpose and activities: LexisNexis makes charitable contributions to nonprofit organizations involved with education for disadvantaged young people and community initiatives of importance to local employees. Support is given primarily in areas of company operations.
Fields of interest: Elementary/secondary education; Education; Legal services; Human services, fund raising/fund distribution; Children/youth, services; Community/economic development Economically disadvantaged.
Program:
LexisNexis Shares Matching Contribution Program: LexisNexis matches contributions made by its employees to nonprofit organizations involved with arts and culture, education, and health and human services on a one-for-one basis from $25 to $250 per employee, per year.
Type of support: Employee volunteer services; General/operating support; In-kind gifts; Pro bono services.
Geographic limitations: Giving primarily in areas of company operations.
Support limitations: No support for fraternal, veterans', religious, political, advocacy, business, trade, professional, social or other membership groups, or for seminaries or theological schools for matching gifts. No grants for athletic funds, tuition, alumni dues, subscriptions or other goods or services for matching gifts.
Number of staff: 2 full-time professional.

Ronald G. Segel Memorial Scholarship Fund Inc.
2 Newton Pl., Ste. 350
Newton, MA 02458-1637 (615) 320-3151

Establishment information: Established in 1992 in DE and MA.
Donors: Cahners Business Information; Cahners Magazine; Reed Elsevier Inc.
Financial data (yr. ended 05/31/12): Assets, $0 (M); gifts received, $2,000; expenditures, $2,000; qualifying distributions, $2,000; giving activities include $2,000 for 2 grants to individuals (high: $1,000; low: $1,000).
Purpose and activities: The foundation awards college scholarships to children of employees of Reed Elsevier Inc.
Type of support: Employee-related scholarships.
Geographic limitations: Giving primarily in areas of company operations, with emphasis on CT, IL, NJ, and NY.
Application information: Applications accepted. Application form required.
Initial approach: Apply online by visiting https://aim.applyists.net/reed
Deadline(s): May 1
Officers and Trustees:* Henry Z. Horbaczewski*, Secy.; Edward R. Comstock*, Treas.
EIN: 223187139

J. Allan Sheehan Scholarship Fund, Inc.
2 Newton Pl., Ste. 350
Newton, MA 02458-1637
E-mail: aglass@applyists.com; Application address: 200 Crutchfield Ave., Nashville, TN 37201, tel.: (615) 627-9686

Establishment information: Established in 1988 in MA.
Donor: Reed Elsevier Inc.
Contact: Andrea Glass
Financial data (yr. ended 12/31/11): Assets, $28,495 (M); gifts received, $2,000; expenditures, $2,060; qualifying distributions, $2,000; giving activities include $2,000 for grants to individuals.
Purpose and activities: The foundation awards college scholarships to children of employees of the Cahners Magazines Division of Reed Elsevier Inc.
Type of support: Employee-related scholarships.
Application information: Applications accepted. Application form required.
Initial approach: E-mail or telephone
Deadline(s): May 1
Officers and Directors:* Henry Z. Horbaczewski*, Secy.; Edward R. Comstock*, Treas.
EIN: 222855930

3162
Reed Engineering Group, Inc.
2424 Stutz, Ste. 400
Dallas, TX 75204-3140 (214) 350-5600

Company URL: http://www.reed-engineering.com
Establishment information: Established in 1988.
Company type: Subsidiary of a private company
Business activities: Provides geotechnical engineering, environmental consulting, and construction observation and testing services.
Business type (SIC): Engineering, architectural, and surveying services; management and public relations services
Corporate officer: Ronald F. Reed, Pres.
Office: Houston, TX
Giving statement: Giving through the Reed Engineering Group Employees Scholarship.

Reed Engineering Group Employees Scholarship
2424 Stutz Dr., Ste. 400
Dallas, TX 75235-6500 (214) 350-5600

Establishment information: Established in 1997 in TX.
Donor: Reed Engineering Group, Inc.
Contact: Yolanda Hawthrone
Financial data (yr. ended 09/30/12): Assets, $227,007 (M); gifts received, $1,725; expenditures, $10,501; qualifying distributions, $6,250; giving activities include $6,250 for 3 grants to individuals (high: $2,500; low: $500).
Purpose and activities: The foundation awards college scholarships to children of employees of Reed Engineering Group.
Fields of interest: Higher education.
Type of support: Employee-related scholarships.
Geographic limitations: Giving limited to TX.
Application information: Applications accepted. Application form required.
Initial approach: Proposal
Deadline(s): Apr. 1
Officers: Ron Reed, Pres.; Sarah Reed, V.P.; Whitney Smith, Secy.-Treas.
EIN: 752728400

3163
Reed Smith LLP
225 5th Ave., Ste. 1200
Reed Smith Ctr.
Pittsburgh, PA 15222-2716 (215) 851-8278

Company URL: http://www.reedsmith.com/
Establishment information: Established in 1877.
Company type: Private company
Business activities: Operates law firm.
Business type (SIC): Legal services
Corporate officers: Gregory B. Jordan, Global Managing Partner; Gary A. Sokulski, C.O.O.; David Duckhouse, C.F.O.
Offices: Los Angeles, Oakland, Palo Alto, San Francisco, CA; Wilmington, DE; Washington, DC; Chicago, IL; Princeton, NJ; New York, NY; Philadelphia, Pittsburgh, PA; Falls Church, Richmond, VA
International operations: China; France; Germany; Greece; United Arab Emirates; United Kingdom
Giving statement: Giving through the Reed Smith LLP Pro Bono Program.

Reed Smith LLP Pro Bono Program
225 5th Ave., Ste. 1200
Reed Smith Ctr.
Pittsburgh, PA 15222-2716 (215) 851-8278
FAX: (215) 851-1420;
E-mail: cwalters@reedsmith.com; Additional tel.: (412) 288-3131; URL: http://www.reedsmith.com/aboutus/probono/

Contact: Christopher K. Walters, Sr. Pro Bono Counsel
Fields of interest: Legal services.
Type of support: Pro bono services - legal.

3164
Reell Precision Manufacturing Corp.
1259 Willow Lake Blvd.
Saint Paul, MN 55110-5103
(651) 484-2447

Company URL: http://www.reell.com
Establishment information: Established in 1970.
Company type: Private company
Business activities: Manufactures laptop computer clutches and hinges.

Business type (SIC): Computer and office equipment
Corporate officers: David Opsahl, Chair.; Kyle Smith, Pres. and C.E.O.; Koning Lai, C.I.O.; Jack M. Field, V.P., Sales; Mike Kemper, V.P., Opers.
Board of directors: David Opsahl, Chair.; Kyle Smith
Giving statement: Giving through the Reell Precision Manufacturing Corporation Contributions Program.

Reell Precision Manufacturing Corporation Contributions Program

1259 Willow Lake Blvd.
St. Paul, MN 55110-5103 (651) 484-2447
FAX: (651) 484-3867; URL: http://www.reell.com/index.php?page=community-involvement

Purpose and activities: Reell makes charitable contributions to nonprofit organizations involved with arts and culture, education, the environment, wildlife, health, human services, community development, youth, disabled people, and religion. Support is given primarily in areas of company operations in Minnesota, and in China, the Netherlands, and Taiwan.
Fields of interest: Arts; Education; Environment, natural resources; Environment; Animals/wildlife, preservation/protection; Health care; Human services; Community/economic development; Religion Youth; Disabilities, people with.
International interests: China; Netherlands; Taiwan.
Type of support: Employee volunteer services; General/operating support.
Geographic limitations: Giving primarily in areas of company operations in MN, and in China, the Netherlands, and Taiwan.
Support limitations: No support for political organizations or candidates. No grants to individuals, or for start-up needs or capital campaigns; no loans; no multi-year grants.
Application information: Applications accepted.
Initial approach: Contact headquarters for application information
Deadline(s): Sept. 1
Final notification: Oct. 31

3165
Norm Reeves, Inc.

18500 Studebaker Rd.
Cerritos, CA 90703 (888) 497-4433

Company URL: http://www.normreeveshonda.com
Establishment information: Established in 1955.
Company type: Subsidiary of a private company
Business activities: Operates car dealership.
Business type (SIC): Motor vehicles—retail
Corporate officers: David M. Conant, Pres.; Dale Ramont, C.I.O.; Armando Diaz, V.P., Human Resources; Marlene Lewis, Treas.
Giving statement: Giving through the Conant Family Foundation.

Conant Family Foundation

20322 S.W. Acacia St., Ste. 100
Newport Beach, CA 92660-1503

Establishment information: Established in 1998 in CA.
Donors: Norm Reeves, Inc.; West Covina Auto Retail, Inc.; Cerritos Auto Retail Co.
Financial data (yr. ended 06/30/12): Assets, $2,018,521 (M); gifts received, $80,125; expenditures, $95,068; qualifying distributions, $77,500; giving activities include $77,500 for grants.
Purpose and activities: The foundation supports organizations involved with education, Parkinson's disease, human services, and Christianity.
Fields of interest: Education; Safety/disasters; Human services.
Type of support: General/operating support.
Support limitations: No grants to individuals.
Application information: Applications not accepted. Unsolicited requests for funds not accepted.
Directors: Catherine Conant; David M. Conant; Marlene Lewis; Jim Mortimer; Lee Stacy.
EIN: 954663527

3166
Regal Entertainment Group

7132 Regal Ln.
Knoxville, TN 37918 (865) 922-1123
FAX: (865) 922-3188

Company URL: http://www.regmovies.com/
Establishment information: Established in 1989.
Company type: Public company
Company ticker symbol and exchange: RGC/NYSE
Business activities: Operates motion picture theaters.
Business type (SIC): Motion picture theaters
Financial profile for 2012: Number of employees, 22,056; assets, $2,209,500,000; sales volume, $2,824,200,000; pre-tax net income, $235,900,000; expenses, $2,490,000,000; liabilities, $2,906,300,000
Fortune 1000 ranking: 2012—742nd in revenues, 660th in profits, and 829th in assets
Corporate officers: Michael L. Campbell, Chair.; Amy E. Miles, C.E.O.; Gregory W. Dunn, Pres. and C.O.O.; David H. Ownby, Exec. V.P., Treas., and C.F.O.; Peter B. Brandow, Exec. V.P., Genl. Counsel, and Secy.
Board of directors: Michael L. Campbell, Chair.; Thomas D. Bell, Jr.; Charles E. Brymer; Stephen A. Kaplan; David H. Keyte; Amy E. Miles; Lee M. Thomas; Jack Tyrrell; Nestor R. Weigand, Jr.; Alex Yemenidjian
Subsidiaries: Edwards Theaters, Inc., Knoxville, TN; National CineMedia, LLC, Centennial, CO; Regal Cinemas Corp., Knoxville, TN; United Artists Theatre Co., Knoxville, TN
Office: Pinellas Park, FL
Giving statement: Giving through the Regal Foundation.
Company EIN: 020556934

Regal Foundation

7132 Regal Ln.
Knoxville, TN 37918-5803 (865) 925-9435
URL: http://www.regmovies.com/About-Regal/Community-Affairs

Establishment information: Established in 2003.
Donor: Regal Entertainment Group.
Financial data (yr. ended 12/31/11): Assets, $7,686,190 (M); gifts received, $4,543,664; expenditures, $3,414,303; qualifying distributions, $3,413,390; giving activities include $3,173,405 for 150 grants (high: $268,513; low: $125).
Purpose and activities: The foundation supports food banks and organizations involved with arts and culture, education, health, cancer, multiple sclerosis, diabetes, child welfare, human services, and children. Special emphasis is directed toward programs designed to benefit economically disadvantaged people or persons suffering economic, social, physical, or educational hardship.
Fields of interest: Media, film/video; Museums (art); Performing arts, theater; Arts; Secondary school/education; Higher education; Education; Hospitals (general); Health care, patient services; Health care; Cancer; Multiple sclerosis; Diabetes; Crime/violence prevention, child abuse; Food banks; Boys & girls clubs; American Red Cross; YM/YWCAs & YM/YWHAs; Human services, gift distribution; Human services; United Ways and Federated Giving Programs Children; Economically disadvantaged.
Type of support: Capital campaigns; General/operating support; In-kind gifts; Program development; Scholarship funds; Sponsorships.
Geographic limitations: Giving primarily in areas of company operations in CA and Knoxville, TN.
Support limitations: No support for political or discriminatory organizations. No grants for travel, operating, or advertising expenses.
Application information: Applications not accepted.
Officers and Directors:* Michael L. Campbell*, Pres.; Gregory W. Dunn; Neal D. Pinsker; Amy E. Miles; Raymond L. Smith, Jr.
EIN: 134249812
Selected grants: The following grants are a representative sample of this grantmaker's funding activity:
$242,860 to University of Tennessee, Knoxville, TN, 2010.
$130,000 to Boys and Girls Clubs of America, Atlanta, GA, 2010.
$130,000 to Boys and Girls Clubs of America, Atlanta, GA, 2010.
$125,000 to Jimmy Fund, Brookline, MA, 2010.
$100,000 to Promise to Protect, Knoxville, TN, 2010.
$50,000 to Multiple Sclerosis Society, National, Los Angeles, CA, 2010.
$30,000 to Adoption Exchange, Aurora, CO, 2010.
$30,000 to Emerald Youth Foundation, Knoxville, TN, 2010.
$30,000 to Will Rogers Motion Picture Pioneers Foundation, Toluca Lake, CA, 2010.
$10,000 to Whiz Kids Tutoring, Denver, CO, 2010.

3167
Regal-Beloit Corporation

200 State St.
Beloit, WI 53511-6254 (608) 364-8800
FAX: (608) 364-8816

Company URL: http://www.regal-beloit.com
Establishment information: Established in 1955.
Company type: Public company
Company ticker symbol and exchange: RBC/NYSE
Business activities: Manufactures mechanical and electrical motion control products.
Business type (SIC): Machinery/general industry; electrical industrial apparatus
Financial profile for 2012: Number of employees, 23,800; assets, $3,569,100,000; sales volume, $3,166,900,000; pre-tax net income, $269,900,000; expenses, $2,854,100,000; liabilities, $1,615,700,000
Fortune 1000 ranking: 2012—682nd in revenues, 584th in profits, and 698th in assets
Corporate officers: Mark J. Gliebe, Chair. and C.E.O.; Jonathan J. Schlemmer, C.O.O.; Chuck A. Hinrichs, V.P. and C.F.O.; John M. Avampato, V.P. and C.I.O.; Peter C. Underwood, V.P., Genl. Counsel, and Secy.; Terry R. Colvin, V.P., Corp. Human Resources
Board of directors: Mark J. Gliebe, Chair.; Stephen Burt; Christopher L. Doerr; Thomas J. Fischer; Dean

A. Foate; Henry W. Knueppel, Jr.; Rakesh Sachdev; Carol N. Skornicka; Curtis W. Stoelting
International operations: British Virgin Islands; China; Germany; Italy; Netherlands; Singapore; United Kingdom
Giving statement: Giving through the Regal-Beloit Corporation Contributions Program and the Regal-Beloit Charitable Foundation.
Company EIN: 390875718

Regal-Beloit Charitable Foundation

200 State St.
Beloit, WI 53511-6254

Establishment information: Established in 1995 in WI.
Donor: Regal-Beloit Corp.
Financial data (yr. ended 12/31/11): Assets, $2,299,517 (M); gifts received, $500,000; expenditures, $320,695; qualifying distributions, $314,000; giving activities include $314,000 for grants.
Purpose and activities: The foundation supports organizations involved with health and recreation.
Fields of interest: Education; Recreation; Human services.
Type of support: Building/renovation; Capital campaigns.
Geographic limitations: Giving primarily in areas of company operations, with emphasis on Beloit, WI.
Support limitations: No grants to individuals.
Application information: Applications not accepted. Unsolicited requests for funds not accepted.
Officers and Trustees:* Henry W. Knoeppel*, Chair.; David A. Barta.
EIN: 391814812

3168
Regence BlueCross BlueShield of Oregon

100 S.W. Market St.
Portland, OR 97201-5766 (503) 225-5336

Company URL: http://www.regence.com/OR/index.jsp
Establishment information: Established in 1941.
Company type: Subsidiary of a private company
Business activities: Operates medical service plan.
Business type (SIC): Insurance/accident and health
Corporate officer: Don Antonucci, Pres.
Subsidiaries: Associated Administrators, Inc., Portland, OR; Regence HMO Oregon, Portland, OR; Regence Life & Health Insurance Co., Portland, OR
Giving statement: Giving through the Regence BlueCross BlueShield of Oregon Corporate Giving Program.

Regence BlueCross BlueShield of Oregon Corporate Giving Program

P.O. Box 1071
Portland, OR 97207-1071
URL: http://www.regence.com/about/community/index.jsp

Purpose and activities: As a complement to its foundation, Regence also makes charitable contributions to nonprofit organizations directly. Support is given primarily in areas of company operations in Oregon.
Fields of interest: Mental health, grief/bereavement counseling; Heart & circulatory diseases; Boys & girls clubs; Human services; Developmentally disabled, centers & services Children.
Type of support: General/operating support.
Geographic limitations: Giving primarily in OR.
Application information: Applications not accepted. Contributes only to pre-selected organizations.

3169
Regence BlueCross BlueShield of Utah

2890 E. Cottonwood Pkwy.
Salt Lake City, UT 84121 (801) 333-2100

Company URL: http://www.regence.com/UT/index.jsp
Establishment information: Established in 1942.
Company type: Subsidiary of a private company
Business activities: Operates medical service plan.
Business type (SIC): Insurance/accident and health
Corporate officers: Mark B. Ganz, Pres. and C.E.O.; Alfred Tredway, V.P., Sales
Offices: Ogden, Provo, UT
Giving statement: Giving through the Regence BlueCross BlueShield of Utah Corporate Giving Program.

Regence BlueCross BlueShield of Utah Corporate Giving Program

P.O. Box 30270
Salt Lake City, UT 84130-0270
URL: http://www.regence.com/about/community/index.jsp

Purpose and activities: Regence BlueCross BlueShield of Utah makes charitable contributions to nonprofit organizations involved with food services and housing. Support is given primarily in Utah.
Fields of interest: Food banks; Housing/shelter; Boys & girls clubs.
Type of support: General/operating support.
Geographic limitations: Giving primarily in UT.
Application information: Applications not accepted. Contributes only to pre-selected organizations.

3170
Reger Associates, Inc.

2124 Jefferson Davis Hwy., Ste. 303A
Stafford, VA 22554-7286 (540) 659-0295
FAX: (540) 659-3945

Company URL: http://www.regerlink.com
Establishment information: Established in 2000.
Company type: Private company
Business activities: Operates a defense contracting company.
Business type (SIC): Management and public relations services
Corporate officers: Rebekah Reger, Pres.; Tom Reger, V.P.; Kathy Bonello, Cont.
Giving statement: Giving through the We Help Them, Inc.

We Help Them, Inc.

Rte. 4
P.O. Box 638B
Buckhannon, WV 26201-9369

Establishment information: Established in 2004 in WV, classified as an independent foundation in 2006.
Donors: Reger Family Owned Business; Maurice J. Bohman; Cynthia A. Bohman; M. Jack Bohman; Stephen J. Bohman; The Reger Group.
Financial data (yr. ended 12/31/11): Assets, $45,461 (M); gifts received, $28,854; expenditures, $28,429; qualifying distributions, $2,050; giving activities include $2,050 for 7 grants to individuals (high: $500; low: $250).
Support limitations: No grants to individuals.
Application information: Applications not accepted. Unsolicited requests for funds not accepted.
Officers: Maurice J. Bohman, Pres.; Cynthia A. Bohman, V.P.; Steve Bohman, Treas.
Board Members: Ken Furl; Rick Rose; Richard D. Trent.
EIN: 550799337

3171
Regions Financial Corporation

(formerly First Alabama Bancshares, Inc.)
1900 5th Ave. N.
Birmingham, AL 35203 (205) 944-1300
FAX: (302) 636-5454

Company URL: https://www.regions.com
Establishment information: Established in 1971.
Company type: Public company
Company ticker symbol and exchange: RF/NYSE
Business activities: Operates bank holding company; operates commercial bank.
Business type (SIC): Banks/commercial; holding company
Financial profile for 2012: Number of employees, 23,427; assets, $121,347,000,000; pre-tax net income, $161,000,000; liabilities, $105,848,000,000
Fortune 1000 ranking: 2012—401st in revenues, 182nd in profits, and 52nd in assets
Forbes 2000 ranking: 2012—1288th in sales, 517th in profits, and 212th in assets
Corporate officers: Earnest W. Deavenport, Jr., Chair.; O.B. Grayson Hall, Jr., Pres. and C.E.O.; David J. Turner, Jr., Sr. Exec. V.P. and C.F.O.; David B. Edmonds, Sr. Exec. V.P. and C.A.O.; Fournier J. Gale III, Sr. Exec. V.P., Genl. Counsel, and Corp. Secy.
Board of directors: Earnest W. Deavenport, Jr., Chair.; Samuel W. Bartholomew, Jr.; George W. Bryan; Carolyn H. Byrd; David J. Cooper, Sr.; Don DeFosset; Eric C. Fast; O.B. Grayson Hall, Jr.; John D. Johns; James R. Malone; Susan W. Matlock; Ruth Ann Marshall; John E. Maupin, Jr.; Charles D. McCrary; John R. Roberts; Lee J. Styslinger III
Subsidiaries: First Alabama Bank, Albertville, AL; Rebsamen Insurance, Inc., Little Rock, AR; Union Planters Bank, N.A., Memphis, TN
Offices: Anniston, Athens, Birmingham, Columbus, Decatur, Dothan, Enterprise, Gadsden, Huntsville, Mobile, Montgomery, Phenix City, Santa Rosa, Selma, Troy, Tuscaloosa, AL
International operations: Bermuda; China; Turks & Caicos Islands
Historic mergers: AmSouth Bancorporation (November 4, 2006)
Giving statement: Giving through the Regions Financial Corporation Contributions Program, the Regions Financial Corporation Foundation, the Regions Foundation, and the Regions/AmSouth Foundation.
Company EIN: 630589368

Regions Financial Corporation Contributions Program

(formerly First Alabama Bancshares, Inc. Corporate Giving Program)
1900 5th Ave. N.
Birmingham, AL 35203-2669 (205) 944-1300
URL: http://www.regions.com/about_regions/sr_charitable_giving.rf

Purpose and activities: As a complement to its foundations, Regions also makes charitable contributions to nonprofit organizations directly. Special emphasis is directed towards financial literacy programs for children and youth, arts and culture, the environment, and community development. Support is limited to areas of company operations in Alabama, Arkansas, Florida, Georgia, Illinois, Indiana, Iowa, Kentucky, Louisiana, Mississippi, Missouri, North Carolina, South Carolina, Tennessee, Texas, and Virginia.
Fields of interest: Arts; Elementary/secondary education; Environment; Health care; Housing/shelter; Youth development; Children, services; Human services, financial counseling; Community development, small businesses; United Ways and Federated Giving Programs Economically disadvantaged.
Type of support: Curriculum development; Employee volunteer services; General/operating support; Program development.
Geographic limitations: Giving limited to areas of company operations in AL, AR, FL, GA, IA, IL, IN, KY, LA, MI, MO, NC, SC, TN, TX, and VA.
Support limitations: No support for political or discriminatory organizations, religious organizations not of direct benefit to the entire community, national organizations with no direct ties to areas of company operations, or alumni associations. No grants to individuals, or for annual operating campaigns of organizations supported by United Way, or athletic scholarships.
Publications: Application guidelines.
Application information: Applications accepted. Proposals should be submitted on organization letterhead and be no longer than 2 pages. Application form not required. Applicants should submit the following:
1) copy of IRS Determination Letter
2) copy of most recent annual report/audited financial statement/990
3) listing of board of directors, trustees, officers and other key people and their affiliations
4) additional materials/documentation

Initial approach: Proposal to local Regions city president
Copies of proposal: 1
Deadline(s): None
Final notification: 30 to 45 days

Regions Financial Corporation Foundation

(formerly Regions Bancorporation Foundation)
c/o Regions Bank
P.O. Box 11426
Birmingham, AL 35202-1647

Establishment information: Established in 1997 in AL.
Donors: AmSouth Bank; AmSouth Bancorporation; Regions Financial Corp.; Regions Morgan Keegan Trust.
Contact: Ann Wells, Treas.
Financial data (yr. ended 12/31/11): Assets, $1,225,152 (M); expenditures, $1,858,048; qualifying distributions, $1,857,048; giving activities include $1,857,048 for 765 grants (high: $200,000; low: $25).
Purpose and activities: The foundation supports organizations involved with health, housing, and human services. Special emphasis is directed toward education and arts and culture.
Fields of interest: Arts; Elementary/secondary education; Higher education; Education; Hospitals (general); Health care, patient services; Health care; YM/YWCAs & YM/YWHAs; Children/youth, services; Human services.
Program:
Matching Gifts Program: The foundation matches contributions made by employees and retirees of Regions Financial Corporation to educational institutions and arts and cultural organizations on a one-for-one basis from $25 to $1,000 per contributor, per year.
Type of support: Continuing support; Employee matching gifts; General/operating support.
Geographic limitations: Giving primarily in AL and FL; some giving also in GA and TN.
Support limitations: No support for religious organizations not of direct benefit to the entire community, political organizations, or alumni groups. No grants to individuals, or for cultural or social events.
Application information: Applications not accepted. Contributes only to pre-selected organizations and through employee matching gifts.
Officers and Directors:* Fournier J. Gale III*, Pres.; Douglas J. Jackson*, V.P.; Dale M. Herbert, Secy.; Ann W. Forney, Treas.; David B. Edmonds; William D. Ritter; Regions Bank.
EIN: 631144265
Selected grants: The following grants are a representative sample of this grantmaker's funding activity:
$200,000 to University of Alabama, Tuscaloosa, AL, 2010.

Regions Foundation

(formerly AmSouth Foundation)
P.O. Box 13906
Jackson, MS 39236-3906
FAX: (601) 510-9287

Establishment information: Incorporated in 1962 in MS.
Donors: Deposit Guaranty National Bank; First American National Bank.
Financial data (yr. ended 12/31/11): Assets, $10,546,652 (M); expenditures, $849,418; qualifying distributions, $755,000; giving activities include $755,000 for grants.
Purpose and activities: The foundation supports hospitals and organizations involved with arts and culture, education, youth development, human services, and Christianity.
Fields of interest: Arts; Education; Hospitals (general); Boys & girls clubs; Boy scouts; Youth development; American Red Cross; Salvation Army; YM/YWCAs & YM/YWHAs; Children/youth, services; Human services; Christian agencies & churches.
Type of support: Annual campaigns; Capital campaigns; Employee matching gifts; General/operating support; Program-related investments/loans; Scholarship funds.
Geographic limitations: Giving limited to MS.
Support limitations: No grants to individuals.
Application information: Applications not accepted. Contributes only to pre-selected organizations.
Board meeting date(s): Annually
Officers and Directors:* Charles L. Irby*, Chair.; James W. Hood*, Vice-Chair. and Pres.; Debbie Purvis, Secy.; Richard D. McRae, Jr., Treas.; Sharon S. Greener; William R. James; James L. Moore; W.R. Newman III; E.B. Robinson, Jr.; Ronnie Smith.
EIN: 646026793
Selected grants: The following grants are a representative sample of this grantmaker's funding activity:
$125,000 to SafeCity Initiative, Jackson, MS, 2008.
$100,000 to Boy Scouts of America, Andrew Jackson Council, Jackson, MS, 2008.
$50,000 to Boys and Girls Clubs of Central Mississippi, Jackson, MS, 2008.
$50,000 to Chamberlain-Hunt Academy, Port Gibson, MS, 2008.
$50,000 to Childrens Scholarship Fund - Metro Jackson, Jackson, MS, 2008.
$50,000 to Mission First, Jackson, MS, 2008.
$50,000 to Young Life Jackson Metro, Jackson, MS, 2008.
$40,000 to New Horizons Ministries, Moss Point, MS, 2008.
$30,000 to Fellowship of Christian Athletes, Kansas City, MO, 2008.
$25,000 to Mississippi Center for Public Policy, Jackson, MS, 2008.

Regions/AmSouth Foundation

(formerly AmSouth/First American Foundation)
c/o Regions Bank, Tr. Dept.
P.O. Box 2886
Mobile, AL 36652-2886

Establishment information: Established in 1994 in TN.
Donors: First American National Bank; AmSouth Bank.
Financial data (yr. ended 12/31/11): Assets, $4,773,188 (M); expenditures, $325,984; qualifying distributions, $282,500; giving activities include $282,500 for grants.
Purpose and activities: The foundation supports organizations involved with arts and culture, education, health, substance abuse treatment, cancer, and youth development.
Fields of interest: Museums (science/technology); Performing arts, ballet; Performing arts, music; Performing arts, orchestras; Historic preservation/historical societies; Arts; Higher education; Education; Health care; Substance abuse, treatment; Cancer; Boy scouts.
Type of support: General/operating support.
Geographic limitations: Giving limited to TN.
Support limitations: No grants to individuals.
Application information: Applications not accepted. Contributes only to pre-selected organizations.
Officers and Directors:* Jim Schmitz*, Pres.; Latrisha Jamison, Treas.; Donna Cheek; Walter Knestrick; Martin Simmons.
EIN: 582071018
Selected grants: The following grants are a representative sample of this grantmaker's funding activity:
$100,000 to Nashville Symphony, Nashville, TN, 2009.
$25,000 to Carson-Newman College, Jefferson City, TN, 2009.
$20,000 to Cumberland Heights Alcohol and Drug Treatment Center, Nashville, TN, 2009.
$10,000 to American Cancer Society, Nashville, TN, 2009.
$10,000 to Mountain States Foundation, Johnson City, TN, 2009.
$10,000 to Tennessee Residence Foundation, Nashville, TN, 2009.
$5,000 to East Tennessee State University, Johnson City, TN, 2009.

3172
Regis Corporation
7201 Metro Blvd.
Minneapolis, MN 55439-2103
(952) 947-7777
FAX: (952) 947-7700

Company URL: http://www.regiscorp.com
Establishment information: Established in 1922.
Company type: Public company
Company ticker symbol and exchange: RGS/NYSE
Business activities: Owns, operates, and franchises hair and hair product salons.
Business type (SIC): Personal services; beauty shops
Financial profile for 2012: Number of employees, 52,000; assets, $1,571,850,000; sales volume, $2,273,780,000; pre-tax net income, -$90,430,000; expenses, $2,341,090,000; liabilities, $682,690,000
Fortune 1000 ranking: 2012—859th in revenues, 929th in profits, and 913th in assets
Corporate officers: Joseph L. Conner, Chair.; Daniel J. Hanrahan, Pres. and C.E.O.; Eric A. Bakken, Exec. V.P., Genl. Counsel, and C.A.O.; Steven M. Spiegel, Exec. V.P. and C.F.O.; Doug Reynolds, Sr. V.P. and C.I.O.; Mark Fosland, Sr. V.P., Finance
Board of directors: Joseph L. Conner, Chair.; Daniel Beltzman; James P. Fogarty; Daniel J. Hanrahan; Michael J. Merriman; Jeffrey C. Smith; Stephen E. Watson; David P. Williams
Offices: Selma, AL; Anchorage, AK; Tucson, AZ; Woodland, CA; Durango, CO; Meriden, CT; Dover, DE; Clearwater, FL; LaGrange, GA; Hilo, HI; Perkin, IL; Bedford, IN; Keokuk, IA; Dodge City, KS; Monroe, LA; Bangor, ME; Waldorf, MD; Hyannis, MA; Port Huron, MI; Eden Prairie, Edina, Roseville, MN
International operations: Canada; France; Germany; Netherlands; United Kingdom
Giving statement: Giving through the Regis Corporation Contributions Program and the Regis Foundation.
Company EIN: 410749934

Regis Corporation Contributions Program
7201 Metro Blvd.
Minneapolis, MN 55439 (952) 947-7777
URL: http://www.regiscorp.com/NA/RegisFoundation/default.asp

The Regis Foundation
7201 Metro Blvd.
Minneapolis, MN 55439-2103 (952) 947-7777

Establishment information: Established in 1981 in MN.
Donors: Regis Corp.; Regis, Inc.
Contact: Paul Finkelstein, Pres.
Financial data (yr. ended 06/30/12): Assets, $744,171 (M); gifts received, $6,000; expenditures, $406,925; qualifying distributions, $404,900; giving activities include $404,900 for grants.
Purpose and activities: The foundation supports organizations involved with arts and culture, education, human services, and Judaism.
Fields of interest: Arts; Elementary/secondary education; Higher education; Libraries (public); Education; Human services; United Ways and Federated Giving Programs; Jewish federated giving programs; Jewish agencies & synagogues.
Type of support: Annual campaigns; Building/renovation; Capital campaigns; General/operating support; Scholarship funds.
Geographic limitations: Giving primarily in the Minneapolis, MN, area.
Application information: Applications accepted. Application form not required.
Initial approach: Proposal
Deadline(s): None
Officers and Directors: Paul Finkelstein, Pres.; Eric A. Bakken, Secy.; Randy Pearce, Treas.
EIN: 411410790
Selected grants: The following grants are a representative sample of this grantmaker's funding activity:
$150,000 to Minneapolis Jewish Federation, Minnetonka, MN, 2011. For general contribution.
$105,000 to Minneapolis Society of Fine Arts, Minneapolis, MN, 2011.
$100,000 to Students in Free Enterprise, Springfield, MO, 2011. For general contribution.
$71,500 to Walker Art Center, Minneapolis, MN, 2011.
$50,000 to United Way, Greater Twin Cities, Minneapolis, MN, 2011. For general contribution.
$15,000 to Ordway Center for the Performing Arts, Saint Paul, MN, 2011. For general contribution.
$10,000 to American Jewish Committee, Chicago, IL, 2011. For general contribution.
$5,000 to Japanese American National Museum, Los Angeles, CA, 2011. For general contribution.
$3,000 to Harvard University, Cambridge, MA, 2011. For general contribution.
$3,000 to University of Pennsylvania, Philadelphia, PA, 2011. For general contribution.

3173
Reid & Riege, P.C.
1 Financial Plz., 21st. Fl.
755 Main St., Ste. 21
Hartford, CT 06103 (860) 278-1150

Company URL: http://www.reidandriege.com/
Establishment information: Established in 1950.
Company type: Private company
Business activities: Provides legal services.
Business type (SIC): Legal services
Corporate officers: John H. Riege, Chair.; Julie Traczyk, C.I.O.; Bruce Lyon, Admin.
Board of director: John H. Riege, Chair.
Giving statement: Giving through the Reid & Riege Foundation.

Reid & Riege Foundation
1 Financial Plz.
Hartford, CT 06103-2608 (860) 278-1150

Donor: Reid & Riege, P.C.
Contact: Suzanne S. Bocchini, Pres.
Financial data (yr. ended 12/31/11): Assets, $529,025 (M); gifts received, $100,020; expenditures, $114,260; qualifying distributions, $111,043; giving activities include $111,043 for grants.
Purpose and activities: The foundation supports art museums and organizations involved with performing arts, health, domestic violence prevention, legal aid, and human services.
Fields of interest: Health care; Recreation; Civil/human rights.
Type of support: Employee matching gifts; General/operating support.
Geographic limitations: Giving limited to the greater Hartford, CT, area.
Application information: Applications accepted. Application form required.
Initial approach: Letter
Deadline(s): None
Officers: Suzanne S. Bocchini, Pres.; Karen L. Brand, V.P.; David L. Sullivan, Secy.-Treas.
Directors: John V. Galiette; Devin M. Karas; Thomas R. Kasper; Jon P. Newton.
EIN: 061077969

3174
Reiff & Nestor Company
50 Reiff St. W.
Lykens, PA 17048 (717) 453-7113

Company URL: http://www.rntap.com
Establishment information: Established in 1912.
Company type: Private company
Business activities: Manufactures taps.
Business type (SIC): Machinery/metalworking
Corporate officers: Patrick J. Savage, Pres.; Mary Nestor, V.P. and Secy.
Giving statement: Giving through the Nestor Charitable Foundation and the Mary Margaret Nestor Foundation.

The Nestor Charitable Foundation
Reiff & West Sts.
P.O. Box 147
Lykens, PA 17048

Establishment information: Established in 1952.
Donors: Reiff & Nestor Co.; Mary Margaret Nestor Charitable Fund.
Financial data (yr. ended 06/30/12): Assets, $51,605 (M); expenditures, $26,147; qualifying distributions, $21,926; giving activities include $21,926 for grants.
Purpose and activities: The foundation supports organizations involved with education, health, hunger, athletics, human services, and Christianity.
Fields of interest: Secondary school/education; Libraries (public); Education; Health care; Food services; Athletics/sports, amateur leagues; Athletics/sports, baseball; YM/YWCAs & YM/YWHAs; Human services; Christian agencies & churches.
Type of support: General/operating support; Scholarship funds.
Geographic limitations: Giving primarily in the Lykens, PA, area.
Support limitations: No loans or program-related investments.
Application information: Applications accepted. Application form required. Applicants should submit the following:
1) brief history of organization and description of its mission
2) descriptive literature about organization
3) detailed description of project and amount of funding requested
Initial approach: Letter
Deadline(s): None
Officers: Donald E. Nestor, Pres.; Robin M. Nestor, Secy.
EIN: 236255983

Mary Margaret Nestor Foundation
c/o Reiff & Nestor Co.
P.O. Box 147
Lykens, PA 17048 (717) 453-7113

Establishment information: Established in 1953 in PA.
Donors: Reiff & Nestor Co.; Nester Charitable Foundation.
Contact: Donald E. Nestor, Pres.

Financial data (yr. ended 06/30/12): Assets, $3,102 (M); gifts received, $4,000; expenditures, $6,995; qualifying distributions, $5,000; giving activities include $5,000 for grants to individuals.
Purpose and activities: The foundation awards scholarships to residents of Dauphin County, Pennsylvania.
Type of support: Scholarships—to individuals.
Geographic limitations: Giving primarily to residents of Dauphin County, PA.
Application information: Applications accepted. Application form required.
Letters of inquiry should include a resume detailing both academic and personal achievements of the candidate.
Initial approach: Letter of inquiry
Deadline(s): None
Officers: Donald E. Nestor, Pres.; Robin M. Nestor, Secy.
EIN: 236277570

3175
Reilly Electrical Contractors, Inc.
14 Norfolk Ave.
South Easton, MA 02375-1907
(508) 230-8001

Company URL: http://www.gorelco.com/aboutus/welcome.php
Establishment information: Established in 1993.
Company type: Private company
Business activities: Provides contract electrical services.
Business type (SIC): Contractors/electrical work
Corporate officers: James J. Reilly, Pres.; Michael McSheffrey, V.P., Opers.; Joseph Fannon, V.P., Finance
Giving statement: Giving through the Reilly Foundation, Inc.

The Reilly Foundation, Inc.
14 Norfolk Ave.
Easton, MA 02375-1907

Establishment information: Established in 2001 in MA.
Donor: Reilly Electrical Contractors, Inc.
Financial data (yr. ended 06/30/12): Assets, $178 (M); expenditures, $112; qualifying distributions, $0.
Purpose and activities: The foundation supports organizations involved with secondary education, health, cancer, recreation, children and youth, and disability services.
Type of support: General/operating support.
Geographic limitations: Giving limited to MA.
Support limitations: No grants to individuals.
Application information: Applications not accepted. Unsolicited requests for funds not accepted.
Officer: James Reilly, Pres.
EIN: 043573745

3176
Reilly Pozner LLP
1900 16th St., Ste. 1700
Denver, CO 80202-5259 (303) 893-6100

Company URL: http://www.rplaw.com/index.php
Company type: Private company
Business activities: Operates law firm.
Business type (SIC): Legal services
Office: Denver, CO
Giving statement: Giving through the Reilly Pozner LLP Pro Bono Program.

Reilly Pozner LLP Pro Bono Program
1900 16th St., Ste. 1700
Denver, CO 80202-5259 (303) 893-6100
E-mail: info@rplaw.com; URL: http://www.rplaw.com/probono/

Contact: John C. Hanley, Exec. Dir.
Fields of interest: Legal services.
Type of support: Pro bono services - legal.

3177
Reily Foods, Co.
(formerly Wm. B. Reily & Co.)
640 Magazine St.
New Orleans, LA 70130-3406
(504) 524-6131

Company URL: http://www.rfoods.com
Establishment information: Established in 1902.
Company type: Subsidiary of a private company
Business activities: Produces coffee, tea, salad dressing, cooking oil, and mayonnaise.
Business type (SIC): Groceries—wholesale; specialty foods/canned, frozen, and preserved; fats and oils; miscellaneous prepared foods
Corporate officers: William B. Reily III, Chair.; James C. McCarthy III, Pres. and C.E.O.; Steve Smith, C.F.O.; Harold Herrmann, Jr., Exec. V.P. and C.F.O.; Tony Doughty, V.P., Opers.; John Sillars, V.P., Mktg.; Jim Dunnigan, V.P., Sales.
Board of director: William B. Reily III, Chair.
Giving statement: Giving through the Reily Foundation.

The Reily Foundation
640 Magazine St.
New Orleans, LA 70130-3406
FAX: (504) 539-5418

Establishment information: Established in 1962.
Donor: Reily Foods Co.
Contact: Robert D. Reily, Dir.
Financial data (yr. ended 12/31/11): Assets, $16,539,729 (M); expenditures, $1,006,275; qualifying distributions, $895,329; giving activities include $895,329 for grants.
Purpose and activities: The foundation supports community foundations and organizations involved with arts and culture, education, health, human services, and civic affairs.
Fields of interest: Performing arts, orchestras; Arts; Education, reform; Charter schools; Higher education; Education; Health care; Children/youth, services; Human services; Foundations (community); United Ways and Federated Giving Programs; Public policy, research; Public affairs.
Type of support: Building/renovation; Capital campaigns; Continuing support; Equipment; General/operating support; Program development.
Geographic limitations: Giving primarily in the greater New Orleans, LA, area.
Support limitations: No support for religious or political organizations. No grants to individuals.
Application information: Applications accepted. Southern Louisiana Grantmakers Forum Common Application Form accepted. Application form required.
Initial approach: Contact foundation for application form
Board meeting date(s): Varies
Deadline(s): None
Directors: Robert Aron; Joan M. Coulter; Robert D. Reily; William B. Reily III; Stephen Usdin.
EIN: 726029179
Selected grants: The following grants are a representative sample of this grantmaker's funding activity:
$80,000 to New Schools for New Orleans, New Orleans, LA, 2010.
$60,000 to Bureau of Governmental Research, New Orleans, LA, 2010. For capital campaign.
$60,000 to Louisiana Philharmonic Orchestra, New Orleans, LA, 2010.
$40,000 to Xavier University of Louisiana, New Orleans, LA, 2010. For capital campaign.
$25,000 to KIPP New Orleans, New Orleans, LA, 2010.
$25,000 to Louisiana Society for the Prevention of Cruelty to Animals, New Orleans, LA, 2010.
$16,000 to New Orleans Opera Association, New Orleans, LA, 2010.
$12,500 to Save the Oaks, New Orleans, LA, 2010.
$12,000 to Greater New Orleans Foundation, New Orleans, LA, 2010.
$8,000 to Committee for a Better New Orleans/Metropolitan Area Committee, New Orleans, LA, 2010.

3178
Reinhart Boerner Van Deuren S.C.
1000 N. Water St.
P.O Box 2965
Milwaukee, WI 53201-2965
(414) 298-1000

Company URL: http://www.reinhartlaw.com
Establishment information: Established in 1894.
Company type: Private company
Business activities: Operates law firm.
Business type (SIC): Legal services
Offices: Scottsdale, AZ; Greenwood Village, CO; Rockford, IL; Madison, Milwaukee, Waukesha, WI
Giving statement: Giving through the Reinhart Boerner Van Deuren S.C. Pro Bono Program.

Reinhart Boerner Van Deuren S.C. Pro Bono Program
1000 N. Water St.
P.O Box 2965
Milwaukee, WI 53201-2965 (414) 298-1000
URL: http://www.reinhartlaw.com/About/Pages/ProBono.aspx

Fields of interest: Legal services.
Type of support: Pro bono services - legal.
Application information: A Pro Bono Committee manages the pro bono program.

3179
Reinsurance Group of America, Incorporated
1370 Timberlake Manor Pkwy.
Chesterfield, MO 63017-6039
(636) 736-7000
FAX: (636) 736-7100

Company URL: http://www.rgare.com
Establishment information: Established in 1973.

Company type: Public company
Company ticker symbol and exchange: RGA/NYSE
Business activities: Operates holding company; sells life and disability reinsurance; sells life and disability insurance.
Business type (SIC): Insurance/accident and health; insurance/life; holding company
Financial profile for 2012: Number of employees, 1,766; assets, $40,360,440,000; sales volume, $9,840,910,000; pre-tax net income, $919,220,000; expenses, $8,921,690,000; liabilities, $33,450,250,000
Fortune 1000 ranking: 2012—275th in revenues, 281st in profits, and 139th in assets
Forbes 2000 ranking: 2012—949th in sales, 916th in profits, and 573rd in assets
Corporate officers: J. Cliff Eason, Chair.; A. Greig Woodring, Pres. and C.E.O.; Donna H. Kinnaird, Sr. Exec. V.P. and C.O.O.; Jack B. Lay, Sr. Exec. V.P. and C.F.O.; William L. Hutton, Exec. V.P., Genl. Counsel, and Secy.; Mark E. Showers, Exec. V.P. and C.I.O.
Board of directors: J. Cliff Eason, Chair.; William J. Bartlett; Arnoud W. A. Boot; John F. Danahy; Alan C. Henderson; Rachel Lomax; Frederick J. Sievert; Stanley B. Tulin; A. Greig Woodring
Giving statement: Giving through the Reinsurance Group of America, Inc. Contributions Program and the Longer Life Foundation.
Company EIN: 431627032

Reinsurance Group of America, Inc. Contributions Program

1370 Timberlake Manor Pkwy.
Chesterfield, MO 63017-6039 (636) 736-7000
URL: http://www.rgare.com

Longer Life Foundation

1370 Timberlake Manor Pkwy.
Chesterfield, MO 63017-6039
E-mail: psmalley@rgare.com; Application address: 161 Bay St., Ste. 4600, P.O. Box 620, Toronto, Ontario, Canada M5J 2S1, tel.: (416) 943-6797, fax: (416) 943-0880; Additional contact: Joan Heins, tel.: (314) 286-1912, e-mail: jheins@dom.wustl.edu; URL: http://www.longerlife.org

Establishment information: Established in 1998 in MO.
Donor: Reinsurance Group of America, Inc.
Contact: Philip S. Smalley M.D., Managing Dir.
Financial data (yr. ended 12/31/11): Assets, $147,127 (M); gifts received, $400,000; expenditures, $374,476; qualifying distributions, $369,150; giving activities include $369,150 for grants.
Purpose and activities: The foundation supports programs designed to study factors that assist in predicting mortality and morbidity of selected populations; and research methods to promote improvements in longevity and health by analyzing the effects of changes in medicine and advances in public health practices.
Fields of interest: Public health; Medical research, institute.
Type of support: Research.
Geographic limitations: Giving primarily in St. Louis, MO.
Publications: Application guidelines; Grants list.
Application information: Applications accepted. Letters of intent should be no longer than 1 to 2 pages. Applicants should also submit an NIH-format biographical sketch. A full application may be requested at a later date. Application form not required. Applicants should submit the following:
1) results expected from proposed grant
2) how project's results will be evaluated or measured
3) explanation of why grantmaker is considered an appropriate donor for project
4) detailed description of project and amount of funding requested

Visit website for detailed application guidelines.
Initial approach: E-mail letter of intent
Deadline(s): Feb. 20
Final notification: Apr. 20
Officers and Directors:* A. Greig Woodring*, Chair.; Larry Shapiro, M.D.*, Vice-Chair.; Sara McCarty, Secy.; Jeffrey Boyer, Treas.
EIN: 431819267
Selected grants: The following grants are a representative sample of this grantmaker's funding activity:
$387,157 to Washington University, Saint Louis, MO, 2010.

3180
William H. Reisner Corporation

33 Elm St.
Clinton, MA 01510-2307 (978) 365-4585

Company URL: http://www.reisner.com/
Establishment information: Established in 1891.
Company type: Private company
Business activities: Recycles copper.
Business type (SIC): Metals and minerals, except petroleum—wholesale
Giving statement: Giving through the William H. Reisner Foundation.

William H. Reisner Foundation

33 Elm St.
Clinton, MA 01510-2307

Establishment information: Established in 1952 in MA.
Donors: William H. Reisner Corp.; Auburn Industrial Development Corp.
Financial data (yr. ended 12/31/11): Assets, $182,098 (M); gifts received, $735; expenditures, $54,476; qualifying distributions, $50,568; giving activities include $50,568 for grants.
Purpose and activities: The foundation supports hospitals and organizations involved with education and Judaism.
Fields of interest: Religion.
Type of support: General/operating support; Scholarship funds.
Geographic limitations: Giving primarily in Clinton, MA.
Application information: Applications not accepted. Unsolicited requests for funds not accepted.
Trustees: Harold H. Reisner; William M. Reisner.
EIN: 046108949

3181
Reitman Industries

10 Patton Dr.
West Caldwell, NJ 07006-6405
(973) 228-5100

Establishment information: Established in 2007.
Company type: Subsidiary of a private company
Business activities: Sells wines and alcoholic beverages wholesale.
Business type (SIC): Beer, wine, and distilled beverages—wholesale
Giving statement: Giving through the Reitman Foundation.

Reitman Foundation

10 Patton Dr.
West Caldwell, NJ 07006-6405

Donor: Reitman Industries.
Financial data (yr. ended 08/31/11): Assets, $2,526,331 (M); expenditures, $106,054; qualifying distributions, $87,972; giving activities include $77,500 for 3 grants (high: $50,000; low: $12,500).
Purpose and activities: The foundation supports organizations involved with arts and culture, education, children and youth, and human services.
Fields of interest: Arts; Higher education; Children/youth, services; Human services; Jewish federated giving programs.
Type of support: General/operating support; Scholarship funds.
Geographic limitations: Giving primarily in NJ.
Support limitations: No grants to individuals.
Application information: Applications not accepted. Unsolicited requests for funds not accepted.
Officers and Trustees:* Margaret Jacobs*, Co-Pres.; Elizabeth Lowenstein*, Co.-Pres.; Kim Jacobs; Kristy Maslin; Dana Siegel.
EIN: 237086130

3182
Reliable Brokerage, Inc.

4 Garfield Rd., Ste. 104
P.O. Box 655
Monroe, NY 10950-6029 (845) 783-6286

Company URL: http://www.reliablebrokerage.com
Establishment information: Established in 1996.
Company type: Private company
Business activities: Operates insurance brokerage company.
Business type (SIC): Insurance agents, brokers, and services
Corporate officers: Henry Kellner, Chair., Co-Pres., and C.E.O.; Sarah Newhouser, Co-Pres.
Board of director: Henry Kellner, Chair.
Giving statement: Giving through the Yachad Monsey Inc.

Yachad Monsey Inc.

80 Herrick Ave.
Spring Valley, NY 10977-3817

Establishment information: Established in 2006 in NY.
Donors: Henry Kellner; Reliable Brokerage, Inc.
Financial data (yr. ended 11/30/11): Assets, $47,138 (M); gifts received, $79,600; expenditures, $59,764; qualifying distributions, $59,020; giving activities include $59,020 for 12 grants (high: $25,000; low: $360).
Fields of interest: Jewish agencies & synagogues.
Geographic limitations: Giving primarily in NY.
Support limitations: No grants to individuals.
Application information: Applications not accepted. Unsolicited requests for funds not accepted.
Officers: Henry Kellner, Pres.; Genesha Kellner, Secy.; Kaila Kellner, Treas.
EIN: 205973211

3183
Remmele Engineering, Inc.
10 Old Hwy. 8
New Brighton, MN 55112 (651) 635-4100

Company URL: http://www.remmele.com
Establishment information: Established in 1949.
Company type: Private company
Business activities: Designs and manufactures specialty machinery.
Business type (SIC): Machinery/general industry; computer and office equipment; machinery/ industrial and commercial; aircraft and parts; search and navigation equipment
Corporate officers: William J. Saul, Chair.; Paul Burton, Pres. and C.E.O.; Vinette Hamm, V.P., Human Resources
Board of director: William J. Saul, Chair.
Giving statement: Giving through the Remmele Foundation.

Remmele Foundation
10 Old Hwy. 8 S.W.
New Brighton, MN 55112-7709

Donor: Remmele Engineering, Inc.
Financial data (yr. ended 12/31/10): Assets, $13,453 (M); expenditures, $2,608; qualifying distributions, $2,608; giving activities include $2,500 for 1 grant to an individual.
Purpose and activities: The foundation awards college scholarships to children of employees and former employees of Remmele Engineering.
Type of support: Employee-related scholarships.
Geographic limitations: Giving limited to MN.
Application information: Applications not accepted. Unsolicited requests for funds not accepted.
Officers: Charles Jungmann, Secy.; Michael Hacknel, Treas.
EIN: 411356088

3184
Rennoc Corporation
3501 South East Blvd.
Vineland, NJ 08360-7780 (856) 327-5400

Company URL: http://www.rennoc.com
Establishment information: Established in 1954.
Company type: Private company
Business activities: Manufactures jackets and pants.
Business type (SIC): Apparel—men's and boys' outerwear
Corporate officer: Michael J. Bruzzese, Pres.
Giving statement: Giving through the Rennoc Corporation Foundation, Inc.

Rennoc Corporation Foundation, Inc.
11 Packer C.T
Sewell, NJ 08080
Application address: P. O. Box 337, Shiloh NJ 08053

Establishment information: Established in 1995 in NJ.
Donors: Michael J. Bruzzese; Carol L. Conner; Deborah L. Conner; Kimberly S. Conner; Samuel R. Conner; Karen B. Iveson; Rennoc Corp.; Kathryn E. Vertolli.
Contact: Samuel R. Conner, Pres.
Financial data (yr. ended 12/31/11): Assets, $2,183,943 (M); expenditures, $104,739; qualifying distributions, $96,300; giving activities include $96,300 for 31 grants (high: $13,000; low: $500).
Purpose and activities: The foundation supports organizations involved with secondary education, the environment, substance abuse treatment, hunger, human services, and Christianity.
Fields of interest: Secondary school/education; Environment; Health care; Substance abuse, treatment; Food services; Residential/custodial care, hospices; Human services; Christian agencies & churches.
Type of support: General/operating support.
Support limitations: No grants to individuals.
Application information: Applications accepted. Application form not required. Applicants should submit the following:
1) name, address and phone number of organization
2) brief history of organization and description of its mission
3) detailed description of project and amount of funding requested

Initial approach: Proposal
Deadline(s): None

Officers: Samuel R. Conner, Pres.; Karen B. Iveson, V.P.; Kathryn E. Vertolli, V.P.
EIN: 223338564
Selected grants: The following grants are a representative sample of this grantmaker's funding activity:
$13,000 to Bayshore Discovery Project, Port Norris, NJ, 2009.
$4,000 to Saint Johns Hospice, Philadelphia, PA, 2009.
$2,000 to IDEA Ministries, Grand Rapids, MI, 2009.

3185
The Renovated Home Ltd.
1477 3rd Ave.
New York, NY 10028-1948 (212) 517-7020

Company URL: http://www.therenovatedhome.com
Establishment information: Established in 1989.
Company type: Private company
Business activities: Operates design and general contracting company.
Business type (SIC): Contractors/miscellaneous special trade
Corporate officer: Lee J. Stahl, Pres.
Board of director: Kristen Hancock
Giving statement: Giving through the Lee J. Stahl and Toby Stahl-Maranga Charitable Foundation.

Lee J. Stahl and Toby Stahl-Maranga Charitable Foundation
1477 3rd Ave., 2nd Fl.
New York, NY 10028-1948

Establishment information: Established in 2004 in NY.
Donor: The Renovated Home.
Financial data (yr. ended 11/30/11): Assets, $811,078 (M); gifts received, $100,000; expenditures, $42,075; qualifying distributions, $39,650; giving activities include $39,650 for 15 grants (high: $3,000; low: $1,000).
Fields of interest: Animal welfare; Boys clubs; Human services, alliance/advocacy; Homeless, human services; International agricultural development.
Support limitations: No grants to individuals.
Application information: Applications not accepted. Unsolicited requests for funds not accepted.
Directors: Toby Maranga; Lee J. Stahl.
EIN: 206379095

3186
The Republic of Tea
5 Hamilton Landing, Ste. 100
Novato, CA 94949-8703 (415) 382-3400
FAX: (415) 382-3401

Company URL: http://www.republicoftea.com
Establishment information: Established in 1992.
Company type: Private company
Business activities: Produces tea.
Business type (SIC): Miscellaneous prepared foods
Financial profile for 2010: Number of employees, 25
Corporate officers: Ronald T. Rubin, Pres. and C.E.O.; Steve Lohmann, C.F.O. and Cont.
Giving statement: Giving through the Republic of Tea Foundation.

The Republic of Tea Foundation
(formerly Central Wholesale Liquor Foundation)
17577 Mockingbird Rd.
Nashville, IL 62263-3407 (618) 478-5520

Establishment information: Established in 1990 in IL as a company-sponsored operating foundation.
Donors: Central Wholesale Liquor Co.; Republic of Tea, Inc.; The Republic of Tea.
Financial data (yr. ended 04/30/11): Assets, $22,401 (M); gifts received, $25,000; expenditures, $24,381; qualifying distributions, $23,981; giving activities include $23,981 for 17 grants to individuals (high: $2,000; low: $155).
Purpose and activities: The foundation awards college scholarships to children of employees of Republic of Tea.
Type of support: Employee-related scholarships.
Application information: Applications not accepted. Contributes only through employee-related scholarships.
Officers: Ronald T. Rubin, Pres. and Treas.; Pamela Rubin, Secy.
EIN: 371264351

3187
Republic Trinidad Corporation
(formerly The Republic Corporation)
5340 Weslwynn St.
P.O. Box 270462
Houston, TX 77277 (713) 993-9200

Company URL: http://www.fnbtrinidad.com
Establishment information: Established in 1955.
Company type: Private company
Business activities: Operates bank holding company; operates commercial bank.
Business type (SIC): Banks/commercial; holding company
Corporate officers: J.E. Eisemann IV, Chair. and C.E.O.; Jeff Mangino, Pres.; Roger D. Eisemann, Secy.-Treas.
Board of directors: J.E. Eisemann, Chair.; Jeff Mangino
Giving statement: Giving through the Republic Corporation Contributions Program.

The Republic Corporation Contributions Program
100 E. Main St.
Trinidad, CO 81082-2709

Contact: Chris Huffman, V.P.
Purpose and activities: Republic makes charitable contributions to nonprofit organizations involved

with historical preservation and community development. Support is given primarily in areas of company operations.
Fields of interest: Historical activities; Community/economic development.
Type of support: General/operating support.
Geographic limitations: Giving primarily in areas of company operations.
Support limitations: No support for religious or political organizations.
Application information: Applications accepted. Telephone calls are not encouraged. Application form not required.
Initial approach: Letter of inquiry to headquarters

3188
Republic Underwriters Insurance Company
5525 LBJ Fwy.
P.O. Box 809076
Dallas, TX 75240-6241 (972) 788-6001

Company URL: http://www.republicgroup.com
Establishment information: Established in 1903.
Company type: Subsidiary of a public company
Business activities: Operates holding company; sells insurance.
Business type (SIC): Holding company; credit institutions/personal; insurance/life; insurance/accident and health
Corporate officers: Bruce W. Schnitzer, Chair.; Parker William Rush, Pres. and C.E.O.; Martin Bruce Cummings, Jr., C.F.O.; Michael Eugene Ditto, V.P. and Genl. Counsel; Glen Rogers, Treas.
Board of directors: Bruce W. Schnitzer, Chair.; Parker W. Rush
Subsidiaries: Blue Ridge Insurance Co., Columbia, MD; Republic Underwriters Insurance Co., Oklahoma City, OK; Republic Vanguard (of Arizona) Insurance Co., Phoenix, AZ; Vanguard Underwriters Insurance Co., Oklahoma City, OK
Giving statement: Giving through the Republic Underwriters Insurance Company Contributions Program.

Republic Underwriters Insurance Company Contributions Program
5525 LBJ Fwy.
Dallas, TX 75240-6241 (972) 788-6001
FAX: (888) 841-8372; URL: https://www.republicgroup.com/about/CommunityInvolvement.aspx

Purpose and activities: Republic makes charitable contributions to nonprofit organizations involved with health, food services, and on a case by case base. Support is given primarily in areas of company operations in Arkansas, Louisiana, Mississippi, New Mexico, Oklahoma, and Texas.
Fields of interest: Health organizations; Food services; United Ways and Federated Giving Programs; General charitable giving.
Type of support: Employee volunteer services; General/operating support.
Geographic limitations: Giving primarily in areas of company operations in AR, LA, MS, NM, OK, and TX.

3189
RESCO, Inc.
455 Twin Lakes Dr., Ste. 100
Oakland, MI 48363-2442 (248) 601-0970

Establishment information: Established in 1985.
Company type: Private company
Business activities: Provides real estate brokerage services.
Business type (SIC): Real estate agents and managers; brokers and bankers/mortgage
Corporate officers: Salvatore Cottone, Pres.; Laura Helms, C.F.O. and Cont.
Giving statement: Giving through the Locations Foundation.

Locations Foundation
614 Kapahulu Ave., 3rd Fl.
Honolulu, HI 96815-3846 (808) 735-4200

Establishment information: Established in 1988 in HI.
Donors: RESCO, Inc.; William Chee.
Financial data (yr. ended 12/31/11): Assets, $726,777 (M); gifts received, $175,349; expenditures, $132,469; qualifying distributions, $105,630; giving activities include $105,630 for grants.
Purpose and activities: The foundation supports organizations involved with health, diabetes, youth, and human services.
Fields of interest: Education, reading; Education; Health care; Cancer; Diabetes; Housing/shelter, development; Big Brothers/Big Sisters; Children, services; Family services; Human services; United Ways and Federated Giving Programs Women.
Type of support: General/operating support; Scholarship funds.
Geographic limitations: Giving primarily in Honolulu, HI.
Support limitations: No grants to individuals.
Application information: Applications accepted. Application form not required.
Initial approach: Proposal
Deadline(s): None
Officers and Trustees:* Mary Edu*, Pres.; George Santoki, V.P.; Noele Kanemoto*, Secy.; Toan Doran*, Co-Treas.; Mikio Sato, Co-Treas.; Dolores Bediones; Stephanie Chan; Jodee Farm; Michael Healy; Zona Jones; Judy Kumano; Kelly Mitchell; Marshall Mower; Russell Nishimoto; Kathy Pang; Greta Richardson; Shannon Smith; Dan Tabori; Jon Yamasato.
EIN: 990267351

3190
Residential Funding Corporation
(doing business as GMAC-RFC)
8400 Normandale Lake Blvd., Ste. 350
Minneapolis, MN 55437-1085
(952) 832-7000

Establishment information: Established in 1982.
Company type: Subsidiary of a private company
Business activities: Provides mortgage banking products and services.
Business type (SIC): Brokers and bankers/mortgage
Corporate officers: Kenneth M. Duncan, Chair.; Bruce J. Paradis, Pres. and C.E.O.; Michael J. Seats, Secy.
Board of director: Kenneth M. Duncan, Chair.
Giving statement: Giving through the Homeownership Preservation Foundation.

Homeownership Preservation Foundation
7645 Lyndale Ave., Ste. 250
Minneapolis, MN 55423-4688
FAX: (952) 857-7535; E-mail: info@hpfonline.org; URL: http://www.hpfonline.org/

Establishment information: Established in 2004 in MN.
Donors: Residential Funding Corp.; Freddie MAC; OCWEN Loan Servicing, Inc.; Chase Manhattan Mortgage Corp.; Countrywide Financial Corp.; Washington Mutual; Wilshire Credit Corp.; Citigroup; HSBC-North America; Fannie MAE; Williams & Williams; American International Group, Inc.; Neighborworks America.
Financial data (yr. ended 12/31/11): Assets, $25,635,858 (M); gifts received, $17,599,494; expenditures, $46,378,957; qualifying distributions, $45,998,949.
Purpose and activities: The foundation partners with consumers, policy makers, and mortgage lenders to deliver innovative homeownership preservation opportunities.
Type of support: Program development.
Geographic limitations: Giving primarily In Washington, DC, New York, NY. and Radcliffe, KY.
Support limitations: No grants to individuals.
Application information: Applications not accepted. Unsolicited requests for funds not accepted.
Officers and Board Members: Bruce Paradis*, Chair.; Colleen Hernandez, C.E.O. and Pres.; Barb Wendt, C.O.O. and Secy.; William Acheson, C.F.O. and Treas.; Bill Acheson; Sharon Sayles Belton; Tom Jacob; Herb Morse; Mary Reilley; Michael Seats; Paul Weech.
EIN: 522403507

3191
Residential Warranty Company, LLC
5300 Derry St.
Harrisburg, PA 17111-3576 (717) 561-4480

Company URL: http://www.rwcwarranty.com
Establishment information: Established in 1981.
Company type: Private company
Business activities: Sells warranty insurance.
Business type (SIC): Insurance/surety
Corporate officers: Suzanne Palkovic, V.P., Mktg.; Lynn Nelson-Probst, V.P., Sales
Giving statement: Giving through the Parmer Family Foundation.

Parmer Family Foundation
911 Grove Rd.
Harrisburg, PA 17111-4674

Establishment information: Established in 2001 in PA.
Donors: Residential Warranty Corp.; Western Pacific Mutual Insurance Co.; George A. Parmer.
Financial data (yr. ended 12/31/11): Assets, $2,078,632 (M); gifts received, $501,500; expenditures, $13,450; qualifying distributions, $8,740; giving activities include $2,500 for 1 grant.
Purpose and activities: The foundation supports organizations involved with K-12 and higher education and Christianity.

Fields of interest: Elementary/secondary education; Higher education; Christian agencies & churches.
Type of support: General/operating support.
Geographic limitations: Giving limited to PA.
Support limitations: No grants to individuals.
Application information: Applications not accepted. Unsolicited requests for funds not accepted.
Officer and Directors:* George A. Parmer*, Pres.; Barbara J. Parmer.
EIN: 251883175

3192
ResMed Inc.

9001 Spectrum Center Blvd.
San Diego, CA 92123-6857
(858) 836-5000
FAX: (858) 836-5501

Company URL: http://www.resmed.com
Establishment information: Established in 1989.
Company type: Public company
Company ticker symbol and exchange: RMD/NYSE
Business activities: Develops, manufactures, and distributes sleep-disordered breathing medical equipment.
Business type (SIC): Medical instruments and supplies
Financial profile for 2012: Number of employees, 3,700; assets, $2,137,870,000; sales volume, $1,368,520,000; pre-tax net income, $331,940,000; expenses, $1,078,120,000; liabilities, $530,240,000
Corporate officers: Peter C. Farrell, Ph.D., Chair.; Robert Douglas, Pres. and C.O.O.; Michael J. Farrell, C.E.O.; Brett Sandercock, C.F.O.; David Pendarvis, C.A.O. and Genl. Counsel; Frank Lacagnina, C.I.O.
Board of directors: Peter C. Farrell, Ph.D., Chair.; Michael J. Farrell; Gary W. Pace, Ph.D.; Michael A. Quinn; Christopher Graham Roberts, Ph.D.; Richard Sulpizio; Ronald R. Taylor; John P. Wareham
International operations: Australia; Finland; France; Germany; Hong Kong; Japan; Malaysia; New Zealand; Singapore; Spain; Sweden; Switzerland; United Kingdom
Giving statement: Giving through the ResMed Foundation.
Company EIN: 980152841

ResMed Foundation

(also known as ResMed Sleep Disordered Breathing Foundation)
7514 Girard Ave., Ste. 1-343
La Jolla, CA 92037-5149 (858) 775-1616
FAX: (858) 459-6557;
E-mail: fiona.tudor@resmedfoundation.org;
Additional e-mail:
resmedsdbfoundation@resmed.com; URL: http://www.resmedfoundation.org/

Establishment information: Established in 2002 in CA.
Donor: ResMed Inc.
Contact: Fiona Tudor, Exec. Dir.
Financial data (yr. ended 12/31/11): Assets, $6,004,335 (M); expenditures, $1,478,104; qualifying distributions, $1,249,574; giving activities include $1,249,574 for grants.
Purpose and activities: The foundation supports programs designed to promote research and public and physician awareness about the importance of sleep and respiratory health.
Fields of interest: Arts; Secondary school/education; Education; Hospitals (general); Public health; Health care; Health organizations; Medical research; Mathematics; Engineering/technology; Science.
Programs:
Clinical Research: The foundation supports programs designed to promote research and public and physician awareness of sleep disordered breathing (SDB), with a primary focus on positive airway pressure therapies and ventilation-based treatments. Special emphasis is directed toward the evaluation, diagnosis, and treatment of SDB and other respiratory disorders; research on other morbidities associated with SDB, including cardiovascular disease, metabolic syndrome, diabetes and morbid obesity; and SDB in conjunction with occupational health safety, asthma and anesthesiology; chronic obstructive pulmonary disease; and pregnancy/preeclampsia. The foundation also supports the application of novel screening and diagnostic tools to identify SDB/OSA, and new and better paradigms to improve patient adherence and compliance with positive airway pressure and ventilation-based treatment methods.
Community Philanthropy: The foundation supports community causes in the areas of primary and secondary education with emphasis on math, science, and technology. The foundation also supports arts and culture in San Diego County.
Physician and Public Awareness: The foundation supports programs designed to further awareness and knowledge of the inherent dangers of untreated sleep disordered breathing and its symptoms, diagnosis, and treatment with sleep specialists, primary care physicians, educator, and the general public. Programs must have a wide outreach to a significant clinical or public population base.
Type of support: Annual campaigns; Continuing support; Publication; Research.
Geographic limitations: Giving primarily in La Jolla and San Diego, CA, Boston, MA, Australia, Canada, France, Norway, and Sweden.
Support limitations: No support for political organizations. No grants to individuals, or for general operating or continuing support, contingencies, deficits, or debt reduction; no loans.
Publications: Application guidelines; Grants list; Program policy statement.
Application information: Applications accepted. Additional information may be requested at a later date. Proposals should be no longer than 5 pages. Organizations receiving support may be asked to provide periodic progress reports and a final report. Applicants should submit the following:
1) role played by volunteers
2) timetable for implementation and evaluation of project
3) how project will be sustained once grantmaker support is completed
4) results expected from proposed grant
5) qualifications of key personnel
6) statement of problem project will address
7) population served
8) name, address and phone number of organization
9) copy of IRS Determination Letter
10) brief history of organization and description of its mission
11) how project's results will be evaluated or measured
12) descriptive literature about organization
13) listing of board of directors, trustees, officers and other key people and their affiliations
14) detailed description of project and amount of funding requested
15) contact person
16) copy of current year's organizational budget and/or project budget
17) listing of additional sources and amount of support

Initial approach: Complete online application or download cover sheet and mail cover sheet and proposal to foundation
Copies of proposal: 1
Deadline(s): Mar. 15 and Sept. 15 for Clinical Research; June 15 and Dec. 15 for Physician and Public Awareness; and May 15 for Community Philanthropy
Final notification: Apr. 30 and Oct. 31 for Clinical Research; July 31 and Jan. 31 for Physician and Pubic Awareness; and July 31 for Community Philanthropy

Officers and Trustees:* Edward Blair*, Chair.; Peter C. Farrell, Ph.D., Secy.; Edward A. Dennis, Ph.D., Treas.; Fiona Tudor, Exec. Dir.; Peter Cistulli, MD, Ph.D.; Charles G. Cochrane, M.D.; Michael P. Coppola, M.D.; Terrence M. Davidson, M.D.; Klaus Schindhelm, BE, Ph.D.
EIN: 020622126
Selected grants: The following grants are a representative sample of this grantmaker's funding activity:
$90,000 to Brigham and Womens Hospital, Boston, MA, 2010.
$40,000 to University Health Network, Toronto, Canada, 2010.
$31,308 to University of Pittsburgh, Pittsburgh, PA, 2010.
$29,978 to University of Chicago, Chicago, IL, 2010.
$10,000 to Athenaeum Music and Arts Library, La Jolla, CA, 2010.
$10,000 to La Jolla Playhouse, La Jolla, CA, 2010.
$10,000 to Monarch School, San Diego, CA, 2010.
$10,000 to Museum of Photographic Arts, San Diego, CA, 2010.
$10,000 to Ocean Discovery Institute, San Diego, CA, 2010.
$8,000 to Salk Institute for Biological Studies, La Jolla, CA, 2010.

3193
Respironics, Inc.

1010 Murry Ridge Ln.
Murrysville, PA 15668-8525
(724) 387-5200

Company URL: http://www.healthcare.philips.com
Establishment information: Established in 1976.
Company type: Subsidiary of a foreign company
Business activities: Designs, develops, manufactures, and markets sleep and respiratory disorder medical devices.
Business type (SIC): Medical instruments and supplies
Financial profile for 2010: Number of employees, 90
Corporate officers: John L. Miclot, Pres. and Co-C.E.O.; Steve Rusckowski, Co-C.E.O.; Craig B. Reynolds, Exec. V.P. and C.O.O.; Han Jansen, C.F.O.
Plant: Wallingford, CT
International operations: Hong Kong
Giving statement: Giving through the Respironics Sleep and Respiratory Research Foundation.

Respironics Sleep and Respiratory Research Foundation

1010 Murry Ridge Ln.
Murrysville, PA 15668-8525

Establishment information: Established in 2003 in PA.
Donor: Respironics, Inc.
Financial data (yr. ended 06/30/12): Assets, $58,143 (M); expenditures, $680,529; qualifying

distributions, $680,529; giving activities include $675,570 for 6 grants (high: $180,000; low: $10,000).
Purpose and activities: The foundation supports programs designed to conduct sleep medicine and respiratory research.
Fields of interest: Higher education; Medical school/education; Hospitals (general); Lung research.
Type of support: General/operating support; Professorships.
Geographic limitations: Giving primarily in MA, NJ, NY, and OH, and in Australia, Canada, Denmark, Germany, and Sweden.
Support limitations: No grants to individuals.
Application information: Applications not accepted. Contributes only to pre-selected organizations.
Officers and Directors:* Craig B. Reynolds*, Pres.; Barbara Hollinshead*, Secy.; Damian Rippole*, Treas.; David White.
EIN: 522421348

3194
Retail Merchants Association, Inc.

2412 Langhorne Rd., Ste. C
Lynchburg, VA 24501-1524 (434) 528-1732

Company URL: http://lynchburgrma.com
Establishment information: Established in 1907.
Company type: Private company
Business activities: Operates a trade association that represents retailers and other businesses in the Central Virginia area.
Business type (SIC): Management and public relations services
Corporate officers: Jerry W. Morcom, Pres.; Gene D. Gallagher, Treas.
Board of directors: Gene D. Gallagher; Danny Givens; Charles W. Hammer; Jerry W. Morcom; Marc A. Schewel; David M. Somers; Rayner V. Snead III; W. Bradley Weaver
Giving statement: Giving through the Retail Merchants Foundation.

Retail Merchants Foundation

2412 Langhorne Rd.
Lynchburg, VA 24501-1545 (434) 528-1732
URL: http://lynchburgrma.com/foundation/about-the-foundation/

Establishment information: Established in 1997 in VA.
Donor: RM Association.
Contact: Debbie Montgomery, Exec. Dir.
Financial data (yr. ended 12/31/11): Assets, $842,982 (M); gifts received, $7,890; expenditures, $153,602; qualifying distributions, $83,965; giving activities include $83,965 for grants.
Purpose and activities: The foundation supports organizations involved with education, health, abuse and rehabilitation issues, employment, hunger, housing, child care, and homelessness.
Fields of interest: Higher education; Education; Health care, financing; Health care; Substance abuse, services; Crime/violence prevention, abuse prevention; Crime/violence prevention, child abuse; Employment, job counseling; Employment, training; Food services; Housing/shelter, development; Housing/shelter, rehabilitation; Housing/shelter; Salvation Army; YM/YWCAs & YM/YWHAs; Children, day care; Homeless, human services; United Ways and Federated Giving Programs.
Type of support: Annual campaigns; General/operating support; Program development; Publication; Scholarship funds.
Geographic limitations: Giving primarily in Amherst, Appomattox, Bedford, Campbell County, and Lynchburg, VA.
Support limitations: No grants to individuals.
Publications: Application guidelines; Grants list.
Application information: Applications accepted. Applicants are asked to submit 8 copies of the letter of inquiry and 1 copy of supporting documentation. All copies must be 3-hole punched. Applicants should submit the following:
1) copy of IRS Determination Letter
2) brief history of organization and description of its mission
3) copy of most recent annual report/audited financial statement/990
4) listing of board of directors, trustees, officers and other key people and their affiliations
5) detailed description of project and amount of funding requested

Initial approach: Letter of inquiry
Copies of proposal: 8
Deadline(s): Oct. 3 to Dec. 2

Officers and Directors: Gene D. Gallagher, Pres.; Charles W. Hammer, V.P.; Jerry W. Morcom, Treas.; Debbie Montogomery, Exec. Dir.; David M. Somers; S. Danny Givens; Marc A. Schewel; Rayner V. Snead, Jr.
EIN: 541824054

3195
REthink Development Corp.

8665 Hayden Pl.
Culver City, CA 90232-2901
(310) 253-9131
FAX: (310) 943-1519

Company URL: http://www.rethinkdev.com
Establishment information: Established in 2005.
Company type: Private company
Business type (SIC): Business services/miscellaneous
Corporate officers: Greg Reitz, Owner; Steve Edwards, Owner
Giving statement: Giving through the REthink Development Corp. Contributions Program.

REthink Development Corp. Contributions Program

8665 Hayden Pl.
Culver City, CA 90232-2901 (310) 253-9131
E-mail: info@rethinkdev.com; URL: http://www.rethinkdev.com

Purpose and activities: REthink Development Corp. is a certified B Corporation that donates a percentage of profits to charitable organizations.

3196
Frank Rewold & Son, Inc.

333 E. 2nd St.
Rochester, MI 48307-2005 (248) 651-7242

Company URL: http://www.frankrewold.com/
Establishment information: Established in 1918.
Company type: Private company
Business activities: Operates construction management company.
Business type (SIC): Contractors/general nonresidential building
Corporate officers: Roy Rewold, Chair.; Frank Rewold, Pres. and C.E.O.; Bill Moesta, C.F.O.; David Dimoff, V.P., Opers.
Board of director: Roy Rewold, Chair.
Giving statement: Giving through the Frank Rewold & Amp Son Foundation.

Frank Rewold & Amp Son Foundation

333 E. Second St.
Rochester, MI 48307 (248) 651-7242

Establishment information: Established in 2005 in MI.
Donor: Frank Rewold and Son, Inc.
Contact: Bill Moesta
Financial data (yr. ended 12/31/11): Assets, $1,598 (M); expenditures, $3,220; qualifying distributions, $1,700; giving activities include $1,700 for grants.
Fields of interest: Health care; Community/economic development; Religion.
Application information: Applications accepted. Application form not required.

Initial approach: Proposal
Deadline(s): None

Officers and Directors:* Frank H. Rewold*, Pres.; Paul Weisenbach*, V.P.; Craig Wolanin*, Secy.-Treas.
EIN: 202376123

3197
Rexam, Inc.

(formerly Rexham Inc.)
4201 Congress St., Ste. 340
Charlotte, NC 28209-4640 (704) 551-1500

Company URL: http://www.rexam.com/index.asp?pageid=2
Establishment information: Established in 1984.
Company type: Subsidiary of a foreign company
Business activities: Manufactures consumer packaging materials.
Business type (SIC): Paper and paperboard/coated, converted, and laminated
Corporate officers: Frank Brown, Pres.; Patrick O'Connell, V.P., Mktg. and Sales; Dallas Stiles, V.P., Sales
Giving statement: Giving through the Rexam Foundation.

The Rexam Foundation

(formerly Rexam Corporation Foundation)
4201 Congress St., Ste. 340
Charlotte, NC 28209-4640

Establishment information: Established in 1958 in DE and NY.
Donors: Rexam Inc.; Rexam Image Products Inc.
Financial data (yr. ended 12/31/11): Assets, $2,682 (M); gifts received, $31,443; expenditures, $28,943; qualifying distributions, $28,943; giving activities include $28,943 for grants.
Purpose and activities: The foundation supports organizations involved with higher education.
Type of support: Employee matching gifts; Employee-related scholarships.
Geographic limitations: Giving primarily in the Southeast, with emphasis on NC and SC.
Support limitations: No grants to individuals (except for employee-related scholarships).
Application information: Applications not accepted. Unsolicited requests for funds not accepted.

Officers: Frank C. Brown, Pres.; Lisa R. Hysko, V.P.; Clinton H. Tumlin, Treas.
EIN: 136165669

3198
Rexnord, LLC

(formerly Rexnord Corp.)
4701 W. Greenfield Ave.
Milwaukee, WI 53214-5310
(414) 643-3000

Company URL: http://www.rexnord.com
Establishment information: Established in 1966.
Company type: Subsidiary of a private company
Business activities: Manufactures and supplies mechanical power transmission components and related products.
Business type (SIC): Machinery/general industry; plastic products/miscellaneous; screw machine products; electronic components and accessories
Financial profile for 2011: Number of employees, 7,400
Corporate officers: Todd A. Adams, Pres. and C.E.O.; Mark W. Peterson, Sr. V.P., and C.F.O.; Patricia M. Whaley, V.P. and Genl. Counsel
Board of director: George C. Moore
Plants: Downers Grove, IL; Indianapolis, IN; Springfield, MA; Morganton, NC; Philadelphia, Warren, PA; Clinton, TN; Grafton, West Milwaukee, WI
Giving statement: Giving through the Rexnord Foundation Inc.
Company EIN: 010752045

Rexnord Foundation Inc.

P.O. Box 2191
Milwaukee, WI 53201-2191 (414) 643-3000

Establishment information: Incorporated in 1953 in WI.
Donor: Rexnord Corp.
Financial data (yr. ended 10/31/11): Assets, $3,788,904 (M); gifts received, $252,000; expenditures, $461,343; qualifying distributions, $458,609; giving activities include $458,609 for 353 grants (high: $90,000; low: $30).
Purpose and activities: The foundation supports organizations involved with arts and culture, education, multiple sclerosis, medical research, and human services.
Fields of interest: Museums (art); Arts; Elementary/secondary education; Higher education; Education; Multiple sclerosis; Medical research; Food services; Children/youth, services; Human services; United Ways and Federated Giving Programs.
Program:
Matching Gift Program: The foundation matches contributions made by employees and directors of Rexnord to charitable, youth-serving, educational, cultural, medical, and civic organizations on a one-for-one basis from $25 to $2,500 per employee, per year.
Type of support: Building/renovation; Employee matching gifts; Employee-related scholarships; Program development.
Geographic limitations: Giving primarily in areas of company operations, with some emphasis on Milwaukee, WI.
Support limitations: No support for religious organizations. No grants to individuals (except for employee-related scholarships), or for endowments.
Publications: Application guidelines.
Application information: Applications accepted. Application form not required.
Initial approach: Proposal
Copies of proposal: 1
Board meeting date(s): 2 or 3 times per year
Officers and Directors:* C. R. Roy*, Pres.; D. Doerr*, V.P.; R. R. Wallis*, Secy.; Todd A. Adams*, Treas.; R. M. MacQueen; W. E. Schauer; D. Taylor.
EIN: 396042029
Selected grants: The following grants are a representative sample of this grantmaker's funding activity:
$100,000 to Menomonee Valley Partners, Milwaukee, WI, 2010.
$90,000 to United Way of Greater Milwaukee, Milwaukee, WI, 2010.
$20,000 to United Performing Arts Fund, Milwaukee, WI, 2010.
$15,000 to Habitat for Humanity, Milwaukee, Milwaukee, WI, 2010.
$15,000 to Milwaukee Public Museum, Milwaukee, WI, 2010.
$15,000 to Milwaukee School of Engineering, Milwaukee, WI, 2010.
$5,000 to Milwaukee Art Museum, Milwaukee, WI, 2010.
$5,000 to Partners Advancing Values in Education, Milwaukee, WI, 2010.
$4,000 to Sharon Lynne Wilson Center for the Arts, Brookfield, WI, 2010.
$1,000 to University of Wisconsin, Milwaukee, WI, 2010.

3199
The Reynolds and Reynolds Company

1 Reynolds Way
Kettering, OH 45430 (937) 485-2000
FAX: (937) 485-2788

Company URL: http://www.reyrey.com
Establishment information: Established in 1866.
Company type: Private company
Business activities: Provides management consulting services.
Business type (SIC): Business forms/manifold; printing/commercial; computer and office equipment; computer services; educational services/miscellaneous
Financial profile for 2012: Number of employees, 4,300
Corporate officers: Robert T. Brockman, Chair. and C.E.O.; Rob Nalley, Vice-Chair.; Ron Lamb, Pres.
Board of directors: Robert T. Brockman, Chair.; Rob Nalley, Vice-Chair.
Subsidiaries: Reyna Financial Corp., Dayton, OH; Shumate Business Forms Co., Lebanon, IN; Wilmer Service Line, Dayton, OH
Divisions: Reynolds and Reynolds-Automotive Systems Div., Dayton, OH; Reynolds and Reynolds-Business Forms Div., Dayton, OH; Reynolds and Reynolds-Business Forms Div., Oklahoma City, OK
Office: Elk Grove Village, IL
International operations: Canada
Giving statement: Giving through the Reynolds and Reynolds Company Foundation and the Reynolds and Reynolds Associate Foundation.
Company EIN: 310421120

The Reynolds and Reynolds Company Foundation

P.O. Box 2608
Dayton, OH 45401-2608 (937) 485-8138
E-mail: alice_davisson@revrey.com; URL: http://www.reyrey.com/company/community/company_foundation.asp
Address for Texas A&M Scholarship: Reynolds and Reynolds Open Undergraduate Scholarship Program, Scholarship Management Services, 1 Scholarship Way, P.O. Box 297, Saint Peter, MN 56082; Contact for Wright State Scholarship: Mary Hutcheson, Enrollment Advisor, Dept. of Computer Science and Engineering, Wright State University, 3640 Colonel Glenn Hwy., Dayton, OH 45435, e-mail: mary.hutcheson@wright.edu

Establishment information: Established in 1986 in OH.
Donor: The Reynolds and Reynolds Co.
Contact: Alice Davisson
Financial data (yr. ended 12/31/11): Assets, $3,424,658 (M); expenditures, $193,738; qualifying distributions, $176,076; giving activities include $176,076 for grants.
Purpose and activities: The foundation supports higher education programs designed to prepare students for key roles in regional communities in which Reynolds has a significant presence; and community based programs that have exceptional benefits for the communities in which Reynolds operates.
Fields of interest: Higher education; Community/economic development.
Programs:
Texas A&M Scholarship: The foundation awards up to three $3,000 scholarships to full-time undergraduate students at Texas A&M University. The program is administered by Scholarship Management Services.
Wright State Scholarship: The foundation awards four-year $2,500 scholarships to up to five incoming first-year computer science or computer engineering students at the College of Engineering and Computer Science at Wright State University. The program is administered by Wright State University.
Type of support: Annual campaigns; Continuing support; Employee-related scholarships; General/operating support; Program development; Scholarship funds; Scholarships—to individuals.
Geographic limitations: Giving primarily in areas of company operations in Dayton, OH.
Support limitations: No support for primary or secondary schools, sectarian organizations, political candidates, fraternal or veterans' organizations, or organizations without adequate accounting records or procedures. No grants to individuals (except for scholarships), or for political parties or offices, tax-supported universities or colleges for operating purposes, deficits or debt retirement, endowments, courtesy events, or capital campaigns.
Publications: Application guidelines.
Application information: Applications accepted. All proposals must be submitted electronically. Support is limited to 1 contribution per organization during any given year. Multi-year funding is not automatic. Application form required. Applicants should submit the following:
1) how project will be sustained once grantmaker support is completed
2) results expected from proposed grant
3) name, address and phone number of organization
4) copy of IRS Determination Letter
5) brief history of organization and description of its mission
6) copy of most recent annual report/audited financial statement/990

7) how project's results will be evaluated or measured
8) list of company employees involved with the organization
9) descriptive literature about organization
10) detailed description of project and amount of funding requested
11) contact person
12) copy of current year's organizational budget and/or project budget
13) listing of additional sources and amount of support
14) statement of problem project will address

Initial approach: E-mail proposal
Copies of proposal: 1
Board meeting date(s): Mar. 1, June 7, Sept. 6, and Dec. 6
Deadline(s): Feb. 10, May 11, Aug. 10, and Nov. 9

Officer and Trustees: Jim Penikas, Treas.; Dave Bates; Robert Burnett; Nicole Case; Willie Daughters; Jon Strawsburg.
EIN: 311168299
Selected grants: The following grants are a representative sample of this grantmaker's funding activity:
$80,000 to Wright State University Foundation, Dayton, OH, 2011.
$70,865 to Scholarship America, Minneapolis, MN, 2011. For scholarship program.
$2,500 to Ohio University, Athens, OH, 2011.
$2,500 to Sinclair Community College, Dayton, OH, 2011.

The Reynolds and Reynolds Associate Foundation

(formerly Reynolds and Reynolds Employee Foundation)
1 Reynolds Way
Kettering, OH 45430-2608 (937) 485-2000
E-mail: alice_davisson@reyrey.com; Tel. for proposal questions: (937) 485-8138; URL: http://www.reyrey.com/

Establishment information: Established in 1979 in OH.
Financial data (yr. ended 12/31/11): Revenue, $184,237; assets, $50,554 (M); gifts received, $188,427; expenditures, $194,823; giving activities include $194,773 for grants.
Purpose and activities: The mission of the foundation is to provide a vehicle for Dayton associates to improve health and human services in the local communities. Focus areas include: health and human services with emphasis on domestic violence/child abuse; youth-at-risk; hunger; issues of the elderly; homelessness; literacy; and life-threatening illness.
Fields of interest: Adult education—literacy, basic skills & GED; Health care; Crime/violence prevention, domestic violence; Crime/violence prevention, child abuse; Food services; Human services; Youth, services; Aging, centers/services Youth; Aging; Economically disadvantaged; Homeless.
Geographic limitations: Giving primarily in the Dayton, OH, area.
Support limitations: No support for non 501(c)(3) organizations, sectarian organizations with a predominately religious purpose, fraternal or veterans' organizations, individual primary or secondary schools (except for occasional special projects), or tax-supported universities and colleges (except for occasional special projects). No grants to individuals, or for endowments, courtesy advertising, fundraising events, deficit or debt retirement, or capital campaigns.
Publications: Grants list.
Application information: Applications accepted. Applicants should submit the following:
1) statement of problem project will address
2) name, address and phone number of organization
3) copy of IRS Determination Letter
4) brief history of organization and description of its mission
5) geographic area to be served
6) copy of most recent annual report/audited financial statement/990
7) listing of board of directors, trustees, officers and other key people and their affiliations
8) detailed description of project and amount of funding requested
9) copy of current year's organizational budget and/or project budget
10) listing of additional sources and amount of support

Initial approach: E-mail proposal
Board meeting date(s): Feb., May, Aug., and Nov.
Deadline(s): Jan. 7, Mar. 14, June 13, and Sept. 12

Officer: LaVon Ferguson, Pres.; Amy Peck, V.P.; Robert Hartings, Treas.
Trustees: Rose Dahlinghaus; Kelly Hall; Chip Hillman; Laura Powell; Diane Trittschuh; Scott Worthington.
EIN: 310976985

3200
R. J. Reynolds Tobacco Company

401 N. Main St.
Winston-Salem, NC 27102-2866
(336) 741-0673

Company URL: http://www.rjrt.com
Establishment information: Established in 1875.
Company type: Subsidiary of a public company
Ultimate parent company: Reynolds American, Inc.
Business activities: Produces cigarettes.
Business type (SIC): Tobacco products—cigarettes
Financial profile for 2010: Number of employees, 100
Corporate officers: Andrew D. Gilchrist, Pres.; Mark A. Peters, C.F.O.; Jeffery S. Gentry, Exec. V.P., Opers.; Tommy L. Hickman, Sr. V.P., Opers.
Giving statement: Giving through the Reynolds American Foundation.

Reynolds American Foundation

(formerly R. J. Reynolds Foundation)
Plaza Bldg., 15th FL
P.O. Box 891
Winston-Salem, NC 27102-2959 (336) 741-5315
URL: http://www.rjrt.com/fndnguide.aspx

Establishment information: Established in 1986 in NC.
Donors: RJR Nabisco Holdings Corp.; R.J. Reynolds Tobacco Co.; Nabisco Brands, Inc.; Planters LifeSavers Co.; RJR Tobacco Intl.; RJR Acquisition Corp.; Reynolds American.
Contact: Stephen R. Strawsburg, Pres.
Financial data (yr. ended 12/31/11): Assets, $62,680,584 (M); expenditures, $3,915,287; qualifying distributions, $3,538,987; giving activities include $3,495,140 for grants.
Purpose and activities: The foundation supports organizations involved with arts and culture, education, community development, and economically disadvantaged people.
Fields of interest: Arts councils; Arts; Child development, education; Elementary school/education; Higher education; Education; Community/economic development; United Ways and Federated Giving Programs Economically disadvantaged.
Program:
Birth-12 Public Education: The foundation supports programs designed to prepare children to enter school ready to learn; and improve academic performance of low-performing and economically disadvantaged students.
Type of support: Annual campaigns; Capital campaigns; Continuing support; Employee matching gifts; Employee-related scholarships; Program development; Scholarship funds.
Geographic limitations: Giving primarily in areas of company operations in KY and NC.
Support limitations: No support for churches or religious organizations not of direct benefit to the entire community, political candidates or organizations, individual day-care centers, or discriminatory organizations. No grants to individuals (except for employee-related scholarships), or for endowments, general operating support, travel expenses, or sponsorships.
Publications: Application guidelines; Program policy statement.
Application information: Applications accepted. Proposals should be no longer than 5 pages. Support is limited to 1 contribution per organization during any given year. Application form not required. Applicants should submit the following:
1) timetable for implementation and evaluation of project
2) signature and title of chief executive officer
3) statement of problem project will address
4) population served
5) name, address and phone number of organization
6) copy of IRS Determination Letter
7) geographic area to be served
8) how project's results will be evaluated or measured
9) listing of board of directors, trustees, officers and other key people and their affiliations
10) detailed description of project and amount of funding requested
11) contact person
12) copy of current year's organizational budget and/or project budget
13) listing of additional sources and amount of support

Initial approach: Proposal
Board meeting date(s): Quarterly
Deadline(s): Feb. 1, May 1, Aug. 1, and Nov. 1
Final notification: Mar. 31, June 30, Sept. 30, and Dec. 31

Officers and Directors: Stephen R. Strawsburg, Pres.; William Nance, V.P.; Fred Franklin, Secy.; Dan Fawley, Treas.; Jim Beckett; Nancy Hawley; Judy Lambeth; Nancy Sturgeon.
Number of staff: 1 full-time professional; 1 full-time support.
EIN: 581681920

3201
RG Industries, Inc.

650 N. State St.
P.O. Box 62744
York, PA 17403-1032 (717) 846-9300

Company URL: http://www.rg-group.com
Establishment information: Established in 1956.
Company type: Private company

Business activities: Manufactures and distributes refrigeration, heating, and cooling equipment parts.
Business type (SIC): Machinery/refrigeration and service industry; industrial machinery and equipment—wholesale; repair shops/ miscellaneous
Corporate officers: Randall A. Gross, C.E.O.; Rich Freeh, Pres. and C.O.O.; Gregory Pitt, Treas.
Giving statement: Giving through the RG Charitable Foundation.

The RG Charitable Foundation

P.O. Box 2824
York, PA 17405-2824

Establishment information: Established in 1989 in PA.
Donors: RG Industries, Inc.; Die-A-Matic, Inc.
Financial data (yr. ended 01/31/12): Assets, $10,313 (M); gifts received, $6,000; expenditures, $10,536; qualifying distributions, $10,500; giving activities include $10,500 for grants.
Purpose and activities: The foundation supports playgrounds and organizations involved with arts and culture, health, and community development.
Fields of interest: Performing arts centers; Arts; Hospitals (general); Health care; Recreation, parks/ playgrounds; Business/industry; Community/ economic development.
Type of support: Capital campaigns; General/ operating support; Sponsorships.
Geographic limitations: Giving primarily in York, PA.
Support limitations: No grants to individuals.
Application information: Applications not accepted. Contributes only to pre-selected organizations.
Trustee: Randall A. Gross.
EIN: 232589813

3202
RGI Group, Inc.

(also known as Revlon)
625 Madison Ave., Frnt. 4
New York, NY 10022-1801 (212) 527-4000

Company URL: http://www.revlon.com
Establishment information: Established in 1932.
Company type: Subsidiary of a private company
Ultimate parent company: MacAndrews & Forbes Holdings Inc.
Business activities: Manufactures, markets, and sells cosmetics, skincare products, fragrances, and personal care products.
Business type (SIC): Soaps, cleaners, and toiletries
Corporate officers: Ronald O. Perelman, Chair. and C.E.O.; David L. Kennedy, Vice-Chair.; Lawrence Elliott, Treas.
Board of directors: Ronald O. Perelman, Chair.; David L. Kennedy, Vice-Chair.
Giving statement: Giving through the Revlon Corporate Giving Program.

Revlon Corporate Giving Program

c/o Revlon Charitable Contribs.
237 Park Ave.
New York, NY 10017-3187 (212) 572-4000
URL: http://www.revlon.com/Revlon-Home/ Revlon-Corporate/RevlonCares.aspx

Purpose and activities: Revlon makes charitable contributions to nonprofit organizations involved with women's health. Support is given on a national basis.
Fields of interest: Health care; Breast cancer; Breast cancer research Women.
Type of support: Sponsorships.
Geographic limitations: Giving on a national basis.

3203
Riceland Foods, Inc.

2120 S. Park Ave.
P.O. Box 927
Stuttgart, AR 72160-6822 (870) 673-5500

Company URL: http://www.riceland.com
Establishment information: Established in 1921.
Company type: Private company
Business activities: Sells rice wholesale.
Business type (SIC): Farm-product raw materials—wholesale
Financial profile for 2010: Number of employees, 227; sales volume, $1,130,000,000
Corporate officers: Thomas C. Hoskyn, Chair.; K. Daniel Kennedy, Pres. and C.E.O.; Harry E. Loftis, V.P. and C.F.O.; Terry L. Richardson, Secy.
Board of director: Thomas C. Hoskyn, Chair.
Giving statement: Giving through the Riceland Foods Foundation.

Riceland Foods Foundation

P.O. Box 927
Stuttgart, AR 72160-0927 (870) 673-5215
Tel: (870) 673-5215

Establishment information: Established in 1998 in AR.
Donor: Riceland Foods, Inc.
Contact: Margaret Oliver
Financial data (yr. ended 07/31/11): Assets, $334,087 (M); gifts received, $105,668; expenditures, $77,805; qualifying distributions, $74,901; giving activities include $72,139 for 75 grants (high: $6,000; low: $50).
Purpose and activities: The foundation supports organizations involved with arts and culture, education, the environment, health, agriculture, children and youth, human services, and community development.
Fields of interest: Arts; Education; Environment; Health care; Agriculture; Youth development; Children/youth, services; Human services; Community/economic development.
Type of support: General/operating support.
Geographic limitations: Giving primarily in areas of company operations, with emphasis on Stuttgart, AR.
Application information: Applications accepted. Application form required.
Initial approach: Proposal
Deadline(s): 20 days prior to board meeting
Officers: Roger E. Pohlner, Chair.; Bill J. Reed, Exec. Dir.
Directors: Wayne Allmon; Linda Dobrovich; Scott Gower; Martin Henry; Don Mccaskill; Rick Rorex.
EIN: 710809367

3204
Rich Products Corporation

1 Robert Rich Way
Buffalo, NY 14213-1714 (716) 878-8000
FAX: (716) 878-8765

Company URL: http://www.richs.com
Establishment information: Established in 1945.
Company type: Private company
Business activities: Produces frozen foods.
Business type (SIC): Specialty foods/canned, frozen, and preserved; bakery products
Financial profile for 2012: Number of employees, 8,000; sales volume, $3,000,000,000
Corporate officers: Robert E. Rich, Jr., Chair.; Melinda R. Rich, Vice-Chair.; William G. Gisel, Jr., Pres. and C.E.O.; Richard M. Ferranti, Exec. V.P. and C.O.O.; James R. Deuschle, Exec. V.P. and C.F.O.; Maureen O. Hurley, Exec. V.P. and C.A.O.; Jill Bond, Sr. V.P., Genl. Counsel; Joe Welsh, Sr. V.P., Human Resources; Paul Klein, V.P., Inf. Systems and C.I.O.; Dwight Gram, V.P., Comms.; Chris Steinmetz, V.P., Mktg.
Board of directors: Robert E. Rich, Jr., Chair.; Melinda R. Rich, Vice-Chair.; William G. Gisel, Jr.
Giving statement: Giving through the Rich Products Corporation Contributions Program and the Rich Family Foundation.

Rich Products Corporation Contributions Program

1150 Niagara St.
Buffalo, NY 14240-0245
FAX: (716) 878-8534; E-mail: btownson@rich.com

Contact: Brian Townson
Purpose and activities: As a complement to its foundation, Rich Products also makes charitable contributions to nonprofit organizations directly. Support is given primarily in western New York.
Fields of interest: Education; Substance abuse, prevention; Cancer; Food services; Children, day care; Family services.
Type of support: Annual campaigns; Donated equipment; Donated products; Employee volunteer services; In-kind gifts; Loaned talent; Matching/ challenge support; Program development; Public relations services; Research; Sponsorships; Use of facilities.
Geographic limitations: Giving primarily in western NY.
Support limitations: No grants for capital campaigns or personal fundraisers.
Publications: Informational brochure; Program policy statement.
Application information: Applications accepted. The Corporate Relations Department handles giving. Application form not required.
Initial approach: Letter
Copies of proposal: 1
Deadline(s): 4 to 6 weeks prior to committee meetings

Rich Family Foundation

(formerly Rich Foundation)
1 Robert Rich Way
P.O. Box 245
Buffalo, NY 14240-0245

Establishment information: Established in 1961.
Donors: Rich Products Corp.; Robert E. Rich, Sr.†.
Contact: Robert E. Rich, Jr.
Financial data (yr. ended 12/31/11): Assets, $5,405,367 (M); gifts received, $2,000,000; expenditures, $1,806,112; qualifying distributions, $1,773,939; giving activities include $1,761,519 for 100 grants (high: $500,000; low: $100).
Purpose and activities: The foundation supports organizations involved with performing arts, education, health, cancer research, fishing, and business and industry.
Fields of interest: Performing arts; Secondary school/education; Education; Health care, clinics/ centers; Health care; Cancer research; Athletics/ sports, fishing/hunting; Business/industry.
Type of support: Annual campaigns; Continuing support; General/operating support; Sponsorships.

Geographic limitations: Giving primarily in FL and Buffalo and Cheektowaga, NY.
Application information: Applications accepted. Application form not required.
Initial approach: Proposal
Deadline(s): None
Officers: Robert E. Rich, Jr., Chair.; Melinda Rich, Pres.; Mary Pat O'Connor, Exec. Dir. and Secy.; Joseph W. Segarra, Treas.
EIN: 166026199
Selected grants: The following grants are a representative sample of this grantmaker's funding activity:
$500,000 to Cleveland Clinic Foundation, Cleveland, OH, 2010. For annual donation.
$200,000 to Cleveland Clinic Foundation, Cleveland, OH, 2010.
$200,000 to Cleveland Clinic Foundation, Cleveland, OH, 2010.
$135,000 to Buffalo Public Schools Foundation, Buffalo, NY, 2010. For annual donation.
$100,000 to Students in Free Enterprise, Springfield, MO, 2010. For annual donation.
$100,000 to Students in Free Enterprise, Springfield, MO, 2010. For annual donation.
$100,000 to Students in Free Enterprise, Springfield, MO, 2010. For annual donation.
$20,000 to Buffalo Public Schools Foundation, Buffalo, NY, 2010.
$10,000 to Roswell Park Alliance Foundation, Buffalo, NY, 2010.
$8,333 to University at Buffalo Foundation, Buffalo, NY, 2010. For annual donation.

3205
P. C. Richard & Son
(doing business as Pcrichard.com)
150 Price Pkwy.
Farmingdale, NY 11735-1315
(631) 843-4300

Company URL: http://www.pcrichard.com
Establishment information: Established in 1909.
Company type: Private company
Business activities: Operates home appliance, consumer electronic, and computer product stores.
Business type (SIC): Appliance stores/household; consumer electronics and music stores
Corporate officers: Gary Richard, C.E.O.; Gregg Richard, Pres.; Thomas Pohmer, V.P. and C.F.O.
Giving statement: Giving through the P.C. Richard Foundation.

The P.C. Richard Foundation
150 Price Pkwy.
Farmingdale, NY 11735-1315

Establishment information: Established in 1994 in NY.
Donors: P.C. Richard & Son; Star Ledger.
Financial data (yr. ended 12/31/11): Assets, $134,925 (M); expenditures, $108,660; qualifying distributions, $106,660; giving activities include $98,050 for 8 grants (high: $25,000; low: $250).
Purpose and activities: The foundation supports Christian agencies and churches and organizations involved with animal welfare and cancer.
Fields of interest: Animal welfare; Cancer; Christian agencies & churches.
Type of support: General/operating support.
Geographic limitations: Giving primarily in NY.
Support limitations: No grants to individuals.
Application information: Applications not accepted. Unsolicited requests for funds not accepted.
Officers: Gregg G. Richard, Pres.; Thomas Pohmer, V.P.; Kevin Hughey, Treas.
EIN: 113213607

3206
Richards, Brandt, Miller & Nelson, PC
299 S. Main St. 15th Fl.
Salt Lake City, UT 84111 (801) 531-2000

Company URL: http://www.rbmn.com
Establishment information: Established in 1977.
Company type: Private company
Business activities: Provides legal services.
Business type (SIC): Legal services
Corporate officer: Matthew C. Barneck, Partner
Giving statement: Giving through the Richards, Brandt, Miller & Nelson Charitable Foundation.

Richards, Brandt, Miller & Nelson Charitable Foundation
299 S. Main St., 15th Fl.
Salt Lake City, UT 84111 (801) 531-2000

Establishment information: Established as a company-sponsored operating foundation; status changed to company-sponsored foundation in 2003.
Donor: Richards, Brandt, Miller & Nelson, PC.
Contact: Brett F. Paulsen, Tr.
Financial data (yr. ended 12/31/11): Assets, $11,159 (M); gifts received, $11,500; expenditures, $8,550; qualifying distributions, $7,850; giving activities include $7,850 for grants.
Purpose and activities: The foundation supports festivals and organizations involved with health, multiple sclerosis, legal aid, and human services.
Fields of interest: Arts; Health care; Human services.
Type of support: General/operating support.
Geographic limitations: Giving primarily in Salt Lake City, UT.
Support limitations: No grants to individuals.
Application information: Applications accepted. Application form required.
Initial approach: Proposal
Deadline(s): None
Trustees: Craig C. Coburn; Elizabeth Hruby-Mills; David H. Tolk.
EIN: 870667132

3207
Richards, Layton & Finger, P.A.
920 N. King St.
1 Rodney Sq.
Wilmington, DE 19801-3361
(302) 651-7849

Company URL: http://www.rlf.com/Home
Establishment information: Established in 1899.
Company type: Private company
Business activities: Operates law firm.
Corporate officers: William J. Wade, Chair.; Robert J. Krapf, Exec. V.P.; Wayne T. Stanford, C.O.O.; Edmund Pierce, C.F.O.; Thomas A. Beck, Sr. V.P.
Office: Wilmington, DE
Giving statement: Giving through the Richards, Layton & Finger, P.A Pro Bono Program.

Richards, Layton & Finger, P.A Pro Bono Program
920 N. King St.
1 Rodney Sq.
Wilmington, DE 19801-3361 (302) 651-7574
E-mail: msmith@rlf.com; Additional tel.: (302) 651-7700; URL: http://www.rlf.com/Community/ProBono

Contact: Melanie George Smith, Assoc.
Fields of interest: Legal services.
Type of support: Pro bono services - legal.
Application information: A Pro Bono Committee manages the pro bono program.

3208
Richards, Watson & Gershon
355 South Grand Ave., 40th Fl.
Los Angeles, CA 90071-3101
(213) 626-8484

Company URL: http://www.rwglaw.com/
Establishment information: \Established in 1954.
Company type: Private company
Business activities: Operates law firm.
Business type (SIC): Legal services
Offices: Brea, Los Angeles, San Francisco, CA
Giving statement: Giving through the Richards, Watson & Gershon Pro Bono Program.

Richards, Watson & Gershon Pro Bono Program
355 South Grand Ave., 40th Fl.
Los Angeles, CA 90071-3101 (213) 626-8484
FAX: (213) 626-0078; URL: http://www.rwglaw.com/recruitment/summer-associate-program.aspx

Fields of interest: Legal services.
Type of support: Pro bono services - legal.

3209
Richardson Sports L.P.
(also known as Carolina Panthers)
800 S. Mint St.
Charlotte, NC 28202-1502 (704) 358-7000

Company URL: http://www.panthers.com
Establishment information: Established in 1993.
Company type: Private company
Business activities: Operates professional football club.
Business type (SIC): Commercial sports
Corporate officers: Danny Morrison, Pres.; Dave Olsen, C.F.O.; Richard M. Thigpen, Genl. Counsel
Giving statement: Giving through the Carolina Panthers Corporate Giving Program.

Carolina Panthers Corporate Giving Program
800 S. Mint St.
Charlotte, NC 28202-1518
URL: http://www.panthers.com/community

Contact: Bernadette Washington
Purpose and activities: The Carolina Panthers make charitable contributions of memorabilia to nonprofit organizations on a case by case basis. Support is given primarily in North Carolina and South Carolina.
Fields of interest: General charitable giving.

Type of support: Donated products; In-kind gifts.
Geographic limitations: Giving primarily in NC and SC.
Support limitations: No grants for fundraising for the benefit of individuals or families; no game ticket donations.
Application information: Applications accepted. Support is limited to 1 contribution per organization during any given year. Proposals should be submitted using organization letterhead. Application form required.
Initial approach: Download application form and mail proposal and application form to headquarters
Copies of proposal: 1
Deadline(s): 2 months prior to need
Final notification: 1 month prior to need

3210
Ricoh Americas Corporation
5 Dedrick Pl.
West Caldwell, NJ 07006-6398
(973) 882-2000

Company URL: http://www.ricoh-usa.com
Establishment information: Established in 1962.
Company type: Subsidiary of a foreign company
Business activities: Sells and markets office automation equipment and electronics wholesale.
Business type (SIC): Professional and commercial equipment—wholesale
Financial profile for 2010: Number of employees, 400; sales volume, $3,030,000,000
Corporate officers: Kazuo Togashi, Chair. and C.E.O.; Tom Salierno, Jr., Pres. and C.O.O.; Martin Brodigan, Exec. V.P. and C.F.O.; Hede Nonaka, Exec. V.P., Mktg.; Tracey J. Rothenberger, Sr. V.P. and C.I.O.; Mark Hershey, Sr. V.P. and Genl. Counsel; Donna Venable, Sr. V.P., Human Resources; Shun Sato, Sr. V.P., Mktg.; Tom Sicarddi, V.P., Finance
Board of director: Kazuo Togashi, Chair.
International operations: Canada
Giving statement: Giving through the Ricoh Corporation Contributions Program.

Ricoh Corporation Contributions Program
5 Dedrick Pl.
West Caldwell, NJ 07006-6304 (973) 882-2000
URL: http://www.ricoh.com/csr/index.html

Purpose and activities: Ricoh makes charitable contributions to nonprofit organizations involved with youth development, health care, poverty, human services fund-raising, and the environment. Support is given primarily in areas of company operations on a national and international basis.
Fields of interest: Environment, forests; Environment; Health care, blood supply; Youth development; Human services, fund raising/fund distribution; United Ways and Federated Giving Programs Economically disadvantaged.
Type of support: Employee matching gifts; Employee volunteer services; General/operating support.
Geographic limitations: Giving primarily in areas of company operations on a national and international basis.
Application information:

3211
Ridgewood Savings Bank
71-02 Forest Ave.
Ridgewood, NY 11385 (718) 240-4778

Company URL: http://www.ridgewoodbank.com
Establishment information: Established in 1920.
Company type: Mutual company
Business activities: Operates savings bank.
Business type (SIC): Savings institutions
Corporate officers: Peter M. Boger, Chair., Pres., and C.E.O.; Leonard Stekol, Exec. V.P. and C.F.O.; Coretta Johnson, V.P. and Treas.
Board of director: Peter M. Boger, Chair.
Giving statement: Giving through the Ridgewood Foundation.

Ridgewood Foundation
71-02 Forest Ave.
Ridgewood, NY 11385

Establishment information: Established in 2003.
Donor: Ridgewood Savings Bank.
Financial data (yr. ended 12/31/11): Assets, $3,280,022 (M); gifts received, $750,000; expenditures, $114,079; qualifying distributions, $113,500; giving activities include $113,500 for grants.
Purpose and activities: The foundation supports organizations involved with Alzheimer's disease, hunger, housing, human services, and Catholicism.
Fields of interest: Education; Human services; Religion.
Type of support: General/operating support.
Application information: Applications not accepted. Contributes only to pre-selected organizations.
Officers: William C. McGarry, Pres.; Peter M. Boger, V.P.; Norman L. McNamme, V.P.; Laura Camelo, Secy.; Leonard Stekol, Treas.
Trustees: Michael A. Agnes; Robert J. Crimmins; James J. Dixon; Robert W. Donohue; Margart Mary Fitzpatrick; Mary A. Ledermann; William A. McKenna, Jr.; Charles J. Ohlig.
EIN: 050584005

3212
Rieke Corporation
(doing business as Rieke Packaging Systems)
500 W. 7th St.
Auburn, IN 46706-2095 (260) 925-3700

Company URL: http://www.riekepackaging.com
Establishment information: Established in 1921.
Company type: Subsidiary of a public company
Business activities: Manufactures steel drum closures, plugs, and sealing rings.
Business type (SIC): Metal containers; gaskets, packing and sealing devices, and rubber hose and belting; metal forgings and stampings; machinery/general industry
Corporate officers: Lynn A. Brooks, Pres.; Don Laipple, C.I.O.
Giving statement: Giving through the Rieke Corporation Foundation.

Rieke Corporation Foundation
(formerly Rieke Corporation Foundation Trust)
9031 Stellhorn Crossing Pkwy.
Fort Wayne, NE 46815-1310 (264) 469-6309

Donor: Rieke Corp.
Contact: Sherri Chaney
Financial data (yr. ended 12/31/11): Assets, $959,060 (M); expenditures, $52,595; qualifying distributions, $43,897; giving activities include $40,500 for 8 grants (high: $10,000; low: $2,000).
Purpose and activities: The foundation supports libraries and organizations involved with health, recreation, children services, and senior citizens.
Fields of interest: Education; Health care; Public affairs.
Type of support: General/operating support.
Support limitations: No grants to individuals.
Application information: Applications accepted. Application form required.
Initial approach: Letter
Deadline(s): Aug. 31
Trustee: Grabill Bank.
EIN: 510158651

3213
J. A. Riggs Tractor Company
9125 Interstate 30
Little Rock, AR 72209-3703
(501) 570-3100

Company URL: http://www.riggs-cat.com/
Establishment information: Established in 1927.
Company type: Private company
Business activities: Operates heavy equipment dealerships.
Business type (SIC): Industrial machinery and equipment—wholesale
Corporate officers: John A. Riggs IV, Pres.; Denny Upton, V.P. and C.F.O.; Mike Andrews, V.P., Sales and Mktg.
Giving statement: Giving through the Riggs Benevolent Fund.

Riggs Benevolent Fund
P.O. Box 831041
Dallas, TX 75283-1041
Application address: c/o Bank of America, N.A., P.C. Group, P.O. Box 1681, Little Rock, AR 72203-1681, tel.: (501) 378-1626

Establishment information: Trust established in 1959 in AR.
Donors: Robert G. Cress; Lamar W. Riggs Trust; J.A. Riggs Tractor Co.; Jack Riggs III; Lamar W. Riggs.
Financial data (yr. ended 12/31/11): Assets, $6,833,356 (M); gifts received, $282,977; expenditures, $580,911; qualifying distributions, $489,600; giving activities include $489,600 for grants.
Purpose and activities: The fund supports museums and hospitals and organizations involved with education, cancer, youth development, children services, and Christianity.
Fields of interest: Museums; Elementary/secondary education; Higher education; Education; Hospitals (general); Cancer; Youth development, agriculture; Youth development; Children, services; United Ways and Federated Giving Programs; Christian agencies & churches.
Type of support: General/operating support; Scholarship funds.
Geographic limitations: Giving primarily in Little Rock, AR.
Support limitations: No grants to individuals.
Application information: Applications accepted. Application form not required. Applicants should submit the following:
1) detailed description of project and amount of funding requested
2) copy of current year's organizational budget and/or project budget

Initial approach: Proposal
Deadline(s): None
Trustees: Robert G. Cress; John A. Riggs III; Bank of America, N.A.
EIN: 716050130
Selected grants: The following grants are a representative sample of this grantmaker's funding activity:
$25,000 to Saint James United Methodist Church, Little Rock, AR, 2010.
$12,500 to Hendrix College, Conway, AR, 2010.
$10,000 to Arkansas Childrens Hospital Foundation, Little Rock, AR, 2010.
$10,000 to Lyon College, Batesville, AR, 2010.
$9,000 to Arkansas Museum of Science and History, Little Rock, AR, 2010.
$5,000 to Philander Smith College, Little Rock, AR, 2010.
$4,000 to Razorback Foundation, Fayetteville, AR, 2010.
$3,000 to Riverfest, Little Rock, AR, 2010.
$2,500 to Arkansas Arts Center, Little Rock, AR, 2010.
$1,800 to University of Arkansas Foundation, Fayetteville, AR, 2010.

3214
Righteous Babe Records, Inc.
341 Delaware Ave., Fl. 2
Buffalo, NY 14202-1871 (716) 852-8020

Company URL: http://www.righteousbabe.com/index.asp
Establishment information: Established in 1990.
Company type: Private company
Business activities: Operates record label.
Business type (SIC): Audio and video equipment/household
Corporate officers: Ani DiFranco, C.E.O.; Scot Fisher, Pres.
Giving statement: Giving through the Righteous Babe Foundation, Inc.

The Righteous Babe Foundation, Inc.
341 Delaware Ave.
Buffalo, NY 14202-1803

Establishment information: Established in 1998 in NY.
Donor: Righteous Babe Records, Inc.
Financial data (yr. ended 06/30/12): Assets, $101 (M); gifts received, $800; expenditures, $1,135; qualifying distributions, $500; giving activities include $500 for grants.
Geographic limitations: Giving primarily in Washington, DC and Buffalo, NY.
Support limitations: No grants to individuals.
Application information: Applications not accepted. Unsolicited requests for funds not accepted.
Officers: Ani DiFranco, Pres.; Scot Fisher, V.P.; Rocco Lucente II, Esq., Secy.
EIN: 161546071

3215
Riker, Danzig, Scherer, Hyland & Perretti LLP
1 Speedwell Ave.
Headquarters Plz.
Morristown, NJ 07962-1981
(973) 451-8417

Company URL: http://www.riker.com/
Establishment information: Established in 1882.
Company type: Private company
Business activities: Operates law firm.
Business type (SIC): Legal services
Corporate officer: Timothy P. Carr, C.F.O.
Offices: Morristown, Trenton, NJ; New York, NY
International operations: United Kingdom
Giving statement: Giving through the Riker, Danzig, Scherer, Hyland & Perretti LLP Pro Bono Program.

Riker, Danzig, Scherer, Hyland & Perretti LLP Pro Bono Program
1 Speedwell Ave.
Headquarters Plz.
Morristown, NJ 07962-1981 (973) 451-8431
E-mail: sfranzblau@riker.com; URL: http://www.riker.com/firm/probono.php

Contact: Sigrid S. Franzblau Esq.
Fields of interest: Legal services.
Type of support: Pro bono services - legal.
Application information: A Pro Bono Committee manages the pro bono program.

3216
The Rima Manufacturing Co.
3850 Munson Hwy.
Hudson, MI 49247-9804 (517) 448-8921

Company URL: http://www.rimamfg.com
Establishment information: Established in 1955.
Company type: Private company
Business activities: Manufactures screw machine products.
Business type (SIC): Screw machine products; machinery/industrial and commercial
Corporate officers: Edward J. Engle, Jr., Pres. and C.E.O.; Jed Engle, Co.-Pres.; Debi Odette, V.P., Opers.
Giving statement: Giving through the Engle Foundation.

The Engle Foundation
3850 Munson Hwy.
Hudson, MI 49247-9800 (517) 448-8921

Establishment information: Established in 1988 in MI.
Donors: The Rima Manufacturing Co.; Edward J. Engle, Jr.
Contact: Edward J. Engle, Jr., Pres. and Treas.
Financial data (yr. ended 08/31/12): Assets, $31,764 (M); expenditures, $20,805; qualifying distributions, $20,385; giving activities include $20,385 for 7 grants (high: $10,000; low: $250).
Purpose and activities: The foundation supports organizations involved with K-12 and higher education and Catholicism.
Fields of interest: Arts; Youth development.
Type of support: General/operating support.
Geographic limitations: Giving primarily in Hudson, MI.
Support limitations: No grants to individuals.
Application information: Applications accepted. Application form required. Applicants should submit the following:
1) name, address and phone number of organization
2) detailed description of project and amount of funding requested
Initial approach: Letter
Deadline(s): None
Officers: Edward J. Engle, Jr., Pres. and Treas.; Jennifer Engle, Secy.
Director: Edward Engle III.
EIN: 382826866

3217
Rimon Law Group, Inc.
220 Sansome St., Ste. 310
San Francisco, CA 94104-2747
(415) 683-5472

Company URL: http://www.rimonlaw.com
Establishment information: Established in 2009.
Company type: Private company
Business activities: Operates virtual law firm.
Business type (SIC): Legal services
Corporate officer: Alexander Hamilton, Owner
Giving statement: Giving through the Rimon Law Group, Inc. Corporate Giving Program.

Rimon Law Group, Inc. Corporate Giving Program
1 Embarcadero Ctr., Ste. 400
San Francisco, CA 94111-3619 (800) 930-7271
URL: http://www.rimonlaw.com

Purpose and activities: Rimon Law Group is a certified B Corporation that donates a percentage of profits to nonprofit organizations.

3218
Rio Tinto America, Inc.
(also known as Rio Tinto Borax)
8051 E. Maplewood Ave., Bldg. 4
Greenwood Village, CO 80111
(303) 713-5000

Company URL: http://www.borax.com
Establishment information: Established in 1872.
Company type: Subsidiary of a foreign company
Business activities: Mines borax.
Business type (SIC): Mining/chemical and fertilizer mineral
Corporate officer: Gary Goldberg, Pres. and C.E.O.
Giving statement: Giving through the Rio Tinto Borax Corporate Giving Program and the Borax Education Foundation.

Rio Tinto Borax Corporate Giving Program
c/o Rio Tinto Minerals
8000 E. Maplewood Ave.
Greenwood Village, CO 80111-4714
URL: http://www.riotinto.com/sustainabledevelopment2011/social/communities.html

Purpose and activities: Rio Tinto Borax makes charitable contributions to nonprofit organizations on a case by case basis. Support is given primarily in areas of company operations in California, Colorado, and Illinois, and in Argentina, Belgium,

Brazil, China, England, France, Germany, Italy, the Netherlands, Singapore, Spain, and Taiwan.
Fields of interest: United Ways and Federated Giving Programs; General charitable giving.
International interests: Argentina; Belgium; Brazil; China; England; France; Germany; Italy; Netherlands; Singapore; Spain; Taiwan.
Type of support: General/operating support.
Geographic limitations: Giving primarily in areas of company operations in CA, CO, and IL, and in Argentina, Belgium, Brazil, China, England, France, Germany, Italy, the Netherlands, Singapore, Spain, and Taiwan.

The Borax Education Foundation

4700 Daybreak Pkwy.
South Jordan, UT 84095-5120

Establishment information: Established in 1963 in CA.
Donor: U.S. Borax Inc.
Financial data (yr. ended 12/31/11): Assets, $6,511 (M); expenditures, $10; qualifying distributions, $0; giving activities include $0 for grants to individuals.
Purpose and activities: The foundation awards college scholarships to children of employees and retirees of Rio Tinto Borax.
Type of support: Employee-related scholarships.
Geographic limitations: Giving primarily in areas of company operations.
Application information: Applications not accepted. Unsolicited requests for funds not accepted.
Officers and Directors:* Gary Goldberg*, Pres.; Jeffrey Olsen*, Treas.; Chris Robison.
EIN: 954497752

3219
Ripplewood Holdings LLC

1 Rockefeller Plz., 32nd Fl.
New York, NY 10020 (212) 582-6700

Establishment information: Established in 1995.
Company type: Private company
Business activities: Operates holding company.
Business type (SIC): Holding company
Corporate officers: Harvey Golub, Chair.; Timothy C. Collins, C.E.O.
Board of director: Harvey Golub, Chair.
Subsidiaries: Dayton/Richmond Corp., Miamisburg, OH; Dur-O-Wal Inc., Aurora, IL; Edwards Baking Co. Inc., Norcross, GA; Gourmet Concepts International Inc., Tucker, GA; Western Country Pies Inc., Salt Lake City, UT; WMC Holding L.L.C., Sunnyvale, CA; WRC Media Inc., New York, NY
International operations: Japan
Giving statement: Giving through the Ripplewood Foundation, Inc.

Ripplewood Foundation, Inc.

1 Rockefeller Plz., 32nd Fl.
New York, NY 10020

Establishment information: Established in 1997 in DE and NY.
Donors: Ripplewood Holdings LLC; Timothy C. Collins.
Financial data (yr. ended 12/31/11): Assets, $139 (M); expenditures, $18,621; qualifying distributions, $17,500; giving activities include $17,500 for grants.
Purpose and activities: The foundation supports organizations involved with arts and culture, education, health, medical research, children services, international affairs, human rights, and civic affairs.
Fields of interest: Arts; Recreation; Human services.
Type of support: General/operating support.
Support limitations: No grants to individuals.
Application information: Applications not accepted. Contributes only to pre-selected organizations.
Officer: Timothy C. Collins, Pres.
EIN: 522036080

3220
Rite Aid Corporation

30 Hunter Ln.
Camp Hill, PA 17011-2400 (717) 761-2633
FAX: (717) 731-3860

Company URL: http://www.riteaid.com
Establishment information: Established in 1962.
Company type: Public company
Company ticker symbol and exchange: RAD/NYSE
Business activities: Operates drug stores.
Business type (SIC): Drug stores and proprietary stores
Financial profile for 2013: Number of employees, 51,300; assets, $7,078,720,000; sales volume, $25,392,260,000; pre-tax net income, $7,500,000; expenses, $25,384,760,000; liabilities, $9,538,150,000
Fortune 1000 ranking: 2012—113th in revenues, 954th in profits, and 475th in assets
Forbes 2000 ranking: 2012—359th in sales, 1867th in profits, and 1651st in assets
Corporate officers: John T. Standley, Chair., Pres., and C.E.O.; Ken Martindale, Sr. Exec. V.P. and C.O.O.; Frank Vitrano, Sr. Exec. V.P., C.F.O., and C.A.O.; Marc A. Strassler, Exec. V.P. and Genl. Counsel; Brian Fiala, Exec. V.P., Human Resources; Doug Donley, Sr. V.P. and C.A.O.; Don P. Davis, Sr. V.P. and C.I.O.; John Learish, Sr. V.P., Mktg.
Board of directors: John T. Standley, Chair.; Joseph B. Anderson; John Baumer; Bruce G. Bodaken; Francois J. Coutu; James L. Donald; David R. Jessick; Michael N. Regan; Mary F. Sammons; Marcy Syms
Subsidiaries: Harco, Inc., Tuscaloosa, AL; Perry Drug Stores, Inc., Pontiac, MI
Giving statement: Giving through the Rite Aid Foundation.
Company EIN: 231614034

The Rite Aid Foundation

P.O. Box 3165
Harrisburg, PA 17105-3165
URL: http://www.riteaid.com/company/community/foundation.jsf

Establishment information: Established in 2001.
Financial data (yr. ended 12/31/11): Revenue, $1,747,162; assets, $1,581,314 (M); gifts received, $1,466,049; expenditures, $2,025,623; giving activities include $1,779,417 for grants and $160,000 for grants to individuals.
Purpose and activities: The foundation supports charitable activities in the various communities that Rite Aid Corporation serves with emphasis on projects that focus on health care, women, and families.
Fields of interest: Health care; Salvation Army; YM/YWCAs & YM/YWHAs; Aging, centers/services; Civil/human rights; Community/economic development; United Ways and Federated Giving Programs Women.
Program:
Grants: The foundation supports programs that focus on health and wellness in the communities in which Rite Aid operates, and which are dedicated to helping people lead healthier and happier lives. Grants are awarded for one year at a time; no organization can receive a grant from the foundation for more than two years in a row.
Geographic limitations: Giving primarily in areas of company operations.
Support limitations: No support for sports teams or fraternal, labor, social, or veteran's organizations; political causes; churches; or religious or sectarian organizations (except for programs that benefit the entire community). No grants to individuals, or for travel, capital campaigns, endowments, or seminars.
Application information: Applications accepted. Applicants should submit the following:
1) population served
2) name, address and phone number of organization
3) copy of IRS Determination Letter
4) geographic area to be served
5) copy of most recent annual report/audited financial statement/990
6) listing of board of directors, trustees, officers and other key people and their affiliations
7) detailed description of project and amount of funding requested
8) contact person
9) copy of current year's organizational budget and/or project budget

Initial approach: Proposal
Deadline(s): None
Final notification: 60 to 90 days
Officers: Mary Sammons, Pres.; John Learish, V.P.; James Mastrian, V.P.; Steve Parsons, V.P.; Robert Sari, Secy.; Karen Rugen, Treas.
Directors: Scott Bernard; Todd McCarty.
EIN: 251892843

3221
RITE-HITE Corporation

8900 N. Arbon Dr.
Milwaukee, WI 53223-2451
(414) 355-2600

Company URL: http://www.ritehite.com/
Establishment information: Established in 1965.
Company type: Subsidiary of a private company
Business activities: Manufactures and sells loading dock and materials handling products.
Business type (SIC): Machinery/construction, mining, and materials handling
Corporate officers: Michael H. White, Chair.; Terry Litz, V.P., Human Resources; Mark S. Kirkish, Cont.
Board of director: Michael H. White, Chair.
Subsidiary: Frommelt Industries, Dubuque, IA
Divisions: Rite-Hite Div., Milwaukee, WI; Rite-Hite Frommelt Div., Milwaukee, WI
Giving statement: Giving through the RITE-HITE Corporation Foundation, Inc.

RITE-HITE Corporation Foundation, Inc.

8900 N. Arbon Dr.
Milwaukee, WI 53223-2451 (414) 355-2600

Establishment information: Established in 1984.
Donors: RITE-HITE Corp.; RITE-HITE Holding Corp.
Contact: Mark S. Kirkish, Treas.
Financial data (yr. ended 12/31/11): Assets, $25,179 (M); gifts received, $1,070,000; expenditures, $1,059,610; qualifying distributions,

$1,059,600; giving activities include $1,059,600 for grants.
Purpose and activities: The foundation supports organizations involved with arts and culture, higher education, health, youth development business, human services, and Christianity.
Fields of interest: Arts; Higher education; Health care, blood supply; Health care; Youth development, business; YM/YWCAs & YM/YWHAs; Human services; United Ways and Federated Giving Programs; Christian agencies & churches.
Type of support: General/operating support.
Application information: Applications accepted. Contributions for unsolicited requests are currently very limited. Application form not required.
Initial approach: Proposal
Deadline(s): None
Officers and Directors:* Michael H. White*, Pres.; Mark G. Petri*, V.P.; Richard M. Esenberg, Secy.; Mark S. Kirkish*, Treas.
EIN: 391522057
Selected grants: The following grants are a representative sample of this grantmaker's funding activity:
$40,000 to United Way of Greater Milwaukee, Milwaukee, WI, 2010.
$25,000 to Lyric Opera of Chicago, Chicago, IL, 2010.
$22,300 to Blood Center of Wisconsin, Milwaukee, WI, 2010.
$5,000 to United Performing Arts Fund, Milwaukee, WI, 2010.
$2,500 to Discovery World, Milwaukee, WI, 2010.
$2,000 to Penfield Childrens Center, Milwaukee, WI, 2010.
$1,000 to Froedtert Hospital Foundation, Milwaukee, WI, 2010.

3222
Ritzville Warehouse Co.
201 E. 1st Ave.
Ritzville, WA 99169-2393 (509) 659-0130

Company URL: http://www.ritzwhse.com
Establishment information: Established in 1893.
Company type: Private company
Business activities: Sells grain wholesale.
Business type (SIC): Farm-product raw materials—wholesale
Corporate officers: Grant Miller, Pres.; John Anderson, C.E.O.; Jeff Milner, C.F.O.; Nancy McRae, Secy.
Board of directors: Don Dirks; Dale Galbreath; Bruce Honn; Jake Klein; Nancy McRae; Grant Miller; Lynn Schmidt; Jay Scrupps; Ron Vold; Jarod Wollweber
Giving statement: Giving through the Ritzville Warehouse Foundation.

Ritzville Warehouse Foundation
201 E. 1st Ave.
Ritzville, WA 99169-0171 (509) 659-0130
Application Address: c/o Scholarship Board, P.O. Box 171, Ritzville, WA 99122.

Establishment information: Established in 2001 in WA.
Donor: Ritzville Warehouse Co.
Financial data (yr. ended 09/30/11): Assets, $0 (M); expenditures, $5,000; qualifying distributions, $5,000; giving activities include $5,000 for 5 grants to individuals (high: $1,000; low: $1,000).
Purpose and activities: The foundation awards college scholarships to high school seniors living in areas of company operations of Ritzville Warehouse Co.
Type of support: Scholarships—to individuals.
Geographic limitations: Giving limited to areas of company operations in WA.
Application information: Applications accepted. Application form required. Applicants should submit the following:
1) name, address and phone number of organization
2) copy of most recent annual report/audited financial statement/990
Initial approach: Letter
Deadline(s): May
Committee Members: Maureen Bourne; Jon Fink; Paul Scheller.
EIN: 753027595

3223
River City Food, Co.
3425 Lake Eastbrook Blvd., S.E.
Grand Rapids, MI 49546-5935
(617) 776-7600

Company URL: http://www.rcfc.com
Establishment information: Established in 1993.
Company type: Private company
Business activities: Operates restaurants.
Business type (SIC): Restaurants and drinking places
Corporate officers: R. Dale Lausch, Pres.; Doug McKinnon, C.O.O.; Matthew Passero, C.I.O.
Giving statement: Giving through the R. Dale Lausch Foundation and the River City Food Company Foundation.

R. Dale Lausch Foundation
3425 Lake Eastbrook Blvd. S.E.
Grand Rapids, MI 49546-5935

Establishment information: Established in 1985 in MI.
Donors: River City Food Co.; R. Dale Lausch.
Financial data (yr. ended 12/31/09): Assets, $44,836 (M); expenditures, $922; qualifying distributions, $505; giving activities include $505 for 1 grant.
Purpose and activities: The foundation supports organizations involved with dance and higher education.
Fields of interest: Education.
Type of support: General/operating support.
Geographic limitations: Giving limited to Grand Rapids, MI.
Support limitations: No grants to individuals.
Publications: Annual report.
Application information: Applications not accepted. Unsolicited requests for funds not accepted.
Officer and Directors:* R. Dale Lausch*, Pres.; Shirley Lausch.
Number of staff: None.
EIN: 382641104

River City Food Company Foundation
3425 Lake Eastbrook Blvd. S.E.
Grand Rapids, MI 49546

Establishment information: Established in 1997 in MI.
Donor: River City Food Co.
Financial data (yr. ended 12/31/10): Assets, $71,418 (M); expenditures, $878; qualifying distributions, $255; giving activities include $255 for 1 grant.
Purpose and activities: The foundation supports the Hearts of West Michigan United Way.
Fields of interest: Education.
Type of support: General/operating support.
Application information: Applications not accepted. Unsolicited requests for funds not accepted.
Officer and Director:* R. Dale Lausch*, Pres.
EIN: 383300379

3224
The River Products Company, Inc.
3273 Dubuque St., N.E.
P.O. Box 2120
Iowa City, IA 52244-2120 (319) 338-1184

Company URL: http://www.riverproducts.com
Establishment information: Established in 1920.
Company type: Private company
Business activities: Produces crushed limestone, sand, and gravel products.
Business type (SIC): Mining/crushed and broken stone; mining/sand and gravel
Financial profile for 2011: Number of employees, 33
Corporate officers: Thomas R. Scott, Pres. and C.E.O.; Matthew C. Banning, V.P. and C.F.O.
Giving statement: Giving through the RPC, Inc. Charitable Foundation.

RPC, Inc. Charitable Foundation
c/o River Products Comapny, Inc.
P.O. Box 2120
Iowa City, IA 52244-2120

Establishment information: Established in 2000.
Donor: River Products Company, Inc.
Financial data (yr. ended 12/31/11): Assets, $1,279 (M); gifts received, $11,500; expenditures, $11,010; qualifying distributions, $11,010; giving activities include $11,010 for grants.
Purpose and activities: The foundation supports organizations involved with education, health, athletics, and human services.
Fields of interest: Arts; Education; Health organizations.
Type of support: General/operating support.
Geographic limitations: Giving limited to IA.
Support limitations: No grants to individuals.
Application information: Applications not accepted. Unsolicited requests for funds not accepted.
Officers: Thomas R. Scott, Pres.; Todd Scott, Secy.; Matthew C. Banning, Treas.
EIN: 421504431

3225
Rivermaid Trading Company
(formerly The Enns Packing Co., Inc.)
6011 E. Pine St.
Lodi, CA 95240-9774 (209) 369-3586
FAX: (209) 369-5465

Company URL: http://www.rivermaid.com/
Establishment information: Established in 1973.
Company type: Private company
Business activities: Produces fruit.
Business type (SIC): Farms/fruit and nut
Corporate officers: Eugene Enns, Chair.; Melvin Enns, Co-Pres. and V.P.; Nick Enns, Co-Pres.; Jim Stewart, Co-Pres.; Patrick Archibeque, C.E.O.; Peter Craig, C.O.O.; Kenneth Enns, C.F.O.

Board of director: Eugene Enns, Chair.
Giving statement: Giving through the Enns Foundation.

Enns Foundation

4572 Ave. 400
Dinuba, CA 93618-9774

Establishment information: Established in 1995 in CA.
Donors: Enns Packing Co., Inc.; Wes Pak Sales, Inc.; Jim Stewart; Terri Stewart.
Financial data (yr. ended 12/31/11): Assets, $125,699 (M); gifts received, $59,200; expenditures, $54,907; qualifying distributions, $52,177; giving activities include $52,177 for grants.
Purpose and activities: The foundation supports food banks.
Fields of interest: Agriculture/food.
Type of support: General/operating support.
Geographic limitations: Giving primarily in Fresno, CA.
Support limitations: No grants to individuals.
Application information: Applications not accepted. Unsolicited requests for funds not accepted.
Officers: Kenneth Enns, Chair.; Rosemary Enns, C.F.O.; Cheryl Herbig, Secy.
EIN: 770385090

3226
Riverway Co.

8400 Normandale Lake Blvd., Ste. 920
Bloomington, MN 55437 (952) 921-3994

Company URL: http://www.riverway.com
Establishment information: Established in 1937.
Company type: Private company
Business activities: Provides water transportation services.
Business type (SIC): Transportation services/water; transportation/water freight
Corporate officers: Henry M. Baskerville, Jr., Chair.; Terry R. Becker, Pres. and C.E.O.; Shirley A. Moen, Exec. Secy.
Board of director: Henry M. Baskerville, Jr., Chair.
Giving statement: Giving through the Riverway Foundation.

The Riverway Foundation

8400 Normandale Lake Blvd., Ste. 920
Bloomington, MN 55437 (952) 921-3994

Establishment information: Established in 1995 in MN.
Donors: Riverway Co.; H.M. Baskerville, Jr.; Terry R. Becker.
Contact: H.M. Baskerville, Jr., Tr.
Financial data (yr. ended 12/31/11): Assets, $3,480,446 (M); expenditures, $225,609; qualifying distributions, $184,155; giving activities include $180,022 for 30 grants (high: $50,000; low: $1,000).
Purpose and activities: The foundation supports organizations involved with Alzheimer's disease, cancer research, domestic violence, housing, children and youth, family counseling, and senior citizens.
Fields of interest: Environment; Human services; Community/economic development.
Type of support: Annual campaigns; Building/renovation; Capital campaigns; Consulting services; Continuing support; Debt reduction; Emergency funds; Endowments; Equipment; General/operating support; Matching/challenge support; Program development; Program evaluation.
Application information: Applications accepted. Application form required.
Initial approach: Letter
Copies of proposal: 1
Deadline(s): None
Trustees: H.M. Baskerville, Jr.; Laura Lee Baskerville Becker; Terry R. Becker.
Number of staff: 1 part-time support.
EIN: 416406915

3227
Riviana Foods, Inc.

2777 Allen Pkwy.
P.O. Box 2636
Houston, TX 77019-2141 (713) 529-3251

Company URL: http://www.riviana.com
Establishment information: Established in 1911.
Company type: Subsidiary of a foreign company
Business activities: Processes, markets, and distributes rice and other food products.
Business type (SIC): Grain mill products, including pet food; food and kindred products
Corporate officers: Antonio Hernandez Callejas, Chair.; Bastiaan G. de Zeeuw, Pres. and C.E.O.; Gregory S. Richardson, V.P. and C.F.O.; Elizabeth B. Woodard, V.P. and Genl. Counsel; Brett L. Beckfield, V.P., Opers.; Tim D. White, V.P., Finance; Paul A. Galvani, V.P., Mktg.; R. Shane Faucett, V.P., Sales; Gerard J. Ferguson, V.P., Human Resources
Board of directors: Antonio Hernandez Callejas, Chair.; Felix Hernandez Callejas; Bastiaan G. de Zeeuw; Pablo Albendea Solis; Elizabeth B. Woodard
Subsidiary: Riviana International Inc., Houston, TX
International operations: Belgium; Costa Rica; Guatemala; United Kingdom
Giving statement: Giving through the Riviana Foods Inc. Corporate Giving Program.

Riviana Foods Inc. Corporate Giving Program

2777 Allen Pkwy.
Houston, TX 77019-2141 (713) 529-3251

Purpose and activities: Riviana Foods makes charitable contributions to nonprofit organizations on a case by case basis. Support is given primarily in areas of company operations in Arkansas, Minnesota, Tennessee, and Texas.
Fields of interest: General charitable giving.
Type of support: Employee matching gifts; In-kind gifts; Scholarships—to individuals.
Geographic limitations: Giving primarily in areas of company operations in AR, MN, TN, and TX.

3228
RJN Group, Inc.

200 W. Front St.
Wheaton, IL 60187-5111

Company URL: http://www.rjn.com
Establishment information: Established in 1975.
Company type: Private company
Business activities: Provides engineering services; provides information technology consulting services.
Business type (SIC): Engineering, architectural, and surveying services; management and public relations services
Corporate officers: Robert North, C.E.O.; Alan J. Hollenbeck, Pres.; Robert J. Januska, C.O.O.
Offices: Fayetteville, AR; Deerfield Beach, FL; Norcross, GA; Collinsville, IL; Boston, MA; St. Louis, MO; Tulsa, OK; Arlington, Austin, Dallas, Fort Worth, San Antonio, TX; Vienna, VA
Giving statement: Giving through the RJN Foundation.

The RJN Foundation

213 S. Wheaton Ave.
Wheaton, IL 60187-5207
URL: http://www.rjn.com/aboutpages.php?id=4

Establishment information: Established in 1994 in IL.
Donors: Richard J. Nogaj; RJN Group, Inc.; Florence Nogaj.
Financial data (yr. ended 12/31/11): Assets, $342,020 (M); gifts received, $24,530; expenditures, $32,614; qualifying distributions, $16,500; giving activities include $16,500 for 23 grants (high: $1,200; low: $500).
Purpose and activities: The foundation supports programs designed to address human welfare. Special emphasis is directed toward programs designed to serve families and children in crisis; people who are economically disadvantaged; people with physical or mental challenges; and people suffering from systemic effects of illiteracy, hunger, poverty, and homelessness.
Fields of interest: Elementary/secondary education; Higher education; Education; Food services; Housing/shelter; Children/youth, services; Family services; Developmentally disabled, centers & services; Homeless, human services; Human services Economically disadvantaged.
Type of support: General/operating support; Scholarship funds.
Geographic limitations: Giving primarily in Wheaton, IL.
Support limitations: No grants to individuals.
Application information: Applications not accepted. Contributes only to pre-selected organizations. Requests are accepted from RJN employees.
Directors: Florence Nogaj; Richard J. Nogaj; Scott Rebman.
EIN: 363963955

3229
Roanoke & Botetourt Telephone Co.

1000 Roanoke Rd.
Daleville, VA 24083-2534 (540) 992-2211

Establishment information: Established in 2001.
Company type: Private company
Business activities: Provides telephone communications services.
Business type (SIC): Telephone communications
Financial profile for 2010: Number of employees, 43
Corporate officers: Ira D. Layman, Chair.; J. Allen Layman, Pres. and C.E.O.
Board of director: Ira D. Layman, Chair.
Giving statement: Giving through the Layman Family Foundation.

Layman Family Foundation

(formerly Roanoke & Botetourt Telephone Foundation)
467 Layman Ln.
Daleville, VA 24083-0174 (540) 992-2211

Establishment information: Established in 1990 in VA.
Donors: Roanoke & Botetourt Telephone Co.; R&B Communications Foundation, Inc.
Contact: J. Allen Layman, Pres.
Financial data (yr. ended 12/31/11): Assets, $519,090 (M); expenditures, $23,440; qualifying distributions, $21,285; giving activities include $21,285 for grants.
Purpose and activities: The foundation supports historical societies and organizations involved with education.
Fields of interest: Education; Human services; Religion.
Type of support: General/operating support.
Geographic limitations: Giving primarily in VA.
Support limitations: No grants to individuals.
Application information: Applications accepted. Application form not required.
Initial approach: Proposal
Deadline(s): None
Officer: J. Allen Layman, Pres.
EIN: 541556638

3230
Robbins & Myers, Inc.

10586 Hwy 75 N.
Willis, TX 77378 (936) 890-1064
FAX: (937) 225-3314

Company URL: http://www.robn.com
Establishment information: Established in 1878.
Company type: Public company
Company ticker symbol and exchange: RBN/NYSE
Business activities: Designs, manufactures, and markets pumping equipment and systems.
Business type (SIC): Machinery/general industry
Financial profile for 2012: Number of employees, 3,473; assets, $1,523,260,000; sales volume, $1,034,780,000; pre-tax net income, $218,510,000; expenses, $816,270,000; liabilities, $446,890,000
Corporate officers: Thomas P. Loftis, Chair.; Peter C. Wallace, Pres. and C.E.O.; Kevin J. Brown, C.F.O., C.A.O., and Cont.; Linn Harson, Secy. and Genl. Counsel; Michael J. McAdams, Treas.; Jeffrey L. Halsey, V.P., Human Resources
Board of directors: Thomas P. Loftis, Chair.; Richard J. Giromini; Stephen F. Kirk; Andrew G. Lampereur; Dale L. Medford; Albert J. Neupaver; Peter C. Wallace
Subsidiaries: Moyno Motor Products, Fairfield, CA; Moyno Oilfield Products, Tulsa, OK; Robbins & Myers, Inc., Fairfield, CA; Robbins & Myers, Inc., Gallipolis, OH; Robbins & Myers, Fluids Handling Group, Springfield, OH; Robbins & Myers/Electro-Craft, Eden Prairie, MN; Robbins & Myers/Moyno Oilfield Products, Inc., Tulsa, OK; Robbins & Myers/Renco, Goleta, CA; Robbins & Myers/RKI, Lumberton, NJ
International operations: Argentina; Australia; Belgium; Brazil; Canada; China; Colombia; France; Germany; India; Italy; Mexico; Netherlands; Singapore; Spain; Venezuela
Giving statement: Giving through the Robbins & Myers Foundation.
Company EIN: 310424220

Robbins & Myers Foundation

51 Plum St., Ste. 260
Dayton, OH 45440-1397

Establishment information: Incorporated in 1966 in OH.
Donor: Robbins & Myers, Inc.
Financial data (yr. ended 08/31/11): Assets, $261,136 (M); expenditures, $0; qualifying distributions, $0.
Purpose and activities: The foundation supports organizations involved with arts and culture, education, housing, and children services.
Type of support: Capital campaigns; Continuing support; Employee matching gifts; General/operating support; Scholarship funds.
Geographic limitations: Giving primarily in areas of company operations, with emphasis on Dayton, OH.
Support limitations: No grants to individuals.
Application information: Applications not accepted. Unsolicited requests for funds not accepted.
Officers: Peter C. Wallace, Pres.; Kevin J. Brown, Treas.; Brenda Wright Walther, Secy.
EIN: 316064597

3231
Lucille Roberts, Inc.

50 E. 42nd St.
New York, NY 10017 (212) 682-8421

Company URL: http://www.lucilleroberts.com
Establishment information: Established in 1969.
Company type: Private company
Business activities: Operates health clubs.
Business type (SIC): Amusement and recreation services/miscellaneous
Financial profile for 2010: Number of employees, 25
Corporate officer: Lucille Roberts, Pres. and C.E.O.
Giving statement: Giving through the Lucille Roberts Foundation for Women, Inc.

Lucille Roberts Foundation for Women, Inc.

4 E. 80th St.
New York, NY 10021-0110

Establishment information: Established in 2003 in NY.
Donor: Bob Roberts.
Financial data (yr. ended 12/31/11): Assets, $15 (M); gifts received, $36,358; expenditures, $36,367; qualifying distributions, $36,358; giving activities include $36,358 for grants.
Purpose and activities: The foundation supports organizations involved with cancer.
Fields of interest: Health care; Employment.
Type of support: General/operating support.
Geographic limitations: Giving primarily in Orange, CT and Syosset, NY.
Application information: Applications not accepted. Unsolicited requests for funds not accepted.
Directors: Kevin Roberts; Kirk Roberts.
Officer: Bob Robert, Pres.
EIN: 134056114

3232
Robins, Kaplan, Miller & Ciresi, L.L.P.

800 Lasalle Ave.
2800 LaSalle Plz.
Minneapolis, MN 55402-2039
(612) 349-8500

Company URL: http://www.rkmc.com/default.aspx
Establishment information: Established in 1938.
Company type: Private company
Business activities: Provides legal services.
Business type (SIC): Legal services
Corporate officers: Martin R. Lueck, Chair.; Patrick Mandile, C.O.O; Dave Rigali, C.I.O.
Board of director: Martin R. Lueck, Chair.
Offices: Los Angeles, San Francisco, CA; Washington, DC; Atlanta, GA; Chicago, IL; Boston, MA; St. Paul, MN
Giving statement: Giving through the Robins, Kaplan, Miller & Ciresi Foundation.

Robins, Kaplan, Miller & Ciresi Foundation

800 LaSalle Ave.
2800 LaSalle Plaza
Minneapolis, MN 55402
URL: http://www.rkmc.com/firm/community/foundations

Establishment information: Established in 1993 in MN.
Donor: Robins, Kaplan, Miller & Ciresi L.L.P.
Contact: Steven A. Schumeister, Dir.
Financial data (yr. ended 08/31/11): Assets, $1,166,635 (M); gifts received, $1,154,589; expenditures, $1,543,334; qualifying distributions, $1,488,922; giving activities include $1,488,922 for 299 grants (high: $51,222; low: $50).
Purpose and activities: The foundation supports organizations involved with arts and culture, education, health, crime and law enforcement, athletics, and human services.
Fields of interest: Media/communications; Performing arts; Arts; Higher education; Law school/education; Education; Hospitals (general); Health care, clinics/centers; Health care; Legal services; Crime/law enforcement; Athletics/sports, Special Olympics; YM/YWCAs & YM/YWHAs; Children, services; Human services; United Ways and Federated Giving Programs.
Type of support: General/operating support; Program development; Scholarship funds; Sponsorships.
Geographic limitations: Giving primarily in areas of company operations, with emphasis on Minneapolis and St. Paul, MN.
Support limitations: No grants to individuals.
Application information: Applications accepted. Application form not required. Applicants should submit the following:
1) detailed description of project and amount of funding requested
Initial approach: Proposal
Deadline(s): None
Officer and Trustees:* Martin R. Lueck*, Chair.; David W. Beehler; Maria R. Butler; James V. Chin; Jan M. Conlin; Christopher W. Madel; Steven A. Schumeister; Ronald J. Schutz; Roman M. Silberfeld.
EIN: 411735325
Selected grants: The following grants are a representative sample of this grantmaker's funding activity:
$200,000 to University of Minnesota, Minneapolis, MN, 2010.
$112,819 to USA Cares, Radcliff, KY, 2010.
$50,000 to William Mitchell College of Law, Saint Paul, MN, 2010.
$37,500 to Equal Justice Works, Washington, DC, 2010.
$35,000 to Fund for the Legal Aid Society, Minneapolis, MN, 2010.
$10,000 to Childrens Theater Company and School, Minneapolis, MN, 2010.
$8,000 to Arch Foundation for the University of Georgia, Athens, GA, 2010.
$5,000 to California Rural Legal Assistance, San Francisco, CA, 2010.

$5,000 to Illusion Theater and School, Minneapolis, MN, 2010.
$3,000 to Think Small, Saint Paul, MN, 2010.

3233
Robins, Kaplan, Miller & Ciresi L.L.P.

2800 Lasalle Plz., 800 Lasalle Ave.
Minneapolis, MN 55402-2015
(612) 349-0885

Company URL: http://www.rkmc.com/
Company type: Private company
Business activities: Operates law firm.
Business type (SIC): Legal services
Offices: Los Angeles, CA; Naples, FL; Atlanta, GA; Boston, MA; Minneapolis, MN; New York, NY
Giving statement: Giving through the Robins, Kaplan, Miller & Ciresi L.L.P. Pro Bono Program.

Robins, Kaplan, Miller & Ciresi L.L.P. Pro Bono Program

2800 Lasalle Plz., 800 Lasalle Ave.
Minneapolis, MN 55402-2015 (612) 349-0885
E-mail: AXNelson@rkmc.com; URL: http://www.rkmc.com/Pro_Bono.htm

Contact: Autumn X. Nelson, Diversity and Pro Bono Mgr.
Fields of interest: Legal services.
Type of support: Pro bono services - legal.
Application information: A Pro Bono Committee manages the pro bono program.

3234
Robinson Bradshaw & Hinson, P.A.

101 N. Tryon St., Ste.1900
Charlotte, NC 28246-0103 (704) 377-2536

Company URL: http://www.rbh.com/
Company type: Private company
Business activities: Operates law firm.
Business type (SIC): Legal services
Corporate officer: Jeanne M. Black, Cont.
Offices: Chapel Hill, Charlotte, NC; Rock Hill, SC
Giving statement: Giving through the Robinson Bradshaw & Hinson, P.A. Pro Bono Program.

Robinson Bradshaw & Hinson, P.A. Pro Bono Program

101 N. Tryon St., Ste.1900
Charlotte, NC 28246-0103 (704) 377-8309
E-mail: djarrell@rbh.com; URL: http://www.rbh.com/pro-bono/

Contact: Douglas M. Jarrell, Partner
Fields of interest: Legal services.
Type of support: Pro bono services - legal.
Application information: An attorney coordinates pro bono projects.

3235
C.H. Robinson Worldwide, Inc.

14701 Charlson Rd.
Eden Prairie, MN 55344 (952) 937-8500
FAX: (952) 937-7703

Company URL: http://www.chrobinson.com
Establishment information: Established in 1905.
Company type: Public company
Company ticker symbol and exchange: CHRW/NASDAQ
Business activities: Arranges freight transportation using trucks, trains, ships, and airplanes belonging to other companies.
Business type (SIC): Transportation services/freight
Financial profile for 2012: Number of employees, 10,929; assets, $2,804,220,000; sales volume, $11,359,110,000; pre-tax net income, $958,460,000; expenses, $10,683,790,000; liabilities, $1,299,850,000
Fortune 1000 ranking: 2012—237th in revenues, 295th in profits, and 771st in assets
Corporate officers: John P. Wiehoff, Chair., Pres., and C.E.O.; Chad M. Lindbloom, Sr. V.P. and C.F.O.; Thomas K. Mahlke, V.P. and C.I.O.; Ben G. Campbell, V.P., Genl. Counsel, and Secy.; Angela K. Freeman, V.P., Human Resources; Troy A. Renner, Treas.
Board of directors: John P. Wiehoff, Chair.; Scott P. Anderson; Robert Ezrilov; Wayne M. Fortun; Mary J. Steele Guifoile; ReBecca Koenig Roloff; Jodee Kozlak; David W. MacLennan; Brian P. Short; James B. Stake; Michael W. Wickham
Giving statement: Giving through the C.H. Robinson Worldwide, Inc. Corporate Giving Program and the C. H. Robinson Worldwide Foundation.
Company EIN: 411883630

C.H. Robinson Worldwide, Inc. Corporate Giving Program

14701 Charlson Rd.
Eden Prairie, MN 55347 (952) 937-8500
E-mail: corporate.giving@chrobinson.com; URL: http://www.chrobinson.com/en/us/About-Us/Corporate-Responsibility/

Purpose and activities: As a complement to its foundation, Robinson Worldwide also makes charitable contributions to local and regional nonprofit organizations in areas of company operations.
Fields of interest: General charitable giving.
Type of support: Employee volunteer services; General/operating support; Sponsorships.
Geographic limitations: Giving primarily in areas of company operations; giving also to national organizations.

C. H. Robinson Worldwide Foundation

401 E. Eighth Street, Ste. 319
Sioux Falls, SD 57103-7031 (952) 683-3432
E-mail: foundation@chrobinson.com; Application address: 14701 Charlson Rd., Ste. 1750, Eden Prairie, MN 55347; URL: http://www.chrobinson.com/en/us/About-Us/Corporate-Responsibility/Foundation/

Establishment information: Established in 2005 in MN.
Donor: C.H. Robinson Worldwide, Inc.
Contact: Kristi Nichols
Financial data (yr. ended 12/31/11): Assets, $10,776,816 (M); expenditures, $634,860; qualifying distributions, $543,253; giving activities include $543,253 for grants.
Purpose and activities: The foundation supports programs designed to expand educational success for at-risk youth; prevent hunger and provide food assistance; improve access to affordable housing; support the immediate living needs of people in crisis; and promote health research, prevention, and treatment.
Fields of interest: Education; Hospitals (general); Health care, clinics/centers; Health care, patient services; Health care; Food services; Food banks; Housing/shelter; American Red Cross; YM/YWCAs & YM/YWHAs; Children/youth, services; Family services; Homeless, human services; Human services; United Ways and Federated Giving Programs Youth.
Type of support: Building/renovation; Capital campaigns; Continuing support; Employee matching gifts; Employee-related scholarships; General/operating support; Program development; Seed money; Technical assistance.
Geographic limitations: Giving primarily in areas of company operations in MN, with emphasis on the Minneapolis-St. Paul metropolitan area.
Support limitations: No support for political organizations or religious organizations not of direct benefit to the entire community.
Publications: Application guidelines; Grants list.
Application information: Applications accepted. Grants range from $1,000 to $25,000. Priority is given to organizations with current C.H. Robinson employee involvement. Applicants should submit the following:
1) timetable for implementation and evaluation of project
2) how project will be sustained once grantmaker support is completed
3) statement of problem project will address
4) copy of IRS Determination Letter
5) brief history of organization and description of its mission
6) copy of most recent annual report/audited financial statement/990
7) how project's results will be evaluated or measured
8) list of company employees involved with the organization
9) detailed description of project and amount of funding requested
10) copy of current year's organizational budget and/or project budget
11) listing of additional sources and amount of support

Initial approach: E-mail letter of inquiry
Copies of proposal: 1
Board meeting date(s): Quarterly
Deadline(s): None

Officers: Angela K. Freeman, Pres.; Ben G. Campbell, Secy.; Troy A. Renner, Treas.
EIN: 680599299
Selected grants: The following grants are a representative sample of this grantmaker's funding activity:
$45,653 to American Red Cross, Des Moines, IA, 2010.
$38,542 to United Way, Greater Twin Cities, Minneapolis, MN, 2010.
$31,229 to Juvenile Diabetes Research Foundation International, New York, NY, 2010.
$20,000 to Produce for Better Health Foundation, Hockessin, DE, 2010.
$15,326 to Leukemia & Lymphoma Society, Natick, MA, 2010.
$14,653 to Minnesota Environmental Fund, Saint Paul, MN, 2010.
$10,000 to Boys and Girls Clubs of the Twin Cities, Saint Paul, MN, 2010.
$10,000 to College Possible, Saint Paul, MN, 2010.
$8,774 to United Arts Fund, Saint Paul, MN, 2010.

$7,500 to People Serving People, Minneapolis, MN, 2010.

3236
Roche Diagnostics, Corp.

(formerly Boehringer Mannheim Corporation)
9115 Hague Rd.
Indianapolis, IN 46250-0457
(317) 521-2000

Company URL: http://www.roche-diagnostics.us
Establishment information: Established in 1896.
Company type: Subsidiary of a foreign company
Business activities: Manufactures medical diagnostic tests and systems.
Business type (SIC): Medical instruments and supplies
Corporate officers: Jack Phillips, Pres.and C.E.O.; Wayne Burris, Sr. V.P. and C.F.O.; Scott D. Wilson, V.P. and Treas.; Chris Wilbur, V.P., Human Resources and Corp. Comms.
Giving statement: Giving through the Roche Diagnostics Corporation Contributions Program.

Roche Diagnostics Corporation Contributions Program

(formerly Boehringer Mannheim Corporation Contributions Program)
9115 Hague Rd.
P.O. Box 50457
Indianapolis, IN 46250-0457
URL: http://www.roche-diagnostics.us/About/Pages/default.aspx

Purpose and activities: Roche Diagnostics makes charitable contributions to nonprofit organizations on a case by case basis. Support is given on a national basis, with emphasis on the Indianapolis, Indiana, area.
Fields of interest: General charitable giving.
Type of support: Employee volunteer services; General/operating support; In-kind gifts; Technical assistance.
Geographic limitations: Giving primarily in areas of company operations, with emphasis on the Indianapolis, IN, area.
Application information: Applications accepted. Application form not required.
Initial approach: Proposal to headquarters

3237
Rochester Gas and Electric Corporation

(formerly Rochester Railway and Light Company)
89 East Ave.
Rochester, NY 14649-0001 (585) 546-2700

Company URL: http://www.rge.com
Establishment information: Established in 1904.
Company type: Subsidiary of a public company
Business activities: Generates, transmits, and distributes electricity; transmits and distributes natural gas.
Business type (SIC): Electric services; gas production and distribution
Financial profile for 2010: Number of employees, 500
Corporate officers: Wesley W. Von Schack, Chair. and C.E.O.; Mark S. Lynch, Pres.; Joseph Syta, V.P., Treas., and Cont.; Michael H. Conroy, Sr. V.P., and C.O.O.
Board of director: Wesley W. Von Schack, Chair.
Giving statement: Giving through the Rochester Gas and Electric Corporation Contributions Program.

Rochester Gas and Electric Corporation Contributions Program

(formerly Rochester Railway and Light Company Contributions Program)
89 East Ave.
Rochester, NY 14649-0001

Purpose and activities: Rochester Gas and Electric makes charitable contributions to nonprofit organizations on a case by case basis. Support is given primarily in areas of company operations in the nine-county greater Rochester, New York, area.
Fields of interest: Environment; General charitable giving.
Type of support: Building/renovation; Cause-related marketing.
Geographic limitations: Giving limited to areas of company operations in the nine-county greater Rochester, NY, area.
Application information:
Number of staff: None.

3238
Rock Bottom Restaurants, Inc.

248 Centennial Pkwy., Ste. 100
Louisville, CO 80027-1346 (303) 664-4000
FAX: (303) 664-4197

Company URL: http://www.rockbottomrestaurantsinc.com/
Establishment information: Established in 1976.
Company type: Private company
Business activities: Operates and franchises restaurants.
Business type (SIC): Restaurants and drinking places
Financial profile for 2010: Number of employees, 8,000
Corporate officers: Frank B. Day, Chair., Pres., and C.E.O.; Gary B. Foreman, Exec. V.P., Opers.; Brian T. Armstrong, Sr. V.P. and C.F.O.; Ted E. Williams, Sr. V.P., Human Resources
Board of director: Frank B. Day, Chair.
Giving statement: Giving through the Rock Bottom Foundation.

Rock Bottom Foundation

248 Centennial Pkwy.
Louisville, CO 80027-1265 (303) 364-4022
FAX: (303) 664-4197; Toll-free tel.: (800) 233-7827; URL: http://craftworksfoundation.org/

Establishment information: Established in 2000 in CO.
Contact: Jessica Newman, Exec. Dir.
Financial data (yr. ended 06/30/11): Revenue, $574,411; assets, $588,105 (M); gifts received, $532,071; expenditures, $647,361; program services expenses, $580,201; giving activities include $268,439 for 15 grants (high: $18,691; low: $5,075).
Purpose and activities: The organization is committed to positively impacting hunger in the community, helping Rock Bottom Restaurants Inc. teammates in crisis, and inspiring a culture of giving and volunteerism.
Fields of interest: Food services Homeless.
Type of support: Emergency funds; General/operating support; Grants to individuals.
Geographic limitations: Giving on a national basis.
Publications: Annual report.
Officers and Directors:* Gary Forman*, Chair. and Pres.; Becca Fischer*, Secy.-Treas.; Jessica Newman, Exec. Dir.; Brian Armstrong; Regan Arntzen; Steve Cominsky; Allen Corey; Sarah Foutch; Diane Greenlee.
Number of staff: 2 full-time professional; 1 part-time professional.
EIN: 841560829

3240
Rocket Ball, Ltd.

(also known as Houston Rockets)
1510 Polk St.
Houston, TX 77002-1099 (713) 758-7200

Company URL: http://www.nba.com/rockets
Establishment information: Established in 1967.
Company type: Private company
Business activities: Operates professional basketball club.
Business type (SIC): Commercial sports
Corporate officers: Leslie L. Alexander, Co-C.E.O.; Thaddeus B. Brown, Co-C.E.O.; Marcus Jolibois, C.F.O.; Rafael Stone, V.P. and Genl. Counsel
Giving statement: Giving through the Houston Rockets Corporate Giving Program and the Clutch City Foundation.

Houston Rockets Corporate Giving Program

1510 Polk St.
Houston, TX 77002-7130
FAX: (713) 758-7358; URL: http://www.nba.com/rockets/community/Community_Donations-256986-34.html

Purpose and activities: As a complement to its foundation, the Houston Rockets also makes charitable contributions of memorabilia to nonprofit organizations. Support is limited to the greater Houston, Texas area.
Fields of interest: General charitable giving.
Type of support: In-kind gifts.
Geographic limitations: Giving limited to the greater Houston, TX area.
Support limitations: No grants to individuals, or for advertising; no monetary contributions.
Publications: Application guidelines.
Application information: Proposals should be submitted using organization letterhead. Personal items to be mailed in or dropped off for signature of players and coaches are not accepted. Applicants should submit the following:
1) copy of IRS Determination Letter
Proposals should include the date, time, and purpose of the event.
Initial approach: Mail, fax, or e-mail proposal
Deadline(s): 4 to 6 weeks prior to need

Clutch City Foundation

1510 Polk St.
Houston, TX 77002-7130 (713) 963-7374
E-mail: sarahj@rocketball.com; URL: http://www.nba.com/rockets/community/Community_Clutch_City_Foundat-277993-822.html

Establishment information: Established in 1996 in TX.
Financial data (yr. ended 12/31/11): Revenue, $428,545; assets, $433,262 (M); gifts received, $371,479; expenditures, $398,425; program services expenses, $392,090; giving activities

include $384,463 for 2 grants (high: $163,408; low: $10,706).
Purpose and activities: The foundation aims to brighten the future of young people through higher education and by promoting social welfare.
Fields of interest: Social work school/education; Youth development, community service clubs.
Geographic limitations: Giving primarily in the Galveston and greater Houston, TX, areas.
Officers and Board of Director:* Tad Brown*, Pres.; Rafael A. Stone*, Secy.; Marcus P. Jolibois*, Treas.; Leslie L. Alexander.
EIN: 760495717

3241
Rockford Acromatic Products Company

(doing business as Aircraft Gear Corporation)
611 Beacon St.
Loves Park, IL 61111 (815) 877-7473

Company URL: http://www.rockfordacromatic.com
Establishment information: Established in 1948.
Company type: Private company
Business activities: Designs and manufactures automotive, truck, and specialty vehicle universal joints.
Business type (SIC): Motor vehicles and equipment
Corporate officers: Dean A. Olson II, Chair.; James Olsen, C.E.O.; Kay Mullins, Secy.-Treas.
Board of director: Dean A. Olson II, Chair.
Giving statement: Giving through the DAO Foundation.

DAO Foundation

611 Beacon St.
Rockford, IL 61111-5902 (815) 964-7226

Establishment information: Established in 1961 in IL.
Donors: Rockford Acromatic Products Co.; Aircraft Gear Corp.; Rockford Constant Velocity.
Contact: Patricia Olson, Tr.
Financial data (yr. ended 03/31/12): Assets, $2,361,966 (M); expenditures, $126,303; qualifying distributions, $110,640; giving activities include $110,640 for 28 grants (high: $20,000; low: $75).
Purpose and activities: The foundation supports organizations involved with arts and culture, education, health, human services, youth, and community development.
Fields of interest: Arts; Youth development; Religion.
Type of support: Building/renovation; Capital campaigns; Endowments; Equipment; Seed money.
Geographic limitations: Giving primarily in the Rockford, IL, area.
Support limitations: No support for political organizations. No grants to individuals.
Publications: Application guidelines.
Application information: Applications accepted. Application form required. Applicants should submit the following:
1) detailed description of project and amount of funding requested
Initial approach: Proposal
Copies of proposal: 1
Board meeting date(s): 4 times per year
Deadline(s): None
Trustees: Amy Olson; Patricia Olson.
EIN: 366101712

Selected grants: The following grants are a representative sample of this grantmaker's funding activity:
$10,300 to Janet Wattles Center, Rockford, IL, 2009.
$10,000 to Rosecrance Foundation, Rockford, IL, 2009.
$10,000 to University of Illinois College of Medicine at Rockford, Rockford, IL, 2009.
$7,000 to Rockford Institute, Rockford, IL, 2009.
$4,825 to Rockford Art Museum, Rockford, IL, 2009.
$3,500 to Carpenters Place, Rockford, IL, 2009.
$1,500 to Rock Valley College, Rockford, IL, 2009.
$1,500 to United Way of Rock River Valley, Rockford, IL, 2009.
$1,000 to Rockford Public Library, Rockford, IL, 2009.

3242
Rockland Trust Company

288 Union St.
Rockland, MA 02370 (781) 878-6100

Company URL: http://www.rocklandtrust.com
Establishment information: Established in 1907.
Company type: Subsidiary of a public company
Business activities: Operates commercial bank.
Business type (SIC): Banks/commercial
Corporate officers: Donna L. Abelli, Chair.; Christopher Oddleifson, Pres. and C.E.O.; Edward F. Jankowski, C.O.O.; Denis K. Sheahan, C.F.O.; David B. Smith, Sr. V.P. and C.I.O.; Barry H. Jensen, Sr. V.P. and Cont.; Raymond G. Fuerschbach, Sr. V.P., Human Resources; Edward H. Seksay, Corp. Secy. and Genl. Counsel
Board of directors: Donna L. Abelli, Chair.; Richard S. Anderson; William P. Bissonnette; Benjamin A. Gilmore II; Kevin J. Jones; Eileen C. Miskell; John J. Morrissey; Daniel F. O' Brien; Christopher Oddleifson; Carlos Ribeiro; Richard H. Sgarzi; John H. Spurr, Jr.; Robert D. Sullivan; Brian S. Tedeschi; Thomas R. Venables
Giving statement: Giving through the Rockland Trust Company Contributions Program and the Rockland Trust Company Charitable Foundation.

Rockland Trust Company Contributions Program

288 Union St.
Rockland, MA 02370-1803
E-mail: ROCKCORP@rocklandtrust.com;
URL: http://www.rocklandtrust.com/OurCommunity/index.aspx

Purpose and activities: As a complement to its foundation, Rockland Trust also makes charitable contributions to nonprofit organizations directly. Support is given primarily in areas of company operations in Massachusetts and Rhode Island.
Fields of interest: Education; Health care; Youth development; Human services; Community/economic development; General charitable giving.
Type of support: Cause-related marketing; Employee volunteer services; General/operating support; Scholarships—to individuals.
Geographic limitations: Giving primarily in areas of company operations in Massachusetts and Rhode Island.

Rockland Trust Company Charitable Foundation

2036 Washington St.
Hanover, MA 02339-1617

Donor: Rockland Trust Co.
Financial data (yr. ended 12/31/11): Assets, $521,665 (M); gifts received, $250,000; expenditures, $272; qualifying distributions, $0.
Purpose and activities: The foundation supports East Bridgewater High School in East Bridgewater, Massachusetts.
Type of support: General/operating support; Scholarship funds.
Geographic limitations: Giving primarily in East Bridgewater, MA.
Support limitations: No grants to individuals.
Application information: Applications not accepted. Unsolicited requests for funds not accepted.
Trustee: Rockland Trust Company.
EIN: 046774373

3243
Rockler Companies, Inc.

4365 Willow Dr.
Medina, MN 55340 (763) 478-8201
FAX: (763) 478-8395

Company URL: http://www.rockler.com
Establishment information: Established in 1954.
Company type: Private company
Business activities: Operates woodworking and hardware retail chain.
Business type (SIC): Hardware stores
Financial profile for 2010: Number of employees, 500
Corporate officers: Ann Rockler Jackson, C.E.O.; David Laporte, Pres. and C.O.O.; David Larson, C.F.O.; Scott Ekman, V.P., Mktg.; Eric Myers, Cont.
Giving statement: Giving through the Rockler Jackson Family Foundation.

Rockler Jackson Family Foundation

c/o Ann Rockler Jackson
900 Partenwood Rd.
Orono, MN 55356

Establishment information: Established in 2002 in MN.
Donors: Rockler Companies, Inc.; Ann Rockler-Jackson.
Financial data (yr. ended 12/31/11): Assets, $528,413 (M); gifts received, $81,070; expenditures, $97,550; qualifying distributions, $93,715; giving activities include $92,590 for 24 grants (high: $43,510; low: $100).
Fields of interest: Education; Recreation; Religion.
Support limitations: No grants to individuals.
Application information: Applications not accepted. Unsolicited requests for funds not accepted.
Officers: Ann Rockler-Jackson, Pres.; David Lebedoff, Secy.-Treas.
Directors: Alexander Jackson; Elizabeth Jackson.
EIN: 412023713

3244
Rocknel Fastener, Inc.

5309 11th St.
Rockford, IL 61109 (815) 873-4000
FAX: (815) 873-4011

Company URL: http://www.rocknel.com
Establishment information: Established in 1989.
Company type: Subsidiary of a foreign company
Business activities: Develops and produces automotive and aerospace fasteners.

Business type (SIC): Business services/miscellaneous
Financial profile for 2011: Number of employees, 115
Corporate officer: Jerry Parsons, Cont.
Giving statement: Giving through the Rocknel Fastener, Inc. Contributions Program.

Rocknel Fastener, Inc. Contributions Program

5309 11th St.
Rockford, IL 61109 (815) 873-4000
URL: http://www.rocknel.com

3239
Rock-Tenn Company

504 Thrasher St.
P.O. Box 4098
Norcross, GA 30071-1967 (770) 448-2193
FAX: (770) 263-3582

Company URL: http://www.rocktenn.com
Establishment information: Established in 1936.
Company type: Public company
Company ticker symbol and exchange: RKT/NYSE
Business activities: Manufactures packaging, merchandising displays, and recycled clay-coated and specialty paperboard and corrugating medium; manufactures laminated paperboard products.
Business type (SIC): Paperboard containers; paperboard mills; paper and paperboard/coated, converted, and laminated
Financial profile for 2012: Number of employees, 26,600; assets, $10,687,100,000; sales volume, $9,207,600,000; pre-tax net income, $389,100,000; expenses, $8,703,500,000; liabilities, $7,281,400,000
Fortune 1000 ranking: 2012—291st in revenues, 524th in profits, and 369th in assets
Forbes 2000 ranking: 2012—992nd in sales, 1515th in profits, and 1432nd in assets
Corporate officers: James A. Rubright, Chair. and C.E.O.; Steven C. Voorhees, Pres. and C.O.O.; Robert B. McIntosh, Exec. V.P., Genl. Counsel, and Secy.; Jennifer Graham-Johnson, Exec. V.P., Human Resources; A. Stephen Meadows, C.A.O.; Paul W. Stecher, Sr. V.P. and C.I.O.; John D. Stakel, Sr. V.P. and Treas.
Board of directors: James A. Rubright, Chair.; Timothy J. Bernlohr; J. Powell Brown; Robert M. Chapman; Terrell K. Crews; Russell M. Currey; G. Stephen Felker; Lawrence L. Gellerstedt III; John W. Spiegel; Bettina M. Whyte
Subsidiary: Southern Container Corp., Hauppauge, NY
International operations: Argentina; Canada; Chile; Mexico
Historic mergers: Smurfit-Stone Container Corporation (May 27, 2011)
Giving statement: Giving through the Rock-Tenn Company Contributions Program.
Company EIN: 620342590

Rock-Tenn Company Contributions Program

c/o Corp. Giving
504 Thrasher St.
Norcross, GA 30071-1967 (770) 448-2193
E-mail: swallace@rocktenn.com; For Volunteer Activities: Tamela Danzey, e-mail: tdanzey@rocktenn.com; URL: http://www.rocktenn.com/about-us/CorporateCitizenship.htm
Contact: Stephanie Wallace
Purpose and activities: Rock-Tenn makes charitable contributions to nonprofit organizations on a case by case basis. Support is given primarily in areas of company operations, with emphasis on Norcross, Georgia.
Fields of interest: General charitable giving.
Type of support: Employee volunteer services; General/operating support.
Geographic limitations: Giving primarily in areas of company operations, with emphasis on Norcross, GA; giving also to national organizations.
Application information:

3245
Rockville Financial, Inc.

25 Park St.
Rockville, CT 06066 (860) 291-3600

Company URL: http://www.rockvillebank.com
Establishment information: Established in 1858.
Company type: Public company
Company ticker symbol and exchange: RCKB/NASDAQ
Business activities: Operates savings bank.
Business type (SIC): Savings institutions; holding company
Financial profile for 2012: Number of employees, 331; assets, $1,998,800,000; pre-tax net income, $22,430,000; liabilities, $1,678,190,000
Corporate officers: Raymond H. Lefurge, Jr., Chair.; Michael A. Bars, Vice-Chair.; William H.W. Crawford IV, Pres. and C.E.O.; Marino J. Santarelli, Exec. V.P. and C.O.O.; John T. Lund, Exec. V.P., C.F.O., and Treas.; Judy L. Keppner, V.P. and Secy.
Board of directors: Raymond H. Lefurge, Jr., Chair.; Michael A. Bars, Vice-Chair.; C. Perry Chilberg; William H. W. Crawford IV; David A. Engelson; Joseph F. Jeamel, Jr.; Kristen A. Johnson; Stuart E. Magdefrau; Rosemarie Novello Papa; Richard M. Tkacz
Giving statement: Giving through the Rockville Bank Foundation, Inc.
Company EIN: 300288470

Rockville Bank Foundation, Inc.

(formerly Rockville Bank Community Foundation, Inc.)
1645 Ellington Rd.
South Windsor, CT 06074-2764 (860) 291-3652
Application address: 25 Park St., P.O. Box 660, Rockville, CT 06066; URL: http://www.rockvillebank.com/category/6522/rockville-bank-foundation.htm

Establishment information: Established in 2005.
Donor: Rockville Bank.
Contact: Judy Keppner, Secy.
Financial data (yr. ended 12/31/11): Assets, $10,386,557 (M); gifts received, $5,041,335; expenditures, $687,500; qualifying distributions, $685,541; giving activities include $633,041 for 292 grants (high: $250,000; low: $25) and $52,500 for 42 grants to individuals (high: $1,250; low: $1,250).
Purpose and activities: The foundation supports organizations involved with education, health, sports, human services, and community development and awards scholarships, vocational, and agricultural awards to high school seniors.
Fields of interest: Secondary school/education; Vocational education; Higher education; Libraries (public); Education, reading; Education; Health care; Agriculture; Athletics/sports, amateur leagues; YM/YWCAs & YM/YWHAs; Children, services; Developmentally disabled, centers & services; Human services; Community/economic development.
Type of support: Annual campaigns; Continuing support; Employee volunteer services; Equipment; General/operating support; Matching/challenge support; Program development; Scholarships—to individuals; Sponsorships.
Geographic limitations: Giving primarily in areas of bank operations in Colchester, Coventry, East Windsor, Ellington, Enfield, Glastonbury, Manchester, Rockville, Somers, South Glastonbury, South Windsor, Suffield, Tolland, and Vernon, CT.
Support limitations: No grants for past deficits or lobbying.
Publications: Application guidelines.
Application information: Applications accepted. Multi-year funding is not automatic. Application form required. Applicants should submit the following:
1) results expected from proposed grant
2) statement of problem project will address
3) name, address and phone number of organization
4) copy of IRS Determination Letter
5) brief history of organization and description of its mission
6) how project's results will be evaluated or measured
7) listing of board of directors, trustees, officers and other key people and their affiliations
8) detailed description of project and amount of funding requested
9) contact person
10) copy of current year's organizational budget and/or project budget
11) listing of additional sources and amount of support

Initial approach: Download application form and mail to foundation; contact foundation for application information for scholarships and awards
Deadline(s): None; varies for scholarships and awards
Final notification: 45 to 60 days

Officers: William H.W. Crawford IV, Chair.; Richard J. Trachimowicz, Pres.; Scott C. Bechtle, Sr. V.P.; Marino J. Santarelli, Sr. V.P.; John T. Lund, V.P., C.F.O., and Treas.; Judy L. Keppner, Secy.
EIN: 203000295
Selected grants: The following grants are a representative sample of this grantmaker's funding activity:
$1,000 to Rebuilding Together, Washington, DC, 2010.

3246
Rockwell Automation, Inc.

(formerly Rockwell International Corporation)
1201 S. 2nd St.
Milwaukee, WI 53204 (414) 382-2000
FAX: (414) 382-4444

Company URL: http://www.rockwellautomation.com
Establishment information: Established in 1928.
Company type: Public company
Company ticker symbol and exchange: ROK/NYSE
International Securities Identification Number: US7739031091
Business activities: Manufactures industrial automation, avionics, and communications systems and automated call distribution systems.
Business type (SIC): Laboratory apparatus; communications equipment; aircraft and parts

Financial profile for 2012: Number of employees, 22,000; assets, $5,636,500,000; sales volume, $6,259,400,000; pre-tax net income, $965,900,000; expenses, $5,293,500,000; liabilities, $3,784,800,000
Fortune 1000 ranking: 2012—403rd in revenues, 259th in profits, and 558th in assets
Forbes 2000 ranking: 2012—1248th in sales, 780th in profits, and 1772nd in assets
Corporate officers: Keith D. Nosbusch, Chair. and C.E.O.; Theodore D. Crandall, Sr. V.P. and C.F.O.; Doug M. Hagerman, Sr. V.P., Genl. Counsel, and Secy.; Marty Thomas, Sr. V.P., Opers.; John McDermott, Sr. V.P., Mktg. and Sales; Susan J. Schmitt, Sr. V.P., Human Resources
Board of directors: Keith D. Nosbusch, Chair.; Betty C. Alewine; J. Phillip Holloman; Verne G. Istock; Barry C. Johnson; Steven R. Kalmanson; James P. Keane; Lawrence D. Kingsley; William T. McCormick, Jr.; Donald R. Parfet
Subsidiary: Allen-Bradley Co., Milwaukee, WI
Plants: Dublin, Duluth, GA; Mayfield Heights, Twinsburg, OH; Mequon, Milwaukee, WI
International operations: Argentina; Australia; Austria; Barbados; Belgium; Bolivia; Brazil; Canada; Chile; China; Czech Republic; Denmark; Ecuador; England; France; Germany; Guatemala; Hong Kong; India; Indonesia; Ireland; Italy; Japan; Malaysia; Mexico; Netherlands; New Zealand; Peru; Philippines; Portugal; Singapore; South Africa; South Korea; Spain; Sweden; Switzerland; Taiwan; Thailand; Trinidad & Tobago; Turkey; United Arab Emirates; United Kingdom; Uruguay; Venezuela
Giving statement: Giving through the Rockwell Automation, Inc. Corporate Giving Program and the Rockwell Automation Charitable Corp.
Company EIN: 251797617

Rockwell Automation, Inc. Corporate Giving Program

(formerly Rockwell International Corporation Contributions Program)
1201 S. Second St.
Milwaukee, WI 53204-2496 (414) 382-2000
URL: http://www.rockwellautomation.com/about_us/neighbor/giving.html

Purpose and activities: As a complement to its foundation, Rockwell Automation also makes charitable contributions to nonprofit organizations directly. Support is given primarily in areas of significant company operations, with emphasis on Cleveland, Ohio, and Milwaukee, Wisconsin.
Fields of interest: Arts; Education; Health care; Disasters, preparedness/services; Human services; Science, formal/general education; Mathematics; Engineering/technology; Public affairs.
Type of support: General/operating support; In-kind gifts; Scholarships—to individuals; Sponsorships.
Geographic limitations: Giving primarily in areas of significant company operations, with emphasis on Cleveland, OH, and Milwaukee, WI.
Application information: Applications not accepted. Unsolicited applications are currently not accepted.

Rockwell Automation Charitable Corp.

c/o Marie Olmsted
1201 S. 2nd St
Milwaukee, WI 53204-2410
E-mail: RACharitable_Corp@ra.rockwell.com; E-mail for Milwaukee, WI: Marie Olmsted, meolmsted@ra.rockwell.com, 414-382-3382; e-mail for Cleveland, OH: Marcia Hendershot, mjhendershot@ra.rockwell.com.; URL: http://www.rockwellautomation.com/rockwellautomation/about-us/community/overview.page?

Establishment information: Established in 2003 in WI.
Donors: Rockwell International Corporation Trust; Rockwell Automation.
Contact: Marie Olmsted
Financial data (yr. ended 09/30/12): Assets, $6,353,434 (M); gifts received, $4,750,000; expenditures, $5,032,966; qualifying distributions, $5,032,212; giving activities include $4,599,098 for 50 grants (high: $785,000; low: $3,230) and $375,158 for employee matching gifts.
Purpose and activities: The foundation supports programs designed to address education and workforce development; health and human services; arts and culture; and civic and disaster relief. Special emphasis is directed toward programs designed to promote K-12 science, technology, engineering, and math education.
Fields of interest: Performing arts; Performing arts, orchestras; Arts; Elementary/secondary education; Education; Disasters, preparedness/services; Boys & girls clubs; Human services; United Ways and Federated Giving Programs; Mathematics; Engineering/technology; Science; Public affairs Women; Economically disadvantaged.
Type of support: Employee matching gifts; General/operating support; Program development; Scholarship funds.
Geographic limitations: Giving in areas of company operations, with emphasis on Greater Cleveland, OH and Milwaukee, WI.
Support limitations: No support for religious organizations for religious purposes, or fraternal or social organizations. No grants to individuals, or for unsolicited capital campaigns, or unsolicited multi-year pledges.
Publications: Application guidelines.
Application information: Applications accepted. Application form required. Applicants should submit the following:
1) how project will be sustained once grantmaker support is completed
2) statement of problem project will address
3) population served
4) copy of IRS Determination Letter
5) brief history of organization and description of its mission
6) geographic area to be served
7) copy of most recent annual report/audited financial statement/990
8) how project's results will be evaluated or measured
9) list of company employees involved with the organization
10) listing of board of directors, trustees, officers and other key people and their affiliations
11) detailed description of project and amount of funding requested
12) plans for cooperation with other organizations, if any
13) copy of current year's organizational budget and/or project budget
14) listing of additional sources and amount of support

Initial approach: Complete online application for organizations located in the U.S.; e-mail application contact for organizations located in Cleveland, OH and Milwaukee, WI
Board meeting date(s): Semi-annually
Deadline(s): Oct. 15 and Apr. 15
Final notification: 3 to 6 months

Officers and Directors:* Keith D. Nosbusch*, Chair.; Doug M. Hagerman, V.P. and Treas.; Theodore D. Crandall, V.P.; Susan J. Schmitt, V.P.; Eileen M. Walter, Secy.
Trustee: BMO Harris Bank, N.A.
EIN: 481307009

3247
Rockwell Collins, Inc.

(formerly Collins Radio)
400 Collins Rd., N.E.
Cedar Rapids, IA 52498 (319) 295-1000
FAX: (319) 295-1523

Company URL: http://www.rockwellcollins.com
Establishment information: Established in 1933.
Company type: Public company
Company ticker symbol and exchange: COL/NYSE
International Securities Identification Number: US7743411016
Business activities: Designs, manufactures, and supports communications and aviation electronics.
Business type (SIC): Communications equipment; search and navigation equipment
Financial profile for 2012: Number of employees, 19,000; assets, $5,314,000,000; sales volume, $4,726,000,000; pre-tax net income, $857,000,000; expenses, $3,869,000,000; liabilities, $4,055,000,000
Fortune 1000 ranking: 2012—511th in revenues, 289th in profits, and 575th in assets
Forbes 2000 ranking: 2012—1429th in sales, 934th in profits, and 1792nd in assets
Corporate officers: Clayton M. Jones, Chair. and C.E.O.; Robert K. (Kelly) Ortberg, Pres.; Patrick E. Allen, Sr. V.P. and C.F.O.; Gary R. Chadick, Sr. V.P., Genl. Counsel, and Secy.; Bruce King, Sr. V.P., Opers.; Ronald W. Kirchenbauer, Sr. V.P., Human Resources
Board of directors: Clayton M. Jones, Chair.; Anthony J. Carbone; Chris A. Davis; Ralph E. Eberhart; John A. Edwardson; David Lilley; Andrew J. Policano; Cheryl L. Shavers; Jeffrey L. Turner
Subsidiary: K-Systems, Inc., San Jose, CA
Plants: Huntsville, AL; Carlsbad, Cypress, Irvine, Los Angeles, Poway, San Francisco, Tustin, CA; Washington, DC; Melbourne, Miami, FL; Atlanta, Warner Robins, GA; Honolulu, HI; Chicago, IL; Bellevue, Coralville, Decorah, Manchester, IA; Wichita, KS; Boston, MA; Ann Arbor, Detroit, MI; Minneapolis, MN; Kansas City, MO; Raleigh, NC; Tulsa, OK; Portland, OR; Dallas, Fort Worth, Houston, Richardson, TX; Kirkland, Renton, Seattle, WA
International operations: Australia; Brazil; Canada; China; France; Germany; Hong Kong; India; Luxembourg; Malaysia; Mexico; Russia; Singapore; United Kingdom
Giving statement: Giving through the Rockwell Collins Community Partnership Fund and the Rockwell Collins Charitable Corporation.
Company EIN: 522314475

Rockwell Collins Community Partnership Fund

400 Collins Rd., N.E., M.S. 126-302
Cedar Rapids, IA 52498-0001
URL: http://www.rockwellcollins.com/Our_Company/Corporate_Responsibility.aspx

Purpose and activities: Through the Rockwell Collins Community Partnership Fund, a direct corporate giving program, Rockwell Collins makes charitable contributions to nonprofit organizations involved with arts, culture, and education. Special emphasis is directed toward programs designed to promote math, science, and engineering education and arts and culture education for young people.

Support is given on a national and international basis in areas of company operations, with some emphasis on Iowa.
Fields of interest: Arts education; Arts; Education; Mathematics; Engineering/technology; Science Youth.
Type of support: Program development; Sponsorships.
Geographic limitations: Giving on a national and international basis in areas of company operations, with some emphasis on IA.
Support limitations: No support for private foundations, religious organizations not of direct benefit to the entire community, fraternal or social organizations, political organizations, or discriminatory organizations. No grants to individuals, or for endowments, debt reduction, political campaigns or candidates, sports teams, events, or scholarships designated for athletes, gifts, door prizes, or raffles, equipment or playground funding, individual classrooms, or school fundraisers.
Publications: Application guidelines.
Application information: Applications accepted. Proposals should be no longer than 3 pages. Submission of promotional materials is not encouraged. The Community Relations Department handles giving. Application form required. Applicants should submit the following:
1) timetable for implementation and evaluation of project
2) how project will be sustained once grantmaker support is completed
3) results expected from proposed grant
4) statement of problem project will address
5) population served
6) name, address and phone number of organization
7) copy of IRS Determination Letter
8) brief history of organization and description of its mission
9) geographic area to be served
10) how project's results will be evaluated or measured
11) list of company employees involved with the organization
12) detailed description of project and amount of funding requested
13) contact person
14) copy of current year's organizational budget and/or project budget
15) listing of additional sources and amount of support

Applications should include the Tax ID number and the website of the organization.
Initial approach: Download application form and mail with proposal to headquarters for organizations located in Cedar Rapids, IA; e-mail application and proposal to the HR manager at nearest Rockwell Collins facility for organizations outside Cedar Rapids, IA
Copies of proposal: 1
Deadline(s): None
Final notification: 6 weeks
Administrators: Cindy Dietz, Mgr., Community Rels.; Melanie Richert, Comms. Specialist, Community Rels.; Ronald W. Kirchenbauer.
Number of staff: 2 full-time professional; 1 part-time support.

Rockwell Collins Charitable Corporation

400 Collins Rd., N.E., M.S. 124-302
Cedar Rapids, IA 52498-0001 (319) 295-8122
FAX: (319) 295-9374;
E-mail: jlbecker@rockwellcollins.com; Additional e-mail: communityrelations@rockwellcollins.com; Contact for Green Communities Prog.: Melanie Richert, Community Rels., tel.: (319) 295-8863, e-mail: mlricher@rockwellcollins.com; URL: http://www.rockwellcollins.com/Our_Company/Corporate_Responsibility/Community_Overview/Charitable_Giving.aspx

Establishment information: Established in 2001 in IA.
Donor: Rockwell Collins, Inc.
Contact: Jennifer Becker, Exec. Dir.
Financial data (yr. ended 09/30/12): Assets, $510,441 (M); gifts received, $4,100,000; expenditures, $4,597,725; qualifying distributions, $4,537,528; giving activities include $4,084,300 for 162 grants (high: $750,000; low: $500) and $453,228 for employee matching gifts.
Purpose and activities: The foundation supports organizations involved with the environment, health, human services, and civic affairs. Special emphasis is directed toward programs designed to promote math, science, engineering, and technology education; and arts and culture with a focus on youth educational initiatives.
Fields of interest: Arts education; Arts; Engineering school/education; Education; Environment, natural resources; Environment, water resources; Environment, land resources; Environment; Youth development; Science, formal/general education; Mathematics; Engineering/technology; Science Youth.
Programs:
Green Communities Program: Through the Green Communities Program, the foundation supports programs designed to improve the environmental condition of the community. Grants range from $500 to $2,500.
Matching Gifts: The foundation matches contributions made by employees of Rockwell Collins to nonprofit organizations involved with arts and culture and education on a one-for-one basis from $25 to $5,000 per employee, per year.
Type of support: Capital campaigns; Continuing support; Employee matching gifts; General/operating support; Program development; Scholarship funds.
Geographic limitations: Giving in the U.S. in areas of company operations, with emphasis on Tustin, CA, Melbourne, FL, IA, Portland, OR, and Richardson, TX; giving also to international organizations in Australia, Canada, France, and the United Kingdom for the Green Communities Program.
Support limitations: No support for private foundations, political candidates or organizations, religious organizations not of direct benefit to the entire community, fraternal or social organizations, or discriminatory organizations. No grants to individuals, or for memorials, endowments, annual campaigns, debt reduction, federated campaigns, political campaigns, sports events or scholarships for designated athletes, gifts, door prizes, or raffles, equipment or playground funding, classroom donations, or school fundraisers.
Publications: Application guidelines.
Application information: Applications accepted. All grant applications should be preceded by an e-mail or telephone inquiry. Applicants for Green Communities Program must be teamed with a Rockwell Collins employee or retiree. Organizations receiving Green Communities grants may be asked to provide interim reports and a final report. Application form required. Applicants should submit the following:
1) how project will be sustained once grantmaker support is completed
2) qualifications of key personnel
3) statement of problem project will address
4) population served
5) copy of IRS Determination Letter
6) brief history of organization and description of its mission
7) geographic area to be served
8) copy of most recent annual report/audited financial statement/990
9) how project's results will be evaluated or measured
10) listing of board of directors, trustees, officers and other key people and their affiliations
11) detailed description of project and amount of funding requested
12) plans for cooperation with other organizations, if any
13) copy of current year's organizational budget and/or project budget
14) listing of additional sources and amount of support

Initial approach: Telephone or e-mail foundation; download application form and mail to foundation for organizations located in IA or mail to nearest company facility for organizations located outside IA; download application form and e-mail form to contact for Green Communities Program
Copies of proposal: 1
Board meeting date(s): Oct. and July
Deadline(s): Apr. 1 to Apr. 30 and Aug. 1 to Aug. 30; Feb. 17 for Green Communities Program
Final notification: 3 months; Apr. for Green Communities Program
Officers and Directors:* Ronald W. Kirchenbauer, Pres.; Gary R. Chadick*, V.P. and Secy.; Patrick E. Allen, V.P. and Treas.; Jennifer Becker, Exec. Dir.; Clayton M. Jones.
Number of staff: None.
EIN: 421526774
Selected grants: The following grants are a representative sample of this grantmaker's funding activity:
$800,000 to US FIRST, Manchester, NH, 2010. For FIRST Lego League (FLL) teams and tournament support.
$500,000 to United Way of East Central Iowa, Cedar Rapids, IA, 2010. For campaign and volunteer program.
$375,000 to Human Services Campus of East Central Iowa, Cedar Rapids, IA, 2010. For new campus.
$120,000 to Georgia Institute of Technology, Atlanta, GA, 2010. For scholarships.
$70,000 to Theater Cedar Rapids, Cedar Rapids, IA, 2010. For Next Act capital campaign.
$50,000 to YMCA of the Cedar Rapids Metropolitan Area, Cedar Rapids, IA, 2010. For Continuing the Quest capital campaign.
$27,500 to LeTourneau University, Longview, TX, 2010. For scholarships and DRM Team project.
$27,500 to United Way of Brevard County, Cocoa, FL, 2010. For campaign support - Melbourne.
$25,000 to Junior Engineering Technical Society, Alexandria, VA, 2010. For engineering career awareness.
$15,000 to Iowa Childrens Museum, Coralville, IA, 2010. For Take Flight aviation exhibit.

3248
The Rockwood Company

20 N. Wacker Dr., Ste. 960
Chicago, IL 60606-2901 (312) 621-2200

Company URL: http://www.rockwoodco.com
Establishment information: Established in 1896.
Company type: Private company

Business activities: Provides insurance brokerage services.
Business type (SIC): Insurance agents, brokers, and services
Corporate officer: David Glaser, C.F.O.
Office: Northbrook, IL
Giving statement: Giving through the Rockwood Foundation.

The Rockwood Foundation

20 N. Wacker Dr., Ste. 960
Chicago, IL 60606-2901 (312) 621-2238

Establishment information: Established in 2004 in IL.
Donor: The Rockwood Co.
Contact: Richard P. Mrotek, Dir.
Financial data (yr. ended 12/31/11): Assets, $114,638 (M); gifts received, $34,890; expenditures, $30,783; qualifying distributions, $15,000; giving activities include $1,000 for 1 grant and $14,000 for 9 grants to individuals (high: $2,000; low: $750).
Purpose and activities: The foundation awards college scholarships to students residing and attending college in Chicago, Illinois.
Type of support: Scholarships—to individuals.
Geographic limitations: Giving primarily in Chicago, IL.
Application information: Applications accepted. Application form required.
Initial approach: Contact foundation for application form
Deadline(s): May 17
Officer: Norman J. Westerhold III, Pres.
Directors: Richard D. Cain; Marshall C. Dahlstrom; David L. Jennings III; Richard P. Mrotek.
EIN: 200248335

3249
Rocky Mountain Natural Gas Company

0096 County Rd. 160
Glenwood Springs, CO 81601
(970) 928-0409

Company type: Subsidiary of a public company
Business activities: Transmits and distributes natural gas.
Business type (SIC): Gas production and distribution
Corporate officers: Michael Morgan, Pres.; Kimberly Allen, C.F.O.
Giving statement: Giving through the Rocky Mountain Natural Gas Memorial Scholarship Fund.

Rocky Mountain Natural Gas Memorial Scholarship Fund

370 Van Gordon St.
Lakewood, CO 80228
Application address: Superintendent, Roading Fork School District Re-1, Glenwood Springs, CO 81601

Establishment information: Established in 1986 in CO.
Donor: Rocky Mountain Natural Gas Co.
Financial data (yr. ended 12/31/09): Assets, $0 (M); expenditures, $1,644; qualifying distributions, $1,644; giving activities include $1,644 for 2 grants to individuals (high: $892; low: $752).
Purpose and activities: The fund awards college scholarships to children of employees of Rocky Mountain Natural Gas, children and grandchildren of employees killed in an explosion at the company, and to students located in Rocky Mountain Natural Gas service territories seeking education beyond high school.
Type of support: Employee-related scholarships; Scholarships—to individuals.
Geographic limitations: Giving limited to areas of company operations in Aspen, Basalt, Delta, Carbondale, Cedaredge, Collbran, Dacono, Eagle, Frederick, Glenwood Springs, Gypsum, Hotchkiss, Montrose, Naturita, Norwood, Nucia, Olathe, Orchard City, Paonia, Snowmass Village, Telluride, Walden, and Wellington, CO.
Publications: Application guidelines.
Application information: Applications accepted. Application form required.
Initial approach: Contact fund or Roaring Fork School District for application form
Deadline(s): May 31
Directors: Daniel E. Watson; Janet Eversman.
EIN: 742442791

3250
The Rodgers & Hammerstein Organization

229 W. 28th St., 11th Fl.
New York, NY 10001 (212) 541-6600

Company URL: http://www.rnh.com
Establishment information: Established in 1944.
Company type: Subsidiary of a foreign company
Business activities: Administers and promotes entertainment copyrights.
Business type (SIC): Investors/miscellaneous
Corporate officers: Theodore Chapin, Pres.; Berk Fink, Sr. V.P., Comms.
Giving statement: Giving through the Rodgers & Hammerstein Foundation.

Rodgers & Hammerstein Foundation

229 West 28th St., 11th Fl.
New York, NY 10001 (212) 541-6600
E-mail: nharman@rnh.com

Establishment information: Established about 1953 in NY.
Donors: Dorothy F. Rodgers†; Hammerstein Music & Theater, Inc.; The Rodgers & Hammerstein Organization; International Cultural Production, Inc.
Contact: Nicole Harman
Financial data (yr. ended 12/31/11): Assets, $42,306 (M); expenditures, $59,088; qualifying distributions, $56,462; giving activities include $55,000 for 24 grants (high: $10,000; low: $500).
Purpose and activities: The foundation supports libraries and organizations involved with performing arts.
Fields of interest: Performing arts; Performing arts, theater; Performing arts, music; Performing arts, opera; Libraries (public).
Type of support: General/operating support.
Geographic limitations: Giving limited to New York, NY.
Support limitations: No grants to individuals.
Application information: Applications not accepted. Contributes only to pre-selected organizations.
Officer: Mary Rodgers Guettel, Co-Pres.; Alice Hammerstein Mathias, Co-Pres.; Theodore S. Chapin, Secy.; Robert Margolies, C.F.O.; R. Andrew Boose; Joshua S. Rubenstein.
EIN: 136084412

3251
Rodman Ford Sales, Inc.

53 Washington St.
Foxboro, MA 02035 (508) 543-3333

Company URL: http://www.rodmancarsandtrucks.com
Establishment information: Established in 1960.
Company type: Private company
Business activities: Operates car dealership.
Business type (SIC): Motor vehicles—retail
Corporate officers: Donald E. Rodman, Pres.; Thomas W. Jackson, C.F.O.; Mike Wagner, V.P., Sales; Linda Tibbetts, Cont.
Giving statement: Giving through the Rodman Ford Sales, Inc. Charitable Trust.

Rodman Ford Sales, Inc. Charitable Trust

Route 1
Foxboro, MA 02035-1388
FAX: (508) 543-7683;
E-mail: cchaplin@rodmanford.com

Establishment information: Established in 1986 in MA.
Donors: R. & R. Realty Co.; Rodman Five Realty Trust; Rodman Ford Sales, Inc.; Donald E. Rodman.
Contact: Donald E. Rodman, Tr.
Financial data (yr. ended 12/31/11): Assets, $43,415 (M); gifts received, $316,820; expenditures, $294,832; qualifying distributions, $277,554; giving activities include $277,554 for grants.
Purpose and activities: The foundation supports organizations involved with arts and culture, education, health, and human services.
Fields of interest: Arts; Education; Health care; Children/youth, services; Human services.
Geographic limitations: Giving primarily in MA.
Support limitations: No grants to individuals.
Application information: Applications not accepted.
Trustees: Donald E. Rodman; Gene D. Rodman.
Number of staff: None.
EIN: 222780804
Selected grants: The following grants are a representative sample of this grantmaker's funding activity:
$5,000 to Greater Boston Food Bank, Boston, MA, 2010.
$2,500 to Jewish National Fund, New York, NY, 2010.
$1,000 to Volunteers of America, Alexandria, VA, 2010.

3252
Rogers & Hardin LLP

229 Peachtree St., N.E.
Atlanta, GA 30303-1601 (404) 522-4700

Company URL: http://www.ralaw.com/index.cfm
Company type: Private company
Business activities: Operates law firm.
Business type (SIC): Legal services
Offices: Fort Lauderdale, Fort Myers, Naples, FL; Chicago, IL; New York, NY; Akron, Cincinnati, Cleveland, Columbus, OH
Giving statement: Giving through the Rogers & Hardin LLP Pro Bono Program.

Rogers & Hardin LLP Pro Bono Program

229 Peachtree St., N.E
2700 International Tower
Atlanta, GA 30303-1601 (404) 522-4700
URL: http://www.rh-law.com/Careers/Attorneys

Fields of interest: Legal services.
Type of support: Pro bono services - legal.
Application information: A Pro Bono Committee manages the pro bono program.

3253
Rogers Corporation

1 Technology Dr.
P.O. Box 188
Rogers, CT 06263-0188 (860) 774-9605
FAX: (860) 779-5509

Company URL: http://www.rogerscorp.com/
Establishment information: Established in 1832.
Company type: Public company
Company ticker symbol and exchange: ROG/NYSE
Business activities: Manufactures polymer composite materials.
Business type (SIC): Plastics and synthetics
Financial profile for 2012: Number of employees, 2,400; assets, $760,020,000; sales volume, $498,760,000; pre-tax net income, $22,650,000; expenses, $473,100,000; liabilities, $325,870,000
Corporate officers: Bruce D. Hoechner, Pres. and C.E.O.; Dennis M. Loughran, V.P., Finance and C.F.O.; Robert M. Soffer, V.P. and Secy.; Terrence W. Mahoney, V.P. and Genl. Counsel; Paul B. Middleton, Corp. Treas.; Ronald J. Pelletier, Corp. Cont.
Board of directors: Michael F. Barry; Charles M. Brennan III; Bruce D. Hoechner; Gregory B. Howey; J. Carl Hsu, Ph.D.; Carol R. Jensen, Ph.D.; William E. Mitchell; Robert G. Paul; Peter C. Wallace
Subsidiary: Bisco Products, Elk Grove Village, IL
Divisions: Business Products Div., Mesa, AZ; Circuit Components Div., Tempe, AZ; Circuit Materials Div., Chandler, AZ; Flexible Circuits Div., Chandler, AZ; Molding Material Div., Manchester, CT; Plymer Products Group-Willimantic Div., Willimantic, CT; Polymer Products Group Atlanta Div., Lithonia, GA; Poron and Composites Div., East Woodstock, CT
International operations: Barbados; Belgium; China; England; France; Germany; Hong Kong; Japan; Luxembourg; South Korea; Taiwan
Giving statement: Giving through the Rogers Corporation Contributions Program.
Company EIN: 060513860

Rogers Corporation Contributions Program

1 Technology Dr.
Rogers, CT 06263-0021 (860) 774-9605
FAX: (860) 779-5509; URL: http://www.rogerscorp.com/about/community.aspx

Purpose and activities: Rogers makes charitable contributions to nonprofit organizations on a case by case basis. Support is given primarily in areas of company operations.
Fields of interest: General charitable giving.
Type of support: Employee volunteer services; General/operating support; Sponsorships.
Geographic limitations: Giving primarily in areas of company operations.

3254
Rolls-Royce North America Inc.

1875 Explorer St., Ste. 200
Reston, VA 20190 (703) 834-1700

Company URL: http://www.rolls-royce.com/northamerica
Establishment information: Established in 2001.
Company type: Subsidiary of a foreign company
Business activities: Manufactures engines.
Business type (SIC): Engines and turbines
Corporate officers: James M. Guyette, Pres. and C.E.O.; William T. Powers III, Exec. V.P. and C.F.O.; Thomas P. Dale, Exec. V.P. and Genl. Counsel; Kirk Larson, Exec. V.P., Human Resources
Giving statement: Giving through the Rolls-Royce North America Inc. Corporate Giving Program.

Rolls-Royce North America Inc. Corporate Giving Program

1875 Explorer St., Ste. 200
Reston, VA 20190 (703) 834-1700
FAX: (703) 709-6087

Contact: Mia Walton, Sr. V.P., Corp. Comms.
Purpose and activities: Rolls-Royce North America makes charitable contributions to nonprofit organizations involved with arts and culture, education, the environment, health, youth development, and on a case by case basis. Support is given on a national and international basis.
Fields of interest: Historical activities; Arts; Education; Environment; Health care; Youth development; General charitable giving.
Type of support: Building/renovation; Conferences/seminars; Employee volunteer services; General/operating support; In-kind gifts; Scholarship funds; Sponsorships.
Application information: Applications accepted. The Corporate Communications Department handles giving. A contributions committee reviews all requests. Application form not required. Applicants should submit the following:
1) timetable for implementation and evaluation of project
2) detailed description of project and amount of funding requested

Initial approach: Proposal to headquarters
Copies of proposal: 1
Committee meeting date(s): Quarterly
Final notification: Following committee meetings

Number of staff: 1 full-time professional.

3255
Roma of New Jersey

1 Roma Blvd.
Piscataway, NJ 08854 (732) 463-7662

Company URL: http://romafood.com
Establishment information: Established in 1955.
Company type: Subsidiary of a private company
Business activities: Operates foodservice distribution businesses.
Business type (SIC): Groceries—wholesale
Corporate officers: Douglas Steenland, Chair. and C.E.O.; James Palazzo, Pres.
Board of directors: Doug Steenland, Chair.; Martin Brand; William Dawson; George Holm; Bruce McEvoy; Prakash Melwani
Giving statement: Giving through the Louis G. Piancone Charitable Foundation, Inc.

Louis G. Piancone Charitable Foundation, Inc.

1 Roma Blvd.
Piscataway, NJ 08854-3726

Establishment information: Established in NJ.
Donors: Roma Food Enterprises, Inc.; Louis G. Piancone; Stephen J. Piancone.
Financial data (yr. ended 12/31/11): Assets, $2,748 (M); expenditures, $930; qualifying distributions, $0.
Purpose and activities: The foundation supports Landmark College in Putney, Vermont.
Type of support: Annual campaigns.
Geographic limitations: Giving primarily in Putney, VT.
Application information: Applications not accepted. Unsolicited requests for funds not accepted.
Trustees: Louis G. Piancone; Louis M. Piancone; Stephen J. Piancone.
EIN: 222405305

3256
Rondys, Inc.

(also known as Idaho Lime)
5647 229th Ave., S.E.
Issaquah, WA 98029-9223 (425) 392-6324

Establishment information: Established in 1970.
Company type: Private company
Business activities: Conducts fishing and crabbing activities; mines lime; mines gold.
Business type (SIC): Fishing/commercial; mining/gold and silver; mining/crushed and broken stone
Corporate officers: Vern W. Hall, Pres.; Bonnie R. Hall Elerding, Secy.
Giving statement: Giving through the Joyce Hall Memorial Music Scholarship.

Joyce Hall Memorial Music Scholarship

14300 N.E. 20th Ave., D-102-204
Vancouver, WA 98686

Establishment information: Established in 2001 in OR.
Donor: Rondys Inc.
Financial data (yr. ended 12/31/11): Assets, $172,892 (M); expenditures, $11,545; qualifying distributions, $10,113; giving activities include $10,000 for 6 grants to individuals (high: $2,000; low: $1,000).
Purpose and activities: The foundation awards college scholarships to students attending Newport High School in Newport, Oregon.
Type of support: Scholarships—to individuals.
Geographic limitations: Giving limited to Newport, OR.
Application information: Applications not accepted. Contributes only to pre-selected individuals.
Officers: Peggy Sabanskas, Pres.; Janet Seavers, V.P.; Bonnie R. Hall-Elerding, Secy.-Treas.
Director: Pat Cowan.
EIN: 931305073

3257
Rood & Riddle, P.S.C.

(also known as Rood & Riddle Equine Hospital)
2150 Georgetown Rd.
P.O. Box 12070
Lexington, KY 40511-9072 (859) 233-0371

Company URL: http://www.roodandriddle.com
Establishment information: Established in 1986.
Company type: Private company
Business activities: Provides veterinary services.
Business type (SIC): Veterinary services
Corporate officers: Deborah Kaufman, C.O.O. and C.F.O.; Sanjay Jeyarajasingham, Cont.
Giving statement: Giving through the Rood & Riddle Foundation Inc.

Rood & Riddle Foundation Inc.

P.O. Box 12070
Lexington, KY 40580-2070 (859) 233-0371

Establishment information: Established in 2003.
Donors: Rood & Riddle, P.S.C.; Rood, Riddle & Partners, P.S.C.; AAEP; AVMA; Bayer Corp.; Boehringer Ingelheim; Butler; Intervet; KTOBA; Live Oak; Luitpold Pharmaceuticals Inc.; MWI; Patterson Companies Inc.; Pfizer Equine Division; Platinum Performance; Merial; Eklin Medical Systems; Alltech; Neogen; Alan Leavitt; Farmers Feed Mill.
Contact: William A. Rood, Dir.
Financial data (yr. ended 12/31/11): Assets, $67,603 (M); gifts received, $536,475; expenditures, $469,986; qualifying distributions, $91,283; giving activities include $91,283 for grants.
Purpose and activities: The foundation supports organizations involved with health, cancer research, housing development, equestrianism, and human services.
Fields of interest: Health care, patient services; Health care; Cancer research; Housing/shelter, development; Athletics/sports, equestrianism; Human services, gift distribution; Homeless, human services; Human services.
Type of support: Building/renovation; General/operating support.
Geographic limitations: Giving primarily in KY.
Application information: Applications accepted. Application form not required.
Initial approach: Proposal
Deadline(s): None
Directors: Lawrence R. Bramlage; Rolf M. Embertson; W. Thomas Riddle; William A. Rood.
EIN: 611446321
Selected grants: The following grants are a representative sample of this grantmaker's funding activity:
$10,428 to Iowa State University, College of Veterinary Medicine, Ames, IA, 2010.

3258
Roosevelt County Electric Cooperative

121 N. Main Ave.
Portales, NM 88130-5961 (575) 356-4491

Company URL: http://www.rcec.org
Establishment information: Established in 1938.
Company type: Cooperative
Business activities: Generates, transmits, and distributes electricity.
Business type (SIC): Electric services
Corporate officers: Pat Boone IV, Pres.; Dave Sanders, Secy.; Bill Cathey, Treas.
Giving statement: Giving through the Roosevelt County Electric Education Foundation.

Roosevelt County Electric Education Foundation

P.O. Box 389
Portales, NM 88130-0389 (575) 356-4491
E-mail: inger@rcec.coop; URL: http://www.rcec.org

Establishment information: Established in 1988 in NM.
Donor: Roosevelt County Electric Cooperative.
Contact: Robin Inge
Financial data (yr. ended 12/31/11): Assets, $554,198 (M); gifts received, $58,219; expenditures, $23,838; qualifying distributions, $19,000; giving activities include $19,000 for grants.
Purpose and activities: The foundation awards scholarships to dependents of members of Roosevelt County Electric Cooperative.
Fields of interest: Higher education.
Programs:
Government in Action Youth Tour: The foundation awards scholarships to sophomore and junior students who are dependents of members of the Roosevelt County Electric Cooperative. Students are asked to submit a 500 word essay on various cooperative topics, and 2 students are chosen to represent the cooperative on an all expense paid trip to Washington, DC for the Government in Action Youth Tour. The trip includes visits to famous landmarks, the U.S. Senate, the House of Representatives, and a visit to the Congressional Representative from their district.
Scholarships: The foundation awards college scholarships to members and dependents of the Roosevelt County Electric Cooperative. The program is designed to assist individuals to further their education, knowledge, and skills to be better prepared to participate in the future employment marketplace. Applicants should be in the current year graduating class or an accredited public or private high school, home schooled or have obtained a New Mexico GED or equivalent. This one year scholarship will be awarded on the basis of funds available and the applicant's eligibility. Applicant must maintain at least a 2.5 GPA on a 4.0 scale and must demonstrate acceptable standards of citizenship and character.
Type of support: Scholarships—to individuals.
Geographic limitations: Giving primarily in areas of company operations.
Publications: Application guidelines; Grants list.
Application information: Applications accepted. Application form required.
Applications should include transcripts and ACT scores, 2 letters of recommendation, and an essay.
Initial approach: Download application form and mail to foundation
Deadline(s): Jan. 31 for scholarships; Dec. 2 for Youth Tour
Officers: Pat Boone, Pres.; Evelyn Ledbetter, V.P.; Dave Sanders, Secy.-Treas.
Trustees: Mack Brown; Wesley Brown; Billy Cathey; Darrell Caviness.
Number of staff: None.
EIN: 850350615

3259
Roosevelt County Rural Telephone Cooperative, Inc.

(also known as Yucca Telecom)
201 W. 2nd St.
P.O. Box 867
Portales, NM 88130-6231 (575) 226-2255

Company URL: http://www.rcrtc.com
Establishment information: Established in 1951.
Company type: Cooperative
Business activities: Provides local telephone communications services.
Business type (SIC): Telephone communications
Corporate officer: Susan Barker, Treas.
Board of directors: Tex Belcher; Lewis Cooper; Jimmy Duncan; Ronny Fouts; Blake Inge; Randy Lieb; Lynn Medlin; David Sanders; Jima Widener
Subsidiary: Yucca Telecommunications Systems, Inc., Portales, NM
Giving statement: Giving through the Roosevelt County Rural Telephone Education Foundation.

Roosevelt County Rural Telephone Education Foundation

P.O. Box 867
Portales, NM 88130 (575) 226-2255
Application address: 201 W. 2nd St., Portales, NM 88130

Establishment information: Established in 1998 in NM.
Donor: Roosevelt County Rural Telephone Cooperative, Inc.
Financial data (yr. ended 12/31/11): Assets, $235,052 (M); expenditures, $7,000; qualifying distributions, $7,000; giving activities include $7,000 for grants to individuals.
Purpose and activities: The foundation awards college scholarships to members of the Roosevelt County Rural Telephone Cooperative and their families.
Type of support: Scholarships—to individuals.
Geographic limitations: Giving limited to Roosevelt County, NM.
Application information: Applications accepted. Application form required.
Initial approach: Proposal
Deadline(s): Feb. 4
Officers: Belcher Tex, Pres.; Windener Jima, V.P.; Lawrence Fouts, Secy.-Treas.
Directors: Jimmy Duncan; Sanders David; Blake Inge; Lynn Medlin; Tharp Nathan; Lieb Randy.
EIN: 850452616

3260
Ropes & Gray LLP

800 Boylston St.
Prudential Tower
Boston, MA 02199-3600 (617) 951-7000

Company URL: http://www.ropesgrayhiring.com/index.asp
Company type: Private company
Business activities: Operates law firm.
Business type (SIC): Legal services
Corporate officer: John Montgomery, Managing Partner
Offices: San Francisco, CA; Washington, DC; Chicago, IL; Boston, MA; New York, NY
International operations: China; Hong Kong; Japan; United Kingdom

Giving statement: Giving through the Ropes & Gray LLP Pro Bono Program.

Ropes & Gray LLP Pro Bono Program

800 Boylston St.
Prudential Tower
Boston, MA 02199-3600 (617) 951-7000
E-mail: rosalyn.nasdor@ropesgray.com;
URL: http://www.ropesgrayhiring.com/pages/practice/probono.htm

Contact: Rosalyn Garbose Nasdor, Sr. Pro Bono Mgr.
Fields of interest: Legal services.
Type of support: Pro bono services - legal.
Application information: A Pro Bono Committee manages the pro bono program.

3261
Rose & Kiernan, Inc.

99 Troy Rd., Ste. 300
East Greenbush, NY 12061-1027
(518) 244-4245

Company URL: http://www.rkinsurance.com
Establishment information: Established in 1869.
Company type: Private company
Business activities: Sells automobile, casualty, life, health, and surety insurance.
Business type (SIC): Insurance/fire, marine, and casualty; insurance/life; insurance/accident and health; insurance/surety
Corporate officers: John F. Murray, Jr., Chair., Pres., and C.E.O.; Joseph F. Vitale, Vice-Chair., Exec. V.P., C.F.O., and Treas.; Carol A. Lewick III, Exec. V.P. and Cont.
Board of directors: John F. Murray, Jr., Chair.; Joseph F. Vitale, Vice-Chair.
Offices: Amherst, Beacon, Glens Falls, Johnson City, Kingston, Pittsford, Plattsburgh, Port Henry, Potsdam, Watertown, NY
Giving statement: Giving through the Rose and Kiernan Charitable Foundation, Inc.

Rose and Kiernan Charitable Foundation, Inc.

99 Troy Rd.
East Greenbush, NY 12061-1027 (518) 244-4245
URL: http://www.rkinsurance.com/community_involvement/rk_charitable_foundation_eventsnews/

Establishment information: Established in 2001 in NY.
Donor: Rose and Kiernan, Inc.
Contact: Joseph F. Vitale, Dir.
Financial data (yr. ended 12/31/11): Assets, $1,702,291 (M); gifts received, $250,925; expenditures, $198,789; qualifying distributions, $198,789; giving activities include $195,589 for 103 grants (high: $10,000; low: $25).
Purpose and activities: The foundation supports organizations involved with higher education, health, cerebral palsy, and human services.
Fields of interest: Higher education; Hospitals (general); Health care, clinics/centers; Health care; Cerebral palsy; YM/YWCAs & YM/YWHAs; Children/youth, services; Family services; Developmentally disabled, centers & services; Human services; United Ways and Federated Giving Programs.
Type of support: General/operating support; Program development; Scholarship funds.
Geographic limitations: Giving primarily in areas of company operations in upstate NY.
Application information: Applications accepted. Application form not required. Applicants should submit the following:
1) detailed description of project and amount of funding requested
Initial approach: Letter of inquiry
Deadline(s): None
Directors: John F. Murray; Joseph F. Vitale; Charles R. Daniels III; Mark C. Nickel.
EIN: 141831866
Selected grants: The following grants are a representative sample of this grantmaker's funding activity:
$12,000 to Glens Falls Hospital Foundation, Glens Falls, NY, 2010.
$10,000 to Center for Disability Services, Albany, NY, 2010.
$9,005 to United Way of the Greater Capital Region, Albany, NY, 2010.
$7,500 to Seton Health Foundation, Troy, NY, 2010.
$7,000 to Albany Medical Center Foundation, Albany, NY, 2010.
$5,000 to Abilities First, Poughkeepsie, NY, 2010.
$5,000 to Ellis Hospital Foundation, Schenectady, NY, 2010.
$5,000 to Mount Saint Mary College, Newburgh, NY, 2010.
$4,000 to Albany College of Pharmacy, Albany, NY, 2010.
$1,000 to Millbrook Central School, Millbrook, NY, 2010.

3262
Rose Hills Memorial Park and Mortuary

(also known as Rose Hills Company)
3888 S. Workman Mill Rd.
Whittier, CA 90601-1626 (562) 699-0921

Company URL: http://www.rosehills.com
Establishment information: Established in 1914.
Company type: Private company
Business activities: Operates cemetery.
Business type (SIC): Real estate subdividers and developers
Corporate officers: Dennis C. Poulsen, Chair.; Kenton C. Woods, C.E.O.; Pat Monroe, Pres.; Mary Guzman, C.F.O.; Gregg M. Williamson, Exec. V.P., Sales and Mktg.
Board of director: Dennis C. Poulsen, Chair.
Giving statement: Giving through the SkyRose Chapel Foundation.

SkyRose Chapel Foundation

(formerly SkyRose Foundation)
3888 Workman Mill Rd.
Whittier, CA 90608 (562) 699-0921

Donors: Rose Hills Co.; Paramount Pictures; WJH Productions LLC; Warner Bros Television.
Contact: Kenton C. Woods, Pres.
Financial data (yr. ended 12/31/11): Assets, $258,796 (M); gifts received, $41,129; expenditures, $45,477; qualifying distributions, $45,402; giving activities include $45,402 for grants.
Purpose and activities: The foundation supports organizations involved with education, health, and human services.
Fields of interest: Arts; Health care; Housing/shelter.
Geographic limitations: Giving primarily in the Whittier, CA, area.
Support limitations: No grants to individuals.
Application information: Applications accepted. Application form required.
Initial approach: Proposal
Deadline(s): None
Officers and Directors:* Kenton C. Woods*, Pres.; Mary C. Guzman*, V.P. and Secy.-Treas.; Patrick C. Monroe*, V.P.; Dennis C. Poulsen.
EIN: 954678354

3263
The Rose Law Firm, P.A.

120 E. 4th St.
Little Rock, AR 72201-2893
(501) 375-9131

Company URL: http://www.roselawfirm.com
Establishment information: Established in 1820.
Company type: Private company
Business activities: Provides legal services.
Business type (SIC): Legal services
Giving statement: Giving through the Rose Law Firm Charitable Trust.

The Rose Law Firm Charitable Trust

120 E. 4th St.
Little Rock, AR 72201-2893

Establishment information: Established in 1987 in AR.
Donor: The Rose Law Firm, P.A.
Financial data (yr. ended 12/31/11): Assets, $31,953 (M); gifts received, $30,091; expenditures, $29,275; qualifying distributions, $28,675; giving activities include $28,675 for grants.
Purpose and activities: The foundation supports bar associations and organizations involved with higher education, health, heart disease, human services, and economic development.
Fields of interest: Mental health/crisis services; Health organizations; Community/economic development.
Type of support: General/operating support; Scholarship funds.
Application information: Applications not accepted. Unsolicited requests for funds not accepted.
Trustees: Bryant K. Cranford; Stephen N. Joiner; W. Wilson Jones.
EIN: 716132107

3264
Rosen's Diversified, Inc.

1120 Lake Ave.
P.O. Box 933
Fairmont, MN 56031-1939 (507) 238-6001

Company URL: http://www.rosensdiversifiedinc.com
Establishment information: Established in 1946.
Company type: Private company
Business activities: Manufactures, markets, and distributes beef products; distributes fertilizers and agricultural chemicals.
Business type (SIC): Non-durable goods—wholesale
Financial profile for 2011: Number of employees, 3,975; sales volume, $2,660,000,000
Corporate officers: Thomas J. Rosen, Chair. and C.E.O.; Robert Hovde, C.F.O.

Giving statement: Giving through the Rosen Family Foundation, Inc.

The Rosen Family Foundation, Inc.

P.O. Box 933
Fairmont, MN 56031-0933

Establishment information: Established in 2002 in MN.
Donors: Rosen's Diversified, Inc.; Roberta A. Rosen.
Financial data (yr. ended 11/30/11): Assets, $1,402,135 (M); gifts received, $253,250; expenditures, $151,155; qualifying distributions, $141,050; giving activities include $141,013 for 133 grants (high: $20,000; low: $500).
Purpose and activities: The foundation supports organizations involved with education, grief counseling, agriculture, children and youth, senior citizens, and Christianity and awards college scholarships.
Fields of interest: Education, early childhood education; Higher education; Education; Mental health, grief/bereavement counseling; Agriculture; Food services; Children/youth, services; Aging, centers/services; Mathematics; Engineering; Christian agencies & churches.
Program:
Rosen's Diversified Inc.'s Scholarship Program: The foundation awards college scholarships to students who plan to pursue careers in agriculture, food science, animal and agricultural science, engineering, or marketing. Recipients are selected based on leadership, civic and extracurricular activities, academics, and community service.
Type of support: General/operating support; Program development; Scholarships—to individuals.
Geographic limitations: Giving primarily in IA, NE, SD, and WI, with emphasis on MN.
Application information: Applications not accepted. Contributes only to pre-selected organizations and individuals.
Officers: Thomas J. Rosen, Pres. and Secy.; Dominick V. Driano, Jr., V.P.; Richard H. Rosen, Treas.
EIN: 412054672
Selected grants: The following grants are a representative sample of this grantmaker's funding activity:
$1,000 to Bellin College of Nursing, Green Bay, WI, 2010.
$1,000 to Mount Marty College, Yankton, SD, 2010.
$1,000 to University of Wisconsin-Green Bay, Green Bay, WI, 2010.

3265
Ross Environmental Services, Inc.

150 Innovation Dr.
Elyria, OH 44035-1674 (440) 366-2000

Company URL: http://www.rossenvironmental.com
Establishment information: Established in 1949.
Company type: Subsidiary of a private company
Business activities: Provides environmental management services.
Business type (SIC): Sanitary services
Corporate officers: Maureen M. Cromling, Chair.; Arthur Hargate, Co-Pres. and C.E.O.
Board of director: Maureen M. Cromling, Chair.
Giving statement: Giving through the Ross Environmental Services, Inc. Corporate Giving Program and the Ross Foundation Inc.

Ross Environmental Services, Inc. Corporate Giving Program

150 Innovation Dr.
Elyria, OH 44035-1672 (440) 366-2076
FAX: (440) 366-2376;
E-mail: mkelch@rossenvironmental.com;
URL: http://www.rossenvironmental.com/index.php?option=com_content&view=ross&layout=ross&id=30&Itemid=41

Contact: Margaret Kelch, Dir., Corp. Comms.
Purpose and activities: As a complement to its foundation, Ross also makes charitable contributions to nonprofit organizations directly. Support is limited to Lorain County, Ohio.
Fields of interest: Education Children/youth.
Type of support: Employee volunteer services; General/operating support.
Geographic limitations: Giving limited to Lorain County, OH.
Support limitations: No support for religious or political organizations, or private schools.
Publications: Informational brochure (including application guidelines).
Application information: Applications accepted. The Corporate Communications Department handles giving. Application form not required. Applicants should submit the following:
1) detailed description of project and amount of funding requested
Initial approach: Proposal to headquarters
Copies of proposal: 1
Final notification: Following review
Number of staff: 1 full-time professional; 1 full-time support.

Ross Foundation Inc.

150 Innovation Dr.
Elyria, OH 44035-1674
FAX: (440) 336-2376;
E-mail: mkelch@rossenvironmental.com;
URL: http://www.rossenvironmental.com/index.php?option=com_content&view=ross&layout=ross&id=30&Itemid=41

Establishment information: Established in 1984 in OH.
Donors: Ross Environmental Services, Inc.; CME Advisory Services, Inc.
Financial data (yr. ended 05/31/12): Assets, $302,850 (M); gifts received, $390,800; expenditures, $88,100; qualifying distributions, $88,000; giving activities include $88,000 for 3 grants (high: $85,000; low: $1,000).
Purpose and activities: The foundation supports organizations involved with education and youth development.
Fields of interest: Education; Public affairs.
Type of support: Program development; Scholarship funds.
Geographic limitations: Giving limited to OH, with emphasis on the Midview Local School District in Lorain County.
Support limitations: No support for religious organizations or fraternal, labor, or veterans' organizations. No grants to individuals, or for courtesy advertising, tickets, or travel.
Application information: Applications not accepted. Unsolicited requests for funds not accepted.
Officers and Directors:* Maureen M. Cromling, Chair., Pres., and Treas.; William E. Cromling II*, Vice-Chair. and V.P.; Jon R. Cromling, V.P.; Daniel Urban, Secy.; Christine M. Cromling; William E. Cromling III.
Number of staff: None.
EIN: 341442262

3266
The Ross Group Construction Corporation

1140 N. 129th East Ave.
Tulsa, OK 74116-1724 (918) 234-7675

Company URL: http://www.trgcc.com
Establishment information: Established in 1979.
Company type: Private company
Business activities: Operates full-service, non-residential general contracting company.
Business type (SIC): Contractors/general nonresidential building
Corporate officers: Warren E. Ross, C.E.O.; Jesse H. Ross, Pres.; Teresa Spelts, V.P., Finance and C.F.O.; David Thomas, V.P., Opers.
Giving statement: Giving through the Ross Charitable Foundation.

The Ross Charitable Foundation

1140 N. 129th E. Ave.
Tulsa, OK 74116-1724

Establishment information: Established in 2006 in OK.
Donor: The Ross Group Construction.
Financial data (yr. ended 12/31/11): Assets, $1,559,551 (M); gifts received, $500,000; expenditures, $189,938; qualifying distributions, $187,981; giving activities include $187,981 for 23 grants (high: $38,471; low: $500).
Fields of interest: Secondary school/education; Higher education, university; Religion.
Geographic limitations: Giving primarily in OK.
Application information: Applications accepted. Application form required. Applicants should submit the following:
1) copy of IRS Determination Letter
2) detailed description of project and amount of funding requested
Initial approach: Letter
Deadline(s): None
Officers and Directors:* Jesse H. Ross, Chair. and Pres.; Warren E. Ross*, Secy.; Teresa A. Spelts*, Treas.
EIN: 205309346
Selected grants: The following grants are a representative sample of this grantmaker's funding activity:
$32,000 to University of Tulsa, Tulsa, OK, 2010.
$10,000 to Bishop Kelley High School, Tulsa, OK, 2010.
$6,000 to University of Oklahoma, Norman, OK, 2010.
$5,000 to Kansas State University, Manhattan, KS, 2010.
$2,500 to Christian Brothers University, Memphis, TN, 2010. For Annual Fund.
$2,500 to Colorado School of Mines, Golden, CO, 2010. For general fund.
$2,500 to Missouri State University, Springfield, MO, 2010.
$2,500 to Oklahoma State University, Stillwater, OK, 2010.
$2,500 to Pittsburg State University, Pittsburg, KS, 2010.
$2,500 to Ronald McDonald House Charities, Oak Brook, IL, 2010. For general fund.

3267
Ross Stores, Inc.
4440 Rosewood Dr.
Pleasanton, CA 94588-3050
(925) 965-4400
FAX: (302) 531-3150

Company URL: http://www.rossstores.com
Establishment information: Established in 1982.
Company type: Public company
Company ticker symbol and exchange: ROST/NASDAQ
Business activities: Operates discount apparel stores.
Business type (SIC): Family apparel and accessory stores
Financial profile for 2013: Number of employees, 57,500; assets, $3,670,560,000; sales volume, $9,721,070,000; pre-tax net income, $1,264,840,000; expenses, $8,456,220,000; liabilities, $1,903,700,000
Fortune 1000 ranking: 2012—278th in revenues, 243rd in profits, and 688th in assets
Forbes 2000 ranking: 2012—952nd in sales, 685th in profits, and 1894th in assets
Corporate officers: Norman A. Ferber, Chair.; Michael A. Balmuth, Vice-Chair. and C.E.O.; Michael B. O'Sullivan, Co-Pres. and C.O.O.; James S. Fassio, Co-Pres.; Michael K. Kobayashi, Exec. V.P. and C.I.O.; Ken Caruana, Exec. V.P., Mktg. and Human Resources; John G. Call, C.F.O.
Board of directors: Norman A. Ferber, Chair.; Michael A. Balmuth, Vice-Chair.; K. Gunnar Bjorklund; Michael J. Bush; Sharon D. Garrett; Larry S. Peiros; George P. Orban; Gregory L. Quesnel
Giving statement: Giving through the Ross Stores, Inc. Corporate Giving Program.
Company EIN: 941390387

Ross Stores, Inc. Corporate Giving Program
4440 Rosewood Dr.
Pleasanton, CA 94588-3050 (925) 965-4400

Purpose and activities: Ross Stores makes charitable contributions to nonprofit organizations on a case by case basis.
Fields of interest: Disasters, preparedness/services; Boys & girls clubs; American Red Cross.
Type of support: Employee volunteer services; General/operating support; Program development.

3268
Rostra Precision Controls, Inc.
2519 Dana Dr.
Laurinburg, NC 28352-4000
(910) 276-4853

Company URL: http://www.rostra.com
Company type: Subsidiary of a private company
Business activities: Manufactures electronic automotive controls, systems, and components.
Business type (SIC): Motor vehicles, parts, and supplies—wholesale
Corporate officers: Thomas P. Petrillo, Chair.; Jim Pineau, C.F.O.; Pete Kallgren, V.P., Sales and Mktg.
Board of director: Thomas P. Petrillo, Chair.
Giving statement: Giving through the Rostra Engineered Component Sunshine Fund.

Rostra Engineered Component Sunshine Fund
(formerly Century Brass Sunshine Fund)
P.O. Box 1802
Providence, RI 02901-1802

Donor: Rostra Precision Controls, Inc.
Financial data (yr. ended 12/31/11): Assets, $44,656 (M); expenditures, $15,832; qualifying distributions, $14,300; giving activities include $14,300 for grants.
Purpose and activities: The fund provides flowers and fruit baskets to employees of Rostra Precision Controls when illness or a death in the family occurs, and small loans for emergencies.
Type of support: Grants to individuals; Loans—to individuals.
Geographic limitations: Giving limited to areas of company operations.
Application information: Applications not accepted. Contributes only through employee-related donations and loans.
Trustee: Bank of America.
EIN: 066219258

3269
Rothgerber Johnson & Lyons LLP
1200 17th St., Ste. 3000
Denver, CO 80202-5839 (303) 623-9000

Company URL: http://www.rothgerber.com/index.aspx
Establishment information: Established in 1903.
Company type: Private company
Business activities: Operates law firm.
Business type (SIC): Legal services
Corporate officers: Barb Mica, C.O.O.; Pattie Coates, Cont.
Offices: Colorado Springs, Denver, CO; Casper, WY
Giving statement: Giving through the Rothgerber Johnson & Lyons LLP Pro Bono Program.

Rothgerber Johnson & Lyons LLP Pro Bono Program
1200 17th St., Ste. 3000
Denver, CO 80202-5839 (303) 623-9000
E-mail: krossman@rothgerber.com; URL: http://www.rothgerber.com/firmprofile.aspx?Show=130

Contact: Kenneth F. Rossman, Partner
Fields of interest: Legal services.
Type of support: Pro bono services - legal.
Application information: An attorney coordinates pro bono projects.

3270
Rothschild Inc.
1251 Ave. of the Americas, 51st Fl.
New York, NY 10020 (212) 403-3500

Company URL: http://www.us.rothschild.com
Establishment information: Established in 1798.
Company type: Subsidiary of a foreign company
Business activities: Provides securities brokerage services.
Business type (SIC): Brokers and dealers/security
Corporate officers: Baron David de Rothschild, Chair.; Roger H. Kimmel, Vice-Chair.; Nigel Higgins, Co-C.E.O.; Olivier Pecoux, Co-C.E.O.
Board of directors: Baron David de Rothschild, Chair.; Roger H. Kimmel, Vice-Chair.
Giving statement: Giving through the Rothschild Inc. Foundation.
Company EIN: 132589894

The Rothschild Inc. Foundation
1251 Ave. of the Americas
New York, NY 10020-1104

Establishment information: Established around 1969.
Donor: Rothschild Inc.
Financial data (yr. ended 12/31/10): Assets, $13,546 (M); expenditures, $0; qualifying distributions, $0.
Purpose and activities: The foundation supports organizations involved with arts and culture, theological education, and other areas.
Fields of interest: Arts; Theological school/education; General charitable giving.
Type of support: General/operating support.
Geographic limitations: Giving primarily in New York, NY.
Support limitations: No grants to individuals.
Application information: Applications not accepted. Unsolicited requests for funds not accepted.
Officer: Christa Schackert, Cont.
EIN: 132618415

3271
Rothstein, Kass & Company, P.C.
4 Becker Farm Rd.
Roseland, NJ 07068-1792 (973) 994-6666

Company URL: http://www.rkco.com
Establishment information: Established in 1959.
Company type: Private company
Business activities: Operates public accounting firm.
Business type (SIC): Accounting, auditing, and bookkeeping services
Corporate officers: Howard Altman, Co-C.E.O.; Steven A. Kass, Co-C.E.O.; Stuart Freiman, C.F.O.
Board of directors: Steven A. Kass; Henry Jia; Robert Levin; Stuart M. Smith; Richard Sumida; Mary C. Wilson
Giving statement: Giving through the Rothstein Kass Foundation Inc.

Rothstein Kass Foundation Inc
c/o Raymond K. Obssuth
4 Becker Farm Rd.
Roseland, NJ 07068-1739
URL: http://www.rkco.com/Site/CorporateCitizenship/CorpContent.aspx

Establishment information: Established in 2007 in NJ.
Donor: Rothstein, Kass & Company, P.C.
Financial data (yr. ended 12/31/11): Assets, $80,477 (M); gifts received, $100,000; expenditures, $141,830; qualifying distributions, $141,800; giving activities include $141,800 for 41 grants (high: $30,000; low: $100).
Purpose and activities: The foundation supports organizations involved with education, animal welfare, breast cancer, multiple sclerosis, and housing development. Special emphasis is directed toward programs designed to promote the environment and children's services.

Fields of interest: Education; Environment; Animal welfare; Breast cancer; Multiple sclerosis; Housing/shelter, development; Children, services.
Type of support: General/operating support; Scholarship funds.
Geographic limitations: Giving primarily in CA, CO, NJ, NY, and TX.
Application information: Applications not accepted. Unsolicited requests for funds not accepted.
Officers and Trustees:* Steven A. Kass*, Pres.; Raymond K. Obssuth*, Secy.; Howard Altman*, Treas.; Stuart Freiman.
EIN: 261592243

3272
Roundy's Supermarkets, Inc.

(formerly Roundy's, Inc.)
875 E. Wisconsin Ave.
Milwaukee, WI 53202 (414) 231-5000

Company URL: http://www.roundys.com
Establishment information: Established in 1872.
Company type: Subsidiary of a public company
Company ticker symbol and exchange: RNDY/NYSE
Business activities: Operates grocery stores; sells meat and meat products, produce, frozen foods, dairy products, and professional equipment and supplies wholesale.
Business type (SIC): Groceries—wholesale
Financial profile for 2012: Number of employees, 7,552; assets, $1,380,090,000; sales volume, $3,890,540,000; pre-tax net income, -$58,490,000; expenses, $3,949,030,000; liabilities, $1,186,820,000
Fortune 1000 ranking: 2012—602nd in revenues, 916th in profits, and 932nd in assets
Corporate officers: Robert A. Mariano, Chair., Pres., and C.E.O.; Darren W. Karst, Exec. V.P. and C.F.O.; Donald S. Rosanova, Exec. V.P., Opers.; Michael P. Turzenski, Group V.P. and C.A.O; Edward G. Kitz, Corp. Secy.
Board of directors: Robert A. Mariano, Chair.; Patrick J. Condon; Ralph W. Drayer; Gregory P. Josefowicz; Christopher F. Larson; Avy H. Stein; John R. Willis
Subsidiary: Pick 'n Save Warehouse Foods, Inc., Milwaukee, WI
Historic mergers: Prescott's Supermarkets, Inc. (January 21, 2003)
Giving statement: Giving through the Roundy's Supermarkets, Inc. Corporate Giving Program and the Roundy's Foundation, Inc.
Company EIN: 390854535

Roundy's Supermarkets, Inc. Corporate Giving Program

875 E. Wisconsin Ave.
Milwaukee, WI 53202-5404
URL: http://www.roundys.com/Home.gsn

Purpose and activities: As a complement to its foundation, Roundy's also makes charitable contributions to nonprofit organizations directly. Support is given primarily in areas of company operations in Illinois, Minnesota, and Wisconsin.
Fields of interest: Education, reading; Food services; Family services, domestic violence.
Type of support: Donated products; General/operating support; In-kind gifts.
Geographic limitations: Giving primarily in areas of company operations in IL, MN, and WI.

Roundy's Foundation, Inc.

c/o Roundy's Supermarkets, Inc.
M.S. 2175
P.O. Box 473
Milwaukee, WI 53201-0473 (414) 231-6159

Establishment information: Established in 2003 in WI.
Donors: Roundy's, Inc.; Roundy's Supermarkets, Inc.
Financial data (yr. ended 12/31/11): Assets, $1,342,093 (M); gifts received, $279,495; expenditures, $1,080,311; qualifying distributions, $792,634; giving activities include $792,634 for grants.
Purpose and activities: The foundation supports programs designed to address literacy, hunger relief, and families in crisis.
Fields of interest: Education, reading; Food services; Food banks; Nutrition; Family services; Family services, domestic violence.
Programs:
Families in Crisis: The foundation supports programs designed to provide assistance and training focused on domestic violence prevention and intervention. Special emphasis is directed toward programs designed to assist families and individuals in conflict or under duress due to abuse or neglect.
Hunger Relief: The foundation supports hunger relief and nutrition initiatives through product and financial donations to organizations and nonprofit food distribution centers. The foundation supports food banks and self-help programs designed to give people long-term solutions to hunger.
Literacy: The foundation supports programs designed to promote literacy. Special emphasis is directed towards in-classroom educational opportunities for students of all ages.
Type of support: Annual campaigns; Capital campaigns; Donated products; General/operating support; In-kind gifts; Program development.
Geographic limitations: Giving primarily in areas of company operations in IL, MN, and WI.
Support limitations: No support for religious organizations not of direct benefit to the entire community, educational institutions for regular programs, foundations, or athletic teams. No grants to individuals, or for capital campaigns or sporting events.
Publications: Annual report (including application guidelines); Application guidelines; Program policy statement.
Application information: Applications accepted. An application form is required for requests over $5,000. Applicants should submit the following:
1) timetable for implementation and evaluation of project
2) population served
3) brief history of organization and description of its mission
4) geographic area to be served
5) how project's results will be evaluated or measured
6) detailed description of project and amount of funding requested
7) copy of current year's organizational budget and/or project budget

Initial approach: Proposal; download application form and mail to foundation for requests over $5,000
Deadline(s): None

Officers and Directors:* Robert A. Mariano*, Pres.; Colleen J. Stenholt*, V.P.; Ed Kitz, Secy.; Darren W. Karst*, Treas.; Flamont T. Butler; Gerardo H. Gonzalez; Sarah Jane Voichcik.
EIN: 200299349
Selected grants: The following grants are a representative sample of this grantmaker's funding activity:
$20,000 to Urban League, Milwaukee, Milwaukee, WI, 2011.
$15,500 to Milwaukee Womens Center, Milwaukee, WI, 2011.
$8,000 to Boys and Girls Clubs of Greater Milwaukee, Milwaukee, WI, 2011.
$5,000 to Hope House of Milwaukee, Milwaukee, WI, 2011.
$5,000 to Junior League of Minneapolis, Minneapolis, MN, 2011.
$5,000 to Saint Vincent de Paul Society of Milwaukee, Milwaukee, WI, 2011.
$4,918 to Hope House of Milwaukee, Milwaukee, WI, 2011.
$4,500 to AIDS Resource Center of Wisconsin, Milwaukee, WI, 2011.
$2,478 to AIDS Resource Center of Wisconsin, Milwaukee, WI, 2011.

3273
Royal Caribbean Cruises Ltd.

1050 Caribbean Way
Miami, FL 33132 (305) 539-6000
FAX: (305) 374-7354

Company URL: http://www.royalcaribbean.com
Establishment information: Established in 1968.
Company type: Public company
Company ticker symbol and exchange: RCL/NYSE
Business activities: Operates cruise ship line.
Business type (SIC): Transportation/water passenger
Financial profile for 2012: Number of employees, 62,000; assets, $19,827,930,000; sales volume, $7,688,020,000; pre-tax net income, $18,290,000; expenses, $7,292,410,000; liabilities, $11,519,180,000
Forbes 2000 ranking: 2012—1117th in sales, 1781st in profits, and 982nd in assets
Corporate officers: Richard D. Fain, Chair. and C.E.O.; Brian J. Rice, Vice-Chair.; Jason Liberty, C.F.O.; Henry Pujol, Sr. V.P. and Cont.
Board of directors: Richard D. Fain, Chair.; Brian J. Rice, Vice-Chair.; Morten Arntzen; Bernard W. Aronson; William L. Kimsey; Ann S. Moore; Gert W. Munthe; Eyal M. Ofer; Thomas J. Pritzker; William K. Reilly; Bernt Reitan; Vagn O. Sorensen; Arne Alexander Wilhelmsen
Giving statement: Giving through the Royal Caribbean Cruises Ltd. Corporate Giving Program.
Company EIN: 980081645

Royal Caribbean Cruises Ltd. Corporate Giving Program

1050 Caribbean Way
Miami, FL 33132-2028 (305) 539-6000
FAX: (305) 579-4738;
E-mail: CommunityRelations@rccl.com; URL: http://www.royalcaribbean.com/ourCompany/community/rcAndTheCommunity.do

Contact: Helen P. O'Connell, Mgr., Community Rels.
Purpose and activities: Royal Caribbean makes charitable contributions to nonprofit organizations involved with children and families, education, and marine conservation. Support is given primarily in areas of company operations in Alaska, California, Florida, Baltimore, Maryland, New Jersey, New York, Texas, and the Caribbean.
Fields of interest: Education; Environment, water pollution; Environmental education; Environment; Safety/disasters; Big Brothers/Big Sisters;

Children/youth, services; Family services; Community/economic development Children; Economically disadvantaged.

Program:

G.I.V.E. for the Holidays: In the weeks and months leading up to the winter holidays, shipboard employees raise money for the charity of their choice in one of their ports of call and Royal Caribbean Cruises Ltd. matches up to $2,500 of the funds raised on each ship. The crew members then purchase items the charity has requested, including mattresses and educational tools for children and families in that city.

Type of support: Donated products; Employee matching gifts; Employee volunteer services; Employee-related scholarships; General/operating support; In-kind gifts; Loaned talent; Scholarship funds; Sponsorships.

Geographic limitations: Giving primarily in AK, CA, FL, Baltimore, MD, NJ, NY, TX, and the Caribbean.

Support limitations: No support for political or religious organizations not of direct benefit to the entire community, animal welfare organizations, museums, bands, orchestras, or art galleries, professional associations, health or human service organizations, local United Ways, individual schools, PTOs, or PTAs. No grants to individuals, or for educational loans, recognition programs, individual opportunities for students and/or teachers, including sponsorship of student ambassador programs, continuing education seminars, or teacher attendance recognition, transportation to and from events or seminars, or health-related causes.

Publications: Application guidelines.

Application information: Applications accepted. Proposals should be no longer than 2 pages. The global Community Relations program handles giving. Requests are not accepted via e-mail. Application form not required. Applicants should submit the following:

1) copy of IRS Determination Letter
2) brief history of organization and description of its mission

Applications should include the date of the event, if applicable.

Initial approach: Proposal
Copies of proposal: 1
Committee meeting date(s): Quarterly
Deadline(s): First Friday of Oct., Jan., Apr., and July
Final notification: End of Oct., Jan., Apr., and July

3274
Royal Neighbors of America

230 16th St.
Rock Island, IL 61201-8645
(309) 788-4561

Company URL: http://www.royalneighbors.org
Establishment information: Established in 1895.
Company type: Fraternal benefit society
Business activities: Operates fraternal benefit society.
Business type (SIC): Insurance/life
Corporate officers: Joyce Elam, Chair.; Patricia Gibford, Vice-Chair.; Cynthia Tidwell, Pres. and C.E.O.; Marc Schoenfeld, C.F.O.; Curt Zeck, C.I.O.; Chris Seistrup, Exec. V.P. and C.O.O.; Bruce Peterson, Genl. Counsel and Secy.
Board of directors: Joyce Elam, Chair.; Patricia Gibford, Vice-Chair.; Nancy Hanna; Patsy Kneller; Justice Ruth McGregor; V. Sue Molina; Chris Seistrup; Benet Spence; Cynthia Tidwell; Estella Vallejo; Susan Waring
Giving statement: Giving through the Royal Neighbors of America Contributions Program and the Royal Neighbors of America Foundation.

Royal Neighbors of America Contributions Program

230 16th St.
Rock Island, IL 61201-8645 (309) 788-4561
E-mail: fraternalservices@royalneighbors.org; URL: http://www.royalneighbors.org/Community/NationOfNeighbors.aspx

Purpose and activities: As a complement to its foundation, Royal Neighbors of America also makes charitable contributions to individuals and nonprofit organizations directly.
Fields of interest: Women.
Type of support: General/operating support; Grants to individuals.
Application information: Applications not accepted. Contributes only to pre-selected individuals.

Royal Neighbors of America Foundation

230 16th St.
Rock Island, IL 61201-8645
Toll-free tel.: (800) 627-4762; URL: http://www.royalneighborsfoundation.org/Home3.aspx

Establishment information: Established in 2002 in IL.
Financial data (yr. ended 12/31/11): Revenue, $65,218; assets, $1,129,659 (M); gifts received, $29,654; expenditures, $96,414; giving activities include $5,935 for grants and $46,000 for 29 grants to individuals.
Purpose and activities: The foundation works to promote charitable and educational causes that empower women to achieve financial security.
Fields of interest: Scholarships/financial aid; Education Women.
Type of support: Scholarships—to individuals.
Officers and Directors :* Cynthia Tidwell*, Pres.; Kristin McDaniel*, V.P.; John Friedrich*, Secy.; Steve Norberg, C.P.A.*, Treas.; Patsy Kneller; Bruce Peterson, J.D., F.L.M.I.; Mary Staver, P.H.R.
EIN: 352164486

3275
Royal Savings Bank

9226 S. Commercial Ave.
Chicago, IL 60617-4508 (773) 768-4800

Company URL: http://www.royalbankweb.com
Establishment information: Established in 1887.
Company type: Subsidiary of a public company
Business activities: Operates savings bank.
Business type (SIC): Savings institutions
Corporate officers: James A. Fitch, Jr., Chair.; Barbara K. Minster, Pres.; Jodi A. Ojeda, Sr. V.P. and C.F.O.; Kelly Wilson, Sr. V.P., Opers.
Board of directors: James A. Fitch, Jr., Chair.; Alan W. Bird; John T. Dempsey; Roger L. Hupe; C. Michael McLaren; Leonard Szwajkowski; Philip J. Timyan
Office: Lansing, IL
Giving statement: Giving through the Royal Charitable Foundation.

Royal Charitable Foundation

9226 S. Commercial Ave.
Chicago, IL 60617-4508

Establishment information: Established in 2005 in IL.
Donor: Royal Savings Bank.
Financial data (yr. ended 06/30/11): Assets, $97,299 (M); expenditures, $3,428; qualifying distributions, $0.
Purpose and activities: The foundation supports organizations involved with education, health, family services, and Catholicism.
Fields of interest: Secondary school/education; Higher education; Education; Hospitals (general); Health care, clinics/centers; Health care; Housing/shelter; Family services; Community/economic development; Catholic agencies & churches.
Type of support: General/operating support.
Geographic limitations: Giving primarily in Chicago, IL.
Application information: Applications not accepted. Unsolicited requests for funds not accepted.
Officer and Directors:* Leonard Szwajkowski*, Secy.; Barbara K. Minster.
EIN: 562496544

3276
Royal Wine Corp.

(doing business as Kedem Food Products Company)
63 Lefante Dr.
Bayonne, NJ 07002-5024 (718) 384-2400

Company URL: http://www.royalwines.com
Establishment information: Established in 1848.
Company type: Private company
Business activities: Produces wine.
Business type (SIC): Beverages
Corporate officers: David Herzog, C.E.O.; Sheldon Ginsberg, Exec. V.P. and C.F.O.; Michael Luftglas, V.P., Mktg. and Public Rels.; Aaron Herzog, Treas.
Giving statement: Giving through the Galanta Foundation, Inc.

Galanta Foundation, Inc.

c/o Royal Wine Corp.
63 Lefante Ln.
Bayonne, NJ 07002-5024

Establishment information: Established in 2003 in NY.
Donor: Royal Wine Corp.
Financial data (yr. ended 12/31/11): Assets, $179,340 (M); gifts received, $500,000; expenditures, $442,210; qualifying distributions, $442,210; giving activities include $442,210 for grants.
Purpose and activities: The foundation supports organizations involved with Judaism.
Fields of interest: Jewish agencies & synagogues.
Type of support: General/operating support.
Geographic limitations: Giving limited to Brooklyn, Monsey, and Spring Valley, NY.
Support limitations: No grants to individuals.
Application information: Applications not accepted. Contributes only to pre-selected organizations.
Officers and Directors:* Judith Buchler, V.P.; Eli Herzog, V.P.; Gary Herzog, V.P.; Herman Herzog, V.P.; Joseph Herzog, V.P.; Michael Herzog*, V.P.; Michael B. Herzog, V.P.; Mordechai Herzog, V.P.; Morris Herzog, V.P.; Nathan Herzog*, V.P.; Phillip Herzog, V.P.; Robert Herzog, V.P.; Aaron Herzog*, Secy.-Treas.
EIN: 030533223
Selected grants: The following grants are a representative sample of this grantmaker's funding activity:

$4,000 to Yeshiva Machzikei Hadas, Brooklyn, NY, 2010.
$4,000 to Yeshiva Shaarei Yosher, Brooklyn, NY, 2010.
$2,100 to Chesed Avraham, Brooklyn, NY, 2010.

3277
Royalnest Corporation

1295 Northern Blvd., Ste. 17
Manhasset, NY 11030-3093
(516) 365-9205

Establishment information: Established in 1977.
Company type: Private company
Business activities: Develops real estate.
Business type (SIC): Real estate subdividers and developers
Corporate officer: Thomas A. Nuzio, V.P. and Cont.
Giving statement: Giving through the Eleanor and Roy Nester Family Foundation.

Eleanor and Roy Nester Family Foundation

1295 N. Blvd., Ste. 17
Manhasset, NY 11030-3002 (516) 365-9205

Establishment information: Established in 1980 in NY.
Donors: Royalnest Corp.; Eleanor D. Nester†; Roy G. Nester†.
Contact: Linda L. Cronin, Secy.-Treas.
Financial data (yr. ended 03/31/12): Assets, $309,359 (M); gifts received, $100,000; expenditures, $31,415; qualifying distributions, $31,350; giving activities include $31,300 for 8 grants (high: $12,500; low: $250).
Purpose and activities: The foundation supports hospitals, Protestant agencies and churches, and organizations involved with education and preventative healthcare.
Fields of interest: Education; Health care; Religion.
Type of support: General/operating support; Scholarship funds.
Geographic limitations: Giving primarily in NY, with emphasis on Long Island.
Support limitations: No grants to individuals.
Application information: Applications accepted. Application form required.
Initial approach: Letter
Copies of proposal: 1
Deadline(s): None
Final notification: Within 2 months
Officers and Directors:* Roy G. Nester*, Pres.; Denis F. Cronin*, V.P.; Peter J. DiConza, Jr.*, V.P.; John W. Nester*, V.P.; Linda L. Cronin*, Co-Secy.-Treas.; Carol A. DiConza*, Co-Secy.
Number of staff: None.
EIN: 112537407

3278
RPM International Inc.

(formerly RPM, Inc.)
2628 Pearl Rd.
P.O. Box 777
Medina, OH 44258 (330) 273-5090

Company URL: http://www.rpminc.com
Establishment information: Established in 1947.
Company type: Public company
Company ticker symbol and exchange: RPM/NYSE
Business activities: Manufactures and markets specialty paints, protective coatings and roofing systems, sealants, and adhesives.
Business type (SIC): Paints and allied products
Financial profile for 2011: Number of employees, 8,873; assets, $3,004,000,000; sales volume, $3,412,700,000
Fortune 1000 ranking: 2012—613th in revenues, 555th in profits, and 699th in assets
Corporate officers: Frank C. Sullivan, Chair. and C.E.O.; Ronald A. Rice, Pres. and C.O.O.; Robert Matejka, Sr. V.P. and C.F.O.; Paul G.P. Hoogenboom, Sr. V.P.and C.I.O.; Edward W. Moore, V.P., Genl. Counsel, and Secy.; Keith R. Smiley, V.P. and Treas.; Barry M. Slifstein, V.P. and Cont.; Randell McShepard, V.P., Public Affairs
Board of directors: Frank C. Sullivan, Chair.; John P. Abizaid; Bruce A. Carbonari; David A. Daberko; James A. Karman; Donald K. Miller; Frederick R. Nance; William A. Papenbrock; Charles A. Ratner; Thomas C. Sullivan; William B. Summers, Jr.; Jerry Sue Thornton; Joseph P. Viviano
International operations: Argentina; Austria; Belgium; Bermuda; Brazil; Canada; Chile; China; Colombia; Czech Republic; Denmark; Dominican Republic; Ecuador; Finland; France; Germany; Hong Kong; Hungary; India; Ireland; Italy; Japan; Luxembourg; Malaysia; Mexico; Namibia; Netherlands; Netherlands Antilles; New Zealand; Norway; Poland; Portugal; Russia; Singapore; South Africa; South Korea; Spain; Sweden; Switzerland; United Arab Emirates; United Kingdom; Venezuela
Giving statement: Giving through the RPM International Inc. Corporate Giving Program.
Company EIN: 020642224

RPM International Inc. Corporate Giving Program

(formerly RPM, Inc. Corporate Giving Program)
2628 Pearl Rd.
P.O. Box 777
Medina, OH 44256-7623
FAX: (330) 273-6169;
E-mail: rmcshepard@rpminc.com

Contact: Randell McShepard, V.P., Public Affairs
Financial data (yr. ended 12/31/11): Total giving, $1,200,000, including $1,200,000 for grants.
Purpose and activities: RPM makes charitable contributions to nonprofit organizations involved with education, health and human services, and civic affairs. Support is given primarily in areas of company operations.
Fields of interest: Elementary/secondary education; Higher education; Education; Health care; Human services; Public affairs.
Type of support: Annual campaigns; Capital campaigns; Cause-related marketing; Continuing support; Curriculum development; Donated products; Employee matching gifts; Employee volunteer services; General/operating support; In-kind gifts; Loaned talent; Matching/challenge support; Program development; Public relations services; Scholarship funds; Sponsorships; Use of facilities.
Geographic limitations: Giving primarily in areas of company operations, with emphasis on the Medina, OH, area.
Support limitations: No support for religious or political organizations.
Publications: Application guidelines; Informational brochure; Program policy statement.
Application information: Applications accepted. The Community Affairs Department handles giving. Application form not required. Applicants should submit the following:
1) detailed description of project and amount of funding requested
Initial approach: Proposal to headquarters
Copies of proposal: 1
Committee meeting date(s): Every 8 weeks
Deadline(s): None
Final notification: 2 months
Administrators: Randell McShepard, V.P., Public Affairs; Diana Riley, Community Affairs Asst. and Special Events Mgr.
Number of staff: 2 full-time professional.

3279
RUAN Transport Management Systems

(formerly Ruan Transportation Corporation)
3200 Ruan Ctr.
666 Grand Ave.
Des Moines, IA 50309 (866) 782-6669

Company URL: http://www.ruan.com
Establishment information: Established in 1932.
Company type: Private company
Business activities: Provides contract transportation services.
Business type (SIC): Trucking and courier services, except by air
Corporate officers: John Ruan III, Chair.; Steve Chapman, Pres. and C.E.O.; Tracey Ball, Sr. V.P. and C.F.O.; Ben McLean, Sr. V.P. and C.I.O.; Roger Mason, Sr. V.P., Sales; Susan Fitzsimmons, V.P. and Genl. Counsel; Tara Meier, V.P., Mktg.; Rachel McLean, V.P., Comms.; Ron Hanson, V.P., Human Resources
Board of directors: John Ruan III, Chair.; Steve Chapman; David Fisher; Jonathan R. Fletcher; Lanny Martin; Suku Radia
Giving statement: Giving through the John Ruan Foundation Trust.

John Ruan Foundation Trust

3200 Ruan Ctr.
666 Grand Ave.
Des Moines, IA 50309-2520 (515) 245-2555

Establishment information: Established in 1955 in IA.
Donors: Ruan Transport Corporation; Elizabeth Ruan Trust; John Ruan.
Contact: John Ruan III, Tr.
Financial data (yr. ended 06/30/12): Assets, $14,659,296 (M); gifts received, $300,000; expenditures, $594,378; qualifying distributions, $580,655; giving activities include $580,655 for grants.
Purpose and activities: The foundation supports community foundations and organizations involved with arts and culture, education, health, mental health, employment, and human services.
Fields of interest: Performing arts; Performing arts, theater; Performing arts, orchestras; Arts; Elementary/secondary education; Higher education; Higher education, college (community/junior); Education; Health care; Mental health/crisis services; Employment, services; Big Brothers/Big Sisters; Children/youth, services; Family services; Residential/custodial care; Developmentally disabled, centers & services; Human services; Foundations (community).
Type of support: Building/renovation; General/operating support.
Geographic limitations: Giving primarily in Des Moines, IA.
Support limitations: No grants to individuals.
Application information: Applications accepted. Application form not required.

Initial approach: Proposal
Deadline(s): None
Trustee: John Ruan III.
EIN: 426059463
Selected grants: The following grants are a representative sample of this grantmaker's funding activity:
$512,500 to Culver Educational Foundation, Culver, IN, 2010.
$20,000 to Des Moines Public Schools, Des Moines, IA, 2010.
$10,000 to Drake University, Des Moines, IA, 2010.
$5,000 to Eaglebrook School, Deerfield, MA, 2010.
$5,000 to Northwestern University, Evanston, IL, 2010.

3280
RubinBrown LLP

(formerly Rubin, Brown, Gornstein & Co., LLP)
1 N. Brentwood Blvd.
St. Louis, MO 63105 (314) 290-3300

Company URL: http://www.rubinbrown.com
Establishment information: Established in 1952.
Company type: Private company
Business activities: Provides accounting services; provides business consulting services.
Business type (SIC): Accounting, auditing, and bookkeeping services; management and public relations services
Corporate officer: James G. Castellano, Chair.
Board of director: James G. Castellano, Chair.
Giving statement: Giving through the RubinBrown Charitable Foundation.

RubinBrown Charitable Foundation

(formerly Rubin, Brown, Gornstein & Co. Charitable Foundation)
1 N. Brentwood Blvd.
St. Louis, MO 63105-3925

Establishment information: Established in 2002 in MO.
Donors: Rubin, Brown, Gornstein & Co., LLP; RubinBrown LLP; Lawrence Rubin.
Financial data (yr. ended 06/30/11): Assets, $450,629 (M); gifts received, $71,515; expenditures, $19,175; qualifying distributions, $19,000; giving activities include $19,000 for 16 grants (high: $5,000; low: $250).
Purpose and activities: The foundation supports parks and playgrounds and organizations involved with education, business and industry, and youth.
Fields of interest: Education; Recreation, parks/ playgrounds; Boy scouts; Youth development, business; Business/industry Youth.
Type of support: General/operating support; Program development.
Geographic limitations: Giving primarily in MO, with emphasis on St. Louis.
Application information: Applications not accepted. Unsolicited requests for funds not accepted.
Trustees: James G. Castellano; Judith Murphy; Lawrence Rubin.
EIN: 331035603

3281
Ruby Tuesday, Inc.

150 W. Church Ave.
Maryville, TN 37801 (865) 379-5700
FAX: (865) 379-5004

Company URL: http://www.rubytuesday.com/
Establishment information: Established in 1972.
Company type: Public company
Company ticker symbol and exchange: RT/NYSE
Business activities: Operates restaurant chain.
Business type (SIC): Restaurants and drinking places
Financial profile for 2012: Number of employees, 36,300; assets, $1,173,540,000; sales volume, $1,325,840,000; pre-tax net income, -$14,940,000; expenses, $1,340,770,000; liabilities, $597,310,000
Corporate officers: Matthew A. Drapin, Chair.; James J. Buettgen III, Pres. and C.E.O.; Kimberly Grant, C.O.O.; Michael Moore, Exec. V.P. and C.F.O.; Scarlett May, Sr. V.P. and Secy.
Board of directors: Matthew A. Drapkin III, Chair.; James J. Buettgen; F. Lane Cardwell, Jr.; Kevin T. Clayton; Matthew A. Drapkin; Bernard Lanigan, Jr.; Jeffrey J. O'Neill; Stephen I. Sadove
Giving statement: Giving through the Ruby Tuesday Team Disaster Response Fund.
Company EIN: 630475239

Ruby Tuesday Team Disaster Response Fund

150 W. Church Ave.
Maryville, TN 37801-4936 (865) 379-5700

Financial data (yr. ended 05/31/11): Revenue, $109,402; assets, $254,011 (M); gifts received, $107,402; expenditures, $172,512; program services expenses, $171,260; giving activities include $171,260 for grants.
Purpose and activities: The fund provides financial assistance to victims of disasters who are employees of Ruby Tuesday, Inc.
Fields of interest: Safety/disasters; Human services, emergency aid.
Type of support: Grants to individuals.
Officers: Andy Scoggins, Pres.; Jud Roper, V.P.; John Doyle, Secy.
Directors: Susan Barlow; Richard Flaherty; Rhonda Sallas.
EIN: 621868105

3282
Ruder Finn Group, Inc.

301 E. 57th St., 3rd Fl.
New York, NY 10022-2900 (212) 593-6400
FAX: (212) 593-6397

Company URL: http://www.ruderfinn.com
Establishment information: Established in 1948.
Company type: Private company
Business activities: Provides public relations, marketing, and advertising services.
Business type (SIC): Management and public relations services; advertising
Financial profile for 2010: Number of employees, 580
Corporate officers: David Finn, Chair.; Dena Merriam, Vice-Chair.; Kathy Bloomgarden, Ph.D., Co-C.E.O.; Peter Finn, Co-C.E.O.; Michael Schubert, C.I.O.
Board of directors: David Finn, Chair.; Dena Merriam, Vice-Chair.
International operations: Australia; China; France; Hong Kong; Israel; Singapore; United Kingdom
Giving statement: Giving through the Ruder Finn, Inc. Corporate Giving Program and the Ruder Finn Fund.

Ruder Finn Fund

c/o Ruder Finn, Inc.
301 E. 57th St.
New York, NY 10022-2905

Establishment information: Established in 1964 in NY.
Donor: Ruder Finn, Inc.
Financial data (yr. ended 08/31/11): Assets, $44,034 (M); expenditures, $2,126; qualifying distributions, $2,000; giving activities include $2,000 for 1 grant.
Purpose and activities: The foundation supports organizations involved with arts and culture.
Fields of interest: Arts councils; Media, print publishing; Arts; Foundations (public).
Type of support: General/operating support.
Geographic limitations: Giving primarily in areas of company operations in CA and NY.
Support limitations: No grants to individuals.
Application information: Applications not accepted. Unsolicited requests for funds not accepted.
Trustee: David Finn.
EIN: 136162874

3283
Rudolph and Sletten, Inc.

1600 Seaport Blvd., Ste. 350
Redwood City, CA 94063-5575
(650) 216-3600

Company URL: http://www.rsconstruction.com
Establishment information: Established in 1960.
Company type: Subsidiary of a public company
Business activities: Provides general contract construction services.
Business type (SIC): Building construction general contractors and operative builders
Financial profile for 2010: Number of employees, 700
Corporate officers: Martin B. Sisemore, Pres. and C.E.O.; Paul A. Aherne, V.P. and Genl. Counsel
Giving statement: Giving through the Rudolph and Sletten, Inc. Corporate Giving Program.

Rudolph and Sletten, Inc. Corporate Giving Program

1600 Seaport Blvd, Ste. 350
Redwood City, CA 94063-5575 (650) 216-3600
URL: http://www.rsconstruction.com/about-us/community-involvement

Purpose and activities: Rudolph and Sletten makes charitable contributions to nonprofit organizations involved with health and welfare. Support is given primarily in areas of company operations, and on a national and international basis.
Fields of interest: Health care; Cancer; Housing/ shelter, volunteer services; Youth development; YM/YWCAs & YM/YWHAs; Aging, centers/services; Homeless, human services.
Type of support: Employee matching gifts; Employee volunteer services; Equipment; General/operating support; Loaned talent.
Geographic limitations: Giving primarily in areas of company operations in CA; giving also to national and international organizations.

3284
Rudy's Food Products, Inc.

9219 Viscount Row
Dallas, TX 75247-5415 (214) 634-7839
FAX: (214) 638-5317

Company URL: http://www.rudystortillas.com/
Establishment information: Established in 1945.
Company type: Private company
Business activities: Produces tortilla products.
Business type (SIC): Miscellaneous prepared foods
Corporate officers: Rudolph Guerra, Sr., Chair.; Louis Guerra, Treas. and C.E.O.; Rudolph Guerra, Jr., Pres.; Rudy Guerra, V.P., Opers.
Board of director: Rudolph Guerra, Sr., Chair.
Giving statement: Giving through the Rudy's Tortillas Foundation.

Rudy's Tortillas Foundation

9219 Viscount Row
Dallas, TX 75247-5415

Establishment information: Established in 2004 in TX.
Donor: Rudy's Food Products, Inc.
Financial data (yr. ended 12/31/11): Assets, $52,065 (M); expenditures, $35,810; qualifying distributions, $35,810; giving activities include $34,500 for 2 grants (high: $24,500; low: $10,000).
Purpose and activities: The foundation provides support for scholarship funds for needy Hispanic students.
Fields of interest: Higher education Hispanics/ Latinos.
Type of support: Scholarship funds.
Geographic limitations: Giving primarily in Dallas and Denton, TX.
Support limitations: No grants to individuals.
Application information: Applications not accepted. Unsolicited requests for funds not accepted.
Directors: Louis J. Guerra; Rudy Guerra, Jr.; Rudy Guerra, Sr.
EIN: 201713196

3285
Chas. E. Rue and Son, Inc.

(doing business as Rue Insurance)
3812 Quakerbridge Rd., Ste. 201
Hamilton, NJ 08619-1004 (609) 586-7474

Company URL: http://www.rueinsurance.com/
Establishment information: Established in 1917.
Company type: Private company
Business activities: Provides insurance brokerage services.
Business type (SIC): Insurance agents, brokers, and services
Corporate officers: Charles L. Rue, Jr., Chair.; William Rue, Pres.; William Rue, Jr., Exec. V.P., Sales; John Warn, V.P., Admin. and Treas.
Board of director: Charles L. Rue, Jr., Chair.
Giving statement: Giving through the Rue Foundation, Inc.

The Rue Foundation, Inc.

3812 Quakerbridge Rd.
Trenton, NJ 08619-1003 (609) 586-7474

Establishment information: Established in 2004 in NJ.
Donors: William M. Rue; Chas E. Rue and Son, Inc.
Contact: William M. Rue, Pres.
Financial data (yr. ended 12/31/11): Assets, $335,691 (M); gifts received, $100,000; expenditures, $77,405; qualifying distributions, $74,500; giving activities include $74,500 for grants.
Purpose and activities: The foundation supports organizations involved with education, health, human services, and economically disadvantaged people.
Fields of interest: Education; Health care; Youth development.
Type of support: General/operating support; Program development.
Geographic limitations: Giving primarily in NJ.
Support limitations: No grants to individuals.
Application information: Applications accepted. Application form required. Applicants should submit the following:
1) detailed description of project and amount of funding requested
Initial approach: Letter
Deadline(s): Dec. 30th
Officers: William M. Rue, Pres.; Joan E. Rue, V.P.; Lisa M. Rue, Secy.; William M. Rue, Jr., Treas.
Trustees: Asley M. Rue; Wesley D. Markham.
EIN: 342007978

3286
Rug & Home, Inc.

4 Factory Shops Blvd.
Gaffney, SC 29341-3321 (864) 488-2383

Company URL: http://www.rugandhome.com
Establishment information: Established in 1995.
Company type: Private company
Business activities: Rug retailer.
Business type (SIC): Furniture and home furnishing stores
Corporate officers: Rakesh Agarwal, C.E.O.; Dolly Agarwal, Pres.
Giving statement: Giving through the Rug & Home Foundation, Inc.

Rug & Home Foundation, Inc.

4 Factory Shops Blvd.
Gaffney, SC 29341-3321

Establishment information: Established in 2007 in SC.
Donors: Rug & Home, Inc.; Art & Decor Kingdom, Inc.
Financial data (yr. ended 12/31/11): Assets, $83,809 (M); gifts received, $1,960; expenditures, $32,200; qualifying distributions, $30,000; giving activities include $30,000 for grants.
Fields of interest: Education; Health care; Religion.
Geographic limitations: Giving primarily in NC.
Support limitations: No grants to individuals.
Application information: Applications not accepted. Unsolicited requests for funds not accepted.
Officers: Rakesh Agarwal, Pres.; Vinita Agarwal, V.P. and Secy.; Aanchal Agarwal, Treas.
EIN: 205173857

3287
Ruradan Corp, Inc.

8 E. 48th St., Ste. 3E
New York, NY 10017-1005 (212) 754-4001
FAX: (212) 754-4479

Establishment information: Established in 1948.
Company type: Private company
Business activities: Operates real estate agency.
Business type (SIC): Real estate agents and managers
Corporate officer: Ralph Elyachar, Pres.
Giving statement: Giving through the Elyachar Welfare Corporation.

Elyachar Welfare Corporation

8 E. 48th St., No. 3E
New York, NY 10017-1005

Establishment information: Established about 1951 in NY.
Donors: Timston Corp.; Gerel Corp.; Ruradan Corp.; Daniel Elyachar; Jonathan Elyachar.
Financial data (yr. ended 12/31/11): Assets, $1,475,271 (M); expenditures, $113,396; qualifying distributions, $97,660; giving activities include $97,660 for grants.
Purpose and activities: The foundation supports general charitable giving.
Fields of interest: General charitable giving.
Type of support: General/operating support.
Geographic limitations: Giving primarily in New York, NY.
Application information: Applications not accepted. Unsolicited requests for funds not accepted.
Officers: Jonathan Elyachar, Pres.; Richard Katz, V.P.
EIN: 136161372

3288
Rusco Fixture Co., Inc.

209 S. Main St.
Oakboro, NC 28129-7718 (704) 485-3339

Company URL: http://ruscofixtures.com
Establishment information: Established in 1976.
Company type: Private company
Business activities: Manufactures store display fixtures.
Business type (SIC): Fixtures/office and store
Corporate officer: Don Russell, Pres.
Giving statement: Giving through the Christian Mission Foundation.

Christian Mission Foundation

P.O. Box 153
Oakboro, NC 28129-0153

Establishment information: Established in 2000.
Donors: Rusco Fixture Co., Inc.; Don Russell.
Financial data (yr. ended 07/31/12): Assets, $514,797 (M); gifts received, $5,500; expenditures, $110,191; qualifying distributions, $103,408; giving activities include $103,408 for grants.
Purpose and activities: The foundation supports organizations involved with reproductive health, international relief, and Christianity.
Fields of interest: Human services; Religion.
Type of support: General/operating support; Grants to individuals.
Application information: Applications not accepted. Unsolicited requests for funds not accepted.
Officers: Don M. Russell, Pres.; Virginia W. Russell, Secy.-Treas.
EIN: 562229925

3289
Russell Investments
1301 2nd Ave., 18th Fl.
Seattle, WA 98101 (206) 505-7877

Company URL: http://www.russell.com
Establishment information: Established in 1936.
Company type: Subsidiary of a mutual company
Business activities: Operates investment firm.
Business type (SIC): Security and commodity services
Corporate officers: Andrew S. Doman, Pres. and C.E.O.; Matt Moss, C.F.O.; Michael Thomas, C.I.O.; George F. Russell, Jr., Chair. Emeritus
Board of director: George F. Russell, Jr.
Offices: San Diego, CA; Tampa, FL; Chicago, IL; New York, NY; Milwaukee, WI
Giving statement: Giving through the Russell Investments Corporate Giving Program.

Russell Investments Corporate Giving Program
c/o Government & Community Relations
1301 Second Ave., 18th Fl.
Seattle, WA 98101-3814 (206) 505-4786
E-mail: communityrelations@russell.com;
URL: http://www.russell.com/US/about_russell/Community/Community_Involvement.asp

Financial data (yr. ended 12/31/08): Total giving, $4,000,000, including $4,000,000 for grants.
Purpose and activities: Russell Investments makes charitable contributions to nonprofit organizations involved with children and improving financial literacy. Special emphasis is directed toward programs that target at-risk children. Support is given primarily in areas of company operations.
Fields of interest: Arts; Education; Human services, financial counseling; Community/economic development Children.
Type of support: Employee matching gifts; Employee volunteer services; General/operating support.

3290
Rutan & Tucker, LLP
611 Anton Blvd., Ste. 1400
Costa Mesa, CA 92626-1931
(714) 641-5100

Company URL: http://www.rutan.com/
Company type: Private company
Business type (SIC): Legal services
Offices: Costa Mesa, Palo Alto, CA
Giving statement: Giving through the Rutan & Tucker, LLP Pro Bono Program.

Rutan & Tucker, LLP Pro Bono Program
611 Anton Blvd., Ste. 1400
Costa Mesa, CA 92626-1931 (714) 641-5100
E-mail: pkohn@rutan.com; URL: http://www.rutan.com/community/

Contact: Philip D. Kohn, Pro Bono Coord.
Fields of interest: Legal services.
Type of support: Pro bono services - legal.
Application information: A Pro Bono Coordinator manages the pro bono program.

3291
Rydell Chevrolet Oldsmobile Cadillac
2700 S. Washington St.
Grand Forks, ND 58201-6720
(701) 772-7211

Company URL: http://www.rydellchev.com
Establishment information: Established in 1954.
Company type: Private company
Business activities: Operates car dealership.
Business type (SIC): Motor vehicles—retail
Corporate officers: Randy J. Nehring, Pres.; Duane Gilleland, Treas.
Giving statement: Giving through the Leonard Rydell Foundation.

The Leonard Rydell Foundation
2700 S. Washington St.
P.O. Box 13398
Grand Forks, ND 58208-3398 (701) 795-3200
Application address: Alerus Financial, 401 Demers Ave., Grand Forks, ND 58201, tel.: (701) 795-3200

Establishment information: Established in 2000 in ND.
Donors: Rydell Chevrolet Oldsmobile Cadillac; Ivan Gandrud Chevrolet, Inc.; Gilleland Chevrolet, Inc.; Lunde Lincoln Mercury; Minot Chrysler Center Inc.; Ressler Chevrolet Inc.; Saturn of St. Paul, Inc.; Sioux Falls Ford, Inc.; Rydell Chevrolet of Waterloo; Sheboygan Chevy; Laramie GM Auto Center; Wes Rydell; Dennis Lunde; Ivan Gandrud; Randy Nehring; Jim Rydell; Team Chevrolet; Team Chevrolet-Toyota Match; Ressler Motor Co.; Norfolk Motor Co.; Owatonna Ford Chrysler; Apple Ford Shakopee.
Contact: Mark Hall
Financial data (yr. ended 12/31/12): Assets, $744,517 (M); gifts received, $80,000; expenditures, $30,802; qualifying distributions, $28,524; giving activities include $26,175 for 15 grants (high: $2,000; low: $268).
Purpose and activities: The foundation supports organizations involved with higher education.
Fields of interest: Education.
Type of support: Scholarship funds.
Geographic limitations: Giving primarily in IA, MN, SD, WI, and WY.
Application information: Applications accepted. Application form required.
Initial approach: Proposal
Deadline(s): July
Officers and Directors:* Wes Rydell*, Pres.; Dennis Lunde*, V.P.; Randy Nehring*, Secy.; Ivan Gandrud*, Treas.; Connie Mondry; Jim Rydell.
EIN: 450459133

3292
Ryder System, Inc.
11690 N.W. 105th St.
Miami, FL 33178-1103 (305) 500-3726
FAX: (305) 593-4731

Company URL: http://www.ryder.com
Establishment information: Established in 1933.
Company type: Public company
Company ticker symbol and exchange: R/NYSE
International Securities Identification Number: US7835491082
Business activities: Provides truck leasing and rental services; transports cars and trucks.
Business type (SIC): Motor vehicle rentals and leasing; trucking and courier services, except by air; transportation services/miscellaneous; motor vehicle repair shops
Financial profile for 2012: Number of employees, 27,700; assets, $8,318,980,000; sales volume, $6,256,970,000; pre-tax net income, $303,120,000; expenses, $5,953,850,000; liabilities, $6,851,490,000
Fortune 1000 ranking: 2012—404th in revenues, 564th in profits, and 445th in assets
Corporate officers: Robert E. Sanchez, Chair., Pres., and C.E.O.; Art A. Garcia, Exec. V.P. and C.F.O.; Gregory F. Greene, Exec. V.P. and C.A.O.; Robert D. Fatovic, Exec. V.P. and Corp. Secy.
Board of directors: Robert E. Sanchez, Chair.; James S. Beard; John M. Berra; Robert J. Eck; L. Patrick Hassey; Michael F. Hilton; Tamara L. Lundgren; Luis P. Nieto, Jr.; Eugene A. Renna; Abbie J. Smith; E. Follin Smith; Hansel E. Tookes II
Subsidiary: Ryder Automotive Carrier, Bloomfield Hills, MI
International operations: Argentina; Australia; Bermuda; Brazil; British Virgin Islands; Canada; China; Germany; Hong Kong; Hungary; Italy; Mauritius; Mexico; Netherlands; Poland; Singapore; United Kingdom
Giving statement: Giving through the Ryder System Charitable Foundation, Inc.
Company EIN: 590739250

The Ryder System Charitable Foundation, Inc.
11690 N.W. 105th St.
Miami, FL 33178-1103 (305) 500-3031
FAX: (305) 500-4579;
E-mail: foundation@ryder.com; URL: http://www.ryder.com/aboutus_cinfo_arc.shtml

Establishment information: Established in 1984 in FL.
Donor: Ryder System, Inc.
Financial data (yr. ended 12/31/11): Assets, $168,828 (M); gifts received, $479,726; expenditures, $1,123,519; qualifying distributions, $1,123,519; giving activities include $1,090,662 for 122 grants (high: $125,000; low: $50) and $32,857 for 51 grants to individuals (high: $2,507; low: $100).
Purpose and activities: The foundation supports organizations involved with arts and culture, education, health, disaster relief, human services, community development, and civic affairs.
Fields of interest: Performing arts; Arts; Higher education; Education; Hospitals (general); Health care; Disasters, preparedness/services; Boy scouts; American Red Cross; Salvation Army; Human services; Community/economic development; United Ways and Federated Giving Programs; Public affairs.
Type of support: Annual campaigns; Building/renovation; Capital campaigns; Employee matching gifts; Employee volunteer services; Employee-related scholarships; General/operating support; Grants to individuals; In-kind gifts; Scholarship funds; Sponsorships.
Geographic limitations: Giving primarily in areas of company operations in Los Angeles, CA, southern FL, Atlanta, GA, St. Louis, MO, Cincinnati, OH, and Dallas, TX.
Publications: Application guidelines; Corporate giving report.
Application information: Applications accepted. Application form not required. Applicants should submit the following:
1) copy of IRS Determination Letter
2) brief history of organization and description of its mission
3) copy of most recent annual report/audited financial statement/990

4) explanation of why grantmaker is considered an appropriate donor for project
5) listing of board of directors, trustees, officers and other key people and their affiliations
6) detailed description of project and amount of funding requested

Initial approach: Proposal
Copies of proposal: 1
Board meeting date(s): Annually and as needed
Deadline(s): None
Final notification: Within 60 days

Officers and Directors:* Gregory T. Swienton*, Chair. and Pres.; Robert D. Fatovic*, V.P. and Secy.; W. Daniel Susik, V.P. and Treas.; Robert E. Sanchez*, V.P.; Robert S. Brunn, C.A.O. and Exec. Dir.
Number of staff: 1 full-time professional; 1 full-time support.
EIN: 592462315
Selected grants: The following grants are a representative sample of this grantmaker's funding activity:
$10,000 to American Heart Association, Dallas, TX, 2010.
$10,000 to Cystic Fibrosis Foundation, Bethesda, MD, 2010.
$10,000 to University of Miami, Coral Gables, FL, 2010.
$5,000 to American Heart Association, Dallas, TX, 2010.
$5,000 to Big Brothers Big Sisters of America, Philadelphia, PA, 2010.
$5,000 to Boston College, Chestnut Hill, MA, 2010.
$4,000 to Inroads, Saint Louis, MO, 2010.
$3,000 to Muscular Dystrophy Association, Tucson, AZ, 2010.
$2,500 to Teach for America, New York, NY, 2010.
$1,100 to Michigan State University, East Lansing, MI, 2010.

3293
Ryerson Inc.

(formerly Ryerson Tull, Inc.)
2621 W. 15th Pl.
Chicago, IL 60608-1712 (773) 762-2121

Company URL: http://www.ryerson.com
Establishment information: Established in 1842.
Company type: Subsidiary of a private company
Business activities: Sells steel wholesale.
Business type (SIC): Metals and minerals, except petroleum—wholesale
Financial profile for 2010: Number of employees, 4,200; sales volume, $3,900,000,000
Corporate officers: Michael C. Arnold, Co-Pres. and C.E.O.; Tom Ziech, C.O.O.; Edward J. Lehner, Exec. V.P. and C.F.O.; Roger W. Lindsay, Sr. V.P., Human Resources; Erich Schnaufer, C.A.O.; M. Louise Turilli, V.P. and Genl. Counsel
International operations: China; India; Mexico
Giving statement: Giving through the Ryerson Foundation.
Company EIN: 363425828

Ryerson Foundation

(formerly Ryerson Tull Foundation)
227 W. Monroe St., 27th Fl.
Chicago, IL 60606
Application address: Ryerson Scholarship Prog., P.O. Box 432, Lansing, IL 60438-0432

Establishment information: Incorporated in 1945 in IL as the Inland Steel Foundation, Inc.
Donors: Ryerson Tull, Inc.; Ryerson Inc.
Contact: Suzan Perry
Financial data (yr. ended 12/31/11): Assets, $17,504 (M); gifts received, $70,000; expenditures, $83,364; qualifying distributions, $83,364; giving activities include $65,000 for 31 grants (high: $5,000; low: $1,000).
Purpose and activities: The foundation awards college scholarships to children of employees of Ryerson Inc.
Fields of interest: Higher education.
Type of support: Employee-related scholarships.
Geographic limitations: Giving limited to areas of company operations, with emphasis on Chicago, IL, and northwest IN.
Application information: Applications not accepted. Contributes only through employee-related scholarships.

Board meeting date(s): Dec.

Officers: Michael C Arnold, Pres. and C.E.O.; Mary Ann Sigler, V.P.; Stephen T. Zollo, V.P.; Eva M. Kalawaski, Secy.; William S. Johnson, C.F.O.; Terence R. Rogers, C.F.O.; Robert J. Joubran, Treas.
Number of staff: 1 part-time professional; 1 part-time support.
EIN: 366046944

3294
Ryman Hospitality Properties, Inc.

(formerly Gaylord Entertainment Company)
1 Gaylord Dr.
Nashville, TN 37214 (615) 316-6000
FAX: (302) 636-5454

Company URL: http://rymanhp.com/
Establishment information: Established in 1925.
Company type: Public company
Company ticker symbol and exchange: GET/NYSE
Business activities: Operates, hotels, resorts, and entertainment attractions.
Business type (SIC): Hotels and motels
Financial profile for 2012: Number of employees, 646; assets, $2,543,140,000; sales volume, $986,590,000; pre-tax net income, -$28,670,000; expenses, $991,350,000; liabilities, $1,689,540,000
Corporate officers: Colin V. Reed, Chair., Pres., and C.E.O.; Mark Fioravanti, Exec. V.P. and C.F.O.; Scott Lynn, Sr. V.P., Genl. Counsel, and Corp. Secy.; Jennifer Hutcheson, Sr. V.P. and Corp. Cont.
Board of directors: Colin V. Reed, Chair.; Michael J. Bender; Edward K. Gaylord II; D. Ralph Horn; Ellen R. Levine; Robert S. Prather, Jr.; Michael D. Rose; Michael I. Roth
Giving statement: Giving through the Gaylord Entertainment Foundation.
Company EIN: 730383730

Gaylord Entertainment Foundation

One Gaylord Dr.
Nashville, TN 37214-1207 (615) 316-6000

Establishment information: Established in 2005 in TN.
Donor: Gaylord Entertainment Co.
Contact: Jacque Layfield
Financial data (yr. ended 12/31/11): Assets, $126,879 (M); gifts received, $507,500; expenditures, $453,405; qualifying distributions, $453,205; giving activities include $453,205 for grants.
Purpose and activities: The foundation supports organizations involved with arts and culture, education, and youth.
Fields of interest: Arts education; Performing arts; Historic preservation/historical societies; Arts; Elementary/secondary education; Higher education; Education; Children/youth, services Youth; Economically disadvantaged.
Type of support: Annual campaigns; General/operating support; Program development.
Geographic limitations: Giving primarily in areas of company operations in TN.
Support limitations: No support for religious, political, veterans', fraternal, labor, lobbying, civic, social, or fraternal organizations. No grants to individuals, or for trusts or endowments.
Application information: Applications accepted. Requests for multi-year commitments are not accepted. Contact hotels directly for in-kind donations. Application form not required. Applicants should submit the following:
1) population served
2) name, address and phone number of organization
3) copy of IRS Determination Letter
4) brief history of organization and description of its mission
5) listing of board of directors, trustees, officers and other key people and their affiliations
6) detailed description of project and amount of funding requested
7) contact person

Initial approach: Proposal
Copies of proposal: 1
Board meeting date(s): Monthly
Deadline(s): None
Final notification: 30 days

Officers: Colin V. Reed, Chair.; David C. Kloeppel, Pres.; Carter R. Todd, Secy.; Rod Connor, Treas.
EIN: 202573370
Selected grants: The following grants are a representative sample of this grantmaker's funding activity:
$10,000 to National Wild Turkey Federation, Edgefield, SC, 2010.
$5,000 to Leukemia & Lymphoma Society, White Plains, NY, 2010.
$2,000 to University of Tennessee, Knoxville, TN, 2010.
$1,000 to Princeton University, Princeton, NJ, 2010.

3295
S & H Builders, Inc.

207 1st St., Apt. 416
Lakewood, NJ 08701-3368 (732) 364-4458

Establishment information: Established in 1984.
Company type: Private company
Business activities: Provides residential general contract construction services.
Business type (SIC): Contractors/general residential building
Corporate officer: Shalom Bauman, Pres.
Giving statement: Giving through the Keren Simcha Foundation.

Keren Simcha Foundation

207 1st St., Ste. 416
Lakewood, NJ 08701-1971 (732) 364-4458
Application address: 115 10th St., Lakewood, NJ 08701

Establishment information: Established in 2004 in NJ.
Donor: S & H Builders, Inc.
Contact: Shalom Bauman, Tr.
Financial data (yr. ended 12/31/11): Assets, $14,072 (M); gifts received, $10,000;

expenditures, $5,370; qualifying distributions, $3,670; giving activities include $3,670 for grants.
Purpose and activities: The foundation supports organizations involved with education and Judaism.
Fields of interest: Arts; Education; Religion.
Type of support: General/operating support; Scholarship funds.
Geographic limitations: Giving primarily in Lakewood, NJ.
Application information: Applications accepted. Application form not required. Applicants should submit the following:
1) detailed description of project and amount of funding requested
Initial approach: Proposal
Deadline(s): None
Trustees: Henna Bauman; Shalom Bauman.
EIN: 202094448

3296
S & S Worldwide, Inc.

75 Mill St.
P.O. Box 513
Colchester, CT 06415-1263
(860) 537-3451

Company URL: http://www.ssww.com
Establishment information: Established in 1906.
Company type: Private company
Business activities: Manufactures craft kits, physical therapy products, physical education products, early learning materials, and games; provides catalog shopping services.
Business type (SIC): Games, toys, and sporting and athletic goods; non-durable goods—wholesale; nonstore retailers
Corporate officers: Stephen L. Schwartz, Chair. and C.E.O.; Adam Schwartz, Co-Pres.; Hy Schwartz, Co-Pres.; Vincent Pescosolido, C.F.O.
Board of director: Stephen L. Schwartz, Chair.
Giving statement: Giving through the Carla and Stephen Schwartz Family Foundation Inc.

The Carla and Stephen Schwartz Family Foundation Inc.

75 Mill St.
Colchester, CT 06415

Establishment information: Established in 1991 in CT.
Donor: S&S Worldwide, Inc.
Financial data (yr. ended 12/31/11): Assets, $522,272 (M); gifts received, $25,000; expenditures, $43,672; qualifying distributions, $41,500; giving activities include $41,500 for grants.
Purpose and activities: The foundation supports museums and organizations involved with health, HIV/AIDS, school athletics, and human services.
Fields of interest: Museums (art); Health care; AIDS; Athletics/sports, school programs; Human services; Jewish federated giving programs AIDS, people with.
Geographic limitations: Giving primarily in CT.
Support limitations: No grants to individuals.
Application information: Applications not accepted. Unsolicited requests for funds not accepted.
Officers: Carla R. Schwartz, Pres.; Stephen L. Schwartz, Secy.
Directors: Adam Schwartz; Hy Schwartz.
EIN: 223148993

3297
S & T Bancorp, Inc.

800 Philadelphia St.
P.O. Box 90
Indiana, PA 15701 (800) 325-2265
FAX: (724) 465-6874

Company URL: http://www.stbank.com
Establishment information: Established in 1902.
Company type: Public company
Company ticker symbol and exchange: STBA/NASDAQ
Business activities: Operates bank holding company; operates commercial bank.
Business type (SIC): Banks/commercial; holding company
Financial profile for 2012: Number of employees, 1,027; assets, $4,526,700,000; pre-tax net income, $41,460,000; liabilities, $3,989,280,000
Corporate officers: James C. Miller, Chair.; Charles G. Urtin, Vice-Chair.; Todd D. Brice, Pres. and C.E.O.; David P. Ruddock, Sr. Exec. V.P. and C.O.O.; Mark Kochvar, Sr. Exec. V.P. and C.F.O.
Board of directors: James C. Miller, Chair.; Charles G. Urtin, Vice-Chair.; John N. Brenzia; Todd D. Brice; John J. Delaney; Michael J. Donnelly; William J. Gatti; Ruth M. Grant; Jeffrey D. Grube; Frank W. Jones; Joseph A. Kirk; David L. Krieger; Fred J. Morelli, Jr.; Alan Papernick; Charles A. Spadafora; Christine J. Toretti
Subsidiary: S&T Bank, Ford City, PA
Giving statement: Giving through the S & T Bancorp Charitable Foundation.
Company EIN: 251434426

S & T Bancorp Charitable Foundation

c/o S&T Bank, Trust Dept.
P.O. Box 220
Indiana, PA 15701-0220
Application address: P.O. Box 190, Indiana, PA 15701, tel.: (724) 465-1443

Establishment information: Established in 1993 in PA.
Donors: S&T Bancorp, Inc.; S&T Bank.
Contact: Todd D. Brice, Pres.
Financial data (yr. ended 12/31/11): Assets, $73,153 (M); gifts received, $375,000; expenditures, $414,452; qualifying distributions, $413,654; giving activities include $413,654 for grants.
Purpose and activities: The foundation supports organizations involved with arts and culture, education, health, athletics, human services, community development, and economically disadvantaged people.
Fields of interest: Arts; Elementary/secondary education; Higher education; Education; Hospitals (general); Health care, clinics/centers; Health care; Athletics/sports, amateur leagues; Athletics/sports, baseball; Boy scouts; American Red Cross; YM/YWCAs & YM/YWHAs; Children/youth, services; Human services; Community/economic development; United Ways and Federated Giving Programs Economically disadvantaged.
Type of support: Annual campaigns; Building/renovation; Capital campaigns; General/operating support; Program development; Scholarship funds; Sponsorships.
Geographic limitations: Giving limited to areas of company operations in Indiana, PA.
Support limitations: No grants to individuals.
Application information: Applications accepted. Application form not required. Applicants should submit the following:
1) detailed description of project and amount of funding requested
Initial approach: Proposal
Deadline(s): None
Officers: Todd D. Brice, Pres.; Edward C. Hauck, V.P.; G. Robert Jorgenson, Treas.
Trustee: S&T Bank.
EIN: 251716950
Selected grants: The following grants are a representative sample of this grantmaker's funding activity:
$39,000 to United Way of Indiana County, Indiana, PA, 2011. For annual campaign.
$20,000 to American Heart Association, Greensburg, PA, 2011.
$20,000 to Clarion University Foundation, Clarion, PA, 2011. For capital campaign.
$17,500 to Kiskiminetas Springs School, Saltsburg, PA, 2011.
$10,000 to Historic Brookville, Brookville, PA, 2011. For capital campaign.
$6,500 to YMCA of Indiana County, Indiana, PA, 2011. For general fund.
$6,000 to United Way of Westmoreland County, Greensburg, PA, 2011. For annual campaign.
$5,000 to Foundation for Indiana University of Pennsylvania, Indiana, PA, 2011.
$5,000 to Indiana Healthcare Foundation, Indiana, PA, 2011.
$2,500 to Economic Growth Connection of Westmoreland, Greensburg, PA, 2011. For general fund.

3298
S.B.E. & S. Clients' Consolidated

2191 Defense Hwy., Ste. 316
Crofton, MD 21114-2456

Company type: Private company
Business activities: Provides legal services.
Business type (SIC): Legal services
Giving statement: Giving through the S.B.E. & S. Clients' Consolidated Charitable Foundation.

S.B.E. & S. Clients' Consolidated Charitable Foundation

2191 Defense Hwy., Ste. 316
Crofton, MD 21114-2456

Establishment information: Established in 1984 in DC.
Donors: S.B.E. & S. Clients' Consolidated; Elizabeth M. Voight†; Paul J. Rohrich†; Hester M. Digges†.
Contact: Thomas J. Egan, Pres.
Financial data (yr. ended 09/30/11): Assets, $3,319,502 (M); expenditures, $148,988; qualifying distributions, $97,061; giving activities include $97,000 for 5 grants (high: $47,000; low: $2,500).
Purpose and activities: The foundation supports bar associations and organizations involved with secondary education, cancer, multiple sclerosis, and disability services.
Fields of interest: Secondary school/education; Cancer; Multiple sclerosis; Legal services; Developmentally disabled, centers & services; Catholic agencies & churches.
Type of support: General/operating support.
Geographic limitations: Giving limited to the greater Washington, DC, area and MD.
Support limitations: No grants to individuals.
Publications: Annual report.
Application information: Applications accepted. Application form not required.

Initial approach: Proposal
Deadline(s): None
Officers and Directors: Thomas J. Egan, Pres.; Thomas J. Egan, Jr., V.P.; Sharon E. Katula, Secy.-Treas.
Directors: Herbert N. Harmon; Maurice J. Montaldo; Walter J. Murphy, Jr.; J. Jude O'Donnell.
EIN: 521306077
Selected grants: The following grants are a representative sample of this grantmaker's funding activity:
$100,000 to Gonzaga College High School, Washington, DC, 2010.
$5,000 to SEEC, Silver Spring, MD, 2010.
$2,500 to Gonzaga College High School, Washington, DC, 2010.

3299
S.J. Electro Systems, Inc.

(also known as SJE-Rhombus Controls)
22650 County Hwy. 6
P.O. Box 1708
Detroit Lakes, MN 56502 (218) 847-1317

Company URL: http://www.sjerhombus.com
Establishment information: Established in 1975.
Company type: Private company
Business activities: Manufactures liquid level controls and motor control panels.
Business type (SIC): Laboratory apparatus; electrical industrial apparatus
Corporate officers: Dave Thomas, C.E.O.; Nathan L. Fetting, C.F.O.
Division: Rhombus Technology Div., Detroit Lakes, MN
Giving statement: Giving through the SJE-Rhombus Controls Corporate Giving Program and the SJE-Rhombus Foundation.

SJE-Rhombus Foundation

(also known as S. J. Electro Systems Foundation)
P.O. Box 1708
Detroit Lakes, MN 56501
URL: http://www.sjerhombus.com/community-involvement.php

Establishment information: Established in 1987 in MN.
Donors: S.J. Electro Systems, Inc.; Stephen P. Johnston.
Financial data (yr. ended 12/31/11): Assets, $699,063 (M); gifts received, $47,963; expenditures, $46,578; qualifying distributions, $39,250; giving activities include $39,250 for grants.
Purpose and activities: The foundation supports programs designed to improve quality of life in the Detroit Lakes and surrounding communities through education, personal growth, community development, and health improvement.
Fields of interest: Higher education; Education; Health care; Heart & circulatory diseases; Boys & girls clubs; Human services; Community/economic development; United Ways and Federated Giving Programs; Psychology/behavioral science.
Program:
Employee-related Scholarships: The foundation awards college scholarships to children of employees of SJE-Rhombus. The program is administered by Scholarship America.
Type of support: Building/renovation; Employee-related scholarships; General/operating support; Program development.
Geographic limitations: Giving primarily in MN, with emphasis on Detroit Lakes.
Publications: Application guidelines.
Application information: Applications accepted. Organizations receiving support are asked to submit progress reports and a final report. Application form required. Applicants should submit the following:
1) how project will be sustained once grantmaker support is completed
2) signature and title of chief executive officer
3) results expected from proposed grant
4) qualifications of key personnel
5) name, address and phone number of organization
6) copy of IRS Determination Letter
7) brief history of organization and description of its mission
8) copy of most recent annual report/audited financial statement/990
9) how project's results will be evaluated or measured
10) listing of board of directors, trustees, officers and other key people and their affiliations
11) detailed description of project and amount of funding requested
12) copy of current year's organizational budget and/or project budget
13) listing of additional sources and amount of support
Initial approach: Proposal
Copies of proposal: 2
Board meeting date(s): Feb., May, Aug., and Nov.
Deadline(s): 2 weeks prior to board meetings
Final notification: 2 weeks following board meetings
Officers: Melissa Lage, Pres.; Laurie Lewandowski, V.P.; Jim Lockrem, Secy.; Nathan L. Fetting, Treas.
EIN: 363556774

3300
SABEResPODER

1849 Sawtelle Blvd., Ste. 630
Los Angeles, CA 90025 (310) 826-3900
FAX: (310) 388-1050

Company URL: http://www.saberespoder.com
Establishment information: Established in 1999.
Company type: Private company
Business type (SIC): Business services/miscellaneous
Corporate officers: Raul Lomeli-Azoubel, Chair.; Amir Hammet, Pres. and C.E.O.
Board of directors: Raul Lomeli-Azoubel, Chair.; Amir Hemmat, Pres. and C.E.O.
Giving statement: Giving through the SABEResPODER Corporate Giving Program.

SABEResPODER Corporate Giving Program

2036 Armacost Ave., 1st Floor
Los Angeles, CA 90025-6113 (310) 826-3900
E-mail: info@saberespoder.com; URL: http://www.saberespoder.com

Purpose and activities: SABEResPODER is a certified B Corporation that donates a percentage of profits to charitable organizations.

3301
Sachs Holdings, Inc.

400 Chesterfield Ctr., Ste. 600
Chesterfield, MO 63017 (636) 537-1000

Company URL: http://www.sachsproperties.com/index.asp
Establishment information: Established in 1950.
Company type: Private company
Business activities: Develops real estate; operates nonresidential buildings.
Business type (SIC): Real estate subdividers and developers; real estate operators and lessors
Financial profile for 2010: Number of employees, 25
Corporate officers: Stephen C. Sachs, Pres.; Ami E. Kutz, C.F.O.
Giving statement: Giving through the Sachs Fund.

Sachs Fund

400 Chesterfield Ctr., Ste. 600
Chesterfield, MO 63017-4890

Establishment information: Established in 1957 in MO.
Donors: Samuel C. Sachs; Sachs Electric Corp.; Sachs Holdings, Inc.; Mary Sachs.
Financial data (yr. ended 04/30/12): Assets, $338,331 (M); gifts received, $1,000,000; expenditures, $1,037,349; qualifying distributions, $1,027,500; giving activities include $1,027,500 for grants.
Purpose and activities: The fund supports hospitals and organizations involved with arts and culture, Parkinson's disease, and Judaism.
Fields of interest: Arts; Hospitals (general); Parkinson's disease; United Ways and Federated Giving Programs; Jewish agencies & synagogues.
Type of support: General/operating support.
Geographic limitations: Giving primarily in MO and NY.
Support limitations: No grants to individuals.
Application information: Applications not accepted. Contributes only to pre-selected organizations.
Trustees: Louis S. Sachs; Mary L. Sachs; Susan E. Sachs.
EIN: 436032385
Selected grants: The following grants are a representative sample of this grantmaker's funding activity:
$14,052 to American Parkinson Disease Association, Staten Island, NY, 2010. For general funding.
$1,000 to United Fund of Talbot County, Easton, MD, 2010. For general funding.

3302
Saco & Biddeford Savings Institution

50 Industrial Park Rd.
Saco, ME 04072-1840 (207) 284-4591

Company URL: http://www.sbsavings.com
Establishment information: Established in 1827.
Company type: Private company
Business activities: Operates savings bank.
Business type (SIC): Savings institutions
Corporate officers: David H. Howe, Chair.; Kevin P. Savage, Pres. and C.E.O.; Robert C. Quinten, V.P. and Treas.
Board of directors: David H. Howe, Chair.; Roland M. Eon; Joan R. Fink; Mark L. Peterson; Kevin P. Savage; Robert F. Wade

Offices: Old Orchard Beach, Scarborough, South Portland, MN
Giving statement: Giving through the Saco & Biddeford Savings Charitable Foundation.

Saco & Biddeford Savings Charitable Foundation

252 Main St.
Saco, ME 04072-1511 (207) 284-4591

Establishment information: Established in 1998 in ME.
Donor: Saco & Biddeford Savings Bank.
Contact: Robert C. Quentin, Secy.-Treas.
Financial data (yr. ended 12/31/11): Assets, $193,690 (M); gifts received, $28,785; expenditures, $96,218; qualifying distributions, $95,650; giving activities include $95,650 for grants.
Purpose and activities: The foundation supports organizations involved with secondary and higher education, health, counseling, domestic violence prevention, human services, and community economic development.
Fields of interest: Arts; Education; Agriculture/food.
Program:
Dollars for Doers: The foundation awards grants to nonprofit organizations with which employees of Saco & Biddeford Savings volunteer, $10 per volunteer hour, up to $200 a year.
Type of support: Employee volunteer services; General/operating support; Sponsorships.
Geographic limitations: Giving primarily in areas of company operations in Saco, ME.
Support limitations: No grants to individuals.
Application information: Applications accepted. Application form required. Applicants should submit the following:
1) population served
2) copy of IRS Determination Letter
3) geographic area to be served
4) detailed description of project and amount of funding requested
Initial approach: Proposal
Deadline(s): None
Directors: Roger S. Elliott; Roland M. Eon; Joan R. Fink; David H. Howe; A. William Kany, Jr.; Mark L. Peterson; Robert F. Wade.
Officers: Kevin P. Savage, Pres.; Robert C. Quentin, Secy.-Treas.
EIN: 010516587

3303
Sacramento Kings, LP

1 Sports Pkwy.
Sacramento, CA 95834-2300
(916) 928-6900

Company URL: http://www.nba.com/kings
Establishment information: Established in 1945.
Company type: Private company
Business activities: Operates professional basketball club.
Business type (SIC): Commercial sports
Corporate officers: John Thomas, Pres.; John Rinehart, Exec. V.P., Opers.; Ruth Hill, V.P., Finance; Jeff David, Sr. V.P. Sales and Mktg.; Donna Ruiz, V.P., Human Resources
Giving statement: Giving through the Sacramento Kings, L.P. Corporate Giving Program and the Sacramento Kings Foundation.

Sacramento Kings, L.P. Corporate Giving Program

Power Balance Pavillion
1 Sports Pkwy.
Sacramento, CA 95834-2300 (916) 928-0000
FAX: (916) 928-0727; URL: http://www.nba.com/kings/community/index.html

Purpose and activities: As a complement to its foundation, the Sacramento Kings also makes charitable contributions of memorabilia to nonprofit organizations directly. Support is given primarily in the Sacramento, California, area.
Fields of interest: Elementary school/education; Student services/organizations; Education, e-learning; Education; Optometry/vision screening; Health care; Recreation, camps; Athletics/sports, basketball.
Type of support: Cause-related marketing; Donated products; Employee volunteer services; In-kind gifts.
Geographic limitations: Giving primarily in the Sacramento, CA, area.

Sacramento Kings Foundation

(formerly The Maloofs & You! Foundation)
1 Sports Pkwy.
Sacramento, CA 95834-2300
URL: http://www.nba.com/kings/community/sacramento-kings-foundation

Establishment information: Established in 1998 in CA.
Donors: Argyle Productions, Inc.; Vlade Divac; Ticketmaster LLC; E&J GALLO Winery; Gawen D. Wells.
Financial data (yr. ended 12/31/11): Assets, $42,161 (M); gifts received, $4,510; expenditures, $26,062; qualifying distributions, $25,164; giving activities include $25,164 for grants.
Purpose and activities: The foundation supports libraries and organizations involved with sports, human services, international relief, and Catholicism.
Fields of interest: Human services.
Type of support: General/operating support.
Geographic limitations: Giving limited to CA.
Application information: Applications not accepted. Unsolicited requests for funds not accepted.
Officers: Matina Kolokotronis, Pres.; Mitch German, Secy.; John Rinehart, Treas.
EIN: 680249718

3304
Sacramento River Cats Baseball Club, LLC

400 Ballpark Dr.
West Sacramento, CA 95691-2824
(916) 376-4700

Company URL: http://www.milb.com/index.jsp?sid=t105
Establishment information: Established in 1999.
Company type: Private company
Business activities: Operates professional baseball club.
Business type (SIC): Amusement and recreation services/miscellaneous
Corporate officers: Alan Ledford, Pres. and C.O.O.; Tom Glick, Sr. V.P., Sales and Mktg.; Dan Vistica, V.P., Finance and Admin.; Matthew LaRose, V.P., Opers.; Bryan Srabian, V.P., Mktg.
Giving statement: Giving through the River Cats Foundation, Inc.

River Cats Foundation, Inc.

400 Ballpark Dr.
West Sacramento, CA 95691-2824 (916) 376-4700
FAX: (916) 376-4710;
E-mail: dvistica@rivercats.com; URL: http://www.rivercats.com/community/foundation/

Establishment information: Established as a company-sponsored foundation in 2000 in CA; status changed to public charity in 2002.
Donors: River City Concessions, LLC; People Reaching Out; Pacific Coast League; Sacramento River Cats Baseball Club, LLC; U.S. Postal Service; Pacific Gas & Electric Co.
Contact: Dan Vistica, Chair.
Financial data (yr. ended 12/31/11): Revenue, $99,016; assets, $170,959 (M); gifts received, $98,885; expenditures, $65,270; giving activities include $63,610 for grants.
Purpose and activities: The foundation supports organizations involved with children, youth, and family activities.
Fields of interest: Children/youth, services; Family services.
Program:
Grants: Grants are available to qualified 501(c)(3) organizations based in the greater Sacramento area that work to provide youth or family activities. Eligible applicants must demonstrate a consistent history of supporting worthy youth and family-based activities in the greater Sacramento are for at least two years prior to the application deadline; applicants must also demonstrate financial stability and support of one or more organizations whose beneficiaries are needy children, youth, or families.
Type of support: Annual campaigns; Program development.
Geographic limitations: Giving limited to the greater Sacramento, CA, area.
Application information: Applications accepted. Organizations receiving support are asked to provide a final report. Application form not required. Applicants should submit the following:
1) timetable for implementation and evaluation of project
2) copy of IRS Determination Letter
3) copy of most recent annual report/audited financial statement/990
4) descriptive literature about organization
5) detailed description of project and amount of funding requested
6) additional materials/documentation
Initial approach: Proposal
Copies of proposal: 2
Board meeting date(s): June
Deadline(s): Mar. 1
Final notification: Late June
Officer and Directors:* Dan Vistica*, Chair.; Grace Bailey; Jennifer Castleberry; John Krivacic; Jess Olivares; Susan Savage; Jeff Savage; Alex Zamansky.
Number of staff: 1 part-time professional.
EIN: 943367617

3305
Saddlehorn, LLC

P.O. Box 1470
Bigfork, MT 59911 (406) 837-6500

Company URL: http://www.saddlehorn.com/
Establishment information: Established in 1945.
Company type: Private company
Business activities: Operates a multi-use housing development company.

Business type (SIC): Real estate operators and lessors
Corporate officer: Doug Averill, Pres.
Giving statement: Giving through the Saddlehorn Community Foundation.

Saddlehorn Community Foundation

P.O. Box 1808
Bigfork, MT 59911-1808 (406) 837-6020

Establishment information: Established in 2007 in MT.
Donor: Saddlehorn, LLC.
Contact: Douglas D. Averill, V.P.
Financial data (yr. ended 12/31/11): Assets, $1,418 (M); expenditures, $463; qualifying distributions, $0.
Purpose and activities: Giving primarily to benefit the community of Bigfork, Montana.
Fields of interest: Community/economic development.
Geographic limitations: Giving limited to Bigfork, MT.
Application information: Applications accepted. Application form not required.
Deadline(s): None
Officers and Directors:* Jim Frizzell*, Pres.; Douglas D. Averill*, V.P.; Joann M. Gould, Secy.-Treas.; Gerald Bygren.
EIN: 208920475

3306
Safeco Insurance Company of America

(formerly Safeco Corporation)
Safeco Plz.
1001 Fourth Ave.
Seattle, WA 98154 (206) 545-5000

Company URL: http://www.safeco.com
Establishment information: Established in 1923.
Company type: Subsidiary of a mutual company
Business activities: Sells automobile and property and casualty insurance.
Business type (SIC): Insurance/fire, marine, and casualty
Financial profile for 2010: Number of employees, 100; sales volume, $4,916,000,000
Corporate officers: Gary R. Gregg, Co-Pres. and C.E.O.; Michael H. Hughes, Co-Pres.; Matthew D. Nickerson, Exec. V.P. and C.O.O.; Kris L. Hill, Sr. V.P., Finance; Michael Joseph Fallon, Treas. and C.F.O.
Offices: Aliso Viejo, CA; Golden, CO; New Britain, CT; Maitland, FL; Duluth, GA; Hoffman Estates, IL; Indianapolis, IN; Sunset Hills, MO; Rochester, NY; Cincinnati, OH; Lake Oswego, OR; Nashville, TN; Plano, TX; Midlothian, VA; Spokane, WA
Giving statement: Giving through the Safeco Corporation Contributions Program and the Safeco Insurance Foundation.
Company EIN: 910742146

Safeco Corporation Contributions Program

Safeco Plz.
1001 Fourth Ave.
Seattle, WA 98154 (206) 545-5000
E-mail: giving@safeco.com; URL: http://www.safeco.com/about-safeco/community

Purpose and activities: As a complement to its foundation, Safeco also makes charitable contributions to nonprofit organizations directly. Support is given on a national basis in areas of company operations.
Fields of interest: Arts; Elementary/secondary education; Education; Safety, education; Safety, automotive safety; Community/economic development Youth; Disabilities, people with.
Programs:
Your Gift Plus: Safeco matches contributions made by its employees to nonprofit organizations on a one-for-one basis up to $500 per employee, per year.
Your Time Plus: Safeco makes charitable contributions to nonprofit organizations with which Safeco employees volunteer at least 25 hours within a 12-month period.
Type of support: Employee volunteer services; General/operating support; Program development; Sponsorships.
Geographic limitations: Giving on a national basis in areas of company operations, with emphasis on Aliso Viejo, CA, Golden, CO, Hartford, CT, Orlando, FL, Atlanta, GA, Chicago, IL, Indianapolis, IN, St. Louis, MO, Rochester, NY, Cincinnati, OH, Portland, OR, Nashville, TN, Dallas, TX, Richmond, VA, and Spokane and the Puget Sound, WA, area.
Support limitations: No support for discriminatory organizations, amateur arts organizations, amateur sports teams, colleges or universities, fraternal or political organizations, hospitals or hospital foundations, individual K-12 schools, national organizations, or religious organizations not of direct benefit to the entire community. No grants to individuals, or for athletic scholarships, capital campaigns, conferences, endowments, film or video production, fundraising or advertising, health education, research, or prevention, debt reduction or emergency needs, research, or theological functions; no loans or investments.
Publications: Application guidelines.
Application information: Applications accepted. Application form required.
Requests for sponsorship support should indicate sponsorship levels and the corresponding benefits.
Initial approach: Complete online application
Committee meeting date(s): Quarterly
Deadline(s): Feb. 1 through Oct. 31 for nominated organizations; 60 days before the date of the event for sponsorships
Final notification: Apr. 30, July 31, and Dec. 1
Administrators: Melissa Brown, Contribs. Specialist; Christopher Wiggins, Contribs. Coord.; Julie Ziegler, Mgr., Contribs.
Number of staff: 4 full-time professional; 1 part-time professional; 1 full-time support.

Safeco Insurance Foundation

1001 4th Ave., Safeco Plaza, Ste. 1800
Seattle, WA 98154-1117 (206) 473-5745
E-mail: Safeco.Foundation@libertymutual.com; URL: http://www.safeco.com/about-safeco/community/foundation

Establishment information: Established in 2006 in WA.
Donors: Safeco Corp.; Safeco Insurance Co.
Contact: Paul Hollie, Fdn. Dir.
Financial data (yr. ended 12/31/11): Assets, $58,038,787 (M); expenditures, $3,228,361; qualifying distributions, $3,100,125; giving activities include $2,694,748 for 138 grants (high: $150,000; low: $5,000) and $405,252 for employee matching gifts.
Purpose and activities: The foundation supports nonprofit organizations involved with arts and culture, hunger, human services, youth, the disabled, economically disadvantaged people, and the homeless. Special emphasis is directed toward programs designed to promote education and health and safety.
Fields of interest: Performing arts; Arts; Elementary school/education; Vocational education; Libraries (public); Education, services; Education, reading; Education; Health care, clinics/centers; Health care; Food services; Safety/disasters; YM/YWCAs & YM/YWHAs; Family services; Developmentally disabled, centers & services; Homeless, human services; Human services; United Ways and Federated Giving Programs Youth; Disabilities, people with; Economically disadvantaged; Homeless.
Programs:
Basic Services Initiative: The foundation supports programs designed to address the immediate capacity of each state's homeless serving-network to meet basic needs of individuals and families. This initiative operates every two years.
Education Initiative: The foundation supports programs designed to improve educational achievements and opportunities for disadvantaged youth and programs designed to build on prior academic successes. Special emphasis is directed toward expanding academic opportunities for low-income and limited English proficient (LEP) students through out-of-school educational programs, extended learning in-school programs, vocational and technical-training, and programs that emphasize the path to further education; elementary programs designed to prevent the "achievement gap" by employing results-based curricula and focusing on basic literacy and/or numeracy; and broadening educational options for LEP students by increasing the number and quality of English language instruction, with a focus on children and adolescents.
Type of support: Capital campaigns; Continuing support; Curriculum development; Employee matching gifts; General/operating support; Program development.
Geographic limitations: Giving primarily in areas of company operations OR and WA.
Support limitations: No support for grantmaking agencies, fraternal, social, labor, or political organizations. No grants to individuals, or for sectarian activities, trips, tours, or transportation, deficit spending or debt liquidation, conferences, forums, or special events.
Publications: Application guidelines; Grants list; Program policy statement.
Application information: Applications accepted. Visit website for Education Initiative and Basic Services Initiative Request for Proposals (RFP) announcement. Support is limited to 1 contribution per organization during any given year. Application form required. Applicants should submit the following:
1) copy of most recent annual report/audited financial statement/990
2) listing of board of directors, trustees, officers and other key people and their affiliations
3) copy of current year's organizational budget and/or project budget
4) listing of additional sources and amount of support
Initial approach: Complete online application
Deadline(s): None
Final notification: 10 weeks
Officers and Directors:* David H. Long*, Chair.; Michael H. Hughes*, Pres.; Dexter K. Legg, V.P. and Secy.; Dennis J. Langwell*, V.P., C.F.O., and Treas.; A. Alexander Fontanes*, V.P. and C.I.O.; Christopher C. Mansfield*, V.P. and Genl. Counsel; Melissa M. MacDonnell, V.P.; Gary J. Ostrow, V.P.
EIN: 204894146

3307
Safeguard Scientifics, Inc.
435 Devon Park Dr., Bldg. 800
Wayne, PA 19087-1945 (610) 293-0600
FAX: (610) 293-0601

Company URL: http://www.safeguard.com
Establishment information: Established in 1953.
Company type: Public company
Company ticker symbol and exchange: SFE/NYSE
Business activities: Operates holding company; develops computer software; provides Internet communications services; provides electronic commerce services.
Business type (SIC): Holding company; security and commodity services; computer services; business services/miscellaneous
Financial profile for 2012: Number of employees, 31; assets, $374,140,000; pre-tax net income, -$39,360,000; expenses, $19,470,000; liabilities, $60,170,000
Corporate officers: Andrew Lietz, Chair.; Stephen T. Zarrilli, Pres. and C.E.O.; Jeffrey B. McGroarty, Sr. V.P. and C.F.O.; Brian J. Sisko, Sr. V.P. and Genl. Counsel; John E. Shave III, V.P., Corp. Comms.; Steven J. Grenfell, C.P.A., V.P., Opers.
Board of directors: Andrew E. Lietz, Chair.; Peter J. Boni; Julie A. Dobson; Keith B. Jarrett; George MacKenzie; George D. McClelland; Jack L. Messman; John J. Roberts; Robert J. Rosenthal, Ph.D.; Stephen T. Zarrilli
Subsidiaries: aligne Inc., Wayne, PA; Arista Knowledge Systems, Inc., Alameda, CA; CompuCom Systems, Inc., Dallas, TX; Sotas, Inc., Gaithersburg, MD; Tangram Enterprise Solutions, Inc., Cary, NC; Technology Leaders Management, Inc., Wayne, PA
Giving statement: Giving through the Safeguard Scientifics Foundation.
Company EIN: 231609753

Safeguard Scientifics Foundation
435 Devon Park Dr., Bldg. 800
Wayne, PA 19087-1945

Establishment information: Established in 1989 in PA.
Donor: Safeguard Scientifics, Inc.
Financial data (yr. ended 12/31/09): Assets, $0 (M); expenditures, $0; qualifying distributions, $0.
Purpose and activities: The foundation supports organizations involved with higher education, animal welfare, breast cancer, and children services.
Fields of interest: Higher education; Animal welfare; Breast cancer; Children, services.
Type of support: Annual campaigns; Continuing support; General/operating support.
Geographic limitations: Giving primarily in CA, PA, TX, and VA.
Support limitations: No grants to individuals.
Application information: Applications not accepted. Unsolicited requests for funds not accepted.
Officers: Steven J. Grenfell, V.P.; Deidre Blackburn, Secy.
EIN: 232571278

3308
Safety Insurance Company
20 Custom House St., Ste. 400
P.O. Box 55089
Boston, MA 02110-3516 (617) 951-0600

Company URL: http://www.safetyinsurance.com
Establishment information: Established in 1979.
Company type: Subsidiary of a public company
Business activities: Provides fire and casualty insurance.
Business type (SIC): Insurance/fire, marine, and casualty
Corporate officers: David F. Brussard, Chair., Pres., and C.E.O.; William J. Bergley, Jr., V.P., C.F.O., and Secy.; Daniel D. Loranger, V.P. and C.I.O.; George M. Murphy, V.P., Mktg.
Board of director: David F. Brussard, Chair.
Giving statement: Giving through the Safety Insurance Charitable Foundation, Inc.

Safety Insurance Charitable Foundation, Inc.
20 Custom House St.
Boston, MA 02110-3513

Establishment information: Established in 2005 in MA.
Donor: Safety Insurance Company, Inc.
Financial data (yr. ended 12/31/11): Assets, $667,065 (M); expenditures, $126,985; qualifying distributions, $112,800; giving activities include $112,800 for grants.
Fields of interest: United Ways and Federated Giving Programs.
Application information: Applications not accepted. Contributes only to pre-selected organizations.
Officers and Directors:* David F. Brussard*, Pres.; Edward N. Patrick, Jr.*, Clerk; William J. Begley, Jr.*, Treas.
EIN: 432091740

3309
Safety-Kleen Systems, Inc.
5360 Legacy Dr., Bldg. 2, Ste. 100
Plano, TX 75024-3132 (972) 265-2000

Company URL: http://www.safety-kleen.com
Establishment information: Established in 1954.
Company type: Subsidiary of a private company
Business activities: Provides industrial equipment cleaning services; provides industrial waste management services; provides oil recycling and re-refining services.
Business type (SIC): Repair shops/miscellaneous; sanitary services
Corporate officers: Ronald W. Haddock, Co-Chair.; Randolph R. Devening, Co-Chair.; Robert M. Craycraft II, Pres. and C.E.O.; Jeffrey O. Richard, Exec. V.P. and C.F.O.; Jean Lee, Sr. V.P., Human Resources
Board of directors: Ronald W. Haddock, Co-Chair.; Randolph R. Devening, Co-Chair.; Robert M. Craycraft II; James Dondero; William Raine; Phillip Raygorodetsky; Joseph Saad
Subsidiaries: Kleen Harbor, Deer Park, TX; Safety-Kleen Envirosystems Co., Elgin, IL; Safety-Kleen Oil Recovery Co., East Chicago, IN
Office: Los Angeles, CA
Giving statement: Giving through the Safety-Kleen Systems, Inc. Corporate Giving Program.

Safety-Kleen Systems, Inc. Corporate Giving Program
(formerly Safety-Kleen Corp. Contributions Program)
5360 Legacy Dr.
Plano, TX 75024-3132 (800) 669-5503

Purpose and activities: Safety-Kleen makes charitable contributions to nonprofit organizations on a case by case basis. Support is given primarily in areas of company operations, with emphasis on Texas.
Fields of interest: Vocational education; Environment; Health organizations Military/veterans.
Type of support: Program development; Sponsorships.
Geographic limitations: Giving primarily in areas of company operations, with emphasis on TX.

3310
Safeway Inc.
5918 Stoneridge Mall Rd.
Pleasanton, CA 94588-3229
(925) 467-3000
FAX: (925) 467-3323

Company URL: http://www.safeway.com
Establishment information: Established in 1915.
Company type: Public company
Company ticker symbol and exchange: SWY/NYSE
International Securities Identification Number: US7865142084
Business activities: Operates grocery stores.
Business type (SIC): Groceries—retail
Financial profile for 2012: Number of employees, 171,000; assets, $14,443,300,000; sales volume, $9,994,000,000; pre-tax net income, $121,400,000; expenses, $9,814,200,000; liabilities, $1,145,280
Fortune 1000 ranking: 2012—62nd in revenues, 294th in profits, and 302nd in assets
Forbes 2000 ranking: 2012—201st in sales, 917th in profits, and 1200th in assets
Corporate officers: Steven A. Burd, Chair. and C.E.O.; Robert L. Edwards, Pres. and C.F.O.; David T. Ching, Sr. V.P. and C.I.O.; Robert A. Gordon, Sr. V.P., Secy., and Genl. Counsel; David F. Bond, Sr. V.P., Finance, and C.A.O.; Russell M. Jackson, Sr. V.P., Human Resources
Board of directors: Steven A. Burd, Chair.; Janet E. Grove; Mohan Gyani; Frank C. Herringer; Kenneth W. Oder; T. Gary Rogers; Arun Sarin; William Y. Tauscher
Subsidiary: The Vons Companies, Inc., Arcadia, CA
Divisions: Denver Div., Englewood, CO; Eastern Div., Lanham, MD; Northern California Div., Pleasanton, CA; Phoenix Div., Tempe, AZ; Portland Div., Clackamas, OR; Seattle Div., Bellevue, WA
International operations: Bermuda; Philippines
Giving statement: Giving through the Safeway Inc. Corporate Giving Program, the Dominick's Foundation, and the Safeway Foundation.
Company EIN: 943019135

Safeway Inc. Corporate Giving Program
5918 Stoneridge Mall Rd.
Pleasanton, CA 94588-3229
URL: http://www.safeway.com/IFL/Grocery/About-CSR

Purpose and activities: As a complement to its foundation, Safeway also makes charitable contributions to nonprofit organizations directly. Support is given primarily in areas of company operations.
Fields of interest: Education; Muscular dystrophy; Autism; Cancer research Disabilities, people with.
Program:
The Art of Dairy: Safeway, in Partnership with Lucerne Foods, support the arts in schools through The Art of Dairy art contest. Using cow imagery as the focal point to promote dairy products as a healthy snack alternative, students in grades 9-12 submit designs based on an annual theme, "Taste

of Moo-sic." After the initial submissions are judged, 30 finalists transfer their designs to a life-sized fiberglass cow. Each school receives a $250 stipend to purchase art supplies their student finalist uses to decorate the cow sculpture. The winning student receives $20,000 for their school's art department, plus $5,000 each for themselves and their art teacher.
Type of support: Cause-related marketing; Employee volunteer services; General/operating support.
Geographic limitations: Giving primarily in areas of company operations.

The Dominick's Foundation

(formerly Dominick's/Omni Foundation)
711 Jorie Blvd., STOP 3900
Oak Brook, IL 60523-4425 (630) 891-5000

Establishment information: Established in 1995 in IL.
Donor: Safeway Co.
Contact: Wynona Redmond, Secy.
Financial data (yr. ended 10/31/09): Revenue, $300,984; assets, $357,509 (M); gifts received, $169,170; expenditures, $248,542; program services expenses, $234,912; giving activities include $234,912 for grants to individuals.
Fields of interest: Arts; Education; Hospitals (specialty); Health organizations, association; Food banks; Human services; YM/YWCAs & YM/YWHAs; Children/youth, services; Women, centers/ services.
Geographic limitations: Giving primarily in IL.
Application information: Applications accepted. Applicants should submit the following:
1) statement of problem project will address
2) population served
3) copy of IRS Determination Letter
4) detailed description of project and amount of funding requested

Initial approach: Letter on organization letterhead
Deadline(s): None

Officers: Don Keprta, Pres.; Brian Baer, V.P. and Treas.; Al Duran, V.P.; Wynona Redmond, Secy.
EIN: 364059130

The Safeway Foundation

5918 Stoneridge Mall Rd.
Pleasanton, CA 94588-3229 (925) 467-3135
E-mail: Christy.Duncan-Anderson@safeway.com; URL: http://www.safewayfoundation.org

Establishment information: Established in 2001 in CA.
Donor: Safeway Inc.
Contact: Christy Duncan Anderson, Exec. Dir.
Financial data (yr. ended 12/31/10): Revenue, $53,412,991; assets, $34,434,947 (M); gifts received, $53,516,413; expenditures, $49,594,088; program services expenses, $47,425,515; giving activities include $47,425,515 for 398 grants (high: $9,827,050; low: $5,000).
Fields of interest: Education; Health care; Agriculture/food; Human services; Community/ economic development.

Programs:

Grants: The Foundation supports nonprofit organization's working in four priority areas: hunger relief; education; health and human services; and assisting people with disabilities. Grant amounts vary for organizations that are national in scope, but a first-time funded organization will typically receive a grant of $10,000 to $25,000. Organizations applying for funding must serve a community where a Safeway store is operating.

Innovative Approaches to Preventing Childhood Obesity Program: This initiative aims to foster collaboration between the medical community and local community-based agencies in geographic areas where Safeway, Vons, Pavilions, Tom Thumb, Randalls, Carrs, and Dominick's have stores or outlets. Grants of up to $100,000 will be awarded to support efforts to expand and enhance services, increase capacity, and/or incorporate new strategies that support healthy body weight among children and/or adolescents; to identify promising approaches that can be replicated, adapted, implemented, and sustained in diverse communities nationwide; and to evaluate the impact of existing programs.
Support limitations: No support for political or religious organizations, advocacy programs, sports teams or athletic competitions, other foundations, for-profit organizations, or granting organizations. No grants to individuals, or for capital or building campaigns, meetings, conferences or workshops, fundraising dinners, galas, or events.
Application information: Applications accepted. Interested organizations are invited to submit a brief letter of introduction to the appropriate operating area if they believe that their mission aligns with the foundation's priority areas of giving. Organizations will be contacted only if the foundation is interested in receiving more information. Application form required. Applicants should submit the following:
1) copy of IRS Determination Letter
2) copy of most recent annual report/audited financial statement/990
3) copy of current year's organizational budget and/ or project budget

Initial approach: Letter of inquiry
Deadline(s): May 15 for Childhood Obesity Program; Open for grants

Officers and Directors:* Larree Renda*, Chair.; David Lee*, Pres.; Mike Minasi*, Pres., Mktg.; Jonathan Mayes*, Sr. V.P.; Kelly Griffith*, Pres., Corp. Merchandising; Brian Dowling*, V.P., Public Affairs.; Christy Duncan Anderson, Exec. Dir.; Bob Bradford.
EIN: 912144510

3311
SAIC, Inc.

(also known as Science Applications International Corporation)
1710 SAIC Dr.
McLean, VA 22102 (703) 676-4300

Company URL: http://www.saic.com
Establishment information: Established in 1969.
Company type: Public company
Company ticker symbol and exchange: SAI/NYSE
International Securities Identification Number: US78390X1019
Business activities: Provides high-technology research and engineering services.
Business type (SIC): Engineering, architectural, and surveying services; computer services; research, development, and testing services
Financial profile for 2013: Number of employees, 40,000; assets, $5,875,000,000; sales volume, $11,173,000,000; pre-tax net income, $658,000,000; expenses, $10,439,000,000; liabilities, $1,793,000,000
Fortune 1000 ranking: 2012—240th in revenues, 325th in profits, and 545th in assets
Forbes 2000 ranking: 2012—860th in sales, 1011th in profits, and 1757th in assets
Corporate officers: John P. Jumper, Chair. and C.E.O.; K. Stuart Shea, C.O.O.; Mark W. Sopp, Exec. V.P. and C.F.O.; Vincent A. Maffeo, Exec. V.P. and Genl. Counsel; Brian F. Keenan, Exec. V.P., Human Resources
Board of directors: John P. Jumper, Chair.; France A. Cordova; Jere A. Drummond; Thomas F. Frist III; John J. Hamre, Ph.D.; Miriam E. John; Anita K. Jones; Harry M. Jansen Kraemer, Jr.; Lawrence C. Nussdorf; Edward J. Sanderson, Jr.; A. Thomas Young
Subsidiary: Telcordia Technologies, Inc., Morristown, NJ
International operations: Australia; Canada; England; France; Germany; India; Scotland
Giving statement: Giving through the SAIC Corporate Giving Program.
Company EIN: 203562868

SAIC Corporate Giving Program

1710 SAIC Dr.
McLean, VA 22102-3703 (703) 676-4300
URL: http://www.saic.com/about/ corporate-responsibility/

Purpose and activities: SAIC makes charitable contributions to nonprofit organizations involved with science, technology, engineering, and mathematics (STEM) education, and the military. Support is given primarily in areas of company operations.
Fields of interest: Elementary/secondary education; Mathematics; Engineering/technology; Science; General charitable giving Military/veterans.
Type of support: Employee matching gifts; Employee volunteer services; General/operating support; Loaned talent; Scholarship funds; Sponsorships.
Geographic limitations: Giving primarily in areas of company operations.

3312
Saint-Gobain Corp.

750 E. Swedesford Rd.
P.O. Box 860
Valley Forge, PA 19482 (610) 341-7000
FAX: (610) 341-7777

Company URL: http:// www.saint-gobain-northamerica.com
Establishment information: Established in 1990.
Company type: Subsidiary of a foreign company
Business activities: Operates holding company.
Business type (SIC): Holding company
Financial profile for 2011: Number of employees, 19,000; assets, $58,800,000,000; sales volume, $54,600,000,000
Corporate officers: Pierre-Andre de Chalendar, Chair. and C.E.O; Timothy Feagans, Sr. V.P. and Genl. Counsel; M. Shawn Puccio, Sr. V.P., Finance; Todd Schock, V.P. and Cont.; Karen Cawkwell, V.P., Comms.; John J. Sweeney, Treas.
Board of director: Pierre-Andre de Chalendar, Chair.
Giving statement: Giving through the Saint-Gobain Corporation Contributions Program and the Saint-Gobain Corporation Foundation.

Saint-Gobain Corporation Foundation

(formerly Norton Company Foundation)
750 E. Swedesford Rd.
P.O. Box 860
Valley Forge, PA 19482-0101
URL: http://www.saint-gobain-northamerica.com/ people/foundation.asp

Establishment information: Trust established in 1953 in MA; incorporated in 1975.

Donors: Norton Co.; Saint-Gobain Corporation.
Contact: William C. Seiberlich, Secy.
Financial data (yr. ended 12/31/11): Assets, $0 (M); gifts received, $1,182,481; expenditures, $1,182,481; qualifying distributions, $1,182,481; giving activities include $1,173,695 for grants.
Purpose and activities: The foundation supports organizations involved with arts and culture, education, health, human services, and other areas. Special emphasis is directed toward programs designed to address housing and community development; energy conservation; and environmental concerns.
Fields of interest: Arts; Education; Environment, energy; Environment; Health care; Housing/shelter; Human services; Community/economic development; General charitable giving.

Programs:
Community Gifts: The foundation support organizations involved with arts and culture, education, housing, and other areas located near a Saint-Gobain facility. The program is designed to enable each facility to target its financial support according to local needs and priorities.
Direct Grants: The foundations supports programs designed to promote housing and community development; energy conservation; and environmental concerns.
Matching Gifts: The foundation matches contributions made by employees of Saint-Gobain to nonprofit organizations.
Type of support: Annual campaigns; Building/renovation; Capital campaigns; Continuing support; Emergency funds; Employee matching gifts; General/operating support; Matching/challenge support; Program development; Seed money.
Geographic limitations: Giving primarily in areas of company operations, with emphasis on MA and PA.
Support limitations: Generally, no support for national or international organizations, national health agencies, or religious, veterans', or fraternal organizations. No grants to individuals, or for endowments, scholarships, fundraising dinners or events, chairs or professorships; no loans.
Publications: Application guidelines; Informational brochure.
Application information: Applications accepted. Application form required. Applicants should submit the following:
1) timetable for implementation and evaluation of project
2) copy of IRS Determination Letter
3) brief history of organization and description of its mission
4) copy of most recent annual report/audited financial statement/990
5) listing of board of directors, trustees, officers and other key people and their affiliations
6) detailed description of project and amount of funding requested
7) copy of current year's organizational budget and/or project budget
8) listing of additional sources and amount of support

Initial approach: Download application form and mail to foundation for Direct Grants
Copies of proposal: 1
Board meeting date(s): Apr. and Sept.
Deadline(s): Feb. 15 and July 15
Final notification: Within 3 weeks

Officers and Directors:* Gilles Colas, Pres.; John J. Sweeney III*, V.P. and Treas.; Karen Cawkwell, V.P.; Tim Feagans, V.P.; M. Shawn Puccio, V.P.; William C. Seiberlich, Secy.; Peter Dachowski; Catherine Ferrante; Rick Poyter; Mark Rayfield; James Thomson.
Number of staff: 1 full-time professional.
EIN: 237423043

Selected grants: The following grants are a representative sample of this grantmaker's funding activity:
$200,000 to YouthBuild USA, Somerville, MA, 2011.
$165,000 to United Way of Central Massachusetts, Worcester, MA, 2011.
$20,000 to Other Carpenter, Philadelphia, PA, 2011.
$11,000 to Genesis Club House, Worcester, MA, 2011.
$10,000 to Baker Industries, Malvern, PA, 2011.
$10,000 to Worcester Historical Museum, Worcester, MA, 2011.
$6,883 to Worcester County Food Bank, Shrewsbury, MA, 2011.
$3,000 to Why Me and Sherrys House, Worcester, MA, 2011.
$2,430 to Boy Scouts of America, Occoneechee Council, Raleigh, NC, 2011.
$2,000 to Garden Grove Community Foundation, Garden Grove, CA, 2011.

3313
Sakar International Inc.

195 Carter Dr.
Edison, NJ 08817 (732) 476-5098
FAX: (732) 248-8082

Company URL: http://www.sakar.com
Establishment information: Established in 1977.
Company type: Private company
Business activities: Designs, manufactures, and markets digital cameras, binoculars, computer accessories, electronic toys, and sports fitness products.
Business type (SIC): Photographic equipment and supplies; computer and office equipment; laboratory apparatus; games, toys, and sporting and athletic goods
Corporate officers: Charles Saka, C.E.O.; Jeffery Saka, Pres.; Ralph Sasson, C.O.O.; Martin Kairey, C.I.O.; Andrea Sobel, V.P., Mktg.; Sammy Saka, Secy.
Giving statement: Giving through the Charles and Brenda Saka Family Foundation.

The Charles and Brenda Saka Family Foundation

195 Carter Dr.
Edison, NJ 08817-2068

Establishment information: Established in 2001 in NJ.
Donor: Sakar International Inc.
Contact: Charles Saka, Tr.
Financial data (yr. ended 12/31/11): Assets, $1,625,517 (M); gifts received, $2,900,000; expenditures, $1,796,669; qualifying distributions, $1,796,226; giving activities include $1,796,226 for grants.
Purpose and activities: The foundation supports organizations involved with education, children and youth, and Judaism.
Fields of interest: Secondary school/education; Higher education; Education; Children/youth, services; Jewish federated giving programs; Jewish agencies & synagogues.
Type of support: General/operating support.
Application information: Applications not accepted. Contributes only to pre-selected organizations.
Trustees: Charles Saka; Jeffrey Saka; Raymond Saka; Sammy Saka.
EIN: 316650219

3314
Saker ShopRites, Inc.

(formerly Foodarama Supermarkets, Inc.)
922 Hwy. 33, Bldg. 6, Ste. 1
P.O. Box 7812
Freehold, NJ 07728-8452 (732) 462-4700

Company URL: http://www.shoprite.com
Establishment information: Established in 1916.
Company type: Private company
Business activities: Operates supermarkets, liquor stores, and garden centers.
Business type (SIC): Groceries—retail; garden supplies—retail; liquor stores
Corporate officers: Joseph J. Saker, Sr., Chair.; Richard J. Saker, Pres. and C.E.O.; Michael Shapiro, C.F.O. and Treas.; Joseph C. Troilo, Sr. V.P., Admin; Carl L. Montanaro, Jr., Sr. V.P., Sales
Board of director: Joseph J. Saker, Sr., Chair.
Subsidiaries: New Linden Price Rite, Inc., Freehold, NJ; ShopRite of Malverne, Inc., Freehold, NJ
Giving statement: Giving through the Foodarama Supermarkets, Inc. Corporate Giving Program.

Foodarama Supermarkets, Inc. Corporate Giving Program

922 Hwy. 33, Bldg. 6, Ste. 1
Freehold, NJ 07728-8439 (732) 462-4700

Contact: Barbara Henriques, Admin. Asst.
Purpose and activities: Foodarama makes charitable contributions of gift certificates to nonprofit organizations on a case by case basis. Support is given primarily in areas of company store operations.
Fields of interest: General charitable giving.
Type of support: Donated products.
Geographic limitations: Giving primarily in areas of company store operations.
Application information: Applications not accepted. Contributes only to pre-selected organizations. The Donations Department handles giving. The company has a staff that only handles contributions.
Number of staff: 1 part-time support.

3315
Saks Incorporated

(formerly Proffitt's, Inc.)
12 E. 49th St.
New York, NY 10017 (212) 753-4000

Company URL: http://www.saksincorporated.com
Establishment information: Established in 1919.
Company type: Public company
Company ticker symbol and exchange: SKS/NYSE
Business activities: Operates department stores; operates furniture stores.
Business type (SIC): Department stores; furniture and home furnishing stores
Financial profile for 2013: Number of employees, 13,900; assets, $2,090,250,000; sales volume, $3,147,550,000; pre-tax net income, $99,390,000; expenses, $3,012,590,000; liabilities, $940,400,000
Fortune 1000 ranking: 2012—685th in revenues, 796th in profits, and 840th in assets
Corporate officers: Stephen I. Sadove, Chair. and C.E.O.; Ronald L. Frasch, Pres.; Kevin Wills, Exec. V.P. and C.F.O.; Micheal Rodgers, Exec. V.P., Opers. and C.I.O.; Michael Brizel, Exec. V.P. and Genl. Counsel; Christine A. Morena, Exec. V.P., Human Resources; Julia Bentley, Sr. V.P., Comms.

Board of directors: Stephen I. Sadove, Chair.; Robert B. Carter; Michael S. Gross; Marguerite W. Kondracke; Jerry W. Levin; Nora P. McAniff; Jack L. Stahl
Subsidiaries: McRae's, Inc., Jackson, MS; Parisian, Inc., Birmingham, AL; Saks Holdings, Inc., New York, NY
Giving statement: Giving through the Saks Incorporated Corporate Giving Program and the Saks Incorporated Foundation.
Company EIN: 620331040

Saks Incorporated Foundation

12 E. 49th St.
New York, NY 10017-1028

Establishment information: Established in 1998 in AL.
Donors: Donald Hess; Saks Inc.; Colonial Properties; Polo Ralph Lauren Corp.; Advance Magazine Group.
Contact: Michael Vincent, V.P. and Treas.
Financial data (yr. ended 01/31/12): Assets, $1,958,738 (M); expenditures, $64,705; qualifying distributions, $61,000; giving activities include $61,000 for 21 grants (high: $10,000; low: $2,000).
Purpose and activities: The foundation supports the American Red Cross and awards scholarships and grants to Saks employees.
Fields of interest: Education; Health care.
Type of support: Employee-related scholarships; General/operating support.
Support limitations: No grants to individuals.
Application information: Applications accepted. Application form not required.
Initial approach: Proposal
Deadline(s): None
Officers: Kevin G. Wills, Pres.; Michael Rodgers, Co-Exec. V.P.; Michael A. Brizel, Co-Exec. V.P.; Michael Vincent, V.P. and Treas.
EIN: 631207483

3316
Salem Co-operative Bank

3 S. Broadway
P.O. Box 67
Salem, NH 03079-0067 (603) 898-2153

Company URL: http://www.salemcoop.com/aboutus.php
Establishment information: Established in 1922.
Company type: Private company
Business activities: Operates savings bank.
Business type (SIC): Savings institutions
Financial profile for 2011: Number of employees, 40; assets, $387,587,000; liabilities, $335,307,000
Corporate officers: David A. Beshara, Chair.; Ann R. Lally, Pres.; Wilbur A. Hyatt, Secy.; Russell Matson, Treas.
Board of director: David A. Beshara, Chair.
Giving statement: Giving through the Salem Co-operative Bank Corporate Giving Program and the Salem Community Benefits, Inc.

Salem Community Benefits, Inc.

3 S. Broadway
Salem, NH 03079-3005 (603) 898-2153

Establishment information: Established in 1998 in NH.
Donor: Salem Co-operative Bank.
Contact: Ann R. Lally, Secy.
Financial data (yr. ended 03/31/12): Assets, $231,132 (M); gifts received, $100,000; expenditures, $79,169; qualifying distributions, $79,165; giving activities include $79,090 for 6 grants (high: $35,000; low: $1,000).
Purpose and activities: The foundation supports organizations involved with dental care and disability services.
Fields of interest: Dental care; Developmentally disabled, centers & services.
Type of support: Equipment; Program development; Sponsorships.
Geographic limitations: Giving limited to the greater Salem, NH, area.
Application information: Applications accepted. Application form required. Applicants should submit the following:
1) detailed description of project and amount of funding requested
Initial approach: Letter
Deadline(s): None
Officers: Nadema Gemmell, Chair.; Ann R. Lally, Secy.
Directors: David Beshara; John Korbey; James Rausch.
EIN: 020499456

3317
Salem Five Cents Savings Bank

210 Essex St.
Salem, MA 01970-3705 (978) 745-5555
FAX: (978) 745-1073

Company URL: http://www.directbanking.com
Establishment information: Established in 1855.
Company type: Private company
Business activities: Operates savings bank.
Business type (SIC): Savings institutions
Financial profile for 2011: Assets, $2,875,184,000
Corporate officers: William H. Mitchelson, Chair.; Joseph M. Gibbons, Pres. and C.E.O.; Ping Yin Chai, Exec. V.P. and C.F.O.; Nancy E. Jones, Sr. V.P., Human Resources
Board of directors: William H. Mitchelson, Chair.; David H. Caldwell; Daniel E. Clasby; Joseph M. Gibbons; Donald S. Glass; Peter C. Gourdeau; Richard R. Gourdeau; Timothy J. Hunt; Martin J. Lawler III; Louise J. Levesque; William J. Lundregan III; A. Carmen Marciano; Mark A. Mitchelson; William H. Mitchelson; Catherine L. Oatway; E. Russell Peach, Jr.; Donald A. Sadoski; John A. Shea, M.D.
Giving statement: Giving through the Heritage/Salem Five Charitable Foundation, Inc. and the Salem Five Charitable Foundation, Inc.

Heritage/Salem Five Charitable Foundation, Inc.

71 Washington St.
Salem, MA 01970 (508) 720-5308
URL: http://www.salemfive.com/index.php/about-salem-five/charitable-foundations

Establishment information: Established in 2006 in MA.
Donor: Salem Five Cents Savings Bank.
Contact: Ping Yin Chai, Treas.
Financial data (yr. ended 12/31/11): Assets, $900,409 (M); expenditures, $61,127; qualifying distributions, $61,127; giving activities include $55,000 for 11 grants (high: $5,000; low: $5,000).
Purpose and activities: The foundation supports nonprofit organizations involved with education, health and human services, youth programs, affordable housing, and community development. Support is limited to areas of company operations in Beverly, Danvers, Marblehead, Peabody and Salem, Massachusetts.
Fields of interest: Education; Health care; Youth development; Community/economic development.
Type of support: General/operating support.
Geographic limitations: Giving limited to areas of company operations in Beverly, Danvers, Marblehead, Peabody, and Salem, MA.
Support limitations: No grants to individuals.
Application information: Applications accepted. Application form required.
Initial approach: Contact foundation for application form
Deadline(s): None
Officers: Donald S. Glass, Pres.; Doris I. Murphy, Secy.; Ping Yin Chai, Treas.
Directors: Daniel E. Clasby; Timothy J. Hunt; William J. Lundregan III; A. Carmen Marciano.
EIN: 204325572

Salem Five Charitable Foundation, Inc.

210 Essex St.
Salem, MA 01970-3705 (978) 720-5322
FAX: (978) 498-0193;
E-mail: karen.lamesa@salemfive.com; Additional contact: Nicolas A. Caporale, Clerk, tel.: (978) 740-5772; URL: https://www.salemfive.com/index.php/in-the-community/charitable-foundations

Establishment information: Established in 1996 in MA.
Donor: Salem Five Cents Savings Bank.
Contact: Karen LaMesa, Mktg. Rep., Community Rels. & Events
Financial data (yr. ended 12/31/11): Assets, $667,158 (M); gifts received, $454,039; expenditures, $284,455; qualifying distributions, $284,376; giving activities include $284,376 for grants.
Purpose and activities: The foundation supports organizations involved with economic self-sufficiency, workforce development, and financial literacy. Support is given primarily in areas of company operations in the North Shore, Massachusetts, area, with emphasis on Salem.
Fields of interest: Education; Employment, training; Human services, financial counseling; Community/economic development.
Type of support: General/operating support; Program development; Sponsorships.
Geographic limitations: Giving primarily in areas of company operations in the North Shore, MA, area, with emphasis on Salem.
Support limitations: No support for discriminatory organizations. No grants for capital campaigns, equipment, or general operating support.
Publications: Application guidelines.
Application information: Applications accepted. Grants range from $50 to $10,000. Application form required. Applicants should submit the following:
1) brief history of organization and description of its mission
2) detailed description of project and amount of funding requested
Initial approach: Complete online application or download application form and e-mail, fax, or mail to foundation
Board meeting date(s): Monthly
Deadline(s): None
Officers and Directors: Joseph M. Gibbons, Pres.; Nicholas A. Caporale, Clerk; Ping Yin Chai, Treas.; David H. Caldwell; Richard Gourdeau; Timothy J.

Hunt; William J. Lundregan III; William H. Mitchelson.
EIN: 043342405
Selected grants: The following grants are a representative sample of this grantmaker's funding activity:
$1,000 to Boston Childrens Theater, Boston, MA, 2009.

3318
salesforce.com, inc.

The Landmark @ 1 Market St., Ste. 300
San Francisco, CA 94105 (415) 901-7000
FAX: (415) 901-7040

Company URL: http://www.salesforce.com
Establishment information: Established in 1999.
Company type: Public company
Company ticker symbol and exchange: CRM/NYSE
International Securities Identification Number: US79466L3024
Business activities: Provides customer relationship management solutions.
Business type (SIC): Computer services
Financial profile for 2013: Number of employees, 9,800; assets, $5,528,960,000; sales volume, $3,050,200,000; pre-tax net income, -$127,790,000; expenses, $3,160,910,000; liabilities, $3,211,320,000
Fortune 1000 ranking: 2012—702nd in revenues, 948th in profits, and 564th in assets
Forbes 2000 ranking: 2012—1628th in sales, 1882nd in profits, and 1783rd in assets
Corporate officers: Marc R. Benioff, Chair. and C.E.O.; Keith G. Block, Co-Vice-Chair. and Pres.; Frank van Veenendaal, Co-Vice-Chair.; George Hu, C.O.O.; Graham V. Smith, Exec. V.P. and C.F.O.
Board of directors: Marc R. Benioff, Chair.; Keith G. Block, Co-Vice-Chair.; Frank van Veenendaal, Co-Vice-Chair.; Craig Conway; Alan G. Hassenfeld; Craig Ramsey; Sanford R. Robertson; Stratton Sclavos; Lawrence Tomlinson; Maynard Webb; Shirley Young
Giving statement: Giving through the salesforce.com Foundation.
Company EIN: 943320693

salesforce.com Foundation

1 Market St., Ste. 300
San Francisco, CA 94105-1315 (415) 901-7000
FAX: (415) 901-8501;
E-mail: foundation@salesforce.com; URL: http://www.salesforcefoundation.org

Establishment information: Established in 1999 in CA.
Donor: salesforce.com, inc.
Contact: Suzanne DiBianca, Exec. Dir.
Financial data (yr. ended 09/30/11): Revenue, $3,228,914; assets, $12,948,114 (M); gifts received, $378,118; expenditures, $7,290,137; program services expenses, $6,864,005; giving activities include $5,070,221 for 66 grants (high: $1,282,841; low: $5,075) and $25,000 for grants to individuals.
Purpose and activities: The foundation educates underserved youth, provides them with exposure to technology, and builds a salesforce.com corporate culture of employee volunteerism in the community.
Fields of interest: Children/youth, services; Engineering/technology Economically disadvantaged.
International interests: Asia; Europe; Japan; Middle East.
Programs:
Community Action Team (CAT) Grants: These grants, open only to salesforce.com employees, are inspired and led by employees who partner with local charitable organizations to identify needs, plan activities, and participate in volunteer activities.
Development Grants: This program provides one application development grant to a nonprofit customer or partner to develop a replicable application for salesforce.com's AppExchange, that is specifically designed for the nonprofit sector and provided at no cost. Proposals must address a specific need that prevails in the nonprofit sector, is not currently being addressed by existing salesforce.com solution partners, and has the ability to be shared via the AppExchange to the nonprofit community with minimal associated costs to nonprofit organizations for implementation and maintenance.
Dollars for Doers: Salesforce.com employees who have volunteered a minimum of ten hours with an organization in any given year are eligible for a grant. For every ten hours volunteered, the foundation will donate $100, with an annual donation cap of $500 per employee.
Technology Grants for Youth Development: These grants are awarded to visionary nonprofit organizations, which focus on youth development, for technology projects or solutions that advance their organization's core mission. Grants are awarded in a range between $5,000 and $15,000, and are funded in $5,000 increments.
Turn It Up Grants: These $10,000 grants are awarded to visionary nonprofit organizations to enable them to develop their use of salesforce.com applications. Successful applicants show that customization and enhanced use of salesforce.com technology support their ability to implement their social change mission. Eligible applicants must be active (at least one login per week for at least one year) users of the salesforce.com application, and be based in Africa, Australia, Europe, Hong Kong, India, Japan, Middle East, New Zealand, Singapore, or Thailand.
Type of support: Employee matching gifts; Equipment; Program development; Technical assistance.
Geographic limitations: Giving on a national and international basis.
Publications: Application guidelines.
Application information: Applications accepted. Application form required.
Initial approach: Complete online application form
Deadline(s): Feb. 27 for Turn It Up Grants
Final notification: Mar. 31 for Turn It Up Grants
Officers and Directors:* Marc R. Benioff*, Chair. and C.E.O.; Suzanne DiBianca, Exec. Dir.; Rebecca Enonchong; Alan Hassenfeld; F. Warren Hellman; Dave Moellenhoff; Laura Scher; Robert Thurman.
Number of staff: 7 full-time professional; 1 part-time support.
EIN: 943347800

3319
Salt River Valley Water Users' Association

(also known as SRP)
1521 N. Project Dr.
Tempe, AZ 85281-1206 (602) 236-5900

Company URL: http://www.srpnet.com
Establishment information: Established in 1903.
Company type: Private company
Business activities: Generates, transmits, and distributes electricity.
Business type (SIC): Electric services
Corporate officers: David Rousseau, Pres.; Mark Bonsall, C.E.O.; Terrill A. Lonon, Corp. Secy.; Dean R. Duncan, Treas.; Mark B. Bonsall, Mgr.
Giving statement: Giving through the SRP Corporate Giving Program.

SRP Corporate Giving Program

1521 N. Project Dr.
Tempe, AZ 85281-1298 (602) 236-5900
FAX: (602) 236-2279; Tel. for employee volunteer services: (602) 236-2488; Application address for donation requests: Corp. Contribs., PAB 337, P.O. Box 52025, Phoenix, AZ 85072-2025.; URL: http://www.srpnet.com/menu/community.aspx

Purpose and activities: SRP makes charitable contributions to nonprofit organizations involved with arts and culture, education, the environment, health, human services, and civic affairs. Support is given primarily in Arizona.
Fields of interest: Arts; Education; Environment; Health care; Food services; Family services; Human services; Public affairs.
Type of support: Employee volunteer services; General/operating support; In-kind gifts.
Geographic limitations: Giving primarily in AZ.
Support limitations: No support for professional schools of art, academic art programs, individual high school or college performing groups, political or lobbying groups or campaigns, fraternal, or veterans' organizations, professional associations, or similar membership groups, or public or commercial broadcasting programs. No grants to individuals, including students and researchers, or for travel expenses, conference fees, endowment programs, medical research projects or individual medical procedures, religious activities that do not benefit the entire community, or debt-reduction campaigns.
Publications: Application guidelines.
Application information: Applications accepted. Form letters and e-mail requests are not accepted. Donations of water, electricity, or equipment are not provided where fees are normally charged. Application form required. Applicants should submit the following:
1) role played by volunteers
2) results expected from proposed grant
3) name, address and phone number of organization
4) brief history of organization and description of its mission
5) geographic area to be served
6) copy of most recent annual report/audited financial statement/990
7) how project's results will be evaluated or measured
8) explanation of why grantmaker is considered an appropriate donor for project
9) listing of board of directors, trustees, officers and other key people and their affiliations
10) detailed description of project and amount of funding requested
11) plans for cooperation with other organizations, if any
12) contact person
13) copy of current year's organizational budget and/or project budget
14) listing of additional sources and amount of support

Volunteer requests should include the name, location, and dates of the project or activity and should be addressed to: SRP VOLUNTEERS, PAB335. Donation requests should include the number of beneficiaries and a Form W-9.
Initial approach: Fax application form to headquarters for volunteer requests; Mail

proposal to headquarters for donation requests
Committee meeting date(s): Annual
Deadline(s): 5 weeks prior to event for volunteer requests
Final notification: 6 weeks for volunteer requests; 8 weeks for donation requests

3320
Samsung Electronics America, Inc.

85 Challenger Rd.
Ridgefield Park, NJ 07660 (201) 229-4000

Company URL: http://www.samsung.com/us
Establishment information: Established in 1977.
Company type: Subsidiary of a foreign company
Business activities: Operates consumer electronics company.
Business type (SIC): Electronic components and accessories
Financial profile for 2009: Number of employees, 1,700; sales volume, $11,210,000,000
Corporate officers: Oh-Hyun Kwon, Vice-Chair. and Co-C.E.O.; Kim Yangkyu, Pres. and Co-C.E.O.
Board of director: Oh-Hyun Kwon, Vice-Chair.
Giving statement: Giving through the Samsung Electronics America, Inc. Contributions Program.

Samsung Electronics America, Inc. Contributions Program

c/o Corp. Giving
105 Challenger Rd.
Ridgefield Park, NJ 07660 (973) 601-6000
URL: http://www.samsung.com/us/aboutsamsung/citizenship/usactivities.html

Purpose and activities: Samsung Electronics America makes charitable contributions to nonprofit organizations involved with children, education, the environment, health, and human services. Support is given primarily in areas of company operations.
Fields of interest: Arts; Education; Environment; Health care; Human services.
Type of support: Donated products; Employee volunteer services; General/operating support; In-kind gifts.
Geographic limitations: Giving primarily in areas of company operations.
Support limitations: No support for organizations not of direct benefit to the entire community, political or lobbying organizations, parent-supported organizations, or private foundations. No grants to individuals.
Application information: Applications accepted. Application form not required.
Initial approach: Proposal to headquarters
Copies of proposal: 1

3321
San Antonio Spurs LLC

1 AT&T Center Pkwy.
San Antonio, TX 78219 (210) 444-5000
FAX: (210) 444-5100

Company URL: http://www.nba.com/spurs
Establishment information: Established in 1967.
Company type: Subsidiary of a private company
Business activities: Operates professional basketball club.
Business type (SIC): Commercial sports
Corporate officers: Peter M. Holt, Chair. and C.E.O.; Rick A. Pych, Exec. V.P., Finance
Board of director: Peter M. Holt, Chair.
Giving statement: Giving through the San Antonio Spurs LLC Corporate Giving Program and the Silver and Black Give Back.

San Antonio Spurs LLC Corporate Giving Program

1 AT&T Ctr.
San Antonio, TX 78219-3604
FAX: (210) 444-5875; URL: http://www.nba.com/spurs/community/donations.html

Purpose and activities: The San Antonio Spurs make charitable contributions to nonprofit organizations involved with education and children and on a case by case basis. Support is given primarily in the San Antonio, Texas, area.
Fields of interest: Secondary school/education; Education, reading; Education; Public health, physical fitness; Nutrition; Athletics/sports, basketball; Children, services; General charitable giving.
Programs:
Read to Achieve: Through Read to Achieve campaign, the Spurs encourage young people to develop a life-long love for reading and adults to read regularly with children. The program includes educational programming, read aloud events with Spurs coaches and player, and free book donations.
Slam Dunk Reading Challenge: Through the Slam Dunk Reading Challenge, the Spurs and IBC Bank challenges sixth, seventh, and eighth grade students to meet and exceed their grade level reading requirement. Winning classes receive game tickets and the grand prize winner receives a Spurs player hosting a read aloud event for their class.
Spurs/CPS Energy Teacher of the Year: The Spurs honors teachers who have had a profound and lasting effect on their students and have gone beyond the call of duty to ensure their students success in school and in life. Honorees receive tickets to a home game and win an commemorative award.
Spurs/Whataburger Winners Circle: The Spurs, in partnership with Whataburger, rewards middle school students who are hard working and who strive to do their best in and out of the classroom. One student is honored per game with game tickets, t-shirt, Whataburger meal for 4, and in-game recognition.
Type of support: Curriculum development; Donated products; In-kind gifts; Income development; Loaned talent; Program development.
Geographic limitations: Giving primarily in areas of company operations within 75 miles of San Antonio, TX.
Publications: Application guidelines.
Application information: Applications accepted. Application form required. Applicants should submit the following:
1) name, address and phone number of organization
2) copy of IRS Determination Letter
3) brief history of organization and description of its mission
4) detailed description of project and amount of funding requested
5) contact person
Initial approach: Complete online application form for memorabilia donations and player/mascot appearances
Copies of proposal: 1
Deadline(s): 30 days prior to need for memorabilia donations and player appearances; 4 weeks prior to need for mascot appearances
Final notification: 10 business days for mascot appearances

Silver and Black Give Back

(formerly The San Antonio Spurs Foundation)
1 AT&T Ctr.
San Antonio, TX 78219-3604 (210) 444-5541
FAX: (210) 444-5875; URL: http://www.nba.com/spurs/community/foundation.html

Establishment information: Established in 1988 in TX.
Contact: Alison Fox, Exec. Dir.
Financial data (yr. ended 06/30/11): Revenue, $1,306,514; assets, $2,073,700 (M); gifts received, $786,761; expenditures, $717,784; giving activities include $227,230 for grants.
Purpose and activities: The foundation supports area disadvantaged youth by encouraging their growth, creativity, development of character, and education and providing opportunities to enjoy a greater quality of life.
Fields of interest: Youth development.
Type of support: Scholarships—to individuals.
Geographic limitations: Giving limited to south TX.
Support limitations: No support for churches, sectarian purposes, schools or sports teams. No grants to individuals (except for scholarships), or for travel, medical research, salaries, or fundraising.
Application information: Applications accepted. Application form not required. Applicants should submit the following:
1) timetable for implementation and evaluation of project
2) copy of IRS Determination Letter
3) brief history of organization and description of its mission
4) listing of board of directors, trustees, officers and other key people and their affiliations
5) copy of current year's organizational budget and/or project budget
Initial approach: Letter of inquiry
Copies of proposal: 15
Deadline(s): Aug. 26
Final notification: Oct. 7
Officer and Directors:* Alison Fox*, Exec. Dir.; Charles Amato; Eric Barbosa; Cory Basso; R.C. Buford; Tino Duran; Pat Frost; Ron Gomez; Gregg Popovich; and 9 additional directors.
EIN: 742509544

3322
San Diego Chargers Football Company

(also known as Chargers Football Company, LLC)
4020 Murphy Canyon Rd.
San Diego, CA 92123 (858) 874-4500

Company URL: http://www.chargers.com
Establishment information: Established in 1959.
Company type: Private company
Business activities: Operates professional football club.
Business type (SIC): Commercial sports
Corporate officers: Dean A. Spanos, Chair. and Pres.; Alexander G. Spanos, C.E.O.; Jim Steeg, Exec. V.P. and C.O.O.; Jeanne M. Bonk, Exec. V.P. and C.F.O.; Marsha Wells, Cont.
Board of director: Dean Spanos, Chair.

Giving statement: Giving through the San Diego Chargers Football Co. Contributions Program and the San Diego Chargers Charities.

San Diego Chargers Football Co. Contributions Program

c/o Community Rels. Donation Request
4020 Murphy Canyon Rd.
San Diego, CA 92123-4407
Contact for Play It Smart: Jim Presby, National Dir., tel.: (800) 486-1865; URL: http://www.chargers.com/community

Purpose and activities: The San Diego Chargers make charitable contributions to nonprofit organizations involved with education, youth sports, and on a case by case basis. Support is given primarily in San Diego, California.
Fields of interest: Libraries (public); Education; Hospitals (general); Public health, physical fitness; Breast cancer; Food services; Athletics/sports, football; Recreation; Youth development; Human services, gift distribution; General charitable giving.
Programs:
Chargers Junior Training Camp: The San Diego Chargers, in partnership with Gatorade, promotes a free football camp in schools and recreation centers, and for nonprofit organizations for summer and fall. The program is designed to teach children the basics of football, exercise, and sportsmanship.
Community Corner: Through Community Corner, San Diego Chargers purchase and donate game tickets to nonprofit organizations serving youth. Participating youth receive tickets to the game, and a free hot dog and soda courtesy of the Chargers.
Play It Smart: Through Play It Smart, high school football teams and their coaches work together to serve young football players from economically underserved communities. The program includes one-on-one mentoring relationships, academic support services, SAT/ACT prep classes, community service events, and team-building activities throughout the year. The program is currently active at San Diego High School.
Type of support: Donated products; In-kind gifts; Income development; Loaned talent.
Geographic limitations: Giving primarily in areas of company operations in CA, with emphasis on San Diego.
Publications: Application guidelines.
Application information: Applications accepted. Proposals should be submitted using organization letterhead. Support is limited to 1 contribution per organization during any given year. The Community Relations Department handles giving. Application form not required. Applicants should submit the following:
1) population served
2) name, address and phone number of organization
3) detailed description of project and amount of funding requested
4) contact person
Proposals should indicate the date of the event and the type of fundraiser.
Initial approach: Mail proposal to headquarters for memorabilia donations, player appearances, and Community Corner
Copies of proposal: 1
Deadline(s): 4 to 6 weeks prior to need for memorabilia donations and player appearances; prior to the start of the season for Community Corner

San Diego Chargers Charities

(also known as The Chargers Community Foundation)
P.O. Box 609609
San Diego, CA 92160-9609 (858) 874-4500

Establishment information: Established in 1995 in CA.
Contact: Ed Trimble, Pres.
Financial data (yr. ended 12/31/11): Revenue, $106,335; assets, $49,823 (M); gifts received, $117,099; expenditures, $110,728; program services expenses, $98,554; giving activities include $70,500 for grants and $19,120 for grants to individuals.
Purpose and activities: The foundation supports, encourages, and creates projects or events that will improve the quality of life for the community of San Diego, California.
Fields of interest: Community/economic development.
Program:
Community Quarterback Award: Winners will receive a $1,000 donation to their youth football or cheer organization; one volunteer will be selected as an overall award winner and receive $2,500 for their organization.
Type of support: Grants to individuals; In-kind gifts.
Geographic limitations: Giving limited to San Diego, CA.
Application information:
Initial approach: Submit nomination form for Community Quarterback Award
Deadline(s): Nov. 9 for Community Quarterback Award
Officers and Directors:* Ed Trimble*, Pres.; Rudy Castruita*, Secy.; Jeanne Bonk*, Treas.; Marilyn Creson Brown; Kimberley Layton; Craig McClellan; Dean A. Spanos.
EIN: 330670086

3323
San Diego Padres Baseball Club L.P.

9449 Friars Rd.
San Diego, CA 92108 (619) 881-6500

Company URL: http://sandiego.padres.mlb.com
Establishment information: Established in 1968.
Company type: Private company
Business activities: Operates professional baseball club.
Business type (SIC): Commercial sports
Corporate officers: Ron Fowler, Chair.; Jeff Moorad, C.E.O.; Tom Garfinkel, Pres. and C.O.O.; Ronda Sedillo, Sr. V.P. and C.F.O; Erik Greupner, Sr. V.P. and Genl. Counsel; Sarah Farnsworth, Sr. V.P., Public Affairs
Board of director: Ron Fowler, Chair.
Giving statement: Giving through the San Diego Padres Baseball Club L.P. Corporate Giving Program.

San Diego Padres Baseball Club L.P. Corporate Giving Program

c/o Community Rels., Charitable Donation
P.O. Box 122000
San Diego, CA 92112-2000 (619) 795-5275
URL: http://sandiego.padres.mlb.com/sd/community/donations.jsp

Purpose and activities: The San Diego Padres make charitable contributions to nonprofit organizations on a case by case basis. Support is given primarily in the greater San Diego, California, area.
Fields of interest: Education; Hospitals (general); Public health, physical fitness; Cancer; Athletics/sports, baseball; Boys & girls clubs; General charitable giving Youth.
International interests: Mexico.
Program:
Charity Ticket Program: The San Diego Padres provides game tickets to nonprofit organizations that serve disadvantaged children who would otherwise not be able to attend a baseball game.
Type of support: Donated products; In-kind gifts; Income development.
Geographic limitations: Giving primarily in area of company operations in the greater San Diego, CA, area, including Imperial and San Diego counties and Baja California, Mexico.
Publications: Application guidelines.
Application information: Applications accepted. Proposals should be submitted using organization letterhead. The Community Relations Department handles giving. Applicants should submit the following:
1) name, address and phone number of organization
2) contact person
3) detailed description of project and amount of funding requested
Proposals should indicate the date of the event and the type of fundraiser.
Initial approach: Proposal to headquarters for memorabilia donations; complete online application form for Charity Ticket Program
Copies of proposal: 1
Deadline(s): 4 to 6 weeks prior to need for memorabilia donations; none for Charity Ticket Program

3324
San Francisco Baseball Associates, L.P.

(also known as San Francisco Giants)
AT & T Park
24 Willie Mays Plz.
San Francisco, CA 94107 (415) 972-2000

Company URL: http://sanfrancisco.giants.mlb.com
Establishment information: Established in 1891.
Company type: Private company
Business activities: Operates professional baseball club.
Business type (SIC): Commercial sports
Financial profile for 2010: Number of employees, 1,240
Corporate officers: Laurence M. Baer, Pres. and C.E.O.; John F. Yee, Sr. V.P. and C.F.O.; Bill Schlough, Sr. V.P. and C.I.O.; Jack F. Bair, Sr. V.P. and Genl. Counsel; Tom McDonald, Sr. V.P., Mktg.; Staci Slaughter, Sr. V.P., Comms.; Lisa Pantages, V.P., Finance; Jeff Tucker, V.P., Sales; Joyce Thomas, V.P., Human Resources; Shana Daum, V.P., Public Affairs; William H. Neukom, Chair. Emeritus
Giving statement: Giving through the San Francisco Giants Corporate Giving Program and the Giants Community Fund.

San Francisco Giants Corporate Giving Program

24 Willie Mays Plz.
San Francisco, CA 94107-2134 (415) 972-2000
Application address for game ticket donations: Take Me Out to the Ballgame c/o Community Rels., 24 Willie Mays Plz., San Francisco, CA 94107; Application address for speaker requests: Speakers

Bureau Prog., 24 Willie Mays Plz., San Francisco, CA 94107; Application address for ballpark community messages requests: "Ballpark Community Messages" San Francisco Giants Community Rels. Dept. AT&T Park, 24 Willie Mays Plz., San Francisco, CA 94107. Application address for clubhouse requests: AT&T Park Community Clubhouse, c/o Community Rels., 24 Willie Mays Plz., San Francisco, CA 94107; URL: http://sanfrancisco.giants.mlb.com/NASApp/mlb/sf/community/index.jsp

Purpose and activities: As a complement to its foundation, the San Francisco Giants make charitable contributions to nonprofit organizations directly. Support is limited to organizations located in the Bay Area and northern California.
Fields of interest: Adult education—literacy, basic skills & GED; Education; Public health; Crime/violence prevention; Recreation, community; Recreation; Youth, services; Community/economic development, volunteer services Economically disadvantaged.
Program:
Take Me Out to the Ballgame: Through the Take Me Out to the Ballgame program, the San Francisco Giants make charitable contributions of game tickets to nonprofit organizations involved with education, community service, and underprivileged people.
Type of support: Donated products; In-kind gifts; Use of facilities.
Geographic limitations: Giving primarily in Support is limited to organizations located in the Bay Area and northern CA.
Support limitations: Generally no donations of community clubhouse space for direct fundraising purposes.
Publications: Application guidelines.
Application information: Applications accepted. Requests for ballpark community board messages and in-kind gifts should be limited to 1 request per organization during any given year. Phone calls are not encouraged. The grantmaker does not accept items to be autographed. Application form required.
Applicants should submit the following:
1) name, address and phone number of organization
2) copy of IRS Determination Letter
3) detailed description of project and amount of funding requested
4) contact person
5) additional materials/documentation
Proposals for game tickets should include the type of organization applying (from six choices), the number of beneficiaries using its services, the age range of the primary beneficiaries of the tickets, whether wheelchair accessible seating is required, and available game dates. Proposals for speaker requests should include date of event, start and end time, event location and address, topics or duties, approximate attendance, age group of beneficiaries, purpose of the request, incentives such as hotels, meals, or honorarium, the date when a reply is needed, an agenda for the event, and driving directions from AT&T Park. Proposals for ballpark community board messages should include a business card, the month requested for posting between April and Sept., and a proposed message of up to 65 characters that raises awareness for a specific organization or cause that is relevant to northern/central California, and contains a phone number and website in the message. Proposals for community clubhouse space should be submitted on the organization's letterhead, along with three available dates for using the space.
Initial approach: Download application form and mail completed proposal and application form to the specified application address
Deadline(s): 6 weeks prior to need for speaker requests; 1 month prior to need for ballpark community board messages, 2 months prior to need for in-kind gifts
Final notification: 2 weeks for game ticket donations

Giants Community Fund

c/o AT&T Park
24 Willie Mays Plz.
San Francisco, CA 94107-2134 (877) 574-4268
FAX: (415) 947-2644;
E-mail: communityfund@sfgiants.com; URL: http://sanfrancisco.giants.mlb.com/sf/community/gcf/index.jsp

Establishment information: Established in CA.
Contact: Sue Petersen, Exec. Dir.
Financial data (yr. ended 12/31/10): Revenue, $1,523,203; assets, $1,030,872 (M); gifts received, $1,518,821; expenditures, $1,310,162; giving activities include $1,065,451 for grants and $25,500 for grants to individuals.
Purpose and activities: The fund assists qualifying local charities that are in need of cash grants for specific programs, primarily education, literacy, health, and violence prevention.
Fields of interest: Education; Health care; Crime/violence prevention; Athletics/sports, baseball.
Type of support: Program development.
Geographic limitations: Giving limited to northern CA.
Publications: Application guidelines; Newsletter.
Application information: Applications accepted. Application form required.
Initial approach: Complete online application form
Board meeting date(s): Quarterly
Officers and Directors:* Peter A. Magowan*, Chair.; Staci Slaughter*, V.P., Public Affairs; Jack F. Bair*, Secy.; John F. Yee*, Treas.; Sue Petersen, Exec. Dir.; Craig Alexander; Mario Alioto; Larry Baer; Julia Bromley; Renel Brooks-Moon; and 23 additional directors.
EIN: 943200061

3325
San Francisco Chronicle

901 Mission St.
San Francisco, CA 94103-2905
(415) 777-1111

Company URL: http://www.sfchron.com
Establishment information: Established in 1865.
Company type: Subsidiary of a private company
Business activities: Publishes newspapers.
Business type (SIC): Newspaper publishing and/or printing
Corporate officers: Frank J. Vega, Chair. and C.E.O.; Mark Adkins, Pres.; Elizabeth A. Cain, C.F.O. and Secy.-Treas.; Todd E. Miller, C.I.O.; Kelly Harville, V.P., Mktg.
Board of director: Frank J. Vega, Chair.
Giving statement: Giving through the Chronicle Season of Sharing Fund.

Chronicle Season of Sharing Fund

P.O. Box 44740
San Francisco, CA 94144-2905 (415) 777-7120
FAX: (415) 546-9291;
E-mail: JKirschenbaum@sfchronicle.com; E-mail for Jennifer Kirschenbaum: JKirschenbaum@sfchronicle.com; URL: http://www.seasonofsharing.org/

Establishment information: Established in 1986.
Donor: San Francisco Chronicle.
Contact: Jennifer Kirschenbaum, Exec. Dir.
Financial data (yr. ended 06/30/11): Revenue, $6,470,280; assets, $2,060,200 (M); gifts received, $6,466,664; expenditures, $6,337,658; giving activities include $6,152,500 for grants and $17,981 for grants to individuals.
Purpose and activities: The fund raises donations for critical family needs, housing assistance, and food programs, and distributes the donations to help people in need throughout the greater San Francisco Bay Area.
Fields of interest: Housing/shelter; Human services Disabilities, people with; Economically disadvantaged.
Type of support: Grants to individuals.
Geographic limitations: Giving primarily in Alameda, Contra Costa, Marin, Napa, San Mateo, San Francisco, Santa Clara, Solano, and Sonoma counties, CA.
Officers and Directors:* Frank Vega*, Pres.; Ward Bushee*, V.P.; Elizabeth Cain*, Secy.-Treas.; Jennifer Kirschenbaum, Exec. Dir.; Ira Hirschfield; George B. Irish.
EIN: 943019992

3326
San Francisco Forty Niners, Ltd.

4949 Centennial Blvd.
Santa Clara, CA 95054-1229
(408) 562-4949

Company URL: http://www.49ers.com
Establishment information: Established in 1946.
Company type: Subsidiary of a private company
Business activities: Operates professional football club.
Business type (SIC): Commercial sports
Corporate officers: John C. York II, Co-Chair.; Denise DeBartolo York, Co-Chair.; Jed York, C.E.O.; Andy Dolich, C.O.O.; Paraag Marathe, C.O.O.; Cipora Herman, C.F.O.; Ethan Casson, V.P., Corp. Sales; Debye Whelchel, Cont.
Board of directors: John C. York II, Co-Chair.; Denise DeBartolo York, Co-Chair.; Kara Berg; Robert Fischbach; Rick Frisbe; Seth Gersch; Jan Katzoff; Mike Latham; Clothilde Hewlett; Keena Turner; Mike Wirth
Giving statement: Giving through the San Francisco Forty Niners Corporate Giving Program and the San Francisco Forty Niners Foundation.

San Francisco Forty Niners Corporate Giving Program

c/o Donations Dept.
4949 Centennial Blvd.
Santa Clara, CA 95054-1229 (408) 562-4949
E-mail: 49ersdonations@niners.nfl.com;
URL: http://www.sf49ers.com/community/donation.php?section=CO%20DonationRequests

Purpose and activities: As a complement to its foundation, the San Francisco Forty Niners also make charitable contributions of memorabilia to nonprofit organizations directly. Support is limited to Alaska, the greater San Francisco Bay and Sacramento area of California, and Hawaii.
Fields of interest: Athletics/sports, amateur leagues; Youth development.
Type of support: Donated products; In-kind gifts.
Geographic limitations: Giving limited to AK, the greater San Francisco Bay and greater Sacramento areas of CA, and HI.

Support limitations: No grants to individuals.
Publications: Application guidelines.
Application information: Applications accepted. Support is limited to 1 contribution per organization during any given year. Fan merchandise for the purpose of autographing is not accepted. No mailed, faxed, or e-mailed requests will be considered. Application form required. Applicants should submit the following:
1) name, address and phone number of organization
2) copy of IRS Determination Letter
3) detailed description of project and amount of funding requested
4) contact person
Applications should include the name, date, and a description of the event, and indicate the type of fundraiser.
Initial approach: Complete online application form
Deadline(s): 6 weeks prior to need
Final notification: 6 weeks

San Francisco Forty Niners Foundation

4949 Centennial Blvd.
Santa Clara, CA 95054-1229 (408) 562-4949
URL: http://www.49ers.com/community/foundation.html

Establishment information: Established in 1991 in CA.
Financial data (yr. ended 12/31/11): Revenue, $3,580,358; assets, $2,993,035 (M); gifts received, $3,575,777; expenditures, $2,574,874; giving activities include $2,431,948 for grants.
Purpose and activities: The foundation raises and allocates funds to nonprofit agencies in the San Francisco Bay Area, California.
Fields of interest: Education; Health care; Youth development.
Program:
Perry/Yonamine Unity Award: The award will honor a San Francisco Bay Area nonprofit agency for exceptional outreach efforts to promote unity in the community. The award is named after former 49ers players Joe Perry and Wally Yonamine. In addition to a monetary grant in the amount of $10,000, the chosen nonprofit will receive recognition at a 49ers home game during the current season, a Perry/Yonamine Unity Award plaque, and tickets for volunteers/employees to attend the game.
Type of support: Continuing support; Equipment; Program development.
Geographic limitations: Giving limited to the San Francisco Bay Area, CA.
Support limitations: No support for political campaigns or religious organizations. No grants for land, building or vehicle purchase, endowments, loans, personal scholarships, travel, drives, or specific individuals.
Application information: Applications not accepted. Contributes only to pre-selected organizations.
Officer: Thomas M. Bowen, Exec. Dir.
Directors: Kara Berg; Robert Fischbach; Rick Frisbie; Seth Gersch; Clothide Hewlett; Jan Katzoff; Mike Latham; Keena Turner; Mike Wirth.
Number of staff: 2 full-time professional.
EIN: 770287514

3327
San Jose Sharks LLC

525 W. Santa Clara St.
San Jose, CA 95113-1520 (408) 287-7070

Company URL: http://sharks.nhl.com/
Establishment information: Established in 1990.
Company type: Subsidiary of a private company
Business activities: Operates professional ice hockey club.
Business type (SIC): Commercial sports
Corporate officers: Greg Jamison, Pres. and C.E.O.; Charlie Faas, Exec. V.P. and C.F.O.; Malcolm Bordelon, Exec. V.P., Opers.; John Tortora, Exec. V.P. and Genl. Counsel; Ken Caveney, V.P., Finance; Fiona Ow Giuffre, V.P., Human Resources
Giving statement: Giving through the Sharks Foundation.

The Sharks Foundation

525 W. Santa Clara St.
San Jose, CA 95113-1520 (408) 287-7070
FAX: (408) 999-5797; E-mail: jcafuir@svse.net.;
URL: http://www.thesharksfoundation.com/

Establishment information: Established in 1997 in CA.
Donors: Compton Family Trust; SONY Playstation; SAP Global Marketing, Inc.; Cadence Design Systems, Inc.; Seagate Technology LLC; Ticketmaster Group, Inc.; WorldCom, Inc.
Contact: Jeff Cafuir, Mgr.
Financial data (yr. ended 07/31/11): Assets, $1,169,887 (M); gifts received, $184,486; expenditures, $787,192; qualifying distributions, $336,744; giving activities include $336,744 for grants.
Purpose and activities: The foundation supports programs designed to benefit youth and their families, with emphasis is directed towards underserved populations and at-risk youth. The foundation also supports programs designed to promote health and safety; education; and character development.
Fields of interest: Education, reading; Education; Health care; Safety/disasters; Athletics/sports, winter sports; Boys & girls clubs; Youth development; Children/youth, services; Family services Youth; Economically disadvantaged.
Type of support: Program development.
Geographic limitations: Giving limited to Santa Clara and Santa Cruz County, CA.
Support limitations: No support for athletic teams, schools, or school-associated 501(c)(3) organizations like PTA's or booster clubs. No grants to individuals, or for general operating deficits, staff salaries, sponsorships or fundraisers, recreational group outings or trips, capital campaigns or building improvement projects, endowments, or reserve funds.
Publications: Application guidelines; Grants list.
Application information: Applications accepted. Grants range from $20,000 to $25,000. Proposals should be no longer than 4 pages. Video and audio submissions are not encouraged. A site visit may be requested. Support is limited to 1 contribution per organizations during any given year. Application form required. Applicants should submit the following:
1) statement of problem project will address
2) population served
3) copy of IRS Determination Letter
4) brief history of organization and description of its mission
5) geographic area to be served
6) how project's results will be evaluated or measured
7) listing of board of directors, trustees, officers and other key people and their affiliations
8) detailed description of project and amount of funding requested
9) copy of current year's organizational budget and/or project budget
10) listing of additional sources and amount of support
11) additional materials/documentation
Initial approach: Download application form and mail proposal and application form to foundation; contact participating schools for 8th Grade Leadership Awards
Copies of proposal: 6
Deadline(s): Postmarked or hand delivered by Sept. 13
Final notification: Jan.
Officers and Directors: Greg Jamison, Pres.; Malcolm Bordelon, V.P.; Charlie Faas, Secy.; Ken Caveney, Treas.; Monte Chavez; Toni Foster; Heather Hunter; Tony Khing; Jim Sparaco; Rosemary Tebaldi; Lynn Wolfe.
EIN: 770374062
Selected grants: The following grants are a representative sample of this grantmaker's funding activity:
$25,000 to Asian Americans for Community Involvement, San Jose, CA, 2010. For general charitable purpose.
$25,000 to Books Aloud, San Jose, CA, 2010. For general charitable purpose.
$25,000 to Bring Me A Book Foundation, Mountain View, CA, 2010. For general charitable purpose.
$25,000 to USA Hockey Foundation, Colorado Springs, CO, 2010. For general charitable purpose.
$24,650 to Hope Rehabilitation Services, San Jose, CA, 2010. For general charitable purpose.
$20,000 to My New Red Shoes, Burlingame, CA, 2010. For general charitable purpose.
$14,500 to UNICEF, New York, NY, 2010. For general charitable purpose.
$3,299 to Sacred Heart Community Service, San Jose, CA, 2010. For general charitable purpose.

3328
Sandusky International, Inc.

(formerly Sandusky Foundry & Machine Company)
615 W. Market St.
Sandusky, OH 44871 (419) 626-5340

Company URL: http://www.sanduskyintl.com
Establishment information: Established in 1904.
Company type: Private company
Business activities: Manufactures paper making machinery.
Business type (SIC): Machinery/special industry
Corporate officers: Edward R. Ryan, Pres. and C.E.O.; Richard A. Hargrave, C.F.O.
International operations: United Kingdom
Giving statement: Giving through the Sandusky International Foundation.

Sandusky International Foundation

(formerly Sandusky Foundry & Machine Company Foundation)
615 W. Market St.
Sandusky, OH 44871-5012

Establishment information: Established in 1967 in OH.
Donors: Sandusky Foundry & Machine Co.; Sandusky International Inc.
Financial data (yr. ended 12/31/11): Assets, $0 (M); gifts received, $200; expenditures, $222;

qualifying distributions, $222; giving activities include $222 for 2+ grants (high: $200).
Purpose and activities: The foundation supports museums and organizations involved with education, heart disease, and human services.
Fields of interest: Education.
Type of support: Annual campaigns; Employee volunteer services; General/operating support; Scholarship funds.
Geographic limitations: Giving primarily in Erie and Sandusky counties, OH.
Support limitations: No grants to individuals.
Application information: Applications not accepted. Unsolicited requests for funds not accepted.
Trustees: R.A. Hargrave; E.R. Ryan.
EIN: 346596951

3329
Sanofi-aventis U.S. LLC

(formerly Aventis Pharmaceuticals Inc.)
55 Corporate Dr.
Bridgewater, NJ 08807 (908) 231-4000

Company URL: http://www.sanofi-aventis.us
Establishment information: Established in 1950.
Company type: Subsidiary of a foreign company
Business activities: Develops, manufactures, and markets pharmaceutical products.
Business type (SIC): Drugs
Financial profile for 2009: Number of employees, 16,508
Corporate officers: Gregory Irace, Pres. and C.E.O.; Laurent Gilhodes, C.F.O.; Philippe Grillet, V.P., Finance and C.F.O.; Judy O'Hagan, V.P., Human Resources
Board of directors: Zan Guerry; Timothy Rothwell
Subsidiaries: Armour Pharmaceutical Co., Tarrytown, NY; Rorer Pharmaceutical Corp., Fort Washington, PA; USV Pharmaceutical Corp., Fort Washington, PA
Historic mergers: Chattem, Inc. (March 11, 2010)
Giving statement: Giving through the sanofi-aventis U.S., LLC. Corporate Giving Program, the Endocrine Fellows Foundation, the Hamico, Inc., and the Sanofi Foundation for North America.

sanofi-aventis U.S., LLC. Corporate Giving Program

(formerly Aventis Pharmaceuticals Inc. Corporate Giving Program)
c/o Corp. Contribs.
55 Corporate Dr.
Bridgewater, NJ 08807
E-mail: US.Philanthropy@sanofi-aventis.com; For Educational Grants: sagrants@sanofi-aventis.com; URL: http://www.sanofi-aventis.us/live/us/en/layout.jsp?scat=EBDE5A81-459C-453D-940E-8E0A2FABEE7E

Purpose and activities: As a complement to its foundation, Aventis Pharmaceuticals also makes charitable contributions to nonprofit organizations directly. Special emphasis is directed toward programs involved with health and human services, education, civic and community development, and the environment. Support is given primarily in areas of company operations in Tucson and Scottsdale, Arizona, Washington, D.C., Atlanta, Georgia, Cambridge, Massachusetts, St. Louis, Missouri, Sparks, Nevada, New York, New York, Malvern/Great Valley, Pennsylvania, and Dallas, Texas, with emphasis on Bridgewater, New Jersey, and its surrounding communities.
Fields of interest: Education; Environment; Health care; Disasters, preparedness/services; Human services; Community/economic development; Public affairs.
Type of support: Employee matching gifts; Employee volunteer services; General/operating support.
Geographic limitations: Giving primarily in areas of company operations in Tucson and Scottsdale, AZ, Washington, DC, Atlanta, GA, Cambridge, MA, St. Louis. MO, Sparks, NV, New York, NY, Malvern/Great Valley, PA, and Dallas, TX, with emphasis on Bridgewater, NJ, and its surrounding communities.
Support limitations: No support for political, religious, fraternal, athletic, or discriminatory organizations, or organizations posing a conflict of interest with Aventis' goals or products, or trade unions, or university-sponsored or free-standing scientific research centers for research on sanofi-aventis related projects or product lines. No grants to individuals, or for deficit financing or debt recovery, capital campaigns, conferences and symposia, or commercial sponsorships or corporate hospitality opportunities.
Application information: Applications not accepted. The Corporate Giving and Philanthropy Department handles giving. The company has a staff that only handles contributions.
Administrators: Amy Dupuis, Corp. Giving Specialist; Melissa Feltmann, Dir., U.S. Community Affairs; Phillip St. James, Mgr., U.S. Community Affairs.
Number of staff: 2 full-time professional; 1 full-time support.

Endocrine Fellows Foundation

P.O. Box 58265
Washington, DC 20037 (877) 877-6515
FAX: (202) 223-1762;
E-mail: info@endocrinefellows.org; E-mail for Anne L. Mercer: amercer@endocrinefellows.org;
URL: http://www.endocrinefellows.org/

Establishment information: Established in 1995 in CA.
Donors: Amylin Pharmaceuticals Inc.; Takeda Pharmaceuticals; Aventis Pharmaceuticals Inc.; Ortho-McNeil Pharmaceutical, Inc.; Sanofi-Aventis; Merck; Novartis; Eli Lilly and Co.; Pfizer; Genzyme; Medtronic; Abbott Laboratories.
Contact: Anne L. Mercer, Exec. Dir.
Financial data (yr. ended 12/31/10): Assets, $626,307 (M); gifts received, $940,337; expenditures, $1,013,345; qualifying distributions, $825,101; giving activities include $327,500 for 22 grants (high: $20,000; low: $7,500) and $708,021 for 4 foundation-administered programs.
Purpose and activities: The foundation supports programs designed to foster the advancement of fellows in endocrinology, diabetes, and metabolism through education and research funding.
Fields of interest: Medical school/education; Hospitals (general); Health care, clinics/centers; Public health, obesity; Nerve, muscle & bone diseases; Diabetes; Medical research, institute; Diabetes research; Medical specialties research.
Programs:

Fellows Development Research Grant Program in Diabetes, Obesity, and Fat Cell Biology: The foundation, in partnership with Amylin Pharmaceuticals, provides four renewable research grants of $12,500 in the areas of cardiometabolic disorders in obesity and diabetes. The grant is designed to foster career development and successful grantees are required to present their research at an EFF scientific forum.

Marilyn Fishman Grant for Diabetes Research: The foundation, in partnership with Bristol-Myers Squibb and AstraZeneca Pharmaceuticals, awards up to eight research grants for $10,000. The grant is limited to metabolism, obesity, and Type 2 diabetes clinical and basic research. Successful grantees are expected to present their research at an EFF scientific diabetes forum for fellows.

Preceptorship Program: The foundation sponsors two-week preceptorships in endocrinology at select institutions to enable fellows to increase their skills in specialized areas. The preceptorships include specialty clinics, research, and techniques that are useful in subspecialty areas of endocrinology and metabolism. The program is limited to second and third year fellows.

The EFF Endocrine Research Grant: The foundation awards up to six $7,500 general endocrinology grants for thyroid, bone, adrenal, growth, and reproductive disorders.

Type of support: Conferences/seminars; Research.
Geographic limitations: Giving primarily in CA, Washington, DC, GA, Chicago, IL, MA, MO, and NY.
Support limitations: No grants to individuals.
Publications: Application guidelines; Newsletter.
Application information: Applications accepted. Application form required. Applicants should submit the following:
1) copy of current year's organizational budget and/or project budget
2) detailed description of project and amount of funding requested

Applications should include a research proposal; graphic material, if applicable; the applicants role in the project; a curriculum vitae; a statement from the applicants mentor; human research committee approval; animal research committee approval; and committee on biohazards approval.
Initial approach: Complete online application form; download application form and mail to foundation for Preceptorships
Deadline(s): Mar. 9 for Fellows Development Research Grant Program, EFF Endocrine Research Grant, and Marilyn Fishman Grant for Diabetes Research; varies for Preceptorships, but generally Mar. 26
Final notification: Apr. 30 for Fellows Development Research Grant Program, EFF Endocrine Research Grant, and Marilyn Fishman Grant for Diabetes Research
Officers and Directors:* John P. Bilezikian, M.D.*, Chair.; Mark Stolar, M.D.*, Pres.; Anne L. Mercer, Exec. Dir.; Ramachandrian Coopan, M.D.*, Editor; Michael Berelowitz, M.D.; Derek LeRoith, M.D., Ph.D.; Ronald Tamler, M.D., Ph.D.
EIN: 954511639
Selected grants: The following grants are a representative sample of this grantmaker's funding activity:
$20,000 to Beth Israel Deaconess Medical Center, Boston, MA, 2010.
$20,000 to Mount Sinai School of Medicine of New York University, New York, NY, 2010.
$20,000 to University of California, Los Angeles, CA, 2010.
$15,000 to Childrens Mercy Hospital, Kansas City, MO, 2010.
$15,000 to Kaiser Permanente, Denver, CO, 2010.
$15,000 to University of Chicago, Chicago, IL, 2010.
$15,000 to University of Michigan, Ann Arbor, MI, 2010.
$15,000 to University of Texas Southwestern Medical Center, Dallas, TX, 2010.
$15,000 to University of Wisconsin System, Madison, WI, 2010.
$7,500 to Yale University, New Haven, CT, 2010.

Hamico, Inc.

1715 W. 38th St.
Chattanooga, TN 37409-1248

Establishment information: Incorporated in 1956 in TN.
Donor: Chattem, Inc.
Financial data (yr. ended 12/31/11): Assets, $54,453,008 (M); expenditures, $3,086,838; qualifying distributions, $2,673,954; giving activities include $2,391,127 for grants.
Purpose and activities: The foundation supports community foundations and festivals and organizations involved with arts and culture, education, health, athletics, and human services.
Fields of interest: Arts; Elementary/secondary education; Higher education; Education; Zoos/zoological societies; Medical care, community health systems; Hospitals (general); Health care; Athletics/sports, school programs; Recreation, fairs/festivals; Athletics/sports, amateur leagues; Athletics/sports, racquet sports; Children/youth, services; Developmentally disabled, centers & services; Human services; Foundations (community); United Ways and Federated Giving Programs.
Type of support: Continuing support; General/operating support.
Geographic limitations: Giving limited to Chattanooga, TN.
Support limitations: No grants to individuals.
Application information: Applications not accepted. Contributes only to pre-selected organizations.
Officers and Directors:* Zan Guerry*, Pres.; Robert E. Bosworth*, Secy.; Herbert Barks; Alexis G. Bogo; John P. Guerry.
EIN: 626040782
Selected grants: The following grants are a representative sample of this grantmaker's funding activity:
$379,499 to Baylor School, Chattanooga, TN, 2007.
$51,000 to Friends of the Festival, Chattanooga, TN, 2007.
$28,200 to Junior League of Chattanooga, Chattanooga, TN, 2007.
$22,540 to Chattanooga Symphony and Opera, Chattanooga, TN, 2007.
$10,000 to Ballet Tennessee, Chattanooga, TN, 2007.
$5,000 to Girls Preparatory School, Chattanooga, TN, 2007.
$4,000 to Allied Arts of Greater Chattanooga, Chattanooga, TN, 2007.
$3,000 to Chattanooga Downtown Partnership, Chattanooga, TN, 2007.
$2,000 to Association for Visual Artists, Chattanooga, TN, 2007.
$1,000 to Boyd-Buchanan School, Chattanooga, TN, 2007.

Sanofi Foundation for North America

(formerly Sanofi-aventis Patient Assistance Foundation)
55 Corporate Dr.
Bridgewater, NJ 08807-2855 (888) 847-4877
FAX: (888) 847-1797; Application address: P.O. Box 759, Somerville, NJ 08876, tel.: (800) 221-4025, fax: (866) 734-7372; Additional tel.: (800) 221-4025; URL: http://www.sanofi.us/l/us/en/layout.jsp?scat=A818CDDB-E4F3-4369-8CC7-C6012BFB3C6A

Establishment information: Established in 1992.
Donors: Marion Merrell Dow Inc.; Hoechst Marion Roussel, Inc.; Aventis Pharmaceuticals Inc.; Sanofi-Aventis US, LLC.
Financial data (yr. ended 12/31/11): Assets, $0 (M); expenditures, $497,491,467; qualifying distributions, $497,491,467; giving activities include $497,491,467 for grants to individuals.
Purpose and activities: The foundation provides medication for patients who are below the federal poverty level and who are not eligible for any third-party medication payments.
Fields of interest: Economically disadvantaged.
Type of support: Donated products; Grants to individuals.
Geographic limitations: Giving on a national basis.
Publications: Application guidelines.
Application information: Applications accepted. Application form required.
Initial approach: Contact foundation for application information
Deadline(s): None
Officers: Gregory Irace, Pres.; Philippe Grillet, V.P.; Stacey Silkworth, Secy.; Richard Thomson, Treas.
EIN: 431614543

3330
Sansar Capital Management, LLC

135 E. 57th St., Ste. 90
New York, NY 10022-2162 (212) 399-8980

Establishment information: Established in 2005.
Company type: Private company
Business activities: Operates investment firm.
Business type (SIC): Investment offices
Financial profile for 2010: Number of employees, 24
Corporate officer: Sanjay Motwani, Owner
Giving statement: Giving through the Sansar Capital Foundation.

The Sansar Capital Foundation

c/o Rothestein Kass
1350 Ave. of the Americas
New York, NY 10019-2050

Establishment information: Established in 2005 in NY.
Donors: Sansar Capital Management, LLC; Sanjay Montwani.
Financial data (yr. ended 12/31/11): Assets, $1,124,706 (M); expenditures, $128,000; qualifying distributions, $128,000; giving activities include $128,000 for grants.
Purpose and activities: The foundation supports organizations involved with education and Indian culture.
Fields of interest: Education.
International interests: India.
Type of support: General/operating support.
Geographic limitations: Giving limited to NY, TX, and India.
Support limitations: No grants to individuals.
Application information: Applications not accepted. Unsolicited requests for funds not accepted.
Trustees: Vincent Guacci; Sanjay Montwani.
EIN: 020761791

3331
Santa Fe Natural Tobacco Company, Inc.

1 Plz. La Prensa
Santa Fe, NM 87504-9702 (505) 473-7617

Company URL: http://www.nascigs.com
Establishment information: Established in 1982.
Company type: Subsidiary of a public company
Business activities: Produces cigarettes.
Business type (SIC): Tobacco products—cigarettes
Financial profile for 2010: Number of employees, 150
Corporate officers: Nicholas A. Bumbacco, Co.-Pres. and C.E.O.; John E. Franzino, Sr. V.P., Finance and C.F.O.; Michael O. Johnson, Sr. V.P. and Genl. Counsel; Michael A. Little, Co.-Pres.; Cressida J. Lozano, V.P., Sales and Mktg.; Mark Smith, V.P., Comms.
Giving statement: Giving through the Santa Fe Natural Tobacco Company Foundation.

Santa Fe Natural Tobacco Company Foundation

(formerly Natural American Spirit Foundation)
P.O. Box 25140
Santa Fe, NM 87504-5140
URL: http://www.sfntcfoundation.org

Establishment information: Established in 1998 in NM.
Donor: Santa Fe Natural Tobacco Co., Inc.
Contact: Nicholas A. Bumbacco, Pres.
Financial data (yr. ended 12/31/11): Assets, $2,886,298 (M); gifts received, $737,863; expenditures, $359,116; qualifying distributions, $275,360; giving activities include $275,360 for grants.
Purpose and activities: The foundation supports programs designed to preserve, promote, and advance American Indian self-sufficiency and culture through the development of American Indian entrepreneurs, the facilitation of American Indian education, and the preservation of American Indian languages.
Fields of interest: Language/linguistics; Historic preservation/historical societies; Higher education; Education; Community/economic development Native Americans/American Indians.
Type of support: General/operating support; Program development.
Geographic limitations: Giving primarily in NM, with some emphasis on Albuquerque, and Porcupine, SD; giving also in CO, NE, NH, and VA.
Support limitations: No grants to individuals.
Publications: Application guidelines.
Application information: Applications accepted. Proposals should be submitted using organization letterhead. Organizations receiving support are asked to provide a final report. Application form required. Applicants should submit the following:
1) signature and title of chief executive officer
2) statement of problem project will address
3) copy of IRS Determination Letter
4) brief history of organization and description of its mission
5) copy of most recent annual report/audited financial statement/990
6) how project's results will be evaluated or measured
7) descriptive literature about organization
8) listing of board of directors, trustees, officers and other key people and their affiliations
9) copy of current year's organizational budget and/or project budget
10) additional materials/documentation
Initial approach: Download application form and mail proposal and application form to foundation
Copies of proposal: 1
Board meeting date(s): Mar., June, Sept., and Dec.
Deadline(s): Feb. 28, May 31, Aug. 31, and Nov. 30
Final notification: 30 days

Officers and Directors: Nicholas A. Bumbacco, Pres.; Susanne R. Farr., V.P.; John E. Franzino, Secy.-Treas.; Russell Means; S. Leigh Park.
EIN: 850448116
Selected grants: The following grants are a representative sample of this grantmaker's funding activity:
$100,000 to American Indian College Fund, Denver, CO, 2009.
$20,000 to Running Strong for American Indian Youth, Alexandria, VA, 2009.

3332
Santrust and Associates, Inc.

(doing business as SanTrust Ltd.)
(formerly W.M. Sanderlin & Associates Inc.)
738 Rugby St.
Orlando, FL 32804-4969 (407) 540-1500

Establishment information: Established in 1989.
Company type: Private company
Business activities: Provides general contract heavy construction services.
Business type (SIC): Heavy construction other than building construction contractors
Corporate officer: W. M. Sanderlin, Pres.
Giving statement: Giving through the Sanderlin Foundation, Inc.

Sanderlin Foundation, Inc.

738 Rugby St.
Orlando, FL 32804-4969 (407) 540-1500

Establishment information: Established in 2003 in FL.
Donor: SanTrust, Ltd.
Contact: Waldron Sanderlin, Pres.
Financial data (yr. ended 12/31/11): Assets, $189,754 (M); expenditures, $2,043; qualifying distributions, $2,000; giving activities include $2,000 for grants.
Purpose and activities: The foundation supports organizations involved with human services and Christianity.
Fields of interest: Human services; Christian agencies & churches.
Type of support: General/operating support.
Geographic limitations: Giving primarily in Orlando, FL.
Application information: Applications accepted. Application form required. Applicants should submit the following:
1) detailed description of project and amount of funding requested
Initial approach: Letter
Deadline(s): None
Officers: Waldron Sanderlin, Pres.; Judith Squillante, V.P.; Joanne Sanderlin, Secy.
Directors: Janet Rouhier; Jacqueline Sanderlin.
EIN: 030437117

3333
SANYO North America Corporation

2055 SANYO Ave.
San Diego, CA 92154 (619) 661-1134

Company URL: http://www.sanyo.com
Establishment information: Established in 1961.
Company type: Subsidiary of a foreign company
Business activities: Provides business services.
Business type (SIC): Management and public relations services
Corporate officers: Masami Murata, Pres.; Aaron S. Fowles, V.P., Corp. Comms.
Board of director: Seiichiro Sano
Giving statement: Giving through the SANYO North America Corporation Contributions Program.

SANYO North America Corporation Contributions Program

2055 Sanyo Ave.
San Diego, CA 92154-6229
URL: http://us.sanyo.com/Social-Responsibility

Purpose and activities: SANYO North America makes charitable contributions to nonprofit organizations involved with music, education, sustainable energy, the environment, and youth development. Support is given primarily in areas of company operations in Arkansas, Georgia, Illinois, Michigan, Missouri, New Jersey, Oregon, and Texas, with emphasis on California.
Fields of interest: Performing arts, music; Education; Environment, energy; Environment; Youth development.
Type of support: Employee volunteer services; In-kind gifts; Program development.
Geographic limitations: Giving primarily in areas of company operations in AR, GA, IL, MI, MO, NJ, OR, and TX, with emphasis on CA.
Application information: Applications not accepted.

3334
SAP America, Inc.

3999 W. Chester Pike
Newtown Square, PA 19073
(610) 661-1000

Company URL: http://www.sap.com/usa
Establishment information: Established in 1988.
Company type: Subsidiary of a foreign company
Business activities: Develops computer software.
Business type (SIC): Computer services
Financial profile for 2010: Number of employees, 1,700; sales volume, $3,170,000,000
Corporate officers: Rodolpho Cardenuto, Pres.; Bill McDermott, Co-C.E.O.; Jim Hagemann Snabe, Co-C.E.O.; Steven Winter, C.O.O.; Mark R. White, C.F.O.; Mary Beth Hanss, Sr. V.P. and Genl. Counsel; Emile Lee, V.P., Comms.; Brigette McInnis-Day, V.P., Human Resources
Board of directors: Werner Brandt; Angelika Dammann; Bill McDermott; Gerhard Oswald; Jim Hagemann Snabe; Vishal Sikka
Offices: Foster City, Irvine, Palo Alto, CA; Denver, CO; Washington, DC; Atlanta, GA; Westchester, IL; Waltham, MA; Southfield, MI; Minneapolis, MN; St. Louis, MO; Morristown, NJ; New York, NY; Cincinnati, Cleveland, OH; Pittsburgh, PA; Austin, Dallas, Houston, Irving, TX; Bellevue, WA
Giving statement: Giving through the SAP America, Inc. Corporate Giving Program.

SAP America, Inc. Corporate Giving Program

3999 West Chester Pike
Newtown Square, PA 19073-2305 (610) 661-1000
E-mail: citizenship@sap.com; SAP Corporate Social Responsibility: csr@sap.com; SAP North America Scholarship Program: SAPScholarship@easymatch.com; Scholarship application URL: http://www.easymatch.com/sapscholarship; URL: http://www.sap.com/company/citizenship/index.epx

Purpose and activities: SAP America makes charitable contributions to nonprofit organizations involved with disabilities, education, science, engineering, mathematics, technology, computer science, military organizations, philanthropy, and volunteerism. Support is given primarily in areas of company operations in Bay Area, California, Washington, DC, Miami, Florida, Atlanta, Georgia, Chicago, Illinois, Boston, Massachusetts, New York, New York, Philadelphia, Pennsylvania, and Dallas and Houston, Texas. Giving also on a national and international basis, including in Germany. Priority is given to long-term initiatives over single events.
Fields of interest: Child development, education; Higher education, university; Adult/continuing education; Scholarships/financial aid; Education; Crime/violence prevention, domestic violence; Business/industry; Philanthropy/voluntarism; Science; Mathematics; Engineering/technology; Computer science; Military/veterans' organizations Children/youth; Disabilities, people with; Economically disadvantaged.
Type of support: Continuing support; Employee matching gifts; Employee volunteer services; Employee-related scholarships; General/operating support.
Geographic limitations: Giving primarily in areas of company operations in Bay Area, CA, Washington, DC, Miami, FL, Atlanta, GA, Chicago, IL, Boston, MA, New York, NY, Philadelphia, PA, and Dallas, and Houston, TX.
Support limitations: No support for organizations that are discriminatory, inconsistent with SAP America's core values, have a bad reputation among the public or stakeholders, or are located in or donate to a country or region where legal requirements have not been followed. No grants in the form of long-term commitments that have no contractual provisions for termination or revisions at short notice, and no possibility of regular assessment, or to individuals who are related to a SAP employee, or who have received a scholarship before.
Publications: Corporate giving report.
Application information: Applications accepted. The Corporate Citizenship Department handles giving. No scholarships for relatives of SAP employees or students who have already received a SAP scholarship. Unsolicited grant requests are not encouraged and are reviewed on an ongoing basis. The maximum for matching gifts is $10,000 per employee, per calendar year, with limited funding provided on a first-come first-serve basis. Scholarship applications must include a transcript, resume, letter of recommendation, and confirmation of community service.
Deadline(s): None for grant requests
Number of staff: 2 full-time professional.

3335
Sartori Food Corporation

107 N. Pleasant View Rd.
P.O. Box 258
Plymouth, WI 53073-0258 (920) 893-6061
FAX: (920) 892-2732

Company URL: http://www.sartorifoods.com
Establishment information: Established in 1939.
Company type: Private company
Business activities: Produces cheese.
Business type (SIC): Dairy products
Financial profile for 2010: Number of employees, 252

Corporate officers: James C. Sartori, C.E.O.; Jeff Schwager, Pres.; Peter Marsing, V.P., Opers.; Frederick M. Bowes II, V.P., Finance; David Leitl, Cont.
Giving statement: Giving through the Sartori Foundation Inc.

The Sartori Foundation Inc.

P.O. Box 258
Plymouth, WI 53073-0258 (920) 893-6061

Establishment information: Established as a company-sponsored operating foundation in 1998.
Donor: Sartori Food Corp.
Contact: Frederick M. Bowes, II, Secy.-Treas.
Financial data (yr. ended 12/31/11): Assets, $962,925 (M); gifts received, $140,000; expenditures, $254,295; qualifying distributions, $242,500; giving activities include $242,500 for grants.
Purpose and activities: The foundation supports hospices and organizations involved with education, health, and civil liberties.
Fields of interest: Secondary school/education; Education; Hospitals (general); Health care; Residential/custodial care, hospices; Civil liberties, right to life.
Type of support: Annual campaigns; General/operating support.
Geographic limitations: Giving primarily in the Sheboygan County, WI, area.
Support limitations: No grants to individuals.
Application information: Applications accepted. Application form not required.
Initial approach: Proposal
Deadline(s): None
Officers: James C. Sartori, Pres.; Janet L. Sartori, V.P.; Frederick M. Bowes II, Secy.-Treas.
EIN: 391933307

3336
SAS Institute Inc.

100 SAS Campus Dr.
Cary, NC 27513-2414 (919) 677-8000

Company URL: http://www.sas.com
Establishment information: Established in 1976.
Company type: Private company
Business activities: Designs, develops, and produces computer software.
Business type (SIC): Computer services
Financial profile for 2011: Number of employees, 11,920; sales volume, $2,750,000,000
Corporate officers: James H. Goodnight, C.E.O.; Don Parker, Sr. V.P. and C.F.O.; John Boswell, Sr. V.P. and Corp. Secy.; Suzanne Gordon, V.P. and C.I.O.; Jennifer Mann, V.P., Human Resources
Offices: Phoenix, AZ; Los Angeles, San Diego, San Francisco, San Jose, CA; Denver, CO; Hartford, CT; Miami, Orlando, FL; Atlanta, GA; Chicago, IL; Kansas City, KS; New Orleans, LA; Rockville, MD; Boston, MA; Detroit, MI; Minneapolis, MN; St. Louis, MO; Bedminster, NJ; New York, NY; Cincinnati, Cleveland, OH; Philadelphia, Pittsburgh, PA; Nashville, TN; Austin, Dallas, Houston, TX; Seattle, WA
International operations: Australia; Belgium; Canada; China; Denmark; Finland; France; Germany; Italy; Japan; Malaysia; Netherlands; New Zealand; Norway; Philippines; Singapore; South Korea; Spain; Sweden; Switzerland; Taiwan; United Kingdom
Giving statement: Giving through the SAS Institute Inc. Corporate Giving Program.

SAS Institute Inc. Corporate Giving Program

SAS Campus Dr.
Cary, NC 27513-2414 (919) 677-8000
FAX: (919) 677-4444;
E-mail: communityrelations@sas.com; URL: http://www.sas.com/corporate/community/index.html

Purpose and activities: SAS makes charitable contributions to nonprofit organizations involved with science, technology, and engineering (STEM) education. Special emphasis is directed towards programs designed to help teens succeed in the classroom and graduate from high school. Support is limited to North Carolina.
Fields of interest: Elementary/secondary education; Education; Youth development; Science; Engineering/technology.
Program:
Employee Volunteer Fund: SAS awards $500 grants to nonprofit organizations with which employees have volunteered an average of eight hours per month for one year.
Type of support: Employee volunteer services; General/operating support; In-kind gifts.
Geographic limitations: Giving primarily in NC.
Support limitations: No support for religious organizations, political organizations or candidates, or organizations not of direct benefit to the entire community. No grants to individuals, or for professional athletic or amateur sports teams, benefit or yearbook advertising, trips or tours, independent film or video production, or single events such as walk-a-thons, fundraisers, workshops, or seminars.
Publications: Application guidelines.
Application information: Applications accepted. Proposals should be no longer than 3 pages. Submitted materials will not be returned. Application form required. Applicants should submit the following:
1) results expected from proposed grant
2) statement of problem project will address
3) population served
4) copy of IRS Determination Letter
5) brief history of organization and description of its mission
6) geographic area to be served
7) copy of most recent annual report/audited financial statement/990
8) how project's results will be evaluated or measured
9) explanation of why grantmaker is considered an appropriate donor for project
10) listing of board of directors, trustees, officers and other key people and their affiliations
11) detailed description of project and amount of funding requested
12) copy of current year's organizational budget and/or project budget

Proposals should include a description of the program's track record; and a description of past support by the SAS Institute with the organization.
Initial approach: Download application form and mail with proposal to headquarters
Copies of proposal: 1
Deadline(s): None

3337
Sasaki Associates, Inc.

64 Pleasant St.
Watertown, MA 02472-2316
(617) 926-3300

Company URL: http://www.sasaki.com
Establishment information: Established in 1953.
Company type: Private company
Business activities: Provides architectural services; provides landscape architectural services.
Business type (SIC): Engineering, architectural, and surveying services; landscape and horticultural services
Corporate officers: James A. Sukeforth, C.E.O.; Dennis Pieprz, Pres.; Steve Roscoe, C.F.O.; Maura Brouillette Haley, V.P., Human Resources
Office: San Francisco, CA
Giving statement: Giving through the Hideo Sasaki Foundation.

The Hideo Sasaki Foundation

64 Pleasant St.
Watertown, MA 02472-2316
E-mail: foundation@sasaki.com; URL: http://www.sasaki.com/about-us/Hideo+Sasaki+Foundation/

Establishment information: Established in 2000 in MA.
Donor: Sasaki Associates, Inc.
Financial data (yr. ended 12/31/11): Assets, $409,804 (M); gifts received, $9,500; expenditures, $35,002; qualifying distributions, $30,000; giving activities include $30,000 for grants.
Purpose and activities: The foundation supports organizations involved with continuing education, research, and writing in the planning and design disciplines; sponsors research; and hosts and supports symposia on planning and design issues.
Fields of interest: Education.
Type of support: Conferences/seminars; General/operating support; Research.
Geographic limitations: Giving primarily in Washington, DC and Boston, MA.
Application information: Applications not accepted. Unsolicited requests for funds not accepted.
Trustees: Elizabeth Meek; James A. Sukeforth; Alan Ward.
EIN: 043534908

3338
Sasol North America, Inc.

(formerly CONDEA Vista Company)
900 Threadneedle, Ste. 100
Houston, TX 77079-2990 (281) 588-3000

Company URL: http://www.sasolnorthamerica.com
Establishment information: Established in 1984.
Company type: Subsidiary of a foreign company
Business activities: Manufactures commodity and specialty chemicals.
Business type (SIC): Chemicals and allied products
Financial profile for 2012: Number of employees, 34,000
Corporate officer: Pat Jernigan, Pres.
Plants: Tucson, AZ; Lake Charles, LA; Baltimore, MD
Office: Austin, TX
Giving statement: Giving through the Sasol North America Inc. Corporate Giving Program and the Showa Shell Sekiyu K.K.

Sasol North America Inc. Corporate Giving Program

(formerly CONDEA Vista Company Contributions Program)
900 Threadneedle
Houston, TX 77079-2990 (337) 494-5301
URL: http://www.sasolswla.com/community.asp

Purpose and activities: Sasol North America makes charitable contributions to nonprofit organizations involved with arts and culture, education, healthcare, civic affairs, and on a case by case basis. Support is given primarily in southwest Louisiana.
Fields of interest: Arts; Education; Animals/wildlife; Health care; United Ways and Federated Giving Programs; Public affairs; General charitable giving.
Type of support: Employee volunteer services; General/operating support.
Geographic limitations: Giving primarily in southwest LA; giving also to national organizations.

3339
Satterlee Stephens Burke & Burke LLP

230 Park Ave., Ste. 1130
New York, NY 10169-0079 (212) 404-8787

Company URL: http://www.ssbb.com/index.php/main
Establishment information: Established in 1894.
Company type: Private company
Business activities: Operates law firm.
Business type (SIC): Legal services
Offices: Iselin, NJ; New York, NY
Giving statement: Giving through the Satterlee Stephens Burke & Burke LLP Pro Bono Program.

Satterlee Stephens Burke & Burke LLP Pro Bono Program

230 Park Ave., Ste. 1130
New York, NY 10169-0079 (212) 404-8787
FAX: (212) 818-9606; E-mail: mfowler@ssbb.com; Additional tel.: (212) 818-9200; URL: http://www.ssbb.com/index.php/firm/entry/4

Contact: Mark A. Fowler Esq., Hiring Partner
Fields of interest: Legal services.
Type of support: Pro bono services - legal.

3340
Saucony, Inc.

191 Spring St.
P.O. Box 9191
Lexington, MA 02420-9191 (617) 824-6000

Company URL: http://www.saucony.com
Establishment information: Established in 1898.
Company type: Subsidiary of a public company
Business activities: Produces running shoes and other athletic footwear.
Business type (SIC): Apparel, piece goods, and notions—wholesale
Financial profile for 2010: Number of employees, 125
Corporate officers: Richard J. Woodworth, Pres.; Sharon Barbano, V.P., Public Rels.
Giving statement: Giving through the Saucony Run For Good, Inc.

Saucony Run For Good, Inc.

(also known as Saucony Run for Good Foundation)
191 Spring St., MD 3185
Lexington, MA 02420-9191 (617) 824-6000
E-mail: RunForGood@saucony.com; URL: http://www.sauconyrunforgood.com/

Establishment information: Established in 2006 in MA.
Financial data (yr. ended 09/30/11): Assets, $8,857 (M); gifts received, $99,416; expenditures, $129,486; qualifying distributions, $121,250; giving activities include $121,250 for grants.
Purpose and activities: The foundation supports programs designed to prevent and reduce childhood obesity; and promote active and healthy lifestyles for children. Special emphasis is directed toward programs designed to improve the lives of children through running.
Fields of interest: Public health, obesity; Public health, physical fitness; Health care Children.
Type of support: Equipment; General/operating support; Program development.
Geographic limitations: Giving primarily in AZ, CA, MA, MD, MI, NY, PA, SC, VA, and WA.
Publications: Application guidelines.
Application information: Applications accepted. Grants of up to $10,000 are awarded. Proposals should be no longer than 4 pages. Support is limited to 1 contribution per organization during any given year. Application form required. Applicants should submit the following:
1) qualifications of key personnel
2) population served
3) copy of IRS Determination Letter
4) brief history of organization and description of its mission
5) detailed description of project and amount of funding requested
6) copy of current year's organizational budget and/or project budget

Initial approach: Download application form and mail proposal and form to foundation
Copies of proposal: 1
Deadline(s): Dec. 13 and June 13
Final notification: Feb. and Aug.

Officers and Directors:* Richard Woodworth*, Pres.; Sharon Barbano*, Secy.; Frank A. Caruso*, Treas.
EIN: 208428900
Selected grants: The following grants are a representative sample of this grantmaker's funding activity:
$2,500 to Childrens Aid Society, New York, NY, 2010.

3341
Savage Services Corp.

(formerly Savage Industries, Inc.)
6340 S. 3000 E., Ste. 600
Salt Lake City, UT 84121-3560
(801) 944-6600

Company URL: http://www.savageservices.com
Establishment information: Established in 1946.
Company type: Subsidiary of a private company
Business activities: Provides materials management and transportation services.
Business type (SIC): Trucking and courier services, except by air; warehousing and storage
Financial profile for 2009: Number of employees, 1,800
Corporate officers: Allen B. Alexander, Chair. and C.E.O.; Kirk Aubry, Pres. and C.O.O; Curtis Dowd, Exec. V.P. and C.F.O.; Kelly Flint, Sr. V.P. and Genl. Counsel
Board of director: Allen B. Alexander, Chair.
Subsidiary: Western Coal Carrier Corp., Castle Dale, UT
Giving statement: Giving through the Kenneth C. Savage Family Foundation, the T. Luke Savage Family Foundation, and the Neal & Sherrie Savage Family Foundation.

Kenneth C. Savage Family Foundation

6340 S. 3000 E., Ste. 600
Salt Lake City, UT 84121-3560

Establishment information: Established in 2000 in UT.
Donors: Savage Industries, Inc.; Savage Services Corp.
Financial data (yr. ended 12/31/11): Assets, $216,697 (M); gifts received, $75,000; expenditures, $30,695; qualifying distributions, $29,495; giving activities include $29,495 for grants.
Purpose and activities: The foundation supports orchestras and organizations involved with education, grief counseling, and human services.
Fields of interest: Arts; Education; Human services.
Type of support: General/operating support.
Geographic limitations: Giving primarily in UT.
Support limitations: No grants to individuals.
Application information: Applications not accepted. Unsolicited requests for funds not accepted.
Officers and Trustees:* John K. Savage*, Pres.; Shannon Savage Magleby*, V.P.; Colleen Savage Smith*, V.P.; Carolyn Savage Wright*, V.P.; Larae T. Savage*, Secy.
EIN: 870651832

The Neal & Sherrie Savage Family Foundation

6340 S. 3000 E., Ste. 600
Salt Lake City, UT 84121 (801) 802-0906
Application address: 42 W. 530 S., Orem, UT 84058, Tel.: (801) 802-0906

Establishment information: Established in 2000 in UT.
Donors: Savage Industries, Inc.; Savage Services Corp.
Contact: Melissa Ann Clayton, Pres. and Tr.
Financial data (yr. ended 12/31/11): Assets, $13,937 (M); gifts received, $75,000; expenditures, $69,148; qualifying distributions, $66,790; giving activities include $66,790 for grants.
Purpose and activities: The foundation supports organizations involved with education, patient services, hunger, and human services.
Fields of interest: Education; Community/economic development; Religion.
International interests: Haiti.
Type of support: General/operating support; Scholarship funds.
Geographic limitations: Giving limited to UT and Haiti.
Support limitations: No grants to individuals.
Application information: Applications accepted. Application form required.

Initial approach: Letter
Deadline(s): None

Officers and Trustees:* Melissa Ann Clayton*, Pres.; Melinda Savage Melville*, Treas.; Anna Savage Benedict; Gregory James Savage; Nathan Neal Savage; Emilee Savage Wright.
EIN: 870651828

The T. Luke Savage Family Foundation

6340 S. 3000 E., Ste. 600
Salt Lake City, UT 84121-3560

Establishment information: Established in 2000 in UT.
Donors: Savage Industries, Inc.; Savage Services Corp.
Financial data (yr. ended 12/31/11): Assets, $163,609 (M); gifts received, $75,000; expenditures, $73,216; qualifying distributions, $72,509; giving activities include $72,509 for grants.
Purpose and activities: The foundation supports organizations involved with education, children services, and residential care.
Fields of interest: Education; Youth development; Religion.
Type of support: General/operating support.
Geographic limitations: Giving primarily in UT.
Support limitations: No grants to individuals.
Application information: Applications not accepted. Unsolicited requests for funds not accepted.
Officers and Trustees:* Todd Savage*, V.P.; Susan Savage*, Secy.-Treas.; Lorrie Savage Gilbert; Lisa Savage Kelly; Matthew Trent Savage; Terrence Savage; Troy Savage; Ty Savage.
EIN: 870651831

3342
Save Mart Supermarkets

1800 Standiford Ave.
Modesto, CA 95350-0180 (209) 577-1600

Company URL: http://www.savemart.com
Establishment information: Established in 1952.
Company type: Private company
Business activities: Operates supermarkets.
Business type (SIC): Groceries—retail
Financial profile for 2011: Number of employees, 20,000; sales volume, $4,800,000,000
Corporate officers: Robert M. Piccinini, Chair. and C.E.O.; Steve Junqueiro, Pres. and C.O.O.; Steve Ackerman, C.F.O.; Mike Silveira, C.A.O.; Cecil Russell, V.P., Mktg.
Board of director: Robert M. Piccinini, Chair.
Subsidiary: Yosemite Express Co., Lathrop, CA
Giving statement: Giving through the Save Mart Supermarkets Corporate Giving Program.

Save Mart Supermarkets Corporate Giving Program

c/o Community Support Team
1800 Standiford Ave.
Modesto, CA 95350-0180 (209) 577-1600
E-mail: eventscharities@savemart.com; Application address: Community Support Team, Save Mart Supermarkets, P.O. Box 4278, Modesto, CA 95352; URL: http://www.savemart.com/index.php?id=108

Purpose and activities: Save Mart makes charitable contributions to nonprofit organizations involved with human services for children, education, health needs, and food for children and families with children. Support is given primarily in areas of company operations.
Fields of interest: Arts; Education; Health care, patient services; Health care; Cancer; Muscular dystrophy; Food services; Recreation; Salvation Army; Children, services; Family services; Human services.
Program:
S.H.A.R.E.S. Program: Through S.H.A.R.E.S., Supporting Humanities, Arts, Recreation, Education, and Sports in the community, Save Mart customers can contribute to schools, churches, and other organizations. Customers receive a S.H.A.R.E.S. card and every time they shop, a registered organization of their choice is awarded a quarterly check for 3% of the qualified purchases.
Type of support: Donated products; General/operating support; In-kind gifts; Sponsorships.
Geographic limitations: Giving primarily in areas of company operations in CA.
Publications: Application guidelines.
Application information: Applications accepted. Proposals should be submitted using organization letterhead. Applicants should submit the following:
1) name, address and phone number of organization
2) contact person
Proposals should include the date and location of the event or program, and the type and amount of funding requested.
Initial approach: Present request at local store for requests valued at $50 or less; proposal to headquarters for requests valued at $50 or more

3343
The Savings Bank

357 Main St.
P.O. Box 30
Wakefield, MA 01880-3993 (781) 224-5341

Company URL: http://www.tsbawake24.com
Establishment information: Established in 1869.
Company type: Mutual company
Business activities: Operates savings bank.
Business type (SIC): Savings institutions
Corporate officers: Brian D. McCoubrey, Pres. and C.E.O.; Robert J. DiBella, Exec. V.P. and C.O.O.; Sally Kaldas, Sr. V.P. and C.F.O.; Raichelle L. Kallery, Sr. V.P., Mktg.; Patricia O'Brien, V.P., Human Resources
Board of directors: Robert DiBella; Glenn Dolbeare; Therese Jarmusik; John MacKay; Susan O'Neill; Karen Sawyer; Brian McCoubrey
Offices: Andover, Lynnfield, Methuen, North Reading, MA
Giving statement: Giving through the Donald E. Garrant Foundation, Inc. and the TSB Charitable Foundation Inc.

Donald E. Garrant Foundation, Inc.

357 Main St.
P.O. Box 30
Wakefield, MA 01880-5027 (781) 224-5428
E-mail: GarrantFoundation@tsbawake24.com; URL: http://www.tsbawake24.com/home/about/charitable/garrant

Establishment information: Established in 2001 in MA.
Donor: The Savings Bank.
Contact: Robert J. DiBella, Treas.
Financial data (yr. ended 12/31/11): Assets, $176,819 (M); gifts received, $1,000; expenditures, $20,639; qualifying distributions, $17,904; giving activities include $16,469 for 3 grants (high: $8,575; low: $1,294).
Purpose and activities: The foundation supports programs designed to promote financial literacy, with emphasis on K-12 schools.
Fields of interest: Elementary/secondary education; Human services, financial counseling.
Type of support: Curriculum development; Equipment.
Support limitations: No grants to individuals.
Publications: Application guidelines.
Application information: Applications accepted. Application form required. Applicants should submit the following:
1) detailed description of project and amount of funding requested
2) population served
3) name, address and phone number of organization
Initial approach: Download application form and mail to foundation
Deadline(s): None
Officers and Directors:* Brian D. McCoubrey*, Pres.; Robert J. DiBella*, Treas.; Scott C. Garrant; Therese Jarmusik; Mark J. Simeola; Vito Vacca.
EIN: 043563155

TSB Charitable Foundation Inc.

357 Main St.
P.O. Box 30
Wakefield, MA 01880-0030 (781) 224-5428
E-mail: TSBCF@tsbawake24.com; URL: http://www.tsbawake24.com/home/about/charitable/tsb

Establishment information: Established in 1997 in MA.
Contact: Robert J. Debella, Treas.
Financial data (yr. ended 12/31/11): Assets, $428,981 (M); expenditures, $29,045; qualifying distributions, $24,244; giving activities include $22,663 for 7 grants (high: $4,000; low: $2,500).
Purpose and activities: The foundation supports programs designed to serve homeless shelters, the poor, and the elderly, and provide family services.
Fields of interest: Health care; Boys & girls clubs; Family services; Homeless, human services Aging; Economically disadvantaged.
Type of support: Building/renovation; Capital campaigns; Program development; Program evaluation.
Geographic limitations: Giving primarily in Andover, Lynnfield, Methuen, North Reading, and Wakefield, MA.
Support limitations: No support for national organizations or state or federal agencies. No grants to individuals or for annual campaigns.
Publications: Application guidelines.
Application information: Applications accepted. Grants range from $1,000 to $5,000. Proposals should be no longer than 10 pages plus appendices. Support is limited to 1 contribution per organization during any given year. Application form not required. Applicants should submit the following:
1) qualifications of key personnel
2) population served
3) name, address and phone number of organization
4) copy of IRS Determination Letter
5) brief history of organization and description of its mission
6) copy of most recent annual report/audited financial statement/990
7) how project's results will be evaluated or measured
8) listing of board of directors, trustees, officers and other key people and their affiliations
9) contact person
10) copy of current year's organizational budget and/or project budget
11) listing of additional sources and amount of support
Initial approach: Cover letter and proposal to foundation
Copies of proposal: 6
Deadline(s): Oct. 1 to Jan. 31
Officers and Directors:* Brian D. McCoubrey*, Pres.; Robert J. DiBella*, Clerk and Treas.; Glenn D. Dolbeare; Therese Jarmusik; John J. MacKay, Jr.; Susan F. O'Neill; Karen A. Sawyer.
EIN: 043370164

3344
Savings Bank of Danbury
220 Main St.
Danbury, CT 06810 (203) 743-3849

Company URL: http://www.sbdanbury.com
Establishment information: Established in 1849.
Company type: Private company
Business activities: Operates savings bank.
Business type (SIC): Savings institutions
Corporate officers: Gary W. Hawley, Chair.; Harold C. Wibling, Pres. and C.E.O.; David H. Woessner, Exec. V.P., C.F.O., and Secy.-Treas.; Kathleen Romagnano, Exec. V.P. and C.O.O.; John Jahne, Sr. V.P. and C.I.O.; Marcia M. Grise, Sr. V.P., Opers.; Judy Haskins-Conde, V.P. and Cont.; Janice Lea, V.P., Mktg.; Bonnie L. Smith, V.P., Human Resources
Board of directors: Gary W. Hawley, Chair.; Paul P. Dinto; Robert S. Feinson; Robert J. Karnhaas, Jr.; Gary W. Kurz; Ralph A. McIntosh, Jr.; Donald D. Mitchell; June A. Renzulli; Harold C. Wibling
Offices: Bethel, Brookfield, New Fairfield, New Milford, Newtown, Waterbury, CT
Giving statement: Giving through the Savings Bank of Danbury Foundation, Inc.

Savings Bank of Danbury Foundation, Inc.
c/o Acctg.
220 Main St.
Danbury, CT 06810-6635 (203) 743-3849
E-mail: web-email@sbdanbury.com

Establishment information: Established in 2003 in CT.
Donor: Savings Bank of Danbury.
Contact: David Woessner, Secy.-Treas.
Financial data (yr. ended 12/31/11): Assets, $1,438,895 (M); expenditures, $134,460; qualifying distributions, $134,460; giving activities include $131,000 for 44 grants (high: $75,000; low: $1,000).
Purpose and activities: The foundation supports organizations involved with arts and culture, education, health, human services, economic development, and community development.
Fields of interest: Arts; Education; Health care; Human services; Economic development; Community/economic development.
Geographic limitations: Giving primarily in areas of company operations.
Application information: Applications accepted. Application form required.
Initial approach: Request application form
Deadline(s): As outlined on apllication
Officers and Directors:* Gary W. Hawley*, Chair.; Harold C. Wibling*, Pres.; Kathleen Romangano*, Exec. V.P.; David H. Woessner, Secy.-Treas.; Philip Cammarano; Karl H. Epple; Donald D. Mitchell; James W. Schmotter; June Renzulli.
EIN: 113709335

3345
SBH Intimates, Inc.
1411 Broadway, 8th Fl.
New York, NY 10018-3496 (212) 354-2400

Establishment information: Established in 1990.
Company type: Private company
Business activities: Sells women's underwear wholesale.
Business type (SIC): Apparel, piece goods, and notions—wholesale
Giving statement: Giving through the SBH Intimates Foundation Inc.

SBH Intimates Foundation Inc.
1411 Broadway, 8th Fl.
New York, NY 10018-3496

Establishment information: Established in 2002 in NY.
Donor: SBH Intimates, Inc.
Financial data (yr. ended 12/31/11): Assets, $3,552 (M); expenditures, $100; qualifying distributions, $0.
Purpose and activities: The foundation supports organizations involved with education and Judaism.
Fields of interest: Secondary school/education; Education, special; Education; Jewish agencies & synagogues.
Geographic limitations: Giving primarily in NY.
Application information: Applications not accepted. Unsolicited requests for funds not accepted.
Officers and Directors:* Jack Beyda*, Pres.; Joseph Harary; Alan Sasson.
EIN: 134199950

3346
SCANA Corporation
1426 Main St.
Columbia, SC 29201-2845 (803) 217-9000
FAX: (803) 748-2344

Company URL: http://www.scana.com
Establishment information: Established in 1846.
Company type: Public company
Company ticker symbol and exchange: SCG/NYSE
Business activities: Operates holding company; generates, transmits, and distributes electricity; transmits and distributes natural gas.
Business type (SIC): Gas production and distribution; electric services; combination utility services; holding company
Financial profile for 2012: Number of employees, 5,842; assets, $14,616,000,000; sales volume, $4,176,000,000; pre-tax net income, $602,000,000; expenses, $3,317,000,000; liabilities, $10,462,000,000
Fortune 1000 ranking: 2012—563rd in revenues, 380th in profits, and 304th in assets
Corporate officers: Kevin B. Marsh, Chair. and C.E.O.; Jimmy E. Addison, Exec. V.P. and C.F.O.; Ronald T. Lindsay, Sr. V.P. and Genl. Counsel; Gina S. Champion, Corp. Secy.; Mark R. Cannon, Treas.; James E. Swan IV, Cont.
Board of directors: Kevin B. Marsh, Chair.; James A. Bennett; D. Maybank Hagood; Joshua W. Martin III; James Michael Micali; Lynne M. Miller; James W. Roquemore; Maceo K. Sloan; Harold C. Stowe
Subsidiaries: SCANA Hydrocarbons, Inc., Columbia, SC; SCANA Petroleum Resources, Inc., Columbia, SC; South Carolina Electric & Gas Company, Columbia, SC
Giving statement: Giving through the SCANA Corporation Contributions Program and the Scana Summer Foundation.
Company EIN: 570784499

SCANA Corporation Contributions Program
220 Operation Way
Cayce, SC 29033-3701 (803) 217-9000
Contact for Community Devel. Grants: John A. Cadena, Mgr., Community/Economic Devel. & Local Govt. & Project Devel., tel.: (803) 217-8837, fax: (803) 933-8225, e-mail: jcadena@scana.com; URL: http://www.scana.com/en/social-responsibility/

Purpose and activities: SCANA makes charitable contributions to nonprofit organizations involved with arts and culture, education, the environment, health, human services, community development, and utilities assistance. Support is limited to Georgia, North Carolina, and South Carolina.
Fields of interest: Arts; Higher education; Education; Environment; Youth development, business; Salvation Army; Utilities; General charitable giving.
Program:
Community Development Grants: SCANA awards capital grants to organizations located in South Carolina to build infrastructure improvements. Special emphasis is directed toward site preparation, extension of water and sewer lines, highway construction, and other public works.
Type of support: Employee volunteer services; General/operating support; In-kind gifts; Loaned talent; Program development.
Geographic limitations: Giving limited to GA, NC, and SC.
Application information: Applications accepted. The Community Affairs Department handles giving.
Initial approach: Contact headquarters for application information for Community Development Grants

Scana Summer Foundation
1525 W. W.T. Harris Blvd., D1114-044
Charlotte, NC 28288-5709 (803) 217-5019
Application address: c/o Scana Corp., Columbia, SC 29218.

Establishment information: Established in 1984 in SC.
Donors: South Carolina Electric & Gas Co.; SCANA Corp.
Contact: Jo Ann Butler
Financial data (yr. ended 12/31/11): Assets, $1,238,105 (M); expenditures, $58,322; qualifying distributions, $46,000; giving activities include $44,000 for 7 grants (high: $25,000; low: $1,500).
Purpose and activities: The foundation supports museums and organizations involved with community development.
Fields of interest: Museums; Community/economic development.
Type of support: General/operating support.
Geographic limitations: Giving limited to SC.
Support limitations: No support for private non-operating foundations.
Application information: Applications accepted. Application form required. Applicants should submit the following:
1) copy of IRS Determination Letter
2) detailed description of project and amount of funding requested
Initial approach: Letter
Board meeting date(s): Quarterly
Deadline(s): None
EIN: 570784136

3347
ScanSource, Inc.

6 Logue Ct.
Greenville, SC 29615-5725 (864) 288-2432
FAX: (864) 288-1165

Company URL: http://www.scansourceinc.com/
Establishment information: Established in 1992.
Company type: Public company
Company ticker symbol and exchange: SCSC/NASDAQ
Business activities: Sells technology products wholesale; provides electronic logistics services.
Business type (SIC): Professional and commercial equipment—wholesale; computer services
Financial profile for 2012: Number of employees, 1,500; assets, $1,201,810,000; sales volume, $3,015,300,000; pre-tax net income, $111,210,000; expenses, $2,901,780,000; liabilities, $549,500,000
Fortune 1000 ranking: 2012—711th in revenues, 781st in profits, and 948th in assets
Corporate officers: Steven R. Fischer, Chair.; Michael L. Baur, C.E.O.; Scott Benbenek, Pres., Opers.; Charles Mathis, C.F.O.; Andrea Meade, Exec. V.P., Opers.; Bobby McLain, Exec. V.P., Corp. Comms.; Gerald Lyons, Sr. V.P., Finance; John J. Ellsworth, V.P., Genl. Counsel, and Corp. Secy.
Board of directors: Steven R. Fischer, Chair.; Michael L. Baur; Michael J. Grainger; Steven H. Owings; Jack Reilly; Randy Whitchurch
International operations: Belgium; Canada; France; Germany; Mexico; United Kingdom
Giving statement: Giving through the ScanSource Charitable Foundation.
Company EIN: 570965380

ScanSource Charitable Foundation

6 Logue Ct.
Greenville, SC 29615-5725 (864) 288-2432
E-mail: joan.dilworth@scansource.com; Additional tel.: (864) 286-4299; URL: http://www.scansourceinc.com/en/About%20ScanSource%20Inc/Charitable%20Foundation.aspx

Establishment information: Established in 1998 in SC.
Donors: ScanSource, Inc.; Owings Family Foundation.
Contact: Joan Dilworth, Pres.
Financial data (yr. ended 12/31/11): Assets, $7,136,193 (M); gifts received, $1,144,114; expenditures, $734,764; qualifying distributions, $615,106; giving activities include $615,106 for grants.
Purpose and activities: The foundation supports organizations involved with education and children. Special emphasis is directed toward programs designed to ensure that children receive the support and education they need to grow up safe, happy, and thriving.
Fields of interest: Education; Children, services.
Program:
Employee Matching Gifts: The foundation matches contributions made by employees of ScanSource to nonprofit organizations on a one-for-one basis.
Type of support: Employee-related scholarships; Program development.
Geographic limitations: Giving primarily in areas of company operations, with some emphasis on AZ, FL, GA, KS, SC, TN, and WA.
Support limitations: No grants to individuals (except for employee-related scholarships).
Application information: Applications not accepted. Contributes only to pre-selected organizations.
Board meeting date(s): 3rd Tue. of every month
Officers and Directors:* Joan Dilworth*, Pres.; Melody Nadeau, V.P.; Jaime Sharp, Secy.; Kathryn Wampole, Treas.; Emily Abernathy; Amanda Caldwell; Crystal Cronin; Will Easley; Misti Fuller; Robin Genzy; Mike Hickey; Kirk Johnson; Sara Maxwell; Karen Mojiea; Constance Mumford; Cory Patrick; Jennifer Pegg; Jordan Shrack; Allean Simmons; Danielle Woodward.
EIN: 571002959
Selected grants: The following grants are a representative sample of this grantmaker's funding activity:
$5,000 to American Heart Association, Dallas, TX, 2011.
$5,000 to Miami Childrens Hospital, Miami, FL, 2011.
$2,000 to Special Olympics, Washington, DC, 2011.
$1,275 to American Diabetes Association, Alexandria, VA, 2011.

3348
Henry Schein, Inc.

135 Duryea Rd.
Melville, NY 11747 (631) 843-5500
FAX: (631) 843-5658

Company URL: http://www.henryschein.com
Establishment information: Established in 1932.
Company type: Public company
Company ticker symbol and exchange: HSIC/NASDAQ
Business activities: Sells health care products and services wholesale; develops and sells practice management computer software.
Business type (SIC): Professional and commercial equipment—wholesale; computer services
Financial profile for 2012: Number of employees, 15,000; assets, $5,334,000,000; sales volume, $8,939,970,000; pre-tax net income, $604,190,000; expenses, $8,321,010,000; liabilities, $2,720,410,000
Fortune 1000 ranking: 2012—296th in revenues, 408th in profits, and 572nd in assets
Forbes 2000 ranking: 2012—1008th in sales, 1531st in profits, and 1792nd in assets
Corporate officers: Stanley M. Bergman, Chair. and C.E.O.; James P. Breslawski, Pres.; Steven Paladino, Exec. V.P. and C.F.O.; Gerald A. Benjamin, Exec. V.P. and C.A.O.
Board of directors: Stanley M. Bergman, Chair.; Barry J. Alperin; Gerald A. Benjamin; James P. Breslawski; Paul Brons; Donald J. Kabat; Philip A. Laskawy; Karyn Mashima; Norman S. Matthews; Mark E. Mlotek; Steven Paladino; Carol Raphael; Bradley T. Sheares, Ph.D.; Louis W. Sullivan, M.D.
Subsidiaries: Bedsole Medical Co. Inc., Birmingham, AL; Caligor South Inc., Birmingham, AL; Columbia Medical Inc., Columbia, MD; Delta Scientific, Inc., Ivyland, PA; General Injectables & Vaccines Inc., Bastian, VA; Insource Inc., Bastian, VA; Sullivan Dental Products, Inc., West Allis, WI; Sullivan Schein Dental Inc., Norcross, GA
International operations: Canada
Giving statement: Giving through the Henry Schein, Inc. Corporate Giving Program and the Henry Schein Cares Foundation, Inc.
Company EIN: 113136595

Henry Schein, Inc. Corporate Giving Program

135 Duryea Rd.
Melville, NY 11747-3834 (631) 843-5500
URL: http://www.henryschein.com/us-en/Corporate/CorporateResponsibility.aspx

Purpose and activities: Henry Schein makes charitable contributions to programs designed to expand healthcare access for underserved and at risk populations, on a national and international basis, by supporting wellness, prevention, and treatment; assisting in emergency preparedness and relief, and enhancing professional training, and delivery of health care services.
Fields of interest: Animal welfare; Health care, support services; Health care, patient services; Health care; Disasters, preparedness/services Economically disadvantaged.
International interests: Australia; Austria; Belgium; Canada; China; Czech Republic; France; Germany; Hong Kong; Iceland; Ireland; Israel; Italy; Luxembourg; Netherlands; New Zealand; Portugal; Saudi Arabia; Slovakia; Spain; Switzerland; Turkey; United Arab Emirates; United Kingdom.
Type of support: Employee volunteer services; In-kind gifts.
Geographic limitations: Giving primarily in areas of company operations, with emphasis on FL, IN, NV, NY, PA, SC, TX, VA, WI, Africa, Canada, France, Germany, New Zealand, and the United Kingdom; giving also to national and international organizations.

Henry Schein Cares Foundation, Inc.

135 Duryea Rd.
Melville, NY 11747-3834 (631) 390-8006
E-mail: contact@hscaresfoundation.org; URL: http://www.hscaresfoundation.org/

Establishment information: Established in 2009 in NY.
Donor: Henry Schein, Inc.
Financial data (yr. ended 12/31/11): Revenue, $1,514,439; assets, $1,543,226 (M); gifts received, $1,511,400; expenditures, $457,596; program services expenses, $457,596; giving activities include $349,103 for 6 grants (high: $100,000).
Purpose and activities: The foundation supports nonprofit organizations that promote dental, medical, and animal health by helping to increase access to care for communities around the world; special emphasis is directed toward community-based programs focused on prevention, wellness, and treatment; disaster preparedness and relief; and capacity building of health institutions that provide training and care.
Fields of interest: Animal welfare; Health care; Health organizations; Disasters, preparedness/services.
Programs:
Global Product Donation Program: The foundation provides a broad selection of health care products and supplies to community medical and dental organizations. Participating organizations will receive a product selection based on the type of service that each organization provides (medical and/or dental) for two years; each participating organization typically receives large pallets of product donations valued from $5,000 to $25,000. Applicants will be evaluated on a variety of criteria, including the size of the community served, the number of health care professionals involved, the ability to use and dispense a large volume of supplies, and the alignment of the applicant's organization with the mission of the foundation.

Healthy Lifestyles, Healthy Communities Program: This program offers grants and supplies to community health organizations to provide free medical and dental services to underserved communities. Eligible applicants must: be public entities (e.g., state or city health departments) or 501(c)(3) organizations; include hypertension, asthma, diabetes, obesity, and oral health screenings; provide participants with educational materials about ways to prevent and treat common health problems, as well as assistance in finding local community health centers where they may receive health care on a regular basis; and demonstrate that the target population is underserved and/or unlikely otherwise to access screenings.
Type of support: Donated products; General/operating support.
Geographic limitations: Giving on a national basis.
Publications: Application guidelines.
Application information: Applications accepted. Application form required.
Initial approach: Contact foundation for application form
Deadline(s): July for Global Product Donation Program; none for Healthy Lifestyles, Healthy Communities Program
Final notification: Sept. for Global Product Donation Program
Officers and Directors:* Stanley Bergman*, Chair.; Steve Kess*, Pres.; Howard Stapler*, V.P.; Susan Vassallo*, V.P. and Exec. Dir.; Michael Ettinger*, Secy.; Ferdinand Jahnel, Treas.; Gerald Benjamin; James Breslawski; Steve Paladino; Steven Paladino.
EIN: 264137268

3349
Schenuit Investments Inc.

102 W. Pennsylvania Ave., Ste. 300
Baltimore, MD 21204-4543
(410) 296-1392

Establishment information: Established in 1912.
Company type: Private company
Business activities: Operates investment company.
Business type (SIC): Investment offices
Corporate officers: Oliver S. Travers, Jr., Co-Pres.; Oliver Travers, Co-Pres.
Giving statement: Giving through the Mary Jean and Oliver Travers Foundation, Inc.

Mary Jean and Oliver Travers Foundation, Inc.

(formerly The Schenuit Foundation, Inc.)
102 W. Pennsylvania Ave., Ste. 300
Towson, MD 21204 (410) 296-1392

Establishment information: Established in MD.
Donor: Schenuit Investment, Inc.
Contact: Nancy Dods, Secy.-Treas. and Dir.
Financial data (yr. ended 04/30/12): Assets, $325,841 (M); expenditures, $33,851; qualifying distributions, $30,825; giving activities include $30,825 for 23 grants (high: $10,000; low: $100).
Fields of interest: Education; Health care; Recreation.
Application information: Applications accepted. Application form required. Applicants should submit the following:
1) copy of IRS Determination Letter
Initial approach: Letter
Deadline(s): None
Officers and Directors:* Oliver S. Travers, Jr.*, Pres.; Mary Jean Travers*, V.P.; Nancy Dods*, Secy.-Treas.
EIN: 526056360

3350
Schiff Hardin LLP

(formerly Schiff Hardin & Waite LLP)
233 S. Wacker Dr., Ste. 6600
Chicago, IL 60606-6473 (312) 258-5500

Company URL: http://www.schiffhardin.com
Establishment information: Established in 1864.
Company type: Private company
Business activities: Provides legal services.
Business type (SIC): Legal services
Corporate officer: Robert H. Riley, Chair.
Board of director: Robert H. Riley, Chair.
Offices: San Francisco, CA; Washington, DC; Atlanta, GA; Lake Forest, IL; Boston, MA; New York, NY
Giving statement: Giving through the Schiff Hardin LLP Pro Bono Assistance Program, the Schiff Hardin LLP Pro Bono Program, and the Schiff Hardin & Waite Foundation.

Schiff Hardin LLP Pro Bono Program

233 S. Wacker Dr., Ste. 6600
Chicago, IL 60606-6473 (312) 258-5500
FAX: (315) 258-5600; URL: http://www.schiffhardin.com/about_us/pro-bono

Contact: Mark C. Zaander, Partner
Fields of interest: Legal services.
Type of support: Pro bono services - legal.
Application information: A Pro Bono Committee manages the pro bono program.

Schiff Hardin & Waite Foundation

(formerly Schiff Hardin & Waite Foundation)
233 S. Wacker Dr., Ste. 6600
Chicago, IL 60606-6360

Establishment information: Established in 1986 in IL.
Donors: Schiff Hardin LLP; Bruce Weisenthal.
Financial data (yr. ended 11/30/11): Assets, $283,429 (M); gifts received, $185,722; expenditures, $183,225; qualifying distributions, $183,225; giving activities include $182,375 for 72 grants (high: $40,000; low: -$5,000).
Purpose and activities: The foundation supports hospitals and organizations involved with education, cancer, crime and law enforcement, automotive safety, and civil rights.
Fields of interest: Education; Hospitals (general); Cancer; Dispute resolution; Legal services; Crime/law enforcement; Safety, automotive safety; YM/YWCAs & YM/YWHAs; Civil/human rights; United Ways and Federated Giving Programs.
Type of support: General/operating support.
Geographic limitations: Giving primarily in Chicago, IL.
Support limitations: No grants to individuals.
Application information: Applications not accepted. Contributes only to pre-selected organizations.
Officer and Directors: Joseph A. Vasquez, Jr., Treas.; Marci A. Eisenstein; Stephen M. Hankins; Robert H. Riley; Kenneth M. Roberts; Peter L. Rossiter; Ronald S. Safer; Bruce P. Weisenthal.
EIN: 363465740
Selected grants: The following grants are a representative sample of this grantmaker's funding activity:
$1,000 to American Cancer Society, Atlanta, GA, 2010.

3351
Schiffenhaus Packaging Corporation

2013 McCarter Hwy.
Newark, NJ 07104-4301 (973) 484-5000

Establishment information: Established in 1895.
Company type: Subsidiary of a public company
Business activities: Manufactures corrugated boxes.
Business type (SIC): Paperboard containers
Corporate officer: Lawrence R. Samples, C.F.O.
Subsidiaries: Schiffenhaus North Inc., Suffern, NY; Schiffenhaus Services Inc., Newark, NJ
Giving statement: Giving through the Schiffenhaus Foundation, Inc.

The Schiffenhaus Foundation, Inc.

40 Devon Rd.
Essex Fells, NJ 07021-1705

Establishment information: Established in 1996 in NJ.
Donors: Schiffenhaus Industries Inc.; Schiffenhaus Packaging, Inc.
Financial data (yr. ended 12/31/11): Assets, $194,681 (M); expenditures, $35,045; qualifying distributions, $32,950; giving activities include $32,950 for grants.
Purpose and activities: The foundation supports organizations involved with arts and culture, education, health, substance abuse, autism, diabetes, medical research, human services, business, and religion.
Fields of interest: Arts; Education; Health care.
Type of support: General/operating support; Scholarship funds.
Geographic limitations: Giving primarily in NJ.
Application information: Applications not accepted. Unsolicited requests for funds not accepted.
Officer: Laurence C. Schiffenhaus, Chair.
EIN: 223428536

3352
Marcus Schloss & Company, Inc.

220 5th Ave., 14th Fl.
New York, NY 10001-7708 (212) 483-1500
FAX: (212) 363-7265

Establishment information: Established in 1959.
Company type: Private company
Business activities: Provides securities brokerage services.
Business type (SIC): Brokers and dealers/security
Corporate officers: Douglas Schloss, Chair. and C.E.O; Richard Schloss, Pres.
Board of director: Douglas Schloss, Chair.
Giving statement: Giving through the Rexford Fund, Inc.

Rexford Fund, Inc.

c/o Marcus Schloss & Co., Inc.
220 5th Ave., 14th Fl.
New York, NY 10001-7708

Establishment information: Established in 1967 in NY.
Donors: Irwin Schloss; Marcus Schloss & Co., Inc.; Rexford Offshore, LLC; Rexford Management, Inc.
Financial data (yr. ended 12/31/11): Assets, $6,862,540 (M); gifts received, $50,000; expenditures, $292,872; qualifying distributions, $289,599; giving activities include $289,599 for grants.
Purpose and activities: The foundation supports organizations involved with arts and culture, education, the environment, health, human services, and Judaism.
Fields of interest: Museums; Arts; Elementary/secondary education; Higher education; Education; Botanical gardens; Environment; Health care; YM/YWCAs & YM/YWHAs; Children/youth, services; Family services; Human services; Jewish agencies & synagogues.
Type of support: Capital campaigns; General/operating support.
Geographic limitations: Giving primarily in CT and New York, NY.
Support limitations: No grants to individuals.
Application information: Applications not accepted. Contributes only to pre-selected organizations.
Officers and Directors:* Douglas Schloss*, Pres.; Richard Schloss*, Secy.; Irwin Schloss.
EIN: 136222049
Selected grants: The following grants are a representative sample of this grantmaker's funding activity:
$100,000 to Saint Pauls School, Concord, NH, 2011.
$25,000 to Princeton University, Princeton, NJ, 2011.
$19,700 to SCO Family of Services, Glen Cove, NY, 2011.
$15,000 to Environmental Defense Fund, New York, NY, 2011.
$10,000 to Duke University, Durham, NC, 2011.
$10,000 to Saint Bernards School, New York, NY, 2011.
$10,000 to Shakespeare Society, New York, NY, 2011.
$7,500 to Planting Fields Foundation, Oyster Bay, NY, 2011.
$7,500 to Planting Fields Foundation, Oyster Bay, NY, 2011.
$7,275 to SCO Family of Services, Glen Cove, NY, 2011.

3353
Schmeling Construction Company

315 Harrison Ave.
Rockford, IL 61104-7051 (815) 399-7800

Company URL: http://www.schmelingconstruction.com/default.asp
Establishment information: Established in 1903.
Company type: Private company
Business activities: Provides building construction and renovation services.
Business type (SIC): Contractors/general nonresidential building
Corporate officers: Roger E. Schmeling, C.E.O.; Stephen E. Schmeling, Pres.
Giving statement: Giving through the Schmeling Construction Company Charitable Trust.

Schmeling Construction Company Charitable Trust

315 Harrison Ave.
Rockford, IL 61104-7051 (815) 399-7800

Establishment information: Established in 1989 in IL.
Donor: Schmeling Construction Co.
Contact: Stephen E. Schmeling, Pres.
Financial data (yr. ended 02/29/12): Assets, $16,622 (M); expenditures, $2,500; qualifying distributions, $2,500; giving activities include $2,500 for 3 grants (high: $1,000; low: $500).
Purpose and activities: The foundation supports organizations involved with education and Alzheimer's disease.
Fields of interest: Education, reading; Education; Alzheimer's disease; United Ways and Federated Giving Programs.
Type of support: General/operating support.
Geographic limitations: Giving primarily in Rockford, IL.
Support limitations: No grants to individuals.
Application information: Applications accepted. Application form not required.
Initial approach: Proposal
Deadline(s): None
Officers: Roger E. Schmeling, C.E.O.; Stephen E. Schmeling, Pres.
EIN: 363654902

3354
Schneider Mills, Inc.

1430 Broadway, 7th Fl., Ste. 1202
New York, NY 10018-3390 (212) 768-7500

Company URL: http://www.schneidermills.com/
Establishment information: Established in 1916.
Company type: Private company
Business activities: Operates fabric mill.
Business type (SIC): Fabrics/broadwoven synthetic and silk
Financial profile for 2010: Number of employees, 12
Corporate officers: Albert Schneider, Pres. and C.E.O.; Bruce Bodinger, Cont.
Office: Taylorsville, NC
Giving statement: Giving through the Samuel Schneider Foundation Inc.

Samuel Schneider Foundation Inc.

P.O. Box 519
Taylorsville, NC 28681

Establishment information: Established in 1951 in NJ.
Donors: Schneider Mills, Inc.; Schneider Trading, Inc.; Albert Schneider; Agnes Schneider.
Financial data (yr. ended 02/28/12): Assets, $1,254,343 (M); gifts received, $3,000; expenditures, $42,425; qualifying distributions, $31,000; giving activities include $31,000 for grants.
Purpose and activities: The foundation supports organizations involved with education.
Fields of interest: Education; Human services; Religion.
Type of support: General/operating support; Program development.
Support limitations: No grants to individuals.
Application information: Applications not accepted. Unsolicited requests for funds not accepted.
Trustees: Jennifer Brinkley; Caroline McPherson; Agnes Schneider.
EIN: 136101811

3355
Schneider National, Inc.

3101 S. Packerland Dr.
P.O. Box 2545
Green Bay, WI 54306-2545 (920) 592-2000

Company URL: http://www.schneider.com
Establishment information: Established in 1935.
Company type: Private company
Business activities: Provides trucking and transportation logistics services.
Business type (SIC): Trucking and courier services, except by air
Financial profile for 2011: Number of employees, 18,185; sales volume, $3,100,000,000
Corporate officers: Thomas Gannon, Vice-Chair. and Secy.; Christopher B. Lofgren, Ph.D., Pres. and C.E.O.; Lori Lutey, C.F.O.; Juidth A. Lemke, Exec. V.P. and C.I.O.; Steve Matheys, Exec. V.P. and C.A.O.; Gail McNutt, Sr. V.P., Finance
Board of directors: Thomas Gannon, Vice-Chair.; Christopher B. Lofgren, Ph.D.
Giving statement: Giving through the Schneider National Foundation, Inc.

Schneider National Foundation, Inc.

P.O. Box 2545
301 S. Packerland Dr.
Green Bay, WI 54306-2545 (920) 592-2000
E-mail: foundation@schneider.com; Additional tel.: (800) 558-6767; URL: http://www.schneider.com/About_Schneider/Schneider_Foundation/index.htm

Establishment information: Established in 1983.
Donor: Schneider National, Inc.
Contact: Mary Gronnert
Financial data (yr. ended 12/31/11): Assets, $97,600 (M); gifts received, $717,572; expenditures, $699,403; qualifying distributions, $699,403; giving activities include $699,403 for grants.
Purpose and activities: The foundation supports organizations involved with arts and culture, education, health, and human services.
Fields of interest: Performing arts, theater; Arts; Higher education; Business school/education; Education; Health care; Housing/shelter, development; Disasters, preparedness/services; Boys & girls clubs; Salvation Army; Children/youth, services; Human services; United Ways and Federated Giving Programs.
Type of support: Capital campaigns; Continuing support; Donated equipment; Emergency funds; Employee volunteer services; Equipment; General/operating support; In-kind gifts; Program development; Scholarship funds; Use of facilities.
Geographic limitations: Giving primarily in areas of company operations, with emphasis on Green Bay, WI; giving also in Canada, China, Mexico, and the Netherlands.
Support limitations: No support for religious organizations. No grants to individuals or for political campaigns.
Publications: Application guidelines.
Application information:
Initial approach: E-mail foundation for application information
Officers: Steve Matheys, Pres.; LuEllen Oskey, Secy.-Treas.
EIN: 391457870

3356
Schnuck Markets, Inc.
11420 Lackland Rd.
P.O. Box 46928
St. Louis, MO 63146-6928 (314) 994-9900

Company URL: http://www.schnucks.com
Establishment information: Established in 1939.
Company type: Private company
Business activities: Operates supermarkets.
Business type (SIC): Groceries—retail
Financial profile for 2009: Number of employees, 15,000; sales volume, $2,600,000,000
Corporate officers: Scott C. Schnuck, Chair. and C.E.O.; Todd R. Schnuck, Pres. and C.O.O.; David Bell, C.F.O.; Ryan Cuba, V.P., Opers.; Bob Howard, V.P., Mktg.; Janice Rhodes, V.P., Human Resources
Board of director: Scott C. Schnuck, Chair.
Giving statement: Giving through the Schnuck Markets, Inc. Corporate Giving Program.

Schnuck Markets, Inc. Corporate Giving Program
c/o Community Rels. Dept.
11420 Lackland Rd.
St. Louis, MO 63146-3559
URL: http://www.schnucks.com/policies.asp

Purpose and activities: Schnuck Markets makes charitable contributions to nonprofit organizations on a case by case basis. Support is given primarily in areas of company operations in Illinois, Indiana, Iowa, Missouri, and Wisconsin.
Fields of interest: General charitable giving.
Program:
eScrip Community Card Program: Through the eScrip Community Card Program, Schnuck makes charitable contributions to nonprofit organizations involved with K-12 education, youth development, and youth for each purchase made by Schnuck shoppers enrolled in the program. Organizations receive up to five percent of each purchase made.
Type of support: Donated products.
Geographic limitations: Giving primarily in areas of company operations in IA, IL, IN, MO, and WI.
Support limitations: No support for third parties or government agencies supported by city, state, or federal taxes. No grants to individuals, or for capital campaigns, golf tournaments, galas, fundraisers for individuals, seminars, conferences, or employee recognition or appreciation events, or reunions or other social events.
Publications: Application guidelines.
Application information: Applications accepted. Proposals should be submitted using organization letterhead. The Community Relations Department handles giving. Application form not required.
Applicants should submit the following:
1) copy of IRS Determination Letter
2) brief history of organization and description of its mission
3) detailed description of project and amount of funding requested
4) listing of additional sources and amount of support

Proposals should specifically note the nature of the request being made.
Initial approach: Proposal to headquarters
Deadline(s): 4 weeks prior to need

3357
Schoeneckers, Inc.
(also known as BI)
7630 Bush Lake Rd.
Minneapolis, MN 55439-2810
(952) 835-4800

Company URL: http://www.biperformance.com
Establishment information: Established in 1950.
Company type: Private company
Business activities: Provides business improvement services.
Business type (SIC): Management and public relations services
Corporate officers: Guy Schoenecker, C.E.O.; Larry Schoenecker, Pres.; Dale Kunz, C.I.O.; Nancy Martinson, V.P., Human Resources
Giving statement: Giving through the Schoeneckers Foundation.

Schoeneckers Foundation
P.O. Box 1610
Minneapolis, MN 55440-1610

Establishment information: Established in 1979 in MN.
Donor: Schoeneckers, Inc.
Contact: Guy Schoenecker, Pres.
Financial data (yr. ended 09/30/11): Assets, $51,101 (M); gifts received, $600,000; expenditures, $601,525; qualifying distributions, $600,000; giving activities include $600,000 for grants.
Purpose and activities: The foundation supports the University of St. Thomas in St. Paul, Minnesota.
Fields of interest: Higher education.
Type of support: General/operating support.
Geographic limitations: Giving primarily in St. Paul, MN.
Support limitations: No grants to individuals.
Application information: Applications not accepted. Contributes only to a pre-selected organization.
Officer and Directors:* Guy Schoenecker, Pres.; James E. O'Brien; Barbara Schoenecker; Larry Schoenecker.
EIN: 411369001
Selected grants: The following grants are a representative sample of this grantmaker's funding activity:
$600,000 to University of Saint Thomas, Saint Paul, MN, 2011.

3358
Scholastic Corporation
557 Broadway
New York, NY 10012-3902 (212) 343-6100

Company URL: http://www.scholastic.com
Establishment information: Established in 1920.
Company type: Public company
Company ticker symbol and exchange: SCHL/ NASDAQ
Business activities: Publishes and distributes children's books, classroom and professional magazines, and other educational materials.
Business type (SIC): Book publishing and/or printing; periodical publishing and/or printing
Financial profile for 2012: Number of employees, 9,200; assets, $1,670,300,000; sales volume, $2,148,800,000; pre-tax net income, $170,700,000; expenses, $1,962,600,000; liabilities, $840,000,000
Fortune 1000 ranking: 2012—900th in revenues, 736th in profits, and 900th in assets
Corporate officers: Richard Robinson, Chair., Pres., and C.E.O.; Maureen O'Connell, Exec. V.P., C.F.O., and C.A.O.; Andrew S. Hedden, Exec. V.P., Genl. Counsel, and Secy.; Kyle Good, Sr. V.P., Corp. Comms.
Board of directors: Richard Robinson, Chair.; James W. Barge; Marianne Caponnetto; John L. Davies; Andrew S. Hedden; Mae C. Jemison, M.D.; Peter M. Mayer; John G. McDonald; Augustus K. Oliver; Richard M. Spaulding; Margaret A. Williams
Subsidiaries: Lectorum Publications, Inc., New York, NY; Scholastic Inc., New York, NY
International operations: Argentina; Australia; Canada; China; England; Hong Kong; India; Mexico; New Zealand; United Kingdom
Giving statement: Giving through the Scholastic Corporation Contributions Program.
Company EIN: 133385513

Scholastic Corporation Contributions Program
c/o Community Affairs Dept.
557 Broadway
New York, NY 10012-3999
URL: http://www.scholastic.com/aboutscholastic/communityprograms.htm

Contact: Keren J. Davis
Purpose and activities: Scholastic makes charitable contributions of books to organizations with literacy programs focused on serving the needs of at-risk children and families. Support is given on a national basis, and on an international basis in areas of company operations.
Fields of interest: Child development, education; Education, reading; Children/youth, services.
Type of support: Donated products; In-kind gifts.
Geographic limitations: Giving on a national basis, and on an international basis in areas of company operations.
Support limitations: No support for political, labor, religious, or fraternal organizations, or for individual schools, or libraries. No grants to individuals, or for fundraisers/auctions, scholarships, or events; no in-kind donations for resale.
Publications: Application guidelines.
Application information: Applications accepted. Support is limited to 1 contribution per organization during any given year. Application form required.
Applicants should submit the following:
1) timetable for implementation and evaluation of project
2) population served
3) name, address and phone number of organization
4) copy of IRS Determination Letter
5) brief history of organization and description of its mission
6) geographic area to be served
7) listing of board of directors, trustees, officers and other key people and their affiliations
8) detailed description of project and amount of funding requested
9) contact person
10) copy of current year's organizational budget and/or project budget
11) listing of additional sources and amount of support
12) list of company employees involved with the organization
13) role played by volunteers

Applications should include the organization's Tax ID Number; and indicate the intended use of the donation, and the grade levels of the children to be served.
Initial approach: Download application form and mail to headquarters

3359
Schoonover Investments, L.P.

5031 Hazel Jones Rd.
Bossier City, LA 71111-5439
(318) 213-2900

Establishment information: Established in 2001.
Company type: Private company
Business activities: Operates holding company.
Business type (SIC): Holding company
Corporate officer: Steven L. Schoonover, Mgr.
Giving statement: Giving through the Schoonover Foundation.

The Schoonover Foundation

333 Texas St., Ste. 2230
Shreveport, LA 71101-5302

Establishment information: Established in 2000 in LA.
Donor: Schoonover Investments, L.P.
Financial data (yr. ended 12/31/11): Assets, $222,688 (M); expenditures, $85,016; qualifying distributions, $82,355; giving activities include $82,355 for grants.
Purpose and activities: The foundation supports hospitals and organizations involved with higher education, multiple sclerosis research, and religion.
Fields of interest: Higher education; Hospitals (general); Multiple sclerosis research; Religion.
Type of support: General/operating support.
Geographic limitations: Giving primarily in LA and OH.
Support limitations: No grants to individuals.
Application information: Applications not accepted. Unsolicited requests for funds not accepted.
Officers: Steven L. Schoonover, Pres. and C.E.O.; Barbara Jean Schoonover, V.P.; Kristen S. Erler, Secy.
Directors: Michelle L. Payne; Brett S. Schoonover; David L. Schoonover.
EIN: 721462460
Selected grants: The following grants are a representative sample of this grantmaker's funding activity:
$505,000 to Ohio University, Athens, OH, 2010.
$75,000 to Kent State University, Kent, OH, 2010.

3360
Schott Magnetics

(formerly Schott Corporation)
1401 Air Wing Rd.
San Diego, CA 92154-7705
(507) 223-5572
FAX: (507) 223-5055

Company URL: http://www.schottcorp.com
Establishment information: Established in 1946.
Company type: Subsidiary of a private company
Business activities: Manufactures specialty electrical equipment.
Business type (SIC): Electronic components and accessories; electric transmission and distribution equipment
Corporate officer: Ross Baldwin, Pres.
Board of director: Owen W. Schott
Giving statement: Giving through the Schott Foundation.

Schott Foundation

9350 Foxford Rd.
Chanhassen, MN 55317-8684

Establishment information: Established in 1981 in MN.
Donor: Schott Corp.
Financial data (yr. ended 03/31/12): Assets, $3,953,609 (M); expenditures, $267,228; qualifying distributions, $242,242; giving activities include $233,500 for 10 grants (high: $60,000; low: $2,000).
Purpose and activities: The foundation supports museums and organizations involved with education, the environment, and the humanities.
Fields of interest: Humanities; Education; Environment, natural resources; Environment.
Type of support: General/operating support; Scholarship funds.
Geographic limitations: Giving primarily in MN.
Application information: Applications accepted. Application form not required. Applicants should submit the following:
1) detailed description of project and amount of funding requested
Initial approach: Letter of inquiry
Deadline(s): None
Officers and Directors:* Owen W. Schott*, C.E.O.; Wendell Schott*, V.P.
EIN: 411392014
Selected grants: The following grants are a representative sample of this grantmaker's funding activity:
$40,000 to Nature Conservancy, Minneapolis, MN, 2011.
$14,000 to Eco Education, Saint Paul, MN, 2011.

3361
A. Schulman, Inc.

3550 W. Market St.
Akron, OH 44333-2658 (330) 666-3751
FAX: (330) 668-7204

Company URL: http://www.aschulman.com
Establishment information: Established in 1928.
Company type: Public company
Company ticker symbol and exchange: SHLM/NASDAQ
Business activities: Sells plastic resins.
Business type (SIC): Plastics and synthetics
Financial profile for 2012: Number of employees, 3,100; assets, $1,193,770,000; sales volume, $2,106,750,000; pre-tax net income, $65,970,000; expenses, $2,034,110,000; liabilities, $692,370,000
Fortune 1000 ranking: 2012—915th in revenues, 821st in profits, and 950th in assets
Corporate officers: Joseph M. Gingo, Chair., Pres., and C.E.O.; Joseph J. Levanduski, V.P., C.F.O., and Treas.; John B. Broerman, V.P. and C.I.O.; Kim L. Whiteman, V.P., Human Resources
Board of directors: Joseph M. Gingo, Chair.; David G. Birney; Howard R. Curd; James A. Mitarotonda; Michael A. McManus, Jr.; Lee D. Meyer; Ernest J. Novak, Jr.; Irvin D. Reid; John B. Yasinsky
Subsidiaries: ASI Investments Holding Co., Akron, OH; ComAlloy International Co., Nashville, TN; The Sunprene Co., Bellevue, OH
Plants: Pasadena, CA; Hockessin, DE; Schaumburg, IL; Evansville, Fort Wayne, IN; Birmingham, Grand Rapids, MI; Eagan, MN; St. Louis, MO; Piscataway, NJ; Sharon Center, OH
International operations: Belgium; Mexico; United Kingdom
Giving statement: Giving through the A. Schulman, Inc. Corporate Giving Program.
Company EIN: 340514850

A. Schulman, Inc. Corporate Giving Program

3550 W. Market St.
Akron, OH 44333-2658

Purpose and activities: A. Schulman makes charitable contributions to nonprofit organizations on a case by case basis. Support is given primarily in Akron and Cleveland, Ohio.
Fields of interest: General charitable giving.
Geographic limitations: Giving primarily in Akron, OH.
Support limitations: No support for political organizations.
Application information: Applications not accepted. The President's office handles giving.

3362
Schulte Roth & Zabel LLP

919 3rd Ave.
New York, NY 10022-3921 (212) 756-2000

Company URL: http://www.srz.com
Establishment information: Established in 1969.
Company type: Private company
Business activities: Operates law firm.
Business type (SIC): Legal services
Offices: Washington, DC; New York, NY
International operations: United Kingdom
Giving statement: Giving through the Schulte Roth & Zabel LLP Pro Bono Program.

Schulte Roth & Zabel LLP Pro Bono Program

919 3rd Ave.
New York, NY 10022-3921
E-mail: danny.greenberg@srz.com; URL: http://www.srz.com/probono/

Contact: Daniel L. Greenberg, Special Counsel, Pro Bono Initiatives
Fields of interest: Legal services.
Type of support: Pro bono services - legal.
Application information: A Pro Bono Committee manages the pro bono program.

3363
The Charles Schwab Corporation

211 Main St.
San Francisco, CA 94105 (415) 667-7000
FAX: (415) 627 8538

Company URL: http://www.aboutschwab.com
Establishment information: Established in 1971.
Company type: Public company
Company ticker symbol and exchange: SCHW/NYSE
Business activities: Provides securities brokerage services.
Business type (SIC): Brokers and dealers/security
Financial profile for 2012: Number of employees, 13,800; assets, $133,637,000,000; sales volume, $4,883,000,000; pre-tax net income, $1,450,000,000; expenses, $3,433,000,000; liabilities, $124,048,000,000
Fortune 1000 ranking: 2012—488th in revenues, 214th in profits, and 45th in assets
Forbes 2000 ranking: 2012—1396th in sales, 630th in profits, and 192nd in assets

Corporate officers: Charles R. Schwab, Chair.; Walter W. Bettinger II, Pres. and C.E.O.; Joseph R. Martinetto, Exec. V.P. and C.F.O.; Jim McGuire, Exec. V.P. and C.I.O.; Carrie E. Dwyer, Exec. V.P., Genl. Counsel, and Corp. Secy.; Jay L. Allen, Exec. V.P., Human Resources
Board of directors: Charles R. Schwab, Chair.; Nancy H. Bechtle; Walter W. Bettinger II; C. Preston Butcher; Stephen A. Ellis; Mark A. Goldfarb; Frank C. Herringer; Stephen T. McLin; Arun Sarin; Paula A. Sneed; Roger O. Walther; Robert N. Wilson
Subsidiaries: Charles Schwab & Co., Inc., San Francisco, CA; Schwab Holdings, Inc., San Francisco, CA; United States Trust Company of New York, New York, NY
Giving statement: Giving through the Charles Schwab Foundation and the Schwab Charitable Fund.
Company EIN: 943025021

Charles Schwab Foundation

211 Main St.
SF211 MN-16-205
San Francisco, CA 94105-1905 (877) 408-5438
FAX: (415) 636-3262;
E-mail: charlesschwabfoundation@schwab.com; URL: http://www.aboutschwab.com/community

Establishment information: Established in 1993 in CA.
Donors: The Charles Schwab Corp.; Charles Schwab & Co., Inc.
Contact: Elinore Robey, Dir. of Progs.; Roger K. Wong, Progs. Mgr.
Financial data (yr. ended 12/31/11): Assets, $3,071,192 (M); gifts received, $3,314,113; expenditures, $4,825,919; qualifying distributions, $4,818,170; giving activities include $4,382,481 for 2,377 grants (high: $500,000; low: $19).
Purpose and activities: Charles Schwab Foundation provides direct grants to select nonprofit organizations that support Schwab's commitment to financial literacy and respond to local cultural and social needs.
Fields of interest: Arts; Disasters, preparedness/services; Boys & girls clubs; Human services, financial counseling; Human services; Community/economic development; Philanthropy/voluntarism; Financial services Children/youth; Adults; Aging; Young adults; Military/veterans; Economically disadvantaged.
Programs:
AARP Foundation Finances 50+: Charles Schwab Foundation and AARP Foundation have launched a new financial capability program. Schwab and AARP volunteers serve as facilitators and money mentors to help adults age 50+ with goal setting, debt reduction, asset building, and creating a financial action plan. Learn more here: http://www.aarp.org/aarp-foundation/our-work/income/finances-50-plus-financial-capability/.
Employee Matching Gifts: The foundation matches contributions made by employees of Charles Schwab to nonprofit organizations on a one-for-one basis from $25 to $1,000 per employee, per year.
Money Matters: Make It Count: The foundation, in collaboration with Boys & Girls Club of America, provides youth ages 13-18 with basic money management skills and practical ways to save, spend, and invest their money. Successful participants receive a certificate of completion and a Money Matters $2,000 scholarship from the foundation.
Type of support: Conferences/seminars; Continuing support; Employee matching gifts; Employee volunteer services; General/operating support; In-kind gifts; Management development/capacity building; Matching/challenge support; Scholarship funds; Sponsorships.
Geographic limitations: Giving on a national basis with emphasis on San Francisco Bay Area, CA, Denver, CO, Orlando, FL, Indianapolis, IN, Richfield, OH, and Austin, TX.
Support limitations: No support for religious, political, or athletic organizations, disease-specific organizations, member-based organizations, discriminatory organizations, organizations with litigious or divisive public agendas, or private foundations; generally, no support for institutions of higher education or hospitals. No grants to individuals (except for Money Matters scholarships), or for advertising or cause-related marketing projects, business development activities, group travel, sponsorships, promotional events, video productions, capital campaigns, or challenge or seed funding; generally, no medical research.
Application information: Applications not accepted. The foundation currently has an invitation only process for giving.
Board meeting date(s): Bi-annual
Officers and Directors:* Charles R. Schwab*, Chair.; Carrie Schwab-Pomerantz, Pres.; Charmel Huffman*, Secy.; Jordan Oliver*, Treas.; Jay L. Allen; Steve Anderson; John Clendening; Patricia Cox; Sherri Kroonenberg; Scott Rhoades; Paul Woolway.
Number of staff: 3 full-time professional; 2 part-time professional.
EIN: 943192615

Schwab Charitable Fund

(formerly Schwab Fund for Charitable Giving)
211 Main St.
San Francisco, CA 94105-1905 (415) 667-9131
FAX: (415) 989-1047;
E-mail: ask@schwabcharitable.org; Toll-free tel.: (800) 746-6216; Toll Free Fax: (877) 535-3852; URL: http://www.schwabcharitable.org

Establishment information: Established in 1999 in CA.
Contact: Kim Laughton, Pres.
Financial data (yr. ended 06/30/11): Revenue, $822,716,213; assets, $3,057,002,991 (M); gifts received, $804,316,091; expenditures, $514,305,128; program services expenses, $510,914,662; giving activities include $504,233,878 for 8,745 grants.
Purpose and activities: The fund educates donors and potential donors about philanthropy, helps them take a strategic approach to their giving, and provides them with tools and resources to develop a lifelong giving program.
Fields of interest: Disasters, 9/11/01; Philanthropy/voluntarism.
Geographic limitations: Giving on a national and international basis.
Publications: Newsletter.
Application information: Applications not accepted. Unsolicited requests for funds not accepted.
Board meeting date(s): Quarterly
Officers and Directors:* Carrie Schwab*, Chair.; Kim Laughton*, Pres.; Nicolas Donatiello, Jr.; Loretta Doon; Sanford R. Robertson; Brooks Walker, Jr.
Number of staff: 25 full-time professional.
EIN: 311640316

3364
Schwabe, Williamson & Wyatt, P.C.

Pacwest Ctr.
1211 SW 5th Ave., Ste. 1900
Portland, OR 97204-3719 (503) 796-2984

Company URL: http://www.schwabe.com/index.aspx
Company type: Private company
Business activities: Operates law firm.
Business type (SIC): Legal services
Offices: Washington, DC; Bend, Eugene, Portland, Salem, OR; Seattle, WA
International operations: Canada
Giving statement: Giving through the Schwabe, Williamson & Wyatt, P.C Pro Bono Program.

Schwabe, Williamson & Wyatt, P.C Pro Bono Program

Pacwest Ctr.
1211 SW 5th Ave., Ste. 1900
Portland, OR 97204-3719 (503) 796-2984
E-mail: dhartwell@schwabe.com; URL: http://www.schwabe.com/values.aspx

Contact: Darius Hartwell, Attorney
Fields of interest: Legal services.
Type of support: Pro bono services - legal.
Application information: A Pro Bono Committee manages the pro bono program.

3365
The Schwan Food Company, Inc.

(formerly Schwan's Sales Enterprises, Inc.)
115 W. College Dr.
Marshall, MN 56258-1747 (507) 532-3274

Company URL: http://www.theschwanfoodcompany.com
Establishment information: Established in 1952.
Company type: Private company
Business activities: Operates holding company; processes, produces, and markets dairy and frozen food products.
Business type (SIC): Holding company; dairy products; specialty foods/canned, frozen, and preserved
Financial profile for 2011: Number of employees, 17,000; sales volume, $3,670,000,000
Corporate officers: Allan Schwan, Chair.; Gregory D. Flack, C.E.O., Pres., and C.O.O.; James P. Dollive, Exec. V.P., Finance and C.F.O.; Brian Sattler, Exec. V.P. and Genl. Counsel; Scott Peterson, Exec. V.P., Human Resources
Board of directors: Alfred Schwan, Chair.; John D. Bowlin; Patrick Bowe; Barbara Fitzgerald; Gregory Flack; Don Miller; Jeannine Rivet; Lorrie Schwan-Okerlund; Steven Sjoblad; Paul M. Schwan
Giving statement: Giving through the Schwan Food Company, Inc. Corporate Giving Program and the Schwan's Corporate Giving Foundation.

The Schwan Food Company, Inc. Corporate Giving Program

(formerly Schwan's Sales Enterprises, Inc. Corporate Giving Program)
115 W. College Dr.
Marshall, MN 56258-1747
URL: http://www.theschwanfoodcompany.com/corporate-citizenship.htm

Purpose and activities: As a complement to its foundation, Schwan also makes charitable contributions and provides sponsorships to nonprofit organizations directly. Support is given primarily in areas of company operations in Florida, Georgia, Kansas, Kentucky, Minnesota, Oklahoma, Pennsylvania, and Texas.
Fields of interest: Education; Public health; Food services; Athletics/sports, amateur leagues; Youth development; Community/economic development; United Ways and Federated Giving Programs.
Type of support: Donated products; Employee matching gifts; Employee volunteer services; Employee-related scholarships; General/operating support; Scholarship funds; Sponsorships.
Geographic limitations: Giving primarily in areas of company operations in FL, GA, KS, KY, MN, OK, PA, and TX.
Application information: Applications accepted. Applicants should submit the following:
1) timetable for implementation and evaluation of project
2) population served
3) what distinguishes project from others in its field
4) contact person
5) listing of additional sources and amount of support

Sponsorship requests should indicate the name, date, and expected attendance of the event.
Initial approach: Complete online application form for sponsorships

Schwan's Corporate Giving Foundation

115 W. College Dr.
Marshall, MN 56258-1747

Establishment information: Established as a company-sponsored operating foundation in 2000 in MN.
Donors: Schwan's Sales Enterprises, Inc.; The Schwan Food Co., Inc.
Financial data (yr. ended 12/31/11): Assets, $10,511,002 (M); expenditures, $170,185; qualifying distributions, $10,157.
Purpose and activities: The foundation supports organizations involved with theater and higher education.
Fields of interest: Performing arts, theater; Higher education.
Type of support: General/operating support.
Geographic limitations: Giving limited to KS and MN.
Application information: Applications not accepted. Contributes only to a pre-selected organization.
Officers: Greg Flack, Chair. and Pres.; Randy Sharbono, Vice-Chair. and Secy.; Scott Peterson, Treas.
EIN: 411990835
Selected grants: The following grants are a representative sample of this grantmaker's funding activity:
$150,000 to Radio America, Arlington, VA, 2010.

3366
SCIenergy, Inc.

(formerly Servidyne, Inc.)
4099 McEwen, Ste. 420
Dallas, TX 75244 (972) 386-5335

Company URL: http://www.scienergy.com
Establishment information: Established in 2007.
Company type: Private company
Business activities: Provides cloud-based energy management solutions.
Business type (SIC): Computer services; real estate operators and lessors
Corporate officers: Steve Gossett, Jr., C.E.O.; Steve Gossett, Sr., Pres. and C.O.O.; Anthony Martin, Sr. V.P., Sales and Opers.
Board of directors: Ricardo Angel; Raj Atluru; Gary Dillabough; John H. N. Fisher; Bill Halter; Michael C. Morgan; Barry Schuler
Subsidiaries: Abrams Construction, Inc., Atlanta, GA; Abrams Fixture Corp., Atlanta, GA; Abrams Properties, Inc., Atlanta, GA
Giving statement: Giving through the Abrams Foundation, Inc.
Company EIN: 580522129

Abrams Foundation, Inc.

1945 The Exchange S.E., Ste. 300
Atlanta, GA 30339-2029

Establishment information: Established in 1957.
Donors: Abrams Fixture Corp.; Abrams Construction, Inc.; Abrams Properties, Inc.; Abrams Industries, Inc.; Dean Fox Foundation Inc.
Financial data (yr. ended 12/31/11): Assets, $838,126 (M); expenditures, $55,993; qualifying distributions, $50,000; giving activities include $50,000 for grants.
Purpose and activities: The foundation supports organizations involved with arts and culture, education, and religion.
Fields of interest: Museums (art); Arts; Higher education; Education; Jewish agencies & synagogues; Religion.
Type of support: General/operating support.
Geographic limitations: Giving limited to Atlanta, GA.
Support limitations: No grants to individuals.
Application information: Applications not accepted. Unsolicited requests for funds not accepted.
Officers: J. Andrew Abrams, Pres.; Alan R. Abrams, V.P.; Rick A. Paternostro, Treas.
EIN: 586036725

3367
Scientific Components Corporation

(doing business as Mini-Circuits)
13 Neptune Ave.
Brooklyn, NY 11235 (718) 934-4500

Company URL: http://www.minicircuits.com
Establishment information: Established in 1969.
Company type: Private company
Business activities: Manufactures microwave components.
Business type (SIC): Electronic components and accessories
Corporate officers: Harvey Kaylie, Pres.; Roberta Kaylie, Secy.; Marc Sweet, Cont.
Board of directors: Alicia Kaylie; Roberta Kaylie
Giving statement: Giving through the Harvey & Gloria Kaylie Foundation, Inc.

The Harvey & Gloria Kaylie Foundation, Inc.

5 Fir Dr.
Kings Point, NY 11024-1528

Establishment information: Established in 1999 in NY.
Donor: Scientific Components Corp.
Financial data (yr. ended 12/31/11): Assets, $13,585,997 (M); gifts received, $2,200,000; expenditures, $2,859,403; qualifying distributions, $2,850,373; giving activities include $2,850,373 for 67 grants (high: $840,000; low: $180).
Purpose and activities: The foundation supports organizations involved with education, health, counseling, human services, and Judaism.
Fields of interest: Secondary school/education; Higher education; Medical school/education; Education, services; Education; Health care; Mental health, counseling/support groups; Children, services; Family services; Human services; Jewish federated giving programs; Jewish agencies & synagogues.
Type of support: General/operating support.
Geographic limitations: Giving primarily in Brooklyn and New York, NY.
Support limitations: No grants to individuals.
Application information: Applications not accepted. Contributes only to pre-selected organizations.
Officers and Directors:* Harvey Kaylie*, Pres.; Gloria W. Kaylie*, V.P.; Alicia Kaylie Yacoby*, Secy.-Treas.; Roberta Kaylie.
EIN: 113502781
Selected grants: The following grants are a representative sample of this grantmaker's funding activity:
$900,000 to City College 21st Century Foundation, New York, NY, 2010. For general operating budget.
$400,000 to Weill Medical College of Cornell University, New York, NY, 2010. For general operating budget.
$100,000 to UJA-Federation of New York, New York, NY, 2010. For general operating budget.
$90,000 to Central Fund of Israel, New York, NY, 2010. For general operating budget.
$68,715 to Orthodox Union - Union of Orthodox Jewish Congregations of America, New York, NY, 2010. For general operating budget.
$42,500 to Ohel Childrens Home and Family Services, Brooklyn, NY, 2010. For general operating budget.
$35,000 to American Friends of Beit Issie Shapiro, New York, NY, 2010. For general operating budget.
$25,000 to Student Advocacy, Elmsford, NY, 2010. For general operating budget.
$14,700 to Palm Beach Orthodox Synagogue, Palm Beach, FL, 2010. For general operating budget.
$4,000 to Realizing the Dream, Atlanta, GA, 2010. For general operating budget.

3368
Scott & Stringfellow, Inc.

Riverfront Plz.-W. Tower
901 E. Bryd St.
Richmond, VA 23219 (804) 643-1811

Company URL: http://www.scottstringfellow.com
Establishment information: Established in 1893.
Company type: Subsidiary of a public company
Business activities: Provides securities brokerage services.
Business type (SIC): Brokers and dealers/security
Financial profile for 2010: Number of employees, 350

Corporate officers: Sidney Buford Scott, Chair.; Walter Spencer Robertson III, Pres. and C.E.O.; George Shipp, C.I.O.
Board of director: Sidney Buford Scott, Chair.
Giving statement: Giving through the Scott and Stringfellow Educational Foundation.

Scott and Stringfellow Educational Foundation

901 E. Byrd. St., Ste. 500
Richmond, VA 23219
FAX: (804) 643-3718

Establishment information: Established in 1993 in VA.
Donors: Scott & Stringfellow, Inc.; Peter R. Kellogg.
Financial data (yr. ended 12/31/11): Assets, $1,043,379 (M); expenditures, $75,456; qualifying distributions, $67,035; giving activities include $64,300 for 5 grants (high: $52,500; low: $600).
Purpose and activities: The foundation supports organizations involved with education and awards grants to teachers and educators.
Fields of interest: Education.
Programs:
Excellence in Education Grant Program: The foundation awards grants to teachers and educators in selected communities who are helping students to think, grow, and develop in today's world.
Scott & Stringfellow Scholarship Program: The foundation awards college scholarships to children of employees of Scott & Stringfellow, Inc.
Type of support: Employee-related scholarships; General/operating support; Grants to individuals.
Geographic limitations: Giving primarily in NC and VA.
Publications: Informational brochure.
Application information: Applications accepted. Application form required.
Initial approach: Proposal
Deadline(s): None
Officers and Directors:* Franklin B. Heiner*, Pres.; Bradley H. Gunter*, Secy.; Robert P. Allen*, Treas.
EIN: 541669283

3369
Scott Bridge Company, Inc.

2641 Interstate Dr.
P.O. Box 2000
Opelika, AL 36804 (334) 749-5045
FAX: (334) 749-3936

Company URL: http://www.scottbridge.com
Establishment information: Established in 1933.
Company type: Private company
Business activities: Provides bridge construction, rehabilitation, and emergency response services.
Business type (SIC): Construction/miscellaneous heavy
Corporate officers: I.J. Scott III, Pres. and C.E.O.; Jack Swarthout, C.O.O.; Michael Terrell, Sr. V.P., Opers.; William M. Scott, V.P., Admin.; Tom Lowrey, Cont.
Giving statement: Giving through the Scott Foundation, Inc.

Scott Foundation, Inc.

2641 Interstate Dr.
Opelika, AL 36804

Establishment information: Established in 2005 in AL.
Donor: Scott Bridge Company, Inc.
Financial data (yr. ended 12/31/11): Assets, $9,509,546 (M); expenditures, $777,975; qualifying distributions, $688,125; giving activities include $688,125 for grants.
Purpose and activities: The foundation supports organizations involved with human services and religion.
Fields of interest: Children/youth, services; Human services; Christian agencies & churches; Protestant agencies & churches; Religion.
Type of support: General/operating support.
Geographic limitations: Giving primarily in AL, CO, FL, and MA, and in Honduras.
Application information: Applications not accepted. Contributes only to pre-selected organizations.
Directors: I.J. Scott III; William M. Scott; Gerard Swarthout III.
EIN: 161744259
Selected grants: The following grants are a representative sample of this grantmaker's funding activity:
$50,000 to Harvest Evangelism, Opelika, AL, 2010.

3370
Scott Technologies, Inc.

(formerly Figgie International Inc.)
1 Chagrin Highlands
2000 Auburn Dr., Ste. 400
Beachwood, OH 44122 (216) 464-6153

Establishment information: Established in 1910.
Company type: Subsidiary of a foreign company
Business activities: Manufactures life support respiratory products.
Business type (SIC): Search and navigation equipment; medical instruments and supplies
Financial profile for 2010: Number of employees, 1,283
Corporate officer: Christopher C. Hopkins, C.E.O.
Plant: Buffalo, NY
Giving statement: Giving through the Scott Technologies, Inc. Corporate Giving Program and the Scott Technologies Foundation.

Scott Technologies Foundation

(formerly Figgie International Foundation)
P.O. Box 8799
Princeton, NJ 08543-8799 (609) 720-4762

Establishment information: Established in 1979 in OH.
Donors: Figgie International Inc.; Rawlings Sporting Goods Co., Inc.; Scott Technologies, Inc.
Financial data (yr. ended 12/31/11): Assets, $1,102,113 (M); expenditures, $84,149; qualifying distributions, $64,353; giving activities include $64,353 for grants.
Purpose and activities: The foundation supports organizations involved with health, safety, and children and youth.
Fields of interest: Health care; Health organizations; Safety/disasters.
Type of support: General/operating support.
Geographic limitations: Giving primarily in AZ, MD, and VA.
Application information: Applications accepted. Application form required.
Initial approach: Proposal
Deadline(s): None
Trustees: John E. Evard; Marc J. Lemberg; Mark Mitchell; George Oliver; Robert M. Roche.
EIN: 341304712

3371
The Scottdale Bank & Trust Company

150 Pittsburgh St.
Scottdale, PA 15683-1733 (724) 887-8330

Company URL: http://www.sbtbank.com/
Establishment information: Established in 1901.
Company type: Private company
Business activities: Operates commercial bank.
Business type (SIC): Banks/commercial
Corporate officers: Donald F. Kiefer, Pres.; Robert B. Ferguson, Secy.
Giving statement: Giving through the Marilyn K. Kiefer Foundation.

Marilyn K. Kiefer Foundation

150 Pittsburgh St.
Scottdale, PA 15683 (724) 887-8330

Establishment information: Established in 1995.
Donors: The Scottdale Bank & Trust Co.; Donald F. Kiefer.
Contact: Marilyn K. Andras, Chair.
Financial data (yr. ended 12/31/11): Assets, $2,244,462 (M); gifts received, $72,395; expenditures, $112,200; qualifying distributions, $112,200; giving activities include $110,000 for 48 grants (high: $15,000; low: $100).
Purpose and activities: The foundation supports public libraries and fire departments and organizations involved with arts and culture, health, youth services, and religion.
Fields of interest: Recreation; Community/economic development; Religion.
Type of support: Building/renovation; Equipment; General/operating support.
Geographic limitations: Giving primarily in Fayette and Westmoreland counties, PA.
Support limitations: No grants to individuals.
Application information: Applications accepted. Application form required. Applicants should submit the following:
1) brief history of organization and description of its mission
2) detailed description of project and amount of funding requested
Initial approach: Letter of inquiry
Deadline(s): Oct. 31
Officers and Director: Marilyn K. Andras*, Chair.; Donald F. Kiefer, V.P.; Lawrence J. Kiefer, Secy.-Treas.
EIN: 251759914

3372
The Scotts Miracle-Gro Company

(formerly The Scotts Company)
14111 Scottslawn Rd.
Marysville, OH 43041 (937) 644-0011
FAX: (937) 578-5754

Company URL: http://www.scotts.com
Establishment information: Established in 1980.
Company type: Public company
Company ticker symbol and exchange: SMG/NYSE
Business activities: Manufactures lawn care fertilizers, control products, and related products; produces grass seeds.
Business type (SIC): Fertilizers and agricultural chemicals; farms, except cash grains/field crop

Financial profile for 2012: Number of employees, 6,100; assets, $2,074,400,000; sales volume, $2,826,100,000; pre-tax net income, $181,800,000; expenses, $2,582,500,000; liabilities, $1,472,500,000
Fortune 1000 ranking: 2012—739th in revenues, 725th in profits, and 845th in assets
Corporate officers: James Hagedorn, Chair. and C.E.O.; Barry W. Sanders, Pres. and C.O.O.; Vincent C. Brockman, Exec. V.P., Genl. Counsel, and Corp. Secy.; Larry Hilsheimer, Exec. V.P. and C.F.O.; Denise S. Stump, Exec. V.P., Human Resources
Board of directors: James Hagedorn, Chair.; Alan H. Barry; Adam Hanft; Stephen L. Johnson; Thomas N. Kelly, Jr.; Katherine Hagedorn Littlefield; Nancy G. Mistretta; Stephanie M. Shern; Michael E. Porter, Ph.D.
Subsidiaries: EG Systems, Inc., Gahanna, OH; Hyponex Corp., Columbus, OH; Sanford Scientific, Inc., Waterloo, NY; Scotts-Sierra Horticultural Products Co., Milpitas, CA
Plants: Bentonville, Hope, AR; Temecula, Valley Center, CA; Lebanon, CT; Apopka, FL; Atlanta, GA; Fort Madison, IA; Burlington, KY; Medway, ME; Rockville, MD; Maryland Heights, MO; Louisburg, NC; Bay Village, OH; Gervais, Molalla, OR; Avondale, PA; Chester, SC; Huntsville, TX; Wakefield, VA; Jackson, WI
Giving statement: Giving through the Scotts Miracle-Gro Company Contributions Program.
Company EIN: 311414921

The Scotts Miracle-Gro Company Contributions Program

(formerly The Scotts Company Contributions Program)
14111 Scottslawn Rd.
Marysville, OH 43041 (937) 644-0011
E-mail: sustainability@scotts.com; URL: http://www.grogood.com/

Purpose and activities: Scotts Miracle-Gro makes charitable contributions to nonprofit organizations involved with community gardens and green spaces, environmental education, and health care. Support is given primarily in areas of company operations, with emphasis on central Ohio. Giving also in Canada and Europe.
Fields of interest: Education, volunteer services; Botanical gardens; Horticulture/garden clubs; Environment, beautification programs; Environmental education; Health care; Nutrition; Recreation, parks/playgrounds; Youth development, volunteer services; United Ways and Federated Giving Programs Economically disadvantaged.
Program:
GRO1000: In 2011, ScottsMiracle-Gro launched GRO1000, a community outreach initiative to create 1,000 community gardens and green spaces by 2018. The program is directed toward neighborhoods, schools, and communities that are under-served. In addition to GRO1000 public garden and green space installations, ScottsMiracle-Gro is also providing GRO1000 Grassroots Grants to help foster community spirit and public service. Grassroots Grants of up to $1,500 are awarded to local communities to help bring edible gardens, flower gardens, and public green spaces to neighborhoods.
Type of support: Advocacy; Annual campaigns; Donated products; Employee volunteer services; General/operating support; In-kind gifts.
Geographic limitations: Giving primarily in areas of company operations, with emphasis on central OH. Giving also in Canada and Europe.
Publications: Application guidelines.
Application information: Applications accepted. Application form required. Applicants should submit the following:
1) name, address and phone number of organization
2) copy of IRS Determination Letter
3) brief history of organization and description of its mission
Applications should specify the company priorities that the grant supports: Gardens/green-spaces, Health and Wellness, Youth Advancement, or Other; and whether the organization is a United Way affiliate.
Initial approach: Complete online application

3373
The Scoular Company

2027 Dodge St.
Omaha, NE 68102 (402) 342-3500

Company URL: http://www.scoular.com/
Establishment information: Established in 1892.
Company type: Private company
Business activities: Trades grain and grain by-products; provides grain storage services; markets popcorn.
Business type (SIC): Farm-product raw materials—wholesale; warehousing and storage; groceries—wholesale
Financial profile for 2011: Number of employees, 660; sales volume, $4,900,000,000
Corporate officers: David Faith, Chair. and Pres.; Marshall Faith, Vice-Chair.; Chuck Elsea, C.E.O.; Randall Foster, C.O.O.; Todd McQueen, Sr. V.P., Opers.; Joan Maclin, Sr. V.P., Genl. Counsel, Comms., and Secy.; Roger L. Barber, V.P. and Treas.
Board of directors: David Faith, Chair.; Marshall Faith, Vice-Chair.
Giving statement: Giving through the Scoular Foundation.

The Scoular Foundation

2027 Dodge St., Ste. 300
Omaha, NE 68102-1229 (402) 342-3500
URL: http://www.scoular.com/about/community-involvement/

Establishment information: Established in 1967 in NE.
Donor: The Scoular Co.
Contact: Marshall E. Faith, Tr.
Financial data (yr. ended 05/31/12): Assets, $385 (M); gifts received, $586,845; expenditures, $590,670; qualifying distributions, $590,670; giving activities include $590,670 for grants.
Purpose and activities: The foundation supports organizations involved with arts and culture, education, public health, and children and youth.
Fields of interest: Museums (art); Performing arts, theater; Arts; Secondary school/education; Higher education; Education; Health care, clinics/centers; Public health; Boy scouts; American Red Cross; Salvation Army; Children/youth, services.
Type of support: Annual campaigns; Building/renovation; Capital campaigns; Equipment; General/operating support; Matching/challenge support; Program development; Scholarship funds; Sponsorships.
Geographic limitations: Giving limited to areas of company operations in IA, KS, MN, MO, Omaha, NE, and SC.
Support limitations: No grants to individuals.
Publications: Application guidelines.
Application information: Applications accepted. Preference is given to organizations with which employees of Scoular are actively involved. Application form not required.
Initial approach: Letter of inquiry to nearest company facility
Deadline(s): None
Trustees: Roger L. Barber; David M. Faith; Marshall E. Faith.
EIN: 363323189
Selected grants: The following grants are a representative sample of this grantmaker's funding activity:
$81,250 to Hope Center, Omaha, NE, 2011.
$46,431 to United Way of the Midlands, Omaha, NE, 2011.
$21,525 to Habitat for Humanity of Omaha, Omaha, NE, 2011.
$20,000 to Boy Scouts of America, Omaha, NE, 2011.
$18,750 to Salina Community Theater, Salina, KS, 2011.
$10,000 to Bellevue University, Bellevue, NE, 2011.
$10,000 to Hidaya Foundation, Santa Clara, CA, 2011.
$10,000 to Project Interfaith, Omaha, NE, 2011.
$6,000 to Emerging Terrain, Omaha, NE, 2011.
$5,650 to American Heart Association, Omaha, NE, 2011.

3374
The E.W. Scripps Company

(also known as Scripps)
312 Walnut St.
2800 Scripps Ctr.
Cincinnati, OH 45202-4024 (513) 977-3000
FAX: (513) 977-3024

Company URL: http://www.scripps.com
Establishment information: Established in 1878.
Company type: Public company
Company ticker symbol and exchange: SSP/NYSE
Business activities: Publishes newspapers; operates broadcast network affiliates; syndicates and licenses comic strips and comic strip characters.
Business type (SIC): Newspaper publishing and/or printing; radio and television broadcasting; nonstore retailers; investors/miscellaneous; motion pictures/production and services allied to
Financial profile for 2012: Number of employees, 4,700; assets, $1,030,770,000; sales volume, $903,460,000; pre-tax net income, $56,910,000; expenses, $829,560,000; liabilities, $493,070,000
Corporate officers: Richard A. Boehne, Chair., Pres., and C.E.O.; Lisa A. Knutson, C.A.O.; Timothy M. Wesolowski, Sr. V.P., C.F.O., and Treas.; William Appleton, Sr. V.P. and Genl. Counsel; Adam P. Symson, Sr. V.P. and Chief Digital Off.; Timothy E. Stautberg, Sr. V.P., Newspapers; Brian Lawlor, Sr. V.P., Television; Robert A. Carson, V.P. and C.I.O.; Julie L. McGehee, V.P. and Corp. Secy.; Douglas F. Lyons, V.P. and Cont.; Carolyn Micheli, V.P., Corp. Comms.; Robin A. Davis, V.P., Strategic Planning and Dev.
Board of directors: Richard A. Boehne, Chair.; Kelly P. Conlin; John W. Hayden; Anne La Dow; Roger Ogden; Mary Peirce; J. Marvin Quin; Paul K. Scripps; Kim Williams
Giving statement: Giving through the Scripps Howard Foundation.
Company EIN: 311223339

Scripps Howard Foundation

P.O. Box 5380
312 Walnut St., 28th Fl.
Cincinnati, OH 45201 (513) 977-3035
FAX: (513) 977-3800;
E-mail: mike.philipps@scripps.com; Contact for Roy W. Howard Scripps Howard Competition, National Journalism Awards and Internships: Susan J. Porter, V.P., Progs., tel.: (800) 888-3000, ext. 3030, e-mail: sue.porter@scripps.com. See Web site for information on specific foundation programs.;
URL: http://www.scripps.com/foundation

Establishment information: Incorporated in 1962 in OH.
Donors: The E.W. Scripps Co.; Jack R. Howard Trust; Robert P. Scripps; Robert A. Buzzelli; Julia & Robert Heidt; Alan & Beverley Horton Fund; Ken Lowe; George & Mary Ann Sanchez; Nackey & Robert Scagliotti; Cindy J. Scripps; Edward W. & Christy Scripps; Henry R. Scripps; William H. & Kathryn Scripps; Donna & Ed Spray; Felicia & Virginia Vasquez.
Contact: Patty Cottingham, V.P., Admin.; Mike Philipps, C.E.O. and Pres.
Financial data (yr. ended 12/31/11): Assets, $60,519,687 (M); gifts received, $3,437,041; expenditures, $6,186,830; qualifying distributions, $5,959,354; giving activities include $4,098,797 for 802 grants (high: $500,000; low: $25) and $351,775 for 140 grants to individuals (high: $35,000; low: $500).
Purpose and activities: The foundation strives to advance the cause of a free press through support of excellence in journalism, quality journalism education, and professional development. The foundation helps build healthy communities and improve the quality of life through support of sound educational programs, strong families, vital social services, enriching arts and culture, and inclusive civic affairs, with emphasis on areas of company operations.
Fields of interest: Media, print publishing; Arts; Journalism school/education; Education, reading; Education; Environment; Family services; Human services; Civil liberties, first amendment; Public affairs; General charitable giving.
Programs:

Community Fund: The foundation supports programs and projects that improve the quality of life in communities where Scripps does business.

Greater Cincinnati Fund: Through the Greater Cincinnati Fund, the Foundation supports organizations involved with arts and culture, education, human services, and civic affairs.

Internships: The foundation awards journalism internship grants program for undergraduates offered in cooperation with their partner schools. The schools recommend internship grant recipients and oversee placement in the best workplace, matching aspirations to job-readiness and helping students move to the next level of their budding journalism careers.

Jack R. Howard Fellowships in International Journalism: Two fellowships are awarded to international journalists for a year of study at Columbia University's Graduate School of Journalism.

Journalism Grants: The foundation supports programs designed to improve journalism through journalism education, mid-career development, content improvement, public forums, conferences, workshops, and programs addressing First Amendment causes, diversity in the workforce, legal issues, and international press freedom. Visit www.scripps.com/foundation for specific program information.

Literacy Grant Program: The foundation supports a range of literacy efforts in Scripps communities.

Roy W. Howard National Collegiate Reporting Competition: Full-time undergraduate journalism students compete for an international study tour. Visit foundation website for program details.

Scripps Howard Awards: The foundation annually awards $175,000 to broadcast and print journalists, and journalism educators in 19 categories to honor outstanding journalistic achievement.

Scripps Howard Foundation Semester in Washington: Student journalists spend a semester learning and reporting from the nation's capital. Visit www.shfwire.com for program details.

Scripps Howard Program in Religion, Journalism and the Spiritual Life: Graduate students of Columbia University's School of Journalism learn about religion and the role it plays in local and global politics through a two-week study tour.

Teen Appeal Newspaper Program: The Teen Appeal Newspaper Program gives students an opportunity to explore career options.

Teen Media Broadcast Program: The Teen Media Broadcast Program gives students an opportunity to explore career options.

Type of support: Building/renovation; Capital campaigns; Conferences/seminars; Curriculum development; Emergency funds; Employee matching gifts; Employee volunteer services; Employee-related scholarships; Endowments; Equipment; Fellowships; General/operating support; Grants to individuals; Internship funds; Matching/challenge support; Professorships; Program development; Research; Scholarships—to individuals; Seed money; Technical assistance.
Geographic limitations: Giving on a national basis, with emphasis on areas of company operations.
Support limitations: No support for religious organizations not of direct benefit to the entire community, political causes or candidates, anti-business organizations, discriminatory organizations, private foundations, or veterans', fraternal, or labor organizations. No grants for courtesy advertising.
Publications: Annual report; Application guidelines.
Application information: Applications accepted. See Foundation website for contact information on specific programs. Application form not required. Applicants should submit the following:
1) qualifications of key personnel
2) brief history of organization and description of its mission
3) copy of most recent annual report/audited financial statement/990
4) how project's results will be evaluated or measured
5) listing of board of directors, trustees, officers and other key people and their affiliations
6) detailed description of project and amount of funding requested
7) listing of additional sources and amount of support

Initial approach: Send Community Fund (including Literacy Grant) proposals to your local Scripps executive; Greater Cincinnati Fund proposals to Patty Cottingham and Journalism Fund proposals to Mike Philipps
Copies of proposal: 1
Board meeting date(s): Semiannually
Deadline(s): None
Final notification: 90 days

Officers and Trustees:* Mike Philipps*, C.E.O. and Pres.; Patty Cottingham, V.P., Admin.; Susan J. Porter, V.P., Progs.; E. John Wolfzorn, Treas.; Charles Barmonde; Rebecca Scripps Brickner; Robin A. Davis; Eduardo Fernandez; Julia Scripps Heidt; Jack Howard-Potter; Lisa A. Knutson; Brian Lawlor; Margaret Scripps Klenzing; Paul K. Scripps*; Virginia Scripps Vasquez; Timothy E. Stautberg; Adam Symson; Timothy M. Wesolowski; Ellen Weiss.
Members: Richard A. Boehne; Kelly Conlin; Anne M. La Dow; John W. Hayden; Roger Ogden; Mary Peirce; Mike Philipps; J. Marvin Quin; Paul K. Scripps; Kim Williams.
Number of staff: 6 full-time professional.
EIN: 316025114
Selected grants: The following grants are a representative sample of this grantmaker's funding activity:
$62,500 to Arizona State University, Tempe, AZ, 2012. For Scripps Howard Innovation Institute.
$50,000 to Florida International University, Miami, FL, 2012. For Scripps Howard Multimedia Center.
$25,000 to Association for Education in Journalism and Mass Communication, Columbia, SC, 2012. For externships to get faculty into newsrooms.
$20,000 to Harvesters-The Community Food Network, Kansas City, MO, 2012. For Fill the Fridge Project.
$15,000 to Carnegie Art Center, North Tonawanda, NY, 2012. For Scripps Howard ArtShop Program.
$10,000 to Rock and Roll Hall of Fame and Museum, Cleveland, OH, 2012. For On the Road Distance Learning Program.
$7,000 to Motor City Blight Busters, Detroit, MI, 2012. For Detroit 2020 Award.
$5,000 to Big Brothers Big Sisters, 2012. For Career Skills Mentoring Program.
$2,400 to Madisonville Emergency Assistance Center, Cincinnati, OH, 2012. For Family Literacy Nights.
$800 to Childrens Theater, Oriental, NC, 2012. For play performance about bullying.

3375
Seaboard, Inc.

150 Day St.
Seymour, CT 06483-3403 (203) 865-1191

Establishment information: Established in 1923.
Company type: Private company
Business activities: Distributes fuel oil.
Business type (SIC): Fuel dealers—retail
Financial profile for 2010: Number of employees, 34
Corporate officers: John W. Bussman, Chair.; William Bussmann, Pres.; Judith Climie, V.P. and Treas.; Donald Wilby, Secy.
Board of director: John W. Bussman, Chair.
Giving statement: Giving through the Bussmann Family Foundation.

The Bussmann Family Foundation

P.O. Box 328
Guilford, CT 06437-0328

Establishment information: Established in 2000.
Donors: Seaboard, Inc.; John W. Bussmann, Sr.; Marion K. Bussmann.
Financial data (yr. ended 06/30/12): Assets, $917,914 (M); expenditures, $50,483; qualifying distributions, $48,750; giving activities include $48,750 for grants.
Purpose and activities: The foundation supports camps and organizations involved with secondary education and higher education, human services, and Christianity.
Fields of interest: Education; Health care; Religion.
Type of support: General/operating support.
Support limitations: No grants to individuals.
Application information: Applications not accepted. Unsolicited requests for funds not accepted.

Officers: John W. Bussmann, Sr., Chair.; George J. Bussmann, Jr., Pres.; Judith A. Climie, Secy.
Directors: James Bussmann; John Bussmann, Jr.; Marion Bussmann; Robert Bussmann.
EIN: 061587076

3376
Seafood Producers Cooperative
2875 Roeder Ave., Ste. 2
Bellingham, WA 98225-2063
(360) 733-0120

Company URL: http://www.spcsales.com
Establishment information: Established in 1944.
Company type: Cooperative
Business activities: Sells salmon, halibut, sablefish, and rockfish wholesale.
Business type (SIC): Groceries—wholesale
Financial profile for 2010: Number of employees, 9; pre-tax net income, $22,800,000
Corporate officers: Jay Haun, Chair.; Bert Bergman, Co.-Vice Chair.; John Skeele, Co.-Vice Chair.; Thomas McLaughlin, Pres. and C.E.O.; George Eliason, Secy.; Rafe Allensworth, Treas.; Jerry Smith, Cont.
Board of directors: Jay Haun, Chair.; Bert Bergman, Co.-Vice-Chair.; John Skeele, Co.-Vice-Chair.; Alan Andersen; Dick Curran; Tom Fisher; Charlie Piercy; Don Seesz; Kathi Warm; Charlie Wilber
Giving statement: Giving through the Seafood Producers Cooperative Foundation.

Seafood Producers Cooperative Foundation
2875 Roeder Ave., Ste. 2
Bellingham, WA 98225-2063

Establishment information: Established in 2004 in WA.
Donor: Seafood Producers Cooperative.
Financial data (yr. ended 12/31/12): Assets, $1,188 (M); gifts received, $3,569; expenditures, $4,516; qualifying distributions, $4,516; giving activities include $4,500 for 3 grants to individuals (high: $1,500; low: $1,500).
Application information: Applications not accepted. Unsolicited requests for funds not accepted.
Directors: Jay Haun; Thomas McLaughlin; Don Seesz.
EIN: 911933552

3377
Seagate Technology PLC
10200 S. De Anza Blvd.
Cupertino, CA 95014 (408) 658-1540

Company URL: http://www.seagate.com
Establishment information: Established in 1979.
Company type: Public company
Company ticker symbol and exchange: STX/NASDAQ
Business activities: Develops and manufactures computer storage technology and products.
Business type (SIC): Computer and office equipment
Financial profile for 2012: Number of employees, 57,900; assets, $8,700,000,000; sales volume, $16,300,000,000; pre-tax net income, $2,882,000,000; expenses, $11,831,000,000; liabilities, $6,609,000,000
Forbes 2000 ranking: 2012—578th in sales, 179th in profits, and 1568th in assets
Corporate officers: Stephen J. Luczo, Chair., Pres., and C.E.O.; Ken Massaroni, Exec. V.P., Genl. Counsel, and C.A.O.; Patrick J. O'Malley, Exec. V.P. and C.F.O.; Dave Mosley, Exec. V.P., Opers.; Mark Brewer, C.I.O.
Board of directors: Stephen J. Luczo, Chair.; Frank J. Biondi, Jr.; Michael R. Cannon; Mei-Wei Cheng; William T. Coleman III; Jay L. Geldmacher; Seh-Woong Jeong; Lydia M. Marshall; Kristen M. Onken; Chong Sup Park; Gregorio Reyes; Edward J. Zander
Subsidiaries: Maxtor Corporation, Milpitas, CA; Seagate Control Data, Oklahoma City, OK; Seagate Recording Media, Fremont, CA; Seagate Tape Technologies, Inc., Santa Maria, CA; Seagate Technologies, Bloomington, MN
International operations: France; Germany; Hong Kong; Italy; Japan; Malaysia; Singapore; South Korea; Taiwan; United Kingdom
Giving statement: Giving through the Seagate Technology LLC Corporate Giving Program.
Company EIN: 980355609

Seagate Technology LLC Corporate Giving Program
(formerly Seagate Technology, Inc. Corporate Giving Program)
920 Disc Dr.
Scotts Valley, CA 95066-4544
E-mail: community.involvement@seagate.com; Community Involvement contacts: For Corporate, Scotts Valley, Fremont, Sunnyvale, and all other regions in California: e-mail: community.involvement@seagate.com; For Longmont, Colorado: Cynthia Martini, e-mail: cynthia.g.martini@seagate.com; For Shrewsbury, Massachusetts, Shakopee, and Normandale, Minnesota, and Pittsburgh, Pennsylvania: Lori Johnson, e-mail: lori.johnson@seagate.com; For Oklahoma City, Oklahoma: Elena Sexton, e-mail: elena.sexton@seagate.com; For China: Audrey Cheah, e-mail: audrey.cheah@seagate.com; For Europe, the Middle East, and Africa: June Coates, e-mail: june.coates@seagate.com; For Malaysia: Audrey Cheah, e-mail: audrey.cheah@seagate.com; For Singapore: Josephine Low, e-mail: josephine.low@seagate.com; For Thailand: Kwanjit Sudsawad, e-mail: kwanjit.sudsawad@seagate.com; URL: http://www.seagate.com/www/en-us/about/global_citizenship/community

Purpose and activities: Seagate makes charitable contributions to nonprofit organizations involved with arts and culture, education, the environment, health, hunger, housing, human services, diversity, science and technology, and civic affairs. Special emphasis is directed toward programs designed to provide K-12 science, math, and technology education to students in low-income and minority communities. Support is given on a national and international basis, with emphasis on areas of company operations.
Fields of interest: Arts; Elementary/secondary education; Education; Environment; Health care; Food services; Housing/shelter; Disasters, preparedness/services; Recreation; Human services; Civil/human rights, equal rights; Science, formal/general education; Mathematics; Engineering/technology; Science; Public affairs Minorities; Economically disadvantaged.
Type of support: Donated equipment; Donated products; Employee matching gifts; Employee volunteer services; General/operating support; In-kind gifts; Scholarship funds.
Geographic limitations: Giving on a national and international basis, with emphasis on areas of company operations.
Support limitations: No support for organizations with overhead expenses exceeding 20 percent of the total operating budget, pass-through organizations, discriminatory organizations, political parties, religious or labor organizations not of direct benefit to the entire community, private foundations, fundraising organizations, special interest groups, or athletic teams. No grants to individuals, or for continuing support, luncheons, banquets, or similar events, endowments, capital campaigns, athletic events, travel, advertising, or multi-year commitments.
Publications: Application guidelines.
Application information: Applications accepted. Proposals should be submitted using organization letterhead. Video, CD, book, and binder submissions are not encouraged. Organizations receiving support are asked to provide a final report. Application form not required. Applicants should submit the following:
1) results expected from proposed grant
2) population served
3) copy of IRS Determination Letter
4) brief history of organization and description of its mission
5) how project's results will be evaluated or measured
6) descriptive literature about organization
7) listing of board of directors, trustees, officers and other key people and their affiliations
8) listing of additional sources and amount of support

Proposals should specifically note the nature of the request being made.
Initial approach: E-mail proposal to nearest Community Involvement contact
Copies of proposal: 1
Committee meeting date(s): Quarterly
Final notification: 4 to 6 weeks

3378
Seagrave Fire Apparatus, LLC
105 E. 12th St.
Clintonville, WI 54929-1518
(715) 823-2141

Company URL: http://www.seagrave.com
Establishment information: Established in 1881.
Company type: Private company
Business activities: Manufactures fire and rescue service apparatus.
Business type (SIC): Motor vehicles and equipment
Corporate officers: A. Joseph Neiner, Chair. and C.E.O.; Nathan Nick, C.O.O.; Mary Jo Wenzel, C.F.O.
Board of director: A. Joseph Neiner, Chair.
Subsidiary: Seagrave Sales and Service of Virginia, Richmond, VA
International operations: Canada
Giving statement: Giving through the Four Wheel Drive Foundation.

Four Wheel Drive Foundation
79 8th St.
Clintonville, WI 54929-1518 (715) 823-7961

Donor: FWD Corp.
Contact: John L. Rosenheim, Secy.
Financial data (yr. ended 09/30/11): Assets, $223,730 (M); gifts received, $117; expenditures, $4,407; qualifying distributions, $0.
Purpose and activities: The foundation awards college scholarships to high school seniors in Clintonville, Wisconsin.
Type of support: Scholarships—to individuals.

Geographic limitations: Giving limited to the Clintonville, WI.
Application information: Applications accepted. Application form required.
Initial approach: Proposal
Deadline(s): May 10
Officers: James M. Green, Pres.; Joseph L. Kaufmann, V.P.; John L. Rosenheim, Secy.
EIN: 396059533

3379
SEAKR Engineering, Incorporated

6221 S. Racine Cir.
Centennial, CO 80111 (303) 790-8499

Company URL: http://www.seakr.com
Establishment information: Established in 1983.
Company type: Private company
Business activities: Manufactures solid state memory systems.
Business type (SIC): Electronic components and accessories
Corporate officers: Ray Anderson, C.E.O. and C.F.O.; Eric Anderson, Co-Pres. and C.O.O.; Scott Anderson, Co-Pres.
Giving statement: Giving through the SEAKR Foundation.

SEAKR Foundation

6221 S. Racine Cir.
Centennial, CO 80111-6427 (303) 790-8499
Additional contact: Melissa Coen, Foundation Rep., tel.: (303) 858-4559; URL: http://www.seakr.com/about/foundation.html

Establishment information: Established in 2004 in CO.
Donors: SEAKR Engineering, Inc.; Raymond E. Anderson.
Contact: Raymond E. Anderson, Chair.
Financial data (yr. ended 12/31/11): Assets, $161,627 (M); gifts received, $198,000; expenditures, $237,140; qualifying distributions, $226,000; giving activities include $226,000 for grants.
Purpose and activities: The foundation awards grants to the families of soldiers killed in the line of duty.
Fields of interest: Family services Military/veterans.
Type of support: Grants to individuals.
Geographic limitations: Giving primarily in CO.
Application information: Applications not accepted. Contributes only to pre-selected individuals.
Officer and Director: Raymond E. Anderson*, Chair.; Lorraine W. Anderson.
EIN: 200979291

3380
Sealaska Corporation

1 Sealaska Plz., Ste. 400
Juneau, AK 99801-1276 (907) 586-1512

Company URL: http://www.sealaska.com
Establishment information: Established in 1972.
Company type: Native corporation
Business activities: Operates native corporation.
Business type (SIC): Logging; mining and quarrying of nonmetallic minerals (except fuels)
Financial profile for 2011: Assets, $3,686,640,000; sales volume, $2,594,870,000; liabilities, $1,065,640,000
Corporate officers: Albert M. Kookesh, Chair.; Rosita F. Worl, Vice-Chair.; Chris E. McNeil, Jr., Pres. and C.E.O.; Sam Landol, C.O.O.; Anthony Mallott, C.I.O. and Treas.; Douglas Morris, V.P. and C.F.O.; Nicole D. Hallingstad, V.P. and Corp. Secy.; Jaeleen Araujo, V.P. and Genl. Counsel; Vicki Soboleff, Corp. Cont.
Board of directors: Albert M. Kookesh, Chair.; Rosita F. Worl, Vice-Chair.; Patrick M. Anderson; Barbara Cadiente-Nelson; Sidney C. Edenshaw; Clarence Jackson, Sr.; J. Tate London; Byron I. Mallott; Jodi M. Mitchell; Joseph G. Nelson; Jacqueline Johnson Pata, Sr.; Bill Thomas; Edward K. Thomas; Ralph Wolfe
Subsidiary: Sealaska Timber Corp., Ketchikan, AK
International operations: Mexico
Giving statement: Giving through the Sealaska Corporate Contributions Program, the Sony Corporation, and the Sealaska Heritage Institute.

Sealaska Heritage Institute

(formerly Sealaska Heritage Foundation)
1 Sealaska Plz., Ste. 301
Juneau, AK 99801-1245 (907) 463-4844
FAX: (907) 586-9293;
E-mail: scholarship@sealaska.com; URL: http://www.sealaskaheritage.org

Establishment information: Established in 1980 in AK.
Donor: Sealaska Corp.
Contact: Deena LaRue, Mgr., Grants
Financial data (yr. ended 12/31/11): Revenue, $3,627,268; assets, $3,783,744 (M); gifts received, $3,468,376; expenditures, $2,665,659; giving activities include $360,730 for grants to individuals.
Purpose and activities: The foundation seeks to harness all available resources to preserve, promote, and maintain the cultures and heritage of the Tlingit, Haida, and Tsimshian people for the benefit of present and future generations and the public; to encourage and support cultural heritage cooperation among all tribes and organizations; to encourage and foster the education of Native Americans so that the public may benefit from their talents; and to cooperate with other heritage programs.
Fields of interest: Arts education; Arts; Business school/education; Engineering school/education; Environment, management/technical assistance; Environment, natural resources; International affairs, goodwill promotion; Civil rights, race/intergroup relations Native Americans/American Indians.
Programs:
Corporate 7(i) Scholarship: Scholarships are available to applicant's whose major field of study relates to Sealaska Corporation's businesses.
Judson L. Brown Endowment Fund: The program awards one scholarship of $5,000 to an outstanding junior or senior college student.
Sealaska Endowment Scholarship: The institute awards academic scholarships for undergraduate, graduate, and vocational studies at accredited institutions.
Type of support: Grants to individuals; Scholarships—to individuals.
Geographic limitations: Giving limited to southeast AK.
Publications: Application guidelines; Informational brochure; Newsletter.
Application information: Applications accepted. Applicants must be Alaska natives who are defined as "Native" under the Alaska Claims Settlement Act 43 U.S.C. 1602(b) and enrolled to Sealaska Corporation or native lineal descendants of Alaska Natives enrolled to Sealaska Corporation, whether or not the applicant owns Sealaska Corporate stock. Application form required.
Initial approach: Download application form
Deadline(s): Mar. 1
Final notification: May 1
Officers and Directors:* Marlene Johnson*, Chair.; Robert Martin*, Vice-Chair.; Dr. Rosita Worl*, Pres.; Joe Nelson*, Secy.; Nancy Barnes; Jeane Breinig; Clarence Jackson; Ethel Lund; Mike Miller.
EIN: 920081844

3381
Sealed Air Corporation

200 Riverfront Blvd.
Elmwood Park, NJ 07407-1033
(201) 791-7600
FAX: (201) 703-4205

Company URL: http://www.sealedair.com
Establishment information: Established in 1960.
Company type: Public company
Company ticker symbol and exchange: SEE/NYSE
International Securities Identification Number: US81211K1007
Business activities: Manufactures and sells food and protective packaging products.
Business type (SIC): Paper and paperboard/coated, converted, and laminated; plastic products/miscellaneous
Financial profile for 2012: Number of employees, 25,000; assets, $9,437,200,000; sales volume, $7,648,100,000; pre-tax net income, -$1,872,000,000; expenses, $9,126,300,000; liabilities, $7,993,400,000
Fortune 1000 ranking: 2012—333rd in revenues, 989th in profits, and 407th in assets
Forbes 2000 ranking: 2012—1134th in sales, 1929th in profits, and 1475th in assets
Corporate officers: William V. Hickey, Chair. and C.E.O.; Jerome A. Peribere, Pres.; Carol P. Lowe, Sr. V.P. and C.F.O.; William G. Stiehl, C.A.O. and Cont.; H. Katherine White, V.P., Genl. Counsel, and Secy.; Tod S. Christie, Treas.
Board of directors: William V. Hickey, Chair.; Hank Brown; Michael Chu; Patrick Duff; Lawrence R. Codey; T.J. Dermot Dunphy; Jacqueline B. Kosecoff; Kenneth P. Manning; William J. Marino; Richard L. Wambold; Jerry R. Whitaker
Subsidiary: Sealed Air (Puerto Rico), Inc., Guaynabo, PR
Plants: Biola, Chula Vista, Hayward, CA; Danbury, CT; Marietta, GA; Hodgkins, Salem, IL; Hyannis, Watertown, MA; Grenada, MS; Fair Lawn, Totowa, NJ; Scotia, NY; Lenoir, Patterson, NC; Sharonville, OH; Hanover, PA; Dallas, Fort Worth, TX
Joint Venture: PolyMask Corp., Conover, NC
International operations: Australia; Barbados; Belgium; Botswana; Brazil; Canada; Cayman Islands; Chile; China; Colombia; Czech Republic; Denmark; Finland; France; Germany; Greece; Guatemala; Hong Kong; Hungary; India; Ireland; Israel; Italy; Luxembourg; Malaysia; Mexico; Netherlands; New Zealand; Norway; Peru; Philippines; Poland; Portugal; Romania; Singapore; South Africa; South Korea; Spain; Sweden; Switzerland; Taiwan; Thailand; Turkey; Ukraine; United Kingdom; Uruguay; Venezuela
Giving statement: Giving through the Sealed Air Corporation Contributions Program.
Company EIN: 650654331

Sealed Air Corporation Contributions Program

200 Riverfront Blvd.
Elmwood Park, NJ 07407-1037 (201) 791-7600
URL: http://www.sealedair.com/Sealed-Air-Sustainability/goals-communities.aspx

Purpose and activities: Sealed Air makes charitable contributions to nonprofit organizations involved with education, the environment, and hunger. Support is given on a national and international basis in areas of company operations.
Fields of interest: Education; Environment; Food services.
Type of support: Consulting services; Donated products; Employee volunteer services; General/operating support.
Geographic limitations: Giving on a national and international basis in areas of company operations.

3382
Sealy Corporation

1 Office Pkwy. Sealy Dr.
Trinity, NC 27370-9449 (336) 861-3500
FAX: (302) 655-5049

Company URL: http://www.sealy.com
Establishment information: Established in 1881.
Company type: Public company
Company ticker symbol and exchange: ZZ/NYSE
Business activities: Licenses its trademark, copyrights and marketing and financial service to manufacturers of Sealy brand products.
Business type (SIC): Investors/miscellaneous; furniture/household
Financial profile for 2012: Number of employees, 4,267; assets, $1,005,340,000; sales volume, $1,347,870,000; pre-tax net income, $8,160,000; expenses, $1,251,010,000; liabilities, $1,062,870,000
Corporate officers: Paul Norris, Chair.; Lawrence J. Rogers, Pres. and C.E.O.; Jeffrey C. Ackerman, Exec. V.P. and C.F.O.; Louis R. Bachicha, Exec. V.P., Sales; Michael Q. Murray, Sr. V.P., Genl. Counsel, and Secy.; Carmen J. Dabiero, Sr. V.P., Human Resources
Board of directors: Paul Norris, Chair.; Simon E. Brown; Deborah G. Ellinger; James W. Johnston; Gary E. Morin; Dean B. Nelson; John B. Replogle; Richard W. Roedel, C.P.A.; Lawrence J. Rogers
International operations: Argentina; Belgium; Brazil; France; Guernsey; Hong Kong; India; Italy; Malaysia; Mexico; Netherlands; Singapore; Spain; Switzerland
Giving statement: Giving through the Sealy Corporation Contributions Program.
Company EIN: 363284147

Sealy Corporation Contributions Program

1 Office Pkwy. at Sealy Dr.
Trinity, NC 27370-9449 (336) 861-3500
URL: http://www.sealy.com/About-Sealy/Community-Involvement.aspx

Purpose and activities: Sealy makes charitable contributions to nonprofit organizations involved with disaster relief, recreation and youth, and fund-raising for human services. Support is given primarily in areas of company operations.
Fields of interest: Housing/shelter, volunteer services; Disasters, preparedness/services; Recreation, camps; Boys & girls clubs; Human services, fund raising/fund distribution; American Red Cross; Salvation Army; YM/YWCAs & YM/YWHAs; Children/youth, services; Children, services; United Ways and Federated Giving Programs.
Type of support: Donated products; Employee volunteer services; General/operating support; In-kind gifts.
Geographic limitations: Giving primarily in areas of company operations.

3383
Seamen's Bank

221 Commercial St.
P.O. Box 659
Provincetown, MA 02657-2100
(508) 487-0035

Company URL: http://www.seamensbank.com
Establishment information: Established in 1851.
Company type: Private company
Business activities: Operates savings bank.
Business type (SIC): Savings institutions
Financial profile for 2011: Number of employees, 25; assets, $291,739,000; pre-tax net income, $1,440,000; liabilities, $259,587,000
Corporate officers: Ernest L. Carreiro, Jr., Chair.; John K. Roderick, Pres. and C.E.O.; Lori F. Meads, V.P., Admin and Mktg.; Jean S. Leonard, V.P., Opers; Laurie Watts-Bumpus, V.P., Human Resources; Paul R. Silva, Clerk; Michael K. Silva, Treas.
Board of directors: Ernest L. Carreiro, Jr., Chair.; George D. Bryant; Ernest L. Carreiro, Jr.; Betsi A. Corea; Christopher E. Enos; John E. Medeiros; Donald E. Murphy; Timothy F. McNulty; Donald R. Reeves; John K. Roderick; Steven E. Roderick; Paul R. Silva; Sandra L. Silva; Paul M. Souza
Giving statement: Giving through the Seamens Long Point Charitable Foundation, Inc.

Seamens Long Point Charitable Foundation, Inc.

350 Route 6
North Truro, MA 02652 (508) 487-0035

Establishment information: Established in 1997 in MA.
Donor: Seamen's Bank.
Contact: John J. Roderick, Pres. and Treas.
Financial data (yr. ended 03/31/12): Assets, $577,878 (M); gifts received, $112,000; expenditures, $91,761; qualifying distributions, $91,611; giving activities include $91,541 for 86 grants (high: $7,500; low: $50).
Purpose and activities: The foundation supports hospices and organizations involved with arts and culture, education, the environment, health, recreation, children and youth, and community development.
Fields of interest: Arts; Education; Health care.
Type of support: General/operating support; Program development; Scholarship funds.
Geographic limitations: Giving limited to the Provincetown, MA, area.
Application information: Applications accepted. Application form required.
Initial approach: Contact foundation for application form
Deadline(s): Varies
Officers and Directors:* John K. Roderick*, Pres. and Treas.; Paul R. Silva*, Clerk; Ernest L. Carreiro, Jr.; Betsi Corea; Christopher Enos; Timothy McNulty; John E. Medeiros; Donald Murphy; Donald R. Reeves; Steven E. Roderick; Sandra Silva; Paul M. Souza.
EIN: 043368515

3384
Sears, Roebuck and Co.

3333 Beverly Rd.
Hoffman Estates, IL 60179-0001
(847) 286-2500

Company URL: http://www.sears.com
Establishment information: Established in 1886.
Company type: Subsidiary of a public company
Business activities: Operates department stores; provides consumer loans; sells insurance.
Business type (SIC): Department stores; credit institutions/personal; insurance carriers
Corporate officers: Lou D'Ambrosio, Pres. and C.E.O.; Michael Collins, Sr. V.P. and C.F.O.; William K. Phelan, Sr. V.P., Cont., and C.A.O.
Subsidiaries: Lands' End, Inc., Dodgeville, WI; Sears Roebuck Acceptance Corp., Greenville, DE
International operations: Canada; Mexico
Giving statement: Giving through the Sears, Roebuck and Co. Contributions Program and the Sears-Roebuck Foundation.

Sears, Roebuck and Co. Contributions Program

3333 Beverly Rd.
Hoffman Estates, IL 60179-0001 (847) 286-2500
URL: http://www.searsholdings.com/communityrelations/

Purpose and activities: Sears supports programs designed to provide home repairs to families in need. Special emphasis is directed towards military and veterans. Support is given on a national basis in areas of company operations.
Fields of interest: Housing/shelter, repairs; Home accessibility modifications; Housing/shelter; Utilities Military/veterans.
Type of support: Donated products; Employee volunteer services; General/operating support; In-kind gifts; Loaned talent.
Geographic limitations: Giving on a national basis in areas of company operations.
Number of staff: 4 full-time professional.

The Sears-Roebuck Foundation

3333 Beverly Rd., Rm. BC097A-A
Hoffman Estates, IL 60179-0001

Establishment information: Incorporated in 1923 in IL as Sears Agricultural Foundation; re-chartered in 1941.
Donors: Sears, Roebuck and Co.; Michele Carlin; Sears Holdings Corp.
Financial data (yr. ended 12/31/11): Assets, $0 (M); expenditures, $5,371; qualifying distributions, $0.
Purpose and activities: The foundation supports organizations involved with families, diversity, and women.
Type of support: Annual campaigns; Capital campaigns; General/operating support; Program development.
Geographic limitations: Giving primarily in Chicago, IL; also giving to national organizations.
Support limitations: No support for religious organizations not of direct benefit to the entire community, political, fraternal, or labor organizations, or colleges providing instruction in technology, religion, or a single profession, or organizations where enrollment is limited by religion. No grants to individuals, or for building or endowments, scholarships, fellowships, or advertisements; no matching gifts.

Application information: Applications not accepted. Unsolicited requests for funds not accepted.
Board meeting date(s): 4 times per year
Officers and Directors:* William R. Harker*, Pres.; James L. Misplon*, V.P.; Dorian R. Williams*, Secy.; Alfred H. Jasser, Treas.; Julie E. Blackburn; Christian E. Brathewaite.
Number of staff: 4 full-time professional.
EIN: 366032266

3385
Seattle Coffee Company

(also known as Seattle's Best Coffee)
2401 Utah Ave. S., Ste. 800
P.O. Box 3717
Seattle, WA 98101-2078 (206) 447-1575

Company URL: http://www.seattlesbest.com
Establishment information: Established in 1971.
Company type: Subsidiary of a public company
Business activities: Operates coffee shops.
Business type (SIC): Restaurants and drinking places
Corporate officer: Steven Schickler, Pres.
Giving statement: Giving through the Vashon Island Coffee Foundation.

Vashon Island Coffee Foundation

P.O. Box 964
Vashon Island, WA 98070-0964
URL: http://www.tvicr.com/coffee/info/foundation.php

Establishment information: Established in 1996 in WA.
Donors: Seattle Coffee Co.; James Stewart; Veloso Trading.
Financial data (yr. ended 12/31/11): Assets, $279,040 (M); gifts received, $57,719; expenditures, $39,785; qualifying distributions, $28,102; giving activities include $28,102 for 4 grants (high: $21,572; low: $100).
Purpose and activities: The foundation supports organizations involved with education, human services, and community development in Central America.
Fields of interest: Education; Human services; Community/economic development.
International interests: Central America; Costa Rica; El Salvador; Guatemala.
Type of support: Building/renovation; General/operating support.
Support limitations: No grants to individuals.
Application information: Applications not accepted. Unsolicited requests for funds not accepted.
Officer: James Stewart, Pres.
EIN: 911704071

3386
The Seattle Times Company

1120 John St.
P.O. Box 70
Seattle, WA 98109 (206) 464-2111

Company URL: http://www.seattletimescompany.com
Establishment information: Established in 1896.
Company type: Subsidiary of a private company
Business activities: Publishes newspapers.
Business type (SIC): Newspaper publishing and/or printing
Financial profile for 2009: Number of employees, 990
Corporate officers: Frank A. Blethen, C.E.O.; Alayne Fardella, C.O.O.; Michael Shepard, Sr. V.P., Opers.; Buster Brown, Sr. V.P., Finance; Jill Mackie, V.P., Public Affairs
Subsidiaries: Walla Walla Union Bulletin, Walla Walla, WA; YAKIMA HERALD, Yakima, WA
Giving statement: Giving through the Seattle Times Company Contributions Program and the Seattle Times Company Fund for the Needy.

The Seattle Times Company Contributions Program

c/o Community Support
P.O. Box 70
Seattle, WA 98111-0070 (206) 464-2111
E-mail: communitysupport@seattletimes.com;
URL: http://www.seattletimescompany.com/community/index.htm

Contact: Suzanne Canino, Dir., Corp. Mktg.
Purpose and activities: The Seattle Times makes charitable contributions to nonprofit organizations involved with arts and culture, youth development, human services, diversity, and women. Support is given primarily in Washington.
Fields of interest: Arts; Youth development; Human services; Civil/human rights, equal rights Women.
Type of support: Capital campaigns; Donated products; Employee volunteer services; General/operating support; Program development; Scholarship funds; Scholarships—to individuals; Sponsorships.
Geographic limitations: Giving primarily in WA, with emphasis on the Puget Sound region of northwestern WA.
Support limitations: No support for religious organizations not of direct benefit to the entire community. No grants to individuals (except for scholarships), or for debt retirement, operating deficits, or team sponsorships or travel.
Publications: Application guidelines.
Application information: Applications accepted. Application form required. Applicants should submit the following:
1) results expected from proposed grant
2) statement of problem project will address
3) population served
4) how project's results will be evaluated or measured
5) list of company employees involved with the organization
6) descriptive literature about organization
7) detailed description of project and amount of funding requested
8) listing of additional sources and amount of support

Requests for sponsorships should include a description of the proposed advertising plan; indicate the benefit to the Seattle Times; and be addressed to the sponsorships manager.
Initial approach: E-mail or mail grant requests to headquarters
Committee meeting date(s): Quarterly
Final notification: 90 days for funding requests; 4 to 6 weeks for sponsorships

Seattle Times Company Fund for the Needy

c/o The Seattle Times Co.
P.O. Box 70
Seattle, WA 98111-0070 (206) 464-2472
URL: http://www.seattletimescompany.com/community/fundforneedy.htm

Establishment information: Established in 1979 in WA.
Donor: The Seattle Times Co.
Financial data (yr. ended 06/30/11): Revenue, $1,004,023; assets, $68,676 (M); gifts received, $1,003,828; expenditures, $973,239; program services expenses, $973,239; giving activities include $968,815 for 15 grants (high: $257,750; low: $19,250).
Purpose and activities: The fund supports organizations that aid needy families and needy individuals.
Fields of interest: Economically disadvantaged.
Geographic limitations: Giving limited to WA.
Officers and Directors:* Frank A. Blethen*, Chair.; Alan A. Fisco*, Pres. and Treas.; Nathaniel T. Brown*, V.P.; Jonathan Michaels*, Secy.; James A. Blethen; Suzanne Canino; Michael B. Shepard.
EIN: 911081445

3387
SeaWorld Parks & Entertainment

(formerly Busch Entertainment Corporation)
9205 S. Park Center Loop, Ste. 400
Orlando, FL 32819 (407) 226-5011

Company URL: http://www.seaworldparksblog.com/
Establishment information: Established in 1979.
Company type: Subsidiary of a public company
Business activities: Operates theme parks.
Business type (SIC): Amusement and recreation services/miscellaneous
Corporate officers: David F. D'Alessandro, Chair.; James D. Atchison, Pres. and C.E.O.; Daniel B. Brown, C.O.O.; James M. Heaney, C.F.O.
Board of directors: David F. D'Alessandro, Chair.; James D. Atchison
Offices: San Diego, CA; Orlando, Tampa, FL; Langhorne, PA; San Antonio, TX; Williamsburg, VA
Giving statement: Giving through the SeaWorld & Busch Gardens Conservation Fund.

SeaWorld & Busch Gardens Conservation Fund

9205 SouthPark Center Loop, Ste. 400
Orlando, FL 32819-8651
E-mail: mail@swbgfund.org; Application address for Environmental Excellence Awards: c/o SeaWorld Orlando Education Dept., 7007 SeaWorld Dr., Orlando, FL 32821, tel.: (877) 792-4332 or (407) 363-2389, *e-mail:* buschgardenseducation@gmail.com; URL: http://www.swbg-conservationfund.org/

Establishment information: Established in 2003 in DE and MO.
Donors: SeaWorld Parks and Entertainment; Busch Entertainment Corp.
Contact: Brad F. Andrews, Pres. and Exec. Dir.
Financial data (yr. ended 12/31/11): Assets, $781,629 (M); gifts received, $614,570; expenditures, $1,114,293; qualifying distributions, $1,088,871; giving activities include $1,088,871 for grants.
Purpose and activities: The foundation supports programs designed to promote species research; habitat protection; animal rescue and rehabilitation; and conservation education.
Fields of interest: Elementary/secondary education; Environment, water resources; Environmental education; Environment; Animals/wildlife, research; Animals/wildlife, public

education; Animal welfare; Animals/wildlife, preservation/protection; Animals/wildlife, fisheries; Animals/wildlife, sanctuaries; Animals/wildlife.

Programs:

Animal Crisis Grants: The fund awards grants to aid wildlife and habitats in peril due to natural or human-caused events.

Environmental Excellence Awards: The fund annually awards eight $10,000 grants to K-12 schools or community groups in recognition of outstanding environmental projects designed to protect and preserve the environment. The award includes an all-expense paid trip for 6 participants to a SeaWorld or Busch Gardens park for a special awards event. This award includes an all-expense paid trip for the honoree and guest to a SeaWorld or Busch Gardens park for a special awards event and an all-expense paid trip to the National Science Teachers Association national conference. Visit URL http://www.seaworld.org/conservation-matters/eea/ for more information.

Environmental Excellence Awards for Individuals: The award of $10,000 recognizes an outstanding youth, adult and environmental educator for individual personal achievements in helping to protect wildlife and wild places.

National Geographic Society Co-Grants: The fund, in partnership with National Geographic Conservation Trust, awards grants to well-deserving projects around the world designed to address co-existing with wildlife.

Type of support: Continuing support; General/operating support; Grants to individuals; Program development; Research.
Geographic limitations: Giving on a national and international basis in areas of company operations.
Support limitations: No grants to individuals (except for Environmental Excellence Awards); generally, no grants for capital campaigns, building, or construction that would outlive the project supported by the Fund or ex-situ captive breeding efforts.
Publications: Annual report; Application guidelines; Financial statement; Newsletter.
Application information: Applications accepted. Grants range from $5,000 to $25,000. A site visit may be requested. Color photographs, brochures, videos, CD's, Websites, news articles, posters, t-shirts, and buttons are encouraged for the Environmental Excellence Awards. Application form required. Applicants should submit the following:
1) results expected from proposed grant
2) qualifications of key personnel
3) detailed description of project and amount of funding requested
4) copy of current year's organizational budget and/or project budget
5) listing of additional sources and amount of support

Initial approach: Complete online application; mail a 300-word letter and a 5 minute video on a CD or flash drive to application address for Environmental Excellence Awards for schools; post and email a video nomination on YouTube for Environmental Excellence Awards for individuals
Board meeting date(s): Once a year in Spring
Deadline(s): Sept. to Dec. 1; Mar. 2 for Environmental Excellence Awards for schools; Mar. 5 for Environmental Excellence Awards for individuals
Final notification: Apr. and May

Officers and Directors: Brad F. Andrews*, Pres. and Exec. Dir.; Howard Demsky, Secy.; Marc G. Swanson, Treas.; James D. Atchison; Virginia M. Busch; Jim Dean; David Grabe; Jack Hanna; Julie Scardina; Hugh Share; Judy St. Leger; Shiela Voss; Glenn Young.
EIN: 113692807
Selected grants: The following grants are a representative sample of this grantmaker's funding activity:
$37,250 to EcoHealth Alliance, New York, NY, 2010. For general support.
$35,000 to World Wildlife Fund, Washington, DC, 2010. For general support.
$30,000 to Fauna and Flora International, Washington, DC, 2010. For general support.
$30,000 to Nature Conservancy, Saint Louis, MO, 2010. For general support.
$30,000 to Wildlife Alliance, Washington, DC, 2010. For general support.
$25,600 to Peregrine Fund, Boise, ID, 2010. For general support.
$15,000 to Audubon Society, National, Ithaca, NY, 2010. For general support.
$15,000 to Coral Reef Alliance, San Francisco, CA, 2010. For general support.
$15,000 to Lands Council, Spokane, WA, 2010. For general support.
$10,000 to Wildlife Alliance, Washington, DC, 2010. For general support.

3388
Securant Bank and Trust

(formerly MWBank)
6001 W. Capitol Dr.
Milwaukee, WI 53216-2196
(414) 442-5800

Company URL: https://www.securantbank.com
Establishment information: Established in 1914.
Company type: Private company
Business activities: Operates commercial bank.
Business type (SIC): Banks/commercial
Corporate officers: David A. Davis, Pres. and C.E.O.; Michael P. Peters, Exec. V.P. and C.O.O.; Jeffrey M. Dereszynski, Sr. V.P. and C.F.O; Ralph M. Garcia, V.P., Opers.; Nicole M. Gmach, Cont.
Board of directors: Emile H. Banks, Jr.; David A. Davis; Daniel B. Druml; William J. Hickmann; Thomas A. Manthy; John E. Perry; Michael P. Peters; Keith C. Pollnow; Michael J. Pretasky, Sr.; William R. Rafferty, Jr.
Giving statement: Giving through the Milwaukee Western Bank Foundation, Inc.

Milwaukee Western Bank Foundation, Inc.

6001 W. Capitol Dr.
Milwaukee, WI 53216-2196

Donors: Milwaukee Western Bank; Securant Bank & Trust.
Financial data (yr. ended 12/31/11): Assets, $7,984 (M); gifts received, $5,000; expenditures, $1,611; qualifying distributions, $1,600; giving activities include $1,600 for grants.
Purpose and activities: The foundation supports organizations involved with education, health, cancer, and youth services.
Fields of interest: Education; Health care; Human services.
Type of support: General/operating support; Scholarship funds.
Geographic limitations: Giving primarily in the Milwaukee, WI, area.
Support limitations: No grants to individuals.
Application information: Applications not accepted. Unsolicited requests for funds not accepted.
Officers and Directors:* David A. Davis*, Pres.; Michael P. Peters*, V.P.; Jeffrey A. Reimer*, Secy.; Jeffrey M. Dereszynski*, Treas.
EIN: 396067854

3389
Securian Financial Group, Inc.

400 Robert St. N.
St. Paul, MN 55101-2098 (651) 665-3500

Company URL: http://www.securian.com
Establishment information: Established in 1880.
Company type: Private company
Business activities: Operates life insurance and investment advisory services company.
Business type (SIC): Insurance/life; security and commodity services
Financial profile for 2011: Number of employees, 5,000; assets, $28,154,600,000; sales volume, $3,056,900,000
Corporate officers: Robert L. Senkler, Chair. and C.E.O.; Randy F. Wallake, Vice-Chair. and Pres.; Warren J. Zaccaro, Exec. V.P. and C.F.O.; Jean Delaney Nelson, Sr. V.P. and C.I.O.; Christopher R. Sebald, Sr. V.P. and C.I.O.; Dwayne C. Radel, Sr. V.P. and Genl. Counsel
Board of directors: Robert L. Senkler, Chair.; Randy F. Wallake, Vice-Chair.; Wilson G. Bradshaw; Mary K. Brainerd; John W. Castro; Sara H. Gavin; John G. Grundhofer; John H. Hooley; Ronald J. Peltier; Trudy A. Rautio; Paul L. Snyder
Subsidiaries: Allied Solutions, Indianapolis, IN; Cherokee National Life, Macon, GA; IA Systems, Albany, NY; Personal Finance Company, Olympia Fields, IL; Securian Casualty Company, Macon, GA; Securian Life Insurance Company, St. Paul, MN; Securian Trust Company, St. Paul, MN
Giving statement: Giving through the Securian Financial Group, Inc. Corporate Giving Program and the Securian Foundation.

Securian Financial Group, Inc. Corporate Giving Program

(formerly Minnesota Life Insurance Company Contributions Program)
c/o Securian Fdn.
400 N. Robert St.
St. Paul, MN 55101-2098
FAX: (651) 665-3551; URL: http://www.securian.com/Securian/About+Us/Securian+Financial+Group/Community+commitment

Contact: Lori J. Koutsky, Mgr., Community Rels.
Purpose and activities: As a complement to its foundation, Securian also makes charitable contributions to nonprofit organizations directly. Support is given primarily in the headquarters community.
Fields of interest: Arts; Higher education; Education; Employment; Human services Economically disadvantaged.
Type of support: Capital campaigns; Employee volunteer services; Employee-related scholarships; General/operating support; In-kind gifts; Loaned talent; Program development; Use of facilities.
Geographic limitations: Giving primarily in areas of company operations, with emphasis on St. Paul, MN.
Support limitations: No support for political, lobbying, fraternal, or veterans' organizations, religious organizations, athletic organizations, start-up organizations, government-supported organizations, international organizations, third party-supported healthcare organizations, or K-12 schools. No grants to individuals (except for

employee-related scholarships), or for fundraising, benefits, sponsorships, or advertising, endowments, trips or tours, conferences, seminars, workshops, or symposiums.
Publications: Application guidelines; Grants list.
Application information: Applications accepted. Proposals should be no longer than 7 pages. Proposals may be submitted using the Minnesota Common Grant Application Form (available on program website). The Community Relations Department handles giving. The company has a staff that only handles contributions. A contributions committee reviews all requests. Application form required. Applicants should submit the following:
1) timetable for implementation and evaluation of project
2) how project will be sustained once grantmaker support is completed
3) results expected from proposed grant
4) qualifications of key personnel
5) statement of problem project will address
6) population served
7) principal source of support for project in the past
8) copy of IRS Determination Letter
9) brief history of organization and description of its mission
10) geographic area to be served
11) copy of most recent annual report/audited financial statement/990
12) how project's results will be evaluated or measured
13) what distinguishes project from others in its field
14) listing of board of directors, trustees, officers and other key people and their affiliations
15) detailed description of project and amount of funding requested
16) plans for cooperation with other organizations, if any
17) copy of current year's organizational budget and/or project budget
18) listing of additional sources and amount of support

Initial approach: Proposal to headquarters
Copies of proposal: 1
Committee meeting date(s): Mar., June, Sept., and Dec.
Deadline(s): Feb. 1, June 1, and Oct. 1
Final notification: Apr., Aug., and Dec.

Number of staff: 1 part-time professional; 1 part-time support.

Securian Foundation

Minnesota Mutual Bldg.
400 Robert St. N
St. Paul, MN 55101-2098 (651) 665-3501
FAX: (651) 665-3551;
E-mail: lori.koutsky@securian.com; URL: http://www.securian.com/Securian/About+Us/Securian+Financial+Group/Community+commitment

Establishment information: Established in 1988 in MN.
Donors: Minnesota Life Insurance Co.; Securian Holding Co.
Contact: Lori J. Koutsky, Mgr.
Financial data (yr. ended 12/31/11): Assets, $37,464,846 (M); expenditures, $1,661,503; qualifying distributions, $1,535,685; giving activities include $1,535,685 for grants.
Purpose and activities: The foundation supports organizations involved with arts and culture, education, employment, youth development, human services, community economic development, and economically disadvantaged people.
Fields of interest: Arts; Higher education; Education; Health care; Employment, services; Employment, training; Employment; Youth development; Human services; Economic development; Business/industry; Community/economic development; United Ways and Federated Giving Programs; Mathematics; Economics Economically disadvantaged.
Programs:

Arts: The foundation supports organizations involved with arts and culture. Special emphasis is directed toward programs designed to provide services to a broad audience and stimulate the cultural vitality of the community.

Economic Independence: The foundation supports programs designed to encourage, develop, and sustain economic independence, including job skill training, job placement services, work readiness, and career development programs for unemployed or underemployed and disadvantaged individuals.

Education: The foundation supports organizations involved with higher education. Special emphasis is directed toward programs designed to promote math, economics, and business and youth development.

Human Services and Special Community Needs: The foundation supports the United Way and organizations involved with health, human services, and community development.

Matching Gifts: The foundation matches contributions made by associates, retirees, and directors of Securian to educational institutions, arts and cultural organizations, and hospitals on a one-for-one basis from $35 to $2,000 per contributor, per year.

Volunteer Plus: The foundation awards $100 grants to nonprofit organizations with which employees and retirees of Securian volunteer at least 50 hours per year.

Type of support: Annual campaigns; Capital campaigns; Employee matching gifts; Employee volunteer services; General/operating support; Program development; Technical assistance.
Geographic limitations: Giving primarily in areas of company operations, with emphasis on MN; giving also to national organizations.
Support limitations: No support for political, lobbying, fraternal, or international organizations, athletic, recreation, or sports-related organizations, religious organizations not of direct benefit to the entire community, or public or private K-12 schools. No grants to individuals, or for scholarships, start-up funds for new organizations, endowments, benefits, sponsorships, fundraising events, advertising, conferences, seminars, workshops, symposiums, trips, or tours.
Publications: Application guidelines; Grants list; Informational brochure; IRS Form 990 or 990-PF printed copy available upon request; Program policy statement.
Application information: Applications accepted. Proposals should be no longer than 7 pages. Proposals may be submitted using the Minnesota Common Grant Application Form. Application form required. Applicants should submit the following:
1) results expected from proposed grant
2) statement of problem project will address
3) population served
4) principal source of support for project in the past
5) copy of IRS Determination Letter
6) brief history of organization and description of its mission
7) geographic area to be served
8) copy of most recent annual report/audited financial statement/990
9) how project's results will be evaluated or measured
10) explanation of why grantmaker is considered an appropriate donor for project
11) what distinguishes project from others in its field
12) listing of board of directors, trustees, officers and other key people and their affiliations
13) detailed description of project and amount of funding requested
14) copy of current year's organizational budget and/or project budget
15) listing of additional sources and amount of support

Proposals should include a description of results from the prior year.

Initial approach: Proposal
Copies of proposal: 1
Deadline(s): Feb. 1, June 1, and Oct. 1
Final notification: Apr., Aug., and Dec.

Officers and Directors:* Robert L. Senkler*, Pres.; Kathleen Pinkett*, V.P.; Dwayne C. Radel*, Secy.; David LePlavy, Treas.
Number of staff: 1 part-time professional; 1 part-time support.
EIN: 363608619
Selected grants: The following grants are a representative sample of this grantmaker's funding activity:
$10,000 to Boys and Girls Clubs of the Twin Cities, Minneapolis, MN, 2010. For annual support.
$7,000 to College Possible, Saint Paul, MN, 2010.
$6,000 to Twin Cities RISE, Minneapolis, MN, 2010.
$5,000 to Minnesota Childrens Museum, Saint Paul, MN, 2010. For annual support.
$5,000 to Minnesota Minority Education Partnership, Saint Paul, MN, 2010.

3390
Securitas Security Services USA, Inc.

(formerly Pinkertons Inc.)
15910 Ventura Blvd.
Encino, CA 91436 (818) 380-1010

Company URL: http://www.securitasinc.com
Establishment information: Established in 1850.
Company type: Subsidiary of a foreign company
Business activities: Provides security solutions.
Business type (SIC): Business services/miscellaneous
Corporate officers: Don W. Walker, Chair.; Santiago Galaz, Pres.; Len Ford, V.P., Sales and Mktg.
Board of director: Don W. Walker, Chair.
Giving statement: Giving through the Securitas Security Services USA, Inc. Corporate Giving Program and the Pinkerton Foundation 2000, Inc.

Pinkerton Foundation 2000, Inc.

(formerly Burns International Foundation, Inc.)
4330 Park Terrace Dr.
Westlake Village, CA 91361-4630

Establishment information: Incorporated in 1953 in IL.
Donors: Borg-Warner Corp.; Borg-Warner Security Corp.; Burns International Services Corp.
Financial data (yr. ended 12/31/11): Assets, $175,267 (M); expenditures, $39,160; qualifying distributions, $35,015; giving activities include $35,000 for 2 grants (high: $25,000; low: $10,000).
Purpose and activities: The foundation supports organizations involved with crime and law enforcement.
Fields of interest: Crime/violence prevention; Crime/law enforcement.
Type of support: General/operating support.

Geographic limitations: Giving limited to Houston, TX and Salt Lake City, UT.
Support limitations: No support for sectarian organizations not of direct benefit to the entire community or foreign-based organizations. No grants to individuals, or for testimonial dinners, fundraising events, advertising, or medical or academic research.
Application information: Applications not accepted. Contributes only to pre-selected organizations.
Officers and Directors:* Don W. Walker, Chair.; Bill Barthelemy*, Pres.; Thomas C. Cantlon*, V.P. and Treas.; Rocco Defelice*, V.P.; Steven A. Lindsey*, V.P.; Stephen L. Moskal, Secy.
Number of staff: 1 full-time professional; 1 full-time support.
EIN: 366051857

3391
Security Benefit Life Insurance Company

1 S.W. Security Benefit Pl.
6th Ave.
Topeka, KS 66636-3704 (785) 438-3000

Company URL: http://www.securitybenefit.com
Establishment information: Established in 1892.
Company type: Subsidiary of a private company
Business activities: Sells life insurance; provides investment advisory services.
Business type (SIC): Insurance/life; security and commodity services
Financial profile for 2012: Number of employees, 600; assets, $15,392,594,076; sales volume, $2,902,815,660; pre-tax net income, $240,088,346; expenses, $2,662,727,225; liabilities, $14,618,627,337
Corporate officers: Michael Kiley, Chair., Pres., and C.E.O.; John Forest Frye, Sr. V.P., C.F.O., and Treas.; John Forrest Guyot, Sr. V.P., Genl. Counsel, and Secy.
Board of directors: Michael Kiley, Chair.; John Forest Frye; John Forrest Guyot
Giving statement: Giving through the Security Benefit Life Insurance Company Contributions Program and the Security Benefit Life Insurance Company Charitable Trust.

Security Benefit Life Insurance Company Charitable Trust

1 Security Benefit Pl.
Topeka, KS 66636-1000

Establishment information: Established in 1976 in KS.
Donor: Security Benefit Life Insurance Co.
Contact: Michael Kiley, Tr.
Financial data (yr. ended 12/31/12): Assets, $56,102 (M); gifts received, $670,000; expenditures, $633,569; qualifying distributions, $633,569; giving activities include $550,269 for 159 grants and $83,300 for 125 employee matching gifts.
Purpose and activities: The foundation supports organizations involved with arts and culture, higher education, cancer, HIV/AIDS research, hunger, human services, women, economically disadvantaged people, and homeless people.
Fields of interest: Performing arts; Arts; Higher education; Cancer; AIDS research; Food services; Children/youth, services; Human services; Voluntarism promotion Youth; Young adults; Physically disabled; Women; Economically disadvantaged; Homeless.
Type of support: Annual campaigns; Capital campaigns; Continuing support; Employee matching gifts; Equipment; Program-related investments/loans.
Geographic limitations: Giving limited to the Topeka, KS, area.
Application information: Applications accepted. Application form not required.
Initial approach: Proposal
Copies of proposal: 1
Deadline(s): None
Trustee: Michael Kiley.
Number of staff: None.
EIN: 486211612
Selected grants: The following grants are a representative sample of this grantmaker's funding activity:
$170,082 to United Way of Greater Topeka, Topeka, KS, 2012.
$50,000 to NEA Foundation for the Improvement of Education, Washington, DC, 2012. For Kansas State Department of Education for improving teaching and learning in public schools, colleges and universities nationwide.
$35,000 to Friends of the Topeka Zoo, Topeka, KS, 2012.
$23,420 to Topeka Performing Arts Center, Topeka, KS, 2012.
$7,820 to Washburn University, Topeka, KS, 2012.

3392
Security Finance Corporation

P.O. Box 811
Spartanburg, SC 29304 (864) 582-8193
FAX: (864) 582-2532

Company URL: http://www.security-finance.com
Establishment information: Established in 1955.
Company type: Subsidiary of a private company
Business activities: Provides consumer loans.
Business type (SIC): Credit institutions/personal
Corporate officers: A. Ray Biggs, Pres. and C.O.O.; A. Greg Williams, C.F.O. and Treas.; Marshall T. Walsh, Secy.
Giving statement: Giving through the Security's Lending Hand Foundation.

Security's Lending Hand Foundation

181 Security Pl.
Spartanburg, SC 29307-5450
URL: http://www.security-finance.com/company_phil.php

Establishment information: Established in 1994 in SC.
Donor: Security Finance Corp.
Financial data (yr. ended 12/31/11): Assets, $158 (M); gifts received, $332,800; expenditures, $337,800; qualifying distributions, $332,800; giving activities include $332,800 for grants.
Purpose and activities: The foundation supports children's hospitals.
Fields of interest: Hospitals (general); Hospitals (specialty); Children, services.
Type of support: General/operating support.
Geographic limitations: Giving primarily in FL, GA, LA, MO, NC, OK, SC, TN, and TX.
Support limitations: No grants to individuals.
Application information: Applications not accepted. Contributes only to pre-selected organizations.
Officers: Susan A. Bridges, Chair.; A. Ray Biggs, Pres.; A. Greg Williams, Secy.-Treas.
EIN: 571012986
Selected grants: The following grants are a representative sample of this grantmaker's funding activity:
$50,000 to Meyer Center for Special Children, Greenville, SC, 2010.
$13,000 to Childrens Hospital of New Mexico, Albuquerque, NM, 2010.
$11,500 to Childrens Hospital Foundation at Saint Francis, Tulsa, OK, 2010.
$5,300 to CHRISTUS Santa Rosa Childrens Hospital, San Antonio, TX, 2010.
$5,300 to Driscoll Childrens Hospital, Corpus Christi, TX, 2010.
$5,000 to American Red Cross, Spartanburg, SC, 2010.
$5,000 to Childrens Medical Center of Dallas, Dallas, TX, 2010.
$5,000 to Primary Childrens Medical Center, Salt Lake City, UT, 2010.
$3,500 to Memorial Health University Medical Center Foundation, Savannah, GA, 2010.
$2,800 to Children Shelter of the Upstate, Spartanburg, SC, 2010.

3393
Security National Bank

601 Pierce St.
P.O. Box 147
Sioux City, IA 51102-6500 (712) 277-6500

Company URL: http://www.snbonline.com
Establishment information: Established in 1884.
Company type: Private company
Business activities: Operates commercial bank.
Business type (SIC): Banks/commercial
Corporate officers: Richard A. Waller, Chair. and C.E.O.; D. Douglas Rice, Pres.
Board of director: Richard A. Waller, Chair.
Office: Dakota Dunes, SD
Giving statement: Giving through the Security National Bank Charitable Foundation.

Security National Bank Charitable Foundation

(formerly SNB Charitable Foundation Trust)
P.O. Box 147
Sioux City, IA 51102-0147

Establishment information: Established in 1995 in IA.
Donor: Security National Bank.
Financial data (yr. ended 12/31/11): Assets, $1,002,784 (M); expenditures, $47,063; qualifying distributions, $45,000; giving activities include $45,000 for grants.
Purpose and activities: The foundation supports organizations involved with arts and culture, education, health, youth development, and community development.
Fields of interest: Education; Youth development; Human services.
Type of support: General/operating support.
Geographic limitations: Giving primarily in Sioux City, IA.
Support limitations: No grants to individuals.
Application information: Applications not accepted. Unsolicited requests for funds not accepted.
Directors: Steve Corrie; D. Douglas Rice; Richard Waller.
EIN: 364063036

3394
Security State Bank
701 E. Howard St.
P.O. Box 279
Hibbing, MN 55746-0279 (218) 263-8855

Company URL: http://www.ssbhibbing.com
Establishment information: Established in 1911.
Company type: Private company
Business activities: Operates commercial bank.
Business type (SIC): Banks/commercial
Corporate officers: Mark Gardeski, Pres. and C.E.O.; Mark Macor, C.F.O.
Board of directors: Michel R. Enich; Gerald R. Erickson; Patrick Gates; Thomas D. Jamar; Edward L. Pajunen; Susan M. Rudberg; John R. Ryan, Jr.
Giving statement: Giving through the Independence Bancshares Charitable Foundation, Inc. and the Security State Bank Foundation.

Independence Bancshares Charitable Foundation, Inc.
231 1st St. E.
Independence, IA 50644-2808

Establishment information: Established in 2003 in IA.
Donors: Security State Bank; Northeast Security Bank.
Financial data (yr. ended 12/31/11): Assets, $11,861 (M); gifts received, $63,500; expenditures, $60,000; qualifying distributions, $59,500; giving activities include $59,500 for grants.
Purpose and activities: The foundation supports museums and organizations involved with education, agriculture, and economic development.
Fields of interest: Education; Environment; Community/economic development.
Type of support: General/operating support.
Geographic limitations: Giving limited to Decorah, Independence, and Sumner, IA.
Support limitations: No grants to individuals.
Application information: Applications not accepted. Unsolicited requests for funds not accepted.
Officers and Directors:* Gary F. Short*, Pres.; James L. Blin*, V.P.; Brian K. Meyer*, Secy.; Benjamin G. Pagel*, Treas.; Willis M. Bywater.
EIN: 201051475

Security State Bank Foundation
701 E. Howard St.
Hibbing, MN 55746-1717

Establishment information: Established in 1996 in MN.
Donors: Security State Bank; Security State Bank of Hibbing.
Financial data (yr. ended 12/31/11): Assets, $299,158 (M); expenditures, $15,809; qualifying distributions, $14,467; giving activities include $14,467 for grants.
Purpose and activities: The foundation supports organizations involved with education, health, domestic violence prevention, mentoring, and human services.
Fields of interest: Health care; Human services; Civil/human rights.
Type of support: General/operating support; Program development; Scholarship funds; Scholarships—to individuals.
Geographic limitations: Giving primarily in Hibbing, MN.
Application information: Applications not accepted. Unsolicited requests for funds not accepted.
Directors: Patrick Gates; Greg Hoag; Don Northagen; Jerry Wallis.
Officers: Greg Hoag, Pres.; Debby Lundquist, Secy.; Mary Jivery, Treas.
EIN: 411830282

3395
Sedgwick LLP
135 Main St., 14th Fl.
San Francisco, CA 94105-1812
(415) 627-1517

Company URL: http://www.sdma.com
Establishment information: Established in 1933.
Company type: Private company
Business activities: Operates law firm.
Business type (SIC): Legal services
Offices: Irvine, Los Angeles, San Francisco, CA; Washington, DC; Ft. Lauderdale, FL; Chicago, IL; Newark, NJ; New York, NY; Austin, Dallas, Houston, TX; Seattle, WA
International operations: Bermuda; France; United Kingdom
Giving statement: Giving through the Sedgwick LLP Pro Bono Program.

Sedgwick LLP Pro Bono Program
135 Main St., 14th Fl.
San Francisco, CA 94105-1812 (213) 426-6900
E-mail: wendy.tucker@sedgwicklaw.com; URL: http://www.sdma.com/firm/culture/probono/

Contact: Wendy Tucker, Partner
Fields of interest: Legal services.
Type of support: Pro bono services - legal.
Application information: A Pro Bono Committee manages the pro bono program.

3396
SEEDS Green Printing and Design, Inc.
P.O. Box 90008
Pittsburgh, PA 15224-0408 (412) 243-9060
FAX: (412) 243-9101

Company URL: http://www.seedsgreenprinting.com/
Establishment information: Established in 1997.
Company type: Private company
Business type (SIC): Business services/miscellaneous
Corporate officers: Jeffrey A. Shaw, Owner; Gayle Giliotti, C.F.O.
Board of director: Jeffrey A. Shaw, Owner
Giving statement: Giving through the SEEDS Green Printing and Design Inc. Contributions Program.

SEEDS Green Printing and Design Inc. Contributions Program
P.O. BOX 90008
Pittsburgh, PA 15224-0408 (412) 243-9060
E-mail: info@seedsgreenprinting.com; URL: http://www.seedsgreenprinting.com/

Purpose and activities: SEEDS Green Printing and Design is a certified B Corporation that donates a percentage of net profits to charitable organizations.

3397
Seldovia Native Association, Inc.
(also known as SNA)
700 E. Diamond Blvd.
P.O. Box L
Anchorage, AK 99515 (907) 868-8006

Company URL: http://www.snai.com
Establishment information: Established in 2001.
Company type: Native corporation
Business activities: Operates native corporation.
Business type (SIC): Government establishments/miscellaneous
Corporate officers: Don Kashevaroff, Jr., Chair.; Leo Barlow, C.E.O.; Fred H. Elvsaas, Pres.; Heather Anderson, C.F.O.; Crystal Collier, Corp. Secy.
Board of directors: Don Kashevaroff, Chair.; Crystal Collier; John L. Crawford; Fred H. Elvsaas; Fred S. Elvsaas, Jr.; Renee Haller; Kimberly Kashevarof; Louis Nagy, Jr.; Harold Yuth
Giving statement: Giving through the SNA Foundation.

SNA Foundation
P.O. Drawer L
Seldovia, AK 99663-0250 (907) 234-7625
FAX: (907) 234-7637; Additional tel.: (800) 478-7898; URL: http://www.snai.com/shareholders/sna-foundation.html

Establishment information: Established in 1996 in AK.
Donor: Seldovia Native Association, Inc.
Financial data (yr. ended 12/31/11): Assets, $0 (M); expenditures, $10,086; qualifying distributions, $9,100; giving activities include $9,100 for grants to individuals.
Purpose and activities: The foundation awards college scholarships to Alaska Native shareholders and lineal descendants and spouses of shareholders of Seldovia Native Association, Inc.
Fields of interest: Native Americans/American Indians.
Type of support: Scholarships—to individuals.
Geographic limitations: Giving limited to AK.
Publications: Application guidelines.
Application information: Applications accepted. Application form required.
Requests should include transcripts, two letters of recommendation, a copy of college acceptance letter, and a photograph.
Initial approach: Download application and mail to foundation
Deadline(s): July 1
Final notification: 20 business days
Officers: Louis Nagy, Jr., Chair.; Alexis Colberg-Nelissen, Pres.; Fred H. Elvsaas, V.P.; Crystal Collier, Secy.
Board Members: Chancelen Collier; Kim Collier; Fred H. Elvsaas, Jr.; Renee Haller; Michele Meehan.
EIN: 920157596

3398
Select Equity Group, Inc.
380 Lafayette St., Fl. 6
New York, NY 10003-6953 (212) 475-8335
FAX: (212) 475-1786

Company URL: http://www.selectequity.com
Establishment information: Established in 1990.
Company type: Private company

Business activities: Provides investment advisory services.
Business type (SIC): Security and commodity services
Corporate officers: George Stabler Loening, Chair.; Robert Joseph Caruso, Pres.; Evan Charles Guillemin, C.O.O. and C.F.O.; Mark B. Jazmin, V.P., Sales
Board of director: George Stabler Loening, Chair.
Giving statement: Giving through the Select Equity Group Foundation.

Select Equity Group Foundation

380 Lafayette St., Ste. 6
New York, NY 10003-6933
E-mail: rwilson@selectequity.com; URL: https://www.selectequity.com/foundation.aspx

Establishment information: Established in 2000 in NY.
Donor: Select Equity Group, Inc.
Contact: Robert Wilson, Exec. Dir.
Financial data (yr. ended 12/31/10): Assets, $5,186,908 (M); gifts received, $2,000,000; expenditures, $1,773,498; qualifying distributions, $1,771,122; giving activities include $1,390,797 for 250 grants (high: $75,000; low: $30).
Purpose and activities: The foundation supports organizations involved with arts and culture, education, the environment, health, cancer, kidney disease, human services, youth development, international economic development, and civil and human rights.
Fields of interest: Arts; Secondary school/education; Education; Environment, water resources; Environment; Health care; Cancer; Kidney diseases; Youth development; Children, services; Human services; International economic development; Civil/human rights.
Program:
Matching Gift Program: The foundation matches contributions made by employees of Select Equity Group to educational institutions and nonprofit organizations involved with culture and the environment up to $25,000, per employee, per calendar year.
Type of support: Employee matching gifts; General/operating support; Program development; Scholarship funds.
Geographic limitations: Giving primarily in AL, CA, MA, IL, NJ, TX, and VA, with emphasis on NY.
Support limitations: No grants to individuals.
Application information: Applications not accepted. Contributes only to pre-selected organizations. Preference is given to organizations endorsed by Select Equity employees.
Board meeting date(s): Four times a year
Trustees: Christopher Arndt; John Britton; George S. Loening; Darren Seirer; Amor Towles.
EIN: 134148796
Selected grants: The following grants are a representative sample of this grantmaker's funding activity:
$75,000 to Charity: Water, New York, NY, 2009.
$75,000 to Posse Foundation, New York, NY, 2009.
$52,500 to Damon Runyon Cancer Research Foundation, New York, NY, 2009.
$25,000 to Publicolor, New York, NY, 2009. For scholarships.
$24,150 to Saint Jude Childrens Research Hospital, New York, NY, 2009.
$21,625 to Multiple Sclerosis Society, National, New York, NY, 2009.
$20,250 to Childrens Aid Society, New York, NY, 2009.
$16,500 to Student Sponsor Partners, New York, NY, 2009.
$14,850 to Harlem RBI, New York, NY, 2009.
$12,300 to Youth Orchestra of the Americas, Arlington, VA, 2009.

3399
Selective Insurance Group, Inc.

(formerly Selected Risks Insurance Company)
40 Wantage Ave.
Branchville, NJ 07890 (973) 948-3000
FAX: (973) 948-0282

Company URL: http://www.selective.com
Establishment information: Established in 1926.
Company type: Public company
Company ticker symbol and exchange: SIGI/NASDAQ
Business activities: Provides property and casualty insurance products and diversified insurance services.
Business type (SIC): Insurance/fire, marine, and casualty
Financial profile for 2012: Number of employees, 2,100; assets, $6,794,220,000; sales volume, $1,734,100,000; pre-tax net income, $37,630,000; expenses, $1,696,470,000; liabilities, $5,703,620,000
Corporate officers: Gregory E. Murphy, Chair., Pres., and C.E.O.; Dale A. Thatcher, Exec. V.P. and C.F.O.; Gordon J. Gaudet, Exec. V.P. and C.I.O.; Michael H. Lanza, Exec. V.P. and Genl. Counsel
Board of directors: Gregory E. Murphy, Chair.; Paul D. Bauer; Annabelle Bexiga; A. David Brown; John C. Burville, Ph.D.; Joan M. Lamm-Tennant, Ph.D.; Michael J. Morrissey; Cynthia S. Nicholson; Ronald L. O'Kelley; William M. Rue; J. Brian Thebault
Giving statement: Giving through the Selective Group Foundation.
Company EIN: 222168890

The Selective Group Foundation

40 Wantage Ave.
Branchville, NJ 07826-5640
FAX: (973) 948-0282;
E-mail: foundation@selective.com; URL: http://www.selective.com

Establishment information: Established in 2005 in NJ.
Donor: Selective Insurance Group, Inc.
Financial data (yr. ended 12/31/11): Assets, $91,201 (M); gifts received, $400,000; expenditures, $386,539; qualifying distributions, $383,665; giving activities include $383,665 for grants.
Purpose and activities: The foundation supports programs designed to provide health and human services; promote civic responsibility; and support home, auto, and business safety.
Fields of interest: Education; Hospitals (general); Health care; Housing/shelter; Disasters, fire prevention/control; Safety, automotive safety; Safety/disasters; YM/YWCAs & YM/YWHAs; Children/youth, services; Family services; Human services; Business/industry; United Ways and Federated Giving Programs; Public affairs Economically disadvantaged.
Program:
President's Club Matching Grant Program: The foundation matches contributions made by employees of Selective to eligible charities in their communities.
Type of support: Building/renovation; Capital campaigns; Employee matching gifts; Employee volunteer services; Equipment; General/operating support; Program development; Scholarship funds.
Geographic limitations: Giving primarily in areas of company operations, with emphasis on NJ.
Support limitations: No support for religious organizations, international organizations, state or federal agencies, discriminatory organizations, political organizations, or animal organizations. No grants to individuals, or for arts or entertainment, advertising, or sponsorships.
Application information: Applications not accepted. Contributes only to pre-selected organizations.
Officers and Directors:* Gail L. Peterson, Pres.; Michael H. Lanza*, Secy.; Dale A. Thatcher*, Treas.; Richard F. Connell.
EIN: 203539039
Selected grants: The following grants are a representative sample of this grantmaker's funding activity:
$2,000 to Ducks Unlimited, Memphis, TN, 2010.
$1,500 to Nature Conservancy, Arlington, VA, 2010.
$1,350 to Susan G. Komen for the Cure, Dallas, TX, 2010.
$1,000 to American Cancer Society, Atlanta, GA, 2010.
$1,000 to Habitat for Humanity International, Americus, GA, 2010.
$1,000 to Special Olympics New Jersey, Lawrenceville, NJ, 2010.

3400
Self Reliance (N.Y.) Federal Credit Union Inc.

108 2nd Ave.
New York, NY 10003-8302 (212) 473-7310

Company URL: http://www.selfrelianceny.org
Establishment information: Established in 1951.
Company type: Federal credit union
Business activities: Operates a not-for-profit, member-owned credit union.
Business type (SIC): Credit unions
Corporate officers: John Flis, Chair.; Jaroslaw Oberyshyn, C.E.O.
Board of director: John Flis, Chair.
Giving statement: Giving through the New York Self Reliance Foundation Ltd.

New York Self Reliance Foundation Ltd.

108 2nd Ave.
New York, NY 10003-8302

Establishment information: Established in 2004 in NY.
Donor: Self Reliance NY FCU.
Financial data (yr. ended 12/31/11): Assets, $3,263,455 (M); gifts received, $325,000; expenditures, $116,250; qualifying distributions, $116,000; giving activities include $116,000 for 12 grants (high: $20,000; low: $1,000).
Fields of interest: Education; Catholic agencies & churches.
Geographic limitations: Giving primarily in CT and NY.
Support limitations: No grants to individuals.
Application information: Applications not accepted. Unsolicited requests for funds not accepted.
Officers: Lubomyr Zielyk, Chair.; Bohdan Kurczak, Secy.
Board Members: Orest Glut; Adam Hapij.
EIN: 202077827

3401
Selig Enterprises, Inc.
1100 Spring St. N.W., Ste. 550
Atlanta, GA 30309-2857 (404) 876-5511

Company URL: http://www.seligenterprises.com
Establishment information: Established in 1918.
Company type: Private company
Business activities: Operates real estate company.
Business type (SIC): Real estate operators and lessors
Corporate officers: Stephen Selig, Chair. and Pres.; Ronald J. Stein, C.P.A., C.F.O.; William J. Dawkins, Sr. V.P., Genl. Counsel, and Secy.
Board of director: Steve Selig, Chair.
Giving statement: Giving through the Gregory and Erica Lewis Family Foundation, Inc., the Stephen Scott Selig Family Foundation, Inc., the Shoulberg Family Foundation Inc., and the SLS Family Foundation.

The Gregory and Erica Lewis Family Foundation, Inc.
1100 Spring St. N.W., Ste. 550
Atlanta, GA 30309-2857 (404) 876-5511

Establishment information: Established in 2005 in GA.
Donor: Selig Enterprises, Inc.
Contact: Gregory Lewis, Mgr.
Financial data (yr. ended 12/31/11): Assets, $1,283 (M); gifts received, $18,000; expenditures, $19,248; qualifying distributions, $18,958; giving activities include $18,958 for grants.
Fields of interest: Education; Human services; Religion.
Geographic limitations: Giving primarily in GA, with emphasis on Atlanta.
Application information: Applications accepted. Application form required.
Initial approach: Letter
Deadline(s): None
Officers: Erica Lewis; Gregory Lewis.
EIN: 202584824

The Stephen Scott Selig Family Foundation, Inc.
1100 Spring St. N.W.
Atlanta, GA 30309-2857 (404) 876-5511

Establishment information: Established in 2005 in GA.
Donor: Selig Enterprises, Inc.
Contact: Stephen Scott Selig, Mgr.
Financial data (yr. ended 12/31/11): Assets, $3,092 (M); gifts received, $18,000; expenditures, $24,624; qualifying distributions, $24,600; giving activities include $24,600 for grants.
Purpose and activities: The foundation supports camps and organizations involved with arts and culture, education, birth defects, cancer, children, and Judaism.
Fields of interest: Arts; Education; Health organizations.
Type of support: General/operating support.
Geographic limitations: Giving primarily in Atlanta, GA.
Application information: Applications accepted. Application form required. Applicants should submit the following:
1) detailed description of project and amount of funding requested
Initial approach: Proposal
Deadline(s): None
Officer: Stephen Scott Selig, Mgr.
EIN: 202424943

The Shoulberg Family Foundation Inc.
1100 Spring St. N.W., Ste. 550
Atlanta, GA 30309-2857 (404) 876-5511

Establishment information: Established in 2005 in GA.
Donor: Selig Enterprises Inc.
Contact: Melinda Shoulberg, Fdn. Mgr.
Financial data (yr. ended 12/31/11): Assets, $1,623 (M); gifts received, $18,000; expenditures, $16,813; qualifying distributions, $16,767; giving activities include $16,767 for grants.
Purpose and activities: The foundation supports camps and organizations involved with education and Judaism.
Fields of interest: Secondary school/education; Higher education; Education; Recreation, camps; Recreation; Family services; Human services; Jewish federated giving programs; Jewish agencies & synagogues.
Type of support: General/operating support; Program development.
Geographic limitations: Giving primarily in Atlanta, GA.
Support limitations: No grants to individuals.
Application information: Applications accepted. Application form not required. Applicants should submit the following:
1) detailed description of project and amount of funding requested
Initial approach: Proposal
Deadline(s): None
EIN: 202424773

The SLS Family Foundation
1100 Spring St. N.W., No. 550
Atlanta, GA 30309-2857 (404) 876-5511

Establishment information: Established in 2005 in GA.
Donor: Selig Enterprises, Inc.
Contact: Bryan R Lewis, Mgr.
Financial data (yr. ended 12/31/11): Assets, $24,441 (M); expenditures, $25,030; qualifying distributions, $25,000; giving activities include $25,000 for grants.
Fields of interest: Education.
Type of support: General/operating support.
Geographic limitations: Giving primarily in Atlanta, GA.
Support limitations: No grants to individuals.
Application information: Applications accepted. Application form required. Applicants should submit the following:
1) detailed description of project and amount of funding requested
2) results expected from proposed grant
Initial approach: Letter
Deadline(s): None
Officer: Brian Lewis, Mgr.
EIN: 202424890

3402
Charles Seligman Distributing Co., Inc.
10885 Clydesdale Ct.
Walton, KY 41094-8386 (859) 344-1881

Establishment information: Established in 1933.
Company type: Private company
Business activities: Sells beer wholesale.
Business type (SIC): Beer, wine, and distilled beverages—wholesale
Corporate officers: Ruth M. Seligman-Doering, Pres. and C.E.O.; Jennifer Doering, C.O.O.; Kristin Tracy, V.P., Inf. Systems; Rick Ludeke, Cont.
Board of director: Ruth M. Seligman-Doering
Giving statement: Giving through the Chas. and Ruth Seligman Family Foundation, Inc.

Chas. and Ruth Seligman Family Foundation, Inc.
10885 Clydesdale Ct.
Walton, KY 41094-8386 (859) 344-1881

Establishment information: Established in 2001 in KY.
Donor: Charles Seligman Distributing Co., Inc.
Contact: Ruth Doering, Tr.
Financial data (yr. ended 09/30/11): Assets, $789,960 (M); expenditures, $96,064; qualifying distributions, $95,875; giving activities include $95,875 for 15 grants (high: $15,000; low: $500).
Purpose and activities: The foundation supports organizations involved with secondary education, mental health, child welfare, and human services.
Fields of interest: Arts; Education; Health care.
Type of support: General/operating support.
Geographic limitations: Giving primarily in KY and Cincinnati, OH.
Application information: Applications accepted. Application form required.
Initial approach: Letter
Copies of proposal: 5
Deadline(s): None
Trustees: Jennifer Doering; Ruth Doering; Chad Seligman; Stacy Staat; Kristin Tracy.
EIN: 611401360

3403
Semiconductor Research Corporation
1101 Slater Rd., Ste. 120
P.O. Box 12053
Durham, NC 27703 (919) 941-9400

Company URL: http://www.src.org
Establishment information: Established in 1982.
Company type: Business league
Business activities: Operates membership organization.
Business type (SIC): Membership organization/miscellaneous
Corporate officers: Larry W. Sumney, Pres. and C.E.O.; Steven J. Hillenius, Exec. V.P. and C.O.O.
Board of director: Steven J. Hillenius
Giving statement: Giving through the S.R.C. Education Alliance.

S.R.C. Education Alliance
P.O. Box 12053
Research Triangle Park, NC 27709-2053 (919) 941-9400
E-mail: EducationAlliance@src.org; Application e-mail for fellowships and scholarships: apply@src.org; URL: http://www.src.org/program/srcea/

Donors: Microelectonics Advanced Research Corp.; Semiconductor Research Corp.; Intel Foundation; IBM; Semiconductor Industry Association.
Financial data (yr. ended 12/31/11): Assets, $550,871 (M); gifts received, $1,314,888; expenditures, $2,089,621; qualifying distributions,

$2,088,025; giving activities include $571,767 for 17 grants (high: $67,000; low: $1,000) and $861,868 for 22 grants to individuals (high: $95,351; low: $2,550).
Purpose and activities: The foundation supports programs designed to promote science and engineering education and the semiconductor industry through university research grants, scholarships, and fellowships.
Fields of interest: Higher education; Engineering school/education; Engineering; Science Minorities; African Americans/Blacks; Hispanics/Latinos; Native Americans/American Indians; Women.
Programs:
Company-Named Fellowships: The foundation awards company-named fellowships to student applicants from the Graduate Fellowship Program whose proposed research matches a cosponsoring company's research interests. The fellowships are named after the companies who provide matching funding for the program. Fellowship recipients are mentored by an industry advisor and is awarded an internship from the cosponsoring company. Fellowships include the AMD/Mahboob Khan/GRC Fellowship, the Robert M. Burger Fellowship, the Peter Verhofstadt Fellowship, and the International Fellowship.
Company-Named Scholarships: The foundation awards company-named scholarships to student applicants whose proposed research matches a cosponsoring company's research interests. The scholarships are named after the companies who provide matching funding for the program. Scholarship recipients are mentored by an industry advisor and is awarded an internship from the cosponsoring company.
GRC Graduate Fellowship Program: The foundation awards graduate fellowships to encourage academically gifted students to pursue graduate degrees in research areas related to SRC, with emphasis on microelectronics; and to develop a pool of high quality doctoral graduates for member companies and universities. Fellowships provide full tuition, a stipend for up to five years of doctoral study, and a $2,000 annual gift for the student's faculty advisor in support of the student.
GRC Master's Scholarship Program: The foundation awards scholarships to encourage academically gifted minority students, including women, African-American, Hispanic, and Native American students, to pursue graduate research related to Global Research Collaboration (GRC), with emphasis on microelectronics; and to develop a pool of high quality minority candidates for doctoral study and hire by GRC companies. The scholarship provides full tuition for up to two years of master's level study and a $2,000 unrestricted gift for use by the student's faculty advisor.
SRC NRI/Hans J. Coufal Fellowship: The foundation awards a fellowship to a graduate student for doctoral study in nanoelectronics-related disciplines, with preference given to nanoelectronic device, technologies, physics, and materials. The fellowship is designed to encourage high-risk research leading to solutions for challenges faced by the semiconductor industry. The fellowship provides full tuition for up to five years of study and a $2,000 annual unrestricted gift for recipient's faculty advisor. The program is administered by the Nanoelectronics Research Initiative.
SRC Undergraduate Research Opportunities (URO): The foundation, in partnership with the Intel Foundation, provides undergraduates with research experience and mentoring. The program is designed to increase academic retention among undergraduates interested in physical sciences and engineering disciplines and includes workshops and resources to assist students with the graduate school application process. The program is currently hosted at participating universities.
Type of support: Fellowships; Research; Scholarships—to individuals.
Geographic limitations: Giving on a national basis, with emphasis on AZ, CA, NC, NY, and OH.
Publications: Application guidelines.
Application information: Applications accepted. Application form required.
Applications should include official transcripts, 3 reference report forms from scientists, engineers, or faculty members, and Graduate Record Examination (GRE) test results.
Initial approach: Download application form or e-mail foundation for application form for fellowships and scholarships
Deadline(s): Mid-Feb for fellowships and scholarships
Final notification: Apr. for fellowships and scholarships
Officers and Directors:* Larry W. Sumney*, C.E.O. and Pres.; Celia I. Merzbacher, V.P., Innovative Partnerships; MaryLisabeth Rich, Exec. Dir.; Steven J. Hillenius; Elizabeth J. Weitzman.
EIN: 581807204
Selected grants: The following grants are a representative sample of this grantmaker's funding activity:
$67,000 to Cornell University, College of Engineering, Ithaca, NY, 2010.
$64,070 to Carnegie Mellon University, Pittsburgh, PA, 2010.
$64,070 to Carnegie Mellon University, Pittsburgh, PA, 2010.
$62,663 to Stanford University, Stanford, CA, 2010.
$60,974 to Purdue University, West Lafayette, IN, 2010.
$59,000 to University of Michigan, Ann Arbor, MI, 2010.
$58,936 to Cornell University, Ithaca, NY, 2010.
$56,585 to University of Arizona, Tucson, AZ, 2010.
$49,500 to University of Washington, College of Engineering, Seattle, WA, 2010.
$39,922 to University of California, Berkeley, CA, 2010.

3404
Seminole Electric Cooperative, Inc.

16313 N. Dale Mabry Hwy.
P.O. Box 272000
Tampa, FL 33688-2000 (813) 963-0994
FAX: (813) 264-7906

Company URL: http://seminole-electric.com
Establishment information: Established in 1948.
Company type: Cooperative
Business activities: Generates and transmits electricity.
Business type (SIC): Electric services
Financial profile for 2010: Assets, $1,844,557,929; expenses, $1,330,879,897
Corporate officers: Timothy S. Woodbury, C.E.O.; Robert W. Strickland, Pres.; John W. Geeraerts, C.F.O.; Floyd Welborn, Sr. V.P., Opers.; Savino A. Garcia, V.P., Admin.; Mark T. Sherman, V.P., Mktg.; W.F. Hart, Secy.-Treas.; Robert A. Mora, Genl. Counsel
Giving statement: Giving through the Seminole Electric Cooperative, Inc. Corporate Giving Program.

Seminole Electric Cooperative, Inc. Corporate Giving Program

P.O. Box 272000
16313 N. Dale Mabry Hwy. 33618
Tampa, FL 33688-2000 (813) 963-0994
E-mail: info@seminole-electric.com; URL: http://www.seminole-electric.com/community_support.php

Purpose and activities: Seminole Electric makes charitable contributions to nonprofit organizations and schools for employee volunteer teams, college scholarships, science fair awards, and energy education programs. Support is given primarily in areas of company operations.
Fields of interest: Higher education, college; Education; Environment, energy; Science.
Type of support: Donated products; Employee volunteer services; General/operating support; In-kind gifts; Scholarship funds; Sponsorships.
Geographic limitations: Giving primarily in areas of company operations in FL.
Application information: The Public Relations Section at Seminole's headquarters handles giving.

3405
Sempra Energy

101 Ash St.
San Diego, CA 92101-3017
(619) 696-2000
FAX: (619) 696-1868

Company URL: http://www.sempra.com
Establishment information: Established in 1998.
Company type: Public company
Company ticker symbol and exchange: SRE/NYSE
International Securities Identification Number: US8168511090
Business activities: Operates holding company; generates, transmits, and distributes electricity; transmits and distributes natural gas.
Business type (SIC): Combination utility services; holding company
Financial profile for 2012: Number of employees, 16,893; assets, $36,499,000,000; sales volume, $9,647,000,000; pre-tax net income, $943,000,000; expenses, $8,088,000,000; liabilities, $26,197,000,000
Fortune 1000 ranking: 2012—281st in revenues, 224th in profits, and 154th in assets
Forbes 2000 ranking: 2012—957th in sales, 631st in profits, and 619th in assets
Corporate officers: Debra L. Reed, Chair. and C.E.O.; Mark A. Snell, Pres.; Joseph A. Householder, Exec. V.P. and C.F.O.; Javade Chaudri, Exec. V.P. and Genl. Counsel; G. Joyce Rowland, Sr. V.P., Human Resources; Randall L. Clark, V.P. and Corp. Secy.; Kathryn J. Collier, V.P. and Co-Treas.; Richard A. Vaccari, V.P. and Co-Treas.; Trevor I. Mihalik, Cont. and C.A.O.
Board of directors: Alan L. Boeckmann; James G. Brocksmith, Jr.; William D. Jones; William G. Ouchi, Ph.D.; Debra L. Reed, Chair.; William C. Rusnack; William P. Rutledge; Hon. Lynn Schenk; Luis Tellez; James C. Yardley; Jack T. Taylor
Subsidiaries: San Diego Gas & Electric Company, San Diego, CA; Southern California Gas Company, Los Angeles, CA
International operations: Netherlands
Giving statement: Giving through the Sempra Energy Corporate Giving Program, the Sempra Energy Foundation, and the Sempra Employee Giving Network.
Company EIN: 330732627

Sempra Energy Corporate Giving Program

c/o Corp. Community Rels. Dept.
101 Ash St.
San Diego, CA 92101-3017 (619) 696-2000
E-mail: gifts@sempra.com; Additional tel.: (877) SEMPRA9; fax: (619) 696-1868; e-mail: sempracommunity@sempra.com. Sempra Employee Giving Network website: Sempraemployeegiving.org; e-mail: SempraEmployeeGiving@sempra.com; SDG&E, tel.: (877) 767-SDGE (7343); e-mail: SDGE_Community@semprautilities.com; Southern California Gas Co., tel.: (877) 344-8509, e-mail: communityrelations@semprautilities.com; Sempra U.S. Gas & Power, e-mail: CommunityRelations@USGP.com; Sempra International, tel.: (888) 843-2464; e-mail: contact@sempraglobal.com.; URL: http://www.sempra.com/responsibility/index.shtml

Contact: Molly Cartmill, Dir., Corp. Community Rels.
Purpose and activities: As a complement to its foundation, Sempra Energy also makes charitable contributions to nonprofit organizations directly. Support is given to organizations involved with education and leadership development, the environment, underserved and communities of color, emergency preparedness, and safety and economic development. Support is given in areas of company operations on a national and international basis.
Fields of interest: Arts; Education; Environment, recycling; Environment, energy; Environment; Health care; Employment, training; Safety/disasters; Minorities/immigrants, centers/services; Human services; Civil/human rights, LGBTQ; Economic development; Business/industry; Community/economic development; Mathematics; Engineering/technology; Social sciences, formal/general education; Public affairs, political organizations; Military/veterans' organizations; Public affairs Economically disadvantaged.

Programs:

Employee Tuition Reimbursement Program: Sempra Energy awards reimbursement scholarships of up to $5,250 per year to full-time employees to be used for tuition, registration costs, required books and software, lab fees, or campus parking. Part-time employees become eligible for up to $800 of scholarship money per year after one year of employment.

Sempra Employee Giving Network: Sempra Employee Giving Network is a 501(c)(3) nonprofit organization run by and for the employees of Sempra Energy. Through the Sempra Employee Giving Network, employees can make direct contributions to any nonprofit group through payroll withholdings.

Type of support: Employee matching gifts; Employee volunteer services; Employee-related scholarships; General/operating support; Sponsorships.
Geographic limitations: Giving in areas of company operations on a national and international basis.
Publications: Corporate giving report; Program policy statement.
Application information: Giving is managed by representatives from individual business units.
Administrators: Molly Cartmill, Dir., Corp. Community Rels.; David Jay, Mgr.; Cathy Lavin, Mgr.
Number of staff: 2 full-time professional; 3 full-time support.

Sempra Energy Foundation

101 Ash St., HQ-07
San Diego, CA 92101-3017 (619) 696-2012
E-mail: SempraEnergyFoundation@sempra.com; Additional tel.: (866) 262-4842; URL: http://www.sempraenergyfoundation.org

Establishment information: Established in 2007 in CA.
Donors: Donald E. Felsinger; Sempra Energy; American Gas Assn.
Financial data (yr. ended 12/31/11): Assets, $6,536,722 (M); expenditures, $2,325,564; qualifying distributions, $2,325,527; giving activities include $2,325,527 for 1,559 grants (high: $106,000; low: $25).
Purpose and activities: The foundation supports programs designed to promote environmental stewardship; advance education; and support communities in need.
Fields of interest: Arts; Education; Environment, natural resources; Environment, water resources; Environment, land resources; Environment, energy; Environmental education; Environment; Health care; Disasters, preparedness/services; Safety/disasters; American Red Cross; Children/youth, services; Family services; Human services; Community/economic development; United Ways and Federated Giving Programs; Mathematics; Engineering/technology; Science.

Programs:

Challenge Grant Program: The foundation provides matching contributions to community events with which employees participate that raises funds for health and human service organizations.

Disaster Response & Safety: The foundation supports programs designed to promote wellness and safety; and provides assistance to communities in times of disaster.

Education: The foundation supports educational programs designed to promote math, science, and technology; and programs designed to advance environmental stewardship in the areas of conservation, habitat restoration, and energy efficiency.

Environment: The foundation supports programs designed to promote sustainability and the advancement of new environmental and energy technologies; infrastructure development in the area of sustainable green technologies; and programs designed to promote conservation, habitat restoration, and energy efficiency.

Environmental Champion Awards: The foundation awards grants to nonprofit organizations making a difference in the environmental arena in the Southwest and Gulf Regions, with a focus on environmental education programs for grades K-12.

Helping People in Need Initiative: The foundation awards grants to programs designed to meet the basic needs of families that continue to struggle with the economic crisis. The program is limited to California and the Gulf Region.

Matching Gift Program: The foundation matches contributions made by employees of Sempra Energy to nonprofit organizations involved with arts and culture and education on a one-for-one basis.

Volunteer Incentive Program (VIP): The foundation awards grants to nonprofit organizations with which employees of Sempra Energy volunteers.

Type of support: Employee matching gifts; Employee volunteer services; General/operating support; Grants to individuals; Matching/challenge support; Program development.
Geographic limitations: Giving primarily in CA; giving also to national organizations.
Support limitations: No support for religious organizations not of direct benefit to the entire community, political or discriminatory organizations, or other private non-operating foundations. No grants to individuals (except for disaster response/relief or company-sponsored scholarship programs), or for capital campaigns, travel expenses, loans or loan guarantees, debt reduction or past operating deficits, or liquidation of an organization.
Publications: Financial statement; Grants list; IRS Form 990 or 990-PF printed copy available upon request.
Application information: Applications not accepted. Unsolicited applications are currently not accepted. The foundation periodically initiates Request for Proposals (RFP) for grants in specific funding areas.
Officers and Directors:* Joseph A. Householder*, Chair.; G. Joyce Rowland*, Vice-Chair. and Pres.; Paul Young, V.P. and Treas.; Diana L. Day, Secy.; Beatriz Palomino Young, Exec. Dir.; Steven D. Davis; Jessie Knight, Jr.; George S. Liparidis; Anne Shen Smith.
EIN: 261325469
Selected grants: The following grants are a representative sample of this grantmaker's funding activity:
$300,000 to Burn Institute, San Diego, CA, 2010. For emergency preparedness and safety.
$250,000 to Foundation for California Community Colleges, Sacramento, CA, 2010. For higher education services.
$200,000 to University of California at San Diego, La Jolla, CA, 2010. For higher education services.
$175,000 to Zoological Society of San Diego, San Diego Zoo, San Diego, CA, 2010. For environmental education.
$100,000 to Hogar de Cristo USA, Miami, FL, 2010. To support individuals in need.
$100,000 to San Diego Historical Society, San Diego, CA, 2010. For education, arts and culture.
$90,793 to University of California at San Diego, La Jolla, CA, 2010. For higher education services.
$60,000 to YMCA of San Diego County, San Diego, CA, 2010. For health and human services.
$50,000 to Info Line of San Diego County, San Diego, CA, 2010. For environmental programs.

Sempra Employee Giving Network

(formerly Energy for Others)
c/o Community Partnerships- Sempra Energy
101 Ash St., HQ-07
San Diego, CA 92101-3017 (877) 696-4999
E-mail: sempraemployeegiving@sempra.com; URL: http://www.sempraemployeegiving.org

Financial data (yr. ended 12/31/11): Revenue, $1,054,606; assets, $325,316 (M); gifts received, $1,054,473; expenditures, $1,000,950; giving activities include $926,083 for grants.
Purpose and activities: The organization supports the areas of health and human services and, on occasion, may choose to contribute to programs that promote public safety and the environment.
Fields of interest: Health care; Human services.

Program:

Grants: The fund accepts grant requests in the areas of health and human services where Sempra Energy employees work and live under its Energy for Others initiative. Eligible organizations must have 501(c)(3) status.

Type of support: General/operating support.
Geographic limitations: Giving primarily in areas of company operations.
Support limitations: No support for programs or activities that are discriminatory based upon age, gender, sexual orientation, marital status, physical or mental disabilities, race, color, religion, national origin or ancestry, or political affiliation. No grants to individuals, or for general operating support, endowment funds, travel, loans, capital or construction campaigns, or overhead costs.

Publications: Application guidelines.
Application information: Applications accepted.
Initial approach: Download application
Officers and Directors:* Frank Urtasun*, Chair.; Jeff Alexander*, V.P.; Kitty Corbin-Teora; Dale Kelly-Cochrane; Mark Nelson; Arturo Romero.
EIN: 710875246

3406
Seneca Foods Corporation

3736 S. Main St.
Marion, NY 14505-9751 (315) 926-8100
FAX: (315) 926-8300

Company URL: http://www.senecafoods.com
Establishment information: Established in 1949.
Company type: Public company
Company ticker symbol and exchange: SENEA/ NASDAQ
Business activities: Produces canned and frozen vegetables.
Business type (SIC): Specialty foods/canned, frozen, and preserved
Financial profile for 2013: Number of employees, 3,500; assets, $803,150,000; sales volume, $1,276,300,000; pre-tax net income, $63,450,000; expenses, $1,205,360,000; liabilities, $435,980,000
Corporate officers: Arthur S. Wolcott, Chair.; Kraig H. Kayser, Pres. and C.E.O.; Paul L. Palmby, Exec. V.P. and C.O.O.; Timothy Benjamin, Sr. V.P., Treas., and C.F.O.; Cynthia L. Fohrd, Sr. V.P. and C.A.O.; Carl A. Cichetti, Sr. V.P. and C.I.O.; Dean E. Erstad, Sr. V.P., Sales and Mktg.; Jeffrey L. Van Riper, V.P., Corp. Cont., and Secy.; John D. Exner, Genl. Counsel
Board of directors: Arthur S. Wolcott, Chair.; Arthur H. Baer; Peter R. Call; John P. Gaylord; Susan A. Henry; Samuel T. Hubbard, Jr.; Kraig H. Kayser; Thomas Paulson; Susan W. Stuart
Plants: Buhl, ID; Buckley, MI; Blue Earth, Le Sueur, Montgomery, Rochester, MN; East Williamson, Geneva, Glencoe, Le Roy, Leicester, Marion, Newark, NY; Covington, NC; Dayton, Othello, Pasco, Yakima, WA; Baraboo, Clyman, Cumberland, Janesville, Mayville, WI
Office: Penn Yan, NY
Giving statement: Giving through the Seneca Foods Corporation Contributions Program, the S. S. Pierce Company Employees Aid Fund, and the Seneca Foods Foundation.
Company EIN: 160733425

S. S. Pierce Company Employees Aid Fund

c/o BNY Mellon, N.A
P.O. Box 185
Pittsburgh, PA 15230-0185

Donor: Seneca Foods Corp.
Financial data (yr. ended 08/31/12): Assets, $17,569 (M); expenditures, $727; qualifying distributions, $420; giving activities include $420 for grants to individuals.
Purpose and activities: The fund awards retirement income supplements to various needy former employees of S.S. Pierce Company.
Fields of interest: Aging; Economically disadvantaged.
Type of support: Grants to individuals.
Geographic limitations: Giving primarily in MA.
Application information: Applications not accepted. Unsolicited requests for funds not accepted.
Trustee: BNY Mellon, N.A.
EIN: 046092670

Seneca Foods Foundation

3736 S. Main St.
Marion, NY 14505-9751 (315) 926-8100
E-mail: foundation@senecafoods.com; URL: http://www.senecafoods.com/Foundation/index.shtml

Establishment information: Established in 1988 in NY.
Donor: Seneca Foods Corp.
Contact: Kraig H. Kayser, C.E.O. and Pres.
Financial data (yr. ended 03/31/12): Assets, $5,908,922 (M); gifts received, $1,000,000; expenditures, $618,705; qualifying distributions, $593,142; giving activities include $593,142 for grants.
Purpose and activities: The foundation supports programs designed to promote education and employment; and youth development.
Fields of interest: Elementary/secondary education; Education, early childhood education; Higher education; Education, services; Education, drop-out prevention; Education; Crime/violence prevention, abuse prevention; Crime/violence prevention, child abuse; Employment, services; Employment, job counseling; Employment; Youth development, adult & child programs; Youth development; Children/youth, services; United Ways and Federated Giving Programs; Leadership development Youth.
Programs:
Education and Employment: The foundation supports pre-school and K-12 programs designed to address academic achievement for at-risk students; early drop-out prevention; and improved decision making and life coping skills. The foundation also supports employment programs designed to enable youth to gain skills to help them become independent and improve their access into modern-day, mainstream society.
Youth Development: The foundation supports programs designed to foster leadership through life skills and enrichment initiatives; provide crisis services for youth in crisis and at-risk for abuse; and promote mentoring through adults supporting youth in one-to-one or small group long-term relationships.
Type of support: Building/renovation; General/ operating support; Program development; Scholarship funds.
Geographic limitations: Giving primarily in areas of company operations in Modesto, CA, Sarasota, FL, Buhl and Payette, ID, Princeville, IL, Arlington, Blue Earth, Glencoe, Rochester, and Montgomery, MN, Geneva, Leicester, Marion, and Penn Yan, NY, Lebanon, PA, Dayton and Yakima, WA, and Baraboo, Cambria, Clyman, Cumberland, Gillett, Janesville, Maryville, Oakfield, Plainfield, and Ripon, WI.
Support limitations: No support for religious organizations not of direct benefit to the entire community, or legislative organizations. No grants to individuals, or for endowments, capital campaigns, fundraising events, sponsorships, or academic, medical, or scientific research; no product donations.
Publications: Application guidelines.
Application information: Applications accepted. Grants are limited to organizations with documented performance results. Organizations applying for support must include performance outcomes and performance data to be eligible for funding. Support is limited to 1 contribution per organization during any given year. Application form required. Applicants should submit the following:
1) role played by volunteers
2) timetable for implementation and evaluation of project
3) results expected from proposed grant
4) qualifications of key personnel
5) population served
6) copy of IRS Determination Letter
7) brief history of organization and description of its mission
8) copy of most recent annual report/audited financial statement/990
9) how project's results will be evaluated or measured
10) explanation of why grantmaker is considered an appropriate donor for project
11) listing of board of directors, trustees, officers and other key people and their affiliations
12) detailed description of project and amount of funding requested
13) copy of current year's organizational budget and/or project budget
14) listing of additional sources and amount of support
Initial approach: Download application form and mail to foundation
Deadline(s): None
Officers and Directors:* Arthur S. Wolcott*, Chair.; Kraig H. Kayser*, C.E.O. and Pres.; Jeffrey L. Van Riper, Secy.; Roland E. Breunig, Treas.; Susan W. Stuart.
EIN: 222996324
Selected grants: The following grants are a representative sample of this grantmaker's funding activity:
$229,000 to Cornell University, Ithaca, NY, 2011.
$1,100 to American Cancer Society, Atlanta, GA, 2011.
$1,000 to Muscular Dystrophy Association, Tucson, AZ, 2011.

3407
Senniger Powers LLP

100 N. Broadway, 17th Fl.
St. Louis, MO 63102-2728 (314) 345-7000

Company URL: http://www.senniger.com
Establishment information: Established in 1919.
Company type: Private company
Business activities: Operates law firm.
Business type (SIC): Legal services
Office: St. Louis, MO
Giving statement: Giving through the Senniger Powers LLP Pro Bono Program.

Senniger Powers LLP Pro Bono Program

100 N. Broadway, 17th Fl.
St. Louis, MO 63102-2728 (314) 345-7000
FAX: (314) 231-4342; URL: http://www.senniger.com/community/

Fields of interest: Legal services.
Type of support: Pro bono services - legal.

3408
Sensient Technologies Corporation

(formerly Universal Foods Corporation)
777 E. Wisconsin Ave.
Milwaukee, WI 53202-5304
(414) 271-6755
FAX: (414) 347-4795

Company URL: http://www.sensient-tech.com
Establishment information: Established in 1882.
Company type: Public company
Company ticker symbol and exchange: SXT/NYSE

Business activities: Manufactures and produces ink-jet inks, technical colors, laser printing and flat screen display chemicals, cosmetic and pharmaceutical additives, and food and beverage colors and fragrances.
Business type (SIC): Chemical preparations/ miscellaneous; beverages; chemicals and allied products; drugs; soaps, cleaners, and toiletries
Financial profile for 2012: Number of employees, 3,983; assets, $1,776,640,000; sales volume, $1,459,050,000; pre-tax net income, $174,310,000; expenses, $1,267,840,000; liabilities, $622,750,000
Corporate officers: Kenneth P. Manning, Chair. and C.E.O.; Paul Manning, Pres. and C.O.O.; Richard F. Hobbs, Sr. V.P. and C.F.O.; John L. Hammond, Sr. V.P., Genl. Counsel, and Secy.; Jeffrey T. Makal, V.P., Cont., and C.A.O.; John F. Collopy, V.P. and Treas.; Stephen J. Rolfs, V.P., Admin.; Christopher M. Daniels, V.P., Human Resources
Board of directors: Kenneth P. Manning, Chair.; Hank Brown; Fergus M. Clydesdale, Ph.D.; James A.D. Croft; William V. Hickey; Peter M. Salmon; Elaine R. Wedral, Ph.D.; Essie Whitelaw
Plants: Turlock, CA; Indianapolis, IN; St. Louis, MO
International operations: Australia; Canada; Mexico; Netherlands; Singapore; United Kingdom
Giving statement: Giving through the Sensient Technologies Foundation, Inc.
Company EIN: 190561070

Sensient Technologies Foundation, Inc.

777 E. Wisconsin Ave.
Milwaukee, WI 53202-5304
FAX: (414) 347-4783

Establishment information: Incorporated in 1958 in WI.
Donors: Sensient Technologies Corp.; Universal Foods Corp.
Contact: Douglas L. Arnold
Financial data (yr. ended 12/31/11): Assets, $12,022,157 (M); expenditures, $543,738; qualifying distributions, $529,522; giving activities include $529,522 for grants.
Purpose and activities: The foundation supports organizations involved with arts and culture, education, health, mental health, medical research, hunger, nutrition, human services, community development, minorities, and homeless people.
Fields of interest: Performing arts; Arts; Education, research; Education, fund raising/fund distribution; Higher education; Education; Hospitals (general); Health care; Mental health/crisis services; Medical research, institute; Food services; Nutrition; Children/youth, services; Family services; Residential/custodial care, hospices; Homeless, human services; Human services; Urban/ community development; Community/economic development; Voluntarism promotion; United Ways and Federated Giving Programs; General charitable giving Minorities; Homeless.
Type of support: Annual campaigns; Capital campaigns; Emergency funds; Endowments; General/operating support; Matching/challenge support; Program development; Research; Scholarship funds.
Geographic limitations: Giving primarily in Indianapolis, IN, St. Louis, MO, and Milwaukee, WI.
Support limitations: No support for sectarian, religious, fraternal, or partisan political organizations. No grants to individuals.
Application information: Applications accepted. Application form not required.
Initial approach: Letter of inquiry
Copies of proposal: 1
Board meeting date(s): Jan. and June/July, or as needed
Deadline(s): 1 month prior to board meetings
Final notification: Prior to Dec.
Officers: Kenneth P. Manning, Pres.; Douglas L. Arnold, V.P.; Richard F. Hobbs, V.P.; Stephen J. Rolfs, Secy.-Treas.
EIN: 396044488
Selected grants: The following grants are a representative sample of this grantmaker's funding activity:
$50,000 to Ronald McDonald House Charities, Oak Brook, IL, 2010.
$25,000 to Milwaukee Public Museum, Milwaukee, WI, 2010.
$15,000 to Boys and Girls Clubs of Greater Milwaukee, Milwaukee, WI, 2010.
$15,000 to Milwaukee Art Museum, Milwaukee, WI, 2010.
$10,000 to American Heart Association, Dallas, TX, 2010.
$10,000 to Milwaukee Public Museum, Milwaukee, WI, 2010.
$8,000 to University of Massachusetts, Amherst, MA, 2010.
$5,000 to Arthritis Foundation, Atlanta, GA, 2010.
$2,500 to University School of Milwaukee, Milwaukee, WI, 2010.
$2,000 to University of Massachusetts, Amherst, MA, 2010.

3409
Sentry Insurance

1800 N. Point Dr.
Stevens Point, WI 54481 (715) 346-6000

Company URL: http://www.sentry.com
Establishment information: Established in 1904.
Company type: Mutual company
Business activities: Operates insurance company.
Business type (SIC): Insurance/life; insurance/fire, marine, and casualty
Financial profile for 2011: Number of employees, 4,273; assets, $11,013,400,000; sales volume, $2,457,800,000
Corporate officers: Dale Robert Schuh, Chair. and C.E.O.; Pete G. McPartland, Pres. and C.O.O.; William James Lohr, Sr. V.P. and Treas.
Board of director: Dale Robert Schuh, Chair.
Subsidiary: Sentry Life Insurance Co., Stevens Point, WI
Giving statement: Giving through the Sentry Insurance Foundation, Inc.

Sentry Insurance Foundation, Inc.

(formerly Sentry Foundation, Inc.)
1800 N. Point Dr.
Stevens Point, WI 54481-1283

Establishment information: Incorporated in 1963 in WI.
Donor: Sentry Insurance.
Financial data (yr. ended 12/31/11): Assets, $10,673,539 (M); gifts received, $1,045,750; expenditures, $3,403,517; qualifying distributions, $3,332,863; giving activities include $2,809,058 for 67 grants (high: $1,549,905; low: $500), $15,000 for 3 grants to individuals (high: $5,000; low: $5,000) and $508,805 for 288 employee matching gifts.
Purpose and activities: The foundation supports organizations involved with fine arts and community services. Special emphasis is directed toward educational initiatives.
Fields of interest: Visual arts; Performing arts; Arts; Higher education; Education, reading; Education; Boys & girls clubs; YM/YWCAs & YM/YWHAs; Children, services; Community/economic development; United Ways and Federated Giving Programs.
Type of support: Continuing support; Employee matching gifts; General/operating support; Scholarship funds; Sponsorships.
Geographic limitations: Giving primarily in areas of company operations in WI.
Support limitations: No support for religious organizations.
Application information: Applications accepted. Application form not required. Applicants should submit the following:
1) detailed description of project and amount of funding requested
Initial approach: Proposal
Copies of proposal: 1
Deadline(s): None
Officers and Directors:* James J. Weishan, Chair. and Pres.; Daniel L. Revai*, V.P.; William M. O'Reilly, Secy.; William James Lohr*, Treas.; Dale Robert Schuh.
EIN: 391037370
Selected grants: The following grants are a representative sample of this grantmaker's funding activity:
$20,000 to Lawrence University, Appleton, WI, 2010.
$15,000 to Milwaukee School of Engineering, Milwaukee, WI, 2010.

3410
Sequa Corporation

(formerly Sun Chemical Corporation)
3000 Bayport Dr., Ste. 880
Tampa, FL 33607 (813) 434-4522

Company URL: http://www.sequa.com
Establishment information: Established in 1929.
Company type: Private company
Business activities: Manufactures aerospace equipment, propulsion equipment, metal coatings, and specialty chemicals.
Business type (SIC): Aircraft and parts; chemicals and allied products; paints and allied products; guided missiles and space vehicles
Financial profile for 2011: Number of employees, 9,400; sales volume, $2,400,000,000
Corporate officers: Peter J. Clare, Chair.; Armand F. Lauzon, Jr., C.E.O.; Donna Costello, C.F.O.; Steven R. Lowson, V.P., Genl. Counsel, and Secy.; Andrew Farrant, V.P., Mktg. and Corp. Comms.; John Bollman, V.P., Human Resources
Board of directors: Peter J. Clare, Chair.; Thomas K. Churbuck; Armand F. Lauzon, Jr.; David M. Marchick; Adam J. Palmer; Mark V. Rosenker; David L. Squier
Subsidiaries: Atlantic Research Corporation, Gainesville, VA; Casco Products Corp., Bridgeport, CT; Chromalloy American Corp., St. Louis, MO; Chromalloy Gas Turbine Corporation, San Antonio, TX
Plants: Amherst, NH; Chester, SC
Giving statement: Giving through the Sequa Foundation of Delaware.
Company EIN: 131885030

Sequa Foundation of Delaware
(formerly Sun Chemical Foundation)
c/o Sequa Corp.
300 Blaisdell Rd.
Orangeburg, NY 10962 (212) 692-2634
Application address: tel.: (212) 692-2634

Establishment information: Established in 1967 in DE.
Donor: Sequa Corp.
Contact: Steven R. Lowson, Tr.
Financial data (yr. ended 12/31/11): Assets, $35,374 (M); expenditures, $10,500; qualifying distributions, $10,500; giving activities include $10,500 for 2 grants (high: $10,000; low: $500).
Purpose and activities: The foundation supports organizations involved with arts and culture, higher education, human services, and Judaism.
Fields of interest: Arts; Human services.
Type of support: Capital campaigns; Continuing support; General/operating support.
Geographic limitations: Giving primarily in NY.
Support limitations: No grants to individuals.
Application information: Applications accepted. Application form required.
Initial approach: Letter
Deadline(s): None
Officers and Trustees:* Armand F. Lauzon, Pres.; Steven R. Lowson*, V.P. and Secy.; James P. Langelotti*, V.P. and Treas.; Donna M. Costello*, V.P. and Cont.; M. Blickensderfer, V.P.
Number of staff: 1 part-time support.
EIN: 237000821

3411
The Serengeti Trading Company, LLC
19100 Hamilton Pool Rd.
Dripping Springs, TX 78620-2871
(512) 358-9595

Company URL: http://www.serengetitrading.com
Establishment information: Established in 2000.
Company type: Private company
Business activities: Manufactures organic and other specialty coffees.
Business type (SIC): Groceries—wholesale
Corporate officers: Bert Von Roemer, Pres.; Marc Carlson, C.F.O.
Giving statement: Giving through the Serengeti Foundation.

The Serengeti Foundation
19100 Hamilton Pool Rd.
Dripping Springs, TX 78620-2871
URL: http://www.serengetiusa.com/

Establishment information: Established in 1997 in TX and CA; funded in 2002.
Donors: The Serengeti Trading Company; Grousbeck Family Foundation; The Prappas Company; Beth Pfeiffer; Silicon Valley Community Foundation; The Max Levinson Foundation; The Anna Levinson Foundation; Rich Hendele.
Financial data (yr. ended 12/31/11): Assets, $6,902,185 (M); gifts received, $2,212,449; expenditures, $406,705; qualifying distributions, $307,120; giving activities include $307,120 for 5 grants (high: $280,000; low: $1,560).
Purpose and activities: The foundation supports land conservation and animal sanctuaries.
Fields of interest: Education; Animals/wildlife; Recreation.
Type of support: General/operating support.
Geographic limitations: Giving primarily in TX, WA, Kenya, Thailand, and Uganda.
Application information: Applications not accepted. Contributes only to pre-selected organizations.
Officer: Marc Carlson, Treas.
Director: Bert Von Roemer.
EIN: 541876544

3412
Servco Pacific Inc.
2850 Pukoloa St., Ste. 300
Honolulu, HI 96819 (808) 564-1300

Company URL: http://www.servco.com
Establishment information: Established in 1919.
Company type: Private company
Business activities: Sells appliances wholesale; operates car and truck dealerships; operates automobile parts and accessories stores; operates tire stores; sells insurance.
Business type (SIC): Electrical goods—wholesale; motor vehicles—retail; auto and home supplies—retail; shopping goods stores/miscellaneous; insurance carriers
Corporate officers: Mark H. Fukunaga, Chair. and C.E.O.; Eric S. Fukunaga, Pres. and C.O.O.; Jeffrey A. Bell, C.F.O. and Sr. V.P.; John W. Harris, C.I.O.; Sandra C.H. Wong, V.P. and Secy.
Board of director: Mark H. Fukunaga, Chair.
Subsidiaries: Pacific Asset Management Corp., Honolulu, HI; Servco Automotive Insurance Co., Inc., Honolulu, HI; Servco California Inc., Los Angeles, CA; Servco Guam Inc., Honolulu, HI; Servco Insurance Agency, Inc., Honolulu, HI; Servco Insurance Services Corp., Honolulu, HI; Servco Investment Corp., Honolulu, HI; Servco Risk Services, Inc., Honolulu, HI; Servco Services Corp., Honolulu, HI; Servco Subaru Inc., Honolulu, HI
Giving statement: Giving through the Servco Foundation.
Company EIN: 990057870

Servco Foundation
P.O. Box 2788
Honolulu, HI 96803-2788
FAX: (808) 523-3937;
E-mail: donations@servco.com

Establishment information: Established in 1986 in HI.
Donor: Servco Pacific Inc.
Contact: Sandra C.H. Wong, Secy.
Financial data (yr. ended 06/30/11): Assets, $5,756,669 (M); expenditures, $356,226; qualifying distributions, $312,867; giving activities include $312,867 for grants.
Purpose and activities: The foundation supports museums and organizations involved with education, youth development, and human services.
Fields of interest: Museums; Higher education; Education; Youth development; Human services.
Program:
Annual Undergraduate Scholarships: The foundation annually awards $4,000 scholarships to spouses and children of Servco Pacific employees to pursue higher education. Applicants must have GPA of 3.0, demonstrated leadership ability through school activities and community service, and financial need.
Type of support: Annual campaigns; Capital campaigns; Employee matching gifts; Employee-related scholarships; General/operating support.
Geographic limitations: Giving limited to HI and the U.S. Pacific region.
Support limitations: No support for political organizations.
Publications: Application guidelines.
Application information: Applications accepted. Application form not required. Applicants should submit the following:
1) copy of IRS Determination Letter
Initial approach: Proposal via e-mail, fax, or postal mail
Copies of proposal: 1
Board meeting date(s): Oct.
Deadline(s): None
Final notification: 1 to 3 weeks
Officers and Directors:* Mark H. Fukunaga*, Chair.; Eric S. Fukunaga*, Pres.; Glenn K. Inouye*, V.P.; Sandra C.H. Wong, Secy.; Jeffrey A. Bell*, Treas.
EIN: 990248256
Selected grants: The following grants are a representative sample of this grantmaker's funding activity:
$20,000 to Salvation Army of Hawaiian Islands, Honolulu, HI, 2009.
$16,000 to Contemporary Museum, Honolulu, HI, 2009.
$10,000 to Chaminade University of Honolulu, Honolulu, HI, 2009.
$10,000 to Hale Kipa, Honolulu, HI, 2009.
$9,000 to Boy Scouts of America, Aloha Council, Honolulu, HI, 2009.
$8,000 to Rehabilitation Hospital of the Pacific, Honolulu, HI, 2009.
$7,500 to Manoa Valley Theater, Honolulu, HI, 2009.
$5,000 to Boys and Girls Club of Hawaii, Honolulu, HI, 2009.
$5,000 to Goodwill Industries of Hawaii, Honolulu, HI, 2009.
$5,000 to Special Olympics Hawaii, Honolulu, HI, 2009.
$5,000 to YMCA of Honolulu, Honolulu, HI, 2009.
$4,400 to Japan-America Society of Hawaii, Honolulu, HI, 2009.
$3,500 to Big Brothers Big Sisters of Honolulu, Honolulu, HI, 2009.
$3,500 to Domestic Violence Legal Hotline, Honolulu, HI, 2009.
$3,000 to Ronald McDonald House Charities of Hawaii, Honolulu, HI, 2009.
$2,500 to U.S.S. Missouri Memorial Association, Aiea, HI, 2009.

3413
Service Corporation International
1929 Allen Pkwy.
Houston, TX 77019 (713) 522-5141
FAX: (713) 525-5586

Company URL: http://www.sci-corp.com
Establishment information: Established in 1962.
Company type: Public company
Company ticker symbol and exchange: SCI/NYSE
Business activities: Owns and operates funeral homes and cemeteries.
Business type (SIC): Funeral services; real estate subdividers and developers
Financial profile for 2012: Number of employees, 20,567; assets, $9,683,570,000; sales volume, $2,410,480,000; pre-tax net income, $245,680,000; expenses, $2,033,400,000; liabilities, $8,340,540,000
Fortune 1000 ranking: 2012—834th in revenues, 641st in profits, and 397th in assets
Corporate officers: Robert L. Waltrip, Chair.; Thomas L. Ryan, Pres. and C.E.O.; Michael R. Webb,

Exec. V.P. and C.O.O.; Eric D. Tanzberger, Sr. V.P., C.F.O., and Treas.; Gregory T. Sangalis, Sr. V.P., Genl. Counsel, and Secy.; Sumner J. Waring III, Sr. V.P., Opers.; Steve A. Tidwell, Sr. V.P., Sales.; Tammy R. Moore, V.P. and Corp. Cont.; Gerry D. Heard, V.P., Sales
Board of directors: Robert L. Waltrip, Chair.; Alan R. Buckwalter III; Anthony L. Coelho; S. Malcolm Gillis, Ph.D.; Victor L. Lund; John W. Mecom, Jr.; Clifton H. Morris, Jr.; Thomas L. Ryan; W. Blair Waltrip; Marc Watts; Edward E. Williams
Subsidiaries: Amedco, Inc., Chesterfield, MO; IFS Industries, Inc., San Diego, CA
Giving statement: Giving through the Service Corporation International Corporate Giving Program.
Company EIN: 741488375

Service Corporation International Corporate Giving Program

1929 Allen Pkwy.
Houston, TX 77019-2506 (713) 522-5141

Contact: Bob Boetticher
Purpose and activities: Through a decentralized corporate giving program, Service Corporation International conducts its philanthropic activities via various company locations that determine local charitable guidelines. At its headquarters in Houston, Texas, Service Corporation International makes charitable contributions of funeral services to nonprofit organizations on a case by case basis.
Fields of interest: General charitable giving.
Type of support: Donated products.
Geographic limitations: Giving in areas of company operations.
Application information: Unsolicited requests are accepted from Service Corporation International officers on behalf of nonprofit organizations only.

3414
The ServiceMaster Company

860 Ridge Lake Blvd.
Memphis, TN 38120 (901) 597-1400

Company URL: http://servicemaster.com/
Establishment information: Established in 1929.
Company type: Subsidiary of a private company
Business activities: Provides housecleaning, termite and pest control, and landscape maintenance services to commercial and residential customers.
Business type (SIC): Services to dwellings
Financial profile for 2011: Number of employees, 27,000; assets, $7,100,000,000; sales volume, $3,370,000,000
Corporate officers: Hank Mullany, C.E.O.; Linda Goodspeed, C.I.O.; Greer G. McMullen, Sr. V.P. and Genl. Counsel; Peter Tosches, Sr. V.P., Corp. Comms.; Jed L. Norden, Sr. V.P., Human Resources; Alison Boyle, Corp. Comms
Subsidiaries: Certified Systems Inc., Dallas, TX; SVM Holding Corp., Downers Grove, IL; The Terminix Corp., Downers Grove, IL; TruGreen-Chemlawn, Memphis, TN
Divisions: American Home Shield Corp., Memphis, TN; CMI Group, Inc., Milwaukee, WI; Merry Maids L.P., Omaha, NE; ServiceMaster Child Care Services, Downers Grove, IL; ServiceMaster Consumer Services Co., Memphis, TN; ServiceMaster Diversified Health Services, Inc., Memphis, TN; ServiceMaster East Management Services, Wayne, PA; ServiceMaster Energy Management, Englewood, CO; ServiceMaster Food Management Services, Downers Grove, IL; ServiceMaster Home Health Care Services, Inc., Downers Grove, IL; ServiceMaster Industrial Commercial Management Services, Inc., Downers Grove, IL; ServiceMaster International & New Business Development, Downers Grove, IL; ServiceMaster Management Services, Downers Grove, IL; ServiceMaster Manufacturing Services, Cairo, IL; ServiceMaster Manufacturing Services, North Aurora, IL; ServiceMaster Manufacturing Services, Lancaster, PA; ServiceMaster Mid-American Management Services, Downers Grove, IL; ServiceMaster Residential/Commercial Services Corp., Memphis, TN; ServiceMaster Southeast Management Services, Tucker, GA; ServiceMaster West Management Services, Irvine, CA
International operations: Canada; United Kingdom
Giving statement: Giving through the ServiceMaster Company Contributions Program and the ServiceMaster Foundation.
Company EIN: 363858106

The ServiceMaster Company Contributions Program

860 Ridge Lake Blvd.
Memphis, TN 38120 (901) 597-1400
E-mail: WeServe@ServiceMaster.com; URL: http://servicemaster.com/about-us/corporate-social-responsibility

Purpose and activities: As a complement to its foundation, ServiceMaster also makes charitable contributions to nonprofit organizations directly. Support is given primarily in areas of company operations; giving also to national organizations.
Fields of interest: Education; Environment; Breast cancer; Medical research, fund raising/fund distribution; Food banks; Housing/shelter, volunteer services.
Type of support: Donated products; Employee volunteer services; General/operating support.
Geographic limitations: Giving primarily in areas of company operations.
Publications: Application guidelines.
Application information: Applications accepted. Telephone calls are not encouraged. Application form not required.
Initial approach: E-mail proposal
Committee meeting date(s): Quarterly
Deadline(s): None
Final notification: 30 to 90 days

The ServiceMaster Foundation

860 Ridgelake Blvd., A3-4019
Memphis, TN 38120-9434 (901) 597-1400

Establishment information: Established in 2002 in IL as successor to the original ServiceMaster Foundation, established in 1987.
Donors: Fairwyn Fund; The ServiceMaster Co.; Harper Collins Publishers.
Contact: Jim Fletcher
Financial data (yr. ended 12/31/11): Assets, $32,682 (M); gifts received, $36,028; expenditures, $8,650; qualifying distributions, $8,650; giving activities include $8,650 for 14 grants to individuals (high: $1,500; low: $250).
Purpose and activities: The foundation awards disaster relief grants to employees affected by natural disasters.
Type of support: Grants to individuals.
Application information: Applications accepted. Application form required.
Attach a Copy of Requesta for Fund and Financial Statement.
Initial approach: Proposal
Deadline(s): None

Officers and Directors:* Greerson G. McMullen*, Pres.; D. Shannon Sparks, V.P.; Krista A. Endres*, Secy.; David W. Martin*, Treas.
EIN: 030503230

3415
Seton Company, Inc.

1000 Madison Ave., Ste. 210
Eagleville, PA 19403-2426 (610) 666-9600

Company URL: http://www.setonleather.com
Establishment information: Established in 1906.
Company type: Subsidiary of a private company
Business activities: Produces tanned and finished cattlehide leather.
Business type (SIC): Leather tanning and finishing
Financial profile for 2009: Number of employees, 4,454
Corporate officers: Philip D. Kaltenbacher, Chair. and C.E.O.; Hermann Kampling, Pres. and C.O.O.; Eric Evans, C.F.O.; Mike Grimm, C.I.O.; Perry Trechak, Treas.; Ken Mitchell, Cont.
Board of director: Philip D. Kaltenbacher, Chair.
Giving statement: Giving through the Seton Company Foundation.

Seton Company Foundation

c/o Seton Co.
310 South St., 2nd Fl.
Morristown, NJ 07960 (973) 455-0181

Establishment information: Established in 1946 in NJ.
Donor: Seton Co.
Contact: Gail K. Kurz, Tr.
Financial data (yr. ended 12/31/11): Assets, $458,492 (M); expenditures, $35,645; qualifying distributions, $31,795; giving activities include $31,715 for 18 grants (high: $15,000; low: $100).
Purpose and activities: The foundation supports organizations involved with arts and culture, education, health, medical research, and human services.
Fields of interest: Arts; Education; Health care; Health organizations, association; Medical research, institute; Human services; United Ways and Federated Giving Programs; Jewish agencies & synagogues.
Type of support: Employee-related scholarships; General/operating support; Scholarship funds.
Support limitations: No support for private non-operating foundations. No grants to individuals (except for employee-related scholarships).
Application information: Applications accepted. Application form not required. Applicants should submit the following:
1) brief history of organization and description of its mission
2) detailed description of project and amount of funding requested
Initial approach: Proposal
Deadline(s): None
Trustees: Philip D. Kaltenbacher; Gail K. Kurz.
EIN: 226029254

3416
Seventh Generation, Inc.

60 Lake St.
Burlington, VT 05401-5218 (802) 658-3773

Company URL: http://www.seventhgeneration.com
Establishment information: Established in 1988.

Company type: Private company
Business activities: Manufactures environmentally friendly and nontoxic household products.
Business type (SIC): Soaps, cleaners, and toiletries
Corporate officers: Peter Graham, Chair.; John B. Replogle, Pres. and C.E.O.; Anita B. Lavoie, Secy.
Board of director: Peter Graham, Chair.
Giving statement: Giving through the Seventh Generation, Inc. Corporate Giving Program.

Seventh Generation, Inc. Corporate Giving Program

60 Lake St.
Burlington, VT 05401-5300 (802) 658-3773
FAX: (802) 658-1771; URL: http://www.seventhgeneration.com/contact-us/donations-and-giving

Purpose and activities: Seventh Generation makes charitable contributions to nonprofit organizations involved with women's issues, environmental sustainability, and human health. Support is given primarily in areas of company operations in Vermont.
Fields of interest: Environment; Health care; Food banks; Women, centers/services.
Programs:
Children's Environmental Health and Wellness: Seventh Generation supports programs designed to directly and positively influence environmental health issues that affect children and provide them with a better quality of life.
Global Cooling: Seventh Generation supports programs designed to promote stewardship, education, and regenerative solutions to global warming.
Type of support: Annual campaigns; Employee volunteer services; Sponsorships.
Geographic limitations: Giving primarily in Support is given primarily in areas of company operations in VT.
Publications: Application guidelines; Corporate giving report.
Application information: Telephone calls are not encouraged. Unsolicited applications for sponsorship requests are not accepted at this time.

3417
Seward & Kissel LLP

1 Battery Park Plz.
New York, NY 10004-1438 (212) 574-1200

Company URL: http://www.sewkis.com
Establishment information: Established in 1890.
Company type: Private company
Business activities: Operates law firm.
Business type (SIC): Legal services
Offices: Washington, DC; New York, NY
Giving statement: Giving through the Seward & Kissel LLP Pro Bono Program.

Seward & Kissel LLP Pro Bono Program

1 Battery Park Plz.
New York, NY 10004-1438 (212) 574-1215
E-mail: yoskowitz@sewkis.com; URL: http://www.sewkis.com/services/xprServiceDetailSymSewardKissel.aspx?xpST=ServiceDetail&service=50

Contact: Jack Yoskowitz, Partner
Fields of interest: Legal services.
Type of support: Pro bono services - legal.
Application information: An attorney coordinates pro bono projects.

3418
Shaklee Corporation

4747 Willow Rd., Ste. P-201
Pleasanton, CA 94588-2763
(925) 924-2000

Company URL: http://www.shaklee.com/index.shtml
Establishment information: Established in 1956.
Company type: Subsidiary of a foreign company
Business activities: Manufactures nutritional, personal care, and household products.
Business type (SIC): Dairy products; drugs; soaps, cleaners, and toiletries; machinery/refrigeration and service industry
Financial profile for 2010: Number of employees, 175
Corporate officers: Roger Barnett, Chair. and C.E.O.; Marjorie Fine, Exec. V.P., Genl. Counsel, and Secy.; Luiz Cerqueria, Sr. V.P. and C.O.O.; Mike Batesole, C.F.O.; Ken Harris, C.I.O.; Cindy Latham, Sr. V.P., Mktg.; Laura Hughes, Sr. V.P., Sales
Board of director: Roger Barnett, Chair.
Subsidiaries: Bear Creek Corp., Medford, OR; Bear Creek Garden, Somis, CA
International operations: Canada; Malaysia; Mexico
Giving statement: Giving through the Shaklee Corporation Contributions Program and the Shaklee Cares.

Shaklee Cares

4747 Willow Rd.
Pleasanton, CA 94588-2763 (925) 924-2003
FAX: (925) 925-2303;
E-mail: shakleecares@shaklee.com; URL: http://www.shakleecares.org/index.html

Establishment information: Established in 1992.
Donor: Shaklee Corp.
Contact: Sibylle Whittam, Pres.
Financial data (yr. ended 03/31/11): Revenue, $161,949; assets, $294,277 (M); gifts received, $161,866; expenditures, $156,077; giving activities include $156,057 for grants.
Purpose and activities: The organization seeks to provide disaster relief when needed to members and employees of Shaklee Corporation and the community.
Fields of interest: Disasters, floods; Disasters, fire prevention/control; Safety/disasters.
Type of support: Grants to individuals; In-kind gifts.
Officers and Directors:* Takashi Bamba, Chair; Bradford Richardson*, Pres.; Roger Barnett*, C.E.O.; Mike Batesole*, C.F.O.; Laura Hughes, V.P.; Cindy Latham, V.P.; Marjorie Fine; Ken Harris; Brad Harrington; Carsten R. Smidt, Ph.D.
EIN: 943169989

3419
Shakopee Mdewakanton Sioux (Dakota) Community

2330 Sioux Trail N.W.
Prior Lake, MN 55372-9077
(952) 445-8900

Company URL: http://www.shakopeedakota.org/
Establishment information: Established in 1969.
Company type: Tribal corporation
Business activities: Operates casino resorts.
Business type (SIC): Amusement and recreation services/miscellaneous
Corporate officers: Stanley R. Crooks, Chair.; Keith B. Anderson, Vice-Chair; Lori K. Watso, Secy.-Treas.
Board of directors: Stanley R. Crooks, Chair.; Keith B. Anderson, Vice-Chair.
Giving statement: Giving through the Shakopee Mdewakanton Sioux (Dakota) Community Contributions Program.

Shakopee Mdewakanton Sioux (Dakota) Community Contributions Program

c/o SMSC Donations
2330 Sioux Trail N.W.
Prior Lake, MN 55372-9077 (952) 445-8900
E-mail: donations@shakopeedakota.org; Donations phone number: (952) 403-5550; URL: http://www.shakopeedakota.org/donations.html

Purpose and activities: The Shakopee Mdewakanton Dakota Community makes charitable contributions to other tribes and Indian and non-Indian organizations directly. Emphasis is given to requests from tribes of the Northern Plains and Minnesota regions.
Fields of interest: Education; Dental care; Health care, EMS; Health care; Mental health/crisis services; Youth development; Human services Native Americans/American Indians.
Program:
Shakopee Mdewakanton Sioux Community (SMSC) Endowed Scholarship: The SMSC scholarship program is designed to recruit and retain talented American Indian students with demonstrated financial need to the University of Minnesota. The SMSC scholarship program is administered by the University's Office for Equity and Diversity. The primary goal of the SMSC scholarship program is to support incoming University of Minnesota freshmen and transfer students with demonstrated financial need. A smaller number of scholarships may also be awarded to newly-admitted graduate and professional students in specific disciplines. Scholarships are renewable for up to four years or until graduation (whichever comes first) for undergraduates, contingent upon academic performance. For graduate and professional students, the length of funding is contingent upon academic performance, the school of enrollment, and degree program, and will be determined on a case-by-case basis.
Type of support: General/operating support; Scholarship funds.
Geographic limitations: Giving primarily in Northern Plains and MN.
Support limitations: No support for adult sports teams. No grants to individuals, or for beauty or beautiful baby contests, modeling, talent, racing, rodeo, music festivals, or People to People Ambassador sponsorships, foreign travel, mass generated requests, film production, start-up costs, fundraising through the sale of advertisements, newsletters with donation envelopes attached, second or third party requests, small business grants or loans, finders' fees, or requests needed in less than two weeks.
Publications: Application guidelines; Corporate giving report.
Application information: Applications accepted. Proposals should be no more than 5 pages. Application form required. Applicants should submit the following:
1) detailed description of project and amount of funding requested

2) copy of current year's organizational budget and/ or project budget
Organizations located on reservations should include a letter of support from their local tribal council. Proposals should be directed to the SMSC Business Council. Organizations located on reservations should include a letter of support from their local tribal council.
Initial approach: Download cover sheet and send with proposal to headquarters
Copies of proposal: 1
Committee meeting date(s): Monthly
Deadline(s): the 25th of each month
Final notification: 30 days or more

3420
Shalam Imports, Inc.
43 W. 33rd St., Ste. 601
New York, NY 10001-3047 (212) 967-6868
FAX: (212) 629-0945

Company URL: http://www.shalamimports.com
Establishment information: Established in 1955.
Company type: Private company
Business activities: Sells backpacks and other travelware.
Business type (SIC): Durable goods—wholesale
Corporate officers: Sasson Shalam, Pres.; Abraham Shalam, V.P.
Giving statement: Giving through the Magen Avraham Fund.

Magen Avraham Fund
1538 Ocean Pkwy.
Brooklyn, NY 11230-7004

Establishment information: Established in 2004 in NY.
Donor: Shalam Imports Inc.
Financial data (yr. ended 12/31/11): Assets, $230 (M); gifts received, $17,190; expenditures, $17,240; qualifying distributions, $17,240; giving activities include $17,240 for 6+ grants (high: $10,220; low: $1,001).
Purpose and activities: The foundation supports organizations involved with Judaism.
Fields of interest: Jewish agencies & synagogues.
Type of support: General/operating support.
Geographic limitations: Giving primarily in Brooklyn, NY.
Support limitations: No grants to individuals.
Application information: Applications not accepted. Unsolicited requests for funds not accepted.
Trustees: Abraham Shalam; Janet Shalam.
EIN: 206374435

3421
M. Shanken Communications, Inc.
387 Park Ave. S.
New York, NY 10016 (212) 684-4224

Company URL: http://www.mshanken.com
Establishment information: Established in 1972.
Company type: Private company
Business activities: Publishes magazines and newsletters; operates related web sites.
Business type (SIC): Periodical publishing and/or printing
Corporate officers: Marvin R. Shanken, Chair., Pres., and C.E.O.; Melvin R. Mannion, M.D., Sr. V.P., Finance and Admin.
Board of director: Marvin R. Shanken, Chair.
Giving statement: Giving through the Shanken Family Foundation and the Wine Spectator California Scholarship Foundation.

Shanken Family Foundation
387 Park Ave. S.
New York, NY 10016-8810 (212) 684-4884
tel.: (212) 684-4884

Establishment information: Established in 1999 in NY.
Donor: M. Shanken Communications, Inc.
Contact: Marvin R. Shanken, Dir.
Financial data (yr. ended 12/31/11): Assets, $2,824,756 (M); gifts received, $318,000; expenditures, $290,250; qualifying distributions, $290,000; giving activities include $290,000 for 17 grants (high: $110,000; low: $1,000).
Purpose and activities: The foundation supports medical centers and organizations involved with education, Autism, diabetes research, disability services, civil and human rights, and Judaism.
Fields of interest: Higher education; Education; Health care, clinics/centers; Autism; Diabetes research; Developmentally disabled, centers & services; Civil/human rights; Jewish federated giving programs; Jewish agencies & synagogues.
Type of support: General/operating support; Program development; Research.
Geographic limitations: Giving primarily in CT, FL, and New York, NY.
Support limitations: No grants to individuals.
Application information: Applications accepted. Application form required. Applicants should submit the following:
1) brief history of organization and description of its mission
2) detailed description of project and amount of funding requested
Initial approach: Proposal
Deadline(s): None
Final notification: Within 2 months
Officer: Melvin Manion, Treas.
Director: Marvin R. Shanken.
EIN: 134027049
Selected grants: The following grants are a representative sample of this grantmaker's funding activity:
$25,000 to Georgetown University, Washington, DC, 2010.
$11,000 to Project ALS, New York, NY, 2010.
$10,000 to Film Society of Lincoln Center, New York, NY, 2010.
$1,200 to Abilities, Inc., Albertson, NY, 2010.

Wine Spectator California Scholarship Foundation
387 Park Ave. S.
New York, NY 10016-8810 (212) 684-4224

Establishment information: Established in 1982 in NY.
Financial data (yr. ended 06/30/11): Revenue, $2,960,398; assets, $11,021,240 (M); expenditures, $1,674,654; giving activities include $144,375 for grants.
Purpose and activities: The foundation provides grants and scholarships to students pursuing careers in the wine industry or other hospitality industry-related vocations.
Fields of interest: Agriculture/food, formal/general education.
Type of support: Scholarships—to individuals.
Geographic limitations: Giving on a national basis.
Officers: Marvin Shanken, Pres.; Mel Mannion, V.P.
EIN: 133129027

3422
Sharp Electronics Corporation
1 Sharp Plz.
Mahwah, NJ 07495-1163 (201) 529-8200

Company URL: http://www.sharp-usa.com
Establishment information: Established in 1962.
Company type: Subsidiary of a foreign company
Business activities: Manufactures consumer and business electronics.
Business type (SIC): Audio and video equipment/ household; computer and office equipment
Corporate officers: Kozo Takahashi, Chair. and C.E.O.; Daisuke Koshima, Pres.; Bill Flynn, Sr., V.P. and C.F.O.
Board of directors: Kozo Takahashi, Chair.; Daisuke Koshima
Subsidiary: Sharp Laboratories of America, Inc., Camas, WA
Divisions: Sharp Latin American Group, Miami, FL; Sharp Manufacturing Co. of America, Memphis, TN; Sharp Systems of America Div., Huntington Beach, CA
Offices: Lawrenceville, GA; Romeoville, IL; Dallas, TX
International operations: Mexico
Giving statement: Giving through the Sharp Electronics Corporation Contributions Program.

Sharp Electronics Corporation Contributions Program
c/o Corp. Contribs.
1 Sharp Plz.
Mahwah, NJ 07430-1163 (201) 529-8200
FAX: (201) 529-8425; URL: http://sharp-world.com/corporate/eco/index.html

Purpose and activities: Sharp makes charitable contributions to nonprofit organizations involved with education, the environment, and social welfare. Support is given primarily in areas of company operations.
Fields of interest: Elementary school/education; Education; Environmental education; Human services.
Program:
Sharp Player of the Month: Sharp makes charitable contributions of electronic products to nonprofit organizations selected by the leading player each month during the professional baseball, basketball, and hockey seasons.
Type of support: Donated products; Employee volunteer services; In-kind gifts; Sponsorships.
Geographic limitations: Giving primarily in areas of company operations.

3423
Shartsis Friese LLP
1 Maritime Plz., 18th Fl.
San Francisco, CA 94111-3404
(415) 421-6500

Company URL: http://www.sflaw.com/index.htm
Company type: Private company
Business activities: Operates law firm.
Business type (SIC): Legal services
Office: San Francisco, CA

Giving statement: Giving through the Shartsis Friese LLP Pro Bono Program.

Shartsis Friese LLP Pro Bono Program

1 Maritime Plz., 18th Fl.
San Francisco, CA 94111-3404 (415) 421-6500
E-mail: ghaynes@sflaw.com; URL: http://www.sflaw.com/pro-bono.htm

Contact: Geoffrey W. Haynes, Chair., Pro Bono Comm.
Fields of interest: Legal services.
Type of support: Pro bono services - legal.
Application information: A Pro Bono Committee manages the pro bono program.

3424
Shatz, Schwartz & Fentin, P.C.

1441 Main St., Ste. 1100
Springfield, MA 01103 (413) 737-1131

Company URL: http://www.ssfpc.com
Establishment information: Established in 1969.
Company type: Private company
Business activities: Provides legal services.
Business type (SIC): Legal services
Corporate officer: Deborah Barton, C.E.O. and C.F.O.
Giving statement: Giving through the Shatz, Schwartz and Fentin Charitable Foundation.

Shatz, Schwartz and Fentin Charitable Foundation

1441 Main St., Ste. 1100
Springfield, MA 01103-1405 (413) 737-1131

Donors: Shatz, Schwartz & Fentin, P.C.; Gary S. Fentin; Timothy P. Mulbern; Steven J. Schwartz; Stephen A. Shatz; James B. Sheils; Ellen W. Freyman; Steven Weiss; Excel Dryer Inc.
Contact: Steven J. Schwartz, Tr.
Financial data (yr. ended 08/31/12): Assets, $4,198 (M); gifts received, $14,000; expenditures, $17,075; qualifying distributions, $17,040; giving activities include $17,040 for 31 grants (high: $5,000; low: $25).
Purpose and activities: The foundation supports organizations involved with music, education, health, legal aid, youth development, and human services.
Fields of interest: Agriculture/food; Human services; Community/economic development.
Type of support: Building/renovation; Capital campaigns; General/operating support.
Geographic limitations: Giving primarily in Springfield, MA.
Support limitations: No grants to individuals.
Application information: Applications accepted. Application form not required.
Initial approach: Proposal
Deadline(s): None
Trustees: Gary S. Fentin; Timothy P. Mulhern; Steven J. Schwartz; Stephen A. Shatz; James B. Sheils.
EIN: 042712836

3425
Shaughnessy Crane Service, Inc.

(doing business as Shaughnessy & Ahern Shaughnessy & Ahern)
346 D St.
Boston, MA 02127-1225 (617) 269-6600

Company URL: http://www.shaughnessy-ahern.com
Establishment information: Established in 1916.
Company type: Subsidiary of a private company
Business activities: Provides rigging services.
Business type (SIC): Contractors/miscellaneous special trade
Corporate officers: Jack Shaughnessy, Sr., C.E.O.; John J. Shaughnessy, Pres. and Treas.; Herbert A. Shaughnessy, Jr., Secy.
Divisions: Shaughnessy Aerialifts, Worcester, MA; Shaughnessy Crane, Boston, MA; Shaughnessy Millwrights, Springfield, MA; Shaughnessy Millwrights, Manchester, NH; Shaughnessy Millwrights, Providence, RI
Giving statement: Giving through the Shaughnessy Charitable Trust.

Shaughnessy Charitable Trust

(formerly John J. and Mary E. Shaughnessy Charitable Trust)
P.O. Box 1802
Providence, RI 02901-1802

Establishment information: Established in 1988 in MA.
Donors: Shaughnessy Crane Service, Inc.; John J. Shaughnessy; Mary E. Shaughnessy; Law Offices of Peter F. Davis; John J. Shaughnessy Trust; Shaughnessy & Ahearn Co.; Second Street Iron & Metal Co., Inc.
Financial data (yr. ended 08/31/11): Assets, $924,426 (M); expenditures, $230,507; qualifying distributions, $217,500; giving activities include $217,500 for grants.
Purpose and activities: The foundation supports organizations involved with education, health, human services, Christianity, and Catholicism.
Fields of interest: Secondary school/education; Adult/continuing education; Education, reading; Education; Hospitals (general); Health care; Children/youth, services; Family services; Women, centers/services; Homeless, human services; Human services; Christian agencies & churches; Catholic agencies & churches.
Type of support: Annual campaigns; Continuing support; General/operating support; Program development; Scholarship funds.
Geographic limitations: Giving limited to Boston, MA.
Support limitations: No grants to individuals.
Application information: Applications not accepted. Contributes only to pre-selected organizations.
Trustees: Susan M. Harrison; Michael P. Shaughnessy; John J. Shaughnessy; Stephen A. Shaughnessy; Bank of America, N.A.
EIN: 046595469

3426
Shaw Industries Group, Inc.

(formerly Shaw Industries, Inc.)
616 E. Walnut Ave.
P.O. Box 2128
Dalton, GA 30721-4409

Company URL: http://www.shawfloors.com
Establishment information: Established in 1967.
Company type: Subsidiary of a public company
Business activities: Manufactures carpet.
Business type (SIC): Carpets and rugs
Corporate officers: Robert E. Shaw, Chair.; Vance D. Bell, C.E.O.; Randy Merritt, Pres.; Hal Long, Exec. V.P., Opers.; Kenneth G. Jackson, C.F.O.; Gerald R. Embry, V.P., Admin., and Cont.
Board of director: Robert E. Shaw, Chair.
Giving statement: Giving through the Shaw Industries Group, Inc. Corporate Giving Program.

Shaw Industries Group, Inc. Corporate Giving Program

616 E. Walnut Ave.
P.O. Box 2128
Dalton, GA 30722-2128 (800) 720-7429
E-mail: info@shawgreenedge.com; URL: http://www.shawgreenedge.com/community_givingback.shtml

Contact: P.O. Box 2128Gerald Embry
Financial data (yr. ended 12/31/10): Total giving, $1,969,335, including $1,239,240 for grants, $683,500 for 1 employee matching gift and $46,595 for in-kind gifts.
Purpose and activities: Shaw Industries makes charitable contributions to nonprofit organizations on a case by case basis. Support is given primarily in areas of company operations.
Fields of interest: General charitable giving.
Type of support: Donated products; General/operating support.
Geographic limitations: Giving primarily in areas of company operations.
Application information: Applications not accepted. Contributes only to pre-selected organizations.

3427
Shaw's Supermarkets, Inc.

750 W. Center St.
West Bridgewater, MA 02379-1518
(508) 313-4000

Company URL: http://www.shaws.com
Establishment information: Established in 1860.
Company type: Subsidiary of a public company
Business activities: Operates supermarkets.
Business type (SIC): Groceries—retail
Financial profile for 2010: Number of employees, 600
Corporate officers: Paul T. Gannon, Co-Pres.and C.E.O.; Mike Stigers, Co-Pres.; Larry Wahlstrom, Co-Pres.; Scott W. Ramsay, Exec. V.P. and C.F.O.; Daniel Zvoneck, C.F.O.; Scott Santos, Sr. V.P., Human Resources
Giving statement: Giving through the Shaw's Supermarkets, Inc. Corporate Giving Program and the Shaw's Supermarket Charitable Foundation.

Shaw's Supermarkets, Inc. Corporate Giving Program

750 West Center St.
West Bridgewater, MA 02379-1518
URL: http://www.shaws.com/about/community.html

Purpose and activities: As a complement to its foundation, Shaw's also makes charitable contributions to nonprofit organizations directly. Support is given primarily in areas of company operations in Maine, Massachusetts, New Hampshire, Rhode Island, and Vermont.
Fields of interest: Environment; Food services; Nutrition.
Type of support: Donated products; Employee volunteer services; General/operating support; In-kind gifts; Program development; Sponsorships.
Geographic limitations: Giving primarily in areas of company operations in MA, ME, NH, RI, and VT.
Support limitations: No support for third-party organizations, organizations that receive more than 30% of their funding through the United Way, or religious, fraternal, or labor organizations. No grants to individuals, or for fees for conferences, seminars, or travel, research, fees for participation in competitive programs, lobbying or political initiatives, school field trips, workforce development programs, travel or academic research, family or individual emergency relief, individual or team fundraising, or lobbying or political initiatives, advertising, parties, or ceremonies or memorials.
Publications: Application guidelines.
Application information: Applications accepted. Mailed, faxed, or e-mailed applications are not accepted. Application form required.
Applications should include a W-9 form.
Initial approach: Complete online application form
Final notification: 4 weeks prior to need

Shaw's Supermarket Charitable Foundation

(formerly Shaw's Market Trust Fund)
P.O. Box 1802
Providence, RI 02901-1802
Application address: c/o Bank of America, 2 Portland Sq., Portland, ME 04104

Establishment information: Trust established in 1959 in ME.
Donor: Shaw's Supermarkets, Inc.
Financial data (yr. ended 07/31/12): Assets, $248,615 (M); expenditures, $324,389; qualifying distributions, $320,311; giving activities include $320,311 for grants.
Purpose and activities: The foundation supports organizations involved with health, cancer, housing accessibility modifications, human services, and military and veterans.
Fields of interest: Health care, clinics/centers; Health care; Cancer; Home accessibility modifications; YM/YWCAs & YM/YWHAs; United Ways and Federated Giving Programs; Military/veterans' organizations.
Type of support: Building/renovation; Capital campaigns; General/operating support.
Geographic limitations: Giving limited to areas of company operations in MA, southern ME, and southern NH.
Support limitations: No grants to individuals.
Application information: Applications accepted. Application form not required.
Initial approach: Proposal
Deadline(s): None
Trustee: Bank of America, N.A.
EIN: 016008389

3428
J. F. Shea Company, Inc.

655 Brea Canyon Rd.
Walnut, CA 91789 (909) 594-9500

Company URL: http://www.jfshea.com
Establishment information: Established in 1881.
Company type: Private company
Business activities: Provides construction and real estate services.
Business type (SIC): Construction/miscellaneous heavy
Corporate officers: John F. Shea, Chair.; Peter O. Shea, Jr., Pres. and C.E.O.; James G. Shontere, C.F.O.
Board of director: John F. Shea, Chair.
Subsidiary: Shea Sand and Gravel, Redding, CA
Giving statement: Giving through the J. F. Shea Company Foundation.

J. F. Shea Company Foundation

655 Brea Canyon Rd.
Walnut, CA 91789-3078

Establishment information: Established in 1967 in CA.
Donor: J.F. Shea Co., Inc.
Financial data (yr. ended 12/31/11): Assets, $5,814,650 (M); expenditures, $258,985; qualifying distributions, $252,105; giving activities include $252,105 for grants.
Purpose and activities: The foundation supports health centers and organizations involved with education, human services, and Catholicism.
Fields of interest: Secondary school/education; Education; Health care, clinics/centers; Children/youth, services; Family services, domestic violence; Human services; United Ways and Federated Giving Programs; Catholic agencies & churches.
Type of support: General/operating support; Program development.
Geographic limitations: Giving primarily in CA.
Support limitations: No grants to individuals.
Application information: Applications not accepted. Contributes only to pre-selected organizations.
Officers: John F. Shea, Pres.; Ronald L. Lakey, V.P.; Edmund H. Shea, Jr., Secy.; Peter O. Shea, Treas.
EIN: 952554052
Selected grants: The following grants are a representative sample of this grantmaker's funding activity:
$89,351 to Archdiocese of Los Angeles, Los Angeles, CA, 2010.
$50,000 to Simpson University, Redding, CA, 2010.
$13,750 to Verbum Dei High School, Los Angeles, CA, 2010.
$9,552 to Diocese of Orange, Orange, CA, 2010.
$1,000 to Natures Hotline, Los Angeles, CA, 2010.

3429
Shearman & Sterling LLP

599 Lexington Ave.
New York, NY 10022-7668 (212) 848-8772

Company URL: http://www.shearman.com
Establishment information: Established in 1873.
Company type: Private company
Business activities: Operates law firm.
Business type (SIC): Legal services
Offices: Palo Alto, San Francisco, CA; Washington, DC; New York, NY
International operations: Belgium; Brazil; Canada; China; France; Germany; Hong Kong; Italy; Japan; Singapore; United Arab Emirates
Giving statement: Giving through the Shearman & Sterling LLP Pro Bono Program.

Shearman & Sterling LLP Pro Bono Program

599 Lexington Ave.
New York, NY 10022-7668 (212) 848-8772
E-mail: scohen@shearman.com; Additional tel.: (212) 848-4000; URL: http://www.shearman.com/about/diversity/diversityglobally/

Contact: Saralyn M. Cohen, Dir. and Counsel, Pro Bono
Fields of interest: Legal services.
Type of support: Pro bono services - legal.
Application information: A Pro Bono Committee manages the pro bono program.

3430
Shell Oil Company

1 Shell Plz.
910 Louisiana St.
Houston, TX 77002 (713) 241-6161

Company URL: http://www.shellus.com
Establishment information: Established in 1953.
Company type: Subsidiary of a foreign company
Business activities: Conducts crude oil and natural gas exploration and production activities; distributes natural gas; operates gasoline service stations; manufactures petrochemicals.
Business type (SIC): Extraction/oil and gas; chemicals/industrial organic; gas production and distribution; gasoline service stations
Financial profile for 2010: Number of employees, 220,000; sales volume, $77,660,000,000
Corporate officers: Jorma Ollila, Chair.; Marvin E. Odum, Pres.; William C. Lowrey, Sr. V.P., Genl. Counsel, and Corp. Secy.
Board of director: Jorma Ollila, Chair.
Giving statement: Giving through the Shell Oil Company Contributions Program and the Shell Oil Company Foundation.

Shell Oil Company Contributions Program

1 Shell Plz.
910 Louisiana St., Ste. 4478A
Houston, TX 77252-2463
FAX: (713) 241-0663;
E-mail: hasting.stewart@shell.com

Contact: Hasting Stewart, Mgr., Social Investment
Purpose and activities: As a complement to its foundation, Shell also makes charitable contributions to nonprofit organizations directly. Support is given on a national basis.
Fields of interest: Environment, water resources; Employment, training.
Programs:
Motive Education Matching Gifts Program: Shell matches contributions made by its employees to nonprofit organizations involved with education on a one-for-one basis.
Shell Education Matching Gifts Program: Shell matches contributions made by its employees to nonprofit organizations involved with education. The first $500 is matched on a two-for-one basis, while the balance is matched one-for-one.
Type of support: Employee volunteer services; Program development; Scholarship funds; Sponsorships.

Geographic limitations: Giving on a national basis, with emphasis on areas of company operations, including Houston, TX; giving also to national organizations.
Support limitations: No support for religious organizations not of direct benefit to the entire community, or fraternal or labor organizations. No grants to individuals, or for operating expenses, conferences or symposia.
Application information: Applications accepted. The Social Investment Department handles giving. A contributions committee reviews all requests. Application form not required. Applicants should submit the following:
1) detailed description of project and amount of funding requested
Initial approach: Proposal to nearest company facility; letter, telephone, email, online application
Copies of proposal: 1
Committee meeting date(s): Weekly
Deadline(s): None
Final notification: Following review
Contributions Committee: Barbara Auzenne, Ext. Affairs Rep.; Debbie Breezoale, Volunteer Coord.; Jayme Cox, Mgr., Govt. Rels.; Dick Francis, Exec. Support; Karan Labat, Coord., Diversity Outreach; J. Pascoe, Issues Mgmt.; Hasting Stewart, Mgr., Social Invest; Frazier Wilson, Prog. Mgr.

Shell Oil Company Foundation

(formerly Shell Companies Foundation, Inc.)
1 Shell Plz., P.O. Box 4749
Houston, TX 77210-4749
FAX: (713) 241-3329;
E-mail: scofoundation@shellus.com

Establishment information: Incorporated in 1953 in NY.
Donors: Shell Oil Co.; Shell Exploration & Production; Motiva.
Financial data (yr. ended 12/31/11): Assets, $114,343,432 (M); gifts received, $247,877; expenditures, $3,672,986; qualifying distributions, $2,706,907; giving activities include $1,206,907 for 1 grant and $1,206,907 for employee matching gifts.
Purpose and activities: The foundation supports organizations involved with community development and through an employee matching gift program.
Fields of interest: Community/economic development; United Ways and Federated Giving Programs.
Program:
Matching Gifts Program: The foundation matches contributions made by employees and pensioners of Shell Oil to nonprofit organizations on a one-for-one basis from $25 to $5,500 per contributor, per year.
Type of support: Employee matching gifts; General/operating support.
Geographic limitations: Giving primarily in areas of company operations with emphasis on Houston, TX.
Support limitations: No support for religious organizations not of direct benefit to the entire community, fraternal or labor organizations, private foundations, or organizations located outside the U.S. No grants to individuals, or for endowments, capital campaigns, or general operating support, or conferences and seminars.
Application information: Applications not accepted. Contributes only to pre-selected organizations.
Officers and Directors:* Bruce Culpepper, Co-Pres.; Marvin E. Odum, Co-Pres.; Frazier Wilson, V.P.; Lynn S. Borgmeier, Secy.; A. M Nolte, Treas.; Smith Deborah, Cont.; Randy Braud; Lisa A. Davis; Cynthia A. P. Deere; Curtis R. Frasier; William C. Lowery; S. P. Methvin; M. Quartemain; Christopher B. Rice; Tom N. Smith.
Number of staff: 7
EIN: 136066583

3431
Shelter Mutual Insurance Company

1817 W. Broadway
Columbia, MO 65218 (573) 445-8441

Company URL: https://
Establishment information: Established in 1945.
Company type: Mutual company
Business activities: Sells casualty and life insurance.
Business type (SIC): Insurance/fire, marine, and casualty; insurance/life
Financial profile for 2011: Number of employees, 3,747; assets, $3,705,787,000; liabilities, $1,025,111,000
Corporate officers: J. Donald Duello, Chair. and Co-C.E.O.; Ann K. Covington, Vice-Chair.; J. David Moore, Pres. and Co-C.E.O.; Rick L. Means, Exec. V.P. and C.O.O.; Francis L. Thompson IV, V.P., Mktg.; Joe L. Moseley, V.P., Public Affairs; Randa C. Rawlins, Secy. and Genl. Counsel
Board of directors: J. Donald Duello, Chair.; Ann K. Covington, Vice-Chair.; Gerald T. Brouder; Randall C. Ferguson, Jr.; Raymond E. Jones; Philip K. Marblestone; Don A. McCubbin; Barry L. McKuin; J. David Moore
Giving statement: Giving through the Shelter Insurance Foundation.

Shelter Insurance Foundation

c/o Shelter Insurance Companies
1817 W. Broadway
Columbia, MO 65218-0001 (573) 214-4324

Establishment information: Established in 1981 in MO.
Donor: Shelter Mutual Insurance Co.
Contact: Joe L. Moseley, V.P. and Secy.
Financial data (yr. ended 06/30/11): Assets, $12,408,364 (M); gifts received, $133,110; expenditures, $698,856; qualifying distributions, $649,048; giving activities include $195,945 for 70 grants (high: $85,000; low: $25) and $453,103 for grants to individuals.
Purpose and activities: The foundation supports hospitals, parks, and organizations involved with education, breast cancer, Alzheimer's disease, child welfare, human services, and Christianity, and awards grants and scholarships to individuals.
Fields of interest: Secondary school/education; Higher education; Business school/education; Education; Hospitals (general); Breast cancer; Alzheimer's disease; Crime/violence prevention, child abuse; Recreation, parks/playgrounds; Big Brothers/Big Sisters; Children/youth, services; Homeless, human services; Human services; United Ways and Federated Giving Programs; Christian agencies & churches.
Programs:
Agent Scholarship Program: The foundation annually awards $1,500 college scholarships to graduating high school seniors in communities where there is a Shelter Mutual Insurance Company agent who participates in the program. The award is selected based on scholastic achievement, participation and leadership in school and community activities, citizenship and moral character, and educational goals.
F.V. Heinkel Award: The foundation awards $2,000 grants to individuals and organizations that have demonstrated excellence in any area of science, medical research, health, education, history, athletics, or any other field designated by the foundation's board of directors. The award is named in honor of Shelter Insurance Companies' founder and first chairman.
William H. Lang Vocational Excellence Award: The foundation annually honors an outstanding vocational-education graduate of Missouri School for the Deaf (MSD). The award is presented at commencement ceremonies and includes a $500 savings bond.
Type of support: Employee matching gifts; Employee-related scholarships; General/operating support; Grants to individuals; Scholarship funds; Scholarships—to individuals.
Geographic limitations: Giving primarily in areas of company operations in AR, CO, IA, IL, IN, KS, KY, LA, MO, MS, NE, NV, OK, and TN.
Application information: Applications accepted. Applicants should submit the following:
1) detailed description of project and amount of funding requested
Initial approach: Proposal; contact foundation or participating school for application form for Agent Scholarship Program
Deadline(s): None; varies for Agent Scholarship Program
Officers and Directors:* J. David Moore*, Pres.; Joe L. Moseley*, V.P. and Secy.; S. Daniel Clapp, Treas.; Don A. McCubbin; Rick L. Means; Mary Lou Mills; Madison M. Moore.
EIN: 431224155
Selected grants: The following grants are a representative sample of this grantmaker's funding activity:
$85,000 to United Way, Heart of Missouri, Columbia, MO, 2011.
$6,500 to Big Brothers Big Sisters of Central Missouri, Columbia, MO, 2011.
$6,450 to Columbia College, Columbia, MO, 2011.
$6,350 to Truman State University, Kirksville, MO, 2011.
$5,000 to Missouri Valley College, Marshall, MO, 2011.
$2,000 to University of Arkansas, School of Business, Fayetteville, AR, 2011.
$1,750 to Missouri State University, Springfield, MO, 2011.
$1,460 to Central Christian College of the Bible, Moberly, MO, 2011.
$1,000 to Intersection, Columbia, MO, 2011.
$1,000 to Youth Entrepreneurs of Kansas, Wichita, KS, 2011.

3432
The Shelton Companies

5955 Carnegie Blvd., Ste. 225
Charlotte, NC 28209 (704) 557-2200

Establishment information: Established in 1978.
Company type: Private company
Business activities: Conducts real estate investment activities.
Business type (SIC): Investors/miscellaneous
Corporate officer: James E. Harris, Sr. V.P. and C.F.O.
Giving statement: Giving through the Shelton Foundation.

The Shelton Foundation

286 Cabernet Ln.
Dobson, NC 27017-6322

Establishment information: Established in 1985 in NC.
Donors: The Shelton Cos.; Charles M. Shelton; R. Edwin Shelton; Ballard G. Norwood.
Financial data (yr. ended 12/31/11): Assets, $1,360,768 (M); gifts received, $82,000; expenditures, $89,998; qualifying distributions, $81,875; giving activities include $81,875 for grants.
Purpose and activities: The foundation supports hospices and hospitals and organizations involved with historic preservation, higher education, and children and youth.
Fields of interest: Education; Youth development; Religion.
Type of support: General/operating support.
Geographic limitations: Giving limited to NC.
Support limitations: No grants to individuals.
Application information: Applications not accepted. Unsolicited requests for funds not accepted.
Officers: Charles M. Shelton, Pres.; R. Edwin Shelton, V.P.; Ballard G. Norwood, Secy.-Treas.
EIN: 581596729

3433
Shenandoah Life Insurance, Co.

2301 Brambleton Ave. S.W.
P. O. Box 12847
Roanoke, VA 24015-4701 (540) 985-4400

Company URL: http://www.shenlife.com
Establishment information: Established in 1914.
Company type: Mutual company
Business activities: Sells life and health insurance.
Business type (SIC): Insurance/life; insurance/accident and health
Corporate officers: Henry C. Wolf, Chair.; Hans L. Carstensen III, Pres. and C.E.O.; Michael W. Coffman, Sr. V.P., C.F.O., and Treas.; Robert R. Peterson, Jr., Sr. V.P. and C.I.O.; Andrew S. Vipperman, V.P. and Cont.; Kathleen M. Kronau, Sr. V.P., Genl. Counsel, and Secy.; Lee B. Mowry III, V.P., Mktg. and Sales; Todd A. Putney, V.P., Human Resources
Board of directors: Henry C. Wolf, Chair.; Gerald L. Baliles; Robert W. Clark; Gordon K. Davies; Ralph B. Everett; W. Heywood Fralin; Alice W. Handy; Kathryn B. McQuade; Charles W. Steger; Joseph H. Vipperman; Karen F. Washabau
Subsidiary: Old Dominion Life Insurance Co., Roanoke, VA
Giving statement: Giving through the Shenandoah Life Insurance Company Contributions Program.

Shenandoah Life Insurance Company Contributions Program

2301 Brambleton Ave. S.W.
Roanoke, VA 24015-4701 (800) 848-5433
E-mail: info@shenlife.com; URL: https://www.shenlife.com/home/wcm/connect/shenlife+public+site/Shenandoah+Life/About+Us/Community+Focused/

Purpose and activities: Shenandoah makes charitable contributions to nonprofit organizations involved with awareness and fund-raising events, senior programs, education, and health services. Support is given primarily in Roanoke, Virginia; giving also to national organizations.
Fields of interest: Education; Health care; Human services, fund raising/fund distribution; Aging, centers/services.
Type of support: Employee volunteer services; General/operating support.
Geographic limitations: Giving primarily in Roanoke, VA, and to national organizations.

3434
Shenandoah Telecommunications Company

500 Shentel Way
Edinburg, VA 22824 (540) 984-4141
FAX: (540) 984-3763

Company URL: http://www.shentel.com
Establishment information: Established in 1902.
Company type: Public company
Company ticker symbol and exchange: SHEN/NASDAQ
Business activities: Operates holding company; provides local telephone communications services.
Business type (SIC): Telephone communications; holding company
Financial profile for 2012: Number of employees, 693; assets, $570,740,000; sales volume, $288,070,000; pre-tax net income, $28,610,000; expenses, $253,420,000; liabilities, $362,890,000
Corporate officers: Christopher E. French, Chair., Pres., and C.E.O.; Earle A. MacKenzie, Exec. V.P. and C.O.O.; Adele M. Skolits, V.P., Finance, and C.F.O.; William L. Pirtle, V.P., Sales and Mktg.; Ann E. Flowers, V.P. and Genl. Counsel; Tom Whitaker, V.P., Opers.
Board of directors: Christopher E. French, Chair.; Ken L. Burch; Tracy Fitzsimmons; John W. Flora; Richard L. Koontz, Jr.; Dales S. Lam; Jonelle St. John; James E. Zerkel II
Giving statement: Giving through the ShenTel Foundation.
Company EIN: 541162807

ShenTel Foundation

P.O. Box 459
Edinburg, VA 22824-0459 (540) 984-5209

Establishment information: Established in 1990 in VA.
Donor: Shenandoah Telecommunications Co.
Contact: Christopher E. French, Pres.
Financial data (yr. ended 12/31/11): Assets, $1,453,593 (M); expenditures, $65,240; qualifying distributions, $65,205; giving activities include $65,205 for grants.
Purpose and activities: The foundation supports organizations involved with arts and culture, education, health, youth development, and human services.
Fields of interest: Education; Health organizations; Human services.
Type of support: General/operating support.
Geographic limitations: Giving primarily in areas of company operations in Edinburgh, VA.
Support limitations: No grants to individuals.
Application information: Applications accepted. Application form required.
Initial approach: Letter
Deadline(s): None
Officers: Christopher E. French, Pres.; Earle A. Mackenzie, Exec. V.P.; Adele M. Skolits, V.P., Finance & Treas.
EIN: 541549765

3435
Sheppard, Mullin, Richter & Hampton LLP

333 S. Hope St., 43rd Fl.
Los Angeles, CA 90071 (213) 617-4101

Company URL: http://careers.sheppardmullin.com/
Establishment information: Established in 1927.
Company type: Private company
Business activities: Operates law firm.
Business type (SIC): Legal services
Corporate officer: Jason Kearnaghan, Chair.
Board of director: Jason Kearnaghan, Chair.
Offices: Costa Mesa, Los Angeles, Palo Alto, San Diego, San Francisco, Santa Barbara, CA; Washington, DC; Chicago, IL; New York, NY
International operations: Belgium; China; England
Giving statement: Giving through the Sheppard, Mullin, Richter & Hampton LLP Pro Bono Program.

Sheppard, Mullin, Richter & Hampton LLP Pro Bono Program

333 S. Hope St., 43rd Fl.
Los Angeles, CA 90071-1406 (212) 634-3095
E-mail: DBrown@sheppardmullin.com; URL: http://careers.sheppardmullin.com/about-probono.html

Contact: Daniel L. Brown Esq., Partner, Pro Bono Chair
Fields of interest: Legal services.
Type of support: Pro bono services - legal.
Application information: A Pro Bono Committee manages the pro bono program.

3436
Sherman & Howard L.L.C.

633 17th St., Ste. 3000
Denver, CO 80202-3622 (303) 297-2900

Company URL: http://www.shermanhoward.com
Establishment information: Established in 1892.
Company type: Private company
Business activities: Operates law firm.
Business type (SIC): Legal services
Offices: Phoenix, AZ; Aspen, Colorado Springs, Denver, Steamboat Springs, Vail, CO; Las Vegas, Reno, NV; Casper, WY
Giving statement: Giving through the Sherman & Howard L.L.C. Pro Bono Program.

Sherman & Howard L.L.C. Pro Bono Program

633 17th St., Ste. 3000
Denver, CO 80202-3622
URL: http://www.shermanhoward.com/AbouttheFirm/ProBono/

Contact: Rebecca Fischer Esq., Member
Fields of interest: Legal services.
Type of support: Pro bono services - legal.
Application information: An attorney coordinates pro bono projects.

3437
The Sherwin-Williams Company
101 W. Prospect Ave.
Cleveland, OH 44115-1075 (216) 566-2000
FAX: (216) 566-3310

Company URL: http://www.sherwin-williams.com
Establishment information: Established in 1866.
Company type: Public company
Company ticker symbol and exchange: SHW/NYSE
Business activities: Manufactures, distributes, and sells house paint and related products.
Business type (SIC): Paints and allied products; chemicals/industrial inorganic; chemicals/industrial organic; chemical preparations/miscellaneous; manufacturing/miscellaneous; paint, glass, and wallpaper stores
Financial profile for 2012: Number of employees, 34,154; assets, $6,234,740,000; sales volume, $9,534,460,000; pre-tax net income, $907,310,000; expenses, $8,627,150,000; liabilities, $4,442,930,000
Fortune 1000 ranking: 2012—282nd in revenues, 282nd in profits, and 531st in assets
Forbes 2000 ranking: 2012—968th in sales, 881st in profits, and 1745th in assets
Corporate officers: Christopher M. Connor, Chair. and C.E.O.; John G. Morikis, Pres. and C.O.O.; Sean P. Hennessy, Sr. V.P., Finance and C.F.O.; Catherine M. Kilbane, Sr. V.P., Genl. Counsel, and Secy.; Robert J. Wells, Sr. V.P., Corp. Comms. and Public Affairs; Steven J. Oberfeld, Sr. V.P., Corp. Planning and Dev.; Thomas E. Hopkins, Sr. V.P., Human Resources; Jeffrey J. Miklich, V.P. and Treas.; Allen J. Mistysyn, V.P. and Corp. Cont.; Richard M. Weaver, V.P., Admin.
Board of directors: Christopher M. Connor, Chair.; Arthur F. Anton; David F. Hodnik; Thomas G. Kadien; Richard J. Kramer; Susan J. Kropf; Richard K. Smucker; John M. Stropki
Plants: Emeryville, Ontario, Victorville, CA; Orlando, Winter Haven, FL; Atlanta, Lawrenceville, Manchester, Morrow, GA; Chicago, Effingham, Flora, Homewood, Rockford, South Holland, IL; Greencastle, Terre Haute, IN; Andover, Coffeyville, KS; Richmond, KY; Baltimore, Beltsville, Crisfield, MD; Holland, MI; Fernley, Reno, NV; Greensboro, NC; Bedford Heights, Cincinnati, Columbus, Grove City, OH; Portland, OR; Fredericksburg, PA; Fountain Inn, SC; Memphis, TN; Arlington, Ennis, Garland, Waco, TX; Portsmouth, VA
International operations: Argentina; Brazil; Canada; Cayman Islands; Chile; China; Curacao; India; Ireland; Jamaica; Japan; Mexico; Peru; Philippines; Portugal; Russia; Singapore; United Kingdom; Uruguay; Venezuela; Vietnam
Historic mergers: M. A. Bruder & Sons, Inc. (June 1, 2007)
Giving statement: Giving through the Sherwin-Williams Foundation.
Company EIN: 340526850

The Sherwin-Williams Foundation
101 Prospect Ave.
1180 Midland
Cleveland, OH 44115-1093 (216) 566-2000

Establishment information: Incorporated in 1964 in OH.
Donor: The Sherwin-Williams Co.
Contact: Maria L. Haller, Dir., Community Engagement
Financial data (yr. ended 12/31/11): Assets, $15,103,723 (M); gifts received, $250,000; expenditures, $828,075; qualifying distributions, $731,311; giving activities include $594,640 for grants (high: $199,000; low: $72) and $136,671 for 375 employee matching gifts.
Purpose and activities: The foundation supports organizations that provide community solutions in the areas of children's health and education leading to economic independence.
Fields of interest: Health care; Disasters, preparedness/services; Children, services; Human services; Community/economic development Children/youth; Economically disadvantaged.
Programs:
Employee Relief Fund: Established after Hurricane Katrina, the Employee Relief Fund allows employees to make donations that will go directly to affected Sherwin-Williams employees in the event of a disaster.
Grants for Volunteers: A donation to a non-profit organization can be made by the Company upon the organization's verification that the employee or retiree has completed at least 50 hours of volunteer service for the organization within one calendar year.
Matching Gifts for Volunteer Leaders: Eligible employees, serving on the governing body of a qualified non-profit organization (i.e., as a Director or Trustee) may submit requests for the Company to match their personal contributions.
Matching Gifts to Education: Eligible employees may submit requests for the Company to match their personal contributions to qualified education institutions, including: four-year colleges and universities, two-year junior and community colleges, graduate and professional schools, and state or national independent college funds.
Scholarships for Employee Dependents: Annually, twelve dependents of employees are selected from a pool of applicants to receive $2,000 scholarships to the college or university of their choice.
The Sherman-Williams Foundation Employee Matching Gifts Program: All active, full-time, salaried employees with at least one year of service and retirees are eligible to participate in the program.
The Sherwin-Williams Grant: The $50,000 Sherwin-Williams Grant is awarded annually by the Foundation to a non-profit organization that exemplifies innovation in one of two primary focus areas and that maximizes the company's impact on the community.
Type of support: Annual campaigns; Capital campaigns; Emergency funds; Employee matching gifts; Employee-related scholarships; General/operating support; Program development.
Geographic limitations: Giving primarily in areas of company operations, with emphasis on Cleveland, OH.
Support limitations: No support for sectarian, labor, veterans', or fraternal organizations, or tax-supported organizations. No grants to individuals, or for endowments, start-up needs, emergency needs, debt reduction, land acquisition, special projects, research, fellowships, publications, advertising, or conferences; no loans.
Application information: Applications not accepted.
Officers and Trustees:* Christopher M. Connor*, Pres.; John G. Morikis*, V.P.; Sean P. Hennessy*, Secy.-Treas.; Thomas E. Hopkins; Catherine Kilbane; Ellen M. Stephens; Robert J. Wells.
EIN: 346555476

3438
Shipman & Goodwin LLP
1 Constitution Plz.
Hartford, CT 06103-1919 (860) 251-5723

Company URL: http://www.shipmangoodwin.com/home.aspx
Company type: Private company
Business activities: Operates law firm.
Business type (SIC): Legal services
Offices: Greenwich, Hartford, Lakeville, Stamford, CT; Washington, DC
Giving statement: Giving through the Shipman & Goodwin LLP Pro Bono Program.

Shipman & Goodwin LLP Pro Bono Program
1 Constitution Plz.
Hartford, CT 06103-1919 (860) 251-5505
E-mail: vfinn@goodwin.com; URL: http://www.shipmangoodwin.com/municipal_law/

Contact: Vaughan Finn, Partner
Fields of interest: Legal services.
Type of support: Pro bono services - legal.
Application information: An attorney coordinates pro bono projects.

3439
Shook, Hardy & Bacon LLP
2555 Grand Blvd.
Kansas City, MO 64108-2613
(816) 559-2380

Company URL: http://www.shb.com/default.aspx
Establishment information: Established in 1889.
Business activities: Operates law firm.
Business type (SIC): Legal services
Corporate officer: John F. Murphy, Chair.
Offices: Irvine, San Francisco, CA; Washington, DC; Miami, Tampa, FL; Kansas City, MO; Houston, TX
International operations: Switzerland; United Kingdom
Giving statement: Giving through the Shook, Hardy & Bacon L.L.P Pro Bono Program.

Shook, Hardy & Bacon L.L.P Pro Bono Program
2555 Grand Blvd.
Kansas City, MO 64108-2613 (816) 559-2380
E-mail: jjustus@shb.com; URL: http://www.shb.com/probono.aspx

Contact: Jolie L. Justus, Dir. Pro Bono Svcs.
Fields of interest: Legal services.
Type of support: Pro bono services - legal.
Application information: A Pro Bono Committee manages the pro bono program.

3440
Shopko Stores Operating Co., LLC
(formerly Shopko Stores, Inc.)
700 Pilgrim Way
Green Bay, WI 54304-9060 (920) 429-2211

Company URL: http://www.shopko.com
Establishment information: Established in 1962.
Company type: Subsidiary of a private company

Business activities: Operates department stores; operates drug stores.
Business type (SIC): Department stores; drug stores and proprietary stores
Financial profile for 2011: Number of employees, 13,500; sales volume, $2,200,000,000
Corporate officers: Michael J. Bettiga, Exec. V.P. and C.O.O.; Gary Gibson, V.P. and Treas.
Historic mergers: Pamida, Inc. (January 4, 2012)
Giving statement: Giving through the ShopKo Stores, Inc. Corporate Giving Program, the Pamida Foundation, and the Shopko Foundation, Inc.

ShopKo Stores, Inc. Corporate Giving Program

P.O. Box 19060
Green Bay, WI 54307-9060 (920) 429-2211
URL: http://www.shopko.com/company/community-giving

Purpose and activities: As a complement to its foundation, ShopKo also makes charitable contributions to nonprofit organizations directly. Support is given primarily in areas of company operations in California, Idaho, Illinois, Iowa, Michigan, Minnesota, Montana, Nebraska, Oregon, South Dakota, Utah, Washington, and Wisconsin.
Fields of interest: Optometry/vision screening; Salvation Army; Children, services; United Ways and Federated Giving Programs.
Type of support: Employee volunteer services; General/operating support; In-kind gifts.
Geographic limitations: Giving primarily in areas of company operations in CA, IA, ID, IL, MI, MN, MT, NE, OR, SD, UT, WA, and WI.

Pamida Foundation

8800 F. St.
Omaha, NE 68127-1507 (402) 596-7492

Establishment information: Established in 1983 in NE.
Donor: Pamida, Inc.
Financial data (yr. ended 01/31/12): Assets, $782,171 (M); gifts received, $1,396,510; expenditures, $1,082,890; qualifying distributions, $1,082,890; giving activities include $733,532 for 1,149 grants (high: $55,637; low: $48).
Purpose and activities: The foundation supports programs designed to encourage and educate youth; help families in need; and enhance quality of life for senior citizens.
Fields of interest: Education; Health care; Food banks; Family services; Aging, centers/services Youth; Aging; Economically disadvantaged.
Type of support: General/operating support; Matching/challenge support; Program development; Sponsorships.
Geographic limitations: Giving limited to areas of company operations in IA, IL, IN, KS, KY, MI, MN, MO, MT, ND, NE, OH, SD, TN, WI, and WY.
Support limitations: No support for religious organizations, for-profit businesses, school cubs, athletic teams, political, labor, or fraternal organizations, or discriminatory organizations. No grants to individuals, or for sports events, advertising in event programs or yearbooks, or mass solicitations by national or international organizations.
Application information: Applications accepted. Proposals should be submitted using organization letterhead. Additional information may be requested at a later date. Support is limited to 1 contribution per organization during any given year. Application form not required. Applicants should submit the following:
1) copy of IRS Determination Letter
2) brief history of organization and description of its mission
3) geographic area to be served
4) descriptive literature about organization
5) detailed description of project and amount of funding requested
Initial approach: Proposal
Copies of proposal: 1
Deadline(s): None
Officers: W. Paul Jones, Pres.; Michael J. Bettiga, V.P.; Chad Frazell, Secy.; Mary Meixelsperger, Treas.; Jessica Strohman, Exec. Dir.
EIN: 470656225
Selected grants: The following grants are a representative sample of this grantmaker's funding activity:
$1,000 to United Way of Greater Cincinnati, Cincinnati, OH, 2009.

Shopko Foundation, Inc.

P.O. Box 19060
Green Bay, WI 54307-9060 (920) 497-2211
E-mail: ShopkoFoundation@Shopko.com;
URL: http://www.shopko.com/company/community-giving-shopko-foundation
Additional email:
ShopkoFamilyScholarship@Shopko.com

Establishment information: Established in 2005 in WI.
Financial data (yr. ended 12/31/11): Revenue, $890,072; assets, $1,148,476 (M); gifts received, $892,202; expenditures, $991,450; program services expenses, $909,656; giving activities include $856,796 for 28 grants and $46,750 for 20 grants to individuals.
Purpose and activities: The foundation supports the wellbeing of Shopko communities, teammates, and the company.
Fields of interest: Education; Athletics/sports, Special Olympics; Youth development; Human services.
Programs:
Community Charitable Grants: Grants are available to support charitable programs and events in Shopko communities.
Green Bay Area Community Grants: This grant program supports programs and projects that enhance the quality of life in the Green Bay Area and northern Wisconsin.
Shopko Teammate and Family Scholarship Program: Scholarships of up to $2,500 are available to full- or part-time Shopko employees and their dependent children (under the age of 24), to attend postsecondary accredited programs, including two- or four-year colleges and universities, as well as vocational and technical schools. Scholarships are awarded based on academic record, leadership, participation in school and community activities, work experience, and recommendations. Applicant must be a U.S. citizen and either a Shopko teammate or a dependent child of Shopko teammate.
Teammate Community Service Grants Program: Grants of up to $1,000 are available to organizations with which Shopko employees (either full- or part-time) have volunteered their time. Eligible organizations must have 501(c)(3) status; Shopko employees must have been an 'active' participant in in the organization, preferably in a leadership role.
Type of support: General/operating support.
Geographic limitations: Giving limited to CA, IA, ID, IL, MI, MN, MT, NE, OR, SD, UT, WA, and WI.
Publications: Application guidelines.
Application information: Applications accepted. Applicants should submit the following:
1) geographic area to be served
2) how project's results will be evaluated or measured
3) detailed description of project and amount of funding requested
Initial approach: Download application online
Deadline(s): Varies
Officers: W. Paul Jones, Pres.; Michael J. Bettiga, V.P.; Chad Frazell, Secy.; Mary Meixelsperger, Treas.
EIN: 200917227
Selected grants: The following grants are a representative sample of this grantmaker's funding activity:
$30,000 to March of Dimes Foundation, White Plains, NY, 2007.
$15,000 to Chamber of Commerce Foundation, Green Bay Area, Green Bay, WI, 2007.
$12,000 to Bellin Foundation, Green Bay, WI, 2007.
$10,000 to New North, Inc., De Pere, WI, 2007.
$5,000 to Boys and Girls Club of Green Bay, Green Bay, WI, 2007.
$2,500 to University of Wisconsin, Eau Claire, WI, 2007.
$2,500 to University of Wisconsin, Eau Claire, WI, 2007.
$2,500 to University of Wisconsin-Fox Valley, Menasha, WI, 2007.
$2,000 to Make-A-Wish Foundation of Idaho, Boise, ID, 2007.
$1,000 to Multiple Sclerosis Society, National, Wisconsin Chapter, Hartland, WI, 2007.

3441
Shuford Development, Inc.

1985 Tate Blvd., S.E., Ste. 54
Hickory, NC 28602-1433 (828) 328-8817

Establishment information: Established in 1995.
Company type: Subsidiary of a private company
Business activities: Operates apartment buildings.
Business type (SIC): Real estate operators and lessors
Corporate officer: C. Hunt Shuford, Jr., Pres.
Giving statement: Giving through the Shuford Industries Foundation Inc.

Shuford Industries Foundation Inc.

(formerly Century Foundation, Inc.)
c/o Richard Reese
P.O. Box 608
Hickory, NC 28603

Establishment information: Established in 1978.
Donors: Shuford Industries, Inc.; CV Industries, Inc.; Shuford Development, Inc.
Financial data (yr. ended 12/31/11): Assets, $29,819 (M); gifts received, $160,000; expenditures, $143,326; qualifying distributions, $142,600; giving activities include $142,600 for 14 grants (high: $62,000; low: $400).
Purpose and activities: The foundation supports organizations involved with arts and culture, education, human services, and Christianity.
Fields of interest: Arts; Higher education; Human services.
Geographic limitations: Giving primarily in Catawba County, NC.
Support limitations: No grants to individuals.
Application information: Applications not accepted. Unsolicited requests for funds not accepted.
Officers: H. F. Shuford, Jr., Pres.; N. S. Dowdy, V.P.; A. A. Shuford II, V.P.; C. H. Shuford, V.P.; Richard L. Reese, Secy.-Treas.
Number of staff: None.
EIN: 581394774

3442
Shugart Enterprises, LLC
221 Jonestown Rd.
Winston-Salem, NC 27104 (336) 765-9661

Company URL: http://www.buyshugart.com/
Establishment information: Established in 1966.
Company type: Private company
Business activities: Builds houses.
Business type (SIC): Operative builders
Corporate officer: Grover F. Shugart, Jr., Pres.
Giving statement: Giving through the Shugart Family Foundation.

Shugart Family Foundation
4004 Long Meadow Ln.
Winston-Salem, NC 27106-6315

Establishment information: Established in 2000 in NC.
Donors: Shugart Enterprises, LLC; Shugart Management Inc.
Financial data (yr. ended 04/30/12): Assets, $782,753 (M); expenditures, $275,425; qualifying distributions, $274,454; giving activities include $274,454 for grants.
Purpose and activities: The foundation supports organizations involved with education, health, hunger, human services, business, and Christianity.
Fields of interest: Education; Health care; Food banks; Food distribution, meals on wheels; Boys & girls clubs; Salvation Army; Children, services; Developmentally disabled, centers & services; Human services; Business/industry; United Ways and Federated Giving Programs; Christian agencies & churches.
Type of support: General/operating support.
Geographic limitations: Giving primarily in NC; giving also to national organizations.
Support limitations: No grants to individuals.
Application information: Applications not accepted. Contributes only to pre-selected organizations.
Directors: Grover F. Shugart, Jr.; Kay W. Shugart.
EIN: 562230054
Selected grants: The following grants are a representative sample of this grantmaker's funding activity:
$4,000 to Feed the Children, Oklahoma City, OK, 2011.
$3,000 to Child Evangelism Fellowship, Warrenton, MO, 2011.
$3,000 to Smile Train, New York, NY, 2011.
$1,500 to Covenant House, New York, NY, 2011.
$1,100 to Special Olympics, Washington, DC, 2011.
$1,000 to American Cancer Society, Atlanta, GA, 2011.
$1,000 to American Heart Association, Dallas, TX, 2011.
$1,000 to Billy Graham Evangelistic Association, Charlotte, NC, 2011.

3443
Shure Manufacturing Corp.
1901 W. Main St.
Washington, MO 63090 (636) 390-7100

Company URL: http://www.shureusa.com
Establishment information: Established in 1940.
Company type: Private company
Business activities: Manufacturers commercial and industrial furniture and steel shelving products.
Business type (SIC): Furniture/office; fixtures/office and store; furniture and fixtures/miscellaneous; metal products/fabricated; manufacturing/miscellaneous
Corporate officers: Daniel E. Richardson, Chair.; Andrew T. Richardson, Pres. and C.E.O.; Peter B. Richardson, V.P., Sales and Mktg.
Board of director: Daniel E. Richardson, Chair.
Giving statement: Giving through the Shure and Richardson Foundation.

The Shure and Richardson Foundation
1901 W. Main St.
Washington, MO 63090-1005

Donor: Shure Manufacturing Corp.
Financial data (yr. ended 09/30/12): Assets, $109,368 (M); expenditures, $2,058; qualifying distributions, $2,050; giving activities include $2,050 for grants.
Purpose and activities: The foundation supports organizations involved with music and education.
Fields of interest: Performing arts, music; Secondary school/education; Higher education; Education.
Type of support: General/operating support.
Geographic limitations: Giving primarily in MO.
Support limitations: No grants to individuals.
Application information: Applications not accepted. Unsolicited requests for funds not accepted.
Trustee: Andrew Richardson.
EIN: 436052003

3444
SI Financial Group, Inc.
803 Main St.
Willimantic, CT 06226 (860) 423-4581

Company URL: http://www.savingsinstitute.com
Establishment information: Established in 1842.
Company type: Public company
Company ticker symbol and exchange: SIFI/NASDAQ
Business activities: Operates bank holding company; operates savings bank.
Business type (SIC): Savings institutions; holding company
Financial profile for 2012: Number of employees, 239; assets, $953,250,000; pre-tax net income, $1,360,000; liabilities, $827,490,000
Corporate officers: Henry P. Hinckley, Chair.; Rheo Arthur Brouillard, Pres. and C.E.O.; Brian J. Hull, Exec. V.P., C.O.O., C.F.O., and Treas.; Laurie L. Gervais, Sr. V.P. and Corp. Secy.
Board of directors: Henry P. Hinckley, Chair.; Mark D. Alliod; Rheo Arthur Brouillard; Donna M. Evan; Roger Engle; Michael R. Garvey; Robert O. Gillard
Subsidiary: Savings Institute Bank and Trust Company, Willimantic, CT
Giving statement: Giving through the SI Financial Group Foundation, Inc.
Company EIN: 841655232

SI Financial Group Foundation, Inc.
803 Main St.
P.O. Box 95
Willimantic, CT 06226 (860) 456-6509
E-mail: sifigfoundation@banksi.com; Application address: 676 Main St., Willimantic, CT 06226, tel.: (860) 456-6509; URL: https://www.savingsinstitute.com/si-group-foundation/

Establishment information: Established in 2004 in CT.
Donor: SI Financial Group, Inc.
Contact: Sandra M. Mitchell, Secy.
Financial data (yr. ended 12/31/11): Assets, $2,389,955 (M); gifts received, $521,720; expenditures, $75,939; qualifying distributions, $73,613; giving activities include $72,025 for 102 grants (high: $6,000; low: $5).
Purpose and activities: The foundation supports programs designed to promote community development through affordable housing, job training, and initiatives that assist economically disadvantaged people; provide basic human and health services for those at risk or in need; advance education through literacy and learning beyond the classroom; promote culture and arts through enrichment initiatives that build audiences for the arts, with emphasis on underserved populations; and promote environmental projects designed to preserve, protect, and revitalize natural resources.
Fields of interest: Arts; Education, reading; Education; Environment, natural resources; Environment; Health care; Employment, training; Housing/shelter, expense aid; Housing/shelter; Human services; Community/economic development Minorities; Economically disadvantaged.
Type of support: Annual campaigns; Capital campaigns; General/operating support; Program development; Scholarship funds; Sponsorships.
Geographic limitations: Giving primarily in areas of company operations in CT.
Support limitations: No support for political or fraternal organizations, or religious organizations not of the direct benefit to the entire community. No grants to individuals, or for political or lobbying activities.
Publications: Application guidelines.
Application information: Applications accepted. Late applications will not be considered. Applicants are asked to submit 10 copies of the application cover sheet, proposal, project budget, and organization current operating budget. Grant awards range from $500 to $25,000. Support is generally given for a period of one year. Application form required. Applicants should submit the following:
1) detailed description of project and amount of funding requested
2) brief history of organization and description of its mission
3) geographic area to be served
4) population served
5) timetable for implementation and evaluation of project
6) qualifications of key personnel
7) how project's results will be evaluated or measured
8) copy of current year's organizational budget and/or project budget
9) listing of additional sources and amount of support
10) copy of IRS Determination Letter
11) copy of most recent annual report/audited financial statement/990
12) listing of board of directors, trustees, officers and other key people and their affiliations

Initial approach: Download application cover sheet and mail proposal and cover sheet to foundation
Copies of proposal: 10
Deadline(s): Mar. 31 and Sept. 30
Final notification: June and Dec.

Officers: Rheo Arthur Brouillard, Chair. and Pres.; Sandra M. Mitchell, Secy.
Directors: William E. Anderson, Jr.; Robert C. Cushman, Sr.; Roger Engle; Donna M. Evan; Laurie L. Gervais; Karen M. Hoke; Brian J. Hull.
Trustee: Savings Institutue Bank & Trust.
EIN: 582683983

Selected grants: The following grants are a representative sample of this grantmaker's funding activity:
$1,000 to American Cancer Society, Atlanta, GA, 2009.

3445
Sidener Supply Company

P.O. Box 28446
St. Louis, MO 63146-0946 (314) 432-4700

Establishment information: Established in 2010.
Company type: Private company
Business activities: Sells waterworks equipment wholesale.
Business type (SIC): Hardware, plumbing, and heating equipment—wholesale; metals and minerals, except petroleum—wholesale; industrial machinery and equipment—wholesale
Giving statement: Giving through the Sidener Foundation.

Sidener Foundation

1829 Borman Circle Dr.
St. Louis, MO 63146-4136 (314) 991-0730
Application address: P.O. Box 28568, St. Louis, MO 63146

Establishment information: Established in 1976.
Donors: Sidener Supply Co.; Lesco Services, Inc.; CJT Enterprises, Inc.
Contact: Jill Gray, Treas.
Financial data (yr. ended 12/31/11): Assets, $1,562,913 (M); gifts received, $500; expenditures, $35,368; qualifying distributions, $30,000; giving activities include $30,000 for grants.
Purpose and activities: The foundation supports hospitals and organizations involved with autism, learning disorders, hunger, and human services.
Fields of interest: Animals/wildlife; Housing/shelter; Human services.
Type of support: General/operating support.
Geographic limitations: Giving primarily in St. Louis, MO.
Support limitations: No grants to individuals.
Application information: Applications accepted. Application form required. Applicants should submit the following:
1) copy of IRS Determination Letter
Initial approach: Letter of inquiry
Copies of proposal: 1
Board meeting date(s): Nov.
Deadline(s): Nov. 1 to Nov. 30
Officers: Roger D. Shannon, Pres.; L.E. Sidener II, Secy.; Jill Arnold, Treas.
EIN: 510189216

3446
Sidley Austin LLP

1 S. Dearborn St.
Chicago, IL 60603-2323 (202) 736-8339

Company URL: http://www.sidley.com/home.aspx
Establishment information: Established in 1914.
Company type: Private company
Business activities: Operates law firm.
Business type (SIC): Legal services
Offices: Los Angeles, Palo Alto, San Francisco, CA; Washington, DC; Chicago, IL; New York, NY; Dallas, TX
International operations: Australia; Belgium; China; Germany; Hong Kong; Japan; Singapore; Switzerland
Giving statement: Giving through the Sidley Austin LLP Pro Bono Program.

Sidley Austin LLP Pro Bono Program

1 S. Dearborn St.
Chicago, IL 60603-2323 (312) 853-7000
URL: http://www.sidley.com/probono/

Contact: Richard O'Malley, Chair., Pro Bono Comm.
Fields of interest: Legal services.
Type of support: Pro bono services - legal.
Application information: A Pro Bono Committee manages the pro bono program.

3447
Sidwell Materials, Inc.

4200 Maysville Pike
Zanesville, OH 43701 (740) 849-2422

Company URL: http://www.sidwellmaterials.com
Establishment information: Established in 1947.
Company type: Private company
Business activities: Provides limestone and related products and services.
Business type (SIC): Lumber and construction materials—wholesale
Financial profile for 2011: Number of employees, 100
Corporate officers: Jeffrey R. Sidwell, Pres.; Drake Prouty, Human Resources
Giving statement: Giving through the Sidwell Foundation.

The Sidwell Foundation

5240 Wortman Rd.
Zanesville, OH 43701-9382 (740) 849-2422

Establishment information: Established in 2006 in OH.
Donor: Sidwell Materials, Inc.
Contact: Jeffrey Sidwell, Pres.
Financial data (yr. ended 12/31/11): Assets, $684,015 (M); gifts received, $100,000; expenditures, $31,769; qualifying distributions, $30,961; giving activities include $30,468 for 19 grants (high: $5,000; low: $100).
Fields of interest: Health organizations; Safety/disasters; Youth development.
Geographic limitations: Giving primarily in OH.
Application information: Applications not accepted. Unsolicited requests for funds not accepted.
Officers: Jeffrey Sidwell, Pres.; Jennie Sidwell, V.P.; Adam Sidwell, Secy.
EIN: 203991810

3448
Siemens Corporation

527 Madison Ave., 8th Fl.
New York, NY 10022-4376 (212) 258-4000

Company URL: http://www.usa.siemens.com
Establishment information: Established in 1847.
Company type: Subsidiary of a foreign company
Business activities: Manufactures electrical and electronic products.
Business type (SIC): Electronic and other electrical equipment and components
Financial profile for 2010: Number of employees, 300; sales volume, $19,900,000,000
Corporate officers: Eric A. Spiegel, Pres. and C.E.O.; Klaus P. Stegemann, C.F.O.; Rose Marie E. Glazer, Sr. V.P., Genl. Counsel, and Secy.; Jim Whaley, Sr. V.P., Comms. and Mktg.; Michael Panigel, Sr. V.P., Human Resources; John Chestnut, V.P. and Cont.; David Getts, V.P., Corp. Finance
Subsidiary: Siemens Automotive, Auburn Hills, MI
Giving statement: Giving through the Siemens Corporation Contributions Program and the Siemens Foundation.

Siemens Corporation Contributions Program

300 New Jersey Ave., NW, Ste. 1000
Washington, DC 20001-2268 (202) 434-4800
FAX: (202) 434-4839; URL: http://www.usa.siemens.com/en/about_us/corporate_responsibility.htm

Purpose and activities: As a complement to its foundation, Siemens also makes charitable contributions to nonprofit organizations directly. Support is given primarily in areas of company operations.
Fields of interest: Arts; Higher education; Education; Environment; Health care; Community/economic development.
Type of support: Employee volunteer services; General/operating support; In-kind gifts.
Geographic limitations: Giving primarily in areas of company operations.

Siemens Foundation

170 Wood Ave. S.
Iselin, NJ 08830-2704 (877) 822-5233
FAX: (732) 603-5890;
E-mail: foundation.us@siemens.com; URL: http://www.siemens-foundation.org

Establishment information: Established in 1998 in NY.
Donor: Siemens Corp.
Financial data (yr. ended 09/30/10): Assets, $51,677,690 (M); gifts received, $4,261,225; expenditures, $7,612,254; qualifying distributions, $7,539,804; giving activities include $752,605 for 13 grants (high: $467,705; low: $1,000) and $874,094 for 146 grants to individuals (high: $23,000; low: $500).
Purpose and activities: The foundation supports programs designed to enhance math and science education.
Fields of interest: Secondary school/education; Higher education; Teacher school/education; Education; Environment; Science, formal/general education; Chemistry; Mathematics; Physics; Engineering/technology; Computer science; Science Children/youth; Minorities.
Programs:
Siemens Competition in Math, Science, and Technology: The foundation fosters individual growth for high school students who are willing to undertake individual or team research projects in science, mathematics, engineering, and technology. Scholarships for winning projects range from $1,000 for regional finalists and up to $100,000 for national winners. The program is administered by the College Board. Visit URL: http://www.collegeboard.com/siemens/ for more information.
Siemens Awards for Advanced Placement: The foundation awards scholarships of $2,000 to students with the greatest number of scores of 5 on AP exams taken in grades 9, 10, and 11 in each of the 50 states and two national winners are awarded a $5,000 scholarship. Eligible exams are Biology, Calculus BC, Chemistry, Computer Science A,

Environmental Science, Physics C: Mechanics, Physics C: Electricity and Magnetism, and Statistics. The College Board identifies eligible students for Siemens Foundation.

Siemens Merit Scholarship Program: The foundation awards $6,000 college scholarships to children of employees of Siemens. The program is administered by National Merit Scholarship Corp.

Siemens STEM Academy: The foundation, in partnership with Discovery Education, provides professional development for teachers of science, technology, engineering, and mathematics (STEM). The academy includes a website of STEM best teaching practices; webinar series featuring leading scientists and experts in their field; the Siemens Teachers as Researchers (STARs) Program, an all expense-paid two-week professional development and research program at the Oak Ridge National Laboratory and the Pacific Northwest National Laboratory; and the STEM Institute, an all expense-paid week-long professional development experience at Discovery Communications. Visit URL: http://www.siemensstemacademy.com/ for more information.

Siemens We Can Change the World Challenge: The foundation awards grants and prizes to students in grades K-12 who uses the fundamentals of scientific methods to address environmental problems in their own backyard. Students, while working with a teacher or mentor, researches, creates green solutions, and shares their results with other students nationwide. Prizes include a grant to the participants school, savings bonds, an appearance on Planet Green, a presentation at the United Nations, a Discovery trip, a pocket video camera, and a Siemens We Can Change the World Challenge green prize pack. Visit URL: http://www.wecanchange.com/ for more information.

Type of support: Employee-related scholarships; General/operating support; Scholarship funds; Scholarships—to individuals.

Geographic limitations: Giving primarily in GA, IL, NV, TX, and VA; giving on a national basis for Siemens Competition in Math, Science.

Publications: Application guidelines; Program policy statement.

Application information: Applications accepted.

Initial approach: Complete online application for Siemens Competition in Math, Science, and Technology and Siemens STARs and Institute; complete online registration for Siemens We Can Change the World Challenge

Copies of proposal: 1

Deadline(s): Oct. 1 for Siemens Competition in Math, Science, and Technology; Feb. 9 for Siemens STARs and Institute; Aug. 24 to Mar. 15 for Siemens We Can Change the World Challenge

Officers and Directors:* Thomas N. McCausland*, Chair.; James Whaley*, Vice-Chair.; Jeniffer Harper-Taylor, Pres.; Ken Cornelius; Daryl Dulaney; Judy Marks; Tom Miller; Michael Panigel; Michael Reitermann; Peter Y. Solmssen; Eric A. Spiegel; Klaus P. Stegeman; Randy H. Zwirn.

EIN: 522136074

Selected grants: The following grants are a representative sample of this grantmaker's funding activity:

$43,000 to Carnegie Mellon University, Pittsburgh, PA, 2010.

$42,100 to University of Notre Dame, Notre Dame, IN, 2010.

$40,000 to University of Texas, Austin, TX, 2010.

$5,000 to Mathematical Association of America, Washington, DC, 2010.

3449

Sierra Alloys Company

5467 Ayon Ave.
Irwindale, CA 91706-2044 (626) 969-6711

Company URL: http://www.sierraalloys.com

Establishment information: Established in 1974.

Company type: Private company

Business activities: Custom hot metal manufacturer.

Business type (SIC): Metal forgings and stampings

Corporate officers: Vicky McGee, V.P., Admin. and Human Resources; Letty Pinard, V.P., Opers.; John Leonard, Cont.

Giving statement: Giving through the Augustyn Foundation Trust.

Augustyn Foundation Trust

(formerly Sierra Alloys Foundation Trust)
5467 Ayon Ave.
Irwindale, CA 91706-2044 (626) 969-8011

Establishment information: Established in 1982 in CA.

Donors: Joseph P. Augustyn†; Sierra Alloys.

Contact: Joseph P. Augustyn, Tr.

Financial data (yr. ended 01/31/12): Assets, $1,878,756 (M); expenditures, $280,369; qualifying distributions, $272,279; giving activities include $264,820 for 64 grants (high: $55,000; low: $370).

Purpose and activities: The foundation supports paleontology museums and organizations involved with cultural awareness, K-12 education, conservation, animals and wildlife, cancer, children services, and Catholicism.

Fields of interest: Arts, cultural/ethnic awareness; Museums (specialized); Elementary/secondary education; Environment, natural resources; Environment, land resources; Animal welfare; Animals/wildlife; Cancer; Children, services; Catholic agencies & churches.

Type of support: General/operating support.

Geographic limitations: Giving primarily in CA.

Support limitations: No grants to individuals.

Application information: Applications accepted. Proposals should be submitted using organization letterhead. Application form required.

Initial approach: Proposal

Deadline(s): None

Trustees: Gretchen J. Augustyn.

EIN: 953673855

Selected grants: The following grants are a representative sample of this grantmaker's funding activity:

$8,000 to National Wildlife Federation, Reston, VA, 2012.

$5,000 to World Wildlife Fund, Washington, DC, 2012.

$4,000 to Nature Conservancy, Arlington, VA, 2012.

$2,000 to American Cancer Society, Atlanta, GA, 2012.

$2,000 to Defenders of Wildlife, Washington, DC, 2012.

$2,000 to Smile Train, New York, NY, 2012.

$1,000 to Special Olympics, Washington, DC, 2012.

3450

Sierra Electric Cooperative, Inc.

610 Hwy. 195
P.O. Box 290
Elephant Butte, NM 87935 (575) 744-5231

Company URL: http://www.sierraelectric.org

Establishment information: Established in 1941.

Company type: Cooperative

Business activities: Generates, transmits, and distributes electricity.

Business type (SIC): Electric services

Corporate officers: Jimmy R. Bason, Pres.; George Biel, V.P. and Treas.; Jay Seitz, Secy.

Board of directors: Jimmy Bason; George Biel; Larry Holmes; Charles McMath; Jay Seitz; Judy Smith; Darryl Sullivan; Walt Toothman; Oscar Lee Wood

Giving statement: Giving through the Sierra Electric Cooperative Education Foundation.

Sierra Electric Cooperative Education Foundation

P.O. Box 290
Elephant Butte, NM 87935-0293 (575) 744-5231

Donor: Sierra Electric Cooperative, Inc.

Contact: Jimmy Capps

Financial data (yr. ended 12/31/11): Assets, $147,699 (M); gifts received, $16,057; expenditures, $8,847; qualifying distributions, $7,950; giving activities include $7,600 for 13 grants to individuals (high: $1,250; low: $500).

Purpose and activities: The foundation awards college scholarships to active members and the immediate family members of active members of Sierra Electric Cooperative.

Fields of interest: Higher education.

Type of support: Scholarships—to individuals.

Geographic limitations: Giving limited to areas of company operations.

Application information: Applications accepted. Application form required.

Initial approach: Contact foundation for application form

Deadline(s): None

Officers: Jimmy R. Bason, Pres.; Walter Toothman, V.P.; Jay Seitz, Secy.; George Biel, Treas.

EIN: 850352648

3451

Sierra Pacific Industries

19794 Riverside Ave.
P.O. Box 496028
Anderson, CA 96007 (530) 378-8000

Company URL: http://www.spi-ind.com

Establishment information: Established in 1920.

Company type: Private company

Business activities: Manufactures lumber and wood products and moldings.

Business type (SIC): Wood products/miscellaneous; wood millwork

Financial profile for 2012: Number of employees, 3,700; sales volume, $1,000,000,000

Corporate officers: Archie Alds Emmerson, Pres.; Mark Emmerson, C.F.O.

Divisions: Sierra Pacific Industries-Arcata Div., Arcata, CA; Sierra Pacific Industries-Burney Div., Burney, CA; Sierra Pacific Industries-Hayfork Div., Hayfork, CA; Sierra Pacific Industries-Loyalton Div., Loyalton, CA; Sierra Pacific Industries-Quincy Div., Quincy, CA; Sierra Pacific Industries-Redding Div.,

Redding, CA; Sierra Pacific Industries-Standard Div., Standard, CA; Sierra Pacific Industries-Susanville Div., Susanville, CA
Plants: Corning, Red Bluff, CA
Giving statement: Giving through the Sierra Pacific Foundation.

Sierra Pacific Foundation

P.O. Box 493842
Redding, CA 96049-3842 (530) 378-8000
FAX: (530) 378-8109;
E-mail: foundation@spi-ind.com; URL: http://www.spi-ind.com/html/spf_foundation.cfm

Establishment information: Established in 1979 in CA.
Donor: Sierra Pacific Industries.
Contact: Carolyn Emmerson Dietz, Pres.
Financial data (yr. ended 06/30/11): Assets, $64,367 (M); gifts received, $500,650; expenditures, $476,716; qualifying distributions, $468,498; giving activities include $191,022 for 148 grants (high: $50,000; low: $150) and $277,476 for 274 grants to individuals (high: $2,500; low: $375).
Purpose and activities: The foundation supports organizations involved with arts and culture, education, forest conservation, animals and wildlife, health, agriculture, recreation, human services, and youth.
Fields of interest: Performing arts, theater; Arts; Secondary school/education; Education; Environment, forests; Animals/wildlife; Health care, clinics/centers; Health care; Agriculture; Athletics/sports, school programs; Recreation, fairs/festivals; Recreation; Human services Youth.
Program:
Sierra Pacific Foundation Scholarships: The foundation awards college scholarships to children of employees of Sierra Pacific Industries.
Type of support: Employee-related scholarships; General/operating support; Program development; Sponsorships.
Geographic limitations: Giving primarily in areas of company operations in CA and WA.
Support limitations: No support for religious organizations or foundations. No grants to individuals (except for employee-related scholarships), or for salaries, general operating support for schools or public agencies, or religious activities.
Publications: Grants list.
Application information: Applications accepted. Application form required. Applicants should submit the following:
1) copy of current year's organizational budget and/or project budget
Initial approach: Contact foundation for application form; mail application form to foundation or nearest company facility
Copies of proposal: 1
Deadline(s): Feb. 28
Final notification: Approximately 2 months
Officers: Carolyn Emmerson Dietz, Pres.; George Emmerson, V.P.; M. D. Emmerson, Secy.
EIN: 942574178
Selected grants: The following grants are a representative sample of this grantmaker's funding activity:
$5,000 to American Cancer Society, Atlanta, GA, 2011.
$2,375 to Pace University, New York, NY, 2011.
$2,250 to University of Colorado, Boulder, CO, 2011.
$2,250 to University of Colorado, Boulder, CO, 2011.
$1,750 to Boise State University, Boise, ID, 2011.
$1,750 to Boise State University, Boise, ID, 2011.
$1,750 to Boise State University, Boise, ID, 2011.
$1,750 to Brigham Young University, Provo, UT, 2011.
$1,750 to Brigham Young University, Provo, UT, 2011.
$1,250 to San Francisco State University, San Francisco, CA, 2011.

3452
SIFCO Industries, Inc.

970 E. 64th St.
Cleveland, OH 44103-1694 (216) 881-8600
FAX: (216) 432-6281

Company URL: http://www.sifco.com
Establishment information: Established in 1916.
Company type: Public company
Company ticker symbol and exchange: SIF/AMEX
Business activities: Provides forging, electroplating, and precision and electrochemical machining services; manufactures gaskets and boiler accessories; repairs and modifies jet engine components.
Business type (SIC): Metal forgings and stampings; metal coating and plating; aircraft and parts
Financial profile for 2012: Number of employees, 565; assets, $106,550,000; sales volume, $125,110,000; pre-tax net income, $9,400,000; expenses, $115,760,000; liabilities, $46,400,000
Corporate officers: Jeffrey P. Gotschall, Chair.; Michael S. Lipscomb, Pres. and C.E.O.; James P. Woidke, C.O.O.; Frank A. Cappello, V.P., Finance and C.F.O.; Remigijus H. Belzinskas, Corp. Cont.
Board of directors: Jeffrey P. Gotschall, Chair.; John G. Chapman, Sr., C.P.A.; Michael S. Lipscomb; Donald C. Molten, Jr.; Alayne L. Reitman; Hudson D. Smith
Subsidiary: SIFCO Custom Machining Co., Minneapolis, MN
Division: SIFCO Forge Group, Cleveland, OH
International operations: Ireland
Giving statement: Giving through the SIFCO Foundation.
Company EIN: 340553950

SIFCO Foundation

970 E. 64th St.
Cleveland, OH 44103-1620 (216) 881-8600

Donor: SIFCO Industries, Inc.
Contact: Jeffrey P. Gotschall, Pres.
Financial data (yr. ended 08/31/11): Assets, $104,978 (M); gifts received, $30,000; expenditures, $40,201; qualifying distributions, $40,100; giving activities include $40,100 for 21 grants (high: $8,000; low: $50).
Purpose and activities: The foundation supports organizations involved with performing arts, education, and community and economic development.
Fields of interest: Performing arts; Performing arts, music; Performing arts, orchestras; Elementary school/education; Higher education; Education; Business/industry; Community/economic development.
Type of support: General/operating support.
Application information: Applications accepted. Application form required. Applicants should submit the following:
1) copy of IRS Determination Letter
2) descriptive literature about organization
3) detailed description of project and amount of funding requested
Initial approach: Proposal
Deadline(s): None
Officers: Jeffrey P. Gotschall, Pres.; Remigijus H. Belzinskas, Secy.; Frank A. Cappello, Treas.
EIN: 346531019

3453
Sigma-Aldrich Corporation

3050 Spruce St.
St. Louis, MO 63103 (314) 771-5765
FAX: (302) 674-5266

Company URL: http://www.sigma-aldrich.com
Establishment information: Established in 1934.
Company type: Public company
Company ticker symbol and exchange: SIAL/NASDAQ
International Securities Identification Number: US8265521018
Business activities: Produces and sells biochemicals, organic and inorganic chemicals, radiolabeled chemicals, diagnostic reagents, chromatography products, and related products; manufactures and sells miscellaneous metal components.
Business type (SIC): Chemicals and allied products—wholesale; metal products/fabricated
Financial profile for 2012: Number of employees, 9,000; assets, $3,820,000,000; sales volume, $2,623,000,000; pre-tax net income, $655,000,000; expenses, $1,964,000,000; liabilities, $1,274,000,000
Fortune 1000 ranking: 2012—784th in revenues, 352nd in profits, and 679th in assets
Forbes 2000 ranking: 2012—1671st in sales, 1128th in profits, and 1888th in assets
Corporate officers: Barrett A. Toan, Chair.; Rakesh Sachdev, Pres. and C.E.O.; Jan A. Bertsch, Exec. V.P., C.F.O., and Treas.; George Lloyd Miller, Sr. V.P., Genl. Counsel, and Secy.; Michael Kanan, V.P. and Corp. Cont.; Douglas W. Rau, V.P., Human Resources
Board of directors: Barrett Toan, Chair.; Rebecca M. Bergman; George M. Church; Michael L. Marberry; W. Lee McCollum; Avi M. Nash; Steven Paul; J. Pedro Reinhard; Rakesh Sachdev; D. Dean Spatz
Subsidiaries: Aldrich Chemical Co., Inc., Milwaukee, WI; Sigma Chemical Co., St. Louis, MO
International operations: Bermuda; Switzerland; United Kingdom
Giving statement: Giving through the Sigma-Aldrich Corporation Contributions Program, the Dan Broida/Sigma-Aldrich Scholarship Fund, Inc., and the Sigma-Aldrich Foundation.
Company EIN: 431050617

Dan Broida/Sigma-Aldrich Scholarship Fund, Inc.

3050 Spruce St.
St. Louis, MO 63103-2530

Establishment information: Established in 1982 in MO as a company-sponsored operating fund.
Donor: Sigma-Aldrich Corp.
Financial data (yr. ended 03/31/11): Assets, $1,078,281 (M); expenditures, $136,735; qualifying distributions, $126,500; giving activities include $126,500 for 19 grants to individuals (high: $7,500; low: $3,000).
Purpose and activities: The foundation awards college scholarships to children of employees of Sigma-Aldrich studying science.
Type of support: Employee-related scholarships.
Geographic limitations: Giving limited to areas of company operations.

Application information: Applications accepted. Application form required.
Initial approach: Letter
Deadline(s): Apr. 10
Officers and Directors:* Joseph Ackerman*, Chair. and Pres.; Teresa Thiel*, Secy.; Ben Sandler*, Treas.; Faith Sandler.
EIN: 431253095

Sigma-Aldrich Foundation

3050 Spruce St.
St. Louis, MO 63103-2530
URL: http://www.sigmaaldrich.com/customer-service/sigma-aldrich-foundation.html

Establishment information: Established in 2004 in MO.
Donor: Sigma-Aldrich Corp.
Contact: Kirk A. Richter, V.P.
Financial data (yr. ended 12/31/11): Assets, $5,021,110 (M); gifts received, $80,000; expenditures, $394,792; qualifying distributions, $379,000; giving activities include $379,000 for grants.
Purpose and activities: The foundation supports organizations involved with education, health, youth development, human services, and science.
Fields of interest: Education; Health care; Youth development; Family services; Human services; United Ways and Federated Giving Programs; Science.
Programs:
Education: The foundation supports programs designed to build and train tomorrow's leaders; and foster the development of well-rounded citizens.
Health and Human Services: The foundation supports programs designed to support youth and strengthen families.
Science: The foundation supports programs designed to advance science in all its forms.
Type of support: Annual campaigns; Continuing support; Employee volunteer services; General/operating support; Research; Scholarship funds.
Geographic limitations: Giving primarily in areas of company operations in St. Louis, MO, and Milwaukee, WI.
Support limitations: No support for discriminatory organizations, political candidates or organizations, athletic teams, or booster or social clubs. No grants to individuals, or for scholarships, supplies or materials for primary or secondary education facilities, political causes or campaigns, fundraising, athletic events, or extracurricular activities for educational institutions.
Publications: Application guidelines.
Application information: Applications accepted. Multi-year funding is not automatic. Organizations receiving support are asked to provide status and evaluation reports. Application form required.
Applicants should submit the following:
1) name, address and phone number of organization
2) list of company employees involved with the organization
3) explanation of why grantmaker is considered an appropriate donor for project
4) detailed description of project and amount of funding requested
5) contact person
Initial approach: Complete online application form
Copies of proposal: 1
Board meeting date(s): 2 or 3 times per year
Deadline(s): None
Final notification: Following board meeting
Officers and Directors: Jai P. Nagarkatti, Pres.; Kirk A. Richter, V.P.; Barbara Branchfield, Secy.; Michael Hollenkemp, Treas.; Joseph D. Ackerman.
Number of staff: None.
EIN: 200884074
Selected grants: The following grants are a representative sample of this grantmaker's funding activity:
$80,000 to United Way of Greater Saint Louis, Saint Louis, MO, 2010.
$42,500 to United Way of Greater Milwaukee, Milwaukee, WI, 2010.
$15,000 to Saint Louis Symphony Orchestra, Saint Louis, MO, 2010.
$10,000 to American Red Cross, Saint Louis, MO, 2010.
$10,000 to Center for Emerging Technologies, Saint Louis, MO, 2010.
$10,000 to Missouri Botanical Garden, Saint Louis, MO, 2010.
$10,000 to Saint Louis Zoo, Saint Louis, MO, 2010.
$5,000 to Cultural Leadership, Saint Louis, MO, 2010.
$5,000 to LAM Treatment Alliance, Cambridge, MA, 2010.
$5,000 to Teach for America, New York, NY, 2010.

3454
Sikorsky Aircraft Corporation

6900 Main St.
Stratford, CT 06614-1358 (203) 386-4000

Company URL: http://www.sikorsky.com
Establishment information: Established in 1925.
Company type: Subsidiary of a public company
Business activities: Designs and manufactures helicopters.
Business type (SIC): Aircraft and parts
Financial profile for 2009: Number of employees, 6,000; sales volume, $6,320,000,000
Corporate officers: Mick Maurer, Pres.; Judith E. Bankowski, V.P. and C.I.O.; Peter J. Graber-Lipperman, V.P. and Genl. Counsel; Richard S. Caswell, V.P., Finance, and C.F.O.; Christian Meisner, V.P., Human Resources; Shade Eddy, Sr. V.P., Opers.
Giving statement: Giving through the Sikorsky Aircraft Corporation Contributions Program.

Sikorsky Aircraft Corporation Contributions Program

6900 Main St.
Stratford, CT 06615-9129
E-mail: shitchcock@sikorsky.com

Contact: Susan Hitchcock
Purpose and activities: Sikorsky makes charitable contributions to nonprofit organizations involved with arts and culture, education, the environment, health and human services, and civic affairs. Support is given primarily in Troy, Alabama, Connecticut, West Palm Beach, Florida, and Milwaukee, Wisconsin.
Fields of interest: Arts; Education; Environment; Health care; Human services; Public affairs.
Programs:
Matching Gift Program: Sikorsky matches contributions made by its employees to educational institutions and organizations involved with arts and culture and the environment on a one-for-one basis from $25 to $10,000 per employee, per year.
Volunteer Grant Program: Through the Volunteer Grant Program, Sikorsky makes charitable contributions of $250 to nonprofit organizations with which employees have volunteered at least 60 hours per year for one year.
Type of support: Employee matching gifts; Employee volunteer services; General/operating support.
Geographic limitations: Giving primarily in Troy, AL, CT, West Palm Beach, FL, and Milwaukee, WI.
Application information: Applications accepted. Application form required.
Initial approach: Complete online application form
Copies of proposal: 1
Deadline(s): June 1
Final notification: 1st quarter

3455
Silicon Valley Bank

3003 Tasman Dr.
Santa Clara, CA 95054-1191
(408) 654-7400

Company URL: http://www.svb.com
Establishment information: Established in 1982.
Company type: Private company
Business activities: Operates commercial bank.
Business type (SIC): Banks/commercial
Corporate officers: Kenneth Wilcox, Chair.; Harry W. Kellogg, Jr., Vice-Chair.; Greg W. Becker, Pres. and C.E.O.; Bruce Wallace, C.O.O.; Michael Descheneaux, C.F.O.; Mary Dent, Genl. Counsel
Board of directors: Kenneth Wilcox, Chair.; Harry W. Kellogg, Jr., Vice-Chair.; Greg W. Becker; Eric A. Benhamou; Joel P. Friedman; Richard C. Kramlich; Lata Krishnan; Jeff N. Maggioncalda; Kate D. Mitchell; John F. Robinson; Garen K. Staglin; Kyung H. Yoon
Giving statement: Giving through the Silicon Valley Bank Foundation.

The Silicon Valley Bank Foundation

3003 Tasman Dr.
Santa Clara, CA 95054-1191 (405) 987-9147
E-mail: svbfoundation@svb.com.; URL: http://www.svb.com/Company/Corporate-Social-Responsibility/Social-Responsibility/

Establishment information: Established in 1995 in CA.
Donor: Silicon Valley Bank.
Financial data (yr. ended 12/31/11): Assets, $1,732,270 (M); gifts received, $1,000,000; expenditures, $182,550; qualifying distributions, $180,750; giving activities include $180,750 for 73 grants (high: $20,000; low: $500).
Purpose and activities: The foundation supports organizations with which employees of Silicon Valley Bank volunteer or serve in leadership positions; and programs designed to serve low-and-moderate income communities.
Fields of interest: Arts; Education; Health care; Employment; Housing/shelter; Homeless, human services; Human services; Community/economic development; United Ways and Federated Giving Programs Economically disadvantaged.
Program:
Community Reinvestment Act (CRA): The foundation awards grants to programs designed to serve low-and-moderate income communities (LMI). Special emphasis directed toward affordable housing for LMI individuals; community services targeted to LMI; financing business or farms in LMI areas or that have a positive employment impact on LMI individuals; and activities that otherwise revitalize or stabilize LMI areas.
Type of support: Capital campaigns; Employee volunteer services; Equipment; General/operating support; Program development.

Geographic limitations: Giving primarily in areas of company operations in northern CA.
Support limitations: No support for religious organizations, discriminatory organizations, or parent teacher associations. No grants to individuals, or for memorial campaigns, fundraising, political activities, research, sponsorship of athletic events or programs, endowments, or advertising.
Publications: Application guidelines.
Application information: Applications accepted. Preference is given to organizations sponsored by a Silicon Valley Bank employee. Grants range from $500 to $2,500. Application form not required.
Applicants should submit the following:
1) copy of IRS Determination Letter
2) brief history of organization and description of its mission
3) geographic area to be served
4) copy of most recent annual report/audited financial statement/990
5) listing of board of directors, trustees, officers and other key people and their affiliations
6) detailed description of project and amount of funding requested
7) copy of current year's organizational budget and/or project budget
8) listing of additional sources and amount of support

Initial approach: Proposal
Board meeting date(s): Quarterly
Deadline(s): None

Officers: Jim Hori, Chair. and Pres.; Scott Bergquist, V.P.; Michelle Churchill, Treas.
Directors: Pamela Aldsworth; Dan Allred; Anne Bongi; Greg Becker; Don Chandler; Susan Garcia; Katie Knepley; Carrie Merritt; Craig Robinson; Brenda Santoro; Jeff Strawn; Mary Toomey.
EIN: 770414630
Selected grants: The following grants are a representative sample of this grantmaker's funding activity:
$20,000 to Best Buddies International, Miami, FL, 2010.
$5,000 to Silicon Valley Education Foundation, San Jose, CA, 2010.
$4,000 to Visual Art Exchange, Raleigh, NC, 2010.
$3,000 to Next Door Solutions to Domestic Violence, San Jose, CA, 2010.
$2,500 to Habitat for Humanity, Austin, Austin, TX, 2010.
$2,500 to Impact on Education, Boulder, CO, 2010.
$2,500 to Save San Francisco Bay Association, Oakland, CA, 2010.
$1,000 to Cystic Fibrosis Foundation, Chicago, IL, 2010.
$1,000 to Food Runners, San Francisco, CA, 2010.
$1,000 to Friends for Youth, Redwood City, CA, 2010.

3456
Sills Cummis & Gross PC

The Legal Center
1 Riverfront Plz.
Newark, NJ 07102 (973) 643-5493

Company URL: http://www.sillscummis.com/
Establishment information: Established in 1971.
Company type: Private company
Business activities: Operates law firm.
Business type (SIC): Legal services
Corporate officer: Steven A. Marks, C.I.O.
Offices: Newark, Princeton, NJ; New York, NY
Giving statement: Giving through the Sills Cummis & Gross P.C Pro Bono Program.

Sills Cummis & Gross P.C Pro Bono Program

The Legal Center
1 Riverfront Plz.
Newark, NJ 07102 (973) 643-5493
E-mail: lriggiola@sillscummis.com; URL: http://www.sillscummis.com/about/community.asp?id=24

Contact: Loryn Riggiola, Member
Fields of interest: Legal services.
Type of support: Pro bono services - legal.
Application information: An attorney coordinates pro bono projects.

3457
Simmons Browder Gianaris Angelides & Barnerd, LLC

1 Court St.
East Alton, IL 62024-1326 (618) 259-2222

Company URL: http://www.simmonsfirm.com
Establishment information: Established in 1999.
Company type: Private company
Business activities: Operates law firm.
Business type (SIC): Legal services
Corporate officers: John Simmons, Chair. and C.E.O.; Peter Rasche, Genl. Counsel
Board of director: John Simmons, Chair.
Giving statement: Giving through the Simmons Employee Foundation.

Simmons Employee Foundation

(also known as SEF)
(formerly SimmonsCooper Employee Charitable Foundation)
1 Court Str.
Alton, IL 62002-1326 (618) 259-2222
FAX: (618) 259-2251;
E-mail: info@simmonsfirm.com; Toll-free tel.: (866)-468-8631; URL: http://www.simmonsfirm.com/f-simmons-employee-foundation.html

Establishment information: Established in 2005 in IL.
Donor: SimmonsCooper.
Financial data (yr. ended 12/31/11): Revenue, $83,134; assets, $70,533 (M); gifts received, $82,679; expenditures, $82,201; giving activities include $81,652 for grants.
Purpose and activities: The foundation supports neighborhood and community development.
Fields of interest: Community/economic development.
Officers: John Simmons, Chair.; David Bamper, Pres.; Theresa Knight, Secy.; Amy Stiebel, Treas.
Trustees: John Barnerd; Amy Bourland; Jennifer Hoernis; Jim Howard; Tim Lowrance; Stephanie Lyons; Yvette Scott; and 9 additional trustees.
EIN: 201927730

3458
Simon Property Group, Inc.

225 W. Washington St.
Indianapolis, IN 46204-3435
(317) 636-1600
FAX: (317) 685-7222

Company URL: http://www.simon.com
Establishment information: Established in 1960.
Company type: Public company
Company ticker symbol and exchange: SPG/NYSE
International Securities Identification Number: US8288061091
Business activities: Operates real estate investment trust.
Business type (SIC): Investors/miscellaneous
Financial profile for 2012: Number of employees, 5,500; assets, $32,586,610,000; sales volume, $4,880,080,000; pre-tax net income, $1,719,630,000; expenses, $2,659,480,000; liabilities, $26,676,000,000
Fortune 1000 ranking: 2012—497th in revenues, 143rd in profits, and 172nd in assets
Forbes 2000 ranking: 2012—1401st in sales, 438th in profits, and 688th in assets
Corporate officers: David Simon, Chair. and C.E.O.; Richard S. Sokolov, Pres. and C.O.O.; Stephen E. Sterrett, Sr. Exec. V.P. and C.F.O.; John Rulli, Sr. Exec. V.P. and C.A.O.; Andrew A. Juster, Exec. V.P. and Treas.; David Schacht, Sr. V.P. and C.I.O.; Steven K. Broadwater, Sr. V.P. and C.A.O.; David Campbell, Sr. V.P., Finance; Liz Zale, Sr. V.P., Comms.; James M. Barkley, Secy. and Genl. Counsel; Lawrence J. Krema, Sr. V.P., Human Resources
Board of directors: David Simon, Chair.; Melvyn E. Bergstein; Larry C. Glasscock; Karen N. Horn, Ph.D.; Allan B. Hubbard; Reuben S. Leibowitz; Herbert Simon; J. Albert Smith, Jr.; Daniel C. Smith, Ph.D.; Richard S. Sokolov
International operations: Bermuda; United Kingdom
Giving statement: Giving through the Simon Youth Foundation, Inc.
Company EIN: 046268599

Simon Youth Foundation, Inc.

225 W. Washington St.
Indianapolis, IN 46204-3420 (317) 263-2361
FAX: (317) 263-2371; E-mail: syf@simon.com; Scholarship application address: Scholarship America, Inc., c/o SYF Scholarship Progs., P.O. Box 297, St. Peter, MN 56082; Toll-free tel.: (800) 537-4180; E-mail for Richard M. Markoff, Ph.D.: markoff@simon.com; URL: http://www.syf.org/

Establishment information: Established in 1997 in IN.
Contact: Richard M. Markoff Ph.D., Exec. V.P.
Financial data (yr. ended 12/31/11): Revenue, $2,343,989; assets, $10,275,320 (M); gifts received, $2,351,535; expenditures, $2,498,219; giving activities include $906,605 for grants to individuals.
Purpose and activities: The foundation fosters and improves educational opportunities, career development, and life skills for "at risk" youth through focused programs and initiatives.
Fields of interest: Secondary school/education; Higher education.
Program:
Community Scholarship Program: Awards scholarships to high school seniors who plan to enroll in a full-time undergraduate course of study at an accredited two- or four-year college, university, or vocational-technical school.
Type of support: Scholarships—to individuals.
Publications: Annual report.
Officers and Directors:* Deborah J. Simon*, Chair.; Richard M. Markoff, Ph.D., Exec. V.P.; Michelle Bellej*, Secy.; Bob Estes*, Treas.; Trudy Banta, Ed.D.; Shari Simon Greenberg; Andy Juster; Richard O. Kissel II; Susan Massela; Michael E. McCarty; Tiffany Olson; Jeffrey H. Patchen; Stephen H. Simon; Richard S. Sokolov; Stephen A. Stitle; James Ward; Cathi Weiner; Eugene White.

Number of staff: 7 full-time professional; 1 part-time professional; 3 full-time support.
EIN: 352035269

3459
J.R. Simplot Company

999 Main St., Ste. 1300
P.O. Box 27
Boise, ID 83702-9000 (208) 336-2110

Company URL: http://www.simplot.com
Establishment information: Established in 1923.
Company type: Private company
Business activities: Produces french fries and potato products; manufacturers fertilizer; manufactures turf and horticultural products; produces cattle feed; produces beef cattle.
Business type (SIC): Specialty foods/canned, frozen, and preserved; farms/livestock; grain mill products, including pet food; fertilizers and agricultural chemicals
Financial profile for 2011: Number of employees, 10,000; sales volume, $4,900,000,000
Corporate officers: Scott R. Simplot, Chair.; William J. Whitacre, C.E.O.; Amber Post, V.P. and Treas.
Board of directors: Scott R. Simplot, Chair.; Steve Beebe; Dale Dunn; Richard M. Hormaechea; Bob Lane; Joe Marshall; Debbie McDonald; Gay C. Simplot; Ted Simplot; William J. Whitacre
International operations: Australia
Giving statement: Giving through the J. R. Simplot Company Contributions Program and the J. R. Simplot Company Foundation, Inc.

J. R. Simplot Company Contributions Program

P.O. Box 27
Boise, ID 83707-0027
FAX: (208) 389-7289;
E-mail: sue.richardson@simpson.com; URL: http://www.simplot.com/community_involvement

Contact: Sue Richardson, Dir., Co. Comms.
Purpose and activities: As a complement to its foundation, J. R. Simplot also makes charitable contributions to nonprofit organizations directly. Support is given in areas of company operations.
Fields of interest: Arts; Education; Youth development; Community/economic development.
Program:
Employee Assistance Program: The company awards scholarship of up to $5,250 per year to full-time employees of Simplot to pursue graduate studies and up to $3,000 to pursue undergraduate studies. The award supports examinations; GED, high school, and undergraduate/graduate degrees from an accredited college/university; certifications; technical skills training; correspondence courses; and self study programs. Applicants are evaluated by managers and human resource personnel.
Type of support: Annual campaigns; Capital campaigns; Conferences/seminars; Donated equipment; Donated products; Emergency funds; Employee-related scholarships; General/operating support; In-kind gifts; Scholarship funds; Sponsorships; Use of facilities.
Geographic limitations: Giving in areas of company operations.
Application information: Applications accepted. The Public Relations Department handles giving. A contributions committee reviews all requests. Application form not required. Applicants should submit the following:
1) descriptive literature about organization
2) detailed description of project and amount of funding requested
Initial approach: Letter of inquiry
Copies of proposal: 1
Committee meeting date(s): Bi-Monthly
Deadline(s): None
Final notification: Following review
Administrators: Adelia Simplot, Coord., Community Rels.; Fred Zerza, V.P., Public Rels.

J. R. Simplot Company Foundation, Inc.

P.O. Box 27
Boise, ID 83707-0027

Establishment information: Established in 2000 in ID.
Donor: J.R. Simplot Co.
Financial data (yr. ended 03/31/11): Assets, $28,866,614 (M); expenditures, $906,603; qualifying distributions, $707,313; giving activities include $707,313 for grants.
Purpose and activities: The foundation supports organizations involved with arts and culture, secondary and higher education, health, agriculture and food, human services, and community development.
Fields of interest: Museums (art); Performing arts, ballet; Performing arts, orchestras; Arts; Secondary school/education; Higher education; Health care, patient services; Health care; Agriculture/food; Boys & girls clubs; YM/YWCAs & YM/YWHAs; Children/youth, services; Human services; Business/industry; Community/economic development; United Ways and Federated Giving Programs.
Type of support: Building/renovation; General/operating support; Scholarship funds.
Geographic limitations: Giving primarily in Boise, ID.
Support limitations: No grants to individuals.
Application information: Applications not accepted. Contributes only to pre-selected organizations.
Officers and Directors:* Gay C. Simplot*, Pres.; John Edward Simplot*, V.P.; Terry T. Uhling, Secy.; Annette Elg, Treas.; Debbie S. McDonald; Scott R. Simplot.
EIN: 820522113
Selected grants: The following grants are a representative sample of this grantmaker's funding activity:
$150,000 to Ballet Idaho, Boise, ID, 2009.
$147,691 to United Way of Treasure Valley, Boise, ID, 2009.
$94,080 to Kids Charities, Rockland, DE, 2009. For grant made through McDonald's LPGA Championship.
$42,482 to United Way of Southwest Wyoming, Rock Springs, WY, 2009.
$36,240 to United Way of Southeastern Idaho, Pocatello, ID, 2009.
$32,500 to Ronald McDonald House Charities, Oak Brook, IL, 2009.
$26,174 to United Way of San Joaquin County, Stockton, CA, 2009.
$10,000 to Boise Art Museum, Boise, ID, 2009.

3460
L. Simpson & Co., Inc.

4922 13th Ave.
Brooklyn, NY 11219-3134 (718) 871-0120

Company URL: http://www.simpsonjewelers.com/
Establishment information: Established in 1959.
Company type: Private company
Business activities: Manufactures costume jewelry.
Business type (SIC): Shopping goods stores/miscellaneous
Corporate officer: Leib Simpson, Pres.
Giving statement: Giving through the Bracha Vehatzlacha Foundation Inc.

Bracha Vehatzlacha Foundation Inc.

4922 13th Ave.
Brooklyn, NY 11219-3134

Establishment information: Established in 2004 in NY.
Donors: L. Simpson & Co., Inc.; Leib Simpson; Simpson Jewelers LLC.
Contact: Leib Simpson, Pres.
Financial data (yr. ended 11/30/11): Assets, $16,263 (M); gifts received, $87,000; expenditures, $72,790; qualifying distributions, $72,646; giving activities include $72,646 for 81 grants (high: $23,500; low: -$36).
Purpose and activities: The foundation supports organizations involved with education and Judaism.
Fields of interest: Education; Jewish agencies & synagogues.
Type of support: General/operating support.
Geographic limitations: Giving primarily in NY.
Application information: Applications accepted. Application form not required.
Initial approach: Proposal
Deadline(s): None
Officers: Leib Simpson, Pres.; Chana Simpson, V.P.; Yosef Simpson, Secy.-Treas.
EIN: 202058937

3461
Simpson Manufacturing Co., Inc.

5956 W. Las Positas Blvd.
P.O. Box 10789
Pleasanton, CA 94588 (925) 560-9030

Company URL: http://www.simpsonmfg.com
Establishment information: Established in 1956.
Company type: Public company
Company ticker symbol and exchange: SSD/NYSE
Business activities: Manufactures building products.
Business type (SIC): Concrete, gypsum, and plaster products; lumber and construction materials—wholesale
Financial profile for 2012: Number of employees, 2,188; assets, $890,320,000; sales volume, $657,240,000; pre-tax net income, $61,920,000; expenses, $595,530,000; liabilities, $100,750,000
Corporate officers: Thomas J. Fitzmyers, Chair.; Karen Colonias, Pres. and C.E.O.; Brian Magstadt, C.F.O. and Secy.-Treas.
Board of directors: Thomas J. Fitzmyers, Chair.; James S. Andrasick; Jennifer A. Chatman; Earl F. Cheit; Gary M. Cusumano; Peter N. Louras, Jr.; Robin Greenway MacGillivray; Barclay Simpson; Barry Lawson Williams
Giving statement: Giving through the Simpson PSB Fund.
Company EIN: 943196943

Simpson PSB Fund

P.O. Box 359
Lafayette, CA 94549-0359
Application address: P.O. Box 359, Lafayette, CA 94549

Establishment information: Established in 1988 in CA.
Donors: Simpson Manufacturing Co., Inc.; Barclay Simpson.
Contact: Barclay Simpson, Chair.; Sharon Simpson
Financial data (yr. ended 12/31/10): Assets, $24,917,725 (M); expenditures, $1,794,127; qualifying distributions, $1,793,767; giving activities include $1,071,500 for 14 grants (high: $1,000,000; low: $1,000).
Purpose and activities: The foundation supports organizations involved with arts and culture, education, rainforests, and domestic violence.
Fields of interest: Museums (art); Performing arts; Performing arts, orchestras; Arts; Elementary school/education; Libraries (public); Education; Environment, forests; Girls clubs; Family services, domestic violence Children; Youth; Minorities; Hispanics/Latinos; Girls; Young adults, female; Boys; Crime/abuse victims.
Type of support: Annual campaigns; General/operating support; Scholarship funds.
Geographic limitations: Giving primarily in CA.
Support limitations: No grants to individuals.
Application information: Applications accepted. Proposal should be submitted on organization letterhead. Application form not required.
Initial approach: Proposal
Copies of proposal: 1
Deadline(s): None
Officer: Barclay Simpson*, Chair.
EIN: 680168017

3462
Simpson Thacher & Bartlett LLP
425 Lexington Ave.
New York, NY 10017-3954 (212) 455-3890

Company URL: http://www.simpsonthacher.com/index.cfm
Company type: Private company
Business activities: Operates law firm.
Business type (SIC): Legal services
Offices: Los Angeles, Palo Alto, CA; Washington, DC; New York, NY; Houston, TX
International operations: Brazil; China; Hong Kong; Japan; United Kingdom
Giving statement: Giving through the Simpson Thacher & Bartlett LLP Pro Bono Program.

Simpson Thacher & Bartlett LLP Pro Bono Program
425 Lexington Ave.
New York, NY 10017-3954 (212) 455-3890
E-mail: hkatzman@stblaw.com; Additional tel.: (212) 455-2000; URL: http://www.simpsonthacher.com/practice_probono.htm

Contact: Harlene Katzman, Pro Bono Counsel & Dir.
Fields of interest: Legal services.
Type of support: Pro bono services - legal.
Application information: A Pro Bono Committee manages the pro bono program.

3463
Singerlewak LLP
(formerly Singer, Lewak, Greenbaum & Goldstein LLP)
10960 Wilshire Blvd., 7th Fl.
Los Angeles, CA 90024-3702
(310) 477-3924

Company URL: http://www.singerlewak.com/
Establishment information: Established in 1959.
Company type: Private company
Business activities: Provides accounting, auditing, and bookkeeping management consulting services.
Business type (SIC): Accounting, auditing, and bookkeeping services
Corporate officers: Harvey A. Goldstein, C.P.A., Chair.; Paula Poundstone, Pres.
Board of director: Harvey A. Goldstein, C.P.A., Chair.
Offices: Irvine, La Jolla, Monterey Park, San Jose, Woodland Hills, CA
Giving statement: Giving through the SLGG Charitable Foundation.

SLGG Charitable Foundation
10960 Wilshire Blvd., Ste. 1100
Los Angeles, CA 90024-3714

Establishment information: Established in 2006 in CA.
Donors: Singer, Lewak, Greenbaum & Goldstein, LLP; Lewis Sharpstone; Steve Cupingood; David Krajanowski.
Financial data (yr. ended 12/31/11): Assets, $85,337 (M); expenditures, $5,208; qualifying distributions, $5,000; giving activities include $5,000 for grants.
Support limitations: No grants to individuals.
Application information: Applications not accepted. Unsolicited requests for funds not accepted.
Officers: Lewis Sharpstone, Chair.; Harvey A. Goldstein, Secy.-Treas.
Director: David Krajanowski.
EIN: 205075098

3464
Singlebrook Technology, Inc.
119 S. Cayuga St., Ste. 202
Ithaca, NY 14850-5580 (607) 330-1493

Company URL: http://www.singlebrook.com
Establishment information: Established in 2006.
Company type: Private company
Business activities: Operates web development firm.
Business type (SIC): Computer services
Corporate officers: Elisa Miller-Out, C.E.O.; Leon Miller-Out, Pres.
Giving statement: Giving through the Singlebrook Technology, Inc. Corporate Giving Program.

Singlebrook Technology, Inc. Corporate Giving Program
119 S. Cayuga St., Ste. 202
Ithaca, NY 14850-5580 (607) 330-1493
URL: http://www.singlebrook.com/about/mission

Purpose and activities: Singlebrook Technology is a certified B Corporation that donates a percentage of profits to nonprofit organizations.
Fields of interest: Environment Children.
Type of support: Employee volunteer services; General/operating support.

3465
Sioux Steel Company
196 1/2 E. 6th St.
P.O. Box 1265
Sioux Falls, SD 57104 (605) 336-1750

Company URL: http://www.siouxsteel.com
Establishment information: Established in 1918.
Company type: Private company
Business activities: Manufactures farm equipment and prefabricated metal buildings.
Business type (SIC): Machinery/construction, mining, and materials handling; plastic products/miscellaneous; steel mill products; metal products/structural
Corporate officers: Scott Rysdon, C.E.O.; Phillip M. Rysdon, Pres.; Jim Peterson, C.O.O.
Board of director: Scott Rysdon
Giving statement: Giving through the Sioux Steel Company Foundation.

Sioux Steel Company Foundation
196 1/2 E. 6th St.
Sioux Falls, SD 57101 (605) 336-1750

Establishment information: Established in 1945 in TN.
Donor: Sioux Steel Co.
Contact: Phillip M. Rysdon, Pres.
Financial data (yr. ended 08/31/12): Assets, $1,964,856 (M); gifts received, $218,279; expenditures, $82,404; qualifying distributions, $40,750; giving activities include $40,750 for grants.
Purpose and activities: The foundation supports organizations involved with higher education, multiple sclerosis, housing development, youth development, and voluntarism promotion.
Fields of interest: Education; Youth development; Human services.
Type of support: Annual campaigns; Building/renovation; Capital campaigns; Equipment; Matching/challenge support.
Geographic limitations: Giving primarily in Sioux Falls, SD.
Support limitations: No grants to individuals.
Application information: Applications accepted. Application form required. Applicants should submit the following:
1) detailed description of project and amount of funding requested
Initial approach: Proposal
Deadline(s): None
Officers: Phillip M. Rysdon, Pres.; Scott Rysdon, V.P.; Jimmie Rysdon, Secy.
EIN: 466012618

3466
Sit Investment Associates, Inc.
3300 IDS Ctr.
80 S. 8th St., Ste. 3300
Minneapolis, MN 55402-2206
(612) 332-3223

Company URL: http://www.sitinvest.com
Establishment information: Established in 1981.
Company type: Private company
Business activities: Provides investment advisory services.
Business type (SIC): Security and commodity services
Financial profile for 2010: Number of employees, 75

Corporate officers: Eugene C. Sit, C.P.A., Chair., C.E.O., and C.I.O.; Michael C. Brilley, Co-Pres.; Peter L. Mitchelson, Co-Pres.; Debra Beaudet, V.P., Human Resources; Robert B. Harrigan, V.P., Mktg.
Board of director: Eugene C. Sit, Chair.
Giving statement: Giving through the Sit Investment Associates Foundation.

Sit Investment Associates Foundation

3300 IDS Ctr.
80 S. 8th St.
Minneapolis, MN 55402-2100

Establishment information: Established in 1984.
Donor: Sit Investment Associates, Inc.
Contact: Debra Beaudet, Dir.
Financial data (yr. ended 12/31/11): Assets, $23,317,082 (M); gifts received, $1,294,858; expenditures, $1,239,982; qualifying distributions, $1,217,990; giving activities include $1,217,990 for grants.
Purpose and activities: The foundation supports organizations involved with arts and culture, education, cancer, hunger, human services, international affairs, and military and veterans.
Fields of interest: Performing arts; Performing arts, orchestras; Historic preservation/historical societies; Arts; Higher education; Education; Cancer; Food services; Food banks; Boy scouts; Salvation Army; Children/youth, services; Homeless, human services; Human services; International affairs, goodwill promotion; United Ways and Federated Giving Programs; Military/veterans' organizations.
Type of support: Annual campaigns; General/operating support.
Geographic limitations: Giving primarily in MN; giving also to national organizations.
Support limitations: No grants to individuals.
Application information: Applications not accepted. Contributes only to pre-selected organizations.
Officer and Director: Paul A. Rasmussen, Secy.; Debra A. Sit.
EIN: 411468021
Selected grants: The following grants are a representative sample of this grantmaker's funding activity:
$200,000 to Minneapolis Society of Fine Arts, Minneapolis, MN, 2011.
$20,000 to Minneapolis Society of Fine Arts, Minneapolis, MN, 2011.
$3,500 to University of Minnesota, Morris, MN, 2011.
$3,000 to University of Chicago, Chicago, IL, 2011.
$2,500 to University of Chicago, Chicago, IL, 2011.
$1,500 to Saint Paul Public Library, Friends of the, Saint Paul, MN, 2011.
$1,500 to University of Notre Dame, Notre Dame, IN, 2011.
$1,000 to Minnesota Public Radio, Saint Paul, MN, 2011.
$1,000 to University of Saint Thomas, Saint Paul, MN, 2011.

3467
Sitnasuak Native Corporation

400 Bering Ave.
P.O. Box 905
Nome, AK 99762-0905 (907) 387-1200

Company URL: http://www.snc.org
Establishment information: Established in 1971.
Company type: Native corporation
Business activities: Operates native corporation.
Business type (SIC): Nonclassifiable establishments
Corporate officers: Jason Evans, Chair.; Gloria A. Karmun, 1st Vice-Chair.; Andrew C. Miller, Jr., 2nd Vice-Chair.; Neal W. Foster, Secy.; Robert K. Evans, Treas.
Board of directors: Jason Evans, Chair.; Gloria A. Karmun, 1st Vice-Chair.; Andrew C. Miller, Jr., 2nd Vice-Chair.; Barbara Amarok; Crystal M. Andersen-Booth; Mark Allred; Helen C. Bell; Janice M. Doherty; Robert K. Evans; Neal W. Foster; Louis H. Green, Jr.; Gloria A. Karmun; Andrew C. Miller, Jr.; Lincoln Trigg
Giving statement: Giving through the Sitnasuak Foundation.

Sitnasuak Foundation

P.O. Box 905
Nome, AK 99762-0905 (907) 443-4305
Applicationj address: c/o BSF, P.O. Box 1008, Nome, AK 99762 tel: (907) 443-4305; URL: http://www.snc.org/foundation

Establishment information: Established in 1994 in AK.
Donors: Gerald Brown; Sitnasauk Native Corporation.
Contact: Moriah Sallaffie
Financial data (yr. ended 12/31/11): Assets, $1,635 (M); gifts received, $89,870; expenditures, $88,945; qualifying distributions, $88,000; giving activities include $88,000 for 1 grant.
Purpose and activities: Scholarship awards to individuals from Nome, Alaska for higher education.
Fields of interest: Higher education Indigenous peoples.
Type of support: Grants to individuals; Scholarships —to individuals.
Geographic limitations: Giving limited to residents of Nome, AK.
Application information: Applications accepted. Application form required.
Initial approach: Proposal
Deadline(s): Apr. 30
Officers: Barbara Amarok, Pres.; Janice Doherty, V.P.; Robert Evans, Treas.
Board Members: Vince Pikoganna; Dawn Salesky.
EIN: 920148088

3468
Siw Thai Silk

4 North Cir.
Yardley, PA 19067-3212 (866) 900-7455
FAX: (215) 295-0190

Company URL: http://www.siwthaisilk.com
Establishment information: Established in 2001.
Company type: Private company
Business type (SIC): Business services/miscellaneous
Corporate officer: Susan Firestone, Pres.
Giving statement: Giving through the Siw Thai Silk Corporate Giving Program.

Siw Thai Silk Corporate Giving Program

4 North Cir.
Yardley, PA 19067-3212 (866) 900-7455
E-mail: info@siwthaisilk.com; URL: http://www.siwthaisilk.com

Purpose and activities: Siw Thai Silk is a certified B Corporation that donates a percentage of net profits to charitable organizations. Support is given primarily in Philadelphia, Pennsylvania.
Fields of interest: Education, reading; Environment, alliance/advocacy; Health care; Disasters, preparedness/services.
Type of support: General/operating support.
Geographic limitations: Giving primarily in Philadelphia, PA.

3469
Sjostrom & Sons, Inc.

1129 Harrison Ave.
P.O. Box 5766
Rockford, IL 61104 (815) 226-0330

Company URL: http://www.sjostromconstruction.com
Establishment information: Established in 1914.
Company type: Private company
Business activities: Provides contract building construction and paving services.
Business type (SIC): Construction/highway and street (except elevated); contractors/general nonresidential building
Financial profile for 2010: Number of employees, 80
Corporate officers: William G. Sjostrom, Chair.; Joel G. Sjostrom, Pres.; David L. Preston, Treas.
Board of directors: William G. Sjostrom, Chair.; Joel G. Sjostrom
Giving statement: Giving through the Sjostrom & Sons Foundation.

Sjostrom & Sons Foundation

P.O. Box 5766
Rockford, IL 61125-0766 (815) 226-0330
Application address: 1129 Harrison Ave., Rockford, IL, 61104-7239

Establishment information: Established in 1983.
Donor: Sjostrom & Sons, Inc.
Contact: Joel Sjostrom, Dir.
Financial data (yr. ended 07/31/12): Assets, $1,002,035 (M); expenditures, $80,275; qualifying distributions, $65,800; giving activities include $65,800 for grants.
Purpose and activities: The foundation supports organizations involved with arts and culture, education, health, and human services.
Fields of interest: Arts; Education; Health care; Salvation Army; Residential/custodial care, hospices; Human services; United Ways and Federated Giving Programs.
Type of support: Building/renovation; General/operating support.
Geographic limitations: Giving primarily in Rockford, IL.
Support limitations: No grants to individuals.
Application information: Applications accepted. Application form not required. Applicants should submit the following:
1) name, address and phone number of organization
Initial approach: Proposal
Deadline(s): None
Directors: Joel Sjostrom; Kristopher Sjostrom.
EIN: 363225935

3470
Skadden, Arps, Slate, Meagher & Flom LLP
4 Times Sq.
New York, NY 10036 (212) 735-3000

Company URL: http://www.skadden.com
Establishment information: Established in 1948.
Company type: Private company
Business activities: Provides legal services.
Business type (SIC): Legal services
Financial profile for 2009: Number of employees, 4,175; sales volume, $2,100,000,000
Corporate officer: Noah J. Puntus, C.F.O.
Offices: Los Angeles, San Francisco, CA; Wilmington, DE; Washington, DC; Chicago, IL; Boston, MA; Newark, NJ; Houston, TX
Giving statement: Giving through the Skadden, Arps, Slate, Meagher & Flom LLP Pro Bono Program and the Skadden Fellowship Foundation, Inc.

Skadden, Arps, Slate, Meagher & Flom LLP Pro Bono Program
4 Times Sq.
New York, NY 10036-6518 (212) 735-2325
E-mail: brenna.devaney@skadden.com; URL: http://www.skadden.com/Index.cfm?contentID=8

Contact: Brenna K. DeVaney, Pro Bono Counsel
Fields of interest: Legal services.
Type of support: Pro bono services - legal.
Application information: A Pro Bono Committee manages the pro bono program.

The Skadden Fellowship Foundation, Inc.
(formerly Skadden, Arps, Slate, Meagher & Flom Fellowship Foundation)
360 Hamilton Ave.
White Plains, NY 10601-1811 (212) 735-2956
FAX: (917) 777-2956;
E-mail: susan.plum@skadden.com; Application address: Skadden Fellowship Program, 4 Times Sq., Rm. 29-218, New York, NY 10036; URL: http://www.skaddenfellowships.org/

Establishment information: Established in 1988 in NY.
Donor: Skadden, Arps, Slate, Meagher & Flom.
Contact: Susan Butler Plum, Dir.
Financial data (yr. ended 12/31/11): Assets, $9,588,665 (M); gifts received, $6,470,927; expenditures, $4,029,309; qualifying distributions, $3,964,931; giving activities include $3,417,885 for 87 grants (high: $116,957; low: $5,000) and $59,773 for 16 grants to individuals (high: $11,681; low: $200).
Purpose and activities: The foundation awards fellowships to graduating law students and outgoing judicial clerks who create projects at public interest organizations designed to provide legal services to the poor, the elderly, the disabled, and those deprived of their civil rights or human rights; and grants to former Skadden Fellows who want to undertake new initiatives on behalf of their clients.
Fields of interest: Law school/education; Civil/human rights, advocacy; Civil/human rights; Leadership development Aging; Disabilities, people with; Economically disadvantaged.
Programs:
Flom Memorial Incubator Grants: The foundation awards $10,000 grants to support creative novel projects undertaken by former Skadden Fellows engaged in public interest work. Proposed projects should identify an evolving need in the community the Fellow serves. Projects can be used to fund outreach to a new population in need of a particular type of service, develop a website to facilitate communication with clients or potential clients, translate materials or brochures into multiple foreign languages, or pilot an innovative approach to a long-standing problem.
Skadden Fellowships: The foundation annually awards fellowships to graduating law students who wish to devote their professional lives to providing legal services that benefit public interest. Fellowships are awarded for a two-year period and grants are made to the public interest organizations chosen by the fellows. Applicants must secure a potential position with a sponsoring public interest organization before applying for a fellowship. Selection is based not only on the qualifications of the applicant, but also on the demonstrated effectiveness of the sponsoring organization. Fellowships include a salary, fringe benefits to which an employee of the sponsoring organization would be entitled, and debt service on law school loans for the duration of the fellowship.
Type of support: Fellowships; Grants to individuals.
Geographic limitations: Giving on a national basis, with emphasis on Berkeley, Los Angeles, Oakland, San Diego, and San Francisco, CA, Washington, DC, Chicago, IL, MA, and Bronx, Brooklyn, and New York, NY.
Support limitations: No grants to individuals who do not secure a potential position with a sponsoring public interest organization.
Publications: Application guidelines.
Application information: Applications accepted. Letters for Flom Memorial Incubator Grants should describe the applicant's career trajectory, the inspiration for the project, and the proposed plan for grant funds. Applicants should submit the following:
1) copy of IRS Determination Letter
Requests for fellowships should include an official law school transcript, two letters of recommendation (from a law school advisor and a former employer), a commitment letter from a potential sponsoring institution, and a resume.
Initial approach: Download application form and mail application form and supporting materials for fellowships; letter to foundation for Flom Memorial Incubator Grants
Copies of proposal: 1
Board meeting date(s): Dec. 3
Deadline(s): Oct. 3 for fellowships; Jan. 15 and July 15 for Flom Memorial Incubator Grants
Final notification: Dec. 7
Officers and Trustees:* Lauren Aguiar, Chair.; Eric J. Friedman*, Pres.; Barry H. Garfinkel*, V.P.; Noah J. Puntus, V.P.; Chris Fulton, Secy.-Treas.; Hon. Judith S. Kaye; Jose Lozano; Suzanne Mckechnie Klahr; Martha Minow; Michael H. Schill; Kurt Schmoke; Robert C. Sheehan; Solomon Watson IV; Marni von Wilpert.
Number of staff: 1 full-time professional; 1 part-time support.
EIN: 133455231

3471
SKB, Inc.
(also known as SKB Environmental)
(formerly SKB Environmental, Inc.)
251 Starkey St., Ste. 228
St. Paul, MN 55107-1821 (651) 224-6329

Company URL: http://www.skbinc.com
Establishment information: Established in 1983.
Company type: Private company
Business activities: Provides waste management solutions.
Business type (SIC): Sanitary services
Corporate officer: Rick O'Gara, Pres.
Giving statement: Giving through the City of Rosemount-SKB Environmental Trust Fund.

City of Rosemount-SKB Environmental Trust Fund
(formerly SKB Environmental, Inc. Rosemount Community Trust)
P.O. Box 392
Rosemount, MN 55068-0392 (651) 454-2533

Establishment information: Established in 1993 in MN as Laidlaw Environmental Services, Inc. Rosemount Community Trust.
Donors: USPCI, Inc.; Laidlaw Environmental Services, Inc.; Safety-Kleen Corp.; SKB Environmental, Inc.; SKB, Inc.
Contact: Donald Chapdelaine, Tr.
Financial data (yr. ended 12/31/11): Assets, $1,567,671 (M); gifts received, $400,567; expenditures, $72,517; qualifying distributions, $68,693.
Geographic limitations: Giving limited to the Rosemount, MN, area.
Support limitations: No grants to individuals, or for political campaigns.
Application information: Applications accepted. Proposals should be submitted using organization letterhead. Application form required.
Initial approach: Proposal
Deadline(s): None
Officers and Trustees: Mary Riley, Pres.; Beth Adams, Secy.; Heather Nosan, Treas.; Donald Chapdelaine; John Domke.
EIN: 411739015
Selected grants: The following grants are a representative sample of this grantmaker's funding activity:
$201,686 to Rosemount, City of, Rosemount, MN, 2009.

3472
Skechers USA, Inc.
228 Manhattan Beach Blvd.,
Manhattan Beach, CA 90266
(310) 318-3100
FAX: (310) 318-5019

Company URL: http://skx.com/
Establishment information: Established in 1992.
Company type: Public company
Company ticker symbol and exchange: SKX/NYSE
Business activities: Operates footwear company.
Business type (SIC): Leather footwear
Financial profile for 2012: Number of employees, 5,666; assets, $1,340,220,000; sales volume, $1,560,320,000; pre-tax net income, $10,470,000; expenses, $1,538,000,000; liabilities, $464,250,000
Corporate officers: Robert Greenberg, Chair.; Michael Greenberg, Pres.; David Weinberg, Exec. V.P., C.O.O., and C.F.O.; Philip Paccione, Exec. V.P., Genl. Counsel, and Corp. Secy.
Board of directors: Robert Greenberg, Chair.; Morton Erlich; Michael Greenberg; Geyer Kosinski; Richard Rappaport; Richard Siskind; Thomas Walsh; David Weinberg
Giving statement: Giving through the Skechers USA, Inc. Contributions Program.
Company EIN: 954376145

Skechers USA, Inc. Contributions Program

228 Manhattan Beach Blvd.
Manhattan Beach, CA 90266 (310) 318-3100
URL: http://skx.com

3473
SKF USA Inc.

890 Forty Foot Rd.
Lansdale, PA 19446-4303 (267) 436-6000
FAX: (267) 436-6001

Company URL: http://www.skf.com/
Establishment information: Established in 1907.
Company type: Subsidiary of a foreign company
Business activities: Manufactures and provides rolling bearing and seal products, solutions, and services.
Business type (SIC): Machinery/general industry; gaskets, packing and sealing devices, and rubber hose and belting
Corporate officers: Poul Jeppesen, Pres. and C.E.O.; Tore Bertilsson, Exec. V.P. and C.F.O.
Board of directors: Martin Bjorkman; Kennet Carlsson; Winnie Fok; Peter Grafoner; Tom Johnstone; Baba Kalyani; Jouko Karvinen; Ulla Litzen; Joe Loughrey; Leif Ostling; Virpi Ring; Niklas Thoresson; Lena Treschow Torell; Lars Wedenborn
Subsidiary: SKF Condition Monitoring Inc., San Diego, CA
Division: SKF Actuation and Motion Control Div., Bethlehem, PA
Plants: Flowery Branch, GA; Plymouth, MI; Hanover, PA
Office: Allentown, PA
Giving statement: Giving through the SKF USA Inc. Corporate Giving Program.

SKF USA Inc. Corporate Giving Program

890 Forty Foot Rd.
P.O. Box 352
Lansdale, PA 19446 (267) 436-6000
URL: http://www.skf.com/portal/skf/home/sustainability?contentId=509046&lang=en

Purpose and activities: SKF makes charitable contributions to nonprofit organizations involved with community development. Special emphasis is directed toward programs that target the economically disadvantaged. Support is given primarily in areas of company operations.
Fields of interest: Community/economic development Economically disadvantaged.
Geographic limitations: Giving primarily in areas of company operations.

3474
Skidmore, Owings & Merrill LLP

224 S. Michigan Ave., Ste. 1000
Chicago, IL 60604-2505 (312) 554-9090

Company URL: http://www.som.com
Establishment information: Established in 1936.
Company type: Private company
Business activities: Provides architectural and engineering services.
Business type (SIC): Engineering, architectural, and surveying services
Corporate officers: John H. Winkler, C.E.O.; Joseph Dailey, C.F.O.
Board of director: Stan Korista
Offices: Los Angeles, San Francisco, CA; Washington, DC; New York, NY
International operations: Hong Kong; United Kingdom
Giving statement: Giving through the Skidmore, Owings & Merrill Foundation.

Skidmore, Owings & Merrill Foundation

224 S. Michigan Ave., Ste. 1000
Chicago, IL 60604-2526 (312) 427-4202
FAX: (312) 360-4545;
E-mail: somfoundation@som.com; URL: http://www.somfoundation.som.com

Establishment information: Established in 1978 in IL.
Donors: Skidmore, Owings & Merrill LLP; Brian Douglas Lee; Leigh Breslau; Paul & Daisy Soros Fellowship; William Baker; Duke University; Gary Haney; Mark Sarkisian; Gene Schnair; College of Creative Studies; New Jersey Society of Architects; Illinois Institute of Technology; Chicago Humanities Festival; Virginia Society American Institute of Architects; Carrie Byles; Philip Enquist; Anthony Vacchione; Stephen Apkin; City National Bank; Emap Support Services, Ltd.; Northwestern University; Mustafa Abadan; T.J. Gottesdiener; Air Force Village, Inc.; Energy BBDO, Inc.
Contact: Nancy Abshire, Exec. Dir.
Financial data (yr. ended 08/31/11): Assets, $3,216,495 (M); gifts received, $38,000; expenditures, $146,809; qualifying distributions, $125,917; giving activities include $71,791 for 7 grants (high: $35,000; low: $750).
Purpose and activities: The foundation awards fellowships to architecture, design, urban design, and structural engineering students.
Fields of interest: Visual arts, architecture; Visual arts, design; Engineering.
International interests: China; United Kingdom.
Programs:
China Prize: The foundation annually awards $20,000 traveling fellowships to outstanding Chinese national students of architecture or urban design from an accredited architecture school in China. Applicants must be in the last year of university in the People's Republic of China as an undergraduate or graduate and must be nominated by a faculty member.
SOM Prize and Travel Fellowship for Architecture, Design, and Urban Design: The foundation annually awards a $50,000 research and travel fellowship to one student to do in-depth research, collaborate with other designers, and pursue independent study outside the realm of established patterns. The winner is expected to disseminate their research and travel experience through a publication, lecture series, exhibits, and other educational means. A $20,000 travel fellowship will also be awarded to the second strongest candidate. Applicant must be an undergraduate or graduate student of accredited U.S. schools of architecture, design, or urban design. Winners are selected based on portfolios, research plans, and travel itineraries.
Structural Engineering Fellowship: The foundation annually awards a $10,000 independent travel fellowship to a student graduating with a Bachelor's, Master's, or Ph.D. degree in structural engineering to pursue the knowledge and experiences of architecture and engineering first hand.
UK Award: The foundation annually awards travel fellowships to students of architecture in the United Kingdom. The award is administered by the Royal Institute of British Architects (RIBA).
Type of support: Fellowships.
Geographic limitations: Giving on a national basis and in China and the United Kingdom.
Support limitations: No grants for scholarships or tuition.
Publications: Application guidelines; Grants list; Newsletter.
Application information: Applications accepted. Applicants receiving support are asked to submit a final report. Application form required. Applicants should submit the following:
1) detailed description of project and amount of funding requested
2) additional materials/documentation
Applications for SOM Prize and Travel Fellowship should include a letter of recommendation, copyright release statement, 12 page portfolio, and research abstract and travel itinerary.
Initial approach: Download Intent to Apply form and mail for SOM Prize and Travel Fellowship
Deadline(s): Apr. 18 for Intent to Apply form for SOM Prize and Travel Fellowship
Final notification: Aug. 5 for SOM Prize and Travel Fellowship
Officers: Mustafa Abadan, Chair.; Ross Wimer, Vice-Chair; William F. Baker, Secy.-Treas.; Nancy Abshire, Exec. Dir.
Directors: Stephen Apking; Roger Duffy; George Efstathiou; Philip Enquist; T.J. Gottesdiener; Gary P. Haney; Graig W. Hartman; Brian Douglas Lee; Peter Magill; Jeffrey J. McCarthy; Mark Regulinski; Peter Ruggiero; Gene Schnair; Richard Tomlinson; Tony Vacchione; Jaime Velez.
Number of staff: 1 part-time professional.
EIN: 362969068

3475
Skinner Corporation

1326 5th Ave., Ste. 717
Seattle, WA 98101-2640 (206) 628-5050

Establishment information: Established in 1916.
Company type: Private company
Business activities: Operates holding company.
Business type (SIC): Holding company
Financial profile for 2010: Number of employees, 3
Corporate officers: Carl G. Behnke, Chair.; Paul W. Skinner, Pres.; Childs Victoria, Secy.-Treas.
Board of director: Carl G Behnke, Chair.
Giving statement: Giving through the Behnke Foundation.

The Behnke Foundation

(formerly Skinner Foundation)
2 Union Sq.
601 Union St., Ste. 3016
Seattle, WA 98101-3913 (206) 623-5449
FAX: (206) 623-6138;
E-mail: behnkefoundation@aol.com; E-mail for Michelle McBride: mmcbride@rebenterprises.com; URL: http://www.behnkefoundation.org/

Establishment information: Trust established in 1956 in WA.
Donors: Skinner Corp.; Alpac Corp.; NC Machinery.
Contact: Michelle McBride, Exec. Dir.
Financial data (yr. ended 12/31/11): Assets, $2,085,602 (M); expenditures, $211,443; qualifying distributions, $147,625; giving activities include $147,625 for grants.
Purpose and activities: The foundation supports organizations involved with arts and culture, education, health, and human services and awards fellowships to artists.
Fields of interest: Visual arts; Visual arts, painting; Museums (art); Arts; Higher education; Education;

Speech/hearing centers; Health care; Boys & girls clubs; Women, centers/services; Human services.

Program:

Neddy Artist Fellowship: The foundation annually awards two $15,000 fellowships in celebration of Robert E. Behnke's life as an artist. The fellowships are awarded to an artist in painting and one in a rotating discipline. Applicants must be nominated by a group of local artists, collectors, and other members of the arts community. Artists are selected based on their commitment to their art and the community. All nominated artists receive $1,000.

Type of support: Building/renovation; Capital campaigns; Endowments; Fellowships; General/operating support; Matching/challenge support; Program development.

Geographic limitations: Giving primarily in areas of company operations in Seattle, WA.

Support limitations: No support for religious organizations not of direct benefit to the entire community or political organizations. No grants to individuals (except for the Neddy Artist Fellowship), or for continuing support, general operating support for the United Way, debt reduction, fundraising events, or conferences; no loans.

Publications: Application guidelines; Informational brochure (including application guidelines).

Application information: The foundation is currently not accepting unsolicited requests for general funding; its focus is on supporting the arts and the Neddy Awards.

Officers and Directors:* Carl G. Behnke*, Chair.; Michelle McBride, Exec. Dir.; John S. Behnke; Marisa W. Behnke; Renee J. Behnke; Sally Skinner Behnke.

Number of staff: 1 full-time professional; 1 part-time support.

EIN: 916025144

3476
SkyWest Airlines, Inc.

444 S. River Rd.
St. George, UT 84790 (435) 634-3000

Company URL: http://www.skywest.com
Establishment information: Established in 1972.
Company type: Subsidiary of a public company
Business activities: Operates passenger airline service.
Business type (SIC): Transportation/scheduled air
Corporate officers: Jerry C. Atkin, Chair. and C.E.O.; Russell A. Childs, Pres. and C.O.O.; Mike Kraupp, C.F.O. and Treas.; Eric Woodward, C.A.O.; Wade Steel, V.P. and Cont.
Board of directors: Jerry C. Atkin, Chair.; J. Ralph Atkin; Margaret S. Billson; Ian M. Cumming; Henry J. Eyring; Robert G. Sarver; Steven F. Udvar-Hazy; James L. Welch
Giving statement: Giving through the SkyWest Airlines, Inc. Corporate Giving Program.

SkyWest Airlines, Inc. Corporate Giving Program

444 S. River Rd.
St. George, UT 84790-2085 (435) 634-3000
URL: http://www.skywest.com/about-skywest-airlines/corporate-giving/

Purpose and activities: SkyWest Airlines makes in-kind donations of travel certificates to nonprofit organizations on a case by case basis. Support is given primarily in areas of company operations.

Fields of interest: General charitable giving.

Type of support: Employee volunteer services; General/operating support; In-kind gifts.

Geographic limitations: Giving primarily in areas of company operations.

Support limitations: No support for individual public or private schools, political or fraternal organizations, or religious institutions. No grants to individuals, or for air transportation for fundraising events, air transportation for individuals, matching gifts, capital or building grants, or development campaigns.

Application information: Applications accepted. Applicants must be designated public charities under the IRS. Application form required. Applicants should submit the following:

1) timetable for implementation and evaluation of project
2) results expected from proposed grant
3) population served
4) name, address and phone number of organization
5) how project's results will be evaluated or measured

Projects must have clearly defined and measureable goals and fit within SkyWest's mission. Letter should include event location, intended use of funds, tickets, and/or volunteers; number of people affected by the grant, and a description of how SkyWest's participation will affect the project's ability to attract other sponsors, contributors, and participants.

Initial approach: Complete online application and proposal
Deadline(s): Two months prior to need

3477
Slant/Fin Corporation

100 Forest Dr.
Greenvale, NY 11548-1205 (516) 484-2600

Company URL: http://www.slantfin.com/
Establishment information: Established in 1949.
Company type: Private company
Business activities: Manufactures heating and air conditioning equipment.
Business type (SIC): Machinery/refrigeration and service industry; metal plumbing fixtures and heating equipment/nonelectric
Corporate officers: Melvin Dubin, Chair.; Donald Brown, Vice-Chair.; Adam Dubin, Pres.; Charles Famoso, C.F.O.; John Svitek, V.P., Finance; Russ Trifilio, V.P., Opers.
Board of directors: Dubin Melvin, Chair.; Donald Brown, Vice-Chair.
International operations: Canada
Giving statement: Giving through the Slant/Fin Foundation, Inc.

The Slant/Fin Foundation, Inc.

100 Forest Dr.
Greenvale, NY 11548-1205 (516) 484-2600

Establishment information: Established in 1985 in NY.
Donors: Melvin Dubin; Slant/Fin Corp.
Contact: Melvin Dubin, Pres.
Financial data (yr. ended 06/30/12): Assets, $104,375 (M); expenditures, $13,062; qualifying distributions, $13,010; giving activities include $13,010 for grants.
Purpose and activities: The foundation supports organizations involved with education, health, youth services, and Judaism.
Fields of interest: Health care; Youth development; Religion.
Type of support: General/operating support.
Geographic limitations: Giving primarily in NY.
Support limitations: No grants to individuals.
Application information: Applications accepted. Application form required.

Initial approach: Proposal
Deadline(s): None

Officers: Melvin Dubin, Pres.; Adam Dubin, V.P.; Donald Brown, Secy.-Treas.
EIN: 112752009

3478
SLM Corporation

(also known as Sallie Mae)
300 Continental Dr.
Newark, DE 19713 (302) 283-8000
FAX: (302) 655-5049

Company URL: https://www.salliemae.com
Establishment information: Established in 1972.
Company type: Public company
Company ticker symbol and exchange: SLM/NYSE
Business activities: Operates holding company; provides higher education loans.
Business type (SIC): Credit institutions/personal; holding company
Financial profile for 2012: Number of employees, 6,800; assets, $181,260,000,000; sales volume, $6,110,000,000; pre-tax net income, $1,433,000,000; expenses, $4,677,000,000; liabilities, $176,200,000,000
Fortune 1000 ranking: 2012—418th in revenues, 212th in profits, and 36th in assets
Corporate officers: Anthony P. Terracciano, Chair.; Albert L. Lord, Vice-Chair. and C.E.O.; John F. Remondi, Pres. and C.O.O.; Laurent C. Lutz, Exec. V.P. and Genl. Counsel; Joni Reich, Exec. V.P., Admin.; Joseph DePaulo, Exec. V.P., Finance
Board of directors: Anthony P. Terracciano, Chair.; Albert L. Lord, Vice-Chair.; Ann Torre Bates; William M. Diefenderfer III; Diane Suitt Gilleland; Earl A. Goode; Ronald F. Hunt; Barry A. Munitz; Howard H. Newman; A. Alexander Porter, Jr.; Frank C. Puleo; Wolfgang Schoellkopf; Steven L. Shapiro; J. Terry Strange; Barry L. Williams
Subsidiary: Nellie Mae Corporation, Braintree, MA
Giving statement: Giving through the Sallie Mae Fund, Inc.
Company EIN: 522013874

The Sallie Mae Fund, Inc.

11100 USA Pkwy.
Fishers, IN 46037
URL: http://www.thesalliemaefund.org

Establishment information: Established in VA.
Donor: The Community Foundation for the National Capital Region.
Financial data (yr. ended 12/31/11): Assets, $4,829 (M); gifts received, $105,000; expenditures, $158,249; qualifying distributions, $155,855.
Purpose and activities: Giving primarily to support programs that encourage higher education and to prepare families for their college investments; giving also to programs that promote early childhood education.
Fields of interest: Education, early childhood education; Higher education; Education, reading; Safety/disasters.
Type of support: Annual campaigns; Employee matching gifts; Employee volunteer services; Program development; Scholarship funds.
Geographic limitations: Giving on a national basis.
Support limitations: No grants to individuals.

Application information: Applications not accepted. Unsolicited requests for funds not accepted.
Officers: April Stercula, Pres.; Jon Kroehler, Sr. V.P.; Catherine Fitzgerald, V.P.; Barbara O'Brien, V.P.; Carol R. Rakatansky, Secy. and Genl. Counsel.
Director: Jack Remondi.
EIN: 522015381

3479
SmartWool Corporation

3495 Airport Cir.
P.O. Box 774928
Steamboat Springs, CO 80477
(888) 879-9665

Company URL: http://www.smartwool.com
Establishment information: Established in 1990.
Company type: Subsidiary of a public company
Business activities: Manufactures wool apparel.
Business type (SIC): Apparel and other finished products made from fabrics and similar materials
Corporate officer: Mark Satkiewicz, Pres.
Giving statement: Giving through the SmartWool Corporation Advocacy Program.

SmartWool Corporation Advocacy Program

c/o Advocacy Prog.
P.O. Box 774928
Steamboat Springs, CO 80477-4928
E-mail: advocacy@smartwool.com

Purpose and activities: SmartWool makes charitable contributions to nonprofit organizations involved with encouraging youths to participate in outdoor activities while promoting environmental stewardship. Support is given on a national basis, with some emphasis on Colorado.
Fields of interest: Environmental education; Environment; Recreation; Youth development.
Type of support: Donated products; Employee volunteer services; General/operating support; Program development; Scholarship funds.
Geographic limitations: Giving on a national basis, with some emphasis on CO.
Support limitations: No support for state agencies, colleges or universities, or religious organizations. No grants to individuals, or for emergency needs, endowments, capital campaigns, land acquisition, or research.
Publications: Application guidelines.
Application information: Applications accepted. Telephone calls are not encouraged. Proposals should include a cover letter and be no longer than 3 pages. Support is limited to one contribution per organization during any given year. Grants generally do not exceed $5,000. Application form required.
Applicants should submit the following:
1) role played by volunteers
2) timetable for implementation and evaluation of project
3) how project will be sustained once grantmaker support is completed
4) results expected from proposed grant
5) qualifications of key personnel
6) population served
7) name, address and phone number of organization
8) copy of IRS Determination Letter
9) brief history of organization and description of its mission
10) copy of most recent annual report/audited financial statement/990
11) how project's results will be evaluated or measured
12) list of company employees involved with the organization
13) descriptive literature about organization
14) listing of board of directors, trustees, officers and other key people and their affiliations
15) detailed description of project and amount of funding requested
16) copy of current year's organizational budget and/or project budget

Proposals should include a description of the organization's capacity and sustainability efforts; the number of youth served; how the project's results will be used and/or disseminated; how the organization promotes environmental stewardship; and the organization's non-discrimination policy. Requests for product donations should specify the type, size, and quantity of the product.
Initial approach: Download application form and mail with proposal to headquarters
Copies of proposal: 1
Committee meeting date(s): Apr.1
Deadline(s): Mar. 1
Final notification: 6 weeks
Number of staff: 1 full-time professional.

3480
SMBC Capital Markets, Inc.

(formerly Sumitomo Bank Capital Markets, Inc.)
277 Park Ave.
New York, NY 10172-0003 (212) 224-5100

Company URL: http://www.smbc-cm.com
Establishment information: Established in 1989.
Company type: Subsidiary of a foreign company
Business activities: Operates foreign bank.
Business type (SIC): Banks/foreign
Corporate officers: Atsuo Konishi, Chair.; Kenichi Morooka, Co-C.E.O.; Tono Lke, Co-C.E.O
Board of director: Atsuo Konishi, Chair.
Giving statement: Giving through the SMBC Global Foundation, Inc.
Company EIN: 133380138

SMBC Global Foundation, Inc.

(formerly Sumitomo Bank Global Foundation)
277 Park Ave., 6th FL
New York, NY 10172-0002
FAX: (212) 224-5193;
E-mail: globalfoundation@smbcgroup.com; E-mail for Maya Zamor: maya_zamor@mbcgroup.com

Establishment information: Established in 1994 in DE and NY.
Donors: Sumitomo Bank Capital Markets, Inc.; SMBC Capital Markets, Inc.
Contact: Maya Zamor
Financial data (yr. ended 12/31/11): Assets, $12,873,642 (M); expenditures, $701,883; qualifying distributions, $444,837; giving activities include $444,837 for grants.
Purpose and activities: The foundation supports organizations involved with arts and culture, education, and human services.
Fields of interest: Arts; Education; Human services.
Program:
SMBC Employee Matching Gift Program: The foundation matches contributions made by employees of SMBC and its subsidiaries to nonprofit organizations on a one-for-one basis from $25 to $1,000 per employee, per year.
Type of support: Annual campaigns; Employee matching gifts; General/operating support; Scholarship funds.
Geographic limitations: Giving primarily in the NY Metro area and Asia.
Support limitations: No support for political, religious, or discriminatory organizations. No grants to individuals directly.
Application information: Applications not accepted.
Officers and Directors:* Kenichi Takahashi, Chair. and Pres.; Jane Hutta, Secy.; Takeshi Fujinuma, Treas.; William Haney; D. Scarborough Smith III; Masaki Tachibana.
EIN: 133766226
Selected grants: The following grants are a representative sample of this grantmaker's funding activity:
$219,800 to Institute of International Education, New York, NY, 2009.
$5,000 to Lincoln Center for the Performing Arts, New York, NY, 2009.
$2,000 to Ronald McDonald House Charities, Oak Brook, IL, 2009.
$1,145 to Autism Speaks, New York, NY, 2009.
$1,000 to Connecticut College, New London, CT, 2009.
$1,000 to Villanova University, Villanova, PA, 2009.

3481
Smelter Service Corp.

400 Arrow Mines Rd.
Mount Pleasant, TN 38474-1605
(931) 379-7765

Company URL: http://www.smelterservice.com/
Establishment information: Established in 1978.
Company type: Private company
Business activities: Distributes and recycles nonferrous scrap and whole metals.
Business type (SIC): Metal refining/secondary nonferrous
Financial profile for 2010: Sales volume, $92,000,000
Corporate officer: Bill Toler, C.E.O.
Giving statement: Giving through the Kids on Stage Foundation of Maury County, Tennessee, Inc.

Kids on Stage Foundation of Maury County, Tennessee, Inc.

P.O. Box 432
Mount Pleasant, TN 38474 (931) 379-7765

Establishment information: Established in 2001 in TN.
Donor: Smelter Service Corp.
Contact: Mike Crane
Financial data (yr. ended 12/31/11): Assets, $96,949 (M); gifts received, $120,884; expenditures, $145,030; qualifying distributions, $116,167; giving activities include $10,000 for 1 grant.
Application information: Applications accepted. Application form not required.
Initial approach: Proposal
Deadline(s): None
Officers: Jim G. Barrier, Pres.; Thomas Hardin, Secy.; Faye Tucker, Treas.
EIN: 621805806

3482
Smith Center Branch
136 S. Main St.
Smith Center, KS 66967-2606
(785) 282-6682

Company URL: http://www.bellebank.com/
Company type: Subsidiary of a private company
Business activities: Operates commercial bank.
Business type (SIC): Banks/commercial
Corporate officer: Steve Mills, Pres.
Giving statement: Giving through the Smith County State Bank and Trust Company Charitable Trust.

Smith County State Bank and Trust Company Charitable Trust
P.O. Box 307
Smith Center, KS 66967-0307

Establishment information: Established in 1991 in KS.
Donor: Smith County State Bank & Trust Co.
Financial data (yr. ended 10/31/12): Assets, $265,528 (M); expenditures, $12,342; qualifying distributions, $12,188; giving activities include $11,674 for 5 grants (high: $5,000; low: $1,000).
Purpose and activities: The foundation supports organizations involved with education and community development.
Fields of interest: Arts; Health care; Community/economic development.
Type of support: General/operating support.
Geographic limitations: Giving limited to Lebanon and Smith Center, KS.
Support limitations: No grants to individuals.
Application information: Applications not accepted. Unsolicited requests for funds not accepted.
Trustee: The Peoples Bank.
EIN: 481106290

3483
C. D. Smith Construction, Inc.
889 E. Johnson St.
P.O. Box 1006
Fond du Lac, WI 54936-1006
(920) 924-2900

Company URL: http://www.cd-smith.com/
Establishment information: Established in 1936.
Company type: Private company
Business activities: Provides general contract construction services.
Business type (SIC): Building construction general contractors and operative builders
Corporate officers: Thomas D. Baker, Chair.; Gary M. Smith, Pres. and C.E.O.; Robert Baker, V.P., Finance; Patrick S. Smith, Secy.; Rob Seibel, Treas.
Board of director: Thomas D. Baker, Chair.
Giving statement: Giving through the C. D. Smith Foundation, Inc.

C. D. Smith Foundation, Inc.
889 E. Johnson St.
Fond du Lac, WI 54936-2933

Establishment information: Established in 1999 in WI.
Donor: C.D. Smith Construction, Inc.
Financial data (yr. ended 12/31/11): Assets, $855,546 (M); gifts received, $760; expenditures, $260,770; qualifying distributions, $260,000; giving activities include $260,000 for grants.
Purpose and activities: The foundation provides charitable donations to the Fond Du Lac Family YMCA in Wisconsin.
Fields of interest: YM/YWCAs & YM/YWHAs.
Type of support: General/operating support.
Geographic limitations: Giving limited to WI.
Support limitations: No grants to individuals.
Application information: Applications not accepted. Contributes only to a pre-selected organization.
Officers and Directors: Gary M. Smith, Pres.; Thomas J. Baker, V.P.; Patrick S. Smith, Secy.; Robert Baker, Treas.; Thomas D. Baker; Mike P. Fortune; Justin Smith; Mary Lou Smith.
EIN: 391972533
Selected grants: The following grants are a representative sample of this grantmaker's funding activity:
$100,000 to Viterbo University, La Crosse, WI, 2010. For operating expenses.

3484
A. O. Smith Corporation
11270 W. Park Pl., Ste. 170
P.O. Box 245008
Milwaukee, WI 53224-9508
(414) 359-4000
FAX: (414) 359-4115

Company URL: http://www.aosmith.com
Establishment information: Established in 1874.
Company type: Public company
Company ticker symbol and exchange: AOS/NYSE
Business activities: Manufactures fractional horsepower, integral horsepower alternating current and direct current, and hermetic electric motors; manufactures gas and electric water heating equipment and copper tube boilers.
Business type (SIC): Electrical industrial apparatus; metal plumbing fixtures and heating equipment/nonelectric
Financial profile for 2012: Number of employees, 10,900; assets, $2,265,200,000; sales volume, $1,939,300,000; pre-tax net income, $233,800,000; expenses, $1,705,500,000; liabilities, $1,071,100,000
Fortune 1000 ranking: 2012—962nd in revenues, 638th in profits, and 825th in assets
Corporate officers: Paul W. Jones, Chair.; Ajita G. Rajendra, Pres. and C.E.O.; John M. Kita, Exec. V.P. and C.F.O.; James F. Stern, Exec. V.P., Genl. Counsel, and Secy.; Randall S. Bednar, Sr. V.P. and C.I.O.; Mark A. Petrarca, Sr. V.P., Human Resources and Public Affairs; Robert J. Heideman, Sr. V.P., Corp. Tech.; Daniel L. Kempken, V.P. and Cont.
Board of directors: Paul W. Jones, Chair.; Ronald D. Brown; Gloster B. Current, Jr.; William P. Greubel; Ajita G. Rajendra; Mathias F. Sandoval; Bruce M. Smith; Mark D. Smith; Idelle K. Wolf; Gene C. Wulf
Plants: Alsip, IL; Monticello, Paoli, IN; Parsons, Wichita, KS; Florence, Mount Sterling, KY; Tipp City, Upper Sandusky, OH; McBee, SC; Winchester, TN; El Paso, Irving, TX; Seattle, WA
International operations: Barbados; Canada; China; France; Germany; Hungary; India; Ireland; Mexico; Netherlands; Singapore; United Arab Emirates; United Kingdom
Giving statement: Giving through the A. O. Smith Foundation, Inc.
Company EIN: 390619790

A. O. Smith Foundation, Inc.
P.O. Box 245008
Milwaukee, WI 53224-9508
URL: http://www.aosmith.com/About/Detail.aspx?id=132&ekmensel=c580fa7b_8_0_132_6

Establishment information: Incorporated in 1955 in WI.
Donor: A.O. Smith Corp.
Contact: Roger S. Smith, Dir.
Financial data (yr. ended 12/31/11): Assets, $4,204,963 (M); gifts received, $1,197,750; expenditures, $1,285,538; qualifying distributions, $1,283,553; giving activities include $1,253,675 for 103 grants (high: $180,000; low: $300) and $29,878 for 39 employee matching gifts.
Purpose and activities: The foundation supports programs designed to strengthen higher education throughout the country; promote the civic, cultural, and social welfare of communities; and advance medical research and improve local health services.
Fields of interest: Arts; Higher education; Hospitals (general); Health care; Medical research; Human services; Community/economic development; United Ways and Federated Giving Programs; Public affairs.
Programs:
Employee-related Scholarships: The foundation awards college scholarships to children of employees of A.O. Smith. The program is administered by Scholarship America.
Matching Gift Program: The foundation matches contributions made by employees of A.O. Smith to educational institutions on a one-for-one basis up to $3,000 per year.
Type of support: Annual campaigns; Building/renovation; Capital campaigns; Continuing support; Employee matching gifts; Employee volunteer services; General/operating support; Program development; Scholarship funds; Sponsorships.
Geographic limitations: Giving primarily in areas of company operations in KY, NC, SC, TN, TX, WA, and WI.
Support limitations: No support for political or lobbying organizations. No grants to individuals.
Publications: Annual report (including application guidelines); Application guidelines.
Application information: Applications accepted. Proposals should be submitted using organization letterhead. Application form not required. Applicants should submit the following:
1) statement of problem project will address
2) population served
3) name, address and phone number of organization
4) copy of IRS Determination Letter
5) brief history of organization and description of its mission
6) geographic area to be served
7) how project's results will be evaluated or measured
8) descriptive literature about organization
9) detailed description of project and amount of funding requested
10) copy of current year's organizational budget and/or project budget
11) listing of additional sources and amount of support

Proposals should include plans for reporting results.
Initial approach: Proposal
Copies of proposal: 1
Board meeting date(s): June and Dec.
Deadline(s): Oct. 30
Officers and Directors:* Bruce M. Smith*, Pres.; Mark A. Petrarca*, Secy.; John J. Kita, Treas.; Paul W. Jones; Edward J. O'Connor; Roger S. Smith.
Number of staff: 1 part-time support.
EIN: 396076924

Selected grants: The following grants are a representative sample of this grantmaker's funding activity:
$180,000 to United Way of Greater Milwaukee, Milwaukee, WI, 2011.
$133,775 to Scholarship America, Saint Peter, MN, 2011.
$111,000 to Boys and Girls Clubs of Greater Milwaukee, Milwaukee, WI, 2011.
$50,000 to Greater Milwaukee Foundation, Milwaukee, WI, 2011.
$35,000 to United Performing Arts Fund, Milwaukee, WI, 2011.
$30,000 to Milwaukee 7 Water Council, Milwaukee, WI, 2011.
$15,000 to Childrens Health System, Milwaukee, WI, 2011.
$12,500 to Goodwill Industries of Southeastern Wisconsin, Milwaukee, WI, 2011.
$10,000 to Childrens Outing Association, Milwaukee, WI, 2011.
$6,000 to Wisconsin Lutheran High School, Milwaukee, WI, 2011.

3485
J M Smith Corporation

101 W. St. John St., Ste. 305
Spartanburg, SC 29306-5150
(864) 542-9419

Company URL: http://www.jmsmith.com/
Establishment information: Established in 1943.
Company type: Private company
Business activities: Sells drugs wholesale; provides data processing services.
Business type (SIC): Drugs, proprietaries, and sundries—wholesale; computer services
Financial profile for 2011: Number of employees, 1,100; assets, $479,000,000; sales volume, $2,430,000,000
Corporate officers: William R. Cobb, Chair. and C.E.O.; Kenneth R. Couch, Pres.; James C. Wilson, Jr., C.F.O. and Treas.
Board of director: William Cobb, Chair.
Giving statement: Giving through the J M Smith Foundation.

J M Smith Foundation

101 W. St. John St., Ste. 305
Spartanburg, SC 29306-5150

Establishment information: Established in 1996 in SC.
Donor: J M Smith Corp.
Financial data (yr. ended 02/29/12): Assets, $301,448 (M); gifts received, $2,212,735; expenditures, $2,499,352; qualifying distributions, $2,499,352; giving activities include $2,499,165 for 396 grants (high: $200,000; low: $200).
Purpose and activities: The foundation supports organizations involved with education, hunger, human services, and Christianity.
Fields of interest: Secondary school/education; Higher education; Education; Food services; Food distribution, meals on wheels; Boys & girls clubs; YM/YWCAs & YM/YWHAs; Human services; United Ways and Federated Giving Programs; Christian agencies & churches.
Type of support: Continuing support; Equipment; General/operating support; Program development; Scholarship funds.
Geographic limitations: Giving primarily in SC; giving also in AR, FL, GA, KY, NC, PA, and VA.
Support limitations: No grants to individuals.
Application information: Applications not accepted. Contributes only to pre-selected organizations.
Officers and Directors: Kenneth R. Couch, Pres.; Tammy Devine, Secy.; James C. Wilson, Jr., Treas.; Henry D. Smith; Mike Webb; Russ Webber.
EIN: 571046595
Selected grants: The following grants are a representative sample of this grantmaker's funding activity:
$157,600 to University of South Carolina Upstate Foundation, Spartanburg, SC, 2010. For unrestricted support.
$100,000 to University of South Carolina Upstate Foundation, Spartanburg, SC, 2010. For unrestricted support.
$71,500 to Converse College, Spartanburg, SC, 2010. For unrestricted support.
$59,500 to Presbyterian College, Clinton, SC, 2010. For unrestricted support.
$58,500 to Wingate University, Wingate, NC, 2010. For unrestricted support.
$56,700 to First Presbyterian Church, Spartanburg, SC, 2010. For unrestricted support.
$37,926 to First Baptist Church, Spartanburg, SC, 2010. For unrestricted support.
$32,701 to Anderson Mill Road Baptist Church, Moore, SC, 2010. For unrestricted support.
$30,800 to Inman First Baptist Church, Inman, SC, 2010. For unrestricted support.
$14,000 to Jackson Baptist Church, Wellford, SC, 2010. For unrestricted support.

3486
Smith, Anderson, Blount, Dorsett, Mitchell & Jernigan, LLP

2500 Wachovia Capitol Ctr.
P.O Box 2611
Raleigh, NC 27602-2611 (919) 821-6629

Company URL: http://www.smithlaw.com/
Establishment information: Established in 1912.
Company type: Private company
Business activities: Operates law firm.
Business type (SIC): Legal services
Office: Raleigh, NC
Giving statement: Giving through the Smith, Anderson, Blount, Dorsett, Mitchell & Jernigan, LLP Pro Bono Program.

Smith, Anderson, Blount, Dorsett, Mitchell & Jernigan, LLP Pro Bono Program

2500 Wachovia Capitol Ctr.
P.O Box 2611
Raleigh, NC 27602-2611 (919) 821-6629
E-mail: rkenyon@smithlaw.com; Additional tel.:(919) 821-1220; URL: http://www.smithlaw.com/about-probono.html

Contact: Rosemary G. Kenyon, Partner
Fields of interest: Legal services.
Type of support: Pro bono services - legal.
Application information: An attorney coordinates pro bono projects.

3487
Smithfield Foods, Inc.

200 Commerce St.
Smithfield, VA 23430 (757) 365-3000

Company URL: http://www.smithfieldfoods.com
Establishment information: Established in 1936.
Company type: Public company
Company ticker symbol and exchange: SFD/NYSE
Business activities: Produces hogs; produces pork products; produces beef products.
Business type (SIC): Meat packing plants and prepared meats and poultry; farms/livestock
Financial profile for 2012: Number of employees, 46,050; assets, $7,422,200,000; sales volume, $13,094,300,000; pre-tax net income, $533,700,000; expenses, $12,383,900,000; liabilities, $4,034,900,000
Fortune 1000 ranking: 2012—213th in revenues, 426th in profits, and 472nd in assets
Forbes 2000 ranking: 2012—739th in sales, 1626th in profits, and 1627th in assets
Corporate officers: Joseph W. Luter III, Chair.; C. Larry Pope, Pres. and C.E.O.; Robert W. Manly IV, Exec. V.P. and C.F.O.; Henry L. Morris, Sr. V.P., Opers.; Kenneth M. Sullivan, Sr. V.P., Finance and C.A.O.; Michael H. Cole, V.P. and Secy.; Mansour T. Zadeh, V.P. and C.I.O.; Timothy Dykstra, V.P. and Corp. Treas.; Jeffrey A. Deel, V.P. and Corp. Cont.
Board of directors: Joseph W. Luter III, Chair.; Carol T. Crawford; Richard T. Crowder; Margaret G. Lewis; Wendell H. Murphy; David C. Nelson; C. Larry Pope; Frank S. Royal, M.D.; John T. Schwieters; Paul S. Trible, Jr.
Subsidiaries: Carroll's Foods, Inc., Warsaw, NC; Patrick Cudahy Inc., Cudahy, WI; Esskay Investments, Inc., Riverwood, MD; Gwaltney of Smithfield, Ltd., Smithfield, VA; Lykes Meat Group, Inc., Plant City, FL; John Morrell & Co., Cincinnati, OH; Murphy Farms LLC, Warsaw, NC; The Smithfield Packing Co., Inc., Smithfield, VA; Sunnyland, Inc., Thomasville, GA
International operations: Bermuda; Germany; Mexico; Netherlands; Poland; Romania; United Kingdom
Giving statement: Giving through the Smithfield Foods, Inc. Corporate Giving Program and the Smithfield-Luter Foundation, Inc.
Company EIN: 520845861

Smithfield Foods, Inc. Corporate Giving Program

200 Commerce St.
Smithfield, VA 23430-1204 (757) 365-3000
URL: http://smithfieldcommitments.com/

Purpose and activities: As a complement to its foundation, Smithfield Foods also makes charitable contributions to nonprofit organizations directly. Support is given on a national basis in areas of company operations.
Fields of interest: Food services; Nutrition; Disasters, preparedness/services; Human services.
Type of support: General/operating support; In-kind gifts.
Geographic limitations: Giving on a national basis in areas of company operations, with some emphasis on Isle of Wight County, VA.
Application information: Applications accepted. Application form not required. Applicants should submit the following:
1) detailed description of project and amount of funding requested
Initial approach: Proposal to headquarters
Final notification: Following review

The Smithfield-Luter Foundation, Inc.

200 Commerce St.
Smithfield, VA 23430-1204 (757) 365-3000
URL: http://www.smithfieldluterfoundation.com/

Establishment information: Established in 2002 in VA and NC.
Donors: Joseph W. Luter III; Smithfield Foods, Inc.
Contact: Stewart Leeth, Deputy Dir.
Financial data (yr. ended 11/30/11): Assets, $2,712,591 (M); gifts received, $3,192,339; expenditures, $3,012,854; qualifying distributions, $3,012,704; giving activities include $3,010,544 for 19 grants (high: $1,000,000; low: $2,300).
Purpose and activities: The foundation supports organizations involved with education and provides scholarships to dependent children and grandchildren of full-time and retired employees of Smithfield and its family of companies to attend select universities.
Fields of interest: Higher education; Scholarships/financial aid; Education; Cancer research Economically disadvantaged.
Type of support: Employee-related scholarships; General/operating support; Program development; Scholarship funds.
Geographic limitations: Giving primarily in areas of company operations in CA, IA, NC, TN, and VA.
Application information: Applications not accepted. Contributes only to pre-selected organizations and through employee-related scholarships.
Officer and Trustees:* Dennis H. Treacy*, Exec. Dir.; Joseph W. Luter IV; Francis Luter.
EIN: 542062029

3488
The J. M. Smucker Company

1 Strawberry Ln.
Orrville, OH 44667-0280 (330) 682-3000
FAX: (330) 684-6410

Company URL: http://www.smucker.com
Establishment information: Established in 1897.
Company type: Public company
Company ticker symbol and exchange: SJM/NYSE
International Securities Identification Number: US8326964058
Business activities: Produces and markets food products; produces jams, jellies, preserves, ice cream toppings, peanut butter, frozen fruits, fruit butters, syrups, food gift boxes, and fruit juices.
Business type (SIC): Specialty foods/canned, frozen, and preserved; beverages; miscellaneous prepared foods
Financial profile for 2012: Number of employees, 4,850; assets, $9,115,230,000; sales volume, $5,525,780,000; pre-tax net income, $701,160,000; expenses, $4,747,500,000; liabilities, $3,951,840,000
Fortune 1000 ranking: 2012—452nd in revenues, 354th in profits, and 419th in assets
Corporate officers: Timothy P. Smucker, Chair.; Richard K. Smucker, C.E.O.; Vincent C. Byrd, Pres. and C.O.O.; Mark R. Belgya, Sr. V.P. and C.F.O.; Barry C. Dunaway, Sr. V.P. and C.A.O.; Christopher P. Resweber, Sr. V.P., Corp. Comms., and Public Affairs; John W. Denman, V.P., Cont., and C.A.O.; Jeannette L. Knudsen, V.P., Genl. Counsel, and Corp. Secy.; Debra A. Marthey, Treas.
Board of directors: Timothy P. Smucker, Chair.; Vincent C. Byrd; R. Douglas Cowan; Kathryn W. Dindo; Paul J. Dolan; Nancy Lopez Knight; Elizabeth Valk Long; Gary A. Oatey; Alex Shumate; Mark T. Smucker; Richard K. Smucker; William H. Steinbrink, Esq.; Paul Smucker Wagstaff
Subsidiaries: California Farm Products, Watsonville, CA; H.B. DeViney Co., New Bethlehem, PA; The Dickinson Family, Inc., Salinas, CA; Mary Ellen, Inc., Salinas, CA; The A.F. Murch Co., Grandview, WA; R-Line Foods, Ripon, WI
Plants: Chico, Oxnard, CA; Havre de Grace, MD; Orrville, OH; Woodburn, OR; Memphis, TN
International operations: Barbados; Canada; China; Hong Kong; Mexico; Scotland
Historic mergers: International Multifoods Corporation (June 18, 2004)
Giving statement: Giving through the J. M. Smucker Company Contributions Program and the Willard E. Smucker Foundation.
Company EIN: 340538550

The J. M. Smucker Company Contributions Program

1 Strawberry Ln.
Orrville, OH 44667-1241 (330) 682-3000
FAX: (330) 684-6410; URL: http://www.smucker.com/family_company/about_us/community.aspx

Purpose and activities: As a complement to its foundation, J.M. Smucker also makes charitable contributions to nonprofit organizations directly. Support is given primarily in areas of company operations in Orrville, Ohio.
Fields of interest: Elementary/secondary education; Boys & girls clubs; Youth development, business; YM/YWCAs & YM/YWHAs; Community development, business promotion; United Ways and Federated Giving Programs.
Type of support: Donated products; Employee volunteer services; General/operating support; In-kind gifts.
Geographic limitations: Giving primarily in areas of company operations, with emphasis on OH.

Willard E. Smucker Foundation

Strawberry Ln.
Orrville, OH 44667-1298

Establishment information: Established in 1968 in OH.
Donor: The J.M. Smucker Co.
Financial data (yr. ended 12/31/11): Assets, $18,027,518 (M); expenditures, $575,247; qualifying distributions, $564,810; giving activities include $564,810 for grants.
Purpose and activities: The foundation supports food banks and organizations involved with arts and culture, education, health, Alzheimer's disease, human services, and Christianity.
Fields of interest: Museums; Arts; Higher education; Education; Hospitals (general); Health care; Alzheimer's disease; Food banks; Salvation Army; Children/youth, services; Family services; Family services, domestic violence; Homeless, human services; Human services; Christian agencies & churches.
Type of support: General/operating support.
Geographic limitations: Giving primarily in AZ, CA, and OH.
Support limitations: No grants to individuals.
Application information: Applications not accepted. Contributes only to pre-selected organizations.
Officers and Trustees:* Timothy P. Smucker*, Pres.; Marcella S. Clark*, Exec. V.P.; Richard K. Smucker*, VP; Jeanette L. Knudson, Secy.; Carole L. Randall; Susan S. Wagstaff.
EIN: 346610889
Selected grants: The following grants are a representative sample of this grantmaker's funding activity:
$30,000 to Institute for American Values, New York, NY, 2010. For general operations.
$25,000 to Banner Alzheimers Foundation, Phoenix, AZ, 2010. For general operations.
$13,000 to Boston Landmarks Orchestra, Cambridge, MA, 2010.
$10,362 to Alzheimers Association, Phoenix, AZ, 2010. For general operations.
$10,000 to Arden Wood Benevolent Association, San Francisco, CA, 2010. For general operations.
$10,000 to Glenmont, Hilliard, OH, 2010. For general operations.
$10,000 to Homeward Bound, Phoenix, AZ, 2010. For general operations.
$10,000 to Monterey Bay Aquarium, Monterey, CA, 2010. For general operations.
$10,000 to Ohio Wesleyan University, Delaware, OH, 2010. For scholarship fund.
$10,000 to Wayne County Community Foundation, Wooster, OH, 2010. For general operations.

3489
Smulekoff Furniture Company, Inc.

97 3rd Ave. S.E.
Cedar Rapids, IA 52401-1410
(319) 362-2181

Company URL: http://www.smulekoffs.com
Establishment information: Established in 1889.
Company type: Private company
Business activities: Operates home furnishings stores.
Business type (SIC): Furniture and home furnishing stores
Corporate officers: Abbott Lipsky, Pres. and C.E.O.; Joan M. Lipsky, Secy.
Board of director: Joan M. Lipsky
Giving statement: Giving through the Smulekoff-Lipsky Fund.

Smulekoff-Lipsky Fund

(formerly Smulekoff-Miller Fund)
97 3rd Ave. S.E.
Cedar Rapids, IA 52401

Donors: Smulekoff Furniture Co.; Smulekoff Investment Co.; Abbott Lipsky; Joan Lipsky; Ann Lipsky.
Financial data (yr. ended 12/31/11): Assets, $637,866 (M); gifts received, $5,000; expenditures, $25,814; qualifying distributions, $22,950; giving activities include $22,950 for grants.
Purpose and activities: The fund supports organizations involved with higher education, human services, and Judaism.
Fields of interest: Higher education; Human services; United Ways and Federated Giving Programs; Jewish agencies & synagogues.
Type of support: General/operating support.
Geographic limitations: Giving primarily in Cedar Rapids, IA.
Support limitations: No grants to individuals.
Application information: Applications not accepted. Contributes only to pre-selected organizations.
Trustees: Abbott Lipsky; Joan Lipsky.
EIN: 426081470

3490
Snell & Wilmer L.L.P.

1 Arizona Ctr.
400 E. Van Buren St., Ste. 1900
Phoenix, AZ 85004-2202 (602) 382-6000

Company URL: http://www.swlaw.com
Establishment information: Established in 1938.
Company type: Private company
Business activities: Provides legal services.
Business type (SIC): Legal services
Financial profile for 2011: Number of employees, 400
Corporate officers: John J. Bouma, Chair.; Michael J. Marrie, C.F.O.
Board of director: John J. Bouma, Chair.
Offices: Phoenix, Tucson, AZ; Irvine, Los Angeles, CA; Denver, CO; Las Vegas, NV; Salt Lake City, UT
Giving statement: Giving through the Snell & Wilmer L.L.P. Corporate Giving Program, the Snell & Wilmer Pro Bono Program, and the Snell & Wilmer Charitable Foundation.

Snell & Wilmer Pro Bono Program

1 Arizona Ctr.
400 E. Van Buren
Phoenix, AZ 85004-2202 (602) 382-6280
E-mail: jgrabel@swlaw.com; URL: http://www.swlaw.com/the-firm/community

Contact: Joshua Grabel, Partner & Pro Bono Chair.
Fields of interest: Legal services.
Type of support: Pro bono services - legal.
Application information: A Pro Bono Committee manages the pro bono program.

Snell & Wilmer Charitable Foundation

c/o Thomas R. Hoecker
1 Arizona Ctr.
Phoenix, AZ 85004-2202
E-mail: thoecker@swlaw.com

Establishment information: Established in 2002 in AZ.
Donors: Snell & Wilmer L.L.P.; John J. Bouma; Jon S. Cohen; Thomas R. Hoecker; Matthew Feeney; Warren E. Platt.
Financial data (yr. ended 12/31/11): Assets, $1,344,455 (M); gifts received, $250,000; expenditures, $203,335; qualifying distributions, $203,335; giving activities include $203,335 for 7 grants (high: $90,000; low: $6,667).
Purpose and activities: The foundation supports museums and organizations involved with education, substance abuse services, and children.
Fields of interest: Museums; Education, early childhood education; Education; Substance abuse, services; Children, services; United Ways and Federated Giving Programs.
Type of support: General/operating support; Program development.
Geographic limitations: Giving primarily in areas of company operations in AZ, CA, and UT.
Support limitations: No grants to individuals.
Application information: Applications not accepted. Contributes only to pre-selected organizations.
Officers: John J. Bouma, Pres.; Jon S. Cohen, V.P. and Secy.; Matthew Feeney, V.P.; Thomas R. Hoecker, V.P.; Warren E. Platt, V.P.
EIN: 470901535
Selected grants: The following grants are a representative sample of this grantmaker's funding activity:
$90,000 to United Way, Valley of the Sun, Phoenix, AZ, 2010.
$25,000 to House of Hope, Salt Lake City, UT, 2010.
$18,333 to Lied Discovery Childrens Museum, Las Vegas, NV, 2010.

3491
Snow, Christensen & Martineau

(formerly Worsley, Snow & Christensen)
10 Exchange Pl., 11th Fl.
Salt Lake City, UT 84111-2824
(801) 322-9000

Company URL: http://www.scmlaw.com/index.php?page_id=2&page_cat_id=2
Establishment information: Established in 1886.
Company type: Private company
Business activities: Provides legal services.
Business type (SIC): Legal services
Corporate officers: David W. Slaughter, Chair.; Paul Walker, Cont.
Board of director: David Slaughter, Chair.
Giving statement: Giving through the Snow, Christensen & Martineau Foundation.

Snow, Christensen & Martineau Foundation

P.O. Box 45000
Salt Lake City, UT 84145-5000

Establishment information: Established in 1988 in UT.
Donor: Snow, Christensen & Martineau.
Financial data (yr. ended 12/31/11): Assets, $436,893 (M); expenditures, $25,162; qualifying distributions, $19,900; giving activities include $19,900 for grants.
Purpose and activities: The foundation supports hospitals and organizations involved with arts and culture, higher education, patient services, children and youth, homelessness, and Christianity.
Fields of interest: Arts; Education; Health care.
Type of support: General/operating support.
Geographic limitations: Giving limited to Salt Lake City, UT.
Support limitations: No grants to individuals.
Application information: Applications not accepted. Unsolicited requests for funds not accepted.
Officer: John E. Gates, Secy.-Treas.
Trustees: Andrew M. Morse; Stanley J. Preston.
EIN: 870450634

3492
Snyder's-Lance, Inc.

(formerly Lance, Inc.)
Charlotte Support Ctr.
13024 Ballantyne Corporate Pl., Ste. 900
Charlotte, NC 28277 (704) 554-1421
FAX: (704) 554-5562

Company URL: http://www.lanceinc.com
Establishment information: Established in 1913.
Company type: Public company
Company ticker symbol and exchange: LNCE/NASDAQ
Business activities: Produces, markets, and sells snack food products.
Business type (SIC): Bakery products
Financial profile for 2012: Number of employees, 5,900; assets, $1,746,730,000; sales volume, $1,618,630,000; pre-tax net income, $99,650,000; expenses, $1,509,490,000; liabilities, $877,230,000
Corporate officers: Michael A. Warehime, Chair.; Carl E. Lee, Jr., Pres., C.E.O., and C.O.O.; Rick D. Puckett, Exec. V.P., C.F.O., and Treas.; Margaret E. Wicklund, V.P. and Corp. Cont.
Board of directors: Michael A. Warehime, Chair.; Jeffrey A. Atkins; Peter P. Brubaker; C. Peter Carlucci, Jr.; John E. Denton; James W. Johnston; Carl E. Lee, Jr.; Wilbur J. Prezzano; Dan C. Swander; Isaiah Tidwell; Patricia A. Warehime
Subsidiaries: Caronuts, Inc., Boykins, VA; Midwest Biscuit Co., Burlington, IA; Nutrition-Pak Co., Mebane, NC; Vista Bakery, Inc., Columbia, SC
Plant: Greenville, TX
Giving statement: Giving through the Lance Foundation.
Company EIN: 560292920

Lance Foundation

P.O. Box 32368
Charlotte, NC 28232-2368 (704) 554-1421

Establishment information: Trust established in 1956 in NC.
Donor: Lance, Inc.
Contact: Sid Levy
Financial data (yr. ended 12/31/11): Assets, $2,138,314 (M); gifts received, $21,070; expenditures, $438,574; qualifying distributions, $415,847; giving activities include $415,847 for grants.
Purpose and activities: The foundation supports hospices and organizations involved with arts and culture, education, hunger, youth development, and business.
Fields of interest: Arts; Higher education; Education; Animals/wildlife, sanctuaries; Breast cancer; Diabetes; Boy scouts; Residential/custodial care, hospices; Homeless, human services; Human services; United Ways and Federated Giving Programs.
Type of support: General/operating support; Scholarship funds.
Geographic limitations: Giving primarily in Charlotte, NC.
Support limitations: No grants to individuals, or for scholarships or fellowships; no loans.
Application information: Applications accepted. Application form not required. Applicants should submit the following:
1) detailed description of project and amount of funding requested
Initial approach: Proposal
Copies of proposal: 1
Board meeting date(s): As required
Deadline(s): None
Final notification: 2 to 3 months
Directors: Rodney Brown; Joe Machicote; Rick D. Puckett.
Trustee: Bank of America, N.A.
Number of staff: 1
EIN: 566039487
Selected grants: The following grants are a representative sample of this grantmaker's funding activity:
$35,000 to United Way of Central Carolinas, Charlotte, NC, 2010. For general use.
$30,000 to Afro-American Cultural Center, Charlotte, NC, 2010. For general use.
$25,000 to Students in Free Enterprise, Springfield, MO, 2010. For general use.
$10,000 to Levine and Dickson Hospice House, Charlotte, NC, 2010. For general use.
$6,000 to Hinds Feet Farm, Huntersville, NC, 2010. For general funds.
$5,000 to Foundation for the Carolinas, Charlotte, NC, 2010. For general funds.

$5,000 to North Carolina Dance Theater, Charlotte, NC, 2010. For general funds.
$5,000 to United Way of Ashland County, Ashland, OH, 2010. For general funds.
$3,500 to Discovery Place, Charlotte, NC, 2010. For general use.
$2,500 to Hope Haven, Rock Valley, IA, 2010. For general funds.

3493
Social Enterprise Associates
1803 Otowi Rd.
Santa Fe, NM 87505-3331 (202) 256-2692

Company URL: http://www.socialenterprise.net
Establishment information: Established in 1969.
Company type: Private company
Business type (SIC): Business services/miscellaneous
Corporate officer: Drew Tulchin, Owner
Giving statement: Giving through the Social Enterprise Associates Corporate Giving Program.

Social Enterprise Associates Corporate Giving Program
1803 Otowi Rd.
Santa Fe, NM 87505-3331 (505) 715-6927
E-mail: info@socialenterprise.net; URL: http://www.socialenterprise.net

Purpose and activities: Social Enterprise Associates is a certified B Corporation that donates a percentage of sales to charitable organizations.

3494
Social(k)
250 Albany St.
Springfield, MA 01105 (866) 929-2525

Company URL: http://www.socialk.com
Company type: Private company
Business activities: Provides a paperless retirement platform for 401(k) and 403(b) plans.
Business type (SIC): Investors/miscellaneous
Corporate officer: Robert M. Thomas, Pres.
Giving statement: Giving through the Social(k) Corporate Giving Program.

Social(k) Corporate Giving Program
250 Albany St.
Springfield, MA 01105-1018 (866) 929-2525
E-mail: info@expertplan.com; URL: http://www.socialk.com

Purpose and activities: Social(k) is a certified B Corporation that donates a percentage of annual pre-tax profits to nonprofit organizations. Special emphasis is directed toward organizations involved with the environment. Support is given primarily in areas of company operations; giving also to national and international organizations.
Fields of interest: Environment.
Type of support: General/operating support.
Geographic limitations: Giving primarily in areas of company operations; giving also to national and international organizations.

3495
SocketLabs, Inc.
650 Naamans Rd., Ste. 307
Claymont, DE 19703-2300 (484) 418-1285
FAX: (484) 693-1371

Company URL: http://www.socketlabs.com
Establishment information: Established in 2007.
Company type: Private company
Business activities: Operates email delivery company.
Business type (SIC): Computer services
Corporate officer: John Alessi, C.E.O.
Giving statement: Giving through the SocketLabs, Inc. Contributions Program.

SocketLabs, Inc. Contributions Program
650 Naamans Rd., Ste. 307
Claymont, DE 19703-2300 (800) 650-1639
URL: http://www.socketlabs.com

3496
Socorro Electric Cooperative, Inc.
215 Manzanares Ave. E.
P.O. Box H
Socorro, NM 87801 (575) 835-0560

Company URL: http://www.socorroelectric.com
Establishment information: Established in 1945.
Company type: Cooperative
Business activities: Generates, transmits, and distributes electricity.
Business type (SIC): Electric services
Financial profile for 2010: Number of employees, 29
Corporate officers: Paul Bustamante, Pres.; Luis Aguilar, Secy.; Leo C. Cordova, Treas.
Board of directors: Luis Aguilar; Leroy Anaya; Paul Bustamante; Leo C. Cordova; Prescilla Mauldin; Milton Ulibarri; David Wade; Charlie Wagner; Donald Wolberg
Giving statement: Giving through the Socorro Electric Foundation.

Socorro Electric Foundation
P.O. Box H
Socorro, NM 87801-0278 (505) 835-0560

Establishment information: Established in 1986 in NM.
Donor: Socorro Electric Cooperative, Inc.
Financial data (yr. ended 12/31/11): Assets, $59,748 (M); expenditures, $12,593; qualifying distributions, $12,163; giving activities include $11,850 for 19 grants to individuals (high: $1,000; low: $500).
Purpose and activities: The foundation awards college scholarships to high school valedictorians in areas of company operations of Socorro Electric Cooperative.
Type of support: Scholarships—to individuals.
Geographic limitations: Giving limited to areas of company operations in NM.
Application information: Applications accepted. Application form required.
Initial approach: Proposal
Deadline(s): None
Officers: Paul Bustamante, Pres.; David Wade, V.P.; Luis Aguilar, Secy.; Milton Ulibarri, Treas.
Trustees: Leroy Anaya; Jack Bruton; Leo C. Cordova; Precilla Mauldin; Charles Wagner; Donald Wolberg.
EIN: 237044964

3497
Sodexo, Inc.
(formerly Sodexho, Inc.)
9801 Washingtonian Blvd.
Gaithersburg, MD 20878 (301) 987-4500

Company URL: http://www.sodexhousa.com
Establishment information: Established in 1966.
Company type: Subsidiary of a foreign company
Business activities: Operates and franchises hotels and senior living communities.
Business type (SIC): Hotels and motels; real estate operators and lessors
Corporate officers: George Chavel, Pres. and C.E.O.; Olivier Poirot, C.F.O.; Lorna Donatone, C.O.O.; Tony Tocco, Sr. V.P. and C.I.O.; Stephen J. Brady, Sr. V.P., Corp. Comms.; Peri Bridger, Sr. V.P., Human Resources; Jaya K. Bohlmann, V.P., Public Rels.
Giving statement: Giving through the Sodexo, Inc. Corporate Giving Program and the Sodexo Foundation, Inc.

Sodexo, Inc. Corporate Giving Program
(formerly Sodexho, Inc. Corporate Giving Program)
9801 Washingtonian Blvd.
Gaithersburg, MD 20878-5355 (301) 987-4500

Contact: Sondra Jenkins
Purpose and activities: As a complement to its foundation, Sodexho also makes charitable contributions to nonprofit organizations directly. Support is given primarily in areas of company operations.
Fields of interest: Food services.
Type of support: Employee volunteer services; In-kind gifts.
Geographic limitations: Giving primarily in areas of company operations.
Application information: Applications not accepted. Contributes only to pre-selected organizations.
Number of staff: 1

Sodexo Foundation, Inc.
(formerly Sodexho Foundation, Inc.)
9801 Washingtonian Blvd.
Gaithersburg, MD 20878-5355 (301) 987-4902
E-mail: stophunger@sodexofoundation.org; URL: http://www.stop-hunger.org
Application email: info@applyists.com, tel.: (615) 320-3149

Establishment information: Established in 1999 in MD.
Donors: Sodexho Marriott Services, Inc.; Sodexho, Inc.
Financial data (yr. ended 12/31/11): Revenue, $2,442,558; assets, $882,784 (M); gifts received, $2,442,124; expenditures, $2,241,796; giving activities include $2,214,302 for grants.
Purpose and activities: The foundation aims to eliminate hunger in the U.S. and assists and supports organizations that provide food and other support to people in need.
Fields of interest: Food banks Economically disadvantaged.
Program:
Stephen J. Brady STOP Hunger Scholarship: The program honors students working to build

awareness and mobilize youth as catalysts for innovative solutions to ending hunger in U.S. communities in their lifetime. To be eligible, students must be enrolled in an accredited education institution in the United States and be able to demonstrate an ongoing commitment to hunger-alleviation activities in their community. Up to five students will be selected as national winners, with each receiving a $5,000 scholarship and a $5,000 grant for their anti-hunger charity of choice. In addition, scholarship recipients and two family members will receive an all-expenses-paid trip to Washington, D.C., for the awards ceremony in June. The Foundation also will recognize twenty regional honorees with a $1,000 donation for their preferred hunger charity.
Type of support: Emergency funds.
Geographic limitations: Giving on a national basis.
Publications: Application guidelines.
Application information: Applications accepted. Application form required.
Initial approach: Submit application
Deadline(s): Feb. 18 for Stephen J. Brady STOP Hunger Scholarship
Officers and Directors:* George Chavel*, V.P.; Lorna Donatone*, V.P.; Shondra Jenkins*, V.P.; Joan Rector McGlockton*, V.P.; Ana Oka*, V.P.; Tom Post*, V.P.; Robert A. Stern*, V.P. and Secy.; Dave Scanlan*, Treas.; Paul Brock; Shondra Jenkins.
EIN: 311652380

3498
Sonic Corp.

300 Johnny Bench Dr.
Oklahoma City, OK 73104 (405) 225-5000
FAX: (302) 655-5049

Company URL: http://www.sonicdrivein.com
Establishment information: Established in 1953.
Company type: Public company
Company ticker symbol and exchange: SONC/NASDAQ
Business activities: Operates and franchises drive-in restaurants.
Business type (SIC): Restaurants and drinking places
Financial profile for 2012: Number of employees, 314; assets, $680,760,000; sales volume, $543,730,000; pre-tax net income, $57,960,000; expenses, $454,790,000; liabilities, $621,510,000
Corporate officers: J. Clifford Hudson, Chair., Pres., and C.E.O.; Stephen C. Vaughan, Exec. V.P. and C.F.O.; Craig Miller, Sr. V.P. and C.I.O.; Claudia San Pedro, V.P. and Treas.; Paige S. Bass, V.P. and Genl. Counsel
Board of directors: J. Clifford Hudson, Chair.; Douglas N. Benham; Kate S. Lavelle; Michael J. Maples; J. Larry Nichols; Federico F. Pena; H.E. Rainbolt; Frank E. Richardson; Robert M. Rosenberg; Jeffrey H. Schutz; Kathryn L. Taylor
Subsidiary: Sonic Industries Inc., Oklahoma City, OK
Giving statement: Giving through the Sonic Corp. Contributions Program.
Company EIN: 731371046

Sonic Corp. Contributions Program

300 Johnny Bench Dr.
Oklahoma City, OK 73104
URL: http://www.sonicdrivein.com/business/giving/corporate.jsp

Contact: Nancy L. Robertson, S.V.P. of Communications
Purpose and activities: Sonic makes charitable contributions to programs designed to provide academic opportunities for Oklahomans ages 4 to 22. Support is limited to Oklahoma.
Fields of interest: Elementary/secondary education; Higher education; Education, drop-out prevention; Education, reading; Health care, blood supply; Safety/disasters, information services; American Red Cross.
Type of support: Donated products; Employee volunteer services; General/operating support; Sponsorships.
Geographic limitations: Giving is limited to OK; giving primarily in areas of company operations for food donations.
Support limitations: No support for private pre-school, primary, or secondary educational institutions, private foundations, health-related organizations, political parties or candidates, sectarian, denominational, or religious organizations, or labor, veterans', or other special interest organizations. No grants to individuals, or for dinners, luncheons, or other forms of indirect support, sporting events including golf tournaments, or sectarian, denominational, or religious causes or events.
Publications: Application guidelines.
Application information: Applications accepted. A detailed proposal may be requested at a later date. Multi-year funding is not automatic. Organizations receiving support are asked to provide a final report. Application form not required. Applicants should submit the following:
1) timetable for implementation and evaluation of project
2) results expected from proposed grant
3) population served
4) copy of IRS Determination Letter
5) brief history of organization and description of its mission
6) how project's results will be evaluated or measured
7) detailed description of project and amount of funding requested
8) plans for acknowledgement

Proposals should indicate when and where the event or program will take place, who will manage the program, whether an in-kind donation will suffice, how many people will benefit, and the immediate and long-term achievement goals of the program and the organization.
Initial approach: Proposal to headquarters; contact nearest company restaurant for food donations
Copies of proposal: 1
Deadline(s): None
Final notification: 8 weeks

3499
Sonlight Curriculum, Ltd.

8042 S. Grant Way
Littleton, CO 80122-2705 (303) 730-6292

Company URL: http://www.sonlight.com
Establishment information: Established in 1999.
Company type: Private company
Business activities: Develops homeschool curriculums.
Business type (SIC): Educational services/miscellaneous
Corporate officer: Sarita Holzmann, Pres.
Giving statement: Giving through the Sonlight Curriculum Foundation.

Sonlight Curriculum Foundation

8024 S. Grant Way
Littleton, CO 80122-2705 (303) 730-8193
FAX: (303) 730-6509;
E-mail: scholarship@sonlight.com; URL: http://www.sonlight.com/scholarships.html

Establishment information: Established in 1999 in CO.
Donors: Sonlight Curriculum, Ltd.; Inquisicorp Corporation.
Contact: John A. Holzmann, Pres.
Financial data (yr. ended 12/31/11): Assets, $153,121 (M); gifts received, $92,000; expenditures, $81,340; qualifying distributions, $80,000; giving activities include $80,000 for 43 grants to individuals (high: $5,000; low: $1,000).
Purpose and activities: The foundation awards college scholarships to individuals who have purchased and used four full Sonlight Curriculum Core programs over at least four years.
Fields of interest: Higher education; Christian agencies & churches.
Program:
Sonlight Scholarships: The foundation annually awards thirteen four-year scholarships, including one $5,000 ($20,000 total), four $2,500 ($10,000 total, each) and eight $1,000 ($4,000 total, each) to students who will attend college in the fall. Applicants must have purchased and used five Sonlight Curriculum Core programs. Applicants are evaluated on creativity, mission mindedness, or acts of kindness, spiritual mindedness, leadership, academic performance, heart for learning, and activities and interests.
Type of support: Scholarships—to individuals.
Geographic limitations: Giving on a national and international basis.
Publications: Application guidelines; Grants list.
Application information: Applications accepted. Application form required.
Applications should include SAT, ACT, or other standardized test scores; a list of extracurricular activities; up to 3 reference letters; a personal essay discussing future plans; a copy of the applicant's best project; a copy of the applicant's best argumentative essay; and a photograph.
Initial approach: Download application form and mail to foundation
Deadline(s): Dec. 7
Final notification: Feb. 15
Officers: John A. Holzmann, Pres.; Sarita Holzmann, Secy.-Treas.
EIN: 841521871

3500
Sonoco Products Company

1 N. 2nd St.
P.O. Box 160
Hartsville, SC 29550-3305 (843) 383-7000
FAX: (843) 383-7008

Company URL: http://www.sonoco.com
Establishment information: Established in 1899.
Company type: Public company
Company ticker symbol and exchange: SON/NYSE
Business activities: Manufactures industrial and consumer paper, paperboard, and metal, plastic, and wood packaging products.
Business type (SIC): Paperboard containers; lumber and wood products; wood products/miscellaneous; paperboard mills; chemical preparations/miscellaneous; plastic products/miscellaneous; machinery/general industry

Financial profile for 2012: Number of employees, 19,600; assets, $4,176,060,000; sales volume, $4,786,130,000; pre-tax net income, $287,070,000; expenses, $4,439,070,000; liabilities, $2,687,080,000
Fortune 1000 ranking: 2012—502nd in revenues, 583rd in profits, and 648th in assets
Corporate officers: Harris E. Deloach, Jr., Chair.; M. Jack Sanders, Pres. and C.E.O.; Barry L. Saunders, V.P. and C.F.O.; Allan H. McLeland, V.P., Human Resources
Board of directors: Harris E. Deloach, Jr., Chair.; M. Jack Sanders; Pamela Lewis Davies; John R. Haley; Edgar H. Lawton III; John E. Linville; James M. Micali; John H. Mullin III; Lloyd W. Newton; Marc D. Oken; Philippe R. Rollier; Thomas E. Whiddon
Subsidiaries: Paper Stock Dealers, Inc., Statesville, NC; Sonoco Containers of Puerto Rico, Las Piedras, PR; Sonoco Fibre Drum, Marietta, GA; Sonoco International, Inc., Hartsville, SC
Plants: Hartselle, AL; Elk Grove, CA; Lavonia, Lithonia, Norcross, GA; Lombard, IL; Edinburgh, IN; Holyoke, MA; Hightstown, NJ; Charlotte, Winston-Salem, NC; Tiffin, OH; Pottstown, PA; Fountain Inn, Hartsville, Stockton, SC; Newport, TN; Sumner, WA; Madison, WI
International operations: Australia; Belgium; Brazil; British Virgin Islands; Canada; Chile; Colombia; Estonia; Finland; France; Germany; Greece; India; Luxembourg; Malaysia; Mexico; Netherlands; New Zealand; Norway; Poland; Russia; Singapore; Spain; Sweden; Switzerland; Taiwan; Thailand; Turkey; United Kingdom; Venezuela
Giving statement: Giving through the Sonoco Products Company Contributions Program, the Cloud Family Foundation, Inc., and the Sonoco Foundation.
Company EIN: 570248420

Sonoco Products Company Contributions Program

1 N. 2nd St.
Hartsville, SC 29550-3305
URL: http://www.sonoco.com/sustainability/communityoverview.aspx

Purpose and activities: As a complement to its foundation, Sonoco also makes charitable contributions to nonprofit organizations directly. Special emphasis is directed toward programs that promote education, health, human services, and the environment. Support is given primarily in areas of company operations.
Fields of interest: Education; Environment; Health care; American Red Cross; Human services; Community/economic development.
Program:
Sonoco Scholarship Program: Sonoco annually awards ten $2,000 college scholarships to the children of U.S. employees renewable for an additional three years for a total award of $8,000.
Type of support: Employee volunteer services; Employee-related scholarships; General/operating support.
Geographic limitations: Giving primarily in areas of company operations.
Publications: Corporate giving report.

Cloud Family Foundation, Inc.

(formerly Walter R. Cloud Foundation, Inc.)
P.O. Box 5876
De Pere, WI 54115-2313

Establishment information: Established in 1984.
Donor: U.S. Paper Mills Corp.
Contact: Robert J. Cloud, Pres.
Financial data (yr. ended 09/30/11): Assets, $5,301,780 (M); expenditures, $463,706; qualifying distributions, $417,596; giving activities include $417,596 for grants.
Purpose and activities: The foundation supports organizations involved with education and hunger.
Fields of interest: Higher education; Education; Food services.
Type of support: General/operating support; Scholarship funds.
Geographic limitations: Giving primarily in areas of plant locations in DePere and Green Bay, WI.
Support limitations: No grants to individuals.
Application information: Applications not accepted. Contributes only to pre-selected organizations.
Officers and Directors: Robert J. Cloud, Pres.; Thomas L. Olson, V.P.; Nancy Gustavson, Secy.; Kathleen T. Riley, Treas.; Walter J. Cloud; Thomas Lemorande; John Rossetti.
EIN: 391432753
Selected grants: The following grants are a representative sample of this grantmaker's funding activity:
$84,196 to ASPIRO, Green Bay, WI, 2011.
$50,000 to New Community Shelter, Green Bay, WI, 2011.
$40,000 to Green Bay Botanical Garden, Green Bay, WI, 2011.
$35,000 to Habitat for Humanity, Greater Green Bay, Green Bay, WI, 2011.
$6,500 to Saint Norbert College, De Pere, WI, 2011. For scholarship.

Sonoco Foundation

1 N. 2nd St., M.S. B04
Hartsville, SC 29550
E-mail: sonoco.foundation@sonoco.com;
URL: http://www.sonocofoundation.com/

Establishment information: Established in 1983 in SC.
Donor: Sonoco Products Co.
Contact: Joyce Beasley
Financial data (yr. ended 12/31/11): Assets, $15,313 (M); gifts received, $1,850,000; expenditures, $1,850,000; qualifying distributions, $0.
Purpose and activities: The foundation supports organizations involved with arts and culture, education, the environment, health and welfare, disaster relief, community economic development, and civic affairs.
Fields of interest: Education; Human services; Community/economic development.
Type of support: Capital campaigns; Continuing support; Employee matching gifts; Employee volunteer services; General/operating support.
Geographic limitations: Giving primarily in areas of company operations, with emphasis on Hartsville, SC.
Support limitations: No support for private foundations, sectarian or denominational religious organizations, missionary groups, organizations with local or regional chapters that are supported by Sonoco, fraternal, social, labor, or veterans' organizations, discriminatory organizations, or intermediary funding agencies (except the United Way). No grants to individuals, or for courtesy advertising, testimonial dinners, loans or investments, political or lobbying campaigns, debt reduction, memorials, endowments, memberships, or conferences, workshops, or seminars.
Publications: Application guidelines.
Application information: Applications accepted. Multi-year funding is not automatic. Organizations receiving support are asked to submit a final report. Application form required. Applicants should submit the following:
1) timetable for implementation and evaluation of project
2) qualifications of key personnel
3) copy of IRS Determination Letter
4) brief history of organization and description of its mission
5) copy of most recent annual report/audited financial statement/990
6) listing of board of directors, trustees, officers and other key people and their affiliations
7) detailed description of project and amount of funding requested
8) copy of current year's organizational budget and/or project budget
9) listing of additional sources and amount of support
10) additional materials/documentation

Initial approach: Letter
Copies of proposal: 1
Board meeting date(s): Quarterly, and as needed
Deadline(s): None

Trustees: R.P. Schrum; Barry L. Saunders; H.E. Deloach, Jr.
Number of staff: 1 part-time professional.
EIN: 570752950
Selected grants: The following grants are a representative sample of this grantmaker's funding activity:
$600,000 to University of South Carolina, Moore School of Business, Columbia, SC, 2008.
$500,000 to Clemson University, Clemson, SC, 2008.
$100,000 to Coker College, Hartsville, SC, 2008.
$34,000 to Trinity Collegiate School, Darlington, SC, 2008.
$30,000 to YMCA of Hartsville, Hartsville, SC, 2008.
$25,000 to Coker College, Hartsville, SC, 2008.
$25,000 to South Carolina Independent Colleges and Universities, Columbia, SC, 2008.
$25,000 to YMCA of Hartsville, Hartsville, SC, 2008.
$20,000 to YMCA of Hartsville, Hartsville, SC, 2008.
$15,000 to YMCA of Hartsville, Hartsville, SC, 2008.

3501
Sonoran Spine Center P.C.

2610 N. 3rd St., Ste. B
Phoenix, AZ 85004-1156 (480) 962-0071

Company URL: http://www.sonoranspine.com
Establishment information: Established in 1999.
Company type: Private company
Business activities: Provides health services.
Business type (SIC): Offices and clinics/doctors'
Corporate officer: Dennis G. Crandall, Pres. and C.E.O.
Office: Mesa, AZ
Giving statement: Giving through the Sonoran Spine Research and Education Foundation.

Sonoran Spine Research and Education Foundation

1432 S. Dobson Rd., Ste. 201
Mesa, AZ 85202-4770 (480) 962-0071
Tel. for Dennis Crandall: (480) 962-0071; Additional tel. for AZ: (602) 443-1424; URL: http://www.spineresearch.org/

Establishment information: Established in 2000 in AZ.
Donors: Dennis Crandall; Medtronic; Depuy Spine Inc.; Dr. Herbert Lewis; Jason Datta.

Contact: Dennis Crandall, Pres.
Financial data (yr. ended 12/31/11): Assets, $103,529 (M); gifts received, $98,782; expenditures, $100,303; qualifying distributions, $76,263; giving activities include $8,000 for 1 grant.
Purpose and activities: The foundation supports public awareness, advocacy groups, and research on spinal disorders; awards spine surgery fellowships; and awards scholarships to students with spinal disorders to attend college in Arizona.
Fields of interest: Spine disorders; Spine disorders research.
Programs:
College Scholarships: The foundation annually awards college scholarships to students who have undergone surgery for spinal deformity and would like to attend college at Arizona State University, University of Arizona, or Northern Arizona University. The program is administered through the financial aid office at Arizona State University.
Spine Surgery Fellowships: The foundation awards clinical and spine research fellowships on adult spinal deformity to physicians who have completed a full residency in orthopedic surgery or neurosurgery.
Type of support: Conferences/seminars; Fellowships; Research; Scholarship funds.
Publications: Application guidelines.
Application information: Applications accepted.
Initial approach: Contact the foundation for fellowship application information; contact the financial aid office at Arizona State University for scholarships
Deadline(s): Varies
Officer: Dennis Crandall, Pres.
Director: Susan Dylo.
EIN: 860982241

3502
Sony Corporation of America

(also known as Sony USA)
550 Madison Ave., 33rd Fl.
New York, NY 10022 (212) 833-6722

Company URL: http://www.sony.com/SCA/corporate.shtml
Company type: Subsidiary of a foreign company
Business activities: Manufactures audio, video, communications, and information technology products; operates record label; produces motion pictures; produces television programming; manufactures computer entertainment products; provides Internet information services.
Business type (SIC): Audio and video equipment/household; computer and office equipment; communications equipment; computer services; motion pictures/production and services allied to
Financial profile for 2010: Number of employees, 250; sales volume, $3,140,000,000
Corporate officers: Michael M. Lynton, Chair. and C.E.O.; Nicole Seligman, Pres.; Steven Kober, Exec. V.P. and C.F.O.; Mark Khalil, Exec. V.P. and Genl. Counsel
Board of director: Michael M. Lynton, Chair.
Subsidiaries: Sony Electronics, Inc., San Diego, CA; Sony Magnetic Products Inc. of America, Dothan, AL; Sony Music Entertainment Inc., New York, NY; Sony Pictures Entertainment Inc., Culver City, CA
Plants: San Diego, CA; Mount Pleasant, PA
Offices: San Jose, CA; Fort Myers, FL
Giving statement: Giving through the Sony USA Corporate Giving Program, the Sony Music Entertainment Inc., and the Sony USA Foundation Inc.

Sony USA Foundation Inc.

550 Madison Ave., 33rd Fl.
New York, NY 10022-3211

Establishment information: Established in 1972 in NY.
Donors: Sony Corp. of America; Sony Electronics, Inc.
Contact: Lisa L. Davis, Dir.
Financial data (yr. ended 12/31/11): Assets, $529,726 (M); expenditures, $150,970; qualifying distributions, $150,595; giving activities include $150,595 for 3 grants (high: $58,480; low: $42,945).
Purpose and activities: The foundation supports organizations involved with education, youth development, and international exchange.
Fields of interest: Education; Youth development; International exchange, students.
Type of support: Continuing support; Curriculum development; General/operating support; Program development; Scholarship funds.
Geographic limitations: Giving primarily in MD and NY; giving also to national and international organizations.
Support limitations: No grants to individuals, or for special projects, research, publications, or conferences; no loans.
Application information: Applications accepted. Application form not required.
Initial approach: Letter of inquiry
Deadline(s): None
Officers and Directors:* Kazushi Ambe*, Chair.; Mark Khalil*, Pres.; Karen E. Kelso, V.P. and Secy.; Edward Wallace, V.P.; Lisa Davis; Ann L. Morfogen; Kenneth L. Nees.
Trustees: Sandra Genelius; Janice Pober; Gary Podorowsky.
EIN: 237181637

3503
Sony Electronics, Inc.

16530 Via Esprillo
San Diego, CA 92127-1708
(858) 942-2400

Company URL: http://news.sel.sony.com
Establishment information: Established in 1960.
Company type: Subsidiary of a public company
Business activities: Operates consumer electronics company.
Business type (SIC): Audio and video equipment/household
Financial profile for 2010: Number of employees, 1,000; sales volume, $3,010,000,000
Corporate officers: Stan Glasgow, Chair.; Phil Molyneux, Pres. and C.O.O.; Rintaro Miyoshi, Exec. V.P. and C.F.O.; Michael T. Williams, Exec. V.P., Genl. Counsel, and Secy.; Michael Fasulo, Exec. V.P., Sales and Opers.; Marjorie Thomas, Sr. V.P. and Corp. Cont.
Board of director: Stan Glasgow, Chair.
Giving statement: Giving through the Sony Electronics, Inc. Corporate Giving Program.

Sony Electronics, Inc. Corporate Giving Program

c/o Community Involvement Council MZ 1028
16530 Via Esprillo
San Diego, CA 92127-1708
E-mail: SelCommunityAffairs@am.sony.com;
URL: http://news.sel.sony.com/en/corporate_information/community

Purpose and activities: Sony Electronics makes charitable contributions to nonprofit organizations involved with education in the classroom, K-12 education, and ecology. Support is given primarily in areas of company operations.
Fields of interest: Elementary/secondary education; Environment, volunteer services; Environment, beautification programs; Environment; Food services; Science, public education.
Type of support: Donated products; Employee volunteer services; In-kind gifts.
Geographic limitations: Giving primarily in areas of company operations.
Support limitations: No grants for fundraising raffles or auctions.
Publications: Application guidelines.
Application information: Applications accepted. The community affairs department handles giving. Community Involvement Councils coordinate programs for local communities. Proposals should be submitted on company letterhead and limited to one to two pages. Application form not required. Applicants should submit the following:
1) copy of IRS Determination Letter
2) brief history of organization and description of its mission
3) list of company employees involved with the organization
4) detailed description of project and amount of funding requested

Proposals should include prior support from Sony, if applicable.
Initial approach: Proposal to headquarters
Deadline(s): None
Final notification: 6 to 8 weeks

3504
Sony Pictures Entertainment Inc.

10202 W. Washington Blvd.
Culver City, CA 90232-3195
(310) 244-4000
FAX: (310) 244-2626

Company URL: http://www.sonypictures.com
Establishment information: Established in 1987.
Company type: Subsidiary of a private company
Business activities: Operates movie, television and digital content production and distribution company.
Business type (SIC): Motion pictures/production and services allied to
Financial profile for 2010: Number of employees, 4,200
Corporate officers: Michael M. Lynton, Co-Chair. and C.E.O.; Amy Pascal, Co-Chair.; Mel Harris, Pres. and C.O.O.; David Hendler, Exec. V.P. and C.F.O.; Peter Iacono, Exec. V.P., Sales; Paul Martin, V.P., Human Resources; Christopher Holt, V.P., Opers.; Jennifer Anderson, V.P., Mktg; Stuart Little, Secy.
Board of directors: Michael M. Lynton, Co-Chair.; Amy Pascal, Co-Chair.
Giving statement: Giving through the Sony Pictures Entertainment Inc. Corporate Giving Program.

Sony Pictures Entertainment Inc. Corporate Giving Program

10202 W. Washington Blvd.
Culver City, CA 90232-3119
URL: http://www.sony.com/SCA/philanthropy.shtml

Purpose and activities: Sony Pictures Entertainment makes charitable contributions to nonprofit organizations involved with helping local

communities, fostering better educational systems, supporting arts and culture, technology, helping disadvantaged youth, disaster response, and protecting and improving the environment. Support is given primarily in areas of company operations, with an emphasis on Culver City, California.
Fields of interest: Arts; Education; Environment; Safety/disasters; Youth, services; Engineering/technology Economically disadvantaged.
Type of support: Employee matching gifts; Employee volunteer services; General/operating support.
Geographic limitations: Giving primarily in in areas of company operations, with an emphasis on Culver City, CA; giving also to national organizations.

3505
Source 44, LLC

514 Via De La Valle, Ste. 203
Solana Beach, CA 92075-2717
(877) 916-6337

Company URL: http://www.source-44.com
Company type: Private company
Business type (SIC): Business services/miscellaneous
Corporate officers: Patrick Blandford, Chair.; Jess F. Kraus, Pres. and C.E.O.; Matt Thorn, C.O.O.
Board of directors: Patrick Blandford, Chair.; Stacy Allen; Christopher S. Gopal, Ph.D; Jess F. Kraus; Ed Viesturs
Giving statement: Giving through the Source 44 LLC Contributions Program.

Source 44 LLC Contributions Program

514 Via De La Valle, Ste. 203
Solana Beach, CA 92075-2717 (877) 916-6337
URL: http://www.source-44.com

Purpose and activities: Source 44 is a certified B Corporation that donates a percentage of sales to charitable organizations. Support is given primarily in Solana Beach, California.
Geographic limitations: Giving primarily in Solana Beach, CA.

3506
SourceMedia Group, Inc.

(formerly Gazette Communications, Inc.)
500 3rd Ave., S.E.
Cedar Rapids, IA 52401-1608
(800) 397-8211

Company URL: http://sourcemedia.net/
Establishment information: Established in 1883.
Company type: Private company
Business activities: Publishes newspapers; broadcasts television.
Business type (SIC): Newspaper publishing and/or printing; radio and television broadcasting
Corporate officers: Joe F. Hladky, Chair.; Chuck Peters, Pres.; Elizabeth Schott, Secy.; Ken Slaughter, Treas.
Board of directors: Joe F. Hladky, Chair.; Don Barry; Jack Evans; Charles Funk; John Hladky
Subsidiaries: Advertiser, Coralville, IA; Database Marketing, Cedar Rapids, IA; DecisionMark, Cedar Rapids, IA; Geographic Decisions Systems, Inc., Cedar Rapids, IA; Interactive Media, Inc., Cedar Rapids, IA; Iowa Farmer Today, Cedar Rapids, IA; KCRG Radio & TV Stations, Cedar Rapids, IA; Penny Saver, Cedar Rapids, IA
Giving statement: Giving through the Gazette Foundation.

The Gazette Foundation

500 3rd Ave. S.E.
Cedar Rapids, IA 52401-1608
E-mail: karla.twedt-ball@gcrcf.org; URL: http://www.gcrcf.org

Establishment information: Established in 1960 in IA.
Donor: Gazette Co. Inc.
Financial data (yr. ended 12/31/11): Assets, $90,556 (M); expenditures, $159,250; qualifying distributions, $159,250; giving activities include $159,250 for 5 grants (high: $72,750; low: $1,500).
Purpose and activities: The foundation supports community foundations, the United Way, and organizations involved with higher education and other areas. The foundation's programs are administered by the Greater Cedar Rapids Community Foundation.
Fields of interest: Higher education; Foundations (community); United Ways and Federated Giving Programs; General charitable giving.
Type of support: Annual campaigns; Building/renovation; Capital campaigns.
Geographic limitations: Giving limited to the Cedar Rapids, IA, area.
Support limitations: No support for public schools or religious organizations. No grants to individuals, or for endowments, advertising, city or municipal projects, fundraising dinners, band uniforms, trips, conferences, group travel, or honoraria for distinguished guests.
Publications: Application guidelines.
Application information: Applications accepted. Grants from the foundation are administered by The Greater Cedar Rapids Community Foundation. Application form required. Applicants should submit the following:
1) role played by volunteers
2) population served
3) copy of IRS Determination Letter
4) brief history of organization and description of its mission
5) geographic area to be served
6) copy of most recent annual report/audited financial statement/990
7) listing of board of directors, trustees, officers and other key people and their affiliations
8) detailed description of project and amount of funding requested
9) plans for cooperation with other organizations, if any
10) copy of current year's organizational budget and/or project budget
Initial approach: See Website
Board meeting date(s): Quarterly or as needed
Deadline(s): See Website
Final notification: 3 months
Officers and Directors:* Joseph F. Hladky III*, Pres.; Ken Slaughter*, V.P. and Secy.-Treas.; Chuck Peters; Elizabeth Hladky.
EIN: 426075177
Selected grants: The following grants are a representative sample of this grantmaker's funding activity:
$56,345 to Greater Cedar Rapids Community Foundation, Cedar Rapids, IA, 2010.
$10,000 to University of Iowa Foundation, Iowa City, IA, 2010. For capital campaign.

3507
South Bend Tribune Corp.

225 W. Colfax Ave.
South Bend, IN 46626-1000
(574) 235-6161

Company URL: http://www.southbendtribune.com
Establishment information: Established in 1873.
Company type: Subsidiary of a private company
Business activities: Publishes newspapers; provides Internet information services.
Business type (SIC): Newspaper publishing and/or printing; computer services
Corporate officers: Kimberly Wilson, Pres.; Kevin Shaw, V.P., Opers.
Giving statement: Giving through the Schurz Communications Foundation, Inc.

Schurz Communications Foundation, Inc.

1301 E. Douglas Rd.
Mishawaka, IN 46545-1732 (574) 235-6243

Establishment information: Incorporated in 1940 in IN.
Donors: Schurz Communications, Inc.; South Bend Tribune Corp.; WSBT, Inc.; West United Way Pledge.
Financial data (yr. ended 12/31/11): Assets, $525,361 (M); gifts received, $158,191; expenditures, $189,034; qualifying distributions, $180,916; giving activities include $180,916 for 8 grants (high: $79,216; low: $600).
Purpose and activities: The foundation supports museums and medical centers and organizations involved with higher education, Christianity, and disabled people.
Fields of interest: Museums; Higher education; Health care, clinics/centers; Recreation, camps; Salvation Army; United Ways and Federated Giving Programs; Christian agencies & churches Disabilities, people with.
Type of support: Annual campaigns; Capital campaigns; Endowments; General/operating support.
Geographic limitations: Giving limited to South Bend, IN.
Application information: Applications accepted. Application form not required.
Initial approach: Proposal
Deadline(s): None
Officers and Directors:* David C. Ray*, Pres.; Sally Brown*, V.P.; Marci Burdick*, Secy.; Charles Pittman*, Treas.
EIN: 356024357

3508
South Dade Toyota

(doing business as Armstrong Motors, Inc.)
(formerly Armstrong Toyota of Homestead)
29330 S. Dixie Hwy.
Homestead, FL 33033 (305) 248-6330

Company URL: http://www.southdadetoyota.com/
Establishment information: Established in 1990.
Company type: Private company
Business activities: Operates car dealership.
Business type (SIC): Motor vehicles—retail
Financial profile for 2009: Number of employees, 65
Corporate officer: William J Armstrong, Pres.
Giving statement: Giving through the Armstrong Toyota and Ford Family Foundation.

Armstrong Toyota and Ford Family Foundation
29330 S. Dixie Hwy.
Homestead, FL 33033-2300

Establishment information: Established in 2003 in FL.
Financial data (yr. ended 12/31/09): Assets, $0 (M); expenditures, $1,689; qualifying distributions, $1,532; giving activities include $1,532 for 1 grant.
Purpose and activities: The foundation supports Catholicism and awards grants to individuals.
Fields of interest: Religion.
Type of support: General/operating support; Grants to individuals.
Application information: Applications not accepted. Unsolicited requests for funds not accepted.
Officer: David Rich, Pres.
EIN: 770612519

3509
South Mississippi Home Health, Inc.
(also known as Deaconess Hospital)
108 Lundy Ln.
Hattiesburg, MS 39401 (601) 268-1842

Company URL: http://www.deaconesshomecare.com
Establishment information: Established in 1969.
Company type: Private company
Business activities: Provides home nursing services.
Business type (SIC): Home healthcare services
Financial profile for 2010: Number of employees, 50
Corporate officer: Ginger Reynolds, Mgr.
Giving statement: Giving through the South Mississippi Home Health Foundation Inc.

South Mississippi Home Health Foundation Inc.
P.O. Box 16841
Hattiesburg, MS 39404 (601) 268-1842
Application address: P.O. Box 15097, Hattiesburg, MS 39401

Donor: South Mississippi Home Health, Inc.
Contact: Elaine Temple, Secy.-Treas.
Financial data (yr. ended 12/31/11): Assets, $1,118,340 (M); gifts received, $42,578; expenditures, $120,027; qualifying distributions, $92,791; giving activities include $92,791 for grants.
Purpose and activities: The foundation supports programs designed to assist indigent patients of South Mississippi Home Health, Inc.
Fields of interest: Education; Health care.
Type of support: General/operating support; Grants to individuals.
Geographic limitations: Giving primarily in areas of company operations in MS.
Application information: Applications accepted. Application form required.
Initial approach: Proposal
Deadline(s): None
Officers: Mary Stainton, Pres.; Elaine Temple, Secy.-Treas.
Director: Lynwood Wheeler, M.D.
EIN: 237079721

3510
South Mountain Company
15 Red Arrow Rd.
P.O. Box 1260
West Tisbury, MA 02575 (508) 693-4850

Company URL: http://www.southmountain.com
Establishment information: Established in 1975.
Company type: Private company
Business activities: Provides architectural services; provides general contract construction services.
Business type (SIC): Engineering, architectural, and surveying services; building construction general contractors and operative builders
Corporate officers: John Adrams, Pres. and C.E.O.; Deirdre Bohan, V.P. and C.O.O.; Michael H. Drezner, Treas.; Siobhan Mullin, Compt.
Giving statement: Giving through the South Mountain Company Foundation.

South Mountain Company Foundation
Red Arrow Rd.
P.O. Box 1260
West Tisbury, MA 02575-1260

Establishment information: Established in 2002 in MA.
Donor: John Abrams.
Financial data (yr. ended 04/30/12): Assets, $6,997 (M); gifts received, $25,503; expenditures, $18,807; qualifying distributions, $18,807; giving activities include $18,772 for grants.
Purpose and activities: The foundation supports organizations involved with housing, mind and body enrichment, and other areas.
Fields of interest: Housing/shelter; Human services, mind/body enrichment; General charitable giving.
Type of support: General/operating support.
Geographic limitations: Giving limited to Vineyard Haven, MA.
Application information: Applications not accepted. Contributes only to pre-selected organizations.
Trustees: John Abrams; Deirdre L. Bohan; Peter D'Angelo; Michael H. Drezner.
EIN: 161628987

3511
South Mountain Company, Inc.
15 Red Arrow Rd.
P.O. Box 1260
West Tisbury, MA 02575 (508) 693-4850
FAX: (508) 693-7738

Company URL: http://www.southmountain.com
Establishment information: Established in 1975.
Company type: Private company
Business type (SIC): Business services/miscellaneous
Corporate officers: John Abrams, Pres. and C.E.O.; Deirdre Bohan, V.P. and C.O.O.
Giving statement: Giving through the South Mountain Company, Inc. Contributions Program.

South Mountain Company, Inc. Contributions Program
15 Red Arrow Rd.
West Tisbury, MA 02575 (508) 693-4850
E-mail: jabrams@southmountain.com; URL: http://www.southmountain.com

Purpose and activities: South Mountain Company is a certified B Corporation that donates a percentage of net profits to charitable organizations. Support is given primarily in Martha's Vineyard, Massachusetts.
Fields of interest: Environment; Housing/shelter; Community/economic development.
Type of support: General/operating support.
Geographic limitations: Giving primarily in Martha's Vineyard, MA.

3512
South Shore Savings Bank
1530 Main St.
South Weymouth, MA 02190-1332
(781) 337-3000

Company URL: http://www.sssb.com
Establishment information: Established in 1997.
Company type: Subsidiary of a private company
Business activities: Operates savings bank.
Business type (SIC): Savings institutions
Corporate officers: Arthur R. Connelly, Chair.; John C. Boucher, Pres. and C.E.O.; Christopher R. Dunn, Exec. V.P. and C.O.O.; Nobo K. Sircar, Exec. V.P. and C.F.O.; Timothy Mitchelson, Genl. Counsel
Board of director: Arthur R. Connelly, Chair.
Giving statement: Giving through the South Shore Savings Charitable Foundation Inc.

South Shore Savings Charitable Foundation Inc.
(formerly 1833 Charitable Foundation, Inc.)
1530 Main St.
South Weymouth, MA 02190-1310 (781) 682-3115
FAX: (781) 331-5881; URL: http://www.sssb.com/about-us/charitable-foundation.aspx

Establishment information: Established in 1996 in MA.
Donors: South Weymouth Savings Bank; South Weymouth Security Corp.; South Shore Savings Bank.
Contact: Kimberly Stoyle, Clerk and Treas.
Financial data (yr. ended 03/31/12): Assets, $1,552,178 (M); gifts received, $278,546; expenditures, $85,587; qualifying distributions, $73,735; giving activities include $73,700 for 18 grants (high: $20,000; low: $700).
Purpose and activities: The foundation supports organizations involved with arts and culture, education, health, human services, and community development.
Fields of interest: Arts; Education; Hospitals (general); Health care; Human services; Community/economic development.
Type of support: Capital campaigns; General/operating support; Program development; Seed money.
Geographic limitations: Giving limited to areas of company operations in southeastern MA.
Application information: Applications accepted. Application form required.
Initial approach: Contact foundation for application form
Copies of proposal: 1
Deadline(s): See application for deadline
Officers and Directors:* John C. Boucher*, Pres.; Christopher R. Dunn*, V.P.; Nobo K. Sircar*, V.P.; Tracey M. Kelley, Clerk and Treas.; Rosemary McGillicuddy; Peter F. McGowan; Pamela O'Leary; Arthur H. Sharp.
Number of staff: None.
EIN: 043356807

3513
Southeastern Bank Financial Corporation

3530 Wheeler Rd.
P.O. Box 1589
Augusta, GA 30909-6710 (706) 738-6990
FAX: (706) 737-3106

Company URL: http://www.georgiabankandtrust.com
Establishment information: Established in 1989.
Company type: Public company
Company ticker symbol and exchange: SBFC/OTC
Business activities: Operates bank holding company.
Business type (SIC): Holding company
Financial profile for 2012: Number of employees, 344; assets, $1,662,500,000; pre-tax net income, $20,920,000; liabilities, $1,526,720,000
Corporate officers: Robert W. Pollard, Jr., Chair.; Edward G. Meybohm, Vice-Chair.; R. Daniel Blanton, Pres. and C.E.O.; Ronald L. Thigpen, Exec. V.P. and C.O.O.; Darrell R. Rains, C.F.O.
Board of directors: Robert W. Pollard, Jr., Chair.; Edward G. Meybohm, Vice-Chair.; William J. Badger; R. Daniel Blanton; W. Marshall Brown; Patrick D. Cunning; Warren A. Daniel; Larry S. Prather, Sr.; Randolph R. Smith, M.D.; John W. Trulock, Jr.; Ronald L. Thigpen
Giving statement: Giving through the Georgia Bank Foundation, Inc.

Georgia Bank Foundation, Inc.

3530 Wheeler Rd.
Augusta, GA 30909-6710

Establishment information: Established in 1999 in GA.
Donor: Georgia Bank & Trust Co.
Contact: Ronald L. Thigpen, Dir.
Financial data (yr. ended 12/31/11): Assets, $859,386 (M); expenditures, $44,320; qualifying distributions, $40,950; giving activities include $40,950 for grants.
Purpose and activities: The foundation supports persons and charitable organizations located in the greater Augusta, Georgia area.
Fields of interest: Education; Health care; Human services.
Type of support: General/operating support.
Geographic limitations: Giving primarily in Augusta, GA.
Application information: Applications accepted. Application form required.
Initial approach: Letter
Deadline(s): None
Directors: William J. Badger; R. Daniel Blanton; Warren A. Daniel; E.G. Maybohn; Robert W. Pollard, Jr.; Randolph R. Smith; Ronald L. Thigpen.
EIN: 582485331

3514
Southern Bancorp, Inc.

605 Main St.
Arkadelphia, AR 71923-5968
(870) 246-3945

Company URL: http://southernbancorp.com
Establishment information: Established in 1986.
Company type: Private company
Business activities: Operates commercial bank.
Business type (SIC): Banks/commercial; holding company
Corporate officer: Walter Smiley, Chair.
Board of director: Walter Smiley, Chair.
Giving statement: Giving through the Southern Bancorp Capital Partners.

Southern Bancorp Capital Partners

(formerly Southern Financial Partners)
1400 W. Markham St., Ste. 400
Little Rock, AR 72201-1845 (501) 372-4201
FAX: (501) 537-1193; E-mail: d0m@southernfp.org; URL: https://banksouthern.com/category/southern-bancorp-capital-partners/

Establishment information: Established in 1988 in AR; changed to current name in 2009.
Contact: Dominik Mjartan, V.P.
Financial data (yr. ended 12/31/11): Revenue, $3,532,792; assets, $23,895,056 (M); gifts received, $1,177,271; expenditures, $3,785,914; giving activities include $1,687,716 for grants.
Purpose and activities: The organization's mission is to revitalize struggling rural communities in the Delta region by promoting comprehensive development: restarting the local economy, rebuilding the civic infrastructure, fostering the emergence of new leadership, addressing health care needs, creating new homeownership and affordable housing opportunities, and supporting quality educational opportunities for residents of all ages.
Fields of interest: Education; Health care; Housing/shelter; Community/economic development; Leadership development Children/youth; Adults; Young adults; Minorities; Economically disadvantaged.
Type of support: Emergency funds; Employee volunteer services; Equipment; General/operating support; In-kind gifts; Program development; Program-related investments/loans; Sponsorships.
Geographic limitations: Giving limited to Arkansas, Ashley, Bradley, Calhoun, Chicot, Clark, Cleveland, Columbia, Crittenden, Cross, Dallas, Desha, Drew, Garland, Grant, Hempstead, Hot Spring, Howard, Jefferson, La Fayette, Lee, Lincoln, Little River, Loanoke, Miller, Mississippi, Monroe, Montgomery, Nevada, Phillips, Pike, Prairie, Pulaski, Quachita, Saline, Siever, St. Francis, Union, and Woodruff counties, AR; and Bolivar, Coahoma, Desoto, Humphreys, Lefore, Quitman, Sunflower, Tallahatchie, Tunica, and Washington counties, MS.
Support limitations: No grants to individuals.
Publications: Newsletter.
Officers and Directors:* Hon. Brian Miller*, Chair.; Joe Black*, Co-Pres.; Ben Steinberg*, Co-Pres.; Phillip N. Baldwin*, C.E.O.; Dominik Mjartan, V.P.; John Edwards; LaVerne Feaster; Dr. Bob Fisher; Dr. Glendell Jones, Jr.; Walt Patterson.
Number of staff: 14
EIN: 581766093

3515
Southern Bank and Trust Company

116 E. Main St.
P.O. Box 729
Mount Olive, NC 28365-2113
(919) 658-7022

Company URL: http://www.southernbank.com
Establishment information: Established in 1901.
Company type: Subsidiary of a public company
Business activities: Operates commercial bank.
Business type (SIC): Banks/commercial
Corporate officers: J. Grey Morgan, Jr., Chair. and C.E.O.; Drew M. Covert, Pres. and C.O.O.; Dan R. Ellis, Jr., Exec V.P. and C.F.O.
Board of directors: J. Grey Morgan, Jr., Chair.; Bynum R. Brown; William H. Bryan; Robert J. Carroll; Hope H. Connell; J. Edwin Drew; Frank B. Holding; G. Rouse Ivey; M.J. McSorley; John C. Pegram, Jr.; W.A. Potts; Charles O. Sykes; Malcolm R. Sullivan
Giving statement: Giving through the Southern Bank Foundation.

Southern Bank Foundation

P.O. Box 729
Mount Olive, NC 28365-0729 (919) 658-7007

Establishment information: Established in 1996 in NC.
Donors: Southern Bank & Trust Co.; Southern Bancshares, Inc.
Contact: David A. Bean, Treas.
Financial data (yr. ended 12/31/11): Assets, $11,203,377 (M); expenditures, $493,544; qualifying distributions, $417,900; giving activities include $417,900 for grants.
Purpose and activities: The foundation supports museums and hospitals and organizations involved with education, human services, community development, and Christianity.
Fields of interest: Museums; Historic preservation/historical societies; Elementary/secondary education; Higher education; Libraries (public); Education; Hospitals (general); Salvation Army; Human services, emergency aid; Residential/custodial care, hospices; Human services; Community/economic development; Christian agencies & churches.
Type of support: Annual campaigns; Building/renovation; Capital campaigns; Debt reduction; Equipment; General/operating support; Program development; Scholarship funds.
Geographic limitations: Giving primarily in eastern NC.
Support limitations: No grants to individuals.
Application information: Application form required. Applicants should submit the following:
1) signature and title of chief executive officer
2) statement of problem project will address
3) name, address and phone number of organization
4) copy of IRS Determination Letter
5) brief history of organization and description of its mission
6) geographic area to be served
7) how project's results will be evaluated or measured
8) detailed description of project and amount of funding requested
9) contact person
10) listing of additional sources and amount of support
Initial approach: Contact foundation for application form
Board meeting date(s): Varies
Deadline(s): None
Officers: Frank B. Holding*, Pres.; John N. Walker*, V.P.; John E. Pegram, Jr., Secy.; David A. Bean, Treas.
Directors: Hope Holding Connell; Charles L. Revelle, Jr.
EIN: 562002871
Selected grants: The following grants are a representative sample of this grantmaker's funding activity:
$380,000 to Mount Olive College, Mount Olive, NC, 2011.
$100,000 to Mount Olive College, Mount Olive, NC, 2011.
$90,000 to Campbell University, Buies Creek, NC, 2011.

$62,500 to Vidant Memorial Hospital Foundation, Greenville, NC, 2011.
$40,000 to Wayne County Development Alliance, Goldsboro, NC, 2011.
$30,000 to Nash Health Care Systems, Rocky Mount, NC, 2011.
$20,000 to Carolinas Gateway Partnership, Rocky Mount, NC, 2011.
$10,000 to Campbell University, Buies Creek, NC, 2011.
$10,000 to Tar River Choral and Orchestral Society, Rocky Mount, NC, 2011.
$5,000 to North Carolina Symphony, Raleigh, NC, 2011.

3516
The Southern Company

30 Ivan Allen, Jr. Blvd., N.W.
Atlanta, GA 30308 (404) 506-5000
FAX: (404) 506-0344

Company URL: http://www.southerncompany.com/
Establishment information: Established in 1945.
Company type: Public company
Company ticker symbol and exchange: SO/NYSE
International Securities Identification Number: US8425871071
Business activities: Generates, transmits, and distributes electricity.
Business type (SIC): Electric services
Financial profile for 2012: Number of employees, 26,439; assets, $63,149,000,000; sales volume, $16,537,000,000; pre-tax net income, $3,749,000,000; expenses, $12,074,000,000; liabilities, $43,770,000,000
Fortune 1000 ranking: 2012—171st in revenues, 86th in profits, and 91st in assets
Forbes 2000 ranking: 2012—566th in sales, 240th in profits, and 374th in assets
Corporate officers: Thomas A. Fanning, Chair., Pres., and C.E.O.; Mark A. Crosswhite, Exec. V.P. and C.O.O.; Art P. Beattie, Exec. V.P. and C.F.O.; G. Edison Holland, Jr., Exec. V.P., Genl. Counsel, and Corp. Secy.
Board of directors: Thomas A. Fanning, Chair.; Juanita Powell Baranco; Jon A. Boscia; Henry A. Clark III; H. William Habermeyer, Jr.; Veronica M. Hagen; Warren A Hood, Jr.; Donald M. James; Dale E. Klein; William G. Smith, Jr.; Steven R. Specker; Larry D. Thompson; Jenner E. Wood III
Subsidiaries: Alabama Power Company, Birmingham, AL; Georgia Power Company, Atlanta, GA; Gulf Power Company, Pensacola, FL; Mississippi Power Company, Gulfport, MS; Southern Power Co., Atlanta, GA
Giving statement: Giving through the Southern Company Contributions Program and the Southern Company Charitable Foundation, Inc.
Company EIN: 580690070

The Southern Company Contributions Program

30 Ivan Allen Jr. Blvd., N.W.
BIN SC1506
Atlanta, GA 30308 (404) 506-5000
E-mail: responsibility@southernco.com; URL: http://www.southerncompany.com/corporateresponsibility/

Financial data (yr. ended 12/31/10): Total giving, $6,570,000, including $6,570,000 for grants.
Purpose and activities: As a complement to its foundation, Southern Company also makes charitable contributions to nonprofit organizations directly. Support is given primarily in areas of company operations.
Fields of interest: Arts, cultural/ethnic awareness; Education; Environment; Health care; Safety/disasters; Youth development; Human services; Community/economic development.
Program:
Employee Matching Gifts: Southern matches contributions made by its employees to nonprofit organizations involved with education.
Type of support: Emergency funds; Employee volunteer services; General/operating support.
Geographic limitations: Giving primarily in areas of company operations.

Southern Company Charitable Foundation, Inc.

241 Ralph McGill Blvd., N.E., BIN 10131
Atlanta, GA 30308-3374 (404) 506-6784
FAX: (404) 506-1485; URL: http://www.southerncompany.com/corporate-responsibility/social-responsibility/communityInvolvement.aspx

Establishment information: Established in 1999 in GA.
Donor: The Southern Co.
Contact: Susan M. Carter, Secy.
Financial data (yr. ended 12/31/11): Assets, $29,338,399 (M); gifts received, $25,000,000; expenditures, $2,024,747; qualifying distributions, $1,873,333; giving activities include $1,873,333 for grants.
Purpose and activities: The foundation supports organizations involved with education, the environment, and disaster relief.
Fields of interest: Education; Environment; Disasters, preparedness/services.
Program:
Disaster Relief Aid Fund: Through the Disaster Relief Aid Fund, the foundation awards emergency assistance grants to employees of the Southern Company displaced by disaster.
Type of support: Annual campaigns; Capital campaigns; Continuing support; Emergency funds; General/operating support; Grants to individuals; Program development.
Geographic limitations: Giving primarily in AL, FL, GA, and MS.
Support limitations: No support for religious organizations or private or secondary schools or non-public foundations. No grants to individuals (except for employee-related emergency assistance grants).
Application information: Applications accepted. Multi-year funding is not automatic. Application form not required. Applicants should submit the following:
1) copy of IRS Determination Letter
2) detailed description of project and amount of funding requested
3) listing of additional sources and amount of support

Initial approach: Proposal
Copies of proposal: 1
Board meeting date(s): May
Deadline(s): None
Final notification: 1 month

Officers and Directors:* G. Edison Holland*, Pres.; Michael K. Anderson*, V.P.; Susan M. Carter, Secy.; Roger S. Steffens, Treas.; Arthur P. Beattie; Christopher C. Womack.
EIN: 582514027
Selected grants: The following grants are a representative sample of this grantmaker's funding activity:
$250,000 to Grady Memorial Hospital Corporation, Grady Health System, Atlanta, GA, 2009. For Greater Grady Campaign.
$250,000 to National Center for Civil and Human Rights, Atlanta, GA, 2009. For design and construction campaign.
$100,000 to University of West Florida, Pensacola, FL, 2009. For multi-culture museum in Pensacola, FL.
$25,000 to American Red Cross, Metropolitan Atlanta Chapter, Atlanta, GA, 2009. For disaster relief assistance related to Georgia floods.
$25,000 to Southern Center for International Studies, Atlanta, GA, 2009. For program support.
$20,000 to Southeast Energy Efficiency Alliance, Atlanta, GA, 2009. For community energy efficiency program in the Southeast.
$20,000 to Youth Development Foundation of SkillsUSA, McDonough, GA, 2009. For National Leadership and Skills Conference.

3517
Southern Furniture Company of Conover, Inc.

1099 2nd Ave. Pl., S.E.
Conover, NC 28613-0307 (828) 464-0311

Company URL: http://www.southernfurniture.net/about.htm
Establishment information: Established in 1884.
Company type: Private company
Business activities: Manufactures upholstered and wood furniture.
Business type (SIC): Furniture/household
Corporate officers: Jerome W. Bolick, Chair., Co-Pres., and C.E.O.; Ken E. Church, Co-Pres.; Ray E. Barnhardt, C.F.O.
Board of director: Ray E. Barnhardt, Chair.
Giving statement: Giving through the Bolick Foundation.

The Bolick Foundation

P.O. Box 307
Conover, NC 28613-0307

Establishment information: Established in 1967 in NC.
Donor: Southern Furniture Co. of Conover, Inc.
Financial data (yr. ended 06/30/12): Assets, $8,688,813 (M); expenditures, $503,303; qualifying distributions, $433,000; giving activities include $433,000 for grants.
Purpose and activities: The foundation supports organizations involved with historical activities, education, health, human services, international relief, and Christianity.
Fields of interest: Historical activities; Elementary/secondary education; Higher education; Theological school/education; Education; Health care; Boy scouts; YM/YWCAs & YM/YWHAs; Residential/custodial care, hospices; Human services; International relief; Christian agencies & churches.
Type of support: Annual campaigns; Building/renovation; Capital campaigns; General/operating support.
Geographic limitations: Giving primarily in NC.
Support limitations: No grants to individuals.
Application information: Applications not accepted. Contributes only to pre-selected organizations.
Trustees: Jerome W. Bolick; Linda B. Bolick.
EIN: 566086348
Selected grants: The following grants are a representative sample of this grantmaker's funding activity:

$10,000 to Boy Scouts of America, Gastonia, NC, 2010.
$10,000 to Salt Block Foundation, Hickory, NC, 2010. For capital campaign.
$5,000 to Sea Level Montessori, Newton, NC, 2010. For capital campaign.
$2,500 to American Heart Association, Charlotte, NC, 2010. For general operating fund.
$2,500 to Newton Depot Authority, Newton, NC, 2010. For general operating fund.
$1,000 to Eastern Catawba Cooperative Christian Ministry, Newton, NC, 2010. For general operating fund.
$1,000 to Independent College Fund of North Carolina, Raleigh, NC, 2010. For general operating fund.

3518
The Southern Kansas Telephone Company, Inc.

112 S. Lee St.
P.O. Box 800
Clearwater, KS 67026-7810
(620) 584-2255

Company URL: http://www.sktmainstreet.com
Establishment information: Established in 1940.
Company type: Private company
Business activities: Provides Internet access services; provides local and long distance telephone communications services; provides cable television services.
Business type (SIC): Telephone communications; cable and other pay television services
Financial profile for 2010: Number of employees, 45
Corporate officers: Dick Lippert, C.E.O.; Bill McVey, C.F.O.; Damon Martin, C.I.O.
Giving statement: Giving through the Mikesell Family Foundation, Inc.

The Mikesell Family Foundation, Inc.

112 S. Lee St.
Clearwater, KS 67026-0800

Establishment information: Established in 2003 in KS.
Donors: Southern Kansas Telephone Co., Inc.; Wichita Community Foundation; William R. McVey; Kendall Mikesell; Gordon Mikesell; Gregory L. Mikesell; Elaine Webb.
Financial data (yr. ended 12/31/11): Assets, $459,940 (M); expenditures, $28,235; qualifying distributions, $24,500; giving activities include $24,500 for 9 grants (high: $7,000; low: $1,000).
Purpose and activities: The foundation supports libraries and community foundations and organizations involved with youth development.
Fields of interest: Youth development; Community/economic development.
Type of support: General/operating support.
Application information: Applications not accepted. Contributes only to pre-selected organizations.
Officers: Gordon G. Mikesell, Chair.; Kendall Mikesell, Pres.; Edwin A. Mikesell, V.P.; William R. McVey, C.F.O.; Gregory L. Mikesell, Treas.
Director: Elaine Webb.
EIN: 320072858

3519
Southern States Cooperative, Inc.

6606 W. Broad St.
P.O. Box 26234
Richmond, VA 23230-1717 (804) 281-1000

Company URL: http://www.southernstates.com
Establishment information: Established in 1923.
Company type: Cooperative
Business activities: Operates feed, seed, fertilizer, farm supplies, and fuel stores.
Corporate officers: John B. East, Chair.; Thomas R. Scribner, Pres. and C.E.O.; Leslie Newton, Exec. V.P. and C.F.O.; Kim Bram, V.P., Genl. Counsel, and Secy.; Philip Miller, V.P. and Cont.; Fred Jezouit, V.P., Finance and Treas.; Betsy Hill, V.P., Human Resources
Board of director: John B. East, Chair.
Giving statement: Giving through the Southern States Cooperative, Inc. Corporate Giving Program.

Southern States Cooperative, Inc. Corporate Giving Program

6606 W. Broad St.
Richmond, VA 23230-1717 (804) 281-1000
URL: http://www.southernstates.com/community/sponsorships/index.aspx

Purpose and activities: Southern States makes charitable contributions to nonprofit organizations involved with agriculture-focused youth development and education. Support is given primarily in areas of company operations in the eastern U.S.
Fields of interest: Agriculture/food, formal/general education; Youth development.
Type of support: General/operating support.
Geographic limitations: Giving primarily in areas of company operations in the eastern U.S.

3520
Southern Union Company

5051 Westheimer Rd.
Houston, TX 77056 (713) 989-2000

Company URL: http://www.sug.com
Establishment information: Established in 1932.
Company type: Public company
Company ticker symbol and exchange: SUG/NYSE
Business activities: Transmits and distributes natural gas.
Business type (SIC): Gas production and distribution
Financial profile for 2011: Number of employees, 2,437; assets, $8,270,860,000; sales volume, $2,665,950,000; pre-tax net income, $359,200,000; expenses, $2,188,100,000; liabilities, $5,631,250,000
Corporate officers: George L. Lindemann, Chair. and C.E.O.; Eric D. Herschmann, Vice-Chair., Pres., and C.O.O.; Richard N. Marshall, Sr. V.P. and C.F.O.; Monica M. Gaudiosi, Sr. V.P. and Genl. Counsel
Board of directors: George L. Lindemann, Chair.; Eric D. Herschmann, Vice-Chair.; David Brodsky; Franklin W. Denius; Kurt A. Gitter, M.D.; Herbert H. Jacobi; Thomas N. McCarter III; George Rountree III; Allan D. Scherer
Subsidiaries: Southern Union Exploration Co., Dallas, TX; Southern Union Financial Corp., Dallas, TX; Southern Union Realty Co., Dallas, TX; Western Gas Interstate Co., Austin, TX
Division: Southern Union Gas Co., Austin, TX
Historic mergers: Providence Energy Corporation (September 28, 2000)
Giving statement: Giving through the Southern Union Company Contributions Program and the Southern Union Charitable Foundation.
Company EIN: 750571592

Southern Union Charitable Foundation

5051 Westheimer Rd.
Houston, TX 77056-5397

Establishment information: Established in 2005 in TX.
Donor: Southern Union Co.
Financial data (yr. ended 12/31/11): Assets, $2,977 (M); gifts received, $3,510; expenditures, $5,248; qualifying distributions, $5,248; giving activities include $1,000 for grants to individuals.
Purpose and activities: The foundation provides scholarships to employees of Southern Union, Texas; and provides disaster relief to victims of recent natural disasters.
Fields of interest: Higher education; Disasters, preparedness/services.
Type of support: Employee-related scholarships; Grants to individuals.
Geographic limitations: Giving primarily in TX; some giving in KS and the Gulf Coast area.
Application information: Applications accepted. Application form required.
Initial approach: Email
Deadline(s): None
Officers: Robert M. Kerngan III, Pres.; Stephen D. McGregor, 1st V.P.; George E. Aldrich, 2nd V.P.; Gary W. Lefelar, 3rd V.P.; Susan Wheeler, Secy.; Michael J. McLaughlin, Treas.
Directors: Monica Gaudiosi; Richard N. Marshall; Larry Stone.
EIN: 203634627

3521
Southern Wine & Spirits of America, Inc.

1600 N.W. 163rd St.
Miami, FL 33169-5641 (305) 625-4171

Company URL: http://www.southernwine.com
Establishment information: Established in 1968.
Company type: Private company
Business activities: Sells wine, spirits, beer, and non-alcoholic beverages wholesale.
Business type (SIC): Beer, wine, and distilled beverages—wholesale; groceries—wholesale
Financial profile for 2012: Number of employees, 13,800; sales volume, $10,800,000,000
Corporate officers: Harvey R. Chaplin, Chair. and C.E.O.; Wayne E. Chaplin, Pres. and C.O.O.; Lee F. Hager, Exec. V.P., Secy., and C.A.O.; Steven R. Becker, Exec. V.P. and Treas.; John R. Preston, V.P., Finance, and Admin.
Board of directors: Harvey R. Chaplin, Chair.; Wayne E. Chaplin
Giving statement: Giving through the Southern Wine & Spirits of America, Inc. Corporate Giving Program and the SWS Charitable Foundation, Inc.

Southern Wine & Spirits of America, Inc. Corporate Giving Program

1600 N.W. 163rd St.
Miami, FL 33169-5641
URL: http://www.southernwine.com/CorporateSocialResponsibility/AboutSocialResponsibility/tabid/90/Default.aspx

Purpose and activities: As a complement to its foundation, Southern Wine & Spirits also makes charitable contributions to nonprofit organizations directly. Support is given on a national basis.
Fields of interest: Higher education; Education; Medical research; Children/youth, services; Business/industry; Science; General charitable giving.
Program:
National Scholarship Program: The company awards college scholarships of up to $2,500 to children of employees.
Type of support: Employee-related scholarships; General/operating support; Sponsorships.
Geographic limitations: Giving on a national basis in areas of company operations, with emphasis on FL.
Application information: Applications not accepted. Contributes only to pre-selected organizations.

SWS Charitable Foundation, Inc.

1600 N.W. 163rd St.
Miami, FL 33169-5641

Establishment information: Established in 2000 in FL.
Donor: Southern Wine & Spirits of America, Inc.
Contact: Robert M. Hersh
Financial data (yr. ended 12/31/12): Assets, $462,333 (M); gifts received, $3,462,108; expenditures, $3,547,272; qualifying distributions, $3,546,094; giving activities include $3,546,094 for grants.
Purpose and activities: The foundation supports organizations involved with arts and culture, education, health, medical research, and human services.
Fields of interest: Arts; Education; Health care; Medical research; Human services.
Type of support: Annual campaigns; Emergency funds; Employee matching gifts; General/operating support; Matching/challenge support; Sponsorships.
Geographic limitations: Giving primarily in KY, NV, NY, PA, SC, and WA, with emphasis on FL.
Support limitations: No grants to individuals (except for employee-related disaster relief grants).
Application information: Applications not accepted. Contributes only to pre-selected organizations.
Officers: Harvey R. Chaplin, Chair.; Wayne E. Chaplin, Pres.; Steven R. Becker, Exec. V.P. and Treas.; Melvin A. Dick, Sr. V.P.; Lee Hager, Secy.
Director: Paul B. Chaplin.
Number of staff: None.
EIN: 651054944
Selected grants: The following grants are a representative sample of this grantmaker's funding activity:
$100,000 to Blessings in a Backpack, Louisville, KY, 2012.
$50,450 to American Cancer Society, Atlanta, GA, 2012.
$50,000 to Food Bank for New York City, New York, NY, 2012.
$40,000 to Child Help, Maui, HI, 2012.
$34,500 to Boys Town of Italy, New York, NY, 2012.
$31,300 to Kids in Distress, Fort Lauderdale, FL, 2012.
$20,000 to Injured Police Officers Fund, Las Vegas, NV, 2012.
$17,500 to American Heart Association, Dallas, TX, 2012.
$15,000 to Florida International University, Miami, FL, 2012.
$10,000 to Make-A-Wish Foundation of Metro New York, Lake Success, NY, 2012.

3522
Southwest Airlines Co.

P.O. Box 36647-1CR
Dallas, TX 75235-1611 (214) 792-4000
FAX: (214) 792-5015

Company URL: http://www.southwest.com
Establishment information: Established in 1971.
Company type: Public company
Company ticker symbol and exchange: LUV/NYSE
International Securities Identification Number: US8447411088
Business activities: Provides air transportation services.
Business type (SIC): Transportation/scheduled air
Financial profile for 2012: Number of employees, 45,861; assets, $18,596,000,000; sales volume, $17,088,000,000; pre-tax net income, $685,000,000; expenses, $16,465,000,000; liabilities, $11,604,000,000
Fortune 1000 ranking: 2012—164th in revenues, 377th in profits, and 255th in assets
Forbes 2000 ranking: 2012—550th in sales, 1300th in profits, and 1017th in assets
Corporate officers: Gary C. Kelly, Chair., Pres., and C.E.O.; Michael G. Van De Ven, Exec. V.P. and C.O.O.; Jeff Lamb, Exec. V.P. and C.A.O.; Randy Sloan, Sr. V.P. and C.I.O.; Tammy Romo, Sr. V.P., Finance and C.F.O.; Greg Wells, Sr. V.P., Opers.; Ginger C. Hardage, Sr. V.P., Comms.; Leah Koontz, V.P. and Cont.; Mark R. Shaw, V.P., Genl. Counsel and Corp. Secy.; Kevin M. Krone, V.P., Mktg. and Sales; Chris Monroe, Treas.
Board of directors: Gary C. Kelly, Chair.; David W. Biegler; J. Veronica Biggins; Douglas H. Brooks; William H. Cunningham, Ph.D.; John G. Denison; Nancy B. Loeffler; John T. Montford; Thomas M. Nealon; Daniel D. Villanueva
Historic mergers: AirTran Holdings, Inc. (May 2, 2011)
Giving statement: Giving through the Southwest Airlines Co. Outreach.
Company EIN: 741563240

Southwest Airlines Co. Outreach

c/o Kati Garrett, Charitable Giving
P.O. Box 36611, HDQ-1CV
2702 Love Field Dr.
Dallas, TX 75235-1611 (214) 792-1300
FAX: (214) 792-4200; URL: http://www.southwest.com/donations/

Financial data (yr. ended 12/31/11): Total giving, $18,239,850, including $1,814,077 for grants and $16,425,773 for in-kind gifts.
Purpose and activities: Southwest Airlines makes charitable contributions of air transportation to nonprofit organizations for fundraisers and transportation requests.
Type of support: Donated products; Employee volunteer services.
Geographic limitations: Giving primarily in areas of company operations.
Publications: Application guidelines.
Application information: Applications accepted. Telephone calls during the application process are not encouraged. All requests for medical transportation must be submitted through Medical Transportation Grant Program participants. Visit website for list of participating hospitals and organizations. The Communications and Strategic Outreach Department handles giving. The company has a staff that only handles contributions. A contributions committee reviews all requests. Applicants should submit the following:
1) name, address and phone number of organization
2) copy of IRS Determination Letter
3) brief history of organization and description of its mission
4) detailed description of project and amount of funding requested
5) contact person
Copy of IRS Determination Letter should be submitted in PDF format. Proposals should indicate the date of the event.
Initial approach: Complete online application
Committee meeting date(s): Monthly
Deadline(s): 45 days prior to event or print deadline (whichever comes first)
Final notification: 2 to 4 weeks before event or by print/RSVP deadline
Administrator: Kati Garrett, Admin. Coord.
Number of staff: 17 full-time professional.

3523
Southwest Business Corporation

(also known as SWBC)
9311 San Pedro Ave., Ste. 600
San Antonio, TX 78216-4458
(210) 635-1231

Company URL: http://www.swbc.com
Establishment information: Established in 1976.
Company type: Private company
Business activities: Provides mortgage loans and other financial services.
Business type (SIC): Insurance agents, brokers, and services
Corporate officers: Charles Amato, Chair.; Gary Dudley, Pres.; John Dallahan, C.O.O.; Craig Carson, Exec. V.P., Sales and Mktg.; Cindy Jorgensen, Sr. V.P. and C.F.O.; Mark Berger, Sr. V.P. and C.I.O.; Kellie Lowder, V.P., Sales; Mystel Duke, V.P., Human Resources; Marvin Cook, Genl. Counsel
Board of director: Charles Amato, Chair.
Giving statement: Giving through the SWBC Foundation.

SWBC Foundation

9311 San Pedro, Ste. 600
San Antonio, TX 78216-4459 (210) 321-7213
URL: http://www.swbc.com/

Establishment information: Established in 2003 in TX.
Donor: Southwest Business Corporation.
Contact: Lisa W. Wilson, Dir.
Financial data (yr. ended 11/30/11): Assets, $12,977,104 (M); expenditures, $908,710; qualifying distributions, $764,866; giving activities include $763,000 for 31 grants (high: $350,000; low: $750).
Purpose and activities: The foundation supports organizations involved with opera, homelessness, and Catholicism.
Fields of interest: Performing arts, opera; Homeless, human services; Catholic agencies & churches.
Type of support: Capital campaigns.
Geographic limitations: Giving primarily in the San Antonio, TX, area.
Application information: Applications accepted. Application form required. Applicants should submit the following:
1) copy of IRS Determination Letter
Initial approach: Proposal
Deadline(s): None
Directors: Charles E. Amato; Gary L. Dudley; Lisa W. Wilson.
EIN: 200511684

3524
Southwest Gas Corporation

5241 Spring Mountain Rd.
P.O. Box 98510
Las Vegas, NV 89193-8510
(702) 876-7237
FAX: (702) 876-7037

Company URL: http://www.swgas.com
Establishment information: Established in 1931.
Company type: Public company
Company ticker symbol and exchange: SWX/NYSE
Business activities: Transmits and distributes natural gas.
Business type (SIC): Gas production and distribution
Financial profile for 2011: Number of employees, 2,245; assets, $4,488,060,000; sales volume, $1,927,780,000; pre-tax net income, $207,910,000; expenses, $1,656,250,000; liabilities, $3,177,880,000
Fortune 1000 ranking: 2012—965th in revenues, 677th in profits, and 626th in assets
Corporate officers: Jeffrey W. Shaw, Pres. and C.E.O.; Roy R. Centrella, Sr. V.P. and C.F.O.; Eric DeBonis, Sr. V.P., Opers.; Gregory J. Peterson, V.P., Cont., and C.A.O.; Karen S. Haller, V.P., Genl. Counsel, and Corp. Secy.; Laura Lopez Hobbs, V.P., Admin. and Human Resources; Kenneth J. Kenny, C.P.A., V.P., Finance, and Treas.
Board of directors: Robert L. Boughner; Jose A. Cardenas; Thomas E. Chestnut; Stephen C. Comer; LeRoy C. Hanneman, Jr.; Michael O. Maffie; Anne L. Mariucci; Michael J. Melarkey; Jeffrey W. Shaw; A. Randall Thoman; Thomas A. Thomas; Terrence L. Wright
Subsidiary: Utility Financial Corp., Las Vegas, NV
Plants: Phoenix, Tucson, AZ; Victorville, CA; Carson City, Las Vegas, NV
Giving statement: Giving through the Southwest Gas Corporation Contributions Program and the Southwest Gas Corporation Foundation.
Company EIN: 880085720

Southwest Gas Corporation Contributions Program

5241 Spring Mountain Rd.
P.O. Box 98510
Las Vegas, NV 89193-8510 (702) 876-7247
FAX: (702) 364-3444; For Tucson and southern Arizona, contact Marty Loreto: (520) 794-6416; for Phoenix and central Arizona, contact Brenda Beckham: (602) 395-4080; for Barstow, Big Bear, and Victorville, California, contact Nancy Keller: (760) 951-4021; and for Carson City and northern Nevada, contact Wendy Walsh: (775) 887-2743

Contact: Suzanne Farinas, Asst. to C.E.O.
Financial data (yr. ended 12/31/09): Total giving, $20,726, including $10,538 for 101 grants (high: $100; low: $50) and $10,188 for 34 in-kind gifts.
Purpose and activities: As a complement to its foundation, Southwest Gas also makes charitable contributions to nonprofit organizations directly. Support is given primarily in areas of company operations.
Fields of interest: Arts; Education; Environment; Health care; Youth development; Human services; Community/economic development.
Type of support: Annual campaigns; Building/renovation; Continuing support; Donated products; Employee volunteer services; General/operating support; In-kind gifts; Program development; Research.
Geographic limitations: Giving primarily in areas of company operations, with emphasis on Phoenix and Tucson, AZ, Barstow, Big Bear, and Victorville, CA, and Carson City and Las Vegas, NV.
Support limitations: No support for churches or athletic organizations. No grants to individuals.
Publications: Informational brochure; Informational brochure (including application guidelines).
Application information: Applications accepted. The C.E.O.'s office handles giving. A contributions committee at each company location reviews all requests originating from that particular area. Application form not required.
Initial approach: Contact nearest company facility for application form
Copies of proposal: 1
Committee meeting date(s): Monthly
Deadline(s): None
Final notification: 4 to 6 weeks
Administrators: Brenda Beckham, Admin., Consumer Affairs, Phoenix; Marty Loreto, Admin., Consumer Affairs, Tucson; Willie Robinson, Admin., Consumer Affairs, Las Vegas.
Number of staff: None.

The Southwest Gas Corporation Foundation

P.O. Box 98510
Las Vegas, NV 89193-8510 (702) 876-7247
Tucson and southern Arizona applications: c/o Marty Loreto, tel.: (520) 794-6416; Phoenix and central Arizona applications: c/o Brenda Beckham, tel.: (602) 395-4084; Barstow, Big Bear, and Victorville, California applications: c/o Nancy Keller, tel.: (760) 951-4021; Carson City and northern Nevada applications: c/o Wendy Walsh, tel.: (775) 887-2743

Establishment information: Established in 1985 in NV.
Donor: Southwest Gas Corp.
Contact: Suzanne Farinas, Asst. to C.E.O.
Financial data (yr. ended 12/31/11): Assets, $1,578,940 (M); gifts received, $742,732; expenditures, $671,569; qualifying distributions, $670,374; giving activities include $670,374 for grants.
Purpose and activities: The foundation supports organizations involved with arts and culture, education, the environment, health, and human services.
Fields of interest: Arts; Education; Environment; Health care; Children/youth, services; Human services.
Program:
Matching Gifts for Higher Education: The foundation matches contributions made by full-time employees and directors of Southwest Gas and its subsidiaries to institutions of higher education on a one-for-one basis from $25 to $2,500 per contributor, per year.
Type of support: Annual campaigns; Building/renovation; Capital campaigns; Continuing support; Emergency funds; Employee matching gifts; General/operating support; Program development; Research.
Geographic limitations: Giving limited to areas of company operations in AZ, San Bernardino County, CA, and NV.
Support limitations: No support for churches, religious or discriminatory organizations, athletic teams, or hospitals. No grants to individuals, or for endowments, trips, or tours.
Publications: Application guidelines; Informational brochure (including application guidelines).
Application information: Applications accepted. Unsolicited applications not accepted in Phoenix or central Arizona. Proposals should be submitted using organization letterhead. Application form required. Applicants should submit the following:
1) results expected from proposed grant
2) population served
3) copy of IRS Determination Letter
4) brief history of organization and description of its mission
5) list of company employees involved with the organization
6) listing of board of directors, trustees, officers and other key people and their affiliations
7) detailed description of project and amount of funding requested
8) copy of current year's organizational budget and/or project budget
9) listing of additional sources and amount of support

Initial approach: Contact foundation for application form
Copies of proposal: 1
Board meeting date(s): As needed
Deadline(s): None
Final notification: Approximately 4 to 6 weeks
Directors: George C. Biehl; Karen Haller; Jeffrey W. Shaw.
Number of staff: None.
EIN: 942988564
Selected grants: The following grants are a representative sample of this grantmaker's funding activity:
$5,000 to American Red Cross, Las Vegas, NV, 2009.
$5,000 to Boy Scouts of America, Las Vegas, NV, 2009.
$2,500 to Big Brothers Big Sisters of Southern Nevada, Las Vegas, NV, 2009.
$2,500 to Girl Scouts of the U.S.A., Las Vegas, NV, 2009.
$1,500 to Arizonas Children Association, Tucson, AZ, 2009.
$1,500 to Salvation Army, Carson City, NV, 2009.
$1,000 to Boys and Girls Clubs of Western Nevada, Carson City, NV, 2009.
$750 to Crossroads Mission, Yuma, AZ, 2009.
$500 to March of Dimes Birth Defects Foundation, Phoenix, AZ, 2009.
$150 to Kids Chance of Arizona, Phoenix, AZ, 2009.

3525
Southwestern Electric Cooperative

216 Main St.
P.O. Box 369
Clayton, NM 88415 (575) 374-2451

Company URL: http://www.swec-coop.org/
Establishment information: Established in 1939.
Company type: Cooperative
Business activities: Transmits and distributes electricity.
Business type (SIC): Electric services
Corporate officers: John Vincent, Pres.; Bob Weese, Secy.-Treas.
Board of directors: Robert Burns; Robert Emery; Larry Harkins; Harry Hopson; Eugene Podzemny; Max Sanchez; Sterlin Shields; Wid Stevenson; John Vincent; Bob Weese
Giving statement: Giving through the Southwestern Electric Cooperative Education Foundation.

Southwestern Electric Cooperative Education Foundation

P.O. Box 369
Clayton, NM 88415 (575) 374-2451

Establishment information: Established in 1998 in NM.
Financial data (yr. ended 05/31/11): Assets, $49,170 (M); gifts received, $700; expenditures, $3,780; qualifying distributions, $3,350; giving activities include $3,000 for 7 grants to individuals (high: $500; low: $250).
Purpose and activities: The foundation awards college scholarships to students living in a residence receiving electric power from Southwestern Electric Cooperative.
Type of support: Scholarships—to individuals.
Geographic limitations: Giving limited to NM.
Application information: Applications accepted. Application form required.
Applications should include a 100-word essay, high school or college transcripts, and three letters of recommendation.
Initial approach: Proposal
Deadline(s): Mar. 15
Final notification: May 1
Officers: John Vincent, Pres.; Eugene Podzemny, V.P.; Bob Weese, Secy.-Treas.
Trustees: Robert Burns; Robert Emery; Harkins Larry; J.M. Poling III; Sterlin Shields; Wid Stevenson.
EIN: 850376832

3526
Southwestern Eye Center, Ltd.

2610 E. University Dr.
Mesa, AZ 85213-8436 (480) 892-8400

Company URL: http://www.sweye.com
Establishment information: Established in 1982.
Company type: Private company
Business activities: Provides ophthalmological services.
Business type (SIC): Offices and clinics/doctors'
Corporate officers: Richard Hinton, C.F.O.; Shane Armstrong, V.P. and Genl. Counsel
Offices: Casa Grande, Cottonwood, Kingman, Lake Havasu City, Lakeside, Nogales, Phoenix, Prescott, Safford, Sierra Vista, Sun City, Yuma, AZ
Giving statement: Giving through the Southwestern Medical Foundation.

Southwestern Medical Foundation

(formerly Southwestern Medical Foundation)
2610 E. University Dr.
Mesa, AZ 85213-8436
URL: http://www.sweye.com/about/charities.php

Establishment information: Established in 1992 in AZ.
Donors: Storz Ophthalmics, Inc.; Bausch & Lomb Inc.
Contact: L. Lothaire Bluth, M.D., Pres.
Financial data (yr. ended 12/31/11): Assets, $22,014 (M); gifts received, $22,255; expenditures, $24,380; qualifying distributions, $24,380.
Purpose and activities: The foundation provides medical and surgical eye care, vision aids, and other services to needy individuals with visual impairments.
International interests: Mexico.
Type of support: Conferences/seminars; General/operating support; Scholarship funds; Use of facilities.
Geographic limitations: Giving primarily in AZ and Chihuahua, Mexico.
Application information: Applications accepted. Application form required. Applicants should submit the following:
1) detailed description of project and amount of funding requested
Initial approach: Proposal
Copies of proposal: 1
Deadline(s): None
Officers and Directors:* L. Lothaire Bluth, M.D.*, Pres.; Connie W. Bluth*, Secy.; John M. Lewis, M.D.
EIN: 860716576

3527
Southwire Company

(also known as Kagan-Dixon Wire Corp)
1 Southwire Dr.
Carrollton, GA 30119 (770) 832-4242
FAX: 800-444-1700

Company URL: http://www.southwire.com
Establishment information: Established in 1937.
Company type: Private company
Business activities: Manufactures and produces electrical wire and cable, aluminum, and copper.
Business type (SIC): Metal products/structural; metal refining/secondary nonferrous
Financial profile for 2011: Number of employees, 4,100; sales volume, $4,300,000,000
Corporate officers: Roy Richards, Jr., Chair.; Stuart Thorn, Pres. and C.E.O.; J. Guyton Cochran, Jr., Exec. V.P. and C.F.O.; Floyd Smith, Exec. V.P. and Genl. Counsel; Jeff Herrin, Exec. V.P., Opers.; Michael Wiggins, Exec. V.P., Human Resources
Board of director: Roy Richards, Jr., Chair.
Subsidiary: Southwire Specialty Products, Osceola, AR
Giving statement: Giving through the Southwire Company Contributions Program.

Southwire Company Contributions Program

1 Southwire Dr.
Carrollton, GA 30119-4400
URL: http://www.southwire.com/ourcompany/Community.htm

Purpose and activities: Southwire makes charitable contributions to nonprofit organizations involved with education, the environment, youth development, human services, and community development. Support is given primarily in areas of company operations, with emphasis on Alabama, Arizona, California, Florida, Georgia, Illinois, Indiana, Kentucky, Mississippi, Pennsylvania, Texas, and Utah, and in Canada and Mexico.
Fields of interest: Education; Environment; Youth development; Human services; Community/economic development.
International interests: Canada; Mexico.
Type of support: Employee volunteer services; General/operating support.
Geographic limitations: Giving primarily in areas of company operations in AL, AZ, CA, FL, GA, IL, IN, KY, MS, PA, TX, and UT, and in Canada and Mexico.

3528
Sovereign Bank

75 State St.
Boston, MA 02109 (617) 346-7200

Company URL: http://www.sovereignbank.com
Establishment information: Established in 1902.
Company type: Subsidiary of a foreign company
Business activities: Operates commercial bank.
Business type (SIC): Banks/commercial
Corporate officers: Paul A. Perrault, Pres. and C.E.O.; Kirk W. Walters, Sr. Exec V.P., C.F.O., and C.A.O
Board of directors: Gonzalo de Las Heras; Ralph V. Whitworth; Brian Hard
Giving statement: Giving through the Sovereign Bank Corporate Giving Program and the Sovereign Bank Foundation.

Sovereign Bank Corporate Giving Program

75 State St.
Boston, MA 02109 (877) 768-2265
URL: http://www.sovereignbank.com/companyinfo/company_information/community_development/default.asp

Purpose and activities: As a complement to its foundation, Sovereign also makes charitable contributions to nonprofit organizations directly. Support is given primarily in areas of company operations.
Fields of interest: Higher education; Education; Food banks; Housing/shelter, volunteer services; Athletics/sports, Special Olympics; Human services, financial counseling; Human services; Economic development; Community/economic development; United Ways and Federated Giving Programs Economically disadvantaged.
Type of support: Employee matching gifts; Employee volunteer services; General/operating support; Loans—to individuals; Scholarship funds.
Geographic limitations: Giving primarily in areas of company operations.

Sovereign Bank Foundation

c/o Sovereign Bank
1130 Berkshire Blvd.
Wyomissing, PA 19610-1200 (610) 526-6343
Additional application addresses: DE, MD, NJ, and PA organizations: CRA Div. Mgr., Sovereign Bank, 20-536-CD2, 2 Aldwyn Lane, Villanova, PA 19085, e-mail: MIDAFoundation@sovereignbank.com; CT, MA, NH, and RI organizations: CRA Division Mgr., Sovereign Bank, MA1-MB2-03-06, 2 Morrissey Blvd., Dorchester, MA 02125, e-mail: NEFoundation@sovereignbank.com; Metro-New York, NY organizations: CRA Division Mgr., Sovereign Bank, NY1-6528-LG12, 195 Montague St., Brooklyn, NY 11201, e-mail: NYFoundation@sovereignbank.com; URL: http://www.sovereignbank.com/companyinfo/company_information/community_development/foundation_guidelines.asp

Establishment information: Established in 1989 in PA.
Donor: Sovereign Bank.
Contact: Craig Williams, V.P.
Financial data (yr. ended 12/31/12): Assets, $0; gifts received, $2,037,050; expenditures, $2,037,050; qualifying distributions, $2,037,050; giving activities include $2,037,035 for grants.
Purpose and activities: The foundation supports organizations involved with arts and culture, education, health, employment, housing, human services, and community and economic development. Special emphasis is directed toward programs targeting low-and moderate-income individuals and communities.
Fields of interest: Media/communications; Visual arts; Museums; Performing arts; Arts; Education, early childhood education; Child development, education; Libraries (public); Education; Environment; Health care; Employment, training;

Housing/shelter, home owners; Housing/shelter, services; Housing/shelter; Children/youth, services; Human services, financial counseling; Human services; Economic development; Community/economic development Economically disadvantaged.

Programs:

Arts and Culture: The foundation supports visual and performing arts opportunities, including museums, libraries, cultural centers, and public radio and television stations that support programs targeting low-and moderate-income communities.

Community Investment and Economic Development: The foundation supports programs designed to promote affordable housing for low-and moderate-income individuals and communities; foster economic development projects designed to improve quality of life, sustain economic development, and support job skills for low-and moderate-income individuals and communities; and promote community development; provide credit counseling, homeownership counseling, home maintenance, and other financial service education; and programs designed to promote the environment.

Health and Human Services: The foundation supports programs designed to revitalize or stabilize low- and moderate-income areas and/or support community services targeting low-and moderate-income individuals.

Youth and Education: The foundation supports programs designed to enrich a child's educational opportunities including school programming, curriculum development from outside organizations, after-school initiatives, early childhood development, and special education programs. Special emphasis is directed toward programs targeting low-and moderate-income communities.

Type of support: Annual campaigns; Building/renovation; Continuing support; Curriculum development; Emergency funds; Employee matching gifts; Employee-related scholarships; General/operating support; Program development.

Geographic limitations: Giving primarily in areas of company operations in CT, New Castle, DE, MA, MD, NH, Central and Southern NJ, NY, Mid-Atlantic, PA, and RI.

Support limitations: No support for political organizations, or organizations traditionally supported by parents, including Little League, Parent Teacher Organizations, and Scouting. No grants to individuals (except for employee-related scholarships), or for capital campaigns, sectarian or religious purposes, pageants, team sponsorships or sporting events, advertising in programs, bulletins, schedules, maps, yearbooks, book covers, or brochures, trips or tours, or walk-a-thon races or similar fundraising events.

Publications: Annual report; Application guidelines; Program policy statement.

Application information: Applications accepted. Proposal narratives should be no longer than 2 pages. Submissions of videos, folders, and plastic covers are not encouraged. Additional information may be requested at a later date. Application form not required. Applicants should submit the following:

1) copy of IRS Determination Letter
2) brief history of organization and description of its mission
3) copy of most recent annual report/audited financial statement/990
4) listing of board of directors, trustees, officers and other key people and their affiliations
5) detailed description of project and amount of funding requested
6) copy of current year's organizational budget and/or project budget
7) listing of additional sources and amount of support

Proposals should include a description of past involvement of the foundation with the organization, if applicable.

Initial approach: Download grant proposal cover sheet and e-mail cover sheet and proposal to foundation

Copies of proposal: 1

Deadline(s): Mar. 7, June 8, and Sept. 7

Final notification: Apr. 30, July 13, and Oct. 31

Officers and Directors:* John V. Killen*, Pres.; Sonia L. Alleyne, V.P.; Patricia Rock, V.P.; Joseph E. Schupp, V.P.; Craig M. Williams, V.P.; Cynthia Kelly, Secy.; Jay Bobb, Treas.; Lawrence F. Delp; Patrick Sullivan.

Number of staff: 1 part-time professional; 1 part-time support.

EIN: 232548113

3529
Spahn & Rose Lumber Company

2175 Southpark Ct.
P.O. Box 149
Dubuque, IA 52003 (563) 582-3606

Company URL: http://www.spahnandrose.com
Establishment information: Established in 1904.
Company type: Private company
Business activities: Operates lumber yards.
Business type (SIC): Lumber and other building materials—retail
Financial profile for 2010: Number of employees, 239
Corporate officers: John P. Hannan, Pres. and C.E.O.; Kenneth L. Funke, C.P.A., V.P., Opers.; Ron E. Gansen, V.P., Finance
Giving statement: Giving through the Spahn & Rose Lumber Company Charitable Foundation.

Spahn & Rose Lumber Company Charitable Foundation

c/o American Trust & Savings Bank
P.O. Box 938
Dubuque, IA 52004-0938

Establishment information: Established in 1975 in IA.
Donor: Spahn & Rose Lumber Co., Inc.
Financial data (yr. ended 01/31/12): Assets, $2,049,930 (M); gifts received, $85,000; expenditures, $112,750; qualifying distributions, $103,600; giving activities include $103,600 for 60 grants (high: $10,000; low: $250).
Purpose and activities: The foundation supports hospitals and organizations involved with arts and culture, education, health, youth development, and human services.
Fields of interest: Arts; Higher education; Education; Hospitals (general); Health care; Youth development; Human services; United Ways and Federated Giving Programs.
Type of support: Annual campaigns; Building/renovation; Capital campaigns; Continuing support; General/operating support.
Geographic limitations: Giving primarily in Dubuque and northeastern IA.
Support limitations: No grants to individuals.
Application information: Applications not accepted. Unsolicited requests for funds not accepted.
Trustee: American Trust & Savings Bank.
EIN: 426234027

3530
Spang and Company

110 Delta Dr.
Pittsburgh, PA 15238-0422 (412) 963-9363

Company URL: http://www.spang.com
Establishment information: Established in 1894.
Company type: Private company
Business activities: Manufactures electronic components, children's games and toys, and electric power transformers.
Business type (SIC): Electronic components and accessories; steel mill products; electric transmission and distribution equipment; games, toys, and sporting and athletic goods
Corporate officers: Frank E. Rath, Jr., Pres.; Bob Harbage, C.F.O.; Brad Yourish, V.P., Mktg.
Subsidiaries: Magnetics, Inc., Butler, PA; Today's Kids, Booneville, AR
Division: Spang Power Electronics Div., Sandy Lake, PA
Giving statement: Giving through the Frank E. Rath * Spang and Company Charitable Trust.

The Frank E. Rath * Spang and Company Charitable Trust

(formerly Spang and Company Charitable Trust)
c/o Spang & Co.
P.O. Box 11422
Pittsburgh, PA 15238-0422 (412) 963-9363

Establishment information: Established in 1972 in PA.
Donors: Spang and Co.; Magnetics, Inc.; F.E. Rath Trust.
Contact: Sandra L. Michael
Financial data (yr. ended 12/31/11): Assets, $6,608,332 (M); expenditures, $350,447; qualifying distributions, $343,300; giving activities include $343,300 for grants.
Purpose and activities: The trust supports zoos and fire departments and organizations involved with performing arts, higher education, health, and cancer.
Fields of interest: Performing arts; Performing arts, orchestras; Performing arts, opera; Higher education; Zoos/zoological societies; Hospitals (general); Health care; Cancer; Cancer research; Disasters, fire prevention/control; Salvation Army.
Type of support: General/operating support.
Geographic limitations: Giving primarily in Butler and Pittsburgh, PA.
Support limitations: No grants to individuals.
Application information: Applications accepted. Application form not required. Applicants should submit the following:

1) name, address and phone number of organization
2) brief history of organization and description of its mission
3) copy of IRS Determination Letter
4) detailed description of project and amount of funding requested

Initial approach: Proposal

Board meeting date(s): Apr., Aug., and Dec.

Deadline(s): 90 days prior to end of calendar quarter

Trustees: David F. Rath; Frank E. Rath, Jr.
EIN: 256020192
Selected grants: The following grants are a representative sample of this grantmaker's funding activity:

$105,000 to Phipps Conservatory and Botanical Gardens, Pittsburgh, PA, 2010.
$25,000 to Shadyside Hospital Foundation, Pittsburgh, PA, 2010.

$10,000 to Pittsburgh Symphony, Pittsburgh, PA, 2010.
$10,000 to Pittsburgh Trust for Cultural Resources, Pittsburgh, PA, 2010.
$10,000 to University of Pittsburgh, Pittsburgh, PA, 2010.
$5,200 to Childrens Hospital of Pittsburgh, Pittsburgh, PA, 2010.
$5,000 to Butler Area Public Library, Butler, PA, 2010.
$5,000 to Butler County Association for the Blind, Butler, PA, 2010.
$5,000 to Pittsburgh Ballet Theater, Pittsburgh, PA, 2010.
$5,000 to Pittsburgh Civic Light Opera, Pittsburgh, PA, 2010.

3531
Spangler Candy Company
400 N. Portland St.
P.O. Box 71
Bryan, OH 43506 (419) 636-4221

Company URL: http://www.spanglercandy.com/
Establishment information: Established in 1906.
Company type: Private company
Business activities: Operates candy company.
Business type (SIC): Sugar, candy, and salted/roasted nut production
Financial profile for 2010: Number of employees, 175
Corporate officers: Dean L. Spangler, Chair.; Kirkland B. Vashaw, Pres. and C.E.O.; William G. Martin, Exec. V.P. and C.F.O.; Kevin Gallagher, C.I.O.; R. Denny Gunter, V.P., Sales; James B. Knight, V.P., Mktg.; Matt Dixon, Cont.
Board of director: Dean L. Spangler, Chair.
Giving statement: Giving through the Spangler Foundation.

Spangler Foundation
P.O. Box 71
Bryan, OH 43506-0071

Establishment information: Established in 2004 in OH.
Donor: Spangler Candy Co.
Financial data (yr. ended 12/31/11): Assets, $207,694 (M); gifts received, $19,200; expenditures, $25,200; qualifying distributions, $25,200; giving activities include $25,200 for 1 grant.
Purpose and activities: The foundation supports the Bryan Area Foundation in Byran, Ohio.
Fields of interest: Foundations (public).
Type of support: General/operating support.
Geographic limitations: Giving primarily in OH.
Support limitations: No grants to individuals.
Application information: Applications not accepted. Unsolicited requests for funds not accepted.
Officers: Dean L. Spangler, Chair.; Kirk Vashaw, Pres. and C.E.O.; William G. Martin, Exec. V.P. and C.F.O.
EIN: 550878475

3532
Spansion Inc.
915 DeGuigne Dr.
P.O. Box 3453
Sunnyvale, CA 94088 (408) 962-2500

Company URL: http://www.spansion.com
Establishment information: Established in 1993.
Company type: Public company
Company ticker symbol and exchange: CODE/NYSE
Business activities: Operates a semiconductor device company that designs, develops, manufactures, markets and sells Flash memory solutions.
Business type (SIC): Electronic components and accessories
Financial profile for 2012: Number of employees, 2,838; assets, $1,172,170,000; sales volume, $915,930,000; pre-tax net income, $37,380,000; expenses, $853,090,000; liabilities, $610,390,000
Corporate officers: Raymond Bingham, Chair.; John H. Kispert, C.E.O.; Randy Furr, Exec. V.P. and C.F.O.; Scot Griffin, Sr. V.P. and Genl. Counsel; Jay Legenhausen, Sr. V.P., Sales; Carmine Renzulli, Sr. V.P., Human Resources
Board of directors: Raymond Bingham, Chair.; Keith Barnes; Hans Geyer; John H. Kispert; William E. Mitchell; Clifton Thomas Weatherford
Giving statement: Giving through the Spansion Inc. Corporate Giving Program.
Company EIN: 203898239

Spansion Inc. Corporate Giving Program
915 DeGuigne Dr.
Sunnyvale, CA 94085-3836 (408) 962-2500
FAX: (408) 962-2502; URL: http://www.spansion.com/About/SocialResponsiblity/Pages/CorporateSocialResponsibility.aspx

Purpose and activities: Spansion makes charitable contributions to nonprofit organizations involved with education, basic needs, and community development. Support is given primarily in areas of company operations in California, and in China, Japan, Malaysia, Singapore, South Korea, Taiwan, and Thailand.
Fields of interest: Elementary/secondary education; Education; Health care; Food services; Housing/shelter; Community/economic development; Science, formal/general education; Mathematics; Leadership development.
International interests: China; Japan; Malaysia; Singapore; South Korea; Taiwan; Thailand.
Type of support: Donated equipment; Employee volunteer services; General/operating support; In-kind gifts; Program development; Sponsorships.
Geographic limitations: Giving primarily in areas of company operations in CA, and in China, Japan, Malaysia, Singapore, South Korea, Taiwan, and Thailand.

3533
Spark Energy, L.P.
2501 Citywest Blvd., Ste. 100
Houston, TX 77042-2836 (713) 977-5645

Company URL: https://www.sparkenergy.com
Establishment information: Established in 1999.
Company type: Private company
Business activities: Operates an electricity and natural gas service company.
Business type (SIC): Electric services
Corporate officers: William Keith Maxwell III, C.E.O.; Nathan Kroeker, Pres.; Christopher Barron, Sr. V.P. and C.I.O.; Mandy Bush, C.F.O.; Denis Vermette, V.P., Finance, and Treas.; Jim Head, V.P., Mktg., and Sales
Giving statement: Giving through the Spark Energy, L.P., Corporate Giving Program.

Spark Energy, L.P., Corporate Giving Program
2501 Citywest Blvd., Ste. # 100
Houston, TX 77042-3019
URL: https://www.sparkenergy.com/Community-Involvement

Purpose and activities: Spark Energy, L.P. makes charitable contributions to nonprofit organizations involved with children, military personnel, the mentally disabled, and homeless families. Support is given primarily in areas of company operations in Arizona, California, Colorado, Connecticut, Florida, Illinois, Indiana, Maryland, Massachusetts, Michigan, Nevada, New Mexico, New York, Ohio, Pennsylvania, and Texas; giving also to national organizations.
Fields of interest: Children, services; Family services; Homeless, human services; International relief; Children's rights Children; Mentally disabled; Military/veterans; Homeless.
Type of support: General/operating support.
Geographic limitations: Giving primarily in areas of company operations in AZ, CA, CO, CT, FL, IL, IN, MA, MD,MI, NM, NV, NY, OH, PA, and TX.
Officer: Frode Helgerud, C.E.O.

3534
Spartan Motors, Inc.
1541 Reynolds Rd.
Charlotte, MI 48813 (517) 543-6400
FAX: (517) 543-7727

Company URL: http://www.spartanmotors.com/
Establishment information: Established in 1975.
Company type: Public company
Company ticker symbol and exchange: SPAR/NASDAQ
Business activities: Manufacturers, markets, and customizes heavy-duty vehicles.
Business type (SIC): Motor vehicles and equipment
Financial profile for 2012: Number of employees, 1,653; assets, $245,150,000; sales volume, $470,580,000; pre-tax net income, -$2,360,000; expenses, $473,170,000; liabilities, $66,420,000
Corporate officers: Hugh W. Sloan, Jr., Chair.; John E. Sztykiel, Pres. and C.E.O.; Thomas W. Gorman, C.O.O.; Thomas T. Kivell, V.P., Genl. Counsel, and Secy.
Board of directors: Hugh W. Sloan, Jr., Chair.; Richard R. Current; Richard F. Dauch; Ronald Harbour; Kenneth Kaczmarek; Andrew M. Rooke; John E. Sztykiel
Giving statement: Giving through the Spartan Motors Private Foundation.
Company EIN: 382078923

The Spartan Motors Private Foundation
1000 Reynolds Rd.
Charlotte, MI 48813 (514) 543-6400

Establishment information: Established in 1995 in MI.
Donor: Spartan Motors, Inc.
Contact: Stacy Guy
Financial data (yr. ended 12/31/10): Assets, $28,466 (M); expenditures, $7,516; qualifying distributions, $7,500; giving activities include $7,500 for grants.
Purpose and activities: The foundation supports general charitable giving and other areas.
Fields of interest: General charitable giving.
Type of support: General/operating support.
Geographic limitations: Giving limited to organizations that benefit Charlotte, MI and the surrounding area.
Application information: Applications accepted. Application form required. Applicants should submit the following:
1) copy of IRS Determination Letter
Initial approach: Letter
Deadline(s): None
Officers: John E. Sztykiel, Pres.; Janine L. Nierenberger, Secy.; Lori Wade, Treas.
Directors: James Knapp; Jim Logan.
EIN: 383212131

3535
Spartan Stores, Inc.

850 76th St., S.W.
P.O. Box 8700
Grand Rapids, MI 49518-8700
(616) 878-2000

Company URL: http://www.spartanstores.com
Establishment information: Established in 1917.
Company type: Public company
Company ticker symbol and exchange: SPTN/NASDAQ
Business activities: Operates regional grocery distributor and retailer.
Business type (SIC): Groceries—retail
Financial profile for 2013: Number of employees, 8,650; assets, $789,670,000; sales volume, $2,608,160,000; pre-tax net income, $43,270,000; expenses, $2,552,240,000; liabilities, $454,010,000
Fortune 1000 ranking: 2012—783rd in revenues, 848th in profits, and 988th in assets
Corporate officers: Craig C. Sturken, Chair.; Dennis Eidson, Pres. and C.E.O.; David M. Staples, Exec. V.P. and C.F.O.; Alex J. DeYonker, Exec. V.P., Genl. Counsel, and Secy.; Alan R. Hartline, Exec. V.P., Mktg.; Thomas A. Van Hall, V.P., Finance
Board of directors: Craig C. Sturken, Chair.; M. Shan Atkins; Wendy A. Beck; Dennis Eidson; Frank M. Gambino; Yvonne R. Jackson; Frederick Morganthall II; Elizabeth A. Nickels; Timothy J. O'Donovan
Giving statement: Giving through the Spartan Stores Foundation.
Company EIN: 380593940

Spartan Stores Foundation

850 76th St., GR761225
P.O. Box 8700
Grand Rapids, MI 49518-8700
URL: http://www.spartanstores.com/internet.nsf/nav/AboutSpartanStores,SpartanStoresFoundation?OpenDocument&category=SpartanStoresFoundation

Establishment information: Established in 2007 in MI.
Donor: Spartan Stores, Inc.
Financial data (yr. ended 12/31/11): Assets, $484,166 (M); gifts received, $1,769,480; expenditures, $1,292,552; qualifying distributions, $1,156,979; giving activities include $1,156,979 for grants.
Purpose and activities: The foundation supports organizations involved with education, health, cancer, hunger, youth development, and human services.
Fields of interest: Higher education; Education, reading; Education; Hospitals (general); Health care; Cancer; Food services; Youth development; Salvation Army; YM/YWCAs & YM/YWHAs; Children, services; Human services; United Ways and Federated Giving Programs.
Type of support: Annual campaigns; Building/renovation; General/operating support.
Geographic limitations: Giving primarily in Grand Rapids, MI.
Support limitations: No grants to individuals.
Application information: Applications not accepted. Contributes only to pre-selected organizations.
Officers: Dennis Edison, Pres.; Alex J. DeYonker, Secy.; Jeanne Norcross, V.P.; David M. Staples, Treas.
EIN: 208767495
Selected grants: The following grants are a representative sample of this grantmaker's funding activity:
$102,000 to United Way, Heart of West Michigan, Grand Rapids, MI, 2010.
$30,000 to Christians Opening Opportunities for Learning, Grand Rapids, MI, 2010.
$22,250 to American Cancer Society, Grand Rapids, MI, 2010.
$10,000 to Western Michigan University Foundation, Kalamazoo, MI, 2010.
$5,100 to Grand Valley State University, Allendale, MI, 2010.
$5,000 to Aquinas College, Grand Rapids, MI, 2010.
$2,500 to ACCESS of West Michigan, Grand Rapids, MI, 2010.
$1,700 to American Diabetes Association, Grand Rapids, MI, 2010.
$1,000 to Food Bank of South Central Michigan, Battle Creek, MI, 2010.

3536
Spear Pharmaceuticals

11924 Fairway Lakes Dr., Ste. 1
Fort Myers, FL 33913 (239) 560-2411

Company URL: http://spearpharma.com
Establishment information: Established in 1993.
Company type: Private company
Business activities: Manufactures branded and bioequivalent dermatological products.
Business type (SIC): Drugs
Corporate officers: K.L. Spear, M.D., Pres.; Stephen Basile, Sr. V.P., Sales and Mktg.
Giving statement: Giving through the ESR Foundation.

The ESR Foundation

15016 Pratolino Way
Naples, FL 34110-2752

Establishment information: Established in 2005 in FL.
Donors: Spear Pharmaceuticals, Inc.; K.L. Spear; Jayne Spear.
Financial data (yr. ended 12/31/11): Assets, $1,603,233 (M); expenditures, $78,408; qualifying distributions, $66,250; giving activities include $66,250 for grants.
Purpose and activities: The foundation supports camps and organizations involved with education, water conservation, animal welfare, diabetes, medical research, abuse prevention, military and veterans, and women.
Fields of interest: Education; Human services.
Type of support: General/operating support.
Geographic limitations: Giving primarily in CO, Washington, DC, FL, IL, and MT; giving also to national organizations.
Support limitations: No grants to individuals.
Application information: Applications not accepted. Unsolicited requests for funds not accepted.
Trustees: Jayne Spear; K. L. Spear.
EIN: 306097971

3537
The Specialty Manufacturing Co.

5858 Centerville Rd.
St. Paul, MN 55127 (651) 653-0599

Company URL: http://www.specialtymfg.com/
Establishment information: Established in 1900.
Company type: Private company
Business activities: Provides contract development and manufacturing services; manufactures lawn and garden products, valves, and metal stampings.
Business type (SIC): Machinery/farm and garden; plastic products/miscellaneous; metal forgings and stampings; metal products/fabricated
Corporate officers: Daniel W. McKeown, Pres. and C.E.O.; Kent Brunner, V.P. and C.F.O.
Giving statement: Giving through the Boss Foundation.

The Boss Foundation

5858 Centerville Rd.
St. Paul, MN 55127-6804 (651) 653-0599

Establishment information: Established around 1957.
Donor: The Specialty Manufacturing Co.
Contact: Daniel W. McKeown, Treas.
Financial data (yr. ended 06/30/12): Assets, $5,625,744 (M); gifts received, $50,000; expenditures, $319,692; qualifying distributions, $280,000; giving activities include $280,000 for grants.
Purpose and activities: The foundation supports zoos and organizations involved with arts and culture, higher education, and human services.
Fields of interest: Museums; Performing arts; Performing arts, theater; Performing arts, opera; Historic preservation/historical societies; Arts; Higher education; Zoos/zoological societies; Youth, services; Human services.
Type of support: General/operating support.
Geographic limitations: Giving primarily in the Minneapolis and St. Paul, MN, metropolitan area.
Support limitations: No grants to individuals.
Publications: Application guidelines.
Application information: Applications accepted. Proposals should be limited to 5 pages. Application form not required. Applicants should submit the following:
1) copy of IRS Determination Letter
2) detailed description of project and amount of funding requested
3) additional materials/documentation
Initial approach: Proposal

Board meeting date(s): June
Deadline(s): June 1
Officers and Trustees:* W. Andrew Boss*, Pres.; Heidi Sandberg McKeown*, Secy.; Daniel W. McKeown, Treas.; Desmond McKeown.
EIN: 416038452

3538
Specialty Restaurants Corporation
8191 E. Kaiser Blvd.
Anaheim, CA 92808-2214 (714) 279-6100
FAX: (714) 998-7574

Company URL: http://www.specialtyrestaurants.com
Establishment information: Established in 1958.
Company type: Private company
Business activities: Operates restaurants.
Business type (SIC): Restaurants and drinking places
Financial profile for 2010: Number of employees, 4,500
Corporate officers: John D. Tallichet, Chair. and Co-Pres.; Vincent E. Kikugawa, Co-Pres.
Board of director: John D. Tallichet, Chair.
Giving statement: Giving through the Specialty Restaurants Corporation Contributions Program.

Specialty Restaurants Corporation Contributions Program
8191 E. Kaiser Blvd.
Anaheim, CA 92808-2214 (714) 279-6100
FAX: (714) 998-7574

Contact: Leslie Moore, Exec. Asst.
Purpose and activities: Specialty Restaurants make charitable contributions to nonprofit organizations involved with arts and culture, the environment, and wildlife preservation, and to museums and on a case by case basis. Support is given primarily in areas of company operations.
Fields of interest: Museums; Arts; Environment; Animals/wildlife, preservation/protection; General charitable giving.
Type of support: Donated products; General/operating support.
Geographic limitations: Giving primarily in areas of company operations.
Application information: Application form not required.
Initial approach: Proposal to headquarters
Deadline(s): None

3539
Spector Gadon & Rosen, P.C.
1635 Market St., Fl. 7
Philadelphia, PA 19103-2290
(215) 241-8888

Company URL: http://www.lawsgr.com
Establishment information: Established in 1974.
Company type: Private company
Business activities: Provides legal services.
Business type (SIC): Legal services
Corporate officer: Sean Sweeney, C.E.O.
Giving statement: Giving through the Spector Gadon & Rosen Foundation.

The Spector Gadon & Rosen Foundation
1635 Market St., 7th Fl.
Philadelphia, PA 19103-2223
URL: http://www.lawsgr.com

Establishment information: Established in 2004 in PA.
Donors: Spector Gadon & Rosen, P.C.; Paul Rosen; Steve Gadon; Edward Fitzgerald.
Financial data (yr. ended 12/31/11): Assets, $1 (M); expenditures, $0; qualifying distributions, $0.
Purpose and activities: The foundation supports organizations involved with arts and culture.
Type of support: General/operating support; Program development.
Geographic limitations: Giving primarily in the southern NJ area and the Delaware Valley, PA.
Support limitations: No support for organizations established less than 2 years ago, religious or political organizations, or umbrella organizations. No grants to.
Application information: Applications not accepted. Unsolicited requests for funds not accepted.
Officers: Paul R. Rosen, Chair. and Pres.; Edward G. Fitzgerald, Secy.-Treas.
EIN: 200342018

3540
Spectra Energy Corp.
5400 Westheimer Ct.
Houston, TX 77056-5310 (713) 627-5400
FAX: (302) 655-5049

Company URL: http://www.spectraenergy.com/
Establishment information: Established in 1911.
Company type: Public company
Company ticker symbol and exchange: SE/NYSE
International Securities Identification Number: US8475601097
Business activities: Provides transportation and storage of natural gas.
Business type (SIC): Gas production and distribution
Financial profile for 2012: Number of employees, 5,600; assets, $30,587,000,000; sales volume, $5,075,000,000; pre-tax net income, $1,415,000,000; expenses, $3,500,000,000; liabilities, $21,357,000,000
Fortune 1000 ranking: 2012—475th in revenues, 210th in profits, and 183rd in assets
Forbes 2000 ranking: 2012—1384th in sales, 669th in profits, and 727th in assets
Corporate officers: William T. Esrey, Chair.; Gregory L. Ebel, Pres. and C.E.O.; Alan N. Harris, C.O.O.; John Patrick Reddy, C.F.O.; Dorothy M. Ables, C.A.O.; Reginald D. Hedgebeth, Jr., Genl. Counsel
Board of directors: William T. Esrey, Chair.; Austin A. Adams; Joseph Alvarado; Pamela L. Carter; Tony Comper; Gregory L. Ebel; Peter B. Hamilton; Dennis R. Hendrix; Michael McShane; Michael G. Morris; Michael E.J. Phelps
Giving statement: Giving through the Spectra Energy Foundation.
Company EIN: 205413139

Spectra Energy Foundation
c/o Community Rels.
5400 Westheimer Ct.
Houston, TX 77056 (713) 627-5036

Contact: Regan Kasman, Mgr., Community Rels.
Purpose and activities: Spectra Energy makes charitable contributions to nonprofit organizations primarily in areas of company operations.
Fields of interest: General charitable giving.
International interests: Canada.
Type of support: Employee matching gifts; Employee volunteer services; Employee-related scholarships; General/operating support.
Geographic limitations: Giving primarily in areas of company operations.
Application information: Applications not accepted. Contributes only to pre-selected organizations.

3541
SpectraCare, Inc.
(also known as SpectraCare Home Health, Inc.)
9000 Wessex Pl., Ste. 100
Louisville, KY 40222-4904 (502) 429-4550

Establishment information: Established in 1988.
Company type: Subsidiary of a public company
Business activities: Provides home health care services; operates bone marrow transplant outpatient clinic.
Business type (SIC): Home healthcare services; miscellaneous health services
Corporate officer: John Dabds, C.F.O., Secy. and Treas.
Giving statement: Giving through the Anthem Foundation, Inc.

Anthem Foundation, Inc.
(formerly Southeastern Group Foundation, Inc.)
120 Monument Cir.
Indianapolis, IN 46204-4903 (317) 488-6058
Additional tel.: (800) 563-5465

Establishment information: Established in 1990 in KY.
Donors: Southeastern Mutual Insurance Co.; SpectraCare, Inc.
Contact: Linda Bloch
Financial data (yr. ended 12/31/11): Assets, $3,996,177 (M); expenditures, $181,138; qualifying distributions, $178,207; giving activities include $178,207 for grants.
Purpose and activities: The foundation supports organizations involved with education, health, and human services.
Fields of interest: Higher education; Education; Health care; Human services Women.
Type of support: General/operating support.
Geographic limitations: Giving limited to KY, with emphasis on Louisville.
Application information: Applications accepted. Application form required.
Initial approach: Contact foundation for application form
Deadline(s): None
Officers: Kathleen S. Kiefer, Secy.; R. David Kretschmer, Treas.; Lance R. Chrisman, Exec. Dir.
Directors: Angela F. Braly; Randal L. Brown; Wayne S. DeVeydt; Bradley M. Fluegel; Lisa Moriyama; Samuel R. Nussbaum, M.D.; Brian A. Sassi.
EIN: 611191499

3542
Spence Accounts Inc.
100 N. 27th St., Ste. 305
Billings, MT 59101-2054 (406) 245-9424
FAX: (406) 248-8493

Establishment information: Established in 1986.
Company type: Private company
Business activities: Provides business services.
Business type (SIC): Business services
Corporate officers: Ralph Spence, Pres.; Deanna Turcotte, Secy.; Tancy W. Spence, Treas.
Giving statement: Giving through the Spence Family Foundation.

The Spence Family Foundation
100 N. 27th St., Ste. 305
Billings, MT 59101-2090 (406) 245-9424

Establishment information: Established in 2001 in MT.
Donors: Ralph Spence, Jr.; Tancy W. Spence; Spence Accounts, Inc.
Contact: Ralph Spencer, Jr., Pres.
Financial data (yr. ended 11/30/11): Assets, $515,414 (M); expenditures, $25,681; qualifying distributions, $25,440; giving activities include $23,500 for 5 grants (high: $17,500; low: $1,000) and $800 for 1 grant to an individual.
Purpose and activities: The foundation supports zoos and hospitals and organizations involved with theater, international affairs, and Christianity.
Fields of interest: Arts; Health care; Human services.
Type of support: General/operating support.
Geographic limitations: Giving primarily in Billings, MT.
Application information: Applications accepted. Application form required.
Initial approach: Contact foundation for application information
Deadline(s): None
Officers: Ralph Spence, Jr., Pres.; Tancy W. Spence, Secy.-Treas.
Directors: Benjamin Spence; Nash Spence; Ralph Spence III.
EIN: 043619122

3543
Spencer Fane Britt & Browne LLP
1000 Walnut St., Ste. 1400
Kansas City, MO 64106-2140
(816) 474-8100

Company URL: http://www.spencerfane.com
Establishment information: Established in 1952.
Company type: Private company
Business activities: Operates law firm.
Business type (SIC): Legal services
Offices: Overland Park, KS; Jefferson City, Kansas City, St. Louis, MO; Omaha, NE
Giving statement: Giving through the Spencer Fane Britt & Browne LLP Pro Bono Program.

Spencer Fane Britt & Browne LLP Pro Bono Program
1000 Walnut St., Ste. 1400
Kansas City, MO 64106-2140 (816) 474-8100
E-mail: swirtel@spencerfane.com; URL: http://www.spencerfane.com

Contact: Sandy Wirtel, Counsel
Fields of interest: Legal services.
Type of support: Pro bono services - legal.
Application information: An attorney coordinates pro bono projects.

3544
Spirit Mountain Gaming, Inc.
(doing business as Spirit Mountain Casino)
27100 S.W. Salmon River Hwy.
P.O. Box 39
Grand Ronde, OR 97347-9753
(503) 879-2350

Company URL: http://www.spiritmountain.com
Establishment information: Established in 1997.
Company type: Tribal corporation
Business activities: Operates casino.
Business type (SIC): Amusement and recreation services/miscellaneous
Financial profile for 2010: Number of employees, 1,500
Corporate officers: Sharon Jackson, Chair.; Rodney Ferguson, C.E.O.; Randy Dugger, C.O.O.; Roy Rhode, C.F.O.
Board of director: Sharon Jackson, Chair.
Giving statement: Giving through the Spirit Mountain Community Fund and the Spirit Mountain Gaming, Inc. Corporate Giving Program.

Spirit Mountain Community Fund
9615 Grand Ronde Rd.
Grand Ronde, OR 97347-9712 (503) 879-1401
FAX: (503) 879-1402;
E-mail: shelley.hanson@thecommunityfund.com; Additional e-mail: communityfund@grandronde.org; URL: http://www.thecommunityfund.com/

Contact: Shelley Hanson, Dir.
Financial data (yr. ended 12/31/10): Total giving, $2,900,000, including $2,900,000 for grants.
Purpose and activities: The foundation supports organizations involved with historic preservation, arts and culture, education, the environment, health, problem gaming, and public safety. Special emphasis is directed toward programs designed to support the aspirations of youth; respect and honor elders; and assist in developing self-sufficiency while sustaining and preserving the air, water, land, and its inhabitants.
Fields of interest: Historic preservation/historical societies; Arts; Education; Environment, natural resources; Environment; Health care; Mental health, gambling addiction; Crime/violence prevention Youth; Native Americans/American Indians.
Type of support: Building/renovation; Curriculum development; Equipment; General/operating support; Matching/challenge support; Program development.
Geographic limitations: Giving primarily in Benton, Clackamas, Lane, Lincoln, Linn, Marion, Multnomah, Polk, Tillamook, Washington, and Yamhill counties, OR; giving limited to Polk and Yamhill counties for nonprofit government agencies.
Support limitations: No support for propaganda or lobbying organizations, pass-through organizations, or discriminatory organizations. No grants to individuals, or for indirect or overhead costs not specifically and essentially related to a project, sectarian or religious projects, activities or materials previously supported by federal, state, or local public funds, annual operating budgets, development office personnel, or annual fundraising activities, continuing support, or sporting complexes or instruction; generally, no grants for economic development or community revitalization; no student loans.
Publications: Annual report; Application guidelines; Corporate giving report; Grants list; Occasional report; Program policy statement.
Application information: Applications accepted. Organizations receiving support are asked to provide a final report. Unsolicited requests for public safety grants from organizations located outside Polk And Yamhill counties, OR, are not accepted. Small Grants are grants less than $10,000; Large Grants are grants greater than $10,000. Unsolicited requests for Small Grants from organizations with an annual operating budget over $250,000 are not accepted. Application form required.
Initial approach: Complete online application form
Copies of proposal: 1
Committee meeting date(s): 4 to 6 times per year
Deadline(s): See website for details
Final notification: 14 days
Officers and Trustees:* Sho Dozono*, Chair.; Camille Mercier, Vice-Chair.; June Sell-Shearer, Secy.; Steve Bobb; Kate Brown; Darlene Hooley; Chip Lazenby; Reynold Leno.
Number of staff: 4 full-time professional.

Spirit Mountain Gaming, Inc. Corporate Giving Program
c/o Sponsorship
P.O. Box 39
Grand Ronde, OR 97347-0039 (503) 879-3054
FAX: (503) 879-6049;
E-mail: sponsorship@spiritmtn.com; URL: http://spiritmountain.com/spirit-mountain-casino-sponsorships/

Purpose and activities: Spirit Mountain makes charitable contributions to nonprofit organizations involved with the environment and tribal arts, culture, and history, and on a case by case basis. Support is given primarily in Oregon.
Fields of interest: Arts, cultural/ethnic awareness; Historical activities; Environment; General charitable giving Native Americans/American Indians.
Type of support: In-kind gifts; Program development; Sponsorships.
Geographic limitations: Giving primarily in OR.
Support limitations: No grants for events not allowing promotion of gaming activities or events with a significant number of underage attendees.
Publications: Application guidelines.
Application information: Applications accepted. In-kind contributions support is limited to 1 contribution per organization during any given year. Applicants should submit the following:
1) population served
2) name, address and phone number of organization
3) brief history of organization and description of its mission
4) descriptive literature about organization
5) detailed description of project and amount of funding requested
6) contact person
7) listing of additional sources and amount of support
8) plans for acknowledgement
9) additional materials/documentation

Proposals should include a W-9 form and media metrics. Requests for in-kind contributions should include a W-9 form and indicate the date of the event.
Initial approach: Mail, e-mail, or fax proposal to headquarters for cash sponsorships; download application form and mail or fax to headquarters for in-kind contributions
Copies of proposal: 1

Committee meeting date(s): Weekly
Final notification: 3 weeks for in-kind contributions

3545
Spirol International Corporation

30 Rock Ave.
Danielson, CT 06239-1434 (860) 774-8571

Company URL: http://www.spirol.com
Establishment information: Established in 1945.
Company type: Private company
Business activities: Manufactures engineered fasteners, shims, pin and insert installation machines, and parts feeding equipment.
Business type (SIC): Screw machine products; metal forgings and stampings; metal products/ fabricated; machinery/special industry
Corporate officers: Jeffrey F. Koehl, Chair. and C.E.O.; William R. Hunt, Pres. and C.O.O.; Patrick Lefebvre, V.P. and Corp. Cont.
Board of director: Jeffrey F. Koehl, Chair.
Subsidiaries: Ascutney Metal Products, Windsor, VT; Spirol West, Inc., Corona, CA
Plant: Stow, OH
International operations: Canada; France; United Kingdom
Giving statement: Giving through the Spirol International Charitable Foundation Inc.

Spirol International Charitable Foundation Inc.

30 Rock Ave.
Danielson, CT 06239-1425
URL: http://www.spirol.com/company/news/ scholarships.php
Contact for Scholarships: Flora Houle, tel.: (860) 774-8571 ext. 4328

Establishment information: Established in 2004 in CT.
Donor: Spirol International Corp.
Contact: John E. Ferdinandi, Treas.
Financial data (yr. ended 12/31/11): Assets, $107,768 (M); expenditures, $53,070; qualifying distributions, $53,070; giving activities include $28,000 for 2 grants (high: $25,000; low: $3,000) and $25,000 for 5 grants to individuals (high: $5,000; low: $5,000).
Purpose and activities: The foundation supports organizations involved with education, conservation, and animal welfare and awards college scholarships.
Fields of interest: Elementary/secondary education; Higher education; Education; Environment, natural resources; Animals/wildlife, preservation/protection.
Program:
SPIROL Scholarship Program: The foundation awards four-year college scholarships of up to $20,000 to high school graduates, for full time students at a two-year or four-year accredited college in California, Connecticut, Ohio, and Vermont pursuing a career in Engineering, Basic Sciences, or Manufacturing Technology. Applicants must have a GPA of 3.0 and demonstrate a commitment to community service/involvement.
Type of support: Building/renovation; Scholarship funds; Scholarships—to individuals.
Geographic limitations: Giving primarily in CA, CT, OH, and VT.
Publications: Application guidelines.
Application information: Applications accepted. Application form not required.
Requests for the SPIROL Scholarship Program should include a personal essay describing education, career, and personal goals; a personal summary describing extracurricular activities, work experience, and special honors received; two letters of recommendation; a narrative summary describing community service/involvement; and a letter supporting the community service event/ involvement.
Initial approach: Proposal; download application form and mail to foundation for SPIROL Scholarship Program
Deadline(s): None; Apr. 16 for SPIROL Scholarship Program
Officers and Trustees: Hans K. Koehl, Chair.; John E. Ferdinandi, Treas.; Jeffrey F. Koehl; James C. Shaw.
EIN: 510494974

3546
Sporting Club

(doing business as Sporting Kansas City)
(formerly Ongoal, LLC)
210 West 19th Terr., Ste. 200
Kansas City, MO 64108 (913) 387-3400

Company URL: http://www.sportingkc.com/
Establishment information: Established in 1996.
Company type: Private company
Business activities: Operates professional soccer club.
Business type (SIC): Commercial sports
Corporate officers: Robb Heineman, C.E.O.; Asim Pasha, C.I.O.; Shawn Quesnell, Cont.
Giving statement: Giving through the Sporting Kansas City Corporate Giving Program.

Sporting Kansas City Corporate Giving Program

(formerly Kansas City Wizards Corporate Giving Program)
210 West 19th Terrace, Ste. 200
Kansas City, MO 64108-2046 (913) 387-3400
URL: http://www.sportingkc.com/community/ welcome

Purpose and activities: The Kansas City Wizards make charitable contributions of autographed team memorabilia to nonprofit organizations for purposes of fundraising. Support is limited to the Kansas City, Kansas area.
Fields of interest: Youth; Economically disadvantaged.
Type of support: Donated products; In-kind gifts.
Geographic limitations: Giving limited to the Kansas City, MO area.
Support limitations: No donations for operating expenses, prizes, or volunteer recognition gifts.
Publications: Application guidelines.
Application information: Applications accepted. Support is limited to 1 contribution per organization during any given year. Applicants should submit the following:
1) name, address and phone number of organization
2) contact person
Applications should include the date, location, description, and expected attendance of the event; and any applicable deadlines.
Initial approach: Complete online application
Deadline(s): 6 weeks prior to event

3547
Sports & Fitness Insurance Corporation, Inc.

214 Key Dr., Ste. 2000
P.O. Box 1967
Madison, MS 39110-6364 (601) 898-8464

Company URL: http://www.sportsfitness.com
Establishment information: Established in 1985.
Company type: Private company
Business activities: Provides insurance brokerage services.
Business type (SIC): Insurance agents, brokers, and services
Financial profile for 2011: Number of employees, 20
Corporate officers: Glynne A. Simpson, Pres. and C.E.O.; Hamp Dye, C.F.O.; Ann Y. Simpson, Treas.
Giving statement: Giving through the Bedford Foundation.

Bedford Foundation

P.O. Box 1967
Madison, MS 39130-1967 (601) 898-8464

Establishment information: Established in 2002 in MS.
Donor: Sports & Fitness Insurance Corp.
Contact: Glynne A. Simpson, Tr.
Financial data (yr. ended 12/31/11): Assets, $6,281 (M); expenditures, $2,895; qualifying distributions, $2,895; giving activities include $2,895 for 1 grant.
Purpose and activities: The foundation supports organizations involved with higher education and human services.
Fields of interest: Higher education; Human services.
Type of support: General/operating support; Scholarship funds; Scholarships—to individuals.
Geographic limitations: Giving primarily in MS.
Application information: Applications accepted. Application form required.
Initial approach: Letter of Inquiry
Deadline(s): None
Trustees: James C. Mingee; Steve Shelton; Collier Simpson; Glynne A. Simpson.
EIN: 611435075

3548
The Sports Authority, Inc.

1050 W. Hampden Ave.
Englewood, CO 80110 (303) 200-5050
FAX: (303) 832-4738

Company URL: http://www.sportsauthority.com
Establishment information: Established in 1987.
Company type: Private company
Business activities: Operates sporting goods stores.
Business type (SIC): Shopping goods stores/ miscellaneous
Financial profile for 2011: Number of employees, 14,250; sales volume, $3,200,000,000
Corporate officers: Darrell D. Webb, Chair. and C.E.O.; Thomas T. Hendrickson, Vice- Chair., Exec. V.P., C.F.O., and Treas.; Tom Wildenberg, Sr. V.P., Finance
Board of directors: Darrell Webb, Chair.; Thomas T. Hendrickson, Vice-Chair.
Giving statement: Giving through the Sports Authority, Inc. Corporate Giving Program and the Oshman Foundation.

Company EIN: 841242802

The Sports Authority, Inc. Corporate Giving Program

1050 W. Hampden Ave.
Englewood, CO 80110-2118 (303) 200-5050
E-mail: donations@sportsauthority.com; For sponsorships: sponsorships@sportsauthority.com; URL: http://www.sportsauthority.com/corp/index.jsp?page=donations

Purpose and activities: As a complement to its foundation, The Sports Authority also makes charitable contributions to nonprofit organizations directly. Special emphasis is directed towards programs designed to promote sports and active lifestyle activities. Support is given on a national basis in areas of company operations.
Fields of interest: Public health, physical fitness; Athletics/sports, amateur leagues; Athletics/sports, professional leagues; Recreation.
Type of support: General/operating support; In-kind gifts; Sponsorships.
Geographic limitations: Giving on a national basis in areas of company operations.
Support limitations: No grants to individuals, or for teams.
Publications: Application guidelines.
Application information:
Initial approach: E-mail request to headquarters

Oshman Foundation

P.O. Box 27969
Houston, TX 77227-7969

Establishment information: Established in 1958.
Donors: Oshman's Sporting Goods, Inc.; Jeanette Oshman Efron.
Financial data (yr. ended 11/30/11): Assets, $6,074,185 (M); expenditures, $257,653; qualifying distributions, $251,256; giving activities include $251,256 for grants.
Purpose and activities: The foundation supports hospitals and organizations involved with arts and culture, education, cancer, human services, and Judaism.
Fields of interest: Visual arts; Performing arts, ballet; Arts; Higher education; Education; Hospitals (general); Cancer; Children/youth, services; Aging, centers/services; Human services; Jewish agencies & synagogues.
Type of support: General/operating support.
Geographic limitations: Giving limited to Houston, TX.
Support limitations: No grants to individuals.
Application information: Applications not accepted. Contributes only to pre-selected organizations.
Officers: Marilyn Oshman, Co-Pres. and Secy.; Judy O. Margolis, Co.-Pres. and Treas.
EIN: 746039864
Selected grants: The following grants are a representative sample of this grantmaker's funding activity:
$50,000 to Baylor College of Medicine, Houston, TX, 2010.
$18,750 to Orange Show Center for Visionary Art, Houston, TX, 2010.
$13,000 to Houston Ballet, Houston, TX, 2010.
$8,000 to Menil Foundation, Houston, TX, 2010.
$5,000 to Methodist Hospital Foundation, Houston, TX, 2010.
$5,000 to University of Texas M.D. Anderson Cancer Center, Houston, TX, 2010.
$2,500 to Camp for All, Houston, TX, 2010.
$2,500 to Kinkaid School, Houston, TX, 2010.
$2,500 to Museum of Fine Arts, Houston, Houston, TX, 2010.
$2,000 to Mesa Verde Foundation, Denver, CO, 2010.

3549
Sports Capital Partners, LLC

(also known as Real Salt Lake)
9256 S. State St.
Sandy, UT 84070 (801) 727-2700

Company URL: http://real.saltlake.mlsnet.com
Establishment information: Established in 1998.
Company type: Private company
Business activities: Operates professional soccer club.
Business type (SIC): Commercial sports
Corporate officers: David Checketts, Chair.; Bill Manning, Pres.; Gary Reimer, Sr. V.P. and C.F.O.; Trey Fitz-Gerald, V.P., Comms.; Nikki Reimer, Cont.
Board of director: David Checketts, Chair.
Giving statement: Giving through the Real Salt Lake Corporate Giving Program.

Real Salt Lake Corporate Giving Program

c/o Community Rels.
9256 South State St.
Sandy, UT 84070-2604
FAX: (801) 727-1459; Contact for player/mascot appearances: Teresa Nelson, tnelson@realsaltlake.com; Contact for Heroes Among Us: heroes@realsaltlake.com, fax: (801) 727-1469; URL: http://www.realsaltlake.com/community

Purpose and activities: Real Salt Lake makes charitable contributions to nonprofit organizations involved with education, youth soccer, and community development. Support is given primarily in Utah.
Fields of interest: Education; Athletics/sports, soccer; Youth development; Children/youth, services; Community/economic development.
Programs:
Heroes Among Us: Through Heroes Among Us, Real Salt Lake and American Express honors everyday people who have made a positive impact to improve the lives of others. The honorees receive game tickets, in game recognition, and a personalized jersey.
Kicks for Kids: Through Kicks for Kids, Real Salt Lake invites nonprofit organizations that benefit at-risk children to a home game. The program is designed to teach youth important skills needed in all aspects of life, including hard work, dedication, commitment, and team effort. The program includes game tickets, a special visit fro Leo the Lion during the game, and in-game recognition on the jumbo-tron.
Type of support: Donated products; In-kind gifts; Income development; Loaned talent.
Geographic limitations: Giving primarily in areas of company operations in UT.
Support limitations: No support for religious organizations not of direct benefit to the entire community.
Publications: Application guidelines.
Application information: Applications accepted. Proposals should be submitted using organization letterhead. Support is limited to 1 contribution per organization during any given year. The Community Relations Department handles giving. Applicants should submit the following:
1) name, address and phone number of organization
2) copy of IRS Determination Letter
3) detailed description of project and amount of funding requested
4) contact person
Proposals should indicate the date, time, location, and alternate location of the event, the expected attendance, the type of fundraiser, and any deadlines.
Initial approach: Mail proposal to headquarters for memorabilia donations; download application form and mail proposal and application form to headquarters for player/mascot appearances; download nomination form and e-mail, mail, or fax to headquarters for Heroes Among Us
Copies of proposal: 1
Deadline(s): 4 weeks prior to need memorabilia donations; 30 days prior to need for player/mascot appearances; none for Heroes Among Us
Final notification: 3 weeks for memorabilia donations; 2 weeks for player/mascot appearances

3550
The Sports Club Company, Inc.

(also known as The Sports Club/LA)
11100 Santa Monica Blvd., Ste. 300
Los Angeles, CA 90025 (310) 479-5200
FAX: (310) 479-4350

Company URL: http://www.thesportsclubla.com
Establishment information: Established in 1977.
Company type: Public company
Company ticker symbol and exchange: SCYL/Pink Sheets
Business activities: Operates sports and fitness clubs.
Business type (SIC): Amusement and recreation services/miscellaneous
Financial profile for 2009: Number of employees, 2,619; assets, $67,150,000; sales volume, $54,520,000; pre-tax net income, -$1,120,000; expenses, $49,790,000; liabilities, $102,940,000
Corporate officers: D. Michael Talla, Chair.; Rex A. Licklider, Vice-Chair. and C.E.O.; Timothy M. O'Brien, C.F.O.
Board of directors: D. Michael Talla, Chair.; Rex A. Licklider, Vice-Chair.; Charles Ferraro; Christopher M. Jeffries; Charles Norris; Andrew L. Turner; George Vasilakos
Giving statement: Giving through the Sports Club/LA for Kids Only.
Company EIN: 954479735

The Sports Club/LA for Kids Only

11151 Missouri Ave.
Los Angeles, CA 90025-3328

Establishment information: Established in 2001 in CA.
Donors: The Sports Club Co., Inc.; L.A./Irvine Sports Club LTD; Sepulveda Realty & Development Co., Inc.
Financial data (yr. ended 12/31/11): Assets, $40,683 (M); gifts received, $12,425; expenditures, $13,520; qualifying distributions, $13,500; giving activities include $13,500 for grants.
Purpose and activities: The foundation supports organizations involved with children and youth.
Fields of interest: Health care; Housing/shelter; Human services.
Geographic limitations: Giving limited to southern CA.
Support limitations: No grants to individuals.

Application information: Applications not accepted. Unsolicited requests for funds not accepted.
Officers and Directors:* Nanette Pattee Francini*, Pres.; Timothy O'Brien, Secy. and C.F.O.; Rex A. Licklider; April Morgan; David Michael Talla.
EIN: 954865162

3551
Sprague Energy Corporation

2 International Dr., Ste. 200
Portsmouth, NH 03801-6809
(603) 431-1000
FAX: (603) 430-5324

Company URL: http://www.spragueenergy.com
Establishment information: Established in 1870.
Company type: Subsidiary of a private company
Business activities: Operates petroleum and petroleum product bulk stations.
Business type (SIC): Petroleum and petroleum products—wholesale
Financial profile for 2010: Number of employees, 500
Corporate officers: David Glendon, Pres. and C.E.O.; Gary Rinaldi, C.O.O. and C.F.O.
Giving statement: Giving through the Draizin Foundation, Inc.

The Draizin Foundation, Inc.

37552 N. 94th St.
Scottsdale, AZ 85262-2536

Establishment information: Established in 1985 in NY.
Donors: RAD Oil Co., Inc.; RAD Energy Corp.
Contact: Stephen S. Draizin, Pres.
Financial data (yr. ended 12/31/11): Assets, $484,768 (M); gifts received, $13,000; expenditures, $38,650; qualifying distributions, $38,430; giving activities include $38,430 for grants.
Purpose and activities: The foundation supports organizations involved with education, children and youth, and Judaism.
Fields of interest: Elementary school/education; Higher education; Education; Children/youth, services; Jewish agencies & synagogues.
Type of support: General/operating support.
Geographic limitations: Giving primarily in AZ, CT, and NY.
Application information: Applications accepted. Application form required. Applicants should submit the following:
1) copy of IRS Determination Letter
Initial approach: Letter
Copies of proposal: 2
Deadline(s): None
Officers: Stephen S. Draizin, Pres.; Donald J. Draizin, V.P.; Jennifer Fuchs, Secy.; Adam Draizin, Treas.
EIN: 133275008

3552
Spraying Systems Co.

780 E. North Ave.
Glendale Heights, IL 60139-3408
(630) 942-9500

Company URL: http://www.spray.com/
Establishment information: Established in 1937.
Company type: Private company
Business activities: Manufactures industrial spray products.
Business type (SIC): Metal products/fabricated
Corporate officers: James E. Bramsen, C.E.O.; David Smith, C.O.O.; Marty Hynes, C.F.O.
Giving statement: Giving through the Opportunity Foundation.

The Opportunity Foundation

(formerly Paula Bramsen Cullen Foundation)
c/o Pederson & Houpt
161 N. Clark St., Ste. 3100
Chicago, IL 60601-3242

Establishment information: Established in 1993 in IL.
Financial data (yr. ended 12/31/11): Assets, $1,912,578 (M); expenditures, $89,674; qualifying distributions, $88,800; giving activities include $88,800 for grants.
Purpose and activities: Giving primarily for public policy research institutes.
Fields of interest: Human services; Community/economic development.
Type of support: General/operating support; Program development.
Support limitations: No grants to individuals.
Application information: Applications not accepted. Contributes only to pre-selected organizations.
Officers: Paula Bramsen Cullen, Pres.; Daniel Cullen, Secy.-Treas.
Director: Mary C. Muehlstein.
EIN: 363835681

3553
The Springer Electric Cooperative, Inc.

408 Maxwell Ave.
P.O. Box 698
Springer, NM 87747 (575) 483-2421

Company URL: http://www.springercoop.com
Establishment information: Established in 1946.
Company type: Cooperative
Business activities: Distributes electricity.
Business type (SIC): Electric services
Corporate officers: Don Schutz, Pres.; Nikki Hooser, Secy.-Treas.
Board of directors: Paul Costa; R.W. Gillespie; Nikki Hooser; Charles Hoy; Tim Morrow; Don Schutz; Gerald Seward; Gary D. Shaw
Giving statement: Giving through the Springer Electric Cooperative Education Foundation.

Springer Electric Cooperative Education Foundation

P.O. Box 698
Springer, NM 87747-0698
Additional tel.: (800) 288-1353; URL: http://www.springercoop.com

Establishment information: Established in 2002; reincorporated in 2003.
Donor: Springer Electric Cooperative, Inc.
Contact: Don Schutz, Pres.
Financial data (yr. ended 12/31/11): Assets, $262,312 (M); gifts received, $12,824; expenditures, $14,850; qualifying distributions, $14,850; giving activities include $14,850 for 18 grants to individuals (high: $1,000; low: $250).
Purpose and activities: The foundation awards college scholarships to dependents of members of Springer Electric Cooperative.
Fields of interest: Higher education; Education.
Type of support: Scholarships—to individuals.
Geographic limitations: Giving limited to NM.
Application information: Applications accepted. Applicants must have a GPA of 2.5. and a minimum ACT score of 15 to apply.
Applications should include transcripts, an essay, and two letters of reference from a teacher, counselor, or employer.
Initial approach: Contact foundation for application form
Deadline(s): Generally Feb., but it varies per year
Officers: Don Schutz, Pres.; Tim Morrow, V.P.; Nikki Hooser, Secy.-Treas.
EIN: 850366101

3554
Springleaf Finance Corporation

(formerly American General Finance, Inc.)
P.O. Box 59
Evansville, IN 47701-0059 (855) 296-9088

Company URL: http://www.springleaffinancial.com/
Establishment information: Established in 1920.
Company type: Subsidiary of a public company
Business activities: Operates holding company; provides consumer loans; sells insurance.
Business type (SIC): Brokers and bankers/mortgage; credit institutions/business; insurance/life; insurance/fire, marine, and casualty
Financial profile for 2010: Number of employees, 6,500; assets, $18,132,960,000; sales volume, $2,216,840,000; liabilities, $16,433,960,000
Corporate officers: Frederick W. Geissinger, Chair., Pres., and C.E.O.; Donald R. Breivogel, Jr., Sr. V.P. and C.F.O.
Board of directors: Frederick W. Geissinger, Chair.; Donald R. Breivogel, Jr.
International operations: United Kingdom
Giving statement: Giving through the American General Finance Foundation, Inc.
Company EIN: 350416090

American General Finance Foundation, Inc.

(formerly American General Finance, Inc.—Richard E. Meier Foundation, Inc.)
601 N.W. 2nd St.
P.O. Box 59
Evansville, IN 47701-0059 (812) 468-5413

Establishment information: Incorporated in 1958 in IN.
Donor: American General Finance, Inc.
Contact: Michelle Dixon, Mgr., Mktg. Prog.
Financial data (yr. ended 12/31/10): Assets, $32,758 (M); gifts received, $335,000; expenditures, $370,538; qualifying distributions, $370,000; giving activities include $370,000 for grants.
Purpose and activities: The foundation supports organizations involved with arts and culture, education, patient services, housing development, children and youth, and community development.
Fields of interest: Museums; Performing arts, orchestras; Arts; Higher education; Education; Health care, patient services; Housing/shelter, development; Boys & girls clubs; YM/YWCAs & YM/YWHAs; Children/youth, services; Community/economic development; United Ways and Federated Giving Programs; Public affairs.

Type of support: Annual campaigns; Building/renovation; Continuing support; General/operating support.
Geographic limitations: Giving primarily in Evansville, IN.
Support limitations: No support for religious organizations not of direct benefit to the entire community or health care organizations. No grants to individuals (except for employee-related scholarships), or for start-up needs, emergency needs or endowments, debt reduction, equipment, land acquisition, special projects, research, publications, tickets or advertising for benefit purposes, or conferences; no loans; no matching or challenge grants.
Publications: Application guidelines.
Application information: Applications accepted. Application form not required. Applicants should submit the following:
1) role played by volunteers
2) timetable for implementation and evaluation of project
3) qualifications of key personnel
4) population served
5) copy of IRS Determination Letter
6) brief history of organization and description of its mission
7) geographic area to be served
8) copy of most recent annual report/audited financial statement/990
9) what distinguishes project from others in its field
10) listing of board of directors, trustees, officers and other key people and their affiliations
11) detailed description of project and amount of funding requested
12) contact person
13) copy of current year's organizational budget and/or project budget
14) listing of additional sources and amount of support
Initial approach: Proposal
Copies of proposal: 1
Board meeting date(s): Quarterly
Deadline(s): None
Final notification: 4 to 6 weeks

Officers and Directors:* Frederick W. Geissinger*, Chair., C.E.O., and Pres.; Donald R. Breivogel, Jr.*, Sr. V.P. and C.F.O.; Timothy M. Hayes, Sr. V.P. and Genl. Counsel; Robert A. Cole, Sr. V.P.; Bryan A. Binyon, V.P. and Treas.; Leonard J. Winiger, V.P. and Cont.; Vincent Ciuffetelli, V.P. and C.I.O.; Brett L. Foster, V.P.; Frederick J. Sujat.
EIN: 356042566
Selected grants: The following grants are a representative sample of this grantmaker's funding activity:
$125,000 to Boys and Girls Club of Evansville, Evansville, IN, 2010.
$10,000 to University of Southern Indiana, Evansville, IN, 2010.

3555
Springs Global US, Inc.

(formerly Springs Industries, Inc.)
205 N. White St.
P.O. Box 70
Fort Mill, SC 29716 (803) 547-1500

Company URL: http://www.springs.com
Establishment information: Established in 1887.
Company type: Subsidiary of a foreign company
Business activities: Manufactures finished fabrics, home furnishings, and industrial fabrics.
Business type (SIC): Fabricated textile products/miscellaneous; fabrics/broadwoven natural cotton; fabrics/broadwoven synthetic and silk; fabric finishing; textile goods/miscellaneous
Corporate officers: Josue Christiano Gomes da Silva, Chair. and C.E.O.; Tom O'Connor, Pres.; Flavio Barbosa, C.F.O.
Board of director: Christiano Josue Gomes da Silva, Chair.
Subsidiaries: Springs Window Fashions Division, Inc., Middleton, WI; Springs Window Fashions LP, Montgomery, PA
Giving statement: Giving through the Springs Global US, Inc. Corporate Giving Program.

Springs Global US, Inc. Corporate Giving Program

(formerly Springs Industries, Inc. Corporate Giving Program)
P.O. Box 70
Fort Mill, SC 29716-0070 (803) 547-1500
URL: http://www.springs.com/social_responsibility/community_involvement.php

Purpose and activities: As a complement to its foundation, Springs Global also makes charitable contributions to nonprofit organizations directly. Support is given primarily in areas of company operations, including South Carolina. Giving also to national and international organizations, including in Brazil.
Fields of interest: Public health school/education; Education; Environment, natural resources; Environment, land resources; Medical care, community health systems; Breast cancer.
Type of support: Cause-related marketing; General/operating support; Sponsorships.
Geographic limitations: Giving primarily in areas of company operations, including SC. Giving also to national and international organizations, including in Brazil.
Number of staff: None.

3556
Sprint Nextel Corporation

(formerly Sprint Corporation)
6391 Sprint Pkwy.
Overland Park, KS 66251-4300
(703) 433-4000

Company URL: http://www.sprintnextel.com
Establishment information: Established in 1938.
Company type: Public company
Company ticker symbol and exchange: S/NYSE
International Securities Identification Number: US8520611000
Business activities: Operates holding company; provides wireless telephone communications services; provides long distance telephone communications services; provide local telephone communications services. At press time, the company is in the process of merging with Softbank Corp.
Business type (SIC): Telephone communications; holding company
Financial profile for 2012: Number of employees, 39,000; assets, $51,600,000,000; sales volume, $35,300,000,000; pre-tax net income, -$4,172,000,000; expenses, $37,165,000,000; liabilities, $44,483,000,000
Fortune 1000 ranking: 2012—87th in revenues, 999th in profits, and 109th in assets
Forbes 2000 ranking: 2012—269th in sales, 1982nd in profits, and 448th in assets
Corporate officers: James H. Hance, Jr., Chair.; Daniel R. Hesse, C.E.O.; Joseph J. Euteneuer, C.F.O.; Charles Wunsch, Sr. V.P., Genl. Counsel, and Corp. Secy.; Bill White, Sr. V.P., Corp. Comms.; Sandra J. Price, Sr. V.P., Human Resources
Board of directors: James H. Hance, Jr., Chair.; Robert R. Bennett; Gordon M. Bethune; Larry C. Glasscock; Daniel R. Hesse; V. Janet Hill; Frank Ianna; Sven-Christer Nilsson; William R. Nuti; Rodney O'Neal
Subsidiaries: Nextel Communications, Inc., Reston, VA; Sprint North Supply Co., New Century, KS; The United Telephone Company of Pennsylvania, Carlisle, PA; United Telephone Company of the Carolinas, Bristol, TN
Division: Local Telecommunications Div., Overland Park, KS
International operations: Bermuda
Historic mergers: Nextel Communications, Inc. (August 12, 2005); Carolina Telephone and Telegraph Company (January 1, 2006); Nextel Partners, Inc. (June 26, 2006)
Giving statement: Giving through the Nextel Community Connect Program, the Sprint Nextel Corporation Contributions Program, and the Sprint Foundation.
Company EIN: 480457967

Nextel Community Connect Program

6200 Sprint Pkwy.
Overland Park, KS 66251-6117
URL: http://shop2.sprint.com/en/about/community/connect.shtml

Purpose and activities: Nextel makes charitable contributions to nonprofit organizations involved with public safety. Support is given primarily in areas of company operations.
Fields of interest: Safety/disasters.
Type of support: Donated products; Employee volunteer services; Sponsorships.
Geographic limitations: Giving primarily in areas of company operations.
Support limitations: No support for religious or denominational organizations, or school athletic organizations. No grants to individuals, or for political causes or candidates, civic sports leagues, tournaments, or office space for permanent operations; no equipment donations other than wireless phones or modems.
Application information: Applicants should submit the following:
1) population served
2) explanation of why grantmaker is considered an appropriate donor for project
3) detailed description of project and amount of funding requested
4) plans for acknowledgement
5) geographic area to be served
Initial approach: Contact headquarters for application information
Deadline(s): None; 2 to 3 months prior to need for sponsorships
Final notification: 30 days

Sprint Nextel Corporation Contributions Program

(formerly Sprint Corporation Contributions Program)
6200 Sprint Pkwy.
Overland Park, KS 66251-6117 (913) 624-6000
E-mail: communityrequests@sprint.com;
URL: http://www.sprint.com/community

Purpose and activities: As a complement to its foundation, Sprint Nextel also makes charitable contributions to nonprofit organizations directly. Special emphasis is directed toward programs that promote K-12 education, youth development, arts and culture, diversity, and civic infrastructure.

Support is given primarily in Los Angeles, California, Denver, Colorado, Washington, DC, Chicago, Illinois, and Kansas City, Kansas, with emphasis on Atlanta, Georgia, New York, New York, and Dallas and Fort Worth, Texas.
Fields of interest: Arts; Elementary/secondary education; Elementary school/education; Environment; Youth development; Community/economic development.
Type of support: Donated products; Employee volunteer services; General/operating support.
Geographic limitations: Giving primarily in areas of company operations in Los Angeles, CA, Denver, CO, Washington, DC, Chicago, IL, and Kansas City, KS, with emphasis on Atlanta, GA, New York, NY, and Fort Worth and Dallas, TX.
Application information: Applications accepted. Application form required.
Initial approach: Complete online application form

Sprint Foundation

(formerly United Telecommunications Foundation)
6220 Sprint Pkwy.
Overland Park, KS 66251-6118
FAX: (913) 624-3490;
E-mail: communityrequests@sprint.com; E-mail for Sprint Local Grant Program:
Local_giving_program@sprint.com; URL: http://www.sprint.com/responsibility/sprint_foundation/index.html

Establishment information: Established in 1989 in KS.
Donors: Sprint Corp.; Sprint Nextel Corp.; The United Telephone Co. of Pennsylvania; Sprint Communications Co., LP.
Financial data (yr. ended 12/31/11): Assets, $3,449,320 (M); gifts received, $5,023,200; expenditures, $4,188,023; qualifying distributions, $4,115,160; giving activities include $4,115,160 for 779 grants (high: $544,213; low: $25).
Purpose and activities: The foundation supports organizations involved with arts and culture, K-12 and business education, environmental stewardship, youth development, community development, and civic affairs.
Fields of interest: Visual arts; Museums; Performing arts; Performing arts, theater; Performing arts, orchestras; Arts; Elementary/secondary education; Business school/education; Environment; Boys & girls clubs; Youth development, adult & child programs; Big Brothers/Big Sisters; Boy scouts; Girl scouts; Camp Fire; Youth development, services; Youth development; American Red Cross; Community/economic development; Leadership development; Public affairs Youth.
Programs:
Arts and Culture: The foundation supports visual and performing arts organizations, theaters, symphonies, and museums and programs designed to contribute to a thriving and diverse community and serve underrepresented communities.
Community Development: The foundation supports regional programs designed to impact the civic infrastructure and health of communities where Sprint employees and customers live and work.
Dollars for Doers: The foundation awards $250 grants to nonprofit organizations with which employees of Sprint volunteer 40 hours during a calendar year.
Education: The foundation supports programs designed to promote urban K-12 education. Special emphasis is directed toward character-education initiatives.
Matching Gift Program: The foundation matches contributions made by employees, directors, and retirees of Sprint to educational institutions and nonprofit organizations involved with arts and culture, public broadcasting, the environment, positive youth development, and the American Red Cross for disaster relief in the U.S. The foundation matches on a one-for-one basis from $25 to $2,500, per donor, per organization.
Sprint Local Grant Program: The foundation annually awards grants to three nonprofit organizations located in the Sprint markets of Atlanta, Dallas and Fort Worth, Denver, and New York City Metro area. The grants supports youth development, including mentoring, leadership, and academic achievement; arts and culture; and environmental stewardship. Grants range from $10,000 to $25,000.
Youth Development: The foundation supports programs designed to promote mentoring; provide leadership training; promote social skills; encourage volunteerism; and promote business and economic education for youth.
Type of support: Annual campaigns; Continuing support; Donated equipment; Employee matching gifts; Employee volunteer services; General/operating support; In-kind gifts; Program development; Scholarship funds.
Geographic limitations: Giving primarily in areas of company operations in Overland Park, KS and Kansas City, MO; giving also in Denver, CO, Atlanta, GA, NJ, and New York, NY, and Dallas and Fort Worth, TX for the Sprint Local Grant Program.
Support limitations: No support for discriminatory organizations, political organizations, religious organizations, private charities or foundations, international organizations, or school-affiliated teams, bands, or choirs. No grants to individuals, or for endowments, capital campaigns, memorials, construction, or renovation projects, travel, film, music, television, video, or media production projects, school-affiliated events, marketing, sports, or event sponsorships; no donations of Sprint products or services.
Publications: Application guidelines; Program policy statement.
Application information: Applications accepted. Finalists for the Sprint Local Grant Program must submit a three-minute video showcasing the program that will receive funding. Application form required. Applicants should submit the following:
1) population served
2) brief history of organization and description of its mission
3) geographic area to be served
4) copy of most recent annual report/audited financial statement/990
5) detailed description of project and amount of funding requested
6) contact person

Initial approach: Complete online application form
Board meeting date(s): Quarterly
Deadline(s): Jan. 3 to Nov. 18; May 1 to June 15 for Spring Local Grant Program
Final notification: 90 days; Sept. 28 for Sprint Local Grant Program
Officers and Directors:* Ralph Reid, Pres. and Exec. Dir.; Scott Andreason, Secy.; Greg Block*, Treas.; Danny Bowman; Steve Gaffney; Bill White.
EIN: 481062018
Selected grants: The following grants are a representative sample of this grantmaker's funding activity:
$544,213 to United Way of Greater Kansas City, Kansas City, MO, 2011.
$217,450 to Kansas University Endowment Association, Lawrence, KS, 2011.
$165,639 to American Red Cross National Headquarters, Washington, DC, 2011.
$102,000 to Nelson Gallery Foundation, Kansas City, MO, 2011.
$40,100 to Boys and Girls Clubs of Greater Kansas City, Kansas City, MO, 2011.
$17,500 to Higher M-Pact, Kansas City, MO, 2011.
$8,678 to United Way of Central Carolinas, Charlotte, NC, 2011.
$5,000 to National Hispanic Media Coalition, Pasadena, CA, 2011.
$5,000 to Ronald McDonald House of New York, New York, NY, 2011.
$2,600 to Barstow School, Kansas City, MO, 2011.

3557
Spurs Sports & Entertainment

(also known as San Antonio Spurs/San Antonio Silver Stars)
1 AT&T Center Pkwy.
San Antonio, TX 78219-3604
(210) 444-5000

Company URL: http://www.wnba.com/silverstars
Establishment information: Established in 2010.
Company type: Private company
Business activities: Operates professional basketball clubs.
Business type (SIC): Commercial sports
Corporate officers: Peter M. Holt, Chair. and C.E.O.; Frank Micelli, Sr. V.P., Sales & Mktg.; Lori Warren, Sr. V.P., Finance and Corp. Admin.; Joe Clark, V.P., Sales; Leo Gomez, V.P., Public Affairs
Board of directors: Peter M. Holt, Chair.; Liza Cartmell; Cathy Coughlin; Charles Ebrom; Bruce Hill; James R. Leininger, M.D.; Larry Mills
Subsidiary: San Antonio Spurs LLC, San Antonio, TX
Division: San Antonio Silver Stars, San Antonio, TX
Giving statement: Giving through the San Antonio Silver Stars Corporate Giving Program.

San Antonio Silver Stars Corporate Giving Program

1 AT&T Ctr.
San Antonio, TX 78219-3604 (210) 444-5000
URL: http://www.wnba.com/silverstars/community

Purpose and activities: The San Antonio Silver Stars make charitable contributions to nonprofit organizations involved with education, recreation, and youth and on a case by case basis. Support is given primarily in the San Antonio, Texas, area.
Fields of interest: Education, reading; Education; Public health, physical fitness; Breast cancer; Heart & circulatory diseases; Nutrition; Athletics/sports, basketball; Recreation; Boys & girls clubs; Children/youth, services; Family services; General charitable giving.
Programs:
Read to Achieve: Through Read to Achieve, the Silver Stars promote the value of reading and encourages families and adults to read regularly with young children. The program includes educational programming, read aloud events with Silver Stars players and coaches, and book donations.
WNBA Fit: Through WNBA FIT, the Silver Stars encourages young girls and women to learn more about their bodies and the importance of physical fitness relating to health, fitness, nutrition, and self-esteem. The program includes player appearances and events throughout the community.
Type of support: Donated products; In-kind gifts; Income development; Loaned talent.
Geographic limitations: Giving primarily in areas of company operations within a 75-mile radius of the San Antonio, TX, area.
Support limitations: No grants for advertising.

Publications: Application guidelines.
Application information: Applications accepted. Application form required. Applicants should submit the following:
1) name, address and phone number of organization
2) copy of IRS Determination Letter
3) brief history of organization and description of its mission
4) detailed description of project and amount of funding requested
5) contact person

Initial approach: Complete online application for memorabilia donations and player/dancer/mascot appearances
Deadline(s): 30 days prior to need for memorabilia donations and player/dancer appearances; 4 weeks prior to need for mascot appearances
Final notification: 10 business days for mascot appearances

3558
SPX Corporation

13515 Ballantyne Corporate Pl.
Charlotte, NC 28277 (704) 752-4400
FAX: (302) 655-5049

Company URL: http://www.spx.com
Establishment information: Established in 1911.
Company type: Public company
Company ticker symbol and exchange: SPW/NYSE
Business activities: Manufactures and provides technical products and systems, industrial products and services, motor vehicle service solutions, and motor vehicle components.
Business type (SIC): Machinery/metalworking; industrial and commercial machinery and computer equipment; electronic and other electrical equipment and components; motor vehicles and equipment
Financial profile for 2012: Number of employees, 15,000; assets, $7,130,100,000; sales volume, $5,100,200,000; pre-tax net income, -$46,500,000; expenses, $5,091,200,000; liabilities, $4,861,400,000
Fortune 1000 ranking: 2012—431st in revenues, 513th in profits, and 484th in assets
Corporate officers: Christopher J. Kearney, Chair., Pres., and C.E.O.; Kevin L. Lilly, Sr. V.P., Genl. Counsel, and Secy.; Jeremy Smeltser, V.P. and C.F.O.
Board of directors: Christopher J. Kearney, Chair.; J. Kermit Campbell; Emerson U. Fullwood; Terry S. Lisenby; David V. Singer; Michael J. Mancuso; Martha B. Wyrsch
Subsidiaries: Advanced Industrial Technologies, Inc., Novi, MI; Advanced Test Products, Inc., Miramar, FL; Flair Corp., Ocala, FL; General Signal Corporation, Stamford, CT; Pearpoint, Inc., Thousand Palms, CA; SPX Cooling Technologies, Inc., Overland Park, KS; SPX Dock Products, Inc., Carrollton, TX; Valley Forge Technical Information Services, Inc., Allen Park, MI; Waukesha Electric Systems, Inc., Waukesha, WI
International operations: Australia; Belgium; Brazil; Canada; China; Czech Republic; Denmark; France; Germany; Hong Kong; India; Ireland; Italy; Japan; Luxembourg; Malaysia; Mauritius; Mexico; Netherlands; New Zealand; Norway; Poland; Scotland; Singapore; South Africa; South Korea; Spain; Sweden; Switzerland; Taiwan; Thailand; United Arab Emirates; United Kingdom
Giving statement: Giving through the SPX Foundation.
Company EIN: 381016240

SPX Foundation

(formerly Sealed Power Foundation)
c/o Foundation For The Carolinas, Client Svcs. Dept.
217 South Tryon St.
Charlotte, NC 28202-3201 (704) 973-4500
E-mail: spxfoundation@fftc.org; Additional address: Jennifer H. Epstein, Dir., Corp. Comms., 13515 Ballantyne Corporate Pl., Charlotte, NC 28277, tel.: (704) 752-4400, e-mail: jennifer.epstein@spx.com

Establishment information: Established in 1982 in MI.
Donors: SPX Corp.; EGS Electrical Group, LLC; O-Z Gedney Co., LLC; Flair Corp.
Financial data (yr. ended 12/31/11): Assets, $81,238 (M); gifts received, $430,000; expenditures, $393,503; qualifying distributions, $336,341; giving activities include $336,341 for grants.
Purpose and activities: The foundation supports organizations involved with arts and culture, education, health, human services, and civic affairs.
Fields of interest: Arts; Education; Health care; Human services; Public affairs.
Type of support: Capital campaigns; Employee matching gifts; General/operating support.
Geographic limitations: Giving primarily in Charlotte, NC.
Publications: Informational brochure (including application guidelines).
Application information: Applications accepted. Application form not required.
Initial approach: Proposal
Copies of proposal: 1
Board meeting date(s): Quarterly
Deadline(s): None
Officers and Trustees:* Robert B. Foreman*, V.P.; Patrick J. O'Leary*, Secy.-Treas.; Christopher J. Kearney.
EIN: 386058308
Selected grants: The following grants are a representative sample of this grantmaker's funding activity:
$37,233 to United Way of Central Carolinas, Charlotte, NC, 2009.
$25,000 to Alexander Youth Network, Charlotte, NC, 2009.
$25,000 to American Diabetes Association, Charlotte, NC, 2009.
$25,000 to Thompson Child and Family Focus, Matthews, NC, 2009.
$25,000 to United Way of Greater Kansas City, Kansas City, MO, 2009.
$10,000 to American Heart Association, Charlotte, NC, 2009.
$10,000 to Muscular Dystrophy Association, Wauwatosa, WI, 2009.
$6,106 to United Way in Waukesha County, Waukesha, WI, 2009.
$5,000 to American Red Cross, Charlotte, NC, 2009.
$5,000 to Foundation for the Carolinas, Charlotte, NC, 2009.

3559
SQA Pharmacy Services Inc.

4700 Wissahickon Ave., Ste. B-108
Philadelphia, PA 19144 (215) 438-3308

Company URL: http://www.sqapharmacy.com
Establishment information: Established in 2005.
Company type: Private company
Business activities: Operates pharmacy.
Business type (SIC): Drug stores and proprietary stores
Corporate officer: Robert Fishman, Pres.
Giving statement: Giving through the SQ Foundation.

The SQ Foundation

4700 Wissahickon Ave., Ste. 126
Philadelphia, PA 19144-4248
E-mail: sspencer@sqfdn.org; URL: http://www.sqfdn.org

Establishment information: Established in PA.
Donors: SQA Pharmacy Services, LLC; Hubex Corp.; Resources for Human Development.
Contact: Steven Spencer, Prog. Dir.
Financial data (yr. ended 12/31/11): Assets, $396 (M); gifts received, $25,000; expenditures, $27,033; qualifying distributions, $27,033; giving activities include $25,000 for 5 grants (high: $5,000; low: $5,000).
Purpose and activities: The foundation supports programs designed to provide healthcare services to low-income individuals and those without health insurance.
Fields of interest: Health care, clinics/centers; Dental care; Health care Economically disadvantaged.
Type of support: Equipment; General/operating support.
Geographic limitations: Giving primarily in CT, DE, NJ, MA, PA, TN, and TX.
Support limitations: No grants to individuals.
Publications: Grants list.
Application information: Grants range from $4,000 to $6,000 and are awarded through a Request for Proposal (RFP) process. Visit website for RFP announcements.
Officers and Directors:* Robert Fishman*, Chair.; Stan Shubilla*, Secy.; Margaret Mowatt*, Treas.
EIN: 208024260

3560
Square D Company

(formerly Fuse and Manufacturing Co.)
1415 S. Roselle Rd.
Palatine, IL 60067-7399 (847) 397-2600

Company URL: http://www.squared.com
Establishment information: Established in 1902.
Company type: Subsidiary of a public company
Business activities: Manufactures and provides electrical distribution and industrial control products, systems, and services.
Business type (SIC): Electric transmission and distribution equipment; electrical industrial apparatus
Plants: Palatine, Schiller Park, IL; Huntington, Peru, IN; Cedar Rapids, IA; Florence, Lexington, KY; Columbia, MO; Lincoln, NE; Asheville, Knightdale, Monroe, NC; Oxford, Westchester, OH; Portland, OR; Columbia, Seneca, SC; Nashville, Smyrna, TN; Salt Lake City, UT; Kent, WA
Giving statement: Giving through the Square D Foundation.

Square D Foundation

1415 S. Roselle Rd.
Palatine, IL 60067-7399
URL: http://www.schneider-electric.us/sites/us/en/company/community/community.page

Establishment information: Incorporated in 1956 in MI.
Donors: Schneider Electric USA, Inc.; Square D Co.
Contact: Aurelie Richard, Treas.

Financial data (yr. ended 12/31/11): Assets, $31,095 (M); gifts received, $4,087,778; expenditures, $4,333,482; qualifying distributions, $4,327,418; giving activities include $4,267,597 for 1,110 grants (high: $675,793; low: $6).
Purpose and activities: The foundation supports organizations involved with arts and culture, education, health, human services, community development, civic affairs, senior citizens, disabled people, and economically disadvantaged people.
Fields of interest: Arts; Education; Hospitals (general); Health care; Housing/shelter, development; Youth, services; Human services; Community/economic development; Public affairs Aging; Disabilities, people with; Economically disadvantaged.
Program:
Employee Matching Gifts: The foundation matches contributions made by employees of Schneider Electric to institutions of higher education, organizations involved with health, and organizations with which employees are involved on a one-for-one basis from $50 to $10,000 per employee, per year.
Type of support: Annual campaigns; Building/renovation; Capital campaigns; Continuing support; Emergency funds; Employee matching gifts; Employee-related scholarships; General/operating support; Matching/challenge support; Professorships; Scholarship funds; Sponsorships.
Geographic limitations: Giving primarily in areas of company operations, with emphasis on IA, IL, IN, KY, MO, NC, NE, OH, SC, TN, and TX; giving also national organizations.
Support limitations: No support for religious organizations, labor unions, or political organizations. No grants to individuals (except for employee-related scholarships).
Application information: Applications not accepted. Telephone calls are not encouraged.
Board meeting date(s): As necessary
Officers and Directors:* George Powers, Pres.; Ted Klee, V.P.; Mary Ann Maclean, Secy.; Aurelie Richard*, Treas.; Allen Breeze; Jeff Dress; Robert Fiorani; Gwen Magner; John Mcpherson; Geraldo Oliuares.
Number of staff: None.
EIN: 366054195

3561
Squire, Sanders & Dempsey LLP
4900 Key Tower
127 Public Sq.
Cleveland, OH 44114-1304 (216) 479-8607

Company URL: http://www.ssd.com/Home.aspx
Establishment information: Established in 1890.
Company type: Private company
Business activities: Operates law firm.
Business type (SIC): Legal services
Offices: Phoenix, AZ; Los Angeles, Palo Alto, San Francisco, CA; Washington, DC; Miami, Tampa, West Palm Beach, FL; Cincinnati, Cleveland, Columbus, OH; Houston, TX; Tysons Corner, VA
International operations: Australia; Belgium; Brazil; China; Czech Republic; Dominican Republic; France; Germany; Hong Kong; Hungary; Japan; Poland; Russia; Slovakia; Spain; Ukraine; United Kingdom
Giving statement: Giving through the Squire, Sanders & Dempsey LLP Pro Bono Program.

Squire, Sanders & Dempsey LLP Pro Bono Program
4900 Key Tower
127 Public Sq.
Cleveland, OH 44114-1304 (216) 479-8607
E-mail: richard.gurbst@ssd.com; Additional tel.: (216) 479-8500; URL: http://www.ssd.com/thefirm/probono/

Contact: Richard S. Gurbst, Partner
Fields of interest: Legal services.
Type of support: Pro bono services - legal.
Application information: A Pro Bono Committee manages the pro bono program.

3562
SRA International, Inc.
4300 Fair Lakes Ct.
Fairfax, VA 22033 (703) 803-1500

Company URL: http://www.sra.com
Establishment information: Established in 1978.
Company type: Private company
Business activities: Provides information technology services and solutions.
Business type (SIC): Computer services
Corporate officers: Ernst Volgenau, Chair.; William L. Ballhaus, C.E.O.; Timothy J. Atkin, Exec. V.P. and C.O.O.; Richard J. Nadeau, Exec. V.P. and C.F.O.; Anne M. Donohue, Esq., Sr. V.P. and Genl. Counsel
Board of directors: Ernst Volgenau, Chair.; William Ballhaus; Chris Ragona
Subsidiary: The Marasco Newton Group , Ltd., Arlington, VA
Giving statement: Giving through the SRA International, Inc. Corporate Giving Program.
Company EIN: 541360804

SRA International, Inc. Corporate Giving Program
4300 Fair Lakes Ct.
Fairfax, VA 22033 (703) 803-1500
FAX: (703) 803-1509; URL: http://www.sra.com/about-us/community/

Purpose and activities: SRA makes charitable contributions to nonprofit organizations involved with education, environmental protection and beautification, health, housing, information technology, law enforcement and justice, disaster relief, and the U.S. military.
Fields of interest: Education, computer literacy/technology training; Education; Environment, beautification programs; Environment; Health care; Crime/law enforcement; Housing/shelter; Safety/disasters; Family services; Military/veterans' organizations.
Type of support: Employee volunteer services.
Geographic limitations: Giving on a national basis.
Application information: The Community Action, Responsibility, Education and Services (CARES) Committee handles volunteerism.

3563
The St. Joe Company
(formerly St. Joe Corporation)
245 Riverside Ave.
133 S. Watersound Pkwy.
Watersound, FL 32413 (904) 301-4200
FAX: (904) 301-4201

Company URL: http://ir.joe.com/overview.cfm
Establishment information: Established in 1936.
Company type: Public company
Company ticker symbol and exchange: JOE/NYSE
Business activities: Builds houses; develops commercial real estate; operates timber tracts.
Business type (SIC): Real estate subdividers and developers; forestry—timber tracts; operative builders
Financial profile for 2012: Number of employees, 74; assets, $6,455,200,000; sales volume, $139,400,000; pre-tax net income, $6,380,000; expenses, $137,260,000; liabilities, $93,500,000
Corporate officers: Bruce R. Berkowitz, Chair.; Park Brady, C.E.O.; Thomas Hoyer, C.F.O.; Kenneth M. Borick, Sr. V.P., Genl. Counsel, and Corp. Secy.; Rhea K. Goff, C.A.O.; Patrick Murphy, V.P., Opers.
Board of directors: Bruce R. Berkowitz, Chair.; Cesar L. Alvarez; Park Brady; Charles J. Crist; Howard S. Frank; Jeffrey C. Keil; Stanley Martin; Thomas P. Murphy, Jr.
Subsidiaries: Apalachicola Northern Railroad Co., Jacksonville, FL; Florida East Coast Industries, Inc., St. Augustine, FL; Jacksonville Properties, Inc., Jacksonville, FL; St. Joe Real Estate Services, Inc., Boca Raton, FL
Giving statement: Giving through the St. Joe Company Contributions Program and the St. Joe Community Foundation Inc.
Company EIN: 590432511

St. Joe Community Foundation Inc.
(formerly Northwest Florida Improvement Foundation, Inc.)
133 S. Watersound Pkwy.
Watersound, FL 32413-7280
FAX: (850) 231-7431; E-mail: sjoffe@stjcf.com; URL: http://www.stjcf.com

Establishment information: Established in 1999 in FL.
Financial data (yr. ended 12/31/11): Assets, $1,929,048 (M); gifts received, $24,573; expenditures, $178,753; qualifying distributions, $79,073; giving activities include $79,073 for 13 grants (high: $25,000; low: $1,000).
Purpose and activities: The foundation seeks to enrich the quality of life of the people who live, work, and play in northwest Florida.
Fields of interest: Arts; Education; Environment; Health care; Human services; Community/economic development Infants/toddlers; Children/youth; Children; Adults; Aging; Young adults; Disabilities, people with; Physically disabled; Blind/visually impaired; Deaf/hearing impaired; Mentally disabled; Minorities; African Americans/Blacks; Hispanics/Latinos; Native Americans/American Indians; Girls; Substance abusers; Economically disadvantaged; Homeless.
Type of support: Building/renovation; Capital campaigns; Curriculum development; Endowments; Equipment; Fellowships; Management development/capacity building; Professorships; Program development; Publication; Research; Scholarship funds; Seed money.
Geographic limitations: Giving limited to Bay, Calhoun, Franklin, Gadsden, Gulf, Jefferson, Leon, Liberty, Wakulla, and Walton counties, FL.

Support limitations: No support for sectarian or religious activities. No grants to individuals, or for fundraising events, health initiatives other than regional healthcare delivery, or individual sports teams.
Application information: Applications not accepted. Unsolicited requests for funds not accepted.
Board meeting date(s): Quarterly
Board Members: Ken Borick; Jorge Gonzalez; Neal Wade.
Number of staff: 1 full-time professional.
EIN: 593576402
Selected grants: The following grants are a representative sample of this grantmaker's funding activity:
$500,000 to Sacred Heart Foundation, Pensacola, FL, 2009. To build Sacred Heart Hospital in Gulf and Franklin Counties.
$100,000 to Sacred Heart Foundation, Pensacola, FL, 2009.
$50,000 to Florida State University, Tallahassee, FL, 2009. For Endowed Scholarship Fund.
$30,000 to College for Every Student, Cornwall, VT, 2009. For Scholars Program in Gulf and Franklin County.
$29,000 to Florida State University, College of Motion Picture, Television and Recording Arts, Tallahassee, FL, 2009. For Chris Coor Award.
$25,000 to Junior Museum of Bay County, Panama City, FL, 2009.
$25,000 to Seaside School Foundation, Santa Rosa Beach, FL, 2009. For Billy Buzzett Award to Seaside Neighborhood School.
$11,962 to Anchorage Childrens Home of Bay County, Panama City, FL, 2009.
$11,962 to Boys and Girls Clubs of Bay County, Panama City, FL, 2009.
$11,962 to Gulf Coast Childrens Advocacy Center, 2009.
$10,000 to Big Brothers Big Sisters of Northwest Florida, Pensacola, FL, 2009. For mentoring program for military children.

3564
St. John Knits International, Inc.

17622 Armstrong Ave.
Irvine, CA 92614 (949) 863-1171

Company URL: http://www.sjk.com/en-us/
Establishment information: Established in 1962.
Company type: Subsidiary of a private company
Business activities: Sells women's apparel, accessories, jewelry, shoes, and home accessories wholesale.
Business type (SIC): Apparel, piece goods, and notions—wholesale
Corporate officers: James P. Kelley, Chair.; Glenn Patrick McMahon, C.E.O.; Bruce A. Fetter, C.O.O; Roger G. Ruppert, Exec. V.P., Finance and C.F.O.; Robert Green, Exec. V.P., Sales and Mktg.
Board of director: James P. Kelley, Chair.
Giving statement: Giving through the St. John Foundation.

The St. John Foundation

17522 Armstrong Ave.
Irvine, CA 92614-5726

Establishment information: Established in CA.
Donor: St. John Knits.
Financial data (yr. ended 10/31/11): Assets, $14,090 (M); expenditures, $1; qualifying distributions, $0.
Purpose and activities: The foundation supports organizations involved with child welfare and other areas.
Type of support: General/operating support.
Geographic limitations: Giving primarily in AZ and CA.
Support limitations: No grants to individuals.
Application information: Applications not accepted. Unsolicited requests for funds not accepted.
Officers: Bruce A. Fetter, Pres.; Tammy Storino, Exec. V.P., C.F.O., and Treas.; Daniel Burke, Secy. and Genl. Counsel.
EIN: 330706594

3565
St. John Properties, Inc.

2560 Lord Baltimore Dr.
Baltimore, MD 21244 (410) 788-0100

Company URL: http://www.sjpi.com
Establishment information: Established in 1971.
Company type: Private company
Business activities: Operates commercial real estate company.
Business type (SIC): Real estate operators and lessors
Corporate officers: Edward St. John, Chair.; Lawrence F. Maykrantz, Pres.
Giving statement: Giving through the Edward St. John Foundation, Inc.

Edward St. John Foundation, Inc.

2560 Lord Baltimore Dr.
Baltimore, MD 21244-2666 (410) 788-0100
FAX: (410) 788-1873;
E-mail: edwardstjohnfoundation@sjpi.com; Contact for Sharon L. Akers: tel.: (410) 369-1273, e-mail: sakers@sjpi.com; URL: http://www.esjfoundation.org/

Donors: Edward A. St. John; St. John Properties, Inc.
Contact: Sharon L. Akers, Exec. Dir.
Financial data (yr. ended 12/31/11): Assets, $228,927 (M); gifts received, $1,250,725; expenditures, $1,296,631; qualifying distributions, $1,226,409; giving activities include $1,226,409 for 61 grants (high: $1,000,000; low: $50).
Purpose and activities: The foundation provides financial assistance to formal education programs through the high school level. The foundation's mission is based on the strong belief that education has the power to transform lives and strengthen communities.
Fields of interest: Secondary school/education; Higher education; Education; Human services; Community/economic development Economically disadvantaged.
Type of support: General/operating support; Program development; Scholarship funds.
Support limitations: No grants for capital campaigns, annual funds, or ongoing operating expenses.
Publications: Application guidelines.
Application information: The foundation budget allocations are committed through 2014. Proposals are currently not accepted.
Officers and Directors:* Lawrence Maykrantz*, Pres.; Kellay St. John*, V.P.; Jerry Wit*, Secy.; Tina Berzins*, Treas.; Sharon Akers, Exec. Dir.
EIN: 201397204

3566
St. Jude Medical, Inc.

1 St. Jude Medical Dr.
St. Paul, MN 55117-9983 (651) 756-2000
FAX: (651) 756-3301

Company URL: http://www.sjm.com
Establishment information: Established in 1976.
Company type: Public company
Company ticker symbol and exchange: STJ/NYSE
Business activities: Develops, manufactures, and distributes cardiovascular medical devices.
Business type (SIC): Medical instruments and supplies
Financial profile for 2012: Number of employees, 15,000; assets, $9,271,000,000; sales volume, $5,503,000,000; pre-tax net income, $1,005,000,000; expenses, $4,403,000,000; liabilities, $5,177,000,000
Fortune 1000 ranking: 2012—457th in revenues, 254th in profits, and 411th in assets
Forbes 2000 ranking: 2012—1333rd in sales, 703rd in profits, and 1525th in assets
Corporate officers: Daniel J. Starks, Chair., Pres., and C.E.O.; Mark W. Murphy, V.P. and C.I.O.; Jason A. Zellers, V.P., Genl. Counsel, and Corp. Secy.; Donald J. Zurbay, V.P., Finance and C.F.O.; Angela D. Craig, V.P., Human Resources
Board of directors: Daniel J. Starks, Chair.; John W. Brown; Richard R. Devenuti; Stuart M. Essig, Ph.D.; Barbara B. Hill; Michael A. Rocca; Wendy L. Yarno
Subsidiaries: Pacesetter, Inc., Sylmar, CA; SJM International, Inc., St. Paul, MN; St. Jude Medical ATG, Inc., Maple Grove, MN; St. Jude Medical Europe, Inc., St. Paul, MN; St. Jude Medical S.C., Inc., St. Paul, MN; St. Jude Medical, Daig Division, Inc., Minnetonka, MN; St. Jude Medical, Inc., Cardiac Assist Division, St. Paul, MN
Division: Cardiac Surgery Div., St. Paul, MN
International operations: Argentina; Australia; Austria; Belgium; Bermuda; Brazil; Canada; China; Colombia; Costa Rica; France; Germany; Hong Kong; Hungary; India; Italy; Japan; Lithuania; Luxembourg; Malaysia; Netherlands; Norway; Portugal; Singapore; Spain; Sweden; Taiwan; Thailand; United Kingdom
Giving statement: Giving through the St. Jude Medical, Inc. Corporate Giving Program and the St. Jude Medical Foundation.
Company EIN: 411276891

St. Jude Medical, Inc. Corporate Giving Program

One St. Jude Medical Dr.
St. Paul, MN 55117-9983 (651) 756-2000
FAX: (651) 756-3301; E-mail: sjmgrants@sjm.com; URL: http://www.sjm.com/companyinformation/grantrequest.aspx

Purpose and activities: As a complement to its foundation, St. Jude Medical also matches contributions made by its employees to nonprofit organizations. Support is given on a national basis.
Fields of interest: General charitable giving.
Type of support: Employee matching gifts.
Geographic limitations: Giving on a national basis.
Application information: Applications not accepted. Contributes only through employee matching gifts.

St. Jude Medical Foundation

1 St. Jude Medical Dr.
St. Paul, MN 55117-1761 (651) 756-2157
FAX: (877) 291-7569;
E-mail: info@sjmfoundation.com; URL: http://www.sjmfoundation.com/

Establishment information: Established in 1997 in MN.
Donor: St. Jude Medical, Inc.
Financial data (yr. ended 12/31/11): Assets, $386,307 (M); gifts received, $4,780,777; expenditures, $4,418,136; qualifying distributions, $4,416,549; giving activities include $4,415,099 for 92 grants (high: $600,000; low: $1,000).
Purpose and activities: The foundation supports organizations involved with arts and culture, K-12 education, health, disaster relief, human services, community development, science, and civic affairs. Special emphasis is directed toward programs designed to improve awareness and treatment of cardiovascular, neurological, and chronic pain conditions.
Fields of interest: Arts; Elementary/secondary education; Health care; Health organizations, public education; Heart & circulatory diseases; Neuroscience; Health organizations; Surgery; Disasters, preparedness/services; Human services; Community/economic development; Mathematics; Engineering/technology; Science; Public affairs.
Programs:
Advancing the State of Medical Knowledge: The foundation supports programs designed to advance cardiovascular and neurological science through education, research, and training.
Community: The foundation supports programs designed to enhance life and vitality of the community. Special emphasis is directed toward programs in the human services, civic, and cultural arenas where a specific tie-in to cardiovascular, neurological, and chronic pain is possible.
Health Awareness: The foundation supports programs designed to improve public awareness of cardiovascular, neurological, and chronic pain conditions, and the device therapy that can change people's lives.
Type of support: Conferences/seminars; Continuing support; Employee matching gifts; Fellowships; General/operating support; Research; Seed money; Sponsorships.
Geographic limitations: Giving on a national basis, with some emphasis on CA, Washington, DC, MA, and MN.
Support limitations: No grants to individuals.
Publications: Application guidelines; Program policy statement.
Application information: Applications accepted. Applications for community outreach, research study, and mission trips are also accepted. Organizations receiving general operating support are asked to submit narrative and financial progress reports near the end of each one-year grant period. Application form required. Applicants should submit the following:
1) name, address and phone number of organization
2) copy of IRS Determination Letter
3) detailed description of project and amount of funding requested
4) contact person
Applications should include a W-9 form.
Initial approach: Complete online application
Copies of proposal: 1
Deadline(s): 60 days prior to need
Officers and Directors:* Angela D. Craig*, Pres.; Daniel J. Starks, V.P.; Pamela S. Krop*, Secy.; Robert Frenz, Treas.; John C. Heinmiller.
EIN: 411868372
Selected grants: The following grants are a representative sample of this grantmaker's funding activity:
$200,000 to Sudden Cardiac Arrest Association, Washington, DC, 2010.
$160,000 to Institute for Health Technology Studies, Washington, DC, 2010. For General Operating Support.
$105,032 to Massachusetts General Hospital, Boston, MA, 2010.
$100,000 to Atrial Fibrillation Association, Stratford Upon Avon, England, 2010. For General Operating Support.
$88,449 to University of Pennsylvania, Philadelphia, PA, 2010.
$84,575 to Cornell University, Ithaca, NY, 2010.
$50,000 to Montefiore Medical Center, Bronx, NY, 2010. For Seymour Furman Electrophysiology and Pacing Fellowship Program.
$50,000 to Mount Sinai School of Medicine of New York University, New York, NY, 2010.
$50,000 to Thoracic Surgery Foundation for Research and Education, Beverly, MA, 2010.
$25,000 to Brigham and Womens Hospital, Boston, MA, 2010.

3567
St. Louis Blues Hockey Club L.L.C.

Scottrade Ctr.
1401 Clark Ave., Brett Hull Way
St. Louis, MO 63103-2700 (314) 622-2500

Company URL: http://www.stlouisblues.com
Establishment information: Established in 1967.
Company type: Subsidiary of a private company
Business activities: Operates professional ice hockey club.
Business type (SIC): Commercial sports
Corporate officers: Tom Stillman, Chair.; Bruce Affleck, C.O.O.; Phil Siddle, Sr. V.P. and C.F.O.; Todd Lambert, Sr. V.P., Sales; Mike Caruso, Sr. V.P., Mktg. and Public Rels.; Karrie Yager, V.P., Mktg.
Board of director: Tom Stillman, Chair.
Giving statement: Giving through the St. Louis Blues Hockey Club L.L.C. Corporate Giving Program and the St. Louis Blues 14 Fund.

St. Louis Blues Hockey Club L.L.C. Corporate Giving Program

c/o Community Rels. Dept.
1401 Clark Ave.
St. Louis, MO 63103-2700 (314) 552-4550
E-mail: communityrelations@stlblues.com; Contact for player appearances: Renah Jones; contact for Blues Bookworm: Randy Girsch, tel.: (314) 589-5998; URL: http://blues.nhl.com/club/page.htm?id=41493

Purpose and activities: The St. Louis Blues make charitable contributions to nonprofit organizations involved with education, health, diversity, youth hockey, and children and youth. Support is given primarily in the greater St. Louis, Missouri, area.
Fields of interest: Education, reading; Education; Hospitals (general); Health care; Cancer; Athletics/sports, winter sports; Recreation; Children/youth, services; Human services, gift distribution; Civil/human rights, equal rights; United Ways and Federated Giving Programs.
Program:
Blue Bookworm: Through Blues Bookworm, the St. Louis Blues rewards K-6 students who spend more of their leisure time reading. Classes that reach or go beyond the goal of reading 250 minutes per month are entered into a drawing for a player appearance. All classes that reach their monthly goal are highlighted on the Blues website, and students that read 1,000 minutes or more receives a game ticket and is recognized on the jumbotron.
Type of support: Donated products; In-kind gifts; Income development; Loaned talent.
Geographic limitations: Giving primarily in areas of company operations in the greater St. Louis, MO, area.
Publications: Application guidelines.
Application information: Applications accepted. Proposal should be submitted using organization letterhead. Telephone calls during the application process are not encouraged. The Community Relations Department handles giving. Application form not required. Applicants should submit the following:
1) population served
2) name, address and phone number of organization
3) copy of IRS Determination Letter
4) descriptive literature about organization
5) detailed description of project and amount of funding requested
6) contact person
Proposals should indicate the date of the event and specifically note the nature of the request being made.
Initial approach: Download application form and mail to headquarters for memorabilia donations; proposal to headquarters for player appearances; complete online application for Blues Bookworm
Copies of proposal: 1
Deadline(s): 6 weeks prior to need for memorabilia donations and player appearances
Final notification: 2 weeks prior to need; 4 weeks prior to need for player appearances

The St. Louis Blues 14 Fund

(formerly The Fourteen Fund)
1401 Clark Ave.
St. Louis, MO 63103-2700 (314) 589-5998
FAX: (314) 622-5410; E-mail: rjones@stlblues.com; URL: http://blues.nhl.com/v2/ext/14fund/index.html

Establishment information: Established in 1998 in MO.
Contact: Randy Girsch
Financial data (yr. ended 12/31/11): Revenue, $772,166; assets, $864,099 (M); gifts received, $770,475; expenditures, $690,983; giving activities include $301,064 for grants.
Purpose and activities: The fund, in conjunction with the St. Louis Blues' community outreach efforts, has a mission to positively impact the community by focusing on collaborative efforts which emphasize cancer awareness, prevention, and intervention; positive youth development through sports; education; and promoting diversity.
Fields of interest: Education; Cancer; Recreation; Youth development Minorities.
Program:
Grants: The foundation makes grants to St. Louis-area organizations that focus on four areas: cancer care and awareness (including prevention and treatment for pediatric and adult cancer patients and their families), health and wellness (including programs that focus on awareness, prevention, and treatment of childhood diseases; programs that promote physical activity, nutrition, and mental well-being of area children; and wellness programs that involve hockey), education (including educational programs that focus on special needs in the community, and programs that present an important initiative to area children, such as diversity and character education), and youth and amateur hockey development (including programs involving learn-to-play programs and scholarships).

Type of support: Building/renovation; Continuing support; Program development.
Geographic limitations: Giving limited to the metropolitan St. Louis, MO area.
Support limitations: No support for organizations lacking 501(c)(3) status. No grants to individuals; no multi-year awards.
Application information: Applications accepted. Application form required.
Initial approach: Download application form
Board meeting date(s): Quarterly
Deadline(s): Jan. 15 and July 15
Trustees: Bruce Affleck; John Davidson; Dennis Hennessy; Scott McCuaig; Phil Siddle; Tom Stillman; James Woodcock.
Number of staff: 1
EIN: 431820447

3568
St. Louis Cardinals L.L.C.

700 Clark St.
St. Louis, MO 63102-1727 (314) 345-9600

Company URL: http://stlouis.cardinals.mlb.com
Establishment information: Established in 1892.
Company type: Private company
Business activities: Operates professional baseball club.
Business type (SIC): Commercial sports
Corporate officers: William O. DeWitt, Jr., Chair. and C.E.O.; Frederick O. Hanser, Vice-Chair.; William O. DeWitt III, Pres.; Brad Wood, Sr. V.P. and C.F.O.; Dan Farrell, Sr. V.P., Sales and Mktg.; Mike Whittle, V.P. and Genl. Counsel
Board of directors: William O. DeWitt, Jr., Chair.; Frederick O. Hanser, Vice-Chair.
Giving statement: Giving through the St. Louis Cardinals L.L.C. Corporate Giving Program and the St. Louis Cardinals Community Fund.

St. Louis Cardinals L.L.C. Corporate Giving Program

c/o Community Rels.Dept.
700 Clark St.
St. Louis, MO 63102-1727 (314) 345-9885
URL: http://stlouis.cardinals.mlb.com/NASApp/mlb/stl/community/index.jsp

Purpose and activities: As a complement to its foundation, the St. Louis Cardinals also make charitable contributions of memorabilia to nonprofit organizations directly. Support is limited to Arkansas, Illinois, Indiana, Kansas, Kentucky, Mississippi, Missouri, and Oklahoma.
Fields of interest: General charitable giving.
Type of support: Donated products; In-kind gifts.
Geographic limitations: Giving limited to AR, IL, IN, KS, KY, MO, MS, and OK.
Publications: Application guidelines.
Application information: Applications accepted. Application form required. Applicants should submit the following:
1) name, address and phone number of organization
2) contact person
Applications should include the Tax ID number of the organization; and the name, date, and a description of the event.
Initial approach: Complete online application form
Deadline(s): 8 weeks prior to need

St. Louis Cardinals Community Fund

(doing business as Cardinals Care)
700 Clark St.
St. Louis, MO 63102-1816 (314) 345-9600
URL: http://stlouis.cardinals.mlb.com/stl/community/index.jsp

Establishment information: Established in 1997 in MO.
Contact: Michael L. Hall, V.P. and Exec. Dir.
Financial data (yr. ended 12/31/11): Revenue, $1,258,774; assets, $2,995,246 (M); gifts received, $788,806; expenditures, $1,350,266; program services expenses, $876,824; giving activities include $876,824 for 40 grants (high: $335,173; low: $500).
Purpose and activities: The fund supports projects that serve or support youth under 20 years old in the St. Louis area.
Fields of interest: Youth development; Children/youth, services.
Program:
Grants: The foundation provides grants to organizations that serve and/or support youth in the greater St. Louis metropolitan area. Eligible applicants must have had 501(c)(3) status for at least one year prior to application, have an organizational budget of up to $2,000,000, and have administration/fundraising expenses that do not exceed 30 percent of its total budget. Grants generally average $3,000 per organization; organizations can only apply and receive funding on a yearly basis.
Type of support: General/operating support; Program development; Scholarship funds.
Geographic limitations: Giving limited to the St. Louis, MO area.
Support limitations: No grants for annual program costs or salaries, operating expenses, fundraising event sponsorships, scholarships/endowment funds, multiple-year pledges, or for individuals.
Publications: Application guidelines; Informational brochure (including application guidelines).
Application information: Applications accepted. Application form required. Applicants should submit the following:
1) copy of IRS Determination Letter
2) copy of most recent annual report/audited financial statement/990
3) listing of board of directors, trustees, officers and other key people and their affiliations
4) contact person
5) copy of current year's organizational budget and/or project budget
Initial approach: Download application form
Copies of proposal: 1
Board meeting date(s): Mar.
Deadline(s): June 9 and Dec. 3
Final notification: Within three months
Officers: William O. Dewitt III*, Pres.; Margot D. Good*, V.P.; Michael Hall*, V.P.; Timothy F. Hanser*, V.P.; Brooke W. Restemayer*, V.P.; Bradford S. Wood*, V.P.; Julie M. Laningham*, Asst. Secy.; Richard Baur*, Treas.
Number of staff: 3 part-time professional; 2 part-time support.
EIN: 431768625

3569
St. Louis Rams Football Co.

(also known as The Rams Football Company, Inc.)
1 Rams Way
St. Louis, MO 63045 (314) 982-7267

Company URL: http://www.stlouisrams.com
Establishment information: Established in 1936.
Company type: Private company
Business activities: Operates professional football club.
Business type (SIC): Commercial sports
Financial profile for 2010: Number of employees, 244
Corporate officers: E. Stanley Kroenke, Chair.; Chip Rosenbloom, Vice-Chair.; Kevin Demoff, V.P. and C.O.O.; Bob Reif, Exec. V.P., Mktg. and Sales; Michael T. Naughton, V.P., Finance; Michael O'Keefe, V.P, Sales; Molly Higgins, V.P., Corp. Comms.; Jeff Brewer, Treas.
Board of directors: E. Stanley Kroenke, Chair.; Chip Rosenbloom, Vice-Chair.; Bill Consoli; Keely Fimbres; Tom Guthrie; Lawrence McCutcheon; Debbie Pollom; Chad Watson; Kanyon West; Michael Yarbrough
Giving statement: Giving through the St. Louis Rams Football Company Contributions Program and the St. Louis Rams Foundation.

St. Louis Rams Football Company Contributions Program

c/o St. Louis Rams Community Outreach, Donation Requests
1 Rams Way
St. Louis, MO 63045-1523
URL: http://www.stlouisrams.com/community

Purpose and activities: As a complement to its foundation, the St. Louis Rams also makes charitable contributions to nonprofit organizations. Support is given primarily within a 120-mile radius of the greater bi-state St. Louis, Missouri, area.
Fields of interest: Education; Health care, infants; Health care, blood supply; Public health, obesity; Cancer; Breast cancer; Food banks; Recreation, public education; Recreation; Youth development; Civil/human rights, equal rights.
Type of support: Continuing support; Employee volunteer services; General/operating support; Income development; Program development; Sponsorships.
Geographic limitations: Giving primarily within a 120-mile radius of the greater bi-state St. Louis, MO area.
Support limitations: No support for card clubs, or adult sports teams. No additional funding for organizations already receiving financial or in-kind support: United Way, St. Jude Children's Research Hospital, and Make-A-Wish Foundation. No grants or donations for business or retail purposes, capital campaigns or start-up funding for new businesses, online auctions, class or family reunions, pageant contests, poker runs, student ambassador exchange programs, non-charity events such as company picnics, employee golf tournaments, employee recognition or incentive programs, car shows, or Chamber of Commerce, city, or neighborhood festivals such as homecoming celebrations and carnivals that are not of benefit to charitable organizations.
Publications: Application guidelines.
Application information: Applications accepted. Proposals should be submitted using organization letterhead. Faxed, e-mailed, or phoned requests will not be accepted. Support is limited to 1 contribution

per organization during any given year. Application form not required. Applicants should submit the following:
1) name, address and phone number of organization
2) copy of IRS Determination Letter
3) contact person
Proposals should indicate the date, type, and beneficiary of the event.
Initial approach: Proposal to headquarters
Copies of proposal: 1
Deadline(s): None
Final notification: At least 6 weeks

St. Louis Rams Foundation

c/o Dir. of Rams Fdn.
1 Rams Way
St. Louis, MO 63045-1523 (314) 982-7267
FAX: (314) 516-8888

Establishment information: Established in 1997 in MO.
Financial data (yr. ended 12/31/10): Revenue, $47,115; assets, $915,596 (M); gifts received, $46,816; expenditures, $142,279; giving activities include $125,000 for grants.
Purpose and activities: The foundation supports efforts and organizations that inspire positive change in youth in the greater St. Louis, Missouri, particularly in the areas of education and literacy, health, and recreation.
Fields of interest: Education, reading; Education; Health care; Recreation; Youth development.
Type of support: Conferences/seminars; Continuing support; Curriculum development; Equipment; General/operating support; In-kind gifts; Matching/challenge support; Program development; Publication; Scholarship funds; Seed money; Technical assistance.
Geographic limitations: Giving primarily in MO and southern IL.
Support limitations: No support for businesses (retail or otherwise). No grants for capital campaigns or start-up funding for new businesses, online auctions, chamber of commerce/city/neighborhood festivals (such as homecoming celebrations or carnivals) that do not directly benefit a charitable organization, class or family reunions, pageant contestants (beauty or otherwise), student ambassador/exchange programs, or non-charity events, such as company picnics, employee golf tournaments, employee recognition/incentive programs, card clubs, car shows, 'poker runs,' and organized adult leisure sports teams.
Officers: John Shaw*, Pres.; Jeff Brewer, Treas.
Directors: E. Stanley Kroenke; Dale Rosenbloom; Lucia Rodriguez.
Number of staff: 2
EIN: 431796215

3570
Stadtmauer Bailkin LLP

850 3rd Ave., 19th Fl.
New York, NY 10022-7233 (212) 751-8600

Company URL: http://www.sbllplaw.com/
Establishment information: Established in 1976.
Company type: Private company
Business activities: Provides legal services.
Business type (SIC): Legal services
Corporate officer: Howard Alan Zipser, Partner
Giving statement: Giving through the N.C.S. Family Foundation, Inc.

N.C.S. Family Foundation, Inc.

c/o Neil A. Simon
5 Michael St.
Spring Valley, NY 10977-2111

Establishment information: Established in 2001 in NY.
Donors: Stadtmauer Bailkin LLP; Neil A. Simon; Carole Simon.
Financial data (yr. ended 12/31/11): Assets, $2,706 (M); gifts received, $300; expenditures, $250; qualifying distributions, $0.
Purpose and activities: The foundation supports organizations involved with Judaism.
Type of support: General/operating support.
Support limitations: No grants to individuals.
Application information: Applications not accepted. Contributes only to pre-selected organizations.
Directors: Carole Simon; Neil A. Simon.
EIN: 134149857

3571
Stafast Products, Inc.

505 Lake Shore Blvd.
Painesville, OH 44077-1121
(440) 357-5546

Company URL: http://www.stafast.com
Establishment information: Established in 1958.
Company type: Private company
Business activities: Manufactures screws, bolts, and fasteners.
Business type (SIC): Screw machine products; industrial machinery and equipment—wholesale
Financial profile for 2010: Number of employees, 40
Corporate officers: Donald S. Selle, Pres.; Joan M. Selle, Secy.-Treas.
Giving statement: Giving through the Stafast Foundation, Inc.

Stafast Foundation, Inc.

(also known as Stay Fast Foundation, Inc.)
505 Lake Shore Blvd.
Painesville, OH 44077-1121 (440) 357-5546

Establishment information: Established in 1985 in OH.
Donors: Stafast Products, Inc.; Donald S. Selle; Joan M. Selle.
Financial data (yr. ended 12/31/11): Assets, $145,338 (M); gifts received, $265,000; expenditures, $230,352; qualifying distributions, $228,120; giving activities include $228,120 for grants.
Purpose and activities: The foundation supports organizations involved with radio, human services, and Christianity.
Fields of interest: Media, radio; Salvation Army; Children, services; Family services; Residential/custodial care; Human services; Christian agencies & churches.
Type of support: General/operating support.
Geographic limitations: Giving primarily in CO, FL, NC, and OH.
Trustees: Donald S. Selle; Joan M. Selle.
EIN: 341485142
Selected grants: The following grants are a representative sample of this grantmaker's funding activity:
$20,000 to Hannahs Home, Mentor, OH, 2010.
$9,786 to Compassion International, Colorado Springs, CO, 2010.
$6,000 to American Family Association, Tupelo, MS, 2010.
$5,000 to Alliance Defense Fund, Scottsdale, AZ, 2010.
$5,000 to Focus on the Family, Colorado Springs, CO, 2010.
$1,000 to Jungle Aviation and Radio Service, Waxhaw, NC, 2010.
$1,000 to Radio Bible Class, Grand Rapids, MI, 2010.

3572
Stage Stores, Inc.

10201 Main St.
Houston, TX 77025 (800) 324-3244

Company URL: http://www.stagestoresinc.com
Establishment information: Established in 1988.
Company type: Public company
Company ticker symbol and exchange: SSI/NYSE
Business activities: Operates department stores.
Business type (SIC): Department stores
Financial profile for 2013: Number of employees, 14,500; assets, $794,870,000; sales volume, $1,645,800,000; pre-tax net income, $60,380,000; expenses, $1,582,410,000; liabilities, $330,000,000
Corporate officers: William Montgoris, Chair.; Michael Glazer, Pres. and C.E.O.; Edward J. Record, C.O.O.; Oded Shein, Exec. V.P. and C.F.O.; Steven L. Hunter, Exec. V.P. and C.I.O.; Ron D. Lucas, Exec. V.P., Human Resources; Richard E. Stasyszen, Sr. V.P., Finance and Cont.
Board of directors: William Montgoris, Chair.; Alan J. Barocas; Diane Ellis; Michael L. Glazer; Gabrielle E. Greene; Earl J. Hesterberg; Lisa Kranc; C. Clayton Reasor; David Y. Schwartz; Ralph Scozzafava
Historic mergers: B. C. Moore & Sons, Inc. (February 27, 2006)
Giving statement: Giving through the Stage Stores, Inc. Corporate Giving Program and the B. C. Moore Foundation.
Company EIN: 911826900

B. C. Moore Foundation

c/o Branch Banking & Trust Co., Trust Tax Dept.
P. O. Box 2907
Wilson, NC 27894-2907 (707) 694-2171
Application address: P.O. Box 72, Wadesboro, NC 28170, tel.: (707) 694-2171

Establishment information: Established in 1951 in AL.
Donor: B.C. Moore & Sons, Inc.
Contact: W. Kirk Crawford
Financial data (yr. ended 01/31/12): Assets, $1,683,831 (M); expenditures, $115,254; qualifying distributions, $94,000; giving activities include $94,000 for 25 grants (high: $35,000; low: $500).
Purpose and activities: The foundation supports arts councils and organizations involved with secondary and higher education, search and rescue, human services, and Christianity.
Fields of interest: Education; Human services; Religion.
Type of support: General/operating support.
Geographic limitations: Giving primarily in NC, SC, and TN.
Application information: Applications accepted. Application form required.
Initial approach: Letter
Deadline(s): None
Trustee: Branch Banking & Trust Co.
Committee Members: Carl E. Bennett; James C. Crawford; W. Kirk Crawford.
EIN: 566062082

3573
Stahl Construction Co.
5755 Wayzata Blvd.
St. Louis Park, MN 55416 (952) 931-9300

Company URL: http://www.stahlconstruction.com
Establishment information: Established in 1981.
Company type: Private company
Business activities: Provides general contract construction services.
Business type (SIC): Building construction general contractors and operative builders
Corporate officer: Wayne Stahl, Pres.
Giving statement: Giving through the Stahl Construction Company Contributions Program.

Stahl Construction Company Contributions Program
5755 Wayzata Blvd.
St. Louis Park, MN 55416-1218 (952) 931-9300
FAX: (952) 931-9941; URL: http://www.stahlconstruction.com/corporate-philanthropy/

Purpose and activities: Stahl makes charitable contributions to nonprofit organizations involved with human services, and on a case by case basis. Support is given primarily in the Des Moines, Iowa, area, and the Twin Cities, Minnesota, area.
Fields of interest: Elementary/secondary education; Human services; Christian agencies & churches; General charitable giving.
Program:
Scholarships: Shahl awards $500 college scholarships to high school students in school districts in areas of company operations planning to pursue a career related to construction.
Type of support: Employee volunteer services; General/operating support.
Geographic limitations: Giving primarily in the Des Moines, IA, area, and the Twin Cities, MN, area.
Application information: Applications not accepted. Contributes only to pre-selected organizations.

3574
StanCorp Financial Group, Inc.
(also known as The Standard)
1100 S.W. 6th Ave.
Portland, OR 97204-1020 (971) 321-7000
FAX: (971) 321-6776

Company URL: http://www.stancorpfinancial.com
Establishment information: Established in 1906.
Company type: Public company
Company ticker symbol and exchange: SFG/NYSE
Business activities: Operates holding company; sells insurance.
Business type (SIC): Insurance/accident and health; insurance carriers; holding company
Financial profile for 2012: Number of employees, 2,875; assets, $19,791,300,000; sales volume, $2,898,400,000; pre-tax net income, $183,400,000; expenses, $2,715,000,000; liabilities, $17,622,300,000
Fortune 1000 ranking: 2012—730th in revenues, 672nd in profits, and 244th in assets
Corporate officers: J. Greg Ness, Chair., Pres., and C.E.O.; Floyd F. Chadee, Sr. V.P. and C.F.O.; Holley Y. Franklin, V.P. and Corp. Secy.; Robert M. Erickson, V.P. and Cont.
Board of directors: J. Greg Ness, Chair.; Virginia L. Anderson; Frederick W. Buckman; Stanley R. Fallis; Duane C. McDougall; Eric E. Parsons; George J. Puentes; Mary F. Sammons; E. Kay Stepp; Michael G. Thorne
Subsidiaries: StanCorp Mortgage Investors, LLC, Portland, OR; Standard Insurance Company, Portland, OR
Giving statement: Giving through the Standard Corporate Giving Program and the Standard Charitable Foundation.
Company EIN: 931253576

The Standard Corporate Giving Program
c/o Public Affairs P12B
1100 S.W. 6th Ave.
Portland, OR 97204 (503) 321-7000
FAX: (503) 321-7935;
E-mail: PublicAffairs@standard.com; Public Affairs tel.: (971) 321-3162, fax.: (971) 321-5243;
URL: http://www.standard.com/community

Financial data (yr. ended 12/31/10): Total giving, $1,720,000, including $1,720,000 for grants.
Purpose and activities: As a complement to its foundation, The Standard makes charitable contributions to nonprofit organizations involved with education, disability and empowerment, cultural development, and healthy communities. Support is given primarily in areas of company operations in Cincinnati, Ohio and Portland, Oregon.
Fields of interest: Arts education; Arts; Education, early childhood education; Secondary school/education; Education; Environment; Medical care, rehabilitation; Employment; Food services; Children, services; Family services; Self-advocacy services, disability; Independent living, disability; Community/economic development Economically disadvantaged.
Programs:
Day of Caring: The Standard regularly offers volunteer opportunities for employees and their families. This includes activities that range from a two- to eight-hour commitment and are scheduled during work hours as well as weekends to accommodate schedules and family activities. All regular full- and part-time employees are eligible to receive up to 8 hours of company-paid time annually to volunteer in their communities.
Dollars for Doers: The Standard supports employees who volunteer their time to community nonprofits by offering corporate contributions to the organizations where employees volunteer. Through the annual Dollars for Doers program, employees who volunteer at least 20 hours a year at an eligible nonprofit can apply for a corporate contribution.
Employee Giving Campaign and Corporate Matching Gift Program: The annual Employee Giving Campaign gives employees and retirees the chance to donate to the eligible 501(c)(3) nonprofit organization or educational institution of their choice and have their donation matched dollar-for-dollar up to $10,000 per employee by The Standard. The program is available to all regular, part-time, and full-time employees and retirees.
Jeans Day Program: The Jeans Day Program allows employees to donate $100 to a nonprofit partner - in exchange they can wear jeans every Friday. The Standard matches each donation dollar for dollar, and in 2011 this partnership raised more than $200,000 for food banks in the U.S.
Volunteer Expo: Each September, The Standard hosts Oregon's largest Volunteer Expo in Portland, OR and Cincinnati, OH, to help connect employees and members of the community with the local volunteer opportunities that match their interests and expertise. Representatives from local and national nonprofits share their mission and volunteer opportunities.
Type of support: Donated products; Employee matching gifts; Employee volunteer services; General/operating support; In-kind gifts; Loaned talent; Program development.
Geographic limitations: Giving primarily in areas of company operations, with emphasis on Cincinnati, OH and Portland, OR.
Support limitations: No support for veterans', labor, religious, athletic, or fraternal groups, discriminatory organizations, pass-through organizations or private foundations, bands or choirs, political candidates or organizations, programs or organizations solely benefitting individuals outside the U.S., or chambers of commerce, service clubs, taxpayer associations, or other similar bodies. No grants to individuals, or for travel, endowments, annual appeals, debt retirement, or operational deficits.
Publications: Application guidelines; Corporate giving report.
Application information: Applications accepted. The Public Affairs Department handles giving. Application form not required. Applicants should submit the following:
1) brief history of organization and description of its mission
2) detailed description of project and amount of funding requested

Proposals should include the date of the event or deadline for receipt of funds.
Initial approach: E-mail or mail proposal
Deadline(s): None
Final notification: 30 days
Number of staff: 1 full-time professional; 2 full-time support.

The Standard Charitable Foundation
1100 S.W. 6th Ave., P11B
Portland, OR 97204-1018 (971) 321-3162
FAX: (971) 321-5243; URL: http://www3.standard.com/

Establishment information: Established in 2005 in OR.
Donor: Stancorp Financial Group, Inc.
Contact: Bob Speltz, Dir., Public Affairs
Financial data (yr. ended 12/31/11): Assets, $2,236,449 (M); gifts received, $24,034; expenditures, $122,866; qualifying distributions, $122,866; giving activities include $106,500 for 6 grants (high: $25,000; low: $10,000).
Purpose and activities: The foundation supports organizations involved with education, health, community development, and the disabled. Special emphasis is directed toward helping individuals and families who have experienced a loss or setback such as a major disability or the loss of a loved one.
Fields of interest: Elementary/secondary education; Education, services; Education, reading; Health care; Employment, training; Employment; Children/youth, services; Human services, financial counseling; Independent living, disability; Human services; Community/economic development Blind/visually impaired; Deaf/hearing impaired; Economically disadvantaged.
Programs:
Community Development: The foundation supports programs designed to build healthy communities; address human services issues affecting children and families; serve disadvantaged populations; develop young people's abilities, knowledge and aptitude for successful futures; increase employment opportunities; strengthen job skills and the workforce; increase entrepreneur financial training and access to capital; and develop financial literacy.

Disability and Health: The foundation supports programs designed to help people with disabilities lead independent and fulfilling lives; promote health and wellness; and help people make informed decisions about their health.

Education Effectiveness: The foundation supports programs designed to strengthen education and develop systems to improve its overall effectiveness, with a focus on K-12 grade levels; promote access to schooling; help low-income and at-risk students succeed in school and prepare for post-secondary education; encourage literacy; promote diversity and inclusion; develop after-school initiatives; and improve education leadership skills and help students achieve high results.

Type of support: Continuing support; General/operating support; Program development.
Geographic limitations: Giving primarily in areas of company operations, with emphasis on OR; giving also to national organizations.
Support limitations: No support for political, labor, religious, athletic, or fraternal groups, discriminatory organizations, memberships in chambers of commerce, service clubs, taxpayer associations or other similar bodies, international organizations, pass-through organizations, private foundations, or bands or choirs. No grants to individuals, or for capital campaigns, advertising or sponsorship, fundraising events, endowments, annual appeals, debt reduction, travel, or general operating support to hospitals or healthcare institutions; no kind-gifts of equipment or property.
Publications: Application guidelines.
Application information: Applications accepted. Candidates will be notified within 30 days of receipt if eligible to formally apply for funding; if accepted, the foundation will provide an application and further instructions. Application form required. Applicants should submit the following:
1) results expected from proposed grant
2) brief history of organization and description of its mission
3) geographic area to be served
4) copy of current year's organizational budget and/or project budget
5) listing of additional sources and amount of support

Initial approach: Complete online letter of inquiry form
Deadline(s): May 1 and Oct.1

Officers and Directors:* J. Greg Ness*, Pres.; Justin R. Delaney*, Secy.; Floyd F. Chadee*, Treas.
EIN: 203997125

3575
Standard Motor Products, Inc.

37-18 Northern Blvd.
Long Island City, NY 11101-1616
(718) 392-0200
FAX: (718) 729-4549

Company URL: http://www.smpcorp.com
Establishment information: Established in 1919.
Company type: Public company
Company ticker symbol and exchange: SMP/NYSE
Business activities: Manufactures, distributes and markets replacement parts for motor vehicles.
Business type (SIC): Electrical equipment and supplies
Financial profile for 2012: Number of employees, 3,500; assets, $576,590,000; sales volume, $948,920,000; pre-tax net income, $67,950,000; expenses, $877,490,000; liabilities, $269,010,000
Corporate officers: Lawrence I. Sills, Chair. and C.E.O.; John P. Gethin, Pres. and C.O.O.; William J. Fazio, C.A.O.; Ray Nicholas, V.P and C.I.O.; James J. Burke, V.P., Finance and C.F.O.; Carmine J. Broccole, V.P., Genl. Counsel, and Secy.; Dale Burks, V.P., Sales and Mktg.; Thomas S. Tesoro, V.P., Human Resources; Robert H. Martin, Treas.
Board of directors: Lawrence I. Sills, Chair.; Pamela Forbes Lieberman; Joseph W. McDonnell; Alisa C. Norris; Arthur S. Sills; Peter J. Sills; Frederick D. Sturdivant; William H. Turner; Richard S. Ward; Roger M. Widmann
Giving statement: Giving through the Fife Family Foundation, Inc.
Company EIN: 111362020

Fife Family Foundation, Inc.

9705 Old Club Trace
Richmond, VA 23238-5733 (804) 740-8261

Establishment information: Established in 1993 in DE; funded in 1994.
Donors: Standard Motor Products, Inc.; Elias and Bertha Fife Foundation, Inc.
Contact: Arthur D. Davis
Financial data (yr. ended 12/31/11): Assets, $1,526,675 (M); expenditures, $96,127; qualifying distributions, $91,311; giving activities include $91,311 for grants.
Purpose and activities: The foundation supports organizations involved with arts and culture, education, conservation, health, human services, community development, and Judaism.
Fields of interest: Arts; Health care; Human services.
International interests: Africa.
Type of support: Annual campaigns; Capital campaigns; General/operating support; Program development.
Application information: Applications accepted. Application form required. Applicants should submit the following:
1) brief history of organization and description of its mission
2) detailed description of project and amount of funding requested

Initial approach: Letter
Deadline(s): None

Officer and Directors:* Arlene Fife*, Pres.; Marilyn Fife Cragin; Susan Fife Davis.
EIN: 113199710

3576
The Standard Register Company

600 Albany St.
Dayton, OH 45417 (937) 221-1000
FAX: (937) 221-1205

Company URL: http://www.standardregister.com
Establishment information: Established in 1912.
Company type: Public company
Company ticker symbol and exchange: SR/NYSE
Business activities: Designs, manufactures, and sells business forms.
Business type (SIC): Business forms/manifold
Financial profile for 2012: Number of employees, 2,200; assets, $259,900,000; sales volume, $601,990,000; pre-tax net income, -$8,540,000; expenses, $607,880,000; liabilities, $386,760,000
Corporate officers: F. David Clarke III, Chair.; Joseph P. Morgan, Jr., Pres. and C.E.O.; Joanne Cummins, C.I.O.; Robert M. Ginnan, V.P., Treas., and C.F.O.; Gerard D. Sowar, V.P., Genl. Counsel, and Secy.
Board of directors: F. David Clarke III, Chair.; David P. Bailis; Roy W. Begley, Jr.; Julie D. Klapstein; R. Eric McCarthey; Joseph P. Morgan, Jr.; John J. Schiff, Jr.; John Q. Sherman II
Subsidiary: SMARTworks.com, Inc., Dayton, OH
International operations: Canada; Mexico
Giving statement: Giving through the Standard Register Company Contributions Program and the Sherman-Standard Register Foundation.
Company EIN: 310455440

The Standard Register Company Contributions Program

c/o Community Contribs. Council
600 Albany St.
Dayton, OH 45417-3405
URL: http://www.standardregister.com/company/community.asp

Purpose and activities: As a complement to its foundation, Standard Register also makes charitable contributions to nonprofit organizations directly. Support is given primarily in Ohio.
Fields of interest: Health care; Children/youth, services; Human services Economically disadvantaged.
Type of support: Donated equipment; Employee volunteer services; General/operating support; Program development.
Geographic limitations: Giving primarily in OH, with emphasis on Dayton.
Application information: Applications accepted. A contributions committee reviews all requests. Application form not required.

Initial approach: Letter of inquiry to headquarters
Copies of proposal: 1
Committee meeting date(s): Monthly
Deadline(s): None

Sherman-Standard Register Foundation

626 Albany St.
Dayton, OH 45408-1405
URL: http://www.standardregister.com/company/community.asp

Establishment information: Incorporated in 1955 in OH.
Donor: The Standard Register Co.
Financial data (yr. ended 11/30/11): Assets, $858,421 (M); expenditures, $71,675; qualifying distributions, $65,094; giving activities include $65,094 for 12 grants (high: $15,000; low: $445).
Purpose and activities: The foundation supports programs designed to serve children, youth, and disadvantaged persons with education and social services.
Fields of interest: Education; Employment; Youth development.
Type of support: General/operating support.
Support limitations: No grants to individuals.
Application information: Applications not accepted. Unsolicited requests for funds not accepted.
Officers and Trustees:* John Q. Sherman II*, Pres.; Kathryn A. Lamme*, Secy.; Robert Ginnan*, Treas.; Roy W. Begley, Jr.; Craig J. Brown; David Clapper; Joe Morgan.
EIN: 316026027

3577
Standard Steel, LLC

(formerly Freedom Forge Corporation)
500 N. Walnut St.
Burnham, PA 17009 (717) 248-4911

Company URL: http://www.standardsteel.com/
Establishment information: Established in 1795.
Company type: Subsidiary of a private company
Business activities: Operates holding company; manufactures railroad wheels and axles, aerospace rings, power generation, mining, and construction equipment, and ingots and billets.
Business type (SIC): Metal forgings and stampings; steel mill products; holding company
Corporate officers: Daniel J. Condon, C.E.O.; Yukinori Akimoto, Pres. and C.O.O.; Alan M. Majewski, Exec. V.P. and C.F.O.; Dana L. Patterson, Sr. V.P. and Admin.; John M. Hilton, Sr. V.P., Sales and Opers.; Craig J. Kaniecki, V.P., Finance
Board of director: Daniel J. Condon
Subsidiaries: American Welding & Manufacturing Co., Warren, OH; Standard Steel, Burnham, PA
Giving statement: Giving through the Freedom Forge Corporation Foundation.

Freedom Forge Corporation Foundation

(formerly American Welding & Manufacturing Company Foundation)
c/o Kish Bank Asset Mgmt.
25 Gateway Dr.
Reedsville, PA 17084-9642

Establishment information: Established about 1956 in OH.
Donor: Freedom Forge Corp.
Financial data (yr. ended 12/31/11): Assets, $1,005,475 (M); expenditures, $99,565; qualifying distributions, $90,191; giving activities include $90,191 for grants.
Purpose and activities: The foundation supports organizations involved with arts and culture, K-12 education, eye diseases, and youth development and awards college scholarships to individuals.
Type of support: Capital campaigns; General/operating support; Scholarships—to individuals.
Application information: Applications accepted. Application form required.
Initial approach: Letter
Deadline(s): None
Trustee: Kish Bank Asset Mgmt.
EIN: 346516721

3578
Stanek Tool Corporation

2500 S. Calhoun Rd.
New Berlin, WI 53151 (262) 786-0120

Company URL: http://www.stanektool.com/
Establishment information: Established in 1924.
Company type: Private company
Business activities: Inspects, gauges, and checks jigs; produces industrial molds and dies; forms plastics.
Business type (SIC): Machinery/metalworking
Corporate officers: Mary Wehrheim, Pres.; Rosemary Bartkowiak, Secy.-Treas.
Giving statement: Giving through the Stanek Foundation, Inc.

Stanek Foundation, Inc.

2500 S. Calhoun Rd.
New Berlin, WI 53151-2712

Donor: Stanek Tool Corp.
Contact: Mary Wehrheim, Pres.
Financial data (yr. ended 06/30/12): Assets, $26,753 (M); gifts received, $10,000; expenditures, $7,225; qualifying distributions, $7,225; giving activities include $7,225 for 20 grants (high: $1,000; low: $50).
Purpose and activities: The foundation supports organizations involved with education, human services, the metalwork industry, and Catholicism.
Fields of interest: Secondary school/education; Higher education; Education; American Red Cross; Homeless, human services; Human services; Business/industry; Catholic agencies & churches.
Type of support: General/operating support; Scholarship funds.
Geographic limitations: Giving primarily in WI.
Support limitations: No grants to individuals.
Application information: Applications accepted. Application form required. Applicants should submit the following:
1) copy of IRS Determination Letter
2) brief history of organization and description of its mission
Initial approach: Letter
Deadline(s): None
Officers: Mary S. Wehrheim, Pres.; Larry Wehrheim, V.P.; Rosemary Bartkowiak, Secy.-Treas.
EIN: 396077475

3579
Stanley Black & Decker, Inc.

(formerly The Black & Decker Corporation)
1000 Stanley Dr.
New Britain, CT 06053 (860) 225-5111
FAX: (860) 827-3895

Company URL: http://www.stanleyblackanddecker.com
Establishment information: Established in 1843.
Company type: Public company
Company ticker symbol and exchange: SWK/NYSE
International Securities Identification Number: US8545021011
Business activities: Manufactures and markets power tools and accessories, hardware and home improvement products, and technology-based fastening systems.
Business type (SIC): Cutlery, hand and edge tools, and hardware; machinery/metalworking
Financial profile for 2012: Number of employees, 45,327; assets, $15,844,000,000; sales volume, $10,190,500,000; pre-tax net income, $527,600,000; expenses, $9,662,900,000; liabilities, $9,176,900,000
Fortune 1000 ranking: 2012—245th in revenues, 220th in profits, and 287th in assets
Forbes 2000 ranking: 2012—920th in sales, 651st in profits, and 1139th in assets
Corporate officers: John F. Lundgren, Chair. and C.E.O.; James M. Loree, Pres. and C.O.O.; Rhonda Gass, V.P. and C.I.O.; Donald Allan, Jr., Sr. V.P. and C.F.O.; Bruce H. Beatt, Sr. V.P., Genl. Counsel, and Secy.; Joe Voelker, Sr. V.P., Human Resources; Craig A. Douglas, V.P. and Treas.
Board of directors: John F. Lundgren, Chair.; Nolan D. Archibald; John G. Breen; George W. Buckley, Ph.D.; Patrick D. Campbell; Carlos M. Cardoso; Virgis W. Colbert; Robert B. Coutts; Benjamin H. Griswold IV; Eileen S. Kraus; Anthony Luiso; Marianne Miller Parrs; Robert L. Ryan
Subsidiaries: DeWalt Industrial Tool Co., Baltimore, MD; Emhart Corporation, Hartford, CT
International operations: Argentina; Australia; Austria; Belgium; Brazil; Canada; Cayman Islands; Chile; China; Colombia; Costa Rica; Czech Republic; Denmark; Ecuador; Finland; France; Germany; Greece; Hong Kong; Hungary; India; Ireland; Italy; Japan; Liechtenstein; Luxembourg; Macau; Malaysia; Mexico; Netherlands; New Zealand; Norway; Panama; Peru; Poland; Singapore; Slovakia; South Korea; Spain; Sweden; Switzerland; Taiwan; Thailand; United Kingdom; Venezuela
Giving statement: Giving through the Stanley Black & Decker, Inc. Corporate Giving Program.
Company EIN: 060548860

Stanley Black & Decker, Inc. Corporate Giving Program

(formerly The Black & Decker Corporation Contributions Program)
1000 Stanley Dr.
New Britain, CT 06053
E-mail: corporatecontributions@stanleyworks.com;
URL: http://www.stanleyblackanddecker.com/company/citizenship

Contact: Natalie A. Shields, V.P. and Corp. Secy.
Purpose and activities: Stanley Black & Decker makes charitable contributions to nonprofit organizations involved with affordable housing construction, reconstruction, and rehabilitation; technical, vocational, mathematics, science, and engineering education; and hospitals and select healthcare-related charities. Support is given primarily in areas of company operations; giving also to national and international organizations.
Fields of interest: Vocational education; Engineering school/education; Hospitals (general); Health care; Housing/shelter, rehabilitation; Housing/shelter; Mathematics; Engineering/technology; Science.
Programs:
Community Revitalization: Black & Decker supports programs designed to promote affordable housing, housing rehabilitation, and ongoing housing renovation. Special emphasis is directed toward programs designed to support home ownership; involve the active participation of neighborhood residents and Black & Decker volunteers; and provide the opportunity for residents to learn home improvement skills.
Education: Black & Decker supports programs designed to promote education and vocational skills important to the company's recruiting and training efforts. Special emphasis is directed toward programs designed to promote engineering study at colleges and universities; school-based math, science and technology that prepare students for a college education; and vocational and skills training for construction and related trades.
Type of support: Employee matching gifts; General/operating support.
Geographic limitations: Giving primarily in areas of company operations.
Support limitations: No grants to individuals.
Publications: Application guidelines.
Application information: Applications accepted. Application form required.
Initial approach: Proposal to headquarters
Deadline(s): None

3580
Stanley Consultants, Inc.

(formerly Stanley Engineering Company, Inc.)
225 Iowa Ave., Stanley Bldg.
Muscatine, IA 52761-3764 (563) 264-6600

Company URL: http://www.stanleyconsultants.com
Establishment information: Established in 1913.
Company type: Subsidiary of a private company
Business activities: Provides engineering, architectural, planning, and management consulting services.
Business type (SIC): Engineering, architectural, and surveying services; management and public relations services
Corporate officers: Gregs G. Thomopulos, Chair. and C.E.O.; Gayle A. Roberts, Pres. and C.O.O.
Board of director: Gregs G. Thomopulos, Chair.
Giving statement: Giving through the Stanley Consultants Charitable Foundation.

Stanley Consultants Charitable Foundation

(formerly Stanley Group Charitable Foundation)
225 Iowa Ave.
Muscatine, IA 52761-3764 (563) 264-6600

Establishment information: Established in 1983 in IA.
Donor: Stanley Consultants, Inc.
Contact: Nancy D. Elliott, Secy.
Financial data (yr. ended 03/31/12): Assets, $348,240 (M); gifts received, $52,000; expenditures, $168,078; qualifying distributions, $168,078; giving activities include $167,917 for 25 grants (high: $50,000; low: $500).
Purpose and activities: The foundation supports organizations involved with education and community development.
Fields of interest: Education; Community/economic development; United Ways and Federated Giving Programs.
Type of support: Annual campaigns; Building/renovation; Capital campaigns; Employee-related scholarships.
Geographic limitations: Giving primarily in areas of company operations, with emphasis on Muscatine, IA.
Support limitations: No grants to individuals (except for employee-related scholarships).
Application information: Applications accepted. Application form not required.
Initial approach: Proposal
Copies of proposal: 1
Board meeting date(s): May
Deadline(s): None
Final notification: Within 2 months
Officers and Directors:* Gregs G. Thomopulos*, Chair.; Gayle A. Roberts*, Pres.; Nancy D. Elliott, Secy.; Richard C. Smith, Treas.
EIN: 421186325

3581
Staples, Inc.

500 Staples Dr.
Framingham, MA 01702 (508) 253-5000

Company URL: http://www.staples.com
Establishment information: Established in 1986.
Company type: Public company
Company ticker symbol and exchange: SPLS/NASDAQ
International Securities Identification Number: US8550301027
Business activities: Operates office products stores; provides catalog shopping services; provides Internet shopping services; provides contract stationer services.
Business type (SIC): Shopping goods stores/miscellaneous; nonstore retailers; mailing, reproduction, commercial art, photography, and stenographic service
Financial profile for 2013: Number of employees, 85,087; assets, $12,280,000,000; sales volume, $24,380,510,000; pre-tax net income, $265,420,000; expenses, $23,927,400,000; liabilities, $6,151,850,000
Fortune 1000 ranking: 2012—122nd in revenues, 941st in profits, and 342nd in assets
Forbes 2000 ranking: 2012—387th in sales, 1871st in profits, and 1322nd in assets
Corporate officers: Ronald L. Sargent, Chair. and C.E.O.; Christine T. Komola, C.F.O.; Cynthia Pevehouse, Sr. V.P. and Genl. Counsel; Stephen Bacica, Corp. Cont.
Board of directors: Ronald L. Sargent, Chair.; Basil L. Anderson; Arthur M. Blank; Drew G. Faust; Justin M. King; Carol M. Meyrowitz; Rowland T. Moriarty; Robert C. Nakasone; Elizabeth A. Smith; Robert Sulentic; Vijay Vishwanath; Paul F. Walsh
Subsidiaries: Medical Arts Press, Philadelphia, PA; Quill, Lincolnshire, IL; SchoolKidz, Woodridge, IL; Smilemakers, Spartanburg, SC
Divisions: Staples Industrial, Framingham, MA; Staples Network Services, Framingham, MA; Staples Promotional Products, Framingham, MA
International operations: Australia; Austria; Belgium; Brazil; Canada; Cayman Islands; China; Denmark; Finland; France; Germany; Greece; Hong Kong; Hungary; India; Ireland; Italy; Luxembourg; Netherlands; New Zealand; Norway; Portugal; Spain; Sweden; Switzerland; United Kingdom
Historic mergers: American Identity Inc. (May 22, 2007)
Giving statement: Giving through the Staples Soul and the Staples Foundation, Inc.
Company EIN: 042896127

Staples Soul

(formerly Staples, Inc. Corporate Giving Program)
500 Staples Dr.
Framingham, MA 01702-4478
E-mail: staplessoul@staples.com; URL: http://www.staples.com/sbd/cre/marketing/staples_soul/index.html

Financial data (yr. ended 12/31/11): Total giving, $18,685,836, including $18,685,836 for grants.
Purpose and activities: As a complement to its foundation, Staples also makes charitable contributions to nonprofit organizations directly. Support is given on a national and international basis in areas of company operations, with some emphasis on Boston, Massachusetts.
Fields of interest: Youth development; Youth, services.
Type of support: Continuing support; Donated products; Employee volunteer services; General/operating support; In-kind gifts; Program development.
Geographic limitations: Giving on a national and international basis in areas of company operations, with some emphasis on Boston, MA.
Support limitations: No grants to individuals.
Application information: Applications accepted.
Initial approach: Contact general manager at nearest company store for application information

Staples Foundation, Inc.

(formerly Staples Foundation for Learning, Inc.)
500 Staples Dr., 4 W.
Framingham, MA 01702-4478 (508) 253-5000
FAX: (508) 253-9600;
E-mail: foundationinfo@staples.com; URL: http://www.staplesfoundation.org/

Establishment information: Established in 2002 in MA.
Donor: Staples, Inc.
Contact: Joy Errico, Dir., Community Rels.
Financial data (yr. ended 01/31/12): Assets, $32,367 (M); gifts received, $3,314,164; expenditures, $3,315,816; qualifying distributions, $3,314,164; giving activities include $3,314,164 for 161 grants (high: $1,000,000; low: $1,000).
Purpose and activities: The foundation supports programs designed to provide education and job skills. Special emphasis is directed toward programs designed to support disadvantaged youth.
Fields of interest: Vocational education; Education, reading; Education; Employment, training; Boys & girls clubs Youth; Economically disadvantaged.
Type of support: Curriculum development; Program development.
Geographic limitations: Giving primarily in CA, CO, GA, MA, NJ, and VA.
Support limitations: No support for public schools without 501(c)(3) status, athletic teams, fiscal sponsors, government agencies, substance abuse agencies, discriminatory organizations, international organizations, political organizations, religious organizations not of direct benefit to the entire community, fraternal or veterans' organizations, professional associations, or similar membership groups. No grants to individuals, or for capital campaigns, athletic events, educational loans, travel, conferences or conventions, books, research papers, or articles in professional journals, medical research, or public or commercial broadcasting.
Publications: Annual report; Corporate giving report; Grants list.
Application information: Applications not accepted. Unsolicited requests for funding are not accepted.
Board meeting date(s): June, Sept., and Jan.
Officers and Directors: Mike Miles, Pres.; Steve Fund, Exec. V.P.; Stephanie Shores Lambert, Clerk; Laura Granahan, Treas.; Steve Bussberg; Jay Mutschler; Paul Mullen; Regis Mulot; Mary Sagat; Amy Shanler; Melissa Shore; Mary Tivnan; Denise Zielecki.
Number of staff: 2
EIN: 470867951

3582
Star Holdings, Inc.

(formerly Star Technologies, Inc.)
216 Brookhollow Industrial Blvd. S.E.
Dalton, GA 30721-9001 (706) 428-9825

Establishment information: Established in 1993.
Company type: Private company
Business activities: Operates computer services company.
Business type (SIC): Computer services
Corporate officers: Charles Cofield, C.E.O.; Thomas Crumley, Pres.; Kevin Harris, C.F.O.; Margaret Smith, Secy.-Treas.
Giving statement: Giving through the Abbotsford Wildlife Foundation, Inc.

Abbotsford Wildlife Foundation, Inc.

P.O. Box 3726
Dalton, GA 30721-0726

Establishment information: Established in GA.
Donors: Bernita P. Cofield; Charles D. Cofield; Star Technologies, Inc.; Star Holdings, Inc.; Arrowstarr, LLC.
Financial data (yr. ended 09/30/11): Assets, $12,470 (M); gifts received, $53,437; expenditures, $55,172; qualifying distributions, $0 and $55,170 for 1 foundation-administered program.
Purpose and activities: The foundation operates a wildlife sanctuary.
Fields of interest: Animals/wildlife, sanctuaries.
Support limitations: No grants to individuals.
Application information: Applications not accepted. Unsolicited requests for funds not accepted.
Officers: Charles D. Cofield, Pres.; Bernita P. Cofield, Secy.-Treas.
EIN: 581739697

3583
Star Industries, Inc.

(formerly Star Liquor, Inc.)
425 Underhill Blvd., Unit 4
Syosset, NY 11791-3413 (516) 921-9300

Company URL: http://www.star-indust.com
Establishment information: Established in 1934.
Company type: Private company
Business activities: Produces and distributes distilled spirits.
Business type (SIC): Beverages; beer, wine, and distilled beverages—wholesale
Corporate officers: Martin S. Silver, Pres. and C.E.O.; Felix Galvez, Mgr.
Giving statement: Giving through the Star Welfare Foundation, Inc.

Star Welfare Foundation, Inc.

c/o Marks, Paneth & Shron, LLP
622 3rd Ave.
New York, NY 10017-6707 (516) 921-9300
Application address: 425 Underhill Blvd., Syosset, NY 11791.

Establishment information: Established in 1944 in NY.
Donors: Star Industries, Inc.; Star Liquor Imports, Inc.
Contact: Martin S. Silver, Pres.
Financial data (yr. ended 12/31/11): Assets, $93,167 (M); gifts received, $10,000; expenditures, $6,681; qualifying distributions, $6,625; giving activities include $6,625 for 15 grants (high: $1,000; low: $25).
Purpose and activities: The foundation supports organizations involved with substance abuse services, cancer, autism, human services, and military and veterans.
Fields of interest: Substance abuse, services; Cancer; Autism; Human services; Military/veterans' organizations.
Type of support: General/operating support.
Geographic limitations: Giving primarily in NY.
Application information: Applications accepted. Application form required. Applicants should submit the following:
1) detailed description of project and amount of funding requested
Initial approach: Letter
Deadline(s): None
Officer: Martin S. Silver, Pres.
EIN: 136110450

3584
Star Lumber & Supply Company, Inc.

325 S. West St.
Wichita, KS 67213-2105 (316) 942-2221

Company URL: http://www.starlumber.com
Establishment information: Established in 1939.
Company type: Private company
Business activities: Operates lumber and building materials stores; operates floor covering stores.
Business type (SIC): Lumber and other building materials—retail; furniture and home furnishing stores
Corporate officers: Christopher J. Goebel, Chair. and C.E.O.; Patrick M. Goebel, Pres. and C.O.O.; Steven Briggs, C.F.O.; Todd Lehman, C.I.O.; Tony Goebel, V.P., Opers.
Board of directors: Christopher J. Goebel, Chair.; Patrick M. Goebel
Giving statement: Giving through the Goebel Family Star Lumber Charitable Foundation.

Goebel Family Star Lumber Charitable Foundation

(formerly Star Lumber & Supply Charitable Foundation)
P.O. Box 7712
Wichita, KS 67277-7712 (316) 942-2221
FAX: (316) 942-0690; Application address: 325 S. West St., Wichita, KS 67213; URL: http://www.starlumber.com/starlumbercharitabletrust.html

Establishment information: Established in 1989 in KS.
Donor: Star Lumber & Supply Co., Inc.
Contact: Robert L. Goebel, Pres.
Financial data (yr. ended 12/31/11): Assets, $905,584 (M); gifts received, $13,500; expenditures, $307,353; qualifying distributions, $305,185; giving activities include $305,185 for grants.
Purpose and activities: The foundation supports medical centers and organizations involved with arts and culture, education, animal welfare, human services, and Catholicism.
Fields of interest: Performing arts, theater; Arts; Higher education; Education; Animal welfare; Health care, clinics/centers; Boy scouts; Children/youth, services; Developmentally disabled, centers & services; Human services; United Ways and Federated Giving Programs; Catholic agencies & churches.
Type of support: Annual campaigns; Building/renovation; Continuing support; Scholarship funds.
Geographic limitations: Giving limited to central KS.
Support limitations: No grants to individuals.
Publications: Grants list.
Application information: Applications accepted. Application form required. Applicants should submit the following:
1) name, address and phone number of organization
2) copy of IRS Determination Letter
3) detailed description of project and amount of funding requested
Initial approach: Complete online application form
Board meeting date(s): Jan., Mar., May, July, Sept., and Nov.
Deadline(s): None
Officers and Trustees: Robert L. Goebel, Pres.; Connie M. Armstrong, Secy.; Jennifer L. Stephens, Treas.; Jess Brearton; Victoria Callen; Kathy Goebel; Patrick M. Goebel; Jacqueline A. Jolly; Jeanette Jones; David McDaneld; Brian Schawe; Allen Spurgeon; Rebecca Stuhlsatz; Jerry Warren.
EIN: 481065296
Selected grants: The following grants are a representative sample of this grantmaker's funding activity:
$60,000 to Rainbows United, Wichita, KS, 2011. For annual fund drive.
$20,000 to United Methodist Open Door, Wichita, KS, 2011. For annual pledge.
$12,500 to Boy Scouts of America, Wichita, KS, 2011. For annual fund drive.
$12,000 to Music Theater of Wichita, Wichita, KS, 2011. For annual fund drive.
$10,000 to Junior League of Wichita, Wichita, KS, 2011. For annual fund drive.
$10,000 to United Way of the Plains, Wichita, KS, 2011. For annual pledge.
$9,274 to Wichita State University, Wichita, KS, 2011. For annual fund drive.
$5,000 to ARC of Sedgwick County, Wichita, KS, 2011. For annual fund drive.
$5,000 to Four-H Foundation, Kansas, Manhattan, KS, 2011. For annual fund drive.
$5,000 to Wichita Symphony Society, Wichita, KS, 2011. For annual fund drive.

3585
Starbucks Corporation

P.O. Box 3717
Seattle, WA 98124-3717 (206) 447-1575
FAX: (206) 318-3432

Company URL: http://www.starbucks.com
Establishment information: Established in 1985.
Company type: Public company
Company ticker symbol and exchange: SBUX/NASDAQ
International Securities Identification Number: US8552441094
Business activities: Operates coffee shops; produces coffee and tea products; produces and sells bottled coffee drinks and ice creams.
Business type (SIC): Restaurants and drinking places; dairy products; beverages; miscellaneous prepared foods
Financial profile for 2012: Number of employees, 160,000; assets, $8,219,200,000; sales volume, $13,299,500,000; pre-tax net income, $2,059,100,000; expenses, $11,302,100,000; liabilities, $3,110,200,000
Fortune 1000 ranking: 2012—208th in revenues, 148th in profits, and 447th in assets
Forbes 2000 ranking: 2012—703rd in sales, 425th in profits, and 1580th in assets
Corporate officers: Howard Schultz, Chair., Pres., and C.E.O.; Troy Alstead, C.F.O. and C.A.O.; Curt Garner, C.I.O.; Lucy Lee Helm, Exec. V.P., Genl. Counsel, and Secy.; Vivek Varma, Exec. V.P., Public Affairs; Marissa Andrada, Sr. V.P., Human Resources
Board of directors: Howard Schultz, Chair.; William W. Bradley; Robert Gates; Mellody Hobson; Kevin Johnson; Olden Lee; Joshua Cooper Ramo; James G. Shennan, Jr.; Clara Shih; Javier G. Teruel; Myron E. Ullman III; Craig E. Weatherup
Plants: Carson Valley, NV; York, PA; Gaston, SC; Kent, WA
International operations: Australia; Brazil; Canada; China; Germany; Japan; Netherlands; Singapore; Switzerland; Thailand; United Kingdom

Giving statement: Giving through the Starbucks Corporation Contributions Program, the Tazo Corporate Giving Program, and the Starbucks Foundation.
Company EIN: 911325671

Starbucks Corporation Contributions Program

c/o Sponsorships and Donations
2401 Utah Ave. S.
Seattle, WA 98134-1436
FAX: (206) 447-3029; URL: http://www.starbucks.com/aboutus/csr.asp

Purpose and activities: Starbucks makes charitable contributions to nonprofit organizations involved with arts and culture, education, and the environment. Support is given primarily in areas of company operations.
Fields of interest: Arts; Education, reading; Education; Children/youth, services.
Programs:
Choose to Give (Matching Gifts): The company matches contributions to charitable organizations made by employees of Starbucks up to $1,000 per year.
Make Your Mark: The company donates $10 for every hour volunteered by Starbucks employees.
Type of support: Continuing support; Donated equipment; Donated products; Employee matching gifts; Employee volunteer services; General/operating support; In-kind gifts; Scholarship funds; Sponsorships.
Geographic limitations: Giving on a national and international basis in areas of company operations.
Support limitations: No support for religious or political organizations. No grants to individuals, or for capital campaigns, scholarships, or fellowships; no scrip donations.
Publications: Corporate giving report; Informational brochure.
Application information: Applications accepted. Applicants must complete an eligibility quiz. Unsolicited faxed or mailed donation or sponsorship requests will not be reviewed. The Corporate Social Responsibility Department handles giving. The company has a staff that only handles contributions.
Initial approach: Complete online application
Deadline(s): 12 weeks in advance of event date for sponsorships
Administrators: Cathie Bachy, Mgr.; Anna Cunningham, Prog. Mgr., Partners Progs.; Joelle Jackie, Project Specialist; Jackie Liau, Int'l. CSR, Giving; Lauren Moore, Dir., Giving.
Number of staff: 5 full-time professional; 1 part-time professional; 1 full-time support.

Tazo Corporate Giving Program

c/o Donations
P.O. Box 66
Portland, OR 97207-0066
URL: http://www.tazo.com/tazo.asp?init=

Purpose and activities: Tazo makes charitable contributions to nonprofit organizations involved with arts and culture, education, the environment, HIV/AIDS, diversity, and children. Support is given on a national and international basis, with emphasis on Portland, Oregon, and India.
Fields of interest: Literature; Arts; Education; Environment; AIDS; Children, services; Civil/human rights, equal rights.
International interests: India.
Type of support: Donated products; General/operating support.
Geographic limitations: Giving on a national and international basis, with emphasis on Portland, OR, and India.
Application information: Applications accepted. Unsolicited requests for monetary contributions are not accepted. Application form required. Applicants should submit the following:
1) population served
2) brief history of organization and description of its mission
3) contact person
Applications should include the organization's Tax ID Number; and the name, location, type, and expected attendance of the event, if applicable.
Initial approach: Download application form and mail to headquarters
Deadline(s): 1 month prior to need

The Starbucks Foundation

c/o Starbucks Corp.
2401 Utah Ave. S.
Seattle, WA 98134-1436
E-mail: foundationgrants@starbucks.com;
URL: http://www.starbucks.com/responsibility/community

Establishment information: Established in 1997 in WA.
Donors: Starbucks Corp.; Starbucks Coffee Co.; Pepsico; Schultz Family Foundation.
Financial data (yr. ended 09/30/11): Assets, $32,316,667 (M); gifts received, $26,883,842; expenditures, $6,223,548; qualifying distributions, $6,216,589; giving activities include $6,177,709 for grants.
Purpose and activities: The foundation supports programs designed to support young people creating change in local communities; water projects through the Ethos Water Fund; and social investments in countries where Starbuck buys coffee, tea, and cocoa.
Fields of interest: Education; Environment, water resources; Public health, clean water supply; Public health, sanitation; Health care; Agriculture; Nutrition; Disasters, preparedness/services; Youth development; International economic development; Social entrepreneurship; Microfinance/microlending; Community/economic development Children/youth.
International interests: Africa; Asia; Canada; China; Europe; Latin America; Middle East; United Kingdom.
Programs:
Community Service Program: Through the Community Service Program, the foundation encourages community partners (employees) and customers to lead community service projects in local communities. Projects range from mentoring students at an after-school program, improving hiking trails, to planning a fundraising event with a qualified organization. Partner-led group projects with at least five members that contribute at least 40 hours of volunteer service are eligible for a Starbucks Community Service Grant of up to $2,500. Funds are directed to the nonprofit organization that benefits from the volunteer service. Visit URL http://community.starbucks.com/index.jspa for more information.
Ethos Water Fund: Through the Ethos Water Fund, the foundation helps children get clean water and raise awareness about the World Water Crisis. For each bottle of Ethos water sold, a contribution of $0.05 US and $0.10 in Canada is directed toward the fund to help finance sustainable water programs.
Partner Match: The foundation matches contributions made by Starbucks partners to nonprofit organizations on a one-for one basis from $20 to $1,000 per employee, per year.
Social Investments in Coffee, Tea, and Cocoa Communities: The foundation, in partnership with nonprofit organizations, supports projects designed to benefit coffee, tea, and cocoa communities. Projects include improving access to education and agricultural training, microfinance and microcredit services, improving biodiversity conservation, and increasing levels of health, nutrition, and water sanitation.
Youth Leadership Grants: The foundation supports programs designed to equip young people ages 15 to 24 to develop business savvy, including the ability to leverage opportunities and make good decisions and achieve results; social conscience, including the impact of an individual and enterprise on a community; and collaborative communication, including the engagement of others in an inclusive manner across teams, functions, and cultures and leveraging new and creative ways to communicate. Grants range from $10,000 to $30,000.
Type of support: Continuing support; Emergency funds; Employee matching gifts; Employee volunteer services; General/operating support; Program development.
Geographic limitations: Giving on a national and international basis in areas of company operations and in countries where the company buys coffee, tea, and cocoa.
Support limitations: No support for private foundations, political, labor, or fraternal organizations, religious organizations not of direct benefit to the entire community, hospitals or medical research institutions, universities or academic research institutions, individual schools or parent teacher associations, or sporting teams. No grants to individuals, or for neighborhood clean-ups or tree plantings, wildlife conservation projects, capital campaigns, capital expenditures or land acquisition, school bands or orchestras or non-literacy art programs, fundraising events, one-time events or programs, event sponsorships, trips or travel, league sports programs, scholarships or fellowships, expeditions, political campaigns, the production of marketing material promoting Starbucks, the production of products to sell in Starbucks stores, endowments, conferences or symposia, contests, festivals, or parades, advertising, tickets to events, or supply drives.
Publications: Application guidelines; Grants list.
Application information: A full proposal may be requested at a later date for Youth Leadership Grants. Priority funding is given to organizations that can demonstrate sustainability. Unsolicited requests are currently not accepted for the Ethos Water Fund and Social Investments in Coffee, Tea, & Cocoa Communities.
Initial approach: Complete online letter of inquiry for Youth Leadership Grants
Deadline(s): Nov. 1 to Dec. 15 for Youth Leadership Grants
Officers and Directors:* Orin Smith*, Pres.; Donna Brooks, Treas.; Rodney Hines, Exec. Dir.; Cliff Burrows; John Culver; Michelle Gass; Lucy Helm; Vivek Varma.
Number of staff: 3 part-time professional; 1 part-time support.
EIN: 911795425
Selected grants: The following grants are a representative sample of this grantmaker's funding activity:
$350,000 to Urban League of Los Angeles, Los Angeles, CA, 2011.
$25,000 to City Year San Jose/Silicon Valley, San Jose, CA, 2011.
$25,000 to City Year Seattle/King County, Seattle, WA, 2011.

$10,000 to Jumpstart for Young Children, Boston, MA, 2011.

3586
Stardust Companies
6730 N. Scottsdale Rd., Ste. 230
Scottsdale, AZ 85253-4416
(408) 607-5800
FAX: (408) 607-5801

Company URL: http://www.stardustco.com
Establishment information: Established in 1986.
Company type: Private company
Business activities: Operates real estate development firm.
Business type (SIC): Real estate subdividers and developers
Corporate officers: Gerald Bisgrove, Chair.; Chris B. Heeter, Pres.
Board of director: Gerald Bisgrove, Chair.
Giving statement: Giving through the Stardust Foundation, Inc.

Stardust Foundation, Inc.
6730 N. Scottsdale Rd., Ste. 230
Scottsdale, AZ 85253-4416 (480) 607-5800
E-mail: contact@stardustco.com; URL: http://www.stardustfoundation.org

Establishment information: Established in 1993 in AZ as successor to the Bisgrove Foundation.
Donors: Gerald Bisgrove; Debra Bisgrove†; Bisgrove Foundation.
Financial data (yr. ended 12/31/11): Assets, $24,774,378 (M); expenditures, $3,526,181; qualifying distributions, $3,470,880; giving activities include $3,453,300 for 29 grants (high: $1,557,500; low: $100).
Purpose and activities: The foundation supports food banks and community foundations and organizations involved with arts and culture, higher education, conservation, cancer, human services, and community development. Special emphasis is directed toward programs designed to link concepts of family and neighborhood stability.
Fields of interest: Museums; Museums (science/technology); Performing arts, orchestras; Arts; Higher education; Environment, natural resources; Botanical gardens; Cancer; Food banks; Children/youth, services; Family services; Homeless, human services; Human services; Community/economic development; Foundations (community); United Ways and Federated Giving Programs.
Type of support: Endowments; General/operating support; Scholarship funds.
Geographic limitations: Giving primarily in Phoenix and Scottsdale, AZ.
Application information: Applications not accepted. Contributes only to pre-selected organizations.
Officers: Gerald Bisgrove*, Pres.; Jon Munson, Secy.-Treas.
EIN: 860735230
Selected grants: The following grants are a representative sample of this grantmaker's funding activity:
$3,729,550 to United Way Foundation, Valley of the Sun, Phoenix, AZ, 2010. For community engagement.
$900,000 to Stardust Foundation of Central New York, Auburn, NY, 2010. For community engagement.
$260,000 to United Way, Valley of the Sun, FireStar Fund, Phoenix, AZ, 2010. For community engagement.
$25,000 to Arizona Planned Giving Institute, Phoenix, AZ, 2010. For community engagement.
$20,000 to Stardust Non-Profit Building Supplies, Mesa, AZ, 2010. For community engagement.
$10,000 to Trends Charitable Fund, Phoenix, AZ, 2010. For community engagement.

3587
Starkey Laboratories, Inc.
6700 Washington Ave., S.
Eden Prairie, MN 55344-3476
(952) 941-6401

Company URL: http://www.starkey.com
Establishment information: Established in 1967.
Company type: Private company
Business activities: Manufactures hearing instruments.
Business type (SIC): Laboratory apparatus
Financial profile for 2010: Number of employees, 1,700
Corporate officers: William F. Austin, C.E.O.; Jerry Ruzicka, Pres.; Scott Nelson, C.F.O.; Keith Guggenberger, Sr. V.P., Opers.; Brandon Sawalich, Sr. V.P., Sales and Mktg.; Larry Miller, Sr. V.P., Human Resources; Kenny Landherr, V.P., Admin; Chris McCormick, V.P., Mktg.; Susan Mussell, Genl. Counsel and Corp. Secy.
Giving statement: Giving through the Starkey Hearing Foundation.

Starkey Hearing Foundation
6700 Washington Ave. S.
Eden Prairie, MN 55344-3405 (866) 354-3254
FAX: (817) 442-8653;
E-mail: executive_director@sotheworldmayhear.org; Toll-free tel.: (800) 769-2799; Admin. Office address: 432 Ball St., Grapevine, TX 76051-5112; URL: http://www.sotheworldmayhear.org

Establishment information: Established in 1984 in MN.
Donor: Starkey Laboratories, Inc.
Contact: Debbie Wright, Exec. Dir.
Financial data (yr. ended 12/31/11): Revenue, $19,732,105; assets, $8,237,880 (M); gifts received, $19,106,950; expenditures, $22,649,072; giving activities include $3,077,378 for grants and $1,151,599 for grants to individuals.
Purpose and activities: The foundation works to promote hearing health awareness while also supporting and conducting research and education on hearing health care.
Fields of interest: Deaf/hearing impaired.
Type of support: Research.
Geographic limitations: Giving on a national and international basis.
Publications: Annual report; Newsletter.
Officers and Directors:* Michael Burton*, Pres.; Tani Austin*, Secy.-Treas.; Debbie Wright, Exec. Dir.; Justin Osmond; Rudy Unterthiner, M.D.
EIN: 363297852

3588
StarKist Co.
225 North Shore Dr., Ste. 400
Pittsburgh, PA 15212 (412) 323-7400

Company URL: http://www.starkist.com
Establishment information: Established in 1918.
Company type: Subsidiary of a foreign company
Business activities: Operates tuna products company.
Business type (SIC): Miscellaneous prepared foods
Corporate officers: Sam Hwi Lee, Pres.; Namjung Kim, C.O.O.
Giving statement: Giving through the StarKist Co. Contributions Program.

StarKist Co. Contributions Program
225 N. Shore Dr., Ste. 400
Pittsburgh, PA 15212 (412) 323-7400
URL: http://www.starkist.com/about-starkist/our-community

3589
Starwood Hotels & Resorts Worldwide, Inc.
1111 Westchester Ave., 3rd Fl.
White Plains, NY 10604 (914) 640-8100

Company URL: http://www.starwoodhotels.com
Establishment information: Established in 1980.
Company type: Public company
Company ticker symbol and exchange: HOT/NYSE
International Securities Identification Number: US85590A4013
Business activities: Operates hotels and resorts.
Business type (SIC): Hotels and motels
Financial profile for 2012: Number of employees, 171,000; assets, $8,861,000,000; sales volume, $6,321,000,000; pre-tax net income, $618,000,000; expenses, $5,537,000,000; liabilities, $5,724,000,000
Fortune 1000 ranking: 2012—400th in revenues, 308th in profits, and 431st in assets
Forbes 2000 ranking: 2012—1243rd in sales, 987th in profits, and 1551st in assets
Corporate officers: Bruce W. Duncan, Chair.; Vasant M. Prabhu, Vice-Chair. and C.F.O.; Frits D. Van Paasschen, Pres. and C.E.O.; Kenneth S. Siegel, Genl. Counsel and C.A.O.; Roger Berry, Sr. V.P. and C.I.O.; Christie Hicks, Sr. V.P. and Sales
Board of directors: Bruce W. Duncan, Chair.; Vasant M. Prabhu, Vice-Chair.; Adam Aron; Amb. Charlene Barshefsky; Thomas E. Clarke, Ph.D.; Clayton C. Daley, Jr.; Lizanne Galbreath; Eric Hippeau; Stephen R. Quazzo; Thomas O. Ryder; Frits Van Paasschen
Giving statement: Giving through the Starwood Hotels & Resorts Worldwide, Inc. Corporate Giving Program and the Starwood Hotels and Resorts Worldwide Foundation, Inc.
Company EIN: 521193298

Starwood Hotels & Resorts Worldwide, Inc. Corporate Giving Program
1111 Westchester Ave.
White Plains, NY 10604-3525 (914) 640-8100
FAX: (914) 640-8310;
E-mail: charitablegiving@starwoodhotels.com; URL: http://www.starwoodhotels.com/corporate/company_values_comm.html

Purpose and activities: As a complement to its foundation, Starwood Hotels & Resorts Worldwide also makes charitable contributions to nonprofit organizations directly. Support is given to national and international organizations.
Fields of interest: General charitable giving.
Type of support: Employee volunteer services; General/operating support; In-kind gifts; Program development; Sponsorships.

Geographic limitations: Giving to national and international organizations.
Publications: Application guidelines.
Application information: Applications accepted. Proposals should specifically note the nature of the request being made. No mailed or telephoned requests will be considered. Additional information may be requested at a later date. A contributions committee reviews all requests. Application form not required. Applicants should submit the following:
1) copy of IRS Determination Letter
2) brief history of organization and description of its mission
3) detailed description of project and amount of funding requested
4) contact person
Initial approach: E-mail letter of inquiry; Contact nearest Starwood Hotel for in-kind requests benefitting local organizations
Committee meeting date(s): Monthly
Deadline(s): None

Starwood Hotels and Resorts Worldwide Foundation, Inc.

(formerly The Sheraton Foundation, Inc.)
155 Federal St., Ste. 700
Boston, MA 02110 (877) 443-4585

Establishment information: Incorporated in 1950 in MA.
Donors: ITT Sheraton Corp.; The Sheraton Corp.; Starwood Hotels & Resorts Worldwide, Inc.
Contact: Jeffery S. Coopersmith
Financial data (yr. ended 12/31/11): Assets, $2,905,675 (M); gifts received, $5,000; expenditures, $435,112; qualifying distributions, $426,462; giving activities include $407,179 for grants.
Purpose and activities: The foundation supports hospitals and organizations involved with performing arts, education, substance abuse, cancer, disaster relief, human services, and volunteerism.
Fields of interest: Health organizations.
Type of support: General/operating support; Scholarship funds.
Geographic limitations: Giving primarily in the Boston, MA area, and in NY.
Support limitations: No grants to individuals, or for endowments, capital campaigns, or research; no matching gifts; no loans.
Application information: Applications accepted. Application form not required. Applicants should submit the following:
1) copy of IRS Determination Letter
2) descriptive literature about organization
Initial approach: Proposal
Deadline(s): None
Officers: Kenneth Siegel, Pres.; Sandy Swider, Clerk; Nicholas Daddario, Treas.
Director: Vansant M. Prabhu.
Number of staff: 2
EIN: 046039510

3590
State Automobile Mutual Insurance Company

(also known as State Auto Insurance Companies)
518 E. Broad St.
Columbus, OH 43215-3901
(614) 464-5000

Company URL: http://www.stateauto.com
Establishment information: Established in 1921.
Company type: Mutual company
Business activities: Sells property and casualty insurance.
Business type (SIC): Insurance/fire, marine, and casualty
Corporate officers: Robert P. Restrepo, Jr., Chair., Pres., and C.E.O.; Mark A. Blackburn, Exec. V.P. and C.O.O.; Steven E. English, V.P. and C.F.O.
Board of directors: Robert P. Restrepo, Jr., Chair.; Mark A. Blackburn
Subsidiary: State Auto Financial Corp., Columbus, OH
Historic mergers: Meridian Mutual Insurance Company (June 1, 2001)
Giving statement: Giving through the State Auto Foundation.

The State Auto Foundation

(formerly Paul R. Gingher State Auto Insurance Companies Foundation)
518 E. Broad St.
Columbus, OH 43215-3901

Establishment information: Established in 1989 in OH.
Donor: State Automobile Mutual Insurance Co.
Financial data (yr. ended 12/31/11): Assets, $1,580,397 (M); gifts received, $250,100; expenditures, $262,793; qualifying distributions, $258,850; giving activities include $258,850 for grants.
Purpose and activities: The foundation supports community foundations and organizations involved with arts and culture, education, human services, and insurance.
Fields of interest: Arts education; Museums; Museums (art); Performing arts, ballet; Arts; Higher education; Education; Youth development, business; Salvation Army; Children/youth, services; Residential/custodial care; Human services; Business/industry; Foundations (community); United Ways and Federated Giving Programs.
Type of support: General/operating support.
Geographic limitations: Giving primarily in Columbus, OH.
Support limitations: No grants to individuals.
Application information: Applications not accepted. Contributes only to pre-selected organizations.
Trustees: Winford L. Logan; Cynthia A. Powell; Robert P. Restrepo, Jr.; Lorranine M. Segworth.
EIN: 311257265
Selected grants: The following grants are a representative sample of this grantmaker's funding activity:
$4,000 to Childrens Museum of Indianapolis, Indianapolis, IN, 2010.

3591
State Farm Mutual Automobile Insurance Company

1 State Farm Plz.
Bloomington, IL 61710-0001
(309) 766-2311

Company URL: http://www.statefarm.com
Establishment information: Established in 1922.
Company type: Mutual company
Business activities: Sells automobile, health, life, casualty, and property insurance; operates savings bank; provides investment advisory services.
Business type (SIC): Insurance/fire, marine, and casualty; savings institutions; security and commodity services; insurance/life; insurance/accident and health
Financial profile for 2011: Number of employees, 65,935; assets, $192,794,000,000; sales volume, $63,176,700,000
Corporate officers: Edward B. Rust, Jr., Chair., Pres., and C.E.O.; Michael L. Tipsord, Co-Vice-Chair. and C.F.O.; James E. Rutrough, Co-Vice-Chair. and C.A.O.; Michael C. Davidson, Co-Vice-Chair.; Kim M. Brunner, Exec. V.P. and Secy; Paul J. Smith, Sr. V.P. and Treas.; Jeffrey W. Jackson, Sr. V.P. and Genl. Counsel
Board of directors: Edward B. Rust, Jr., Chair.; Michael C. Davidson, Co-Vice-Chair.; Michael L. Tipsord, Co-Vice-Chair.; James E. Rutrough, Co-Vice-Chair.; Dan E. Arvizu; Gerald M. Czarnecki; Michael C. Davidson; Christopher C. DeMuth; W.H. Knight, Jr.; Judith A. Muhlberg; Susan M. Phillips; Paul T. Stecko; Pamela B. Strobel; John D. Zeglis
Subsidiaries: State Farm County Mutual Insurance Co. of Texas, Dallas, TX; State Farm Fire and Casualty Co., Bloomington, IL; State Farm General Insurance Co., Bloomington, IL; State Farm Indemnity Co., Bloomington, IL; State Farm Life and Accident Assurance Co., Bloomington, IL; State Farm Life Insurance Co., Bloomington, IL
Offices: Birmingham, AL; Tempe, AZ; Bakersfield, Rohnert Park, CA; Greeley, CO; Jacksonville, Winter Haven, FL; Alpharetta, Duluth, GA; West Lafayette, IN; Monroe, LA; Frederick, MD; Marshall, Portage, MI; Woodbury, MN; Columbia, Hazelwood, St. Louis, MO; Lincoln, NE; Parsippany, Wayne, NJ; Ballston Spa, NY; Columbus, Newark, OH; Tulsa, OK; Salem, OR; Concordville, PA; Murfreesboro, TN; Austin, TX; Charlottesville, VA; DuPont, WA
International operations: Bermuda; Canada
Giving statement: Giving through the State Farm Mutual Automobile Insurance Company Contributions Program and the State Farm Companies Foundation.

State Farm Mutual Automobile Insurance Company Contributions Program

One State Farm Plaza
Bloomington, IL 61710-0001
Contact for Project Ignition: NYLC Project Ignition Dir., 1667 Snelling Ave. N., Ste. D300, Saint Paul, MN 55108, tel.: (888) 856-7026, fax: (651) 631-2955, e-mail: mvankeulen@nylc.org;
URL: http://www.statefarm.com/about/part_spos/community/community.asp

Purpose and activities: As a complement to its foundation, State Farm also makes charitable contributions to nonprofit organizations directly. Support is given on a national basis and in Canada in areas of company operations; and on a national basis to high schools for teen driver safety public awareness campaigns.
Fields of interest: Education, public education; Elementary/secondary education; Education; Housing/shelter, home owners; Housing/shelter; Disasters, preparedness/services; Safety, education; Safety, automotive safety; Community development, neighborhood development; Community/economic development; Financial services.
International interests: Canada.
Programs:
Community Development: State Farm supports programs designed to provide affordable quality housing; assist first-time homeowners; and promote sustainable communities.
Education: State Farm supports programs designed to improve teacher quality; integrate core classroom curriculum with service to the community; and incorporate system improvement programs at the K-12 level.

Project Ignition: Through the Project Ignition program, in partnership with the National Youth Leadership Council (NYLC), State Farm annually awards 25 $2,000 grants to high schools for students to create and produce public awareness, service-learning campaigns addressing the issue of teen driver safety. Up to ten finalist schools receive grants of up to $5,000 for travel to the NYLC's annual National Service-Learning Conference. One overall winning school receives a $10,000 grant.

Safety: State Farm supports programs designed to promote automobile, home, and personal financial safety; and provide disaster recovery services.

Type of support: Curriculum development; Employee volunteer services; In-kind gifts; Sponsorships.
Geographic limitations: Giving on a national basis and in Canada in areas of company operations; giving on a national basis for Project Ignition; giving also to national organizations.
Support limitations: No support for religious or political organizations. No grants to individuals, or for scholarships.
Publications: Application guidelines.
Application information: Applications accepted. Support is limited to one contribution per organization during any given year. Application form required. Applicants should submit the following:
1) results expected from proposed grant
2) statement of problem project will address
3) population served
4) name, address and phone number of organization
5) copy of IRS Determination Letter
6) how project's results will be evaluated or measured
7) detailed description of project and amount of funding requested
8) plans for cooperation with other organizations, if any
9) contact person
10) plans for acknowledgement
11) additional materials/documentation
Project Ignition proposals from high schools should include the number of students enrolled.
Initial approach: Complete online application form for Grants; complete online application form for Project Ignition
Copies of proposal: 1
Administrators: Mike Fernandez, V.P., Corp. Comms. and Ext. Rels.; Kristy Funk, Asst. Dir., Corp. Comms. and Ext. Rels.
Number of staff: 7 full-time professional; 3 full-time support.

State Farm Companies Foundation

1 State Farm Plz.
Bloomington, IL 61710-0001 (309) 766-2161
FAX: (309) 766-2314; Additional e-mail: home.sf-foundation.494b00@statefarm.com;
URL: http://www.statefarm.com/aboutus/community/grants/foundation/foundation.asp

Establishment information: Incorporated in 1963 in IL.
Donor: State Farm Mutual Automobile Insurance Co.
Contact: Karen Mayfield, Asst. Secy., Fdn Board of Mgrs.
Financial data (yr. ended 12/31/11): Assets, $7,890,769 (M); gifts received, $15,433,646; expenditures, $16,591,038; qualifying distributions, $16,393,065; giving activities include $13,082,228 for 802 grants (high: $3,000,000), $80,000 for 8 grants to individuals (high: $10,000; low: $10,000) and $3,230,837 for employee matching gifts.
Purpose and activities: The foundation supports key initiatives and scholarships, as well as associate-directed programs, including grants supporting volunteerism and matching gifts to two- and four-year colleges and universities.
Fields of interest: Higher education; Education, drop-out prevention; Education; Voluntarism promotion.
International interests: Canada.
Programs:
Good Neighbor Grant Program: Through foundation awards $500 grants on behalf of each eligible State Farm associate, agent, or retiree who volunteers a minimum of 40 hours a year to an eligible nonprofit organization.
Matching Gift Program: The Foundation Matching Gift Program encourages State Farm associates to support higher education. The foundation matches limited individual charitable contributions made by State Farm eligible employees, agents and retirees to eligible colleges and universities.
National Merit $2,500 Scholarship Program: The foundation awards $2,500 college scholarships to high school seniors who qualify as top finalists in the annual National Merit Scholarship Program. The program is administered by the National Merit Scholarship Corporation.
State Farm Companies Foundation Scholarship Program: The foundation annually awards 100 four-year college scholarships of $3,000 to $8,000 to academically talented dependents of employees, retirees, and agents of State Farm. The program is administered by the National Merit Scholarship Corporation.
State Farm Good Neighbor Scholarship Program: The foundation awards scholarships to 26 high school seniors who plan to attend college, technical, or vocational school, but do not qualify for other scholarships. The program is administered by Scholarship America. Visit URL http://www.26seconds.com/ for more information.
Type of support: Employee matching gifts; Employee volunteer services; Employee-related scholarships; General/operating support; Scholarship funds.
Geographic limitations: Giving on a national basis and in Canada.
Support limitations: No support for Houses of Worship or organizations established for religious, political, or special interest purposes, veterans', fraternal, or social organizations under Section 501 (c)(4), professional organizations under Section 501 (c)(6), discriminatory organizations, or nonprofit, tax-exempt organizations under Section 501(c)(3) of the U.S. Internal Revenue Code that are not private foundations because they are described in Code Section 509(a)(3) or 509(a)(4). No grants to individuals.
Application information: Applications accepted. Application form required.
Initial approach: Letter
Copies of proposal: 1
Deadline(s): None
Final notification: 60 days
Officers and Directors:* Edward B. Rust, Jr.*, Chair. and Pres.; Mary Crego, V.P. and Secy.; David Beigie, V.P., Progs.; Don Heltner, V.P., Fixed Income; Joseph P. Young, V.P., Fixed Income; Duane Farrington, V.P.; Michael L. Tipsord, V.P.; Paul J. Smith, Treas.; Brian V. Boyden; Kellie Clapper; W.H. Knight, Jr.; Karen Mayfield; Susan M. Phillips; Debra L. Wheeler; Ed Woods.
EIN: 366110423
Selected grants: The following grants are a representative sample of this grantmaker's funding activity:
$3,000,000 to Illinois Wesleyan University, Bloomington, IL, 2011.
$1,850,024 to National Merit Scholarship Corporation, Evanston, IL, 2011.
$1,000,000 to Americas Promise - The Alliance for Youth, Washington, DC, 2011.
$915,230 to Illinois State University Foundation, Normal, IL, 2011.
$465,000 to University of Illinois at Urbana-Champaign, Urbana, IL, 2011.
$395,422 to United Way of McLean County, Bloomington, IL, 2011.
$330,000 to National Board for Professional Teaching Standards, Arlington, VA, 2011.
$247,436 to United Way of McLean County, Bloomington, IL, 2011.
$203,911 to United Way of McLean County, Bloomington, IL, 2011.
$3,344 to United Way of the Columbia-Willamette, Portland, OR, 2011.

3592
State Street Corporation

(formerly State Street Boston Corporation)
1 Lincoln St.
Boston, MA 02111-2900 (617) 786-3000
FAX: (617) 654-3386

Company URL: http://www.statestreet.com
Establishment information: Established in 1792.
Company type: Public company
Company ticker symbol and exchange: STT/NYSE
International Securities Identification Number: US8574771031
Business activities: Operates financial holding company; operates commercial bank; provides investment advisory services.
Business type (SIC): Banks/commercial; security and commodity services; holding company
Financial profile for 2012: Number of employees, 29,660; assets, $222,582,000,000; pre-tax net income, $2,766,000,000; liabilities, $201,713,000,000
Fortune 1000 ranking: 2012—268th in revenues, 95th in profits, and 25th in assets
Forbes 2000 ranking: 2012—924th in sales, 278th in profits, and 124th in assets
Corporate officers: Joseph L. Hooley, Chair., Pres., and C.E.O.; Joseph C. Antonellis, Vice-Chair.; Edward J. Resch, Exec. V.P. and C.F.O.; James J. Malerba, Exec. V.P., C.A.O., and Cont.; Christopher (Chris) Perretta, Exec. V.P. and C.I.O.; Jeffrey N. Carp, Exec. V.P. and Secy.; David C. Phelan, Exec. V.P. and Genl. Counsel
Board of directors: Joseph L. Hooley, Chair.; Kennett F. Burnes; Peter Coym; Dame Amelia C. Fawcett; David P. Gruber; Linda A. Hill; Robert S. Kaplan; Patrick De Saint-Aignan; Richard P. Sergel; Ronald L. Skates; Gregory L. Summe; Robert E. Weissman; Thomas J. Wilson
Subsidiary: State Street Bank and Trust Company, Boston, MA
Offices: Alameda, Los Angeles, San Francisco, CA; Denver, CO; Greenwich, Hartford, Westport, CT; Clearwater, Jacksonville, Naples, FL; Atlanta, GA; Chicago, IL; Des Moines, IA; Portland, ME; Milton, Osterville, Westborough, Westwood, MA; Lansing, MI; Bloomington, MN; Kansas City, St. Louis, MO; Manchester, NH; Princeton, NJ; New York, Purchase, NY; Providence, RI; Arlington, VA
Joint Venture: Boston Financial Data Services, Quincy, MA
International operations: Cayman Islands; France; Germany; Ireland; Luxembourg; United Kingdom
Giving statement: Giving through the State Street Corporation Contributions Program and the State Street Foundation, Inc.
Company EIN: 042456637

State Street Corporation Contributions Program

(formerly State Street Boston Corporation Contributions Program)
c/o Community Affairs Dept.
225 Franklin St.
Boston, MA 02110-2801
URL: http://www.statestreet.com/wps/portal/internet/corporate/home/aboutstatestreet/corporatecitizenship/overview

Financial data (yr. ended 12/31/10): Total giving, $5,200,000, including $3,200,000 for grants and $2,000,000 for employee matching gifts.
Purpose and activities: As a complement to its foundation, State Street also makes charitable contributions to nonprofit organizations directly. Support is given on a national and international basis.
Fields of interest: Health care; Employment, training; Youth development; Human services; Community/economic development; General charitable giving.
Type of support: Employee matching gifts; Employee volunteer services; General/operating support; Sponsorships.
Geographic limitations: Giving primarily on a national and international basis in areas of company operations, with emphasis on MA.
Publications: Corporate giving report.
Application information: Applications accepted. The Community Affairs Department handles giving. A contributions committee reviews all requests. Application form not required.
Initial approach: Proposal to headquarters

State Street Foundation, Inc.

1 Lincoln St
Boston, MA 02111-2900
E-mail: StateStreetFoundation@statestreet.com; E-mail address for international applicants: statestreet@cafoline.org; statestreet@give2asia.org for organizations located in the Asia Pacific; URL: http://www.statestreet.com/wps/portal/internet/corporate/home/aboutstatestreet/corporatecitizenship/globalphilanthropy/statestreetfoundation/

Establishment information: Established in 2006 in MA.
Donor: State Street Bank & Trust Co.
Contact: Amanda Northrop, V.P., North America and Asia Pacific Grants
Financial data (yr. ended 12/31/11): Assets, $47,681,833 (M); gifts received, $32,000,000; expenditures, $21,093,649; qualifying distributions, $21,090,059; giving activities include $20,998,165 for 670 grants (high: $750,000; low: $500).
Purpose and activities: The mission of State Street Foundation's strategic grantmaking program is to contribute to the sustainability of communities where State Street operates, primarily by investing in education as it relates to employability for disadvantaged populations. Limited funding is also provided, by invitation only, to organizations and programs that deliver critical services to help people along the path to economic self-sufficiency.
Fields of interest: Secondary school/education; Vocational education; Vocational education, post-secondary; Adult education—literacy, basic skills & GED; Education, services; Education, drop-out prevention; Education; Crime/violence prevention, youth; Employment, services; Employment, training; Employment; Youth development; Community development, neighborhood development; Community/economic development Youth; Disabilities, people with; Immigrants/refugees; Economically disadvantaged.
Programs:
Credentials and Employability: The foundation supports initiatives designed to increase access to industry-recognized credential programs, including college, vocational, and technical training that will open doors to future employment; enable attainment of industry-recognized credentials, including disadvantaged individuals that complete educational programs and attain a recognized credential relating to the achievement of educational skills; promote basic job-readiness skills needed to succeed in a workplace; and increase employment experience and opportunities for disadvantaged individuals.
Disaster Relief Emergency Assistance Fund: The foundation provides grants in response to large-scale disasters around the world that have a significant, lasting impact and require a concerted relief and rebuilding effort.
Education: The foundation supports programs designed to enable success in basic education. Special emphasis is directed toward programs that allow disadvantaged individuals to gain access to basic skills, including a high school or secondary degree and language literacy for non-native speakers.
Employment: The foundation supports programs designed to increase job placement and job retention for disadvantaged individuals.
Matching Gift Program: The foundation matches contributions made by employees of State Street to educational institutions and charitable organizations; awards grants to nonprofit organizations with which employees volunteer; and matches fulfilled pledges raised by an individual employee for an organized fundraising event.
Workforce Development Sector Improvement: The foundation supports educational sector programs designed to increase the effectiveness of the education system and improve student outcomes through eliminated disparities in educational opportunities, enhanced school culture, and/or increased teacher effectiveness; and employment sector programs designed to improve the effectiveness of the workforce system through increased investment, improved coordination, and enhanced capacity that contribute to a skilled workforce.
Type of support: Annual campaigns; Building/renovation; Capital campaigns; Continuing support; Emergency funds; Employee matching gifts; Employee volunteer services; General/operating support; In-kind gifts; Program development; Sponsorships.
Geographic limitations: Giving primarily in areas of company operations in CA, GA, IL, Boston and Quincy, MA, MO, NJ, NY, and PA and in Australia, Austria, Belgium, Canada, Cayman Islands, Europe, France, Germany, India, Ireland, Italy, Japan, Luxembourg, the Middle East, Netherlands, Poland, Qatar, Singapore, South Africa, South Korea, Switzerland, Taiwan, and the United Kingdom.
Support limitations: No support for political candidates or organizations, lobbying, labor, or fraternal organizations, or religious organizations not of direct benefit to the entire community. No grants to individuals, or for endowments, political causes or campaigns, sectarian activities for religious organizations, travel, team sponsorships, or sporting events, or medical research or disease specific initiatives.
Publications: Application guidelines; Grants list.
Application information: Applications accepted. Applicants may be asked to submit a full grant application. Organizations receiving support are asked to provide a final report. Visit website for nearest community contact information. Applicants should submit the following:
1) timetable for implementation and evaluation of project
2) results expected from proposed grant
3) population served
4) copy of IRS Determination Letter
5) brief history of organization and description of its mission
6) copy of most recent annual report/audited financial statement/990
7) listing of board of directors, trustees, officers and other key people and their affiliations
8) detailed description of project and amount of funding requested
9) copy of current year's organizational budget and/or project budget

Initial approach: Complete online preliminary grant application; e-mail preliminary grant applications for organizations located in the Asia Pacific, Canada, the Cayman Islands, Europe, Middle East, and South Africa
Deadline(s): None for preliminary grant applications
Final notification: 8 weeks for preliminary grant applications
Officers and Directors:* George A. Russell, Jr.*, Pres.; Simon Zornoza*, Clerk; James J. Malebra*, Treas.
EIN: 562615567
Selected grants: The following grants are a representative sample of this grantmaker's funding activity:
$591,700 to United Way of Massachusetts Bay, Boston, MA, 2011. For corporate support for United Way Campaign.
$500,000 to New Profit, Cambridge, MA, 2011. To provide interventions to assist in transition from high school to post-secondary education/employment.
$300,000 to Womens Lunch Place, Boston, MA, 2011. For capital campaign to renovate Resource Center that will enable it to expand job readiness program.
$100,000 to Asian American Civic Association, Boston, MA, 2011. For operating support for Adult Education and Workforce Development Center.
$100,000 to Boys and Girls Clubs of Boston, Boston, MA, 2011. For Life After the Club program, expanding outcomes measurement work and for AmeriCorps volunteer position.
$18,430 to Charities Aid Foundation UK, West Malling, England, 2011. To support Eva's Initiatives for Homeless Youth's Life Skills Program, which includes a number of programs, supported by a variety of life skills initiatives, to help youth succeed in developing long-term self-sufficiency in housing and employment. Eva's Initiatives is in Toronto, Canada.
$16,839 to Charities Aid Foundation UK, West Malling, England, 2011. To support Pathways to Education Canada's delivery of programs to youth, including mentoring, advocacy and counseling support, financial assistance with food and travel and bursary to assist with postgraduate programs following graduation.
$12,000 to Charities Aid Foundation UK, West Malling, England, 2011. For work of Podkarpackie Hospice for Children Foundation in Rzeszow, Poland, as they support a training course for medical volunteers wishing to work at the hospice.
$8,248 to Charities Aid Foundation UK, West Malling, England, 2011. For Schools without Borders, to support capacity workshop series to train SWB staff and to strengthen their platform.

3593
Station Casinos, Inc.

1505 S. Pavilion Center Dr.
Las Vegas, NV 89102-4343
(702) 495-3000

Company URL: http://www.stationcasinos.com
Establishment information: Established in 1976.
Company type: Private company
Business activities: Operates casino hotels; operates casinos; provides casino management services.
Business type (SIC): Hotels and motels; amusement and recreation services/ miscellaneous; management and public relations services
Financial profile for 2011: Sales volume, $1,180,000,000; pre-tax net income, $316,000,000
Corporate officers: Frank J. Fertitta III, Chair., Pres., and C.E.O.; Lorenzo Fertitta, Vice-Chair.; Kevin L. Kelley, Exec. V.P. and C.O.O.; Marc J. Falcone, Exec. V.P. and C.F.O.; Thomas M. Friel, Exec. V.P., Treas., and C.A.O.; Curtis Ching, Cont.
Board of directors: Frank J. Fertitta III, Chair.; Lorenzo Fertitta, Vice-Chair.
Subsidiaries: Boulder Station, Inc., Las Vegas, NV; Fiesta Station, Inc., Las Vegas, NV; Palace Station Hotel & Casino, Inc., Las Vegas, NV; Santa Fe Station, Inc., Las Vegas, NV; Sunset Station, Inc., Henderson, NV; Texas Station, LLC, North Las Vegas, NV
Giving statement: Giving through the Station Casinos, Inc. Corporate Giving Program.
Company EIN: 880136443

Station Casinos, Inc. Corporate Giving Program

c/o Corp. and Govt. Rels.
1505 S. Pavilion Center Dr.
Las Vegas, NV 89135-1403 (702) 367-2411
FAX: (702) 495-3310; URL: http://www.stationcasinos.com/corp/community/

Purpose and activities: Station Casinos makes charitable contributions to nonprofit organizations involved with youth, education, community betterment, and diversity. Support is given primarily in southern Nevada.
Fields of interest: Elementary/secondary education; Higher education; Education; Children/ youth, services; Children, foster care; Family services; Family services, domestic violence; Aging, centers/services; Homeless, human services; Human services; Civil/human rights, equal rights Youth.
Programs:
Caring for Community: Through Caring for Community, the company donates employee volunteers and money to local nonprofit organizations each month. The program includes a public awareness campaign and a $50,000 donation.
Community Betterment: The company supports programs designed to provide basic services to those in need, including food, shelter, clothing, or other social service needs. Special emphasis is directed toward domestic violence shelters, education, and prevention; homeless shelters; senior citizens; and foster parent outreach and recruitment.
Diversity: The company supports programs designed to enhance economic opportunities within minority communities.
Education: The company supports programs designed to strengthen K-12 public education and improve access to higher education.
Smart Start School Partnership: Through Smart Start School Partnership, the company annually supports and partners with Clark County's economically challenged primary schools. The program includes employee volunteers and resources to ensure that kids with challenging financial situations at home are given access to tools and opportunities that will help them become successful adults.
Youth: The company supports programs designed to provide services to children.
Type of support: Employee volunteer services; General/operating support; Sponsorships.
Geographic limitations: Giving primarily in areas of company operations in southern NV.
Support limitations: No support for discriminatory organizations. No grants to individuals.
Publications: Application guidelines; Program policy statement.
Application information: Applications accepted. The Corporate and Government Relations Department handles giving. Application form not required.
Applicants should submit the following:
1) name, address and phone number of organization
2) copy of IRS Determination Letter
3) contact person
4) detailed description of project and amount of funding requested
Initial approach: Proposal to headquarters
Deadline(s): None

3594
Stearns Lending, Inc.

4 Hutton Centre Dr., Ste. 500
Santa Ana, CA 92707 (714) 513-7777

Company URL: http://www.stearns.com
Establishment information: Established in 1989.
Company type: Private company
Business activities: Provides real estate financing and business management services.
Business type (SIC): Brokers and bankers/ mortgage
Financial profile for 2010: Number of employees, 122
Corporate officers: Glenn B. Stearns, C.E.O.; Katherine Le Le, Pres.; Robert Telles, C.F.O. and Secy.; Kim Day, Sr. V.P., Opers.; Richard S. Donine, V.P., Mktg.
Giving statement: Giving through the Stearns Family Charitable Foundation.

The Stearns Family Charitable Foundation

c/o Foundation Source
501 Silverside Rd.
Wilmington, DE 19809-1377

Establishment information: Established in 2004 in DE.
Donors: Stearns Lending, Inc.; Celebrity Fight Night.
Financial data (yr. ended 12/31/11): Assets, $5,744 (M); expenditures, $42,538; qualifying distributions, $37,500; giving activities include $37,500 for grants.
Fields of interest: Arts; Human services.
Geographic limitations: Giving primarily in CA.
Support limitations: No grants to individuals.
Application information: Applications not accepted. Unsolicited requests for funds not accepted.
Officer and Director:* Glenn B. Stearns*, Pres. and Secy.
EIN: 201650072

3595
Steel Dynamics, Inc.

(also known as SDI)
7575 W. Jefferson Blvd.
Fort Wayne, IN 46804 (260) 969-3500
FAX: (260) 969-3590

Company URL: http://www.steeldynamics.com
Establishment information: Established in 1993.
Company type: Public company
Company ticker symbol and exchange: STLD/ NASDAQ
Business activities: Operates carbon steel products company.
Business type (SIC): Steel mill products
Financial profile for 2012: Number of employees, 6,670; assets, $5,815,420,000; sales volume, $7,290,230,000; pre-tax net income, $204,070,000; expenses, $6,899,070,000; liabilities, $3,409,950,000
Fortune 1000 ranking: 2012—354th in revenues, 630th in profits, and 547th in assets
Corporate officers: Keith E. Busse, Chair.; Mark Millett, Pres. and C.E.O.; Theresa E. Wagler, Exec. V.P. and C.F.O.; Robert Francis, V.P. and C.I.O.; Richard A. Poinsatte, V.P. and Treas.; Ben Eisbart, V.P., Human Resources
Board of directors: Keith E. Busse, Chair.; John C. Bates; Frank D. Byrne, M.D.; Traci Dolan; Paul B. Edgerley; Jurgen Kolb; James C. Marcuccilli; Mark D. Millett; Gabriel L. Shaheen; Richard P. Teets; James A. Trethewey
Giving statement: Giving through the Steel Dynamics Foundation, Inc.
Company EIN: 351929476

The Steel Dynamics Foundation, Inc.

7575 W. Jefferson Blvd.
Fort Wayne, IN 46804-4131

Donor: Steel Dynamics, Inc.
Contact: Beth Burke
Financial data (yr. ended 12/31/11): Assets, $8,627,911 (M); expenditures, $1,984,768; qualifying distributions, $1,963,800; giving activities include $1,963,800 for grants.
Purpose and activities: The foundation supports organizations involved with children and family services. Special emphasis is directed toward programs designed to promote economic development, including education in business and technology fields.
Fields of interest: Business school/education; Children/youth, services; Family services; Economic development.
Type of support: Building/renovation; Capital campaigns; Equipment; General/operating support; Sponsorships.
Geographic limitations: Giving primarily in areas of company operations.
Application information: Applications not accepted. Contributes only to pre-selected organizations.
Directors: Keith E. Busse; Joseph A. Ruffolo; Theresa E. Wagler.
Number of staff: None.
EIN: 263012038
Selected grants: The following grants are a representative sample of this grantmaker's funding activity:
$1,131,355 to Indiana University-Purdue University Fort Wayne, Fort Wayne, IN, 2010.

$300,000 to Trine University, Angola, IN, 2010.
$100,000 to Indiana University-Purdue University Fort Wayne, Fort Wayne, IN, 2010.
$50,000 to Youth for Christ, Fort Wayne, IN, 2010.
$33,333 to Fort Wayne Childrens Zoo, Fort Wayne, IN, 2010.
$30,000 to Matthew 25 Health and Dental Clinic, Fort Wayne, IN, 2010. For general operating expenses.
$15,000 to Center for Whitley County Youth, Columbia City, IN, 2010.
$10,000 to SCAN, Fort Wayne, IN, 2010.

3596
Steel Technologies Inc.

15415 Shelbyville Rd.
Louisville, KY 40245-4137 (502) 245-2110

Company URL: http://www.steeltechnologies.com/
Establishment information: Established in 1971.
Company type: Subsidiary of a foreign company
Business activities: Processes flat-rolled steel.
Business type (SIC): Steel mill products
Corporate officers: Michael J. Carroll, Pres. and C.E.O.; Roger D. Shannon, C.F.O. and Treas.; Richard P. Furber, Exec. V.P., Opers.; Joseph M. Kamer, V.P., Genl. Counsel and Secy.; Patrick M. Flanagan, V.P., Human Resources
Giving statement: Giving through the Steel Foundation, Inc.

The Steel Foundation, Inc.

15415 Shelbyville Rd.
Louisville, KY 40245-4137

Establishment information: Established in 2004 in KY.
Donors: Steel Technologies, Inc.; Bradford T. Ray; Michael Carroll.
Financial data (yr. ended 12/31/11): Assets, $869,036 (M); gifts received, $142,101; expenditures, $205,933; qualifying distributions, $174,741; giving activities include $170,071 for grants.
Fields of interest: Safety/disasters; Recreation; Human services.
Geographic limitations: Giving primarily in Louisville, KY.
Support limitations: No grants to individuals.
Application information: Applications not accepted. Contributes only to pre-selected organizations.
Officers and Directors:* Stuart Ray*, Pres.; Pat Flanagan*, Secy.; Bradford Ray*, Treas.
EIN: 562468607

3597
Steelcase Inc.

901 44th St., S.E.
Grand Rapids, MI 49508-7594
(616) 247-2710
FAX: (616) 475-2270

Company URL: http://www.steelcase.com
Establishment information: Established in 1912.
Company type: Public company
Company ticker symbol and exchange: SCS/NYSE
Business activities: Designs and manufactures office architecture, furniture, and technology; refurbishes furniture; manufactures marine accessories; provides business consulting services.
Business type (SIC): Furniture/office; repair shops/reupholstery and furniture; management and public relations services
Financial profile for 2013: Number of employees, 10,400; assets, $1,689,600,000; sales volume, $2,868,700,000; pre-tax net income, $54,900,000; expenses, $2,809,400,000; liabilities, $1,021,600,000
Fortune 1000 ranking: 2012—758th in revenues, 805th in profits, and 893rd in assets
Corporate officers: Robert C. Pew III, Chair.; James P. Hackett, C.E.O.; James P. Keane, Pres. and C.O.O.; David C. Sylvester, Sr. V.P. and C.F.O.; Nancy W. Hickey, Sr. V.P. and C.A.O.; Lizbeth S. O'Shaughnessy, Sr. V.P. and Secy.
Board of directors: Robert C. Pew III, Chair.; Lawrence J. Blanford; William P. Crawford; Connie K. Duckworth; James P. Hackett; R. David Hoover; David W. Joos; Elizabeth Valk Long; Cathy D. Ross; Peter M. Wege II; P. Craig Welch, Jr.; Kate Pew Wolters
Subsidiaries: Brayton International Inc., High Point, NC; Office Details Inc., Grand Rapids, MI; PolyVision Corp., Atlanta, GA; Steelcase Financial Services Inc., Grand Rapids, MI
Divisions: Steelcase Design Partnership Div., Grand Rapids, MI; Steelcase International Div., Grand Rapids, MI; Steelcase North America Div., Grand Rapids, MI
Plants: Athens, AL; City of Industry, CA
International operations: Canada; France; Germany; Spain
Giving statement: Giving through the Steelcase Inc. Corporate Giving Program and the Steelcase Foundation.
Company EIN: 380819050

Steelcase Inc. Corporate Giving Program

c/o Community Rels.
901 44th St., SE
Grand Rapids, MI 49508-7575
E-mail: cr@steelcase.com; URL: http://www.steelcase.com/na/in_the_community_ourcompany.aspx?f=18478

Purpose and activities: As a complement to its foundation, Steelcase also makes charitable contributions to nonprofit organizations directly. Support is given on a national and international basis in areas of company operations.
Fields of interest: Arts; Education; Environment; Community/economic development Minorities.
Type of support: Donated products; Employee volunteer services; General/operating support; In-kind gifts.
Geographic limitations: Giving on a national and international basis in areas of company operations.
Application information: Applications accepted.
Initial approach: E-mail headquarters for application information
Deadline(s): None
Final notification: 3 weeks
Number of staff: 1 full-time professional.

Steelcase Foundation

P.O. Box 1967, GH-4E
Grand Rapids, MI 49501-1967
FAX: (616) 475-2200;
E-mail: pgebben@steelcase.com; URL: http://www.steelcase.com/en/company/who/steelcase-foundation/pages/steelcasefoundation.aspx

Establishment information: Established in 1951 in MI.
Donor: Steelcase Inc.
Contact: Phyllis Gebben, Donations Coord.
Financial data (yr. ended 11/30/11): Assets, $83,798,547 (M); expenditures, $4,939,526; qualifying distributions, $4,069,503; giving activities include $3,569,880 for 61 grants (high: $425,000; low: $900) and $479,623 for employee matching gifts.
Purpose and activities: The foundation supports organizations involved with arts and culture, education, the environment, health, human services, and community development. Special emphasis is directed toward programs designed to assist youth, the elderly, people with disabilities, and economically disadvantaged people.
Fields of interest: Arts; Education, early childhood education; Education; Environment; Health care; Homeless, human services; Human services; Economic development; Community/economic development Youth; Aging; Disabilities, people with; Economically disadvantaged.
Programs:
Employee Matching Gifts: The foundation matches contributions made by employees, retirees, and directors of Steelcase to nonprofit organizations involved with arts and culture, education, and the environment and conservation up to $10,000 per contributor, per year.
Scholarships: The foundation awards college scholarships to children of employees of Steelcase and Steelcase subsidiaries. The program is administered by the National Merit Scholarship Corp.
Type of support: Building/renovation; Capital campaigns; Employee matching gifts; Employee-related scholarships; Equipment; General/operating support; Management development/capacity building; Program development; Scholarship funds; Seed money.
Geographic limitations: Giving limited to areas of company operations, with emphasis on Athens, AL and Grand Rapids, MI.
Support limitations: No support for churches or religious organizations not of direct benefit to the entire community, or discriminatory organizations. No grants to individuals (except for employee-related scholarships), or for endowments or conferences or seminars.
Publications: Annual report; Application guidelines; Grants list.
Application information: Applications accepted. Letters of inquiry should be submitted using organization letterhead. A full proposal may be requested at a later date. Support is limited to 1 contribution per organization during any given year. Application form required. Applicants should submit the following:
1) signature and title of chief executive officer
2) results expected from proposed grant
3) copy of IRS Determination Letter
4) detailed description of project and amount of funding requested
Initial approach: Letter of inquiry for application form
Copies of proposal: 1
Board meeting date(s): Quarterly
Deadline(s): Quarterly
Final notification: At least 90 days
Officers and Trustees:* Kate Pew Wolters*, Chair.; Julie Ridenour, Pres.; James P. Hackett; Mary Anne Hunting; Elizabeth Welch Lykins; Mary Goodwillie Nelson; Robert C. Pew III; Craig Niemann.
Number of staff: 1 full-time professional; 1 full-time support.
EIN: 386050470
Selected grants: The following grants are a representative sample of this grantmaker's funding activity:

$450,000 to United Way, Heart of West Michigan, Grand Rapids, MI, 2010. For 2010 Campaign.
$250,000 to John Ball Zoological Society, Grand Rapids, MI, 2010. For Phase I. Restore the Roar.
$200,000 to Michigan State University, East Lansing, MI, 2010. For MSU West Michigan Medical School.
$200,000 to Urban Institute for Contemporary Arts, Grand Rapids, MI, 2010. For "Where Art Happens" capital campaign.
$150,000 to Cherry Street Health Services, Grand Rapids, MI, 2010. For Heart of the City Health Center.
$150,000 to Grand Rapids Art Museum, Grand Rapids, MI, 2010. For Centennial Year - Art - Legacy - Vision.
$100,000 to Grand Valley State University, Grand Rapids, MI, 2010. For Mary Idema Pew Library Learning and Information Commons.
$100,000 to United Way, Heart of West Michigan, Grand Rapids, MI, 2010. For 2010 Campaign.
$75,000 to Grand Action Foundation, Grand Rapids, MI, 2010. For Grand Rapids Urban Market.
$75,000 to Kent Intermediate School District, Grand Rapids, MI, 2010. For Kent School Services Network.

3598
Stephens, Inc.

111 Center St.
Little Rock, AR 72201 (501) 377-2000

Company URL: http://www.stephens.com
Establishment information: Established in 1933.
Company type: Subsidiary of a private company
Business activities: Operates investment banking firm.
Business type (SIC): Brokers and dealers/security
Corporate officers: Warren A. Stephens, Chair., Pres., and C.E.O.; Curt Bradbury, C.O.O.; Mark Doramus, C.F.O.; David Knight, Exec. V.P. and Genl. Counsel
Board of director: Warren A. Stephens, Chair.
Giving statement: Giving through the Jane Howard Foundation.

The Jane Howard Foundation

c/o Doug Martin and Melanie Masino
3800 Hill Rd.
Little Rock, AR 72205-3930

Establishment information: Established in 2006 in AR.
Donors: Melanie Masino; Stephens, Inc.; Doug Martin.
Financial data (yr. ended 05/31/12): Assets, $1,296,249 (M); expenditures, $66,537; qualifying distributions, $62,558; giving activities include $62,558 for grants.
Purpose and activities: The foundation supports health clinics and festivals and organizations involved with arts and culture, higher education, heart disease, and neuroscience.
Fields of interest: Education; Animals/wildlife; Health care.
Type of support: General/operating support.
Geographic limitations: Giving primarily in AR.
Support limitations: No grants to individuals.
Application information: Applications not accepted. Unsolicited requests for funds not accepted.
Trustees: Doug Martin; Melanie Masino.
EIN: 736361836

3599
Steptoe & Johnson LLP

1330 Connecticut Ave., N.W.
Washington, DC 20036-1795
(202) 429-6258

Company URL: http://www.steptoe.com/
Establishment information: Established in 1945.
Company type: Private company
Business activities: Operates law firm.
Business type (SIC): Legal services
Corporate officer: Philip L. Malet, Vice-Chair.
Offices: Phoenix, AZ; Los Angeles, CA; Washington, DC; Chicago, IL; New York, NY
International operations: Belgium; China
Giving statement: Giving through the Steptoe & Johnson LLP Pro Bono Program.

Steptoe & Johnson LLP Pro Bono Program

1330 Connecticut Ave., N.W.
Washington, DC 20036-1795 (202) 429-6258
E-mail: bkagan@steptoe.com; Additional tel.: (202) 429-3000; URL: http://www.steptoe.com/about-service.html

Contact: Barbara K. Kagan, Public Svc. Counsel
Fields of interest: Legal services.
Type of support: Pro bono services - legal.
Application information: A Pro Bono Committee manages the pro bono program.

3600
STERIS Corporation

5960 Heisley Rd.
Mentor, OH 44060-1834 (440) 354-2600
FAX: (440) 639-4457

Company URL: http://www.steris.com
Establishment information: Established in 1985.
Company type: Public company
Company ticker symbol and exchange: STE/NYSE
Business activities: Develops, manufactures, and markets infection prevention, contamination prevention, microbial reduction, and medical, surgical, and therapy support systems, products, services, and technologies.
Business type (SIC): Medical instruments and supplies
Financial profile for 2013: Number of employees, 6,000; assets, $1,761,110,000; sales volume, $1,501,900,000; pre-tax net income, $227,100,000; expenses, $1,259,070,000; liabilities, $814,130,000
Corporate officers: John P. Wareham, Chair.; Walter M. Rosebrough, Jr., Pres. and C.E.O.; Michael J. Tokich, Sr. V.P. and C.F.O.; Mark D. McGinley, Sr. V.P., Genl. Counsel, and Secy.; William L. Aamoth, V.P. and Corp. Treas.
Board of directors: John P. Wareham, Chair.; Richard C. Breeden; Cynthia L. Feldmann; Jacqueline B Kosecoff, Ph.D.; David B. Lewis; Kevin M. McMullen; Walter M. Rosebrough, Jr.; Mohsen M. Sohi; Loyal W. Wilson; Michael B. Wood, M.D.
Subsidiaries: American Sterilizer Company, Horsham, PA; Ecomed, Inc., Indianapolis, IN; Hausted, Inc., Medina, OH; STERIS FoodLabs, Inc., Manhattan, KS; STERIS USA Distribution Corp., Mentor, OH; STERISOnline Inc., Mentor, OH
Plant: Montgomery, AL
International operations: Belgium; Canada; Finland; Japan; Sweden; United Kingdom
Giving statement: Giving through the Founders Memorial Fund of the American Sterilizer Company and the STERIS Foundation.
Company EIN: 341482024

Founders Memorial Fund of the American Sterilizer Company

5960 Heisley Rd.
Mentor, OH 44060-1834

Establishment information: Established in 1938 in PA.
Donors: George F. Hall; J. Everett Hall.
Contact: Hilary Morton
Financial data (yr. ended 12/31/11): Assets, $1,759,653 (M); expenditures, $96,491; qualifying distributions, $89,153; giving activities include $84,800 for 99 grants to individuals (high: $3,500; low: $400).
Purpose and activities: The foundation awards college scholarships to children of employees and retirees of American Sterilizer Co.
Fields of interest: Higher education.
Type of support: Employee-related scholarships.
Geographic limitations: Giving limited to areas of company operations.
Application information: Applications not accepted. Contributes only through employee-related scholarships.
Trustees: Bill Aamoth; Dennis Patton; PNC Bank, N.A.
EIN: 256062068

The STERIS Foundation

5960 Heisley Rd.
Mentor, OH 44060-1834
URL: http://www.steris.com/about/HSE/sustainability.cfm

Establishment information: Established in 1995 in OH.
Donor: STERIS Corp.
Financial data (yr. ended 03/31/12): Assets, $152,335 (M); expenditures, $337,529; qualifying distributions, $337,000; giving activities include $337,000 for grants.
Purpose and activities: The foundation supports organizations involved with arts and culture, health, human services, heart disease, diabetes, and human services.
Fields of interest: Performing arts, theater; Arts; Hospitals (general); Nursing care; Health care; Heart & circulatory diseases; Diabetes; American Red Cross; Human services; United Ways and Federated Giving Programs.
Type of support: General/operating support.
Geographic limitations: Giving primarily in areas of company operations in OH.
Support limitations: No grants to individuals.
Application information: Applications not accepted. Contributes only to pre-selected organizations.
Officers: Gerard J. Reis, Pres.; Dennis Patton, Secy.; John R. Schloss, Treas.
EIN: 341807803
Selected grants: The following grants are a representative sample of this grantmaker's funding activity:
$50,000 to Colorado State University, Fort Collins, CO, 2011.
$10,000 to American Heart Association, Dallas, TX, 2011.
$5,000 to United Way of Greater Saint Louis, Saint Louis, MO, 2011.

3601
Sterling Mets, L.P.

(doing business as New York Mets)
123-01 Roosevelt Ave.
Flushing, NY 11368-1699 (718) 507-8449

Company URL: http://newyork.mets.mlb.com
Establishment information: Established in 1962.
Company type: Private company
Business activities: Operates professional baseball club.
Business type (SIC): Commercial sports
Corporate officers: Fred Wilpon, Chair. and C.E.O.; Saul Katz, Pres.; Jeff Wilpon, C.O.O.; David Cohen, Exec. V.P. and Genl. Counsel; Mark Peskin, C.F.O.; David Newman, Sr. V.P., Mktg. and Comms.; Paul Asencio, Sr. V.P., Corp. Sales; Leonard Labita, V.P. and Cont.
Board of directors: Fred Wilpon, Chair.; Steve Greenberg; David Katz; Micheal Katz; Saul Katz; Tom Osterman; Ivan G. Seidenberg; Staurt Sucherman; Steven H. Temares; Marvin Tepper; Jeff Wilpon; Richard Wilpon
Giving statement: Giving through the New York Mets Foundation, Inc.

New York Mets Foundation, Inc.

Citi Field
Flushing, NY 11368-1699 (718) 507-6387
FAX: (718) 507-6395; URL: http://newyork.mets.mlb.com/NASApp/mlb/nym/community/index.jsp

Establishment information: Established in NY.
Donor: Sterling Mets LP.
Contact: Leonard S. Labita
Financial data (yr. ended 10/31/11): Revenue, $2,521,355; assets, $2,236,744 (M); gifts received, $2,521,355; expenditures, $2,323,938; giving activities include $2,323,938 for grants.
Purpose and activities: The foundation promotes athletes and athletics through scholarship funds, public parks, improvement projects, and various social service organizations.
Fields of interest: Athletics/sports, baseball; Recreation.
Type of support: Scholarship funds.
Officers and Trustees:* Jeffrey Wilpon*, Exec. V.P.; Dave Howard, V.P.; David Cohen, Secy.; Mark Peskin, Treas.; Saul Katz; Fred Wilpon.
EIN: 136159029

3602
Sterne, Agee & Leach, Inc.

800 Shades Creek Pkwy., Ste. 700
Birmingham, AL 35209-4532
(205) 949-3500

Company URL: http://www.sterneagee.com
Establishment information: Established in 1901.
Company type: Subsidiary of a private company
Business activities: Provides securities brokerage services.
Business type (SIC): Brokers and dealers/security
Financial profile for 2010: Number of employees, 600
Corporate officers: James A. Stivender Holbrook, Jr., Chair., Pres., and C.E.O.; Brian Barze, C.F.O.
Board of director: James A. Stivender Holbrook, Jr., Chair.
Giving statement: Giving through the Sterne, Agee & Leach Charitable Foundation, Inc.

Sterne, Agee & Leach Charitable Foundation, Inc.

800 Shades Creek Pkwy., Ste. 125
Birmingham, AL 35209-4538

Establishment information: Established as a company-sponsored operating foundation in 1999 in AL.
Donors: Sterne, Agee & Leach, Inc.; Charles D. Carlisle; Sterne Agee.
Financial data (yr. ended 12/31/11): Assets, $604,714 (M); gifts received, $100,525; expenditures, $219,523; qualifying distributions, $219,523; giving activities include $215,000 for 5 grants (high: $100,000; low: $5,000).
Purpose and activities: The foundation supports hospitals and organizations involved with arts and culture, education, patient services, children and youth, disability services, and women.
Fields of interest: Performing arts, ballet; Arts; Education; Hospitals (general); Health care, patient services; Big Brothers/Big Sisters; YM/YWCAs & YM/YWHAs; Children/youth, services; Developmentally disabled, centers & services Women.
Type of support: General/operating support; Program development; Scholarship funds.
Geographic limitations: Giving primarily in Birmingham, AL.
Support limitations: No grants to individuals.
Application information: Applications not accepted. Unsolicited requests for funds not accepted.
Officers: James S. Holbrook, Chair.; Brian Barze, Secy.; Linda M. Daniel, Treas.
EIN: 631234814

3603
Steve's Lake View Pavilion, Inc.

45 Lakeview Rd.
Foxboro, MA 02035-1739 (508) 543-9099

Company URL: http://www.lakeviewpavilion.com
Company type: Private company
Business activities: Operates reception hall.
Business type (SIC): Restaurants and drinking places
Corporate officer: Anastia Kourtidis, Pres.
Giving statement: Giving through the Lake View Pavilion Charitable Foundation.

Lake View Pavilion Charitable Foundation

45 Lakeview Rd.
Foxborough, MA 02035-1739 (508) 543-9099

Donor: Steve's Lake View Pavilion, Inc.
Contact: Anastasia Tsoumbanos, Dir.
Financial data (yr. ended 12/31/11): Assets, $12,617 (M); gifts received, $10,800; expenditures, $6,985; qualifying distributions, $6,950; giving activities include $5,450 for 2 grants (high: $3,950; low: $1,500) and $1,500 for 3 grants to individuals (high: $500; low: $500).
Purpose and activities: The foundation supports libraries and organizations involved with performing arts and secondary education and awards college scholarships to Foxborough, Massachusetts, residents.
Fields of interest: Education; Housing/shelter.
Type of support: General/operating support; Scholarships—to individuals.
Geographic limitations: Giving limited to the Foxborough, MA, area.
Application information: Applications accepted. An application form is required for scholarships. Application form required.
Initial approach: Contact local high school for application form for scholarships
Deadline(s): Apr. 1 for scholarships
Officers: Efstathios Kourtidis, Pres.; Christos Kourtidis, Clerk.
Directors: Natalia Kapourelakos; Anastasia Tsoumbanos.
EIN: 043116285

3604
W. P. Stewart & Co., Ltd.

527 Madison Ave., 20th Fl.
New York, NY 10022-4362 (212) 750-8585

Company URL: http://www.wpstewart.com
Establishment information: Established in 1975.
Company type: Subsidiary of a foreign company
Business activities: Provides investment advisory services.
Business type (SIC): Security and commodity services
Corporate officers: William P. Stewart, Chair.; Mark I. Phelps, Pres. and C.E.O.; Mark D. Bergen, C.O.O. and C.F.O.; James T. Tierney, Jr., C.I.O.; Seth L. Pearlstein, Secy. and Genl. Counsel
Board of directors: William P. Stewart, Chair.; Alfred J. Mulder; Mark I. Phelps; Charles H. Price; Mal Serure; Alexandre Von Furstenberg
Giving statement: Giving through the W. P. Stewart & Co. Foundation Inc.

W. P. Stewart & Co. Foundation Inc.

527 Madison Ave.
New York, NY 10022-4304

Establishment information: Established in 1998 in NY and DE.
Donors: W.P. Stewart & Co., Inc.; WPS Advisors.
Financial data (yr. ended 12/31/11): Assets, $348 (M); gifts received, $16,750; expenditures, $18,915; qualifying distributions, $17,000; giving activities include $17,000 for grants.
Purpose and activities: The foundation supports art museums and community foundations and organizations involved with education, health, substance abuse, cancer, and human services.
Fields of interest: Museums (art); Secondary school/education; Higher education; Education; Hospitals (general); Health care; Substance abuse, services; Cancer; Human services; Foundations (community); United Ways and Federated Giving Programs.
Type of support: General/operating support.
Geographic limitations: Giving on a national basis, with some emphasis on New York, NY.
Support limitations: No grants to individuals.
Application information: Applications not accepted. Unsolicited requests for funds not accepted.
Officers and Directors:* Mark Phelps*, Pres.; Mark Bergen, V.P. and Treas.; Seth L. Pearlstein, Secy.; William P. Stewart, Jr.
EIN: 134034704

3605
Stewart Builders, Ltd.
(doing business as Keystone Concrete Placement)
16575 Village Dr.
Houston, TX 77040 (713) 983-8002

Company URL: http://www.keystoneconcrete.com/
Establishment information: Established in 1992.
Company type: Private company
Business activities: Provides concrete and construction services.
Business type (SIC): Contractors/concrete work
Financial profile for 2011: Number of employees, 1,500
Corporate officers: Donald G. Stewart, Pres.; Rodney J. Horn, V.P., Sales; Mark Stewart, Secy.-Treas.
Giving statement: Giving through the Stewart Family Catholic Education Scholarship Foundation.

The Stewart Family Catholic Education Scholarship Foundation
17535 Seidel Cemetary Rd.
Tomball, TX 77377-5987 (713) 983-8002

Establishment information: Established in 2006 in TX.
Donors: Stewart Builders, Inc.; Donald G. Stewart; Bradley S. Stewart; Sandy Stewart; Mark A. Stewart; Lisa Stewart; Craig Stewart; Brandy Stewart; Roger Jarvis; Jamie Jarvis; Stewart Builders Enterprises.
Contact: Mark A. Stewart, V.P.
Financial data (yr. ended 12/31/11): Assets, $373,687 (M); expenditures, $52,083; qualifying distributions, $50,000; giving activities include $50,000 for 4 grants (high: $19,000; low: $5,000).
Fields of interest: Christian agencies & churches.
Application information: Applications accepted. Application form not required.
Initial approach: Proposal
Deadline(s): None
Officers: Donald G. Stewart, Pres.; Bradley Stewart, V.P.; Donald C. Stewart, V.P.; Mark A. Stewart, V.P.; Timothy Stewart, Treas.
EIN: 204943153

3606
Stewart Information Services Corporation
1980 Post Oak Blvd., Ste. 2000
P.O. Box 2029
Houston, TX 77056-3826 (713) 625-8100
FAX: (713) 552-9523

Company URL: http://www.stewart.com/
Establishment information: Established in 1893.
Company type: Public company
Company ticker symbol and exchange: STC/NYSE
Business activities: Provides real estate information and transaction management services, including title insurance.
Business type (SIC): Insurance/title
Financial profile for 2012: Number of employees, 6,300; assets, $1,291,180,000; sales volume, $1,910,410,000; pre-tax net income, $89,340,000; expenses, $1,821,070,000; liabilities, $722,370,000
Fortune 1000 ranking: 2012—973rd in revenues, 718th in profits, and 938th in assets
Corporate officers: Edward Douglas Hodo, Chair.; Malcolm S. Morris, Vice-Chair.; Stewart Morris, Jr., Vice-Chair.; Matthew W. Morris, C.E.O.; Allen Berryman, C.F.O.; Murshid Khan, C.I.O.
Board of directors: Edward Douglas Hodo, Ph.D., Chair.; Malcolm S. Morris, Vice-Chair.; Stewart Morris, Jr., Vice-Chair.; Catherine A. Allen; Thomas G. Apel; Robert L. Clarke; Paul W. Hobby; Frank Keating; Laurie Moore-Moore; Matt Morris; W. Arthur Porter, Ph.D.
Giving statement: Giving through the M. Max Crisp Stewart Scholarship Foundation.
Company EIN: 741677330

M. Max Crisp Stewart Scholarship Foundation
1980 Post Oak Blvd., Ste. 910
Houston, TX 77056-3899 (713) 625-8076

Establishment information: Established in TX.
Donor: Stewart Information Services Corporation.
Contact: Debbie Wilson, Pres.
Financial data (yr. ended 12/31/11): Assets, $175 (M); gifts received, $37,500; expenditures, $37,500; qualifying distributions, $37,500; giving activities include $37,500 for grants.
Purpose and activities: The foundation awards scholarships to children of employees of Stewart Information Services Corp. and its subsidiaries to attend an accredited state college.
Type of support: Employee-related scholarships.
Geographic limitations: Giving primarily in areas of company operations in AR, CA, ME, OH, TX, and VA.
Application information: Applications not accepted. Unsolicited requests for funds not accepted.
Officers: Debbie Wilson, Pres.; Alison Evers, V.P. and Treas.; Liz Henshaw, V.P.; Natalie Lancaster, Secy.
EIN: 760462905

3607
Stiles Corporation
301 E. Las Olas Blvd.
Fort Lauderdale, FL 33301 (954) 627-9300
FAX: (954) 627-9288

Company URL: http://www.stiles.com
Establishment information: Established in 1951.
Company type: Private company
Business activities: Develops real estate.
Business type (SIC): Real estate subdividers and developers
Corporate officers: Terry W. Stiles, Chair. and C.E.O.; Douglas P. Eagon, Pres.; Stephen R. Palmer, C.O.O.; Robert Esposito, C.F.O.; Rocco Ferrera, C.I.O.; Denny O'Shea, Genl. Counsel
Board of director: Terry W. Stiles, Chair.
Giving statement: Giving through the Stiles Corporation Corporate Giving Program and the Stiles Family Foundation, Inc.

Stiles Corporation Corporate Giving Program
301 East Las Olas Blvd.
Fort Lauderdale, FL 33301-2295 (954) 627-9300
FAX: (954) 627-9288; URL: http://www.stiles.com/about

Purpose and activities: As a complement to its foundation, Stiles also makes charitable contributions to nonprofit organizations directly. Support is given primarily in areas of company operations in Florida.
Fields of interest: Animal welfare; Housing/shelter; Youth development; General charitable giving.
Type of support: Employee volunteer services; General/operating support; In-kind gifts.
Geographic limitations: Giving primarily in areas of company operations in FL.

The Stiles Family Foundation, Inc.
300 S.E. 2nd St.
Fort Lauderdale, FL 33301-1923

Establishment information: Established in 2001 in FL.
Donors: Stiles Corp.; Terry W. Stiles.
Financial data (yr. ended 12/31/11): Assets, $384 (M); gifts received, $28,000; expenditures, $28,134; qualifying distributions, $5,000; giving activities include $5,000 for grants.
Purpose and activities: The foundation supports museums and organizations involved with education, cancer, child welfare, housing development, school athletics, and Christianity.
Fields of interest: Museums; Higher education; Education; Cancer; Crime/violence prevention, child abuse; Housing/shelter, development; Athletics/sports, school programs; Christian agencies & churches.
Type of support: Capital campaigns; General/operating support.
Geographic limitations: Giving primarily in Fort Lauderdale, FL.
Application information: Applications not accepted. Contributes only to pre-selected organizations.
Officer: Terry W. Stiles, Pres.
EIN: 311808921

3608
Stinson Morrison Hecker LLP
1201 Walnut St., Ste. 2900
Kansas City, MO 64106-2178
(816) 691-2479

Company URL: http://www.stites.com/home.php
Establishment information: Established in 1878.
Company type: Private company
Business activities: Operates law firm.
Business type (SIC): Legal services
Corporate officers: Mark D. Hinderks, Managing Partner; Terry E. Brummer, C.O.O.; Doug Doerfler, C.F.O.; Vic A. Peterson, C.I.O.
Offices: Phoenix, AZ; Washington, DC; Overland Park, Wichita, KS; Jefferson City, Kansas City, St. Louis, MO; Omaha, NE
Giving statement: Giving through the Stinson Morrison Hecker LLP Pro Bono Program.

Stinson Morrison Hecker LLP Pro Bono Program
1201 Walnut St., Ste. 2900
Kansas City, MO 64106-2178 (816) 842-8600
E-mail: lmoore@stinson.com; URL: http://www.stinson.com/Meet_Us/In_the_Community/Pro_Bono.aspx

Contact: Lynda Moore, Dir., Professional Dev. & Recruiting
Fields of interest: Legal services.
Type of support: Pro bono services - legal.
Application information: A Pro Bono Committee manages the pro bono program.

3609
Stites & Harbison, PLLC
400 W. Market St., Ste. 1800
Louisville, KY 40202-3352 (502) 587-3400

Company URL: http://www.stites.com/home.php
Establishment information: Established in 1897.
Company type: Private company
Business activities: Operates law firm.
Business type (SIC): Legal services
Corporate officer: Kennedy Helm III, Chair.
Offices: Atlanta, GA; Jeffersonville, IN; Frankfort, Lexington, Louisville, KY; Franklin, Nashville, TN; Alexandria, VA
Giving statement: Giving through the Stites & Harbison, PLLC Pro Bono Program.

Stites & Harbison, PLLC Pro Bono Program
400 W. Market St., Ste. 1800
Louisville, KY 40202-3352 (502) 587-3400
URL: http://www.stites.com/about/3/pro-bono

Fields of interest: Legal services.
Type of support: Pro bono services - legal.
Application information: An attorney at each office coordinates pro bono projects.

3610
Stock Yards Bank and Trust Company
(also known as Stock Yards Bank)
1040 E. Main St.
Louisville, KY 40206-1888 (502) 582-2571

Company URL: http://www.syb.com
Establishment information: Established in 1904.
Company type: Subsidiary of a public company
Business activities: Operates commercial bank.
Business type (SIC): Banks/commercial
Corporate officers: David P. Heintzman, Chair. and C.E.O.; James A. Hillebrand, Pres.; Nancy B. Davis, C.F.O.
Board of director: David P. Heintzman, Chair.
Giving statement: Giving through the Stock Yards Bank Foundation Inc.

Stock Yards Bank Foundation Inc.
P.O. Box 34290
Louisville, KY 40232-4290

Establishment information: Established in 2001.
Donor: Stock Yards Bank & Trust Co.
Financial data (yr. ended 12/31/11): Assets, $205,454 (M); gifts received, $65,700; expenditures, $177,517; qualifying distributions, $176,175; giving activities include $176,175 for 23 grants (high: $25,000; low: $1,000).
Purpose and activities: The foundation supports organizations involved with arts and culture, education, health, and human services.
Fields of interest: Arts; Higher education; Education; Hospitals (general); Health care; Children/youth, services; Human services.
Type of support: Annual campaigns; Capital campaigns; Endowments; Sponsorships.
Application information: Applications not accepted. Unsolicited requests for funds not accepted.
Officers: David P. Heintzman, Pres.; Nancy B. Davis, Secy.-Treas.
Director: Kathy C. Thompson.
EIN: 611380342

Selected grants: The following grants are a representative sample of this grantmaker's funding activity:
$30,000 to Junior Achievement of Kentuckiana, Louisville, KY, 2010.
$25,000 to Saint Xavier High School, Louisville, KY, 2010.
$15,000 to Trinity High School, Louisville, KY, 2010.
$5,000 to Church Home and Infirmary Episcopal Church Home, Louisville, KY, 2010. For capital campaign.
$5,000 to Kentucky Opera, Louisville, KY, 2010.

3611
Stoel Rives LLP
900 S.W. 5th Ave., Ste. 2600
Portland, OR 97204-1268 (503) 224-3380

Company URL: http://www.stoel.com/index.aspx
Establishment information: Established in 1907.
Company type: Private company
Business activities: Operates law firm.
Business type (SIC): Legal services
Corporate officer: Darryl C. Hair, C.O.O.
Offices: Anchorage, AK; Sacramento, San Diego, San Francisco, Truckee, CA; Boise, ID; Minneapolis, MN; Portland, OR; Salt Lake City, UT; Seattle, Vancouver, WA
Giving statement: Giving through the Stoel Rives LLP Pro Bono Program.

Stoel Rives LLP Pro Bono Program
900 S.W. 5th Ave., Ste. 2600
Portland, OR 97204-1268 (503) 224-3380
E-mail: ajpedersen@stoel.com; URL: http://www.stoel.com/about.aspx?show=1519

Contact: Amy Joseph Pedersen, Partner
Fields of interest: Legal services.
Type of support: Pro bono services - legal.
Application information: An attorney coordinates pro bono projects.

3612
Stoelting, Inc.
502 Hwy. 67
Kiel, WI 53042 (920) 894-2293

Company URL: http://www.stoelting.com/
Establishment information: Established in 1905.
Company type: Subsidiary of a private company
Business activities: Manufactures cheese making equipment and systems, industrial parts, washing machines, and soft serve, shake, and slush machines.
Business type (SIC): Machinery/special industry; metal products/fabricated
Corporate officers: David Sachse, Pres.; Tom Dinolfo, C.F.O
Giving statement: Giving through the SBC Foundation, Inc.

SBC Foundation, Inc.
(formerly Stoelting Brothers Company Foundation, Inc.)
P.O. Box 127
Kiel, WI 53042-0127

Donor: Stoelting, Inc.
Financial data (yr. ended 09/30/12): Assets, $221,035 (M); expenditures, $11,682; qualifying distributions, $11,682; giving activities include $11,160 for 3 grants (high: $3,830; low: $3,500).
Purpose and activities: The foundation supports St. Peter's United Church of Christ in Kiel, Wisconsin.
Fields of interest: Religion.
Type of support: General/operating support; Scholarships—to individuals.
Geographic limitations: Giving limited to Kiel, WI.
Application information: Applications not accepted. Unsolicited requests for funds not accepted.
Officers: Frederick Stoelting, Pres.; John F. Stoelting, V.P.; Robert A. Voigt, Secy.-Treas.
EIN: 396123893

3613
Stoll Keenon Ogden PLLC
2000 PNC Plz.
500 W. Jefferson St.
Louisville, KY 40202-2874 (502) 333-6000

Company URL: http://www.skofirm.com/Home
Establishment information: Established in 1897.
Company type: Private company
Business activities: Operates law firm.
Business type (SIC): Legal services
Offices: Frankfort, Henderson, Lexington, Louisville, Morganfield, KY
Giving statement: Giving through the Stoll Keenon Ogden PLLC Pro Bono Program.

Stoll Keenon Ogden PLLC Pro Bono Program
2000 PNC Plz.
500 W. Jefferson St.
Louisville, KY 40202-2874 (859) 231-3000
E-mail: palmer.vance@skofirm.com; URL: http://www.skofirm.com/CommunityOrganizations

Contact: P. Gene Vance, Member
Fields of interest: Legal services.
Type of support: Pro bono services - legal.
Application information: A Pro Bono Committee manages the pro bono program.

3614
Stone Energy Corporation
625 E. Kaliste Saloom Rd.
Lafayette, LA 70508-2540 (337) 237-0410
FAX: (337) 521-2072

Company URL: http://www.stoneenergy.com/
Establishment information: Established in 1993.
Company type: Public company
Company ticker symbol and exchange: SGY/NYSE
Business activities: Conducts oil and gas acquisition, exploration, and development activities.
Business type (SIC): Extraction/oil and gas
Financial profile for 2012: Number of employees, 386; assets, $2,776,430,000; sales volume, $951,490,000; pre-tax net income, $234,020,000; expenses, $689,500,000; liabilities, $1,904,300,000
Corporate officers: David H. Welch, Chair., Pres., and C.E.O.; Kenneth H. Beer, Exec. V.P. and C.F.O.; Jerome F. Wenzel, Jr., Exec. V.P., Opers.; J. Kent Pierret, Sr. V.P., Treas. and C.A.O.; Andrew L. Gates III, Sr. V.P., Genl. Counsel, and Secy.; Florence M. Ziegler, V.P., Human Resources, Comms., and Admin.

Board of directors: David H. Welch, Chair.; George R. Christmas; B.J. Duplantis; Peter D. Kinnear; John P. Laborde; Robert S. Murley; Richard A. Pattarozzi; Donald E. Powell; Kay G. Priestly; Phyllis M. Taylor
Giving statement: Giving through the Stone Energy Corporation Contributions Program.
Company EIN: 721235413

Stone Energy Corporation Contributions Program

625 E. Kaliste Saloom Rd.
Lafayette, LA 70508-2540 (337) 237-0410
URL: http://www.stoneenergy.com/links/corporateGiving.aspx?hid=1

Purpose and activities: Stone Energy makes charitable contributions to nonprofit organizations involved with arts and culture, education, health, youth development, human services, and civic affairs. Support is given primarily in areas of company operations in New Orleans, Louisiana, Houston, Texas, and Morgantown, West Virginia, with emphasis on the greater Lafayette, Lousiana, area.
Fields of interest: Arts; Education; Health care; Youth development; Human services; Public affairs.
Type of support: Employee volunteer services; General/operating support.
Geographic limitations: Giving primarily in areas of company operations in New Orleans, LA, Houston, TX, and Morgantown, WV, with emphasis on the greater Lafayette, LA, area.

3615
Stonecutter Mills Corporation

400 Spindale St.
Spindale, NC 28160-1646 (828) 286-2341

Company URL: http://www.stonecuttermills.com
Establishment information: Established in 1920.
Company type: Private company
Business activities: Develops real estate.
Business type (SIC): Real estate subdividers and developers
Financial profile for 2012: Assets, $4,692,866
Corporate officers: C.R. Bridges, Chair. and Secy.-Treas.; James Cowan, C.E.O.; Ray Bridges, Corp. Secy.
Board of director: C.R. Bridges, Chair.
Giving statement: Giving through the Stonecutter Foundation, Inc.

Stonecutter Foundation, Inc.

230 Spindale St.
Spindale, NC 28160-1604
E-mail: tbarringer@stonecuttermills.com;
Application address: P.O. Box 157, Spindale, NC 28160

Establishment information: Incorporated in 1944 in NC.
Donors: Stonecutter Mills Corp.; Ivy Cowan.
Contact: Terri C. Barringer, Secy.-Treas.
Financial data (yr. ended 03/31/12): Assets, $8,833,629 (M); expenditures, $442,720; qualifying distributions, $297,200; giving activities include $297,200 for grants.
Purpose and activities: The foundation supports arts councils and organizations involved with K-12 and higher education, fire safety, golf, community and economic development, and religion and awards student loans.
Fields of interest: Arts councils; Elementary/secondary education; Higher education; Disasters, fire prevention/control; Athletics/sports, golf; Community/economic development; Religion.
Type of support: Building/renovation; General/operating support; Student loans—to individuals.
Geographic limitations: Giving primarily in NC; giving in Rutherford and Polk County, NC, for student loans.
Application information: Applications accepted. Application form required.
Initial approach: Contact foundation for application form for student loans
Deadline(s): None
Officers and Directors:* Z. E. Dobbins, Jr.*, Pres.; C. Ray Bridges, V.P.; James R. Cowan, V.P.; Terri C. Barringer, Secy. and Treas.; D. Daniel Briscoe; Dillard Morrow; M. L. Summey.
EIN: 566044820
Selected grants: The following grants are a representative sample of this grantmaker's funding activity:
$25,000 to Asheville School, Asheville, NC, 2012.
$25,000 to Isothermal Community College, Spindale, NC, 2012.
$25,000 to Isothermal Community College Foundation, Spindale, NC, 2012.
$10,000 to Rutherford County Arts Council, Forest City, NC, 2012.
$10,000 to Rutherford County Arts Council, Forest City, NC, 2012.
$5,000 to Boy Scouts of America, Piedmont Council, Gastonia, NC, 2012.
$5,000 to Rutherford Housing Partnership, Rutherfordton, NC, 2012.
$5,000 to Rutherford Lifeservices, Spindale, NC, 2012.
$5,000 to Youth Empowerment, Spindale, NC, 2012.
$2,500 to Rutherfordton Enrichment Council, Rutherfordton, NC, 2012.

3616
Stoneham Savings Bank

359 Main St.
Stoneham, MA 02180-3513
(781) 438-9400

Company URL: http://www.stonesav.com/
Establishment information: Established in 1855.
Company type: Private company
Business activities: Operates savings bank.
Business type (SIC): Savings institutions
Corporate officers: Donat Fournier, Pres. and C.E.O.; Jeffrey A. Worth, Exec. V.P. and C.O.O.; Ruth J. Rogers, V.P. and C.F.O.; Teresa Harrington, V.P., Human Resources
Giving statement: Giving through the Stoneham Savings Charitable Foundation, Inc.

Stoneham Savings Charitable Foundation, Inc.

359 Main St.
Stoneham, MA 02180-0998
URL: http://www.stonesav.com/about-us/our-community.aspx

Establishment information: Established in 2005 in MA.
Donor: Stoneham Savings Bank.
Financial data (yr. ended 12/31/11): Assets, $423,722 (M); expenditures, $45,635; qualifying distributions, $45,635; giving activities include $42,750 for 10 grants (high: $10,000; low: $500).
Purpose and activities: The foundation supports theaters and organizations involved with education, mental health, human services, and military and veterans.
Fields of interest: Performing arts, theater; Secondary school/education; Education, ESL programs; Education; Mental health/crisis services, rape victim services; Residential/custodial care, senior continuing care; Aging, centers/services; Human services; Military/veterans' organizations.
Type of support: Continuing support; General/operating support.
Geographic limitations: Giving primarily in MA.
Support limitations: No grants to individuals.
Application information: Applications not accepted. Unsolicited requests for funds not accepted.
Officers and Directors:* Donat Fournier*, Pres.; Joanne M. Anderson, Clerk; Ruth J. Rogers, Treas.; John L. Bracciotti; August S. Niewenhous III; George Riccardelli; Jeffrey A. Worth.
EIN: 202717192

3617
Stonyfield Farm, Inc.

(doing business as Stonyfield Yogurt)
10 Burton Dr.
Londonderry, NH 03053-7436
(603) 437-4040

Company URL: http://www.stonyfield.com
Establishment information: Established in 1983.
Company type: Subsidiary of a foreign company
Business activities: Produces yogurt, frozen yogurt, and ice cream.
Business type (SIC): Dairy products
Financial profile for 2010: Number of employees, 200
Corporate officers: Gary Hirshberg, Chair.; Walt Freese, Pres. and C.E.O.; Diane Carhart, C.O.O.; Alice Markowitz, V.P., Comms.
Board of director: Gary Hirshberg, Chair.
Giving statement: Giving through the Stonyfield Farm, Inc. Corporate Giving Program.

Stonyfield Farm, Inc. Corporate Giving Program

10 Burton Dr.
Londonderry, NH 03053-7436
URL: http://www.stonyfield.com/about_us/stonyfield_profits_for_planet/index.jsp

Purpose and activities: Stonyfield Farm makes charitable contributions to nonprofit organizations involved with family farming, slowing or reversing climate change, organic agriculture and reduction of toxins in agriculture and the food supply, and avoiding adverse health impacts from environmental and agricultural practices. Support is given on a national basis.
Fields of interest: Environment, toxics; Environment, climate change/global warming; Environmental education; Environment; Agriculture, sustainable programs; Nutrition.
Program:
Profits for the Planet Program: Through the Profits for the Planet Program, Stonyfield Farm supports programs designed to help protect and restore the environment.
Type of support: Donated products; General/operating support; Scholarship funds; Sponsorships.
Geographic limitations: Giving on a national basis.
Publications: Application guidelines; Grants list.
Application information: Applications accepted.
Initial approach: Visit website for application guidelines for monetary contributions;

complete online application form for product donations
Deadline(s): 6 weeks prior to need for product donations

3618
The Stop & Shop Supermarket Company LLC

(formerly The Stop & Shop Supermarket Company)
1385 Hancock St.
Quincy, MA 02169-5100 (781) 380-8000

Company URL: http://www.stopandshop.com
Establishment information: Established in 1914.
Company type: Subsidiary of a foreign company
Business activities: Operates supermarkets.
Business type (SIC): Groceries—retail
Financial profile for 2010: Number of employees, 900; sales volume, $4,550,000,000
Corporate officers: William J Grize, Pres. and C.E.O.; Paula Price, C.F.O.
Giving statement: Giving through the Stop & Shop Supermarket Company LLC Corporate Giving Program and the Stop & Shop/Giant Family Foundation.

The Stop & Shop Supermarket Company LLC Corporate Giving Program

(formerly The Stop & Shop Supermarket Company Contributions Program)
c/o Community Affairs
P.O. Box 55888
Boston, MA 02205-5888 (617) 770-6050
Application address for organizations in Massachusetts, New Hampshire, Rhode Island, and Connecticut (except New Haven and Fairfield Counties): Community Affairs, Stop & Shop Supermarket New England Division, 1385 Hancock St., Quincy, MA 02169; For organizations in New Jersey, New York, and Connecticut (New Haven and Fairfield counties only): Community Affairs, Stop & Shop Supermarket New York Metro Division, 287 Bowman Ave., Purchase, NY 10577; URL: http://www.stopandshop.com/about_us/community/index.htm

Purpose and activities: As a complement to its foundation, Stop & Shop also makes charitable contributions to nonprofit organizations directly. Support is given primarily in areas of company operations in Connecticut, Maine, Massachussets, New Hampshire, New Jersey, New York, and Rhode Island.
Fields of interest: Education; Health care, fund raising/fund distribution; Cancer; Cancer research; Food services; Nutrition; Athletics/sports, training; Children, services.
Type of support: Donated products; General/operating support; Scholarship funds.
Geographic limitations: Giving primarily in areas of company operations in CT, MA, ME, NH, NJ, NY, and RI.
Publications: Application guidelines.
Application information: Applications accepted. Giving is limited to one contribution per organization in any given year. Application letter should be submitted using company letterhead. Proposals for requests of $1,000 or more should be limited to 5 pages. Application form required. Applicants should submit the following:
1) results expected from proposed grant
2) population served
3) name, address and phone number of organization
4) copy of IRS Determination Letter
5) geographic area to be served
6) listing of board of directors, trustees, officers and other key people and their affiliations
7) detailed description of project and amount of funding requested
8) contact person
9) copy of current year's organizational budget and/or project budget
10) plans for acknowledgement
Proposals should include a list of company stores within ten miles, event date, whether the company has donated to the organization before, a deadline for the decision, a copy of the organization's Form W-9, and, for requests of $1,000 or more, the number of people served.
Initial approach: Download application form and mail to headquarters
Committee meeting date(s): Monthly for requests of $1,000 or more
Deadline(s): 6 weeks prior to need for requests of up to $1,000; 8 weeks prior to need for requests of more than $1,000
Final notification: 8 weeks

Stop & Shop/Giant Family Foundation

(formerly The Stop & Shop Family Foundation)
1385 Hancock St.
Quincy, MA 02169-5103

Establishment information: Established in 2002.
Donors: The Stop & Shop Supermarket Co.; The Stop & Shop Supermarket Co. LLC; Ahold Financial Services, LLC.
Financial data (yr. ended 12/31/10): Assets, $7,763,189 (M); gifts received, $389,312; expenditures, $1,712,813; qualifying distributions, $637,425; giving activities include $637,425 for grants.
Purpose and activities: The foundation supports organizations involved with education, health, hunger, and children.
Fields of interest: Education; Public health, obesity; Health care; Food services; Food banks; YM/YWCAs & YM/YWHAs Children.
Type of support: General/operating support.
Geographic limitations: Giving primarily in areas of company operations in CT, Washington, DC, MA, NJ, and NY.
Application information: Applications not accepted. Contributes only to pre-selected organizations.
Officers and Directors:* Carl Schlicker, Pres.; Faith Weiner*, V.P.; Thomas Hippler*, Secy.; Patricia King*, Treas.; Paula Price.
EIN: 043548392
Selected grants: The following grants are a representative sample of this grantmaker's funding activity:
$138,334 to Greater Boston Food Bank, Boston, MA, 2010.
$75,800 to Capital Area Food Bank, Washington, DC, 2010.
$75,000 to Boys and Girls Club of Pawtucket, Pawtucket, RI, 2010.
$62,500 to YMCA of Greater Boston, Boston, MA, 2010.
$40,000 to Community Food Bank of New Jersey, Hillside, NJ, 2010.
$40,000 to Long Island Cares, Hauppauge, NY, 2010.
$39,800 to Maryland Food Bank, Baltimore, MD, 2010.
$38,333 to Rhode Island Community Food Bank Association, Providence, RI, 2010.
$30,833 to Foodshare, Bloomfield, CT, 2010.
$10,000 to Food Bank of Western Massachusetts, Hatfield, MA, 2010.

3619
Stout Industries, Inc.

6425 W. Florissant Ave.
St. Louis, MO 63136-3622 (314) 385-4600

Company URL: http://www.stoutmarketing.com
Establishment information: Established in 1886.
Company type: Private company
Business activities: Manufactures metal advertising signs and indoor-outdoor point of purchase advertising displays.
Business type (SIC): Manufacturing/miscellaneous; metal products/structural; machinery/refrigeration and service industry
Corporate officers: Patrick Connors, Pres.; Jerry Schultz, V.P., Opers.
Giving statement: Giving through the Stout Industries Charitable Foundation.

Stout Industries Charitable Foundation

6425 W. Florissant Ave.
St. Louis, MO 63136-3622 (314) 385-4600
E-mail: john-woods@stoutmarketing.com

Establishment information: Established in 1990 in MO.
Donor: Stout Industries, Inc.
Contact: Judith Woods, Pres.
Financial data (yr. ended 12/31/11): Assets, $202,842 (M); gifts received, $1,500; expenditures, $15,511; qualifying distributions, $7,000; giving activities include $7,000 for grants.
Purpose and activities: The foundation supports organizations involved with theological education, cancer, human services, and Christianity.
Fields of interest: Education; Health organizations; Religion.
Type of support: General/operating support.
Geographic limitations: Giving primarily in St. Louis, MO.
Support limitations: No grants to individuals.
Application information: Applications accepted. Application form not required. Applicants should submit the following:
1) name, address and phone number of organization
2) detailed description of project and amount of funding requested
Initial approach: Letter of inquiry
Deadline(s): Dec. 1
Officers: Judith Woods, Pres.; John R. Woods, Jr., V.P.; Carol S. Milburn, Secy.
EIN: 431530116

3620
Stradley Ronon Stevens & Young, LLP

2600 1 Commerce Sq.
Philadelphia, PA 19103-7098
(215) 564-8000

Company URL: http://www.stradley.com/index.php
Business activities: Operates law firm.
Business type (SIC): Legal services
Corporate officers: William R. Sasso, Chair.; Jeffrey A. Lutsky, Managing Partner; James H. Jenkins, C.F.O.
Offices: Wilmington, DE; Washington, DC; Cherry Hill, NJ; Harrisburg, Malvern, Philadelphia, PA
Giving statement: Giving through the Stradley Ronon Stevens & Young, LLP Pro Bono Program.

Stradley Ronon Stevens & Young, LLP Pro Bono Program

2600 1 Commerce Sq.
Philadelphia, PA 19103-7098 (215) 564-8609
E-mail: egonzalez@stradley.com; URL: http://www.stradley.com/community-service.php#Pro

Contact: Erica S. Gonzalez, Mgr., Recruitment
Fields of interest: Legal services.
Type of support: Pro bono services - legal.

3621
Stradling Yocca Carlson & Rauth

660 Newport Ctr., Dr., Ste. 1600
P.O Box 7680
Newport Beach, CA 92660-6422
(949) 725-4000

Company URL: http://www.sycr.com/content/view/188/763/
Company type: Private company
Business activities: Operates law firm.
Business type (SIC): Legal services
Offices: Newport Beach, Sacramento, San Diego, San Francisco, Santa Barbara, CA
Giving statement: Giving through the Stradling Yocca Carlson & Rauth Pro Bono Program.

Stradling Yocca Carlson & Rauth Pro Bono Program

660 Newport Ctr., Dr., Ste. 1600
P.O Box 7680
Newport Beach, CA 92660-6422 (949) 725-4137
E-mail: mschneider@sycr.com; URL: http://www.sycr.com/content/view/355/1148/

Contact: Marc Schneider, Genl. Counsel
Fields of interest: Legal services.
Type of support: Pro bono services - legal.

3622
Stram, Inc.

703 Palomar Airport Rd., Ste. 100
Carlsbad, CA 92011-1040 (760) 602-9460

Establishment information: Established in 1950.
Company type: Private company
Business activities: Owns and operates gasoline service stations.
Business type (SIC): Gasoline service stations
Financial profile for 2011: Number of employees, 9
Corporate officers: Robert E. Boyer, Pres.; Sean Copeland, V.P. and C.F.O.
Giving statement: Giving through the Marvin Boyer Scholarship Foundation.

Marvin Boyer Scholarship Foundation

(formerly The Marvin Boyer Memorial Scholarship Fund)
3737 Camino del Rio S., Ste. 109
San Diego, CA 92108-4007
Application address: P.O. Box 412, Potosi, MO 63664

Donor: Stram, Inc.
Contact: John C. Mowry, Tr.
Financial data (yr. ended 12/30/11): Assets, $0 (M); gifts received, $5,000; expenditures, $5,000; qualifying distributions, $5,000; giving activities include $5,000 for 1 grant to an individual.
Purpose and activities: The foundation annually awards a college scholarship to a qualified student to attend the University of Missouri.
Type of support: Scholarships—to individuals.
Geographic limitations: Giving limited to MO.
Application information: Applications accepted. Application form required.
Proposals should include proof of admission to the University of Missouri.
Initial approach: Letter
Deadline(s): Dec. 15
Trustees: John C. Mowry; William B. Treitler; Marguerite Wilson.
EIN: 330245562

3623
Strategy Arts

447 Beaumont Cir.
P.O. Box 2052
West Chester, PA 19380-2052
(610) 701-7050
FAX: (484) 693-1360

Company URL: http://www.strategyarts.com
Establishment information: Established in 2004.
Company type: Private company
Business type (SIC): Business services/miscellaneous
Corporate officer: Scott Wheeler, Mgr.
Giving statement: Giving through the Strategy Arts Corporate Giving Program.

Strategy Arts Corporate Giving Program

P.O. Box 2052
West Chester, PA 19380-2052 (610) 701-7050
E-mail: Info@strategyarts.com; URL: http://www.strategyarts.com

Purpose and activities: Strategy Arts is a certified B Corporation that donates a percentage of net profits to charitable organizations.

3624
Levi Strauss & Co.

1155 Battery St.
San Francisco, CA 94111-1230
(415) 501-6000

Company URL: http://www.levistrauss.com
Establishment information: Established in 1853.
Company type: Subsidiary of a public company
Business activities: Operates brand-name clothing company.
Business type (SIC): Apparel, piece goods, and notions—wholesale
Financial profile for 2011: Number of employees, 16,200; assets, $3,135,200,000; sales volume, $4,410,600,000
Fortune 1000 ranking: 2012—520th in revenues, 664th in profits, and 733rd in assets
Corporate officers: Richard L. Kauffman, Chair.; Chip Bergh, Pres. and C.E.O.; Blake Jorgensen, Exec. V.P. and C.F.O.; Tom Peck, Sr. V.P. and C.I.O.; Cathy Unruh, Sr. V.P., Human Resources; Robert D. Haas, Chair. Emeritus
Board of directors: Richard L. Kauffman, Chair.; Fernando Aguirre; Chip Bergh; Vanessa J. Castagna; Robert A. Eckert; Peter E. Haas, Jr.; Robert D. Haas; Leon J. Level; Stephen C. Neal; Patricia Sales Pineda
Plants: Little Rock, AR; Hebron, KY; Canton, MS; Henderson, NV
Offices: Bentonville, AR; Weston, FL; Hoffman Estates, IL; Minneapolis, MN; St. Louis, MO; New York, NY; Eugene, OR; Knoxville, TN; Frisco, Westlake, TX; Milwaukee, WI
International operations: Canada
Giving statement: Giving through the Levi Strauss & Co. Contributions Program, the Levi Strauss Foundation, and the Red Tab Foundation.

Levi Strauss & Co. Contributions Program

1155 Battery St.
San Francisco, CA 94111-1203 (415) 501-6000
FAX: (415) 501-7112; URL: http://www.levistrauss.com/sustainability/people/community-engagement

Contact: Stuart C. Burden, Dir., Community Affairs, The Americas
Purpose and activities: As a complement to its foundation, Levi Strauss also makes charitable contributions to nonprofit organizations directly. Support is given on a national and international basis in areas of company operations, with some emphasis on South Africa.
Fields of interest: Education, public education; AIDS; Employment, services; Civil/human rights.
Type of support: Advocacy; Employee volunteer services; General/operating support; In-kind gifts; Sponsorships.
Geographic limitations: Giving on a national and international basis in areas of company operations, with some emphasis on South Africa.
Number of staff: 12 full-time professional; 5 full-time support; 2 part-time support.

Levi Strauss Foundation

1155 Battery St.
Levi Plaza
San Francisco, CA 94111-1203 (415) 501-3577
FAX: (415) 501-6575;
E-mail: LeviStraussFoundation@levi.com; E-mail for Daniel Jae-Won Lee: dlee4@levi.com; URL: http://www.levistrauss.com/about/foundations/levi-strauss-foundation

Establishment information: Incorporated in 1952 in CA.
Donors: Levi Strauss & Co.; Peter E. Haas, Jr.; F. Warren Hellman.
Contact: Daniel Jae-Won Lee, Exec. Dir.
Financial data (yr. ended 11/30/11): Assets, $61,457,895 (M); gifts received, $1,257,465; expenditures, $8,759,442; qualifying distributions, $8,626,882; giving activities include $8,433,418 for 196 grants (high: $335,833; low: $300).
Purpose and activities: The foundation supports organizations involved with education, health, HIV/AIDS prevention, HIV/AIDS research, legal aid, employment, disaster relief, human services, community development, civic affairs, and women. Special emphasis is directed toward programs designed to advance the human rights and well-being of underserved people.
Fields of interest: Education; Reproductive health; Public health; Public health, hygiene; Health care; AIDS; AIDS research; Legal services; Employment, equal rights; Employment; Disasters, preparedness/services; American Red Cross; Human services, financial counseling; Human services; Civil/human rights, equal rights; Civil/human rights, advocacy; Business/industry; Community development, small businesses;

Community/economic development; Public policy, research; Financial services; Public affairs Women; Economically disadvantaged.
International interests: Africa; Asia; Canada; China; Europe; Haiti; Latin America.
Programs:
Asset Building: The foundation supports programs designed to enable low-income working people to accumulate and build financial assets. Special emphasis is directed toward programs designed to drive asset building innovation to scale and sustainability; advance asset-based policy to promote savings and protect assets for low-income working people; encourage the asset building field to pay attention to disparities based on race, ethnicity, and immigration; endorse emerging international asset building networks; and promote financial literacy and access to financial products for apparel and textile workers and fair trade producers.
Employee Matching Gifts: The foundation matches contributions made by employees of Levi Strauss to nonprofit organizations on a one-for-one basis from $20 to $1,200 per employer, per year.
Employee Volunteer Grants: The foundation awards grants to nonprofit organizations with which employees and retirees of Levi Strauss volunteer or serve on boards.
HIV/AIDS: The foundation supports programs designed to address the needs of workers; improve the workplace environment; and promote the social change necessary to improve access to HIV/AIDS prevention, treatment, and care. Special emphasis is directed toward addressing stigma and discrimination in laws, policies, and social settings; building advocacy capacity of HIV/AIDS organizations and vulnerable groups; and providing prevention, testing, treatment, and care for apparel workers.
Pioneers in Justice: Through Pioneers in Justice, the foundation brings together next-generation leaders who are poised to shape social justice work for peer learning and to equip them with new tools, strategies, and ways of working to create change. The program is designed to promote and invest in collaboration and alliance building among "unlikely allies;" and accelerate learning and action in the field about how to transition to "Social Justice Version 2.0," which includes social media to engage constituents and building a broader base to create change.
Workers' Rights: The foundation supports programs designed to advance the human rights and well-being of apparel workers in communities where Levi Strauss products are manufactured. Special emphasis is directed toward programs designed to educate workers and factory management about labor rights and responsibilities; improve the health of workers including hygiene, reproductive health, and HIV/AIDS; provide asset building opportunities for workers; and support factory-level dispute resolution mechanisms, legal aid, and arbitration channels to build local capacity to enforce labor laws.
Type of support: Capital campaigns; Continuing support; Employee matching gifts; Employee volunteer services; Equipment; General/operating support; Management development/capacity building; Program development; Publication; Research; Scholarship funds; Sponsorships; Technical assistance.
Geographic limitations: Giving on a national and international basis in areas of company operations, with emphasis on CA, NY, Africa, Asia, Canada, China, Europe, Latin America, and Mexico.
Support limitations: No support for political, sectarian, religious, or discriminatory organizations, or sports teams. No grants to individuals, or for capital, endowment, or building funds, athletic competition, or advertising.
Application information: Applications not accepted. Contributes only to pre-selected organizations.
Officers and Directors:* Robert D. Haas*, Pres.; Hilary K. Krane, V.P.; Daniel Jae-Won Lee, Secy. and Exec. Dir.; Roger Fleischmann, Treas.; R. John Anderson; Sandrine Besnard-Corblet; Dorota Gotkowska; Peter E. Haas, Jr.; Jennifer Haas-Dehejia; Jeff Harlowe; Michael Kobori; Amy Leonard; Daniel Lurie; Babur Rifiq.
Number of staff: 14
EIN: 946064702
Selected grants: The following grants are a representative sample of this grantmaker's funding activity:
$250,000 to Water.org, Kansas City, MO, 2011. To fund sustainable water programs that will provide at least 200 million liters of water to communities in need of reliable access.
$170,000 to CARE USA, Atlanta, GA, 2011. For renewal support to enhance and expand the scope of the Sewing for a Brighter Future program for women garment workers in Cambodia.
$150,000 to Apparel Lesotho Alliance to Fight AIDS, Maseru, Lesotho, 2011. For industry-wide workplace initiative to combat the HIV/AIDS epidemic among apparel workers in Lesotho, payable over 2.00 years.
$100,000 to San Francisco Convention and Visitors Bureau, San Francisco, CA, 2011. For our partnership with SF Travel.
$100,000 to United Way Worldwide, Alexandria, VA, 2011. For Central Community Chest of Japan. For relief and recovery efforts in wake of the earthquake and tsunami in Japan.
$70,000 to Women Organized to Respond to Life-threatening Disease, Oakland, CA, 2011. To build advocacy capacity to reduce stigma and discrimination for women living with HIV/AIDS in the U.S. and sponsor WORLD's 20-year anniversary celebration.
$60,000 to Stichting Mama Cash, Amsterdam, Netherlands, 2011. For General support - human rights leadership grant, payable over 3.00 years.
$25,000 to Blue Planet Run Foundation, Redwood City, CA, 2011. For the Ride for Your Life 2011.
$25,000 to Global Fund for Women, San Francisco, CA, 2011. For General support - human rights leadership grant.
$21,150 to HandsOn Bay Area, San Francisco, CA, 2011. For Community Day projects in San Francisco.

The Red Tab Foundation

c/o Levi Strauss & Co.
1155 Battery St., LS7
San Francisco, CA 94120-6906 (415) 501-6554
FAX: (415) 501-1859;
E-mail: RedTabFoundation@levi.com; Toll-free tel. : (800)-544-5498; e-mail for Mary Palafox : mpalafox@levi.com; URL: http://www.redtabfoundation.org/

Establishment information: Established as a company-sponsored foundation in 1981 in CA; status changed to public charity.
Donors: Gerald O'Shea‡; Claire O'Shea.
Contact: Mary Palafox, Exec. Dir.
Financial data (yr. ended 05/31/11): Revenue, $1,352,072; assets, $15,867,200 (M); gifts received, $697,738; expenditures, $2,120,589; program services expenses, $1,806,361; giving activities include $1,246,110 for 1,071 grants to individuals and $465,592 for foundation-administered programs.
Purpose and activities: The foundation provides financial assistance, education, and preventative programs to help individuals in their own efforts to maintain their financial, physical, and emotional health.
Fields of interest: Economically disadvantaged.
Type of support: Grants to individuals; Student loans—to individuals.
Geographic limitations: Giving on a national basis.
Application information: Applications not accepted. Contributes only through employee-related emergency grants and student loans.
Officers and Directors:* Peter E. Haas, Jr.*, Pres.; Mary Jane Luck, V.P.; Mary Palafox*, Secy. and Exec. Dir.; Susan Brennan; Jim Chriss; Shannon Di Donato; Diane Ellsworth; Tom Fanoe; Mary Jane Luck; and 4 additional directors.
EIN: 942779937

3625
The Stride Rite Corporation

191 Spring St.
Lexington, MA 02421-8049 (617) 824-6000

Company URL: http://www.strideritecorp.com
Establishment information: Established in 1919.
Company type: Subsidiary of a public company
Business activities: Manufactures and sells children's and men's footwear.
Business type (SIC): Shoe stores; leather footwear; apparel, piece goods, and notions—wholesale
Corporate officers: Gregg S. Ribatt, Pres. and C.E.O.; Frank A. Caruso, Sr. V.P. and C.A.O.; Yusef Akyuz, Sr. V.P. and C.I.O.; Charles W. Redepenning, Jr., Genl. Counsel and Secy.; Gordon W. Johnson, Jr., Treas.
Subsidiaries: The Keds Corp., Cambridge, MA; Sperry Top-Sider, Inc., Cambridge, MA; Stride Rite Children's Group, Inc., Cambridge, MA
Plants: Boston, Brockton, Lawrence, MA; Fulton, Hamilton, Tipton, MO
International operations: Canada
Giving statement: Giving through the Stride Rite Philanthropic Foundation.
Company EIN: 041399290

The Stride Rite Philanthropic Foundation

191 Spring St.
Lexington, MA 02421-8045

Establishment information: Established in 1993 in MA.
Donors: The Stride Rite Corp.; The Stride Rite Charitable Foundation, Inc.
Financial data (yr. ended 09/30/11): Assets, $985,371 (M); gifts received, $200,000; expenditures, $104,370; qualifying distributions, $104,120; giving activities include $104,120 for 12 grants (high: $50,000; low: $495).
Purpose and activities: The foundation supports organizations involved with education, health, youth development, disability services, and the footwear and fashion industry. Special emphasis is directed toward programs designed to serve children.
Fields of interest: Public health, obesity; Public health, physical fitness; Health care, patient services; Health care; Athletics/sports, Special Olympics; Youth development; Developmentally disabled, centers & services; Business/industry Children.
Type of support: General/operating support.
Geographic limitations: Giving primarily in the greater Boston, MA, area.
Support limitations: No grants to individuals.
Application information: Applications accepted. Application form required.

Initial approach: Proposal
Deadline(s): None
Officers and Directors:* Gregg Ribatt*, Pres.; Angela Bass*, Secy.; Frank A. Caruso*, Treas.
EIN: 043183600

3626
Stride Tool Inc.

30333 Emerald Valley Pkwy.
Glenwillow, OH 44139-4934
(440) 247-4600

Company URL: http://www.stridetool.com
Establishment information: Established in 1980.
Company type: Private company
Business activities: Designs, manufactures, and markets hand tools.
Business type (SIC): Cutlery, hand and edge tools, and hardware
Financial profile for 2010: Number of employees, 150
Corporate officers: Lori Northrup, Chair.; Ron Ortiz, C.E.O.; Gary Medved, Pres.; Peg Adams, C.F.O.
Board of director: Lori Northrup, Chair.
Subsidiary: Toolsource LLC, Ellicottville, NY
Divisions: Imperial Div., Niles, IL; Milbar Div., Chagrin Falls, OH
Giving statement: Giving through the Bares Foundation.

The Bares Foundation

5 Park Ave.
Ellicottville, NY 14731-9705

Establishment information: Established in 1977 in OH.
Donors: Stride Tool Inc.; Jack A. Bares; Milbar Corp.
Financial data (yr. ended 06/30/11): Assets, $148,198 (M); gifts received, $100; expenditures, $105,981; qualifying distributions, $76,664; giving activities include $6,305 for 2 grants (high: $6,285; low: $20).
Purpose and activities: The foundation supports organizations involved with radio, orchestras, education, computer science, Christianity, and children.
Fields of interest: Human services.
International interests: El Salvador.
Type of support: General/operating support.
Support limitations: No grants to individuals.
Application information: Applications not accepted. Unsolicited requests for funds not accepted.
Officers: Michael Hoffman, Chair.; Jack A. Bares, Pres.; Alice W. Bares, V.P.; Lori Northrup, Secy.-Treas.
Trustees: Kent Bares; John Bares.
EIN: 341211995

3627
Stryker Corporation

2825 Airview Blvd.
Kalamazoo, MI 49002-1802
(269) 385-2600
FAX: (269) 385-1062

Company URL: http://www.stryker.com
Establishment information: Established in 1941.
Company type: Public company
Company ticker symbol and exchange: SYK/NYSE
Business activities: Operates a medical technology company.
Business type (SIC): Medical instruments and supplies
Financial profile for 2012: Number of employees, 22,010; assets, $13,206,000,000; sales volume, $8,657,000,000; pre-tax net income, $1,705,000,000; expenses, $6,916,000,000; liabilities, $4,609,000,000
Fortune 1000 ranking: 2012—305th in revenues, 156th in profits, and 324th in assets
Forbes 2000 ranking: 2012—1021st in sales, 482nd in profits, and 1268th in assets
Corporate officers: William U. Parfet, Chair.; Kevin A. Lobo, Pres. and C.E.O.; William R. Jellison, V.P. and C.F.O.; Tony M. McKinney, V.P. and C.A.O.; Dean H. Bergy, V.P. and Corp. Secy.; Jeanne M. Blondia, V.P. and Treas.; Curtis E. Hall, Esq., V.P. and Genl. Counsel; Yin C. Becker, V.P., Comms., and Public Affairs; Steven P. Benscoter, V.P., Human Resources
Board of directors: William U. Parfet, Chair.; Howard E. Cox, Jr.; Srikant M. Datar, Ph.D.; Roch Doliveux; Louise L. Francesconi; Allan C. Golston; Howard L. Lance; Kevin A. Lobo; Ronda E. Stryker
Giving statement: Giving through the Stacy and David Markel Charitable Foundation.

Stacy and David Markel Charitable Foundation

(formerly David and Stacy Markel Charitable Foundation)
3060 Dover Pl.
Ann Arbor, MI 48104-1816

Establishment information: Established in 2004 in MI.
Donors: David Markel; Stacy Markel; Stryker Corporation.
Financial data (yr. ended 12/31/11): Assets, $134,152 (M); gifts received, $13,000; expenditures, $44,588; qualifying distributions, $42,454; giving activities include $42,454 for grants.
Geographic limitations: Giving primarily in MI, with some giving in IL and NY.
Support limitations: No grants to individuals.
Application information: Applications not accepted. Unsolicited requests for funds not accepted.
Officers: David Markel, Pres.; Stacy Markel, V.P.
EIN: 202000896

3628
Stupp Bridge Company

3800 Weber Rd.
St. Louis, MO 63125 (314) 638-5000

Company URL: http://www.stuppbridge.com
Establishment information: Established in 1856.
Company type: Subsidiary of a private company
Business activities: Fabricates structural steel.
Business type (SIC): Metal products/structural
Corporate officers: Robert P. Stupp, Chair.; Kenneth J. Kubacki, Vice-Chair; John P. Stupp, Jr., Exec. V.P. and C.O.O.; Thomas L. Turner, Treas. and C.F.O.; John Clark, Sr. V.P., Sales
Board of directors: Robert P. Stupp, Chair.; Kenneth J. Kubacki, Vice-Chair.
Giving statement: Giving through the Stupp Bros. Bridge & Iron Company Foundation.

Stupp Bros. Bridge & Iron Company Foundation

3800 Weber Rd.
St. Louis, MO 63125-1160

Establishment information: Trust established about 1952 in MO.
Donors: Stupp Bros. Bridge & Iron Co.; Stupp Bridge Co.
Financial data (yr. ended 10/31/11): Assets, $8,290,697 (M); expenditures, $502,417; qualifying distributions, $457,721; giving activities include $457,721 for grants.
Purpose and activities: The foundation supports organizations involved with education, health, children and youth, business, and religion.
Fields of interest: Elementary/secondary education; Higher education; Education; Hospitals (general); Health care; Boy scouts; YM/YWCAs & YM/YWHAs; Children/youth, services; Business/industry; United Ways and Federated Giving Programs; Religion.
Type of support: Annual campaigns; General/operating support; Program development; Scholarship funds.
Geographic limitations: Giving primarily in St. Louis, MO.
Application information: Applications not accepted. Unsolicited requests for funds not accepted.
Trustees: John P. Stupp, Jr.; Robert P. Stupp.
EIN: 237412437
Selected grants: The following grants are a representative sample of this grantmaker's funding activity:
$12,000 to University of Arizona Foundation, Tucson, AZ, 2011.
$5,000 to Duke University, Durham, NC, 2011.
$5,000 to Lehigh University, Bethlehem, PA, 2011.
$1,000 to United Negro College Fund, Fairfax, VA, 2011.
$1,000 to University of Colorado Foundation, Boulder, CO, 2011.

3629
Joseph S. Sturniolo & Associates, Inc.

7535 E. Hampden Ave., Ste. 501
Denver, CO 80231-4838 (303) 695-4363

Company URL: http://www.jsturniolo.com
Establishment information: Established in 1995.
Company type: Private company
Business activities: Provides investment advisory services.
Business type (SIC): Security and commodity services
Corporate officers: Joseph S. Sturniolo, C.E.O.; Steve D. Arrigan, Pres.
Board of directors: Erin Daugherty; Holly Glass
Giving statement: Giving through the Transition Kids.

Transition Kids

7535 E. Hampden Ave., Rm. 501
Denver, CO 80231-4838 (303) 883-3083

Establishment information: Established as a company-sponsored operating foundation in 2004 in CO.
Donor: Joseph S. Sturniolo & Associates, Inc.
Contact: Joseph S. Sturniolo, Chair.
Financial data (yr. ended 12/31/11): Assets, $17,948 (M); gifts received, $1,541; expenditures, $450; qualifying distributions, $150; giving activities include $150 for grants.
Purpose and activities: The foundation supports programs designed to serve at risk children.
Type of support: General/operating support; Program development.

Geographic limitations: Giving primarily in Denver, CO.
Application information: Applications accepted. Application form required.
Initial approach: Letter of inquiry
Deadline(s): None
Officer: Joseph S. Stumiolo, Chair.
EIN: 201159460

3631
Subaru of America, Inc.

Subaru Plz.
P.O. Box 6000
Cherry Hill, NJ 08002 (856) 488-8500

Company URL: http://www.subaru.com
Establishment information: Established in 1968.
Company type: Subsidiary of a foreign company
Business activities: Markets automobiles.
Business type (SIC): Motor vehicles, parts, and supplies—wholesale
Corporate officers: Takeshi Tachimori, Chair., Pres., and C.E.O.; Thomas J. Doll, Exec. V.P., C.O.O., and C.F.O.; Bill Cyphers, Sr. V.P., Sales
Board of director: Takeshi Tachimori, Chair.
Plants: Aurora, CO; Austell, GA; Itasca, IL; Cherry Hill, NJ; Portland, OR; Moorestown, PA
Giving statement: Giving through the Subaru of America Foundation, Inc.

Subaru of America Foundation, Inc.

P.O. Box 6000
Cherry Hill, NJ 08034-6000 (856) 488-5099
FAX: (856) 488-3300;
E-mail: foundation@subaru.com; Application address: 2235 Rte. 70 W., Cherry Hill, NJ 08002; Additional tel.: (856) 488-8500; URL: http://www.subaru.com/company/soa-foundation/index.html

Establishment information: Established in 1984 in NJ.
Donor: Subaru of America, Inc.
Contact: Sandra Capell, Community Svcs. Mgr.
Financial data (yr. ended 03/31/12): Assets, $2,238,699 (M); gifts received, $500,000; expenditures, $495,743; qualifying distributions, $495,318; giving activities include $495,318 for grants.
Purpose and activities: The foundation supports programs designed to promote youth-based environmental stewardship and enhance the academic learning experience for youth.
Fields of interest: Elementary/secondary education; Teacher school/education; Education, services; Education, reading; Education; Environment, natural resources; Environmental education; Environment; Human services; Science, formal/general education; Mathematics; Science Children/youth.
Programs:
Matching Gifts: The foundation matches contributions made by employees of Subaru of America to nonprofit organizations on a one-for-one basis up to $2,000 per employee, per year.
Memorial Grants: The foundation awards grants to charitable organizations in lieu of sending flowers when a Subaru employee loses an immediate family member.
Partnership Grants: The foundation seeks partnerships designed to engage youth and encourage active participation in the learning experience through professional development for educators, enhanced math and science education, and improved literacy and education; promote environmental stewardship through school gardens and science exploration; and partnerships designed to benefit youth through grade 12.
Subaru Scholars: The foundation awards college scholarships to children of employees of Subaru of America. Scholarship awards range from $1,000 to $5,000. The program is administered by The Scholarship Foundation.
Type of support: Continuing support; Employee matching gifts; Employee-related scholarships; General/operating support; Program development.
Geographic limitations: Giving limited to areas of company operations in Phoenix, AZ, Los Angeles, San Diego, and San Francisco, CA, Denver, CO, Washington, DC, Orlando, FL, Atlanta, GA, Chicago and Itasca, IL, Minneapolis, MN, Burlington, Camden, and Westhampton, NJ, Columbus, OH, Portland, OR, Philadelphia, PA, Dallas, TX, and Seattle, WA.
Support limitations: No support for veterans', fraternal, or labor organizations, government agencies, churches, religious, or sectarian organizations, public or private schools, charter schools, or school districts, social, membership, or other organizations not of direct benefit to the entire community, political organizations or candidates, discriminatory organizations, or national organizations. No grants to individuals (except for employee-related scholarships), or for advertising, sponsorships of special events, table purchases, athletic campaigns, capital campaigns, or political campaigns; no vehicle donations.
Publications: Application guidelines.
Application information: Applications accepted. Grants range up to $5,000 in regional locations. Grants in the Subaru of America corporate headquarters area may be higher. Faxed or e-mailed applications are not accepted. Support is limited to 1 contribution per organization during any given year. Organizations receiving support are asked to submit a grant evaluation form. Application form required. Applicants should submit the following:
1) timetable for implementation and evaluation of project
2) qualifications of key personnel
3) statement of problem project will address
4) population served
5) copy of IRS Determination Letter
6) brief history of organization and description of its mission
7) geographic area to be served
8) copy of most recent annual report/audited financial statement/990
9) how project's results will be evaluated or measured
10) explanation of why grantmaker is considered an appropriate donor for project
11) listing of board of directors, trustees, officers and other key people and their affiliations
12) detailed description of project and amount of funding requested
13) contact person
14) copy of current year's organizational budget and/or project budget
15) listing of additional sources and amount of support
Initial approach: Download application form and mail proposal and application form to foundation
Copies of proposal: 2
Board meeting date(s): Twice per year
Deadline(s): Feb. 15 for educational requests; July 31 for environmental requests
Final notification: May for educational requests; Nov. for environmental requests
Officers and Trustees:* Thomas Doll, Pres.; Joseph T. Scharff*, Secy.-Treas.; Daniel Dalton; Sheila Galluci-Davis; Fumio Iwashita.
EIN: 222531774

3632
Subaru of Indiana Automotive, Inc.

(formerly Subaru-Isuzu Automotive Inc.)
5500 State Rd., 38 E.
P.O. Box 5689
Lafayette, IN 47905 (765) 449-1111

Company URL: http://www.subaru-sia.com
Establishment information: Established in 1987.
Company type: Subsidiary of a foreign company
Business activities: Manufactures automobiles.
Business type (SIC): Motor vehicles and equipment
Corporate officers: Masahiro Kasai, Pres. and C.E.O.; T. Nishizawa, Exec. V.P., Secy., and C.F.O.
Giving statement: Giving through the Subaru of Indiana Automotive, Inc. Corporate Giving Program and the SIA Foundation, Inc.

SIA Foundation, Inc.

P.O. Box 6470
Lafayette, IN 47903-6479 (765) 449-6565
FAX: (765) 449-6952;
E-mail: shannon.walker@subaru-sia.com;
URL: http://www.siafoundation.org/

Establishment information: Established in 1997 in IN.
Donors: Subaru-Isuzu Automotive Inc.; Subaru of Indiana Automotive, Inc.
Financial data (yr. ended 12/31/11): Assets, $1,464,877 (M); expenditures, $91,257; qualifying distributions, $82,767; giving activities include $69,652 for 89 grants (high: $7,394; low: $25) and $10,219 for 38 employee matching gifts.
Purpose and activities: The foundation supports organizations involved with arts and culture, education, health, and human services.
Fields of interest: Arts; Education; Health care; Human services.
Program:
Matching Gift Program: The foundation matches contributions made by employees of SIA to nonprofit organizations.
Type of support: Building/renovation; Capital campaigns; Employee matching gifts; Equipment.
Geographic limitations: Giving limited to IN.
Support limitations: No support for political, lobbying, religious, fraternal, or discriminatory organizations. No grants to individuals, or for general operating costs, routine expenses, debt reduction, endowments, memorials, fundraising events, conferences, meals, travel, or annual fund drives.
Publications: Application guidelines; Grants list.
Application information: Applications accepted. Application form required. Applicants should submit the following:
1) copy of IRS Determination Letter
2) detailed description of project and amount of funding requested
Initial approach: Proposal
Copies of proposal: 1
Deadline(s): Jan. 1 to Mar. 31 and July 1 to Sept. 30
Directors: Thomas Vernon Easterday; Douglas Robert Meyer; David Rausch; Sue Scholer; Edward Wulbrect.
EIN: 352033162

3630
Sub-Zero, Inc.
(formerly Sub-Zero Freezer Company, Inc.)
4717 Hammersley Rd.
Madison, WI 53711-2798 (608) 271-2233

Company URL: http://www.subzero.com
Establishment information: Established in 1945.
Company type: Private company
Business activities: Manufactures freezers.
Business type (SIC): Appliances/household
Financial profile for 2010: Number of employees, 600
Corporate officers: James J. Bakke, Pres. and C.E.O.; Ed Murphy, C.F.O.; Scott LaFleur, V.P., Opers.; Charles Verri, V.P., Human Resources; Michele Bedard, V.P., Mktg.
Plant: Phoenix, AZ
Giving statement: Giving through the Sub-Zero Foundation, Inc.

Sub-Zero Foundation, Inc.
c/o Sub-Zero Wolf, Inc.
4717 Hammersley Rd.
Madison, WI 53711 (608) 271-2233

Establishment information: Established in 1998 in WI.
Donor: Sub-Zero Freezer Co., Inc.
Contact: Marge Bien
Financial data (yr. ended 04/30/12): Assets, $110,162 (M); expenditures, $89,590; qualifying distributions, $89,590; giving activities include $89,590 for 43 grants (high: $47,250; low: $150).
Purpose and activities: The foundation supports zoos and organizations involved with arts and culture, education, conservation, health, Alzheimer's disease, diabetes, athletics, human services, and business promotion.
Fields of interest: Medical research; Human services; Community/economic development.
Type of support: General/operating support; Program development.
Geographic limitations: Giving primarily in Madison, WI.
Application information: Applications accepted. Application form required. Applicants should submit the following:
1) detailed description of project and amount of funding requested
Initial approach: Letter
Deadline(s): None
Trustees: Helen A. Bakke; James J. Bakke; Deborah A. Schwartz.
EIN: 391918462
Selected grants: The following grants are a representative sample of this grantmaker's funding activity:
$100,000 to Boys and Girls Club of Dane County, Madison, WI, 2010.
$45,000 to United Way of Dane County, Madison, WI, 2010.
$2,500 to Society of Saint Vincent de Paul, Madison, WI, 2010.
$1,000 to Aldo Leopold Nature Center, Monona, WI, 2010.
$1,000 to Alzheimers Association, Denville, NJ, 2010.

3633
Suitter Axland & Hanson, P.C.
(formerly Suitter Axland Armstrong & Hanson, P.C.)
175 S. West Temple, Ste. 700
Salt Lake City, UT 84101-1480
(801) 532-7300

Company type: Private company
Business activities: Provides legal services.
Business type (SIC): Legal services
Giving statement: Giving through the LeRoy S. Axland Memorial Foundation.

LeRoy S. Axland Memorial Foundation
(formerly The Suitter Axland Foundation)
8 E. Broadway, Ste. 200
Salt Lake City, UT 84111-2246

Donor: Suitter Axland & Hanson, P.C.
Financial data (yr. ended 03/31/12): Assets, $79,337 (M); expenditures, $95; qualifying distributions, $0.
Purpose and activities: The foundation supports historical societies, day care, and service clubs.
Fields of interest: Historic preservation/historical societies; Children, day care; Community development, service clubs.
Type of support: General/operating support; Program development.
Geographic limitations: Giving primarily in Salt Lake City, UT.
Support limitations: No grants to individuals.
Application information: Applications not accepted. Unsolicited requests for funds not accepted.
Trustees: Michael W. Homer; Carl F. Huefner.
EIN: 870484418

3634
Sullivan & Cromwell LLP
125 Broad St.
New York, NY 10004-2498 (212) 558-4000

Company URL: http://www.sullcrom.com
Establishment information: Established in 1879.
Company type: Private company
Business activities: Provides legal services.
Business type (SIC): Legal services
Corporate officers: Joseph Shenker, Chair.; Robert Howard, C.F.O.
Board of director: Joseph Shenker, Chair.
Offices: Los Angeles, Palo Alto, CA; Washington, DC
International operations: Australia; China; England; France; Germany; Hong Kong; Japan
Giving statement: Giving through the Sullivan & Cromwell LLP Pro Bono Program and the Sullivan & Cromwell Foundation.

The Sullivan & Cromwell Foundation
125 Broad St., Ste. 2533
New York, NY 10004-2498

Establishment information: Established in 2001 in NY.
Donors: Sullivan & Cromwell LLP; Banco Popular.
Financial data (yr. ended 12/31/11): Assets, $82,412 (M); gifts received, $1,031,971; expenditures, $966,033; qualifying distributions, $965,875; giving activities include $965,875 for grants.
Type of support: Emergency funds; General/operating support.
Support limitations: No grants to individuals.
Application information: Applications not accepted. Unsolicited requests for funds not accepted.
Officers and Directors:* H. Rodgin Cohen*, Chair. and Pres.; Ricardo A. Mestres, Jr.*, Secy.; John E. Merow*, Treas.
EIN: 311809780
Selected grants: The following grants are a representative sample of this grantmaker's funding activity:
$50,000 to Operation USA, Los Angeles, CA, 2010.
$25,000 to Appropriate Infrastructure Development Group, Weston, MA, 2010.
$25,000 to Project Medishare for Haiti, Miami, FL, 2010.
$20,000 to World Vision, Tacoma, WA, 2010.
$10,000 to Hope for Haiti, Naples, FL, 2010.
$1,000 to Operation REACH, New Orleans, LA, 2010.

3635
Sullivan & McLaughlin Companies, Inc.
74 Lawley St.
Boston, MA 02122-3608 (617) 474-0500

Company URL: http://www.sullymac.com
Establishment information: Established in 1966.
Company type: Private company
Business activities: Provides contract electrical and communications services.
Business type (SIC): Contractors/electrical work
Corporate officers: Hugh McLaughlin, C.E.O.; John Mc Laughlin, Pres.; Larry Richmond, C.O.O.; Joseph Gates, C.F.O.

Ballybreen-Drumaville Charitable Foundation, Inc.
74 Lawley St.
Boston, MA 02122-3608
Application address: 162 Monroe Rd., Quincy, MA 02169

Establishment information: Established as a company-sponsored operating foundation in 2000 in MA.
Donors: Sullivan & McLaughlin Electrical Contractors, Inc.; Sullivan & McLaughlin Companies, Inc.
Contact: Hugh McLaughlin, Pres.
Financial data (yr. ended 06/30/12): Assets, $193,036 (M); gifts received, $25,500; expenditures, $15,563; qualifying distributions, $14,000; giving activities include $14,000 for grants.
Purpose and activities: The foundation supports organizations involved with secondary education, disease, and human services and awards grants to individuals.
Fields of interest: Education; Health care; Health organizations.
Type of support: General/operating support; Grants to individuals.
Application information: Applications accepted. Application form not required.
Initial approach: Proposal
Deadline(s): None
Officers: Hugh McLaughlin, Pres.; Catherine Rudicus, Clerk; John Garvin McLaughlin, Treas.
Directors: Daniel J. McDevitt; Kathleen A. McLaughlin.
EIN: 043530867

3636
Sullivan & Worcester LLP

1 Post Office Sq.
Boston, MA 02109-2129 (617) 338-2817

Company URL: http://www.sandw.com
Company type: Private company
Business activities: Operates law firm.
Business type (SIC): Legal services
Corporate officer: Dianne C. Hertneky, C.O.O.
Offices: Washington, DC; Boston, MA; New York, NY
Giving statement: Giving through the Sullivan & Worcester LLP Pro Bono Program.

Sullivan & Worcester LLP Pro Bono Program

1 Post Office Sq.
Boston, MA 02109-2129 (617) 338-2817
FAX: (617) 338-2880;
E-mail: pdinardo@sandw.com; Additional tel.: (617) 338-2800; URL: http://www.sandw.com/firm-involvement.html

Contact: Patrick Dinardo, Chair, Pro Bono Comm.
Fields of interest: Legal services.
Type of support: Pro bono services - legal.
Application information: A Pro Bono Committee manages the pro bono program.

3637
Sulphur Springs Valley Electric Cooperative, Inc.

(also known as SSVEC)
350 N. Haskell Ave.
Willcox, AZ 85643-1718 (520) 384-2221

Company URL: http://www.ssvec.org
Establishment information: Established in 1938.
Company type: Cooperative
Business activities: Distributes electricity.
Business type (SIC): Electric services
Corporate officers: Creden W. Huber, C.E.O.; Kathy Thatcher, Pres.; Kirby Chapman, C.F.O. and C.A.O.; Anselmo Torres, C.O.O.
Board of directors: Dan Barrera; Pat English; Joseph Furno; Harold L. Hinkley; Don Kyte; David Luna; Gene Manring; Curtis Nolan; Joe Smith; Kathy Thatcher; Les Thompson
Giving statement: Giving through the Sulphur Springs Valley Electric Cooperative Foundation, Inc.

Sulphur Springs Valley Electric Cooperative Foundation, Inc.

(also known as SSVEC Foundation)
P.O. Box 820
Willcox, AZ 85644-0820 (520) 384-5510
E-mail: waynec@ssvec.com; URL: http://www.ssvec.org/scholarship-program/

Establishment information: Established in 1985.
Donors: Sulphur Springs Valley Electric Cooperative, Inc.; Armed Forces Communication and Electronics Assn.
Contact: Wayne Crane
Financial data (yr. ended 12/31/11): Assets, $782,800 (M); gifts received, $156,105; expenditures, $102,311; qualifying distributions, $101,863; giving activities include $5,000 for 1 grant and $17,000 for 32 grants to individuals (high: $5,000; low: $500).
Purpose and activities: The foundation supports programs designed to promote youth; and awards college scholarships to students and grants to students and advisors for educational tours and science fairs.
Fields of interest: Education; Youth development; Engineering; Science Youth.
Programs:
SSVEC Foundation Scholarship Program: The foundation awards twenty $1,000 college scholarships to high school seniors who are children of members of Sulphur Springs Valley Electric Cooperative. One graduate from Benson, Bowie, Buena, Patagonia, San Simon, St. David, Tombstone, Valley Union, and Willcox high schools will each be awarded a scholarship. One scholarship will also be awarded to 12th grade graduates of home schools, charter schools, and private or public high schools in Cochise, Pima, Graham, or Santa Cruz counties.
Washington Youth Tour: The foundation sponsors six junior high school students from Benson, Bowie, Buena, Patagonia, St. David, San Simon, Tombstone, Valley Union, or Willcox high schools to attend a one-week educational tour of Washington, D.C.
YES Fair: The foundation awards grants, equipment, and travel expenses to students and advisors for the Youth Engineering Science Fair (YES Fair), where students in grades 5-12 compete in up to 14 science categories to receive cash awards and prizes. Two grand prize winners in the 9-12 divisions are also selected to compete at the Intel International Science and Engineering Fair.
Type of support: Conferences/seminars; Equipment; Grants to individuals; Scholarship funds; Scholarships—to individuals.
Geographic limitations: Giving limited to areas of company operations in AZ.
Publications: Application guidelines.
Application information: Applications accepted. Applicants should submit the following:
1) qualifications of key personnel
2) copy of IRS Determination Letter
3) copy of most recent annual report/audited financial statement/990
4) listing of board of directors, trustees, officers and other key people and their affiliations
5) detailed description of project and amount of funding requested
6) contact person
7) copy of current year's organizational budget and/or project budget

Initial approach: Complete online application or request application from participating high school counselors for scholarships; download entry form for Youth Engineering Science Fair; contact selected high schools for Washington Youth Tour
Deadline(s): Mar. 4 for scholarships; Feb. 7 for Youth Engineering Science Fair

Officers: Daniel Barrera, Pres.; Pat English, V.P.; Joe Smith, Secy.; Harold Hinkley, Treas.
Directors: Cecil O. Carlile; Joseph Furno; Donald Kyte; David Luna; Gene Manring; Andrew Mayberry; Curtis Nolan; Kathryn Thatcher.
EIN: 860488826

3638
SUMCO Phoenix Corporation

(formerly Mitsubishi Silicon America Corp.)
19801 N. Tatum Blvd.
Phoenix, AZ 85050 (480) 473-6000

Company URL: http://www.sumcousa.com
Establishment information: Established in 1995.
Company type: Subsidiary of a foreign company
Business activities: Manufactures electronic-grade silicon wafers.
Business type (SIC): Electronic components and accessories
Corporate officers: Kazumasa Shoji, Pres. and C.E.O.; Chuck Wallace, C.I.O.
Plants: Albuquerque, NM; Cincinnati, OH; Salem, OR
Giving statement: Giving through the SUMCO Phoenix Corporation Contributions Program.

SUMCO Phoenix Corporation Contributions Program

(formerly Mitsubishi Silicon America Corp. Contributions Program)
19801 N. Tatum Blvd.
Phoenix, AZ 85050-4201 (480) 473-6000
URL: http://www.sumcousa.com/about_community.htm

Purpose and activities: SUMCO Phoenix makes charitable contributions to nonprofit organizations involved with the environment. Support is given primarily in areas of company operations in New Mexico and Ohio, with some emphasis on Phoenix, Arizona.
Fields of interest: Environment.
Type of support: Employee volunteer services; General/operating support.
Geographic limitations: Giving primarily in areas of company operations in NM and OH, with some emphasis on Phoenix, AZ.

3639
Sumitomo Corporation of America

600 3rd Ave.
New York, NY 10016-2001 (212) 207-0700

Company URL: http://www.sumitomocorp.com
Establishment information: Established in 1952.
Company type: Subsidiary of a foreign company
Business activities: Conducts trading and investment activities.
Business type (SIC): Investors/miscellaneous
Financial profile for 2010: Number of employees, 175; assets, $6,430,000,000; sales volume, $5,470,000,000; pre-tax net income, $82,970,000
Corporate officers: Michihisa Shinagawa, Pres. and C.E.O.; Masato Sugimori, Exec V.P. and C.F.O.; Brian Carolin, Sr. V.P., Sales and Mktg.
Subsidiaries: Sumitrans Corporate, Jamaica, NY; Treadway Corp., South San Francisco, CA
Giving statement: Giving through the Sumitomo Corporation of America Corporate Giving Program and the Sumitomo Corporation of America Foundation.

Sumitomo Corporation of America Foundation

600 3rd Ave.
New York, NY 10016-2001
URL: http://www.sumitomocorp.com/about/community.html

Establishment information: Established in 2004 in NY.
Donor: Sumitomo Corporation of America "SCOA".
Financial data (yr. ended 03/31/11): Assets, $9,442,253 (M); expenditures, $609,158; qualifying distributions, $559,500; giving activities include $559,500 for grants.

Purpose and activities: The foundation supports organizations involved with arts and culture, education, relief assistance, and social services. Special emphasis is directed toward programs designed to enhance understanding in the United States of Japan, its people, culture, and society through research, education, and cultural initiatives.
Fields of interest: Arts, cultural/ethnic awareness; Performing arts; Arts; Higher education; Education; Disasters, preparedness/services; Children/youth, services; Human services; Community/economic development.
Type of support: General/operating support; Research; Sponsorships.
Geographic limitations: Giving primarily in areas of company operations, with emphasis on NY.
Support limitations: No grants to individuals.
Application information: Applications not accepted. Contributes only to pre-selected organizations.
Officers: Toshifumi Shibuya, Pres.; Elizabeth Peters, Secy.; Masao Hirota, Treas.
EIN: 202103634
Selected grants: The following grants are a representative sample of this grantmaker's funding activity:
$75,000 to Columbia University, Graduate School of Business, New York, NY, 2009.
$75,000 to Columbia University, Graduate School of Business, New York, NY, 2009.
$75,000 to Columbia University, Graduate School of Business, New York, NY, 2009.
$25,000 to Lincoln Center for the Performing Arts, New York, NY, 2009.
$15,000 to American Museum of Natural History, New York, NY, 2009.
$15,000 to Metropolitan Museum of Art, New York, NY, 2009.
$10,000 to Columbia University, Graduate School of Business, New York, NY, 2009.
$10,000 to Japanese American National Museum, Los Angeles, CA, 2009.
$5,000 to Japanese American National Museum, Los Angeles, CA, 2009.
$5,000 to Music From Japan, New York, NY, 2009.

3640
Sumitomo Electric Wiring Systems, Inc.

(also known as SEWS)
1018 Ashley St.
P.O. Box 90031
Bowling Green, KY 42102-9031
(270) 782-7397

Company URL: http://www.sewsus.com
Establishment information: Established in 1986.
Company type: Subsidiary of a foreign company
Business activities: Manufactures automotive wiring harnesses and connecting components.
Business type (SIC): Lighting and wiring equipment/electric
Financial profile for 2012: Number of employees, 12,000
Corporate officers: Yoshio Ebihara, Chair.; Toru Kuwahara, C.E.O.
Board of director: Yoshio Ebihara, Chair.
Giving statement: Giving through the SEWS Spirit for Education Foundation, Inc.

The SEWS Spirit for Education Foundation, Inc.

1018 Ashley St.
Bowling Green, KY 42103-2499 (270) 782-7397

Establishment information: Established in 1997 in KY.
Donor: Sumitomo Electric Wiring Systems, Inc.
Contact: Tammy Monday
Financial data (yr. ended 12/31/11): Assets, $78,114 (M); expenditures, $8,932; qualifying distributions, $6,000; giving activities include $6,000 for grants.
Purpose and activities: The foundation awards college scholarships to dependents of non-management employees of Sumitomo Electric Wiring Systems and its affiliates.
Type of support: Employee-related scholarships.
Geographic limitations: Giving primarily in areas of company operations in KY.
Application information: Applications accepted. Application form required.
Initial approach: Proposal
Deadline(s): Feb. 16
Officera and Trustees:* Lewis Burke; Cecile Garmon; Wade Markham; Sharon Woodward.
EIN: 611315218

3641
Summit Electric Supply Company, Inc.

2900 Stanford N.E.
Albuquerque, NM 87107-1814
(505) 346-9000
FAX: (505) 346-1616

Company URL: http://www.summit.com
Establishment information: Established in 1977.
Company type: Private company
Business activities: Distributes electrical equipment.
Business type (SIC): Electrical goods—wholesale
Corporate officers: Victor R. Jury, Jr., Pres. and C.E.O.; Russ Hiller, V.P., Finance and C.F.O.; David Wascom, C.I.O.; Dan Long, V.P. and Genl. Counsel; Cole Harrison, V.P., Opers.; Sheila Hernandez, V.P., Mktg.
Giving statement: Giving through the Summit Electric Supply Co., Inc., Contributions Program.

Summit Electric Supply Co., Inc., Contributions Program

2900 Stanford NE
Albuquerque, NM 87107-1814
E-mail: info@summit.com; Additional tel.: (505) 346-9000; URL: http://www.summit.com/about-us/Community-Involvement.php

3642
Summit Tool Company

(doing business as Ken-Tool Company)
(formerly Warren Tool Corporation)
768 E. North St.
Akron, OH 44305-1164 (330) 535-7177

Company URL: http://www.summittoolcompany.com/
Establishment information: Established in 1938.
Company type: Private company
Business activities: Manufactures forged hand tools.
Business type (SIC): Cutlery, hand and edge tools, and hardware
Corporate officers: H. Alexander Pendleton, Chair.; Douglas M. Romstadt, Pres.
Board of director: H. Alexander Pendleton, Chair.
Subsidiary: Ken-Tool Co., Akron, OH
Giving statement: Giving through the Pendleton Foundation.

Pendleton Foundation

(formerly Warren Tool Foundation, Inc.)
768 E. North St.
Akron, OH 44305-1164 (330) 535-7177

Establishment information: Established around 1975 in OH.
Donors: Summit Tool Co.; Elaine Hadden.
Contact: H. Alexander Pendleton, Pres.
Financial data (yr. ended 12/31/09): Assets, $10,397 (M); gifts received, $10,200; expenditures, $2,935; qualifying distributions, $2,935; giving activities include $1,750 for 2 grants (high: $1,250; low: $500).
Purpose and activities: The foundation supports organizations involved with theater and higher education.
Fields of interest: Arts; Education.
Type of support: General/operating support.
Geographic limitations: Giving primarily in OH.
Support limitations: No grants to individuals.
Application information: Applications accepted. Application form required.
Initial approach: Letter
Deadline(s): None
Officers: H. Alexander Pendleton, Pres.; Tamara B. Pendleton, Secy.; Doug Romstadt, Treas.
EIN: 347254279

3643
Sun Life Assurance Company of Canada (U.S.)

1 Sun Life Executive Park
Wellesley Hills, MA 02481 (781) 237-6030

Company URL: http://www.sunlife-usa.com
Establishment information: Established in 1970.
Company type: Subsidiary of a foreign company
Business activities: Sells life insurance.
Business type (SIC): Insurance/life
Corporate officers: James H. Sutcliffe, Chair.; Donald A. Stewart, C.E.O.; C. James Prieur, Pres. and C.O.O.
Board of directors: James H. Sutcliffe, Chair.; Donald A. Stewart, C.E.O; William D. Anderson; Richard H. Booth; John H. Clappison; David A. Ganong; Martin J. G. Glynn; Krystyna T. Hoeg; David W. Kerr; Idalene F. Kesner; Mitchell M. Merin; Hugh D. Segal; Barbara G. Stymiest
Giving statement: Giving through the Sun Life Assurance Company of Canada (U.S.) Corporate Giving Program.

Sun Life Assurance Company of Canada (U.S.) Corporate Giving Program

1 Sun Life Executive Park, SC 2132
Wellesley Hills, MA 02481 (781) 263-6306
E-mail: Kaitlin.Jaquez@sunlife.com; For Sun Life Rising Star Award: risingstar@sunlife.com; URL: http://www.sunlife.com/us/Get+to+know+us/Our+community+involvement?vgnLocale=en_CA

Contact: Kaitlin Jaquez, Sr. Philanthropy Prog. Mgr.
Purpose and activities: Sun Life makes charitable contributions to nonprofit organizations involved with arts and culture, education, health, financial

literacy, and human services. Support is given primarily in areas of company operations in Los Angeles, California, Broward, Collier, Hendry, Lee, Miami-Dade, Monroe, and Palm Beach counties, Florida, Boston, Massachusetts, Detroit, Michigan, and Philadelphia, Pennsylvania, and in Canada, Hong Kong, Indonesia, and the Philippines.
Fields of interest: Arts; Secondary school/education; Education; Children/youth, services; Civil/human rights, disabled Economically disadvantaged.
Programs:
Arts and Culture: Sun Life supports programs designed to make arts accessible to audiences of varying economic means. Special emphasis is directed toward program designed to enhance the cultural life of the community, including performing and visual arts, encouraging new audience development, and participation of young people.
Education: Sun Life supports programs designed to improve literacy; provide professional development and training; and assist the educationally disadvantaged improve their quality of life.
Health: Sun Life supports programs designed to promote health-related initiatives. Special emphasis is directed toward programs designed to promote the treatment and rehabilitation of patients who suffer from disabling illnesses; services with long-term, measurable results; programs that focus on improving the health of communities, with a focus on wellness and healthy lifestyles; and initiatives that are preventive in nature and actively moving from short-term remedies to long-term solutions.
Matching Gifts Program: Sun Life matches contributions made by its employees to nonprofit organizations.
Social Services: Sun Life supports programs designed to provide direct services to people in need, including sheltering the homeless; hunger relief; and youth development.
Type of support: Employee matching gifts; Employee volunteer services.
Geographic limitations: Giving primarily in areas of company operations in Los Angeles, CA, Broward, Collier, Hendry, Lee, Miami-Dade, Monroe, and Palm Beach counties, FL, Boston, MA, Detroit, MI, and Philadelphia, PA, and in Canada, Hong Kong, Indonesia, and the Philippines.
Support limitations: No support for discriminatory organizations.
Publications: Application guidelines; Corporate giving report.
Application information: Applications accepted. Contributions are currently limited to the Sun Life Rising Star Awards program. Application form not required.
Initial approach: Check website for geographic focus areas and application deadline
Copies of proposal: 1

3644
Sun Light & Power

1035 Folger Ave.
Berkeley, CA 94710-2819 (510) 845-2997

Company URL: http://www.sunlightandpower.com
Establishment information: Established in 1976.
Company type: Private company
Business activities: Operates solar power integrator company.
Business type (SIC): Electric services
Corporate officers: Lisa Takeuchi Takeuchi Cullen, C.E.O.; Gary Gerber, Pres.; Martin Pedley, C.O.O.; Mark Mumm, Cont.
Giving statement: Giving through the Sun Light & Power Corporate Giving Program.

Sun Light & Power Corporate Giving Program

1035 Folger Ave.
Berkeley, CA 94710-2819 (510) 845-2997
URL: http://www.sunlightandpower.com

Purpose and activities: Sun Light & Power is a certified B Corporation that donates a percentage of profits to nonprofit organizations. Special emphasis is directed toward organizations involved with affordable housing, community development, and green building. Support is given primarily in the San Francisco Bay Area, California.
Fields of interest: Environment; Housing/shelter; Community/economic development.
Type of support: Employee volunteer services; General/operating support.
Geographic limitations: Giving primarily in the San Francisco Bay area, CA.

3645
Sun Lumber Company, Inc.

22 Main Ave.
P.O. Box 590
Weston, WV 26452-1943 (304) 269-1000

Establishment information: Established in 1905.
Company type: Private company
Business activities: Operates timber tracts.
Business type (SIC): Forestry—timber tracts
Corporate officers: Frank Brewester, Co-Pres.; Billy D. Lake, Co-Pres.; Barbara L. Elliott, Secy. and Treas.
Giving statement: Giving through the Sun Lumber Company Education Foundation.

The Sun Lumber Company Education Foundation

P.O. Box 590
Weston, WV 26452-0590 (304) 269-1000

Establishment information: Established in 2000 in WV.
Donors: Sun Lumber Co.; Frank L. Brewster; June Brewster.
Contact: Frank L. Brewster, Tr.
Financial data (yr. ended 12/31/11): Assets, $36,764 (M); expenditures, $2,000; qualifying distributions, $2,000; giving activities include $2,000 for 1 grant.
Purpose and activities: The foundation awards college scholarships to children of employees of Sun Lumber Company, graduates from certain counties in West Virginia attending Glenville State College and enrolled in forestry education, and West Virginia high school graduates enrolled in forestry education.
Fields of interest: Education.
Type of support: Employee-related scholarships; Scholarships—to individuals.
Application information: Applications accepted. Application form required.
Initial approach: Letter or telephone call
Deadline(s): None
Trustee: Frank L. Brewster.
EIN: 550780820

3646
Sun Products Corporation

60 Danbury Rd.
Wilton, CT 06897 (203) 254-6700

Company URL: http://www.sunproductscorp.com
Establishment information: Established in 1975.
Company type: Private company
Business activities: Manufactures laundry detergents, softeners, and other fabric care products.
Business type (SIC): Soaps, cleaners, and toiletries
Financial profile for 2011: Number of employees, 3,500; sales volume, $2,000,000,000
Corporate officers: Neil P. DeFeo, Chair.; Jeffrey P. Ansell, Pres. and C.E.O.; Kris Kelley, Exec. V.P. and C.F.O.; Michael Pellegrino, C.I.O.; Beth Hecht, Sr. V.P., Genl. Counsel, and Secy.; Gretchen Crist, Sr. V.P., Human Resources, and Comms.
Board of directors: Neil DeFeo, Chair.; Lawernce Benjamin
Plants: Bowling Green, KY; Baltimore, MD; Dyersburg, TN; Houston, TX; Salt Lake City, UT
Office: Trumbull, CT
International operations: Canada
Giving statement: Giving through the Community Cares Foundation.

Community Cares Foundation

(formerly Playtex Cares Foundation)
1720 Post Road Rd. E., Ste. 215
Westport, CT 06880

Establishment information: Established in 2005 in CT, DE, and NJ.
Donor: Playtex Products, Inc.
Contact: Becky Troiano, Secy.
Financial data (yr. ended 12/31/09): Assets, $0 (M); expenditures, $237,814; qualifying distributions, $237,664; giving activities include $237,664 for 7 grants (high: $100,000; low: $29).
Fields of interest: Human services.
Geographic limitations: Giving primarily in DE.
Support limitations: No grants to individuals.
Application information: Applications accepted. Application form required. Applicants should submit the following:
1) name, address and phone number of organization
2) descriptive literature about organization
3) detailed description of project and amount of funding requested
4) contact person
Initial approach: Proposal
Deadline(s): None
Officers and Directors:* Neil P. DeFeo*, Pres.; Becky Troiano, Secy.; Gretchen R. Crist*, Treas.
EIN: 203555247
Selected grants: The following grants are a representative sample of this grantmaker's funding activity:
$100,000 to Westport Country Playhouse, Westport, CT, 2009. For general fund.
$77,635 to Manhattan College, Riverdale, NY, 2009.
$25,000 to FSW, Inc., Bridgeport, CT, 2009. For general fund.
$25,000 to International Crisis Group, New York, NY, 2009. For general fund.
$5,000 to Agape Society, Fairfield, CT, 2009. For general fund.

3647
Sunbeam Properties, Inc.
1401 79th St. Causway
Miami, FL 33141-4104 (305) 795-2617

Establishment information: Established in 1983.
Company type: Subsidiary of a private company
Business activities: Operates real estate agency.
Business type (SIC): Real estate agents and managers
Corporate officers: Edmund N. Ansin, Pres. and C.E.O.; Roger G. Metcalf, Secy.
Giving statement: Giving through the Ansin Foundation.

Ansin Foundation
P.O. Box 610727
Miami, FL 33261-0727

Establishment information: Established in 1957.
Donors: Sunbeam Television Corp.; WHDH-TV, Inc.; Sunbeam Development Corp.; Sunbeam Properties, Inc.; Edmund N. Ansin.
Financial data (yr. ended 12/31/11): Assets, $31,827,993 (M); gifts received, $3,900,000; expenditures, $1,242,663; qualifying distributions, $1,211,492; giving activities include $1,211,492 for 40 grants (high: $330,000; low: $100).
Purpose and activities: The foundation supports hospitals and organizations involved with arts and culture, education, youth development, and community development.
Fields of interest: Performing arts, ballet; Performing arts, theater; Arts; Secondary school/education; Higher education; Education; Hospitals (general); Boys & girls clubs; Community/economic development; United Ways and Federated Giving Programs.
Type of support: General/operating support; Scholarship funds.
Geographic limitations: Giving primarily in FL and Boston, MA.
Support limitations: No grants to individuals.
Application information: Applications not accepted. Contributes only to pre-selected organizations.
Trustee: Edmund N. Ansin.
EIN: 046046113
Selected grants: The following grants are a representative sample of this grantmaker's funding activity:
$10,000 to Brown University, Providence, RI, 2010.

3648
The Sundt Companies, Inc.
2015 W. River Rd., Ste. 101
Tucson, AZ 85704 (520) 750-4600

Company URL: http://www.sundt.com
Establishment information: Established in 1890.
Company type: Private company
Business activities: Operates construction companies.
Business type (SIC): Construction/miscellaneous heavy
Corporate officers: J. Douglas Pruitt, Chair.; David S. Crawford, Pres. and C.E.O.; Raymond C. Bargull, Exec. V.P. and C.F.O.; Randy Nye, Sr. V.P. and Genl. Counsel
Giving statement: Giving through the Sundt Foundation.

Sundt Foundation
2015 W. River Rd., Ste. 101
Tucson, AZ 85704-1676 (520) 750-4600
E-mail: caboyd@sundt.com; URL: http://www.sundt.com/sundt-foundation

Establishment information: Established in 1998 in AZ.
Contact: Charles Boyd, Exec. Dir.
Financial data (yr. ended 09/30/11): Revenue, $762,393; assets, $329,313 (M); gifts received, $762,094; expenditures, $764,399; program services expenses, $726,601; giving activities include $726,601 for 21 grants (high: $50,000; low: $5,500).
Purpose and activities: As the fundraising arm of Sundt, the foundation works to support the needs of disadvantaged children and adults in the communities in which it does business.
Fields of interest: Community/economic development Children; Adults; Disabilities, people with.
Program:
Grants: The foundation awards grants, ranging from $1,000 to $10,000 to nonprofit organizations that work to improve the quality of life in the communities where Sundt has an established office. Grants must address one of the following two areas: children's issues (programs that improve the lives of disadvantaged children) or community issues (programs that improve the quality of life for disadvantaged adults).
Geographic limitations: Giving limited to Phoenix and Tucson, AZ; Los Angeles, Sacramento, and San Diego, CA; Cary, NC; and El Paso and San Antonio, TX.
Publications: Annual report; Application guidelines.
Application information: Applications accepted. Application form required. Applicants should submit the following:
1) copy of IRS Determination Letter
2) listing of board of directors, trustees, officers and other key people and their affiliations

Initial approach: Complete online application
Board meeting date(s): Quarterly
Deadline(s): Mar. 15, June 15, Sept. 15, and Dec. 15

Officers and Directors:* Tom Crohurst*, Pres.; Lisa White*, V.P.; Michelle Ashmore*, Secy.; John Parsons*, Treas.; Charles Boyd, Exec. Dir.; Rich Block; Tom Camden; Richard Condit; Dave Crawford; Eric Hedlund; Jacquelyn Hoppes; Abigail Shaver.
EIN: 860935586

3649
Sunkist Growers, Inc.
14130 Riverside Dr.
Sherman Oaks, CA 91423-2313
(818) 986-4800

Company URL: http://www.sunkist.com
Establishment information: Established in 1893.
Company type: Cooperative
Business activities: Cooperative marketer of fresh citrus and citrus by-products.
Business type (SIC): Groceries—wholesale
Financial profile for 2010: Number of employees, 500; assets, $189,790,000; sales volume, $1,010,000,000
Corporate officers: Nicholas L. Bozick, Chair.; Craig Armstrong, Co-Vice-Chair.; James P. Finch, Co-Vice-Chair.; Mark G. Gillette, Co-Vice-Chair.; Timothy J. Lindgren, Pres. and C.E.O.; Charles L. Woltmann, Sr. V.P. and Genl. Counsel; James A. Padden, V.P. and C.O.O.; Richard G. French, V.P. and C.F.O.; Kevin P. Fiori, V.P., Sales and Mktg.; John R. McGovern, V.P., Human Resources
Board of directors: Nicholas L. Bozick, Chair.; Craig Armstrong, Co-Vice-Chair.; James P. Finch, Co-Vice-Chair.; Mark G. Gillette, Co-Vice-Chair.; Caroline K. Alfheim; Lee C. Bailey; Nicholas L. Bozick; William E. Chaney; Steve H. Cutting; Donald E. Dames; Robert C. Davis III; Gerald M. Denni; Harold S. Edwards; James P. Finch; Mark D. Gillette; John M. Grether; Russell Katayama; Gary T. Laux; Samuel G. Mayhew; Tom L. Mazzetti; Eric M. Meling; Martin Mittman; Dick R. Neece; Cecilia A. Perry; Richard W. Pidduck; Kevin R. Riddle; Gary M. Romoff; Charles H. Sheldon; Randy Veeh; Henry F. Vega; Bruce D. Wileman
International operations: China; Japan; Switzerland
Giving statement: Giving through the Sunkist Growers, Inc. Corporate Giving Program and the A. W. Bodine—Sunkist Memorial Foundation.

Sunkist Growers, Inc. Corporate Giving Program
6500 Wilshire Blvd., Ste. 1900
Los Angeles, CA 90048-4920
Application for A.W. Bodine - Sunkist Memorial Scholarship Program: Sunkist Growers, P.O. Box 7888, Van Nuys, CA, 91409-7888; URL: http://www.sunkist.com/about/bodine_scholarship.aspx

Purpose and activities: Sunkist awards college scholarships to undergraduate college students. Support is given on a national basis.
Fields of interest: Education; Community development, neighborhood development; General charitable giving.
Type of support: Cause-related marketing; Continuing support; Employee matching gifts; General/operating support; In-kind gifts; Scholarships—to individuals; Sponsorships.
Geographic limitations: Giving on a national basis and in Canada.
Publications: Application guidelines.
Application information: Applications accepted. Application form required. Applicants should submit the following:
1) listing of additional sources and amount of support
2) copy of current year's organizational budget and/or project budget
3) copy of most recent annual report/audited financial statement/990
4) name, address and phone number of organization
5) additional materials/documentation

Proposals should include proof of financial need, family or personal involvement in California or Arizona agriculture, transcripts with grade point average, college board test scores, extracurricular activities, references, and an essay.
Initial approach: Download application form and mail to application address
Deadline(s): Apr. 30

A. W. Bodine—Sunkist Memorial Foundation
P.O. Box 7888
Van Nuys, CA 91409-7888

Establishment information: Established in 1984.
Donors: Sunkist Growers, Inc.; Ralph E. Bodine; Helen Bodine; Max Cardey; The Marlin Group, Inc.
Contact: Claire H. Smith, V.P.
Financial data (yr. ended 12/31/11): Assets, $446,938 (M); expenditures, $36,952; qualifying distributions, $30,000; giving activities include $30,000 for 15 grants to individuals (high: $2,000; low: $2,000).

Purpose and activities: The foundation awards college scholarships to students with a personal or family involvement in Arizona or California agriculture.
Fields of interest: Higher education; Agriculture.
Type of support: Scholarships—to individuals.
Geographic limitations: Giving primarily in AZ and CA.
Publications: Application guidelines.
Application information: Applications accepted. Application form required.
Applications should include personal and financial information including most recent tax return; an essay; transcripts and college board test scores; and two references from teachers, school administrators, employers, or community organizers.
Initial approach: Download application form and mail to foundation
Deadline(s): Apr. 30
Officers: Ralph E. Bodine, Pres.; Claire H. Smith, V.P.; John Caragozian, Secy.; Shannon Gleason, Treas.
Director: Helen Bodine.
EIN: 953958439

3650
Sunoco, Inc.

(formerly Sun Company, Inc.)
1735 Market St. Ste. LL
Philadelphia, PA 19103-7583
(215) 977-3000
FAX: (215) 977-3409

Company URL: http://www.sunocoinc.com
Establishment information: Established in 1886.
Company type: Subsidiary of a public company
Company ticker symbol and exchange: SUN/NYSE
Business activities: Refines and markets petroleum; produces coke; mines coal; conducts real estate investment activities.
Business type (SIC): Petroleum refining; mining/coal and lignite surface; real estate subdividers and developers
Financial profile for 2011: Number of employees, 10,500; assets, $11,982,000,000; sales volume, $49,616,000,000; pre-tax net income, -$2,404,000,000; expenses, $49,320,000,000; liabilities, $11,089,000,000
Corporate officers: Brian P. MacDonald, Chair., Pres., and C.E.O.; Stacy L. Fox, Sr. V.P., Genl. Counsel, and Corp. Secy.; Robert W. Owens, Sr. V.P., Mktg.; Michael J. Colavita, V.P. and C.F.O.; Daniel J. Platt, Treas.; Joseph P. Krott, Compt.
Board of directors: Brian P. MacDonald, Chair.; Irene C. Britt; Chris C. Casciato; William H. Easter III; Gary W. Edwards; Ursula O. Fairbairn; John P. Jones III; James G. Kaiser; John K. Wulff
Subsidiaries: Aristech Chemical Corporation, Pittsburgh, PA; Elk River Resources, Inc., Knoxville, TN; Helios Capital Corp., Radnor, PA; Radnor Corp., Radnor, PA; Sun Refining and Marketing Co., Philadelphia, PA
Giving statement: Giving through the Sunoco, Inc. Corporate Giving Program and the Sunoco Foundation.
Company EIN: 231743282

Sunoco, Inc. Corporate Giving Program

(formerly Sun Company, Inc. Corporate Giving Program)
c/o Sunoco, Inc.
1735 Market St., Ste. LL
Philadelphia, PA 19103-7583
URL: https://www.sunocoinc.com/about-sunoco/social-responsibility/index

Contact: Ed Hazzouri, Dir., Public Affairs, Delaware Valley
Purpose and activities: As a complement to its foundation, Sunoco makes charitable contributions to nonprofit organizations directly.
Fields of interest: Environment, energy; Human services; Economic development.
Type of support: Donated products; General/operating support; In-kind gifts; Sponsorships.
Geographic limitations: Giving primarily in areas of company operations.
Support limitations: Generally, no support for national or international organizations, religious organizations, fraternal organizations, athletic organizations, schools, colleges, or universities, or disease-specific organizations. Generally, no grants to individuals, or for debt reduction.
Publications: Application guidelines; Informational brochure (including application guidelines).
Application information: Multi-year funding is not automatic. The Public Affairs - Community Relations Department handles giving. Proposal should be submitted on organization letterhead. Proposals are not accepted by e-mail or fax. Application form not required. Applicants should submit the following:
1) timetable for implementation and evaluation of project
2) signature and title of chief executive officer
3) population served
4) copy of IRS Determination Letter
5) detailed description of project and amount of funding requested
6) copy of current year's organizational budget and/or project budget
Initial approach: Proposal to headquarters
Copies of proposal: 1
Deadline(s): None
Final notification: Positive responses only
Number of staff: 2 full-time professional; 1 full-time support.

The Sunoco Foundation

1735 Market St., Ste. LL
Philadelphia, PA 19103-7583
FAX: (866) 231-7702;
E-mail: raclauser@sunocoinc.com; URL: http://www.sunocoinc.com/about-sunoco/social-responsibility/index

Establishment information: Established in 2005 in PA.
Donor: Sunoco, Inc.
Contact: Ruth A. Clauser, Pres.
Financial data (yr. ended 12/31/11): Assets, $28,452,280 (M); expenditures, $1,833,079; qualifying distributions, $1,810,515; giving activities include $1,803,015 for 55 grants.
Purpose and activities: The foundation supports programs designed to promote projects that educate and develop skills for the workforce; promote environmental stewardship and responsibility; and help communities become better places to live and work.
Fields of interest: Education; Environment; Community/economic development; United Ways and Federated Giving Programs.
Type of support: Program development.
Geographic limitations: Giving primarily in areas of company operations, with emphasis on Philadelphia, PA.
Support limitations: No support for athletic teams, bands, or choirs, religious organizations, pass-through organizations, discriminatory organizations, political parties, candidates, or partisan-political groups, fraternal or war veteran organizations, or private schools. No grants to individuals, or for fundraising events or sponsorships, single diseases or disease related causes, equipment (unless part of a community outreach program), athletic events, memorial grants, or travel.
Publications: Application guidelines.
Application information: Applications accepted. Application form required. Applicants should submit the following:
1) timetable for implementation and evaluation of project
2) how project will be sustained once grantmaker support is completed
3) signature and title of chief executive officer
4) population served
5) copy of IRS Determination Letter
6) copy of most recent annual report/audited financial statement/990
7) listing of board of directors, trustees, officers and other key people and their affiliations
8) detailed description of project and amount of funding requested
9) copy of current year's organizational budget and/or project budget
10) listing of additional sources and amount of support
Initial approach: Complete online application
Deadline(s): None
Officers and Directors:* Dennis Zeleny*, Chair.; Ruth Clauser, Pres.; Charmian Uy, Treas.
EIN: 203459268
Selected grants: The following grants are a representative sample of this grantmaker's funding activity:
$200,000 to Kimmel Center for the Performing Arts, Philadelphia, PA, 2011. For endowment fund.
$200,000 to United Way of Greater Philadelphia and Southern New Jersey, Philadelphia, PA, 2011.
$100,000 to City Year, Boston, MA, 2011.
$50,000 to Partnership for the Delaware Estuary, Wilmington, DE, 2011.
$50,000 to Philadelphia Academies, Philadelphia, PA, 2011.
$34,791 to United Way of Southeast Delaware County, Chester, PA, 2011.
$30,000 to Philabundance, Philadelphia, PA, 2011.
$26,000 to Greater Philadelphia Chamber of Commerce Regional Foundation, Philadelphia, PA, 2011.
$25,000 to Congreso de Latinos Unidos, Philadelphia, PA, 2011.
$25,000 to Philadelphia Museum of Art, Philadelphia, PA, 2011.

3651
SunPower Builders

80 Pechins Mill Rd.
Collegeville, PA 19426-3222
(610) 489-1105
FAX: (610) 489-6608

Company URL: http://www.sunpowerbuilders.com
Establishment information: Established in 1972.
Company type: Private company
Business type (SIC): Business services/miscellaneous

Corporate officer: Jon Costanza, Pres.
Giving statement: Giving through the SunPower Builders Corporate Giving Program.

SunPower Builders Corporate Giving Program

80 Pechins Mill Rd.
Collegeville, PA 19426-3222 (610) 489-1105
E-mail: info@sunpowerbuilders.com; URL: http://www.sunpowerbuilders.com

Purpose and activities: SunPower Builders is a certified B Corporation that donates a percentage of net profits to charitable organizations.

3652
Sunrise Securities Corp.

600 Lexington Ave., 23rd Fl.
New York, NY 10022-4570 (212) 421-1616
FAX: (212) 750-7277

Company URL: http://www.sunrisecorp.com/
Establishment information: Established in 1992.
Company type: Private company
Business activities: Operates investment bank.
Business type (SIC): Brokers and dealers/security
Corporate officers: Michael Brill, Vice-Chair.; Nathan A. Low, Pres.; Marcia Kucher, C.F.O.
Board of director: Michael Brill, Vice-Chair.
Giving statement: Giving through the Sunrise Charitable Foundation, Inc.

Sunrise Charitable Foundation, Inc.

c/o Sunrise Securities
641 Lexington Ave., 25th Fl.
New York, NY 10022-4503

Establishment information: Established in 2006 in NY.
Donors: Lisa Low; Nathan A. Low; Sunrise Securities Inc.
Financial data (yr. ended 12/31/11): Assets, $2,131,267 (M); gifts received, $232,700; expenditures, $392,221; qualifying distributions, $391,837; giving activities include $391,837 for grants.
Purpose and activities: The foundation supports nonprofit organizations involved with Judaism and Israel.
Fields of interest: Jewish agencies & synagogues.
Type of support: General/operating support.
Geographic limitations: Giving primarily in New York, NY.
Application information: Applications not accepted. Contributes only to pre-selected organizations.
Officer and Director:* Nathan A. Low*, Pres.
EIN: 510568537
Selected grants: The following grants are a representative sample of this grantmaker's funding activity:
$60,000 to Yad Avraham Institute, New York, NY, 2010. For general purposes.
$55,000 to Jewish Center, New York, NY, 2010. For general purposes.
$25,000 to American Friends of Ramot Torah Schools, Brooklyn, NY, 2010. For general purposes.
$20,000 to Chevrat Pinto, Spring Valley, NY, 2010. For general purposes.
$10,000 to Chai Lifeline, New York, NY, 2010. For general purposes.
$10,000 to Kollel of Greater Boston, Brighton, MA, 2010. For general purposes.
$2,300 to Congregation Kehilath Jeshurun, New York, NY, 2010. For general purposes.
$1,800 to Jewish Center of Atlantic Beach, Atlantic Beach, NY, 2010. For general purposes.
$1,500 to Youth Renewal Fund, New York, NY, 2010. For general purposes.
$1,000 to Abraham Joshua Heschel School, New York, NY, 2010. For general purposes.

3653
Sunshine Makers, Inc.

(doing business as Simple Green)
15922 Pacific Coast Hwy.
Huntington Beach, CA 92649
(562) 795-6000
FAX: (562) 592-3830

Company URL: http://www.simplegreen.com
Establishment information: Established in 1979.
Company type: Private company
Business activities: Manufactures cleaning products.
Business type (SIC): Soaps, cleaners, and toiletries
Financial profile for 2009: Number of employees, 78
Corporate officers: Bruce P. FaBrizio, Pres. and C.E.O.; Bill Sample, Chair.; Richard White, C.O.O.; Patrick Sheehan, Exec. V.P., Sales; Rose Concilio, C.F.O.; Robert J. Snetsinger, V.P., Finance.; Charles P. Leo, Ph.D., V.P., Admin. and Human Resources; Linda Dayyat, Secy.
Giving statement: Giving through the EGBAR Foundation.

EGBAR Foundation

15922 Pacific Coast Hwy.
Huntington Beach, CA 92649-1806 (562) 795-6000
FAX: (562) 592-1124; URL: http://www.egbar.org

Establishment information: Established in 1989 in CA.
Donor: Sunshine Makers, Inc.
Contact: Chelsea Bryan
Financial data (yr. ended 11/30/11): Assets, $75,207 (M); gifts received, $153,089; expenditures, $124,030; qualifying distributions, $95,000; giving activities include $95,000 for 47 grants (high: $47,000; low: $1,000).
Purpose and activities: The foundation supports programs designed to promote clean environments. Special emphasis is directed toward programs designed to educate children throughout the world about the importance of recycling and protecting the environment; promote greater awareness of community environmental clean-up needs and what can be done to meet them; challenge all segments of communities, both young and old, to be responsive to those needs; provide and raise funds to effect action on projects that address environmental clean-up needs; and promote "Making a Difference" throughout the world.
Fields of interest: Environment, fund raising/fund distribution; Environment, public education; Environment, recycling; Environment, natural resources; Environmental education; Environment Children.
Type of support: General/operating support; Sponsorships.
Geographic limitations: Giving primarily in CA.
Support limitations: No grants to individuals.
Application information: Applications accepted. Application form required.
Initial approach: Letter
Deadline(s): None
Directors: Bruce P. Fabrizio; De Serres; John A. Todhunter.
EIN: 330386889

3654
SunTrust Bank

303 Peachtree St., N.E., 26th Fl.
P.O. Box 4418
Atlanta, GA 30302-4418 (404) 588-7711

Company URL: http://www.suntrust.com
Company type: Subsidiary of a public company
Ultimate parent company: SunTrust Banks, Inc.
International Securities Identification Number: US8679141031
Business activities: Operates commercial bank.
Business type (SIC): Banks/commercial
Financial profile for 2009: Number of employees, 28,001; sales volume, $10,420,030,000
Corporate officers: William H. Rogers, Jr., Chair. and C.E.O.; Aleem Gillani, C.F.O.; Anil T. Cheriyan, C.I.O.; Raymond D. Fortin, Genl. Counsel and Secy.
Board of director: William H. Rogers, Jr., Chair.
Giving statement: Giving through the SunTrust Bank Corporate Giving Program, the SunTrust Bank Charitable Trust, and the SunTrust Foundation.

SunTrust Bank Corporate Giving Program

P.O. Box 4418, Dept. 041
Atlanta, GA 30302-4418 (404) 588-8250

Contact: Raymond B. King, Sr. V.P., Community and Govt. Rels.
Purpose and activities: As a complement to its foundation, SunTrust also makes charitable contributions to nonprofit organizations directly. Support is given primarily in the metropolitan Atlanta, Georgia, area.
Fields of interest: Arts; Education.
Type of support: Building/renovation; Capital campaigns; Program development.
Geographic limitations: Giving primarily in the metropolitan Atlanta, GA, area.
Support limitations: No support for churches, tax-supported educational institutions, or political organizations. No grants to individuals, or for general operating or continuing support.
Application information: Applications accepted. Application form required.
Initial approach: Contact headquarters for application form
Copies of proposal: 1
Deadline(s): Nov. 30, Mar. 31, and Aug. 31
Final notification: 3 to 4 weeks following review

SunTrust Bank Charitable Trust

(formerly Crestar Bank Charitable Trust)
P.O. Box 1908
Orlando, FL 32802-1908
Application address: 919 E. Main St., Richmond, VA 23219

Establishment information: Established in 1964 in VA.
Donor: Crestar Bank.
Contact: Cheryl Hechler
Financial data (yr. ended 12/31/11): Assets, $11,338,343 (M); expenditures, $210,531; qualifying distributions, $144,930; giving activities include $115,000 for 5 grants (high: $50,000; low: $5,000).
Purpose and activities: The trust supports corporate foundations and organizations involved

with historic preservation and community economic development.
Fields of interest: Historic preservation/historical societies; Community/economic development; Foundations (corporate).
Type of support: Continuing support; General/operating support.
Geographic limitations: Giving primarily in VA.
Support limitations: No support for government-supported organizations or political, religious, or national health organizations. No grants to individuals, or for scholarships or fellowships; no loans.
Publications: Application guidelines.
Application information: Applications accepted. Application form required. Applicants should submit the following:
1) results expected from proposed grant
2) detailed description of project and amount of funding requested
Initial approach: Proposal
Copies of proposal: 1
Board meeting date(s): Semiannually, and as required
Deadline(s): Oct.
Trustee: SunTrust Bank.
Number of staff: 3
EIN: 546054608
Selected grants: The following grants are a representative sample of this grantmaker's funding activity:
$25,000 to Florida Community Loan Fund, Orlando, FL, 2011. For general charitable purpose.

SunTrust Foundation

(formerly SunTust Mid-Atlantic Foundation)
c/o SunTrust Banks, Inc.
919 E. Main St.
Richmond, VA 23219-4625 (804) 782-7907
URL: https://www.suntrust.com/AboutUs/CommunityCommitment/Philanthropy

Establishment information: Established in 1973 in VA.
Donors: Crestar Bank; SunTrust Bank.
Contact: Brenda L. Skidmore, Pres.
Financial data (yr. ended 12/31/11): Assets, $224,755,326 (M); expenditures, $11,032,491; qualifying distributions, $10,463,188; giving activities include $10,379,612 for grants.
Purpose and activities: The foundation supports organizations involved with arts and culture, education, health, cancer, human services, community and economic development, voluntarism promotion, and civic affairs.
Fields of interest: Museums; Museums (art); Performing arts centers; Performing arts, music; Performing arts, orchestras; Historic preservation/historical societies; Arts; Elementary/secondary education; Higher education; Business school/education; Theological school/education; Education, reading; Education; Medical care, community health systems; Hospitals (general); Health care; Cancer; American Red Cross; Salvation Army; YM/YWCAs & YM/YWHAs; Children, services; Human services, financial counseling; Human services; Urban/community development; Community development, business promotion; Community development, men's clubs; Community/economic development; Voluntarism promotion; United Ways and Federated Giving Programs; Leadership development; Public affairs.
Program:
Matching Gifts Program: The foundation matches contributions made by employees of SunTrust Bank to educational institutions and nonprofit organizations involved with arts and culture from $25 to $3,000 per employee, per year.
Type of support: Annual campaigns; Building/renovation; Capital campaigns; Employee matching gifts; Equipment; General/operating support.
Geographic limitations: Giving limited to areas of company operations, with emphasis on Washington, DC, FL, GA, MD, NC, TN, SC, and VA.
Support limitations: No support for government-supported, political, religious, or national organizations. No grants to individuals, or for research, scholarships, or fellowships; no loans.
Application information: Applications accepted. Application form not required. Applicants should submit the following:
1) results expected from proposed grant
2) descriptive literature about organization
3) detailed description of project and amount of funding requested
Initial approach: Proposal
Copies of proposal: 1
Board meeting date(s): Semiannually, and as required
Deadline(s): Sept. 1
Officers and Directors:* Brenda L. Skidmore*, Pres.; Jane A. Markins, Secy.-Treas.; Mark A. Chancy; C.T. Hll; Thomas G. Kuntz; William H. Rogers, Jr.; James M. Wells III; Jenner Wood.
Trustee: SunTrust Bank.
Number of staff: 2 full-time professional.
EIN: 237336418
Selected grants: The following grants are a representative sample of this grantmaker's funding activity:
$900,000 to United Way of Metropolitan Atlanta, Atlanta, GA, 2010.
$400,000 to New World Symphony, Miami Beach, FL, 2010.
$300,000 to Volunteer USA Foundation, Tallahassee, FL, 2010.
$175,000 to Henry W. Grady Health System Foundation, Atlanta, GA, 2010.
$66,667 to Chamber Foundation of Chattanooga, Chattanooga, TN, 2010.
$50,000 to Consumer Credit Counseling Service of Greater Atlanta, Atlanta, GA, 2010.
$6,738 to Community Foundation of Greater Chattanooga, Chattanooga, TN, 2010.
$5,000 to Broward Performing Arts Foundation, Fort Lauderdale, FL, 2010.
$5,000 to Middle Tennessee State University Foundation, Murfreesboro, TN, 2010.
$5,000 to YMCA, Peninsula Metropolitan, Yorktown, VA, 2010.

3655
Sunwest Bank

2050 Main St., Ste. 300
Irvine, CA 92614-8255 (714) 730-4444
FAX: (714) 832-0258

Company URL: http://www.sunwestbank.com/
Establishment information: Established in 1970.
Company type: Public company
Company ticker symbol and exchange: SWBC/OTC
Business activities: Operates state commercial bank.
Business type (SIC): Banks/commercial
Corporate officers: Eric D. Hovde, Chair.; Chris Walsh, Pres. and C.E.O.
Board of directors: Eric D. Hovde, Chair.; Ron Howarth; Edward Kellogg; Glen R. Mozingo, Esq.; John D. Strockis; Jeffery M. Thomas; Chris Walsh; Russ Wertz
Giving statement: Giving through the Sunwest Bank Charitable Foundation.

The Sunwest Bank Charitable Foundation

2050 Main St., Ste. 300
Irvine, CA 92614-8279 (714) 881-3039
E-mail: jboyd@sunwestbank.com; URL: http://www.sunwestbankfoundation.org/

Establishment information: Established in 2009 in CA.
Donor: Sunwest Bank.
Contact: Jeffrey Boyd, Exec. Dir.
Financial data (yr. ended 12/31/11): Assets, $1,855,261 (M); gifts received, $500,000; expenditures, $853,133; qualifying distributions, $819,393; giving activities include $819,393 for grants.
Purpose and activities: The foundation supports programs designed to assist poor, needy, and vulnerable populations, and children. Special emphasis is directed toward programs that provide food, shelter, housing, healthcare, and other primary needs.
Fields of interest: Health care; Food services; Food banks; Housing/shelter, development; Housing/shelter; Homeless, human services; Human services Children; Economically disadvantaged.
Type of support: Building/renovation; Continuing support; General/operating support.
Geographic limitations: Giving primarily in Flagstaff and Phoenix, AZ and Orange County and San Diego County, CA; limited giving in Ghana.
Support limitations: No support for political candidates. No grants to individuals, or for political campaigns, scholarships, or sponsorships.
Publications: Application guidelines; Grants list.
Application information: Applications accepted. Extra consideration is given to organizations with which Sunwest Bank employees serve as volunteers. Application form required. Applicants should submit the following:
1) copy of IRS Determination Letter
2) copy of most recent annual report/audited financial statement/990
3) listing of board of directors, trustees, officers and other key people and their affiliations
4) detailed description of project and amount of funding requested
5) copy of current year's organizational budget and/or project budget
Initial approach: Download application form and mail to foundation
Board meeting date(s): Quarterly
Deadline(s): None
Officers: Eric D. Hovde, Chair.; Jeffrey Boyd, Exec. Dir.
Trustees: Glenn Gray; Jason Raefski.
EIN: 271607730
Selected grants: The following grants are a representative sample of this grantmaker's funding activity:
$100,000 to Orangewood Childrens Foundation, Santa Ana, CA, 2010.
$50,000 to Flagstaff Medical Center, Flagstaff, AZ, 2010.
$10,000 to Family Assistance Ministries, San Clemente, CA, 2010.
$10,000 to Kids in Need of Defense, Washington, DC, 2010.
$10,000 to Old Town Mission, Cottonwood, AZ, 2010.
$5,200 to Orange County Rescue Mission, Tustin, CA, 2010.
$5,000 to Olive Crest Treatment Center, Santa Ana, CA, 2010.

3656
Super Fresh Food Markets, Inc.
2 Paragon Dr.
Montvale, NJ 07645 (201) 573-9700

Company URL: http://www.superfreshfood.com
Establishment information: Established in 1982.
Company type: Subsidiary of a public company
Business activities: Operates grocery stores.
Business type (SIC): Groceries—retail
Corporate officer: Harry Austin, Pres.
Giving statement: Giving through the Super Fresh Food Markets, Inc. Corporate Giving Program.

Super Fresh Food Markets, Inc. Corporate Giving Program
2 Paragon Dr.
Montvale, NJ 07645-1718 (201) 573-9700
URL: http://www.superfreshfood.com/pages_aboutUs.asp

Purpose and activities: SuperFresh makes charitable contributions of store gift cards to nonprofit organizations involved with the education, health, and welfare of children. Support is given primarily in areas of company operations.
Fields of interest: Education; Health care; Human services Children.
Type of support: Donated products; In-kind gifts.
Geographic limitations: Giving primarily in areas of company operations.
Support limitations: No support for political or discriminatory organizations. No grants to individuals, or for journal ads.
Publications: Application guidelines.
Application information: Applications accepted. Support is limited to 1 contribution per organization during any given year. Proposals should be submitted using organization letterhead. Application form required. Applicants should submit the following:
1) descriptive literature about organization
2) detailed description of project and amount of funding requested
3) plans for acknowledgement

Proposals should indicate the date by which a donation is needed, the organization's Tax I.D. number, and a bonus card number.
Initial approach: Download application form and deliver completed proposal and application form to nearest company store
Copies of proposal: 1
Deadline(s): 4 weeks prior to need
Final notification: 4 weeks

3657
Superior Essex Inc.
6120 Powers Ferry Rd, Ste. 150
Atlanta, GA 30339 (770) 657-6000

Company URL: http://www.essexgroup.com
Establishment information: Established in 1954.
Company type: Subsidiary of a foreign company
Business activities: Manufactures wire and cable products.
Business type (SIC): Primary metal industries
Corporate officers: Justin F. Deedy, Pres. and C.E.O.; David S. Aldridge, Exec. V.P., C.F.O., and Treas.; Mary Love Sullenberger, Sr. V.P., Genl. Counsel, and Corp. Secy.; Debbie Baker-Oliver, Sr. V.P., Corp. Admin.; Tracye C. Gilleland, Sr. V.P., Finance and Corp. Cont.
Divisions: Electrical Group, Fort Wayne, IN; OEM Group, Fort Wayne, IN
Giving statement: Giving through the Superior Essex Inc. Corporate Giving Program.

Superior Essex Inc. Corporate Giving Program
6120 Powers Ferry Rd., Ste. 150
Atlanta, GA 30339-2999 (770) 657-6000
E-mail: corporate.giving@spsx.com; URL: http://www.essexgroup.com/news.aspx?id=74

Purpose and activities: Superior Essex makes charitable contributions to nonprofit organizations involved with education and the environment. Special emphasis is directed toward programs that reach the underserved areas of our communities. Support is given primarily in areas of company operations.
Fields of interest: Education; Environment; Youth development, centers/clubs; Youth development Economically disadvantaged.
Type of support: Employee matching gifts; Employee volunteer services; General/operating support; In-kind gifts; Scholarships—to individuals; Sponsorships.
Geographic limitations: Giving primarily in areas of company operations.
Support limitations: No support for political organizations or religious organizations.
Application information: Application form not required.
Copies of proposal: 1

3658
Superior Metal Products, Inc.
(also known as American Trim)
1005 W. Grand Ave.
Lima, OH 45801-3429 (419) 228-1145

Company URL: http://www.amtrim.com
Establishment information: Established in 1948.
Company type: Private company
Business activities: Manufactures fabricated metal and plastic components and assemblies.
Business type (SIC): Fabricated metal products (except machinery and transportation equipment); plastic products/miscellaneous
Corporate officers: Leo J. Hawk, Chair.; Henry Hawk, Vice-Chair.; Jeffrey A. Hawk, C.E.O.
Board of directors: Leo J. Hawk, Chair.; Henry Hawk, Vice-Chair.
Subsidiary: Cullman Products, Cullman, AL
Giving statement: Giving through the Ar-Hale Family Foundation, Inc.

Ar-Hale Family Foundation, Inc.
(formerly Ar-Hale Foundation, Inc.)
P.O. Box 210
Lima, OH 45802-0210 (419) 991-7624
E-mail: bprueter@woh.rr.com; Additional contact: Leo Hawk, Pres., tel.: (419) 331-1040

Establishment information: Established in 1990 in OH.
Donor: Superior Metal Products, Inc.
Contact: Beverly J. Prueter
Financial data (yr. ended 12/31/11): Assets, $741,236 (M); expenditures, $250,513; qualifying distributions, $230,747; giving activities include $230,747 for grants.
Purpose and activities: The foundation supports organizations involved with family issues, health, and education. Special emphasis is directed toward initiatives working to personally impact the lives of families and children. Support is given primarily to communities where the family member conducts their business and in the communities where the foundation shareholders reside.
Fields of interest: Performing arts, orchestras; Secondary school/education; Higher education; Education; Health care; Athletics/sports, baseball; YM/YWCAs & YM/YWHAs; Family services; Human services; Christian agencies & churches; Catholic agencies & churches.
Type of support: Annual campaigns; Building/renovation; Capital campaigns; Consulting services; Continuing support; Curriculum development; Emergency funds; Endowments; Fellowships; Film/video/radio; General/operating support; Management development/capacity building; Matching/challenge support; Program development; Scholarships—to individuals; Seed money; Technical assistance.
Geographic limitations: Giving primarily in communities where the foundation shareholders reside, with emphasis on Louisville, KY; Allen, Auglaize, and Shelby counties, and the cities of Cincinnati and Lima, OH; and Shawnee, OK.
Support limitations: No grants to individuals (except for scholarships).
Application information: Applications accepted. Application form not required. Applicants should submit the following:
1) copy of most recent annual report/audited financial statement/990
2) detailed description of project and amount of funding requested
3) contact person
4) copy of current year's organizational budget and/or project budget

Initial approach: Proposal
Copies of proposal: 2
Board meeting date(s): Jan. 29, May 8, July 25, and Sept. 17
Deadline(s): None
Final notification: 6 weeks

Officers: Leo Hawk, Pres.; Arlene F. Hawk, V.P.
EIN: 341644337

3659
SUPERVALU INC.
11840 Valley View Rd.
Eden Prairie, MN 55344-3643
(952) 828-4000

Company URL: http://www.supervalu.com
Establishment information: Established in 1870.
Company type: Public company
Company ticker symbol and exchange: SVU/NYSE
International Securities Identification Number: US8685361037
Business activities: Sells groceries wholesale; operates grocery stores.
Business type (SIC): Groceries—wholesale; groceries—retail
Financial profile for 2013: Number of employees, 35,000; assets, $11,034,000,000; sales volume, $17,097,000,000; pre-tax net income, -$426,000,000; expenses, $17,254,000,000; liabilities, $12,449,000,000
Fortune 1000 ranking: 2012—86th in revenues, 983rd in profits, and 347th in assets
Forbes 2000 ranking: 2012—274th in sales, 1895th in profits, and 1348th in assets
Corporate officers: Robert Miller, Chair.; Sam Duncan, Pres. and C.E.O.; Sherry M. Smith, Exec. V.P. and C.F.O.; Randy Burdick, Exec. V.P. and C.I.O.; Karla Robertson, Exec. V.P., Genl. Counsel ,

and Secy.; Mark Van Buskirk, Exec. V.P., Mktg.; Michele Murphy, Exec V.P., Human Resources and Corp. Comms.
Board of directors: Robert Miller, Chair.; Donald R. Chappel; Irwin Cohen; Mark Neporent; Philip L. Francis; Matthew E. Rubel; Wayne C. Sales; John T. Standley; Lenard Tessler
Subsidiaries: Albertsons LLC, Boise, ID; Charley Brothers Co., New Stanton, PA; Cub Foods, Stillwater, MN; Food Giants, Inc., Atlanta, GA; J.M. Jones Co., Urbana, IL; The Lewis Grocer Co., Indianola, MS; Plainmark, Inc., Eden Prairie, MN; Preferred Products, Inc., Chaska, MN; Springfield Sugar & Products Co., Windsor Locks, CT; Sweet Life Foods, Inc., Suffield, CT; Wetterau Properties, Inc., Hazelwood, MO
Plants: Anniston, AL; Aurora, CO; Des Moines, IA; Minneapolis, MN; Bismarck, Fargo, ND; Green Bay, WI
International operations: Bermuda; Cayman Islands
Giving statement: Giving through the SUPERVALU INC. Corporate Giving Program, the Albertson's Stores Charitable Foundation Inc., the Dart Group Foundation, Inc., the Dart Group II Foundation, Inc., and the SUPERVALU Foundation.
Company EIN: 410617000

SUPERVALU INC. Corporate Giving Program

11840 Valley View Rd.
Eden Prairie, MN 55344-3643 (952) 828-4000
URL: http://www.supervalu.com/sv-webapp/community/community.jsp

Purpose and activities: As a complement to its foundation, SUPERVALU also makes charitable contributions to nonprofit organizations directly. Support is given to organizations involved with hunger relief, health and nutrition, and environmental stewardship. Support is given primarily in areas of company operations, and to national organizations.
Fields of interest: Education, information services; Education, early childhood education; Environment; Health care; Diabetes; Heart & circulatory research; Food services; Nutrition; Human services, fund raising/fund distribution; United Ways and Federated Giving Programs.
Type of support: Annual campaigns; Donated products; Employee volunteer services; General/operating support; In-kind gifts; Sponsorships.
Geographic limitations: Giving primarily in areas of company operations, and to national organizations.
Application information:
Initial approach: For local or regional giving, contact manager at nearest distribution facility, support office, or grocery store. National giving is handled by the foundation.

Albertson's Stores Charitable Foundation Inc.

(formerly Albertson's Charitable Foundation, Inc.)
P.O. Box 20, Corp. Tax 70428
Boise, ID 83726
Application address: P.O. Box 990, Minneapolis, MN 55440, tel.: (952) 903-1731

Establishment information: Established in 2003 in ID.
Donors: General Mills, Inc.; Rocky Mountain PGA Foundation; PepsiCo, Inc.
Financial data (yr. ended 01/31/13): Assets, $0 (M); expenditures, $34,213; qualifying distributions, $34,213; giving activities include $34,213 for 1 grant.
Purpose and activities: The foundation supports programs designed to promote environmental stewardship; health and nutrition; and hunger relief.
Fields of interest: Agriculture/food; Human services; Religion.
Program:
Hurricanes Katrina and Rita Assistance Fund: The foundation awards $2,500 grants to associates of Albertson's affected by hurricanes Katrina and Rita.
Type of support: Capital campaigns; General/operating support; Program development.
Geographic limitations: Giving on a national basis in area of company operations.
Application information: Applications accepted. Application form required. Applicants should submit the following:
1) role played by volunteers
2) population served
3) copy of IRS Determination Letter
4) detailed description of project and amount of funding requested
5) contact person
Initial approach: Contact foundation for application form
Deadline(s): None
Officer and Directors:* John F. Boyd*, V.P. and Treas.; Michael Erlandson; David E. Pylipow.
EIN: 200051735
Selected grants: The following grants are a representative sample of this grantmaker's funding activity:
$150,000 to Citizenship Education Fund, Chicago, IL, 2008. For community outreach.
$150,000 to Metropolitan Family Services, Chicago, IL, 2008. For community outreach.
$100,000 to Northern Illinois Food Bank, Geneva, IL, 2008. For capital campaign.
$75,000 to Chicago 2016 Exploratory Committee, Chicago, IL, 2008. For community outreach.
$45,000 to Midwestern University, Bright Star Program, Downers Grove, IL, 2008. For scholarships.
$25,500 to National Association of Chain Drug Stores Pharmacy Education Foundation, Alexandria, VA, 2008. For scholarships.
$20,000 to California State Parks Foundation, San Francisco, CA, 2008. For community outreach.
$20,000 to Casa Central, Chicago, IL, 2008. For community outreach.
$12,000 to Idaho Foodbank Warehouse, Boise, ID, 2008. For capital campaign.
$12,000 to La Salle University, Philadelphia, PA, 2008. For scholarships.

Dart Group Foundation, Inc.

1255 22nd St. N.W., Ste. 600
Washington, DC 20037-1225 (202) 293-4500

Establishment information: Established in 1987 in MD.
Donor: Dart Group Corp.
Contact: Ronald Haft, Dir.
Financial data (yr. ended 12/31/11): Assets, $1,803,742 (M); expenditures, $138,428; qualifying distributions, $130,500; giving activities include $130,500 for grants.
Purpose and activities: The foundation supports organizations involved with arts and culture, health, employment, hunger, housing, human services, and Judaism.
Fields of interest: Education; Human services; Religion.
Type of support: General/operating support.
Geographic limitations: Giving primarily in CA, Washington, DC, and MD.
Support limitations: No support for political organizations. No grants to individuals.
Application information: Applications accepted. Application form required. Applicants should submit the following:
1) statement of problem project will address
2) copy of IRS Determination Letter
3) brief history of organization and description of its mission
Initial approach: Proposal
Copies of proposal: 1
Deadline(s): None
Directors: Elliot Arditti; Ronald S. Haft.
Number of staff: None.
EIN: 521497671
Selected grants: The following grants are a representative sample of this grantmaker's funding activity:
$25,000 to GLSEN, New York, NY, 2009.
$12,500 to Enterprise Community Partners, Columbia, MD, 2009.
$12,500 to Museum of Contemporary Art, Los Angeles, CA, 2009.
$2,000 to Feed the Children, Oklahoma City, OK, 2009.
$1,500 to AIDS Project Los Angeles, Los Angeles, CA, 2009.

Dart Group II Foundation, Inc.

(formerly Crown Books Foundation, Inc.)
1255 22nd St. N.W., Ste. 600
Washington, DC 20037-1225

Establishment information: Established in 1988 in MD.
Donor: Crown Books Corp.
Financial data (yr. ended 12/31/11): Assets, $2,394,654 (M); expenditures, $195,727; qualifying distributions, $185,750; giving activities include $185,750 for grants.
Purpose and activities: The foundation supports organizations involved with arts and culture, education, health, and human services.
Fields of interest: Arts; Education; Hospitals (general); Health care; Children/youth, services; Human services; Protestant agencies & churches.
Type of support: General/operating support.
Geographic limitations: Giving primarily in CA, Washington, DC, MD, and VA.
Support limitations: No support for political organizations. No grants to individuals.
Application information: Applications accepted. Application form not required. Applicants should submit the following:
1) statement of problem project will address
2) copy of IRS Determination Letter
3) brief history of organization and description of its mission
4) detailed description of project and amount of funding requested
Initial approach: Proposal
Copies of proposal: 1
Deadline(s): None
Directors: Elliot Arditti; Ronald S. Haft.
Number of staff: None.
EIN: 521590726
Selected grants: The following grants are a representative sample of this grantmaker's funding activity:
$14,500 to Delaware Pet Adoption Center, Rehoboth Beach, DE, 2007.
$12,000 to Treatment and Learning Centers, Rockville, MD, 2007.
$10,000 to Childrens National Medical Center, Washington, DC, 2007.
$5,000 to Cystic Fibrosis Foundation, Washington, DC, 2007.
$5,000 to Pathfinders for Autism Resource Center, Cockeysville, MD, 2007.

$4,000 to Bread for the City, Washington, DC, 2007.
$4,000 to Learning Ally, Washington, DC, 2007.

SUPERVALU Foundation

P.O. Box 990
Minneapolis, MN 55440-0990
URL: http://www.supervalu.com/sv-webapp/community/community.jsp

Establishment information: Established in 1993 in MN.
Donors: General Mills; SUPERVALU INC.
Contact: Sherry Smith, Sr. V.P. and Co-Treas.
Financial data (yr. ended 02/29/12): Assets, $2,019,171 (M); gifts received, $1,680,962; expenditures, $1,554,712; qualifying distributions, $1,554,712; giving activities include $1,546,437 for 316 grants (high: $468,000; low: $25).
Purpose and activities: The foundation supports programs designed to promote environmental stewardship; health and nutrition; and hunger relief.
Fields of interest: Environment, natural resources; Environment; Public health; Health care; Heart & circulatory diseases; Diabetes; Food services; Nutrition.
Programs:
Dietary Health and Nutrition: The foundation supports programs designed to promote nutrition education and healthy lifestyles through diet.
Environmental Stewardship: The foundation supports programs designed to promote environmental stewardship, sustainable operations, and local efforts toward sustainability.
Hunger Relief: The foundation supports programs designed to provide hunger relief; and distribute food.
Type of support: Employee matching gifts; General/operating support; Program development; Scholarship funds.
Geographic limitations: Giving primarily in areas of company operations in MN.
Support limitations: No support for United Way-supported organizations (over 30 percent of budget) or veterans', fraternal, or labor organizations. No grants to individuals, or for conferences, seminars, or travel, advertising, fundraising, academic research, parties, ceremonies, or memorials, lobbying or political initiatives, school field trips, or workforce development.
Publications: Application guidelines.
Application information: Applications accepted. Application form required. Applicants should submit the following:
1) qualifications of key personnel
2) copy of IRS Determination Letter
3) brief history of organization and description of its mission
4) copy of most recent annual report/audited financial statement/990
5) how project's results will be evaluated or measured
6) listing of board of directors, trustees, officers and other key people and their affiliations
7) detailed description of project and amount of funding requested
8) copy of current year's organizational budget and/or project budget
9) listing of additional sources and amount of support

Applications must include a signed and dated IRS W-9.
Initial approach: Complete online application for organizations located near Minneapolis, MN; visit local websites for organizations located outside of Minneapolis, MN
Board meeting date(s): Quarterly
Deadline(s): Varies
Final notification: Within 90 days
Officers and Directors: Stacey Nelson-Kumar, Pres.; John F. Boyd, Group V.P. and Treas.; Mary Vander Leest, Secy.; Shannon Bennett; Mike Erlandson; Joel Guth; Diane Harper; Dave Pylipow; Janet Sparkman.
EIN: 411752955
Selected grants: The following grants are a representative sample of this grantmaker's funding activity:
$1,972,000 to Minneapolis Foundation, Minneapolis, MN, 2005.
$167,132 to United Way, 2005.
$158,124 to United Way of Greater Saint Louis, Saint Louis, MO, 2005.
$27,000 to United Way of Greater Saint Louis, Saint Louis, MO, 2005.
$25,000 to United Way, 2005.
$22,028 to United Way of Westmoreland County, Greensburg, PA, 2005.
$15,063 to United Way of Central Georgia, Macon, GA, 2005.
$10,000 to United Way of Champaign County, Champaign, IL, 2005.
$10,000 to United Way of Spokane County, Spokane, WA, 2005.
$6,410 to United Way of Ashtabula County, Ashtabula, OH, 2005.

3660
The Survis Group

(formerly A & A Services, Inc.)
2136 W. Park Place Blvd., Ste. B
Stone Mountain, GA 30087-3538
(678) 476-3600

Company URL: http://www.survisgroup.com/
Establishment information: Established in 1991.
Company type: Private company
Business activities: Provides employment services; provides consulting services.
Business type (SIC): Personnel supply services; management and public relations services
Corporate officers: Anita L. Hall, Chair.; Art Hall, C.E.O.; Gary Epp, Pres.
Board of director: Anita L. Hall, Chair.
Subsidiary: Competitive Resources Group, Inc., Lawrenceville, GA
Giving statement: Giving through the Christian Marketing Alliance, Inc.

Christian Marketing Alliance, Inc.

(formerly Educational Alliance Fund, Inc.)
5555 Oakbrook Pkwy., Ste. 345
Norcross, GA 30093

Establishment information: Established in 2001 in GA.
Donors: A&A Services, Inc.; The Survis Group; Art Hall; Anita L. Hall.
Financial data (yr. ended 06/30/12): Assets, $0 (M); expenditures, $0; qualifying distributions, $0.
Purpose and activities: The foundation supports organizations involved with higher education and Christianity.
Geographic limitations: Giving primarily in GA.
Support limitations: No grants to individuals.
Application information: Applications not accepted. Unsolicited requests for funds not accepted.
Officers: Arthur M. Hall, Pres.; Anita L. Hall, Secy.
EIN: 582661636

3661
Susquehanna Pfaltzgraff Company

140 E. Market St.
P.O. Box 2026
York, PA 17401-1219 (717) 848-5500

Establishment information: Established in 1941.
Company type: Subsidiary of a private company
Business activities: Manufactures ceramic dinnerware and giftware; broadcasts radio; provides cable television services.
Business type (SIC): Pottery; radio and television broadcasting; cable and other pay television services
Financial profile for 2010: Number of employees, 1,900
Corporate officer: Louis J. Appell, Jr., Chair.
Board of director: Louis J. Appell, Chair.
Subsidiaries: Casco Cable Television, Inc., Brunswick, ME; The Pfaltzgraff Co., York, PA; Radio Indianapolis, Inc., Indianapolis, IN; Susquehanna Radio Corp., Virginia Beach, VA; Syracuse China Corp., Syracuse, NY; WARM Broadcasting Co., Avoca, PA; WSBA AM/FM, York, PA
Giving statement: Giving through the Susquehanna Pfaltzgraff Foundation.

Susquehanna Pfaltzgraff Foundation

140 E. Market St.
P.O. Box 2026
York, PA 17405-2026 (717) 848-5500

Establishment information: Established in 1966 in PA.
Donors: Susquehanna Pfaltzgraff Co.; Susquehanna Radio Corp.; The Pfaltzgraff Co.; Susquehanna Cable Co.; York Cable Television Co.; Louis J. Appell, Jr.
Contact: John L. Finlayson, Treas.
Financial data (yr. ended 12/31/11): Assets, $11,395,255 (M); gifts received, $300,000; expenditures, $114,258; qualifying distributions, $12,500; giving activities include $12,500 for grants.
Purpose and activities: The foundation supports botanical gardens and organizations involved with preservation, land conservation, mental health, youth, and residential care.
Type of support: Capital campaigns; Program development.
Geographic limitations: Giving in the U.S., primarily in Washington, DC, ME, and York, PA; giving also in Australia.
Application information: Applications accepted. Application form not required. Applicants should submit the following:
1) copy of IRS Determination Letter
2) detailed description of project and amount of funding requested
Initial approach: Proposal
Copies of proposal: 1
Deadline(s): None

Officers and Directors:* Louis J. Appell, Jr.*, Pres.; Helen A. Norton*, V.P.; William H. Simpson, Secy.; John L. Finlayson*, Treas.
EIN: 236420008

3662
Sustainable Harvest Coffee Importers
The Natural Capital Ctr.
721 N.W. 9th Ave., Ste. 350
Portland, OR 97209-3451 (503) 235-1119
FAX: (503) 296-2349

Company URL: http://www.sustainableharvest.com
Establishment information: Established in 1997.
Company type: Private company
Business type (SIC): Business services/ miscellaneous
Corporate officers: David Griswold, Pres.; Mack Stilson, Cont.
Giving statement: Giving through the Sustainable Harvest Coffee Importers Corporate Giving Program.

Sustainable Harvest Coffee Importers Corporate Giving Program
Natural Capital Ctr.
721 N.W. 9th Ave., Ste. 235
Portland, OR 97209-3451 (503) 235-1119
E-mail: info@sustainableharvest.com; URL: http://www.sustainableharvest.com

Purpose and activities: Sustainable Harvest Coffee Importers is a certified B Corporation that donates a percentage of profits to charitable organizations. Support is given primarily in Oaxaca, Mexico, Lima, Peru, and Moshi, Tanzania.
Fields of interest: Agriculture/food, formal/general education; Agriculture, sustainable programs.
International interests: Mexico; Peru; Tanzania, Zanzibar and Pemba.
Geographic limitations: Giving primarily in Oaxaca, Mexico, Lima, Peru, and Moshi, Tanzania.

3663
Sutherland Asbill & Brennan LLP
999 Peachtree St. NE
Atlanta, GA 30309-3915 (404) 853-8067

Company URL: http://www.sutherland.com
Establishment information: Established in 1924.
Company type: Private company
Business activities: Operates law firm.
Business type (SIC): Legal services
Offices: Sacramento, CA; Washington, DC; Atlanta, GA; New York, NY; Austin, Houston, TX
International operations: United Kingdom
Giving statement: Giving through the Sutherland Asbill & Brennan LLP Pro Bono Program.

Sutherland Asbill & Brennan LLP Pro Bono Program
999 Peachtree St. NE
Atlanta, GA 30309-3915 (404) 853-8067
E-mail: terri.hendley@sutherland.com; URL: http://www.sutherland.com/publicservice/

Contact: Terri A. Hendley, Supvr. of Pro Bono and Community Svc.
Fields of interest: Legal services.
Type of support: Pro bono services - legal.
Application information: A Pro Bono Committee manages the pro bono program.

3664
Sutter Health
2200 River Plaza Dr.
Sacramento, CA 95833-4134
(916) 733-8800
FAX: (916) 554-6771

Company URL: http://www.sutterhealth.org
Establishment information: Established in 1996.
Company type: Private company
Business activities: Operates network of medical and surgical hospitals.
Business type (SIC): Hospitals
Corporate officer: Patrick E. Fry, Pres. and C.E.O.
Board of directors: Geraldine R. Brinton; Mary Brown; Patrick Fry; Michael R. Gaulke; Peter Jacobi; Richard M. Levy, Ph.D.; Sharon L. McCollam; Todd Murray; David G. Nasaw; Andrew Pansini; Robert R. Peabody, Jr., M.D.; Michael A. Roosevelt; Joan Smith-Maclean, M.D.; Todd Smith; Barry L. Williams
Giving statement: Giving through the Sutter Health Corporate Giving Program.

Sutter Health Corporate Giving Program
c/o Community Benefit Dept.
2200 River Plaza Dr.
Sacramento, CA 95833 (916) 733-8800
E-mail: Communitygiving@sutterhealth.org; URL: http://www.sutterhealth.org/about/comben/index.html

3665
Sweetbay Supermarket
(formerly Kash n' Karry Food Stores, Inc.)
3801 Sugar Palm Dr.
Tampa, FL 33619 (813) 620-1139

Company URL: http://www.sweetbaysupermarket.com/
Establishment information: Established in 1946.
Company type: Subsidiary of a foreign company
Business activities: Operates grocery stores.
Business type (SIC): Groceries—retail
Corporate officers: Michael T. Vail, Pres. and C.O.O.; Karen Fernald, Sr. V.P., Opers.; Steve Campbell, V.P., Human Resources
Division: Sweetbay Supermarket Div., Tampa, FL
Giving statement: Giving through the Sweetbay Supermarket Corporate Giving Program.

Sweetbay Supermarket Corporate Giving Program
c/o Sweetbay Supports
3801 Sugar Palm Dr.
Tampa, FL 33619-8301
URL: http://www.sweetbaysupermarket.com/home.jsp

Purpose and activities: Sweetbay makes charitable contributions to nonprofit organizations involved with nutrition and wellness, hunger relief, and on a case by case basis. Special emphasis is directed toward programs designed to involve Sweetbay associates and customers. Support is given primarily in areas of company operations.
Fields of interest: Education; Public health; Health care; Food services; Nutrition; General charitable giving.
Programs:
Hunger Relief: The company supports programs designed to provide food to those who can't afford it; and programs designed to end hunger.
Nutrition and Wellness: The company supports programs designed to promote nutrition, health education, and preventative medicine.
Type of support: Capital campaigns; Donated products; Employee volunteer services; General/operating support; In-kind gifts; Program development; Sponsorships.
Geographic limitations: Giving primarily in areas of company operations, with emphasis on FL.
Support limitations: No support for organizations veterans', fraternal, religious, or other organizations not of direct benefit to the entire community, tax-supported organizations, political organizations, sports teams, public and private K-12 institutions, or animal welfare organizations. No grants to individuals, or for fundraising events or golf tournaments, or athletic events.
Publications: Application guidelines.
Application information: Applications accepted. Additional information may be requested at a later date. Application form required. Applicants should submit the following:
1) population served
2) name, address and phone number of organization
3) copy of IRS Determination Letter
4) brief history of organization and description of its mission
5) geographic area to be served
6) copy of most recent annual report/audited financial statement/990
7) detailed description of project and amount of funding requested
8) contact person
9) listing of additional sources and amount of support

Proposals should include a letter confirming the organization's tax-exempt status, and a list of potential funding sources.
Initial approach: Download application form and mail proposal and application form to nearest company store for request of up to $500; download application form and mail proposal and application form to headquarters for requests over $500
Copies of proposal: 1
Deadline(s): None
Final notification: 30 days

3666
John S. Swift Company, Inc.
(also known as JSSCO)
999 Commerce Ct.
Buffalo Grove, IL 60089-2375
(847) 465-3300

Company URL: http://www.johnswiftprint.com/about.html
Establishment information: Established in 1912.
Company type: Private company
Business activities: Provides lithography and printing services; publishes catalogs and forms.
Business type (SIC): Printing/commercial; book publishing and/or printing; publishing/miscellaneous
Financial profile for 2010: Number of employees, 50
Corporate officers: John S. Swift III, Chair. and C.E.O.; Michael Ford, Pres.; Deane Fraser, Sr. V.P., Opers.
Board of director: John S. Swift III, Chair.

Giving statement: Giving through the John S. Swift Company Inc. Charitable Trust.

John S. Swift Company Inc. Charitable Trust

1525 W. WT Harris Blvd., D1114-044
Charlotte, NC 28288-1161 (336) 047-8169
Application address: 1248 Research Dr., St. Louis, MO 63103, tel.: (336) 747-8169

Establishment information: Trust established in 1952 in MO.
Donor: John S. Swift Co., Inc.
Contact: Bryan M. Swift, Tr.
Financial data (yr. ended 12/31/11): Assets, $1,696,529 (M); expenditures, $96,938; qualifying distributions, $89,378; giving activities include $87,000 for 79 grants (high: $10,000; low: $95).
Purpose and activities: The trust supports hospitals and organizations involved with education, animals and wildlife, multiple sclerosis, pediatrics research, and children services.
Fields of interest: Secondary school/education; Higher education; Education; Animals/wildlife, preservation/protection; Animals/wildlife, sanctuaries; Animals/wildlife; Hospitals (general); Multiple sclerosis; Pediatrics research; Girl scouts; Children, services.
Type of support: General/operating support; Program development.
Geographic limitations: Giving primarily in Chicago, IL, and St. Louis, MO.
Support limitations: No grants to individuals.
Application information: Applications accepted. Application form not required.
Initial approach: Letter of inquiry
Deadline(s): Varies
Trustees: Bryan M. Swift; Hampden M. Swift; Wells Fargo Bank, N.A.
EIN: 436020812

3667
Swift Energy Company

16825 Northchase Dr., Ste. 400
Houston, TX 77060-6098 (281) 874-2700
FAX: (281) 874-2808

Company URL: http://www.swiftenergy.com
Establishment information: Established in 1979.
Company type: Public company
Company ticker symbol and exchange: SFY/NYSE
Business activities: Produces, refines, and markets crude oil and natural gas.
Business type (SIC): Extraction/oil and gas
Financial profile for 2012: Number of employees, 332; assets, $2,444,060,000; sales volume, $557,290,000; pre-tax net income, $36,580,000; expenses, $520,710,000; liabilities, $1,407,200,000
Corporate officers: Terry E. Swift, Chair. and C.E.O.; Bruce H. Vincent, Pres.; Robert J. Banks, Exec. V.P. and C.O.O.; Alton D. Heckaman, Jr., Exec. V.P. and C.F.O.; Laurent A. Baillargeon, V.P. and Genl. Counsel; Steven B. Yakle, V.P., Corp. Admin.; Adrian D. Shelley, Treas.; Christopher M. Abundis, Corp. Secy.
Board of directors: Terry E. Swift, Chair.; Deanna L. Cannon; Douglas J. Lanier; Greg Matiuk; Clyde W. Smith, Jr.; Charles J. Swindells; Bruce H. Vincent
Giving statement: Giving through the Swift Energy Charitable Fund.
Company EIN: 203940661

Swift Energy Charitable Fund

16825 Northchase Dr., Ste. 400
Houston, TX 77060

Establishment information: Established in 2005 in TX.
Donors: Swift Energy Company; A. Earl Swift†; Terry E. Swift; Joseph A. D'Amico; Alton D. Heckaman, Jr.; James M. Kitterman; Victor R. Moran; Bruce H. Vincent; Tara L. Seaman; and 5 additional donors.
Financial data (yr. ended 12/31/11): Assets, $5,400 (M); gifts received, $40,831; expenditures, $0; qualifying distributions, $40,830; giving activities include $40,830 for 3 grants (high: $37,830; low: $1,000).
Purpose and activities: Giving to assist displaced employees and contractors working from Swift Energy Company's field office in the presidential-declared disaster zone of Hurricane Katrina in Louisiana.
Fields of interest: Environment; Health care; Human services.
Type of support: General/operating support; Grants to individuals.
Application information: Applications not accepted. Unsolicited requests for funds not accepted.
Officers and Directors:* Terry E. Swift*, Pres.; Bruce H. Vincent*, V.P.; Alton D. Heckman, Jr.*, C.F.O.
EIN: 203402113

3668
Swinerton Incorporated

260 Townsend St.
San Francisco, CA 94107-1719
(415) 421-2980

Company URL: http://www.swinerton.com
Establishment information: Established in 1888.
Company type: Private company
Business activities: Provides general contract construction services.
Business type (SIC): Contractors/general nonresidential building
Financial profile for 2009: Number of employees, 1,325; assets, $5; sales volume, $1,240,000,000
Corporate officers: Mike Re, Chair. and C.E.O.; Jeffrey C. Hoopes, Pres.; Gary Rafferty, Exec. V.P. and C.O.O.; Roxanne Watson, Cont.
Board of director: Mike Re, Chair.
Giving statement: Giving through the Swinerton Foundation.

The Swinerton Foundation

P.O. Box 77048
San Francisco, CA 94107-0048 (415) 984-1372
FAX: (415) 984-1384;
E-mail: swinertonfoundation@swinerton.com;
URL: http://www.swinerton.com/web/do/content/about/swinertonFoundation

Establishment information: Established in 2002 in CA.
Donors: Swinerton Inc.; Swinerton Builders.
Financial data (yr. ended 12/31/11): Assets, $814,853 (M); gifts received, $491,352; expenditures, $425,854; qualifying distributions, $301,575; giving activities include $301,575 for grants.
Purpose and activities: The foundation supports organizations involved with arts and culture, construction education, the environment, health, human services, and community development.
Fields of interest: Arts; Education; Environment; Health care; Youth, services; Human services; Business/industry; Community/economic development.
Type of support: Employee volunteer services; Equipment; Program development; Sponsorships.
Geographic limitations: Giving primarily in areas of company operations in CA.
Support limitations: No grants to individuals.
Application information: Applications not accepted. Contributes only to pre-selected organizations.
Officers and Directors:* Charles P. Kuffner*, Chair.; Luke P. Argilla*, Pres.; Phyllis M. Smith*, Secy.; Linda G. Schowalter*, Treas.; Gayle M. Cooper; W.J. Dysart; Frank Foellmer; Charles R. Moore; Lucille Morris-Tyndall; Gary J. Rafferty.
EIN: 030490864
Selected grants: The following grants are a representative sample of this grantmaker's funding activity:
$15,000 to American Heart Association, Dallas, TX, 2011.
$10,000 to Trust for Public Land, San Francisco, CA, 2011.
$7,320 to Hawaii Foodbank, Honolulu, HI, 2011.
$5,000 to Arizona State University Foundation for a New American University, Tempe, AZ, 2011.
$5,000 to Mission Hiring Hall, San Francisco, CA, 2011.
$5,000 to Rebuilding Together Seattle, Seattle, WA, 2011.
$5,000 to Sierra Forever Families, Sacramento, CA, 2011.
$4,000 to Community Service Programs, Santa Ana, CA, 2011.
$3,500 to Architectural Foundation of San Francisco, San Francisco, CA, 2011.
$3,000 to Great Aloha Run, Honolulu, HI, 2011.

3669
Symantec Corporation

350 Ellis St.
Mountain View, CA 94043 (650) 527-8000

Company URL: http://www.symantec.com
Establishment information: Established in 1982.
Company type: Public company
Company ticker symbol and exchange: SYMC/NASDAQ
International Securities Identification Number: US8715031089
Business activities: Develops Internet security technology solutions.
Business type (SIC): Computer services
Financial profile for 2013: Number of employees, 21,500; assets, $14,379,000,000; sales volume, $6,906,000,000; pre-tax net income, $1,023,000,000; expenses, $5,783,000,000; liabilities, $8,958,000,000
Fortune 1000 ranking: 2012—379th in revenues, 173rd in profits, and 329th in assets
Forbes 2000 ranking: 2012—1199th in sales, 555th in profits, and 1226th in assets
Corporate officers: Daniel H. Schulman, Chair.; Stephen Bennett, Pres. and C.E.O.; Stephen Gillett, Exec. V.P. and C.O.O.; James Beer, Exec. V.P. and C.F.O.; Scott Taylor, Exec. V.P., Genl. Counsel, and Secy.
Board of directors: Daniel H. Schulman, Chair.; Stephen Bennett; Michael A. Brown; Frank E. Dangeard; Geraldine B. Laybourne; David L. Mahoney; Robert S. Miller; Paul Unruh
Offices: Culver City, Mountain View, CA; Heathrow, FL; Roseville, MN; Beaverton, Springfield, OR
International operations: Ireland

Giving statement: Giving through the Symantec Corporation Contributions Program and the Symantec Foundation.
Company EIN: 770181864

Symantec Corporation Contributions Program

c/o Symantec Community Rels.
350 Ellis St.
Mountain View, CA 94043-2202 (650) 527-8000
E-mail: cr@symantec.com; E-mail address for Symantec Software Scholarship (Utah): symantec_scholarship@symantec.com; E-mail address for Symantec Research Labs Graduate Fellowships: SRLFellowship@Symantec.com; URL: http://www.symantec.com/about/profile/responsibility/community/index.jsp

Financial data (yr. ended 03/31/12): Total giving, $23,978,000, including $3,467,517 for grants, $694,483 for employee matching gifts and $19,816,000 for in-kind gifts.
Purpose and activities: As a complement to its foundation, Symantec also makes charitable contributions to nonprofit organizations directly. Special emphasis is directed toward organizations involved with science, technology, engineering, and math education, as well as equal access to educational opportunities; online safety; diversity; and environmental responsibility. Through a partnership with TechSoup Global, Symantec makes software donations to organizations in 23 countries.
Fields of interest: Education, reading; Education; Environment; Safety/disasters, public education; Safety/disasters; International affairs, equal rights; Civil/human rights, equal rights; Civil/human rights, minorities; Civil/human rights, LGBTQ; Mathematics; Engineering/technology; Science Women; Girls.
Programs:
Dollars for Doers Program: Symantec donates $15 for every hour of volunteer service (up to $1,000 per employee annually) that an employee contributes to a nonprofit through the Dollars for Doers program. In Fiscal Year 2012, Symantec paid $170,000 to match employees' time contributions through the Dollars for Doers program.
Employee Matching Gift Program: Symantec matches contributions made by its employees to nonprofit organizations on a one-for-one basis up to $1,000 per employee per year.
Symantec Research Labs Graduate Fellowships: Symantec Research Labs Graduate Fellowships are open to Ph.D. and M.S. students with a focus on technology research. A key goal of the program is to fund innovative research that has real-world value in areas of Symantec's business interests in information security, availability, and integrity. Fellowship participants gain research and development experience through guidance and mentorship from a top scientist of Symantec Research Labs during the fellowship period. Each participant is also encouraged to spend a summer working with their mentor at Symantec on a research project in their area of interest. A stipend is provided to cover educational, travel and living expenses for visits to conduct research on our campuses (i.e. reasonable costs up to $20,000 are reimbursed). All recipients will be encouraged to take a salaried internship with Symantec.
Symantec Software Scholarship (Utah): The Symantec Software Scholarship program is intended to encourage high school students (grades 9-12) to pursue education in math and science. Students are eligible to win one of four $10,000 Symantec Software Scholarship Awards by creating and entering a software-based science project into a Utah regional science fair. One scholarship will be awarded at each of the four science fairs: Richey Science Fair (Weber State University); Salt Lake Science and Engineering Fair (University of Utah); Central Utah Science and Engineering Fair (Brigham Young University); and Southern Utah Science and Engineering Fair (Southern Utah University).
Type of support: Donated products; Employee matching gifts; Employee volunteer services; Fellowships; General/operating support; In-kind gifts; Scholarship funds; Sponsorships.
Geographic limitations: Giving on a national and international basis in areas of company operations, including Mountain View, CA, Ireland, Japan, and Singapore.
Publications: Application guidelines.
Application information: Applications accepted. Application form required. Applicants should submit the following:
1) name, address and phone number of organization
2) contact person
Applications for the Symantec Research Labs Graduate Fellowships should include a personal statement of research interests of up to 500 words, standardized test scores, three letters of recommendation, a resume or C.V., and a thesis proposal (optional).
Initial approach: E-mail completed application form with personal statement for Symantec Research Labs Graduate Fellowships
Deadline(s): Applications for Symantec Research Labs Graduate Fellowships are due at 8 a.m., Feb. 25, 2013
Number of staff: 1 full-time professional.

Symantec Foundation

(formerly VERITAS Software Foundation)
350 Ellis St.
Mountain View, CA 94043
URL: http://www.symantec.com/about/profile/responsibility/community/index.jsp

Establishment information: Established in 2000 in CA.
Donors: VERITAS Software Corp.; Mark Leslie; Fred Van Den Bosch; Symantec Corp.
Financial data (yr. ended 12/31/11): Assets, $1,374,532 (M); gifts received, $250,000; expenditures, $173,670; qualifying distributions, $172,035; giving activities include $172,000 for 1 grant.
Purpose and activities: The foundation supports organizations involved with education. Special emphasis is directed toward programs designed to promote math, science, technology, and engineering education; incorporate technology in teaching; and engage minorities and women in the technological sciences.
Fields of interest: Education; Human services.
Type of support: General/operating support; Program development; Scholarship funds.
Geographic limitations: Giving on a national basis within 50 miles of areas of company operations; giving also to national organizations and U.S.-based international organizations located within 50 miles of areas of company operations.
Support limitations: No support for religious organizations not of direct benefit to the entire community, veterans' organizations, or fraternal organizations, political candidates, organizations deemed detrimental to Symantec's business goals or that can be classified as "anti-business", private foundations, K-12 schools, or for-profit organizations. No grants to individuals, or for political causes, courtesy advertising, fundraising events, capital campaigns, or conferences or symposia.
Publications: Corporate giving report.
Application information: Applications not accepted. Unsolicited requests for funds not accepted.
Board meeting date(s): Mar., June, Sept., and Dec.
Officers and Directors:* Rebecca Ranninger*, Pres.; Scott Taylor*, Secy.; Drew Delmato, Treas.; Steve Trilling.
Number of staff: None.
EIN: 770542613

3670
Symmco Incorporated

40 S. Park St.
P.O. Box F
Sykesville, PA 15865-1199 (814) 894-2461

Company URL: http://www.symmco.com
Establishment information: Established in 1952.
Company type: Private company
Business activities: Manufactures and distributes powdered metal bearings and structural parts.
Business type (SIC): Machinery/general industry
Financial profile for 2010: Number of employees, 110
Corporate officers: John W. Bean, Chair.; John Mosco, Pres. and C.E.O.; Alvin Rodgers, C.F.O.
Board of director: John W. Bean, Chair.
Giving statement: Giving through the Symmco Foundation.

Symmco Foundation

c/o S & T Wealth Management
256 Main St.
Brookville, PA 15825-1251 (814) 894-2461
Application address: c/o Symmco, Inc. Sykesville, PA

Establishment information: Established in 1983 in PA.
Donor: Symmco Inc.
Contact: Betty D. Hoare, Tr.
Financial data (yr. ended 12/31/11): Assets, $1,814,620 (M); gifts received, $50,000; expenditures, $98,537; qualifying distributions, $76,700; giving activities include $76,700 for grants.
Purpose and activities: The foundation supports libraries and organizations involved with higher education, human services, and Christianity.
Fields of interest: Education; Health organizations; Human services.
Type of support: Annual campaigns; General/operating support.
Support limitations: No grants to individuals.
Application information: Applications accepted. Application form required. Applicants should submit the following:
1) geographic area to be served
Initial approach: Proposal
Deadline(s): None
Trustees: John W. Bean; Betty D. Hoare.
Number of staff: None.
EIN: 251480507

3671
Syngenta Seeds, Inc.

(formerly Rogers Brothers Company)
600 North Armstrong Pl.
P.O. Box 4188
Boise, ID 83704 (208) 322-7272

Company URL: http://www.rogersadvantage.com
Establishment information: Established in 1876.
Company type: Subsidiary of a foreign company
Business activities: Produces vegetable seeds.
Business type (SIC): Horticultural specialties
Financial profile for 2010: Number of employees, 72
Corporate officers: Rick Mitchell, Pres.; Jeffrey Beard, C.O.O.; Edward C. Resler, Secy.
Plants: Longmont, CO; Boise, ID; Downers Grove, IL
International operations: Canada
Giving statement: Giving through the Rogers Brothers Foundation.

Rogers Brothers Foundation

c/o The Bank of Commerce
P.O. Box 1887
Idaho Falls, ID 83403-1887 (208) 523-2020
Application address: Rogers Seed Co., Foundation Admin. Committee, 600 N. Armstrong Pl., Boise, ID 41888, tel.: (800) 574-1553

Donors: Rogers Brothers Co.; Syngenta Seeds, Inc.
Financial data (yr. ended 06/30/12): Assets, $1,187 (M); gifts received, $5,000; expenditures, $10,335; qualifying distributions, $9,500; giving activities include $9,500 for grants to individuals.
Purpose and activities: The foundation awards college scholarships to children of employees and retirees of Syngenta Seeds, Inc., Rogers NK Seed Company, and their subsidiaries.
Type of support: Employee-related scholarships.
Geographic limitations: Giving primarily in ID.
Application information: Applications not accepted. Unsolicited requests for funds not accepted.
Committee Members: Kathleen Schindler; John Sorenson; Jess Wilson.
Trustee: The Bank of Commerce.
EIN: 826012018

3672
Syniverse Technologies, Inc.

(formerly TSI Telecommunication Services Inc.)
8125 Highwoods Palm Way
Tampa, FL 33647-1765 (813) 637-5000

Company URL: http://www.syniverse.com
Establishment information: Established in 1987.
Company type: Subsidiary of a private company
Business activities: Provides communications technology solutions.
Business type (SIC): Communications equipment
Corporate officers: Robert J. Marino, Chair.; Tony Holcombe, Vice-Chair.; Jeffrey S. Gordon, Pres. and C.E.O.; Alfred de Cardenas, C.O.O.; David W. Hitchcock, C.F.O., Admin; Laura E. Binion, Sr. V.P. and Genl. Counsel
Board of directors: Robert J. Marino, Chair.; Tony G. Holcombe, Vice-Chair.; Kevin L. Beebe; Stephen C. Gray; Jeffrey S. Gordon; Mark J. Johnson; Raymond Ranelli
Giving statement: Giving through the Syniverse Technologies, Inc. Corporate Giving Program.
Company EIN: 061262301

Syniverse Technologies, Inc. Corporate Giving Program

(formerly TSI Telecommunication Services Inc. Corporate Giving Program)
8125 Highwoods Palm Way
Tampa, FL 33647-1776 (813) 637-5000
URL: http://www.syniverse.com/corporate-social-responsibility.htm

Purpose and activities: Syniverse makes charitable contributions to nonprofit organizations involved with safety, pregnant mothers, human services, and technology education. Support is given primarily in areas of company operations, with emphasis on Tampa Bay, Florida.
Fields of interest: Reproductive health, prenatal care; Disasters, preparedness/services; Boys & girls clubs; Human services; Children/youth, services; United Ways and Federated Giving Programs; Engineering/technology.
Type of support: Donated products; Employee volunteer services; In-kind gifts; Program development.
Geographic limitations: Giving primarily in areas of company operations, with emphasis on Tampa Bay, FL.

3673
Synopsys, Inc.

700 E. Middlefield Rd.
Mountain View, CA 94043-4033
(650) 584-5000
FAX: (302) 636-5454

Company URL: http://www.synopsys.com
Establishment information: Established in 1986.
Company type: Public company
Company ticker symbol and exchange: SNPS/NASDAQ
Business activities: Develops electronic design automation software; provides integrated circuit design consulting services.
Business type (SIC): Computer services; management and public relations services
Financial profile for 2012: Number of employees, 8,138; assets, $4,147,660,000; sales volume, $1,756,020,000; pre-tax net income, $201,130,000; expenses, $1,565,990,000; liabilities, $1,645,970,000
Corporate officers: Aart J. de Geus, Chair. and Co-C.E.O.; Chi-Foon Chan, Pres. and Co-C.E.O.; Brian Beattie, C.F.O.; John Chilton, Sr. V.P., Mktg.; Joe Logan, Sr. V.P., Sales; Jan Collinson, Sr. V.P., Human Resources; Brian Cabrera, V.P., Genl. Counsel, and Secy.
Board of directors: Aart J. De Geus, Ph.D., Chair.; Alfred J. Castino; Chi-Foon Chan; Bruce R. Chizen; Deborah A. Coleman; Chrysostomos L. Nikias; John G. Schwarz; Roy Vallee; Steven C. Walske
Historic mergers: Avant! Corporation (June 6, 2002)
Giving statement: Giving through the Avant! Foundation, the Synopsys Foundation, and the Synopsys Silicon Valley Science & Technology Outreach Foundation.
Company EIN: 561546236

The Avant! Foundation

4320 Stevens Creek Blvd., Ste. 168
San Jose, CA 95129-1281 (408) 551-0322
FAX: (408) 551-0324;
E-mail: info@avantifoundation.org; Additional tel.: (408) 737-7168

Establishment information: Established in 1998 in CA.
Donor: Avant! Corp.
Financial data (yr. ended 12/31/11): Assets, $2,565,937 (M); expenditures, $815,125; qualifying distributions, $763,100; giving activities include $456,514 for 18 grants (high: $50,000; low: $150) and $139,067 for 24 grants to individuals (high: $12,023; low: $315).
Purpose and activities: The foundation supports programs designed to promote education; improve the lives of disadvantaged individuals; and provide financial assistance for college tuition and expenses.
Fields of interest: Higher education; Education Economically disadvantaged.
Type of support: General/operating support; Program development; Scholarships—to individuals.
Geographic limitations: Giving limited to CA.
Application information: Applications not accepted. Contributes only to pre-selected organizations and individuals.
Directors: Kamne M. Thomas, Exec. Dir.; Jayne Booker; Charles St. Clair; Reginald Swilley.
EIN: 943290664

The Synopsys Foundation

(formerly Synopsys Technology Education Opportunity Foundation)
700 E. Middlefield Rd.
Mountain View, CA 94043-4024 (650) 694-5000
E-mail: community-relations@synopsys.com; URL: http://www.synopsys.com/Company/CommunityInvolvement/CommunityRelations/Pages/SynopsysFoundation.aspx

Establishment information: Established in 1998 in CA.
Donor: Synopsys, Inc.
Contact: Erin Brennock, Pres.
Financial data (yr. ended 12/31/11): Assets, $2,152,191 (M); gifts received, $1,600,000; expenditures, $1,513,784; qualifying distributions, $1,505,149; giving activities include $1,505,149 for grants.
Purpose and activities: The foundation supports programs designed to promote K-12 science and math education.
Fields of interest: Elementary/secondary education; Education; American Red Cross; Science, formal/general education; Mathematics; Science.

Programs:

Employee Matching Gifts: The foundation matches contributions made by employees of Synopsys to educational institutions and nonprofit organizations.

Team Match: Through the Team Match Program, employee teams of 5 or more participate in charitable fundraising events that help raise awareness and funds for causes or projects and have their registration fee matched.

Type of support: Annual campaigns; Employee matching gifts; Fellowships; Program development; Scholarship funds; Sponsorships.
Geographic limitations: Giving primarily in CA.
Application information: Applications not accepted. Unsolicited applications are not accepted.
Officers and Directors: Arte de Geus*, Chair.; Erin Brennock, C.E.O. and Pres.; Ericka Varga, Secy.; Karen Brocher, Treas. and C.F.O.; Brian Beattle; Deirdre Hanford.
EIN: 770488629
Selected grants: The following grants are a representative sample of this grantmaker's funding activity:

$305,000 to Silicon Valley Community Foundation, Mountain View, CA, 2010.
$2,847 to Second Harvest Food Bank of Santa Clara and San Mateo Counties, San Jose, CA, 2010.
$1,515 to Crohns and Colitis Foundation of America, San Francisco, CA, 2010.
$1,150 to Saratoga Education Foundation, Saratoga, CA, 2010.

Synopsys Silicon Valley Science & Technology Outreach Foundation

700 E. Middlefield Rd.
Mountain View, CA 94043 (415) 306-1764
FAX: (707) 996-9855;
E-mail: robinson@synopsys.com; URL: http://www.outreach-foundation.org

Establishment information: Established as a company-sponsored operating foundation in 1999 in CA.
Donors: Synopsys Technology Education Opportunity Foundation; Industry Initiatives; Synopsys Community Fund; Synopsys Foundation; Kaiser Permanente.
Contact: Gary Robinson, Pres.
Financial data (yr. ended 12/31/11): Assets, $373,354 (M); gifts received, $915,725; expenditures, $923,105; qualifying distributions, $840,137; giving activities include $271,308 for 9 grants (high: $125,208; low: $1,450).
Purpose and activities: The foundation awards grants to teachers and students developing science projects at K-12 schools; and sponsors programs, competitions, fairs, and seminars involved with science.
Fields of interest: Elementary/secondary education; Science, formal/general education; Engineering; Science.
Programs:
i 3: initiate. investigate. innovate: Through this program, the foundation inspires and rewards 4th, 5th, and 6th graders to learn about science by participating in local, outside-the-classroom activities.
Sciberpalooza!: The foundation sponsors an online science fair for students in 6th grade who submit YouTube video presentations of their science projects.
Sciencepalooza!: The foundation sponsors a science fair for students in grades 9-12 in the East Side Union High School District in San Jose.
SuperSchool Teacher Training: The foundation provides free grade-specific teacher training seminars that are tied to California's Science Content Standards and approved for Continuing Education Units through San Jose State University.
Synopsys Championship: The foundation sponsors an annual science fair for students in grades 6-12 in Santa Clara County, CA. Winning participants advance to the California State Science Fair and the Intel International Science and Engineering Fair.
Synopsys Outreach Foundation n + 1 Prize: The foundation annually awards a prize to the Santa Clara County high school student or teams of students competing in the Synopsys Silicon Valley Science & Technology Championship whose project best exemplifies "the next breakthrough" in science or engineering.
Type of support: Conferences/seminars; Equipment; Program development; Sponsorships.
Geographic limitations: Giving limited to Santa Clara County, CA, and areas of field office operations.
Support limitations: No grants for technical papers.
Publications: Application guidelines.
Application information: Applications accepted. Application form required.
Initial approach: Complete online application form; see website www.outreach-foundation.org
Deadline(s): Oct. 1
Directors: Dana Ditmore; Tom Ferry; Richard Goldman; Zahra Karami; Michael Keating; Roy Okuda; Murlin Marks; Judy Peterson; Venkata Ravella; Larke Reeber; Lynn Shannon; Jaci Spross.
Officers: Erin Brennock, Chair.; Gary Robinson, Pres.; Erika Varga McEnroe, Secy.; Anna Garcia, Treas.
EIN: 770520414
Selected grants: The following grants are a representative sample of this grantmaker's funding activity:
$285,589 to East Side Union High School District, San Jose, CA, 2008.

3674
Synovus Financial Corp.

1111 Bay Ave., Ste. 500
P.O. Box 120
Columbus, GA 31902-4298 (706) 649-2311
FAX: (706) 641-6555

Company URL: http://www.synovus.com
Establishment information: Established in 1888.
Company type: Public company
Company ticker symbol and exchange: SNV/NYSE
Business activities: Operates bank holding company; operates commercial bank.
Business type (SIC): Banks/commercial; holding company
Financial profile for 2012: Number of employees, 4,963; assets, $26,760,010,000; pre-tax net income, $31,480,000; liabilities, $23,190,580,000
Forbes 2000 ranking: 2012—1874th in sales, 714th in profits, and 806th in assets
Corporate officers: Kessel D. Stelling, Jr., Chair. and C.E.O.; Allen J. Gula, Jr., Exec. V.P. and C.O.O.; Thomas J. Prescott, Exec. V.P. and C.F.O.; Samuel F. Hatcher III, Exec. V.P., Genl. Counsel, and Secy.; Liliana McDaniel, C.A.O.; Renee Roth, C.I.O.
Board of directors: Kessell D. Stelling, Jr., Chair.; Catherine A. Allen; Stephen T. Butler; Elizabeth W. Camp; T. Michael Goodrich; V. Nathaniel Hansford; Mason H. Lampton; Jerry W. Nix; Joseph J. Prochaska, Jr.; J. Neal Purcell; Barry L. Storey; Melvin T. Stith; Phillip W. Tomlinson; James D. Yancey
Subsidiaries: Athens First Bank & Trust Co., Athens, GA; Bank of Coweta, Newnan, GA; Bank of Hazlehurst, Hazlehurst, GA; Bank of North Georgia, Alpharetta, GA; Bank of Pensacola, Pensacola, FL; The Bank of Tuscaloosa, Tuscaloosa, AL; CB&T Bank of Middle Georgia, Warner Robins, GA; CB&T Bank of Russell County, Phenix City, AL; Charter Bank & Trust Co., Marietta, GA; Citizens & Merchants State Bank, Douglasville, GA; The Citizens Bank, Fort Valley, GA; Citizens Bank and Trust of West Georgia, Carrollton, GA; The Citizens Bank of Cochran, Cochran, GA; Citizens First Bank, Rome, GA; The Coastal Bank of Georgia, Brunswick, GA; The Cohutta Banking Co., Chatsworth, GA; Columbus Bank and Trust Company, Columbus, GA; Commercial Bank, Thomasville, GA; Commercial Bank and Trust Co. of Troup County, LaGrange, GA; Community Bank and Trust of Southeast Alabama, Enterprise, AL; First Coast Community Bank, Fernandina Beach, FL; First Commercial Bank of Birmingham, Birmingham, AL; First Commercial Bank of Huntsville, Huntsville, AL; First Community Bank of Tifton, Tifton, GA; First National Bank of Jasper, Jasper, AL; First State Bank and Trust Co. of Valdosta, Valdosta, GA; Georgia Bank and Trust, Calhoun, GA; Mountain National Bank, Tucker, GA; National Bank of South Carolina, Columbia, SC; The National Bank of Walton County, Monroe, GA; Peachtree National Bank, Peachtree City, GA; pointpath bank, N.A., Columbus, GA; ProCard, Inc., Golden, CO; Quincy State Bank, Quincy, FL; Sea Island Bank, Statesboro, GA; Security Bank and Trust Co. of Albany, Albany, GA; Sterling Bank, Montgomery, AL; Sumter Bank and Trust Co., Americus, GA; The Tallahassee State Bank, Tallahassee, FL; TSYS Total Debt Management, Inc., Norcross, GA; Vanguard Bank and Trust Co., Valparaiso, FL
Giving statement: Giving through the Synovus Foundation.
Company EIN: 581134883

The Synovus Foundation

(formerly CB&T Charitable Trust)
c/o Synovus Trust Co.
P.O. Box 23024
Columbus, GA 31902-3024 (706) 644-3496
FAX: (706) 649-5986

Establishment information: Established in 1969.
Donors: Columbus Bank & Trust Co.; Synovus Financial Corp.; Total System Services, Inc.
Contact: Fray McCormick, Treas.
Financial data (yr. ended 12/31/11): Assets, $1,049,441 (M); gifts received, $648,000; expenditures, $687,400; qualifying distributions, $686,000; giving activities include $686,000 for grants.
Purpose and activities: The foundation supports museums and organizations involved with education, health, human services, and community economic development.
Fields of interest: Museums; Performing arts, opera; Secondary school/education; Higher education; Libraries (public); Education; Hospitals (general); Health care; YM/YWCAs & YM/YWHAs; Children/youth, services; Human services; Community/economic development; United Ways and Federated Giving Programs.
Type of support: Annual campaigns; Building/renovation; Capital campaigns; General/operating support.
Geographic limitations: Giving primarily in the Columbus, GA area.
Support limitations: No support for religious organizations. No grants to individuals.
Application information: Applications accepted. Application form not required. Applicants should submit the following:
1) copy of IRS Determination Letter
2) detailed description of project and amount of funding requested
Initial approach: Proposal
Board meeting date(s): Monthly
Deadline(s): None
Officers and Directors:* Calvin Smyre*, Chair.; Steve Melton*, Secy.; Fray McCormick, Treas.; Billy Blanchard; Lee Lee James.
Number of staff: 7
EIN: 237024198
Selected grants: The following grants are a representative sample of this grantmaker's funding activity:
$200,000 to Columbus Technical College, Columbus, GA, 2010.
$120,000 to United Way of the Chattahoochee Valley, Columbus, GA, 2010.
$100,000 to Pastoral Institute, Columbus, GA, 2010.

$50,000 to Columbus State University, Columbus, GA, 2010.
$50,000 to Georgia Meth Project, Atlanta, GA, 2010.
$50,000 to MidTown, Inc., Columbus, GA, 2010.
$30,000 to Brookstone School, Columbus, GA, 2010.
$15,000 to Albany State University, Albany, GA, 2010.
$10,000 to Alabama State University Foundation, Montgomery, AL, 2010.

3675
Syracuse Convention & Visitors Bureau

572 South Salina St.
Syracuse, NY 13202 (315) 470-1910
FAX: (3150 471-8545

Company URL: http://www.visitsyracuse.org
Company type: Private company
Business activities: Operates destination marketing organization.
Business type (SIC): Business services/ miscellaneous
Corporate officers: David Holder, Pres.; Carol Eaton, V.P., Mktg; Tracey Kegebein, V.P., Sales
Giving statement: Giving through the Syracuse Sports Corporation.

Syracuse Sports Corporation

(also known as SSC)
572 South Salina St.
Syracuse, NY 13202 (315) 699-6595
E-mail: jonnoj24@aol.com; URL: http://www.visitsyracuse.org/sports-corp

Establishment information: Established in 1985.
Contact: Jon Cooley
Financial data (yr. ended 12/31/09): Assets, $13,156; expenditures, $550.
Purpose and activities: The Syracuse Sports Corporation Small Grants Program provides up to $500 in funding to organizations developing or expanding sporting events and competitions in the Greater Syracuse area.
Fields of interest: Recreation; Community/ economic development.
Type of support: General/operating support.
Geographic limitations: Giving limited to the Greater Syracuse, NY, area.
Support limitations: No support for political organizations or for completed events or events not taking place within 12 months of the award. No grants to individuals.
Publications: Application guidelines.
Application information: Proposals should be submitted using the Syracuse Sports Corp. Grant Application Form. Criteria for funding encourages multiple day programs in which a representative portion of participants are from out-of-town.
Applicants should submit the following:
1) name, address and phone number of organization
2) listing of board of directors, trustees, officers and other key people and their affiliations
3) contact person
4) copy of current year's organizational budget and/ or project budget
Proposal should also include event description, competition structure, and schedule Identification of free promotional opportunities for the SSC and its business.
Initial approach: Proposal
Deadline(s): None
Final notification: 2 months
Officers and Directors:* Bill Motto, Pres.; David Kasouf, V.P.; Peter Waack, Secy.; David Holder, Treas.; Michael Folsom; Barb Henderson; Mark Hills.
EIN: 161264443

3676
Syre Realty Corp.

975 E. 24th St.
Brooklyn, NY 11210 (718) 677-6215

Establishment information: Established in 1983.
Company type: Private company
Business activities: Operates real estate agency.
Business type (SIC): Real estate agents and managers
Corporate officer: Samuel Gluck, Pres. and C.E.O.
Giving statement: Giving through the Amber Foundation.

The Amber Foundation

975 E. 24th St.
Brooklyn, NY 11210-3611

Establishment information: Established in 2005 in NY.
Donors: Syre Realty Corp.; GRW Properties, LLC; Samuel Gluck; Livia Gluck.
Financial data (yr. ended 12/31/10): Assets, $670,860 (M); gifts received, $55,000; expenditures, $54,290; qualifying distributions, $54,290; giving activities include $53,650 for grants.
Fields of interest: Human services.
Support limitations: No grants to individuals.
Application information: Applications not accepted. Unsolicited requests for funds not accepted.
Trustees: Livia Gluck; Samuel Gluck.
EIN: 206738476

3677
Sysco Corporation

1390 Enclave Pkwy.
Houston, TX 77077-2099 (281) 584-1390
FAX: (281) 584-1737

Company URL: http://www.sysco.com
Establishment information: Established in 1969.
Company type: Public company
Company ticker symbol and exchange: SYY/NYSE
Business activities: Sells food and food-related products wholesale.
Business type (SIC): Groceries—wholesale
Financial profile for 2012: Number of employees, 47,800; assets, $12,094,970,000; sales volume, $42,380,940,000; pre-tax net income, $1,784,000,000; expenses, $40,490,310,000; liabilities, $7,409,930,000
Fortune 1000 ranking: 2012—65th in revenues, 181st in profits, and 346th in assets
Forbes 2000 ranking: 2012—207th in sales, 558th in profits, and 1317th in assets
Corporate officers: Manuel A. Fernandez, Chair.; William J. DeLaney III, Pres. and C.E.O.; Robert Chris Kreidler, Exec. V.P. and C.F.O.; G. Mitchell Elmer, Sr. V.P., Cont., and C.A.O.; Twila M. Day, Sr. V.P. and C.I.O.; Russell T. Libby, Sr. V.P., Genl. Counsel, and Secy.; Ajoy H. Karna, Sr. V.P., Finance; William W. Goetz, Sr. V.P., Mktg.; Scott A. Sonnemaker, Sr. V.P., Sales; Paul T. Moskowitz, Sr. V.P., Human Resources; Mark Wisnoski, V.P., Human Resources; Charles H. Wilson, V.P., Corp. Comms.
Board of directors: Manuel A. Fernandez, Chair.; John M. Cassaday; Judith B. Craven; William J. DeLaney III; Larry C. Glasscock; Jonathan Golden; Joseph A. Hafner, Jr.; Hans-Joachim Koerber, Ph.D.; Nancy S. Newcomb; Richard G. Tilghman; Jacquelyn M. Ward
International operations: Canada; United Kingdom
Giving statement: Giving through the Sysco Corporation Contributions Program.
Company EIN: 741648137

Sysco Corporation Contributions Program

1390 Enclave Pkwy.
Houston, TX 77077-2099 (281) 584-1390
URL: http://sysco.com/about-sysco/corporate-responsibility.html

Purpose and activities: Through a decentralized corporate giving program, Sysco conducts its philanthropic activities via various company locations that determine local charitable guidelines. At its headquarters in Houston, Texas, Sysco makes charitable contributions to nonprofit organizations involved with arts and culture, educational development, food services, and on a case by case basis.
Fields of interest: Arts; Higher education; Food services; General charitable giving Minorities.
Programs:
John F. and Eula Mae Baugh Scholarship Program: SYSCO Corp. annually awards seven four-year college scholarships valued up to $10,000 to dependents of its full-time employees with at least five years of service. The program is administered by the Citizens' Scholarship Foundation of America, Inc.
Matching Gifts to Higher Education Program: SYSCO Corp. matches contributions made by full-time employees and members of the Board of Directors to U.S. and Canadian colleges and universities and other eligible organizations on a one-for-one basis up to $5,000 per contributor, per year.
Type of support: Cause-related marketing; Donated products; Employee volunteer services; General/ operating support; In-kind gifts; Scholarship funds; Sponsorships.
Geographic limitations: Giving in areas of company operations, with emphasis on Houston, TX; giving also to national organizations.

3678
Systel, Inc.

1655 Industrial Blvd.
Sugar Land, TX 77478-2579
(281) 313-3600
FAX: (281) 495-2121

Company URL: http://www.systelusa.com
Establishment information: Established in 1988.
Company type: Private company
Business activities: Designs and integrates rugged industrial computer systems.
Business type (SIC): Computer and office equipment
Corporate officers: Vimal Kothari, Pres. and C.E.O.; Venkat Nadella, C.O.O.; Jeff Saleeby, C.F.O.
Giving statement: Giving through the Prema Foundation.

Prema Foundation

15827 River Roads Dr.
Houston, TX 77079-5041 (281) 206-7620

Establishment information: Established in 2004 in TX.
Donors: Vimal Kothari; Charndra Shekhar; Ravi Konde; Devdutt Nagarkar; Systel, Inc.; GP Ktronics, Inc.; Ravikant Varanasi; Sangeeta Varanasi.
Financial data (yr. ended 12/31/10): Assets, $393,907 (M); gifts received, $642,898; expenditures, $383,836; qualifying distributions, $382,712; giving activities include $380,776 for 4 grants (high: $311,276; low: $500).
Purpose and activities: The foundation supports organizations involved with cultural awareness, health, Hinduism, and economically disadvantaged people.
Fields of interest: Arts, cultural/ethnic awareness; Health care, clinics/centers; Health care; Hinduism Economically disadvantaged.
Type of support: General/operating support.
Geographic limitations: Giving primarily in Houston, TX and India.
Support limitations: No grants to individuals.
Application information: Applications accepted. Application form not required. Applicants should submit the following:
1) detailed description of project and amount of funding requested
Initial approach: Proposal
Deadline(s): None
Directors: Hansa Kothari; Vimal Kothari; Imitiaz Munshi.
EIN: 206070206
Selected grants: The following grants are a representative sample of this grantmaker's funding activity:
$5,000 to Saint Agnes Academy, Houston, TX, 2009.
$1,000 to Lighthouse for the Blind of Houston, Houston, TX, 2009.
$1,000 to Star of Hope Mission, Houston, TX, 2009.

3679
Taco Bell Corp.

1 Glen Bell Way
Irvine, CA 92618 (949) 863-4500

Company URL: http://www.tacobell.com
Establishment information: Established in 1962.
Company type: Subsidiary of a public company
Business activities: Operates restaurants.
Business type (SIC): Restaurants and drinking places
Corporate officers: Greg Creed, Pres. and C.E.O.; Thomas E. Davin, C.O.O.; Melissa Lora, C.F.O.; Bob Fulmer, V.P., Mktg.
Giving statement: Giving through the Taco Bell Corp. Contributions Program and the Taco Bell Foundation.

Taco Bell Corp. Contributions Program

1 Glen Bell Way
Irvine, CA 92618 (949) 863-4579
E-mail: TBFTGrantInquiries@tacobell.com; URL: http://www.tacobell.com/careers/communitygrants

Purpose and activities: As a complement to its foundation, Taco Bell also makes charitable contributions to nonprofit organizations directly. Emphasis is given to organizations involved with teen education, hunger relief, and community building.
Fields of interest: Secondary school/education; Food services; Food banks; Community/economic development.
Type of support: General/operating support.
Geographic limitations: Giving primarily is limited to Orange County, CA.
Publications: Application guidelines.
Application information: Applications accepted. Contributions are limited to one donation per organization in any given year. Grants generally range from $5,000 to $20,000. Grantees are expected to complete an online progress report detailing how funds were used. Application form required. Applicants should submit the following:
1) population served
2) name, address and phone number of organization
3) copy of IRS Determination Letter
4) how project's results will be evaluated or measured
5) detailed description of project and amount of funding requested
6) contact person
7) copy of current year's organizational budget and/or project budget
8) additional materials/documentation
Applications should include website address, and program or event name, date, and location.
Initial approach: Complete online application
Deadline(s): Aug. 17, 2012
Final notification: Oct. 2012

Taco Bell Foundation

1 Glen Bell Way
Irvine, CA 92618-3344 (949) 863-4312
E-mail: tacobellfoundationforteens@tacobell.com; URL: http://www.tacobellfoundationforteens.org/

Establishment information: Established in 1992 in CA.
Donor: Taco Bell Corp.
Contact: Fulmer Bob, Exec. Dir.
Financial data (yr. ended 12/31/11): Revenue, $7,638,509; assets, $8,608,923 (M); gifts received, $7,628,438; expenditures, $6,358,616; program services expenses, $5,319,940; giving activities include $4,267,640 for 3 grants (high: $2,273,388; low: $450,000).
Purpose and activities: The foundation seeks to improve the lives of young people and help them to reach their full potential as productive, caring, and educated adults.
Fields of interest: Boys & girls clubs Youth.
Geographic limitations: Giving primarily in Atlanta, GA.
Application information: Applications not accepted. Contributes only to pre-selected organizations.
Board meeting date(s): Fall
Officers and Board Members:* Greg Creed*, Chair.; Langel Craig*, Vice-Chair.; Van Hersett Lynn*, Treas.; Fulmer Bob, Exec. Dlr.; Bill Allmon; Linda Alvarado; Dirk Dozier; Lee Engler; Farzin Ferdowsi; Craig Langel; Lee Mitchell; Mark Peterson; Rob Savage; Clint Smith; Jerome Thomas; Mike Valdron.
Number of staff: 2 full-time professional.
EIN: 330523542

3680
Tacoma News, Inc.

(doing business as News Tribune)
1950 S. State St.
Tacoma, WA 98405-2817 (253) 597-8742

Company URL: http://www.thenewstribune.com
Establishment information: Established in 1880.
Company type: Subsidiary of a public company
Business activities: Publishes newspapers.
Business type (SIC): Newspaper publishing and/or printing
Financial profile for 2010: Number of employees, 300
Corporate officers: Cheryl Dell, Pres.; Elaine Lintecum, Treas.
Giving statement: Giving through the News Tribune Scholarship Foundation.

News Tribune Scholarship Foundation

1950 S. State St.
Tacoma, WA 98411

Establishment information: Established in 1989 in WA.
Donor: Tacoma News Inc.
Contact: Jerald L. Allen, Pres.
Financial data (yr. ended 12/31/11): Assets, $81,049 (M); expenditures, $6,932; qualifying distributions, $6,000; giving activities include $5,600 for 4 grants to individuals (high: $2,200; low: $1,000).
Purpose and activities: The foundation awards college scholarships to children of employees of Morning News Tribune.
Type of support: Employee-related scholarships.
Geographic limitations: Giving limited to Tacoma, WA.
Application information: Applications accepted. Application form required.
Initial approach: Proposal
Deadline(s): Jan.
Officers: Jerald L. Allen, Pres.; Shelley Beroth, Treas.
Director: David Zeeck.
EIN: 943082120

3681
Taiyo Birdair Corporation

65 Lawrence Bell Dr., Ste 100
Amherst, NY 14221-7075 (716) 633-9500

Company URL: http://www.taiyobirdair.com
Establishment information: Established in 1956.
Company type: Subsidiary of a foreign company
Business activities: Provides lightweight tensile membrane and cable roof system construction services.
Business type (SIC): Contractors/general nonresidential building
Corporate officers: Mitsuo Sugimoto, Pres.; Thomas Wuerch, Sr. V.P., Opers.
Giving statement: Giving through the Taiyo Birdair Corporation Contributions Program.

Taiyo Birdair Corporation Contributions Program

65 Lawrence Bell Dr., Ste. 200
Amherst, NY 14221-7075

Contact: Kimberly Boeheim, Mgr., Human Resources

Purpose and activities: Taiyo Birdair makes charitable contributions to nonprofit organizations on a case by case basis. Support is given on a national basis.
Fields of interest: General charitable giving.
Type of support: General/operating support.
Geographic limitations: Giving on a national basis, with emphasis on NY.
Application information: Applications accepted. Application form not required.
Initial approach: Proposal to headquarters
Deadline(s): None
Final notification: Following review

3682
The Talbots, Inc.

1 Talbots Dr.
Hingham, MA 02043 (781) 749-7600
FAX: (302) 655-5049

Company URL: http://www.talbots.com
Establishment information: Established in 1947.
Company type: Public company
Company ticker symbol and exchange: TLB/NYSE
Business activities: Operates women's and children's apparel, accessories, and shoe stores; provides catalog shopping services; provides Internet shopping services.
Business type (SIC): Women's apparel stores; women's specialty and accessory stores; children's apparel and accessory stores; shoe stores; nonstore retailers; computer services
Financial profile for 2012: Number of employees, 8,737; assets, $644,180,000; sales volume, $1,141,250,000; pre-tax net income, -$109,690,000; expenses, $1,243,830,000; liabilities, $628,210,000
Corporate officers: Gary M. Pfeiffer, Chair.; Trudy F. Sullivan, Pres. and C.E.O.; Michael Scarpa, C.O.O., C.F.O., and Treas.; Benedetta I. Casamento, Exec. V.P., Finance
Board of directors: Gary M. Pfeiffer, Chair.; Marjorie L. Bowen; John W. Gleeson; Andrew H. Madsen; Trudy F. Sullivan; Susan M. Swain
Historic mergers: The J. Jill Group, Inc. (May 3, 2006)
Giving statement: Giving through the Talbots, Inc. Contributions Program and the Talbots Charitable Foundation, Inc.
Company EIN: 411111318

The Talbots, Inc. Contributions Program

c/o Community Relations
1 Talbots Dr.
Hingham, MA 02043-1551
E-mail: community@talbots.com; URL: http://www.talbotsinc.com/corp_resp.asp

Purpose and activities: As a complement to its foundation, Talbots makes charitable contributions to nonprofit organizations directly. Special emphasis is directed toward women's education, health and well being. Support is given primarily in areas of company operations in Tampa, Florida, Hingham and Lakeville, Massachusetts (greater Boston area), New York, New York, and Knoxville, Tennessee.
Fields of interest: Women, centers/services Women.
Type of support: Donated products; In-kind gifts.
Geographic limitations: Giving primarily in areas of company operations in Tampa, FL, Hingham and Lakeville, MA (greater Boston area), New York, NY, and Knoxville, TN.
Support limitations: No grants to individuals.
Publications: Application guidelines.
Application information: Applications accepted. Videos, DVDs or glossy photos are not accepted and cannot be returned.
Proposal should include organization's tax ID/EIN number.
Initial approach: Proposal
Deadline(s): None
Final notification: 60 days

Talbots Charitable Foundation, Inc.

c/o Donations Coord.
1 Talbots Dr.
Hingham, MA 02043-1551
E-mail: foundation@talbots.com; URL: http://www.talbotsinc.com/brands/talbots/charitable.asp

Establishment information: Established in 2001.
Donors: The Talbots, Inc.; Arnold B. Zetcher.
Financial data (yr. ended 01/31/12): Assets, $448,729 (M); gifts received, $45,404; expenditures, $289,496; qualifying distributions, $219,000; giving activities include $219,000 for grants.
Purpose and activities: The foundation supports programs designed to promote the education, health, and cultural enrichment of women; and awards college scholarships.
Fields of interest: Arts; Education; Health care; Human services; United Ways and Federated Giving Programs Women.
Programs:
Associate Award of Excellence: The foundation awards 10 college scholarships to high school seniors who are children of Talbots associates. The award includes nine $2,000 scholarships and one $5,000 scholarship for the top applicant receiving the Zetcher Excellence Award. The program is administered by Scholarship America.
Talbots Scholarship Foundation: The foundation annually awards ten $15,000 college scholarships to women pursuing a college education later in life, and one $30,000 Nancy Talbot Scholarship Award to a finalist that demonstrates courage, conviction, and entrepreneurial spirit. The program is administered by Scholarship America.
Type of support: Building/renovation; General/operating support; Program development; Research; Scholarships—to individuals.
Geographic limitations: Giving primarily in areas of company operations in Tampa, FL, Hingham and Lakeville, MA, New York, NY, and Knoxville, TN.
Support limitations: No support for political candidates, athletes, or beauty pageant contestants, religious or sectarian organizations not of direct benefit to the entire community, or discriminatory organizations. No grants to individuals (except for scholarships), or for merchandise.
Publications: Application guidelines.
Application information: Applications accepted. An application form is required for scholarships. Telephone calls during the application process are not encouraged. Support is limited to 1 contribution per organization during any given year. Multi-year funding is not automatic. Applicants should submit the following:
1) name, address and phone number of organization
2) copy of IRS Determination Letter
3) brief history of organization and description of its mission
4) detailed description of project and amount of funding requested
5) contact person
Initial approach: E-mail proposal; download application form for scholarships
Deadline(s): None; Jan. 5 for scholarships
Final notification: 6 to 8 weeks; spring for scholarships
Officers and Directors:* Trudy F. Sullivan*, Chair. and Pres.; Richard T. O'Connell, Jr.*, Sr. V.P. and Secy.; Michael Scarpa*, Sr. V.P. and Treas.; Edward L. Larsen*, Sr. V.P. and Treas.; John Fiske III, Sr. V.P.; Carol Gordon Stone*, V.P.; Warren J. Casey.
EIN: 043547221
Selected grants: The following grants are a representative sample of this grantmaker's funding activity:
$180,000 to Scholarship America, Saint Peter, MN, 2012. For scholarship awards.
$23,000 to Scholarship America, Saint Peter, MN, 2012. For scholarship awards.

3683
TALX Corporation

11432 Lackland Rd.
St. Louis, MO 63146 (314) 214-7000

Company URL: http://www.talx.com/
Establishment information: Established in 1971.
Company type: Subsidiary of a public company
Business activities: Provides outsourcing solutions to Human Resources, Payroll, and Tax departments of companies, public sector and non-profit organizations.
Business type (SIC): Computer services
Corporate officers: William W. Canfield, Chair. and C.E.O.; J. Dann Adams, Pres.; L. Keith Graves, C.F.O.
Board of director: William W. Canfield, Chair.
Giving statement: Giving through the TALX Charitable Foundation.

TALX Charitable Foundation

c/o John Elwood
1550 Peachtree St. N.E.
Atlanta, GA 30309-2402
URL: http://www.talx.com/aboutus/foundation.asp

Establishment information: Established in 2004 in MO.
Donor: TALX Corporation.
Financial data (yr. ended 03/31/12): Assets, $2,448,853 (M); gifts received, $2,116; expenditures, $166,440; qualifying distributions, $145,013; giving activities include $145,000 for 9 grants (high: $40,000; low: $2,500).
Purpose and activities: The foundation supports programs designed to enhance the education of disadvantaged youth in the St. Louis area.
Fields of interest: Charter schools; Higher education; Education; Youth development, business; Homeless, human services Youth; Economically disadvantaged.
Type of support: General/operating support.
Geographic limitations: Giving primarily in St. Louis, MO.
Support limitations: No grants to individuals.
Publications: IRS Form 990 or 990-PF printed copy available upon request.
Application information: Applications not accepted. Contributes only to pre-selected organizations.
Officers and Directors:* J. Dann Adams*, Pres.; Ellen A. Stanko*, V.P.; William F. Barge, Secy.-Treas.; Robert Kamerschen; Kenneth Marshall.
EIN: 202021573
Selected grants: The following grants are a representative sample of this grantmaker's funding activity:

$40,000 to College Summit, Saint Louis, MO, 2012. For unrestricted funds.
$40,000 to Haven of Grace, Saint Louis, MO, 2012. For unrestricted funds.
$15,000 to Teach for America, Saint Louis, MO, 2012. For unrestricted funds.
$2,500 to Youth for Christ, Central Ohio, Columbus, OH, 2012. For unrestricted funds.

3684
Tamar Fink, Inc.

3033 Excelsior Blvd., Ste. 575
Minneapolis, MN 55416-4527
(612) 922-3113

Company URL: http://www.tamarfink.com
Establishment information: Established in 1986.
Company type: Private company
Business activities: Operates life insurance and wealth management company.
Business type (SIC): Insurance/life
Corporate officers: Kenneth Chaim Fink, Pres. and C.E.O.; Michael Abrams, V.P., Mktg.
Giving statement: Giving through the Tamar Fink Family Foundation.

Tamar Fink Family Foundation

3033 Excelsior Blvd., Ste. 575
Minneapolis, MN 55416-5185

Establishment information: Established in 2007 in MN.
Donors: Tamar Fink, Inc.; Kenneth Fink.
Financial data (yr. ended 12/31/11): Assets, $226,460 (M); gifts received, $1,770; expenditures, $279,242; qualifying distributions, $277,408; giving activities include $276,560 for 23 grants (high: $95,000; low: $100).
Purpose and activities: The foundation supports organizations involved with education and Judaism.
Fields of interest: Education; Jewish federated giving programs; Jewish agencies & synagogues.
Type of support: General/operating support.
Geographic limitations: Giving primarily in St. Louis Park, MN, Brooklyn, NY, and Israel.
Support limitations: No grants to individuals.
Application information: Applications not accepted. Contributes only to pre-selected organizations.
Officer and Directors:* Kenneth Chaim Fink*, Pres. and Secy.; Nicole Benjamin Fink; David Gotlieb; Robert Karon.
EIN: 261513383
Selected grants: The following grants are a representative sample of this grantmaker's funding activity:
$20,000 to Ohr Somayach International, Brooklyn, NY, 2010.
$10,000 to Torah Academy of Minneapolis, Saint Louis Park, MN, 2010.
$4,000 to Minneapolis Jewish Federation, Minnetonka, MN, 2010.
$3,600 to American Friends of Migdal Torah, Brooklyn, NY, 2010.
$1,800 to National Conference of Synagogue Youth, New York, NY, 2010.
$1,350 to Beth Jacob Congregation, Mendota Heights, MN, 2010.
$1,000 to Microgrants, Minneapolis, MN, 2010.

3685
TAMKO Building Products, Inc.

220 W. 4th St.
P.O. Box 1404
Joplin, MO 64801 (417) 624-6644
FAX: (800) 760-7954

Company URL: http://www.tamko.com
Establishment information: Established in 1944.
Company type: Private company
Business activities: Manufactures roofing, siding and insulation.
Business type (SIC): Lumber and construction materials—wholesale
Corporate officers: Ethelmae C. Humphreys, Chair.; David Craig Humphreys, Pres. and C.E.O.; Jeff Beyer, V.P. and C.F.O.; Robert L. Bradley, V.P. and Genl. Counsel; Stephen A. McNally, V.P., Sales and Mktg.; Sandy Betebenner, Treas.
Board of director: Ethelmae C. Humphreys, Chair.
Giving statement: Giving through the TAMKO Building Products, Inc. Contributions Program.

TAMKO Building Products, Inc. Contributions Program

220 W. 4th St.
P.O. Box 1404
Joplin, MO 64802 (417) 624-6644
URL: http://www.tamko.com

3686
Tampa Bay Rays Baseball, Ltd.

(formerly Tampa Bay Devil Rays, Ltd.)
1 Tropicana Dr.
St. Petersburg, FL 33705 (727) 825-3137
FAX: 727-825-3111

Company URL: http://tampabay.rays.mlb.com
Establishment information: Established in 1994.
Company type: Private company
Business activities: Operates professional baseball club.
Business type (SIC): Commercial sports
Corporate officers: Meghan Maloney, Chair.; Matthew P. Silverman, Pres.; John Higgins, Sr. V.P., Admin. and Genl. Counsel; Rick Nafe, V.P., Opers.; Rob Gagliardi, V.P., Finance; Tom Hoof, V.P., Mktg.; Brian Richeson, V.P., Sales; Rick Vaughn, V.P., Comms.; Patrick Smith, Cont.
Board of director: Meghan Maloney, Chair.
Giving statement: Giving through the Tampa Bay Rays Baseball Corporate Giving Program.

Tampa Bay Rays Baseball Corporate Giving Program

(formerly Tampa Bay Devil Rays, Ltd. Corporate Giving Program)
c/o Community Rels.
Tropicana Field
1 Tropicana Dr.
St. Petersburg, FL 33705-1703
E-mail: community@raysbaseball.com; URL: http://tampabay.rays.mlb.com/tb/community/index.jsp

Purpose and activities: The Tampa Bay Devil Rays make charitable contributions to nonprofit organizations on a case by case basis. Support is given primarily in the 10-county Tampa Bay, Florida, area.
Fields of interest: Elementary school/education; Education; Breast cancer; Athletics/sports, baseball; Boys & girls clubs; YM/YWCAs & YM/YWHAs; General charitable giving Youth.
Programs:
Rays Community Corner: Through Rays Community Corner, nonprofit organizations raise awareness for their causes during games. Representatives from the organizations pass out information to promote their local programs and share stories and answer questions. Participants receive 2 complimentary game tickets, a kiosk on the main concourse, 2 fifteen second public address announcements, and a premium Rays item for a free giveaway.
Speakers Bureau: Through Speakers Bureau, members of Ray's front office or broadcast teams speak at local events including player information, baseball operations, community programs, and sales and advertising.
Type of support: Donated products; Employee volunteer services; In-kind gifts; Loaned talent.
Geographic limitations: Giving primarily in areas of company operations in the 10-county Tampa Bay, FL, area.
Publications: Application guidelines.
Application information: Applications accepted. Proposals should be submitted using organization letterhead. Support is limited to 1 contribution per organization during any given year. The Community Relations Department handles giving. Applicants should submit the following:
1) name, address and phone number of organization
2) descriptive literature about organization
3) detailed description of project and amount of funding requested
4) contact person
Proposals should indicate the type, date, and location of the event, if applicable, and how the donation will be used.
Initial approach: Mail proposal to headquarters for memorabilia donations and Speakers Bureau; complete online application for Rays Community Corner
Copies of proposal: 1
Deadline(s): 5 weeks prior to need for memorabilia donations; 8 weeks prior to need for Speakers Bureau; none for Rays Community Corner

3687
Tanadgusix Corporation

(also known as TDX)
615 E. 82nd Ave., Ste. 200
Anchorage, AK 99518 (907) 278-2312

Company URL: http://www.tanadgusix.com/
Company type: Native corporation
Business activities: Operates native corporation.
Business type (SIC): Nonclassifiable establishments
Corporate officers: Ron P. Philemonoff, C.E.O.; Julie Shane, Pres.; Doug Koprowski, C.F.O.; Curt Wang, Cont.
Giving statement: Giving through the TDX Foundation.

TDX Foundation

615 E. 82nd Ave., Ste. 200
Anchorage, AK 99518 (907) 278-2312
URL: http://www.tanadgusix.com/

Establishment information: Established in 1992 in AK.
Donors: American Seafoods Co.; Central Bering Sea Fishermens Assn.; Icicle Seafoods, Inc.; Trident

Seafoods Corp.; Department of Commerce; U.S. Department of Energy; Trident Seapoods.
Financial data (yr. ended 09/30/11): Assets, $56,814 (M); gifts received, $102,175; expenditures, $55,614; qualifying distributions, $55,614; giving activities include $50,960 for 36 grants to individuals (high: $3,000; low: $1,000).
Purpose and activities: The foundation awards college scholarships to owners and descendents of owners of Tanadgusix Corporation common stock.
Type of support: Scholarships—to individuals.
Geographic limitations: Giving limited to AK.
Application information: Applications accepted. Application form required.
Initial approach: Letter
Deadline(s): Aug. 1
Officers: Kurt Wong, Pres.; Carol Barnes, V.P.; Rena Kudrin, Treas.
Directors: Daria Dirks; Hedy Christensen; Julianna Shane.
EIN: 920144730

3688
Tanner Companies

(formerly Doncaster Collar and Shirt Co.)
581 Rock Rd.
Rutherfordton, NC 28139-8104
(828) 287-4205

Company URL: https://www.doncaster.com
Establishment information: Established in 1931.
Company type: Private company
Business activities: Manufactures women's, juniors', and misses' dresses, sportswear, and ready-to-wear apparel.
Business type (SIC): Apparel—women's outerwear; women's apparel stores
Corporate officers: Allison Pell Tanner, C.E.O.; Laura C. Kendall, Pres.; Randall W. Reavis, C.I.O.; David Pocock, V.P., Mktg.; Jeff Steelman, Cont.
Giving statement: Giving through the Tanner Foundation, Inc.

Tanner Foundation, Inc.

P.O. Box 1139
Rutherfordton, NC 28139-2115 (828) 288-5139
URL: https://www.doncaster.com/DoncasterEcommerce/TannerFoundation.aspx

Establishment information: Established around 1975 in NC.
Donor: Tanner Cos.
Contact: Laura Kendall, Dir.
Financial data (yr. ended 12/31/11): Assets, $1,811 (M); expenditures, $33,034; qualifying distributions, $33,000; giving activities include $33,000 for grants.
Purpose and activities: The foundation supports community centers and organizations involved with arts and culture, education, health, housing development, and human services. Special emphasis is directed toward programs designed to benefit women and families.
Fields of interest: Arts councils; Museums; Arts; Education; Health care, clinics/centers; Health care; Housing/shelter, development; YM/YWCAs & YM/YWHAs; Children/youth, services; Family services; Residential/custodial care, hospices; Human services; Community development, civic centers; United Ways and Federated Giving Programs Women.
Type of support: Capital campaigns; Continuing support; General/operating support; Matching/challenge support; Research.
Geographic limitations: Giving primarily in areas of company operations in NC, with emphasis on Rutherford County.
Support limitations: No grants to individuals.
Application information: Applications accepted. Application form not required. Applicants should submit the following:
1) copy of IRS Determination Letter
2) brief history of organization and description of its mission
3) detailed description of project and amount of funding requested
4) copy of current year's organizational budget and/or project budget

Initial approach: Proposal
Copies of proposal: 1
Board meeting date(s): Varies
Deadline(s): Dec. 1
Officers and Directors: James T. Tanner, Pres.; Michael S. Tanner, V.P.; Laura C. Kendall; Charlie Nickels; Allison Pell Tanner.
EIN: 510151695

3689
Tap Packaging Solutions

(formerly The Chilcote Company)
2160 Superior Ave. E.
Cleveland, OH 44114-2184 (216) 781-6000
FAX: (800) 276-2572

Company URL: http://www.tap-usa.com
Establishment information: Established in 1906.
Company type: Private company
Business activities: Provides printing services; binds books; manufactures photo albums and mounts.
Business type (SIC): Book publishing and/or printing; paper and paperboard/coated, converted, and laminated; blankbooks, bookbinding, and looseleaf binders; metal products/fabricated
Financial profile for 2011: Number of employees, 200
Corporate officers: David B. Chilcote, Chair.; David Hein, Vice-Chair.; J. Anthony Hyland, Pres. and C.E.O.; Matthew Moir, V.P., Opers.; Douglas P. Roof, Jr., Corp. Cont.
Board of directors: David B. Chilcote, Chair.; David Hein, Vice-Chair.
Giving statement: Giving through the Chilcote Company Charitable Trust.

The Chilcote Company Charitable Trust

2160 Superior Ave.
Cleveland, OH 44114-2102 (216) 781-6000

Establishment information: Established in 1989 in OH.
Donor: The Chilcote Co.
Contact: David Chilcote, Pres.
Financial data (yr. ended 12/31/11): Assets, $131,116 (M); expenditures, $2,879; qualifying distributions, $1,846; giving activities include $1,700 for 2 grants (high: $1,500; low: $200).
Purpose and activities: The foundation supports organizations involved with arts and culture, education, health, cancer research, and human services.
Fields of interest: Museums (art); Performing arts, orchestras; Arts; Elementary school/education; Education; Health care, patient services; Health care; Cancer research; Housing/shelter, development; Youth development, business; Children, services; Human services; United Ways and Federated Giving Programs.
Type of support: General/operating support.
Geographic limitations: Giving primarily in Cleveland, OH.
Support limitations: No grants to individuals.
Application information: Applications accepted. Application form required. Applicants should submit the following:
1) detailed description of project and amount of funding requested

Initial approach: Letter
Deadline(s): None
Officer: David Chilcote, Pres.
EIN: 341637597

3690
TAP Publishing

174 4th St.
P.O. Box 509
Crossville, TN 38555-4303 (931) 484-5137

Company URL: http://www.tappublishing.com/
Establishment information: Established in 1937.
Company type: Private company
Business activities: Publishes newspapers and periodicals.
Business type (SIC): Periodical publishing and/or printing
Corporate officers: Jack Dykstra, Pres.; Cosby Stone, C.E.O.; Gene Kahle, C.F.O.; Paul Dykstra, V.P. and Secy.
Giving statement: Giving through the 4-C's Foundation.

4-C's Foundation

(also known as 4 C's Foundation)
294 Cleveland St.
Crossville, TN 38555-4854
Application address: c/o Cumberland County High School, 660 Stanley St., Crossville, TN 38555

Establishment information: Established in 2004 in TN.
Donor: TAP Publishing.
Financial data (yr. ended 09/30/11): Assets, $13,227 (M); gifts received, $11,625; expenditures, $10,500; qualifying distributions, $10,350; giving activities include $10,350 for 12 grants to individuals (high: $1,100; low: $250).
Purpose and activities: The foundation supports organizations involved with education and awards scholarships to graduates of Cumberland County High School and Stone Memorial High School in Crossville, Tennessee.
Fields of interest: Secondary school/education; Higher education; Education.
Type of support: General/operating support; Scholarships—to individuals.
Geographic limitations: Giving limited to Crossville, TN.
Application information: Applications accepted. Application form required.
Initial approach: Proposal
Deadline(s): Apr. 1
Officers: Fran Young, Pres.; Leslie McCoy, V.P.; Nancy J. Hyder, Secy.-Treas.
EIN: 721586790

3691
Target Corporation
(formerly Dayton Hudson Corporation)
1000 Nicollet Mall
Minneapolis, MN 55403-2467
(612) 304-6073
FAX: (612) 761-5555

Company URL: http://www.target.com/
Establishment information: Established in 1902.
Company type: Public company
Company ticker symbol and exchange: TGT/NYSE
International Securities Identification Number: US87612E1064
Business activities: Operates general merchandise stores.
Business type (SIC): Variety stores; general merchandise stores
Financial profile for 2013: Number of employees, 361,000; assets, $48,163,000,000; sales volume, $73,301,000,000; pre-tax net income, $4,568,000,000; expenses, $67,971,000,000; liabilities, $31,605,000,000
Fortune 1000 ranking: 2012—36th in revenues, 63rd in profits, and 114th in assets
Forbes 2000 ranking: 2012—102nd in sales, 189th in profits, and 474th in assets
Corporate officers: Gregg W. Steinhafel, Chair., Pres., and C.E.O.; John J. Mulligan, Exec. V.P. and C.F.O.; Beth M. Jacob, Exec. V.P. and C.I.O.; Timothy R. Baer, Exec. V.P., Genl. Counsel, and Corp. Secy.; Jodeen A. Kozlak, Exec. V.P., Human Resources
Board of directors: Gregg W. Steinhafel, Chair.; Roxanne S. Austin; Douglas M. Baker, Jr.; Calvin Darden; Henrique De Castro; Mary N. Dillon; James A. Johnson; Mary E. Minnick; Anne M. Mulcahy; Derica W. Rice; John G. Stumpf; Solomon D. Trujillo
Subsidiaries: Target Bank, Salt Lake City, UT; Target National Bank, Sioux Falls, SD; Target Stores, Inc., Minneapolis, MN
Giving statement: Giving through the Target Corporation Contributions Program and the Target Foundation.
Company EIN: 410215170

Target Corporation Contributions Program
1000 Nicollet Mall
Minneapolis, MN 55403-2530 (612) 338-0085
E-mail: Community.Relations@target.com;
URL: https://corporate.target.com/corporate-responsibility

Purpose and activities: As a complement to its foundation, Target also makes charitable contributions to nonprofit organizations directly. Emphasis is given to organizations involved with education, the arts, public safety, the environment, and health and well-being. Support is limited to areas of company operations.
Fields of interest: Arts, cultural/ethnic awareness; Arts education; Visual arts, design; Museums; Performing arts, theater; Arts; Elementary/secondary education; Education, early childhood education; Libraries/library science; Libraries (public); Education, reading; Education; Public health; Crime/violence prevention; Crime/law enforcement; Safety/disasters, management/technical assistance; Safety/disasters; Youth development; Children, services.
Programs:
Forensics Labs and Investigations Centers: Target shares its safety resources with community partners whenever possible, including its two forensics labs, located in Minneapolis, MN and Las Vegas, NV and its Investigations Centers across the country. These facilities support law enforcement investigations - approximately 30 percent of Target's forensics labs' work is unrelated to Target, and the company offers those services to partners for free.
Take Charge of Education: Target donates 1% of a customer's purchases with a Target REDcard to the eligible K-12 school of their choosing.
Target & Blue: The Target & BLUE program was started in 1990 to form connections with law enforcement, public safety, and criminal justice agencies, and to share the company's programs, resources, and ideas. Through programs like National Night Out, Heroes & Helpers, and the company's public safety grants - and resources like forensics labs - Target helps communities make strides toward a higher standard of safety.
Type of support: Donated products; Employee volunteer services; Equipment; General/operating support; In-kind gifts; Sponsorships.
Geographic limitations: Giving is limited to areas of company operations.
Support limitations: No support for religious organizations for religious purposes, educational institutions for regular instructional programs, treatment programs such as substance or alcohol abuse, athletic teams or events, or advocacy or research groups, from education grants. No education grants to individuals, or for fundraising or gala events, capital or building construction projects, or endowment campaigns.
Publications: Application guidelines; Grants list.
Application information: Applications accepted. Organizations must be within 100 miles of a Target store to apply for a grant. Applications are accepted online only; hard-copy applications are not accepted. Recipients will be asked to complete a survey at the end of the grant program year. Applicants should submit the following:
1) population served
2) copy of current year's organizational budget and/or project budget

Initial approach: Complete online application form; contact local store's Assets Protection team for public safety grants.
Deadline(s): Aug. 1 to Sept. 30 for Field Trip Grants; Mar. 1 to Apr. 30 for Early Childhood Reading Grants and Arts, Culture & Design in Schools Grants
Final notification: Aug. 31 for Education Grants; Jan. 1 for Field Trip Grants
Number of staff: 70 full-time professional.

Target Foundation
(doing business as Target Foundation)
(formerly Dayton Hudson Foundation)
c/o Community Rels.
1000 Nicollet Mall, TPN1144
Minneapolis, MN 55403-2467 (800) 388-6740
FAX: (612) 696-4706;
E-mail: community.relations@target.com;
URL: https://corporate.target.com/corporate-responsibility/grants

Establishment information: Incorporated in 1918 in MN.
Donors: Dayton Hudson Corp.; Target Corp.
Contact: Jeanne Kavanaugh, Sr. Specialist
Financial data (yr. ended 01/28/12): Assets, $20,903,916 (M); gifts received, $11,750,000; expenditures, $9,769,533; qualifying distributions, $9,757,496; giving activities include $9,750,000 for 174 grants (high: $1,225,000; low: $5,000).
Purpose and activities: The foundation supports programs designed to promote arts and culture accessibility; and provide for basic needs of individuals and families at risk. Support is limited to the Minneapolis/St. Paul, Minnesota 7-county metropolitan area.
Fields of interest: Museums; Arts; Food services; Housing/shelter; Salvation Army; Family services; Human services; Community/economic development; United Ways and Federated Giving Programs.
Programs:
Arts: The foundation supports programs designed to provide accessible and affordable art and cultural experiences to the community.
Social Services: The foundation supports programs designed to provide food, clothing, and housing to communities and families at-risk.
Type of support: General/operating support.
Geographic limitations: Giving limited to the Minneapolis/St. Paul, MN 7-county metropolitan area.
Support limitations: No support for religious organizations not of direct benefit to the entire community; generally, no support for health organizations. No grants to individuals, or for endowments, national ceremonies, memorials, conferences, fundraising dinners, testimonials, or similar events, recreation, therapeutic programs, or living subsidies.
Publications: Annual report; Application guidelines; Grants list; Program policy statement.
Application information: Applications accepted. Applicants are required to register through the Minnesota Cultural Data Project. Application form required. Applicants should submit the following:
1) listing of board of directors, trustees, officers and other key people and their affiliations
2) detailed description of project and amount of funding requested
3) copy of current year's organizational budget and/or project budget
4) listing of additional sources and amount of support

Initial approach: Complete online application
Board meeting date(s): Varies
Deadline(s): Jan 1. to Feb. 1 for Arts; Mar. 1 to May 1 for Social Services
Final notification: Usually within 90 days
Officers and Trustees:* Gregg W. Steinhafel*, Chair.; Laysha Ward*, Pres.; Timothy R. Baer*, Secy.; John J. Mulligan, Treas.; John D. Griffith; Beth M. Jacob; Jodeen A. Kozlak; Terrance J. Scully; Kathee Tesjia.
Number of staff: 1 full-time professional.
EIN: 416017088
Selected grants: The following grants are a representative sample of this grantmaker's funding activity:
$5,000,000 to Minnesota Orchestral Association, Minneapolis, MN, 2011. For capital campaign for Hall renovations.
$1,225,000 to United Way, Greater Twin Cities, Minneapolis, MN, 2011. For general operating support.
$415,500 to Musical Instrument Museum, Phoenix, AZ, 2011. For general operating support.
$275,000 to Catholic Charities of the Archdiocese of Saint Paul and Minneapolis, Minneapolis, MN, 2011. For general operating support.
$200,000 to Bridge for Youth, Minneapolis, MN, 2011. For general operating support.
$200,000 to People Serving People, Minneapolis, MN, 2011. For general operating support.
$50,000 to Avenues for Homeless Youth, Minneapolis, MN, 2011. For general operating support.
$30,000 to House of Charity, Minneapolis, MN, 2011. For general operating support.
$27,000 to Charities Review Council of Minnesota, Saint Paul, MN, 2011. For general operations.
$25,000 to Twin Cities Community Gospel Choir, Minneapolis, MN, 2011. For general operating support.

3692
Tastefully Simple, Inc.
1920 Turning Leaf Ln. S.W.
P.O. Box 3006
Alexandria, MN 56308-3006
(320) 763-0695

Company URL: http://www.tastefullysimple.com
Establishment information: Established in 1995.
Company type: Private company
Business activities: Operates direct sales company.
Business type (SIC): Nonstore retailers
Corporate officers: Jill Blashack Strahan, C.E.O.; Joani Nielson, C.O.O.; Bill R. Finley, C.F.O; Joseph Smoliga, Jr., V.P., Opers.; Darrin Johnson, V.P., Sales
Giving statement: Giving through the Tastefully Simple Corporate Giving Program.

Tastefully Simple Corporate Giving Program
c/o Community Rels.
1920 Turning Leaf Ln. S.W.
Alexandria, MN 56308-3006 (320) 763-0695
FAX: (320) 763-2144; URL: http://www.tastefullysimple.com/whoweare/givingwithgratitude.aspx

Purpose and activities: Tastefully Simple makes charitable contributions to nonprofit organizations involved with strengthening families, empowering women, entrepreneurship, the environment, and arts and culture. Support is limited to areas of company operations in Douglas, Grant, Otter Tail, Pope, Stearns, and Todd counties, Minnesota, with emphasis on Douglas County.
Fields of interest: Arts; Environment; Employment, training; Food services; Housing/shelter; Family services; Family services, domestic violence; Community development, small businesses; Leadership development Women; Girls.
Type of support: Program development.
Geographic limitations: Giving limited to areas of company operations in Douglas, Grant, Otter Tail, Pope, Stearns, and Todd counties, MN, with emphasis on Douglas County.
Support limitations: No support for political, lobbying, religious, fraternal, labor, veterans', or controversial organizations, or churches, or sports teams. No grants to individuals, or for general operating expenses, travel, competitions, or similar sports-related activities.
Publications: Application guidelines.
Application information: Applications accepted. Additional documentation or videos not accepted unless requested by the Community Relations department after an initial review of the request. Application form required. Applicants should submit the following:
1) timetable for implementation and evaluation of project
2) results expected from proposed grant
3) statement of problem project will address
4) name, address and phone number of organization
5) copy of IRS Determination Letter
6) brief history of organization and description of its mission
7) detailed description of project and amount of funding requested
8) copy of current year's organizational budget and/or project budget
9) listing of additional sources and amount of support

Initial approach: Mail or fax application to headquarters
Deadline(s): Nov. 1
Final notification: Dec. 31

3693
Tasty Baking Company
3 Crescent Dr., Ste. 200
Philadelphia, PA 19112 (215) 221-8500

Company URL: http://www.tastykake.com
Establishment information: Established in 1914.
Company type: Subsidiary of a public company
Business activities: Produces and sells cakes, pies, cookies, pretzels, brownies, pastries, doughnuts, and snack bars.
Business type (SIC): Bakery products
Financial profile for 2010: Number of employees, 870; assets, $189,470,000; sales volume, $180,560,000; pre-tax net income, -$6,430,000; expenses, $186,990,000; liabilities, $161,690,000
Corporate officers: James E. Ksansnak, Chair.; Charles P. Pizzi, Pres. and C.E.O.; Paul D. Ridder, Sr. V.P. and C.F.O.; Laurence Weilheimer, Sr. V.P., Genl. Counsel, and Corp. Secy.; Robert V. Brown, Sr. V.P., Sales; Eugene P. Malinowski, V.P. and Corp. Treas.; Brenden O'Malley, V.P., Sales; Jonathan L. Silvon, V.P., Mktg.; David A. Vidovich, V.P., Human Resources
Board of directors: James E. Ksansnak, Chair.; Mark G. Conish; James C. Hellauer; Ronald J. Kozich; James E. Nevels; Charles P. Pizzi; Mark T. Timbie; Judith M. von Seldeneck; David J. West
Giving statement: Giving through the Tasty Baking Foundation.
Company EIN: 231145880

Tasty Baking Foundation
c/o Flowers Foods
1919 Flowers Cir.
Thomasville, GA 31757-1137 (215) 221-8500

Establishment information: Established in 1955 in PA.
Donor: Tasty Baking Co.
Contact: Eugene P. Malinowski, Secy.-Treas.
Financial data (yr. ended 12/31/11): Assets, $11,928 (M); gifts received, $35,000; expenditures, $38,940; qualifying distributions, $38,900; giving activities include $38,900 for 21 grants (high: $5,000; low: $500).
Purpose and activities: The foundation supports organizations involved with journalism, secondary and higher education, nursing care, autism, food services, children services, business promotion, Judaism, and the visually impaired.
Fields of interest: Arts; Education; Human services.
Type of support: General/operating support.
Geographic limitations: Giving limited to the greater Philadelphia, PA, area.
Application information: Applications accepted. Application form required. Applicants should submit the following:
1) copy of IRS Determination Letter
2) brief history of organization and description of its mission
3) copy of most recent annual report/audited financial statement/990
4) listing of board of directors, trustees, officers and other key people and their affiliations

Initial approach: Proposal.
Copies of proposal: 1
Deadline(s): 2 days prior to board meetings

Officers and Trustees:* Nelson G. Harris*, Chair.; Eugene P. Malinowski*, Secy.-Treas.; Charles R. Pizzi; Laurence Weilheimer.
EIN: 236271018

3694
The Tatitlek Corporation
561 E. 36th Ave.
Anchorage, AK 99503-4137
(907) 278-4000

Company URL: http://www.tatitlek.com
Establishment information: Established in 1973.
Company type: Native corporation
Business activities: Operates native corporation.
Business type (SIC): Nonclassifiable establishments
Corporate officers: Lloyd Allen, Chair.; Roy Totemoff, Pres. and C.E.O.; Peter Giannini, C.O.O.; Carolyn Smithhisler, C.F.O.; Kristel Komakhuk, Secy.; Sheri Buretta, Treas.
Board of directors: Lloyd Allen, Chair.; Sheri Buretta; Kristel Komakhuk; Roy Totemoff; Klen Vlasoff
Giving statement: Giving through the Copper Mountain Foundation.

Copper Mountain Foundation
P.O. Box 650
Cordova, AK 99574-0650 (907) 278-4000
URL: https://ttcshservices.tatitlek.com/Default.aspx

Donors: The Tatitlek Corp.; Alyeska Pipeline Co.; Chugach Alaska Corp.
Financial data (yr. ended 12/31/11): Assets, $118,283 (M); gifts received, $138,634; expenditures, $117,624; qualifying distributions, $105,334; giving activities include $36,343 for 20 grants to individuals (high: $10,000; low: $210).
Purpose and activities: The foundation awards college scholarships and career enhancement grants to individuals who are Alaska Natives or descendants of Alaska Natives with ancestral ties to the Native Village of Tatitlek.
Fields of interest: Native Americans/American Indians.
Type of support: Grants to individuals; Scholarships—to individuals.
Geographic limitations: Giving primarily in AK.
Application information: Applications accepted. Application form required.

Initial approach: Proposal
Deadline(s): None

Officers: Lloyd Allen, Chair.; Sheri Buretta, V.P.; Kristel Komakhuk, Secy.-Treas.
Board Member: Ken Vlasoff.
EIN: 920137461

3695
TCF National Bank
200 Lake St. E.
Wayzata, MN 55391-1693 (612) 661-6500

Company URL: http://www.tcfbank.com
Establishment information: Established in 1923.
Company type: Subsidiary of a public company
Business activities: Operates commercial bank.
Business type (SIC): Banks/commercial
Financial profile for 2009: Number of employees, 7,573; sales volume, $1,484,040,000

Corporate officers: William A. Cooper, Chair. and C.E.O.; Craig R. Dahl, Co-Vice-Chair.; Thomas F. Jasper, Co-Vice-Chair.
Board of directors: William A. Cooper, Chair.; Craig R. Dahl, Co-Vice-Chair.; Thomas F. Jasper, Co-Vice-Chair.
Giving statement: Giving through the TCF Foundation.

TCF Foundation

200 Lake St. E., EXO-01-C
Wayzata, MN 55391-1693
FAX: (952) 745-2775; E-mail: dpete@tcfbank.com; URL: http://www.tcfbank.com/About/about_community_relations.jsp

Establishment information: Established in 1989 in MN.
Donors: TCF National Bank Minnesota; TCF National Bank; TCF Financial Corp.
Contact: Denise Peterson, Community Affairs Off.
Financial data (yr. ended 12/31/11): Assets, $223,824 (M); gifts received, $1,802,800; expenditures, $1,979,614; qualifying distributions, $1,979,614; giving activities include $1,979,614 for grants.
Purpose and activities: The foundation supports organizations involved with education, human services, community development, and the arts; and programs designed to improve the economic and social well-being of the community. Support is limited to areas of company operations and only to nonprofit organizations where there are TCF employees actively involved.
Fields of interest: Arts; Education; Housing/shelter, rehabilitation; Housing/shelter; Youth development; Human services, financial counseling; Human services; Community/economic development; Financial services Economically disadvantaged.
Programs:
Matching Gifts Program: The foundation matches contributions made by employees of TCF to nonprofit organizations on a one-for-one basis from $25 to $5,000 per employee, per year.
Scholarship Programs: The foundation supports nonprofit community organizations, elementary and secondary schools, vocational and technical schools, and accredited 2 or 4 year colleges and universities managing programs providing direct financial support to students. Support is limited to the greater Chicago, Illinois, area, northwest Indiana, and southeastern Wisconsin.
TCF Employee's Fund: Through the TCF Employee's Fund, TCF employees make donations to nonprofit organizations through automatic payroll deductions and the deductions are matched on a one-for-one basis by the foundation. Grants are based on employee involvement through volunteerism.
Type of support: Annual campaigns; Capital campaigns; Continuing support; Employee matching gifts; Employee volunteer services; Employee-related scholarships; General/operating support; Loaned talent; Program development; Scholarship funds.
Geographic limitations: Giving limited to areas of company operations in CO, MI, and MN, the greater Chicago, IL, area, northwest IN, and southeastern WI, including Kenosha, the greater Milwaukee area, and Racine.
Support limitations: No support for political parties or candidates, churches, religious organizations not of direct benefit to the entire community, lobbying organizations, or social organizations. No grants to individuals (except for employee-related scholarships), or for social events, fundraising activities, or advertising or publications.
Publications: Application guidelines; Corporate report.
Application information: Applications accepted. The foundation accepts full proposals by invitation only. Only nonprofit organizations where there are TCF employees actively involved are considered.
Initial approach: Letter of inquiry
Copies of proposal: 1
Board meeting date(s): Quarterly
Deadline(s): None
Final notification: Up to 3 months
Officers and Directors:* William A. Cooper*, Chair.; Jason E. Korstange*, Vice-Chair.; Gregory J. Pulles*, Secy.; Thomas F. Jasper, Treas.; Mark L. Jeter.
Number of staff: 1 full-time professional.
EIN: 411659826

3696
TD Bank, N.A.

(doing business as TD Banknorth)
(formerly TD Banknorth)
2 Portland Sq.
P.O. Box 9540
Portland, ME 04112-9540 (207) 761-8500

Company URL: http://www.tdbank.com
Establishment information: Established in 1986.
Company type: Subsidiary of a foreign company
Business activities: Operates commercial bank.
Business type (SIC): Banks/commercial; holding company
Corporate officers: W. Edmund Clark, Chair.; Bharat B. Masrani, Pres. and C.E.O.; Stephen J. Boyle, Exec. V.P., Finance and C.F.O.
Board of directors: W. Edmund Clark, Chair.; William E. Bennett; P. Kevin Condron; Stanley E. Grayson; Dana S. Levenson; Bharat B. Masrani; Thomas J. Mullin; Peter G. Vigue; Natica Von Althann
Subsidiaries: Bank of New Hampshire, Manchester, NH; Peoples Heritage Bank, Portland, ME
Historic mergers: American Financial Holdings, Inc. (February 14, 2003); TD Commerce Bank (March 31, 2008)
Giving statement: Giving through the TD Bank, N.A. Corporate Giving Program and the TD Charitable Foundation.

TD Bank, N.A. Corporate Giving Program

(formerly TD Banknorth Inc. Corporate Giving Program)
2 Portland Square
P.O. Box 9540
Portland, ME 04112-9540 (800) 462-3666
E-mail: CommunitySponsorships@YesBank.com; URL: http://www.tdbank.com/community/our_community.html

Purpose and activities: As a complement to its foundation, TD Bank also makes charitable contributions to nonprofit organizations directly. Emphasis is given to programs that provide affordable housing, education, or financial literacy, have broad support, and offer an opportunity for employee volunteerism. Support is limited to areas of company operations.
Fields of interest: Arts; Education; Environment; Health care; Housing/shelter, expense aid; Athletics/sports, Special Olympics; Recreation; Human services, financial counseling; Human services; Community development, small businesses; United Ways and Federated Giving Programs Economically disadvantaged.
Type of support: Employee volunteer services; General/operating support; In-kind gifts; Loaned talent; Sponsorships.
Geographic limitations: Giving limited to areas of company operations.
Support limitations: No support for religious, fraternal, political, advocacy, government, labor, or veterans' organizations, public or private educational institutions for grades K-12, including associated teams, groups, events or scholarships, single issue organizations, or organizations not of direct benefit to the entire community. No grants to individuals or families, or for trips, tours, transportation or travel, golf outings or tournaments, national conferences, professional fundraising, annual appeals or annual operating support, membership fees or dues, research projects, memorials, pageants, yearbook ads, or other advertising.
Publications: Application guidelines; Corporate giving report.
Application information: Applications accepted. Support is limited to 1 contribution per organization during any given year. Regional community sponsorship committees handle giving. Event or program descriptions should be limited to 3 pages. Applicants should submit the following:
1) copy of IRS Determination Letter
2) copy of most recent annual report/audited financial statement/990
3) detailed description of project and amount of funding requested
4) copy of current year's organizational budget and/or project budget
5) listing of additional sources and amount of support

Proposals should contain a Form W-9, and a 12-month schedule of events.
Initial approach: Complete online eligibility quiz and online application
Committee meeting date(s): Monthly
Deadline(s): 3 months prior to need
Final notification: 30 days following board meetings

TD Charitable Foundation

(formerly TD Banknorth Charitable Foundation)
P.O. Box 9540
1 Portland Sq.
Portland, ME 04112-9540 (207) 756-6947
E-mail: CharitableGiving@TDBanknorth.com; E-mail for Michael Rayder: Michael.Rayder@TDBanknorth.com; URL: http://www.tdbank.com/community/grants.html

Establishment information: Established in 2002 in ME.
Donors: Carolina First Foundation; Banknorth Group, Inc.; TD Banknorth Inc.; American Savings Bank; Cape Cod Bank and Trust Co.; Interchange Bank; Commerce Bancorp, Inc.
Contact: Michael L. Rayder, Jr., Mgr.
Financial data (yr. ended 12/31/11): Assets, $83,686,928 (M); gifts received, $7,774,110; expenditures, $14,515,858; qualifying distributions, $14,164,398; giving activities include $13,824,674 for 1,468 grants.
Purpose and activities: The foundation supports organizations involved with affordable housing; education and financial literacy; and the environment. Special emphasis is directed toward programs designed to support low- to moderate-income individuals by providing services, training, or education that improves the quality of life and provides opportunities for advancement.
Fields of interest: Education, ESL programs; Education, services; Education, reading; Education; Environment, natural resources; Environment,

energy; Environment; Food banks; Housing/shelter, development; Housing/shelter, rehabilitation; Housing/shelter; Youth development, adult & child programs; Youth development; Human services, financial counseling; Human services; Community development, small businesses; Community/ economic development; United Ways and Federated Giving Programs; Mathematics Economically disadvantaged.

Programs:

Affordable Housing: The foundation supports programs designed to promote community revitalization and the preservation and development of affordable housing.

Education/Financial Literacy: The foundation supports programs designed to promote reading, writing, math, and financial literacy for all ages; pre- and after-school initiatives that reinforce basic learning skills; English as a second language; tutoring and mentorship; and education-focused youth development programs and initiatives.

Environment: The foundation supports programs designed to improve the environment through energy-saving and sustainability; promote environmental awareness and education; and engage the community in active preservation of natural surroundings.

Housing for Everyone Grant Competition: The foundation annually awards grants to nonprofit organizations designed to make a meaningful difference in meeting the affordable housing needs in their community. A different theme aiming to improve affordable housing is announced every year. Grants range from $10,000 to $100,000.

Non-Profit Training Resource Fund: The foundation awards grants of up to $1,000 to nonprofit organizations for employees to attend approved classes and courses designed to enhance job performance. Special emphasis is directed toward organizations designed to promote affordable housing for low-to-moderate income individuals; increase economic and small business development; provide financial literacy programming to low- and moderate-income youth, individuals, or families; and promote afterschool or extracurricular programming for children from low-to-moderate income households.

Type of support: Annual campaigns; Employee matching gifts; Employee volunteer services; Management development/capacity building; Program development; Sponsorships.

Geographic limitations: Giving limited to areas of company operations in CT, Washington, DC, DE, FL, MA, MD, ME, NC, NH, NJ, NY, PA, RI, SC, VA, and VT.

Support limitations: No support for private foundations, political candidates, lobbying, advocacy, research, or discriminatory organizations, fraternal, labor, or veterans' groups, religious organizations not of direct benefit to the entire community, or athletic teams or social groups. No grants to individuals, or for fundraising events, scholarships, memberships, advertising, annual campaigns, travel or conferences, debt reduction, trips or tours, endowments, or capital campaigns; no general operating support.

Publications: Application guidelines; Corporate giving report; Grants list; Program policy statement.

Application information: Applications accepted. Organizations receiving support for the Non-Profit Training Resource Fund are required to provide a certificate of completion or other evidence of the employee's attendance of the training. Support is limited to 1 contribution per organization during any given year. Visit website for application deadlines. Application form required. Applicants should submit the following:

1) timetable for implementation and evaluation of project
2) statement of problem project will address
3) population served
4) copy of IRS Determination Letter
5) brief history of organization and description of its mission
6) geographic area to be served
7) copy of most recent annual report/audited financial statement/990
8) how project's results will be evaluated or measured
9) listing of board of directors, trustees, officers and other key people and their affiliations
10) contact person
11) copy of current year's organizational budget and/or project budget
12) listing of additional sources and amount of support

Requests for the Non-Profit Training Resource Fund should include a description of the organization's size and capacity, the course's impact on the organization and community, and how the information will be used to impact the organization or provide a new service; descriptive literature on the course; and the documented approval of the organization's executive director.

Initial approach: Complete online application
Board meeting date(s): Quarterly
Deadline(s): Varies by state; July 5 to Sept 2 for Housing for Everyone Grant Competition; None for Non-Profit Training Resource Fund
Final notification: 2 weeks following committee meeting; Nov. for Housing for Everyone Grant Competition; 2 to 6 weeks for Non-Profit Training Resource Fund

Officers and Directors: Elizabeth K. Warn, Pres.; Mark Crandall, V.P.; John R. Opperman, Clerk; Paul Young, Treas.; Michael Carbone; Joseph Fico; Fred Graziano; Scott Mullin.

EIN: 141864317

Selected grants: The following grants are a representative sample of this grantmaker's funding activity:
$500,000 to ACCION USA, New York, NY, 2011. For Maine to Miami Microlending and Financial Education Initiative.
$320,000 to United Way of Greater Portland, Portland, ME, 2010. For United Way Community Campaign.
$272,000 to United Way of Greater Portland, Portland, ME, 2011. For United Way Community Campaign.
$200,000 to Neighborhood Reinvestment Corporation, NeighborWorks America, Washington, DC, 2010. For NeighborWorks Training Institute.
$127,500 to Boys and Girls Clubs in New Jersey, Clifton, NJ, 2011. For Project Learn.
$125,000 to World Trade Center Memorial Foundation, New York, NY, 2010. For 9/11 Initiative.
$120,000 to New Jersey Citizen Action Education Fund, Newark, NJ, 2010. For Housing, Community and Economic Development Projects.
$120,000 to New Jersey Citizen Action Education Fund, Newark, NJ, 2011. For Housing, Community and Economic Development.
$100,000 to Asian Americans for Equality, New York, NY, 2011. For Chinatown Tenements Energy Efficiency Initiative.
$100,000 to Cooper Foundation, Camden, NJ, 2010. For Bright Beginnings - Neonatal Follow Up Program.
$100,000 to Moorestown Ecumenical Neighborhood Development, Moorestown, NJ, 2010. For Leriola Green Energy Efficiency Initiative.
$100,000 to Osceola County Council on Aging, Kissimmee, FL, 2011. For Buen Vecino Landings Project.
$68,268 to New Hampshire Food Bank, Manchester, NH, 2010. For Emergency Food Purchase Program.
$50,000 to First Book, Washington, DC, 2011. For Banking on Books Program.
$50,000 to Harlem Educational Activities Fund, New York, NY, 2010. For HEAF Continuum.
$50,000 to Lutheran Medical Center, Brooklyn, NY, 2011. For Electronic Medical Record Training.
$7,500 to Latin American Economic Development Association, Camden, NJ, 2011. For Entrepreneurial Development Training.
$7,500 to Milford Housing Development Corporation, Milford, DE, 2010. For Kent County Self-Help Program.
$5,000 to Project Paul, Keansburg, NJ, 2010. For Educational Support Program.
$5,000 to United Way of Broward County, Fort Lauderdale, FL, 2011. For United Way Community Campaign.

3697
Teachers Credit Union

(also known as TCU)
110 S. Main St.
P.O. Box 1395
South Bend, IN 46601-1805
(574) 232-8012

Company URL: https://www.tcunet.com
Establishment information: Established in 1931.
Company type: Private company
Business activities: Operates state credit union.
Business type (SIC): Credit unions
Corporate officers: David Sage, Chair.; Richard Rice, Pres.; Amy Sink, Sr. V.P. and C.F.O.; Valerie Miller, V.P. and Genl. Counsel; Todd Brown, V.P., Finance
Board of director: David Sage, Chair.
Giving statement: Giving through the TCU Foundation, Inc.

TCU Foundation, Inc.

110 S. Main St.
South Bend, IN 46601-1805
Application address: P.O. Box 1395, South Bend, IN, 46624; URL: https://www.tcunet.com/News_Info/AboutTCU/TCUFoundation/

Establishment information: Established in 1995 in IN.
Donors: Teachers Credit Union; Community Foundation of St. Joseph County.
Financial data (yr. ended 12/31/11): Assets, $626,774 (M); gifts received, $163,044; expenditures, $206,155; qualifying distributions, $206,155; giving activities include $206,155 for grants.
Purpose and activities: The foundation supports organizations involved with education and other member-driven initiatives. Special emphasis is directed toward programs that promote life-long learning and financial literacy.
Fields of interest: Museums (art); Arts; Education, reading; Education; Health care; Children/youth, services; Voluntarism promotion.
Type of support: Curriculum development; Donated equipment; Employee matching gifts; Endowments; Matching/challenge support; Program development; Research; Scholarship funds; Scholarships—to individuals.

Geographic limitations: Giving limited to areas of company operations in IN.
Application information: Applications accepted. Application form not required.
Initial approach: Complete online form; telephone
Copies of proposal: 1
Deadline(s): 1 month prior to board meetings
Officers: David Sage, Chair.; William Hojnacki, Vice-Chair.; Al Bias, Secy.; Rick Rice, Treas.
Directors: Alfred Bias; Shirley Golichowski; Vincent Henderson; Juan Manigault; Jeanette Moeller; John Myers; William Schlundt; Roger Thornton.
Number of staff: None.
EIN: 351939838
Selected grants: The following grants are a representative sample of this grantmaker's funding activity:
$14,600 to Indiana University, Bloomington, IN, 2010. For general support.
$10,000 to Holy Cross College, Notre Dame, IN, 2010. For general support.
$5,000 to Girl Scouts of the U.S.A., Fort Wayne, IN, 2010. For general support.
$5,000 to Indiana Council for Economic Education, West Lafayette, IN, 2010. For general support.
$5,000 to Studebaker National Museum, South Bend, IN, 2010. For general support.
$3,000 to Bethel College, Mishawaka, IN, 2010. For general support.
$3,000 to University of Notre Dame, Notre Dame, IN, 2010.
$2,500 to Center for Leadership Development, Indianapolis, IN, 2010. For general support.
$2,500 to Teens Organized, Unified, Goal-Oriented, Helpful, Indianapolis, IN, 2010. For general support.
$2,000 to Fischoff National Chamber Music Association, Notre Dame, IN, 2010. For general support.

3698
TeamQuest Corporation

1 TeamQuest Way
P.O. Box 1125
Clear Lake, IA 50428 (641) 357-2700

Company URL: http://www.teamquest.com
Establishment information: Established in 1991.
Company type: Private company
Business activities: Provides information technology performance optimization and capacity planning services.
Business type (SIC): Computer services
Corporate officers: Jerred D. Ruble, Pres. and C.E.O.; Terry A. Wisner, Exec. V.P. and C.F.O.; Renee Ritter, V.P. of Sales.; Cathy Kent, Corp. Cont.; Kathleen Koranda, Human Resources
Giving statement: Giving through the TeamQuest Foundation.

TeamQuest Foundation

1 TeamQuest Way
Clear Lake, IA 50428-2296 (641) 357-2700

Establishment information: Established in 2002 in IA.
Donors: TeamQuest Corporation; Terry B. Cobb.
Financial data (yr. ended 12/31/11): Assets, $335,031 (M); gifts received, $35,000; expenditures, $14,551; qualifying distributions, $13,050; giving activities include $13,050 for grants.
Purpose and activities: The foundation supports programs designed to promote the advancement of technologies used by nonprofit and educational programs for daily operations and for the implementation of community-based programs.
Fields of interest: Arts; Recreation; Public affairs.
Type of support: Program development.
Geographic limitations: Giving primarily in northern IA.
Support limitations: No grants to individuals.
Application information: Applications accepted. Application form required.
Initial approach: Contact foundation for application form
Board meeting date(s): June
Deadline(s): Jan. 1 and Apr. 30
Officers: Terry B. Cobb, Pres.; Terry A. Wisner, V.P. and Secy.; Cathy A. Kent, Treas.
Directors: Steven A. Hild; Jerred D. Ruble.
EIN: 721538400

3699
Techni-Core, Inc.

7426 Linder Ave.
Skokie, IL 60077-3219 (847) 673-8300

Establishment information: Established in 1984.
Company type: Private company
Business activities: Manufactures precision control actuators.
Business type (SIC): Machinery/industrial and commercial
Corporate officers: Dennis Benning, Pres.; James Zangrilli, C.F.O.; Stephen R. Roberti, Secy.
Giving statement: Giving through the Grace Roberti Foundation.

Grace Roberti Foundation

3708 Alden Rd.
Woodstock, IL 60098-9707 (815) 337-3500

Establishment information: Established in 2000 in IL.
Donors: Techni-Core, Inc.; Joseph M. Roberti; Vincent V. Roberti.
Contact: Dominick Roberti, Pres. and Treas.
Financial data (yr. ended 12/31/11): Assets, $1,527,431 (M); expenditures, $107,208; qualifying distributions, $90,000; giving activities include $90,000 for grants.
Purpose and activities: The foundation supports organizations involved with K-12 education, health, birth defects, human services, and Christianity.
Type of support: Building/renovation; Equipment; General/operating support.
Geographic limitations: Giving primarily in IL and NJ; giving also to national organizations.
Support limitations: No grants to individuals.
Application information: Applications accepted. Application form required. Applicants should submit the following:
1) copy of IRS Determination Letter
2) descriptive literature about organization
Initial approach: Letter
Deadline(s): None
Officers: Dominick Roberti, Pres. and Treas.; Michael Roberti, Secy.
EIN: 364401144

3700
Teck Resources Limited

(formerly Teck Cominco American Incorporated)
501 N. Riverpoint Blvd., Ste. 300
Spokane, WA 99202 (509) 747-6111

Company URL: http://www.teck.com
Establishment information: Established in 1913.
Company type: Subsidiary of a foreign company
Business activities: Conducts mineral exploration and mining activities.
Business type (SIC): Mining/lead and zinc; mining/gold and silver; fertilizers and agricultural chemicals
Corporate officers: Norman B. Keevil, Chair.; Donald R. Lindsay, Pres. and C.E.O.; Ronald A. Millos, Sr. V.P., Finance, and C.F.O.; John F. Gingell, V.P. and Cont.; Dean Winsor, V.P., Human Resources
Board of director: Norman B. Keevil, Chair.
International operations: Chile; Peru
Giving statement: Giving through the Teck Resources Limited Corporate Giving Program.

Teck Resources Limited Corporate Giving Program

(formerly Teck Cominco American Incorporated Corporate Giving Program)
501 North Riverpoint Blvd., Ste. 300
Spokane, WA 99202-1649 (509) 747-6111
URL: http://www.teck.com/Generic.aspx?PAGE=Teck+Site/Responsibility&portalName=tc

Purpose and activities: Teck Resources makes charitable contributions to nonprofit organizations involved with arts and culture, education, the environment, medical research and health, and community development. Support is given primarily in Washington State.
Fields of interest: Arts; Education; Environment; Community/economic development.
Type of support: General/operating support; In-kind gifts.
Geographic limitations: Giving primarily in WA.
Support limitations: No support for religious, political, lobbying, or for-profit organizations. No grants to individuals, or for advertising, promotions, debt reduction campaigns, telephone or commercial solicitations, contests, raffles, or other activities centered around tickets/prizes.
Application information: Applications accepted. Applicants should submit the following:
1) brief history of organization and description of its mission
2) listing of board of directors, trustees, officers and other key people and their affiliations
3) detailed description of project and amount of funding requested
4) contact person
5) copy of current year's organizational budget and/or project budget
Initial approach: Complete online application

3701
TECO Energy, Inc.

Teco Plz., 702 N. Franklin St.
Tampa, FL 33602 (813) 228-4111
FAX: (813) 228-1670

Company URL: http://www.tecoenergy.com
Establishment information: Established in 1899.
Company type: Public company
Company ticker symbol and exchange: TE/NYSE

Business activities: Generates, transmits, and distributes electricity; produces coal and natural gas.
Business type (SIC): Electric services; mining/coal and lignite surface; trucking and courier services, except by air; warehousing and storage; transportation/deep sea domestic freight; transportation services/water
Financial profile for 2012: Number of employees, 3,900; assets, $7,356,500,000; sales volume, $2,996,600,000; pre-tax net income, $383,800,000; expenses, $2,441,300,000; liabilities, $5,064,700,000
Fortune 1000 ranking: 2012—692nd in revenues, 560th in profits, and 476th in assets
Corporate officers: Sherrill W. Hudson, Chair.; John B. Ramil, Pres. and C.E.O.; Sandra W. Callahan, Sr. V.P., Finance, C.F.O., and C.A.O.; Charles A. Attal III, Sr. V.P. and Genl. Counsel
Board of directors: Sherrill W. Hudson, Chair.; James L. Ferman, Jr.; Evelyn V. Follit; Joseph P. Lacher; Loretta A. Penn; John B. Ramil; Thompson L. Rankin; William D. Rockford; Paul L. Whiting
Giving statement: Giving through the TECO Energy, Inc. Corporate Giving Program and the TECO Energy Foundation, Inc.
Company EIN: 592052286

TECO Energy, Inc. Corporate Giving Program

702 N. Franklin St.
Tampa, FL 33602-4429 (813) 228-4111
URL: http://www.tecoenergy.com/csr/

Purpose and activities: As a complement to its foundation, TECO Energy also makes charitable contributions to nonprofit organizations involved with education, performing arts, housing, and cultural institutions. Support is given primarily in areas of company operations, with emphasis on Florida, and Kentucky. Giving also in Guatemala.
Fields of interest: Museums; Performing arts; Education, public education; Secondary school/education; Higher education, college; Business school/education; Environment, public education; Hospitals (general); Housing/shelter, volunteer services; Athletics/sports, school programs; Salvation Army; Women, centers/services; United Ways and Federated Giving Programs Aging.
Type of support: Employee volunteer services; General/operating support.
Geographic limitations: Giving primarily in areas of company operations in FL, KY, and Guatemala.
Publications: Corporate giving report.
Number of staff: None.

TECO Energy Foundation, Inc.

702 N. Franklin St.
Tampa, FL 33602-4429 (813) 228-1111
Application address: P.O. Box 111, Tampa, FL 33601-0111, tel.: (813) 228-4497; URL: http://www.tecoenergy.com/csr/community/communityinvolvement/

Establishment information: Established as a company-sponsored operating foundation.
Donor: TECO Energy, Inc.
Contact: Jack Amor, Exec. Dir.
Financial data (yr. ended 12/31/11): Assets, $527,556 (M); expenditures, $552,746; qualifying distributions, $551,480; giving activities include $551,480 for 7 grants (high: $180,000; low: $10,000).
Purpose and activities: The foundation supports museums and performing art centers and organizations involved with higher education.
Fields of interest: Museums; Museums (art); Museums (history); Performing arts centers; Higher education.
Type of support: Capital campaigns; Matching/challenge support.
Geographic limitations: Giving primarily in Tampa, FL.
Application information: Applications accepted. Application form not required. Applicants should submit the following:
1) detailed description of project and amount of funding requested
2) timetable for implementation and evaluation of project

Initial approach: Proposal
Deadline(s): None

Officers and Directors: Sandra W. Callahan*, V.P.; David Schwartz, Secy.; Kim Caruso, Treas.; Jack Amor, Exec. Dir.; Valerie Strickland, Tax Off.; Chuck Attal; Gordon Gillete; Bruce Narzissenfeld; John B. Ramil.
EIN: 010598444
Selected grants: The following grants are a representative sample of this grantmaker's funding activity:
$160,000 to University of South Florida Foundation, Tampa, FL, 2010.
$125,000 to Tampa Bay History Center, Tampa, FL, 2010.
$115,000 to David A. Straz, Jr. Center for the Performing Arts, Tampa, FL, 2010.
$86,020 to Saint Leo University, Saint Leo, FL, 2010.
$50,000 to Hillsborough Educational Partnership Foundation, Tampa, FL, 2010.
$10,000 to Chamber of Commerce of Florida, Tallahassee, FL, 2010.

3702
Tedco, Inc.

738 Well Rd.
West Monroe, LA 71292-0138
(318) 325-4265

Establishment information: Established in 1983.
Company type: Private company
Business activities: Manufactures soaps and detergents.
Business type (SIC): Soaps, cleaners, and toiletries
Corporate officer: Byron K. Tedeton, Pres.
Giving statement: Giving through the Easy Tedeton Memorial Scholarship Foundation.

Easy Tedeton Memorial Scholarship Foundation

738 Well Rd.
West Monroe, LA 71292-0138

Establishment information: Established in 2006 in LA.
Donors: Tedco, Inc.; Miracle II, LLC.
Financial data (yr. ended 06/30/12): Assets, $10,186 (M); gifts received, $60,800; expenditures, $57,526; qualifying distributions, $57,492; giving activities include $57,492 for grants to individuals.
Purpose and activities: The foundation provides scholarship awards to residents of West Monroe, Louisiana.
Fields of interest: Higher education.
Type of support: Scholarships—to individuals.
Geographic limitations: Giving primarily to residents of West Monroe, LA.
Application information: Applications not accepted. Unsolicited requests for funds not accepted.
Officers: Byron Kirk Tedeton, Pres.; Pamela Sue Tedeton, Secy.-Treas.
Director: Byron Kirk Tedeton, Jr.
EIN: 205297277

3703
Tees At Risk, LLC

2720 W. Chew St.
Allentown, PA 18104-5350 (610) 435-4198

Company URL: http://teesatrisk.com
Establishment information: Established in 2010.
Company type: Private company
Business type (SIC): Business services/miscellaneous
Corporate officers: Richard Kligman, Founder; Ben Wiener, Founder
Board of director: Toby Smith
Giving statement: Giving through the Tees At Risk LLC Contributions Program.

Tees At Risk LLC Contributions Program

2720 W Chew St.
Allentown, PA 18104-5350 (610) 435-4198
URL: http://teesatrisk.com

Contact: Toby Smith, Dir.
Purpose and activities: Tees At Risk is a certified B Corporation that donates a percentage of sales to charitable organizations.
Fields of interest: Youth development; Children/youth, services.
Type of support: General/operating support.

3704
Teichert, Inc.

3500 American River Dr.
Sacramento, CA 95864-5802
(916) 484-3011

Company URL: http://www.teichert.com
Establishment information: Established in 1887.
Company type: Subsidiary of a private company
Business activities: Manufactures and provides construction products and services.
Business type (SIC): Heavy construction other than building construction contractors; concrete, gypsum, and plaster products
Financial profile for 2010: Number of employees, 1,800
Corporate officers: Judson T. Riggs, Pres. and C.E.O.; Patrick Pathipati, Exec. V.P. and C.F.O.; Robert S. Bryant, V.P., Human Resources
Giving statement: Giving through the Teichert Foundation.

Teichert Foundation

3500 American River Dr.
Sacramento, CA 95864-5802 (916) 484-3255
Additional address: P.O. Box 15002, Sacramento, CA 95851-1002; URL: http://www.teichert.com/index.cfm?pageid=486

Establishment information: Established in 1990 in CA.
Donors: A. Teichert & Son, Inc.; Teichert, Inc.; Ruth Tucker.
Contact: Emily Begay, Prog. Assoc.
Financial data (yr. ended 03/31/12): Assets, $9,929,811 (M); gifts received, $6,439;

expenditures, $753,109; qualifying distributions, $650,964; giving activities include $650,964 for grants.
Purpose and activities: The foundation supports organizations involved with arts and culture, education, environmental planning and preservation, health, youth development, human services, community development, transportation and planning, civic affairs, and senior citizens. Special emphasis is directed toward programs designed to focus on children and youth.
Fields of interest: Historic preservation/historical societies; Arts; Education; Environment; Medical care, rehabilitation; Health care; Boys & girls clubs; Youth development; Children/youth, services; Human services; Community/economic development; Transportation; Public affairs Children; Youth; Aging.
Program:
Employee Matching Grants: The foundation matches contributions made by employees of Teichert to schools and nonprofit organizations on a one-for-one basis up to $250 per employee, per year.
Type of support: Capital campaigns; Continuing support; Employee matching gifts; General/operating support.
Geographic limitations: Giving primarily in areas of company operations in Amador, Calaveras, Colusa, El Dorado, Mariposa, Merced, Nevada, North Solano, Placer, Sacramento, San Joaquin, Stanislaus, Sutter, Tuolumne, Yolo, and Yuba counties, CA.
Support limitations: No support for religious organizations not of direct benefit to the entire community, political organizations, or fraternal organizations, societies, or orders. No grants to individuals, or for political campaigns, courtesy advertising or tickets for benefits, telephone solicitations, or national fundraising campaigns.
Publications: Application guidelines; Grants list.
Application information: Applications accepted. Grants range from $3,000 to $7,500. Mailed, late, or incomplete submissions are not accepted. Organizations applying for support are encouraged to register with GuideStar. Support is limited to 1 contribution per organization during any given year. Organizations receiving support are asked to submit a final report. Application form not required.
Applicants should submit the following:
1) role played by volunteers
2) timetable for implementation and evaluation of project
3) how project will be sustained once grantmaker support is completed
4) qualifications of key personnel
5) statement of problem project will address
6) population served
7) principal source of support for project in the past
8) copy of IRS Determination Letter
9) copy of most recent annual report/audited financial statement/990
10) how project's results will be evaluated or measured
11) listing of board of directors, trustees, officers and other key people and their affiliations
12) detailed description of project and amount of funding requested
13) plans for cooperation with other organizations, if any
14) copy of current year's organizational budget and/or project budget

Initial approach: Complete online application
Board meeting date(s): Biannually
Deadline(s): Feb. 24 and Aug. 24
Final notification: June 1 and Dec. 3

Officers and Directors:* Anne S. Haslam*, Secy.; Norman Eilert, C.F.O.; Frederick A. Teichert*, Exec. Dir.; Thomas J. Hammer; Judson T. Riggs; Melita M. Teichert.
Number of staff: 1 full-time professional; 1 full-time support.
EIN: 680212355
Selected grants: The following grants are a representative sample of this grantmaker's funding activity:
$150,000 to Sutter Medical Center Foundation, Sacramento, CA, 2012.
$15,000 to Sacramento Ballet Association, Sacramento, CA, 2012.
$10,000 to Sacramento City Unified School District, Sacramento, CA, 2012.
$8,500 to Inter-Faith Ministries of Greater Modesto, Modesto, CA, 2012.
$7,500 to Boy Scouts of America, Modesto, CA, 2012.
$7,500 to Stanislaus Community Foundation, Modesto, CA, 2012.
$7,500 to Yolo Basin Foundation, Davis, CA, 2012.
$7,500 to Yolo Family Service Agency, Woodland, CA, 2012.
$5,000 to Sacramento Steps Forward, Sacramento, CA, 2012.
$5,000 to Special Recreation Services, Reno, NV, 2012.

3705
Teitler & Teitler, L.L.P.

1114 Ave. of the Americas, Fl. 45
New York, NY 10036-7772 (212) 997-4400

Company URL: http://www.teitlerteitler.com
Establishment information: Established in 1963.
Company type: Private company
Business activities: Provides legal services.
Business type (SIC): Legal services
Corporate officer: Michael F. Teitler, Partner
Giving statement: Giving through the Teitler Foundation, Inc.

Teitler Foundation, Inc.

c/o Teitler & Teitler
1114 Ave. of the Americas, 45th Fl.
New York, NY 10036-7703

Donor: Teitler & Teitler.
Financial data (yr. ended 12/31/11): Assets, $64,656 (M); expenditures, $2,213; qualifying distributions, $1,800; giving activities include $1,800 for grants.
Purpose and activities: The foundation supports organizations involved with higher education and Judaism.
Fields of interest: Human services; Religion.
Type of support: General/operating support.
Geographic limitations: Giving primarily in PA.
Support limitations: No grants to individuals.
Application information: Applications not accepted. Unsolicited requests for funds not accepted.
Director: Michael F. Teitler.
EIN: 237123347

3706
Tektronix, Inc.

14150 S.W. Karl Braun Dr.
P.O. Box 500
Beaverton, OR 97077-0001
(503) 627-7111

Company URL: http://www.tek.com/
Establishment information: Established in 1946.
Company type: Subsidiary of a public company
Business activities: Manufactures, markets, services, and provides test, measurement, and monitoring products and solutions.
Business type (SIC): Laboratory apparatus
Financial profile for 2010: Number of employees, 1,600
Corporate officers: Amir Aghdaei, Pres.; Colin Slade, C.F.O.; Robert W. Blaskowsky, V.P. and C.I.O.; James F. Dalton, V.P., Genl. Counsel, and Secy.; Karsten Beutnagel, V.P., Human Resources; Susan G. Kirby, Treas.
Subsidiary: Tektronix Development Co., Beaverton, OR
Giving statement: Giving through the Tektronix Foundation.
Company EIN: 930343990

Tektronix Foundation

P.O. Box 500, M.S. 50-237
Beaverton, OR 97077-0001 (503) 627-7088
URL: http://www.tek.com/about/foundation.html

Establishment information: Incorporated in 1952 in OR.
Donor: Tektronix, Inc.
Contact: Joanne Maxwell
Financial data (yr. ended 12/31/11): Assets, $338,365 (M); gifts received, $480,000; expenditures, $677,242; qualifying distributions, $663,566; giving activities include $663,566 for grants.
Purpose and activities: The foundation supports organizations involved with arts and culture, education, conservation, and human services.
Fields of interest: Arts; Elementary/secondary education; Higher education; Business school/education; Engineering school/education; Education; Environment, natural resources; Human services; United Ways and Federated Giving Programs.
Program:
Employee Matching Gifts: The foundation matches contributions made by employees, directors, and retirees of Tektronix to educational institutions and nonprofit organizations involved with arts and culture, conservation, and human services from $20 to $2,000 per contributor, per year.
Type of support: Annual campaigns; Continuing support; Employee matching gifts; Equipment; General/operating support; Program development.
Geographic limitations: Giving primarily in OR.
Support limitations: No grants to individuals, or for emergency needs or endowments, demonstration projects, debt reduction, research, publications, or conferences; no loans; no challenge grants.
Application information: Applications not accepted. Contributes only to pre-selected organizations.
Officer and Trustees:* Amie Aghdaei, Chair.; Treasure Bailey; Robert W. Blaskowsky; Robin Burnham; Martyn Etherington.
EIN: 936021540
Selected grants: The following grants are a representative sample of this grantmaker's funding activity:

$85,000 to Oregon State University, Corvallis, OR, 2010.
$85,000 to Oregon State University, Corvallis, OR, 2010.

3707
Teleflex Incorporated

155 S. Limerick Rd.
Limerick, PA 19468-1699 (610) 948-5100
FAX: (610) 948-5101

Company URL: http://www.teleflex.com
Establishment information: Established in 1943.
Company type: Public company
Company ticker symbol and exchange: TFX/NYSE
Business activities: Manufactures industrial, medical, and aerospace products.
Business type (SIC): Medical instruments and supplies; industrial and commercial machinery and computer equipment; aircraft and parts
Financial profile for 2012: Number of employees, 11,600; assets, $3,739,500,000; sales volume, $1,551,010,000; pre-tax net income, -$165,370,000; expenses, $1,648,380,000; liabilities, $1,960,550,000
Corporate officers: Benson F. Smith, Chair., Pres., and C.E.O.; Laurence G. Miller, Exec. V.P., C.A.O., Genl. Counsel, and Secy.; Thomas E. Powell, Sr. V.P. and C.F.O.; Timothy F. Duffy, V.P. and C.I.O.; Jake Elguicze, V.P. and Treas.; Melissa J. Manion, V.P., Human Resources
Board of directors: Benson F. Smith, Chair.; George G. Babich, Jr.; Patricia C. Barron; William R. Cook; W. Kim Foster; Jeffrey A. Graves; Stephen K. Klasko; Sigismundus W.W. Lubsen; Stuart A. Randle; Harold L. Yoh III; James W. Zug
Subsidiaries: Capro Inc., Willis, TX; Cetrek Inc., Limerick, PA; Pilling Weck Inc., Fort Washington, PA; Sermatech International Inc., Limerick, PA; Techsonic Industries, Inc., Eufaula, AL; Teleflex Automotive Manufacturing Corp., Van Wert, OH; Teleflex Control Systems, Inc., Oxnard, PA; Teleflex Fluid Systems, Inc., Suffield, CT; TFX Equities Inc., Plymouth Meeting, PA; TFX Medical Inc., Blue Bell, PA
Plants: Compton, CA; Manchester, CT; Boynton Beach, FL; Biddeford, ME; Sugar Land, TX
International operations: Australia; Austria; Barbados; Belgium; Canada; Czech Republic; Denmark; France; Germany; Greece; Hong Kong; Hungary; India; Italy; Japan; Luxembourg; Malaysia; Mexico; Netherlands; New Zealand; Norway; Poland; Singapore; Slovakia; South Africa; Spain; Sweden; Switzerland; United Kingdom; Uruguay
Giving statement: Giving through the Arrow International Inc., Scholarship Fund and the Teleflex Foundation.
Company EIN: 231147939

Arrow International Inc., Scholarship Fund

c/o Kim Marks-Wachovia Bank, N.A.
1525 W. WT Harris Blvd.
Charlotte, NC 28288-5709

Establishment information: Established in 1994 in PA.
Donors: Arrow International Inc.; Arrow Precision Products, Inc.
Financial data (yr. ended 12/30/09): Assets, $0 (M); expenditures, $1,739,711; qualifying distributions, $1,737,495; giving activities include $1,737,122 for 1 grant.
Purpose and activities: The foundation awards scholarships to children, grandchildren and more remote lineal descendants of individuals employed at Arrow International Inc., or its subsidiary.
Fields of interest: Higher education; Scholarships/financial aid.
Type of support: Employee-related scholarships.
Geographic limitations: Giving primarily in PA.
Application information: Applications not accepted.
Trustee: Wachovia Bank, N.A.
EIN: 232801942

Teleflex Foundation

155 S. Limerick Rd.
Limerick, PA 19468-1603
E-mail: foundation@teleflex.com; URL: http://www.teleflex.com/en/aboutUs/teleflexFoundation/index.html

Establishment information: Established in 1980 in PA.
Donor: Teleflex Inc.
Financial data (yr. ended 12/31/11): Assets, $3,130,221 (M); expenditures, $208,976; qualifying distributions, $209,116; giving activities include $189,418 for 222 grants (high: $7,500; low: $50).
Purpose and activities: The foundation supports programs designed to promote arts and culture, education, and human services.
Fields of interest: Performing arts; Arts; Elementary school/education; Higher education; Education, reading; Education; Animals/wildlife; Health care; Housing/shelter, development; Boys & girls clubs; Big Brothers/Big Sisters; YM/YWCAs & YM/YWHAs; Children/youth, services; Human services.
Type of support: Curriculum development; Employee matching gifts; Program development; Scholarship funds.
Application information: Applications not accepted. Unsolicited requests for funds not accepted.
Directors: Christine Brady; Cathy Bucci; Matt Howald; Lisa Ramsey; Laura Sancineto.
Number of staff: 1 part-time professional.
EIN: 232104782
Selected grants: The following grants are a representative sample of this grantmaker's funding activity:
$5,000 to Girl Scouts of the U.S.A., Chicago, IL, 2010.
$2,000 to University of Michigan, Ann Arbor, MI, 2010.

3708
TeleTech Holdings, Inc.

9197 S. Peoria St.
Englewood, CO 80112-5833
(303) 397-8100
FAX: (303) 397-8199

Company URL: http://www.teletech.com/en-US/
Establishment information: Established in 1982.
Company type: Public company
Company ticker symbol and exchange: TTEC/NASDAQ
Business activities: Operates global business process outsourcing company.
Business type (SIC): Business services/miscellaneous
Financial profile for 2012: Number of employees, 43,000; assets, $847,170,000; sales volume, $1,162,980,000; pre-tax net income, $73,860,000; expenses, $1,084,440,000; liabilities, $360,880,000
Corporate officers: Kenneth D. Tuchman, Chair. and C.E.O.; James E. Barlett, Vice-Chair.; Martin DeGhetto, C.O.O.; Regina Paolillo, Exec. V.P. and C.F.O.
Board of directors: Kenneth D. Tuchman, Chair.; James E. Barlett, Vice-Chair.; Gregory A. Conley; Robert Frerichs; Shrikant Mehta; Anjan Mukherjee; Robert M. Tarola; Shirley A. Young
Giving statement: Giving through the TeleTech Community Foundation.
Company EIN: 841291044

TeleTech Community Foundation

(formerly TeleTech Foundation)
c/o Foundation Source
501 Silverside Rd., No. 123
Wilmington, DE 19809-1374
E-mail: TeleTechFoundation@TeleTech.com; E-mail for Emily Eikelberner: emilyeikelberner@teletech.com; URL: http://www.teletech.com/corporate-responsibility/foundation

Establishment information: Established in 2007 in DE.
Donor: TeleTech Holdings, Inc.
Contact: Emily Eikelberner, Exec. Dir.
Financial data (yr. ended 12/31/11): Assets, $14,261 (M); gifts received, $301,000; expenditures, $353,268; qualifying distributions, $279,760; giving activities include $279,760 for grants.
Purpose and activities: The foundation supports orchestras and organizations involved with health, heart disease, Multiple sclerosis, breast cancer, hunger, and human services. Special emphasis is directed toward programs designed to maximize the educational experience for students who demonstrate the greatest need.
Fields of interest: Performing arts, orchestras; Education, management/technical assistance; Elementary/secondary education; Education, reading; Education; Breast cancer; Heart & circulatory diseases; Multiple sclerosis; Food services; Food banks; Big Brothers/Big Sisters; YM/YWCAs & YM/YWHAs; Family services, domestic violence; Human services Youth.
Type of support: Donated products; Employee volunteer services; General/operating support; Program development; Sponsorships.
Geographic limitations: Giving primarily in areas of company operations in CO, MT, NJ, WA, WV, Europe, Latin America, and Switzerland.
Support limitations: No support for discriminatory organizations, grantmaking foundations, religious organizations not of direct benefit to the entire community, lobbying, political, or fraternal organizations, or sports teams. No grants to individuals, or for debt financing, endowments, memorials, advertising, sporting events, festivals, or parades.
Application information: Applications not accepted. Contributes only to organizations pre-selected by employees. All organizations seeking grants must have sponsorship from a minimum of 25 TeleTech employees.
Board meeting date(s): Quarterly
Officer and Directors:* Emily Eikelberner*, Pres., Secy., and Exec. Dir.; Mike Jossi; Kenneth D. Tuchman; John Troka.
EIN: 208954966
Selected grants: The following grants are a representative sample of this grantmaker's funding activity:
$250,000 to Hope for Haiti, Naples, FL, 2010.
$25,000 to New Jersey Symphony Orchestra, Newark, NJ, 2010.
$25,000 to Teach for America, Denver, CO, 2010.
$16,000 to American Heart Association, Seattle, WA, 2010. For charitable event.

$15,000 to Multiple Sclerosis Society, National, Denver, CO, 2010. For charitable event.
$7,500 to American Red Cross, Charlotte, NC, 2010. For charitable event.
$5,000 to American Heart Association, Indianapolis, IN, 2010. For charitable event.
$5,000 to American Heart Association, Seattle, WA, 2010. For charitable event.
$5,000 to Family Tree, Wheat Ridge, CO, 2010.
$5,000 to Safehouse Denver, Denver, CO, 2010.

3709
Tellabs, Inc.

1 Tellabs Ctr.
1415 W. Diehl Rd.
Naperville, IL 60563-2349 (630) 798-8800
FAX: (630) 798-2000

Company URL: http://www.tellabs.com
Establishment information: Established in 1976.
Company type: Public company
Company ticker symbol and exchange: TLAB/NASDAQ
Business activities: Designs, manufactures, provides, markets, and services optical networking, broadband access, and voice-quality enhancement products, solutions, and services.
Business type (SIC): Communications equipment
Financial profile for 2012: Number of employees, 2,525; assets, $1,638,100,000; sales volume, $1,052,600,000; pre-tax net income, -$148,600,000; expenses, $1,209,300,000; liabilities, $536,800,000
Corporate officers: Vincent H. Tobkin, Chair.; Daniel P. Kelly, Pres. and C.E.O.; James M. Sheehan, Exec. V.P., Genl. Counsel, and C.A.O.; John M. Brots, Exec. V.P., Opers.; Roger J. Heinz, Exec. V.P., Sales; Thomas P. Minichiello, V.P., Finance and C.F.O.
Board of directors: Vincent H. Tobkin, Chair.; Bo Hedfors; Frank Ianna; Vincent D. Kelly; Michael E. Lavin; Stephanie Pace Marshall; Alex Mashinsky; Gregory J. Rossman; Dennis F. Strigl; Jan H. Suwinski; Mikel H. Williams
International operations: China; Finland
Historic mergers: Advanced Fibre Communications, Inc. (November 30, 2004)
Giving statement: Giving through the Tellabs, Inc. Corporate Giving Program and the Tellabs Foundation.
Company EIN: 363831568

Tellabs, Inc. Corporate Giving Program

1 Tellabs Ctr.
1415 W. Diehl Rd.
Naperville, IL 60563-2349 (630) 798-8800
E-mail: corporate.responsibility@tellabs.com; URL: http://www.tellabs.com/about/corpresp.shtml

Financial data (yr. ended 12/31/11): Total giving, $186,304, including $38,769 for grants and $147,535 for employee matching gifts.
Purpose and activities: As a complement to its foundation, Tellabs matches contributions made by its employees to programs and nonprofit organizations in areas of company operations.
Fields of interest: General charitable giving.
Type of support: Employee matching gifts; Sponsorships.
Geographic limitations: Giving primarily in areas of company operations, with emphasis on Santa Clara, CA, Dallas, TX, and in China and Finland.
Support limitations: No support for political and religious organizations, or for fraternities and sororities, or business associations. No grants to individuals.
Publications: Corporate giving report.
Application information: Applications accepted. The Corporate Communications Department handles giving. A contributions committee reviews all requests. Application form not required.
Initial approach: Letter of inquiry
Copies of proposal: 1
Committee meeting date(s): Varies
Deadline(s): None
Final notification: 6 to 8 weeks
Officers and Directors:* Michael J. Birk; Denise Callarman; Carol C. Gavin; Stephanie Pace Marshall; Timothy J. Wiggens.

Tellabs Foundation

1415 W. Diehl Rd.
Naperville, IL 60563-2349
FAX: (630) 798-4778;
E-mail: meredith.hilt@tellabs.com; URL: http://www.tellabs.com/about/foundation.shtml

Establishment information: Established in 1997 in IL.
Donor: Tellabs, Inc.
Contact: Meredith Hilt, Exec. Dir.
Financial data (yr. ended 12/31/11): Assets, $24,260,505 (M); expenditures, $1,561,346; qualifying distributions, $1,315,976; giving activities include $1,315,976 for 15 grants (high: $145,000; low: $12,070).
Purpose and activities: The foundation supports organizations involved with education, the environment, and health.
Fields of interest: Engineering school/education; Education; Environment, waste management; Environment, natural resources; Environment, water resources; Environment, land resources; Environmental education; Environment; Hospitals (general); Health care, clinics/centers; Public health; Health care; Mathematics; Science.
International interests: China; Finland.
Programs:
Education: The foundation supports programs designed to focus on engineering, science, mathematics, and technology education.
Environment: The foundation supports programs designed to encourage understanding and the protection of the environment. Special emphasis is directed toward environmental education, land and water protection, and waste reduction.
Health and Wellness: The foundation supports programs designed to engage in health and wellness-related research, education, and treatment. Special emphasis is directed toward programs designed to involve hospitals and healthcare facilities.
Type of support: Building/renovation; Conferences/seminars; Curriculum development; Management development/capacity building; Program development; Research; Seed money.
Geographic limitations: Giving primarily in areas of company operations, with emphasis on Santa Clara, CA, Chicago, and Naperville, IL, and Dallas, TX, and in China and Finland.
Support limitations: No support for political or lobbying organizations, labor unions or organizations, service organizations raising money for community purposes, local or national alumni groups, clubs or fraternities, individual churches or synagogues or other religious organizations, or organizations not of direct benefit to the entire community, or discriminatory organizations. No grants to individuals, or for local athletic or sports programs, travel, tours, expeditions, or trips, institutional memberships or subscription fees for publications, or benefit events, raffle tickets, or fundraising efforts returning value to the donor; no product or equipment donations.
Publications: Application guidelines; IRS Form 990 or 990-PF printed copy available upon request.
Application information: Applications accepted. Letters of inquiry should be no longer than 1 to 2 pages. Letters of inquiry are not accepted by fax or e-mail. A full proposal may be requested at a later date. Application form not required. Applicants should submit the following:
1) results expected from proposed grant
2) copy of IRS Determination Letter
3) brief history of organization and description of its mission
4) geographic area to be served
5) explanation of why grantmaker is considered an appropriate donor for project
6) detailed description of project and amount of funding requested
7) plans for cooperation with other organizations, if any
8) contact person
9) copy of current year's organizational budget and/or project budget
10) plans for acknowledgement
Initial approach: Letter of inquiry
Board meeting date(s): Jan., Apr., July, and Oct.
Deadline(s): Jan. 1, Apr. 1., July 1, and Oct. 1
Officers: Michael J. Birck, Pres. and Treas.; Denise Callarman, V.P.; Carol Gavin, V.P.; Stephanie Pace Marshall, V.P.; Meredith Hilt*, Secy. and Exec. Dir.
Number of staff: 1 part-time support.
EIN: 364037547

3710
Telligen

1776 W. Lakes Pkwy.
West Des Moines, IA 50266
(515) 223-2900
FAX: (515) 222-2407

Company URL: http://www.telligen.org
Establishment information: Established in 1972.
Company type: Private company
Business activities: Operates a healthcare information technology and quality management company.
Business type (SIC): Computer services
Corporate officers: Jeffery Chungath, C.E.O.; Denise Sturm, C.F.O.; Doug Ventling, V.P., Human Resources
Board of directors: Stephanie Altman; R. Ried Boom, M.D.; Ruth Cox, Sr., Ph.D.; Larry Goetz, M.D.; Carlotta Rinke, M.D.; Victoria Sharp, M.D.; David Swieskowski, M.D.; David L. Thomas, M.D.
Offices: Oak Brook, IL; Elkridge, MD; Bloomington, MN; Syracuse, NY; Oklahoma City, OK
Giving statement: Giving through the Telligen Community Initiatives Program.

Telligen Community Initiatives Program

1776 West Lakes Pkwy.
West Des Moines, IA 50266-8239 (515) 223-2900
FAX: (515) 222-2407; E-mail: grants@telligen.org; URL: http://www.telligen.org/community

Contact: Greg Stone, Co-Lead; Erik Thompson, Co-Lead
Financial data (yr. ended 12/31/11): Total giving, $150,000, including $150,000 for grants.

Purpose and activities: Telligen makes charitable contributions to nonprofit organizations involved with health-related projects aimed at improving the health, social well-being, and educational attainment of society. Special emphasis is directed toward programs serving the elderly, homeless, and underserved populations. Support is limited to areas of company operations in Illinois and Iowa.
Fields of interest: Higher education; Health care, public policy; Health care, equal rights; Health care, formal/general education; Health care; Community/economic development.
Type of support: General/operating support.
Geographic limitations: Giving limited to areas of company operations in IA and IL.
Support limitations: No support for religious, political, or discriminatory organizations, organizations that redistribute funds to other tax-exempt organizations, organizations in which a Telligen board member or his/her spouse has significant involvement, United Way organizations seeking support for United Way-funded programs, or hospitals or hospital foundations. No grants to individuals, or for capital campaigns, deficit reduction, retirement of debt, general endowments, construction projects, or athletics or athletic events.
Publications: Application guidelines.
Application information: Additional documentation should be submitted in MS Word, MS Excel, JPEG or Adobe PDF format. Grants do not exceed $25,000 per organization per year; organizations are eligible to receive one grant award per year. Application form required. Applicants should submit the following:
1) copy of IRS Determination Letter
2) copy of most recent annual report/audited financial statement/990
3) listing of board of directors, trustees, officers and other key people and their affiliations

Submission should also include letters of support.
Initial approach: Download application and e-mail completed form and additional documentation to headquarters
Deadline(s): Sept. 30

3711
Temple-Inland Inc.
1300 S. MoPac Expwy.
Austin, TX 78746-6933 (512) 434-5800

Company URL: http://www.templeinland.com
Establishment information: Established in 1983.
Company type: Subsidiary of a public company
Business activities: Operates holding company; manufactures corrugated packaging products; manufactures building products; operates timber tracts; operates savings bank; provides mortgages; develops real estate; sells insurance.
Business type (SIC): Paperboard mills; forestry—timber tracts; lumber and wood products (except furniture); savings institutions; brokers and bankers/mortgage; insurance carriers; real estate subdividers and developers
Financial profile for 2011: Number of employees, 10,500; assets, $5,909,000,000; sales volume, $3,799,000,000; pre-tax net income, $128,000,000; expenses, $3,605,000,000; liabilities, $4,980,000,000
Subsidiaries: Gaylord Container Corporation, Deerfield, IL; Inland Paperboard and Packaging, Inc., Indianapolis, IN; Temple-Inland Forest Products Corp., Diboll, TX
Giving statement: Giving through the Temple-Inland Foundation.
Company EIN: 121903917

Temple-Inland Foundation
6400 Poplar Ave.
Memphis, TN 38197-0100 (512) 434-3160
FAX: (512) 434-2566; Application address: c/o Karen Lee, 1300 S. Mopac Expwy., FL 3N, Austin, TX 78746, tel.: (512) 434-3160.; URL: http://www.templeinland.com/OurMission/CorporateCitizenship/social.asp

Establishment information: Established in 1985 in TX.
Donors: Temple-Inland Inc.; Temple-Inland Forest Products Corp.
Financial data (yr. ended 06/30/12): Assets, $24,995 (M); gifts received, $1,444,454; expenditures, $1,427,189; qualifying distributions, $1,422,669; giving activities include $1,422,669 for 824 grants (high: $80,610; low: $25).
Purpose and activities: The foundation supports organizations involved with arts and culture, education, health, youth development, and human services.
Fields of interest: Museums; Performing arts; Arts; Elementary/secondary education; Higher education; Education; Medical care, rehabilitation; Health care; Youth development, centers/clubs; Boys & girls clubs; Children/youth, services; Human services.
Program:
Temple-Inland Foundation Scholarship Program: The foundation annually awards four-year college scholarships to children of active, retired, or deceased employees of Temple-Inland. The program is designed to recognize students who demonstrate outstanding academic ability, leadership, and other significant qualities.
Type of support: Employee-related scholarships; General/operating support; Research.
Geographic limitations: Giving primarily in areas of company operations, with emphasis on TX.
Support limitations: No grants to individuals (except for employee-related scholarships).
Application information: Applications accepted.
Initial approach: Proposal
Copies of proposal: 1
Board meeting date(s): Quarterly
Deadline(s): None
Officers and Directors:* Patricia Neuhoff, Pres.; Deano Orr, V.P.; Maria F. Adair, Secy.; Carol Tusch, Treas.; Terri L. Herrington; Paul J. Karre; Franz J. Marx; Carol L. Roberts; Mark S. Sutton; Fred A. Towler.
EIN: 751977109

3712
Ten West Apparel Inc.
10 W. 33rd St., Rm. 216
New York, NY 10001-3306 (212) 564-1007

Company URL: http://www.tenwestapparel.com
Establishment information: Established in 1975.
Company type: Private company
Business activities: Sells men's, women's, and children's apparel wholesale.
Business type (SIC): Apparel, piece goods, and notions—wholesale
Corporate officers: Solomon Gadeh, Chair., Pres., and C.E.O.; Joey Lando, Cont.
Board of director: Solomon Gadeh, Chair.
Giving statement: Giving through the Mordechai Gadeh Foundation.

Mordechai Gadeh Foundation
10 W. 33rd St., Ste. 216
New York, NY 10001-3306

Establishment information: Established in 2003 in NY.
Donors: Mid Newark, LLP; Ten West Apparel, Inc.
Financial data (yr. ended 12/31/11): Assets, $148 (M); gifts received, $37,001; expenditures, $36,901; qualifying distributions, $36,201; giving activities include $36,201 for grants.
Fields of interest: Religion.
Application information: Applications not accepted. Unsolicited requests for funds not accepted.
Trustees: Solomon Gadeh; Teddy Gadeh.
EIN: 300202039

3713
Tenet Healthcare Corporation
(formerly National Medical Enterprises, Inc.)
1445 Ross Ave., Ste. 1400
Dallas, TX 75240-2703 (469) 893-2200

Company URL: http://www.tenethealth.com
Establishment information: Established in 1960.
Company type: Public company
Company ticker symbol and exchange: THC/NYSE
Business activities: Operates hospitals.
Business type (SIC): Hospitals
Financial profile for 2012: Assets, $9,044,000,000; sales volume, $9,119,000,000; pre-tax net income, $334,000,000; expenses, $8,374,000,000; liabilities, $7,901,000,000
Fortune 1000 ranking: 2012—269th in revenues, 643rd in profits, and 423rd in assets
Forbes 2000 ranking: 2012—996th in sales, 1690th in profits, and 1545th in assets
Corporate officers: Edward A. Kangas, Chair.; Trevor Fetter, Pres. and C.E.O.; Daniel J. Cancelmi, C.F.O.; Audrey Andrews, Sr. V.P. and Genl. Counsel; Daniel Waldmann, Sr. V.P., Public Affairs; Cathy Fraser, Sr. V.P., Human Resources
Board of directors: Edward A. Kangas, Chair.; John Ellis Bush; Trevor Fetter; Brenda J. Gaines; Karen M. Garrison; J. Robert Kerrey; Richard R. Pettingill; Ronald A. Rittenmeyer; James A. Unruh
International operations: Cayman Islands; United Kingdom
Giving statement: Giving through the Tenet Healthcare Corporation Contributions Program.
Company EIN: 952557091

Tenet Healthcare Corporation Contributions Program
(formerly National Medical Enterprises, Inc. Corporate Giving Program)
1445 Ross Ave
Dallas, TX 75202 (469) 893-2000
E-mail: sustainability@tenethealth.com; URL: http://www.tenethealth.com/Community/Pages/default.aspx

Purpose and activities: As a complement to its foundation, Tenet also makes charitable contributions to nonprofit organizations directly. Support is given primarily in areas of company operations.
Fields of interest: Health care; Human services.
Type of support: Annual campaigns; Employee volunteer services; General/operating support; Sponsorships.
Geographic limitations: Giving primarily in areas of company operations.

3714
Tennant Company
701 N. Lilac Dr.
P.O. Box 1452
Minneapolis, MN 55440 (763) 540-1200
FAX: (763) 513-2142

Company URL: http://www.tennantco.com
Establishment information: Established in 1870.
Company type: Public company
Company ticker symbol and exchange: TNC/NYSE
Business activities: Manufactures industrial floor maintenance and resurfacing machinery, waxes, sealants, detergents, and allied products.
Business type (SIC): Machinery/refrigeration and service industry; chemicals and allied products—wholesale; services to dwellings
Financial profile for 2012: Number of employees, 2,816; assets, $420,760,000; sales volume, $738,980,000; pre-tax net income, $59,890,000; expenses, $676,280,000; liabilities, $185,710,000
Corporate officers: H. Chris Killingstad, Pres. and C.E.O.; Thomas J. Paulson, V.P. and C.F.O.; Karen A. Durant, V.P., Cont.; Heidi M. Wilson, V.P., Genl. Counsel, and Secy.; Thomas J. Dybsky, V.P., Admin.; Don B. Westman, V.P., Opers.; Rusty Zay, V.P., Mktg.; Patrick J. O'Neill, Treas.
Board of directors: Azita Arvani; William F. Austen; Carol S. Eicher; James T. Hale; H. Chris Killingstad; David Mathieson; Donal Leo Mulligan; Stephen G. Shank; Steven A. Sonnenberg; David S. Wichmann
Subsidiary: Castex Inc., Holland, MI
International operations: Austria; Belgium; Brazil; Bulgaria; China; Denmark; Germany; India; Italy; Netherlands; New Zealand; Singapore; Spain; Sweden; United Kingdom; Uruguay
Giving statement: Giving through the Tennant Foundation.
Company EIN: 410572550

Tennant Foundation
(formerly Tennant Company Foundation)
701 N. Lilac Dr.
P.O. Box 1452
Minneapolis, MN 55440
URL: http://www.tennantco.com/am-en/Pages/SustainabilityDetails.aspx?itemid=9

Establishment information: Established in 1973 in MN.
Donor: Tennant Co.
Financial data (yr. ended 12/31/11): Assets, $149,181 (M); expenditures, $433,391; qualifying distributions, $433,366; giving activities include $405,866 for 312 grants (high: $40,000; low: $25).
Purpose and activities: The foundation supports programs designed to improve the quality of life in communities through environmental initiatives and social services; promote workforce readiness through education, vocational rehabilitation and other related services; and contribute to cultural and arts organizations.
Fields of interest: Performing arts; Performing arts, theater; Performing arts, orchestras; Arts; Higher education; Education; Environment; Hospitals (general); Employment, services; Employment, training; Employment; Food banks; Housing/shelter, development; Human services; United Ways and Federated Giving Programs.
Type of support: Capital campaigns; Continuing support; Employee matching gifts; Employee volunteer services; General/operating support; Matching/challenge support.
Geographic limitations: Giving primarily in areas of company operations, with emphasis on the Minneapolis, MN, area and its western suburb.
Support limitations: No support for United Way-supported organizations, umbrella organizations, lobbying or political organizations, national organizations without active local chapters, religious organizations not of direct benefit to the entire community, or elementary or secondary schools. No grants to individuals or for trips or tours, tickets, tables, advertising, or benefit purposes.
Publications: Application guidelines.
Application information: Applications accepted. Applications may be submitted using the Minnesota Common Grant Application Form. A site visit may be requested. Application form not required. Applicants should submit the following:
1) how project will be sustained once grantmaker support is completed
2) results expected from proposed grant
3) statement of problem project will address
4) name, address and phone number of organization
5) copy of IRS Determination Letter
6) brief history of organization and description of its mission
7) copy of most recent annual report/audited financial statement/990
8) how project's results will be evaluated or measured
9) explanation of why grantmaker is considered an appropriate donor for project
10) listing of board of directors, trustees, officers and other key people and their affiliations
11) detailed description of project and amount of funding requested
12) contact person
13) copy of current year's organizational budget and/or project budget
14) listing of additional sources and amount of support

Initial approach: Download application form and mail to foundation
Copies of proposal: 1
Board meeting date(s): Biannually
Deadline(s): None

Officers and Directors:* Heidi M. Wilson, Pres.; Dana Stromlund, Treas.; Karen A. Durant; Thomas J. Dybsky; H. Chris Killingstad; Kathryn Lovik; Thomas J. Paulson.
Number of staff: 1 part-time professional; 1 part-time support.
EIN: 237297045
Selected grants: The following grants are a representative sample of this grantmaker's funding activity:
$4,200 to Minnesota Public Radio, Saint Paul, MN, 2010.
$1,500 to AIDS Foundation of Chicago, Chicago, IL, 2010.
$1,500 to Indiana University Foundation, Bloomington, IN, 2010.

3715
Tenneco Inc.
(formerly Tenneco Automotive Inc.)
500 N. Field Dr.
Lake Forest, IL 60045-2595
(847) 482-5000
FAX: (847) 482-5940

Company URL: http://www.tenneco.com
Establishment information: Established in 1987.
Company type: Public company
Company ticker symbol and exchange: TEN/NYSE
Business activities: Manufactures automotive emissions control and ride control products and systems.
Business type (SIC): Motor vehicles and equipment
Financial profile for 2012: Number of employees, 25,000; assets, $3,608,000,000; sales volume, $7,363,000,000; pre-tax net income, $323,000,000; expenses, $6,928,000,000; liabilities, $3,362,000,000
Fortune 1000 ranking: 2012—349th in revenues, 498th in profits, and 696th in assets
Corporate officers: Gregg M. Sherrill, Chair. and C.E.O.; Hari N. Nair, C.O.O.; Kenneth R. Trammell, Exec. V.P. and C.F.O.; James Harrington, Sr. V.P., Genl. Counsel, and Corp. Secy.; Gregg A. Bolt, Sr. V.P., Human Resources and Admin.; H. William Haser, V.P. and C.I.O.; John Kunz, V.P. and Treas.; Paul D. Novas, V.P. and Cont.; Jane Ostrander, V.P., Comms.; Jane Ostrander, V.P., Comms.
Board of directors: Gregg M. Sherrill, Chair.; Dennis J. Letham; Hari N. Nair; Roger B. Porter; David B. Price, Jr.; Paul T. Stecko; Mitsunobu Takeuchi; Jane L. Warner
Plants: Paragould, AR; Long Beach, CA; Hartwell, GA; Angola, Elkhart, Ligonier, IN; Grass Lake, Jackson, Litchfield, Marshall, Monroe, Sterling Heights, MI; Fenton, Kansas City, MO; Cozad, Seward, NE; Milan, Napoleon, OH; Smithville, TN; Harrisonburg, Virginia Beach, VA
International operations: Argentina; Australia; Belgium; Brazil; China; Czech Republic; Denmark; France; Germany; Hong Kong; India; Italy; Jamaica; Luxembourg; Mauritius; Mexico; Netherlands; New Zealand; Poland; Portugal; Romania; South Africa; South Korea; Spain; Sweden; Thailand; Turkey; United Kingdom
Giving statement: Giving through the Tenneco Inc. Corporate Giving Program and the Monroe Auto Equipment Company Foundation.
Company EIN: 760515284

Tenneco Inc. Corporate Giving Program
(formerly Tenneco Automotive Inc. Corporate Giving Program)
500 North Field Dr.
Lake Forest, IL 60045-2595
FAX: (847) 482-5940

Contact: Jane Ostrander, Dir., Global Comms.
Purpose and activities: Tenneco makes charitable contributions to nonprofit organizations involved with healthcare and human services. Support is given on a national and international basis in areas of company operations.
Fields of interest: Health care; Disasters, preparedness/services; Big Brothers/Big Sisters; Human services; United Ways and Federated Giving Programs; General charitable giving.
Type of support: Employee volunteer services; General/operating support.
Geographic limitations: Giving on a national and international basis in areas of company operations.

3716
Tennessee Football, Inc.
(also known as Tennessee Titans)
460 Great Circle Rd.
Nashville, TN 37228 (615) 565-4000

Company URL: http://www.titansonline.com
Establishment information: Established in 1959.
Company type: Private company
Business activities: Operates professional football club.
Business type (SIC): Commercial sports
Financial profile for 2010: Number of employees, 100

Corporate officers: K.S. Bud Adams, Jr., Chair., Pres., and C.E.O.; Don MacLachlan, Exec. V.P., Admin.; Elza Bullock, Sr. V.P. and Genl. Counsel; Jenneen Kaufman, V.P. and C.F.O.; Ralph Ockenfels, V.P., Mktg.; Stuart Spears, V.P., Opers. and Sales
Board of director: K.S. Bud Adams, Jr., Chair.
Giving statement: Giving through the Tennessee Titans Corporate Giving Program and the Tennessee Titans Foundation.

Tennessee Titans Corporate Giving Program

c/o Community Rels. Dept., Donation Requests
460 Great Circle Rd.
Nashville, TN 37228-1404
FAX: (615) 565-4015; URL: http://www.titansonline.com/community/index.html

Purpose and activities: The Tennessee Titans make charitable contributions of memorabilia to nonprofit organizations on a case by case basis. Support is given primarily in northern Alabama, southern Kentucky, and Tennessee.
Fields of interest: Elementary school/education; Education; Hospitals (general); Public health, physical fitness; Athletics/sports, football; United Ways and Federated Giving Programs; General charitable giving Youth.
Program:
Titan Tuesdays: Through Titan Tuesdays, the Titans surprises students on Tuesdays during the season with a school assembly featuring a Titans player. The players share experiences about growing up, give advice, and promotes NFL's Play 60 and What Moves U campaign, which encourages students to get at least 60 minutes of physical activity every day in an effort to fight childhood obesity. Participating schools are selected though Metro Nashville Schools and the American Heart Association. Titan Tuesday also consists of visits to local hospitals.
Type of support: Donated products; In-kind gifts; Income development; Loaned talent.
Geographic limitations: Giving primarily in areas of company operations in the Mid-South, including northern AL, southern KY, and TN.
Support limitations: No grants to individuals, or for sponsorships; no game ticket donations.
Publications: Application guidelines.
Application information: Applications accepted. Support is limited to 1 contribution per organization during any given year. Telephone calls are not encouraged. Proposals should be submitted using organization letterhead. The Community Relations Department handles giving. Application form required. Applicants should submit the following:
1) name, address and phone number of organization
2) detailed description of project and amount of funding requested
3) contact person
Initial approach: Complete online application form or mail proposal to headquarters for memorabilia donations
Copies of proposal: 1
Deadline(s): 3 weeks prior to need for memorabilia donations

Tennessee Titans Foundation

P.O. Box 844
Houston, TX 77001-0844
URL: http://www.titansonline.com/community/foundation.html

Establishment information: Established in 1999 in TN.
Donors: Tennessee Football, Inc.; K.S. Adams, Jr.; Garth Brooks Teammates for Kids Foundation.
Contact: K.S. Adams, Jr., Pres.
Financial data (yr. ended 12/31/11): Assets, $2,023,766 (M); gifts received, $143,377; expenditures, $410,634; qualifying distributions, $401,731; giving activities include $401,731 for grants.
Purpose and activities: The foundation supports hospitals, camps, and community foundations and organizations involved with arts and culture, higher education, football, youth development, and human services.
Fields of interest: Arts; Secondary school/education; Higher education; Hospitals (general); Recreation, camps; Athletics/sports, football; Boys & girls clubs; Boy scouts; Girl scouts; Youth development; Children/youth, services; Human services; Foundations (community); United Ways and Federated Giving Programs.
Program:
Titan Community Quarterback Award: The foundation honors community volunteers who demonstrate leadership and dedication to bettering their hometowns. The foundation awards grants to nonprofit organizations on behalf of finalists and the winner.
Type of support: Annual campaigns; Building/renovation; Capital campaigns; Employee volunteer services; Equipment; General/operating support; Program development; Scholarship funds.
Geographic limitations: Giving limited to TN.
Support limitations: No grants to individuals.
Application information: Applications not accepted. Unsolicited applications are currently not accepted.
Officers: K.S. Adams, Jr., Pres.; K.S. Adams IV, Corp. Secy.
EIN: 760611503
Selected grants: The following grants are a representative sample of this grantmaker's funding activity:
$83,333 to Baptist Hospital Foundation, Nashville, TN, 2009.
$16,695 to Jason Foundation, Hendersonville, TN, 2009.
$16,694 to Boy Scouts of America, Nashville, TN, 2009.

3717
Tension Envelope Corporation

819 E. 19th St.
Kansas City, MO 64108-1781
(816) 471-3800

Company URL: http://www.tension.com
Establishment information: Established in 1886.
Company type: Private company
Business activities: Manufactures envelopes.
Business type (SIC): Paper and paperboard/coated, converted, and laminated
Corporate officers: E. Bertram Berkley, Chair.; Bill Berkley, Pres. and C.E.O.; Brad Bradley, C.I.O.; Dick Berkley, Secy.-Treas.
Board of director: E. Bertram Berkley, Chair.
Subsidiaries: TransCoast Envelope Co., San Francisco, CA; Transo Envelope Co., Glendale, CA
Plants: Santa Fe Springs, CA; Des Moines, IA; Marysville, KS; Minneapolis, MN; St. Louis, MO; Hackensack, NJ; Winston-Salem, NC; Memphis, TN; Fort Worth, TX
Giving statement: Giving through the Tension Envelope Foundation.

Tension Envelope Foundation

819 E. 19th St., 5th Fl.
Kansas City, MO 64108-1781 (816) 471-3800

Establishment information: Incorporated in 1954 in MO.
Donor: Tension Envelope Corp.
Contact: William Berkley, Dir.
Financial data (yr. ended 11/30/11): Assets, $1,645,934 (M); expenditures, $263,392; qualifying distributions, $255,170; giving activities include $255,170 for 7 grants (high: $162,900; low: $1,100).
Purpose and activities: The foundation supports organizations involved with arts and culture, education, human services, and community development.
Fields of interest: Arts; Higher education; Libraries (public); Education; Health care; Human services; Business/industry; Community/economic development; United Ways and Federated Giving Programs; Jewish federated giving programs.
Type of support: General/operating support; Scholarships—to individuals.
Geographic limitations: Giving primarily in areas of company operations.
Application information: Applications accepted. Application form not required.
Initial approach: Letter
Deadline(s): Feb. 15th for scholarships
Directors: E. Bertram Berkley; Eliot S. Berkley; Richard L. Berkley; William Berkley.
EIN: 446012554

3718
Teradyne, Inc.

600 Riverpark Dr.
North Reading, MA 01864 (978) 370-2700
FAX: (617) 451-1984

Company URL: http://www.teradyne.com
Establishment information: Established in 1960.
Company type: Public company
Company ticker symbol and exchange: TER/NYSE
International Securities Identification Number: US8807701029
Business activities: Manufactures automatic test equipment and related software.
Business type (SIC): Laboratory apparatus; computer services
Financial profile for 2012: Number of employees, 3,600; assets, $2,429,340,000; sales volume, $1,656,750,000; pre-tax net income, $265,980,000; expenses, $1,369,380,000; liabilities, $650,990,000
Corporate officers: Albert Carnesale, Chair.; Mark E. Jagiela, Pres.; Michael A. Bradley, C.E.O.; Gregory R. Beecher, C.F.O.; Charles Gray, V.P., Genl. Counsel, and Secy.
Board of directors: Albert Carnesale, Chair.; James W. Bagley; Michael A. Bradley; Daniel W. Christman; Edwin J. Gillis; Timothy E. Guertin; Paul J. Tufano; Roy A. Vallee
Subsidiaries: GenRad, Inc., Westford, MA; Kinetrix, Inc., Bedford, NH; Softbridge, Inc., Burlington, MA
Plant: Walnut Creek, CA
International operations: Hong Kong; Ireland; Japan
Giving statement: Giving through the Teradyne, Inc. Corporate Giving Program.
Company EIN: 042272148

Teradyne, Inc. Corporate Giving Program

600 Riverpark Dr.
North Reading, MA 01864-2634 (978) 370-2700
URL: http://www.teradyne.com/hr/pages/community.html

Purpose and activities: Teradyne makes charitable contributions to nonprofit organizations involved with science and technical education in grades K-12. Support is given primarily in areas of company operations.
Fields of interest: Elementary/secondary education; Education, computer literacy/technology training; Science, public education; General charitable giving.
Type of support: Employee matching gifts; Employee volunteer services; Employee-related scholarships; General/operating support.
Geographic limitations: Giving primarily in areas of company operations, with some emphasis on Boston, MA.

3719
Terex Corporation

200 Nyala Farm Rd.
Westport, CT 06880-6261 (203) 222-7170
FAX: (203) 222-7976

Company URL: http://www.terex.com
Establishment information: Established in 1925.
Company type: Public company
Company ticker symbol and exchange: TEX/NYSE
Business activities: Manufactures construction, demolition, and mining machinery and equipment.
Business type (SIC): Machinery/construction, mining, and materials handling; motor vehicles and equipment
Financial profile for 2012: Number of employees, 21,300; assets, $6,746,200,000; sales volume, $7,348,400,000; pre-tax net income, $155,600,000; expenses, $7,032,800,000; liabilities, $4,738,500,000
Fortune 1000 ranking: 2012—351st in revenues, 727th in profits, and 499th in assets
Corporate officers: Ronald M. DeFeo, Chair. and C.E.O.; Phillip C. Widman, Sr. V.P. and C.F.O.; Eric I. Cohen, Sr. V.P., Genl. Counsel, and Secy.; Brian J. Henry, Sr. V.P., Finance; Kevin A. Barr, Sr. V.P., Human Resources; Mark Clair, V.P., Cont., and C.A.O.
Board of directors: Ronald M. DeFeo, Chair.; G. Chris Andersen; Paula H.J. Cholmondeley; Donald DeFosset; Thomas J. Hansen; David A. Sachs; Oren G. Shaffer; David C. Wang; Scott W. Wine
Subsidiaries: Koehring Cranes & Excavators, Waverly, IA; Mark Industries, Waverly, IA; Northwest Engineering Co., Waverly, IA
Plants: Hudson, OH; Tulsa, OK
International operations: Australia; Canada; Czech Republic; France; Germany; Italy; United Kingdom
Giving statement: Giving through the Terex Corporation Contributions Program.
Company EIN: 341531521

Terex Corporation Contributions Program

c/o Corp. Secy.
200 Nyala Farms Rd.
Westport, CT 06880-6265 (203) 222-7170
URL: http://www.terex.com/en/

Purpose and activities: Terex makes charitable contributions to nonprofit organizations involved with education, health, youth services, and programs designed to provide services to those who are in need or underprivileged. Support is given primarily in areas of company operations.
Fields of interest: Education; Health care; Youth, services; General charitable giving Economically disadvantaged.
Type of support: Employee volunteer services; General/operating support.
Geographic limitations: Giving primarily in areas of company operations in Westport, CT.

3720
The Terlato Wine Group

2401 Waukegan Rd.
Bannockburn, IL 60015 (847) 444-5500
FAX: (847) 236-0848

Company URL: http://www.terlatowinegroup.com/
Establishment information: Established in 1938.
Company type: Private company
Business activities: Operates vineyards and wineries; sells and markets premium domestic and international wines.
Business type (SIC): Beer, wine, and distilled beverages—wholesale
Financial profile for 2010: Number of employees, 370
Corporate officers: Anthony J. Terlato, Chair.; John A. Terlato, Vice-Chair., Exec. V.P., and C.A.O.; William A. Terlato, Pres. and C.E.O.; David Lane, C.O.O.; Jeffrey N. Gruber, V.P., Human Resources; Susan Fleischman, V.P., Corp. Comms.; Richard Dasher, Cont.
Board of directors: Anthony Terlato, Chair.; John Terlato, Vice-Chair.
Giving statement: Giving through the Terlato Family Foundation.

Terlato Family Foundation

900 Armour Dr.
Lake Bluff, IL 60044-1926

Establishment information: Established in 2003 in IL.
Donor: Terlato Wine Group, Ltd.
Financial data (yr. ended 12/31/11): Assets, $699,738 (M); gifts received, $200,000; expenditures, $151,214; qualifying distributions, $151,214; giving activities include $151,214 for grants.
Purpose and activities: The foundation supports organizations involved with education, health, golf, and youth development.
Fields of interest: Education; Health care; Youth development.
Type of support: Annual campaigns; General/operating support; Program development; Sponsorships.
Geographic limitations: Giving primarily in CA and IL.
Support limitations: No grants to individuals.
Application information: Applications not accepted. Unsolicited requests for funds not accepted.
Officers: Anthony J. Terlato, Pres.; Josephine P. Terlato, V.P.; William A. Terlato, Treas.
Director: John A. Terlato.
EIN: 364527896
Selected grants: The following grants are a representative sample of this grantmaker's funding activity:
$25,000 to College Success Foundation, Issaquah, WA, 2010.
$6,000 to Duke University, Durham, NC, 2010.
$2,500 to Northwestern Lake Forest Hospital, Lake Forest, IL, 2010.
$1,500 to Womans Board of Rush University Medical Center, Chicago, IL, 2010.
$1,000 to Lake Forest Country Day School, Lake Forest, IL, 2010.

3721
Terra Coastal Properties, Inc.

23405 Pacific Coast Hwy.
Malibu, CA 90265-4824 (310) 456-6431

Establishment information: Established in 2008.
Company type: Private company
Business activities: Operates real estate agency.
Business type (SIC): Real estate agents and managers
Corporate officers: Michael Novotny, C.E.O.; Cynthia Schmon, Pres.; Lea Johnson, Secy.
Giving statement: Giving through the Malibu Realty Charitable Foundation.

Malibu Realty Charitable Foundation

23405 Pacific Coast Hwy.
Malibu, CA 90265-4824

Establishment information: Established in 2002 in CA.
Donor: Terra Coastal Properties, Inc.
Financial data (yr. ended 12/31/11): Assets, $2,061 (M); gifts received, $3,943; expenditures, $2,506; qualifying distributions, $2,496; giving activities include $800 for 2 grants (high: $500; low: $300).
Fields of interest: Education.
Support limitations: No grants to individuals.
Application information: Applications not accepted. Unsolicited requests for funds not accepted.
Officers: Michael Novotny, Pres.; Kate E. Craig-Novotny, V.P.; Lea Johnson, Secy.; Barry Kinyon, Treas.
Directors: Marcus Beck; Leon Johnson; Alan Paul Mark*; Jonathan A. Saver; Lisa Saver; Cynthia Schmon.
EIN: 920179460

3722
Terre Haute Gas Corporation

(also known as Indiana Gas Company, Inc.)
632 Cherry St.
Terre Haute, IN 47808 (317) 321-0320

Company type: Private company
Business activities: Manufactures industrial and foundry coke, tar, and light oils.
Business type (SIC): Gas production and distribution
Giving statement: Giving through the Indiana Chemical Trust.
Company EIN: 350793669

Indiana Chemical Trust

c/o Old National Trust Co.
P.O. Box 1447
Terre Haute, IN 47808-1447 (812) 462-7459

Establishment information: Established in 1953 in IN.
Donors: Terre Haute Gas Corp.; Indiana Gas and Chemical Corp.; Tribune-Star Publishing Co.

Contact: Julie Schlosser
Financial data (yr. ended 12/31/11): Assets, $9,335,181 (M); expenditures, $451,910; qualifying distributions, $406,000; giving activities include $406,000 for grants.
Purpose and activities: The foundation supports museums and hospitals and organizations involved with historic preservation, education, animal welfare, patient services, housing development, and human services.
Fields of interest: Museums (art); Museums (children's); Historic preservation/historical societies; Higher education; Engineering school/education; Education; Animals/wildlife, preservation/protection; Hospitals (general); Health care, patient services; Housing/shelter, development; Children, services; Residential/custodial care; Developmentally disabled, centers & services; Human services.
Type of support: General/operating support.
Geographic limitations: Giving primarily in areas of company operations in Terre Haute, IN.
Support limitations: No grants to individuals.
Application information: Applications accepted. Application form not required.
Initial approach: Proposal
Board meeting date(s): Dec.
Deadline(s): None
Committee Members: W. Curtis Brighton; Anton Hulman George; Mari Hulman George.
Trustee: Old National Trust Co.
EIN: 356024816
Selected grants: The following grants are a representative sample of this grantmaker's funding activity:
$5,000 to Archdiocese of Indianapolis, Indianapolis, IN, 2010.
$5,000 to Best Buddies International, Miami, FL, 2010.

3723
Tesoro Corporation

(formerly Tesoro Petroleum Corporation)
19100 Ridgewood Pkwy.
San Antonio, TX 78259-1828
(210) 626-6000
FAX: (210) 636-5454

Company URL: http://www.tsocorp.com
Establishment information: Established in 1968.
Company type: Public company
Company ticker symbol and exchange: TSO/NYSE
Business activities: Refines crude oil; sells petroleum products wholesale; operates gasoline service stations; operates convenience stores.
Business type (SIC): Petroleum refining; petroleum and petroleum products—wholesale; groceries—retail; gasoline service stations
Financial profile for 2012: Number of employees, 5,700; assets, $10,702,000,000; sales volume, $8,156,000,000; pre-tax net income, $162,000,000; expenses, $7,964,000,000; liabilities, $6,451,000,000
Fortune 1000 ranking: 2012—95th in revenues, 257th in profits, and 368th in assets
Corporate officers: Steven H. Grapstein, Chair.; Gregory J. Goff, Pres. and C.E.O.; Charles S. Parrish, Exec. V.P., Genl. Counsel, and Secy.; Dan Romasko, Exec. V.P., Opers.; G. Scott Spendlove, Sr. V.P. and C.F.O.; Claude P. Moreau, Sr. V.P., Mktg.; Tracy D. Jackson, V.P. and Treas.; Arlen Glenewinkel, Jr., V.P. and Cont.
Board of directors: Steven H. Grapstein, Chair.; Rodney Frank Chase; Gregory J. Goff; Robert W. Goldman; David Lilley; Mary Pat McCarthy; James W. Nokes; Susan Tomasky; Michael E. Wiley; Patrick Y. Yang, Ph.D.
Subsidiaries: Tesoro Alaska Co., Anchorage, AK; Tesoro Hawaii Corporation, Honolulu, HI
Giving statement: Giving through the Tesoro Corporation Contributions Program.
Company EIN: 950862768

Tesoro Corporation Contributions Program

(formerly Tesoro Petroleum Corporation Contributions Program)
19100 Ridgewood Pkwy.
San Antonio, TX 78259-1834 (210) 626-6000
For requests in Alaska, mail application to: Steve Hansen, V.P., Refining, 54741 Tesoro Rd., P.O. Box 3369, Kenai, AK 99611; For requests in California, mail application to: Kenneth Dami, Rep., Gov. Rels., 150 Solano Way, Martinez, CA 94553, or Brissa Sotelo, Public and Gov. Affairs Rep., 2101 E. Pacific Coast Hwy., Wilmington, CA 90744; For requests in Hawaii, mail application to: Lance N. Tanaka, Mgr., Gov. & Community Rels., 91-325 Komohana St., Kapolei, HI 96707; For requests in North Dakota, mail application to: David Schollars, Mgr., Human Resources, 900 Old Red Trail N.E., Mandan ND 58554; For requests in Texas, mail applications to: Carrie Bulsiewicz, Mgr., Corp. Comms. & Community Investment, 19100 Ridgewood Pkwy., San Antonio, TX 78259; For requests in Washington, mail application to: John McDarment, Mgr., Human Resources, P.O. Box 700, Anacortes, WA 98221; URL: http://www.tsocorp.com/TSOCorp/SRR/CommunityOutreach/index.htm

Purpose and activities: Tesoro makes charitable contributions to nonprofit organizations involved with the environment, education, community vitality, and quality of life issues. Support is given in areas of company operations in Kenai, Alaska, Martinez, California, Hawaii, Mandan, North Dakota, San Antonio, Texas, Salt Lake City, Utah, and Anacortes, Washington.
Fields of interest: Education, public education; Education, volunteer services; Education, special; Education; Environment; Agriculture/food, volunteer services; Food distribution, meals on wheels; Housing/shelter, volunteer services; Housing/shelter, development; Athletics/sports, Special Olympics; Boys & girls clubs; Youth development, services; Aging, centers/services; Minorities/immigrants, centers/services; Community/economic development; United Ways and Federated Giving Programs Economically disadvantaged.
Type of support: Cause-related marketing; Continuing support; Employee matching gifts; Employee volunteer services; General/operating support; In-kind gifts; Sponsorships.
Geographic limitations: Giving in areas of company operations in Kenai, AK, Martinez, CA, HI, Mandan, ND, San Antonio, TX, Salt Lake City, UT, and Anacortes, WA.
Support limitations: No support for religious, or political organizations, or government agencies. No grants to individuals, or for travel, sporting events, research programs, meetings, conferences, seminars, advertising, or marketing sponsorships, or capital projects.
Publications: Application guidelines.
Application information: Applications accepted. A contributions committee reviews all requests. Application form required. Applicants should submit the following:
1) results expected from proposed grant
2) population served
3) name, address and phone number of organization
4) copy of IRS Determination Letter
5) brief history of organization and description of its mission
6) geographic area to be served
7) how project's results will be evaluated or measured
8) list of company employees involved with the organization
9) listing of board of directors, trustees, officers and other key people and their affiliations
10) detailed description of project and amount of funding requested
11) contact person
12) copy of current year's organizational budget and/or project budget
13) listing of additional sources and amount of support
14) additional materials/documentation
Requests should include the number of employees and volunteers, a list of key staff, date of incorporation, and/or the name and address of parent organization. If the organization is seeking renewed support, the application should include a final report or evaluation.
Initial approach: Complete online application form, or download and mail application to contributions committee in each state
Copies of proposal: 1
Deadline(s): Ongoing
Number of staff: 1 full-time professional.

3725
Texas Brine Company, LLC

4800 San Felipe St.
Houston, TX 77056-3908 (713) 877-2700

Company URL: http://www.texasbrine.com/index.html
Establishment information: Established in 1926.
Company type: Subsidiary of a private company
Business activities: Produces brine; operates brine pipelines.
Business type (SIC): Chemical preparations/miscellaneous; pipelines (except natural gas/operation of)
Financial profile for 2010: Number of employees, 36
Corporate officers: Ted Grabowski, Pres.; Bruce E. Martin, V.P., Opers.; R. Wayne Sneed, Secy.-Treas.
Giving statement: Giving through the Iris and Lloyd Webre Foundation.

The Iris and Lloyd Webre Foundation

4800 San Felipe St., Ste. 100
Houston, TX 77056-3908

Establishment information: Established in 1987 in TX.
Donors: Texas Brine Co., LLC; Iris Paine Webre†.
Financial data (yr. ended 09/30/11): Assets, $5,742,437 (M); expenditures, $405,688; qualifying distributions, $330,000; giving activities include $330,000 for grants.
Purpose and activities: The foundation supports museums and women's clubs and organizations involved with television, education, health, human services, voluntarism promotion, and Catholicism.
Fields of interest: Media, television; Museums; Secondary school/education; Higher education; Education; Health care, clinics/centers; Health care; Children, services; Human services; Community development, women's clubs; Voluntarism promotion; Catholic agencies & churches.

Type of support: Capital campaigns; Equipment; General/operating support; Program development; Scholarship funds.
Geographic limitations: Giving limited to Houston, TX.
Support limitations: No grants to individuals.
Application information: Applications not accepted. Contributes only to pre-selected organizations.
Officers: Robert W. Sneed*, Pres.; Roberta Rude, V.P.; Mary Iris Webre, V.P.; Marjorie Pribyl, Secy.-Treas.
EIN: 760240169
Selected grants: The following grants are a representative sample of this grantmaker's funding activity:
$150,000 to Saint Thomas High School, Houston, TX, 2010.
$25,000 to University of Saint Thomas, Houston, TX, 2010.
$20,000 to Junior League of Houston, Houston, TX, 2010.
$10,000 to Basilian Fathers Missions, Sugar Land, TX, 2010.
$10,000 to Covenant House Texas, Houston, TX, 2010.
$10,000 to K U H T-TV Channel 8, Houston, TX, 2010.
$10,000 to Saint Thomas High School, Houston, TX, 2010.
$10,000 to San Jose Clinic, Houston, TX, 2010.
$10,000 to Star of Hope Mission, Houston, TX, 2010. For operating fund.
$5,000 to Duchesne Academy of the Sacred Heart, Houston, TX, 2010.

3726
Texas Credit Union League

4455 LBJ Freeway
Farmers Branch, TX 75244 (469) 385-6400

Company URL: http://www.tcul.coop/
Establishment information: Established in 1934.
Company type: Business league
Business activities: Operates state trade association serving credit unions in Texas.
Business type (SIC): Membership organization/ miscellaneous
Corporate officers: Paul A. Trylko, Chair.; Robert Peterson, Vice-Chair.; James L. Boyd, Secy.; James S. Tuggle, Treas.
Giving statement: Giving through the Texas Credit Union Foundation.

Texas Credit Union Foundation

4455 LBJ Freeway, Ste. 1100
Framers Branch, TX 75244-5998 (800) 953-8283
E-mail: cmoran@tcuf.coop; URL: http://www.tcuf.coop/

Establishment information: Established in 1965 in TX.
Contact: Courtney Moran, Exec. Dir.
Financial data (yr. ended 12/31/11): Revenue, $666,134; assets, $1,800,924 (M); gifts received, $694,209; expenditures, $573,574; giving activities include $146,486 for grants and $129,444 for grants to individuals.
Purpose and activities: The organization is dedicated to progressive professional development of credit union staff and volunteers, financial education programs for youth and adults, and creating valuable resources for Texas credit unions and the communities they serve.
Fields of interest: Safety/disasters; Human services, emergency aid.
Programs:
Community Investment Fund Grants: These grants come from a shared investment program that strengthens the credit union movement throughout Texas, across the US, and worldwide. Grants to develop credit unions of all sizes may include but are not limited to, various audits, software conversions, planning sessions, equipment, and technical assistance.
General Grants: The Foundation provides grants and scholarships in support of three focus areas: financial education and community outreach; credit union professional development education; and disaster relief for credit union communities.
Phase One Disaster Relief Grants: These grants are provided to credit union employees to assist with immediate disaster relief needs, such as out of pocket costs that may result from being evacuated. These grants are up to $500 per credit union employee, up to 60 days after disaster struck. The intent of these grants is to help stabilize the credit union employee's individual situation so they can return to work.
Phase Three Disaster Relief Grants: These grants are intended to follow-up with those credit union employees who suffered catastrophic loss and are still needing assistance after Phase Two grants have been distributed. Phase Three will begin 180 days after the respective disaster.
Phase Two Disaster Relief Grants: These grants are intended to assist credit union employees with significant needs. Phase two will be implemented following the distribution of Phase One Grants. Amounts of grants will be dependent on the amount of disaster relief funds available, but usually range from $1,000 - $5,000. The Foundation will notify affected credit unions about Phase Two Grant applications, beginning 90 days after disaster has struck. Phase Two Grants could be distributed sooner if insurance claims have been received prior.
Officers and Trustees:* Arna Reynolds*, Chair.; Chris O'Conner*, Vice-Chair.; Tim McCoy*, Secy.; Maria Martinez*, Treas.; Courtney Moran, Exec. Dir.; Tim Haegelin*; Art Hornell*; Scott Rose*; Ken Thomason*; Randall Dixon*; Donna Neal*; Dale Hansard, Jr.*; Nancy Renneker*; Mandy Clayton*.
EIN: 756039968

3727
Texas Industries, Inc.

(also known as TXI)
1341 W. Mockingbird Ln., Ste. 700W
Dallas, TX 75247-6913 (972) 647-6700
FAX: (972) 647-3964

Company URL: http://www.txi.com
Establishment information: Established in 1951.
Company type: Public company
Company ticker symbol and exchange: TXI/NYSE
Business activities: Manufactures, produces, and sells structural steel and specialty bar products and cement, aggregate, and concrete products.
Business type (SIC): Steel mill products; cement/ hydraulic; concrete, gypsum, and plaster products
Financial profile for 2012: Number of employees, 1,630; assets, $1,576,930,000; sales volume, $647,000,000; pre-tax net income, $8,470,000; expenses, $638,530,000; liabilities, $880,660,000
Corporate officers: Robert D. Rogers, Chair.; Mel G. Brekhus, Pres. and C.E.O.; James B. Rogers, V.P. and C.O.O.; Kenneth R. Allen, V.P., Finance, Treas., and C.F.O.; T. Lesley Vines, V.P., Corp. Cont., and Treas.; Frederick G. Anderson, V.P., Genl. Counsel, and Secy.; Michael P. Collar, V.P., Human Resources; Terry Marshall, V.P., Inf. Systems
Board of directors: Robert D. Rogers, Chair.; Melvin G. Brekhus; John D. Baker II; Eugenio Santiago Clariond Reyes-Retana; Sam Coats; Sean P. Foley; Bernard Lanigan, Jr.; Thomas R. Ransdell; Thomas L. Ryan; Ronald G. Steinhart; Dorothy C. Weaver
Subsidiaries: Athens Brick Co., Athens, TX; Brookhollow Corp., Dallas, TX; Chaparral Steel Co., Midlothian, TX; TXI Aviation, Inc., Dallas, TX; TXI Cement Co., Dallas, TX; TXI Transportation Co., Dallas, TX
Plants: Alexandria, Bossier City, Monroe, Perryville, LA
Giving statement: Giving through the Texas Industries Foundation.
Company EIN: 750832210

Texas Industries Foundation

1341 W. Mockingbird Ln., Ste. 700
Dallas, TX 75247-6913 (972) 647-6700

Establishment information: Incorporated in 1965 in TX.
Donors: Texas Industries, Inc.; TXI Operations LP.
Financial data (yr. ended 12/31/11): Assets, $4,988 (M); gifts received, $25,000; expenditures, $25,982; qualifying distributions, $25,982; giving activities include $25,000 for 5 grants (high: $5,000; low: $5,000).
Purpose and activities: The foundation awards college scholarships to children of employees of Texas Industries, Inc.
Fields of interest: Higher education.
Type of support: Employee-related scholarships.
Geographic limitations: Giving primarily in areas of company operations in TX.
Support limitations: No grants to individuals (except for employee-related scholarships).
Application information: Applications accepted. Application form required.
Initial approach: Letter
Deadline(s): Mar. 31
Officers and Directors:* Mel G. Brekhus*, Pres.; Kenneth R. Allen*, V.P., Finance; Frederick G. Anderson, Secy.; T. Lesley Vines, Cont.; Robert D. Rogers.
EIN: 756043179

3728
Texas Instruments Incorporated

12500 TI Blvd.
P.O. Box 660199
Dallas, TX 75266-0199 (972) 995-2011
FAX: (302) 655-5049

Company URL: http://www.ti.com
Establishment information: Established in 1953.
Company type: Public company
Company ticker symbol and exchange: TXN/NYSE
International Securities Identification Number: US8825081040
Business activities: Designs, manufactures, and sells semiconductors and sensors and controls; provides educational and productivity solutions.
Business type (SIC): Electronic components and accessories; computer and office equipment
Financial profile for 2012: Number of employees, 34,151; assets, $20,021,000,000; sales volume, $12,825,000,000; pre-tax net income, $1,935,000,000; expenses, $10,852,000,000; liabilities, $9,060,000,000

Fortune 1000 ranking: 2012—218th in revenues, 117th in profits, and 240th in assets
Forbes 2000 ranking: 2012—758th in sales, 337th in profits, and 973rd in assets
Corporate officers: Richard K. Templeton, Chair., Pres., and C.E.O.; Joseph F. Hubach, Sr. V.P., Genl. Counsel, and Secy.; Kevin P. March, Sr. V.P. and C.F.O.; John Szczsponik, Sr. V.P., Sales and Mktg.; Terri West, Sr. V.P., Comms.; Darla H. Whitaker, Sr. V.P., Human Resources
Board of directors: Richard K. Templeton, Chair.; Ralph W. Babb, Jr.; Daniel A. Carp; Carrie S. Cox; Pamela H. Patsley; Robert E. Sanchez; Wayne R. Sanders; Ruth J. Simmons; Christine Todd Whitman
Subsidiary: Unitrode Corporation, Merrimack, NH
Plants: Tucson, AZ; San Diego, San Jose, CA; Germantown, MD; Attleboro, MA; Houston, Plano, Sherman, TX
International operations: Australia; Austria; Barbados; Belgium; Bermuda; Brazil; Canada; China; Czech Republic; Denmark; Finland; France; Germany; Hong Kong; India; Ireland; Luxembourg; Malaysia; Mexico; Netherlands; Panama; Philippines; Singapore; South Korea; Spain; United Kingdom
Historic mergers: Burr-Brown Corporation (August 24, 2000); National Semiconductor Corporation (September 23, 2011)
Giving statement: Giving through the Texas Instruments Incorporated Corporate Giving Program and the Texas Instruments Foundation.
Company EIN: 750289970

Texas Instruments Incorporated Corporate Giving Program

12500 TI Blvd
Dallas, TX 75243-0592
URL: http://www.ti.com/giving

Purpose and activities: As a complement to its foundation, Texas Instruments also makes charitable contributions to nonprofit organizations directly. Support is given primarily in the greater Dallas, TX, area.
Fields of interest: Arts; Secondary school/education; Education; Public health; Human services; Civil/human rights, equal rights; Business/industry; Community/economic development; Mathematics; Engineering/technology; Science.
Type of support: General/operating support; In-kind gifts; Sponsorships.
Geographic limitations: Giving primarily in areas of company operations, with emphasis on the greater Dallas, TX, area.
Support limitations: No support for private foundations, or religious, veterans, fraternal, labor, or political organizations, hospitals, or sports teams. No grants to individuals, including sponsorships, or for travel or tours, golf tournaments, sporting events, endowments, unrestricted gifts to national or international organizations, table sponsorships, courtesy advertising, including program books and yearbooks, entertainment events, scholarships, or conferences.
Publications: Application guidelines.
Application information: Applications accepted. Applicants should submit the following:
1) copy of IRS Determination Letter
2) name, address and phone number of organization
Initial approach: Complete online eligibility quiz
Copies of proposal: 1
Number of staff: 1 full-time professional; 1 full-time support.

Texas Instruments Foundation

P.O. Box 650311, M.S. 3998
Dallas, TX 75265-0199 (214) 480-6873
FAX: (214) 480-6820; E-mail: giving@ti.com; Additional tel.: (214) 480-3221; URL: http://www.ti.com/corp/docs/csr/giving.shtml

Establishment information: Trust established in 1951 in TX; incorporated in 1964.
Donor: Texas Instruments Inc.
Contact: Ann Pomykal, Exec. Dir.
Financial data (yr. ended 12/31/11): Assets, $43,269,142 (M); gifts received, $12,000,000; expenditures, $11,258,849; qualifying distributions, $11,082,291; giving activities include $9,430,931 for 53 grants (high: $1,575,200; low: $15,000) and $1,547,370 for employee matching gifts.
Purpose and activities: The foundation supports organizations involved with arts and culture, education, health, human services, community development, and science.
Fields of interest: Museums (science/technology); Performing arts; Performing arts, orchestras; Arts; Education, management/technical assistance; Elementary/secondary education; Secondary school/education; Teacher school/education; Education; Health care; Human services; Community/economic development; United Ways and Federated Giving Programs; Science, formal/general education; Mathematics; Engineering/technology; Science.
Programs:
Arts and Culture: The foundation supports arts and cultural institutions designed to attract and retain employees and boost the economic growth of communities located in areas in which Texas Instruments operates.
Community Services: The foundation supports health and human services organizations designed to meet community needs and contributes to the United Way.
Education: The foundation supports programs designed to promote math and science education, with emphasis on STEM (science, technology, engineering, and math) teacher effectiveness.
Employee Matching Gift Program: The foundation matches contributions made by employees, retirees, and directors of Texas Instruments to K-12 and higher education institutions and arts and cultural organizations on a one for one basis from $50 to $10,000 per employee, per year.
Type of support: Annual campaigns; Building/renovation; Capital campaigns; Continuing support; Curriculum development; Employee matching gifts; General/operating support; Program development; Research; Scholarship funds.
Geographic limitations: Giving primarily in areas of company operations in Dallas, TX.
Support limitations: No support for private foundations, sectarian, denominational, or religious organizations, political parties or candidates, veterans', fraternal, or labor organizations, or sport teams. No grants to individuals, or for sponsorships, endowments, political activities, courtesy advertising, program books, yearbooks, entertainment events, scholarships, or conferences, sporting events, golf tournaments, or travel or tours; no product donations.
Publications: Application guidelines; Program policy statement.
Application information: Applications accepted. Application form required.
Initial approach: Complete online eligibility quiz and application
Board meeting date(s): Mar., June, Sept., and Dec.
Deadline(s): None
Final notification: 3 weeks following board meetings
Officers and Directors:* Sam Self*, Chair.; Terri West*, V.P.; Bart Thomas*, Secy.; Kevin P. March*, Treas.; Ann Pomykal, Exec. Dir.; David K. Heacock; Rafael R. Lizardi; Lewis H. McMahan; Venu Menon; Julie M. VanHaren; Darla H. Whitaker.
Number of staff: 1 full-time professional.
EIN: 756038519
Selected grants: The following grants are a representative sample of this grantmaker's funding activity:
$1,725,000 to Museum of Nature and Science, Dallas, TX, 2011.
$1,575,200 to United Way of Metropolitan Dallas, Dallas, TX, 2011. For operating support.
$1,500,000 to United Way of Metropolitan Dallas, Dallas, TX, 2010. For operating support.
$861,050 to Advanced Placement Strategies, Austin, TX, 2011. For 22nd Annual Hiram W. Lettingwell Hat Luncheon.
$659,175 to Advanced Placement Strategies, Austin, TX, 2010. For operating support.
$500,000 to Dallas Arboretum and Botanical Society, Dallas, TX, 2010. For operating support.
$428,424 to American Red Cross, Dallas Area Chapter, Dallas, TX, 2011. For operating support.
$400,000 to Dallas Center for the Performing Arts Foundation, Dallas, TX, 2010. For operating support.
$372,500 to University of Texas at Dallas, Richardson, TX, 2011. For Uteach.
$362,000 to Laying the Foundation, Dallas, TX, 2010. For operating support.
$250,000 to Teach for America, Dallas, TX, 2010. For operating support.
$244,140 to New Teacher Project, Brooklyn, NY, 2011. For operating support.
$200,000 to American Red Cross, Dallas Area Chapter, Dallas, TX, 2010. For operating support.
$141,050 to University of Texas at San Antonio, San Antonio, TX, 2011. For TexPREP.
$140,000 to United Way of Grayson County, Sherman, TX, 2011. For operating support.
$128,808 to United Way of Grayson County, Sherman, TX, 2010. For operating support.
$100,000 to Dallas Black Dance Theatre, Dallas, TX, 2011.
$50,000 to Dallas Children's Theater, Dallas, TX, 2010. For operating support.
$25,000 to CitySquare, Dallas, TX, 2011. For operating support.
$25,000 to First Presbyterian Church, Dallas, TX, 2010. For operating support of Stewpot.

3729
The Texas Rangers, Ltd.

1250 Copeland Rd., Ste. 1100
Arlington, TX 76011-1310 (817) 436-5400

Company URL: http://texas.rangers.mlb.com
Establishment information: Established in 1961.
Company type: Subsidiary of a private company
Business activities: Operates professional baseball club.
Business type (SIC): Commercial sports
Corporate officers: Ray C. Davis, Co-Chair.; Bob R. Simpson, Co-Chair.; Nolan Ryan, Pres and C.E.O.; Rick George, C.O.O.; Kellie Fischer, Exec. V.P. and C.F.O.; John Blake, Exec. V.P., Comms.; Terry Turner, Sr. V.P., Human Resources; Starr Pritchard, V.P. and Cont.; Becky Kimbro, V.P., Mktg.
Board of directors: Ray C. Davis, Co-Chair.; Bob R. Simpson, Co-Chair.

Giving statement: Giving through the Texas Rangers Baseball Foundation.

Texas Rangers Baseball Foundation

P.O. Box 90111
Arlington, TX 76004-3111 (817) 273-5287
URL: http://texas.rangers.mlb.com/tex/community/foundation.jsp

Establishment information: Established in 1991 in TX.
Financial data (yr. ended 12/31/11): Revenue, $1,993,929; assets, $1,898,238 (M); gifts received, $2,317,636; expenditures, $1,865,654; giving activities include $569,631 for grants and $900,111 for grants to individuals.
Purpose and activities: The foundation makes contributions to various charities, establishes and maintains area youth baseball facilities, provides scholarships to Dallas-Fort Worth area students, and provides tickets for Texas Rangers games to underprivileged children.
Fields of interest: Higher education; Athletics/sports, baseball; Youth development; Children, services; Youth, services; Human services.
Programs:
Johnny Oates Scholarships: The foundation awards scholarships to employees and the children of employees of the Texas Rangers and Sportservice.
Mark Holtz Scholarships: Four $2,000 scholarships will be awarded to seniors studying journalism at Texas Christian University and University of Texas - Austin.
Mentorship Program: This program, sponsored in conjunction with Chesapeake Energy and Volunteers of America, helps ten aspiring young students from Polytechnic High School in Fort Worth Independent School District, by matching them with a mentor to guide them throughout the school year. Mentors and students meet at Rangers Ballpark each month during the school year for special sessions, including interviewing and applying for jobs, financial literacy, the importance of community service, etiquette, goal-setting, and healthy living.
Nolan Ryan Scholarships: Two scholarships are awarded annually to one female and one male graduating senior from Alvin High School. Awards are based on academics, school and community activities, and financial need, and require that the recipients have participated in a high school sport for four years.
Richard Greene Scholars: Six scholarships will be awarded annually to students in the Arlington Independent School District.
Type of support: Donated products; Employee-related scholarships; Scholarships—to individuals.
Geographic limitations: Giving primarily in the Dallas-Fort Worth, TX area.
Application information: Applications accepted. Contact organization for application deadlines.
Initial approach: Telephone; contact high school counselor for Richard Greene Scholars Program
Officers: Casey Coffman, Pres.; Dale Petroskey, Secy.; Kellie Fischer, Treas.
Directors: John Blake; Jon Daniels; Lauri Greer; Thomas O. Hicks; Thomas O. Hicks, Jr.; Kevin Millwood; Nolan Ryan; Ruth Ryan; Jim Sundberg.
EIN: 752404714

3730
Texor Petroleum Company

3340 S. Harlem Ave.
Riverside, IL 60546-2126 (708) 447-1999
FAX: (708) 447-1047

Company URL: http://www.texor.com
Establishment information: Established in 1974.
Company type: Private company
Business activities: Sells petroleum wholesale.
Business type (SIC): Petroleum and petroleum products—wholesale
Corporate officers: Thomas E. Gleitsman, C.E.O.; Anthony E. Speiser, Pres.; Michael Lins, C.F.O.
Giving statement: Giving through the Speiser Family Foundation.

The Speiser Family Foundation

135 S. Kensington Ave.
La Grange, IL 60525-2214

Establishment information: Established in 1996 in IL.
Donors: Texor Petroleum Co.; Anthony Speiser; Christine Speiser; Exron Capital, Inc.
Financial data (yr. ended 12/31/11): Assets, $1,052,260 (M); gifts received, $159,056; expenditures, $183,632; qualifying distributions, $178,320; giving activities include $178,320 for grants.
Purpose and activities: The foundation supports organizations involved with K-12 education, housing, youth development, and human services.
Fields of interest: Education; Housing/shelter; Youth development.
Geographic limitations: Giving primarily in IL.
Support limitations: No grants to individuals.
Application information: Applications not accepted. Unsolicited requests for funds not accepted.
Officers and Directors:* Christine Speiser*, Pres.; Anthony Speiser, Secy.-Treas.; Matthew B. Spieser.
EIN: 364117679

3731
Textron Inc.

40 Westminster St.
Providence, RI 02903-2525 (401) 421-2800

Company URL: http://www.textron.com
Establishment information: Established in 1923.
Company type: Public company
Company ticker symbol and exchange: TXT/NYSE
International Securities Identification Number: US8832031012
Business activities: Provides aerospace technology, commercial products, and financial services.
Business type (SIC): Aircraft and parts; engines and turbines; electrical equipment and supplies; guided missiles and space vehicles; search and navigation equipment; insurance/accident and health
Financial profile for 2012: Number of employees, 33,000; assets, $13,033,000,000; sales volume, $12,237,000,000; pre-tax net income, $841,000,000; expenses, $11,396,000,000; liabilities, $10,042,000,000
Fortune 1000 ranking: 2012—225th in revenues, 296th in profits, and 328th in assets
Corporate officers: Scott C. Donnelly, Chair., Pres., and C.E.O.; Frank T. Connor, Exec. V.P. and C.F.O.; E. Robert Lupone, Exec. V.P., Genl. Counsel, and Corp. Secy.; Cheryl H. Johnson, Exec. V.P., Human Resources; Richard L. Yates, Sr. V.P. and Corp. Cont.; Diane K. Schwarz, V.P. and C.I.O.; Mary F. Lovejoy, V.P. and Treas.; Adele J. Suddes, V.P., Comms.; Cathy Streker, V.P., Human Resources
Board of directors: Scott C. Donnelly, Chair.; Kathleen M. Bader; R. Kerry Clark; James T. Conway; Ivor J. Evans; Lawrence K. Fish; Paul E. Gagne; Dain M. Hancock; Lord Powell; Lloyd G. Trotter; James L. Ziemer
Subsidiaries: Aircraft Engine Components Textron, Newington, CT; Airfoil Textron, Thomasville, GA; Bell Helicopter Textron Inc., Hurst, TX; Camcar Textron, Rockford, IL; The Cessna Aircraft Company, Wichita, KS; Cherry Textron, Santa Ana, CA; Cone Drive Textron, Traverse City, MI; CWC Castings Textron, Muskegon, MI; E-Z-GO Textron, Augusta, GA; Elco Textron Inc., Rockford, IL; Fuel Systems Textron, Zeeland, MI; Greenlee Textron, Rockford, IL; HR Textron, Valencia, CA; Jacobsen Textron, Racine, WI; McCord Winn Textron, Troy, MI; Micromatic Textron, Holland, MI; Textron Aerostructures, Nashville, TN; Textron Defense Systems, Wilmington, MA; Textron Financial Corp., Providence, RI; Textron Lycoming Reciprocating Engines, Williamsport, PA; Textron Marine & Land Systems, New Orleans, LA; Textron Specialty Materials, Lowell, MA
International operations: Canada; Singapore
Giving statement: Giving through the Textron Inc. Corporate Giving Program and the Textron Charitable Trust.
Company EIN: 050315468

Textron Inc. Corporate Giving Program

40 Westminster
Providence, RI 02903-2525
URL: http://www.textron.com/about/commitment/corp-giving/index.php

Contact: Karen Warfield, Community Affairs Mgr.
Purpose and activities: As a complement to its foundation, Textron also makes charitable contributions to nonprofit organizations. Support is given primarily in areas of company operations, with emphasis on Rhode Island.
Fields of interest: Arts; Higher education; Education, ESL programs; Education, services; Education, reading; Public health; Health care; Employment, training; Employment; Food banks; Housing/shelter, development; Housing/shelter, homeless; Housing/shelter; Youth development; Human services; Community/economic development; Engineering/technology Minorities; Women.
Type of support: Employee volunteer services; General/operating support; Program development; Sponsorships.
Geographic limitations: Giving primarily in areas of company operations, with emphasis on RI.
Support limitations: No support for discriminatory, political, fraternal, or veterans' organizations, or for religious organizations not of benefit to the entire community. No grants to individuals.
Publications: Application guidelines; Corporate giving report.
Application information: Applications accepted. Proposals should be no longer than 5 pages. Support is limited to 1 contribution per organization during any given year. The Associated Grant Makers Common Proposal form is accepted. Application form required. Applicants should submit the following:
1) qualifications of key personnel
2) population served
3) name, address and phone number of organization
4) copy of IRS Determination Letter
5) how company employees can become involved with the organization
6) brief history of organization and description of its mission

7) geographic area to be served
8) how project's results will be evaluated or measured
9) explanation of why grantmaker is considered an appropriate donor for project
10) listing of board of directors, trustees, officers and other key people and their affiliations
11) detailed description of project and amount of funding requested
12) plans for cooperation with other organizations, if any
13) contact person
14) copy of current year's organizational budget and/or project budget

Initial approach: Download application form and mail with proposal to headquarters
Deadline(s): Mar. 1 and Sept. 1

The Textron Charitable Trust

c/o Textron Inc.
40 Westminster St.
Providence, RI 02903-2525
URL: http://www.textron.com/about/commitment/corp-giving/

Establishment information: Trust established in 1953 in VT.
Donors: Textron Inc.; Cessna Foundation, Inc.
Contact: Karen Warfield, Mgr., Community Affairs
Financial data (yr. ended 12/31/11): Assets, $21,453,811 (M); expenditures, $3,166,426; qualifying distributions, $3,126,224; giving activities include $2,445,862 for 122 grants (high: $350,000; low: $1,000) and $451,732 for 522 employee matching gifts.
Purpose and activities: The foundation supports organizations involved with arts and culture, education, the environment, animals and wildlife, health, workforce development, hunger, housing, youth development, human services, community revitalization, minorities, women, and low-income individuals.
Fields of interest: Arts; Education, early childhood education; Higher education; Education, ESL programs; Education, services; Education, reading; Education; Environment; Animals/wildlife; Hospitals (general); Public health; Health care; Employment, training; Employment; Food services; Food banks; Housing/shelter; Youth development, adult & child programs; Youth development; Family services; Homeless, human services; Human services; Economic development; Community/economic development; United Ways and Federated Giving Programs; Engineering/technology Minorities; Women; Economically disadvantaged.
Programs:

Employee Matching Gifts: The foundation matches contributions made by employees and directors of Textron to institutions of secondary and higher education, hospitals, and nonprofit organizations involved with arts and culture, the environment, and animals and wildlife on a two-for-one basis from $25 to $7,500 per contributor, per year.

Healthy Families and Vibrant Communities: The foundation supports programs and organizations designed to improve quality of life in communities where Textron has a business presence. Special emphasis is directed toward arts and culture, including outreach programs designed to enhance learning and target low- and moderate income individuals; community revitalization, including affordable housing and economic development in low-income areas; and health and human service organizations, including food pantries, homeless shelters, health education, and services for low-income residents.

Textron Scholarship Program: The foundation awards college scholarships of up to $2,000 to children of employees of Textron. The program is administered by National Merit Scholarship Corp.

Workforce Development and Education: The foundation supports programs designed to help adults and young people achieve employment and success in the workplace. Special emphasis is directed toward job training and employment development, including school-to-work programs, job training for underserved audiences, literacy, and ESL; enrichment and mentoring programs for youth, including after-school programs and youth development initiatives; and college and university support, including scholarship funds and internships for women and minorities with a focus on technology, manufacturing, and engineering.
Type of support: Building/renovation; Capital campaigns; Continuing support; Employee matching gifts; Employee-related scholarships; Equipment; General/operating support; Internship funds; Matching/challenge support; Program development; Scholarship funds; Technical assistance.
Geographic limitations: Giving on a national basis in areas of company operations, with emphasis on Washington, DC, KS, NJ, RI, and VA.
Support limitations: No support for political, fraternal, or veterans' organizations, religious institutions, or discriminatory organizations. No grants to individuals (except for employee-related scholarships), or for endowments, land acquisition, debt reduction, or demonstration projects; no loans.
Publications: Application guidelines; Program policy statement.
Application information: Applications accepted. Proposals should be no longer than 5 pages. The Associated Grant Makers (AGM) Common Proposal Form is also accepted. Support is limited to 1 contribution per organization during any given year. Multi-year commitments will be considered but are limited. Application form required. Applicants should submit the following:
1) timetable for implementation and evaluation of project
2) how project will be sustained once grantmaker support is completed
3) qualifications of key personnel
4) statement of problem project will address
5) population served
6) copy of IRS Determination Letter
7) brief history of organization and description of its mission
8) geographic area to be served
9) copy of most recent annual report/audited financial statement/990
10) how project's results will be evaluated or measured
11) listing of board of directors, trustees, officers and other key people and their affiliations
12) detailed description of project and amount of funding requested
13) plans for cooperation with other organizations, if any
14) copy of current year's organizational budget and/or project budget

Initial approach: Download application form and mail proposal and application form to foundation
Copies of proposal: 1
Board meeting date(s): Quarterly
Deadline(s): Mar. 1 and Sept. 1

Officers: John D. Butler, Exec. V.P., Admin.; Terry O' Donnell, Exec. V.P. and Genl. Counsel; Robert Rowland, V.P., Govt. Affairs; Adele Suddes, V.P., Comms.; Dick Yates, Corp. Cont.
Trustee: State Street Bank & Trust Co.
Number of staff: 1 full-time professional.
EIN: 256115832

Selected grants: The following grants are a representative sample of this grantmaker's funding activity:
$242,500 to United Way of the Plains, Wichita, KS, 2009.
$150,000 to John F. Kennedy Center for the Performing Arts, Washington, DC, 2009.
$110,000 to United Way of Rhode Island, Providence, RI, 2009.
$100,000 to Textron Chamber of Commerce Academy, Providence, RI, 2009.
$66,000 to Women and Infants Hospital of Rhode Island, Providence, RI, 2009.
$50,000 to Injured Marine Semper Fi Fund, Oceanside, CA, 2009.
$33,334 to Gracemed Health Clinic, Wichita, KS, 2009.
$25,000 to Festival Ballet Providence, Providence, RI, 2009.
$20,000 to Air Force Aid Society, Arlington, VA, 2009.
$20,000 to Chamber Education Foundation, Warwick, RI, 2009.

3724
Tex-Trude, Inc.

2001 Sheldon Rd.
P.O. Box 58
Channelview, TX 77530 (281) 452-5961

Company URL: http://www.tex-trude.com
Establishment information: Established in 1952.
Company type: Private company
Business activities: Manufactures polyethylene sheathing and tubing.
Business type (SIC): Plastic products/miscellaneous
Financial profile for 2011: Number of employees, 150
Corporate officers: Charlie Nettles, Jr., Pres.; Kyle Harding, Cont.
Giving statement: Giving through the Tex-Trude Charities, Inc.

Tex-Trude Charities, Inc.

2001 Sheldon Rd.
Channelview, TX 77530-2685 (713) 481-3405

Establishment information: Established in 1988 in TX.
Donor: Tex-Trude, Inc.
Contact: Dennis K. Harding, Tr.
Financial data (yr. ended 12/31/11): Assets, $205,771 (M); gifts received, $25,000; expenditures, $25,000; qualifying distributions, $25,000; giving activities include $25,000 for grants.
Purpose and activities: The foundation supports organizations involved with higher and medical education, epilepsy, and Alzheimer's disease.
Type of support: General/operating support; Research.
Application information: Applications accepted. Application form required. Applicants should submit the following:
1) copy of IRS Determination Letter
2) brief history of organization and description of its mission
3) detailed description of project and amount of funding requested

Initial approach: Letter
Deadline(s): None

Trustees: Dennis K. Harding; Charles M. Nettles.
EIN: 760250950

3732
TFS Financial Corporation

7007 Broadway Ave.
Cleveland, OH 44105 (216) 441-6000
FAX: (216) 441-7050

Company URL: http://www.thirdfederal.com/
Establishment information: Established in 1938.
Company type: Public company
Company ticker symbol and exchange: TFSL/NASDAQ
Business activities: Operates bank holding company.
Business type (SIC): Holding company; savings institutions
Financial profile for 2012: Number of employees, 896; assets, $11,518,120,000; pre-tax net income, $13,610,000; liabilities, $9,711,270,000
Corporate officers: Marc A. Stefanski, Chair., Pres., and C.E.O.; Paul J. Huml, Co-C.O.O. and C.A.O.; Meredith S. Weil, Co-C.O.O.; David S. Huffman, C.F.O.; Ralph M. Betters, C.I.O.; Bernard S. Kobak, Secy.
Board of directors: Mark A. Stefanski, Chair.; Anthony J. Asher; Martin J. Cohen; Robert A. Fiala; Robert B. Heisler, Jr.; Bernard S. Kobak; William Charles Mulligan; Terrence R. Ozan; Marianne Piterans; Paul W. Stefanik; Ben S. Stefanski, III
Subsidiary: Third Federal Savings and Loan Association, Cleveland, OH
Giving statement: Giving through the Third Federal Foundation.
Company EIN: 522054948

Third Federal Foundation

7007 Broadway Ave.
Cleveland, OH 44105-1441 (216) 641-7270

Establishment information: Established in 2007 in OH.
Donors: Third Federal Savings and Loan Association, MHC; TFS Financial Corp.
Contact: Kurt Karakul, Pres. and Exec. Dir.
Financial data (yr. ended 12/31/11): Assets, $41,533,332 (M); gifts received, $1,272; expenditures, $3,304,641; qualifying distributions, $2,946,946; giving activities include $2,946,946 for grants.
Purpose and activities: The foundation supports nonprofit organizations involved with education and community development. Special emphasis is directed toward programs designed to raise the aspirations of students in the community and enhance knowledge of specific areas, including economics, communications, business, and public speaking.
Fields of interest: Elementary school/education; Secondary school/education; Higher education; Business school/education; Boys & girls clubs; Youth development; Community development, neighborhood development; Economic development; Community/economic development; Economics Economically disadvantaged.
Type of support: General/operating support; Program development.
Geographic limitations: Giving primarily in areas of company operations in OH, with emphasis on Cleveland.
Support limitations: No grants to individuals.
Application information: Applications accepted. Application form not required. Applicants should submit the following:
1) copy of IRS Determination Letter
2) detailed description of project and amount of funding requested
3) brief history of organization and description of its mission

Initial approach: Proposal
Deadline(s): None
Final notification: Following review

Officers and Directors:* Marc A. Stefanski*, C.E.O.; Kurt Karakul, Pres. and Exec. Dir.; Meredith Weil, V.P. and Treas.; Ralph M. Betters, Secy.; Robert A. Fiala; John Marino.
EIN: 208467212
Selected grants: The following grants are a representative sample of this grantmaker's funding activity:
$780,338 to Cleveland Central Catholic High School, Cleveland, OH, 2010.
$200,000 to University Hospitals Health System, Cleveland, OH, 2010.
$100,000 to University Settlement, Cleveland, OH, 2010.
$70,000 to Slavic Village Development, Cleveland, OH, 2010.
$50,000 to Partnership for a Safer Cleveland, Cleveland, OH, 2010.
$46,200 to Ideastream, Cleveland, OH, 2010.
$25,000 to Cleveland Foundation, Cleveland, OH, 2010.
$25,000 to East Side Organizing Project, Cleveland, OH, 2010.
$25,000 to Stella Maris, Cleveland, OH, 2010.
$14,000 to Literacy Cooperative of Greater Cleveland, Cleveland, OH, 2010.

3733
Thermo Fisher Scientific Inc.

(formerly Thermo Electron Corporation)
81 Wyman St.
Waltham, MA 02454 (781) 622-1000
FAX: (781) 622-1207

Company URL: http://www.thermofisher.com/global/en/home.asp
Company type: Public company
Company ticker symbol and exchange: TMO/NYSE
International Securities Identification Number: US8835561023
Business activities: Manufactures process equipment, analytical instruments, measuring and controlling devices, and heating and air conditioning equipment; constructs power plants.
Business type (SIC): Laboratory apparatus; construction/miscellaneous heavy; machinery/special industry; machinery/refrigeration and service industry; electric services
Financial profile for 2012: Number of employees, 38,900; assets, $27,444,600,000; sales volume, $12,509,900,000; pre-tax net income, $1,269,400,000; expenses, $11,027,800,000; liabilities, $11,979,900,000
Fortune 1000 ranking: 2012—220th in revenues, 171st in profits, and 196th in assets
Forbes 2000 ranking: 2012—773rd in sales, 483rd in profits, and 787th in assets
Corporate officers: Jim P. Manzi, Chair.; Marc N. Casper, Pres. and C.E.O; Peter M. Wilver, Sr. V.P. and C.F.O.
Board of directors: Jim P. Manzi, Chair.; Marc N. Casper; Nelson J. Chai; C. Martin Harris, M.D.; Tyler Jacks, Ph.D.; Judy C. Lewent; Thomas J. Lynch; William G. Parrett; Lars Rebien Sorensen; Scott M. Sperling; Elaine S. Ullian
Subsidiary: Fisher Scientific International Inc., Hampton, NH
Plants: Delano, Mendota, Woodland, CA; Albuquerque, NM
Giving statement: Giving through the Thermo Fisher Scientific Inc. Contributions Program.
Company EIN: 042209186

Thermo Fisher Scientific Inc. Contributions Program

(also known as Thermo Fisher Foundation for Science)
81 Wyman St.
Waltham, MA 02454 (781) 622-1000
FAX: (781) 622-1207; URL: http://www.thermofisher.com/global/en/about/responsibility/responsibility.html

Purpose and activities: As a complement to its foundation, Thermo Fisher Scientific supports science students and promotes interest in the STEM subjects: science, technology, engineering and math; also matches employee gifts and encourages employee volunteerism.
Fields of interest: Teacher school/education; Disasters, preparedness/services; Community/economic development; Science, formal/general education; Mathematics; Engineering/technology; Science.
Program:
Matching Program: Thermo Fisher matches half of every dollar that company employees donate to nonprofits, up to $1,000 annually per employee.
Type of support: Employee matching gifts; Employee volunteer services; Faculty/staff development; General/operating support; Program development; Scholarships—to individuals; Sponsorships.
Geographic limitations: Giving primarily in areas of company operations on a national and international basis.
Application information: Employee volunteerism is handled by employee-led Community Action Councils (CACs).

3734
Thinkshift Communications

1325 3rd Ave., Ste. 5
San Francisco, CA 94122-2763
(415) 848-9181
FAX: (4150 593-7560

Company URL: http://www.thinkshiftcom.com/
Establishment information: Established in 2001.
Company type: Private company
Business type (SIC): Business services/miscellaneous
Corporate officers: Carolyn McMaster, Principal; Sandra Stewart, Principal
Giving statement: Giving through the Thinkshift Communications Corporate Giving Program.

Thinkshift Communications Corporate Giving Program

1325 Third Ave., Ste.5
San Francisco, CA 94122-2763 (415) 848-9181
E-mail: start@thinkshiftcom.com; URL: http://www.thinkshiftcom.com/

Purpose and activities: Thinkshift Communications is a certified B Corporation that donates a percentage of sales to charitable organizations. Support is given primarily in San Francisco, California.
Fields of interest: Environment.
Type of support: General/operating support.
Geographic limitations: Giving primarily in San Francisco, CA; giving also to national organizations.

3735
Third Federal Savings and Loan Association
7007 Broadway Ave.
Cleveland, OH 44105-1441 (216) 641-6000

Company URL: http://www.thirdfederal.com
Establishment information: Established in 1938.
Company type: Subsidiary of a public company
Business activities: Operates savings bank.
Business type (SIC): Savings institutions
Corporate officers: Marc A. Stefanski, Chair., Pres., and C.E.O.; Meredith S. Weil, C.O.O.; David S. Huffman, C.F.O.; Ralph M. Betters, C.I.O.
Board of director: Marc A. Stefanski, Chair.
Giving statement: Giving through the Ben S. and Gerome R. Stefanski Foundation.

The Ben S. and Gerome R. Stefanski Foundation
7007 Broadway Ave.
Cleveland, OH 44105-1490 (216) 441-7318

Establishment information: Established in 2005 in OH.
Donor: Third Federal Savings and Loan Association, MHC.
Contact: Marc A. Stefanski, Pres.
Financial data (yr. ended 12/31/11): Assets, $99,494 (M); expenditures, $2,819; qualifying distributions, $2,500; giving activities include $2,500 for grants.
Purpose and activities: The foundation supports organizations involved with education and housing.
Fields of interest: Education; Health care; Housing/shelter.
Type of support: General/operating support.
Geographic limitations: Giving primarily in the Cleveland, OH, area.
Application information: Applications accepted. Application form not required.
Initial approach: Letter or telephone
Deadline(s): Sept. 30
Officers and Trustees:* Marc A. Stefanski*, Pres.; Floyd E. Stefanski*, V.P.; Bernard S. Kobak*, Secy.-Treas.
EIN: 202372000

3736
Thomaston Savings Bank
203 Main St.
P.O. Box 907
Thomaston, CT 06787-1721
(860) 283-1874

Company URL: http://www.thomastonsavingsbank.com
Company type: Private company
Business activities: Operates savings bank.
Business type (SIC): Savings institutions
Corporate officers: George P. Seabourne, Chair.; David V. Merchant, Vice-Chair.; Stephen L. Lewis, Pres. and C.E.O.; James R. Nichol, Exec. V.P. and C.O.O.; Mark J. Blum, Sr. V.P. and C.F.O.; Jack Lynn, Sr. V.P. and C.I.O.
Board of directors: George P. Seabourne, Chair.; David V. Merchant, Vice Chair.; Paul C. Broomhead, M.D.; David J. Carlson; Bradford P. Erickson; James S. Kaniewski; Stephen L. Lewis; Thomas G. Parisot; Carrie A. Zimyeski
Offices: Bethlehem, Harwinton, Terryville, Waterbury, Watertown, CT
Giving statement: Giving through the Thomaston Savings Bank Foundation, Inc.

Thomaston Savings Bank Foundation, Inc.
P.O. Box 907
Thomaston, CT 06787-0907 (860) 283-4373
Application address: 203 Main St., Thomaston, CT 06787; URL: https://www.thomastonsavingsbank.com/about-thomaston-savings-bank/foundation.aspx

Establishment information: Established in 1997 in CT.
Donor: Thomaston Savings Bank.
Contact: James Nichol, Secy.
Financial data (yr. ended 12/31/11): Assets, $4,110,062 (M); gifts received, $200,000; expenditures, $269,142; qualifying distributions, $251,596; giving activities include $251,596 for grants.
Purpose and activities: The foundation supports fire departments and organizations involved with arts and culture, education, health, safety, human services, and religion.
Fields of interest: Arts; Libraries (public); Education, services; Education, reading; Education; Health care, EMS; Health care; Disasters, fire prevention/control; Safety/disasters; Athletics/sports, amateur leagues; Youth, services; Aging, centers/services; Developmentally disabled, centers & services; Human services; Christian agencies & churches; Religion.
Type of support: Building/renovation; Equipment; General/operating support; Program development.
Publications: Application guidelines.
Application information: Applications accepted. Application form required. Applicants should submit the following:
1) copy of IRS Determination Letter
2) copy of current year's organizational budget and/or project budget
Initial approach: Letter
Deadline(s): Jun. 30
Officers and Trustees:* George Seabourne*, Chair.; David Carlson*, Pres.; James Nichol, Secy.; Stephen Lewis, Treas.; Walter Barber; Bradford Erickson; James Kaniewski; David Merchant; Roger Perreault.
EIN: 061483909
Selected grants: The following grants are a representative sample of this grantmaker's funding activity:
$4,264 to Thomaston Volunteer Fire Department, Thomaston, CT, 2010.
$3,500 to Watertown Library Association, Watertown, CT, 2010.
$3,335 to Central Naugatuck Valley Help, Waterbury, CT, 2010.
$3,196 to Morris Volunteer Fire Department, Morris, CT, 2010.
$2,883 to Saint Mary Magdalen School, Science Lab, Oakville, CT, 2010.
$2,711 to Plymouth Community Food Pantry, Terryville, CT, 2010.
$2,000 to McCall Foundation, Torrington, CT, 2010.
$2,000 to Northwest Connecticut Association for the Arts, Torrington, CT, 2010.
$2,000 to Safe Haven of Greater Waterbury, Education Materials, Waterbury, CT, 2010.
$1,657 to Saint Mary School, Waterbury, CT, 2010.

3737
Thomasville Furniture Industries, Inc.
401 E. Main St.
Thomasville, NC 27361 (336) 472-4000

Company URL: http://www.thomasville.com
Establishment information: Established in 1904.
Company type: Subsidiary of a public company
Business activities: Manufactures furniture.
Business type (SIC): Furniture/household
Corporate officer: Edward D. Teplitz, Pres.
Subsidiaries: Fayette Enterprises Inc., Fayette, MS; Gordon's Inc., Johnson City, TN; Thomasville Upholstery, Inc., Hickory, NC
Giving statement: Giving through the Thomasville Furniture Industries Foundation.

Thomasville Furniture Industries Foundation
1525 W. W.T. Harris Blvd.
Charlotte, NC 28288-5709 (336) 732-6010

Establishment information: Trust established in 1960 in NC.
Donors: Thomasville Furniture Industries, Inc.; Interco.
Contact: Sherald Cratch
Financial data (yr. ended 12/31/11): Assets, $7,919,322 (M); gifts received, $240,298; expenditures, $374,123; qualifying distributions, $304,490; giving activities include $304,490 for grants.
Purpose and activities: The foundation supports hospices and organizations involved with education, health, cancer, youth development, child welfare, and community economic development.
Fields of interest: Elementary/secondary education; Higher education; Scholarships/financial aid; Education; Health care; Cancer; Crime/violence prevention, child abuse; Youth development, business; Residential/custodial care, hospices; Community development, business promotion; Community/economic development; United Ways and Federated Giving Programs.
Type of support: Employee-related scholarships; General/operating support; Matching/challenge support; Program development; Scholarship funds.
Geographic limitations: Giving primarily in NC.
Support limitations: No grants to individuals (except for employee-related scholarships).
Application information: Applications not accepted. Contributes only to pre-selected organizations.
Administrative Committee: Frederick B. Starr, Chair.; Carlyle A. Nance, Jr., Secy.; Frank B. Burr; Charles G. O'Brien.
Trustee: Wachovia Bank, N.A.
EIN: 566047870
Selected grants: The following grants are a representative sample of this grantmaker's funding activity:
$10,000 to YMCA, Tom A. Finch Community, Thomasville, NC, 2010.
$2,451 to YMCA, Tom A. Finch Community, Thomasville, NC, 2010.
$2,363 to YMCA, Tom A. Finch Community, Thomasville, NC, 2010.
$2,000 to Girl Scouts of the U.S.A., Saint Louis, MO, 2010.
$1,250 to University of Miami, Coral Gables, FL, 2010.
$1,000 to Saint Patrick Center, Saint Louis, MO, 2010.

3738
Thompson & Knight LLP
1 Arts Plz.
1722 Routh St., Ste. 1500
Dallas, TX 75201-2532 (214) 969-1700

Company URL: http://www.tklaw.com/home.cfm
Establishment information: Established in 1887.
Company type: Private company
Business activities: Operates law firm.
Business type (SIC): Legal services
Corporate officer: Jeffrey A. Zlotky, Managing Partner
Giving statement: Giving through the Thompson & Knight LLP Pro Bono Program and the Thompson & Knight Foundation.

Thompson & Knight LLP Pro Bono Program
1 Arts Plz.
1722 Routh St., Ste.1500
Dallas, TX 75201-2532
E-mail: John.Cohn@tklaw.com; URL: http://www.tklaw.com/pro_bono.cfm

Contact: John Cohn, Chair of Pro Bono Committee
Fields of interest: Legal services.
Type of support: Pro bono services - legal.
Application information: A Pro Bono Committee manages the pro bono program.

Thompson & Knight Foundation
1722 Routh St., Ste. 1500
Dallas, TX 75201-2532

Establishment information: Established in 1991.
Contact: Pauline Saucedo
Financial data (yr. ended 12/31/11): Revenue, $760,872; assets, $394,988 (M); gifts received, $751,035; expenditures, $798,580; giving activities include $797,313 for grants.
Purpose and activities: The foundation supports a wide range of civic and charitable organizations, with a focus on the YMCA, the United Way, Goodwill, and March of Dimes.
Fields of interest: YM/YWCAs & YM/YWHAs; United Ways and Federated Giving Programs.
Geographic limitations: Giving limited to TX.
Officers and Directors:* David M. Rosenberg*, Chair.; Scott Stolley, Vice-Chair.; Sam P. Burford, Jr.*, Secy.; Diane Scheffler*, Treas.; David M. Bennett; Susan E. Coleman; Anne Marie Cowdrey; Greg W. Curry; Barry Davis; Andy Flint; J. Holt Foster III; Sharon Fountain; Craig A. Haynes; Bill McDonald, Jr.; James W. McKellar; Pauline Saucedo.
EIN: 752371851

3739
J. Walter Thompson Company
466 Lexington Ave.
New York, NY 10017-3176 (212) 210-7000

Company URL: http://www.jwt.com
Establishment information: Established in 1864.
Company type: Subsidiary of a foreign company
Business activities: Provides advertising services.
Business type (SIC): Advertising
Corporate officers: Bob Jeffrey, Chair. and C.E.O.; Michael Maedel, Pres.; Lewis J. Trencher, Exec. V.P. and C.F.O.
Board of director: Bob Jeffrey, Chair.
Offices: Phoenix, AZ; Los Angeles, Sacramento, San Diego, San Francisco, CA; Denver, CO; Miami, FL; Atlanta, GA; Chicago, IL; Indianapolis, IN; New Orleans, LA; Baltimore, MD; Detroit, MI; Minneapolis, MN; Kansas City, St. Louis, MO; Newark, NJ; Rochester, NY; Charlotte, NC; Cincinnati, Cleveland, OH; Tulsa, OK; Philadelphia, PA; Memphis, TN; Dallas, Houston, TX; Salt Lake City, UT; Richmond, VA; Seattle, WA
International operations: Argentina; Australia; Austria; Bangladesh; Belgium; Bolivia; Bosnia-Herzegovina; Brazil; Bulgaria; Canada; Chile; China; Colombia; Costa Rica; Croatia; Czech Republic; Dominican Republic; Ecuador; Egypt; El Salvador; Estonia; Finland; France; Germany; Ghana; Greece; Guatemala; Honduras; Hungary; India; Indonesia; Ireland; Israel; Italy; Ivory Coast; Japan; Kenya; Kuwait; Latvia; Lebanon; Lithuania; Macedonia; Malaysia; Mexico; Morocco and the Western Sahara; Mozambique; Nepal; Netherlands; New Zealand; Nicaragua; Nigeria; Pakistan; Panama; Paraguay; Peru; Philippines; Poland; Portugal; Romania; Russia; Saudi Arabia; Serbia; Singapore; Slovakia; Slovenia; South Africa; South Korea; Spain; Sri Lanka; Sweden; Switzerland; Syria; Taiwan; Thailand; Tunisia; Turkey; Ukraine; United Arab Emirates; United Kingdom; Uruguay; Venezuela; Vietnam; Zimbabwe
Giving statement: Giving through the J. Walter Thompson Company Contributions Program and the J. Walter Thompson Company Fund, Inc.

J. Walter Thompson Company Fund, Inc.
c/o WPP Group USA, Inc.
100 Park Ave., 4th Fl.
New York, NY 10017
Application address: 466 Lexington Ave., New York, NY 10017

Establishment information: Incorporated in 1953 in NY.
Donor: J. Walter Thompson Co., Inc.
Contact: Richard Pollet, Secy.
Financial data (yr. ended 11/30/11): Assets, $1,217,460 (M); expenditures, $30,827; qualifying distributions, $30,827; giving activities include $18,580 for 25 grants (high: $2,600; low: $25).
Purpose and activities: The foundation supports organizations involved with education.
Fields of interest: Education.
Type of support: Employee matching gifts; General/operating support; Scholarship funds.
Geographic limitations: Giving primarily in Durham, NC; giving also in CT, IN, ME, NJ, and NY for employee matching gifts.
Support limitations: No grants to individuals.
Application information: Applications accepted. Application form required. Applicants should submit the following:
1) copy of IRS Determination Letter
Initial approach: Letter
Copies of proposal: 1
Board meeting date(s): Mar. to Apr.
Deadline(s): None
Officers and Directors:* Lewis J. Trencher*, Chair.; Robert L. Jeffrey*, Pres.; Richard Pollet*, Secy.; Donna Matteo Rabinowitz*, Treas.
EIN: 136020644

3740
Thompson Hine LLP
3900 Key Ctr.
127 Public Sq.
Cleveland, OH 44114-1291 (216) 566-5500

Company URL: http://www.thompsonhine.com/home/
Establishment information: Established in 1911.
Company type: Private company
Business activities: Operates law firm.
Business type (SIC): Legal services
Corporate officers: David J. Hooker, Managing Partner; Frank A. LaManna, C.O.O.; Michael E. Goldberg, C.F.O.
Offices: Washington, DC; Atlanta, GA; New York, NY; Cincinnati, Cleveland, Columbus, Dayton, OH
Giving statement: Giving through the Thompson Hine LLP Pro Bono Program.

Thompson Hine LLP Pro Bono Program
3900 Key Ctr.
127 Public Sq.
Cleveland, OH 44114-1291 (216) 566-5543
E-mail: Stacey.Greenwell@ThompsonHine.com; Additional tel.:(216) 566-5500; URL: http://www.thompsonhine.com/about/pro_bono/

Contact: Stacey Greenwell, Assoc.
Fields of interest: Legal services.
Type of support: Pro bono services - legal.
Application information: A Pro Bono Committee manages the pro bono program.

3741
Thomson Reuters Corporation
(formerly Thomson U.S. Holdings Inc.)
3 Times Sq.
New York, NY 10036 (646) 223-4000

Company URL: http://thomsonreuters.com
Establishment information: Established in 1851.
Company type: Subsidiary of a foreign company
Business activities: Provides financial and other data to businesses and professionals.
Business type (SIC): Computer services
Financial profile for 2012: Assets, $32,600,000,000; sales volume, $13,300,000,000
Forbes 2000 ranking: 2012—725th in sales, 289th in profits, and 688th in assets
Corporate officers: David K. R. Thomson, Chair.; W.Geoffrey Beattie, Vice-Chair.; James C. Smith, Pres. and C.E.O.; Stephane Bello, Exec. V.P. and C.F.O.
Board of directors: David K.R. Thomson, Chair.; W.Geoffrey Beattie, Vice-Chair.; Manvinder S. Banga; Mary Cirillo; Steven A. Denning; Lawton W. Fitt; Deryck Maughan; Roger L. Martin; Ken Olisa; Vance K. Opperman; Wulf von Schimmelmann; James C. Smith; John M. Thompson; Peter J. Thompson
Giving statement: Giving through the Thomson Reuters Corporation Contributions Program and the Thomson Reuters Foundation Inc.

Thomson Reuters Foundation Inc.
c/o Thomson Reuters
3 Times Sq., 20th Fl.
New York, NY 10036-6564
URL: http://www.trust.org/

Establishment information: Established in 2001 in NY.
Financial data (yr. ended 12/31/10): Revenue, $1,820; assets, $123,462 (M); gifts received, $1,820; expenditures, $14,535.
Purpose and activities: The organization aims to raise funds to support programs aimed at providing humanitarian relief of hardship, need, and/or distress.
Trustees: David Craig; Stephen Dando; Geert Linnebank; Elizabeth Maclean; Lisa Silver.
EIN: 134192037

3742
Thomson Reuters, Legal

(also known as Thomson West)
(formerly West Publishing Corporation)
610 Opperman Dr.
Eagan, MN 55123-1340 (651) 687-7000

Company URL: http://thomsonreuters.com/products_services/legal
Establishment information: Established in 1872.
Company type: Subsidiary of a foreign company
Business activities: Provides database information services; publishes books and electronic products.
Business type (SIC): Computer services; book publishing and/or printing
Corporate officers: Peter Warwick, Pres. and C.E.O.; Helen Owers, C.O.O.; Stephane Bello, C.F.O.; Edward Friedland, Genl. Counsel
Giving statement: Giving through the Thomson Reuters Legal Corporate Giving Program.

Thomson Reuters Legal Corporate Giving Program

(formerly Thomson West Community Partnership Program)
c/o Community Rels.
610 Opperman Dr.
Eagan, MN 55123-1340 (651) 848-5926
E-mail: martha.field@thomsonreuters.com; Additional application address: c/o West Group Community Partnership Prog., 50 E. Broad St., Rochester, NY 14694; URL: http://thomsonreuters.com/products_services/legal/corporate_responsibility/

Contact: Martha Field, Mgr., Community Rels.
Purpose and activities: Thomson Reuters Legal makes charitable contributions to nonprofit organizations involved with educating the future workforce, strengthening youth and families, and advancing legal services. Support is given primarily in areas of company operations in California, Illinois, Maryland, Massachusetts, Minnesota, New Jersey, New Mexico, and New York, and in Argentina, Australia, Belgium, Brazil, Canada, France, Hong Kong, India, Ireland, Japan, Malaysia, the Netherlands, New Zealand, Singapore, Spain, Sweden, and the United Kingdom.
Fields of interest: Education; Legal services; Employment, training; Youth development; Youth, services; Family services; Community/economic development.
International interests: Argentina; Australia; Belgium; Brazil; Canada; France; Hong Kong; India; Ireland; Japan; Malaysia; Netherlands; New Zealand; Singapore; Spain; Sweden; United Kingdom.
Type of support: Employee volunteer services; General/operating support; Pro bono services - legal; Program development; Sponsorships.
Geographic limitations: Giving primarily in areas of company operations in CA, IL, MA, MD, MN, NJ, NM, and NY, and in Argentina, Australia, Belgium, Brazil, Canada, France, Hong Kong, India, Ireland, Japan, Malaysia, the Netherlands, New Zealand, Singapore, Spain, Sweden, and the United Kingdom.
Publications: Corporate giving report.
Application information: Applications accepted. Application form required. Applicants should submit the following:
1) how project will be sustained once grantmaker support is completed
2) staff salaries
3) population served
4) name, address and phone number of organization
5) copy of IRS Determination Letter
6) brief history of organization and description of its mission
7) copy of most recent annual report/audited financial statement/990
8) how project's results will be evaluated or measured
9) list of company employees involved with the organization
10) listing of board of directors, trustees, officers and other key people and their affiliations
11) detailed description of project and amount of funding requested
12) contact person
13) copy of current year's organizational budget and/or project budget
14) listing of additional sources and amount of support
15) plans for acknowledgement

Applications should include the organization's Tax ID Number. Sponsorship requests should include a description of past support by Thomson Reuters Legal with the organization, the name and date of the event, how the funds will be used, how the event will be promoted, and sponsorship levels and benefits of each.
Initial approach: Download application form and mail to headquarters

3743
Thorntons Inc.

10101 Linn Station Rd., Ste. 200
Louisville, KY 40223 (502) 425-8022

Company URL: http://www.thorntonsinc.com
Establishment information: Established in 1952.
Company type: Private company
Business activities: Operates convenience stores; operates gasoline service stations.
Business type (SIC): Groceries—retail; gasoline service stations
Financial profile for 2010: Number of employees, 2,500; sales volume, $1,400,000,000
Corporate officers: Matthew A. Thornton, Pres. and C.E.O.; Tony Harris, C.O.O.; Christopher Kamer, C.F.O.; Pat Thomasson, C.I.O.; David Bridgers, V.P. and Genl. Counsel; Mike Woerner, V.P., Human Resources; John Zikias, V.P., Mktg.
Giving statement: Giving through the Thorntons Inc. Corporate Giving Program and the Thornton's Foundation, Inc.

Thorntons Inc. Corporate Giving Program

c/o Sponsorships & Donations
10101 Linn Station Rd., Ste. 200
Louisville, KY 40233-3819 (502) 339-8385
FAX: (502) 327-7297;
E-mail: givingback@thorntonsinc.com; URL: http://www.thorntonsinc.com/Giving-Back.html

Purpose and activities: As a complement to its foundation, Thorntons makes charitable contributions to nonprofit organizations directly. Support is given primarily in areas of company operations; giving also to national organizations.
Fields of interest: Breast cancer research Children; Youth.
Type of support: General/operating support; Sponsorships; Technical assistance.
Geographic limitations: Giving primarily in areas of company operations in IL, IN, KY, OH, and TN.
Publications: Application guidelines.
Application information: Applications accepted. Application form required. Applicants should submit the following:
1) name, address and phone number of organization
2) copy of IRS Determination Letter
3) descriptive literature about organization
4) detailed description of project and amount of funding requested
5) contact person
6) plans for acknowledgement

Application should include event details, and the items requested.
Initial approach: Download application form and mail completed form to headquarters
Final notification: 4 weeks

The Thornton's Foundation, Inc.

Thorton Park Plz.
10101 Linn Station Rd., Ste. R200
Louisville, KY 40223-3848

Establishment information: Established in 2003 in KY.
Donor: Thorntons Inc.
Financial data (yr. ended 09/30/10): Assets, $3,864 (M); gifts received, $20,000; expenditures, $25,000; qualifying distributions, $25,000; giving activities include $25,000 for 1 grant.
Purpose and activities: The foundation supports the Salvation Army.
Fields of interest: Youth development; Salvation Army.
Type of support: General/operating support; Scholarship funds.
Geographic limitations: Giving limited to KY.
Support limitations: No grants to individuals.
Application information: Applications not accepted. Unsolicited requests for funds not accepted.
Officers and Directors:* Matthew A. Thornton*, Pres.; Christopher R. Kamer*, Treas.; Brenda M. Stackhouse.
EIN: 020629729

3744
C. Thorrez Industries, Inc.

4909 W. Michigan Ave.
Jackson, MI 49201-7909 (517) 750-3160
FAX: (517) 750-1792

Company URL: http://www.thorrez.com
Establishment information: Established in 1919.
Company type: Private company

Business activities: Manufactures screw machine products.
Business type (SIC): Screw machine products
Financial profile for 2009: Number of employees, 125
Corporate officers: Albert F. Thorrez, Chair.; Camiel E. Thorrez, Pres.; Al Thorrez, C.F.O.; Michael Thorrez, V.P.; Morris C. Thorrez, Secy.
Board of director: Albert F. Thorrez, Chair.
Giving statement: Giving through the Manufacturing Academy.

The Manufacturing Academy
4909 W. Michigan Ave.
Jackson, MI 49201-7909

Establishment information: Established in 2002 in MI.
Donors: C. Thorrez Industries, Inc.; Thorrez Foundation.
Financial data (yr. ended 12/31/11): Assets, $33,073 (M); gifts received, $25,064; expenditures, $14,337; qualifying distributions, $0.
Purpose and activities: The foundation supports organizations involved with manufacturing.
Fields of interest: Youth development, business; Community/economic development.
Type of support: General/operating support; Sponsorships.
Application information: Applications not accepted. Unsolicited requests for funds not accepted.
Officers: Camiel Thorrez, Pres.; Steve Lazaroff, V.P.
Directors: Tom Bartol; Scott Brockie; Jim Carpenter; Bill Wilson.
EIN: 383103954

3745
Three Rivers Home Health Services, Inc.
205 Foster St.
P.O. Box 640
Eastman, GA 31023-6239 (478) 374-2027

Company URL: http://www.123rivers.com
Establishment information: Established in 1979.
Company type: Private company
Business activities: Provides home health care services.
Business type (SIC): Home healthcare services
Corporate officers: Kaye B. Smith, Pres.; LaMae Smith Williams, V.P. and C.F.O.
Offices: Abbeville, Cochran, Dublin, Helena, Soperton, GA
Giving statement: Giving through the James R. & Lamae S. Williams Private Foundation, Inc.

The James R. & Lamae S. Williams Private Foundation, Inc.
766 Cochran Hwy.
Eastman, GA 31023-3672

Donor: Three Rivers Home Health Services, Inc.
Financial data (yr. ended 12/31/11): Assets, $176,893 (M); expenditures, $12,950; qualifying distributions, $12,400; giving activities include $12,400 for grants.
Purpose and activities: The foundation supports organizations involved with cancer, higher education, children and youth, and Christianity.
Fields of interest: Education; Recreation; Religion.
Type of support: General/operating support; Scholarship funds.
Support limitations: No grants to individuals.
Application information: Applications not accepted. Contributes only to pre-selected organizations.
Officers and Directors:* Lamae S. Williams*, Pres.; James R. Williams*, Secy.-Treas.
EIN: 582217634

3746
Three Z Printing Co.
902 W. Main St.
Teutopolis, IL 62467-1329 (217) 857-3153

Company URL: http://www.threez.com
Establishment information: Established in 1978.
Company type: Private company
Business activities: Provides commercial offset printing services.
Business type (SIC): Printing/commercial
Financial profile for 2011: Number of employees, 420
Corporate officers: Daniel Zerrusen, Pres.; Kurt Zerrusen, Secy.; Lorraine Zerrusen, Treas.
Giving statement: Giving through the Zerrusen Family Foundation.

Zerrusen Family Foundation
902 W. Main St.
Teutopolis, IL 62467-1329

Establishment information: Established in 2003 in IL.
Donor: Three Z Printing Co.
Financial data (yr. ended 12/31/11): Assets, $8,000,920 (M); expenditures, $629,254; qualifying distributions, $622,940; giving activities include $622,940 for grants.
Purpose and activities: The foundation supports organizations involved with human services and Christianity.
Fields of interest: Human services; Christian agencies & churches.
Type of support: General/operating support.
Geographic limitations: Giving primarily in IL.
Support limitations: No grants to individuals.
Application information: Applications not accepted. Contributes only to pre-selected organizations.
Trustee: Lorraine E. Zerrusen.
EIN: 200484359
Selected grants: The following grants are a representative sample of this grantmaker's funding activity:
$150,000 to Divine Word Missionaries, Techny, IL, 2010.
$10,000 to University of Illinois Foundation, Urbana, IL, 2010.

3747
Thrivent Financial for Lutherans
(formerly Aid Association for Lutherans)
625 4th Ave. S.
Minneapolis, MN 55415-1624
(612) 340-7000

Company URL: http://www.thrivent.com
Establishment information: Established in 1902.
Company type: Fraternal benefit society
Business activities: Sells insurance; provides investment advisory services; operates commercial bank.
Business type (SIC): Insurance carriers; banks/commercial; security and commodity services
Financial profile for 2011: Number of employees, 2,926; assets, $62,759,900,000; sales volume, $7,470,500,000
Corporate officers: Kurt M. Senske, Chair.; Bradford L. Hewitt, Pres. and C.E.O.; Randall L. Boushek, Sr. V.P. and C.F.O.; Russell W. Swansen, Sr. V.P. and C.I.O.; Teresa J. Rasmussen, Sr. V.P., Genl. Counsel, and Secy.; Marie A. Uhrich, Sr. V.P., Comms.
Board of directors: Kurt M. Senske, Chair.; Addie J. Butler; Bradford L. Hewitt; Mark A. Jeske; Kirk Farney; Frederick G. Kraegel; F. Mark Kuhlmann; Richard C. Lundell; Paul W. Middeke; Frank H. Moeller; Bonnie E. Raquet; Alice M. Richter; James H. Scott; Allan R. Spies; Adrian M. Tocklin
Subsidiaries: Thrivent Financial Corp., Minneapolis, MN; Thrivent Investment Management Inc., Minneapolis, MN; Thrivent Real Estate Products Co., Minneapolis, MN; Thrivent Research Corp., Minneapolis, MN; Thrivent Securities Corp., Minneapolis, MN; Thrivent Variable Insurance Products Co., Minneapolis, MN
Giving statement: Giving through the Thrivent Financial for Lutherans Corporate Giving Program and the Thrivent Financial for Lutherans Foundation.
Company EIN: 390123480

Thrivent Financial for Lutherans Foundation
(formerly Lutheran Brotherhood Foundation)
4321 N. Ballard Rd.
Appleton, WI 54919-0001 (800) 236-3736
FAX: (920) 628-5448;
E-mail: foundation@thrivent.com; E-mail for Corporate Communities: CommunityGrants@thrivent.com; URL: https://www.thrivent.com/foundations/tflfoundation/index.html

Establishment information: Established in 1982 in MN.
Donors: Lutheran Brotherhood; Lutheran Brotherhood Research Corp.; Aid Association for Lutherans; Thrivent Financial for Lutherans.
Financial data (yr. ended 12/31/11): Assets, $85,554,945 (M); gifts received, $9,913,784; expenditures, $15,298,411; qualifying distributions, $15,167,647; giving activities include $15,148,544 for grants.
Purpose and activities: The foundation supports organizations involved with education, health, employment, housing, youth developing, human services, volunteerism, the Lutheran community, and economically disadvantaged people.
Fields of interest: Elementary/secondary education; Education, early childhood education; Education; Health care; Employment, services; Employment; Housing/shelter, homeless; Housing/shelter, home owners; Housing/shelter; Youth development, business; Youth development; Family services, parent education; Human services, financial counseling; Homeless, human services; Human services; Religion, management/technical assistance; Religion, fund raising/fund distribution; Protestant agencies & churches Economically disadvantaged.
Programs:
Corporate Communities - Early Childhood Education: The foundation supports programs designed to provide basic skills and learning preparation to achieve long-term success and a productive workforce. Special emphasis is directed toward early childhood education organizations and programs that adequately prepare preschoolers for kindergarten; organizations that ensure affordable, quality childcare is available to all, particularly the working poor; and programs that equip parents with

information on school readiness and early childhood development parenting skills. Support is limited to the Twin Cities, Minnesota, and the Fox Cities, Wisconsin.

Corporate Communities - Ending Homelessness: The foundation supports programs designed to help resolve physical, economic, and social needs; and ensure safe and stable places to live. Special emphasis is directed toward affordable long-term housing for those of low and moderate incomes aimed at self-sufficiency; transitional housing and related holistic/supportive services for homeless and precariously housed individuals and families, aimed at self-sufficiency; and work readiness and job support. Support is limited to the Twin Cities, Minnesota, and the Fox Cities, Wisconsin.

Corporate Communities - Financial Wellness: The foundation supports programs designed to help people make informed financial decisions. Special emphasis is directed toward personal financial education to encourage home ownership, informed investing, and educated financial choices; youth education that teaches responsible money management skills during the K-12 years; and affordable financial services as an alternative to predatory financial programs. Support is limited to the Twin Cities, Minnesota, and the Fox Cities, Wisconsin.

Employee Giving Campaign Matching Grants: The foundation matches contributions made by employees of Thrivent Financial to the United Way and the Lutheran Community Foundation during the company's annual employee giving campaign.

Lutheran Grant Program: The foundation supports programs designed to improve the health and vitality of the Lutheran communities; and promote economic security and sustainability.

Thrivent Gift Multiplier Program: The foundation matches contributions made by employees, field members, and retirees of Thrivent Financial to nonprofit organizations on a one-for-one basis from $25 to $10,000 per contributor, per year. The foundation provides a double match to contributions made by directors of Thrivent Financial to nonprofit organizations up to $20,000 per contributor, per year.

Type of support: Conferences/seminars; Curriculum development; Employee matching gifts; Employee volunteer services; General/operating support; Management development/capacity building; Matching/challenge support; Program development; Research; Seed money.

Geographic limitations: Giving on a national basis to Lutheran communities for the Lutheran Grant Program; giving limited to the Twin Cities, MN, including Minneapolis and St. Paul, and the Fox Cities, WI for Corporate Communities Grants.

Support limitations: No support for national or international organizations or churches or church organizations for expenses normally regarded as church responsibility for Corporate Communities Grants. No grants to individuals, or for political activities or causes, debt reduction, capital costs involving the purchase of major equipment including technological equipment such as computers or associated software, furnishings, vehicles, facility construction or renovation, consultation services (except for feasibility studies), or publications; no grants for services duplicated by other organizations, religious causes, or endowments for Corporate Communities Grants; no loans or investments for Corporate Communities Grants.

Publications: Application guidelines; Informational brochure (including application guidelines).

Application information: Applications accepted. Funding preference is given to Challenge Grant requests. Organizations receiving support are asked to submit a final report. Application form required.

Applicants should submit the following:

1) timetable for implementation and evaluation of project
2) how project will be sustained once grantmaker support is completed
3) results expected from proposed grant
4) qualifications of key personnel
5) statement of problem project will address
6) copy of IRS Determination Letter
7) brief history of organization and description of its mission
8) copy of most recent annual report/audited financial statement/990
9) how project's results will be evaluated or measured
10) list of company employees involved with the organization
11) explanation of why grantmaker is considered an appropriate donor for project
12) listing of board of directors, trustees, officers and other key people and their affiliations
13) detailed description of project and amount of funding requested
14) copy of current year's organizational budget and/or project budget
15) listing of additional sources and amount of support
16) plans for acknowledgement

Initial approach: Download application form and e-mail to foundation for Lutheran Grant Program requests under $25,000; e-mail concept proposal for Lutheran Grant Program requests over $25,000; download application form and e-mail for Corporate Communities

Copies of proposal: 1

Board meeting date(s): Monthly

Deadline(s): None for Lutheran Grant Program; Feb. 1, May 1, Aug. 1, and Nov. 1 for Corporate Communities

Final notification: 8 weeks for Lutheran Grant Program requests under $25,000; 4 weeks for Lutheran Grant Program requests over $25,000

Officers and Trustees:* Marie A. Uhrich*, Chair. and Pres.; Timothy T. Schwan*, V.P.; Randall L. Boushek*, Treas.; Teresa J. Rasmussen; Anne Sample.

EIN: 411449680

Selected grants: The following grants are a representative sample of this grantmaker's funding activity:

$1,450,000 to Evangelical Lutheran Church in America, Chicago, IL, 2010. For Churchwide Grant.

$1,150,000 to Lutheran Church-Missouri Synod, Saint Louis, MO, 2010. For Churchwide Grant.

$275,000 to United Way Fox Cities, Menasha, WI, 2010. For Lutheran Community Economic Outreach Bridge Grant.

$125,000 to Family Housing Fund, Minneapolis, MN, 2010. For Family Housing Fund - Performance to Outcomes Initiative.

$123,500 to Lutheran Educational Conference of North America, Sioux Falls, SD, 2010. For Connecting Colleges and Congregational Ministry.

$100,000 to LEAVEN, Menasha, WI, 2010. For Emergency Assistance Program.

$25,000 to CommonBond Communities, Saint Paul, MN, 2010. For Family Advantage Centers.

$16,000 to Pacific Lutheran University, Tacoma, WA, 2010. For Grant Recommendation Program.

$10,000 to Cross Lutheran Church, Milwaukee, WI, 2010. For Lutheran Community Economic Outreach Bridge Grant.

$8,391 to Trinity Lutheran Church, Eau Claire, WI, 2010. For Lutheran Community Economic Outreach Bridge Grant.

3748
Tidewater Inc.

Pan American Life Ctr.
601 Poydras St., Ste. 1900
New Orleans, LA 70130 (504) 568-1010
FAX: (504) 566-4582

Company URL: http://www.tdw.com
Establishment information: Established in 1956.
Company type: Public company
Company ticker symbol and exchange: TDW/NYSE
Business activities: Provides offshore water transportation and marine support services.
Business type (SIC): Water transportation; transportation services/water
Financial profile for 2013: Number of employees, 7,900; assets, $4,168,060,000; sales volume, $1,244,160,000; pre-tax net income, $195,160,000; expenses, $1,037,930,000; liabilities, $1,606,300,000
Corporate officers: Dean E. Taylor, Chair.; Jeffrey M. Platt, Pres. and C.E.O.; Jeff A. Gorski, Exec. V.P. and C.O.O.; Quinn P. Fanning, Exec. V.P. and C.F.O.; Bruce D. Lundstrom, Exec. V.P., Genl. Counsel, and Secy.; Darren J. Vorst, V.P. and Treas.; Craig J. Demarest, V.P. and Cont.
Board of directors: Dean E. Taylor, Chair.; M. Jay Allison; James C. Day; Richard T. Du Moulin; Morris E. Foster; J. Wayne Leonard; Jon C. Madonna; Joseph H. Netherland; Richard A. Pattarozzi; Jeffrey M. Platt; Nicholas J. Sutton; Cindy B. Taylor; Jack E. Thompson
Subsidiaries: Pan-Marine International, Inc., New Orleans, LA; Pental Insurance Co., Ltd., New Orleans, LA; Point Marine, Inc., New Orleans, LA; Seafarer Boat Corp., New Orleans, LA; Tidewater Marine, Inc., Amelia, LA; Tidewater Marine International, Inc., New Orleans, LA; Tidewater Marine Service, Inc., New Orleans, LA; Tidewater Marine Western, Inc., New Orleans, LA; Tidewater Offshore Services, Inc., New Orleans, LA; Tidex Nigeria Ltd., New Orleans, LA; Twenty Grand Offshore, New Orleans, LA
International operations: Australia; Bahamas; Barbados; Bermuda; Brazil; Canada; Cayman Islands; Chile; Cyprus; England; India; Kazakhstan; Liberia; Malaysia; Mexico; Netherlands; Netherlands Antilles; Nigeria; Panama; Russia; Singapore; Turks & Caicos Islands; Vanuatu; Venezuela
Giving statement: Giving through the Tidewater Inc. Corporate Giving Program.
Company EIN: 720487776

Tidewater Inc. Corporate Giving Program

2000 W. Sam Houston Pkwy., Ste. 1218
Houston, TX 77042-3615 (713) 470-5300
URL: http://www.tdw.com/about/social-responsibility/

Purpose and activities: Tidewater makes charitable contributions to nonprofit organizations on a case by case basis. Support is given primarily in areas of company operations in California, Louisiana, and Texas.
Fields of interest: General charitable giving.
Type of support: General/operating support.
Geographic limitations: Giving primarily in areas of company operations in CA, LA, and TX; giving also to national organizations.
Application information:

3749
Tidewater Transit Company, Inc.

6174 US Hwy 70 W.
P.O. Box 189
Kinston, NC 28502 (252) 523-4103

Company URL: http://www.tidewater-transit.com/
Establishment information: Established in 1949.
Company type: Private company
Business activities: Operates dry and liquid bulk materials transportation company.
Business type (SIC): Trucking and courier services, except by air
Corporate officers: Frank Famularo, Pres.; Kim Tucker, C.F.O.; Kendra Warren, V.P., Admin.; Dave Arnold, V.P., Opers.
Giving statement: Giving through the Harvey-McNairy Foundation Inc.

The Harvey-McNairy Foundation Inc.

P.O. Box 189
Kinston, NC 28502-0189

Establishment information: Established in 2007 in NC.
Donors: Tidewater Transit Company; Harvey Enterprises Inc.; Mallard Oil Company.
Financial data (yr. ended 12/31/11): Assets, $3,360,394 (M); gifts received, $60,000; expenditures, $167,376; qualifying distributions, $141,500; giving activities include $141,500 for 19 grants (high: $51,000; low: $1,000).
Application information: Applications not accepted. Unsolicited requests for funds not accepted.
Officers: Leigh H. McNairy, Pres.; John O. McNairy, Secy.-Treas.
EIN: 208686982
Selected grants: The following grants are a representative sample of this grantmaker's funding activity:
$30,000 to Alpha USA, Bannockburn, IL, 2010.

3750
Tiffany & Co.

727 5th Ave.
New York, NY 10022 (212) 755-8000

Company URL: http://www.tiffany.com
Establishment information: Established in 1837.
Company type: Public company
Company ticker symbol and exchange: TIF/NYSE
International Securities Identification Number: US8865471085
Business activities: Operates jewelry stores.
Business type (SIC): Shopping goods stores/ miscellaneous
Financial profile for 2013: Number of employees, 9,900; assets, $4,630,850,000; sales volume, $3,794,250,000; pre-tax net income, $643,580,000; expenses, $3,097,030,000; liabilities, $2,032,120,000
Fortune 1000 ranking: 2012—611th in revenues, 385th in profits, and 616th in assets
Forbes 2000 ranking: 2012—1535th in sales, 1222nd in profits, and 1839th in assets
Corporate officers: Michael J. Kowalski, Chair. and C.E.O.; James N. Fernandez, Exec. V.P. and C.O.O.; Patrick F. McGuiness, Sr. V.P. and C.F.O.; Patrick B. Dorsey, Sr. V.P., Genl. Counsel, and Secy.; John S. Petterson, Sr. V.P., Opers.; Victoria Berger-Gross, Sr. V.P., Human Resources
Board of directors: Michael J. Kowalski, Chair.; Rose Marie Bravo; Gary E. Costley, Ph.D.; Lawrence K. Fish; Abby F. Kohnstamm; Charles K. Marquis; Peter May; William A. Shutzer; Robert S. Singer
International operations: British Virgin Islands
Giving statement: Giving through the Tiffany & Co. Corporate Giving Program and the Tiffany & Co. Foundation.
Company EIN: 133228013

Tiffany & Co. Corporate Giving Program

727 5th Ave.
New York, NY 10022 (212) 755-8000
URL: http://www.tiffany.com/csr/

Financial data (yr. ended 12/31/11): Total giving, $8,000,000, including $7,685,000 for grants and $315,000 for employee matching gifts.
Purpose and activities: As a complement to its foundation, Tiffany & Co. also makes charitable contributions to nonprofit organizations directly. Support is limited to areas of company operations.
Fields of interest: Arts; Education; Environment; Health care; Human services.
Programs:
Employee Matching Gift Program: Through the Employee Giving Program, Tiffany matches U.S. employee charitable donations at a ratio of 1:1 up to $1,000 per employee per year.
Volunteer Matching Program: Through the Volunteer Matching Program, Tiffany will donate $100 for every 10 hours volunteered at nonprofit organizations by its employees up to $1,000 per employee per year.
Type of support: Donated products; Emergency funds; Employee matching gifts; Employee volunteer services.
Geographic limitations: Giving limited to areas of company operations.

The Tiffany & Co. Foundation

200 Fifth Ave.
New York, NY 10010-3302
FAX: (212) 230-5341;
E-mail: foundation@tiffany.com; URL: http://www.tiffanyandcofoundation.org

Establishment information: Established in 2000 in NY.
Donor: Tiffany & Co.
Contact: Anisa Kamadoli Costa, Pres.
Financial data (yr. ended 01/31/11): Assets, $25,578,645 (M); gifts received, $4,000,000; expenditures, $4,412,448; qualifying distributions, $4,181,000; giving activities include $4,181,000 for 35 grants (high: $500,000; low: $10,000).
Purpose and activities: The foundation supports programs designed to protect the beauty of nature and the creativity of human nature. Special emphasis is directed toward programs designed to preserve the arts and promote environmental conservation.
Fields of interest: Arts education; Visual arts; Visual arts, design; Museums; Arts; Environment, research; Environment, natural resources; Environment, water resources; Environment, land resources; Botanical/horticulture/landscape services; Environment, beautification programs; Environment; Recreation, parks/playgrounds; Urban/community development; Geology.
Programs:
Coral Conservation: The foundation supports healthy oceans and the coral conservation in the ecosystem. Special emphasis is directed toward programs designed to promote the preservation of precious corals and healthy marine ecosystems through research and outreach.
Excellence in Design: The foundation supports programs designed to enhance the field of decorative arts through preservation and innovation, especially jewelry. Special emphasis is directed toward programs designed to promote design through scholarship and education; showcase design in the field of decorative arts; and promote excellence in design at the world's great cultural institutions.
Responsible Mining: The foundation supports programs designed to promote responsible mining of precious metals, diamonds, and gemstones and the communities with which mining occurs. Special emphasis is directed toward programs designed to promote the development of standards for responsible mining at the large-scale level; remediate areas where both small- and large-scale mining have occurred; protect places of natural and historic importance from the threat of mining; and promote economic and social development in areas where mining occurs in an effort to support and strengthen mining communities.
Urban Parks: The foundation supports programs designed to meet the needs of local communities through strategic design improvements of urban parks and gardens. Special emphasis is directed toward rehabilitation, protection, and creation of public urban green spaces and the enhancement of the visitor experience.
Type of support: Continuing support; General/ operating support; Program development; Research; Sponsorships.
Geographic limitations: Giving primarily in CA, CO, Washington, DC, MA, MT, NY, RI, VA, Mexico, and the United Kingdom.
Support limitations: No support for religious, political, social, or fraternal organizations or athletic teams. No grants to individuals, or for capital campaigns, fundraising benefits or events, or athletic events; no product donations.
Publications: Application guidelines; Program policy statement.
Application information: Applications accepted. Additional information may be requested at a later date. Application form required. Applicants should submit the following:
1) qualifications of key personnel
2) copy of IRS Determination Letter
3) brief history of organization and description of its mission
4) explanation of why grantmaker is considered an appropriate donor for project
5) detailed description of project and amount of funding requested
6) copy of current year's organizational budget and/ or project budget

Initial approach: Complete online letter of inquiry
Board meeting date(s): Twice annually
Deadline(s): Rolling
Final notification: 3 months

Officers and Directors:* Fernanda M. Kellogg*, Chair.; Anisa Kamadoli Costa, Pres.; Michael W. Connolly, Treas.; Patrick B. Dorsey; James N. Fernandez; Michael J. Kowalski; James E. Quinn.
EIN: 134096178
Selected grants: The following grants are a representative sample of this grantmaker's funding activity:
$500,000 to Trust for Public Land, San Francisco, CA, 2011. For Campaign to Save Cathuenga Park, Home of Hollywood Sign and for permanent protection of Cathuenga Park to become part of Griffin Park.
$200,000 to Environmental Defense Fund, New York, NY, 2011. For Coral Wildlife Campaign.

$200,000 to Trout Unlimited, Arlington, VA, 2011. For Abandoned Hard Rock Mine Restoration Program in the American West.
$150,000 to Wildlife Conservation Society, Bronx, NY, 2011. For continued support of Global Coral Reef Conservation Program in Coral Triangle community-based management strategic for global protection of coral and climate change adaptation strategies.
$150,000 to World Wildlife Fund, Washington, DC, 2011. For Mining and Sustainable Land use Management in and around Protected and Sensitive Ecosystems Project.
$100,000 to Alaska Conservation Foundation, Anchorage, AK, 2011. For Bristol Bay Regional Vision Project.
$75,000 to World Monuments Fund, New York, NY, 2011. For general operating support.
$50,000 to Bard College, Annandale on Hudson, NY, 2011. For publication, A History of the Decorative and Applied Arts and Design, 1400-2000 comprehensive history of decorative arts.
$40,000 to African Wildlife Foundation, Washington, DC, 2011. To design and plan phase of education center at Chobe National Park, which seek to serve meeting place for land and wildlife conservation in Africa's Kazungula Heartland.
$26,000 to Metropolitan Museum of Art, New York, NY, 2011. For Tiffany & Co Foundation Curatorial Internship in American Decorative Arts.

3751
Tikigaq Corporation
2121 Abbott Rd., Ste. 202
Anchorage, AK 99507 (907) 365-6299

Company URL: http://www.tikigaq.com
Establishment information: Established in 1971.
Company type: Native corporation
Business activities: Operates construction and logistics services company.
Business type (SIC): Management and public relations services
Corporate officers: Sayers Tuzroyluk, Sr., Chair.; Kinneeveauk Herbert, Jr., Pres. and C.E.O.; Troy Izatt, C.O.O.; Janelle Cobb, C.F.O.; Daisy Sage, Secy.; Violet Attungana, Treas.
Board of directors: Sayers Tuzroyluk, Sr., Chair.; Violet Attungana; Herbert Kinneeveauk, Jr.; Clark Lane, Sr.; Masuk M. Lane; Martin Oktollik; Alzred Oomittuk; Daisy Sage
Giving statement: Giving through the Tigara Educational Foundation Inc.

Tigara Educational Foundation Inc.
P.O. Box 9
Point Hope, AK 99766-0009 (907) 368-2235

Establishment information: Established in 2000 in AK.
Donors: Tikigaq Corporation; Arctic Slope Regional Corporation; Skew Eskimos Inc.
Financial data (yr. ended 06/30/12): Assets, $29,242 (M); gifts received, $4,669; expenditures, $29,060; qualifying distributions, $19,689; giving activities include $19,689 for 38 grants to individuals (high: $1,389; low: $500).
Purpose and activities: Scholarship awards to natives of the Point Hope, Alaska, region and their descendants who maintain a 2.0 GPA to promote education, pride and to preserve the Inupiat culture.
Type of support: Scholarships—to individuals.
Geographic limitations: Giving limited to AK, primarily in the Point Hope region.
Application information: Applications accepted. Application form required.
Initial approach: Letter
Deadline(s): None
Officers: George Kingik, Pres.; Jack Schaefer, V.P.; Sayers Tuzroyluk, Secy.; Violet Attungana, Treas.
EIN: 920158717

3752
The Tillman Company, Inc.
160 W. Clayton St.
Athens, GA 30601-2710 (706) 548-5201

Establishment information: Established in 1920.
Company type: Private company
Business activities: Develops real estate.
Business type (SIC): Real estate subdividers and developers
Corporate officer: Thomas Tillman, Jr., C.E.O.
Giving statement: Giving through the Thomas McKey Tillman Foundation, Inc.

Thomas McKey Tillman Foundation, Inc.
P.O. Box 1308
Athens, GA 30603

Donor: The Tillman Co., Inc.
Financial data (yr. ended 05/31/12): Assets, $478,114 (M); expenditures, $21,826; qualifying distributions, $20,300; giving activities include $20,000 for 9 grants (high: $10,000; low: $500).
Purpose and activities: The foundation supports cemeteries and orchestras and organizations involved with K-12 education, health, and Christianity.
Fields of interest: Performing arts, orchestras; Elementary/secondary education; Health care, clinics/centers; Health care; YM/YWCAs & YM/YWHAs; Christian agencies & churches; Cemeteries/burial services, cemetery company.
Type of support: Capital campaigns; General/operating support; Program development; Scholarship funds.
Geographic limitations: Giving limited to Athens, GA.
Support limitations: No grants to individuals.
Application information: Applications not accepted. Unsolicited requests for funds not accepted.
Trustees: Louise T. Adams; Marie T. Eisenberg; Joseph E. Tillman.
EIN: 586055331

3753
Tim Hortons Inc.
4150 Tuller Rd., Unit 236
Dublin, OH 43017 (614) 791-4200

Company URL: http://www.timhortons.com
Establishment information: Established in 1964.
Company type: Subsidiary of a foreign company
Business activities: Operates chain of coffee and donut shops.
Business type (SIC): Restaurants and drinking places
Financial profile for 2012: Assets, $2,300,000,000; sales volume, $3,100,000,000
Forbes 2000 ranking: 2012—1603rd in sales, 1195th in profits, and 1968th in assets
Corporate officers: Paul D. House, Chair., Pres. and C.E.O.; David F. Clanachan, C.O.O.; Cynthia J. Devine, C.F.O.; R. Scott Toop, Exec. V.P., Genl. Counsel and Corp. Secy.; Brigid V. Pelino, Exec. V.P., Human Resources
Board of directors: Paul D. House, Chair.; Frank Iacobucci; Donald B. Schroeder
Offices: Brighton, MI; West Greenwich, RI
Giving statement: Giving through the Tim Hortons Inc., Corporate Giving Program.

Tim Hortons Inc., Corporate Giving Program
4150 Tuller Rd.
Dublin, OH 43017 (614) 791-4200
URL: http://www.timhortons.com/us/en/difference/donation.html

Purpose and activities: Tim Hortons makes charitable donations to nonprofit organizations in areas of company operations. Special emphasis is directed toward programs that serve children, including local sports teams and leagues, and community festivals.
Fields of interest: Recreation, fairs/festivals; Athletics/sports, amateur leagues Children.
Type of support: Donated products; In-kind gifts; Sponsorships.
Geographic limitations: Giving primarily in areas of company operations in CT, KY, ME, MA, MI, NY, OH, PA, RI, and WV.
Support limitations: No support for political or religious organizations, or traveling sports teams. No grants to individuals, or for book endorsements.
Publications: Application guidelines.
Application information: Applications accepted. Proposals should be limited to 2 MB. Application form required. Applicants should submit the following:
1) name, address and phone number of organization
2) copy of IRS Determination Letter
3) brief history of organization and description of its mission
4) geographic area to be served
5) detailed description of project and amount of funding requested
6) contact person

Applications should include a sponsorship proposal, list of affiliations, event date, description of what the funds raised will be used for, expected attendance of the event, if applicable, and the type of donation being requested.
Initial approach: Complete online application
Deadline(s): 12 weeks prior to event for sponsorships

3754
The Timberland Company
200 Domain Dr.
Stratham, NH 03885-2575 (603) 772-9500

Company URL: http://www.timberland.com
Establishment information: Established in 1952.
Company type: Private company
Business activities: Designs, develops, engineers, manufactures, markets, and sells footwear, apparel, and accessories.
Business type (SIC): Leather footwear; apparel and other finished products made from fabrics and similar materials
Financial profile for 2011: Number of employees, 5,789
Corporate officers: Sidney W. Swartz, Chair.; Jeffrey B. Swartz, Pres. and C.E.O.; Carden N. Welsh, Sr. V.P. and C.A.O.; Carrie W. Teffner, V.P. and C.F.O.; John J. Fitzgerald, Jr., V.P., Corp. Cont., and C.A.O.; Danette Wineberg, V.P., Genl. Counsel, and Secy.
Board of director: Sidney W. Swartz, Chair.

Subsidiaries: The Outdoor Footwear Co., Isabela, PR; SmartWool Corporation, Steamboat Springs, CO; Timberland Aviation, Inc., Londonderry, NH; Timberland Direct Sales, Inc., Stratham, NH; Timberland Europe, Inc., Stratham, NH; Timberland International Sales Corp., Stratham, NH; Timberland Manufacturing Co., Stratham, NH; Timberland Netherlands, Inc., Stratham, NH; The Timberland World Trading Co., Stratham, NH
International operations: Dominican Republic; France; Germany; Hong Kong; Netherlands; Singapore; Spain; United Kingdom
Giving statement: Giving through the Timberland Company Contributions Program.
Company EIN: 020312554

The Timberland Company Contributions Program

200 Domain Dr.
Stratham, NH 03885-2575 (603) 772-9500
E-mail: csrinfo@timberland.com; URL: http://responsibility.timberland.com/

Financial data (yr. ended 12/31/11): Total giving, $1,749,238, including $739,692 for grants and $1,009,546 for in-kind gifts.
Purpose and activities: Timberland makes charitable contributions to nonprofit organizations involved with recreation, camps, and festivals, the environment, disabilities, community development, housing, safety and disasters, and food services. Support is given primarily in areas of company operations, and on a national and international basis.
Fields of interest: Environment, natural resources; Environment; Food services; Housing/shelter, volunteer services; Safety/disasters; Recreation, camps; Recreation, fairs/festivals; Family resources and services, disability; Community/economic development.
Type of support: Annual campaigns; Building/renovation; Donated products; Employee volunteer services; General/operating support.
Geographic limitations: Giving primarily in areas of company operations, and on a national and international basis.
Support limitations: No support for fraternal, veterans', labor, or political organizations, sectarian or religious organizations not of direct benefit to the entire community, sports teams, or discriminatory organizations.
Application information:
Initial approach: E-mail inquiry to learn more about the donations program

3755
Time Warner Cable Inc.

60 Columbus Cir.
New York, NY 10023 (212) 364-8200
FAX: (302) 655-5049

Company URL: http://www.timewarnercable.com
Establishment information: Established in 1989.
Company type: Public company
Company ticker symbol and exchange: TWC/NYSE
International Securities Identification Number: US8873173038
Business activities: Operates national cable television company.
Business type (SIC): Cable and other pay television services
Financial profile for 2012: Number of employees, 510,000; assets, $49,809,000,000; sales volume, $21,386,000,000; pre-tax net income, $2,683,000,000; expenses, $17,594,000,000; liabilities, $42,530,000,000
Fortune 1000 ranking: 2012—134th in revenues, 91st in profits, and 111th in assets
Forbes 2000 ranking: 2012—439th in sales, 270th in profits, and 462nd in assets
Corporate officers: Glenn A. Britt, Chair. and C.E.O.; Robert D. Marcus, Pres. and C.O.O.; Arthur T. Minson, Jr., Exec. V.P. and C.F.O.; Marc Lawrence-Apfelbaum, Exec. V.P., Genl. Counsel, and Secy.
Board of directors: Glenn A. Britt, Chair.; Carole Black; Thomas H. Castro; David C. Chang, Ph.D.; James E. Copeland, Jr.; Peter R. Haje; Donna A. James; Don Logan; N.J. Nicholas, Jr.; Wayne H. Pace; Edward D. Shirley; John E. Sununu
Giving statement: Giving through the Time Warner Cable Inc. Corporate Giving Program.
Company EIN: 841496755

Time Warner Cable Inc. Corporate Giving Program

60 Columbus Cir.
New York, NY 10019 (212) 364-8200
URL: http://www.timewarnercable.com/Corporate/about/community/default.html
Additional URL: http://www.connectamillionminds.com/

Purpose and activities: Time Warner Cable supports nonprofit organizations involved with education. Special emphasis is directed toward programs that inspire young people to build the skills they need - science, technology, engineering, and math - to become the problem solvers of tomorrow. Support is limited to areas of company operations.
Fields of interest: Elementary/secondary education; Education; Environment; Mathematics; Science.
Program:
Connect a Million Minds (CAMM): Through the Connect a Million Minds (CAMM) program, Time Warner Cable introduces youth to opportunities and resources that inspire them to develop the important science, technology, engineering and math skills they need to solve the economic, environmental and community challenges of the future.
Type of support: Curriculum development; Donated products; Employee volunteer services; General/operating support; In-kind gifts; Program development.
Geographic limitations: Giving limited to areas of company operations in CA, HI, IN, KY, ME, MO, NC, NE, NH, NJ, NY, OH, SC, TX, and WI.
Support limitations: No support for political, fraternal, or discriminatory organizations, or religious organizations not of direct benefit to the entire community, or social clubs, or private foundations. No grants to individuals, or for capital campaigns.
Publications: Application guidelines.
Application information: Applications accepted. Application form required.
Initial approach: Complete online application
Deadline(s): Rolling

3756
Time Warner Entertainment Company, L.P.

(doing business as Oceanic Time Warner Cable)
200 Akamainui St.
Mililani, HI 96789-3912 (808) 625-2100

Company URL: http://www.oceanic.com/about_us
Company type: Subsidiary of a public company
Ultimate parent company: Time Warner Inc.
Business activities: Provides cable television services; provides data telephone communications services; produces motion pictures and television programs; broadcasts television.
Business type (SIC): Motion pictures/production and services allied to; telephone communications; radio and television broadcasting; cable and other pay television services
Corporate officers: Glenn A. Britt, Chair. and C.E.O.; Nate Smith, Pres.
Board of director: Glenn A. Britt, Chair.
Division: Oceanic Time Warner Cable, Mililani, HI
Giving statement: Giving through the Oceanic Time Warner Cable Corporate Giving Program.

Oceanic Time Warner Cable Corporate Giving Program

200 Akamainui St.
Mililani, HI 96789-3912
URL: http://www.timewarner.com/corp/citizenship/community/index.html

Purpose and activities: Oceanic Time Warner Cable makes charitable contributions to nonprofit organizations involved with K-12 education, and on a case by case basis. Support is given primarily in areas of company operations in Hawaii.
Fields of interest: Education, public education; Elementary/secondary education; General charitable giving.
Type of support: Employee volunteer services; In-kind gifts.
Geographic limitations: Giving primarily in areas of company operations in HI.

3757
Time Warner Inc.

(formerly AOL Time Warner Inc.)
1 Time Warner Ctr.
New York, NY 10019 (212) 484-8000
FAX: (302) 655-5049

Company URL: http://www.timewarner.com
Establishment information: Established in 1985.
Company type: Public company
Company ticker symbol and exchange: TWX/NYSE
Business activities: Provides Internet information services; provides cable television services; produces motion pictures; broadcasts television; operates record label; publishes magazines and books.
Business type (SIC): Computer services; periodical publishing and/or printing; book publishing and/or printing; audio and video equipment/household; radio and television broadcasting; cable and other pay television services; motion pictures/production and services allied to
Financial profile for 2012: Number of employees, 34,000; assets, $68,304,000,000; sales volume, $28,729,000,000; pre-tax net income, $4,542,000,000; expenses, $22,811,000,000; liabilities, $38,427,000,000

Fortune 1000 ranking: 2012—105th in revenues, 61st in profits, and 84th in assets
Forbes 2000 ranking: 2012—329th in sales, 185th in profits, and 350th in assets
Corporate officers: Jeffrey L. Bewkes, Chair. and C.E.O.; Paul T. Cappuccio, Exec. V.P. and Genl. Counsel; Gary L. Ginsberg, Exec. V.P., Corp. Mktg. and Comms.; John K. Martin, Jr., C.F.O. and C.A.O.
Board of directors: Jeffrey L. Bewkes, Chair.; James L. Barksdale; William P. Barr; Stephen F. Bollenbach; Robert C. Clark; Mathias Dopfner; Jessica P. Einhorn; Fred Hassan; Kenneth J. Novack; Paul D. Wachter; Deborah C. Wright
Subsidiaries: Atlanta National League Baseball Club, Inc., Atlanta, GA; Historic TW Inc., New York, NY; Time Warner Entertainment Company, L.P., Mililani, HI; Turner Broadcasting System, Inc., Atlanta, GA
Giving statement: Giving through the Time Warner Inc. Corporate Giving Program and the Time Warner Foundation, Inc.
Company EIN: 134099534

Time Warner Inc. Corporate Giving Program

(formerly AOL Time Warner Inc. Corporate Giving Program)
1 Time Warner Ctr.
New York, NY 10019-6038 (212) 484-8000
FAX: (212) 489-6183; URL: http://www.timewarner.com/our-company/corporate-responsibility/in-the-community/

Contact: Lisa Quiroz, Sr. V.P., Corp. Responsibility
Purpose and activities: As a complement to its foundation, Time Warner also makes charitable contributions to nonprofit organizations directly. Support is given primarily in the New York, New York, area.
Fields of interest: Arts education; Media/communications; Media, film/video; Media, television; Performing arts, theater; Arts; Elementary/secondary education; Education; Youth development.
Type of support: Employee matching gifts; Employee volunteer services; General/operating support; Program development; Scholarship funds.
Geographic limitations: Giving primarily in the New York, NY, area.
Support limitations: No support for religious organizations, political organizations, or government-supported organizations.
Application information: Applications not accepted. The company utilizes an invitation only Request For Proposal (RFP) process. Unsolicited requests are not accepted.

Time Warner Foundation, Inc.

(formerly AOL Time Warner Foundation)
1 Time Warner Ctr.
New York, NY 10019-6038
E-mail: corporate.responsibility@timewarner.com; URL: http://www.timewarner.com/our-company/corporate-responsibility/investing-in-our-communities/community-investments/

Establishment information: Established in 1997 in VA.
Donors: America Online, Inc.; AOL Time Warner Inc.; Time Warner Inc.
Contact: Lisa Quiroz, Pres.
Financial data (yr. ended 12/31/11): Assets, $10,634,325 (M); expenditures, $4,264,300; qualifying distributions, $4,264,300; giving activities include $4,260,000 for 15 grants (high: $1,000,000; low: $10,000).
Purpose and activities: The foundation supports programs designed to create, develop, and produce work that reflects the voices and experiences of the world, which is critical to sustaining a culturally rich, vibrant and informed community; and promote college access and college advocacy.
Fields of interest: Media/communications; Media, film/video; Media, television; Media, journalism; Museums; Higher education; Education; Disasters, 9/11/01.
Type of support: Building/renovation; General/operating support; Program development.
Geographic limitations: Giving primarily in Washington, DC and New York, NY.
Support limitations: No support for political, labor, religious, or fraternal organizations or amateur or professional sports groups. No grants to individuals, or for book publication, or film or music production.
Application information: Applications not accepted. Contributes only to pre-selected organizations.
Officers and Directors:* Lisa Quiroz*, Pres.; Brenda C. Karickhoff, V.P. and Secy.; Daniel J. Osheyack, V.P.; Rosa Olivares, Treas.; Pascal Desroches, C.F.O.; Philip Sanchez, Assoc. Dir.; Molly Battin; Peter Castro; Teri Everett; Sue Fleishman; Gary L. Ginsberg; Lisa Gregorian; Karen Magee; Henry McGee; Quentin Shaffer; Misty Skedgell.
EIN: 541886827

3758
Times Publishing Company

(doing business as Erie Times News)
490 1st Ave. S.
St. Petersburg, FL 33701 (727) 893-8111

Company URL: http://www.tampabay.com
Establishment information: Established in 1888.
Company type: Private company
Business activities: Publishes newspaper.
Business type (SIC): Newspaper publishing and/or printing
Financial profile for 2010: Number of employees, 3,600
Corporate officers: Paul C. Tash, Chair. and C.E.O.; Jana L. Jones, C.F.O.
Board of director: Paul C. Tash, Chair.
Giving statement: Giving through the Erie Times Needy Fund of the Times Publishing Company.

Erie Times Needy Fund of the Times Publishing Company

205 W. 12th St.
Erie, PA 16534-0001 (814) 870-1765

Financial data (yr. ended 12/31/11): Revenue, $93,619; assets, $130,344 (M); gifts received, $91,357; expenditures, $88,585; giving activities include $86,365 for grants.
Fields of interest: Community/economic development.
Type of support: Grants to individuals.
Officer and Board Members:* James Englert, Pres.; Mike Borzon, V.P.; Tom Chido, Past Pres.; Holly Baldauf, Secy.; William McCall, Treas.; John Kossibel; Michael Mead; Edward Mead; David Stolar; Donald Young.
EIN: 256070411

3759
Times-Journal, Inc.

(also known as Marietta Daily Journal)
580 S. Fairground St., S.E.
P.O. Box 449
Marietta, GA 30060 (770) 428-9411

Company URL: http://www.mdjonline.com
Establishment information: Established in 1866.
Company type: Private company
Business activities: Publishes newspaper.
Business type (SIC): Newspaper publishing and/or printing
Corporate officers: Hap Smith, Chair.; Otis A. Brumby, Jr., C.E.O.; Terry Smith, Pres.; Wade Stephens, V.P., Sales and Mktg.
Board of director: Hap Smith, Chair.
Giving statement: Giving through the Marietta Daily Journal Community Foundation.

Marietta Daily Journal Community Foundation

580 Fairground St.
Marietta, GA 30060-1575
Application address: P.O. Box 449, Marietta, GA 30061, tel.: (770) 428-9411

Establishment information: Established in GA.
Donor: Times-Journal, Inc.
Contact: Otis A. Brumby, Jr., C.E.O.
Financial data (yr. ended 12/31/11): Assets, $503,512 (M); expenditures, $29,282; qualifying distributions, $27,600; giving activities include $27,600 for grants.
Purpose and activities: The foundation supports orchestras and organizations involved with higher education.
Fields of interest: Arts; Health organizations; Civil/human rights.
Type of support: General/operating support.
Geographic limitations: Giving primarily in GA.
Application information: Applications accepted. Application form required. Applicants should submit the following:
1) detailed description of project and amount of funding requested
2) copy of current year's organizational budget and/or project budget
Initial approach: Letter
Deadline(s): None
Officer and Trustees:* Otis A. Brumby*, C.E.O.; F. T. Davis; Spain Brumby Gregory.
EIN: 030532316

3760
The Timken Company

1835 Dueber Ave., S.W.
Canton, OH 44706-0932 (330) 438-3000
FAX: (330) 458-6006

Company URL: http://www.timken.com
Establishment information: Established in 1899.
Company type: Public company
Company ticker symbol and exchange: TKR/NYSE
Business activities: Manufactures tapered roll bearings and specialty alloy steel.
Business type (SIC): Machinery/general industry; steel mill products
Financial profile for 2012: Number of employees, 20,000; assets, $4,244,700,000; sales volume, $4,987,000,000; pre-tax net income, $766,000,000; expenses, $4,186,100,000; liabilities, $2,012,500,000

Fortune 1000 ranking: 2012—493rd in revenues, 337th in profits, and 642nd in assets
Corporate officers: Ward J. Timken, Jr., Chair.; James W. Griffith, Pres. and C.E.O.; Glenn A. Eisenberg, Exec. V.P., Finance and Admin.; Daniel E. Muller, Sr. V.P. and C.I.O.; John Theodore Mihaila, Sr. V.P. and Cont.; William R. Burkhart, Sr. V.P. and Genl. Counsel; Donald L. Walker, Sr. V.P., Human Resources; Scott A. Scherff, V.P. and Corp. Secy.; Kari Groh, V.P., Comms.
Board of directors: Ward J. Timken, Jr., Chair.; John M. Ballbach; Phillip R. Cox; Diane C. Creel; James W. Griffith; John A. Luke, Jr.; Joseph W. Ralston; John P. Reilly; Frank C. Sullivan; John M. Timken, Jr.; Ward J. Timken; Jacqueline F. Woods
Subsidiaries: Latrobe Steel Co., Latrobe, PA; MPB Corporation, Keene, NH; MPB Export Corp., Keene, NH
Plants: North Little Rock, AR; Carlyle, IL; Lenexa, KS; Lebanon, NH; Asheboro, Columbus, Lincolnton, NC; Ashland, Bucyrus, Columbus, Eaton, New Philadelphia, St. Clair, Wooster, OH; Franklin, PA; Gaffney, SC; Knoxville, TN; Ogden, UT; Altavista, Richmond, VA
International operations: Australia; Brazil; Canada; Cayman Islands; China; Czech Republic; England; France; Germany; Hong Kong; India; Italy; Japan; Luxembourg; Mexico; Netherlands; North Korea; Poland; Russia; Singapore; South Africa; Spain; Sweden; Venezuela
Giving statement: Giving through the Timken Company Charitable and Educational Fund, Inc. and the Timken Company Charitable Trust.
Company EIN: 340577130

The Timken Company Charitable and Educational Fund, Inc.

(formerly The Timken Company Educational Fund, Inc.)
1835 Dueber Ave. S.W.
Canton, OH 44706-2728
URL: http://www.timken.com/EN-US/ABOUT/CITIZENSHIP/SCHOLARSHIP/Pages/Scholarship.aspx

Establishment information: Established in 1957.
Donor: The Timken Co.
Financial data (yr. ended 12/31/11): Assets, $2,494,524 (M); expenditures, $1,077,323; qualifying distributions, $1,076,711; giving activities include $951,978 for grants.
Purpose and activities: The foundation awards college scholarships to children of associates and retirees of the Timken Company, its subsidiaries, and joint ventures.
Fields of interest: Higher education.
International interests: Asia; Brazil; China; Eastern & Central Europe; India; Latin America; Poland; Romania; South Africa.
Type of support: Employee-related scholarships.
Geographic limitations: Giving primarily in areas of company operations, with emphasis on Brazil, China, Poland, and Romania.
Application information: Applications not accepted. Contributes only through employee-related scholarships.
Board meeting date(s): Quarterly
Officers and Trustees:* G. A. Eisenberg*, Exec. V.P.; Donald L. Walker*, Sr. V.P.; K. L. Groh*, V.P., Comms.
EIN: 346520257

The Timken Company Charitable Trust

1835 Dueber Ave., S.W.
P.O. Box 6927
Canton, OH 44706-2728 (330) 471-3071
FAX: (330) 471-4381;
E-mail: timken.trust@timken.com; URL: http://www.timken.com/en-us/about/citizenship/CharitableTrust/Pages/default.aspx

Establishment information: Trust established in 1947 in OH.
Donor: The Timken Co.
Contact: Kathy Schooley, Admin.
Financial data (yr. ended 12/31/10): Assets, $2,719,763 (M); expenditures, $950,285; qualifying distributions, $943,375; giving activities include $931,450 for 103 grants (high: $255,000; low: $250).
Purpose and activities: The foundation supports organizations involved with arts and culture, education, and community and economic development and programs designed to improve quality of life in communities where Timken associates live and work.
Fields of interest: Performing arts; Arts; Higher education; Libraries (public); Education; Housing/shelter, development; Youth development, business; Salvation Army; Community/economic development; United Ways and Federated Giving Programs.
Type of support: Building/renovation; General/operating support; Income development.
Geographic limitations: Giving primarily in areas of company operations, with some emphasis on GA, IL, NC, NH, OH, SC, and VA.
Support limitations: No grants to individuals, or for health-related research, capital projects, or national programs.
Publications: Application guidelines; Corporate report.
Application information: Applications accepted. Application form required. Applicants should submit the following:
1) name, address and phone number of organization
2) copy of IRS Determination Letter
3) brief history of organization and description of its mission
4) copy of most recent annual report/audited financial statement/990
5) how project's results will be evaluated or measured
6) list of company employees involved with the organization
7) listing of board of directors, trustees, officers and other key people and their affiliations
8) detailed description of project and amount of funding requested
9) contact person
10) copy of current year's organizational budget and/or project budget
Initial approach: Complete online application form
Deadline(s): Sept. 1; 60 days prior to need for fundraising events
Officers and Advisors:* Ward J. Timken, Jr., Pres.; Elizabeth Engels, V.P.; Robert J. Lapp, Secy.; Philip D. Fracassa, Treas.; William R. Burkhart; Glenn A. Eisenberg; Kari L. Groh; Ronald J. Myers; Donald L. Walker*.
Number of staff: 3 full-time professional; 3 full-time support.
EIN: 346534265
Selected grants: The following grants are a representative sample of this grantmaker's funding activity:
$255,000 to United Way of Greater Stark County, Canton, OH, 2010. For general operations.
$150,000 to Arts in Stark, Canton, OH, 2010. For general operations.
$75,000 to Ohio Foundation of Independent Colleges, Columbus, OH, 2010. For general operations.
$30,500 to United Way of the Piedmont, Spartanburg, SC, 2010. For general operations.
$27,500 to Walsh University, North Canton, OH, 2010. For general operations.
$18,000 to United Way, Bucyrus Area, Bucyrus, OH, 2010. For general operations.
$12,000 to United Way, Monadnock, Keene, NH, 2010. For general operations.
$5,000 to Bucyrus Area Community Foundation, Bucyrus, OH, 2010. For general operations.
$2,500 to Union County Historical Society, Union, SC, 2010. For general operations.
$1,000 to City Center Ballet, Lebanon, NH, 2010. For general operations.

3761
Tindall Corporation

(formerly Tindall Concrete Pipe Company)
3076 N Blackstock Rd.
Spartanburg, SC 29301-5566
(864) 576-3230

Company URL: http://www.tindallcorp.com
Establishment information: Established in 1963.
Company type: Private company
Business activities: Manufactures structural precast concrete products.
Business type (SIC): Concrete, gypsum, and plaster products
Corporate officers: William Lowndes III, Chair. and C.E.O.; William Lowndes IV, Vice-Chair.; Gregory F. Force, Pres. and C.O.O.; Cheryl O. Lang, C.P.A., V.P. and C.F.O.; David Britt, V.P., Sales; Donnie Brown, V.P., Human Resources; Clancy Fretwell, C.P.A., Cont.
Board of directors: William Lowndes III, Chair.; William Lowndes IV, Vice-Chair.
Giving statement: Giving through the Lowndes Foundation, Inc.

The Lowndes Foundation, Inc.

c/o Atlantic Trust Co., N.A.
100 Federal St., 37th Fl.
Boston, MA 02110-1802

Establishment information: Established in 1997.
Donors: William Lowndes III; Tindall Corp.; Lowndes III Trust.
Financial data (yr. ended 12/31/11): Assets, $13,391,547 (M); gifts received, $109,457; expenditures, $819,897; qualifying distributions, $643,004; giving activities include $643,004 for grants.
Purpose and activities: The foundation supports organizations involved with education, civil liberties, economic development, public policy, and government and public administration.
Fields of interest: Higher education; Education; Civil liberties, advocacy; Economic development; Public policy, research; Government/public administration.
Type of support: General/operating support.
Geographic limitations: Giving primarily in Washington, DC, Hillside, MI, Irvington-on-Hudson, NY, and Spartanburg, SC.
Support limitations: No grants to individuals.
Application information: Applications not accepted. Contributes only to pre-selected organizations.
Officers and Trustee:* William Lowndes III, Pres. and Treas.; Henrietta M. Lowndes*, Secy.
EIN: 571027898

Selected grants: The following grants are a representative sample of this grantmaker's funding activity:
$70,000 to Cato Institute, Washington, DC, 2011.
$50,000 to Atlas Economic Research Foundation, Washington, DC, 2011. For general charitable purposes.
$25,000 to Hillsdale College, Hillsdale, MI, 2011.
$25,000 to Independent Institute, Oakland, CA, 2011. For general charitable purposes.
$20,000 to Ludwig von Mises Institute for Austrian Economics, Auburn, AL, 2011.
$20,000 to Mercatus Center, Arlington, VA, 2011. For general charitable purposes.
$20,000 to State Policy Network, Arlington, VA, 2011. For general charitable purposes.
$15,000 to Foundation for Research on Economics and the Environment, Bozeman, MT, 2011. For general charitable purposes.
$15,000 to Institute for Justice, Arlington, VA, 2011.
$12,000 to Heritage Foundation, Washington, DC, 2011.

3762
Tireco, Inc.

500 W. 190th St., Ste. 600, 6th Fl.
Gardena, CA 90248-4265 (310) 767-7990

Company URL: http://www.tireco.com
Establishment information: Established in 1976.
Company type: Private company
Business activities: Operates tire distribution company.
Business type (SIC): Motor vehicles, parts, and supplies—wholesale
Corporate officers: Robert Liu, Chair.; Charlie Juang, C.I.O.
Board of directors: Robert Liu, Chair.; Victor Li
Giving statement: Giving through the RM Liu Foundation.

The RM Liu Foundation

500 W. 190th St., 6th Fl.
Gardena, CA 90248-4265

Establishment information: Established in 2007 in CA.
Donors: Justin Liu; Emily Liu; Tireco, Inc.
Financial data (yr. ended 12/31/11): Assets, $2,123,804 (M); gifts received, $1,755,000; expenditures, $1,658,208; qualifying distributions, $1,644,557; giving activities include $1,642,182 for 4 grants (high: $1,250,000; low: $2,000).
Fields of interest: Higher education; International affairs.
Geographic limitations: Giving primarily in CA.
Support limitations: No grants to individuals.
Application information: Applications not accepted. Contributes only to pre-selected organizations.
Officers: Justin R. Liu, Pres.; Robert W. Liu, V.P.; Emily F. Liu, Secy.; Mimi W. Liu, C.F.O.
EIN: 208643551
Selected grants: The following grants are a representative sample of this grantmaker's funding activity:
$1,250,000 to University of Notre Dame, Notre Dame, IN, 2010.
$10,000 to Los Angeles Parks Foundation, Los Angeles, CA, 2010.
$4,131 to Pacific Council on International Policy, Los Angeles, CA, 2010.

3763
Titan Industrial Corporation

555 Madison Ave.
New York, NY 10022 (212) 421-6700

Company type: Private company
Business activities: Manufactures, markets, imports, and exports steel products.
Business type (SIC): Steel mill products; iron and steel foundries; metals and minerals, except petroleum—wholesale
Corporate officer: Michael S. Levin, Chair. and C.E.O.
Board of director: Michael S. Levin, Chair.
Giving statement: Giving through the Ruth and Jerome A. Siegel Foundation.

Ruth and Jerome A. Siegel Foundation

1175 Old White Plains Rd.
Mamaroneck, NY 10543-1018

Establishment information: Incorporated in 1951 in NY.
Donors: Titan Industrial Corp.; Jerome Siegel; Ruth Siegel.
Financial data (yr. ended 11/30/11): Assets, $63,424 (M); gifts received, $119,630; expenditures, $192,173; qualifying distributions, $189,673; giving activities include $186,942 for 69 grants (high: $25,000; low: $100).
Purpose and activities: The foundation supports museums and organizations involved with performing arts, education, health, human services, and Judaism.
Fields of interest: Museums; Performing arts; Higher education; Medical school/education; Education; Hospitals (general); Health care; Big Brothers/Big Sisters; YM/YWCAs & YM/YWHAs; Children, services; Human services; Jewish federated giving programs; Jewish agencies & synagogues.
Type of support: General/operating support; Program development.
Geographic limitations: Giving limited to New York, NY.
Support limitations: No grants to individuals.
Application information: Applications not accepted. Contributes only to pre-selected organizations.
Officer and Directors: Jerome A. Siegel*, Pres. and Treas.; Henry Siegel; Ruth Siegel.
EIN: 136066216
Selected grants: The following grants are a representative sample of this grantmaker's funding activity:
$25,000 to Big Brothers Big Sisters of New York City, New York, NY, 2011.
$25,000 to UJA-Federation of New York, New York, NY, 2011.
$10,000 to UJA-Federation of New York, New York, NY, 2011.
$5,000 to Westchester Community College Foundation, Valhalla, NY, 2011.
$2,000 to UJA-Federation of New York, New York, NY, 2011.
$1,000 to Caramoor Center for Music and the Arts, Katonah, NY, 2011.

3764
TIV Operations Group, Inc.

5300 Town and Country Blvd.
P.O. Box 3053
McKinney, TX 75070 (972) 624-7000

Company URL: http://www.tiv.com
Establishment information: Established in 1987.
Company type: Private company
Business activities: Provides telecommunications consulting services.
Business type (SIC): Management and public relations services
Corporate officers: David W. Larsen, Chair. and C.E.O.; Louis A. Martinelli, Pres. and C.O.O.; Michael Ladwig, Cont.
Board of director: David W. Larsen, Chair.
Giving statement: Giving through the Hauferma Foundation.

Hauferma Foundation

206 E. Louisiana St.
McKinney, TX 75069-4312

Establishment information: Established in 2000 in TX.
Donors: TIV Operations Group, Inc.; David Wayne Larsen; Victoria Coates Larsen; Michael Andrew Ladwig.
Financial data (yr. ended 12/31/11): Assets, $1 (M); gifts received, $23,400; expenditures, $23,785; qualifying distributions, $23,200; giving activities include $23,200 for grants.
Purpose and activities: The foundation supports Christian agencies and churches.
Fields of interest: Religion.
Type of support: Program development.
Geographic limitations: Giving primarily in TX.
Support limitations: No grants to individuals.
Application information: Applications not accepted. Unsolicited requests for funds not accepted.
Officers: David Wayne Larsen, Pres.; Michael Andrew Ladwig, V.P.; Victoria Coates Larsen, V.P.
EIN: 752854354

3765
The TJX Companies, Inc.

770 Cochituate Rd.
Framingham, MA 01701 (508) 390-1000

Company URL: http://www.tjx.com
Establishment information: Established in 1919.
Company type: Public company
Company ticker symbol and exchange: TJX/NYSE
Business activities: Operates apparel and home fashions stores.
Financial profile for 2011: Number of employees, 166,000; assets, $7,971,800,000; sales volume, $21,942,200,000; pre-tax net income, $2,164,090,000; expenses, $19,778,100,000; liabilities, $4,871,860,000
Fortune 1000 ranking: 2012—115th in revenues, 111th in profits, and 402nd in assets
Corporate officers: Bernard Cammarata, Chair.; Carol M. Meyrowitz, C.E.O.; Ernie L. Herrman, Pres.; Jeffrey G. Naylor, Sr. Exec. V.P., C.F.O., and C.A.O.
Board of directors: Bernard Cammarata, Chair.; Jose B. Alvarez; Alan M. Bennett; David A. Brandon; David T. Ching; Michael F. Hines; Amy B. Lane; Carol Meyrowitz; John F. O'Brien; Willow B. Shire; Fletcher H. Wiley
Subsidiaries: HomeGoods, Inc., Milford, MA; Marmaxx Operating Corp., Chicago, IL

Plants: Bloomfield, Meriden, CT; Decatur, GA; Brownsburg, Evansville, South Bend, IN; Fall River, Woburn, Worcester, MA; Las Vegas, NV; New York, NY; Charlotte, NC; Philadelphia, Pittston Township, PA; Bridgewater, VA
International operations: Canada; Germany; Hong Kong; United Kingdom
Giving statement: Giving through the TJX Companies, Inc. Corporate Giving Program and the TJX Foundation, Inc.
Company EIN: 042207613

The TJX Companies, Inc. Corporate Giving Program

770 Cochituate Rd.
Framingham, MA 01701-4666 (508) 390-1000
URL: http://www.tjx.com/corporate_community_initiatives.asp

Purpose and activities: As a complement to its foundation, TJX also makes charitable contributions to nonprofit organizations directly. Support is given primarily in areas of company operations on a local, national, and international basis.
Fields of interest: Education; Public health, physical fitness; Health care; Cancer; Employment, services; Nutrition; Disasters, preparedness/services; Human services, fund raising/fund distribution; Family services; Family services, domestic violence; Family resources and services, disability; Community/economic development Children; Women; Economically disadvantaged.
Type of support: Cause-related marketing; Employee volunteer services; General/operating support; In-kind gifts; Sponsorships.
Geographic limitations: Giving primarily in areas of company operations on a local, national, and international basis.
Application information: The Community Relations department handles giving. Application form not required.
Copies of proposal: 1

The TJX Foundation, Inc.

(formerly Zayre Foundation, Inc.)
c/o The TJX Cos., Inc.
770 Cochituate Rd., Rte. X4S
Framingham, MA 01701-4666 (508) 390-3199
FAX: (508) 390-5722;
E-mail: TJX_Foundation@TJX.com; URL: http://www.tjx.com/corporate_community_foundation.asp

Establishment information: Incorporated in 1966 in MA.
Donors: The TJX Cos., Inc.; Marshalls of MA, Inc.
Contact: Christine A. Strickland, Mgr.
Financial data (yr. ended 01/28/12): Assets, $16,267,172 (M); gifts received, $499,452; expenditures, $8,695,629; qualifying distributions, $8,394,204; giving activities include $8,394,204 for 1,406 grants (high: $333,000; low: $700).
Purpose and activities: The foundation supports programs designed to provide basic-need services to disadvantaged women, children, and families. Special emphasis is directed toward programs designed to promote strong families; provide emergency shelter; enhance education and job readiness; and build community ties.
Fields of interest: Vocational education; Adult education—literacy, basic skills & GED; Education, ESL programs; Education; Health care, infants; Reproductive health, prenatal care; Substance abuse, services; Mental health, counseling/support groups; Genetic diseases and disorders; Alzheimer's disease; Medical research; Crime/violence prevention, domestic violence; Food services; Housing/shelter, temporary shelter; Disasters, preparedness/services; Youth development; Children, adoption; Children, services; Family services; Family services, domestic violence; Residential/custodial care; Residential/custodial care, hospices; Developmentally disabled, centers & services; Independent living, disability; Civil/human rights Children; Disabilities, people with; Women; AIDS, people with; Economically disadvantaged.
Programs:
Civic/Community: The foundation supports programs designed to teach disadvantaged persons independent living skills; and improve race/cultural relations.
Domestic Violence Prevention: The foundation supports programs designed to provide emergency services and shelter accommodations for victims and family members affected by abusive situations; and programs designed to break the cycle of violence.
Education: The foundation supports programs designed to provide academic and vocational opportunities for the disadvantaged, including early-intervention, mentoring, tutoring, GED, and college coursework; and programs designed to teach people to speak, read, and write English.
Health: The foundation supports programs designed to provide early prenatal services and healthy baby education. The foundation also provides funding for medical research that furthers the treatment of, or eliminated the impact of, congenital or chronic diseases.
Social Services: The foundation supports programs designed to benefit disadvantaged children and families; strengthen the family unit, along with the parent-child relationship; offer food and clothing assistance; provide counseling, youth development, and adoption services; and programs designed to directly help those with mental or physical impairments.
Type of support: Continuing support; General/operating support; Program development.
Geographic limitations: Giving on a national basis in areas of company operations, with emphasis on MA.
Support limitations: No support for political, fraternal, or international organizations. No grants to individuals, or for capital campaigns, cash reserves, computer purchases, conferences, seminars, consultant fees, salaries, conventions, education loans, endowments, fellowships, films, photography, renovation, new construction, publications, public policy research, advocacy, seed money, travel, or transportation.
Publications: Application guidelines; Corporate giving report; Program policy statement.
Application information: Applications accepted. Additional information may be requested at a later date. Application form required.
Initial approach: Complete online eligibility quiz and application form
Copies of proposal: 1
Board meeting date(s): Week of Apr. 1, June 17, and Oct. 21
Deadline(s): Dec. 10, Feb. 25, and July 1
Final notification: 4 weeks following board meeting
Officers and Directors:* Bernard Cammarata, Chair. and Pres.; Scott Goldenberg, V.P.; Paul Kangas, V.P.; Carol M. Meyrowitz, V.P.; Mary B. Reynolds, V.P.; Ann McCauley, Secy.; Jeffrey G. Naylor*, Treas.
Number of staff: 3 full-time professional.
EIN: 042399760
Selected grants: The following grants are a representative sample of this grantmaker's funding activity:
$270,432 to Save the Children Federation, Westport, CT, 2011.
$150,000 to National Domestic Violence Hotline, Austin, TX, 2011.
$100,000 to Boys and Girls Clubs of America, Atlanta, GA, 2011.
$50,000 to Catholic Schools Foundation, Boston, MA, 2011.
$40,000 to Easter Seals Massachusetts, Boston, MA, 2011.
$10,000 to Inter-Care Family Foundation, New York, NY, 2011.
$5,000 to Center for Teen Empowerment, Boston, MA, 2011.
$5,000 to Freedom House, Washington, DC, 2011.
$5,000 to InnVision the Way Home, San Jose, CA, 2011.
$5,000 to Misericordia University, Dallas, PA, 2011.

3766
A.M. Todd Company

1717 Douglas Ave.
Kalamazoo, MI 49007-1600
(269) 343-2603

Company URL: http://www.amtodd.com
Establishment information: Established in 1869.
Company type: Subsidiary of a private company
Business activities: Produces essential oils and food ingredients.
Business type (SIC): Fats and oils; food and kindred products
Corporate officers: Raymond J. Hughes, Pres. and C.E.O.; Catherine B. Hnatin, C.O.O. and C.F.O.; Steven M. Buell, V.P., Finance; Tony Willard, V.P., Sales and Mktg.
Subsidiaries: Flavorite Laboratories, Horn Lake, MS; Folexco/EEH, Montgomery, PA; Zink & Triest, Montgomeryville, PA
Giving statement: Giving through the A. M. Todd Company Foundation.

A. M. Todd Company Foundation

P.O. Box 3636
Grand Rapids, MI 49501-3636 (269) 567-7864
Application address: 136 E. Michigan Ave., Kalamazoo, MI 49007, tel.: (269) 567-7881

Establishment information: Established in 1962 in MI.
Donors: A.M. Todd Co.; Zink & Triest Co.
Contact: Pat Llewellyn
Financial data (yr. ended 12/31/11): Assets, $10,590 (M); expenditures, $66,453; qualifying distributions, $64,500; giving activities include $64,500 for grants.
Purpose and activities: The foundation supports organizations involved with arts and culture, education, the environment, health, human services, community development, and Christianity.
Fields of interest: Mental health/crisis services; Human services.
Type of support: Annual campaigns; Building/renovation; Capital campaigns; Continuing support.
Geographic limitations: Giving limited to Kalamazoo County, MI.
Support limitations: No grants to individuals.
Application information: Applications accepted. Application form required. Applicants should submit the following:
1) copy of IRS Determination Letter
Initial approach: Proposal
Deadline(s): None
Trustees: Ian D. Blair; A.J. Todd III; Fifth Third Bank.
EIN: 386055829

3767
Toeniskoetter & Breeding, Inc.
1960 The Alameda, Ste. 20
San Jose, CA 95126-1447 (408) 246-7500

Company URL: http://toeniskoetterdevelopment.com/index.htm
Establishment information: Established in 1983.
Company type: Private company
Business activities: Provides general contract construction services.
Business type (SIC): Building construction general contractors and operative builders
Corporate officers: Charles J. Toeniskoetter, Chair.; Brad W. Krouskup, Pres. and C.E.O.; Yvonne Siko, V.P., Finance
Board of director: Charles J. Toeniskoetter, Chair.
Giving statement: Giving through the Toeniskoetter Family Foundation.

Toeniskoetter Family Foundation
(formerly Toeniskoetter & Breeding Foundation, Inc.)
1960 The Alameda, Ste. 20
San Jose, CA 95126-1441

Establishment information: Established in 1989 in CA.
Donors: Toeniskoetter & Breeding, Inc.; Chuck Toeniskoetter; Linda Toeniskoetter.
Financial data (yr. ended 12/31/11): Assets, $309,338 (M); gifts received, $17,500; expenditures, $36,269; qualifying distributions, $32,000; giving activities include $32,000 for grants.
Purpose and activities: The foundation supports EMS and organizations involved with higher education, conservation, and stroke awareness.
Fields of interest: Arts; Animals/wildlife; Health care.
Type of support: General/operating support.
Geographic limitations: Giving primarily in areas of company operations in San Jose, CA.
Support limitations: No grants to individuals.
Application information: Applications not accepted. Unsolicited requests for funds not accepted.
Officers: Charles J. Toeniskoetter, Pres.; Steven Hallgrimson, Secy.; Brad Krouskup, Treas.
EIN: 770252552

3768
Tofias PC
350 Massachusetts Ave., Ste. 5
Cambridge, MA 02139 (617) 761-0600

Company URL: http://www.tofias.com
Establishment information: Established in 1966.
Company type: Subsidiary of a private company
Business activities: Provides accounting and consulting services.
Business type (SIC): Accounting, auditing, and bookkeeping services; management and public relations services
Board of director: David Rocco
Offices: New Bedford, MA; Newport, Providence, RI
Giving statement: Giving through the Tofias PC Charitable Foundation.

Tofias PC Charitable Foundation
c/o Richard M. Simon et al
500 Boylston St.
Boston, MA 02116 (617) 761-0600

Establishment information: Established in 2001 in MA.
Donor: Tofias PC.
Contact: Katherine Finucci
Financial data (yr. ended 12/31/11): Assets, $0 (M); gifts received, $3,750; expenditures, $8,664; qualifying distributions, $8,664; giving activities include $8,664 for 8 grants (high: $5,000; low: $50).
Purpose and activities: The foundation supports museums and organizations involved with education, children services, senior citizens, and Judaism.
Fields of interest: Education; Human services; Religion.
Type of support: Management development/capacity building; Program development.
Support limitations: No support for political organizations. No grants to individuals, or for scholarships or endowments.
Application information: Applications accepted. Application form required. Applicants should submit the following:
1) copy of IRS Determination Letter
2) copy of most recent annual report/audited financial statement/990
3) listing of board of directors, trustees, officers and other key people and their affiliations

Initial approach: Proposal
Copies of proposal: 1
Deadline(s): None

Trustees: Tracy Gallagher; Richard M. Simon.
Number of staff: 1
EIN: 043572076

3769
Toll Brothers, Inc.
250 Gibraltar Rd.
Horsham, PA 19044 (215) 938-8000
FAX: (302) 655-5049

Company URL: http://www.tollbrothers.com
Establishment information: Established in 1967.
Company type: Public company
Company ticker symbol and exchange: TOL/NYSE
Business activities: Designs, builds, markets and arranges financing for single-family detached and attached homes in luxury residential communities.
Business type (SIC): Operative builders
Financial profile for 2012: Number of employees, 2,396; assets, $6,181,040,000; sales volume, $1,882,780,000; pre-tax net income, $112,940,000; expenses, $1,817,040,000; liabilities, $3,059,340,000
Fortune 1000 ranking: 2012—979th in revenues, 341st in profits, and 533rd in assets
Forbes 2000 ranking: 2012—1774th in sales, 1037th in profits, and 1751st in assets
Corporate officers: Robert I. Toll, Chair.; Bruce Toll, Vice-Chair.; Douglas C. Yearley, Jr., C.E.O.; Richard T. Hartman, Pres. and C.O.O.; Martin P. Connor, Treas. and C.F.O.
Board of directors: Robert I. Toll, Chair.; Bruce E. Toll, Vice-Chair.; Robert S. Blank; Edward G. Boehne; Richard J. Braemer; Christine N. Garvey; Carl B. Marbach; Stephen A. Novick; Paul E. Shapiro; Douglas C. Yearley, Jr.
Giving statement: Giving through the Toll Brothers, Inc. Corporate Giving Program.
Company EIN: 232416878

Toll Brothers, Inc. Corporate Giving Program
250 Gibraltar Rd.
Horsham, PA 19044-2323 (215) 938-8000
URL: http://www.tollbrothers.com/homesearch/servlet/HomeSearch?app=aboutcharity_home

Purpose and activities: Toll Brothers makes charitable contributions to nonprofit organizations on a case by case basis. Support is given primarily in areas of company operations in Arizona, California, Colorado, Connecticut, Delaware, Florida, Illinois, Maryland, Massachusetts, Michigan, Minnesota, Nevada, New Jersey, New York, North Carolina, Pennsylvania, South Carolina, Texas, and Virginia.
Fields of interest: General charitable giving.
Type of support: Employee matching gifts; Employee volunteer services; General/operating support; In-kind gifts; Sponsorships.
Geographic limitations: Giving primarily in areas of company operations in AZ, CA, CO, CT, DE, FL, IL, MA, MD, MI, MN, NC, NJ, NV, NY, PA, SC, TX, and VA; giving also to national organizations.

3771
Tomkins Industries, Inc.
(formerly Philips Industries, Inc.)
4801 Springfield St.
Dayton, OH 45431-1084 (937) 476-0434

Establishment information: Established in 1957.
Company type: Subsidiary of a foreign company
Business activities: Manufactures conveyors and conveying equipment, commercial and industrial blowers and fans, motor vehicle parts, hot tubs and shower stalls, and plastic building panels and other building components.
Business type (SIC): Machinery/construction, mining, and materials handling; plastic products/miscellaneous; machinery/general industry; appliances/household; motor vehicles and equipment
Subsidiaries: Arrowhead Conveyor Co., Inc., Oshkosh, WI; Dearborn Fabricating and Engineering Co., Detroit, MI; J & J Register, El Paso, TX; Lasco Products Group, Anaheim, CA; Mayfran International, Inc., Cleveland, OH; Mid-West Conveyor Co., Inc., Kansas City, KS; The Residential Products Group, Malta, OH; Shelby Advanced Automotive Technologies, McKinney, TX; Shelter Products Group, Elkhart, IN
Division: Ruskin Div., Grandview, MO
Plants: Tucson, AZ; Mount Sterling, OH; Richardson, TX
International operations: Netherlands
Giving statement: Giving through the Tomkins Corporation Foundation.

Tomkins Corporation Foundation
(formerly Philips Industries Foundation)
1551 Wewatta St., MS 9N A4
Denver, CO 80202

Establishment information: Established in 1986 in OH.
Donors: Tomkins Industries, Inc.; David Newlands.
Financial data (yr. ended 04/30/12): Assets, $6,305,208 (M); expenditures, $174,622; qualifying distributions, $169,376; giving activities include $169,376 for 134 grants (high: $68,020; low: $25).

Purpose and activities: The foundation supports organizations involved with education, cancer, human services, and Christianity.
Fields of interest: Higher education; Scholarships/financial aid; Education; Cancer; Human services; Christian agencies & churches.
Type of support: Employee matching gifts; General/operating support; Scholarship funds.
Geographic limitations: Giving primarily in Denver, CO, Chicago, IL, KS, MI, and OH; giving also to national organizations.
Support limitations: No grants to individuals.
Application information: Applications not accepted. Contributes only to pre-selected organizations.
Officers and Trustees:* Thomas C. Reeve*, V.P. and Secy.; John Barker*, V.P.; Sylvia Church*, V.P.; Daniel J. Disser, V.P.; Robert F. Hayes, V.P.
EIN: 311207183
Selected grants: The following grants are a representative sample of this grantmaker's funding activity:
$5,575 to American Cancer Society, Atlanta, GA, 2011.
$3,620 to Wake Forest University, Winston-Salem, NC, 2011.
$3,500 to Denver Rescue Mission, Denver, CO, 2011.
$2,820 to World Vision, Federal Way, WA, 2011.
$1,447 to Leukemia & Lymphoma Society, White Plains, NY, 2011.

3770
Tom's of Maine, Inc.

302 Lafayette Ctr.
P.O. Box 1873
Kennebunk, ME 04043-6870
(207) 985-2944

Company URL: http://www.tomsofmaine.com
Establishment information: Established in 1970.
Company type: Subsidiary of a public company
Business activities: Manufactures personal health care products.
Business type (SIC): Soaps, cleaners, and toiletries
Financial profile for 2010: Number of employees, 95
Corporate officers: Thomas M. Chappell, C.E.O.; Bill F. McGonagle, C.F.O.
Giving statement: Giving through the Tom's of Maine, Inc. Corporate Giving Program.

Tom's of Maine, Inc. Corporate Giving Program

302 Lafayette Ctr.
Kennebunk, ME 04043-6870 (800) 985-1188
FAX: (207) 985-2196;
E-mail: donations@tomsofmaine.com; E-mail address for Dental Health For All applications and questions: Sponsorships@tomsofmaine.com; URL: http://www.tomsofmaine.com/community-involvement

Purpose and activities: Tom's of Maine makes charitable contributions to nonprofit organizations involved with the arts, education, human services, and the environment. Support for Dental Health for All is limited to dental clinics in Alabama, Washington, DC, Kentucky, Mississippi, and New Mexico.
Fields of interest: Arts; Dental school/education; Education; Environment; Dental care; Human services Economically disadvantaged.
Type of support: Continuing support; Donated products; Employee volunteer services; General/operating support; In-kind gifts; Sponsorships.
Geographic limitations: Giving primarily in Support for Dental Health for All is limited to dental clinics in AL, Washington, DC, KY, MS, and NM.
Support limitations: No support for organizations that conduct animal testing, or discriminatory organizations. No grants to individuals.
Publications: Application guidelines; Grants list.
Application information: Applications accepted. Currently contributes grant funding only to pre-selected organizations, except for Dental Health For All. A contributions committee reviews all requests. No proposals accepted that contain obscene, sexual, misleading, or defamatory material. Application form required. Applicants should submit the following:
1) timetable for implementation and evaluation of project
2) results expected from proposed grant
3) name, address and phone number of organization
4) copy of IRS Determination Letter
5) what distinguishes project from others in its field
6) detailed description of project and amount of funding requested
7) contact person
8) copy of current year's organizational budget and/or project budget
9) additional materials/documentation

Dental Health For All applications should include the number of patients served monthly, the number of additional patient exams or services that would be provided with the grant, the frequency with which the organization provides free or low-cost dental care, and a success story showing the organization's impact in the community. It should demonstrate how the project will make an enduring positive change in the community. Finalists for Dental Health For All will be required to submit a photo of their dental clinic helping the community, and the organization's logo. Tom's of Maine may display information from applications that are chosen as finalists in future website posts.
Initial approach: Download application form and submit completed proposal as an attachment by e-mail for Dental Health for All
Deadline(s): Mar. 15 for Dental Health for All
Final notification: Apr. 1 for Dental Health for All
Number of staff: 1 part-time professional.

3772
Tonkon Torp LLP

1600 Pioneer Tower
888 S.W. 5th Ave.
Portland, OR 97204-2099 (503) 221-1440

Company URL: http://www.tonkon.com/
Establishment information: Established in 1974.
Company type: Private company
Business activities: Operates law firm.
Business type (SIC): Legal services
Offices: Washington, DC; Portland, OR
Giving statement: Giving through the Tonkon Torp LLP Pro Bono Program.

Tonkon Torp LLP Pro Bono Program

1600 Pioneer Tower
888 S.W. 5th Ave.
Portland, OR 97204-2099 (503) 802-2129
E-mail: james.hein@tonkon.com; URL: http://www.tonkon.com/Careers/-ProBono.html

Contact: James Hein, Pro Bono Comm. Chair
Fields of interest: Legal services.
Type of support: Pro bono services - legal.
Application information: A Pro Bono Committee manages the pro bono program.

3773
Tony Hawaii Automotive Group Ltd.

94-1299 Ka Uka Blvd.
Waipahu, HI 96797-6206 (808) 680-7100
FAX: (808) 483-5443

Company URL: http://www.tony-group.com
Establishment information: Established in 1990.
Company type: Private company
Business activities: Operates car dealerships.
Business type (SIC): Motor vehicles—retail
Corporate officers: Stan Masamitsu, Pres.; Mike Koga, C.F.O.; Yuriko Sugimura, Secy.
Giving statement: Giving through the Tony Group Foundation.

Tony Group Foundation

(formerly Masamitsu Foundation)
94-1299 Ka Uka Blvd.
Waipahu, HI 96797-4495

Establishment information: Established in 1989 in HI.
Donors: Tony Hawaii Automotive Group Ltd.; Pacific Nissan Inc.; Tony Hawaii Corp.; Tony Hyundai; Tony Motors, Inc.
Financial data (yr. ended 06/30/12): Assets, $324,631 (M); gifts received, $38,740; expenditures, $44,274; qualifying distributions, $41,362; giving activities include $38,862 for 27 grants (high: $13,000; low: $50).
Purpose and activities: The foundation supports food banks and organizations involved with orchestras, secondary education, liver disorders, muscular dystrophy, school athletics, and golf.
Fields of interest: Arts; Education; Human services.
Type of support: General/operating support; Scholarship funds.
Geographic limitations: Giving primarily in Honolulu, HI.
Support limitations: No grants to individuals.
Application information: Applications not accepted. Unsolicited requests for funds not accepted.
Officers and Directors:* Norie Masamitsu*, Pres.; Tony Masamitsu*, V.P.; Yuriko Jane Sugimura*, Secy.; Stan Masamitsu*, Treas.
EIN: 990277167

3774
Tops Markets LLC

(formerly Tops Markets Inc.)
5274 Main & Union
P.O. Box 1027
Williamsville, NY 14221 (716) 632-7411

Company URL: http://www.topsmarkets.com
Establishment information: Established in 1920.
Company type: Subsidiary of a foreign company
Business activities: Operates grocery stores.
Business type (SIC): Groceries—retail
Financial profile for 2011: Number of employees, 12,700; assets, $680,000,000; sales volume, $2,260,000,000
Corporate officers: Frank Curci, Co.-Pres. and C.E.O.; Schuyler Lininger, Co.-Pres.; Kevin

Darrington, C.O.O.; Peter Labbe, Exec. V.P., Opers.; Diane Colgan, V.P., Sales ad Mktg.
Giving statement: Giving through the Tops Markets LLC Corporate Giving Program.

Tops Markets LLC Corporate Giving Program

(formerly Tops Markets Inc. Corporate Giving Program)
c/o Community Rels. Dept.
P.O. Box 1027
Buffalo, NY 14240-1027 (800) 522-2522
FAX: (716) 635-5987; URL: http://www.topsmarkets.com/Community/Pages/CommunityOverview_S.las?-token.S=

Purpose and activities: Tops Markets makes charitable contributions to nonprofit organizations involved with hunger, children's services including education, sports, and healthcare, and cultural and ethnic awareness. Support given primarily in areas of company operations, with emphasis on New York and Pennsylvania.
Fields of interest: Arts, cultural/ethnic awareness; Education; Health care; Diabetes; Food services; Food banks; Athletics/sports, amateur leagues; Human services, fund raising/fund distribution; Salvation Army; Children/youth, services; United Ways and Federated Giving Programs.
Type of support: Annual campaigns; Cause-related marketing; Donated products; General/operating support; In-kind gifts.
Geographic limitations: Giving primarily in areas of company operations, with emphasis on NY and PA.
Support limitations: No grants to individuals, or for private fundraisers.
Publications: Application guidelines.
Application information: Applications accepted. Proposals should be submitted using organization letterhead. The Community Relations Department handles giving. Application form not required.
Applicants should submit the following:
1) name, address and phone number of organization
2) contact person
Proposals for cash donations should include name, date, and reason for event; amount requested; and organization's W-9 form.
Initial approach: Proposal to headquarters; contact local store manager for requests of less than $50
Copies of proposal: 1
Deadline(s): 4 to 6 weeks prior to event
Number of staff: 1 full-time professional.

3775
The Toro Company

8111 Lyndale Ave. S.
Bloomington, MN 55420-1196
(952) 888-8801

Company URL: http://www.thetorocompany.com
Establishment information: Established in 1914.
Company type: Public company
Company ticker symbol and exchange: TTC/NYSE
Business activities: Designs, manufactures, and markets professional turf maintenance equipment, turf and agricultural irrigation systems, landscaping equipment, and residential yard products.
Business type (SIC): Machinery/farm and garden; metal plumbing fixtures and heating equipment/nonelectric
Financial profile for 2012: Number of employees, 5,066; assets, $935,200,000; sales volume, $1,958,690,000; pre-tax net income, $196,260,000; expenses, $1,753,110,000; liabilities, $622,800,000
Fortune 1000 ranking: 2012—956th in revenues, 686th in profits, and 976th in assets
Corporate officers: Michael J. Hoffman, Chair., Pres., and C.E.O.; Renee J. Peterson, V.P., Finance and C.F.O.; Thomas J. Larson, V.P. and Treas.; Timothy P. Dordell, V.P., Secy., and Genl. Counsel; Blake M. Grams, V.P. and Corp. Cont.; Judy L. Altmaier, V.P., Opers.; Peter M. Ramstad, V.P., Human Resources
Board of directors: Michael J. Hoffman, Chair.; Robert C. Buhrmaster; Janet K. Cooper; Gary L. Ellis; Jeffrey M. Ettinger; Katherine J. Harless; James O'Rourke; Gregg W. Steinhafel; Christopher A. Twomey
Subsidiary: Exmark Manufacturing Co. Inc., Beatrice, NE
Plants: El Cajon, Riverside, CA; Shakopee, Windom, MN; Abilene, El Paso, TX; Baraboo, Plymouth, Tomah, WI
International operations: Australia; Belgium; Bermuda; Canada; France; Gibraltar; Italy; Luxembourg; Mexico; Switzerland; United Kingdom
Giving statement: Giving through the Toro Company Contributions Program and the Toro Foundation.
Company EIN: 410580470

The Toro Company Contributions Program

c/o Toro Giving Program
8111 Lyndale Ave. S.
Bloomington, MN 55420-1196 (952) 887-8870
E-mail: judson.mcneil@toro.com; Additional e-mail: community@thetorocompany.com; URL: http://www.thetorocompany.com/community/index.html

Contact: Judson M. McNeil, Mgr., Community Relations
Purpose and activities: As a complement to its foundation, Toro also makes charitable contributions to nonprofit organizations directly. Support is given primarily in areas of company operations in California, Minnesota, Nebraska, Texas, Wisconsin, Australia, and New Mexico.
Fields of interest: Higher education; Education; Environment, natural resources; Environment, beautification programs; Environmental education; Environment; Disasters, preparedness/services; Athletics/sports, soccer; Athletics/sports, golf; Business/industry; Community/economic development.
Programs:
Kendrick B. Melrose Family Foundation Scholarship: The foundation awards college scholarships to children of employees of Toro. Awards range from $500 to $2,000. The program is administered by Scholarship America, Inc.
Toro Employee Scholarship Program: The foundation awards college scholarships of up to $2,000 to children of employees of Toro. The program is administered by Scholarship America, Inc.
Type of support: Annual campaigns; Donated equipment; Donated products; Employee volunteer services; Employee-related scholarships; General/operating support; In-kind gifts; Program development; Research; Scholarship funds.
Geographic limitations: Giving primarily in areas of company operations in El Cajon and Riverside, CA, Bloomington, Shakopee, and Windom, MN, Beatrice, NE, El Paso, TX, Tomah, WI, Australia, and Juarez, Mexico.
Support limitations: No support for religious organizations or churches or political organizations. No grants for capital campaigns, endowments, or sponsorships.
Publications: Corporate giving report.
Application information: The company has a staff that only handles contributions. A contributions committee reviews all requests.
Committee meeting date(s): Quarterly
Contributions Committee: Judson M. Tharin, Jr., Community Rels. Specialist; David Aikere; Tim Baube; Stacy Bogart; Phil Burkhart; Mike Drazen; Mike Happe; Dave Irvin; Connie Kotke; Rick Rodieo; Mark Stinson; Tom Swain; Darren Vedetake; Keith Wanttaja; John Wright; Dana Lonn.
Number of staff: 1 full-time professional; 1 part-time professional; 1 part-time support.

The Toro Foundation

8111 Lyndale Ave. S.
Bloomington, MN 55420-1196
E-mail: community@thetorocompany.com; URL: http://www.thetorocompany.com/community/foundation.html

Establishment information: Established in 1988 in MN.
Donor: The Toro Co.
Contact: Judson McNeil, Pres.
Financial data (yr. ended 12/31/11): Assets, $3,722,336 (M); gifts received, $1,169,000; expenditures, $881,182; qualifying distributions, $848,652; giving activities include $848,652 for grants.
Purpose and activities: The foundation supports organizations involved with arts and culture, education, the environment, health, human services, and civic affairs. Special emphasis is directed toward programs designed to promote turf maintenance, water management, and agronomy.
Fields of interest: Media/communications; Arts; Higher education; Education; Environment, water resources; Environment, land resources; Environment; Health care; Agriculture; Children/youth, services; Human services; United Ways and Federated Giving Programs; Public affairs.
International interests: Australia; Mexico.
Programs:
Dollars for Doers: The foundation awards $300 to nonprofit organizations with which employees of Toro volunteer at least 30 hours.
Dr. James Watson Fellowship Program: The foundation awards up to four $5,000 fellowships to students and researchers in the sports turf industry. The program is administered by the Golf Course Superintendents Association of America.
Employee Volunteer Grant Program: The foundation awards $300 grants to nonprofit organizations with which employees and directors of Toro volunteer at least 30 hours per year.
Matching Gifts: The foundation matches contributions made by employees of Toro to organizations involved with public broadcasting, education, and the environment on a one-for-one basis from $25 to $1,000 per employee, per year.
Type of support: Annual campaigns; Continuing support; Employee matching gifts; Employee volunteer services; Employee-related scholarships; Fellowships; General/operating support; In-kind gifts; Matching/challenge support; Program development; Scholarship funds; Sponsorships.
Geographic limitations: Giving primarily in areas of company operations in El Cajon and Riverside, CA, Minneapolis and Windom, MN, Beatrice, NE, El Paso, TX, Tomah and western WI, and in Australia and Mexico.
Support limitations: No support for political or religious organizations. No grants for capital campaigns.
Publications: Application guidelines; Corporate giving report.

Application information: Applications accepted. Requests may be submitted using the Minnesota Common Grant Application Form. Support is limited to 1 contribution per organization during any given year. Multi-year funding is not automatic. Telephone calls during the application process are not encouraged. Application form required. Applicants should submit the following:
1) copy of IRS Determination Letter
2) brief history of organization and description of its mission
3) copy of most recent annual report/audited financial statement/990
4) how project's results will be evaluated or measured
5) detailed description of project and amount of funding requested
6) copy of current year's organizational budget and/or project budget
7) listing of additional sources and amount of support

Initial approach: Contact foundation via mail for application form
Board meeting date(s): Quarterly
Final notification: 3 months

Officers and Directors:* Judson McNeil*, Pres.; Nancy McGrath, Secy.; Blake M. Grams*, Treas.; Timothy P. Dordell; Michael D. Drazen; Michael J. Hoffman; Peter M. Ramstad; Kurt Svendsen; Stephen P. Wolfe.
Number of staff: 1 part-time professional; 1 full-time support; 1 part-time support.
EIN: 363593618
Selected grants: The following grants are a representative sample of this grantmaker's funding activity:
$55,000 to First Tee, Saint Augustine, FL, 2011. For program support.
$10,000 to Minneapolis Park and Recreation Board, Minneapolis, MN, 2011.

3776
Toshiba America, Inc.

1251 Ave. of the Americas, Ste. 4100
New York, NY 10020-1104 (212) 596-0600

Company URL: http://www.toshiba.com
Establishment information: Established in 1965.
Company type: Subsidiary of a foreign company
Business activities: Operates holding company; manufactures and sells electronic products.
Business type (SIC): Electronic and other electrical equipment and components
Corporate officers: Yoshihide Fujii, Chair. and C.E.O.; Hiromitsu Igarashi, Pres.; Shigeru Takase, C.I.O.; Duncan Kane, Sr., V.P., Human Resources; Mark Mathews, V.P. and Mktg.; Larry White, V.P., Sales
Board of director: Yoshihide Fujii, Chair.
Giving statement: Giving through the Toshiba America Inc. Corporate Giving Program and the Toshiba America Foundation.

Toshiba America Inc. Corporate Giving Program

1251 Ave. of the Americas, Ste. 4110
New York, NY 10020
URL: http://www.toshiba.com/csr/

Purpose and activities: As a complement to its foundation, Toshiba America also makes charitable contributions to nonprofit organizations involved with community relations, the environment, and education, with an emphasis on math and science. Support is given primarily in areas of company operations on a national basis, and in Canada.
Fields of interest: Education; Environment; Community/economic development; Mathematics; Science.
Type of support: Employee volunteer services; Employee-related scholarships; General/operating support; Sponsorships.
Geographic limitations: Giving primarily in areas of company operations on a national basis, and in Canada.
Publications: Corporate giving report.

Toshiba America Foundation

c/o Prog. Office
1251 Ave. of the Americas, 41st Fl.
New York, NY 10020-4110 (212) 596-0620
FAX: (212) 221-1108;
E-mail: foundation@tai.toshiba.com; URL: http://www.taf.toshiba.com

Establishment information: Established in 1990 in NY.
Donors: Toshiba America, Inc.; Toshiba Corporation.
Contact: Laura Cronin, Dir.
Financial data (yr. ended 03/31/12): Assets, $9,921,459 (M); expenditures, $400,152; qualifying distributions, $349,502; giving activities include $349,502 for grants.
Purpose and activities: The foundation supports schools and organizations involved with K-12 science and mathematics education.
Fields of interest: Elementary/secondary education; Science, formal/general education; Mathematics.
Programs:
6-12 Grants: The foundation supports projects designed by classroom teachers to improve instruction for students in grades 6-12. Special emphasis is directed toward programs designed by math and science teachers to make their own classrooms more exciting and successful for students.
K-5 Grants: The foundation awards grants of up to $1,000 for projects designed to improve teaching and learning in K-5 science and mathematics. Special emphasis is directed toward innovative programs designed by individual teachers, and small teams of teachers, for use in their own classrooms.
Type of support: Equipment; Program development.
Geographic limitations: Giving on a national basis, with some emphasis on areas of company operations in CA, IL, NJ, NY, TN, and TX.
Support limitations: No support for religious or political organizations, teacher training institutes, or discriminatory organizations. No grants to individuals, or for professional development, capital campaigns, endowments, start-up needs, general operating support, conferences, building, computer hardware or materials, audio-visual equipment, videos, textbooks, independent study, fundraising, dinners, special events, educational research, after-school programs, or educational summer programs.
Publications: Application guidelines; Corporate giving report; Grants list; Informational brochure (including application guidelines); Newsletter; Occasional report.
Application information: Applications accepted. Applicants are encouraged to contact the foundation to discuss project ideas prior to applying. Organizations receiving support are asked to submit a final report. Application form required. Applicants should submit the following:
1) timetable for implementation and evaluation of project
2) how project's results will be evaluated or measured
3) detailed description of project and amount of funding requested
4) copy of current year's organizational budget and/or project budget

Initial approach: Download application form and mail to foundation
Copies of proposal: 2
Board meeting date(s): Mar. and Sept.
Deadline(s): Oct. 1 for K-5 Grant Program; None for 6-12 Grant Program requests of up to $5,000; Feb. 1 and Aug. 2 for 6-12 Grant Program requests over $5,000
Final notification: 3 months; Mar. and Sept. for 6-12 Grant Program requests over $5,000

Officers and Directors:* John A. Anderson, Jr.*, Pres.; Thomas Gallatin, Secy.; Wayne Chau, Treas.; Shinichiro Akiba; Yoshihide Fuji; Tetsuo Kadoya; Mark Mathews; Toshiya Miyaguchi; Hideya Sakaida; Mark Simons; Atsushi Tanaka.
Number of staff: 2 full-time professional.
EIN: 133596612

3777
TOSOH Quartz, Inc.

(formerly Weiss Scientific Glass Blowing Co.)
14380 N.W. Science Park Dr.
Portland, OR 97229-5419 (503) 605-5600

Company URL: http://www.tosohquartz.com
Establishment information: Established in 1957.
Company type: Subsidiary of a foreign company
Business activities: Manufactures industrial glassware.
Business type (SIC): Glass/pressed or blown
Corporate officers: Gunther Weiss, Chair.; Roger Wood, Pres. and C.E.O.; Robert Jarrett, C.F.O.
Board of director: Gunther Weiss, Chair.
Giving statement: Giving through the Tosoh Quartz Education Foundation.

Tosoh Quartz Education Foundation

(also known as Weiss Scientific Foundation)
14380 N.W. Science Park Dr.
Portland, OR 97229-5419 (503) 605-5600

Establishment information: Established in 1984 in OR.
Donors: Weiss Scientific Glass Blowing Co.; TOSOH Quartz, Inc.
Contact: Robert Jarrett
Financial data (yr. ended 12/31/11): Assets, $369,905 (M); expenditures, $143,567; qualifying distributions, $129,511; giving activities include $129,511 for 21 grants (high: $15,833; low: $260).
Purpose and activities: The foundation awards college scholarships to children of employees of TOSOH Quartz, Inc.
Fields of interest: Higher education.
Type of support: Employee-related scholarships.
Application information: Applications accepted. Application form required.

Initial approach: Letter
Deadline(s): On or around July. 1

Trustees: Graham Hindley; Jim Shaffer; Jeff Wessel; Rogger Wood.
EIN: 930879802

3778
Total Petrochemicals USA, Inc.

(formerly Atofina Petrochemicals, Inc.)
1201 Louisiana St., Ste. 1800
P.O. Box 674411
Houston, TX 77002 (713) 483-5000

Company URL: http://www.totalpetrochemicalsusa.com
Establishment information: Established in 1956.
Company type: Subsidiary of a foreign company
Business activities: Manufactures polyethylene, polypropylene, polystyrene, elastomers, and poly vinyl chloride.
Business type (SIC): Plastics and synthetics
Financial profile for 2009: Number of employees, 1,550
Corporate officers: Geoffroy Petit, C.E.O.; Bernard Claude, Pres.; Lee O'Shields, V.P. and C.I.O.; Bertrand de La Noue, C.F.O.
Plants: Carville, LA; Tulsa, OK; Deer Park, Grapevine, Pasadena, Port Arthur, TX
Giving statement: Giving through the Total Petrochemicals USA Foundation.

Total Petrochemicals USA Foundation

(formerly Atofina Petrochemicals Foundation)
P.O. Box 674411, Ste. 1800
Houston, TX 77267-4411
Application address: 1201 Louisiana St., Ste. 1800, Houston, TX 77002

Establishment information: Incorporated in 1974 in TX.
Donor: FINA, Inc.
Contact: Carolyn Sanders, V.P.
Financial data (yr. ended 12/31/11): Assets, $2,741,408 (M); expenditures, $134,652; qualifying distributions, $133,800; giving activities include $133,800 for grants.
Purpose and activities: The foundation supports organizations involved with arts and culture, education, the environment, health, civic affairs, and minorities.
Fields of interest: Arts; Education; Environment; Health care; United Ways and Federated Giving Programs; Public affairs Minorities.
Program:
Employee Matching Gifts: The foundation matches contributions made by employees of Total Petrochemicals USA to their alma maters from $50 to $5,000 per employee, per year.
Type of support: Employee matching gifts; General/operating support.
Geographic limitations: Giving primarily in areas of company operations, with emphasis on LA and TX.
Support limitations: No support for religious organizations. No grants to individuals.
Publications: Application guidelines.
Application information: Applications accepted. Application form not required.
Initial approach: Proposal
Board meeting date(s): Annually
Deadline(s): None
Officers and Directors:* Geoffrey Petit, Pres.; Robert D. Kilpatrick, V.P. and Genl. Counsel; Carolyn Sanders*, V.P.; Karyn Grace, Secy.; Jim Parks, Treas.; Richard L. Charter II.
Number of staff: 1 part-time professional.
EIN: 237391423

3779
Totem Ocean Trailer Express, Inc.

(doing business as Tote)
32001 32nd Ave. S., Ste. 200
Federal Way, WA 98001 (253) 449-8100

Company URL: http://www.totemocean.com/
Establishment information: Established in 1975.
Company type: Subsidiary of a private company
Business activities: Operates cargo vessel fleet.
Business type (SIC): Transportation/deep sea domestic freight
Corporate officers: John Parrott, Pres.; Phil Morrell, V.P., Opers.; Stephanie Holthaus, V.P., Sales; Maria Campbell, V.P., Human Resources
Giving statement: Giving through the Totem Ocean Trailer Express, Inc. Corporate Giving Program.

Totem Ocean Trailer Express, Inc. Corporate Giving Program

32001 32nd Avenue S., Ste. 200
Federal Way, WA 98001-9601
FAX: (253) 449-8225; For Lower 48: Contribs. Comm., tel.: (253) 449-8100; For Alaska.: Cindy Curtis, Community Rels. Coord., tel.: (907) 265-7232; For Fairbanks: Stuart Zimmerman, Fairbanks Mgr., tel.: (907) 265-7262; URL: http://www.totemocean.com/corporate-giving

Purpose and activities: Totem Ocean Trailer Express makes charitable contributions to nonprofit organizations involved with arts and culture, education, the environment, health, youth development, and human services. Support is limited to Alaska and Washington, with emphasis on Anchorage, Fairbanks, and Kenai, Alaska, and Seattle and Tacoma, Washington.
Fields of interest: Arts; Education; Health care; Youth development; Human services; Community/economic development.
Type of support: Capital campaigns; Employee volunteer services; Endowments; General/operating support; In-kind gifts; Sponsorships; Technical assistance.
Geographic limitations: Giving limited to AK and WA, with emphasis on Anchorage, Fairbanks, and Kenai, AK, and Seattle and Tacoma, WA.
Support limitations: No support for religious, political, labor, or fraternal organizations. No grants to individuals, or for sporting events or teams, or political events.
Publications: Application guidelines.
Application information: Applications accepted. Application form required. Applicants should submit the following:
1) name, address and phone number of organization
2) copy of IRS Determination Letter
3) brief history of organization and description of its mission
4) descriptive literature about organization
5) listing of board of directors, trustees, officers and other key people and their affiliations
6) detailed description of project and amount of funding requested
7) contact person
8) population served
9) additional materials/documentation

Applications should include the date, sponsorship levels, and expected attendance of the event if applicable; and the organization or event logo.
Initial approach: Complete online application form
Deadline(s): None

3780
Totsy Manufacturing Co., Inc.

1 Bigelow St.
P.O. Box 509
Holyoke, MA 01040-5744 (413) 536-0510

Establishment information: Established in 1984.
Company type: Private company
Business activities: Manufactures dolls, doll clothing, and novelty toys.
Business type (SIC): Games, toys, and sporting and athletic goods
Giving statement: Giving through the Totsy Foundation.

Totsy Foundation

c/o Steven M. Feldman
99 Twin Hills Dr.
Longmeadow, MA 01106

Establishment information: Established in 1982 in MA.
Donors: Totsy Manufacturing Co., Inc.; Shefford S. Golband Charitable Gift Annuity.
Financial data (yr. ended 03/31/12): Assets, $318,856 (M); expenditures, $37,792; qualifying distributions, $22,800; giving activities include $22,800 for 11 grants (high: $5,600; low: $200).
Purpose and activities: The foundation supports organizations involved with performing arts, education fundraising, early childhood education, early childhood development, human services, community development, and Judaism.
Fields of interest: Human services; Religion.
Type of support: Annual campaigns; Building/renovation; Capital campaigns; Conferences/seminars; Emergency funds; Endowments.
Geographic limitations: Giving primarily in western MA.
Support limitations: No grants to individuals.
Application information: Applications not accepted. Unsolicited requests for funds not accepted.
Board meeting date(s): May and Sept.
Trustees: Donna G. Feldman; Steven M. Feldman; Helen H. Goldband.
EIN: 042785460

3781
Towerbrook Capital Partners L.P.

Park Ave. Twr.
65 E. 55th St., Fl. 27
New York, NY 10022-3362 (212) 699-2200
FAX: (917) 591-9851

Company URL: http://www.towerbrook.com
Establishment information: Established in 2000.
Company type: Private company
Business activities: Operates private equity investment firm.
Business type (SIC): Security and commodity services
Corporate officers: Neal Moszkowski, Co-C.E.O.; Ramez Sousou, Co-C.E.O.; Filippo Cardini, C.O.O. and Genl. Counsel; Jennifer Ternoey Glassman, C.F.O.
Giving statement: Giving through the Towerbrook Foundation.

Towerbrook Foundation
Park Ave. Tower
65 E. 55th St., 27 Fl.
New York, NY 10022-3362 (212) 699-2200
FAX: (917) 591-9851;
E-mail: contact@towerbrook.com; Additional tel.: (212) 699-2278; URL: http://
www.towerbrook.com/foundation/

Establishment information: Established in 2006 in NY.
Donor: Towerbrook Capital Partners LP.
Contact: Jennifer Glassman, Treas.; Filippo Cardini, Secy.
Financial data (yr. ended 12/31/11): Assets, $9,268,333 (M); gifts received, $1,810,941; expenditures, $2,032,691; qualifying distributions, $1,930,606; giving activities include $1,930,606 for grants.
Purpose and activities: The foundation supports organizations involved with education, health, bone diseases, allergies research, employment, youth development, human services, international development, philanthropy, and military and veterans.
Fields of interest: Education, management/technical assistance; Elementary/secondary education; Higher education; Business school/education; Engineering school/education; Education; Public health; Health care; Nerve, muscle & bone diseases; Allergies research; Employment; Youth development; American Red Cross; Human services; International development; Voluntarism promotion; Venture philanthropy; Philanthropy/voluntarism; Military/veterans' organizations.
Type of support: Annual campaigns; Equipment; General/operating support; Program development; Scholarship funds.
Geographic limitations: Giving primarily in areas of company operations in CT, MA , and NY, and in Finland, Italy, and the United Kingdom.
Application information:
Initial approach: Contact foundation for application information
Officers and Directors:* Neal Moszkowski*, Co-Chair.; Ramez Sousou, Co-Chair.; Filippo Cardini, Secy.; Jennifer Glassman*, Treas.; Jonathan Bilzin; Robin Esterson; Niclas Gabran; Winston Ginsberg; Gordon Holmes; Brian Jacobsen; Axel Meyersiek; Travis Nelson; Andrew Rolfe; Ian Sacks; Karim Saddi; Patrick Smulders; John Sinik.
EIN: 743182897
Selected grants: The following grants are a representative sample of this grantmaker's funding activity:
$90,000 to Princeton University, Princeton, NJ, 2010.
$88,600 to Pat Tillman Foundation, Tempe, AZ, 2010. For general operating support.
$75,000 to Food Allergy Initiative, New York, NY, 2010. For general operating support.
$55,000 to Osteogenesis Imperfecta Foundation, Gaithersburg, MD, 2010.
$50,000 to Teach for America, San Francisco, CA, 2010.
$50,000 to Year Up Bay Area, San Francisco, CA, 2010. For general operating support.
$30,000 to Charities Aid Foundation America, Alexandria, VA, 2010.
$30,000 to Ubuntu Education Fund, New York, NY, 2010. For general operating support.
$10,000 to Partners in Health, Boston, MA, 2010.
$5,000 to Tufts University, Medford, MA, 2010.

3782
R. M. Towill Corporation
2024 N. King St., Ste. 200
Honolulu, HI 96819-3494 (808) 842-1133
FAX: (808) 842-1937

Company URL: http://www.rmtowill.com
Establishment information: Established in 1930.
Company type: Subsidiary of a private company
Business activities: Provides civil engineering and surveying services.
Business type (SIC): Engineering, architectural, and surveying services
Corporate officers: Russell Figueroa, Chair. and C.E.O.; Greg Hiyakumoto, Pres.; Nancy Matsuno, Compt.
Board of director: Russell Figueiroa, Chair.
Giving statement: Giving through the R. M. Towill Foundation.

R. M. Towill Foundation
2024 N. King St., Ste. 200
Honolulu, HI 96819-3456 (808) 842-1133

Establishment information: Established in 2004 in HI.
Donors: R.M. Towill Corporation; Russell Figueiroa; Bert R. Toba; Nancy K. Matsuno; Greg H. Hiyakumoto; Chester Koga; Leighton Lum; James Yamamoto.
Contact: Russell Figueiroa, Chair.
Financial data (yr. ended 12/31/11): Assets, $117,118 (M); gifts received, $129,095; expenditures, $86,196; qualifying distributions, $84,750; giving activities include $84,750 for grants.
Purpose and activities: Giving primarily for Hawaii schools and school teachers, and nonprofit educational and community support organizations.
Fields of interest: Arts; Education; Human services.
Type of support: General/operating support.
Geographic limitations: Giving primarily in HI.
Application information: Applications accepted. Application form required. Applicants should submit the following:
1) detailed description of project and amount of funding requested
Initial approach: Proposal
Deadline(s): None
Officers and Directors:* Russell Figueiroa*, Chair. and Pres.; Bert R. Toba, V.P.; Greg H. Hiyakumoto, Secy.; Nancy K. Matsuno, Treas.; Leighton Lum; James Yamamoto.
EIN: 830397737

3783
Town Sports International Holdings, Inc.
5 Penn Plz., 4th Fl.
New York, NY 10001 (212) 246-6700
FAX: (302) 655-5049

Company URL: http://www.mysportsclubs.com
Establishment information: Established in 1973.
Company type: Public company
Company ticker symbol and exchange: CLUB/NASDAQ
Business activities: Operates physical fitness centers.
Business type (SIC): Amusement and recreation services/miscellaneous
Financial profile for 2012: Number of employees, 7,800; assets, $403,910,000; sales volume, $478,980,000; pre-tax net income, $18,290,000; expenses, $438,560,000; liabilities, $459,410,000
Corporate officers: Thomas J. Galligan, Chair.; Robert J. Giardina, Pres. and C.E.O.; Terry G. Kew, C.O.O.; Daniel Gallagher, C.F.O.; Paul Barron, C.I.O.; David M. Kastin, Sr. V.P., Genl. Counsel, and Secy.; Scott Milford, Sr. V.P., Human Resources; Kieran Sikso, V.P., Finance; Kelley Bubolo, V.P., Sales
Board of directors: Thomas J. Galligan, III, Chair.; Paul N. Arnold; Bruce C. Bruckmann; J. Rice Edmonds; Robert J. Giardina; Kevin McCall
Giving statement: Giving through the Town Sports International Holdings, Inc. Contributions Program.
Company EIN: 200640002

Town Sports International Holdings, Inc. Contributions Program
5 Penn Plz., 4th Fl.
New York, NY 10001 (212) 246-6700
URL: http://www.mysportsclubs.com

3784
Toyota Motor Manufacturing North America, Inc.
(also known as TMMNA)
25 Atlantic Ave.
Erlanger, KY 41018-3151 (859) 746-4000

Company URL: http://www.toyota.com
Establishment information: Established in 1996.
Company type: Subsidiary of a foreign company
Business activities: Manufactures automobiles.
Business type (SIC): Motor vehicles and equipment
Corporate officers: Atsushi Niimi, Chair. and C.E.O.; Tetsuo Agata, Pres. and C.O.O.; Charles Brown, V.P., Finance, and Secy.; Millie Marshall, V.P., Human Resources
Board of director: Atsushi Niimi, Chair.
Subsidiaries: Bodine Aluminum, Inc., St. Louis, MO; Toyota Motor Manufacturing, West Virginia, Inc., Buffalo, WV
Giving statement: Giving through the Toyota Motor Manufacturing North America, Inc. Corporate Giving Program, the Toyota Motor Engineering & Manufacturing Scholarship Foundation, Inc., and the Toyota USA Foundation.

Toyota Motor Manufacturing North America, Inc. Corporate Giving Program
25 Atlantic Ave., M.C. EA-NA
Erlanger, KY 41018-3151
E-mail: philanthropy@tmmna.com; URL: http://
www.toyota.com/about/our_commitment/
philanthropy/guidelines/index.html

Purpose and activities: Toyota Motor Manufacturing makes charitable contributions to nonprofit organizations involved with arts and culture, education, the environment, health and human services, mental health, diversity, community development, civic affairs, and minorities. Special emphasis is directed toward programs designed to target young people. Support is given primarily in northern Kentucky and the greater Cincinnati, Ohio, area.
Fields of interest: Arts; Education; Environment; Health care; Mental health/crisis services; Human services; Civil/human rights, equal rights; Community/economic development; Leadership development; Public affairs Youth; Minorities.

Type of support: Annual campaigns; Continuing support; Program development; Sponsorships.
Geographic limitations: Giving primarily in northern KY and the greater Cincinnati, OH, area.
Support limitations: No support for political, fraternal, veterans' or military, political, or religious organizations, individual or private schools, United Way-supported organizations, or organizations already supported by the company. No grants to individuals, or for beauty pageants or athletic events, fundraising events directing more than 40 percent of funds raised to administrative, operating, or fundraising costs, or general operating support or debt reduction; no vehicle donations.
Publications: Application guidelines.
Application information: Applications accepted. Organizations receiving support are asked to provide annual progress reports. A contributions committee reviews all requests. Application form required.
Applicants should submit the following:
1) copy of IRS Determination Letter
Initial approach: Complete online application form
Copies of proposal: 1
Committee meeting date(s): Feb., May, Aug., and Nov.
Deadline(s): Postmarked by Jan. 1, Apr. 1, July 1, and Oct. 1
Final notification: 2 weeks following committee meetings

Toyota Motor Engineering & Manufacturing Scholarship Foundation, Inc.

(formerly Toyota Motor Manufacturing Scholarship Foundation, Inc.)
25 Atlantic Ave., ACCTTAX
Erlanger, KY 41018-3151
URL: http://sms.scholarshipamerica.org/tema/

Establishment information: Established in 2002 in DE and KY.
Donor: Toyota Motor Manufacturing North America, Inc.
Financial data (yr. ended 12/31/11): Assets, $1,009,935 (M); expenditures, $83,605; qualifying distributions, $83,605; giving activities include $71,250 for 57 grants to individuals.
Purpose and activities: The foundation awards college scholarships to children of employees of Toyota Motor Manufacturing North America, New United Motor Manufacturing, and their subsidiaries. The program is administered by Scholarship America, Inc.
Fields of interest: Higher education.
Type of support: Employee-related scholarships.
Geographic limitations: Giving primarily in areas of company operations.
Application information: Applications accepted. Application form required.
Initial approach: Proposal
Deadline(s): None
Officers: Mike Price, Pres.; Pat Nepute, Secy.; Charles Brown, Treas.
EIN: 300150685

Toyota USA Foundation

c/o Fdn. Admin.
601 Lexington Ave., 49th Fl.
New York, NY 10022-4611 (212) 715-7486
Tel. for questions about online applications: (212) 715-7490; URL: http://www.toyota.com/foundation

Establishment information: Established in 1987 in CA.
Donors: Toyota Motor Sales, U.S.A., Inc.; Toyota Motor Manufacturing North America, Inc.
Financial data (yr. ended 06/30/12): Assets, $103,052,108 (M); expenditures, $5,911,294; qualifying distributions, $5,175,610; giving activities include $5,156,919 for 25 grants (high: $1,800,000; low: $20,000).
Purpose and activities: The foundation supports organizations involved with K-12 education. Special emphasis is directed toward math, science, and environmental science.
Fields of interest: Elementary/secondary education; Higher education; Environment, natural resources; Environment; Youth, services; Science, formal/general education; Mathematics; Science.
Type of support: Curriculum development; Equipment; Program development; Program evaluation.
Geographic limitations: Giving primarily in areas of major company operations in AZ, CA, Washington, DC, IL, MD, NM, NY, and TX; giving also to national organizations.
Support limitations: No support for discriminatory organizations, government agencies, private or public K-12 schools, religious, fraternal, or lobbying organizations, or political parties or candidates. No grants to individuals, or for general operating support, annual campaigns, or debt reduction, endowments, capital campaigns, fundraising events, or construction or equipment, conferences, meals, or travel, or publication subsidies, advertising, or mass mailings.
Publications: Application guidelines; Grants list.
Application information: Grants range from $50,000 to $200,000. A site visit may be requested. Additional information may be requested at a later date. Applicants should submit the following:
1) population served
2) name, address and phone number of organization
3) copy of IRS Determination Letter
4) brief history of organization and description of its mission
5) geographic area to be served
6) detailed description of project and amount of funding requested
7) copy of current year's organizational budget and/or project budget
8) plans for acknowledgement
Initial approach: Complete online application
Board meeting date(s): Twice per year
Deadline(s): None
Final notification: Up to 6 months
Officers and Directors:* Yoshimi Inaba*, Pres.; Dian Ogilvie*, Secy.; Hiroshi Nishida*, Treas.; Tetsuo Agata; Chuck Brown; Barbra Cooper; Robert C. Daly; Katsuyuki Kusakawa; Jim Lentz; Patricia Salas Pineda; Steve St. Angelo; Shigeki Terashi; James Weisman.
Number of staff: 2 full-time professional; 1 full-time support.
EIN: 953255038
Selected grants: The following grants are a representative sample of this grantmaker's funding activity:
$800,000 to Nature Conservancy, Arlington, VA, 2010. To establish the first nationwide network for environmental high schools and provide students from these schools with real world, paid summer internships in the conservation field, ultimately servicing over 17,000 students.
$552,000 to Earthecho International, Washington, DC, 2010. To help youth restore and protect the water on the planet by providing both science-based environmental education materials and service-learning tools and resources to improve the health of the environment.
$340,000 to Robin Hood Foundation, New York, NY, 2010. To cut in half the failure rates of students in poor middle schools by developing creative and integrated science-based curricula that capture the attention of middle-school students, motivating them to remain in school and stay on track to graduate high school.
$299,794 to University of Kentucky Research Foundation, Lexington, KY, 2010. For outreach professors and teachers to partner in data supported analyses of school challenges, build teacher leadership capacity to design and implement school reform, and strengthen teacher training at partner colleges and universities.
$260,000 to California State Parks Foundation, San Francisco, CA, 2010. To support the PORTS (Parks Online Resources for Teachers and Students) program, which allows state park interpreters to make live presentations to classrooms via videoconferencing.
$250,000 to Western Kentucky University Foundation, Bowling Green, KY, 2010. To increase student achievement and teacher efficiency in math and technology.
$207,000 to National Council for Science and the Environment, Washington, DC, 2010. To support the establishment of a high school teacher training component for the EnvironMentors program. EnvironMentors seeks to increase interest in the environment among under-represented youth by matching each participant to mentors working in environmental fields.
$205,000 to National Wildlife Federation, Gulf States Natural Resource Center, Austin, TX, 2010. To improve science learning for students in grades K-8 within the Austin Independent School District by expanding its Schoolyard Habitats Program and increasing teachers' capacity to use these outdoor classrooms.
$175,000 to Black Rock Forest Consortium, Cornwall, NY, 2010. To develop The Digital Forest, a web-based application that allows students to draw on data sets and mathematical models embedded in a "virtual" simulation of Black Rock Forest to analyze environmental changes over time.
$150,000 to Rochester Institute of Technology, Kate Gleason College of Engineering, Rochester, NY, 2010. To enable the TPS (Toyota Production Systems) Lab to partner with WE@RIT (Women Engineers at the Rochester Institute of Technology) to provide K-12 programs focused on production, distribution, and supply chain concepts for the delivery of high-quality, cost effective products and services to over 745 girls annually.

3785
Toyota Motor Manufacturing, Indiana, Inc.

(also known as TMMI)
4000 Tulip Tree Dr.
P.O. Box 4000
Princeton, IN 47670-4000 (812) 387-2000

Company URL: http://www.toyota.com
Establishment information: Established in 1996.
Company type: Subsidiary of a foreign company
Business activities: Manufactures pickup trucks, sport utility vehicles, and minivans.
Business type (SIC): Motor vehicles and equipment
Corporate officers: Kazumori Oi, Pres.; Randy Reynolds, V.P., Admin.
Giving statement: Giving through the Toyota Motor Manufacturing, Indiana, Inc. Corporate Giving Program.

Toyota Motor Manufacturing, Indiana, Inc. Corporate Giving Program

c/o Public Affairs
4000 Tulip Tree Dr.
Princeton, IN 47670-2300 (812) 387-2000
FAX: (812) 387-2001; URL: http://www.toyota.com/about/community/fundguidelines/tmmi-contribution-app.pdf

Purpose and activities: Toyota Motor Manufacturing, Indiana makes charitable contributions to nonprofit organizations involved with arts and culture, education, the environment, health and human services, youth development, diversity, community development, and civic affairs. Support is given primarily in Wabash and White counties, Illinois, Daviess, Dubois, Gibson, Knox, Pike, Posey, Spencer, Warrick, and Vanderburg counties, Indiana, and Daviess and Henderson, Kentucky.
Fields of interest: Arts, cultural/ethnic awareness; Arts; Education; Environment; Health care; Youth development, formal/general education; Human services; Civil/human rights, equal rights; Community/economic development; Public affairs.
Type of support: Employee volunteer services; General/operating support; Sponsorships.
Geographic limitations: Giving primarily in areas of company operations in Wabash and White counties, IL, Daviess, Dubois, Gibson, Knox, Pike, Posey, Spencer, Warrick, and Vanderburg counties, IN, and Daviess and Henderson, KY.
Support limitations: No support for discriminatory, religious, or labor organizations, or political parties or candidates. No grants to individuals, or for publication, lobbying activities, advertising, capital campaigns, or endowments.
Publications: Application guidelines.
Application information: Applications accepted. Toyota prefers to support programs, rather than sponsor events. Organizations must apply for each new grant requested, and subsequent funding is contingent upon evaluation of previous activities. Toyota does not donate vehicles. Applications are not accepted by mail. Application form required. Applicants should submit the following:
1) population served
2) name, address and phone number of organization
3) copy of IRS Determination Letter
4) brief history of organization and description of its mission
5) geographic area to be served
6) listing of board of directors, trustees, officers and other key people and their affiliations
7) detailed description of project and amount of funding requested
8) contact person
9) copy of current year's organizational budget and/or project budget
10) listing of additional sources and amount of support
11) plans for acknowledgement
12) additional materials/documentation
Proposals should contain the program or event title, three objectives for the program or event, and the number of beneficiaries.
Initial approach: Complete online application
Committee meeting date(s): Monthly for sponsorships
Deadline(s): Feb. 15, May 15, Aug. 15, and Nov. 15
Final notification: End of the month following the deadline; or 45 days

3786
Toyota Motor Manufacturing, Kentucky, Inc.

1001 Cherry Blossom Way
Georgetown, KY 40324 (502) 868-3027

Company URL: http://www.toyota.com/about/operations/manufacturing/tmmk
Establishment information: Established in 1986.
Company type: Subsidiary of a foreign company
Business activities: Manufactures automobiles; manufactures engines and powertrain parts.
Business type (SIC): Motor vehicles and equipment
Corporate officers: Wilbert W. James, Jr., Pres.; Takao Gonno, V.P., Admin., and Secy.-Treas.
Giving statement: Giving through the Toyota Motor Manufacturing, Kentucky, Inc. Corporate Giving Program.

Toyota Motor Manufacturing, Kentucky, Inc. Corporate Giving Program

1001 Cherry Blossom Way
Georgetown, KY 40324-9564 (502) 868-2000
E-mail: nila.wells@tema.toyota.com; URL: http://www.toyotageorgetown.com/comm3.asp

Contact: Nila Wells, Community Rels. Specialist
Purpose and activities: Toyota Motor Manufacturing, Kentucky makes charitable contributions to nonprofit organizations involved with arts and culture, education, the environment, health and human services, diversity, community development, civic affairs, and minorities. Special emphasis is directed toward programs designed to target young people and that are sustainable. Support is limited to Kentucky.
Fields of interest: Arts; Education; Environment; Health care; Safety/disasters; Human services; Civil/human rights, equal rights; Community/economic development; Leadership development Youth; Minorities.
Programs:
Arts and Culture: Toyota Motor Manufacturing, Kentucky supports programs designed to preserve and advance arts and culture, particularly for children; and provide events that bring a variety of art programs to the community.
Civic and Community Progress: Toyota Motor Manufacturing, Kentucky supports programs designed to address local and state issues; and provide leadership programs for developing human capital.
Education: Toyota Motor Manufacturing, Kentucky supports programs designed to provide education for people of all ages. Special emphasis is directed toward programs designed to help ensure the success of Kentucky's reform-related programs.
Environment: Toyota Motor Manufacturing, Kentucky supports programs designed to provide environmental education; and promote the sustainability and preservation of the environment.
Health and Human Services: Toyota Motor Manufacturing, Kentucky supports programs designed to advance physical and mental health for people of all ages; and strengthen the quality of individual and family life by providing opportunities for personal growth and development.
Minorities and Diversity: Toyota Motor Manufacturing, Kentucky supports programs designed to promote the advancement and growth of opportunity, inclusion, respect, equality, and justice for all people.
Type of support: Continuing support; Donated equipment; Employee matching gifts; Employee volunteer services; Employee-related scholarships; In-kind gifts; Program development; Sponsorships.
Geographic limitations: Giving limited to KY.
Support limitations: No support for political, fraternal, veterans' or military, political, or religious organizations, individual or private schools, United Way-supported organizations, or organizations already supported by the company. No grants to individuals, or for beauty pageants or athletic events, fundraising events directing more than 40 percent of funds raised to operating costs, or general operating support or debt reduction.
Publications: Application guidelines.
Application information: Applications accepted. Organizations receiving support are asked to provide a final report. The Community Relations Department handles giving. A contributions committee reviews all requests. Application form required. Applicants should submit the following:
1) name, address and phone number of organization
2) how project's results will be evaluated or measured
3) list of company employees involved with the organization
4) contact person
5) copy of current year's organizational budget and/or project budget
6) listing of additional sources and amount of support
7) plans for acknowledgement
8) detailed description of project and amount of funding requested
Initial approach: Complete online application form
Copies of proposal: 1
Committee meeting date(s): Mar., June, Sept., and Dec.
Deadline(s): Feb. 1, May 1, Aug. 1, and Nov. 1
Final notification: 45 days

3787
Toyota Motor Manufacturing, West Virginia, Inc.

(also known as TMMWV)
1 Sugar Maple Ln.
Buffalo, WV 25033-9430 (304) 937-7000

Company URL: http://www.toyota.com/about/operations/manufacturing/tmmwv
Establishment information: Established in 1996.
Company type: Subsidiary of a foreign company
Business activities: Manufactures automobile engines and transmissions.
Business type (SIC): Motor vehicles and equipment
Corporate officer: Petfuji Okuda, C.E.O.
Giving statement: Giving through the Toyota Motor Manufacturing, West Virginia, Inc. Corporate Giving Program.

Toyota Motor Manufacturing, West Virginia, Inc. Corporate Giving Program

1 Sugar Maple Ln.
Buffalo, WV 25033-9430 (304) 937-7403
FAX: (304) 937-7299; URL: http://www.toyota.com/about/philanthropy/guidelines/

Purpose and activities: Toyota Motor Manufacturing, West Virginia makes charitable contributions to nonprofit organizations involved with math, science, and computer education, the environment, wildlife preservation, health and human services, families, community development, and on a case by case basis. Support is given

primarily in Cabell, Jackson, Kanawha, Lincoln, Mason, and Punam counties, West Virginia.
Fields of interest: Elementary/secondary education; Education; Environment, air pollution; Environment, natural resources; Environment; Animals/wildlife, preservation/protection; Health care; Family services; Human services; Economic development; Community/economic development; Public affairs; General charitable giving.
Type of support: General/operating support; Sponsorships.
Geographic limitations: Giving primarily in areas of company operations in Cabell, Jackson, Kanawha, Lincoln, Mason, and Putnam counties, WV, with emphasis on Putnam County; giving also to statewide organizations.
Support limitations: No support for discriminatory organizations, fraternal organizations, pageants, labor organizations, religious groups, or political candidates. No grants for political parties.
Publications: Application guidelines.
Application information: Applications accepted. Additional information may be requested at a later date. A presentation may be requested. Organizations receiving support are asked to submit a final report. A contributions committee reviews all requests. Application form required. Applicants should submit the following:
1) detailed description of project and amount of funding requested
2) contact person
3) name, address and phone number of organization
4) brief history of organization and description of its mission
5) copy of current year's organizational budget and/or project budget
6) listing of additional sources and amount of support
7) population served
8) copy of IRS Determination Letter

Initial approach: Complete online application form
Copies of proposal: 1
Committee meeting date(s): Quarterly
Deadline(s): Jan. 1, Mar. 1, June 1, and Oct. 1
Final notification: 45 days

3788
Toyota Motor North America, Inc.

9 W. 57th St., Ste. 4900
New York, NY 10019-2701 (212) 223-0303

Company URL: http://www.toyota.com
Establishment information: Established in 1996.
Company type: Subsidiary of a private company
Business activities: Provides business services.
Business type (SIC): Management and public relations services
Financial profile for 2011: Number of employees, 8,950; assets, $358,607,000,000; liabilities, $227,278,000,000
Corporate officers: Shigeki Terashi, Pres. and C.O.O.; Dian D. Ogilvie, Sr. V.P. and Secy.; Barbara Jones, V.P., Admin.
Office: Washington, DC
Giving statement: Giving through the Toyota Motor North America, Inc. Corporate Giving Program.

Toyota Motor North America, Inc. Corporate Giving Program

601 Lexington Ave., 49th Fl.
New York, NY 10022-2701 (212) 223-0303
URL: http://www.toyota.com/about/philanthropy/

Contact: Jennifer Rochkind, Mgr., Corp. Philanthropy
Purpose and activities: Toyota makes charitable contributions to programs with a focus on education, the environment, and safety. Support is given primarily in areas of company operations.
Fields of interest: Education; Environment; Safety, automotive safety.
Type of support: Program development.
Geographic limitations: Giving primarily in the New York, NY, metropolitan area.
Support limitations: No support for religious or political organizations. No grants to individuals.
Publications: Application guidelines.
Application information: Applications accepted. The Community Relations Department handles giving. Application form required. Applicants should submit the following:
1) copy of IRS Determination Letter
2) detailed description of project and amount of funding requested
3) copy of current year's organizational budget and/or project budget

Initial approach: Complete online application
Copies of proposal: 1
Deadline(s): None
Final notification: 45 days

3789
Toyota Motor Sales, U.S.A., Inc.

19001 S. Western Ave.
Torrance, CA 90501-1106 (310) 468-4000

Company URL: http://www.toyota.com
Establishment information: Established in 1957.
Company type: Subsidiary of a foreign company
Business activities: Manufactures automobiles.
Business type (SIC): Motor vehicles and equipment
Corporate officers: Yoshimi Inaba, Chair. and C.E.O.; James E. Lentz III, Pres. and C.O.O.; Tracey C. Doi, Group V.P. and C.F.O.; Randall J. Pflughaupt, Group V.P., Sales and Admin.; Katsuyuki Kusakawa, Sr. V.P. and Treas.
Board of director: Yoshimi Inaba, Chair.
Giving statement: Giving through the Toyota Motor Sales, U.S.A., Inc. Corporate Giving Program.

Toyota Motor Sales, U.S.A., Inc. Corporate Giving Program

19001 S. Western Ave., Dept. WC11
Torrance, CA 90501-1106 (800) 331-4331
URL: http://www.toyota.com/about/philanthropy/index.html

Purpose and activities: Toyota Motor Sales makes charitable contributions to nonprofit organizations involved with education, the environment, safety, arts and culture, civic and community issues, health and human services, and diversity. Support is given primarily in areas of company operations.
Fields of interest: Arts; Education; Environment; Health care; Safety/disasters; Civil/human rights, equal rights; Community/economic development; Public affairs.
Type of support: Employee volunteer services; General/operating support; Program development.
Geographic limitations: Giving is limited to Torrance, CA.
Support limitations: No support for discriminatory organizations, political parties or candidates, or organizations that serve only their own memberships, such as fraternal organizations, labor organizations, or religious groups. No grants to individuals, or for publications, lobbying activities, advertising, capital campaigns or endowments.
Publications: Application guidelines.
Application information: Applications accepted. Toyota prefers to support programs, rather than sponsor events. Organizations must apply for each new grant requested, and subsequent funding is contingent upon evaluation of previous activities. Applications are not accepted by mail. Applicants may call (212) 715-7490 for questions regarding the proposal process. Applicants should submit the following:
1) timetable for implementation and evaluation of project
2) results expected from proposed grant
3) name, address and phone number of organization
4) how project's results will be evaluated or measured
5) listing of board of directors, trustees, officers and other key people and their affiliations
6) detailed description of project and amount of funding requested
7) contact person
8) copy of current year's organizational budget and/or project budget
9) listing of additional sources and amount of support
10) plans for acknowledgement

Proposals should include an EIN number, program or event title, total administrative cost for the project, an explanation of three target objectives for the program, and the expected number of program or event participants.

Initial approach: Complete online application form
Final notification: 45 days

3790
Toys "R" Us, Inc.

1 Geoffrey Way
Wayne, NJ 07470 (973) 617-3500

Company URL: http://www.toysrusinc.com
Establishment information: Established in 1948.
Company type: Private company
Business activities: Operates toy stores.
Business type (SIC): Shopping goods stores/miscellaneous; department stores
Financial profile for 2011: Number of employees, 70,000; assets, $8,832,000,000; sales volume, $13,864,000,000
Corporate officers: Gerald L. Storch, Chair. and C.E.O.; Claire Babrowski, Exec. V.P. and C.O.O.; F. Clay Creasey, Jr., Exec. V.P. and C.F.O.; Deborah M. Derby, Exec. V.P. and C.A.O.; David J. Schwartz, Exec. V.P., Genl. Counsel, and Corp. Secy.; Daniel Caspersen, Exec. V.P., Human Resources; Thomas J. Reinebach, Sr. V.P. and C.I.O.; Charles D. Knight, Sr. V.P. and Corp. Cont.
Board of director: Gerald L. Storch, Chair.
International operations: Australia; Austria; Belgium; Canada; France; Germany; Hong Kong; Japan; Portugal; Spain; Switzerland; United Kingdom
Giving statement: Giving through the Toys "R" Us Children's Fund, Inc.
Company EIN: 223260693

Toys "R" Us Children's Fund, Inc.

1 Geoffrey Way
Wayne, NJ 07470-2030 (973) 617-3500
E-mail: lucass@toysrus.com; URL: http://www4.toysrus.com/about/corpPhilanthropy.cfm

Establishment information: Established in 1992 in DE.
Donor: Toys "R" Us, Inc.

Contact: Sloane Lucas, Mgr., Corp. Philanthropy
Financial data (yr. ended 01/31/11): Revenue, $8,290,228; assets, $10,980,429 (M); gifts received, $5,570,847; expenditures, $8,071,609; program services expenses, $8,071,609; giving activities include $4,292,546 for 51 grants (high: $500,000; low: $7,500).
Purpose and activities: The fund makes charitable contributions to nonprofit organizations involved with children's health and welfare.
Fields of interest: Health care; Disasters, 9/11/01; Children, services Children.
Type of support: Continuing support; Employee matching gifts; In-kind gifts; Matching/challenge support; Research; Seed money.
Geographic limitations: Giving on a national basis.
Support limitations: No grants for advertising, fundraising, conferences, or agency building campaigns; no loans.
Publications: Corporate report.
Application information: Applications accepted. Application form not required. Applicants should submit the following:
1) copy of IRS Determination Letter
2) copy of most recent annual report/audited financial statement/990
3) descriptive literature about organization
4) detailed description of project and amount of funding requested

Initial approach: Proposal
Copies of proposal: 1
Deadline(s): Sept. 1
Final notification: Nov. 15

Officers and Directors:* Kathleen Waugh*, Chair.; Deborah Derby*, Pres.; Peter W. Weiss*, Treas.; David J. Schwartz*, Secy.; Greg Ahearn; Daniel Caspersen; David J. Schwartz; Gerald Storch.
Number of staff: 2 full-time professional; 1 full-time support.
EIN: 223200892

3791
Tractor & Equipment Company, Inc.

5336 Messer-Airport Hwy.
Birmingham, AL 35212 (205) 591-2131

Company URL: http://www.tractor-equipment.com
Establishment information: Established in 1943.
Company type: Private company
Business activities: Sells construction and mining equipment wholesale.
Business type (SIC): Industrial machinery and equipment—wholesale
Corporate officers: James W. Waitzman, Jr., Chair. and C.E.O.; Dan Stracener, Pres.; Lloyd Adams, Exec. V.P. and C.F.O.
Board of director: James W. Waitzman, Jr., Chair.
Giving statement: Giving through the Tractor & Equipment Company Foundation.

The Tractor & Equipment Company Foundation

5336 Airport Hwy.
Birmingham, AL 35212-1599 (205) 591-2131

Establishment information: Established in 1977 in AL.
Donor: Tractor & Equipment Co., Inc.
Contact: Lloyd Adams, Secy.-Treas.
Financial data (yr. ended 12/31/11): Assets, $80,549 (M); expenditures, $109,546; qualifying distributions, $108,590; giving activities include $46,475 for 14 grants (high: $10,000; low: $275) and $62,115 for 15 grants to individuals (high: $11,225; low: $568).
Purpose and activities: The foundation supports organizations involved with education, health, recreation, youth development, human services, and Christianity.
Fields of interest: Higher education; Education; Health care; Recreation; Youth development; Human services; United Ways and Federated Giving Programs; Christian agencies & churches.
Type of support: Employee-related scholarships; General/operating support.
Geographic limitations: Giving primarily in AL.
Support limitations: No grants to individuals (except for employee-related scholarships).
Application information: Applications accepted. Application form required.

Initial approach: Proposal
Deadline(s): Mar. 1

Officers: James W. Waitzman, Jr., Pres.; Lloyd Adams, Secy.-Treas.
EIN: 630718825

3792
Tradition Mortgage LLC

6800 France Ave. S., Ste. 310
Minneapolis, MN 55435-2004
(952) 920-5100

Company URL: http://www.traditionllc.com
Establishment information: Established in 1999.
Company type: Private company
Business activities: Provides mortgage brokerage services.
Business type (SIC): Brokers and bankers/ mortgage
Corporate officer: Erik Hendrikson, Pres.
Giving statement: Giving through the Tradition Family Foundation.

Tradition Family Foundation

16972 Brandtjen Farm Dr.
Lakeville, MN 55044 (952) 920-5100

Establishment information: Established in 1999 in MN.
Donors: Tradition Ventures, LLC; Robert H. Enebak; Doris M. Enebak; Enebak Construction Co.; Tradition Mortgage, LLC; Tradition Development, LLC.
Contact: Leah D. Hendrikson, Dir.
Financial data (yr. ended 12/31/11): Assets, $357,040 (M); expenditures, $25,363; qualifying distributions, $25,304; giving activities include $23,591 for 22 grants (high: $4,974; low: $100).
Fields of interest: Arts; Education; Human services.
Type of support: General/operating support.
Application information: Applications accepted. Minnesota Common Grant Application Form accepted. Application form required.

Initial approach: Proposal
Deadline(s): None

Directors: Diane L. Enebak; Rebecca L. Enebak; Leah D. Hendrikson.
EIN: 411958548

3793
Trail Blazers, Inc.

(also known as Portland Trail Blazers)
1 Center Ct., Ste. 200
Portland, OR 97227-2103 (503) 234-9291

Company URL: http://www.nba.com/blazers
Establishment information: Established in 1970.
Company type: Subsidiary of a private company
Business activities: Operates professional basketball club.
Business type (SIC): Commercial sports
Corporate officers: Chris McGowan, Pres. and C.E.O.; Gregg Olson, Exec. V.P. and C.F.O.; Michael Fennell, Sr. V.P. and Genl. Counsel; Chris Dill, V.P. and C.I.O.; Bill Christensen, V.P., Finance; Traci Richardson, V.P., Mktg.; Traci Rose, V.P., Comms.; Traci Reandeau, V.P., Human Resources; Larry Weinberg, Chair. Emeritus
Board of directors: Jeff Dunn; Bert Kolde; Peter McLoughlin
Giving statement: Giving through the Portland Trail Blazers Corporate Giving Program.

Portland Trail Blazers Corporate Giving Program

c/o Blazers Community Rels.
1 Center Ct., Ste. 200
Portland, OR 97227-2103 (503) 797-9997
URL: http://www.nba.com/blazers/community/community_overview.html

Purpose and activities: The Portland Trail Blazers makes charitable contributions to nonprofit organizations involved with education, health, and fitness programs for children and youth. Priority for ticket giveaways is given to organizations that are focused on improving the lives of disadvantaged children. Support is limited to areas of company operations in Oregon and southwest Washington.
Fields of interest: Performing arts, education; Language (foreign); Elementary/secondary education; Education, early childhood education; Education, reading; Hospitals (specialty); Public health, physical fitness; Crime/law enforcement, police agencies; Housing/shelter, rehabilitation; Housing/shelter, repairs; Housing/shelter; Athletics/sports, training; Youth development, fund raising/fund distribution; Boys clubs; Girls clubs; Youth development; Salvation Army; Children/youth, services; Human services, gift distribution Economically disadvantaged.
Program:

Blazers Community Builders Youth Corps (BCBYC): This program works to empower youth to change the world one community at a time through the four Boys & Girls Clubs of Portland, Oregon. Fashioned after the award-winning Blazers Community Builders, BCBYC mentors teens in charitable giving and hands-on community outreach - a curriculum designed to cultivate the next generation of philanthropists. In its first year, BCBYC groups performed community service projects, solicited and researched grant requests and donated a total of $40,000 to non-profits in all four communities served by the Youth Corps.

Type of support: Donated products; Employee volunteer services; General/operating support; In-kind gifts; Sponsorships.
Geographic limitations: Giving limited to OR and southwest WA.
Support limitations: No support for private schools, political organizations, campaigns, or candidates for public office, religious, fraternal, or discriminatory organizations, organizations that receive 20% or more of their budgets from United Way, private

foundations, or foundations that are grantmaking bodies. No grants to individuals, or for prizes or giveaways, trips or tours, seminars, debt retirement or operational deficits, or general operating budgets of tax-supported institutions.
Publications: Application guidelines.
Application information: Applications accepted. Proposals should be as brief as possible in explaining the applying organization and the project or event for which support is being sought. Contributions are limited to one donation per organization per year from July 1 through June 30. Requests for autographed memorabilia or Blazers merchandise are limited to auction and/or raffle activities organized to raise funds for nonprofit organizations. Application form not required. Applicants should submit the following:
1) name, address and phone number of organization
2) copy of IRS Determination Letter
3) brief history of organization and description of its mission
4) copy of most recent annual report/audited financial statement/990
5) listing of board of directors, trustees, officers and other key people and their affiliations
6) detailed description of project and amount of funding requested
7) contact person
8) copy of current year's organizational budget and/or project budget
9) listing of additional sources and amount of support

Requests for in-kind support should include the number of people served. Organizations receiving a non-financial donations are asked to submit a follow-up document to the Blazers specifying the dollar amount raised from the donated product.
Initial approach: Proposal to headquarters
Copies of proposal: 1
Deadline(s): 1 month prior to need for in-kind auction or raffle donations; 4 weeks prior to event or start of fundraising campaign for in-kind donations.

3794
Trane Inc.

(formerly American Standard Companies Inc.)
1 Centennial Ave.
Piscataway, NJ 08855 (732) 652-7100
FAX: (732) 980-6300

Company URL: http://www.trane.com
Establishment information: Established in 1885.
Company type: Subsidiary of a public company
Business activities: Manufactures air conditioning systems, bathroom and kitchen fixtures and fittings, and braking and control systems.
Business type (SIC): Machinery/refrigeration and service industry; pottery; motor vehicles and equipment
Financial profile for 2009: Number of employees, 29,000
Corporate officers: Frederic M. Poses, Chair. and Co-C.E.O.; Douglas Cohn, Co-C.E.O.; Jay Allison, Pres.; John Hodson, C.F.O.; David Gregory, C.I.O.; Lawrence Costello, Sr. V.P., Human Resources; Mary Elizabeth Gustafsson, Sr. V.P., Genl. Counsel, and Secy.; David S. Kuhl, V.P. and Treas.
Board of director: Frederic M. Poses, Chair.
Subsidiary: The Trane Co., La Crosse, WI
Giving statement: Giving through the Trane Foundation of New York.

Trane Foundation of New York

(formerly American Standard Foundation)
1 Centennial Ave.
Piscataway, NJ 08855-3921 (732) 652-7100
E-mail: slondon@trane.com

Establishment information: Trust established in 1952 in PA as Westinghouse Air Brake Foundation; name changed in 1977.
Donors: American Standard Inc.; American Standard Cos., Inc.; Trane U.S. Inc.
Contact: David Kuhl, Tr.
Financial data (yr. ended 12/31/11): Assets, $0 (M); expenditures, $2,526; qualifying distributions, $2,526; giving activities include $2,526 for grants.
Purpose and activities: The foundation supports community foundations and organizations involved with arts and culture, education, and other areas.
Fields of interest: Arts; Education, special; Higher education; Education; American Red Cross; Foundations (community); United Ways and Federated Giving Programs; General charitable giving.
Type of support: Employee matching gifts; General/operating support.
Geographic limitations: Giving primarily in areas of significant company operations.
Application information: Applications accepted. Application form required. Applicants should submit the following:
1) brief history of organization and description of its mission
2) copy of most recent annual report/audited financial statement/990
3) detailed description of project and amount of funding requested

Initial approach: Letter
Deadline(s): None
Officers: Barbara A. Santoro, Secy.
Trustees: Robert L. Katz; David S. Kuhl; Lawrence R. Kurland.
EIN: 256018911

3796
Transammonia, Inc.

320 Park Ave.
New York, NY 10022-6987 (212) 223-3200

Company URL: http://www.transammonia.com
Establishment information: Established in 1965.
Company type: Private company
Business activities: Operates fertilizer and fertilizer raw materials merchandising and trading company.
Business type (SIC): Fertilizers and agricultural chemicals
Financial profile for 2011: Number of employees, 403; sales volume, $8,420,000,000
Corporate officers: Ronald P. Stanton, Chair. and C.E.O.; Edward G. Weiner, Sr. V.P. and C.F.O.; Benjamin Tan, C.I.O.; Oliver K. Stanton, Secy.
Board of director: Ronald P. Stanton, Chair.
Giving statement: Giving through the Transammonia Disaster Relief Fund.

Transammonia Disaster Relief Fund

c/o Transammonia
320 Park Ave.
New York, NY 10022-6815

Establishment information: Established in 2005 in NY.
Donors: Transammonia, Inc.; Peter Baumann; Khalil Itani.
Financial data (yr. ended 12/31/11): Assets, $44 (M); expenditures, $25; qualifying distributions, $0.
Purpose and activities: The foundation supports New York Presbyterian Hospital.
Fields of interest: Health care; Housing/shelter.
Type of support: General/operating support.
Geographic limitations: Giving primarily in New York, NY.
Application information: Applications not accepted. Unsolicited requests for funds not accepted.
Trustees: Peter Baumann; Fred M. Lowenfels; Ronald P. Stanton; Edward G. Weiner.
EIN: 203431705

3797
Transco Inc.

55 E. Jackson Blvd., Ste. 2100
Chicago, IL 60604-4166 (312) 427-2818

Company URL: http://www.transcoinc.com/
Establishment information: Established in 1936.
Company type: Private company
Business activities: Manufactures railroad equipment; manufactures and installs thermal insulation systems.
Business type (SIC): Railroad equipment; abrasive, asbestos, and nonmetallic mineral products
Corporate officers: Charles Andersen, C.E.O.; Ellen M. Smith, V.P. and C.F.O.; Peggy M. Damm, Cont.
Subsidiaries: Advance Thermal Corp., Bensenville, IL; Europa Management Inc., Chicago, IL; National Thermal Insulation, Chicago, IL; Transco Products Inc., Chicago, IL; Transco Railway Products Inc., Bucyrus, OH; Transco Realty Inc., Chicago, IL; Transcoat Inc., Chicago, IL
Giving statement: Giving through the Transco Inc. Charitable Foundation.

Transco Inc. Charitable Foundation

55 E. Jackson Blvd., Ste. 2100
Chicago, IL 60604-4166 (312) 896-8512
Tel.:(312) 896-8512

Establishment information: Established in 1986 in IL.
Donor: Transco Inc.
Contact: Ellen M. Smith, Dir.
Financial data (yr. ended 03/31/12): Assets, $33,605 (M); gifts received, $30,000; expenditures, $25,630; qualifying distributions, $25,615; giving activities include $25,615 for 11 grants (high: $9,000; low: $100).
Purpose and activities: The foundation supports organizations involved with music, cancer, ALS, brain research, human services, and Judaism.
Fields of interest: Performing arts, music; Cancer; ALS; Brain research; Children/youth, services; Human services; United Ways and Federated Giving Programs; Jewish federated giving programs; Jewish agencies & synagogues.
Type of support: General/operating support.
Geographic limitations: Giving primarily in IL.
Support limitations: No grants to individuals.
Application information: Applications accepted. Application form required. Applicants should submit the following:
1) detailed description of project and amount of funding requested

Initial approach: Letter
Deadline(s): None
Directors: Charles P. Anderson; Jay S. Berlinsky; Ellen M. Smith.
EIN: 363504296

3795
Trans-High, Corp.
235 Park Ave. S.
New York, NY 10003-1405 (212) 475-7845

Establishment information: Established in 2009.
Company type: Private company
Business activities: Publishes alternative lifestyle books and magazines; distributes videos and clothing.
Business type (SIC): Book publishing and/or printing; periodical publishing and/or printing
Corporate officer: Judy L. Baker, Chair.
Board of director: Judy L. Baker, Chair.
Giving statement: Giving through the High Hopes Foundation, Inc.

High Hopes Foundation, Inc.
419 Park Ave. S., 16th Fl.
New York, NY 10016-8411

Establishment information: Established in 1989 in NY.
Donor: Trans-High Corp.
Financial data (yr. ended 05/31/11): Assets, $0 (M); gifts received, $16,500; expenditures, $13,625; qualifying distributions, $13,500; giving activities include $13,500 for 7 grants (high: $3,500; low: $500).
Purpose and activities: The foundation supports organizations involved with media, education, horses, civil rights, and civic affairs.
Fields of interest: Mental health/crisis services; Health organizations; Religion.
Type of support: General/operating support; Scholarship funds.
Geographic limitations: Giving primarily in New York, NY.
Support limitations: No grants to individuals.
Application information: Applications not accepted. Contributes only to pre-selected organizations.
Directors: Judith Baker; Michael Kennedy.
EIN: 133527256

3798
Transit Mix Concrete Company
444 E. Costilla St.
Colorado Springs, CO 80903-3761
(719) 475-0700

Company URL: http://www.transitmix.com
Establishment information: Established in 1939.
Company type: Subsidiary of a public company
Business activities: Manufactures building construction supplies.
Business type (SIC): Concrete, gypsum, and plaster products; construction/highway and street (except elevated)
Corporate officers: Jerald Schanbel, Pres.; John Bertrand, C.I.O.
Giving statement: Giving through the Transit Mix Concrete Company Trust.

Transit Mix Concrete Company Trust
(formerly Transmix Concrete Company Trust)
c/o Wells Fargo Bank N.A.
P.O. Box 53456, MAC S4101-22G
Phoenix, AZ 85072-3456

Donor: Transit Mix Concrete Co.
Financial data (yr. ended 12/31/11): Assets, $15,768 (M); gifts received, $6,000; expenditures, $10,729; qualifying distributions, $8,476; giving activities include $7,000 for 5 grants (high: $2,000; low: $1,000).
Purpose and activities: The foundation awards college scholarships to children of employees of Transit Mix Concrete Company who are high school graduates having resided in El Paso County, Colorado, for at least two years.
Fields of interest: Education.
Type of support: Employee-related scholarships.
Geographic limitations: Giving limited to Colorado Springs, CO, and areas of company operations in El Paso County, CO.
Application information: Applications not accepted. Unsolicited requests for funds not accepted.
Trustee: Wells Fargo Bank, N.A.
EIN: 846042789

3799
TransUnion Corp.
555 W. Adams St.
Chicago, IL 60661-3614 (312) 985-2860

Company URL: http://www.transunion.com
Establishment information: Established in 1968.
Company type: Private company
Business activities: Provides credit reporting services.
Business type (SIC): Credit reporting and collection agencies
Financial profile for 2011: Number of employees, 3,000; assets, $1,005,800,000; sales volume, $1,024,000,000; pre-tax net income, $67,100,000; expenses, $771,300,000; liabilities, $1,830,200,000
Corporate officers: Penny S. Pritzker, Chair.; Siddharth N. Mehta, Pres. and C.E.O.; Samuel Allen Hamood, Exec. V.P. and C.F.O.
Board of director: Penny S. Pritzker, Chair.
Subsidiaries: TransUnion Interactive, Inc., Chicago, IL; TransUnion Settlement Solutions, Inc., Charlotte, NC
Giving statement: Giving through the TransUnion Corp. Contributions Program.
Company EIN: 743135689

TransUnion Corp. Contributions Program
555 W. Adams St.
Chicago, IL 60661-3719
URL: http://www.transunion.com/corporate/about-transunion/who-we-are/community-affairs.page

Purpose and activities: TransUnion makes charitable contributions to nonprofit organizations involved with financial education and services. Support is given primarily in areas of company operations.
Fields of interest: Higher education; Youth development, business; Human services, financial counseling; Community/economic development.
Type of support: General/operating support.
Geographic limitations: Giving primarily in areas of company operations.

3800
Transwestern Investment Realty
2801 N. Tenaya Way, Ste. C
Las Vegas, NV 89128-1400
(702) 851-9000

Establishment information: Established in 2003.
Company type: Private company
Business activities: Operates real estate investment company.
Business type (SIC): Investors/miscellaneous
Corporate officer: Jeffrey A. Pori, Pres.
Giving statement: Giving through the Neusport Football Club.

Neusport Football Club
(formerly Revolution Athletic Club, Inc.)
7250 Peak Dr., Ste. 100
Las Vegas, NV 89128-1400
E-mail: jbrown@neusport.com; URL: http://www.neusport.com

Establishment information: Established in 2006 in NV.
Donor: Transwestern Investments Realty.
Financial data (yr. ended 07/31/10): Revenue, $1,115,062; assets, $204,021 (M); gifts received, $321,015; expenditures, $976,801; program services expenses, $87,342; giving activities include $2,170 for grants to individuals.
Directors: Jessica Brown; Christine Johnsong.
EIN: 412207419

3801
Travel Advantage Network, Inc.
(also known as TAN)
672 Old Mill Rd., Ste. 311
P.O. Box 64220
Millersville, MD 21108-1363
(800) 223-0088

Company URL: http://www.planwithtan.com
Establishment information: Established in 1992.
Company type: Private company
Business activities: Operates travel agency.
Business type (SIC): Travel and tour arrangers
Corporate officer: Bradley S. Callahan, C.E.O.
Giving statement: Giving through the TAN Corporate Giving Program.

TAN Corporate Giving Program
c/o Mktg. Dept.
672 Old Mill Rd.
Millersville, MD 21108-1363
URL: http://www.planwithtan.com/TANCharities.aspx

Purpose and activities: TAN makes charitable contributions of week-long condominium vacations to nonprofit organizations on a case by case basis. Three vacations are donated monthly. Support is given on a national basis.
Fields of interest: General charitable giving.
Type of support: Donated products; Employee volunteer services.
Geographic limitations: Giving on a national basis.
Application information: Applications accepted. Application form not required. Applicants should submit the following:
1) name, address and phone number of organization
2) contact person

Proposals should indicate the date of the event.
Initial approach: Proposal to headquarters

3802
The Travelers Companies, Inc.

(formerly The St. Paul Companies, Inc.)
485 Lexington Ave.
New York, NY 10017 (917) 778-6000

Company URL: http://www.travelers.com/
Establishment information: Established in 1853.
Company type: Public company
Company ticker symbol and exchange: TRV/NYSE
International Securities Identification Number: US89417E1091
Business activities: Operates holding company; sells property casualty insurance for auto, home, and business.
Business type (SIC): Holding company; security and commodity services; insurance/fire, marine, and casualty; insurance/surety
Financial profile for 2012: Number of employees, 30,600; assets, $104,938,000,000; sales volume, $25,740,000,000; pre-tax net income, $3,166,000,000; expenses, $22,574,000,000; liabilities, $79,533,000,000
Fortune 1000 ranking: 2012—116th in revenues, 78th in profits, and 63rd in assets
Forbes 2000 ranking: 2012—363rd in sales, 227th in profits, and 243rd in assets
Corporate officers: Jay S. Fishman, Chair. and C.E.O.; Jay S. Benet, Vice-Chair. and C.F.O.; William H. Heyman, Vice-Chair. and C.I.O.; Charles J. Clarke, Vice-Chair.; Irwin R. Ettinger, Vice-Chair.; Alan D. Schnitzer, Vice-Chair.; Doreen Spadorcia, Vice-Chair.; Brian W. MacLean, Pres. and C.O.O.; Andy F. Bessette, Exec. V.P. and C.A.O.; Madelyn Lankton, Exec. V.P. and C.I.O.; Maria Olivo, Exec. V.P. and Corp. Treas.; Kenneth F. Spence III, Exec. V.P. and Genl. Counsel; Lisa Caputo, Exec. V.P., Mktg. and Comms.; Joan Kois Woodward, Exec. V.P., Public Policy; John P. Clifford, Jr., Exec. V.P., Human Resources
Board of directors: Jay S. Fishman, Chair.; Jay S. Benet, Vice-Chair.; Charles Clarke, Vice-Chair.; Irwin R. Ettinger, Vice-Chair.; William H. Heyman, Vice-Chair.; Alan D. Schnitzer, Vice-Chair.; Alan L. Beller; John H. Dasburg; Janet M. Dolan; Kenneth M. Duberstein; Lawrence G. Graev; Patricia L. Higgins; Thomas R. Hodgson; William J. Kane; Cleve L. Killingsworth, Jr.; Donald J. Shepard; Doreen Spadorcia; Laurie J. Thomsen
Historic mergers: USF&G Corporation (April 24, 1998)
Giving statement: Giving through the Travelers Companies, Inc. Corporate Giving Program and the Travelers Foundation.
Company EIN: 410518860

The Travelers Companies, Inc. Corporate Giving Program

1 Tower Sq. - 2MS
Hartford, CT 06183 (651) 310-7757
FAX: (651) 310-2327;
E-mail: lcolanin@travelers.com; For questions within the state of CT: contact Tara Spain, e-mail: TNSPAIN@travelers.com; for Minnesota, contact Mike Newman, e-mail: MNEWMAN@travelers.com; URL: http://www.travelers.com/community/

Contact: Marlene Ibsen, V.P., Community Rels.; Lisa Colaninno, Opers. Mgr.
Financial data (yr. ended 12/31/12): Total giving, $8,343,699, including $8,343,699 for grants.
Purpose and activities: As a complement to its foundation, Travelers also makes charitable contributions to nonprofit organizations directly. Support is given primarily in areas of company operations.
Fields of interest: Arts; Education; Community/economic development Minorities; Economically disadvantaged.
Programs:
Employee Matching Gifts: The company matches contributions made by employees of Travelers to nonprofit organizations on a one-for-one basis up to $500 per employee, per year.
Volunteer Match: The company awards $500 grants to nonprofit organizations with which employees of Travelers volunteer at least 24 hours.
Type of support: Capital campaigns; Employee volunteer services; General/operating support; Program development; Scholarship funds; Sponsorships.
Geographic limitations: Giving primarily in areas of significant company operations, with emphasis on Hartford, CT, and St. Paul, MN; limited giving to national organizations.
Support limitations: No support for discriminatory, sectarian or religious, political, lobbying, fraternal, health or disease-specific organizations, or hospitals or other health service organizations generally supported by third-part reimbursement mechanisms.
Publications: Application guidelines; Corporate giving report; Corporate report; Grants list.
Application information: Applications accepted. The Community Relations Department handles giving. Application form required.
Initial approach: Complete online pre-application form
Committee meeting date(s): Quarterly
Deadline(s): Sept. 6
Final notification: 120 days
Number of staff: 5 full-time professional; 3 full-time support; 1 part-time support.
Selected grants: The following grants are a representative sample of this grantmaker's funding activity:
$510,650 to University of Connecticut Foundation, Storrs, CT, 2012. For program support for education initiative to improve access to post-secondary education for underserved communities and to build awareness of potential careers in insurance and finances.
$253,000 to Metropolitan State University Foundation, Saint Paul, MN, 2012. For program support for Travelers Pathways Program and Insurance Minor Program provides scholarships and post-secondary education aspirations and career preparation for risk management and insurance industry.
$200,000 to Capital Community College, Hartford, CT, 2012. For travelers EDGE to provide outreach and educational opportunities to underserved students to increase pipeline to college and careers through select education partners.

Travelers Foundation

385 Washington St.
St. Paul, MN 55102-1309 (651) 310-7757
FAX: (651) 310-2327;
E-mail: lcolanin@travelers.com; Additional contacts: Michael Newman, V.P., Travelers Foundation, tel.: (651) 310-7263; Tara N. Spain, V.P., Travelers Foundation, tel.:(860) 277-7015; and Lisa Colaninno, Opers. Mgr., tel.: (860) 277-3761; URL: http://www.travelers.com/corporate-info/about/community/foundation.aspx

Establishment information: Established in 1998 in MN.
Donors: The St. Paul Companies, Inc.; The St. Paul Travelers Companies, Inc.; The Travelers Companies, Inc.
Contact: Marlene Ibsen, Pres. and C.E.O.
Financial data (yr. ended 12/31/12): Assets, $142,626 (M); gifts received, $7,404,532; expenditures, $7,904,532; qualifying distributions, $7,904,532; giving activities include $7,893,699 for 475 grants (high: $350,000; low: $500).
Purpose and activities: The foundation supports organizations involved with arts and culture, education, employment, housing, youth, community development, leadership development, and economically disadvantaged people.
Fields of interest: Arts, cultural/ethnic awareness; Arts education; Arts; Elementary/secondary education; Education; Employment, training; Employment; Housing/shelter; Youth, services; Community development, small businesses; Community/economic development; Leadership development Minorities; Economically disadvantaged.
Programs:
Arts and Culture: The foundation supports organizations that build communities and enrich lives through arts and cultural activities and contribute directly to enhanced academic learning and access for low-income and underserved communities.
Community Development: The foundation supports organizations that help to create and maintain safety, stability, and vitality in local neighborhoods.
Education: The foundation supports initiatives that improve academic and career success for underrepresented youth, specifically targeted at public school children in grades 5 through 12, students in transition to post-secondary education, and students in a post-secondary learning environment.
Type of support: Capital campaigns; Employee matching gifts; Employee volunteer services; General/operating support; Program development; Scholarship funds; Sponsorships.
Geographic limitations: Giving primarily in areas of significant company operations, with emphasis on Hartford, CT and St. Paul, MN; limited giving to national organizations.
Support limitations: No support for discriminatory organizations, sectarian religious organizations, political, lobbying, or fraternal organizations, health or disease-specific organizations, or hospitals or other health services organizations generally supported by third-party reimbursement mechanisms, or environmental programs. No grants to individuals, or for scholarships, benefits, fund-raisers, walk-a-thons, telethons, galas or other revenue generating events, advertising, medical research, medical equipment, hospital capital or operating funds, replacement of government funding, human services such as counseling, chemical abuse treatment or family programs, or special events.
Application information: Applications not accepted. Contributes only to pre-selected organizations.
Board meeting date(s): Quarterly
Officers and Directors:* Andy F. Bessette*, Vice-Chair.; Marlene M. Ibsen*, C.E.O and Pres.; Michael Newman, V.P.; Tara N. Spain, V.P.; Kurt Schwartzkopf, Corp. Secy.; Jay S. Benet*, C.F.O. and Treas.; John P. Clifford, Jr.; Ron James; Michael F. Klein; Brian MacLean; Scott W. Rynda; Doreen Spadorcia; Kenneth F. Spence III; Joan K. Woodword.
Number of staff: None.
EIN: 411924256

Selected grants: The following grants are a representative sample of this grantmaker's funding activity:
$1,350,000 to Saint Paul Public Schools, Saint Paul, MN, 2012. To expand Advancement Via Individual Determination Initiative, national program to encourage students to enroll in courses that prepare them for college.
$780,000 to Hartford Public Schools, Hartford, CT, 2012. For program support for academic year including High School Inc, Asian Studies Academy, and Hartford Promise.
$500,000 to Habitat for Humanity International, Americus, GA, 2012.
$500,000 to United Way of Central and Northeastern Connecticut, Hartford, CT, 2012. For program support.
$80,000 to Ordway Center for the Performing Arts, Saint Paul, MN, 2012. For programs and events.

3803
Treasure Valley Business Group
439 E. Shore Dr., Ste. 200
P.O. Box 7067
Boise, ID 83707 (208) 383-9600

Company URL: http://www.treasurevalley.com
Establishment information: Established in 1994.
Company type: Private company
Business activities: Operates frozen foods company.
Business type (SIC): Groceries—wholesale
Corporate officer: Gary Lim, Pres. and C.E.O.
Giving statement: Giving through the Burke Family Foundation and the Transfer the Power Foundation, Inc.

Burke Family Foundation
P.O. Box 2536
Eagle, ID 83616-9119

Establishment information: Established in 2002 in ID.
Donors: Treasure Valley Sales & Marketing, Inc.; Timothy J. Burke; Dotty's Co., LLC.
Financial data (yr. ended 12/31/11): Assets, $99,912 (M); expenditures, $25,961; qualifying distributions, $25,236; giving activities include $25,236 for 7 grants (high: $10,000; low: $100).
Purpose and activities: The foundation supports Christian agencies and churches.
Fields of interest: Education; Religion.
International interests: Mexico.
Support limitations: No grants to individuals.
Application information: Applications not accepted. Unsolicited requests for funds not accepted.
Directors: Mary E. Burke; Timothy J. Burke.
EIN: 820517542

Transfer the Power Foundation, Inc.
P.O. Box 2536
Eagle, ID 83616-9119 (208) 383-0757
E-mail: info@transferthepower.com; Toll-free tel.: (208) 850-6800; URL: http://www.transferthepower.com

Establishment information: Established in 2002 in ID; funded in 2005.
Donor: Treasure Valley Business Group, Inc.
Financial data (yr. ended 12/31/11): Revenue, $31,434; assets, $208,346 (M); expenditures, $183,428; program services expenses, $168,403.
Officers: Timothy J. Burke, Pres.; Mary E. Burke, Secy.
Director: Ronald D. Coate.
EIN: 201593796

3804
Trends International, LLC
5188 W. 74th St.
Indianapolis, IN 46268 (317) 388-1212

Company URL: http://www.trendsinternational.com
Establishment information: Established in 1987.
Company type: Private company
Business activities: Manufactures and publishes posters, calendars, coloring activity kits and social stationery.
Business type (SIC): Non-durable goods—wholesale
Corporate officers: Phil St. Jean, Pres. and C.E.O.; Dave Kenna, C.I.O.; Bill Barrow, V.P., Sales and Mktg.; Darren Bowlby, Cont.
Giving statement: Giving through the Trends International Charitable Foundation Inc.

Trends International Charitable Foundation Inc.
5188 W. 74th St.
Indianapolis, IN 46268 (317) 388-1212

Establishment information: Established in 2003 in IN.
Donor: Trends International, Inc.
Contact: Steve Townley, V.P. and Treas.
Financial data (yr. ended 03/31/12): Assets, $31,178 (M); expenditures, $51,890; qualifying distributions, $49,500; giving activities include $49,500 for grants.
Fields of interest: Health care; Recreation; Human services.
Geographic limitations: Giving primarily in central IN and NY.
Application information: Applications accepted. Application form required. Applicants should submit the following:
1) detailed description of project and amount of funding requested
Initial approach: Letter
Deadline(s): None
Officers: Phil S. St. Jean, Pres. and Secy.; Steve Townley, V.P. and Treas.
EIN: 421590143

3806
Tribune-Review Publishing Company
622 Cabin Hill Dr.
Greensburg, PA 15601-1692
(724) 626-0513

Company URL: http://www.pittsburghlive.com/x/tribune-review
Establishment information: Established in 1924.
Company type: Private company
Business activities: Publishes newspapers; provides Internet information services.
Business type (SIC): Newspaper publishing and/or printing; computer services
Financial profile for 2010: Number of employees, 1,400
Corporate officers: Richard Mellon Scaife, Chair.; Ralph J. Martin, C.E.O.; Edward H. Harrel, Pres.; Nickolas F. Monico, C.O.O.; Raymond A. Hartung, Jr., Sr. V.P. and C.F.O.; Todd Tansimore, V.P., Finance; Bonnie Dake, V.P., Mktg.; H. Yale Gutnick, Secy.; Mark Berkowitz, Cont.
Board of director: Richard Mellon Scaife, Chair.
Subsidiary: T-R Printing & Publishing, Greensburg, PA
Giving statement: Giving through the Tribune-Review Charities.

Tribune-Review Charities
503 Martindale St., 3rd Fl.
Pittsburgh, PA 15212-5746

Establishment information: Established in 2000 in PA.
Donors: Trib Total Media, Inc.; Tribune-Review Publishing Co.; Richard J. Scaife Journalism Foundation.
Contact: Raymond A. Hartung, Jr., Treas.
Financial data (yr. ended 12/31/12): Assets, $5,506 (M); expenditures, $0; qualifying distributions, $0.
Purpose and activities: The foundation supports organizations involved with higher education, boxing, and disability services.
Fields of interest: Education; Recreation.
Type of support: Conferences/seminars; General/operating support; Sponsorships.
Geographic limitations: Giving primarily in Pittsburgh, PA.
Support limitations: No grants to individuals.
Application information: Applications accepted. Application form not required.
Initial approach: Proposal
Deadline(s): None
Officers: Ralph Martin, Pres.; H. Yale Gutnick, V.P.; Jennifer Bertetto, Secy.; Raymond A. Hartung, Jr., Treas.
Directors: Jennifer Walters.
EIN: 251848276

3807
Trico Electric Cooperative, Inc.
8600 W. Tangerine Rd.
P.O. Box 930
Marana, AZ 85658 (520) 744-2944

Company URL: http://www.trico.org
Establishment information: Established in 1945.
Company type: Cooperative
Business activities: Generates, transmits, and distributes electricity.
Business type (SIC): Electric services
Corporate officers: George P. Davies, Chair.; Vincent Nitido, Co-C.E.O.; Marv Athey, Co-C.E.O.; Kevin Rittler, C.A.O.; Barbara Stockwell, Secy.
Board of directors: Don Black; L. Nick Buckelew; George P. Davies; Brad DeSpain; Lawrence Hinchliffe; Barbara Stockwell; Marsha Thompson
Giving statement: Giving through the Trico Foundation.

The Trico Foundation
c/o Trico Electric Cooperative
P.O. Box 930
Marana, AZ 85653-0930 (520) 744-2944
E-mail: mpugno@trico.coop; URL: http://www.trico.coop/index.php?option=com_content&view=article&id=107&Itemid=109

Establishment information: Established in 1986 in AZ.
Donors: Cyprus Pima Mining Co.; Trico Electric Cooperative, Inc.

Financial data (yr. ended 12/31/11): Assets, $1,741,681 (M); gifts received, $39,332; expenditures, $73,706; qualifying distributions, $71,022; giving activities include $69,920 for 34 grants to individuals (high: $4,600; low: $920).
Purpose and activities: The foundation awards college scholarships to members and children and spouses of members of Trico Electric Cooperative.
Fields of interest: Higher education.
Program:
Scholarships: The foundation awards college scholarships to Trcico members and to the immediate family of Trico members. Students attending two-year schools are awarded $1,840 ($920 per semester) and students attend four-year schools are awarded $4,600 ($2,300 per semester). Applicants must have a 2.5 GPA or greater.
Type of support: Scholarships—to individuals.
Geographic limitations: Giving limited to AZ.
Publications: Application guidelines.
Application information: Applications accepted. Application form required.
Requests should include high school transcripts, at least one letter of recommendation, and financial statements.
Initial approach: Download application form and mail to foundation
Deadline(s): Varies, visit website for deadline
Officers: Marsha Thompson, Pres.; Charles B. DeSpain, V.P.; Don Black, Secy.; L. Nick Buckelew, Treas.
Trustees: George P. Davies; Barbara Stockwell.
EIN: 942941045

3805
Tri-County Electric Membership Corporation

4255 Alt. U.S. Hwy. 117 S.
P.O. Box 130
Dudley, NC 28333 (919) 735-2611

Company URL: http://www.tcemc.com
Establishment information: Established in 1940.
Company type: Cooperative
Business activities: Distributes electricity.
Business type (SIC): Electric services
Corporate officers: Carl W. Kornegay, Jr., Pres.; William Farmer, Jr., Secy.; Richard R. Grady, Treas.
Board of directors: Keith R. Beavers; William Farmer, Jr.; Dallace Grady; Richard R. Grady; Leland Heath; Carl W. Kornegay, Jr.; Randy McCullen; Worth Overman, Jr.; McKinley Price; Janice W. Smith; C. Coolidge Turner
Giving statement: Giving through the Tri-County Electric Foundation, Inc.

Tri-County Electric Foundation, Inc.

P.O. Box 130
Dudley, NC 28333-0130 (919) 735-2611

Establishment information: Established as a company-sponsored operating foundation.
Financial data (yr. ended 12/31/11): Assets, $38,733 (M); gifts received, $120,799; expenditures, $118,633; qualifying distributions, $118,461; giving activities include $69,631 for 23 grants (high: $10,000; low: $250) and $48,830 for 28 grants to individuals (high: $5,000; low: $300).
Purpose and activities: The foundation supports fire departments and organizations involved with higher education, health, football, and human services and awards grants to individuals and families in need of financial assistance for shelter, clothing, food, healthcare, or other emergencies.
Fields of interest: Health care; Housing/shelter; Human services.
Type of support: Equipment; Grants to individuals; Program development; Scholarship funds.
Geographic limitations: Giving primarily in NC.
Support limitations: No grants for general operating support, salaries, or political purposes.
Application information: Applications accepted. Application form required.
Initial approach: Contact foundation for application form
Deadline(s): None
Directors: Gloria Bass; Kathy Creech; Cindy Davis; Amy Fishcer; Carl Kornegay, Jr.; Ronnie Parks.
Officers: Ronnie Parks, Pres.; Gail Cottle, V.P.; Gloria Bass, Secy.; Jennings Outlaw, Treas.
EIN: 621838433

3808
Trident Systems Incorporated

10201 Fairfax Blvd., Ste. 300
Fairfax, VA 22030-2222 (703) 273-1012

Company URL: http://www.tridsys.com
Establishment information: Established in 1985.
Company type: Private company
Business activities: Operates military technology company.
Business type (SIC): Computer services
Corporate officers: Nicholas Karangelen, Pres.; John Broglio, Exec. V.P., Opers.
Giving statement: Giving through the Trident Foundation.

Trident Foundation

10201 Fairfax Blvd., Ste. 300
Fairfax, VA 22030-2222

Establishment information: Established in 2005.
Donors: Nicholas E. Karangelen; Trident Systems.
Financial data (yr. ended 09/30/11): Assets, $294,574 (M); expenditures, $15,743; qualifying distributions, $15,600; giving activities include $15,600 for 1 grant.
Purpose and activities: The foundation supports the Special Operations Warrior Foundation in Tampa, Florida.
Fields of interest: Education.
Type of support: General/operating support.
Support limitations: No grants to individuals.
Application information: Applications not accepted. Unsolicited requests for funds not accepted.
Officer: Nicholas E. Karangelen, Pres.
Directors: Megan Fitzsimmons; Richard K. Gallagher.
EIN: 030575923

3809
TriLibrium

111 S.W. Columbia St., Ste.250
Portland, OR 97201 (503) 546-2050
FAX: (503) 546-8970

Company URL: http://www.TriLibrium.com
Establishment information: Established in 2008.
Company type: Private company
Business type (SIC): Business services/ miscellaneous
Corporate officers: Andre Furin, Co-Founder; Brian C. Setzler, Co-Founder
Giving statement: Giving through the TriLibrium Corporate Giving Program.

TriLibrium Corporate Giving Program

2100 NE Broadway, Ste. 205
Portland, OR 97232 (503) 546-2050
URL: http://www.TriLibrium.com

Purpose and activities: TriLibrium is a certified B Corporation that donates a percentage of net profits to charitable organizations. Support is given primarily in Portland, Oregon.
Type of support: General/operating support.
Geographic limitations: Giving primarily in Portland, OR.

3810
Trim Masters Inc.

1090 Industry Rd.
Harrodsburg, KY 40330-9140
(859) 734-6969

Company URL: http://www.trimmasters.com
Establishment information: Established in 1987.
Company type: Joint venture
Business activities: Manufactures automotive interior trim.
Business type (SIC): Fabricated textile products/ miscellaneous
Corporate officer: Tadashi Naito, Pres.
Giving statement: Giving through the Trim Masters Charitable Foundation, Inc.

Trim Masters Charitable Foundation, Inc.

401 Enterprise Dr.
Nicholasville, KY 40356-2294

Donor: Trim Masters Inc.
Financial data (yr. ended 06/30/12): Assets, $1,910,267 (M); expenditures, $395,577; qualifying distributions, $393,790; giving activities include $393,790 for grants.
Purpose and activities: The foundation supports festivals and parks and organizations involved with arts and culture, education, health, cancer, child welfare, agriculture, athletics, and human services.
Fields of interest: Arts, cultural/ethnic awareness; Arts; Elementary/secondary education; Higher education; Libraries (public); Education; Health care; Cancer; Crime/violence prevention, child abuse; Agriculture; Recreation, parks/playgrounds; Recreation, fairs/festivals; Athletics/sports, amateur leagues; Boy scouts; YM/YWCAs & YM/YWHAs; Children, services; Human services; United Ways and Federated Giving Programs.
Type of support: Building/renovation; Capital campaigns; Equipment; General/operating support; Matching/challenge support; Program development; Scholarship funds; Sponsorships.
Geographic limitations: Giving primarily in KY.
Support limitations: No grants to individuals.
Application information: Applications not accepted. Contributes only to pre-selected organizations.
Officers and Directors: Dale Kihlman, Pres.; Steve Hesselbrock, V.P.; Beth Rohrback, Secy.-Treas.; Larry Carter; Anji Dodd; Julie Frank; Mike French; Scarlett Ingram; Mark Jennings.
EIN: 611225606
Selected grants: The following grants are a representative sample of this grantmaker's funding activity:
$155,000 to United Way, Heart of Kentucky, Danville, KY, 2010.

$25,000 to United Way of Delaware County, Muncie, IN, 2010. For general operations.
$10,000 to American Cancer Society, Oklahoma City, OK, 2010.
$10,000 to Anderson Dean Community Park, Harrodsburg, KY, 2010. For general operations.
$10,000 to Mercer County Public Library, Harrodsburg, KY, 2010. For general operations.
$3,000 to American Heart Association, Dallas, TX, 2010. For research.
$2,000 to Big Brothers Big Sisters of the Bluegrass, Lexington, KY, 2010. For general operations.
$1,000 to American Diabetes Association, Alexandria, VA, 2010. For research.
$1,000 to American Red Cross, Lexington, KY, 2010. For general operations.
$1,000 to Ball State University, Muncie, IN, 2010. For scholarships.

3811
Tripifoods, Inc.

1427 William St.
P.O. Box 1107
Buffalo, NY 14240 (716) 853-7400

Company URL: http://www.tripifoods.com
Establishment information: Established in 1911.
Company type: Private company
Business activities: Sells groceries, cigarettes, candy, frozen foods, and cosmetic and personal care items wholesale.
Business type (SIC): Groceries—wholesale; drugs, proprietaries, and sundries—wholesale; non-durable goods—wholesale
Corporate officer: Gregory Tripi, Chair., Pres., and C.E.O.
Board of director: Gregory Tripi, Chair.
Giving statement: Giving through the Tripifoods Foundation.

Tripifoods Foundation

c/o Hodgson Russ LLP
The Guaranty Bldg.
140 Pearl St., Ste. 100
Buffalo, NY 14202-4014

Establishment information: Established in 1986 in NY.
Donor: Tripifoods, Inc.
Financial data (yr. ended 06/30/12): Assets, $323,756 (M); gifts received, $70,000; expenditures, $14,546; qualifying distributions, $14,250; giving activities include $14,250 for grants.
Purpose and activities: The foundation supports hospitals and organizations involved with education, hunger, human services, and Catholicism.
Fields of interest: Secondary school/education; Theological school/education; Education; Hospitals (general); Food services; Human services; Catholic agencies & churches.
Type of support: General/operating support; Program development.
Geographic limitations: Giving primarily in western NY.
Support limitations: No grants to individuals.
Application information: Applications not accepted. Unsolicited requests for funds not accepted.
Trustees: Ted Cwudzinski; Gregory G. Tripi; Robert Wolski.
EIN: 133399842

3812
Triumph Modular, Inc.

(formerly Triumph Leasing Corporation)
194 Ayer Rd.
Littleton, MA 01460 (978) 486-0120

Company URL: http://www.triumphleasing.com
Establishment information: Established in 1981.
Company type: Private company
Business activities: Leases storage containers, over-the-road trailers, office trailers, and modular buildings.
Business type (SIC): Motor vehicle rentals and leasing
Corporate officers: Clifford Cort, Pres.; Gary Eason, C.F.O.; J. R. Hartley, V.P., Opers.; Mark Gaboury, V.P., Sales; Glenn A. Cort, Secy.-Treas.; Dave Treveloni, Cont.
Giving statement: Giving through the Arthur H. Cort Family Foundation.

Arthur H. Cort Family Foundation

c/o Ronald Cort
96 Jericho Road
Weston, MA 02493-1220

Establishment information: Established in 1972.
Donors: Plymouth Rock Transportation Corp.; Triumph Leasing Corp.; Arthur H. Cort†.
Financial data (yr. ended 11/30/11): Assets, $264,592 (M); expenditures, $38,162; qualifying distributions, $38,105; giving activities include $38,105 for grants.
Purpose and activities: The foundation supports hospitals and organizations involved with higher education, patient services, leukemia, learning disorders, and children and youth.
Fields of interest: Health care; Recreation; Youth development.
Type of support: Annual campaigns; General/operating support; Scholarship funds.
Geographic limitations: Giving primarily in MA.
Support limitations: No grants to individuals.
Application information: Applications not accepted. Contributes only to pre-selected organizations.
Trustees: Ronald Cort; Clifford Cort; Glenn Cort; Jack Cort; Lorna Macleod.
EIN: 237267248

3813
Tropicana Products, Inc.

1001 13th Ave. E.
P.O. Box 049003
Bradenton, FL 34208-2699 (941) 747-4461

Company URL: http://www.tropicana.com
Establishment information: Established in 1947.
Company type: Subsidiary of a public company
Business activities: Produces orange and grapefruit juice products.
Business type (SIC): Specialty foods/canned, frozen, and preserved
Corporate officers: Neil Campbell, Pres.; Dennis F. Hareza, Sr. V.P. and C.F.O.; Melinda Brown, Cont.
Giving statement: Giving through the Tropicana Products, Inc. Corporate Giving Program.

Tropicana Products, Inc. Corporate Giving Program

c/o Contribs. Comm.
1001 13th Ave. E.
Bradenton, FL 34208-2656
E-mail: tropicana.contributionscommittee@tropicana.com; URL: http://cr.tropicana.com/usen/tropusen.cfm?link=donations&date=20110502

Purpose and activities: Tropicana makes charitable contributions to nonprofit organizations on a case by case basis. Support is limited to California, Florida, and New Jersey.
Fields of interest: General charitable giving.
Type of support: Employee volunteer services; General/operating support.
Geographic limitations: Giving limited to areas of company operations in CA, FL, and NJ.
Application information: Applications accepted. A contributions committee reviews all requests. Application form not required. Applicants should submit the following:
1) name, address and phone number of organization
2) copy of IRS Determination Letter
3) detailed description of project and amount of funding requested

Initial approach: E-mail proposal to headquarters
Copies of proposal: 1
Deadline(s): 4 weeks prior to need
Final notification: Following review

3814
True Oil, LLC

455 N. Poplar
P.O. Box 2360
Casper, WY 82602 (307) 237-9301

Company URL: http://www.truecos.com/True_Oil
Establishment information: Established in 1953.
Company type: Private company
Business activities: Conducts crude petroleum exploration and production activities; produces natural gas.
Business type (SIC): Extraction/oil and gas
Corporate officers: H.A.'Hank' True III, Pres.; R.E. Dobbins, Treas.
Giving statement: Giving through the True Foundation.

True Foundation

P.O. Drawer 2360
Casper, WY 82602-2360

Establishment information: Established in 1958 in WY.
Donors: True Oil LLC; H. A. True, Jr.†; Jean D. True.
Contact: Cherie Miller, Exec. Secy.
Financial data (yr. ended 11/30/11): Assets, $2,457,869 (M); expenditures, $320,521; qualifying distributions, $306,511; giving activities include $306,511 for grants.
Purpose and activities: The foundation supports organizations involved with arts and culture, education, health, substance abuse services, legal aid, agriculture, and human services.
Fields of interest: Museums; Arts; Higher education; Education; Hospitals (general); Health care, clinics/centers; Medical care, rehabilitation; Health care; Substance abuse, services; Legal services; Agriculture; Agriculture, livestock issues; Children, services; Residential/custodial care, hospices; Developmentally disabled, centers & services; Human services; United Ways and Federated Giving Programs.

Type of support: Employee-related scholarships; General/operating support; Program development; Scholarship funds.
Geographic limitations: Giving primarily in WY and the Rocky Mountain area.
Application information: Applications accepted. Applicants should submit the following:
1) detailed description of project and amount of funding requested
Initial approach: Proposal
Deadline(s): None
Trustee: H. A. True III.
EIN: 836004596
Selected grants: The following grants are a representative sample of this grantmaker's funding activity:
$66,256 to United Way of Natrona County, Casper, WY, 2010.
$50,000 to 12-24 Club, Casper, WY, 2010.
$20,000 to National Cowboy and Western Heritage Museum, Oklahoma City, OK, 2010.
$10,000 to Child Development Center of Natrona County, Casper, WY, 2010.
$8,500 to Natrona County Public Library Foundation, Casper, WY, 2010.
$5,678 to Buffalo Bill Memorial Association, Cody, WY, 2010.
$2,500 to Childrens Advocacy Project, Casper, WY, 2010.
$2,250 to Dickinson State University, Dickinson, ND, 2010.
$2,000 to Craig and Susan Thomas Foundation, Cheyenne, WY, 2010.
$1,500 to Troopers Drum and Bugle Corps, Casper, WY, 2010.

3815
True Value Company

(formerly TruServ Corporation)
8600 W. Bryn Mawr Ave.
Chicago, IL 60631-3505 (773) 695-5000

Company URL: http://www.truevaluecompany.com
Establishment information: Established in 1910.
Company type: Cooperative
Business activities: Sells hardware and related products wholesale; manufactures and sells paint and paint applicators.
Business type (SIC): Hardware, plumbing, and heating equipment—wholesale; paints and allied products; manufacturing/miscellaneous
Financial profile for 2011: Number of employees, 2,466; assets, $693,300,000; sales volume, $1,804,000,000
Corporate officers: Brian A. Webb, Chair.; Lyle Heidemann, Pres. and C.E.O.; David A. Shadduck, Sr. V.P. and C.F.O.; Cathy Anderson, Sr. V.P., Human Resources, Genl. Counsel, and Secy.; Rosalee Hermens, V.P. and C.I.O.; Barbara Wagner, V.P. and Corp. Treas.
Board of directors: Brian A. Webb, Chair.; M. Shan Atkins; Cheryl Bachelder; Brent A. Burger; Richard E. George, Jr.; Michael S. Glode; Thomas S. Hanemann; Lyle Heidemann; Gregory Josefowicz; Kenneth A. Niefeld; Charles M. Welch
Subsidiary: Warner Industrial Supply, Inc., Minneapolis, MN
Divisions: General Paint & Chemical Div., Cary, IL; General Power Equip. Co., Harvard, IL
Historic mergers: ServiStar Coast to Coast Corporation (July 1, 1997)
Giving statement: Giving through the True Value Company Contributions Program and the True Value Foundation.
Company EIN: 362099896

True Value Foundation

8600 Bryn Mawr Ave.
Chicago, IL 60631-3579 (773) 695-5000
URL: http://truevaluecompany.com/about_true_value/true-value-foundation.asp

Financial data (yr. ended 12/31/11): Revenue, $628,618; assets, $397,310 (M); gifts received, $628,618; expenditures, $520,243; giving activities include $400,148 for grants and $84,500 for grants to individuals.
Purpose and activities: The charity supports nonprofit organizations involved with children and youth, elementary and secondary education, community development, and disaster preparedness.
Fields of interest: Elementary/secondary education; Disasters, preparedness/services; Community/economic development Children/youth.
Type of support: Donated products; Employee-related scholarships.
Officers and Directors:* Brian A. Webb, Pres.; Brent A. Burger, V.P.; Susan M. Radde, Secy.; Barbara L. Wagner, Treas.; Cathy C. Anderson; Lyle G. Heidemann; Christine Taylor.
EIN: 261897927

3816
Truefit Solutions Inc.

800 Cranberry Woods Dr., Ste. 120
Cranberry Township, PA 16066-5209
(724) 772-5959

Company URL: http://www.truefitsolutions.com/
Establishment information: Established in 1997.
Company type: Private company
Business activities: Customizes and develops computer software.
Business type (SIC): Computer services
Corporate officers: Louis Schaab, Chair.; Gary Griffin, C.F.O.
Board of director: Louis Schaab, Chair.
Giving statement: Giving through the Truefit Kingdom Builders Foundation.

Truefit Kingdom Builders Foundation

800 Cranberry Woods Dr., Ste. 120
Cranberry Township, PA 16066-5210 (724) 772-5959

Establishment information: Established in 2005 in PA.
Donor: Truefit Solutions.
Contact: Trevor Norris, Tr.
Financial data (yr. ended 12/31/12): Assets, $231,292 (M); expenditures, $34,665; qualifying distributions, $33,270; giving activities include $33,270 for 11 grants (high: $10,920; low: $100).
Fields of interest: Education; Human services; Religion.
Support limitations: No grants to individuals.
Application information: Applications accepted. Application form not required.
Initial approach: Proposal
Deadline(s): None
Trustees: Darrin Grove; Christopher S. Lasswell; Trevor J. Norris.
EIN: 256887993

3817
Truland Systems Corporation

1900 Oracle Way, Ste. 700
Reston, VA 20190-4733 (703) 464-3000

Company URL: http://www.truland.com/
Establishment information: Established in 1977.
Company type: Private company
Business activities: Provides contract electrical services.
Business type (SIC): Contractors/electrical work
Corporate officers: Robert W. Truland, Chair., Pres., and C.E.O.; John Jordan, C.F.O.
Board of director: Robert W. Truland, Chair.
Giving statement: Giving through the Truland Foundation.

The Truland Foundation

1900 Oracle Way, Ste. 700
Reston, VA 20190-4733 (703) 464-3000
E-mail: rtruland@truland.com

Establishment information: Established in 1954 in VA.
Donor: Truland Systems Corp.
Contact: Robert W. Truland, Pres.
Financial data (yr. ended 03/31/12): Assets, $158,175 (M); gifts received, $196,182; expenditures, $621,480; qualifying distributions, $588,108; giving activities include $588,108 for grants.
Purpose and activities: The foundation supports maritime museums and organizations involved with education, health, cystic fibrosis, cancer, heart disease, and Christianity.
Fields of interest: Museums (marine/maritime); Historic preservation/historical societies; Elementary/secondary education; Higher education; Education; Hospitals (general); Health care; Cystic fibrosis; Cancer; Heart & circulatory diseases; Christian agencies & churches.
Type of support: Capital campaigns; General/operating support.
Geographic limitations: Giving primarily in Washington, DC, MD, and VA; some giving in Bermuda.
Support limitations: No grants to individuals.
Application information: Applications accepted. Application form not required. Applicants should submit the following:
1) detailed description of project and amount of funding requested
Initial approach: Proposal
Deadline(s): None
Officers and Directors:* Robert W. Truland*, Pres.; Ingrid A. Moini, Secy.; Mary W. Truland.
EIN: 546037172
Selected grants: The following grants are a representative sample of this grantmaker's funding activity:
$100,000 to George Washington University, Washington, DC, 2011. For general operating support.
$50,000 to Washington Drama Society, Washington, DC, 2011. For general operating support.
$10,000 to Cystic Fibrosis Foundation, Bethesda, MD, 2011. For general operating support.
$10,000 to Saint Anselms Abbey School, Washington, DC, 2011. For general operating support.
$5,500 to American Cancer Society, Vienna, VA, 2011. For general operating support.

3818
Trustmark Insurance Company
400 Field Dr.
Lake Forest, IL 60045 (847) 615-1500

Company URL: http://www.trustmarkins.com
Establishment information: Established in 1913.
Company type: Private company
Business activities: Sells life and health insurance.
Business type (SIC): Insurance/life; insurance/accident and health
Financial profile for 2011: Assets, $1,850,762,790; sales volume, $1,035,284,912; liabilities, $1,285,135,042
Corporate officers: J. Grover Thomas, Jr., Chair.; Joseph L. Pray, Pres. and C.E.O.; Phil Goss, Sr. V.P. and C.F.O.
Board of director: J. Grover Thomas, Jr., Chair.
Giving statement: Giving through the Trustmark Foundation.

Trustmark Foundation
(formerly BTL Foundation)
400 Field Dr.
Lake Forest, IL 60045-4809
Contact for Impact Educator Grant Program: Cindy Gallaher, tel.: (847) 283-4065,
E-mail: cindy.gallaher@trustmarkins.com;
URL: http://www.trustmarkins.com/internet/corporate/aboutus_205.html

Establishment information: Established in 1985.
Donor: Trustmark Insurance Co.
Financial data (yr. ended 12/31/11): Assets, $565,397 (M); gifts received, $846,368; expenditures, $1,185,513; qualifying distributions, $1,185,498; giving activities include $1,185,498 for grants.
Purpose and activities: The foundation supports organizations involved with arts and culture, education, health, safety, and human services.
Fields of interest: Arts; Education; Health care, clinics/centers; Health care; Pediatrics; Nutrition; Safety/disasters; Children/youth, services; Residential/custodial care, hospices; Human services; United Ways and Federated Giving Programs.
Program:
Impact Educator Grant Program: The foundation, in partnership with Lake Forest Hospital, awards grants of up to $1,000 to teachers in Lake County public and private schools who promote healthy lifestyles through innovative educational programs. The program is limited to Lake County, Illinois.
Type of support: Employee volunteer services; Employee-related scholarships; General/operating support; In-kind gifts; Program development.
Geographic limitations: Giving primarily in IL.
Support limitations: No grants to individuals (except for employee-related scholarships).
Publications: Application guidelines.
Application information: Applications accepted. Application form not required. Applicants should submit the following:
1) results expected from proposed grant
2) name, address and phone number of organization
3) how project's results will be evaluated or measured
4) detailed description of project and amount of funding requested
5) copy of current year's organizational budget and/or project budget

Initial approach: Complete online application for Impact Educator Grant Program
Deadline(s): Oct. 24. for Impact Educator Grant Program
Final notification: Dec. for Impact Educator Grant Program

Officer and Trustees:* Nancy Eckrich*, Chair.; John Patton Hollow; Kathy Machak; David M. McDonough; Elizabeth O'Brien; Karen Preusker; Lloyd Sarrel; J. Grover Thomas, Jr.
EIN: 363330631
Selected grants: The following grants are a representative sample of this grantmaker's funding activity:
$30,000 to Interfaith House, Chicago, IL, 2010.
$20,000 to Feeding America, Chicago, IL, 2010.
$15,000 to Kennedy Krieger Foundation, Baltimore, MD, 2010.
$15,000 to Recreation Unlimited Foundation, Ashley, OH, 2010.
$10,000 to Actuarial Foundation, Schaumburg, IL, 2010.
$10,000 to American Cancer Society, Atlanta, GA, 2010.
$10,000 to Midwest Palliative and Hospice CareCenter, Glenview, IL, 2010.
$5,000 to Ravinia Festival Association, Highland Park, IL, 2010.
$5,000 to Rockhurst University, Kansas City, MO, 2010.
$1,803 to Save-A-Pet, Grayslake, IL, 2010.

3819
Tucson Electric Power Company
(also known as TEP)
1 S. Church Ave., Ste. 100
Tucson, AZ 85701-1612 (520) 571-4000

Company URL: http://www.tucsonelectric.com
Establishment information: Established in 1892.
Company type: Subsidiary of a public company
Business activities: Generates, transmits, and distributes electricity.
Business type (SIC): Electric services
Corporate officers: Paul J. Bonavia, Chair. and C.E.O.; David G. Hutchens, Pres.; Kevin P. Larson, Sr. V.P., C.F.O., and Treas.; Michael J. DeConcini, Sr. V.P., Opers.; Todd C. Hixon, V.P. and Genl. Counsel; Karen G. Kissinger, V.P. and Cont.; Kentton C. Grant, V.P., Finance; Catherine E. Ries, V.P., Human Resources; Herlinda H. Kennedy, Corp. Secy.
Board of directors: Paul J. Bonavia, Chair.; Lawrence J. Aldrich; Barbara M. Baumann; Larry W. Bickle; Harold W. Burlingame; Robert A. Elliott; Daniel W.L. Fessler; Louise L. Francesconi; Warren Y. Jobe; Ramiro G. Peru; Gregory A. Pivirotto; Joaquin Ruiz
Giving statement: Giving through the TEP Corporate Giving Program.

TEP Corporate Giving Program
P.O. Box 711, UE102
Tucson, AZ 85702-0711 (520) 884-3740
FAX: (520) 884-3606; E-mail: sfoltz@tep.com;
Application address for employee volunteer services: c/o TEP CAT Clearinghouse Subcommittee, Anna M. Cunes, P.O. Box 711, M.S. ID UE102, Tucson, AZ 85702, tel.: (520) 884-3741, e-mail: acunes@tep.com; URL: http://www.tucsonelectric.com/Community

Contact: Sharon Foltz
Purpose and activities: TEP makes charitable contributions to nonprofit organizations involved with education, energy conservation, environmental education, safety, economic development, and community development. Support is given primarily in Pima County and the White Mountain, Arizona, area.
Fields of interest: Education; Environment, energy; Environmental education; Safety, education; Economic development; Community/economic development.
Type of support: Capital campaigns; Employee volunteer services; General/operating support; In-kind gifts.
Geographic limitations: Giving primarily in areas of company operations in Pima County and the White Mountain, AZ, area.
Support limitations: No support for religious organizations, or political organizations or candidates, fraternal, social, or veterans' organizations, or individual K-12 schools. No grants to individuals, or for capital campaigns, endowments, fundraisers, sponsorships, travel, medical research, or adult sports; no electric service donations.
Publications: Application guidelines; Grants list.
Application information: Applications accepted. Proposals should be submitted unstapled using organization letterhead. Videos, brochures, CDs, and other ancillary materials are not accepted. Support is limited to 1 contribution per organization during any given year. An application form is required for employee volunteer services. The Community Relations Department handles giving. A contributions committee at each locale reviews all requests. Application form required. Applicants should submit the following:
1) role played by volunteers
2) timetable for implementation and evaluation of project
3) signature and title of chief executive officer
4) results expected from proposed grant
5) statement of problem project will address
6) population served
7) copy of IRS Determination Letter
8) brief history of organization and description of its mission
9) copy of most recent annual report/audited financial statement/990
10) how project's results will be evaluated or measured
11) listing of board of directors, trustees, officers and other key people and their affiliations
12) detailed description of project and amount of funding requested
13) listing of additional sources and amount of support
14) plans for acknowledgement

Organization should be at least three years old.
Initial approach: Mail proposal to headquarters for grants; download application form and mail to application address for employee volunteer services
Copies of proposal: 1
Committee meeting date(s): Sept. to Nov.
Deadline(s): Sept. 16 for grants. As early as possible for employee volunteer services
Final notification: Nov. for grants. 1 week following committee meetings for employee volunteer services

3820
Tulalip Casino
10200 Quil Ceda Blvd.
Tulalip, WA 98271-9163 (360) 716-7162

Company URL: http://www.tulalipcasino.com
Establishment information: Established in 1992.
Company type: Tribal corporation
Business activities: Operates casino.
Business type (SIC): Amusement and recreation services/miscellaneous
Corporate officers: Melvin R. Sheldon, Jr., Chair.; Deborah Parker, Vice Chair.; Glen Gobin, Secy.; Chuck James, Treas.
Board of directors: Melvin R. Sheldon, Jr., Chair.; Deborah Parker, Vice Chair.; Marlin Fryberg, Jr.; Mark Hatch; Don Hatch, Jr.
Giving statement: Giving through the Tulalip Tribes Charitable Fund.

Tulalip Tribes Charitable Fund
8802 27th Ave. N.E.
Tulalip, WA 98271-8063 (360) 716-5000
FAX: (360) 716-0126;
E-mail: msheldon@tulaliptribes-nsn.gov;
URL: http://www.quilcedavillage.org/charitable_fund/index.asp

Contact: Marilyn Sheldon, Charitable Contribs.
Purpose and activities: The fund supports organizations involved with arts and culture, pre-K and K-12 education, youth athletics, environment, and wildlife conservation.
Fields of interest: Performing arts, music; Arts; Elementary/secondary education; Education, early childhood education; Environment; Animals/wildlife; Health care; Recreation; Human services; International affairs; Public affairs; Religion Youth; Native Americans/American Indians.
Type of support: Capital campaigns; Conferences/seminars; Consulting services; Curriculum development; General/operating support; Matching/challenge support; Program development; Scholarship funds.
Geographic limitations: Giving limited to WA, with emphasis on King, Skagit, and Snohomish counties.
Support limitations: No support for political candidates or organizations. No grants to individuals, or for memorials or endowments, travel expenses, or legal fees.
Publications: Application guidelines; Grants list.
Application information: Applications accepted. The Charitable Contributions Department handles giving and reviews all requests. The company has a staff that only handles contributions. Application form required. Applicants should submit the following:
1) timetable for implementation and evaluation of project
2) results expected from proposed grant
3) qualifications of key personnel
4) statement of problem project will address
5) population served
6) copy of IRS Determination Letter
7) brief history of organization and description of its mission
8) geographic area to be served
9) copy of most recent annual report/audited financial statement/990
10) how project's results will be evaluated or measured
11) listing of board of directors, trustees, officers and other key people and their affiliations
12) detailed description of project and amount of funding requested
13) copy of current year's organizational budget and/or project budget
14) listing of additional sources and amount of support

Proposals should indicate the number of full-time staff, part-time staff, and volunteers; the organization's relationships with other organizations working to meet the same needs or providing similar services and how the organization differs from these other organizations; and other organizations solicited for support.
Initial approach: Download application form and mail proposal and application form to foundation
Copies of proposal: 1
Committee meeting date(s): Quarterly
Deadline(s): Mar. 1, June 1, Sept. 1, and Dec. 1
Final notification: 60 days following deadline if approved
Number of staff: 1 full-time professional.

3821
Tupperware Brands Corporation
14901 S. Orange Blossom Trail
Orlando, FL 32837-6600 (407) 826-5050
FAX: (302) 655-5049

Company URL: http://www.tupperwarebrands.com
Establishment information: Established in 1989.
Company type: Public company
Company ticker symbol and exchange: TUP/NYSE
Business activities: Manufactures and sells consumer products.
Business type (SIC): Plastic products/miscellaneous
Financial profile for 2012: Number of employees, 13,000; assets, $1,821,800,000; sales volume, $2,583,800,000; pre-tax net income, $272,800,000; expenses, $2,277,300,000; liabilities, $1,342,700,000
Fortune 1000 ranking: 2012—790th in revenues, 589th in profits, and 872nd in assets
Corporate officers: E. V. Goings, Chair. and C.E.O.; Simon C. Hemus, Pres. and C.O.O.; Michael Poteshman, Exec. V.P. and C.F.O.; Thomas M. Roehlk, Exec. V.P. and Secy.; Edward R. Davis III, V.P. and Treas.; Nick Poucher, V.P. and Cont.
Board of directors: E. V. Goings, Chair.; Catherine A. Bertini; Susan M. Cameron; Kriss Cloninger III; Antonio Monteiro De Castro; Joe R. Lee; Angel R. Martinez; Robert J. Murray; David R. Parker; Joyce M. Roche; M. Anne Szostak
Giving statement: Giving through the Tupperware Brands Corporation Contributions Program and the Tupperware Brands Foundation.
Company EIN: 364062333

Tupperware Brands Corporation Contributions Program
c/o Corp. Contribs.
14901 S. Orange Blossom Trail
Orlando, FL 32837-6600 (407) 826-5050
E-mail: YolandaLondono@tupperware.com;
URL: http://tupperware.csrroom.com/

Contact: Yolanda LondoNo, V.P., Global Social Responsibility
Purpose and activities: As a complement to its foundation, Tupperware also makes charitable contributions to nonprofit organizations directly. Support is given on a national and international basis.
Fields of interest: Children, services; Community/economic development.
Type of support: Capital campaigns; Cause-related marketing; Donated products; Employee matching gifts; Employee volunteer services; General/operating support; In-kind gifts; Matching/challenge support; Program development.
Geographic limitations: Giving on a national and international basis in areas of company operations.
Support limitations: No support for religious organizations, political organizations, or controversial organizations.
Application information: Application form not required. Applicants should submit the following:
1) detailed description of project and amount of funding requested
Initial approach: Proposal to headquarters
Copies of proposal: 1
Final notification: Following review

Tupperware Brands Foundation
(formerly Tupperware Children's Foundation)
c/o Tupperware Corp.
14901 S. Orange Blossom Trail
Orlando, FL 32837-6600

Establishment information: Established in 2003 in FL.
Donors: Tupperware U.S., Inc.; Tupperware Brands Corp.
Financial data (yr. ended 12/31/11): Assets, $467,776 (M); gifts received, $917,845; expenditures, $614,625; qualifying distributions, $614,000; giving activities include $614,000 for grants.
Purpose and activities: The foundation supports programs designed to educate and empower women and girls.
Fields of interest: Boys & girls clubs; Youth development, business Women; Girls.
Type of support: Capital campaigns; General/operating support.
Geographic limitations: Giving primarily in Lakeland and Orlando, FL.
Support limitations: No grants to individuals.
Application information: Applications not accepted. Contributes only to pre-selected organizations.
Officers and Directors:* Thomas M. Roehlk*, Pres.; Josef Hajek, Secy.; Michael Poteshman*, Treas.; Yolanda Londono, Exec. Dir.; Lillian D. Garcia.
EIN: 550824285

3822
Turf Paradise, Inc.
1501 W. Bell Rd.
Phoenix, AZ 85023-3411 (602) 942-1101

Company URL: http://www.turfparadise.com/
Establishment information: Established in 1954.
Company type: Private company
Business activities: Operates horse racing facilities.
Business type (SIC): Commercial sports; amusement and recreation services/miscellaneous
Corporate officers: Jerry Simms, Chair.; Eugene Joyce, Pres.; Patty Chakour, C.F.O.
Board of directors: Jerry Simms, Chair.; Frank Abbate; Amelia Blanco; Del Blondin; Gareth Jones; Sondra Reisinger; Serena Simms; Shawn Swartz; Tony Toporek
Giving statement: Giving through the Turf Paradise Foundation.

Turf Paradise Foundation
1501 W. Bell Rd.
Phoenix, AZ 85023-3411

Establishment information: Established in 1986.

Donors: Turf Paradise, Inc.; Ryan Family Foundation; T.P. Racing, LLP; Arizona H.B.P.A.
Contact: Vincent Francia, Chair.
Financial data (yr. ended 12/31/11): Assets, $15,568 (M); gifts received, $83,390; expenditures, $83,824; qualifying distributions, $83,824; giving activities include $9,800 for 1+ grant and $58,859 for 102 grants to individuals (high: $48,480).
Purpose and activities: The foundation supports organizations involved with equestrianism and awards grants to individuals associated with horse racing.
Fields of interest: Athletics/sports, equestrianism.
Type of support: General/operating support; Grants to individuals.
Application information: Applications accepted. Application form required. Applicants should submit the following:
1) brief history of organization and description of its mission
2) detailed description of project and amount of funding requested

Initial approach: Proposal
Deadline(s): None

Officers: Vincent Francia, Chair.; David W. Johnson, Vice.-Chair.
Director: John K. Mangum.
EIN: 742442775

3823
Turner Broadcasting System, Inc.

(also known as TBS)
1 CNN Ctr., N.W.
Atlanta, GA 30303-2762 (404) 827-1700

Company URL: http://www.turner.com
Establishment information: Established in 1970.
Company type: Subsidiary of a public company
Ultimate parent company: Time Warner Inc.
Business activities: Provides cable television services.
Business type (SIC): Cable and other pay television services; real estate subdividers and developers; commercial sports
Financial profile for 2013: Number of employees, 10,000
Corporate officers: Philip I. Kent, Chair. and C.E.O.; John Kampfe, Exec. V.P. and C.F.O.; Kelly Regal, Exec. V.P.
Board of director: Philip I. Kent, Chair.
Subsidiaries: Cable News Network, Inc., Atlanta, GA; The Cartoon Network LP, LLLP, Atlanta, GA; Peachtree TV, Atlanta, GA; Turner Broadcasting Sales, Inc., Atlanta, GA; Turner Classic Movies LP, LLLP, Atlanta, GA; Turner Network Television LP, LLLP, Atlanta, GA; Turner Sports, Inc., Atlanta, GA
Offices: Burbank, CA; Washington, DC; Miami, FL; Atlanta, GA; Chicago, IL; Detroit, MI; New York, NY
Giving statement: Giving through the TBS Corporate Giving Program.

TBS Corporate Giving Program

c/o Corp. Affairs Dept.
1 CNN Ctr., 11 N.
Atlanta, GA 30303-2762
FAX: (404) 827-5924;
E-mail: corporate.contributions@turner.com;
URL: http://www.turner.com/community

Contact: Kristina Christy, Dir., Corp. Responsibility
Purpose and activities: TBS makes charitable contributions to nonprofit organizations involved with arts and culture and secondary education. Special emphasis is directed toward programs designed to involve TBS executives and employees. Support is given primarily in Atlanta, Georgia.
Fields of interest: Arts; Secondary school/ education.
Programs:
Matching Grants: Turner will match up to $500 of an employee donation made to an educational institution or arts related nonprofit.
Turner Voices: Through the Turner Voices program, Turner supports organizations focused on high school-aged youth and the arts.
Volunteer Project Grants: When a Turner employee spends 30 hours or more volunteering with a nonprofit, they may apply for a monetary grant to support the organization.
Type of support: Cause-related marketing; Donated equipment; Donated products; Employee matching gifts; Employee volunteer services; In-kind gifts; Matching/challenge support; Program development; Sponsorships; Use of facilities.
Geographic limitations: Giving primarily in Atlanta, GA.
Support limitations: No support for religious organizations, fraternal organizations, athletic organizations, or veterans' organizations. No grants to individuals, or for continuing support, courtesy or journal advertising campaigns, seminars, conferences, or trips.
Application information: Applications not accepted. Contributes only to pre-selected organizations. The Corporate Responsibility Department handles giving and reviews all requests. The company has a staff that only handles contributions.
Committee meeting date(s): Jan.
Number of staff: 1 full-time professional; 1 full-time support; 1 part-time support.
Selected grants: The following grants are a representative sample of this grantmaker's funding activity:
$70,000 to Alliance Theater Company, Atlanta, GA, 2012.
$70,000 to Junior Achievement of Georgia, Atlanta, GA, 2012.
$60,000 to 21st Century Leaders, Decatur, GA, 2012.
$30,000 to VOX Teen Communications, Atlanta, GA, 2012.
$25,000 to Teach for America, Atlanta, GA, 2012.
$10,000 to Center for Puppetry Arts, Atlanta, GA, 2012.
$10,000 to Dads Garage, Atlanta, GA, 2012.
$10,000 to Georgia Center for Nonprofits, Atlanta, GA, 2012.
$10,000 to Theatrical Outfit, Atlanta, GA, 2012.

3824
Turner Construction Company

375 Hudson St.
New York, NY 10014-3658 (212) 229-6000

Company URL: http://www.turnerconstruction.com
Establishment information: Established in 1902.
Company type: Subsidiary of a foreign company
Business activities: Provides building construction services.
Business type (SIC): Contractors/general nonresidential building
Financial profile for 2010: Number of employees, 200; sales volume, $7,403,130,000
Corporate officers: Peter J. Davoren, Pres. and C.E.O.; John A. DiCiurcio, C.O.O.; Karen O. Gould, Sr. V.P., C.F.O., and Treas.; Mike Murphy, V.P. and Corp. Secy.; Chris McFadden, V.P., Comms.
Subsidiaries: The Lathrop Co., Inc., Maumee, OH; Turner Construction Co. of Texas, Dallas, TX
Giving statement: Giving through the Turner Construction Company Contributions Program and the Turner Construction Company Foundation.

Turner Construction Company Contributions Program

375 Hudson St.
New York, NY 10014 (212) 229-6000
URL: http://www.turnerconstruction.com/about-us/community-involvement

Purpose and activities: Turner makes charitable contributions to nonprofit organizations on a case by case basis. Support is given primarily in the New York, New York, area.
Fields of interest: Food banks; Housing/shelter, volunteer services; Youth development; Salvation Army.
Program:
YouthForce 2020: In New York City, YouthForce 2020 offers many opportunities and programs, one of which is an $8,000 scholarship/ internship to five students each year. To be eligible, the student must maintain a 2.80 GPA and major in Civil/Electrical/ Environmental/Mechanical Engineering, Construction Management or Architecture. The four-year internship at Turner begins immediately following the first full year of college. The scholarship program has been established to encourage minorities and women who have a strong, sincere desire to pursue an education that will result in a career in the Building Industry.
Type of support: General/operating support; Scholarship funds; Sponsorships.
Geographic limitations: Giving primarily in the New York, NY, area.
Publications: Application guidelines.
Application information: Applications accepted. Proposals for YouthForce 2020 should include a high school transcript, SAT or ACT transcript, essay, resume or biographical statement, two letters of reference, and confirmation of financial need. Application form required. Applicants should submit the following:
1) additional materials/documentation

Initial approach: Download online application form and mail with proposal to headquarters
Deadline(s): Apr. 30 for YouthForce 2020

Turner Construction Company Foundation

375 Hudson St., 6th Fl.
New York, NY 10014-3658

Establishment information: Established in 1980 in NY.
Donors: Turner Construction Co.; Garner USA LP; Sauer Group Inc.
Financial data (yr. ended 12/31/10): Assets, $291,567 (M); gifts received, $1,191,545; expenditures, $1,279,928; qualifying distributions, $1,279,928; giving activities include $826,839 for 98 grants (high: $110,000; low: $75).
Purpose and activities: The foundation supports organizations involved with education, health, heart disease, cancer research, children and youth, domestic violence, and international relief.
Fields of interest: Higher education; Education; Health care, volunteer services; Hospitals (general); Health care; Heart & circulatory diseases; Cancer research; American Red Cross; Children/youth, services; Family services, domestic violence; International relief.

Type of support: General/operating support; Program development; Scholarship funds.
Geographic limitations: Giving primarily in FL and IL.
Support limitations: No grants to individuals.
Application information: Applications not accepted. Contributes only to pre-selected organizations.
Officers: Peter J. Davoren, Pres.; Stephen Christo, Sr. V.P. and Secy.; John Onnembo, Jr., V.P.; Debi Herman, Treas.; Wilfried Eckert, C.F.O.
EIN: 133072570
Selected grants: The following grants are a representative sample of this grantmaker's funding activity:
$110,000 to American Heart Association, Dallas, TX, 2010.
$40,000 to Save the Children Federation, Westport, CT, 2010.
$25,000 to Yale-New Haven Hospital, New Haven, CT, 2010.
$15,000 to Childrens Memorial Foundation, Chicago, IL, 2010.
$15,000 to Florida A & M University Foundation, Tallahassee, FL, 2010.
$15,000 to Horizons for Youth, Chicago, IL, 2010.
$10,000 to Northern Westchester Hospital, Mount Kisco, NY, 2010.
$10,000 to Tutoring Chicago, Chicago, IL, 2010.
$6,439 to American Heart Association, Dallas, TX, 2010.
$5,000 to Inspiration Corporation, Chicago, IL, 2010.

3825
Turner Industries Group, L.L.C.

(also known as Turner Industries Ltd.)
8687 United Plaza Blvd., 5th Fl.
P.O. Box 2750
Baton Rouge, LA 70809 (225) 922-5050

Company URL: http://www.turner-industries.com
Establishment information: Established in 1961.
Company type: Private company
Business activities: Provides industrial building construction services; repairs, rents, and leases industrial machinery and equipment.
Business type (SIC): Contractors/general nonresidential building; equipment rental and leasing/miscellaneous; repair shops/miscellaneous
Financial profile for 2010: Number of employees, 400; sales volume, $1,600,000,000
Corporate officers: Roland M. Toups, Chair. and C.E.O.; Thomas H. Turner, Vice-Chair. and C.O.O.; Lester J. Griffon, Jr., V.P., Finance, and C.F.O.
Board of directors: Roland M. Toups, Chair.; Thomas H. Turner, Vice-Chair.
Giving statement: Giving through the Turner Foundation.

The Turner Foundation

c/o JPMorgan Chase Bank, N.A.
P.O. Box 3038
Milwaukee, WI 53201-3038
Application address: JPMorgan Chase Bank, N.A., 450 Laurel St., N. Tower, Ste. 200, Baton Rouge, LA 70801, tel.: (225) 332-4443

Establishment information: Established in 1989 in LA.
Donors: Turner Industries, Inc.; National Maintenance Corp.; International Piping Systems; Nichols Construction; International Maintenance Corp.; Burt S. Turner; Suzanne W. Turner.
Financial data (yr. ended 12/31/11): Assets, $4,490,839 (M); expenditures, $273,784; qualifying distributions, $219,171; giving activities include $219,171 for grants.
Purpose and activities: The foundation supports organizations involved with historic preservation, education, recreation, and Catholicism.
Fields of interest: Historic preservation/historical societies; Education; Recreation, parks/playgrounds; Recreation; Catholic agencies & churches.
Type of support: Program development.
Geographic limitations: Giving primarily in Washington, DC, Baton Rouge, LA, and New York, NY.
Support limitations: No grants to individuals.
Application information: Application form not required.
Initial approach: Contact foundation for application information
Deadline(s): None
Trustee: JPMorgan Chase Bank, N.A.
EIN: 581875562
Selected grants: The following grants are a representative sample of this grantmaker's funding activity:
$175,000 to BREC Foundation, Baton Rouge, LA, 2010. For program support.
$10,000 to Teach for America, New York, NY, 2010. For program support.
$6,000 to Cultural Landscape Foundation, Washington, DC, 2010. For program support.

3826
Tutor Perini Corporation

(formerly Perini Corporation)
15901 Olden St
Sylmar, CA 91342 (818) 362-8391

Company URL: http://www.tutorperini.com
Establishment information: Established in 1918.
Company type: Public company
Company ticker symbol and exchange: TPC/NYSE
Business activities: Provides construction services; develops real estate.
Business type (SIC): Construction/miscellaneous heavy; contractors/general residential building; real estate subdividers and developers
Financial profile for 2012: Number of employees, 11,016; assets, $3,296,410,000; sales volume, $4,111,470,000; pre-tax net income, -$267,840,000; expenses, $4,333,280,000; liabilities, $2,152,550,000
Fortune 1000 ranking: 2012—570th in revenues, 946th in profits, and 725th in assets
Corporate officers: Ronald N. Tutor, Chair. and C.E.O.; Michael R. Klein, Vice-Chair.; Robert Band, Pres.; Moichael Kershaw, Exec. V.P. and C.F.O.; William B. Sparks, Exec. V.P. and Secy.-Treas.
Board of directors: Ronald N. Tutor, Chair.; Michael R. Klein, Vice-Chair.; Marilyn A. Alexander; Peter Arkley; Robert Band; Anthony R. Coscia; Martin Melone; Robert L. Miller; Raymond R. Oneglia; Donald D. Snyder; Dickran Tevrizian
Offices: Phoenix, AZ; Southfield, MI; Hawthorne, NY
Giving statement: Giving through the Perini Corporation Contributions Program and the Charles B. & Louis R. Perini Family Foundation, Inc.
Company EIN: 041717070

The Charles B. & Louis R. Perini Family Foundation, Inc.

(formerly Perini Memorial Foundation, Inc.)
P.O. Box 1802
Providence, RI 02901-1802
Application address: c/o David B. Perini, 3 Donnelly Dr., Dover, MA 02030

Establishment information: Incorporated in 1953 in MA.
Donor: Perini Corp.
Contact: David B. Perini, Pres.
Financial data (yr. ended 12/31/11): Assets, $1,234,081 (M); expenditures, $63,690; qualifying distributions, $48,000; giving activities include $48,000 for grants.
Purpose and activities: The foundation supports organizations involved with education, boating, health, birth defects, cancer, and human services.
Fields of interest: Education; Environment; Human services.
Type of support: General/operating support.
Application information: Applications accepted. Application form not required. Applicants should submit the following:
1) copy of most recent annual report/audited financial statement/990
Initial approach: letter
Deadline(s): Nov. 1
Officer: Charles B. Perini, V.P.
Trustees: Bank of America; Bart W. Perini; Heather Perini; Timothy Perini.
EIN: 046118587

3827
Twins Sports Inc.

(also known as Minnesota Twins)
34 Kirby Puckett Pl.
Minneapolis, MN 55415-1523
(612) 375-1366

Company URL: http://minnesota.twins.mlb.com
Establishment information: Established in 1901.
Company type: Private company
Business activities: Operates professional baseball club.
Business type (SIC): Commercial sports
Corporate officers: Jerry Bell, Chair.; Jim Pohlad, C.E.O.; David St. Peter, Pres.; Kip Elliott, Exec. V.P. and C.F.O.; Matt Hoy, V.P., Opers.; Raenell Dorn, V.P., Human Resources
Board of directors: Jerry Bell, Chair.; Howard Fox; Bill Pohlad; Bob Pohlad; Jim Pohlad; David St. Peter
Giving statement: Giving through the Minnesota Twins Corporate Giving Program and the Minnesota Twins Community Fund.

Minnesota Twins Corporate Giving Program

c/o Community Rels. Dept.
1 Twins Way
Minneapolis, MN 55403-1418 (612) 659-3400
URL: http://minnesota.twins.mlb.com/min/community/index.jsp

Purpose and activities: As a complement to its foundation, the Minnesota Twins also makes charitable contributions of memorabilia to nonprofit organizations on a case by case basis. Support is limited to southwest Florida, Iowa, Minnesota, North Dakota, South Dakota, and Wisconsin.
Fields of interest: General charitable giving.
Type of support: In-kind gifts.

Geographic limitations: Giving limited to southwest FL, IA, MN, ND, SD, and WI.
Publications: Application guidelines.
Application information: Applications accepted. Application form required. Applicants should submit the following:
1) contact person
Proposals should indicate the date of the event, if applicable, and the date by which the donation is needed.
Deadline(s): 6 weeks prior to need
Final notification: 2 weeks prior to need

Minnesota Twins Community Fund

1 Twins Way
Minneapolis, MN 55403-1418 (612) 659-3407
FAX: (612) 573-6725; URL: http://mlb.mlb.com/min/community/index.jsp

Establishment information: Established in 1991 in MN.
Financial data (yr. ended 12/31/11): Revenue, $1,610,952; assets, $881,367 (M); gifts received, $1,512,984; expenditures, $1,526,276; program services expenses, $1,462,685; giving activities include $1,029,492 for 50 grants (high: $175,000; low: $5,339).
Purpose and activities: The fund seeks to enrich local and regional communities by providing resources for the healthy development of children and families through an association with baseball, softball, and the Minnesota Twins.
Fields of interest: Education; Athletics/sports, baseball; Recreation; Youth development.
Programs:
Diamonds and Dreams Scholarship Program: This program supports upper Midwest and southwest Florida youth in their pursuit of post-secondary education by providing up to 20 awards of $1,000 each to eligible applicants. Eligible applicants must: be U.S. residents who reside in Minnesota, Iowa, North Dakota, South Dakota, Wisconsin, or southwest Florida; be high school seniors who plan to enroll in a full-time, undergraduate course of study at an accredited two- or four-year college, university, or vocational-technical school; have a minimum GPA of 2.0; and participate, either as a player or volunteer, with an organized youth baseball or softball organization.
Fields for Kids: The fund provides financial support (between $1,000 and $5,000) to improve baseball and/or softball facilities for children in the upper Midwest and southwestern Florida. It makes matching grants to small nonprofit organizations and local governments that operate baseball and/or softball programs.
Tournament Grant Program: The fund will distribute grants of $100 to $1,000 to assist youth baseball and softball organizations administer national, regional, or statewide tournaments. Grant funds should be used to reduce the operating expenses of the tournament.
Youth Baseball and Softball Camp Scholarship Program: The fund will distribute scholarships of $100 to $500 for underprivileged upper Midwest youth to attend a baseball or softball instructional camp. The program is open to any upper Midwest youth involved in an organized youth baseball or softball program.
Type of support: Building/renovation; Equipment; General/operating support; In-kind gifts; Program development; Scholarships—to individuals.
Geographic limitations: Giving primarily in southwestern FL, IA, MN, ND, SD, and WI.
Publications: Application guidelines; Financial statement; Informational brochure; Informational brochure (including application guidelines); Newsletter.
Application information: Applications accepted. Application form required.
Initial approach: Download application form
Board meeting date(s): Quarterly
Officer and Directors:* Kevin Merkle*, Chair.; Paul Asao*, Vice-Chair.; Sharow Euerle*, Vice-Chair.; Jay Kim*, Vice-Chair.; Kevin Smith*, Secy.; Tom Larson*, C.F.O.; Duane Arens; Duane Reed; David E. St. Peter; and 12 additional directors.
EIN: 411697280

3828
Ty, Inc.

280 Chestnut Ave.
Westmont, IL 60559-1139 (630) 920-1515
FAX: (630) 920-1980

Company URL: http://www.ty.com
Establishment information: Established in 1986.
Company type: Private company
Business activities: Operates toy company.
Business type (SIC): Games, toys, and sporting and athletic goods
Corporate officers: Harold Warner, Chair. and C.E.O.; Tania Lundeen, Sr. V.P., Sales; Richard Jeffrey, C.F.O.
Board of director: H. Ty Warner, Chair.
Giving statement: Giving through the Ty, Inc. Contributions Program.

Ty, Inc. Contributions Program

280 Chestnut Ave.
Westmont, IL 60559-1139 (630) 920-1515
E-mail: tlundeen@tymail.com; URL: http://world.ty.com/

3829
Tyco Electronics Corporation

P.O. Box 3608
MS 140-10
Harrisburg, PA 17105-3608 (717) 592-4869

Company URL: http://www.tycoelectronics.com
Establishment information: Established in 1941.
Company type: Subsidiary of a foreign company
Business activities: Manufactures passive electronic components.
Business type (SIC): Electronic and other electrical equipment and components
Financial profile for 2009: Assets, $16,280,000,000; sales volume, $10,440,000,000
Corporate officers: Tom Lynch, C.E.O.; Joe Donahue, Exec. V.P. and C.O.O.; Robert Hau, Exec. V.P. and C.F.O.; John Jenkins, Exec. V.P. and Genl. Counsel; Jane Leipold, Sr. V.P., Human Resources; Joan Wainwright, Sr. V.P., Comms., and Mktg.
Board of director: Tom Lynch
International operations: Argentina; Australia; Austria; Brazil; Canada; Czech Republic; Denmark; Finland; France; Germany; Hong Kong; Hungary; Ireland; Italy; Malaysia; Mexico; Netherlands; New Zealand; Norway; Philippines; Poland; Singapore; South Korea; Spain; Sweden; Switzerland; Taiwan; Thailand; Turkey; United Kingdom
Giving statement: Giving through the Tyco Electronics Foundation.

Tyco Electronics Foundation

(formerly AMP Foundation)
c/o Tyco Electronics Corp.
P.O. Box 3608, M.S. 140-10
Harrisburg, PA 17105-3608 (717) 592-4869
FAX: (717) 592-4022;
E-mail: mjrakocz@tycoelectronics.com; Additional e-mail address: TEfoundation@te.com; URL: http://www.tycoelectronics.com/aboutus/community

Establishment information: Established in 1977 in PA.
Donor: AMP Inc.
Contact: Mary J. Rakoczy, Exec. Dir.
Financial data (yr. ended 12/31/10): Assets, $13,444,559 (M); gifts received, $135,406; expenditures, $697,106; qualifying distributions, $651,628; giving activities include $590,893 for 95 grants (high: $100,000; low: $110).
Purpose and activities: The foundation supports programs designed to promote education; energy and the environment; community development; and ethical business practices and conduct. Special emphasis is directed toward programs designed to address math, science, and engineering.
Fields of interest: Elementary/secondary education; Education; Environment, energy; Business/industry; Community/economic development; United Ways and Federated Giving Programs; Mathematics; Engineering; Science.
Programs:
Community Impact: The foundation supports local United Way chapters and organizations with which employees of Tyco Electronics volunteer.
Education: The foundation supports programs designed to address business and community concerns of Tyco Electronics. Special emphasis is directed toward programs designed to promote pre-college math and science education.
Type of support: Employee volunteer services; General/operating support; Program development; Research.
Geographic limitations: Giving primarily in areas of company operations, with emphasis on Menlo Park and northern CA, Boston, MA, NC, Harrisburg and central PA, and SC.
Support limitations: No support for private foundations, national organizations, service clubs, or fraternal, social, labor, or trade organizations, discriminatory organizations, or religious organizations not of direct benefit to the entire community. No grants to individuals, or for administrative or overhead expenses for research, political campaigns, or programs posing a potential conflict of interest; no loans or investments.
Publications: Application guidelines.
Application information: Applications accepted. A contributions committee reviews all requests. Organizations receiving support are asked to provide a final report. Application form not required.
Applicants should submit the following:
1) statement of problem project will address
2) population served
3) name, address and phone number of organization
4) copy of IRS Determination Letter
5) brief history of organization and description of its mission
6) copy of most recent annual report/audited financial statement/990
7) how project's results will be evaluated or measured
8) list of company employees involved with the organization
9) explanation of why grantmaker is considered an appropriate donor for project
10) listing of board of directors, trustees, officers and other key people and their affiliations

11) detailed description of project and amount of funding requested
12) plans for cooperation with other organizations, if any
13) contact person
14) copy of current year's organizational budget and/or project budget
15) listing of additional sources and amount of support

Proposals should include the organization's fax number, if available, and a description of past involvement by the foundation with the organization.
Initial approach: Proposal
Copies of proposal: 1
Deadline(s): None
Final notification: 4 to 6 weeks following board meetings

Officer: Mary J. Rakoczy, Exec. Dir.
Trustee: M&T Bank.
Number of staff: 1 full-time professional.
EIN: 232022928

3830
W. S. Tyler, Inc.

200 Peach Orchard Rd.
Salisbury, NC 28147-8323 (704) 633-5384
FAX: (704) 633-5392

Company URL: http://www.wstyler.ca/
Establishment information: Established in 2009.
Company type: Private company
Business activities: Manufactures fabricated wire and electric screening equipment.
Business type (SIC): Metal products/fabricated; machinery/special industry
Corporate officer: Florian Festge, Pres.
Giving statement: Giving through the Marion C. Tyler Foundation.

Marion C. Tyler Foundation

c/o KeyBank
4900 Tiedeman Rd.
Brooklyn, OH 44144-2302

Establishment information: Established in 1931 in OH.
Donor: W.S. Tyler, Inc.
Financial data (yr. ended 12/31/11): Assets, $1,105,524 (M); expenditures, $51,149; qualifying distributions, $37,566; giving activities include $37,566 for grants.
Purpose and activities: The foundation awards grants to supplement the pensions of indigent retirees of W.S. Tyler, Inc.
Type of support: Grants to individuals.
Geographic limitations: Giving primarily in areas of company operations in OH.
Support limitations: No loans or program-related investments.
Application information: Applications not accepted. Unsolicited requests for funds not accepted.
Trustee: KeyBank, N.A.
EIN: 346525274

3831
Tyler Technologies, Inc.

(formerly Tyler Corporation)
5949 Sherry Ln., Ste. 1400
Dallas, TX 75225-8010 (972) 713-3700
FAX: (972) 713-3741

Company URL: http://www.tylertech.com
Establishment information: Established in 1966.
Company type: Public company
Company ticker symbol and exchange: TYL/NYSE
Business activities: Provides data warehousing, Web hosting, electronic document management, information management outsourcing, title plant and property record database information, and real estate appraisal products and services.
Business type (SIC): Computer services
Financial profile for 2012: Number of employees, 2,388; assets, $338,310,000; sales volume, $363,300,000; pre-tax net income, $53,870,000; expenses, $306,730,000; liabilities, $193,020,000
Corporate officers: John M. Yeaman, Chair.; John S. Marr, Jr., Pres. and C.E.O.; Brian K. Miller, Exec. V.P., C.F.O., and Treas.; H. Lynn Moore, Jr., Exec. V.P. and Genl. Counsel; W. Michael Smith, V.P. and C.A.O.; Matthew Bieri, V.P. and C.I.O.; Robert Sansone, V.P., Human Resources; Terri L. Alford, Cont.
Board of directors: John M. Yeaman, Chair.; Donald R. Brattain; J. Luther King, Jr.; John S. Marr, Jr.; G. Stuart Reeves; Michael D. Richards; Dustin R. Womble
Subsidiaries: Business Resources Corp., Dallas, TX; CMS Holdings, Inc., Ames, IA; Eagle Computer Systems, Inc., Eagle, CO; FundBalance, Inc., Ann Arbor, MI; Gemini Systems Inc., Falmouth, ME; Interactive Computer Designs, Inc., Lubbock, TX; NationsData.com, Inc., Dallas, TX; Process Inc., Falmouth, ME; The Software Group, Inc., Plano, TX
Giving statement: Giving through the Tyler Foundation.
Company EIN: 752303920

Tyler Foundation

5949 Sherry Ln., Ste. 1400
Dallas, TX 75225-6532 (972) 713-3700

Establishment information: Established in 1971 in TX.
Donors: Tyler Corp.; Tyler Technologies, Inc.
Contact: Terri L. Alford, Secy.
Financial data (yr. ended 12/31/11): Assets, $2,574,388 (M); expenditures, $163,300; qualifying distributions, $144,615; giving activities include $144,615 for 46 grants (high: $18,780; low: $75).
Purpose and activities: The foundation supports hospitals and services clubs and organizations involved with education, patient services, cystic fibrosis, breast cancer, diabetes, housing development, golf, and human services.
Fields of interest: Education, early childhood education; Higher education; Education; Health care, patient services; Cystic fibrosis; Breast cancer; Diabetes; Housing/shelter, development; Athletics/sports, golf; Big Brothers/Big Sisters; American Red Cross; Children/youth, services; Human services, gift distribution; Human services; Community development, service clubs.
Type of support: General/operating support.
Geographic limitations: Giving primarily in areas of company operations, with emphasis on ME and Dallas, TX.
Support limitations: No grants to individuals, or for scholarships or fellowships; no loans; no matching gifts.
Application information: Applications accepted. Application form not required.
Initial approach: Proposal
Copies of proposal: 1
Board meeting date(s): As required
Deadline(s): None
Final notification: 3 to 4 weeks

Officers and Trustee:* John M. Yeaman, Pres.; Brian K. Miller, V.P. and Treas.; Terri L. Alford, Secy.
EIN: 237140526
Selected grants: The following grants are a representative sample of this grantmaker's funding activity:
$15,000 to Cystic Fibrosis Foundation, Dallas, TX, 2010.
$15,000 to Operation Tribute, Gorham, ME, 2010.
$14,000 to American Red Cross, Des Moines, IA, 2010.
$13,250 to Salesmanship Club of Dallas, Dallas, TX, 2010.
$10,000 to Lubbock Christian School, Lubbock, TX, 2010.
$5,000 to South Texas Academic Rising Scholars, McAllen, TX, 2010.
$2,500 to Boy Scouts of America, Circle Ten Council, Dallas, TX, 2010.
$2,000 to American Cancer Society, Topsham, ME, 2010.
$1,560 to Texas Stampede, Dallas, TX, 2010.
$1,000 to Cancer Community Center, South Portland, ME, 2010.

3832
Tyson Foods, Inc.

2200 Don Tyson Pkwy.
P.O. Box 2020
Springdale, AR 72762-6999
(479) 290-4000
FAX: (479) 290-7973

Company URL: http://www.tyson.com
Establishment information: Established in 1935.
Company type: Public company
Company ticker symbol and exchange: TSN/NYSE
Business activities: Produces, markets, and distributes chicken, beef, pork, prepared foods, and related allied products.
Business type (SIC): Meat packing plants and prepared meats and poultry; food and kindred products
Financial profile for 2012: Number of employees, 11,500; assets, $11,896,000,000; sales volume, $33,278,000,000; pre-tax net income, $927,000,000; expenses, $32,197,000,000; liabilities, $5,884,000,000
Fortune 1000 ranking: 2012—93rd in revenues, 300th in profits, and 353rd in assets
Forbes 2000 ranking: 2012—284th in sales, 940th in profits, and 1348th in assets
Corporate officers: John H. Tyson, Chair.; Donald Smith, Pres. and C.E.O.; James V. Lochner, C.O.O.; Dennis Leatherby, Exec. V.P. and C.F.O.; David L. Van Bebber, Exec. V.P. and Genl. Counsel; Curt T. Calaway, Sr. V.P., Cont., and C.A.O.; Gary Cooper, Sr. V.P. and C.I.O.; Kenneth J. Kimbro, Sr. V.P., Human Resources; R. Read Hudson, V.P. and Secy.; Matt Ellis, V.P. and Treas.
Board of directors: John H. Tyson, Chair.; Kathleen M. Bader; Gaurdie E. Banister, Jr.; Jim D. Kever; Kevin McNamara; Brad T. Sauer; Robert C. Thurber; Barbara A. Tyson; Albert C. Zapanta
Subsidiaries: Foodbrands America, Inc., Oklahoma City, OK; Tyson Fresh Meats, Inc., Dakota Dunes, SD

International operations: Argentina; Bermuda; British Virgin Islands; Canada; Cayman Islands; China; France; Hong Kong; India; Italy; Mauritius; Mexico; Netherlands; Poland; Turkey
Giving statement: Giving through the Bridge Capital, LLC Contributions Program, the Tyson Foods, Inc. Corporate Giving Program, and the Tyson Foods Foundation, Inc.
Company EIN: 710225165

Tyson Foods, Inc. Corporate Giving Program

c/o Community Rels.
2200 Don Tyson Pkwy.
Springdale, AR 72762-6901 (479) 290-4000
URL: http://www.tyson.com/Consumer/AboutTyson/TysonCares/Default.aspx

Purpose and activities: As a complement to its foundation, Tyson also makes charitable contributions to nonprofit organizations directly. Support is given primarily in areas of company operations in Alabama, Arizona, Arkansas, California, Georgia, Hawaii, Illinois, Indiana, Iowa, Kansas, Kentucky, Maryland, Mississippi, Missouri, Nebraska, New Jersey, New Mexico, New York, North Carolina, Oklahoma, Pennsylvania, South Carolina, South Dakota, Tennessee, Texas, Virginia, Washington, and Wisconsin.
Fields of interest: Education; Food services; General charitable giving.
Type of support: Building/renovation; Donated products; Employee volunteer services; General/operating support; In-kind gifts; Program development; Scholarship funds; Sponsorships.
Geographic limitations: Giving primarily in areas of company operations in AL, AR, AZ, CA, GA, HI, IA, IL, IN, KS, KY, MD, MO, MS, NC, NE, NJ, NM, NY, OK, PA, SC, SD, TN, TX, VA, WA, and WI.

Tyson Foods Foundation, Inc.

(formerly The IBP Foundation, Inc.)
c/o Robin Wages
P.O. Box 2020
Springdale, AR 72765-2020 (479) 290-2876

Establishment information: Established in 1979 in NE.
Donors: IBP, Inc.; Tyson Foods, Inc.
Contact: Annetta Young, Admin.
Financial data (yr. ended 12/31/11): Assets, $4,907,792 (M); expenditures, $707,072; qualifying distributions, $691,666; giving activities include $691,666 for grants.
Purpose and activities: The foundation supports community foundations and organizations involved with health, equestrianism, and boys.
Fields of interest: Youth development.
Type of support: General/operating support.
Geographic limitations: Giving in areas of company operation with emphasis on AR, Waterloo, IA, and Lexington, NE.
Support limitations: No support for churches or athletic teams. No grants to individuals, or for contests, or conferences.
Application information: Applications accepted. Application form required. Applicants should submit the following:
1) population served
2) name, address and phone number of organization
3) copy of IRS Determination Letter
4) detailed description of project and amount of funding requested
5) copy of current year's organizational budget and/or project budget

Initial approach: Contact foundation for application form
Board meeting date(s): Quarterly
Deadline(s): None

Officer: Robin A. Wages, Secy.
Directors: Archie Schaffer; John Tyson.
EIN: 476014039

3834
U.M. Holding Limited

(formerly United Medical Corporation)
56 N. Haddon Ave., Ste. 300
P.O. Box 200
Haddonfield, NJ 08033-2438
(856) 354-2200

Company URL: http://www.umholdings.com
Establishment information: Established in 1972.
Company type: Private company
Business activities: Manufactures fitness equipment; provides medical examination services; provides pharmaceutical research services.
Business type (SIC): Miscellaneous health services; medical offices and clinics/miscellaneous; research, development, and testing services; management and public relations services
Corporate officers: John Aglialoro, Chair. and C.E.O.; Joan Carter, Pres.; Arthur W. Hicks, Jr., V.P. and C.F.O.
Board of director: John Aglialoro, Chair.
Subsidiaries: Cardio Data Services, Haddonfield, NJ; Life Extension, Inc., New York, NY; Research Data Corp., Haddonfield, NJ; Trotter, Millis, MA
Giving statement: Giving through the U.M. Holdings Foundation.

U.M. Holdings Foundation

(formerly The United Medical Philanthropic Foundation)
56 N. Haddon Ave.
Haddonfield, NJ 08033-0288

Establishment information: Established in 1988 in NJ.
Donors: U.M. Holding Ltd.; Executive Health Exams Intl.
Contact: Rebecca H. Price, Tr.
Financial data (yr. ended 12/31/11): Assets, $33,459 (M); gifts received, $100,000; expenditures, $103,597; qualifying distributions, $103,500; giving activities include $103,500 for 6 grants (high: $40,000; low: $1,000).
Purpose and activities: The foundation supports service clubs and organizations involved with opera, health, hockey, and youth services.
Fields of interest: Performing arts, opera; Health care; Athletics/sports, winter sports; Youth, services; Community development, service clubs.
Type of support: General/operating support.
Geographic limitations: Giving primarily in southern NJ.
Support limitations: No grants to individuals.
Application information: Applications accepted. Application form required.

Initial approach: Letter
Copies of proposal: 1
Deadline(s): None

Officer: John Aglialoro, Chair. and Pres.
Trustees: Joan P. Carter; Arthur W. Hicks; Rebecca H. Price.
EIN: 521599160

3835
U.S. Bancorp

(also known as U.S. Bank)
(formerly First Bank System, Inc.)
800 Nicollet Mall
Minneapolis, MN 55402 (651) 466-3000
FAX: (612) 303-0782

Company URL: http://www.usbank.com
Establishment information: Established in 1863.
Company type: Public company
Company ticker symbol and exchange: USB/NYSE
Business activities: Operates bank holding company; operates commercial bank.
Business type (SIC): Banks/commercial; holding company
Financial profile for 2012: Number of employees, 64,486; assets, $353,855,000,000; pre-tax net income, $7,726,000,000; liabilities, $314,857,000,000
Fortune 1000 ranking: 2012—132nd in revenues, 35th in profits, and 16th in assets
Corporate officers: Richard K. Davis, Chair., Pres., and C.E.O.; Andrew Cecere, Vice-Chair. and C.F.O.; James L. Chosy, Exec. V.P., Genl. Counsel, and Corp. Secy.; Jennie P. Carlson, Exec. V.P., Human Resources
Board of directors: Richard K. Davis, Chair.; Douglas M. Baker, Jr.; Y. Marc Belton; Victoria Buyinski Gluckman; Arthur D. Collins, Jr.; Roland A. Hernandez; Doreen Woo Ho; Joel W. Johnson; Olivia F. Kirtley; Jerry W. Levin; David B. O'Maley; O'dell M. Owens, M.D.; Craig D. Schnuck, Jr.; Patrick T. Stokes
Subsidiaries: FBS Capital I, Minneapolis, MN; First Building Corp., Minneapolis, MN; First Group Royalties, Inc., Minneapolis, MN; First System Services, Inc., Minneapolis, MN; U.S. Bancorp Capital I, Wilmington, DE; U.S. Bancorp Card Services, Inc., Minneapolis, MN; U.S. Bancorp Community Development Corp., Minneapolis, MN; U.S. Bancorp Equity Capital, Inc., Minneapolis, MN; U.S. Bancorp Information Services, Inc., St. Paul, MN; U.S. Bancorp Insurance Services, Inc., Minneapolis, MN; U.S. Bancorp Investments, Inc., Minneapolis, MN; U.S. Bancorp Venture Capital Corp., Minneapolis, MN; U.S. Bank N.A., Minneapolis, MN; U.S. Bank N.A. MT, Billings, MT; U.S. Bank N.A. ND, Fargo, ND; U.S. Bank N.A. OR, Canby, OR; U.S. Bank Trust Co., N.A., Portland, OR; U.S. Bank Trust N.A., St. Paul, MN; U.S. Bank Trust N.A. MT, Billings, MT; U.S. Trade Services, Inc., Portland, OR
International operations: Ireland
Historic mergers: U.S. Bancorp (August 1, 1997); Piper Jaffray Companies Inc. (May 1, 1998); Firstar Corporation (February 27, 2001); Downey Savings and Loan Association (November 21, 2008)
Giving statement: Giving through the U.S. Bancorp Foundation, Inc.
Company EIN: 410255900

U.S. Bancorp Foundation, Inc.

U.S. Bank BC-MN-H21B
800 Nicollet Mall
Minneapolis, MN 55402 (612) 303-4000
FAX: (612) 303-0787;
E-mail: USBancorp@Easymatch.com; Additional address: U.S. Bancorp Foundation Grant Prog., P.O. Box 8857, Princeton, NJ 08543-8857, tel.: (866) 243-6925; URL: http://www.usbank.com/cgi_w/cfm/about/community_relations/charit_giving.cfm

Establishment information: Established in 1979.
Donors: First Bank System, Inc.; U.S. Bancorp; U.S. Bank, N.A.

Contact: John Pacheco, Dir.
Financial data (yr. ended 12/31/11): Assets, $35,410,950 (M); gifts received, $30,000,000; expenditures, $22,605,548; qualifying distributions, $22,373,819; giving activities include $21,939,542 for grants.
Purpose and activities: The foundation supports organizations involved with arts and culture, economic opportunity (see website for definition), education, and United Way. Special emphasis is directed toward programs designed to improve the educational and economic opportunities of low- and moderate-income individuals and families; and enhance the cultural and artistic lives of communities.
Fields of interest: Arts, multipurpose centers/ programs; Arts education; Museums; Performing arts; Historic preservation/historical societies; Arts; Elementary/secondary education; Higher education; Education; Employment, training; Employment; Housing/shelter, development; Housing/shelter, rehabilitation; Housing/shelter, home owners; Housing/shelter; Youth development, adult & child programs; Youth development; Human services, financial counseling; Economic development; Community development, small businesses; Community/economic development; United Ways and Federated Giving Programs Children/youth; Children; Youth; Adults; Young adults; Economically disadvantaged.
Programs:
Cultural and Artistic Enrichment: The foundation supports programs designed to build audiences for the arts, especially among underserved populations; bring select and limited civic amenities to underserved, rural communities; and promote the arts in education.
Economic Opportunity - Affordable Housing: The foundation supports programs designed to preserve, rehabilitate, and construct quality affordable housing that assists low- and moderate-income populations; and provide home buyer counseling and related economic education to individuals and families with low and moderate incomes.
Economic Opportunity - Economic Development: The foundation supports programs designed to promote small business development and expansion, commercial revitalization, and job creation.
Economic Opportunity - Self-Sufficiency: The foundation supports programs designed to assist low- and moderate-income individuals in development of work and life skills essential to self-sufficiency, with a focus on work-entry programs, specific skills training, employment retention, and personal financial management training; and help people transition from welfare to work by addressing child care and transportation issues.
Education: The foundation supports programs designed to help low-income and at-risk students succeed in school and prepare for post-secondary education; provide financial literacy training; and engage in effective mentoring programs. Special emphasis is directed toward programs designed to reach a broad number of students; bring together community resources; support curriculum innovation; and be replicated.
Employee Matching Gifts: The foundation matches contributions made by eligible employees of U.S. Bank to institutions of higher education and nonprofit organizations on a one-for-one basis from $50 to $1,000 per contributor, per year.
Type of support: Capital campaigns; Employee matching gifts; General/operating support; In-kind gifts; Program development; Scholarship funds.
Geographic limitations: Giving primarily in AR, AZ, CA, CO, IA, ID, IL, IN, KS, KY, MN, MO, MT, ND, NE, NM, NV, OH, OR, SD, TN, UT, WA, WI, and WY.
Support limitations: No support for fraternal organizations, merchant associations, or 501(c)(4) or (6) organizations, 509(a)(3) supporting organizations, pass-through organizations or private foundations, religious organizations, political organizations or lobbying organizations, or sponsorships. No grants to individuals, or for fundraising events or sponsorships, travel, endowments, debt reduction, or chamber memberships or programs.
Publications: Annual report; Application guidelines; Corporate report; Grants list.
Application information: Applications accepted. Unsolicited applications accepted from organizations located in communities served by U.S. Bank. Visit website for state charitable giving contacts and various application deadlines. Application form required. Applicants should submit the following:
1) copy of IRS Determination Letter
2) copy of most recent annual report/audited financial statement/990
3) listing of board of directors, trustees, officers and other key people and their affiliations
4) copy of current year's organizational budget and/ or project budget
5) additional materials/documentation

Initial approach: Complete online application
Board meeting date(s): 5 times per year
Deadline(s): Deadlines vary by state; Check website for deadlines for local area; Feb. 1 for Arts and Culture, Apr. 1 for Economic Opportunity, and July 1 for Education for organizations located in Twin Cities, Minnesota

Officers and Directors:* Deborah M. Burke*, Chair. and Pres.; James L. Chosy*, Secy.; Andrew Cecere*, Treas.; Jennie P. Carlson; Richard K. Davis*; Terrance Dolan; John Elmore; Elliot Jaffee; Barry Martin; Richard Payne; Kent Stone; Jeffry H. von Gillern.
EIN: 411359579
Selected grants: The following grants are a representative sample of this grantmaker's funding activity:
$850,000 to United Way, Greater Twin Cities, Minneapolis, MN, 2010. For general operating support.
$850,000 to United Way, Greater Twin Cities, Minneapolis, MN, 2011. For general operating support.
$200,000 to Minnesota Orchestral Association, Minneapolis, MN, 2010. For general operating support.
$200,000 to Minnesota Orchestral Association, Minneapolis, MN, 2011. For general operating support.
$150,000 to Saint Louis University, Saint Louis, MO, 2010. For general operating support.
$150,000 to Saint Louis University, Saint Louis, MO, 2011. For general operating support.
$100,000 to American Red Cross, Bismarck, ND, 2010. For general operating support.
$100,000 to American Red Cross National Headquarters, Washington, DC, 2011. For general operating support.
$100,000 to Greenlining Institute, Berkeley, CA, 2010. For general operating support.
$100,000 to Local Initiatives Support Corporation, New York, NY, 2011. For general operating support.
$90,000 to Sioux Empire Housing Partnership, Sioux Falls, SD, 2011. For general operating support.
$65,000 to Minnesota Home Ownership Center, Saint Paul, MN, 2010. For general operating support.
$50,000 to Big Brothers Big Sisters of Metropolitan Milwaukee, Milwaukee, WI, 2010. For general operating support.
$50,000 to Big Brothers Big Sisters of Metropolitan Milwaukee, Milwaukee, WI, 2011. For general operating support.
$5,500 to United Way of the Greater Clarksville Region, Clarksville, TN, 2011. For general operating support.
$5,000 to Association for the Advancement of Contemporary Dance, Boise, ID, 2011. For general operating support.
$5,000 to Elements of Education Partners, Tacoma, WA, 2011. For general operating support.
$5,000 to Northeast Community College Foundation, Norfolk, NE, 2010. For general operating support.
$4,500 to Field Museum of Natural History, Chicago, IL, 2010. For general operating support.
$4,500 to United Way of Columbia County, Rainier, OR, 2010. For general operating support.

3836
U.S. Bank N.A.

800 Nicollett Mall
Minneapolis, MN 55402 (651) 466-3000

Company URL: http://www.usbank.com
Establishment information: Established in 1853.
Company type: Subsidiary of a public company
Business activities: Operates commercial bank.
Business type (SIC): Banks/commercial
Corporate officers: Richard K. Davis, Chair., Co-Pres., and C.E.O.; Dan Arrigoni, Co-Pres.
Board of director: Richard K. Davis, Chair.
Giving statement: Giving through the U.S. Bank N.A. Corporate Giving Program and the U.S. Bank Charitable Foundation.

U.S. Bank N.A. Corporate Giving Program

c/o Community Affairs
800 Nicollett Mall
Minneapolis, MN 55402-7000
Contacts for Sponsorship Managers: Troy Morrison for AZ, CA, CO, NV, and UT, tel.: (858) 523-4216; Dan Bernert for AR, IL, IN, KY, OH, TN, and WI, tel.: (513) 632-2989; Dennis Bash for ID, MT, NE, OR, WA, WY, and national sponsorships, tel.: (503) 275-5244; Leslie Berkshire for KS, MN, MO, ND, SD, and national sponsorships, tel.: (612) 973-2391; URL: http://www.usbank.com/cgi_w/cfm/about/community_relations/sponsorship_event.cfm

Purpose and activities: U.S. Bank makes charitable contributions to nonprofit organizations involved with arts and culture, education, employment, housing, youth development, and community economic development. Support is given primarily in areas of company operations.
Fields of interest: Historic preservation/historical societies; Arts; Secondary school/education; Education; Employment, services; Employment, training; Housing/shelter, development; Housing/ shelter; Youth development; Salvation Army; Human services, financial counseling; Business/industry; Community/economic development; United Ways and Federated Giving Programs.
Programs:
Five Star Volunteer Award: Through the Five Star Volunteer Award, the company honors their most exceptional employee volunteers. The employee

receives recognition and a financial contribution to the organization cited in their nomination.

Make It Happen Program: Through Make It Happen, the company invites U.S. Bank Visa credit and debit cardholders to submit stories that would help a charity, friend, or the local community if they had $5,000. Cardholders use social media platforms like Facebook, Twitter, and LinkedIn to encourage the public to vote for their story. The cardholder with the most votes at the end of the promotion period receives $5,000 for their cause and $5,000 for themselves. Cardholders also receive an entry to win $5,00 every time the make a purchase during the promotion using their U.S. Bank Visa debit or credit card.
Type of support: Annual campaigns; Building/renovation; Capital campaigns; Continuing support; Curriculum development; Donated equipment; Donated products; Employee volunteer services; Equipment; General/operating support; In-kind gifts; Loaned talent; Management development/capacity building; Matching/challenge support; Professorships; Program development; Sponsorships.
Geographic limitations: Giving primarily in areas of company operations in AR, AZ, CA, CO, IA, ID, IL, IN, KS, KY, MN, MO, MT, ND, NE, NV, OH, OR, SD, TN, UT, WA, WI, and WY.
Support limitations: No support for national organizations. No grants to individuals, or for out-of-state travel, purchase of event tickets or program ads, tables at events or golf-hole purchases, civic or other memberships, or seminars or trade shows.
Publications: Application guidelines; Corporate giving report.
Application information: Applications accepted. The Community Development Department handles giving. The company has a staff that only handles contributions.
Initial approach: Contact local Sponsorship Manager for sponsorships
Copies of proposal: 1
Deadline(s): Varies for sponsorships
Final notification: Following review
Number of staff: 1 full-time professional; 1 full-time support.

U.S. Bank Charitable Foundation

(formerly First Bank Charitable Foundation)
c/o Trust Tax Services
P.O. Box 64713
St. Paul, MN 55164-0713

Establishment information: Trust established in 1962 in NE.
Donor: FirsTier Bank, N.A., Omaha.
Financial data (yr. ended 12/31/11): Assets, $46,113 (M); expenditures, $2,646; qualifying distributions, $2,106; giving activities include $1,596 for 1 grant.
Purpose and activities: The foundation supports the Madonna Foundation in Lincoln, Nebraska.
Fields of interest: Hospitals (general); Health care.
Type of support: General/operating support.
Geographic limitations: Giving primarily in Lincoln, NE.
Support limitations: No grants to individuals.
Application information: Applications not accepted. Unsolicited requests for funds not accepted.
Trustee: U.S. Bank, N.A.
EIN: 476020716

3837
U.S. Fiduciary Services, Inc.

801 Warrenville Rd., Ste. 500
Lisle, IL 60532-1396 (888) 647-4282

Company URL: http://www.usfiduciaryservices.com/
Establishment information: Established in 2003.
Company type: Private company
Business activities: Operates custom fiduciary services company.
Business type (SIC): Depository banking/functions related to
Corporate officers: Michael Welgat, Pres. and C.E.O.; Mark A. Elste, C.O.O; Timothy D. Weber, C.F.O.
Giving statement: Giving through the U.S. Fiduciary Services Charitable Foundation, Inc.

U.S. Fiduciary Services Charitable Foundation, Inc.

11270 W. Park Pl.
Milwaukee, WI 53224
Application address: c/o Linda Jelineck, U.S. Fiduciary Services, Inc., 801 Warrenville Rd., Ste. 500, Lisle, IL 60532, tel.: (630) 810-4500.

Establishment information: Established in 2006 in WI.
Donor: U.S. Fiduciary Services, Inc.
Contact: Lauren McAfee, Secy.
Financial data (yr. ended 12/31/11): Assets, $4,642 (M); expenditures, $8,840; qualifying distributions, $8,840; giving activities include $7,800 for 17 grants (high: $500; low: $100).
Purpose and activities: The foundation supports service clubs and organizations involved with education, diabetes, and breast cancer research.
Fields of interest: Higher education; Education; Diabetes; Breast cancer research; Community development, service clubs.
Type of support: Program development; Research; Scholarship funds.
Geographic limitations: Giving primarily in IL and WI.
Support limitations: No grants to individuals.
Application information: Applications accepted. Application form required.
Initial approach: Proposal
Deadline(s): None
Officers and Directors:* Mark A. Elste*, Pres.; Bradley K. Rinsem*, V.P.; Vaughn Gordy*, V.P.; Scott Harding*, V.P.; James Staruck*, V.P.; Arlene Westbrook, Secy.; Linda Jelinek*, Treas.
EIN: 204540416

3838
U.S. Foodservice, Inc.

9755 Patuxent Woods Dr.
Columbia, MD 21046-2286 (410) 312-7100

Company URL: http://www.usfoodservice.com
Establishment information: Established in 1989.
Company type: Private company
Business activities: Sells food wholesale.
Business type (SIC): Groceries—wholesale
Financial profile for 2011: Number of employees, 25,000; sales volume, $18,860,000,000
Corporate officers: Edward M. Liddy, Chair.; John A. Lederer, Pres. and C.E.O.; Stuart Schuette, C.O.O.; Allan Swanson, C.F.O.; Keith Roland, C.I.O.; Juliette Pryor, Exec. V.P. and Genl. Counsel; Milke Jester, V.P., Sales; David Lee, V.P., Opers.; Emily Gilbert, V.P., Human Resources
Board of director: Edward M. Liddy, Chair.
Subsidiary: Stock Yards Packing Co., Inc., Chicago, IL
Giving statement: Giving through the U.S. Foodservice Corporate Giving Program.

U.S. Foodservice Corporate Giving Program

9399 W. Higgins Rd.
Rosemont, IL 60018 (847) 720-8000
URL: http://www.usfoods.com/about-us/corporate-citizenship.html

Purpose and activities: U.S. Foodservice makes charitable contributions to programs designed to end hunger in America. Support is given on a national basis.
Fields of interest: Food services; Food banks; Human services, fund raising/fund distribution.
Type of support: Donated products; Employee volunteer services; In-kind gifts.
Geographic limitations: Giving on a national basis.

3839
U.S. Poultry & Egg Association, Inc.

1530 Cooledge Rd.
Tucker, GA 30084-7303 (770) 493-9401

Company URL: http://www.uspoultry.org/
Establishment information: Established in 1947.
Company type: Business league
Business activities: Produces and processes broilers, turkeys, ducks, eggs, and breeding stock.
Business type (SIC): Business association
Corporate officers: James Adams, Chair.; Elton Maddox, Vice-Chair.; Paul Hill, Secy.; Sherman Miller, Treas.
Board of directors: James Adams, Chair.; Elton Maddox, Vice-Chair.; Bill Bradley; Lyman Campbell; Gary Cooper; Tom Hensley; Mark Hickman; Greg Hinton; Jay Houchin; Kenton Kreager; Don Mabe; Pete Martin; Sherman Miller; Wes Morris; Shawn Nicholas; John Prestage; Walt Shafer; Mark Waller
Giving statement: Giving through the U.S. Poultry & Egg/Harold E. Ford Foundation, Inc.

U.S. Poultry & Egg/Harold E. Ford Foundation, Inc.

(formerly Southeastern Poultry & Egg/Harold E. Ford Foundation)
1530 Cooledge Rd.
Tucker, GA 30084-7303 (770) 493-9401
FAX: (770) 493-9257;
E-mail: bjenkins@poultryegg.org; URL: http://www.poultryfoundation.org/

Establishment information: Established in 1994 in GA.
Donors: U.S. Poultry & Egg Association; CTB, Inc.
Contact: Donald Dalton, Pres.
Financial data (yr. ended 09/30/11): Assets, $4,982,136 (M); gifts received, $57,818; expenditures, $650,974; qualifying distributions, $497,266; giving activities include $497,266 for grants.
Purpose and activities: The foundation supports programs and research designed to promote the poultry and egg industry.
Fields of interest: Higher education; Agriculture.
Program:
Poultry Science Education Fund: The foundation annually awards student recruitment grants of up to

$7,500 to colleges and universities with poultry science courses that do not have a full department with a poultry science degree.
Type of support: General/operating support; Program development; Research.
Geographic limitations: Giving primarily in AL, AR, CA, GA, MS, and TX.
Support limitations: No grants to individuals.
Publications: Application guidelines.
Application information: Applications accepted. Application form required. Applicants should submit the following:
1) detailed description of project and amount of funding requested
Initial approach: Download application form and e-mail or mail to foundation for the Poultry Science Education Fund
Deadline(s): Aug. 1 for the Poultry Science Education Fund
Officers: Steve Willardsen, Chair.; Gary Cooper, Vice-Chair.; James Adams, Secy.; Mark Waller, Treas.
Directors: James Denton; Elton Maddox; Wallace Morgan.
EIN: 582098298
Selected grants: The following grants are a representative sample of this grantmaker's funding activity:
$134,188 to Auburn University, Auburn, AL, 2011.
$132,941 to North Carolina State University, Raleigh, NC, 2011.
$53,432 to Ohio State University, Columbus, OH, 2011.
$29,499 to Texas A & M University, College Station, TX, 2011.
$19,043 to University of Arkansas, Fayetteville, AR, 2011.
$16,334 to University of Georgia, Athens, GA, 2011.
$15,295 to Texas A & M University, College Station, TX, 2011.
$7,000 to Jones County Junior College, Ellisville, MS, 2011.
$6,500 to Modesto Junior College, Modesto, CA, 2011.
$5,422 to Louisiana State University and A & M College, Baton Rouge, LA, 2011.

3840
U.S. Silica Company

UPS - 2496 Hancock Rd.
P.O. Box 187
Berkeley Springs, WV 25411
(304) 258-2500
FAX: (304) 258-8295

Company URL: http://www.u-s-silica.com
Establishment information: Established in 1987.
Company type: Private company
Business activities: Produces silica sand, kaolin clay, aplite, and related industrial minerals.
Business type (SIC): Mining/sand and gravel; mining/clay, ceramic, and refractory mineral
Corporate officers: Bryan A. Shinn, Pres. and Co-C.E.O.; Brian Slobodow, Co-C.E.O. and C.A.O.; Don Merril, V.P. and C.F.O.; Michael L. Winkler, V.P., Opers.; Michael L. Thompson, Treas.; Christine Marshall, Genl. Counsel and Corp. Secy.
Subsidiaries: Better Materials Corp., Woodbine, NJ; George F. Pettinos, Inc., Wayne, PA
Plants: Hurtsboro, AL; Ottawa, IL; Dubberly, LA; Rockwood, MI; Pacific, MO; Buena Vista Township, Mauricetown, Newport, Port Elizabeth, NJ; Dundee, OH; Mill Creek, OK; Mapleton Depot, PA; Columbia, SC; Jackson, TN; Kosse, TX; Montpelier, VA
Giving statement: Giving through the U.S. Silica Company Education Foundation.

The U.S. Silica Company Education Foundation

8490 Progress Dr., Ste. 300
Frederick, MD 21701 (800) 243-7500

Establishment information: Established in 1998.
Donors: U.S. Silica Company; Better Minerals & Aggregates Co.
Contact: Richard A. Johnson
Financial data (yr. ended 12/31/11): Assets, $36,002 (M); gifts received, $22,000; expenditures, $22,000; qualifying distributions, $22,000; giving activities include $22,000 for 4 grants to individuals (high: $6,000; low: $4,000).
Purpose and activities: The foundation awards college scholarships to children of employees of Better Minerals & Aggregates Company.
Type of support: Employee-related scholarships.
Geographic limitations: Giving limited to areas of company operations.
Application information: Applications accepted. Application form required.
Initial approach: Proposal
Deadline(s): Jan.
Officers and Directors: Brian Slobodow*, Pres.; Richard A. Johnson*, V.P. and Treas.; James Manion, V.P.; Yvonne M. Wood, Secy.; David Murray.
EIN: 550760222

3841
U.S. Smokeless Tobacco Company LLC

(formerly UST Inc.)
100 W. Putnam Ave.
Greenwich, CT 06830 (203) 661-1100

Company URL: http://www.ussmokeless.com
Establishment information: Established in 1822.
Company type: Subsidiary of a public company
Business activities: Produces and markets smokeless tobacco products.
Business type (SIC): Tobacco products—chewing, smoking, and snuff; beverages
Corporate officer: Peter P. Paoli, Pres. and C.E.O.
Subsidiaries: International Wine & Spirits Ltd., Greenwich, CT; Stimson Lane Ltd., Woodinville, WA; UST Enterprises Inc., Greenwich, CT
Plants: Franklin Park, IL; Hopkinsville, KY; Nashville, TN; Paterson, WA
Giving statement: Giving through the U.S. Smokeless Tobacco Company LLC Corporate Giving Program.
Company EIN: 061193986

U.S. Smokeless Tobacco Company LLC Corporate Giving Program

(formerly UST Inc. Corporate Giving Program)
P.O. Box 18583
Pittsburgh, PA 15236-0583 (800) 650-7411
URL: http://www.ussmokeless.com/en/cms/Responsibility/Investing_in_Communities/default.aspx

Purpose and activities: U.S. Smokeless Tobacco Company makes charitable contributions to nonprofit organizations involved with arts and culture, education, the environment, and youth development, as a subsidiary of the Altria Group. Support is given in areas of company operations.
Fields of interest: Arts, cultural/ethnic awareness; Elementary/secondary education; Education; Environment, natural resources; Environment; Youth development.
Program:
USSTC Operation Ranger Program: U.S. Smokeless Tobacco awards rugged, off-road utility vehicles to emergency responders. The program is designed to enhance emergency response capability at the community level.
Type of support: Employee matching gifts; Employee volunteer services.
Geographic limitations: Giving in areas of company operations.
Application information: Applications accepted.
Initial approach: Visit the Altria Group website for application guidelines

3842
UBS Financial Services Inc.

(formerly UBS PaineWebber Inc.)
1285 Ave. of the Americas, 12th Fl.
New York, NY 10019 (212) 713-2000

Company URL: http://financialservicesinc.ubs.com
Establishment information: Established in 1879.
Company type: Subsidiary of a foreign company
Business activities: Provides securities brokerage services.
Business type (SIC): Brokers and dealers/security
Financial profile for 2009: Number of employees, 15,505
Corporate officers: Robert J. McCann, C.E.O.; Anita M. Sands, C.O.O.
Subsidiary: Rotan Mosle Financial Corp., Houston, TX
International operations: United Kingdom
Giving statement: Giving through the UBS Financial Services Inc. Corporate Giving Program and the UBS Foundation U.S.A.

UBS Financial Services Inc. Corporate Giving Program

(formerly UBS PaineWebber Inc. Corporate Giving Program)
1285 Ave. of the Americas
New York, NY 10019-6028
E-mail: communityaffairs@ubs.com; URL: http://financialservicesinc.ubs.com/wealth/CommunityInvolvement.html

Purpose and activities: As a complement to its foundation, UBS also makes charitable contributions to nonprofit organizations directly. Support is given primarily in areas of company operations.
Fields of interest: Visual arts; Museums; Performing arts; Performing arts, orchestras; Arts; Higher education; Education; Cancer; Recreation, fairs/festivals; Athletics/sports, golf; Big Brothers/Big Sisters; YM/YWCAs & YM/YWHAs; Children/youth, services; Family services; Human services.
Type of support: Curriculum development; Donated equipment; Employee matching gifts; Employee volunteer services; Employee-related scholarships; General/operating support; In-kind gifts; Income development; Management development/capacity building; Matching/challenge support; Program development; Publication; Research; Sponsorships; Use of facilities.
Geographic limitations: Giving primarily in areas of company operations, with emphasis on FL, Chicago, IL, Boston, MA, New York, NY, Cleveland, OH,

Philadelphia, PA, Houston, TX, and Salt Lake City, UT; giving also to national organizations.
Application information: Applications not accepted. Contributes only to pre-selected organizations. The Community Affairs Department handles giving.
Number of staff: 1 full-time professional; 2 full-time support.

3833
U-Haul International, Inc.

2727 N. Central Ave.
Phoenix, AZ 85004 (602) 263-6645

Company URL: http://www.uhaul.com
Establishment information: Established in 1945.
Company type: Subsidiary of a public company
Business activities: Rents moving trucks and trailers; provides self-storage services.
Business type (SIC): Motor vehicle rentals and leasing; warehousing and storage
Financial profile for 2011: Number of employees, 18,000
Corporate officers: Edward J. Shoen, Chair. and C.E.O.; John C. Taylor, Pres.; Robert T. Peterson, C.F.O.; James H. Greer, V.P., Human Resources
Board of directors: Edward J. Shoen, Chair.; John C. Taylor
Giving statement: Giving through the U-Haul International, Inc. Corporate Giving Program.
Company EIN: 860663060

U-Haul International, Inc. Corporate Giving Program

c/o Community Rels., Attn.: Donations
2727 N. Central Ave.
Phoenix, AZ 85004-1158
FAX: (602) 263-6772;
E-mail: publicrelations@uhaul.com; URL: http://www.uhaul.com/About/Philanthropy.aspx

Purpose and activities: U-Haul makes charitable contributions to nonprofit organizations involved with food, shelter, and clothing and provides self-storage services to people affected by natural disasters. Support is given on a national basis in areas of company operations, with some emphasis on Phoenix, Arizona, and in Canada.
Fields of interest: Food services; Housing/shelter; Disasters, preparedness/services; Human services, emergency aid.
International interests: Canada.
Type of support: Donated products; Grants to individuals; Sponsorships.
Geographic limitations: Giving on a national basis in areas of company operations, with some emphasis on Phoenix, AZ, and in Canada.
Support limitations: No grants for beauty pageants or individual competitions, race teams or car clubs, school activities or sports teams.
Application information: Applications accepted. Application form not required. Applicants should submit the following:
1) name, address and phone number of organization
2) copy of IRS Determination Letter
3) contact person
Proposals should specifically note the nature of the request being made; for equipment donations indicate the size, type, locations, and preferred dates.
Initial approach: Mail, fax, or e-mail proposal to headquarters; e-mail or telephone for self-storage facilities
Copies of proposal: 1
Deadline(s): 3 weeks prior to need

3843
Ukpeagvik Inupiat Corporation

3201 C St., Ste. 801
P.O. Box 890
Anchorage, AK 99503 (907) 677-5200

Company URL: http://www.ukpik.com
Establishment information: Established in 1973.
Company type: Native corporation
Business activities: Operates native corporation.
Business type (SIC): Nonclassifiable establishments
Corporate officers: Price E. Brower, Chair.; Grant B. Thompson, Jr., Vice-Chair.; Anthony E. Edwardsen, Pres.; Richard Ungarook, Sr., Secy.; Forrest D. Olemaun, Treas.
Board of directors: Price E. Brower, Chair.; Grant B. Thompson, Jr., Vice-Chair.; Herman L. Ahsoak; Ned T. Arey, Sr.; Anthony E. Edwardsen; Raynita B. Hepa; David Maasak Leavitt, Jr.; Forrest D. Olemaun; Richard Ungabrook, Sr.
Office: Anchorage, AK
Giving statement: Giving through the UIC Foundation, Inc.

UIC Foundation, Inc.

3201 C St., Ste. 801
Anchorage, AK 99503 (907) 852-4460
FAX: (907) 852-4459; E-mail: mkaleak@ukpik.com; Additional tel.: (907) 852-7438; additional e-mail: UICFoundation@Ukpik.com; URL: http://www.ukpik.com/ShareholderProgramsAndServices.htm

Establishment information: Established in 1994 in AK.
Donors: Ukpeagvik Inupiat Corp.; National Park Svc.; UIC Construction LLC.
Contact: Mabel J. Kaleak
Financial data (yr. ended 12/31/11): Assets, $22,676 (M); gifts received, $128,383; expenditures, $115,202; qualifying distributions, $115,125; giving activities include $115,125 for grants to individuals.
Purpose and activities: The foundation supports organizations in various areas and awards college scholarships to shareholders and descendents of shareholders of Ukpeagvik Inupiat Corporation.
Type of support: Scholarships—to individuals.
Geographic limitations: Giving primarily in AK, with emphasis on Barrow.
Support limitations: No support for organizations that do not benefit shareholders and descendents of shareholders of Ukpeagvik Inupiat Corporation.
Publications: Application guidelines; Financial statement.
Application information: Applications accepted. Grants generally do not exceed $5,000. Application form required.
Scholarship applications must include a letter of acceptance from a post-secondary institution, recent transcripts, 3 letters of recommendation, and a personal essay.
Initial approach: Letter of inquiry; download application form and mail to foundation for scholarships
Copies of proposal: 1
Board meeting date(s): 3rd Thur. of each quarter
Deadline(s): Dec. 1, Mar. 1, May 1, and Aug. 1 for scholarships
Final notification: 2 weeks following deadlines
Officers and Directors: Anthony Edwardsen*, Pres.; Max Angeak*, V.P.; Larry Cooper*, Secy.-Treas.; Doreen Knodel; Roy Nageak.
Number of staff: 1 full-time support.
EIN: 920157584

3844
UL LLC

(also known as Underwriters Laboratories)
333 Pfingsten Rd.
Northbrook, IL 60062-2096 (847) 272-8800

Company URL: http://ul.com
Establishment information: Established in 1894.
Company type: Private company
Business activities: Operates product safety and certification testing services company.
Business type (SIC): Research, development, and testing services
Corporate officers: Keith E. Williams, Pres. and C.E.O.; Michael Saltzman, Sr. V.P. and C.F.O.; Christian Anschuetz, Sr. V.P. and C.I.O.
Giving statement: Giving through the UL Corporate Giving Program.

UL Corporate Giving Program

333 Pfingsten Rd.
Northbrook, IL 60062-2096 (847) 272-8800
URL: http://ul.com/global/eng/pages/corporate/careers/why/csr/

Purpose and activities: UL makes charitable contributions to nonprofit organizations involved with safety and education. Support is given primarily in areas of company operations.
Fields of interest: Education; Safety/disasters.
Type of support: Employee volunteer services; General/operating support.
Geographic limitations: Giving primarily in areas of company operations.

3845
Ulmer & Berne LLP

1660 W. 2nd St., Ste.1100
Cleveland, OH 44113-1448 (216) 583-7000

Company URL: http://www.ulmer.com/Pages/default.aspx
Establishment information: Established in 1908.
Company type: Private company
Business activities: Operates law firm.
Business type (SIC): Legal services
Corporate officer: Kip Reader, Managing Partner
Offices: Chicago, IL; Cincinnati, Cleveland, Columbus, OH
Giving statement: Giving through the Ulmer & Berne LLP Pro Bono Program.

Ulmer & Berne LLP Pro Bono Program

1660 W. 2nd St., Ste.1100
Cleveland, OH 44113-1448 (216) 583-7052
E-mail: jadams@ulmer.com; Additional tel.: (216) 583-7000; URL: http://www.ulmer.com/insideub/Pages/ProBono.aspx

Contact: Jennifer Lawry Adams, Partner
Fields of interest: Legal services.
Type of support: Pro bono services - legal.
Application information: By the attorney coordinating pro bono projects.

3846
UMB Financial Corporation

(formerly United Missouri Bancshares, Inc.)
1010 Grand Blvd.
Kansas City, MO 64106-2008
(816) 860-7000
FAX: (816) 860-4642

Company URL: http://www.umb.com
Establishment information: Established in 1913.
Company type: Public company
Company ticker symbol and exchange: UMBF/ NASDAQ
Business activities: Operates bank holding company; operates commercial bank.
Business type (SIC): Holding company; banks/ commercial
Financial profile for 2011: Number of employees, 3,448; assets, $14,927,200,000; pre-tax net income, $170,220,000; liabilities, $13,647,850,000
Corporate officers: J. Mariner Kemper, Chair. and C.E.O.; Michael D. Hagedorn, Vice-Chair., C.F.O., and C.A.O.; Peter J. DeSilva, Pres. and C.O.O.
Board of directors: J. Mariner Kemper, Chair.; Michael Hagedorn, Vice-Chair.; Paul D. Bartlett, Jr.; Thomas E. Beal; David R. Bradley, Jr.; Nancy K. Buese, C.P.A.; Peter J. DeSilva; Terrence P. Dunn; Kevin C. Gallagher; Peter J. Genovese; Gregory M. Graves; Alexander C. Kemper; Crosby R. Kemper, Jr.; Kris Alan Robbins; Thomas D. Sanders; L. Joshua Sosland; Paul Uhlmann III; J. Lyle Wells, Jr.; Thomas J. Wood III
Subsidiaries: United Missouri Bank of Boonville, Boonville, MO; United Missouri Bank of Brookfield, Brookfield, MO; United Missouri Bank of Carthage, Carthage, MO; United Missouri City Bank, Kansas City, MO
Giving statement: Giving through the UMB Financial Corporation Contributions Program.
Company EIN: 430903811

UMB Financial Corporation Contributions Program

(formerly United Missouri Bancshares, Inc. Corporate Giving Program)
c/o Community Involvement
P.O. Box 419226
Kansas City, MO 64141-6226
URL: https://www.umb.com/AboutUMB/Company/CommunityInvolvement/index.htm

Purpose and activities: UMB makes charitable contributions to nonprofit organizations involved with the arts, agriculture, economic development, and health and wellness. Support is given primarily in Los Angeles, California, Denver, Colorado, Washington, DC, Chicago, Illinois, and Kansas City, Kansas, with emphasis on Atlanta, Georgia, New York, New York, and Dallas and Fort Worth, Texas.
Fields of interest: Arts; Public health; Agriculture; Economic development.
Type of support: Employee volunteer services; General/operating support; In-kind gifts.
Geographic limitations: Giving primarily in Los Angeles, CA, Denver, CO, Washington, DC, Chicago, IL, and Kansas City, KS, with emphasis on Atlanta, GA, New York, NY, and Fort Worth and Dallas, TX.
Support limitations: No support for religious or fraternal, labor, political, or veterans' organizations, primary or secondary schools, or athletic groups. No grants to individuals, or for non-educational affiliated programs or events, or political campaigns; no in-kind gifts for events other than those sponsored by UMB.
Publications: Application guidelines.
Application information: Application form not required. Applicants should submit the following:
1) role played by volunteers
2) population served
3) name, address and phone number of organization
4) copy of IRS Determination Letter
5) brief history of organization and description of its mission
6) list of company employees involved with the organization
7) listing of board of directors, trustees, officers and other key people and their affiliations
8) detailed description of project and amount of funding requested
9) copy of current year's organizational budget and/ or project budget

Proposals should include the organization's website and indicate the organization's relationship to UMB banking, United Way affiliation, information about tax credits, and any deadlines, if applicable. Requests for in-kind donations should specify the quantity and intended use of the items.
Initial approach: Proposal to headquarters
Final notification: 4 to 6 weeks

3847
Umpqua Bank

445 S.E. Main St.
Roseburg, OR 97470-4900 (866) 486-7782

Company URL: http://umpquabank.com
Establishment information: Established in 1953.
Company type: Subsidiary of a public company
Business activities: Operates commercial bank.
Business type (SIC): Banks/commercial
Corporate officers: Allyn Ford, Chair.; Ray Davis, Pres. and C.E.O.
Giving statement: Giving through the Umpqua Bank Corporate Giving Program.

Umpqua Bank Corporate Giving Program

445 S.E. Main St.
Rosenberg, OR 97470-4900 (503) 727-4287
FAX: (541) 440-3961;
E-mail: community@umpquabank.com; URL: http://umpquabank.com/1.0/pages/ulCommunity.aspx?prodCAT=ulSupport

3848
Unaka Company, Inc.

1500 Industrial Rd.
Greeneville, TN 37745-3541
(800) 251-7558

Company URL: http://www.unaka.com
Establishment information: Established in 1950.
Company type: Private company
Business activities: Produces packaged foods; provides warehousing services.
Business type (SIC): Food and kindred products; warehousing and storage
Corporate officers: Robert Austin, Jr., C.E.O.; Gary Landes, Pres.; Buddy Yonz, C.F.O.
Subsidiaries: Crown Point Ltd., Mullins, SC; Sopakco Inc., Greeneville, TN
Giving statement: Giving through the Unaka Foundation, Inc.

The Unaka Foundation, Inc.

(formerly Unaka Scholarship Foundation, Inc.)
1500 Industrial Rd.
Greeneville, TN 37745-3541
E-mail: budd44@meco.net

Donors: Sopakco Inc.; Unaka Co., Inc.
Contact: L.A. Yonz, Secy.
Financial data (yr. ended 06/30/11): Assets, $16,838 (M); gifts received, $465,000; expenditures, $457,769; qualifying distributions, $457,679; giving activities include $457,679 for grants.
Purpose and activities: The foundation supports organizations involved with orchestras, education, and children.
Fields of interest: Performing arts, orchestras; Education; Children, services.
Programs:
Employee-Related Scholarships: The foundation awards college scholarships to children of full-time and seasonal employees of Unaka.
Matching Charitable Gifts: The foundation matches contributions made by employees of Unaka to nonprofit organizations.
Type of support: Capital campaigns; Employee matching gifts; Employee-related scholarships; General/operating support; Program development.
Geographic limitations: Giving primarily in TN.
Support limitations: No grants to individuals (except for employee-related scholarships).
Application information: Applications accepted. Application form required.
Initial approach: Contact foundation for application form
Deadline(s): None
Officers and Directors:* Dominick Jackson*, Pres.; L.A. Yonz, Secy.; Dean A. Nebben; Rayburn H. Tankersley; Harry D. Wade.
EIN: 621530053
Selected grants: The following grants are a representative sample of this grantmaker's funding activity:
$4,000 to University of Tennessee, Knoxville, TN, 2011.
$2,928 to American Cancer Society, Atlanta, GA, 2011.
$2,775 to Multiple Sclerosis Society, National, New York, NY, 2011.
$1,600 to University of Tennessee, Knoxville, TN, 2011.
$1,000 to American Diabetes Association, Alexandria, VA, 2011.
$1,000 to Life University, Marietta, GA, 2011.
$1,000 to Life University, Marietta, GA, 2011.
$1,000 to Tusculum College, Greeneville, TN, 2011.
$1,000 to Tusculum College, Greeneville, TN, 2011.

3849
UncommonGoods, LLC

140 58th St., Bldg B, Ste. 5A
Brooklyn, NY 11220-2521 (888) 365-0056

Company URL: http://www.uncommongoods.com
Establishment information: Established in 1999.
Company type: Private company
Business activities: Operates online and catalog retailer of products for the home.
Business type (SIC): Nonstore retailers
Corporate officers: David Bolotsky, C.E.O.; Thomas Epting, C.O.O.
Giving statement: Giving through the UncommonGoods Corporate Giving Program.

UncommonGoods Corporate Giving Program

140 58th St.
Bldg. B, Ste. 5A
Brooklyn, NY 11220-2523 (888) 365-0056
URL: http://www.uncommongoods.com/about/better.jsp

Purpose and activities: UncommonGoods is a certified B Corporation that donates a percentage of profits to nonprofit organizations.
Fields of interest: Environment, forests; Health care; Mental health/crisis services, rape victim services; Food services; Children/youth, services; Anti-slavery/human trafficking.
Type of support: Continuing support.
Application information: Applications not accepted. Contributes only to pre-selected organizations.

3850
Underground Elephant, Inc.

600 B St., Ste. 1300
San Diego, CA 92101 (800) 466-4178
FAX: (619) 923-2607

Company URL: http://undergroundelephant.com
Establishment information: Established in 2008.
Company type: Private company
Business activities: Operates online marketing company.
Business type (SIC): Management and public relations services
Corporate officers: Jason Kulpa, C.E.O.; William Huff, C.F.O.; Michael Norman, Sr. V.P., Mktg.; Keola Malone, Sr. V.P., Tech.
Giving statement: Giving through the Underground Elephant, Inc. Contributions Program.

Underground Elephant, Inc. Contributions Program

715 J St., Ste. 200
San Diego, CA 92101-7136 (858) 815-5324
URL: http://undergroundelephant.com

3851
Ungaretti & Harris LLP

3500 3 First National Plz.
70 W. Madison Ste., 3500
Chicago, IL 60602-4252 (312) 977-4400

Company URL: http://www.uhlaw.com/home.aspx
Company type: Private company
Business activities: Operates law firm.
Business type (SIC): Legal services
Corporate officer: Thomas M. Fahey, Managing Partner
Offices: Washington, DC; Chicago, Springfield, IL
Giving statement: Giving through the Ungaretti & Harris LLP Pro Bono Program.

Ungaretti & Harris LLP Pro Bono Program

3500 3 First National Plz.
70 W. Madison Ste., 3500
Chicago, IL 60602-4252 (312) 977-4400
E-mail: jtruskusky@uhlaw.com; URL: http://www.uhlaw.com/about/probono/

Contact: John T. Ruskusky, Chair, Pro Bono Comm.
Fields of interest: Legal services.
Type of support: Pro bono services - legal.
Application information: A Pro Bono Committee manages the pro bono program.

3852
UniGroup, Inc.

1 Premier Dr.
Fenton, MO 63026 (636) 305-5000

Company URL: http://www.unigroupinc.com
Establishment information: Established in 1987.
Company type: Private company
Business activities: Provides moving services.
Business type (SIC): Trucking and courier services, except by air
Financial profile for 2009: Number of employees, 1,050; sales volume, $1,600,000,000
Corporate officers: H. Daniel McCollister, Chair. and C.E.O.; Richard H. McClure, Pres. and C.O.O.; John M. Lograsso, Exec. V.P., Sales and Mktg.; Randall C. Poppell, C.I.O.; Mark Schroeder, Sr. V.P. and C.F.O.; Jan R. Alonzo, Sr. V.P. and Genl. Counsel; Cathy Malear, Sr. V.P., Human Resources; Carl O. Walter, V.P., Comms., and Mktg.
Board of director: H. Daniel McCollister, Chair.
Subsidiary: Mayflower Transit, LLC, Fenton, MO
Giving statement: Giving through the UniGroup, Inc. Corporate Giving Program and the UniGroup, Inc. Scholarship Foundation.

UniGroup, Inc. Corporate Giving Program

1 Premier Dr.
Fenton, MO 63026-2989 (636) 326-3100

Contact: George Mitch, Asst. to Pres.
Purpose and activities: UniGroup makes charitable contributions to nonprofit organizations on a case by case basis. Support is given primarily in areas of company operations.
Fields of interest: General charitable giving.
Type of support: General/operating support.
Geographic limitations: Giving primarily in areas of company operations; giving also to national organizations.
Application information: Application form not required.
Initial approach: Proposal to headquarters
Final notification: Following review

UniGroup, Inc. Scholarship Foundation

1 United Dr., Ste. R-3
Fenton, MO 63026-2535
FAX: (314) 349-2503

Establishment information: Established as a company-sponsored operating foundation in 1998 in MO.
Donor: UniGroup, Inc.
Financial data (yr. ended 12/31/11): Assets, $167,767 (M); gifts received, $13,090; expenditures, $58,671; qualifying distributions, $50,000; giving activities include $50,000 for 14 grants to individuals (high: $5,000; low: $3,000).
Purpose and activities: The foundation awards college scholarships to children of employees of UniGroup and its affiliated companies.
Fields of interest: Higher education.
Type of support: Employee-related scholarships.
Geographic limitations: Giving primarily in MO.
Application information: Applications accepted. Application form required.
Initial approach: Proposal
Deadline(s): Feb. 25
Officers and Director:* Michael A. DiRaimondo*, V.P. and Treas.; Linda Nosko, Secy.
EIN: 431806966

3853
Unilever United States, Inc.

700 Sylvan Ave.
Englewood Cliffs, NJ 07632-3113
(877) 995-4483

Company URL: http://www.unileverusa.com/
Establishment information: Established in 1890.
Company type: Subsidiary of a foreign company
Business activities: Manufactures and produces chemicals, soaps, detergents, shortenings, margarines, pancake syrup, and other household and institutional products.
Business type (SIC): Miscellaneous prepared foods; fats and oils; soaps, cleaners, and toiletries
Financial profile for 2009: Number of employees, 13,000
Corporate officers: Michael Treschow, Chair.; Kevin Havelock, Pres. and Group V.P.; Henry Schirmer, Sr. V.P., Finance and C.F.O.
Board of director: Michael Treschow, Chair.
Subsidiaries: Chesebrough-Pond's USA Co., Greenwich, CT; Conopco, Inc., New York, NY; Lever Bros. Company, New York, NY; Thomas J. Lipton Company, Englewood Cliffs, NJ; Van Den Bergh Foods Co., Lisle, IL
International operations: Canada
Giving statement: Giving through the Unilever United States Foundation, Inc.

Unilever United States Foundation, Inc.

c/o Unilever United States, Inc.
800 Sylvan Ave.
Englewood Cliffs, NJ 07632-3113 (201) 894-2450
Additional contact: Philip Cohen, tel.: (201) 894-2236

Establishment information: Incorporated in 1952 in NY.
Donors: Unilever United States, Inc.; Lever Bros. Co.; Van den Bergh Foods Co.; Unilever Research.
Contact: Greg Postian, Asst. V.P.
Financial data (yr. ended 12/31/11): Assets, $29,990 (M); gifts received, $1,057,706; expenditures, $3,100,614; qualifying distributions, $3,093,283; giving activities include $2,339,605 for 243 grants (high: $321,985; low: $100) and $753,678 for 1,516 employee matching gifts.
Purpose and activities: The foundation supports programs designed to promote healthier lifestyles for families and children with a focus on good nutrition, active healthy lifestyles, self-esteem, and hunger relief; and environmental issues with a focus on climate change, water conservation, waste and packaging, and environmental preservation.
Fields of interest: Education; Environment, waste management; Environment, climate change/global warming; Environment, natural resources; Environment, water resources; Environment; Public health, physical fitness; Food services; Food banks; Nutrition; Children/youth, services; Human services; Community/economic development.
Type of support: Employee matching gifts; Employee-related scholarships; General/operating support; Program development; Scholarship funds.

Geographic limitations: Giving primarily in areas of company operations, with emphasis on Washington, DC, IL, NJ, and NY.
Support limitations: No support for religious, labor, political, or veterans' organizations. No grants to individuals (except for employee-related scholarships), or for goodwill advertising, fundraising events or testimonial dinners, or capital campaigns; no loans.
Publications: Application guidelines.
Application information: Applications accepted. Application form not required. Applicants should submit the following:
1) copy of IRS Determination Letter
Initial approach: Proposal
Copies of proposal: 1
Board meeting date(s): May, Oct., and Dec.
Deadline(s): None
Final notification: 1 month following board meetings
Officers and Directors:* Jonathan Atwood*, Pres.; Sharon Rossi*, V.P.; David A. Schwartz, V.P.; Lauren Beck, Secy.; Henry Schirmer*, Treas.
Number of staff: 1 part-time professional.
EIN: 136122117

3854
Union Bank, N.A.

(formerly Union Bank of California, N.A.)
400 California St., 15th Fl.
San Francisco, CA 94104 (415) 765-3434

Company URL: https://www.unionbank.com
Establishment information: Established in 1864.
Company type: Subsidiary of a foreign company
Business activities: Operates commercial bank.
Business type (SIC): Banks/commercial
Corporate officers: John F. Woods, Vice-Chair and C.F.O.; John C. Erickson, Vice-Chair.; Mark W. Midkiff, Vice-Chair.; Timothy H. Wennes, Vice-Chair.; Masashi Oka, Pres. and C.E.O.; John Itokazu, Sr. Exec. V.P., C.I.O., and C.O.O.; Morris W. Hirsch, Sr. Exec. V.P. and Genl. Counsel; Erin Selleck, Sr. Exec. V.P. and Treas.; Annemieke van der Werff, Sr. Exec. V.P., Human Resources
Board of directors: John C. Erickson, Vice-Chair.; Mark W. Midkiff, Vice-Chair.; Timothy H. Wennes, Vice-Chair.; John F. Woods, Vice-Chair.
Offices: New York, NY; Dallas, TX
Giving statement: Giving through the Union Bank, N.A. Corporate Giving Program and the Union Bank Foundation.

Union Bank, N.A. Corporate Giving Program

(formerly Union Bank of California, N.A. Corporate Giving Program)
c/o Area Contrib. Comm.
400 California St., MC 1-001-08
San Francisco, CA 94104 (415) 765-3870
San Diego/Riverside/San Bernardino application address: c/o J.R. Raines, Donations Admin., 530 B St., MC S-650, San Diego, CA 92101, tel.: (619) 230-3043; Los Angeles/Orange Counties application address: c/o Anabel Gutierrez, Donations Admin., 445 S. Figueroa St., MC G04-010, Los Angeles, CA 90071, tel.: (213) 236-5540; URL: https://www.unionbank.com/company_information/company_information/community_reinvestment/charitable_contributions/index.jsp

Financial data (yr. ended 12/31/11): Total giving, $6,704,750, including $6,704,750 for grants.
Purpose and activities: As a complement to its foundation, Union Bank also makes charitable contributions to nonprofit organizations directly. Support is given primarily in areas of company operations.
Fields of interest: Arts; Education; Environment; Health care; Housing/shelter; Human services; Urban/community development; Community/economic development Homeless.
Type of support: Employee volunteer services; General/operating support; Scholarship funds; Sponsorships.
Geographic limitations: Giving primarily in areas of company operations, with emphasis on CA, OR, and WA.
Support limitations: No support for political, veterans', military, fraternal, or professional organizations, or individual K-12 schools; generally, no support for United Way-supported organizations or private foundations. No grants to individuals, or for dinner or luncheon tickets, advertising, video or film production unless distribution and screening are guaranteed, capital campaigns, service club activities, general operating support for hospitals, healthcare institutions, or educational institutions, or beauty or talent contests.
Publications: Application guidelines.
Application information: Applications accepted. The company has a staff that only handles contributions. A contributions committee reviews all requests. Application form not required. Applicants should submit the following:
1) copy of IRS Determination Letter
2) brief history of organization and description of its mission
3) copy of most recent annual report/audited financial statement/990
4) listing of board of directors, trustees, officers and other key people and their affiliations
5) detailed description of project and amount of funding requested
6) copy of current year's organizational budget and/or project budget
7) listing of additional sources and amount of support

Requests exceeding $10,000 must include performance measurement criteria. Sponsorship requests should include event invitations or brochures.
Initial approach: Proposal to headquarters
Copies of proposal: 1
Committee meeting date(s): Monthly
Deadline(s): None
Final notification: 2 to 3 months
Administrators: Gabriela Martinez, Off., Union Bank of California Fdn.; Karen Murakami, Off., Union Bank of California Fdn.; Kathy Patoff, V.P. and Community Devel. Off.

Union Bank Foundation

P.O. Box 45174
San Francisco, CA 94145-0174 (619) 230-3105
E-mail: charitablegiving@unionbank.com; Contact for J.R. Raines: Union Bank, N.A., 530 B Street, M.C. S-1450, San Diego, CA 92101, e-mail: jr.raines@unionbank.com; Contact for Northern CA, Central CA, and Pacific Northwest: Karen Murakami, Asst. V.P., Union Bank, N.A., 400 California Street, Mail Code 1-001-08, San Francisco, CA 94104, tel.: (415) 765-3890; URL: https://www.unionbank.com/global/about/corporate-social-responsibility/foundation/foundation-grants.jsp

Establishment information: Established in 1953.
Donors: Union Bank of California, N.A.; Union Bank.
Contact: J.R. Raines, Asst. V.P.
Financial data (yr. ended 12/31/11): Assets, $2,012,872 (M); gifts received, $4,515,854; expenditures, $4,459,907; qualifying distributions, $4,459,907; giving activities include $4,395,250 for 404 grants (high: $250,000; low: $750).
Purpose and activities: The foundation supports nonprofit organizations involved with affordable housing, community economic development, education, and the environment. Special emphasis is directed toward programs designed to benefit low-to-moderate income populations.
Fields of interest: Museums; Business school/education; Adult education—literacy, basic skills & GED; Education, ESL programs; Scholarships/financial aid; Education, services; Education, reading; Education, computer literacy/technology training; Education; Environment, waste management; Environment, recycling; Environment, natural resources; Environment, energy; Botanical gardens; Environmental education; Environment; Aquariums; Substance abuse, treatment; Crime/violence prevention; Crime/violence prevention, youth; Dispute resolution; Employment, services; Employment, training; Agriculture; Housing/shelter, aging; Independent housing for people with disabilities; Housing/shelter, temporary shelter; Housing/shelter, homeless; Housing/shelter; Children, day care; Youth, services; Human services, financial counseling; Community development, small businesses; Microfinance/microlending; Community/economic development Economically disadvantaged.
Programs:
Affordable Housing: The foundation supports programs designed to promote for-sale housing; rental housing; special needs housing; senior housing; transitional living facilities; emergency and homeless shelters; youth housing; self-help housing; farmworker housing; predevelopment funding to nonprofit developers; and capacity building for nonprofit housing organizations.
Community Economic Development: The foundation supports programs designed to promote community economic development. Special emphasis is directed toward small business development, including microenterprise development, technical assistance and entrepreneurial training, organizations that encourage access to capital for business or farms, and job creation; individual development, including job training and apprenticeship, welfare to work, wealth accumulation and asset building, life skills training, financial literacy and credit counseling, mortgage credit counseling, business education, and intervention and prevention programs for at-risk youth; and neighborhood development, including gang prevention and intervention, crime intervention, dispute resolution and mediation, reduction of liquor outlets, improved quality of food in local markets, childcare and daycare, drug and alcohol rehabilitation programs, independent living, and organizational capacity building.
Education: The foundation supports programs designed to encourage education. Special emphasis is directed toward scholarship programs; tutoring; GED preparation; ESL programs; computer education; teacher training; literacy; parent education; outreach initiatives for visual and performing arts organizations targeting low-to-moderate income populations; enrichment programs targeting low-to-moderate income populations; and capacity building for nonprofits.
Environment: The foundation supports programs designed to promote brownfield remediation; science and education related to green building; energy system upgrade and conservation; rehabilitation and cleanup; coastal/creek and reserve cleanup and preservation; urban green

space projects; environmental education; aquariums and museums; state parks, nature centers, conservancy centers, botanical gardens, and wildlife centers; and ecology and recycling centers.
Type of support: Continuing support; General/operating support; Management development/capacity building; Program development; Scholarship funds.
Geographic limitations: Giving primarily in areas of company operations in CA.
Support limitations: No support for political, religious, veterans, military, fraternal, or professional organizations, service clubs, individual elementary or secondary level schools, or intermediary foundations. No grants to individuals, or for capital campaigns, or educational institution operating funds.
Publications: Application guidelines; Corporate giving report.
Application information: Applications accepted. Grant requests exceeding $10,000 must include performance measurement criteria and the requester must submit a report of achievement annually. Multi-year funding is not automatic. Application form required. Applicants should submit the following:
1) results expected from proposed grant
2) population served
3) copy of IRS Determination Letter
4) brief history of organization and description of its mission
5) copy of most recent annual report/audited financial statement/990
6) listing of board of directors, trustees, officers and other key people and their affiliations
7) detailed description of project and amount of funding requested
8) copy of current year's organizational budget and/or project budget
9) listing of additional sources and amount of support

Initial approach: Complete online application
Board meeting date(s): Bi-Monthly
Deadline(s): None

Officers: Carl A. Ballton, Pres.; Gabriela Martinez, Secy.
EIN: 542178792

3855
Union County Savings Bank

320 N. Broad St.
Elizabeth, NJ 07208-3703 (908) 354-4600

Establishment information: Established in 1883.
Company type: Private company
Business activities: Operates savings bank.
Business type (SIC): Savings institutions
Corporate officers: Donald C. Sims, Pres. and C.E.O.; Frank Zabita, Treas.
Board of director: Donald C. Sims
Giving statement: Giving through the UCSB Charitable Foundation, Inc.

UCSB Charitable Foundation, Inc.

320 N. Broad St.
Elizabeth, NJ 07207

Establishment information: Established in 2002 in NJ.
Donor: Union County Savings Bank.
Financial data (yr. ended 12/31/11): Assets, $1,061,672 (M); gifts received, $540; expenditures, $52,540; qualifying distributions, $52,000; giving activities include $52,000 for 12 grants (high: $10,000; low: $2,000).
Purpose and activities: The foundation supports organizations involved with secondary education and human services.
Fields of interest: Secondary school/education; Boys & girls clubs; Residential/custodial care, hospices; Developmentally disabled, centers & services; Human services.
Type of support: General/operating support.
Geographic limitations: Giving primarily in Elizabeth, Newark, South Plains, and Union, NJ.
Application information: Applications not accepted. Unsolicited requests for funds not accepted.
Officers and Trustees:* Donald C. Sims*, Pres.; John K. Donahue*, V.P.; Kathleen H. Doyle*, Secy.; Joseph A. Manfredi; Tina A. Fredella.
EIN: 061665773

3856
Union Oil Company of California

(doing business as Chevron Corporation)
6001 Bollinger Canyon Rd.
San Ramon, CA 94583 (925) 842-1000

Company URL: http://www.chevron.com/
Establishment information: Established in 1890.
Company type: Subsidiary of a public company
Business activities: Conducts crude oil and natural gas exploration, production, and marketing activities; produces geothermal energy; generates, transmits, and distributes electricity; operates pipelines; operates natural gas storage facilities.
Business type (SIC): Extraction/oil and gas; pipelines (except natural gas/operation of); electric services; gas production and distribution
Corporate officers: Charles R. Williamson, Co-Chair. and C.E.O.; John S. Watson, Co-Chair.; Joe D. Cecil, V.P. and Compt.
Board of directors: John S. Watson, Co-Chair.; Charles R. Williamson, Co-Chair.
Giving statement: Giving through the Unocal Foundation.
Company EIN: 951315450

Unocal Foundation

6001 Bollinger Canyon Rd.
San Ramon, CA 94583-2324

Establishment information: Incorporated in 1962 in CA.
Donors: Unocal Corp.; Union Oil Co. of California.
Financial data (yr. ended 12/31/11): Assets, $499,244 (M); expenditures, $16,967; qualifying distributions, $0.
Purpose and activities: The foundation supports organizations involved with education, the environment, health, international affairs, and community development.
Fields of interest: Education; Environment, natural resources; Environment; Health care, clinics/centers; Health care; International affairs; Community/economic development.
Program:
Unocal Foundation Scholarship Program: The foundation annually awards up to 30 college scholarships to children of employees and retirees of Unocal. The program is administered by Scholarship America, Inc.
Type of support: Annual campaigns; Continuing support; Curriculum development; Scholarship funds.
Geographic limitations: Giving primarily in Washington, DC, ME, and VA; giving also in HI.
Support limitations: No support for veterans', fraternal, sectarian, social, religious, or athletic organizations, choral, band, or similar groups, trade or business associations, or state agencies or departments. No grants to individuals (except for employee-related scholarships), or for general operating support, capital campaigns for education, secondary education, endowments, courtesy advertising, conferences, or trips or tours; no loans.
Application information: Applications not accepted. Unsolicited requests for funds not accepted.
Directors: Ramiro Estrada*; Kari Endries; Matthew Lonner*; James Lyness; Rhonda Zygocki.
Number of staff: 1 full-time professional; 1 full-time support; 2 part-time support.
EIN: 956071812

3857
Union Pacific Corporation

1400 Douglas St.
Omaha, NE 68179 (402) 544-5000
FAX: (402) 271-6408

Company URL: http://www.up.com
Establishment information: Established in 1863.
Company type: Public company
Company ticker symbol and exchange: UNP/NYSE
International Securities Identification Number: US9078181081
Business activities: Provides railroad transportation services.
Business type (SIC): Transportation/railroad
Financial profile for 2012: Number of employees, 45,928; assets, $47,153,000,000; sales volume, $20,926,000,000; pre-tax net income, $6,318,000,000; expenses, $14,187,000,000; liabilities, $27,276,000,000
Fortune 1000 ranking: 2012—138th in revenues, 49th in profits, and 118th in assets
Forbes 2000 ranking: 2012—453rd in sales, 144th in profits, and 489th in assets
Corporate officers: James R. Young, Chair.; John J. Koraleski, Pres. and C.E.O.; Robert M. Knight, Jr., Exec. V.P., Finance and C.F.O.; Diane K. Doren, Exec. V.P. and Secy.; Lyndon L. Tennison, Sr. V.P. and C.I.O.; Gayla Thal, Sr. V.P. and Genl. Counsel; Mary Sanders Jones, V.P. and Treas.; Jeffrey P. Totusek, V.P. and Cont.
Board of directors: James R. Young, Chair.; Andrew H. Card, Jr.; Erroll B. Davis, Jr.; Thomas J. Donohue; Archie W. Dunham; Judith Richards Hope; John J. Koraleski; Charles C. Krulak; Michael R. McCarthy; Michael W. McConnell; Thomas F. McLarty III; Steven R. Rogel; Jose H. Villarreal
Subsidiaries: Southern Pacific Rail Corporation, San Francisco, CA; Union Pacific Railroad Co., Omaha, NE
Giving statement: Giving through the Union Pacific Corporation Contributions Program and the Union Pacific Foundation.
Company EIN: 132626465

Union Pacific Corporation Contributions Program

1400 Douglas St., Stop 1560
Omaha, NE 68179-1001 (402) 544-5034
FAX: (402) 501-2291; E-mail: dfmyers@up.com; URL: http://www.uprr.com/aboutup/community/contacts.shtml

Contact: Darlynn Myers, Dir., Corp. Rels.
Financial data (yr. ended 12/31/12): Total giving, $5,441,000, including $5,441,000 for grants.

Purpose and activities: As a complement to its foundation, Union Pacific also makes charitable contributions to nonprofit organizations directly. Support is given primarily in areas of company operations.
Fields of interest: Education; Community/economic development Children/youth; Youth; Military/veterans.
Type of support: Advocacy; Employee matching gifts; Equipment; In-kind gifts; Program development; Scholarship funds; Sponsorships.
Geographic limitations: Giving primarily in areas of company operations.
Support limitations: No support for religious organizations or political organizations.
Application information: Applications accepted. The Corporate Relations Department handles giving. The company has a staff that only handles contributions. Visit website to find state contact information. Application form not required. Applicants should submit the following:
1) detailed description of project and amount of funding requested
Initial approach: Complete online application
Copies of proposal: 1
Deadline(s): None
Final notification: Following review if approved
Number of staff: 1 full-time professional.

Union Pacific Foundation

1400 Douglas St., Stop 1560
Omaha, NE 68179-1001 (402) 544-5600
FAX: (402) 501-2291; E-mail: upf@up.com;
URL: http://www.up.com/found

Establishment information: Incorporated in 1959 in UT.
Donor: Union Pacific Corp.
Contact: Darlynn Myers, Dir.
Financial data (yr. ended 12/31/11): Assets, $454,221 (M); gifts received, $7,532,500; expenditures, $7,318,695; qualifying distributions, $7,182,796; giving activities include $7,182,796 for 794 grants (high: $518,705; low: $500).
Purpose and activities: The foundation supports zoos and aquariums and organizations involved with arts and culture, education, the environment, health, human services, community development, and civic affairs.
Fields of interest: Media, television; Media, radio; Museums; Museums (science/technology); Historic preservation/historical societies; Education, public education; Libraries (public); Education, services; Education; Botanical gardens; Environment; Zoos/zoological societies; Aquariums; Hospitals (general); Health care; Boys & girls clubs; Children, services; Human services; Community/economic development; Public affairs.
Program:
Community-Based Grant Program: The foundation annually awards grants to nonprofit organizations located in Union Pacific Communities. Special emphasis is directed toward the capacity building of nonprofits to increase their impact and effectiveness; community and civic engagement organizations designed to enrich general quality of life, including aquariums, botanical gardens, children's museums, history/science museums, public libraries, and public television and radio; and health and human service organizations designed to improve the level of health care or provide human services in the community.
Type of support: Building/renovation; Capital campaigns; Continuing support; Equipment; General/operating support; Management development/capacity building; Program development.
Geographic limitations: Giving on a national basis in areas of company operations, with emphasis on AR, AZ, CA, CO, IA, ID, IL, KS, LA, MN, MO, MT, NE, NM, NV, OK, OR, TX, UT, WA, WI, and WY.
Support limitations: No support for pass-through organizations, political or lobbying organizations, religious organizations not of direct benefit to the entire community, fraternal or veterans' organizations, local affiliates of national health and disease-specific organizations, animal rights organizations, elementary or secondary schools, volunteer fire departments or other emergency response organizations, labor organizations, or organizations whose programs are national or international in scope. No grants to individuals, or for debt reduction, salaries, athletic programs or events, conventions, conferences, or seminars, sponsorship of dinners, benefits or other special events, fellowships or research; no railroad equipment donations; no loans.
Publications: Application guidelines; Program policy statement.
Application information: Applications accepted. A full application may be requested at a later date. Support is limited to 1 contribution per organization during any given year. Application form required.
Initial approach: Complete online Stage One preliminary application
Board meeting date(s): Late Jan.
Deadline(s): May 1 to Aug. 15 for Stage One and Stage Two applications
Final notification: 2 business days for Stage One; Feb. for Stage Two
Officers and Trustees:* John J. Koraleski*, Chair.; Robert W. Turner*, Pres.; C. R. Eisele, Sr. V.P., Strategic Planning and Admin.; Robert M. Knight, Jr.*, V.P., Finance; P. J. O'Malley, V.P., Taxes; Barbara W. Schaefer*, Secy.; J. Michael Hemmer*, Genl. Counsel; S. A. Oiness, Treas.; Jeffrey P. Totusek, Cont.
Number of staff: 1 full-time professional.
EIN: 136406825
Selected grants: The following grants are a representative sample of this grantmaker's funding activity:
$3,200,000 to Educational Partnerships, Fairfield, CT, 2010.
$518,705 to Educational Partnerships, Fairfield, CT, 2011.
$476,155 to Educational Partnerships, Fairfield, CT, 2011.
$360,000 to Durham Museum, Omaha, NE, 2010.
$360,000 to Durham Museum, Omaha, NE, 2011.
$315,000 to United Way of the Midlands, Omaha, NE, 2010.
$315,000 to United Way of the Midlands, Omaha, NE, 2011.
$75,000 to Joslyn Art Museum, Omaha, NE, 2010.
$50,000 to Joslyn Art Museum, Omaha, NE, 2011.
$25,000 to Salvation Army of Omaha, Omaha, NE, 2010.
$12,000 to USO Fort Riley, Fort Riley, KS, 2011.
$10,000 to Big Shoulders Fund, Chicago, IL, 2010.
$7,000 to Texas Christian University, Fort Worth, TX, 2011.
$5,000 to Assistance League of Long Beach, Long Beach, CA, 2010.
$5,000 to Friends of Central Arkansas Libraries, Little Rock, AR, 2010.
$5,000 to Marfa Studio of Arts, Marfa, TX, 2011.
$4,500 to Stanfield Community Center, Stanfield, OR, 2011.
$4,000 to Heartland Museum Foundation, Clarion, IA, 2010.
$2,500 to United Way of Southeastern Idaho, Pocatello, ID, 2011.
$2,500 to United Way, Fremont Area, Fremont, NE, 2010.

3858
Union Savings Bank

226 Main St.
Danbury, CT 06810-6635 (203) 830-4200

Company URL: http://www.unionsavings.com
Establishment information: Established in 1866.
Company type: Private company
Business activities: Operates savings bank.
Business type (SIC): Savings institutions
Financial profile for 2011: Assets, $2,495,954,000; liabilities, $2,495,954,000
Corporate officers: Jack T. Tyransky, C.P.A., Chair.; Donald T. Studley, C.P.A., Vice-Chair.; Francis G. Dattalo, Pres. and C.E.O.; David A. Birkins, Exec. V.P. and C.F.O.; William J. McNamara, Exec. V.P. and C.I.O.; Lynne A. Beardsley, Exec. V.P., Human Resources
Board of directors: Jack T. Tyransky, C.P.A., Chair.; Donald T. Studley, C.P.A., Vice-Chair.; Ray P. Boa; John A. Brighenti; Arnold E. Finaldi, Jr.; David S. Hawley; Jeff M. Levine; John M. Murphy, M.D.; Gregory S. Oneglia; Stephen G. Rosentel; Cynthia Stevens; H. Ray Underwood, Jr.; Lucie H. Voves
Giving statement: Giving through the Union Savings Bank Corporate Giving Program and the Union Savings Bank Foundation, Inc.
Company EIN: 060570800

Union Savings Bank Foundation, Inc.

226 Main St.
Danbury, CT 06810-6635 (203) 830-4242
FAX: (203) 830-4225;
E-mail: usbfoundation@unionsavings.com;
Additional tel.: (203) 803-4202; URL: http://www.unionsavings.com/page.cfm?p=459

Establishment information: Established in 1998 in CT.
Donor: Union Savings Bank.
Contact: Marie O'Neil, Sr. V.P., Mktg.
Financial data (yr. ended 12/31/11): Assets, $2,610,621 (M); gifts received, $10,050; expenditures, $245,933; qualifying distributions, $214,300; giving activities include $214,300 for grants.
Purpose and activities: The foundation supports organizations involved with health, hunger, and human services. Special emphasis is directed toward programs designed to promote education and youth development.
Fields of interest: Education, reading; Education; Health care, clinics/centers; Health care, home services; Health care; Food services; Food banks; Food distribution, meals on wheels; Youth development; Salvation Army; YM/YWCAs & YM/YWHAs; Children/youth, services; Family services; Human services, financial counseling; Developmentally disabled, centers & services; Human services.
Type of support: Annual campaigns; Building/renovation; Conferences/seminars; Equipment; General/operating support; Program development.
Geographic limitations: Giving primarily in areas of company operations in CT.
Support limitations: No support for public entities, municipalities, or sectarian organizations. No grants to individuals, or for capital expenses, multi-year funding, endowments, or start-up or first-year programs.
Publications: Application guidelines; Grants list.
Application information: Applications accepted. Grants range from $2,500 to $10,000. Mailed applications are not accepted. Applications are reviewed by The Grants Committee. Additional information may be requested at a later date.

Application form required. Applicants should submit the following:
1) name, address and phone number of organization
2) brief history of organization and description of its mission
3) geographic area to be served
4) copy of most recent annual report/audited financial statement/990
5) list of company employees involved with the organization
6) listing of board of directors, trustees, officers and other key people and their affiliations
7) detailed description of project and amount of funding requested
8) copy of current year's organizational budget and/or project budget
9) listing of additional sources and amount of support

Initial approach: Download application form and e-mail to foundation
Copies of proposal: 1
Board meeting date(s): Oct.
Deadline(s): June 1 to Aug. 31
Final notification: Oct.

Officers and Trustees:* Jack T. Tyransky*, Chair.; John C. Kline*, Pres.; Elizabeth B. Durkin, Secy.; David A. Birkins, Treas.; Thomas A. Frizzell; Lynne A. Beardsley; Ray P. Boa; Abner Burgos-Rodriquez; Arnold E. Finaldi, Jr.; Mary Ann Frede; Thomas R. Green; David S. Hawley; Maryann S. Kiely; Jay C. Lent*; Jeffrey M. Levine; John M. Murphy; Stephen G. Rosentel; Cynthia Stevens; Donald T. Studley; Lucie H. Voves.
EIN: 061508286

3859
Unisys Corporation
801 Lakeview Dr., Ste 100
Blue Bell, PA 19424 (215) 986-4011
FAX: (302) 655-5049

Company URL: http://www.unisys.com
Establishment information: Established in 1986.
Company type: Public company
Company ticker symbol and exchange: UIS/NYSE
Business activities: Provides computer systems integration and server technology services and solutions; provides information technology consulting services.
Business type (SIC): Computer services; management and public relations services
Financial profile for 2011: Number of employees, 22,800; assets, $2,420,400,000; sales volume, $3,706,400,000; pre-tax net income, $254,100,000; expenses, $3,417,800,000; liabilities, $4,020,600,000
Fortune 1000 ranking: 2012—621st in revenues, 659th in profits, and 812th in assets
Corporate officers: J. Edward Coleman, Chair. and C.E.O.; Janet B. Haugen, Sr. V.P. and C.F.O.; Suresh Mathews, Sr. V.P. and C.I.O.; Nancy S. Sundheim, Sr. V.P., Genl. Counsel, and Secy.; Patricia A. Bradford, Sr. V.P., Human Resources; Scott A. Battersby, V.P. and Treas.; Scott W. Hurley, V.P. and Corp. Cont.
Board of directors: J. Edward Coleman, Chair.; Alison Davis; Nathaniel A. Davis; James J. Duderstadt; Henry C. Duques; Matthew J. Espe; Denise K. Fletcher; Leslie F. Kenne; Charles B. McQuade; Lee D. Roberts; Paul E. Weaver
International operations: United Kingdom
Giving statement: Giving through the Unisys Corporation Contributions Program.
Company EIN: 380387840

Unisys Corporation Contributions Program
801 Lakeview Dr., Ste. 100
Blue Bell, PA 19422-1901 (215) 986-4011
URL: http://www.unisys.com/unisys/about/sr/detail.jsp?id=10500002&pid=207

Purpose and activities: Unisys makes charitable contributions to nonprofit organizations involved with business and technology higher education, health, and human services. Support is given primarily in areas of company operations in Alabama, California, Illinois, Michigan, Minnesota, Missouri, New Jersey, New York, North Dakota, Pennsylvania, Puerto Rico, Utah, Virginia, and Washington.
Fields of interest: Museums (science/technology); Higher education; Business school/education; Health care; Human services; Civil/human rights, equal rights; United Ways and Federated Giving Programs; Science; Engineering/technology; Public affairs, political organizations.
Type of support: Employee volunteer services; General/operating support.
Geographic limitations: Giving primarily in areas of company operations with emphasis on AL, CA, IL, MI, MN, MO, ND, NJ, NY, PA, PR, UT, VA, and WA.

3860
United Air Lines, Inc.
1200 E. Algonquin Rd.
Arlington Heights, IL 60005-4712
(847) 700-7826

Company URL: http://www.ual.com
Establishment information: Established in 1968.
Company type: Subsidiary of a public company
Business activities: Provides air transportation services.
Business type (SIC): Transportation/scheduled air
Financial profile for 2006: Number of employees, 55,000; assets, $25,581,000,000; sales volume, $17,880,000,000; expenses, $17,369,000,000; liabilities, $22,988,000,000
Corporate officer: Angie Peterson, Mgr.
Subsidiaries: Covia, LLC, Elk Grove Village, IL; Mileage Plus Holdings, Inc., Elk Grove Village, IL; United Air Lines Credit Corp., Elk Grove Village, IL; United Aviation Fuels Corp., Elk Grove Village, IL; United Cogen, Inc., San Francisco, CA; United GHS Inc., Elk Grove Village, IL; United Vacations, Inc., Elk Grove Village, IL
Historic mergers: Continental Airlines, Inc. (October 1, 2010)
Giving statement: Giving through the United Air Lines, Inc. Corporate Giving Program, the United Airlines Foundation, and the Continental Scholarship Fund.
Company EIN: 362675206

United Air Lines, Inc. Corporate Giving Program
77 W. Wacker Dr.
Chicago, IL 60601 (312) 997-8000
URL: http://www.united.com/web/en-US/content/company/globalcitizenship/community.aspx

Purpose and activities: As a complement to its foundation, United also makes charitable contributions to nonprofit organizations directly. Support is given primarily in areas of company operations, with emphasis on Los Angeles and San Francisco, California, Denver, Colorado, Chicago, Illinois, Newark, New Jersey, New York, New York, Cleveland, Ohio, and Houston, Texas.
Type of support: Employee volunteer services; In-kind gifts; Sponsorships.
Geographic limitations: Giving primarily in areas of company operations, with emphasis on Los Angeles and San Francisco, CA, Denver, CO, Chicago, IL, Newark, NJ, New York, NY, Cleveland, OH, and Houston, TX.
Support limitations: No support for political, religious, discriminatory, evangelical, or fraternal organizations, individual public or private schools, fraternities or sororities, alumni associations, athletic teams or leagues or their booster organizations, or international organizations (unless they have a location and are incorporated in the U.S.). No grants for capital or building campaigns, thrill sports, or beauty pageants.
Application information: As a newly merged company, United is reviewing and evaluating its combined portfolio of existing community partnerships. At this time the company is not accepting any new applications for support. Additional information will be posted on the website. Applicants should submit the following:
1) name, address and phone number of organization
2) copy of IRS Determination Letter
3) listing of board of directors, trustees, officers and other key people and their affiliations
4) detailed description of project and amount of funding requested
5) contact person
6) listing of additional sources and amount of support
7) plans for acknowledgement

Proposals should include the event or activity date and location, number of tickets requested, intended use of requested support, expected number of attendees, and a copy of promotional materials from the prior year.
Deadline(s): 90 days prior to event
Final notification: 30 days (minimum)

United Airlines Foundation
(formerly UAL Foundation)
P.O. Box 66100
Chicago, IL 60666-0100
FAX: (847) 700-7345; Application address: c/o United Airlines - HDQPR, Corp. Social Investment, 77 W. Wacker Dr., Chicago, IL 60601, tel.: (312) 997-8034; URL: http://www.united.com/web/en-US/content/company/globalcitizenship/community.aspx

Establishment information: Incorporated in 1951 in IL.
Donor: United Air Lines, Inc.
Financial data (yr. ended 12/31/11): Assets, $3,146,521 (M); gifts received, $2,002,970; expenditures, $1,788,947; qualifying distributions, $1,764,952; giving activities include $1,764,952 for grants.
Purpose and activities: The foundation supports organizations involved with disaster relief and humanitarian aid. Special emphasis is directed toward programs designed to address youth potential, arts and culture, and health initiatives.
Fields of interest: Museums; Performing arts, ballet; Performing arts, theater; Performing arts, music; Arts; Education; Health care; Food services; Disasters, preparedness/services; Youth development, business; Youth development; Human services Youth.
Program:
Volunteer Impact Grants: The foundation awards grants to nonprofit organizations with which employees of United Airlines volunteer.

Type of support: Annual campaigns; Employee volunteer services; General/operating support; Program development; Research; Scholarship funds.
Geographic limitations: Giving primarily in areas of company operations in Los Angeles and San Francisco, CA, Denver, CO, Chicago, IL, Newark, NJ, New York, NY, Cleveland, OH, and Houston, TX.
Support limitations: No support for political or fraternal organizations, United Way-supported organizations, religious organizations, or individual public or private schools. No grants to individuals, or for capital campaigns or development campaigns; no air transportation for fundraising events.
Publications: Corporate giving report.
Application information: Applications not accepted. The foundation is not accepting grant proposals at this time.
Board meeting date(s): Mar., June, Sept., and Dec.
Officers and Directors:* Mark Anderson*, Chair.; Sonya Y. Jackson, Pres.; Jeffrey T. Foland, V.P.; Peter D. McDonald, V.P.; Thomas J. Sabatino, Jr., Secy.; John R. Gebo, Treas.; John H. Walker.
Number of staff: 2
EIN: 366109873
Selected grants: The following grants are a representative sample of this grantmaker's funding activity:
$118,352 to Feeding America, Chicago, IL, 2010.
$105,000 to Museum of Science and Industry, Chicago, IL, 2010.
$100,000 to San Francisco Opera, San Francisco, CA, 2010.
$75,000 to Breast Cancer Network of Strength, Chicago, IL, 2010.
$70,000 to Chicago Childrens Theater, Chicago, IL, 2010.
$50,000 to American Red Cross, Chicago, IL, 2010.
$40,000 to Lincoln Park Zoo, Chicago, IL, 2010.
$25,000 to After School Matters, Chicago, IL, 2010.
$25,000 to American Cancer Society, Chicago, IL, 2010.
$25,000 to Chicago Public Schools, Chicago, IL, 2010.

Continental Scholarship Fund
c/o HQSTX
1600 Smith St.
Houston, TX 77002-7362 (713) 324-2130

Establishment information: Established in 2001 in TX.
Donors: Amec; Aviation Constructors, Inc.; The Chase Manhattan Bank; CTSI Logistics; Electronic Data Systems Corp.; Rockwell Collins, Inc.; Tan's Holding Corp.
Contact: William K. Crouch, Chair.
Financial data (yr. ended 12/31/10): Revenue, $1,067,452; assets, $2,653,307 (M); gifts received, $1,002,976; expenditures, $704,488; program services expenses, $704,488; giving activities include $696,810 for grants to individuals.
Purpose and activities: The foundation awards college scholarships to children and spouses of employees of Continental Airlines and its subsidiaries.
Type of support: Employee-related scholarships.
Geographic limitations: Giving primarily in areas of company and subsidiary operations.
Application information: Applications not accepted. Contributes only through employee-related scholarships.
Officers and Directors:* William K. Crouch*, Chair.; Frank Star*, V.P. and Treas.; Douglas P. Kelley*, Secy.; Lori Gobillot; Katrina Manning; Roosevelt Nesbitt.
EIN: 760691086

3861
United Bank
200 E. Nashville Ave.
P.O. Box 8
Atmore, AL 36504 (251) 446-6100

Company URL: http://www.ubankal.com
Establishment information: Established in 1904.
Company type: Subsidiary of a private company
Business activities: Operates commercial bank.
Business type (SIC): Banks/commercial
Corporate officers: David Swift, Chair.; William J. Justice, Vice-Chair.; Robert R. Jones III, Pres. and C.E.O.; Mitchell D. Staples, Sr. V.P., C.F.O., and Cont.
Board of directors: David Swift, Chair.; William J. Justice, Vice-Chair.
Giving statement: Giving through the United Bank Charitable Foundation.

United Bank Charitable Foundation
200 E. Nashville Ave.
Atmore, AL 36502-2536

Establishment information: Established in 1997 in AL.
Donor: United Bank.
Contact: Robert R. Jones III, Pres.
Financial data (yr. ended 12/31/11): Assets, $169,948 (M); expenditures, $13,445; qualifying distributions, $12,705; giving activities include $12,705 for grants.
Purpose and activities: The foundation supports organizations involved with arts and culture, education, health, human services, civic affairs, and Christianity.
Fields of interest: Education; Health organizations; Human services.
Type of support: General/operating support.
Geographic limitations: Giving primarily in areas of company operations in AL.
Support limitations: No grants to individuals.
Application information: Applications not accepted. Unsolicited requests for funds not accepted.
Officers: Robert R. Jones III, Pres.; Tina N. Brooks, Secy.; Allen W. Jones, Treas.
Trustees: David W. Swift; William J. Justice.
EIN: 631192797

3862
United Brass Works, Inc.
714 S. Main St.
Randleman, NC 27317-2102
(336) 498-2661

Company URL: http://www.ubw.com
Establishment information: Established in 1910.
Company type: Private company
Business activities: Manufactures plumbing supplies.
Business type (SIC): Metal plumbing fixtures and heating equipment/nonelectric; rubber products/fabricated; plastic products/miscellaneous; pottery; cutlery, hand and edge tools, and hardware; metal forgings and stampings; metal products/fabricated
Corporate officers: Edward Benson, Chair. and C.E.O.; Michael Berkelhammer, Pres.
Board of director: Edward Benson, Chair.
Giving statement: Giving through the United Brass Foundation, Inc.

The United Brass Foundation, Inc.
714 S. Main St.
Randleman, NC 27317-2102

Donor: United Brass Works, Inc.
Financial data (yr. ended 12/31/11): Assets, $94,201 (M); gifts received, $72,000; expenditures, $65,318; qualifying distributions, $65,300; giving activities include $65,300 for 5 grants (high: $52,500; low: $300).
Purpose and activities: The foundation supports organizations involved with Judaism.
Fields of interest: Jewish federated giving programs; Jewish agencies & synagogues.
Type of support: General/operating support.
Geographic limitations: Giving limited to Greensboro, NC.
Support limitations: No grants to individuals.
Application information: Applications not accepted. Contributes only to pre-selected organizations.
Directors: Edward Benson; Michael Berkelhammer.
EIN: 581489756

3863
United Business Media LLC
(formerly CMP Media LLC)
600 Community Dr.
Manhasset, NY 11030-3847
(516) 562-5000

Company URL: http://ubmtechnology.com
Establishment information: Established in 1971.
Company type: Subsidiary of a foreign company
Business activities: Publishes newspapers and magazines; provides Internet information services; provides trade show and conference services; provides printing services.
Business type (SIC): Newspaper publishing and/or printing; periodical publishing and/or printing; printing/commercial; computer services; business services/miscellaneous
Corporate officers: Donald Pazour, C.E.O.; Adam K. Marder, Exec. V.P. and C.F.O.; Paul Miller, Sr. V.P.
Giving statement: Giving through the United Business Media Community Connection Foundation.

United Business Media Community Connection Foundation
(formerly CMP Community Connection Foundation)
600 Community Dr.
Manhasset, NY 11030

Establishment information: Established in 1988 in DE.
Donors: CMP Media Inc.; CMP Media, LLC; Gerard G. Leeds; Mrs. Gerard G. Leeds; CMP Publications, Inc.; Caroline and Sigmund Schott Foundation, Inc.; United Business Media PLC; United Business Media Ltd.
Financial data (yr. ended 12/31/11): Assets, $23,549 (M); gifts received, $100,000; expenditures, $111,217; qualifying distributions, $97,040; giving activities include $97,040 for 216 grants (high: $16,647; low: $5).
Purpose and activities: The foundation supports local nonprofit organizations through employee-driven programs. Special emphasis is directed toward organizations involved with arts and culture, education, the environment, health, transitional housing, youth, and senior citizens. Support is given primarily in areas of company operations.
Fields of interest: Arts; Education; Environment; Health care; Housing/shelter Youth; Aging.

Type of support: Building/renovation; Curriculum development; Emergency funds; Employee matching gifts; Employee volunteer services; Equipment; General/operating support; In-kind gifts; Program development; Seed money; Technical assistance.
Application information: Applications not accepted. Unsolicited requests for funds not accepted.
Officers: Alison Brown, Pres.; Michael A. Russak, Jr., V.P.
Directors: Jackie Alexander; Joshua Auger; Ozgur Aytar; Sandy Cipriano; Ed Day; Allison Doyle; Carol Flanagan; Brian Lynn; Marie Myers; Illysa Ortsman; and 5 additional directors.
Number of staff: 1 full-time professional.
EIN: 112945655
Selected grants: The following grants are a representative sample of this grantmaker's funding activity:
$80,043 to Feeding America, Chicago, IL, 2010.
$2,000 to Boys Hope Girls Hope, Bridgeton, MO, 2010.
$1,672 to American Cancer Society, Atlanta, GA, 2010.

3864
United Coal Company, Inc.

(also known as UC)
1005 Glenway Ave.
Bristol, VA 24201 (276) 466-3322

Company URL: http://www.unitedco.net/ucc.html
Establishment information: Established in 1970.
Company type: Subsidiary of a private company
Business activities: Mines coal.
Business type (SIC): Mining/coal and lignite surface
Giving statement: Giving through the United Company Charitable Foundation.

The United Company Charitable Foundation

(formerly United Coal Company Charitable Foundation)
1005 Glenway Ave.
Bristol, VA 24201-3473 (276) 645-1458
FAX: (276) 645-1420;
E-mail: mmgayle@unitedco.net
Scholarship address: Rose Hurley, Mountain Mission School, 1760 Edgewater Dr., Grundy VA 24614, tel.: (276) 791-1514, e-mail: rhurley@unitedco.net

Establishment information: Established in 1986 in VA.
Donors: United Coal Co., Inc.; Burton Fletcher; The Summit Fund, LLC.
Contact: Martha M. Gayle, Pres.
Financial data (yr. ended 12/31/11): Assets, $39,394,045 (M); gifts received, $1,100; expenditures, $2,963,482; qualifying distributions, $2,769,396; giving activities include $2,138,236 for 119 grants (high: $400,000; low: $100) and $386,166 for 3 foundation-administered programs.
Purpose and activities: The foundation supports organizations involved with arts and culture, education, health, disaster relief, school athletics, hunger, human services, and the economically disadvantaged.
Fields of interest: Museums; Museums (art); Performing arts, theater; Arts; Higher education; Education; Health care, clinics/centers; Health care; Food services; Food banks; Disasters, preparedness/services; Athletics/sports, school programs; Boys & girls clubs; Boy scouts; Salvation Army; YM/YWCAs & YM/YWHAs; Children/youth, services; Residential/custodial care; Homeless, human services; Human services.
Program:
Scholarship Program: The foundation awards scholarships to graduates of Mountain Mission School in Grundy, Virginia to pursue higher education. The scholarship is designed to cover the cost of tuition, fees, room, board, books, and supplies. Applicants must demonstrate financial need and a GPA of 2.75.
Type of support: Building/renovation; Capital campaigns; General/operating support; Program development; Scholarship funds; Scholarships—to individuals; Sponsorships.
Geographic limitations: Giving primarily in TN and VA.
Support limitations: No grants to individuals (except for scholarships) or for political or related causes; no loans.
Application information: Applications accepted. Application form not required.
Scholarship applications should include transcripts, a copy of the applicants college acceptance letter, and a copy of the applicant's financial aid award letter.
Initial approach: Contact foundation for application information for grants; contact foundation for application form for scholarships
Deadline(s): Jan. 20 and July 1 for scholarships
Final notification: 3 to 4 weeks for scholarships
Officers and Directors:* James W. McGlothlin*, Chair.; Martha McGlothlin-Gayle*, Pres.; Nicholas Street*, Secy.; Lois A. Clarke*, Treas.; Frances McGlothlin; David Street; Fay Street.
EIN: 541390453
Selected grants: The following grants are a representative sample of this grantmaker's funding activity:
$1,500,000 to Mountain Mission School, Grundy, VA, 2009.
$601,000 to Virginia Intermont College, Bristol, VA, 2009.
$400,000 to Virginia Tech Foundation, Blacksburg, VA, 2009.
$200,000 to Virginia Museum of Fine Arts, Richmond, VA, 2009.
$100,000 to Childrens Museum of Naples, Naples, FL, 2009.
$60,000 to William King Regional Arts Center, Abingdon, VA, 2009.
$56,880 to University of Pennsylvania, Philadelphia, PA, 2009.
$55,207 to George Mason University, Fairfax, VA, 2009.
$27,536 to Milligan College, Milligan College, TN, 2009.
$6,000 to Barter Theater, Abingdon, VA, 2009.

3865
United Community Bancorp Inc.

92 Walnut St.
Lawrenceburg, IN 47025 (812) 537-4822
FAX: (302) 655-5049

Company URL: https://www.bankucb.com
Establishment information: Established in 1999.
Company type: Private company
Company ticker symbol and exchange: UCBA/NASDAQ
Business activities: Operates commercial bank.
Business type (SIC): Banks/commercial; savings institutions
Financial profile for 2012: Number of employees, 114; assets, $495,900,000; pre-tax net income, $2,780,000; liabilities, $440,920,000
Corporate officers: Ralph B. Sprecher, Chair.; William F. Ritzmann, Pres. and C.E.O.; Elmer G. McLaughlin, Exec. V.P. and C.O.O.; W. Michael McLaughlin, Sr. V.P., Opers.; Vicki A. March, Sr. V.P., Finance and C.F.O.; Brenda I. Wheat, V.P., Opers.
Board of directors: Ralph B. Sprecher, Chair.; Robert J. Ewbank; Jerry W. Hacker; James D. Humphrey; Elmer G. McLaughlin; William F. Ritzmann; Eugene B. Seitz II; George Michael Seitz; Richard C. Strzynski
Giving statement: Giving through the UCB Charitable Foundation.
Company EIN: 364587081

UCB Charitable Foundation

92 Walnut St.
Lawrenceburg, IN 47025-1836 (812) 537-4822

Establishment information: Established in 2006 in IN.
Donor: United Community Bancorp.
Financial data (yr. ended 06/30/12): Assets, $1,019,665 (M); expenditures, $59,918; qualifying distributions, $55,462; giving activities include $55,462 for 47 grants (high: $5,892; low: $75).
Purpose and activities: The foundation supports art councils and community foundations and organizations involved with historic preservation, education, muscular dystrophy, athletics, and youth development.
Fields of interest: Arts; Education; Public affairs.
Type of support: General/operating support.
Geographic limitations: Giving primarily in IN.
Support limitations: No support for political or fraternal organizations. No grants to individuals.
Application information: Applications accepted. Application form required.
Initial approach: Letter
Deadline(s): None
Directors: Robert J. Ewbank; Jerry W. Hacker; Frederick L. McCarter; Elmer G. McLaughlin; William F. Ritzman; Eugene B. Seitz.
EIN: 204604858

3866
United Community Banks, Inc.

59 Hwy. 515
PO Box 398
Blairsville, GA 30514 (706) 781-2265

Company URL: http://www.ucbi.com
Establishment information: Established in 1950.
Company type: Public company
Company ticker symbol and exchange: UCBI/NASDAQ
Business activities: Operates commercial banks.
Business type (SIC): Banks/commercial
Financial profile for 2011: Number of employees, 1,706; assets, $7,443,200,000; pre-tax net income, -$432,290,000; liabilities, $6,807,680,000
Corporate officers: W. C. Nelson, Jr., Chair.; Jimmy C. Tallent, Pres. and C.E.O.; H. Lynn Harton, C.O.O.; Rex S. Schuette, Exec. V.P. and C.F.O.
Board of directors: W. C. Nelson, Jr., Chair.; Robert H. Blalock; Clifford V. Brokaw; Cathy Cox; Steven J. Goldstein; Robert L. Head; Thomas A. Richlovsky; John D. Stephens; Jimmy C. Tallent; Tim Wallis
Giving statement: Giving through the United Community Charitable Foundation, Inc.
Company EIN: 581807304

United Community Charitable Foundation, Inc.

63 Hwy. 515
Blairsville, GA 30512-3569

Establishment information: Established in 2005 in GA.
Donor: United Community Bank.
Financial data (yr. ended 12/31/11): Assets, $157 (M); expenditures, $0; qualifying distributions, $0.
Fields of interest: Health care.
Support limitations: No grants to individuals.
Application information: Applications not accepted. Unsolicited requests for funds not accepted.
Officers and Directors:* Jimmy C. Tallent*, Chair. and Pres.; Brad Miller*, V.P. and Secy.; Rex S. Schuette*, V.P. and Treas.; Guy W. Freeman*, V.P.; Alan H. Kumler*, V.P.; David Shearrow.
EIN: 203735711

3867
United Conveyor Corporation

2100 Norman Dr. W.
Waukegan, IL 60085-6753 (847) 473-5900

Company URL: http://www.unitedconveyor.com
Establishment information: Established in 1920.
Company type: Private company
Business activities: Manufactures pneumatic, hydraulic, and mechanical conveying systems.
Business type (SIC): Machinery/construction, mining, and materials handling
Corporate officers: Donald N. Basler, Chair.; Douglas S. Basler, Pres.; Mark Stringer, C.F.O.; Fred Schroeder, Cont.
Board of director: Donald N. Basler, Chair.
Giving statement: Giving through the United Conveyor Foundation.

United Conveyor Foundation

2100 Norman Dr. W.
Waukegan, IL 60085-6752 (847) 473-5900
E-mail: davidhoyem@unitedconveyor.com

Establishment information: Established about 1957 in IL.
Donor: United Conveyor Corp.
Contact: Mary Nelson
Financial data (yr. ended 12/31/11): Assets, $4,146,871 (M); gifts received, $60,000; expenditures, $164,065; qualifying distributions, $164,025; giving activities include $128,125 for 31 grants (high: $25,000; low: $25) and $35,900 for 10 grants to individuals (high: $5,000; low: $300).
Purpose and activities: The foundation supports festivals and organizations involved with arts and culture, education, child welfare, and human services.
Fields of interest: Media, television; Performing arts, music; Performing arts, orchestras; Arts; Elementary/secondary education; Higher education; Medical school/education; Crime/violence prevention, child abuse; Recreation, fairs/festivals; Salvation Army; YM/YWCAs & YM/YWHAs; Children/youth, services; Family services, domestic violence; Human services; United Ways and Federated Giving Programs.
Type of support: Employee matching gifts; Employee-related scholarships; General/operating support.
Geographic limitations: Giving primarily in IL.
Application information: Applications accepted. Application form required.
Initial approach: Proposal
Deadline(s): July 1
Trustees: Donald N. Basler; David S. Hoyem.
EIN: 366033638
Selected grants: The following grants are a representative sample of this grantmaker's funding activity:
$8,000 to Chicago Symphony Orchestra, Chicago, IL, 2010.
$5,000 to YMCA, North Suburban, Northbrook, IL, 2010.
$3,500 to Chicago Youth Centers, Chicago, IL, 2010.
$3,500 to Ravinia Festival Association, Highland Park, IL, 2010.
$3,000 to Juvenile Protective Association, Chicago, IL, 2010.
$3,000 to W F M T Fine Arts Circle, Chicago, IL, 2010.
$2,000 to Chicago Botanic Garden, Glencoe, IL, 2010.
$2,000 to Northland College, Ashland, WI, 2010.
$2,000 to Salvation Army, Chicago, IL, 2010.
$1,500 to United Way of Saint Joseph County, South Bend, IN, 2010.

3868
United Finance Co.

515 E. Burnside St.
Portland, OR 97214-1183 (503) 232-5153

Company URL: http://www.unitedfinance.com
Establishment information: Established in 1922.
Company type: Subsidiary of a private company
Business activities: Provides consumer loans; sells credit insurance.
Business type (SIC): Credit institutions/personal; insurance/surety
Financial profile for 2010: Number of employees, 15
Corporate officers: Richard H. Parker, Jr., Chair.; Richard H. Parker III, Pres. and C.E.O.; Marcus Holling, Exec. V.P. and Treas.; Deanna V. Kooy, V.P. and Secy.; Brent Lay, Cont.
Board of director: Richard H. Parker, Jr., Chair.
Giving statement: Giving through the R. H. Parker/United Foundation.

R. H. Parker/United Foundation

P.O. Box 4487
515 E. Burnside
Portland, OR 97208-4487 (503) 238-6464
URL: http://www.unitedfinance.com/charitableDonations.aspx

Establishment information: Established in 1994 in OR.
Donors: Richard H. Parker; United Finance Co.
Financial data (yr. ended 12/31/11): Assets, $4,177,576 (M); gifts received, $525,000; expenditures, $157,197; qualifying distributions, $154,472; giving activities include $151,117 for 44 grants (high: $40,000; low: $100).
Purpose and activities: The foundation supports museums and organizations involved with higher education, youth, and other areas.
Fields of interest: Museums; Museums (children's); Higher education; Higher education, college; Boy scouts; Youth, services; United Ways and Federated Giving Programs.
Type of support: Building/renovation; General/operating support; Program development; Scholarship funds.
Geographic limitations: Giving primarily in the Pacific Northwest, with emphasis on OR and WA.
Support limitations: No grants to individuals.
Publications: Grants list.
Application information: Applications accepted. Application form not required. Applicants should submit the following:
1) statement of problem project will address
2) copy of IRS Determination Letter
3) detailed description of project and amount of funding requested
Initial approach: Proposal
Copies of proposal: 1
Deadline(s): July 31
Officers and Directors:* Richard H. Parker, Jr., Pres.; Marcus W. Holling*, V.P.; Richard H. Parker III*, V.P.; Lorine G. Cox*, Secy.; Judy Ann Parker.
EIN: 931155287
Selected grants: The following grants are a representative sample of this grantmaker's funding activity:
$20,000 to High Desert Museum, Bend, OR, 2010.
$5,000 to Jesuit High School, Portland, OR, 2010.
$2,500 to Saint Andrew Nativity School, Portland, OR, 2010. For scholarship program.
$2,000 to De La Salle North Catholic High School, Portland, OR, 2010.
$1,400 to Beaver Athletic Student Fund, Corvallis, OR, 2010.
$1,000 to AFSA Education Foundation, Washington, DC, 2010.
$1,000 to Mayo Foundation, Scottsdale, AZ, 2010.
$1,000 to Oregon Historical Society, Portland, OR, 2010.
$1,000 to REACH Community Development, Portland, OR, 2010.
$1,000 to Rockaway Beach, City of, Rockaway Beach, OR, 2010.

3869
United Fire & Casualty Company

(also known as United Fire Group)
118 2nd Ave. S.E.
P.O. Box 73909
Cedar Rapids, IA 52407-3909
(319) 399-5700

Company URL: http://www.unitedfiregroup.com
Establishment information: Established in 1946.
Company type: Public company
Company ticker symbol and exchange: UFCS/NASDAQ
Business activities: Sells property and casualty insurance.
Business type (SIC): Insurance/fire, marine, and casualty
Financial profile for 2011: Number of employees, 909; assets, $3,694,650,000; sales volume, $813,240,000; pre-tax net income, $46,070,000; expenses, $767,170,000; liabilities, $2,965,480,000
Corporate officers: Jack B. Evans, Chair.; John A. Rife, Vice-Chair.; Randy A. Ramlo, Pres. and C.E.O.; Michael T. Wilkins, Exec. V.P., Corp. Admin.; Dianne M. Lyons, V.P. and C.F.O.; Barrie W. Ernst, V.P. and C.I.O.; Neal R. Scharmer, V.P., Genl. Counsel, and Corp. Secy.; Timothy G. Spain, V.P., Human Resources; David A. Lange, Corp. Secy.; Janice A. Martin, Treas.; Kevin W. Helbing, Cont.
Board of directors: Jack B. Evans, Chair.; John A. Rife, Vice-Chair.; Scott L. Carlton; Christopher R. Drahozal; Douglas M. Hultquist; Casey D. Mahon; George D. Milligan; James W. Noyce; Michael W. Phillips; Mary K. Quass; Randy A. Ramlo; Kyle D. Skogman

Subsidiaries: Addison Insurance Co., Lombard, IL; Lafayette Insurance Co., New Orleans, LA; United Life Insurance Co., Cedar Rapids, IA
Giving statement: Giving through the United Fire Group Corporate Giving Program and the United Fire Group Foundation.
Company EIN: 420644327

United Fire Group Foundation

118 2nd Ave. S.E.
Cedar Rapids, IA 52401-1212

Establishment information: Established in 2001 in IA.
Donor: United Fire & Casualty Co.
Financial data (yr. ended 12/31/11): Assets, $9,049 (M); gifts received, $37,774; expenditures, $747,985; qualifying distributions, $747,985; giving activities include $747,985 for 47 grants (high: $175,000; low: $25).
Purpose and activities: The foundation supports museums and organizations involved with theater, education, employment, and human services and awards grants to individuals for higher education and disaster relief.
Fields of interest: Museums; Performing arts, theater; Higher education; Business school/ education; Libraries (public); Education; Goodwill Industries; YM/YWCAs & YM/YWHAs; Children, services; Residential/custodial care; Residential/ custodial care, hospices; Developmentally disabled, centers & services; Human services; United Ways and Federated Giving Programs.
Type of support: Emergency funds; General/ operating support; Grants to individuals; Program development.
Geographic limitations: Giving primarily in IA.
Application information: Applications not accepted. Contributes only to pre-selected organizations and individuals.
Officers: Randy A. Ramlo, Pres.; Michael T. Wilkens, Secy.; Dianne M. Lyons, Treas.
EIN: 421492320
Selected grants: The following grants are a representative sample of this grantmaker's funding activity:
$33,000 to Theater Cedar Rapids, Cedar Rapids, IA, 2010.
$10,000 to Cedar Rapids Museum of Art, Cedar Rapids, IA, 2010.
$6,000 to Cedar Rapids Opera Theater, Cedar Rapids, IA, 2010.
$5,000 to American Diabetes Association, Alexandria, VA, 2010.

3870
The United Illuminating Company

157 Church St., Ste. 16
P.O. Box 1564
New Haven, CT 06510 (203) 499-2000

Company URL: http://www.uinet.com
Establishment information: Established in 1899.
Company type: Subsidiary of a public company
Business activities: Transmits and distributes electricity.
Business type (SIC): Electric services
Corporate officers: Nathaniel D. Woodson, Chair.; Anthony J. Vallillo, Pres. and C.O.O.; Richard J. Nicholas, C.F.O.; W. Marie Zanavich, V.P. and C.I.O.
Board of director: Nathaniel D. Woodson, Chair.
Giving statement: Giving through the United Illuminating Company Contributions Program and the United Illuminating Foundation.

The United Illuminating Company Contributions Program

157 Church St.
New Haven, CT 06510-2103 (203) 499-2000
URL: http://www.uinet.com/uinet/connect/UINet/Top+Navigator/About+UI/UI+in+the+Community/

Purpose and activities: As a complement to its foundation, The United Illuminating Company also makes charitable contributions to nonprofit organizations directly. Support is given primarily in areas of company operations in Connecticut.
Fields of interest: Community/economic development; General charitable giving.
Programs:
Arts: United Illuminating supports programs designed to reflect the cultural diversity and values of the entire community.
Community Development: United Illuminating supports programs designed to highlight the community's strengths and promote its citizens. Special emphasis is directed toward programs designed to address workforce development, cultural diversity, and neighborhood initiatives.
Environment: United Illuminating supports programs designed to address the proper use of energy, pollution prevention, and natural resources conservation.
Youth Development: United Illuminating supports programs designed to address the well-being of children and improve the educational system. Special emphasis is directed toward programs designed to address math, science, and technology skills, literacy skills, parental involvement, at-risk youth, and health.
Type of support: Employee volunteer services; General/operating support; In-kind gifts.
Geographic limitations: Giving primarily in areas of company operations in CT.
Number of staff: 2 full-time professional; 1 full-time support.

The United Illuminating Foundation

P.O. Box 1564, Tax Section 1-15F
New Haven, CT 06506-0901

Establishment information: Established in 1990 in CT.
Donor: The United Illuminating Co.
Financial data (yr. ended 12/31/11): Assets, $2,196,731 (M); gifts received, $500,000; expenditures, $283,111; qualifying distributions, $282,756; giving activities include $282,756 for grants.
Purpose and activities: The foundation supports hospitals and organizations involved with arts and culture, human services, children and youth services, and community development.
Fields of interest: Museums; Performing arts, orchestras; Arts; Higher education; Hospitals (general); Human services; Children/youth, services; Community/economic development; United Ways and Federated Giving Programs.
Type of support: Capital campaigns; General/ operating support.
Geographic limitations: Giving limited to CT.
Support limitations: No grants to individuals.
Application information: Applications not accepted. Contributes only to pre-selected organizations.
Trustees: Richard J. Nicholas; James Torgerson; Anthony J. Vallillo.
EIN: 061310455
Selected grants: The following grants are a representative sample of this grantmaker's funding activity:
$30,000 to United Way of Coastal Fairfield County, Bridgeport, CT, 2010. For general operating budget.
$30,000 to United Way of Greater New Haven, New Haven, CT, 2010. For general operating budget.
$25,050 to University of New Haven, West Haven, CT, 2010. For capital contribution.
$25,000 to Amistad Academy, New Haven, CT, 2010. For capital contribution.
$19,624 to Operation Fuel, Bloomfield, CT, 2010. For general operating budget.
$5,000 to United Way of Milford, Milford, CT, 2010. For general operating budget.
$2,700 to Fairfield University, Fairfield, CT, 2010. For general operating budget.
$2,500 to Clarkson University, Potsdam, NY, 2010. For general operating budget.
$1,498 to American Red Cross, Ct Chapter, Farmington, CT, 2010. For capital contribution.
$1,000 to Gateway Community College, New Haven, CT, 2010. For general operating budget.

3871
United Merchants and Manufacturers, Inc.

1650 Palisade Ave.
Teaneck, NJ 07666 (201) 837-1700

Establishment information: Established in 1922.
Company type: Private company
Business activities: Produces fabric and yarn; operates women's clothing and accessory stores.
Business type (SIC): Fabrics/broadwoven natural cotton; fabrics/broadwoven synthetic and silk; yarn and thread mills; jewelry and notions/costume; women's apparel stores; women's specialty and accessory stores
Financial profile for 2011: Number of employees, 650
Corporate officers: Uzi Ruskin, Chair., Pres., and C.O.O.; Sidney O. Margolis, Exec. V.P., Admin.; Judith A. Nadzick, C.F.O.; Norman R. Forson, Sr. V.P. and Compt.
Board of director: Uzi Ruskin, Chair.
Subsidiaries: Decora, Fort Edward, NY; Jonathan Logan Overseas Development Corp., New York, NY; Victoria Creations, Inc., Warwick, RI
Giving statement: Giving through the U.M.R. Foundation Inc.

U.M.R. Foundation Inc.

(also known as United Merchants Foundation, Inc.)
P.O. Box 2477
Sarasota, FL 34230

Establishment information: Incorporated in 1944 in NY.
Donor: United Merchants and Manufacturers, Inc.
Contact: Uzi Ruskin, Pres.
Financial data (yr. ended 06/30/12): Assets, $1,556,495 (M); expenditures, $76,777; qualifying distributions, $70,350; giving activities include $70,350 for grants.
Purpose and activities: The foundation supports organizations involved with arts and culture, education, conservation, health, Crohn's and Colitis disease, human services, and Judaism.
Fields of interest: Environment; Medical research; Religion.
Type of support: General/operating support; Program development.
Support limitations: No grants to individuals.

Application information: Applications accepted. Application form required.
Initial approach: Letter
Deadline(s): None
Officers: Uzi Ruskin, Pres.; Varda Ruskin, V.P.; Jules Blackman, Secy.
Directors: Elan Ruskin; Amos Sapir.
EIN: 136077135

3872
United Parcel Service, Inc.

(also known as UPS)
55 Glenlake Pkwy., N.E.
Atlanta, GA 30328 (404) 828-6000
FAX: (404) 828-7666

Company URL: http://www.ups.com
Establishment information: Established in 1907.
Company type: Public company
Company ticker symbol and exchange: UPS/NYSE
Business activities: Provides package delivery and specialized transportation and logistics services.
Business type (SIC): Trucking and courier services, except by air; transportation/scheduled air
Financial profile for 2012: Number of employees, 399,000; assets, $38,863,000,000; sales volume, $54,127,000,000; pre-tax net income, $974,000,000; expenses, $52,784,000,000; liabilities, $34,210,000,000
Fortune 1000 ranking: 2012—53rd in revenues, 239th in profits, and 144th in assets
Forbes 2000 ranking: 2012—158th in sales, 712th in profits, and 588th in assets
Corporate officers: D. Scott Davis, Chair. and C.E.O.; David P. Abney, C.O.O.; Kurt P. Kuehn, C.F.O.; David A. Barnes, Sr. V.P. and C.I.O.; Teri Plummer McClure, Sr. V.P., Genl. Counsel, and Secy.; Christine M. Owens, Sr. V.P., Comms.; John McDevitt, Sr. V.P., Human Resources
Board of directors: D. Scott Davis, Chair.; F. Duane Ackerman; Michael J. Burns; Stuart E. Eizenstat; Michael L. Eskew; William R. Johnson; Candace Kendle; Ann M. Livermore; Rudy H.P. Markham; Clark T. Randt, Jr.; John W. Thompson; Carol B. Tome; Kevin M. Warsh
Subsidiary: United Parcel Service of America, Inc., Atlanta, GA
Offices: Ontario, CA; Rockford, IL; Philadelphia, PA; Columbia, SC; Dallas, TX
International operations: Canada
Giving statement: Giving through the UPS Corporate Giving Program, the UPS Store, Inc., the UPS Foundation, and the MBE Foundation for Children's Initiatives.
Company EIN: 582480149

UPS Corporate Giving Program

c/o Corp. Contribs.
55 Glenlake Pkwy., N.E.
Atlanta, GA 30328-3474
URL: http://www.upssponsorships.com

Purpose and activities: As a complement to its foundation, UPS also makes charitable contributions to nonprofit organizations directly. Support is given primarily in areas of company operations on a national and international basis.
Fields of interest: Arts, cultural/ethnic awareness; Athletics/sports, amateur leagues; Community/ economic development.
Program:
UPS Neighbor to Neighbor Program: Through the UPS Neighbor to Neighbor Program, UPS employees volunteer their time to philanthropic causes in their local communities. The program is designed to promote volunteerism and an awareness of community need. Volunteer projects range from food drives and soup kitchens to employee mentorship of youth.
Type of support: Sponsorships.
Geographic limitations: Giving primarily in areas of company operations, nationally and internationally.
Publications: Application guidelines.
Application information: Applications accepted. Hard copy applications are not accepted. Application form required.
Initial approach: Complete online eligibility quiz and application for sponsorships
Deadline(s): 90 days prior to need for sponsorships
Final notification: 30 days for sponsorships

The UPS Foundation

55 Glenlake Pkwy., N.E.
Atlanta, GA 30328-3474 (404) 828-6374
FAX: (404) 828-7435; URL: http:// community.ups.com/UPS+Foundation

Establishment information: Incorporated in 1951 in DE.
Donor: United Parcel Service of America, Inc.
Financial data (yr. ended 12/31/11): Assets, $1,478,913 (M); gifts received, $39,583,896; expenditures, $42,724,737; qualifying distributions, $39,848,304; giving activities include $39,833,790 for 1,813 grants (high: $6,670,250; low: $100).
Purpose and activities: The foundation supports programs designed to promote economic and global literacy; environmental sustainability; nonprofit effectiveness; diversity; and community safety.
Fields of interest: Higher education; Business school/education; Education, reading; Education; Environment, climate change/global warming; Environment, natural resources; Environment, energy; Environment, forests; Environment; Food services; Disasters, preparedness/services; Safety, automotive safety; Safety/disasters; Boys & girls clubs; Youth development, adult & child programs; Girl scouts; American Red Cross; Salvation Army; Children/youth, services; Human services, financial counseling; Human services; International relief; Civil/human rights, equal rights; Civil/human rights; Social entrepreneurship; Microfinance/microlending; Nonprofit management; Community/economic development; Voluntarism promotion; United Ways and Federated Giving Programs; Leadership development Minorities; Economically disadvantaged.
International interests: Brazil; Canada; China; Mexico; South Africa.
Programs:
Community Safety: The foundation supports programs deigned to improve the safety and well-being of communities. Special emphasis is directed toward improving road safety; and enhancing the strategies and efficiencies of organizations involved with disaster and humanitarian relief.
Diversity: The foundation supports programs designed to promote economic empowerment, educational opportunity, leadership, mentorship, and inclusion for underserved and underrepresented populations.
Employee Matching Gifts: The foundation matches contributions made by employees of UPS to educational institutions and cultural and arts organizations on a one-for-one basis from $25 to $3,000 per employee, per year.
Environmental Sustainability: The foundation supports programs designed to foster protection and conservation of the natural world for future generations, including climate change and carbon reduction; energy and resource conservation; education and awareness; and research.
James E. Casey Scholarship Program: The foundation awards college scholarships to children of employees of UPS who plan to enter four-year degree programs at colleges and universities. The scholarship was established in honor of the UPS founder James E. Casey. Scholarships range from $2,000 to $6,000.
The George D. Smith Scholarship Program: The foundation awards scholarships to children of employees of UPS who are high school seniors planning to enroll in full-time courses of study of two years or less. Eligible programs include business schools, vocational-technical schools, and associate degree programs at four-year colleges and universities. Scholarships range from $500 to $2,000.
UPS Road Code: The foundation, in partnership with the Boys and Girls Clubs of America, offers a four-session training program to educate new and aspiring teen drivers about UPS's safe driving methods. At the sessions, UPS volunteers present two hours of instruction to young people ages 13-18 at their local Boys and Girls Club.
Volunteerism: The foundation supports nonprofit partners through volunteerism capacity building, improving nonprofit effectiveness, leadership development, and technology enhancements.
Type of support: Continuing support; Employee matching gifts; Employee volunteer services; Employee-related scholarships; Endowments; In-kind gifts; Management development/capacity building; Program development; Publication; Research; Scholarship funds; Technical assistance.
Geographic limitations: Giving on a national basis and in Brazil, Canada, China, England, Mexico, the Philippines, and South Africa; giving also to statewide, regional, national, and international organizations.
Support limitations: No support for religious organizations not of direct benefit to the entire community. No grants to individuals (except for employee-related scholarships); generally, no grants for capital campaigns, endowments, or general operating support.
Publications: Annual report; Informational brochure.
Application information: Applications not accepted. Contributes only to pre-selected organizations.
Board meeting date(s): Oct. and Nov.
Officers and Trustees:* Allen E. Hill*, Chair.; Eduardo Martinez, Pres.; Frank Romeo, V.P., Fdn. Progs. and Corporate Rels.; David P. Abney*, Secy.; Kurt P. Kuehn*, Treas.; Dan Brutto; D. Scott Davis; Teri Plummer McClure; Christine M. Owens.
Number of staff: 7 full-time professional; 4 full-time support.
EIN: 136099176
Selected grants: The following grants are a representative sample of this grantmaker's funding activity:
$7,148,082 to United Way, 2010.
$6,670,250 to United Way Worldwide, Alexandria, VA, 2011.
$1,729,750 to National Merit Scholarship Corporation, Evanston, IL, 2010.
$1,647,374 to National Merit Scholarship Corporation, Evanston, IL, 2011.
$1,005,000 to Boys and Girls Clubs of America, Atlanta, GA, 2011.
$750,000 to National Council of La Raza, Washington, DC, 2010.
$625,000 to Urban League, National, New York, NY, 2010.
$625,000 to Urban League, National, New York, NY, 2011.
$600,000 to HandsOn Network, Atlanta, GA, 2011.

$450,000 to Nature Conservancy, Arlington, VA, 2010.
$400,000 to World Association of Girl Guides and Girl Scouts, London, England, 2010.
$300,000 to HandsOn Network, Atlanta, GA, 2010.
$10,000 to National Badge of Honor Memorial Foundation, Washington, DC, 2010.
$10,000 to United Way of Central and Northeastern Connecticut, Hartford, CT, 2010.
$8,600 to Sweet Dreamzzz Detroit, Farmington, MI, 2011.
$5,000 to United Way of Greenville County, Greenville, SC, 2011.

3873
United Services Automobile Association

(also known as USAA)
9800 Fredricksburg Rd.
San Antonio, TX 78288-0001
(210) 456-1800

Company URL: http://www.usaa.com
Establishment information: Established in 1922.
Company type: Mutual company
Business activities: Sells automobile, property, and life insurance; provides investment advisory services; operates savings bank; provides direct mail advertising services; operates travel agency.
Business type (SIC): Insurance/fire, marine, and casualty; travel and tour arrangers; savings institutions; security and commodity services; insurance/life; mailing, reproduction, commercial art, photography, and stenographic service
Financial profile for 2011: Number of employees, 22,832; assets, $94,262,400,000; sales volume, $17,946,100,000
Corporate officers: Josue Robles, Jr., Pres. and C.E.O.; Kristi Ann Matus, Exec. V.P. and C.F.O.; Kevin J. Bergner, Exec. V.P. and C.A.O.; Steven Alan Bennett, Exec. V.P., Genl. Counsel, and Corp. Secy.; Wendi E. Strong, Exec. V.P., Corp. Comms.; Dawn M. Johnson, V.P., Mktg.; Micheal J. Broll, Secy.; James J. Vitali, Treas.
Board of directors: John P. Abizaid; Patricia C. Barron; Herman E. Bulls; Thomas P. Carney; Eileen M. Collins; Stephen B. Croker; Thomas B. Fargo; Fredrick M. Hamilton; Lester L. Lyles; John H. Moellering; Josue Robles, Jr.; Michael E. Ryan; Joseph C. Strasser, Sr.
Offices: Phoenix, AZ; Colorado Springs, CO; Tampa, FL; Norfolk, VA
Giving statement: Giving through the USAA Corporate Giving Program, the USAA Educational Foundation, and the USAA Foundation, Inc.

The USAA Educational Foundation

9800 Fredericksburg Rd.
San Antonio, TX 78288-0026 (800) 531-6196
FAX: (210) 498-9590; URL: https://www.usaaedfoundation.org/Misc/edufdn_about_us

Establishment information: Established in 1998 in TX as a company-sponsored operating foundation.
Donor: United Services Automobile Assn.
Financial data (yr. ended 12/31/11): Assets, $66,904,063 (M); expenditures, $4,792,576; qualifying distributions, $4,778,423 and $3,798,874 for foundation-administered programs.
Purpose and activities: The foundation provides publications on financial management, safety concerns, and significant live events to help consumers make informed decisions.
Fields of interest: Education; Safety, automotive safety; Safety/disasters; Family services; Business/industry; Military/veterans' organizations.
Type of support: Publication.
Geographic limitations: Giving primarily in San Antonio, TX.
Application information: Applications not accepted. Contributes only to a pre-selected organization.
Officers and Directors:* Josue Robles, Jr.*, Chair.; Barbara B. Gentry, Vice-Chair. and Pres.; Steven Alan Bennett*, Exec. V.P. and Secy.; Edwin T. McQuiston, Sr. V.P. and Treas.; Kenneth W. Smith, Sr. V.P.; Patrick A. Wageman, V.P. and Tax Officer; Kristi Ann Matus; Stuart B. Parker; Wendi E. Strong.
Number of staff: 14 full-time professional.
EIN: 742411017

The USAA Foundation, Inc.

9800 Fredericksburg Rd., D-03-E
San Antonio, TX 78288-3500 (210) 498-1225

Establishment information: Established in 2004 in TX as successor to the USAA Foundation, a Charitable Trust.
Donors: Barbara B. Gentry; The USAA Educational Foundation.
Contact: Barbara B. Gentry, Vice-Chair.
Financial data (yr. ended 06/30/11): Assets, $133,924,343 (M); gifts received, $100; expenditures, $8,918,013; qualifying distributions, $8,827,932; giving activities include $8,827,932 for 541 grants (high: $3,431,118; low: $200).
Purpose and activities: The foundation supports organizations involved with arts and culture, education, health, human services, and economic development.
Fields of interest: Arts; Higher education; Education; Hospitals (general); Health care; Food banks; American Red Cross; Homeless, human services; Human services; Economic development; United Ways and Federated Giving Programs.
Type of support: General/operating support.
Geographic limitations: Giving primarily in Phoenix, AZ, Colorado Springs, CO, Tampa, FL, San Antonio, TX, and Norfolk, VA.
Support limitations: No grants for capital campaigns (for colleges or universities) or for monuments or memorials.
Publications: Annual report (including application guidelines).
Application information: Applications accepted. Application form not required.
Initial approach: Proposal
Copies of proposal: 1
Deadline(s): None
Officers and Directors:* Josue Robles, Jr., Chair.; Barbara B. Gentry*, Vice-Chair.; Steve Speakes, Pres.; Steven Alan Bennett*, Exec. V.P. and Secy.; Edwin T. McQuiston, Sr. V.P. and Treas.; Kenneth W. Smith, Sr. V.P.; Patrick A. Wageman, V.P. and Tax Off.; Kristi Ann Matus; Stuart B. Parker; Wendi E. Strong.
EIN: 202303140
Selected grants: The following grants are a representative sample of this grantmaker's funding activity:
$3,431,118 to United Way of San Antonio and Bexar County, San Antonio, TX, 2011.
$220,500 to University of Texas at San Antonio, San Antonio, TX, 2011.
$175,000 to Alamo Community College District Foundation, San Antonio, TX, 2011.
$100,000 to American Red Cross, San Antonio, TX, 2011.
$100,000 to San Antonio Area Foundation, San Antonio, TX, 2011.
$90,000 to CHRISTUS Santa Rosa Childrens Hospital Foundation, San Antonio, TX, 2011.
$10,000 to Charity Ball Association of San Antonio, San Antonio, TX, 2011.
$7,500 to University of Tampa, Tampa, FL, 2011.
$5,000 to Chrysalis Shelter for Victims of Domestic Violence, Phoenix, AZ, 2011.
$5,000 to Returning Heroes Home, San Antonio, TX, 2011.

3874
United Space Alliance, LLC

600 Gemini St.
Houston, TX 77058-2708 (281) 212-6200

Company URL: http://www.unitedspacealliance.com
Establishment information: Established in 1996.
Company type: Joint venture
Business activities: Manages and conducts space flight operations.
Business type (SIC): Transportation services/miscellaneous
Corporate officers: Virginia A. Barnes, Pres. and C.E.O.; William R. Capel, V.P., C.F.O., and Compt.; Rochelle L. Cooper, V.P. and Genl. Counsel; Sherri K. Lee, V.P., Human Resources, Comms., and Public Rels.
Giving statement: Giving through the United Space Alliance Foundation.

United Space Alliance Foundation

c/o Bank of New York Mellon Corp.
P.O. Box 185
Pittsburgh, PA 15230-0185
Application address: 1150 Gemini St., Houston, TX 77058-2708

Establishment information: Established in 2001 in AL, DE, FL, and TX.
Donor: United Space Alliance, LLC.
Contact: Eileen A. Groves Esq., Dir.
Financial data (yr. ended 12/31/11): Assets, $61,280 (M); gifts received, $319,500; expenditures, $338,041; qualifying distributions, $338,041; giving activities include $338,041 for grants.
Purpose and activities: The foundation supports museums and community foundations and organizations involved with education, human services, and space and aviation.
Fields of interest: Museums (science/technology); Higher education; Engineering school/education; Scholarships/financial aid; Education; American Red Cross; Children/youth, services; Human services; Foundations (community); United Ways and Federated Giving Programs; Space/aviation.
Type of support: General/operating support; Scholarship funds.
Geographic limitations: Giving primarily in AL, FL, and TX.
Application information:
Initial approach: Contact foundation for application information
Officers and Directors: Eileen Groves, Esq., Co-Secy.; Vanessa Rincones, Co-Secy.; Virginia A. Barnes; Daniel C. Brandenstein; William R. Capel; Rochelle L. Cooper; Kim Doering; Kari Fluegel; Norm Gookins; Scott Hartwig; Kate B. Kronmiller; Mark Nappi.
EIN: 760668924
Selected grants: The following grants are a representative sample of this grantmaker's funding activity:

$62,500 to United Way of Brevard County, Cocoa, FL, 2010.
$25,000 to Information Technology and Innovation Foundation, Washington, DC, 2010.
$12,250 to Florida Institute of Technology, Melbourne, FL, 2010.
$7,500 to Crosswinds Youth Services, Cocoa, FL, 2010.
$5,000 to Arts Alliance Center at Clear Lake, Nassau Bay, TX, 2010.
$5,000 to Circles of Care, Melbourne, FL, 2010.
$5,000 to Genesys Works, Houston, TX, 2010.
$5,000 to Girl Scouts of the U.S.A., Houston, TX, 2010.
$5,000 to Huntsville Hospital Foundation, Huntsville, AL, 2010.
$2,500 to American Cancer Society, Huntsville, AL, 2010.

3875
The United States Achievement Academy

(also known as USSA)
2528 Palumbo Dr.
Lexington, KY 40509-1203 (859) 269-5671

Company URL: http://www.usaa-academy.com
Establishment information: Established in 1978.
Company type: Private company
Business activities: Operates directory publishing company.
Business type (SIC): Book publishing and/or printing
Corporate officer: Jeffrey Fraley, Pres. and C.E.O.
Giving statement: Giving through the United States Achievement Academy Scholarship Foundation, Inc.

United States Achievement Academy Scholarship Foundation, Inc.

2528 Palumbo Dr.
Lexington, KY 40509-1203 (859) 269-5671
URL: http://www.usaa-academy.com/schfacts.html

Establishment information: Established in 2003 in KY.
Donor: Unitied States Achievement Academy, LLC.
Financial data (yr. ended 12/31/11): Assets, $2,424 (M); gifts received, $198,137; expenditures, $198,073; qualifying distributions, $86,000; giving activities include $86,000 for 449 grants to individuals (high: $10,000; low: $100).
Purpose and activities: The foundation awards scholarships to members of the U.S. Achievement Academy, Kentucky.
Fields of interest: Education.
Programs:

The Dr. George A. Stevens Founder's Award: The foundation awards a $10,000 scholarship to a student nominated to the USAA by an educator. The award is given in honor of USAA foundation Dr. George A. Stevens and is designed to enhance the intellectual and personal growth of students who demonstrate a genuine interest in learning.

USAA Educational Cash Grants: The foundation awards educational scholarships of up to $1,500 to students nominated to the USAA by an educator. The grants are based on GPA; scores on SAT's; honors and awards; school activities, leadership positions, and sports involvement; and special interests, hobbies, and community service.

Type of support: Scholarships—to individuals.
Geographic limitations: Giving primarily in KY.
Application information: Applications accepted. Application form required.
Initial approach: Complete online application form
Deadline(s): Quarterly beginning Oct. 1 thru May 15.
Directors: James H. Booth; Angela B. Fraley; Jeffrey Fraley; Craig S. Preece.
EIN: 200145934

3876
United States Cellular Corporation

(also known as U.S. Cellular)
8410 W. Bryn Mawr Ave., Ste. 700
Chicago, IL 60631-3463 (773) 399-8900
FAX: (773) 399-8936

Company URL: http://www.uscc.com
Establishment information: Established in 1983.
Company type: Public company
Company ticker symbol and exchange: USM/NYSE
Business activities: Provides wireless telephone communications services.
Business type (SIC): Telephone communications
Financial profile for 2012: Number of employees, 8,100; assets, $6,587,450,000; sales volume, $4,452,080,000; pre-tax net income, $205,050,000; expenses, $4,295,430,000; liabilities, $2,853,590,000
Corporate officers: Leroy T. Carlson, Jr., Chair.; Mary N. Dillon, Pres. and C.E.O.; Steven T. Campbell, Exec. V.P., Finance, C.F.O., and Treas.; Carter S. Elenz, Exec. V.P., Sales; Edward Perez, V.P., Sales and Mktg.
Board of directors: Leroy T. Carlson, Jr., Chair.; James Barr III; Leroy T. Carlson; J. Samuel Crowley; Walter C.D. Carlson; Ronald E. Daly; Paul-Henri Denuit; Mary N. Dillon; Harry J. Harczak, Jr.; Gregory P. Josefowicz; Kenneth R. Meyers; Cecelia D. Stewart
Giving statement: Giving through the United States Cellular Corporation Contributions Program.
Company EIN: 621147325

United States Cellular Corporation Contributions Program

c/o Public Affairs and Comms. Dept.
8410 W. Bryn Mawr, Ste. 700
Chicago, IL 60631-3463 (733) 399-8900
E-mail: publicaffairs&communications@uscellular.com; URL: http://www.uscellular.com/about/community-outreach/index.html

Purpose and activities: U.S. Cellular makes charitable contributions to nonprofit organizations involved with economically disadvantaged youth, families, and seniors. Support is given primarily in areas of company operations.
Fields of interest: Education; Youth, services; Family services; Aging, centers/services Economically disadvantaged.
Programs:

Associate Matching Gifts: U.S. Cellular matches contributions made by its employees on a one-for-one basis.

Community Phone Program: Through the Community Phone Program, U.S. Cellular provide wireless and voicemail services to organizations that support disadvantaged youth, families and seniors.

Type of support: Donated products; Employee matching gifts; Employee volunteer services; Program development; Sponsorships.
Geographic limitations: Giving primarily in areas of company operations in IA, IL, KS, ME, MO, NC, NE, OK, OR, TN, VA, WI, and WV.
Support limitations: No support for discriminatory organizations, political organizations or candidates, lobbying, advocacy, social, labor, or alumni organizations, fraternal or religious organizations not of direct benefit to the entire community, primary, secondary, or charter schools, or local athletic or sports organizations. No grants to individuals, or for endowments or memorials, construction or renovation, special occasion, goodwill, or single-interest magazines, walk-a-thons, travel, or general operating support.
Application information: Applications accepted.
Copies of proposal: 1

3877
United States Steel Corporation

600 Grant St.
Pittsburgh, PA 15219-2800 (412) 433-1121
FAX: (302) 674-5266

Company URL: http://www.ussteel.com
Establishment information: Established in 1901.
Company type: Public company
Company ticker symbol and exchange: X/NYSE
International Securities Identification Number: US9129091081
Business activities: Manufactures and sells steel products; produces coke; mines iron ore and taconite.
Business type (SIC): Steel mill products; mining/iron
Financial profile for 2012: Number of employees, 39,000; assets, $15,217,000,000; sales volume, $19,328,000,000; pre-tax net income, $6,000,000; expenses, $19,081,000,000; liabilities, $11,740,000,000
Fortune 1000 ranking: 2012—147th in revenues, 930th in profits, and 297th in assets
Forbes 2000 ranking: 2012—485th in sales, 1845th in profits, and 1170th in assets
Corporate officers: John P. Surma, Chair. and C.E.O.; Mario Longhi, Exec. V.P. and C.O.O.; Gretchen R. Haggerty, Exec. V.P. and C.F.O.; James D. Garraux, Sr. V.P. and Genl. Counsel; John J. Quaid, V.P. and Treas.; Gregory A. Zovko, C.P.A., V.P. and Cont.; Joseph R. Scherrbaum, Jr., V.P., Sales; Susan M. Suver, V.P., Human Resources
Board of directors: John P. Surma, Jr., Chair.; Dan O. Dinges; John G. Drosdick; John J. Engel; Richard A. Gephardt; Charles R. Lee; Frank J. Lucchino; Glenda G. McNeal; Seth E. Schofield; Murry S. Gerber; David S. Sutherland; Patricia A. Tracey
International operations: Austria; Belgium; Brazil; Canada; France; Germany; Mexico; Serbia; Thailand; United Kingdom
Historic mergers: Lone Star Technologies, Inc. (June 14, 2007)
Giving statement: Giving through the United States Steel Foundation, Inc.
Company EIN: 251897152

United States Steel Foundation, Inc.

(formerly USX Foundation, Inc.)
600 Grant St., Rm. 675
Pittsburgh, PA 15219-2800 (412) 433-5237
FAX: (412) 433-2792; URL: http://www.ussteel.com/uss/portal/home/aboutus/foundation

Establishment information: Incorporated in 1953 in DE.
Donor: United States Steel Corp.
Contact: Susan M. Kapusta, Pres.
Financial data (yr. ended 11/30/11): Assets, $1,729,076 (M); gifts received, $1,426,500;

expenditures, $1,837,973; qualifying distributions, $1,782,934; giving activities include $1,694,500 for 104 grants (high: $166,500; low: $1,500) and $88,434 for 122 employee matching gifts.
Purpose and activities: The foundation supports organizations involved with arts and culture, higher education, the environment, health, violence prevention, legal aid, safety, human services, science, and civic affairs.
Fields of interest: Performing arts; Arts; Higher education; Business school/education; Engineering school/education; Environment; Public health; Health care; Crime/violence prevention; Legal services; Safety, education; Human services; Engineering; Science; Public policy, research; Public affairs.
Programs:
Education: The foundation supports institutions of higher education. Special emphasis is directed toward institutions with programs designed to provide engineering, science, and business education.
Employee Matching Gifts: The foundation matches contributions made by employees and directors of U.S. Steel to institutions of higher education on a one-for-one basis and 50 cents to the dollar to nonprofit organizations involved with private secondary education, special education, arts and culture, the environment, and the American Red Cross. Matching gifts range from $50 to $10,000 per contributor, per year.
Public, Cultural, and Scientific Affairs: The foundation supports public policy, legal, business, and community organizations; major performing arts organizations and culture institutions designed to enhance quality of life in U.S. Steel communities; and science and environmental organizations whose programs relate to the business interests of U.S. Steel.
Safety, Health, and Human Services: The foundation supports programs designed to promote safe and healthy communities by promoting violence and injury prevention, providing health education and promotion, and training first responders.
U.S. Steel Endowed Scholarships: The foundation supports endowed scholarships at selected universities. The scholarships are available to entering first-year students who have been accepted for full-time study toward a baccalaureate degree in a business-related major such as (but not limited to) engineering, accounting, finance, computer science, business, or natural sciences. Preference will be given to students who are children of employees of U.S. Steel. Scholarships are administered by selected universities.
U.S. Steel Scholarship Program: The foundation annually awards renewable $2,500 college scholarships to children of employees of U.S. Steel. The program is administered by Scholarship America, Inc.
Type of support: Capital campaigns; Employee matching gifts; Employee-related scholarships; General/operating support; Scholarship funds.
Geographic limitations: Giving primarily in areas of company operations, with an emphasis on AL, IL, IN, and PA.
Support limitations: No support for religious organizations for religious purposes, hospitals or nursing homes, or grantmaking foundations. No grants to individuals (except for employee-related scholarships), or for pre-collegiate education (unless U.S. Steel employees are directly involved), individual research projects, economic development, conferences, seminars, or symposia, travel, sponsorship of special events or fundraising events, publication of papers, books, or magazines, production of films, videotapes, or other audio-visual materials, or general operating support for organizations that receive operating funds from United Ways.
Publications: Application guidelines; Program policy statement.
Application information: Applications accepted. Support is limited to 1 contribution per organization during any given year. Application form required.
Applicants should submit the following:
1) signature and title of chief executive officer
2) copy of IRS Determination Letter
3) brief history of organization and description of its mission
4) copy of most recent annual report/audited financial statement/990
5) listing of board of directors, trustees, officers and other key people and their affiliations
6) detailed description of project and amount of funding requested
7) copy of current year's organizational budget and/or project budget
8) listing of additional sources and amount of support

Applications for capital requests should include the campaign goal or total cost of the specific capital need.
Initial approach: Complete online application
Copies of proposal: 1
Board meeting date(s): July and Nov.
Deadline(s): Apr. 13 for Education; June 1 for Public, Cultural, and Scientific Affairs and Safety, Health, and Human Services
Final notification: Following board meetings
Officers and Trustees:* David H. Lohr*, Chair.; Susan M. Kapusta, Ph.D.*, Pres.; John J. Quaid, V.P. and Treas.; William Donovan, V.P., Investments; James D. Garraux*, Secy. and Genl. Counsel; Gretchen R. Haggerty*, C.F.O.; Gregory A. Zovko, Compt.; Darin R. Hoffner, Tax Counsel; John P. Surma; Susan M. Suver.
Number of staff: 1 full-time professional; 1 part-time professional; 2 full-time support.
EIN: 136093185
Selected grants: The following grants are a representative sample of this grantmaker's funding activity:
$250,000 to Pennsylvania State University, University Park, PA, 2010.
$200,000 to Carnegie Mellon University, Pittsburgh, PA, 2010.
$162,500 to United Way of Allegheny County, Pittsburgh, PA, 2010.
$162,500 to United Way of Allegheny County, Pittsburgh, PA, 2010.
$112,500 to United Way, Lake Area, Griffith, IN, 2010.
$112,500 to United Way, Lake Area, Griffith, IN, 2010.
$100,000 to Purdue University, West Lafayette, IN, 2010.
$100,000 to Robert Morris University, School of Business, Moon Township, PA, 2010.
$22,500 to United Way of Northeastern Minnesota, Chisholm, MN, 2010.
$2,500 to Wayne State University, Detroit, MI, 2010.

3878
United States Sugar Corporation

111 Ponce de Leon Ave.
Clewiston, FL 33440-3032 (863) 983-8121

Company URL: http://www.ussugar.com
Establishment information: Established in 1931.
Company type: Private company
Business activities: Produces sugarcane; produces orange juice.
Business type (SIC): Farms, except cash grains/field crop; specialty foods/canned, frozen, and preserved
Corporate officers: Robert H. Buker, Jr., Pres. and C.E.O.; Carl Stringer, C.I.O.; Gerard A. Bernard, Sr. V.P. and C.F.O.; Robert E. Coker, Sr. V.P., Public Affairs; Charles F. Shide, V.P., Human Resources
Subsidiaries: South Central Florida Express, Inc., Clewiston, FL; Southern Gardens Citrus, Clewiston, FL
Giving statement: Giving through the United States Sugar Corporation Charitable Trust.

United States Sugar Corporation Charitable Trust

c/o United States Sugar Corp.
111 Ponce de Leon Ave.
Clewiston, FL 33440

Establishment information: Trust established in 1952 in FL.
Donor: United States Sugar Corp.
Financial data (yr. ended 10/31/11): Assets, $3,926 (M); expenditures, $0; qualifying distributions, $0.
Purpose and activities: The trust supports fairs and festivals and organizations involved with education, animal training, community development, civic affairs, and African-Americans.
Fields of interest: Education; Human services.
Type of support: Annual campaigns; General/operating support; Program development; Scholarship funds.
Support limitations: No grants to individuals, or for scholarships or fellowships; no loans.
Application information: Applications not accepted. Unsolicited requests for fundsa are not accepted.
Trustees: Robert H. Buker; Robert Coker; Malcolm Wade, Jr.
EIN: 596142825
Selected grants: The following grants are a representative sample of this grantmaker's funding activity:
$15,000 to Glades Day School, Belle Glade, FL, 2010. For unrestricted grant.

3879
United States Tennis Association

(also known as USTA)
70 W. Red Oak Ln.
White Plains, NY 10604 (914) 696-7000

Company URL: http://www.usta.com
Establishment information: Established in 1881.
Company type: Business league
Business activities: Operates national governing body for sport of tennis.
Business type (SIC): Business association; commercial sports; amusement and recreation services/miscellaneous
Corporate officers: Lucy S. Garvin, Chair. and Pres.; Gordon A. Smith, C.O.O.; Ed Neppl, C.F.O.; Lawrence Bonfante, C.I.O.; Andrea S. Hirsch, C.A.O. and Genl. Counsel; Vincent Lowndes, Treas.; Joseph Healy, Cont.
Board of director: Lucy S. Garvin, Chair.
Giving statement: Giving through the United States Tennis Association Contributions Program and the USTA Serves - Foundation for Academics. Character. Excellence.

United States Tennis Association Contributions Program

70 W. Red Oak Ln.
White Plains, NY 10604-3602 (914) 696-7000
E-mail: grants@usta.com; E-mail for Facilities Assistance Prog.: facilities@usta.com. Application contact for Pancho Gonzalez Scholar Athlete Grant: c/o The USTA Office of Diversity. National contact for Multicultural Excellence Prog. Grant, and Multicultural Individual Player Grant for National Competition & Training: Jean Desdunes, Sr. Dir., Diversity, tel.: (305) 481-1491; e-mail: JDesdunes@usta.com. Application contact for Multicultural Excellence Prog. Grant: c/o Diversity and Inclusion Dept.; National contact for Okechi Womeodu Scholar Athlete Grant, and Althea Gibson Leadership Award: Stefanie Lennaco, Coord., Diversity, tel.: (914) 696-7203, e-mail stefanie.iennaco@usta.com; e-mail for Public Facility Assistance: national contact: Facility Team (914) 696-7291, technical@usta.com; National contact for CTA & NJTL Community Tennis Devel. Workshop Scholarship: Emily Sandor (NJTL), (914) 696-7037, sandor@usta.com, or David Slade (CTA), tel.: (914) 696-7241, e-mail: slade@usta.com; URL: http://www.usta.com/About-USTA/USTA-Awards/AwardsandGrants/

Purpose and activities: As a complement to its foundation, the United States Tennis Association supports organizations and individuals that help to grow the game of tennis. Special emphasis is directed toward programs that promote diversity. Support is given on a national basis.
Fields of interest: Recreation, community; Recreation, parks/playgrounds; Athletics/sports, racquet sports; Recreation; Youth development.

Programs:

Althea Gibson Leadership Award: Through the Althea Gibson Leadership Award, USTA honors the memory, life, and achievements of Althea Gibson. The program rewards players who work to excel in leading others on and off the court.

CTA & NJTL Community Tennis Development Workshop Scholarship: This scholarship is available to all USTA registered CTA and NJTL Chapter/Program Leaders who have demonstrated continued excellence in community development and/or youth programming. Priority will be given to applicants from organizations that have never received a scholarship. District and Section Staff are not eligible to apply.

Multicultural Excellence Program Grant: Through the Multicultural Excellence Program, USTA provides funding to competitive junior development programs that train youngsters aspiring to achieve national and/or international rankings. Funding will be based on number of players with sectional and national rankings in a specific program. Participating programs must be year-round; provide a high level of on-court instruction and off-court training opportunities; and have a history of developing tournament level players.

Multicultural Individual Player Grant for National Competition & Training: Through the Multicultural Individual Player Grant for National Competition & Training Program, USTA provides funding to competitive junior players aspiring to achieve national and/or international rankings. Funding will be based on the success level of the player in the previous year. Players must be training and competing in tournaments year-round and have a history of strong national tournament results.

Okechi Womeodu Scholar Athlete Grant: Through the Okechi Womeodu Scholar Athlete Grant program, USTA honors the memory, life, and achievements of Okechi Womeodu, on and off the court. The grant reward players who work to excel as much in the classroom as in sports. Players must be training and competing in tournaments year-round, have a history of strong national tournament results, and a minimum GPA of 3.0.

Pancho Gonzalez Scholar Athlete Grant: In honor of Pancho Gonzalez, the Mexican-American who won two U.S. Championships' men's singles titles, USTA annually awards $2,500 grants to one male player and one female player who work to excel in leading others on and off the court. The grant funding is intended to be awarded to junior players aspiring to achieve a national and/or international ranking. The recipients should have a history of strong national tournament results. The recipients must be actively training and competing in tournaments in the award year.

Public Facility Assistance Program: Through the Public Facility Assistance Program, USTA assists community tennis organizations and their clients. Special emphasis is directed toward programs that have a significant impact on the growth of tennis.
Type of support: Advocacy; Building/renovation; Equipment; General/operating support; Scholarships—to individuals; Technical assistance.
Geographic limitations: Giving on a national basis.
Publications: Application guidelines.
Application information: Applications accepted. Full grant applications are accepted by invitation only for the Facility Assistance Program. Organizations seeking grants are limited to one application per year. If the project is not completed within 12 months, grant funds may be distributed to another community. Application form required. Applicants should submit the following:
1) timetable for implementation and evaluation of project
2) population served
3) name, address and phone number of organization
4) brief history of organization and description of its mission
5) copy of most recent annual report/audited financial statement/990
6) detailed description of project and amount of funding requested
7) contact person
8) copy of current year's organizational budget and/or project budget

Applications for the Pancho Gonzalez Scholar Athlete Grant must include two letters of recommendation, school transcript, a tournament and training schedule, a recent photograph, and an essay of 750 words or less. Applications for Multicultural Excellence Program Grant must include program and training details.

Initial approach: Download application form and mail to headquarters; Complete online application for Facility Assistance Program
Deadline(s): None for Facility Assistance Program; Dec. 31, 2012 for Pancho Gonzalez Scholar Athlete Grant and Okechi Womeodu Scholar Athlete Grant; Nov. 9, 2012 for Multicultural Excellence Program Grant. and Multicultural Individual Player Grant for National Competition & Training; June 1 for Multicultural Excellence Program Grant
Final notification: For Facility Assistance Program: 30 days for first contact, 60 days for final decision; March for Pancho Gonzalez Scholar Athlete Grant, and Okechi Womeodu Scholar Athlete Grant; Dec. 31 for Multicultural Excellence Program Grant

USTA Serves - Foundation for Academics. Character. Excellence.

(formerly USTA Tennis and Education Foundation)
70 W. Red Oak Ln.
White Plains, NY 10604-3602 (914) 696-7223
FAX: (914) 697-2307;
E-mail: foundation@usta.com; URL: http://www.usta.com/about-usta/usta-serves/

Establishment information: Established in 1994 in NY.
Contact: Karen Ford
Financial data (yr. ended 12/31/11): Revenue, $1,700,019; assets, $2,793,299 (M); gifts received, $1,658,464; expenditures, $1,747,649; program services expenses, $1,507,386; giving activities include $920,175 for 65 grants (high: $40,000; low: $7,250) and $397,750 for grants to individuals.
Purpose and activities: The foundation supports organizations and programs that enhance the lives of people through tennis and education.
Fields of interest: Education; Athletics/sports, racquet sports.

Programs:

Aces for Kids: The program awards grants to nonprofit organizations that support efforts in tennis and education to help disadvantaged, at-risk youth, and people with disabilities. Special consideration will be given to organizations that promote the foundation's "Aces for Kids" initiative, which strives to promote healthy lifestyles and combat childhood and adult obesity through providing disadvantaged, at-risk children the opportunity to learn to play tennis and improve their academic skills in a structured format. Awards may be used to fund programs for underserved youth, college scholarships, and programs for special-needs populations.

Dwight F. Davis Memorial Scholarship: A $7,500 scholarship will be awarded over four years to two students who are entering a four-year college or university program. The scholarship is available to high school seniors who have performed with distinction and actively participated in extracurricular activities, community service, and an organized tennis program.

Dwight Mosley Scholarship Award: A $10,000 scholarship will be awarded over four years to one male and one female student of diverse ethnic backgrounds who are entering a four-year college or university program. The scholarship is available to U.S. Tennis Association-ranked high school seniors of ethnically-diverse heritage who have excelled academically and participated extensively in an organized community tennis program. Applicants must demonstrate sportsmanship on and off the court.

Eve Craft Education & College Scholarship: A $2,500 scholarship will be awarded to one male and one female student entering a four-year college or university program. The scholarship is available to two high school seniors, one male and one female, who have excelled academically, demonstrated community service, played tennis in an organized program, and who reside in an economically-disadvantaged community.

Marian Wood Baird Scholarship Award: A scholarship award of $15,000 is available to high school seniors who have excelled academically, demonstrated achievements in leadership, and participated extensively in an organized community tennis program (such as USTA School Tennis, USTA National Junior Tennis League, USTA Team Tennis, USTA High Performance, or other such qualified programs as determined by the foundation's scholarship committee). Applicants must demonstrate sportsmanship on and off the court.

Player Incentive Awards: One-time grants of $500 each are available to encourage the development of United States Tennis Association (USTA) youth tennis program participants who demonstrate great potential and a commitment to academic excellence. Grants can be used for such expenses as tournament fees, indoor/winter lessons, summer tennis programs, and/or participation in USTA or other tennis organization programs. Eligible applicants must: currently be enrolled in grades 6 to 199; show financial need for all tennis-related fees; demonstrate a strong commit to academic achievement; and be a middle-school player with high-school varsity team potential, or be a high school varsity player.

USTA Tennis & Education Foundation College Education Scholarship: A $6,000 scholarship will be awarded over four years to students entering a two or four-year college or university. The scholarship is available to high school seniors who have excelled academically, demonstrated community service and participated in an organized tennis program.

USTA Tennis & Education USTA T&EF College Textbook Scholarship: A $1,000 scholarship will be awarded to students entering a two- or four-year college or university program. The scholarship provides a one-time award to assist students in purchasing textbooks or supplies.

Type of support: Grants to individuals; Scholarships—to individuals.
Geographic limitations: Giving on a national basis.
Publications: Annual report; Application guidelines; Grants list; Newsletter.
Application information: Applications accepted. Applicants may apply for all scholarship programs offered by the foundation; however, individuals will not be awarded more than one scholarship. Applicants should submit the following:
1) how project will be sustained once grantmaker support is completed
2) results expected from proposed grant
3) qualifications of key personnel
4) statement of problem project will address
5) population served
6) name, address and phone number of organization
7) copy of IRS Determination Letter
8) brief history of organization and description of its mission
9) geographic area to be served
10) copy of most recent annual report/audited financial statement/990
11) how project's results will be evaluated or measured
12) detailed description of project and amount of funding requested
13) plans for cooperation with other organizations, if any
14) contact person
15) copy of current year's organizational budget and/or project budget
16) listing of additional sources and amount of support

Initial approach: Download application
Deadline(s): Feb. 5 for Player Incentive Awards and all scholarships; Mar. 15 and Oct. 15 for Aces for Kids
Final notification: May and Dec. for Aces for Kids

Officers and Directors:* Lawrence A. Rand*, Chair.; Mary Carillo*, Pres.; Missie Rennie*, V.P.; Tiina Bougas Smith*, V.P.; Elizabeth L. Mathieu, Esq.*, Treas.; Katrina M. Adams; Howard B. Cowan; Anne Marie Davis; David N. Dinkins; Benjamin Doller; Jamshid Ehsani; Andre Hawaux; John B. Hess; and 17 additional directors.
EIN: 133782331

3880
United Supermarkets LLC

7830 Orlando Ave.
Lubbock, TX 79423-1942 (806) 791-0220

Company URL: http://www.unitedtexas.com
Establishment information: Established in 1916.
Company type: Private company
Business activities: Operates supermarkets.
Business type (SIC): Groceries—retail
Financial profile for 2011: Number of employees, 10,000; sales volume, $1,300,000,000
Corporate officers: Robert Taylor, C.E.O.; Joni Andrews, Co-Pres.; Matt Bumstead, Co-Pres.; R. Gantt Bumstead, Co-Pres.; Sidney Hopper, Exec. V.P., and C.O.O.; SuzAnn Kirby, C.F.O.; Peter Wellman, C.I.O.; Wes Jackson, Sr. V.P., Sales
Giving statement: Giving through the United Supermarkets, Inc. Corporate Giving Program.

United Supermarkets, Inc. Corporate Giving Program

7830 Orlando Ave.
Lubbock, TX 79423-1942 (877) 848-6483
For technical assistance with sponsorship application: e-mail: service@sponsor.com; tel.: (514) 393-8767 or (877) 776-6767;
URL: http://www.unitedtexas.com/our-community

Contact: Deonna Anderson
Purpose and activities: United Supermarkets makes charitable contributions to nonprofit organizations involved with education, hunger, sports, art, recreation, human services, community development, environmental beautification, housing, and civic affairs. Support is limited to areas of company operations in north and west Texas.
Fields of interest: Arts; Elementary school/education; Higher education; Higher education, university; Education; Environment, beautification programs; Food services; Food banks; Housing/shelter, volunteer services; Athletics/sports, amateur leagues; Children, services; Human services; Community/economic development; United Ways and Federated Giving Programs; Public affairs; Religion.
Type of support: Donated products; Employee volunteer services; General/operating support; In-kind gifts; Sponsorships.
Geographic limitations: Giving limited to areas of company operations in north and west TX.
Support limitations: No support for third parties raising funds for organizations that the company directly supports. No grants to individuals or families.
Publications: Application guidelines.
Application information: Applications accepted. Support is limited to 1 contribution per organization during any given year. Proposals should be submitted using only one method: online or in person. Merchandise donations usually range from $10 to $30 in gift cards or product. Proposals are not accepted via fax, e-mail, or mail. Application form required. Applicants should submit the following:
1) name, address and phone number of organization
2) detailed description of project and amount of funding requested
3) contact person
4) copy of IRS Determination Letter

Initial approach: Complete online application; Contact local store for volunteer requests
Deadline(s): 4 weeks prior to event, six months prior to event or sports season start if the marketing department is required
Final notification: Several weeks

3881
United Talent Agency, Inc.

9336 Civic Center Dr.
Beverly Hills, CA 90212-2401
(310) 273-6700

Company URL: http://www.unitedtalent.com
Establishment information: Established in 1991.
Company type: Private company
Business activities: Operates talent and literary agency.
Business type (SIC): Bands, orchestras, and entertainers
Corporate officers: James Berkus, Chair. and C.E.O.; Andrew Thau, C.O.O. and Genl. Counsel
Board of director: James Berkus, Chair.
Giving statement: Giving through the UTA Foundation.

UTA Foundation

9560 Wilshire Blvd., Ste. 500
Beverly Hills, CA 90211-2404
URL: http://www.unitedtalent.com/#foundation/

Establishment information: Established in 2004 in CA.
Donor: United Talent Agency, Inc.
Financial data (yr. ended 12/30/11): Assets, $185,614 (M); gifts received, $303,316; expenditures, $195,357; qualifying distributions, $168,039; giving activities include $168,039 for 26 grants (high: $35,361; low: $1,000).
Purpose and activities: The foundation supports food banks and organizations involved with media, education, conservation, mental health, gun control, and human services.
Fields of interest: Media/communications; Secondary school/education; Education, services; Education, reading; Education; Environment, natural resources; Environment, water resources; Mental health/crisis services, rape victim services; Crime/violence prevention, gun control; Food banks; Children/youth, services; Homeless, human services; Human services.
Type of support: Employee volunteer services; General/operating support; Scholarship funds.
Geographic limitations: Giving primarily in CA.
Support limitations: No grants to individuals.
Publications: Grants list.
Application information: Applications not accepted. Contributes only to pre-selected organizations.
Officers: James Berkus, C.E.O.; Peter Benedek, V.P.; Jeremy Zimmer, Secy.; Jay Sures, C.F.O.
EIN: 201130740
Selected grants: The following grants are a representative sample of this grantmaker's funding activity:
$7,023 to Saint Joseph Center, Venice, CA, 2009.
$6,600 to Brady Center to Prevent Gun Violence, Washington, DC, 2009.
$1,600 to Project Angel Food, Los Angeles, CA, 2009.
$1,000 to Writers Guild Foundation, Los Angeles, CA, 2009.

3882
United Technologies Corporation
(also known as UTC)
1 Financial Plz.
Hartford, CT 06103 (860) 728-7000
FAX: (302) 655-5049

Company URL: http://www.utc.com
Establishment information: Established in 1925.
Company type: Public company
Company ticker symbol and exchange: UTX/NYSE
International Securities Identification Number: US9130171096
Business activities: Manufactures building systems and aerospace high technology products.
Business type (SIC): Aircraft and parts; machinery/construction, mining, and materials handling; machinery/refrigeration and service industry
Financial profile for 2012: Number of employees, 218,000; assets, $89,409,000,000; sales volume, $57,708,000,000; pre-tax net income, $6,911,000,000; expenses, $50,024,000,000; liabilities, $63,495,000,000
Fortune 1000 ranking: 2012—50th in revenues, 38th in profits, and 67th in assets
Forbes 2000 ranking: 2012—140th in sales, 113th in profits, and 273rd in assets
Corporate officers: Louis R. Chenevert, Chair. and C.E.O.; Gregory J. Hayes, Sr. V.P. and C.F.O.; Charles D. Gill, Sr. V.P. and Genl. Counsel; Elizabeth B. Amato, Sr. V.P., Human Resources; Nancy Davis, V.P. and C.I.O.
Board of directors: Louis R. Chenevert, Chair.; John V. Faraci; Jean-Pierre Garnier, Ph.D.; Jamie S. Gorelick; Edward A. Kangas; Ellen J. Kullman; Marshall O. Larsen; Harold W. McGraw III; Richard B. Myers; H. Patrick Swygert; Andre Villeneuve; Christine Todd Whitman
Subsidiaries: Carrier, Corp., Farmington, CT; Hamilton Sundstrand Corp., Windsor Locks, CT; International Comfort Products, LLC, Indianapolis, IN; Otis Elevator Company, Farmington, CT; Pratt & Whitney Power Systems, Inc., East Hartford, CT; Sikorsky Aircraft Corporation, Stratford, CT
Divisions: UTC Fire & Security, Farmington, CT; UTC Power, South Windsor, CT
International operations: Australia; Canada; China; England; France; Germany; Hong Kong; Ireland; Japan; Luxembourg; Mexico; Netherlands; Poland; Singapore; South Korea; Spain; United Kingdom
Historic mergers: Sundstrand Corporation (June 10, 1999)
Giving statement: Giving through the United Technologies Corporation Contributions Program.
Company EIN: 060570975

United Technologies Corporation Contributions Program
1 Financial Plz.
Hartford, CT 06103-2608 (860) 728-7000
URL: http://www.utc.com/Corporate+Responsibility

Contact: Andrea Doane, Dir., Corp. Citizenship and Community Investment
Purpose and activities: UTC makes charitable contributions to programs designed to build sustainable cities; support vibrant communities; advance STEM (science, technology, engineering, and math) education; and invest in emerging markets. Support is given on a national and international basis in areas of company operations.
Fields of interest: Museums; Arts; Secondary school/education; Education; Environment, natural resources; Environment; Health care; Housing/shelter, development; Athletics/sports, Special Olympics; Human services; Community/economic development; United Ways and Federated Giving Programs; Mathematics; Engineering/technology; Science Minorities; Women.
International interests: China; India.
Programs:

Advancing STEM Education: UTC supports programs designed to advance the education of science, technology, engineering, and mathematics to develop the next generation of engineers and scientists. Special emphasis is directed toward programs that include employee volunteerism to spark students' interest and inspire innovation especially for minorities and women.

Building Sustainable Cities: UTC supports programs designed to build environmentally sustainable cities that are safe and energy efficient to protect people, assets, and natural resources. Special emphasis is directed toward sustainable building practices, urban green space, and the preservation of natural habitats to offset green-house gas emissions.

Investing in Emerging Markets: UTC supports programs designed to lay the foundation for responsible citizenship from the inception of expanding business opportunities.

Matching Gift Program: UTC matches contributions made by its full-time employees and directors to educational institutions and nonprofit organizations involved with arts and culture, the environment, community enrichment, health, and human services on a one-for-one basis from $25 to $10,000 per contributor, per year.

Support Vibrant Communities: UTC support programs designed to promote community revitalization, health and human services, and arts and culture.

Volunteer Grant Program: UTC awards $250 grants to nonprofit organizations with which its full-time employees and the full-time employees of its domestic divisions and subsidiaries volunteer at least 60 hours per year.

Type of support: Capital campaigns; Conferences/seminars; Continuing support; Curriculum development; Donated products; Employee matching gifts; Employee volunteer services; General/operating support; In-kind gifts; Program development; Sponsorships; Technical assistance.
Geographic limitations: Giving on a national and international basis in areas of company operations, with emphasis on Hartford, CT, New York, NY, China, and India.
Support limitations: No support for religious organizations, municipalities, booster clubs, sororities or fraternities, political groups, or organizations engaged in or advocating illegal action. No grants to individuals, or for religious activities, or publications or merchandise.
Publications: Application guidelines.
Application information: Applications accepted. UTC administers grants for its corporate headquarters and its business units including Carrier, Hamilton Sundstrand, Otis, Pratt & Whitney, Sikorsky, United Technologies Research Center, UTC Fire & Security, and UT Power. Nonproft organizations may apply to only one UTC business during any given year. The Community Affairs Department handles giving. The company has a staff that only handles contributions. Application form required.
Initial approach: Complete online eligibility quiz and application form
Copies of proposal: 1
Deadline(s): None for corporate headquarters grants; Mar. 1 to June 1 for business unit grants
Final notification: Up to 3 months
Number of staff: 3 full-time professional; 1 part-time professional; 1 full-time support.

3883
United Telephone Mutual Aid Corporation
(also known as Turtle Mountain Communications Inc.)
411 7th Ave.
P.O. Box 729
Langdon, ND 58249-2517 (701) 256-5156

Company URL: http://www.utma.com
Establishment information: Established in 1952.
Company type: Private company
Business activities: Provides telephone communications services; provides cable television services; provides Internet access services.
Business type (SIC): Telephone communications; cable and other pay television services
Corporate officer: Kenneth Carlson, Mgr.
Giving statement: Giving through the United Telephone Educational Foundation, Inc.

United Telephone Educational Foundation, Inc.
P.O. Box 729
Langdon, ND 58249-0729 (701) 256-5156
E-mail: utcfound@utma.com

Establishment information: Established in 1991 in ND.
Donor: United Telephone Mutual Aid Corp.
Contact: Kenneth Carlson, Secy.-Treas.
Financial data (yr. ended 12/31/11): Assets, $683,145 (M); expenditures, $72,174; qualifying distributions, $48,750; giving activities include $48,750 for grants to individuals.
Purpose and activities: The foundation awards college scholarships to children of members receiving telephone service from United Telephone Mutual Aid Corporation and Turtle Mountain Communications.
Type of support: Scholarships—to individuals.
Geographic limitations: Giving limited to areas of company operations.
Application information: Applications accepted. Application form required.
Initial approach: Contact foundation for application form
Deadline(s): Mar. 31
Directors: Marlin Swanson; Nancy Belanus; William Brooks; Arlaine Delebo; Nancy Haraseth; Guy Mitchell; Gene Narum.
Officers: Allyn Hart, Pres.; Bernard Schommer, V.P.; Kenneth Carlson, Secy.-Treas.
EIN: 450414760

3884
UnitedHealth Group Incorporated
(formerly United HealthCare Corporation)
UnitedHealth Group Ctr.
9900 Bren Rd. E.
Minnetonka, MN 55343 (952) 936-1300

Company URL: http://www.unitedhealthgroup.com
Establishment information: Established in 1977.
Company type: Public company
Company ticker symbol and exchange: UNH/NYSE

Business activities: Sells health insurance.
Business type (SIC): Insurance/accident and health
Financial profile for 2012: Number of employees, 133,000; assets, $80,885,000,000; sales volume, $110,618,000,000; pre-tax net income, $8,622,000,000; expenses, $101,364,000,000; liabilities, $49,707,000,000
Fortune 1000 ranking: 2012—17th in revenues, 36th in profits, and 74th in assets
Forbes 2000 ranking: 2012—48th in sales, 103rd in profits, and 301st in assets
Corporate officers: Richard T. Burke, Chair.; Stephen J. Hemsley, Pres. and C.E.O.; David S. Wichmann, Exec. V.P. and C.F.O.; Eric S. Rangen, Sr. V.P. and C.A.O.
Board of directors: Richard T. Burke, Chair.; William C. Ballard, Jr.; Edson Bueno, M.D.; Robert J. Darretta; Stephen J. Hemsley; Michele J. Hooper; Rodger A. Lawson; Douglas W. Leatherdale; Glenn M. Renwick; Kenneth I. Shine, M.D.; Gail R. Wilensky, Ph.D.
International operations: Argentina; Australia; Belgium; Bermuda; Brazil; Bulgaria; Canada; Cayman Islands; Chile; Costa Rica; Croatia; Czech Republic; Finland; France; Germany; Hong Kong; Hungary; India; Ireland; Italy; Japan; Mauritius; Mexico; Netherlands; Peru; Poland; Romania; Russia; Serbia; Singapore; Spain; Sweden; Switzerland; Ukraine; United Kingdom; Uruguay
Historic mergers: Oxford Health Plans, Inc. (July 29, 2004); PacifiCare Health Systems, Inc. (December 20, 2005)
Giving statement: Giving through the UnitedHealth Group Incorporated Contributions Program, the United Health Foundation, and the UnitedHealthcare Children's Foundation.
Company EIN: 411321939

UnitedHealth Group Incorporated Contributions Program

UnitedHealth Group Ctr.
9900 Bren Rd. E.
Minnetonka, MN 55343 (952) 936-1300
URL: http://www.unitedhealthgroup.com/main/SocialResponsibility.aspx

United Health Foundation

9900 Bren Rd. E., MN008-W150
Minnetonka, MN 55343-9664
FAX: (952) 936-1675;
E-mail: unitedhealthfoundationinfo@uhc.com;
URL: http://www.unitedhealthfoundation.org

Establishment information: Established in 1999 in MN.
Donors: United Healthcare Services, Inc.; UnitedHealth Group Inc.; Accenture, LLP; Pacificare Health Systems Foundation; Homecall Hospice.
Contact: Shelly Espinosa, Dir., Community Affairs
Financial data (yr. ended 12/31/11): Assets, $67,405,508 (M); gifts received, $1,838,301; expenditures, $11,316,000; qualifying distributions, $11,536,806; giving activities include $9,838,607 for 62 grants (high: $1,375,000; low: $5,000) and $8,217,903 for 4 foundation-administered programs.
Purpose and activities: The foundation supports programs designed to create healthier communities; expand access to healthcare services; nurture the future health workforce; and improve medical outcomes.
Fields of interest: Medical school/education; Health care, clinics/centers; Health care, patient services; Health care Economically disadvantaged.
Programs:
Advancing Clinical Evidence: The foundation supports up-to-date scientific and clinical evidence as a direct pathway to quality patient care; and partners with health research agencies and medical societies that play a key role in improving clinical care delivery. Online resources and commentaries that address the translation of the best science into applied clinical practice is available on the foundation's website.
America's Health Rankings: Through America's Health Rankings, the foundation aims to stimulate public conversation and debate on the health of individuals, communities, states, and the nation as a whole. Rankings are based on annual state-by-state analysis of health outcomes and determinants. Visit URL http://www.americashealthrankings.org/ for more information.
Caregivers of Veterans: The foundation, in partnership with the National Alliance for Caregiving, gives voices to caregivers who are caring for veterans across the age spectrum through the study Caregivers of Veterans - Serving on the Homefront. The study reveals how providing care affects caregivers' lives; the organizations and information sources that have been helpful to hem; and programs and services that provide support and assistance. The full study is available on the foundation's website.
Community Health Centers of Excellence: The foundation expands access to quality healthcare through multi-year partnerships with community health centers in economically-challenged communities in Washington, DC, New York, Miami, and New Orleans. The program is designed to transform clinics into "Centers of Excellence" in healthcare access and delivery. Special emphasis is directed toward preventative care, coordination of care, and the use of nationally-recognized standards of treatment, tailored to the unique needs of each community.
Diverse Scholars Initiative: The foundation awards scholarship funds to programs designed to develop healthcare professionals from diverse, multicultural backgrounds to increase the number of qualified yet underrepresented healthcare professionals entering the workforce. The scholarships are administered through partnerships with a variety of ethnically-based nonprofit and civic organizations.
Type of support: Continuing support; Program development; Publication; Scholarship funds; Technical assistance.
Geographic limitations: Giving on a national basis in areas of company operations, with emphasis on Washington, DC, FL, MN, and NY.
Support limitations: No support for private foundations, fiscal agents, political candidates, athletic associations, or religious organizations not of direct benefit to the entire community. No grants to individuals, or for scholarships (except for the Diverse Scholar Program), general operating support, capital campaigns, building or renovation, equipment (unless related to a request for project support), endowments, fundraising events, development campaigns, political causes, lobbying efforts, recreational or sporting events, basic or biomedical research, or travel.
Publications: Annual report; Corporate giving report.
Application information: Applications not accepted. The foundation is currently not accepting unsolicited requests.
Officers and Directors:* James R. Campbell*, Chair.; Kate Rubin, Pres.; Jeanette Pfotenhauer, Secy.; Robert Oberrender, Treas.; William A. Munsell; Larry Renfro; Jeannine Rivet; Reed V. Tuckson, M.D.; Anthony Welters.
Number of staff: None.
EIN: 411941615
Selected grants: The following grants are a representative sample of this grantmaker's funding activity:
$1,375,000 to Daughters of Charity Services of New Orleans, New Orleans, LA, 2011. For Centers of Excellence.
$1,000,000 to Childrens Health Fund, New York, NY, 2011. For Centers of Excellence.
$1,000,000 to Unity Health Care, Washington, DC, 2011. For Centers of Excellence.
$825,000 to Distance Learning Center, Philadelphia, PA, 2011. For StemPrep Project.
$500,000 to Marys Center for Maternal and Child Care, Washington, DC, 2011. For mobile dentistry vehicle.
$500,000 to University of Miami, Coral Gables, FL, 2010. For Centers of Excellence.
$499,747 to RAND Corporation, Santa Monica, CA, 2010. For Compare Initiative, which provides information and tools to help policymakers, the media and other interested parties understand, design and evaluate health policies.
$482,618 to Campaign for Tobacco-Free Kids, Washington, DC, 2011. For Youth by Youth Initiative and Youth Advocacy Symposium.
$385,906 to National Association of School Nurses, Silver Spring, MD, 2011. For School Nurse Childhood Obesity Prevention Education (SCOPE) Program.
$350,000 to Project HOPE - The People-to-People Health Foundation, Millwood, VA, 2011. For issue on diabetes.
$275,000 to Daughters of Charity Services of New Orleans, New Orleans, LA, 2010. For Centers of Excellence.
$275,000 to Daughters of Charity Services of New Orleans, New Orleans, LA, 2010. For Centers of Excellence.
$250,000 to Childrens Health Fund, New York, NY, 2010. For Centers of Excellence.
$250,000 to Childrens Health Fund, New York, NY, 2010. For Centers of Excellence.
$250,000 to Childrens Health Fund, New York, NY, 2010. For Centers of Excellence.
$250,000 to Childrens Health Fund, New York, NY, 2010. For Centers of Excellence.
$250,000 to Childrens Health Fund, New York, NY, 2010. For Centers of Excellence.
$100,000 to Association of Minority Health Professions Schools, Atlanta, GA, 2011. For 28th Annual Symposium.
$60,000 to Alliance for Health Reform, Washington, DC, 2010. To support Capitol Hill Luncheon briefings.
$60,000 to National Association of Area Agencies on Aging, Washington, DC, 2011. For Hearing Loss Education and Awareness Initiative.

UnitedHealthcare Children's Foundation

MN012-S286
P.O. Box 41
Minneapolis, MN 55440-0041 (952) 992-4459
Toll-free tel.: (800) 328-5979, ext. 24459;
URL: http://www.uhccf.org

Establishment information: Established in 1999 in MD.
Financial data (yr. ended 12/31/11): Revenue, $3,809,665; assets, $9,720,389 (M); gifts received, $3,920,248; expenditures, $3,087,756; giving activities include $2,577,507 for grants to individuals.
Purpose and activities: The foundation works to provide medically necessary services for families and children who have gaps in their commercial

health benefit plan coverage, and greater access to health-related services that have the potential to significantly enhance either the clinical condition or the quality of life of children.
Fields of interest: Medical care, community health systems; Health care, insurance; Health care; Children/youth, services Children/youth.

Program:
Grants Program: Grants are available to provide financial assistance for families who have children with medical needs not covered or not fully covered by their commercial health benefit plan. Eligible applicants must be sixteen years old or younger and live in the U.S.; and must be covered by a commercial health benefit plan (as defined by the foundation) and limits for the requested service are either exceeded, or no coverage is available and/or the co-payments are a serious financial burden on the family. Amount awarded to an individual within a 12-month period is limited to either $5,000 or 85 percent of the fund balance, whichever amount is less; awards to any one individual are limited to a lifetime maximum of $7,500. Grant applications requesting assistance for dental or orthodontic treatment unrelated to a serious medical condition are excluded from grant consideration.
Type of support: Emergency funds; Grants to individuals.
Geographic limitations: Giving on a national basis.
Publications: Application guidelines; Informational brochure.
Application information: Applications accepted.
Initial approach: Complete online application
Board meeting date(s): Monthly
Final notification: One to two months after submission of application
Directors: Thomas P. Barbera; David S. Hefner, M.P.A.; Jeannine Rivet, R.N., M.P.H.; Dr. Reed Tuckson; David S. Wichmann.
EIN: 522177891

3885
Unitil Corporation

6 Liberty Ln. W.
Hampton, NH 03842-1720 (603) 772-0775
FAX: (603) 773-6605

Company URL: http://www.unitil.com
Establishment information: Established in 1984.
Company type: Public company
Company ticker symbol and exchange: UTL/NYSE
Business activities: Operates holding company; generates, transmits, and distributes electricity; transmits and distributes natural gas.
Business type (SIC): Combination utility services; holding company
Financial profile for 2012: Number of employees, 467; assets, $886,600,000; sales volume, $353,100,000; pre-tax net income, $29,200,000; expenses, $305,600,000; liabilities, $626,000,000
Corporate officers: Robert G. Schoenberger, Chair., Pres., and C.E.O.; Thomas P. Meissner, Jr., Sr. V.P. and C.O.O.; Mark H. Collin, Sr. V.P. and C.F.O.; George E. Long, Jr., V.P., Admin.; Sandra L. Whitney, Corp. Secy.
Board of directors: Robert G. Schoenberger, Chair.; William D. Adams; Robert V. Antonucci; David P. Brownell; Lisa Crutchfield; Albert H. Elfner III; Edward F. Godfrey; Michael B. Green; Eben S. Moulton; M. Brian O'Shaughnessy; Sarah P. Voll; David A. Whiteley
Subsidiaries: Fitchburg Gas and Electric Light Co., Fitchburg, MA; Unitil Energy Systems, Inc., Kensington, NH; Unitil Power Corp., Hampton, NH; Unitil Realty Corp., Hampton, NH; Unitil Resources, Inc., Hampton, NH; Unitil Service Corp., Hampton, NH
Giving statement: Giving through the Unitil Corporation Contributions Program.
Company EIN: 020381573

Unitil Corporation Contributions Program

c/o Community Devel.
6 Liberty Ln. W.
Hampton, NH 03842-1704 (603) 773-6540
E-mail: community@unitil.com; URL: http://www.unitil.com/our-community/donations-sponsorships

Purpose and activities: Unitil makes charitable contributions to nonprofit organizations on a case by case basis. Support is limited to areas of company operations in Massachusetts, Maine, and New Hampshire.
Fields of interest: General charitable giving.
Type of support: Annual campaigns; Capital campaigns; Continuing support; Donated equipment; Donated products; Employee volunteer services; General/operating support; In-kind gifts; Loaned talent; Scholarship funds; Sponsorships; Use of facilities.
Geographic limitations: Giving limited to areas of company operations in MA, ME, and NH.
Publications: Application guidelines.
Application information: Applications accepted. Application form not required. Applicants should submit the following:
1) results expected from proposed grant
2) name, address and phone number of organization
3) brief history of organization and description of its mission
4) detailed description of project and amount of funding requested
5) contact person
6) additional materials/documentation

Initial approach: Download application form and mail to headquarters
Final notification: 4 to 8 weeks

3886
Univar USA Inc.

(formerly CHEMCENTRAL Corporation)
17425 N.E. Union Hill Rd.
Redmond, WA 98052 (425) 889-3400

Company URL: http://www.univarusa.com
Establishment information: Established in 1924.
Company type: Subsidiary of a foreign company
Business activities: Operates industrial chemical distribution company.
Business type (SIC): Chemicals and allied products—wholesale
Financial profile for 2010: Number of employees, 350
Corporate officers: Dave M. Strizzi, Pres.; John J. Zillmer, C.E.O.
Plants: Mesa, AZ; Hayward, Santa Fe Springs, CA; Denver, CO; Coral Springs, Orlando, FL; Doraville, GA; Fort Wayne, Indianapolis, IN; Louisville, KY; Jefferson, LA; Romulus, Wyoming, MI; Lakeville, MN; Kansas City, Maryland Heights, MO; Nashua, NH; Tonawanda, NY; Jamestown, NC; Hamilton, Strongsville, Toledo, OH; Oklahoma City, Tulsa, OK; Portland, OR; Coraopolis, Morrisville, PA; Dallas, Houston, Odessa, San Antonio, TX; Woods Cross, UT; Kent, Spokane, WA; New Berlin, WI
Offices: Mobile, AL; Conway, AR; Granger, IN; Fallston, MD; Springfield, MO; Baldwinsville, NY; Huntersville, NC; Westerville, OH; Simpsonville, SC; Collierville, Franklin, Knoxville, TN; El Paso, TX; Powhatan, VA
Giving statement: Giving through the Univar USA Inc. Corporate Giving Program, the CHEMCENTRAL Charitable Trust, and the Univar Foundation.

Univar USA Inc. Corporate Giving Program

(formerly CHEMCENTRAL Corporation Contributions Program)
17425 NE Union Hill Rd.
Redmond, WA 98052 (425) 889-3400

Purpose and activities: The company supports general and higher education programs on a case by case basis. Support is given on a national basis primarily in areas of company operations.
Fields of interest: Higher education; Education; Crime/violence prevention, domestic violence; Homeless, human services.
Type of support: General/operating support.
Geographic limitations: Giving on a national basis in areas of company operations.
Application information: Applications accepted.
Initial approach: Proposal to headquarters
Committee meeting date(s): As needed
Deadline(s): None

CHEMCENTRAL Charitable Trust

17425 N.E. Union Hill Rd.
Redmond, WA 98052-3375

Establishment information: Established in 1993 in IL.
Donor: CHEMCENTRAL Corp.
Financial data (yr. ended 12/31/11): Assets, $0 (M); expenditures, $22,807; qualifying distributions, $22,807; giving activities include $22,792 for 1 grant.
Purpose and activities: The foundation awards college scholarships to children of employees of CHEMCENTRAL.
Type of support: Employee-related scholarships.
Geographic limitations: Giving limited to areas of company operations.
Application information: Applications not accepted. Unsolicited requests for funds not accepted.
Trustees: Meg Medlin; Laurie Saint.
EIN: 363803848

Univar Foundation

(formerly Van Waters & Rogers Foundation)
17425 NE Union Hill Rd.
Redmond, WA 98052-3375

Establishment information: Established in 1967.
Donors: Van Waters & Rogers Inc.; Vopak USA Inc.; Univar Inc.
Contact: John J. Zillmer, Pres.
Financial data (yr. ended 12/31/10): Assets, $0 (M); gifts received, $213,092; expenditures, $237,025; qualifying distributions, $237,025; giving activities include $237,000 for 8 grants (high: $67,000; low: $5,000).
Purpose and activities: The foundation supports organizations involved with higher education, business education, substance abuse treatment, disaster relief, human services, and science.
Fields of interest: Higher education; Business school/education; Substance abuse, treatment; Disasters, preparedness/services; Children/youth, services; Human services, gift distribution; Human services; Chemistry; Science.

Type of support: Annual campaigns; Building/renovation; Capital campaigns; Continuing support; Emergency funds; Program development.
Geographic limitations: Giving primarily in WA.
Support limitations: No grants to individuals.
Application information: Applications not accepted. Contributes only to pre-selected organizations.
Officers and Directors:* John J. Zillmer*, Pres.; Edward A. Evans*, V.P.; Amy E. Weaver, Secy.; Steven M. Nielson, Treas.
EIN: 910826180
Selected grants: The following grants are a representative sample of this grantmaker's funding activity:
$50,000 to University of Washington, Seattle, WA, 2009.
$2,500 to University of Washington, Seattle, WA, 2009.

3887
Universal American Corp.

44 S. Broadway Ste. 1200
White Plains, NY 10601-4411
(914) 934-5200
FAX: (914) 934-0700

Company URL: http://www.universalamerican.com
Establishment information: Established in 1981.
Company type: Public company
Company ticker symbol and exchange: UAM/NYSE
Business activities: Operates insurance and managed care company.
Business type (SIC): Insurance/accident and health
Financial profile for 2012: Number of employees, 2,300; assets, $2,531,300,000; sales volume, $2,177,500,000; pre-tax net income, $77,630,000; expenses, $2,089,640,000; liabilities, $1,518,800,000
Fortune 1000 ranking: 2012—888th in revenues, 813th in profits, and 800th in assets
Corporate officers: Richard A. Barasch, Chair. and C.E.O.; Robert A. Waegelein, C.P.A., Pres. and C.F.O.; Steven H. Black, C.A.O.; Anthony L. Wolk, Sr. V.P., Genl. Counsel and Corp. Secy.; Dan Lieber, Sr. V.P., Opers.
Board of directors: Richard A. Barasch, Chair.; Barry W. Averill; Sally W. Crawford; Matthew W. Etheridge; Mark K. Gormley; Mark M. Harmeling; David S. Katz; Linda H. Lamel; Patrick J. McLaughlin; Richard Perry; Thomas A. Scully; Robert A. Spass; Sean M. Traynor; Christopher E. Wolfe
Giving statement: Giving through the Universal American Corp. Contributions Program.
Company EIN: 112580136

Universal American Corp. Contributions Program

(also known as Collaborating for Good Health Giving Back Program)
6 International Dr., Ste. 190
Rye Brook, NY 10573-1068 (914) 934-5200
URL: http://www.universalamerican.com/giving-back-program.aspx

Purpose and activities: Universal American Corp. makes charitable contributions to nonprofit organizations with programs designed to improve the health and healthcare of older Americans. Support is given primarily in areas of company operations.
Fields of interest: Aging, centers/services Aging.
Type of support: General/operating support; Program evaluation.
Geographic limitations: Giving in areas of company operations.
Support limitations: No grants to individuals.
Application information: Applications accepted. Requests may not exceed $50,000 for one year, though most are in the $5,000 to $10,000 range. The Giving Back Program will consider national and regional proposals in key geographic areas.

3888
Universal Care, Inc.

1600 E. Hill St.
Signal Hill, CA 90755-3682 (562) 424-6200

Company URL: http://www.universalcare.com
Establishment information: Established in 1983.
Company type: Private company
Business activities: Operates medical service plan.
Business type (SIC): Insurance/accident and health
Corporate officers: Howard E. Davis, Pres. and C.E.O.; Jeffrey V. Davis, C.O.O.; Mark Gunter, C.F.O.
Board of director: Robert Myers
Giving statement: Giving through the Center for a Brand New Day.

Center for a Brand New Day

1600 E. Hill St.
Signal Hill, CA 90755-3682
URL: http://c4bnd.org/

Establishment information: Established in 2000 in CA.
Donors: Universal Care, Inc.; Elaine Davis; Howard Davis.
Financial data (yr. ended 12/31/11): Assets, $27,899 (M); gifts received, $9,412; expenditures, $12,927; qualifying distributions, $23,507.
Purpose and activities: The foundation provides services to individuals with mental illness.
Application information: Applications not accepted. Unsolicited requests for funds not accepted.
Officers: Elaine Davis, Pres.; Pat Taylor, V.P.; Dianne U-Ming, V.P.; Dawn McCormack, Secy.; Steven B. Siskin, Treas.
Directors: Marillyn Brame; Lucy Brimbuela; Lois Labahn; Timothy Murray; Tom Purkiss; Bob Rossen; Gloria Shanks.
EIN: 912083280

3889
Universal City Development Partners, Ltd.

(doing business as Universal Orlando Resort)
1000 Universal Studios Plz.
Orlando, FL 32819-7610 (407) 363-8000

Company URL: http://www.universalorlando.com
Establishment information: Established in 1987.
Company type: Private company
Business activities: Operates entertainment resort.
Business type (SIC): Amusement and recreation services/miscellaneous
Corporate officers: Thomas Williams, Chair. and Co-C.E.O.; John R. Sprouls, Co-C.E.O.; William A. Davis, Pres. and C.O.O.; Alice A. Norsworthy, Exec. V.P., Mktg. and Sales; Tracey L. Stockwell, C.F.O.; Catherine A. Roth, Sr. V.P. and Genl. Counsel; William McCorey, Sr. V.P. and C.I.O.; Sherry Wheelock, V.P., Finance and Treas.; Daniel Neal, V.P., Finance and Cont.
Board of director: Thomas Williams, Chair.
Giving statement: Giving through the Universal Orlando Resort Corporate Giving Program and the Universal Orlando Foundation.

Universal Orlando Resort Corporate Giving Program

c/o Community & Diversity Rels. Correspondence Dept.
1000 Universal Studios Plz.
Orlando, FL 32819-7601 (407) 368-8000
URL: http://cr.ucdp.net/charitable_contributions.html

Purpose and activities: As a complement to its foundation, Universal Orlando Resort also make charitable contributions to nonprofit organizations directly. Special emphasis is directed toward programs that focus on arts and culture, strengthening communities, youth development, and education. Support is given primarily in central Florida.
Fields of interest: Arts; Elementary school/education; Youth development; Community/economic development Economically disadvantaged.
Type of support: Donated products; Employee volunteer services; General/operating support; In-kind gifts.
Geographic limitations: Giving primarily in central FL.
Publications: Application guidelines.
Application information: Applications accepted. Universal primarily donates theme park tickets. Application form required.
Initial approach: Complete online application for theme park passes
Deadline(s): Nov. 1, Feb. 1, May 1, and Aug. 1

Universal Orlando Foundation

1000 Universal Studios Plz.
Orlando, FL 32819-7601 (407) 224-5690

Establishment information: Established in 1998 in FL.
Contact: Diane O'Dell, Exec. Dir.
Financial data (yr. ended 12/31/11): Revenue, $1,647,170; assets, $1,676,504 (M); gifts received, $1,678,034; expenditures, $1,282,026; program services expenses, $1,163,722; giving activities include $1,022,679 for grants.
Purpose and activities: The organization aims to promote quality of life in the central Florida community, addressing needs and concerns primarily in the areas of education, children, and families.
Fields of interest: Education; Human services Children.
Geographic limitations: Giving primarily in the central FL region.
Officers and Directors:* John Sprouls*, Pres.; Judith Luengas*, Secy.; Tracey Stockwell*, Treas.; Diane O'Dell, Exec. Dir.; Ric Florell; Peter Giacalone; Charlie Gundacker; Alice Norsworthy; Rhonda Rhodes; Cathy Roth.
EIN: 593510383

3890
Universal Forest Products, Inc.
2801 E. Beltline N.E.
Grand Rapids, MI 49525 (616) 364-6161
FAX: (616) 361-7534

Company URL: http://www.ufpi.com
Establishment information: Established in 1955.
Company type: Public company
Company ticker symbol and exchange: UFPI/NASDAQ
Business activities: Sells softwoods wholesale.
Business type (SIC): Lumber and construction materials—wholesale
Financial profile for 2012: Number of employees, 5,200; assets, $860,540,000; sales volume, $2,054,930,000; pre-tax net income, $41,060,000; expenses, $2,010,400,000; liabilities, $260,770,000
Fortune 1000 ranking: 2012—932nd in revenues, 860th in profits, and 984th in assets
Corporate officers: William G. Currie, Chair.; Matthew J. Misad, C.E.O.; Patrick M. Webster, Pres. and C.O.O.; Michael R. Cole, C.F.O. and Treas.
Board of directors: William G. Currie, Chair.; John M. Engler; John W. Garside; Gary F. Goode; Bruce Merino; Mark A. Murray; Thomas W. Rhodes; Louis A. Smith
International operations: Bermuda; Canada; Mexico
Giving statement: Giving through the Robert & Joan Hill Family Foundation and the Universal Forest Products Education Foundation.
Company EIN: 381465835

Robert & Joan Hill Family Foundation
5974 Watson Dr.
Fort Collins, CO 80528-8877

Establishment information: Established in 2005 in CO.
Donors: Universal Forest Products; Robert K. Hill; Joan P. Hill.
Financial data (yr. ended 12/31/11): Assets, $163,521 (M); expenditures, $48,162; qualifying distributions, $47,182; giving activities include $47,182 for 11 grants (high: $10,100; low: $500).
Purpose and activities: The foundation supports organizations involved with higher education, cancer, Alzheimer's disease, school athletics, and children services.
Fields of interest: Higher education; Cancer; Alzheimer's disease; Athletics/sports, school programs; Athletics/sports, basketball; Children, services.
Type of support: General/operating support.
Geographic limitations: Giving primarily in CA and CO.
Support limitations: No grants to individuals.
Application information: Applications not accepted. Contributes only to pre-selected organizations.
Officers: Robert K. Hill, Pres.; Amanda R. Campion, V.P.; Mark Campion, V.P.; Angela M. Parman, V.P.; James E. Parman, V.P.; Joan P. Hill, Secy.
EIN: 201919268

Universal Forest Products Education Foundation
(formerly Universal Companies, Inc. Education Foundation)
2801 E. Beltline Ave. N.E.
Grand Rapids, MI 49525-9680

Establishment information: Established in 1990 in MI.
Donor: Universal Forest Products, Inc.
Contact: Nancy DeGood, Dir.
Financial data (yr. ended 12/31/11): Assets, $563,684 (M); expenditures, $35,579; qualifying distributions, $32,680; giving activities include $32,680 for grants.
Purpose and activities: The foundation awards college scholarships to children and adopted children of full-time employees of Universal Forest Products.
Type of support: Employee-related scholarships.
Application information: Applications accepted. Application form required.
Initial approach: Letter
Deadline(s): None
Officer and Directors:* Michael R. Cole*, Pres.; Nancy DeGood; Glenda Glenn; Ronald J. Schollaart.
EIN: 382945715

3891
Universal Leaf Tobacco Company, Inc.
9201 Forest Hill Ave., Fl. 1
Richmond, VA 23235-6885 (804) 359-9311

Company URL: http://www.universalcorp.com/
Establishment information: Established in 1918.
Company type: Subsidiary of a public company
Business activities: Sells leaf tobacco wholesale.
Business type (SIC): Farm-product raw materials—wholesale
Corporate officers: Henry H. Harrell, Chair. and C.E.O.; Allen B. King, Pres. and C.O.O.; David C. Moore, Sr. V.P. and C.F.O.; William J. Coronado, V.P. and Cont.; James M. White III, V.P. and Genl. Counsel
Board of director: Henry H. Harrell, Chair.
Subsidiaries: Dunnington-Beach Tobacco Co., Farmville, VA; K.R. Edwards Leaf Tobacco Co., Inc., Smithfield, NC; Imperial Processing Corp., Kenbridge, VA; Lancaster Leaf Tobacco, Lancaster, PA; Macliu-Zimmer-McGill Tobacco Co., Mc Kenney, VA; Southern Processors, Inc., Danville, VA; Southwestern Tobacco Co., Lexington, KY; J.P. Taylor Co. Inc., Henderson, NC; Thorpe-Greenville Export Tobacco, Rocky Mount, NC; Tobacco Processors, Inc., Wilson, NC; R.P. Watson Co., Wilson, NC
Giving statement: Giving through the Universal Leaf Foundation.

Universal Leaf Foundation
P.O. Box 25099
Richmond, VA 23260-5099 (804) 359-9311
URL: http://www.universalcorp.com/SCIP/SCIP-CommunityInvolvement.asp?Menu=

Establishment information: Established in 1975 in VA.
Donor: Universal Leaf Tobacco Co., Inc.
Contact: H. Michael Ligon, V.P.
Financial data (yr. ended 06/30/12): Assets, $15,258,219 (M); expenditures, $788,391; qualifying distributions, $641,423; giving activities include $641,423 for grants.
Purpose and activities: The foundation supports organizations involved with arts and culture, education, conservation, health, cancer, hunger, human services, and community development.
Fields of interest: Performing arts; Historic preservation/historical societies; Arts; Higher education; Education; Environment, natural resources; Hospitals (general); Health care; Cancer; Food services; American Red Cross; YM/YWCAs & YM/YWHAs; Children/youth, services; Residential/custodial care; Aging, centers/services; Human services; Community/economic development; United Ways and Federated Giving Programs.
Type of support: Annual campaigns; Capital campaigns; General/operating support; Program development; Scholarship funds.
Geographic limitations: Giving primarily in Richmond, VA.
Support limitations: No grants to individuals.
Application information: Applications accepted. Application form not required. Applicants should submit the following:
1) copy of IRS Determination Letter
2) brief history of organization and description of its mission
3) copy of most recent annual report/audited financial statement/990
4) descriptive literature about organization

Initial approach: Letter of inquiry
Deadline(s): None
Officers and Directors:* George C. Freeman III*, Pres.; H. Michael Ligon*, V.P.; Catherine H. Claiborne*, Secy. and Assoc. Genl. Counsel; J. S. Rowe*, Treas.; David C. Moore; H. B. Smith.
Number of staff: 1 full-time professional; 1 part-time support.
EIN: 510162337
Selected grants: The following grants are a representative sample of this grantmaker's funding activity:
$100,000 to VCU Massey Cancer Center, Richmond, VA, 2011.
$25,000 to CenterStage Foundation, Richmond, VA, 2011.
$25,000 to United Way of Greater Richmond and Petersburg, Richmond, VA, 2011.
$25,000 to Virginia Foundation for Independent Colleges, Richmond, VA, 2011.
$22,937 to United Way of Greater Richmond and Petersburg, Richmond, VA, 2011.
$10,000 to Nature Conservancy, Charlottesville, VA, 2011.
$10,000 to YMCA, Lancaster Family, Lancaster, PA, 2011.
$5,000 to Better Housing Coalition, Richmond, VA, 2011.
$4,500 to Childrens Hospital, Richmond, VA, 2011.
$2,000 to Hampden-Sydney College, Development Office, Hampden Sydney, VA, 2011.

3892
Universal Refractories, Inc.
915 Clyde St.
Wampum, PA 16157-4403 (724) 535-4374

Establishment information: Established in 1984.
Company type: Private company
Business activities: Manufactures clay refractories.
Business type (SIC): Clay structural products
Corporate officers: Walter Sylvester, Pres.; Tom Sylvester, C.F.O.
Board of director: Walter Sylvester
Giving statement: Giving through the Walter R. Sylvester Memorial Scholarship Fund.

Walter R. Sylvester Memorial Scholarship Fund
101 Jane Kirk Ct.
Aliquippa, PA 15001
Application address: c/o Center Area Senior High School, Attn.: Guidance Counselor Office, 160 Baker Rd. Ext., Monaca, PA, 15061-2571

Establishment information: Established in 2005 in PA.
Donor: Universal Refractories, Inc.

Financial data (yr. ended 12/31/11): Assets, $192,391 (M); gifts received, $60,000; expenditures, $10,068; qualifying distributions, $10,000; giving activities include $10,000 for 5 grants to individuals (high: $2,000; low: $2,000).
Purpose and activities: The foundation awards scholarships to graduating seniors from Center Area Senior High School, Monaca, Pennsylvania, with a GPA 3.0 or better and must attend a 4-year accredited college.
Type of support: Scholarships—to individuals.
Geographic limitations: Giving primarily in Monaca, PA.
Application information: Applications accepted. Application form required.
Initial approach: Contact foundation for application form
Deadline(s): Mar. 1
Directors: Kimberly McKenzie; Lois Sylvester; Michael Sylvester; Thomas Sylvestor; Walter Sylvester.
EIN: 206365186

3893
Universal Studios, Inc.

100 Universal City Plz., Bldg. 2160/8H
Universal City, CA 91608-1002
(800) 864-8377

Company URL: http://www.universalstudios.com
Establishment information: Established in 1958.
Company type: Subsidiary of a public company
Ultimate parent company: General Electric Company
Business activities: Produces motion pictures and home videos; operates theme parks; produces television programming.
Business type (SIC): Motion pictures/production and services allied to; amusement and recreation services/miscellaneous
Financial profile for 2010: Number of employees, 15,000; sales volume, $1,000,000,000
Corporate officers: Ronald Meyer, Pres. and C.O.O.; Sean Gamble, Exec. V.P. and C.F.O.
Board of directors: Michael Jackson; Donna Langley
Giving statement: Giving through the Universal Studios, Inc. Corporate Giving Program, the Jurassic Foundation Inc., the Lew Wasserman Scholarship, and the Discover A Star Foundation.

Universal Studios, Inc. Corporate Giving Program

100 Universal City Plz.
Universal City, CA 91608-1002 (818) 866-3099
URL: http://www.universalstudioshollywood.com/com_rel/index.html

Purpose and activities: As a complement to its foundations, Universal Studios also makes charitable contributions to nonprofit organizations directly. Support is given primarily in the Los Angeles, California, area.
Fields of interest: Children.
Type of support: Donated products; Employee volunteer services; In-kind gifts.
Geographic limitations: Giving primarily in the Los Angeles, CA, area.
Support limitations: No support for athletic organizations. No grants to individuals, or for film or video projects.
Number of staff: 2

The Jurassic Foundation Inc.

c/o Braver P.C.
117 Kendrick St., Ste. 800
Needham, MA 02494
E-mail: lamannam@carnegiemnh.org; URL: http://jurassicfoundation.org/

Establishment information: Established in 1999 in MA.
Donor: Universal Studios, Inc.
Financial data (yr. ended 12/31/11): Assets, $134,734 (M); expenditures, $42,702; qualifying distributions, $40,000; giving activities include $40,000 for 13 grants (high: $5,000; low: $1,000).
Purpose and activities: The foundation awards grants of up to $5,000 to qualified research scientists and students for research on aspects of dinosaur paleobiology. Special emphasis is directed toward students, postdoctoral researchers, and other researchers with limited funding opportunities.
Fields of interest: Biology/life sciences; Anatomy (animal); Science.
Type of support: Fellowships; Research.
Geographic limitations: Giving on a national and international basis, with emphasis on CA, MA, NY, PA, TX, Argentina, and Canada.
Application information: Applications not accepted. Unsolicited requests for funds not accepted.
Officers and Directors:* Mathew C. Lamanna*, Pres.; Eva Koppelhus*, Treas.; Anusuya Chinsamy-Turan; Patrick M. O'Connor; David J. Varricchio.
EIN: 043448123

The Lew Wasserman Scholarship

100 Universal City Plz.
Universal City, CA 91608-1002

Donors: NBC Universal, Inc.; Universal Studios, Inc.
Financial data (yr. ended 12/31/10): Assets, $570,335 (M); gifts received, $31,370; expenditures, $55,760; qualifying distributions, $35,761; giving activities include $21,026 for 1 grant.
Purpose and activities: The foundation awards college scholarships. The program is administered by Scholarship America, Inc.
Type of support: Scholarships—to individuals.
Application information: Applications not accepted. Unsolicited requests for funds not accepted.
Officers and Directors:* Ron Meyer, Pres.; Maren Christensen, Exec. V.P. and Secy.; Christy Rupert Shibata, Exec. V.P. and Treas.; Lynn A. Calpeter, Exec. V.P.; Richard Cotton, Exec. V.P.; Cindy Gardner, Sr. V.P.; Marc Palotay, Sr. V.P.; John Apadula, V.P.; James Degnan, V.P.; Todd F. Davis, V.P.; Thomas N. Jones, V.P.; David H. Meyers, V.P.; Jennifer Dawn Mayhew, V.P.; Brian J. O'Leary, Jr., V.P.
EIN: 954479463

Discover A Star Foundation

100 Universal City Plz., Bldg. 1280
Universal City, CA 91608-1002 (818) 622-3948
FAX: (818) 622-3083;
E-mail: Dorothea.Scattaglia@nbcuni.com;
URL: http://www.universalstudioshollywood.com/com_rel/das.html

Establishment information: Established in 1993.
Contact: Dorothea Scattaglia, Exec. Dir.
Financial data (yr. ended 12/31/10): Revenue, $341,086; assets, $248,042 (M); gifts received, $394,257; expenditures, $304,301; giving activities include $257,400 for grants.
Purpose and activities: The foundation supports nonprofit organizations involved with children's health and well-being, and homeless intervention.
Fields of interest: Housing/shelter, homeless Children.
Type of support: General/operating support.
Application information: Applications accepted.
Initial approach: Complete online application
Officers and Directors:* Larry Kurzweil*, Chair.; Dorothea G. Scattaglia, Exec. Dir.; Brian Bacica; Jennifer Cabalquinto; Cindy Gardner; Virginia Tanawong; Michael Taylor.
EIN: 954495513

3894
Universal Supply Co., Inc.

852 S. White Horse Pike
Hammonton, NJ 08037-2017
(609) 561-6300

Company URL: http://www.universalsupply.com
Establishment information: Established in 1965.
Company type: Private company
Business activities: Sells building materials wholesale.
Business type (SIC): Lumber and construction materials—wholesale
Corporate officer: Jeff Umosella, Pres.
Giving statement: Giving through the Joseph F. Umosella Family Foundation.

The Joseph F. Umosella Family Foundation

2400 Del Lago Dr.
Fort Lauderdale, FL 33316-2307 (609) 561-3000

Establishment information: Established in 2004 in DE and NJ.
Donor: Universal Supply Co., Inc.
Contact: Joseph F. Umosella, Jr.
Financial data (yr. ended 12/31/11): Assets, $1,854,132 (M); gifts received, $74,604; expenditures, $89,146; qualifying distributions, $71,336; giving activities include $71,336 for grants.
Purpose and activities: The foundation supports organizations involved with cystic fibrosis research and cancer research.
Type of support: General/operating support.
Geographic limitations: Giving primarily in Bethesda, MD and Philadelphia, PA.
Application information: Applications accepted. Application form not required.
Initial approach: Proposal
Deadline(s): None
Officers: Joseph F. Umosella, Jr., Pres.; Sheila Presti, V.P.; John Umosella, V.P.; Jeffrey Umosella, Secy.; Joseph F. Umosella III, Treas.
EIN: 202041985

3895
Universal Uclick

1130 Walnut St.
Kansas City, MO 64106 (816) 581-7340

Company URL: http://universaluclick.com
Establishment information: Established in 1970.
Company type: Subsidiary of a private company
Business activities: Operates newspaper syndication company.

Business type (SIC): Business services/ miscellaneous
Financial profile for 2009: Number of employees, 200
Corporate officers: John P. McMeel, Chair.; Lee Salem, Pres.; Randy Herr, V.P. and Cont.; John Vivona, V.P., Sales
Board of director: John P. McMeel, Chair.
Giving statement: Giving through the Andrews McMeel Universal Foundation.

Andrews McMeel Universal Foundation

(formerly Andrews & McMeel Foundation)
1130 Walnut St.
Kansas City, MO 64106-2109

Establishment information: Established in 1991 in MO.
Donor: United Press Syndicate.
Contact: Kathleen W. Andrews, V.P. and Secy.
Financial data (yr. ended 12/31/11): Assets, $2,855,658 (M); expenditures, $309,128; qualifying distributions, $276,315; giving activities include $276,315 for grants.
Purpose and activities: The foundation supports organizations involved with arts and culture, education, health, cancer, ALS, housing, human services, and community development.
Fields of interest: Visual arts; Museums (art); Performing arts; Performing arts centers; Arts; Secondary school/education; Higher education; Education; Hospitals (general); Health care; Cancer; ALS; Housing/shelter; Children/youth, services; Human services; Community/economic development.
Type of support: Employee matching gifts; General/ operating support; Scholarship funds.
Geographic limitations: Giving primarily in KS and MO, with emphasis on the bi-state Kansas City area.
Application information: Applications accepted. Application form not required. Applicants should submit the following:
1) detailed description of project and amount of funding requested
Initial approach: Proposal
Deadline(s): None
Officers and Directors:* John P. McMeel*, Pres. and Treas.; Kathleen W. Andrews, V.P. and Secy.; Hugh T. Andrews; James C. Andrews; Suzanne M. Glynn; Bridget J. McMeel; Maureen McMeel; Susan S. McMeel.
EIN: 431570308
Selected grants: The following grants are a representative sample of this grantmaker's funding activity:
$50,000 to University of Notre Dame, Notre Dame, IN, 2010.
$7,000 to Nelson Gallery Foundation, Kansas City, MO, 2010.
$6,300 to Bishop Ward High School, Kansas City, KS, 2010.
$5,000 to Books for Africa, Saint Paul, MN, 2010.
$5,000 to Child Advocacy Services Center, Kansas City, MO, 2010.
$3,750 to Kansas City Symphony, Kansas City, MO, 2010.
$3,000 to Saint Lukes Hospital Foundation, Kansas City, MO, 2010.
$2,000 to Mary Atkins Trust, Kansas City, MO, 2010.
$1,750 to Caritas Clinics, Leavenworth, KS, 2010.
$1,500 to Heart to Heart International, Olathe, KS, 2010.

3896
University Mechanical Contractors, Inc.

11611 49th Pl. W.
P.O. Box 67
Mukilteo, WA 98275-4255 (206) 364-9900

Company URL: http://www.umci.com
Establishment information: Established in 1920.
Company type: Private company
Business activities: Operates mechanical contracting company specializing in large commercial and industrial projects.
Business type (SIC): Construction/miscellaneous heavy
Corporate officers: Jerry Bush, Pres. and C.E.O.; Douglas L. Smith, V.P. and C.F.O.; Patrick Damitio, V.P., Opers.; Marj Schmidt, Secy.
Giving statement: Giving through the UMC Charitable Foundation.

UMC Charitable Foundation

11611 49th Pl. W.
P.O. Box 67
Mukilteo, WA 98275-0067 (206) 364-9900
E-mail: info@umccf.org; URL: http://www.umccf.org

Establishment information: Established in 2005 in WA.
Donor: University Mechanical Contractors, Inc.
Contact: Marj Schmidt, Secy.
Financial data (yr. ended 12/31/11): Revenue, $45,090; assets, $20,172 (M); gifts received, $45,090; expenditures, $48,472; giving activities include $47,867 for grants.
Purpose and activities: The foundation supports a variety of causes, in particular those that focus on childhood illness, disease, and underprivileged youths, that are important to employees of University Mechanical Contractors, Inc.
Fields of interest: Children/youth, services; Philanthropy/voluntarism.
Program:
Scholarships: Ten scholarships of up to $250 each are available to employees of University Mechanical Contractors, Inc. to support their children's school or sports team fundraisers.
Geographic limitations: Giving primarily in WA.
Support limitations: No grants to individuals.
Publications: Application guidelines.
Application information: Application form required.
Initial approach: Submit application for scholarships
Deadline(s): None
Officers: Jerry Bush*, Pres.; Marj Schmidt*, Secy.; Doug Smith*, Treas.
EIN: 201868301

3897
Untours

(formerly Idyll, Ltd.)
415 E. Jasper St.
Media, PA 19063 (888) 868-6871

Company URL: http://www.untours.com
Establishment information: Established in 1975.
Company type: Private company
Business activities: Operates European travel company.
Business type (SIC): Travel and tour arrangers
Corporate officer: Hal Taussig, Pres.
Giving statement: Giving through the Untours Foundation.

Untours Foundation

P.O. Box 405
Media, PA 19063-0405
URL: http://www.untoursfoundation.org

Establishment information: Established in 1993 in PA.
Donor: Harold E. Taussig.
Financial data (yr. ended 12/31/11): Assets, $1,746,256 (M); gifts received, $53,748; expenditures, $104,457; qualifying distributions, $74,994; giving activities include $74,994 for grants.
Purpose and activities: The foundation supports the Greiner Family Foundation and provides low interest loans to organizations in order to create jobs, build low-income housing, and support "Fair Trade" products.
Fields of interest: Employment, services; Housing/ shelter; Business/industry; General charitable giving.
Type of support: General/operating support; Program-related investments/loans.
Application information: Applications not accepted. Unsolicited requests for funds not accepted.
Officers: Harold E. Taussig, Pres.; Norma L. Taussig, V.P.
EIN: 232703497

3898
Unum Group

(formerly UnumProvident Corporation)
1 Fountain Sq.
Chattanooga, TN 37402-1307
(423) 294-1011
FAX: (302) 636-5454

Company URL: http://www.unum.com
Establishment information: Established in 1848.
Company type: Public company
Company ticker symbol and exchange: UNM/NYSE
International Securities Identification Number: US91529Y1064
Business activities: Operates holding company; sells life and health insurance.
Business type (SIC): Holding company; insurance/ life; insurance/accident and health
Financial profile for 2012: Number of employees, 9,100; assets, $62,236,100,000; sales volume, $10,515,400,000; pre-tax net income, $1,249,500,000; expenses, $9,265,900,000; liabilities, $53,623,500,000
Fortune 1000 ranking: 2012—257th in revenues, 219th in profits, and 92nd in assets
Forbes 2000 ranking: 2012—897th in sales, 678th in profits, and 378th in assets
Corporate officers: William J. Ryan, Chair.; Thomas R. Watjen, Pres. and C.E.O.; Kevin P. McCarthy, Exec. V.P. and C.O.O.; Richard P. McKenney, Exec. V.P. and C.F.O.; Liston Bishop III, Exec. V.P. and Genl. Counsel; Breege A. Farrell, Sr. V.P. and C.I.O.; Diane Garofalo, Sr. V.P., Human Resources
Board of directors: William J. Ryan, Chair.; E. Michael Caulfield; Pamela H. Godwin; Ronald E. Goldsberry; Kevin T. Kabat; Timothy F. Keaney; Thomas Kinser; Gloria C. Larson; A.S. MacMillan, Jr.; Edward J. Muhl; Michael J. Passarella; Thomas R. Watjen
Subsidiaries: Providence National Assurance Co., Chattanooga, TN; Provident Life and Accident Insurance Co., Chattanooga, TN; Provident Life and Casualty Insurance Co., Chattanooga, TN
Offices: Atlanta, GA; New York, NY; Charlotte, NC; Columbia, SC; Nashville, TN

International operations: Argentina; United Kingdom
Historic mergers: UNUM Corporation (June 30, 1999)
Giving statement: Giving through the UnumProvident Corporation Contributions Program.
Company EIN: 621598430

UnumProvident Corporation Contributions Program

(formerly Provident Companies, Inc. Corporate Giving Program)
1 Fountain Sq.
Chattanooga, TN 37402-1306 (423) 755-1011
FAX: (423) 755-3194;
E-mail: CommunityRelations@unum.com;
Application addresses: Portland, ME: Susan Austin, 2211 Congress St., B118, Portland, ME 04122; and Worcester, MA: Meghan Maceiko, 18 Chestnut St., Worcester, MA 01608; Tel. for Cathy Barrett: (423) 294-7579, FAX: (423) 755-3194, E-mail: cbarrett@unum.com; URL: http://www.unum.com/aboutus/Responsibility/CommunityGiving.aspx

Contact: Cathy Barrett, Community Rels. Mgr.
Purpose and activities: UnumProvident makes charitable contributions to nonprofit organizations involved with arts and culture; public education; health and wellness; and disability services. Support is given in areas of company operations.
Fields of interest: Arts; Elementary/secondary education; Education; Hospitals (general); Health care; Food services; Boys & girls clubs; Children, services; Independent living, disability; Human services; United Ways and Federated Giving Programs Disabilities, people with.
International interests: Canada; United Kingdom.
Programs:
Arts and Culture: UnumProvident supports arts organizations that have a charter, program, and vision that closely aligns with UnumProvident's corporate giving strategy.
Disability: UnumProvident supports programs designed to help people with disabilities lead independent and fulfilling lives.
Health and Wellness: UnumProvident supports programs designed to improve the wellness of individuals and communities.
Matching Gifts Program: UnumProvident matches contributions made by its employees to educational institutions on a two-for-one basis, and to nonprofit organizations on a one-for-one basis from $50 to $7,500 per employee, per year. The company also provides a $50 match for employees' participation in walks and other "a-thon" events.
Public Education: UnumProvident supports programs designed to promote public education, with emphasis on grades K-12. The company provides funds to bring programs to schools that help students achieve high results.
Unum Strong Schools Grant Program: UnumProvident, in partnership with Chattanooga, TN schools, awards mini-grants of up to $1,000 for classroom or school-based projects and lessons in the Hamilton County school system, grades K-12. Special emphasis is directed toward projects that integrate career preparation with academic content.
Volunteer Service Grants: UnumProvident provides matching gifts for employee volunteer services. The company matches $1 for each hour an employee volunteers, from a minimum of 50 hours for $50 up to 500 hours for $500 per year.
Type of support: Employee matching gifts; Employee volunteer services; Employee-related scholarships; General/operating support; Program development; Scholarships—to individuals; Sponsorships.
Geographic limitations: Giving in areas of company operations, with emphasis on Worcester, MA, Portland, ME, SC, Chattanooga, TN, and in Canada and the United Kingdom.
Support limitations: No support for political organizations or political candidates, or religious organizations not of direct benefit to the entire community. No grants for general operating support for higher education.
Publications: Application guidelines; Corporate giving report.
Application information: Applications accepted. Proposal should be submitted using organization letterhead. Support is limited to 1 contribution per organization during any given year. Applicants should submit the following:
1) copy of IRS Determination Letter
2) copy of most recent annual report/audited financial statement/990
3) listing of board of directors, trustees, officers and other key people and their affiliations
4) detailed description of project and amount of funding requested
5) copy of current year's organizational budget and/or project budget
Initial approach: Proposal to local community relations representative; download application form and mail for headquarters for Unum Strong Schools Grants Program
Deadline(s): None; Jan. 9 for Unum Strong Schools Grants Program
Final notification: Feb. for Unum Strong Schools Grants Program

3899
Updike, Kelly & Spellacy, P.C.

100 Pearl St., 17th Fl.
P.O. Box 231277
Hartford, CT 06103-3100 (860) 548-2600

Company URL: http://www.uks.com
Establishment information: Established in 1967.
Company type: Private company
Business activities: Provides legal services.
Business type (SIC): Legal services
Corporate officers: David E. Sturgess, Pres.; Deneen Seifel, C.A.O.; Frank Mauri, C.I.O.; Robert J. Martino, Treas.
Giving statement: Giving through the Updike, Kelly and Spellacy, P.C. Charitable Foundation, Inc.

Updike, Kelly and Spellacy, P.C. Charitable Foundation, Inc.

100 Pearl St. 17th Fl.
P.O. Box 231277
Hartford, CT 06123-1277

Establishment information: Established in 1995 in CT.
Donors: Updike, Kelly & Spellacy, P.C.; R. Alisha Verdone; Katherine C. Blancaflor; Robert M. Decrescenzo; Robert J. Martino; David J. Monz; John F. Wolter.
Financial data (yr. ended 12/31/11): Assets, $16,225 (M); gifts received, $37,700; expenditures, $31,690; qualifying distributions, $31,690; giving activities include $31,690 for grants.
Purpose and activities: The foundation supports organizations involved with arts and culture, education, the environment, and health.
Fields of interest: Arts; Education; Health care.
Type of support: General/operating support; Scholarship funds.
Geographic limitations: Giving primarily in CT.
Support limitations: No grants to individuals.
Application information: Applications not accepted. Unsolicited requests for funds not accepted.
Officers: Robert J. Martino, Pres.; John F. Wolter, Secy.
EIN: 061409387

3900
Upper Crust Enterprises, Inc.

411 Center St.
Los Angeles, CA 90012-3435
(213) 625-0038

Company URL: http://uppercrustent.com
Establishment information: Established in 2006.
Company type: Private company
Business activities: Manufactures Panko Japanese breadcrumbs.
Business type (SIC): Bakery products
Corporate officers: Gary Kawaguchi, Pres. and C.E.O.; Edward Shelley, C.F.O.; Thomas Shea, V.P., Sales and Mktg.; Migule Araujo, Cont.
Giving statement: Giving through the Kawaguchi-Kihara Memorial Foundation.

Kawaguchi-Kihara Memorial Foundation

411 Center St.
Los Angeles, CA 90012-3435 (213) 217-4221

Establishment information: Established in 1979 in CA.
Donors: Fishking Processors, Inc.; Upper Crust Enterprises, Inc.
Contact: Gary Kawaguchi, Pres. and Treas.
Financial data (yr. ended 03/31/11): Assets, $240,949 (M); expenditures, $50,960; qualifying distributions, $50,960; giving activities include $46,600 for 5 grants (high: $23,000; low: $3,600).
Purpose and activities: The foundation supports organizations involved with Japanese culture, theater, health, nutrition, senior citizens, and Buddhism.
Fields of interest: Arts, cultural/ethnic awareness; Performing arts, theater; Health care; Nutrition; Residential/custodial care, senior continuing care; Aging, centers/services; Buddhism.
Type of support: General/operating support.
Geographic limitations: Giving primarily in Los Angeles, CA.
Support limitations: No grants to individuals.
Application information: Applications accepted. Application form not required. Applicants should submit the following:
1) copy of IRS Determination Letter
2) detailed description of project and amount of funding requested
Initial approach: Proposal
Deadline(s): None
Officers: Gary Kawaguchi, Pres. and Treas.; Mirei Kagawa, Secy.
Directors: Kenneth Kawaguchi; Mayumi Morishita.
Number of staff: 1 part-time professional; 1 part-time support.
EIN: 953397616
Selected grants: The following grants are a representative sample of this grantmaker's funding activity:
$5,000 to Japanese American National Museum, Los Angeles, CA, 2011.

3901
Urban Partnership Bank

7936 S. Cottage Grove
P.O. Box 19260
Chicago, IL 60619-0260 (773) 420-5050

Company URL: http://www.upbnk.com
Establishment information: Established in 2010.
Company type: Private company
Business activities: Operates community development bank.
Business type (SIC): Banks/commercial
Financial profile for 2011: Assets, $1,400,000,000
Corporate officers: David Vitale, Chair.; William Farrow III, Pres. and C.E.O.
Board of director: David Vitale, Chair.
Offices: Detroit, MI; Cleveland, OH
Giving statement: Giving through the Urban Partnership Bank Corporate Giving Program.

Urban Partnership Bank Corporate Giving Program

Urban Partnership Bank
7936 S. Cottage Grove
Chicago, IL 60619 (773) 420-5050
URL: https://www.upbnk.com/nonprofit/sri/

Contact: Suzzane Griffith, V.P., Dir. of Corp. Responsibility & Community Engagement; Valerie Hill, Community Rels. Specialist
Purpose and activities: Urban Partnership Bank supports nonprofit organizations involved with education, arts and culture, and community development. Special emphasis is directed toward programs that target underserved urban areas.
Fields of interest: Arts, multipurpose centers/programs; Arts, cultural/ethnic awareness; Arts education; Visual arts; Performing arts; Elementary/secondary education; Middle schools/education; Elementary school/education; Secondary school/education; Education, gifted students; Charter schools; Education, computer literacy/technology training; Education, e-learning; Youth development, centers/clubs; Community development, neighborhood development; Community development, public/private ventures; Economic development; Urban/community development; Social entrepreneurship; Community development, small businesses; Microfinance/microlending; Community development, real estate; Community/economic development.
Type of support: Continuing support; General/operating support; In-kind gifts; Program development; Sponsorships.
Geographic limitations: Giving primarily in Chicago and Cook County, IL, Midtown Detroit and Wayne County, MI, East Cleveland and Cuyahoga County, OH.
Application information: Applications accepted.
Initial approach: Letter and brief proposal
Copies of proposal: 1
Committee meeting date(s): Ongoing
Deadline(s): Sept. 30
Final notification: Quarterly

3902
US Airways Group, Inc.

111 W. Rio Salado Pkwy.
Tempe, AZ 85281 (480) 693-0800
FAX: (302) 655-5049

Company URL: http://www.usairways.com
Establishment information: Established in 1939.
Company type: Public company
Company ticker symbol and exchange: LCC/NYSE
Business activities: Operates air transportation services company. At press time, the company is in the process of merging with AMR Corp.
Business type (SIC): Holding company; transportation/scheduled air
Financial profile for 2012: Number of employees, 31,200; assets, $9,396,000,000; sales volume, $13,831,000,000; pre-tax net income, $637,000,000; expenses, $12,836,000,000; liabilities, $8,606,000,000
Fortune 1000 ranking: 2012—199th in revenues, 279th in profits, and 408th in assets
Forbes 2000 ranking: 2012—700th in sales, 983rd in profits, and 1519th in assets
Corporate officers: W. Douglas Parker, Chair and Co-C.E.O.; Bruce R. Lakefield, Vice-Chair; J. Scott Kirby, Pres.; Robert D. Isom, Jr., Exec. V.P. and C.O.O.; Derek J. Kerr, Exec. V.P. and C.F.O.; Elise Eberwein, Exec. V.P., Comms.; Brad Jensen, Sr. V.P. and C.I.O.; David Seymour, Sr. V.P., Opers.; Keith Bush, Sr. V.P., Finance; David Seymour, Sr. V.P., Opers.; Andrew Nocella, Sr. V.P., Mktg.; Tom Weir, V.P. and Treas.; Michael R. Carreon, V.P. and Cont.; John McDonald, V.P., Corp. Comms.; Ryan Price, V.P., Human Resources
Board of directors: W. Douglas Parker, Chair.; Matthew J. Hart; Richard C. Kraemer; Cheryl Gordon Krongard; Denise M. O'Leary; George M. Philip; William Post
Subsidiaries: America West Airlines, Inc., Phoenix, AZ; Material Services Co., Inc., Middletown, PA; Piedmont Airlines, Inc., Salisbury, MD; PSA Airlines, Inc., Dayton, OH; US Airways, Inc., Tempe, AZ
Office: Phoenix, AZ
International operations: Bermuda
Giving statement: Giving through the US Airways Group, Inc. Corporate Giving Program, the US Airways Community Foundation, and the US Airways Education Foundation, Inc.
Company EIN: 541194634

US Airways Group, Inc. Corporate Giving Program

4000 E. Sky Harbor Blvd.
Phoenix, AZ 85034
E-mail: community.relations@usairways.com;
URL: http://www.usairways.com/corporategiving

Contact: Kelly Balthazor, Mgr., Community Rels.
Purpose and activities: As a complement to its foundation, US Airways also makes charitable contributions to nonprofit organizations directly. Support is limited to organizations that are located and provide services in the major metropolitan areas of Phoenix, Arizona, Washington, DC., Charlotte, North Carolina, and Philadelphia, Pennsylvania.
Fields of interest: Arts; Education; Health care; Human services; Community/economic development.
Type of support: Employee volunteer services; General/operating support; In-kind gifts.
Geographic limitations: Giving is limited to organizations that are located and provide services in the major metropolitan areas of Phoenix, AZ, Washington, DC., Charlotte, NC, and Philadelphia, PA.
Support limitations: No support for political, labor or fraternal organizations; associations or service clubs (i.e. Junior League, Lions, Rotary, Kiwanis); auxiliary organizations, third party/ pass-through fundraisers or organizations fundraising on behalf of a nonprofit organization; individual schools or universities including their support organizations (i.e. Boosters, clubs, PTA/PTO's, athletic teams, bands, performing arts groups, alumni associations or reunions); religious organizations, churches that are purely denominational in purpose; foundations or organizations which are grant-making entities; organizations funded 50% or more by government sources; organizations whose primary mission is funding medical or scientific research; organizations that primarily provide advocacy for issue-related topics; or discriminatory organizations. No grants to individuals, or for scholarships or camperships; competitions, beauty pageants or talent contests; endowments, debt reduction, capital or building campaigns; video or film production costs or sponsorship; purchase of advertising; or discounted or waived baggage fees.
Publications: Application guidelines; Grants list.
Application information: Applications accepted. All written requests must be submitted using organization letterhead at least 60 days prior to the event and any print deadlines. No status calls are accepted. Faxed, e-mailed, or incomplete requests will not be considered. The Community Relations Department handles giving. The company has a staff that only handles contributions. A contributions committee reviews all requests. Application form not required. Applicants should submit the following:
1) name, address and phone number of organization
2) copy of IRS Determination Letter
3) brief history of organization and description of its mission
4) listing of board of directors, trustees, officers and other key people and their affiliations
5) detailed description of project and amount of funding requested
6) contact person
7) copy of current year's organizational budget and/or project budget

Requests for events should include information on sponsorship levels and benefits for each level, a 5-year history of previous support received from America West and/or U.S. Airways, and a list of other airline partners including pending requests.
Initial approach: Complete online application
Copies of proposal: 1
Committee meeting date(s): Bi-Monthly
Deadline(s): None
Final notification: 8 weeks
Number of staff: 3 full-time professional.

US Airways Community Foundation

(formerly America West Community Foundation)
4000 E. Sky Harbor Blvd.
Phoenix, AZ 85034-3802 (480) 693-3652
FAX: (480) 693-3715;
E-mail: community.relations@usairways.com;
URL: http://www.usairways.com/corporategiving/

Establishment information: Incorporated in 1995 in AZ.
Donor: America West Airlines, Inc.
Contact: Julie Coleman, V.P.
Financial data (yr. ended 12/31/11): Assets, $9,346,261 (M); expenditures, $572,295; qualifying distributions, $560,000; giving activities include $560,000 for grants.
Purpose and activities: The foundation supports organizations involved with arts and culture, education, health, and human services. Support is limited to areas of company operations within 100 miles of hub and focus cities.

Fields of interest: Museums; Performing arts, theater; Arts; Education; Health care, clinics/centers; Health care; Goodwill Industries; Youth development, business; Human services; United Ways and Federated Giving Programs.
Type of support: Building/renovation; Capital campaigns.
Geographic limitations: Giving limited to areas of company operations within 100 miles of Phoenix, AZ, Washington, DC, Charlotte, NC, and Philadelphia, PA.
Support limitations: No support for professional associations, service clubs, religious, political, labor, fraternal, sports, or discriminatory organizations, hospitals or medical centers, YMCAs, organizations funded 50% or more by government sources, or organizations whose primary mission is funding medical or scientific research, or foundations or organizations which are grant-making entities, sports teams, scouting troops, individual schools, or animal shelters or agencies. No grants to individuals, or for hardware, software, equipment, or infrastructure support, general operating support, debt reduction, endowments, staff or consultant fees, scholarships or camperships, beauty pageants, or talent contests.
Publications: Application guidelines.
Application information: Applications accepted. Application form required. Applicants should submit the following:
1) role played by volunteers
2) timetable for implementation and evaluation of project
3) how project will be sustained once grantmaker support is completed
4) results expected from proposed grant
5) population served
6) copy of IRS Determination Letter
7) brief history of organization and description of its mission
8) geographic area to be served
9) copy of most recent annual report/audited financial statement/990
10) how project's results will be evaluated or measured
11) listing of board of directors, trustees, officers and other key people and their affiliations
12) detailed description of project and amount of funding requested
13) copy of current year's organizational budget and/or project budget
14) listing of additional sources and amount of support

Initial approach: Complete online application
Copies of proposal: 1
Board meeting date(s): Twice per year
Deadline(s): Apr. 1 and Oct. 1
Final notification: June and Dec.

Officers and Directors: C.A. Howlett, Pres.; Julie Coleman, V.P.; Caroline B. Ray, Secy.; Michael R. Carreon, Treas. and Cont.; Chuck F. Allen; W. Douglas Parker; Christopher J. Sever.
Number of staff: None.
EIN: 860825827
Selected grants: The following grants are a representative sample of this grantmaker's funding activity:
$250,000 to Franklin Institute Science Museum, Philadelphia, PA, 2011.
$200,000 to Pennsylvania Ballet, Philadelphia, PA, 2011.
$50,000 to Red Wiggler Community Farm, Clarksburg, MD, 2011.
$40,000 to Smith Farm, Washington, DC, 2011.
$20,000 to CityDance Ensemble, Washington, DC, 2011.

US Airways Education Foundation, Inc.

(formerly America West Airlines Education Foundation, Inc.)
c/o Community Rels.
4000 E. Sky Harbor Blvd.
Phoenix, AZ 85034-3802 (480) 693-5748
FAX: (480) 693-3715;
E-mail: community.relations@usairways.com;
URL: http://www.usairways.com/awa/content/aboutus/corporategiving/educationfoundation.aspx

Establishment information: Incorporated as a company-sponsored foundation in 1990 in AZ; status changed to public charity.
Contact: Sue Glawe, Pres.
Financial data (yr. ended 12/31/11): Revenue, $524,011; assets, $748,197 (M); gifts received, $224,619; expenditures, $460,023; program services expenses, $460,000; giving activities include $170,000 for 17 grants (high: $10,000) and $290,000 for grants to individuals.
Purpose and activities: The foundation supports initiatives in communities U.S. Airways serves by funding community education grants to nonprofit organizations.
Fields of interest: Education.
Program:
Grants: This program provides grants of $10,000 to nonprofit organizations with educational programs located in and providing services within the major metropolitan area of the airline's hub cities of Charlotte, Philadelphia Phoenix, and Washington, D.C. that meet at least one of the following criteria: Educational programs that focus on learning and academic achievement for economically disadvantaged children age 18 and younger; educational programs that focus on learning and academic achievement for developmentally disabled children age 18 and younger; and programs that increase student interest and academic achievement in Science, Technology, Engineering and Math (STEM) for children age 18 and younger.
Type of support: Curriculum development; Employee-related scholarships; Equipment; Program development.
Geographic limitations: Giving primarily in areas of company operations.
Support limitations: No support for grantmaking foundations, start-up organizations, or discriminatory organizations. No grants to individuals (except for employee-related scholarships), or for travel expenses, transportation costs, capital or building projects, debt retirement, operational costs, endowments, general operating budgets, conference fees, program advertisements, tickets or tables for dinners or benefits, stipends for personal expenses, research or conference fees, programs that are purely denominational in purpose, or political campaigns or activities; no air transportation donations.
Publications: Application guidelines.
Application information: Applications accepted. Applications are made available after May 1 of each year. Application form required. Applicants should submit the following:
1) copy of IRS Determination Letter

Initial approach: Download application form
Copies of proposal: 1
Board meeting date(s): Bi-monthly
Deadline(s): July 1

Officers and Trustees:* Sue Glawe*, Pres.; Michael R. Carreon*, Treas.; Debbie Castaldo; Karen Conway; Gene D'Adamo; Elise Eberwein; Matt Eggers; Michael Hawley; Steven Helfgot; Don Honeycutt; Paul Kinsey; Dr. Laura Martin; Patrick Meenan; Tim Newman; Ashley Oster; Jim Pitman; Daniel Pearson; Terri Pope; Barbara Ryan; Sheryl Rothberg; Judy Schueler; Neil Boyden Tanner; Carl Ulrich.
EIN: 860670438
Selected grants: The following grants are a representative sample of this grantmaker's funding activity:
$3,500 to Boston Local Development Corporation, Boston, MA, 2007. For ReadBoston Family Literacy Project.
$3,500 to Boys Hope Girls Hope of Arizona, Phoenix, AZ, 2007. For community-based program.
$3,500 to Brooklyn Childrens Museum, Brooklyn, NY, 2007. For museum team.
$3,500 to Childhelp USA, Scottsdale, AZ, 2007. For child abuse prevention.
$3,500 to Childrens Theater of Charlotte, Charlotte, NC, 2007. For Drama for Healthy Living: Alcohol and Substance Abuse Prevention Program.
$3,500 to Civitan Foundation of Arizona, Phoenix, AZ, 2007. For Better Together Program.
$3,500 to Hopeworks N Camden, Camden, NJ, 2007. For Hope Through School.
$3,500 to Philadelphia Education Fund, Philadelphia, PA, 2007. For College Access Program.
$3,500 to Spread the Word Nevada, Henderson, NV, 2007. For Kids to Kids.
$2,500 to Stepping Stone Foundation, Phoenix, AZ, 2007. For Preschool and Family Literacy project.

3903
USA Gasoline Corporation

5000 Kanan Rd.
Agoura Hills, CA 91301-2516
(818) 991-3401

Company URL: http://www.tsocorp.com
Company type: Private company
Business activities: Operates gasoline service stations.
Business type (SIC): Gasoline service stations
Corporate officer: Gregory J. Goff, Pres. and C.E.O.
Giving statement: Giving through the John J. Moller Family Foundation.

John J. Moller Family Foundation

6591 Collins Dr. E-11
Moorpark, CA 93021-1493

Establishment information: Established in 2003 in CA.
Donors: USA Gasoline Corp.; USA Petroleum Corp.; Dansk Investment Group, Inc.
Financial data (yr. ended 12/31/11): Assets, $158,848 (M); expenditures, $8,330; qualifying distributions, $7,500; giving activities include $7,500 for 1 grant.
Purpose and activities: The foundation supports organizations involved with elementary education, environmental education, and the U.S. Navy.
Fields of interest: Arts; Animals/wildlife; Community/economic development.
Type of support: General/operating support; Program development.
Geographic limitations: Giving primarily in CA, HI, and MA.
Application information: Applications not accepted. Unsolicited requests for funds not accepted.
Officers and Directors: Kristopher Moller*, Pres.; Kriston D. Qualls*, Secy.; Nancy Conant, Treas.; Danielle Tokai Moller Martinez, Family Dir.; Austin Moller, Family Dir.; John J. Moller, Family Dir.
EIN: 352208959

3904
USEC Inc.

2 Democracy Ctr.
6903 Rockledge Dr.
Bethesda, MD 20817 (301) 564-3200
FAX: (301) 564-3201

Company URL: http://www.usec.com
Establishment information: Established in 1998.
Company type: Public company
Company ticker symbol and exchange: USU/NYSE
Business activities: Supplier of low enriched uranium for commercial nuclear power plants.
Business type (SIC): Mining and quarrying of nonmetallic minerals (except fuels)
Financial profile for 2011: Number of employees, 1,885; assets, $3,549,300,000; sales volume, $1,671,800,000; pre-tax net income, -$258,500,000; expenses, $1,919,200,000; liabilities, $2,796,900,000
Fortune 1000 ranking: 2012—969th in revenues, 987th in profits, and 824th in assets
Corporate officers: James R. Mellor, Chair.; John K. Welch, Pres. and C.E.O.; Robert Van Namen, Sr. V.P. and C.O.O.; John C. Barpoulis, Sr. V.P. and C.F.O.; Peter B. Saba, Sr. V.P., Genl. Counsel, and Secy.; J. Tracy Mey, V.P. and C.A.O.; Stephen S. Greene, V.P., Finance and Treas.; John Donelson, V.P., Mktg. and Sales; Richard V. Rowland, V.P., Human Resources
Board of directors: James R. Mellor, Chair.; Sigmund L. Cornelius; Joseph T. Doyle; George Dudich; H. William Habermeyer, Jr.; William J. Madia; W. Henson Moore; Hiroshi Sakamoto; Walter E. Skowronski; M. Richard Smith; John K. Welch
Giving statement: Giving through the USEC Inc. Corporate Giving Program.
Company EIN: 522107911

USEC Inc. Corporate Giving Program

6903 Rockledge Dr.
Bethesda, MD 20817-1818 (301) 564-3200
E-mail: Giving@usec.com; URL: http://www.usec.com/company/corporate-citizenship/charitable-giving

Purpose and activities: USEC Inc. makes charitable contributions to nonprofit organizations involved with education, social services and support programs, medical research, the environment, and arts and culture. Support is given primarily in areas of company operations in Washington, DC, western Kentucky, southern Ohio, and eastern Tennessee.
Fields of interest: Museums; Performing arts centers; Education; Environment; Medical research; Food services; Housing/shelter; Aging, centers/services; Human services; Mathematics; Science Economically disadvantaged.
Type of support: Employee volunteer services; General/operating support; In-kind gifts; Scholarship funds.
Geographic limitations: Giving primarily in areas of company operations in Washington, DC, western KY, southern OH, and eastern TN.
Support limitations: No support for discriminatory or political organizations. No grants to individuals, teams, or organizations raising funds to benefit other organizations.
Publications: Application guidelines.
Application information: Applications accepted. Use Short Form for requests of $1,000 or less and Long Form for requests of more than $1,000. Application form required. Applicants should submit the following:
1) results expected from proposed grant
2) population served
3) name, address and phone number of organization
4) copy of IRS Determination Letter
5) brief history of organization and description of its mission
6) geographic area to be served
7) copy of most recent annual report/audited financial statement/990
8) how project's results will be evaluated or measured
9) list of company employees involved with the organization
10) explanation of why grantmaker is considered an appropriate donor for project
11) descriptive literature about organization
12) listing of board of directors, trustees, officers and other key people and their affiliations
13) detailed description of project and amount of funding requested
14) contact person
15) copy of current year's organizational budget and/or project budget
16) listing of additional sources and amount of support
17) plans for acknowledgement
18) additional materials/documentation

Proposals should include the date the donation and decision are needed by, whether the request is associated with an event, a description of the organization's financial accountability practices, size and makeup of the organization, program allocations to be made using the donation, any past or existing relationship with USEC Inc., a list of other entities where the organization has requested support, dates the program will run, and the fundraising target for the program.
Initial approach: Download application form and email completed proposal

3905
USG Corporation

550 W. Adams St.
Chicago, IL 60661-3676 (312) 436-4000
FAX: (302) 655-5049

Company URL: http://www.usg.com
Establishment information: Established in 1902.
Company type: Public company
Company ticker symbol and exchange: USG/NYSE
Business activities: Operates holding company; manufactures diverse building materials.
Business type (SIC): Holding company; chemical preparations/miscellaneous; concrete, gypsum, and plaster products; abrasive, asbestos, and nonmetallic mineral products; metal products/structural
Financial profile for 2012: Number of employees, 8,500; assets, $3,723,000,000; sales volume, $3,224,000,000; pre-tax net income, -$170,000,000; expenses, $3,192,000,000; liabilities, $3,717,000,000
Fortune 1000 ranking: 2012—663rd in revenues, 931st in profits, and 685th in assets
Corporate officers: James S. Metcalf, Chair., Pres., and C.E.O.; Matthew F. Hilzinger, Exec. V.P. and C.F.O.; Stanley L. Ferguson, Exec. V.P. and Genl. Counsel, Secy.; Christopher R. Griffin, Exec. V.P., Opers.; Brian J. Cook, Sr. V.P., Human Resources
Board of directors: James S. Metcalf, Chair.; Jose Armario; Matthew Carter, Jr.; W. Douglas Ford; Gretchen R. Haggerty; William H. Hernandez; Brian A. Kenney; Richard P. Lavin; Steven F. Leer
Subsidiaries: L&W Supply Corp., Chicago, IL; United States Gypsum Co., Chicago, IL; USG Corp., Chicago, IL; USG Interiors, Inc., Chicago, IL; USG International, Ltd., Chicago, IL
Giving statement: Giving through the United States Gypsum Foundation, Inc.
Company EIN: 363329400

United States Gypsum Foundation, Inc.

(formerly USG Foundation, Inc.)
550 W. Adams St.
Chicago, IL 60661-3676 (312) 436-4021
E-mail: usgfoundation@usg.com; URL: http://www.usg.com/company/corporate-responsibility.html

Establishment information: Incorporated in 1978 in IL.
Donors: USG Corp.; Chicago Tourism Fund.
Contact: Jeff P. Rodewald, Pres.
Financial data (yr. ended 12/31/11): Assets, $759,686 (M); expenditures, $634,570; qualifying distributions, $634,555; giving activities include $551,261 for 54 grants (high: $69,793; low: $500) and $83,294 for employee matching gifts.
Purpose and activities: The foundation supports organizations involved with arts and culture, higher education, health, human services, community development, and civic affairs.
Fields of interest: Performing arts; Arts; Higher education; Hospitals (general); Health care; Heart & circulatory diseases; American Red Cross; Children/youth, services; Human services; Community/economic development; United Ways and Federated Giving Programs; Public affairs.
Type of support: Annual campaigns; Building/renovation; Capital campaigns; Continuing support; Employee matching gifts; Equipment; General/operating support; Program development; Research; Scholarship funds; Technical assistance.
Geographic limitations: Giving primarily in areas of company operations.
Support limitations: No support for sectarian organizations not of direct benefit to the entire community, political organizations, fraternal or veterans' organizations, or primary or secondary schools; generally, no support for united fund-supported organizations. No grants to individuals, or for courtesy advertising; no loans.
Publications: Application guidelines.
Application information: Applications accepted. Multi-year funding is not automatic. Application form not required. Applicants should submit the following:
1) results expected from proposed grant
2) statement of problem project will address
3) copy of IRS Determination Letter
4) copy of most recent annual report/audited financial statement/990
5) explanation of why grantmaker is considered an appropriate donor for project
6) listing of board of directors, trustees, officers and other key people and their affiliations
7) detailed description of project and amount of funding requested
8) additional materials/documentation

Initial approach: Proposal
Copies of proposal: 1
Board meeting date(s): Quarterly
Deadline(s): None

Officers and Directors:* Jeffrey P. Rodewall*, Pres.; Stanley L. Ferguson*, V.P. and Secy.; Brian J. Cook*, V.P.; Brendan J. Deely*, V.P.; Richard H. Fleming*, V.P.; James S. Metcalf, V.P.
Number of staff: 1 full-time professional.
EIN: 362984045
Selected grants: The following grants are a representative sample of this grantmaker's funding activity:
$50,000 to Ronald McDonald House Charities, Oak Brook, IL, 2011.
$20,000 to Chicago United, Chicago, IL, 2011.
$17,500 to Chicago Cares, Chicago, IL, 2011.

$14,000 to American Heart Association, Dallas, TX, 2011.
$10,000 to Junior Achievement of Chicago, Chicago, IL, 2011.
$6,500 to Special Olympics, Washington, DC, 2011.
$4,255 to Art Institute of Chicago, Chicago, IL, 2011.
$1,000 to Greater Chicago Food Depository, Chicago, IL, 2011.

3906
Usibelli Coal Mine, Inc.

100 Cushman St., Ste. 210
P.O. Box 1000
Fairbanks, AK 99701-4674 (907) 452-2625

Company URL: http://www.usibelli.com
Establishment information: Established in 1943.
Company type: Private company
Business activities: Mines coal.
Business type (SIC): Coal mining
Financial profile for 2011: Number of employees, 130
Corporate officers: Joseph E. Usibelli, Sr., Chair.; Joseph E. Usibelli, Jr., Pres.; Glen Weaver, V.P., Finance, and C.F.O.; Alan Renshaw, V.P., Opers.
Board of director: Joseph E. Usibelli, Sr., Chair.
Giving statement: Giving through the Usibelli Foundation.

Usibelli Coal Mine, Inc. Corporate Giving Program

P.O. Box 1000
Healy, AK 99743-1000 (907) 683-2226
FAX: (907) 683-2253; E-mail: info@usibelli.com; URL: http://www.usibelli.com/Community_corp.php

Purpose and activities: As a complement to its foundation, Usibelli Coal Mine also makes charitable contributions to nonprofit organizations directly. Support is given primarily in areas of company operations in Alaska.
Fields of interest: Museums; Arts; Higher education; Youth development; General charitable giving.
Type of support: Employee matching gifts; Employee-related scholarships; Endowments; General/operating support; Research.
Geographic limitations: Giving primarily in areas of company operations in AK.

The Usibelli Foundation

100 Cushman St., Ste. 210
Fairbanks, AK 99701-4674 (907) 452-2625
E-mail: info@usibelli.com; URL: http://www.usibelli.com/Community_found.php

Establishment information: Established in 1991 in AK.
Donor: Usibelli Coal Mine, Inc.
Contact: Bill Brophy, Exec. Dir.
Financial data (yr. ended 12/31/11): Assets, $2,078,398 (M); gifts received, $500; expenditures, $118,961; qualifying distributions, $111,960; giving activities include $111,960 for grants.
Purpose and activities: The foundation supports organizations involved with arts and culture, education, health, human services, and civic affairs.
Fields of interest: Arts; Human services; Public affairs.
Programs:
Emil Usibelli Distinguished Teaching, Research, and Service Awards: The foundation annually awards three $10,000 scholarships to individuals who display extraordinary excellence in teaching, research, or public service.
Honors Scholarships: The foundation awards college scholarships to honor students at University of Alaska Fairbanks.
Tri-Valley High School Scholarships: The foundation annually awards college scholarships to five graduates of Tri-Valley high school based on academic excellence and class standing. The foundation awards an Emil Usibelli Scholarship for $1,500, a Cecil Lester Memorial Scholarship for $1,250, and three Usibelli Coal Mine Scholarships for $750.
Usibelli Mining Scholarships: The foundation annually awards college scholarships of $500 to University of Alaska Fairbanks School of Mineral Engineering students enrolled in mining and geological engineering programs.
Type of support: Continuing support; Endowments; General/operating support; Research; Scholarship funds; Scholarships—to individuals.
Geographic limitations: Giving primarily in Fairbanks and Healy, AK.
Support limitations: No support for political organizations, national health or social service organizations without a local chapter, or discriminatory organizations. No grants to individuals (except for scholarships), or for travel, pageants, campaigns, book publication, video, film, or homepage production.
Publications: Application guidelines; Program policy statement.
Application information: Applications accepted. Multi-year funding is not automatic. Application form not required. Applicants should submit the following:
1) timetable for implementation and evaluation of project
2) population served
3) copy of IRS Determination Letter
4) brief history of organization and description of its mission
5) geographic area to be served
6) detailed description of project and amount of funding requested
7) plans for cooperation with other organizations, if any
8) copy of current year's organizational budget and/or project budget
9) listing of additional sources and amount of support

Initial approach: Proposal
Copies of proposal: 1
Board meeting date(s): Quarterly
Deadline(s): Feb. 28, May 31, Aug. 31, and Nov. 30
Final notification: Mar. 31, June 30, Sept. 30, and Dec. 31

Officers and Directors:* Joseph E. Usibelli, Sr.*, Chair.; Joseph E. Usibelli, Jr., Pres.; Rosalie A. Whyel, V.P.; A. Kirk Lanterman, Secy.-Treas.; Bll Brophy, Exec. Dir.; R. Marc Langland; Richard A. Wien.
EIN: 943152617

3907
Fred Usinger, Inc.

1030 N. Old World 3rd St.
Milwaukee, WI 53203-1302
(414) 276-9105

Company URL: http://www.usinger.com
Establishment information: Established in 1880.
Company type: Private company
Business activities: Produces sausages.
Business type (SIC): Meat packing plants and prepared meats and poultry
Corporate officers: Frederick Usinger IV, Pres.; Allen J. Weidler, V.P., Finance; John Gabe, V.P., Sales and Mktg.
Giving statement: Giving through the Usinger Foundation, Inc.

Usinger Foundation, Inc.

1030 N. Old World 3rd St.
Milwaukee, WI 53203-1302 (414) 276-9100

Donor: Fred Usinger, Inc.
Contact: Debra L. Usinger, Pres.
Financial data (yr. ended 12/31/11): Assets, $85,785 (M); expenditures, $12,093; qualifying distributions, $11,600; giving activities include $11,600 for grants.
Purpose and activities: The foundation supports zoological societies and organizations involved with arts and culture, environmental education, health, hunger, human services, and business.
Fields of interest: Arts; Environment; Human services.
Type of support: General/operating support.
Geographic limitations: Giving primarily in Milwaukee, WI.
Support limitations: No grants to individuals.
Application information: Applications accepted. Application form required. Applicants should submit the following:
1) brief history of organization and description of its mission

Initial approach: Letter
Deadline(s): Dec. 1

Officers and Directors:* Debra L. Usinger*, Pres.; Frederick D. Usinger*, V.P.; Allen W. Weidler*, Secy.-Treas.
EIN: 396066333

3908
UTC Aerospace Systems

(formerly Goodrich Corporation)
4 Coliseum Ctr.
2730 W. Tyvola Rd.
Charlotte, NC 28217-4578 (704) 423-7000
FAX: (704) 423-7002

Company URL: http://utcaerospacesystems.com/
Establishment information: Established in 1870.
Company type: Subsidiary of a public company
Business activities: Manufactures and provides aviation components, systems, and services; manufactures military and space systems and products. At press time, the company is in the process of merging with United Technologies Corporation.
Business type (SIC): Guided missiles and space vehicles; aircraft and parts
Corporate officer: Michael Dumais, Pres.
Plants: Phoenix, AZ; Burnsville, MN; Charlotte, NC; Brecksville, OH; Arlington, VA

International operations: Australia; Germany; Hong Kong; Japan; Netherlands
Giving statement: Giving through the Goodrich Foundation.
Company EIN: 340252680

Goodrich Foundation

(formerly The Goodrich Foundation, Inc.)
4 Coliseum Centre
2730 W. Tyvola Rd.
Charlotte, NC 28217-4578 (704) 423-7489
FAX: (704) 423-7011;
E-mail: grantinfo@goodrich.com; URL: http://utcaerospacesystems.com/Company/Pages/goodrich-foundation.aspx

Establishment information: Established in 1989 in OH.
Donors: The B.F.Goodrich Co.; Goodrich Corp.
Contact: Kelly Chopus, Secy.
Financial data (yr. ended 12/31/11): Assets, $6,904,108 (M); expenditures, $1,930,484; qualifying distributions, $1,878,619; giving activities include $1,158,015 for 55 grants (high: $100,000; low: $1,051) and $695,001 for 1,475 employee matching gifts.
Purpose and activities: The foundation supports programs designed to advance K-12 and higher education science, technology, engineering, and math initiatives focused on the next generation of engineering scientists; promote vibrant communities through community revitalization, health and social services, and arts and culture; and build sustainable cities through environmental sustainable practices, projects, and urban green space.
Fields of interest: Museums (science/technology); Arts; Education, reform; Elementary/secondary education; Higher education; Adult/continuing education; Education, services; Education; Environment; Health care; Disasters, preparedness/services; Human services; Community/economic development; United Ways and Federated Giving Programs; Space/aviation; Mathematics; Engineering/technology; Science.
Type of support: Annual campaigns; Continuing support; Employee matching gifts; Employee volunteer services; Employee-related scholarships; General/operating support; In-kind gifts; Management development/capacity building; Matching/challenge support; Program development; Research; Scholarship funds; Sponsorships; Use of facilities.
Geographic limitations: Giving on a national basis in areas of company operations, with emphasis on Charlotte, NC.
Support limitations: No support for private foundations, churches, fraternal, social, labor groups with high fundraising or administrative expenses, political parties or candidates, discriminatory organizations, organizations primarily funded through municipal, country, state, or federal dollars, individual United Way agencies already supported by Goodrich, and international organizations. No grants to individuals, or for endowments, religious programs, lobbying activities, travel, tours, exhibitions, trips, local athletics, sports programs, equipment, courtesy advertising benefits, tables, or tickets.
Publications: Application guidelines.
Application information: Applications accepted. Multi-year funding is not automatic. Multi-year funding requests should not exceed 5 years. Telephone calls are not encouraged. Application form required. Applicants should submit the following:
1) copy of IRS Determination Letter
2) copy of most recent annual report/audited financial statement/990
3) listing of board of directors, trustees, officers and other key people and their affiliations
4) copy of current year's organizational budget and/or project budget
Initial approach: Complete online application form
Board meeting date(s): Quarterly
Deadline(s): Mar. 1 and Aug. 1
Final notification: 90 days
Officers: Terrence G. Linnert, Pres.; Jack Carmola, V.P.; Kelly Chopus, Secy.; Scott Kuechle, Treas.
Number of staff: 1 full-time professional; 1 full-time support.
EIN: 261195329
Selected grants: The following grants are a representative sample of this grantmaker's funding activity:
$100,000 to American Red Cross, Charlotte, NC, 2011. For Japan Earthquake Pacific Tsunami Disaster.
$100,000 to Charlotte Bridge Home, Charlotte, NC, 2011. For pilot project.
$50,000 to Communities in Schools of Charlotte-Mecklenburg, Charlotte, NC, 2011. For Communities In Schools at Westerly Hills.
$50,000 to Wounded Warrior Project, Jacksonville, FL, 2011. For general operating support.
$35,000 to Habitat for Humanity of Charlotte, Charlotte, NC, 2011. For Adopt-A-Home.

3909
UTI Technology, Inc.

2304 La Mirada Dr.
Vista, CA 92081 (760) 295-2917

Company URL: http://www.utitechnology.com
Establishment information: Established in 1980.
Company type: Private company
Business activities: Sells computer monitors wholesale.
Business type (SIC): Professional and commercial equipment—wholesale
Corporate officer: Keith Kim, Owner
Giving statement: Giving through the UTI Foundation, Inc.

The UTI Foundation, Inc.

c/o Thomas I. Hara
10650 County Rd. 81; Ste. 103
Maple Grove, MN 55369-4080

Establishment information: Established in 1996 in MN.
Donors: Keith K. Kim; Helen L. Kim; UTI Technology Inc.
Financial data (yr. ended 05/31/12): Assets, $882,378 (M); gifts received, $330,000; expenditures, $172,250; qualifying distributions, $160,100; giving activities include $160,100 for grants.
Purpose and activities: The foundation supports organizations involved with higher education and Christianity.
Fields of interest: Arts; Civil/human rights; Religion.
Type of support: General/operating support.
Geographic limitations: Giving primarily in San Diego, CA, St. Louis, MO, and Burke and Lynchburg, VA.
Support limitations: No grants to individuals.
Application information: Applications not accepted. Unsolicited requests for funds not accepted.
Directors: Thomas I. Hara; Helen L. Kim; Keith K. Kim.
EIN: 411859780

3910
Utica Mutual Insurance Company

180 Genesee St.
P.O. Box 530
New Hartford, NY 13413-2299
(315) 734-2000

Company URL: http://www.uticanational.com
Establishment information: Established in 1914.
Company type: Mutual company
Business activities: Sells property, fire, casualty, and liability insurance.
Business type (SIC): Insurance/fire, marine, and casualty
Corporate officers: J. Douglas Robinson, Chair. and C.E.O.; Brian P. Lytwynec, Pres. and C.O.O.; James P. Carhart, Sr. V.P. and C.I.O.; Raymond E. Cox, Sr. V.P., C.F.O., and Treas.; Kristen H. Martin, Sr. V.P. and Corp. Secy.; W. Craig Heston, Chair. Emeritus
Board of directors: J. Douglas Robinson, Chair.; Russell A. Acevedo; C. William Bachman; Alfred E. Calligaris; Roy A. Cardia; Paul A. Hagstrom; W. Craig Heston; Gregory M. Harden; Jerry J. Hartman; Zelda J. Holcomb; Brian Lytwynec; Nicholas O. Matt; Alan J. Pope; Timothy R. Reed; Linda E. Romano; Eric K. Scholl
Subsidiaries: Graphic Arts Mutual Insurance Co., Utica, NY; Republic Franklin Insurance Co., Columbus, OH; Utica Lloyds of Texas, Dallas, TX; Utica National Insurance Co. of Texas, Dallas, TX; Utica National Life Insurance Co., Inc., New Hartford, NY
Giving statement: Giving through the Utica National Group Foundation, Inc.

Utica National Group Foundation, Inc.

c/o Screening Committee Chair.
P.O. Box 530
Utica, NY 13503-0530
E-mail: michael.austin@uticanational.com; URL: http://www.uticanational.com/company/corporatecitizenship.asp

Establishment information: Established in 1987 in NY.
Donor: Utica Mutual Insurance Co.
Contact: Michael C. Austin, V.P., Corp. Comms.
Financial data (yr. ended 12/31/11): Assets, $5,604,854 (M); gifts received, $2,000; expenditures, $243,528; qualifying distributions, $231,329; giving activities include $231,329 for grants.
Purpose and activities: The foundation supports organizations involved with education, substance abuse treatment, human services, and community development. Special emphasis is directed toward programs that support the healthy development of children and families; and that address the root causes of social problems.
Fields of interest: Higher education; Education; Health care; Substance abuse, treatment; American Red Cross; Salvation Army; YM/YWCAs & YM/YWHAs; Children/youth, services; Family services; Human services; Community/economic development; United Ways and Federated Giving Programs.
Type of support: Annual campaigns; Building/renovation; Employee matching gifts; Employee-related scholarships; Equipment; General/operating support; Matching/challenge support; Program development; Scholarship funds; Seed money.
Geographic limitations: Giving primarily in the greater Utica, NY, area, with emphasis on Herkimer, Madison, and Oneida counties.

Support limitations: No grants for political activities or voter registration activity.
Publications: Annual report (including application guidelines); Application guidelines.
Application information: Applications accepted. Proposals should be submitted using organization letterhead. A site visit may be requested. Application form not required. Applicants should submit the following:
1) signature and title of chief executive officer
2) results expected from proposed grant
3) name, address and phone number of organization
4) copy of IRS Determination Letter
5) brief history of organization and description of its mission
6) listing of board of directors, trustees, officers and other key people and their affiliations
7) detailed description of project and amount of funding requested
8) contact person
9) copy of current year's organizational budget and/ or project budget
Initial approach: Proposal
Copies of proposal: 10
Board meeting date(s): Quarterly
Deadline(s): Jan. 15, Apr. 15, July 15, and Oct. 15
Final notification: 1 month following deadlines
Officers and Directors:* J. Douglas Robinson*, Pres.; George P. Wardley III, Secy.; C. William Bachman; Alfred B. Calligaris; Roy A. Cardia; Jerry J. Hartman; Zelda J. Holcomb; Brian P. Lytwynec; Nicholas O. Matt; Alan J. Pope; Timothy R. Reed; Linda E. Romano; John R. Zapisek.
EIN: 161313450
Selected grants: The following grants are a representative sample of this grantmaker's funding activity:
$5,219 to United Way of Massachusetts Bay, Boston, MA, 2010.
$5,000 to Economic Development Growth Enterprises Corporation, Rome, NY, 2010.
$3,209 to United Way of Long Island, Deer Park, NY, 2010.
$3,000 to College of Saint Rose, Albany, NY, 2010.
$2,510 to Boston Conservatory of Music, Boston, MA, 2010. For program services.
$1,500 to United Way of Buffalo and Erie County, Buffalo, NY, 2010.
$1,500 to United Way of Central Ohio, Columbus, OH, 2010.
$1,500 to United Way of Metropolitan Atlanta, Atlanta, GA, 2010.

3911
Uticon, Inc.
6420 Reading Rd.
Rosenberg, TX 77471-5654
(281) 341-9500

Company URL: http://
Establishment information: Established in 1984.
Company type: Private company
Business activities: Provides general contract construction services.
Business type (SIC): Building construction general contractors and operative builders
Corporate officer: Donald Wenzel, Pres.
Giving statement: Giving through the Wenzel Family Foundation.

Wenzel Family Foundation
14140 Frances St.
Needville, TX 77461-7500

Establishment information: Established in 2002 in TX.
Donors: Uticon, Inc.; Don Wenzel.
Financial data (yr. ended 12/31/12): Assets, $529,759 (M); gifts received, $24,750; expenditures, $27,562; qualifying distributions, $24,750; giving activities include $24,750 for 6 grants (high: $6,500; low: $1,000).
Purpose and activities: The foundation supports organizations involved with education and Catholicism.
Fields of interest: Education; Religion.
Type of support: General/operating support; Scholarship funds.
Geographic limitations: Giving limited to Needville and Rosenberg, TX.
Support limitations: No grants to individuals.
Application information: Applications not accepted. Unsolicited requests for funds not accepted.
Officers and Directors:* Donald P. Wenzel*, Pres.; Dustin Wenzel*, V.P.; Angela Wenzel-Davlin*, Secy.-Treas.
EIN: 270020985

3913
V.F. Corporation
105 Corporate Center Blvd.
Greensboro, NC 27408 (336) 424-6000
FAX: (336) 547-7634

Company URL: http://www.vfc.com
Establishment information: Established in 1899.
Company type: Public company
Company ticker symbol and exchange: VFC/NYSE
International Securities Identification Number: US9182041080
Business activities: Manufactures clothing.
Business type (SIC): Apparel—men's and boys' outerwear; hosiery and knitted fabrics; apparel—women's outerwear
Financial profile for 2012: Number of employees, 57,000; assets, $9,633,020,000; sales volume, $10,879,850,000; pre-tax net income, $1,421,880,000; expenses, $9,414,590,000; liabilities, $4,507,400,000
Fortune 1000 ranking: 2012—250th in revenues, 188th in profits, and 399th in assets
Corporate officers: Eric C. Wiseman, Chair., Pres., and C.E.O.; Robert K. Shearer, Sr. V.P. and C.F.O.; Scott A. Roe, V.P., Cont., and C.A.O.; Martin Schneider, V.P. and C.I.O.; Laura C. Meagher, V.P., Genl. Counsel, and Secy.; Susan Larson Williams, V.P., Human Resources
Board of directors: Eric C. Wiseman, Chair.; Richard T. Carucci; Juliana L. Chugg; Juan Ernesto De Bedout; Ursula O. Fairbairn; George Fellows; Robert J. Hurst; Laura W. Lang; W. Alan McCollough; Clarence Otis, Jr.; Matthew J. Shattock; Raymond G. Viault
Subsidiaries: JanSport, Inc., Appleton, WI; The H. D. Lee Company, Inc., Merriam, KS; Red Kap Apparel Corp., Nashville, TN; The Timberland Company, Stratham, NH; Vanity Fair, Inc., Alpharetta, GA; Vanity Fair Intimates, Inc., New York, NY; Wrangler Apparel Corp., Greensboro, NC
International operations: Argentina; Belgium; Brazil; Canada; Chile; France; Germany; Hong Kong; Italy; Luxembourg; Mauritius; Mexico; Portugal; Scotland; Switzerland; Turkey; United Kingdom
Giving statement: Giving through the VF Corporation Contributions Program, the Blue Bell Foundation, and the VF Foundation.
Company EIN: 231180120

VF Corporation Contributions Program
105 Corporate Center Blvd.
Greensboro, NC 27408-3194 (336) 424-6000
URL: http://www.vfc.com/corporate-responsibility

Purpose and activities: As a complement to its foundation, VF also makes charitable contributions to nonprofit organizations directly. Support is given primarily in areas of company operations.
Fields of interest: Education; Environment, water pollution; Environment, natural resources; Health care, research; Hospitals (general); Health care; Breast cancer; Crime/violence prevention, child abuse; Crime/violence prevention, sexual abuse; Employment; Food banks; Recreation, camps; Athletics/sports, baseball; Recreation; Youth development, centers/clubs; Children/youth, services Disabilities, people with.
Type of support: Cause-related marketing; Employee volunteer services; General/operating support; Sponsorships.
Geographic limitations: Giving primarily in areas of company operations.
Application information: Applications accepted.

Blue Bell Foundation
1525 W. WT Harris Blvd.
Charlotte, NC 28288-5709
Application address: c/o Sam Tucker, V.P., Human Resources, P.O. Box 21488, Greensboro, NC 27420, tel.: (910) 373-3412

Establishment information: Trust established in 1944 in NC.
Donors: Blue Bell, Inc.; Wrangler Apparel Corp.
Financial data (yr. ended 12/31/11): Assets, $5,318,974 (M); expenditures, $359,641; qualifying distributions, $317,457; giving activities include $317,457 for grants.
Purpose and activities: The foundation supports organizations involved with arts and culture, education, health, athletics, human services, and community development.
Fields of interest: Arts councils; Museums; Performing arts, orchestras; Arts; Elementary/ secondary education; Higher education; Education; Hospitals (general); Health care; Athletics/sports, Special Olympics; Children, foster care; Human services; Community/economic development; United Ways and Federated Giving Programs.
Type of support: Employee matching gifts; General/ operating support; Scholarship funds.
Geographic limitations: Giving primarily in areas of company operations, with emphasis on NC.
Support limitations: No grants to individuals.
Application information: Applications accepted. Application form not required.
Initial approach: Proposal
Advisory Committee: D. P. Laws; Robert H. Matthews; T. L. Weatherford.
Trustee: Wachovia Bank, N.A.
EIN: 566041057
Selected grants: The following grants are a representative sample of this grantmaker's funding activity:
$22,700 to Scholarship America, Saint Peter, MN, 2010. For general purpose.
$3,000 to Ronald McDonald House Charities, Oak Brook, IL, 2010. For general purpose.
$3,000 to Summit House, Greensboro, NC, 2010. For general purpose.
$2,000 to Wake Forest University, Winston-Salem, NC, 2010. For general purpose.
$1,000 to American Diabetes Association, Alexandria, VA, 2010. For general purpose.

VF Foundation

105 Corporate Center Blvd.
Greensboro, NC 27408-3194
URL: http://www.vfc.com/corporate-responsibility/social/vf-in-the-community

Establishment information: Established in 2002 in NC.
Donor: V.F. Corp.
Financial data (yr. ended 12/31/11): Assets, $10,299,272 (M); gifts received, $1,395,000; expenditures, $1,742,985; qualifying distributions, $1,741,166; giving activities include $1,741,166 for 164 grants (high: $250,800; low: $50).
Purpose and activities: The foundation supports camps and organizations involved with arts and culture, higher education, multiple sclerosis, housing development, sexual abuse, human services, and economic development.
Fields of interest: Museums; Arts; Higher education; Multiple sclerosis; Crime/violence prevention, sexual abuse; Housing/shelter, development; Recreation, camps; American Red Cross; Children/youth, services; Residential/custodial care, hospices; Human services; Economic development; United Ways and Federated Giving Programs.
Programs:
Employee Matching Gift Program: The foundation matches contributions made by employees of VF Corp. to universities and public television stations.
VF 100 Program: The foundation annually awards grants to 100 VF associates selected as winners based on the number of volunteer hours they contributed to their communities. The foundation awards $1,000 to the qualified charity of each associates choice.
Type of support: Capital campaigns; Employee matching gifts; Employee volunteer services; General/operating support.
Geographic limitations: Giving primarily in areas of company operations in Greensboro, NC.
Support limitations: No support for religious or political organizations. No grants to individuals.
Application information: Applications not accepted. Contributes only to pre-selected organizations.
Officers and Directors:* Eric C. Wiseman*, Chair.; Candace E. Cummings*, Secy.; Susan Larson Williams*, Treas.
EIN: 562322084
Selected grants: The following grants are a representative sample of this grantmaker's funding activity:
$197,500 to United Way of Greater Greensboro, Greensboro, NC, 2011.
$131,666 to Action Greensboro, Greensboro, NC, 2011.
$25,000 to Four-H Council, National, Chevy Chase, MD, 2011.
$25,000 to Greensboro Childrens Museum, Greensboro, NC, 2011.
$25,000 to Students in Free Enterprise, Springfield, MO, 2011.
$23,150 to American Jewish Committee, New York, NY, 2011.
$22,000 to Multiple Sclerosis Society, National, New York, NY, 2011.
$21,500 to UJA-Federation of New York, New York, NY, 2011.
$13,150 to Kids in Distressed Situations, New York, NY, 2011.
$12,300 to Wake Forest University, Winston-Salem, NC, 2011.

3914
Valassis Communications, Inc.

19975 Victor Pkwy.
Livonia, MI 48152-7001 (734) 591-3000
FAX: (734) 591-4503

Company URL: http://www.valassis.com/
Establishment information: Established in 1970.
Company type: Public company
Company ticker symbol and exchange: VCI/NYSE
Business activities: Prints and publishes coupons and promotional materials.
Business type (SIC): Advertising
Financial profile for 2012: Number of employees, 6,400; assets, $1,589,040,000; sales volume, $2,162,080,000; pre-tax net income, $184,870,000; expenses, $1,948,790,000; liabilities, $1,115,470,000
Fortune 1000 ranking: 2012—893rd in revenues, 703rd in profits, and 911th in assets
Corporate officers: Alan F. Schultz, Chair.; Robert A. Mason, Pres. and C.E.O.; Ronald Goolsby, C.O.O.; Robert L. Recchia, Exec. V.P., C.F.O.; Suzanne C. Brown, Exec. V.P., Sales and Mktg.; Todd L. Wiseley, Genl. Counsel and Corp. Secy.
Board of directors: Alan F. Schultz, Chair.; Joseph B. Anderson, Jr.; Kenneth V. Darish; Rob Mason; Robert L. Recchia; Thomas J. Reddin; Wallace S. Snyder; Luis A. Uninas; Amb. Faith Whittlesey
Plants: Los Angeles, CA; Wilton, CT; Atlanta, GA; Chicago, IL; Wichita, KS; Boston, MA; Minneapolis, MN; Durham, NC; Dallas, TX
International operations: Canada; Mexico
Giving statement: Giving through the Valassis Communications, Inc. Corporate Giving Program.
Company EIN: 382760940

Valassis Communications, Inc. Corporate Giving Program

c/o Valassis Giving Comms.
19975 Victor Pkwy.
Livonia, MI 48152-7001 (734) 591-3000
URL: http://www.valassis.com/1024/Company/citizen.aspx

Purpose and activities: Valassis makes charitable contributions to nonprofit organizations involved with education, animal welfare, food services, human services, and abducted children. Support is given primarily in areas of company operations.
Fields of interest: Education; Animal welfare; Health care; Food banks; Food distribution, meals on wheels; Children, services; Human services; General charitable giving Military/veterans.
Type of support: Employee volunteer services; General/operating support.
Geographic limitations: Giving primarily in areas of company operations.
Application information: Applications accepted. Application form not required.
Initial approach: Proposal to headquarters
Deadline(s): None
Final notification: Following review

3915
Valero Energy Corporation

(formerly Valero Refining & Marketing Co.)
1 Valero Way
San Antonio, TX 78249 (210) 345-2000
FAX: (302) 655-5049

Company URL: http://www.valero.com
Establishment information: Established in 1980.
Company type: Public company
Company ticker symbol and exchange: VLO/NYSE
Business activities: Refines and markets petroleum.
Business type (SIC): Petroleum refining; petroleum and petroleum products—wholesale
Financial profile for 2012: Number of employees, 21,671; assets, $44,477,000,000; sales volume, $133,925,000,000; pre-tax net income, $3,706,000,000; expenses, $135,240,000,000; liabilities, $26,445,000,000
Fortune 1000 ranking: 2012—9th in revenues, 94th in profits, and 121st in assets
Forbes 2000 ranking: 2012—25th in sales, 275th in profits, and 518th in assets
Corporate officers: William R. Klesse, Chair., and C.E.O.; Joe Gorder, Pres. and C.O.O.; Michael S. Ciskowski, Exec. V.P. and C.F.O.; Jay D. Browning, Sr. V.P. and Genl. Counsel; Michael Crownover, Sr. V.P., Human Resources; Cheryl Thomas, V.P. and C.I.O.; Donna Marie Titzman, V.P. and Treas.; Mark Schmeltekopf, V.P. and Cont.
Board of directors: William R. Klesse, Chair.; Ronald K. Calgaard; Jerry D. Choate; Ruben M. Escobedo; Deborah Platt Majoras; Bob Marbut; Donald L. Nickles; Philip J. Pfeiffer; Robert A. Profusek; Susan Kaufman Purcell; Stephen M. Waters; Randall J. Weisenburger; Rayford Wilkins, Jr.
Subsidiaries: Basis Petroleum Inc., Houston, TX; National Convenience Stores Incorporated, Houston, TX; The Premcor Refining Group Inc., St. Louis, MO
Plants: Armstrong, Clear Lake, Corpus Christi, Delmita, Gilmore, San Martin, Shilling, Shoup, Sonora, Thompsonville, TX
International operations: Canada; Cayman Islands; Luxembourg; United Kingdom
Historic mergers: Ultramar Diamond Shamrock Corporation (December 31, 2001)
Giving statement: Giving through the Valero Energy Corporation Contributions Program, the Valero Energy Foundation, and the Valero Scholarship Trust.
Company EIN: 741828067

Valero Energy Foundation

(formerly Ultramar Diamond Shamrock Foundation)
1 Valero Way
P.O. Box 696000
San Antonio, TX 78269-6000 (210) 345-2615
FAX: (210) 345-2103;
E-mail: valeroenergyfoundation@valero.com; E-mail address for Sylvia Rodriguez: Sylvia.Rodriguez@valero.com; URL: http://www.valero.com/Community/Community_Giving/Pages/Home.aspx

Establishment information: Established in 1999 in TX.
Donors: Ultramar Diamond Shamrock Corp.; Valero Energy Corp.
Contact: Sylvia Rodriguez, Exec. Dir.
Financial data (yr. ended 12/31/11): Assets, $33,770,047 (M); gifts received, $24,907,052; expenditures, $23,413,820; qualifying distributions, $23,365,959; giving activities include $20,726,061 for grants.
Purpose and activities: The foundation supports zoos and food banks and organizations involved with arts and culture, education, health, muscular dystrophy, multiple sclerosis, recreation, human services, and military and veterans.
Fields of interest: Museums; Museums (art); Arts; Elementary/secondary education; Higher education; Libraries (public); Education; Zoos/zoological societies; Hospitals (general); Reproductive health; Health care, patient services; Health care; Muscular

dystrophy; Multiple sclerosis; Food banks; Athletics/sports, amateur leagues; Recreation; Boys & girls clubs; Big Brothers/Big Sisters; Boy scouts; Girl scouts; American Red Cross; Salvation Army; YM/YWCAs & YM/YWHAs; Children/youth, services; Family services; Family services, domestic violence; Residential/custodial care; Developmentally disabled, centers & services; Homeless, human services; Human services; United Ways and Federated Giving Programs; Military/veterans' organizations.
Type of support: Building/renovation; Capital campaigns; General/operating support; Program development; Sponsorships.
Geographic limitations: Giving primarily in areas of company operations, with emphasis on TX.
Support limitations: No grants to individuals.
Publications: Application guidelines.
Application information: Applications accepted. Application form required. Applicants should submit the following:
1) signature and title of chief executive officer
2) name, address and phone number of organization
3) detailed description of project and amount of funding requested
4) copy of IRS Determination Letter
Initial approach: Download application form and E-mail or mail to foundation
Deadline(s): None
Officers: William R. Kleese*, Chair. and C.E.O.; Michael S. Ciskowski, Exec V.P. and C.F.O.; Jay D. Browning, Sr. V.P. and Secy.; Clayton E. Killinger, Sr. V.P. and Cont.; Stephanie A. Rosales, V.P. and Tax Dir.; Donna Marie Titzman, V.P. and Treas.; Eric A. Fisher, V.P.; J. Stephen Gilbert, V.P.; Sylvia C. Rodriguez, Exec. Dir.
EIN: 742904514
Selected grants: The following grants are a representative sample of this grantmaker's funding activity:
$1,000,000 to University of Texas Health Science Center, San Antonio, TX, 2010.
$983,638 to United Way of San Antonio and Bexar County, San Antonio, TX, 2010.
$800,000 to Witte Museum, San Antonio, TX, 2010.
$100,000 to American Red Cross, San Antonio, TX, 2010.
$50,000 to Boys and Girls Clubs of San Antonio, San Antonio, TX, 2010.
$10,000 to Girls Inc. of San Antonio, San Antonio, TX, 2010.
$10,000 to Guadalupe Cultural Arts Center, San Antonio, TX, 2010.
$10,000 to LULAC Rey Feo Scholarship Committee, San Antonio, TX, 2010.
$10,000 to Texas Foundation of Hope, San Antonio, TX, 2010.
$10,000 to United Way of Saint Charles, Luling, LA, 2010.

Valero Scholarship Trust

P.O. Box 696000
San Antonio, TX 78269-6000

Establishment information: Established in 1996 in TX.
Donor: Valero Energy Corp.
Financial data (yr. ended 12/31/11): Assets, $183,783 (M); gifts received, $255,000; expenditures, $262,785; qualifying distributions, $256,853; giving activities include $256,853 for 109 grants (high: $3,750; low: $1,103).
Purpose and activities: The trust awards college scholarships to the children of employees of Valero Energy and its affiliates.
Fields of interest: Higher education.
Type of support: Employee-related scholarships.
Geographic limitations: Giving limited to areas of company operations.
Application information: Applications not accepted. Contributes only through employee-related scholarships.
Trustee: Frost National Bank.
EIN: 746437579
Selected grants: The following grants are a representative sample of this grantmaker's funding activity:
$4,000 to Texas State University, San Marcos, TX, 2006.
$2,500 to Arizona State University, Tempe, AZ, 2006.
$2,500 to Arizona State University, Tempe, AZ, 2006.
$2,500 to Arizona State University, Tempe, AZ, 2006.
$2,500 to Austin College, Sherman, TX, 2006.
$2,500 to Baylor University, Waco, TX, 2006.
$2,500 to Bob Jones University, Greenville, SC, 2006.
$2,500 to Oklahoma State University, Stillwater, OK, 2006.
$2,500 to University of California, Los Angeles, CA, 2006.
$2,500 to University of California, Los Angeles, CA, 2006.

3916
Valley National Bancorp

1455 Valley Rd.
Wayne, NJ 07470 (973) 305-8800
FAX: (973) 305-1605

Company URL: http://www.valleynationalbank.com
Establishment information: Established in 1927.
Company type: Public company
Company ticker symbol and exchange: VLY/NYSE
Business activities: Operates bank holding company; operates commercial bank.
Business type (SIC): Banks/commercial; holding company
Financial profile for 2012: Number of employees, 2,910; assets, $16,012,650,000; pre-tax net income, $210,380,000; liabilities, $14,510,270,000
Corporate officers: Gerald H. Lipkin, Chair., Pres., and C.E.O.; Peter Crocitto, Sr. Exec. V.P. and C.O.O.; Alan D. Eskow, C.P.A., Sr. Exec. V.P., C.F.O., and Corp. Secy.
Board of directors: Gerald H. Lipkin, Chair.; Andrew B. Abramson; Pamela Bronander; Eric P. Edelstein; Alan D. Eskow; Graham O. Jones; Walter H. Jones III; Gerald Korde; Michael L. LaRusso; Marc J. Lenner; Robinson Markel; Richard S. Miller; Barnett Rukin; Suresh L. Sani; Mary J. Steele Guilfoile
Subsidiary: Valley National Bank, Wayne, NJ
Giving statement: Giving through the Valley National Bancorp Contributions Program, the Greater Community Educational Foundation, Inc., the Valley Foundation, Inc., and the Valley National Bancorp Charitable Foundation, Inc.
Company EIN: 222477875

Valley National Bancorp Contributions Program

1455 Valley Rd.
Wayne, NJ 07470-2089
URL: https://www.valleynationalbank.com/About/Community.aspx

Contact: Garret G. Nieuwenhuis, 1st Sr. V.P.
Purpose and activities: As a complement to its foundation, Valley National Bancorp also makes charitable contributions to nonprofit organizations directly. Support is given primarily in central and northern New Jersey and New York, New York.
Fields of interest: Breast cancer research; Housing/shelter; General charitable giving.
Type of support: Employee volunteer services; General/operating support; Pro bono services - real estate and facilities.
Geographic limitations: Giving primarily in central and northern NJ and New York, NY.
Publications: Financial statement; Program policy statement.
Application information: Applications accepted. Proposals should be submitted using organization letterhead. The Marketing Department handles giving. A contributions committee reviews all requests. Application form not required. Applicants should submit the following:
1) copy of IRS Determination Letter
2) copy of most recent annual report/audited financial statement/990
3) descriptive literature about organization
4) detailed description of project and amount of funding requested
5) copy of current year's organizational budget and/or project budget
Initial approach: Proposal to headquarters
Copies of proposal: 1
Committee meeting date(s): As needed
Deadline(s): None
Final notification: 2 weeks
Number of staff: 1 full-time professional; 1 full-time support.

Greater Community Educational Foundation, Inc.

1455 Valley Rd.
Wayne, NJ 07470-2089 (973) 305-8506
Application address: 1195 Hamburg Tpke., Wayne, NJ 07470

Establishment information: Established in 1998 in NJ.
Donor: Greater Community Bancorp.
Contact: Anthony M. Bruno, Jr., Pres.
Financial data (yr. ended 12/31/11): Assets, $164,230 (M); expenditures, $15,630; qualifying distributions, $15,630; giving activities include $15,500 for 7 grants to individuals (high: $3,500; low: $1,250).
Purpose and activities: The foundation awards scholarships to first year college students.
Type of support: Scholarships—to individuals.
Application information: Applications accepted. Application form required.
Applications should include a typed essay.
Initial approach: Contact foundation for application form
Deadline(s): Dec. 31 prior to first year of college
Officers: Anthony M. Bruno, Jr., Pres.; Dianne M. Grenz, 1st. Sr. V.P.; Jeanette M. Chardavoyne, Secy.
EIN: 223705689

The Valley Foundation, Inc.

1455 Valley Rd.
Wayne, NJ 07470-0558

Establishment information: Established in 1996 in NJ.
Donor: Valley National Bancorp.
Financial data (yr. ended 12/31/11): Assets, $55,891 (M); expenditures, $205; qualifying distributions, $0.
Purpose and activities: The foundation supports organizations involved with housing.

Fields of interest: Housing/shelter.
Type of support: General/operating support.
Geographic limitations: Giving limited to NJ.
Application information: Applications not accepted. Contributes only to pre-selected organizations.
Officers and Directors:* Gerald H. Lipkin*, Pres.; Peter Crocito, V.P.; Dianne Grenz, V.P.; Alan D. Eskow*, Treas.
EIN: 223473532

Valley National Bancorp Charitable Foundation, Inc.

(formerly Greater Community Bancorp Charitable Foundation, Inc.)
1455 Valley Rd.
Wayne, NJ 07470-2089 (973) 305-8506
Application address: 1195 Hamburg Tpke., Wayne, NJ 07470

Establishment information: Established in 2005 in NJ.
Donors: Greater Community Bank; Bergen Community Bank.
Contact: Anthony M. Bruno, Jr., Pres.
Financial data (yr. ended 12/31/11): Assets, $395,933 (M); expenditures, $1,130; qualifying distributions, $1,000; giving activities include $1,000 for grants.
Purpose and activities: The foundation supports organizations involved with education.
Type of support: General/operating support.
Geographic limitations: Giving primarily in areas of company operations in NJ.
Application information: Applications accepted. Application form required.
Initial approach: Contact foundation for application information
Deadline(s): None
Officers: Anthony M. Bruno, Jr., Pres.; Dianne M. Grenz, 1st Sr. V.P.; Jeannette M. Chardavoyne, Secy.
EIN: 203760448

3917
Valley News Company

1305 Stadium Rd.
Mankato, MN 56001-5397 (507) 345-4819

Company URL: http://www.valleynewscompany.com
Establishment information: Established in 1940.
Company type: Private company
Business activities: Sells magazines wholesale.
Business type (SIC): Non-durable goods—wholesale; nonstore retailers
Corporate officer: Troy Leiferman, Pres.
Giving statement: Giving through the Valley News Charity Fund.

Valley News Charity Fund

1305 Stadium Rd.
Mankato, MN 56001-5355

Establishment information: Established in 1985 in MN.
Donor: Valley News Co.
Financial data (yr. ended 12/31/11): Assets, $771,307 (M); gifts received, $1,600; expenditures, $23,371; qualifying distributions, $21,000; giving activities include $21,000 for grants.
Purpose and activities: The fund supports community foundations and organizations involved with K-12 and higher education, health, school athletics, and human services.
Fields of interest: Education; Health care; Human services.
Type of support: Building/renovation; General/operating support; Program development; Sponsorships.
Geographic limitations: Giving primarily in Mankato, MN.
Support limitations: No grants to individuals.
Application information: Applications not accepted. Unsolicited requests for funds not accepted.
Officers: Troy Leiferman, Pres.; Margaret Leiferman, Secy.
EIN: 363339339

3918
Valley Telephone Cooperative, Inc.

752 E. Maley St.
P.O. Box 970
Willcox, AZ 85643-1303 (520) 384-2231

Company URL: http://www.vtc.net/page.php?page=contact
Establishment information: Established in 1962.
Company type: Private company
Business activities: Provides local telephone communications services.
Business type (SIC): Telephone communications
Corporate officers: Steve Metts, C.E.O.; Troy Judd, C.F.O; Kristi Lee, C.I.O
Board of directors: Thomas Kuykendall; John Lacy; Carrol Miller; George May; Joe Chapin; Jyme Stoner; Ruby Sipes; Candace Roll; William Swift; David Thompson
Giving statement: Giving through the Valley Telephone Cooperative Foundation.

Valley Telephone Cooperative Foundation

P.O. Box 970
Willcox, AZ 85644-0970 (520) 384-2231
FAX: (520) 384-2831; URL: http://www.vtc.net/

Establishment information: Established in 1991 in AZ.
Donor: Valley Telephone Cooperative, Inc.
Financial data (yr. ended 12/31/12): Assets, $1,541,536 (M); gifts received, $124,649; expenditures, $73,355; qualifying distributions, $70,035; giving activities include $5,155 for 9 grants (high: $880; low: $500) and $62,500 for 39 grants to individuals (high: $2,500; low: $1,250).
Purpose and activities: The foundation awards college scholarships to members, patrons, and family members of patrons of Valley Telephone Cooperative, Inc.
Type of support: Scholarships—to individuals.
Publications: Application guidelines.
Application information: Applications accepted. Application form required.
Applications should include official transcripts, an essay, and 2 letters of recommendation.
Initial approach: Proposal
Deadline(s): Mar. 11
Officers: David Thompson, Pres.; William Swift, V.P.; Joseph Chapin, Secy.-Treas.
Directors: Joseph Chapin; George May; Carrol Miller; Candace Roll; Ruby Sipes; Jyme Stoner.
EIN: 742613547

3919
Valmont Industries, Inc.

1 Valmont Plz.
13815 First National Bank Pkwy.
Omaha, NE 68154-5215 (402) 963-1000
FAX: (402) 963-1198

Company URL: http://www.valmont.com
Establishment information: Established in 1946.
Company type: Public company
Company ticker symbol and exchange: VMI/NYSE
Business activities: Manufactures mechanized irrigation equipment, engineered poles, towers, and structures, and other fabricated metal products.
Business type (SIC): Metal products/structural; metal products/fabricated; machinery/farm and garden; industrial machinery and equipment—wholesale
Financial profile for 2012: Number of employees, 10,543; assets, $2,568,550,000; sales volume, $3,029,540,000; pre-tax net income, $359,290,000; expenses, $2,647,240,000; liabilities, $1,218,640,000
Fortune 1000 ranking: 2012—706th in revenues, 540th in profits, and 796th in assets
Corporate officers: Mogens C. Bay, Chair. and C.E.O.; Todd Atkinson, Exec. V.P. and Corp. Secy.; Richard P Heyse, Sr. V.P. and C.F.O.; Mark C. Jaksich, V.P. and Cont.; Vanessa K. Brown, V.P., Human Resources
Board of directors: Mogens C. Bay, Chair.; Glen A. Barton; Kaj R. Den Daas; James B. Milliken; Daniel P. Neary; Catherine James Paglia; Amb. Clark T. Randt, Jr.; Walter Scott, Jr.; Kenneth E. Stinson
Subsidiary: Cascade Earth Sciences, Ltd., Albany, OR
Plants: Bay Minette, Tuscaloosa, AL; Long Beach, Los Angeles, CA; Commerce City, CO; Bartow, FL; Claxton, GA; Chicago, IL; Elkhart, Plymouth, IN; Sioux City, IA; El Dorado, KS; Farmington, Minneapolis, MN; McCook, Valley, West Point, NE; Tulsa, OK; Salem, Tualatin, OR; Jasper, TN; Brenham, Mansfield, TX; Lindon, UT
International operations: Australia; Brazil; China; Estonia; Finland; France; Germany; Mexico; Morocco and the Western Sahara; Netherlands; Poland; South Africa; Spain; Turkey; United Arab Emirates; United Kingdom
Giving statement: Giving through the Valmont Industries, Inc. Corporate Giving Program and the Valmont Foundation.
Company EIN: 470351813

The Valmont Foundation

1 Valmont Plz., 5th Fl.
Omaha, NE 68154-5215
FAX: (402) 963-1095;
E-mail: ed.burchfield@valmont.com

Establishment information: Established in 1976.
Donor: Valmont Industries, Inc.
Contact: Mogen Bay, Tr.; Terry McClain, Tr.
Financial data (yr. ended 02/29/12): Assets, $0 (M); expenditures, $0; qualifying distributions, $0.
Purpose and activities: The foundation supports organizations involved with arts and culture, K-12 and higher education, health, and human services.
Fields of interest: Arts; Elementary/secondary education; Higher education; Health care; Children/youth, services; Family services; Human services.
Geographic limitations: Giving primarily in NE.
Publications: Corporate report.
Application information: Applications accepted. Application form not required.
Initial approach: Proposal
Copies of proposal: 1

Board meeting date(s): Varies
Deadline(s): None
Final notification: Varies
Trustees: Mogens C. Bay; Terry J. McClain.
EIN: 362895245

3920
The Valspar Corporation

901 3rd Ave., S.
P.O. Box 1461
Minneapolis, MN 55440-1461
(612) 851-7000
FAX: (612) 851-7408

Company URL: http://www.valspar.com
Establishment information: Established in 1806.
Company type: Public company
Company ticker symbol and exchange: VAL/NYSE
Business activities: Manufactures and distributes paint and coatings.
Business type (SIC): Paints and allied products
Financial profile for 2012: Number of employees, 9,800; assets, $3,626,840,000; sales volume, $4,020,850,000; pre-tax net income, $417,220,000; expenses, $3,538,580,000; liabilities, $2,403,310,000
Fortune 1000 ranking: 2012—584th in revenues, 480th in profits, and 693rd in assets
Corporate officers: Gary E. Hendrickson, Chair., Pres., and C.E.O.; Rolf Engh, Exec. V.P., Genl. Counsel, and Secy.; James L. Muehlbauer, Exec. V.P., C.F.O., and C.A.O.; Anthony L. Blaine, Sr. V.P., Human Resources
Board of directors: Gary E. Hendrickson, Chair.; Jack J. Allen; John M. Ballach; John S. Bode; William M. Cook; Jeffrey H. Curler; Ian R. Friendly; Janel Haugarth; Mae C. Jemison, M.D.; Gregory P. Palen
Plants: Azusa, Los Angeles, CA; Tampa, FL; Covington, GA; Carol Stream, Chicago, Kankakee, Marengo, Rockford, Wheeling, IL; Fort Wayne, IN; Louisville, KY; Hagerstown, MD; Picayune, MS; High Point, Statesville, NC; Medina, OH; Pittsburgh, Rochester, PA; Jackson, TN; Garland, Grand Prairie, TX
International operations: Australia; Brazil; Canada; China; France; Germany; Japan; Malaysia; Mexico; South Africa; Switzerland; United Kingdom
Giving statement: Giving through the Valspar Corporation Contributions Program and the Valspar Foundation.
Company EIN: 362443580

The Valspar Corporation Contributions Program

P.O. Box 1461
Minneapolis, MN 55440-1461 (612) 851-7000
URL: http://valsparglobal.com/corp/about/community_involvement_matters.jsp

Purpose and activities: As a complement to its foundation, Valspar also makes charitable contributions to nonprofit organizations directly. Support is given primarily in areas of company operations, with emphasis on Minneapolis, Minnesota.
Fields of interest: Housing/shelter, rehabilitation; Housing/shelter; Urban/community development.
Type of support: General/operating support; In-kind gifts.
Geographic limitations: Giving primarily in areas of company operations, with emphasis on Minneapolis, MN.
Application information: Application form not required.

The Valspar Foundation

P.O. Box 1461
Minneapolis, MN 55440-1461 (612) 337-5903
FAX: (612) 337-5904; URL: http://www.valsparglobal.com/corp/about/valspar_foundation.jsp

Establishment information: Established in 1979.
Donor: The Valspar Corp.
Contact: Gwen Leifeld, Mgr.
Financial data (yr. ended 09/30/11): Assets, $85,513 (M); gifts received, $275,000; expenditures, $1,151,868; qualifying distributions, $1,151,843; giving activities include $1,031,843 for 264 grants (high: $325,000; low: $34) and $120,000 for 79 grants to individuals (high: $1,500; low: $1,500).
Purpose and activities: The foundation supports organizations involved with arts and culture, education, health, housing, poison prevention, human services, and community development.
Fields of interest: Media, radio; Museums (science/technology); Performing arts, orchestras; Arts; Education; Health care; Housing/shelter, development; Housing/shelter; Safety, poisons; American Red Cross; YM/YWCAs & YM/YWHAs; Children/youth, services; Family services; Human services; Community/economic development; United Ways and Federated Giving Programs Economically disadvantaged.
Type of support: Annual campaigns; Building/renovation; Employee matching gifts; Employee-related scholarships; General/operating support; In-kind gifts; Program development; Sponsorships.
Geographic limitations: Giving limited to areas of company operations, with emphasis on the Twin Cities, MN, metropolitan area.
Support limitations: No support for religious, ethnic, fraternal, labor, or veterans' organizations.
Officers: M. I. Dougherty, Pres.; Anthony L. Blaine, V.P.; William L. Mansfield, V.P.; Rolf Engh, Secy.
Number of staff: 1 full-time professional; 1 part-time support.
EIN: 411363847

3921
Vandor Corporation

4251 W. Industries Rd.
Richmond, IN 47374-1435 (765) 966-7676

Company URL: http://www.vandorcorp.com
Establishment information: Established in 1985.
Company type: Private company
Business activities: Manufactures vacuumformed, injection molded, and custom die cut plastic products; manufactures funeral products.
Business type (SIC): Plastic products/miscellaneous; manufacturing/miscellaneous
Corporate officers: Alan H. Elder, Chair.; Gerald Davis, Pres. and C.E.O.; Mark Harrington, C.F.O.; Mark Elder, V.P., Sales
Board of directors: Alan H. Elder, Chair.; Mark Harrington
Giving statement: Giving through the Elder Foundation.

Elder Foundation

4251 W. Industries Rd.
Richmond, IN 47374-1385

Establishment information: Established in 1994 in IN.
Donors: Elder Groups, Inc.; Vandor Corp.; Bruce E. Elder Trust.
Financial data (yr. ended 06/30/12): Assets, $873,728 (M); gifts received, $6,000; expenditures, $165,385; qualifying distributions, $159,000; giving activities include $159,000 for 2 grants (high: $153,000; low: $6,000).
Purpose and activities: The foundation supports organizations involved with youth development and Christianity.
Fields of interest: Boys & girls clubs; Christian agencies & churches.
Type of support: General/operating support.
Geographic limitations: Giving primarily in Richmond, IN and Rochester, MI.
Application information: Applications not accepted. Contributes only to pre-selected organizations.
Trustees: Alan H. Elder; Amy Elder; Jack E. Elder; Julie Elder; Louise Elder; Paul A. Elder.
EIN: 351944291

3922
Varnum LLP

333 Bridget St., N.W.
P.O. Box 352
Grand Rapids, MI 49501-0352
(616) 262-0011

Company URL: http://www.varnumlaw.com/
Company type: Private company
Business activities: Operates law firm.
Business type (SIC): Legal services
Offices: Grand Rapids, Kalamazoo, Lansing, Novi, MI
Giving statement: Giving through the Varnum LLP Pro Bono Program.

Varnum LLP Pro Bono Program

333 Bridget St., N.W.
P.O. Box 352
Grand Rapids, MI 49501-0352 (616) 336-6532
E-mail: msallard@varnumlaw.com; Additional tel.: (616) 262-0011; URL: http://www.varnumlaw.com/about-varnum/pro-bono-work/

Contact: Mark Allard, Partner
Fields of interest: Legal services.
Type of support: Pro bono services - legal.
Application information: A Pro Bono Coordinator manages the pro bono program.

3923
Varnum, Riddering, Schmidt & Howlett LLP

333 Bridge St., N.W., Ste. 1300
P.O. Box 352
Grand Rapids, MI 49501-0352
(616) 336-6000

Company URL: http://www.varnumlaw.com
Establishment information: Established in 1888.
Company type: Private company
Business activities: Provides legal services.
Business type (SIC): Legal services
Offices: Grand Haven, Kalamazoo, Lansing, MI; Milwaukee, WI
Giving statement: Giving through the Varnum, Riddering, Schmidt & Howlett LLP Corporate Giving Program.

Varnum, Riddering, Schmidt & Howlett LLP Corporate Giving Program

Bridgewater Pl.
P.O. Box 352
Grand Rapids, MI 49501-0352 (616) 336-6000
URL: http://www.varnumlaw.com/diversity-and-inclusion-at-varnum/varnum-in-the-community/

Purpose and activities: Varnum makes charitable contributions to nonprofit organizations involved with art and culture, education, and community and economic development. Support is given primarily in areas of company operations in Michigan.
Fields of interest: Arts; Education; Human services; Community/economic development Economically disadvantaged.
Type of support: Employee volunteer services; General/operating support; Pro bono services - strategic management.
Geographic limitations: Giving primarily in areas of company operations in MI.
Contributions Committee: Larry J. Titley, Chair.; Randy Boileau; Dirk Hoffius; Pete Livingston; Kent Vana.

3924
Vaughan Furniture Company, Inc.

816 Glendale Rd.
P.O. Box 1489
Galax, VA 24333 (276) 236-6111

Company URL: http://www.vaughanfurniture.com
Establishment information: Established in 1923.
Company type: Private company
Business activities: Manufactures wood household furniture.
Business type (SIC): Furniture/household
Corporate officers: Taylor C. Vaughan, Chair., Pres., and C.E.O.; Michael E. Stevens, Sr. V.P., Admin., and Secy.; David Miller, Sr. V.P., Sales; Pete Hall, Treas.
Board of director: Taylor C. Vaughan, Chair.
Giving statement: Giving through the Vaughan Foundation.

Vaughan Foundation

P.O. Box 1489
Galax, VA 24333-1489 (276) 236-6111

Donor: Vaughan Furniture Co., Inc.
Contact: Taylor Vaughan, Pres.
Financial data (yr. ended 09/30/12): Assets, $509,403 (M); expenditures, $12,520; qualifying distributions, $11,000; giving activities include $11,000 for 7 grants (high: $3,000; low: $500).
Purpose and activities: The foundation supports organizations involved with health, human services, and Christianity.
Fields of interest: Education; Health care; Human services.
Type of support: General/operating support.
Geographic limitations: Giving primarily in VA.
Support limitations: No grants to individuals.
Application information: Applications accepted. Application form required. Applicants should submit the following:
1) copy of IRS Determination Letter
2) brief history of organization and description of its mission
3) detailed description of project and amount of funding requested

Initial approach: Letter
Deadline(s): None

Officers and Directors:* Taylor Vaughan*, Pres.; John David Vaughan*, V.P.; Raymond L. Hall, Jr.*, Secy.; Michael E. Stevens.
EIN: 541295313

3925
Vectren Corporation

1 Vectren Sq.
P.O. Box 209
Evansville, IN 47708 (812) 491-4000

Company URL: http://www.vectren.com
Establishment information: Established in 2000 from the merger of Indiana Energy, Inc. with SIGCORP, Inc.
Company type: Public company
Company ticker symbol and exchange: VVC/NYSE
Business activities: Operates holding company; transmits and distributes natural gas; generates, transmits, and distributes electricity.
Business type (SIC): Combination utility services; holding company
Financial profile for 2012: Number of employees, 5,400; assets, $5,089,100,000; sales volume, $2,232,800,000; pre-tax net income, $241,500,000; expenses, $1,877,600,000; liabilities, $3,563,000,000
Fortune 1000 ranking: 2012—867th in revenues, 637th in profits, and 593rd in assets
Corporate officers: Carl L. Chapman, Chair., Pres., and C.E.O.; Jerome A. Benkert, Jr., Exec. V.P. and C.F.O.; Robert E. Heidorn, V.P. and Genl. Counsel; Robert L. Goocher, V.P. and Treas.; M. Susan Hardwick, V.P. and Cont.; Douglas Petitt, V.P., Mktg.; Michael Roeder, V.P., Comms.; Ellis Redd, V.P., Human Resources
Board of directors: Carl L. Chapman, Chair.; James H. DeGraffenreidt, Jr.; Neil C. Ellerbrook; John D. Engelbrecht; Anton H. George; Martin C. Jischke; Robert G. Jones; J. Timothy McGinley; R. Daniel Sadlier; Michael L. Smith; Jean L. Wojtowicz
Subsidiaries: Energy Systems Group LLC, Evansville, IN; Indiana Gas Company, Inc., Indianapolis, IN; Southern Indiana Gas and Electric Company, Evansville, IN; Southern Indiana Properties, Inc., Evansville, IN; Vectren Communications Svcs., Evansville, IN
Giving statement: Giving through the Vectren Corporation Contributions Program and the Vectren Foundation, Inc.
Company EIN: 352086905

Vectren Corporation Contributions Program

(formerly SIGCORP, Inc. Corporate Giving Program)
1 Vectren Sq.
Evansville, IN 47708
URL: http://www.vectren.com/web/holding/discover/community/connection_i.jsp

Contact: Mark Miller
Purpose and activities: As a complement to its foundation, Vectren also makes charitable contributions to nonprofit organizations directly. Support is given primarily in areas of company operations.
Fields of interest: Arts; Education; Health care; Human services; Community/economic development; Public affairs.
Type of support: General/operating support; Sponsorships.
Geographic limitations: Giving primarily in areas of company operations.
Application information: Applications accepted. Application form required.

Initial approach: Download application form

Vectren Foundation, Inc.

(formerly Indiana Energy Foundation, Inc.)
1 Vectren Sq.
Evansville, IN 47708-1251 (812) 491-4176
E-mail: mmiller@vectren.com; Additional application address and contact: Lynda Hoffman, Community Affairs, Mgr., Vectren Corp., 120 W. 2nd St., Ste. 1212, Dayton, OH 45402-1685, tel.: (937) 222-2936, e-mail:lkhoffman@vectren.com; URL: http://www.vectrenfoundation.org/

Establishment information: Established in 2000 in IN.
Donors: Indiana Energy, Inc.; Vectren Corp.
Contact: Mark Miller, Mgr., Community Affairs
Financial data (yr. ended 12/31/11): Assets, $857,367 (M); gifts received, $13,640; expenditures, $1,997,183; qualifying distributions, $1,992,878; giving activities include $1,992,878 for grants.
Purpose and activities: The foundation supports programs designed to promote community development; energy conservation and environmental stewardship; and education. Special emphasis is directed toward programs designed to contribute to sustainable future.
Fields of interest: Elementary/secondary education; Higher education; Education, services; Education, reading; Education; Environment, natural resources; Environment, energy; Environmental education; Environment; Health care, clinics/centers; Health care; Employment; Housing/shelter, development; Housing/shelter; Youth development, adult & child programs; American Red Cross; YM/YWCAs & YM/YWHAs; Children/youth, services; Economic development; Community/economic development; United Ways and Federated Giving Programs; Leadership development; Public affairs.
Programs:

Community Development: The foundation supports programs designed to build strong communities. Special emphasis is directed toward programs designed to advance community improvement, economic development, energy efficiency, affordable housing, and civic planning; restore and maintain neighborhoods through company resources and sustainable economic and community projects that encourages communities to grow and prosper; and promote community re-building and renovation.

Education: The foundation supports programs designed to advance a skilled and educated workforce. Special emphasis is directed toward programs designed to improve the quality and quantity of an educated workforce through strategies that advance life-long learning and professional development; enhance student performance, grade-level readiness, literacy, mentoring, and experiential learning; and foster innovation and developing future leaders.

Ellerbrook Spirit of Community Awards: The foundation annually honors a Vectren employee who demonstrates a strong commitment to community service. The award includes a $5,000 grant to the nonprofit organization chosen by the honoree.

Employee Volunteer Grants: The foundation awards $2,500 grants to nonprofit organizations with which groups of 15 or more employees of Vectren volunteer at least four hours toward an approved community project; $200 grants to nonprofit organizations with which employees volunteer at least 40 hours per year; and $10 per employee for any team of five or more employees who participate in a fundraising event for a tax exempt agency.

Energy Conservation and Environmental Stewardship: The foundation supports programs designed to promote the preservation of natural resources and energy conservation. Special emphasis is directed toward programs designed to assist Vectren customers address the rise in energy costs through smart energy choices that lowers the impact on the environment; drive long-term conservation behaviors and practices; preserve or restore natural resources; increase access to natural resource areas throughout Vectren's service areas; and foster responsible stewardship of natural and environmental resources.
Type of support: Capital campaigns; Employee matching gifts; Employee volunteer services; Equipment; General/operating support; Program development; Sponsorships.
Geographic limitations: Giving limited to areas of company operations in IN and OH.
Support limitations: No support for political, religious, fraternal, labor, or veterans' organizations or issue-oriented organizations. No grants to individuals or for scholarships.
Publications: Annual report; Application guidelines.
Application information: Applications accepted. Application form required. Applicants should submit the following:
1) results expected from proposed grant
2) copy of IRS Determination Letter
3) copy of most recent annual report/audited financial statement/990
4) listing of board of directors, trustees, officers and other key people and their affiliations
5) copy of current year's organizational budget and/or project budget
6) listing of additional sources and amount of support

Initial approach: Download application form and e-mail or mail to foundation
Deadline(s): None
Final notification: 90 days

Officers and Directors:* Jeffrey W. Whiteside*, Pres.; Ronald E. Christian*, V.P. and Secy.; Jerome A. Benkert, Jr.; Carl L. Chapman.
EIN: 351950691
Selected grants: The following grants are a representative sample of this grantmaker's funding activity:
$100,000 to University of Evansville, Evansville, IN, 2011.
$50,690 to United Way of Southwestern Indiana, Evansville, IN, 2011.
$50,000 to Japan-America Society of Indiana, Indianapolis, IN, 2011.
$35,000 to Nature Conservancy, Arlington, VA, 2011.
$25,000 to Habitat of Evansville, Evansville, IN, 2011.
$25,000 to Hollys House, Evansville, IN, 2011.
$19,600 to Dayton Art Institute, Dayton, OH, 2011.
$15,000 to Boys and Girls Club of Evansville, Evansville, IN, 2011.
$15,000 to Evansville Christian Life Center, Evansville, IN, 2011.
$10,000 to American Gas Foundation, Washington, DC, 2011.

3926
Vedante Corp.

P.O. Box 19391
Boulder, CO 80302 (303) 938-4040

Company URL: http://vedante.com
Establishment information: Established in 2006.
Company type: Private company
Business type (SIC): Business services/miscellaneous
Corporate officer: Barbara Kantor, C.E.O.
Giving statement: Giving through the Vedante Corp. Contributions Program.

Vedante Corp. Contributions Program

P.O. Box 19391
Boulder, CO 80308-2391 (303) 938-4040
E-mail: customerservice@vedante.com; URL: http://vedante.com

Purpose and activities: Vedante Corp. is a certified B Corporation that donates a percentage of net profits to charitable organizations.

3927
Veev Spirits, LLC

5979 W. 3rd St., Ste. 204
Los Angeles, CA 90036-2834
(323) 937-0345

Company URL: http://www.VeeVlife.com
Establishment information: Established in 2008.
Company type: Private company
Business type (SIC): Business services/miscellaneous
Corporate officers: Courtney Reum, Co-Founder; Carter Reum, Co-Founder; Bryan Crowley, C.O.O.
Giving statement: Giving through the Veev Spirits LLC Contributions Program.

Veev Spirits LLC Contributions Program

5979 West 3rd St.
Los Angeles, CA 90036-2834 (323) 937-0345
E-mail: info@veevlife.com; URL: http://www.VeeVlife.com

Purpose and activities: Veev Spirits is a certified B Corporation that donates a percentage of net profits to charitable organizations.
Fields of interest: Environment, forests; Environment.
Type of support: General/operating support.

3928
Velting Contractors, Inc.

3060 Breton Rd.
Grand Rapids, MI 49512-1748
(616) 949-6660
FAX: (616) 949-8168.

Company URL: http://www.velting.com
Establishment information: Established in 1921.
Company type: Private company
Business activities: Provides road construction and excavation services.
Business type (SIC): Construction/highway and street (except elevated); construction/miscellaneous heavy; contractors/miscellaneous special trade
Corporate officers: Scott Velting, Pres.; Abe Moerland, Jr., Treas.
Giving statement: Giving through the Velting Foundation.

Velting Foundation

3060 Breton Rd. S.E.
Grand Rapids, MI 49512-1748

Establishment information: Established in 1980 in MI.
Donors: Velting Contractors, Inc.; James Velting; David L. Velting.
Financial data (yr. ended 11/30/10): Assets, $9,735 (M); expenditures, $20; qualifying distributions, $0.
Purpose and activities: The foundation supports organizations involved with health, human services, and Christianity.
Type of support: General/operating support.
Geographic limitations: Giving primarily in Grand Rapids, MI.
Support limitations: No grants to individuals.
Application information: Applications not accepted. Unsolicited requests for funds not accepted.
Officers: Scott A. Velting, Pres.; Kevin Velting, V.P.; Abraham Moerland, Jr., Secy.-Treas.
EIN: 381859282

3929
Venable LLP

750 E. Pratt St., Ste. 900
Baltimore, MD 21202-3157
(410) 244-7400

Company URL: http://www.venable.com/
Company type: Private company
Business activities: Operates law firm.
Business type (SIC): Legal services
Corporate officers: James L. Shea, Chair.; Karl A. Racine, Managing Partner
Offices: Los Angeles, CA; Washington, DC; Baltimore, Rockville, Towson, MD; New York, NY; Tysons Corner, VA
Giving statement: Giving through the Venable LLP Pro Bono Program.

Venable LLP Pro Bono Program

750 E. Pratt St., Ste. 900
Baltimore, MD 21202-3157 (202) 344-4741
E-mail: sarosenthal@venable.com; Additional tel.: (410)244-7400; URL: http://www.venable.com/probono/

Contact: Seth A. Rosenthal, Chair, Pro Bono Committee
Fields of interest: Legal services.
Type of support: Pro bono services - legal.
Application information: A Pro Bono Committee manages the pro bono program.

3930
Vendome Capital LLC

325 Front St., PMB 410
Evanston, WY 82930

Establishment information: Established in 1996.
Company type: Private company
Business activities: Operates holding company.
Business type (SIC): Holding company

Giving statement: Giving through the McKinley Family Foundation.

McKinley Family Foundation

3921 Clay St.
San Francisco, CA 94118-1623

Establishment information: Established in 2000 in CA.
Donors: Vendome Capital, LLC; Thomas G. McKinley; McKinley Revocable Trust; Vincent Worms.
Financial data (yr. ended 12/31/11): Assets, $620,607 (M); expenditures, $139,736; qualifying distributions, $133,789; giving activities include $130,651 for 8 grants (high: $72,320; low: $1,000).
Purpose and activities: The foundation supports organizations involved with education.
Fields of interest: Education.
Geographic limitations: Giving primarily in CA.
Support limitations: No grants to individuals.
Application information: Applications not accepted. Unsolicited requests for funds not accepted.
Trustees: Janet B. McKinley; Sara M. McKinley; Thomas G. McKinley.
EIN: 943381422

3931
Ventas, Inc.

353 N. Clark St., Ste. 3300
Chicago, IL 60654 (877) 483-6827

Company URL: http://www.ventasreit.com/
Establishment information: Established in 1983.
Company type: Public company
Company ticker symbol and exchange: VTR/NYSE
Business activities: Operates healthcare real estate investment trust.
Business type (SIC): Investors/miscellaneous
Financial profile for 2012: Number of employees, 439; assets, $18,980,000,000; sales volume, $2,485,300,000; pre-tax net income, $298,270,000; expenses, $2,205,190,000; liabilities, $9,786,320,000
Fortune 1000 ranking: 2012—807th in revenues, 424th in profits, and 252nd in assets
Corporate officers: Debra A. Cafaro, Chair. and C.E.O.; Raymond J. Lewis, Pres.; Richard A. Schweinhart, Exec. V.P. and C.F.O.; John D. Cobb, Exec. V.P. and C.I.O.; T. Richard Riney, Exec. V.P., C.A.O., and Genl. Counsel; Robert J. Brehl, C.A.O. and Cont.; John K. Hart, Sr. V.P. and C.I.O.
Board of directors: Debra A. Cafaro, Chair.; Douglas Crocker II; Ronald G. Geary; Jay M. Gellert; Richard I. Gilchrist; Matthew J. Lustig; Douglas M. Pasquale; Robert D. Reed; Sheli Z. Rosenberg; Glenn J. Rufrano; James D. Shelton
Office: Louisville, KY
Giving statement: Giving through the Ventas Charitable Foundation, Inc.
Company EIN: 611055020

Ventas Charitable Foundation, Inc.

10350 Ormsby Park Pl., Ste. 300
Louisville, KY 40223

Establishment information: Established in 2005 in KY.
Financial data (yr. ended 12/31/11): Assets, $11,482,668 (M); gifts received, $10,000,000; expenditures, $162,461; qualifying distributions, $155,092; giving activities include $155,092 for 19 grants (high: $50,000; low: $1,000).
Fields of interest: Education; Recreation; Human services.
Support limitations: No grants to individuals.
Application information: Applications not accepted. Contributes only to pre-selected organizations.
Officers and Directors:* Richard A. Schweinhart, Pres.; Kristen M. Benson, Secy.; Brian K. Wood, Treas.
EIN: 203959500

3932
Venture Founders, LLC

12 Wildflower Ln.
Putney, VT 05346-8640 (802) 536-4663

Company URL: http://startupowl.com/
Establishment information: Established in 2006.
Company type: Private company
Business type (SIC): Business services/ miscellaneous
Corporate officer: William Keyser, Owner
Giving statement: Giving through the Venture Founders LLC Contributions Program.

Venture Founders LLC Contributions Program

12 Wildflower Ln.
Putney, VT 05346-8640 (802) 536-4663
E-mail: info@startupowl.com; URL: http://startupowl.com/

Purpose and activities: Venture Founders is a certified B Corporation that donates a percentage of net profits to charitable organizations.

3933
Venturedyne, Ltd.

Prairie Preserve
600 College Ave.
Pewaukee, WI 53072-3572 (262) 691-9900
FAX: (262) 691-9901

Company URL: http://www.venturedyne.com/home/
Establishment information: Established in 1986.
Company type: Private company
Business activities: Manufactures industrial machinery, material handling equipment, and environmental test chambers.
Business type (SIC): Machinery/special industry; machinery/construction, mining, and materials handling; machinery/refrigeration and service industry; laboratory apparatus
Corporate officers: Brian L. Nahey, Chair., Pres., and C.E.O.; Robert E. Smith, C.F.O. and Secy.-Treas.
Board of director: Brian L. Nahey, Chair.
Subsidiaries: Advanced Detection Systems, Milwaukee, WI; Chisholm, Boyd & White Co., Alsip, IL; Climet Instruments Co., Redlands, CA; Dings Dynamics Co., Milwaukee, WI; Dings Magnetic Co., Milwaukee, WI; Scientific Dust Collectors, Milwaukee, WI; Thermotron Industries, Inc., Holland, MI
Giving statement: Giving through the Venturedyne, Ltd. Foundation.

Venturedyne, Ltd. Foundation

(formerly Wehr Corporation Foundation)
600 College Ave.
Pewaukee, WI 53072-3572

Donor: Venturedyne, Ltd.
Contact: Brian L. Nahey, Pres. and Treas.
Financial data (yr. ended 12/31/11): Assets, $74,298 (M); expenditures, $4,300; qualifying distributions, $4,300; giving activities include $4,300 for grants.
Purpose and activities: The foundation supports hospices and organizations involved with higher education, cancer, children and youth services, and Christianity.
Fields of interest: Education.
Type of support: General/operating support; Scholarship funds.
Geographic limitations: Giving primarily in MI and WI.
Support limitations: No grants to individuals.
Application information: Applications accepted. Application form not required.
Initial approach: Proposal
Deadline(s): None
Officers and Directors:* Brian L. Nahey*, Pres. and Treas.; Nicole J. Daniels*, V.P.; Nancy L. Nahey*, Secy.
EIN: 396096050

3934
H. Verby Company, Inc.

18614 Jamaica Ave.
Jamaica, NY 11423-2494 (718) 454-5522

Company URL: http://www.vherby.com
Establishment information: Established in 2003.
Company type: Private company
Business activities: Sells building material products wholesale.
Business type (SIC): Lumber and construction materials—wholesale
Corporate officer: Steve Finburg, C.F.O.
Plants: Hauppauge, Holbrook, NY
Giving statement: Giving through the Stanley M. & Marjorie S. Verby Foundation Inc.

Stanley M. & Marjorie S. Verby Foundation Inc.

218 Albon Rd.
Hewlett Harbor, NY 11557-2635

Donors: H. Verby Co. Inc.; H. Verby Holding Co.; Thermo Realty.
Financial data (yr. ended 10/31/11): Assets, $100,913 (M); expenditures, $26,539; qualifying distributions, $26,000; giving activities include $26,000 for 1 grant.
Purpose and activities: The foundation supports senior centers and organizations involved with higher education and Judaism.
Fields of interest: Higher education; Aging, centers/services; Jewish federated giving programs; Jewish agencies & synagogues.
Type of support: General/operating support.
Geographic limitations: Giving limited to FL and NY.
Support limitations: No grants to individuals.
Application information: Applications not accepted. Unsolicited requests for funds not accepted.
Officers: Stanley H. Verby, Pres.; Marjorie S. Verby, V.P.
EIN: 116010298

3935
Veridyne, Inc.

(formerly Shepard-Patterson and Associates)
370 Reed Rd., Ste. 105
Broomall, PA 19008-4002 (610) 328-7971
FAX: (610) 325-1599

Company URL: http://www.veridyneinc.com
Establishment information: Established in 1986.
Company type: Private company
Business activities: Provides information technology and technical consulting services.
Business type (SIC): Computer services
Corporate officer: Samuel J. Patterson, Pres. and C.E.O.
Giving statement: Giving through the Sam and Deidre Patterson Foundation.

The Sam and Deidre Patterson Foundation

(formerly The Veridyne Private Foundation, Inc.)
c/o Foundation Source
501 Silverside Rd.
Wilmington, DE 19809-1377

Establishment information: Established in 2003 in DE.
Donors: Veridyne, Inc.; Sam Patterson.
Financial data (yr. ended 12/31/11): Assets, $172,123 (M); expenditures, $17,079; qualifying distributions, $9,000; giving activities include $9,000 for grants.
Purpose and activities: The foundation supports fraternities and organizations involved with human services, urban development, and African Americans.
Fields of interest: Human services; Community/economic development; Religion.
Type of support: General/operating support; Program development; Scholarship funds.
Support limitations: No grants to individuals.
Application information: Applications not accepted. Contributes only to pre-selected organizations.
Officers and Director:* Samuel J. Patterson, Pres. and Secy.; Deidre Patterson, V.P.; Anthony Patterson.
EIN: 020709431

3936
Verizon Communications Inc.

(formerly Bell Atlantic Corporation)
140 West St., 29th Fl.
New York, NY 10007 (212) 395-1000

Company URL: http://www22.verizon.com
Establishment information: Established in 1983.
Company type: Public company
Company ticker symbol and exchange: VZ/NYSE
International Securities Identification Number: US92343V1044
Business activities: Provides local and long distance telephone communications services; provides wireless telephone communications services; publishes directories.
Business type (SIC): Telephone communications; publishing/miscellaneous
Financial profile for 2012: Number of employees, 183,400; assets, $225,222,000,000; sales volume, $115,846,000,000; pre-tax net income, $9,897,000,000; expenses, $102,686,000,000; liabilities, $192,065,000,000
Fortune 1000 ranking: 2012—16th in revenues, 223rd in profits, and 23rd in assets
Forbes 2000 ranking: 2012—44th in sales, 673rd in profits, and 122nd in assets
Corporate officers: Lowell C. McAdam, Chair. and C.E.O.; Francis J. Shammo, Exec. V.P. and C.F.O.; Marc C. Reed, Exec. V.P. and C.A.O.; Roger Gurnani, Exec. V.P. and C.I.O.; Randal S. Milch, Exec. V.P. and Genl. Counsel; Thomas J. Tauke, Exec. V.P., Public Affairs and Comms.; William L. Horton, Jr., Sr. V.P. and Corp. Secy.; Matthew D. Ellis, Sr. V.P. and Treas.; Robert J. Barish, Sr. V.P. and Cont.
Board of directors: Lowell C. McAdam, Chair.; Richard L. Carrion; Melanie L. Healey; Martha Frances Keeth; Robert W. Lane; Sandra O. Moose; Joseph Neubauer; Donald T. Nicolaisen; Clarence Otis, Jr.; Hugh B. Price; Rodney Earl Slater; Kathryn A. Tesija; Gregory D. Wasson
Subsidiaries: Cellco Partnership, Basking Ridge, NJ; Verizon Delaware Inc., Wilmington, DE; Verizon Maryland Inc., Baltimore, MD; Verizon New England Inc., Boston, MA; Verizon New Jersey Inc., Newark, NJ; Verizon New York Inc., New York, NY; Verizon Pennsylvania Inc., Philadelphia, PA; Verizon Virginia Inc., Richmond, VA; Verizon Washington, DC Inc., Washington, DC; Verizon West Virginia Inc., Charleston, WV
Historic mergers: NYNEX Corporation (August 15, 1997); MCI, Inc. (January 6, 2006); ALLTEL Corporation (January 9, 2009)
Giving statement: Giving through the Verizon Communications Inc. Pro Bono Assistance Program, the Verizon Foundation, and the Verizon Reads, Inc.
Company EIN: 232259884

Verizon Communications Inc. Pro Bono Assistance Program

1 Verizon Way, VC54N067
Basking Ridge, NJ 07920 (908) 559-5731
E-mail: john.frantz@verizon.com; URL: http://responsibility.verizon.com/community-impact/pro-bono/

Contact: John P. Frantz, V.P. and Assoc. Genl. Counsel
Purpose and activities: As a complement to its foundation, Verizon Communications provides free legal services to nonprofit organizations and individuals in need on a case by case basis. Special emphasis is directed toward programs that support education, victims of domestic violence, and returning veterans. Support is given primarily to current philanthropic partners of Verizon Communications.
Fields of interest: Education; Legal services; Family services, domestic violence Military/veterans.
Type of support: Pro bono services - legal.

Verizon Foundation

(formerly Bell Atlantic Foundation)
1 Verizon Way, VC34W539B
Basking Ridge, NJ 07920-1025
FAX: (908) 630-2660; Contact for Verizon Foundation Progs.: Binta Vann-Joseph, Dir. of Mktg. Strategy, tel.: (908) 559-1300, e-mail: binta.d.vann-joseph@verizon.com; Ellen Yu, Verizon Media Rels., tel.: (908) 559-2818, e-mail: ellen.yu@verizon.com; URL: http://foundation.verizon.com

Establishment information: Established in 1985 in NY.
Donors: NYNEX Corp.; Bell Atlantic Corp.; Verizon Communications Inc.
Financial data (yr. ended 12/31/11): Assets, $144,451,318 (M); gifts received, $853,566; expenditures, $66,315,521; qualifying distributions, $65,847,672; giving activities include $56,282,791 for 23,494 grants (high: $2,459,727; low: $25).
Purpose and activities: The foundation supports programs designed to use technology to solve critical social issues in the areas of education, healthcare, and sustainability.
Fields of interest: Museums (specialized); Arts; Elementary/secondary education; Higher education; Libraries (public); Education, services; Education, reading; Education, e-learning; Education; Environment, energy; Environmental education; Environment; Health care, information services; Public health; Health care; Crime/violence prevention, domestic violence; Crime/law enforcement; Children/youth, services; Family services, parent education; Family services, domestic violence; Community/economic development; Mathematics; Engineering/technology; Computer science; Science; Public affairs Children; Aging; Disabilities, people with; Women; Economically disadvantaged.
Programs:
Disaster Relief Incentive Program (DRIP): The foundation matches contributions made by employees of Verizon to disaster relief organizations for natural disasters including floods, hurricanes, fires, and other extraordinary human disaster events on a one-for-one basis up to $1,000 per employee, per year. This program is activated in times of natural disaster and other events.
Education: The foundation support programs designed to leverage mobile technology, digital content, and teacher training to increase student interest and achievement in science, technology, engineering, and math. Special emphasis in directed toward Verizon Innovative Learning Schools, a free online content and mobile application; Verizon Innovative Learning Community, a free online community; and Thinkfinity, a online resource for lesson plans and educational activities.
Healthcare: The foundation supports programs designed to use technology-based partnerships to address disparities in healthcare and improve quality and access for those affected by chronic disease. Special emphasis is directed toward using technology to connect children to better healthcare; increased access to care and chronic disease management for underserved women; connecting healthcare providers, patients, and caregivers to create care models and enable seniors with chronic disease to "age in place"; and programs designed to provide education, prevention, victim relief and empowerment resources for domestic violence prevention.
Matching Incentive Program (MIP): The foundation matches contributions made by employees and retirees of Verizon to nonprofit organizations involved with arts and culture, education, the environment, health, and human services on a one-for-one basis from $25 to $1,000 per employee, per year and to institutions of higher education from $25 to $5,000 per employee or retiree, per year.
Sustainability: The foundation supports programs designed to foster smart energy practice in communities and universities and build awareness while inspiring good environmental citizens among schools and communities. Special emphasis is toward leveraging technology to promote energy reduction; and foster environmental citizens who can apply their skills and knowledge to take action and promote sustainability.
Team Fundraising Program: The foundation matches funds raised by teams of ten or more eligible employees for nonprofit organizations involved with education, healthcare, and sustainability, up to $10,000 per team, per event.

Thinkfinity: The foundation, in partnership with educational and literacy organizations, provides a free online portal to educational resources for teachers, trainers, and students including standards-based, grade-specific, K-12 lesson plans and other interactive tools. The online portal is designed to improve educational attainment and student achievement through multidisciplinary classroom materials, time-saving searches, and comprehensive professional development resources. Visit URL http://www.thinkfinity.org/welcome for more information.

Verizon Scholarship Program: The foundation annually awards up to 250 four-year $5,000 college scholarships to high school seniors who are children of employees of Verizon. The program is administered by Scholarship America, Inc.

Volunteer Incentive Program (VIP): The foundation awards $750 grants to nonprofit organizations with which employees of Verizon volunteer 50 hours or more.

Type of support: Building/renovation; Curriculum development; Employee matching gifts; Employee volunteer services; Employee-related scholarships; Equipment; General/operating support; Program development; Scholarship funds; Sponsorships; Technical assistance.

Geographic limitations: Giving on a national basis, with emphasis on CA, Washington DC, MN, NJ, and NY.

Support limitations: No support for private charities or foundations, religious organizations not of direct benefit to the entire community, religious organizations duplicating the work of other organizations in the same community, political candidates or organizations, discriminatory organizations, or lobbying organizations. No grants to individuals (except for employee-related scholarships), or for political causes or campaigns, endowments or capital campaigns, film, music, television, video, or media production or broadcast underwriting, research studies (unless related to projects already being supported by Verizon), sports sponsorships, performing arts tours, or association memberships, or field trips for secondary or elementary schools; no product donations.

Publications: Application guidelines; Corporate giving report; Financial statement; Informational brochure (including application guidelines); IRS Form 990 or 990-PF printed copy available upon request; Program policy statement.

Application information: Applications accepted. The average grant ranges from $5,000 to $10,000. Applicants are welcome to contact a Community Relations Manager in their state with questions. Support is limited to 1 contribution per organization during any given year for 3 years in length. Organizations receiving support are asked to submit quarterly reports and a final report. Application form required. Applicants should submit the following:

1) results expected from proposed grant
2) statement of problem project will address
3) population served
4) name, address and phone number of organization
5) brief history of organization and description of its mission
6) geographic area to be served
7) how project's results will be evaluated or measured
8) list of company employees involved with the organization
9) detailed description of project and amount of funding requested
10) copy of current year's organizational budget and/or project budget
11) listing of additional sources and amount of support

Initial approach: Complete online application form
Board meeting date(s): Annually
Deadline(s): Jan. 1 to Oct. 14
Final notification: 90 days

Officers and Directors: Thomas J. Tauke, Vice-Chair. and Secy.; Rose Stuckey Kirk, Pres.; Neil D. Olson, V.P. and Treas.; Michael W. Morrell, V.P. and Cont.; James G. Mullaney, C.I.O.; Lowell C. McAdam; Francis J. Shammo.

Number of staff: 8 full-time professional.

EIN: 133319048

Selected grants: The following grants are a representative sample of this grantmaker's funding activity:

$3,156,724 to Scholarship America, Saint Peter, MN, 2010.
$2,000,000 to World Trade Center Memorial Foundation, New York, NY, 2010.
$665,553 to Urban League, National, New York, NY, 2010.
$600,000 to Pace University, New York, NY, 2010.
$562,000 to Smithsonian Institution, Washington, DC, 2010.
$428,000 to International Reading Association, Newark, DE, 2010.
$271,326 to Food for the Poor, Coconut Creek, FL, 2010.
$10,000 to Advot Project, Los Angeles, CA, 2010.
$10,000 to Ferd and Gladys Alpert Jewish Family and Childrens Service of Palm Beach County, West Palm Beach, FL, 2010.
$4,000 to Frostburg State University Foundation, Frostburg, MD, 2010.

Verizon Reads, Inc.

1 Verizon Way, 3rd Fl.
Basking Ridge, NJ 07920-1025 (908) 559-4457
Toll-free tel.: (877) 483-READS; URL: http://www.verizonreads.net
Additional URL: http://foundation.verizon.com

Establishment information: Established in 1999 in DE.

Contact: Rose M. Kirk, Pres.

Financial data (yr. ended 12/31/11): Revenue, $464,508; assets, $2,485,752 (M); gifts received, $464,240; expenditures, $630,574; giving activities include $630,574 for 87 grants.

Purpose and activities: The organization aims to raise literacy funding, promote community awareness, and support a wide diversity of literacy programs.

Fields of interest: Adult education—literacy, basic skills & GED; Education, reading.

Programs:

Grants Program: Grants are available to elementary and secondary schools (public and private) that are registered with the National Center for Education Statistics, as well as eligible tax-exempt organizations, whose proposals focus on literacy, education, domestic violence prevention, healthcare and accessibility, and Internet safety. Average grant sizes range from $5,000 - $10,000.

Verizon Scholarship Program: Scholarship grants are available to children of Verizon employees who plan to attend four-year colleges and universities. Scholarships are highly competitive and based on financial need, academic performance, and extracurricular leadership activities.

Type of support: Scholarships—to individuals.

Geographic limitations: Giving on a national basis.

Support limitations: No support for organizations lacking 501(c)(3) status, religious organizations, or discriminatory organizations. No grants to individuals, or for endowments, capital campaigns, research studies, or political causes.

Publications: Application guidelines.

Application information: Applications accepted.
Initial approach: Complete online application
Deadline(s): Feb. 1 for Verizon Scholarship Program; Nov. 1 for Grants Program
Final notification: 90 days

Officers: Rose M. Kirk*, Pres.; Robert J. Burden*, V.P., Taxes; Scott L. Cordy*, V.P., Taxes; Janet M. Garrity*, V.P. and Treas.; Carrie C. Hughes*, V.P.; Richard P. Jankun*, V.P., Taxes; Karrie E. Schweikert*, V.P.

EIN: 061558490

3937
Vermeer Manufacturing Company

1210 Vermeer Rd. E.
P.O. Box 200
Pella, IA 50219-7660 (641) 628-3141

Company URL: http://www.vermeer.com

Establishment information: Established in 1948.

Company type: Private company

Business activities: Designs and manufactures underground construction equipment, environmental equipment, and agricultural equipment.

Business type (SIC): Machinery/construction, mining, and materials handling; machinery/farm and garden

Corporate officers: Robert L. Vermeer, Chair. and C.E.O.; Mary Vermeer Andringa, Pres. and C.O.O.; Steve Van Dusseldorp, V.P., Finance and Secy.-Treas.; Vince Newendorp, V.P., Admin

Board of director: Robert L. Vermeer, Chair.

Giving statement: Giving through the Vermeer Charitable Foundation, Inc.

Vermeer Charitable Foundation, Inc.

1210 Vermeer Rd. E.
Pella, IA 50219-7660
E-mail: charitablefoundation@vermeer.com; Application address: P.O. Box 200, Pella, IA 50219; URL: http://www2.vermeer.com/pls/apex/f?p=114:1:3288483616510404

Establishment information: Established in 1977 in IA.

Donors: Vermeer Manufacturing Co.; Vermeer Farms, Inc.

Contact: Lois J. Vermeer, Secy.

Financial data (yr. ended 12/31/11): Assets, $5,787,430 (M); gifts received, $3,209,000; expenditures, $1,135,055; qualifying distributions, $1,113,450; giving activities include $1,113,450 for 152 grants (high: $250,000; low: $100).

Purpose and activities: The foundation supports projects designed to bring honor and praise to God. Special emphasis is directed toward projects designed to promote the quality of life for Vermeer employees and communities; inspire Vermeer employees to use their skills and resources; and utilize Vermeer products and expertise.

Fields of interest: Elementary/secondary education; Higher education; Christian agencies & churches.

Program:

Scholarships: The foundation awards scholarships to children of employees of Vermeer.

Type of support: Building/renovation; Employee-related scholarships; Scholarship funds; Seed money; Sponsorships.

Geographic limitations: Giving primarily in the Pella, IA, area.

Support limitations: No grants to individuals (except for employee-related scholarships), or for endowments; no loans.

Publications: Application guidelines.
Application information: Applications accepted. Additional information may be requested at a later date. Application form required.
Initial approach: E-mail or mail letter of introduction and complete online application form
Copies of proposal: 2
Board meeting date(s): Apr., Oct., and as required
Deadline(s): Apr. and Nov.
Officers and Directors:* Robert Vermeer*, Pres.; Lois J. Vermeer*, Secy.; Mindi Vanden Bosch*, Treas.; Dale J. Andringa; Mary Vermeer Andringa; David Vermeer; Matilda Vermeer; Tricia Vermeer; Allison Van Wyngarden.
Number of staff: 1 part-time professional; 2 part-time support.
EIN: 421087640
Selected grants: The following grants are a representative sample of this grantmaker's funding activity:
$165,000 to Pella Regional Health Center, Pella, IA, 2009.
$150,000 to Central College, Pella, IA, 2009.
$100,000 to Calvin College, Grand Rapids, MI, 2009.
$100,000 to Dordt College, Sioux Center, IA, 2009.
$100,000 to Northwestern College, Orange City, IA, 2009.
$81,000 to Rehoboth Christian School, Rehoboth, NM, 2009.
$70,000 to Fuller Theological Seminary, Pasadena, CA, 2009.
$50,000 to Calvin Theological Seminary, Grand Rapids, MI, 2009.
$20,000 to Ascending Leaders, Sugar Land, TX, 2009.
$13,300 to Crown Broadcasting Company, Pella, IA, 2009.

3938
Vermeer Mid Atlantic, Inc.
10900 Carpet St.
Charlotte, NC 28273 (704) 588-3238

Company URL: http://www.vermeermidatlantic.com
Establishment information: Established in 1985.
Company type: Private company
Business activities: Operates a full-service heavy equipment dealership.
Business type (SIC): Industrial machinery and equipment—wholesale
Corporate officers: David C. Hann, Pres.; Christine A. Vos, Secy.-Treas.
Giving statement: Giving through the John Vos Family Foundation, Inc.

John Vos Family Foundation, Inc.
c/o Katherine A. Grice
14409 Greenview Dr., Ste. 201
Laurel, MD 20708-4240

Establishment information: Established in 2007 in MD.
Donors: John L. Vos; Vermeer Mid Atlantic, Inc.; Christine A. Vos.
Financial data (yr. ended 12/31/11): Assets, $713,005 (M); gifts received, $200,000; expenditures, $37,960; qualifying distributions, $34,500; giving activities include $34,500 for grants.
Fields of interest: Education; Housing/shelter; Human services.
Geographic limitations: Giving primarily in MD.
Support limitations: No grants to individuals.
Application information: Applications not accepted. Unsolicited requests for funds not accepted.
Officers: John L. Vos, Pres.; Robin M. Vos, V.P.; Tricia J. Vos, V.P.; Christine A. Vos, Secy.-Treas.
EIN: 261587229

3939
Vermillion Consulting Inc.
6160 Oakmont Ln.
Gurnee, IL 60031-5352 (847) 548-5737

Company URL: http://www.vermillionconsulting.com
Establishment information: Established in 1995.
Company type: Private company
Business activities: Provides banking and finance consulting services.
Business type (SIC): Management and public relations services
Financial profile for 2010: Number of employees, 500,000
Corporate officer: Dale R. Vermillion, Pres. and C.E.O.
Giving statement: Giving through the Mortgage Professionals Providing Hope Inc.

Mortgage Professionals Providing Hope Inc.
495 Grand Blvd., Ste. 206
Miramar Beach, FL 32550
URL: http://www.mpph.org

Establishment information: Established in 2006 in IL.
Donor: Vermillion Consulting, Inc.
Financial data (yr. ended 12/31/10): Assets, $409 (M); expenditures, $335; qualifying distributions, $0.
Purpose and activities: Giving to provide food, water, shelter, education, medical services and hope for the impoverished children and families of rural India.
Geographic limitations: Giving primarily in India.
Support limitations: No grants to individuals.
Application information: Applications not accepted. Unsolicited requests for funds not accepted.
Officers: Dale Vermillion, Pres.; Laurel A. Vermillion, Secy.; Douglas B. Rowland, Treas.
EIN: 205051856

3940
Vermont Alpine Racing Association
(doing business as VARA)
2167 Main St.
P.O. Box 145
Cavendish, VT 05142 (802) 226-8188

Company URL: http://www.vara.org
Establishment information: Established in 1971.
Company type: Business league
Business activities: Operates hotels and motels.
Business type (SIC): Business services/miscellaneous
Corporate officers: Tao Smith, Pres.; Kirk B. Dwyer, Secy.; Lynne Sullivan, Treas.
Board of directors: Tom Aicher; Marty Bak; Stever Bartlett; Marilyn Cochran Brown; Fred Coriell; Peter Cornish; Abby Copeland; Kirk Dwyer; Lori Furrer; Eric Harlow; Chuck Hughes; Dave Iverson; Adam Julius; Steve Kelley; Peter Mackey; Neal McNealus; Wendy Neal; Tom Parks; Ron Quensel; Chris Reynolds; Tao Smith; Dylan Snell; Lynn Sullivan; Igor Vanovac; Steve Wry
Giving statement: Giving through the VARA Educational Foundation, Inc.

VARA Educational Foundation, Inc.
P.O. Box 82
Cavendish, VT 05142 (802) 226-8188

Establishment information: Established in VT.
Donor: Vermont Alpine Racing Association.
Financial data (yr. ended 07/31/11): Assets, $165,348 (M); gifts received, $18,750; expenditures, $32,990; qualifying distributions, $30,656; giving activities include $30,656 for 34 grants to individuals (high: $2,500; low: $300).
Purpose and activities: Grants awarded to individuals to offset expenses of national skiing contests and coaching.
Fields of interest: Athletics/sports, winter sports.
Type of support: Grants to individuals.
Geographic limitations: Giving limited to residents of VT.
Application information: Applications accepted. Application form required.
Initial approach: See website www.vara.org for application
Deadline(s): Oct. 15
Officers: Thomas Aicher, Pres.; Tao Smith, V.P.; Lori Furrer, Secy.; Lynn Sullivan, Treas.
EIN: 237336991

3941
Vernier Software & Technology LLC
13979 S.W. Millikan Way
Beaverton, OR 97005-2886
(503) 277-2299
FAX: (503) 277-2440

Company URL: http://www.vernier.com
Establishment information: Established in 1981.
Company type: Private company
Business activities: Develops computer software.
Business type (SIC): Computer services
Corporate officers: David L. Vernier, Pres. and C.E.O.; Christine Vernier, C.F.O.
Giving statement: Giving through the Vernier Software & Technology LLC Corporate Giving Program.

Vernier Software & Technology LLC Corporate Giving Program
13979 S.W. Millikan Way
Beaverton, OR 97005-2886
URL: http://www.vernier.com/company/philanthropy/

Purpose and activities: Vernier awards grants to K-12 science teachers and college instructors. Support is given primarily in Oregon.
Fields of interest: Education; Science; Engineering/technology.
Programs:
Employee Matching Gift Program: Vernier matches contributions made by its employees to nonprofit organizations on a one-for-one basis up to $1,000 per employee, per year.
Vernier/NSTA Technology Awards: Through the Vernier/NSTA Technology Awards program, Vernier annually awards seven $3,000 grants to K-12 and

college science instructors recognized for the innovative use of data-collection technology using a computer, graphing calculator, or other handheld in the science classroom. Each grant consists of $1,000 in cash, $1,000 in Vernier products, and $1,000 toward expenses to attend the National Science Teachers Association (NSTA) national convention. One grant is awarded to an elementary school instructor, two grants are awarded to middle school instructors, three grants are awarded to high school instructors, and one grant is awarded to a college instructor.
Type of support: Employee matching gifts; Employee volunteer services; General/operating support; Grants to individuals.
Geographic limitations: Giving primarily in OR.
Application information: Applications accepted. Application form required.
Initial approach: Visit website for Vernier Technology Awards application information
Deadline(s): Nov. 30 for Vernier Technology Awards

3942
Vesco Oil Corporation

(also known as Vesco Industrial Lubricants)
16055 W. 12 Mile Rd.
P.O. Box 525
Southfield, MI 48076 (248) 557-1600

Company URL: http://www.vesco-oil.com
Establishment information: Established in 1947.
Company type: Private company
Business activities: Distributes wholesale brand lubricants and provides bulk and hazardous waste management.
Business type (SIC): Fuel dealers—retail
Corporate officers: Donald R. Epstein, Pres. and C.E.O.; Cheryl Reitzloff, C.F.O.; Carol Pajak, Cont.
Giving statement: Giving through the Marjory and Donald Epstein Family Charitable Foundation.

Marjory and Donald Epstein Family Charitable Foundation

16055 W. 12 Mile Rd.
Southfield, MI 48076-2909

Establishment information: Established in 1997 in MI.
Donor: Vesco Oil Corp.
Financial data (yr. ended 12/31/11): Assets, $516,168 (M); gifts received, $60,000; expenditures, $19,410; qualifying distributions, $19,410; giving activities include $19,410 for 5 grants (high: $5,000; low: $1,000).
Purpose and activities: The foundation supports organizations involved with theater, elementary education, Epilepsy, family services, and Judaism.
Fields of interest: Arts; Religion.
Type of support: General/operating support.
Geographic limitations: Giving primarily in MI.
Support limitations: No grants to individuals.
Application information: Applications not accepted. Unsolicited requests for funds not accepted.
Directors: Donald R. Epstein; Lillian J. Epstein; Marjory Epstein.
EIN: 383350806

3943
Vestcor Equities, Inc.

3020 Hartley Rd., Ste. 300
Jacksonville, FL 32257-8207
(904) 260-3030

Company URL: http://www.vestcor.com
Establishment information: Established in 1983.
Company type: Private company
Business activities: Operates real-estate development company.
Business type (SIC): Real estate subdividers and developers
Corporate officers: John Darrell Rood, Chair.; Mark T. Farrell, Pres. and Secy.; C. Stephens Moore, V.P. and C.F.O.
Board of director: John Darrell Rood, Chair.
Giving statement: Giving through the Vestcor Family Foundation, Inc.

The Vestcor Family Foundation, Inc.

3020 Hartley Rd., Ste. 300
Jacksonville, FL 32257

Establishment information: Established in FL.
Donor: The Vestcor Companies.
Financial data (yr. ended 12/31/11): Assets, $8,083 (M); gifts received, $22,562; expenditures, $26,664; qualifying distributions, $21,350; giving activities include $21,350 for 8 grants (high: $10,000; low: $100).
Purpose and activities: Giving primarily for the benefit of disadvantaged and needy persons in the northeast Florida area and in the Bahamas, through the distribution of funds to public charities, and through the administration of various initiatives that focus on literacy, tutoring, self-esteem building, career development, scholarship funding, vocational training, family self-sufficiency, and disaster relief.
Fields of interest: Education; Health care.
Support limitations: No grants to individuals.
Application information: Applications not accepted. Contributes only to pre-selected organizations.
Officer: William L. Morgan, Pres.
Directors: Jaime A. Rodd; Kim A. Taylor.
EIN: 651197315

3944
VHA Inc.

(also known as Very Healthy America)
220 Las Colinas Blvd. E.
P.O. Box 140909
Irving, TX 75039-5503 (972) 830-0626

Company URL: http://www.vha.com
Establishment information: Established in 1977.
Company type: Private company
Business activities: Provides health care management consulting services.
Business type (SIC): Management and public relations services
Corporate officers: Joseph A. Zaccagnino, Chair.; Peter Csapo, Pres. and C.E.O.; Scott Downing, Exec. V.P., Sales; Colleen Risk, Exec. V.P., Human Resources
Board of directors: Joseph A. Zaccagnino, Chair.; Jeffrey W. Bolton; Marna Borgstrom; Julian L. Carr; Gary Duncan; Patrick Fry; Bobbie Gerhart; John B. Grotting; Russell D. Harrington, Jr.; Jeffrey H. Hillebrand; Steven P. Johnson; John F. Koster; Kelby Krabbenhoft; Gerald Miller; Jerry K. Myers; Curt Nonomaque; Alfred G. Stubblefield; Penny Wheeler; Gary R. Yates
Subsidiaries: HPPI LLC, Irving, TX; Novation LLC, Irving, TX; Solucients Inc., Bellevue, WA; VHA Central Atlantic Inc., Charlotte, NC; VHA Metro Inc., Armonk, NY; VHA Mountain States, LLC, Denver, CO; VHA Oklahoma Arkansas LLC, Oklahoma City, OK; VHA Upper Midwest Inc., Minneapolis, MN; VHA West Coast Inc., Pleasanton, CA
Giving statement: Giving through the VHA Foundation, Inc.

VHA Foundation, Inc.

(formerly The VHA Health Foundation, Inc.)
220 E. Las Colinas Blvd.
Irving, TX 75039-5500
FAX: (972) 830-0332;
E-mail: vhahealthfoundation@vha.com

Donors: VHA Inc.; VHA Gulf States; Blessing Hospital Foundation; Parrish Meducal Center; VHA Southeast; Aspirus Wausau Hospital; Carolina East Medical Center; Center Care Health; Cox Health; Doblin Group, Inc.; Fairmont Olympic Hotel; FMOL Health System; Grand View Hospital; Health East Care Bethesda Hospital; Karla Strange; Marion General Hospital; Maritan Memorial Hospital; Stormont-Vail Foundation; The Queen's Medical; University Hospital od Eastern Carolina; Yale New Haven Health.
Financial data (yr. ended 12/31/11): Assets, $883,557 (M); gifts received, $557,394; expenditures, $1,782,742; qualifying distributions, $1,750,250; giving activities include $1,734,183 for 47 grants (high: $264,000; low: $250).
Purpose and activities: The foundation supports programs designed to improve individual and community health. Special emphasis is directed toward programs designed to promote patient safety and provide disaster relief.
Fields of interest: Hospitals (general); Health care, clinics/centers; Public health; Health care, patient services; Health care; Disasters, preparedness/services; American Red Cross.
Type of support: General/operating support; Grants to individuals; Program development.
Geographic limitations: Giving on a national basis.
Publications: Financial statement; Grants list.
Application information: Applications not accepted. Contributes only to pre-selected organizations.
Board meeting date(s): Feb. 19, Apr. 15, Oct. 16, and Dec. 11
Officers: Curt Nonomaque, Chair.; Michael J. Regier, Secy.; Franco Dooley, Treas.
Director: Colleen M. Risk*.
Number of staff: 1 full-time professional; 1 part-time professional.
EIN: 222710552
Selected grants: The following grants are a representative sample of this grantmaker's funding activity:
$56,750 to MeritCare Health System, Fargo, ND, 2009.
$4,000 to Lawrence General Hospital, Lawrence, MA, 2009.

3945
Viacom Inc.

1515 Broadway
New York, NY 10036 (212) 258-6000
FAX: (302) 636-5454

Company URL: http://www.viacom.com
Establishment information: Established in 1971.
Company type: Public company
Company ticker symbol and exchange: VIA/NASDAQ

Business activities: Provides cable television services; provides Internet entertainment services; produces motion pictures; licenses music.
Business type (SIC): Cable and other pay television services; investors/miscellaneous; computer services; motion pictures/production and services allied to
Financial profile for 2012: Number of employees, 9,880; assets, $22,250,000,000; sales volume, $13,887,000,000; pre-tax net income, $3,470,000,000; expenses, $10,007,000,000; liabilities, $14,802,000,000
Forbes 2000 ranking: 2012—737th in sales, 271st in profits, and 923rd in assets
Corporate officers: Sumner M. Redstone, Chair. and Founder; Shari E. Redstone, Vice-Chair.; Philippe P. Dauman, Pres. and C.E.O.; Thomas E. Dooley, C.O.O.; Wade Davis, Exec. V.P. and C.F.O.; Michael D. Fricklas, Exec. V.P., Genl. Counsel, and Secy.; Scott M. Mills, Exec. V.P., Human Resources and Admin.; Carl D. Folta, Exec. V.P., Corp. Comms
Board of directors: Sumner M. Redstone, Chair.; Shari E. Redstone, Vice-Chair.; George S. Abrams; Philippe P. Dauman; Thomas E. Dooley; Alan C. Greenberg; Robert K. Kraft; Blythe J. McGarvie; Charles E. Phillips, Jr.; Frederic V. Salerno; William Schwartz
Subsidiaries: BET Holdings LLC, Washington, DC; Famous Music LLC, New York, NY; MTV Networks Company, New York, NY; Paramount Pictures Corp., Los Angeles, CA; Viacom Consumer Products Inc., Los Angeles, CA; Viacom International Inc., New York, NY
International operations: Argentina; Australia; Bahamas; Belgium; Bermuda; Brazil; Canada; Cayman Islands; Denmark; Finland; France; Germany; Hong Kong; Hungary; India; Italy; Japan; Malaysia; Mauritius; Mexico; Netherlands; Netherlands Antilles; New Zealand; Nigeria; Norway; Philippines; Poland; Portugal; Singapore; South Africa; South Korea; Spain; Sweden; Switzerland; United Kingdom
Giving statement: Giving through the Viacom, Inc. Contributions Program.
Company EIN: 203515052

Viacom, Inc. Contributions Program

1515 Broadway
New York, NY 10036 (212) 258-6000
URL: http://www.viacommunity.com/

3946
Viad Corp

(formerly The Dial Corp)
1850 N. Central Ave., Ste. 1900
Phoenix, AZ 85004-4545 (602) 207-1000
FAX: (302) 655-5049

Company URL: http://www.viad.com
Establishment information: Established in 1914.
Company type: Public company
Company ticker symbol and exchange: VVI/NYSE
Business activities: Provides money order issuance services; provides trade show arrangement services.
Business type (SIC): Business services/ miscellaneous; depository banking/functions related to
Financial profile for 2012: Number of employees, 3,930; assets, $650,580,000; sales volume, $1,025,230,000; pre-tax net income, $26,800,000; expenses, $998,430,000; liabilities, $262,520,000
Corporate officers: Paul B. Dykstra, Chair., Pres., and C.E.O.; Ellen M. Ingersoll, C.F.O.; G. Michael Latta, C.A.O. and Cont.; George N. Hines, C.I.O.; Deborah J. DePaoli, Genl. Counsel and Secy.
Board of directors: Paul B. Dykstra, Chair.; Wayne G. Allcott; Daniel Boggan, Jr.; Isabella Cunningham, Ph.D.; Richard H. Dozer; Jess T. Hay; Robert C. Krueger; Robert E. Munzenrider; Margaret E. Pederson; Albert M. Teplin
Subsidiaries: GES Exposition Services, Inc., Las Vegas, NV; Glacier Park, Inc., Phoenix, AZ
Division: Exhibitgroup/Giltspur Div., Roselle, IL
International operations: Canada; Germany; United Kingdom
Giving statement: Giving through the Viad Corp Contributions Program and the Viad Corp Fund.
Company EIN: 361169950

The Viad Corp Fund

(formerly The Dial Corp Fund)
1850 N. Central Ave., Ste. 800
Phoenix, AZ 85004-4545

Establishment information: Established in 1987 in AZ.
Donors: The Dial Corp; Viad Corp.
Financial data (yr. ended 12/31/11): Assets, $407 (M); expenditures, $0; qualifying distributions, $0.
Purpose and activities: The fund supports organizations involved with health and human services.
Application information: Applications not accepted. Unsolicited requests for funds not accepted.
Officers: David C. Roberston, Pres.; Ellen M. Ingersoll, V.P.; Scott E. Sayre, Secy.
EIN: 742499884

3947
The Vianova Group, LLC

P.O. Box 3788
San Diego, CA 92163-1788
(619) 446-6780
FAX: ((619) 793-4837

Company URL: http://www.thevianovagroup.com
Establishment information: Established in 2005.
Company type: Private company
Business type (SIC): Business services/ miscellaneous
Corporate officer: Frank G. Scarpaci, Pres.
Giving statement: Giving through the Vianova Group, LLC Contributions Program.

The Vianova Group, LLC Contributions Program

P. O. Box 3788
San Diego, CA 92163-1788 (619) 446-6780
E-mail: info@thevianovagroup.com; URL: http://thevianovagroup.com/about/mission-values/

Purpose and activities: The Vianova Group is a certified B Corporation that donates a percentage of profits to charitable organizations.

3948
Victaulic Co.

4901 Kesslersville Rd.
P.O. Box 31
Easton, PA 18044-0031 (610) 559-3300

Company URL: http://www.victaulic.com
Establishment information: Established in 1925.
Company type: Private company
Business activities: Develops and manufactures mechanical pipe joining systems.
Business type (SIC): Metal products/fabricated
Corporate officers: John F. Malloy, Chair., Pres., and C.E.O.; Joe Savage, Exec. V.P. and C.F.O.
Board of director: John F. Malloy, Chair.
Subsidiaries: Aquamine, LLC, Bristol, TN; Coastline Plastics L.L.C., Yulee, FL; Victaulic Depend-O-Lok, Inc., Doraville, GA; Victaulic Fire Safety Co. LLC, Easton, PA; Victaulic Intl., Easton, PA; Victaulic Tool Co., Easton, PA
International operations: Belgium; Canada; United Arab Emirates
Giving statement: Giving through the Frederick H. Bedford, Jr. and Margaret S. Bedford Charitable Foundation.

Frederick H. Bedford, Jr. and Margaret S. Bedford Charitable Foundation

c/o Victaulic Co.
4901 Kesslersville Rd.
Easton, PA 18040-6714

Establishment information: Established in 1989 in DE.
Donor: Victaulic Co.
Financial data (yr. ended 09/30/11): Assets, $4,644,245 (M); gifts received, $400,000; expenditures, $323,299; qualifying distributions, $321,599; giving activities include $321,599 for grants.
Purpose and activities: The foundation supports organizations involved with performing arts, education, the environment, health, human services, children, and women.
Fields of interest: Performing arts, theater; Elementary/secondary education; Higher education; Education; Hospitals (general); Health care; Children/youth, services; Residential/custodial care; United Ways and Federated Giving Programs.
Type of support: General/operating support.
Geographic limitations: Giving on primarily in NC, NJ, NY, TX, with an emphasis on PA.
Support limitations: No grants to individuals.
Application information: Applications not accepted. Contributes only to pre-selected organizations.
Officers: John F. Malloy, Pres.; Pierre D'Arenberg*, V.P.; Pat Fisher, Secy.; Muffie B. Murray, Treas.
EIN: 133544702
Selected grants: The following grants are a representative sample of this grantmaker's funding activity:
$133,168 to United Way of the Greater Lehigh Valley, Bethlehem, PA, 2011. For general charitable contribution.
$35,000 to New York-Presbyterian Hospital, New York, NY, 2011. For general charitable contribution.
$5,000 to Childrens Home of Easton, Easton, PA, 2011. For general charitable contribution.
$5,000 to Lafayette College, Easton, PA, 2011. For general charitable contribution.
$5,000 to Memorial Sloan-Kettering Cancer Center, New York, NY, 2011. For general charitable contribution.
$5,000 to Saint Baldricks Foundation, Monrovia, CA, 2011.

$5,000 to Suffolk University, Boston, MA, 2011. For general charitable contribution.
$2,500 to American Society for the Prevention of Cruelty to Animals, New York, NY, 2011. For general charitable contribution.
$2,500 to ProJeCt of Easton, Easton, PA, 2011. For general charitable contribution.
$2,500 to State Theater Center for the Arts, Easton, PA, 2011. For general charitable contribution.

3949
Victor Envelope Company

301 Arthur Ct.
Bensenville, IL 60106-3381
(630) 616-2750
FAX: (630) 616-9371

Company URL: http://www.victorenvelope.com
Establishment information: Established in 1959.
Company type: Private company
Business activities: Manufactures and prints envelopes.
Business type (SIC): Paper and paperboard/coated, converted, and laminated
Corporate officers: Ken Seroka, C.E.O.; Kent Dahlgren, Co-Pres.; Richard Eckaus, Co-Pres.; Ken Gundalch, Co-Pres. and V.P.; Mary Lynn Leland, Cont.
Giving statement: Giving through the Burgess Family Foundation, Inc.

The Burgess Family Foundation, Inc.

(formerly The Victor Foundation, Inc.)
c/o Griffith & Jacobson
55 W. Monroe St., Ste. 3550
Chicago, IL 60603-5020 (312) 803-5940

Establishment information: Established in 1996 in IL.
Donor: Victor Envelope Co., Inc.
Contact: Suzanne C. Burgess, Secy.-Treas.
Financial data (yr. ended 06/30/12): Assets, $339,292 (M); expenditures, $26,850; qualifying distributions, $20,000; giving activities include $20,000 for 5 grants (high: $5,000; low: $1,000).
Purpose and activities: The foundation supports organizations involved with television, education, autism, hunger, and voluntarism.
Fields of interest: Education; Health organizations; Human services.
Type of support: General/operating support; Scholarship funds.
Geographic limitations: Giving primarily in IL.
Support limitations: No grants to individuals.
Application information: Applications accepted. Application form required. Applicants should submit the following:
1) detailed description of project and amount of funding requested
Initial approach: Letter
Copies of proposal: 1
Deadline(s): None
Officers: Kirk Burgess, Pres.; Suzanne C. Burgess, Secy.-Treas.
Director: Lou Rascia.
EIN: 364118705

3950
Victorinox Swiss Army, Inc.

(formerly Swiss Army Brands, Inc.)
1 Research Dr.
P.O. Box 874
Shelton, CT 06484-0874 (203) 929-6391

Company URL: http://www.victorinox.com
Establishment information: Established in 1884.
Company type: Subsidiary of a foreign company
Business activities: Markets and sells cutlery, sunglasses, and watches.
Business type (SIC): Hardware, plumbing, and heating equipment—wholesale; durable goods—wholesale
Financial profile for 2010: Number of employees, 168
Corporate officers: Carl Elsener, C.E.O.; Patrick Cooper, V.P., Sales
Giving statement: Giving through the Victorinox—Swiss Army Knife Foundation.

Victorinox—Swiss Army Knife Foundation

445 Park Ave., 9th Fl.
New York, NY 10022-4108

Establishment information: Established in 1993 in NY.
Donors: The Forschner Group, Inc.; Swiss Army Brands, Inc.; Victorinox Cutlery Co.; Louis Marx, Jr.; Brae Group, Inc.; Victorinox AG; Brae Capital Corp.; Victorinox Swiss Army, Inc.
Financial data (yr. ended 12/31/11): Assets, $508,329 (M); gifts received, $550,000; expenditures, $83,351; qualifying distributions, $81,257; giving activities include $81,257 for 4 grants (high: $50,000; low: $1,257).
Purpose and activities: The foundation supports organizations involved with music, education, health, cancer research, tennis, and youth services.
Fields of interest: Education; Health care; Human services.
Type of support: Building/renovation; General/operating support; Program development; Research.
Geographic limitations: Giving primarily in NY.
Support limitations: No grants to individuals.
Application information: Applications not accepted. Unsolicited requests for funds not accepted.
Directors: John Bradford Barnes; Thomas R. Chudy; Louis Marx, Jr.
EIN: 133692303

3951
Viejas Enterprises

5000 Willows Rd., Ste. 229
Alpine, CA 91901-1656 (619) 569-5400

Company URL: http://www.viejasbandofkumeyaay.org/
Establishment information: Established in 1991.
Company type: Tribal corporation
Business activities: Operates casino, shopping center, and bank.
Business type (SIC): Amusement and recreation services/miscellaneous
Corporate officers: Lyn Baxter, C.E.O.; Holly O'Brien, V.P., Mktg.; Laura Brown, V.P., Human Resources
Giving statement: Giving through the Viejas Enterprises Corporate Giving Program.

Viejas Enterprises Corporate Giving Program

c/o Viejas Band of Kumeyaay Indians
5000 Willows Rd.
Alpine, CA 91901-1656 (619) 659-5400
FAX: (619) 659-5401;
E-mail: community@viejas.com; URL: http://www.viejasbandofkumeyaay.org/html/community_support/community_support.html

Purpose and activities: Viejas Enterprises makes charitable contributions to nonprofit organizations involved with diversity, the environment, youth and seniors, education, and cultural preservation.
Fields of interest: Arts, cultural/ethnic awareness; Education; Substance abuse, services; Crime/law enforcement; Youth, services; Aging, centers/services; Human services; Community/economic development Native Americans/American Indians; Military/veterans.
Type of support: Program development; Sponsorships.
Geographic limitations: Giving on a national basis in areas of company operations.
Support limitations: No support for private foundations, discriminatory organizations, sectarian or denominational religious organizations not of direct benefit to the entire community, government entities (other than schools), or organizations that re-grant to other groups or causes. No grants to individuals, or for tuition, general operating expenses, travel, loans or loan guarantees, debt reduction, or liquidation.
Publications: Application guidelines.
Application information: Applications accepted. Proposals must be on official organization letterhead or personal stationary, sent to the attention of the V.P. of Community and Public Rels.
Initial approach: Mail, fax, or e-mail proposal to headquarters
Deadline(s): 60 days prior to need

3952
ViewSonic Corporation

381 Brea Canyon Rd.
Walnut, CA 91789-0708 (909) 444-8888

Company URL: http://www.viewsonic.com
Establishment information: Established in 1987.
Company type: Private company
Business activities: Manufactures computer monitors, flat panel displays, and projectors.
Business type (SIC): Computer and office equipment; photographic equipment and supplies
Corporate officers: James Chu, Chair. and C.E.O.; Jeff Volpe, Pres.; Sung Yi, C.F.O.
Board of director: James Chu, Chair.
International operations: Canada; China; Denmark; Finland; France; Germany; Italy; Japan; Norway; Singapore; Spain; Sweden; Taiwan; United Kingdom
Giving statement: Giving through the ViewSonic Corporation Contributions Program.
Company EIN: 954120606

ViewSonic Corporation Contributions Program

381 Brea Canyon Rd.
Walnut, CA 91789-3060 (909) 444-8800
Additional tel. for corp. office: (877) 247-3748.; URL: http://www.viewsonic.com/us/company/community

Purpose and activities: ViewSonic makes charitable contributions to nonprofit organizations involved

with adoption and family services, gifts for underprivileged children and children with medical conditions, and cultural festivals. Support is given in areas of company operations.
Fields of interest: Arts; Recreation, fairs/festivals; Athletics/sports, water sports; Children, adoption; Children, services; Family services; Human services, gift distribution.
Type of support: General/operating support; Sponsorships.
Geographic limitations: Giving primarily in areas of company operations, with emphasis on CA.

3953
G&K Vijuk Intern, Corp.

(formerly Vijuk Equipment, Inc.)
715 N. Church Rd.
Elmhurst, IL 60126-1415 (630) 530-2203

Company URL: http://www.vijukequip.com
Establishment information: Established in 1967.
Company type: Private company
Business activities: Manufactures binding equipment.
Business type (SIC): Machinery/special industry
Corporate officers: Stephen Remke, Pres.; Luis B. Campos, V.P., Sales
Giving statement: Giving through the Joseph & Drenda Vijuk Foundation.

Joseph & Drenda Vijuk Foundation

c/o Vijuk Equipment, Inc.
6 Cascade Ct. W.
Burr Ridge, IL 60527

Establishment information: Established in 2000 in IL.
Donors: Vijuk Equipment, Inc.; Joseph M. Vijuk; Drenda Vijuk.
Financial data (yr. ended 03/31/12): Assets, $1,233,622 (M); gifts received, $503,535; expenditures, $264,086; qualifying distributions, $260,500; giving activities include $260,500 for 6 grants (high: $250,000; low: $1,000).
Purpose and activities: The foundation supports organizations involved with higher education, leukemia research, and human services.
Fields of interest: Higher education; Cancer, leukemia research; Boys & girls clubs; YM/YWCAs & YM/YWHAs; Aging, centers/services; Human services.
Type of support: General/operating support; Scholarship funds.
Geographic limitations: Giving primarily in FL, IL, and Ontario, Canada.
Support limitations: No grants to individuals (except for scholarships).
Application information: Applications not accepted. Contributes only to pre-selected organizations.
Directors: Angie B. Rottinger; Drenda Vijuk; Joseph M. Vijuk.
EIN: 364390632

3954
Village Automotive Group Inc.

700 Providence Hwy.
Norwood, MA 02062 (781) 762-5900

Company URL: http://villageautomotive.com
Establishment information: Established in 1963.
Company type: Private company
Business activities: Operates dealerships.
Business type (SIC): Motor vehicles—retail
Corporate officer: Raymond J. Ciccolo, Pres.
Giving statement: Giving through the Ciccolo Family Foundation, Inc.

Ciccolo Family Foundation, Inc.

75 N. Beacon St.
Boston, MA 02134-1912 (617) 560-1700

Establishment information: Established in MA.
Donors: Cadillac Village; Honda Village; Charles River Saab; Saab City of Framingham; Volvo Village; Nissan Village; Village Motors South.
Contact: Raymond J. Ciccolo, Pres.
Financial data (yr. ended 12/31/11): Assets, $87,636 (M); gifts received, $19,757; expenditures, $93,256; qualifying distributions, $92,732; giving activities include $92,732 for grants.
Fields of interest: Arts; Education; Human services.
Support limitations: No grants to individuals.
Application information: Applications accepted. Application form required. Applicants should submit the following:
1) copy of IRS Determination Letter
2) detailed description of project and amount of funding requested
Initial approach: Letter
Deadline(s): None
Officers and Trustees:* Raymond J. Ciccolo*, Pres. and Treas.; Peter E. Mullane*, Clerk.
EIN: 222975713

3955
Maurice Villency, Inc.

200 Robbins Ln., Ste. D
Jericho, NY 11753 (516) 653-2210

Establishment information: Established in 1932.
Company type: Private company
Business activities: Operates home furnishing stores.
Business type (SIC): Furniture and home furnishing stores
Corporate officers: Robert D. Villency, Chair. and C.E.O.; John Lombardi, Sr. V.P., Opers.
Board of director: Robert D. Villency, Chair.
Giving statement: Giving through the Maurice Villency Foundation.

Maurice Villency Foundation

200 Robbins Ln.
Jericho, NY 11753-2265

Establishment information: Established in 1988 in NY.
Donors: Maurice Villency, Inc.; Robert Villency; The David Everett Foundation; The Kids Fund.
Financial data (yr. ended 05/31/09): Assets, $17 (M); gifts received, $200; expenditures, $230; qualifying distributions, $230.
Purpose and activities: The foundation awards grants to needy individuals.
Type of support: Grants to individuals.
Geographic limitations: Giving primarily NY.
Application information: Applications not accepted. Unsolicited requests for funds not accepted.
Directors: Stuart Kessler; Robert Villency.
EIN: 133487733

3956
Vilter Manufacturing Corporation

(also known as Vilter Manufacturing, LLC)
5555 S. Packard Ave.
Cudahy, WI 53110 (414) 744-0111

Company URL: http://www.emersonclimate.com/
Establishment information: Established in 1867.
Company type: Subsidiary of a public company
Business activities: Manufactures industrial refrigeration, heat exchange, and air conditioning equipment.
Business type (SIC): Machinery/refrigeration and service industry
Corporate officers: Ronald F. Prebish, Pres., C.E.O., and C.O.O.; Gloria Spudowski, C.F.O.; Richard Cundy, V.P. and C.F.O.; Mark T. Stencel, V.P., Mktg. and Sales.; John Barry, V.P., Opers.
Subsidiaries: Filbert Corp., Altamonte Springs, FL; Filbert Corp. (Main Office), Miami, FL; Gebhardt Industrial Refrigeration, Inc., Milwaukee, WI; Vilter Export Corp., Milwaukee, WI
Giving statement: Giving through the Vilter Foundation Inc.

Vilter Foundation Inc.

5555 S. Packard Ave.
Cudahy, WI 53110-2623 (414) 744-0111

Establishment information: Incorporated in 1961 in WI.
Donor: Vilter Manufacturing Corp.
Contact: John Csepella, Secy.-Treas.
Financial data (yr. ended 07/31/12): Assets, $3,028,636 (M); expenditures, $185,167; qualifying distributions, $145,880; giving activities include $117,380 for 82 grants (high: $3,100; low: $500).
Purpose and activities: The foundation supports organizations involved with arts and culture, education, animals, health, hunger, and human services. Special emphasis is directed toward programs designed to promote education and research relating to the refrigeration and air conditioning industry.
Fields of interest: Arts; Education; Health care.
Type of support: General/operating support; Program development; Scholarship funds.
Geographic limitations: Giving primarily in Milwaukee, WI.
Support limitations: No grants to individuals.
Application information: Applications accepted. Application form not required.
Initial approach: Proposal
Deadline(s): None
Officer: J.D. Csepella, Secy.-Treas.
Director: G.F. Reinders.
EIN: 390678640

3957
Vinson & Elkins L.L.P.

First City Tower
1001 Fannin St., Ste. 2500
Houston, TX 77002-6760 (713) 758-2222

Company URL: http://www.vinson-elkins.com/home.aspx
Establishment information: Established in 1917.
Company type: Private company
Business activities: Provide legal services.
Business type (SIC): Legal services
Corporate officer: Timothy W. Armstrong, C.F.O.

Offices: Washington, DC; Austin, Dallas, TX
Giving statement: Giving through the Vinson & Elkins L.L.P. Scholarship Foundation.

Vinson & Elkins L.L.P. Scholarship Foundation

1001 Fannin St., Ste. 2500
Houston, TX 77002-6760 (713) 758-2222
E-mail: jtran@velaw.com; URL: http://www.vinson-elkins.com/overview/scholarships.aspx?id=476

Establishment information: Established in 1994 in TX.
Donor: Vinson & Elkins L.L.P.
Contact: Julie Tran
Financial data (yr. ended 12/31/11): Assets, $1,249 (M); gifts received, $73,518; expenditures, $74,769; qualifying distributions, $74,769; giving activities include $74,769 for 20 grants to individuals (high: $3,795; low: $2,500).
Purpose and activities: The foundation awards college scholarships to high school students who are African-American, Hispanic, Native Americans, or Pacific Islanders from low income families in Austin, Dallas, and Houston, Texas who are interested in pursuing a career in law.
Fields of interest: Asians/Pacific Islanders; African Americans/Blacks; Hispanics/Latinos; Native Americans/American Indians.
Type of support: Scholarships—to individuals.
Geographic limitations: Giving limited to Austin, Dallas, and Houston, TX.
Publications: Application guidelines.
Application information: Applications accepted. Application form required.
Requests should include an essay, high school transcripts, 2 letters of recommendation, a photograph, and copies of applications for financial aid.
Initial approach: Download application form and mail to foundation
Deadline(s): Apr. 1
Officer: Ellyn Josef, Secy.
Directors: Roxanne T. Almaraz; Timothy W. Armstrong; Josiah M. Daniel III; Mark Early; Gilian A. Hobson; Milam Foster Newby; James A. Reeder, Jr.; Mark R. Spradling.
EIN: 760428361

3958
Vinson & Elkins LLP

1001 Fannin St., Ste. 2500
Houston, TX 77002-6760 (713) 758-2222

Company URL: http://www.velaw.com/
Establishment information: Established in 1917.
Company type: Private company
Business activities: Operates law firm.
Business type (SIC): Legal services
Offices: Palo Alto, CA; Washington, DC; New York, NY; Austin, Dallas, Houston, TX
International operations: China; Hong Kong; Japan; Saudi Arabia; Soviet Union (Former); United Arab Emirates; United Kingdom
Giving statement: Giving through the Vinson & Elkins LLP Pro Bono Program.

Vinson & Elkins LLP Pro Bono Program

1001 Fannin St., Ste. 2500
Houston, TX 77002-6760 (713) 758-2091
E-mail: ejosef@velaw.com; Additional tel.:(713) 758-2222; URL: http://www.velaw.com/overview/overview.aspx?id=34

Contact: Ellyn Josef, Pro Bono Counsel
Fields of interest: Legal services.
Type of support: Pro bono services - legal.
Application information: A Pro Bono Committee manages the pro bono program.

3959
Virginia Scrap Iron & Metal Co., Inc.

1620 S. Jefferson St.
P.O. Box 8278
Roanoke, VA 24016-4908 (540) 343-3667

Establishment information: Established in 1935.
Company type: Private company
Business activities: Sells scrap metal wholesale.
Business type (SIC): Durable goods—wholesale
Corporate officer: Mary Ann Ward, Pres.
Giving statement: Giving through the Sam and Marion Golden Helping Hand Foundation, Inc.

The Sam and Marion Golden Helping Hand Foundation, Inc.

(formerly Virginia Scrap Iron & Metal Co. Charitable Foundation, Inc.)
P.O. Box 8278
Roanoke, VA 24014-0278 (540) 343-3667

Donors: Virginia Scrap Iron & Metal Co., Inc.; Industrial & Mill Suppliers, Inc.; Robin Wohlleban; Samuel Golden.
Contact: Mary Ann Ward, Pres.
Financial data (yr. ended 12/31/11): Assets, $14,258,812 (M); gifts received, $94,710; expenditures, $598,404; qualifying distributions, $492,000; giving activities include $492,000 for grants.
Purpose and activities: The foundation supports food banks and organizations involved with arts and culture, education, health, recreation, human services, and Judaism.
Fields of interest: Museums (art); Arts; Education; Health care, clinics/centers; Health care; Food banks; Recreation; Salvation Army; Children/youth, services; Homeless, human services; Human services; United Ways and Federated Giving Programs; Jewish agencies & synagogues.
Type of support: General/operating support; Program development.
Geographic limitations: Giving primarily in VA.
Support limitations: No grants to individuals.
Application information: Applications accepted. Application form not required.
Initial approach: Proposal
Deadline(s): None
Officer and Directors: Mary Ann Ward, Pres.; John Lichenstein; David Tenzer.
EIN: 546050920
Selected grants: The following grants are a representative sample of this grantmaker's funding activity:
$110,000 to Beth Israel Synagogue, Roanoke, VA, 2011.
$110,000 to Temple Emanuel, Roanoke, VA, 2011.
$50,000 to Taubman Museum of Art, Roanoke, VA, 2011.
$25,500 to Roanoke Area Ministries, Roanoke, VA, 2011.
$11,000 to West End Center, Roanoke, VA, 2011.
$7,000 to Apple Ridge Farm, Roanoke, VA, 2011.
$6,000 to Child Health Investment Partnership, Roanoke, VA, 2011.
$5,000 to Western Virginia Foundation for the Arts and Sciences, Roanoke, VA, 2011.
$4,000 to Greenvale School, Roanoke, VA, 2011.
$2,000 to Virginia Foundation for Independent Colleges, Richmond, VA, 2011.

3960
Visa Inc.

P.O. Box 8999
San Francisco, CA 94128-8999
(415) 932-2100

Company URL: http://corporate.visa.com
Establishment information: Established in 1958.
Company type: Public company
Company ticker symbol and exchange: V/NYSE
Business activities: Operates retail electronic payments network.
Business type (SIC): Business services/miscellaneous
Financial profile for 2012: Number of employees, 8,500; assets, $40,013,000,000; sales volume, $10,421,000,000; pre-tax net income, $2,207,000,000; expenses, $8,282,000,000; liabilities, $12,383,000,000
Fortune 1000 ranking: 2012—260th in revenues, 92nd in profits, and 141st in assets
Forbes 2000 ranking: 2012—888th in sales, 241st in profits, and 627th in assets
Corporate officers: Robert W. Matschullat, Chair.; Charles W. Scharf, C.E.O.; Ryan McInerney, Pres.; Byron H. Pollitt, C.F.O.; Joshua R. Floum, Genl. Counsel
Board of directors: Robert W. Matschullat, Chair.; Gary Coughlan; Mary B. Cranston; Francisco Javier Fernandez-Carbajal; Cathy Elizabeth Minehan; Suzanne Nora Johnson; David J. Pang; Charles W. Scharf; William Shanahan; John A. Swainson
Giving statement: Giving through the Visa Inc. Corporate Giving Program.
Company EIN: 260267673

Visa Inc. Corporate Giving Program

P.O. Box 8999, MS M1-11J
San Francisco, CA 94128-8999 (415) 932-2100
URL: http://corporate.visa.com/corporate-responsibility/index.shtml

Purpose and activities: Visa Inc. makes charitable contributions to nonprofit organizations involved with international humanitarian aid and disaster relief programs, local communities, financial self-sufficiency, literacy, hunger, and poverty. Support is given on a national and international basis.
Fields of interest: Adult education—literacy, basic skills & GED; Food services; Disasters, preparedness/services; Human services; Human services, financial counseling; International economic development; International migration/refugee issues; Microfinance/microlending; Community/economic development Economically disadvantaged.
Program:
Matching Gift Program: The global Matching Gift program supports the charitable interests of eligible employees. Under this program, employees donate to an eligible charitable organization, and Visa matches the donation one-to-one, up to $5,000 each year.
Type of support: Employee matching gifts; Employee volunteer services; General/operating support; Sponsorships.
Geographic limitations: Giving on a national and international basis.

3961
Vision Service Plan, Inc.
(also known as VSP)
3333 Quality Dr.
Rancho Cordova, CA 95670-7985
(916) 851-5000

Company URL: http://www.vsp.com
Establishment information: Established in 1955.
Company type: Private company
Business activities: Operates vision medical service plan.
Business type (SIC): Insurance/accident and health
Corporate officers: Timothy Jankowski, Chair.; Rob Lynch, Pres. and C.E.O.; Donald J. Ball, Jr., C.F.O.
Board of director: Tim Jankowski, Chair.
Offices: Phoenix, AZ; Long Beach, San Francisco, CA; Denver, CO; Hartford, CT; Tampa, FL; Atlanta, GA; Honolulu, HI; Chicago, IL; Indianapolis, IN; Kansas City, KS; Columbia, MD; Boston, MA; Southfield, MI; Minneapolis, MN; St. Louis, MO; Parsippany, NJ; Charlotte, NC; Canton, Columbus, OH; Portland, OR; Philadelphia, PA; Greenville, SC; Dallas, Houston, TX; Seattle, WA
Giving statement: Giving through the VSP Corporate Giving Program.

VSP Corporate Giving Program
1 Gatehall Dr., Ste. 303
Parsippany, NJ 07054-4514
E-mail for Mobile Eyes e-mail: MobileClinic@vsp.com; fax: (916) 463-9051; URL: https://vspglobal.com/cms/vspglobal-outreach.html

Purpose and activities: VSP makes charitable contributions to nonprofit organizations involved with vision care and disaster relief, with an emphasis on children's services. Support is given primarily in areas of company operations with emphasis on Sacramento, CA; giving also to national organizations.
Fields of interest: Health care, fund raising/fund distribution; Diabetes; Housing/shelter, volunteer services; Disasters, preparedness/services; Boys & girls clubs; Children, services Economically disadvantaged.
Program:
Paid Volunteer Program: VSP also encourages company employees, including part-time, to take up to eight hours of paid time off each year to volunteer for their charity of choice. VSP also makes charitable contributions to nonprofit organizations with which employees volunteer.
Type of support: Annual campaigns; Employee volunteer services; General/operating support; Loaned talent; Sponsorships.
Geographic limitations: Giving primarily in areas of company operations, with emphasis on Sacramento, CA; giving also to national organizations.
Publications: Application guidelines.
Application information: Applications accepted. Application form required. Applicants should submit the following:
1) results expected from proposed grant
2) name, address and phone number of organization
3) detailed description of project and amount of funding requested

Applications for Mobile Eyes should include the type of event and services needed, the number of attendees expected and their age groups, and the primary language spoken by patients.
Initial approach: Download application form and fax or e-mail completed form for Mobile Eyes
Deadline(s): 8 weeks prior to event

3962
Vista Metals Corporation
13425 Whittram Ave.
Fontana, CA 92335 (909) 823-4278

Company URL: http://www.vistametals.com/index.html
Establishment information: Established in 1968.
Company type: Private company
Business activities: Manufactures aluminum billets and ingots.
Business type (SIC): Metal refining/primary nonferrous
Corporate officers: Jake J. Farber, Chair.; Andrew Primack, Pres.
Board of director: Jake J. Farber, Chair.
Giving statement: Giving through the Alpert & Alpert Foundation.

The Alpert & Alpert Foundation
1815 S. Soto St.
Los Angeles, CA 90023-4210

Establishment information: Established in 1974 in CA.
Donors: Raymond Alpert; Jake J. Farber; Alpert & Alpert Iron & Metal, Inc.; Vista Metals Corp.; V.S. Trading.
Financial data (yr. ended 06/30/12): Assets, $0 (M); gifts received, $1,109,520; expenditures, $731,104; qualifying distributions, $727,500; giving activities include $727,500 for grants.
Purpose and activities: The foundation supports family foundations and organizations involved with arts and culture, cancer, human services, and Judaism.
Fields of interest: Arts; Cancer; Human services; Foundations (private grantmaking); Jewish federated giving programs; Jewish agencies & synagogues; Religion.
Type of support: General/operating support.
Geographic limitations: Giving primarily in CA.
Support limitations: No grants to individuals.
Application information: Applications not accepted. Unsolicited requests for funds not accepted.
Officers and Directors:* Jake J. Farber*, Pres.; Alan Alpert*, V.P.; Howard Farber*, V.P.; Raymond Alpert*, Secy.-Treas.
EIN: 237388729
Selected grants: The following grants are a representative sample of this grantmaker's funding activity:
$6,500 to Piece by Piece, Los Angeles, CA, 2011. For general charitable use.
$3,000 to Concern Foundation, Los Angeles, CA, 2011. For general charitable use.
$2,500 to Jewish Vocational Service, Los Angeles, CA, 2011. For general charitable use.
$2,500 to Valley Beth Shalom, Encino, CA, 2011. For general charitable use.
$1,250 to Gabriella Axelrad Education Foundation, Los Angeles, CA, 2011. For general charitable use.
$1,000 to Jewish Federation Council of Greater Los Angeles, Los Angeles, CA, 2011. For general charitable use.
$1,000 to Links, The, Washington, DC, 2011. For general charitable use.

3963
Vista Property Management, LLC
2-8 Hawley St.
Binghamton, NY 13901-3114
(607) 722-4469

Company URL: http://www.vistaleasing.com/index2.html
Establishment information: Established in 1999.
Company type: Private company
Business activities: Operates hotels.
Business type (SIC): Hotels and motels
Corporate officer: Ashok Sury, Corp. Cont.
Giving statement: Giving through the Sherali Fazal Visram Memorial Foundation, Inc.

Sherali Fazal Visram Memorial Foundation, Inc.
c/o Holiday Inn
2-8 Hawley St.
Binghamton, NY 13901-3114

Establishment information: Established in 2000 in MA.
Donors: Vista Property Management, LLC; S&S Kissimmee, LLC.
Financial data (yr. ended 12/31/11): Assets, $9,748 (M); gifts received, $10,426; expenditures, $1,292; qualifying distributions, $0.
Purpose and activities: The foundation supports the Life Institute for Girls in India.
Fields of interest: Children, services.
International interests: India.
Geographic limitations: Giving primarily in India.
Support limitations: No grants to individuals.
Application information: Applications not accepted. Unsolicited requests for funds not accepted.
Officers: Amin Sherali Visram, Pres.; Ally Visram, V.P.
Director: Azim Visram.
Number of staff: None.
EIN: 043279667

3964
Visteon Corporation
(doing business as Visteon Automotive)
1 Village Center Dr.
Van Buren Township, MI 48111
(800) 847-8366
FAX: (302) 655-5049

Company URL: http://www.visteon.com
Establishment information: Established in 1997.
Company type: Public company
Company ticker symbol and exchange: VSTNQ/Pink Sheets
Business activities: Manufactures automotive systems, modules, and components.
Business type (SIC): Motor vehicles and equipment
Financial profile for 2012: Number of employees, 22,000; assets, $5,156,000,000; sales volume, $6,857,000,000; pre-tax net income, $291,000,000; expenses, $6,757,000,000; liabilities, $3,771,000,000
Corporate officers: Francis M. Scricco, Chair.; Timothy D. Leuliette, Pres. and C.E.O.; Jeff Stafeil III, Exec. V.P. and C.F.O.; Michael K. Sharnas, Sr. V.P. and Genl. Counsel
Board of directors: Francis M. Scricco, Chair.; Duncan H. Cocroft; Jeffrey D. Jones; Timothy D. Leuliette; Robert J. Manzo; David L. Treadwell; Harry J. Wilson

Giving statement: Giving through the Visteon Fund.
Company EIN: 383519512

The Visteon Fund

P.O. Box 850
Belleville, MI 48112-0850

Establishment information: Established in 1999 in MI.
Donor: Visteon Corp.
Financial data (yr. ended 12/31/11): Assets, $566,453 (M); expenditures, $112,925; qualifying distributions, $111,463; giving activities include $110,000 for 2 grants (high: $100,000; low: $10,000).
Purpose and activities: The fund supports organizations involved with education, water conservation, health, youth development, children, civil rights, and community development.
Fields of interest: Education; Environment, water resources; Health care; Boys & girls clubs; Big Brothers/Big Sisters; Youth development, business; Children, services; Civil/human rights; Community/economic development.
Type of support: General/operating support; Program development.
Geographic limitations: Giving primarily in MI.
Support limitations: No grants to individuals.
Application information: Applications not accepted. Unsolicited requests for funds not accepted.
Officers and Trustees:* Donald J. Stebbins*, Chair. and Pres.; Heidi Sepanik*, Secy.; Michael P. Lewis*, Treas.; Willaim G. Quigley III; Michael K. Sharnas; Dorothy L. Stephenson.
EIN: 383566029
Selected grants: The following grants are a representative sample of this grantmaker's funding activity:
$200,000 to Focus: HOPE, Detroit, MI, 2010. For general fund.

3965
Vodafone Americas Inc.

(formerly AirTouch Communications, Inc.)
275 Shoreline Dr. Ste. 400
Redwood City, CA 94065 (650) 832-6611

Company URL: http://www.vodafone.com/hub_page.html
Establishment information: Established in 1994.
Company type: Subsidiary of a foreign company
Business activities: Operates mobile telecommunications company.
Business type (SIC): Telephone communications
Corporate officers: Nick Land, Chair.; Arun Sarin, Pres. and C.O.O.; Samiel L. Ginn, C.E.O.; Mohanbir Singh Gyani, Exec. V.P. and C.F.O.
Board of director: Nick Land, Chair.
Giving statement: Giving through the Vodafone Americas Foundation.

Vodafone Americas Foundation

(formerly Vodafone-US Foundation)
999 18th St., Ste. 1750
Denver, CO 80202-2404
E-mail: americasfoundation@vodafone.com; Application address: 275 Shoreline Dr., Ste. 400, Redwood City, CA 94065, tel.: (925) 210-3870, fax: (925) 210-3852; e-mail for Julie Sugiyama, Dir.: June.Sugiyama@vodafone.com; e-mail for Genevieve Sublette, Assoc.; genevieve.sublette@vodafone.com; e-mail for Wireless Innovation Project: project@vodafone.com; URL: http://www.vodafone-us.com/

Establishment information: Established in 1993 as a spin-off of Pacific Telesis Foundation; current name adopted in Jan. 2000.
Donors: AirTouch Communications, Inc.; Vodafone Americas Inc.
Contact: June Sugiyama, Dir.
Financial data (yr. ended 12/31/11): Assets, $19,917,695 (M); expenditures, $1,582,239; qualifying distributions, $1,150,183; giving activities include $1,150,183 for grants.
Purpose and activities: The foundation supports programs designed to strengthen families; serve children and youth; foster leadership development; address civic participation and urban issues; promote the arts; and promote technology.
Fields of interest: Performing arts; Arts; Higher education; Teacher school/education; Education; Environment; Health care; Substance abuse, prevention; Housing/shelter; Youth development, adult & child programs; Youth development; Children/youth, services; Youth, pregnancy prevention; Family services; Human services; Community/economic development; Engineering/technology; Public policy, research; Public affairs, citizen participation; Leadership development; Public affairs.
Programs:

Civic Participation & Urban Issues: The foundation supports programs designed to address inner city issues, including traffic, graffiti, overcrowding, affordable housing needs, and retention of open space; promote an understanding of civic issues and the political process; develop public policy to create positive change; and programs designed to encourage the public to be contributing members of the community and society.

Leadership Development: The foundation supports programs designed to prepare youth for future leadership roles; provide young people with tools and knowledge to be well-informed leaders; and promote economic education, teacher preparation, professional development, and mentorship.

mHealth Alliance Award: The foundation, in partnership with mhealth Alliance, and as part of the Wireless Innovation Project, awards a grant to the developer of an innovative wireless technology with the most potential to address critical health challenges, with a focus on developing regions. The winner is awarded a cash prize, benefits of up to $50,000, and the opportunity to participate in Santa Clara University's Center for Science, Technology, and Society's Global Social Benefit Incubator Program (GSBI). Visit URL: http://www.mhealthalliance.org/ for more information.

Strengthening Families: The foundation supports programs designed to address the social breakdown in families; strengthen communication between parents and their children; foster the well-being of families through initiatives like teen pregnancy prevention and drug and alcohol prevention; and programs designed to give young people alternatives to criminal and violent behavior and prepare youth to make positive life choices.

Supporting Children and Youth: The foundation supports programs designed to promote potential in youth; and help cultivate and develop special talents. Special emphasis is directed toward programs designed to serve young people who are motivated, yet otherwise would not be able to pursue their talents and dreams.

The Arts: The foundation supports traditional arts organizations through outreach, education, and presentations for families and youth; and programs designed to use creative ways to expand their services to those who would not otherwise be able to experience their arts programs.

Vodafone Wireless Innovation Project: Through the Vodafone Wireless Innovation Project, the foundation seeks to identify and fund the best innovations using wireless related technology to address critical social issues around the world. Project proposals must demonstrate significant advancement in the field of wireless-related technology applied to social benefit use. The competition is open to projects from universities and nonprofit organizations based in the United States. Although organizations must be based in the United States, projects may operate and help people outside of the United States. Grants of up to $300,000 are awarded and winners are annually announced at the Global Philanthropy Forum in April. Visit URL: http://project.vodafone-us.com/ for more information.

Type of support: Continuing support; Employee matching gifts; General/operating support; Program development; Scholarship funds.
Geographic limitations: Giving primarily in areas of company operations in CA, with emphasis on the San Francisco Bay Area and Denver, CO metro area; giving in the U.S. for the Wireless Innovation Project.
Support limitations: No support for political organizations or religious organizations not of direct benefit to the entire community, fraternal, veterans', or labor groups, individual K-12 schools or school districts, or discriminatory organizations. No grants to individuals, or for capital campaigns, endowments, sports programs, fundraising events, goodwill advertising, cause-related marketing, health-related programs, memberships, administrative services, emergency appeals, or large national projects; no product or service donations.
Publications: Application guidelines; Grants list.
Application information: Applications accepted. Unsolicited applications for general funding are not accepted, but the foundation will keep all inquiries on file and contact applying organizations if opportunities arise within the grantmaking cycle. Organizations receiving Vodafone Wireless Innovation Project funds are asked to submit a progress report twice a year. Application form not required.

Initial approach: Complete online eligibility quiz and application for Vodafone Wireless Innovation Project
Deadline(s): Oct. to Dec. 31 for Vodafone Wireless Innovation Project
Final notification: Feb. 3 for Vodafone Wireless Innovation Project

Officers and Directors:* Megan Doberneck*, Secy.; Fay Arjomandi; William Keever; Arun Sarin; Paul Martin; Peters Suh.
Number of staff: 1 part-time professional; 1 full-time support.
EIN: 205900761
Selected grants: The following grants are a representative sample of this grantmaker's funding activity:
$50,000 to Columbia University, New York, NY, 2010.
$25,000 to World Affairs Council of Northern California, San Francisco, CA, 2010.
$15,000 to Bnai Brith International, Washington, DC, 2010. For general operating support.
$15,000 to Food Bank of the Rockies, Denver, CO, 2010.
$15,000 to Glide Foundation, San Francisco, CA, 2010.
$12,000 to Berkeley Repertory Theater, Berkeley, CA, 2010.
$10,000 to Larkin Street Youth Services, San Francisco, CA, 2010.
$10,000 to Prevent Child Abuse America, Chicago, IL, 2010.

$10,000 to Project AVARY, Novato, CA, 2010. For general operating support.
$10,000 to Sewall Child Development Center, Denver, CO, 2010. For general operating support.

3966
Henry Vogt Machine Company

1000 W. Ormsby Ave.
Louisville, KY 40210-1873 (502) 634-1500

Company URL: http://
Establishment information: Established in 1902.
Company type: Private company
Business activities: Manufactures valves and fittings and heat transfer and ice making equipment.
Business type (SIC): Metal products/fabricated; metal products/structural; machinery/refrigeration and service industry
Corporate officers: Henry V. Heuser, Jr., C.E.O.; Margaret S. Culver, Secy.
Giving statement: Giving through the Henry Vogt Foundation, Inc.

Henry Vogt Foundation, Inc.

1000 W. Ormsby Ave.
Louisville, KY 40210-1918 (502) 634-1500
FAX: (502) 635-3022

Establishment information: Incorporated in 1958 in KY.
Donor: Henry Vogt Machine Co.
Contact: Henry V. Heuser, Jr., Pres.
Financial data (yr. ended 06/30/12): Assets, $1,091,876 (M); expenditures, $1,073,332; qualifying distributions, $1,047,429; giving activities include $1,044,500 for 8 grants (high: $1,000,000; low: $1,000).
Purpose and activities: The foundation supports organizations involved with education, the environment, children and youth, human services, and community development.
Fields of interest: Education; Environment; Community/economic development.
Type of support: Building/renovation; Capital campaigns; Continuing support; Equipment.
Geographic limitations: Giving primarily in KY, with emphasis on the Jefferson County and Louisville areas.
Support limitations: No grants to individuals, or for endowments, scholarships, or fellowships; no matching gifts; no loans.
Application information: Applications accepted. Application form not required. Applicants should submit the following:
1) detailed description of project and amount of funding requested
Initial approach: Proposal
Copies of proposal: 1
Board meeting date(s): June 30
Deadline(s): None
Officers and Director:* Henry V. Heuser, Jr.*, Pres.; Margaret S. Culver, Secy.-Treas.
EIN: 237416717
Selected grants: The following grants are a representative sample of this grantmaker's funding activity:
$20,000 to Gildas Club Louisville, Louisville, KY, 2009.
$20,000 to Wayside Christian Mission, Louisville, KY, 2009.
$5,000 to Greater Louisville Inc., Economic Development, Louisville, KY, 2009.

3967
Volkswagen Group of America, Inc.

(formerly Volkswagen of America, Inc.)
2200 Ferdinand Porsche Dr.
Herndon, VA 20171 (248) 754-5000

Company URL: http://www.volkswagengroupamerica.com
Establishment information: Established in 1955.
Company type: Subsidiary of a foreign company
Business activities: Manufactures automobiles and motor vehicles.
Business type (SIC): Motor vehicles and equipment
Corporate officers: Jonathan Browning, Pres. and C.E.O.; Mark Barnes, C.O.O.; David Geanacopoulos, Exec. V.P., Genl. Counsel, and Public Affairs; Frank Trivieri, Exec. V.P., Sales; Mike Beamish, Exec. V.P., Human Resources; Kevin Mayer, V.P., Mktg.
Subsidiary: VW Credit, Inc., Libertyville, IL
Giving statement: Giving through the Volkswagen of America, Inc. Corporate Giving Program and the Volkswagen of America Foundation.

Volkswagen of America Foundation

2200 Ferdinand Porche Dr.
Herndon, VA 20171-5884

Establishment information: Established in 2001 in MI.
Donor: Volkswagen of America, Inc.
Financial data (yr. ended 12/31/11): Assets, $1,692,925 (M); expenditures, $100,000; qualifying distributions, $100,000; giving activities include $100,000 for 2 grants (high: $50,000; low: $50,000).
Purpose and activities: The foundation awards disaster relief grants to individuals.
Fields of interest: Disasters, preparedness/services; Disasters, Hurricane Katrina.
Type of support: Grants to individuals.
Support limitations: No grants to individuals (except for disaster relief grants).
Application information: Applications not accepted. Unsolicited requests for funds not accepted.
Officers and Directors:* David Geanacopoulus*, Pres.; Kevin Duke, Secy.; Martin Luedtke, Treas.; Mike Beamish; Tony Cervone.
EIN: 383628606

3968
Volvo Trucks North America, Inc.

7900 National Service Rd.
P.O. Box 26115
Greensboro, NC 27409-9416
(336) 393-2000

Company URL: http://www.volvotrucksnorthamerica.com
Establishment information: Established in 1981.
Company type: Subsidiary of a foreign company
Business activities: Manufactures trucks and truck parts and accessories.
Business type (SIC): Motor vehicles and equipment; motor vehicles, parts, and supplies—wholesale
Corporate officer: Dennis Slagle, Pres. and C.E.O.
Giving statement: Giving through the Volvo Trucks North America, Inc. Corporate Giving Program.

Volvo Trucks North America, Inc. Corporate Giving Program

P.O. Box 26115
Greensboro, NC 27402-6115 (336) 393-2000
E-mail: robin.crawford@volvo.com; URL: http://www.volvotrucks.com/trucks/na/en-us/about_us/corporate_social_responsibility/Pages/corporate_social_responsibility.aspx

Purpose and activities: Volvo Trucks North America makes charitable contributions to organizations involved with health and welfare, education, civic and community improvement, and arts and culture. Support is given in areas of company operations, and on a national basis to organizations in the transportation industry.
Fields of interest: Arts, cultural/ethnic awareness; Education; Health care; Safety, automotive safety; Community/economic development; United Ways and Federated Giving Programs; Transportation; Public affairs.
Type of support: Donated equipment; General/operating support; In-kind gifts.
Geographic limitations: Giving primarily in Support is given in areas of company operations, and on a national basis to organizations in the transportation industry.
Application information: Application form not required.

3969
Dan Vos Construction Company

(also known as DVCC)
6160 E. Fulton St.
P.O. Box 189
Ada, MI 49301-0189 (616) 676-9169

Company URL: http://www.danvosconstruction.com/
Establishment information: Established in 1951.
Company type: Private company
Business activities: Provides general contract residential construction services.
Business type (SIC): Contractors/general residential building
Financial profile for 2009: Number of employees, 75
Corporate officer: Steve Huisjen, C.F.O.
Giving statement: Giving through the Gary and Mary Vos Foundation.

Gary and Mary Vos Foundation

6160 E. Fulton St.
P.O. Box 189
Ada, MI 49301-0189

Establishment information: Established in 2001 in MI.
Donor: Dan Vos Construction Co.
Financial data (yr. ended 12/31/11): Assets, $158,704 (M); gifts received, $25,000; expenditures, $15,513; qualifying distributions, $15,000; giving activities include $15,000 for grants.
Purpose and activities: The foundation supports organizations involved with Christianity.
Fields of interest: Christian agencies & churches.
Type of support: General/operating support.
Support limitations: No grants to individuals.
Application information: Applications not accepted. Contributes only to pre-selected organizations.

Officers and Trustee: Gary Vos, Pres.; John Sellman, V.P.; Gordon De Young, Secy.; Everett Vander Tuin, Treas.; Mary Vos.
EIN: 383615658

3912
V-T Industries Inc.

1000 Industrial Pk.
P.O. Box 490
Holstein, IA 51025-7730 (712) 368-4381

Company URL: http://www.vtindustries.com
Establishment information: Established in 1956.
Company type: Private company
Business activities: Manufactures laminate countertops and architectural wood doors.
Business type (SIC): Plastic products/ miscellaneous
Financial profile for 2010: Number of employees, 280
Corporate officers: Douglas E. Clausen, Pres. and C.F.O.; Richard Liddell, Sr. V.P., Sales and Mktg.
Giving statement: Giving through the Clausen Family Foundation.

Clausen Family Foundation

685 Indian Wells Ct.
Dakota Dunes, SD 57049-5121

Establishment information: Established in 2007 in SD.
Donor: V-T Industries, Inc.
Financial data (yr. ended 12/31/11): Assets, $0 (M); expenditures, $61,954; qualifying distributions, $59,750; giving activities include $59,750 for 2 grants (high: $50,000; low: $9,750).
Purpose and activities: The foundation supports the Galva-Holstein Community School Foundation in Holstein, Iowa and awards college scholarships to individuals for post-secondary education.
Fields of interest: Education.
Program:
Clausen Family Scholarship Program: The foundation awards $1,500 scholarships to individuals for postsecondary education. The program is administered by Scholarship America.
Type of support: General/operating support; Scholarships—to individuals.
Geographic limitations: Giving primarily in Holstein, IA.
Application information: Applications accepted. Application form required.
Initial approach: Letter
Deadline(s): May 15 for scholarships
Officers and Directors:* Douglas J. Clausen*, Pres.; Joanie S. Clausen*, Secy.; Randall S. Gerritsen*, Treas.
EIN: 331158977
Selected grants: The following grants are a representative sample of this grantmaker's funding activity:
$350,000 to Galva-Holstein Community School District Foundation, Holstein, IA, 2009. To construct school auditorium.
$18,598 to Scholarship America, Saint Peter, MN, 2009. For post-secondary education scholarships.

3970
Vulcan, Inc.

505 5th Ave. S., Ste. 900
Seattle, WA 98104-3821 (206) 342-2000

Company URL: http://www.vulcan.com
Establishment information: Established in 1986.
Company type: Private company
Business activities: Operates holding company.
Business type (SIC): Holding company
Corporate officers: Paul G. Allen, Chair.; Jody Allen, Pres. and C.E.O.; Bill Benack, V.P., Finance
Board of director: Paul G. Allen, Chair.
Subsidiaries: First and Goal Inc., Seattle, WA; Vulcan Capital Inc., Seattle, WA
Giving statement: Giving through the Vulcan Inc. Corporate Giving Program.
Company EIN: 911374788

Vulcan Inc. Corporate Giving Program

505 5th Ave. S., Ste. 900
Seattle, WA 98104-3821
E-mail: sponsorships@vulcan.com; URL: http://www.vulcan.com/TemplateGeneric.aspx?contentId=33

Contact: Tony White
Purpose and activities: Vulcan makes charitable contributions to nonprofit organizations and educational institutions involved with arts and culture, education, health, affordable housing, youth development, diversity, and community development. Support is given primarily in areas of company operations in the Pacific Northwest.
Fields of interest: Humanities; Arts; Education; Health care; Housing/shelter; Youth development; Civil/human rights, equal rights; Community/economic development.
Type of support: Conferences/seminars; Sponsorships.
Geographic limitations: Giving primarily in areas of company operations in the Pacific Northwest.
Support limitations: No support for organizational programming, general operating expenses, annual campaigns, capital campaigns, land purchases, building, or equipment.
Publications: Application guidelines.
Application information: Applications accepted. Support is limited to 1 contribution per organization during any given year. A community affairs committee reviews all requests.
Initial approach: E-mail or telephone headquarters for application information
Committee meeting date(s): Every three weeks

3971
Vulcan, Inc.

410 E. Berry Ave.
P.O. Box 1850
Foley, AL 36535-1850 (251) 943-7000
FAX: 1-251-943-9270

Company URL: http://www.vulcaninc.com
Establishment information: Established in 1935.
Company type: Private company
Business activities: Manufactures aluminum sheet, blanks, and extrusions; manufactures metal stampings; manufactures metal signs; manufactures lawn mowers; manufactures aluminum coils.
Business type (SIC): Metal rolling and drawing/ nonferrous; metal forgings and stampings; machinery/farm and garden; manufacturing/ miscellaneous
Financial profile for 2009: Number of employees, 236
Corporate officers: Cater C. Lee, Chair.; Robert W. Lee, Pres. and C.E.O.
Board of director: Cater C. Lee, Chair.
Subsidiary: Southland Mower Corp., Selma, AL
Giving statement: Giving through the Vulcan Scholarships, Inc.

Vulcan Scholarships, Inc.

P.O. Box 1850
Foley, AL 36536-1850 (251) 943-2645
URL: http://www.vulcaninc.com

Establishment information: Established in 1984.
Donors: Cater Lee; Vulcan, Inc.
Contact: Thomas M. Lee, Secy.-Treas.
Financial data (yr. ended 10/31/12): Assets, $333,488 (M); gifts received, $20,400; expenditures, $15,702; qualifying distributions, $15,600; giving activities include $15,600 for 12 grants to individuals (high: $2,100; low: $750).
Purpose and activities: The foundation awards college scholarships to students attending Foley, Gulf Shores, and Robertsdale high schools in Alabama who are planning to study chemistry, physics, or engineering.
Type of support: Scholarships—to individuals.
Geographic limitations: Giving limited to Baldwin County, AL.
Application information: Applications accepted. Application form required.
Initial approach: Proposal
Deadline(s): Mid-Feb.
Officers: James E. Stewart, Jr., Chair.; Thomas M. Lee, Secy.-Treas.
Directors: John Koniar; Robert W. Lee.
EIN: 630887786

3972
Vulcan Materials Company

(formerly Virginia Holdco, Inc.)
1200 Urban Center Dr.
P.O. Box 385014
Birmingham, AL 35242-5014
(205) 298-3000
FAX: (205) 298-2960

Company URL: http://www.vulcanmaterials.com
Establishment information: Established in 1909.
Company type: Public company
Company ticker symbol and exchange: VMC/NYSE
Business activities: Manufactures construction materials and chemicals.
Business type (SIC): Concrete, gypsum, and plaster products; mining/crushed and broken stone; chemicals/industrial inorganic
Financial profile for 2012: Assets, $8,126,600,000; sales volume, $2,567,310,000; pre-tax net income, -$120,420,000; expenses, $2,482,530,000; liabilities, $436,554
Fortune 1000 ranking: 2012—797th in revenues, 907th in profits, and 451st in assets
Corporate officers: Donald M. James, Chair. and C.E.O.; Daniel F. Sansone, Exec. V.P. and C.F.O.; Robert A. Wason IV, Sr. V.P. and Genl. Counsel; J. Wayne Houston, Sr. V.P., Human Resources; Ejaz A. Khan, V.P., Cont., and C.I.O.; C. Wes Burton, Jr., V.P. and Treas.; Jerry F. Perkins, Jr., Secy.
Board of directors: Donald M. James, Chair.; Phillip W. Farmer; H. Allen Franklin; Ann McLaughlin Korologos; Douglas J. McGregor; Richard T. O'Brien; James T. Prokopank; Donald B. Rice; Vincent J. Trosino; Kathleen Wilson-Thompson

Subsidiary: Florida Rock Industries, Inc., Jacksonville, FL
Plants: Washington, DC; Miami, FL; Atlanta, GA; Chicago, IL; Monon, IN; Cedar Rapids, Robins, IA; Wichita, KS; Fort Knox, Lake City, KY; Geismar, LA; Iuka, MS; Boone, Winston-Salem, NC; Liberty, Lyman, SC; Athens, Chattanooga, Knoxville, TN; San Antonio, TX; Manassas, VA; Port Edwards, WI
International operations: Bahamas; Canada
Giving statement: Giving through the Vulcan Materials Company Contributions Program and the Vulcan Materials Company Foundation.
Company EIN: 630366371

Vulcan Materials Company Contributions Program

1200 Urban Center Dr.
Birmingham, AL 35242 (205) 298-3000
E-mail: giving@vmcmail.com; URL: http://www.vulcanmaterials.com/social.asp

Purpose and activities: As a complement to its foundation, Vulcan also matches contributions made by its employees to nonprofit organizations, and provides scholarship funds.
Fields of interest: Arts; Education; Hospitals (general).
Type of support: Employee matching gifts; Employee-related scholarships; Scholarship funds.
Geographic limitations: Giving primarily in areas of company operations.
Application information: Applications not accepted. Contributes only through employee matching gifts and scholarship funds.

Vulcan Materials Company Foundation

P.O. Box 385014
Birmingham, AL 35238-5014 (205) 298-3222
E-mail: giving@vmcmail.com; Additional tel.: (205) 298-3229; URL: http://www.vulcanmaterials.com/sustainability/community/vulcan-foundation

Establishment information: Established in 1987 in AL.
Donors: Vulcan Materials Co.; Vulcan Lands Inc.; Calmat Co.; Legacy Vulvan Corp.-Western.
Contact: Carol B. Maxwell, Secy.-Treas.
Financial data (yr. ended 11/30/11): Assets, $4,803,174 (M); gifts received, $2,175,000; expenditures, $2,460,923; qualifying distributions, $2,350,913; giving activities include $2,350,913 for 538 grants (high: $144,000; low: $100).
Purpose and activities: The foundation supports programs designed to work with schools; support environmental stewardship; and encourage employee involvement.
Fields of interest: Education, reform; Elementary/secondary education; Higher education; Engineering school/education; Environment, natural resources; Environment; Animals/wildlife, preservation/protection; Animals/wildlife; Business/industry; Science, formal/general education; Mathematics.
Programs:
Elementary/Secondary Education: The foundation supports programs designed to provide public education authorities with the tools necessary to help all students; improve educational systems and individual schools by partnering with schools located in Vulcan's operating areas; encourage students' curiosity and excitement about math, science, and business; link the math and science taught in classrooms to society and disciplines in the workplace; and educate students about the vital role of business and industry in society.
Environmental Stewardship: The foundation supports programs designed to promote an understanding of the connection between environmental stewardship and sustainable development; and adhere to fact-based, balanced environmental principles.
Higher Education: The foundation supports programs designed to focus on science and engineering, and improve public education.
Type of support: Annual campaigns; Capital campaigns; Continuing support; Employee volunteer services; Employee-related scholarships; Endowments; General/operating support; Matching/challenge support; Program development; Scholarship funds; Seed money.
Geographic limitations: Giving primarily in areas of company operations, with emphasis on Birmingham, AL.
Support limitations: No support for political organizations, athletic, labor, fraternal, or veterans' organizations, discriminatory organizations, or private foundations. No grants to individuals (except for employee-related scholarships), or for telephone or mass mail appeals, testimonial dinners, or sectarian religious activities.
Publications: Annual report (including application guidelines); Application guidelines.
Application information: Applications accepted. E-mail foundation for local Charitable Contributions Officer contact information. Proposals should be no longer than 1 to 2 pages. Application form not required. Applicants should submit the following:
1) timetable for implementation and evaluation of project
2) statement of problem project will address
3) copy of IRS Determination Letter
4) copy of most recent annual report/audited financial statement/990
5) how project's results will be evaluated or measured
6) listing of board of directors, trustees, officers and other key people and their affiliations
7) detailed description of project and amount of funding requested
8) copy of current year's organizational budget and/or project budget

Initial approach: Proposal to nearest Charitable Contributions Officer; proposal to foundation for organizations located in the Birmingham, AL, area
Copies of proposal: 1
Board meeting date(s): Quarterly
Deadline(s): None

Officers and Trustees:* Donald M. James*, Chair.; David A. Donaldson, V.P.; Carol B. Maxwell, Secy.-Treas.; Daniel F. Sansone; Danny R. Shepherd; J. Wayne Houston.
Number of staff: 1 full-time professional; 1 part-time support.
EIN: 630971859
Selected grants: The following grants are a representative sample of this grantmaker's funding activity:
$144,000 to United Way of Central Alabama, Birmingham, AL, 2010.
$120,000 to University of North Florida, Jacksonville, FL, 2010.
$100,000 to Childrens Hospital of Alabama, Birmingham, AL, 2010.
$50,000 to Alabama Symphonic Association, Birmingham, AL, 2010.
$50,000 to Tarrant Redevelopment Authority, Tarrant, AL, 2010.
$30,000 to YWCA of Birmingham, Birmingham, AL, 2010.
$8,000 to Innovation Depot, Birmingham, AL, 2010.
$5,000 to Fernbank Museum of Natural History, Atlanta, GA, 2010.
$5,000 to Samford University, Alabama Governors School, Birmingham, AL, 2010.
$2,000 to United Way of Henderson County, Hendersonville, NC, 2010.

3973
Wachtell, Lipton, Rosen & Katz

51 W. 52nd St.
New York, NY 10019 (212) 403-1000

Company URL: http://www.wlrk.com
Establishment information: Established in 1965.
Company type: Private company
Business activities: Provides legal services.
Business type (SIC): Legal services
Corporate officers: Edward M. Herlihy, Co-Chair.; Daniel A. Neff, Co-Chair.; Edward F. Diyanmi, C.O.O.
Board of directors: Edward M. Herlihy, Co-Chair.; Daniel A. Neff, Co-Chair.
Office: New York, NY
Giving statement: Giving through the Wachtell, Lipton, Rosen & Katz Pro Bono Program, the Lipton Foundation, and the Wachtell, Lipton, Rosen & Katz Foundation.

Wachtell, Lipton, Rosen & Katz Pro Bono Program

51 W. 52nd St.
New York, NY 10019-6150 (212) 403-1000
E-mail: MWolinsky@wlrk.com; URL: http://www.wlrk.com/Page.cfm/Thread/The%20Firm/SubThread/Pro%20Bono

Contact: Marc Wolinsky, Partner
Fields of interest: Legal services.
Type of support: Pro bono services - legal.
Application information: All attorneys may bring pro bono matters of interest to the firm.

The Lipton Foundation

c/o Wachtell, Lipton, Rosen & Katz
51 W. 52nd St.
New York, NY 10019-6119

Establishment information: Established in 2001 in NY.
Donor: Wachtell, Lipton, Rosen & Katz.
Financial data (yr. ended 12/31/10): Assets, $8,555,085 (M); expenditures, $473,936; qualifying distributions, $384,500; giving activities include $384,500 for grants.
Purpose and activities: The foundation supports museums and food banks and organizations involved with higher and law education, wildlife preservation, human services, and Judaism.
Fields of interest: Museums; Higher education; Law school/education; Animals/wildlife, preservation/protection; Food banks; Children, services; Family services; Homeless, human services; Human services; Jewish federated giving programs; Jewish agencies & synagogues.
Type of support: General/operating support; Program development.
Geographic limitations: Giving primarily in NY.
Support limitations: No grants to individuals.
Application information: Applications not accepted. Contributes only to pre-selected organizations.
Officers: Susan L. Lipton, Pres.; Martin Lipton, V.P. and Secy.; Katherine B. Lipton, V.P.; Samantha D. Lipton, V.P.; Constance Monte, Treas.
EIN: 582629617
Selected grants: The following grants are a representative sample of this grantmaker's funding activity:

$50,000 to University of Pennsylvania, Philadelphia, PA, 2009.
$50,000 to Wildlife Conservation Society, Bronx, NY, 2009.
$17,000 to Food Bank for New York City, Bronx, NY, 2009.
$15,000 to Project Renewal, New York, NY, 2009.
$15,000 to University of Miami, Coral Gables, FL, 2009.
$14,000 to Partnership with Children, New York, NY, 2009.
$10,000 to Jewish Museum, New York, NY, 2009.
$10,000 to New York University, School of Medicine, New York, NY, 2009.
$10,000 to New Yorkers for Children, New York, NY, 2009.
$2,500 to New Press, New York, NY, 2009.

The Wachtell, Lipton, Rosen & Katz Foundation

51 W. 52nd St.
New York, NY 10019-6119

Establishment information: Established in 1981 in NY.
Donor: Wachtell, Lipton, Rosen & Katz.
Financial data (yr. ended 09/30/11): Assets, $10,349,203 (M); gifts received, $2,500,000; expenditures, $1,876,585; qualifying distributions, $1,857,600; giving activities include $1,857,100 for 27 grants (high: $303,600; low: $5,000).
Purpose and activities: The foundation supports medical centers and organizations involved with education, 9/11 memorials, justice, law, Judaism, and people of color.
Fields of interest: Elementary/secondary education; Higher education; Law school/education; Education; Health care, clinics/centers; Palliative care; Courts/judicial administration; Legal services; Disasters, 9/11/01; Jewish federated giving programs; Jewish agencies & synagogues African Americans/Blacks.
Type of support: Annual campaigns; General/operating support; Scholarship funds.
Geographic limitations: Giving limited to New York, NY.
Support limitations: No grants to individuals.
Application information: Applications not accepted. Contributes only to pre-selected organizations.
Board meeting date(s): As necessary
Officers and Directors:* Martin Lipton*, Pres.; Herbert M. Wachtell*, V.P. and Secy.; Constance Monte, V.P. and Treas.; Edward D. Herlihy*, V.P.; Daniel A. Neff*, V.P.; Jodi D. Schwartz, V.P.
EIN: 133099901
Selected grants: The following grants are a representative sample of this grantmaker's funding activity:
$1,000,000 to New York University, New York, NY, 2004. For Neuroscience Program.
$1,000,000 to New York University, New York, NY, 2004. For President's Endowment Fund.
$750,000 to UJA-Federation of New York, New York, NY, 2004. For general support.
$400,000 to Prep for Prep, New York, NY, 2004. For general support.
$200,000 to New York City Leadership Academy, Long Island City, NY, 2004. For general support.
$200,000 to University of Pennsylvania, Philadelphia, PA, 2004.
$100,000 to University of Chicago, School of Law, Chicago, IL, 2004.
$97,000 to Harvard University, Cambridge, MA, 2004. For Law School Fund.
$50,000 to Jewish Theological Seminary of America, New York, NY, 2004. For general support.
$50,000 to Mount Sinai School of Medicine of New York University, New York, NY, 2004.

3974
Wadsworth Brothers Construction Company, Inc.

1350 E. Draper Pkwy.
Draper, UT 84020-8567 (801) 576-1453

Company URL: http://www.wadsbro.com/
Establishment information: Established in 1991.
Company type: Private company
Business activities: Operates construction company.
Business type (SIC): Construction/highway and street (except elevated)
Corporate officers: Guy L. Wadsworth, Pres.; Helene Candi Wadsworth, Secy.
Giving statement: Giving through the Wadsworth Brothers Charitable Foundation.

Wadsworth Brothers Charitable Foundation

1350 E. Draper Pkwy.
Draper, UT 84020-8567
URL: http://www.wadsbro.com/charities/

Establishment information: Established in 2006 in UT.
Donor: Wadsworth Brothers Construction Company, Inc.
Financial data (yr. ended 12/31/11): Assets, $620,872 (M); expenditures, $165,927; qualifying distributions, $165,767; giving activities include $165,767 for grants.
Purpose and activities: The foundation supports organizations involved with mental health, cancer, housing development, children and youth, gift distribution, the disabled, and the economically disadvantaged.
Fields of interest: Mental health/crisis services; Cancer; Housing/shelter, development; Children/youth, services; Human services, gift distribution; Developmentally disabled, centers & services Economically disadvantaged.
Type of support: General/operating support.
Geographic limitations: Giving primarily in Salt Lake City, UT.
Support limitations: No grants to individuals.
Application information: Applications not accepted. Contributes only to pre-selected organizations.
Director: Guy L. Wadsworth.
EIN: 208096411

3975
Waffle House, Inc.

5986 Financial Dr.
Norcross, GA 30071-2949 (770) 729-5700

Company URL: http://www.wafflehouse.com
Establishment information: Established in 1955.
Company type: Private company
Business activities: Operates and franchises restaurants; sells food and food industry equipment wholesale.
Business type (SIC): Restaurants and drinking places; professional and commercial equipment—wholesale; groceries—wholesale; investors/miscellaneous
Corporate officers: Joe W. Rogers, Jr., Chair. and C.E.O.; Bert Thornton, Pres. and C.O.O.
Board of director: Joe W. Rogers, Jr., Chair.
Giving statement: Giving through the Waffle House Foundation, Inc.

Waffle House Foundation, Inc.

(formerly GFF Educational Foundation, Inc.)
5986 Financial Dr.
Norcross, GA 30071-2949 (770) 729-5780
Application address: P.O. Box 6450, Norcross, GA 30071; URL: http://www.wafflehouse.com/in-the-community/waffle-house-foundation

Establishment information: Established in 1982 in GA.
Donor: Waffle House, Inc.
Contact: Jenny Wilson
Financial data (yr. ended 05/31/11): Assets, $356,682 (M); gifts received, $230,269; expenditures, $207,500; qualifying distributions, $207,500; giving activities include $182,500 for 26 grants (high: $25,000; low: $200) and $25,000 for 5 grants to individuals (high: $5,000; low: $5,000).
Purpose and activities: The foundation supports organizations involved with education, health, human services, civic affairs, youth, and economically disadvantaged people and awards college scholarships to students in financial need.
Fields of interest: Secondary school/education; Education; Health care; Salvation Army; YM/YWCAs & YM/YWHAs; Developmentally disabled, centers & services; Independent living, disability; Human services; Public affairs Youth; Economically disadvantaged.
Type of support: Equipment; Program development; Scholarship funds; Scholarships—to individuals.
Geographic limitations: Giving primarily in the metropolitan Atlanta, GA, area, including Butts, Cherokee, Clayton, Cobb, Coweta, DeKalb, Douglas, Fayette, Forsyth, Fulton, Gwinnett, Henry, Paulding, and Rockdale counties.
Support limitations: No support for religious organizations not of direct benefit to the entire community or political candidates. No grants for capital campaigns, endowments, debt reduction, general operating support, or sponsorships of charity balls, dinner, golf outings, etc.
Publications: Application guidelines.
Application information: Applications accepted. Telephone calls during the application process are not encouraged. Application form not required. Applicants should submit the following:
1) copy of most recent annual report/audited financial statement/990
2) descriptive literature about organization
3) listing of board of directors, trustees, officers and other key people and their affiliations
4) detailed description of project and amount of funding requested
5) copy of current year's organizational budget and/or project budget
6) listing of additional sources and amount of support

Initial approach: Proposal
Deadline(s): None

Officers: Elizabeth Bailey, Pres.; Tracy Bradshaw, V.P.; Mike Howard, Treas.
EIN: 581477023
Selected grants: The following grants are a representative sample of this grantmaker's funding activity:
$5,000 to Teach for America, New York, NY, 2010.
$2,500 to American Cancer Society, Atlanta, GA, 2010.
$2,000 to Empty Stocking Fund, Atlanta, GA, 2010.

3976
E. R. Wagner Manufacturing Company
4611 N. 32nd St.
Milwaukee, WI 53209-6023
(414) 871-5080

Company URL: http://www.erwagner.com
Establishment information: Established in 1900.
Company type: Private company
Business activities: Manufactures casters and wheels, hinges and stampings, and tubular products.
Business type (SIC): Metal forgings and stampings; cutlery, hand and edge tools, and hardware; metal products/structural; metal products/fabricated
Corporate officers: Frank M. Sterner, Pres. and C.E.O.; Brian Glynn, Sr. V.P. and Co-C.F.O.; Lew Schildkraut, V.P and Co-C.F.O.
Giving statement: Giving through the E. R. Wagner Manufacturing Company Foundation, Inc.

E. R. Wagner Manufacturing Company Foundation, Inc.
4611 N. 32nd St.
Milwaukee, WI 53209-6023

Establishment information: Established in 1955.
Donor: E.R. Wagner Manufacturing Co.
Contact: Mark Hart, Treas.
Financial data (yr. ended 12/31/11): Assets, $558,584 (M); expenditures, $6,472; qualifying distributions, $3,679.
Purpose and activities: The foundation supports hospitals and organizations involved with arts and culture, education, mental health, lung disease, employment, and human services.
Fields of interest: Arts; Medical school/education; Education; Hospitals (general); Mental health/crisis services; Lung diseases; Goodwill Industries; Children, services; Human services; United Ways and Federated Giving Programs.
Type of support: General/operating support.
Geographic limitations: Giving primarily in Milwaukee, WI.
Support limitations: No grants to individuals.
Application information: Applications accepted. Application form not required.
Initial approach: Proposal
Deadline(s): None
Officers and Directors:* Marna W. Fullerton, Pres.; Bernard S. Kubale, V.P. and Secy.; Mark Hart, Treas.; Cynthia W. Kahler.
EIN: 396037097

3977
Wahl Clipper Corporation
(formerly Wahl Clipper Corp.)
2900 N. Locust St.
P.O. Box 578
Sterling, IL 61081 (815) 625-6525

Company URL: http://www.wahlclipper.com
Establishment information: Established in 1911.
Company type: Private company
Business activities: Manufactures hair clippers, trimmers, shavers, and massagers.
Business type (SIC): Manufacturing/miscellaneous
Corporate officers: Gregory S. Wahl, Pres. and C.E.O.; Scott Hamilton, C.F.O. and Treas.; Bruce Kramer, V.P., Sales and Mktg.; Melissa Woessner, Cont.
Giving statement: Giving through the Leo J. Wahl Foundation.

Leo J. Wahl Foundation
2902 N. Locust St.
Sterling, IL 61081-9501 (815) 625-6525

Establishment information: Established in 1985 in IL.
Donor: Wahl Clipper Corp.
Contact: Clipper C. Wahl
Financial data (yr. ended 12/31/11): Assets, $263,823 (M); gifts received, $50,000; expenditures, $49,288; qualifying distributions, $49,250; giving activities include $49,250 for grants.
Purpose and activities: The foundation awards college scholarships to children of employees of Wahl Clipper Corp.
Fields of interest: Higher education.
Type of support: Employee-related scholarships.
Geographic limitations: Giving limited to Sterling, IL.
Application information: Applications accepted. Application form required.
Initial approach: Proposal
Deadline(s): None
Officers: Greg Wahl, Pres.; John A. Van Osdol, Secy.; Donna Rosenthal, Treas.
Director: Mary Jane Gearns.
EIN: 363447061

3978
Wake Electric Membership Corporation
414 E. Wait St.
P.O. Box 1229
Wake Forest, NC 27588-1229
(919) 863-6300

Company URL: http://www.wemc.com
Establishment information: Established in 1940.
Company type: Cooperative
Business activities: Distributes electricity.
Business type (SIC): Electric services
Corporate officers: Jim Mangum, C.E.O.; Roy Jones, Pres.; Phil Price, C.O.O.; Joe Eddins, Secy.; Howard Conyers, Treas.
Board of directors: Bill Bailey; Howard Conyers; Mike Dickerson; Joe Eddins; Joe Hilburn; Roy Jones; Reuben Matthews; Suzy Morgan; Allen Nelson
Giving statement: Giving through the Wake Electric Care, Inc.

Wake Electric Care, Inc.
414 E. Wait St.
Wake Forest, NC 27588-1229
Application address: Wake Electric Care, Inc., P.O. Box 1229, Wake Forest, NC 27588

Establishment information: Established in 2002 in NC.
Contact: Fred Keller
Financial data (yr. ended 12/31/11): Assets, $191,376 (L); gifts received, $146,461; expenditures, $142,418; qualifying distributions, $142,418; giving activities include $142,418 for 66 + grants (high: $15,000; low: $175).
Purpose and activities: The foundation supports organizations involved with education, recreation, and human services.
Fields of interest: Secondary school/education; Higher education; Education; Recreation; Boys & girls clubs; Human services.
Type of support: Equipment; General/operating support; Program development; Scholarship funds.
Geographic limitations: Giving primarily in areas of company operations in Durham, Franklin, Granville, Johnston, Nash, Wake, and Vance, NC.
Application information: Applications accepted. Application form required. Applicants should submit the following:
1) statement of problem project will address
2) copy of IRS Determination Letter
3) how project's results will be evaluated or measured
4) detailed description of project and amount of funding requested
5) copy of current year's organizational budget and/or project budget
6) listing of additional sources and amount of support
Initial approach: Proposal
Deadline(s): None
Directors: Carolyn Barnes; Molly Bostic; Hubert L. Gooch, Jr.; Jan Hopkins; Cedric Jones; Robert Lanier; Michelle McGhee; Frances McIver; Frank Pearce.
EIN: 561938901

3979
Wakefern Food Corp.
5000 Riverside Dr.
P.O. Box 7812
Keasbey, NJ 08832 (908) 527-3300

Company URL: http://www.shoprite.com/wakefern/
Establishment information: Established in 1946.
Company type: Cooperative
Business activities: Operates retailer owned cooperative.
Business type (SIC): Groceries—wholesale
Financial profile for 2010: Number of employees, 400; sales volume, $11,800,000,000
Corporate officers: Joseph S. Colalillo, Chair. and C.E.O.; Joseph Sheridan, Pres. and C.O.O.; Douglas Wille, C.F.O.; Jeff Reagan, Sr. V.P., Mktg.; Cheryl Williams, V.P., Mktg.; Ann Marie Burke, V.P., Human Resources
Board of director: Joseph S. Colalillo, Chair.
Giving statement: Giving through the Wakefern Food Corp. Contributions Program.

Wakefern Food Corp. Contributions Program
5000 Riverside Dr.
Keasbey, NJ 08832-1209 (908) 527-3300
URL: http://www.shoprite.com/wakefern/cnt/wakefern/WFC_Sustainability.html

Purpose and activities: Wakefern Corp. makes charitable contributions to nonprofit organizations involved with hunger, poverty, health and wellness, and education. Support is given primarily in New Jersey.
Fields of interest: Education; Health care; Food services; Food banks Economically disadvantaged.
Type of support: Donated products; Employee volunteer services; General/operating support; In-kind gifts; Sponsorships.
Geographic limitations: Giving primarily in NJ.

3981
Walgreen Co.
200 Wilmot Rd.
Deerfield, IL 60015-4620 (847) 315-2500
FAX: (847) 914-2804

Company URL: http://www.walgreens.com
Establishment information: Established in 1901.
Company type: Public company
Company ticker symbol and exchange: WAG/NYSE
Business activities: Operates drug stores.
Business type (SIC): Drug stores and proprietary stores
Financial profile for 2012: Number of employees, 240,000; assets, $33,462,000,000; sales volume, $71,633,000,000; pre-tax net income, $3,376,000,000; expenses, $68,169,000,000; liabilities, $15,226,000,000
Fortune 1000 ranking: 2012—37th in revenues, 93rd in profits, and 167th in assets
Forbes 2000 ranking: 2012—108th in sales, 280th in profits, and 633rd in assets
Corporate officers: James A. Skinner, Chair.; Gregory D. Wasson, Pres. and C.E.O.; Wade D. Miquelon, Exec. V.P. and C.F.O.; Thomas J. Sabatino, Jr., Exec. V.P., Genl. Counsel, and Corp. Secy.; Timothy J. Theriault, Sr. V.P. and C.I.O.; Mia M. Scholz, Sr. V.P., and C.A.O.; Jason M. Dubinsky, V.P. and Treas.; Ted Heidloff, Cont.
Board of directors: James A. Skinner, Chair.; Janice M. Babiak; David J. Brailer, M.D., Ph.D.; Steven A. Davis; William C. Foote; Mark P. Frissora; Ginger L. Graham; Alan G. McNally; Dominic Murphy; Stefano Pessina; Nancy M. Schlichting; David Y. Schwartz; Alejandro Silva; Gregory D. Wasson
Subsidiaries: Drugstore.com, Inc., Bellevue, WA; Duane Reade Holdings, Inc., New York, NY
International operations: China; Hong Kong; India; Mauritius
Historic mergers: Option Care, Inc. (September 12, 2007)
Giving statement: Giving through the Walgreen Co. Contributions Program, the Walgreen Benefit Fund, and the Walgreens Assistance, Inc.
Company EIN: 361924025

Walgreen Co. Contributions Program
200 Wilmot Rd.
Deerfield, IL 60015-4620
URL: http://www.walgreens.com/topic/sr/social_responsibility_home.jsp

Purpose and activities: As a complement to its foundations, Walgreen also makes charitable contributions to nonprofit organizations directly. Emphasis is given to programs that address access to health and wellness in the community, pharmacy education and mentoring, civic and community outreach, and emergency and disaster relief. Support is given primarily in areas of company operations.
Fields of interest: Elementary/secondary education; Pharmacy/prescriptions; Health care; Cancer; Heart & circulatory diseases; Health organizations; Immunology; Cancer research; Heart & circulatory research; Diabetes research; Medical research; Safety/disasters; Community/economic development; United Ways and Federated Giving Programs; Public affairs.
Type of support: Annual campaigns; Employee volunteer services; General/operating support; In-kind gifts.
Geographic limitations: Giving primarily in areas of company operations.
Support limitations: No support for religious organizations not of direct benefit to the entire community, lobbying, partisan, or denominational groups, or individual elementary or secondary schools. No grants for advertising, promotional events, or sponsorship of athletic teams, endowment or capital campaigns, sponsorships for individuals participating in cause-related events such as walks, runs, or conferences, sponsorships submitted by a third party on behalf of an organization, or educational or travel grants for contests, pageants, trips, or conventions.
Publications: Application guidelines.
Application information: Applications accepted. Telephone inquiries and faxed requests are not accepted. Application form required. Applicants should submit the following:
1) population served
2) name, address and phone number of organization
3) copy of IRS Determination Letter
4) brief history of organization and description of its mission
5) copy of most recent annual report/audited financial statement/990
6) list of company employees involved with the organization
7) listing of board of directors, trustees, officers and other key people and their affiliations
8) detailed description of project and amount of funding requested
9) contact person
10) copy of current year's organizational budget and/or project budget
11) listing of additional sources and amount of support
12) plans for acknowledgement

Proposals should include a list of accrediting agencies, if applicable.
Initial approach: Complete online application for grants; for auction items, merchandise, or gift cards (not exceeding $20), contact nearest district office.

Administrators: John F. Gremer, Dir., Community Affairs; Martha O'Bryan, Mgr., Community Affairs.
Number of staff: 1 full-time professional; 3 part-time support.

Walgreen Benefit Fund
104 Wilmot Rd., MS No. 1410
Deerfield, IL 60015-5121 (847) 315-4662
URL: http://www.walgreens.com/topic/sr/sr_walgreens_benefit.jsp

Establishment information: Incorporated in 1939 in IL.
Donors: Touro University; Walgreen Co.; C.R. Walgreen, Jr.; L. Daniel Jorndt; Ohio Northwestern University; Texas Tech University.
Contact: John Gremer, V.P.
Financial data (yr. ended 04/30/12): Assets, $22,480,827 (M); gifts received, $115,653; expenditures, $1,438,824; qualifying distributions, $1,415,516; giving activities include $1,415,516 for grants to individuals.
Purpose and activities: The fund awards grants to employees and former employees and the family members of employees and former employees of Walgreen who have experienced hardship cause by long illnesses, accidents, natural disasters, and other situations.
Fields of interest: Economically disadvantaged.
Type of support: Grants to individuals.
Geographic limitations: Giving primarily in areas of company operations in Deerfield, IL.
Publications: Annual report; Application guidelines.
Application information: Applications accepted. Application form not required. Applicants should submit the following:
1) copy of IRS Determination Letter
2) copy of most recent annual report/audited financial statement/990
3) listing of board of directors, trustees, officers and other key people and their affiliations
4) detailed description of project and amount of funding requested
5) copy of current year's organizational budget and/or project budget
6) listing of additional sources and amount of support

Initial approach: Contact fund for application information
Copies of proposal: 1
Board meeting date(s): Monthly
Deadline(s): None
Final notification: 4 to 6 weeks

Officers and Directors:* K. E. Dimitriou*, Pres.; John Gremer*, V.P.; R. M. Silverman*, V.P.; N. J. Godfrey*, Secy.-Treas.; R. J. Hans; C.O. Knupp; M. D. Oettinger; C. A. Spitz; M. A. Wattley.
Number of staff: 1 part-time professional; 1 part-time support.
EIN: 366051130

Walgreens Assistance, Inc.
104 Wilmot Rd., M.S. 1444
Deerfield, IL 60015-5121
URL: http://www.walgreens.com/topic/sr/sr_giving_back_flu_shot.jsp

Donor: Walgreen Co. and Subsidiaries.
Financial data (yr. ended 08/31/11): Assets, $0 (M); gifts received, $2,096,100; expenditures, $2,096,100; qualifying distributions, $2,096,100; giving activities include $2,096,100 for grants to individuals.
Purpose and activities: The foundation provides flu shot vouchers to the uninsured or underinsured ill, needy, and infants to prevent influenza and improve health.
Fields of interest: Health care.
Type of support: Donated products; Grants to individuals; In-kind gifts.
Geographic limitations: Giving on a national basis.
Application information: The foundation partners with the U.S. Department of Health and Human Services to distribute flu vaccine vouchers to local health agencies and community partners.
Officers and Directors:* John Gremer*, Pres.; John Mann*, V.P.; Robert Silverman*, Secy.; Rick Hans*, Treas.
EIN: 274521750

3982
Cecil I. Walker Machinery Company
1400 E. Dupont Ave.
Belle, WV 25015-1217 (304) 949-6400

Company URL: http://www.walker-cat.com
Establishment information: Established in 1950.
Company type: Subsidiary of a private company
Business activities: Manufactures construction and mining machinery.
Business type (SIC): Machinery/construction, mining, and materials handling
Financial profile for 2010: Number of employees, 580
Corporate officers: Richard Walker, C.E.O.; Steve Walker, Pres. and C.O.O.; A. S. Southworth, Treas.
Giving statement: Giving through the Cecil I. Walker Machinery Company Charitable Trust.

Cecil I. Walker Machinery Company Charitable Trust

10 S. Dearborn St., Il1-0117
Chicago, IL 60603-2300

Donor: Cecil I. Walker Machinery Co.
Financial data (yr. ended 05/31/12): Assets, $4,270,461 (M); expenditures, $594,064; qualifying distributions, $538,586; giving activities include $536,000 for 11 grants (high: $250,000; low: $2,500).
Purpose and activities: The foundation supports organizations involved with arts and culture, higher education, and Christianity.
Fields of interest: Performing arts; Arts; Higher education; Girl scouts; YM/YWCAs & YM/YWHAs; Christian agencies & churches.
Type of support: Annual campaigns; Continuing support; General/operating support; Scholarship funds; Sponsorships.
Geographic limitations: Giving limited to Charleston, WV.
Support limitations: No grants to individuals.
Application information: Applications not accepted. Contributes only to pre-selected organizations.
Directors: D. Stephen Walker; Richard B. Walker.
Trustees: JPMorgan Chase Bank, N.A.
EIN: 556050733

3983
Wallace Associates, Inc.

291 Southhall Ln., Ste. 103
Maitland, FL 32751-7278 (407) 629-4055

Establishment information: Established in 1975.
Company type: Private company
Business activities: Provides management consulting services.
Business type (SIC): Management and public relations services
Corporate officers: William N. Wallace, Pres.; Anna Wallace, Secy.; Christena Black, Cont.
Giving statement: Giving through the Ann & Bill Wallace Foundation, Inc.

Ann & Bill Wallace Foundation, Inc.

291 Southhall Ln., Ste. 103
Maitland, FL 32751

Establishment information: Established in 2003 in FL.
Donors: Wallace Associates, Ltd.; Wilburn N. Wallace; Bill Wallace; Ann Wallace.
Financial data (yr. ended 12/31/11): Assets, $1,424,175 (M); expenditures, $74,148; qualifying distributions, $67,557; giving activities include $67,500 for 10 grants (high: $10,000; low: $5,000).
Purpose and activities: The foundation supports food banks and organizations involved with higher education, health and human services, and Christianity.
Fields of interest: Health care; Agriculture/food; Human services.
Type of support: General/operating support; Scholarship funds.
Support limitations: No grants to individuals.
Application information: Applications not accepted. Contributes only to pre-selected organizations.
Directors: Christina Black; Ann Wallace; Bill Wallace; Judith Wallace; William N. Wallace II.
EIN: 331062280

3980
Wal-Mart Stores, Inc.

(also known as Walmart)
702 S.W. 8th St.
Bentonville, AR 72716-8611
(479) 273-4000
FAX: (479) 277-1830

Company URL: http://www.walmartstores.com
Establishment information: Established in 1945.
Company type: Public company
Company ticker symbol and exchange: WMT/NYSE
International Securities Identification Number: US9311421039
Business activities: Operates variety stores.
Business type (SIC): Variety stores
Financial profile for 2013: Number of employees, 2,200,000; assets, $203,105,000,000; sales volume, $469,162,000,000; pre-tax net income, $25,737,000,000; expenses, $441,361,000,000; liabilities, $126,762,000,000
Fortune 1000 ranking: 2012—1st in revenues, 7th in profits, and 29th in assets
Forbes 2000 ranking: 2012—1st in sales, 16th in profits, and 135th in assets
Corporate officers: S. Robson Walton, Chair.; Michael T. Duke, Pres. and C.E.O.; Charles M. Holley, Jr., Exec. V.P. and C.F.O.; Rollin L. Ford, Exec. V.P. and C.A.O.; Karenann K. Terrell, Exec. V.P. and C.I.O.; Jeffrey J. Gearhart, Exec. V.P. and Corp. Secy.; Jeff Davis, Exec. V.P. and Treas.; Karen Roberts, Exec. V.P. and Genl. Counsel; Steven P. Whaley, Sr. V.P. and Cont.
Board of directors: S. Robson Walton, Chair.; Aida M. Alvarez; James W. Breyer; M. Michele Burns; James I. Cash, Jr.; Roger Campbell Corbett; Douglas Neville Daft; Michael T. Duke; Timothy P. Flynn; Marissa A. Mayer; Gregory Boyd Penner; Steven S. Reinemund; H. Lee Scott, Jr.; Arne M. Sorenson; Jim C. Walton; Christopher J. Williams; Linda S. Wolf
Plants: Wasilla, AK; Flippin, AR; City of Industry, CA; Mililani, HI; Crawfordsville, IN; Pella, IA; Chanute, Lawrence, KS; St. Roberts, MO; Minot, NC; Jay, Moore, OK; Philadelphia, PA
Offices: Turlock, CA; Tallahassee, FL; Boise, ID; Alton, IL; Ankeny, IA; Aberdeen, WA
International operations: England
Giving statement: Giving through the Wal-Mart Stores, Inc. Corporate Giving Program, the Wal-Mart Foundation, Inc., and the Wal-Mart Associates in Critical Need Fund.
Company EIN: 710415188

Wal-Mart Stores, Inc. Corporate Giving Program

(also known as Walmart Corporate Giving Program)
702 S.W. 8th St.
Bentonville, AR 72716-8611 (479) 273-4000
URL: http://walmartstores.com/CommunityGiving/

Financial data (yr. ended 01/31/13): Total giving, $775,000,000, including $775,000,000 for in-kind gifts.
Purpose and activities: As a complement to its foundation, Wal-Mart Stores also makes charitable contributions to nonprofit organizations directly. Support is given primarily in areas of company operations.
Fields of interest: Education, services; Education; Hospitals (general); Food services; Food banks; Disasters, preparedness/services; American Red Cross; Salvation Army; Children, services; Human services, gift distribution.
Program:
Teacher Rewards Program: Through the Teacher Rewards Program, Wal-Mart and Sam's Club rewards teachers and schools in need. The company selects one local K-8 school in each location, and randomly selects 10 teachers per school to receive a $100 Teacher Reward card to purchase classroom supplies from a Wal-Mart store, Sam's Club, or online at walmart.com or samsclub.com.
Type of support: Donated products; Employee volunteer services; General/operating support; In-kind gifts.
Geographic limitations: Giving on a national basis in areas of company operations; giving also to national organizations.
Application information: Applications accepted. Application form not required.
Initial approach: Contact nearest company Walmart Store or Sam's Club for product donations
Deadline(s): None for product donations

The Wal-Mart Foundation, Inc.

(also known as The Walmart Foundation)
(formerly Wal-Mart Foundation)
702 S.W. 8th St., Dept. 8687, No. 0555
Bentonville, AR 72716-0555 (800) 530-9925
FAX: (479) 273-6850; URL: http://walmartfoundation.org

Establishment information: Established in 1979 in AR.
Donor: Wal-Mart Stores, Inc.
Contact: Julie Gehrki, Sr. Dir., Business Integration
Financial data (yr. ended 01/31/12): Assets, $30,057,516 (M); gifts received, $173,622,222; expenditures, $175,680,474; qualifying distributions, $175,680,474; giving activities include $175,680,474 for 10,577 grants (high: $9,329,774; low: $1).
Purpose and activities: The foundation supports programs designed to promote hunger relief and healthy eating; sustainability; women's economic empowerment; and career opportunity. The foundation also funds disaster relief, women, military and veterans, and economically disadvantaged people.
Fields of interest: Middle schools/education; Elementary school/education; Secondary school/education; Higher education; Teacher school/education; Adult education—literacy, basic skills & GED; Education, ESL programs; Education, services; Education, drop-out prevention; Education, reading; Education; Health care, equal rights; Hospitals (general); Health care, clinics/centers; Public health; Health care; Employment, services; Employment, training; Employment, retraining; Goodwill Industries; Employment; Agriculture, sustainable programs; Agriculture, farmlands; Food services; Food banks; Food distribution, meals on wheels; Nutrition; Housing/shelter; Disasters, preparedness/services; Boys & girls clubs; Youth development, business; American Red Cross; Salvation Army; Children, services; Human services, financial counseling; Human services, mind/body enrichment; Developmentally disabled, centers & services; Community development, business promotion; Community development, small businesses; Community/economic development; United Ways and Federated Giving Programs; Military/veterans' organizations Minorities; Women; Military/veterans; Economically disadvantaged.
Programs:
Fighting Hunger Together Initiative: Through the Fighting Hunger Together Initiative, Wal-Mart and the foundation support programs designed to help end hunger in America through 2015. The initiative includes in-kind food donations from Wal-Mart stores, distribution centers, and Sam's Club locations; grants to hunger relief organizations at the national, state, and local level from the

foundation; volunteerism efforts from Wal-Mart associates and customers; and collaboration with government, food manufacturers, and other corporations to increase impact and reach a greater number of families in need. Visit URL: http://fightinghunger.walmart.com for more information.

Global Women's Economic Empowerment Initiative: Through the Global Women's Economic Empowerment Initiative, Wal-Mart and the foundation support programs designed to empower women across the global supply chain. Special emphasis is directed toward programs designed to increase sourcing from women-owned businesses; empower women on farms and in factories; empower women through training and education; increase gender diversity among major suppliers; and programs designed to make significant philanthropic giving toward women's economic empowerment. Visit URL: http://walmartstores.com/women/ for more information.

Local Giving Program: The foundation awards grants of $250 to $2,500 to nonprofit organizations recommended by Wal-Mart Stores, Sam's Club, and Logistics Facilities to support the needs of local communities. Special emphasis is directed toward programs designed to promote hunger relief and healthy eating; sustainability; women's economic empowerment; and career opportunity.

Local Giving Program - Sam's Club: Through the Sam's Club Giving Program, Sam's Club and the foundation supports small businesses at the national, state, and local level, including advanced training that empowers, particularly women- and minority-owned businesses. Special emphasis is directed toward hunger relief and healthy eating; sustainability; women's economic empowerment; career opportunity; education; and youth success.

National Giving Program: The foundation awards grants of $250,000 and higher to organizations that are implementing programs in multiple sites across the country or have innovative initiatives that are ready for replication nationally. Special emphasis is directed toward programs designed to promote hunger relief and healthy eating; sustainability; women's economic empowerment; or career opportunity.

State Giving Program: The foundation awards grants of $25,000 to $250,000 to nonprofit organizations that serve a particular state or region. State Advisory Councils made up of local Wal-Mart associates determine the needs within each state, review grant applications, and make recommendations to the foundation. The foundation encourages requests that support hunger relief and healthy eating; sustainability; women's economic empowerment; and career opportunity.

State Giving Program - Northwest Arkansas: The foundation awards grants starting at $5,000 to nonprofit organizations designed to serve Benton and Washington counties, Arkansas. Special emphasis is directed toward hunger relief and healthy eating; health care; and quality of life.

Volunteerism Always Pays (VAP): Through the Volunteerism Always Pays (VAP) program, Wal-Mart associates may request charitable contributions on behalf of eligible organizations where they volunteer.

Wal-Mart Associate Scholarship: The foundation annually awards renewable college scholarships of up to $16,000 to Wal-Mart and Sam's Club associates to pursue postsecondary education at American Public University, a two-year institution, or a four-year institution. The program is administered by ACT, Inc.

Wal-Mart Dependent Scholarship: The foundation annually awards renewable college scholarships of up to $13,000 to dependents of associates of Wal-Mart who are graduating high school with a 2.5 cumulative GPA and a demonstrated financial need. The program is administered by ACT, Inc.

Type of support: Emergency funds; Employee matching gifts; Employee volunteer services; Employee-related scholarships; Grants to individuals; Management development/capacity building; Matching/challenge support; Program development; Scholarship funds; Sponsorships.

Geographic limitations: Giving on a national basis in areas of company operations, with emphasis on AR, Washington, DC, DE, GA, MA. MD, NY, TN, TX, UT, and VA.

Support limitations: No support for faith-based organizations not of direct benefit to the entire community, political candidates or organizations, athletic teams, or discriminatory organizations. No grants to individuals (except for scholarships), or for multi-year funding, annual meetings, contests or pageants, political causes or campaigns, advertising, film, or video projects, research, athletic sponsorships or events, tickets for contests, raffles, or any other activities with prizes, travel, capital campaigns, endowments, association or chamber memberships, or registration fees, research, salaries, stipends, trips, rewards, construction costs, or projects that send products or people to a foreign country.

Publications: Application guidelines; Program policy statement.

Application information: Applications accepted. A full proposal may be requested at a later date for National Giving Program. Organizations receiving support are asked to submit an impact report detailing what outcomes were achieved. Applicants should submit the following:

1) statement of problem project will address
2) population served
3) name, address and phone number of organization
4) copy of IRS Determination Letter
5) detailed description of project and amount of funding requested
6) contact person
7) copy of current year's organizational budget and/or project budget

Initial approach: Complete online application for State Giving Program and Local Giving Program; complete online letter of inquiry for National Giving Program

Board meeting date(s): Mar., May, Aug., and Nov.

Deadline(s): None for State Giving Program; Dec. 1 for Local Giving Program; None for National Giving Program

Final notification: 90 days for Local Giving Program; 8 weeks for State Giving Program - Northwest Arkansas; 6 to 8 weeks for National Giving Program

Officers and Directors:* Michael T. Duke, Chair.; Sylvia Mathews Burwell, Pres.; Michelle Gilliard, V.P.; Michael Spencer, Secy.; Tim Culp, Treas.; Eduardo Castro-Wright; M. Susan Chambers; Matt Cockrell; Leslie A. Dach; Cindy Davis; Tom Mars; Margaret McKenna; Gisel Ruiz; Cathy Smith.

Number of staff: 31 full-time professional.

EIN: 205639919

Selected grants: The following grants are a representative sample of this grantmaker's funding activity:

$9,659,762 to ACT, Inc., Iowa City, IA, 2011.
$6,451,407 to Feeding America, Chicago, IL, 2011.
$5,797,922 to United e-Way, Alexandria, VA, 2011.
$3,400,000 to Boys and Girls Clubs of America, Atlanta, GA, 2011.
$3,000,000 to YMCA of the U.S.A., Chicago, IL, 2011.
$43,680 to Meals on Wheels of Fayetteville, Fayetteville, AR, 2011.
$4,750 to Cherokee County Crisis Center, Jacksonville, TX, 2011.
$2,500 to Inland Northwest Musicians, Hermiston, OR, 2011.
$2,000 to White County Public Library, Searcy, AR, 2011.

Wal-Mart Associates in Critical Need Fund

(also known as Walmart Associates in Critical Need Fund)
702 S.W. 8th St., Dept. 8687
M.S. No. 0555
Bentonville, AR 72716-0555 (800) 530-9925

Establishment information: Established in 2001 in AR.

Financial data (yr. ended 01/31/12): Revenue, $16,254,181; assets, $13,022,238 (M); gifts received, $16,228,271; expenditures, $10,092,265; giving activities include $10,092,265 for grants to individuals.

Purpose and activities: The fund assists Wal-Mart associates in need.

Fields of interest: Human services.

Trustees: Yvonne Cooper; Jennifer May-Brust; Margaret Mekenna; Deborah Neria; Rita Seckington; Erron Smith; Jennifer White.

EIN: 710858484

3984
Walter Energy, Inc.

(formerly Walter Industries, Inc.)
3000 Riverchase Galleria, Ste. 1700
Birmingham, AL 35244 (205) 745-2000
FAX: (302) 655-5049

Company URL: http://www.walterenergy.com/

Establishment information: Established in 1946.

Company type: Public company

Company ticker symbol and exchange: WLT/NYSE

Business activities: Manufactures water infrastructure and flow control products; mines coal; produces natural gas; builds houses; provides mortgages; produces furnace and foundry coke; manufactures chemicals; manufactures slag fiber.

Business type (SIC): Contractors/general residential building; coal mining; extraction/oil and gas; chemicals and allied products; petroleum and coal products/miscellaneous; abrasive, asbestos, and nonmetallic mineral products; machinery/industrial and commercial; brokers and bankers/mortgage

Financial profile for 2012: Number of employees, 4,100; assets, $5,768,420,000; sales volume, $2,399,890,000; pre-tax net income, -$1,164,760,000; expenses, $3,413,020,000; liabilities, $4,757,850,000

Fortune 1000 ranking: 2012—836th in revenues, 984th in profits, and 548th in assets

Corporate officers: Michael T. Tokarz, Chair.; Walter J. Scheller III, C.E.O.; William Harvey, C.F.O.; Thomas J. Lynch, Sr. V.P., Human Resources; Earl H. Doppelt, V.P., Genl. Counsel, and Secy.; Robert P. Kerley, V.P., Corp. Cont., and C.A.O.

Board of directors: Michael T. Tokarz, Chair.; David R. Beatty; Jerry W. Kolb; Patrick A. Kriegshauser; Joseph B. Leonard; Graham Mascall; Bernard G. Rethore; Walter J. Scheller III; A.J. Wagner; Mary R. Henderson

Subsidiaries: Best Insurors, Inc., Tampa, FL; Cardem Insurance Co., Ltd., Tampa, FL; Dixie Building Supplies, Inc., Tampa, FL; The Georgia Marble Co., Atlanta, GA; Hamer Properties, Inc., Tampa, FL; Mid-State Homes, Inc., Tampa, FL; Shore Oil Corp., Tampa, FL; United States Pipe &

Foundry, Birmingham, AL; J.W. Walter, Inc., Tampa, FL; Jim Walter Homes, Inc., Tampa, FL; Walter Land Co., Tampa, FL; Jim Walter Papers, Inc., Jacksonville, FL; Jim Walter Resources, Inc., Birmingham, AL
International operations: Bermuda
Giving statement: Giving through the Walter Energy, Inc. Corporate Giving Program and the Walter Foundation.
Company EIN: 133429953

Walter Energy, Inc. Corporate Giving Program

4211 W. Boy Scout Blvd.
Tampa, FL 33607 (813) 871-4811
FAX: (813) 871-4399;
E-mail: corporatecommunications@walterenergy.com; For Alabama inquiries: Dennis Hall, tel.: (205) 554-6905, e-mail: publicrelations@jwrinc.com; URL: http://www.walterenergy.com/citizenshipcenter/corp_giving.html

Contact: Michael A. Monahan, Dir., Corp. Comms.
Purpose and activities: As a complement to its foundation, Walter Energy also makes charitable contributions to nonprofit organizations directly. Special emphasis is directed toward programs that support children and families, health, education, and arts and culture. Support is given primarily in areas of company operations in Alabama, and Tampa, Florida.
Fields of interest: Arts; Education; Health care; Family services Children.
Type of support: Employee volunteer services; General/operating support.
Geographic limitations: Giving primarily in areas of company operations in AL and Tampa, FL.
Support limitations: No support for political, labor, religious, fraternal, sports, or discriminatory organizations. No grants to individuals, or for capital campaigns, construction and renovation projects, fundraising events such as raffles, telethons, walk-a-thons or auctions, chairs, endowments or scholarships sponsored by academic or nonprofit institutions, or special events such as conferences, symposia or sporting competitions.
Publications: Application guidelines.
Application information: Applications accepted. Priority is assigned to requests involving the volunteer efforts of Walter Energy employees. Applicants should submit the following:
1) results expected from proposed grant
2) copy of IRS Determination Letter
3) brief history of organization and description of its mission
4) detailed description of project and amount of funding requested
5) contact person
Initial approach: Proposal
Deadline(s): None
Final notification: 4 weeks

The Walter Foundation

(formerly Jim Walter Corporation Foundation)
13623 N. Florida Ave.
Tampa, FL 33613-3216 (813) 961-0530

Establishment information: Established in 1966 in FL.
Donor: Walter Industries, Inc.
Contact: W.K. Baker, Tr.
Financial data (yr. ended 08/31/12): Assets, $15,618,613 (M); expenditures, $911,232; qualifying distributions, $760,250; giving activities include $760,250 for grants.
Purpose and activities: The foundation supports hospitals and organizations involved with orchestras, historical activities, secondary and higher education, mental health and crisis services, hunger, human services, and Christianity.
Fields of interest: Performing arts, orchestras; Historical activities; Secondary school/education; Higher education; Hospitals (general); Mental health/crisis services; Food distribution, meals on wheels; Boys & girls clubs; Salvation Army; Children, services; Residential/custodial care; Developmentally disabled, centers & services; Human services; Christian agencies & churches.
Type of support: General/operating support.
Geographic limitations: Giving primarily in FL.
Support limitations: No grants to individuals.
Application information: Applications accepted. Application form not required.
Initial approach: Proposal
Deadline(s): None
Trustees: W. K. Baker; S. L. Myers; R. A. Walter.
EIN: 596205802
Selected grants: The following grants are a representative sample of this grantmaker's funding activity:
$100,000 to University of Tampa, Tampa, FL, 2010.
$100,000 to University of Tampa, Tampa, FL, 2011.
$75,000 to Florida Orchestra, Saint Petersburg, FL, 2011.
$50,000 to Idlewild Baptist Church, Lutz, FL, 2010.
$37,000 to Idlewild Baptist Church, Lutz, FL, 2011.
$30,000 to Tampa General Hospital Foundation, Tampa, FL, 2011.
$25,000 to American Red Cross, Tampa, FL, 2010.
$25,000 to Florida Orchestra, Saint Petersburg, FL, 2010.
$25,000 to Tampa Bay History Center, Tampa, FL, 2010.
$25,000 to Tampa Bay History Center, Tampa, FL, 2011.
$25,000 to Tampa General Hospital Foundation, Tampa, FL, 2010.
$15,000 to University of South Florida Foundation, Tampa, FL, 2010.
$15,000 to University of South Florida Foundation, Tampa, FL, 2011.
$10,000 to HARC, Tampa, FL, 2010.
$10,000 to HARC, Tampa, FL, 2011.
$10,000 to Metropolitan Ministries, Tampa, FL, 2011.
$10,000 to Tampa General Hospital Foundation, Tampa, FL, 2010.
$10,000 to Tampa Lighthouse for the Blind, Tampa, FL, 2010.
$10,000 to Tampa Lighthouse for the Blind, Tampa, FL, 2011.
$10,000 to Vanderbilt University, Nashville, TN, 2011.

3985
Warburg Pincus Partners LLC

450 Lexington Ave.
New York, NY 10017-3147 (212) 878-0600

Company URL: http://www.warburgpincus.com
Establishment information: Established in 1939.
Company type: Private company
Business activities: Operates venture capital company.
Business type (SIC): Investors/miscellaneous
Financial profile for 2010: Number of employees, 200; sales volume, $1,330,000,000
Corporate officers: James C. Smith, Chair. and C.E.O.; William H. Janeway, Vice-Chair.; John L. Vogelstein, Vice-Chair.; Charles R. Kaye, Co-Pres.; Joseph P. Landy, Co-Pres.
Board of directors: James C. Smith, Chair.; William H. Janeway, Vice-Chair.; John L. Vogelstein, Vice-Chair.
International operations: United Kingdom
Giving statement: Giving through the Warburg Pincus Partners LLC Corporate Giving Program and the Warburg Pincus Foundation.

The Warburg Pincus Foundation

450 Lexington Ave., 32nd Fl.
New York, NY 10017-3200

Establishment information: Established in 2000 in NY.
Donor: Warburg Pincus Partners LLC.
Financial data (yr. ended 11/30/11): Assets, $4,160,229 (M); gifts received, $6,155,300; expenditures, $2,320,659; qualifying distributions, $2,260,269; giving activities include $2,260,269 for grants.
Purpose and activities: The foundation supports parks and organizations involved with arts and culture, education, health, human services, and international affairs.
Fields of interest: Arts, cultural/ethnic awareness; Performing arts, theater; Arts; Higher education; Education, reading; Education; Health care, volunteer services; Hospitals (general); Health care, clinics/centers; Health care; Recreation, parks/playgrounds; Youth, services; Human services; International development; International relief; International affairs.
Type of support: Annual campaigns; General/operating support; Program development.
Geographic limitations: Giving primarily in CA, CT, GA, MA, New York, NY, and PA.
Support limitations: No grants to individuals.
Application information: Applications not accepted. Contributes only to pre-selected organizations.
Officers and Directors:* Charles R. Kaye*, Co-Pres.; Joseph P. Landy*, Co-Pres.; Scott A. Arenare*, Secy.; Timothy J. Curt*, Treas.; Steve G. Glenn.
EIN: 134148834

3986
C. P. Ward, Inc.

100 West River Rd.
Scottsville, NY 14546 (585) 889-8800

Company URL: http://cpward.com/
Establishment information: Established in 1921.
Company type: Private company
Business activities: Operates construction company.
Business type (SIC): Construction/highway and street (except elevated); construction/miscellaneous heavy; lumber and construction materials—wholesale; equipment rental and leasing/miscellaneous
Corporate officer: Dick Ash, Pres.
Giving statement: Giving through the C.P. Ward Charitable Foundation.

C.P. Ward Charitable Foundation

100 River Rd.
Scottsville, NY 14546-0900

Donor: C.P. Ward, Inc.
Financial data (yr. ended 12/31/11): Assets, $9,496 (M); gifts received, $10,000; expenditures, $5,870; qualifying distributions, $5,845; giving activities include $5,845 for grants.

Fields of interest: Education; Health organizations; Public affairs.
Type of support: General/operating support.
Geographic limitations: Giving limited to the Scottsville, NY, area.
Application information: Applications not accepted. Unsolicited requests for funds not accepted.
Officers: Richard A. Ash, Pres. and Treas.; William Keihl, V.P. and Secy.
EIN: 166098244

3987
Ward/Kraft, Inc.

2401 Cooper St.
P.O. Box 938
Fort Scott, KS 66701-3033 (620) 223-5500
FAX: (620) 223-1751

Company URL: http://www.wardkraft.com
Establishment information: Established in 1972.
Company type: Subsidiary of a private company
Business activities: Manufactures business forms and labels.
Business type (SIC): Business forms/manifold
Corporate officers: Harold E. Kraft, Chair; Roger E. Kraft, C.E.O.; Mark Tucker, Pres.
Board of director: Harold E. Kraft, Chair.
Giving statement: Giving through the Christian Learning Center Foundation.

The Christian Learning Center Foundation

3200 Liberty Bell Rd., Ste. 100
Fort Scott, KS 66701-7600

Establishment information: Established in 2005 in KS.
Donor: Ward Kraft, Inc.
Financial data (yr. ended 12/31/11): Revenue, $453,469; assets, $482,288 (M); gifts received, $360,000; expenditures, $464,664.
Purpose and activities: The foundation works to educate and encourage students to obtain the skills to meet the demands of the world.
Fields of interest: Education; Christian agencies & churches.
Support limitations: No grants to individuals.
Application information: Applications not accepted. Contributes only to pre-selected organizations.
Officers: Roger Kraft, Pres.; Janet S. Byler, Secy.-Treas.
Trustees: Diana Davis; Wanda Kraft.
EIN: 202114756

3988
The Warnaco Group, Inc.

501 Seventh Ave.
New York, NY 10018 (212) 287-8000

Company URL: http://www.warnaco.com
Establishment information: Established in 1874.
Company type: Subsidiary of a public company
Parent company: PVH Corp.
Business activities: Manufactures apparel for men, women, and children. At press time, the company is in the process of merging with PVH Corp.
Business type (SIC): Apparel—men's and boys' outerwear; hosiery and knitted fabrics; apparel—women's outerwear; apparel—women's, girls', and children's undergarments
Financial profile for 2011: Number of employees, 6,400; assets, $1,653,300,000; sales volume, $2,297,100,000
Plants: Bridgeport, CT; New York, NY; Portland, OR
Giving statement: Giving through the Warnaco Foundation.
Company EIN: 954032739

The Warnaco Foundation

c/o Warnaco Inc.
470 Wheelers Farm Rd.
Milford, CT 06461-9137

Establishment information: Established in 2007 in DE.
Donor: Warnaco, Inc.
Contact: Brent Landquist
Financial data (yr. ended 12/31/11): Assets, $195,229 (M); gifts received, $334,472; expenditures, $423,818; qualifying distributions, $388,288; giving activities include $388,288 for grants.
Fields of interest: Breast cancer; Athletics/sports, water sports; Youth development, centers/clubs.
Geographic limitations: Giving primarily in CA and CO.
Application information: Applications not accepted. Contributes only to pre-selected organizations.
Officers and Directors:* Elizabeth Wood*, Pres.; Ericka Alford, Secy.; Jay A. Galluzzo; Joseph R. Gromek; Lawrence R. Rutkowski.
EIN: 562675524
Selected grants: The following grants are a representative sample of this grantmaker's funding activity:
$167,000 to Save the Children Federation, Westport, CT, 2009.
$100,000 to Save the Children Federation, Westport, CT, 2009.
$10,000 to Boys and Girls Club, Madison Square, New York, NY, 2009.
$10,000 to New York Cares, New York, NY, 2009.
$1,250 to Multiple Sclerosis Society, National, Pittsburgh, PA, 2009.
$1,200 to Dreams Go On, Hollidaysburg, PA, 2009.

3989
Warner Bros. Home Entertainment Group

4000 Warner Blvd.
Burbank, CA 91522-0001 (818) 954-6000
FAX: (212) 954-7667

Company URL: http://www.warnerbros.com
Establishment information: Established in 2005.
Company type: Subsidiary of a private company
Business activities: Produces and distributes motion picture videos.
Business type (SIC): Motion picture and video tape distribution
Corporate officers: Barry M. Meyer, Chair.; Kevin Tsujihara, Pres. and C.E.O.; Edward A. Romano, Exec. V.P. and C.F.O.; John Rogovin, Exec. V.P. and Genl. Counsel; Susan Nahley Fleishman, Exec. V.P., Comms. and Public Affairs; Kiko Washington, Exec. V.P., Human Resources
Board of director: Barry M. Meyer, Chair.
Giving statement: Giving through the Warner Bros. Home Entertainment Group Corporate Giving Program.

Warner Bros. Home Entertainment Group Corporate Giving Program

4000 Warner Blvd.
Burbank, CA 91522-0001 (818) 954-6000
URL: http://www.warnerbros.com/#/page=company-info/

3990
Warner Music Group Corp.

75 Rockefeller Plz.
New York, NY 10019 (212) 275-2000

Company URL: http://www.wmg.com/
Establishment information: Established in 1811.
Company type: Subsidiary of a private company
Business activities: Operates recorded music and music publishing company.
Business type (SIC): Audio and video equipment/household
Financial profile for 2011: Number of employees, 3,700; assets, $3,779,000,000; sales volume, $2,984,000,000
Fortune 1000 ranking: 2012—753rd in revenues, 926th in profits, and 578th in assets
Corporate officers: Lyor Cohen, Chair. and C.E.O.; Brian Roberts, Exec. V.P. and C.F.O.; Paul M. Robinson, Exec. V.P. and Genl. Counsel; Will Tanous, Exec. V.P., Mktg. and Comms.; Mark Ansorge, Exec. V.P., Human Resources
Board of director: Lyor Cohen, Chair.
Giving statement: Giving through the Warner Music Group Charitable Foundation.
Company EIN: 134271875

Warner Music Group Charitable Foundation

75 Rockefeller Plz., 12th Fl.
New York, NY 10019-6908 (212) 275-3482

Establishment information: Established in 2005 in NY.
Donor: Warner Music Group.
Financial data (yr. ended 09/30/11): Assets, $767 (M); gifts received, $1,754; expenditures, $1,764; qualifying distributions, $1,764.
Geographic limitations: Giving primarily in LA, with some giving in FL.
Application information: Applications accepted. Application form required. Applicants should submit the following:
1) copy of IRS Determination Letter
2) detailed description of project and amount of funding requested
3) additional materials/documentation
Initial approach: Letter
Deadline(s): None
Officers: Edgar Bronfman, Jr.*, Pres.; Christopher Papandrew, V.P.; Kevin Conway*, Secy.
Directors: Mark Ansorge; Will Tanous.
EIN: 203562379

3991
The Warrell Corporation

(formerly Pennsylvania Dutch Company, Inc.)
1250 Slate Hill Rd.
Camp Hill, PA 17011 (717) 761-5440
FAX: (717) 761-5702

Company URL: http://www.warrellcorp.com/
Establishment information: Established in 1965.
Company type: Private company

Business activities: Produces candy and snack foods.
Business type (SIC): Sugar, candy, and salted/roasted nut production; miscellaneous prepared foods
Financial profile for 2011: Number of employees, 240
Corporate officers: Lincoln A. Warrell, Chair.; Patrick Huffman, Pres. and C.O.O.; Kevin Silva, Sr., Sr. V.P., Admin.; Osher Yam, V.P., Finance; Arny Strom, V.P., Mktg.; Tom Yantis, Corp. Cont.
Board of director: Lincoln A. Warrell, Chair.
Giving statement: Giving through the Warrell Corporation Foundation.

The Warrell Corporation Foundation

(formerly The Pennsylvania Dutch Company Foundation)
366 Belvedere St.
Carlisle, PA 17013-3503

Establishment information: Established in 1976.
Donors: Pennsylvania Dutch Co., Inc.; Jonas E. Warrell; The Warrell Corporation.
Financial data (yr. ended 10/31/11): Assets, $25,267 (M); gifts received, $32,000; expenditures, $32,113; qualifying distributions, $31,550; giving activities include $31,550 for 31 grants (high: $5,000; low: $100).
Purpose and activities: The foundation supports organizations involved with arts and culture, secondary and higher education, homelessness, civic affairs, and Catholicism.
Fields of interest: Arts; Secondary school/education; Higher education; Homeless, human services; Leadership development; Public affairs; Catholic agencies & churches.
Type of support: Annual campaigns; Building/renovation; Capital campaigns; General/operating support; Program development.
Application information: Applications not accepted. Unsolicited requests for funds not accepted.
Officer: Marilyn E. Warrell, Mgr.
EIN: 232022526

3992
Warren Pharmaceuticals, Inc.

712 Kitchawan Rd.
Ossining, NY 10562-1118 (914) 762-7586

Company URL: http://www.warrenpharma.com
Establishment information: Established in 2001.
Company type: Private company
Business activities: Develops tissue-protective biotech technologies.
Business type (SIC): Drugs
Corporate officers: Anthony Cerami, Ph.D., Chair. and C.E.O.; Frans Wuite, M.D., C.O.O.
Board of directors: Anthony Cerami, Ph.D., Chair.; Michael Brines, M.D., Ph.D.; John D. Macomber; Jesper Zuethen
Giving statement: Giving through the Kenneth S. Warren Laboratories, Inc.

The Kenneth S. Warren Laboratories, Inc.

(formerly Drug and Vaccine Development Corporation)
712 Kitchawan Rd.
Ossining, NY 10562-1118 (914) 762-7668

Establishment information: Established in NY.
Donors: Johnson & Johnson Services, Inc.; Ortho Biotech Inc.; Ortho Biotech Products, L.P.; Warren Pharmaceuticals, Inc.; Carla Cerami Hand; Thomas Donnelly.
Financial data (yr. ended 12/31/10): Assets, $3,250,408 (M); expenditures, $81,364; qualifying distributions, $40,937.
Purpose and activities: The foundation facilitates the discovery and development of new therapeutics to alleviate health problems of the world's poorest people, with emphasis on the fields of parasitology and tropical medicine.
Support limitations: No grants to individuals.
Application information: Applications not accepted. Unsolicited requests for funds not accepted.
Officer: Carla Cerami Hand, Pres. and Treas.; Thomas Donnelly, Secy.
EIN: 133054365

3993
Warren Transport, Inc.

210 Beck Ave.
P.O. Box 420
Waterloo, IA 50704 (319) 233-6113

Company URL: http://www.warrentransport.com
Establishment information: Established in 1949.
Company type: Private company
Business activities: Operates trucking company; transports specialized equipment and machinery.
Business type (SIC): Trucking and courier services, except by air
Corporate officers: Robert J. Molinaro, Co-Pres. and C.E.O.; Richard Donnelly, Co-Pres.; Shirley Schweertman, C.I.O.; Arthur Hellum, V.P. and Cont.
Giving statement: Giving through the WTI Charitable Foundation.

WTI Charitable Foundation

P.O. Box 420
Waterloo, IA 50704-0420 (319) 233-6113
Application address: 3545 Augusta Circle, Waterloo, IA 50701

Establishment information: Established in 1998 in IA.
Donor: Warren Transport, Inc.
Contact: Robert J. Molinaro, Pres.
Financial data (yr. ended 12/31/11): Assets, $3,561,111 (M); gifts received, $820,500; expenditures, $353,454; qualifying distributions, $332,500; giving activities include $332,500 for grants.
Purpose and activities: The foundation supports food banks and organizations involved with higher education, animal welfare, mental health, human services, and Catholicism.
Fields of interest: Higher education; Education; Animal welfare; Mental health/crisis services; Food banks; Salvation Army; Homeless, human services; Human services; Catholic agencies & churches.
Type of support: General/operating support.
Geographic limitations: Giving primarily in IA.
Application information: Applications accepted. Application form not required. Applicants should submit the following:
1) name, address and phone number of organization
2) detailed description of project and amount of funding requested
Initial approach: Proposal
Deadline(s): None
Officers: Robert J. Molinaro, Pres.; Mary Ellen Molinaro, V.P.; Shirley Schweertman, Secy.; Tunis Den Hartog, Treas.
EIN: 421480934

3994
The Washington Corporations

101 International Dr.
P.O. Box 16630
Missoula, MT 59808-1549 (406) 523-1300

Company URL: http://www.washcorp.com
Establishment information: Established in 1964.
Company type: Private company
Business activities: Provides business services.
Business type (SIC): Management and public relations services
Corporate officer: Lawrence R. Simkins, Pres.
Giving statement: Giving through the Dennis & Phyllis Washington Foundation, Inc.

Dennis & Phyllis Washington Foundation, Inc.

(formerly Dennis R. Washington Foundation, Inc.)
P.O. Box 16630
Missoula, MT 59808-6630 (406) 523-1300
URL: http://www.dpwfoundation.org/

Establishment information: Established in 1988 in MT.
Donors: Dennis & Phyllis Washington; Washington Corporations; Montana Rail Link, Inc.; Montana Resources, L.L.P; Dennis Washington; Phyllis J. Washington; Modern Machinery, Inc.
Contact: Mike Halligan, Exec. Dir.
Financial data (yr. ended 12/31/11): Assets, $436,814,858 (M); gifts received, $78,134,276; expenditures, $21,653,216; qualifying distributions, $20,942,995; giving activities include $20,388,792 for 291 grants (high: $10,000,000; low: $500).
Purpose and activities: The foundation supports organizations involved with arts and culture, education, health, human services, and community services, and awards college scholarships and fellowships. Special emphasis is directed toward programs designed to provide a direct service to economically and socially disadvantaged youth and their families, at-risk or troubled youth, and individuals with special needs.
Fields of interest: Performing arts, theater; Performing arts, music; Arts; Education, early childhood education; Higher education; Scholarships/financial aid; Education, services; Education; Dental care; Health care; Food banks; Athletics/sports, Special Olympics; Youth development; Human services; Community/economic development Infants/toddlers; Children/youth; Children; Youth; Disabilities, people with; Physically disabled; Native Americans/American Indians; Economically disadvantaged; Homeless.
Programs:
Arts and Culture: The foundation supports programs designed to bring people together from all walks of life to share their creative talents, intellects, passions, customs, and bold initiatives to explore new ways of doing things, with emphasis on theatre, art, and music.
Community Service: The foundation supports programs designed to promote community service and organizations that fortify the connection between community service and the common interest to do more for the places we call home.
Dennis and Phyllis Washington Native American Graduate Fellowship: The foundation awards a graduate fellowship of up to $10,000 to a member of a Montana Indian Tribe who is accepted into a Master's or Doctoral Degree program at the Graduate School of The University of Montana or Montana State University. The program is administered by the graduate school admissions

office at Montana State University and The University of Montana.

Dennis R. Washington Achievement Scholarship: The foundation annually awards scholarships of up to $30,000 for up to 3 years to State and National Horatio Alger Scholar Alumni who have exhibited integrity and perseverance in overcoming personal adversity and who is working towards a post-graduate degree in education.

Education: The foundation supports programs designed to reach children through early childhood education, after-school learning, post-secondary scholarships, and graduate fellowships that help young people get the start they deserve.

Health and Human Services: The foundation supports programs designed to ensure access to basic healthcare services to the most vulnerable members of the community. Special emphasis is directed toward groups that provide physical or psychological care for those in need; and experiential programs that offer disabled or disadvantaged people the chance to do something they may not have otherwise.

Helen B. Miller Horatio Alger Scholarship: The foundation awards college scholarships to students who attend Montana State University, demonstrate financial need, and demonstrate the ability to overcome adversity in their young lives. The program is administered by Montana State University.

Horatio Alger Montana Undergraduate Scholarship Program: The foundation annually awards 50 $10,000 college scholarships to Montana high school seniors planning to attend The University of Montana, The University of Montana-Western, The University of Montana-Missoula College of Technology, Helena College of Technology of the University of Montana, or Montana Tech of the University of Montana. The scholarship was expanded to include Montana State University and its affiliate campuses.

Washington Companies Employee Family Scholarship Program: The foundation awards college scholarships of up to $8,000 to children or spouses of employees who are attending an accredited university, college, vocational technical school, community college of technology, or trade school. Employees must work full-time within an eligible Washington Company.

Type of support: Annual campaigns; Building/renovation; Employee-related scholarships; Fellowships; Matching/challenge support; Program development; Scholarship funds; Scholarships—to individuals.

Geographic limitations: Giving primarily in areas of company operations, with emphasis on MT.

Support limitations: No support for discriminatory organizations, sectarian or religious organizations not of direct benefit to the entire community, veterans' or fraternal organizations not of direct benefit to the entire community, private or public foundations, or political action or legislative advocacy groups. No grants to individuals (except for scholarships), or for debt reduction, general operating support, travel expenses or trips, endowments, sponsorships including auctions, dinners, tickets, advertising, or annual fundraising events, curriculum development for educational institutions, or motor vehicle or other transportation equipment purchases; generally, no grants for capital campaigns; no loans.

Publications: Application guidelines.

Application information: Applications accepted. Organizations receiving support are asked to submit a post-grant evaluation. An interview may be required for graduate level scholarships. Application form required. Applicants should submit the following:

1) copy of IRS Determination Letter
2) copy of most recent annual report/audited financial statement/990
3) detailed description of project and amount of funding requested
4) copy of current year's organizational budget and/or project budget

Requests for scholarships should include transcripts, GPA, letters of recommendation, and an essay.

Initial approach: Complete online application form
Board meeting date(s): Quarterly
Deadline(s): None; Apr. 1 for Dennis R. Washington Achievement Scholarship; Apr. 15 for Horatio Alger Montana Undergraduate Scholarship Program (apply directly to Horatio Alger Association via their website)
Final notification: 90 days

Officers and Directors:* Phyllis J. Washington*, Chair.; Lawrence R. Simkins, Pres.; Mike Halligan, Exec. Dir.; William H. Brodsky; Rolin Erickson; Brian Sheridan.

Number of staff: 1 full-time professional.

EIN: 363606913

Selected grants: The following grants are a representative sample of this grantmaker's funding activity:

$16,000,000 to Washington Family Ranch, Antelope, OR, 2010. For program support.
$2,095,000 to University of Montana Foundation, Missoula, MT, 2010. For program support.
$50,000 to Missoula County High Schools, Missoula, MT, 2010. For program support.
$37,000 to Special Olympics Montana, Great Falls, MT, 2010. For program support.
$25,000 to Butte Archives, Friends of the, Butte, MT, 2010. For program support.
$20,000 to Polson School District, Polson, MT, 2010. For program support.
$15,000 to Childrens Oncology Camp Foundation, Missoula, MT, 2010. For program support.
$10,000 to Maroon Athletic Center, Butte, MT, 2010. For program support.
$10,000 to Missoula Law Enforcement Youth Camp, Missoula, MT, 2010. For program support.
$5,500 to Education Foundation for Billings Public Schools, Billings, MT, 2010. For program support.

3995
Washington Division of URS Corporation

(doing business as Washington Group)
(formerly Washington International Group, Inc.)
720 Park Blvd.
P.O. Box 73
Boise, ID 83712-7714 (208) 386-5000

Company URL: http://www.urscorp.com/
Establishment information: Established in 1912.
Company type: Subsidiary of a public company
Business activities: Provides design, engineering, construction, construction management, facilities and operations management, environmental remediation, and mining services.
Business type (SIC): Heavy construction other than building construction contractors; oil and gas field services; engineering, architectural, and surveying services; management and public relations services
Corporate officer: H. Thomas Hicks, Chair.
Board of director: H. Thomas Hicks, Chair.
Giving statement: Giving through the Manulife Financial Corp. Contributions Program and the Boise Legacy Constructors Foundation, Inc.
Company EIN: 690565601

Boise Legacy Constructors Foundation, Inc.

(formerly Washington Group Foundation)
102 S. 17th St., Ste. 200
Boise, ID 83702-5172
FAX: (208) 424-7627;
E-mail: blcfoundation@qwestoffice.net; URL: http://boiselegacyconstructorsfoundation.com/

Establishment information: Established in 1947 in ID as a company-sponsored operating foundation.
Donors: Morrison Knudsen Corp.; Washington Group International, Inc.; WGI Holdings England.
Contact: Marlene M. Puckett, Secy. and Exec. Dir.
Financial data (yr. ended 12/31/11): Assets, $6,723,301 (M); gifts received, $200; expenditures, $328,009; qualifying distributions, $325,080; giving activities include $58,200 for 19 grants (high: $15,000; low: $100) and $156,697 for 205 grants to individuals (high: $10,781).
Purpose and activities: The foundation supports programs designed to promote health and human services, civic and community issues, education, and culture and arts, and awards grants to needy individuals to assist with basic necessities.
Fields of interest: Visual arts; Performing arts; Arts; Education; Environment; Health care; Salvation Army; Human services; Community/economic development; Mathematics; Engineering/technology; Science; Public affairs Youth; Aging; Economically disadvantaged.

Programs:

Civic and Community: The foundation supports programs designed to benefit the public at large by unifying the community, solving problems, and enhancing quality of life with social activities to build good neighborhoods.

Culture and Arts: The foundation supports programs designed to provide performing and cultural arts experience to underserved communities and underprivileged individuals, with emphasis on youth and elderly.

Education: The foundation supports high-impact educational programs designed to further knowledge of math, science, the environment, communications, and technology to help build a future workforce.

Health and Human Services: The foundation supports programs designed to provide relief to the poor, elderly, and disabled, and solutions for others who are experiencing crisis.

Type of support: Emergency funds; Equipment; Grants to individuals; Program development; Sponsorships.
Geographic limitations: Giving limited to Boise, ID.
Support limitations: No support for political, labor, or fraternal organizations, merchant associations, civic clubs, memberships, lobbying, or discriminatory organizations, or churches or religious organizations. No grants for trust funds, sporting events, seminars, contests, sponsorships, travel, student trips or tours, books, films, television or video production, research or feasibility studies, or tickets for raffles or other prize-oriented activities.
Application information: Applications not accepted. Individuals must be referred by a social service agency.
Officers and Directors:* Frank Finlayson*, Pres.; Marlene M. Puckett*, Secy. and Exec. Dir.; Russ Strong*, Treas.; Mary Ann Arnold; Frank Finlayson; Mac Hartley; James McCallum; Matthew Reece; Tony Sander; Scott Wilson; Dawn Yantek.
Number of staff: 1 full-time professional.
EIN: 826005410

3996
Washington Financial Bank

(formerly Washington Federal Savings Bank)
190 N. Main St., Ste. 400
Washington, PA 15301-4395
(724) 222-3120

Company URL: http://www.washfed.com
Establishment information: Established in 1899.
Company type: Private company
Business activities: Operates savings bank.
Business type (SIC): Savings institutions
Financial profile for 2011: Assets, $821,793,519; liabilities, $728,926,962
Corporate officers: William M. Campbell, Chair.; D. Jackson Milhollan, Vice-Chair.; Brian J. Smith, Pres. and C.E.O.; Michael P. Pirih, Exec. V.P. and C.I.O.; John S. Milinovich, Exec. V.P., Treas., and C.F.O.; Suzanne L. Taylor, Sr. V.P. and Secy.; Janet L. Brandtonies, V.P. and Cont.; Elizabeth I. Guerrieri, V.P., Mktg.
Board of directors: William M. Campbell, Chair.; D. Jackson Milhollan, Vice-Chair.; David R. Andrews; Martin P. Beichner, Jr.; Mary Lyn Drewitz; James R. Proudfit; Brian J. Smith; Telford W. Thomas; Louis E. Waller
Giving statement: Giving through the Washington Financial Charitable Foundation.

Washington Financial Charitable Foundation

190 N. Main St.
Washington, PA 15301-4349
E-mail: info@washfed.com; URL: http://www.washfed.com/building-our-community/charitable-support.aspx

Establishment information: Established in 1991 in PA.
Donors: Washington Federal Savings Bank; Washington Financial Bank.
Financial data (yr. ended 06/30/12): Assets, $68,217 (M); gifts received, $44,564; expenditures, $25,450; qualifying distributions, $24,975; giving activities include $24,500 for 20 grants (high: $3,750; low: $500).
Purpose and activities: The foundation supports organizations involved with health and human services, community development, and education.
Fields of interest: Education; Health care; Human services.
Programs:
Customer Choice Awards: Through Customer Choice Awards, customers vote for the nonprofit organization or community development project they would like to see funded. The foundation awards grants to those organizations based on total votes received.
Washington Financial Scholarship Fund: The foundation awards 10 $1,000 college scholarships to customers of Washington Financial Bank. Selection is based primarily on community service with priority given to those demonstrating the most significant financial need.
Type of support: Building/renovation; Capital campaigns; Equipment; Matching/challenge support; Scholarships—to individuals.
Geographic limitations: Giving primarily in Washington County, PA, and surrounding market areas.
Support limitations: No support for political, religious, fraternal, or national organizations or private foundations. No grants to individuals (except for scholarships), or for conferences or seminars or specialized health campaigns; no loans.
Publications: Application guidelines; Informational brochure (including application guidelines).
Application information: Applications accepted. Application form required. Applicants should submit the following:
1) statement of problem project will address
2) population served
3) copy of IRS Determination Letter
4) brief history of organization and description of its mission
5) geographic area to be served
6) how project's results will be evaluated or measured
7) detailed description of project and amount of funding requested
8) copy of current year's organizational budget and/or project budget
Initial approach: Proposal
Copies of proposal: 1
Board meeting date(s): Quarterly
Deadline(s): None
Officers: William M. Campbell, Chair.; Mary Lyn Drewitz, Secy.; D. Jackson Milhollan, Treas.
Trustees: David R. Andrews; Martin P. Beichner; Joseph M. Jefferson; James R. Proudfit; Brain J. Smith; Telford W. Thomas; Louis E. Waller; Richard L. White.
Number of staff: None.
EIN: 256395164

3997
Washington Gas Light Company

(also known as Washington Gas Company)
101 Constitution Ave. N.W.
Washington, DC 20080 (703) 750-4440

Company URL: http://www.washgas.com
Establishment information: Established in 1848.
Company type: Subsidiary of a public company
Business activities: Transmits and distributes natural gas.
Business type (SIC): Gas production and distribution; contractors/general residential building; steam and air-conditioning supply services
Financial profile for 2011: Number of employees, 1,399; assets, $3,809,034,000
Corporate officers: Terry D. McCallister, Jr., Chair. and C.E.O.; Adrian P. Chapman, Pres. and C.O.O.; Vincent L. Ammann, Jr., V.P. and C.F.O.; Leslie T. Thornton, V.P. and Genl. Counsel; Douglas A. Staebler, V.P., Opers.; Luanne S. Gutermuth, V.P., Human Resources; Arden T. Phillips, Corp. Secy.; Anthony M. Nee, Treas.; William R. Ford, Cont.
Board of directors: Terry D. McCallister, Jr., Chair.; Michael D. Barnes; James W. Dyke, Jr.; Melvyn J. Estrin; Nancy C. Floyd; James F. Lafond; Debra L. Lee; Terry D. McCallister
Subsidiaries: Advanced Mechanical Technology, Inc., Newton, MA; Davenport Insulation, Inc., Springfield, VA
Giving statement: Giving through the Washington Gas Light Company Contributions Program.

Washington Gas Light Company Contributions Program

c/o Corp. Contribs.
101 Constitution Avenue, NW, 3rd Fl.
Washington, DC 20080 (202) 624-6696
E-mail: tfunn@washgas.com; Contact for applications covering entire metro area of Washington, DC, Virginia, and Maryland: Lynn Battle, Corp. Rels., Washington Gas Light Company; Contact for applications covering any single jurisdiction in the metro area: Steven Jumper, Regional Public Policy, Washington Gas Light Company; URL: http://www.washgas.com/pages/CharitableGiving

Contact: Tracye Funn
Purpose and activities: Washington Gas Light makes charitable contributions to nonprofit organizations involved with education, air quality, and health. Support is given primarily in areas of company operations.
Fields of interest: Elementary/secondary education; Education; Environment, air pollution; Health care.
Type of support: Employee volunteer services; In-kind gifts.
Geographic limitations: Giving primarily in areas of company operations in Washington, DC, MD, and VA.
Support limitations: No support for religious organizations for sectarian purposes, political associations, organizations with a strictly sports focus, or organizations lacking 501(c)(3) status. No grants to individuals, or for general operating expenses, capital campaigns, or endowments.
Application information: Applications accepted. Application form not required. Applicants should submit the following:
1) copy of IRS Determination Letter
2) brief history of organization and description of its mission
3) how project's results will be evaluated or measured
4) explanation of why grantmaker is considered an appropriate donor for project
5) listing of board of directors, trustees, officers and other key people and their affiliations
6) detailed description of project and amount of funding requested
7) contact person
8) copy of current year's organizational budget and/or project budget
Initial approach: Proposal (no more than 5 pages) to headquarters
Copies of proposal: 1
Deadline(s): May 30
Final notification: 6 to 8 weeks

3998
Washington Nationals Baseball Club, LLC

(doing business as Washington Nationals)
(formerly Baseball Expos, L.P.)
1500 S. Capitol St., S.E.
Washington, DC 20003-1507
(202) 675-6287

Company URL: http://washington.nationals.mlb.com
Establishment information: Established in 2005.
Company type: Private company
Business activities: Operates professional baseball club.
Business type (SIC): Commercial sports
Financial profile for 2010: Number of employees, 99
Corporate officers: Marla Lerner Tanenbaum, Chair.; Stanley H. Kasten, Pres.; Andrew Feffer, C.O.O.; Lori A. Creasy, C.F.O.; Elise Holman, Sr. V.P., Admin; Damon T. Jones, V.P. and Genl. Counsel; Ted Towne, V.P., Finance; John Guagliano, V.P., Mktg.; Lara Potter, V.P., Comms.; Alexa Herndon, V.P., Human Resources
Board of director: Marla Lerner Tanenbaum, Chair.

Giving statement: Giving through the Washington Nationals Corporate Giving Program and the Washington Nationals Dream Foundation.

Washington Nationals Corporate Giving Program

c/o Community Rels., Donation Request
Nationals Park
1500 S. Capital Street SE
Washington, DC 20003-3599
E-mail: community.relations@nationals.com; E-mail for Speakers Request: speakers@nationals.com; URL: http://washington.nationals.mlb.com/NASApp/mlb/was/community/index.jsp

Purpose and activities: The Washington Nationals make charitable contributions to nonprofit organizations on a case by case basis. Support is given primarily in the greater Washington, DC, area.
Fields of interest: Elementary school/education; Libraries (public); Education, reading; Cancer; Breast cancer; Food banks; Athletics/sports, baseball; Boys & girls clubs; Children/youth, services; Military/veterans' organizations; General charitable giving Youth.
Programs:
In-game Military Appreciation: The Washington Nationals provide 19 Lexus President Club game tickets at every home game to wounded soldiers and other active military groups. The program includes a gourmet buffet, complimentary in-seat food and beverage service, views of underground battling cages and post-game press conference, and military groups are recognizes with a standing ovation by fans and players at the bottom of the third inning.
Season Ticket Donation Program: Through a partnership with Most Valuable Kids, season ticket holders of the Washington Nationals mail their unused tickets to be donated to area nonprofit organizations.
Speakers Request: Through Speakers Request, members of the Nationals' Front Office and friends in the community share knowledge and experience through a presentation.
The Commissioner's Community Initiative: The Washington Nationals, in partnership with MLB, awards game tickets to community and civic groups who would not otherwise be able to attend a Major League Baseball game. The program is designed to support the development of well-rounded youth and to reward the accomplishments of young people.
Type of support: Donated products; Employee volunteer services; In-kind gifts; Income development; Loaned talent.
Geographic limitations: Giving primarily in areas of company operations in the greater Washington, DC, area.
Support limitations: No grants for general operating support.
Publications: Application guidelines; Newsletter.
Application information: Applications accepted. Proposals should be submitted using organization letterhead. Support is limited to 1 contribution per organization during any given year. The Community Relations Department handles giving. Applicants should submit the following:
1) name, address and phone number of organization
2) copy of IRS Determination Letter
3) detailed description of project and amount of funding requested
4) contact person
Proposals should indicate the date of the event.
Initial approach: Mail proposal to headquarters for memorabilia donations; complete online application for speakers request and Commissioner's Community Initiative
Copies of proposal: 1
Deadline(s): 45 days prior to need for memorabilia donations; 6 weeks prior to need for speakers requests

The Washington Nationals Dream Foundation

1500 South Capitol St., S.E.
Washington, DC 20003-1507 (202) 541-1753
FAX: (202) 547-7057;
E-mail: vera.maher@nationals.com; URL: http://washington.nationals.mlb.com/was/community/foundation/index.jsp

Establishment information: Established in 2005 in DC as the Washington Nationals Foundation; current name adopted in 2007.
Contact: Vera Maher, Managing Coord.
Financial data (yr. ended 12/31/10): Revenue, $879,887; assets, $3,362,930 (M); gifts received, $1,073,121; expenditures, $505,862; giving activities include $337,022 for grants.
Purpose and activities: The foundation is committed to creating and maintaining community partnerships that improve the lives of children and families across the Washington Capital Region, especially in the fields of children's education, health, and recreation.
Fields of interest: Education; Athletics/sports, baseball; Recreation; Youth development; Community/economic development Children/youth.
Program:
Grants Program: The foundation will make available limited financial support to organizations in the Washington capital region whose programs are aligned with the foundation's focus on children's education, health, and recreation. Priority will be given to programs where: the foundation's commitment of resources has a significant impact on the projects or programs that align with its values; the project or program affords the foundation the opportunity to develop alliances and/or partnerships; the impact of the project or program and the foundation's involvement in it are measurable; and the foundation supports, but does not operate, the project or program.
Type of support: Program development.
Geographic limitations: Giving limited to Washington, DC.
Application information: Applications accepted. Applicants should submit the following:
1) contact person
2) detailed description of project and amount of funding requested
3) brief history of organization and description of its mission
Initial approach: Letter
Officers and Directors:* Marla L. Tanenbaum*, Chair.; Alphonso Maldon, Jr.*, Pres.; Debra L. Cohen; Matthew Cutts; Mark D. Lerner; Theodore N. Lerner.
EIN: 342034830

3999
The Washington Post Company

1150 15th St. N.W.
Washington, DC 20071-0001
(202) 334-6000
FAX: (202) 334-4536

Company URL: http://www.washpostco.com
Establishment information: Established in 1947.
Company type: Public company
Company ticker symbol and exchange: WPO/NYSE
Business activities: Publishes newspapers and magazines in print and online; provides educational services; also broadcast and cable television.
Business type (SIC): Newspaper publishing and/or printing; periodical publishing and/or printing; radio and television broadcasting; cable and other pay television services; vocational schools
Financial profile for 2012: Number of employees, 17,000; assets, $5,105,070,000; sales volume, $3,995,620,000; pre-tax net income, $122,280,000; expenses, $3,849,420,000; liabilities, $2,507,950,000
Fortune 1000 ranking: 2012—580th in revenues, 679th in profits, and 589th in assets
Corporate officers: Donald E. Graham, Chair. and C.E.O.; Hal S. Jones, Jr., Sr. V.P., Finance and C.F.O.; Veronica Dillon, Sr. V.P., Genl. Counsel, and Secy.; Wallace R. Cooney, V.P., Finance and C.A.O.; Daniel J. Lynch, V.P. and Treas.; Rima Calderon, V.P., Comms.; Denise Demeter, V.P., Human Resources
Board of directors: Donald E. Graham, Chair.; Lee C. Bollinger; Christopher C. Davis; Barry Diller; Thomas S. Gayner; Dave Goldberg; Anne M. Mulcahy; Ronald L. Olson; Larry D. Thompson; G. Richard Wagoner; Katharine Weymouth
Subsidiaries: Cable One, Inc., Phoenix, AZ; The Daily Herald Co., Everett, WA; Greater Washington Publishing, Inc., Fairfax, VA; Kaplan, Inc., New York, NY; Post-Newsweek Media, Inc., Gaithersburg, MD; Post-Newsweek Stations, Inc., Detroit, MI
International operations: Australia; Canada; China; Ireland; Israel; Singapore; United Kingdom
Giving statement: Giving through the Washington Post Company Contributions Program and the Washington Post Company Educational Foundation.
Company EIN: 530182885

The Washington Post Company Contributions Program

1150 15th St. N.W.
Washington, DC 20071-0001
FAX: (202) 334-4536;
E-mail: calderonr@washpost.com; URL: http://www.washpostco.com/phoenix.zhtml?c=62487&p=irol-ourcompanycommunity

Contact: Rima Calderon, V.P., Comms. and External Rels.
Financial data (yr. ended 12/31/11): Total giving, $2,813,839, including $2,813,839 for grants.
Purpose and activities: The Washington Post Company makes charitable contributions to nonprofit organizations involved with education, journalism, human services, and civic affairs. Support is given primarily in Washington, DC.
Fields of interest: Media, print publishing; Visual arts; Performing arts; Education; Children/youth, services; Human services; Public affairs.
Type of support: Annual campaigns; Employee matching gifts; General/operating support; In-kind gifts.
Geographic limitations: Giving primarily in Washington, DC.
Support limitations: No support for fraternal, political, or religious organizations or national or international organizations. No grants for conferences, special exhibitions, theater productions, or museum exhibitions.
Application information: Applications accepted. Washington Regional Association of Grantmakers' Common Grant Application Format accepted. The Corporate Communications Department handles giving. A contributions committee reviews all requests. Application form not required. Applicants should submit the following:
1) copy of IRS Determination Letter

2) copy of most recent annual report/audited financial statement/990
3) listing of board of directors, trustees, officers and other key people and their affiliations
4) copy of current year's organizational budget and/ or project budget
5) additional materials/documentation

Proposals should include a cover letter.

Initial approach: Proposal to headquarters
Copies of proposal: 1
Deadline(s): None
Final notification: 2 months

Number of staff: 1 part-time professional; 1 part-time support.

The Washington Post Company Educational Foundation

1150 15th St. N.W.
Washington, DC 20071-0001
FAX: (202) 334-4963;
E-mail: morsecm@washpost.com; URL: http:// www.washingtonpost.com/community

Establishment information: Established in 1988 in Washington, DC.
Donor: The Washington Post Co.
Contact: Carrie Morse
Financial data (yr. ended 12/31/11): Assets, $20,069 (M); gifts received, $384,000; expenditures, $402,685; qualifying distributions, $402,685; giving activities include $71,791 for 31 grants (high: $5,291; low: $1,000) and $63,000 for 21 grants to individuals (high: $3,000; low: $3,000).
Purpose and activities: The foundation supports organizations involved with education and awards grants for educational leadership and excellence in teaching.
Fields of interest: Secondary school/education; Higher education; Education.

Programs:

Distinguished Educational Leadership Awards: The foundation honors one principal from a private school and 19 principals from local public school systems in Washington, D.C., Maryland, and Virginia. The award is designed to recognize principals who go beyond the day-to-day demands of their position to create an exceptional educational environment and to encourage excellence in school leadership. The award includes a reception at The Post and participation in an educational seminar.

The Agnes Meyer Outstanding Teacher Awards: The foundation awards $3,000 to an outstanding teacher selected in each of the 19 local public systems, and one award to a teacher from a private school in the metropolitan area. The award is limited to school systems in Washington, D.C., Maryland, and Virginia. The award is designed to recognize excellence in teaching and to encourage creative and quality instruction.

Type of support: Grants to individuals; Scholarship funds; Scholarships—to individuals.
Geographic limitations: Giving primarily in the greater metropolitan Washington, DC, area, including MD and VA.
Publications: Application guidelines.
Application information: Applications accepted. Application form required.

Initial approach: Contact foundation for application form
Deadline(s): None

Officers: James A. McLaughlin, Secy.; Margaret Scott Schiff, Treas.
Directors: Donald E. Graham; David Jones; Lionel Neptune; Katharine Weymouth.
EIN: 521545926

4000
Washington Sports & Entertainment, L.P.

(also known as Washington Wizards/Washington Mystics)
601 F St., N.W.
Washington, DC 20004-1605
(202) 628-3200

Company URL: http://www.nba.com/wizards
Establishment information: Established in 1961.
Company type: Private company
Business activities: Operates professional basketball clubs.
Business type (SIC): Commercial sports
Corporate officers: Abe Pollin, Chair.; Ernie Grunfeld, Pres.; Matt Williams, Sr. V.P., Comms.
Board of director: Abe Pollin, Chair.
Divisions: Washington Mystics, Washington, DC; Washington Wizards, Washington, DC
Giving statement: Giving through the Washington Mystics Corporate Giving Program, the Washington Wizards Corporate Giving Program, and the Washington Sports & Entertainment Charities, Inc.

Washington Mystics Corporate Giving Program

c/o Community Rels. Dept.
601 F St., N.W., 3rd FL
Washington, DC 20004-1605
FAX: (202) 527-7539; URL: http://www.wnba.com/ mystics/

Purpose and activities: The Washington Mystics make charitable contributions to nonprofit organizations involved with health and fitness, breast cancer awareness, reading, and youth basketball, and on a case by case basis. Support is given primarily in Washington, DC, Maryland, and Virginia.
Fields of interest: Education, reading; Hospitals (general); Public health, physical fitness; Health care; Genetic diseases and disorders; Breast cancer; Athletics/sports, basketball; General charitable giving Youth.
Type of support: Donated products; In-kind gifts; Income development; Loaned talent.
Geographic limitations: Giving primarily in areas of company operations in Washington, DC metropolitan area.
Publications: Application guidelines.
Application information: Applications accepted. Proposals should be submitted using organization letterhead. Support is limited to 1 contribution per organization during any given year. Organizations receiving support are asked to submit a final report. The Community Relations Department handles giving. Application form not required. Applicants should submit the following:

1) name, address and phone number of organization
2) copy of IRS Determination Letter
3) detailed description of project and amount of funding requested
4) contact person

Requests for memorabilia donations should indicate the date, time, and location of the event.

Initial approach: Mail or fax proposal to headquarters for memorabilia donations, player appearances, and promotional items
Copies of proposal: 1
Deadline(s): 4 weeks prior to need for memorabilia donations and player appearances; 3 weeks prior to need for promotional items

Washington Wizards Corporate Giving Program

c/o Community Rels. Dept.
601 F St., N.W.
Washington, DC 20004-1605
URL: http://www.nba.com/wizards/community/ index.html

Purpose and activities: The Washington Wizards make charitable contributions to nonprofit organizations involved with youth, homelessness, and the underserved and on a case by case basis. Support is given primarily in the metropolitan Washington, DC, area.
Fields of interest: Education, reading; Education; Food services; Food banks; Youth, services; Human services, gift distribution; Homeless, human services; General charitable giving Economically disadvantaged.

Program:

Timeout With The Wizards: Through Reading Timeouts, the Wizards select local classrooms to go on a field trip to the Verizon Center where a Wizards player reads aloud with the students and talk about the importance of reading.

Type of support: Donated products; In-kind gifts; Income development; Loaned talent.
Geographic limitations: Giving primarily in areas of company operations in the metropolitan Washington, DC, area.
Publications: Application guidelines.
Application information: Applications accepted. Proposals should be submitted using organization letterhead. Support is limited to 1 contribution per organization during any given year. The Community Relations Department handles giving. Application form not required. Applicants should submit the following:

1) population served
2) name, address and phone number of organization
3) copy of IRS Determination Letter
4) descriptive literature about organization
5) detailed description of project and amount of funding requested
6) contact person

Proposals for memorabilia donations should indicate the date, time, and location of the event. Proposals for ticket donations should indicate the number of tickets needed.

Initial approach: Proposal to headquarters for memorabilia donations, promotional items, and ticket donations; complete online application for player appearances
Copies of proposal: 1
Deadline(s): 4 to 6 weeks prior to need for memorabilia donations; 3 weeks prior to need for promotional items; 5 to 6 weeks for player appearances; none for ticket donations
Final notification: 2 weeks prior to need for player appearances

Washington Sports & Entertainment Charities, Inc.

821 Capital Centre Blvd.
Largo, MD 20774-4811 (202) 661-5099

Financial data (yr. ended 12/31/11): Revenue, $66,552; assets, $274,517 (M); gifts received, $54,465; expenditures, $33,094; giving activities include $9,059 for grants.
Purpose and activities: The organization aims to relieve distressed and underprivileged youth in the Washington, DC area.
Fields of interest: Youth development; Human services Youth; Economically disadvantaged.
Type of support: Grants to individuals.

Geographic limitations: Giving primarily in the metropolitan Washington, DC area.
Officer and Directors:* Peter Biche, C.F.O.; Mary Davis; Gary Handleman; Judy Holland; William Tomoff.
EIN: 521627622

4001
The Washington Trust Company
23 Broad St.
Westerly, RI 02891-1879 (401) 348-1200

Company URL: http://www.washtrust.com
Establishment information: Established in 1800.
Company type: Subsidiary of a public company
Business activities: Operates commercial bank.
Business type (SIC): Banks/commercial
Corporate officers: Joseph J. MarcAurele, Chair.; David V. Devault, C.F.O.; Barbara J. Perino, Exec. V.P., Opers.
Board of director: Joseph J. MarcAurele, Chair.
Giving statement: Giving through the Washington Trust Charitable Foundation.

The Washington Trust Charitable Foundation
c/o The Washington Trust Co.
23 Broad St.
Westerly, RI 02891-1879 (401) 348-1207
URL: http://www.washtrust.com/home/about/community

Establishment information: Established in 1994 in RI.
Donor: The Washington Trust Co.
Contact: Dennis L. Algiere, Dir., Community Affairs
Financial data (yr. ended 12/31/11): Assets, $2,492,327 (M); gifts received, $989,649; expenditures, $401,998; qualifying distributions, $400,834; giving activities include $400,834 for grants.
Purpose and activities: The foundation supports programs designed to promote affordable housing and revitalization; business and economic development; youth and family services; health and human services; arts and culture; colleges, universities, and libraries; and conservation and the environment.
Fields of interest: Museums; Arts; Higher education; Libraries (public); Education; Environment, natural resources; Environment; Hospitals (general); Health care; Housing/shelter; YM/YWCAs & YM/YWHAs; Youth, services; Family services; Human services; Business/industry; Community/economic development; United Ways and Federated Giving Programs.
Type of support: Building/renovation; Capital campaigns; Continuing support; General/operating support; Program development.
Geographic limitations: Giving primarily in areas of company operations in southeastern CT, MA, and RI.
Support limitations: No grants to individuals.
Publications: Application guidelines.
Application information: Applications accepted. Application form not required. Applicants should submit the following:
1) detailed description of project and amount of funding requested
2) copy of IRS Determination Letter
Initial approach: Proposal
Copies of proposal: 1
Board meeting date(s): Dec.
Deadline(s): Oct. 1
Final notification: Jan.
Trustee: The Washington Trust Co.
EIN: 050477294
Selected grants: The following grants are a representative sample of this grantmaker's funding activity:
$51,000 to United Way of Rhode Island, Providence, RI, 2010. For operations.
$25,000 to YMCA, Ocean Community, Westerly, RI, 2010. For operations.
$20,000 to University of Rhode Island, Kingston, RI, 2010. For operations.
$10,000 to Westerly Hospital Foundation, Westerly, RI, 2010. For operations.
$7,000 to Rhode Island for Community and Justice, Providence, RI, 2010. For operations.
$5,000 to Boy Scouts of America, East Providence, RI, 2010. For operations.
$5,000 to Kent Center for Human and Organizational Development, Warwick, RI, 2010. For operations.
$2,500 to Grow Smart Rhode Island, Providence, RI, 2010. For operations.
$2,500 to Local Initiatives Support Corporation, Providence, RI, 2010. For operations.
$2,000 to Westerly Area Rest Meals, Westerly, RI, 2010. For operations.

4002
Waterford Group, L.L.C.
914 Hartford Tpke.
P.O. Box 715
Waterford, CT 06385 (860) 442-4559

Company URL: http://waterfordhotelgroup.com/
Establishment information: Established in 1986.
Company type: Private company
Business activities: Operates hotels; develops casinos; provides residential and nonresidential general contract construction services; provides public facility management services; operates restaurants.
Business type (SIC): Hotels and motels; contractors/general residential building; contractors/general nonresidential building; restaurants and drinking places; real estate subdividers and developers; management and public relations services
Corporate officers: Len Wolman, Chair. and C.E.O.; Robert W. Winchester, Pres. and C.O.O.; David Rebich, C.F.O.; Michael Heaton, V.P., Opers.; Brien Fox, V.P., Sales and Mktg.; Lisa Beers, V.P., Corp. Public Rels.; Judith Moran, V.P., Human Resources
Board of director: Len Volmen, Chair.
Subsidiaries: Waterford Gaming, L.L.C., Waterford, CT; Waterford Hotel Group, Inc., Waterford, CT; Wolman Construction, Waterford, CT
Giving statement: Giving through the Waterford Group Charitable Foundation, Inc.

Waterford Group Charitable Foundation, Inc.
914 Hartford Tpke.
Waterford, CT 06385-4229 (860) 442-4559
E-mail: lbeers@waterfordgroup.net

Establishment information: Established in 2004 in CT.
Donor: Waterford Group.
Contact: Lisa Beers
Financial data (yr. ended 12/31/11): Assets, $34,582 (M); gifts received, $91,177; expenditures, $71,613; qualifying distributions, $71,612; giving activities include $67,385 for 209 grants (high: $2,500; low: -$1,000).
Purpose and activities: The foundation supports hospitals and health centers and organizations involved with ballet, education, housing, and human services.
Fields of interest: Education; Housing/shelter; Human services.
Type of support: Annual campaigns; Employee volunteer services; General/operating support; In-kind gifts; Program development; Sponsorships.
Geographic limitations: Giving primarily in areas of company operations in southeastern and central CT.
Application information: Applications accepted. Application form required. Applicants should submit the following:
1) copy of IRS Determination Letter
2) detailed description of project and amount of funding requested
Initial approach: Letter
Deadline(s): Monthly
Officers and Directors:* Len Wolman*, Pres.; Mark Wolman*, V.P.; Del J. Lauria*, Secy.; Alan D. Angel*, Treas.
EIN: 550851570

4003
Waters Corporation
34 Maple St.
Milford, MA 01757 (508) 478-2000
FAX: (508) 872-1990

Company URL: http://www.waters.com
Establishment information: Established in 1958.
Company type: Public company
Company ticker symbol and exchange: WAT/NYSE
International Securities Identification Number: US9418481035
Business activities: Operates holding company; manufactures and sells liquid chromatography instruments and chromatography columns, mass spectrometry instruments, and thermal analysis and rheology instruments.
Business type (SIC): Laboratory apparatus; holding company
Financial profile for 2012: Number of employees, 5,900; assets, $3,168,150,000; sales volume, $1,843,640,000; pre-tax net income, $487,620,000; expenses, $1,332,150,000; liabilities, $1,700,790,000
Fortune 1000 ranking: 2012—991st in revenues, 350th in profits, and 735th in assets
Corporate officers: Douglas A. Berthiaume, Chair., Pres., and C.E.O.; John Ornell, V.P. and C.F.O., Finance and Admin.; Mark T. Beaudouin, V.P. and Genl. Counsel; Elizabeth B. Rae, V.P., Human Resources
Board of directors: Douglas A. Berthiaume, Chair.; Joshua Bekenstein; Michael J. Berendt, Ph.D.; Edward Conard; Laurie H. Glimcher, M.D.; Christopher A. Kuebler; William J. Miller; JoAnn A. Reed; Thomas P. Salice
International operations: Argentina; Australia; Austria; Brazil; Chile; Czech Republic; Denmark; Estonia; Finland; France; Germany; Greece; Hungary; Iceland; India; Indonesia; Ireland; Israel; Jordan; Latvia; Lithuania; Malaysia; Malta; Mexico; Netherlands; New Zealand; Norway; Poland; Romania; Saudi Arabia; South Africa; Sweden; Syria; Taiwan; Thailand; Ukraine; United Kingdom; Vietnam
Giving statement: Giving through the Waters Corporation Contributions Program.
Company EIN: 133668640

Waters Corporation Contributions Program

34 Maple St.
Milford, MA 01757-3604 (508) 478-2000
E-mail: CharitableGiving@waters.com; URL: http://www.waters.com/waters/nav.htm?locale=en_US&cid=134614727

Purpose and activities: Waters makes charitable contributions to nonprofit organizations involved with the arts, the environment, recreation, human services, science, education, and health care. Support is given primarily in areas of company operations in Massachusetts.
Fields of interest: Arts; Education; Health care; Recreation; Human services; Science.
Program:
Employee Matching Gifts: Waters supports individual employee contributions through a Matching Gift Program which matches employee contributions to qualified nonprofit organizations.
Type of support: Employee matching gifts; General/operating support.
Geographic limitations: Giving primarily in areas of company operations in MA.
Application information: Applications not accepted. Contributes only to pre-selected organizations.

4004
Watershed Capital, LLC

113 W. Fleetwood Dr.
Lookout Mountain, TN 37350-1431
(423) 825-6715

Company URL: http://www.watershedcapital.net
Establishment information: Established in 2007.
Company type: Private company
Business type (SIC): Business services/miscellaneous
Corporate officers: Michael Whelchel, Owner; Shawn Lesser, Owner
Board of directors: Peter Adriaens; Ronit Erlitzki; Ben Taube
Giving statement: Giving through the Watershed Capital LLC Contributions Program.

Watershed Capital LLC Contributions Program

113 W Fleetwood Dr.
Lookout Mountain, TN 37350-1431 (423) 825-6715
E-mail: info@watershedcapital.com; URL: http://www.watershedcapital.net

Purpose and activities: Watershed Capital is a certified B Corporation that donates a percentage of profits to charitable organizations.

4005
WaterStone Bank

(formerly Wauwatosa Savings and Loan Association)
11200 W. Plank Ct.
Wauwatosa, WI 53226 (414) 761-1000

Company URL: http://www.wsbonline.com
Establishment information: Established in 1921.
Company type: Subsidiary of a public company
Business activities: Operates savings bank.
Business type (SIC): Savings institutions
Corporate officers: Patrick S. Lawton, Chair.; Douglas S. Gordon, Pres. and C.E.O.; Richard C. Larson, Sr. V.P. and C.F.O.; William F. Bruss, Sr. V.P., Genl. Counsel, and Secy.; Don P. Bray, V.P. and C.I.O.; Mark R. Gerke, V.P. and Cont.
Board of director: Patrick S. Lawton, Chair.
Giving statement: Giving through the WaterStone Bank Corporate Giving Program and the Wauwatosa Savings and Loan Foundation.

WaterStone Bank Corporate Giving Program

11200 W. Plank Ct.
Wauwatosa, WI 53226-3250
URL: http://www.wsbonline.com/CommunitySupport.aspx

Purpose and activities: As a complement to its foundation, WaterStone Bank also makes charitable contributions to nonprofit organizations directly. Support limited to areas of company operations in southeastern Wisconsin.
Fields of interest: Education; Youth development; Youth, services; Community/economic development.
Type of support: General/operating support; Sponsorships.
Geographic limitations: Giving limited to areas of company operations in southeastern WI.
Application information: Applications accepted. Application form not required.
Initial approach: Proposal to headquarters

Wauwatosa Savings and Loan Foundation

(formerly Wauwatosa Savings Bank Foundation)
1360 Greenway Terr.
Elm Grove, WI 53122-1607

Establishment information: Established in 1985 in WI.
Donor: Wauwatosa Savings Bank.
Contact: Charles A. Perry, Tr.
Financial data (yr. ended 12/31/11): Assets, $2,000,000 (M); expenditures, $104,804; qualifying distributions, $103,716; giving activities include $103,716 for grants.
Purpose and activities: The foundation supports service clubs and organizations involved with arts and culture, education, health, cancer, children and youth, and Christianity.
Fields of interest: Arts; Education; Health care.
Type of support: General/operating support.
Geographic limitations: Giving primarily in the metropolitan Milwaukee, WI, area.
Support limitations: No grants to individuals.
Application information: Applications accepted. Application form required. Applicants should submit the following:
1) detailed description of project and amount of funding requested
Initial approach: Letter
Copies of proposal: 1
Deadline(s): None
Trustees: Charles A. Perry; Marilyn J. Perry.
EIN: 391548588

4006
Watson Clinic LLP

1600 Lakeland Hills Blvd.
Lakeland, FL 33805-3065 (863) 680-7560

Company URL: http://www.watsonclinic.com
Establishment information: Established in 1941.
Company type: Private company
Business activities: Provides health services.
Business type (SIC): Offices and clinics/doctors'
Corporate officers: Louis S. Saco, C.E.O.; Heather Shinall, C.F.O.; Robert Marmol, Cont.
Giving statement: Giving through the Watson Clinic Foundation, Inc.

Watson Clinic Foundation, Inc.

100 S. Kentucky Ave., Ste. 255
Lakeland, FL 33801-5089 (863) 802-6221
FAX: (863) 668-3857;
E-mail: cbamberg@watsonclinic.com; URL: http://www.watsonclinic.com/wcf/default.aspx

Establishment information: Established in 1960 in FL; status changed to a public charity in 2002.
Donors: Watson Clinic LLP; Lakeland Regional Medical; Hilda Blanton; Earleen Field; State of Florida.
Contact: Cauney S. Bamberg, Exec. Dir.
Financial data (yr. ended 12/31/11): Revenue, $337,912; assets, $1,339,878 (M); gifts received, $315,415; expenditures, $254,339; giving activities include $11,750 for grants and $5,550 for grants to individuals.
Purpose and activities: The foundation acquires charitable gifts and other resources exclusively to support medical research, education, and service.
Fields of interest: Health care; Medical research, institute.
Type of support: In-kind gifts; Scholarships—to individuals.
Geographic limitations: Giving primarily to FL.
Application information: Applications accepted. Application form not required.
Officers and Directors:* Louis Saco, M.D.*, Chair.; Richard J. Cardosi, M.D.*, Pres. and C.E.O.; Stanley Piotrowski*, Secy.-Treas.; Cauney S. Bamberg, Exec. Dir.; Glen Barden, M.D.; Kamal Haider, M.D.; Adil R. Khan; Pranay Patel, M.D.; Angelo Spoto, Jr., M.D.; Jeffrey Scott Swygert, M.D.
EIN: 591100876

4007
Watson Pharmaceuticals, Inc.

311 Bonnie Cir.
Corona, CA 92880 (951) 270-1400

Company URL: http://www.watsonpharm.com
Establishment information: Established in 1984.
Company type: Public company
Company ticker symbol and exchange: WPI/NYSE
Business activities: Develops, produces, markets, and distributes pharmaceutical products.
Financial profile for 2011: Number of employees, 6,030; assets, $5,827,300,000; sales volume, $3,566,900,000
Corporate officers: Allen Chao, Ph.D., Chair.; Paul M. Bisaro, Pres. and C.E.O.; Joseph Papa, C.O.O.; Mark W. Durand, Sr. V.P. and C.F.O.; Thomas W. Giordano, Sr. V.P. and C.I.O.; David A. Buchen, Sr. V.P., Genl. Counsel, and Secy.; Clare Carmichael, Sr. V.P., Human Resources; Maria Chow, V.P., Opers.; Chato Abad, V.P., Finance; R. Todd Joyce, Corp. Cont.
Board of directors: Allen Chao, Ph.D., Chair.; Paul M. Bisaro; Michael J. Fedida; Michel J. Feldman; Albert F. Hummel; Catherine M. Klema; Jack Michelson; Ronald R. Taylor; Andrew L. Turner; Fred G. Weiss
Subsidiary: Watson Laboratories, Inc., Corona, CA
Joint Venture: Somerset Pharmaceuticals, Inc., Tampa, FL

Giving statement: Giving through the Watson Pharmaceuticals, Inc. Corporate Giving Program.
Company EIN: 953872914

Watson Pharmaceuticals, Inc. Corporate Giving Program

Morris Corporate Center III
400 Interpace Pkwy.
Parsippany, NJ 07054-1120 (862) 261-7000
Additional tel.: (951) 493-5300; URL: http://www.actavis.com/en/Responsibility/Community/default.htm

Purpose and activities: Watson Pharmaceuticals makes charitable contributions to nonprofit organizations involved with health, welfare, community needs, and quality of life. Support is given primarily in areas of company operations in Corona, CA, Morristown, NJ, Copiague, NY, and Salt Lake City, UT. Giving also on a national and international basis.
Fields of interest: Health care, blood supply; Pharmacy/prescriptions; Health care; AIDS; Safety/disasters; American Red Cross; Children/youth, services; Children, services; Human services, gift distribution; Community/economic development.
Type of support: Donated products; Employee matching gifts; Employee volunteer services; General/operating support; In-kind gifts.
Geographic limitations: Giving primarily in areas of company operations in Corona, CA, Morristown, NJ, Copiague, NY, and Salt Lake City, UT. Giving also on a national and international basis.

4008
Wausau Paper Corp.

(formerly Wausau-Mosinee Paper Corporation)
100 Paper Pl.
Mosinee, WI 54455-6000 (715) 693-4470
FAX: (715) 692-2082

Company URL: http://www.wausaupaper.com
Establishment information: Established in 1899.
Company type: Public company
Company ticker symbol and exchange: WPP/NYSE
Business activities: Manufactures, converts, and sells paper and paper products.
Business type (SIC): Paper mills
Financial profile for 2012: Number of employees, 1,900; assets, $700,720,000; sales volume, $822,170,000; pre-tax net income, -$7,510,000; expenses, $826,310,000; liabilities, $495,210,000
Corporate officers: Thomas J. Howatt, Chair.; Henry C. Newell, Pres. and C.E.O.; Sherri L. Lemmer, Sr. V.P. and C.F.O.; Patrick J. Medvecz, Sr. V.P., Opers.; Curtis R. Schmidt, Sr. V.P., Human Resources
Board of directors: Thomas J. Howatt, Chair.; Michael C. Burandt; Londa J. Dewey; Gary W. Freels; Charles E. Hodges; G. Watts Humphrey, Jr.; John S. Kvocka; George P. Murphy; Henry C. Newell
Giving statement: Giving through the Wausau Paper Corp. Contributions Program and the Wausau Paper Foundation, Inc.
Company EIN: 390690900

Wausau Paper Foundation, Inc.

(formerly Wausau Paper Mills Foundation, Inc.)
100 Paper Pl.
Mosinee, WI 54455-9099 (715) 693-4470

Establishment information: Established in 1958.
Donors: Rhinelander Paper Mills Co.; Wausau Paper Mills Co.; Wausau-Mosinee Paper Corp.; Wausau Paper Corp.
Contact: Curtis R. Schmidt, V.P., Human Resources
Financial data (yr. ended 12/31/11): Assets, $26,476 (M); gifts received, $140,000; expenditures, $198,479; qualifying distributions, $198,479; giving activities include $183,970 for 33 grants (high: $25,000; low: $100) and $14,378 for 17 employee matching gifts.
Purpose and activities: The foundation supports organizations involved with arts and culture, higher education, health, recreation, youth development, and public policy research.
Fields of interest: Museums (art); Arts; Higher education; Hospitals (general); Health care; Recreation; Boys & girls clubs; Youth development, business; YM/YWCAs & YM/YWHAs; United Ways and Federated Giving Programs; Public policy, research.
Type of support: Continuing support; Employee matching gifts; General/operating support; Scholarship funds.
Application information: Applications accepted. Application form required. Applicants should submit the following:
1) detailed description of project and amount of funding requested
Initial approach: Letter
Deadline(s): None

Officers and Directors:* San W. Orr, Jr., Chair.; Thomas J. Howatt, Pres. and C.E.O.; Scott P. Doescher, Exec. V.P. and Secy.-Treas.; Londa J. Dewey; Gary W. Freels; G. Watts Humphrey, Jr.; Dennis J. Kuester.
EIN: 396080502
Selected grants: The following grants are a representative sample of this grantmaker's funding activity:
$49,200 to United Way of Marathon County, Wausau, WI, 2010.
$16,500 to United Way of Mercer County, Harrodsburg, KY, 2010.
$13,700 to United Way of Greater Cincinnati, Cincinnati, OH, 2010.
$9,000 to Leigh Yawkey Woodson Art Museum, Wausau, WI, 2010.
$7,500 to WMC Foundation, Madison, WI, 2010.
$7,100 to United Way of Crow Wing County, Brainerd, MN, 2010.
$5,000 to Boy Scouts of America, Samoset Council, Weston, WI, 2010.
$5,000 to Girl Scouts of the U.S.A., Wausau, WI, 2010.
$5,000 to United Negro College Fund, Fairfax, VA, 2010.
$2,500 to Wausau Dance Theater, Wausau, WI, 2010.

4009
Wawa, Inc.

260 W. Baltimore Pike
Red Roof Baltimore Pike
Wawa, PA 19063-5620 (610) 358-8000

Company URL: http://www.wawa.com
Establishment information: Established in 1964.
Company type: Private company
Business activities: Operates convenience food stores.
Business type (SIC): Groceries—retail
Financial profile for 2011: Number of employees, 18,000; assets, $1,570,000,000; sales volume, $6,990,000,000
Corporate officers: Richard D. Wood, Jr., Chair.; Howard B. Stoeckel, Pres. and C.E.O.; David Johnston, Exec. V.P. and C.O.O.
Board of director: Richard D. Wood, Jr., Chair.
Giving statement: Giving through the Wawa, Inc. Corporate Giving Program.

Wawa, Inc. Corporate Giving Program

c/o Corp. Charities Comm., Grant Request Application
260 W. Baltimore Pike
Wawa, PA 19063-5620 (610) 358-8000
URL: http://www.wawa.com/WawaWeb/Community.aspx

Purpose and activities: Wawa makes charitable contributions to nonprofit organizations involved with children's health, breast cancer, heart disease, cancer research, HIV/AIDS research, domestic violence, sexual violence, and hunger. Support is limited to areas of company operations in Delaware, Flordia, Maryland, New Jersey, Pennsylvania, and Virginia.
Fields of interest: Health care; Heart & circulatory diseases; Cancer research; AIDS research; Crime/violence prevention, domestic violence; Crime/violence prevention, sexual abuse; Food services Children.
Program:
Wawa Hoagie Fundraising: Wawa provides community-based nonprofit organizations with coupons for Wawa Short Hoagies at a retail price of $3.00 for fundraising. Organizations can resell the coupons for $4.19 to raise funds. Coupons will be shipped in packs of 25, with a minimum order of 150, and a maximum of 2,000 per quarter per organization.
Type of support: Donated products; Employee matching gifts; Employee volunteer services; General/operating support; In-kind gifts; Income development; Program development.
Geographic limitations: Giving limited to areas of company operations in DE, FL, MD, NJ, PA, and VA.
Publications: Application guidelines.
Application information: Applications accepted. An interview, presentation, or site visit may be requested. Telephone calls and personal visits are not encouraged. The Corporate Charities Committee handles giving. The Delaware Valley Grantmakers' common grant application form is accepted. Application form not required. Applicants should submit the following:
1) timetable for implementation and evaluation of project
2) results expected from proposed grant
3) population served
4) copy of IRS Determination Letter
5) brief history of organization and description of its mission
6) copy of most recent annual report/audited financial statement/990
7) listing of board of directors, trustees, officers and other key people and their affiliations
8) detailed description of project and amount of funding requested
9) contact person
10) copy of current year's organizational budget and/or project budget
11) listing of additional sources and amount of support

Proposals should indicate the percentage of funds budgeted for administrative costs; include the resume of the project officer; indicate any relationship between the organization and Wawa; and state capital expenses.
Initial approach: Proposal to headquarters
Copies of proposal: 1
Committee meeting date(s): Jan. and July

Deadline(s): Apr. 15 and Oct. 15
Final notification: 2 months following committee meetings
Corporate Charities Committee: Lori Bruce, Chair.; Kathleen Betchner; Jared G. Culolta; Michele Dougherty; Salvatore J. Mattera; Mark N. Suprenant.

4010
WB Enterprises, Inc.

(also known as Ksm Industries, Inc.)
N. 115 W. 19025 Edison Dr.
Germantown, WI 53022-3023
(262) 251-9510

Company URL: http://http://www.ksmindustries.com/
Establishment information: Established in 1903.
Company type: Subsidiary of a private company
Business activities: Operates holding company.
Business type (SIC): Holding company
Corporate officers: James Keyes, Chair.; David Oechsner, Pres.; Phil Davis, V.P., Opers.
Board of director: James Keyes, Chair.
Giving statement: Giving through the James E. and John A. Keyes Families Foundation, Inc.

James E. and John A. Keyes Families Foundation, Inc.

788 N. Jefferson St., Ste. 900
Milwaukee, WI 53202-3739

Establishment information: Established in 1999 in WI.
Donor: WB Enterprises, Inc.
Financial data (yr. ended 12/31/11): Assets, $601,284 (M); expenditures, $42,335; qualifying distributions, $36,550; giving activities include $36,550 for grants.
Purpose and activities: The foundation supports hospitals, youth centers, and organizations involved with secondary and higher education, children and youth, homelessness, and Christianity.
Fields of interest: Education; Human services; Religion.
Type of support: General/operating support.
Geographic limitations: Giving primarily in IN and WI.
Support limitations: No grants to individuals.
Application information: Applications not accepted. Unsolicited requests for funds not accepted.
Officers: James E. Keyes, Pres.; John A. Keyes, V.P.; John P. Miller, Secy.
EIN: 391963274

4011
WD-40 Company

1061 Cudahy Pl.
P.O. Box 80607
San Diego, CA 92110-3929
(619) 275-1400
FAX: (619) 275-5823

Company URL: http://www.wd-40.com
Establishment information: Established in 1953.
Company type: Public company
Company ticker symbol and exchange: WDFC/NASDAQ
Business activities: Manufactures lubricants, hand cleaners, and household cleaning products.
Business type (SIC): Chemical preparations/miscellaneous; soaps, cleaners, and toiletries; petroleum and coal products/miscellaneous
Financial profile for 2012: Number of employees, 347; assets, $300,870,000; sales volume, $342,780,000; pre-tax net income, $50,910,000; expenses, $291,060,000; liabilities, $115,410,000
Corporate officers: Neal E. Schmale, Chair.; Garry O. Ridge, Pres. and C.E.O.; Jay Rembolt, V.P., Finance, C.F.O., and Treas.
Board of directors: Neal E. Schmale, Chair.; Giles H. Bateman; Peter D. Bewley; Richard A. Collato; Mario L. Crivello; Linda A. Lang; Garry O. Ridge; Gregory A. Sandfort
International operations: Australia; Canada; United Kingdom
Giving statement: Giving through the WD-40 Community Involvement Program.
Company EIN: 951797918

WD-40 Community Involvement Program

1061 Cudahy Pl.
San Diego, CA 92110-3929
URL: http://www.wd40company.com/about/community/

Contact: Maria M. Mitchell, V.P., Corp. and Investor Rels.
Purpose and activities: WD-40 makes charitable contributions to nonprofit organizations involved with arts and culture, education, health and human services, employment training and retraining, youth development, community development, civic affairs, and economically disadvantaged people. Support is given on a national and international basis.
Fields of interest: Arts; Elementary/secondary education; Higher education; Education, drop-out prevention; Education; Health care; Employment, training; Employment, retraining; Youth development; Family services; Human services; Economic development; Urban/community development; Community/economic development; Public affairs Infants/toddlers; Children/youth; Children; Youth; Adults; Aging; Young adults; Disabilities, people with; Physically disabled; Blind/visually impaired; Deaf/hearing impaired; Mentally disabled; Minorities; Asians/Pacific Islanders; African Americans/Blacks; Hispanics/Latinos; Native Americans/American Indians; Indigenous peoples; Women; Infants/toddlers, female; Girls; Young adults, female; Infants/toddlers, male; Boys; Young adults, male; Military/veterans; Substance abusers; AIDS, people with; Single parents; Crime/abuse victims; Terminal illness, people with; Economically disadvantaged; Homeless; Migrant workers.
Type of support: Donated equipment; Donated products; Employee matching gifts; Employee volunteer services; General/operating support.
Geographic limitations: Giving on a national and international basis in areas of company operations.
Support limitations: No support for political organizations or candidates, labor organizations, or religious or sectarian organizations not of direct benefit to the entire community. No grants to individuals, or for golf tournaments or dinner tables.
Publications: Application guidelines.
Application information: Applications accepted. Proposals should be brief. Corporate Management handles giving. A contributions committee reviews all requests. Application form not required.
Applicants should submit the following:
1) name, address and phone number of organization
2) copy of IRS Determination Letter
3) copy of most recent annual report/audited financial statement/990
4) descriptive literature about organization
5) listing of board of directors, trustees, officers and other key people and their affiliations
6) detailed description of project and amount of funding requested
7) contact person
8) listing of additional sources and amount of support

Proposals should include a description of past involvement by WD-40 with the organization; and indicate the percentage of funds budgeted for administrative costs and programs.
Initial approach: Proposal to headquarters
Copies of proposal: 1
Committee meeting date(s): Twice per year
Deadline(s): None

4012
The Weather Company, Inc.

300 Interstate North Pkwy. S.E.
Atlanta, GA 30339-2404 (770) 226-0000

Company URL: http://www.weather.com/
Establishment information: Established in 1982.
Company type: Private company
Business activities: Operates cable network.
Business type (SIC): Cable and other pay television services
Corporate officer: David W. Kenny, Chair. and C.E.O.
Giving statement: Giving through the Weather Company, Inc. Contributions Program.

The Weather Company, Inc. Contributions Program

300 Interstate North Pkwy. S.E.
Atlanta, GA 30339-2404 (770) 226-0000
URL: http://www.weather.com

4013
Weather Shield Manufacturing, Inc.

1 Weather Shield Plz.
P.O. Box 309
Medford, WI 54451 (715) 748-2100

Company URL: http://www.weathershield.com
Establishment information: Established in 1955.
Company type: Private company
Business activities: Manufactures and sells wooden window frames, plastic windows, and doors.
Business type (SIC): Wood millwork; plastic products/miscellaneous
Corporate officers: Edward Lee Schield, C.E.O.; John Kuhn, C.F.O.; Mark A. Schield, V.P., Sales and Mktg.
Giving statement: Giving through the Schield Companies Foundation, Inc. and the Weather Shield LITE Foundation.

Schield Companies Foundation, Inc.

(formerly Weather Shield Manufacturing Foundation, Inc.)
P.O. Box 309
Medford, WI 54451-0309

Donor: Weather Shield Manufacturing, Inc.
Financial data (yr. ended 12/31/11): Assets, $456,033 (M); expenditures, $26,400; qualifying

distributions, $24,500; giving activities include $24,500 for grants.
Purpose and activities: The foundation awards college scholarships to children of employees of Weather Shield Manufacturing.
Fields of interest: Higher education; Education.
Type of support: Employee-related scholarships.
Geographic limitations: Giving limited to WI.
Support limitations: No grants to individuals (except for employee-related scholarships).
Application information: Applications not accepted. Unsolicited requests for funds not accepted.
Officers: Edward L. Schield, Pres.; Kevin L. Schield, V.P.; Mark A. Schield, V.P.; Starla M. Ruesch, Secy.-Treas.
EIN: 391362989

Weather Shield LITE Foundation

1 Weather Shield Plz.
Medford, WI 54451-2206
FAX: (715) 748-6508;
E-mail: litefoundation@weathershield.com;
URL: http://www.weathershield.com/WhyWS/OurStory/LITEFoundation.aspx

Establishment information: Established in 1999 in WI.
Donor: Weather Shield Manufacturing, Inc.
Contact: Kevin Schield, Pres.
Financial data (yr. ended 12/31/11): Revenue, $44,927; assets, $7,092 (M); gifts received, $39,900; expenditures, $44,750; giving activities include $35,910 for grants and $8,840 for grants to individuals.
Purpose and activities: The foundation supports various community endeavors of interest to employees of Weather Shield Manufacturing, Inc.
Fields of interest: Community/economic development.
Program:
Grants: The foundation provides grants to organizations that are based in central Wisconsin, and that provide for emergency services, youth activities, the care of the elderly or indigent, or environmental programs. Both non-profit and for-profit organizations are eligible for grants under this program.
Type of support: Employee matching gifts; Grants to individuals; In-kind gifts.
Publications: Application guidelines.
Application information: Applications accepted. Application form required.
Initial approach: Contact foundation for application form
Deadline(s): Mar.
Officers and Directors:* Kevin Schield*, Pres.; Sally Thomas*, Secy.; Starla Ruesch*, Treas.; Vicki Ahles; Jill Dassow; Clarice Schield; Edward Schield; Mike Tingo.
EIN: 391978784

4014
Weaver and Tidwell, L.L.P.

(doing business as Weaver)
2821 W. 7th St., Ste. 700
Fort Worth, TX 76107-8913 (817) 332-7905

Company URL: http://www.weaverllp.com
Establishment information: Established in 1950.
Company type: Subsidiary of a foreign company
Business activities: Operates certified public accounting firm.
Business type (SIC): Accounting, auditing, and bookkeeping services
Corporate officers: W.M. Lawhon, Chair.; Tommy D. Lawler, C.E.O.; Kerry D. Caves, C.O.O.
Board of director: W.M. Lawhon, Chair.
Offices: Austin, Dallas, Houston, San Antonio, TX
Giving statement: Giving through the Weaver and Tidwell Private Foundation.

Weaver and Tidwell Private Foundation

2821 W. 7th St., Ste. 700
Fort Worth, TX 76107
E-mail: wtfoundation@weaverandtidwell.com;
URL: http://www.weaverllp.com/Careers/Experienced/CorporateResponsibility.aspx

Establishment information: Established in 2007 in TX.
Donor: Weaver and Tidwell, LLP.
Financial data (yr. ended 05/31/12): Assets, $18,242 (M); gifts received, $93,130; expenditures, $77,000; qualifying distributions, $77,000; giving activities include $77,000 for grants.
Purpose and activities: The foundation sponsors organizations, events, and programs in the communities in which Weaver and Tidwell employees live and work.
Fields of interest: Performing arts; Health care, patient services; Youth development; Human services; Family services.
Geographic limitations: Giving primarily in Dallas, Fort Worth, and Houston, TX.
Support limitations: No grants to individuals.
Application information: Applications not accepted. Unsolicited requests for funds not accepted.
Directors: Tracy Elms; James Fitts; Andy Freundlich; Gary McIntosh; Laura McNutt.
Officers: Tommy Lawler, Chair.; Jana L. Volkman, Secy.; William M. Mack Lawhon, Treas.
EIN: 208574509

4015
Weaver Popcorn Company, Inc.

14470 Bergen Blvd., Ste. 100
Noblesville, IN 46060-3377
(765) 934-2101

Company URL: http://www.weaverpopcorn.com
Establishment information: Established in 1928.
Company type: Private company
Business activities: Manufactures and sells popcorn.
Business type (SIC): Miscellaneous prepared foods
Corporate officers: Michael E. Weaver, Pres. and C.E.O.; Rebecca Weaver, Secy.
Giving statement: Giving through the Weaver Popcorn Foundation, Inc.

Weaver Popcorn Foundation, Inc.

14470 Bergen Blvd., Ste. 100
Noblesville, IN 46060-3377 (317) 915-4763

Establishment information: Established in 1997 in IN.
Donor: Weaver Popcorn Co., Inc.
Contact: Brian Hamilton
Financial data (yr. ended 12/31/11): Assets, $2,915,132 (M); gifts received, $389,275; expenditures, $379,116; qualifying distributions, $371,703; giving activities include $371,703 for 60 grants (high: $75,000; low: $75).
Purpose and activities: The foundation supports organizations involved with education, health, youth development, and human services, and awards educational scholarships to residents of Huntington, IN.
Fields of interest: Secondary school/education; Higher education; Education; Health care; Boy scouts; YM/YWCAs & YM/YWHAs; Children/youth, services; Family services, domestic violence; Human services.
Type of support: General/operating support; Scholarships—to individuals.
Geographic limitations: Giving primarily in IN.
Application information: Applications accepted. Bob Straight Scholarships are limited to graduating seniors of Huntington North High School in Huntington, IN. Other scholarships are open to Indiana residents to pursue higher education. Application form not required. Applicants should submit the following:
1) brief history of organization and description of its mission
2) detailed description of project and amount of funding requested
Scholarship applications should include transcripts, description of financial need, an essay, and letters of recommendation.
Initial approach: Proposal; contact foundation or Huntington North High School for scholarships
Deadline(s): None; varies for scholarships
Officers and Directors:* Michael E. Weaver*, Chair.; William E. Weaver*, V.P.; Rebecca J. Weaver*, Secy.; Thomas M. Shoaff.
EIN: 352026043
Selected grants: The following grants are a representative sample of this grantmaker's funding activity:
$7,500 to Marian University, Indianapolis, IN, 2009.
$2,500 to American Cancer Society, Fort Wayne, IN, 2009.
$2,500 to Ball State University, Muncie, IN, 2009.
$2,500 to Hoosier Veterans Assistance Foundation, Indianapolis, IN, 2009.
$2,500 to Indiana University, Bloomington, IN, 2009.
$2,500 to Indiana University, Bloomington, IN, 2009.
$2,500 to Purdue University, West Lafayette, IN, 2009.
$2,500 to University of Saint Francis, Fort Wayne, IN, 2009.
$2,500 to Waukesha County Technical College, Pewaukee, WI, 2009.
$2,000 to Damien Center, Indianapolis, IN, 2009.

4016
Webster Bank

145 Bank St.
Waterbury, CT 06702-2211 (203) 578-2253

Company URL: http://www.websterbank.com
Establishment information: Established in 1935.
Company type: Subsidiary of a public company
Business activities: Operates commercial bank.
Business type (SIC): Banks/commercial
Corporate officers: James C. Smith, Chair. and C.E.O.; Gerald P. Plush, Pres. and C.O.O.; Harriet Munrett Wolfe, Esq., Exec. V.P., Genl. Counsel, and Secy.; Jeffrey N. Brown, C.A.O.; Glenn MacInnes, C.F.O.
Board of directors: James C. Smith, Chair.; Gerald P. Plush
Giving statement: Giving through the Webster Bank Corporate Giving Program and the Harold Webster Smith Foundation, Inc.

Webster Bank Corporate Giving Program

c/o Community Affairs
145 Bank St. - M0410
Waterbury, CT 06702-2211 (203) 578-2253
FAX: (203) 578-2507;
E-mail: CommAffairs@websterbank.com;
URL: https://www.websteronline.com/about-webster/webster/community/community-partnerships.html

Purpose and activities: As a complement to its foundation, Webster also makes charitable contributions to nonprofit organizations directly. Support is given primarily in areas of company operations, with emphasis on Connecticut, Massachusetts, Westchester County, New York, and Rhode Island. Priority will be given to organizations that collaborate with existing community resources, have Webster employee involvement, incorporate approaches and evaluation measures that ensure positive results, and where there is a business relationship.
Fields of interest: Performing arts; Arts; Education; Public health; Human services; Family services; Human services, financial counseling; United Ways and Federated Giving Programs; Financial services Economically disadvantaged.
Type of support: Employee volunteer services; General/operating support; Sponsorships.
Geographic limitations: Giving primarily in areas of company operations, with emphasis on CT, MA, Westchester County, NY, and RI.
Support limitations: Generally no support for organizations with limited availability to the general public, religious organizations other than those serving Webster's priority areas, or single disease or national health research or service organizations. Generally no grants to individuals, or for operating expenses for hospitals or educational institutions, programs that benefit specific individuals, golf events, third-party solicitations, endowments, or capital campaigns.
Publications: Application guidelines.
Application information: Applications accepted. Past recipients should limit requests to one per year. Support is limited to organizations that serve low and moderate income individuals and families. Proposals should be submitted using organization letterhead. Application form required. Applicants should submit the following:
1) detailed description of project and amount of funding requested
2) listing of additional sources and amount of support
3) copy of current year's organizational budget and/or project budget
4) contact person
5) listing of board of directors, trustees, officers and other key people and their affiliations
6) descriptive literature about organization
7) how project's results will be evaluated or measured
8) copy of most recent annual report/audited financial statement/990
9) geographic area to be served
10) brief history of organization and description of its mission
11) copy of IRS Determination Letter
12) name, address and phone number of organization

Proposals should include a cover letter, sponsorship details, name of chief executive officer or executive director, amount requested, a list of sponsorship opportunities, if applicable, an explanation of the organization's relationship with Webster, and its past success rate.
Initial approach: Contact local branch for requests of up to $250. Download application form and mail completed proposal and form to application address for other requests
Copies of proposal: 1
Deadline(s): None
Number of staff: 1 full-time professional; 1 part-time support.

Harold Webster Smith Foundation, Inc.

(formerly Webster Bank Foundation, Inc.)
145 Bank St. (FA 201)
Waterbury, CT 06702-2211

Establishment information: Established in 1988 in CT.
Donors: Bristol Savings Bank; Webster Bank, N.A.; Webster Financial Corp.
Financial data (yr. ended 12/31/11): Assets, $2,887,512 (M); gifts received, $133,000; expenditures, $545,525; qualifying distributions, $522,500; giving activities include $522,500 for grants.
Purpose and activities: The foundation supports organizations involved with theater, housing, and community development.
Fields of interest: Arts.
Type of support: General/operating support.
Application information: Applications not accepted. Unsolicited requests for funds not accepted.
Officers and Directors:* James C. Smith*, Chair.; Jeffrey N. Brown*, Pres.; Gregory S. Madar, Sr. V.P. and Treas.; Kathryn T. Luna*, V.P.; Mark S. Lyon, Secy.; Robert L. Guenther; Nitin J. Mhatre; William E. Wrang.
EIN: 222947047

4017 Webster Five Cents Savings Bank

136 Thompson Rd.
Webster, MA 01570-1416 (508) 943-9401

Company URL: http://www.web5.com/
Establishment information: Established in 1868.
Company type: Subsidiary of a private company
Business activities: Operates savings bank.
Business type (SIC): Savings institutions
Financial profile for 2011: Assets, $558,872,000; liabilities, $490,208,000
Corporate officers: Daniel W. Ivascyn, Chair.; Richard T. Leahy, Pres. and C.E.O.; Joseph D. Radovanic, C.O.O.; Edward Gaudette, C.I.O.; David S. Bayer II, Clerk; Brian S. Westerlind, Treas.
Board of director: Daniel W. Ivascyn, Chair.
Giving statement: Giving through the Webster Five Foundation, Inc.

Webster Five Foundation, Inc.

10 A St.
Auburn, MA 01501-2102 (508) 943-9401

Establishment information: Established in 1995 in MA.
Donor: Webster Five Cents Savings Bank.
Contact: Karen M. Kempskie-Aquino, Treas. and Exec. Dir.
Financial data (yr. ended 10/31/11): Assets, $89,615 (M); gifts received, $123,456; expenditures, $128,995; qualifying distributions, $128,695; giving activities include $128,550 for grants.
Purpose and activities: The foundation supports nonprofit organizations involved with arts and culture, education, health, human services, community economic development, and senior citizens.
Fields of interest: Arts; Education; Human services.
Type of support: Annual campaigns; Emergency funds; General/operating support; Program development.
Geographic limitations: Giving primarily in areas of company operations in MA.
Support limitations: No support for political organizations or candidates, churches or synagogues or any affiliated organizations, fraternal organizations, employment unions, or tax-supported entities. No grants to individuals or for capital campaigns.
Publications: Application guidelines.
Application information: Applications accepted. Application form required.
Initial approach: Contact foundation for application form
Deadline(s): None
Officers and Directors: Richard T. Leahy*, Pres.; Benjamin A. Craver, Clerk; Karen M. Kempskie-Aquino, Treas. and Exec. Dir.; Maura E. Aniello; David S. Bayer.
EIN: 043303760

4018 Webster Industries, Inc.

325 Hall St.
Tiffin, OH 44883-1419 (419) 447-8232
FAX: (419) 448-1618

Company URL: http://www.websterchain.com
Establishment information: Established in 1876.
Company type: Private company
Business activities: Manufactures conveyor and power transmission equipment and malleable iron castings.
Business type (SIC): Machinery/construction, mining, and materials handling; iron and steel foundries; machinery/general industry
Corporate officers: Fredric C. Spurck, Chair. and C.E.O.; Andrew J. Felter, Pres. and C.O.O.; Christopher D. English, V.P., Finance; Dean E. Bogner, V.P., Sales
Board of director: Fredric C. Spurck, Chair.
Giving statement: Giving through the Webster Foundation, Inc.

Webster Foundation, Inc.

325 Hall St.
Tiffin, OH 44883-1419

Establishment information: Established in 1975 in OH.
Donor: Webster Industries, Inc.
Contact: Christopher D. English, Tr.
Financial data (yr. ended 12/31/11): Assets, $36,750 (M); gifts received, $25,000; expenditures, $23,605; qualifying distributions, $23,510; giving activities include $23,510 for grants.
Purpose and activities: The foundation supports hospitals and organizations involved with education, legal aid, and youth development. Special emphasis is directed toward programs designed to serve children and young adults of Seneca County, Ohio.
Fields of interest: Education; Health care; Human services.
Type of support: Capital campaigns; Equipment; Program development.

Geographic limitations: Giving primarily in Seneca County, OH.
Support limitations: No grants to individuals.
Application information: Applications accepted. Application form required. Applicants should submit the following:
1) detailed description of project and amount of funding requested
Initial approach: Letter
Deadline(s): July 1 and Dec. 1
Trustees: Christopher D. English; Jim Getz; Brent T. Howard; Fredric C. Spurck; G.K. Tolford.
EIN: 237446923

4019
Webster's United Food Services Inc.

1188 W. Fond Du Lac St.
P.O. Box 367
Ripon, WI 54971-9210 (920) 748-5498

Establishment information: Established in 1983.
Company type: Private company
Business activities: Operates grocery store chain.
Business type (SIC): Groceries—retail
Corporate officers: Robert Webster, Pres.; Kathleen Webster, V.P. and Secy.
Giving statement: Giving through the Webster Foundation, Inc.

Webster Foundation, Inc.

8001 Radke Rd.
Ripon, WI 54971-9607 (920) 748-5498
Application address: 1188 W. Fond du Lac St., Ripon, WI 54971

Establishment information: Established in 2002.
Donor: Webster's United Food Service, Inc.
Contact: Stephanie Sauerbrei, Secy.
Financial data (yr. ended 12/31/11): Assets, $308,379 (M); gifts received, $60,000; expenditures, $95,458; qualifying distributions, $79,380; giving activities include $79,380 for 38 grants (high: $14,300; low: $279).
Purpose and activities: Giving to organizations for humanitarian purpose; grants to individuals for educational purposes.
Fields of interest: Higher education, college; Human services.
Type of support: General/operating support; Scholarships—to individuals.
Geographic limitations: Giving primarily in WI.
Application information: Applications accepted. Application form required.
Initial approach: Proposal
Deadline(s): Apr. 1 for scholarships; Nov. 1 for grants
Officers: Robert Webster, Pres.; Stephanie Sauerbrei, Secy.
Directors: Linda Kinziger; Allen Stibb.
EIN: 743053295

4020
WEDGE Group Incorporated

WEDGE International Twr., 1415 Louisiana St., Ste. 3000
P.O. Box 130688
Houston, TX 77002 (713) 739-6500

Company URL: http://www.wedgegroup.com/
Company type: Private company
Business activities: Provides investment services.
Business type (SIC): Investors/miscellaneous
Financial profile for 2010: Number of employees, 25
Corporate officers: Issam M. Fares, Chair.; James M. Tidwell, Pres. and C.E.O.; Wilfred M. Krenek, V.P. and C.F.O.; Richard E. Blohm, Jr., V.P. and Genl. Counsel
Board of directors: Issam M. Fares, Chair.; Fares I. Fares
Giving statement: Giving through the WEDGE Foundation.

The WEDGE Foundation

1415 Louisiana St., Ste. 3000
Houston, TX 77002-7351

Establishment information: Established in 2001 in TX.
Donors: WEDGE Group Incorporated; WEDGE Holdings, Inc.
Financial data (yr. ended 12/31/11): Assets, $107,305 (M); gifts received, $805,000; expenditures, $800,347; qualifying distributions, $800,000; giving activities include $800,000 for grants.
Purpose and activities: The foundation supports organizations involved with cultural awareness, higher education, health, children and youth, public policy, and Christianity.
Fields of interest: Arts, cultural/ethnic awareness; Higher education; Health care, association; Health care, clinics/centers; Health care, patient services; Health care; American Red Cross; Children/youth, services; Public policy, research; Christian agencies & churches.
Type of support: Building/renovation; Endowments; Fellowships; General/operating support; Sponsorships.
Geographic limitations: Giving primarily in Washington, DC, MA, MN, NJ, NY, and TX.
Application information: Applications not accepted. Contributes only to pre-selected organizations.
Officers: Fares I. Fares, Pres.; Richard E. Blohm, Jr., Secy.; Jim M. Tidwell, Treas.
EIN: 760533546
Selected grants: The following grants are a representative sample of this grantmaker's funding activity:
$208,097 to Middle East Institute, Washington, DC, 2010.
$105,000 to American University of Beirut, New York, NY, 2010.
$100,000 to Mayo Foundation, Rochester, MN, 2010.
$10,000 to Rice University, Houston, TX, 2010.

4021
Wegmans Food Markets, Inc.

1500 Brooks Ave.
P.O. Box 30844
Rochester, NY 14603-0844 (585) 328-2550

Company URL: http://www.wegmans.com
Establishment information: Established in 1916.
Company type: Private company
Business activities: Operates supermarkets.
Business type (SIC): Groceries—retail
Financial profile for 2011: Number of employees, 41,771; sales volume, $5,600,000,000
Corporate officers: Daniel R. Wegman, Chair. and C.E.O.; Paul S. Speranza, Jr., Vice-Chair., Genl. Counsel and Secy.; James J. Leo, Sr. V.P. and C.F.O.; Donald Reeve, C.I.O.; Jack DePeters, Exec. V.P., Opers.; Gerard Pierce, Sr. V.P., Human Resources
Board of director: Daniel R. Wegman, Chair.
Giving statement: Giving through the Wegmans Food Markets, Inc. Corporate Giving Program.

Wegmans Food Markets, Inc. Corporate Giving Program

c/o Contrib. Comm.
1500 Brooks Ave.
Rochester, NY 14603-0844 (585) 328-2550
Application addresses: Buffalo, NY: Attn. Theresa Jackson, Buffalo Contrib. Committee, 651 Dick Rd., Depew, NY 14043, tel.: (716) 685-8170; Syracuse: Attn. Evelyn Carter, Syracuse Contrib. Committee, 7519 Oswego Rd., Syracuse, NY 13090, tel.: (315) 546-1110; URL: http://www.wegmans.com

Contact: Linda Lovejoy, Mgr., Community Rels.
Purpose and activities: Wegmans makes charitable contributions to nonprofit organizations designed to promote food for the hungry; healthy eating and activity; neighborhoods; and youth. Support is given primarily in areas of company operations.
Fields of interest: Higher education; Education, reading; Education; Public health, physical fitness; Food services; Food banks; Food distribution, groceries on wheels; Nutrition; Children/youth, services; Community/economic development; United Ways and Federated Giving Programs; General charitable giving.
Program:
Wegmans Scholarship Program: Wegmans Food Markets annually awards scholarships to employees to pursue their educational goals. Part-time employees are awarded up to $1,500 a year for four years (up to $6,000 total) and full-time employees are awarded up to $2,200 a year for four years (up to $8,800 total). The program is designed to encourage and build the future of employees through strong work performance and academic achievement.
Type of support: Donated products; Employee volunteer services; Employee-related scholarships; General/operating support; In-kind gifts; Income development; Program development; Public relations services; Sponsorships.
Geographic limitations: Giving primarily in areas of company operations in MD, NJ, NY, PA, and VA.
Support limitations: No support for organizations without a 501(c) 3 status or political organizations. No grants to individuals, or for scholarships (except for employee-related scholarships), professional development seminars or conferences, employee recognition events, pageants, or travel expenses for educational or extracurricular events.
Publications: Application guidelines.
Application information: Applications accepted. Proposals should be submitted using organization letterhead. Application form not required. Applicants should submit the following:
1) name, address and phone number of organization
2) copy of IRS Determination Letter
3) brief history of organization and description of its mission
4) detailed description of project and amount of funding requested
5) contact person
Proposals should indicate the date of the event, if applicable, and specifically note the nature of the request being made.
Initial approach: Proposal to headquarters for organizations in Rochester; proposal to application address for organizations located in Buffalo and Syracuse; proposal to service desk of local stores for small contributions and

organizations located in MD, NJ, PA, and VA and the Southern Tier of NY
Copies of proposal: 1
Deadline(s): 6 months prior to need for large sponsorships; None for small contributions
Final notification: 4 weeks for large sponsorships; 2 weeks for small contributions

4022
Weil, Gotshal & Manges, L.L.P.
767 5th Ave.
New York, NY 10153 (212) 310-8000

Company URL: http://www.weil.com
Business activities: Provides legal services.
Business type (SIC): Legal services
Financial profile for 2009: Number of employees, 1,700; sales volume, $1,233,000,000
Corporate officers: Stephen Dannhauser, Chair.; Norman LaCroix, C.F.O.
Board of director: Stephen Dannhauser, Chair.
Offices: Menlo Park, CA; Washington, DC; Miami, FL; Dallas, Houston, TX
Giving statement: Giving through the Weil, Gotshal & Manges Foundation.

Weil, Gotshal & Manges Foundation
c/o Weil, Gotshal & Manges LLP
767 5th Ave.
New York, NY 10153-0001 (212) 310-6813

Establishment information: Established in 1983 in NY.
Donors: Weil, Gotshal & Manges LLP; Robert Todd Lang; Ira M. Millstein; Harvey R. Miller.
Contact: Dennis Foley, Treas.
Financial data (yr. ended 12/31/11): Assets, $6,030,612 (M); gifts received, $1,573,014; expenditures, $1,761,390; qualifying distributions, $1,760,815; giving activities include $1,760,815 for grants.
Purpose and activities: The foundation supports museums and organizations involved with education, legal services, disaster relief, children and youth, international relief, civil and human rights, business, and Judaism.
Fields of interest: Museums; Elementary school/education; Higher education; Law school/education; Education; Legal services; Disasters, 9/11/01; American Red Cross; Children/youth, services; International relief; Civil/human rights; Business/industry; United Ways and Federated Giving Programs; Jewish federated giving programs; Jewish agencies & synagogues.
Type of support: General/operating support; Scholarship funds.
Geographic limitations: Giving primarily in NJ and NY.
Support limitations: No grants to individuals.
Application information: Applications accepted. Application form not required. Applicants should submit the following:
1) brief history of organization and description of its mission
2) copy of most recent annual report/audited financial statement/990
3) detailed description of project and amount of funding requested
4) copy of current year's organizational budget and/or project budget

Initial approach: Proposal
Copies of proposal: 1
Deadline(s): Nov. 1

Officer and Directors:* Dennis Foley*, Treas.; Stephen Dannhauser; Richard Davis; Thomas Roberts.
EIN: 133158325
Selected grants: The following grants are a representative sample of this grantmaker's funding activity:
$71,500 to University of Pennsylvania, Law School, Philadelphia, PA, 2009. For general support.
$55,000 to Cornell University, Law School, Ithaca, NY, 2009. For general support.
$50,000 to Georgetown University, Law School, Washington, DC, 2009. For general support.
$50,000 to Syracuse University, College of Law, Syracuse, NY, 2009. For general support.
$50,000 to Syracuse University, College of Law, Syracuse, NY, 2009. For general support.
$50,000 to Yale University, Law School, New Haven, CT, 2009. For general support.
$30,000 to Pro Bono Partnership, White Plains, NY, 2009. For general support.
$27,000 to Greater Boston Legal Services, Boston, MA, 2009. For general support.
$25,000 to Downtown Brooklyn Partnership, Brooklyn, NY, 2009. For general support.
$12,561 to National Minority Supplier Development Council, New York, NY, 2009. For general support.

4023
Weil, Gotshal & Manges LLP
767 5th Ave.
New York, NY 10153-0119 (212) 310-8000

Company URL: http://www.weil.com/
Company type: Private company
Business activities: Operates law firm.
Business type (SIC): Legal services
Offices: Redwood Shores, CA; Wilmington, DE; Washington, DC; Miami, FL; Boston, MA; New York, NY; Providence, RI; Dallas, Houston, TX
International operations: China; Czech Republic; France; Germany; Hungary; Poland; United Kingdom
Giving statement: Giving through the Weil, Gotshal & Manges LLP Pro Bono Program.

Weil, Gotshal & Manges LLP Pro Bono Program
767 5th Ave.
New York, NY 10153-0119 (212) 310-8056
E-mail: miriam.buhl@weil.com; Additional tel.: (212) 310-8000; URL: http://www.weil.com/probono/

Contact: Miriam Buhl, Pro Bono Counsel
Fields of interest: Legal services.
Type of support: Pro bono services - legal.
Application information: A Pro Bono Committee manages the pro bono program.

4024
Weis Markets, Inc.
1000 S. 2nd St.
P.O. Box 471
Sunbury, PA 17801-0471 (570) 286-4571
FAX: (570) 286-3286

Company URL: http://www.weismarkets.com/
Establishment information: Established in 1912.
Company type: Public company
Company ticker symbol and exchange: WMK/NYSE
Business activities: Operates grocery stores; operates pet shops.
Business type (SIC): Groceries—retail; retail stores/miscellaneous
Financial profile for 2012: Number of employees, 17,400; assets, $1,090,440,000; sales volume, $2,701,410,000; pre-tax net income, $130,910,000; expenses, $2,574,370,000; liabilities, $294,750,000
Fortune 1000 ranking: 2012—770th in revenues, 767th in profits, and 960th in assets
Corporate officers: Robert F. Weis, Chair.; Jonathan H. Weis, Vice-Chair. and Secy.; David Jerome Hepfinger, Pres. and C.E.O.; Scott F. Frost, CPA, Sr. V.P., C.F.O., and Treas.; James E. Marcil, Sr. V.P. Human Resources; John J. Ropietski, Jr., Sr. V.P., Opers.; Kurt A. Schertle, Sr. V.P., Sales
Board of directors: Robert F. Weis, Chair.; Jonathan H. Weis, Vice-Chair.; Harold G. Graber, Jr.; David J. Hepfinger; Edward J. Lauth III; Gerrald B. Silverman; Glenn D. Steele, Jr., M.D., Ph.D.
Giving statement: Giving through the Weis Markets, Inc. Corporate Giving Program.
Company EIN: 240755415

Weis Markets, Inc. Corporate Giving Program
c/o Weis Markets Donations
1000 S. 2nd St.
P.O. Box 471
Sunbury, PA 17801-3318 (866) 999-9347
E-mail: weis_donations@weismarkets.com; Weis Markets Corp. Donation Hotline: 1-800-662-5370, ext. 3199; URL: http://www.weismarkets.com/about-weis/community/

Purpose and activities: Weis Markets makes charitable contributions to organizations icluding food banks, community-based health care organizations, schools, and pet shelters. Most donations are made in the form of Weis Markets Gift Cards. Support is limited to areas of company operations in Maryland, New Jersey, New York, Pennsylvania, and West Virginia.
Fields of interest: Education; Animal welfare; Health care, clinics/centers; Health care; Food services; Food banks; United Ways and Federated Giving Programs.
Type of support: General/operating support; In-kind gifts.
Geographic limitations: Giving limited to areas of company operations, with emphasis on MD, NJ, NY, PA, and WV.
Support limitations: No support for fraternal, labor, or political organizations; or organizations already supported by the company. No grants to individuals requesting donations for trips, sports sponsorships, or pageants; individuals requesting direct assistance with catastrophic health and financial needs; or for advertising in school yearbooks or programs for parties and benefit performances, or associate incentives.
Application information: Applications accepted. Applications are not accepted via fax. Follow-up calls and emails are not encouraged. Application form not required.
Applications should include the Weis Markets store location closest to the applicant's residence, a Weis Markets Preferred Shoppers Club Card number, and a daytime phone number.
Initial approach: E-mail proposal
Deadline(s): Two weeks prior to event

4025
Welch Foods, Inc.
3 Concord Farms, 575 Virginia Rd.
Concord, MA 01742-9101 (978) 371-1000

Company URL: http://www.welchs.com
Establishment information: Established in 1869.
Company type: Subsidiary of a cooperative
Business activities: Produces grape juice, jam, and jelly.
Business type (SIC): Specialty foods/canned, frozen, and preserved
Corporate officers: Joseph C. Falcone, Chair.; Bradley C. Irwin, Pres. and C.E.O.; Michael J. Perda III, V.P. and C.F.O.; David J. Lukiewski, Sr. V.P., Sales and Mktg.; Thomas E. Gettig, V.P., Human Resources and Admin.; Vivian S.Y. Tseng, Esq., V.P., Genl. Counsel, and Secy.; David F. Engelkemeyer, V.P., Opers.; Damon G. Hart, V.P., Sales
Board of directors: Joseph Falcone, Chair.; Charles J. Chapman; Jerry A. Czebotar; Douglas R. Forraht; Daniel A. Grady; Timothy E. Grow; David J. Lukiewski; Stephen B. Morris; Joseph J. Schena; Stephen H. Warhover; Thomas G. Wilkinson III; James T. Winton
Divisions: Food Service Div., Concord, MA; Food Store Div., Concord, MA; International Div., Concord, MA
Plants: Lawton, MI; Westfield, NY; North East, PA; Grandview, Kennewick, Yakima Valley, WA
Giving statement: Giving through the Welch Foods Inc. Corporate Giving Program.

Welch Foods Inc. Corporate Giving Program
3 Concord Farms
575 Virginia Rd.
Concord, MA 01742-9101 (978) 371-1000

Purpose and activities: Welch Foods makes charitable contributions to nonprofit organizations involved with education, agriculture, and on a case by case basis. Support is given primarily in areas of company operations and areas of grape growers.
Fields of interest: Education; Agriculture; General charitable giving.
Type of support: Employee matching gifts; General/operating support; In-kind gifts.
Geographic limitations: Giving primarily in areas of company operations, with emphasis on Concord, MA, and areas of grape growers.
Support limitations: No support for national organizations or political or religious organizations. No grants to individuals.
Application information: Applications accepted. The Marketing Department handles giving. Application form not required. Applicants should submit the following:
1) detailed description of project and amount of funding requested
Initial approach: Proposal to headquarters
Copies of proposal: 1
Final notification: Following review
Number of staff: 1 full-time professional.

4026
Wellmark, Inc.
(doing business as Wellmark Blue Cross and Blue Shield of Iowa)
636 Grand Ave.
P.O. Box 9232
Des Moines, IA 50309-2565
(515) 245-4500
FAX: (515) 248-5617

Company URL: http://www.wellmark.com
Establishment information: Established in 1939.
Company type: Private company
Business activities: Operates medical service plan.
Business type (SIC): Insurance/accident and health
Financial profile for 2010: Number of employees, 1,909; assets, $2,129,214,000; liabilities, $1,016,604,000
Corporate officers: John D. Forsyth, Chair. and C.E.O.; David Brown, Exec. V.P., C.F.O., and Treas.; Timothy Peterson, Exec. V.P. and C.I.O.; Marcelle J. Chickering, Exec. V.P., Human Resources; Cory R. Harris, Sr. V.P. and Genl. Counsel
Board of directors: John D. Forsyth, Chair.; Thomas M. Cink; Melanie C. Dreher; Daryl K. Henze; William C. Hunter; Paul E. Larson; Angeline M. Lavin; Kenton K. Moss; Terrence J. Mulligan; Dave Neil
Office: Sioux Falls, SD
Giving statement: Giving through the Wellmark, Inc. Corporate Giving Program and the Wellmark Foundation.

Wellmark, Inc. Corporate Giving Program
c/o Community Rels. Dept.
1331 Grand Ave.
Des Moines, IA 50309-2901 (515) 376-4500
E-mail: inthecommunity@wellmark.com;
URL: http://www.wellmark.com/AboutWellmark/Community/Contributions.aspx

Purpose and activities: As a complement to its foundation, Wellmark also makes charitable contributions to nonprofit organizations involved with the arts, health, diversity and inclusion, civic affairs, and human services. Support is limited to Iowa and South Dakota.
Fields of interest: Arts; Public health; Human services; Civil/human rights, equal rights; Community/economic development; Public affairs.
Programs:
Employee Matching Gifts Program: Wellmark matches contributions made by its employees to educational institutions on a one-for-one basis up to $10,000 per employee, per year.
Employee Volunteer Program: Wellmark awards grants to nonprofit organizations with which its employees volunteer 24 hours.
Type of support: Employee matching gifts; Employee volunteer services; General/operating support; Sponsorships.
Geographic limitations: Giving limited to IA and SD.
Support limitations: No support for discriminatory organizations, religious organizations, or political organizations. No grants to individuals, or for endowments or memorials, membership dues, travel expenses, or youth groups, teams, choirs, bands, clubs, etc.
Publications: Application guidelines.
Application information: Applications accepted. Contributions generally do not exceed $5,000. Multi-year funding is not automatic. Support is limited to 1 grant per organization during any given year. The Community Relations Department handles giving. A contributions committee reviews all requests for grants. Application form required. Applicants should submit the following:
1) timetable for implementation and evaluation of project
2) results expected from proposed grant
3) statement of problem project will address
4) population served
5) name, address and phone number of organization
6) brief history of organization and description of its mission
7) how project's results will be evaluated or measured
8) listing of board of directors, trustees, officers and other key people and their affiliations
9) detailed description of project and amount of funding requested
10) contact person
11) copy of current year's organizational budget and/or project budget
12) plans for acknowledgement
Applications should include the Tax ID Number of the organization.
Initial approach: Complete online application form
Committee meeting date(s): Quarterly
Deadline(s): 4 months prior to need
Final notification: 3 months
Number of staff: 2 full-time professional; 2 part-time professional.

The Wellmark Foundation
(formerly The IASD Health Care Foundation)
1331 Grand Ave., Station 3W751
Des Moines, IA 50309-2551 (515) 376-4819
FAX: (515) 376-9082;
E-mail: wmfoundation@wellmark.com; E-mail for Matt McGarvey: mcgarveym@wellmark.com; Additional contact: Cheryl Clarke, Sr. Prog. Mgr., tel.: (515) 245-4997, e-mail: clarkec@wellmark.com; URL: http://www.wellmark.com/foundation/index.asp

Establishment information: Established in 1991 in IA.
Donors: Blue Cross and Blue Shield of Iowa; Blue Cross and Blue Shield of South Dakota; Wellmark, Inc.
Contact: Matt McGarvey, Dir.
Financial data (yr. ended 12/31/11): Assets, $33,282,007 (M); expenditures, $2,555,457; qualifying distributions, $2,209,413; giving activities include $2,209,413 for grants.
Purpose and activities: The foundation supports programs designed to improve the health of Iowans, South Dakotans, and their communities. Special emphasis is directed toward childhood obesity prevention; and community-based wellness and prevention.
Fields of interest: Elementary/secondary education; Dental care; Reproductive health; Reproductive health, prenatal care; Public health; Public health, obesity; Public health, physical fitness; Health care; Food services; Nutrition; Family services, parent education; United Ways and Federated Giving Programs Children.
Program:
Healthy Communities Grant Program: The foundation supports programs designed to target childhood obesity prevention and community-based wellness and prevention. The foundation awards grants of up to $25,000 for small projects and new collaborations that address upstream health issues influenced by the environment, social, and economic conditions of the community. The foundation also awards large grants up to $150,000 for projects with larger resource needs and more mature initiatives.
Type of support: Continuing support; Curriculum development; Management development/capacity

building; Program development; Publication; Seed money.
Geographic limitations: Giving limited to IA and SD.
Support limitations: No grants to individuals, or for biomedical research not of direct benefit to local residents, uncompensated care for direct clinical services, or services that are billable for third-party reimbursement, capital campaigns, equipment, organizations indirect/overhear costs, debt reduction, annual campaigns, fundraising events, or endowments.
Publications: Annual report; Application guidelines; Grants list; Newsletter.
Application information: Applications accepted. Letters of interest should be no longer than 3 pages. Applicants may be invited to submit a full proposal at a later date. Applicants should submit the following:
1) results expected from proposed grant
2) statement of problem project will address
3) population served
4) copy of IRS Determination Letter
5) geographic area to be served
6) copy of most recent annual report/audited financial statement/990
7) listing of board of directors, trustees, officers and other key people and their affiliations
8) detailed description of project and amount of funding requested
9) copy of current year's organizational budget and/or project budget

Initial approach: Download cover page and mail letter of interest
Copies of proposal: 4
Board meeting date(s): Mar. 30, May 24, Aug. 11, and Nov. 1
Deadline(s): Apr. 12 for requests of $25,000 and under for Healthy Communities Grant Program; Aug. 2 for requests of $25,001 to $150,000 for Healthy Communities Grant Program

Officers and Directors: John D. Forsyth, Chair.; Janet Griffin, Secy.; Christa Kuennen, Treas.; Mary Ann Abrams; Theodore J. Boesen, Jr.; Eldon E. Huston; Ruth Litchfield; Edward R. Lynn; Robert E. O'Connell; Robert J. Richard; Sheila Riggs; Roberta Wattlesworth.
Number of staff: 2 full-time professional; 1 part-time professional.
EIN: 421368650
Selected grants: The following grants are a representative sample of this grantmaker's funding activity:
$90,000 to Community HealthCare Association of the Dakotas, Sioux Falls, SD, 2009. To provide oral health screening and preventive dental treatment via Delta Dental's Dakota Smiles mobile dental program.
$90,000 to Iowa Department of Public Health, Des Moines, IA, 2009. For the Data Warehouse program, which creates an efficient, effective tool to disseminate health data and make positive health improvements in Iowa communities.
$90,000 to Youth and Family Services, Rapid City, SD, 2009. For the Choose to Move Childhood Obesity Prevention Project, which will integrate physical activity and wise nutrition choices into daily routines.
$87,983 to South Dakota State University, Brookings, SD, 2009. For agencies to implement food backpack projects to provide grocery items to elementary school children in low-income families. The backpacks would be accompanied by interactive nutrition and cooking lessons to increase children's awareness of healthy eating behaviors. The resulting changes in eating patterns will be analyzed.
$86,847 to Iowa Department on Aging, Des Moines, IA, 2009. To expand Chronic Disease Self-Management Program into additional Iowa counties, with an emphasis on wellness and prevention.
$86,640 to Iowa Department of Education, Des Moines, IA, 2009. To support schools in implementing nutrition standards for foods and beverages sold on school grounds during the school day with the goal of improving overall school wellness.
$70,059 to Van Buren, County of, Keosauqua, IA, 2009. For Creating Wellness Through Lasting Leadership, designed to address two of the weakest links in most health and wellness efforts: keeping leaders and participants motivated and funding. Focuses on leadership development and ongoing fundraising techniques.
$57,000 to University of Northern Iowa Foundation, Cedar Falls, IA, 2009. To work with food services staff, teachers, students, school administrators, and farmers in public schools to develop and implement strategies that will result in healthier school lunch programs. The lessons learned in these pilot school settings will be documented to enhance project replication potential.
$56,135 to Burgess Foundation, Onawa, IA, 2009. For the Monona County childhood obesity prevention project, which will add indoor and outdoor fitness equipment to the local school, park, city, library and community center, and develop programs and activities to educate students and families about fitness and nutrition to reduce the risk of childhood obesity.
$55,085 to Pathfinders Resource Conservation and Development Area, Fairfield, IA, 2009. To provide outreach to public schools in southeast Iowa to establish a fresh foods program using only locally grown fruits, vegetables and other food products.

4027
WellPoint, Inc.

(formerly Anthem, Inc.)
120 Monument Cir.
Indianapolis, IN 46204 (317) 488-6000
FAX: (317) 488-6260

Company URL: http://www.wellpoint.com
Establishment information: Established in 1936.
Company type: Public company
Company ticker symbol and exchange: WLP/NYSE
Business activities: Operates health benefits company.
Business type (SIC): Insurance/accident and health; insurance/life; pension, health, and welfare funds; insurance agents, brokers, and services
Financial profile for 2012: Number of employees, 43,500; assets, $58,955,400,000; sales volume, $61,711,700,000; pre-tax net income, $3,865,500,000; expenses, $57,846,200,000; liabilities, $35,152,700,000
Fortune 1000 ranking: 2012—47th in revenues, 73rd in profits, and 94th in assets
Forbes 2000 ranking: 2012—130th in sales, 212th in profits, and 399th in assets
Corporate officers: Joseph R. Swedish, Pres. and C.E.O.; Wayne S. DeVeydt, Exec. V.P. and C.F.O.; John Cannon, Exec. V.P., Legal, Genl. Counsel, and Secy.
Board of directors: Lenox D. Baker, Jr.; Susan B. Bayh; Sheila P. Burke; Robert L. Dixon, Jr.; Julie A. Hill; Warren Y. Jobe; Ramiro G. Peru; William J. Ryan; George A. Schaefer
Subsidiaries: AMERIGROUP Corporation, Virginia Beach, VA; SpectraCare, Inc., Louisville, KY
Historic mergers: Trigon Healthcare, Inc. (July 31, 2002); WellPoint Health Networks Inc. (November 30, 2004); Anthem Health Plans, Inc. (December 1, 2004); Anthem Insurance Companies, Inc. (December 1, 2004)
Giving statement: Giving through the WellPoint Foundation, Inc.
Company EIN: 352145715

WellPoint Foundation, Inc.

(formerly Anthem Foundation, Inc.)
120 Monument Cir.
Indianapolis, IN 46204-4906
E-mail: wellpoint.foundation@wellpoint.com; Additional e-mail: communityrelations@wellpoint.com; URL: http://www.wellpointfoundation.org/home.html

Establishment information: Established in 2000 in IN.
Donors: Anthem Insurance Cos., Inc.; Anthem Health Plans of New Hampshire, Inc.; Anthem, Inc.; WellPoint, Inc.; Howard Cashion Living Trust.
Contact: Lance Chrisman, Exec. Dir.
Financial data (yr. ended 12/31/11): Assets, $117,269,801 (M); expenditures, $10,922,906; qualifying distributions, $10,952,293; giving activities include $7,391,013 for 61 grants (high: $1,846,402; low: $2,000) and $1,930,565 for employee matching gifts.
Purpose and activities: The foundation supports programs designed to enhance the health and well-being of individuals and families. Special emphasis is directed toward programs designed to promote healthy generations.
Fields of interest: Health care, infants; Reproductive health, prenatal care; Public health; Public health, communicable diseases; Public health, obesity; Public health, physical fitness; Health care, insurance; Health care; Mental health, smoking; Heart & circulatory diseases; Diabetes; Disasters, preparedness/services; Boys & girls clubs; American Red Cross; YM/YWCAs & YM/YWHAs; Public policy, research.
Programs:
Associate Giving Campaign: The foundation matches contributions made by associates of WellPoint to non-profit organizations on a two-for-one basis up to $25,000, per campaign year.
Director's Fund: The foundation matches contributions made by directors of WellPoint to heath-related nonprofit organizations for up to $10,000 per contributor, per year.
Healthy Generations: The foundation supports programs designed to improve public health in the 14 states where WellPoint serves. Special emphasis is directed toward programs designed to reduce children's obesity levels; reduce adult risk for cardiac mortality; improve and sustain healthy physical activity levels; decrease the prevalence of diabetes in adults; encourage at-risk expectant mothers to engage in sustained prenatal care in their first trimesters; help at-risk expectant mothers commit to behaviors that reduce the risk of having low birth-weight babies; improve influenza prevention and immunization rates for adults; improve pneumococcal prevention and immunization rates for adults; and help individuals adopt and sustain smoking cessation behaviors.
Type of support: Continuing support; Emergency funds; Employee matching gifts; Employee volunteer services; General/operating support; Program development; Research; Scholarship funds; Sponsorships.
Geographic limitations: Giving primarily in areas of company operations in CA, CO, CT, GA, IN, KY, ME, MO, NV, NY, NH, OH, VA, and WI; giving also to national organizations.
Support limitations: No support for private charities or foundations, religious organizations not of direct

benefit to the entire community, political candidates or organizations, discriminatory organizations, or association memberships. No grants to individuals, or for political causes or campaigns, lobbying activities, endowments, film, music, TV, video, or media production projects or broadcast program underwriting, fundraising events, sports sponsorships, performing arts tours, or requests that provide benefit to WellPoint, Inc. or WellPoint employees.
Publications: Application guidelines; Grants list.
Application information: Applications accepted. Organizations receiving support are asked to submit an interim and a final report. Unsolicited applications for capital projects, initiatives, or campaigns are not accepted. Research and policy grants are by invitation only and must align with the Healthy Generations signature initiative. Organizations with research or policy projects should e-mail the foundation with a brief summary. Application form required. Applicants should submit the following:
1) results expected from proposed grant
2) copy of IRS Determination Letter
3) copy of most recent annual report/audited financial statement/990
4) listing of board of directors, trustees, officers and other key people and their affiliations
5) copy of current year's organizational budget and/or project budget
6) detailed description of project and amount of funding requested
7) contact person
8) how project's results will be evaluated or measured
9) geographic area to be served
10) population served
Initial approach: Complete online eligibility quiz and application
Board meeting date(s): Quarterly
Deadline(s): Apr. 19 and Sept. 13
Final notification: 4 to 6 months
Officers and Directors:* Kathleen S. Kiefer, Secy.; Wayne S. DeVeydt*, C.F.O.; R. David Kretschmer, Treas.; Lance Chrisman, Exec. Dir.; Angela F. Braly; Randal L. Brown; Lisa Moriyama; Samuel R. Nussbaum, M.D.; Brian A. Sassi.
EIN: 352122763
Selected grants: The following grants are a representative sample of this grantmaker's funding activity:
$1,845,402 to American Heart Association, Dallas, TX, 2011. For Hands-Only Cardiopulmonary Resuscitation (CPR) White Surf Campaign.
$1,743,128 to Boys and Girls Clubs of America, Atlanta, GA, 2010. For Healthy Generations, Youth Health Promotion.
$1,266,029 to OASIS Institute, Saint Louis, MO, 2010. For Healthy Generations, adult activity.
$1,000,000 to March of Dimes Foundation, White Plains, NY, 2010. For Healthy Generations, parental care.
$750,000 to American Cancer Society, Atlanta, GA, 2011. For Patient Navigator Programs.
$500,000 to American Diabetes Association, Alexandria, VA, 2010. For Healthy Generations, diabetes.
$500,000 to American Diabetes Association, Alexandria, VA, 2011. For Healthy Generations Diabetes Prevention.
$374,600 to California Council on Physical Fitness and Sports, Santa Monica, CA, 2010. For Healthy Generations, Youth Health Promotion.
$295,387 to Brookings Institution, Washington, DC, 2010. For Engelberg Center's public policy research.
$288,475 to Arthritis Foundation, Los Angeles, CA, 2011. For Health Generations adults activity.
$275,000 to National Coalition for Women with Heart Disease, Washington, DC, 2011. For Healthy Generations.
$271,792 to HealthMPowers, Atlanta, GA, 2010. For Healthy Generations, Youth Health Promotion.
$250,000 to Dartmouth College, Hanover, NH, 2011. For healthcare improvement.
$250,000 to HealthCorps, New York, NY, 2011. For peer mentoring program.
$210,000 to Nurse-Family Partnership, Denver, CO, 2010. For Healthy Generations, low birth weight.
$207,470 to Los Angeles Lakers Youth Foundation, El Segundo, CA, 2010. For Healthy Generations, Youth Health Promotion.
$75,000 to Providence Speech and Hearing Center, Orange, CA, 2010. For uninsured support/access to care.
$54,800 to Blue Ridge Health Center, Arrington, VA, 2011. For Latino community health promoters in Action Program.
$50,000 to Alzheimers Association, Rocky Mountain Chapter, Denver, CO, 2011. For program support.

4028
Wells Fargo & Company

420 Montgomery St.
San Francisco, CA 94163 (866) 249-3302

Company URL: http://www.wellsfargo.com
Establishment information: Established in 1852.
Company type: Public company
Company ticker symbol and exchange: WFC/NYSE
International Securities Identification Number: US9497461015
Business activities: Operates financial holding company; operates commercial bank.
Business type (SIC): Banks/commercial; holding company
Financial profile for 2012: Number of employees, 269,200; assets, $1,422,968,000,000; pre-tax net income, $28,471,000,000; liabilities, $1,265,414,000,000
Fortune 1000 ranking: 2012—25th in revenues, 5th in profits, and 6th in assets
Forbes 2000 ranking: 2012—72nd in sales, 14th in profits, and 23rd in assets
Corporate officers: John G. Stumpf, Chair., Pres., and C.E.O.; Timothy J. Sloan, Sr. Exec. V.P. and C.F.O.; Patricia R. Callahan, Sr. Exec. V.P. and C.A.O.; Kevin A. Rhein, Sr. Exec. V.P. and C.I.O.; Richard D. Levy, Exec. V.P. and Cont.; James M. Strother, Exec. V.P. and Genl. Counsel
Board of directors: John G. Stumpf, Chair.; John D. Baker II; Elaine L. Chao; John S. Chen; Lloyd H. Dean; Susan E. Engel; Enrique Hernandez, Jr.; Donald M. James; Cynthia H. Milligan; Federico F. Pena; Howard V. "Rick" Richardson; Judith M. Runstad; Stephen W. Sanger; Susan G. Swenson
International operations: Aruba; Barbados; Bermuda; Brazil; Canada; Cayman Islands; China; Hong Kong; India; Ireland; Japan; Mauritius; Netherlands; Philippines; Singapore; South Korea; United Kingdom; Uruguay
Historic mergers: Greater Bay Bancorp (October 1, 2007); Wachovia Corporation (December 31, 2008)
Giving statement: Giving through the Wells Fargo & Company Contributions Program, the First Security Foundation, the Sarasota County Foundation, the Scholarship Fund for South Carolina State College, the Wachovia Regional Community Development Corporation, Inc., the Wachovia Wells Fargo Foundation, Inc., the Wells Fargo Foundation, and the Wells Fargo Regional Foundation.
Company EIN: 410449260

Wells Fargo & Company Contributions Program

MAC A0112-073
550 California St., 7th Fl.
San Francisco, CA 94104-1004
URL: https://www.wellsfargo.com/about/csr

Contact: Tim Hanlon, Sr. V.P., Corp. Community Devel. Group
Purpose and activities: As a complement to its foundation, Wells Fargo also makes charitable contributions to nonprofit organizations directly. Support is given primarily in areas of company operations.
Fields of interest: Elementary/secondary education; Human services; Economic development; Community/economic development.
Type of support: Curriculum development; Employee volunteer services; General/operating support; Program development; Sponsorships; Technical assistance.
Geographic limitations: Giving primarily in areas of company operations.
Support limitations: No support for fraternal, military, professional, or other membership organizations, political parties, lobbying organizations, athletic organizations, or religious organizations. No grants to individuals, or for endowments, conferences or seminars, trips, or tours, equipment, research, film or video production, literary projects, or advertising.
Publications: Application guidelines.
Application information: Applications accepted. Proposals should be no longer than 5 pages in length. Application form not required. Applicants should submit the following:
1) timetable for implementation and evaluation of project
2) copy of IRS Determination Letter
3) brief history of organization and description of its mission
4) copy of most recent annual report/audited financial statement/990
5) how project's results will be evaluated or measured
6) listing of board of directors, trustees, officers and other key people and their affiliations
7) detailed description of project and amount of funding requested
8) copy of current year's organizational budget and/or project budget
Initial approach: Visit website for guidelines and contact information for local contribution managers
Copies of proposal: 1
Deadline(s): 3 months prior to need
Final notification: 90 days

First Security Foundation

76 S. Main St., 2nd Fl.
Salt Lake City, UT 84101-1558

Establishment information: Established in 1952 in UT.
Donor: First Security Corp.
Financial data (yr. ended 12/31/11): Assets, $3,122,134 (M); expenditures, $191,060; qualifying distributions, $175,000; giving activities include $175,000 for grants.
Purpose and activities: The foundation supports organizations involved with higher education.
Fields of interest: Higher education.
Type of support: General/operating support; Scholarship funds.
Geographic limitations: Giving limited to ID, UT, and WY.
Support limitations: No grants to individuals.

Application information: Applications not accepted. Contributes only to pre-selected organizations.
Officers and Trustee:* Spencer F. Eccles*, Chair.; Eileen C. Hansen, Secy.; Verna Lee Johnston, Treas.
EIN: 876118149
Selected grants: The following grants are a representative sample of this grantmaker's funding activity:
$26,300 to University of Utah, Salt Lake City, UT, 2009.
$17,000 to Utah State University, Logan, UT, 2009.
$13,000 to Idaho State University, Pocatello, ID, 2009.
$13,000 to University of Idaho, Moscow, ID, 2009.
$10,600 to Boise State University, Boise, ID, 2009.
$7,000 to Weber State University, Ogden, UT, 2009.
$5,300 to College of Idaho, Caldwell, ID, 2009.
$4,300 to College of Eastern Utah, Price, UT, 2009.
$4,300 to Southern Utah University, Cedar City, UT, 2009.
$4,300 to Westminster College, Salt Lake City, UT, 2009.

Sarasota County Foundation

c/o Wachovia Bank, N.A.
P.O. Box 267
Sarasota, FL 34230-0267 (941) 361-5803
E-mail: communityaffairs@wachovia.com; Application address: 1819 Main St., Ste. 230, Sarasota, FL 34236; URL: https://www.wachovia.com/foundation/v/index.jsp?vgnextoid=41da8372b4b8c110VgnVCM2000005d7d6fa2RCRD&vgnextfmt=default

Establishment information: Established in 1958 in FL; funded in 1967.
Donors: Palmer First National Bank and Trust; Wachovia Bank, N.A.
Contact: Joan Greenwood
Financial data (yr. ended 12/31/11): Assets, $1,254,550 (M); expenditures, $65,780; qualifying distributions, $52,073; giving activities include $44,000 for 7 grants (high: $10,000; low: $3,600).
Purpose and activities: The foundation supports community foundations and organizations involved with education, mental health, and human services.
Fields of interest: Health care; Human services; Civil/human rights.
Type of support: Equipment; Matching/challenge support; Program development.
Geographic limitations: Giving limited to Sarasota County, FL.
Support limitations: No support for grantmaking foundations. No grants to individuals, or for endowments, travel, research, annual campaigns, debt reduction, deficit financing, operating or program expenses, marketing materials or advertising, conferences, workshops, or seminars; no multi-year support.
Publications: Application guidelines.
Application information: Applications accepted. Application form required. Applicants should submit the following:
1) results expected from proposed grant
2) statement of problem project will address
3) name, address and phone number of organization
4) copy of IRS Determination Letter
5) brief history of organization and description of its mission
6) copy of most recent annual report/audited financial statement/990
7) how project's results will be evaluated or measured
8) listing of board of directors, trustees, officers and other key people and their affiliations
9) contact person
10) copy of current year's organizational budget and/or project budget
11) geographic area to be served
12) listing of additional sources and amount of support

Initial approach: Download application form and mail proposal and application from to application address
Board meeting date(s): Jan.
Deadline(s): Jan. 15
Final notification: Mar. 15

Trustee: Wells Fargo Bank, N.A.
EIN: 596169723

Scholarship Fund for South Carolina State College

1525 W. W.T. Harris Blvd. D1114-044
Charlotte, NC 28288-5709 (866) 601-0001

Establishment information: Established in 1990 in SC.
Donors: First Union National Bank of South Carolina; First Union Corp.; Wachovia Corp.
Financial data (yr. ended 10/31/12): Assets, $59,353 (M); expenditures, $3,384; qualifying distributions, $3,103; giving activities include $3,103 for 1 grant.
Purpose and activities: The foundation awards college scholarships to juniors enrolled in the School of Business at South Carolina State College. The program is administered by the South Carolina Foundation of Independent Colleges.
Type of support: Scholarships—to individuals.
Geographic limitations: Giving limited to SC.
Application information: Applications accepted. Application form required.

Initial approach: Contact foundation for application information
Deadline(s): Aug. 31

Trustee: Wells Fargo Bank, N.A.
EIN: 586239696

Wachovia Regional Community Development Corporation, Inc.

(formerly First Union Regional Community Development Corporation, Inc.)
123 S. Broad St., PA 4360
Philadelphia, PA 19109-1029 (215) 670-4307
FAX: (215) 670-4313

Establishment information: Established in 1993 in PA.
Donors: CoreStates Financial Corp; First Union Corp.; Wachovia Corp.
Contact: Kimberly J. Allen, V.P. and Sr. Prog. Off.
Financial data (yr. ended 12/31/11): Assets, $7,252,797 (M); expenditures, $57,560; qualifying distributions, $15,000; giving activities include $15,000 for grants.
Purpose and activities: The foundation provides loans to organizations with programs designed to promote housing and community development in low-income communities.
Type of support: Program-related investments/loans.
Geographic limitations: Giving primarily in DE, NJ, and the eastern half of PA.
Application information: Applications accepted. Application form not required. Applicants should submit the following:
1) copy of most recent annual report/audited financial statement/990

Initial approach: Proposal
Deadline(s): None

Officers and Board Members:* Eleanor V. Horne*, Chair.; C. Kent McGuire, Ph.D., Vice-Chair.; Denise McGregor Armbrister*, Exec. Dir.; Austin Burke; Fernando Chang-Muy; Ed Covington; Doug Dimmig; Lucia Gibbons; Judith H. Hoopes; Ernie Jones; Stephanie W. Naidoff, Esq.*; John Petillo, Ph.D.; Mike Rizer, Esq.; Ralph Smith, Esq.; Susanne Svizeny.
EIN: 232735410

Wells Fargo Foundation

333 S. Grant Ave., 12th Fl.
Los Angeles, CA 90071
FAX: (310) 789-8989;
E-mail: thanlon@wellsfargo.com; URL: http://www.wellsfargo.com/donations

Establishment information: Established in 1979 in MN.
Donors: Norwest Corp.; Wells Fargo & Co.; Norwest Ltd.
Contact: Timothy G. Hanlon, Pres.
Financial data (yr. ended 12/31/11): Assets, $531,481,108 (M); gifts received, $8,818,226; expenditures, $113,079,653; qualifying distributions, $107,542,374; giving activities include $107,542,374 for 10,714+ grants (high: $3,000,000).
Purpose and activities: The foundation supports organizations involved with education, job creation and job training, housing, financial literacy, human services, and community economic development.
Fields of interest: Elementary/secondary education; Education; Employment, services; Employment, training; Housing/shelter, development; Housing/shelter, home owners; Housing/shelter, services; Housing/shelter; Human services, financial counseling; Human services; Economic development; Community/economic development Economically disadvantaged.
Programs:

Educational Matching Gift Program: The foundation matches contributions made by employees and directors of Wells Fargo to educational institutions on a one-for-one basis from $25 to $5,000 per employee, per year.

Wells Fargo Housing Foundation - Home Ownership Grant Program: The foundation supports programs designed to create sustainable homeownership opportunities for low- to moderate-income individuals. Special emphasis is directed toward first-time homebuyer counseling; pre and post-purchase counseling; and foreclosure counseling and prevention activities. Formerly a separate company-sponsored foundation, the Wells Fargo Housing Foundation is a program of the Wells Fargo Foundation.

Wells Fargo Housing Foundation - Team Volunteer Program: The foundation awards grants to nonprofit organizations with which employees of Wells Fargo volunteer to help build, renovate, paint, or repair a home for low-to moderate-income individuals. Grants of up to $30,000 per home are available. Projects that serve the military, use green products, or work on foreclosed or abandoned properties are eligible for additional funds. Formerly a separate company-sponsored foundation, the Wells Fargo Housing Foundation is a program of the Wells Fargo Foundation.

Type of support: Annual campaigns; Continuing support; Employee matching gifts; Employee volunteer services; General/operating support; Management development/capacity building; Program development.
Geographic limitations: Giving primarily in areas of company operations.
Support limitations: No support for religious organizations not of direct benefit to the entire community, lobbying organizations, or fraternal organizations. No grants to individuals, or for political campaigns, advertising purchases including booths and tickets, fundraising dinners, video or film productions, club memberships, or endowments.

Publications: Application guidelines; Corporate giving report.
Application information: Applications accepted. Application form not required. Applicants should submit the following:
1) copy of IRS Determination Letter
Visit website for detailed application guidelines by state.
Initial approach: Varies by state. Visit website for details
Copies of proposal: 1
Deadline(s): Varies
Final notification: 90 to 120 days
Officers and Directors:* Timothy G. Hanlon*, Pres.; Richard D. Levy, Sr. V.P. and Treas.; Timothy R. Chinn, V.P.; James A. Horton, V.P.; Mary E. Schaffner, Secy.; John R. Campbell; Georgette "Gigi" Dixon; Alejandro J. Hernandez; Cynthia E. Ishigaki; Tami B. Simmons; John G. Stumpf; Dean L. Thorp.
Number of staff: None.
EIN: 411367441
Selected grants: The following grants are a representative sample of this grantmaker's funding activity:
$1,245,200 to Scholarship America, Saint Peter, MN, 2011.
$932,260 to United Way of Central Iowa, Des Moines, IA, 2011.
$500,000 to American Red Cross, 2011.
$250,000 to National Community Reinvestment Coalition, Washington, DC, 2011.
$150,000 to Palm Springs Art Museum, Palm Springs, CA, 2011.
$24,000 to United Way of the Midlands, Omaha, NE, 2011.
$15,000 to Eureka Schools Foundation, Granite Bay, CA, 2011.
$15,000 to Rebuilding Together of the Carolinas, Charlotte, NC, 2011.
$15,000 to YMCA of Metropolitan Fort Worth, Fort Worth, TX, 2011.

Wells Fargo Regional Foundation

(formerly Wachovia Regional Foundation)
123 S. Broad St.
MAC Y1379-030
Philadelphia, PA 19109-1029 (215) 670-4300
FAX: (215) 670-4313;
E-mail: communityaffairs@wachovia.com; Contact for Neighborhood Implementation and Planning Grants: Kimberly Allen, Prog. Off., tel.: (215) 670-4307, Crystal Dundas, Prog. Off., tel.: (215) 670-4311; URL: https://www.wellsfargo.com/about/regional-foundation/index

Establishment information: Established in 1998.
Donors: CoreStates Financial Corp; First Union Corp.; Wachovia Corp.
Contact: Denise McGregor Armbrister, Exec. Dir.
Financial data (yr. ended 12/31/11): Assets, $74,265,761 (M); expenditures, $5,654,439; qualifying distributions, $5,380,164; giving activities include $5,255,500 for 132 grants (high: $100,000; low: $1,000).
Purpose and activities: The foundation supports organizations involved with neighborhood planning and development.
Fields of interest: Employment, job counseling; Employment, training; Housing/shelter, development; Housing/shelter; Children, services; Family services; Community development, neighborhood development; Economic development; Urban/community development.
Programs:
Neighborhood Implementation Grants: The foundation awards grants from $100,000 to $750,000 for comprehensive community development projects that target specific neighborhoods and are based on current resident-driven neighborhood plans. Special emphasis is directed towards projects designed to address children and families; economic development; affordable housing and housing counseling; and neighborhood building.
Neighborhood Planning Grants: The foundation awards grants from $25,000 to $100,000 for resident-driven neighborhood plans that take comprehensive approaches to revitalization. Special emphasis is directed toward plans designed to address children and families; economic development; affordable housing and housing counseling; and neighborhood building.
Type of support: Equipment; Program development; Program evaluation; Technical assistance.
Geographic limitations: Giving primarily in Kent, New Castle, and Sussex, DE, Atlantic, Bergen, Burlington, Camden, Cape May, Cumberland, Essex, Hudson, Hunterdon, Gloucester, Mercer, Middlesex, Monmouth, Morris, Ocean, Passaic, Salem, Somerset, Sussex, Union, and Warren, NJ, and Adams, Berks, Bradford, Bucks, Carbon, Centre, Chester, Clinton, Columbia, Cumberland, Dauphin, Delaware, Juniata, Lackawanna, Lancaster, Lebanon, Lehigh, Lycoming, Luzerne, Mifflin, Monroe, Montgomery, Montour, Northampton, Northumberland, Perry, Philadelphia, Pike, Potter, Schuylkill, Snyder, Sullivan, Susquehanna, Tioga, Union, Wayne, Wyoming, and York, PA.
Support limitations: No support for political organizations or national or international organizations; generally, no support for K-12 private schools, colleges or universities, veterans' or fraternal organizations, arts or cultural organizations, hospitals or medical centers, or health- or disease-related organizations. No grants to individuals, or for general operating support, strategic or business plans, "bricks and mortar" projects, political causes, endowments, capital campaigns, debt reduction, or special events; generally, no grants for religious programs or activities.
Publications: Application guidelines; Grants list; Program policy statement.
Application information: Applications accepted. Neighborhood Planning and Implementation Grants have two phases. Phase two of the application process is by invitation only. A site visit may be requested. Application form required. Applicants should submit the following:
1) timetable for implementation and evaluation of project
2) population served
3) name, address and phone number of organization
4) copy of IRS Determination Letter
5) brief history of organization and description of its mission
6) geographic area to be served
7) copy of most recent annual report/audited financial statement/990
8) how project's results will be evaluated or measured
9) detailed description of project and amount of funding requested
10) contact person
11) copy of current year's organizational budget and/or project budget
12) listing of additional sources and amount of support
Initial approach: Complete online eligibility quiz and application form
Board meeting date(s): Jan., Apr., July, and Oct.
Deadline(s): Sept. 6 for phase one and Oct. 11 for phase two for Neighborhood Planning Grants; Apr. 12 and Oct. 25 for phase one and June 21 and Jan. 17 for phase two for Neighborhood Implementation Grants
Final notification: Jan. 31 for Neighborhood Planning Grants; Nov. 1 and Apr. 30 for Neighborhood Implementation Grants
Officers and Directors:* C. Kent McGuire, Ph.D.*, Chair.; Austin J. Burke, Vice-Chair.; Denise McGregor Armbrister, Sr. V.P. and Exec. Dir.; Lois W. Greco, Sr. V.P. and Evaluation Off.; Kimberly Allen, V.P. and Prog. Off.; Fernando Chang-Muy; Lucia Gibbons; Stacy Holland; Maria Matos; John Petillo, Ph.D.; Mike Rizer, Esq.; Ralph Smith, Esq.; Susanne Svizeny; John Thurber, Esq.; Robert Torres, Esq.
Number of staff: 4 full-time professional; 1 full-time support.
EIN: 222625990
Selected grants: The following grants are a representative sample of this grantmaker's funding activity:
$100,000 to Catholic Charities, Diocese of Metuchen, Perth Amboy, NJ, 2009.
$100,000 to Cramer Hill Community Development Corporation, Camden, NJ, 2009.
$100,000 to Ironbound Community Corporation, Newark, NJ, 2009.
$100,000 to Ironbound Community Corporation, Newark, NJ, 2009.
$83,500 to Enterprise Center, Philadelphia, PA, 2009.
$75,000 to Chester Community Improvement Project, Chester, PA, 2009.
$75,000 to Chester Community Improvement Project, Chester, PA, 2009.
$75,000 to Community Action Committee of the Lehigh Valley, Bethlehem, PA, 2009.
$50,000 to Interfaith Housing Development Corporation of Bucks County, Bristol, PA, 2009.
$45,000 to Pencader Hundred Community Center, Newark, DE, 2009.

4029
Wendel, Rosen, Black & Dean LLP

1111 Broadway, 24th Fl.
P.O. Box 2047
Oakland, CA 94607 (510) 834-6600

Company URL: http://wendel.com
Establishment information: Established in 1909.
Company type: Private company
Business activities: Operates law firm.
Business type (SIC): Legal services
Corporate officer: Daniel Rapaport, Managing Partner
Office: Modesto, CA
Giving statement: Giving through the Wendel, Rosen, Black & Dean LLP Corporate Giving Program.

Wendel, Rosen, Black & Dean LLP Corporate Giving Program

1111 Broadway, 24th Fl.
Oakland, CA 94607 (510) 834-6600
E-mail: marketing@wendel.com; URL: http://wendel.com/index.cfm?fuseaction=content.contentDetail&id=8752

Purpose and activities: Support is given primarily in areas of company operations in Oakland, California.
Fields of interest: Environment; Community/economic development.
Type of support: Employee volunteer services; General/operating support; Sponsorships.
Geographic limitations: Giving primarily in areas of company operations in Oakland, CA.

Application information: Applications accepted.
Initial approach: Proposal e-mailed to headquarters

4030
The Wendy's Company

(formerly Wendy's/Arby's Group, Inc.)
1 Dave Thomas Blvd.
Dublin, OH 43017 (614) 764-3100

Company URL: http://www.wendysarbys.com
Establishment information: Established in 1969.
Company type: Public company
Company ticker symbol and exchange: WEN/NASDAQ
Business activities: Operates holding company; operates and franchises restaurants.
Business type (SIC): Restaurants and drinking places; holding company; investors/miscellaneous
Financial profile for 2012: Number of employees, 44,000; assets, $4,303,200,000; sales volume, $2,505,240,000; pre-tax net income, -$13,120,000; expenses, $2,457,570,000; liabilities, $2,317,340,000
Fortune 1000 ranking: 2012—809th in revenues, 874th in profits, and 636th in assets
Corporate officers: Nelson Peltz, Chair.; Peter W. May, Vice-Chair.; Emil J. Brolick, Pres. and C.E.O.; Stephen E. Hare, Sr. V.P. and C.F.O.; Steven B. Graham, Sr. V.P. and C.A.O.; R. Scott Toop, Sr. V.P., Genl. Counsel, and Secy.; John N. Peters, Sr. V.P., Opers.
Board of directors: Nelson Peltz, Chair.; Peter W. May, Vice-Chair.; Emil J. Brolick; Clive Chajet; Edward P. Garden; Janet Hill; Joseph A. Levato; J. Randolph Lewis; Peter H. Rothschild; David E. Schwab II; Roland C. Smith; Raymond S. Troubh; Jack G. Wasserman
Subsidiaries: National Propane Corp., New Hyde Park, NY; Wendy's International, Inc., Dublin, OH
International operations: Canada
Giving statement: Giving through the Wendy's Company Contributions Program.
Company EIN: 380471180

The Wendy's Company Contributions Program

(formerly The Wendy's Company Controbutions Program)
1 Dave Thomas Blvd.
Dublin, OH 43017-5452 (614) 764-3100
URL: http://www.aboutwendys.com/responsibility/

Purpose and activities: As a complement to its foundation, Wendy's also makes charitable contributions to nonprofit organizations and awards scholarships to high school seniors directly. Support is given on a national basis, with emphasis on areas of company operations.
Fields of interest: Education; Animal welfare; Health care, research; Children, adoption; Children, foster care; Children, services; Military/veterans' organizations.
Type of support: Employee volunteer services; General/operating support; Scholarship funds.
Geographic limitations: Giving on a national basis, with emphasis on areas of company operations.
Publications: Application guidelines.
Application information: Applications accepted. Applications for the Wendy's High School Heisman Program should include information about the applicant's learning, performance and leadership activities in their school and community. Application form required.
Initial approach: Complete online application for Wendy's High School Heisman Program
Deadline(s): Oct. 2 for Wendy's High School Heisman Program

4031
Wendy's International, Inc.

(also known as Wendy's)
1 Dave Thomas Blvd.
Dublin, OH 43017-0256 (614) 764-3100

Company URL: http://www.wendys.com
Establishment information: Established in 1969.
Company type: Subsidiary of a public company
Business activities: Operates and franchises restaurants.
Business type (SIC): Restaurants and drinking places; investors/miscellaneous
Corporate officers: Nelson Peltz, Chair.; Peter W. May, Vice-Chair.; Emil J. Brolick, Pres. and C.E.O.; Stephen D. Farrar, C.O.O.; Stephen E. Hare, Sr. V.P. and C.F.O.; Steven B. Graham, Sr. V.P. and C.A.O.
Board of directors: Nelson Peltz, Chair.; Peter W. May, Vice-Chair.; Emil J. Brolick; Clive Chajet; Edward P. Garden; Janet Hill; Jeseph A. Levato; J. Randolph Lewis; Peter H. Rothschild; David E. Schwab II; Roland C. Smith; Raymond S. Troubh; Jack G. Wasserman
International operations: Canada
Giving statement: Giving through the Wendy's International, Inc. Corporate Giving Program and the Wendy's International Foundation.

Wendy's International Foundation

1 Dave Thomas Blvd.
Dublin, OH 43017 (614) 764-3100
Application address: P.O. Box 256, Dublin, OH 43017

Establishment information: Established in 2002.
Donor: Wendy's International, Inc.
Contact: Dennis L. Lynch, Pres.
Financial data (yr. ended 12/31/12): Assets, $672,980 (M); expenditures, $1,780; qualifying distributions, $1,780.
Purpose and activities: The foundation supports hospitals and organizations involved with golf and human services.
Fields of interest: Hospitals (general); Athletics/sports, golf; Children, adoption; Children, services; Human services, gift distribution; Human services.
Type of support: General/operating support; Scholarship funds.
Geographic limitations: Giving primarily in OH.
Application information: Applications accepted. Application form required. Applicants should submit the following:
1) descriptive literature about organization
2) detailed description of project and amount of funding requested
Initial approach: Letter
Deadline(s): None
Officers and Directors:* Dennis L. Lynch*, Pres.; Kimberly Butler, Sr. V.P.; Mark S. Inzetta*, Secy.; Stephen E. Hare, Treas.; Emil J. Brolick.
EIN: 311807834

4032
Wendy's of Montana, Inc.

2906 2nd Ave. N., Ste. 210
Billings, MT 59101-2099 (406) 252-5125

Establishment information: Established in 1976.
Company type: Private company
Business activities: Operates restaurants.
Business type (SIC): Restaurants and drinking places
Corporate officers: Sam McDonald, Jr., Chair. and C.E.O.; Gregory C. McDonald, Pres. and C.E.O.; Deborah McDonald, Treas.
Board of director: Sam McDonald, Jr., Chair.
Giving statement: Giving through the Wendy's of Montana Foundation Inc.

Wendy's of Montana Foundation Inc.

2906 2nd Ave. N.
Billings, MT 59101-2026 (406) 252-5125

Establishment information: Established in 1998 in NV.
Donors: Wendy's of Montana, Inc.; Sam E. McDonald, Jr.; Martin Family Foundation; Food Services of America.
Contact: Gregory C. McDonald, Pres.
Financial data (yr. ended 12/31/11): Assets, $36,118 (M); gifts received, $254,556; expenditures, $227,250; qualifying distributions, $225,717; giving activities include $193,879 for 24 grants (high: $58,439; low: $250).
Purpose and activities: The foundation supports organizations involved with arts and culture, education, athletics, adoption, and community development.
Fields of interest: Museums (art); Performing arts, theater; Performing arts, orchestras; Arts; Higher education; Education; Athletics/sports, amateur leagues; Athletics/sports, baseball; Boys & girls clubs; YM/YWCAs & YM/YWHAs; Children, adoption; Community/economic development.
Type of support: General/operating support; Program development; Sponsorships.
Geographic limitations: Giving primarily in Billings, MT.
Application information: Applications accepted. Application form required. Applicants should submit the following:
1) how project will be sustained once grantmaker support is completed
2) copy of IRS Determination Letter
3) copy of most recent annual report/audited financial statement/990
4) how project's results will be evaluated or measured
5) explanation of why grantmaker is considered an appropriate donor for project
6) listing of board of directors, trustees, officers and other key people and their affiliations
7) plans for cooperation with other organizations, if any
8) listing of additional sources and amount of support
Initial approach: Proposal
Deadline(s): None
Officers: Gregory C. McDonald, Pres.; John Wilcox, Secy.-Treas.
Directors: John T. Jones; Sam E. McDonald, Jr.
EIN: 880393923
Selected grants: The following grants are a representative sample of this grantmaker's funding activity:
$43,600 to Dave Thomas Foundation for Adoption, Columbus, OH, 2009.
$15,000 to Billings, City of, Billings, MT, 2009.
$5,000 to Carroll College, Helena, MT, 2009.

$5,000 to Yellowstone Art Museum, Billings, MT, 2009.
$5,000 to YMCA of Sheridan County, Sheridan, WY, 2009.
$5,000 to YMCA, Scottsbluff Family, Scottsbluff, NE, 2009.
$4,000 to Alberta Bair Theater, Billings, MT, 2009.
$4,000 to Billings, City of, Billings, MT, 2009.
$3,750 to Dickinson State University, Dickinson, ND, 2009.
$2,000 to Billings Public Schools, Billings, MT, 2009.

4033
Wenger Corp.

555 Park Dr.
P.O. Box 448
Owatonna, MN 55060-0448
(507) 455-4100

Company URL: http://www.wengercorp.com
Establishment information: Established in 1946.
Company type: Private company
Business activities: Designs, manufactures, and sells music-related products.
Business type (SIC): Musical instruments
Corporate officers: Jerry A. Wenger, Chair.; Kenneth L. Pizel, V.P., Finance, Treas., and C.F.O.; Dave Bullard, V.P., Mktg.; Mary Ann Smith, Secy.; Brian Paulson, Cont.
Board of director: Jerry A. Wenger, Chair.
Giving statement: Giving through the Wenger Foundation.

Wenger Foundation

P.O. Box 142
Navarre, MN 55392-0142 (952) 467-3667

Establishment information: Established in 1982 in MN.
Donor: Wenger Corp.
Contact: Wendy Dankey, Exec. Dir.
Financial data (yr. ended 12/31/11): Assets, $7,397,234 (M); gifts received, $992,211; expenditures, $453,172; qualifying distributions, $438,910; giving activities include $438,910 for grants.
Purpose and activities: The foundation supports hospitals and organizations involved with arts and culture, higher education, and children and youth.
Fields of interest: Performing arts, theater; Performing arts, music; Performing arts, orchestras; Historic preservation/historical societies; Arts; Higher education; Hospitals (general); Children/youth, services; United Ways and Federated Giving Programs.
Type of support: Annual campaigns; Capital campaigns; General/operating support; Matching/challenge support; Scholarship funds; Scholarships—to individuals.
Geographic limitations: Giving primarily in Minneapolis and Owatonna, MN.
Support limitations: No grants to individuals (except for scholarships).
Application information: Applications accepted. Application form not required.
Initial approach: Letter of inquiry
Copies of proposal: 1
Deadline(s): None
Officers and Directors: Jerry A. Wenger, Pres.; Wendy Dankey, Exec. Dir.; Nancy Benjamin; Kirsten Johnson; Kari Wenger; Sonja H. Wenger.
Number of staff: 1 part-time support.
EIN: 411436658
Selected grants: The following grants are a representative sample of this grantmaker's funding activity:
$22,500 to Minnesota Private College Fund, Saint Paul, MN, 2010.
$15,000 to Minnesota Opera, Minneapolis, MN, 2010.
$10,000 to Guthrie Theater, Minneapolis, MN, 2010.
$10,000 to Minnesota Orchestral Association, Minneapolis, MN, 2010.
$8,500 to VocalEssence, Minneapolis, MN, 2010.
$5,000 to American Composers Forum, Saint Paul, MN, 2010.
$5,000 to BestPrep, Brooklyn Park, MN, 2010.
$5,000 to Walker Art Center, Minneapolis, MN, 2010.
$4,000 to Rose Ensemble, Saint Paul, MN, 2010.
$3,596 to Minnesota Orchestral Association, Minneapolis, MN, 2010.

4034
West Bank

1601 22nd St., Ste. 100
P.O. Box 65020
West Des Moines, IA 50266-1408
(515) 222-2300

Company URL: http://www.westbankiowa.com
Establishment information: Established in 1893.
Company type: Subsidiary of a public company
Business activities: Operates commercial bank.
Business type (SIC): Banks/commercial
Corporate officers: David R. Milligan, Chair.; Robert G. Pulver, Vice-Chair.; Brad L. Winterbottom, Pres.; Douglas R. Gulling, C.F.O.
Board of directors: David R. Milligan, Chair.; Robert G. Pulver, Vice-Chair.
Giving statement: Giving through the West Bancorporation Foundation, Inc.

The West Bancorporation Foundation, Inc.

1601 22nd St.
West Des Moines, IA 50266-1408 (515) 222-2300

Establishment information: Established in 2003 in IA.
Donor: West Bank.
Contact: Jill Hansen, Exec. Dir.
Financial data (yr. ended 12/31/11): Assets, $1,110,945 (M); gifts received, $300,100; expenditures, $231,937; qualifying distributions, $221,250; giving activities include $221,250 for 76 grants (high: $40,000; low: $500).
Purpose and activities: The foundation supports organizations involved with arts and culture, education, and human services. Special emphasis is directed toward programs designed to benefit low- and moderate-income individuals.
Fields of interest: Arts; Elementary/secondary education; Higher education; Education; Human services Economically disadvantaged.
Type of support: Annual campaigns; Building/renovation; Capital campaigns; General/operating support; Program development; Scholarship funds; Sponsorships.
Geographic limitations: Giving primarily in central and eastern IA.
Support limitations: No support for athletic organizations, fraternal organizations, K-12 schools, pass-through organizations (with the exception of United Way and independent college funds), political organizations, private foundations, sectarian, religious or denominational organizations, social organizations, tax-supported city, county, or state organizations, trade, industry, or professional organizations, United Way organizations for United Way-funded programs, or veterans' organizations. No grants to individuals, or for conference or seminar attendance, courtesy or goodwill advertising in benefit publications, endowments or memorials, fellowships, festival participation, or capital campaigns for hospitals or healthcare facilities.
Publications: Application guidelines.
Application information: Applications accepted. Application form required. Applicants should submit the following:
1) copy of IRS Determination Letter
2) copy of most recent annual report/audited financial statement/990
3) listing of board of directors, trustees, officers and other key people and their affiliations
4) copy of current year's organizational budget and/or project budget
Initial approach: Download application form and E-mail or mail to foundation
Deadline(s): Jan. 1, Apr. 1, July 1, and Oct. 1
Officers and Directors:* Alice A. Jensen, Secy.; Douglas R. Gulling*, Treas.; Jill T. Hansen, Exec. Dir.; Peggy J. Fleming; Steve R. Hall; Kaye R. Lozier; David D. Nelson; Sharen K. Surber; Ashley L. Wear; Rodney S. Wiekert; Brad L. Winterbottom.
EIN: 200523259
Selected grants: The following grants are a representative sample of this grantmaker's funding activity:
$40,200 to United Way of Central Iowa, Des Moines, IA, 2010. For annual fundraising.
$21,000 to American Red Cross, Des Moines, IA, 2010.
$10,000 to Des Moines Symphony, Des Moines, IA, 2010.
$6,000 to Dowling Catholic High School, West Des Moines, IA, 2010.
$5,000 to Eddie Davis Community Center, West Des Moines, IA, 2010.
$2,500 to Amyotrophic Lateral Sclerosis Association, Johnston, IA, 2010.
$2,500 to Chrysalis Foundation, Des Moines, IA, 2010.
$2,000 to Prevent Blindness Iowa, Des Moines, IA, 2010.
$2,000 to Science Center of Iowa, Des Moines, IA, 2010.
$1,000 to West Des Moines Community Schools Foundation, West Des Moines, IA, 2010.

4035
West Corporation

11808 Miracle Hills Dr.
Omaha, NE 68154 (402) 963-1200

Company URL: http://www.west.com/
Establishment information: Established in 1986.
Company type: Private company
Business activities: Provides business process outsourcing services.
Business type (SIC): Business services/miscellaneous
Financial profile for 2011: Number of employees, 33,400; assets, $3,000,000,000; sales volume, $2,388,210,000
Corporate officers: Thomas B. Barker, Chair. and C.E.O.; Nancee Shannon R. Berger, Pres. and C.O.O.; Paul M. Mendlik, Exec. V.P., Treas., and C.F.O.; Mark V. Lavin, Exec. V.P. and C.A.O.; Dave Mussman, Exec. V.P., Genl. Counsel, and Secy.

Board of director: Thomas B. Barker, Chair.
Giving statement: Giving through the West Education Foundation.

West Education Foundation

11808 Miracle Hills Dr.
Omaha, NE 68154-4403 (402) 963-1200
URL: http://sms.scholarshipamerica.org/west/

Establishment information: Established in 2006 in NE.
Donor: West Corporation.
Financial data (yr. ended 12/31/11): Assets, $573,292 (M); gifts received, $200,004; expenditures, $183,422; qualifying distributions, $174,738; giving activities include $168,000 for 76 grants to individuals (high: $3,000; low: $1,000).
Purpose and activities: The foundation provides scholarship awards to dependent children, under the age of 24, of employees of United States West Corporation, St. Peter, Minnesota. The program is administered by Scholarship America.
Fields of interest: Higher education.
Type of support: Scholarships—to individuals.
Geographic limitations: Giving primarily in areas of company operations.
Application information: Applications accepted. The program is closed at this time. Revisit the site in Feb., 2014 to access the guidelines and application form for the 2014 program. Application form required.
Initial approach: Proposal
Deadline(s): Mar. 15
Directors: Thomas B. Barker; Nancee Shannon R. Berger; Paul M. Mendlik.
EIN: 204763223

4036
West Manor Construction Corp.

19304 Horace Harding Expwy., Ste. 2
Fresh Meadows, NY 11365-2800
(718) 264-1420

Establishment information: Established in 1999.
Company type: Private company
Business activities: Operates general contracting company.
Business type (SIC): Contractors/general residential building
Corporate officer: Steven Bluestone, Pres.
Giving statement: Giving through the Bluestone Family Foundation.

The Bluestone Family Foundation

141 James St.
Hastings on Hudson, NY 10706-3406
Application address: P.O. Box 604523, Bayside NY 11360

Establishment information: Established in 2006.
Donor: West Manor Construction.
Contact: Ira Lichtiger, Dir.
Financial data (yr. ended 12/31/11): Assets, $0 (M); expenditures, $238; qualifying distributions, $0.
Purpose and activities: The foundation supports organizations involved with the environment, heart disease, and disability services.
Fields of interest: Environment; Heart & circulatory diseases; Developmentally disabled, centers & services.
Type of support: General/operating support.
Geographic limitations: Giving limited to the five boroughs of New York City.
Support limitations: No grants to individuals.
Application information: Applications not accepted. Unsolicited requests for funds not accepted.
Directors: Eric Bluestone; Sara Herbstman; Ira Lichtiger.
EIN: 204046711

4037
West Marine, Inc.

500 Westridge Dr.
Watsonville, CA 95076-4100
(831) 728-2700
FAX: (302) 655-5049

Company URL: http://www.westmarine.com
Establishment information: Established in 1968.
Company type: Public company
Company ticker symbol and exchange: WMAR/NASDAQ
Business activities: Operates recreational and commercial boating supplies and apparel stores; provides Internet shopping services; provides catalog shopping services; sells recreational and commercial boating supplies and apparel wholesale.
Business type (SIC): Boats—retail; industrial machinery and equipment—wholesale; nonstore retailers; computer services
Financial profile for 2012: Number of employees, 4,043; assets, $354,270,000; sales volume, $675,250,000; pre-tax net income, $24,330,000; expenses, $650,080,000; liabilities, $75,860,000
Corporate officers: Randolph K. Repass, Chair.; Matt Hyde, Pres. and C.E.O.; Brad Willis, C.I.O.; Tom Moran, Sr. V.P., Finance and C.F.O.; Pam Fields, Sr. V.P., Genl. Counsel, and Secy.; Debra Radcliff, Sr. V.P., Mktg.; Linda Kennedy, V.P., Human Resources
Board of directors: Randolph K. Repass, Chair.; Matthew Hyde; Dennis Madsen; Jamie Nordstrom; Robert Olsen; Barbara L. Rambo; Alice M. Richter; Christiana Shi
Giving statement: Giving through the West Marine BlueFuture.
Company EIN: 770355502

West Marine BlueFuture

(formerly West Marine, Inc. Corporate Giving Program)
c/o Donations and Sponsorships
500 Westridge Dr.
Watsonville, CA 95076-4171
FAX: (831) 768-5750; URL: http://www.westmarine.com/bluefuture

Purpose and activities: West Marine makes charitable contributions to nonprofit organizations involved with water conservation, boating, youth boating, and human services. Support is given primarily in areas of company operations.
Fields of interest: Environment, water resources; Safety/disasters, public education; Athletics/sports, water sports; Youth development.
Programs:
Marine Conservation Grants: West Marine supports programs designed to maintain waterways and ensure that they remain pristine and ecologically viable for future generations.
Youth Boating Grants: West Marine supports programs designed to encourage young people to enjoy boating as a recreational activity that's both fun and educational.
Type of support: Employee volunteer services; In-kind gifts; Program development; Sponsorships.
Geographic limitations: Giving on a national basis.
Support limitations: No support for political organizations. No grants to individuals, or for conventions or conferences, scholarships, team sponsorship or travel, production of films, videotapes, or recordings, capital campaigns, publications or displays, general operating support, seed money, salaries, transportation, meals, lodging, or debt repayment or reimbursement.
Publications: Application guidelines.
Application information: Applications accepted. Marine Environment contributions do not exceed $5,000 in value; Youth Boating contributions do not exceed $1,000 in value. Application form required. Applicants should submit the following:
1) how project will be sustained once grantmaker support is completed
2) name, address and phone number of organization
3) brief history of organization and description of its mission
4) detailed description of project and amount of funding requested
5) contact person
6) copy of current year's organizational budget and/or project budget
7) listing of additional sources and amount of support

Applications for Marine Environment Grants should include the Tax ID Number of the organization, the number of paid staff and volunteers, and a description of past support by West Marine with the organization. Applications for Youth Boating Grants should include the Tax ID Number of the organization, the start and end dates of the program, and the number of children/youths enrolled in the program.
Initial approach: Download application form and e-mail to headquarters for Marine Conservation Grants; download application form and fax to headquarters for Youth Boating Grants
Deadline(s): May 1 for Marine Conservation Grants; June 1 for Youth Boating Grants
Final notification: May 30 for Marine Conservation Grants

4038
West Pharmaceutical Services, Inc.

(formerly The West Company, Incorporated)
530 Herman O. W. Dr.
Exton, PA 19341 (610) 594-2900

Company URL: http://www.westpharma.com
Establishment information: Established in 1923.
Company type: Public company
Company ticker symbol and exchange: WST/NYSE
Business activities: Provides drug formulation research and development services; provides clinical research and laboratory services; designs, develops, and manufactures pharmaceutical, health care, and consumer product dispensing and delivering components and systems.
Business type (SIC): Rubber products/fabricated; medical instruments and supplies; laboratories/medical and dental; research, development, and testing services
Financial profile for 2012: Number of employees, 6,700; assets, $1,564,000,000; sales volume, $1,266,400,000; pre-tax net income, $108,600,000; expenses, $1,142,900,000; liabilities, $835,100,000
Corporate officers: Donald E. Morel, Jr., Ph.D., Chair. and C.E.O.; William J. Federici, Sr. V.P. and C.F.O.; John R. Gailey III, V.P., Genl. Counsel, and Secy.; Michael A. Anderson, V.P. and Treas.; Daniel

Malone, V.P. and Cont.; Richard D. Luzzi, V.P., Human Resources
Board of directors: Donald E. Morel, Jr., Ph.D., Chair.; Mark Buthman, Ph.D.; William F. Feehery, Ph.D.; Thomas W. Hofmann; L. Robert Johnson; Paula A. Johnson, M.D.; Douglas A. Michels; John H. Weiland; Anthony Welters; Patrick J. Zenner
Subsidiary: Tech Group, Inc., Scottsdale, AZ
Plants: Phoenix, Tempe, AZ; Clearwater, St. Petersburg, FL; Frankfort, IN; Grand Rapids, MI; Kearney, NE; Kinston, NC; Jersey Shore, Lititz, Upper Darby, Williamsport, PA; Cayey, PR
Offices: San Francisco, CA; Delton, MI; Peterborough, NH; Cincinnati, Cleveland, Loveland, OH; Palmyra, PA
International operations: Argentina; Australia; Brazil; China; Colombia; Denmark; England; France; Germany; India; Ireland; Israel; Italy; Japan; Mexico; Singapore; Spain; Venezuela
Giving statement: Giving through the H. O. West Foundation.
Company EIN: 231210010

The H. O. West Foundation

(also known as The Herman O. West Foundation)
530 Heilman O. West Dr.
Exton, PA 19341 (610) 594-2945
E-mail: maureen.goebel@westpharma.com;
URL: http://www.westpharma.com/en/about/Pages/CharitableGiving.aspx

Establishment information: Established in 1972 in PA.
Donors: The West Co., Inc.; West Pharmaceutical Services, Inc.
Contact: Richard D. Luzzi, Tr.; Maureen B. Goebel, Admin.
Financial data (yr. ended 12/31/12): Assets, $3,447,277 (M); expenditures, $788,480; qualifying distributions, $788,480; giving activities include $697,290 for grants, $62,023 for 49 grants to individuals and $28,350 for 122 employee matching gifts.
Purpose and activities: The foundation supports organizations involved with arts and culture, education, health, human services, community development, and science and technology. Support is given primarily in areas of company operations in Arizona, Florida, Michigan, North Carolina, Nebraska, and Pennsylvania.
Fields of interest: Arts; Education, fund raising/fund distribution; Higher education; Education; Hospitals (general); Health care; Human services; Community/economic development; United Ways and Federated Giving Programs; Engineering/technology; Science.
Programs:
H.O. West Foundation Scholarship Program: The foundation annually awards up to seven college scholarships to children and dependents of employees of West Pharmaceutical Services and its subsidiaries. Winners are selected on the basis of character, maturity, leadership, extra-curricular activities, motivation, interest and desire, patriotism, predicted success in college, and academic achievement. Each scholarship is renewable for 4 years with a maximum of $10,000.
Matching Gifts to Education Program: The foundation matches contributions made by employees, retirees, and directors of West Pharmaceutical Services and its domestic subsidiaries to institutions of higher education on a one-for-one basis from $25 to $1,000 per contributor, per year.
Matching Gifts to Nonprofit Organizations: The foundation matches contributions made by H. O. West employees to nonprofit organizations of their choice on a dollar-for-dollar basis from $25 to $500 per contribution per year.
Type of support: Annual campaigns; Building/renovation; Capital campaigns; Continuing support; Emergency funds; Employee matching gifts; Employee-related scholarships; General/operating support; Matching/challenge support; Research; Scholarships—to individuals.
Geographic limitations: Giving primarily in areas of company operations in AZ, FL, MI, NC, NE, and PA.
Publications: Application guidelines.
Application information: Applications accepted. Application form not required. Applicants should submit the following:
1) copy of IRS Determination Letter
2) copy of most recent annual report/audited financial statement/990
3) detailed description of project and amount of funding requested
4) listing of additional sources and amount of support

Initial approach: Proposal or letter
Copies of proposal: 1
Board meeting date(s): Spring and fall
Deadline(s): 1 week prior to board meetings
Final notification: Varies

Officer and Trustees:* George R. Bennyhoff, Chair.; Paula A. Johnson, M.D.; Richard D. Luzzi.
Number of staff: None.
EIN: 383674460
Selected grants: The following grants are a representative sample of this grantmaker's funding activity:
$50,000 to YMIC Foundation, West Chester, PA, 2012.
$46,000 to Fox Chase Cancer Center, Philadelphia, PA, 2012.
$10,000 to American Red Cross, Southeastern Pennsylvania Chapter, Philadelphia, PA, 2012. For Hurricane Sandy.
$10,000 to Franklin Institute Science Museum, Philadelphia, PA, 2012.
$5,000 to Academy of Natural Sciences of Philadelphia, Philadelphia, PA, 2012.
$5,000 to American Red Cross, Southeastern Pennsylvania Chapter, Philadelphia, PA, 2012.
$5,000 to Cancer Care, New York, NY, 2012.
$5,000 to Downingtown STEM Academy, Downingtown, PA, 2012.
$5,000 to Philadelphia Museum of Art, Philadelphia, PA, 2012.
$5,000 to Zoological Society of Philadelphia, Philadelphia Zoo, Philadelphia, PA, 2012.
$3,500 to YMIC Foundation, West Chester, PA, 2012.

4039
Westar Energy, Inc.

(formerly Western Resources, Inc.)
818 S. Kansas Ave.
P.O. Box 889
Topeka, KS 66612-1203 (785) 575-6300
FAX: (785) 575-6596

Company URL: http://www.westarenergy.com/
Establishment information: Established in 1924.
Company type: Public company
Company ticker symbol and exchange: WR/NYSE
Business activities: Generates, transmits, and distributes electricity; provides security services.
Business type (SIC): Electric services; business services/miscellaneous
Financial profile for 2012: Number of employees, 2,313; assets, $9,265,230,000; sales volume, $2,261,470,000; pre-tax net income, $408,600,000; expenses, $1,699,340,000; liabilities, $6,369,090,000
Fortune 1000 ranking: 2012—860th in revenues, 497th in profits, and 412th in assets
Corporate officers: Charles Q. Chandler IV, Chair.; Mark A. Ruelle, Pres. and C.E.O.; James Ludwig, Exec. V.P., Public Affairs; Douglas Sterbenz, Exec. V.P. and C.O.O.; Tony Somma, Sr. V.P., C.F.O., and Treas.; Larry Irick, V.P., Genl. Counsel, and Corp. Secy.; Leroy P. Wages, V.P. and Cont.; Jerl Banning, V.P., Human Resources
Board of directors: Charles Q. Chandler IV, Chair.; Mollie Hale Carter; R.A. Edwards III; Jerry B. Farley; Richard L. Hawley; B. Anthony Isaac; Arthur B. Krause; Sandra A.J. Lawrence; Michael F. Morrissey; Mark A. Ruelle; S. Carl Soderstrom, Jr.
Subsidiary: Kansas Gas and Electric Company, Wichita, KS
Giving statement: Giving through the Westar Energy Foundation.
Company EIN: 480290150

Westar Energy Foundation

(formerly Western Resources Foundation, Inc.)
818 S. Kansas Ave.
Topeka, KS 66612-1203 (785) 575-1544
FAX: (785) 575-8119; Application address: P.O. Box 889, Topeka, KS 66601-0089; URL: http://www.westarenergy.com/wcm.nsf/content/foundation

Establishment information: Established in 1991 in KS.
Donors: Western Resources, Inc.; Westar Energy, Inc.
Contact: Cynthia McCarvel, Pres.
Financial data (yr. ended 12/31/11): Assets, $735,266 (M); expenditures, $683,577; qualifying distributions, $673,974; giving activities include $673,974 for grants.
Purpose and activities: The foundation supports programs designed to improve academic performance of youth; and prepare youth for the world of work and community leadership.
Fields of interest: Education; Employment; Children/youth, services Youth.
Program:
Matching Gift Program: The foundation matches contributions made by its employees to institutions of higher education on a one-for-one basis from $100 to $1,000 per household, per year.
Type of support: Employee matching gifts; General/operating support; Program development; Scholarship funds.
Geographic limitations: Giving primarily in areas of company operations in KS.
Support limitations: No support for organizations supported by the United Way, tax-supported institutions, fraternal, ethnic, church, or social organizations, local youth or athletic groups including scout troops, 4-H clubs, or athletic teams, or political organizations. No grants to individuals, or for building fund drives, capital campaigns, primary or secondary school-related functions, medical research, disease campaigns, fundraising walks, or conferences, conventions, or meeting sponsorships.
Publications: Application guidelines; Informational brochure.
Application information: Applications accepted. Support is limited to 1 contribution per organization during any given year. Application form required. Applicants should submit the following:
1) copy of IRS Determination Letter
2) detailed description of project and amount of funding requested
3) listing of additional sources and amount of support

4) listing of board of directors, trustees, officers and other key people and their affiliations
5) copy of current year's organizational budget and/or project budget
6) statement of problem project will address
7) how project will be sustained once grantmaker support is completed

Applications should include a letter of endorsement from a Westar Energy employee or retiree.
Initial approach: Download application form and mail to foundation
Copies of proposal: 1
Deadline(s): None
Final notification: 4 to 6 weeks
Officers: Cynthia McCarvel, Pres.; Carlene Barkley, Secy.; John M. Grace, Treas.
Directors: Bruce A. Akin; C. Michael Lennen; James J. Ludwig; Caroline A. Williams.
Number of staff: 2 full-time professional; 1 full-time support.
EIN: 481099341
Selected grants: The following grants are a representative sample of this grantmaker's funding activity:
$80,000 to American Red Cross, Wichita, KS, 2011.
$79,960 to United Way of the Plains, Wichita, KS, 2011.
$15,000 to Kansas Childrens Discovery Center, Topeka, KS, 2011. For capital campaign.
$10,000 to Big Brothers Big Sisters, Kansas, Wichita, KS, 2011.
$8,940 to United Way of the Flint Hills, Emporia, KS, 2011.
$7,750 to Court Appointed Special Advocates of Shawnee County, Topeka, KS, 2011.
$7,000 to Boys and Girls Club of Topeka, Topeka, KS, 2011.
$6,000 to Topeka Youth Project, Topeka, KS, 2011.
$5,000 to Heartspring, Wichita, KS, 2011.
$5,000 to Topeka Association for Retarded Citizens, Topeka, KS, 2011.

4040
The Western & Southern Life Insurance Company

400 Broadway St.
Cincinnati, OH 45202-3312 (513) 629-1800

Company URL: http://www.westernsouthernlife.com
Establishment information: Established in 1888.
Company type: Subsidiary of a mutual company
Business activities: Sells life insurance.
Business type (SIC): Insurance/life
Corporate officers: John Finn Barrett, Chair., Pres., and C.E.O.; William Olds, Sr. V.P. and C.O.O.; Robert Walker, Sr. V.P. and C.F.O.; Nicholas P. Sargen, Sr. V.P. and C.I.O.; Don Wuebbling, Sr. V.P. and Genl. Counsel; Noreen J. Hayes, Sr. V.P., Human Resources; Bradley Hunkler, V.P. and C.A.O.; Michael J. Laatsch, V.P., Public Rels. and Corp. Comms.
Board of director: John Finn Barrett, Chair.
Giving statement: Giving through the Western & Southern Life Insurance Company Contributions Program and the Western & Southern Financial Fund, Inc.
Company EIN: 310487145

The Western & Southern Life Insurance Company Contributions Program

400 Broadway
Cincinnati, OH 45202-3312
URL: http://www.westernsouthernlife.com/aboutUs/wsfg/communityinvolvement.asp

Purpose and activities: As a complement to its foundation, Western & Southern Life also makes charitable contributions to nonprofit organizations directly. Support is given primarily in the greater Cincinnati, Ohio area.
Fields of interest: Education; Health care.
Type of support: Employee volunteer services; General/operating support; Sponsorships.
Geographic limitations: Giving primarily in the greater Cincinnati, OH, area.

Western & Southern Financial Fund, Inc.

(formerly Western-Southern Foundation, Inc.)
400 Broadway, MS 28
Cincinnati, OH 45202-3312 (513) 629-1464
URL: http://www.westernsouthernlife.com/aboutUs/wsfg/communityinvolvement.asp

Establishment information: Established in 1988 in OH.
Donors: The Western & Southern Life Insurance Co.; Columbus Life Insurance Co.
Contact: Edward J. Babbit, Secy.-Treas.
Financial data (yr. ended 12/31/12): Assets, $4,175,726 (M); expenditures, $2,949,655; qualifying distributions, $2,939,655; giving activities include $2,937,426 for 252+ grants (high: $481,676).
Purpose and activities: The fund supports organizations involved with arts and culture, education, health, mental health, cancer, multiple sclerosis, human services, and community development.
Fields of interest: Museums; Arts; Higher education; Business school/education; Education; Health care, patient services; Health care; Mental health/crisis services; Cancer; Multiple sclerosis; Boy scouts; American Red Cross; Salvation Army; Children/youth, services; Human services; Community development, neighborhood development; Business/industry; Community/economic development; United Ways and Federated Giving Programs.
Program:
Employee Matching Gifts: The fund matches contributions made by full-time associates of Western & Southern Financial to colleges and universities on a one-for-one basis.
Type of support: Annual campaigns; Building/renovation; Capital campaigns; Continuing support; Employee matching gifts; General/operating support; Program development; Scholarship funds; Sponsorships.
Geographic limitations: Giving primarily in Cincinnati, OH.
Publications: Application guidelines.
Application information: Applications accepted. Application form not required.
Initial approach: Proposal
Deadline(s): None
Officers and Trustees:* Thomas L. Williams*, Chair.; John Finn Barrett*, Pres.; Edward J. Babbit, Secy.-Treas.
EIN: 311259670

4041
Western Asset Management Company

385 E Colo Blvd., Ste. 250
Pasadena, CA 91101 (626) 844-9400

Establishment information: Established in 1986.
Company type: Subsidiary of a public company
Business activities: Operates asset management company; provides investment management and related services to institutional and individual clients, company-sponsored mutual funds and other pooled investment vehicles.
Business type (SIC): Security and commodity services
Giving statement: Giving through the Western Asset Management Company Charitable Foundation.

Western Asset Management Company Charitable Foundation

385 E. Colorado Blvd.
Pasadena, CA 91101-1923

Establishment information: Established in 2005 in CA.
Donors: Western Asset Mgmt. Co.; Legg Mason, Inc.
Financial data (yr. ended 03/31/12): Assets, $6,045,816 (M); gifts received, $6,549,758; expenditures, $538,736; qualifying distributions, $533,580; giving activities include $533,580 for grants.
Purpose and activities: The foundation supports organizations involved with arts and culture, education, health, water sports, and human services.
Fields of interest: Media, radio; Performing arts, orchestras; Arts; Higher education; Education; Hospitals (general); Health care, clinics/centers; Health care; Athletics/sports, water sports; American Red Cross; Children/youth, services; Children, foster care; Human services.
Type of support: General/operating support.
Geographic limitations: Giving primarily in CA.
Support limitations: No grants to individuals.
Application information: Applications not accepted. Contributes only to pre-selected organizations.
Officers: James W. Hirschmann, Pres.; Tracey A. Hutson, Secy.; Bruce D. Alberts, C.F.O.
Director: Paul White.
EIN: 202589546
Selected grants: The following grants are a representative sample of this grantmaker's funding activity:
$30,000 to Pasadena Community Foundation, Pasadena, CA, 2011.
$30,000 to Pasadena Community Foundation, Pasadena, CA, 2011.
$25,000 to Los Angeles Chamber Orchestra Society, Los Angeles, CA, 2011.
$25,000 to UCLA Foundation, Los Angeles, CA, 2011.
$20,000 to AAF Rose Bowl Aquatics Center, Pasadena, CA, 2011.
$15,000 to Pasadena Hospital Association, Pasadena, CA, 2011.
$10,000 to Hillsides, Pasadena, CA, 2011.
$7,000 to Los Angeles Philharmonic Association, Los Angeles, CA, 2011.
$1,000 to Saint Mary Medical Center Foundation, Langhorne, PA, 2011.
$1,000 to San Marino Schools Foundation, San Marino, CA, 2011.

4042
Western Digital Corporation

3355 Michelson Dr., Ste. 100
Irvine, CA 92612 (949) 672-7000

Company URL: http://www.wdc.com
Establishment information: Established in 1970.
Company type: Public company
Company ticker symbol and exchange: WDC/ NASDAQ
International Securities Identification Number: US9581021055
Business activities: Designs, develops, manufactures, and markets computer hard drives.
Business type (SIC): Computer and office equipment
Financial profile for 2012: Number of employees, 103,111; assets, $14,206,000,000; sales volume, $12,478,000,000; pre-tax net income, $1,757,000,000; expenses, $10,707,000,000; liabilities, $6,537,000,000
Fortune 1000 ranking: 2012—222nd in revenues, 129th in profits, and 307th in assets
Forbes 2000 ranking: 2012—602nd in sales, 276th in profits, and 1234th in assets
Corporate officers: Thomas E. Pardun, Chair.; Michael D. Cordano, Co-Pres.; Timothy M. Layden, Co-Pres.; Stephen D. Mulligan, Pres. and C.E.O; Wolfgang U. Nickl, V.P. and C.F.O.
Board of directors: Thomas E. Pardun, Chair.; Kathleen A. Cote; Henry T. DeNero; William L. Kimsey; Michael D. Lambert; Len J. Lauer; Matthew E. Massengill; Stephen D. Miligan; Roger H. Moore; Kensuke Oka; Arif Shakeel; Masahiro Yamamura
International operations: Canada; Cayman Islands; England; France; Germany; Hong Kong; Ireland; Japan; Malaysia; Netherlands; Philippines; Singapore; South Korea; Taiwan; United Kingdom
Giving statement: Giving through the Western Digital Corporation Contributions Program and the Western Digital Foundation.
Company EIN: 330956711

Western Digital Corporation Contributions Program

3355 Michelson Dr., Ste. 100
Irvine, CA 92612-5694 (949) 672-7000
URL: http://www.wdc.com/en/company/communityrelations/

Contact: Rose Krupp, Dir., WD Foundation & Community Rels.
Purpose and activities: As a complement to its foundation, Western Digital makes charitable contributions to organizations directly. Emphasis is given to organizations involved with education, basic needs, and civic and community issues. Support is limited to areas of company operations.
Fields of interest: Education, public education; Education, computer literacy/technology training; Education; Environment; Health care; Family services; Human services, financial counseling; Homeless, human services; Human services; Community/economic development; Science, public education; Mathematics; Engineering/technology; Military/veterans' organizations; Public affairs Economically disadvantaged.
Program:
Matching Gift Programs: Western Digital provides a matching gifts program, through a partnership with United Way, for employee donations made to educational institutions. Private educational institutions may qualify for WD funding through the Matching Gifts Program rather than through Foundation grants.
Type of support: Donated products; Employee matching gifts; Employee volunteer services; In-kind gifts.
Geographic limitations: Giving is limited to areas of company operations in Alameda, Orange, and Santa Clara counties, CA, and Boulder County, CO.
Support limitations: No support for sports teams, discriminatory organizations, grantmaking foundations, or religious organizations for programs that do not serve the general public, and no repetitive annual grants, multi-year donations, or continuing support. No grants to individuals, or for capital programs or fundraising events.
Publications: Application guidelines.
Application information: Applications accepted. The Contributions Committee handles requests. Proposals should be submitted using organization letterhead. Neither video or audio will be accepted as part of the application process. Application form required. Applicants should submit the following:
1) role played by volunteers
2) how project will be sustained once grantmaker support is completed
3) name, address and phone number of organization
4) copy of IRS Determination Letter
5) copy of most recent annual report/audited financial statement/990
6) how project's results will be evaluated or measured
7) descriptive literature about organization
8) listing of board of directors, trustees, officers and other key people and their affiliations
9) detailed description of project and amount of funding requested
10) contact person
11) copy of current year's organizational budget and/or project budget
12) listing of additional sources and amount of support

Applicants must submit a WD Grant Impact Report for any previous WD-funded projects two months prior to submitting a new application.
Initial approach: Proposal to headquarters
Committee meeting date(s): Semi-annual
Deadline(s): July 15 and Jan. 15

Western Digital Foundation

3355 Michelson Dr., Ste. 100
Irvine, CA 92612-5964
FAX: (949) 672-9676;
E-mail: Rosemary.Krupp@wdc.com; E-mail for Milissa Bedell: Milissa.bedell@wdc.com;
URL: http://www.wdc.com/en/company/communityrelations/

Establishment information: Established in 1997 in CA.
Donors: Western Digital Corp.; Texas Instruments Inc.; Western Digital Technologies, Inc.
Contact: Rosemary Krupp, Dir.; Milissa Bedell, Mgr., Community Rels.
Financial data (yr. ended 07/31/11): Assets, $350,040 (M); gifts received, $1,895,647; expenditures, $1,774,263; qualifying distributions, $1,774,263; giving activities include $1,769,113 for 133 grants (high: $254,220; low: $250).
Purpose and activities: The foundation supports organizations involved with education, the environment, disaster relief, human services, community development, science, civic affairs, economically disadvantaged people and veterans.
Fields of interest: Education, computer literacy/technology training; Education; Environment, natural resources; Environment; Disasters, preparedness/services; Family services; Homeless, human services; Community/economic development; United Ways and Federated Giving Programs; Mathematics; Engineering/technology; Computer science; Science Military/veterans; Economically disadvantaged.
Programs:
Basic Needs: The foundation supports programs designed to counter economic hardship, provide economic progress, and lead to economic self-sufficiency. Special emphasis is directed toward programs designed to promote homeless prevention and crisis intervention; and basic health care and basic needs services.
Civic and Community: The foundation supports programs designed to promote long-term betterment and permanent improvement of a community. Special emphasis is directed toward environmental protection and preservation; and community volunteer projects benefiting low income families and/or veterans. The program is limited to Alameda, Orange, and Santa Clara counties, CA and Boulder county, CO.
Education: The foundation supports programs designed to serve primary through graduate education. Special emphasis is directed towards innovation in engineering including electrical, mechanical, chemical, and solid state physics; and personal computing literacy and science discovery.
Type of support: Donated products; Employee matching gifts; Employee volunteer services; In-kind gifts.
Geographic limitations: Giving limited to areas of company operations, with emphasis on Alameda, Orange, and Santa Clara, CA and Boulder County, CO.
Support limitations: No support for religious organization not of direct benefit to the entire community, sports teams, discriminatory organizations, grantmaking foundations, political organizations, hospitals, or museums. No grants to individuals, or for capital campaigns, athletic events, fundraising, conferences or seminars, research, scholarships or stipends, or start-up funds; no multi-year grants.
Publications: Application guidelines; Program policy statement.
Application information: Applications accepted. Proposals should be submitted using organization letterhead. Requests for multi-year funding are not accepted. Support is limited to 1 contribution per organization during any given year. Video and audio submissions are not accepted. Application form required. Applicants should submit the following:
1) name, address and phone number of organization
2) copy of IRS Determination Letter
3) brief history of organization and description of its mission
4) copy of most recent annual report/audited financial statement/990
5) how project's results will be evaluated or measured
6) listing of board of directors, trustees, officers and other key people and their affiliations
7) detailed description of project and amount of funding requested
8) contact person
9) copy of current year's organizational budget and/or project budget
10) listing of additional sources and amount of support

Initial approach: Download application form and mail with proposal to foundation
Copies of proposal: 1
Board meeting date(s): Semi-annual
Deadline(s): Jan. 15 and July 15
Final notification: 3 months

Officers: Michael D. Cordano; Jacqueline M. DeMana; Timothy M. Leyden; Stephen D. Miligan; Wolfgang Nickl.

Number of staff: 1 full-time professional; 1 part-time professional.
EIN: 330769372
Selected grants: The following grants are a representative sample of this grantmaker's funding activity:
$77,367 to United Way Silicon Valley, San Jose, CA, 2009.
$50,000 to K O C E-TV Foundation, Costa Mesa, CA, 2009.
$25,000 to THINK Together, Santa Ana, CA, 2009.
$20,000 to Project Tomorrow, Irvine, CA, 2009.
$17,680 to Boys and Girls Club of the Harbor Area, Club Technical, Costa Mesa, CA, 2009.
$10,000 to American Red Cross, Orange County Chapter, Santa Ana, CA, 2009.
$10,000 to Rebuilding Together Silicon Valley, San Jose, CA, 2009.
$10,000 to Silicon Valley Independent Living Center, San Jose, CA, 2009.
$10,000 to Women Helping Women, Costa Mesa, CA, 2009.
$10,000 to Womens Initiative for Self Employment, San Francisco, CA, 2009.
$5,000 to American Heart Association, Start O.C Heart Walk, Irvine, CA, 2009.
$5,000 to Boys and Girls Club of Anaheim, Anaheim, CA, 2009.
$5,000 to Stop-Gap, Costa Mesa, CA, 2009.

4043
Western Oilfields Supply Company

(doing business as Rain for Rent)
4001 State Rd.
P.O. Box 2248
Bakersfield, CA 93308-4537
(661) 399-9124
FAX: (661) 392-9427

Company URL: http://www.rainforrent.com/default.htm
Establishment information: Established in 1934.
Company type: Private company
Business activities: Manufactures irrigation equipment.
Business type (SIC): Machinery/farm and garden
Corporate officers: Keith Mittan, C.E.O.; John W. Lake, Pres.; John Staab, C.I.O.; Robert Lake, Co.-C.F.O.; Anthony E. Schoen, Co.-C.F.O.
Giving statement: Giving through the Diane S. Lake Charitable Trust.

Diane S. Lake Charitable Trust

P.O. Box 1737
Bakersfield, CA 93302-1737

Establishment information: Established in 1999 in CA.
Donors: Western Oilfield Supply Co.; Diane S. Lake.
Financial data (yr. ended 12/31/11): Assets, $744,201 (M); gifts received, $1,010,328; expenditures, $698,650; qualifying distributions, $698,500; giving activities include $698,500 for grants.
Purpose and activities: The foundation supports museums and zoos and organizations involved with performing arts, higher education, health, substance abuse, and youth services.
Fields of interest: Museums; Performing arts, theater; Performing arts, orchestras; Higher education; Zoos/zoological societies; Hospitals (general); Health care, clinics/centers; Speech/hearing centers; Health care; Substance abuse, services; Boys & girls clubs; Youth, services.
Type of support: General/operating support.
Geographic limitations: Giving limited to Bakersfield, CA.
Support limitations: No grants to individuals.
Application information: Applications not accepted. Contributes only to pre-selected organizations.
Trustees: Christopher Lake; Diane S. Lake.
EIN: 776166455
Selected grants: The following grants are a representative sample of this grantmaker's funding activity:
$65,000 to California State University Bakersfield Foundation, Bakersfield, CA, 2010.
$60,000 to California Living Museum, Bakersfield, CA, 2010.
$25,000 to Bakersfield Memorial Hospital Foundation, Bakersfield, CA, 2010.
$25,000 to Kern Veterans Memorial Foundation, Bakersfield, CA, 2010.
$20,000 to Boys and Girls Clubs of Kern County, Bakersfield, CA, 2010.
$20,000 to Castilleja School, Palo Alto, CA, 2010.
$15,000 to American Cancer Society, Washington, DC, 2010.
$15,000 to Golden Empire Gleaners, Bakersfield, CA, 2010.
$10,000 to Bakersfield Museum of Art, Bakersfield, CA, 2010.
$10,000 to Junior League of Bakersfield, Bakersfield, CA, 2010.

4044
Western Refining, Inc.

123 W. Mills Ave.
El Paso, TX 79905 (915) 775-3300
FAX: (302) 655-5049

Company URL: http://www.wnr.com
Establishment information: Established in 1993.
Company type: Public company
Company ticker symbol and exchange: WNR/NYSE
Business activities: Refines petroleum.
Business type (SIC): Petroleum refining
Financial profile for 2012: Number of employees, 3,800; assets, $2,480,410,000; sales volume, $9,503,130,000; pre-tax net income, $617,090,000; expenses, $8,791,240,000; liabilities, $1,571,340,000
Fortune 1000 ranking: 2012—283rd in revenues, 399th in profits, and 805th in assets
Forbes 2000 ranking: 2012—965th in sales, 1234th in profits, and 1961st in assets
Corporate officers: Paul L. Foster, Chair.; Jeff A. Stevens, Pres. and C.E.O.; Gary R. Dalke, C.F.O.; William R. Jewell, C.A.O.; Jeffrey S. Beyersdorfer, Sr. V.P. and Treas.; Lowry Barfield, Sr. V.P., Genl. Counsel, and Secy.
Board of directors: Paul L. Foster, Chair.; Carin Marcy Barth; Sigmund Cornelius; L. Frederick Francis; Brian J. Hogan; William D. Sanders; Ralph A. Schmidt; Jeff A. Stevens; Scott D. Weaver
Subsidiary: Western Refining Co., L.P., El Paso, TX
Giving statement: Giving through the Western Refining, Inc. Corporate Giving Program.
Company EIN: 203472415

Western Refining, Inc. Corporate Giving Program

123 W. Mills Ave.
El Paso, TX 79901-1339
URL: http://www.westernrefining.com/Index.aspx?Level=AboutWestern&Page=Community

Purpose and activities: Western Refining makes charitable contributions to nonprofit organizations involved with the arts, education, health, and social and civic affairs. Support is given primarily in areas of company operations in Arizona, California, Colorado, Nevada, New Mexico, Texas, and Virginia.
Fields of interest: Arts; Education; Health care; Family services; Community/economic development; Public affairs.
Type of support: Employee volunteer services; General/operating support.
Geographic limitations: Giving primarily in areas of company operations in AZ, CA, CO, NM, NV, TX, and VA.

4045
The Western Union Company

(formerly New York and Mississippi Valley Printing Telegraph Company)
12500 E. Belford Ave.
Englewood, CO 80112 (720) 332-1000
FAX: (302) 655-5049

Company URL: http://www.westernunion.com
Establishment information: Established in 1851.
Company type: Public company
Company ticker symbol and exchange: WU/NYSE
Business activities: Provides global money transfer and messaging services.
Business type (SIC): Depository banking/functions related to; telegraph and other communications services
Financial profile for 2012: Number of employees, 9,000; assets, $9,465,700,000; sales volume, $5,664,800,000; pre-tax net income, $1,168,800,000; expenses, $4,334,800,000; liabilities, $8,525,100,000
Fortune 1000 ranking: 2012—445th in revenues, 196th in profits, and 404th in assets
Forbes 2000 ranking: 2012—1314th in sales, 566th in profits, and 1509th in assets
Corporate officers: Jack M. Greenberg, Chair.; Hikmet Ersek, Pres. and C.E.O.; Scott T. Scheirman, Exec. V.P. and C.F.O.; John R. Dye, Exec. V.P., Genl. Counsel, and Secy.; John David Thompson, Exec. V.P., Opers. and C.I.O.; Richard Williams, Sr. V.P. Human Resources
Board of directors: Jack M. Greenberg, Chair.; Dinyar S. Devitre; Hikmet Ersek; Richard A. Goodman; Betsy D. Holden; Linda Fayne Levinson; Roberto G. Mendoza; Micheal A. Miles, Jr.; Solomon D. Trujillo; Wulf Von Schimmelmann
International operations: Algeria; Argentina; Australia; Austria; Barbados; Belgium; Bermuda; Brazil; Canada; Chile; Costa Rica; France; Germany; Greece; Hong Kong; India; Ireland; Italy; Luxembourg; Mexico; Morocco and the Western Sahara; Netherlands; New Zealand; Norway; Panama; Peru; Philippines; Russia; Singapore; Spain; Sweden
Giving statement: Giving through the Western Union Company Corporate Giving Program and the Western Union Foundation.
Company EIN: 204531180

The Western Union Company Corporate Giving Program

c/o Community Rels.
12500 E. Belford Ave., M1G
Englewood, CO 80112-5939
FAX: (720) 332-4761;
E-mail: eventsponsorship@westernunion.com;
URL: http://www.westernunion.com/info/aboutUsCommunity.asp

Purpose and activities: As a complement to its foundation, Western Union also makes charitable contributions to nonprofit organizations directly. Support is given on a national and international basis in areas of company operations.
Fields of interest: Education; Health care; Employment; Disasters, preparedness/services; Minorities/immigrants, centers/services; Human services; Social entrepreneurship; Community development, small businesses; Financial services.
Type of support: Sponsorships.
Geographic limitations: Giving on a national and international basis in areas of company operations; giving also to regional, national, and international organizations.
Application information: Applications accepted. Application form not required. Applicants should submit the following:
1) name, address and phone number of organization
2) copy of IRS Determination Letter
3) brief history of organization and description of its mission
4) detailed description of project and amount of funding requested
5) contact person
Proposals should indicate the date and time of the event, the levels of sponsorship available, and sponsorship benefits; and include a W-9 form.
Initial approach: Proposal to headquarters
Copies of proposal: 1
Deadline(s): None

Western Union Foundation

12500 E. Belford Ave., Ste. M1-I
Englewood, CO 80112-5939 (720) 332-6606
FAX: (720) 332-4772;
E-mail: foundation@westernunion.com; Scholarship application address: Institute of International Education, 475 17th St., Ste. 800, Denver, CO 80202, tel.: (303) 837-0788, fax: (303) 837-1409, e-mail: wufamily@iie.org; URL: http://foundation.westernunion.com/

Establishment information: Established as a company-sponsored operating foundation in 2000 in CO.
Donors: First Data Corp.; Western Union Co.
Financial data (yr. ended 12/31/11): Assets, $2,954,244 (M); gifts received, $9,554,528; expenditures, $9,753,230; qualifying distributions, $9,747,343; giving activities include $7,990,611 for 138 grants (high: $769,987; low: $84) and $435,288 for employee matching gifts.
Purpose and activities: The foundation supports programs designed to provide individuals with better access to educational opportunities, promote economic development, and provide basic human services to communities in developing countries. Special emphasis is directed toward programs designed to promote job training, life skills and small business development, financial literacy, community integration, and assistance to migrants and immigrants.
Fields of interest: Secondary school/education; Vocational education; Education, ESL programs; Education; Employment, training; Disasters, preparedness/services; Human services, financial counseling; Human services; International affairs, U.N.; Economic development; Business/industry; Social entrepreneurship; Community development, small businesses; Community/economic development; Engineering/technology; Public affairs Children; Adults; Minorities; Immigrants/refugees; Economically disadvantaged; Migrant workers.
International interests: Brazil; China; Global programs; India; Mexico; Philippines.
Programs:
Agent Giving Program: Through the Agent Giving Program, Western Union agents identify a geography, issue, or program that warrants special attention. Giving to those issues or programs are matched by the foundation on a one-for-one basis.
Donations for Doers: The foundation awards $500 grants to nonprofit organizations with which employees of Western Union volunteer 50 hours within a calendar year.
Education for Better: Through the three-year Education for Better initiative, Western Union and its foundation provides an average of $10,000 per day for more than 1,000 days to nonprofits and NGO's working to improve global education, with a focus on secondary and vocational training. The initiative includes "shared value" education products that help move education funds to underserved communities with speed and accuracy; advocacy for education; cause marketing; grants; and employee engagement with emphasis on volunteerism.
Employee Gift Match: The foundation matches contributions made by employees of Western Union to nonprofit organizations on a one-for-one basis up to $25,000 per employee, per calendar year.
Family Scholarship Program: The foundation awards scholarships of $1,000 to $5,000 to immigrant and migrant workers and their families. The scholarships can be used for tuition for college/university language acquisition classes, technical/skill training, and/or financial literacy; and are awarded to two members of the same family to encourage economic development through education. Priority is given to applicants who have lived in the U.S for less than 7 years. The program is administered by the Institute of International Education (IIE).
Our World, Our Family: The foundation promotes the Our World, Our Family initiative designed to empower migrant families through education and global economic opportunity. Special emphasis is directed toward programs designed to provide economic opportunity to help those most in need, connect new migrant families with vital local resources, boost language skills, and promote job readiness, civic engagement, and access to education; support entrepreneurship and personal finance to help make migration a choice rather than a necessity; and engage in dialogue between global leaders about the issues that affect migrant communities.
Type of support: Building/renovation; Continuing support; Employee matching gifts; Employee volunteer services; Equipment; Matching/challenge support; Program development; Scholarship funds; Scholarships—to individuals.
Geographic limitations: Giving on a national and international basis, with emphasis on Phoenix, AZ, Los Angeles and San Francisco, CA, Denver, CO, Washington, DC, Miami, FL, Chicago, IL, New York, NY, Argentina, Australia, Austria, Brazil, Canada, China, Costa Rica, Egypt, Ghana, Guatemala, Haiti, India, Indonesia, Kenya, Lithuania, Mexico, Morocco, New Zealand, Nigeria, Pakistan, Peru, Philippines, Romania, Russia, South Africa, Uganda, and United Arab Emirates.
Support limitations: No support for pass-through organizations, health organizations, arts, media, or humanities organizations, or religious or political organizations. No grants for general operating support, endowments, special events, capital campaigns, post-secondary scholarship programs, early childhood education, debt reduction, disease research, environmental causes, sports, or athletics.
Publications: Annual report; Application guidelines; Financial statement; Grants list; Newsletter.
Application information: Unsolicited requests for general grants are not accepted at this time. The foundation is working with its current NGO partners and will solicit proposals from NGOs that align with its giving platform. Application form required.
Initial approach: Complete online application for Family Scholarship Program
Copies of proposal: 1
Board meeting date(s): Quarterly
Deadline(s): Oct. 19 for Family Scholarship Program
Final notification: Nov. 30 for Family Scholarship Program
Officers and Directors:* John Dye*, Chair.; Patrick Gaston, Pres.; Jo-Anne Scharmann, Treas.; Odilon Almeida; Jean Claude Farah; Davida Fedeli; Paul Foster; Christopher Kawula; Diane Scott; Drina Yue.
Number of staff: 3 full-time professional; 2 full-time support.
EIN: 311738614
Selected grants: The following grants are a representative sample of this grantmaker's funding activity:
$769,987 to American Red Cross National Headquarters, Washington, DC, 2011. For restricted support.
$567,741 to United States Fund for UNICEF, New York, NY, 2011. For restricted support.
$470,067 to American Red Cross National Headquarters, Washington, DC, 2011. For restricted support.
$400,000 to Fundacion Banco do Brasil, Brasilia, Brazil, 2011. For restricted support.
$250,000 to Massachusetts Institute of Technology, Cambridge, MA, 2011. For restricted support.
$186,811 to Mercy Corps, Portland, OR, 2011. For restricted support.
$42,650 to CARE International UK, Sierra Leone, London, England, 2011. For restricted support.
$32,371 to Caritas Athens-Refugee Program, Athens, Greece, 2011. For restricted support.
$25,000 to Denver Scholarship Foundation, Denver, CO, 2011. For unrestricted support.
$15,000 to Grantmakers Concerned with Immigrants and Refugees, Sebastopol, CA, 2011. For unrestricted support.

4046
The Westervelt Company

(formerly Gulf States Paper Corporation)
1400 Jack Warner Pkwy. N.E.
P.O. Box 48999
Tuscaloosa, AL 35404-1002
(205) 562-5000
FAX: (205) 562-5012

Company URL: http://www.westervelt.com/
Establishment information: Established in 1884.
Company type: Private company
Business activities: Produces forest products; manufactures wood products; manufactures pulp and paperboard; manufactures paperboard packaging.
Business type (SIC): Logging; lumber and wood products (except furniture); pulp mills; paperboard mills; paperboard containers
Financial profile for 2010: Number of employees, 650
Corporate officers: Michael E. Case, Pres. and C.E.O.; Gary Dailey, V.P., Finance and C.F.O.; Ray Robbins, V.P., Secy., and Genl. Counsel
Subsidiaries: GSD Packaging, LLC, Hazleton, PA; Livingston Box Co., Livingston, AL; Resolution Packaging, Marion, NC

Plants: Cuba, Demopolis, Moundville, Ralph, AL; Nicholasville, KY; Joplin, MO; Claremont, Conover, NC; Waco, TX
Offices: Aliceville, Columbiana, Gordo, AL
Giving statement: Giving through the Jack Warner Foundation, Inc.

Jack Warner Foundation, Inc.

2705 Battlement Dr.
Tuscaloosa, AL 35406
URL: http://www.warnerfoundation.org/

Establishment information: Established in 2000 in AL.
Donors: Gulf States Paper Corp.; Jack W. Warner; Jonathan W. Warner, Jr.
Financial data (yr. ended 12/31/11): Assets, $26,799 (M); gifts received, $84; expenditures, $494,612; qualifying distributions, $399,061; giving activities include $399,061 for grants.
Purpose and activities: The foundation operates the Westervelt-Warner Museum of American Art in Tuscaloosa, Alabama.
Support limitations: No grants to individuals.
Application information: Applications not accepted. Unsolicited requests for funds not accepted.
Officers and Directors:* Jonathan W. Warner*, Chair.; Susan G. Austin*, Pres.; James B. Boone, Jr.*, V.P.; Dean J. Barry Mason*, Treas.; William Hibbard; Shelley Jones; Donald L. Stein.
EIN: 912004069

4047
Westfield Insurance Company

1 Park Cir.
P.O. Box 5001
Westfield Center, OH 44251-9700
(330) 887-0101

Company URL: http://www.westfieldinsurance.com
Establishment information: Established in 1848.
Company type: Subsidiary of a private company
Business activities: Sells property, casualty, and title insurance; operates commercial bank.
Business type (SIC): Insurance/fire, marine, and casualty; banks/commercial; insurance/title
Corporate officers: Jon Park, Chair.; James R. Clay, C.E.O.; Robert Krisowaty, Treas.; Frank Anthony Carrino, Secy.
Board of directors: Jon Park, Chair.; Michael J. Bernaski; James C. Boland; James Clay; Fariborz Ghadar; Gary D. Hallman; Susan J. Insley; Deborah D. Pryce; John Watson; Thomas E. Workman
Offices: Middletown, DE; Lancaster, PA
Giving statement: Giving through the Westfield Insurance Company Contributions Program and the Westfield Insurance Foundation.

Westfield Insurance Company Contributions Program

1 Park Cir.
P.O. Box 5001
Westfield Center, OH 44251-5001
E-mail: community@westfieldgrp.com; URL: http://www.westfieldinsurance.com/community/pg.jsp?page=community

Contact: Jani Davis, Dir., Community Investment
Purpose and activities: Westfield makes charitable contributions to nonprofit organizations involved with education, safety, human services, and community revitalization. Support is given primarily in areas of company operations, with emphasis on Ohio.
Fields of interest: Education; Housing/shelter; Safety/disasters; Human services; Community/economic development.
Type of support: Employee volunteer services; In-kind gifts; Program development.
Geographic limitations: Giving primarily in areas of company operations, with emphasis on OH.
Application information: Applications not accepted. Grantmaking is currently suspended.

The Westfield Insurance Foundation

(doing business as Westfield Group Foundation)
1 Park Cir.
P.O. Box 5001
Westfield Center, OH 44251-5001
E-mail: community@westfieldgrp.com; URL: http://www.westfieldinsurance.com/community/pg.jsp?page=community

Establishment information: Established in 2005 in OH.
Donors: Westfield Insurance Co.; Westfield National Insurance Co.; Westfield Group Foundation.
Financial data (yr. ended 12/31/11): Assets, $12,665,972 (M); expenditures, $475,596; qualifying distributions, $435,307; giving activities include $435,307 for grants.
Purpose and activities: The foundation supports programs designed to promote community revitalization, safety, education, and human services.
Fields of interest: Arts; Higher education; Education; Housing/shelter, development; Housing/shelter; Safety, automotive safety; Human services; Community/economic development; United Ways and Federated Giving Programs.
Program:
Volunteer Grant Program: The foundation awards $500 to nonprofit organizations with which employees of Westfield volunteers 50 hours within a year.
Type of support: Building/renovation; Capital campaigns; Employee volunteer services; Equipment; General/operating support; Program development.
Geographic limitations: Giving limited to areas where Westfield conducts business, with emphasis on IN, OH, and PA.
Support limitations: No support for organizations outside of Westfield operating territories, annual operating budgets for United Way agencies, membership organizations (unless they benefit the public), religious, fraternal or labor organizations, or for youth and adult athletic teams and associations. No grants to individuals, or for scholarship/student exchange programs, advertising, fundraising benefits or events, or conferences or seminars.
Application information: The foundation has suspended its community grant program until further notice.
Directors: Frank Carrino; James Clay; Jani Davis; Troy Gail; Robert J. Joyce; Robert Krisowaty; Edward Largent; Patricia Schiesswohl.
EIN: 203816760
Selected grants: The following grants are a representative sample of this grantmaker's funding activity:
$300,000 to Playhouse Square Foundation, Cleveland, OH, 2011.
$100,000 to University of Akron Foundation, Akron, OH, 2011.
$40,000 to United Way of Medina County, Medina, OH, 2011. For general operations.
$33,000 to Fund for Our Economic Future, Cleveland, OH, 2011.
$15,000 to Governors Highway Safety Association, Washington, DC, 2011.
$15,000 to Pennsylvania State University, University Park, PA, 2011.
$10,000 to Saint Baldricks Foundation, Monrovia, CA, 2011. For general operations.
$7,500 to Habitat for Humanity of Charlotte, Charlotte, NC, 2011.
$6,830 to United Way of Medina County, Medina, OH, 2011.
$5,000 to United Way of Medina County, Medina, OH, 2011.

4048
Westinghouse Air Brake Technologies Corporation

(doing business as Wabtec Corporation)
1001 Air Brake Ave.
Wilmerding, PA 15148 (412) 825-1000
FAX: (412) 825-1019

Company URL: http://www.wabtec.com
Establishment information: Established in 1869.
Company type: Public company
Company ticker symbol and exchange: WAB/NYSE
Business activities: Manufactures braking equipment and other parts for locomotives, freight cars, and passenger railcars.
Business type (SIC): Railroad equipment
Financial profile for 2012: Number of employees, 9,253; assets, $2,351,540,000; sales volume, $2,391,120,000; pre-tax net income, $377,360,000; expenses, $1,998,840,000; liabilities, $1,074,710,000
Fortune 1000 ranking: 2012—838th in revenues, 522nd in profits, and 817th in assets
Corporate officers: William E. Kassling, Chair.; Emilio A. Fernandez, Vice-Chair.; Albert J. Neupaver, Pres. and C.E.O.; Raymond T. Betler, C.O.O.; Alvaro Garcia-Tunon, Exec. V.P. and C.F.O.; David L. DeNinno, Sr. V.P., Genl. Counsel. and Secy.; Patrick D. Dugan, Sr. V.P., Finance. and Cont.; Scott E. Wahlstrom, Sr. V.P., Human Resources; Keith P. Hildum, V.P. and Treas.; Timothy R. Wesley, V.P., Corp. Comms.
Board of directors: William E. Kassling, Chair.; Emilio A. Fernandez, Vice-Chair.; Robert J. Brooks; Lee B. Foster II; Brian P. Hehir; Michael W.D. Howell; Albert J. Neupaver; Gary C. Valade; Nickolas W. Vande Steeg
Giving statement: Giving through the Wabtec Foundation.
Company EIN: 251615902

Wabtec Foundation

1001 Air Brake Ave.
Wilmerding, PA 15148

Establishment information: Established in 2007 in PA.
Donor: Westinghouse Air Brake Technologies Corp.
Contact: Scott E. Walhstrom, V.P. and Dir.
Financial data (yr. ended 12/31/11): Assets, $3,874,340 (M); expenditures, $213,917; qualifying distributions, $185,743; giving activities include $182,428 for 69 grants (high: $32,495; low: $50).
Fields of interest: Education; Human services; Community/economic development.
Support limitations: No grants to individuals, religious organizations.
Application information: Applications accepted. Application form required. Applicants should submit the following:
1) copy of IRS Determination Letter

2) detailed description of project and amount of funding requested
Initial approach: Proposal
Deadline(s): 1 week prior to foundation meeting

Officers and Directors:* Albert J. Neupaver*, Pres.; Scott E. Walhstrom*, V.P.; David M. Seitz, Secy.; Keith P. Hildum, Treas.; Lee B. Foster II; William E. Kassling.
EIN: 141994641

4049
Westinghouse Electric Company

(formerly Westinghouse Electric Company LLC)
150 John Downey Dr.
New Britain, CT 06051-2904
(860) 826-4100

Company URL: http://www.westinghousenuclear.com/
Establishment information: Established in 1886.
Company type: Subsidiary of a foreign company
Business activities: Manufactures and provides nuclear electric power equipment and services.
Business type (SIC): Industrial and commercial machinery and computer equipment
Financial profile for 2010: Number of employees, 27
Corporate officers: Shigenori Shiga, Chair.; Aris Candris, Pres. and C.E.O.; Masayoshi Hirata, Sr. V.P. and C.F.O.; Mike Sweeney, Sr. V.P. and Genl. Counsel; Anthony D. Greco, Sr. V.P., Human Resources
Board of directors: Shigenori Shiga, Chair.; Ramsey Coates; Aris Candris; Tony Greco; Masayoshi Hirata; Kiyoshi Okamura; Akihiro Takubo
Plants: New Britain, Windsor, CT; Burr Ridge, Lake Bluff, IL; Rockville, MD; Newington, NH; Blairsville, Cheswick, Churchill, Madison, PA; Columbia, Spartanburg, SC; Chattanooga, TN; Ogden, UT; Richland, WA
International operations: Belgium; Germany
Giving statement: Giving through the Westinghouse Electric Company Corporate Giving Program.

Westinghouse Electric Company Corporate Giving Program

(formerly Westinghouse Electric Company LLC Corporate Giving Program)
1000 Westinghouse Dr.
Cranberry Township, PA 16066-5228
Application address: Tracey Rapali, Westinghouse Charitable Giving Program, Ste. 170, Bay 517F, 1000 Westinghouse Dr., Cranberry Township, PA 16066; URL: http://www.westinghousenuclear.com/Community/Charitable_Giving/

Purpose and activities: Westinghouse makes charitable contributions to nonprofit organizations involved with educational programs that emphasize math, science and technology, civil and social services, and health and welfare. Special emphasis is directed toward programs designed to help meet the needs of populations such as the disadvantaged, youth, seniors, minorities, and people with disabilities. Support is given primarily in areas of company operations, with emphasis on southwestern Pennsylvania.
Fields of interest: Education, computer literacy/technology training; Education; Environment, natural resources; Public health; Safety/disasters; Children/youth, services; Self-advocacy services, disability; Aging, centers/services; Civil/human rights, minorities; Community development, civic centers; Community/economic development; Mathematics; Science Economically disadvantaged.
Type of support: General/operating support.
Geographic limitations: Giving primarily in areas of company operations, with emphasis on southwestern PA.
Support limitations: No support for religious, or discriminatory organizations, hospitals, United Way-affiliated organizations, colleges, universities, or two-year institutions, fine arts organizations, or organizations operated by a religiously affiliated organization without their own nonprofit status. No grants to individuals, or for political purposes, highly specialized health, medical, or welfare programs, capital improvements, or building projects, liberal arts, fine arts, or similar educational programs, graduate, or medical education, chairs, or professorships, general endowment, tickets, memberships, equipment purchases at universities, or educational research programs.
Publications: Application guidelines.
Application information: Applications accepted. Support is limited to 2 contributions per organization during any given five-year period. Contributions generally do not exceed $5,000. The Charitable Giving Advisory Board reviews all requests. Application form not required. Applicants should submit the following:
1) population served
2) copy of IRS Determination Letter
3) copy of most recent annual report/audited financial statement/990
4) how project's results will be evaluated or measured
5) listing of board of directors, trustees, officers and other key people and their affiliations
6) detailed description of project and amount of funding requested
7) copy of current year's organizational budget and/or project budget
8) contact person
9) statement of problem project will address
10) timetable for implementation and evaluation of project
11) additional materials/documentation

All proposals must include a W-9 Form, and the organization's mission statement, if applicable.
Initial approach: Proposal to headquarters or nearest company facility
Copies of proposal: 1
Committee meeting date(s): Quarterly

4050
Westport Corporation

(doing business as Mundi Westport Corporation)
331 Changebridge Rd.
P.O. Box 2002
Pine Brook, NJ 07058-9182
(973) 575-0110

Company URL: http://www.mundiwestport.com
Establishment information: Established in 1969.
Company type: Private company
Business activities: Manufactures men's and women's leather goods and accessories.
Business type (SIC): Leather goods/personal
Corporate officers: Richard Florin, Chair.; Jay Kevin Ross, Pres. and C.E.O; Anthony J. Brain, C.F.O.
Board of director: Richard Florin, Chair.
Giving statement: Giving through the Florin Family Foundation, Inc.

The Florin Family Foundation, Inc.

331 Changebridge Rd.
P.O. Box 189
Pine Brook, NJ 07058-9581

Establishment information: Established in 1995 in NJ.
Donor: Westport Corp.
Contact: Richard Florin, Pres. and Treas.
Financial data (yr. ended 12/31/11): Assets, $1,392,445 (M); gifts received, $300,000; expenditures, $296,216; qualifying distributions, $281,399; giving activities include $281,399 for grants.
Purpose and activities: The foundation supports community foundations and organizations involved with higher education, domestic violence prevention, family services, and Judaism.
Fields of interest: Higher education; Crime/violence prevention, domestic violence; Family services; Foundations (community); Jewish federated giving programs; Jewish agencies & synagogues.
Type of support: General/operating support.
Geographic limitations: Giving primarily in MA, NJ, and NY.
Support limitations: No grants to individuals.
Application information: Applications not accepted. Contributes only to pre-selected organizations.
Officers and Trustee: Richard Florin, Pres. and Treas.; Thelma Florin, Secy.; John Florin.
EIN: 223347455
Selected grants: The following grants are a representative sample of this grantmaker's funding activity:
$3,816 to Jewish Community Center of Metrowest, West Orange, NJ, 2011. For general support.
$3,000 to American Jewish Committee, Millburn, NJ, 2011. For general support.
$2,200 to Lasell College, Newton, MA, 2011. For general support.
$1,528 to Rachel Coalition, Florham Park, NJ, 2011. For general support.
$1,000 to Jewish Historical Society of Metrowest, Whippany, NJ, 2011. For general support.
$1,000 to University of Richmond, Richmond, VA, 2011. For general support.

4051
Weyco Group, Inc.

(formerly Weyenberg Shoe Manufacturing Company)
333 W. Estabrook Blvd.
P.O. Box 1188
Milwaukee, WI 53201-1188
(414) 908-1600
FAX: (414) 908-1603

Company URL: http://www.weycogroup.com
Establishment information: Established in 1906.
Company type: Public company
Company ticker symbol and exchange: WEYS/NASDAQ
Business activities: Markets men's footwear.
Business type (SIC): Apparel, piece goods, and notions—wholesale
Financial profile for 2012: Number of employees, 633; assets, $285,320,000; sales volume, $293,470,000; pre-tax net income, $30,930,000; expenses, $263,670,000; liabilities, $111,160,000
Corporate officers: Thomas W. Florsheim, Jr., Chair. and C.E.O.; John W. Florsheim, Pres. and C.O.O.; John F. Wittkowske, Sr. V.P., C.F.O., and Secy.; Judith Anderson, V.P., Finance and Treas.

Board of directors: Thomas W. Florsheim, Jr., Chair.; Tina Chang; Robert Feitler; John W. Florsheim; Thomas W. Florsheim, Sr.; Cory L. Nettles; Frederick P. Stratton, Jr.
Subsidiaries: Stacy Adams Shoe Co., Milwaukee, WI; Nunn-Bush Shoe Co., Milwaukee, WI
Giving statement: Giving through the Weyco Group Charitable Trust.
Company EIN: 390702200

Weyco Group Charitable Trust
P.O. Box 1188
Milwaukee, WI 53201-1188 (414) 908-1880

Establishment information: Established in 1996 in WI.
Donor: Weyco Group, Inc.
Contact: John F. Wittkowske, Tr.
Financial data (yr. ended 12/31/11): Assets, $234,403 (M); expenditures, $179,351; qualifying distributions, $179,320; giving activities include $179,320 for grants.
Purpose and activities: The trust supports civic centers and organizations involved with arts and culture, education, human services, the footwear industry, and leadership development.
Fields of interest: Museums (art); Arts; Secondary school/education; Higher education; Education, services; Education, reading; Education; YM/YWCAs & YM/YWHAs; Children/youth, services; Human services; Community development, civic centers; Business/industry; United Ways and Federated Giving Programs; Leadership development.
Type of support: General/operating support; Program development; Scholarship funds.
Geographic limitations: Giving primarily in Milwaukee, WI.
Support limitations: No grants to individuals.
Application information: Applications accepted. Application form required. Applicants should submit the following:
1) copy of IRS Determination Letter
Initial approach: Letter
Deadline(s): None
Trustees: John W. Florsheim, Sr.; Thomas W. Florsheim, Sr.; Thomas W. Florsheim, Jr.; John F. Wittkowske.
EIN: 396645370
Selected grants: The following grants are a representative sample of this grantmaker's funding activity:
$16,000 to Childrens Outing Association, Milwaukee, WI, 2010. For general support.
$13,370 to United Performing Arts Fund, Milwaukee, WI, 2010. For general support.
$11,500 to Milwaukee Art Museum, Milwaukee, WI, 2010. For general support.
$8,000 to YMCA Youth Leadership Academy, Milwaukee, WI, 2010. For general support.
$5,000 to College Possible Milwaukee, Milwaukee, WI, 2010. For general support.
$5,000 to Marquette University, Milwaukee, WI, 2010. For general support.
$5,000 to Milwaukee College Preparatory School, Milwaukee, WI, 2010. For general support.
$2,500 to Milwaukee Symphony Orchestra, Milwaukee, WI, 2010. For general support.
$1,750 to Wisconsin Historical Foundation, Madison, WI, 2010. For general support.
$1,230 to Jewish Family Services, Milwaukee, WI, 2010. For general support.

4052
Weyerhaeuser Company
33663 Weyerhaeuser Way S.
Federal Way, WA 98063-9777
(253) 924-2345
FAX: (253) 924-3543

Company URL: http://www.weyerhaeuser.com
Establishment information: Established in 1900.
Company type: Public company
Company ticker symbol and exchange: WY/NYSE
International Securities Identification Number: US9621661043
Business activities: Conducts logging activities; produces, distributes, and sells forest products; develops real estate.
Business type (SIC): Lumber and wood products (except furniture); logging; real estate subdividers and developers
Financial profile for 2012: Number of employees, 13,200; assets, $12,592,000,000; sales volume, $7,059,000,000; pre-tax net income, $439,000,000; expenses, $6,324,000,000; liabilities, $8,522,000,000
Fortune 1000 ranking: 2012—363rd in revenues, 413th in profits, and 336th in assets
Forbes 2000 ranking: 2012—1177th in sales, 1299th in profits, and 1300th in assets
Corporate officers: Charles R. Williamson, Chair.; Daniel S. Fulton, Pres. and C.E.O.; Patricia M. Bedient, Exec. V.P. and C.F.O.; Jerry Richards, C.A.O.; Sandy D. McDade, Sr. V.P. and Genl. Counsel; John A. Hooper, Sr. V.P., Human Resources; Claire S. Grace, V.P. and Secy.; Jeanne Hillman, V.P. and Cont.
Board of directors: Charles R. Williamson, Chair.; Debra A. Cafaro; Mark A. Emmert; Daniel S. Fulton; John I. Kieckhefer; Wayne W. Murdy; Nicole W. Piasecki; Doyle R. Simons; Richard H. Sinkfield; D. Michael Steuert; Kim Williams
Subsidiaries: DeQueen & Eastern Railroad Co., De Queen, AR; Golden Triangle Railroad, Columbus, MS; Mississippi & Skuna Valley Railroad Co., Bruce, MS; Westwood Shipping Lines, Inc., Tacoma, WA; Weyerhaeuser Real Estate Co., Tacoma, WA
Office: Washington, DC
International operations: Uruguay
Historic mergers: Willamette Industries, Inc. (February 11, 2002)
Giving statement: Giving through the Weyerhaeuser Giving Fund and the Weyerhaeuser Company Foundation.
Company EIN: 910470860

Weyerhaeuser Giving Fund
c/o Public Affairs
P.O. Box 9777
Federal Way, WA 98063-9777 (253) 924-2345
E-mail: anne.leyva@weyerhaeuser.com; Additional e-mail: karen.veitenhans@weyerhaeuser.com; URL: http://www.weyerhaeuser.com/Sustainability/People/Communities/WeyerhaeuserGivingFund

Financial data (yr. ended 12/31/09): Total giving, $1,100,000, including $1,100,000 for grants.
Purpose and activities: As a complement to its foundation, Weyerhaeuser also makes charitable contributions to nonprofit organizations, public education institutions, and government entities directly. Emphasis is given to programs that support youth development, promote sustainable communities, and nurture quality of life. Support is given primarily in areas of company operations in Alabama, Arkansas, Louisiana, Mississippi, North Carolina, Oklahoma, Oregon, and Washington; giving also on a national and international basis, with emphasis on Canada.
Fields of interest: Arts, cultural/ethnic awareness; Elementary/secondary education; Environment, climate change/global warming; Environment, natural resources; Environment, energy; Environment, forests; Environmental education; Environment; Housing/shelter, expense aid; Housing/shelter; Safety/disasters; Recreation, parks/playgrounds; Youth development; Family services; Homeless, human services; Human services; Community development, neighborhood development; Community/economic development; Public affairs Economically disadvantaged.
Type of support: General/operating support; In-kind gifts.
Geographic limitations: Giving primarily in areas of company operations in AL, AR, LA, MS, NC, OK, OR, and WA; giving also on a national and international basis, with emphasis on Canada.
Support limitations: No support for fraternal, social, labor, or political organizations, disease-specific support, including national health-related organizations or their local affiliates, sports teams or athletic events, or national campaigns or programs. No grants to individuals, including direct scholarship or bursary assistance, or for activities that provide a direct or tangible benefit to Weyerhaeuser or its employees, conferences, forums, or special events, activities that influence legislation, theological purposes, sponsorships, the purchase of tickets or tables at fundraising benefits, operating deficits or debt liquidation, hospital building or equipment campaigns resulting in higher costs to health-care users, services the public sector is reasonably expected to provide, endowments, memorials, capital campaigns, research or conferences unrelated to the forest products or homebuilding industries, or multi-year requests.
Publications: Application guidelines.
Application information: Applications accepted. Employees in company locations serve as advisors to the Weyerhaeuser Giving Fund. Local giving is limited to communities within a 50 mile/80 kilometer radius of a major Weyerhaeuser facility with 50 or more employees in the U.S. or Canada, and programs that support a state-wide issue of interest to the company in its key states. Giving to national and international organizations and in the headquarters area of Seattle/Tacoma/Federal Way, WA, are by invitation only. The minimum grant awarded is $1,000. Applicants should submit the following:
1) name, address and phone number of organization
2) copy of IRS Determination Letter
3) detailed description of project and amount of funding requested
4) contact person
5) copy of current year's organizational budget and/or project budget
Initial approach: Contact nearest company facility to assess interest, then complete online application
Deadline(s): Aug. 1
Final notification: 6-8 weeks after an Advisory Committee recommends funding the request; by late fall

Weyerhaeuser Company Foundation
P.O. Box 9777
CH 3E22
Federal Way, WA 98063-9777 (253) 924-3159
FAX: (253) 924-3658;
E-mail: bruce.amundson@weyerhaeuser.com; Additional contacts: Karen Veitenhans, Exec. Dir., e-mail: karen.veitenhans@weyerhaeyser.com; Anne Leyva, Secy., e-mail:

anne.leyva@weyerhaeuser.com; URL: http://www.weyerhaeuser.com/Sustainability/People/Communities

Establishment information: Incorporated in 1948 in WA.
Donors: Weyerhaeuser NR Company; Weyerhaeuser Co.; Gareth Curtiss.
Contact: Bruce Amundson, Pres.
Financial data (yr. ended 12/31/11): Assets, $4,473,730 (M); gifts received, $4,000,000; expenditures, $646,655; qualifying distributions, $238,538; giving activities include $231,000 for 1 grant.
Purpose and activities: The foundation supports organizations involved with the education, the environment, affordable housing and shelter, and the forest products industry. Support is given primarily in areas of company operations.
Fields of interest: Higher education; Education; Environment, research; Environment, public policy; Environment, natural resources; Environment, forests; Environmental education; Food banks; Housing/shelter, temporary shelter; Housing/shelter; Youth development; Human services; Business/industry; United Ways and Federated Giving Programs Children.
Programs:
Making WAVES (Weyerhaeuser Active Volunteer Employees): Through Making WAVES, the foundation awards grants from $1,000 to $5,000 to nonprofit organizations with which teams of at least ten employees, retirees, and the families and friends of employees and retirees of Weyerhaeuser volunteer at least 50 hours.
Matching Gift Program for Education: The foundation matches contributions made by employees and directors of Weyerhaeuser to educational institutions on a one-for-one basis from $25 to $5,000 per contributor, per year.
Scholarship Program: The foundation annually awards up to 65 college scholarships to children of employees of Weyerhaeuser. The program is administered by Scholarship America, Inc.
Type of support: Building/renovation; Capital campaigns; Conferences/seminars; Curriculum development; Emergency funds; Employee matching gifts; Employee volunteer services; Employee-related scholarships; Equipment; General/operating support; Program development; Research.
Geographic limitations: Giving on a national and international basis primarily in areas of company operations, with emphasis on Washington, DC, GA, MN, OR, WA, Canada, and China.
Support limitations: No support for religious organizations not of direct benefit to the entire community; generally, no support for disease-specific organizations. No grants to individuals (except for employee-related scholarships), or for political campaigns, lobbying activities, general operating support for organizations indirectly receiving Weyerhaeuser Foundation support through a federated organization or combined campaign, tickets or tables, or activities providing benefits to Weyerhaeuser or employees of Weyerhaeuser; generally, no grants for services the public sector should be reasonably expected to provide, endowments or memorials, research or conferences unrelated to the forest products industry, hospital capital campaigns resulting in higher costs to healthcare users, or debt reduction.
Application information: Applications not accepted. Grantmaking is suspended until further notice. All charitable contributions are made through the direct corporate giving program.
Officers and Trustees:* Ernesta Ballard*, Chair.; Bruce Amundson, Pres.; Karen L. Veitenhans, V.P. and Exec. Dir.; Anne Leyva, Secy.; Jeffrey W. Nitta, Treas.; Jeanne M. Hillman, Cont.; Patricia M. Bedient; Mike Branson; Lawrence Burrows; Miles Drake; Daniel S. Fulton; Thomas F. Gideon; Sandy D. McDade.
Number of staff: 4 full-time professional; 2 full-time support.
EIN: 916024225
Selected grants: The following grants are a representative sample of this grantmaker's funding activity:
$296,500 to North Carolina Agricultural Foundation, Raleigh, NC, 2010. For ongoing water footprint and sustainability platform underlying the range of biomass production and use for food, fiber and fuels in Uruguay.
$172,565 to Scholarship America, Saint Peter, MN, 2010. For 2010 Weyerhaeuser Company Foundation Scholarship Program.
$100,000 to United Way of King County, Seattle, WA, 2010. For 2010 - 2011 Campaign.
$40,000 to Dierks, City of, Dierks, AR, 2010. For new community education center which will house the Dierks Chamber of Commerce, a large community room and kitchen, multi-purpose classrooms, computer lab and community education center.
$30,000 to Habitat for Humanity of East King County, Redmond, WA, 2010. For La Fortuna, Renton Development - Phase 1, payable over 1.50 years.
$30,000 to United Way of Linn County, Albany, OR, 2010. For 2010 Annual United Way Campaign.
$20,000 to Family Finance Resource Center, Longview, WA, 2010. For Foreclosure Prevention Counseling Program, payable over 1.50 years.
$18,000 to Washington Pulp and Paper Foundation, Seattle, WA, 2010. For scholarships for qualified students from the Longview region enrolled in Paper Science and Engineering at the University of Washington, including students choosing a 5th year dual-degree option with Chemical Engineering Paper Science and Engineering.
$16,000 to Hands on Childrens Museum, Olympia, WA, 2010. To create the Fabulous Forest Gallery in The New Hands On Children's Museum on East Bay, payable over 8.00 years.
$10,925 to Treutlen House at New Ebenezer, Rincon, GA, 2010. For replacement of porch railing and wood flooring.

4053
Wheeler Trigg O'Donnell LLP

1801 California St., Ste. 3600
Denver, CO 80202-2617 (303) 244-1800

Company URL: http://www.wtotrial.com/index.aspx
Establishment information: Established in 1998.
Company type: Private company
Business activities: Operates law firm.
Business type (SIC): Legal services
Corporate officers: Mike O'Donnell, Chair; Hugh Gottschalk, Managing Partner
Office: Denver, CO
Giving statement: Giving through the Wheeler Trigg O'Donnell LLP Pro Bono Program.

Wheeler Trigg O'Donnell LLP Pro Bono Program

1801 California St., Ste. 3600
Denver, CO 80202-2617 (303) 244-1800
E-mail: barker@wtotrial.com; Additional tel.: (303) 244-1800; URL: http://www.wtotrial.com/3418

Contact: Scott Barker, Chair, Pro Bono Committee
Fields of interest: Legal services.
Type of support: Pro bono services - legal.
Application information: A Pro Bono Committee manages the pro bono program.

4054
Whip Mix Corporation

361 Farmington Ave.
P.O. Box 17183
Louisville, KY 40217 (502) 637-1451

Company URL: http://www.whipmix.com
Establishment information: Established in 1919.
Company type: Private company
Business activities: Produces dental compounds; manufactures dental equipment.
Business type (SIC): Medical instruments and supplies
Corporate officers: Allen F. Steinbock, Chair. and C.E.O.; James W. Myers, Pres.
Board of director: Allen F. Steinbock, Chair.
Giving statement: Giving through the Capricorn Foundation Charitable Trust.

Capricorn Foundation Charitable Trust

c/o Allen F. Steinbock
P.O. Box 17183
Louisville, KY 40217-0183 (502) 584-9793
Application address: Margaret H. Anderson, C.P.A., c/o Anderson, Bryant, Lasky, & Winslow, PSC, 943 S. 1st St., Louisville, KY 40203

Establishment information: Established in 1983.
Donor: Whip-Mix Corp.
Contact: Margaret H. Anderson
Financial data (yr. ended 12/31/11): Assets, $1,371,629 (M); expenditures, $104,642; qualifying distributions, $78,100; giving activities include $78,100 for grants.
Purpose and activities: The foundation supports organizations involved with arts and culture, education, and school athletics.
Fields of interest: Arts; Education; Human services.
Type of support: General/operating support.
Geographic limitations: Giving primarily in KY.
Support limitations: No grants to individuals.
Application information: Applications accepted. Application form required. Applicants should submit the following:
1) copy of IRS Determination Letter
Initial approach: Contact foundation for application form
Deadline(s): None
Trustees: Rowland Hutchinson; Grover Potts; Allen F. Steinbock; Anne Steinbock; David J. Steinbock; R. Ted Steinbock; Stuart Steinbock.
EIN: 311096396

4055
Whirl Wind Propellers Corp.

(also known as Whirl Wind Aviation, Inc.)
1800 Joe Crosson Dr., Ste. C
El Cajon, CA 92020-1230 (619) 562-3725

Company URL: http://www.whirlwindpropellers.com
Establishment information: Established in 1995.
Company type: Private company
Business activities: Manufactures aircraft parts and equipment.
Business type (SIC): Aircraft and parts
Corporate officer: Patricia Platt-Rust, Pres.
Giving statement: Giving through the Blue Sky Foundation.

The Blue Sky Foundation

9625 Mission Gorge Rd., Ste. B2-312
Santee, CA 92071

Establishment information: Established in 2004 in CA.
Donor: Whirl Wind Propellers Corp.
Financial data (yr. ended 12/31/11): Assets, $122,976 (M); gifts received, $30,000; expenditures, $45,796; qualifying distributions, $31,120; giving activities include $31,120 for grants.
Purpose and activities: The foundation supports organizations involved with music and cancer.
Fields of interest: Arts; Recreation; Religion.
Type of support: General/operating support; Sponsorships.
Geographic limitations: Giving primarily in Santee, CA and Bellingham, WA.
Support limitations: No grants to individuals.
Application information: Applications not accepted. Unsolicited requests for funds not accepted.
Officers: James Rust, C.E.O.; Patricia Platt-Rust, Secy.
EIN: 200502651

4056
Whirlpool Corporation

2000 N. M63
Benton Harbor, MI 49022-2692
(269) 923-5000
FAX: (302) 636-5454

Company URL: http://www.whirlpoolcorp.com
Establishment information: Established in 1911.
Company type: Public company
Company ticker symbol and exchange: WHR/NYSE
International Securities Identification Number: US9633201069
Business activities: Manufactures and markets major home appliances.
Business type (SIC): Appliances/household
Financial profile for 2012: Number of employees, 68,000; assets, $15,400,000,000; sales volume, $18,100,000,000; pre-tax net income, $558,000,000; expenses, $17,274,000,000; liabilities, $11,136,000,000
Fortune 1000 ranking: 2012—154th in revenues, 396th in profits, and 295th in assets
Forbes 2000 ranking: 2012—514th in sales, 1296th in profits, and 1160th in assets
Corporate officers: Jeff M. Fettig, Chair. and C.E.O.; Larry Venturelli, Exec. V.P. and C.F.O.; Kirsten Hewitt, Sr. V.P. and Genl. Counsel; David A. Binkley, Sr. V.P., Human Resources
Board of directors: Jeff M. Fettig, Chair.; Samuel R. Allen; Gary T. DiCamillo; Diane M. Dietz; Michael F. Johnston; William T. Kerr; John D. Liu; Harish Manwani; William D. Perez; Michael A. Todman; Michael D. White
Plants: Fort Smith, AR; Evansville, La Porte, IN; Oxford, MS; Clyde, Findlay, Greenville, Marion, OH; Knoxville, La Vergne, TN
Offices: Pleasanton, CA; Denver, CO; Boca Raton, FL; Naperville, IL; Lenexa, KS; Dayton, OH; Ben Salem, PA
International operations: Argentina; Australia; Austria; Belgium; Bermuda; Brazil; British Virgin Islands; Bulgaria; Canada; Cayman Islands; Chile; China; Colombia; Croatia; Ecuador; El Salvador; England; Estonia; Finland; France; Germany; Greece; Guatemala; Hong Kong; India; Ireland; Isle of Man; Italy; Kazakhstan; Lithuania; Luxembourg; Malaysia; Mauritius; Mexico; Morocco and the Western Sahara; Netherlands; Netherlands Antilles; New Zealand; Norway; Peru; Poland; Portugal; Romania; Russia; Singapore; Slovakia; Slovenia; South Africa; Spain; Sweden; Switzerland; Thailand; Turkey; Ukraine; United Kingdom; Uruguay
Historic mergers: Maytag Corporation (March 31, 2006)
Giving statement: Giving through the Whirlpool Corporation Contributions Program, the Maytag Corporation Foundation, and the Whirlpool Foundation.
Company EIN: 381490038

Maytag Corporation Foundation

2000 N. M-63, MD 2900
Benton Harbor, MI 49022

Establishment information: Incorporated in 1952 in IA.
Donor: Maytag Corp.
Financial data (yr. ended 12/31/11): Assets, $551,005 (M); expenditures, $300; qualifying distributions, $300; giving activities include $300 for grants.
Purpose and activities: The foundation supports organizations involved with education and the YMCA of Greater Cleveland.
Fields of interest: Education.
Program:
Scholarship Program: The foundation annually awards up to 40 college scholarships of up to $2,500 to children of employees of Maytag. The program is administered by the National Merit Scholarship Corporation.
Type of support: Employee-related scholarships; General/operating support.
Support limitations: No support for health agencies, churches, or fraternal organizations. No grants to individuals (except for employee-related scholarships), or for benefit dinners, complimentary advertising, or sponsorships, conferences, seminars, endowments, religious causes, or international relations; no loans.
Application information: Applications not accepted. Contributes only to pre-selected organizations.
Board meeting date(s): Jan., July, and Nov.
Officers and Directors:* D. Jeffrey Noel*, Chair. and Pres.; Larry Prange, V.P.; John Geddes, Secy.-Treas.
Number of staff: 1 full-time professional; 1 full-time support.
EIN: 426055722
Selected grants: The following grants are a representative sample of this grantmaker's funding activity:
$20,000 to University of Tennessee, Chattanooga, TN, 2007.

Whirlpool Foundation

2000 N. M-63, MD 3106
Benton Harbor, MI 49022 (269) 923-5580
FAX: (269) 925-0154;
E-mail: whirlpool_foundation@whirlpool.com; Tel. for Candice Garman: (269) 923-5584; URL: http://www.whirlpoolcorp.com/responsibility/building_communities/whirlpool_foundation.aspx

Establishment information: Incorporated in 1951 in MI.
Donor: Whirlpool Corp.
Contact: Candice Garman, Mgr.
Financial data (yr. ended 12/31/11): Assets, $315,559 (M); gifts received, $12,000,000; expenditures, $12,514,966; qualifying distributions, $12,235,387; giving activities include $12,156,254 for grants.
Purpose and activities: The foundation supports programs designed to promote lifelong learning, quality family life, and cultural diversity; and partnerships and collaborations designed to address community issues.
Fields of interest: Arts, cultural/ethnic awareness; Arts; Elementary/secondary education; Higher education; Business school/education; Education; Disasters, preparedness/services; Boys & girls clubs; Youth development, business; American Red Cross; YM/YWCAs & YM/YWHAs; Family services; Human services; Community/economic development; United Ways and Federated Giving Programs.
Programs:
Dollars for Doers: The foundation awards $500 grants to nonprofit organizations with which employees of Whirlpool volunteer. Nonprofit organizations must have a focus on quality family life, cultural diversity, and/or lifelong learning issues.
Matching Gifts: The foundation matches contributions made by directors, employees, and retirees of Whirlpool to United Way campaigns, disaster relief initiatives, and nonprofit organizations involved with the foundation's focus areas on a one-for-one basis from $50 to $10,000 per contributor, per year.
Whirlpool Foundation Sons and Daughters Scholarship Program: The foundation awards college scholarships to the children of employees of Whirlpool and its subsidiaries in the U.S. and Canada. The foundation awards four-year $16,000 scholarships, one-time honor awards of $2,500, and one-time incentive awards of $1,000.
Type of support: Continuing support; Employee matching gifts; Employee volunteer services; Employee-related scholarships; General/operating support; Matching/challenge support; Program development; Research; Scholarship funds.
Geographic limitations: Giving primarily in areas of company operations, with emphasis on Benton Harbor, MI.
Support limitations: No support for social, labor, veterans', alumni, or fraternal organizations, athletic associations, or national groups whose local chapters have already received funding. No grants to individuals (except for employee-related scholarships), or for conferences or seminars, political causes, capital campaigns or endowments, sporting events, goodwill advertisements for fundraising benefits or program books, tickets for testimonials or similar benefit events, or general operating support for United Way agencies.
Application information: Applications not accepted. The foundation is not accepting new requests for grantmaking at this time.
Board meeting date(s): Quarterly

Officers and Trustees:* D. Jeffrey Noel*, Pres.; David A. Binkley, V.P.; John Geddes, Secy.-Treas.; Alan Holaday; Robert LaForest; Tim Reynolds.
Number of staff: 1 full-time professional; 1 full-time support.
EIN: 386077342
Selected grants: The following grants are a representative sample of this grantmaker's funding activity:
$4,799,950 to Renaissance Development Nonprofit Housing Corporation, Detroit, MI, 2011.
$2,000,000 to Renaissance Development Nonprofit Housing Corporation, Detroit, MI, 2010.
$2,000,000 to Renaissance Development Nonprofit Housing Corporation, Detroit, MI, 2010.
$2,000,000 to Renaissance Development Nonprofit Housing Corporation, Detroit, MI, 2010.
$1,500,000 to Renaissance Development Nonprofit Housing Corporation, Detroit, MI, 2010.
$1,000,000 to Renaissance Development Nonprofit Housing Corporation, Detroit, MI, 2010.
$1,000,000 to Renaissance Development Nonprofit Housing Corporation, Detroit, MI, 2011.
$1,000,000 to Renaissance Development Nonprofit Housing Corporation, Detroit, MI, 2011.
$1,000,000 to Renaissance Development Nonprofit Housing Corporation, Detroit, MI, 2011.
$1,000,000 to Renaissance Development Nonprofit Housing Corporation, Detroit, MI, 2011.
$825,000 to Renaissance Development Nonprofit Housing Corporation, Detroit, MI, 2011.
$758,416 to United Way of Southwest Michigan, Saint Joseph, MI, 2010.
$500,000 to Cornerstone Alliance, Benton Harbor, MI, 2010.
$500,000 to Cornerstone Alliance, Benton Harbor, MI, 2010.
$425,000 to Renaissance Development Nonprofit Housing Corporation, Detroit, MI, 2011.
$375,000 to Renaissance Development Nonprofit Housing Corporation, Detroit, MI, 2011.
$228,837 to United Way of Sandusky County, Fremont, OH, 2010.
$200,000 to Renaissance Development Nonprofit Housing Corporation, Detroit, MI, 2011.
$60,032 to United Way of Fort Smith Area, Fort Smith, AR, 2010.
$50,000 to Habitat for Humanity International, Ann Arbor, MI, 2011.

4057
Whitaker Bank Corporation of Kentucky

2937 Paris Pike
Lexington, KY 40512-4037 (859) 299-5246

Company URL: http://www.whitakerbank.com
Establishment information: Established in 1992.
Company type: Private company
Business activities: Operates savings bank.
Business type (SIC): Banks/commercial
Corporate officers: Elmer Whitaker, C.E.O.; Wallace Warfield, C.F.O.
Giving statement: Giving through the Whitaker Foundation, Inc.

Whitaker Foundation, Inc.

2937 Paris Pike
P.O. Box 14037
Lexington, KY 40512-4037

Establishment information: Established in 2004 in KY.
Donors: Elmer Whitaker; Elmer Whitaker Revocable Trust; Elmer Whitaker Foundation; Whitaker Bank Corp. of Kentucky.
Financial data (yr. ended 12/31/11): Assets, $870,046 (M); gifts received, $3,750; expenditures, $49,103; qualifying distributions, $40,334; giving activities include $40,334 for grants.
Fields of interest: Education; Health care; Human services.
Support limitations: No grants to individuals.
Application information: Applications not accepted. Unsolicited requests for funds not accepted.
Officers: Elmer Whitaker, Pres.; Jack E. Whitaker, Secy.; Wallace Warfield, Treas.
Director: Beverly R. Whitaker.
EIN: 300262001

4058
White & Case LLP

1155 Ave. of the Americas
New York, NY 10036-2787 (212) 819-8200

Company URL: http://www.whitecase.com/
Establishment information: Established in 1901.
Company type: Private company
Business activities: Operates law firm.
Business type (SIC): Legal services
Offices: Los Angeles, Palo Alto, CA; Washington, DC; Miami, FL; New York, NY
International operations: Belgium; Brazil; China; Czech Republic; Finland; France; Germany; Hong Kong; Hungary; Italy; Japan; Kazakhstan; Mexico; Poland; Qatar; Romania; Saudi Arabia; Singapore; Slovakia; South Africa; Soviet Union (Former); Sweden; Turkey; United Arab Emirates; United Kingdom
Giving statement: Giving through the White & Case LLP Pro Bono Program.

White & Case LLP Pro Bono Program

1155 Ave. of the Americas
New York, NY 10036-2787 (212) 819-7805
FAX: (212) 354-8113;
E-mail: prickerfor@whitecase.com; URL: http://www.whitecase.com/about/probono-1/

Contact: Patrick Rickerfor, Pro Bono Coord.
Fields of interest: Legal services.
Type of support: Pro bono services - legal.

4059
White and Williams LLP

1 Liberty Pl., Ste. 1800
1650 Market St
Philadelphia, PA 19103-7304
(215) 864-7000

Company URL: http:///
www.whiteandwilliams.com/
Establishment information: Established in 1899.
Company type: Private company
Business activities: Operates law firm.
Business type (SIC): Legal services
Offices: Wilmington, DE; Boston, MA; Cherry Hill, Paramus, NJ; New York, Pleasantville, NY; Berwyn, Center Valley, Conshohocken, Philadelphia, PA
International operations: China
Giving statement: Giving through the White and Williams LLP Pro Bono Program.

White and Williams LLP Pro Bono Program

1 Liberty Pl., Ste. 1800
1650 Market St.
Philadelphia, PA 19103-7304 (856) 317-3600
E-mail: oneillk@whiteandwilliams.com; Additional tel.:(215) 864-7000; URL: http://www.whiteandwilliams.com/firm-probono.html

Contact: Kathy A. O'Neill, Partner
Fields of interest: Legal services.
Type of support: Pro bono services - legal.
Application information: A Pro Bono Committee manages the pro bono program.

4060
R. H. White Construction Company, Inc.

6 Wright Ave.
Merrimack, NH 03054 (508) 832-3295

Company URL: http://www.rhwhite.com
Establishment information: Established in 1923.
Company type: Subsidiary of a private company
Business activities: Provides general contract construction services.
Business type (SIC): Construction/miscellaneous heavy
Corporate officers: Leonard H. White, Chair.; David H. White, Pres. and C.E.O.
Board of director: Leonard H. White, Chair.
Giving statement: Giving through the White Companies Charitable Trust.

The White Companies Charitable Trust

41 Central St.
Auburn, MA 01501-2300

Establishment information: Established in 1981 in MA.
Donors: R.H. White Construction Co., Inc.; L.H. White and Sons; R.H. White Contracting; Laurel Hill Realty; White Development; R.H. White Companies, Inc.
Financial data (yr. ended 04/30/12): Assets, $718,709 (M); expenditures, $230,017; qualifying distributions, $228,280; giving activities include $228,280 for 50 grants (high: $150,000; low: $50).
Purpose and activities: The foundation supports organizations involved with education, health, children and youth services, human services, and religion.
Fields of interest: Education; Human services; Religion.
Type of support: General/operating support.
Geographic limitations: Giving primarily in MA.
Support limitations: No grants to individuals.
Application information: Applications not accepted. Unsolicited requests for funds not accepted.
Trustees: Sumner B. Tilton, Jr.; David H. White; Leonard H. White.
EIN: 042731784

4061
Whiteman Osterman & Hanna LLP
1 Commerce Plz.
Albany, NY 12260-1000 (518) 487-7600

Company URL: http://www.woh.com/
Company type: Private company
Business activities: Operates law firm.
Business type (SIC): Legal services
Offices: Albany, Plattsburgh, NY
Giving statement: Giving through the Whiteman Osterman & Hanna LLP Pro Bono Program.

Whiteman Osterman & Hanna LLP Pro Bono Program
1 Commerce Plz.
Albany, NY 12260-1000 (518) 487-7600
E-mail: cbuckey@woh.com; URL: http://www.woh.com/about_woh/

Contact: Christopher Buckey, Partner
Fields of interest: Legal services.
Type of support: Pro bono services - legal.
Application information: A Pro Bono Coordinator manages the pro bono program.

4062
WhiteWave Foods Company
(formerly White Wave, Inc.)
12002 Airport Way
Broomfield, CO 80021-2546
(303) 635-4000

Company URL: http://www.whitewave.com
Establishment information: Established in 1977.
Company type: Subsidiary of a public company
Business activities: Produces soy milk, dairy, and dairy-related products.
Business type (SIC): Dairy products; miscellaneous prepared foods
Financial profile for 2010: Number of employees, 350; sales volume, $2,050,000,000
Corporate officers: Gregg L. Engles, Chair. and C.E.O.; Blaine E. McPeak, Pres.; Kelly J. Haecker, C.F.O.; Thomas N. Zanetich, Exec. V.P., Human Resources; Doug Behrens, Sr. V.P., Sales; Scott Toth, Sr. V.P., Opers.
Board of director: Gregg L. Engles, Chair.
Division: Horizon Organic Dairy Div., Longmont, CO
Giving statement: Giving through the WhiteWave Foods Partners for Better.

WhiteWave Foods Partners for Better
(formerly Horizon Organic Dairy Corporate Giving Program)
12002 Airport Way
Broomfield, CO 80021-2546 (303) 635-4000
URL: http://www.whitewave.com/partners-for-better/

Purpose and activities: WhiteWave Foods makes charitable contributions to nonprofit organizations involved with hunger, nutrition, and sustainable farming. Support is given primarily in Colorado.
Fields of interest: Agriculture, sustainable programs; Food services; Food banks; Nutrition Children.
Type of support: Donated products; General/operating support.
Geographic limitations: Giving primarily in CO; giving also to national organizations.

4063
The Whiting-Turner Contracting Company
300 E. Joppa Rd.
Baltimore, MD 21286-3020
(410) 821-1100
FAX: (410) 337-5570

Company URL: http://www.whiting-turner.com
Establishment information: Established in 1909.
Company type: Private company
Business activities: Provides general contract construction services.
Business type (SIC): Building construction general contractors and operative builders
Financial profile for 2011: Number of employees, 1,839; sales volume, $3,232,000,000
Corporate officers: Willard Hackerman, Pres. and C.E.O.; Charles A. Irish, Sr. Exec. V.P. and C.F.O.; Maynard Grizzard, V.P. and Secy.
Offices: Irvine, San Francisco, CA; New Haven, CT; Newark, DE; Washington, DC; Fort Lauderdale, Orlando, FL; Atlanta, GA; Boston, MA; Las Vegas, NV; Somerset, NJ; Cleveland, OH; Allentown, PA; Dallas, TX; Chantilly, Richmond, VA
Giving statement: Giving through the Whiting-Turner Contracting Company Contributions Program.

The Whiting-Turner Contracting Company Contributions Program
300 E. Joppa Rd.
Baltimore, MD 21286
URL: http://www.whiting-turner.com/about_us/about_us.html

Purpose and activities: Whiting-Turner makes charitable contributions to nonprofit organizations on a case by case basis. Support is given primarily in areas of company operations, and to national organizations.
Fields of interest: Education; Health care; Cancer; Medical research; Food banks; Housing/shelter; Big Brothers/Big Sisters; United Ways and Federated Giving Programs.
Type of support: Employee volunteer services; General/operating support.
Geographic limitations: Giving on a national basis in areas of company operations, and on a national basis.

4064
The Whitley Group
(formerly The Whitley Printing Company)
4129 Commercial Center Dr., Ste. 400
Austin, TX 78744-1026 (512) 476-7101

Company URL: http://www.whitleyco.com
Establishment information: Established in 1952.
Company type: Private company
Business activities: Operates commercial printing company.
Business type (SIC): Printing/commercial
Corporate officer: Kevin B. Cassis, Pres.
Giving statement: Giving through the Whitley Charitable Foundation.

The Whitley Charitable Foundation
8911 N. Capital of Texas Hwy., Bldg. 3, No. 3120
Austin, TX 78759-7247 (512) 476-7101

Establishment information: Established in 1990 in TX.
Donors: Stephine Jones Dent; Matthew Jones; Ronald Jones; Whitley Company, LP.
Contact: Ronald Jones, Pres.
Financial data (yr. ended 12/31/11): Assets, $2,233,917 (M); expenditures, $118,993; qualifying distributions, $104,500; giving activities include $104,500 for 12 grants (high: $50,000; low: $250).
Purpose and activities: The foundation supports organizations involved with higher education, hunger, athletics, human services, and Christianity.
Fields of interest: Higher education; Food distribution, meals on wheels; Athletics/sports, amateur leagues; Women, centers/services; Human services; Christian agencies & churches.
Type of support: General/operating support.
Geographic limitations: Giving primarily in TX.
Support limitations: No grants to individuals.
Application information: Applications accepted. Application form not required.
Initial approach: Proposal
Deadline(s): None
Officers: Ronald Jones, Pres.; Matthew Jones, V.P. and Secy.-Treas.
Director: Stephanie Jones Dent.
EIN: 742588216
Selected grants: The following grants are a representative sample of this grantmaker's funding activity:
$50,000 to Baylor University, Waco, TX, 2011.
$5,000 to Saint Marys Episcopal School, Memphis, TN, 2011.
$1,250 to Friends of the Governors Mansion, Austin, TX, 2011.
$1,000 to American Cancer Society, Atlanta, GA, 2011.

4065
Whitney National Bank
228 St. Charles Ave.
New Orleans, LA 70130-2601
(504) 586-7421

Company URL: http://www.whitneybank.com
Establishment information: Established in 1883.
Company type: Subsidiary of a public company
Business activities: Operates commercial bank.
Business type (SIC): Banks/commercial
Corporate officers: Joseph S. Exnicios, Pres.; Richard C. Abbott, Sr. V.P. and C.O.O.; Francisco Dearmas, Exec. V.P., Opers.
Giving statement: Giving through the Whitney National Bank Corporate Giving Program.

Whitney National Bank Corporate Giving Program
228 St. Charles Ave.
New Orleans, LA 70130-2601
URL: http://www.whitneybank.com/CorporatePhilanthropy/index.asp

Purpose and activities: Whitney National Bank makes charitable contributions to nonprofit organizations involved with arts and culture, education, the environment, housing, health and human services, and public service. Support is given primarily in areas of company operations in Alabama, Florida, Louisiana, Mississippi, and Texas.
Fields of interest: Arts; Education; Environment; Health care; Housing/shelter; Human services; Public affairs; General charitable giving.
Type of support: General/operating support; Program development; Sponsorships.

Geographic limitations: Giving primarily in areas of company operations in AL, FL, LA, MS, and TX; giving also to national organizations.
Support limitations: No support for political organizations or religious organizations not of direct benefit to the entire community. No grants to individuals, or for operating costs of organizations that receive funds from a Whitney-supported United Way.
Publications: Application guidelines.
Application information: Applications accepted. Proposals should include a 1 to 2 page cover letter. Proposals must not exceed 5 single-spaced typed and numbered pages. Binders are not accepted. Multi-year funding is not automatic. Application form not required. Applicants should submit the following:
1) how project will be sustained once grantmaker support is completed
2) results expected from proposed grant
3) population served
4) name, address and phone number of organization
5) copy of IRS Determination Letter
6) brief history of organization and description of its mission
7) copy of most recent annual report/audited financial statement/990
8) how project's results will be evaluated or measured
9) what distinguishes project from others in its field
10) listing of board of directors, trustees, officers and other key people and their affiliations
11) detailed description of project and amount of funding requested
12) listing of additional sources and amount of support

Guideline requirements should be included in cover letter or submitted as attachments. Proposals should include a description of past support by Whitney with the organization.
Initial approach: Proposal to nearest regional headquarters
Copies of proposal: 1
Committee meeting date(s): Monthly
Deadline(s): None
Final notification: 6 weeks

4066
Whole Foods Market, Inc.

550 Bowie St.
Austin, TX 78703 (512) 477-4455
FAX: (512) 482-7000

Company URL: http://www.wholefoodsmarket.com
Establishment information: Established in 1980.
Company type: Public company
Company ticker symbol and exchange: WFM/NASDAQ
International Securities Identification Number: US9668371068
Business activities: Operates natural foods grocery stores.
Business type (SIC): Groceries—retail
Financial profile for 2012: Number of employees, 53,100; assets, $5,294,220,000; sales volume, $11,698,830,000; pre-tax net income, $752,040,000; expenses, $10,955,320,000; liabilities, $1,491,750,000
Fortune 1000 ranking: 2012—232nd in revenues, 349th in profits, and 576th in assets
Forbes 2000 ranking: 2012—790th in sales, 1021st in profits, and 1810th in assets
Corporate officers: John B. Elstrott, Chair.; John P. Mackey, Co-C.E.O.; Walter E. Robb IV, Co-C.E.O.; A.C. Gallo, Pres. and C.O.O.; Glenda F. Flanagan, Exec. V.P. and C.F.O.; David Lannon, Co-Exec. V.P., Opers.; Ken Meyer, Co-Exec. V.P., Opers.; Sam Ferguson, V.P. and Cont.; Roberta Lang, V.P. and Genl. Counsel; Sirr Less, V.P., Comms.; Margaret Wittenberg, V.P., Public Affairs
Board of directors: John B. Elstrott, Chair.; Gabriele E. Greene; Hass Hassan; Stephanie Kugelman; John P. Mackey; Walter Robb; Jonathan A. Seiffer; Morris J. Siegel; Jonathan D. Sokoloff; Ralph Z. Sorenson; William A. Tindell III
Subsidiary: Amrion, Inc., Boulder, CO
International operations: Canada; England; Wales
Historic mergers: Wild Oats Markets, Inc. (August 28, 2007)
Giving statement: Giving through the Whole Foods Market, Inc. Corporate Giving Program, the Global Animal Partnership, the Whole Kids Foundation, and the Whole Planet Foundation.
Company EIN: 741989366

Whole Foods Market, Inc. Corporate Giving Program

550 Bowie St.
Austin, TX 78703-4644 (512) 477-4455
URL: http://www.wholefoodsmarket.com/company/giving.php

Purpose and activities: As a complement to its foundation, Whole Foods makes charitable contributions via various company locations that determine local charitable guidelines. Support is limited to areas of company operations in Alabama, Arizona, Arkansas, California, Colorado, Connecticut, District of Columbia, Florida, Georgia, Hawaii, Illinois, Indiana, Kansas, Kentucky, Louisiana, Maine, Maryland, Massachusetts, Michigan, Minnesota, Missouri, Nebraska, Nevada, New Jersey, New Mexico, New York, North Carolina, Ohio, Oklahoma, Oregon, Pennsylvania, Rhode Island, South Carolina, Tennessee, Texas, Utah, Virginia, Washington, and Wisconsin, and in Canada and the United Kingdom.
Fields of interest: Food services; Food banks; General charitable giving.
Type of support: Donated products; Employee volunteer services; General/operating support; Sponsorships.
Geographic limitations: Giving limited to areas of company operations in AK, AL, AR, AZ, CA, CO, CT, DC, FL, GA, HI, IL, IN, KS, KY, LA, MA, MD, ME, MI, MN, MO, NC, NE, NJ, NM, NV, NY, OH, OK, OR, PA, RI, SC, TN, TX, UT, VA, WA, and WI, and in Canada and the United Kingdom.
Application information: Applications accepted.
Initial approach: Contact Marketing Director at nearest company store or visit website for application information

Global Animal Partnership

(formerly Animal Compassion Foundation)
P.O. Box 21484
Washington, DC 20009-0984
E-mail: info@globalanimalpartnership.org; URL: http://www.globalanimalpartnership.org/

Establishment information: Established in 2005 in TX.
Donors: Whole Foods Market Services, Inc.; Vanguard Charitable Endowment Program; Stefan Muth; Miyun Park; The Humane Society of the United States; Whole Foods Market.
Financial data (yr. ended 12/31/11): Assets, $561,643 (M); gifts received, $249,706; expenditures, $215,417; qualifying distributions, $0.
Purpose and activities: The foundation is dedicated to improving the lives of farm animals and supports best practices that enhance animal needs and behaviors through a worldwide network of producers and researchers, and funding on-farm research and producer workshops.
Fields of interest: Animals/wildlife; Agriculture; Agriculture, livestock issues.
Application information: Applications not accepted. Unsolicited requests for funds not accepted.
Officers: Joyce D'Silva, Chair.; Ian Duncan, Vice-Chair.; Margaret Wittenberg, Secy.-Treas.; Miyun Park, Exec. Dir.
Directors: Steve Gross; John Mackey; Sara Miller; George Siemon; Jim Webster.
EIN: 202234609

Whole Kids Foundation

550 Bowie St.
Austin, TX 78703-4644
E-mail: whole.kids@wholefoods.com; Additional e-mail: info@gardengrants.com; URL: http://www.wholekidsfoundation.org

Establishment information: Established in 2011.
Contact: Nona Evans, Exec. Dir.
Purpose and activities: The foundation works to increase the availability and consumption of nutritious food in schools, and create and support tools that enable schools and parents to establish healthy eating environments and engage children in making good food choices.
Fields of interest: Teacher school/education; Health sciences school/education; Nutrition.
Programs:
Nutrition Education for Teachers: Through the Nutrition Education for Teachers, the foundation is piloting nutrition and cooking education for teachers with the goal of improving their nutrition, health and wellness. Initially, the pilot program will be limited to the Austin, Texas Independent School District.
School Garden Grant Program: Through the School Garden Grant Program, a collaboration between Whole Kids Foundation, Whole Foods Market and FoodCorps, the Foundation provide grants of $2,000 to support school garden projects in the US, UK and Canada. Funds will be disbursed to recipients as a one-time, one-year award. Completion of an end-of-grant survey will be required for all recipients.
Type of support: Curriculum development; Program development.
Geographic limitations: Giving on a national basis and in Canada and the U.K.
Publications: Application guidelines; Newsletter.
Application information: Applications accepted. Application form required. Applicants should submit the following:
1) timetable for implementation and evaluation of project
2) copy of IRS Determination Letter
3) copy of current year's organizational budget and/or project budget
4) listing of additional sources and amount of support

Submission should include a letter of authorization and support from the school principal on school letterhead; photo of the garden site; information on local, city, state policies related to school gardens; plan for the garden; plans for the harvest and for sustaining the garden over multiple years; and the applicant's and Tax ID.
Initial approach: Complete online application for School garden grants
Deadline(s): Dec. 31 for School garden grants
Final notification: Feb.
Officers and Directors:* Walter Robb, Chair.; Nona Evans, Exec. Dir.; Scott Allshouse; Glenda Flanagan; Cindy McCann; Ken Meyer; Jim Sud; Margaret Wittenberg.

Whole Planet Foundation

550 Bowie St.
Austin, TX 78703-4677 (512) 542-3834
FAX: (512) 482-7000;
E-mail: general_info@wholeplanetfoundation.org;
URL: http://www.wholeplanetfoundation.org

Establishment information: Established in 2005 in DE and TX.
Donors: Whole Foods Market Services, Inc.; Pepsico; Seventh Generation; ITO EN.
Financial data (yr. ended 12/31/11): Assets, $6,779,764 (M); gifts received, $8,416,152; expenditures, $7,306,312; qualifying distributions, $7,300,072; giving activities include $5,982,031 for 38 grants (high: $402,539; low: $3,550) and $7,300,072 for foundation-administered programs.
Purpose and activities: The foundation creates and supports economic partnerships with the poor in developing-world communities that supply Whole Foods stores with product. Special emphasis is directed toward microfinance institutions in Latin America, Africa and Asia who in turn develop and offer microenterprise loan programs, training and other financial services to the self-employed poor.
Fields of interest: International development; International economic development; Economic development; Community development, business promotion; Social entrepreneurship; Community development, small businesses; Microfinance/microlending Economically disadvantaged.
International interests: Africa; Asia; Latin America.
Type of support: Capital campaigns; General/operating support.
Geographic limitations: Giving primarily in NY and in developing communities in Africa, Argentina, Asia, Bangladesh, Costa Rica, Ethiopia, Guatemala, Haiti, Honduras, India, Indonesia, Kenya, Latin America, Nepal, Nicaragua, Peru, and Thailand.
Support limitations: No grants to individuals.
Publications: Annual report; Financial statement; IRS Form 990 or 990-PF printed copy available upon request; Newsletter.
Application information: Applications not accepted. Contributes only to pre-selected organizations.
Officers and Directors:* John P. Mackey*, Co-Chair.; Lee Valkenaar*, Co-Chair.; Philip Sansone*, Pres. and Exec. Dir.; Roberta Lang*, V.P. and Treas.; Scott Allshouse; Michael Besancon; Glenda F. Flanagan; Ken Meyer; Will Paradise; Walter E. Robb IV; Jeff Teter.
Number of staff: 6 full-time professional.
EIN: 202376273

4067
Whyte Hirschboeck Dudek S.C.

555 E. Wells St., Ste. 1900
Milwaukee, WI 53202-2837
(414) 273-2100

Company URL: http://www.whdlaw.com/index.aspx
Establishment information: Established in 1943.
Company type: Private company
Business activities: Operates law firm.
Business type (SIC): Legal services
Offices: Madison, Milwaukee, WI
Giving statement: Giving through the Whyte Hirschboeck Dudek S.C. Pro Bono Program.

Whyte Hirschboeck Dudek S.C. Pro Bono Program

555 E. Wells St., Ste. 1900
Milwaukee, WI 53202-2837 (414) 273-2100
E-mail: amaher@whdlaw.com; URL: http://www.whdlaw.com/community.aspx

Contact: Ann Maher, Shareholder
Fields of interest: Legal services.
Type of support: Pro bono services - legal.
Application information: An attorney who coordinates pro bono projects as an ancillary duty to other work.

4068
Wiggin and Dana LLP

1 Century Tower
265 Church St.
New Haven, CT 06510-7013
(203) 498-4400

Company URL: http://www.wiggin.com/index.aspx
Establishment information: Established in 1934.
Company type: Private company
Business activities: Operates law firm.
Business type (SIC): Legal services
Offices: Greenwich, Hartford, New Haven, Stamford, CT; New York, NY; Philadelphia, PA
Giving statement: Giving through the Wiggin and Dana LLP Corporate Giving Program.

Wiggin and Dana LLP Corporate Giving Program

1 Century Tower
265 Church St.
New Haven, CT 06510-7013
E-mail: rlanger@wiggin.com; For Pro Bono information: Alan Schwartz, Partner, tel.: (203) 498-4332, fax:(203) 782-2889; URL: http://www.wiggin.com/about.aspx?Show=154

Contact: Alan Schwartz, Partner
Fields of interest: Legal services.
Type of support: Pro bono services - legal.

4069
Wigwam Mills, Inc.

3402 Crocker Ave.
P.O. Box 818
Sheboygan, WI 53081 (920) 457-5551

Company URL: http://www.wigwam.com
Establishment information: Established in 1905.
Company type: Private company
Business activities: Manufactures socks.
Business type (SIC): Hosiery and knitted fabrics
Corporate officers: Robert Chesebro, Jr., Chair. and C.E.O.; Gerald Vogel, Pres. and C.O.O.; James G. Einhauser, V.P., Sales and Mktg.
Board of director: Robert Chesebro, Jr., Chair.
Giving statement: Giving through the Wigwam Mills Fund Inc.

Wigwam Mills Fund Inc.

P.O. Box 818
Sheboygan, WI 53082-0818

Donor: Wigwam Mills, Inc.
Financial data (yr. ended 11/30/12): Assets, $24,010 (M); gifts received, $40,000; expenditures, $34,514; qualifying distributions, $34,514; giving activities include $34,500 for 3 grants (high: $30,000; low: $500).
Purpose and activities: The foundation supports camps and organizations involved with orchestras, cancer, youth development, and family services.
Fields of interest: Human services; Religion.
Type of support: General/operating support.
Application information: Applications not accepted. Unsolicited requests for funds not accepted.
Officers: Robert E. Chesebro, Jr., Pres.; James B. Einhauser, V.P.; Terry B. Ver Straate, Treas.
EIN: 396053425

4070
Wilbur-Ellis Company

(also known as WECO)
345 California St., Fl. 27
San Francisco, CA 94104-2644
(415) 772-4000

Company URL: http://www.wilburellis.com/pages/Home.aspx
Establishment information: Established in 1921.
Company type: Private company
Business activities: Sells agricultural and industrial products wholesale.
Business type (SIC): Farm-product raw materials—wholesale; chemicals and allied products—wholesale
Financial profile for 2011: Number of employees, 3,100; assets, $1,160,000,000; sales volume, $2,340,000,000
Corporate officers: Herbert B. Tully, Chair.; Carter P. Thacher, Vice-Chair.; John P. Thacher, Pres. and C.E.O.; Jerry Coupe, C.I.O.; David P. Granoff, V.P. and Genl. Counsel
Board of directors: Herbert B. Tully, Chair.; Carter Thacher, Vice-Chair.
Giving statement: Giving through the Brayton Wilbur Foundation.

Brayton Wilbur Foundation

345 California St., 27th Fl.
San Francisco, CA 94104-2644

Establishment information: Incorporated in 1947 in CA.
Donors: Brayton Wilbur, Jr.‡; Wilbur-Ellis Co.; Judy Wilbur.
Financial data (yr. ended 12/31/11): Assets, $3,571,620 (M); expenditures, $168,786; qualifying distributions, $149,500; giving activities include $149,500 for grants.
Purpose and activities: The foundation supports aquariums and organizations involved with arts and culture, secondary education, and civic affairs.
Fields of interest: Arts; Health care; Human services.
Geographic limitations: Giving primarily in San Francisco, CA.
Support limitations: No grants to individuals.
Application information: Applications not accepted. Contributes only to pre-selected organizations.
Officers: Judy Wilbur, Pres.; Claire W. Pollini, V.P.; Michael D. Wilbur, V.P.; Jaye G. Stedman, Secy.; Susan W. Harrington, Treas.
EIN: 946088667

4071
Wilentz, Goldman & Spitzer P.A.

90 Woodbridge Ctr., Dr.
P.O. Box 10
Woodbridge, NJ 07095-1163
(732) 855-6176

Company URL: http://ww.wilentz.com/
Establishment information: Established in 1919.
Company type: Private company
Business activities: Operates law firm.
Business type (SIC): Legal services
Corporate officer: David T. Wilentz, Founding Partner
Offices: Eatontown, Woodbridge, NJ; New York, NY; Philadelphia, PA
Giving statement: Giving through the Wilentz, Goldman & Spitzer P.A. Pro Bono Program.

Wilentz, Goldman & Spitzer P.A. Pro Bono Program

90 Woodbridge Ctr., Dr.
P.O. Box 10
Woodbridge, NJ 07095-1163 (732) 855-6055
E-mail: sbarcan@wilentz.com; URL: http://www.wilentz.com/Public_Service_Record.aspx

Contact: Stephen Barcan, Administrative Shareholder
Fields of interest: Legal services.
Type of support: Pro bono services - legal.
Application information: On a rotation basis through our Pro Bono Coordinator.

4072
John Wiley & Sons, Inc.

111 River St.
Hoboken, NJ 07030-5774 (201) 748-6000
FAX: (201) 748-6088

Company URL: http://www.wiley.com
Establishment information: Established in 1807.
Company type: Public company
Company ticker symbol and exchange: JW.A/NYSE
Business activities: Publishes scientific, technical, and medical, professional and consumer, and educational print and electronic products.
Business type (SIC): Book publishing and/or printing
Financial profile for 2012: Number of employees, 5,200; assets, $2,532,950,000; sales volume, $1,782,740,000; pre-tax net income, $272,100,000; expenses, $1,502,320,000; liabilities, $1,515,380,000
Corporate officers: Peter Booth Wiley, Chair.; Stephen M. Smith, Pres. and C.E.O.; Ellis E. Cousens, Exec. V.P., C.O.O., and C.F.O.; Gary M. Rinck, Sr. V.P. and Genl. Counsel; Clay Stobaugh, Sr. V.P., Mktg.; William J. Arlington, Sr. V.P., Human Resources; Edward J. Melando, V.P., Corp. Cont., and C.A.O.; Vincent Marzano, V.P. and Treas.; Michael L. Preston, Corp. Secy.
Board of directors: Peter Booth Wiley, Chair.; Mari J. Baker; Jean-Lou Chameau; Linda P.B. Katehi; Matthew S. Kissner; Raymond W. McDaniel, Jr.; Eduardo R. Menasce; William J. Pesce; William B. Plummer; Kalpana Raina; Stephen M. Smith; Jesse C. Wiley
Offices: San Francisco, CA; DeKalb, IL; Indianapolis, IN; Ames, IA; Malden, MA; Edison, Somerset, NJ; New York, NY; Cleveland, OH; Austin, TX; Charlottesville, Harrisonburg, VA
International operations: Australia; Canada; Germany; Singapore; United Kingdom
Giving statement: Giving through the John Wiley & Sons, Inc. Corporate Giving Program and the Wiley Foundation, Inc.
Company EIN: 135593032

John Wiley & Sons, Inc. Corporate Giving Program

111 River St.
Hoboken, NJ 07030-5773 (201) 748-6000
FAX: (201) 748-6940; URL: http://www.wiley.com/WileyCDA/Section/id-380789.html

Contact: Susan Spilka, V.P., Corp. Comms.
Financial data (yr. ended 04/30/12): Total giving, $1,750,375, including $1,750,375 for grants.
Purpose and activities: John Wiley makes charitable contributions to libraries and nonprofit organizations involved with arts and culture, business and industry, and science and technology. Support is given primarily in the greater New Jersey and New York, New York, area.
Fields of interest: Museums; Performing arts; Performing arts, theater; Performing arts, music; Arts; Libraries/library science; Business/industry; Chemistry; Physics; Engineering/technology; Biology/life sciences; Science.
Programs:
Matching Gift Program: John Wiley matches contributions made by its employees and directors and the spouses of its employees and directors to nonprofit organizations involved with arts and culture, education, wildlife preservation, and land conservation on a three-for-one basis up to $500 and on a one-for-one basis from $500 to $2,000 per contributor, per organization, per calendar year.
ServiceMatch Program: John Wiley makes charitable contributions of $250 to nonprofit organizations with which employees volunteer from 12 to 30 hours during a calendar year and $500 to nonprofit organizations with which employees volunteer at least 30 hours during a calendar year.
Type of support: Annual campaigns; Capital campaigns; Conferences/seminars; Curriculum development; Donated equipment; Donated products; Emergency funds; Employee matching gifts; Employee volunteer services; Endowments; Fellowships; General/operating support; Matching/challenge support; Publication; Scholarship funds.
Geographic limitations: Giving primarily in the greater NJ and New York, NY, area, with emphasis on Hoboken, NJ.
Support limitations: No support for religious or political organizations.
Publications: Application guidelines; Program policy statement.
Application information: Applications accepted. The Corporate Communications Department handles giving. Application form not required. Applicants should submit the following:
1) detailed description of project and amount of funding requested
Initial approach: Proposal to headquarters
Copies of proposal: 1
Deadline(s): None
Final notification: Following review
Administrators: Denise Giglio, Coord., Matching Gifts; Susan Spilka, Sr. V.P., Corp. Comms.

The Wiley Foundation, Inc.

c/o D. Wiley, Wiley & Sons
111 River St.
Hoboken, NJ 07030-5773
FAX: (201) 748-6940; E-mail: dwiley@wiley.com; URL: http://www.wiley.com/legacy/wileyfoundation/

Establishment information: Established in 2001 in NY.
Donor: John Wiley & Sons, Inc.
Contact: Deborah E. Wiley, Chair.; Alicia Baldo, Secy.
Financial data (yr. ended 04/30/12): Assets, $1,065,382 (M); gifts received, $151,000; expenditures, $105,969; qualifying distributions, $99,778; giving activities include $50,000 for 1 grant and $36,001 for 5 grants to individuals (high: $11,667; low: $500).
Purpose and activities: The foundation awards grants to Ph.D. and M.D. scientists.
Fields of interest: Graduate/professional education; Biomedicine; Science.
Program:
Wiley Prize in Biomedical Sciences: Through the Wiley Prize in Biomedical Sciences program, the foundation annually awards one $35,000 grant to a Ph.D. or M.D. scientist who has opened new fields of research or advanced novel concepts or their applications in a particular biomedical discipline. The award recognizes a specific contribution or series of contributions that demonstrate the nominee's leadership in the development of research concepts or their clinical application.
Type of support: Grants to individuals.
Geographic limitations: Giving on an national basis and in Germany, the Netherlands, and the United Kingdom.
Publications: Application guidelines; Grants list.
Application information: Applications accepted. Nominations for the Wiley Prize in Biomedical Sciences should be submitted by someone other than the nominee. More than one nomination can be made from the same organization. Application form required.
Nominations for the Wiley Prize in Biomedical Sciences should include letters of support from colleagues familiar with the nominee's work and a curriculum vitae.
Initial approach: Complete online nomination form for the Wiley Prize in Biomedical Sciences or submit form via e-mail or mail
Deadline(s): July 31 for the Wiley Prize in Biomedical Sciences
Officers: Deborah E. Wiley, Chair. and Pres.; Guenter Blobel, V.P.; Denise Giglio, Secy.-Treas.
Directors: Elizabeth Cox; Mike Davis; Patrick Kelly; Kaye Pace.
EIN: 134163744

4073
Wiley Rein LLP

1776 K St., N.W.
Washington, DC 20006-2398
(202) 719-7000

Company URL: http://www.wileyrein.com/index.cfm
Establishment information: Established in 1983.
Business activities: Operates law firm.
Business type (SIC): Legal services
Corporate officer: Richard E. Wiley, Managing Partner
Offices: Washington, DC; McLean, VA

Giving statement: Giving through the Wiley Rein LLP Pro Bono Program.

Wiley Rein LLP Pro Bono Program

1776 K St., N.W.
Washington, DC 20006-2398 (202) 719-7346
E-mail: pkhoury@wileyrein.com; Additional tel.: (202) 719-7000; URL: http://www.wileyrein.com/about.cfm?sp=probono

Contact: Paul Khoury, Partner/Chair, Pro Bono Comm.
Fields of interest: Legal services.
Type of support: Pro bono services - legal.
Application information: A Pro Bono Committee manages the pro bono program.

4074
Wilkes Artis, Chartered

(formerly Wilkes, Artis, Hedrick & Lane)
1825 I St., N.W., Ste. 300
Washington, DC 20006 (202) 457-7800

Company URL: http://www.wilkesartis.com/about.html1926
Establishment information: Established in 1926.
Company type: Private company
Business activities: Provides legal services.
Business type (SIC): Legal services
Financial profile for 2009: Number of employees, 137
Corporate officer: Charles A. Kamil III, Pres.
Giving statement: Giving through the Wilkes Artis, Chartered.

Wilkes Artis, Chartered

1825 I Street N.W., Ste. 300
Washington, DC 20036-5403

Establishment information: Established in 1982 in DC.
Donors: Stanley J. Fineman; Allen Jones, Jr.; Norman M. Glasgow, Sr.; Albert L. Ledgard, Jr.; Whayne S. Quin; Wilkes, Artis, Hedrick & Lane; Robert L. Gorham; Charles A. Camalier III; C. Francis Murphy; Maureen E. Dwyer; Joseph B. Whitebread, Jr.
Contact: Stanley J. Fineman, Pres.
Financial data (yr. ended 09/30/11): Assets, $6,969 (M); gifts received, $9,000; expenditures, $6,080; qualifying distributions, $4,900; giving activities include $4,900 for 9 grants (high: $1,000; low: $100).
Purpose and activities: The foundation supports organizations involved with heart disease, brain disorders, courts and judicial administration, football, and human services.
Fields of interest: Heart & circulatory diseases; Brain disorders; Courts/judicial administration; Athletics/sports, football; Residential/custodial care, hospices; Human services.
Type of support: General/operating support; Scholarship funds.
Geographic limitations: Giving primarily in Washington, DC, MD, and VA.
Support limitations: No grants to individuals.
Application information: Applications accepted. Application form required.
Initial approach: Letter
Deadline(s): None
Officers and Directors:* Stanley J. Fineman, Pres.; Charles A. Camalier, V.P.; Eric S. Kassoff, Secy.-Treas.
EIN: 521272246

4075
Willdan Group, Inc.

2401 E. Katella Ave., Ste. 300
Anaheim, CA 92806-6073 (714) 940-6300
FAX: (714) 940-4920

Company URL: http://www.willdan.com/
Establishment information: Established in 1964.
Company type: Public company
Company ticker symbol and exchange: WLDN/NASDAQ
Business activities: Provides municipal engineering services.
Business type (SIC): Engineering, architectural, and surveying services
Financial profile for 2011: Number of employees, 562; assets, $64,310,000; sales volume, $107,170,000; pre-tax net income, $3,330,000; expenses, $103,760,000; liabilities, $30,020,000
Corporate officers: Win Westfall, Chair.; Thomas D. Brisbin, Ph.D., Pres. and C.E.O.; Kimberly D. Grant, Sr. V.P., Treas., and C.F.O.
Board of directors: Win Westfall, Chair.; Thomas D. Brisbin, Ph.D.; Raymond W. Holdsworth; Douglas J. McEachern; Keith W. Renken; John M. Toups
Giving statement: Giving through the Willdan Group of Companies Foundation.
Company EIN: 141951112

The Willdan Group of Companies Foundation

2401 E. Katella Ave., Ste. 300
Anaheim, CA 92806-5909
URL: http://wgifoundation.org/

Establishment information: Established in 2005 in CA.
Donor: The Wildan Group of Companies.
Financial data (yr. ended 12/31/11): Assets, $0 (M); gifts received, $26,455; expenditures, $26,455; qualifying distributions, $26,430; giving activities include $26,430 for grants.
Purpose and activities: The foundation supports organizations involved with education, breast cancer, HIV/AIDS, athletics, human services, civic affairs, and the visually impaired.
Fields of interest: Education; Human services; Public affairs.
Type of support: General/operating support; Scholarship funds.
Geographic limitations: Giving primarily in CA.
Support limitations: No grants to individuals.
Application information: Applications accepted. Application form required.
Initial approach: See website for application form
Deadline(s): See website for deadline
Directors: Jean Blythe; Tracy Lenocker; Win Westfall.
EIN: 342045559

4076
Williams & Connolly LLP

725 12th St., N.W.
Washington, DC 20005-3901
(202) 434-5000

Company URL: http://www.wc.com/
Establishment information: Established in 1967.
Company type: Private company
Business activities: Operates law firm.
Business type (SIC): Legal services
Corporate officers: Lynda Schuler, Partner and Exec. Dir.; Nicole G. Minnick, C.I.O.
Office: Washington, DC
Giving statement: Giving through the Williams & Connolly LLP Pro Bono Program.

Williams & Connolly LLP Pro Bono Program

725 12th St., N.W.
Washington, DC 20005-3901 (202) 434-5804
E-mail: thentoff@wc.com; URL: http://www.wc.com/about.html

Contact: Thomas G. Hentoff, Partner
Fields of interest: Legal services.
Type of support: Pro bono services - legal.
Application information: A Pro Bono Committee manages the pro bono program.

4077
The Williams Companies, Inc.

1 Williams Ctr.
Tulsa, OK 74172 (918) 573-2000
FAX: (918) 573-6714

Company URL: http://co.williams.com
Establishment information: Established in 1908.
Company type: Public company
Company ticker symbol and exchange: WMB/NYSE
Business activities: Conducts natural gas exploration and production activities; transmits natural gas.
Business type (SIC): Gas production and distribution; extraction/oil and gas
Financial profile for 2012: Assets, $24,300,000,000; sales volume, $7,500,000,000
Fortune 1000 ranking: 2012—342nd in revenues, 224th in profits, and 212th in assets
Forbes 2000 ranking: 2012—1139th in sales, 670th in profits, and 865th in assets
Corporate officers: Frank T. McInnis, Chair.; Alan S. Armstrong, Pres. and C.E.O.; Donald R. Chappel, Sr. V.P. and C.F.O; Craig L. Rainey, Sr. V.P. and Genl. Counsel; Robyn L. Ewing, Sr. V.P., Admin., and C.A.O.
Board of directors: Frank T. MacInnis, Chair.; Alan S. Armstrong; Joseph R. Cleveland; Kathleen B. Cooper; John A. Hagg; Juanita H. Hinshaw; Steven W. Nance; Murray D. Smith; Janice D. Stoney; Laura A. Sugg; John H. Williams; Joseph H. Williams
Subsidiaries: Texas Gas Transmission Corporation, Owensboro, KY; Transco Energy Company, Houston, TX; Transcontinental Gas Pipe Line Corporation, Houston, TX; Williams Energy Co., Texas City, TX; Williams Pipe Line Co., LLC, Doniphan, NE
International operations: Argentina; Austria; Barbados; Bermuda; Canada; Cayman Islands; England; South Africa; Spain; United Kingdom
Giving statement: Giving through the Williams Companies Foundation, Inc.
Company EIN: 730569878

The Williams Companies Foundation, Inc.

1 Williams Ctr., M.D. 45
Tulsa, OK 74172-0140 (918) 573-9676
FAX: (918) 573-6006;
E-mail: communityrelationstulsa@williams.com

Establishment information: Incorporated in 1974 in OK.
Donor: The Williams Cos., Inc.
Contact: Alison Anthony, Pres.
Financial data (yr. ended 12/31/11): Assets, $16,016,913 (M); gifts received, $6,900,000; expenditures, $6,629,840; qualifying distributions,

$6,629,840; giving activities include $6,629,840 for 1 grant.
Purpose and activities: The foundation supports organizations involved with arts and culture, education, health, human services, community development, and civic affairs.
Fields of interest: Media/communications; Museums; Humanities; Arts; Libraries (public); Education; Health care; Family services; Human services; Economic development; Community/economic development; United Ways and Federated Giving Programs; Public affairs.
Program:
Williams Foundation Scholarship Program: The foundation annually awards ten four-year $1,500 college scholarships to children of employees and retirees of Williams Companies. The program is administered by the National Merit Scholarship Corp.
Type of support: Building/renovation; Capital campaigns; Employee-related scholarships; General/operating support; Matching/challenge support; Research; Scholarship funds.
Geographic limitations: Giving primarily in areas of company operations, with emphasis on Tulsa, OK; giving also to statewide and national organizations.
Support limitations: No grants to individuals (except for employee-related scholarships).
Application information: Applications accepted. Contact foundation for nearest company facility. Application form not required. Applicants should submit the following:
1) copy of IRS Determination Letter
2) copy of most recent annual report/audited financial statement/990
3) listing of board of directors, trustees, officers and other key people and their affiliations
4) copy of current year's organizational budget and/or project budget

Initial approach: Proposal to nearest company facility
Copies of proposal: 1
Board meeting date(s): Varies
Deadline(s): None
Final notification: Approximately 1 month

Officers and Directors:* Robyn L. Ewing*, Chair.; Alison Anthony, Pres.; Sarah C. Miller, Secy.; Alan S. Armstrong; Randall Lee Barnard; Donald R. Chappel; Rory L. Miller; Craig L. Rainey; Phillip D. Wright.
EIN: 237413843
Selected grants: The following grants are a representative sample of this grantmaker's funding activity:
$6,629,840 to Tulsa Community Foundation, Tulsa, OK, 2011. To support health and welfare charities and scholarships and Education programs.

4078
Williams Mullen

William Mullen Ctr.
200 S. 10th St., Ste. 1600
Richmond, VA 23219-4061 (804) 420-6000

Company URL: http://www.williamsmullen.com/
Establishment information: Established in 1909.
Company type: Private company
Business activities: Operates law firm.
Business type (SIC): Legal services
Corporate officers: James V. Meath, Chair.; M. Keith Kapp, Vice-Chair.; Thomas R. Frantz, Pres. and C.E.O.; Craig L. Rascoe, V.P. and C.O.O.; R. Brian Ball, V.P. and Genl. Counsel; Julious P. Smith, Jr., Chair. Emeritus
Board of directors: James V. Meath, Chair.; M. Keith Kapp, Vice-Chair.; Farhad Aghdami; R. Brian Ball; Wyatt S. Beazley IV; David C. Burton; Arlene J. Diosegy; Howard W. Dobbins; Calvin W. Fowler, Jr.; Jonathan A. Frank; Thomas R. Frantz; J. Conrad Garcia; A. Brooks Hock; Danny W. Jackson; William A. Old, Jr.; Elizabeth Davenport Scott; Evelyn M. Suarez; Julious P. Smith, Jr.
Offices: Washington, DC; Durham, Raleigh, Wilmington, NC; Charlottesville, Newport News, Norfolk, Portsmouth, Richmond, Tysons Corner, Virginia Beach, VA
International operations: United Kingdom
Giving statement: Giving through the Williams Mullen Pro Bono Program and the Williams Mullen Foundation.

Williams Mullen Pro Bono Program

William Mullen Ctr.
200 S. 10th St., Ste. 1600
Richmond, VA 23219-4061 (804) 420-6403
FAX: (804) 420-6507;
E-mail: anea@williamsmullen.com; URL: http://www.williamsmullen.com/story/values/community/pro-bono

Contact: G. Andrew Nea, Jr., Pro Bono Partner
Fields of interest: Legal services.
Type of support: Pro bono services - legal.

Williams Mullen Foundation

(formerly WMCD Charitable Foundation)
P.O. Box 1320
Richmond, VA 23218-1320
URL: http://www.williamsmullen.com/story/values/community/foundation

Establishment information: Established in 1994 in VA.
Donor: Julious P. Smith, Jr.
Financial data (yr. ended 01/31/12): Assets, $114,230 (M); gifts received, $345,800; expenditures, $349,470; qualifying distributions, $349,270; giving activities include $349,270 for grants.
Fields of interest: Museums; Performing arts, theater; Arts; Higher education; Aquariums; Health organizations, association; Health organizations; Recreation, parks/playgrounds; Human services; American Red Cross; Business/industry; Engineering/technology.
Geographic limitations: Giving primarily in VA.
Support limitations: No grants to individuals.
Application information: Applications not accepted. Contributes only to pre-selected organizations.
Officer and Directors:* John L. Walker*, Pres.; Craig L. Rascoe; Julious P. Smith, Jr.
EIN: 541700227
Selected grants: The following grants are a representative sample of this grantmaker's funding activity:
$6,700 to Business Consortium for Arts Support, Norfolk, VA, 2012.
$6,000 to Virginia Foundation for Independent Colleges, Richmond, VA, 2012.
$5,890 to Foodbank of Southeastern Virginia, Norfolk, VA, 2012.
$5,798 to Richmond Forum, Richmond, VA, 2012.
$5,500 to Hampton Roads Partnership, Norfolk, VA, 2012.
$4,550 to FORKids, Norfolk, VA, 2012.
$4,000 to World Pediatric Project, Richmond, VA, 2012.
$3,600 to American Heart Association, Glen Allen, VA, 2012.
$3,500 to Horizons Hampton Roads, Norfolk, VA, 2012.
$1,600 to American Red Cross, Raleigh, NC, 2012.

4080
Williamsburg Pottery Factory, Inc.

6692 Richmond Rd., Rte. 60 W.
P.O. Box 123
Williamsburg, VA 23188 (757) 564-3326

Company URL: http://www.williamsburgpottery.com
Establishment information: Established in 1938.
Company type: Private company
Business activities: Operates pottery and home furnishings retail complex.
Business type (SIC): Furniture and home furnishing stores
Corporate officer: Kimberley A. Maloney, Chair., C.E.O., Pres., and Secy.
Board of director: Kimberley A. Maloney, Chair.
Giving statement: Giving through the James Maloney Foundation.

The James Maloney Foundation

1009 Lightfoot Rd.
Williamsburg, VA 23188-9020 (757) 229-2393

Establishment information: Established in 2005 in VA.
Donor: Williamsburg Pottery Factory.
Financial data (yr. ended 12/31/11): Assets, $771,419 (M); expenditures, $39,769; qualifying distributions, $35,500; giving activities include $20,500 for 6 grants (high: $6,000; low: $1,000) and $15,000 for 6 grants to individuals (high: $2,500; low: $2,500).
Fields of interest: Education; Human services.
Type of support: Scholarships—to individuals.
Geographic limitations: Giving limited to the Williamsburg, VA, area.
Application information: Applications accepted. Application form required.
Initial approach: Letter
Deadline(s): None
Officers: Kimberly A. Maloney, Pres.; Peter J. Kao, V.P. and Secy.-Treas.
Directors: Ronald Kleveland; Shin Murphy.
EIN: 203957354

4079
Williams-Sonoma, Inc.

3250 Van Ness Ave.
San Francisco, CA 94109 (415) 421-7900
FAX: (302) 636-5454

Company URL: http://www.williams-sonomainc.com/
Establishment information: Established in 1956.
Company type: Public company
Company ticker symbol and exchange: WSM/NYSE
Business activities: Specialty retailer of home furnishings.
Business type (SIC): Home furniture, furnishings, and equipment stores
Financial profile for 2013: Number of employees, 26,800; assets, $2,187,680,000; sales volume, $4,042,870,000; pre-tax net income, $409,960,000; expenses, $3,633,710,000; liabilities, $878,540,000
Fortune 1000 ranking: 2012—582nd in revenues, 517th in profits, and 835th in assets
Corporate officers: Adrian D.P. Bellamy, Chair.; Laura J. Alber, Pres. and C.E.O.; Julie Whalen, Exec. V.P. and C.F.O.

Board of directors: Adrian D.P. Bellamy, Chair.; Laura J. Alber; Rose Marie Bravo; Patrick Connolly; Mary Ann Casati; Adrian T. Dillon; Anthony A. Greener; Ted W. Hall; Michael R. Lynch; Lorraine Twohill; Julie P. Whalen
Giving statement: Giving through the Williams Sonoma Foundation.
Company EIN: 942203880

Williams Sonoma Foundation

3250 Van Ness Ave.
San Francisco, CA 94109-1012

Establishment information: Established in 2006 in CA also reports in AL, AK, AZ, AR, CT, CO, FL, GA, IL, KS, KY, ME, MD, MA, MI, MN, MS, NH, NM, NY ND, OH, OK, OR, PA, RI, SC, TN, UT, VA, WA, WI, and WV.
Donor: Williams Sonoma, Inc.
Financial data (yr. ended 01/31/12): Assets, $75,091 (M); gifts received, $50,000; expenditures, $75; qualifying distributions, $0.
Purpose and activities: The foundation awards disaster relief grants to employees of Williams Sonoma in response to Hurricane Katrina.
Fields of interest: Disasters, Hurricane Katrina.
Type of support: Scholarships—to individuals.
Geographic limitations: Giving primarily in CA.
Application information: Applications not accepted. Unsolicited requests for funds not accepted.
Officers: Howard Lester, Pres. and C.E.O.; Sharon McCollan, Exec. V.P., Treas., and C.F.O.; Seth Jaffe, Secy.
Director: Pat Connolly.
EIN: 203424952

4081
Willkie Farr & Gallagher LLP

The Equitable Ctr.
787 7th Ave.
New York, NY 10019-6099 (212) 728-8000

Company URL: http://www.willkie.com/home.aspx
Establishment information: Established in 1888.
Company type: Private company
Business activities: Operates law firm.
Business type (SIC): Legal services
Offices: Washington, DC; New York, NY
International operations: Belgium; France; Germany; Italy; United Kingdom
Giving statement: Giving through the Willkie Farr & Gallagher LLP Pro Bono Program.

Willkie Farr & Gallagher LLP Pro Bono Program

The Equitable Ctr.
787 7th Ave.
New York, NY 10019-6099 (212) 728-8621
E-mail: sparadise@willkie.com; Additional tel.: (212) 728-8000; URL: http://www.willkie.com/recruiting/recruiting_page.aspx?iOffice_ID=323140605&iPage_ID=325531005

Contact: Stacey E. Paradise, Director of Attorney Training & Pro Bono
Fields of interest: Legal services.
Type of support: Pro bono services - legal.
Application information: A Pro Bono Committee manages the pro bono program.

4082
Willow Springs Enterprises

5591 Willow Wood Dr.
Morrison, CO 80465-2169

Establishment information: Established in 1972.
Company type: Private company
Business activities: Builds houses.
Business type (SIC): Contractors/general residential building
Giving statement: Giving through the Spurgeon Memorial Foundation.

Spurgeon Memorial Foundation

5591 Willow Wood Dr.
Morrison, CO 80465-2291

Establishment information: Established in 1998.
Donors: Willow Springs Enterprises; Vance Harwood; Stanley A. Harwood.
Financial data (yr. ended 12/31/11): Assets, $131,308 (M); expenditures, $12,515; qualifying distributions, $11,500; giving activities include $11,500 for 15 grants (high: $1,200; low: $240).
Purpose and activities: The foundation supports Christian agencies and churches.
Fields of interest: Theological school/education; Human services; Christian agencies & churches.
Type of support: General/operating support.
Geographic limitations: Giving primarily in CO.
Support limitations: No grants to individuals.
Application information: Applications not accepted. Contributes only to pre-selected organizations.
Officers: Stanley A. Harwood, Pres.; Rodene L. Harwood, V.P.
Directors: Shawn Harwood; Vance R. Harwood.
EIN: 846021017

4083
Wilson Sonsini Goodrich & Rosati

650 Page Mill Rd.
Palo Alto, CA 94304-1050 (650) 493-9300

Company URL: http://www.wsgr.com/WSGR/index.aspx
Company type: Private company
Business activities: Operates law firm.
Business type (SIC): Legal services
Corporate officer: Sunil Bhardwaj, Sr. V.P.
Offices: Palo Alto, San Diego, San Francisco, CA; Georgetown, DE; Washington, DC; New York, NY; Austin, TX; Seattle, WA
International operations: Belgium; China; Hong Kong
Giving statement: Giving through the Wilson Sonsini Goodrich & Rosati Pro Bono Program.

Wilson Sonsini Goodrich & Rosati Pro Bono Program

650 Page Mill Rd.
Palo Alto, CA 94304-1050 (650) 493-9300
E-mail: probono@wsgr.com; URL: http://www.wsgr.com/WSGR/Display.aspx?SectionName=probono

Contact: Mark G. Parnes, Assistant General Counsel
Fields of interest: Legal services.
Type of support: Pro bono services - legal.
Application information: A Pro Bono Committee manages the pro bono program.

4084
Wilsonart International, Inc.

(formerly Ralph Wilson Plastics Co.)
2400 Wilson Pl.
P.O. Box 6110
Temple, TX 76503-6110 (254) 207-7000

Company URL: http://www.wilsonart.com
Establishment information: Established in 1956.
Company type: Subsidiary of a public company
Business activities: Manufactures countertops and decorative laminates.
Business type (SIC): Plastic products/miscellaneous
Corporate officers: Bill DiGaetano, Pres.; Susan Simpson, C.F.O.; Tim Atkinson, V.P., Sales
Giving statement: Giving through the Ralph Wilson Plastics Employees Scholarship Fund and the Ralph Wilson Plastics Scholarship Fund, Inc.

Ralph Wilson Plastics Employees Scholarship Fund

600 General Bruce Dr.
Temple, TX 76504-2402 (254) 774-5832
Application address: P.O. Box 625, Temple, TX 76503-0625, tel.: (254) 774-5832

Establishment information: Established in 1966 in TX.
Donor: Ralph Wilson Plastics Co.
Financial data (yr. ended 06/30/12): Assets, $1,163,426 (M); gifts received, $500; expenditures, $69,272; qualifying distributions, $58,500; giving activities include $58,500 for grants to individuals.
Purpose and activities: The foundation awards college scholarships to children of employees of WI-Temple.
Fields of interest: Higher education.
Type of support: Employee-related scholarships.
Geographic limitations: Giving limited to Temple, TX.
Application information: Applications accepted. Application form required.
Initial approach: Proposal
Deadline(s): Apr. 13
Officers: Brenda White, Pres.; Eric Worley, V.P.; Charlene Harvey, Secy.; Dale Arnett, Treas.
Board Members: Peter Barajas; Donna Stone; Laurie Steger.
EIN: 746245026

Ralph Wilson Plastics Scholarship Fund, Inc.

P.O. Box 1118
Fletcher, NC 28732-1118

Donors: Ralph Wilson Plastics Co.; Service America Corp.
Financial data (yr. ended 12/31/11): Assets, $691,844 (M); expenditures, $41,091; qualifying distributions, $30,000; giving activities include $30,000 for grants.
Purpose and activities: The foundation awards college scholarships to dependents of employees of Ralph Wilson Plastics' WilsonArt-Fletcher plant in North Carolina.
Fields of interest: Higher education.
Type of support: Employee-related scholarships.
Geographic limitations: Giving limited to NC.
Application information: Applications not accepted. Unsolicited requests for funds not accepted.
Officers: Dennis Clark, Pres.; Wanda McFadden, V.P.; Fran Patton, Secy.; David Whiteside, Treas.
EIN: 581576914

4085
A. Wimpfheimer & Bro., Inc.

(doing business as American Velvet Company)
22 Bayview Ave.
Stonington, CT 06378-1148
(860) 535-1050

Company URL: http://www.wimpvel.com
Establishment information: Established in 1845.
Company type: Private company
Business activities: Manufactures velvet.
Business type (SIC): Fabrics/broadwoven synthetic and silk
Corporate officer: Fred Leigsky, Pres.
Giving statement: Giving through the Wimpfheimer Foundation, Inc.

The Wimpfheimer Foundation, Inc.

P.O. Box 472
Stonington, CT 06378-1148

Establishment information: Established in 1949 in CT.
Donors: A. Wimpfheimer & Bro., Inc.; Jacques D. Wimpfheimer.
Financial data (yr. ended 12/31/11): Assets, $881,023 (M); expenditures, $48,309; qualifying distributions, $45,000; giving activities include $45,000 for grants.
Purpose and activities: The foundation supports libraries and organizations involved with K-12 education, spine disorders research, hunger, fire safety, equestrianism, youth development, and community development.
Fields of interest: Education; Youth development; Community/economic development.
Type of support: General/operating support.
Geographic limitations: Giving primarily in CT and FL.
Support limitations: No grants to individuals.
Application information: Applications not accepted. Unsolicited requests for funds not accepted.
Officers: James Wimpfheimer, Pres.; Fred Liskey, V.P.
Directors: Susan Barber; Donald Wimpfheimer.
EIN: 066036353

4086
Windway Capital Corporation

630 Riverfront Dr., Ste. 200
Sheboygan, WI 53081-4629
(920) 457-8600

Company URL: http://www.windway.com
Establishment information: Established in 1988.
Company type: Private company
Business activities: Operates holding company; manufactures sails; manufactures food service products.
Business type (SIC): Fabricated textile products/ miscellaneous; cutlery, hand and edge tools, and hardware; holding company
Corporate officers: Terry J. Kohler, Pres. and C.E.O.; Eric Zufel, Genl. Counsel
Subsidiaries: Composite Rigging, North Kingstown, RI; Edgewater Power Boats LLC, Edgewater, FL; North Sails, Milford, CT; The Vollrath Co., Sheboygan, WI
Giving statement: Giving through the Windway Foundation, Inc.

Windway Foundation, Inc.

P.O. Box 897
Sheboygan, WI 53081 (920) 457-8600
Application address: c/o Windway Capital, 630 Riverfront Dr., Ste. 200, Sheboygan, WI 53081

Donors: The Vollrath Co., LLC; Windway Capital Corp.
Contact: Terry Kohler, Pres.
Financial data (yr. ended 09/30/11): Assets, $65,615 (M); gifts received, $180,000; expenditures, $157,189; qualifying distributions, $157,189; giving activities include $156,100 for 31 grants (high: $25,000; low: $500).
Purpose and activities: The foundation supports organizations involved with arts and culture, education, human services, civil rights, and civic affairs.
Fields of interest: Arts; Higher education; Education; Youth, services; Human services; Civil/ human rights; Public affairs.
Type of support: Equipment; In-kind gifts; Program development; Research; Scholarship funds.
Geographic limitations: Giving primarily in areas of company operations.
Support limitations: No grants to individuals.
Application information: Applications accepted. Application form required. Applicants should submit the following:
1) copy of IRS Determination Letter
Initial approach: Letter of inquiry
Deadline(s): None
Officers and Directors:* Terry J. Kohler*, Pres.; Mary S. Kohler*, V.P.; Mary Ten Tenhaken*, Secy.; Roland M. Neumann, Jr.*, Treas.
EIN: 396046987

4087
Winn-Dixie Stores, Inc.

5050 Edgewood Ct.
Jacksonville, FL 32254-3699
(904) 783-5000
FAX: (904) 783-5235

Company URL: http://www.winndixiegrocerystores.com/
Establishment information: Established in 1925.
Company type: Public company
Company ticker symbol and exchange: WINN/ NASDAQ
Business activities: Operates grocery stores.
Business type (SIC): Groceries—retail; groceries—wholesale
Financial profile for 2011: Number of employees, 47,000; assets, $1,799,790,000; sales volume, $6,880,780,000; pre-tax net income, -$33,020,000; expenses, $6,908,580,000; liabilities, $936,280,000
Corporate officers: Peter L. Lynch, Chair., Pres., and C.E.O.; Maura Hart, C.I.O.; Bennett L. Nussbaum, Sr. V.P. and C.F.O.; Timothy Williams, Sr. V.P., Genl. Counsel, and Corp. Secy.; Larry B. Appel, Sr. V.P., Opers.; Anita Dahlstrom-Gutel, Sr. V.P., Human Resources.
Board of directors: Peter L. Lynch, Chair.; Evelyn V. Follit; Charles P. Garcia; Jeffrey C. Girard; Yvonne R. Jackson; Gregory P. Josefowicz; James P. Olson; Terry Peets; Richard E. Rivera
Plants: Montgomery, AL; Orlando, Pompano Beach, Tampa, FL; Atlanta, GA; Louisville, KY; Charlotte, Raleigh, NC; Fort Worth, TX
Giving statement: Giving through the Winn-Dixie Stores, Inc. Corporate Giving Program and the Winn-Dixie Stores Foundation.
Company EIN: 590514290

Winn-Dixie Stores, Inc. Corporate Giving Program

5050 Edgewood Ct.
Jacksonville, FL 32254-3699 (904) 783-5000
URL: http://www.winndixie.com/Community/ Community.asp

Purpose and activities: As a complement to its foundation, Winn-Dixie also makes charitable contributions of gift cards to nonprofit organizations directly. Support is limited to areas of company operations in Alabama, Florida, Georgia, Louisiana, and Mississippi.
Fields of interest: Food banks; Housing/shelter; Athletics/sports, school programs; General charitable giving.
Type of support: Cause-related marketing; In-kind gifts; Sponsorships.
Geographic limitations: Giving limited to areas of company operations in AL, FL, GA, LA, and MS.
Application information: Applications accepted. Application form required. Applicants should submit the following:
1) population served
2) name, address and phone number of organization
3) geographic area to be served
4) contact person
5) plans for acknowledgement
Sponsorship applications should specifically note the nature of the request being made; the name, date, expected attendance, and a description of the event; and the employee referral name, if applicable.
Initial approach: Contact local Winn-Dixie store director for gift card donations; complete online application form for sponsorships
Deadline(s): Feb. 1 for sponsorships

Winn-Dixie Stores Foundation

5050 Edgewood Ct.
Jacksonville, FL 32254-3601 (904) 783-5000
URL: https://www.winndixie.com/CO/Community%20Events/Default.aspx

Establishment information: Incorporated in 1943 in FL.
Donors: PGA Tour Charities, Inc.; Winn-Dixie Stores, Inc.
Contact: Beth Goldberg, Secy.
Financial data (yr. ended 12/31/11): Assets, $1,284,943 (M); gifts received, $1,248,810; expenditures, $1,105,104; qualifying distributions, $1,097,186; giving activities include $1,097,186 for grants.
Purpose and activities: The foundation supports organizations involved with education, health, hunger, and women.
Fields of interest: Elementary school/education; Higher education; Education; Hospitals (general); Health care, clinics/centers; Health care; Cancer; Food services; Food banks Women.
Program:
Employee Matching Gifts: The foundation matches contributions made by employees, directors, and retirees of Winn-Dixie to educational institutions and hospitals and nonprofit organizations involved with human services on a one-for-one basis from $50 to $2,500 per contributor, per institution, per year up to $10,000 per contributor, per year.
Type of support: Annual campaigns; Building/ renovation; Conferences/seminars; Continuing support; Employee matching gifts; Equipment; Matching/challenge support; Program development; Research; Scholarship funds.
Geographic limitations: Giving primarily in areas of company operations in AL, FL, GA, LA, and MS.

Support limitations: No support for religious or political organizations or schools. No grants to individuals, or for capital campaigns, general operating support, multi-year commitments, capital campaigns, fundraising, or sponsorships.
Publications: Application guidelines; Grants list.
Application information: Applications accepted. Proposals should be no longer than 6 pages. Organizations receiving support are asked to provide a final report. Application form required. Applicants should submit the following:
1) how project will be sustained once grantmaker support is completed
2) results expected from proposed grant
3) statement of problem project will address
4) population served
5) copy of IRS Determination Letter
6) brief history of organization and description of its mission
7) geographic area to be served
8) how project's results will be evaluated or measured
9) listing of board of directors, trustees, officers and other key people and their affiliations
10) detailed description of project and amount of funding requested
11) plans for acknowledgement
Initial approach: Download application form and mail proposal and application form to foundation
Copies of proposal: 3
Board meeting date(s): As required
Deadline(s): July 31
Officers and Directors:* Mary Kellmanson*, Pres.; Chris Vukich*, V.P.; Beth Golderg, Secy.; D. Michael Byrum*, Treas.
EIN: 590995428

4088
Winnebago Industries, Inc.
605 W. Crystal Lake Rd.
P.O. Box 152
Forest City, IA 50436 (641) 585-3535
FAX: (641) 585-6966

Company URL: http://www.winnebagoind.com
Establishment information: Established in 1958.
Company type: Public company
Company ticker symbol and exchange: WGO/NYSE
Business activities: Manufactures motor homes.
Business type (SIC): Motor vehicles and equipment
Financial profile for 2012: Number of employees, 2,380; assets, $286,070,000; sales volume, $581,680,000; pre-tax net income, $10,110,000; expenses, $572,150,000; liabilities, $141,380,000
Corporate officers: Randy J. Potts, Chair., Pres., and C.E.O.; Sarah N. Nielsen, V.P. and C.F.O.; Scott C. Folkers, V.P., Genl. Counsel, and Secy.; Robert L. Gossett, V.P., Admin.; Scott S. Degnan, V.P., Sales
Board of directors: Randy J. Potts, Chair.; Irvin E. Aal; Robert M. Chiusano; Jerry N. Currie; Lawrence A. Erickson; Robert J. Olson; Martha Tomson Rodamaker; Mark Schroepfer
Giving statement: Giving through the Winnebago Industries Foundation.
Company EIN: 420802678

Winnebago Industries Foundation
P.O. Box 152
Forest City, IA 50436-0152

Establishment information: Established in 1972 in IA.
Donor: Winnebago Industries, Inc.
Contact: Kathy Bonjour
Financial data (yr. ended 02/28/12): Assets, $2,035,285 (M); expenditures, $105,212; qualifying distributions, $95,083; giving activities include $95,083 for 43 grants (high: $15,000; low: $100).
Purpose and activities: The foundation supports health centers and day care centers and organizations involved with education, animals and wildlife, sports, and community development.
Fields of interest: Education; Recreation; Human services.
Type of support: Annual campaigns; Building/renovation; Equipment; General/operating support; Matching/challenge support; Scholarship funds; Sponsorships.
Geographic limitations: Giving primarily in areas of company operations in IA.
Application information: Applications accepted. Application form required.
Initial approach: Letter
Copies of proposal: 1
Deadline(s): None
Trustees: Raymond M. Beebe; Randy Potts; William J. O'Leary; Robert J. Olson.
EIN: 237174206

4089
Winston & Strawn LLP
35 W. Wacker Dr.
Chicago, IL 60601-9703 (312) 558-5600

Company URL: http://www.winston.com
Establishment information: Established in 1853.
Company type: Private company
Business activities: Provides legal services.
Business type (SIC): Legal services
Corporate officers: Dan Web, Chair.; David S. McDonald, C.F.O.
Board of director: Dan Webb, Chair.
Offices: Los Angeles, San Francisco, CA; Washington, DC; Chicago, IL; Newark, NJ; New York, NY; Charlotte, NC; Houston, TX
International operations: China; France; Hong Kong; Soviet Union (Former); Swaziland; United Kingdom
Giving statement: Giving through the Winston & Strawn LLP Pro Bono Program and the Winston & Strawn Foundation.

Winston & Strawn LLP Pro Bono Program
35 W. Wacker Dr.
Chicago, IL 60601-9703 (312) 558-8068
E-mail: gmcconnell@winston.com; Additional tel.: (312) 558-5600; URL: http://www.winston.com/index.cfm?contentID=5

Contact: Greg McConnell, Pro Bono Counsel
Fields of interest: Legal services.
Type of support: Pro bono services - legal.
Application information: A Pro Bono Committee manages the pro bono program.

Winston & Strawn Foundation
35 W. Wacker Dr.
Chicago, IL 60601-9703 (312) 558-5636
FAX: (312) 558-5700; URL: http://www.winston.com/index.cfm?contentid=184&itemid=309&displaymore=1

Establishment information: Established in 1990 in IL.
Financial data (yr. ended 01/31/12): Revenue, $75,588; assets, $2,383,542 (M); expenditures, $175,549; giving activities include $158,353 for grants.
Purpose and activities: The foundation provides support to a wide variety of organizations, with specific interests in education, arts, social welfare, and law-related issues.
Fields of interest: Arts; Education; Legal services.
Type of support: Employee matching gifts.
Geographic limitations: Giving primarily in Washington, DC, IL, and NY.
Application information:
Board meeting date(s): Monthly
Officers and Directors:* Susan Benton-Powers*, Chair.; James M. Neis*, Pres.; Wayne D. Boberg, V.P.; Samuel Mendenhall, Secy.-Treas.; Zoe Ashcroft; Thomas M. Buchanan; Jonathan Goldstein; David A. Honig; Lee T. Paterson; Kurt L. Schultz; James R. Thompson.
Number of staff: 1 part-time professional.
EIN: 363685819

4090
The Winter Construction Company
(also known as The Winter Group of Companies)
191 Peachtree St, N.E. , Ste. 2100
Atlanta, GA 30303 (404) 588-3300

Company URL: http://www.wintercompanies.com
Establishment information: Established in 1978.
Company type: Private company
Business activities: Provides general contract construction services.
Business type (SIC): Contractors/general residential building; contractors/general nonresidential building
Corporate officers: Robert L. Silverman, Chair. and Pres.; Ralph Mumme, Exec. V.P. and C.F.O.; Brandi Coggia, V.P. and Cont.
Board of director: Robert L. Silverman, Chair.
Giving statement: Giving through the Winter Group of Companies Contributions Program.

The Winter Group of Companies Contributions Program
191 Peachtree St., NE
Ste. 2100
Atlanta, GA 30303-1770 (404) 588-3300
URL: http://www.wintercompanies.com/giving-back.html

Purpose and activities: Winter makes charitable contributions to nonprofit organizations. Support is given primarily to Special Olympics Georgia in Georgia.
Fields of interest: Athletics/sports, golf; Athletics/sports, Special Olympics.
Type of support: Employee volunteer services; Sponsorships.
Geographic limitations: Giving primarily in GA.

4091
Wipfli LLP
11 Scott St.
Wausau, WI 54403 (715) 845-3111

Company URL: http://www.wipfli.com
Establishment information: Established in 1930.
Company type: Private company

Business activities: Provides accounting and business consulting services.
Business type (SIC): Accounting, auditing, and bookkeeping services
Corporate officers: Dale Muehl, C.O.O.; Mark Faanes, C.F.O.; Mark Baker, C.I.O.
Giving statement: Giving through the Wipfli Foundation, Inc.

Wipfli Foundation, Inc.

P.O. Box 8010
Wausau, WI 54402-8010 (715) 845-3111
Application address: 11 Scott St., Wausau, WI 54403, tel.: (715) 845-3111

Establishment information: Established in 2005 in WI.
Donor: Wipfli, LLP.
Contact: Kathy Labrake, Pres.
Financial data (yr. ended 05/31/12): Assets, $591,889 (M); gifts received, $122,100; expenditures, $125,638; qualifying distributions, $122,050; giving activities include $122,050 for grants.
Fields of interest: Education.
Support limitations: No grants for individuals.
Application information: Applications accepted. Application form required. Applicants should submit the following:
1) descriptive literature about organization
2) detailed description of project and amount of funding requested
Initial approach: Proposal
Deadline(s): None
Officers and Directors:* Kathy Labrake*, Pres.; Kenneth Krueger*, V.P.; Lauri Roberts*, Secy.-Treas.
EIN: 202901635

4092
Wisconsin Centrifugal

905 E. St. Paul Ave.
Waukesha, WI 53188-3804 (262) 544-7700

Company URL: http://www.metaltek.com/
Establishment information: Established in 1945.
Company type: Subsidiary of a private company
Business activities: Operates copper foundries, blast furnaces, and steel mills; manufactures non-ferrous die castings, fabricated plate-work, bronze bushings, bearings, rings and gear blanks, stainless steel, monel and high temperature alloy rings, and vacuum melted centrifugally cast parts.
Business type (SIC): Metal foundries/nonferrous
Corporate officers: Andrew Cope, Chair.; Robert J. Smickley, C.E.O.; Rick Danning, Treas. and C.F.O.; Robert Johnston, Secy.
Board of directors: Andrew Cope, Chair.; Rick Danning; Robert Johnston; Robert J. Smickley
Giving statement: Giving through the Wisconsin Centrifugal Charitable Foundation Inc.

Wisconsin Centrifugal Charitable Foundation Inc.

905 E. St. Paul Ave.
Waukesha, WI 53188-3898

Establishment information: Established in 1987 in WI.
Donors: Wisconsin Centrifugal; Metaltek International Inc.
Financial data (yr. ended 06/30/12): Assets, $7,011 (M); gifts received, $86,000; expenditures, $79,076; qualifying distributions, $78,234; giving activities include $78,234 for 2 grants (high: $74,901; low: $3,333).
Purpose and activities: The foundation supports clinics and organizations involved with education, dental care, hunger, and Christianity.
Fields of interest: Education; Health care; Human services.
Type of support: Endowments; General/operating support; Scholarship funds.
Geographic limitations: Giving limited to Waukesha and Watertown, WI.
Support limitations: No grants to individuals.
Application information: Applications not accepted. Unsolicited requests for funds not accepted.
Officer: Robert J. Smickley, Pres.
EIN: 391591534

4093
Wisconsin Energy Corporation

231 W. Michigan St.
P.O. Box 1331
Milwaukee, WI 53201 (414) 221-2345
FAX: (414) 221-2008

Company URL: http://www.wisconsinenergy.com
Establishment information: Established in 1987.
Company type: Public company
Company ticker symbol and exchange: WEC/NYSE
International Securities Identification Number: US9766571064
Business activities: Operates holding company; generates, transmits, and distributes electricity; transmits and distributes natural gas; produces and distributes steam.
Business type (SIC): Holding company; electric services; gas production and distribution; combination utility services; real estate subdividers and developers
Financial profile for 2012: Number of employees, 4,504; assets, $14,285,000,000; sales volume, $4,246,400,000; pre-tax net income, $852,600,000; expenses, $3,426,100,000; liabilities, $10,119,500,000
Fortune 1000 ranking: 2012—557th in revenues, 317th in profits, and 306th in assets
Forbes 2000 ranking: 2012—1489th in sales, 997th in profits, and 1218th in assets
Corporate officers: Gale E. Klappa, Chair., Pres., and C.E.O.; Susan H. Martin, Exec. V.P., Genl. Counsel, and Secy.; J. Patrick Keyes, Exec. V.P. and C.F.O; Scott J. Lauber, V.P. and Treas.; Stephen P. Dickson, V.P. and Cont.
Board of directors: Gale E. Klappa, Chair.; John F. Bergstrom; Barbara L. Bowles; Patricia W. Chadwick; Curt S. Culver; Thomas J. Fischer; Ulice Payne, Jr.; Mary Ellen Stanek; Henry W. Knueppel
Subsidiaries: Edison Sault Electric Co., Sault Sainte Marie, MI; Minergy, L.L.C., Winneconne, WI; W.E. Power, L.L.C., Milwaukee, WI; Wisconsin Electric Power Co., Milwaukee, WI; Wisconsin Energy Capital Corp., Milwaukee, WI; Wisconsin Gas, L.L.C., Milwaukee, WI; Wispark, L.L.C., Milwaukee, WI
Giving statement: Giving through the Wisconsin Energy Corporation Foundation, Inc.
Company EIN: 391391525

Wisconsin Energy Corporation Foundation, Inc.

(formerly Wisconsin Electric System Foundation, Inc.)
231 W. Michigan St., Rm. P409A
Milwaukee, WI 53203-0001 (414) 221-2107
FAX: (414) 221-2412;
E-mail: wec.foundation@we-energies.com; E-mail for Patricia L. McNew: patti.mcnew@we-energies.com; URL: http://www.wec-foundation.com/

Establishment information: Incorporated in 1982 in WI.
Donors: State of Wisconsin Dept. of Adm.; Wisconsin Energy Corp.
Contact: Patricia L. McNew, Fdn. Admin.
Financial data (yr. ended 12/31/11): Assets, $31,343,231 (M); gifts received, $2,666,700; expenditures, $9,374,201; qualifying distributions, $9,760,541; giving activities include $9,091,869 for 1,227 grants (high: $1,666,700; low: $25) and $545,238 for loans/program-related investments.
Purpose and activities: The foundation supports organizations involved with arts and culture, economic health, education, and the environment.
Fields of interest: Museums; Performing arts; Arts; Higher education; Libraries (public); Education; Environment, natural resources; Environmental education; Environment; Employment, services; Goodwill Industries; Employment; Disasters, preparedness/services; Boys & girls clubs; YM/YWCAs & YM/YWHAs; Children, services; Human services; Economic development; Business/industry; Community/economic development; United Ways and Federated Giving Programs.
Programs:
Arts: The foundation supports programs designed to expand and increase accessibility to the arts through outreach; and promote creative expression in children through educational activities.
Economic Health: The foundation supports programs designed to stimulate economic growth and development of communities located in areas of Wisconsin Energy operations. Special emphasis is directed toward programs designed to strengthen the regions economic base; encourage and retain world-class businesses and talent; and create high-value employment and a sustainable quality of life.
Education: The foundation supports educational systems designed to educate and empower students to embrace opportunity, achieve future success, and become contributing members of the workforce.
Employee Matching Gifts: The foundation matches contributions made by employees and retirees of Wisconsin Energy to educational institutions and nonprofit organizations involved with arts and culture on a one-for-one basis from $25 to $20,000 per contributor, per year.
Environment: The foundation supports programs designed to promote environmental education, resource preservation, and conservation, which will guide communities toward an environmentally responsible future.
Type of support: Capital campaigns; Employee matching gifts; Endowments; Equipment; General/operating support; In-kind gifts; Program development; Scholarship funds; Sponsorships.
Geographic limitations: Giving limited to areas of company operations in the Upper Peninsula, MI, area and WI.
Support limitations: No support for political action or legislative advocacy organizations or veterans' or fraternal organizations. No grants to individuals, or for trips, tours, pageants, team or extra-curricular school events, or student exchange programs, programs whose primary purpose is the promotion of religious doctrine or tenets, or programs whose purpose is solely athletic in nature; no renewable energy projects.
Publications: Application guidelines; Program policy statement.
Application information: Applications accepted. Additional information may be requested at a later date. Requests by telephone are not accepted. A

site visit may be requested. Application form required. Applicants should submit the following:
1) statement of problem project will address
2) copy of IRS Determination Letter
3) brief history of organization and description of its mission
4) copy of most recent annual report/audited financial statement/990
5) listing of board of directors, trustees, officers and other key people and their affiliations
6) detailed description of project and amount of funding requested
7) copy of current year's organizational budget and/ or project budget
8) listing of additional sources and amount of support
9) plans for acknowledgement

Initial approach: Complete online application form
Board meeting date(s): Quarterly
Deadline(s): Jan. 31, Apr. 30, July 31, and Oct. 31
Final notification: 90 days

Officers and Directors:* Gale E. Klappa*, Pres.; Kristine A. Rappe*, V.P.; Keith H. Ecke, Secy.; Jeffrey P. West, Treas.; Kevin Fletcher; Frederick D. Kuester; Allen L. Leverett; Thelma A. Sias.
EIN: 391433726
Selected grants: The following grants are a representative sample of this grantmaker's funding activity:
$1,666,700 to Marquette University, Milwaukee, WI, 2011. For State of Wisconsin 'Study of Engineering Grant'.
$1,000,000 to UWM Real Estate Foundation, Milwaukee, WI, 2011. For UWM Innovation Park Contribution.
$500,000 to United Performing Arts Fund, Milwaukee, WI, 2011. For Contribution to UPAF.
$270,546 to Scholarship America, Saint Peter, MN, 2011. For WEC Daughters and Sons Scholarship Awards.
$253,806 to United Way of Greater Milwaukee, Milwaukee, WI, 2011. For United Way campaign year.
$25,000 to Saint Joan Antida High School Foundation, Milwaukee, WI, 2011. For Four Year Engineering Program.
$6,350 to United Way of Dickinson County, Iron Mountain, MI, 2011. For United Way Contribution.
$5,000 to Waukesha County Economic Development Corporation, Pewaukee, WI, 2011. For President's Challenge, Legacy Strategic Sponsor.
$3,100 to Pius XI High School, Milwaukee, WI, 2011.
$3,000 to Metropolitan Opera, Lincoln Center, New York, NY, 2011.

4094
Wisconsin Physicians Service Insurance Corporation

(also known as WPS Health Insurance)
1717 W. Broadway
P.O. Box 8190
Madison, WI 53708-8190 (608) 221-4711
FAX: (608) 223-3626

Company URL: http://www.wpsic.com
Establishment information: Established in 1946.
Company type: Private company
Business activities: Operates medical service plan.
Business type (SIC): Insurance/accident and health
Financial profile for 2012: Number of employees, 4,000
Corporate officers: Michael Hamerlik, Pres. and C.E.O.; Tom Nelson, C.F.O.; David L. Vogel, Secy.
Subsidiaries: Administrative & Technical Services, Inc., Madison, WI; The EPIC Life Insurance Co., Madison, WI
Offices: Appleton, Eau Claire, Green Bay, Milwaukee, Wausau, WI
Giving statement: Giving through the WPS Charitable Foundation Inc.

WPS Charitable Foundation Inc.

(formerly Ray Koenig Charitable Foundation of WPS Inc.)
1717 W. Broadway
Monona, WI 53713-1834 (608) 221-5117
E-mail: kim.olsen@wpsic.com; Application address: P.O. Box 7786, Madison, WI 53707-7786

Establishment information: Established in WI.
Donors: Wisconsin Physicians Service Insurance Corp.; The Epic Life Insurance Company.
Contact: William C. Beisenstein, Secy.-Treas.
Financial data (yr. ended 12/31/11): Assets, $1,188,360 (M); gifts received, $290,970; expenditures, $51,725; qualifying distributions, $49,642; giving activities include $47,350 for 41 grants (high: $5,000; low: $500).
Purpose and activities: The foundation supports organizations involved with education, youth, business, and minorities.
Fields of interest: Higher education; Education; Youth, services; Business/industry Minorities.
Type of support: Employee-related scholarships; General/operating support; Scholarship funds.
Geographic limitations: Giving primarily in Madison, WI.
Application information: Applications accepted. Application form required.

Initial approach: Proposal
Deadline(s): None

Officers and Trustees:* James R. Riordan*, Chair.; Eugene J. Nordby, M.D.*, Pres.; William C. Beisenstein*, Secy.-Treas.; Martin V. Timmins, V.P.
EIN: 391568111

4095
Wisconsin Power and Light Company

4902 N. Biltmore Ln., Ste. 1000
Madison, WI 53718 (608) 458-3311

Company URL: https://www.alliantenergy.com
Establishment information: Established in 1924.
Company type: Subsidiary of a public company
Business activities: Generates, transmits, and distributes electricity; transmits and distributes natural gas; distributes water.
Business type (SIC): Combination utility services
Corporate officers: Patricia L. Kampling, Chair., Pres., and C.E.O.; Thomas L. Hanson, V.P., C.F.O., and Treas.; Robert J. Durian, C.A.O. and Cont.; Peggy Howard Moore, V.P., Finance; Dean E. Ekstrom, V.P., Sales
Board of directors: Patricia L. Kampling, Chair., Pres., and C.E.O.; Patrick E. Allen; Michael L. Bennett; Darryl B. Hazel; Singleton B. McAllister; Ann K. Newhall; Dean C. Oestreich; David A. Perdue, Jr.; Judith D. Pyle; Carol P. Sanders
Subsidiary: South Beloit Water, Gas & Electric Co., South Beloit, IL
Giving statement: Giving through the Riverland Conservancy, Inc.

Riverland Conservancy, Inc.

(formerly Wisconsin Power and Light Land Stewardship Trust, Inc.)
P.O. Box 95
Sauk City, WI 53583
E-mail: riverlandconservancy@alliantenergy.com; URL: http://www.riverlandconservancy.org/ Index.html

Establishment information: Classified as a company-sponsored operating foundation in 1998.
Donors: Wisconsin Power and Light Co.; Interstate Power and Light Co.; Alliant Energy Corp.; U.S. Dept. of Agriculture; Wisconsin Dept. of Natural Resources.
Financial data (yr. ended 12/31/11): Assets, $5,811,762 (M); gifts received, $3,250; expenditures, $165,699; qualifying distributions, $156,711; giving activities include $3,090 for 3 grants (high: $2,500; low: $290).
Purpose and activities: The foundation supports organizations involved with photography and the environment and manages and maintains Lansing Preserve, Iowa, and Merrimac Preserve, Wisconsin.
Fields of interest: Human services.
Type of support: General/operating support; Scholarship funds.
Application information: Applications not accepted. Contributes only to pre-selected organizations.
Officers: Tom Hanson, Pres.; Linda Lynch, Secy.; Kathy Lipp, Treas.
Directors: Tom Aller; Bob Bartlett; Joyce Hanes; Barb Swan; Randy Zogarum.
EIN: 391914563

4096
Wisconsin Public Service Corporation

700 N. Adams St.
P.O. Box 19003
Green Bay, WI 54307-9003 (800) 450-7280

Company URL: http://www.wisconsinpublicservice.com
Establishment information: Established in 1883.
Company type: Subsidiary of a public company
Company ticker symbol and exchange: WIPSO/OTC
Business activities: Generates, transmits, and distributes electricity; transmits and distributes natural gas.
Business type (SIC): Electric services; gas production and distribution
Financial profile for 2012: Assets, $3,521,900,000; sales volume, $1,499,200,000; pre-tax net income, $197,400,000; expenses, $1,275,000,000; liabilities, $2,349,200,000
Corporate officers: Lawrence T. Borgard, Chair. and C.E.O.; Charles A. Cloninger, Pres.; Joseph P. O'Leary, Sr. V.P. and C.F.O.; Diane L. Ford, V.P. and Corp. Cont.; Barth J. Wolf, Secy.; William J. Guc, Treas.
Board of director: Lawrence T. Borgard, Chair.
Subsidiary: WPS Leasing, Inc., Green Bay, WI
Giving statement: Giving through the Wisconsin Public Service Foundation, Inc.

Wisconsin Public Service Foundation, Inc.

(formerly WPS Foundation, Inc.)
700 N. Adams St.
P.O. Box 19001
Green Bay, WI 54307-9001 (920) 433-1433
E-mail: kmlemke@wisconsinpublicservice.com;
URL: http://www.wisconsinpublicservice.com/company/foundation.aspx

Establishment information: Incorporated in 1964 in WI.
Donor: Wisconsin Public Service Corp.
Contact: Karmen Lemke, Mgr., Community Rels.
Financial data (yr. ended 12/31/11): Assets, $20,438,327 (M); gifts received, $500,000; expenditures, $1,080,142; qualifying distributions, $1,057,490; giving activities include $1,057,490 for grants.
Purpose and activities: The foundation supports programs designed to promote arts and culture; education; the environment; human services and health; community and neighborhood; and awards college scholarships.
Fields of interest: Arts, cultural/ethnic awareness; Museums; Performing arts; Arts; Vocational education; Higher education; Business school/education; Engineering school/education; Adult/continuing education; Education; Environment, natural resources; Environment, energy; Environment, forests; Environment; Animals/wildlife; Hospitals (general); Health care; Mental health/crisis services; Employment; Agriculture; Youth development, adult & child programs; Aging, centers/services; Developmentally disabled, centers & services; Human services; Community/economic development Minorities; Women.
Programs:

Adult Student Technical College Scholarship Program: Non-renewable scholarships of $250 to $500 will be awarded to adults who are entering or returning to school after a number of years in the workforce. Applicants must be accepted into a two-year associate degree program at Fox Valley Technical College, Lakeshore Technical College, Northcental Technical College, Nicolet Technical College, Mid-Sate Technical College, or Northeast Wisconsin Technical College.

Agribusiness/Forestry Scholarship: Awards scholarships to children of employees of WPS or children of a customer with a primary residence in WPS territory to attend select universities or technical colleges. The program is designed to help young people develop skills, leadership, and technical knowledge to meet the challenges of forestry, farming, and farm-related activities. Recipients are awarded $500 for a two-year technical college and $1,000 for a four-year college.

Arts and Culture: The foundation supports arts and culture organizations with broad exposure, including theater, dance, music, drama, and museums; and programs designed to promote diversity, and make the arts accessible to all people.

Business and Technology Scholarships: Awards $1,500 renewable college scholarships to women and minorities majoring in the area of business or engineering, including electrical, mechanical, civil, industrial, chemical, computer, or environmental engineering. Applicants must be a full-time junior or senior in college; attend a four-year institution in Illinois, Indiana, Iowa, Michigan, Minnesota, or Wisconsin; and have a GPA of 2.8.

College Scholarship: College scholarships of up to $1,500 per year for four years to high school seniors who are children of WPS employees or children of a customer with a primary residence in WPS territory. Applicants must be in the upper 10 percent of his or graduation class and plan to attend a college or university listed in the latest edition of the "Higher Education Directory".

Community & Neighborhood Development: The foundation supports programs designed to promote community improvement and well-being, including downtown revitalization and economic growth.

Dollars for Doers: The foundation awards grants of up to $100 to nonprofit organizations with which employees of Wisconsin Public Service volunteers at least 20 hours.

Education: The foundation supports programs designed to enhance Wisconsin Public Services' educational initiatives, including opportunities for minorities and women; and programs designed to demonstrate a partnership between the business and educational communities, career planning, pre-employment preparations, youth mentoring, and community service.

Environment: The foundation supports programs designed to protect and encourage the wise use of natural resources; and programs designed to promote betterment of fish and wildlife, water and air quality, forests, energy efficiency, renewable energy, and recycling.

Human Services & Health: The foundation supports programs designed to provide basic critical needs to ensure a healthy community; the United Way; social service programs designed to serve low-income, senior, and handicapped individuals; and programs designed to preserve physical and mental health, with emphasis on wellness and prevention.

Innovative Educator Grant: Grants of up to $1,000 to middle school, junior high, or high school educators or teams of educators with projects designed to improve student achievement. Special emphasis is directed toward projects in the areas of math, science, or technology. Grants may be used to purchase equipment or curriculum materials, field trips that are a supplemental learning tool to classroom curriculum, robotics programs, community gardens, engineering mentoring programs, workshops for science teachers, props for energy lessons, history of energy workshops, and marketing energy projects.

Linus M. Stoll Grant: Two grants at $1,000 each will be awarded for the academic year to high school seniors who are children of employees of WPS or children of a customer with a primary residence in WPS territory. The grants will be renewable for the second year, provided the students maintain at least a 3.0 GPA and are in good standing with their technical college. Applicants must demonstrate high academic standards, exemplary community services, and leadership in extracurricular activities while in high school. Applicant must also plan to attend Fox Valley Technical College, Lakeshore Technical College, Northcentral Technical College, Nicolet Technical College, Mid-State Technical College, or Northeast Wisconsin Technical College.

Matching Gifts: The foundation matches contributions made by employees and retirees of Wisconsin Public Service to nonprofit organizations involved with arts and culture, the environment, health and human services, and community and neighborhood development on a one-for-one basis from $50 to $2,000 per contributor, per year.

Minority and/or Female Northeast Wisconsin Technical College Grant: Awards a non-renewable $500 grants to three non-traditional minority/female students who plan to enroll in technical programs at Northeast Wisconsin Technical College. Applicants must be a high school senior or an adult returning to school. The program is limited to children of employees of WPS or children of a customer with a primary residence in WPS territory.

Paul D. Ziemer Scholarship: Annual awards of $2,000 college scholarships to children of employees of WPS or children of a customer with a primary residence in WPS territory. Applicants must be in the upper 10 percent of his or her graduation class; plan to attend the University of Wisconsin-Madison; and major in business or engineering.

Tim Howard Memorial Scholarship: One $1,000 non-renewable scholarship to a high school senior or returning adult student who is a child of a WPS employee or child of a customer with a primary residence in WPS territory. Applicant must plan to attend Northeast Wisconsin Technical College and pursue a degree in Electrical Power Distribution. The scholarship was established in honor of Tim Howard who endured fatal injuries while restoring electricity in the Wausaukee area.

UW-Marinette Grant for Returning Adults: These awards are $250 per semester for part-time students and $500 per semester for full-time students, to a maximum of $2,000 to returning adult students who demonstrate financial need, show academic promise and are planning to earn a bachelor's degree. Applicants must be 22 years of age or older when returning to college, entering as a freshman or sophomore at the University of Wisconsin - Marinette and reside in a WPS territory.

Wayne J. Peterson Memorial Scholarship: Annual awards of $2,000 college scholarships to children of employees of WPS or children of a customer with a primary residence in WPS territory. Applicants must have a GPA of 3.0; plan to attend Marquette University or St. Norbert College; and major in engineering or business.

Wisconsin Technical Grant: Awards a $500 one-year, non-renewable grant to graduating high school seniors who are children of employees of WPS or children of a customer with a primary residence in WPS territory to attend Fox Valley Technical College, Lakeshore Technical College, Northcentral Technical College, Nicolet Technical College, Mid-State Technical College, or Northeast Wisconsin Technical College.
Type of support: Annual campaigns; Building/renovation; Capital campaigns; Continuing support; Employee matching gifts; Employee volunteer services; Employee-related scholarships; Equipment; General/operating support; Program development; Research; Scholarship funds; Scholarships—to individuals.
Geographic limitations: Giving generally limited to areas of company operations in upper MI and northeastern WI.
Support limitations: No support for churches and other religious organizations, political organizations, discriminatory organizations, or public or private K-12 schools. No grants to individuals (except for scholarships), or for natural gas or electric service, moving of poles, or utility construction.
Publications: Application guidelines; Grants list; Informational brochure.
Application information: Applications accepted. Application form required. Applicants should submit the following:
1) copy of IRS Determination Letter
2) copy of most recent annual report/audited financial statement/990
3) list of company employees involved with the organization
4) explanation of why grantmaker is considered an appropriate donor for project
5) listing of board of directors, trustees, officers and other key people and their affiliations
6) detailed description of project and amount of funding requested
7) copy of current year's organizational budget and/or project budget
8) listing of additional sources and amount of support

9) plans for acknowledgement
Initial approach: Complete online application form or mail proposal to foundation
Copies of proposal: 1
Board meeting date(s): May and as required
Deadline(s): None; varies for Innovative Educator Grant; visit website for various scholarship deadlines
Final notification: 4 months; 6 weeks for Innovative Educator Grant
Officers: James F. Schott, Pres.; Charles A. Schrock, V.P.; Barth J. Wolf, Secy.; Joseph P. O'Leary, Treas.
EIN: 396075016
Selected grants: The following grants are a representative sample of this grantmaker's funding activity:
$105,000 to United Way of Brown County, Green Bay, WI, 2011.
$20,000 to Bellin College of Nursing, Green Bay, WI, 2011.
$20,000 to Bellin Foundation, Green Bay, WI, 2011.
$15,000 to American Gas Foundation, Washington, DC, 2011.
$15,000 to ASPIRO, Green Bay, WI, 2011.
$15,000 to Green Bay Botanical Garden, Green Bay, WI, 2011.
$10,000 to N.E.W. Zoological Society, Green Bay, WI, 2011.
$5,000 to Ability Building Center, Rochester, MN, 2011.
$5,000 to Iron County Historical and Museum Society, Caspian, MI, 2011.
$3,500 to United Way of Portage County, Stevens Point, WI, 2011.

4097
Wishart, Norris, Henninger & Pittman, P.A.
3120 S. Church St.
Burlington, NC 27215-9114
(336) 584-3388

Company URL: http://www.wnhplaw.com
Establishment information: Established in 1976.
Company type: Private company
Business activities: Provides legal services.
Business type (SIC): Legal services
Corporate officer: Robert B. Norris, Pres.
Giving statement: Giving through the Wishart, Norris, Henninger & Pittman Charitable Foundation Inc.

Wishart, Norris, Henninger & Pittman Charitable Foundation Inc.
3120 S. Church St.
Burlington, NC 27215-9114 (336) 584-3388
Additional address: P.O. Box 1995, Burlington, NC 27216; URL: http://www.wnhplaw.com/index.php?option=com_content&view=article&id=19&Itemid=18

Establishment information: Established as a company-sponsored operating foundation in 2001 in NC.
Donors: Wishart, Norris, Henninger & Pittman, P.A.; J. Wade Harrison.
Contact: Sharon Dent, Chair.
Financial data (yr. ended 12/31/11): Assets, $192,506 (M); gifts received, $33,706; expenditures, $40,171; qualifying distributions, $34,883; giving activities include $34,883 for 35 grants (high: $5,900; low: $300).
Purpose and activities: The foundation supports organizations involved with secondary and higher education, birth defects, breast cancer, human services, children's rights, and Christianity.
Fields of interest: Education; Health care; Religion.
Type of support: General/operating support.
Geographic limitations: Giving primarily in Burlington and Charlotte, NC.
Support limitations: No grants to individuals.
Application information: Applications accepted. Application form required.
Initial approach: Contact foundation
Deadline(s): Contact foundation
Officers: Sharon Dent, Chair.; Nathan Adams, Pres., Alamance Div.; Megan Sandler, Pres., Mecklenburg Div.
Board Members: Trey Baker; Jane Black; Kelly Caudill; Brenda Fairbrother; Herdicine Garrick; Sarah Lucente; Molly Whitlatch.
EIN: 562243215

4098
The Wittern Group
8040 University Blvd.
Des Moines, IA 50325 (515) 274-3641

Company URL: http://www.wittern.com/index.asp
Establishment information: Established in 1931.
Company type: Private company
Business activities: Manufactures vending machines.
Business type (SIC): Machinery/refrigeration and service industry
Corporate officers: Francis Arthur Wittern, Chair.; Heidi Chico, Pres.; Tony Wayne, C.F.O.
Board of director: Francis Arthur Wittern, Chair.
Giving statement: Giving through the F.A. Wittern Charitable Foundation.

F.A. Wittern Charitable Foundation
8040 University Blvd.
Des Moines, IA 50325-1118

Donors: The Wittern Group; American Machine Corp.; Modern Leasing Corp.; F. A. Wittern, Jr.; Inland Finance; 8040 Holdings, Inc.; F.A. Wittern III; John Bruntz.
Financial data (yr. ended 03/31/12): Assets, $1,500,682 (M); gifts received, $525,000; expenditures, $41,128; qualifying distributions, $35,300; giving activities include $35,300 for grants.
Purpose and activities: The foundation supports organizations involved with secondary and higher education, animals and wildlife, health, birth defects, and human services.
Fields of interest: Education; Agriculture/food.
Type of support: General/operating support.
Support limitations: No grants to individuals.
Application information: Applications not accepted. Unsolicited requests for funds not accepted.
Officers: F.A. Wittern, Jr., Pres.; F.A. Wittern III, V.P.; John Bruntz, Mgr.
EIN: 421114774

4099
WKBN
(formerly WKBN Broadcasting Corporation)
3930 Sunset Blvd.
Youngstown, OH 44512 (330) 782-1144

Company URL: http://www.wkbn.com
Establishment information: Established in 1926.
Company type: Subsidiary of a private company
Business activities: Broadcasts television.
Business type (SIC): Radio and television broadcasting
Corporate officers: John Heinen, Pres. and C.O.O.; Eric Simontis, C.F.O.
Giving statement: Giving through the Williamson Family Foundation.

Williamson Family Foundation
8399 Tippecanoe Rd.
Canfield, OH 44406-8106

Donors: Martha J. Stewart; Lowry A. Stewart; Warren P. Williamson III; WKBN Broadcasting Corp.
Financial data (yr. ended 12/31/10): Assets, $2,053,880 (M); gifts received, $18,000; expenditures, $140,758; qualifying distributions, $100,095; giving activities include $100,095 for 19 grants (high: $83,195; low: $150).
Purpose and activities: The foundation supports historical societies and hospitals and organizations involved with education, animals and wildlife, and Huntington's disease.
Fields of interest: Historic preservation/historical societies; Higher education; Education; Aquariums; Animals/wildlife; Hospitals (general); Health organizations; United Ways and Federated Giving Programs.
Type of support: General/operating support.
Geographic limitations: Giving primarily in CA and OH.
Support limitations: No grants to individuals.
Application information: Applications not accepted. Unsolicited requests for funds not accepted.
Officers: Warren P. Williamson III, Chair.; John D. Williamson II, Vice-Chair.; Martha Stewart, Secy.-Treas.
Trustees: Susan Brownless; Lowry Stewart; Lynn Williamson; Warren P. Williamson IV.
EIN: 346568495

4100
WKS Restaurant Corporation
2735 Carson St., Ste. 200
Lakewood, CA 90712 (562) 425-1402

Company URL: http://www.wkscorp.biz/
Establishment information: Established in 1987.
Company type: Private company
Business activities: Operates as franchisee of restaurant chain.
Business type (SIC): Restaurants and drinking places
Giving statement: Giving through the WKS Foundation.

The WKS Foundation
2735 Carson St.
Lakewood, CA 90712-4036

Donors: WKS Restaurant Co.; Roland C. Spongberg.
Financial data (yr. ended 12/31/11): Assets, $0 (M); expenditures, $0; qualifying distributions, $0.
Application information: Applications not accepted. Unsolicited requests for funds not accepted.
Trustees: Roland C. Spongberg; Sandra Spongberg.
EIN: 208255795

4101
Woerner Management, Inc.
777 S. Flagler Dr., Ste. 1100 E.
West Palm Beach, FL 33401-6153
(561) 835-3747

Establishment information: Established in 1996.
Company type: Private company
Business activities: Provides management services.
Business type (SIC): Management and public relations services
Corporate officer: Lester Woerner, C.E.O.
Board of director: Lester Woerner
Giving statement: Giving through the Woerner World Ministries, Inc.

Woerner World Ministries, Inc.
275 S.W. 3rd Ave.
South Bay, FL 33493-2221

Establishment information: Established as a company-sponsored operating foundation in 1998 in FL.
Donors: Woerner Management, Inc.; Lester J. Woerner.
Financial data (yr. ended 06/30/11): Assets, $80,931 (M); gifts received, $89,000; expenditures, $158,236; qualifying distributions, $146,443; giving activities include $78,500 for 2 grants (high: $44,500; low: $34,000).
Purpose and activities: The foundation supports organizations involved with child welfare, athletics, human services, and Christianity.
Fields of interest: Crime/violence prevention, child abuse; Athletics/sports, amateur leagues; Children/youth, services; Human services; Christian agencies & churches.
Type of support: General/operating support.
Geographic limitations: Giving primarily in FL.
Application information: Applications not accepted. Unsolicited requests for funds not accepted.
Officers: Lester J. Woerner, Chair.; Kathy Miller, Pres.; Dave Williams, Secy.; Christina Wiemer, Treas.
EIN: 650907241
Selected grants: The following grants are a representative sample of this grantmaker's funding activity:
$18,000 to Place of Hope, Palm Beach Gardens, FL, 2009.
$2,900 to Kings Academy, West Palm Beach, FL, 2009.
$1,500 to Kings Academy, West Palm Beach, FL, 2009.

4102
Wolf & Company, P.C.
99 High St., 21st. Fl.
Boston, MA 02110-2352 (617) 439-9700
FAX: (617) 542-0400

Company URL: http://www.wolfandco.com
Establishment information: Established in 1911.
Company type: Private company
Business activities: Operates a certified public accounting and business consulting firm.
Business type (SIC): Accounting, auditing, and bookkeeping services
Corporate officers: Daniel P. DeVasto, C.P.A., Pres. and C.E.O.; Thomas Vocatura, V.P.
Giving statement: Giving through the Wolf & Company Charitable Foundation, Inc.

Wolf & Company Charitable Foundation, Inc.
99 High St., 21st Fl.
Boston, MA 02110-2352 (617) 439-9700

Establishment information: Established in 2006 in MA.
Donors: Daniel P. Devasto; Gerard F. Boudreau; Jana B. Bacon; Martin M. Caine; Anthony T. Carideo, Jr.; Gerald R. Gagne; Scott M. Goodwin; Jean M. Joy; James P. Kenney; Mark A. O'Connell; Margery L. Piercey; Michael J. Tetrault; Denise M. Toomey; Carol E. Tully; Thomas J. Vocatura; Wolf and Company PC.
Contact: Daniel P. Devasto, Pres.
Financial data (yr. ended 12/31/11): Assets, $42,030 (M); gifts received, $26,405; expenditures, $31,820; qualifying distributions, $31,820; giving activities include $31,785 for 45 grants (high: $5,000; low: $50).
Purpose and activities: The foundation supports organizations involved with education, health, golf, and human services.
Fields of interest: Education; Youth development; Human services.
Type of support: General/operating support; Sponsorships.
Geographic limitations: Giving primarily in MA.
Support limitations: No grants to individuals.
Application information: Applications accepted. Application form not required.
Initial approach: Proposal
Deadline(s): None
Officers and Directors:* Daniel P. Devasto*, Pres.; Scott M. Goodwin*, Clerk; Anthony T. Carideo, Jr.*, Treas.
EIN: 205817793

4103
Wolf Distributing Company
20 W. Market St., Ste. 200
York, PA 17401-1203 (717) 852-4800

Company URL: http://www.wolfdistributingco.com/
Establishment information: Established in 1843.
Company type: Subsidiary of a private company
Business activities: Distributes lumber and building materials.
Business type (SIC): Lumber and other building materials—retail
Financial profile for 2011: Number of employees, 90
Corporate officers: Thomas W. Wolf, Chair. and C.E.O.; David R. Confer, Vice-Chair.; Craig Danielson, Co-Pres.; Brad Kostelich, Co-Pres.; Michael Newsome, Exec. V.P. and C.F.O.
Board of directors: Thomas W. Wolf, Chair.; David R. Confer, Vice-Chair.; Craig Danielson
Giving statement: Giving through the Wolf Foundation.

The Wolf Foundation
P.O. Box 1267
York, PA 17405-1267 (717) 852-4800

Establishment information: Established in 1969 in PA.
Donors: Wolf Distributing, Inc.; The Lumber Yard; Thomas W. Wolf; George W. Hodges.
Financial data (yr. ended 12/31/11): Assets, $460 (M); gifts received, $12,586; expenditures, $231,877; qualifying distributions, $227,095; giving activities include $227,095 for grants.
Purpose and activities: The foundation supports community foundations and organizations involved with arts and culture, education, conservation, animal welfare, housing development, human services, and Christianity.
Fields of interest: Arts, cultural/ethnic awareness; Media/communications; Museums (history); Arts; Higher education; Libraries (public); Education; Environment, natural resources; Animal welfare; Housing/shelter, development; Boy scouts; YM/YWCAs & YM/YWHAs; Human services; Foundations (community); United Ways and Federated Giving Programs; Christian agencies & churches.
Type of support: Building/renovation; Capital campaigns; General/operating support.
Geographic limitations: Giving primarily in York, PA.
Support limitations: No grants to individuals.
Application information: Applications accepted. Application form not required. Applicants should submit the following:
1) population served
2) brief history of organization and description of its mission
Initial approach: Proposal
Deadline(s): None
Officers: George W. Hodges*, Pres.; Leon M. Kopec, V.P.; David R. Confer, Secy.; Ronald J. Blevins, Treas.
EIN: 237028494
Selected grants: The following grants are a representative sample of this grantmaker's funding activity:
$200,000 to Crispus Attucks Association, York, PA, 2009.
$100,000 to YMCA of York and York County, York, PA, 2009.
$47,000 to United Way of York County, York, PA, 2009.
$45,000 to Cultural Alliance of York County, York, PA, 2009.
$20,000 to York County Community Foundation, York, PA, 2009.
$15,000 to Dream Wrights Youth and Family Theater, York, PA, 2009.
$1,334 to YWCA of York, York, PA, 2009.
$1,000 to Habitat for Humanity of Chester County, Coatesville, PA, 2009.

4104
Wolf, Greenfield & Sacks, P.C.
Federal Reserve Plz.
600 Atlantic Ave.
Boston, MA 02210-2206 (617) 646-8000

Company URL: http://ww.wolfgreenfield.com/
Establishment information: Established in 1927.
Company type: Private company
Business activities: Operates law firm.
Business type (SIC): Legal services
Corporate officer: Timothy J. Oyer, Pres. and Managing Partner
Office: Boston, MA
Giving statement: Giving through the Wolf, Greenfield & Sacks, P.C. Pro Bono Program.

Wolf, Greenfield & Sacks, P.C. Pro Bono Program
Federal Reserve Plz.
600 Atlantic Ave.
Boston, MA 02210-2206 (617) 646-8000
E-mail: Robert.Abrahamsen@WolfGreenfield.com;
URL: http://www.wolfgreenfield.com/careers/firm/44

Contact: Robert Abrahamsen, Shareholder
Fields of interest: Legal services.
Type of support: Pro bono services - legal.
Application information: A Pro Bono Committee manages the pro bono program.

4105
Wolff Shoe Company

(formerly Wolf Shoe Manufacturing Company)
1705 Larkin Williams Rd.
Fenton, MO 63026-2006 (636) 326-6711

Establishment information: Established in 1918.
Company type: Private company
Business activities: Manufactures shoes.
Business type (SIC): Apparel, piece goods, and notions—wholesale; shoe stores
Corporate officers: William Wolff, Chair.; Gary Wolff, Pres.; Mark Selemyer, C.I.O.; Tracy L. Hartman, Secy.; Timothy M. Roshiem, Treas.
Board of director: William Wolff, Chair
Giving statement: Giving through the Wolff Shoe Foundation.

Wolff Shoe Foundation

1705 Larkin Williams Rd.
Fenton, MO 63026-2024

Establishment information: Established in 1984 in MO.
Donors: Wolff Shoe Co.; Elaine Wolff; William Wolff; William Wolff Trust.
Financial data (yr. ended 12/31/11): Assets, $11,405 (M); gifts received, $196,008; expenditures, $239,150; qualifying distributions, $239,150; giving activities include $239,150 for grants.
Purpose and activities: The foundation supports organizations involved with education, health, and Judaism.
Fields of interest: Elementary/secondary education; Higher education; Theological school/education; Education; Hospitals (general); Health care; Jewish federated giving programs; Jewish agencies & synagogues.
Type of support: General/operating support; Scholarship funds.
Geographic limitations: Giving primarily in the St. Louis, MO, area.
Support limitations: No grants to individuals.
Application information: Applications not accepted. Contributes only to pre-selected organizations.
Officers and Directors: Elaine Wolff*, Mgr.; William Wolf*, Mgr.; Gary Wolff*, Mgr.
EIN: 431345719
Selected grants: The following grants are a representative sample of this grantmaker's funding activity:
$25,000 to Jewish Federation of Saint Louis, Saint Louis, MO, 2009.

4106
Wolverine World Wide, Inc.

9341 Courtland Dr. N.E.
Rockford, MI 49351-0001 (616) 866-5500
FAX: (616) 866-5550

Company URL: http://www.wolverineworldwide.com
Establishment information: Established in 1883.
Company type: Public company
Company ticker symbol and exchange: WWW/NYSE
Business activities: Manufactures leather footwear.
Business type (SIC): Leather footwear
Financial profile for 2012: Number of employees, 8,299; assets, $2,614,400,000; sales volume, $1,640,840,000; pre-tax net income, $94,180,000; expenses, $1,532,310,000; liabilities, $1,972,000,000
Corporate officers: Blake W. Krueger, Chair., Pres., and C.E.O.; Donald T. Grimes, Sr. V.P., C.F.O., and Treas.; Pamela L. Linton, Sr. V.P., Human Resources; R. Paul Guerre, V.P., Genl. Counsel, and Secy.; Michael D. Stornant, V.P., Finance; Douglas M. Jones, Corp. Cont.
Board of directors: Blake W. Krueger, Chair.; Jeffrey M. Boromisa; William K. Gerber; Alberto Luis Grimoldi; Joseph R. Gromek; David T. Kollat; Brenda J. Lauderback; Nicholas T. Long; Timothy J. O'Donovan; Shirley D. Peterson; Michael A. Volkema
Subsidiaries: Hush Puppies Retail, Inc., Rockford, MI; Hy-Test, Inc., Kirksville, MO; Wolverine Outdoors, Inc., Rockford, MI
Giving statement: Giving through the Wolverine World Wide, Inc. Corporate Giving Program and the Wolverine World Wide Foundation.
Company EIN: 381185150

Wolverine World Wide Foundation

c/o Wolverine World Wide, Inc.
9341 Courtland Dr. N.E.
Rockford, MI 49351-0001 (616) 866-5500
URL: http://www.wolverineworldwide.com/about-us/causes/

Establishment information: Established in MI.
Donor: Wolverine World Wide.
Contact: Christi Cowdin, V.P.
Financial data (yr. ended 12/31/10): Assets, $3,825,964 (M); gifts received, $1,000,000; expenditures, $786,607; qualifying distributions, $763,332; giving activities include $763,332 for grants.
Purpose and activities: The foundation supports organizations involved with arts and culture, education, the environment, cancer, muscular dystrophy, diabetes, housing development, youth and family services, and urban development.
Fields of interest: Museums; Performing arts, orchestras; Arts; Higher education; Medical school/education; Education; Environment, natural resources; Environment, land resources; Environment; Cancer; Muscular dystrophy; Diabetes; Housing/shelter, development; Youth development, business; YM/YWCAs & YM/YWHAs; Children/youth, services; Family services; Urban/community development; United Ways and Federated Giving Programs.
Type of support: Employee matching gifts; General/operating support; Scholarship funds.
Geographic limitations: Giving primarily in areas of company operations in MI.
Application information: Applications accepted. Application form not required. Applicants should submit the following:
1) name, address and phone number of organization
2) detailed description of project and amount of funding requested
3) contact person
4) brief history of organization and description of its mission

Initial approach: Proposal
Deadline(s): None

Officers and Trustees:* Blake W. Krueger*, Pres.; Christi L. Cowdin, V.P.; Kenneth A. Grady*, Secy.; Donald T. Grimes*, Treas.; James D. Zwiers.
EIN: 320140361
Selected grants: The following grants are a representative sample of this grantmaker's funding activity:
$15,000 to Trout Unlimited, Arlington, VA, 2010.
$5,000 to Grand Valley State University, Allendale, MI, 2010.
$5,000 to Teach for America, New York, NY, 2010.

4107
Wonder Transport Co.

2204 Brodhead Rd.
Aliquippa, PA 15001-4536 (724) 378-3780

Company type: Private company
Business activities: Provides trucking services.
Business type (SIC): Trucking and courier services, except by air
Corporate officers: David Faulk, Co-Pres.; Kenneth N. Faulk, Co-Pres.
Giving statement: Giving through the Signs & Wonders Ministries.

Signs & Wonders Ministries

286 Shafer Rd.
Moon Township, PA 15108-1095

Establishment information: Established as a company-sponsored operating foundation.
Donors: Wonder Transport, Inc.; Geri Faulk; Kenneth N. Faulk.
Financial data (yr. ended 12/31/11): Assets, $62,444 (M); gifts received, $59,120; expenditures, $43,083; qualifying distributions, $43,083; giving activities include $13,768 for 20 grants (high: $2,500; low: $100) and $9,424 for 9 grants to individuals (high: $3,400; low: $172).
Purpose and activities: The foundation supports organizations involved with Christianity and awards grants to individuals.
Fields of interest: Christian agencies & churches.
Type of support: General/operating support; Grants to individuals.
Geographic limitations: Giving primarily in PA.
Application information: Applications not accepted. Unsolicited requests for funds not accepted.
Officers: Kenneth N. Faulk, Pres.; David Faulk, V.P.; Geraldine T. Faulk, Secy.-Treas.
EIN: 251641538

4108
Wood County National Bank

181 2nd St. S.
Wisconsin Rapids, WI 54494-4100
(715) 423-7600

Company URL: http://www.wcnbank.com
Establishment information: Established in 1969.
Company type: Subsidiary of a private company
Business activities: Operates commercial bank.
Business type (SIC): Banks/commercial
Corporate officers: Steven C. Bell, Chair. and C.E.O.; Mary D. Ironside, Exec. V.P. and C.F.O.
Board of director: Steven C. Bell, Chair.
Giving statement: Giving through the Woodtrust-Bell Foundation Inc.

Woodtrust-Bell Foundation Inc.

(formerly Bell Family Charitable Foundation, Inc.)
181 2nd St. S.
Wisconsin Rapids, WI 54494-4100

Establishment information: Established in 1992 in WI.
Donors: Steven C. Bell; Margaret L. Bell; Wood County National Bank; WCN Bancorp; Paula J. Bell; Wood County Trust Co.; Woodtrust Financial Corp.; Margaret L. Bell Administrative Trust.
Financial data (yr. ended 12/31/11): Assets, $3,533,402 (M); gifts received, $50,000; expenditures, $183,845; qualifying distributions, $156,183; giving activities include $150,515 for 24 grants (high: $25,000; low: $250).
Purpose and activities: The foundation supports recreation centers and community foundations and organizations involved with secondary and higher education, health, employment, and children services.
Fields of interest: Secondary school/education; Higher education; Health care; Employment; Recreation, centers; YM/YWCAs & YM/YWHAs; Children, services; Foundations (community).
Type of support: Building/renovation; Capital campaigns; Endowments; Equipment; General/operating support; Program development; Scholarship funds; Sponsorships.
Application information: Applications not accepted. Unsolicited requests for funds not accepted.
Officers: Steven C. Bell, Co-Chair.; Chad D. Kane, Co-Chair.; Paula J. Bell, Pres.; Rebecca L. Kettleson, V.P.; Sandra L. Oleson, Secy.; Deborah N. Kane, Treas.
Directors: Margaret S. Bell; Elizabeth A. Bell Killian.
EIN: 396572208
Selected grants: The following grants are a representative sample of this grantmaker's funding activity:
$25,000 to Opportunity Development Centers, Wisconsin Rapids, WI, 2010. For operations.
$25,000 to Riverview Health Care Foundation, Wisconsin Rapids, WI, 2010. For operations.
$25,000 to YMCA of South Wood County, Port Edwards, WI, 2010. For operations.
$15,500 to Lincoln High School, Wisconsin Rapids, WI, 2010. For scholarships.
$10,000 to Humane Society, South Wood County, Wisconsin Rapids, WI, 2010. For operations.
$10,000 to McMillan Memorial Library, Wisconsin Rapids, WI, 2010. For operations.
$10,000 to YMCA, Wausau-Woodson, Wausau, WI, 2010.
$5,000 to Family Center, Wisconsin Rapids, WI, 2010. For operations.
$3,000 to Performing Arts Foundation, Wausau, WI, 2010. For operations.
$2,000 to Assumption High School, Wisconsin Rapids, WI, 2010. For scholarships.

4109
Woodard & Curran

41 Hutchins Dr.
Portland, ME 04102 (207) 774-2112
FAX: (207) 774-4751

Company URL: http://www.woodardcurran.com/
Establishment information: Established in 1979.
Company type: Private company
Business activities: Operates an engineering and environmental management company.
Business type (SIC): Engineering, architectural, and surveying services
Corporate officers: Douglas McKeown, Chair. and C.E.O.; Guy William Vaillancourt, Pres.; David Remick, C.F.O.
Board of directors: Douglas McKeown, Chair.; Eric Carlson; Carolyn Chin; R. Duff Collins; Michael Curato; Steve Guttenplan; Leroy Kendricks; Guy William Vaillancourt; Bruce Wagner
Giving statement: Giving through the Woodard and Curran Foundation.

Woodard and Curran Foundation

41 Hutchins Dr.
Portland, ME 04102-1973
FAX: (207) 774-6635; Toll-free tel.: (800) 426-4262; URL: http://woodardcurranfoundation.org

Establishment information: Established in 2010 in ME.
Financial data (yr. ended 12/31/12): Revenue, $65,503; assets, $73,712 (M); gifts received, $64,489; expenditures, $5,410; program services expenses, $5,000; giving activities include $5,000 for 1 grant.
Purpose and activities: The foundation is dedicated to directing endowment resources to nonprofits with environmental missions focused on creating a healthier world.
Fields of interest: Environment.
Program:
Grants: The foundation awards grants to nonprofit organizations that focus on environmental causes, and that incorporate health or educational missions or components to their projects. Eligible projects must support the public at-large.
Geographic limitations: Giving primarily to ME.
Support limitations: No support for for-profit organizations; organizations that directly benefit Woodard and Curran Inc.'s business, marketing, or recruitment operations; houses of worship; political organizations; or political action committees.
Publications: Application guidelines.
Application information: Applications accepted. Application form required.
Initial approach: Submit application
Deadline(s): June 1
Final notification: Fall
Officers and Directors:* Tom Francoeur*, Pres.; Barry Sheff*, V.P.; Celeste Labadie*, Secy.; Joe Geary*, Treas.; Kelly Camp; Duff Collins; Kelly Cowan; Althea Masterson; Bruce Nicholson; Jay Sheehan.
EIN: 272130228

4110
Woodforest Financial Group, Inc.

1330 Lake Robbins, Ste. 100
P.O. Box 7889
The Woodlands, TX 77380 (832) 375-2000
FAX: (832) 375-3001

Company URL: http://www.woodforest.com/
Establishment information: Established in 1980.
Company type: Private company
Business activities: Operates bank holding company.
Business type (SIC): Holding company
Corporate officers: Robert E. Marling, Jr., Chair. and C.E.O.; Michael H. Richmond, C.F.O.; M. Ann Thomas, C.O.O.
Board of director: Robert E. Marling, Jr., Chair.
Giving statement: Giving through the Woodforest Charitable Foundation.

The Woodforest Charitable Foundation

1330 Lake Robbins Dr., Ste. 100
The Woodlands, TX 77380-3267
E-mail: info@woodforestcharitablefoundation.org; URL: http://www.woodforestcharitablefoundation.org/

Establishment information: Established in 2005 in TX.
Donors: Woodforest National Bank; Southern States Brokerage; Mike Rose; Guy Lewis; Robert Marling; Michael H. Richmond; George Sowers; Fred Greene.
Financial data (yr. ended 12/31/11): Assets, $16,651,705 (M); gifts received, $4,430,805; expenditures, $660,998; qualifying distributions, $523,860; giving activities include $523,860 for grants.
Purpose and activities: The foundation supports food banks and organizations involved with health, human services, and community development. Special emphasis is directed toward programs designed to address social issues; and promote public service.
Fields of interest: Health care, clinics/centers; Health care, patient services; Health care; Food banks; Boys & girls clubs; Children/youth, services; Aging, centers/services; Women, centers/services; Homeless, human services; Human services; Community/economic development.
Type of support: General/operating support; Program development.
Geographic limitations: Giving primarily in areas of company operations in AL, FL, GA, IL, IN, KY, LA, MD, MS, NC, NY, OH, PA, SC, VA, and WV, with emphasis on TX.
Support limitations: No grants to individuals.
Publications: Grants list.
Application information: Applications not accepted. Contributes only to pre-selected organizations.
Officers and Directors:* Robert E. Marling, Jr.*, Pres.; Kim Marling*, V.P. and Exec. Dir.; Vicki Richmond*, Secy.-Treas.
EIN: 202516951
Selected grants: The following grants are a representative sample of this grantmaker's funding activity:
$30,000 to Houston Food Bank, Houston, TX, 2010.
$27,500 to Montgomery County Womens Center, The Woodlands, TX, 2010.
$25,000 to Boys and Girls Country of Houston, Hockley, TX, 2010.
$18,260 to North Texas Food Bank, Dallas, TX, 2010.
$12,000 to Regional East Texas Food Bank, Tyler, TX, 2010.
$10,000 to Montgomery County Emergency Assistance, Conroe, TX, 2010.
$10,000 to San Antonio Food Bank, San Antonio, TX, 2010.
$8,500 to Montgomery County Youth Services, Conroe, TX, 2010.
$5,000 to Helping a Hero, Houston, TX, 2010.
$3,000 to Eastern Illinois Foodbank, Urbana, IL, 2010.

4111
Woods Rogers PLC

10 S. Jefferson St., Ste. 1400
Roanoke, VA 24011-1331 (540) 983-7600

Company URL: http://www.woodsrogers.com/
Company type: Private company
Business activities: Operates law firm.

Business type (SIC): Legal services
Corporate officers: Nicholas C. Conte, Chair.; Thomas R. Bagby, Pres.
Offices: Charlottesville, Danville, Richmond, Roanoke, VA
Giving statement: Giving through the Woods Rogers PLC Corporate Giving Program.

Woods Rogers PLC Corporate Giving Program

10 S. Jefferson St., Ste. 1400
Roanoke, VA 24011-1331
E-mail: sponsorship@woodsrogers.com;
URL: http://www.woodsrogers.com/about-us/community-support/

Fields of interest: Legal services.
Type of support: Pro bono services - legal.

4112
Woodward Inc.

(formerly Woodward Governor Company)
1000 E. Drake Rd.
Fort Collins, CO 80525 (970) 482-5811
FAX: (970) 498-3050

Company URL: http://www.woodward.com
Establishment information: Established in 1870.
Company type: Public company
Company ticker symbol and exchange: WWD/NASDAQ
Business activities: Designs, manufactures, and sells aircraft propeller governors, diesel engines, aircraft control valves, turbines and turbine parts, internal combustion engine parts, and speed changers.
Business type (SIC): Aircraft and parts; metal products/fabricated; engines and turbines; machinery/general industry
Financial profile for 2012: Number of employees, 6,600; assets, $1,859,960,000; sales volume, $1,865,630,000; pre-tax net income, $197,810,000; expenses, $1,667,820,000; liabilities, $851,850,000
Fortune 1000 ranking: 2012—985th in revenues, 665th in profits, and 868th in assets
Corporate officers: Thomas A. Gendron, Chair. and C.E.O.; Robert F. Welch, Jr., Vice-Chair., C.F.O., and Treas.; A. Christopher Fawzy, Corp. V.P., Genl. Counsel, and Corp. Secy.; Steven J. Meyer, Corp. V.P., Human Resources
Board of directors: Thomas A. Gendron, Chair.; Robert F. Weber, Jr., Vice-Chair.; John D. Cohn; Paul Donovan; John A. Halbrook; Larry E. Rittenberg, Ph.D.; James R. Rulseh; Ronald M. Sega; Gregg C. Sengstack; Michael T. Yonker
Divisions: Aircraft Engine Systems, Rockford, IL; Industrial Controls, Fort Collins, CO
Giving statement: Giving through the Woodward Governor Company Charitable Trust.
Company EIN: 361984010

Woodward Governor Company Charitable Trust

5001 N. 2nd St.
Rockford, IL 61125-7001

Establishment information: Established in 1947 in IL.
Donors: Woodward, Inc.; Woodward Governor Co.
Contact: Pam Cappitelli, Chair., Contribs. Comm.
Financial data (yr. ended 12/31/11): Assets, $20,982,431 (M); gifts received, $200,000; expenditures, $1,171,578; qualifying distributions, $1,110,970; giving activities include $1,110,970 for grants.
Purpose and activities: The trust supports organizations involved with arts and culture, education, health, mental health, hunger, housing, human services, community development, disabled people, homeless people, and economically disadvantaged people.
Fields of interest: Museums; Arts; Higher education; Education; Health care, clinics/centers; Health care; Substance abuse, services; Mental health/crisis services; Food services; Food banks; Housing/shelter; YM/YWCAs & YM/YWHAs; Children/youth, services; Family services, domestic violence; Homeless, human services; Human services; Community/economic development; United Ways and Federated Giving Programs Disabilities, people with; Economically disadvantaged; Homeless.
Type of support: Annual campaigns; Capital campaigns; Continuing support; Emergency funds; Equipment; General/operating support; Seed money.
Geographic limitations: Giving primarily in areas of company operations, with emphasis on Fort Collins, CO, Rockford, IL, and Stevens Point, WI.
Support limitations: No grants to individuals, or for endowments, research, scholarships, fellowships, special projects, publications, or conferences; no loans; no matching gifts.
Application information: Application form not required. Applicants should submit the following:
1) copy of IRS Determination Letter
2) detailed description of project and amount of funding requested

Initial approach: Proposal
Copies of proposal: 1
Board meeting date(s): As required
Deadline(s): Mar. or July is preferred
Final notification: 8 weeks

Trustees: Julia Buchanan; Jay Evans; A. Christopher Fawzy; Marty Glass; Dan Loescher; Phil Turner.
EIN: 846025403
Selected grants: The following grants are a representative sample of this grantmaker's funding activity:
$4,000 to Muscular Dystrophy Association, Tucson, AZ, 2010.

4113
Woodward-Graff Wines

P.O. Box 1753
Sonoma, CA 95476 (707) 935-2102

Company URL: http://www.woodward-graffwinefoundation.org/wines.html
Establishment information: Established in 1974.
Company type: Private company
Business activities: Operates winery.
Business type (SIC): Beverages
Corporate officer: W. Philip Woodward, Pres.
Giving statement: Giving through the Woodward/Graff Wine Foundation.

Woodward/Graff Wine Foundation

(formerly Chalone Wine Foundation)
P.O. Box 1753
Sonoma, CA 95476-1753 (707) 935-2102
FAX: (707) 935-2105;
E-mail: info@woodward-graffwinefoundation.org;
URL: http://www.woodward-graffwinefoundation.org

Establishment information: Established in 1998 in CA.
Financial data (yr. ended 03/31/10): Revenue, $12,037; assets, $448,534 (M); gifts received, $11,935; expenditures, $20,873; program services expenses, $16,200; giving activities include $16,200 for grants to individuals.
Purpose and activities: The foundation awards scholarships to deserving students of the art and science of wine, food and hospitality.
Fields of interest: Vocational education; Food services.
Program:
The Richard H. Graff Scholarship: Scholarships are awarded to students of the art and science of wine, food and hospitality.
Type of support: Scholarships—to individuals.
Geographic limitations: Giving with emphasis on the wine-making communities in CA.
Officers and Directors:* Constance A. Majoy*, Pres.; Honorio Della*, Secy.; W. Philip Woodward*, Treas.; David Graff; James H. Niven.
EIN: 943297049

4114
Woori America Bank

1250 Broadway
New York, NY 10001-3752 (212) 244-1500

Company URL: http://www.wooriamericabank.com/eng/
Establishment information: Established in 1984.
Company type: Subsidiary of a foreign company
Business activities: Operates commercial bank.
Business type (SIC): Banks/commercial
Financial profile for 2007: Assets, $1,075,000,000
Corporate officer: Yong-Heung Cho, Pres. and C.E.O.
Giving statement: Giving through the Woori America Bank Scholarship Foundation, Inc.

Woori America Bank Scholarship Foundation, Inc.

1250 Broadway, 16th Fl.
New York, NY 10001-3701
E-mail: daejin.choi@wooriamericabank.com; Additional contact: Kyunghan Chung, tel.: (212) 244-3000 ext. 223, e-mail: kyunghan.chung@wooriamericabank.com;
URL: http://www.wooriamericabank.com/eng/about/Scholarship.asp

Establishment information: Established in 2004 in NY.
Donor: Woori America Bank.
Contact: Daejin Choi
Financial data (yr. ended 12/31/11): Assets, $98,809 (M); gifts received, $100,000; expenditures, $113,473; qualifying distributions, $100,000; giving activities include $4,000 for 1 grant and $96,000 for 49 grants to individuals (high: $2,000; low: $2,000).
Purpose and activities: The foundation awards college scholarship to graduating high school seniors in the operating area of Woori American Bank branches.
Fields of interest: Higher education.
Program:
Scholarships: The foundation awards $2,000 college scholarships to high school graduate students residing in California, Maryland, New Jersey, New York, Pennsylvania, Virginia, and Washington D.C. Applicants must demonstrate academic excellence, strong leadership, and financial need.

Type of support: Scholarships—to individuals.
Geographic limitations: Giving primarily to residents in CA, Washington, DC, MD, NY, NJ, PA, and VA.
Publications: Application guidelines.
Application information: Applications accepted. Application form required.
Applications should include transcripts, SAT scores, college letter of acceptance, and family income tax return. Household income must be less than $68,000 and the applicant's GPA must be 3.2 or higher.
Initial approach: Complete online application
Deadline(s): Mar. 15 to Apr. 30
Final notification: May
Officer and Directors: Yong Heung Cho, Pres.; John Song Yook Hung; Kwang Hyun Chung.
EIN: 201916285

4115
The WorkflowOne Company

(formerly The Relizon Company)
220 E. Monument Ave.
Dayton, OH 45402-1223 (937) 228-5800

Company URL: http://www.workflowone.com
Establishment information: Established in 2004.
Company type: Subsidiary of a private company
Business activities: Prints promotional products.
Business type (SIC): Printing trade services
Corporate officers: Tatman Tim, Pres. and C.E.O.; Thomas J. Koenig, C.F.O.; Jeff Noffsinger, C.I.O.; Kelly Whitt, V.P., Human Resources
Giving statement: Giving through the WorkflowOne Employee Foundation.

WorkflowOne Employee Foundation

(formerly The Relizon Employee Foundation)
220 E. Monument Ave.
Dayton, OH 45402-1223 (937) 630-8054
FAX: (937) 630-8968;
E-mail: sharon.williamson@workflowone.com

Establishment information: Established in 2000 in OH as the Relizon Employee Foundation; changed to current name in 2005 with the purchasing of the Relizon Company by Workflow Management, Inc.
Contact: Mary Ann Kabel, Secy.
Financial data (yr. ended 12/31/11): Revenue, $33,975; assets, $86,956 (M); gifts received, $33,969; expenditures, $57,528; giving activities include $57,403 for grants.
Purpose and activities: The foundation supports health and human services needs in the Miami Valley area.
Fields of interest: Arts, public policy; Elementary school/education; Secondary school/education; Education, reading; Crime/violence prevention, domestic violence; Food banks; Children/youth, services; Human services.
Type of support: Continuing support; Program development.
Geographic limitations: Giving primarily to Montgomery County, OH.
Support limitations: No support for religious or political organizations. No grants for economic development.
Application information:
Officers and Directors:* Nathan Jenkin*, Pres.; Brian Winner*, V.P.; Mary Ann Kabel*, Secy.; Benjamin Cutting; Jennifer Fett; Christopher Jauch.
Number of staff: None.
EIN: 311739852

4116
Working Assets Funding Service, Inc.

101 Market St., Ste. 700
San Francisco, CA 94105 (415) 369-2000

Company URL: http://www.workingassets.com
Establishment information: Established in 1985.
Company type: Private company
Business activities: Provides long distance telephone, paging, credit card, and online services.
Business type (SIC): Communications services/miscellaneous; telephone communications; business services/miscellaneous
Corporate officers: Laura Scher, Chair. and C.E.O.; Michael Kieschnick, Pres.; Steve Gunn, V.P., Opers.
Board of director: Laura Scher, Chair.
Giving statement: Giving through the Working Assets Funding Service, Inc. Corporate Giving Program.

Working Assets Funding Service, Inc. Corporate Giving Program

c/o Donations Mgr.
101 Market St.
San Francisco, CA 94105 (415) 369-2000
E-mail: donations.info@workingassets.com; Toll-free tel. for Working Assets and CREDO: (800) 668-9253; URL: http://www.workingassets.com/Recipients.aspx

Purpose and activities: Working Assets makes charitable contributions to nonprofit organizations involved with civil rights, economic and social justice, voting affairs and civic participation, peace and international freedom, human rights, and the environment. Support is limited to national and international organizations.
Fields of interest: Environment, pollution control; Environment; Animals/wildlife; Reproductive health; Health care; Women, centers/services; International peace/security; International human rights; Civil/human rights, equal rights; Civil/human rights, LGBTQ; Civil rights, voter education; Civil liberties, reproductive rights; Civil liberties, first amendment; Freedom from violence/torture; Civil/human rights; Public affairs.
Type of support: Advocacy; General/operating support.
Geographic limitations: Giving to national and international organizations.
Support limitations: No support for disease-specific organizations, religious organizations, or organizations established less than one year ago.
Publications: Grants list.
Application information: Contributes only to organizations nominated by the company's customers and chosen by the board of directors. All nominated organizations must be national or international in scope. Application form not required.
Applicants should submit the following:
1) name, address and phone number of organization
2) contact person
Nominations should include the development director's name (or a person in a similar role), the development director's e-mail address and phone number, and the organization's website.
Initial approach: Complete online nomination form

4117
Working Excellence, LLC

11654 Plaza America Dr., Ste. 555
Reston, VA 20190-4700 (202) 587-1200
FAX: (202) 587-1200

Company URL: http://www.workingexcellence.com
Company type: Private company
Business type (SIC): Business services/miscellaneous
Corporate officer: James F. Kenefick, Owner
Giving statement: Giving through the Working Excellence, LLC Contributions Program.

Working Excellence, LLC Contributions Program

7921 Jones Branch Rd., Ste. 106
McLean, VA 22102-3332 (202) 587-1200
URL: http://www.workingexcellence.com/triple-bottom-line

Purpose and activities: Working Excellence is a certified B Corporation that donates a percentage of profits to charitable organizations.

4118
World Centric

2121 Staunton Ct.
Palo Alto, CA 94306-1439 (650) 283-3797
FAX: (866) 850-9732

Company URL: http://www.worldcentric.org
Establishment information: Established in 2004.
Company type: Private company
Business type (SIC): Business services/miscellaneous
Corporate officer: Aseem Das, C.E.O.
Giving statement: Giving through the World Centric Corporate Giving Program.

World Centric Corporate Giving Program

2121 Staunton Ct.
Palo Alto, CA 94306-1439 (650) 283-3797
URL: http://www.worldcentric.org

Purpose and activities: World Centric is a certified B Corporation that donates a percentage of net profits to charitable organizations.
Fields of interest: Environment.
Type of support: General/operating support.

4119
World of Chantilly, Inc.

4302 Farragut Rd.
Brooklyn, NY 11203 (718) 859-1110
FAX: (718) 859-1303

Company URL: http://www.chantilly.com
Establishment information: Established in 1991.
Company type: Private company
Business activities: Produces kosher French desserts.
Business type (SIC): Bakery products
Corporate officers: Daniel Faks, Chair.; Alberto Faks, Pres.
Board of director: Daniel Faks, Chair.
Giving statement: Giving through the Aouni Faks Foundation.

Aouni Faks Foundation

4302 Farragut Rd.
Brooklyn, NY 11203-6520

Establishment information: Established in 2001 in NY.
Donors: World of Chantilly, Inc.; Chambord, LLC.
Financial data (yr. ended 12/31/10): Assets, $497,436 (M); gifts received, $60,000; expenditures, $15,800; qualifying distributions, $15,700; giving activities include $15,700 for 3 grants (high: $12,500; low: $1,200).
Purpose and activities: The foundation supports organizations involved with Judaism.
Fields of interest: Jewish agencies & synagogues.
Type of support: General/operating support.
Application information: Applications not accepted. Unsolicited requests for funds not accepted.
Officers: Ibrahim Faks, V.P.; Freddy Faks, Secy.; Daniel Faks, Treas.
EIN: 306004475

4120
World Products, L.L.C.

19654 8th St. E.
P.O. Box 517
Sonoma, CA 95476-0517 (707) 996-5201

Company URL: http://www.worldproducts.com/ContactUs.htm
Establishment information: Established in 1970.
Company type: Private company
Business activities: Sells electronic parts and equipment wholesale.
Business type (SIC): Electrical goods—wholesale
Corporate officers: Bob Stone, Chair. and C.E.O.; Mark Beynon, Pres.
Board of director: Bob Stone, Chair.
Giving statement: Giving through the World Products Inc. Foundation.

World Products Inc. Foundation

c/o Jesse R. Stone
4741 Fremont Ave. S.
Minneapolis, MN 55409-2206

Establishment information: Established in 1987 in CA and MN.
Donor: World Products, Inc.
Financial data (yr. ended 11/30/12): Assets, $113 (M); gifts received, $265; expenditures, $351; qualifying distributions, $0.
Purpose and activities: The foundation supports organizations involved with arts and culture, education, health, and children and youth.
Fields of interest: Arts; Elementary/secondary education; Education; Hospitals (general); Health care; Youth development, centers/clubs; Children/youth, services.
Geographic limitations: Giving primarily in Sonoma, CA.
Support limitations: No grants to individuals.
Application information: Applications not accepted. Unsolicited requests for funds not accepted.
Officers: Jesse R. Stone, Pres.; R. D. Estes, V.P.; Carolyn J. Stone, Secy.-Treas.
EIN: 411599604

4121
World Wrestling Entertainment, Inc.

1241 E. Main St.
Stamford, CT 06902 (203) 352-8600
FAX: (302) 655-5049

Company URL: http://corporate.wwe.com
Establishment information: Established in 1980.
Company type: Public company
Company ticker symbol and exchange: WWE/NYSE
Business activities: Produces television and pay-per-view programming; produces live sports entertainment events; licenses entertainment properties.
Business type (SIC): Motion pictures/production and services allied to; investors/miscellaneous; bands, orchestras, and entertainers
Financial profile for 2012: Number of employees, 721; assets, $381,380,000; sales volume, $484,010,000; pre-tax net income, $42,680,000; expenses, $440,820,000; liabilities, $86,660,000
Corporate officers: Vincent K. McMahon, Chair. and C.E.O.; Michael Luisi, Pres. and Genl. Counsel; George A. Barrios, C.F.O.
Board of directors: Vincent K. McMahon, Chair.; Basil DeVito; Kevin Dunn; Patricia A. Gottesman; Stuart U. Goldfarb; David Kenin; Joseph H. Perkins; Frank A. Riddick III; Jeffrey R. Speed
Giving statement: Giving through the World Wrestling Entertainment, Inc. Corporate Giving Program.
Company EIN: 042693383

World Wrestling Entertainment, Inc. Corporate Giving Program

c/o In Your Corner
1241 E. Main St.
Stamford, CT 06902-3520
E-mail: InYourCorner@wwecorp.com; URL: http://corporate.wwe.com/community/overview.jsp

Purpose and activities: World Wrestling Entertainment makes charitable contributions to nonprofit organizations involved with literacy, civic engagement, military affairs, and children's services. Support is given on a national basis, with emphasis on areas of company operations.
Fields of interest: Education, equal rights; Education, reading; Education; Children, services; Public affairs, citizen participation; Military/veterans' organizations.
Type of support: Employee volunteer services; In-kind gifts; Publication; Sponsorships.
Geographic limitations: Giving on a national basis, with emphasis on areas of company operations.
Application information: Applications not accepted. Contributes only to pre-selected organizations.

4122
World-Wide Holdings Corporation

950 3rd Ave., Fl. 18
New York, NY 10022-2897 (212) 486-2000

Establishment information: Established in 1987.
Company type: Private company
Business activities: Operates holding company.
Business type (SIC): Holding company
Corporate officers: Victor Elmaleh, Chair. and C.E.O.; Jim Stanton, Pres.; David Lowenfeld, Exec. V.P.; Eleenore Pienitz, Secy.
Board of director: Victor Elmaleh, Chair.
Giving statement: Giving through the Frank and Domna Stanton Foundation.

The Frank and Domna Stanton Foundation

112 E. 74th St., Rm. 9N
New York, NY 10021-3535

Establishment information: Established in 1987 in NY.
Donors: World-Wide Holdings Corp.; Donna Stanton.
Financial data (yr. ended 12/31/10): Assets, $339,530 (M); expenditures, $51,055; qualifying distributions, $48,943; giving activities include $48,943 for 15 grants (high: $23,293; low: $75).
Purpose and activities: The foundation supports libraries and organizations involved with arts and culture, Parkinson's disease, and civil liberties.
Fields of interest: Media/communications; Performing arts, opera; Arts; Libraries (public); Parkinson's disease; Civil liberties, first amendment.
Type of support: General/operating support.
Geographic limitations: Giving primarily in NY.
Support limitations: No grants to individuals.
Application information: Applications not accepted. Unsolicited requests for funds not accepted.
Officers: Domna Stanton, V.P.; James Stanton, Secy.; Michael Stanton, Treas.
EIN: 133416233

4123
Worthen Industries, Inc.

3 E. Spit Brook Rd.
Nashua, NH 03060-5783 (603) 888-5443

Company URL: http://www.worthenindustries.com
Establishment information: Established in 1866.
Company type: Private company
Business activities: Manufactures coated, non-rubberized fabrics and adhesives.
Business type (SIC): Chemical preparations/miscellaneous; textile goods/miscellaneous
Corporate officer: Eileen Morin, C.E.O.
Giving statement: Giving through the FP Worthen Foundation.

FP Worthen Foundation

3 E. Spit Brook Rd.
Nashua, NH 03060-5783 (603) 888-5443

Donors: Worthen Industries, Inc.; Frederic P. Worthen; Helen F. Worthen.
Contact: David S. Worthen, Treas.
Financial data (yr. ended 04/30/11): Assets, $1,197,343 (M); expenditures, $59,628; qualifying distributions, $50,000; giving activities include $50,000 for 14 grants (high: $10,000; low: $1,000).
Purpose and activities: The foundation supports organizations involved with K-12 education, health, housing development, equestrianism, and the disabled.
Fields of interest: Animals/wildlife; Recreation; Youth development.
Type of support: General/operating support; Program development; Scholarship funds.
Application information: Applications accepted. Application form required. Applicants should submit the following:
1) detailed description of project and amount of funding requested

Initial approach: Letter
Deadline(s): None
Officers and Trustees:* Helen W. Berns*, Pres.; David S. Worthen*, Treas.; Frederic P. Worthen, Jr.; Susan B. Worthen.
EIN: 046050139

4124
Worthington Industries, Inc.

200 Old Wilson Bridge Rd.
Columbus, OH 43085 (614) 438-3210
FAX: (614) 438-3136

Company URL: http://www.worthingtonindustries.com
Establishment information: Established in 1955.
Company type: Public company
Company ticker symbol and exchange: WOR/NYSE
Business activities: Manufactures metal and plastic products.
Business type (SIC): Steel mill products; iron and steel foundries
Financial profile for 2012: Number of employees, 10,500; assets, $1,877,800,000; sales volume, $2,534,700,000; pre-tax net income, $177,260,000; expenses, $2,433,090,000; liabilities, $1,180,620,000
Fortune 1000 ranking: 2012—801st in revenues, 711th in profits, and 865th in assets
Corporate officers: John P. McConnell, Chair. and C.E.O.; Mark A. Russell, Pres. and C.O.O.; Eric M. Smolenski, C.I.O.; B. Andrew Rose, V.P. and C.F.O.; Matthew A. Lockard, V.P. and Treas.; Dale T. Brinkman, V.P., Admin., Genl. Counsel, and Secy.; Cathy M. Lyttle, V.P., Comms.; Terry M. Dyer, V.P., Human Resources.; Richard G. Welch, Cont.
Board of directors: John P. McConnell, Chair.; Kerrii B. Anderson; John B. Blystone; Mark C. Davis; Michael J. Endres; Ozey K. Horton; Peter Karmanos, Jr.; Carl A. Nelson, Jr.; Sidney A. Ribeau; Mary F. Schiavo
Subsidiaries: Buckeye Steel Castings Co., Columbus, OH; Capital Die, Tool and Machine Co., Columbus, OH; London Industries, Inc., London, OH; I.H. Schlezinger, Inc., Columbus, OH; TWB Co., Taylor, MI; Worthington Armstrong Venture, Sparrows Point, MD; Worthington Custom Plastics, Inc., St. Matthews, SC; Worthington Cylinder Corp., Jefferson, OH; Worthington Precision Metals, Inc., Franklin, TN; Worthington Specialty Processing, Jackson, MI; The Worthington Steel Co., Columbus, OH
Plants: Citronelle, AL; Midland, GA; Porter, IN; Louisville, KY; Baltimore, MD; Jackson, MI; Mason, Mentor, Monroe, Salem, Upper Sandusky, OH; Claremore, OK; Malvern, PA; Rock Hill, SC
Giving statement: Giving through the Worthington Industries, Inc. Corporate Giving Program.
Company EIN: 311189815

Worthington Industries, Inc. Corporate Giving Program

200 Old Wilson Bridge Rd.
Columbus, OH 43085-2247 (614) 438-3210
E-mail: WIFoundation@WorthingtonIndustries.com; URL: http://www.worthingtonindustries.com/corporate-information/corporate-giving

Purpose and activities: Worthington makes charitable contributions to nonprofit organizations involved with education, civic organizations, health and human services, and arts and culture. Support is given primarily in areas of company operations, with emphasis on central Ohio.
Fields of interest: Arts; Education; Health care; Human services; Community/economic development; Public affairs.
Type of support: Donated products; Employee volunteer services; General/operating support; In-kind gifts.
Geographic limitations: Giving primarily in areas of company operations, with emphasis on central OH.
Support limitations: No support for religious, ethnic, fraternal, or labor organizations. No grants to individuals, or for debt reduction.
Publications: Application guidelines.
Application information: Applications accepted.
Initial approach: E-mail proposal

4125
Wm. Wrigley Jr. Company

410 N. Michigan Ave.
Chicago, IL 60611 (312) 644-2121

Company URL: http://www.wrigley.com
Establishment information: Established in 1891.
Company type: Subsidiary of a private company
Business activities: Produces and markets confectionery products.
Business type (SIC): Sugar, candy, and salted/roasted nut production
Financial profile for 2011: Number of employees, 16,400
Corporate officers: William Wrigley, Jr., Chair.; Martin Radvan, Pres. and C.E.O.; Reuben Gamoran, Exec. V.P. and C.F.O.; Ellen Kollar, Sr. V.P. and Genl. Counsel; Howard Malovany, Secy.
Board of director: William Wrigley, Jr., Chair.
Subsidiaries: Amurol Confections Co., Naperville, IL; L.A. Dreyfus Co., South Plainfield, NJ; Four-Ten Corp., Chicago, IL
International operations: Australia; Austria; Canada; China; Czech Republic; Finland; France; Germany; Hungary; India; Japan; Kenya; Malaysia; New Zealand; Philippines; Poland; Slovenia; Spain; Sweden; Taiwan; United Kingdom
Giving statement: Giving through the Wm. Wrigley Jr. Company Contributions Program and the Wm. Wrigley Jr. Company Foundation.
Company EIN: 361988190

Wm. Wrigley Jr. Company Contributions Program

410 N. Michigan Ave.
Chicago, IL 60611-4211 (312) 644-2121
URL: http://www.wrigley.com/global/principles-in-action/people.aspx

Purpose and activities: As a complement to its foundation, Wm. Wrigley Jr. also makes charitable contributions to nonprofit organizations directly. Support is limited to areas of company operations in Gainesville, Georgia; Chicago and Yorkville, Illinois; and Chattanooga, Tennessee.
Fields of interest: Arts; Dental school/education; Education; Environmental education; Environment; Dental care; Health care; Crime/violence prevention, child abuse; Nutrition; Children, services; Human services; Civil/human rights, equal rights; Community/economic development; Public affairs; General charitable giving Children.
Type of support: Employee volunteer services; In-kind gifts; Sponsorships.
Geographic limitations: Giving limited to areas of company operations in Gainesville, GA, Chicago and Yorkville, IL, and Chattanooga, TN.
Support limitations: No support for political, religious, discriminatory, or military organizations. Generally no grants to individuals, or for social events, silent auctions or raffles, or military requests.
Publications: Application guidelines.
Application information: Applications accepted. Unsolicited sponsorship requests are generally not accepted. Application form required. Applicants should submit the following:
1) statement of problem project will address
2) name, address and phone number of organization
3) contact person
Applications for product donations should include the date and description of the event, the anticipated percentage of participants under 12 years of age, and any applicable deadlines.
Initial approach: Complete online application form for product donations
Deadline(s): 30 days prior to need

Wm. Wrigley Jr. Company Foundation

410 N. Michigan Ave.
Chicago, IL 60611-4213
FAX: (312) 644-0015; URL: http://www.wrigley.com/global/principles-in-action/foundation.aspx

Establishment information: Established in 1986 in IL.
Donor: Wm. Wrigley Jr. Co.
Contact: Maureen Jones, Prog. Dir.
Financial data (yr. ended 12/31/11): Assets, $62,867,986 (M); expenditures, $4,607,580; qualifying distributions, $4,562,778; giving activities include $4,174,001 for 43 grants (high: $935,550; low: $100) and $358,777 for employee matching gifts.
Purpose and activities: The foundation supports programs designed to improve the health of people and the planet through sustainable initiatives focused on oral health, environmental stewardship, and healthy communities.
Fields of interest: Elementary/secondary education; Higher education; Education; Environment, waste management; Environment, natural resources; Environment, land resources; Environmental education; Environment; Dental care; Public health, physical fitness; Health care; Nutrition; Disasters, preparedness/services; Youth development; American Red Cross; Children/youth, services; United Ways and Federated Giving Programs.
Programs:
Matching Grant Program: The foundation matches contributions made by associates, retirees, and directors of Wrigley to nonprofit organizations on a two-for-one basis up to $1,500 per employee, per year.
WAVE Grants: The foundation awards $250 grants to nonprofit organizations with which associates of Wrigley volunteers at least 25 hours of service.
Type of support: Building/renovation; Continuing support; Employee matching gifts; Employee volunteer services; General/operating support; Program development; Scholarship funds.
Geographic limitations: Giving on a national basis in areas of company operations with emphasis on IL, MD, and VA; giving also internationally in Australia, China, India, and Ireland.
Support limitations: No support for athletic teams or hospitals. No grants to individuals, or for artistic or cultural activities (unless related to educational programming), sports, or research or support services related to specific medical conditions or diseases.
Application information: Applications not accepted. Unsolicited applications are currently not accepted.
Officers and Directors:* Martin Radvan*, Pres.; Andrew Pharaoh*, V.P.; Ritu Vig, Secy.; Anthony

Gedeller, Treas.; Mary Haupt, Exec. Dir.; Ian Burton; Casey Keller; Martin Schlatter; Tomek Suchecki; Samson Suen; Denise Young.
EIN: 363486958

4126
WSA Fraternal Life

11265 Decatur St., Ste. 100
P.O. Box 351920
Westminster, CO 80234 (303) 451-1494

Company URL: http://www.wsa-life.com
Establishment information: Established in 1908.
Company type: Fraternal benefit society
Business activities: Sells life insurance; provides investment advisory services.
Business type (SIC): Insurance/life; security and commodity services
Corporate officers: John J. Kogovsek, Chair.; Diana J. Bartolo, Vice-Chair.; Randy R. Fuss, Pres. and C.E.O.
Board of directors: John J. Kogovsek, Chair.; Diana Bartolo, Vice-Chair.; Cynthia Conte; Randy R. Fuss; Roger P. Lewis; Gary Moore; Micheal R. Osborn; Lisa Povich; Rocco Santangelo
Giving statement: Giving through the WSA Fraternal Life Corporate Giving Program.

WSA Fraternal Life Corporate Giving Program

11265 Decatur St., Ste. 100
Westminster, CO 80234-4795
URL: http://www.wsalife.com/community.php

Purpose and activities: WSA Fraternal Life makes charitable contributions to nonprofit organizations on a case by case basis. Support is given primarily in areas of company operations.
Fields of interest: General charitable giving.
Program:
Lodge Activity Funding Program: Through the Lodge Activity Funding Program, the company makes funds available to each active lodge on an annual basis to donate to worthy causes.
Type of support: Employee volunteer services; General/operating support.
Geographic limitations: Giving primarily in areas of company operations.

4127
WSFS Financial Corporation

500 Delaware Ave.
Wilmington, DE 19801 (302) 792-6000
FAX: (302) 571-6842

Company URL: http://www.wsfsbank.com
Establishment information: Established in 1832.
Company type: Public company
Company ticker symbol and exchange: WSFS/NASDAQ
Business activities: Operates bank holding company; operates savings bank.
Business type (SIC): Savings institutions; holding company
Financial profile for 2012: Number of employees, 763; assets, $4,375,150,000; pre-tax net income, $48,290,000; liabilities, $3,954,090,000
Corporate officers: Marvin N. Schoenhals, Chair.; Charles G. Cheleden, Vice-Chair.; Mark A. Turner, Pres. and C.E.O.; Stephen A. Fowle, Exec. V.P. and C.F.O.
Board of directors: Marvin N. Schoenhals, Chair.; Charles G. Cheleden, Vice-Chair.; Anat M. Bird; Jennifer Wagner Davis; Donald W. Delson; Eleuthere I. Du Pont; Zissimos A. Frangopoulos; Calvert A. Morgan, Jr.; David G. Turner; Mark A. Turner
Subsidiary: Wilmington Savings Fund Society, FSB, Wilmington, DE
Giving statement: Giving through the WSFS Financial Corporation Contributions Program and the WSFS Foundation.
Company EIN: 222866913

WSFS Financial Corporation Contributions Program

500 Delaware Ave.
Wilmington, DE 19801-1490
E-mail: dmitchell@wsfsbank.com; URL: http://www.wsfsbank.com/about-wsfs.aspx?id=2004

Purpose and activities: As a complement to its foundation, WSFS also makes charitable contributions to nonprofit organizations directly. Support is given primarily in Delaware.
Fields of interest: General charitable giving.
Type of support: Employee volunteer services; General/operating support; Program development; Sponsorships.
Geographic limitations: Giving primarily in DE.
Publications: Application guidelines.
Application information: Applications accepted. Application form required. Applicants should submit the following:
1) name, address and phone number of organization
2) copy of IRS Determination Letter
3) brief history of organization and description of its mission
4) list of company employees involved with the organization
5) listing of board of directors, trustees, officers and other key people and their affiliations
6) detailed description of project and amount of funding requested
7) contact person
8) copy of current year's organizational budget and/or project budget

Applications should indicate the date and time of the event; and whether the organization has a banking relationship with WSFS.
Initial approach: Download application form and mail with supporting materials to headquarters
Deadline(s): None
Final notification: Following review
Corporate Contributions Committee: Janis Julian, Chair.; Scott Baylis; Cindy Compton-Barone; Steve Fowl; Susan List; Pam McCuthceon; Lynn Schaefer; Michael Skipper; Kathy Uni.

WSFS Foundation

500 Delaware Ave.
Wilmington, DE 19801-1490

Establishment information: Established in 2003 in DE.
Donor: Wilmington Savings Fund Society.
Contact: Michael Skipper, Secy.
Financial data (yr. ended 12/31/11): Assets, $1,476,691 (M); expenditures, $84,155; qualifying distributions, $75,000; giving activities include $75,000 for 5 grants (high: $25,000; low: $10,000).
Purpose and activities: The foundation supports organizations involved with education and business.
Fields of interest: Education; Business/industry.
Type of support: General/operating support; Program development.
Geographic limitations: Giving limited to DE.
Support limitations: No grants to individuals.
Application information: Applications accepted. Application form not required.
Initial approach: Proposal
Copies of proposal: 1
Board meeting date(s): Apr.
Deadline(s): None
Officers and Directors:* Rodger Levenson*, Pres.; Stephanie Heist*, V.P.; Michael Skipper, Secy.; Robert F. Mack*, Treas.
EIN: 134229063

4128
Wurster Oil Co., Inc.

2500 4th St.
Jonesville, LA 71343-2009 (318) 339-7246

Establishment information: Established in 1952.
Company type: Private company
Business activities: Operates gasoline service stations.
Business type (SIC): Gasoline service stations
Corporate officers: Diane Thornton, Pres.; David Thornton, Secy.
Giving statement: Giving through the Harvest Foundation, Inc.

Harvest Foundation, Inc.

P.O. Box 38
Jonesville, LA 71343-0038

Establishment information: Established in 2001 in LA.
Donors: Wurster Oil Co., Inc.; James E. Thornton Testamentary Trust.
Financial data (yr. ended 12/31/11): Assets, $707 (M); expenditures, $76,309; qualifying distributions, $74,812; giving activities include $74,812 for 63 grants (high: $37,850; low: $28).
Purpose and activities: The foundation supports Christian agencies and churches.
Fields of interest: Health care; Human services; Religion.
Type of support: General/operating support.
Support limitations: No grants to individuals.
Application information: Applications not accepted. Unsolicited requests for funds not accepted.
Officers: Diane W. Thornton, Pres.; J.R. Ayres, V.P.; Steve Ayres, Secy.-Treas.
EIN: 721517384

4129
Wurzburg, Inc.

710 S. 4th St.
Memphis, TN 38126-3713 (800) 492-0014

Establishment information: Established in 1908.
Company type: Subsidiary of a private company
Business activities: Sells packaging and shipping supplies wholesale.
Business type (SIC): Paper and paper products—wholesale
Subsidiaries: Artcraft Converters, Inc., Memphis, TN; Multiform, Inc., Memphis, TN
Offices: Birmingham, Madison, AL; Macon, GA; Frankfort, KY; Harahan, Shreveport, LA; Jackson, MS; Greer, SC; Knoxville, Nashville, TN
Giving statement: Giving through the Warren S. Wurzburg, Sr. and Marjorie O. Wurzburg Foundation.

The Warren S. Wurzburg, Sr. and Marjorie O. Wurzburg Foundation

P.O. Box 1908
Orlando, FL 32802-1908
Application address: c/o Warren Wurzburg, 710 S. 4th St., Memphis, TN 38101-0710

Establishment information: Established in 1984 in TN.
Donors: Wurzburg, Inc.; Steven M. Shapiro; Warren Wurzburg, Jr.
Contact: Warren Wurzburg
Financial data (yr. ended 12/31/11): Assets, $184,345 (M); expenditures, $35,819; qualifying distributions, $30,980; giving activities include $30,980 for grants.
Purpose and activities: The foundation supports organizations involved with Judaism.
Fields of interest: Religion.
Type of support: General/operating support.
Geographic limitations: Giving limited to Memphis, TN.
Support limitations: No grants to individuals.
Application information: Applications accepted. Application form required. Applicants should submit the following:
1) detailed description of project and amount of funding requested
Initial approach: Letter
Deadline(s): None
Trustee: SunTrust Bank.
EIN: 581544786

4130
Wyatt, Tarrant & Combs, LLP

PNC Plz.
500 W. Jefferson St., Ste. 2800
Louisville, KY 40202-2898 (502) 562-7159

Company URL: http://www.wyattfirm.com
Company type: Private company
Business activities: Operates law firm.
Business type (SIC): Legal services
Offices: Fort Collins, CO; New Albany, IN; Lexington, Louisville, KY; Jackson, MS; Memphis, Nashville, TN
Giving statement: Giving through the Wyatt, Tarrant & Combs, LLP Pro Bono Program.

Wyatt, Tarrant & Combs, LLP Pro Bono Program

PNC Plz.
500 W. Jefferson St., Ste. 2800
Louisville, KY 40202-2898 (502) 589-5235
E-mail: dkelly@wyattfirm.com; Additional tel.: (502) 562-7159; URL: http://www.wyattfirm.com/about-wyatt/pro-bono

Contact: Don Kelly, Partner
Fields of interest: Legal services.
Type of support: Pro bono services - legal.
Application information: A Pro Bono Committee manages the pro bono program.

4131
Wyche, P.A.

44 E. Camperdown Way
P.O. Box 728
Greenville, SC 29602-0728 (864) 242-8200

Company URL: http://www.wyche.com/
Company type: Private company
Business activities: Operates law firm.
Business type (SIC): Legal services
Offices: Columbia, Greenville, SC
Giving statement: Giving through the Wyche, P.A. Pro Bono Program.

Wyche, P.A. Pro Bono Program

44 E. Camperdown Way
P.O. Box 728
Greenville, SC 29602-0728
URL: http://www.wyche.com/community

Fields of interest: Legal services.
Type of support: Pro bono services - legal.
Application information: An attorney who coordinates pro bono projects as an ancillary duty to other work.

4132
Wyndham Worldwide Corporation

22 Sylvan Way
Parsippany, NJ 07054 (973) 753-6000
FAX: (302) 636-5454

Company URL: http://www.wyndhamworldwide.com
Establishment information: Established in 1990.
Company type: Public company
Company ticker symbol and exchange: WYN/NYSE
International Securities Identification Number: US98310W1080
Business activities: Operates hospitality company.
Business type (SIC): Hotels and lodging places/ membership organization
Financial profile for 2012: Number of employees, 32,500; assets, $9,463,000,000; sales volume, $4,534,000,000; pre-tax net income, $628,000,000; expenses, $3,790,000,000; liabilities, $7,533,000,000
Fortune 1000 ranking: 2012—528th in revenues, 398th in profits, and 405th in assets
Forbes 2000 ranking: 2012—1461st in sales, 1255th in profits, and 1509th in assets
Corporate officers: Stephen P. Holmes, Chair. and C.E.O.; Thomas G. Conforti, Exec. V.P. and C.F.O.; Scott G. McLester, Exec. V.P. and Genl. Counsel; Nicola Rossi, Sr. V.P. and C.A.O.
Board of directors: Stephen P. Holmes, Chair.; Myra J. Biblowit; James E. Buckman; George Herrera; Brian Mulroney; Pauline D.E. Richards; Michael H. Wargotz
Giving statement: Giving through the Wyndham Worldwide Corporation Contributions Program.
Company EIN: 200052541

Wyndham Worldwide Corporation Contributions Program

22 Sylvan Way
Parsippany, NJ 07054-3801 (973) 753-6000
URL: http://www.wyndhamworldwide.com/about/corporate-responsibility.cfm

Purpose and activities: Wyndham Worldwide Corporation makes charitable contributions to nonprofit organizations involved with women, children, and the environment. Support is given primarily in areas of company operations.
Fields of interest: Environment Children; Women.
Type of support: Employee matching gifts; Employee volunteer services; General/operating support.
Geographic limitations: Giving primarily in areas of company operations.

4133
Wynne Building Corporation

12804 S.W. 122nd Ave.
Miami, FL 33186-6203 (305) 235-3175
FAX: (305) 378-9716

Establishment information: Established in 1983.
Company type: Private company
Business activities: Operates mobile home site; developer.
Business type (SIC): Real estate operators and lessors
Corporate officers: Joel F. Wynne, Pres.; Eric P. Wynne, V.P. and Secy.; Matthew L. Wynne, V.P. and Treas.
Giving statement: Giving through the Wynne Charitable Foundation.

Wynne Charitable Foundation

12804 S.W. 122nd Ave.
Miami, FL 33186-6203

Establishment information: Established in 2007 in FL.
Donors: Wynne Building Corporation; Joel F. Wynne.
Financial data (yr. ended 09/30/11): Assets, $423,400 (M); gifts received, $325,000; expenditures, $176,929; qualifying distributions, $329,140; giving activities include $170,450 for 51 grants (high: $127,500; low: $50).
Purpose and activities: The foundation supports organizations involved with education and human services.
Fields of interest: Higher education; Education, services; Education; Salvation Army; Children, services; Aging, centers/services; Human services; United Ways and Federated Giving Programs.
Type of support: General/operating support; Program development.
Geographic limitations: Giving primarily in FL.
Support limitations: No grants to individuals.
Application information: Applications not accepted. Unsolicited requests for funds not accepted.
Trustees: Deena L. Wynne; Dorothy Wynne; Eric P. Wynne; Joel F. Wynne; Matthew Lyle Wynne.
EIN: 261583201
Selected grants: The following grants are a representative sample of this grantmaker's funding activity:
$15,000 to United Way of Saint Lucie County, Fort Pierce, FL, 2011. For general support.
$10,000 to Allegheny College, Meadville, PA, 2011. For general support.
$2,000 to Save the Children Federation, Westport, CT, 2011. For general support.
$1,000 to Saint Edwards School, Vero Beach, FL, 2011. For general support.
$1,000 to Treasure Coast Food Bank, Fort Pierce, FL, 2011. For general support.
$1,000 to University of California, Berkeley, CA, 2011. For general support.

4134
X.L. America, Inc.

70 Seaview Ave., Ste.7
Stamford, CT 06902-6040 (203) 964-5200
FAX: (203) 602-7739

Company URL: http://www.xlgroup.com/
Establishment information: Established in 1986.
Company type: Subsidiary of a foreign company
Business activities: Operates insurance company.
Business type (SIC): Insurance agents, brokers, and services

Corporate officers: Michael S. McGavick, C.E.O.; Dennis Kane, C.O.O; Peter R. Porrino, Exec. V.P. and C.F.O.; Kirstin Roman Gould, Exec. V.P., Genl. Counsel and Secy.
Giving statement: Giving through the XL America Foundation, Inc.

XL America Foundation, Inc.

(formerly NRC Foundation, Inc.)
100 Constitution Plz., 12th Fl.
Hartford, CT 06103 (203) 964-5200

Establishment information: Established in 1999 in CT and DE.
Donors: XL Global Services, Inc.; Nicholas Brown; Ron Bornhuetter; Daniel J. McNamara.
Contact: Elizabeth Reeves, Chair. and Pres.
Financial data (yr. ended 12/31/11): Assets, $139,605 (M); gifts received, $12,500; expenditures, $25,150; qualifying distributions, $25,000; giving activities include $25,000 for grants.
Purpose and activities: Scholarship awards to children of employees of XL America, CT, for one year of study.
Type of support: Scholarships—to individuals.
Geographic limitations: Giving on a national basis.
Application information: Applications accepted. Application form required.
Initial approach: Proposal
Deadline(s): Aug.
Officers: Elizabeth Reeves, Chair. and Pres.; Michael Davi, V.P.; Richard McCarty, Secy.; Gabriel Carino, Treas.
Directors: Gary Bakalar; Edward Heffeman; John Welch.
EIN: 061559574

4135
Xcel Energy Inc.

(formerly Northern States Power Company)
414 Nicollet Mall
Minneapolis, MN 55401-1993
(612) 330-5500
FAX: (612) 330-5878

Company URL: http://www.xcelenergy.com
Establishment information: Established in 1909.
Company type: Public company
Company ticker symbol and exchange: XEL/NYSE
International Securities Identification Number: US98389B1008
Business activities: Generates, transmits, and distributes electricity; transmits and distributes natural gas.
Business type (SIC): Combination utility services
Financial profile for 2012: Number of employees, 11,198; assets, $31,140,690,000; sales volume, $10,128,220,000; pre-tax net income, $1,355,400,000; expenses, $8,305,540,000; liabilities, $22,266,610,000
Fortune 1000 ranking: 2012—266th in revenues, 216th in profits, and 179th in assets
Forbes 2000 ranking: 2012—923rd in sales, 655th in profits, and 721st in assets
Corporate officers: Benjamin G.S. Fowke III, Chair., Pres., and C.E.O.; Teresa S. Madden, Sr. V.P. and C.F.O.; Marvin E. McDaniel, Jr., Sr. V.P. and C.A.O.; Scott Wilensky, Sr. V.P. and Genl. Counsel; Kent T. Larson, Sr. V.P., Opers.; Cathy James Hart, V.P. and Corp. Secy.; George E. Tyson II, V.P. and Treas.; Jeff Savage, V.P. and Cont.
Board of directors: Benjamin G.S. Fowke III, Chair.; Gail Koziara Boudreaux; Fredric W. Corrigan; Richard K. Davis; Albert F. Moreno; Richard T. O'Brien; Christopher J. Policinski; A. Patricia Sampson; J. Joseph Sheppard; David A. Westerlund; Kim Williams; Timothy V. Wolf
Subsidiaries: Cormorant Corp., Helena, MT; First Midwest Auto Park, Inc., Minneapolis, MN; LaPaz, Minneapolis, MN; Northern States Power Company, Minneapolis, MN; Public Service Co. of Colorado, Denver, CO; Southwestern Public Service Co., Amarillo, TX; United Power & Land Co., Minneapolis, MN
Offices: Mankato, St. Cloud, MN; Grand Forks, ND; Sioux Falls, SD
Historic mergers: New Century Energies, Inc. (August 18, 2000)
Giving statement: Giving through the Xcel Energy Inc. Corporate Giving Program and the Xcel Energy Foundation.
Company EIN: 410448030

Xcel Energy Foundation

414 Nicollet Mall
Minneapolis, MN 55401-1927 (612) 215-5317
FAX: (612) 215-4522;
E-mail: foundation@xcelenergy.com; Jeanne Fox, Michigan and Wisconsin, e-mail: jean.fox@xcelenergy.com; James R. Garness, Sr. Fdn. Rep., Minnesota, e-mail: james.r.garness@xcelenergy.com; Judy Paukert, North and South Dakota, e-mail: judith.n.paukert@xcelenergy.com; Terry Price, Sr. Fdn. Rep., New Mexico and Texas, e-mail: terry.price@xcelenergy.com; Shanda Vangas, Sr. Fdn. Rep., Colorado, e-mail: Shanda.L.Vangas@excelenergy.com; URL: http://www.xcelenergy.com/About_Us/Community/Corporate_Giving

Establishment information: Established in 2001.
Donor: Xcel Energy Inc.
Contact: Monique Lovato, Dir., Corp. Philanthropy
Financial data (yr. ended 12/31/11): Assets, $2,866,161 (M); gifts received, $7,734,084; expenditures, $7,753,902; qualifying distributions, $7,750,657; giving activities include $7,647,073 for grants.
Purpose and activities: The foundation supports organizations involved with arts and culture, education, the environment, animals and wildlife, employment, and economic sustainability.
Fields of interest: Arts, equal rights; Arts education; Arts; Elementary/secondary education; Business school/education; Scholarships/financial aid; Education; Environment, alliance/advocacy; Environment, public education; Environment, water resources; Environment, land resources; Environment, energy; Environment, beautification programs; Environmental education; Environment; Animals/wildlife, alliance/advocacy; Animals/wildlife, public education; Animals/wildlife, preservation/protection; Employment, training; Employment, retraining; Employment; Boy scouts; Economic development; Business/industry; Community/economic development; United Ways and Federated Giving Programs; Science, formal/general education; Mathematics Economically disadvantaged.
Programs:
Arts and Culture: The foundation supports programs designed to increase accessibility to artistic and cultural activities that enable all members of communities to participate in the arts. Special emphasis is directed toward programs designed to provide free or reduced admission to artistic and cultural activities for people who otherwise could not afford to attend; engage the public in art and cultural events; enhance music education/performing arts in schools by offering concerts, musician or performer visits, family workshops, or teacher training; and address social issues, concerns, and challenges facing communities.
Dollars for Doing: The foundation awards grants of $5 per hour to nonprofit organizations with which employees of Xcel Energy volunteer at least 100 hours.
Economic Sustainability: The foundation supports programs designed to assist individuals in obtaining employment; and provides funding to organizations that support job creation. Special emphasis is directed toward community development projects designed to improve the economic well-being and sustainability of a community, such as programs that create attract or retain business especially in economically depressed areas; transitional and supportive programs designed to provide educational employment, and job placement services for low-income populations; and programs designed to promote personal skill development, including job entry skills and retraining of unemployed and underemployed workers.
Education: The foundation supports programs designed to promote math, science, and economic education for students in kindergarten through college. Special emphasis is directed toward programs designed to enrich and improve student performance in math and science, in combination with core academic curriculum; establish endowments for scholarships focused on mathematics, science, technical, or environmental areas of study, as they relate to the energy industry; provide scholarships and internships for the same areas of study; encourage students with economic education and practical business/technical skills to compete effectively in the job market; support district, state, and/or national educational standards in math and science; and promote student participation in math and science curriculum through programs that involve participation and partnership among students, educators, business, and nonprofit entities.
Environment: The foundation supports programs designed to promote environmental education, awareness, and partnerships. Special emphasis is directed toward programs designed to train and support K-12 educators in teaching curriculum focused on energy and the environment; emphasize dialogue and consensus building in the areas of energy efficiency, renewable technologies, and wildlife stewardship; display exhibits at museums and other public community-based facilities, with an emphasis on interactive and demonstration displays that build awareness for energy efficiency, renewable technologies, and wildlife stewardship; preserve, restore, and improve wildlife habitat, open lands, wetlands, parks, trail systems, or recreational areas; and meet the stated goal of producing environmental improvement through neighborhood cleanup and beautification efforts that provide volunteer opportunities for employees and retirees of Xcel Energy.
Matching Gifts: The foundation matches contributions made by employees of Xcel Energy to nonprofit organizations on a one-for-one basis up to $750 per employee, per year and to institutions of higher education up to $2,000 per employee, per year.
Volunteer Energy: The foundation awards $500 grants to nonprofit organizations with which teams of six or more employees of Xcel Energy volunteer.
Type of support: Employee matching gifts; Employee volunteer services; General/operating support; Program development.
Geographic limitations: Giving limited to areas of company operations in CO, MI, MN, ND, NM, SD, TX, and WI.

Support limitations: No support for national organizations, government agencies, religious, political, veterans', or fraternal organizations not of direct benefit to the entire community or disease-specific organizations. No grants to individuals, or for research programs, endowments, athletic or scholarship competitions, benefits or fundraising activities, sports or athletic programs, or capital campaigns.
Publications: Application guidelines; Grants list; Informational brochure; Program policy statement.
Application information: Applications accepted. Applicants may be invited to submit a full proposal. Organizations receiving support are asked to submit a final report. Application form required.
Initial approach: Complete online letter of intent form
Deadline(s): Dec. 15 to Jan. 20 for Education and Environment; Apr. 23 to May 11 for Arts & Culture and Economic Sustainability
Final notification: Within 3 weeks following deadlines
Officers and Directors:* Ben Fowke*, Chair. and Pres.; Roy Palmer*, Secy.; Geroge E. Tyson II, Treas.; David L. Eves; Cathy J. Hart; C. Riley Hill; Judy M. Poferl; Mark E. Stoering.
EIN: 412007734
Selected grants: The following grants are a representative sample of this grantmaker's funding activity:
$201,891 to United Way, Greater Twin Cities, Minneapolis, MN, 2009.
$125,000 to Salvation Army, Northern Division, Roseville, MN, 2009.
$80,000 to Minnesota Private College Fund, Saint Paul, MN, 2009.
$50,000 to Volunteers for Outdoor Colorado, Denver, CO, 2009.
$30,000 to Science Museum of Minnesota, Saint Paul, MN, 2009.
$10,000 to Sustainable Revolution Project, Minneapolis, MN, 2009.
$8,636 to 4Charity Foundation, Honolulu, HI, 2009.
$7,500 to Dakota Area Resources and Transportation for Seniors, West Saint Paul, MN, 2009.
$7,500 to Denver Public Schools Foundation, Denver, CO, 2009.
$5,000 to Lake Superior Big Top Chautauqua, Washburn, WI, 2009.

4136
Xerox Corporation

45 Glover Ave.
P.O. Box 4505
Norwalk, CT 06856-4505 (203) 849-2478
FAX: (203) 968-3218

Company URL: http://www.xerox.com
Establishment information: Established in 1906.
Company type: Public company
Company ticker symbol and exchange: XRX/NYSE
International Securities Identification Number: US9841211033
Business activities: Develops, manufactures, and distributes document processing products and solutions.
Business type (SIC): Computer and office equipment; photographic equipment and supplies
Financial profile for 2012: Number of employees, 147,600; assets, $30,015,000,000; sales volume, $22,390,000,000; pre-tax net income, $1,348,000,000; expenses, $21,042,000,000; liabilities, $18,145,000,000
Fortune 1000 ranking: 2012—131st in revenues, 168th in profits, and 186th in assets
Forbes 2000 ranking: 2012—423rd in sales, 506th in profits, and 738th in assets
Corporate officers: Ursula M. Burns, Chair. and C.E.O.; Kathryn Mikells, Exec. V.P., and C.F.O; Don H. Liu, Sr. V.P., Genl. Counsel, and Secy.; Joseph H. Mancini,, Jr., V.P. and C.A.O.; Carol Zierhoffer, V.P. and C.I.O.; Rhonda L. Seegal, V.P. and Treas.; Leslie F. Varon, V.P., Finance, and Cont.
Board of directors: Ursula M. Burns, Chair.; Glenn A. Britt; Richard J. Harrington; William Curt Hunter; Robert J. Keegan; Robert A. McDonald; Charles O. Prince III; Ann N. Reese; Sara Martinez Tucker; Mary Agnes Wilderotter
Plants: El Segundo, CA; Webster, NY
International operations: Austria; Barbados; Belgium; Bermuda; Brazil; Bulgaria; Canada; Chile; China; Colombia; Czech Republic; Denmark; Ecuador; Egypt; Finland; France; Germany; Greece; Guatemala; Haiti; Honduras; Hong Kong; India; Ireland; Israel; Japan; Kazakhstan; Luxembourg; Malaysia; Mauritius; Mexico; Morocco and the Western Sahara; Netherlands; Norway; Peru; Poland; Portugal; Romania; Russia; Scotland; Singapore; Slovenia; Spain; Sweden; Switzerland; Trinidad & Tobago; Turkey; Ukraine; United Kingdom; Venezuela
Giving statement: Giving through the Xerox Foundation.
Company EIN: 160468020

The Xerox Foundation

45 Glover Ave.
P.O. Box 4505
Norwalk, CT 06856-4505 (203) 849-2453
E-mail: mark.conlin@xerox.com; URL: http://www.xerox.com/foundation

Establishment information: Incorporated in 1979 in DE as successor to the Xerox Fund.
Donor: Xerox Corp.
Contact: Mark J. Conlin, Pres.
Financial data (yr. ended 12/31/11): Assets, $340 (M); gifts received, $438,295; expenditures, $440,595; qualifying distributions, $440,595; giving activities include $277,595 for 21 grants (high: $30,000; low: $20) and $163,000 for 125 grants to individuals (high: $10,000; low: $1,000).
Purpose and activities: The foundation supports organizations involved with arts and culture, education, including the application of information technology, the environment, workforce preparedness, human services, science and technology, national public policy issues, civic affairs, minorities, women, and economically disadvantaged people.
Fields of interest: Arts; Higher education; Adult education—literacy, basic skills & GED; Education; Environment; Employment; Children/youth, services; Family services; Human services; United Ways and Federated Giving Programs; Engineering/technology; Science; Public policy, research; Public affairs Children/youth; Youth; Disabilities, people with; Physically disabled; Blind/visually impaired; Deaf/hearing impaired; Mentally disabled; Minorities; African Americans/Blacks; Hispanics/Latinos; Native Americans/American Indians; Indigenous peoples; Women; Military/veterans; Economically disadvantaged; Homeless.
Programs:
Xerox Community Involvement Program: The foundation provides seed money for qualified activities and programs with which Xerox Corp. employees are involved.
Xerox Employee Matching Gifts Program: The foundation matches contributions made by current employees, directors, or retired employees of Xerox to four-year educational institutions, two-year community colleges, and junior colleges on a one-for-one basis from $25 to $1,000 per contributor, per institution.
Xerox Social Service Leave Program: Through the Social Service Leave Program, Xerox employees take fully-paid sabbaticals of up to one year to volunteer full-time on social action projects of their own design and choosing.
Type of support: Continuing support; Curriculum development; Emergency funds; Employee matching gifts; Employee volunteer services; Employee-related scholarships; General/operating support; Professorships; Program development; Research; Scholarship funds; Seed money; Sponsorships; Technical assistance.
Geographic limitations: Giving on a national basis primarily in areas of company operations.
Support limitations: No support for political organizations or candidates, religious or sectarian organizations, or municipal, county, state, federal, or quasi-government agencies. No grants to individuals (Except for Technical Minority Scholarships), or for endowments or endowed chairs; no product donations.
Publications: Annual report; Application guidelines; Corporate giving report (including application guidelines); Corporate report; Informational brochure (including application guidelines); Program policy statement (including application guidelines).
Application information: Applications accepted. Proposals should be brief. Multi-year funding is not automatic. Organizations that have previously received support on an annual basis from the foundation must re-submit requests each year to be considered for continued support. Application form not required. Applicants should submit the following:
1) results expected from proposed grant
2) name, address and phone number of organization
3) copy of IRS Determination Letter
4) copy of most recent annual report/audited financial statement/990
5) how project's results will be evaluated or measured
6) descriptive literature about organization
7) detailed description of project and amount of funding requested
8) contact person
9) copy of current year's organizational budget and/or project budget
10) listing of additional sources and amount of support
11) additional materials/documentation
Initial approach: Proposal or letter of inquiry
Copies of proposal: 1
Board meeting date(s): Monthly contributions meetings; quarterly board meetings
Deadline(s): None
Final notification: 30 to 45 days
Officer: Mark J. Conlin, Pres.
Trustees: Ursula Burns.
Number of staff: 3 full-time professional; 2 part-time professional; 2 full-time support.
EIN: 060996443

4137
Xilinx, Inc.

2100 Logic Dr.
San Jose, CA 95124-3400 (408) 559-7778
FAX: (408) 559-7114

Company URL: http://www.xilinx.com
Establishment information: Established in 1984.
Company type: Public company

Company ticker symbol and exchange: XLNX/NASDAQ
Business activities: Operates a semiconductor company.
Business type (SIC): Electronic components and accessories
Financial profile for 2013: Number of employees, 3,329; assets, $4,729,450,000; sales volume, $2,168,650,000; pre-tax net income, $547,010,000; expenses, $1,587,920,000; liabilities, $1,766,150,000
Fortune 1000 ranking: 2012—864th in revenues, 320th in profits, and 627th in assets
Corporate officers: Philip T. Gianos, Chair.; Moshe Gavrielov, Pres. and C.E.O.; Jon Olson, Sr. V.P. and C.F.O.; Raja Petrakian, Sr. V.P., Opers.; Frank Tornaghi, Sr. V.P., Sales; Kevin Cooney, Corp. V.P. and C.I.O.; Scott Hover-Smoot, Corp. V.P., Genl. Counsel, and Secy.; Marilyn Stiborek Meyer, Corp. V.P., Human Resources
Board of directors: Philip T. Gianos, Chair.; John L. Doyle; Moshe N. Gavrielov; William G. Howard, Jr.; J. Michael Patterson; Albert A. Pimentel; Marshall C. Turner, Jr.; Elizabeth W. Vanderslice
Giving statement: Giving through the Xilinx, Inc. Contributions Program.
Company EIN: 770188631

Xilinx, Inc. Contributions Program

c/o Community Rels.
2100 Logic Dr.
San Jose, CA 95124-3400 (408) 559-7778
FAX: (408) 559-7114; URL: http://www.xilinx.com/about/community-relations/index.htm

Purpose and activities: Xilinx makes charitable contributions to nonprofit organizations involved with arts and culture, education, healthcare, and community and social services. Support is given primarily in areas of company operations in California, Colorado, New Mexico, and Oregon, and in China, India, Ireland, Japan, and Singapore.
Fields of interest: Arts; Elementary/secondary education; Education, special; Health care; Human services; Science, formal/general education; Mathematics; Engineering/technology.
International interests: China; India; Ireland; Japan; Singapore.
Type of support: Employee volunteer services; General/operating support; In-kind gifts; Program development.
Geographic limitations: Giving primarily in areas of company operations in CA, CO, NM, and OR, and in China, India, Ireland, Japan, and Singapore.
Support limitations: No support for religious organizations not of direct benefit to the entire community, political organizations, fraternal organizations, or discriminatory organizations. No grants for athletic programs, athletic scholarships, tournaments, youth and adult sports leagues, or recreational activities.

4138
XTEK, Inc.

11451 Reading Rd.
Cincinnati, OH 45241 (513) 733-7800

Company URL: http://www.xtek.com/
Establishment information: Established in 1909.
Company type: Private company
Business activities: Manufactures hardened steel machine components, custom gearing, crane wheels, steel mill work rolls, and power transmission parts.
Business type (SIC): Machinery/industrial and commercial; machinery/metalworking; machinery/general industry; electronic components and accessories
Corporate officers: Kyle H. Seymour, Pres., and C.E.O.; Roger Miller, C.O.O.; Ed Plavko, Exec. V.P. and C.F.O.; Edward R. Plavko, V.P., Finance; Tom Ryan, V.P., Mktg.; James J. Raible, V.P., Sales; Jennifer King, V.P., Human Resources
Giving statement: Giving through the XTEK Foundation.
Company EIN: 250447969

XTEK Foundation

P.O. Box 1118, ML CN-OH-W10X
Cincinnati, OH 45201-1118

Establishment information: Incorporated in 1962 in OH.
Donors: XTEK, Inc.; James D. Kiggen.
Financial data (yr. ended 12/31/11): Assets, $53,590 (M); gifts received, $60,000; expenditures, $34,800; qualifying distributions, $34,350; giving activities include $33,750 for 2 grants (high: $28,750; low: $5,000).
Purpose and activities: The foundation supports organizations involved with arts and culture and the United Way.
Fields of interest: Arts; United Ways and Federated Giving Programs.
Type of support: Annual campaigns.
Geographic limitations: Giving primarily in the greater Cincinnati, OH, area.
Application information: Applications not accepted. Unsolicited requests for funds not accepted.
Trustees: Jennifer Gill King; Kyle H. Seymour.
EIN: 316029606

4139
Xylem, Inc.

(formerly ITT WCO, Inc.)
1133 Westchester Ave., Ste. N200
White Plains, NY 10604 (914) 323-5700
FAX: (914) 323-5800

Company URL: http://www.xyleminc.com
Establishment information: Established in 2011.
Company type: Public company
Company ticker symbol and exchange: XYL/NYSE
International Securities Identification Number: US98419M1009
Business activities: Operates water technology company.
Business type (SIC): Machinery/general industry
Financial profile for 2012: Number of employees, 12,700; assets, $4,679,000,000; sales volume, $3,791,000,000; pre-tax net income, $388,000,000; expenses, $3,348,000,000; liabilities, $2,605,000,000
Fortune 1000 ranking: 2012—612th in revenues, 476th in profits, and 612th in assets
Corporate officers: Markos I. Tambakeras, Chair.; Gretchen W. McClain, Pres. and C.E.O.; Mike Speetzen, Sr. V.P. and C.F.O.; Nicholas R. Colisto, Sr. V.P. and C.I.O.; Christian S. Na, Sr. V.P., Genl. Counsel, and Secy.
Board of directors: Markos I. Tambakeras, Chair.; Curtis J. Crawford, Ph.D.; Robert F. Friel; Victoria D. Harker; Sten E. Jakobsson; Steven R. Loranger; Edward J. Ludwig; Gretchen W. McClain; Surya N. Mohapatra, Ph.D.; Jerome A. Peribere; James P. Rogers
Giving statement: Giving through the Xylem Inc. Contributions Program.
Company EIN: 452080495

Xylem Inc. Contributions Program

1133 Westchester Ave.
White Plains, NY 10604 (914) 323-5700
FAX: (914) 323-5800;
E-mail: michaelc.fields@xyleminc.com; URL: http://www.xyleminc.com/en-us/sustainability/global-citizenship/Pages/default.aspx

Contact: Michael Fields, Dir., Xylem Watermark
Purpose and activities: Xylem makes charitable contributions to nonprofit organizations that provide and protect safe water resources in communities around the world through its signature charitable program, Xylem Watermark, and other efforts. Support is given on a national basis, with emphasis on areas of company operations; and on an international basis, including China and Latin America, with emphasis on developing countries.
Fields of interest: Public health school/education; Education; Environment, water resources; Public health, clean water supply; Health care; Disasters, preparedness/services; Women, centers/services; Public utilities, water; Public utilities, sewage Economically disadvantaged.
Programs:
Stockholm Junior Water Prize: The Stockholm Junior Water Prize is a global competition started more than 15 years ago that engages high school students in more than 30 countries to come forward with ideas on how to improve the world's water quality. Xylem is the global sponsor of the international competition that is held annually in Sweden. The company also supports the qualifying competitions in nine countries through funding and volunteer judges. Finalists from each country earn a trip to World Water Week where they interact with the biggest names in the water arena.
Xylem Watermark: Through Watermark, and in association with several key nonprofit partners, Xylem brings safe water, sanitation, and hygiene education to schools and communities in developing countries. The program also provides relief - in the form of funding and equipment donations - in the aftermath of disasters where clean and safe water is an issue. And Xylem funds disaster risk reduction projects that secure water resources in vulnerable communities. Through strategic partnerships, employee engagement, and innovative water solutions, Xylem Watermark helped 500,000 people globally in its first three years, and will reach a million more people by the end of 2013.
Type of support: Employee matching gifts; Employee volunteer services; Equipment; General/operating support; Sponsorships.
Geographic limitations: Giving on a national basis, with emphasis on areas of company operations; and on an international basis, including China and Latin America, with emphasis on developing countries.

4140
Yahoo! Inc.

701 1st Ave.
Sunnyvale, CA 94089-1019 (408) 349-3300
FAX: (408) 349-3301

Company URL: http://www.yahoo.com
Establishment information: Established in 1994.
Company type: Public company
Company ticker symbol and exchange: YHOO/NASDAQ
International Securities Identification Number: US9843321061
Business activities: Provides Internet information services.
Business type (SIC): Computer services

Financial profile for 2012: Number of employees, 11,700; assets, $17,103,300,000; sales volume, $4,986,600,000
Fortune 1000 ranking: 2012—494th in revenues, 48th in profits, and 268th in assets
Forbes 2000 ranking: 2012—1400th in sales, 143rd in profits, and 1071st in assets
Corporate officers: Maynard G. Webb, Jr., Chair.; Marissa Ann Mayer, Pres. and C.E.O.; Henrique de Castro, C.O.O.; Kenneth A. Goldman, C.F.O.; Ron Bell, Genl. Counsel and Secy.
Board of directors: Maynard G. Webb, Jr., Chair.; John Hayes; Susan James; Daniel S. Loeb; Peter Liguori; Marrisa Mayer; Thomas McInerney; Harry J. Wilson; Michael J. Wolf
International operations: Argentina; Australia; Brazil; Canada; Denmark; France; Germany; Hong Kong; India; Italy; Japan; Mexico; Singapore; South Korea; Spain; Taiwan; United Kingdom
Giving statement: Giving through the Yahoo! Employee Foundation and the Yahoo! for Good.
Company EIN: 770398689

Yahoo! Employee Foundation

(also known as YEF)
701 1st Ave.
Sunnyvale, CA 94089-1019
URL: http://forgood.yahoo.com/

Purpose and activities: The Yahoo! Employee Foundation is an employee-driven philanthropic organization. All monies are donated by employees, and all activities are run by a volunteer committee of Yahoo! employees.
Fields of interest: General charitable giving.
Type of support: Employee volunteer services; General/operating support.
Application information: Applications not accepted. Contributes only to pre-selected organizations.

Yahoo! for Good

701 1st Ave.
Sunnyvale, CA 94089-1019 (408) 349-3300
FAX: (408) 349-3301; URL: http://forgood.yahoo.com

Purpose and activities: As a complement to its foundation, Yahoo! also makes charitable contributions to nonprofit organizations directly.
Fields of interest: Education; Environment; Breast cancer; Safety/disasters, fund raising/fund distribution; Safety/disasters; Engineering/technology.
Program:
Employee Matching Gifts: Yahoo! matches contributions made by its employees to nonprofit organizations up to $1,000 per employee, per year.
Type of support: Cause-related marketing; Donated products; Employee volunteer services.
Number of staff: 1

4141
Yamaha Motor Corporation, U.S.A.

6555 Katella Ave.
Cypress, CA 90630 (714) 761-7300

Company URL: http://www.yamaha-motor.com
Establishment information: Established in 1977.
Company type: Subsidiary of a foreign company
Business activities: Markets motorcycles, outboard motors, ATVs, personal watercraft, snowmobiles, boats, outdoor power equipment, and race kart engines.
Business type (SIC): Motor vehicles, parts, and supplies—wholesale; industrial machinery and equipment—wholesale; durable goods—wholesale
Financial profile for 2010: Number of employees, 400
Corporate officers: Masato Adachi, Pres.; Nicky Mizuta, C.F.O.; Michael Grbic, V.P. and Genl. Counsel
Giving statement: Giving through the Yamaha Motor Corporation, U.S.A. Corporate Giving Program.

Yamaha Motor Corporation, U.S.A. Corporate Giving Program

6555 Katella Ave.
Cypress, CA 90630-5101 (714) 761-7740

Purpose and activities: Yamaha makes charitable contributions to nonprofit organizations on a case by case basis. Support is given on a national basis.
Fields of interest: General charitable giving.
Type of support: Donated products; General/operating support.
Support limitations: No grants to individuals (except for scholarships).

4142
W. G. Yates & Sons Construction Company

1 Gully Ave.
Philadelphia, MS 39350 (601) 656-5411
FAX: (601) 656-8958

Company URL: http://www.wgyates.com
Establishment information: Established in 1964.
Company type: Subsidiary of a private company
Business activities: Operates nonresidential construction company.
Business type (SIC): Contractors/general nonresidential building
Corporate officers: William G. Yates III, Chair., Pres., and C.E.O.; Kenny Bush, V.P., Human Resources; Brandon R. Dunn, C.F.O.; Marvin Blanks III, Treas. and C.F.O.
Board of director: William G. Yates III, Chair.
Giving statement: Giving through the Yates Emergency Relief Foundation.

Yates Emergency Relief Foundation

P.O. Box 456
Philadelphia, MS 39350-0456

Financial data (yr. ended 06/30/09): Assets, $55,566 (M); expenditures, $7,000; giving activities include $7,000 for grants to individuals.
Purpose and activities: The foundation provides financial assistance to employees of W.G. Yates & Sons Construction Company who suffered a substantial loss due to a tragedy.
Fields of interest: Human services, emergency aid.
Type of support: Emergency funds; Grants to individuals.
Officer: Carolyn Y. Voyles, Pres.
Directors: William G. Yates, Jr.; William G. Yates III.
EIN: 203449198

4143
The YGS Group, Inc.

(formerly York Graphic Services, Inc.)
3650 W. Market St.
York, PA 17404-5813 (717) 505-9701

Company URL: http://www.theygsgroup.com/
Establishment information: Established in 1953.
Company type: Private company
Business activities: Provides commercial printing, offsetting, color separation, and typesetting services.
Business type (SIC): Printing/commercial; printing trade services
Corporate officers: James Kell, C.E.O.; Brad Altman, Pres.; Thomas Grentz, C.F.O.
Giving statement: Giving through the Hellenic Foundation.

The Hellenic Foundation

12051 Rosemount Dr.
Fort Myers, FL 33913-8380 (801) 322-1814

Donors: York Graphic Services, Inc.; John F. Grove, Jr.
Contact: John F. Grove, Jr., Tr.
Financial data (yr. ended 06/30/11): Assets, $291,829 (M); expenditures, $17,214; qualifying distributions, $9,941; giving activities include $7,750 for 5 grants (high: $5,000; low: $250).
Purpose and activities: The foundation supports organizations involved with education, health, and autism, and awards college scholarships.
Fields of interest: Higher education; Theological school/education; Education; Health care; Autism.
Type of support: Annual campaigns; General/operating support; Scholarships—to individuals.
Geographic limitations: Giving primarily in ID, PA, and UT.
Application information: Applications accepted. Application form required.
Requests for scholarships should include academic records, recommendations, and a statement of financial needs.
Initial approach: Letter
Deadline(s): None
Trustees: John F. Grove, Jr.; Teresa I. Grove.
EIN: 222536161

4144
YIKES, Inc.

204 E. Girard Ave.
Philadelphia, PA 19125-3909
(215) 238-8801

Company URL: http://www.yikesinc.com
Establishment information: Established in 1996.
Company type: Private company
Business activities: Operates Web design and development company.
Business type (SIC): Business services/miscellaneous
Corporate officers: Mia Levesque, Co-Owner; Tracy Levesque, Co-Owner
Giving statement: Giving through the YIKES, Inc. Corporate Giving Program.

YIKES, Inc. Corporate Giving Program

305 Brown St.
Philadelphia, PA 19123 (215) 238-8801
URL: http://www.yikesinc.com/company/social-responsibility/

Purpose and activities: Yikes, Inc. is a certified B Corporation that donates a percentage of profits to nonprofit organizations.

4145
York Container Company

138 Mount Zion Rd.
P.O. Box 3008
York, PA 17402-0008 (717) 757-7611

Company URL: http://www.yorkcontainer.com
Establishment information: Established in 1954.
Company type: Private company
Business activities: Operates packaging company.
Business type (SIC): Paperboard containers
Corporate officers: Dennis E. Willman, Chair.; Alan S. King, C.E.O.; Steve Tansey, Pres. and C.O.O.; William C. Ludwig, C.F.O. and Treas.; Constance L. Wolf, Secy.
Board of director: Dennis E. Willman, Chair.
Giving statement: Giving through the York Container Foundation.

York Container Foundation

138 Mount Zion Rd.
York, PA 17402-8985

Establishment information: Established in 1983 in PA.
Donor: York Container Co.
Financial data (yr. ended 12/31/11): Assets, $167 (M); expenditures, $875; qualifying distributions, $0.
Purpose and activities: The foundation supports hospitals and organizations involved with higher education, children and youth, and Christianity.
Fields of interest: Arts; Health organizations; Human services.
Type of support: Annual campaigns; Building/renovation; Capital campaigns; Debt reduction; Endowments.
Geographic limitations: Giving primarily in PA, with emphasis on York.
Support limitations: No grants to individuals.
Application information: Applications not accepted. Unsolicited requests for funds not accepted.
Officers: Dennis W. Willman, Chair.; Charles S. Wolf, Jr., Pres.; Constance L. Wolf, Secy.; William Ludwig, Treas.
EIN: 222473590
Selected grants: The following grants are a representative sample of this grantmaker's funding activity:
$25,000 to Logos Academy, York, PA, 2009. For general purpose.
$25,000 to YWCA of York, York, PA, 2009. For general purpose.
$5,000 to York College of Pennsylvania, York, PA, 2009. For general purpose.
$1,000 to Leadership York, York, PA, 2009. For general purpose.
$1,000 to York, City of, York, PA, 2009. For general purpose.

4146
The Young Agency, Inc.

500 Plum St., Ste. 200
Syracuse, NY 13204-1480 (315) 474-3374
FAX: (315) 474-7039

Company URL: http://www.youngagency.com
Establishment information: Established in 1905.
Company type: Subsidiary of a public company
Business activities: Provides insurance brokerage services.
Business type (SIC): Insurance agents, brokers, and services
Corporate officers: George J. Schunck, Chair. and C.E.O.; Roy S. Moore III, Pres.
Board of director: George J. Schunck, Chair.
Giving statement: Giving through the Young Agency Foundation.

Young Agency Foundation

Bridgewater Pl.
500 Plum St., Ste. 200
Syracuse, NY 13204-1480

Establishment information: Established in 1987 in NY.
Donor: The Young Agency, Inc.
Financial data (yr. ended 12/31/11): Assets, $731 (M); gifts received, $10,000; expenditures, $10,000; qualifying distributions, $10,000; giving activities include $10,000 for grants.
Purpose and activities: The foundation supports hospitals and organizations involved with patient services, children, and senior citizen services.
Fields of interest: Hospitals (general); Health care, patient services; Boy scouts; YM/YWCAs & YM/YWHAs; Children, services; Aging, centers/services; United Ways and Federated Giving Programs.
Type of support: General/operating support.
Geographic limitations: Giving primarily in Syracuse, NY.
Support limitations: No grants to individuals.
Application information: Applications not accepted. Unsolicited requests for funds not accepted.
Trustees: Nicholas J. Dereszynski; Roy S. Moore III; George J. Schunck.
EIN: 161298185

4147
Young Contracting, Inc.

8215 Roswell Rd., Bldg. 400
Atlanta, GA 30350-2808 (770) 522-9270

Company URL: http://www.youngcontracting.com
Establishment information: Established in 1991.
Company type: Private company
Business activities: Operates general contracting company.
Business type (SIC): Contractors/general residential building
Corporate officer: Gary W. Young, Pres.
Office: Tampa, FL
Giving statement: Giving through the Young Contracting Company Foundation, Inc.

Young Contracting Company Foundation, Inc.

8215 Roswell Rd., Bldg. 400
Atlanta, GA 30350-2808 (770) 522-9270

Establishment information: Established in 2007 in GA.
Donor: Young Contracting/SE, Inc.
Contact: Gary W. Young, C.E.O. and C.F.O.
Financial data (yr. ended 12/31/11): Assets, $282,511 (M); expenditures, $41,081; qualifying distributions, $38,755; giving activities include $38,755 for grants.
Fields of interest: Animals/wildlife; Health care; Youth development.
Geographic limitations: Giving primarily in GA.
Application information: Applications accepted. Application form required.
Initial approach: Proposal
Deadline(s): None
Officers: Gary W. Young, C.E.O. and C.F.O.; Benjamin R. Peacock, Secy.
EIN: 261558530

4148
Young Steel Products Co.

17819 Foxborough Ln.
Boca Raton, FL 33496-1320
(561) 477-9080

Establishment information: Established in 2000.
Company type: Private company
Business activities: Provides investment services.
Business type (SIC): Investment offices
Corporate officer: Maury Young, Owner
Giving statement: Giving through the M. A. Young Foundation.

M. A. Young Foundation

17819 Foxborough Ln.
Boca Raton, FL 33496-1320

Donor: Young Steel Products Co.
Financial data (yr. ended 03/31/12): Assets, $1,273,665 (M); expenditures, $67,448; qualifying distributions, $63,633; giving activities include $63,633 for grants.
Fields of interest: Health care; Human services; Religion.
Support limitations: No grants to individuals.
Application information: Applications not accepted. Contributes only to pre-selected organizations.
Officer and Directors:* M. A. Young*, Pres.; Babette S. Young; Robert A. Young.
EIN: 510365021

4149
YSI Incorporated

1725 Brannum Ln., Ste. 1700
Yellow Springs, OH 45387-1106
(937) 767-7241

Company URL: http://www.ysi.com
Establishment information: Established in 1948.
Company type: Private company
Business activities: Designs and manufactures precision measurement sensors and control instruments.
Business type (SIC): Laboratory apparatus
Corporate officers: Malte Von Matthiessen, Chair.; Richard J. Ormlor, Pres. and C.E.O.; Leon Erdman, C.F.O.
Board of director: Malte Van Matthiessen, Chair.
International operations: Hong Kong
Giving statement: Giving through the YSI Foundation, Inc.

YSI Foundation, Inc.

P.O. Box 279
Yellow Springs, OH 45387-0279
E-mail: smiller@ysi.com

Establishment information: Established in 1990 in OH.
Donor: YSI Inc.
Contact: Deb Stottlemyer, Treas.

Financial data (yr. ended 12/31/11): Assets, $56,973 (M); gifts received, $155,087; expenditures, $177,623; qualifying distributions, $174,673; giving activities include $174,673 for 32 grants (high: $30,903; low: $50).
Purpose and activities: The foundation supports organizations involved with arts and culture, education, disaster relief, human services, community development, and life sciences. Special emphasis is directed to programs designed to promote global environmental stewardship.
Fields of interest: Arts; Higher education; Education; Environment, water pollution; Environment, natural resources; Environment, water resources; Environment; Disasters, preparedness/services; Human services; Community/economic development; United Ways and Federated Giving Programs; Science.
Programs:
Graduate Student Scholarship and Equipment Loan Program: The foundation annually awards four scholarships and loans equipment free of charge to graduate students for original research projects created by the student or in response to a YSI Research Proposal. Special emphasis is directed to the study of environmental variables in oceans, estuaries, rivers, lakes, or laboratory settings. Scholarships of up to $10,000 are awarded and each proposal is eligible for a $1,000 travel grant to a national conference to present the results of investigations.
Minding the Planet Grants: The foundation awards grants of up to $25,000 to projects designed to promote sustainability of earth, its habitants, and its natural resources; and projects designed to preserve or restore natural habitats. The environmental focus for Minding the Planet Grant changes on a yearly basis. A request for proposal is announced in June.
YSI Scholarships: The foundation awards scholarships to a local high school student and a YSI employee's child to pursue a two or four-year post-high school continuing education program.
Type of support: Building/renovation; Capital campaigns; Continuing support; Curriculum development; Emergency funds; Employee matching gifts; Employee-related scholarships; Endowments; Equipment; Matching/challenge support; Program development; Publication; Scholarship funds; Scholarships—to individuals; Seed money; Technical assistance.
Geographic limitations: Giving primarily in OH.
Support limitations: Generally, no support for large national or local organizations. No grants for general operating support or annual campaigns.
Publications: Application guidelines; Occasional report (including application guidelines).
Application information: Applications accepted. Proposals should be no longer than 5 pages for Mind the Planet Grants and 10 pages for the Graduate Student Scholarship and Equipment Loan Program. Organizations receiving support are asked to submit a final report. Application form not required.
Initial approach: Letter
Copies of proposal: 1
Board meeting date(s): Quarterly
Deadline(s): None
Final notification: May 15 for Graduate Student Scholarship and Equipment Loan Program
Officers: Deb Stottlemyer, Treas.
Trustees: Anita Brown; Michael Fields; Tim Finegan; Malte Von Matthiessen; Christopher McIntire; Charlene Miller; Susan Miller; Fred Tolliver.
EIN: 311292180
Selected grants: The following grants are a representative sample of this grantmaker's funding activity:
$25,000 to North American Lake Management Society, Madison, WI, 2010.
$15,000 to Baltimore Harbor Waterkeeper, Baltimore, MD, 2010.
$5,000 to Kids Ecology Corps, Fort Lauderdale, FL, 2010.
$3,500 to Places, Dayton, OH, 2010.
$3,000 to Daybreak, Dayton, OH, 2010.
$2,500 to Antioch University, Yellow Springs, OH, 2010.
$2,500 to Ohio State University, Columbus, OH, 2010. For scholarship.
$2,500 to Ohio University, Athens, OH, 2010. For scholarship.
$2,500 to River Network, Portland, OR, 2010.
$2,500 to Washington University, Saint Louis, MO, 2010. For scholarship.

4150
Yum! Brands, Inc.

(formerly Tricon Global Restaurants, Inc.)
1900 Colonel Sanders Ln.
Louisville, KY 40213 (502) 874-8300
FAX: (502) 454-2410

Company URL: http://www.yum.com
Establishment information: Established in 1997.
Company type: Public company
Company ticker symbol and exchange: YUM/NYSE
International Securities Identification Number: US9884981013
Business activities: Operates fast-food restaurants.
Business type (SIC): Restaurants and drinking places
Financial profile for 2012: Number of employees, 523,000; assets, $9,011,000,000; sales volume, $13,633,000,000; pre-tax net income, $2,145,000,000; expenses, $11,339,000,000; liabilities, $6,857,000,000
Fortune 1000 ranking: 2012—201st in revenues, 131st in profits, and 425th in assets
Forbes 2000 ranking: 2012—706th in sales, 386th in profits, and 1545th in assets
Corporate officers: David C. Novak, Chair. and C.E.O.; Samuel Jing-Shyh Su, Vice-Chair.; Richard T. Carucci, Pres.; Roger Eaton, C.O.O.; Patrick Grismer, C.F.O.; Christian L. Campbell, Sr. V.P., Genl. Counsel, and Secy.; W. Lawrence Gathof, V.P. and Treas.; David Russell, V.P. and Corp. Cont.
Board of directors: David C. Novak, Chair.; Samuel Jing-Shyh Su, Vice-Chair.; Michael J. Cavanagh; David W. Dorman; Massimo Ferragamo; Mirian M. Graddick-Weir; J. David Grissom; Bonnie G. Hill; Jonathan S. Linen; Thomas C. Nelson; Thomas M. Ryan; Robert D. Walter
Subsidiaries: KFC Corporation, Louisville, KY; Long John Silver's, Inc., Lexington, KY; Pizza Hut, Inc., Dallas, TX; Taco Bell Corp., Irvine, CA
International operations: Australia; Bahrain; Brazil; Canada; Cayman Islands; Chile; China; France; Germany; Hong Kong; India; Luxembourg; Malta; Mauritius; Mexico; Netherlands; New Zealand; Poland; Russia; Singapore; South Africa; South Korea; Spain; Taiwan; Thailand; United Kingdom; Venezuela
Giving statement: Giving through the Yum! Brands, Inc. Corporate Giving Program and the Yum! Brands Foundation, Inc.
Company EIN: 133951308

Yum! Brands, Inc. Corporate Giving Program

1441 Gardiner Ln.
Louisville, KY 40213-1914 (502) 874-8300
URL: http://www.yum.com/responsibility/default.asp

Purpose and activities: As a complement to its foundation, Yum! Brands also makes charitable contributions to nonprofit organizations involved with hunger relief. Support is given on a national and international basis.
Fields of interest: Food services; International relief.
Type of support: Cause-related marketing; Donated products; Employee volunteer services; General/operating support; In-kind gifts; Public relations services.
Geographic limitations: Giving on a national and international basis.
Application information: International donations made via United Nations World Food Program.

Yum! Brands Foundation, Inc.

(formerly Tricon Foundation, Inc.)
P.O. Box 35910
Louisville, KY 40232-5910 (502) 874-8294
Application address: 1441 Gardiner Ln., Louisville, KY 40213-5910; URL: http://www.yum.com/responsibility/foundation.asp

Establishment information: Established in 1998 in KY and TX.
Donors: Tricon Global Restaurants, Inc.; Yum! Brands, Inc.
Contact: Mary Dossett, Mgr., Community Affairs
Financial data (yr. ended 12/31/11): Assets, $16,163,513 (M); gifts received, $8,206,250; expenditures, $6,123,197; qualifying distributions, $6,120,307; giving activities include $6,120,307 for 394 grants (high: $1,977,500; low: $25).
Purpose and activities: The foundation supports programs designed to promote hunger relief, youth development, and the arts.
Fields of interest: Performing arts, theater; Arts; Higher education; Education; Diabetes; Food services; Food banks; Disasters, preparedness/services; Youth, services; Human services; United Ways and Federated Giving Programs.
Programs:
Employee Matching Gifts Program: The foundation matches contributions made by associates of Yum! Brands to nonprofit organizations on a one-for-one basis up to $10,000 per associate, per year.
Foundation Board Support Program: The foundation awards grants to nonprofit organizations with which employees of Yum! Brands serve as directors.
Type of support: Annual campaigns; Continuing support; Employee matching gifts; Employee volunteer services; General/operating support; Program development.
Geographic limitations: Giving primarily in areas of company operations, with some emphasis on Louisville, KY; giving also to national organizations.
Application information: Applications not accepted. Unsolicited applications are currently not accepted.
Officers and Directors:* David C. Novak*, Chair. and C.E.O.; Jonathan Blum, Pres.; Christian L. Campbell*, V.P. and Secy.; Richard T. Carrucci*, V.P. and Treas.; Donald Phillips, V.P.; W. Lawrence Gathof, C.F.O.; Laura Melilo Barnum, Exec. Dir. and Admin.; Anne Byerlein.
EIN: 611327140
Selected grants: The following grants are a representative sample of this grantmaker's funding activity:

$1,977,500 to Friends of the World Food Program, Friends of World Hunger, Washington, DC, 2011. For unrestricted support.
$885,573 to World Food Program USA, Washington, DC, 2011. For unrestricted support.
$723,363 to United Way, Metro, Louisville, KY, 2011. For unrestricted support.
$488,154 to Fund for the Arts, Louisville, KY, 2011. For unrestricted support.
$225,000 to Long Island Cares, Hauppauge, NY, 2011. For unrestricted support.
$133,995 to Muhammad Ali Museum and Education Center, Louisville, KY, 2011. For unrestricted support.
$100,000 to Friends of the World Food Program, Washington, DC, 2011. For unrestricted support.
$70,000 to Actors Theater of Louisville, Louisville, KY, 2011. For unrestricted support.
$15,000 to Alliance to End Hunger, Washington, DC, 2011. For unrestricted support.
$5,000 to Stage One: The Louisville Childrens Theater, Louisville, KY, 2011. For unrestricted support.

4151
Zale Corporation

901 W. Walnut Hill Ln.
Irving, TX 75038-1003 (972) 580-4000
FAX: (972) 580-5266

Company URL: http://www.zalecorp.com
Establishment information: Established in 1924.
Company type: Public company
Company ticker symbol and exchange: ZLC/NYSE
Business activities: Operates jewelry stores and kiosks.
Business type (SIC): Shopping goods stores/miscellaneous
Financial profile for 2012: Number of employees, 12,500; assets, $1,171,000,000; sales volume, $1,866,900,000; pre-tax net income, -$25,530,000; expenses, $1,847,760,000; liabilities, $992,100,000
Fortune 1000 ranking: 2012—983rd in revenues, 898th in profits, and 953rd in assets
Corporate officers: Terry Burman, Chair.; Theophlius Killion, C.E.O.; Matthew W. Appel, C.A.O.; Thomas A. Haubenstricker, Sr. V.P. and C.F.O.; Brad Furry, Sr. V.P. and C.I.O.; Toyin Ogun, Sr. V.P., Human Resources
Board of directors: Terry Burman, Chair.; Neale Attenborough; Yuval Braverman; David F. Dyer; Kenneth B. Gilman; Theophlius Killion; John B. Lowe, Jr.; Joshua Olshansky; Beth M. Pritchard
Subsidiary: Zale Delaware, Inc., Irving, TX
Giving statement: Giving through the Zale Corporation Contributions Program.
Company EIN: 750675400

Zale Corporation Contributions Program

901 W. Walnut Hill Ln.
Irving, TX 75038-1003 (972) 580-4000
URL: http://www.zalecorp.com/communityprograms.aspx

Purpose and activities: Zale makes charitable contributions to nonprofit organizations involved with breast cancer and autism. Support is given on a national basis in areas of company operations, with emphasis on Texas.
Fields of interest: Vocational education; Breast cancer; Autism; Salvation Army; Human services; Philanthropy/voluntarism, volunteer services.
Type of support: Employee volunteer services; General/operating support.
Geographic limitations: Giving on a national basis in areas of company operations, with emphasis on TX; giving also to national and international organizations.

4152
Zallie Supermarkets, Inc.

1230 Blackwood Clementon Rd.
Clementon, NJ 08021-5632
(856) 627-6501

Establishment information: Established in 1981.
Company type: Private company
Business activities: Operates supermarkets.
Business type (SIC): Groceries—retail
Corporate officers: George Zallie, Pres.; Micheal Donald, C.F.O. and Secy.
Giving statement: Giving through the ZSI Foundation Inc.

ZSI Foundation Inc.

1230 Blackwood Clementon Rd.
Clementon, NJ 08021-5632

Establishment information: Established in 1998 in NJ.
Donors: Zallie Supermarkets, Inc.; Berat Corp.
Financial data (yr. ended 12/31/11): Assets, $8,462 (M); expenditures, $10,030; qualifying distributions, $10,000; giving activities include $10,000 for 1 grant.
Purpose and activities: The foundation supports organizations involved with education, heart disease, and baseball.
Fields of interest: Human services.
Type of support: General/operating support; Scholarship funds.
Geographic limitations: Giving primarily in NJ.
Application information: Applications not accepted. Contributes only to pre-selected organizations.
Officers: George J. Zallie, Secy.
EIN: 522001708

4153
Zappos.com, Inc.

2280 Corporate Cir.
Henderson, NV 89074 (702) 943-7777

Company URL: http://www.zappos.com
Establishment information: Established in 1999.
Company type: Subsidiary of a public company
Parent company: Amazon.com, Inc.
Business activities: Operates online shoe retailing company.
Business type (SIC): Shoe stores
Financial profile for 2010: Sales volume, $1,640,000,000
Corporate officers: Tony Hsieh, C.E.O.; Chris Nielsen, C.O.O. and C.F.O.
Giving statement: Giving through the Zappos.com Corporate Giving Program.

Zappos.com Corporate Giving Program

2280 Corporate Cir.
Henderson, NV 89074 (702) 943-7777
URL: http://about.zappos.com/our-unique-culture/zappos-community-involvement

Purpose and activities: Zappos.com makes charitable contributions to nonprofit organizations. Support is given in areas of company operations in Kentucky and Nevada, and on a national basis.
Fields of interest: Cancer; Muscular dystrophy; AIDS; Crime/violence prevention, sexual abuse; Housing/shelter, temporary shelter; Housing/shelter; Athletics/sports, Special Olympics; Boys clubs; Girls clubs; Human services, fund raising/fund distribution; Children, services; Family services; Human services, gift distribution; Women, centers/services Economically disadvantaged.
Type of support: Annual campaigns; Donated products; Employee volunteer services; General/operating support; In-kind gifts.
Geographic limitations: Giving primarily in areas of company operations in KY and NV, and on a national basis.
Application information: Applications accepted. Application form required. Applicants should submit the following:
1) name, address and phone number of organization
2) copy of IRS Determination Letter
3) brief history of organization and description of its mission
4) list of company employees involved with the organization
5) detailed description of project and amount of funding requested
6) contact person

Applications should include a 250-word proposal abstract.
Initial approach: Complete online application form

4154
Roger Zatkoff Company

(doing business as Zatkoff Seals & Packings)
23230 Industrial Park Dr.
Farmington Hills, MI 48335-2850
(248) 478-2400
FAX: (248) 478-3392

Company URL: http://www.zatkoff.com
Establishment information: Established in 1959.
Company type: Private company
Business activities: Sells seals and sealing technologies wholesale.
Business type (SIC): Gaskets, packing and sealing devices, and rubber hose and belting
Corporate officers: Roger Zatkoff, C.E.O.; Gary A. Zatkoff, Pres.; Larry Cholody, C.O.O.; Denise Staudt, Secy.
Giving statement: Giving through the Zatkoff Family Foundation.

Zatkoff Family Foundation

23230 Industrial Park Dr.
Farmington Hills, MI 48335-2850

Establishment information: Established in 2000 in MI.
Donor: Roger Zatkoff Company.
Financial data (yr. ended 12/31/11): Assets, $9,428,885 (M); gifts received, $3,400,000; expenditures, $200,716; qualifying distributions, $194,260; giving activities include $194,260 for 31 grants (high: $107,210; low: $100).
Purpose and activities: The foundation supports organizations involved with education, health, and Christianity.
Fields of interest: Higher education; Education; Health care; United Ways and Federated Giving Programs; Christian agencies & churches.
Geographic limitations: Giving limited to MI.
Support limitations: No grants to individuals.

Application information: Applications not accepted. Unsolicited requests for funds not accepted.
Officer: Gary Zatkoff, Pres.
EIN: 383574982
Selected grants: The following grants are a representative sample of this grantmaker's funding activity:
$58,708 to University of Michigan, Ann Arbor, MI, 2010.
$35,000 to University of Michigan, Ann Arbor, MI, 2010.
$19,000 to University of Michigan, Ann Arbor, MI, 2010.
$8,000 to Mercy High School, Farmington Hills, MI, 2010.
$3,000 to Detroit Country Day School, Beverly Hills, MI, 2010.
$3,000 to University of Toledo Foundation, Toledo, OH, 2010.
$2,000 to University of Michigan, Ann Arbor, MI, 2010.
$2,000 to Walsh Jesuit High School, Cuyahoga Falls, OH, 2010.
$1,000 to Teach for America, New York, NY, 2010.

4155
Zeta Associates Incorporated

10302 Eaton Pl., Ste. 500
Fairfax, VA 22030-2229 (703) 385-7050

Company URL: http://www.zai.com
Establishment information: Established in 1984.
Company type: Private company
Business activities: Provides complex communications signals collection and processing systems.
Business type (SIC): Communications services/ miscellaneous
Corporate officer: John Nelson, Pres.
Giving statement: Giving through the Zeta Associates Foundation.

Zeta Associates Foundation

10302 Eaton Pl., 5th Fl.
Fairfax, VA 22030-2215

Establishment information: Established in 2005 in VA.
Donor: Zeta Associates Incorporated.
Financial data (yr. ended 12/31/11): Assets, $87,932 (M); gifts received, $5,700; expenditures, $25,542; qualifying distributions, $25,500; giving activities include $25,500 for 3 grants to individuals (high: $8,500; low: $8,500).
Type of support: Scholarships—to individuals.
Geographic limitations: Giving primarily in VA.
Application information: Applications not accepted. Unsolicited requests for funds not accepted.
Officers and Directors:* John Nelson*, Chair.; Tony Pappas*, Vice-Chair.; Steven Sprague*, Pres.; Catherine Golik*, Secy.; John Behrens*, Treas.
EIN: 203382239

4156
Zilkha & Sons, Inc.

450 Park Ave., Ste. 2102
New York, NY 10022-2675 (212) 758-7750

Establishment information: Established in 1941.
Company type: Private company
Business activities: Provides investment advisory services.
Business type (SIC): Security and commodity services
Corporate officers: Ezra K. Zilkha, Pres.; Cecile Zilkha, V.P. and Secy.
Giving statement: Giving through the Zilkha Foundation, Inc.

The Zilkha Foundation, Inc.

450 Park Ave., Ste. 2102
New York, NY 10022-2675

Establishment information: Incorporated in 1948 in NY.
Donors: Zilkha & Sons, Inc.; Ezra K. Zilkha; Cecile E. Zilkha.
Contact: Ezra K. Zilkha, Pres. and Treas.
Financial data (yr. ended 08/31/12): Assets, $821,845 (M); expenditures, $1,119,016; qualifying distributions, $1,111,640; giving activities include $1,111,640 for grants.
Purpose and activities: The foundation supports hospitals and organizations involved with opera, K-12 and higher education, human services, international affairs, public policy research, and Judaism.
Fields of interest: Performing arts, opera; Elementary/secondary education; Higher education; Hospitals (general); Human services; International affairs, foreign policy; Jewish federated giving programs; Public policy, research; Jewish agencies & synagogues.
Type of support: General/operating support.
Geographic limitations: Giving primarily in Washington, DC and New York, NY.
Support limitations: No grants to individuals.
Application information: Applications not accepted. Contributions only to pre-selected organizations.
Board meeting date(s): Dec.
Officers: Ezra K. Zilkha, Pres. and Treas.; Cecile E. Zilkha, V.P. and Secy.
EIN: 136090739
Selected grants: The following grants are a representative sample of this grantmaker's funding activity:
$379,500 to Brookings Institution, Washington, DC, 2011.
$123,660 to Metropolitan Opera, New York, NY, 2011.
$95,000 to Wesleyan University, Middletown, CT, 2011.
$93,000 to Lycee Francais de New York, New York, NY, 2011.
$55,000 to Council on Foreign Relations, New York, NY, 2011.
$20,500 to UJA-Federation of New York, New York, NY, 2011.
$20,000 to American Hospital of Paris Foundation, New York, NY, 2011.
$3,000 to French Institute Alliance Francaise, New York, NY, 2011.
$1,000 to French-American Foundation, New York, NY, 2011.
$1,000 to Weill Medical College of Cornell University, New York, NY, 2011.

4157
Zimmer Holdings, Inc.

345 E. Main St.
Warsaw, IN 46580-2746 (574) 267-6131
FAX: (302) 636-5454

Company URL: http://www.zimmer.com
Establishment information: Established in 1927.
Company type: Public company
Company ticker symbol and exchange: ZMH/NYSE
International Securities Identification Number: US98956P1021
Business activities: Manufactures and distributes orthopedic implants and surgical, hospital, patient, and other health care products.
Business type (SIC): Medical instruments and supplies; professional and commercial equipment —wholesale
Financial profile for 2012: Number of employees, 9,300; assets, $9,012,400,000; sales volume, $4,471,700,000; pre-tax net income, $990,100,000; expenses, $3,424,300,000; liabilities, $3,151,500,000
Fortune 1000 ranking: 2012—534th in revenues, 252nd in profits, and 424th in assets
Forbes 2000 ranking: 2012—1455th in sales, 693rd in profits, and 1545th in assets
Corporate officers: John L. McGoldrick, Chair.; David C. Dvorak, Pres. and C.E.O.; James T. Crines, Exec. V.P., Finance and C.F.O.; Chad F. Phipps, Sr. V.P., Genl. Counsel, and Secy.; Richard C. Stair., Sr. V.P., Opers.; William P. Fisher, Sr. V.P., Human Resources; Derek Davis, V.P., Finance, Corp. Cont., and C.A.O.
Board of directors: John L. McGoldrick, Chair.; Christopher B. Begley; Betsy J. Bernard; David C. Dvorak; Larry C. Glasscock; Robert A. Hagemann; Arthur J. Higgins; Cecil B. Pickett, Ph.D.
Divisions: Hall Surgical Div., Carpinteria, CA; Prosthetic Implant Div., Warsaw, IN; Zimmer Orthopaedic Implant Div., Warsaw, IN; Zimmer Patient Care Div., Dover, OH
Giving statement: Giving through the Zimmer Holdings, Inc. Corporate Giving Program.
Company EIN: 134151777

Zimmer Holdings, Inc. Corporate Giving Program

c/o Public Affairs Dept.
P.O. Box 708
Warsaw, IN 46581-0708 (574) 267-6131
For external research funding requests: research.requests@zimmer.com; URL: http://www.zimmer.com/en-US/corporate/community.jspx

Purpose and activities: Zimmer makes charitable contributions to nonprofit organizations and programs that promote professional medical education.
Fields of interest: Medical school/education; Health care; Medical research; Disasters, preparedness/services; General charitable giving.
Type of support: Donated products; Employee matching gifts; General/operating support; In-kind gifts.
Geographic limitations: Giving primarily in areas of company operations, with emphasis on Warsaw, IN.
Publications: Application guidelines.
Application information: Applications accepted. Requests for charitable donations from Zimmer must be made in connection with a general fundraising effort by the charitable entity, rather than a request directed only to Zimmer. Proposals should be submitted using organization letterhead. Application form required. Applicants should submit the following:
1) copy of IRS Determination Letter
2) brief history of organization and description of its mission
3) listing of board of directors, trustees, officers and other key people and their affiliations
4) contact person
5) copy of current year's organizational budget and/ or project budget

Proposal should include a valid e-mail address for communications.

Initial approach: Proposal to headquarters
Deadline(s): None

4158
Zions Bancorporation

(formerly Keystone Insurance and Investment Co.)
1 S. Main St., 15th Fl.
Salt Lake City, UT 84133 (801) 524-4787
FAX: (801) 524-2129

Company URL: http://www.zionsbancorporation.com
Establishment information: Established in 1873.
Company type: Public company
Company ticker symbol and exchange: ZION/NASDAQ
Business activities: Operates bank holding company; operates commercial bank.
Business type (SIC): Holding company; banks/commercial
Financial profile for 2012: Number of employees, 10,368; assets, $55,511,920,000; pre-tax net income, $541,570,000; liabilities, $49,459,850,000
Fortune 1000 ranking: 2012—823rd in revenues, 434th in profits, and 100th in assets
Forbes 2000 ranking: 2012—1690th in sales, 1497th in profits, and 418th in assets
Corporate officers: Harris Henry Simmons, Chair., Pres., and C.E.O.; Doyle L. Arnold, Vice-Chair. and C.F.O.; Joe Reilly, Exec. V.P. and C.I.O.; Thomas E. Laursen, Exec. V.P. and Genl. Counsel; Alexander J. Hume, Sr. V.P. and Cont.
Board of directors: Harris Henry Simmons, Chair.; Doyle L. Arnold, Vice-Chair.; Jerry C. Atkin; R. Don Cash; Patricia Frobes; James David Heaney; Roger B. Porter; Stephen D. Quinn; Laurence E. Simmons; Steven C. Wheelwright; Shelley Thomas Williams
Subsidiaries: Amegy Corp., Houston, TX; Cash Access, Inc., Las Vegas, NV; The Commerce Bank of Oregon, Portland, OR; The Commerce Bank of Washington, Seattle, WA; Great Western Financial Corp., Chatsworth, CA; MP Technology, Inc., San Clemente, CA; National Bank of Arizona, Phoenix, AZ; NetDeposit, L.L.C., Salt Lake City, UT; Nevada State Bank, Las Vegas, NV; Vectra Bank Colorado, Denver, CO; Welman Holdings, Inc., Berkeley, CA; Zions First National Bank, Salt Lake City, UT; Zions Insurance Agency, Inc., Salt Lake City, UT; Zions Insurance Agency, Inc., Salt Lake City, UT; Zions Management Services Co., Salt Lake City, UT
Giving statement: Giving through the Zions Bancorporation Contributions Program and the Zions Bancorporation Foundation.
Company EIN: 870227400

The Zions Bancorporation Foundation

1 S. Main St., 15th Fl.
Salt Lake City, UT 84133-1109

Establishment information: Established in 1997 in UT.
Donor: Zions Bancorporation.
Financial data (yr. ended 12/31/11): Assets, $2,572,344 (M); expenditures, $5,427; qualifying distributions, $5,200; giving activities include $5,200 for 1 grant.
Purpose and activities: The foundation supports organizations involved with performing arts, the environment, health, cancer, legal aid, and community development.
Fields of interest: Performing arts; Performing arts, orchestras; Botanical gardens; Environment; Health care; Cancer; Legal services; Housing/shelter; Community/economic development; United Ways and Federated Giving Programs.
Type of support: General/operating support; Program development.
Geographic limitations: Giving limited to CA, Las Vegas, NV, Portland, OR, Houston, TX, and Salt Lake City, UT.
Support limitations: No grants to individuals.
Application information: Applications not accepted. Unsolicited requests for funds not accepted.
Officers and Trustee:* Harris H. Simmons*, Pres.; W. David Hemingway, Treas.
EIN: 841411938

4159
Zotos International Inc.

100 Tokeneke Rd.
Darien, CT 06820-4825 (203) 655-8911

Company URL: http://www.zotos.com
Establishment information: Established in 1929.
Company type: Subsidiary of a foreign company
Business activities: Manufactures and distributes beauty aid products.
Business type (SIC): Soaps, cleaners, and toiletries
Financial profile for 2010: Number of employees, 300
Corporate officers: Ron Krassin, Pres. and C.E.O.; Herb Nieporent, Sr., Sr. V.P., Treas., and C.F.O.; Elizabeth Kenny, V.P., Mktg.
Giving statement: Giving through the Zotos International Inc. Corporate Giving Program.

Zotos International Inc. Corporate Giving Program

100 Tokeneke Rd.
Darien, CT 06820-4825 (203) 655-8911

Purpose and activities: Zotos International makes charitable contributions to nonprofit organizations involved with education, community development, civic affairs, and on a case by case basis. Support is given primarily in areas of company operations.
Fields of interest: Education; Community/economic development; Public affairs; General charitable giving.
Type of support: Donated products; General/operating support; In-kind gifts; Sponsorships.
Geographic limitations: Giving primarily in areas of company operations, with emphasis on Darien, CT.
Application information:
Initial approach: Proposal
Deadline(s): None
Final notification: 2 to 3 weeks

4160
Zurich Capital Markets Inc.

105 E. 17th St., 44th Fl.
New York, NY 10003-2015 (917) 534-4900

Company URL: http://
Establishment information: Established in 1996.
Company type: Subsidiary of a foreign company
Business activities: Provides investment advisory services.
Business type (SIC): Security and commodity services
Corporate officers: Richard Price, C.E.O.; Joseph Clough, C.F.O.
Giving statement: Giving through the Zurich Foundation, Inc.

The Zurich Foundation, Inc.

c/o Zurich Alternative Asset Mgt., LLC
105 E. 17th St., 3rd Fl.
New York, NY 10003-2105

Establishment information: Established in 2000 in NY.
Donor: Zurich Capital Markets Inc.
Financial data (yr. ended 12/31/11): Assets, $2,412 (M); expenditures, $1,085; qualifying distributions, $0.
Purpose and activities: The foundation supports organizations involved with education, the environment, and human services.
Fields of interest: Education; Environment; Children/youth, services; Human services.
Support limitations: No grants to individuals.
Application information: Applications not accepted. Unsolicited requests for funds not accepted.
Officers: Grant Murray, Pres.; George Childs, V.P. and Secy.; Joanne Smith, V.P. and Treas.
EIN: 134147153

APPENDIX

The following is a list of corporate giving programs and foundations published in the last edition of the *Directory* that are no longer eligible for inclusion for the reasons noted.

AFC Foundation, Inc., The
Atlanta, GA
Current information not available.

Akzo America Foundation, The
Chicago, IL
The foundation terminated June 12, 2012.

Alchemia Consulting LLC Corporate Giving Program
Seattle, WA
Current information not available.

American Specialty Foundation
Roanoke, IN
The foundation terminated in 2010 and transferred it's assets to the Fort Wayne Philharmonic.

AMR Corporation Contributions Program
Fort Worth, TX
Current information not available.

Amylin Pharmaceuticals, Inc. Corporate Giving Program
San Diego, CA
The corporate giving program has terminated.

Aquamantra, Inc. Corporate Giving Program
Dana Point, CA
Current information not available.

Armstrong Teasdale LLP Pro Bono Program
St. Louis, MO
Current information not available.

Ashford & Wriston Pro Bono Program
Honolulu, HI
Current information not available.

Ater Wynne LLP Pro Bono Program
Portland, OR
Current information not available.

Atlanta Thrashers Corporate Giving Program
Atlanta, GA
The corporate giving program terminated in 2011.

Autobahn Motorcar Group Youth Scholarship Tour
See Sand Dollar Foundation

Baach Robinson & Lewis PLLC Pro Bono Program
See Lewis Baach PLLC Pro Bono Program

Babst Calland Clements & Zomnir, P.C. Pro Bono Program
Pittsburgh, PA
Current information not available.

Baker Manock & Jensen, PC Pro Bono Program
Fresno, CA
Current information not available.

Bank of Granite Foundation
Hickory, NC
The foundation terminated.

Barley Snyder LLC Pro Bono Program
Lancaster, PA
Current information not available.

Bay State Gas Company Contributions Program
Brockton, MA
Current information not available.

Belin McCormick, P.C. Pro Bono Program
Des Moines, IA
Current information not available.

BeOn Holdings, Inc. Contributions Program
Santa Monica, CA
Current information not available.

Berkeley Patients Group Contributions Program
Berkeley, CA
Current information not available.

Betterworldbuys.com Corporate Giving Program
Pottstown, PA
Current information not available.

Beveridge & Diamond, P.C. Pro Bono Program
Washington, DC
Current information not available.

Beyond The Bottom Line Corporate Giving Program
Arlington, VA
Current information not available.

Bikestation Contributions Program
Long Beach, CA
Current information not available.

Bilzin Sumberg Baena Price & Axelrod LLP Pro Bono Program
Miami, FL
Current information not available.

Bingham Greenebaum Doll LLP Pro Bono Program
(Formerly Bingham McHale LLP Pro Bono Program)
Indianapolis, IN
Current information not available.

Bingham McHale LLP Pro Bono Program
See Bingham Greenebaum Doll LLP Pro Bono Program

Blank Rome LLP Pro Bono Program
Philadelphia, PA
Current information not available.

Blueprint Research & Design, Inc. Corporate Giving Program
San Francisco, CA
Current information not available.

Bondurant, Mixson & Elmore, LLP Pro Bono Program
Atlanta, GA
Current information not available.

Bristol Bay Native Corporation Contributions Program
Anchorage, AK
Current information not available.

Brooks, Pierce, McLendon, Humphrey & Leonard, L.L.P. Pro Bono Program
Greensboro, NC
Current information not available.

Brouse McDowell, LPA Pro Bono Program
Akron, OH
Current information not available.

Brown & Sons Charitable Foundation, Inc., Alex.
Baltimore, MD
Current information not available.

Bruder Foundation, Michael A.
Broomall, PA
The foundation terminted Dec. 31, 2011 and transferred its assets to Neumann College.

Buchanan Ingersoll & Rooney PC Pro Bono Program
Pittsburgh, PA
Current information not available.

Build-A-Future Foundation
Houston, TX
Current information not available.

Butler, Snow, O'Mara, Stevens, & Cannada, PLLC Pro Bono Program
Ridgeland, MS
Current information not available.

Byrider Foundation, Inc., J. D.
Carmel, IN
The foundation terminated on July 28, 2011.

CACI International Inc. Corporate Giving Program
Arlington, VA
Current information not available.

Calfee, Halter & Griswold LLP Pro Bono Program
Cleveland, OH
Current information not available.

Cara Foundation, Inc., The
(Formerly Milwaukee Insurance Foundation, Inc.)
Brookfield, WI
Current information not available.

Carlsmith Ball LLP Pro Bono Program
Honolulu, HI
Current information not available.

Carlton Fields Pro Bono Program
Tampa, FL
Current information not available.

Century—Clarke M. Williams Charitable Foundation
See CenturyTel-Clark M. Williams Charitable Foundation

CenturyTel-Clark M. Williams Charitable Foundation
(Formerly Century—Clarke M. Williams Charitable Foundation)
Monroe, LA
The CenturyTel-Clark M. Williams Charitable Foundation merged with The CenturyLink-Clarke M. Williams Foundation on 5/31/2012.

Chaka MarketBridge Corporate Giving Program
Arlington, VA
Current information not available.

Chesapeake Corporation Foundation
West Point, VA
The foundation has merged into The Community Foundation, Inc.

Chicago Tribune Company Community Giving Program
Schaumburg, IL
Current information not available.

Christensen O'Connor Johnson Kindness PLLC Pro Bono Program
Seattle, WA
Current information not available.

Clifford Chance US LLP Pro Bono Program
New York, NY
Current information not available.

Coalition to Protect Americas Elders, Inc.
Tampa, FL
Current information not available.

Cohen and Wolf, P.C. Pro Bono Program
Bridgeport, CT
Current information not available.

Conexant Systems, Inc. Corporate Giving Program
Newport Beach, CA
Current information not available.

Connolly Bove Lodge & Hutz LLP Pro Bono Program
Wilmington, DE
Current information not available.

Conscious Planet Media Corporate Giving Program
Chicago, IL
Current information not available.

Constangy, Brooks & Smith, LLP Pro Bono Program
Atlanta, GA
Current information not available.

Contraception Foundation, The
(Formerly Norplant Foundation)
Tracy, CA
Current information not available.

Cooley LLP Pro Bono Program
Palo Alto, CA
Current information not available.

Corey Charitable Foundation, Inc.
Cicero, IL
The foundation terminated on Mar. 5, 2012.

Countrywide Foundation, The
Charlotte, NC
The foundation terminated Mar. 5, 2010.

Covington & Burling LLP Pro Bono Program
Washington, DC
Current information not available.

CP&L Corporate Giving Program
See Progress Energy, Inc. Corporate Giving Program

Cravath, Swaine & Moore LLP Pro Bono Program
New York, NY
Current information not available.

Crowe & Dunlevy, APC Pro Bono Program
Oklahoma City, OK
Current information not available.

Cullen and Dykman LLP Pro Bono Program
Brooklyn, NY
Current information not available.

Cullman Savings Foundation
Cullman, AL
The Cullman Savings Foundation merged with The Cullman Savings Bank Foundation on 12/31/2011.

Cummings & Lockwood LLC Pro Bono Program
Stamford, CT
Current information not available.

CVPS Corporate Giving Program
Rutland, VT
The corporate giving program terminated.

Daniel Technology Group Inc. Contributions Program
West Chester, PA
Current information not available.

DCB Foundation, Inc.
Jasper, IN
Current information not available.

Dexter Apache Holdings, Inc. Corporate Contributions Program, The
(Formerly Dexter Company Contributions Program, The)
Fairfield, IA
Current information not available.

Dexter Company Contributions Program, The
See Dexter Apache Holdings, Inc. Corporate Contributions Program, The

Diamond McCarthy LLP Pro Bono Program
Houston, TX
Current information not available.

Dickinson Wright PLLC Pro Bono Program
Detroit, MI
Current information not available.

Dickinson, Mackaman, Tyler & Hagen PC Pro Bono Program
Des Moines, IA
Current information not available.

Direct Foundation, Inc., The
Williston, VT
The foundation terminated in 2010.

DLA Piper LLP Pro Bono Program
Baltimore, MD
Current information not available.

Dorf Foundation, Inc., The
New York, NY
Current information not available.

Dorris Family Foundation, Albert and Nancy
Edina, MN
The foundation terminated on Dec. 31, 2011.

Dragonfly Designs Studio Corporate Giving Program
South San Francisco, CA
Current information not available.

Duval & Stachenfeld LLP Pro Bono Program
New York, NY
Current information not available.

Dzambuling Imports LLC Contributions Program
El Cerrito, CA
Current information not available.

Edgewood Partners, LLC Corporate Giving Program
Yardley, PA
Current information not available.

Edwards Angell Palmer & Dodge LLP Pro Bono Program
See Edwards Wildman Palmer LLP Pro Bono Program

Edwards Wildman Palmer LLP Pro Bono Program
(Formerly Edwards Angell Palmer & Dodge LLP Pro Bono Program)
Boston, MA
Current information not available.

Elliott Greenleaf & Siedzikowski, P.C. Pro Bono Program
Blue Bell, PA
Current information not available.

Emerald Valley Kitchen Corporate Giving Program
Kent, WA
Current information not available.

Empire State Charity Fund
Brooklyn, NY
Current information not available.

Employees Community Fund of Boeing
Huntsville, AL
Current information not available.

Epstein Becker & Green, P.C. Pro Bono Program
Washington, DC
Current information not available.

Euro Brokers Relief Fund, Inc.
New York, NY
Current information not available.

Fab-Steel Products Foundation, Inc.
Clovis, NM
Current information not available.

Fair Trade Sports, Inc. Corporate Giving Program
Bainbridge Island, WA
Current information not available.

Fall River Knitting Mills Community Improvement Foundation
See Reitzas Family Foundation

Family Radio Foundation, Inc.
Fairfax, VA
The foundation terminated in 2011.

Farmington Bank Foundation, Inc.
See Farmington Bank Foundation Community Foundation Inc.

Farmington Bank Foundation Community Foundation Inc.
(Formerly Farmington Bank Foundation, Inc.)
Farmington, CT
Current information not available.

Faruki Ireland & Cox P.L.L. Pro Bono Program
Dayton, OH
Current information not available.

Fatwallet Charitable Foundation
Roscoe, IL
Current information not available.

Ferris, Baker Watts Foundation
Silver Spring, MD
Current information not available.

Fifty Men and Women of Toledo, Inc., The
Toledo, OH
Status Changed to Private Foundation.

First Washington Community Foundation
Windsor, NJ
The foundation terminated on Dec. 31, 2010.

Fisher & Phillips LLP Pro Bono Program
Atlanta, GA
Current information not available.

Fitch Even Tabin & Flannery Pro Bono Program
Chicago, IL
Current information not available.

Foote Mineral Company Charitable Trust
Milwaukee, WI
The trust terminated on Sept. 10, 2009 and transferred its assets to the United Way of Cleveland County.

Forbes Foundation
New York, NY
The foundation terminated Dec. 23, 2011.

Foremost Insurance Company Grand Rapids, Michigan Corporate Giving Program
Caledonia, MI
Current information not available.

Forest City Enterprises Charitable Foundation, Inc.
Cleveland, OH
The grantmaker is inactive.

Foster, Swift, Collins & Smith, P.C. Pro Bono Program
Lansing, MI
Current information not available.

Foundation, Oldfather, The
(Formerly Schlesinger Foundation, Robert A., The)
Tucson, AZ
The foundation terminated Mar. 3, 2011 and transferred its assets to the Glassman foundation.

Fox Rothschild LLP Pro Bono Program
Philadelphia, PA
Current information not available.

Fragomen, Del Rey, Bernsen & Loewy, LLP Pro Bono Program
New York, NY
Current information not available.

Franklin Family Charitable Foundation, Inc., The
Stoughton, MA
The foundation terminated on Feb. 8, 2011.

Freeport-McMoRan Foundation
New Orleans, LA
The foundation terminated.

Funkhouser Vegosen Liebman & Dunn LTD. Pro Bono Program
Chicago, IL
Current information not available.

Gardere Wynne Sewell LLP Pro Bono Program
Dallas, TX
Current information not available.

Gelson's Markets Corporate Giving Program
Encino, CA
Current information not available.

Generations Foundation
Traverse City, MI
The Generations Foundation merged with The Rock Charitable Foundation on 6/9/2011.

Gentry Locke Rakes & Moore Pro Bono Program
Roanoke, VA
Current information not available.

Glaser Educational Foundation
Mill Valley, CA
The foundation terminated in 2010.

Goodsill Anderson Quinn & Stifel LLP Pro Bono Program
Honolulu, HI
Current information not available.

Gordon Silver Pro Bono Program
Las Vegas, NV
Current information not available.

Gordon Thomas Honeywell LLP Pro Bono Program
Tacoma, WA
Current information not available.

Goulston & Storrs, P.C. Pro Bono Program
Boston, MA
Current information not available.

Graves, Dougherty, Hearon & Moody, P.C. Pro Bono Program
Austin, TX
Current information not available.

Gray Plant Mooty Pro Bono Program
Minneapolis, MN
Current information not available.

Graydon Head & Ritchey LLP Pro Bono Program
Cincinnati, OH
Current information not available.

Greenbaum, Rowe, Smith & Davis LLP Pro Bono Program
Iselin, NJ
Current information not available.

Greenberg Glusker Fields Claman & Machtinger LLP Pro Bono Program
Los Angeles, CA
Current information not available.

Greenebaum Doll & McDonald PLLC Pro Bono Program
Louisville, KY
Current information not available.

Greenlab Creative Ltd. Corporate Giving Program
Hollywood, CA
Current information not available.

Gresham Savage Nolan & Tilden, PC Pro Bono Program
San Bernardino, CA
Current information not available.

Gunderson Dettmer Stough Villeneuve Franklin & Hachigian, LLP Pro Bono Program
Redwood City, CA
Current information not available.

Hahn & Hessen LLP Pro Bono Program
New York, NY
Current information not available.

Hall, Estill, Hardwick, Gable, Golden & Nelson, P.C.
Tulsa, OK
Current information not available.

Hancock Estabrook, LLP Pro Bono Program
Syracuse, NY
Current information not available.

Harris Beach PLLC Pro Bono Program
Rochester, NY
Current information not available.

Harrity & Harrity, LLP Pro Bono Program
Fairfax, VA
Current information not available.

Harter Secrest & Emery LLP Pro Bono Program
Rochester, NY
Current information not available.

Hartmarx Charitable Foundation
Chicago, IL
Current information not available.

Harwell Howard Hyne Gabbert & Manner, P.C. Pro Bono Program
Nashville, TN
Current information not available.

Hawkins Delafield & Wood LLP Pro Bono Program
New York, NY
Current information not available.

Haynes & Boone, LLP Pro Bono Program
Dallas, TX
Current information not available.

Hedrick Gardner Kincheloe & Garofalo, LLP Pro Bono Program
Charlotte, NC
Current information not available.

Hegeman Memorial Trust Fund
New York, NY
The trust terminated on July 28, 2011.

Hirschler Fleischer, A.P.C. Pro Bono Program
Richmond, VA
Current information not available.

Holland & Hart LLP Pro Bono Program
Denver, CO
Current information not available.

Holland & Knight LLP Pro Bono Program
Tampa, FL
Current information not available.

Hotfrog, LLC Contributions Program
Great Barrington, MA
Current information not available.

Howard Rice Nemerovski Canady Falk & Rabkin, PC Pro Bono Program
San Francisco, CA
Current information not available.

Hudson Charitable Foundation, A.B.
Topeka, KS
The foundation terminated Aug. 31, 2010 and transferred its assets to the victims of the Greensburg, KS tornado.

Hughes Hubbard & Reed LLP Pro Bono Program
New York, NY
Current information not available.

Human Investing Corporate Giving Program
Lake Oswego, OR
Current information not available.

Hunter, Maclean, Exley & Dunn, P.C. Pro Bono Program
Savannah, GA
Current information not available.

Hunton & Williams LLP Pro Bono Program
Richmond, VA
Current information not available.

I Found Freedom International, Inc.
Murphy, NC
The foundation terminated on Dec. 15, 2011.

iContact Corporation Contributions Program
Morrisville, NC
Current information not available.

IMC Global Inc. Corporate Giving Program
See Mosaic Global Holdings Inc. Corporate Giving Program

In Every Language Corporate Giving Program
Louisville, KY
Current information not available.

ING DIRECT Corporate Giving Program
Wilmington, DE
Current information not available.

Iron Horse Foundation, Inc.
Whitefish, MT
The foundation terminated May 27, 2011 and transferred its assets to the Iron Horse Donor Advised Fund created with the Whitefish Community Foundation.

Irwin Financial Foundation
Columbus, IN
Current information not available.

ISO International LLC. Contributions Program
De Pere, WI
Current information not available.

Jackson Lewis LLP Pro Bono Program
White Plains, NY
Current information not available.

Jaffe Raitt Heuer & Weiss A.P.C. Pro Bono Program
Southfield, MI
Current information not available.

Jaydor Foundation, The
See Silverman Family Foundation, Inc.

JFK Medical Center Auxillary, Inc.
See JFK Medical Center Foundation, Inc.

JFK Medical Center Foundation, Inc.
(Formerly JFK Medical Center Auxillary, Inc.)
Atlantis, FL
The foundation terminated in May 2011.

Johnston Barton Proctor & Rose LLP Pro Bono Program
Birmingham, AL
Current information not available.

Kaye Scholer LLP Pro Bono Program
New York, NY
Current information not available.

Keker & Van Nest LLP Pro Bono Program
San Francisco, CA
Current information not available.

Keller Foundation, Inc.
See Keller Foundation, Inc., J. J.

Keller Foundation, Inc., J. J.
(Formerly Keller Foundation, Inc.)
Neenah, WI
Current information not available.

Kellmer Company Foundation, Jack
Philadelphia, PA
Current information not available.

Kelly Services, Inc. Foundation, The
Troy, MI
The foundation terminated on Feb. 12, 2012.

Kenny Nachwalter P.A. Pro Bono Program
Miami, FL
Current information not available.

Knobbe Martens Olson & Bear, LLP Pro Bono Program
Irvine, CA
Current information not available.

Kupelian Ormond & Magy, P.C. Pro Bono Program
Southfield, MI
Current information not available.

Laham Family Charitable Foundation, Inc., Gregory and Deborah
Westwood, MA
The foundation terminated in 2011 and transferred its assets to the Boston Foundation.

Laird Norton Family Fund
Seattle, WA
The fund terminated on June 26, 2012 and transferred its assets to the Laird Norton Family Foundation.

Law Weathers Pro Bono Program
Grand Rapids, MI
Current information not available.

Lerman Senter PLLC Pro Bono Program
Washington, DC
Current information not available.

Levine Sullivan Koch & Schulz, L.L.P. Pro Bono Program
Washington, DC
Current information not available.

Lewis Baach PLLC Pro Bono Program
(Formerly Baach Robinson & Lewis PLLC Pro Bono Program)
Washington, DC
Current information not available.

Lewis, Rice & Fingersh, L.C. Pro Bono Program
Saint Louis, MO
Current information not available.

Lindquist & Vennum P.L.L.P. Pro Bono Program
Minneapolis, MN
Current information not available.

Lionel Sawyer & Collins Pro Bono Program
Las Vegas, NV
Current information not available.

Locke Lord Bissell & Liddell LLP Pro Bono Program
Dallas, TX
Current information not available.

Lord Bissell & Brook Foundation
Chicago, IL
Current information not available.

Los Angeles Sparks Corporate Giving Program
El Segundo, CA
Current information not available.

Lowenstein Sandler PC Pro Bono Program
Roseland, NJ
Current information not available.

Luce, Forward, Hamilton & Scripps LLP Pro Bono Program
San Diego, CA
The pro bono program has terminated.

Lyman Lumber Company Foundation, The
Excelsior, MN
The foundation terminated.

Machen Advisory Group Corporate Giving Program
Charlotte, NC
Current information not available.

Manatt, Phelps & Phillips, LLP Pro Bono Program
Los Angeles, CA
Current information not available.

Manning Curtis Bradshaw & Bednar LLC Pro Bono Program
Salt Lake City, UT
Current information not available.

Mantria Foundation
Bala Cynwyd, PA
Current information not available.

Marathon Oil Company Foundation
Houston, TX
The foundation terminated Nov. 30, 2011.

Marshall & Ilsley Bank Foundation, Inc.
See Marshall & Ilsley Foundation, Inc.

Marshall & Ilsley Corporation Contributions Program
Milwaukee, WI
The corporate giving program terminated.

Marshall & Ilsley Foundation, Inc.
(Formerly Marshall & Ilsley Bank Foundation, Inc.)
Milwaukee, WI
The foundation terminated.

Marten Law Pro Bono Program
Seattle, WA
Current information not available.

May Employees Trust Fund, David
Cincinnati, OH
The trust terminated Dec., 2010 and transferred its assets to the United Way of Greater St Louis.

McAndrews, Held & Malloy, Ltd. Pro Bono Program
Chicago, IL
Current information not available.

McBride Fund
(Formerly McBride Fund, Pierre)
(Also known as Porcelain Metals Foundation)
Cleveland, OH
Current information not available.

McBride Fund
(Formerly McBride Fund, Pierre)
(Also known as Porcelain Metals Foundation)
Cleveland, OH
Current information not available.

McBride Fund, Pierre
See McBride Fund

McCarter & English LLP Pro Bono Program
Newark, NJ
Current information not available.

McCormick Barstow Sheppard Wayte & Carruth LLP Pro Bono Program
Fresno, CA
Current information not available.

McKool Smith, P.C. Pro Bono Program
Dallas, TX
Current information not available.

McNees Wallace & Nurick LLC Pro Bono Program
Harrisburg, PA
Current information not available.

Medin Foundation, The
Brooklyn, NY
Current information not available.

Merck-Schering Plough Patient Assistance Program, Inc.
Whitehouse Station, NJ
The Merck-Schering Plough Patient Assistance Program terminated.

MGLAW, PPLC Pro Bono Program
Nashville, TN
The pro bono program terminated.

MicrobiaLogic LLC Product Donation Program
Mesa, AZ
Current information not available.

Mid-Wisconsin Foundation, Inc.
Medford, WI
The foundation is in the process of terminating.

Milford Automatics Foundation, Inc.
Seymour, CT
Current information not available.

Miller & Chevalier, Chartered Pro Bono Program
Washington, DC
Current information not available.

Miller & Martin PLLC Pro Bono Program
Chattanooga, TN
Current information not available.

Milwaukee Insurance Foundation, Inc.
See Cara Foundation, Inc., The

Minyard Food Stores, Inc. Corporate Giving Program
Coppell, TX
Current information not available.

Mitchell Silberberg & Knupp LLP Pro Bono Program
Los Angeles, CA
Current information not available.

MJ Everson Financial Corporate Giving Program
Santa Rosa, CA
Current information not available.

Modell Foundation, Arthur B. & Patricia B.
Houston, TX
The foundation terminated on Dec. 28, 2011.

Monroe Auto Equipment Company Foundation
Detroit, MI
Current information not available.

Moosehead Manufacturing Company Trust
Providence, RI
The trust terminated.

Morris James LLP Pro Bono Program
Wilmington, DE
Current information not available.

Mosaic Global Holdings Inc. Corporate Giving Program
(Formerly IMC Global Inc. Corporate Giving Program)
Plymouth, MN
Current information not available.

Moses & Singer LLP Pro Bono Program
New York, NY
Current information not available.

MPI Coin Foundation, Inc.
Grafton, WI
The foundation terminated on Sept. 30, 2011.

Nebeling Scholarship Fund, Jacob
San Francisco, CA
The fund terminated in 2011.

Nest Collective Corporate Giving Program, The
Emeryville, CA
Current information not available.

New Orleans Hornets NBA L.P. Corporate Giving Program
New Orleans, LA
Current information not available.

New York Knicks Corporate Giving Program
New York, NY
Current information not available.

Nixon Peabody LLP Pro Bono Program
New York, NY
Current information not available.

Norplant Foundation
See Contraception Foundation, The

Norris, Mclaughlin & Marcus, P.A. Pro Bono Program
Bridgewater, NJ
Current information not available.

Northwest Airlines, Inc. Corporate Giving Program
Eagan, MN
The corporate giving program terminated.

Nossaman LLP Pro Bono Program
Los Angeles, CA
Current information not available.

O'Melveny & Meyers LLP Pro Bono Program
New York, NY
Current information not available.

Ocean Spray Cranberries, Inc. Corporate Giving Program
Lakeville, MA
Current information not available.

Old Mutual Asset Management Charitable Foundation, Inc.
(Formerly UAM Charitable Foundation, Inc.)
Boston, MA
Current information not available.

Oracle Education Foundation
(Formerly Oracle Help Us Help Foundation)
Redwood City, CA
Status Changed to Private Foundation.

Oracle Help Us Help Foundation
See Oracle Education Foundation

Orchard Foundation, The
South Portland, ME
Current information not available.

Pacesetter Corporation Foundation, The
Omaha, NE
Current information not available.

PaineWebber Foundation
See UBS Foundation U.S.A.

Parable Renovations, Inc. Contributions Program
Silverdale, PA
Current information not available.

Parker, Hudson, Rainer & Dobbs LLP Pro Bono Program
Atlanta, GA
Current information not available.

Phelps Dunbar LLP Pro Bono Program
New Orleans, LA
Current information not available.

Pitney Bowes Literacy and Education Fund, Inc.
Stamford, CT
Current information not available.

Plastic Packaging Foundation, Inc.
Hickory, NC
The foundation terminated Sept. 29, 2010 and transferred its assets to the United Way of Catawba County.

Plunkett Cooney Pro Bono Program
Bloomfield Hills, MI
Current information not available.

Porcelain Metals Foundation
See McBride Fund

Premier Foundation
Sioux Center, IA
The Premier Foundation merged with The Premier Communications Foundation on 12/31/2009.

Prime Healthcare Services Foundation, Inc.
Ontario, CA
The foundation is in 60-month termination process.

ProAction Foundation
Pleasanton, CA
The foundation terminated in 2009.

Progress Energy, Inc. Corporate Giving Program
(Formerly CP&L Corporate Giving Program)
Raleigh, NC
The corporate giving program terminated.

Pugh, Jones & Johnson, P.C. Pro Bono Program
Chicago, IL
Current information not available.

Pullman & Comley LLC Pro Bono Program
Bridgeport, CT
Current information not available.

Red Lion Hotels Corporation Contributions Program
(Formerly WestCoast Hospitality Corporation Contributions Program)
Spokane, WA
Current information not available.

Reitzas Family Foundation
(Formerly Fall River Knitting Mills Community Improvement Foundation)
Fall River, MA
Current information not available.

Republic Beverage Company Foundation, The
See RNDC Foundation

Respironics Charitable Foundation
Murrysville, PA
The foundation terminated on Jan. 19, 2012 and transferred its assets to the American Red Cross.

Rhoades McKee PC Pro Bono Program
Grand Rapids, MI
Current information not available.

Riddell Williams P.S. Pro Bono Program
Seattle, WA
Current information not available.

RNDC Foundation
(Formerly Republic Beverage Company Foundation, The)
Atlanta, GA
The foundation terminated on Dec. 31, 2011 and transferred its assets to the Republic National Distributing Company Foundation, Inc.

Robinson & Cole LLP Pro Bono Program
Hartford, CT
Current information not available.

Rockford Products Corporation Foundation
Belvidere, IL
The foundation terminated on Feb. 28, 2011 and transferred its assets to the Community Foundation of Northern Illinois.

Rogers Towers, P.A. Pro Bono Program
Jacksonville, FL
Current information not available.

Rosenbaum Family Foundation, Inc., Ronnie and Jerrold
Jacksonville, FL
Current information not available.

Rothwell, Figg, Ernst & Manbeck, P.C. Pro Bono Program
Washington, DC
Current information not available.

Russell Educational Foundation
Pittsburgh, PA
The foundation terminated in 2010.

Ryan, Swanson & Cleveland, PLLC Pro Bono Program
Seattle, WA
Current information not available.

Sachs Electric Foundation, The
Fenton, MO
Current information not available.

Salomon Scholarship Fund, William R.
New York, NY
The fund terminated on June 30, 2012.

Samuel Family Foundation
Effingham, IL
The foundation terminated on Dec. 31, 2011.

Sand Dollar Foundation
Autobahn Motorcar Group Youth Scholarship Tour
Fort Worth, TX
Current information not available.

Sara Lee Foundation
Downers Grove, IL
The foundation terminated on June 28, 2012.

Saul Ewing LLP Pro Bono Program
Philadelphia, PA
Current information not available.

ScalePassion Corporate Giving Program
North Palm Beach, FL
Current information not available.

Schiff Hardin LLP Pro Bono Assistance Program
Chicago, IL
Current information not available.

Schlesinger Foundation, Robert A., The
See Foundation, Oldfather, The

Schnader Harrison Segal & Lewis LLP Pro Bono Program
Philadelphia, PA
Current information not available.

Schottenstein, Zox & Dunn Co., LPA Pro Bono Program
Columbus, OH
The pro bono program terminated.

Scientific-Atlanta Foundation, Inc.
Lawrenceville, GA
The foundation terminated Aug. 2, 2010 and transferred its assets to the Cisco Foundation, Inc.

SDialogue, LLC Corporate Giving Program
Kingston, NY
Current information not available.

Security Benefit Group Charitable Trust
Topeka, KS
The trust terminated June 30, 2011 and transferred its assets to Washburn University of Topeka.

Seyfarth Shaw LLP Pro Bono Program
Chicago, IL
Current information not available.

Shumaker & Sieffert, PA Pro Bono Program
Woodbury, MN
Current information not available.

Shute, Mihaly & Weinberger LLP Pro Bono Program
San Francisco, CA
Current information not available.

Silverman Family Foundation, Inc.
(Formerly Jaydor Foundation, The)
Carlstadt, NJ
The foundation terminated on Sept. 21, 2011.

Simmons Perrine Moyer Bergman PLC Pro Bono Program
Cedar Rapids, IA
Current information not available.

Smith Debnam Narron Drake Saintsing & Myers,LLP Pro Bono Program
Raleigh, NC
Current information not available.

Smith, Gambrell & Russell, LLP Pro Bono Program
Atlanta, GA
Current information not available.

SNC Foundation
Oshkosh, WI
The foundation terminated on June 30, 2011 and transferred its assets to the Oshkosh Area Community Foundation.

Social Good Consulting Corporate Giving Program
Ventura, CA
Current information not available.

Sonesta Charitable Foundation, Inc.
Boston, MA
The foundation terminated in 2012.

SourceCut Foundation, Inc.
Osseo, WI
Current information not available.

Speak Shop LLC Contributions Program
Beaverton, OR
Current information not available.

Spiegel & McDiarmid LLP Pro Bono Program
Washington, DC
Current information not available.

Spirit of America Foundation, Inc.
Mentor, OH
No grantmaking activity for 3+ years Status changed to a public charity.

Starn O'Toole Marcus & Fisher Pro Bono Program
Honolulu, HI
Current information not available.

Stearns Weaver Miller Weissler Alhadeff & Sitterson, P.A. Pro Bono Program
Miami, FL
Current information not available.

Sterne, Kessler, Goldstein & Fox P.L.L.C. Pro Bono Program
Washington, DC
Current information not available.

Stewart Living Omnimedia Foundation, Martha, The
New York, NY
Status Changed to Private Foundation.

Strasburger & Price, LLP Pro Bono Program
Dallas, TX
Current information not available.

Strickland Scholarship Foundation, Inc., Charles Brantley
Goldsboro, NC
Current information not available.

Stroock & Stroock & Lavan LLP Pro Bono Program
New York, NY
Current information not available.

Strumwasser & Woocher LLP Pro Bono Program
Los Angeles, CA
Current information not available.

STUDIOetc Corporate Giving Program
Exton, PA
Current information not available.

Sullivan & Cromwell LLP Pro Bono Program
New York, NY
Current information not available.

Sunstein Kann Murphy & Timbers LLP Pro Bono Program
Boston, MA
Current information not available.

Sutin Thayer & Browne Pro Bono Program
Albuquerque, NM
Current information not available.

T.S. Designs Corporate Giving Program
Burlington, NC
Current information not available.

Taco Johns Foundation
Cheyenne, WY
Current information not available.

Taft Stettinius & Hollister LLP Pro Bono Program
Cincinnati, OH
Current information not available.

Tampa Bay Buccaneers Charities, Inc.
Tampa, FL
Current information not available.

Tate Family Foundation, Inc., Robert and Joyce, The
(Formerly Tate Industries Foundation, Inc.)
Sarasota, FL
Current information not available.

Tate Industries Foundation, Inc.
See Tate Family Foundation, Inc., Robert and Joyce, The

Teramana Enterprises Charitable Foundation
Steubenville, OH
The foundation terminated on Oct. 5, 2011 and transferred its assets to the American Legion Post 33 Teramana Baseball Association.

Thompson Coburn LLP Pro Bono Program
St. Louis, MO
Current information not available.

Thompson, Coe, Cousins & Irons, L.L.P. Pro Bono Program
Dallas, TX
Current information not available.

Thorp Reed & Armstrong, LLP Pro Bono Program
Pittsburgh, PA
Current information not available.

Trilogy Employee Foundation
Austin, TX
Current information not available.

Troutman Sanders LLP Pro Bono Program
Atlanta, GA
Current information not available.

Turtle Love Co. Contributions Program
Portland, ME
Current information not available.

UAM Charitable Foundation, Inc.
See Old Mutual Asset Management Charitable Foundation, Inc.

UBS Foundation U.S.A.
(Formerly PaineWebber Foundation)
Weehawken, NJ
The grantmaker is in the process of terminating.

Ukrop's Educational Foundation
Richmond, VA
The foundation terminated Apr. 7, 2010 and distributed its assets to Ukrop's Homestyle Food Foundation and the Tesco Foundation.

University Kidney Disease Research Associates
See University Kidney Research Organization

University Kidney Research Organization
(Formerly University Kidney Disease Research Associates)
Los Angeles, CA
Current information not available.

Updike, Kelly & Spellacy, P.C. Pro Bono Program
Hartford, CT
Current information not available.

Van Ness Feldman, P.C. Pro Bono Program
Washington, DC
Current information not available.

Vanguard Group Foundation, The
Malvern, PA
Status Changed to Private Foundation.

Vedder Price, P.C. Pro Bono Program
Chicago, IL
Current information not available.

Verrill Dana, LLP Pro Bono Program
Portland, ME
Current information not available.

Von Briesen & Roper, S.C. Pro Bono Program
Milwaukee, WI
Current information not available.

Vorys, Sater, Seymour and Pease LLP Pro Bono Program
Columbus, OH
Current information not available.

W.S. Badger Company, Inc. Contributions Program
Gilsum, NH
Current information not available.

Wachovia Foundation, Inc., The
See Wachovia Wells Fargo Foundation, Inc., The

Wachovia Wells Fargo Foundation, Inc., The
(Formerly Wachovia Foundation, Inc., The)
Charlotte, NC
The foundation is in the process of terminating.

Waller Lansden Dortch & Davis, LLP Pro Bono Program
Nashville, TN
Current information not available.

Ward and Smith, P.A. Pro Bono Program
New Bern, NC
Current information not available.

Warner Norcross & Judd LLP Pro Bono Program
Grand Rapids, MI
Current information not available.

Warshafsky Law Firm Foundation, Inc.
Milwaukee, WI
Current information not available.

Wayne County National Bank Foundation
See Wayne National City Foundation

Wayne National City Foundation
(Formerly Wayne County National Bank Foundation)
Cleveland, OH
The foundation terminated in 2009.

WestCoast Hospitality Corporation Contributions Program
See Red Lion Hotels Corporation Contributions Program

White City Scholarship Association
Stanton, IA
The association terminated on Nov. 21, 2011.

Wildman, Harrold, Allen & Dixon LLP Pro Bono Program
Chicago, IL
The pro bono program terminated.

Williams Kastner Pro Bono Program
Seattle, WA
Current information not available.

Wilmer Cutler Pickering Hale and Dorr LLP Pro Bono Program
Washington, DC
Current information not available.

Winthrop & Weinstine, P.A. Pro Bono Program
Minneapolis, MN
Current information not available.

Withers Bergman LLP Pro Bono Program
New Haven, CT
Current information not available.

Wolff & Samson PC Pro Bono Program
West Orange, NJ
Current information not available.

Woodcock Washburn LLP Pro Bono Program
Philadelphia, PA
Current information not available.

Woods Oviatt Gilman LLP Pro Bono Program
Rochester, NY
Current information not available.

XTRA Corporation Charitable Foundation
St. Louis, MO
The foundation terminated on June 6, 2011 and transferred its assets to XTRA Corporation.

Young Conaway Stargatt & Taylor, LLP Pro Bono Program
Wilmington, DE
Current information not available.

YourVive Corporate Giving Program
Fairfield, IA
Current information not available.

Zelle Hofmann Voelbel & Mason LLP Pro Bono Program
Minneapolis, MN
Current information not available.

INDEX OF OFFICERS, DONORS, TRUSTEES, AND ADMINISTRATORS

This index is an alphabetical listing of the names of corporate officers, donors, trustees, and administrators listed in the Descriptive Directory. Corporations are identified only by the sequence numbers assigned in the Descriptive Directory.

1345 Cleaning Service Co. II LP, 1431
13th Regional Corp., The, 1
1820 Security Corp., 1946
1820 Security Corporation, 1946
1834 Realty Inc., 666
1st Alaskans Foundation, 1
1st Source Bank, 2
1st Source Bank Charitable Trust, 2

299 Cleaning Service Co. II LP, 1431

3 A Holdings, LLC, 723
373-381 Park Avenue South, LLC, 1775
3M Co., 3

4514 Realty Trust, 3044

605 Cleaning Service Co. II LP, 1431

8040 Holdings, Inc., 4098

A&A Services, Inc., 3660
A&B Properties, Inc., 85
A&E Inc., 6
A&R Enterprises, 580
A. Duda & Sons, Inc., 1188
A. Poliner, Gary, 2749
A.F. Holding Co., 2595
A.J. Facts Inc., 8
AAA Minnesota/Iowa, 3015
Aadnesen, Christopher, 76
AAEP, 3257
Aal, Irvin E., 4088
Aamodt, Patsy, 234
Aamoth, Bill, 3600
Aamoth, William L., 3600
Aanensen, Theodore J., 2108
Aarons, Martha, 422
Aarons, Orvile, 2646
Aarsen, Bert, 1198
Aasand, Henry, 2773
Abad, Chato, 4007
Abadan, Mustafa, 3474
Aballo, Paul G., 1119
ABARTA Inc., 10
Abba Technologies, Inc., 11
Abbate, Frank, 3822
Abbate, Mark L., 1207
Abbe, Charles J., 1016
Abbe, Larry, 130
Abbey, Richard W., 1306
Abbot Machine Co., 12
Abbotsford State Bank, 15
Abbott Laboratories, 13, 3329
Abbott, Deb, 1905
Abbott, Greg, 1821
Abbott, James A., 2488
Abbott, Kristin, 213
Abbott, Mark, 2347
Abbott, Neil F., 1329
Abbott, Richard C., 4065
Abbott, Thomas, 2915
Abbott, Tilli G., 1887
Abbott, Tom, 1248
Abboud, Andy, 2225
Abby's Inc., 14
AbbyBank, 15
Abdalla, Zein, 2935
Abdoo, Richard A., 67, 2715
Abdoulah, Colleen, 2625
Abdul-Latif, Saad, 2935
Abe, Kazuharu, 2074
Abel, Alice V., 2653
Abel, Cabrelle, 1180
Abel, Elizabeth N., 2653
Abel, Gregory E., 2504, 2860
Abel, James J., 965
Abel, James P., 178, 2653, 2660
Abel, John C., 2653
Abel, Mary C., 2653
Abele, John, 540
Abelli, Donna L., 1927, 3242
Abelman, Judy, 297
Abercrombie, George, 1823
Aberdeen Creek Corp., 18
Abernathy, Emily, 3347
Abeyta, Leandro, 744
Abi-Karam, Leslie, 2926
Abizaid, John P., 3278, 3873
Ables, Dorothy M., 3540
Abney, David, 2050
Abney, David P., 3872
Abood, M., 1366
Abraham, E. Spencer, 2756
Abraham, Karen, 500
Abraham, Spencer, 1563, 2780
Abraham, William J., 3091
Abraham, William J., Jr., 2879
Abram, Peggy S., 1324
Abram, Sam, 2603
Abramowitz, Barry J., 2262
Abrams Construction, Inc., 3366
Abrams Fixture Corp., 3366
Abrams Industries, Inc., 3366
Abrams Properties, Inc., 3366
Abrams, Alan R., 3366
Abrams, Denis S., 2565
Abrams, Floyd, 651
Abrams, George S., 3945
Abrams, J. Andrew, 3366
Abrams, James, 2451
Abrams, James D., 2451
Abrams, Jim, 2451
Abrams, John, 3510, 3511
Abrams, Karen, 642
Abrams, Mary Ann, 4026
Abrams, Michael, 3684
Abramson, Andrew B., 3916
Abravanel, Roger, 2319
Abreu, Claudio, 381
Abrial, Francois, 62
Abry Partners, LLC, 1140
Absher, Ron, 826
Abshire, Nancy, 3474
Abt Electronics, Inc., 20
Abt, Jon, 20
Abt, Michael, 20
Abt, Richard L., 20
Abt, Robert J., 20
Abt, William P., 20
Abundis, Christopher M., 3667
AC Coin & Slot, Inc., 281
AC Houston Lumber Co., 1870
Acacia Life Insurance Co., 21
Academy Ford, Inc., 2298
Acadia Insurance Company, 426
Accenture, LLP, 3884
Accordino, Daniel T., 704
Accupac, Inc., 23
ACE American Insurance Co., 24
Ace World Companies, Ltd., 25
Aceto, Peter, 1937
Acevedo, Russell A., 3910
ACF Industries LLC, 26
ACF Industries, Inc., 26
Acheson, Bill, 3190
Acheson, William, 3190
Achtmeyer, William F., 565
Achuff, Stephen C., 333
Acker, Gordy, 1269
Acker, Jean, 1269
Acker, Marian, Jr., 362
Acker, William B., 2123
Ackerman, Christina, 83
Ackerman, F. Duane, 107, 1842, 3872
Ackerman, Jeffrey C., 3382
Ackerman, Joel, 2154
Ackerman, Joseph, 3453
Ackerman, Joseph D., 3453
Ackerman, Phillip C., 2628
Ackerman, Steve, 2401, 3342
Ackerman, Thomas F., 764, 990
Ackermann, Jakob, 2343
Ackley, Lilly, 515
Ackley, Sprague, 2401
Ackman, William, 2925
Acme Machine Automatics, Inc., 28
Acme-McCrary Corp., 29
Acosta, Arcilia C., 1273
Acosta, Joe, 2920
ACP Loan Repayment, 1219
Action Building Contractors, 1314
Action Energy, Inc., 2641
Activision Blizzard, Inc., 30
Activision, Inc., 30
Acton, Susan E., 1481
Acuity Management, Inc., 31
Acuity Mutual Insurance Co., 32
Acuity, A Mutual Insurance Co., 1165
Adachi, Joe, 672
Adachi, Masato, 4141
Adair, Charles E., 3074
Adair, Danielle, 1053
Adair, Kemmie, 151
Adair, Lyle, 923
Adair, Maria F., 3711
Adair, Marla, 1968
Adair, Marsha A., 1307
Adair, Paul H., 1307
Adam, George F., Jr., 2268
Adam, Helmut M., 2879
Adamack, Randy, 367
Adamo, Victor T., 2455
Adams and Reese, LLP, 34
Adams, Austin A., 1190, 3540
Adams, Beckie, 1203
Adams, Ben C., 325
Adams, Ben R., 570
Adams, Beth, 3471
Adams, Charles E., 1188
Adams, Clayton R., 2394
Adams, Clint B., 61
Adams, Courtney, 417
Adams, David G., 569
Adams, Derick W., 177
Adams, Diana N., 123
Adams, Edward, 1281
Adams, Ellen, 1525
Adams, Frank, Sr., 2615
Adams, Harold L., 893, 2245
Adams, J. Dann, 1288, 3683
Adams, J. Dinsmore, Jr., 440, 1010
Adams, Jacob, Sr., 234
Adams, James, 3839
Adams, Jeff, 402

Alexander, Stuart, 2711
Alexander, Susan, 465
Alexander, Susan H., 465
Alexander, Tim, 2293
Alexander, Wes, 131
Alexandre, Kristin, 2197
Alexas, Richard, 1670
Alexion Pharmaceuticals, Inc., 86
Alfa Mutual Fire Insurance Co., 87
Alfa Mutual Insurance Co., 87
Alfano, Michael C., 1089
Alfheim, Caroline K., 3649
Alfonsa, Michele D., 1368
Alfonso, Fatima, 2514
Alfonso, Humberto P., 1213
Alford, A.L., Jr., 3017
Alford, Brad A., 297
Alford, Bradley A., 2663
Alford, Ericka, 3988
Alford, Sandra E., 324
Alford, Terri L., 3831
Alhambra Foundry Co., Ltd., 88
Ali, Nadeem S., 1663
Aliabadi, Karen, 1430
Alice Manufacturing Co., Inc., 89
Alice Marie, Sister, 3080
Alioto, Mario, 3324
All, Matthew D., 495
All-Players Golf Tournament, 562
Allamanno, Marsha, 1007
Allan, Donald, Jr., 3579
Allardice, Robert B., III, 1742
Allcott, Wayne G., 3946
Allegheny Technologies Inc., 91
Allegheny Teledyne Inc., 91
Allegiance Corp., 377
Allegis Group, Inc., 92
Allegre, Raul, 3052
Allegretti, Jon A., 201
Allemang, Arnold A., 1160, 1161
Allen Canning Co., 98
Allen Company, W.R., 511
Allen Furniture Co., Ivan, LLC, 96
Allen Workspace, Ivan, LLC, 96
Allen, Andrew, 760, 3047
Allen, Barry K., 729
Allen, Benjamin F., 2385
Allen, Berry K., 1732
Allen, Betty, 2293
Allen, Bruce, 3054
Allen, Bryan D., 1724
Allen, Catherine A., 3606, 3674
Allen, Chuck F., 3902
Allen, Dean, 2435
Allen, Dean C., 2435
Allen, E. Thomas, 882
Allen, Frederick L., 95
Allen, G. Ashley, 2525
Allen, George, 2435
Allen, Gregory S., 145
Allen, H. Inman, 96
Allen, Herbert A., 862
Allen, Herbert Anthony, III, 93
Allen, Hubert, 2913
Allen, Hubert L., 13
Allen, Inman, 96
Allen, Jack, 760, 2647
Allen, Jack B., 760
Allen, Jack J., 3920
Allen, Jack, Jr., 760
Allen, James S., 2550
Allen, Jay L., 3363
Allen, Jerald L., 3680
Allen, Jody, 3970
Allen, John L., 814
Allen, Joshua C., 98
Allen, Kenneth R., 3727
Allen, Kimberly, 3249, 4028
Allen, Lloyd, 3694
Allen, Martin, 1763
Allen, Martin J., 1628
Allen, Michael P., 1628
Allen, Patrick E., 104, 3247, 4095
Allen, Paul G., 1460, 3970
Allen, Quincy L., 1541
Allen, Robert, 52
Allen, Robert P., 3368
Allen, Roderick L., 98
Allen, Ronald W., 862
Allen, Samuel R., 1061, 4056
Allen, Sharon L., 1070
Allen, Stacy, 3505
Allen, Stacy P., 2303
Allen, Stephen, 1628
Allen, Susan J., 1628
Allen, Vicki, 2435
Allen, William B., 2010
Allen-Edmonds Shoe Corp., 97
Allendale Mutual Insurance Co., 1323
Allender, Patrick W., 552
Allensworth, Rafe, 3376
Aller, Thomas L., 104
Aller, Tom, 4095
Allergan, Inc., 99
Allessio, Robert M., 912
ALLETE, Inc., 100
Alley, Brayton B., 2740
Alley, James M., III, 495
Alleyne, Sonia L., 3528
Allfirst Bank, 2323
Allford, Allan, 1077
Allhoff, Henry, 839
Alliant Credit Union, 103
Alliant Energy Corp., 104, 4095
Alliod, Mark D., 3444
Allison, Bob, 106
Allison, Clyde H., Jr., 2725
Allison, Henry J., Jr., 106
Allison, James, 2419
Allison, James R., 106
Allison, Jay, 3794
Allison, John A., IV, 385
Allison, M. Jay, 3748
Allison, Michael J., 588
Allison, Michael, Jr., 2785
Allison, R. Dirk, 61
Allison, Rhonda, 106
Allison, Robert J., Jr., 1494
Allison-Erwin Co., 106
Allman, Jim, 1918
Allmon, Bill, 3679
Allmon, Wayne, 3203
Allred, C. Stephen, 1907
Allred, Dan, 3455
Allred, Mark, 3467
Allshouse, Scott, 4066
Allstate Corp., The, 107
Allstate Insurance Co., 107
Allstate New Jersey Insurance Co., 107
AllStyle Coil Co., L.P., 108
Alltech, 3257
Alm, John R., 2150
Almandinger, Travis, 2246
Almar Sales Co. Inc., 110
Almaraz, Roxanne T., 3957
Almeda, Mark E., 2563
Almeida, David, 202
Almeida, Jose E., 956
Almeida, Odilon, 4045
Almeida, Richard J., 1942
Almgren, Raymond, 2632
Almon, Robert C., 2304
Almond, Trey, 876
Alnoor, Shalal, 1108
Aloj, Salvatore, Dr., 1978
Alonzo, Annette, 1470
Alonzo, Jan R., 3852
Alpac Corp., 3475
Alpenrose Dairy, Inc., 111
Alper, Max V., 1065
Alperin, Barry J., 3348
Alpern, Robert J., 13
Alpert & Alpert Iron & Metal, Inc., 3962
Alpert, Alan, 3962
Alpert, Benjamin, 866
Alpert, Peter H., 866
Alpert, Raymond, 3962
Alpert, Richard, 866
Alpeter, James A., 2997
Alpha Bancorp, 2731
Alpha I Marketing Corp, 2192
Alpha Industries, 723
Alpha Systems, 1666
Alphamill Trust, 637
Alphin, Lewis J., 2639
Alpine Bank & Trust Co., 2081
Alro Steel Corp., 113
Alsan Realty Co., 114
Alsco Inc., 115
Alspaugh, Robert W., 328
Alstead, Troy, 3585
Alston, Alyce, 1233
Altabef, Peter A., 406
Altaf, Tariq, 2731
Altair Learning Management I, Inc., 117
Altavilla, Alfredo, 801
Altec Industries, Inc., 118
Altemeyer, Donald B., 597
Altenau, Jeanette M., 1532
Altenbaumer, Larry, 129
Alter, Richard, 1859
Altieri, Michael, 2306
Altieri, Mike, 2306
Altmaier, Judy L., 3775
Altman Co., The, 119
Altman, Brad, 4143
Altman, Howard, 3271
Altman, James P., 119
Altman, Jon, 119
Altman, Jonathan S., 119
Altman, Norm J., 119
Altman, Norman J., III, 119
Altman, Randall S., 595
Altman, Stephanie, 3710
Altman, Steven R., 3095
Altman, William M., 2154
Altobello, Nancy A., 1293
Alton, Gregg H., 1582
Alton, Robert, Jr., 1797
Altschuler, Steven M., 2443
Altstadt, Manfred, 2605
Aluminum Co. of America, 82
Alutto, Joseph Anthony, 2325
Alvarado, Donna M., 997
Alvarado, Joseph, 893, 3540
Alvarado, Linda, 3679
Alvarado, Linda G., 3, 2984
Alvarado, Maria Teresa, 1608
Alvarado, Robert, 200
Alvarez, Aida M., 3980
Alvarez, Antonio, 2459
Alvarez, Cesar L., 1654, 3563
Alvarez, Jose B., 3765
Alvarez, Ralph, 2274
Alvarez, Raul, 1191, 2312
Alvarez, Sergio, 803
Alvater, Paul, 23
Alves, Jay E., 879
Alves, Paget L., 1964
Alyea, Mark, 113
Alyea, Nancy, 3038
Alyeska Pipeline Co., 657, 2184, 3694
AM Society for Surgery of the Hand, 1875
Amado, Joseph S., 120
Amaitis, Edward, 2114
Amalfi, Peter, 473
Amar Industries, Inc., 731
Amaral, John E., 1824
Amarok, Barbara, 3467
Amatisto, Frank, 939
Amato, Charles, 3321, 3523
Amato, Charles E., 3523
Amato, Elizabeth B., 3882
Ambani, Mukesh Dhirubhai, 340
Ambe, Kazushi, 3502
Amberg, Deborah A., 100
Ambesi-Impiombato, S., Dr., 1978
Amble, Joan, 592
Ambler, John O., 618
Amboy National Bank, 124
Ambrose, Affie, 33
Ambrosi, Thomas G., 1946
Ambrosio, Anthony G., 727
AMCOL International Corp., 127
Amec, 3860
Amelio, Gilbert F., 273
Amen, Robert M., 1962
Amendola, Michael, 698
Ameren Corp., 128
America First Cos. L.L.C., 616
America Online, Inc., 3757
America West Airlines, Inc., 3902
American Appraisal Associates, Inc., 132
American Biltrite, Inc., 133
American Biosystems, 1804
American Building Supply, Inc., 134
American Buildings Co., 135
American Campus Communities Services, Inc., 136
American Century Cos., Inc., 137
American Civil Liberties Union, 248
American Direct Mail Marketing, Inc., 138
American Dredging Co., 139
American Eagle Outfitters, Inc., 140
American Electric Power Co., Inc., 141
American Electric Power Service Corp., 141
American Equity Mortgage, 142
American Express, 143, 1538
American Express Co., 143
American Express Foundation, 3125
American Family Life Assurance Co. of Columbus, 54
American Fidelity Assurance Co., 145
American Future Systems, Inc., 146
American Gas Assn., 3405
American General Finance, Inc., 3554
American Health Care Centers, Inc., 152
American Healthways, 496
American Honda Motor Co., Inc., 150
American Hospice, Inc., 151
American Hospital Supply Corp., 377
American Industrial Center, 154

American Industries, Inc., 155
American Insulated Wire Corp., 2255
American International Group, Inc., 156, 3190
American Legacy Foundation, 504
American Legion, 3015
American Machine Corp., 4098
American Manufacturing Corp., 157
American Mutual Life Insurance Co., 302
American Optical Corp., 159
American Paper & Twine Co., 160
American Product Distributors, Inc., 162
American Ramallah Federation, 3124
American Retail Group, Inc., 163
American Retail Properties, Inc., 163
American Savings Bank, 3696
American Schlafhorst Co., 164
American Seafoods Co., 3687
American Seafoods Company, 1586
American Snuff Co., 165
American Standard Cos., Inc., 3794
American Standard Inc., 3794
American State Bank, 166
American Trend Life Insurance Co., 750
American Trust & Savings Bank, 3529
American United Life Insurance Co., 169
American Woodmark Corp., 170
AMERIGROUP Corp., 171
AmeriPlan Corp., 172
Ameristar East Chicago, 176
Amerisure Mutual Insurance Co., 177
Ameritas Life Insurance Corp., 178
Ameritec Corp., 179
AmerUs Group Co., 302
Amery, Brian F., 557
Ames, Carmen Holding, 1395
Ames, Marshall, 2250
Ames, Richard, 524
Ames, Robert A., 334
Amestoy, Jay, 2414
AMETEK, Inc., 181
Amgen Inc., 182
Amica Mutual Insurance Co., 183
Amick, Bill L., 498
Amin, Dhruvika Patel, 475
Amis, Richard M., 1401
Ammann, Daniel, 1555
Ammann, Vincent L., Jr., 3997
Ammerman, Brian J., 2492
Ammerman, Robert T., 135
Amnews Corp., 185
Amoco Corp., 234, 547
Amoco Production Co., 547
Amor, Jack, 3701
Amoroso, Joseph A., Jr., 1208
Amos, Daniel P., 54
Amos, John Shelby, II, 54
Amos, Kathleen V., 54
Amos, Paul S., II, 54
Amos, Robert T., III, 697
AMP Inc., 3829
AMPCO-Pittsburgh Foundation, 186
Amprey, Andrea M., 687
AMR Corp., 187
Amshoff, Phil, 1053
AmSouth Bancorporation, 3171
AmSouth Bank, 1679, 3171
Amsted Industries Inc., 188
AmTrust Financial Corp., 2791
Amundson, Audrey, 2743
Amundson, Bruce, 4052
Amundson, Joy A., 956
AMVESCAP, 1983
Amylin Pharmaceuticals Inc., 3329
Anable, Susan, 2968
Anand, Krishnan, 50
Anastasio, Curtis V., 2763
Anastasion, Steven M., 318
Anaya, Leroy, 3496
Anchor Fabricators, Inc., 192
AnchorBank, FSB, 193
Andahazy, Denise, 996
Andaya, Bryan, 2202
Andelman, David R., 727
Anderegg, Gregory L., 2049
Anderl, Richard C., 2607
Anders, Bruce, 934
Anders, Jerry, 1637
Andersen Corp., 194
Andersen, Alan, 3376
Andersen, Bill, 2137
Andersen, Charles, 3797
Andersen, G. Chris, 3719
Andersen, Joseph B., Jr., 3093
Andersen, Nevin N., 2759
Andersen, Paul H., 199
Andersen-Booth, Crystal M., 3467
Anderson Packaging, Inc., 195
Anderson, Anthony K., 297, 1389
Anderson, Arthur T., 1918
Anderson, Basil L., 398, 1747, 2563, 3581
Anderson, Brad, 693
Anderson, Bradbury H., 442, 1554
Anderson, Bradford L., 1496
Anderson, Brian P., 716, 1626, 3083
Anderson, Bruce, 802
Anderson, Bruce K., 101
Anderson, Calvin, 507
Anderson, Carl G., Jr., 700
Anderson, Cathy, 3815
Anderson, Cathy C., 3815
Anderson, Charles G., 934
Anderson, Charles P., 3797
Anderson, Charlotte Jones, 1022, 2626
Anderson, Christy Duncan, 3310
Anderson, Connie, 1397
Anderson, Darrel T., 1907
Anderson, David, 265, 1762
Anderson, David C., 2850
Anderson, David G., 1762
Anderson, David Hugo, 2747
Anderson, David J., 141, 195, 1852, 2544
Anderson, David R., 144
Anderson, Davis, 1674
Anderson, Dennis, 1045
Anderson, Derrick, 1699
Anderson, Donna, 946
Anderson, Douglas E., 558
Anderson, Douglas L., 2504, 2860
Anderson, Douglas R., 1078
Anderson, Douglas W., 353
Anderson, Eric, 3379
Anderson, Eric J., 1513
Anderson, Erik, 1995
Anderson, Erik J., 301
Anderson, Fred D., 1217
Anderson, Frederick G., 3727
Anderson, Gary, 939, 1678
Anderson, Gary E., 774, 1213, 3060
Anderson, Gene H., 1800
Anderson, Gerald M., 1183
Anderson, Gerard M., 1183
Anderson, Gordon, 1397
Anderson, Heather, 3397
Anderson, James M., 178
Anderson, Jason, 2570
Anderson, Jeffrey R., 195
Anderson, Jennifer, 3504
Anderson, Jennifer A., 1084
Anderson, Jerald, 2588
Anderson, Joanne M., 3616
Anderson, Johanna Edens, 403
Anderson, John, 3222
Anderson, John A., Jr., 3776
Anderson, John R., 195, 1732
Anderson, Jonathon, 878
Anderson, Joseph B., 3220
Anderson, Joseph B., Jr., 2473, 2765, 3914
Anderson, Judith, 4051
Anderson, Julie, 1167
Anderson, Keith B., 3419
Anderson, Kerrii B., 795, 4124
Anderson, Laurie, 1430
Anderson, Linda, 195
Anderson, Lorraine W., 3379
Anderson, Mark, 3860
Anderson, Martin, 72
Anderson, Mary Jane, 2613
Anderson, Melissa M., 1799
Anderson, Michael A., 4038
Anderson, Michael J., 1424
Anderson, Michael K., 1567, 3516
Anderson, Michael W., 807
Anderson, Mike, 805
Anderson, Patricia, 2862
Anderson, Patrick M., 3380
Anderson, Philip M., 700
Anderson, R. John, 3624
Anderson, Ray, 3379
Anderson, Raymond E., 3379
Anderson, Reuben V., 273, 2195
Anderson, Richard, 926, 2190
Anderson, Richard D., 2954
Anderson, Richard E., 1139
Anderson, Richard H., 691, 1073, 2453
Anderson, Richard S., 1927, 3242
Anderson, Rick, 2581
Anderson, Robert L., 1404
Anderson, Rodney J., 614
Anderson, S. Dan, 2433
Anderson, Sabrina, 1490
Anderson, Scott, 3379
Anderson, Scott P., 3235
Anderson, Steve, 1002, 2862, 3363
Anderson, Steven C., 2622
Anderson, Steven G., 990
Anderson, Susan A., 934
Anderson, Thomas I., 2997
Anderson, Urton, 913
Anderson, Virginia L., 3574
Anderson, Will, 2184
Anderson, William D., 3643
Anderson, William E., Jr., 3444
Anderson, William, Jr., 2184
Andracchio, Eugenie Dunn, 1681
Andracchio, Vincent C., II, 1681
Andrada, Marissa, 3585
Andrade, Anthony F., 349
Andrade, Robert P., 2902
Andras, Marilyn K., 3371
Andrasick, James S., 3461
Andre, Kenneth B., 1663
Andreason, Scott, 3556
Andreessen, Marc L., 1217, 1794
Andreotti, Lamberto, 578, 1184
Andretti, Michael, 197
Andrew, Peter, Jr., 576
Andrews, Ann Marie, 2813
Andrews, Audrey, 3713
Andrews, Brad F., 3387
Andrews, David R., 2952, 3996
Andrews, Earl, 711
Andrews, Hugh T., 3895
Andrews, James C., 3895
Andrews, Joni, 3880
Andrews, Kathleen W., 3895
Andrews, Kirkland B., 2756
Andrews, Mary Linda, 1588
Andrews, Mike, 3213
Andrews, Nathan, 1070
Andrews, Patricia Totemoff, 776
Andrews, Sally, 1835
Andrews, Susan, 2865
Andringa, Dale J., 3937
Andringa, Mary Vermeer, 2517, 3937
Andrist, Sally, 2527
Androscoggin Bank, 199
Andrulonis, Gregory S., 956
Andruszkiewicz, Peter, 491
Anfuso, Joseph, 1445
Angaiack, John, 657
Angaiak, John P., 657
Angeak, Max, 3843
Angehrn, David, 2649
Angel, Alan D., 4002
Angel, Ricardo, 3366
Angel, Stephen F., 3025, 3029
Angelakis, Michael, 2649
Angelakis, Michael J., 887
Angelastro, Philip J., 2808
Angelica, Robert E., 2245
Angelini, Michael P., 1724
Angell, Laura, 2236
Angelle, Evelyn M., 1706
Angelos, Georgia K., 334
Angelos, John Peter, 334
Angelos, Louis Francis, 334
Angelos, Peter G., 334
Angelotti, Barbara, 1148
Angileri, Joseph, 902
Anglin, Scott W., 171
Angner, Dennis P., 1993
Angoco, Vic S., Jr., 85
Anheuser Busch, 2684
Anheuser-Busch Cos., Inc., 202
Aniello, Maura E., 4017
Ankerholz, Bradford G., 1635
Ann's Trading Co., Inc., 203
Annala, Jennifer S., 2855
Anne Citrino, Mary, 1766
Annenberg Foundation Grant, The, 2340
Annenberg Foundation, The, 385
Annibale, Bob, 821
Annis, Amy, 31
Annis, Michael R., 618
Anocoil Corp., 204
Ansari, Jon, 2341
Ansari, Jon R., 2341
Anschuetz, Christian, 3844
Anschutz D.C. Soccer, LLC, 1018
Ansell, Jeffrey P., 3646
Ansin, Edmund N., 3647
Ansley, Nancy, 1958
Ansorge, Mark, 3990
Anstice, Martin, 2214
Anstice, Martin B., 2214
Anthem Health Plans of New Hampshire, Inc., 4027
Anthem Insurance Cos., Inc., 4027
Anthem, Inc., 4027
Anthony Timberlands, Inc., 206
Anthony, Alison, 4077
Anthony, Donald, 802

Anthony, John E., 206
Anthony, Steven M., 206
Antolock, Rodney C., 1738
Anton, Arthur F., 1467, 3437
Anton, John J., 903
Anton, William C., 2638
Antoncic, Madelyn, 1959
Antonellis, Joseph C., 3592
Antonetti, Chris, 847
Antonorsi, Michael, 803
Antonorsi, Richard, 803
Antonucci, Don, 3168
Antonucci, Robert V., 3885
Antoun, Adel, 1348
ANZA, Inc., 208
Anzaldua, Ricardo, 2481
AOC Ambulatory Surgery Center, 1875
Aoki, Shoichi, 306
AOL Services, Inc., 263
AOL Time Warner Inc., 3757
Aon Corp., 210
Apadula, John, 3893
Apatech, Inc., 2829
Apatoff, Robert S., 2437
Apel, Thomas G., 3606
Apex Aridyne Corp., 212
Apex Construction, 136
Apex CoVantage, LLC, 213
Apex Data Services, Inc., 213
Apex Oil Co., Inc., 214
APEX Properties, Inc., 553
Apkin, Stephen, 3474
Apking, Stephen, 3474
Apodaca, Patrick, 3076
Apoliona, S. Haunani, 342
Apollo Group, Inc., 216
Apostolico, Frank E., 505
Appel, Larry B., 4087
Appel, Matthew W., 4151
Appel, Robert J., 186
Appelbaum, Malcolm, 23
Appell, Jeffrey, 1773
Appell, Louis J., 3661
Appell, Louis J., Jr., 3661
Apple, Jim B., 1395
Applebaum, Charles, 2977
Applebaum, Stanley A., 2741
Applebaum, Stuart, 2922
Applegate, Don, 2714
Applera Corp., 2268
Appleton, William, 3374
Applied Materials, Inc., 220
AptarGroup, Inc., 221
Apte, Shirish, 821
Aragon, Ismael, 1211
Aragon, Marilyn, 2038
Arakas, Peter, 2247
Arakawa, Minoru, 367
ARAMARK Corp., 334
Aramony, Diane Marie, 2605
Aranguren-Trellez, Luis, 1942
Araskog, Rand V., 641
Araujo, Jaeleen, 3380
Araujo, Jeremy, 2928
Araujo, Migule, 3900
Arbabi, Deborah E., 986
Arbas, Anne, 2045
Arbeit & Co., 225
Arbeit Investment, 225, 2820
Arbella, Inc., 226
Arbough, Daniel K., 2260
Arbulu, Luis, 1613
Arby's Restaurant Group, 228
Arcay, Arnaldo, 820
Arce, Jorge, 1099
ArcelorMittal USA, Inc., 229
Arch Chemicals, Inc., 962
Archambeau, Shellye, 227
Archer, Dennis W., 902, 2050, 2393
Archer, Galen, 1266
Archer, James, 2010
Archer, Michael A., 1149
Archer, Timothy M., 2214
Archibald, Nolan D., 595, 1895, 2292, 3579
Archibald, Simon, 1947
Archibald, Valerie, 672
Archibeque, Patrick, 3225
Archie, Joseph Patrick, 1058
Architectural Woodwork Corp., 581
Archuleta, Steve, 705
Arciero-Craig, Patricia A., 1589
Arctic Slope Regional Corp., 234
Arctic Slope Regional Corporation, 3751
Ardiff, Ralph, 2928
Ardisana, Lizabeth A., 827
Arditti, Elliot, 3659
Arduini, Peter J., 1947
Arehart, Kurt, 1565
Arellano, Cliff, 896
Arellano, Clifford I., 896
Arellano, Nancy M., 896
Arenare, Scott A., 3985
Arendall, Jane Rast, 3012
Arens, Duane, 3827
Arey, Ned T., Sr., 3843
Argidius Foundation, 163
Argilla, Luke P., 3668
Arguello, Alfredo, 1552
Arguello, David, 705
Argyelan, Mark, 1848
Argyle Productions, Inc., 3303
Argyropolous, James, 1527
Argyros, George L., 1389
Arias, Libby, 2028
Arias, Victor, Jr., 50
Ariel Corporation, 237
Ariens Co., 238
Ariens Corp., 238
Ariens Memorial, Francis, 238
Ariens, Daniel T., 238, 1651
Ariens, Mary M., 238
Ariens, Michael, 238
Ariosa, Cindy, 2482
Arison, Micky, 696
Arison, Nick, 1767
Arisumi, Alan H., 1405
Arizona Dental Insurance Services, Inc., Inc., 1077
Arizona H.B.P.A., 3822
Arizona Public Service Co., 239
Arizpe, A. Steve, 1944
Arjomandi, Fay, 3965
Ark-Les Corp., 2000
Arkansas Blue Cross and Blue Shield, 240
Arkansas Steel Assocs., 241
Arkell, Betty, 1833
Arkema Inc., 242
Arkin, Marilyn, 96
Arkley, Peter, 3826
Arledge, Curtis Y., 344
Arlington, William J., 4072
Armacost, Mike, 3105
Armacost, Samuel H., 660, 1487
Armario, Jose, 3905
Armbrister, Denise McGregor, 4028
Armbrust Chain Co., 243
Armbrust, Donald, 243
Armbrust, Donald G., 243
Armbrust, Howard, 243
Armbrust, Howard W., 243
Armbrust, Richard, 2793
Armbust, Steven, 243
Armco Insurance Group, Inc., 2750
Armed Forces Communication and Electronics Assn., 3637
Armel, Wendy W., 170
Armes, Roy V., 936, 2355
Armistead, David H., 1730
Armitage, Richard Lee, 913
Armitage, Robert A., 2274
Armold, Thomas E., 219
Armstrong Communications, Inc., 245
Armstrong Telephone Co. of Maryland, 245
Armstrong Telephone Co. of West Virginia, 245
Armstrong Utilities, Inc., 245
Armstrong World Industries, Inc., 246
Armstrong, Alan S., 4077
Armstrong, Barbara Blount, 687
Armstrong, Bill G., 1271
Armstrong, Brian, 3238
Armstrong, Brian T., 3238
Armstrong, C. Michael, 2887
Armstrong, Charles G., 367
Armstrong, Chuck, 367
Armstrong, Connie M., 3584
Armstrong, Craig, 3649
Armstrong, Jeffrey R., 2153
Armstrong, Kathie, 3108
Armstrong, Keith J., 1953
Armstrong, Otis, 657
Armstrong, Ron, 2850
Armstrong, Ronald E., 2850
Armstrong, Shane, 3526
Armstrong, Steve, 2593
Armstrong, Tim, 209
Armstrong, Timothy W., 3957
Armstrong, Trace, 2626
Armstrong, Whit, 71
Armstrong, William J, 3508
Armstrong, William L., 1774
Arnaboldi, Nicole, 980
Arndt, Christopher, 3398
Arndt, Thomas D., 1651
Arndt, Tom, 1651
Arneson, Linda, 878
Arneson, Linda M., 878
Arnett, Dale, 4084
Arney, Rex, 503
Arnold & Porter, 248
Arnold Industries, Inc., 2680
Arnold, Chuck, 1460
Arnold, Clark S., 1131
Arnold, Colleen F., 685
Arnold, Craig, 956, 1216
Arnold, Dave, 3749
Arnold, Douglas L., 3408
Arnold, Doyle L., 4158
Arnold, Ed, 200
Arnold, Eldon R., 1008
Arnold, Ethan, 768
Arnold, Gary, 30
Arnold, Jill, 3445
Arnold, John H., 2947
Arnold, John M., 2947
Arnold, Kara Hanlon, 2947
Arnold, Katharine G., 2947
Arnold, Kay Kelley, 1279
Arnold, Mary Ann, 3995
Arnold, Michael C, 3293
Arnold, Michael C., 3293
Arnold, Michael J., 1465, 1494
Arnold, Paul N., 946, 3783
Arnold, Phyllis H., 385
Arnold, Robert M., 2947
Arnold, Scott, 2298
Arnold, Stephen D., 2316
Arnold, Susan E., 1127, 2427
Arnold, Tim, 874
Arntzen, Morten, 3273
Arntzen, Regan, 3238
Aron, Adam, 2957, 3589
Aron, Robert, 3177
Aronin, Jeffrey S., 1125
Aronson, Arnold H., 3123
Aronson, Bernard W., 1376, 3273
Arora, Nikesh, 869
Arpey, Gerard J., 2049
Arpin, Lori, 1555
Arrendale, Thomas A., III, 1373
Arresta, John D., 2645
Arri, Michael, 2418
Arriagada, Ivan, 455
Arrigan, Steve D., 3629
Arrigoni, Dan, 3836
Arrison, Jerome P., 1421
Arrison, Jerry P., 1421
Arrow International Inc., 3707
Arrow Precision Products, Inc., 3707
Arrowhead Properties, L.P., 250
Arrowstarr, LLC, 3582
Arroyo Paloma, Inc., 252
Arroyo, Elva P., 2870
Arroyo, F. Thaddeus, 274
Arroyo, Vicky, 2415
Arsenault, Robert, 1620
Art & Decor Kingdom, Inc., 3286
Arthur's Enterprises, Inc., 253
Arthur, C. Alan, 1374
Arthur, Thomas D., 2981
Artichoke Joe's, Inc., 254
Artigue, Ray, 2968
Artzt, Russell M., 638
Arvani, Azita, 3714
Arvia, Anne L., 1542
Arvin, James, 2025
ArvinMeritor, Inc., 2473
Arvizu, Dan E., 3591
Arway, Pamela, 1791
Arway, Pamela M., 1044
Asand, Matsuhiro, 2103
Asano, Matsuhiro, 2103
Asao, Paul, 3827
Asbury, Kevin, 2311
Asbury, Valerie, 2271
Ascheim, Thomas, 2703
Ascher, Erin, 2807
Aseltine, Ronald, 199
Asencio, Paul, 3601
ASG Equities LLC, 748
Ash Grove Cement Co., 256
Ash, Dick, 3986
Ash, George E., Sr., 1716
Ash, Jackie, 110
Ash, Karen Artz, 2101
Ash, Mary Kay, 2392
Ash, Richard A., 3986
Ashapura, Inc., Inc., 1191
Ashburn, John F., Jr., 2550
Ashby, Lawrence C., 257
Ashby, Lisa, 685
Ashby, O'Conner G., 385
Ashcraft, Stephen Patrick, 1917

Baekgaard, Barbara Bradley, 551
Baer, Arthur H., 3406
Baer, Brian, 3310
Baer, John M., 1410
Baer, Larry, 3324
Baer, Laurence M., 3324
Baer, Luke, 529
Baer, Richard N., 2264
Baer, Timothy R., 3691
Baerg, Dan, 1344
Baerman, Cynthia, 1635
Baerman, Cynthia A., 1635
Baert, Steven, 2753
Baeur, Robert, 2136
Baeza, Mario L., 63, 591
Bag Arts, LLC, 2328
Bagby, Thomas R., 4111
Bagget, Vernon, 72
Baggett, Art, Jr., 2853
Baghkhanian, Arzhang, 88
Bagian, James P., 1139
Baginski, Steven, 2121
Bagkhanian, Mike, 88
Bagley, Freddie J., 897
Bagley, James W., 3718
Bagley, Lester, 2530
Bagley, Martha R., Esq., 1207
Bagley, Ralph R., Esq., 1207
Bagley, Ross, 918
Baglivo, Mary, 3088
Bague, Hugo, 2061
Bahler, Gary M., 1459
Baicker, Katherine, 2274
Baier, Frank W., 926
Baier, Lucinda M., 521
Bailey Nurseries, Inc., 315
Bailey, A. Robert D., 376
Bailey, Bill, 3978
Bailey, Bob, 758, 3028
Bailey, David G., 1156
Bailey, Elizabeth, 3975
Bailey, Elizabeth E., 120
Bailey, Forrest D., 1170
Bailey, G. Alan, 2604
Bailey, Gordon, 315
Bailey, Gordon, Jr., 315
Bailey, Grace, 3304
Bailey, Greg, 544
Bailey, H. Shephard, 1054
Bailey, Holly A., 1411
Bailey, Irwin W., II, 1867
Bailey, Jack, 72
Bailey, John P., 315
Bailey, Joseph, 3041
Bailey, Lee C., 3649
Bailey, Martha A., 2125
Bailey, Michael, 395
Bailey, Michael C., 395
Bailey, Patricia B., 226
Bailey, Rich, 2360
Bailey, Robert L., 2500
Bailey, Rodney P., 315
Bailey, S. Graham, 495
Bailey, Sallie B., 2310
Bailey, Susan, 474
Bailey, Treasure, 3706
Bailey, Vicky A., 1287
Bailis, David P., 3576
Baillargeon, Laurent A., 3667
Bain, John H., 1849
Bain, Judith S., 1286
Bain, Travis W., II, 1082
Bainum, Stewart W., Jr., 798
Bainum, Stewart, Jr., 798
Baio, Derrick, 2691
Bair, Jack F., 3324
Bair, Michael, 2336
Baird & Warner, Inc., 316
Baird and Co., Robert W., 317
Baird, Brent D., 2323
Baird, Bruce C., 1078
Baird, Dick, 1573
Baird, Gilbert, 3140
Baird, John, 316
Baird, John W., 316
Baird, Patrick S., 45
Baird, Richard L., Jr., 663
Baird, Robert, 3116
Baird, Stephen W., 316
Baird, W. Blake, 2404
Baird, Zoe, 804
Bak, Marty, 3940
Bakalar, Gary, 4134
Bakalar, John S., 2439
Bakane, John L., 907
Baker & Hostetler LLP, 319
Baker and Baker Real Estate Developer, LLC, 318
Baker Coarsey Enterprises, Inc., 322
Baker Corporation, Michael, 323
Baker Hughes Inc., 324
Baker, Alton, 1680
Baker, Alton F., III, 1680
Baker, Brad, 510
Baker, Brendan, 689
Baker, Bridget, 2649
Baker, Charles E., 328
Baker, Dave, 134, 3154
Baker, Debra, 3071
Baker, Donald, 1077
Baker, Douglas M., Jr., 1220, 3691, 3835
Baker, Edward L., 1444
Baker, Edwin M., 1680
Baker, Jack H., Fr., 1078
Baker, Jeffrey A., 1038
Baker, John, 318, 1444
Baker, John D., II, 3727, 4028
Baker, Johny, 2846
Baker, Judith, 3795
Baker, Judy L., 3795
Baker, Larry F., 2634
Baker, Lee, 2573
Baker, LeighAnne, 1792
Baker, Lenox D., Jr., 4027
Baker, Mari J., 4072
Baker, Marianna, 769
Baker, Mark, 4091
Baker, Mary C., 322
Baker, Mary G., 322
Baker, Patricia M., 318
Baker, Raymond T., 2324
Baker, Richard A., 2302
Baker, Richard A., Jr., 1680
Baker, Rick, 1146, 1680, 1790
Baker, Robert, 809, 3483
Baker, Robert W., 1239
Baker, Shane, 1567
Baker, Stephen L., 322
Baker, Thomas D., 3483
Baker, Thomas E., 1419
Baker, Thomas J., 243, 3483
Baker, Tom, 898, 1273
Baker, Trey, 4097
Baker, Vernon G., II, 2473
Baker, W. K., 3984
Baker, William, 3474
Baker, William A., 875
Baker, William A., Jr., 875
Baker, William F., 3474
Baker, William T., 769
Baker-Oliver, Debbie, 3657
Bakewell Corp., 326
Bakewell Lii, Edward L., 326
Bakewell, Edward L., III, 326
Bakewell, Edward L., Jr., 326
Bakke, Helen A., 3630
Bakke, James J., 3630
Bakken, Eric A., 3172
Balagia, S. Jack, 1315
Balbach, John J., 1053
Balboni, John N., 1968, 2749
Balch, Chris, 1833
Balco Holdings, Inc., 378
Baldauf, Holly, 3758
Baldridge, Kevin, 1992
Baldridge, Sharon, 1307
Balducci, Don, 446
Baldwin, Barbara L., 1666
Baldwin, George, 2971
Baldwin, Gerald, 2916
Baldwin, H. Furlong, 1623, 2617
Baldwin, James L., Jr., 1169
Baldwin, John C., 3103
Baldwin, Leah, 1248
Baldwin, Michael, 2818
Baldwin, Phillip N., 3514
Baldwin, Robert H., 2489
Baldwin, Ronald C., 1084
Baldwin, Ross, 3360
Bale, Peter, 265
Bales, Maria, 1427
Baliles, Gerald L., 120, 3433
Baliszewski, Rabin, 2912
Balkema, Gary S., 552
Ball, Andrew L., 157
Ball, David, 2156
Ball, Donald J., Jr., 3961
Ball, F. Michael, 1867
Ball, G. Thomas, 319
Ball, George L., 2887
Ball, Larry, 3052
Ball, R. Brian, 4078
Ball, Russell C., III, 157
Ball, Russell D., 2550
Ball, Scott, 544
Ball, Tracey, 3279
Ballach, John M., 3920
Ballantine, Elizabeth A., 2422
Ballantine, John W., 3010
Ballantyne, Mark, 134
Ballantyne, Sharee, 134
Ballard, Ernesta, 4052
Ballard, Eugene G., 426
Ballard, James, 2455
Ballard, Joe N., 1518
Ballard, Melissa G., 1538
Ballard, Shari L., 1458
Ballard, William C., Jr., 3884
Ballbach, John M., 3760
Ballester, Alejandro M., 3003
Ballew, Christa, 2410
Ballhaus, William, 3562
Ballhaus, William F., Jr., 1171
Ballhaus, William L., 3562
Ballmer, Steve, 2501
Ballmer, Steven A., 2501
Ballot, Alissa E., 1443
Ballou, Bill, 511
Ballou, Roger H., 101
Ballton, Carl A., 3854
Ballweg, Annie, 1269
Ballweg, Ben, 1269
Ballweg, Diane, 1269
Ballweg, Jackie, 1269
Ballweg, Ken, 1269
Ballweg, Nick, 1269
Ballweg, Sam, 1269
Balmuth, Michael A., 3267
Balog, James, 1647
Balser, David, 1256
Balson, Andrew B., 487, 1151
Baltes, John, 1790
Baltimore Community Foundation, The, 2596
Baltimore Equitable Society, The, 332
Baltimore Gas and Electric Co., 1309
Baltimore Orioles L.P., 334
Baltimore, David, 182
Baltimore, Thomas J., Jr., 3072
Baltz, Jeffrey D., 214
Bamba, Takashi, 3418
Bamberg, Cauney S., 4006
Bame, Tracy L., 1494
Bamke, Reed, 991
Bammann, Linda B., 1348
Bamper, David, 3457
Bamrick, Mike, 2007
Ban, Stephen D., 1270
BancFirst, 750
Banco Popular, 3634
Banco Popular Foundation, Inc., 3003
Banco Popular North America, 3003
BancorpSouth, Inc., 336
Bancroft, Charles, 578
Bancroft, Natalie, 2700
BancWest Corp., 1405
Band, Jonathon, 696
Band, Robert, 3826
Bandera, Janet, 2557
Bandes, Jed, 1382
Bandlow, Robert E., 2174
Bandriwsky, Pavlo T., 1422
Bane, Richard C., 1209
Bane, Sandra N., 57
Banerji, Shumeet, 1794
Banfield, Simon, 719
Banga, Ajay, 1160, 1161, 2399
Banga, Manvinder S., 1130, 3741
Bangor Savings Bank, 338
Banholzer, Bill, 1161
Baniel, Paul, 1651
Banister, Gaurdie E., Jr., 3832
Banister, Michael, 1464
Bank of America, 1776, 3149, 3268, 3826
Bank of America Corp., 340, 2679
Bank of America National Trust and Savings Assn., 339
Bank of America, N.A., 106, 128, 339, 340, 516, 632, 907, 1163, 1619, 1692, 2265, 2663, 3213, 3425, 3427, 3492
Bank of Commerce, The, 3671
Bank of Greene County, The, 341
Bank of Hawaii, 342
Bank of New York Mellon Corp. Foundation, 344
Bank of New York Mellon, N.A., The, 82
Bank of New York Mellon, The, 1150
Bank of New York, The, 344
Bank of Stockton, 345
Bank of Tokyo-Mitsubishi Trust Co., 347
Bank of Tokyo-Mitsubishi UFJ Trust Co., 347
Bank of Utica, 348

Barshefsky, Charlene, Amb., 1950, 3589
Barsness, Cheryl, 130
Barsness, Richard A., 130
Barstad, Melanie W., 816
Barta, David A., 935, 3167
Bartek, Brad, 770
Bartel, Tony D., 1530
Bartel, Warren E., 2839
Bartell, George D., 2622
Bartelt, Dale R., 1668
Bartelt, Glenn, 2361
Barth, Carin Marcy, 4044
Barth, Dan, 2795
Barth, Danny, 370
Barth, Kevin G., 890
Barth, Robert, 21
Barthelemy, Bill, 3390
Bartholdson, John A., 2776
Bartholomay, William C., 280
Bartholomew, Samuel W., Jr., 3171
Bartkovich, Jennifer D., 1841
Bartkowiak, Rosemary, 3578
Bartlett and Co., 365
Bartlett, Bob, 104, 4095
Bartlett, Bruce R., 365
Bartlett, Katharine T., 540
Bartlett, Mark B., 7
Bartlett, Paul D., Jr., 365, 3846
Bartlett, Stever, 3940
Bartlett, Tom, 167
Bartlett, William J., 3179
Bartlitt, Fred H., Jr., 2164
Bartmess, Sheila, 1952
Bartol, Tom, 3744
Bartolacci, J. C., 2406
Bartolacci, Joseph C., 2406
Bartolo, Diana, 4126
Bartolo, Diana J., 4126
Bartolotto, Margaret, 2843
Barton Malow Company, 366
Barton, Amy Lynn, 1865
Barton, Bernard, 1834
Barton, Bradford, 932
Barton, Colin M., 2725
Barton, Deborah, 3424
Barton, Glen A., 3919
Barton, Jacqueline K., 1160, 1161
Barton, James F., 3133
Barton, Jeremy, 535
Barton, Tracey, 1790
Barton-Malow Enterprises, Inc., 366
Bartow, Gene, 1857
Bartram, Thomas L., 1399
Bartz, Carol A., 818
Barwick, R. Brian, 1966
Barz, Richard J., 1993
Barze, Brian, 3602
Barzi, Silvio, 2399
Basan, Patricia, 2415
Basha, Edward N., Jr., 369
Basha, Johnny, 369
Basham, Bob, 487
Basham, Robert D., 487
Bashinsky, Joann, 1601
Bashinsky, Joann F., 1601
Bashinsky, Sloan Y., Sr., 1601
Basier, Frank, 1191
Basile, Stephen, 3536
Basilio, Paulo, 1772
Baskerville, H.M., Jr., 3226
Baskerville, Henry M., Jr., 3226
Basler, Donald N., 3867
Basler, Douglas S., 3867
Bason, Jimmy, 3450
Bason, Jimmy R., 3450
Bass Electric, 1570
Bass, Angela, 3625
Bass, Carl, 289, 2417
Bass, Gloria, 3805
Bass, James K., 2469
Bass, Ladd, 1587
Bass, Michael, 2623
Bass, Paige S., 3498
Bass, Paul M., 473
Bass, Robert, 802
Bass, Robert Muse, 2138
Bass, William, 1143
Bassett Furniture Industries, Inc., 372
Bassett, John K., 2550
Bassham, Terry, 890
Bassingthwaite, Dwight, 1339
Basso, Cory, 3321
Bastean, Todd A., 612
Bastiaens, F. Guillaume, 1153
Bastian, Edward H., 1073
Bastien, Kevin, 2055, 2059
Baston, Bryan, 57
Batch, Charlie, 2627
Batchelder, Herbert W., 530
Batcheler, Colleen, 904
Batcheler, Colleen R., 904
Batchelor Enterprises, 1958
Batchelor, George E., 1958
Batchelor, Jon, 1958
Batchelor, Karen, 177
Batchelor-Robjohns, Anne O., 1958
Bate, Eugene, 1930
Bate, Kenneth M., 999
Bateh & Brothers Foundation, Eissa A., Inc., 3124
Bateh, James A., 3124
Bateh, Robert, 3124
Bateh, Robert A., 3124
Bateman, Giles H., 2269, 4011
Bateman, Justin, 2785
Bateman, Maureen S., 1279
Bates, Ann Torre, 3478
Bates, Charles, 809
Bates, Dave, 3199
Bates, James, 1478
Bates, Jesse Dan, 2763
Bates, John C., 1770, 3595
Bates, Mark, 79
Bates, Michael, 2226
Bates, Michelle F., 452
Bates, Paul, 1601
Bates, Paul R., 1601
Bates, Roger, 2738
Bates, Sarah J., 1770
Bates, Yasmin, 1739
Batesole, Mike, 3418
Bath, Margaret, 2120
Bathco (The Navy Yard), 3123
Bathgate, Lawrence E., II, 1910
Batista, Carlos S., 2646
Batistatos, Speros A., 2344
Batkin, Alan R., 1747, 2808
Batool, Ansar, 3097
Batory, Ronald L., 914
Batson, Amanda, 2126
Batson-Cook Co., 373
Batten, Frank, Jr., 2218
Battersby, Scott A., 3859
Battin, Molly, 3757
Battle, A. George, 1311
Battles, Lynn, 2361
Batts Group, Ltd., The, 374
Batts, James L., 374
Batts, John H., 374
Batts, John T., 374
Batts, Michael A., 374
Batts, Robert H., 374
Battye, Kenneth S., 2245
Baube, Tim, 3775
Baude, Bruce, 857
Bauder, Lillian, 1183
Baudo, Susan, 2879
Bauer USA Foundation, 382
Bauer, Chris Michael, 193
Bauer, David P., 2628
Bauer, Dianne E., 2320
Bauer, Dick, 1607
Bauer, Fred D., 219
Bauer, Jim, 2994
Bauer, Julie, 104
Bauer, Kristen, 752
Bauer, Laurie, 194
Bauer, Matt, 449
Bauer, Nancy, 2565
Bauer, Paul D., 3399
Bauer, Rich, 2968
Bauer, Richard, 3039
Bauer, William H., Jr., 1470
Bauernfeind, George G., 1886
Bauernhuber, Charles, 664
Baugh, Terry, 1279
Baughin, Charles M., 1813
Baughman, Corinne, 2581
Baughman, Derek A., 342
Baum Co., Otto, Inc., 375
Baum, Craig R., 375, 941
Baum, Herb, 2948
Baum, J. Robert, 1799
Baum, Jane Goodman, 1610
Baum, Kenneth D., 375, 941
Baum, Kurt L., 375
Baum, Marc, 2617
Baum, Richard, 551
Baum, Terry, 941
Baum, Terry L., 375, 941
Baum, Wayne, 941
Baum, Wayne E., 375, 941
Bauman, Deb, 2543
Bauman, Elizabeth, 1427
Bauman, Henna, 3295
Bauman, Marvin J., 2205
Bauman, Robert J., 2591
Bauman, Shalom, 3295
Baumann, Barbara M., 3819
Baumann, Peter, 3796
Baumbach, Martha, 3136
Baumeister, Michel, 2193
Baumer, John, 3220
Baumeyer, Bill, 563
Baumgartner, J. A., 722
Baumgartner, Tracy J., 887
Baumier, Barbara, 2482
Baune, Steven, 860
Baur, Michael L., 3347
Baur, Richard, 3568
Baurer, Barbara A., 951
Bausch & Lomb Inc., 376, 3526
Bavasi, Margaret, 2136
Bawek, Rick, 3154
Bax, John, 2290
Baxt, Leonard J., 1164
Baxter Allegiance Foundation, The, 685
Baxter International Inc., 377
Baxter, Jeremy, 835
Baxter, Lyn, 3951
Baxter, Ralph H., Jr., 2826
Baxter, Terry L., 2629
Bay Alarm Co., 378
Bay Chevrolet, 379
Bay State Savings Bank, 380
Bay, Mogens C., 904, 3919
Bayazit, Soledad, 163
Bayer Corp., 381, 3257
Bayer Healthcare Pharmaceuticals Inc., 382
Bayer, David S., 4017
Bayer, David S., II, 4017
Bayers, William, 1869
Bayh, Evan, 2365
Bayh, Susan B., 1259, 4027
Bayless, William, 136
Bayless, William C., Jr., 136
Baylinson, Ilene, 2410
Baylis, Robert M., 2688
Baylis, Scott, 4127
Bayly, George V., 1635
Baynham, Frank, 2251
Bays, A. Bernard, 383
Bays, Robert L., 544
Bayside Development of Miami, 1236
Bayt, Phillip, 1905
BayView Financial Trading Group, L.P., 384
BB&T Corp., 385
BC International Group, Inc., 387
BDP International, Inc., 388
Beach, Dana, 475
Beach, Darlene E., 1904
Beach, Rick, 1981
Beach, Tim, 2686
Beadles, Gregory, 277
Beahm, John, 2037
Beahm, Paul E., 2622
Beal, Bruce A., 139
Beal, David, 878
Beal, Thomas E., 3846
Beale, John J., 830
Beall's Department Stores, Inc., 389
Beall's, Inc., 389
Beall, Beverly, 389
Beall, Pamela K., 2362
Beall, Pamela K.M., 2365
Beall, Robert M., II, 389
Beamish, Mike, 3967
Beamon, Tina Clark, 515
Bean & Sons Co., D.D., Inc., 391
Bean, Christopher V., 391
Bean, David A., 3515
Bean, Delcie, 391
Bean, Delcie D., 391
Bean, John W., 3670
Bean, Mark C., 391
Bean, Vernon, 391
Beane, Claire, 1927
Beans, Robert L., 657
Bear Co., Lewis, The, 393
Bear, Belle Y., 393
Bear, Lewis, III, 393
Bear, Lewis, Jr., 393
Beard, James, 2513
Beard, James R., 2513
Beard, James S., 1559, 3292
Beard, Jeffrey, 3671
Beard, Richard A., III, 1188
Beard, Ronald S., 660
Beard, Susan, 2733
Bearden Lumber Co., Inc., 206
Bearden, Stacie, 1842
Beardsley, Lynne A., 3858
Beardsworth, James A., 45

Bearse, Stacy V., 485
Beath, Richard W., 1957
Beatt, Bruce H., 3579
Beattie, Art P., 3516
Beattie, Arthur P., 3516
Beattie, Brian, 3673
Beattie, Richard I., 1732
Beattie, W. Geofrey, 1552
Beattie, W.Geoffrey, 3741
Beattle, Brian, 3673
Beatty, David R., 3984
Beatty, Mark, 1734
Beatty, Sean, 251
Beauchamp, Robert E., 508
Beaudet, Debra, 3466
Beaudouin, Mark T., 4003
Beaumont, Scott A., 996
Beaver Street Fisheries, Inc., 394
Beaver, Donald, 2948
Beaver, Thomas A., 2635
Beaver, William H., Jr., 1951
Beavers, Keith R., 3805
Beavers, Robert M., Jr., 1655
Beazley, Wyatt S., IV, 4078
Bebbington, Claire, 547
Bebis, Stephen, 586
Beccalli, Nani, 1552
Becerra, Manuel, 268
Becher, Michael R., 1410
Becher, Richard, 1788
Bechner Foundation, Paul, 127
Becht, Bart, 950
Bechtel Corp., 395
Bechtel Group, Inc., 395
Bechtel Power Corp., 395
Bechtel Systems of Infrastructure, Inc., 395
Bechtel, Riley, 395
Bechtel, Riley P., 395
Bechtel, Steve, Jr., 395
Bechtle, Nancy H., 3363
Bechtle, Scott C., 3245
Bechtold, Monty, 1080
Beck Charitable Lead Trust, Henry C., 396
Beck Company, The, 396
Beck, Barbara J., 1220
Beck, David, 1512
Beck, David F., 2406
Beck, Ed, 2638
Beck, G. Douglas, 1081
Beck, Henry C., III, 396
Beck, Jeannine, 142
Beck, Jim, 915
Beck, Kendra, 2361
Beck, Lauren, 3853
Beck, Marcus, 3721
Beck, Robert R., 1126
Beck, Ronald, 2026
Beck, S. Fred, 1906
Beck, Sheryl, 678
Beck, Teresa, 3104
Beck, Thomas A., 3207
Beck, Tom, 2979
Beck, Wendy A., 3535
Becker, Charlie, 2991
Becker, Douglas L., 2231
Becker, Greg, 3455
Becker, Greg W., 3455
Becker, Harold M., 1679
Becker, Howard C., 2790
Becker, Jan, 289
Becker, Jeff, 2282
Becker, Jeffery, 1938
Becker, Jennifer, 3247
Becker, Laura Lee Baskerville, 3226
Becker, Margaret, 1258
Becker, Martin, 1195
Becker, Robert D., 1679
Becker, Scott, 2716
Becker, Steve, 1602
Becker, Steven R., 3521
Becker, Terry R., 3226
Becker, Thomas, 2287
Becker, Todd, 1809
Becker, Ulrich, 3159
Becker, Yin C., 3627
Beckerle, Mary C., 1895
Beckerman, Dan, 2306, 2308
Beckerman, Ken, 2401
Beckers, Pierre-Olivier, 1458
Beckert, Richard, 638
Beckett, Jim, 3200
Beckett, Steven J., 159
Beckfield, Brett L., 3227
Beckham, Brenda, 3524
Beckler, Edward, 2643
Beckler, Gregory S., 2643
Beckler, Janet, 2643
Beckler, Janet J., 2643
Beckler, Mathew, 216
Beckler, Philip A., 2643
Beckman Coulter, Inc., 397
Beckman, Jill, 1981
Beckman, Joel S., 1795
Beckman, Karen, 1460
Beckman, Paul, 2883
Beckwitt, Rick, 2250
Becky, Walter W., II, 2579
Becton, Henry P., Jr., 398, 406
Bedard, Kipp A., 2500
Bedard, Michele, 3630
Bedard, Paul, 382
Bedi, Gurminder S., 902
Bedient, Patricia M., 74, 4052
Bedingfield, Kenneth L., 2744
Bediones, Dolores, 3189
Bednar, Randall S., 3484
Bednarek, James K., 537
Beebe, Bruce, 2168
Beebe, Cheryl K., 1942, 2861
Beebe, Kevin L., 2709, 3672
Beebe, Lydia I., 780
Beebe, Raymond M., 4088
Beebe, Steve, 3459
Beeber, Ronald L., 1071
Beecher, Gregory R., 3718
Beedle, Joseph, 2743
Beegle, Ronald R., 46
Beehler, David W., 3232
Beeler, Ralph B., 438
Beeler, W. Christopher, 1855
Beeman, Robert L., 3066
Beer, James, 3669
Beer, Kenneth H., 3614
Beer, Robert A., 1399
Beerhalter, Mary, 742
Beernink, Howard, 3035
Beers, Kerri L., 839
Beers, Lisa, 4002
Beers, Stephen, 2110
Beery, Joe, 2268
Begeman, Gary, 2709
Begemann, Brett D., 1213, 2559
Beggs, Richard, 1020
Begley, Christopher B., 1809, 1867, 4157
Begley, Roy W., Jr., 3576
Begley, William J., Jr., 3308
Behar, Robert I., 1661
Behling, Lisa, 1314
Behnke, Carl G, 3475
Behnke, Carl G., 3475
Behnke, John S., 3475
Behnke, Marisa W., 3475
Behnke, Renee J., 3475
Behnke, Sally Skinner, 3475
Behrens, Doug, 4062
Behrens, Gregg D., 2740
Behrens, John, 4155
Behrens, Roger R., 1817
Behring, Alexandre, 613
Behrman, Grant, 2689
Behrman, Michael J., 1785
Behrman, Philip G., 1287
Beichner, Martin P., 3996
Beichner, Martin P., Jr., 3996
Beier, David, 182
Beigie, David, 3591
Beijing Industrial Development Co. Ltd., 3123
Beiler, Samuel R., 287
Beilman, Ted, 2114
Beirlein, Debbie, 1196
Beisenstein, William C., 4094
Beital, Sandy, 2184
Beithon, Patricia A., 215
Beitz, Robert, 301
Beitzel, Jeremiah, 2948
Bekenstein, Joshua, 566, 4003
Bekins Distribution Center Co., 401
Bekins Investments, 401
Belair, Scott A., 1880
Belak, Michael, 2482
Belanger, David, 899
Belanger, Keith M., 2323
Belanger, Linda, 1565
Belanus, Nancy, 3883
Belcher, Tex, 3259
Belda, Alain J.P., 1960
Belden Brick Co., 402
Belden Holding & Acquisition Co., 402
Belden, Doug, 876
Belden, John, 402
Belden, Peter, 195
Belden, Robert F., 402
Belden, Robert T., 402
Belden, William H., Jr., 402
Belec, Anne E., 595
Belechak, Joseph G., 1194
Belgya, Mark R., 3488
Beliveau, Russell A., 2410
Belk Department Stores, The, 403
Belk Enterprises, 403
Belk, H.W. McKay, 403, 861
Belk, Inc., 403
Belk, John R., 403
Belk, Matthews, 403
Belk, Thomas M., Jr., 403, 404
Belk-Simpson Co., 404
Belknap, Robert, Jr., 2622
Bell Administrative Trust, Margaret L., 4108
Bell Atlantic Corp., 3936
Bell Helmets, 30
Bell, A.I., 2639
Bell, David, 2912, 3356
Bell, G. Russell, 397
Bell, Helen C., 3467
Bell, James A., 1160, 1161, 2071
Bell, James D., Jr., 317
Bell, Jane A., 642
Bell, Jeffrey A., 3412
Bell, Jerry, 3827
Bell, John Irving, 1549
Bell, Ken, 1146
Bell, Leonard, 86
Bell, Margaret L., 4108
Bell, Margaret S., 4108
Bell, Mary H., 1817
Bell, Paula J., 4108
Bell, Peggy, 2920
Bell, Rex, 2522
Bell, Rex L., 2522
Bell, Ron, 4140
Bell, Sharon, 2620
Bell, Steven C., 4108
Bell, Susan, 76
Bell, Susan M., 128
Bell, Thomas D., Jr., 57, 2725, 3166
Bell, Vance D., 3426
Bell, Victor E., III, 1396
Bell, William J., 641
Bellairs, Chris, Jr., 1054
Bellamy, Adrian D.P., 1533, 4079
Belle Tire, 1095
Belle, Diane, 1075
Bellej, Michelle, 3458
Beller, Alan L., 3802
Belleville Shoe Manufacturing Company, 405
Bellin, Richard, 1734
Bellin, Richard C., 1734
Bellini, Francesco, 2549
Bello, Stephane, 3741, 3742
Bellomy, Perry, 3121
Bellora, Mauricio, 2555
Bellotti, Frances X., 226
Bellows, Christopher, 1834
Bellows, Jeff, 501
Belmont, Michael J., 2533
Belo Corp., 406
Belo Corp., A.H., 406
Belon, Philippe, 519
Belshaw-Jones, Sharon, 1496
Belskus, Jeffrey G., 1555, 1885
Belsky, Joel A., 2333
Beltax Corp., 2174
Belton, Marc, 1554
Belton, Sharon Sayles, 3190
Belton, Y. Marc, 3835
Belts, Robert E., 1093
Beltzman, Daniel, 3172
Belvidere, 1963
Belvidere National Bank & Trust Co., 2081
Belzinskas, Remigijus H., 3452
Bemis Co., Inc., 407
Bemis Manufacturing Co., 408
Bemis, Erin, 408
Bemis, Peter, 408
Bemis, Peter F., 408
Ben & Jerry's Corp., 409
Ben & Jerry's Homemade, Inc., 409
Bena, Chuck, 835
Benack, Bill, 3970
Benanav, Gary G., 362, 1313
Benard, Yohann, 81
Benbenek, Scott, 3347
Bence, Craig, 2840
Bench, Sherice P., 1233
Bendapudi, Neeli, 2216
Bender, Bob, 2927
Bender, David E., 34
Bender, Dwain, 809
Bender, Michael J., 3294

Bender, Ralph, 977
Bender, Stephen G., 1788
Bendheim, John M., 145
Bene, Robert Del, 1960
Bene, Stephen G., 1242
Benecke, Lars, 381
Benecke, Mary Lou, 1162
Benedek, Peter, 3881
Benedetti, Dante B., 1306
Benedetti, Joseph C., 2676
Benedict, Anna Savage, 3341
Benedict, John P., 410
Benedict, Larry, 747
Beneficial Corp., 411
Beneficial Mutual Bancorp, Inc., 412
Beneficial New Jersey, 411
Benenson, Clement, 1935
Benenson, Clement C., 1935
Benenson, James, 1935
Benenson, James, III, 1935
Benenson, James, Jr., 1935
Benet, Jay S., 3802
Benetti, Joe, 939
Benevento & Mayo Partners, 414
Bengochea, Chuck, 1790
Bengu, Hasan, 3125
Benham, Douglas N., 3498
Benhamou, Eric A., 3455
Benioff, Marc, 818
Benioff, Marc R., 3318
Benito, Javier, 2139
Benjamin, Alan G., 2826
Benjamin, Christopher J., 85
Benjamin, Gerald, 3348
Benjamin, Gerald A., 3348
Benjamin, Jeff, 305
Benjamin, Jeffrey D., 775
Benjamin, Lawernce, 3646
Benjamin, Lawrence S., 1376
Benjamin, Lucas, 2572
Benjamin, Mark, 2572
Benjamin, Matthew, 2572
Benjamin, Michael, 2912
Benjamin, Nancy, 4033
Benjamin, Timothy, 3406
Benjamin-Brown, Hether, 661
Benjamins, Ed, 1674
Benkert, Jerome A., Jr., 3925
Benmosche, Robert H., 156
Bennack, Frank A., Jr., 3123
Bennard, Edward, 3040
Benner, Chris, 415
Bennett, Alan M., 1448, 1706, 3765
Bennett, Beth, 2530
Bennett, Bonnie B., 391
Bennett, Bruce, 3071
Bennett, Carl E., 3572
Bennett, Christie, 2991
Bennett, David, 1174
Bennett, David M., 3738
Bennett, Hank, 529
Bennett, James A., 3346
Bennett, Jim, 1252
Bennett, Joanna, 7
Bennett, Joanna Makepeace, 7
Bennett, John E., 417
Bennett, Jon S., 2344
Bennett, Louise Gaylord, 2795
Bennett, Michael, 747
Bennett, Michael L., 104, 4095
Bennett, Paul, 780
Bennett, Richard J., 1590
Bennett, Robert R., 1126, 3556
Bennett, Shannon, 3659
Bennett, Stephen, 3669
Bennett, Stephen M., 187
Bennett, Steven Alan, 3873
Bennett, Tanya, 626
Bennett, Twila, 2462
Bennett, William E., 3696
Bennett-Smith, Nicole, 1327
Benning, Dennis, 3699
Bennink, Jan, 863
Bennyhoff, George R., 4038
Benoist, Gray G., 2801
Benoit, D. Ben, 772
Benoliel, D. Jeffrey, 3093
Benoliel, Joel, 948
Benscoter, Steven P., 3627
Bense, Allan, 1689
Bensel, Greg, 2679
Bensen, Peter J., 2427
Bensford, John L., 2935
Benson, David, 1026, 1349
Benson, Dea, 3145
Benson, Douglas P., 2826
Benson, Edward, 3862
Benson, James, 291
Benson, James S., 990
Benson, Jim, 68
Benson, John, 1808
Benson, Kris, 334
Benson, Kristen M., 3931
Benson, Laurie, 1394
Benson, Luke, 431
Benson, Marilyn, 2638
Benson, Mark J., 3017
Benson, P. Douglas, 2826
Benson, P. George, 3045
Benson, Rene, 2679
Benson, Richard T., 182
Benson, Robert J., 2814
Benson, Robert K., 183
Benson, Tom, 2679
Bentas, Lily Haseotes, 1003
Benten, R. Anthony, 2690
Bentley Manufacturing Co., Inc., 416
Bentley, Charles W., Jr., 3086
Bentley, Julia, 3315
Bentley, Ronald M., 2681
Benton, Lurner O., III, 3087
Benton-Powers, Susan, 4089
Bentson, N. Larry, 2505
Bentz, Robert, 2330
Benvel, Paulette, 2562
Benveniste, Lawrence M., 101
Benziger, John M., 715
BEPCO, LP, 2138
Beracha, Barry H., 1792
Beran, David R., 120
Beran, Robin D., 722
Berardesco, Charles A., 1309
Berardinis, Roger A., 1302
Berardino, Joseph F., 3108
Berat Corp., 4152
Berberich, Bill, 591
Berce, Daniel E., 1556
Berchtold, Scott, 606
Bereday, Mari, 2204
Berelowitz, Michael, 3329
Berenbaum, Stan, 1915
Berendt, Michael J., Ph.D., 4003
Beresford, Dennis R., 2245
Berg, Al, 2369
Berg, Brad, 1081
Berg, Charles G., 1044
Berg, David P., 1919
Berg, Donald C., 592, 2471
Berg, Eric A., 1964
Berg, Jeffrey S., 2821
Berg, Kara, 3326
Berg, Kevin, 1062
Berg, Mark S., 2981
Berg, Mark Stephen, 2981
Berg, Michael J., 1831
Bergami, Samuel S., Jr., 2513
Bergan, John W., 2568
Bergdoll, Brian, 508
Bergen Community Bank, 3916
Bergen, Andre, 2769
Bergen, John (Jack) D., 82
Bergen, Mark, 3604
Bergen, Mark D., 3604
Berger, Cindy, 239
Berger, Gillett, 396
Berger, Irving, 1882
Berger, Jeffrey P., 460
Berger, John R., 349
Berger, Mark, 3523
Berger, Nancee Shannon R., 4035
Berger, Stephen, 2784
Berger, William, 1882
Berger-Gross, Victoria, 3750
Berges, David E., 1795
Berges, James G., 3025
Bergeson, Scott, 1450
Bergevin, Denise, 496
Bergey, Rachelle, 2368
Bergh, Chip, 3624
Berghammer Construction Corp., 418
Bergin, Mary, 2175
Bergley, William J., Jr., 3308
Berglund Chevrolet, 419
Bergman, Bert, 3376
Bergman, Garrett E., 993
Bergman, Rebecca M., 3453
Bergman, Stanley, 3348
Bergman, Stanley M., 3348
Bergmann, Thomas E., 188
Bergner, Kevin J., 3873
Bergquist, Carl R., Jr., 420
Bergquist, Carl R., Sr., 420
Bergquist, Scott, 3455
Bergren, Byron L., 521
Bergren, Scott O., 2988
Bergson, Simon, 2354
Bergstein, Melvyn E., 3458
Bergstrom Climate Systems, Inc., 421
Bergstrom Inc., 421
Bergstrom Manufacturing Co., Inc., 421
Bergstrom, Craig A., 2199
Bergstrom, John C., 1140
Bergstrom, John F., 39, 261, 1651, 2150, 4093
Bergum, Lester N., 1410
Bergum, William R., 313
Bergy, Dean H., 3627
Berick, James H., 846
Beriont, Susan, 1190
Berisford, John, 2429
Berk, Howard M., 1120
Berk-Tek, Inc., 423
Berke, Matt, 2570
Berke, Zachary, 1316
Berkel & Company Contractors, Inc., 424
Berkel, Charles J., 424
Berkelhammer, Michael, 3862
Berkery, Rosemary T., 1448
Berkey, Douglas, 878
Berkheimer Oursourcing, Inc., 425
Berkheimer, H.A., Inc., 425
Berkheimer, John, 425
Berkheimer, John D., 425
Berkhouse, Julie B., 2925
Berkley Aviation LLC, 426
Berkley Corp., W.R., 426
Berkley Risk Administrators Company, LLC, 426
Berkley, Bill, 3717
Berkley, Dick, 3717
Berkley, E. Bertram, 3717
Berkley, Eliot S., 3717
Berkley, Richard L., 3717
Berkley, Thomas, 7
Berkley, W. Robert, 426
Berkley, W. Robert, Jr., 426
Berkley, William, 3717
Berkley, William R., 426
Berkley, William R., Jr., 426
Berkman, Lance, 1871
Berkman, William L., 1871
Berkowitz, Alice, 1930
Berkowitz, Alice R., 1930
Berkowitz, Arthur M., 427
Berkowitz, Bruce R., 3563
Berkowitz, Carolyn S., 679
Berkowitz, Edwin J., 427
Berkowitz, J.E., L.P., 427
Berkowitz, Leonard M., 1930
Berkowitz, Mark, 3806
Berkshire Bank, 428
Berkshire Hathaway Inc., 429
Berkson, Steven, 853
Berkus, James, 3881
Berlex Inc., 382
Berlex Laboratories, Inc., 382
Berlin, Arnold M., 1510
Berlin, Michael D., 3050
Berlinger, Liz, 2062
Berlinsky, Jay S., 3797
Berman, Ann E., 2296
Berman, Bruce, 488
Berman, Frank, 488
Berman, Michael A., 2324
Berman, Richard, 2335
Berman, Scott A., 434
Berman, Walter S., 174
Bermas, Stephen, 915
Bermudez, Jorge A., 2563
Bernacchi, Jeffrey M., 853
Bernados, Tony, 2573
Bernard, Betsy J., 3047, 4157
Bernard, Gerard A., 3878
Bernard, Scott, 3220
Bernard, William J., 1488
Bernardes, Oscar, 3029
Bernardi, Anthony, 1716
Bernardi, Renzo, 2272
Bernardin, Thomas, 619
Bernasek, Brian A., 1792
Bernaski, Michael J., 4047
Bernauer, David W., 2312
Bernbach, John L., 2807
Berndt, Richard O., 332, 2996, 2997
Bernecker's Nursery, Inc., 431
Bernecker, Donald, 431
Bernecker, Robert, 431
Berner, G. Gary, 2681
Berner, Kyle R., 1354
Berner, Mary, 3141
Bernhard, Brenda, 2010
Bernhard, Brenner, 2175
Bernhard, G. Kenneth, 2088
Bernhard, Linda M., 1668
Bernhard, Robert J., 1007
Bernhardt Furniture Company, 432

Binion, Laura E., 3672
Binkley, David A., 4056
Binkley, John, 76
Binney & Smith, Inc., 973
Binns, Robert R., 1592
Binstock, Joan Anne, 2303
Binswanger Corp., 464
Binswanger Glass Co., 27
Binswanger, Betsy W., 27
Binswanger, David R., 464, 2958
Binswanger, Elizabeth, 464
Binswanger, Frank G., III, 464
Binswanger, Frank G., Jr., 464
Binswanger, John K., 464
Binswanger, Millard I., 27
Binswanger, Robert B., 464
Bintz, Mary C., 2681
Binyon, Bryan A., 3554
Biogen, Inc., 465
Biomet, Inc., 466
Biondi, Frank J., Jr., 182, 641, 1747, 3377
Bionetics Corp., The, 467
Birchfield, J. Kermit, 1957
Birck, Michael J., 3709
Bird, Alan W., 3275
Bird, Anat M., 4127
Bird, Brian B., 2748
Bird, J. Richard, 1265
Bird, Peter F., Jr., 1762
Bird, Shelley, 685
Bird, Shirley, 685
Bird, Thomas W., 1333
Bird-in-Hand Corp., 468
Birdhouse, 30
Birdseye Foods, 469
Birdsong Corp., 470
Birdsong Lii, Thomas H., 470
Birdsong, George Y., 470
Birdsong, Thomas H., III, 470
Birk, Michael J., 3709
Birkenholz, Robert E., 2445
Birkhead, L. Keith, 1335
Birkins, David A., 3858
Birkland, Roderick C., 111
Birkland, Wendall R., 111
Birmingham Hide & Tallow, Inc., 471
Birnbaum, Roger, 2479
Birnbaum, Scott K., 46
Birnberg, Diane Mix, 1864
Birney, David G., 3361
Bisaro, Paul M., 4007
Bisbee, Gerald E., Jr., 754
Bischel, David A., 2853
Bischmann, Joanne M., 1732
Bischof, Jens, 2041
Bischoff, J. Michael, 2385
Bischoff, Scott J., 2051
Bischoff, Winfried F. W., 2274
Bischoff, Winfried F. W., Sir, 2429
Bisciotti, Stephen J., 92
Bisetti, Robert, 1846
Bisgrove Foundation, 3586
Bisgrove, Debra, 3586
Bisgrove, Gerald, 3586
Bishkin, S. James, 3117
Bishop, Dana, 1409
Bishop, John J., 2584
Bishop, Liston, III, 3898
Bishop, Marie, 2130
Bishop, Mark, 2151
Bishop, Nicholas J., 2130
Bishop, Paul R., 1047
Bishop, Ted, 2953
Bishop, Teresa A., 1635
Bishop, Terri C., 216
Bishop, Thomas P., 1567
Bisignano, Frank J., 1400, 2072
Bisio, Gabriel, 1107
Bisselberg, Stephanie S., 67
Bissett, Hallie, 934
Bissett, Hallie L., 934
Bissey, Jeff, 2824
Bisson, Kevin M., 2469
Bissonnette, William P., 1927, 3242
Bitsberger, Timothy S., 853
Bitterman, Mary G.F., 342
Bittner, Ryan J., 60
Bitto, George G., 63
Bitzer, Astrid S., 10
Bitzer, John F., III, 10
Bitzer, Michelle R., 10
Biumi, Bonnie, 2133
BJ's Wholesale Club, Inc., 473
Bjorge, Dale, 1952
Bjork, Annette, 1452
Bjork, Claes G., 1632
Bjorklund, K. Gunnar, 3267
Bjorkman, Martin, 3473
Bjornholt, J. Eric, 2499
Bjornson, Sandy P., 1079
Bjornsonc, Sandy, 1079
Black Hills Corp., 474
Black, Carole, 3755
Black, Christena, 3983
Black, Christina, 3983
Black, Don, 3807
Black, James R., 2407
Black, Jane, 4097
Black, Jeanne M., 3234
Black, Jim, 2407
Black, Joe, 3514
Black, Kenneth A., 1396
Black, Natalie A., 2050, 2182
Black, Pat, 962
Black, Steven D., 2617
Black, Steven H., 3887
Black, Theodore N., 1819
Black, William D., 887
Black, William H., 502
Blackbaud, Inc., 1302
Blackburn, Deidre, 3307
Blackburn, Frank, 1211
Blackburn, Julie E., 3384
Blackburn, Mark A., 3590
Blackburn, Rex, 1907
Blackey, Brent G., 1832
Blackford, David, 653
Blackford, David E., 2324
Blackford, Dean, 1734
Blackhurst, Jan Jones, 650
Blackman, Jules, 3871
Blackmar, Alfred O., 54
Blackmer, Dennis, 1452
Blackmon, R. Charles, 135
Blackmon, Richard W., 1395
Blackmore, Peter, 2459
Blackmore, R. Gregoire, 2507
Blackstone, Kathy C., 1429
Blackwell, Allison, 397
Blackwood, C. Michael, 1799
Blackwood, Lindsay K., 812
Blade Communications, Inc., 481
Blade, Christy, 3015
Blaine, Anthony L., 3920
Blaine, Gregory W., 756
Blair & Co., Inc., Isaac, 2382
Blair & Co., William, L.L.C., 478
Blair Construction, Inc., 479
Blair, Amy M., 2263
Blair, Brenda M., 479
Blair, Bryce, 3083
Blair, Donald W., 2710
Blair, Edward, 3192
Blair, Frank, 1136
Blair, Fred A., 479
Blair, Gary J., 481
Blair, Ian D., 3766
Blair, Jim, 2557
Blair, John S., 1225
Blair, Michael W., 1055
Blair, Randy, 1429
Blair, Scott G., 2873
Blais, Dave, 3091
Blais, Roger, 913
Blaise, Nicole, 2474
Blake, Allen H., 1393
Blake, Francis S., 1842
Blake, H. Scott, 1854
Blake, John, 3729
Blake, Kent, 2260
Blake, Kristianne, 301
Blake, Norman P., Jr., 2842
Blake, Patrick, 2434
Blakely, Carolyn, 240
Blakely, Matt, 2586
Blakesley, Leonard E., 922
Blakey, Marion C., 74
Blalock, Jo, 1146
Blalock, Robert H., 3866
Blancaflor, Katherine C., 3899
Blanchard, Billy, 3674
Blanchard, Brenda, 2752
Blanchard, Cayce, 2538
Blanchard, James H., 273
Blanchard, Mark E., 1883
Blanchet, Lesile, 131
Blanchet, Leslie, 131
Blanco, Amelia, 3822
Bland, Billy, 859
Bland, Kim, 1490
Blandford, Patrick, 3505
Blanding, Robert James, 2301
Blandino, David A., 1799
Blanford, Lawrence J., 1653, 3597
Blank, Arthur M., 277, 959, 2589, 3581
Blank, Robert S., 3769
Blank, Steven A., 2763
Blankenship, Bill, 1664
Blankenship, Carlene, 1855
Blankenship, Coni, 1005
Blankenship, David, 45
Blankenship, Mark H., 2007
Blankfein, Lloyd C., 1603, 1604
Blankfield, Bryan J., 2833
Blanks, Dennis, 2525
Blanks, Marvin, III, 4142
Blanton, Hilda, 4006
Blanton, R. Daniel, 3513
Blanton, Thomas K., 2044
Blanton, Wendall, 1296
Blase, Eric, 3050
Blase, William A., Jr., 273
Blaser, Lon, 2173
Blasetto, James, 272
Blashack Strahan, Jill, 3692
Blasini, Kevin A., 2424
Blaskowsky, Robert W., 3706
Blaszak, Shelley, 2548
Blaszka, Greg, 2040
Blatt, Gregory R., 1903
Blatz, Kathleen A., 496
Blaufuss, William F., Jr., 1559
Blausey, William W., 1216
Blausey, William W., Jr., 1216
Blauvelt, Gene, 44
Blaylock, Ronald E., 426
Blazar, Paul, 298
Blazek, David, 667
Blefari, Gino, 1973
Bleier, Edward, 483
Blencoe, Harry A., 1404
Blessing Hospital Foundation, 3944
Blethen, Frank A., 3386
Blethen, James A., 3386
Blettner, Brad, 814
Bleuer, T. Cory, 508
Bleustein, Jeffrey L., 595
Blevins, Ronald J., 4103
Blevins, Teresa F., 2218
Blew, C.J., 802
Blew, Clinton J., 802
Blickensderfer, M., 3410
Blin, James L., 3394
Blinn, Mark A., 1447
Blitzer, Michael, 1781
Blitzer, Michael J., 2128
Blobel, Guenter, 4072
Bloch, Henry W., 1695
Blocher, Mitch, 287
Block Communications, Inc., 481
Block Electric Co., Inc., 482
Block, Alan, 2625
Block, Allan, 481
Block, Arthur R., 887
Block, Cyrus, 481
Block, Greg, 3556
Block, Jack G., 482
Block, John G., 482
Block, John R., 481
Block, Keith G., 3318
Block, Rich, 3648
Block, Tom, 1454
Bloem, James H., 1886
Blohm, Donald E., 2205
Blohm, Richard E., Jr., 4020
Blom, Suzanne M., 562
Blomgren, Stuart, 1973
Blommer Chocolate Co., Inc., 484
Blommer, Henry J., Jr., 484
Blommer, Joseph, 484
Blommer, Peter, 484
Blommer, Steve, 484
Blondia, Jeanne M., 3627
Blondin, Del, 3822
Blood-Horse, Inc., The, 485
Bloodworth, Carolyn A., 854, 921
Bloom, Daniel, 172
Bloom, Dennis, 172
Bloom, Gary L., 508
Bloom, Michael K., 1330
Bloomer, Donald E., 826
Bloomfield, Doug, 2723
Bloomgarden, Kathy, 3282
Bloss, Bob, 1707
Blossman, David, 19
Blount, Daniel J., 1635
Blount, Sally, 13
Blount, Susan L., 3072
Blount, W. Frank, 2106
Blue Bell, Inc., 3913
Blue Chip Casino, Inc., 489
Blue Cross and Blue Shield of Alabama, Inc., 492
Blue Cross and Blue Shield of Florida, Inc., 493

Blue Cross and Blue Shield of Iowa, 4026
Blue Cross and Blue Shield of Kansas, Inc., 495
Blue Cross and Blue Shield of Massachusetts, Inc., 501
Blue Cross and Blue Shield of Michigan, 502
Blue Cross and Blue Shield of Minnesota, 496
Blue Cross and Blue Shield of Mississippi, 490
Blue Cross and Blue Shield of North Carolina, Inc., 497
Blue Cross and Blue Shield of South Carolina, 498
Blue Cross and Blue Shield of South Dakota, 4026
Blue Cross and Blue Shield of Tennessee, 507
Blue Cross and Blue Shield of Wyoming, 503
Blue Cross Blue Shield of Louisiana, 2309
Blue Cross of Idaho Health Service, Inc., 504, 2500
Blue Cross of Northeastern Pennsylvania, 505
Blue Shield of California, 1275
Blue Water Environmental, 3014
Blue, Frank W., 2600
Blue, Robert M., 1150
Blue, Suzanne, 3154
Bluechoice Health Plan of SC, Inc., 498
Bluedorn, Todd, 1216
Bluestone, Eric, 4036
Bluestone, Steven, 4036
Bluhm, Robert L., 1714
Blum, Eva T., 2997
Blum, James A., 588
Blum, Jonathan, 4150
Blum, Jonathan D., 2154
Blum, Mark J., 3736
Blum, Paul, 2128
Blum, Ray, 937
Blum, Ray N., 937
Blum, Richard C., 725
Blum, Steve, 289
Blumenschein, Joel R., 1382
Blumenthal, Judith, 1685
Blunden, Craig G., 3071
Bluth, Connie W., 3526
Bluth, L. Lothaire, 3526
Blystone, John B., 4124
Blythe, Jean, 4075
BMG Music, 439
BMO Harris Bank, N.A., 3246
BMS/Sanofi Pharmaceuticals Partnership, 578
BNSF Railway, 618
BNY Capital Corp., 344
BNY Mellon, N.A., 3406
Boa, Ray P., 3858
Boak, Dick, 2390
Boals, Richard L., 500
Board of Trade of the City of Chicago, Inc., 853
Board, Virginia M., 1150
Boardman, D. Dixon, 2819
Boardman, Thomas A., 3
Boas, Bill, 11
Boaz, Katherine H., 1855
Bob's Discount Furniture of Mass., LLC, 511
Bob's Discount Furniture, Inc., 511
Bob's Discount Furniture, LLC, 511
Bob, Fulmer, 3679
Bobb, Jay, 3528
Bobb, Steve, 3544
Bobby, Theodore N., 1772
Boberg, Wayne D., 4089
Bobins, Norman R., 57, 787
Bobo, John T., 2419
Bobsin, Geoffrey, 658
Boccadoro, Steven M., 1216
Bocchini, Suzanne S., 3173
Bocchino, Lisa Duda, 1188
Boccio, Frank, 2688
Boccio, Frank M., 2688
Bochart, Jessica, 957
Bock, Kurt F., 951
Bodager, Brian R., 261
Bodaken, Bruce G., 3220
Bodam, Gary, 1990
Bodden, Walter P., Jr., 801
Bode, Christopher D., 1087
Bode, Clive D., 2138
Bode, John S., 3920
Bodenhofer, Eric, 3159
Bodfish, Paul, Sr., 234
Bodford, Alvin, 1283
Bodford, Alvin M., 1283
Bodford, Brenda S., 1283
Bodford, Jason M., 1283
Bodine, Christopher W., 2619
Bodine, Helen, 3649
Bodine, Ralph E., 3649
Bodinger, Bruce, 3354
Bodman, Samuel W., III, 1793
Bodner, Jeff, 2685
Bodner, Larry E., 1065
Boeckmann, Alan, 233
Boeckmann, Alan L., 3405
Boehlen, Mark, 1538
Boehne, Edward G., 412, 3769
Boehne, Richard A., 3374
Boehringer Ingelheim Pharmaceuticals, Inc., 515
Boehringer Ingelheim USA Corp., 515
Boeing Co., The, 516
Boens, Debra D., 2647
Boersig, Clemens A.H., 1257
Boeschenstein, Harold, 2844
Boesel, Stephen W., 3040
Boesen, Theodore J., Jr., 4026
Boessen, Douglas G., 871
Boettcher, James H., 637
Bogan, Thomas, 2878
Bogart, Stacy, 3775
Bogart, Stacy L., 2999
Bogeajis, Kay L., 2916
Boger, Peter M., 3211
Boggan, Daniel, Jr., 852, 871, 3946
Boggs, E. Jackson, 1479
Boggs, N. Cornell, III, 1162
Boggs, Thomas Hale, Jr., 2898
Bogle, Robert W., 1926
Bogner, Dean E., 4018
Bogo, Alexis G., 3329
Bogus, Donald W., 2801
Boguth, Terry Ann, 2455
Boh Bros. Construction Co., L.L.C., 517
Boh, Robert H., 517
Boh, Robert S., 517
Bohan, Deirdre, 3510, 3511
Bohan, Deirdre L., 3510
Bohan, James, 2805
Bohannan, Miles, 2141
Bohannon, Terri, 3140
Bohbrink, Marshall, 1674
Bohlmann, Jaya K., 3497
Bohm, Friedrich K. M., 2325
Bohman, Cynthia A., 3170
Bohman, M. Jack, 3170
Bohman, Maurice J., 3170
Bohman, Stephen J., 3170
Bohman, Steve, 3170
Bohn, Karen M., 2836
Bohn, Karina, 310
Bohn, Robert G., 2461, 2833, 2886
Bohnsack, Christie, 1275
Boies, Jeffrey E., 2378
Boigegrain, Barbara A., 1413
Boike, Brian D.J., 827
Boileau, Randy, 3923
Boillat, Pascal, 1349
Boiron, Christian, 519
Boiron, Thierry, 519
Boiron-Borneman Co., 519
Bojalad, Ronald, 1032
Boland, Elizabeth, 566
Boland, Elizabeth J., 566
Boland, James C., 4047
Boland, Mary M., 140
Boland, William E., Jr., 1325
Bolen, Dianne, 1347
Bolens, Barbara, 552
Boler Co., Inc., The, 520
Boler, James W., 520
Boler, John M., 520
Boler, Matthew J., 520
Boler, Michael J., 520
Boles, Donna M., 398
Bolger, David P., 2415
Boliba, Jeff, 624
Bolick, J. Bruce, 1665
Bolick, Jerome W., 3517
Bolick, Linda B., 3517
Bolinder, William H., 1565
Boling, Michael R., 934
Bolker, Cynthia, 2688
Bolla, Gianluca, 1685
Bolland, David, 2993
Bolland, David S., 2993
Bolland, Marc J., 2358
Bollenbach, Stephen F., 2105, 2333, 2556, 3757
Bollinger, Bernard, 600
Bollinger, Lee C., 3999
Bollman, John, 3410
Bolognini, Louis T., 1922
Bolotin, Irving, 2250
Bolotsky, David, 3849
Bolt, Bretton J., 2705
Bolt, Gregg A., 3715
Bolte, John H., 2634
Bolte, John M., 388
Bolte, Richard J., Jr., 388
Bolten, Joshua B., 1257
Bolton, J. Mark, 859
Bolton, Jeffrey W., 3944
Bolton, William J., 407
Bomian, Leo, 72
Bomstein, Brian E., 384
Bon Jovi, Jon, 53
Bon-Ton Stores, Inc., The, 521
Bonach, Edward J., 857
Bonanni, Fabrizio, 182
Bonanno, Phyllis, 528
Bonanno, Phyllis O., 528
Bonarti, Michael A., 291
Bonavia, Paul J., 3819
Boncher, John, 1009
Bond, David F., 3310
Bond, Elton, 2431
Bond, Jill, 3204
Bond, John M., Jr., 1518
Bond, John R. H., 2740
Bond, Nani, 516
Bond, Ray, 1513
Bond, Robert T., 2165
Bondan, Sandy, 2369
Bondar, Lori J., 297
Bonderman, David, 1273, 1555
Bondi, John, 2595
Bone, Theresa Z., 1287
Boneal Inc., 523
Bonello, Kathy, 3170
Boneparth, Peter, 2041, 2181
Bonetto, Frank, 346
Bonfante, Lawrence, 3879
Bonfield, Gordon B., 2056
Bonfield, Peter, 2462
Bong, Francis S. Y., 42
Bongard, Carey L., 268
Bongi, Anne, 3455
Boni, Eric N., 258
Boni, Peter J., 3307
Bonitz of South Carolina, Inc., 524
Bonk, Jeanne, 3322
Bonk, Jeanne M., 3322
Bonner, Cindi Bear, 393
Bonner, Michael A., 2565
Bonnevier, Bruce J., 2467
Bonney, Michael W., 999
Bonomo, Charles, 2593
Bonovitz, Sheldon M., 887
Bonsall, Mark, 3319
Bonsall, Mark B., 3319
Bontempo, C. Angela, 2323
Bontempo, Robert N., 323
Bonzani, Andrew, 1960, 1974
Boocock, Richard, 63
Book, Eldon, 1956
Booker, Jayne, 3673
Booker, Jennifer, 1890
Booker, Marilyn, 2570
Bookman, Stuart, 785
Boom, R. Ried, 3710
Boone, Douglas, 3035
Boone, Douglas A., 3035
Boone, Eileen Howard, 1014
Boone, James B., Jr., 4046
Boone, Michael M., 1759
Boone, Pat, 3258
Boone, Pat, IV, 3258
Boone, Torrence, 1383
Boor, David A., 997
Boor, Leon J., 495
Boorman, Mary, 2977
Boose, R. Andrew, 3250
Boot, Arnoud W. A., 3179
Booth, Dan, 2540
Booth, Debbie, 719
Booth, James H., 3875
Booth, Lewis W.K., 2556
Booth, Richard H., 2737, 3643
Booth-Barbarin, Ann V., 272
Boothby, Lee K., 2695
Boots, Ian G., 438
Boots, Ira G., 438
Boozer, Greg, 1576
Boragno, Richard, 848
Borcherding Enterprises, Inc., 526
Borcherding, John, 526
Borcherding, Kim, 526

Bord, Marie L., 348
Bordelon, Malcolm, 3327
Borden Manufacturing Co., 527
Borden, Edwin B., III, 527
Borden, Michael, 1883
Borden, Ralph, 527
Borden, Robert H., 527
Borden, W. Lee, 527
Borenin, Jessica, 84
Borg, Jennifer A., 2733
Borg, Malcolm A., 2733
Borg, Sandra A., 2733
Borg, Stephen A., 2733
Borg-Warner Corp., 3390
Borg-Warner Security Corp., 3390
Borgard, Lawrence T., 2735, 4096
Borgmeier, Lynn S., 3430
Borgstrom, Marna, 3944
BorgWarner Inc., 528
Borick, Ken, 3563
Borick, Kenneth M., 3563
Borick, Steven J., 2324
Borin, Mark C., 2926
Boring, Marilyn, 2019
Borjesson, Rolf L., 297
Borlinghaus, Scott R., 1321
Born, Ross J., 2077
Borne, Dan, 2309
Borneman, J. Ralph, Jr., 1291
Borner, Thomas A., 3086
Bornheimer, Deborah H., 1209
Bornheimer, Deborah Hill, 1209
Bornhuetter, Ron, 4134
Bornstein, Steve, 2626
Borok, Gil, 725
Boromisa, Jeffrey M., 4106
Borrego, Kenneth T., 2034
Borrego, Kenny, 2034
Borrell, Anthony, 487
Borror, David, 1149
Borror, Douglas D., 1149
Borror, Douglas G., 1149
Borst, Elizabeth S., 2879
Bortoli, Mario, 3098
Bortoli, Matt, 3098
Boryczka, Margaret, 213
Borzon, Mike, 3758
Bosacker, Lyle, 1797
Bosch, Joseph A., 1124
Bosch, Mindi Vanden, 3937
Boscia, Jon A., 3516
BOSE Corp., 530
Bose, Amar G., 530
Boskin, Michael J., 1315, 2821
Boskofsky, Peter, 2184
Bosman, Ruud H., 1323
Boss, Greg, 993
Boss, James, 2482
Boss, W. Andrew, 3537
Bosse, Jeffrey A., 2179
Bosserman, David, 2611
Bossidy, Lawrence A., 428
Bossong Hosiery Mills, Inc., 532
Bossong, F.Huntley, 532
Bossong, Joseph C., 532
Bost, Glenn E., II, 3025
Bost, Robert G., 2947
Bostic, Molly, 3978
Bostock, Roy J., 1073
Boston Beer Co., The, 606
Boston Capital Holdings, LP, 534
Boston Sand & Gravel Co., 539
Boston Scientific Corp., 540
Bostrom, Brent, 1674
Bostrom, Brent B., 1674
Bostrom, Susan L., 646
Boswell Charitable Lead Trust, Lois K., The, 1928
Boswell Foundation, Amie, 1928
Boswell Foundation, Joe, 1928
Boswell Foundation, Johnathon, 1928
Boswell Foundation, Julie, 1928
Boswell, Brad, 1928
Boswell, Gina R., 2358
Boswell, John, 3336
Boswell, John J., 1928
Bosworth, Robert E., 3329
Bosworth, Stephen W., 1971
Botas, Luis, 2122
Botham, Lydia, 2217
Bothe, Richard, 1470
Botta, G. Andrea, 1635
Bottemiller, Donald L., 1847
Bottemiller, Mark, 1847
Bottger, Graeme W., 82
Bottini, Mark, 2904
Bottling Group, LLC, 2935
Bottoli, Marcello, 1962
Bottomley, Kevin T., 2928
Botts, Patrick C., 2603
Bouchard, Angelee F., 1766
Bouchard, Caren, 2645
Bouchard, Karen, 2993
Boucher, Douglas, 170
Boucher, John C., 3512
Boucher, Peter, 1400
Bouchut, Pierre, 1458
Boudazin, Janick, 519
Boudreau, Gerard F., 4102
Boudreau, Helen, 2752
Boudreaux, Daniel, 2978
Boudreaux, Gail Koziara, 4135
Bouffard, Joseph J., 331
Boughner, Robert L., 546, 3524
Bouillion, Harold, 2678
Boukai, Akhram, 925
Boukai, Amer, 925
Boukai, Amer A., 925
Boukai, Ziad, 925
Bouki, Amer, 925
Bouki, Issam, 925
Bouki, Ziad, 925
Bouknight, J.A., Jr., 3077
Bouldin, Steven H., 2229
Boulet, Virginia, 751
Boulier, Charles J., III, 2645
Boulos, Paul F., 2608
Bouma, John J., 3490
Bouman, Rosemarie, 2415
Bound To Stay Bound Books, Inc., 541
Bourdo, Douglas, 947
Bourdukofsky, Tara, 84
Bourgeois, Henry, 2659
Bourke, Anita, 1917
Bourland, Amy, 3457
Bourne, Maureen, 3222
Bourne, Tom, 2581
Bourns, Gordon L., 542
Bourns, Gordon L., II, 542
Bourns, Inc., 542
Bousbib, Ari, 1842, 1924
Boushek, Randall L., 3747
Bousquet-Chavanne, Patrick, 592
Boutin, Jeff, 476
Boutwell, David A., 1726
Bowater, Ben, 1248
Bowden, Jen, 870
Bowden, Mathew W., 71
Bowe, Patrick, 3365
Bowen, Dan, 2594
Bowen, Jeffrey, 1026
Bowen, John R., 2741
Bowen, Marjorie L., 3682
Bowen, Nancy, 945
Bowen, Thomas M., 3326
Bower, Charles W., 411
Bower, Curtis A., 2887
Bower, Joseph L., 2296
Bower, Kevin, 2852
Bower, Mark, 1846
Bower, Ralph W., 50
Bower, Robert, 142
Bowers, G. Thomas, 1419
Bowers, Patrick, 2634
Bowers, Robert E., Jr., 2394
Bowers, Tom, 1312
Bowers, W. Paul, 1567
Bowes, Frederick M., II, 3335
Bowes, Jim, 2401
Bowie, Paul, 92
Bowlby, Darren, 3804
Bowlen, John, 2906
Bowlen, Pat, 2906
Bowler, Keith, 1196
Bowles, Barbara L., 1867, 4093
Bowles, Crandall C., 1061, 2071
Bowles, Erskine B., 2570, 2725
Bowles, James E., 26
Bowles, Rice, McDavid, Graff & Love, 544
Bowlin, John D., 3365
Bowman, Becky, 566
Bowman, Danny, 3556
Bowman, Gary, 2800
Bowman, Harry W., 2149
Bowman, Nancy, 774
Bowman, Paul B., 1016
Bowman, Valli, 763
Bowser, Mark F., 958
Bowsher, Charles A., 1382
Box, Mimi, 53
Boxer, Mark L., 812
Boxleitner, Jerry, 195
Boyan, Craig, 628
Boyanovsky, Harold D., 856
Boyce, Ann Allston, 3040
Boyce, Donna J., 1723
Boyce, Edward, 241
Boyce, Gregory H., 2364, 2907
Boyce, Jefferson C., 2688
Boyce, Kevin M., 1252
Boyce, Mark C., 2681
Boyd Coffee Co., 545
Boyd, Brenda, 545
Boyd, Charles, 3648
Boyd, Christopher, 545
Boyd, Colin, 2050
Boyd, David, 545
Boyd, David D., 545
Boyd, Debbie, 1470
Boyd, James L., 3726
Boyd, James R., 1706
Boyd, Jeffrey, 3655
Boyd, Jody, 545
Boyd, John F., 3659
Boyd, Judy, 545
Boyd, Karri, 545
Boyd, Katherine M., 1391
Boyd, Kelsey, 545
Boyd, Larry C., 1941
Boyd, Michael, 545
Boyd, Ralph F., Jr., 1124, 1348
Boyd, Richard, 545
Boyd, Richard D., 545
Boyd, Stephen, 545
Boyd, William, 489
Boyd, William R., 546
Boyd, William S., 546
Boyden, Brian V., 3591
Boyea, Bruce W., 2681
Boyer, Brooks, 790
Boyer, David, 588
Boyer, Dewayne, 1988
Boyer, Earl, 2361
Boyer, Guy, 499
Boyer, H. Stacey, 2561
Boyer, Jeffrey, 3179
Boyer, John F., 2410
Boyer, K. David, Jr., 385
Boyer, Paul, 2456
Boyer, Robert E., 3622
Boyer, Stacey H., 2561
Boyke, Dale C., 2793
Boykin, Edward P. (Pete), 2650
Boykin, Frank, 2545
Boykin, Frank A., 2545
Boylan, Dean M., 539
Boylan, Dean M., Jr., 539
Boylan, Dean M., Sr., 539
Boylan, Jeanne-Marie, 539
Boylan, John L., 2216
Boyle, Alison, 3414
Boyle, Frederick J., 1047
Boyle, Kevin, 2319
Boyle, Kristin, 140
Boyle, Patrick, 2769
Boyle, Stephen J., 3696
Boyle, Steven, 421
Boyle, Timothy P., 2747
Boylson, Michael J., 2925
Boyne, Jack, 381
Boynton, Paul G., 571, 3134
Boze, Brandon B., 725
Bozer, Ahmet C., 862
Bozesky, Margaret, 2820
Bozich, Frank, 368
Bozick, Nicholas L., 3649
Bozman, Blake, 1177
BP Alaska, 234
BP America Inc., 547
BP Amoco Corp., 547
BP Corp. North America Inc., 547
BP Products North America, Inc., 547
BPI Technology, Inc., 548
Brabeck-Letmathe, Peter, 1315
Bracciotti, John L., 3616
Bracco, Michael, 346
Brace, Frederic F., 1457
Bracke, James, 1797
Bracken, Brenda, 1639, 2896
Bracken, Charles H.R., 2263
Bracken, Julie H., 1051
Bracken, Richard M., 1762
Bracken, Richard M., Jr., 1762
Brackett, Mark, 2162
Brackman, Adam, 2677
Braco, Holly, 2716
Bradbury, Curt, 3598
Braddock, Michael G., 2362, 2365
Braddock, Richard S., 1214
Bradford, Bob, 238, 3310
Bradford, Darryl M., 1309
Bradford, David T., 917
Bradford, James W., 966, 1559
Bradford, James W., Jr., 1632
Bradford, Jay, 2343

Bradford, Jay H., 2343
Bradford, Patricia A., 3859
Bradford, Steven M., 1817
Bradley Foundation, Lynde and Harry, Inc., The, 1201
Bradley, Alison, 2003
Bradley, Bill, 3839
Bradley, Brad, 3717
Bradley, C.G., 913
Bradley, Craig, 310
Bradley, David R., Jr., 3846
Bradley, Denise, 752
Bradley, Dorothy M., 2748
Bradley, James, 2003
Bradley, Jo, 499
Bradley, Joseph W., 795
Bradley, Kathleen G., 2176
Bradley, Kerry, 2251
Bradley, Michael A., 304, 3718
Bradley, Michelle, 2003
Bradley, Phillip A., 1186
Bradley, Robert L., 3685
Bradley, William W., 3585
Bradley-Wells, Kathy, 735
Bradshaw, Chuck, 1279
Bradshaw, James, 699
Bradshaw, Jami L., 1410
Bradshaw, John F., 1946
Bradshaw, Tracy, 3975
Bradshaw, Wilson G., 3389
Bradway, Randy, 752
Bradway, Robert A., 182, 2725
Brady Corporation, 552
Brady, Barrett, 1800
Brady, Christine, 3707
Brady, Debra L., 1926
Brady, Ed, 553
Brady, James T., 2423, 3040
Brady, Jerome D., 1484
Brady, Larry D., 324
Brady, Nicholas F., 1793
Brady, Park, 3563
Brady, Pat Foy, 697
Brady, Robert T., 2323, 2628
Brady, Sharon M., 1916
Brady, Stephen J., 3497
Brady, Steven E., 2781
Brady, Suzanne M., 1490
Brae Capital Corp., 3950
Brae Group, Inc., 3950
Braemer, Richard J., 3769
Braet, Christine, 1049
Braet, Joseph, 1049
Brafman, Reisa, 1433
Bragg Live Food Products, Inc., 554
Bragg, Patricia, 554
Braginsky, Sidney, 1134
Brailer, David J., 3981
Brailey, John, 315
Brain, Anthony J., 4050
Brainerd, Mary K., 3389
Brake, Edwin R., 1251
Braly, Angela F., 3055, 3541, 4027
Bram, Kim, 3519
Brama, Elizabeth M., 564
Bramante, Christina, 642
Bramble, Frank P., Sr., 340
Bramblett, George W., 1759
Bramco, Inc., 555
Brame, Marillyn, 3888
Bramlage, Lawrence R., 3257
Bramlage, Stephen, 2844
Bramlage, Stephen P., Jr., 2844
Bramley, John, 499
Bramsch, Susan, 131
Bramsen, James E., 3552
Bramson, Jim, 2290
Bramstedt, Susan, 74
Branch Banking & Trust Co., 385, 1776, 3572
Branch, David, 1081
Branch, David W., 1081
Branch, Debbie, 1417
Branchfield, Barbara, 3453
Brand, Jacques, 1099
Brand, Karen L., 3173
Brand, Martin, 2938, 3255
Brandenberger, Alena, 744
Brandenstein, Daniel C., 3874
Brandes, JoAnne, 566
Brandman, Andrew, 819
Brandman, Andrew T., 2769
Brandon, Adrienne, 285
Brandon, David, 1183, 2517
Brandon, David A., 1151, 3765
Brandon, Edward B., 936
Brandon, Russ, 606
Brandow, Peter B., 3166
Brandt, Carol, 129
Brandt, Donald E., 239
Brandt, Eric K., 579, 1089, 2214
Brandt, Werner, 3334
Brandt, William F., Jr., 170
Brandtjen, H.A., III, 1634
Brandtonies, Janet L., 3996
Braniff, Juan Carlos, 1239
Brannan, Joe, 265, 2729
Brannon, Randy, 72
Brannon, Timothy H., 3134
Bransfield, John R., Jr., 2683
Branson, Mike, 4052
Brant, Terri, 3133
Branter, Linda, 1074
Branter, Linda L., 1074
Brantl, Rita, 865
Brantley, Hugh H., 561
Brantley, Thomas M., 340
Brantner, Linda, 1074
Brasher's Salt Lake Auto Auction, 1538
Brasseler USA Dental, LLC, 556
Brasseur, Bernard, 346
Brasuell, Thomas C., 2345
Braswell, Fred O., 72
Brathewaite, Christian E., 3384
Bratic, Alexander, 2604
Bratic, Caroline, 2604
Bratic, Caroline D., 1370
Bratic, Walter, 2604
Bratlien, Mark K., 1824
Brattain, Donald R., 3831
Brattleboro Paper Products, Inc., 1294
Bratton, William J., 2586
Braud, Randy, 3430
Braun, Alan W., 2179, 2798
Braun, Edward H., 1016
Braun, James E., 2431
Braun, Janis L., 3141
Braverman, Alan, 1127
Braverman, Beverly, 1553
Braverman, Eva, 1553
Braverman, Yuval, 4151
Bravo Natural Resources, 2641
Bravo, Rose Marie, 2230, 3750, 4079
Brawley, S. Mark, 128
Bray, Don P., 4005
Bray, Steve, 1193
Bray, Steven L., 547
Bray, Thomas L., 564
Bready, Richard L., 349
Brearton, David, 2556
Brearton, Jess, 3584
Brearton, Robert D., 145
Breaux, Gary, 2484
Breaux, John, 1578
Breaux, Senator John B., 997
Breeden, Richard C., 3600
Breedlove, James T., 3029
Breedlove, John P., 1919
Breen, John G., 3579
Breen, Maura C., 1313
Breen, Yellow Light, 338
Breerwood, Roy, 1688
Breeze, Allen, 3560
Breezoale, Debbie, 3430
Breffeilh, Richard, 2768
Brehl, Robert J., 3931
Brehm, John R., 1988
Brehm, Julie, 1568
Breidenthal, R. J., Jr., 1335
Breidinger, Dave R., 887
Breier, Benjamin A., 2154
Breinig, Jeane, 3380
Breitenbach, Thomas, 690
Breitman, Leo R., 133
Breivik, Mike, 1586
Breivogel, Donald R., Jr., 3554
Brekhus, Mel G., 3727
Brekhus, Melvin G., 3727
Brekhus, Todd R., 684
Brekken, Kathleen A., 100
Breme, Patricia, 1490
Bremman, Sean, 2685
Bremner, Georgie, 260
Bren, Donald L., 1992
Brenco L.P., 2175
Brenizer, Bruce, 2538
Brennan, Charles M., III, 3253
Brennan, Ciaran, 659
Brennan, David, 853
Brennan, Edward J., 1104
Brennan, Eleanor, 1100
Brennan, Eleanor F., 1100
Brennan, George G., 124
Brennan, Jacqueline E., 1419
Brennan, John J., 1382, 1552, 1683, 1724
Brennan, John P., 41
Brennan, John T., Jr., 986
Brennan, Michael, 555, 2684
Brennan, Nora, 1947
Brennan, Patrick J., 1292
Brennan, Paul F., 157
Brennan, Susan, 3624
Brenneman, Gregory D., 291, 1842
Brenner, Bernhard J., 2175
Brenner, Colleen, 2175
Brenner, Mark, 216
Brenner, Richard, 2751
Brenninkmeyer, Hans, 163
Brennock, Erin, 3673
Brenzia, John N., 3297
Bresch, Heather, 2610
Breslau, Leigh, 3474
Breslawski, James, 3348
Breslawski, James P., 3348
Breslawsky, Marc C., 358, 571
Bresler, Charles, 2460
Breslin, Chris, 981
Breslin, Danielle, 497
Breslow, John, 963
Bresnahan, Paul D., 2734
Bress, Drew, 2627
Brestal, Kim, 516
Bresten, Theresa M., 1854
Brestle, Daniel J., 1120
Brestle, George, 664
Brett, John, 229
Brett, Stephen M., 1550
Breul, Jonathan D., 1960
Breunig, Roland E., 3406
Brevic, Scott, 2466
Brewer Foods Inc., 558
Brewer Trust, Lucy, 558
Brewer, Janet J., 2650
Brewer, Jeff, 3569
Brewer, Joe B., Jr., 558
Brewer, Joseph B., III, 558
Brewer, Joseph B., Jr., 558
Brewer, Larry, 1179
Brewer, Lucy Ann, 558
Brewer, Mark, 3377
Brewer, Mike, 1657
Brewer, Rosalind G., 2292
Brewer, Virginia H., 558
Brewer, William A., III, 457
Brewester, Frank, 3645
Brewington, Jeff, 1587
Brewington, Jeffrey R., 1587
Brewster, Frank L., 3645
Brewster, June, 3645
Breyer, James W., 1068, 2700, 3980
Breyfogle, Jon, 1671
Breyfogle, Nancy, 2217
Breza, John A., 1078
Brezovec, Daniel T., 219
Briad, Cris, 2570
Brian M. Stolar, Esq., 2977
Brice, Todd D., 3297
Brickenden Speakers Bureau, Inc., 1953
Brickner, Rebecca Scripps, 3374
Bridge Manufacturing, Inc., 702
Bridgeford, Gregory M., 2312
Bridgeman, Junior, 2953
Bridgeman, Ulysses Lee, 807
Bridger, Peri, 3497
Bridgers, David, 3743
Bridges, C. Ray, 3615
Bridges, C.R., 3615
Bridges, Ray, 3615
Bridges, Susan A., 3392
Bridgestone Americas Holding, Inc., 560
Bridgestone Americas, Inc., 560
Bridgestone/Firestone, Inc., 560
Bridgewater Candle Co., LLC, The, 561
Bridgewater Savings Bank, 562
Bridgeway Capital Management, Inc., 563
Bridgman, Gary, 159
Bridgman, Richard S., Jr., 2394
Bridwell, C. Kenneth, 1392
Brierton, Dan, 2949
Briggs & Stratton Corp., 565
Briggs, David, 703
Briggs, John C., 1900
Briggs, Joseph, 3129
Briggs, Kendice K., 2990
Briggs, Robert D., 1047
Briggs, Scott, 2795
Briggs, Steven, 3584
Brighenti, John A., 3858
Brighitbill, David E., 2929
Brighton, W. Curtis, 1555, 1885, 3722
Brightpoint North America, LP, 636
Brightwell, Laura, 863
Briley, Judith, 119
Brill, Beth, 1762

Brill, Michael, 3652
Brilley, Michael C., 3466
Brillion Iron Works, Inc., 569
Brimbuela, Lucy, 3888
Brin, Bob, 2864
Brin, Sergey, 1613
Brinckerhoff & Neuville, Inc., 570
Brinckerhoff Gentsch, Margaret, 570
Brinckerhoff, Beverly B., 570
Brinckerhoff, Mary, 570
Brinckerhoff, Mary E., 570
Brines, Michael, 3992
Brink's Co., The, 571
Brinkley, Amy Woods, 340, 708
Brinkley, Christine, 2407
Brinkley, Diane C., 2928
Brinkley, Jennifer, 3354
Brinkman, Dale T., 4124
Brinks, Brent, 611
Brinks, Greg A., 2205
Brinkster, 574
Brinkster Communications, Inc., 574
Brinton, Geraldine R., 3664
Brinzo, John S., 67, 1073
Brisbin, Thomas D., 4075
Briscoe, D. Daniel, 3615
Briseno, Jesse, 1470
Brisimitzakis, Angelo C., kis, 112
Briskman, Louis J., 727
Brisky, Lauren J., 17
Brister, Patricia, 1347
Bristol Bay Native Corp., 576
Bristol County Savings Bank, 577
Bristol Savings Bank, 4016
Bristol-Myers Squibb Co., 578
Bristow, Peter M., 1395
Bristow, William S., Jr., 362
Britell, Jenne K., 988, 3103
Brito Perez, Maria, 272
Brito, Archie, 2204
Britt, David, 3761
Britt, Glenn A., 685, 3755, 3756, 4136
Britt, Irene C., 3650
Brittain, Randolph W., 2997
Brittain, Susan, 240
Brittenham, Harry M., 1172
Britto, Vanessa, 1528
Britton, Bill, 2906
Britton, Jerry, 744
Britton, John, 3398
Brizel, Michael, 3315
Brizel, Michael A., 3315
Brlas, Laurie, 850, 2943
Broad, Matt, 2786
Broad, Matthew R., 2786
Broad, Molly Corbett, 2887
Broadbent, Peregrine C., 2030
Broadcom Corp., 579
Broaddus, J. Alfred, Jr., 3040
Broader, Shelley G., 2021
Broadman, Dorothy, 679
Broadwater, Steven K., 3458
Broatch, Robert E., 1683
Brocchini Farms, Inc., 580
Brocchini, Kristine, 580
Brocchini, Robert, 580
Brocchini, Stephen, 580
Broccole, Carmine J., 3575
Brocher, Karen, 3673
Brochstein, Deborah, 581
Brochstein, Joel, 581
Brochstein, Lynn, 581
Brochstein, Raymond D., 581
Brochstein, Raymond. D., 581
Brochsteins, Inc., 581
Brock, Charles E., 1132
Brock, Doug, 2594
Brock, J. Don, 1132
Brock, John F., 863
Brock, Lindsey C., III, 1764
Brock, Macon F., Jr., 1145
Brock, Nancy E., 2323
Brock, Paul, 3497
Brock, Rochelle, 2344
Brockbank, Mark E., 426
Brockelman, Mark, 1147
Brockelmeyer, Scott, 1365
Brockett, Susan P., 827
Brockhoff, Glynda, 2485
Brockie, Scott, 3744
Brockman, Carla, 1102
Brockman, Dorothy K., 1052
Brockman, Robert T., 1052, 3199
Brockman, Vincent C., 3372
Brocksmith, James G., Jr., 3405
Brockton Wholesale Beverage Co., Inc., 1862
Broderick, Denise, 1900
Broderick, Dennis J., 2333
Brodie, Nancy S., 333
Brodigan, Martin, 3210
Brodsky, David, 3520
Brodsky, Howard, 2685
Brodsky, Jeff, 2570
Brodsky, Julian A., 887
Brodsky, William H., 3994
Brody, Christopher W., 1982
Brody, Martin, 2015
Brody, Nina, 2689
Brody, William R., 1960
Broeckel, Julie, 1651
Broenen, James S., 1359
Broerman, John B., 3361
Brogan, Stephen J., 2058
Brogdon, Gino, 2112
Broglio, John, 3808
Brokaw, Clifford V., 3866
Brolick, Emil J., 4030, 4031
Broll, Micheal J., 3873
Bromark, Raymond J., 638
Bromelkamp, Henry A., 582
Bromley, C. Thomas, III, 899
Bromley, Craig, 1717
Bromley, James H., 996
Bromley, Julia, 3324
Bromwell, Paul, 1511
Bronander, Pamela, 3916
Bronczek, David J., 1968
Brondeau, Pierre, 1449, 2364
Brondeau, Pierre R., 1449
Bronfin, Kenneth A., 1747
Bronfman, Edgar M., Jr., 1903
Bronfman, Edgar, Jr., 3990
Bronicki, Yoram, 2822
Brons, Paul, 3348
Bronson, Anne L., 22
Bronson, David, 3074
Bronson, David M., 3074
Bronson, John S., 1524
Bronson, Joseph R., 2016
Bronwell, Thomas, 2633
Brook, Bruce, 510
Brook, Bruce R., 2698
Brooke, Beth, 1293
Brooke, Beth A., 1293
Brooker, Kimball T., 354
Brooker, T. Kimball, 354
Brooker, Thomas K., 354
Brooker, Wes, 135
Brooklawn Gardens, Inc., 1782
Brookline Bancorp, MHC, 583
Brooks Resources Corp., 585
Brooks, Bruce M., 2501
Brooks, Carl, 176
Brooks, Carolyn, 2786
Brooks, Coby G., 1858
Brooks, Conley, 585
Brooks, Conley, Jr., 585
Brooks, Donna, 3585
Brooks, Douglas H., 572, 3522
Brooks, Heidi, 3137
Brooks, Janine, 1346
Brooks, Johnny, 464
Brooks, Kelly, 1167, 2190
Brooks, Laura L., 3069
Brooks, Lois, 1113
Brooks, Lynn A., 3212
Brooks, Martha F., 1732, 2006
Brooks, Michael T., 1542
Brooks, Rhonda L., 2461, 2473
Brooks, Robert, 2366
Brooks, Robert J., 4048
Brooks, Robert L., 314
Brooks, Ronnie, 2054
Brooks, Tina N., 3861
Brooks, William, 3883
Brooks, Zafar, 1902
Brooks-Moon, Renel, 3324
Brooks-Scanlon, Inc., 585
Broom, Charles, 2995
Broom, Charles F., 2995
Broome, Richard, 1792
Broome, Russel A., 1603
Broomhead, Malcolm, 455
Broomhead, Paul C., 3736
Brophy, Bll, 3906
Brosch, Sharon, 1088
Brosnan, Deborah, 678
Brosnick, Richard B., 629
Brossart, Darcie, 2925
Brossart, Darcie M., 2925
Brostrom, Tracy, 263
Brothen, Jason, 615
Brotherhood Mutual Insurance Co., 588
Brothers, Ellen L., 1809
Brothers, Robert V., 240
Brotherton, Carmen K., 2828
Brotherton, David L., 2828
Brotman, Jeffrey H., 948
Brots, John M., 3709
Brouder, Gerald T., 3431
Brough, M. Joseph, 1906
Brougher, Jefferson W., 1966
Brougher, Joseph L., 1966
Broughton, George W., 2929
Brouillard, John C., 39
Brouillard, Rheo Arthur, 3444
Broussard, Bruce D., 1886
Brouwer, Steve, 2282
Browdy, Michelle H., 1960
Brower, C. Eugene, 234
Brower, Eugene, 234
Brower, Price E., 3843
Brown & Root, Inc., 1706
Brown Brothers Harriman & Co., 589
Brown Group, Inc., 591
Brown Shoe Co., Inc., 591
Brown, A. David, 3399
Brown, Alex, 40
Brown, Alison, 3863
Brown, Allyson, 2212
Brown, Amanda, 2130
Brown, Andrew A., 380
Brown, Anita, 4149
Brown, Arthur, 127
Brown, Bart R., 1541
Brown, Bates, 2409
Brown, Brien, 2815
Brown, Buster, 3386
Brown, Bynum R., 3515
Brown, C. David, II, 1014, 3134
Brown, Carl Beau, 654
Brown, Carole Ann, 1963
Brown, Cathy, 1365
Brown, Charles, 3784
Brown, Chuck, 3784
Brown, Clay, 1842
Brown, Clayton, 1963
Brown, Coleen, 1430
Brown, Colin, 2044
Brown, Colleen B., 1430
Brown, Craig J., 3576
Brown, Daniel, 590
Brown, Daniel B., 3387
Brown, David, 529, 4026
Brown, David A., 2991
Brown, David A. B., 1255
Brown, David J., 2130
Brown, David T., 528, 1484
Brown, Deborah S., 2211
Brown, Dennis, 1076
Brown, Donald, 3477
Brown, Donnie, 3761
Brown, Douglass J., 1309
Brown, Edward J., III, 1776
Brown, Edward J., Jr., 1016
Brown, Elizabeth C., 1963
Brown, Ellyn L., 857, 1382, 2769
Brown, Frances A., 875
Brown, Francis A., 875
Brown, Frank, 3197
Brown, Frank C., 3197
Brown, Fred E., 1963
Brown, Fred E., III, 1963
Brown, Garvin, 592
Brown, Gary, 1961
Brown, George Garvin, IV, 592
Brown, Gerald, 3467
Brown, Greg, 439, 818
Brown, Gregory A., 683
Brown, Gregory Q., 2586
Brown, Hank, 3381, 3408
Brown, Harold, 1851, 2962
Brown, J. Frank, 1842
Brown, J. Hyatt, 1970
Brown, J. Powell, 3239
Brown, J. Terrell, 977
Brown, J.Terrell, 977
Brown, Jack E., 2790
Brown, James, 1464
Brown, James M., 677
Brown, Jay, 1136, 2416
Brown, Jeffrey N., 4016
Brown, Jessica, 1031, 2670, 3800
Brown, Joe, 2626
Brown, John Seely, 122, 945
Brown, John W., 3566
Brown, Joseph, 2159
Brown, Joyce F., 3123
Brown, Judy L., 2943
Brown, Kate, 3544
Brown, Katherine, 3070
Brown, Kathy, 937
Brown, Keith, 148
Brown, Kevin, 690
Brown, Kevin J., 3230

Brown, Laura, 3951
Brown, Laura D., 1626
Brown, Lloyd, 2552
Brown, Lucy, 2200
Brown, Mack, 3258
Brown, Marcus V., 1279
Brown, Marilyn, 764
Brown, Marilyn Cochran, 3940
Brown, Marilyn Creson, 3322
Brown, Marshall, 2585
Brown, Martin S., Jr., 592
Brown, Mary, 3664
Brown, Mary Rose, 2763
Brown, Melinda, 3813
Brown, Melinda J., 1171
Brown, Melissa, 3306
Brown, Melvin C., 576
Brown, Michael, 813
Brown, Michael A., 3669
Brown, Michael G., 1378
Brown, Michael W., 1253, 1944
Brown, Michelle, 452
Brown, Mike, 240
Brown, Morris L., 690
Brown, Nathaniel T., 3386
Brown, Nicholas, 4134
Brown, Paul J., 1695
Brown, Peter C., 751
Brown, Peter D., 1459
Brown, Peter G., 1060
Brown, Peter S., 249
Brown, Peter W., 372, 1150
Brown, Randal L., 3541, 4027
Brown, Rebecca, 1521
Brown, Richard C., 1366
Brown, Richard G., Jr., 956
Brown, Richard H., 1184
Brown, Richard K., 709
Brown, Richard King, 709
Brown, Robert, 52, 2691
Brown, Robert A., 1184
Brown, Robert D., 265
Brown, Robert J., 292
Brown, Robert L., Jr., 1567
Brown, Robert V., 3693
Brown, Rodney, 3492
Brown, Rodney L., Jr., 3010
Brown, Roger, 510
Brown, Roger H., 566
Brown, Ronald D, 2348
Brown, Ronald D., 3484
Brown, Roni, 2673
Brown, Sally, 3507
Brown, Sandra L., 1630
Brown, Sharon Shiroma, 1405
Brown, Shelaghmichael, 901
Brown, Shona L., 2935
Brown, Simon E., 1065, 3382
Brown, Sondra, 2208
Brown, Suzanne C., 3914
Brown, Tad, 3240
Brown, Thaddeus B., 3240
Brown, Thomas D., 3107
Brown, Timothy W., 1938
Brown, Todd, 3697
Brown, Todd C., 1130
Brown, Tom, 1136, 2702
Brown, Vanessa K., 3919
Brown, W. Marshall, 3513
Brown, W. Thacher, 1733
Brown, Wesley, 3258
Brown, William M., 1736
Brown-Forman, 1858
Browne, Chuck, 1602
Browne, Jeanette Y., 1490
Browne, Joe, 2626
Browne, John P., 2711
Browne, Karalee, 2853
Browne, Michael L., 1733
Browne, Nancy D., 1603
Browne, Philip M., 521
Browne, William A., Jr., 3129
Brownell, David P., 3885
Brownell, Thomas H., 2633
Browning, Jay D., 3915
Browning, Jonathan, 3967
Browning, Michael G., 1189
Browning, Peter C., 2312, 2760
Brownless, Susan, 4099
Brownley, Louise Slator, 918
Brownstein, Norman, 593
Bru, Abelardo E., 1124, 2150
Brubaker, Jeffrey R., 852
Brubaker, Kimberly A., 1523
Brubaker, Lynn, Jr., 1795
Brubaker, Peter P., 3492
Bruce, Kofi, 1554
Bruce, Lori, 4009
Bruce, Maryann, 2416
Bruce, Peter W., 313
Bruch, Ruth E., 344
Bruckmann, Bruce C., 2545, 3783
Bruder, Ann J., 893
Bruder, Gordon, 1966
Bruder, Thomas A., 2342
Brueckner, Richard F., 1382
Bruehlman, Ronald, 1924
Bruffett, Stephen L., 903
Bruggeman, Kelly, 1409
Bruggeworth, Robert A., Jr., 2529
Brull, Randy, 569
Brumback, Emerson L., 1645
Brumback, Karl, 2398
Brumby, Otis A., 3759
Brumby, Otis A., Jr., 3759
Brumfield, Bruce J., 1082
Brumfield, Byron, 135
Brumfield, Catherine, 2338
Brummel, Lisa, 370
Brummer, Terry E., 3608
Brun, Leslie A., 291, 2466
Brunck, Robert, 423
Brundage, Maureen A., 804
Brune, Catherine S., 128
Brunel, Patrick, 2962
Bruner, Hugh, 1074
Bruni, Victoria H., 1880
Brunk, Chris, 612
Brunk, James F., 2545
Brunn, Robert S., 3292
Brunner, Hugh, 1074
Brunner, James E., 854, 921
Brunner, Kent, 3537
Brunner, Kim M., 3591
Brunner, Robert E., 2246
Brunner-Salter, Lillian, 3071
Bruno Assocs., G.L., Inc., 594
Bruno, Anthony, 2691
Bruno, Anthony M., Jr., 3916
Bruno, Brad, 682
Bruno, Gabriel, 2279
Bruno, Gary L., 594
Bruno, Mark, 3042
Bruno, Michael B., 2309
Bruns, Kathy B., 588
Brunson, Donald E., 899
Brunson, Philip, 1070
Brunstad, James Wade, 3012
Brunstad, Margaret Hayes, 3012
Brunstead, John, 2173
Brunswick Corp., 595
Brunswick, Paul L., 2875
Bruntz, John, 4098
Bruss, William F., 4005
Brussard, David F., 3308
Brust, Robert H., 956
Brutge, Alan, 2589
Brutoco, Rinaldo S., 2460
Bruton, Jack, 3496
Brutto, Dan, 3872
Brutto, Daniel J., 1916
Bruzzese, Michael J., 3184
Bryan, George W., 3171
Bryan, Glynis A., 2926
Bryan, Lourd, 975
Bryan, Stephanie, 2998
Bryan, William H., 2594, 3515
Bryant, Andy D., 1950, 2434
Bryant, Curt, 2738
Bryant, David J., 2101
Bryant, Douglas C., 3107
Bryant, Dwane, 456
Bryant, Forrest, 1533
Bryant, Gary S., 1765
Bryant, George D., 3383
Bryant, John A., 2120
Bryant, Karen, 370
Bryant, Lewis, 1417
Bryant, R. Jeep, 344
Bryant, Robert S., 3704
Bryant, Warren, 2786
Bryant, Warren F., 1143
Brymer, Charles E., 3166
Brzezinski, Rob, 2530
BSA Design, Inc., 597
BSA LifeStructures, Inc., 597
BT Capital Corp., 1099
Bubalo Construction Co., Steve, Inc., 598
Bubalo, Louise, 598
Bubalo, Louise Esther, 598
Bubalo, Steve, 598
Bubolo, Kelley, 3783
Bubp, Gregory, 1219
Buccaneer L.P., 599
Buccella, Steve, 2401
Bucci, Cathy, 3707
Bucci, Mary D., 590
Bucciarelli, Gary W., III, 2452
Bucek, Michael, 2093
Buch, James D., 1668
Buchalter, Gilbert, 2955
Buchalter, Irwin R., 600
Buchalter, Nemer, Fields, & Younger, 600
Buchalter, Stewart, 600
Buchanan, Edison C., 2981
Buchanan, John, 455
Buchanan, Julia, 4112
Buchanan, Margaret E., 1532
Buchanan, Richard, 2623
Buchanan, Thomas M., 4089
Buchband, Richard, 2358
Buchen, David A., 4007
Buchholz, Karen Dougherty, 412, 887
Buchholz, Rose, 2838
Buchholz, Scott A., 474
Buchholz, William R., 135
Buchi, J. Kevin, 752
Buchler, Judith, 3276
Buchman, Diana, 1376
Buchmann, Josef, 2294
Buchta, Glen, 1317
Buchwald Wright, Karen, 237
Buchwald, Herbert T., 2324
Buchwald, Maureen, 2881
Buchwaldt, Felix Von, 2721
Buck, David, 2964
Buck, Fred, 891
Buck, Linda B., 1962
Buck, Robert R., 3100
Buckalew, B. Stevens, 1674
Buckelew, L. Nick, 3807
Buckeye Diamond Logistics, Inc., 601
Buckingham, Lisa M., 2281
Buckingham, Lorie, 2711
Buckler, Jan, 1350
Buckley Associates, Inc., 602
Buckley II, Robert L., 602
Buckley, F. Reid, 973
Buckley, George W., 3, 233, 2935, 3579
Buckley, Jean C., 1158
Buckley, Jerry S., 669
Buckley, John, 1158
Buckley, Matt, 2353
Buckley, Robert L., II, 602
Buckley, Sarah, 1687
Buckman, Floyd, 2487
Buckman, Frederick W., 3574
Buckman, James E., 4132
Buckman, Timothy, 660
Buckmaster, James, 968
Buckmaster, Jim, 968
Buckner, David, 2536
Buckner, Quinn, 2852
Buckner, Simon B., IV, 365
Bucknor, J. Kofi, 2698
Bucksbaum, Matthew, 1961
Buckstead, Kevin, 2487
Buckwalter, Alan R., III, 3413
Budd, Wayne A., 2434
Budde, Gerald, 2651
Budnik, Shaun L., 1070
Budweiser of Anderson, Inc., 605
Budweiser of Columbia, Inc., 605
Budweiser of Greenville, Inc., 605
Buechler, Kenneth F., 3107
Buechler, Steve, 1080
Buehler, Kevin J., 83
Buehler, Michael, 2462
Buehler, William F., 3103
Bueker, Paul, 1552
Buell, Bernadette, 1113
Buell, Jack A., 3017
Buell, Mark, 2865
Buell, Steven M., 3766
Buelsing, Norbert M., 85
Bueno, Edson, 3884
Buer, Bob, 608
Bueretta, Sherri D., 805
Buese, Nancy K., 3846
Buettgen, James J., 3281
Buettgen, James J., III, 3281
Bufalino, Sebastian J., 377
Bufano, Kathryn, 403
Buffalo Bills Inc., 606
Buffardi, James S., 1364
Buffardi, Louis J., 1364
Buffett, George, 429
Buffett, George, II, 429
Buffett, Howard G., 429, 862
Buffett, Jeanett, 429
Buffett, Jeannette, 429
Buffett, Jennifer, 2710
Buffett, John, 429
Buffett, Patricia M., 429

Buffett, Peter, 2710
Buffett, Warren E., 429
Buffkin, Buron, 1271
Bufftree Building Co., Inc., 607
Buford, C. Robert, 1981
Buford, R.C., 3321
Buford, T. Mark, 900
Bugbee, James H., 792
Buggeln, Kate, 255
Buhl, G. Lawrence, 1733
Buhler, Michael O., 2796
Buhr, James, 369
Buhrmaster, Robert C., 3775
Build-A-Bear Workshop Canada Ltd, 608
Build-A-Bear Workshop, Inc., 608
Builders, Inc., 609
Building 19, Inc., 610
Buist Electric, Inc., 611
Buist, Larry, 611
Bujarski, Robert Joseph, 3107
Bujese, David M., 204
Buker, Robert H., 3878
Buker, Robert H., Jr., 3878
Bukowsky, Bob, 1908
Bull, Marcia, Dr., 1399
Bulla, Robert B., 500
Bullard, Dave, 4033
Bullard, Lyman G., Jr., 3011
Bullen, Bruce M., 501
Bulling, Keith D., 1532
Bullis, Eugene M., 1139
Bullock, Elza, 3716
Bullock, Ray, 2413
Bulls, Herman E., 3873
Bulman, Lyn, 1357
Bumbacco, Nicholas A., 3331
Bump, Larry J., 1255
Bumpus, John P., 2270
Bumstead, Matt, 3880
Bumstead, R. Gantt, 3880
Bunce, Lynn S., 1712, 1713
Bunce, Lynn Stevens, 1713
Bunch, C. Robert, 2801
Bunch, Charles E., 2996, 2997, 3025
Bunch, Joe, 72
Bunch, Kerian, 1298
Bundock, Marjory, 1978
Bundy, David, 1053
Bundy, David C., 1053
Bundy, John, 1586
Bunge North America, Inc., 612
Bunn, Christopher R., 761
Bunn, Donna Chaney, 761
Bunn, Eric, 947
Bunn, Georgia, 947
Bunney, Kenneth E., 1052
Bunson, Steven M., 1603
Bunten, Paul, 3113
Bunting, George L., Jr., 332
Bunting, Robert, 2581
Bunting, Theodore H., Jr., 1280
Bunting, Theodore, Jr., 1278, 1919
Buonadonna, Joseph, 2416
Buonconti, Gregory E., 2984
Buoncore, Richard J., 1845
Buongiorno, Michael J., 2342
Burak, Mark A., 342
Burandt, Michael C., 4008
Burbridge, Martin S., 981
Burch, Bruce K., 2601
Burch, Ken L., 3434
Burchell, Ed, 335
Burchilli, Jefferey A., 1323
Burck, R.D., 136
Burd, Loretta M., 1008
Burd, Nancy, 2961
Burd, Steven A., 2181, 3310
Burden, Robert J., 3936
Burdett, Barbara J., 3040
Burdick, Marci, 3507
Burdick, Randy, 3659
Burdick, Randy G., 2786
Burdick, Rick L., 292
Burdman, Lee J., 1845
Buretta, Sheri, 3694
Buretta, Sheri D., 805
Buretta, Sherri D., 805
Burford, Sam P., Jr., 3738
Burgdoerfer, Stuart, 2277
Burgdoerfer, Stuart B., 3057
Burger Ozark Country Cured Hams, 614
Burger, Barbara, 519
Burger, Brent A., 3815
Burger, Martha A., 777
Burger, Steven F., 614
Burgeson, John C., 1264
Burgess, D.J., 1634
Burgess, Dana, 1969
Burgess, Kathy, 611
Burgess, Kirk, 3949
Burgess, Melanie A., 2044
Burgess, Melissa P., 581
Burgess, Richard, 562
Burgess, Richard, Jr., 562
Burgess, Robert K., 38, 177, 2767
Burgess, Shari L., 2237
Burgess, Suzanne C., 3949
Burgess, Tyler, 1969
Burgess, Will, 2692
Burgmann, Frederick F., 786
Burgos-Rodriquez, Abner, 3858
Burgoyne, John H., 2973
Burgstahler, Robert, 832
Burguieres, Philip J., 1872
Burgunder, Amelie B., 2090
Burgunder, B. Bernei, Jr., 2090
Burgunder, B. Bernei, Sr., 2090
Burgunder, Bernei, 2090
Burgunder, Selma K., 2090
Buri, James J., 930
Burian, Lawrence, 2336
Burke Centre Automotive, Inc., 138
Burke, Ann Marie, 3979
Burke, Austin, 4028
Burke, Austin J., 4028
Burke, Christine, 2373
Burke, Cindy S., 1388
Burke, Daniel, 3564
Burke, Daniel J., 1729
Burke, Deborah M., 3835
Burke, Donald, 301
Burke, Franklin L., 1446
Burke, J. Timothy, 2742
Burke, James J., 3575
Burke, Jeffrey A., 2832
Burke, John, 2502, 2832
Burke, John E., 2042
Burke, John M., 2832
Burke, Joseph J., 2782
Burke, Kenneth M., 1287
Burke, Kevin, 916, 1852
Burke, Lawrence J., 2373
Burke, Lawrence J., II, 2373
Burke, Lewis, 3640
Burke, Linda M., 7
Burke, Mary E., 3803
Burke, Matthew, 562
Burke, Michael S., 42
Burke, Peter M., 2506
Burke, Richard T., 3884
Burke, Rita Moschovidis, 131
Burke, Sheila P., 804, 4027
Burke, Sheryl A., 48
Burke, Stephen B., 429, 2071, 2649
Burke, Thomas, 2923
Burke, Thomas A., 2544
Burke, Timothy J., 3803
Burke, Timothy L., 478
Burke, William A., III, 2694
Burkett, Charles G., 1406
Burkhamer, Rick, 1466
Burkhard, Phyllis, 798
Burkhart, Joan, 1552
Burkhart, Phil, 3775
Burkhart, William R., 3760
Burkle, Ron, 30
Burks, Dale, 3575
Burks, Ellis, 847
Burlingame, Harold W., 3819
Burlington Capital Group LLC, The, 616
Burlington Industries LLC, 1971
Burlington Industries, Inc., 1971
Burlington Northern Santa Fe Corp., 618
Burman, Terry, 4151
Burmeister, Neil J., 2687
Burmeister-Smith, Christy, 301
Burmeister-Smith, Christy M., 301
Burnes, Kennett F., 3592
Burnett Co., Leo, Inc., 619
Burnett USA, Leo, Inc., 619
Burnett, Charles Vance, 2622
Burnett, Dale A., 2681
Burnett, Jason, 717
Burnett, Robert, 1052, 3199
Burnett, Robert D., 1052
Burnette, Michele, 939
Burnette, Mike, 2729
Burnham, Donald, 2475
Burnham, Rebecca L., 500
Burnham, Richard B., 1531
Burnham, Robin, 3706
Burnison, Jeffrey L., 2980
Burns & McDonnell, Inc., 620
Burns International Services Corp., 3390
Burns, Angie, 2461
Burns, Brent D., 2044
Burns, Clay, 672
Burns, Daniel J., 2323
Burns, Donald A., 2521
Burns, Karen, 2767
Burns, Karon M., 214
Burns, Kevin R., 246
Burns, Laurie, 1032
Burns, M. Anthony, 1895, 2950
Burns, M. Michael, 1603
Burns, M. Michele, 818, 1604, 3980
Burns, Michael B., 988
Burns, Michael J., 3872
Burns, Mike, 880
Burns, Owen F., 2681
Burns, Patrick A., 2605
Burns, Robert, 3525
Burns, Robert T., 3085
Burns, Ronald, 859
Burns, Sara J., 741
Burns, Stephanie A., 945
Burns, Terry, 502
Burns, Truman, 2853
Burns, Ursala M., 1315
Burns, Ursula, 4136
Burns, Ursula M., 143, 4136
Burns, William M., 1549
Burns-McNeill, Robin R., 2049
Burr, Anna Monteleone, 2675
Burr, Cole, 622
Burr, Douglas H., 1441
Burr, Frank B., 3737
Burr, Michael, 2528
Burrece, Lois A., 2837
Burrell, Chet, 687
Burress, Tom, 2139
Burris, Jeffrey W., 990
Burris, Jerry W., 2926
Burris, Wayne, 3236
Burritt, David B., 2292
Burroughs & Chapin, 1776
Burroughs, John R., 2343
Burroughs, Julia, 2475
Burrows, Cliff, 3585
Burrows, Keith, 2280
Burrows, Lawrence, 4052
Burrows, Roy, 1292
Burrus, John E., 1297
Bursch Travel, 3015
Bursch, H. Dean, 917
Burt's Bees, 623
Burt, Brady T., 2881
Burt, Stephen, 3167
Burton Foundation, 1538
Burton Snowboards, 624
Burton, Alan, 808
Burton, Amanda, 849
Burton, C. Wes, Jr., 3972
Burton, David C., 4078
Burton, Eric James, 2971
Burton, Ian, 4125
Burton, Jack, 76
Burton, Jake, 624
Burton, James E., 1382
Burton, Michael, 3587
Burton, Patrick, 1304
Burton, Paul, 3183
Burton, Robert O., 3066
Burton, Stanley, 1968
Burton, Thomas R., 1712
Burville, John C., 3399
Burwell, Mike, 3042
Burwell, Sylvia Mathews, 2481, 3980
Burwick, David A., 533
Burwitz, Jacqueline E., 1271
Burza, Eileen F., 2936
Burzik, Catherine M., 398
Busby, A. Patrick, 1289
Busby, John S., 2789
Busch Entertainment Corp., 3387
Busch, August A., III, 1257
Busch, Dick, 2505
Busch, Doug, 655
Busch, Ralph B., III, 437
Busch, Robert L., 272
Busch, Virginia M., 3387
Buschmann, Raymond P., 2579
Buse, John, 272
Bush, Craig E., 3093
Bush, Gregory J., 2421
Bush, Jack, 2421
Bush, Jerry, 3896
Bush, John Ellis, 3134, 3713
Bush, John L., 2421
Bush, Keith, 3902
Bush, Kenny, 4142
Bush, Mandy, 3533
Bush, Mary K., 1125, 2383, 3040
Bush, Michael J., 3267
Bush, Patricia M., 2421
Bush, Steven C., 218

Bush, Wesley, 2744
Bush, Wesley G., 2725
Bush, William E., Jr., 437
Bushby, Philip A., Dr., 2948
Bushee, Ward, 3325
Bushey, Chris, 3099
Bushey, Chris C., 3099
Bushman, J. L., 3
Bushman, Julie L., 2050
Bushman, Michael, 2613
Bushnell, James, 2612
Business Impact Group, LLC, 625
Busko, Mary Bernhardt, 432
Busquet, Anne M., 2984
Buss, Eric, 2269
Buss, Jeanie, 2307
Buss, Jerry H., 2307
Bussberg, Steve, 3581
Busse, Keith E., 3595
Bussenger, John, 1572
Bussiere, Michel, 2491
Bussman, John W., 3375
Bussman, Paul D., 1001
Bussmann, George J., Jr., 3375
Bussmann, James, 3375
Bussmann, John W., Sr., 3375
Bussmann, John, Jr., 3375
Bussmann, Marion, 3375
Bussmann, Marion K., 3375
Bussmann, Robert, 3375
Bussmann, William, 3375
Bussone, Mary Z., 1998
Bustamante, Paul, 3496
Buster, H. Clifford, III, 1144
Buster, Steven K., 2446
Bustillo, Rafael, 901
Bustle, John W., 1061
Butcher, C. Preston, 3363
Buth, Douglas P., 3091
Buth, Jay S., 2737
Buthman, Mark, 4038
Buthman, Mark A., 2150
Butier, Mitchell R., 297
Butler, 3257
Butler Capital Corp., 475
Butler Manufacturing Co., 626
Butler, Addie J., 3747
Butler, Christopher D., 1926
Butler, Deborah H., 2725
Butler, Denise J., 2667
Butler, Flamont T., 3272
Butler, Fred, 475
Butler, Gary C., 291
Butler, Gilbert, 475
Butler, Gregory B., 2737, 3075
Butler, Ildiko, 475
Butler, James Brian, 2693
Butler, James G., Jr., 424
Butler, Jeffrey D., 2737
Butler, John D., 3731
Butler, John M., 854, 921
Butler, Kevin M., 1071
Butler, Kimberly, 4031
Butler, Maria R., 3232
Butler, Michael J., 1276
Butler, Robert C., 79
Butler, Stephen G., 904, 935, 1464
Butler, Stephen T., 3674
Butler, Thomas W., Jr., 1350
Butt Grocery Co., H.E., 628
Butt, Barbara Dan, 628
Butt, Charles C., 628
Butt, Howard E., Jr., 628
Butt, Howard E., Sr., 628
Butterfield, Stephen F., 2660
Butterfield, Steve, 2660
Butterworth, David C., 828
Button, Darryl D., 45
Butts, John, 820
Butvilas, George J., 827
Butzel Long, 629
Butzlaff, Stephen H., 2740
Buyinski Gluckman, Victoria, 3835
Buzard, Tim, 790
Buzard, Timothy, 790
Buzzard, James A., 2445
Buzzelli, Robert A., 3374
Byala, Brian, 2610
Byant, R. Jeep, 344
Byars, Michael D., 456
Bybee, Amanda, 2614
Byerlein, Anne, 4150
Byers Choice, Ltd., 630
Byers, Jeffrey D., 630
Byers, Joyce F., 630
Byers, Robert L., 630, 1421
Byers, Robert L., Jr., 630, 1421
Byerwalter, Mariann, 616
Bygren, Gerald, 3305
Byler, Janet S., 3987
Byles, Carrie, 3474
Bylsma, Gregory J, 2517
Bylsma, Gregory J., 2517
Bynoe, Linda Walker, 2740
Bynoe, Peter C.B., 1508
Bynum, Bruce, 947
Byorum, Martha L., 2747
Byrd Cookie Co., 631
Byrd, Beth, 636
Byrd, Beth C., 636
Byrd, Carolyn, 1348
Byrd, Carolyn H., 1348, 3171
Byrd, Carolyn Hogan, 50
Byrd, Dennis, 2126
Byrd, Edward R., 2855
Byrd, Judith I., 2335
Byrd, Kim Gunshinan, 1873
Byrd, Vincent C., 1110, 3488
Byrne, Dana W., 850
Byrne, Frank D., 3595
Byrne, Kevin, 335
Byrne, Patrick J., 2500
Byrne, Richard, 2689
Byrne, Samuel T., 51
Byrnes, Brian M., 370
Byrnes, Bruce L., 540, 592, 1112
Byrnes, Doreen R., 1984
Byrnes, James J., 2681
Byrnes, Jonathan L.S., 2593
Byron-Weston Co., 969
Byrum, D. Michael, 4087
Bywater, Willis M., 1808, 3394

C & C Ford, 632
C&C Metal Products Corp., 633
C.M. Capital Corp., 637
CAB, 1963
Cabalquinto, Jennifer, 3893
Caban-Owen, Catalina, 2262
Cabaniss, Thomas E., 2430
Cabe, Robert D., 240
Cabeza de Vaca, Susana, 1266
Cabezas, Ximena, 1266
Cabiallavetta, Mathis, 2962
Cable, Greg, 2480
Cablevision of Michigan, Inc., 640
Cablik, Anna R., 385, 1567
Cabot Corp., 642
Cabot, Amanda, 1031
Cabot, Samuel, III, 643
Cabrera, Angel, 2948
Cabrera, Brian, 3673
Cabrera, Fenando, 2122
Caccini, Gianpaolo, 423
Cacciotti, Dawn, 2638
Cachinero-Sanchez, Benito, 1184
Cacique Distributors, U.S., 644
Cacique, Inc., 644
CACO Services Co., 3119
Cada, Deanna, 1908
Cadanau, Carl, III, 111
Cadavid, Sergio A., 2006
Caddell Construction Co., Inc., 645
Caddell, Cathy L., 645
Caddell, Christopher P., 645
Caddell, J. Kirby, 645
Caddell, Jeffrey P., 645
Caddell, John A., 645
Caddell, John K., 645
Caddell, Joyce K., 645
Caddell, Michael A., 645
Cade, Christopher R., 2057
Cadence Design Systems, Inc., 3327
Cadiente-Nelson, Barbara, 3380
Cadieux, Chester, III, 3109
Cadillac Products Inc., 648
Cadillac Village, 3954
Cadonau, Anita J., 111
Cadonau, Carl H., Jr., 111
Cadonau, Randall E., 111
Caesars Entertainment Operating Company, Inc., 650
Cafaro, Debra A., 3931, 4052
Caffey Distributing Co., I.H., Inc., 2523
Caffey Distributors, I.H., 2523
Caffey, Kip R., 692
Caffrey, Jack, 905
Caforio, Giovanni, 578
Cagley, Lon, 3078
Cahill, Chris J., 2225
Cahill, Dennis, 251
Cahill, John J., 3067
Cahill, John T., 869, 2245
Cahill, Michael B., 830
Cahn, Robert, 959
Cahners Business Information, 3161
Cahners Magazine, 3161
Cahshill, Robert M., 1984
Cain, Barry S., 1219
Cain, Brennan, 1317
Cain, Elizabeth, 3325
Cain, Elizabeth A., 3325
Cain, Richard D., 3248
Cain, Susan O., 2287
Cain-Pozzo, Diane, 2462
Caine, Martin M., 4102
Cajun Constructors, Inc., 652
Calabrese, Joe, 1737
Calabrese, Thomas, 2683
Calabrese, Vincent J., 1318
Calado, Miguel M., 1817
Calaiacovo, William, 2989
Calandro, Michele, 2309
Calantzopoulos, Andre, 2962
Calarco, Vincent A., 2698
Calaway, Curt T., 3832
Calaway, Tonit M., 1732
Calbert, Michael M., 1143
Calder, Debbie, 1689
Calderado, Cheryl, 1118
Calderado, Cheryl A., 1118
Calderara, William C., 2646
Calderon, Jorge Familiar, 1959
Calderon, Rima, 3999
Calderone, Tom, 2596
Calderoni, Frank, 38
Calderoni, Frank A., 818
Calderoni, Robert M., 2075, 2165
Caldwe, Bernard L., II, 345
Caldwell, Amanda, 3347
Caldwell, Chris, 2603
Caldwell, David H., 3317
Caldwell, Desiree, 1450
Caldwell, Donald R., 3093
Caldwell, John E., 40
Caldwell, Kim, 297
Caldwell, Kirbyjon, 563
Caldwell, Kirbyjon H., 2756
Caldwell, Robert E., Jr., 561
Caldwell, Robert E., Sr., 561
Caldwell, Robert, Sr., 561
Caldwell, Royce S., 1512
Caldwell, Sarah R., 561
Caldwell, Sylvia R., 561
Caldwell, T. Dodd, 561
Caley, Bobby, 2379
Calfee, William R., 850
Calgaard, Ronald K., 3915
Calhoun, David L., 516, 722
Calhoun, Robert B., Jr., 2303
Calhoun, Stephen T., 2861
Califano, Joseph A., Jr., 727
California Department of Fish and Game, 1992
California Physicians' Service Agency Inc., 655
California Pizza Kitchen, Inc., 656
Calista Corporation, 657
Calkain Realty, Inc., 658
Calkins, Larry D., 1835
Call, J. Douglas, 2048
Call, John G., 3267
Call, Laurel, 267
Call, Peter R., 3406
Callahan, Bradley S., 3801
Callahan, Jack F., Jr., 2429
Callahan, Jack R., 2553
Callahan, John P., 1618
Callahan, Meredith C., 3040
Callahan, Patricia R., 4028
Callahan, Sandra W., 3701
Callahoan, Mathew, 1828
Callarman, Denise, 3709
Callaway Golf Co., 660
Callaway, Cindy, 660
Callaway, E. Reeves, III, 2088
Callaway, Edward C., 1953
Callaway, Ely R., Jr., 660
Callaway, Ronald E., 2553
Calle, Craig, 1541
Callejas, Antonio Hernandez, 3227
Callejas, Felix Hernandez, 3227
Callen, Victoria, 3584
Callicrate, Maggie, 2974
Calligaris, Alfred B., 3910
Calligaris, Alfred E., 3910
Callis, David, 2486
Calmat Co., 3972
Calpeter, Lynn A., 3893
Calpine Corp., 661
Calpine Corporation, 661
Calumet Enterprises Inc., 662
Calvano, Gregory, 1186
Calvert, Jim, 1644
Calvert, Lisa, 1569

Calvi Electric Co., 664
Calvo, Felix, 1811
Cama, Domenick A., 1984
Camacho, Frank, 998
Camalier, Charles A., 4074
Camalier, Charles A., III, 4074
Cambre, Ronald C., 1623
Cambria, Christopher C., 1548
Cambria, Dennis J., 772
Cambridgeport Bank, 3137
Cambron, Michael S., 178
Camden, Tom, 3648
Camelo, Laura, 3211
Cameron, Andrew D., 2995
Cameron, Dennis, 1525
Cameron, Jo Carol, 145
Cameron, Lynda L., 145
Cameron, Peter, 31
Cameron, Ronald M., 2590
Cameron, Rose, 2253
Cameron, Susan M., 1155, 3821
Cameron, Wendy, 2610
Cameron, William M., 145
Camilleri, Louis C., 2962
Camilleri, Michael J., 590
Camiolo, Karen M., 2628
Cammaker, Sheldon I., 1255
Cammarano, Philip, 3344
Cammarata, Bernard, 3765
Cammarata, William, 487
Cammiso, Valerie, 1961
Camp, Elizabeth W., 3674
Camp, John, 420
Camp, Kelly, 4109
Camp, Randolph W., 1634
Camp, William H., 795
Campana, Deena, 416
Campanella, Joseph, 2790
Campanella, Joseph A., 2790
Campaniano, Robin K., 1405
Campanile, Rita P., 1048
Campbell Soup Co., 669
Campbell, Alan, 1495
Campbell, Alice J., 377
Campbell, Ben G., 3235
Campbell, Beth Newlands, 1723
Campbell, Bob, 2096
Campbell, Boyd, 2482
Campbell, Bruce L., 1126
Campbell, Carl, 2952
Campbell, Charley, 2199
Campbell, Cheryl, 1433
Campbell, Christian L., 4150
Campbell, Daniel W., 2759
Campbell, David, 3458
Campbell, David D., 1635
Campbell, Dennis, 2005
Campbell, Donald, 1785
Campbell, Donald H., 1785
Campbell, Eric, 2541
Campbell, George, Jr., 360
Campbell, J. Kermit, 3558
Campbell, James R., 3884
Campbell, Jeffrey C., 1795, 2434
Campbell, Jill, 958
Campbell, John R., 4028
Campbell, Kirby J., 245
Campbell, Kristin, 1812
Campbell, Lewis B., 578
Campbell, Lloyd E., 1683
Campbell, Lyman, 3839
Campbell, Maria, 3779
Campbell, Mark, 640
Campbell, Michael, 2619
Campbell, Michael A., 3062
Campbell, Michael E., 2445
Campbell, Michael H., 1073, 1621
Campbell, Michael L., 3166
Campbell, Mike, 1621
Campbell, Myrtle, 2344
Campbell, Neil, 3813
Campbell, Patrick D., 3579
Campbell, Paul, 3123
Campbell, Paul V., 2577
Campbell, Phyllis J., 74, 2724
Campbell, Reid T., 2813
Campbell, Robert D., 2715
Campbell, Ronald, 905
Campbell, Ronald J., 737
Campbell, Steve, 3665
Campbell, Steven T., 3876
Campbell, Thomas E., 2847
Campbell, Tina, 2096
Campbell, W. Patrick, 2030
Campbell, William B., 1318
Campbell, William M., 3996
Campbell, William V., 217, 1982
Campell, Ronald J., 737
Campion, Amanda R., 3890
Campion, Mark, 3890
Campisi, David J., 460
Campos, Dannielle C., 340
Campos, Luis B., 3953
Campos, R. Yvonne, 1799
Camus, Philippe, 81
Canaday, Shawn M., 437
Cancelmi, Daniel J., 3713
Candini, Suzanne M., 1445
Candlesticks, Inc., 670
Candris, Aris, 4049
Candris, Aristides S., 2715
Canepa, Stephen, 182
Canevari, Paul J., 505
Canfield, William W., 3683
Cangemi, Thomas R., 2682, 2683
Cangiolosi, Ryan, 2018
Canino, Suzanne, 3386
Cannaday, Jennifer, 665
Cannataro, Jim, 2712
Canning, Charles F., Jr., 2976
Canning, Charlotte H., 1821
Canning, Gena R., 338
Canning, John A., Jr., 945, 1309
Canning, Richard, 7
Cannon Valley Cellular, Inc., 671
Cannon Valley Telecom, Inc., 671
Cannon, Benjamin E., 547
Cannon, Deanna L., 3667
Cannon, John, 4027
Cannon, Marc, 292
Cannon, Mark R., 3346
Cannon, Michael R., 38, 2214, 3377
Cannon, Stephen, 984, 2463
Cano, Angel, 901
Canoles, Chris, 1842
Canon-USA, Inc., 672
Cantara, Daniel E., 1419
Canter, Charles W. "Nick", 2312
Cantlon, Angelica T., 1962
Cantlon, Thomas C., 3390
Cantor, Diana F., 1151
Cantor, Michael, 2977
Cantor, Richard, 2564
Cantrell, Edith M., 424
Cantrell, Hugh, 1088
Canzano, Anna, 1430
Caouette, John, 2416
Capati, Maria, 998
Cape Cod Bank and Trust Co., 3696
Cape Cod Five Cents Savings Bank, 674
Capel, William R., 3874
Capellas, Michael D., 818
Capello, Jeffrey D., 540
Caperton, Gaston, 3072
Caperton, W. Gaston, III, 1272
Capezio/Ballet Makers Inc., 675
Capezza, Joseph C., 1766
Capiraso, Michael, 2689
Capital Bank & Trust Co., 677
Capital City Bank, 676
Capital City First National Bank, 676
Capital Gazette Communications, Inc., 2218
Capital Group Cos., Inc., The, 677
Capital International, 677
Capital Investments & Ventures Corp., 678
Capital Management Services, 677
Capital Research & Management Co., 677
Capitol Federal Financial, 680
Capizzi, Tom, 1134
Caplanson, Nicholas, 1118
Caplin, Mortimer M., 1027
Capo, Thomas P., 936, 1144, 2237
Capone, Christopher M., 757
Capone, Gary J., 1486
Capone, Michael, 291
Capone, Michael L., 291
Caponigro, John, 197
Caponnetto, Marianne, 3358
Caporale, Nicholas A., 3317
Capozzi, Barbara A., 888
Capp, Stephen H., 2978
Cappaert, Steven M., 2471
Cappelli, Gregory W., 216
Cappello, Frank A., 3452
Cappello, Gerard, 30
Capps, John R., 890
Capps, Thomas E., 171
Capps, Vickie L., 1134
Cappuccio, Paul T., 3757
Caprario, Steven, 511
Capri, Inc., 682
Caprio, Patricia D., 2814
Caprio, Tony, 685
Capron, Philippe G.H., 30
Capuano, Linda A., 2364
Caputo, Lisa, 3802
Caputo, Lisa M., 442
Caputo, Louise, 743
Caracappa, Joe, 634
Caradec, Philippe, 1030
Caragozian, John, 3649
Caratan, Tina, 2581
Carbert, Jennifer, 2999
Carbonari, Bruce A., 3278
Carbone, Anthony J., 3247
Carbone, Michael, 3696
Carbone, Paul, 1191
Carboneau, David K., 3010
Carcieri, Sara, 3160
Card, Andrew H., Jr., 3857
Card, Robert G., 758
Card, Wesley R., 2057
Cardella, Thomas J., 1651
Carden, Joel, 2858
Cardenas, Alfred de, 3672
Cardenas, Jose A., 3524
Cardenas-Raptis, Ana de, 644
Cardenuto, Rodolpho, 3334
Cardey, Max, 3649
Cardia, Roy A., 3910
Cardiello, Sam, 1025
Cardillo, Sara A., 2323
Cardinal Health, Inc., 685
Cardini, Filippo, 3781
Cardis, John T., 297
Cardon, Wilford A., 1077
Cardone, Angelo, 2959
Cardosi, Richard J., 4006
Cardoso, Carlos M., 2125, 3579
Cardozo, Richard N., 2636
Cardwell, F. Lane, Jr., 3281
Cardwell, Patrick, 1973
Care Now, 3043
CareFusion 303, Inc., 688
Caremore Medical Enterprises, 689
Carendi, Jan, 1385
CareSource Management Group, 690
Carey, Albert, 1842
Carey, Bryan, 2401
Carey, Charles P., 853
Carey, Chase, 2700
Carey, Christopher J., 830
Carey, John M., 1770
Carey, Matthew A., 1842
Carey, Maver, 2200
Carey, Robert S., Jr., 910
Carey, W. David P., III, 668
Carfagna, Peter, 2209
Carfora, Jeffrey J., 2909
Carfora, Joseph J., 2711
Cargill Charitable Trust, 691
Cargill, Emmanuel, 2942
Cargill, Inc., 691
Carhart, Diane, 3617
Carhart, James P., 3910
Caribou Coffee Co., 692
Carideo, Anthony T., Jr., 4102
Carillo, Mary, 3879
Carillon Importers, Ltd., 2381
Carino, Gabriel, 4134
Carleton, Mark D., 360
Carley, Patrick, Rev., 2127
Carlile, Cecil O., 3637
Carlin, Leo, 53
Carlin, Michele, 3384
Carlin, Michele Aguilar, 2586
Carlini, Anthony, 914
Carlini, Barbara, 1653
Carlini, Barbara D., 1054, 1107
Carlino, Catherine A., 251
Carlino, Peter M., 2923
Carlisle Overstreet, J., 2573
Carlisle, Charles D., 3602
Carlisle, Dave, 2792
Carlo, Walter, 1167
Carlock, Chester, 2138
Carlos, Ruth Ann, 2448
Carlsmith, Laura, 2742
Carlson 2000 BCG Charitable Annuity Trust, Arleen M., 693
Carlson 2000 MCN Charitable Annuity Trust, Arleen M., 693
Carlson Companies, Inc., 693
Carlson, Arleen M., 693
Carlson, Carroll, 2173
Carlson, Christopher A., 2790
Carlson, Curtis L., 693
Carlson, David, 3736
Carlson, David J., 3736
Carlson, Dennis, 802
Carlson, Eric, 4109
Carlson, Gary L., 1817
Carlson, Gerry, 1432

Carlson, James G., 171
Carlson, Jan, 528
Carlson, Jennie P., 3835
Carlson, Jon, 1074
Carlson, Kenneth, 3883
Carlson, Leroy T., 3876
Carlson, Leroy T., Jr., 3876
Carlson, Lon, 1867
Carlson, Marc, 3411
Carlson, Rob, 1525
Carlson, Robert, 1339
Carlson, Robert W., 3092
Carlson, Robert W., Jr., 3092
Carlson, Ronald P., 1103
Carlson, Steven G., 528
Carlson, Tim, 1029
Carlson, Walter C.D., 3876
Carlsson, Kennet, 3473
Carlton, Donald M., 2632
Carlton, Scott L., 3869
Carlucci, C. Peter, Jr., 3492
Carlucci, David R., 2399
Carmack, Gwen, 1235
CarMax Auto Superstores, Inc., 694
CarMax Business Services, LLC, 694
Carmen-Jones, Tracy, 1563
Carmichael, Clare, 4007
Carmichael, Dan R., 2789
Carmichael, Greg D., 1377
Carmichael, James, 2184
Carmichael, John A., 2323
Carmichael, Paula F., 2734
Carmichael, William P., 1383
Carmody, Timothy R., 695
Carmola, Jack, 3908
Carmona, Richard H., 852
Carmouche, Charles H., 1375
Carnaghi, Sharon, 1413
Carnarse, Drew, 2813
Carnation Co., 2663
Carneal, Jeffrey J., 1201
Carnes, Dennis L., 2110
Carnesale, Albert, 3718
Carney, Brian P., 456
Carney, Sean D., 376
Carney, Thomas, 2875
Carney, Thomas P., 3873
Carnwath, Alison J., 2850
Caro, James, 2622
Carolin, Brian, 3639
Carolina Beer and Beverage, LLC, 2523
Carolina Casualty Insurance Company, 426
Carolina Containers Co., 697
Carolina East Medical Center, 3944
Carolina First Foundation, 3696
Carolina Ice Co., Inc., 699
Carolina Power & Light Co., 1189
Carolina Premium, 2523
Carolina Renaissance LP, 2523
Caroln, Dennis, 343
Carosone, Mike, 516
Carousel Snack Bars of Minnesota, Inc., 2266
Carp, Daniel A., 1073, 2725, 3728
Carp, Jeffrey N., 3592
Carpenter, Alvin R., 3074
Carpenter, Ben, 3138
Carpenter, Benjamin, 3138
Carpenter, Craig M., 567
Carpenter, Dan, 1271
Carpenter, David R., 145
Carpenter, Donna, 624
Carpenter, Edmund M., 669
Carpenter, Flave, 1278
Carpenter, George C., III, 1264
Carpenter, George T., 362
Carpenter, Jake Burton, 624
Carpenter, Jim, 3744
Carpenter, Mary Ellen, 1488
Carpenter, Randall R., 565
Carpenter, Rob, 1477
Carpenter, Robert, 859
Carpenter, Thomas S., 226
Carpenter, W. Geoffrey, 2423
Carpenter, William F., III, 2270
Carper, John T., 1884
Carpino, John, 200
Carr, Dave, 129, 2945
Carr, Elliott, 674
Carr, J. Craig, 1420
Carr, Jim, 2250
Carr, John, 1842
Carr, Julian L., 3944
Carr, Julie, 1407
Carr, Lauren A., 2499
Carr, Robert, 1915
Carr, Robert E., 1096, 2506
Carr, Timothy P., 3215
Carrabba, Joseph, 2698
Carrabba, Joseph A., 850
Carrara, George M., 1376
Carreiro, Ernest L., Jr., 3383
Carreon, Michael R., 3902
Carrick, Shaun, 2512
Carrigan-McCurdy, Clantha, 1528
Carrillo, Arturo, 27
Carrillo, Doug, 2853
Carrillo, Jesse, 1813
Carrington, H. G., Jr., 656
Carrington, John D., 1225
Carrino, Frank, 4047
Carrino, Frank Anthony, 4047
Carrion, Richard L., 3003, 3936
Carris Financial Corp., 702
Carris Reels of California, Inc., 702
Carris Reels of Connecticut, Inc., 702
Carris Reels, Inc., 702
Carris, William H., 702
Carroll Enterprises, Inc., 703
Carroll, Brian K., 703
Carroll, Christopher F., 1974
Carroll, Christopher O., 660
Carroll, David C., 2628
Carroll, Ed, 126
Carroll, Francis, 703
Carroll, Francis R., 703
Carroll, J. Martin, 515
Carroll, James, 1142
Carroll, John, 849
Carroll, John A., 1207
Carroll, Kevin, 1674
Carroll, Leo P., 910, 2513
Carroll, Leonard M., 186
Carroll, Lisa, 703
Carroll, Loren K., 2106
Carroll, Mary C., 222
Carroll, Mary M., 703
Carroll, Michael, 3596
Carroll, Michael J., 2098, 3596
Carroll, Milton, 738, 739, 1706
Carroll, Pat, 1427
Carroll, Penny, 966
Carroll, Robert J., 3515
Carroll, Russell L., 2310
Carroll, William J., 1624
Carrucci, Richard T., 4150
Carruthers, Brian, 1432
Carruthers, Thomas, III, 2482
Carruthers, Wendy, 540
Carson Electric Cooperative, Kit, Inc., 705
Carson, Benjamin S., Sr., 948, 2120
Carson, Craig, 3523
Carson, John, 1790
Carson, Mike, 2964
Carson, Randolph W., 2723
Carson, Robert A., 3374
Carson, Sandra M., 3081
Carson, William, 425
Carstanjen, Julia, 807
Carstanjen, William C., 807
Carstens, Godfrey H., Jr., 2683
Carstensen, Hans L., III, 3433
Cartee, Joseph B., 901
Carter Sullivan, William, III, 589
Carter, Amon G., 1472
Carter, Andrea, 278, 279
Carter, C. Michael, 1141
Carter, Charles R., 1631
Carter, Ellis McGehee, 706
Carter, George P., 2928
Carter, Joan, 3834
Carter, Joan P., 3834
Carter, John, 3042
Carter, John D., 2747
Carter, Kimberly, 859
Carter, Larry, 3810
Carter, Larry R., 818
Carter, Lynn A., 679
Carter, Lynne A., 2693
Carter, Marshall N., 2769
Carter, Mary D., 194
Carter, Matthew, Jr., 216, 3905
Carter, Michael A., 2973
Carter, Mollie Hale, 233, 4039
Carter, Pamela L., 997, 3540
Carter, Powhatan, 1211
Carter, Renee, 1748
Carter, Robert B., 1352, 1406, 3315
Carter, Sue, 2106
Carter, Susan K., 63
Carter, Susan M., 1567, 3516
Carter, Theresa, 2809
Carter, Tim, 1347
Carter, Timothy L., 2983
Carter, William, 616
Carter, William H., 2325
Carter, Zachary W., 641, 2385
Carter-Miller, Jocelyn, 1974
Carter-Miller, Jocelyn E., 3047
Cartmell, Liza, 3557
Cartmill, Molly, 3405
Cartoon Network, 30
Cartwright, Carol A., 1424
Cartwright, James E., 3135
Carty, Donald J., 1068
Carty, Penny L., 934
Caruana, Ken, 3267
Carucci, Richard T., 3913, 4150
Caruso Kitchen Designs, 709
Caruso, Andrea, 709
Caruso, Anthony F., Jr., 1937
Caruso, Dominic J., 2048
Caruso, Frank A., 3340, 3625
Caruso, Gerard, 709
Caruso, Jared, 709
Caruso, Jared A., 709
Caruso, Jerry, 709
Caruso, Joe, 640
Caruso, John A., 709
Caruso, Karen, 709
Caruso, Kim, 3701
Caruso, Mike, 3567
Caruso, Robert Joseph, 3398
Carvalho, Kristin T., 2514
Carvalho, Marcelo Baptista, 1961
Carvalho, Ricardo, 2896
Carver Federal Savings Bank, 711
Carver, Howard L., 266
Carver, Judith G., 1060
Carver, Robert, 2380
Cary Oil Co., Inc., 712
Cary, A. Bray, Jr., 1287
Casa Ford, Inc., 1464
Casabona, Joseph E., 1272
Casabonne, Mike, 2920
Casabonne, Mike G., 2920
Casady, Mark S., 1382
Casagrande, John, 298
Casale, Carl M., 802
Casale, Robert J., 2397
Casamento, Benedetta I., 3682
Casarella, Frank P., 2902
Casati, Mary Ann, 4079
Casavant, Arthur F., 2928
Casazza, William J., 48
Casbeer, George, 960
Casbeer, George H., 960, 961
Cascade Chrysler, Inc., 2096
Cascade Controls, Inc., 1009
Cascade Natural Gas Corp., 2441
Cascade Utilities, 1045
Cascepara, Judy, 2663
Casciato, Chris C., 3650
Cascone, Michael, Jr., 493
Case, Daniel, 1672
Case, Gregory C., 210, 1125
Case, Jack, 747
Case, Joe, 2487
Case, Michael E., 4046
Case, Nathan, 117
Case, Nicole, 3199
Casellas, Gilbert F., 3072
Casey, Daniel P., 127
Casey, David, 2410
Casey, Helen Hanna, 1722
Casey, Kevin M., 887
Casey, Leah, 2853
Casey, Lynn, 2864
Casey, Michael D., 708, 732
Casey, Suzanne E., 183
Casey, Thomas W., 842
Casey, Timothy, 2592
Casey, Warren J., 3682
Casey, William, 2401
Cash, James I., Jr., 804, 1552, 3980
Cash, Jeff, 3037
Cash, Kevin L., 319
Cash, Larry S., 2743
Cash, R. Don, 2628, 3104, 4158
Cash, W. Larry, 900
Cashill, Robert M., 1984
Cashin, Arthur D., Jr., 2769
Cashin, Harry X., III, 2645
Cashin, Steve, 225
Cashion Living Trust, Howard, 4027
Cashman, Chistopher, 1926
Cashman, Gideon, 3073
Cashman, Kristina K., 372
Cashmere Capital, 2597
Casiano, Kimberly A., 1464, 2443, 2605
Casino Queen, Inc., 714
Casner Family Fund, 2113
Caspall, Ken, 2486, 2487
Casparino, Michael J., 2928

Casper, Marc N., 3733
Caspersen, Daniel, 3790
Caspersen, Finn M. W., Jr., 2909
Caspersen, Finn M.W., 411
Caspersen, Finn M.W., Jr., 411, 2909
Cass, Richard, 335
Cass, Richard W., 335
Cassaday, John M., 3677
Cassel, Christine K., 2086
Cassetti, Robert K., 945
Cassidy & Pinkard, Inc., 715
Cassidy, Brendan, 715
Cassidy, Christopher J., 778
Cassidy, Frank, 661
Cassidy, Kathryn A., 1552
Cassis, Glynis, 2088
Cassis, Kevin B., 4064
Cassity, Mike, 1762
Casson, Ethan, 3326
Castagna, Eugene A., 399
Castagna, Robert, 540
Castagna, Vanessa J., 708, 3624
Castaldo, Debbie, 3902
Casteel, Chip, 1313
Casteen, John T., III, 120
Castellani, Robert, 2728
Castellani, Robert A., 2728
Castellano, Christine M., 1942
Castellano, James G., 3280
Castellano, John, 1833
Castellano, Thomas J., 1799
Castelli, Ralph A., Jr., 2123
Castelli, Romie, 1716
Castellini, Bob, 814
Castellini, Phil, 814
Castellini, Phillip J., 814
Castellini, Robert H., 814
Castillo, Jay E., 2341
Castillo, Maya, 1275
Castino, Alfred J., 3673
Castle & Co., A.M., 716
Castle & Cooke, Inc., 717
Castleberry, Jennifer, 3304
Casto, Don M., III, 1894
Castor, Richard L., 1561
Castro, Henrique de, 4140
Castro, Hollie S., 508
Castro, John W., 3389
Castro, Peter, 3757
Castro, Thomas H., 3755
Castro-Wright, Eduardo, 3980
Castruita, Rudy, 3322
Caswell, Richard S., 3454
Catalane, Bart, 1569
Catalano, Anna C., 775, 2443
Cataldo, Karen, 3160
Catalina Marketing Corp., 719
Catania, Angelo, 2782
Catapillar, Inc., 722
Catawissa Lumber & Specialty Co., Inc., 720
Catell, Robert B., 2335, 2630
Catellus Land & Development Corporation and Subsidiaries, 3060
Caterpillar Inc., 722
Cates, Andrew F., 2981
Cates, Andy, 1857
Cates, Hunter, 131
Cates, Staley, 1857
Cathay Bank, 723
Cathcart, Alun, 299
Cathey, Bill, 3258
Cathey, Billy, 3258
Cathey, Dale C., 967
Cathy, Dan T., 791
Cathy, Donald M., 791
Cathy, S. Truett, 791
Catino, Annette, 2741
Catone, Robert, 1692
Cattaneo, Mario, 2319
Catz, Safra A., 2821
Caudiano, Annette, 2541
Caudill, Kelly, 4097
Caudle, Robert, 2235
Cauffman, Lewis, 2677
Caulfield, Alex, 1018
Caulfield, E. Michael, 3898
Caulfield, Gary L., 1405
Caulton-Harris, Helen, 501
Cava, Gregory J., 910
Cavalier, Lynn M., 1424
Cavalier, Michael D., 815
Cavanagh, Michael J., 4150
Cavanagh, Richard E., 1683
Cavanagh, Toni, 2342
Cavanaugh, James W., 1866
Cavanaugh, Paul, 2963
Cavanaugh, Robert B., 2925
Cavanaugh, Robert F., 1791
Cavanaugh, Steven M., 1763
Cavanaugh, Terrence W., 1291
Cavatorta, Enrico, 2319
Caveney Family Enterprises, LP, 2872
Caveney, Gerald W., 2872
Caveney, Jack E., 2872
Caveney, John E., 2872
Caveney, Ken, 3327
Caves, Kerry D., 4014
Caviness, Darrell, 3258
Cawkwell, Karen, 3312
Cawley, Thomas P., 2916
Cayce, Eugenia Topple, 2896
Caylor, Mark A., 2744
Cayrac Corp., 799
Cazala, Beatrice, 578
Cazalot, Clarence P., Jr., 324, 2363, 2364
Cazer, Michael, 189
CB Richard Ellis Group, Inc., 725
CB Richard Ellis Services, Inc., 725
CBS Corp., 727
CBS Inc., 727
CDM Holdings, Inc., 982
Cebular, John, 920
Cebulon, John, 920
Ceccarelli, Jeff, 2765
Cecere, Andrew, 3835
Cech, Thomas R., 2466
Cecil, Joe D., 3856
Cecil, Robin, 2876
Cederna, James A., 2529
Cederoth, Andrew J., 2647
Cefaly, James, 2306
Ceglar, Frank J., Jr., 1338
Celanese Americas Corp., 730
Celebrity Fight Night, 3594
Celebrity International, Inc., 731
Celebrity Salute to Boston Garden, A, 534
Celentano, John E., 578
Celestine, Von, 563
Cellino, A.M., 2628
Cellular South, Inc., 636
CEMEX Corp., 734
Cenac, Connie, 1764
Cenac, Dwight, 1764
Cendant Corp., 299
Cenex Harvest States Cooperatives, 802
CENEX, Inc., 802
Centaur, Inc., 1770
Centene Charitable Foundation, The, 735
Centene Management Company, LLC, 735
Centene Managment Co., LLC, 735
Center Care Health, 3944
Center for Siouxland, 1541
Center, Steve, 150
Centerior Energy Corp., 1424
CentiMark Corp., 740
Cento, Juan N., 266
Central Bering Sea Fishermens Assn., 3687
Central Maine Power Co., 1904
Central National Bank, 742
Central National-Gottesman, Inc., 743
Central New Mexico Electric Cooperative, 744
Central Pennsylvania Investment Company, 1318
Central State Bank, 745
Central Stearns Comsis, Inc., 77
Central Storage & Warehouse Co., 746
Central Valley Electric Cooperative, Inc., 747
Central Wholesale Liquor Co., 3186
Centrella, Roy R., 3524
Century 21, Inc., 748
Century Construction Co., Inc., 749
Century Life Assurance Co., 750
Cepek, Gretchen, 105
Cerami, Anthony, 3992
Ceran, Jennifer, 1217
Ceresino, Gordon J., 1351
Cermak, Mark E., 853
Cernak, Kenneth S., 1212
Cerner Corp., 754
Cerny, Melissa, 763
Cerqueria, Luiz, 3418
Cerritos Auto Retail Co., 3165
Cerrone, Judy, 888
Cerrone, Pamela, 1607
Cerruti, Dominique, 2769
Cerutti, Dominique, 2769
Cervenka, Debbie, 2966
Cervenka, Robert, 2966
Cervone, Tony, 3967
Ceryanec, Joseph H., 2471
Cesan, Raul E., 2690
Cesare, Denise S., 505
Cesare, Joseph G., 2924
Cesaro, Jerry, 2135
Cessna Foundation, Inc., 3731
Cestare, Thomas D., 412
Cestra, Annie H., 1722
Cestra, Annie Hanna, 1722
Ceverha, Mary E., 1347
CEW Asset Trust, 3044
CFA Properties, Inc., 791
CFPO, Inc., 976
CFS Bancorp, Inc., 756
CFW Communications Co., 2758
Ch Robinson Company, 663
CH2M Hill, 758
Cha, Johnson M.D., 637
Cha, Lucia, 637
Cha, Selina, 637
Chabraja, Nicholas D., 1551, 2740
Chadbourne & Parke LLP, 759
Chadee, Floyd F., 3574
Chaden, Lee A., 693, 1155, 1720
Chadick, Gary R., 3247
Chadis, Lucy, 1828
Chadwick, Claire M., 283
Chadwick, Jay, 2238
Chadwick, John W., 2782
Chadwick, Jonathan, 2417
Chadwick, Patricia W., 183, 4093
Chadwick, Peter, 1046
Chafetz, Irwin, 2225
Chafey, Rick, 2968
Chaffin, Janice, 1964
Chagnon, Rick, 1881
Chai, Ling, 2037
Chai, Nelson J., 819, 3733
Chai, Ping Yin, 3317
Chaib, Al, 2871
Chait, Gerald, 1571
Chaityn, Carl, 1075
Chajet, Clive, 4030, 4031
Chakmak, Paul J., 546
Chakour, Patty, 3822
Chaldler, Russ, 888
Chalendar, Pierre-Andre de, 3312
Chalfin, Mitchell, 633
Chaloner, Peter, 831
Chaltiel, Victor, 2225
Chamarthi, Mamatha, 854, 921
Chamberlain Group, Inc., 1187
Chamberlin, Glenn, 188
Chambers, Anne Cox, 959
Chambers, Caroline E., 889
Chambers, Caroline M., 1624
Chambers, James R., 460
Chambers, John T., 818
Chambers, Julius L., 1588
Chambers, Karla S., 947
Chambers, M. Susan, 3980
Chambers, Thomas P., 211
Chambless, Robert G., 861
Chambliss, Wendell J., 1348
Chambord, LLC, 4119
Chameau, Jean-Lou, 4072
Chamillard, George W., 2469
Champion, Gina S., 3346
Champion, Madeleine L., 827
Champions Pipe & Supply, Inc., 2138
Champlin, Byron, 2281
Champman, James N., 2656
Chan, Cherie, 2853
Chan, Chi-Foon, 3673
Chan, Stephanie, 3189
Chan, Tom, 2664
Chancy, Mark A., 3654
Chand, Riz, 618
Chandler, Anderson, 1981
Chandler, Arthur E., 1733
Chandler, Charles Q., IV, 1981, 4039
Chandler, Don, 3455
Chandler, Joy, 2125
Chandler, Kerry D., 2623
Chandler, Mark, 818
Chandler, Mary, 1007
Chandler, Russ, 888
Chandler-Frates & Reitz, Inc., 760
Chandor, Stebbins B., Jr., 2758
Chaney Enterprises, L.P., 761
Chaney, Francis H., II, 761
Chaney, G. Mark, 687
Chaney, Hulet, 507
Chaney, Hulet M., 507
Chaney, Kim J., 1001
Chaney, Tanna, 1952
Chaney, William E., 3649
Chang, Andrew, 1172, 1755
Chang, Charles K., 1202

Chang, David C., 3755
Chang, Do Won, 1469
Chang, Enrique, 137
Chang, Gigi Lee, 2992
Chang, Jaw-Kang, 2967
Chang, Ray, 2995
Chang, Ray D., 2995
Chang, Tina, 4051
Chang, Vanessa, 655
Chang, Vanessa C.L., 1228
Chang, Warren, 228
Chang-Diaz, Franklin R., 1007
Chang-Muy, Fernando, 4028
Chanter, Nigel, 2937
Chao, Allen, 4007
Chao, Elaine L., 1141, 2700, 3066, 4028
Chapdelaine, Donald, 3471
Chapelard, Frederic, 81
Chapin, Bill, 2091
Chapin, David C., 583
Chapin, Joe, 3918
Chapin, Joseph, 3918
Chapin, Sarah Palisi, 692
Chapin, Theodore, 3250
Chapin, Theodore S., 3250
Chaplin, C. Edward, 2416
Chaplin, Chuck, 2416
Chaplin, Ernest, 2117
Chaplin, Harvey R., 3521
Chaplin, Paul B., 3521
Chaplin, Wayne E., 3521
Chapman & Associates, 763
Chapman and Cutler, 285
Chapman Auto Group, 632
Chapman High School, 1943
Chapman, Adrian P., 3997
Chapman, Allan, 722
Chapman, Andrew, 3081
Chapman, Bre, 1347
Chapman, Carl L., 3925
Chapman, Charles J., 4025
Chapman, Charles J., III, 2873
Chapman, Constance, 1955
Chapman, Gerald S., 763
Chapman, Gil, 2741
Chapman, Gregory, 763
Chapman, Gregory S., 763
Chapman, Jennifer, 1381
Chapman, John G., Sr., 3452
Chapman, Julie D. S., 577
Chapman, Kirby, 3637
Chapman, Matthew W., 2499
Chapman, Michael D., 632
Chapman, Norman H., 1943
Chapman, Paul, 16
Chapman, Randolph, 3015
Chapman, Randy, 3015
Chapman, Richard E., 2154
Chapman, Richard P., Jr., 583
Chapman, Robert H., III, 1943
Chapman, Robert M., 3239
Chapman, Steve, 3279
Chapman, Steven G., 1998
Chapman, Steven M., 936
Chapman, Thomas W., 2086
Chappel, Donald R., 3659, 4077
Chappell, Inajo Davis, 2448
Chappell, Robert E., 996, 3093
Chappell, Thomas M., 3770
Charanjiva, Lakshman, 1443
Charbonnet, Marques, 335
Chard, Joseph, 367
Chardavoyne, Jeanette M., 3916
Chardavoyne, Jeannette M., 3916
Charette, George J., III, 2902
Charity Folks, Inc., Inc., 2769
Charles River Laboratories, Inc., 764
Charles River Saab, 3954
Charles, David M., 1139
Charles, Elisabeth, 2945
Charles, Kris, 2120
Charles, Lynn, 2556
Charlestein, Gary, 3036
Charlestein, Julie, 3036
Charlestein, Morton L., 3036
Charleston, Kevin Patrick, 2301
Charlier, Christophe, 584
Charlier, Jean-Yves, 30
Charlotte Hornets, The, 2678
Charlton, Scott, 634
Charreton, Didier, 324
Charron, David, 2482
Charron, Paul R., 669
Charter Manufacturing Co., Inc., 766
Charter One Bank, 3137
Charter, Richard L., II, 3778
Chartis Group, LLC, 768
Chase Manhattan Bank, The, 439, 2071, 3860
Chase Manhattan Mortgage Corp., 3190
Chase Oil Co., 770
Chase, Deb, 770
Chase, Karla, 770
Chase, Lynn, 769
Chase, Mack C., 770
Chase, Marilyn Y., 770
Chase, Richard, 770
Chase, Robert, 770
Chase, Robert C., 770
Chase, Rodney Frank, 3723
Chase, Warren W., Jr., 2734
Chasey, Jacqueline, 439
Chasin, Charlie, 2570
Chatham Ventures, Inc., 2071
Chatila, Ahmad R., 2459
Chatman, Jennifer A., 3461
Chatmon, Bryan, 516
Chatmon, Katie, 989
Chatmon, R.D., 989
Chatmon, R.D. & Katie, 989
Chattem, Inc., 3329
Chau, Micheline, 2316
Chau, Wayne, 3776
Chau, Windon, 2925
Chaudri, Javade, 3405
Chaufferin, Gilles, 519
Chavel, George, 3497
Chaves, Arthur J., 2506
Chavez, Asdrubal, 820
Chavez, Christina, 2349
Chavez, Monte, 3327
Chavez, Robert B., 46
Chavez, Sandra J., 481
Chazanoff, Lucille, 2741
Chazen, Jerome, 1376
Chazen, Stephen I., 2780
Checketts, David, 3549
Checketts, David W., 2041
Chee, William, 3189
Chee, William S., 1753
Cheek, Donna, 3171
Cheeseman, Kelly, 2306
Cheetham, Robert, 309
Cheever, Sharon A., 2855
Cheit, Earl F., 3461
Cheleden, Charles G., 4127
Chelette, David, 1892
Chellgren, Paul W., 2996, 2997
Chelsea Groton Savings Bank, 772
CHEMCENTRAL Corp., 3886
Chemed Corp., 773
Chemers, Joel W., 1219
Chemical Investments, Inc., 2071
Chen, Benjamin, 3102
Chen, Eric, 42
Chen, Heng W., 723
Chen, John S., 1127, 4028
Chen, Thomas, 992
Chenault, Kenneth I., 143, 1960, 3055
Chender, Amy, 16
Chenega Corp., 776
Chenevert, Louis R., 3882
Cheney, Jeffrey P., 2182
Cheng, Andrew, 1582
Cheng, Bob, 1358
Cheng, Clifford, 1358
Cheng, Dunson K., 723
Cheng, George, 1358
Cheng, Jean, 1358
Cheng, Linda Y.H., 2853, 2952
Cheng, Mei-Wei, 3377
Chenoweth, Chris, 1496
Cheong, Melissa, 58
Cheong, Thian C., 2994
Chereskin, Benjamin D., 729
Cherian, Corina Polk, 1390
Cherington, Gretchen, 2394
Cheriyan, Anil T., 3654
Cherney, Richard, 1036
Cherng, Andrew, 2871
Cherng, Peggy T., 2871
Chernick, Richard J., 1651
Chernick, Rick, 1651
Chernin, Peter, 143
Chernoff, Alex, 2799
Cherrier, Steve, 497
Cherry, Kim, 1406
Cherry, Kimberley C., 1406
Cherrytree Investments, 1140
Chersi, Robert J., 1450
Cherubini, Paul B., 851
Chesebro, Robert E., Jr., 4069
Chesebro, Robert, Jr., 4069
Chesler, Randall M., 1232
Chesley, Walter T., 496
Chess, Robert B., 2658
Chessen, Robert M., 586
Chesser, Michael J., 2092
Chestnov, Richard, 2015
Chestnov, Robert, 2015
Chestnut, John, 3448
Chestnut, Thomas E., 3524
Cheston, Sheila C., 2744
Cheston, Shelia, 2744
Chetnani, Jairaj, 3100
Chevassus, Alain, 221
Cheviot Savings Bank, 779
Chevrolet, Gordon, 2573
Chevron Corp., 780
Chevron U.S.A., Inc., 234
ChevronTexaco Corp., 780
Chew, Ching-Meng, 1220
Chew, Clinton, 2446
Chew, Lewis, 2952
Chew, Paul J., 333
Cheyne, David, 2283
Chhina, Ivar, 3150
Chi, Vivian, 665
Chia, Douglas K., 2048
Chiarelli, Peter W., 1736
Chiasera, August J., 2323
Chibe, Paul, 202
Chicago Board of Trade, 853
Chicago Charities, 187
Chicago Humanities Festival, 3474
Chicago Mercantile Exchange, Inc., 853
Chicago Sun-Times, Inc., 786
Chicago Title and Trust Co., 787
Chicago Tourism Fund, 3905
Chicago Tribune Co., 788
Chicago White Metal Casting Co., Inc., 789
Chick-fil-A, Inc., 791
Chickering, Marcelle J., 4026
Chico Pardo, Jaime, 1852
Chico, Heidi, 4098
Chicoine, David L., 2559
Chicopee Bancorp, Inc., 792
Chiddick, Gerald K., 177
Chido, Tom, 3758
Chidoni, Anthony, 1685
Chidsey, John W., 613
Chief Industries, Inc., 793
Chiefs Red Coat / Red Friday, 2091
Chilberg, C. Perry, 3245
Chilcote Co., The, 3689
Chilcote, David, 3689
Chilcote, David B., 3689
Child, Jeffrey B., 171
Child, Martha, 2346
Child, William F., IV, 761
Childress, Brad, 2530
Childs, Andrew, 2904
Childs, David, 849
Childs, George, 4160
Childs, Russell A., 3476
Childs, William F., IV, 761
Chiles, Joy, 2013
Chiles, Mark, 1956
Chilson, Mark, 690
Chilton, John, 3673
Chilton, Kevin P., 190
Chilton, Nelle Ratrie, 385
Chimahusky, Karen, 3099
Chiminski, John, 1134
Chin, Carolyn, 4109
Chin, Daniel, 1570
Chin, James V., 3232
Chinese Healing Institute, 794
Ching, Catherine H.Q., 2198
Ching, Christina, 42
Ching, Curtis, 3593
Ching, David T., 3310, 3765
Ching, Deborah, 723
Ching, Lawrence S.L., 2198
Ching, Meredith J., 85
Chinloy, Aida, 2640
Chinn, Timothy R., 4028
Chinsamy-Turan, Anusuya, 3893
Chinski, Arthur, 600
Chip, William, 3052
Chipman, Stephen, 1633
Chiquita Brands International, Inc., 795
Chirico, Emanuel, 1110, 1801, 3088
Chiricosta, Rick, 2448
Chironna, John, 2593
Chisholm, Robert A., 2084
Chiusano, Robert M., 4088
Chiusolo, Eric, 2449
Chizen, Bruce R., 2821, 3673
Chlebowski, John F., Jr., 1413, 2756
Chmielinski, Jane, 42
Cho, Yong Heung, 4114
Cho, Yong-Heung, 4114
Cho, Young-Chan, 1379

Choate, Chris A., 1556
Choate, Jerry D., 3915
Choggiung Ltd., 797
Choi, Audrey, 2570
Choi, Hank H., 3102
Choi, Hannah, 3102
Choi, Hyun Ho, 3102
Choi, Joe Y., 3102
Choi, Paul, 386
Choi, Roy, 2664
Choice Hotels International, Inc., 798
Chokachi, Susan, 1684
Choksi, Mary C., 299, 2808
Cholestech Corporation, 3074
Cholmondeley, Paula H.J., 1089, 3719
Cholnoky, I. John, 1558
Cholody, Larry, 4154
Chon, Gloria M., 2123
Chong, Arthur, 579
Chong, Rachael, 721
Chong, Wei-Li, 2177
Chookaszian, Dennis H., 853
Chopra, Deepak, 2460
Chopus, Kelly, 3908
Choquette, Paul J., Jr., 1581
Chorbajian, Herbert G., 2681
Chorey, William L., 470
Chornyei, Ernest J., Jr., 349
Choski, Umesh, 26
Chosy, James L., 3835
Chotin Group Corp., The, 799
Chotin, Robin, 799
Chotin, Steven B., 799
Chou, John G., 175
Chou, Priscilla, 637
Chouchani, Victor, 8
Chow, Henry W. K., 40
Chow, Hsichao, 947
Chow, Maria, 4007
Chow, William, 1256
Chow, Winston K.H., 1405
Chowdhry, Sheru, 1869
Chrestman, Flossie, 234
Chrin, John R., 271
Chrisman, Kenneth R., 1139
Chrisman, Lance, 4027
Chrisman, Lance R., 3541
Chriss, Jim, 3624
Christensen, Bill, 3793
Christensen, Christopher R., 1275
Christensen, David A., 1797
Christensen, Debra J., 3082
Christensen, Harold K., 15
Christensen, Hedy, 3687
Christensen, James M., 1651
Christensen, Kelley, 286
Christensen, Maren, 2649, 3893
Christensen, Robert J., 2850
Christensen, Roy E., 1275
Christensen, Sarah, 286
Christenson, Glenn C., 2765
Christenson, James, 2517
Christenson, James E., 2517
Christenson, Nancy K., 2441
Christenson, Norma, 2067
Christian, David A., 1150
Christian, Dick, 487
Christian, Fredric V., 491
Christian, Ronald E., 3925
Christiansen, Dale, 2714
Christiansen, Donald B., 306
Christiansen, Emil, Sr., 2797
Christiansen, Freddie, 2797
Christiansen, Freddy, 2797
Christiansen, Larry, 469
Christianson, Anton J., 1140
Christianson, Shawn M., 600
Christianson, Wei Sun, 2230
Christie Family Foundation, 2684
Christie, Tod S., 3381
Christjansen, Miranda, 2797
Christman, Daniel W., 3718
Christmas, George R., 3614
Christo, Stephen, 3824
Christon, Anthony C., 2015
Christopher, William T., 2262
Christopherson, Lisa A., 1764
Christopherson, Mark, 1227
Christy, John William, 2842
Christy, Stephen F., 2394
Chronis, Amy, 1070
Chrysler Corp., 801
Chrysler Group LLC, 801
CHS Inc., 802
Chu, Chinh E., 1134
Chu, J. Michael, 487
Chu, James, 3952
Chu, Michael, 3381
Chu, Roberta F., 1754
Chubb, Stephen D., 764
Chubb, Thomas C., III, 2847
Chudy, Thomas R., 3950
Chugach Alaska Corp., 805, 3694
Chugach Alaska Regional Corp., 805
Chugg, Juliana L., 3913
Chugh, Nalini, 2398
Chun, Grant Y.M., 85
Chun, Landon H. W., 668
Chun, Michael J., 342, 2404
Chun, Patrick, 1381
Chung, Kwang Hyun, 4114
Chungath, Jeffery, 3710
Churay, Daniel J., 2431
Churbuck, Thomas K., 3410
Church of Jesus Christ of LDS, 1538
Church, George M., 3453
Church, John R., 1554
Church, Ken E., 3517
Church, Steve A., 2179
Church, Steven A., 2179
Church, Sylvia, 3771
Churchill Downs Inc., 807
Churchill, Clinton R., 342
Churchill, Dwight D., 51
Churchill, Michelle, 3455
Churchwell, Don, 1846
Chwat, Anne, 1962
Chya, Mitch, 2797
Chyatte, Scott, 810
Chythlook, Joseph L., 576
Ciaccia, Peter, 2689
Cialone, Brenda Cook, 549
Ciampa, Dominick, 2682, 2683
Cianbro Corp., 808
Ciavarra, Christopher A., 966
Ciba Insurance Services, Inc., 809
Ciccarelli, Robert G., 2506
Ciccolo, Raymond J., 3954
Ciccone, J. A., 2406
Ciccone, Jennifer A., 2406
Cicconi, James W., 273
Cicero, Lisa B., 2350
Cichetti, Carl A., 3406
Cicio, Tony, 1030
Ciempa, Jason, 747
Cieutat, Barrett, 1292
Cigarran, Thomas, 2620
CIGNA Corp., 812
Ciliberto, Tricia, 2781
Cilio, Kellyann, 23
Cilio, Kimberly, 23
Cimerola, Patrick, 798
Cimino, Jay, 2298
Cimino, Mike, 2298
Cimral, John, 665
Cincinnati Enquirer, The, 1532
Cincinnati, New Orleans and Texas Pacific Railway Co., The, 2725
Cindrich, Robert J., 2610
Cinergy Foundation, 1189
Cink, Thomas M., 4026
Cinque, John, 1190
Cintani, Marilyn, 2360
Cintani, William R., 269, 2360, 2660
Ciochon, Alan W., 2492
Ciolek, Anne, 1232
Ciongoli, Adam G., 2281
Cipoletti, Bryan, 245
Cipriano, Carmela, 2183
Cipriano, Enio, 2380
Cipriano, Giovanna, 1459
Cipriano, Sandy, 3863
Ciprich, Paula M., 2628
Cirame, Graceann B., 1329
Ciraulo, John, 2398
Ciraulo, John F., 2398
CIRI, Inc., 934
Cirillo, A. C., Jr., 3
Cirillo, Mary, 3741
Cirone, John C., 3106
Cirujano, Jose Maria, 1904
Cischke, Susan M., 1464
Cisco Systems, Inc., 818
Cisiewski, Mary, 516
Ciskowski, Michael S., 3915
Cisnero, Claudia, 1236
Cistulli, Peter, 3192
Ciszewski, John, 1095, 1096, 2866
Citation Homes Central, 276
CITC, 934
CITGO Petroleum Corporation, 820
Citibank, N.A., 821, 2525
Citicorp, 821
Citigroup, 3190
Citigroup Inc., 821
Citigroup Venture Capital Ltd., 821
Citizens Bank, 947
Citizens Bank Mid-Atlantic Charitable Foundation, The, 3137
Citizens Bank of Rhode Island, 3137
Citizens Bank, N.A., 827
Citizens Banking Co., 827
Citizens Charitable Foundation, 3137
Citizens Financial Bank, 756
Citizens First National Bank Foundation, 825
Citizens Helping Citizens Fund, 756
Citizens National Bank, 826
Citizens National Bank of Evans City, PA, 2706
Citizens Savings Bank, 3137
Citizens Savings Bank, SSB, 385
Citizens State Bank, 828
Citizens Trust Co., 3137
Citizens Union Bank, 350
Citrino, Mary Anne, 1145
Citrone, Neil, 853
City Carton Co. Inc., 829
City National Bank, 3474
Ciuffetelli, Vincent, 3554
Ciupak, Susan M., 1360
Civello, Anthony N., 2622
Civgin, Don, 107
Civiello, Catheen, 1620
Civiello, Cathleen, 1620
Civitella, Michael J., 1603
CJT Enterprises, Inc., 3445
Clabaugh, Sandra, 896
Claflin, Bruce L., 40
Claiborne Inc., Liz, 1376
Claiborne, Catherine H., 3891
Clair, Mark, 3719
Clanachan, David F., 3753
Clancey, John P., 65
Clancy, Brenda K., 45
Clancy, Mary Anne, 1946
Clancy, Maureen E., 2682, 2683
Clancy, Paul, 465
Clancy, Paul J., 465
Clancy, Thomas L., Jr., 334
Clanon, Paul, 2853
Clanton, B. Shane, 901
Clapp Irrevocable Trust, Mary Lee, 2211
Clapp, Dale S., 2344
Clapp, S. Daniel, 3431
Clapper, David, 3576
Clapper, Kellie, 3591
Clappison, John H., 3643
CLARCOR Inc., 832
Clardy, Amanda, 2268
Clare, Dan, 1690
Clare, Jack, 1191
Clare, Peter, 525
Clare, Peter J., 3410
Claremont Savings Bank, 833
Clarey, Patricia, 1766
Clark Associates, Inc., 662
Clark Electric Appliance & Satellite, 835
Clark, Alan, 2523
Clark, Allen O., 1576
Clark, Barry, 2359
Clark, Bonnie, 2964
Clark, Candace A., 2088
Clark, Carol, 1748
Clark, Celeste A., 2120, 2443
Clark, Christopher T., 1089
Clark, Dan, 1418
Clark, Darlene, 2138
Clark, David W., 2333
Clark, Del, 2200
Clark, Dennis, 4084
Clark, Donald L., 1419
Clark, Elizabeth A., 662
Clark, Etta, 1213
Clark, Eugene, 2923
Clark, Frank, 1309
Clark, Frank M., 48
Clark, Fred E., 662
Clark, Gene, 2923
Clark, Henry A., III, 3516
Clark, Ian T., 1549
Clark, J. Coley, 2558
Clark, J. Mark, 2009
Clark, Jane B., 2563
Clark, Janet F., 1068, 2363, 2364
Clark, Joe, 3557
Clark, John, 72, 3628
Clark, Jonathan, 2659
Clark, Karen A., 1167
Clark, Kelly P. W., 1835
Clark, Kevin P., 1071
Clark, Kristen, 1772
Clark, Linda A., 937
Clark, Linda Ann, 937
Clark, M., 662
Clark, Marcella S., 3488

Clark, Margaret, 663
Clark, Mark T., 1424
Clark, Matthew J., 235
Clark, Maxine, 608, 1459
Clark, Midge, 388
Clark, Murray W., 2734
Clark, Paul N., 56
Clark, R. Kerry, 304, 376, 1554, 3731
Clark, Ralph W., 2246
Clark, Randall L., 3405
Clark, Richard T., 291, 945, 2466
Clark, Robert C., 3757
Clark, Robert Charles, 2808
Clark, Robert J., 576
Clark, Robert W., 3433
Clark, Ronald K., 3018
Clark, Sattie, 1243
Clark, Stephen L., 1981
Clark, Susan F., 2765
Clark, Thomas F., 2348
Clark, Timothy J., 479
Clark, Tony, 2346
Clark, Vernon E., 3135
Clark, W. Edmund, 3696
Clark-Morey, Timothy, 2143
Clarke Environmental Mosquito Management, Inc., 837
Clarke, Brian, 446
Clarke, Carolyn, 2321
Clarke, Charles, 3802
Clarke, Charles J., 3802
Clarke, F. David, III, 3576
Clarke, Glenn, 2541
Clarke, Hubert P., 2909
Clarke, J. Dwaine, 2141
Clarke, J. Lyell, III, 837
Clarke, James J., Jr., 139
Clarke, Janet M., 1541
Clarke, Janet Morrison, 959
Clarke, Jeffrey W., 1068
Clarke, John C., 2124
Clarke, John L., III, 837
Clarke, Lois A., 3864
Clarke, Mark, 1228
Clarke, Mary Kemp, 837
Clarke, Mary Rob, 837
Clarke, Michael A., 3108
Clarke, Peter J., 2737
Clarke, Robert L., 2607, 3606
Clarke, Sheilagh M., 1459
Clarke, Theodore J., 937
Clarke, Thomas E., 2694, 3589
Clarke, Troy, 2647
Clarkeson, John S., 642, 2737
Clarks Companies, N.A., The, 838
Clarkson, Rich, 2711
Claro, Cesar J., 2683
Clasby, Daniel E., 3317
Clason, Bob, 1466
Classen, Peter K., 2997
Classic Leather, Inc., 840
Classon, Rolf A., 1804
Claude, Bernard, 3778
Clausen, Douglas E., 3912
Clausen, Douglas J., 3912
Clausen, Joanie S., 3912
Clausen, John, 1080
Clausen, Patricia A., 2745
Clauser, Ruth, 3650
Claussen, W. Henry, 345
Clavette, Alan C., 2704
Clavette, Alan J., 2704
Clavins, Vicki, 316
Clawson, Grant, 923
Claxton, Robert, 460
Clay, James, 4047
Clay, James R., 4047
Clayton, Annette K., 2999
Clayton, Bret K., 3029
Clayton, Gretchen, 1603
Clayton, James A., 1430
Clayton, James H., 1347
Clayton, Janet, 1228
Clayton, Kevin T., 841, 3281
Clayton, Mandy, 3726
Clayton, Melissa Ann, 3341
CLD Investments, Ltd., 635
Clear Channel Communications, Inc., 842
Cleary, James J., 1239
Cleary, John F., 806
Cleary, Kevin, 848
Cleberg, Anthony S., 474
Clecak, Vivian, 655
Clegg, Jackie, 853
Clemence, Richard R., 1103
Clemens Markets, Inc., 844
Clemens, Abram S., 844
Clemens, Jack S., 844
Clemens, James C., 844
Clemens, Jill, 844
Clemens, Lillian H., 844
Clemens, Mark, 844
Clemens, Paul F., 1413
Clement, Cristi, 2914
Clemente, C. L., 2950
Clements Foods Co., 845
Clements, Edward B., 845
Clements, Michelle, 3150
Clements, Richard, 845
Clements, Richard H., 845
Clements, Richard L., 845
Clements, Robert H., 845
Clemmens, Daniel L., 1800
Clemmer, Dennis, 2732
Clemmer, Dennis M., 2732
Clemmer, Richard L., 2650
Clemmons, Mark, 2886
Clemons, Scott, 589
Clemons, Sheila, 507
Clendening, John, 3363
Clerico, John A., 900
Cleveland Electric Illuminating Co., The, 1424
Cleveland Indians Baseball Co., Inc., 847
Cleveland, Cotton M., 2629, 2737
Cleveland, Joseph R., 4077
Cleveland, Levi, 2615
Cleveland-Cliffs Inc., 850
Cleverly, A. Bruce, 708
Click, Betty J., 871
Click, Kevin, 2962
Clif Bar & Co., 848
Clifford Chance US LLP, 849
Clifford, James, 1064
Clifford, John P., Jr., 3802
Clifford, Leigh, 395
Clifford, William J., 2923
Cliffs Natural Resources, 850
Clifton Forge-Waynesboro Telephone Co., 2758
Clifton, Mitch, 2730
Clifton, Steven E., 1765
Climie, Judith, 3375
Climie, Judith A., 3375
Cline, Claudia, 933
Cline, Jerry D., 2622
Cline, Michael W., 2094
Clinton Savings Bank, 851
Clinton, Amanda, 131
Clinton, Chelsea, 1903
Cloninger, Charles A., 4096
Cloninger, Kriss, III, 54, 3821
Cloonan, Brian, 3072
Clopton, Nancy, 885
Clorox Co., The, 852
Close, Kristi A., 2929
Close, Stephen P., 1149
Closing Network, The, 3041
Clositers Donations, The, 1236
Clossin, Todd, 1377
Closson, Steven A., 199
Clothier, Brad, 1074
Clothier, Kevin C., 988
Clothier, Sharon R., 2964
Cloud, Robert J., 3500
Cloud, Sanford, Jr., 2737
Cloud, Walter J., 3500
Cloudt, William, 885
Cloudt, William J., 885
Clough, Charles I., Jr., 2265
Clough, Ian D., 1106
Clough, Joseph, 4160
Clouser, Dennis R., 521
Cloverdale Equipment Co., 366
Cloyd, Mary Ann, 3042
Clubb, Susan, 2104
Cluster, Darryl, 148
Clydesdale, Fergus M., 3408
CME Advisory Services, Inc., 3265
Cmiel, David F., 1673
CMP Media Inc., 3863
CMP Media, LLC, 3863
CMP Publications, Inc., 3863
CMRCC, Inc., 2071
CMS Energy Corp., 854
CMW Inc., 2027
CNA Financial Corp., 855
Coach, Inc., 858
Coady, Roxanne J., 1419
Coan, Gaylord O., 1922
Coastal Wholesale, Inc., 699
Coate, Ronald D., 3803
Coates, David R., 2633
Coates, Pamela, 1287
Coates, Pattie, 3269
Coates, Ramsey, 4049
Coats American Inc., 860
Coats, Sam, 3727
Coba, Tony, 1767
Cobb, Alice A., 2765
Cobb, D. Keith, 101
Cobb, Janelle, 3751
Cobb, John D., 3931
Cobb, Kevin W., 1555
Cobb, Pat, 1679
Cobb, Terry B., 3698
Cobb, William, 3485
Cobb, William C., 1695
Cobb, William R., 3485
Coben, Lawrence S., 2756
Cobian, Darlene M., 564
Coburn, Craig C., 3206
Coburn, John, 2710
Coburn, John F., III, 2710
Coburn, Q.J., 2650
Coca Cola Bottling Company NY, 1186
Coca-Cola, 2112
Coca-Cola Co., The, 862
Coca-Cola Company/Coca-Cola Enterprises, The, 2622
Coca-Cola Enterprises Inc., 863
CocaCola, 185
Cochenour, David, 1499
Cochran, J. Guyton, Jr., 3527
Cochran, John R., 1425
Cochran, Kenneth D., 231
Cochran, Mark, 2417
Cochran, Patricia, 2446
Cochran, Paula, 1235
Cochran, Phyllis E., 2580
Cochran, Rick, 2067
Cochran, Sandra B., 966, 1143
Cochrane, Charles G., 3192
Cochrane, Luther P., 176
Cocklin, Kim, 285
Cocklin, Kim R., 285
Cockrell, Matt, 3980
Cocroft, Duncan H., 3964
Coder, Gary, 626
Coder, Stacie A., 2388
Codey, Lawrence R., 1863, 3381
Codina, Armando, 1842
Codina, Armando M., 187
Cody, James R., 1737
Cody, John E., 1532
Cody, Thomas G., 2790
Cody, William M., 3057
Coe, Jonathan, 2952
Coe, Vicki, 2110
Coel, Kevin S., 903
Coelho, Anthony L., 3413
Coen, Beverly J., 2723
Coen, Bill, 2486
Coes, Putnam, 2582
Cofer, Cathy, 1875
Coffey, Connie, 1556
Coffey, John F., 2335
Coffin, Gregory R., 2332
Coffman, Casey, 1023, 3729
Coffman, Michael W., 3433
Coffman, Vance D., 3, 182, 1061
Cofield, Bernita P., 3582
Cofield, Charles, 3582
Cofield, Charles D., 3582
Cofield, Ronald M., 3042
Cogan, Andrew B., 170, 2176
Cogan, John F., 1582
Cogen, Jeff, 1023, 2620
Coggia, Brandi, 4090
Coggin, Michael S., 2270
Coggins, John, 2137
Coggins, John J., 2137
Coghill, Craig, 1458
Coghlan, Alicia, 578
Coghlin Construction Services, Inc., 865
Coghlin Cos., Inc., 864
Coghlin Electrical Contractors Inc., 865
Coghlin, Christopher, 864
Coghlin, Edwin B., Jr., 865
Coghlin, James W., 864
Coghlin, James W., Jr., 864
Coghlin, James W., Sr., 864
Cognetti, Richard, 2162
Cognis Corp., 368
Cogswell-Wojtecki, Lourdes, 2654
Cohan, Angela, 728
Cohasset Ltd., 2409
Cohen Family Foundation, Inc., The, 1383
Cohen, Abraham, 1342
Cohen, Albert, 1342
Cohen, Babette Goodman, 1610
Cohen, Bennett, 409
Cohen, Betsy Z., 48

Cohen, Brian, 2401
Cohen, Burton M., 2489
Cohen, Dan, 1126
Cohen, David, 3601
Cohen, David L., 887
Cohen, Debra L., 3998
Cohen, Dennis, 964
Cohen, Douglas A., 590
Cohen, Eileen Phillips, 2636
Cohen, Eileen R., 2630
Cohen, Eric I., 3719
Cohen, Erle, 1539
Cohen, Gray M., 2943
Cohen, H. Rodgin, 3634
Cohen, Harold M., 50
Cohen, Irwin, 3659
Cohen, Jeffrey, 724
Cohen, Jon S., 3490
Cohen, Jonathan, 1610
Cohen, Jonathan Goodman, 1610
Cohen, K. P., 1315
Cohen, Larry, 2596
Cohen, Lyor, 3990
Cohen, Marshall, 1589
Cohen, Martin J., 3732
Cohen, Maryjo R., 2636
Cohen, Michele L., 2512
Cohen, Mitch, 1191
Cohen, Moshe, 1342
Cohen, Murray, 1072
Cohen, Raymond, 1342
Cohen, Richard B., 634
Cohen, Rick, 634
Cohen, Robert L., 1917
Cohen, Robert S., 915
Cohen, Roberta, 1072
Cohen, Ross N., 1748
Cohen, Stephen J., 3050
Cohen, Steve, 1407
Cohen, Steven A., 1859
Cohen, Suzanne, 3050
Cohen, William C., Jr., 1917
Cohen, William S., 727
Cohen, Zach, 2100
Cohenour, Bruce R., 372
Cohn & Co., J.H., 866
Cohn, Douglas, 3794
Cohn, Gary D., 1603, 1604
Cohn, John D., 4112
Cohn, Mary Louise, 2310
Cohoes Savings Bank, 1419
Cohon, Jared L., 344, 2258
Cohrs, Torben, 650
Coia, Gerald D., 1210
Coile, Jon, 2482
Coker, Robert, 3878
Coker, Robert E., 3878
Colaianne, Melonie B., 2393
Colalillo, Joseph S., 3979
Colangelo, Jerry, 2968
Colangelo, Ron, 1097
Colaruotolo, Frank D., 1419
Colas, Gilles, 3312
Colasacco, Domenic, 2873
Colatrella, Brenda D., 2466
Colavita, Michael J., 3650
Colberg, Alan B., 266
Colberg, Stig, 934
Colberg-Nelissen, Alexis, 3397
Colbert, Celia A., 2466
Colbert, Marie, 1773
Colbert, Thomas W., 897
Colbert, Virgis W., 340, 1809, 2304, 3579
Colburn, Keith W., 917
Colburn, Martin, 2396
Cole Haan Holdings, Inc., 867
Cole National Foundation, 2319
Cole Productions, Kenneth, Inc., 2128
Cole, Alan D., 1855
Cole, Billy, 1567
Cole, Christine B., 2847
Cole, David, 1088
Cole, Jason, 9
Cole, John P., Jr., 2263
Cole, Kenneth D., 2128
Cole, Mandy, 2290
Cole, Michael H., 3487
Cole, Michael R., 3890
Cole, Norborne P., Jr., 2876
Cole, Paulette, 16
Cole, Richard A., 1640
Cole, Richard J., 1729
Cole, Richard R., 2241
Cole, Robert A., 3554
Cole, Sue W., 2391
Cole, Thomas L., 2333
Cole, Timothy A., 1065
Coleman, Barbara, 2573
Coleman, Barbara Bell, 1863
Coleman, C. Joseph, 1479
Coleman, Dan C., 500
Coleman, Deborah A., 3673
Coleman, Dorothy, 1972
Coleman, J. Edward, 2258, 3859
Coleman, James E., 1529
Coleman, James J., Jr., 1972
Coleman, James J., Sr., 1972
Coleman, Jonathan D., 2024
Coleman, Julie, 3902
Coleman, Kristin M., 595
Coleman, Leonard S., 299, 1242
Coleman, Leonard S., Jr., 807, 2808
Coleman, Lewis, 2744
Coleman, Lewis W., 1172
Coleman, Mary Sue, 2048, 2471
Coleman, Michael J., 1089
Coleman, Russell F., 406
Coleman, Scott, 1184
Coleman, Susan E., 3738
Coleman, Thomas B., 1972
Coleman, William T., III, 3377
Coles, Tom, 2299
Coletti, Julie, 2452
Coley, Bill G., 2242
Coley, Britt, 1283
Coley, Dottie, 2242
Coley, Malcomb D., 1293
Coley, Norman, 2242
Coley, William A., 2907
Colgan, Diane, 3774
Colgate Investments, 2169
Colgate-Palmolive Co. Consumer Products Division, 2622
Colin, Robert L., 567
Colina, Alonso, 1266
Colinear, Janine, 1799
Colisto, Nicholas R., 4139
Coll, J. Peter, 2826
Collar, Michael P., 3727
Collat, Charles A., 2412
Collat, Charles A., Jr., 2412
Collat, Charles A., Sr., 2412
Collato, Richard A., 4011
College of Creative Studies, 3474
Coller, Andrea, 3142
Coller, Jim, 335
Colleran, Lisa, 2156
Collett, James R., Jr., 432
Collett, William C., 1174
Collette Travel Service, Inc., 872
Colley, James, 520
Collier, Brice, 2678
Collier, Chancelen, 3397
Collier, Chris, 1437
Collier, Christopher, 1437
Collier, Crystal, 3397
Collier, Kathryn J., 3405
Collier, Kim, 3397
Collier, M. H., 722
Collier, Scott, 166
Collier, W.R., 166
Colligan, Thomas J., 856, 2785
Collin, Mark H., 3885
Collins Development Corp., 873
Collins, Arthur D., Jr., 82, 516, 691, 3835
Collins, Atwood, III, 2323
Collins, Betty L., 1944
Collins, Bruce, 2625
Collins, Christine, 694
Collins, David, 2250
Collins, Dennis, 2112
Collins, Duff, 4109
Collins, Eileen M., 3873
Collins, Harry A., 873
Collins, John, 499, 2631
Collins, John F., 2497
Collins, Joseph J., 887
Collins, Karen Jones, 1390
Collins, Keith L., 1940
Collins, M. James, 1083
Collins, Mark, 396
Collins, Michael, 3150, 3384
Collins, Michael G., 2536
Collins, R. Duff, 4109
Collins, Rebecca L., 1946
Collins, Rick, 848
Collins, Steve, 2648
Collins, Timothy C., 3219
Collins, Tom, 2136
Collins, William, 1839
Collins, William C., 774
Collins, William M., 715
Collinson, Jan, 3673
Collis, Steven H., 175
Collomb, Bertrand P., 1184
Collopy, John F., 3408
Colloredo-Mansfeld, Franz F., 1581
Colman, Wes, 2710
Colombo, William J., 1110
Colonial Oil Industries, Inc., 875
Colonial Properties, 3315
Colonias, Karen, 3461
Colonis, Harry, 772
Colorado State Bank and Trust, 880
Colorado Steel Contractors, 1344
Colorado Steel Systems, 1344
Colosi, Michael F., 2128
Colpitts, Guthrie S., 1488
Colpo, Charles C., 2841
Colt Investments, Inc., 881
Colt, Inc., The, 1450
Colt, Mack V., 881
Colt, Sara C., 881
Colten, Marsha L., 915
Colter, Gary F., 2844
Columbia Cleaning, 1431
Columbia Energy Group, 2715
Columbia Financial Inc., 882
Columbia Gas of Ohio, Inc., 2715
Columbia Gas System, Inc., The, 2715
Columbia/HCA Healthcare Corp., 1762
Columbine Cody Corp., 2215
Columbus Bank & Trust Co., 3674
Columbus Electric Cooperative, Inc., 885
Columbus Life Insurance Co., 4040
Columbus Southern Power Co., 141
Colvin, Greyson, 1340
Colvin, John B., 3105
Colvin, Robert E., 1225
Colvin, Stephen, 2703
Colvin, Terry R., 3167
Colwell, Scott, 710
Colwin, Dawn, 2503
Colwin, Joseph P., 2503
Comar, Terrence R., 1078
Comas, Daniel L., 1027
Comb, David, 2670
Combret, Francois Polge de, 423
Combs, Donald G., 2670
Combs, Katherine, 1309
Combs, Sean John "Diddy", 30
Combs, Sue, 1833
Combs, Timothy, 3133
Comcast CICG, LP, 887
Comcast QVC, Inc., 887
Comcast-Spectator, 888
Comeau, Douglas W., 2763
Comeau, Paul R., 1820
Comer, James P., 2659
Comer, Stephen, 2978
Comer, Stephen C., 3524
Comerica Bank, 889, 1711, 2393
Comerica Inc., 889
Cominsky, Steve, 3238
Comm, Harry, 1716
Comma, Lenny, 2007
Commanditer Finance, Ltd., 3125
Commerce Bancorp, Inc., 3696
Commerce Bancshares, Inc., 890
Commerce Construction, 2343
Commercial Bank, 891
Commercial Bank of Grayson, The, 891
Commercial Brick Corp., 892
Commercial Federal Bank, FSB, 346
Commercial Stainless, Inc., 662
Commes, Thomas A., 219
Commisso, Rocco, 2625
Communication Products Inc., 896
Communication Technology Services, LLC, 2672
Community Bancshares of Mississippi, Inc., 897
Community Bank of Texas, 136
Community Bank, N.A., 898
Community Foundation for the National Capital Region, The, 3478
Community Foundation of St. Joseph County, 3697
Community Health Systems, 900
Community Service Foundation, 1116
Como, Robert L., 2681
Companion Healthcare Corp., 498
Companion, Lydia, 321
Compass Bank, 901
Comper, Tony, 3540
Compton Family Trust, 3327
Compton, H. Ray, 1145
Compton, Jeffrey B., 523
Compton, Jen, 537
Compton, John C., 1406
Compton, Ken, 1576
Compton, Kevin, 1737
Compton, Lisa, 826
Compton, Michael, 2982

Compton, Randy, 2982
Compton, Walter K., 2600
Compton-Barone, Cindy, 4127
Comstock, Edward R., 3161
Comstock, Elizabeth J., 2710
Comstock, Jerry, 613
ConAgra Foods, Inc., 904
ConAgra, Inc., 904
Conant, Catherine, 3165
Conant, David M., 3165
Conant, Doglas R., 305
Conant, Douglas R., 175, 305
Conant, Nancy, 3903
Conard, Edward, 4003
Conaty, William J., 1612
Concannon, Chris, 2618
Concepcion, Lisa, 344
Concept Mining, Inc., 905
Concilio, Rose, 3653
Concorde Group Corp., 1177
Condioti, Steve, 2316
Condiotti, Steve, 2316
Condit, Richard, 3648
Conditioned Air Systems, Inc., 906
Condon, Daniel J., 3577
Condon, Donald Marion, Jr., 2355
Condon, Freeman J., 1946
Condon, Patrick J., 3272
Condon, Thomas J., 677
Condon, Tom, 2168
Condos, George M., 228
Condron, P. Kevin, 1724, 3696
Cone Mills Corp., 907
Cone, Carol A., 2394
Conefry, John J., Jr., 271
Conely, Chris W., 1548
Conerly, Tracy T., 337
Cones, Patty, 2169
Confer, David R., 4103
Conforti, Thomas G., 4132
Confranceso, Elaine R., 48
Conigliaro, Laura, 1068
Conine, C.Kent, 1347
Conish, Mark G., 3693
Conklin, Laura J., 32
Conklin, Michael, 2926
Conklin, Ronald, 2159
Conklin, Tom, 2178
Conlee, Robert, 2692
Conley, Barbara, 1394
Conley, Gregory A., 3708
Conley, Joan C., 2617, 2618
Conley, Kari, 2824
Conley, Mike, 1857
Conley, Renae, 1279
Conley, Renea, 1279
Conlin, Jan M., 3232
Conlin, Kelly, 3374
Conlin, Kelly P., 3374
Conlin, Kevin P., 1863
Conlin, Mark J., 4136
Conlon, James J., 338
Conn Appliances, Inc., 908
Conn, C., 908
Conn, W. Lance, 765
Connair, Thomas, 833
Connair, Thomas P., 833
Connally, Stan, 1689
Connaughton, James L., 1309
Connaughton, John, 1762
Connecticut Attorneys Title Insurance Co., 910
Connecticut Bank and Trust Co., The, 428
Connecticut Light and Power Co., The, 2737
Connecticut Natural Gas Corp., 912
Connell, Hope H., 3515
Connell, Hope Holding, 1396, 3515
Connell, Mark, 298
Connell, Richard F., 3399
Connell, Wayne, 744
Connell, William J., 1187
Connelly, Arthur R., 3512
Connelly, Deirdre P., 2333
Connelly, Diedre P., 1588
Connelly, Jeffery A., 1265
Connelly, Jeffrey A., 1265
Connelly, Patricia D., 1946
Connelly, Peter, 2246
Connelly, Renee, 2344
Connelly, Serena Simmons, 928
Connelly, Thomas M., Jr., 1184
Conner, Carol L., 3184
Conner, Deborah L., 3184
Conner, Joseph L., 3172
Conner, Kimberly S., 3184
Conner, Marjorie L., 1035
Conner, Richard H., Jr., 2674
Conner, Samuel R., 3184
Conner, Terry, 1083
Conner, Terry W., 1759
Conners, Maureen, 1059
Conney, Matthew T., Jr., 3031
Connolly, Brian M., 502
Connolly, Landon, 740
Connolly, Michael W., 3750
Connolly, Pat, 4079
Connolly, Patrick, 4079
Connolly, Paul M., 1209
Connolly, Scott, 3068
Connolly, Sean, 1809
Connolly, Tim, 1651
Connor, Christopher M., 1216, 3437
Connor, Denis, 1149
Connor, Frank T., 3731
Connor, Geoffrey M., 3069
Connor, James T., 412
Connor, Josh, 2570
Connor, Martin P., 3769
Connor, Rod, 3294
Connor, W. Robert, 1588
Connors, Colleen, 496
Connors, Holly A., 851
Connors, John G., 2710
Connors, John M., Jr., 956, 1747
Connors, John P., Jr., 2741
Connors, Michael P., 1213
Connors, Nelda J., 540
Connors, Patrick, 3619
Connors, Robert R., 1410
Connors, William, 388, 887
Connstep, Inc., 1953
ConocoPhillips Co., 913
Cononelos, Louis J., 2127
Conover, Robert V., 2144
Conrad, Andrew J., 1141
Conrad, Caryn, 628
Conrad, Christine, 199
Conrad, Deborah S., 1950
Conrad, Katie, 2410
Conrad, Ken, 2638
Conrad, Peter J., 1271
Conrad, Phillip G., 1257
Conrades, George, 68
Conrades, George H., 68, 1732, 2821
Conradi, Charles R., 852
Conrail Inc., 914
Conroy, Don, 420
Conroy, Kevin, 2694
Conroy, Michael H., 3237
Consell, Dominique, 295
Consi, Anthony J., II, 2909
Considine, Jill M., 1974
Considine, Terry, 1980
Conslato, Laurie, 2980
Consoli, Bill, 3569
Consolidated Electrical Distributors, Inc., 917
Consolidated Natural Gas Co., 1150
Consolidated Supermarket Supply, 2192
Consolidated Systems, Inc., 918
Constable, David E., 1448
Constant, Guy, 572
Constantakis, Nicholas P., 323
Constellation Energy Group, Inc., 1309
Conston, Charles, 920
Conston, Elizabeth, 920
Conston, Inc., 920
Conston, Shirley, 920
Conston, Stuart, 920
Construction Assocs., 749
Constructors, Inc., 2653
Consumers Energy Co., 921
Consumers Power Co., 921
Conte, Cynthia, 4126
Conte, Nicholas C., 4111
Contero, Enrique A., 2274
Conti, Anthony, 181
Conti, Emanuele A., 1190
Conti, Fulvio, 210
Conti, Philip P., 1287
ContiGroup Cos., Inc., 926
Continental Can Co., Inc., 915
Continental Development Corporation, 922
Continental Divide Electric Cooperative, Inc., 923
Continental Electric Construction Co., 924
Continental Food Mgmt., 925
Continental General Tire, Inc., 927
Continental Grain Co., 926
Continental Tire North America, Inc., 927
Continental Western Insurance Company, 426
Contran Corp., 928
Control Air Conditioning Corp., 929
Control Assemblies Co., 3119
Control Systems International, Inc., 930
Convalescent Services, Inc., 931
Convergys Corp., 933
Convery, Edward P., 1988
Convery, Joseph, 1514
Convery, Tim, 476
Conway, Chip, 2906
Conway, Chris, 832
Conway, Christopher L., 832
Conway, Craig, 3318
Conway, Craig A., 40
Conway, James T., 3731
Conway, James V., 452
Conway, John W., 988, 3026
Conway, Karen, 3902
Conway, Kellyanne E., 1201
Conway, Kevin, 3990
Conway, Kevin J., 1635
Conway, Marian, 2683
Conway, Mike, 452
Conway, Paul D., 691
Conway, R. Stan, 2343
Conway, Ronald J., 914
Conway, William S., 2605
Conwood Co., 165
Conyers, Howard, 3978
Coogan, J. Jerome, 577
Cook Living Trust, Charles and Dorothy, 898
Cook Residuary Trust, Charles and Dorothy, 898
Cook, Amy D., 679
Cook, Brian J., 3905
Cook, Caren, 278, 279
Cook, Charles D., 1395
Cook, Charles E., 898
Cook, Chris, 2603
Cook, Christopher D., 2603
Cook, Donald G., 970
Cook, E. Gary, 2310
Cook, Errol M., 2808
Cook, Garry, 2031
Cook, Ian M., 869, 2935
Cook, J. Michael, 887, 1962
Cook, Jennifer, 2392
Cook, Jill E., 1007
Cook, John, 76
Cook, John D., 592
Cook, John R., 2968
Cook, Linda Z., 516, 2106
Cook, Linda Zarda, 691, 2364
Cook, Marvin, 3523
Cook, Paul T., 1951
Cook, Ralph D., 71
Cook, Randall, 41
Cook, Scott D., 1217, 1982, 3055
Cook, Stephen B., 3158
Cook, Steven M., 3083
Cook, Susan J., 1216
Cook, Timothy, 217
Cook, Timothy D., 2710
Cook, Vince, 1627
Cook, William M., 1153, 3920
Cook, William R., 3093, 3707
Cook, Yvonne, 1799
Cooke, Kenneth L., 2216
Cookson, David S., 246
Cooley, Charles P., 2544
Cooley, John L., 588
Cooley, Shrair, Labovitz, 461
Coolidge, E. David, 478
Coolidge, E. David, III, 478
Coolley, William A., 2300
Coombs, Ron, 2044
Coomes, Michelle, 1552
Coon, Ken, 1438
Coon, Marcia M., 2468
Coonan, Cathleen E., 865
Coonelly, Frank, 2985
Cooney, Ed, 2333
Cooney, Edward J., 1581
Cooney, Kevin, 4137
Cooney, Wallace R., 3999
Coons, Margaret M., 1863
Coons, Nancy B., 520
Coopan, Ramachandrian, 3329
Cooper Industries, Inc., 935
Cooper Tire & Rubber Co., 936
Cooper, Aaron, 611
Cooper, Adam, 1095
Cooper, Alan S., 775
Cooper, Barbra, 3784
Cooper, Barry, 1400
Cooper, Cindy, 2088
Cooper, Coyte, 2797
Cooper, David J., Sr., 71, 3171
Cooper, Edward S., 1926

Cooper, Ellen, 2281
Cooper, Garrett W., 588
Cooper, Gary, 3832, 3839
Cooper, Gayle M., 3668
Cooper, James A., 1393
Cooper, Jane, 1790
Cooper, Janet K., 3775
Cooper, Janet Linden, 2608
Cooper, Kathleen B., 4077
Cooper, Larry, 3843
Cooper, Lewis, 3259
Cooper, Nancy E., 2580
Cooper, Patrick, 3950
Cooper, Rochelle L., 3874
Cooper, Steven, 1716
Cooper, Thomas P., 2154
Cooper, William A., 3695
Cooper, Yvonne, 3980
Cooper-Boyer, Karen, 1088
Cooperating for food safety, Inc., 548
Cooperrider, Keith, 2701
Coor, Lattie F., 500
Coors, Jeffrey H., 1635
Coors, Peter H., 1272, 2523, 2549
Coors-Ficeli, Christein, 2549
Cope, Andrew, 4092
Cope, Bruce, 1889
Cope, Glen, 2486
Copelan, Ann H., 2930
Copelan, Jesse, 2930
Copeland, Abby, 3940
Copeland, James E., Jr., 913, 3755
Copeland, Jananne A., 722
Copeland, Jr., James E., 1288
Copeland, Margot James, 2136
Copeland, Mark G., 2743
Copeland, Michael, 1326
Copeland, Mike, 1326
Copeland, Sean, 3622
Copenhaver, Don, 2486
COPIC Insurance Company, 937
Copley Press Inc., The, 938
Copley, David C., 938
Copley, Helen K., 938
Copple, Robert D., 815
Coppola, Michael P., 3192
Coquille Economic Development Corp., 939
Coral Chemical Co., 940
Coral International, Inc., 940
Corbacho, Marc, 2462
Corbat, Michael L., 821
Corbeil, Charles F., 1738
Corbet, Kathleen A., 2397
Corbett, Luke R., 190
Corbett, Roger Campbell, 3980
Corbett, S. Mark, 1647
Corbin, Anderw C., 495
Corbin, Andrew C., 495
Corbin, Jerry E., 1947
Corbin, Larry C., 1300
Corbin, William R., 903
Corbin-Teora, Kitty, 3405
Corcoran, Bob, 2649
Corcoran, Mark T., 52
Corcoran, Robert L., 1552
Corcoran, Thomas A., 1548
Corcoran, Timothy J., 2639
Corcoran, William M., 1623
Cordani, David M., 812
Cordano, Michael D., 4042
Cordeiro, Carlos, 455
Cordeiro, Eduardo E., 642, 1449
Cordero, Abel, 644
Cordes, James F., 141
Cordova, France A., 1228, 3311
Cordova, Francis, 705
Cordova, Leo C., 3496
Cordova, Lu M., 2094
Cordova, Lucas, Jr., 2034
Cordy, Scott L., 3936
CORE Construction Services of Illinois, Inc., 941
Corea, Betsi, 3383
Corea, Betsi A., 3383
Coremin, Scott, 1847
CoreStates Financial Corp, 4028
Corey, Allen, 3238
Coriell, Fred, 3940
Coriz, Elias, 2034
Corkery, Ann M., 1201
Corkrean, John J., 1220
Corless, Gary, 3074
Corless, Gary A., 3074
Corlett, Glenn E., 1631, 3032
Cornelio, Charles C., 2281
Cornelison, Albert O., Jr., 1706
Cornelius, James M., 578, 2443
Cornelius, Ken, 3448
Cornelius, Marcia, 3031
Cornelius, Sigmund, 4044
Cornelius, Sigmund L., 2715, 3904
Cornell, Alison A., 955
Cornell, Brian, 2999
Cornely, William G., 1149
Cornerstone Bank, N.A., 942, 943
Cornerstone Winter Park Holdings, LLC, 944
Corning Inc., 945
Cornish, Charlie, 2991
Cornish, Mark, 260
Cornish, Peter, 3940
Cornwell, Darwyn, 25
Cornwell, Diane, 894
Cornwell, W. Don, 156, 305, 2950
Coronado, William J., 3891
Correnti, John D., 2647
Corrie, Steve, 3393
Corrigan, Fredric W., 4135
Corrigan, Mark H., 999
Corriher, Jon, 1458
Corry Savings Bank, 2746
Corso, Cliff, 2416
Corso, Clifford D., 2416
Cort, Arthur H., 3812
Cort, Clifford, 3812
Cort, Glenn, 3812
Cort, Glenn A., 3812
Cort, Jack, 3812
Cort, Ronald, 3812
Cortese, Denis A., 754
Cortez, Daniel, 820
Corti, Robert J., 30, 305
Cortinas, Dora, 572
Corvallis Clinic, 947
Corvallis Radiology, PC, 947
Corvi, Carolyn, 91
Corvino, John, 790
Corvino, Robert, 853
Corwin, Bruce C., 2483
Corwin, David, 2483
Corwin, Debbie, 1079
Coryell, Edward, 1926
Coscia, Anthony R., 3826
Cosentino, Eric F., 1910
Cosentino, Philip, 570
Cosgrove, Howard E., 2756
Cosgrove, Michael J., 1552
Cosgrove, Peter, 1419
Cosgrove, Stephen J., 2048
Cosgrove, William V., 1984
Coslet, Jonathan J., 466
Cosse, Steven A., 2600
Costa, Anisa Kamadoli, 3750
Costa, Mark J., 1213
Costa, Paul, 3553
Costa, Scott W., 607
Costamagna, Claudio, 2319
Costanza, Dennis, 1824
Costanza, Jon, 3651
Costanzo, Dennis P., 1113
Costco Wholesale Corp., 948
Costello, Donna, 3410
Costello, Donna M., 3410
Costello, Ellen M., 1739
Costello, Francis W., 2074
Costello, Kevin, 534
Costello, Lawrence, 3794
Costley, Gary E., 955, 3047, 3750
Cote, David M., 1852, 2071
Cote, Kathleen A., 4042
Cote, Stephen P., 1946
Cotese, Casey, 2024
Cotham, W. Robert, 2138
Cothran, Paul, 2596
Cotter, James, 2646
Cotter, Jeffrey Louis, 1524
Cotter, Lisa, 2913
Cotter, Paula M., 1207
Cotter, Richard J., 1806
Cotter, William D., 159
Cottingham, Patty, 3374
Cottingham, Walter C., 1395
Cottle, Daren, 1215
Cottle, Gail, 3805
Cottle, William T., 1424
Cotton, Bob, 2633
Cotton, Howard E., 2101
Cotton, Kate H., 3066
Cotton, Peter, Dr., 2804
Cotton, Richard, 2649, 3893
Cotton, Robert, 2633
Cottone, Salvatore, 3189
Cottrell, Paul, 2976
Cottrell, Sophie, 1696
Couch, Genevieve R., 2590
Couch, John C., 637
Couch, Kenneth R., 3485
Coughenour, Katherine N., 3093
Coughlan, Gary, 3960
Coughlan, James P., 684
Coughlan, Robert J., 684
Coughlin, Catherine, 273
Coughlin, Cathy, 3557
Coughlin, Christopher J., 956, 1190
Coughlin, Edward James, 2031
Coughlin, Edward John, 2031
Coughlin, Jeg, 2031
Coughlin, Jeg Anthony, 2031
Coughlin, Laura, 516
Coughlin, Michael Allen, 2031
Coughlin, Phillip Troy, 2031
Coukos, Stephen J., 666
Coules, Blake, 698
Coulter, David A., 2416
Coulter, Joan M., 3177
Coulter, Patricia, 2958
Counceller, April Laktonen, 2184
Counsell, Craig, 2346
Country Financial, 1131
Countryman, Gary L., 727, 2265
Countryman, Tom, 1035
Countrywide Financial Corp., 3190
County Bank, The, 952
Coupe, Jerry, 4070
Couper, John M., 766
CouponsToGo.com, 138
Coupounas, Demetrios G. C., 1606
Coupounas, Kim Reither, 1606
Coupounas, Kim Riether, 1606
Courain, Jennifer R., 3148
Courain, Robert C., III, 3148
Courain, Robert C., Jr., 3148
Courain, Ruth D., 3148
Courcel, Georges Chodron de, 423
Courduroux, Pierre, 2559
Coursen, Sam, 1495
Courtemanche, Betty C., 2506
Courtemanche, Dan, 2347
Courter, Craig E., 2940
Courtney, C. Douglas, 3132
Courtney, Dan, 957
Courtney, H. Mark, 1446
Courtney, Richard D., 1972
Courtney, Thomas P., 1591
Courtright, Joe, 2622
Coury, Robert J., 2610
Cousens, Ellis E., 4072
Cousins Real Estate Corp., 953
Cousins Submarines, Inc., 954
Cousins, Michael S., 1921
Cousins, Scott, 2114
Coutts, Robert B., 3579
Coutu, Francois J., 3220
Coutu, Pete, 2991
Covance Inc., 955
Covert, Drew M., 3515
Covey, Michael J., 3017
Covey, Patrick M., 1035
Covey, Richard, 3140
Covey, Steven K., 2647
Covington, Alec C., 2619
Covington, Ann K., 3431
Covington, Ed, 4028
Covington, Edward H., 697, 1740
Covington, Ned, 1740
Covington, Peter J., 2430
Covington, Wendy, 1031
Cowan, Donald, 2945
Cowan, Howard B., 3879
Cowan, Ivy, 3615
Cowan, James, 3615
Cowan, James R., 3615
Cowan, Jill, 2483
Cowan, Kelly, 4109
Cowan, Laurie, 993
Cowan, Michael R., 156
Cowan, Pat, 3256
Cowan, R. Douglas, 1035, 3488
Coward, Teri, 2622
Cowboys Wives Association, 1022
Cowdin, Christi L., 4106
Cowdrey, Anne Marie, 3738
Cowen, Randolph L., 1253
Cowen, Scott S., 149, 1467, 2694
Cowenhoven, Anna, 340
Cowger, Gary L., 1071
Cowhig, Michael T., 2694
Cowie, James J., 646
Cowles Media Co., 2422
Cowles, David S., 350
Cowles, Jim, 821
Cowsert, Susan, 1227
Cox & Smith Inc., 960
Cox Charitable Lead Trust, 501
Cox Enterprises, Inc., 959

Cox Health, 3944
Cox Smith Matthews Incorporated, 960
Cox Wood Preserving Co., 962
Cox, Bill, Jr., 962
Cox, C. Lee, 2952
Cox, Carol, 2268
Cox, Carrie S., 685, 732, 3728
Cox, Cathy, 3866
Cox, David, 228
Cox, Donna O., 2445
Cox, Donna Owens, 2445
Cox, Elizabeth, 4072
Cox, George, 2769
Cox, H. Adrian, 331
Cox, Harold D., 1083
Cox, Heather M., 679
Cox, Howard E., Jr., 3627
Cox, James M., 959
Cox, James R., 2081
Cox, James S., 41
Cox, Jay, 3087
Cox, Jayme, 3430
Cox, Julie Coppola, 2628
Cox, Lorine G., 3868
Cox, Matthew, 2404
Cox, Matthew J., 2404
Cox, Maurine, 1464
Cox, Patricia, 3363
Cox, Patrick, 2914
Cox, Philip G., 3026
Cox, Phillip R., 1112, 3760
Cox, Raymond E., 3910
Cox, Robert M., Jr., 1257
Cox, Ruth, Sr., 3710
Cox, Thomas, 2593
Cox, Tom, 957
Cox, William B., 962
Cox., Matthew J., 2404
Coxe, John, 1587
Coxe, Samuel Makepeace, 7
Coxe, Tench, 2767
Coxhead, Andrew B., 1155
Coye, Molly J., 48
Coyle, Dennis L., 3070
Coyle, Maurice J., 1415
Coym, Peter, 3592
Coyne, John F., 2016
Coyne, Martin J., Jr., 2427
Coyne, Martin M., II, 68
Cozen, Stephen A., 964
Cozyn, Martin A., 2780
Cozzens, Tyler, 1982
Cozzone, Robert D., 1927
CP Kelco, Inc., 1953
CPI Corp., 965
Crabb, Gregory J., 177
Crabtree, Ashley M., 61
Crabtree, Dan, 2093
Cracchiolo, James M., 174
Cracker Barrel Old Country Store, Inc., 966
Cracknell, Neil, 1602
Craddock, R. Frank, Jr., 734
Craft Brothers Co., Inc., 967
Craft, Don, 2054
Craft, Rocky, 2807
Cragin, Marilyn Fife, 3575
Craig, Angela D., 3566
Craig, David, 3741
Craig, Guillermo Luksic, 423
Craig, Hubert M., III, 1396
Craig, Jeffrey A., 2473
Craig, Joan M., 2506
Craig, Langel, 3679
Craig, Lee C., 1208
Craig, Mary Ellen, 143
Craig, Mary P., 2088
Craig, Myrita, 1797
Craig, Myrita J., 1797
Craig, Pamela J., 22, 68
Craig, Peter, 3225
Craig-Novotny, Kate E., 3721
Craighead, Martin, 324
Craighead, Martin S., 324
Craigie, James R., 2471
Craigmile, Mark, 55
Craigslist, Inc., 968
Craime, William C., 3031
Crain, Alan R., 324
Crain, Alan R., Jr., 324
Crain, Andrew, 1508
Crall, Darrell, 2953
Cram, Betsy C., 1414
Cram, Ole R., 1414
Cramblit, Miggie E., 1047
Cramer, Harold, 2923
Cramer, William C., Jr., 1689
Crampton, Kevin, 416
Crampton, Kevin P., 416
Crampton, Kristine M., 416
Cranch, Laurence, 849
Cranch, Laurence E., 102
Crandall, Dennis, 3501
Crandall, Dennis G., 3501
Crandall, J. Taylor, 2138
Crandall, Mark, 3696
Crandall, Pyles, Haviland & Turner, LLP, 3089
Crandall, Pyles, Haviland, Turner & Smith, LLP, 3089
Crandall, Richard L., 1112, 1155
Crandall, Robert W., 333
Crandall, Roger W., 2397
Crandall, Theodore D., 3246
Crane & Co., Inc., 969
Crane Co., 970
Crane, Ann B., 1894
Crane, Christopher M., 1309
Crane, David W., 1239, 2756
Crane, Jameson, 2277
Crane, Jane E., 3017
Crane, Jim, 1871
Crane, Lynn, 2606
Crane, Nancy, 737
Crane, Stephen A., 1264
Craney, Jeff, 1767
Cranford, Bryant K., 3263
Cranford, Michael S., 2899
Crankshaw, Marc, 766
Cranor, John M., III, 50
Cransberg, Alan, 82
Cranston Print Works Co., 972
Cranston, Mary B., 2075, 3960
Cranston, Thomas R., 333
Crapol, Heidi, 1565
Cratty, Al, Jr., 2797
Craven, Judith B., 3677
Craven, Judith L., 406
Craven, Julie H., 1866
Craven, Thomas J., 3042
Craver, Benjamin A., 4017
Craver, Theodore F., Jr., 1228, 1766
Crawford, Barry, 1449
Crawford, Bruce, 2808
Crawford, Candace T., 833
Crawford, Carol T., 3487
Crawford, Curtis J., 1184, 4139
Crawford, Dave, 3648
Crawford, David, 455
Crawford, David S., 3648
Crawford, Frederick J., 857, 2281
Crawford, Heather, 2141
Crawford, Jack, 2638
Crawford, James C., 3572
Crawford, John L., 3397
Crawford, Kathleen F., 848
Crawford, Kermit R., 107, 2622
Crawford, Robert M., 462
Crawford, Sally W., 3887
Crawford, Stephanie, 415
Crawford, Stephen G., 337
Crawford, Steve, 1668
Crawford, Steven R., 1668
Crawford, Terry W., 125
Crawford, Timothy, 7
Crawford, Victor, 2935
Crawford, W. Kirk, 3572
Crawford, William H. W., IV, 3245
Crawford, William H.W., IV, 3245
Crawford, William P., 3597
Crawley, A. Bruce, 1926
Craycraft, Robert M., II, 3309
Crayola, LLC, 1707
Crayton, Sandra Austin, 1366
Creamer & Son, J. Fletcher, Inc., 974
Creamer, Dale A., 974
Creamer, Glenn M., 729
Creamer, J. Fletcher, 974
Creamer, J. Fletcher, Jr., 974
Creamer, Sean R., 227
Creasey, F. Clay, Jr., 3790
Creasy, Lori A., 3998
Creative Artists Agency, LLC, 30, 975
Creative Financial Group, Ltd., 976
Creative Hairdressers, Inc., 3130
Credit Bureau of Baton Rouge, 977
Credit Bureau of Clarksville, 978
Credit Bureau of Nashville, Inc., 811
Credit Marketing & Management Assn., 979
Credit Suisse First Boston, 2267
Credit Suisse First Boston Corp., 980
Credit Suisse First Boston LLC, 980
Credit Suisse USA, 980
Creech, Carter, 2409
Creech, Kathy, 3805
Creed, Greg, 1964, 3679
Creed, Thomas R., 428
Creek, Phillip G., 2325
Creekman, James E., 1396
Creekmore, James H., Sr., 636
Creekmore, Meredith, 636
Creekmore, Wade, 636
Creel, Diane C., 91, 3760
Creel, Jerry, 841
Creel-Harrison Foundation, 2573
Cregg, Roger A., 889
Crego, Mary, 3591
Cremers, Eric J., 3017
Cremers, Noelle, 2853
Cremin, Robert, 3034
Crenshaw, William E., 3079
Crepin, Frederic Raymond, 30
Crescent Electric Supply Co., 981
Crescent Iron Works Inc., 982
Crescent Operating, Inc., 2570
Crescent Plastics, Inc., 983
Crescent Stock Match Fund, 2570
Cresline Plastics Pipe Co., Inc., 983
Cress, Robert G., 3213
Cressman, Walter H., 1421
Cressman, Warren, 1607
Crestar Bank, 3654
Crews, Anne, 2392
Crews, Mark S., 71
Crews, Michael C., 2907
Crews, Sidney, 636
Crews, Terrell K., 233, 1866, 3239
Crewson, Scott N., 1845
Cribbs, Jeffery S., Sr., 1921
Cricchio, Mary Ann, 2638
Crichlow, Rhonda, 2753
Crider, Karen S., 2740
Crilly, Tim J., 503
Crimmins, Robert J., 3211
Crimmins, Steve, 2662
Crimmins, Thomas P., 1179
Crimmins, Timothy, 2928
Crimmins, Timothy P., Jr., 2928
Crines, James T., 4157
Crinnion, Mark A., 26
Cripe, Julie, 1347
Crisan, Jeff, 2447
Crisp, Charles R., 57, 1282
Crispo, Arthur, 3123
Criss, KB, 2553
Crist, Charles J., 3563
Crist, Gretchen, 3646
Crist, Gretchen R., 3646
Critelli, Michael J., 1216
Crivelli, Charles, III, 506
Crivello, Mario L., 4011
Crocco, M. Scott, 63
Crocito, Peter, 3916
Crocitto, Peter, 3916
Crockard, James E., III, 1287
Crocker, Charles, 1487
Crocker, Douglas, II, 3931
Crockett, John R., III, 1511
Croffy, Bruce, 504
Croft, James A.D., 3408
Croft, Jane Aurell, 985
Croft, Kent G., 985
Croft, Kent Gordon, 985
Croft, L. Gordon, 985
Croggon, Charles C., 1070
Croghan, Raymond, 984
Crohurst, Tom, 3648
Croker, Stephen B., 3873
Cromling, Christine M., 3265
Cromling, Jon R., 3265
Cromling, Maureen M., 3265
Cromling, William E., II, 3265
Cromling, William E., III, 3265
Cronin, Brian, 678
Cronin, Charles F., 1724
Cronin, Crystal, 3347
Cronin, Denis F., 3277
Cronin, Joseph, 1234
Cronin, Joseph M., 1234
Cronin, Joseph, Jr., 1234
Cronin, Kathleen M., 853
Cronin, Linda L., 3277
Cronin, Patrick J., 3067
Cronin, Tim, 97
Crooks, Carolyn, 1620
Crooks, Stanley R., 3419
Croom, Marshall A., 2312
Cropp-Metcalfe, 138
Cropper, Stephen L., 437
Crosby, Bob, 991
Crosby, Elizabeth J., 1628
Crosby, Gary M., 1419
Crosby, James S., 1628
Crosby, John, 1628
Crosby, John F., 1628

Crosby, Peter, 499
Crosby, Ralph D., Jr., 141
Crosby, Tom, 1466
Croskey, Charles, 1682
Cross, Andy, 2582
Cross, Gregory, 2309
Cross, Iris M., 547
Cross, John, 2761
Cross, L. Jay, 2687
Cross, Leslie H., 1134
Crossett, Susan M., 2630
Crosswhite, Mark A., 3516
Crosswhite, R. Joe, 2323
Crotty, Cindy P., 2136
Crotty, Eileen, 1820
Crotty, Gerald C., 2057
Crotty, W. Garrett, 1970, 2621
Crouch, Charles L., III, 3078
Crouch, Robert F., 938
Crouch, William K., 3860
Crovitz, L. Gordon, 1869
Crow, Timothy M., 1842
Crowder, Carolyn, 422
Crowder, Richard T., 3487
Crowe, Barbara L., 2991
Crowe, Jeffrey C., 3074
Crowe, Maria, 2274
Crowell & Moring LLP, 986
Crowley, Bryan, 3927
Crowley, J. Samuel, 3876
Crowley, Jeff, 7
Crowley, Michael, 276
Crowley, Peter T., 2699
Crowley, Ruth M., 261
Crowley, William C., 292
Crowley, William J., Jr., 112
Crown Books Corp., 3659
Crown Roofing Services, Inc., 989
Crown, James S., 1551, 2071
Crown, Janet, 30
Crown, Lester, 2402
Crown, Susan, 1916
Crown, Susan M., 2740
Crownhart, Stacy, 3154
Crownover, James, 3051
Crownover, James W., 775
Crownover, Michael, 3915
Crudo, Francine, 2781
Cruickshank, Donald G., 3095
Cruise, Daniel, 82
Crull, Linn A., 2603
Crum, Gary T., 1983
Crum, Scott, 305
Crumb, Dan, 2091
Crumley, Thomas, 3582
Crump, Chris, 2692
Crump, Faith H., 1053
Crump, Harold, 1877
Crump-Caine, Lynn, 1524
Crusan, Donna Grace, 2168
Crutchfield, Kevin S., 112
Crutchfield, Lisa, 3885
Crutchfield, Scott, 984
Cruz, Edward, 2683
Crystal Print, Inc., 991
Crystal Window & Door Systems, Ltd., 992
Crystal, Clayton, 2008
Crystal, Elaine, 2008
Crystal, Emanuel, 2008
Crystal, Gerald P., 2008
Crystal, Lynn, 2008
Crystal, Richard P., 1383
Crystal, Shannon, 2008
Csapo, Peter, 3944
Csepella, J.D., 3956
Csiba-Womersley, Maria, 1895
CSL Behring, 993
CSS Industries, Inc., 996
Csuka, Anne G., 910
CSW Foundation, 141
CT Health Foundation, 501
CTB, Inc., 3839
CTSI Logistics, 3860
Cuba, Ryan, 3356
Cuban, Brian, 1021
Cuban, Jeff, 1021
Cuban, Kim, 1021
Cubbin, Robert S., 827
Cudd, Sonia, 1653
Cuddy, Daniel H., 1415
Cuddy, Gerard P., 412
Cudlip, Brittain B., 359
Cuene, Casey, 1651
Cuhlane, Michael, 2302
Cukierski, Gerald P., 1969
Culbertson, Leslie S., 1950
Culhane, Steve, 1080
Cullen & Sons, J.P., Inc., 1000
Cullen, Brian C., 2159
Cullen, Daniel, 3552
Cullen, Daniel F., 464
Cullen, David J., 1000
Cullen, Gavin, 2940, 2941
Cullen, James G., 56, 2048, 3072
Cullen, John P., 1000
Cullen, Lisa Takeuchi Takeuchi, 3644
Cullen, Mark A., 1000
Cullen, Paula Bramsen, 3552
Cullen, Richard, 2430
Cullen, Richard F., 1000
Cullinan, Kevin A., 703
Cullman Savings Bank, 1001
Cullum Davis Foundation, Shelby, 1201
Culmer, Lynn, 1563
Culmone, Josephine R., 2513
Culolta, Jared G., 4009
Culp, H. Lawrence, Jr., 1027
Culp, Jacqueline, 2251
Culp, Richard, 283
Culp, Richard W., 283
Culp, Tim, 3980
Culpepper, Bruce, 3430
Culver Franchising System Inc., 1002
Culver, Craig C., 1002
Culver, Curt S., 2488, 4093
Culver, John, 3585
Culver, Leola, 1002
Culver, Margaret S., 3966
Cumberland Gravel & Sand Co., 1768
Cummin, Pearson C., III, 533
Cumming, Ian M., 3476
Cummings & Lockwood, 1004
Cummings, Alexander B., 862
Cummings, Alexander Benedict, Jr., 861
Cummings, Bruce, 1682
Cummings, Candace E., 3913
Cummings, Dan, 506
Cummings, Don, 1735
Cummings, Julie, 2127
Cummings, Kevin, 1984
Cummings, Kurt P., 306
Cummings, Martin Bruce, Jr., 3188
Cummings, Richard F., 1260
Cummings, Robert F., Jr., 945
Cummins Construction Co., Inc., The, 1005
Cummins Engine Co., Inc., 1007
Cummins Filtration, 1006
Cummins Inc., 1007
Cummins, Brendan, 258
Cummins, Dan, 2863
Cummins, Joanne, 3576
Cummins, Mark R., 1733
Cummins, Robert L., 1005
Cummins, Robert L., Jr., 1005
Cummins, Willa Jane, 1005
Cummiskey, Susan W., 3141
CUNA Mutual Insurance Society, 1008
Cundiff, Kellie, 1552
Cundiff, Richard M., 1603
Cundy, Richard, 3956
Cuneo, Dennis C., 67, 528
Cunha, Paul, 1050
Cunniffe, Jane, 159
Cunniffe, Maurice, 159
Cunniffe, Maurice J., 159
Cunning, Patrick D., 3513
Cunningham, Anna, 3585
Cunningham, C. Baker, 667
Cunningham, Curt, 759
Cunningham, Isabella, 3946
Cunningham, J. Dawson, 1035
Cunningham, John, 1123
Cunningham, John E., IV, 3144
Cunningham, Kristen N., 1054
Cunningham, Larry, 1268
Cunningham, Meredith A., 363
Cunningham, Michael J., 46
Cunningham, Sandy, 1314
Cunningham, Sarah, 67
Cunningham, Susan M., 850
Cunningham, T. Jefferson, III, 2323
Cunningham, Ted, 1790
Cunningham, William H., 2281, 3522
Cupertino Electric, Inc., 1009
Cuperus, Ron, 1416
Cupingood, Steve, 3463
Curato, Michael, 4109
Curatola, MaryGrace, 267
Curb, B. Scott, 1416
Curci, Frank, 3774
Curci, John V., 1935
Curci-Turner Company LLC, 2343
Curd, Howard R., 3361
Curd, Richard, 1326
Curl, Benny, 631
Curl, Kay, 631
Curl, Yvonne M., 2639
Curlee, J. Cecil, Jr., 3032
Curler, Jeffrey H., 3920
Curless, Michael S., 3060
Curley, Robert M., 428, 2681
Curley, Stephen C., 2801
Curran, Bentley, 552
Curran, Bentley N., 552
Curran, Connie R., 1867
Curran, Dick, 3376
Curran, Joseph F., 2751
Curran, Michael, 702
Curran, Michael H., 922
Curran, Randall, 3141
Curran, Randall E., 3141
Curren, Meredith, 491
Curren, Meredith A., 349
Current, Gloster B., Jr., 3484
Current, Richard R., 3534
Currey, Russell M., 3239
Currie, Jerry N., 4088
Currie, Jim, 2377
Currie, Laura, 2620
Currie, Peter, 382
Currie, Peter W., 1951
Currie, William G., 3890
Currier, Barbara, 896
Currier, James, 896
Currow, James C., 2573
Curry, Charles, 2967
Curry, Greg W., 3738
Curry, Kelly E., 1765
Curry, Mimi, 1031
Curry, Philomena, 1031
Curt, Timothy J., 3985
Curtin, Michael F., 1129
Curtis, Alfred B., Jr., 2683
Curtis, Becky, 1403
Curtis, Charlie, 2615
Curtis, David M., 3104
Curtis, Donna, 2137
Curtis, Gary, 2127
Curtis, L.B., 1272
Curtis, Miranda, 2263
Curtis, Ron, 2592
Curtiss, Gareth, 4052
Curtiss, Jeffrey E., 2106
Curves International, Inc., 1011
Cushing, Brenda J., 302
Cushing, Brenda Jean, 302
Cushman, Anne Adams, 666
Cushman, John C., III, 660
Cushman, Robert C., Sr., 3444
Cusick, Charles, 1094
Cusumano, Gary M., 1632, 3461
Cutbirth, Jason F., 1944
Cutco Corporation, 1012
Cutco Cutlery, 1012
Cutco Cutlery Corp., 1012
Cuthbert-Millett, Elizabeth, 2694
Cuticelli, John J., Jr., 1609
Cutie Pie Baby Inc., 1013
Cutler, Alan B., 2295
Cutler, Alexander M., 1184, 1216
Cutler, Sarah S., 936
Cutler, Stephen M., 2071
Cutsforth, David, 947
Cutshaw, Finley, 1432
Cutting, Benjamin, 4115
Cutting, Steve H., 3649
Cutts, Matthew, 3998
CV Industries, Inc., 3441
CVS Corp., 1014
CVS Pharmacy, Inc., 1014
Cwudzinski, Ted, 3811
Cyan Worlds, Inc., 1015
Cyan, Inc., 1015
Cygnus Business Media, Inc., 1634
Cymerys, Ed, 655
Cynical, Thomas, 1441
Cyphers, Bill, 3631
Cyprus Pima Mining Co., 3807
Cyprus, Nick, 3141
Cyr, Annette, 567
Cyr, Kevin, 423
Cyr, Martha, 392
Cywinski, John, 2139
Czarnecki, Gerald M., 3591
Czarnecki, Mark J., 2323
Czarnecki, Mark K., 2323
Czebotar, Jerry A., 4025
Czelada, Laura L., 1078
Czerniakowski, Peter J., 211
Czerniakowski, Rita, 1770
Czinege, Michael, 125
Czopek, Joseph C., 827

D & K Insurance Agency, 1170
D&M Equipment Co., 1570
D'Adamo, Gene, 3902
D'Agostino, Sharon, 2048
D'Alessandro, D. Beatty, 1640
D'Alessandro, David F., 3387
D'Alessio, M. Walter, 1926
D'Allessandro, Joe, 3160
D'Aloia, G. Peter, 1449, 1999
D'Amato, Janice M., 2850
D'Amato, Joseph, 1261
D'Amato, Joseph A., 1261
D'Amato, Louis J., 2513
D'Ambra, Michael V., 491
D'Ambrose, Michael, 233
D'Ambrosio, Karl, 1310
D'Ambrosio, Lou, 3384
D'Ambrosio, Louis J., 2172
D'Ambrosio, Maria, 798
D'Amelio, Frank, 2950
D'Amelio, Frank A., 1886
D'Amico, Joseph A., 3667
D'Amico, Paul, 2535
D'Amore, Robert R., 2928
D'Amour, Charles L., 461
D'Amour, Donald H., 461
D'Amour, Michael, 461
D'Amour-Daley, Claire, 461
D'Angelo, Peter, 3510
D'Anniballe, Nick, 1960
D'Annunzio & Sons, Inc., 1017
D'Annunzio, David, 453
D'Annunzio, James, 1017
D'Annunzio, James J., 1017
D'Annunzio, Joseph P., 1017
D'Annunzio, Michael, 453, 1017
D'Annunzio, Michael A., 1017
D'Annunzio, Stephen D., 1017
D'Annunzio, Vincent, 453
D'Annunzio, Vincent F., 453
D'Antoni, David J., 2809
D'Aquila, Jean M., 2262
D'Arenberg, Pierre, 3948
D'Armond, Dan, 508
D'Arrigo, Daniel J., 2489
D'Aurelio, Brian, 1260
D'Emic, Susana, 1508
D'Orso, Chris, 2824
D'Orta, James A., 687
D'Silva, Joyce, 4066
da Silva, Luis Maria Viana Palha, 2769
Dab, John M., 2716
Dabagia, Hassan, 489
Dabds, John, 3541
Dabek, Bozena, 1212
Daberko, David A., 2365, 3278
Dabiero, Carmen J., 3382
Dabill, Phillip A., 588
Dach, Leslie A., 3980
Dachowski, Peter, 3312
Dachs, Alan, 395
Dachs, Alan M., 1497
Dacier, Paul T., 1253
Dacy, Bob, 1050
Daddario, Nicholas, 3589
Dady, Dominique, 2968
Daffy's, Inc., 1019
Daft, Douglas Neville, 3980
Dagen, Dale, 1666
Dagg, Rolf A., 934
Daggett, John, 2833
Daglio, Robert J., 725
Dagostino, S., 2048
Dague, James, 1466
Daher, Nancy, 640
Dahir, Victor W., 2558
Dahl, Craig R., 3695
Dahl, Lawrence W., 2278
Dahl, Richard J., 668, 1120, 1907
Dahlback, Claes, 1603, 1604
Dahlberg Foundation, Ken and Betty, 2535
Dahlberg, Inc., 2535
Dahlberg, Kenneth C., 2586
Dahlgren, Kent, 3949
Dahlin, Jeff, 615
Dahlinghaus, Rose, 3199
Dahlstrom, Marshall C., 3248
Dahlstrom-Gutel, Anita, 4087
Dahm, Wendy A., 316
Dahya, Hanif "wally", 2683
Dahya, Hanif W., 2682
Daichendt, Gary J., 2650
Daigle, Nancy, 2556
Daigneault, Daniel R., 1391
Dailey, Gary, 4046
Dailey, George, Jr., 3069
Dailey, Jeffrey J., 1338
Dailey, Jeffrey John, 1338
Dailey, Joseph, 3474
Dailey, Mark D., 1447
Daily, Elgin, 1412
Daily, Genevieve, 1412
Daimler Chrysler, 1131
DaimlerChrysler Corp., 801
Dain Rauscher Inc., 3136
Dairy House Co., 1963
Daiss, Daniel M., 2446
Daiwa Securities America Inc., 1020
Dake, Bonnie, 3806
Dakovich, Milt, 2282
Dal Bello, Michael, 466
Dalby, Linda S., 1046
Dalchow, M.A., 2361
Dale, Angela Henkels, 1779
Dale, Lenore Hawk, 30
Dale, Robert V., 966
Dale, Thomas P., 3254
Daleo, Robert D., 1288
Daley, Charles J., Jr., 2245
Daley, Clayton C., Jr., 2760, 3589
Daley, Dorian E., 2821
Daley, Erica, 2521
Daley, James E., 38, 1683
Daley, Michael J., 853
Daley, Pamela, 1552
Daley, Richard M., 862
Daley, Tor, 1317
Dalke, Gary R., 4044
Dall, Marcia A., 1291
Dallahan, John, 3523
Dallas Basketball Ltd., 1021
Dallas Cowboys Football Club, Ltd., 1022
Dallas Cowboys Merchandising, 1022
Dallas Mavericks Foundation, The, 1021
Dallas, H. James, 2453
Dallas, Terry G., 1563, 2756
Dallob, Naomi C., 773
Dally, Craig A., 1518
Dally, Martha M., 170
Dalton, Christopher, 1979
Dalton, Daniel, 3631
Dalton, Donna, 2577
Dalton, James F., 3706
Dalton, Nathaniel, 51
Dalton, Robert, Jr., 2011
Dalton, Sharon C., 48
Dalton, Tom, 1936
Dalton, Wesley Roberts, 1167
Daly, Aileen, 2958
Daly, Ann, 1172
Daly, Charles, 3160
Daly, Colin, 1300
Daly, George G., 426
Daly, Kathleen C., 2477
Daly, Michael P., 428
Daly, Robert C., 3784
Daly, Ronald E., 3876
Daly, Sandra S., 1703
Daly, William, 2631
Dalzell, Richard L., 209
Damar Machine Co., Inc., 1024
Damas, Raul, 2689
Damato, Jennifer, 2171
Dambach, Mike, 465
Dambrine, Francois, 346
Damcott, John H., 1799
Dames, Donald E., 3649
Damholt, Sandra, 1347
Damicone, Jim, 1191
Damitio, Patrick, 3896
Damm, Peggy M., 3797
Dammann, Angelika, 3334
Dammeyer, Rod F., 3107
Damonti, John L., 578
Damron, Rick D., 2312
Dan's Supreme Supermarkets, Inc., 1025, 2135
Dan, Michael T., 3047
Dana Corporation, 1026
Dana, Matt, 2968
Danahy, John F., 3179
Danchak, Peter J., 505
Dancy, Desiree, 2690
Dando, Stephen, 3741
Danforth Co., John W., 1028
Danforth, John C., 754
Dang, Kimberly Allen, 2153
Dangeard, Frank E., 3669
Dangoor, David E.R., 2304
Daniel Industries, Inc., 1257
Daniel, J. Michael, 372
Daniel, Josiah M., III, 3957
Daniel, Laree R., 54
Daniel, Linda M., 3602
Daniel, Nicole C., 78
Daniel, Warren A., 3513
Daniels, Brian, 578
Daniels, Charles R., III, 3261
Daniels, Christopher M., 3408
Daniels, Claire, 976
Daniels, Gary E., 976
Daniels, Jennifer, 2650
Daniels, Jon, 3729
Daniels, Laird K., 1014
Daniels, Michael A., 2469
Daniels, Nicole J., 3933
Daniels-Carter, Valerie, 1651
Danielson, Craig, 4103
Danielson, Doug, 1466
Danielson, Sue, 1248
Danilewitz, Dale, 175
Danis Building Construction Co., 1029
Danis, John, 1029
Danis, Tom, 1029
Danka Office Imaging Co., 2185
Dankenbrink, Kristine A., 887
Dankers, Paul, 2542
Dankey, Wendy, 4033
Dann, Robert, 1179
Danner, Denise R., 239
Dannhauser, Stephen, 4022
Dannies, Robert B., Jr., 2928
Danning, Rick, 4092
Dannon Co., Inc., The, 1030
Danos, Paul, 1554
Dansby, Darrick, 814
Dansk Investment Group, Inc., 3903
Dansko, LLC, 1031
Dansky, Ira M., 2057
Danversbank, 2928
Danzig, David, 1969
Darbee, Peter A., 2853
Darby, Joyce, 2891
Darby, Joyce L., 2891
Darby, Terry, 72
Darcy, Stathy, 855
Darcy, Thomas, 2417
Darden Restaurants, Inc., 1032
Darden, Calvin, 685, 863, 3691
Darden, Glenn F., 3106
Darden, Glenn M., 3106
Darden, Mary, 1032
Darden, Thomas F., 3106
Dardess, Margaret B., 1588
Dare, Josh, 1921
Dareus, Marcel, 606
Darish, Kenneth V., 3914
Darland, Tye, 1568
Darley, Michael L., 2344
Darnell, David C., 340
Darragh, Lucy, 501
Darrah, Mathew G., 1281
Darrell, Mark C., 2207, 2208
Darretta, Robert J., 3884
Darrigrand, Maritxu, 3108
Darrington, Kevin, 3774
Darrington, Susan, 1460
Darrow, Betsy, 341
Darrow, Chris, 1186
Darrow, Kurt L., 2205
Darrow, Scott, 2064
Dart Container Corporation, 1033
Dart Container Corporation of Georgia, 1033
Dart Container Corporation of Kentucky, 1033
Dart Container Sales Co., LLC, 1033
Dart Group Corp., 3659
Dart, Ariane, 1033
Dart, Justin M., 1034
Dart, Kenneth B., 1033
Dart, Robert C., 1033
Dart, William A., 1033
Das, Aseem, 4118
Dasburg, John H., 3802
Dasher, Richard, 3720
Dasis, John, 228
Dassow, Jill, 4013
Dastoor, Michael K., 2006
Datar, Srikant M., 3627
Datatel, Inc., 1252
Datta, Jason, 3501
Dattalo, Francis G., 3858
Dattilo, Thomas A., 1736
Dauch, Richard F., 3534
Daucsavage, Bruce, 2783
Daugherty, Erin, 3629
Daughhetee, Deanna, 142
Daughters, Willie, 3199
Dauler, L. Van V., Jr., 2667
Daum, Martin, 1093
Daum, Shana, 3324
Dauman, Philippe P., 3945
Dauphinee, Joan, 2112

Dauten, Kent P., 1765
Dauterman, Dudley, 1590
Dauterman, Dudley L., 1590
Davanzo, Christopher, 2593
Dave, Pierson, 2251
Davenport, Dave, 251
Davenport, David M., 251
Davenport, Glenn, 966
Davern, Alexander M., 2632
Daversa, Michael, 1045
Davey Tree Expert Co., The, 1035
Davey, Bob, 2018
Davey, Deirdre N., 174
Davey, James P., 2123
Davi, Michael, 4134
David, Jeff, 3303
David, Lorraine B., 1167
David, Sanders, 3259
Davidson, Carol Anthony, 1044
Davidson, Chris, 957
Davidson, Daryl, 265
Davidson, Donnie, 135
Davidson, Gordon K., 1362
Davidson, Janet G., 81
Davidson, John, 3567
Davidson, Lisa, 3122
Davidson, Megan L., 2668
Davidson, Michael C., 3591
Davidson, Park R., 1971
Davidson, Peggy, 2392
Davidson, Robert C., Jr., 2016
Davidson, Sarah, 135
Davidson, Sheila K., 2688
Davidson, Ted, 103
Davidson, Terrence M., M.D., 3192
Davie, Anita, 2435
Davie, Earl, 2435
Davies, Andrew, 733
Davies, Christa, 210
Davies, Duane, 2561
Davies, George P., 3807
Davies, Gordon K., 3433
Davies, Holly, 1031
Davies, Howard J., 2570
Davies, Joe, 3105
Davies, John L., 3358
Davies, Pamela L., 1330
Davies, Pamela Lewis, 3500
Davies, Pat, 455
Davies, Simon, 2283
Davignon, Etienne F., 1582
Davin, Thomas E., 3679
Davis Auto World, Don, Inc., 1037
Davis Brothers Construction, 136
Davis Foundation, Shelby Cullum, 1201
Davis, Alison, 3859
Davis, Anne, 2668
Davis, Anne M., 2668
Davis, Anne Marie, 3879
Davis, Barbara, 859
Davis, Barry, 3738
Davis, Betty, 2043
Davis, Bradley T., 55
Davis, Brenda, 3150
Davis, Brett, 265
Davis, Charles A., 1791, 3057
Davis, Chris A., 3247
Davis, Christopher C., 3999
Davis, Cindy, 3805, 3980
Davis, Cindy L., 2125
Davis, Clay Parker, 826
Davis, D. Scott, 1852, 3872
Davis, David A., 3388
Davis, Derek, 4157
Davis, Diana, 3987
Davis, Don H., Jr., 1916
Davis, Don P., 3220
Davis, Don W., 1339
Davis, Donald L., 1037
Davis, Edward, 1887
Davis, Edward R., III, 3821
Davis, Elaine, 3888
Davis, Elliot S., 91
Davis, Erika T., 2841
Davis, Erroll B., Jr., 1555, 3857
Davis, F. T., 3759
Davis, Gary, 2043
Davis, Gary L., 2043
Davis, George S., 220, 3095
Davis, Gerald, 3921
Davis, Greg, 1383
Davis, Henry, 1649
Davis, Henry R., 2094
Davis, Howard, 3888
Davis, Howard E., 3888
Davis, Ian E.L., 2048
Davis, J. Kimbrough, 676
Davis, J. Mark, 862
Davis, Jack E., 3010
Davis, James C., 92
Davis, James G., Jr., 170
Davis, James P., 1077
Davis, James S., 2668
Davis, James W., 2043
Davis, Jana, 1762
Davis, Jana Joustra, 1762
Davis, Jani, 4047
Davis, Jeff, 3980
Davis, Jeffrey V., 3888
Davis, Jeffrey W., 2638
Davis, Jennifer Wagner, 4127
Davis, Jerome L., 215, 1530
Davis, Jim, 698
Davis, John, 428, 1037, 3059
Davis, John M., 851
Davis, Judith M., 498
Davis, June, 2043
Davis, Kelly, 3059
Davis, Kenneth D., 2639
Davis, Lisa, 3502
Davis, Lisa A., 3430
Davis, Marcia, 657
Davis, Mark, 1319
Davis, Mark C., 4124
Davis, Martha, 2465
Davis, Mary, 4000
Davis, Mary Anne, 1043
Davis, Matthew, 1037
Davis, Max, 72
Davis, Michael L., 1554
Davis, Mike, 4072
Davis, Morgan W., 2813
Davis, Nancy, 3882
Davis, Nancy B., 3610
Davis, Nathaniel A., 3859
Davis, Ozie, III, 814
Davis, Paul, 2991
Davis, Paula, 82, 2935
Davis, Phil, 4010
Davis, Phyllis, 891
Davis, Ray, 3847
Davis, Ray C., 3729
Davis, Richard, 4022
Davis, Richard K., 3835, 3836, 4135
Davis, Robert C., III, 3649
Davis, Robert M., 377
Davis, Robert T., 2414
Davis, Robin, 1267
Davis, Robin A., 3374
Davis, Ronald A., 2743
Davis, Ronald R., 1074
Davis, Shannon Sedgwick, 563
Davis, Shawn C., 2561
Davis, Shelva J., 2880
Davis, Sonya Meyers, 2559
Davis, Steve, 2043
Davis, Steven, 751
Davis, Steven A., 1300, 3981
Davis, Steven D., 3405
Davis, Steven J., 2043
Davis, Sue, 1326
Davis, Susan F., 2050, 3100
Davis, Susan Fife, 3575
Davis, Terry, 2235
Davis, Thomas C., 1054
Davis, Todd, 1326
Davis, Todd F., 3893
Davis, Tom, 2480
Davis, Tony, 751
Davis, W. Derek, 1132
Davis, Wade, 3945
Davis, Wilbur R., 2603
Davis, Will, 1887
Davis, William A., 3889
Davis, William L., 2365
Davis, William L., III, 63
Davis, Willie D., 2489
Davish, Patrick, 2466
Davison Iron Works, Inc., 1042
Davison, Brian, 2246
Davison, Dale, 2483
Davison, J. Scott, 169
Davison, John, 1476
DaVita Inc., 1044
Davlin, James A., 1555
Davoren, Peter J., 3824
Dawkins, Brian, 2627
Dawkins, William J., 3401
Dawley, Bob, 511
Dawley, John T., 2928
Dawn, Keith, 2781
Dawson, Carole, 939
Dawson, Dennis, 1088
Dawson, G. Steven, 136
Dawson, J. Hallam, 289
Dawson, Jerry L., 3148
Dawson, Peter, 395
Dawson, Peter A., 395
Dawson, William, 2938, 3255
Day Management Corp., 1045
Day, Curtis, 15
Day, David M., 1077
Day, Dawn, 991
Day, Dennis G., 1668
Day, Diana L., 3405
Day, Ed, 3863
Day, Edward, VI, 2536
Day, Frank B., 3238
Day, James C., 1282, 2815, 3748
Day, Jim, 3098
Day, Kevin R., 1441
Day, Kim, 3594
Day, L.B., 2499
Day, Raymond F., 1464
Day, Robert A., 1494
Day, Susan Oakley, 3110
Day, Suzanne F., 2315
Day, Twila M., 3677
Dayal, Duke, 346
Daybarian, Mark, 2255
Dayton Foundation, 1345
Dayton Hudson Corp., 3691
Dayton Power and Light Co., The, 1047
Dayton, Paul K., 678, 2133
Dayyat, Linda, 3653
de Alonso, Marcela Perez, 1794
De Bedout, Juan Ernesto, 3913
de Brier, Donald P., 2780
De Carbonnel, Francois, 182
De Cardenas, Gilbert L., 644
de Cardenas, Gilbert L., Jr., 644
de Cardenas, Gilbert, Sr., 644
De Castro, Antonio Monteiro, 3821
De Castro, Henrique, 3691
De Cock, Frans G., 2545
De Cook, J. Mark, 1784
De Gasperis, Francois, 2381
de Geus, Aart J., 220, 3673
de Geus, Arte, 3673
De Jesus, David D., 2484
de la Vauvre, Herve, 1667
de la Vega, Ralph, 273, 274, 2688
De Laney, David C., 337
De May, Stephen G., 1189
De Maynadier, Patrick D., 1804
de Mishaan, Solita Cohen, 1236
De Montaner, Pedro, 2449
de Rothschild, Baron David, 3270
de Rothschild, Lynn Forester, 2230
De Rycker, Sonali, 1903
De Sole, Domenico, 1533, 2694
de Toledo, Philip, 677
de Vaucleroy, Jacques, 1458
De Vries, Randall J., 1644
De Young, Dave, 2073
De Young, Gordon, 3969
de Zeeuw, Bastiaan G., 3227
Deacon, Steven D., 1050
Dead River Co., 1051
Deal, Clifford M., III, 861
Deal, Ronald E., 385
Deal, Tom, 1279
Dealer Computer Services, Inc., 1052
Dealy, Richard P., 2981
Dean Foods Corporation, 1054
Dean Fox Foundation Inc., 3366
Dean Management Corp., 1054
Dean, Danny, 1383
Dean, Dorton & Ford, 1053
Dean, Doughlas, 1053
Dean, Douglas P., 1053
Dean, Gordon, 2570
Dean, Jim, 3387
Dean, Lloyd H., 4028
Deane, Shelley W., 1488
DeArk, Melissa G., 1053
Dearmas, Francisco, 4065
Deason, Bob, 2424
Deatherage, David, 2485
Deaton, Chad C., 324
Deaton, Chadwick C., 63
Deavenport, Earnest W., Jr., 3171
deBalmann, Yves C., 1309
Debbie, Dube, 2234
DeBenedictis, Nicholas, 222, 1309, 1926
Deblaere, Jo, 22
DeBlois Oil Co., 1056
DeBlois, Constance A., 1056
DeBlois, Robert E., 1056
Debode, Gary, 1229
DeBoer, Bryan B., 2287
DeBoer, Sidney B., 2287
DeBolt, Scott, 886
DeBonis, Eric, 3524
DeBonis, Richard L., 1712

Deborah, Smith, 3430
DeBriyn, Paul A., 59
Debrowski, Thomas A., 2405
DeBruce Grain, Inc., 1057
DeBruce, Paul E., 1057
Dec, Katherine, 1200
DeCanniere, Dan, 2107
Decarlo, Steve, 1025
DeCarolis, D.L., 2628
Decenzo, David A., 306
DeCesare, Michael, 2417
Decherd, Robert W., 406, 2150
Decker, Kathy, 959
Decker, Patrick K., 1741
Decker, Sharon A., 861
Decker, Sharon Allred, 1330
Decker, Susan L., 429, 948, 1950
Decker, Thomas A., 964
Deckert, Elizabeth C., 881
DeCocco, Philip, 1632
Decoff, Thomas R., 2475
DeConcini, Michael J., 3819
DeCook, J. Mark, 1784
Decor Cabinets, 709
Decrescenzo, Robert M., 3899
DeCrona, Bruce E., 1306
Dedham Institution for Savings, 1060
Dedrick, Gregg R., 1087
Dee Foundation, 1538
Dee, James D., 700
Dee, Mike, 1147
Deedy, Justin F., 3657
Deegan, Gail, 1253
Deel, Jeffrey A., 3487
Deely, Brendan J., 3905
Deeney, Gerald D., 1877
Deep, Said, 640
Deere & Co., 1061
Deere, Cynthia A. P., 3430
Deerfield Management Company, 1062
Deese, George E., 1446
Deese, Willie A., 1089
DeFabrizio, Francesca, 1208
DeFalco, Stephen, 969
Defares, Robert H., 1920
Defaur, Piere, 62
DeFazio, Gary M., 398
DeFelice, Gene, 360
Defelice, Genevieve, 1276
Defelice, Rocco, 3390
Defenders of Wildlife, 930
DeFeo, Neil, 3646
DeFeo, Neil P., 3646
DeFeo, Ronald M., 2125, 3719
Deffner, David L., 2553
Deffner, Roger, 15
Defiance Publishing Company, LLC, 1063
DeFosset, Don, 3171
DeFosset, Don, Jr., 1999
DeFosset, Donald, 3719
DeFrancesco, Anne, 226
Deger, Michael J., 482
Deger, Ralph, 2401
Degerth, Martin, 2839
DeGhetto, Martin, 3708
Degliomini, Charles A., 1261
Degnan, James, 3893
Degnan, Scott S., 4088
Degnan, Stephen, 2662
DeGol, David A., 1465
DeGolia, Rick, 2288
DeGood, Nancy, 3890
DeGraan, Edward F., 183, 398
DeGraffenreidt, James H., Jr., 2397, 3925
Degrandpre, Peter, 1212
Dehn, William, 758
Dehn, William T., 758
Dehne, Tanuja, 2756
Deidiker, Jim D., 661
Deily, James T., 1994
Deily, Linnet F., 780, 1852
Dekema, Kyle, 1248
Dekker, David, 1064
Dekker, Harriett, 1064
Dekker, Marcel, 1064
Dekker, Marcel, Inc., 1064
Dekker, Marcell, 1064
Dekker, Russell, 1064
Dekkers, Marijn, 382
Dekkers, Marijn E., 1552
Del Bene, Robert F., 1960
Del Giudice, Michael J., 2335
Del Moral-Niles, Christopher J., 261
Del Sol, Carlos M., 669
Del Vecchio, Claudio, 2319
Del Vecchio, Jules A., 1653
Del Vecchio, Leonardo, 2319
Del Vecchio, Mark A., 2441
DeLaMater, Chester C., 1419
Deland, Daniel F., 2205
Delaney, John A., 2629
Delaney, John J., 3297
Delaney, Justin R., 3574
Delaney, Kevin P., 3100
Delaney, Peter B., 2794
Delaney, Rich, 2935
DeLaney, William J., 1313
DeLaney, William J., III, 3677
DeLano, Mike, 2538
Delaurenti, Charles J., II, 1404
Delaware National Bank of Delhi, The, 1518
DeLawder, C. Daniel, 2881
DeLawder, Charles Daniel, 2881
Delebo, Arlaine, 3883
Delehanty, Martha, 733
Delekta, Peter A., 2145
Delfiner, Hannah, 1657
Delfiner, Michael, 1657
Delfiner, Ruth, 1657
Delgado, William, 1634
Delhi Harmony Ranch, 1445
Delie, Vincent J., Jr., 1318
Delker, Wayne L., 852
Delkoski, M. P., 3
Dell'Osso, Domenic J., Jr., 777
Dell, Cheryl, 3680
Dell, Michael S., 1068
Dell, Robert M., 2228
Della, Honorio, 4113
Dellaquilla, Frank J., 1257
Deller, Michael, 2136
Delly, Gayla J., 1447
Delman, Debra, 227
Delmato, Drew, 3669
Deloach, H.E., Jr., 3500
Deloach, Harris E., Jr., 1189, 3500
Deloitte & Touche LLP, 1070
Deloitte & Touche USA LLP, 1070
Deloitte Haskins & Sells, 1070
Deloitte LLP, 1070
Delong, John, 1620
DeLorenzo, David A., 1141
Delorenzo, Lou, 1458
Delorme, Claude, 2491
Delp, Lawrence F., 3528
Delphi Automotive Systems Corp., 1071
Delphi Corp., 1071
Delphos Herald, Inc., 1072
Delsanto, John L., 22
Delson, Donald W., 4127
Delta Air Lines, Inc., 1073
Delta Dental of Colorado, 878
Delta Dental Plan of Kansas, Inc., 1074
Delta Dental Plan of Massachusetts, 1083
Delta Dental Plan of Oklahoma, Inc., 1079
Delta Dental Washington Dental Svc., 1081
Delta Fresh, LLC, 3002
Delta Industries, Inc., 1082
Deltek Systems, Inc., 1285
Deluca, Bill, 2354
DeLuca, Francis, 1399
DeLuca, Frederick A., 1138
Delucca, John J., 1268
Deluxe Corp., 1084
Delvaux, Tracy Rossetti, 1722
Delzer, Dennis, 2883
Deman, Greg, 401
DeMana, Jacqueline M., 4042
Demarest, Craig J., 3748
DeMaris, Shari J., 1808
DeMartini, Robert, 2668
DeMatteis, Claire, 719
DeMatteo, Daniel A., 1530
Demchak, William S., 2996, 2997
Demere, Robert H., Jr., 875
Demeritt, Stephen R., 1213
Demeter, Denise, 3999
Demicco, Lewis J., 2042
Demicco, Louis J., 2042
Demientieff, Laverna, 2797
Deming, Claiborne P., 2600
Demoff, Kevin, 3569
Demoulas Super Markets, Inc., 1085
Demoulas, Arthur T., 1085
DeMoura, Robert J., 577
Dempsey, Bill, 2991
Dempsey, John, 155
Dempsey, John T., 3275
Dempsey, Patrick J., 362
Dempsey, Ray C., 547
Dempsey, William G., 1867
Demsey, John D., 2057
Demsien, Steve, 238
Demsky, Howard, 3387
DeMuth, Christopher C., 3591
Den Daas, Kaj R., 3919
Den Hartog, Grace R., 2841
DeNale, Carol A., 1014
DeNaples, Louis A., 505
Denault, Leo, 1279
Denault, Leo P., 1278, 1279
Denend, Leslie G., 2417
DeNero, Henry T., 4042
Denham, Grey, 1585
Denham, Robert E., 780, 2690
Denholm, Robyn, 2075
DeNicola, T. Kevin, 889
Denigan, Susan, 2662
DeNinno, David L., 323, 4048
Denison, John G., 3522
Denison, Susan S., 2808
Denius, Franklin W., 3520
Denman, John W., 3488
Dennen, Joe, 536
Denner, Alexander J., 465
Denni, Gerald M., 3649
Denning, Steven A., 3741
Denninger, William C., 2088
Dennis & Phyllis Washington, 3994
Dennis, Edward A., 3192
Dennis, Jack S., 2251
Dennis, Pat, 2795
Dennis, Patricia Diaz, 2397
Dennis, Robert J., 1559
Dennis, Shirley M., 1419
Dennis, William, 2231
Dennison, Wayne, 590
Denniston, Brackett, 1552
Denniston, Brackett B., III, 1552
Denny, James, 3109
Deno, David, 487
Deno, David J., 2916
Denomme, Thomas G., 2393
Denot, Gerard, 346
Densmore, Doug W., 979
Densmore, Ken, 2010
DENSO International America, Inc., 1088
Denson, Charlie D., 2710
Dent, Mary, 3455
Dent, Sharon, 4097
Dent, Stephanie Jones, 4064
Dent, Stephine Jones, 4064
Dent, Tom, 2486
Dental Components, Inc., 1049
Dental Delivery Systems, Inc., 1370
Dental Delivery, Inc., 1370
Dental Services of Massachusetts Inc., 1083
Dentice, Aggie, 2427
Dentinger, Mark P., 2165
Denton, David M., 1014
Denton, Gus B., 507
Denton, James, 3839
Denton, John E., 3492
DENTSPLY International Inc., 1089
Denuit, Paul-Henri, 3876
Denys, Judi, 1560
Denzel, Bonnie, 2883
DePaoli, Deborah J., 3946
Department of Commerce, 3687
Department of Justice, State of California, 678
DePaulo, Joseph, 3478
DePeters, Jack, 4021
DePierro, John, 2741
DePierro, John J., 2741
DePinto, Joseph, 5, 2786
DePinto, Joseph M., 5, 572
Deposit Guaranty National Bank, 3171
DePuy Mitek, Inc., 2048
DePuy Orthopaedics, Inc., 2048
Derby, Deborah, 3790
Derby, Deborah M., 3790
Derby, Steven R., 2342
Derbyshire, John, 2106
Derderian, John, 2894
Derendoff, Shane, 1167
Dereszynski, Jeffrey M., 3388
Dereszynski, Nicholas J., 4146
Derickson, Sandra L., 1795
DeRienzis, Joshua H., 3074
Dering, Garrett W., 894
Dermody Properties, Inc., 1168
Dermody, Michael C., 1168
DeRodes, Robert P., 2650
DeRosa, Christina, 2611
DeRose, Robert, 1232
Derossi, Antonio, 1385
Derrick, Brian, 2462
Derrington, Ken R., 2154

Derrough, Lee A., 2091
Derry, John E., 2094
DeSanctis, Ellen, 913
DeSantis, Paul F., 1300
Descheneaux, Michael, 3455
Deseret Trust Company, 2862
Deshong, J.K., 395
Design One One, 947
DeSilva, Peter J., 3846
DeSisto, Rena M., 340
Desjardins, Leslie A., 221
DesLauriers, Charles T., 2671
Desmond, Laura, 38
Desmond-Hellmann, Susan, 3055
DeSoto, Pete, 2478
Desoto, Peter, 2478
DeSousa, Joseph, 2631
DeSpain, Brad, 3807
DeSpain, Charles B., 3807
Despeaux, Kim, 1279
Desroches, Pascal, 3757
DesRosier, Thomas J., 999
Dessner, Randy, 1452
DeStefano, Gary, 2710
DeStefano, Robert J., 271
Dethmers Manufacturing Co., 1091
DeTrane, Sal, 2447
Detroit Diesel Corp., 1093
Detroit Edison Co., The, 1183
Detroit Pistons Basketball Co., 1095
Dettmer, Eric, 2926
Dettmer, Ted, 2418
DeTurk, Nanette P., 1799
Deuel, Elizabeth, 1726
Deuschle, James R., 3204
Deutch, John M., 3135
Deutsch Co., The, 1098
Deutsch, Carl, 1098
Deutsch, Eleanor, 1098
Deutsch, James F., 3070
Deutsch, Lester, 1098
Deutsch, Michael J., 2183
Deutsch-Adler, Alexis, 1098
Deutsch-Zakarin, Gina, 1098
Deutsche Bank Americas Holding Corp., 1099
Deutsche-Zakarin, Gina, 1098
Devanny, Earl H., III, 890
DeVard, Jerri L., 403
Devasto, Daniel P., 4102
Devaul, Frank, 771
Devault, David V., 4001
DeVeau, David R., 2153
Development Services Trust, 3060
Devening, Randolph R., 3309
Devenuti, Richard R., 933, 3566
Devereaux Corp., Robert J., 1100
Devereaux, Harry, 1846
Devereaux, Jack, Jr., 1846
Devereaux, Michael F., 1100
Devereaux, Robert J., 1100
DeVeydt, Wayne S., 3541, 4027
DeVinck, Steven Q., 100
Devine, Brian K., 2945
Devine, Cynthia J., 3753
Devine, Donald, 2409
Devine, Marty, 1054
Devine, Michael F., III, 1059
Devine, Tammy, 3485
DeVinney, Betty W., 507
DeVito, Basil, 4121
Devitre, Dinyar S., 120, 4045
Devitt, Blake E., 377
Devitt, F. Edward, 2681
Devlin, Patrick J., 502
Devlin, Robert M., 935
DeVoe Buick Cadillac Inc., Dick, 1101
DeVoe, Barbara J., 1101
DeVoe, David F., 1480, 2700
DeVoe, Mark A., 1101
Devoe, Richard H., 1101
Devonshire, David W., 227, 2473
DeVore, Lynne, 2524
DeVos, Dan, 2824
DeVos, Doug, 189
Devos, Pam, 2824
DeVos, Rich, Sr., 2824
DeVos, Richard M., 2824
Devriendt, Beverly, 3020
DeVries, Betsy, 2475
DeVries, James, 2723
DeVries, Matt, 611
Dew, Bruce J., Jr., 1113
Dew, Donald F., 1113
Dew, Donald F., Sr., 1113
Dew, Donald H., 1113
Dew, Thomas H., 1113
DeWalt, David, 2417
DeWalt, David G., 2417
DeWalt, Michael, 722
Dewar, Patrick M., 2292
DeWatt, David G., 1073
Dewbrey, Diane, 1797
Dewbrey, Diane L., 1797
Dewey, Kenneth W., 1270
Dewey, Londa J., 144, 4008
DeWitt, Arnie, 2966
DeWitt, Carey A., 629
Dewitt, William O., III, 3568
DeWitt, William O., Jr., 3568
Dexter-Russell Inc., 1103
Dexter-Russell, Inc., 1103
DeYonker, Alex J., 3535
Dhanda, Anuj, 2997
Dhein, Jere, 3061
Dhillon, Janet, 2925
Di Donato, Shannon, 3624
Di Leo, Burno V., 1960
Diageo North America, Inc., 1107
Diagnos-Techs., Inc., 1108
Dial Corp, The, 3946
Diamandis, Peter, 1951
Diamente, Christine, 81
Diamond Resort Hawaii, 1868
Diamond Ridge Development, LLC, 723
Diamond Technology Partners Inc., 2759
Diamond Vogel North, Inc., 1198
Diamond, David A., 2607
Diamond, Gene, 756
Diamond, Matthew C., 1559
Diamond, Robin, 1139
Diamond, Susan, 1680
Diana, Andrew J., 381
Dias, Fiona P., 39
Diaz, Armando, 3165
Diaz, Eddie, 885
Diaz, Fred, 801
Diaz, Laura, 2209
Diaz, Nelson A., 1309
Diaz, Paul J., 1044, 2154
Diaz, Thelma, 1959
Diaz-Rosario, Luis, 3103
DiBella, Robert, 3343
DiBella, Robert J., 3343
DiBianca, Suzanne, 3318
DiBiasio, Bob, 847
DiBiasio, Robert A., 847
DiBlasi, D.J., 459
Dibuono, Nicholas, Jr., 2380
DiCamillo, Gary T., 4056
DiCamillo, Marietta, 2346
Dicciani, Nance K., 1706, 3029
Dice, Jeffrey M., 2719
DiCesare, Thor, 740
DiCesare, Thor D., 740
DiCiaccio, Rhonda, 1557
DiCiurcio, John A., 3824
Dick's Sporting Goods, Inc., 1110
Dick, Frank, 1590
Dick, Jimmy, IV, 1464
Dick, John W., 2263
Dick, Melvin A., 3521
Dick, Russell, 1887
Dick, Wesley, 3021
Dickason, Richard R., 1307
Dicke, James F., 987
Dicke, James F., II, 987
Dicke, James F., III, 987
Dickens, Helen M., 799
Dickens, Marty G., 1559
Dickerson, Gary, 1438
Dickerson, Gary E., 220
Dickerson, Mike, 3978
Dickey, Boh A., 3017
Dickey, Eileen D., 411
Dickinson, Daniel M., 722
Dickinson, David, 2548
Dickinson, Mary, 2548
Dickson, E. Rolland, 1141
Dickson, John T., 2165
Dickson, Stephen P., 4093
Dickson, Thomas W., 1738
DiConza, Carol A., 3277
DiConza, Peter J., Jr., 3277
DiCroce, Anthony J., 2782
Dicus, John B., 680
Dicus, Mary Woodley, 1189
Didesch, Bruce, 939
DiDonato, Tom, 140
Die-A-Matic, Inc., 3201
Diebold, Inc., 1112
Diederich, Gene Michael, 2557
Diedrich, Dan, 2949
Diefenderfer, William M., III, 3478
Diehl, Jay, 2329
Diehl, Scott, 1680
Diehl, Willie, 2620
Diemolding Corp., 1113
Dierberg, James F., 1393
Dierberg, James F., II, 1393
Dierberg, Mary W., 1393
Dierberg, Michael J., 1393
Dierking, Will, 2651
Diesen, David, 15
Diestel, David, 1426
Dieterle, Daniel, 1728
Dieterle, Michael M., 177
Dietrick, Martin A., 3031
Dietz & Watson, Inc., 1114
Dietz, Carolyn Emmerson, 3451
Dietz, Cindy, 3247
Dietz, Deborah Rybicki, 1075
Dietz, Diane M., 4056
Dietz, Kit D., 2304
Dietz, Ryan, 763
Dietz, W. Ronald, 679
Dietze, Katherine Elizabeth, 2406
Dietzler, David A., 3010
Difazio, V. James, 1946
DiFranco, Ani, 3214
DiFronzo, Pascal W., 289
DiGaetano, Bill, 4084
DiGanci, Todd T., 1382
Digby, Jeffrey, 909
DiGenova, Jerry, 704
DiGeso, Amy, 2230
Digges, Hester M., 3298
Diggs, Alisa, 1077
Diggs, James C., 91
Diggs, Shauna Ryder, 502
Digiacomo, David, 1914
DiGiacomo, Kara, 465
Digilio, Monica, 2133
Digiusto, Alessandra, 1099
Dignum, Dale, 487
DiGrazia, G. Gino, 3079
Diker, Charles M., 2296
Dilbeck, 1116
Dilbeck, Mark, 1116
Dileo, Paul, 1099
Dill, Chris, 3793
Dill, David M., 2270
Dillabough, Gary, 3366
Dillard Investment Corp., 2796
Dillard, Gary, 240
Dillard, Gray, 240
Dillard, James E., 120
Dillard, William T., II, 360
Diller Telephone Co., 1117
Diller, Barry, 862, 1311, 1903, 3999
Diller, Jack, 2620
Dilley, Margarita K., 757
Dillin, Carol, 3010
Dillion, Eileen M., 1604
Dillman, Linda, 3112
Dillman, Linda M., 754
Dillon, Adrian T., 4079
Dillon, David B., 1124, 2195
Dillon, Donald F., 1427
Dillon, Eileen M., 1603
Dillon, James, 603
Dillon, Jenni, 1383
Dillon, John M., 508
Dillon, John T., 2120
Dillon, John W., 1087
Dillon, Mary N., 3691, 3876
Dillon, Michael, 38
Dillon, Molly, 2465
Dillon, Veronica, 3999
Dillon-Ridgley, Diane, 1953
Dilsaver, Evelyn, 46, 655
Dilworth, Joan, 3347
DiManna, Sara E., 1272
DiMarco, Stephanie G., 41
Dime Bank, 1118
Dime Savings Bank of Norwich, 1118
Dimeo, Bradford S., 1119
DiMicco, Daniel R., 1189, 2760
Dimick, Neil F., 2610
Dimitriou, K. E., 3981
Dimling, John A., 227
Dimmig, Doug, 4028
Dimock, Rodney C., 428
Dimoff, David, 3196
Dimon, James, 2071, 2072
Dimond, Robert B., 2619
Dimos, Chris T., 2622
DiMuccio, Robert A., 183
Dinan, Curtis L., 2815
Dindo, Kathryn M., 100
Dindo, Kathryn W., 3488
Dineen, Patrick J., 1081
Dingemans, Simon, 1588
Dinges, Dan O., 3877
Dinges, Jim, 1666
Dingmann, Duane, 2966

Dingwell, Mark Edward, 1188
Dinh, Viet D., 2700
Dinion, Eva, 162
Dinkins Trust, C.L., 635
Dinkins, Brad, 635
Dinkins, David N., 3879
Dinkins, Michael, 635
DiNola, Ralph, 1652
Dinolfo, Tom, 3612
DiNovi, Anthony, 1191
Dinsmore, Gordon G., 430
Dinsmore, Robert, 544
Dinto, Paul P., 3344
Dionisio, John M., 42
DiOrio, Rana, 2288
Diosegy, Arlene J., 4078
Dipaola, Robert, 2166
DiPaolo, Nicholas, 1459
DiPiazza, Samuel A., Jr., 1124
Dipietro, Gil, 1620
Dipietro, Gilbert, 1620
DiPietro, Kenneth, 465
Dippin Dots Franchising, Inc., 1122
Dir, Rodney D., 2758
Diraddo, Donald, 335
DiRaimo, Carol A., 2007
DiRaimondo, Michael A., 3852
Director, David, 2262
DIRECTV Group, Inc., The, 1124
DiRisio, Derek M., 3077
Dirks, Daria, 3687
Dirks, Don, 3222
Dirksen, Bill, 1464
Dirkx, Ryan, 242
DiSanto, Edmund, 167
Discovery Communications, Inc., 1126
DiSepio, Marguerite, 124
Disera, David, 1408
Dishaw, Michael, 366
Disher, Linda, 1383
Dishman, Tammy, 680
DiSilvestro, Anthony P., 669
Disney Co., Walt, The, 1127
Dispatch Printing Co., The, 1129
Disser, Daniel J., 3771
Disser, Peter T., 2739
Dissinger, Ronald L., 2120
DiStasio, James S., 1253, 2737
Distaso, John C., 2981
Ditch, Amanda J., 839
Ditkoff, James H., 1027
Ditmore, Dana, 3673
Ditmore, Robert K., 735
Ditrolio, Jospeh F., 887
Dittamore, Raymond V., 2268, 3095
Dittberner, Jason, 1077
Dittenhafer, Brian D., 1984
Dittmann, David, 2689
Ditto, Michael Eugene, 3188
Divac, Vlade, 3303
Dively, Joseph R., 1411, 1412
Diversey, Inc., 2049
Diversified Buildings, Inc., 941
Diversified Technology, Inc., 1289
Diversityinc Media, 1131
DiVittorio, Tom, 1561
Dix, Albert E., 1063
Dix, David E., 1063
Dix, G. Charles, II, 1063
Dix, R. Victor, 1063
Dix, Robert C., Jr., 1063
Dix, Ronald H., 313
Dixie Group, Inc., The, 1132
Dixie Yarns, Inc., 1132
Dixit, Vishva, 1549
Dixon Hughes Goodman, 1133
Dixon, Charles D., 840
Dixon, Christopher B., 2751
Dixon, G. Lowell, 2427
Dixon, Gene, Jr., 2201
Dixon, Georgette "Gigi", 4028
Dixon, Guy B., 2201
Dixon, James J., 3211
Dixon, Leslie H., 317
Dixon, Leslie W., 3148
Dixon, Mark, 172
Dixon, Matt, 3531
Dixon, Randall, 3726
Dixon, Robert, 2935
Dixon, Robert L., Jr., 4027
Dixon, Robert M., Jr., 337
Dixon, Ronard F., 162
Dixon, Steven C., 777
Dixon, Thomas H., 2814
Diyanmi, Edward F., 3973
Djerejian, Edward P., Amb., 2780
DjerejianIrani, Edward P., 2780
Djonovic, Navy E., 3070
DJR Holding Corp., 1135
DKB Foundation, 2542
Dlugokecki, Frederick A., 2646
Doan, Andrea, 963
Doan, Kathleen, 839
Doane, W. Allen, 85, 1405
Dobbins, Howard W., 4078
Dobbins, R.E., 3814
Dobbins, Z. E., Jr., 3615
Dobbs, S. B., 1448
Dobbs, Stephen B., 1007
Doberneck, Megan, 3965
Dobkin, Richard J., 966
Doblin Group, Inc., 3944
Dobos, John A., 912
Dobrovich, Linda, 3203
Dobsky, Paul, 415
Dobson Telephone Co., 1137
Dobson, Julie A., 3307
Dobson, Karen, 503
Dobson, Terry, 823
Dobson, W. Terry, 823
Docherty, Susan E., 1555
Docken, Paula, 2619
Dockendorff, Charles J., 956
Doctoroff, Daniel L., 486
Doctors Co., The, 1139
Dodd, Anji, 3810
Dodd, Jeanne D., 1162
Dodds, Hamish, 1727
Dodds, Hamish A., 1727, 2973
Dodds, Jay P., 1403
Dodge, George, Jr., 1337
Dods, Nancy, 3349
Dods, Walter A., Jr., 85, 346, 2404
Dodson, Blane, 715
Dodson, Jennifer Parker, 2884
Dodson, Mark S., 2747
Dodson, Paulette, 2948
Dodson, Zeke, 715
Doelle, Kurt, 640
Doenng, Mark, 2641
Doerfler, Doug, 3608
Doerhoff, Claudia, 3122
Doerhoff, Neil, 3122
Doering, Jennifer, 3402
Doering, Kim, 3874
Doering, Ruth, 3402
Doering, Shannon, 2653
Doermer, Richard, 551
Doerr, Chris, 2629
Doerr, Christopher L., 3167
Doerr, D., 3198
Doerr, L. John, 1613
Doerr, R. Chris, 493
Doerr, Thomas L., 2188
Doescher, Scott P., 4008
Doggendorf, Daniel, 1023
Doggett, William B., 1216
Doheny, Edward I., II, 2070
Doherty, Courtney M., 1051
Doherty, Edmund J., 226
Doherty, Janice, 3467
Doherty, Janice M., 3467
Doherty, Patrick, 221
Doherty, Peter J., 756
Doherty, Shawn, 1292
Dohle, Markus, 2922
Doi, Tracey C., 3789
Doiron, Craig, 839
Doiron, Mark, 1723
Dolan, Brian T., 2550
Dolan, Charles F., 641, 2336
Dolan, Charles P., 2336, 2769
Dolan, James L., 641, 2336
Dolan, James P., 1140
Dolan, Janet M., 1153, 3802
Dolan, Jim, 1140
Dolan, John F. X., 1382
Dolan, Kathleen M., 641
Dolan, Kevin, 13
Dolan, Kristin A., 641, 2336
Dolan, Mark V., 1904
Dolan, Michael J., 2405
Dolan, Patrick F., 641
Dolan, Paul J., 847, 3488
Dolan, Raymond P., 167
Dolan, Ronald J., 2790
Dolan, Scott, 716
Dolan, Terrance, 3835
Dolan, Thomas C., 641, 2336
Dolan, Traci, 3595
Dolan, Victoria, 869
Dolan, Vincent M., 1189
Dolan-Sweeney, Deborah, 641
Dolan-Sweeney, Deborah A., 2336
Dolbeare, Glenn, 3343
Dolbeare, Glenn D., 3343
Dolby, Edward C., 1330
Dole Food Co., Inc., 717
Doleshek, Richard, 3104
Doleshek, Richard J., 3104
Dolfi, D. Scott, 1683
Dolfi, Roxanne, 1317
Dolgen, Jonathan L., 1311
Dolich, Andy, 3326
Doliveux, Roch, 3627
Doll, Dixon, 1124
Doll, Mark G., 2749
Doll, Norman, 2972
Doll, Thomas, 3631
Doll, Thomas J., 3631
Dollar Bank, FSB, 1142
Dollar General Corp., 1143
Doller, Benjamin, 3879
Dollive, James P., 3365
Dolloff, Christopher, 831
Dolsky, Mark G., 495
Dolvin, Neal, 350
Doman, Andrew S., 3289
Dombach, Brian, 1676
Dombeck, Michael P., 2049
Dombkowski, Kristy R., 1749
Dombrowski, David, 1097
Dombrowski, Louis, 1549
Domeck, Brian, 3057
Domeck, Brian C., 3057
Domico, Greg, 205
Dominguez, Cari, 2358
Dominguez, Carlos, 818
Dominguez, Michael J., 729
Dominion Chevrolet Co., 1148
Dominion Energy New England, 1150
Dominion Energy, Inc., 1150
Dominion Resources, Inc., 1150
Dominion Transmission, 1150
Domino, Joseph F., 1280
Dominquez, Joseph, 1309
Domke, John, 3471
Donahoe, Ernest N., 385
Donahoe, John J., 1217, 1950
Donahue, J. Christopher, 1351
Donahue, Jim, 3016
Donahue, Joe, 3829
Donahue, John F., 1351
Donahue, John K., 3855
Donahue, Ken, 613
Donahue, Kevin M., 3090
Donahue, Michael J., 63
Donahue, Robert J., 2751
Donahue, Thomas R., 1351, 1799
Donahue, Timothy J., 988
Donahue, Timothy M., 1214
Donald & Linda Gross Foundation, 2135
Donald, Arnold W., 696, 988, 2208
Donald, James L., 3220
Donald, Micheal, 4152
Donaldson Co., Inc., 1153
Donaldson, David A., 3972
Donaldson, James A., 853
Donaldson, Michael P., II, 1282
Donaldson, Phil, 194
Donaldson, Philip E., 194
Donaldson, Steve, 1317
Donargo, Vincent, 567
Donatelli, Joyce, 46
Donatiello, Nicolas, Jr., 3363
Donatone, Lorna, 3497
Donatuti, Bruce, 2984
Donavan, James J., 2323
Dondero, James, 3309
Dondlinger and Sons Construction Co., Inc., 1154
Dondlinger, James M., 1154
Dondlinger, Thomas E., 1154
Dondlinger, Tom E., 1154
Donegan, Thomas G., 2482
Donelson, John, 3904
Donine, Richard S., 3594
Donkis, Michael, 1267
Donleavy, John J., 2630
Donley, Doug, 3220
Donley, Max, 2450
Donlin Creek, LLC, 657
Donlon, Hugh J., 2681
Donnalley, Joseph T., 2057
Donnell, Cydney, 136
Donnell, Terry O', 3731
Donnellan, Brain, 2482
Donnellan, Brian, 2482
Donnelley & Sons Co., R.R., 1155
Donnelley, Reuben Simpson, 716
Donnelly, Chris, 1267
Donnelly, John J., 1176
Donnelly, Michael J., 3297
Donnelly, Richard, 3993
Donnelly, Richard M., 2833
Donnelly, Scott C., 3731

Donnelly, Terence, 895
Donnelly, Thomas, 3992
Donnelly, Thomas J., 887
Donnini, Scott, 2618
Donofrio, Nicholas M., 40, 344, 1071, 2265
Donohoe, John J., 1217
Donohue, Anne M., 3562
Donohue, Fay, 1083
Donohue, John F., 226
Donohue, Nicholas C., 2659
Donohue, Robert W., 3211
Donohue, Thomas J., 3857
Donohue, Thomas J., Jr., 912
Donovan Marine, Inc., 1156
Donovan, Dennis P., 2958
Donovan, Edward, 2751
Donovan, Mark, 2091
Donovan, Nancy S., 2241
Donovan, Paul, 832, 4112
Donovan, Thomas C., 2872
Donovan, Tim, 650
Donovan, Walter C., 3085
Donovan, William, 3877
Doochin, Jerald, 1975
Doochin, Julie, 160
Doochin, Michael, 1975
Doochin, Robert S., 160
Doodian, Rob, 126
Doody, Joseph D., 2904
Dooley, Christopher P., 1880
Dooley, Franco, 3944
Dooley, John T., 1382
Dooley, Richard G., 2030
Dooley, Thomas E., 3945
Doolin, Wallace B., 692
Doolittle, Lea Anne, 2747
Doon, Loretta, 3363
Dopfner, Mathias, 3757
Doppelt, Earl H., 3984
Dorado, Raymond, 344
Doramus, Mark, 3598
Doran, Brian F., 3003
Doran, Carl, 1463
Doran, Charles, 126
Doran, Stephen E., 2171
Doran, Thomas, 1823
Doran, Toan, 3189
Dorch, Verona A., 1741
Dordell, Timothy P., 3775
Dordelman, William E., 887
Dorduncu, Ahmet C., 1968
Doren, Diane K., 3857
Dorer, Benno, 852
Dorey, William G., 1632
Dorfman, Mark A., 1179
Doria, Denise C., 1399
Dorman, D. E., 1715
Dorman, David, 1715
Dorman, David W., 1014, 2586, 4150
Dorman, Margaret K., 1287
Dorn, Megan, 1565
Dorn, Nancy, 1552
Dorn, Raenell, 3827
Dorner, Irene, 1876
Dorney, Kevin, 2410
Dorny, D. Matthew, 2759
Dorrance, Bennett, 669
Dorris, Gary A., 2606
Dorris, William E., 2147
Dorsa, Caroline, 3077
Dorsa, Caroline D., 465, 3077
Dorschel, Jay A., 2616
Dorsey, James, 1491
Dorsey, Patrick B., 3750
Dorsman, Peter, 2650
Dorsman, Peter A., 219
Dorton, Richard O., 1053
Doshi, Chandrika, 1305
Doshi, Hasmukh M., 1305
Doshi, Vashal, 1305
Doss, J. Matthew, 479
Doss, Matt, 479
Dossman, Curley M., Jr., 1568
Dot Foods, Inc., 1158
Doti, James L., 1389
Dotson, Darlene B., 1770
Dotson, David C., 1146
Dotterer, Herb, 461
Dotty's Co., LLC, 3803
Doty, Mark A., 2991
Doty, Michael, 1300
Doucette, James W., 900
Doucette, Kathleen, 2262
Doucette, Steve, 476
Dougherty, David F., 933
Dougherty, M. I., 3920
Dougherty, Michele, 4009
Dougherty, Neil, 56
Dougherty, Robert A., 65
Doughty, Tony, 3177
Douglas Corp., 1159
Douglas Hodo, Edward, 3606
Douglas, Bill, 863
Douglas, Bruce J., 2224
Douglas, Chester W., 1083
Douglas, Craig A., 3579
Douglas, Elyse, 1792
Douglas, Elyse B., 266
Douglas, J.A.M., Jr., 862
Douglas, James H., 2633
Douglas, Laura M., 2260
Douglas, Laurie Zeitlin, 3079
Douglas, Mark A., 3093
Douglas, Richard W., 285
Douglas, Robert, 3192
Douglas, Scott S., 2246
Douglas, William W., III, 863
Douglas, William, III, 862
Douglass, Ann Megan, 2573
Douglass, Lee, 240
Douglass, Ollen, 2582
Douglass, William P., 1297
Douhan, Zelinda Makepeace, 7
Dovberg, Dana, 146
Dove, Carol L., 2639
Dove, Chris, 1458
Dove, Timothy L., 2981
Dover, Robert A., 775
Dow Chemical Co., The, 1161
Dow Corning Corp., 1162
Dow Jones & Co., Inc., 1163
Dow, Ben, 2991
Dow, Gabrielle, 335
Dow, Robert Stanley, 2303
Dow, Roger, 3140
Dow, Stafford, 3146
Dowd, Brian, 24
Dowd, Curtis, 3341
Dowda, Tanya, 2217
Dowding, Alyssa C., 2855
Dowdy, N. S., 3441
Dowell, Greg, 136
Dowell, Greg A., 136
Dower, Roger C., 2049
Dowler, Chris, 267
Dowling & Partners Securities, LLC, 1165
Dowling, Brian, 3310
Dowling, J. Robert, 226
Dowling, Michael J., 2736
Dowling, Steven, 2912
Dowling, Vincent J., Jr., 1165, 1918
Downe, William, 2358
Downer, E. Michael, 2446
Downer, Edward M., III, 2446
Downes, Laurence M., 3104
Downey, Bruce L., 685
Downey, J. Michael, 2845
Downey, Matthew J., 607
Downey, Shannon, 2987
Downey, Thomas J., 516
Downey, William H., 2092
Downing, Lynn, 2966
Downing, Scott, 3944
Downs, John H., 863
Doyal, Steve, 1707
Doyle Foundation, 30
Doyle, Allison, 3863
Doyle, Dan, 2349
Doyle, Daniel A., 3081
Doyle, Don, 83
Doyle, Francis A., 2737
Doyle, Francis A., III, 2265
Doyle, J. Patrick, 1151, 1524
Doyle, James, 855
Doyle, John, 3281
Doyle, John D., 2265
Doyle, John J., Jr., 583
Doyle, John L., 4137
Doyle, Joseph E., 2863
Doyle, Joseph T., 3904
Doyle, Kathleen H., 3855
Doyle, Kevin M., 725
Doyle, Michael, 1466
Doyle, Noreen, 2698
Doyle, Patrick, 1124
Doyle, Patrick T., 1124
Doyle, Susan M., 1263
Doyle, Thomas J., 1356
Doyon Ltd., 1167
Dozer, Richard H., 216, 500, 3946
Dozier, Bill L., 345
Dozier, Dirk, 3679
Dozono, Sho, 3544
Dozoretz, Beth, 1368
Dozoretz, Ronald I., 1368
DP Advisors LLC, 1168
DP Homes LLC, 1168
DPC Midstream, 1189
Drabek, Anthony, 2743
Dragas, Helen E., 1150
Drago, Joseph, 837
Drahozal, Christopher R., 3869
Draizin, Adam, 3551
Draizin, Donald J., 3551
Draizin, Stephen S., 3551
Drake Industries, LLC, 1777
Drake, Ann M., 716
Drake, C. David, 1661
Drake, Carol L., 1631
Drake, Darin, 1777
Drake, Michael L., 1777
Drake, Miles, 4052
Drake, Pansy L., 1777
Drake, Peter, 484
Drake, Rodman L., 732
Drake, Shelley C., 2323
Drake, Shelly C., 2323
Dralle, Jeffrey, 2282
Draper & Kramer, Inc., 1170
Draper, E. Linn, Jr., 101, 112, 2748
Draper, Michael J., 616
Drapin, Matthew A., 3281
Drapkin, Matthew A., 3281
Drapkin, Matthew A., III, 3281
Draughn, Vicki, 1169
Draut, Eric J., 1955
Drayer, Ralph W., 3272
Drayna, Jon, 261
Drazen, Michael D., 3775
Drazen, Mike, 3775
DreamWorks Animation SKG, Inc., 1172
Dreasler, Brady E., 3110
Dreher, Melanie C., 4026
Dreier, Stephen I., 566
Dreiling, Richard W., 1143, 2312
Dreisbach, James, 937
Dreisig, W. Patrick, 629
Drendel, Dale, 1466
Dress Barn, Inc., The, 255
Dress, Jeff, 3560
Dressel, Melanie J., 3081
Dresser, 1173
Dresser Industries, 1173
Drew, Dennis M., 1824
Drew, J. Edwin, 3515
Drew, Pamela J., 2126
Drewes, Alfred H., 2935
Drewitz, Mary Lyn, 3996
Drewry, William, 3141
Drexel, Janie, 2307
Drexler, John T., 231
Drexler, Millard S., 217
Dreyer's Grand Ice Cream, Inc., 1174
Dreyfus, Andrew, 501
Dreyfus, Andrew C., 501
Drezner, Michael H., 3510
Driano, Dominick V., Jr., 3264
Driessnack, Robert, 1955
Driessnack, Robert J., 1955
Driggers, Timothy K., 1282
Drinan, Helen G., 501
Drinko, John D., 319
Dripchak, Dave, 2963
Driscoll, Brent, 1012
Driscoll, James C., III, 2704
Driscoll, Maggie, 2213
Driscoll, William L., 3017
Drive Financial Services LP, 1177
Driver, B. Kenneth, 942
Driver, Walter W., Jr., 1288
Droppa, Jane W.I., 1810
Drosdick, John G., 3877
Drossaert, Wim, 2608
Drossner, Audrey B., 2245
Drow, Frederick B., 1765
Drozd, Taras, 1422
DRS Technologies Inc., 1179
drugstore.com, inc., 1180
Druml, Daniel B., 3388
Drummond, David C., 1613
Drummond, Jere, 528
Drummond, Jere A., 528, 3311
Drury, David J., 2749
Druten, Robert J., 2094
DRW Holdings LLC., 1181
Dryer, Jackie, 2903
DTE Energy Ventures, Inc., 1183
Du Moulin, Richard T., 3748
Du Plessis Currie, John Alexander, 567
Du Pont, Eleuthere I., 1184, 4127
DUB, 30
Dubai Municipality, 1953
Dube, Eric, 1588

Duberstein, Kenneth M., 516, 1068, 3802
DuBiago, Nicholas, 1399
Dubin, Adam, 3477
Dubin, James, 1259
Dubin, Melvin, 3477
Dubinsky, Jason M., 3981
Dublon, Dina, 2501, 2935
Dubois, Carey, 893
Dubos, Jean-Francois, 30
Dubose, Art, 62
Dubow, Craig A., 1532
Dubow, Lawrence J., 2014
Ducan, E.Townes, 566
Ducap Electronics, Inc., 1045
Duchossois Industries, Inc., 1187
Duchossois Technology Partners, LLC, 1187
Duchossois, Craig J., 807, 1187
Duchossois, Kimberly, 1187
Duchossois, R. Bruce, 1187
Duchossois, Richard L., 807, 1187
Duckett, Michael R., 32
Duckhouse, David, 2595, 3163
Duckworth, Connie K., 2749, 3597
Ducrest, Thomas L., 2879
Duda & Sons, A., Inc., 1188
Duda, Andy L., 1188
Duda, Andy, Jr., 1188
Duda, Dan, 1188
Duda, David J., 1188
Duda, Ferdinand S., 1188
Duda, Joseph A., 1188
Duda, Sammy, 1188
Duda-Chapman, Tracy, 1188
Dudding, Theresa, 2431
Dudek, Patricia L., 786
Duderstadt, James J., 3859
Dudiak, Rose, 1477
Dudich, George, 3904
Dudley, Bill, 395
Dudley, Gary, 3523
Dudley, Gary L., 3523
Dudley, Jay, 3010
Dudley, William N., Jr., 395
Duell, Caroline, 1244
Duello, J. Donald, 3431
Duenas, Rayna, 934
Duennes, Doug, 334
Duerden, John H., 2776
Duerrner, Cindy A., 554
Dues, John J., 464
Duesenberg, Mark H., 1366
Duess, Robert, 3153
Duey, Maria C., 2393
Duff, Andrew S., 2983
Duff, Patrick, 3381
Duff, Paul, 1082
Dufficy, Nancy, 2774
Duffie, Darrell, 2563
Duffy Homes, 1235
Duffy, Bill, 279, 512
Duffy, Catherine, 1602
Duffy, James E., 564
Duffy, Robert L., 1736
Duffy, Roger, 3474
Duffy, Terrance A., 853
Duffy, Terrence A., 853
Duffy, Timothy F., 3707
Duffy, William T., 512
Dufour, Alfred, 2552
Dufour, Pierre, 233
Dugan, A.W., 2727
Dugan, Albert W., 2727
Dugan, Lydia P., 2727
Dugan, Patrick D., 4048
Dugan, Patrick W., 2727
Dugas, Richard J., Jr., 3083
Duggal, Elizabeth Gold, 1598
Duggan, Michael, 1158
Dugger, Randy, 3544
Duginski, Michael, 437
Duhamel, Scott, 491
Duke Energy Business Services, 1189
Duke Energy Corp., 1189
Duke Energy Field Services, LP, 1189
Duke Power Co., 1189
Duke University, 3474
Duke, Kevin, 3967
Duke, Michael T., 3980
Duke, Mike, 1001
Duke, Mystel, 3523
Duke, Patrick, 934
Duke, Patrick W., 1167
Dukes, David E., 1395
Dulaney, Daryl, 3448
Dumais, Michael, 3908
Dumas, Bryan, 2716
Dumas, David, 560
Dumont-McCafferty, Yvonne, 957
DuMouchel, William H., 226
Dun & Bradstreet Corp., The, 1190
Dunaway, Barry C., 3488
Dunaway, Cambria W., 595
Dunbar, M., 2047
Dunbar, Mary L., 1477
Dunbar, W. Roy, 1886, 2258
Duncan, Alan H., 2590
Duncan, Allison Fouch, 2209
Duncan, Amani, 2390
Duncan, Bridget Downey, 2122
Duncan, Bruce W., 3589
Duncan, Chris, 1858
Duncan, Dean R., 3319
Duncan, Deborah L., 1497, 1683
Duncan, Douglas G., 1892
Duncan, Gary, 3944
Duncan, Ian, 4066
Duncan, Jimmy, 3259
Duncan, Kenneth M., 3190
Duncan, Mark D., 2500
Duncan, Moria, 1234
Duncan, Robert D., 114
Duncan, Ronald A., 1550
Duncan, Sam, 3659
Duncan, Thurman, 2235
Duncomb, Vicki J., 1140
Dundon, Thomas, 1177
Dundrea, Matthew W., 211
Dunford, Michael P., 956
Dunham, Archie W., 777, 2310, 3857
Dunham, Linda, 2427
Dunham, Paul, 2851
Dunigan, Larry E., 2798
Dunkin Brands Inc., 1191
Dunkin' Donuts Inc., 1191
Dunlaevy, J. Williar, 428
Dunlaevy, James Williar, 428
Dunlap, Edward B., 740
Dunlap, Edward B., Jr., 740
Dunlap, Michael, 1283
Dunlap, Michael S., 2660
Dunlap, Pamela L., 2963
Dunlap, R. Thornwell, III, 952
Dunlap, R.T., III, 952
Dunlap, R.T., Jr., 952
Dunlap, Timothy M., 740
Dunlap, William H., 2474
Dunleavy, Michael F., 988
Dunlevy, James, 512
Dunlop, Becky Norton, 1201
Dunlop, Eleanor, 1248
Dunlop, Walker, 1314
Dunn Investment Company, 1192
Dunn, Allison, 2474
Dunn, Brandon R., 4142
Dunn, Byron W., 3106
Dunn, Christopher R., 3512
Dunn, Clay, 1884
Dunn, Dale, 3459
Dunn, Donald L., 793
Dunn, Dons L., 1338
Dunn, E. Paul, Jr., 1368
Dunn, Geoffrey, 1165
Dunn, George, 2695
Dunn, Gregory W., 3166
Dunn, Jeff, 3793
Dunn, Jeffrey D., 149
Dunn, Kevin, 4121
Dunn, Lucy, 2250
Dunn, Michael, 669
Dunn, Micheal G., 2860
Dunn, Norma, 661
Dunn, Pattie M., 1681
Dunn, Pattie McCay, 1681
Dunn, Sarah, 858
Dunn, Steve, 196
Dunn, Terrence P., 2094, 3846
Dunn, Wallace, 1133
Dunn, William P., Jr., 287
Dunne, Richard, 1065
Dunne, Tiffany, 901
Dunnigan, Jim, 3177
Dunphy, Cecilia, 1683
Dunphy, T.J. Dermot, 3381
Dunsire, Deborah L., 99
Dunsmore, Lorri Anne, 2501
Dunston, S. Cary, 170
Dunton, Frank W., 331
Duperreault, Brian, 2385
Dupilka, Cynthia, 341
Duplantis, B.J., 3614
duPont, A.I., 970
Dupont, Augustus, 969
DuPont, Augustus I., 970
Dupont, Brenda K., 170
Dupont, Kevin, 2757
Dupps Co., 1193
Dupps, David M., 1193
Dupps, Frank N., 1193
Dupps, Frank, Jr., 1193
Dupps, John, 1193
Dupps, John A., Jr., 1193
DuPre, John L., 1710
Dupree, Donald R., 1713
Dupuis, Amy, 3329
DuPuy, Robert A., 2345
Duques, Henry C., 3859
Duquette, Lisa A., 380
Duquette, Robert B., 380
Dur, Philip A., 2125
Dura Medical Inc., 3043
Duran, Al, 3310
Duran, Chris, 705
Duran, Tino, 3321
Durand, Mark W., 4007
Durant, Karen A., 3714
Durante, Katherine B., 2782
Durazo, Felix, 1077
Durbin, John, 2431
Durcan, D. Mark, 2500
Durcanin, Joseph A., 427
Durham, H. Lee, Jr., 1396
Durham, Michael J., 1792
Durian, Robert J., 104, 4095
Durkin, Bryan T., 853
Durkin, Dennis, 30
Durkin, Elizabeth B., 3858
Durkin, Marian M., 301
Duro-Last Roofing, 1196
Duron, Rosalie, 3010
Durrett, Beth A., 444
Durrett, William E., 145
Dutch Gold Honey, Inc., 1197
Dutcher, Judi H., 496
Dutkowsky, Robert, 1564
Dutt, John, 545
Dutt, Katy, 545
Duval, Cyrille, 423
Duvall, Carol, 83
Duvall, Lewis, 350
Duvick, David F., 1220
Duvvru, Shiva, 3065
Duvvuru, Shiva, 3065
Duxbury, Elizabeth J., 2991
DVK, Inc., 1198
Dvorak, Bernard G., 2263
Dvorak, David C., 4157
Dwight, Diana T., 2056
Dwight, John K., 2928
Dworak, Cathy A., 1651
Dworman Foundation, Inc., 1098
Dwyer, Ann, 2444
Dwyer, Carrie E., 3363
Dwyer, Dean P., 938
Dwyer, Ellen, 986
Dwyer, James, 1081
Dwyer, James E., Jr., 2493
Dwyer, Jim, 1081
Dwyer, Jim F., 2444
Dwyer, John J., Jr., 2671
Dwyer, Kirk, 3940
Dwyer, Kirk B., 3940
Dwyer, Maureen E., 4074
Dwyer, Richard M., 2129
Dybsky, Thomas J., 3714
Dye, Hamp, 3547
Dye, John, 4045
Dye, John R., 4045
Dye, Karey D., 1603
Dye, Robert J., 211
Dyer, Colin, 2061
Dyer, David F., 4151
Dyer, Harold, 283
Dyer, John, 2162
Dyer, John M., 959
Dyer, Rick, 1026
Dyer, Terry M., 4124
Dyess, Kirby A., 3010
Dygert, Justin, 210
Dygon, Anne M., 2514
Dyke, James W., Jr., 3997
Dyke, Pete, 2926
Dyke, Shannon Van, 1545
Dykes, Jamie, 455
Dykes, Ronald M., 167
Dykhouse, Dana J., 2748
Dykhouse, Richard R., 765
Dykshorn, Owen, 3035
Dykstra, Jack, 3690
Dykstra, Karen, 209
Dykstra, Paul, 3690
Dykstra, Paul B., 3946
Dykstra, Timothy, 3487
Dylo, Susan, 3501
Dymond, William T., Jr., 2313

Dynacraft BSC, Inc., 30
Dynamet Inc., 1200
Dynatek, Inc., 1995
Dysart, W.J., 3668
Dyson, David E., 3062
Dyson, David E., Jr., 3062
Dyson, Jim, 1445
Dyson, Steven, 2156
Dzau, Victor J., 2453, 2935
Dziedzic, Joseph W., 571
Dzielak, Robert, 1311
Dzledzic, Joseph W., 571
Dzwonczyk, Christine, 717

E&J GALLO Winery, 3303
E.ON U.S. LLC, 2260
Eads, Misha, 1660
Eads, Thomas, 1660
Eagan, Brain C., 2742
Eagan, Gail, 226
Eagin, Mary, 1821
Eagin, Mary Hoffer, 1821
Eagin, Sara, 1821
Eagle Gate College, 1538
Eagle West, LLC, 1203
Eagle, Jevin S., 708
Eagletech International, Inc., 1202
Eagon, Douglas P., 3607
Eaker, Norman, 2059
Earhart, Cindy C., 2725
Earl, James F., 1741
Earley, Anthony F., Jr., 1464, 2952
Earley, James, 912
Earley, James E., 912
Earley, Nancy J., 945
Early, Mark, 3957
Early, Mike, 608
Early, W. B., 2032
Earnest, Steve, 1790
Earnhardt, Teresa, 1205
Earth, Inc., 838
Easley, Will, 3347
Eason, Gary, 3812
Eason, J. Cliff, 3179
East Boston Savings Bank, 1207
East Cambridge Savings Bank, 1208
East Maui Irrigation Co., Ltd., 85
East Rock Village, Inc., 1782
East, John B., 3519
Easter Unlimited Inc., 3038
Easter, Chris, 2111
Easter, William H., III, 3650
Easterbrook, Robert, 957
Easterday, Thomas Vernon, 3632
Eastern American Energy Corp., 1272
Eastern Bank, 1209
Eastern Federal Bank, 1210
Eastern New Mexico Rural Telephone Cooperative, 1211
Eastern Savings and Loan Assn., 1210
Easthampton Savings Bank, 1212
Eastman Chemical Co., 1213
Eastman Kodak Co., 1214
Eastman, Lance, 2178
Eastman, Lance E., 2178
Easton Aluminum, Inc., 1215
Easton Development, Inc., 1215
Easton Technical Products, Inc., 1215
Easton, Gregory J., 1215
Easton, James L., 1215
Easton, Lynn E., 1215
Easton, Robin E., 2850
Easton, Robin J., 2850
Eaton Corp., 1216
Eaton, Carol, 3675
Eaton, George F., II, 338
Eaton, Perry, 1415, 2184
Eaton, Richard A., 2693
Eaton, Roger, 2139, 4150
Eaton, Roger G., 2549
Eaves, John W., 231
Ebanks, Michelle M., 2724
eBay Inc., 1217
Ebbrecht, David R., 2094
Ebeid, Russell J., 1682
Ebel, Gregory L., 2580, 3540
Eber, Norris R., 1961
Eberhard Equipment, 1218
Eberhard, Ken D., 1218
Eberhard, Sandra, 1218
Eberhardt, Douglass M., 345
Eberhardt, Douglass M., II, 345
Eberhardt, Mary D., 345
Eberhardt, Nancy K., 1921
Eberhardt-Sandstrom, Mary Elizabeth, 345
Eberhart, H. Paulett, 40, 190
Eberhart, James P., 2810
Eberhart, Marcie, 140
Eberhart, Ralph E., 2016, 3247
Eberle, Karl, 1732
Ebersol, Charles R., Jr., 910
Ebert, Robert F., 1441
Eberwein, Elise, 3902
Ebihara, Yoshio, 3640
Ebinger, Phil, 278, 279
Ebinger, Phill, 278
Ebling, Keith J., 1313
Ebrom, Charles, 3557
Ebsworth, Barney A., 608
Eccles Foundation, 1538
Eccles, Spencer F., 4028
Echolds, Leslie, 1602
Echolds, Mike, 1602
Eck, Robert J., 3292
Eckart, John W., 2600
Eckaus, Richard, 3949
Ecke, Keith H., 4093
Eckel, Keith W., 2639
Eckelberry, Jim, 2792
Ecker, Bart E., 505
Ecker, William D., 1744
Eckerson, William, 415
Eckert, Bret, 285
Eckert, Robert A., 182, 2427, 3624
Eckert, Wilfried, 3824
Eckholdt, Eric, 980
Eckleberry, Mark, 1716
Eckrich, Nancy, 3818
Eckroth, Joseph F., 1792
Eclipse, Inc., 1219
Eco Duct, Inc., 929
Ecolab Inc., 1220
Econoco Corp., 1222
Eddings, Chris, 3016
Eddington, Roderick I., 2700
Eddins, Andy, 6
Eddins, Heidi J., 100
Eddins, Joe, 3978
Eddy, Kathy G., 1741
Eddy, Robert W., 473
Eddy, Shade, 3454
Edeker, Randy B., 1900
Edelman, Daniel J., 1224
Edelman, David P., 2128
Edelman, Harriet, 572
Edelman, Martin, 40, 1147
Edelman, Paul S., 2193
Edelman, Richard, 1224
Edelson, David B., 292
Edelstein, Eric P., 3916
Edens, Steve, 2459
Edens, Tom, 524
Edens, Wesley Robert, 2923
Edenshaw, Cheryl, 2615
Edenshaw, Sidney C., 3380
Eder, J. Stephen, 2477
Edgar County Bank & Trust Co., 1225
Edge, Gary, 2538
Edge, Jayne, 2037
Edgerley, Paul B., 3595
Edgerton, Jerry A., 1550
Edgington Oil Co., 214
Edgmon, Bryce, 797
Edible Arrangements Franchise Group, Inc., 1226
Edina Realty, Inc., 1227
Edison Intl., 1228
Edison, Coit, 2490
Edison, Dennis, 3535
Edison, Sheri H., 407
Edmond, Luiz Fernando, 202
Edmonds, David B., 3171
Edmonds, J. Rice, 3783
Edmonds, Ron, 1161
Edmund A Cyrol Trust, 2274
Edmund, Dan, 1629
Edmundson, Chad, 1383
Edrei, Daniel, 2454
Edrei, Mary, 2454
Edrei, Michael, 2454
Edrei, Sharon, 2454
EDS Foundation, 1794
Edsim Leather Co., Inc., 1230
Edson, Gregory P., 1403
Edson, Jill M., 833
Edu, Mary, 3189
Education Lending Group, Inc., 1232
Educational Communications, Inc., 1233
Edvisors Network, Inc., 1234
Edwab, David H., 2460
Edwards Industries, Inc., 1235
Edwards Insulation, 1235
Edwards Investment Group, LLC, 699
Edwards, Bob, 1383
Edwards, Bruce A., 1663
Edwards, Dan, 2014
Edwards, David C., 699
Edwards, David N., 297
Edwards, Dawn N., 362
Edwards, Deborah, 2877
Edwards, Denis, 2358
Edwards, E. Merle, 699
Edwards, Edwin M., 699
Edwards, Elena, 1565
Edwards, Gary R., 986
Edwards, Gary W., 1279, 3650
Edwards, Greg, 1966
Edwards, Harold S., 3649
Edwards, James O., 213
Edwards, Jeff, 394
Edwards, Jeffrey L., 99
Edwards, Jeffrey W., 1235
Edwards, John, 3514
Edwards, Julie H., 2815
Edwards, Merle W., 699
Edwards, Mike, 1406
Edwards, Ollie W., 699
Edwards, Patricia L., 1282
Edwards, Peter H, Jr., 1235
Edwards, Peter H., 1235
Edwards, R.A., III, 4039
Edwards, Robert L., 3310
Edwards, Steve, 3195
Edwards, Stuart M., 699
Edwards, Thomas L., 699
Edwards, Thomas L., Jr., 699
Edwards, Trevor, 2405, 2710
Edwardsen, Anthony, 3843
Edwardsen, Anthony E., 3843
Edwardson, Andy, 1335
Edwardson, Francesca Maher, 1892
Edwardson, John A., 1352, 3247
Eems, William J. Vander, 283
EFC Bancorp, Inc., 2997
EFC Holdings, Inc., 1236
Efird, Claire, 404
Efron, Jeanette Oshman, 3548
Efstathiou, George, 3474
EG&G, Inc., 2939
Egan, Dale, 132
Egan, James, 496
Egan, John R., 1253
Egan, Kevin P., 2879
Egan, Michael, 538
Egan, Peter J., 1
Egan, Thomas J., 3298
Egan, Thomas J., Jr., 3298
Egan, William P., 752
Egasti, Jamie, 719
Egawa, Keishi, 2414
Egger, Harry O., 2881
Egger, Terrance C.Z., 2989
Eggers, David, 2729
Eggers, Helen B., 340
Eggers, Matt, 3902
Eggers, Tara, 1031
Eggert, Mary, 735
Eggleston, Alan P., 271
Egnaty, Lorraine, 2200
Egnotovich, Cynthia M., 2355
EGS Electrical Group, LLC, 3558
Ehly, Marvin P., 269
Ehrlich, Clifford A., 1261
Ehrlich, Donald J., 1027
Ehrline, Leo, 584
Ehrman, Daniel S., 1532
Ehsani, Jamshid, 3879
EI Technologies, LLC, 1237
Eiche, Jocelyn K., 12
Eiche, Stuart B., 12
Eichelman, Paul, 619
Eicher, Carol S., 3714
Eichler, Rodney J., 211
Eichman, Eric, 2290
Eiding, Patrick J., 1926
Eidson, Dennis, 3535
Eiferman, Jack, 1528
Eigen, Steven, 743
Eigendorff, Rich, 2596
Eigner, Richard, 637
Eihusen, D. J., 793
Eihusen, Marilyn, 793
Eihusen, Robert G., 793
Eikelberner, Emily, 3708
Eilermann, John, 2418
Eilermann, John F., Jr., 2418
Eilert, Norman, 3704
Einhauser, James B., 4069
Einhauser, James G., 4069
Einhorn, Edward M., 790
Einhorn, Jessica P., 3757
Einsidler, Lee R., 1482
Eisbart, Ben, 3595
Eischens, Curt, 802

Eisele, C. R., 3857
Eisele, Mark O., 219
Eisele, Thomas L., 2707
Eiseman, Byron, 1501
Eiseman, Byron M., Jr., 1501
Eisemann, J.E., 3187
Eisemann, J.E., IV, 3187
Eisemann, Roger D., 3187
Eisen, Stacey, 1867
Eisenband, Neil, 31
Eisenberg, G. A., 3760
Eisenberg, Glenn A., 112, 1330, 3760
Eisenberg, Marie T., 3752
Eisenberg, Warren, 399
Eisenreich, Bobbi Jo, 1651
Eisenstein, Marci A., 3350
Eisman, Robert B., 123
Eisner, Michael, 1903
Eitel, Charles R., 145
Eitel, Maria S., 2710
Eiting, James E., 2507
Eiting, Mitchell, 2507
Eiting-Klamar, Anne, 2507
Eizenstat, Stuart E., 3872
Ekholm, Borje, 2617
Eklin Medical Systems, 3257
Ekman, Scott, 3243
Ekstrom, Dean E., 4095
El Dorado Motors, Inc., 1238
El Paso Corp., 1239
El Paso Energy Corp., 1239
El Paso Natural Gas Co., 1239
El-Mansy, Youseff A., 2214
Elam, Joyce, 3274
Elam, Patricia, 2573
Elam, Theodore M., 145
Eland, Alan, 1677
Elaree, Thompson, 1858
Elbrock, Edward, 885
Elcock, Walter B., 340
Elder Groups, Inc., 3921
Elder Trust, Bruce E., 3921
Elder, Alan H., 3921
Elder, Amy, 3921
Elder, Jack E., 3921
Elder, Julie, 3921
Elder, Louise, 3921
Elder, Mark, 3921
Elder, Paul A., 3921
Elder, R. J., 801
Eldred, Charles, 3076
Eldred, Don, 547
Eldredge, James W., 3081
Eldridge, Barry J., 850
Eldridge, Brad, 886
Eldridge, Nancy, 499
Electric Power Equipment Co., 1240
Electronic Data Systems Corp., 3860
Elenz, Carter S., 3876
Elf Atochem North America, Inc., 242
Elfner, Albert H., III, 2629, 3885
Elg, Annette, 3459
Elgin Financial Savings Bank, 2997
Elgin Riverboat Resort, 1629
Elgin Sweeper Co., 1246
Elguicze, Jake, 3707
Eliades, David J., 2734
Elias Industries, Inc., 1247
Elias, Howard D., 1532
Elias, Moses, 1250
Elias, Norman, 1247
Elias, Sylvia M., 1247
Eliason Corp., 1248
Eliason, Fredrik, 997
Eliason, George, 3376
Eliason, Wanda M., 1248
Elicker, John, 578
Eline, William G., 2886
Elite Spice, Inc., 1249
Elizabeth Nursing Home, 1250
Elizabeth Ruan Trust, 3279
Elkin, James, 2752
Elkin, Jim, 2752
Elkin, Lisa, 902
Elkington, Karol Sue, 2028
Elkins, Ronald Charles, 990
Elkins, Sam, 2920
Elkins, Sam M., 2920
Ellard, Heidi, 2670
Ellard, James V., 2670
Ellen Stanek, Mary, 317
Ellen, David, 641
Ellen, Martin M., 1169
Ellenberger, John, 2217
Eller, Bob, 335
Ellerbrook, Neil C., 2798, 3925
Elliman, Christopher J., 475
Ellin & Tucker, Chartered, 1251
Ellinger, Deborah G., 2633, 3382
Ellinghausen, James R., 3083
Ellingstad, Paul, 1794
Elliot, Donald H., 2630
Elliot, Greg W., 2647
Elliot, John B., 1867
Elliott, Anita C., 1143
Elliott, Barbara L., 3645
Elliott, Chris A., 1980
Elliott, Denise M., 2163
Elliott, G. Warren, 1336
Elliott, Gregory W., 2647
Elliott, James N., 1645
Elliott, Jerry V., 2758
Elliott, Jim, 421
Elliott, Kip, 3827
Elliott, Lawrence, 3202
Elliott, Michael, 2026
Elliott, Nancy D., 3580
Elliott, Robert A., 3819
Elliott, Roger S., 3302
Elliott, Stephanie Leigh H., 1079
Elliott, Steven, 1894
Elliott, Steven G., 344, 3026
Ellis Real Estate Holdings, LLC, 929
Ellis, C. Lee, 87
Ellis, Carol Murphy, 2599
Ellis, Clyde E., 2887
Ellis, Dan R., Jr., 3515
Ellis, Diane, 3572
Ellis, Eileen, 929
Ellis, Gary L., 2453, 3775
Ellis, Gregory S., 929
Ellis, James, 3108
Ellis, James O., 1150
Ellis, James O., Jr., 2292
Ellis, Joe, 2906
Ellis, John, 367
Ellis, Jon S., 929
Ellis, Josiah, 2906
Ellis, Kathy, 2420
Ellis, Kendrick G., 929
Ellis, Kenneth M., 929
Ellis, Matt, 3832
Ellis, Matthew D., 3936
Ellis, Nicholas, 2151
Ellis, Stanley J., 929
Ellis, Stephen A., 3363
Ellis, Tod, 2606
Ellis, William B., 2397
Ellison, Amy, 1074
Ellison, C. Samuel, 396
Ellison, Lawrence J., 2821
Ellison, Marvin, 1842
Ellison, Marvin R., 1695
Ellman, David W., 964
Ells, Catherine A., 2394
Ellspermann, Richard, 1455
Ellsworth, Diane, 3624
Ellsworth, H. Anderson, 2635
Ellsworth, John J., 3347
Ellsworth, Steve, 3103
Ellyn, Lynne, 1183
Elmaleh, Victor, 4122
Elmer, G. Mitchell, 3677
Elmore, John, 3835
Elmore, Leonard J., 2241
Elmore, Roger, 1404
Elmore, William B., 861
Elms, Tracy, 4014
Elovitz, Debra, 610
Elovitz, Elaine, 610
Elovitz, Gerald, 610
Elovitz, William, 610
Elsea, Chuck, 3373
Elsener, Carl, 3950
Elsenhans, Lynn, 324
Elson, Jeff, 1495
Elste, Mark A., 3837
Elstrott, John B., 4066
Elvin, Mark, 2410
Elvsaas, Fred H., 3397
Elvsaas, Fred H., Jr., 3397
Elvsaas, Fred S., Jr., 3397
Ely, James S., III, 900
Elyachar, Daniel, 3287
Elyachar, Jonathan, 3287
Elyachar, Ralph, 3287
Elyas, Nagui, 2375
Emanuel, Areil Z., 1267
Emap Support Services, 3474
Embertson, Rolf M., 3257
Embler, Michael J., 819
Embry, David, 1666
Embry, Gerald R., 3426
Embry, Melissa, 1023
Emco Chemical Distributions, Inc., 1254
Emerick, Albert D., 1465
Emerson Electric Co., 1257
Emerson Ventures, 1257
Emerson, Dan, 1932
Emerson, David B., 3031
Emerson, Frances B., 1061
Emerson, Ralph W., Jr., 2323
Emery, David R., 474
Emery, Robert, 3525
Emery, Sidney W., Jr., 100
Emhart Glass Sweden AB, 945
Emhoff, Laurena L., 2690
EMI Christian Music Group, Inc., 1258
Emirgil, Nur, 3125
Emkes, Mark A., 560, 832, 1406, 1663
Emma, Edward C., 2045
Emma, Philip B., 2474
Emmenegger, Chuck, 673
Emmerson, Archie Alds, 3451
Emmerson, George, 3451
Emmerson, M. D., 3451
Emmerson, Mark, 3451
Emmert, John C., Jr., 1961
Emmert, Mark A., 2807, 4052
Emmetsberger, Brock, 2398
Emmett, Denis, 1294
Emmett, Denis L., 1294
Emmett, Richard, 1191
Emmis Radio Corp., 1260
Emmis Radio, LLC, 1260
Empedocles, Marianne, 2370
Empire Iron Mining Partnership, 850
Empire Southwest Co., 1262
Empire Southwest, LLC, 1262
Empire State Certified Development Corporation, 2681
Employers Mutual Casualty Co., 1264
Emrey, Tom, 1120
Emslie, Robert, 1399
Emslie, Robert D., 1399
Encana Corporation, 1266
Encana Oil & Gas (USA), Inc., 1266
Endeavor Agency, L.L.C., The, 1267
Enders, Randall J., 1407
Endres Manufacturing Co., 1269
Endres, Charlie, 1269
Endres, John, 3039
Endres, John J., 1607
Endres, Krista A., 3414
Endres, Laura, 1269
Endres, Michael, 1894
Endres, Michael J., 4124
Endres-Ballweg, Diane, 1269
Endries, Kari, 3856
Enebak Construction Co., 3792
Enebak, Diane L., 3792
Enebak, Doris M., 3792
Enebak, Rebecca L., 3792
Enebak, Robert H., 3792
Energen Corporation, 1270
Energizer Holdings, Inc., 1271
Energy BBDO, Inc., 3474
Energy Corp. of America, 1272
Eng, Wai-Ling, 2427
Engebretson, Douglas, 792
Engebretson, Douglas K., 792
Engel, Glenn, 2409
Engel, Hans, 368
Engel, John J., 3877
Engel, Mark, 2061
Engel, Susan E., 4028
Engel, Susan S., 1416
Engelbrecht, John D., 3925
Engelkemeyer, David F., 4025
Engelman, Robert S., Jr., 2415
Engels, Elizabeth, 3760
Engelson, David A., 3245
Engelstad, Kurt, 1
Engelstad, Ronald E., 1535
Engeman, John, 1376
Engemann, Tim, 2486
Engh, Rolf, 3920
Engibous, Thomas, 2925
England, J. Herb, 1265
England, Louise C., 2088
Englander, Shoshana, 2597
Engle, Edward J., Jr., 3216
Engle, Edward, III, 3216
Engle, Jed, 3216
Engle, Jennifer, 3216
Engle, Jerry R., 1410
Engle, Roger, 3444
Englefield, F. William, IV, 2881
Engler, John M., 3890
Engler, Lee, 3679
Englert, James, 3758
Engles, Gregg L., 1054, 4062
Englese, James R., 654
English, Carl L., 141
English, Christopher D., 4018
English, Courtney, 2668

English, Edmond J., 511
English, John, 652
English, Kelly, 605
English, Pat, 3637
English, Roderick, 1410
English, Steven E., 3590
Engstrom, Erik, 3161
Engwall, Mark, 1188
Eni, Christopher W., 1114
Eni, Louis, 1114
Eni, Louis J., Jr., 1114
Eni, Ruth, 1114
Eni, Ruth Deitz, 1114
Eni, Ruth Dietz, 1114
Enich, Michel R., 3394
Enk International/wsa, 838
Enloe, Robert Ted, III, 2246
Enly, Marvin P., 269
EnMark Gas Gathering, L.P., 1274
Ennico, Dolores J., 2801
Ennis, Sandy, 1183
Enns Packing Co., Inc., 3225
Enns, Eugene, 3225
Enns, Kenneth, 3225
Enns, Melvin, 3225
Enns, Nick, 3225
Enns, Rosemary, 3225
Enoch, Leslie B., II, 811
Enonchong, Rebecca, 3318
Enos, Christopher, 3383
Enos, Christopher E., 3383
Enquist, Philip, 3474
Enrico, Roger A., 1172
Enright, J. Scott, 1259
Enright, Scott, 1260
Enriquez-Cabot, Juan, 642
Enser, Matt, 1045
Ensign Facility Services, Inc., 1275
Ensign-Bickford Industries, Inc., 1276
Ensing, Mike, 2177
Ensor, Kenneth, 1859
Entelco Corp., 1277
Entergy Arkansas, Inc., 839
Entergy Corp., 1279
Entergy, Corp., 1279
Enterprise Holdings Foundation, 1538
Enterprise Holdings, Inc., 1281
Enterprise Rent-A-Car Co., 1281
Environmental Systems Research Institute, 1992
Environova, LLC, 1570
Envirosense Consortium, Inc., 1953
Enzerra, David J., 2315
Eon, Roland M., 3302
Epes Carriers, Inc., 1283
Epic Life Insurance Company, The, 4094
Epling, Bill, 1380
Epp, Gary, 3660
Eppel, James, Jr., 496
Epperson, Leigh Ann K., 101
Eppinger, Frederick H., 1724
Eppinger, Frederick H., Jr., 735
Eppink, Stephen G., 2232
Epple, Karl H., 3344
Eppler, Klaus, 255, 399
Epps, Michael F., 166
Epps, Roselyn P., 2605
Eppstein Uhen Architects, Inc., 1285
Eppstein, Sam, 1285
Eppstein, Samuel, 1285
Epstein, Donald M., 2403
Epstein, Donald R., 3942
Epstein, Jonathan G., 1379
Epstein, Lillian J., 3942
Epstein, Marjory, 3942
Epstein, Robert, 352, 1862
Epstein, Stuart J., 2649
Epstein, Thomas W., 655
Epting, Thomas, 3849
EQD Holdings Co., LLC, 1287
Equifax Inc., 1288
Equitable Cos. Inc., The, 307
Equitable Life Assurance Society of the U.S., The, 307
Equitable Production Co., 1287
ERB, Bruce, 1318
Erb, Lynn F., 1361
Erbrick, Michael F., 791
Ercolani, Robert M., 2380
Ercolani, Theresa, 2380
Erdeman, Joseph E., 268
Erdman, Leon, 4149
Erdman, Warren K., 2094
Erdos, Barry, 608
Erede, Sergio, 2319
Ergon Asphalt & Emulsions, Inc., 1289
Ergon Exploration, Inc., 1289
Ergon Nonwovens, Inc., 1289
Ergon Refining, Inc., 1289
Ergon, Inc., 1289
Ergon-West Virginia, Inc., 1289
Erickson & Sons, C., Inc., 1290
Erickson, Andrew M., 183
Erickson, Bernard B., Jr., 1637
Erickson, Bernie, 1637
Erickson, Bill, 2387
Erickson, Bradford, 3736
Erickson, Bradford P., 3736
Erickson, Charles, 1290
Erickson, Charles G., III, 1290
Erickson, Constance, 1689
Erickson, Debra, 2133
Erickson, Donald, 1232
Erickson, Gary J., 848
Erickson, Gerald A., 1832
Erickson, Gerald R., 3394
Erickson, Gregory, 1637
Erickson, Jeff, 2994
Erickson, Jennifer Weyrauch, 2585
Erickson, Jim, 2184
Erickson, John C., 3854
Erickson, John D., 2836
Erickson, Jon, 802
Erickson, Lawrence A., 4088
Erickson, Peter C., 1554
Erickson, Randall J., 261
Erickson, Robert M., 3574
Erickson, Rolin, 3994
Erickson, Ronald A., 1832
Erickson, Suzanne, 1290
Ericson, James D., 2049, 2371
Ericson, Lois G., 1669
Ericson, Rebecca, 770
Ericson, Steven L., 1669
Erikson, Cindy, 3137
Erikson, Sheldon R., 667
Erkkila, John, 947
Erlandson, Michael, 3659
Erlandson, Mike, 3659
Erler, Kristen S., 3359
Erlich, Morton, 3472
Erlich, Paula, 2008
Erlitzki, Ronit, 4004
Ermers, Gary J., 1053
Erne, David A., 2749
Ernest, Ronald W., 979
Ernst, Barrie W., 3869
Ernst, Mark A., 1427
Ernst, Robert, 2651
Ersek, Hikmet, 4045
Erstad, Dean E., 3406
Ertel, Beth, 384
Ertel, David, 384
Ervin, Michael E., 690
Erving Industries, Inc., 1294
Erving Paper Mills, Inc., 1294
Erwin, Tim, 969
ESB Securities Corp., 1212
Esbenshade's Greenhouses, Inc., 1295
Esbenshade, Fred, 1295
Esbenshade, Roger, 1295
Esbenshade, Scott, 1295
Esbenshade, Terry, 1295
Escarra, Vicki B., 1766
Escheated Funds, 2914
Eschenburg, Marc R., 1282
Escobar, Michael, 107
Escobedo, Ruben M., 1512, 3915
Esenberg, Richard M., 3221
Eskew, Michael L., 3, 1960, 2274, 3872
Eskildsen, Aileen M., 1251
Eskow, Alan D., 3916
Esleeck, S. Hugh, 1800
Esler, Susan B., 258
Espe, Marchell, 805
Espe, Matthew J., 246, 1914, 3859
Espeland, Curt E., 1213
Espeland, Curtis E., 1213
Espich, Jeffery K., 2379
Espinosa, John, 511
Esplin, J. Kimo, 1895
Esposito, Anthony G., 2790
Esposito, Domenick, 866
Esposito, James, 3138
Esposito, Liliana M., 1054
Esposito, Michael P., Jr., 1467
Esposito, Robert, 3607
Esque, Shelly M., 1950
Esquenazi, Mayra, 2321
Esquivel, Ruben E., 285
Esrey, William T., 1554, 3540
ESSA Bancorp, Inc., 1297
Essa, Joe, 3080
Essary, Shellee, 2154
Essaye, Anthony, 849
Esser, Pat, 2625
Esser, Patrick J., 958
Essex, Amy E., 1402
Essig, Stuart, 1947
Essig, Stuart M., 1947, 3566
Essner, Robert A., 2397
Esson, Robert, 2299
Estate of Emma Irvine, 476
Estep, Roger, 2022
Estep, Sandra J., 3079
Ester, Todd V., 1078
Esterson, Robin, 3781
Estes, Bob, 1174, 3458
Estes, Debbie, 2530
Estes, R. D., 4120
Esteva, Marc, 1566
Estey, William A., 2332
Esther, Chet, Jr., 1674
Estrada, Ramiro, 3856
Estrin, Edward Z., 3050
Estrin, Judith L., 1127
Estrin, Melvyn J., 3997
Etchart, Eric P., 1624
Etess, Mitchell, 2546
Etheredge, James R., 981
Etheridge, Matthew W., 3887
Etherington, Martyn, 3706
Ethridge, William T., 2911
Ettelson, John R., 478
Etter, Delores M., 1171
Ettinger, Irwin R., 3802
Ettinger, Jeffrey M., 1866, 3775
Ettinger, Michael, 3348
Ettinger, Ronald S., 3093
Etzinga, Jim, 611
Eubanks, Douglas, 1741
Eubanks, Gail, 1170
Euchner, John, 2714
Euclide, Kristine A., 2334
Euerle, Sharow, 3827
Eugster, Jack W., 474, 1624, 2269
Eulberg, Joseph, 1300
Eurich, Juliet A., 332
European Imports, LLC, 2298
Eurton, Gus, 280
Euson, David A., 1524
Euteneuer, Joseph J., 3556
Evan, Donna M., 3444
Evangelisti, Molly Maloney, 2422
Evanko, Paul, 2401
Evans, Andrew W., 57
Evans, Bill, 173
Evans, Bob, 2938
Evans, Caswell A., Jr., 1083
Evans, Cynthia, 878
Evans, Cynthia A., 878
Evans, Daniel J., 948
Evans, Deborah, 64
Evans, Donald L., 1273
Evans, Douglas L., 1301
Evans, Edward A., 3886
Evans, Eric, 3415
Evans, Gay Huey, 913
Evans, Gerald W., Jr., 1720
Evans, Gregory P., 1933
Evans, Heidi, 1168
Evans, Hugh M., III, 3040
Evans, Ivor J., 935, 2473, 3731
Evans, Ivor J., Jr., 2473
Evans, J. Thomas, 1082
Evans, Jack, 3506
Evans, Jack B., 3869
Evans, Jason, 422, 3467
Evans, Jay, 4112
Evans, Jim, 2830
Evans, John, 2625
Evans, Kim, 2538
Evans, Larry, 1414
Evans, Linda R., 474
Evans, M. Christopher, 2606
Evans, Mark C., 549
Evans, Mike, 1248
Evans, Nancy, 1679
Evans, Nona, 4066
Evans, Ralph L., 2461
Evans, Richard A., 1301
Evans, Richard B., 543
Evans, Richard H., 2270
Evans, Richard W., Jr., 1512
Evans, Robert, 3467
Evans, Robert K., 3467
Evans, Robert L., 807
Evans, Robert S., 970
Evans, Susan R., 2508
Evans, Tom, 1082
Evans, Willard S., Jr., 2735, 2931
Evans-Lombe, Nicholas, 1569
Evard, John E., 3370
Evavold, Norbert, 2883
Evening Post Publishing Co., 1302
Evenson, Brian, 2351

Evenson, Jeffrey, 945
Evenson, Jeffrey W., 945
Everest, Christine Gaylord, 2795
Everets, John, 343
Everets, John W., 343
Everett Foundation, David, The, 3955
Everett Mutual Savings Bank, 2136
Everett, Bob, 2625
Everett, Gregory, 1610
Everett, Malcolm E., III, 2971
Everett, Morgan H., 861
Everett, Nora, 3047
Everett, Ralph B., 3433
Everett, Richard, III, 2734
Everett, Susan, 2117
Everett, Teri, 3757
Evergreen Bancorp, Inc., 2919
Evergreen Bank, N.A., 2919
Everhart, Deborah H., 861
Everist, Thomas, 2441
Everitt, David C., 595, 1061, 1741
Evers, Alison, 3606
Evers, Tony, 1314
Evers-Manly, Sandra, 2744
Eversman, Janet, 3249
Everson, Carolyn, 1792
Everton, Marsha M., 521
Everts, John, 3133
Eves, David L., 4135
Ewbank, Robert J., 3865
Ewert, Cliff, 1455
Ewert, Douglas S., 2460
Ewing Irrigation, Inc., 1303
Ewing, Carrie, 2937
Ewing, Charles, Sr., 1857
Ewing, Ed, 1021
Ewing, John, 499
Ewing, R. Stewart, Jr., 751
Ewing, Robyn L., 4077
Ewing, Stephen E., 854, 921, 2628
Excel Dryer Inc., 3424
Excel Industries, Inc., 1195
Excell Mktg., 1304
Excellium Pharmaceutical, Inc., 1305
Exchange Bank, 1306
Exchange Bankshares Corp., 1307
Exchange National Bank & Trust Co., 1307
Executive Health Exams Intl., 3834
Executive Lodging Ltd., Inc., 1308
Exelon Corporation, 1309
Exely, Jessica, 1153
Exner, John D., 3406
Exnicios, Joseph S., 4065
Exon, Charles S., 3108
Exotic Metals Forming Co., 1310
Exponential, Inc., 1312
Express Scripts, Inc., 1313
Exron Capital, Inc., 3730
Extendicare Health Services, Inc., 1314
Exxon Corp., 1315
Exxon Mobil Corp., 1315
Exxon Mobile, 2184
Eyak Corp., The, 1317
Eyak Technology, LLC, 1317
Eyring, Henry J., 3476
Ezell, David W., 256
Ezell, DeWitt, 507
Ezell, DeWitt, Jr., 507, 2270
Ezell, Mark E., 1748
Ezrilov, Robert, 3235

F.A. Kohler, Inc., 1235
Faanes, Mark, 4091
Faas, Charlie, 3327
Faasen, William C. Van, 2737
Faber Brother, Inc., 1319
Faber, Timothy J., 2277
Fabiano Brothers, Inc., 1320
Fabiano, Evangeline L., 1320
Fabiano, James C., 1320
Fabiano, James C., II, 1320
Fabiano, Joseph R., II, 1320
Fabick Tractor Co., John, 1321
Fabick, Douglas R., 1321
Fabick, Harry, 1321
Fabri-Kal Corp., 1322
FaBrizio, Bruce P., 3653
Fabry, Jeff, 1996
Facchini, Sam J., 2638
Factory Mutual Insurance Co., 1323
Fada, Joe, 599
Fader, Brian, 1784
Fader, Steven B., 1784
Faerber, Dennis, 1955
Fagan, Shirley, 2771
Fagerbakke, Erin, 615
Fagerland-Tubbs Trust, 2361
Fagg, Karen B., 2441
Fagler, Rose, 2991
Fagnani, Laurie, 2184
Fagundes, Heather L., 2422
Fahey Construction Co., J.M., 454
Fahey, Bridget K., 454
Fahey, Joseph T., 454
Fahey, Kevin F., 454
Fahey, Mark, 1709
Fahey, Peter M., 1603, 1604
Fahey, Thomas M., 3851
Fahrer, Belle, 983
Failor, Crystal, 1418
Faimann, Gabriel, 201
Fain, Richard D., 3273
Fainor, Scott V., 2635
Fair, Arthur B., III, 2506
Fairbairn, Ursula O., 63, 3650, 3913
Fairbank, Richard D., 679
Fairbrother, Brenda, 4097
Faircloth, Molly, 953
Fairey, Richard, 2573
Fairfax State Savings Bank, 1325
Fairfield National Bank, 1326, 2881
Fairley-Barlow, Trina, 986
Fairmont Olympic Hotel, 3944
Fairmount Tire & Rubber Inc., 1328
Fairweather Foundation, 2138
Fairwyn Fund, 3414
Faith, David, 3373
Faith, David M., 3373
Faith, Marshall, 3373
Faith, Marshall E., 3373
Fajarito, Joey, 2768
Fakhouri, Haifa, 502
Faks, Alberto, 4119
Faks, Daniel, 4119
Faks, Freddy, 4119
Faks, Ibrahim, 4119
Falck, David P., 239
Falck, Donald P., 239
Falcone Charitable Foundation, Nola Maddox, 2573
Falcone, Joseph, 4025
Falcone, Joseph C., 4025
Falcone, Marc J., 3593
Falcone, Mark, 2531
Falcone, Philip, 2531
Falconer, Richard D., 543
Falero, Ralph, 2730
Falgoust, Dean T., 1494
Falk, Jack, 1958
Falk, Stephen, 685
Falk, Steve, 685
Falk, Thomas J., 2150, 2292
Faller, Marcia R., 184
Fallert, James A., 2207
Falletta, John M., 2427
Fallis, Stanley R., 3574
Fallon Co., LLC, The, 1329
Fallon, Bill, 2416
Fallon, David, 832
Fallon, Elizabeth J., 1329
Fallon, Joseph F., 1329
Fallon, Michael J., 1329
Fallon, Michael Joseph, 3306
Fallon, Susan G., 1329
Fallon, William C., 2416
Falls, Spencer, 1274
Falsetti, Dennis, 1116
Falzarano, Anthony, 2040
Falzon, Robert, 3072
Fameco, 2357
Famiglietti, Eileen M., 1382
Famiglietti, Richard M., 2646
Famoso, Charles, 3477
Famularo, Frank, 3749
Fanandakis, Nicholas C., 1184
Fandrich, William, 501
Faneuil, Edward J., 1593
Fanjul, Oscar, 2385
Fannie MAE, 3190
Fanning, Quinn P., 3748
Fanning, Thomas A., 71, 1567, 3516
Fannon, Joseph, 3175
Fanoe, Tom, 3624
Fante, Richard, 272
Fantini, Rick J., 2461
Faraci, John V., 1968, 3025, 3882
Faraci, Philip J., 1214
Farah, Andrew E., 1651
Farah, Jean Claude, 4045
Farah, Roger, 3123
Farah, Roger N., 48, 3057, 3123
Farb, Gretchen Hoffer, 1821
Farber, Anna, 2570
Farber, Erica, 227
Farber, Hilliard, 1806
Farber, Howard, 3962
Farber, Jack, 996
Farber, Jake J., 3962
Farber, Steven W., 593
Fardella, Alayne, 3386
Farello, Thomas A., 2945
Fares, Fares I., 4020
Fares, Issam M., 4020
Fargo, Jill, 793
Fargo, Thomas B., 1755, 3873
Fargo, Thomas B., ADM., 2404
Fargotstein, Phillip F., 1360
Farhat, Camille, 158
Farhat, Jamal M., 528
Farias, Brandt G., 1405
Farid, Kamran, 1226
Farid, Tariq, 1226
Farina, Amanda, 1018
Farish, William S., 2113
Farkosh, Randall, 1272
Farley, Andrew D., 2106
Farley, Jane M., 1745
Farley, Jerry B., 4039
Farley, John W., 1201
Farley, Kevin, 2465
Farley, Paul J., 2734
Farley, Suzie T., 1297
Farley, William F., 496
Farm, Jodee, 3189
Farmer, Dennis, 1674
Farmer, Jeremy G.O., 210
Farmer, Phillip W., 3972
Farmer, Richard T., 816
Farmer, Scott D., 816
Farmer, William, Jr., 3805
Farmers & Mechanics Bank, The, 745
Farmers & Merchants Trust Company of Chambersburg, 1336
Farmers Alliance Mutual Insurance Company, 1335
Farmers and Merchants Bank, 3087
Farmers and Merchants Bank & Trust Co., 1334
Farmers Bank, The, 3087
Farmers Feed Mill, 3257
Farmers Group, Inc., 1338
Farmers Merchants Bank, 1334
Farmers Trust Co., 1845
Farmers Union Central Exchange, Inc., 802
Farmers Union Marketing & Processing Assoc., 1339
Farmers' Electric Cooperative, Inc. of New Mexico, 1337
Farner, Thomas E., 1986
Farner, Tom, 1986
Farnesi, Frank, 412
Farney, Kirk, 3747
Farnham, Robert E., 1765
Farnsworth, Alan H., 376
Farnsworth, Sarah, 3323
Farr, David N., 1257, 1960
Farr, Kevin, 2405
Farr, Kevin M., 2405
Farr, Paul A., 3026
Farr, Tom, 1687
Farr., Susanne R., 3331
Farragher, Robert M., 851
Farrands, Louise, 476
Farrant, Andrew, 3410
Farrant, M. A., 1315
Farrar, Stephen D., 4031
Farrell & Co., 1341
Farrell, Anne, 3150
Farrell, Anne V., 3150
Farrell, Benny, 2487
Farrell, Breege A., 3898
Farrell, Bruce M., 419
Farrell, Dan, 3568
Farrell, Don, 123
Farrell, Gretchen A., 2279
Farrell, Kathleen A., 2660
Farrell, Kathy, 2660
Farrell, Larry C., 1341
Farrell, Mark T., 3943
Farrell, Mary C., 426
Farrell, Michael J., 1341, 1351, 3192
Farrell, Patricia C., 910
Farrell, Peter, 715
Farrell, Peter C., 3192
Farrell, Peter J., 715
Farrell, Robert S., 2683
Farrell, Shane, 419
Farrell, Thomas E., II, 1150
Farrell, Thomas F., II, 120, 1150
Farrell, W. James, 3, 13, 107
Farrell, William J., 505
Farrelly, Joseph W., 1974
Farrington, Duane, 3591

Farrington, Hugh G., 1458
Farrington, Tom, 2943
Farris, G. Steven, 211
Farris, Lora, 1023
Farrow, Kathryn Ann, 2028
Farrow, Margaret A., 32
Farrow, Peter, 2173
Farrow, William, III, 3901
Farshchian, Nasser, 2431
Farthing, William P., Jr., 2885
Farver, Charles, 2917
Farver, Joan, 2917
Fasano, Jim, 2156
Fasano, Philip, 2086
Fasano, Ronald D., 1841
Fashion Trend LLC, 1342
Fasold, Mark, 392
Fasolo, Peter M., 2048
Fasseas, Alexis, 2731
Fasseas, Drew, 2731
Fasseas, Paula, 2731
Fasseas, Peter A., 2731
Fassio, James S., 3267
Fast Trac Buildings, Inc., 1344
Fast, Eric C., 291, 970, 3171
Fasulo, Michael, 3503
Fatal, Peter, 2497
Fate, Jennifer, 1167
Fate, Lisa Wu, 886
Fatovic, Robert D., 3292
Fauber, Robert, 2563
Faucett, R. Shane, 3227
Faulk, David, 4107
Faulk, Geraldine T., 4107
Faulk, Geri, 4107
Faulk, Kenneth N., 4107
Faulkner, Colin, 1023
Faulkner, Jon A., 1132
Faulkner, Larry R., 1315
Faull, Gary F., 1404
Faulstich, Anne S., 1865
Faulstich, Blair D., 1865
Faulstich, George L., Jr., 1865
Faulstich, George, Jr., 1865
Faulstich, Kendall P., 1865
Fauntleroy, Elizabeth M., 89
Faurot, Barbara, 1565
Fausel, Stephen A., 2215
Fauss, Ronnie, 1021
Faust, Drew G., 3581
Faust, Lynn, 456
Favre, Kristin, 516
Favrot Fund, Thomas B., 1156
Fawcett, Dame Amelia C., 3592
Fawcett, John, 3137
Fawley, Dan, 3200
Fawzy, A. Christopher, 4112
Faxon, Brad, 2954
Fay, Charles, 2132
Fayard, Gary P., 862
Fayock, Daniel, 3025
Fazio, Joseph M., 2519
Fazio, Victor H., 2744
Fazio, William J., 3575
Fazzolari, Salvatore D., 1741
FBR Capital Markets, Inc., 1345
Feagans, Tim, 3312
Feagans, Timothy, 3312
Feagin, Moses, 2536
Feagin, Moses H., 2536
Fealing, Burt, 1999
Fealy, Robert L., 807, 1187
Fearon, Richard H., 1216
Feasel, Gregory D., 879
Feaster, LaVerne, 3514
Feather, Jeffrey, 2635
Feather, Jeffrey P., 2635
Featherstone, Mari, 2952
Feazelle, Anne, 419
FEB Investments, 1963
Feddersen, James A., 32
Fedeli, Davida, 4045
Feder, Franklin L., 82
Federal Home Loan Mortgage Corp., 1348
Federal Screw Works, 1350
Federated Department Stores, Inc., 2333
Federated Investors, Inc., 1351
Federici, William J., 4038
Federico, Richard A., 1151
Fedida, Michael J., 4007
Fee, Laura, 915
FEECO International, Inc., 1353
Feeheley, Tim, 2022
Feehery, William F., 4038
Feely, Terri, 2611
Feeney, Christopher J., 1066
Feeney, Kevin M., 62
Feeney, Matthew, 3490
Feeny, Curtis F., 725
Feeser, Robert A., 2445
Fefel, Jeremy, 334
Feffer, Andrew, 3998
Feffer, Andy, 512
Feick, John E., 2780
Feidler, Mark L., 1288, 2688
Feig, Erik M., 2482
Feiger, Mitchell, 2415
Feilmeier, Steven J., 2180
Feinberg, Ann Merriam, 2645
Feinberg, Anna Merriam, 2645
Feinberg, David M., 141
Feinblum, Barnet M., 1527
Feinblum, Julieus, 511
Feinson, Robert S., 3344
Feinstein, Leonard, 399
Feist, Howard N., III, 133
Feitler, Robert, 4051
Fekete, Frank L., 3069
Felchner, Edward L., 32
Feld, Kenneth, 1355
Feld, Leonard G., 1863
Feldberg, Meyer, 2333
Felder, Larry, 265
Feldhausen, Audry, 1796
Feldman, Alan D., 1459
Feldman, Donna G., 3780
Feldman, Lawrence, 2082
Feldman, Michel J., 4007
Feldman, Sheila, 913
Feldman, Steven M., 3780
Feldmann, Cynthia L., 3600
Feldpausch, James, 1523
Feldpausch, Mark S., 1523
Feldpausch, Parker T., 1523
Feldstein, Kathleen Foley, 2422
Feldstein, Robert, 40
Felerhoff, Susan, 1698
Felice, Stephen J., 1068
Felix, Karen, 207
Felker, G. Stephen, 3239
Fell, Nick, 2523
Feller, Robert E., 2866
Fellerhoff, Randall, 1698
Fellerhoff, Randy D., 1698
Fellerhoff, Susan, 1698
Fellowes, James E., 1357
Fellowes, John E., II, 1357
Fellows, George, 3913
Felmer, Thomas J., 552
Felpausch Co., G&R, 1523
Fels, Samantha, 2250
Felsher, Steven G., 2758
Felsinger, Donald E., 233, 2744, 3405
Felt, Tim, 876
Felten, Ronald, 2487
Felten, Ronnie, 2487
Felter, Andrew J., 4018
Felter, Timothy L., 2693
Feltes, Karen S., 301
Feltman, Doug, 2689
Feltmann, Melissa, 3329
Felton, Dianne Daiss, 2446
Feltz, Steve, 2747
Fema Electronics Corp., 1358
Fenaroli, Albert, 388
Fenaroli, Albert J., 388
Fencl, Eric R., 608
Fender, Jeff, 2938
Fendrich, Steve, 2407
Fenich, Randy, 2581
Fenimore, William M., Jr., 827
Fennell, Barbara, 1079
Fennell, Laura A., 1982
Fennell, Michael, 3793
Fennig, Greg, 1988
Fenter, Thomas C., 490
Fentiman, Gary, 2298
Fentin, Gary S., 3424
Fenton Art Glass Co., 1361
Fenton Gift Shops, Inc., 1361
Fenton, Bob, 2298
Fenton, Dave, 5
Fenton, Dennis M., 1867
Fenton, George W., 1361
Fenton, Michael D., 1361
Fenton, Randall R., 1361
Fenton, Rick, 1915
Fenton, Scott K., 1361
Fenton, Thomas K., 1361
Fenton, Tim, 2427
Fenwick, Lex, 1163
Feragen, Jody H., 1866
Ferber, Norman A., 3267
Ferdinandi, John E., 3545
Ferdowsi, Farzin, 3679
Fergel, Melissa M., 1485
Ferguson Electric Construction Co., Inc., 1363
Ferguson Electric Service Co., Inc., 1363
Ferguson Family Foundation, Inc., 1363
Ferguson, April, 576
Ferguson, David L., 3140
Ferguson, Gary, 84
Ferguson, Gerald, 2601
Ferguson, Gerald P., Jr., 2601
Ferguson, Gerard J., 3227
Ferguson, Gerene Dianne Chase, 770
Ferguson, J. Brian, 2842, 2965
Ferguson, Jerry L., 466
Ferguson, Jerry L., Mrs., 466
Ferguson, Joel I., 502
Ferguson, Kim, 335
Ferguson, LaVon, 3199
Ferguson, Mark, 405
Ferguson, Patricia A., 1946
Ferguson, Randall C., Jr., 3431
Ferguson, Rhonda S., 1424
Ferguson, Robert B., 3371
Ferguson, Rodney, 3544
Ferguson, Roger W., Jr., 1962
Ferguson, Sam, 4066
Ferguson, Stanley L., 3905
Ferguson, Ted, 2099
Ferguson, Thomas D., 1273
Ferguson, Trey, 1726
Ferguson, W. Dennis, 1382
Fergusson, Frances D., 2405, 2950
Ferlic, Randolph M., 211
Ferm, Robert M., 1703
Ferman, James L., Jr., 3701
Fernald, Karen, 3665
Fernandes, Anthony G., 324
Fernandes, Gary J., 483, 638
Fernandez G., Carlos, 1257
Fernandez, Eduardo, 3374
Fernandez, Emilio A., 4048
Fernandez, Frank, 496
Fernandez, Idalia P., 1382
Fernandez, James N., 1190, 3750
Fernandez, Judith, 2048
Fernandez, Manuel A., 595, 1446, 3677
Fernandez, Michael Anthony, 812
Fernandez, Mike, 3591
Fernandez, Raul, 2280
Fernandez, Raul J., 1376
Fernandez, Sam, 2305
Fernandez, Santiago, 2305
Fernandez-Carbajal, Francisco Javier, 3960
Fernelius, Alan Blaine, 2028
Ferragamo, Massimo, 4150
Ferrales, Sid, 3144
Ferrando, Jonathan P., 292
Ferrante, Catherine, 3312
Ferranti, Richard M., 3204
Ferrara Pan Candy Company, 1364
Ferrara, Albert E., Jr., 67
Ferrara, Nello V., 1364
Ferrara, Salvatore, II, 1364
Ferrara, Todd, 2853
Ferrarell, Timothy M., 1626
Ferraresi, Daniel J., 1958
Ferrari, Catherine, 1716
Ferrari, Pierre, 409
Ferrari, Vinny, 2059
Ferraro, Charles, 3550
Ferraro, David, 702
Ferraro, John, 1293
Ferrato, Donna, 2711
Ferre, Maria Luisa, 3003
Ferreer, Michael F., 1208
Ferreira, Nelson, 2684
Ferrell, James E., 1365
Ferrell, Randy, 686
Ferrer, Barbara, 501
Ferrera, Rocco, 3607
Ferriola, John J., 2760
Ferris, Robert R., 2730
Ferro Corp., 1366
Ferro, Dennis H., 3047
Ferro, Pedro, 2473
Ferry, Michael J., 428
Ferry, Tom, 3673
Fertitta, Frank J., III, 3593
Fertitta, Lorenzo, 3593
Fertitta, Paige, 2219
Fertitta, Tilman, 3120
Fertitta, Tilman J., 2219, 3120
Feruness, Samuel, 1887
Fessler, Daniel W.L., 3819
Festa, Alfred E., 1623
Festa, Fred E., 1623
Festge, Florian, 3830
Fetherston, Richard A., 144

Fogarty, Kenneth, 3161
Fogarty, Mark P., 2461
Fogel, Jordan, 1062
Fogelman, Amy, 1525
Fogg, David H., 1551
Fogg, Lindy, 199
Fogg, Mark, 937
Fogg, Richard E., 2841
Fogle, Jarrod, 1050
Foglesong, Robert H., 323
Foglesong, William Greg, 708
Fohn, Dick, 2581
Fohrd, Cynthia L., 3406
Fohrer, Alan, 655
Fohrer, Alan J., 2608
Foith, Scot A., 1177
Fok, Winnie, 3473
Foland, Jeffrey T., 3860
Foldcraft, Co., 1452
Foletta, Mark G., 184
Foley Hoag LLP, 1454
Foley, Bill, 2548
Foley, Dennis, 4022
Foley, Hoag & Eliot LLP, 1454
Foley, Jay, 44
Foley, John, 288
Foley, John V., 2484
Foley, Michelle, 1095
Foley, Patrick, 1766
Foley, Rita V., 2948
Foley, Sean P., 3727
Foley, William P., II, 1371
Folio, James M., 2690
Folkers, Scott C., 4088
Folkerson, Jennifer G., 1538
Folkerson, Richard, 1538
Folkwein, Kristy, 1162
Follett Corp., 1455
Follett, Dwight W., 1455
Follett, Mildred, 1455
Folliard, Thomas J., 3083
Folliard, Tom, 694
Follis, Daniel S., Jr., 902
Follit, Evelyn V., 3701, 4087
Follo, James F., 1594
Follo, James M, 2690
Follo, James M., 2690
Folsom, Michael, 3675
Folta, Carl D., 3945
Foltyn, David, 1853
Fondse, Kevin, 506
Fong, Arthur S.K., 1753
Fong, Date, 1381
Fong, Diane M., 2497
Fong, Ivan K., 3
Fong, Pearl, 1381
Fons, Jerome, 2564
Fontaine, R. Richard, 1530
Fontanals-Cisneros, Ella, 1236
Fontanes, A. Alexander, 2265, 3306
Fonteyne, Paul, 515
Fonteyne, Paul R., 515
Fonville & Co., 1456
Fonville, Charles, 1456
Fonville, Charles L., 1456
Fonville, Doris, 1456
Food Lion LLC, 1458
Food Services of America, 4032
Foodmaker, Inc., 2007
Foot, Silas B., III, 3154
Foote, William C., 3981
Foote-Hudson, Marilyn E., 1588
Foothills Brewing Co., 2523
Foran, Margaret M., 2780
Forbes, Emily Hunt, 1890
Forbes, Glenn S., 1866
Forbes, H. Scott, 2794
Forbes, J. Michael, 1272
Forbes, Karrie, 2407
Forbes, Kay P., 1813
Forbes, Keith, 2487
Force, Gregory F., 3761
Forcier-Rowe, Claire, 1490
Ford Chrysler, Owatonna, 3291
Ford Meter Box Co., Inc., The, 1463
Ford Motor Co., 1464
Ford Motor Credit Co., 1464
Ford Shakopee, Apple, 3291
Ford, Alfred B., 1464
Ford, Allyn, 3847
Ford, Ann, 2451
Ford, Ben, 2418
Ford, Brian, 599
Ford, Chris, 2781
Ford, Daniel H., 1463
Ford, Diane L., 2735, 4096
Ford, Edsel B., II, 1464, 1970
Ford, Frederick C., 1170
Ford, Gerald J., 1494
Ford, James B., 285
Ford, Len, 3390
Ford, Lynne, 663
Ford, Mark S., 1463
Ford, Michael, 3666
Ford, Rollin L., 3980
Ford, Ronald, 2732
Ford, Scott T., 273
Ford, Steven R., 1463
Ford, Thomas, 2928
Ford, W. Douglas, 63, 3905
Ford, William C., Jr., 1217
Ford, William Clay, 1094
Ford, William Clay, Jr., 1094, 1464
Ford, William L., 2815
Ford, William R., 3997
Ford-Hutchinson, Anthony W., 2466
Forde, Joseph, 1108
Fordyce, James H., 42
Fordyce, Michael J., 1668
Fore John Committee, 1486
Fore, Henrietta H., 1315
Fore, Stephanie, 1813
Forehand, Joe W., 22, 1400
Foreman, Gary B., 3238
Foreman, Phillip G., 1465
Foreman, Robert B., 3558
Foreman, Stephen A., 2323
Forero, Antonio, 2321
Forest City Ratner Companies, 584
Forest City Ratner Companies Foundation, 584
Foret, Mickey P., 1073, 2619
Forlenza, Vincent A., 398
Forman, Charles D., 2225
Forman, Gary, 3238
Forman, Gwen, 1003
Formosa Plastics Corp., Texas, 1470
Fornarola, Andrew, 1419
Forney, Ann W., 3171
Forraht, Douglas R., 4025
Forrest, Lynne, 1222
Forrest, Stephen R., 220
Forrestel, Margaret, 2048
Forrester, M. Rankine, 1979
Forrester, Robert H., 2697
Forrester, W. Thomas, 3057
Forrester, William Thomas, 1349
Forschler, Richard A., 1324
Forschner Group, Inc., The, 3950
Forsgren, John H., 1189, 2656
Forson, Norman R., 3871
Forst, Doug, 3033
Forster, Andrea, 2935
Forsyte, Carol, 2585
Forsyth, Don M., 1541
Forsyth, John D., 377, 4026
Forsyth, Norman, 771
Forsyth, Stephen C., 775
Forsyth, Susan Marie, 10
Forsyth, William D., 1510
Forsyth, William D., III, 1510
Forsythe, Alan, 2139
Forsythe, Christopher T., 285
Forsythe, Daryl R., 2681
Forsythe, Gary V., 811
Forsythe, Ralph C., 87
Fort Myer Construction Corporation, 1471
Fort Worth Star-Telegram, 1472
Fortanet, Francisco, 1962
Forte, Linda D., 889
Forte, Richard S., 970
Fortin, Raymond D., 3654
Fortino-Duchossois, Dayle, 1187
Fortis Benefits Insurance Co., 266
Fortis Insurance Co., 266, 267
Fortis, Inc., 266
Fortugno, Dominick, 2159
Fortun, Wayne M., 1524, 3235
Fortunak, Mathew, 2842
Fortune, Mike P., 3483
Forward, Frank D., 473
Foschi, Pier Luigi, 696
Fosdick, Linda, 1490
Fosdick, Michael, 2606
Foshee, Douglas L., 667, 1239
Foshee, Steve, 72
Fosland, Mark, 3172
Fosler, Gail D., 377
Foss, Eric J., 223, 812, 2935
Foss, John H., 2205
Foss, Joseph E., 334
Foss, Madeline, 420
Foss, Michael, 2945
Foss, Warren, 2655
Fossard, Jessica, 131
Foster, Bradley A., 1102
Foster, Brett L., 3554
Foster, Colin, 1079
Foster, Daria L., 2303
Foster, Don P., 1799
Foster, Donald A., 2332
Foster, J. Holt, III, 3738
Foster, James C., 764
Foster, Jonathan F., 775, 2237
Foster, Kent, 2925
Foster, Kent B., 2688
Foster, L. Colin, 1079
Foster, Lee B., II, 4048
Foster, Michael, 689
Foster, Morris E., 3748
Foster, Neal W., 422, 3467
Foster, Parran, 2967
Foster, Paul, 4045
Foster, Paul L., 4044
Foster, Paul W., 2482
Foster, Randall, 3373
Foster, Robert W., 2332
Foster, Rock, 2662
Foster, Rock A., 2662
Foster, Ronald C., 2500
Foster, Tim, 1929
Foster, Toni, 3327
Foster, W. Kim, 1795, 3707
Fotiades, George L., 221, 3060
Foudy, James, 2702
Foulkes, Fred K., 566, 2873
Foundation Fence, Inc., 1577
Fountain, Jillian E., 1314
Fountain, Sharon, 3738
Fountain, W. Frank, 1183
Four Seasons Securities, Inc., 2573
Four Winds Casino Resort, 1477
Fournier, Donat, 3616
Fournier, Laura, 902
Fouse, Jacqualyn A., 732, 1110
Fousek, Linda L., 2448
Foust, Curt R., 2024
Foutch, Randy A., 1774
Foutch, Sarah, 3238
Fouts, Lawrence, 3259
Fouts, Ronny, 3259
Fowden, Jerry, 919
Fowke, Ben, 4135
Fowke, Benjamin G.S., III, 4135
Fowl, Steve, 4127
Fowle, Stephen A., 4127
Fowler Packing Co., 1478
Fowler, Calvin W., Jr., 4078
Fowler, Donald W., 1836
Fowler, Fred J., 2952
Fowler, John C., 3091
Fowler, John P., 1581
Fowler, Mike, 2480
Fowler, Peggy Y., 1755, 3010
Fowler, Ron, 3323
Fowler, Ted M., Jr., 2638
Fowler, Tom, 2151
Fowles, Aaron S., 3333
Fox, Alan R., 60
Fox, Alison, 3321
Fox, Bill C., 3119
Fox, Brien, 4002
Fox, Bruce, 2629
Fox, Chester W., 2809
Fox, David, 1548
Fox, David K., 3119
Fox, Gregory C., 618
Fox, Howard, 3827
Fox, James, 1031
Fox, Jeffrey H., 933
Fox, Jennifer E., 725
Fox, Jerry D., 2068
Fox, Jim, 2306
Fox, Kelly, 993
Fox, M. Carol, 884
Fox, Margene B., 3119
Fox, Marty, 2369
Fox, Mary Anne, 1623
Fox, Richard P., 3034
Fox, Robert L., 2216
Fox, Stacy L., 3650
Fox, William C., 1271
Foxworth, Domonique, 2627
Foy, David T., 2813
Foy, Henry G., 697
Foyle, Adonal, 2624
Foyt, Casey, 1932
Fracassa, Philip D., 3760
Fracassi, Joseph, 2858
Fracassini, Paul J., 1255
Fradin, Roger, 2593, 2984
Fradin, Russ, 442
Fradkin, Andy, 640
Fragie, Jack W., 2622
Frahm, Sheila, 1335

Fraioli, Edward D., 1508
Fraizer, Patrick, 2868
Fraleigh, Christopher J., 1032
Fraley, Angela B., 3875
Fraley, Jeffrey, 3875
Fralin, W. Heywood, 3433
Framingham Co-Operative Bank, 1481
Francavilla, Luigi, 2319
France, Brian Z., 1970, 2621
France, James C., 1970, 2621
Francesconi, Louise L., 3627, 3819
Francia, Vincent, 3822
Francini, Nanette Pattee, 3550
Franciosa, Marc A., 3029
Francis, Ben, 2552
Francis, Charles T., 725
Francis, Cheryl A., 210, 1817
Francis, Dana, 993
Francis, David R., 2410
Francis, Dick, 3430
Francis, Jay Kent, 2028
Francis, L. Frederick, 4044
Francis, Michael R., 2983
Francis, Philip L., 688, 2948, 3659
Francis, Robert, 3595
Francis, Robert D., 1139
Francis, Shay, 1822
Francis, Steve, 1851
Francis, Timothy, 616
Franco, Yvette, 2392
Francoeur, Tom, 4109
Frangopoulos, Zissimos A., 4127
Frank & Roslyn Grobman Foundation, 2135
Frank Rewold and Son, Inc., 3196
Frank, Charles, 2722
Frank, Charley, 814
Frank, Deborah R., 1635
Frank, Dolores, 1786
Frank, Dolores M., 1786
Frank, Eugene D., 1482
Frank, Faith, 307
Frank, Howard S., 696, 3563
Frank, John, 1482
Frank, Jonathan A., 4078
Frank, Julie, 3810
Frank, Stephen E., 2744, 2765
Frank, Udo, 3139
Frankel, Barbara, 1131
Frankel, Herman, 1483
Frankel, Laurie, 1483
Frankel, Matthew, 126
Franken, Linda A., 2689
Frankfort, Lew, 858
Frankfurt, Michael, 2689
Frankiewicz, Dan, 2478
Franklin Bancorp, Benjamin, Inc., 1927
Franklin Electric Co., Inc., 1484
Franklin Federal Savings & Loan, 1485
Franklin Financial Corporation, 1485
Franklin Holdings, Inc., 915
Franklin Homeowners Assurance Company, 2604
Franklin Mutual Insurance Co., The, 1486
Franklin Savings Bank, 1488
Franklin, Barbara Hackman, 48
Franklin, Christopher H., 222
Franklin, Douglas E., 1385
Franklin, Fred, 3200
Franklin, H. Allen, 3972
Franklin, Holley Y., 3574
Franklin, Jack R., 1392
Franklin, Jerry, 1337, 2928
Franklin, Larry J., 2873
Franklin, Roy, 510
Franklin, Scott B., 910
Franklin, Shirley C., 1073
Frankowski, Tom, 3091
Franks, Brian, 2052
Franks, Martin D., 727
Franlovich, Bertha, 1887
Franshaw, Inc., 1489
Frantz, Thomas R., 4078
Franulovich, Bertha M., 1887
Franzen, Reinhart, 382
Franzino, John E., 3331
Frasch, Ronald, 984
Frasch, Ronald L., 3315
Fraser, Cathy, 3713
Fraser, Darryl M., 2744
Fraser, Deane, 3666
Fraser, E. W., 1552
Fraser, Simon, 3139
Fraser-Liggett, Claire M., 398
Frasier, Curtis R., 3430
Fratianni, Michael, 1888
Fratto, Tanya, 510
Frattura, Kevin, 2684
Frauhiger, Rudy, 2379
Frayser, William E. W., Jr., 1485
Frazel, Francis J., 2223
Frazel, Jerome A., Jr., 2223
Frazel, Jerome V., 2223
Frazel, Joanne K., 2223
Frazel, Mark J., 2223
Frazell, Chad, 3440
Frazer, Dale, 1205
Frazer, John B., Jr., 3017
Frazier, A.D., Jr., 211
Frazier, D. Mell Meredith, 2471
Frazier, Don, 2401
Frazier, Gregory R., 2190
Frazier, Kenneth C., 1315, 2466
Frazier, Mell Meredith, 2471
Frazier, Sandra A., 592
Frazier, W. Edwin, III, 3134
Frazier-Coleman, Christie, 369
Freda, Fabrizio, 2230
Freddie MAC, 3190
Frede, Mary Ann, 3858
Fredella, Tina A., 3855
Frederick, David D., 799
Frederick, Douglas J., 2636
Frederick, Edward, 2290
Frederick, William C., 2682, 2683
Fredericksburg Area Association of Realtors, 1490
Fredericksen, John, 2543
Fredrick, Charles J., 1532
Free, Scott D., 1318
Freed, Dean, 2462
Freed, Dean MacLean, 2462
Freeders, J. Chris, 2833
Freedman & Sons, S., Inc., 1493
Freedman, Larry, 696
Freedman, Lawrence, 675
Freedman, Mark, 1493
Freedman, Mark S., 1493
Freedom Forge Corp., 3577
Freeh, Rich, 3201
Freels, Gary W., 4008
Freeman, Angela K., 3235
Freeman, Bradford M., 725, 1228
Freeman, Bruce, 718
Freeman, Cathy S., 336
Freeman, David, 2629
Freeman, George C., III, 1485, 3891
Freeman, Guy W., 3866
Freeman, James W., 169
Freeman, Jody, 913
Freeman, Kenneth W., 1762
Freeman, Ronald B., 1940
Freeman, Willard O., 1126
Freeman, William M., 819
Freer, Patrick J., 1518
Freese, Walt, 3617
Freiberg, Steven J., 2399
Freidland, Sheila, 1503
Freiling, Don, 2762
Freiman, Daniel E., 2709
Freiman, Stuart, 3271
Freimuth, Stanley E., 1514
Freitag, Jerry T., 1535
Freitag, Randal J., 2281
Freiwald, Gregory M., 1161
Fremming, Michele, 1227
Fremont Bank, 1496
Fremont Sequoia Holding, L.P., 1497
French, Beverly A., 1651
French, Christopher E., 3434
French, Douglas D., 2517
French, Greg, 576
French, Irvin, 2816
French, James S. M., 1192
French, Janel W., 1624
French, Joe, 1192
French, Kindy, 1345
French, Mary Dunn, 1192
French, Mike, 3810
French, Richard G., 3649
French, William, 1192
French, William D., 1192
Frenkel, Jacob A., 2296
Frenz, Robert, 3566
Freres Lumber Co., Inc., 1498
Freres Timber Co., 1498
Freres, Robert T., 1498
Freres, Robert T., Jr., 1498
Freres, Robert T., Sr., 1498
Freres, Theodore F., 1498
Frerichs, Robert, 3708
Frerking, Melissa, 754
Fresh Mark, Inc., 1499
Freston, Thomas E., 1172
Fretwell, Clancy, 3761
Fretz, Deborah M., 112
Fretz, Joseph H., 2324
Freudenthal, David D., 231
Freundlich, Andy, 4014
Frey, Shellie, 1602
Freyer, Patrick, 2816
Freyer, Patrick D., 2816
Freyman, Ellen W., 3424
Freyman, Thomas C., 13
Frias, James D., 2760
Fribourg, Charles A., 926
Fribourg, Paul J., 926, 2230, 2296
Frick, Joseph A., 1926
Frick, Mark, 1483
Frick, Travis C., 1053
Fricke, Kim, 2968
Fricklas, Michael D., 3945
Fricks, William P., 1551
Friday, Eldredge & Clark, LLP, 1501
Fridy, John, 2644
Fried, Albert, Jr., 1255
Fried, Tammy D., 143
Friedell, Gerald H., 2224
Friedery, John R., 1447
Friedland Realty, Inc., 1503
Friedland, Edward, 3742
Friedland, Robert, 1503
Friedland, Robert L., 1503
Friedland, Sheila G., 1503
Friedman, Aaron, 2530
Friedman, Alan, 2462
Friedman, Billings, Ramsey & Co., Inc., 1345
Friedman, Brian, 2687
Friedman, Brian P., 2030
Friedman, Emanuel, 1345
Friedman, Eric J., 3470
Friedman, Ezra, 58
Friedman, Joel P., 3455
Friedman, Margo, 138
Friedman, Michael A., 732
Friedman, Philip, 2638
Friedman, Robert L., 477
Friedman, Samuel D., 3044
Friedman, Shari D., 1368
Friedman, Stephen, 1603, 1604
Friedman, Tod, 886
Friedman, Tully M., 852
Friedmann, Margo, 138
Friedrich, John, 3274
Friedt, Karen, 152
Friel, Beth A., 1733
Friel, Robert F., 688, 2939, 4139
Friel, Thomas M., 3593
Friend, David, 2711
Friendly, Ian R., 1554, 3920
Frier, Rick, 719
Frierson, D. Kennedy, Jr., 1132
Frierson, Daniel K., 1132, 2310
Frierson, Paul K., 1132
Fries, Michael T., 2263
Friesen Lumber Co., 1505
Friesen Timber, LLC, 1505
Friesen, Harlan, 1505
Friesen, Jon, 1505
Friesen, Jon T., 1505
Friesman, Bryan, 2368
Friesner, Jackie, 613
Friess, Robert M., 220
Frigo, Gary, 2716
Frisbe, Rick, 3326
Frisbie, Rick, 3326
Frisbie, Ron, 688
Frisbie, Susan, 2874
Frisbie, Susan P., 2874
Frisby, Jeffrey D., 3093
Frisch, Adam, 394
Frisch, Benjamin P., 394
Frisch, Diane J., 1942
Frisch, Hans, 394
Frisch, Harry, 394
Frisch, John B., 2512
Frisch, Mark, 394
Frissora, Mark P., 1071, 1792, 3981
Frist, Thomas F., III, 1762, 3311
Frist, William R., 1762
Fristoe, Drew, 1490
Fritel, Steve, 802
Fritel, Steven, 802
Fritsch, Edward J., 1800
Fritz, Jim, 2824
Fritz, Martin A., 1287
Fritzky, Edward V., 2016
Fritzson, Paul A., 1723
Frizzell, Jim, 3305
Frizzell, Thomas A., 3858
Frobes, Cynthia A., 2123
Frobes, Patricia, 1992, 4158
Frock, Scott, 1083
Froehle, Thomas, Jr., 1324

Frohlich, Julia Ann, 1405
Fromberg, Barry A., 919
Fromm, Ronald A., 591
Fromson, Howard A., 204
Fromson, Michael, 204
Frontczak, Steven Robert, 2557
Frontier Partners, Inc., 1510
Frooman, Thomas, 816
Frost National Bank, 1512, 3915
Frost, Bert, 755
Frost, Carolyn Barry, 210
Frost, Duane, 744
Frost, Greg, 2024
Frost, Gregory Alan, 2024
Frost, Pat, 3321
Frost, Richard, 2184
Frost, Scott F., 4024
Frostad, Erik I., 934
Fru-Con Corp., 1513
Frucher, Meyer, 2617
Frucher, Sandy, 2618
Fruin & Co. General Contractors, 1513
Fruin-Colnon Contracting Co., 1513
Fruth, Lynne, 2622
Fry, Amy, 515
Fry, Bryan, 2942
Fry, Darrel K., 2573
Fry, John A., 900
Fry, Patrick, 3664, 3944
Fry, Patrick E., 3664
Fry, Stephen F., 2274
Fry, Susan, 1077
Fryberg, Marlin, Jr., 3820
Frye, Darrell L., 1740
Frye, John Forest, 3391
Frye, Shirley T., 1588
Frye, Stephen F., 2274
Fryling, James R., 3158
Fryman, Tony, 1015
Frywald, J. Erik, 2613
FSAR Fee Associates, 1431
Fuccillo, Ralph, 1083
Fuchs, Anne Sutherland, 2984
Fuchs, Jennifer, 3551
Fuchs, Mark, 2310
Fuchs, Ralf-Rainer, 1513
Fudge, Ann M., 1552
Fuel, 30
Fuentes, Thomas A., 1201
Fuerer, Cornel B., 1184
Fuerschbach, Raymond G., 3242
Fugate, Mark C., 1785
Fugere, Sally A., 2064
Fugleberg, Hugh, 1646
Fugo, Denise, 2638
Fuhrman, Gary, 2336
Fuhrmann, David E., 1466
Fuji, Yoshihide, 3776
Fujie, Holly J., 600
Fujii, Yoshihide, 3776
Fujimoto, Michael K., 1405, 1754
Fujimoto, Mike, 1136
Fujimoto, Robert M., 1754
Fujinuma, Takeshi, 3480
Fujioka, Robert T., 1405
Fujisankei Communications International, Inc., 1515
Fujita, Scott, 2627
Fujiwara, Chiaki, 1816
Fujiyama, Ian, 525
Fukadome, Yoshiyuki, 2713
Fukui, Masaki, 2654
Fukunaga, Eric S., 3412
Fukunaga, Mark H., 1359, 3412
Fulconis, Thibault, 346
Fulford, Eric, 1988
Fulgham, Tina, 2351
Fuller Co., H.B., 1517
Fuller, Eric, 2697
Fuller, Holly J., 1212
Fuller, JoAnn, 72
Fuller, Joseph B., 3088
Fuller, Kathryn S., 82
Fuller, Leland, 72
Fuller, Misti, 3347
Fullerton, Marna W., 3976
Fullerton, Scott, 3108
Fullmer, Jeff, 608
Fullmer, John D., 2224
Fullwood, Emerson U., 171, 3558
Fulmer, Bob, 3679
Fulton Financial Advisors, 1518
Fulton Financial Corp., 1518
Fulton, Chris, 3470
Fulton, Daniel S., 4052
Fulton, Paul, 372, 708
Fulton, Richard, 1986
Fulton, Rita E., 3066
Fulton, Rufus A., Jr., 1799
Fulton, Rufus Ayers, Jr., 1518
Fulton, Stuart W., 3042
Fulwiler, Terrence R., 1651
Fund, Steve, 3581
Fundacion Salvi Columbia, 2321
Funderburg Farms, Inc., 2081
Funderburg, John K., Jr., 2081
Funderburg, R. Robert, 2081
Funderburg, R. Robert, Jr., 2081
Funderburg, Sally D., 2081
Funk, Bradley C., 2577
Funk, Charles, 3506
Funk, Charles N., 2508
Funk, Christine, 2466
Funk, Kristy, 3591
Funke, Kenneth L., 3529
Furber, Richard P., 3596
Furber, Rick P., 2098
Furek, Robert M., 2397
Furgatch, Andrew L., 3078
Furin, Andre, 3809
Furl, Ken, 3170
Furlong, Andrew T., Jr., 2126
Furlong, Chad, 867
Furlong, Dave, 401
Furman, David M., 3133
Furman, Jeff, 409
Furman, Jeffrey, 409
Furman, Matt, 442
Furniture Auctions of America, 511
Furniture Brands International, Inc., 1519
Furno, Joseph, 3637
Furr Investments, Ltd., 1520
Furr, John, 1520
Furr, Paula, 1520
Furr, Randy, 3532
Furrer, Lori, 3940
Furry, Brad, 4151
Furst, Gury, 1136
Fusco, Andy, 544
Fusco, Frank E., 271
Fusco, Jack A., 661
Fuson, Rick, 2852
Fuss, Daniel J., 2301
Fuss, Daniel Joseph, 2301
Fuss, Randy R., 4126
Fussel, Stephen R., 13
Fussell, David G., 942
Fussell, Stephen R., 13
Fuster, Sergio, 1030
Futcher, Jack, 395
Futcher, Katie, 2209
Futter, Ellen V., 2071
FWD Corp., 3378
Fyke, Jim, 2620
Fyrwald, J. Erik, 2274

G&K Services, 1524
Gaalswyk, Kathy, 496
Gabbert, Joseph, 2417
Gabbert, Suzanne K., 990
Gabbert, Vince, 2113
Gabe, John, 3907
Gable & Gotwals P.C., 1525
Gable, Carl I., 1953
Gaboury, Mark, 3812
Gabran, Niclas, 3781
Gabriel, Clarence J., Jr., 1699
Gabriele, Eileen, 2429
Gabriele, Mary Eileen, 2429
Gabrys, Richard M., 854, 921
Gabrys, Richard Marcel, 2205
Gaburick, John F., 333
Gaby, Debbie, 2968
Gach, Gregory H., 1776
Gackle, George D., 3118
Gad, Albert, 1109
Gadbois, Richard A., III, 3108
Gadeh, Solomon, 3712
Gadeh, Teddy, 3712
Gadek, Stanley, 2543
Gadek, Stanley J., 2543
Gadin, Deborah M., 3100
Gadon, Steve, 3539
Gaer, Steve K., 3114
Gaff, Tom P., 1555
Gaffaney, Lawrence, 1887
Gaffner, Arlin E., 725
Gaffney, James, 1413
Gaffney, James J., 246, 1922
Gaffney, Mark T., 502
Gaffney, Steve, 3556
Gaffney, Thomas J., 2136
Gafford, Ronald J., 288
Gafner, Meldon K., 508
Gage, Barbara Carlson, 693
Gage, Edwin C., 693
Gage, Geoffrey, 693
Gage, Geoffrey Carlson, 693
Gage, Rick Carlson, 693
Gage, Scott C., 693
Gage, Scott Carlson, 693
Gagliardi, Rob, 3686
Gagne, Gerald R., 4102
Gagne, Paul E., 3731
Gagnon, Diane, 2465
Gail, Troy, 4047
Gailey, John R., III, 4038
Gaillard, Patricia J.W., 2320
Gain, Judith K., 297
Gaines, Brenda J., 57, 1349, 2785, 3713
Gaines, Donald E., 3081
Gainey, Alesha, 1776
Gaio, Edward J., 1729
Gaither, James C., 2767
Galanis, Themis G., 1455
Galante, Bill, 1147
Galante, Edward G., 3029
Galanti, Richard A., 948
Galaz, Santiago, 3390
Galbraith, Gary R., 166
Galbraith, Steve, 2409
Galbreath, Dale, 3222
Galbreath, Lizanne, 3589
Gale, Booth, 2413
Gale, Brent E., 2860
Gale, Cynthia Barber, 355
Gale, Fournier J., III, 3171
Gale, William C., 816
Galgan, Frank S., 1350
Galgano, Carol, 1806
Galgano, Cheryl A., 1806
Galgano, Gerald, 1806
Galgano, Jim, 1806
Galgon, Michael T., 3144
Galia, Gary C., 1322
Galiette, John V., 3173
Galiette, Mark, 1165
Galik, Jeffrey, 578
Galin, Tomi, 900
Galla, Ronald M., 2088
Gallagher, Arthur J., 1528
Gallagher, Barbara, 2968
Gallagher, Beth, 210
Gallagher, Daniel, 3783
Gallagher, Donald J., 127, 850
Gallagher, Gavin L., 628
Gallagher, Gene D., 3194
Gallagher, J. Patrick, 1528
Gallagher, James, 1717
Gallagher, Jamie, 126
Gallagher, John E., 398
Gallagher, Kevin, 3531
Gallagher, Kevin C., 3846
Gallagher, Michael E., 2447
Gallagher, Michael R., 99
Gallagher, Richard K., 3808
Gallagher, Richard S., 313
Gallagher, Terence, 3069
Gallagher, Thomas W., 827
Gallagher, Tracy, 3768
Gallagher, William J., 1139
Gallagher, William M., 1465
Gallagher, William T., 988
Gallahue, Kieran T., 688
Gallard, Andrew P., 1046
Gallardo, Juan, 722
Gallatin, Thomas, 3776
Gallegos, James H., 104
Gallegos, Merlinda, 2489
Gallenstein, Mike, 485
Gallery, Grant, 1382
Gallery, Robert E., 340
Gallett, Scott D., 528
Galligan, Thomas J., 3783
Galligan, Thomas, III, 1083
Gallion, Thomas T., III, 1748
Gallitano, David J., 1724
Gallivan, Karen Park, 1624
Gallo, A.C., 4066
Gallo, Ernest, 1529
Gallo, Joseph E., 1529
Gallo, Joseph Y., 1129
Gallogly, James L., 2322
Gallogly, Mark T., 1026
Gallopoulos, Gregory, 1551
Gallot, Jerome, 423
Galloway, Harvey L., 498
Galloway, Jean, 1392
Galloway, Scott, 1541
Galloway, Terry L., 2896
Galluci-Davis, Sheila, 3631
Galluzzo, Jay A., 3988
Galpin, Greg, 2991

Galvani, Paul A., 3227
Galvani, Paul V., 1481
Galvanoni, Matthew R., 1942
Galvez, Felix, 3583
Galvin, John, 872
Galvin, Walter J., 128, 1323
Galyean, Tommy, 2010
Gambale, Virginia, 2041
Gamber Glass Container, Inc., 1197
Gamber, Kitty L., 1197
Gamber, Luella M., 1197
Gamber, Marianne M., 1197
Gamber, Nancy, 1197
Gamber, Nancy J., 1197
Gamber, W. Ralph, 1197
Gamber, W.R., II, 1197
Gambet, Daniel G., 2635
Gambill, Regina, 3038
Gambino, Frank M., 3535
Gamble, John W., Jr., 2258
Gamble, Rory, 1078
Gamble, Sean, 3893
Gamble-Booth, Gwyneth, 3010
Gambrell, Sarah Belk, 403
Gambrinus Enterprises, 2240
Gammage, Grady, Jr., 1531
Gammon, Jeanne, 74
Gamoran, Reuben, 2384, 4125
Gamper, Albert R., Jr., 3077
Gandrud Chevrolet, Inc., Ivan, 3291
Gandrud, Ivan, 3291
Gangolli, Julian S., 99
Gangwal, Rakesh, 2786, 2948
Ganley, Ching-Ching, 11
Gannett Co., Inc., 1532
Gannett Outdoor, 633
Gannon, Christopher R., 499
Gannon, Georgetta H., 523
Gannon, Georgetta Hollon, 523
Gannon, Keith, 523
Gannon, Kristin F., 668
Gannon, Maureen, 3076
Gannon, O. Keith, 523
Gannon, Paul T., 3427
Gannon, Thomas, 3355
Ganong, David A., 3643
Gansen, Ron E., 3529
Gansheimer, Jan, 1851
Gansler, Jayne M., 1566
Gansner, Katherine, 2461
Ganss, Beth, 464
Gantt, Harvey B., 2760
Gantz, Charles, 2276
Gantz, Eric J., 2276
Gantz, James P., 2276
Gantz, Rosemary, 2276
Ganz, Mark, 665
Ganz, Mark B., 665, 3010, 3169
Ganz, Peter, 258
Ganzi, Victor F., 2954
Gao Yao Chung Jye Shoes Mfg., 838
Gap, Inc., The, 1533
Gappa, John A., 2351
Garaud, Jean-Jacques, 1823
Garbarino, John R., 2782
Garbe, Thomas F., 2997
Garber, Amanda, 2923
Garberding, Scott R., 801
Garcia C., Elisa D., 2785
Garcia, Anna, 3673
Garcia, Art A., 3292
Garcia, Astrid, 2961
Garcia, Charles P., 4087
Garcia, Christian, 1706
Garcia, Daniel P., 2086
Garcia, Fabian T., 2150
Garcia, G. Gary, 2756
Garcia, J. Conrad, 4078
Garcia, Kip M., 1693
Garcia, Lillian D., 3821
Garcia, Manuel, 2034
Garcia, Miguel, 179
Garcia, Paul R., 1190
Garcia, Ralph, 2034
Garcia, Ralph M., 3388
Garcia, Raul, 1083
Garcia, Savino A., 3404
Garcia, Susan, 3455
Garcia, Yolie, 2914
Garcia-Lathrop, Angie, 340
Garcia-Molina, Hector, 2821
Garcia-Tunon, Alvaro, 2406, 4048
Gard, Karen, 2324
Gard, Michael, 103
Garden Valley Telephone Co., 1535
Garden, Edward P., 1330, 4030, 4031
Gardent, Paul B., 2394
Gardes, Derek, 1614
Gardeski, Mark, 3394
Gardiner Savings Institution, F.S.B., 343
Gardiner, Kent, 986
Garding, Ed, 1409
Gardinier, Michael, 469
Gardise, John, 2243
Gardner Architects, Donald A., Inc., 1536
Gardner Designs, Donald A., LLC, 1536
Gardner Interactive, Donald A., LLC, 1536
Gardner, Brian E., 1707
Gardner, Catherine, 590
Gardner, Cindy, 2649, 3893
Gardner, David, 2582
Gardner, David W., 1440
Gardner, David Wayne, 1440
Gardner, Donald A., 1536
Gardner, Donald A., Inc., 1536
Gardner, Ed, 393
Gardner, Ed, Jr., 393
Gardner, Jenny, 814
Gardner, Lewis B., 1287
Gardner, M. Alan, 733
Gardner, Mary, 1440
Gardner, Pamela J., 1871, 2695
Gardner, R. Hartwell, 2981
Gardner, Robert, 760
Gardner, Sharyl S., 2507
Gardner, Timothy J., 272
Gardner, Tom, 2582
Garduno, Catherine, 705
Garelick Manufacturing Co., Inc., 1537
Garelick, David, 1537
Garelick, Herbert, 1537
Garelick, Kenneth D., 1537
Garelick, Richard, 1537
Garelick, Richard J., 1537
Garelick, Saul S., 1537
Garff Enterprises, Inc., 1538
Garff, John K., 1538
Garff, Katherine B., 1538
Garff, Matthew B., 1538
Garff, Robert H., 1538
Garfinkel, Barry H., 3470
Garfinkel, Tom, 3323
Gargalli, Claire W., 324, 3029
Gargano, Anthony J., 1624
Gargano, Lynn Marie, 2303
Gargaro, Eugene A., Jr., 2393
Gargiulo, Andrea, 226
Garibaldi, James J., 1984
Garich, Russell, 13
Garimalla, Nagaraj, 3065
Garimalla, Satish, 3065
Garimella, Suresh V., 2544
Garland, Alex, 2614
Garland, Greg C., 2965
Garland, Greg. C., 2965
Garmendia, Jenny Miller, 678
Garmon, Cecile, 3640
Garmon-Brown, Ophelia, 403
Garneau, Richard, 543
Garner USA LP, 3824
Garner, Curt, 3585
Garner, David, 2582
Garner, Eric L., 441
Garner, M. Craig, Jr., 1395
Garner, Michael, 1009
Garner, Terry, 1590
Garner, Terry L., 1590
Garner, Tom, 2582
Garnett, Kenneth R., 1449
Garnett, Robert, 2236
Garnier, Jean-Pierre, 3882
Garofalo, Diane, 3898
Garrant, Scott C., 3343
Garraux, James D., 3877
Garrels, John C., III, 133
Garren, Robert E., 1971
Garrett, Broox G., Jr., 337
Garrett, Donald, 939
Garrett, Douglas R., 490
Garrett, Ezra, 2952
Garrett, Gary, 2759
Garrett, Kati, 3522
Garrett, Mark, 38
Garrett, Michael W.O., 1747
Garrett, Scott, 2010
Garrett, Sharon D., 3267
Garrett, Stanley, 2066
Garrett, Stephen P., 145
Garrett, William A., 1592
Garrick, Herdicine, 4097
Garriques, Ronald G., 227
Garrison, Karen M., 2088, 3713
Garrison, Milton, 2238
Garrison, Richard C., 501
Garrison, Wayne, 1892
Garrity, Janet M., 3936
Garrone, Cynthia, 202
Garside, John W., 3890
Garson, Gary W., 2296
Garst, Elizabeth, 286, 1846, 3116
Garst, Jennifer, 286, 1846
Garst, Mary, 1846
Garst, Sarah, 3116
Garten, Jeffrey E., 48
Garth Brooks Teammates for Kids Foundation, 3716
Gartland, Bill, 284
Gartland, Greg, 284
Gartland, James M., Jr., 284
Gartland, Joseph C., 284
Gartmann, Pamela, 1076
Garton, Aaron, 2052
Garton, Shawn, 2052
Garvey, Christine N., 3060, 3769
Garvey, James W., 609
Garvey, Marc, 1902
Garvey, Maria Regina, 163
Garvey, Michael J., 2232
Garvey, Michael R., 3444
Garvey, Mike, 609
Garvin, J. Guthrie, 2398
Garvin, Lucy S., 3879
Garvin, Sam, 2968
Garvin, Vail P., 1926
Garwood, Keith D., 2215
Garza, Antonio O., 2558
Garza, Antonio O., Jr., 2094
Garza, David, 2274
Gas Turbine Efficiency, 661
Gasaway, Sharilyn S., 1892
Gasbarro, Eric, 491
Gascoigne, Richard R., 3032
Gasdaska, William, Jr., 1558
Gasparovic, John J., 528
Gasper, Joseph J., 1008
Gass, Michelle, 3585
Gass, Rhonda, 3579
Gasser, Michael J., 1300, 1663
Gassmann, Tim, 2524
Gast, Steven D., 2680
Gast, Thomas C., 32
Gaston, Patrick, 4045
Gaston, Patrick R., 399
Gaston, Sterling, 570
Gates, Andrew L., III, 3614
Gates, Brad J., 1567
Gates, John E., 3491
Gates, Joseph, 3635
Gates, Patrick, 3394
Gates, Robert, 3585
Gates, W. Gary, 2607
Gates, William, 2010
Gates, William H., III, 429, 2501
Gates, William H., Sr., 948
Gateway 2000, Inc., 1541
Gateway, Inc., 1541
Gatewood, Robert C., 894
Gathers, Tom, 1032
Gathof, W. Lawrence, 4150
Gatta, Allison, 1552
Gatti, William J., 3297
Gatto, Patricia, 1163
GATX Corp., 1542
Gaudean, Faith M., 2123
Gaudet, Gordon J., 3399
Gaudette, Edward, 4017
Gaudiosi, Monica, 3520
Gaudiosi, Monica M., 3520
Gaul, J. Herbert, Jr., 437
Gauld, William, 1939
Gaulding, John, 2560
Gaulin, Laura, 476
Gaulke, Michael R., 1016, 3664
Gault, Polly L., 1228
Gaumond, Mark E., 3134
Gaunce Management Inc., 1543
Gaunce, Chapatcha, 1543
Gaunce, Patrick, 1543
Gaunce, Wayne, 1543
Gaunch, C. Edward, 385
Gauron, Paul R., 2668
Gavaert, John, 1024
Gavagan, George R., 1532
Gavegnano, Richard J., 1207
Gavin, Carol, 3709
Gavin, Carol C., 3709
Gavin, James R., III, 377
Gavin, John J., 996
Gavin, Sara H., 3389
Gavin, Timothy F., 701
Gavrielov, Moshe, 4137
Gavrielov, Moshe N., 4137
Gavronski, Dan, 991
Gaw, Maria, 131

Gawlak, Tom, 2984
Gaworski, Juli, 2258
Gawryk, Terry, 1422
Gay, Linda, 476
Gay, Robert C., 1906
Gayhardt, Donald F., Jr., 412
Gayle, Helene D., 862, 869
Gayle, Jacob A., 2453
Gaylord Entertainment Co., 3294
Gaylord, Edward K., II, 3294
Gaylord, John P., 3406
Gaylord, Tim, 2396
Gayner, Thomas S., 3999
Gaynor, John M., 520
Gaynor, Mitchell, 2075
Gazette Co. Inc., 3506
Gazette Newspapers, 3016
Gazette-Times, Carvallis, 947
Gaziano, Angelo, 2373
Gazzillo, Lori, 428
GE, 1383
GE Capital Corp., 1275
Geanacopoulos, David, 3967
Geanacopoulus, David, 3967
Gear Motions Inc., 1544
Gearhart, Jeffrey J., 3980
Gearns, Mary Jane, 3977
Geary, Jim, 2674
Geary, Joe, 4109
Geary, Marie, 1552
Geary, Ronald G., 3931
Gebert, Ned, 2435
Gebhardt, Susan G., 2554
Gebhardt, William, 2554
Gebo, John, 103
Gebo, John R., 3860
Gedaka, Kenneth A., 1449
Geddes, John, 4056
Gedeller, Anthony, 4125
Gee, E. Gordon, 1300, 2277
Gee, Kenny, 906
Geekie, Mathew W., 1640
Geekie, Matthew W., 1640
Geelan, John W., 2983
Geenbeg, Maurice, 147
Geeraerts, John W., 3404
Gegenheimer, Rick, 2377
Gehl Co., 1545
Gehlsen, Anne, 1407
Gehman, David W., 2998
Gehring, Fred, 1801, 3088
Gehring, John F., 904
Geiger, Drew, 530
Geile, Rob, 1818
Geisel, Gary N., 2323
Geisler, John E., 691
Geissinger, Frederick W., 3554
Geissler, Werner, 1612
Geist, Jerry D., 758
Geist, John C., 533
Geitzen, Barbara, 1403
Gelatt, C. Daniel, 3047
Gelb, Joel, 2629
Gelco Construction, 1546
Gelco Supply, Inc., 1546
Geldmacher, Jay L., 2844, 3377
Geller, Alison, 44
Geller, Kenneth S., 2411
Geller, Mitch, 3152
Geller, Sheldon M., 2135
Gellerstedt, Larry L., III, 953
Gellerstedt, Lawrence L., III, 953, 3239
Gellert, Jay M., 1766, 3931
Gelmick, Bob, 2915
Gelnaw, Bill, 796
Geltzeiler, Michael S., 2769
Gemini Industries, Inc., 1547
Gemkow, Stephan, 2041
Gemmell, Nadema, 3316
Gemmill, Elizabeth H., 412
Gems Motorsports, 1776
Gemuend, Markus, 1549
Gemunder, Joel F., 773
Genco, Christopher M., 2497
GenCorp Foundation Inc., 1548, 2809
Gender, Robert, 156
Gendron, Thomas A., 1795, 4112
Genelius, Sandra, 3502
Genentech, Inc., 1549
General Accident Insurance Co. of America, 2813
General Dynamics Corp., 1551
General Electric Co., 1552
General Iron Industries, Inc., 1553
General Mills, 3659
General Mills, Inc., 1554, 2619, 3659
General Motors Corp., 1555
General Motors Foundation, Inc., 1071
General Procument Inc., 925
General Railway Signal Corp., 1557
Generous, Eric, 1345
Geneseo Communications, Inc., 1560
Genesis Apparel, Inc., 3063
Genna, Richard A., 2769
Gennaro, Paul J., 42
Genney, Guy, 1565
Genovese, Peter J., 3846
GENPHARM, L.P., 2622
GenRad, Inc., 1564
Genshaft Trust, Leona, 1499
Genshaft, Neil, 1499
Gentilcore, Dorothy, 1370
Gentilozzi, Kathy, 46
Gentilozzi, Kathy E., 46
Gentry, Barbara B., 3873
Gentry, Jeffery S., 3200
Gentry, Jesse, 2995
Gentzler, Roland G., 1866
Gentzler, Ronald G., 1866
Genworth Financial, Inc., 1565
Genzler, Cathy, 1359
Genzy, Robin, 3347
Genzyme Corp., 1566
Genzyne, 3329
Geoffrey, Robert, 277
Georgantas, Aristides W., 1863
George, Anton H., 3925
George, Anton Hulman, 1555, 1885, 3722
George, Arthur L., Jr., 2723
George, Deborah S., 258
George, Don, 499
George, Don C., 499
George, Gary C., 1892
George, Katherine M., 1885
George, M. Josephine, 1885
George, Mari Hulman, 1555, 1885, 3722
George, Michael, 3112
George, Michael A., 2264
George, Mike, 572
George, Nancy L., 1885
George, Richard, 1645
George, Richard Dick, 1645
George, Richard E., Jr., 3815
George, Richard L., 190
George, Rick, 3729
George, Terry E., 1149
George, Thomas A., 1059
George, William M., 1799
George, William W., 1315, 1603, 1604
Georgens, Thomas, 289
Georgia Bank & Trust Co., 3513
Georgia Council for the arts, 2573
Georgia Financial, LLC, 2880
Georgia Gas Co., 57
Georgia Power Co., 1567
Georgia-Pacific Corp., 1568
Georgiadis, Margaret H., 2057
Georgieff, Gregory, 1917
Georgoff, Thomas, 2522
Gephardt, Richard A., 735, 751, 1464, 3877
Gephart, Gerard, 1552
Gepsman, Martin J., 853
Geraghty, Patrick, 496
Geraghty, Susan, 993
Gerard, Jamie, 2697
Gerard, Julie W., 433
Gerard, Robert, 1589
Gerard, Robert A., 1695
Gerard, Steven L., 2070, 2250
Gerber, Gary, 3644
Gerber, Murry S., 1706, 3877
Gerber, Robert I., 2303
Gerber, Terry, 2
Gerber, William K., 67, 4106
Gerdelman, John W., 2841
Gerdes, Larry G., 853
Gerel Corp., 3287
Geren, Preston M., III, 190
Gerene Furguson, 770
Gergen, David, 566
Gerhart, Bobbie, 3944
Gerke, Mark R., 4005
Gerlach, John B., Jr., 1894, 2216
Gerlits, Francis J., 2164
Germ, John F., 507
German, Mitch, 3303
Germano, Don, 1110
Germano, Karen A., 534
Gerritsen, Randall S., 3912
Gerry, Paul J., Jr., 2506
Gersack, Robert, 1423
Gersch, Nicole V., 889
Gersch, Seth, 3326
Gersh, Lisa, 1747
Gershon, Norm, 957
Gershon, Peter, 2630
Gershowitz, Diane Marcus, 2371
Gershwind, Erik, 2593
Gerson, Mathew, 1223
Gerson, Ralph J., 1682
Gerspach, John C., 821
Gerstein, Beth, 568
Gerstle, Michael, 2687
Gerstman, Ned I., 804
Gerstner, Karen, 563
Gertsen, Greg, 1080
Gertz, H. F., 2205
Gervais, Laurie L., 3444
Gervais, Stephen L., 2734
Gervasi, Martha, 1742
Geschke, Charles M., 38
Geschwindt, Philip, 3142
Gessay, Scott, 2755
Gesseck, Richard H., 2645
Gethin, John P., 3575
Gettig, Thomas E., 4025
Gettman, James A., 396
Getts, David, 3448
Getty Images, 2711
Getty, Mark, 1569
Getz, Jim, 4018
Geyer, Hans, 3532
Geyer, Rob, 655
Geyer-Sylvia, Zelda, 504
Ghadar, Fariborz, 4047
Ghanemi, Ace, 25
Ghanemi, Camron, 25
Ghanemi, Linda S., 25
Ghilotti Brothers Construction, Inc., 1570
Ghilotti Brothers, Inc., 1570
Ghilotti Construction Co., 1570
Ghilotti Construction, Inc., 1570
Ghilotti, Dante, 1570
Ghilotti, Dante W., 1570
Ghilotti, Eva, 1570
Ghilotti, Eva R., 1570
Ghilotti, Michael, 1570
Ghilotti, Michael M., 1570
Ghilotti, Richard Dick, 1570
Ghoddousi, Shahriar, 1780
Ghosh, Bishalakhi, 81
Giacalone, Peter, 3889
Giaccia, Andrew A., 759
Giacoio, Anthony, Sr., 675
Giacomin, Jon, 685
Giacomini, Andrew, 1725
Giallongo, Reyno A., Jr., 1399
Giambastiani, Edmund P., Jr., Adm., 516
Giampa, Diane M., 380
Giancamilli, Andrew A., 2622
Giangrande, Paul, 382
Giangrasso, Chris, 242
Giannantonio, Frank, 2220
Giannini, Duane, 2704
Giannini, Duane H., 2704
Giannini, Peter, 3694
Gianos, Philip T., 4137
Giant Eagle, Inc., 1571
Giard, Sharlene, 3140
Giardina, Robert J., 3783
Gibb, Russ, 640
Gibbons, David T., 2943
Gibbons, John M., 1059
Gibbons, Joseph M., 3317
Gibbons, Lucia, 4028
Gibbons, Michael, 2638
Gibbons, Michael E., 3032
Gibbons, Michael J., 1971
Gibbons, Mike, 2638
Gibbons, Thomas P., 344
Gibbs Die Casting Corp., 2179
Gibbs International, Inc., 1576
Gibbs Racing, Joe, 1776
Gibbs, David, 2988
Gibbs, Jimmy I., 1576
Gibbs, Joseph E., 933
Gibbs, Marsha H., 1576
Gibbs, Stephen L., 1653
Giberson, Karen, 1578
Gibford, Patricia, 3274
Giblin, John, 507
Giblin, Vincent J., 1863
Gibney, Charles W., 2733
Gibraltar Cable Barrier Systems, 1577
Gibraltar Material Distribution, 1577
Gibson Plumbing Co., Inc., 1579
Gibson, Bill, 1579
Gibson, Charles Scott, 2747
Gibson, Christopher R., 232
Gibson, Dale, 1080
Gibson, Donald E., 341
Gibson, Gary, 3440

Gibson, Hank, 1106
Gibson, Jodi M., 2925
Gibson, Jodie, 2925
Gibson, John W., 2815
Gibson, Lee R., 1347
Gibson, Martyn, 3147
Gibson, Pam, 1579
Gibson, Scott, 1579
Gibson, William L., 1878
Giddens, Gregg, 2284
Giddens, Keith B., 2284
Giddings & Lewis, Inc., 2337
Giddings & Lewis, LLC, 2337
Gideon, Thomas F., 4052
Gidley, Marta D., 1463
Gidwani, Bahar, 994
Giedgowd, Joe, 630
Gielen, Elizabeth Moody, 2562
Giertz, James R., 1517, 1804
Gifford Foundation, The, 276
Gifford, Chad, 538
Gifford, Charles K., 340, 727, 2737
Gifford, David W., 1420
Gifford, William F., Jr., 2574
Gifford-Lundberg, Anisia R., 2506
Giftos, P. Michael, 112
Giga, Aziz S., 3025
Giggey, Brenan, 106
Giglio, Denise, 4072
Giglio, Lawrence R., 1640
Giguere, Craig, 1103
Gikoas, William J., 792
Gilbane, Robert V., 1581
Gilbane, Thomas F., III, 1581
Gilbane, Thomas F., Jr., 1581
Gilbane, William J., Jr., 1581
Gilbert, Daniel R., 724
Gilbert, Emily, 3838
Gilbert, J. Stephen, 3915
Gilbert, Jarobin, Jr., 1459
Gilbert, Lorrie Savage, 3341
Gilbert, Michael, 1819
Gilbert, Steven J., 2416
Gilbert-Davis, Grace T., 2671
Gilbertson, John S., 306
Gilbertstein, Michael, 1444
Gilbreth, Edward M., 1302
Gilchrist, Andrew D., 3200
Gilchrist, Corydon J., 1406
Gilchrist, Daniel R., 3142
Gilchrist, Malcolm Lan Grant, 2264
Gilchrist, Richard I., 3931
Gildea, John, 1971
Gilder, Ginny, 370
Gildody, Paul D., 380
Gilead Sciences, Inc., 1582
Giles, Bill, 2964
Giles, Cheryl, 412
Giles, Clark P., 3131
Giles, Jody, 1737
Giles, Robert, 2941
Giles, William T., 294, 572
Giles-Klein, Lisa, 613
Gilhodes, Laurent, 3329
Giliotti, Emil, 2437
Giliotti, Gayle, 3396
Gilkey, Glenn C., 1448
Gill, Charles D., 3882
Gill, Jeremy, 323
Gill, Matthew J., 1881
Gill, Phupinder S., 853, 1413
Gillani, Aleem, 3654
Gillard, Robert O., 3444
Gilleland Chevrolet, Inc., 3291
Gilleland, Diane Suitt, 3478
Gilleland, Duane, 3291
Gilleland, Tracye C., 3657
Gilles, Joe, 1263
Gillespie, David, 84
Gillespie, Patrick B., 1926
Gillespie, R.W., 3553
Gillete, Gordon, 3701
Gillett, Stephen, 442, 3669
Gillette, Eleanor, 1100
Gillette, Howard, 2886
Gillette, Mark D., 3649
Gillette, Mark G., 3649
Gilley, R. Stevens, 2198
Gilliam, Franklin D., Jr., 655
Gilliam, Theron I., Jr., 2250
Gilliam, Thomas, 2605
Gillian, John, 2666
Gillian, Roy, 2781
Gilliard, Michelle, 3980
Gilligan, Chris, 415
Gilligan, Edward P., 143
Gilligan, J. Kevin, 1624
Gilligan, Kevin, 1517
Gillilan, John S., Jr., 2666
Gilliland, Sam, 3117
Gillis, Edwin J., 3718
Gillis, Ruth Ann M., 1309, 3017
Gillis, S. Malcolm, 42, 3413
Gillis, S. Malcom, 1706
Gillis, Timothy H., 2190
Gillman, Brian, 1592
Gillmore, Scott, 1259
Gillow, Paul, 3141
Gilman, Alfred G., 2274
Gilman, Kenneth B., 1376, 4151
Gilmartin, Raymond V., 1554
Gilmartin, Thomas, 2335
Gilmer, Mark, 1979
Gilmore, Barry, 2203
Gilmore, Benjamin A., II, 1927, 3242
Gilmore, Bob, 2250
Gilmore, Dennis J., 1389, 1390
Gilmore, Jay C., 1087
Gilmore, Karen, 2860
Gilmore, Ray, 2699
Gilmore, Richie, 1205
Gilroy, Beth, 347
Gilsinn, John P., 612
Gilstrap, Mark, 137
Giltner, Thomas R., 273
Gin, Sue Ling, 1309
Gindi, Abraham, 748
Gindi, Raymond, 748
Gingell, John F., 3700
Gingerich, Philip E., 1318
Gingo, Joseph M., 3361
Gingras, Mark R., 2262
Ginivan, William J., 1345
Ginn, Samiel L., 3965
Ginn, William J., 1035
Ginnan, Robert, 3576
Ginnan, Robert M., 3576
Ginsberg, David, 538
Ginsberg, Gary L., 3757
Ginsberg, Sheldon, 3276
Ginsberg, Winston, 3781
Ginsburg Trust, Abe, 2015
Ginsburg, Abe, 2015
Ginsburg, Abraham, 2015
Ginsburg, Allan, 2015
Ginsburg, Howard, 2015
Gioia, Bradford, 285
Giokas, William J., 792
Giordano, Nicholas A., 1926
Giordano, Thomas W., 4007
Giraldo, John P., 126
Girard, Jeffrey C., 4087
Girard, Sara, 742
Girardi, Thomas V., 546
Giroi, Raymond, 748
Giromini, Richard J., 3230
Girsch, Emily, 2282
Girsky, Stephen J., 1555
Gisel, William G., Jr., 3204
Gisnburg Trust, Silvia, 2015
Gispanski, Thomas, 1727
Gitter, Kurt A., 3520
Giuffre, Fiona Ow, 3327
Giuffre, Linda, 563
Giuliano, Tony, 2786
Giunta, David L., 1450
Gius, Richard J., 285
Givan, Kevin, 2692
Givens, Danny, 3194
Givens, Kaye, 1577
Givens, S. Danny, 3194
Gjertson, Douglas, 2366
GJF Construction Corp., 1584
Glaccum, Joann, 2565
Glacier Fish Company, LLC, 1586
Gladden, Brian T., 1068
Gladden, John E., 1079
Glades Electric Cooperative, Inc., 1587
Gladstone, Henry A., 964
Glahn, John Van, 2166
Glaister, Thomas, 766
Glanton, Richard, 222
Glascow, Pat, 2439
Glaser, Bill, 1617
Glaser, Daniel E., 497
Glaser, Daniel S., 2385
Glaser, David, 3248
Glaser, Rob, 367
Glaser, Robert, 3144
Glasgow, Norman M., Sr., 4074
Glasgow, Stan, 3503
Glasgow, William P., 1550
Glasier, Richard J., 696
Glass, Dan, 2093
Glass, David D., 2093
Glass, Dennis R., 2281
Glass, Don, 2093
Glass, Donald S., 3317
Glass, Holly, 3629
Glass, Joel, 2824
Glass, Kevin, 2573
Glass, Marty, 4112
Glass, Milton, 501
Glass, Ruth, 2093
Glass, Tyler A., 3142
Glasscock, Larry C., 3458, 3556, 3677, 4157
Glasser, Marcy E., 879
Glassford, Jim, 2104
Glassman, Cynthia A., 1125
Glassman, Jennifer, 3781
Glassman, Karl G., 2246
Glassman, Robert A., 1209
Glast, Phillips & Murray, 136
Glauber, Robert R., 2563
Glaus, R. Wayne, 1084
Glavin, William, 24
Glavin, William F., Jr., 2818
Glawe, Sue, 3902
Glaxo Wellcome Americas Inc., 1588
GlaxoSmithKline, 2622
GlaxoSmithKline Holdings (Americas) Inc., 1588
GlaxoSmithKline LLC F.K.A. SmithKline, 1588
Glaze, Bill, 2300
Glaze, Brett, 2552
Glazer, Bruce, 2194
Glazer, Bryan, 599
Glazer, Edward, 599
Glazer, Joel, 599
Glazer, Malcolm, 599
Glazer, Margie, 838
Glazer, Michael, 965, 3572
Glazer, Michael L., 3572
Glazer, Rose Marie E., 3448
Glazerman, Ellan, 1293
Glazier, Ronald B., 469
Gleacher, Eric, 1589
Gleaner Life Insurance Society, 1590
Gleason Corp., 1591
Gleason Foundation, 1591
Gleason, Dave, 566
Gleason, James S., 1591
Gleason, Shannon, 3649
Gleeson, John W., 3682
Gleim, Michael L., 521
Gleitsman, Thomas E., 3730
Glendinning, Stewart, 2523
Glendon, David, 3551
Glenewinkel, Arlen, Jr., 3723
Glenn, Glenda, 3890
Glenn, J. Kirk, Jr., 403
Glenn, Joel, 2138
Glenn, Michael S., 471
Glenn, Richard Savik, 234
Glenn, Stephen, 1079
Glenn, Steve G., 3985
Glenn, T. Michael, 1352, 2926
Glick, Alvin L., 113
Glick, Barry J., 113
Glick, Carl, 113
Glick, Carlton L., 113
Glick, Marty, 728
Glick, Randal L., 113
Glick, Randy, 113
Glick, Tom, 3304
Glickman, Daniel R., 853
Glidden, Jeffrey D., 2878
Glidewell, C. Douglas, 1468
Gliebe, Mark J., 3167
Gliedman, Michael S., 2623
Glimcher, Laurie H., 578, 4003
Glimcher, Michael P., 2325
Glispin, Arthur, 3090
Glisson, Patrick C., 2157
Global Cornerstone Healthcare Services, Inc., 1686
Global Education Excellance, 1997
Global Green Solutions, 2597
Global Industrial Technologies, Inc., 201
Global Link Solutions, Inc., 925
Global Petroleum Corp., 1593
Global Rental Co., 118
Globe Vending Corp., 281
Globus Medical, Inc., 2171
Glocer, Thomas H., 2466, 2570
Glode, Michael S., 3815
Glossman, Diane B., 123
Glotzbach, Edward L., 2208
Glover, Daniel K., 71
Glover, Edmund C., 373
Glover, J. Littleton, Jr., 373, 385
Glover, S. Taylor, 959
Glowiak, Brian G., 801

Goodwin, Thomas R., 1272
Goodwyn, Monica, 2482
Goodyear Tire & Rubber Co., The, 1612
Goodyear, Charles W., 190
Google Inc., 1613
Gookins, Norm, 3874
Gooldrup, Michael, 2771
Goolis, Jennifer, 1548
Goolsby, Allen C., III, 3148
Goolsby, Ronald, 3914
Gootee General Contractors, Ryan, LLC, 1614
Gootee, Ryan P., 1614
Gootee, Sara M., 1614
Gopal, Christopher S., 3505
Gora, Jo Ann M., 1410
Gorder, Joe, 3915
Gordon, Anne, 2958
Gordon, Bancroft S., 2383
Gordon, Brad, 755
Gordon, Bruce S., 727, 2744
Gordon, Chris, 1762
Gordon, Dan, 1615
Gordon, Daniel L., 1590
Gordon, David A., 2228
Gordon, Douglas S., 4005
Gordon, George E., 1415
Gordon, Ian K., 497
Gordon, Ilene S., 1942, 1968
Gordon, Jeffrey S., 3672
Gordon, Jim, 1615
Gordon, John, 1615
Gordon, John A., 1171
Gordon, John M., 1615
Gordon, John R., 190
Gordon, Marc C., 143
Gordon, Marc D., 442
Gordon, Michael S., 1120
Gordon, Mike, 538
Gordon, Neal, 2005
Gordon, Richard E., 57
Gordon, Richard K., 285
Gordon, Robert A., 3310
Gordon, Sara, 663
Gordon, Suzanne, 3336
Gordon, William B., 122
Gordy, Carol F., 337
Gordy, Vaughn, 3837
Gore, Albert A., Jr., 217
Gore, Arun, 1639
Gore, Cecelia, 2527
Gore, Diane, 503
Gorecki, Christopher, 655
Gorelick, Jamie S., 122, 3882
Gorelick, Richard D., 1947
Goren, Bella, 1533
Goren, Isabella D., 187
Gorga, Joseph L., 1971
Gorham, Robert L., 4074
Gorin, Nathen, 2720
Gorish, Frances M., 3070
Gorlin, Robert H., 1682
Gorman, Christopher M., 2136
Gorman, James P., 2570
Gorman, Joseph J., Jr., 833
Gorman, Leon A., 392
Gorman, Monica, 140
Gorman, Peter, 403
Gorman, Stephen E., 1073
Gorman, Thomas W., 3534
Gormley, Mark K., 3887
Gorn, Stephen, 3105
Gorn, Stephen M., 3105
Gorry, James A., III, 1145
Gorski, Jeff A., 3748
Gorsky, Alex, 2048
Gorss, Steve J., 2262
Gorsuch, Kristin L., 2453
Gorup, Patrick J., 256
Gose, Kristin, 1388
Goshgarian, George, 506
Gosiger Haley, Jane, 1617
Gosiger, Inc., 1617
Gosline, Don W., 2663
Goss, Jennifer M., 1791
Goss, Marjorie, 1009
Goss, Phil, 3818
Gossett, Robert L., 4088
Gossett, Steve, Jr., 3366
Gossett, Steve, Sr., 3366
Gossweiler, Albert E., 2108
Got2b, 30
Gotham, Rich, 352
Gothorpe, William G., 1060
Gotkowska, Dorota, 3624
Gotlieb, David, 3684
Goto, Masaaki, 1020
Goto, Noriaki, 347
Gotro, Jerry, 2137
Gotschall, Jeffrey P., 3452
Gotta, John H., 2088
Gottdenker, Michael I., 1730
Gottesdiener, T.J., 3474
Gottesfeld, Stephen P., 2698
Gottesman, Jerome, 1229
Gottesman, Margery, 1229
Gottesman, Patricia A., 4121
Gottfried, Pat, 216
Gottfried, Ran, 2943
Gottlieb, Keith, 923
Gottschalk, Hugh, 4053
Gottschalk, John, 2806
Gottschalk, Thomas A., 2164
Gottung, Lizanne C., 2310
Goulart, Janet A., 1590
Goulart, Steven J., 2481
Gould Electronics Inc., 1618
Gould, Anne L., 2742
Gould, Brad, 2968
Gould, Brian, 1628
Gould, Christopher K.K., 442
Gould, Gilbert, 44
Gould, James M., 608
Gould, Joann M., 3305
Gould, John E., 757
Gould, Karen O., 3824
Gould, Kirstin Roman, 4134
Gould, Michael, 488
Gould, Paul A., 186, 1126, 2263
Gould, Stephen A., 586
Goulden, David I., 1253
Goulds Pumps, Inc., 1619
Goulet, Beverly K., 187
Goupil, Dominique Philippe, 1380
Gourdeau, Peter C., 3317
Gourdeau, Richard, 3317
Gourdeau, Richard R., 3317
Gove, Sue E., 294
Government Employees Benefit Assoc., Inc., 1620
Government Employees Insurance Co., 1621
Gow, George, 2031
Goward, Abigail, 340
Gowdy, Michelle, 2980
Gowen, Brian, 2830
Gowen, Jim, Sr., 241
Gower, Scott, 3203
Goyette, Dominic, 1438
Gozon, Richard C., 175
GP Ktronics, Inc., 3678
GPS Construction Services, LLC, 136
GPU Service, Inc., 1424
Grabe, David, 3387
Grabe, William O., 902
Graber, Harold G., Jr., 4024
Graber, William R., 2086, 2580
Graber-Lipperman, Peter J., 3454
Grabill Bank, 3212
Grabill, Galen, 2714
Grable, Robert C., 285
Grabovac, Greg R., 1429
Grabow, Karen, 2217
Grabowski, Ted, 3725
Grabowsky, Lou J., 1633
Graboys, Ken, 768
Grace & Co., W.R., 1623
Grace, Barbara F., 2064
Grace, Claire S., 4052
Grace, John M., 4039
Grace, Karyn, 3778
Grace, Patrick P., 773
Grace, Robert P., 1420
Grace, Ted, 1528
Graceffa, Al C., 343
Gracey, Paul C., Jr., 1964
Gracey, William M., 507
Graco Inc., 1624
Graddick-Weir, Mirian M., 1733, 2466, 4150
Gradishar, Randy, 2298
Grady, Dallace, 3805
Grady, Daniel A., 530, 4025
Grady, James F., 654
Grady, Kenneth A., 4106
Grady, Lois W., 2813
Grady, Richard R., 3805
Grady-Troia, Christopher, 360
Graef, Eric R., 3032
Graeser, Mark R., 1029
Graev, Lawrence G., 3802
Graf, Alan B., Jr., 1352, 2710
Graf, Jonathan, 136
Graf, Jonathan A., 136
Graf, Mark R., 1125
Graf, Robert T., 2315
Graff Chevrolet, Inc., 1238
Graff, Christopher, 2633
Graff, David, 4113
Graff, Scott H., 2702
Graff, Stanley V., 1238
Grafoner, Peter, 3473
Grafton, Susan S., 442
Gragg, Donna, 1225
Graham Architectural Products, 1625
Graham Capital Corp., 1625
Graham Engineering Corp., 1625
Graham Packaging Co., L.P., 1625
Graham Packaging Holdings Co., 1625
Graham, Bill, 860
Graham, Christopher A., 806
Graham, Dan, 434
Graham, Donald C., 1625
Graham, Donald E., 3999
Graham, Ginger L., 3981
Graham, H. Devon, Jr., 1494
Graham, Ingrid A., 1625
Graham, John, 380, 2235
Graham, John H., 505
Graham, Jonathan P., 1027
Graham, Kristin, 1625
Graham, Kristine, 1153
Graham, Mary, 682
Graham, Meredith M., 1519
Graham, Patricia Albjerg, 211
Graham, Peter, 3416
Graham, Robert H., 1983
Graham, Steven B., 4030, 4031
Graham, Stuart E., 1741, 3026
Graham, Terri, 2007
Graham, Timothy, 1520
Graham, Tom, 261
Graham, Wayne, 75
Graham-Johnson, Jennifer, 3239
Grahame, Heather H., 2748
Graig, Keith, 2762
Graig, Kim, 1318
Grainge, Lucian, 30
Grainger, Michael J., 3347
Gram, Dwight, 3204
Gramelspacher, Glenn, II, 2026
Gramelspacher, Mark B., 2027
Gramelspacher, Nicholas, 2026
Gramelspacher, Phillip, 2025
Gramigna, Edward A., Jr., 2909
Grams, Blake M., 3775
Granado, Alejandro, 820
Granahan, Laura, 3581
Granat, Jill, 613
Grand Bank for Savings, FSB, 2578
Grand Circle Corp., 1627
Grand Circle Travel, 1627
Grand Circle Trust, 1627
Grand Rapids Area Chamber of Commerce, 1131
Grand Rapids Label Co., 1628
Grand Victoria Casino, 1629
Grand View Hospital, 3944
Granderson, Curtis, 2346
Grandma Brown's Beans, Inc., 1630
Graner, James A., 1624
Granetz, Marc D., 980
Granfors, Donna, 1552
Grangaard, Paul D., 97
Granger, Catherine D., 2342
Granger, Danyelle, 2798
Granger, L. Keith, 492
Graning, Michael, 409
Granito, Frank H., III, 2193
Granito, Frank H., Jr., 2193
Granoff, David P., 4070
Granquist, Bruce, 55
Granquist, Deborah, 499
Grant Thornton LLP, 1633
Grant, Adrienne, 30
Grant, Denise M., 1276
Grant, Edward A., 2776
Grant, Hugh, 2559, 3025
Grant, Hugh M., 2559
Grant, Jennifer L., 63
Grant, John A., 322
Grant, Kentton C., 3819
Grant, Kimberly, 3281
Grant, Kimberly D., 4075
Grant, Leslie E., 1083
Grant, Marilee, 540
Grant, Maureen, 2064
Grant, Ruth M., 3297
Grant, Veva M., 2146
Grant, W. Thomas, II, 890
Graphic Arts Show Co., Inc., 1634
Graphic Packaging International, Inc., 1635
Graphics Atlanta Inc, 1186
Graphix Unlimited, Inc., 1637
Grapstein, Steven H., 3723

Gras, Horst E., 313
Grasee, Kari E., 144
Grass, Gayle C., 2919
Grassi, Anthony P., 475
Grassmyer, K. Scott, 2847
Grassmyer, K. Scott, Jr., 2847
Grater, Paul A., 2058
Grauer, Peter T., 486, 1044
Gravelle, Michael, 1371
Graves, Earl G., Jr., 294
Graves, Gary A., 692
Graves, Gregory M., 620, 3846
Graves, Jeffrey A., 1795, 3707
Graves, Joel, 1952
Graves, L. Keith, 3683
Graves, Paul, 1449
Graves, William P., 1970
Gray, Ann Maynard, 1189
Gray, Bobby, 2738
Gray, Charles, 3718
Gray, Faver, 136
Gray, Gavin, 2940, 2941
Gray, Glenn, 3655
Gray, Gloria, 2484
Gray, Herb, 972
Gray, John L., 228
Gray, Johnnie, 1651
Gray, Johnnie L., 1651
Gray, Jonathan D., 477
Gray, Lee, 1833
Gray, Matthew, 1641
Gray, Matthew J., 1641
Gray, Melvin, 1641
Gray, Sean, 428
Gray, Stephen C., 3672
Gray, Steve, 1804
Gray, Steven F., 1641
Gray, Susanne, 1641
Gray, Tim, 2450
Gray, Victor, 814
Gray, William H., III, 1068, 2950, 3072
Graybar Electric Company, Inc., 1640
Graycor, Inc., 1641
Graye, Mitchell T.G., 1647
Grayson, Robert C., 2128
Grayson, Stanley E., 3696
Graziadei, Frank, 185
Graziano, Fred, 3696
Graziano, Judith O., 505
Grbic, Michael, 4141
Greaf, Jack, 2538
Great American Group, 511
Great American Insurance Co., 1165
Great Lakes Bank, N.A., 1644
Great Lakes Castings Corp., 1643
Great Lakes Financial Resources, 1644
Great Plains Natural Gas Co., 2441
Greater Augusta Arts Council, 2573
Greater Community Bancorp, 3916
Greater Community Bank, 3916
Greater Construction Corp., The, 1648
Greater Miami Jewish Federation, 2398
Greater Omaha Packing Co., 1649
Greaves, Roger F., 1766
Grebe, Michael W., 806, 2833
Greco, Al, 2354
Greco, Anthony D., 4049
Greco, Larry, 2162
Greco, Lois W., 4028
Greco, Tom R., 1506
Greco, Tony, 4049
Greczyn, Robert J., Jr., 497
Greed, John R., 2605
Greehey, Bill, 2763
Greehey, William E., 2763
Green Bay Packers, 1651
Green, Christy S., 2270
Green, Darrell, 2626
Green, Darryl, 2358
Green, David, 2312
Green, David R., 2312
Green, Harriet, 1257
Green, James, 1545
Green, James E., 1053
Green, James M., 3378
Green, James R., 206
Green, Jennifer, 814
Green, John D., 325
Green, Judson C., 2648
Green, Julian, 784
Green, Kevin R., 496
Green, Louis H., Jr., 3467
Green, Louis, Jr., 422
Green, Maria C., 1916
Green, Maria C., Jr., 1916
Green, Mel E., 2951
Green, Michael B., 3885
Green, Michael S., 1186
Green, Myra, 1083
Green, Philip D., 1512
Green, Phillip D., 1512
Green, R. Scott, 2381
Green, Richard, 1258
Green, Richard R., 2263
Green, Rick, 206
Green, Robert, 3564
Green, Ronald J., 2870
Green, Sandra L., 2588
Green, Scott, 2381
Green, Stephen S., 1567
Green, Stephen W., 780
Green, Steve, 1258
Green, Steven B., 2690
Green, Steven J., 2984
Green, Susan M., 850
Green, Thomas R., 3858
Green, Tweed & Co., 1657
Green, William D., 2429
Greenacre, Martyn D., 752
Greenberg Foundation, The, 945
Greenberg, Alan C., 3945
Greenberg, Daniel, 945, 2533
Greenberg, David I., 1921
Greenberg, Evan, 24
Greenberg, Evan G., 862
Greenberg, Jack M., 107, 1747, 2358, 4045
Greenberg, Jonathan, 1495
Greenberg, Kenneth, 2533
Greenberg, Lon R., 174, 222
Greenberg, Michael, 2533, 3472
Greenberg, Norman, 610
Greenberg, Richard, 3128
Greenberg, Robert, 3472
Greenberg, Roger, 2533
Greenberg, Shari Simon, 3458
Greenberg, Steve, 3601
Greenblatt, Sherwin, 1171
Greenburg, Dick, 3128
Greene & Assocs., W.H., Inc., 1656
Greene, A. Hugh, 3074
Greene, Bill, 1656
Greene, Caitlin E., 1656
Greene, Dennis, 3054
Greene, Diane B., 1613, 1982
Greene, Fred, 4110
Greene, Gabriele E., 4066
Greene, Gabrielle, 566
Greene, Gabrielle E., 3572
Greene, Gregory F., 3292
Greene, Jeffrey M., 915
Greene, Jennifer L., 1656
Greene, Jerry W., Jr., 1719
Greene, Jesse J., Jr., 722
Greene, Kevin, 3145
Greene, Kristie A., 1656
Greene, Lora, 1402
Greene, Marie N., 2615
Greene, Mary Jane, 1656
Greene, Michelle D., 2769
Greene, Richard L., 1824
Greene, Richard T., Jr., 711
Greene, Stephen S., 3904
Greene, Terrence G., 1656
Greene, Terry, 1656
Greene, Thomas, 347
Greene, Thomas E., 2448
Greene, Tom, 869
Greene, William H., III, 1656
Greenebaum, L.M., 2245
Greener, Anthony A., 4079
Greener, Sharon S., 3171
Greenfield, Danny L., 91
Greenfield, David, 1724
Greenfield, David W., 2125
Greenfield, Jerry, 409
Greenhill, Becky M., 959
Greenhill, H. Gaylon, 32
Greeniaus, H. John, 1974
Greenlaw, Patricia A., 703
Greenleaf, Peter S., 2450
Greenleaf, Stewart J., 1419
Greenlee, Diane, 3238
Greenlee, Douglas A., 1729
Greenlees, Michael E., 17
Greenough, Donald M., 1946
GreenPoint Bank, 679
Greensboro News Co., 2218
Greenspan, Brad, 30
Greenspon, Carolyn D., 2690
Greenstein, Ira A., 1910
Greenthal, Jill, 68, 1869
Greenwald, Gordon, 1887
Greenwald, Taylor J., 933
Greenway, Lumina V., 2551
Greenway, Mark, 240
Greenwich Capital Markets, Inc., 3138
Greenwood Dermatology, Inc., 1660
Greenwood Gardens, Inc., 1782
Greenwood, Charles F., 2393
Greenwood, Donald F., 620
Greer, Bob, Jr., 977
Greer, C. Scott, 1449
Greer, Deborah H., 2022
Greer, James H., 3833
Greer, John, 2820
Greer, Lauri, 3729
Greer, R. Scott, 2658
Greffin, Judith P., 107
Gregg, Charles W., 1648
Gregg, Gary R., 3306
Gregg, Judd, 1852
Gregg, Kirk P., 945
Gregg, Vicky, 507
Gregg, Vicky B., 507, 1406
Gregoire, Chris, 2292
Gregoire, Michael P., 638
Gregor, Jim, 1195
Gregor, Joie A., 904
Gregorian, Lisa, 3757
Gregorits, Victor, 847
Gregory Enterprises Inc., Carl, 1661
Gregory Galvanizing & Metal Processing, Inc., 1662
Gregory Industries, 1662
Gregory, Carl L., 1661
Gregory, David, 2200, 3794
Gregory, Jason, 1661
Gregory, John L., III, 1855
Gregory, Louis P., 285
Gregory, Raymond T., 1662
Gregory, Robert B., 1391
Gregory, Spain Brumby, 3759
Gregory, T. Stephen, 1662
Gregurich, Doug, 2798
Greifeld, Robert, 2617
Greig, Andy, 395
Greig, Paul G., 1425
Grein, Thomas W., 2274
Greiner, Julie, 2333
Greis, Leslie, 2209
Greisch, John J., 1804
Gremer, John, 3981
Gremer, John F., 3981
Gremley, Robert, 1655
Gremley, Robert C., 2878
Gremp, John T., 2070
Grenfell, Steven J., 3307
Grennier, Scott R., 2833
Grenrock, Gwyn L., 99
Grentz, Thomas, 4143
Grenz, Dianne, 3916
Grenz, Dianne M., 3916
Gresh, William, 1101
Gresham, Carol, 2738
Gretencord, Laura, 2387
Grether, John M., 3649
Gretta, John W., 1367
Greubel, William P., 3484
Greupner, Erik, 3323
Greve, Bryan, 2714
Greve, James, Sr., 2138
Grevelding, Bill, 1248
Greving, Robert C., 857
Grewcock, Bruce E., 2142
Grey, Robert J., 3026
Greystone Funding Corp., 1665
Grich, Bobby, 200
Griego, Alex, 923
Griego, Linda M., 42, 727
Griepentrog, Wilmer, 835
Grier, Marjorie N., 1150
Grier, Mark B., 3072
Grierson, Donald K., 2878
Gries, Charles J., 2415
Griesbaum, Kathy, 84
Griesman, Mark, Mr., 1296
Griesman, Mark, Mrs., 1296
Griff, Christine, 2935
Griff, John, 1589
Griffey, Mike, 978
Griffin, Archie M., 17, 2584
Griffin, Bobby J., 1720
Griffin, Christopher R., 3905
Griffin, David, 724
Griffin, Debra, 199
Griffin, Gary, 3816
Griffin, Hayne, 823
Griffin, Hayne P., Jr., 823
Griffin, Janet, 4026
Griffin, John C., 2119
Griffin, John P., 2119
Griffin, Kim, 2119
Griffin, Lisa, 1210
Griffin, Lisa Posada, 1409
Griffin, Mark E., 2622

Griffin, Phil, 1415
Griffin, Polly, 2119
Griffin, R.A., Jr., 1790
Griffin, Ronald B., 294
Griffin, Scot, 3532
Griffin, Shawn Stelow, 2925
Griffith Laboratories U.S.A., Inc., 1667
Griffith Laboratories, Inc., 1667
Griffith Labs Worldwide, 1667
Griffith Micro Science, Inc., 1667
Griffith, Brett R., 1666
Griffith, Dean L., 1667
Griffith, Helga L., 1666
Griffith, Inc., 1666
Griffith, J. Brian, 2486
Griffith, James W., 1916, 3760
Griffith, John, 939
Griffith, John B., 2
Griffith, John D., 3691
Griffith, Kelly, 3310
Griffith, Lois J., 1667
Griffith, Michael J., 30
Griffith, Richard S., 1666
Griffith, Richard S., Jr., 1666
Griffith, Richard S., Sr., 1666
Griffith, Scott, 140
Griffith, Scott M., 1666
Griffith, Timothy T., 2362, 2365
Griffiths, William C., 3100
Griffon, Lester J., Jr., 3825
Griffy, Timothy T., 1293
Griggs, Kenneth, 1981
Grigsby, Dawn, 652
Grigsby, J. Eugene, III, 2086
Grigsby, Jennifer M., 777
Grigsby, L. Lane, 652
Grigsby, Lane, 652
Grigsby, Lisa, 690
Grigsby, Todd William, 652
Grillet, Philippe, 3329
Grilli, Henry G., 296
Grimaldi, Megan, 3159
Grimaldo, Joseph, 2380
Grimes, David, 382
Grimes, Donald T., 4106
Grimes, Robert, 2763
Grimm, Donald W., 2268
Grimm, Mike, 3415
Grimm, Miranda, 3070
Grimm, Patti, 2281
Grimm, Richard E., 2924
Grimoldi, Alberto Luis, 4106
Grimshaw, Eric, 2815
Grimstad, Gary, 2581
Grimwood, Paul, 2663
Grindinger, Dennis J., 1889
Grinnell Mutual Reinsurance Co., 1668
Grinney, Jay, 1270
Grinstead, Steve, 3053
Gripentrog, Wilmer, 835
Grise, Cheryl W., 2481, 3083
Grise, Marcia M., 3344
Grismer, Patrick, 4150
Grissom, J. David, 4150
Grissom, Steven L., 1411
Griswell, J. Barry, 2517
Griswold Industries, 1669
Griswold Industries, Inc., 1669
Griswold, Benjamin H., IV, 333, 1446, 3579
Griswold, David, 3662
Griswold, David E., 1669
Griswold, Marjorie S., 1669
Griswold, Scott A., 717
Gritter, Barry E., 337
Grize, William J, 3618
Grizzard, Maynard, 4063
Groark, Eunice S., 2928
Groat, Jonathan S., 1078
Grobman, Richard, 1025
Grobstein, Michael, 578
Groch, Jim, 725
Groenhuysen, Wilco, 752
Groeniger & Co., 1670
Groeniger, Beverly J., 1670
Groeniger, Michael H., 1670
Groeniger, Michael H., Sr., 1670
Groeniger, Richard, 1670
Groff, Dave, 1346
Grogan, Kevin, 2573
Grogan, Sheila, 490
Groh, K. L., 3760
Groh, Kari, 3760
Groh, Kari L., 3760
Groleau, Gary, 2674
Grollman, Evelyn, Dr., 1978
Gromek, Joseph R., 3988, 4106
Gromoff, Elary, Jr., 84
Groningen, Dale Van, 506
Gross, Allen, 1019
Gross, Bruce E., 2250
Gross, Donald, 1025
Gross, Kenneth, 1025
Gross, Keralyn, 1517
Gross, Linda, 1025
Gross, Michael, 2689
Gross, Michael S., 3315
Gross, Patrick W., 679
Gross, Randall A., 3201
Gross, Steve, 4066
Gross, Thomas S., 1216
Gross, Uwe, 2184
Grossberg, Adam, 376
Grossberg, Eric, 568
Grosse, Wayne N., 446
Grosser, Sharon, 2335
Grosser, Shawn, 21
Grosser, Steven E., 2505
Grossman, Jerry, 2711
Grossman, Mindy, 487
Groszewski, Martha, 2892
Groth, Terri L., 2337
Groth, Terry, 2337
Groth, Thomas, 2993
Grotting, John B., 3944
Grounds, William, 2489
Group Health Cooperative of Eau Claire, 2173
Group W Cable, Inc., 640
Grousbeck Family Foundation, 3411
Grousbeck, H. Irving, 352
Grousbeck, Wyc, 352
Grousbeck, Wycliffe, 352
Grove Farm Co., Inc., 1672
Grove, Darrin, 3816
Grove, Janet E., 46, 3310
Grove, John F., Jr., 4143
Grove, Teresa I., 4143
Grover, Fred, 140
Grover, Sarah Goldsmith, 656
Groves and Sons Co., S.J., 1673
Groves, C. T., 1673
Groves, Eileen, Esq., 3874
Groves, Frank N., 1673
Groves, Franklin N., 1673
Groves, Laura, 152
Groves, Ray J., 937
Groves, Ronald, 2081
Groves, Vaughn R., 112
Grow, Polly, 2507
Grow, Timothy E., 4025
Growcock, Terry D., 1736, 1741
Growing Family, Inc., 2838
Growmark, Inc., 1674
Grubb Construction, Stephen R., Inc., 1675
Grubb, Katherine, 27
Grubb, Kristin, 225
Grubb, Stephen R., 1675
Grubbs, Melinda H., 1745
Grube, Jeffrey D., 3297
Grubel, Stanley J., 757
Gruber, David P., 3592
Gruber, Jeffrey N., 3720
Gruen, Marcy, 2051
Grumbacher, Thomas M., 521
Grunberg, Greg, 1359
Grundhofer, Jerry A., 1220
Grundhofer, John G., 3389
Grunfeld, Ernie, 4000
Grunstein, Laurence R., 822
Grusky, Robert R., 292
GRW Properties, LLC, 3676
Grypp, Keith A., 2121
GSF Asset Trust, 3044
GSM Industrial, Inc., 1676
GSM Roofing, 1676
Guacci, Vincent, 3330
Guagliano, John, 3998
Guarantee Electric Co., 1678
Guaranty Bank and Trust Co., 1679
Guarasci, Michael Ernest, 1934
Guarascio, Philip, 227, 2876
Guard Publishing Co., 1680
Guard, Tim, 2906
Guardian Corp., 1681
Guardian Holdings, Inc., 1681
Guardian Industries Corp., 1095, 1682
Guardian Life Insurance Co. of America, The, 1683
Guardian Protection Services, Inc., 245
Guarnaccia, Giacomo T., Jr., 910
Guazza, Keith, 1077
Guber, Peter, 728
Gubernick, Alan, 632
Guc, William J., 4096
Gucci America, Inc., 1684
Gudas, Viki, 1477
Gudipati, Rao, 2497
Gue, Kevin, 2401
Guelfi, Hillary Hedinger, 155
Guempel, Alyssa, 131
Guengerich, Gary, 1083
Guennewig, Victoria B., 935
Guenther, Paul B., 1683, 2335
Guenther, Robert L., 4016
Guernsey, Evelyn E., 2303
Gueron, Judith M., 82
Guerra, Andrea, 2319
Guerra, Joao, 202
Guerra, Louis, 3284
Guerra, Louis J., 3284
Guerra, Rudolph, Jr., 3284
Guerra, Rudolph, Sr., 3284
Guerra, Rudy, 3284
Guerra, Rudy, Jr., 3284
Guerra, Rudy, Sr., 3284
Guerra, Stephen, 2675
Guerre, R. Paul, 4106
Guerrero, Anthony R., Jr., 1405
Guerrieri, Elizabeth I., 3996
Guerry, John P., 3329
Guerry, Zan, 3329
Guertin, Ralph, 2380
Guertin, Shawn M., 48
Guertin, Timothy E., 3718
Guess ?, Inc., 1685
Guettel, Mary Rodgers, 3250
Guffey, John G., Jr., 663
Guggenberger, Keith, 3587
Guichard, Kent B., 170
Guided Alliance Healthcare Services, 1686
GuideOne Life Insurance Co., 1687
Guido, Robert L., 893
Guifarro, Jan, 869
Guifoile, Mary J. Steele, 3235
Guilbert, Rob, 267
Guillemin, Evan Charles, 3398
Guillot-Pelpel, Veronique, 423
Guimaraes, Enderson, 294
Guinan, Mark, 1804
Guiness Bass Import Co., 2523
Guinn, Ginger, 1001
Guinn, Jennifer, 608
Guinn, Max A., 1061
Guinness UDV North America, Inc., 1107
Guinnessey, Kathleen, 1190
Guion, Kathleen, 1143
Guiterrez, Carol, 2920
Gula, Allen J., Jr., 3674
Gulati, Lisa, 2017
Gulay, Carole, 1609
Guldeman, Philip E., 386
Gulf Power Co., 1689
Gulf States Paper Corp., 4046
Gulig, Susan, 2948
Gulino, Rick, 752
Gulledge, Michael R., 2241
Gullett, Mark, 2957
Gulley, Joan L., 2997
Gulling, Douglas R., 4034
Gulmi, James S., 1559
Gumienny, Frank, 2958
Gumina, William J., 2156
Gund, Gordon, 2120
Gundacker, Charlie, 3889
Gundalch, Ken, 3949
Gunder, Peter C., 144
Gunderson, Cory, 1153
Gunkel, Thomas F., 2577
Gunn, Steve, 4116
Gunnigle, Grant, 2141
Gunnigle, Ryan, 2141
Gunnigle, Ryan T., 2141
Gunnin, Mark, 1889
Gunning, Tom, 1256
Gunsett, Daniel J., 1663
Gunst, Robert A., 1534
Gunter, Bradley H., 3368
Gunter, Gar, 2251
Gunter, Mark, 3888
Gunter, R. Denny, 3531
Gunter, William D., Jr., 2629
Guobao, Zhang, 47
Guon, Jane M., 2855
Gupta, Mahendra, 591
Gupta, Rajiv L., 1071, 1794
Gupta, Shailendra, 1995
Gupta, Shalabh, 305
Gupta, Shashikant, 213
Guptill, George H., Jr., 1486
Gurganous, Thomas S., 1640
Gurgovits, Stephen J., Sr., 1318
Gurke, James C., 1569
Gurnani, Roger, 3936

Gurwitch, Janet L., 2205
Gurwitz, Norman H., 1383
Gusha, John, 1083
Gust, Lynn, 2485
Gustafson, Barbara A., 1585
Gustafson, Lynda S., 1693
Gustafson, Susan, 3130
Gustafsson, Mary Elizabeth, 3794
Gustavel, Jack W., 504
Gustavsen, Ken, 2466
Gustavson, Nancy, 3500
Gutermuth, Luanne S., 3997
Guth Lighting Systems, Inc., 1692
Guth, Joel, 3659
Guth, Robert E., 3141
Guthart, Leo, 221
Guthrie, Debbie, 3071
Guthrie, Donald, 2709
Guthrie, Donald S., 2342
Guthrie, Sarah Walker, 2478
Guthrie, Tom, 3569
Gutierezz, Carol, 2920
Gutierrez, Carlos M., 2780
Gutierrez, Jose M., 1087
Gutierrez, Mauricio, 2756
Gutierrez, Oswaldo, 1608
Gutnick, H. Yale, 3806
Guttenplan, Steve, 4109
Guttman, Tim G., 175
Guttmann, Craig, 2401
Guy, Andrew J., 657
Guy, George, 657
Guy, Janice P., 2506
Guy, Stephen B., 1296
Guyan, Rick, 511
Guyaux, Joseph C., 1799, 2997
Guyer, Jocelyn, 690
Guyette, James M., 3254
Guyette, Michael, 496
Guyman, Charlotte, 429
Guynn, George C., 2847
Guyot, John Forrest, 3391
Guyton, Jean, 1833
Guyton, Sam, 1833
Guzman, Brian, 1934
Guzman, Mary, 3262
Guzman, Mary C., 3262
Guzzi, Anthony J., 1255, 1879
Guzzi, Paul, 501
Guzzo, Dana F., 2391
Gwaltney, Julia, 1266
Gwathmey, Bette-Ann, 3123
Gwin, Robert G., 190
Gwizdala, Lori A., 774
Gwynn, Michael, 2903
Gyani, Mohan, 3310
Gyani, Mohanbir Singh, 3965
Gybel, Thomas P., 123
Gyenes, Lawrence A., 2437
Gyland, Rosellen, 1764
Gzesh, Irwin I., 103

H&K Inc., 1694
H&R Block, Inc., 1695
Haack, Calvin D., 2504
Haack, Susan E., 2584
Haag, Natalie G., 680
Haag, William H., III, 3032
Haas, Peter E., Jr., 3624
Haas, Richard, 2786
Haas, Robert D., 3624
Haas, Ronald D., 3042
Haas, Vernon B., 2636
Haas-Dehejia, Jennifer, 3624
Haase, Bronson J., 2371
Habegger, Ronald J., 588
Habel, George, 698
Haben, Mary Kay, 1300
Haber, Thomas R., 1588
Haberlandt, Frederick R., 1551
Haberli, Ernst A., 1542
Habermeyer, H. William, Jr., 2021, 3516, 3904
Habib, Philippe, 270
Habib, Warren, 316
Habig, Christopher, 1099
Habig, Douglas A., 2149
Hachigian, Kirk S., 935, 2850
Hachman, Timothy J., 345
Hackenson, Elizabeth, 47
Hacker, Douglas A., 2619
Hacker, Jerry W., 3865
Hackerman, Harold I., 1251
Hackerman, Willard, 4063
Hackett, Ann Fritz, 390, 679, 1474
Hackett, Dennis, 2195
Hackett, James P., 2749, 3597
Hackett, James T., 667, 1448
Hackett, John A., 583
Hackett, Lee, 132
Hackman, Dale, 1466
Hackman, Steve, 2811
Hackmann, Glen F., 317
Hacknel, Michael, 3183
Hackney, Allan T., 1717
Hackstock, Anne, 1697
Hackstock, Nich J., 1697
Hackstock, Nick J., 1697
Hackstock, Nick J., Inc., 1697
Hacobian, Mossik, 1454
Hadden, Elaine, 3642
Hadden, Stephen J., 437
Haddock, Ronald W., 3309
Hadeed Carpet Cleaning, Inc., 138
Hadley, Lester, 2615
Hadley, Stephen, 3135
Hadlock, Kevin W., 3104
Hadrych, Thomas J., 502
Haecker, Kelly J., 4062
Haeffner, Peter C., Jr., 271
Haefner, Michael E., 285
Haegelin, Tim, 3726
Haerr, Sally, 3116
Haffernman, Thomas, 2733
Haffke, Christopher W., 149
Haffner, David S., 407, 1719, 2246
Hafner, Joseph A., Jr., 3677
Hafner, Travis, 847
Haft, Ronald S., 3659
Haft, Ted, 2294
Hagan-Sohn, Jacky, 957
Hagedorn, James, 3372
Hagedorn, Michael, 3846
Hagedorn, Michael D., 3846
Hagel, Charles T., 780
Hageman, Jonathan, 2398
Hagemann, Robert A., 3103, 4157
Hagen, Jonathan Hirt, 1291
Hagen, Sue, 1141
Hagen, Susan Hirt, 1291
Hagen, Thomas B., 1291
Hagen, Veronica, 2698
Hagen, Veronica M., 3516
Hagenbuch, Diane S., 2790
Hagenlocker, Edward E., 175
Hager, David A., 1102
Hager, George V., Jr., 1561
Hager, Jim, 2217
Hager, Lee, 3521
Hager, Lee F., 3521
Hagerman, Doug M., 3246
Hagerty Brothers Company, 1698
Hagerty, Thomas M., 1371, 2488, 2558
Hagerud, Tony, 447
Hagey, Mary Beth, 1044
Hagg, John A., 4077
Haggard, James, 1133
Hagge, Stephen J., 221
Haggerty, Charles A., 1084, 2314, 2926
Haggerty, Fred, 2162
Haggerty, Gretchen R., 3877, 3905
Haggin, L.L., III, 2113
Hagood, D. Maybank, 3346
Hagstrom, Paul A., 3910
Hagy, Paul A., 210
Hahn, Arthur W., 2101
Hahn, Gene, 1861
Hahn, John, 1915
Hahn, Michelle, 1829
Haider, Kamal, 4006
Haidet, Jeffrey K., 2433
Haight, Lisa, 1255
Haigis, Brian, 2251
Hailey, Ann V., 1626
Hailey, V. Ann, 305
Haimovitz, Jules, 483
Haines & Haines, Inc., 1701
Haines, Holly, 1701
Haines, James S., Jr., 100
Haines, John J., 1484
Haines, Kellie M., 1749
Haines, Nadine, 1701
Haines, Samuel R., 1544
Haines, William S., 1701
Haines, William S., Jr., 1701
Hair, Darryl C., 3611
Haiti Relief Donations, 3014
Haje, Peter R., 3755
Hajek, Josef, 3821
Hake, Ralph F., 2842
Haken, Bernadette, 1062
Halasz, Michelle M., 694
Halbert, Frederic L., 1749
Halbert, Margaret, 3045
Halbreich, Jeremy, 786
Halbrook, John A., 4112
Haldeman, Charles E., Jr., 2429
Haldewang, Mildred M., 1929
Haldewang, William A., 1929
Haldewang, William J., 1929
Hale, Brett, 807
Hale, Danny L., 107
Hale, Glen, 1961
Hale, James K., 476
Hale, James T., 3714
Hale, Richard J., 490
Hale, Roger W., 258, 1867
Halenda, John J., 542
Hales, Ben, 2679
Haley, Charles, 2930
Haley, Jane Gosiger, 1617
Haley, Joanie, 1872
Haley, John J., 2410
Haley, John R., 1617, 3500
Haley, Maura Brouillette, 3337
Haley, Michael P., 2270
Haley, Peter G., 1617
Halfon, Jean-Michel, 2950
Halkyard, Jonathan S., 650, 2765
Hall & Evans L.L.C, 1703
Hall Elerding, Bonnie R., 3256
Hall Town Paperboard Co., 2796
Hall, Amy, 1433
Hall, Anita L., 3660
Hall, Anson C., 428
Hall, Anthony W., 2153
Hall, Anthony W., Jr., 1239
Hall, Art, 3660
Hall, Arthur M., 3660
Hall, Bruce, 2945
Hall, Bruce C., 2945
Hall, Bryan H., 2263
Hall, Christoper E., 226
Hall, Cindy, 2344
Hall, Conrad M., 1145
Hall, Curtis E., 3627
Hall, Dave, 2174
Hall, David E., 1707
Hall, Derrick M., 310
Hall, Donald J., Jr., 1707
Hall, Donald J., Sr., 1707
Hall, Douglas K., 1035
Hall, Edward E., Inc., 1702
Hall, Frank W., 2981
Hall, George F., 3600
Hall, Ira D., 3029
Hall, J. Everett, 3600
Hall, James G., 687
Hall, Jeffrey, 1313
Hall, John, 92
Hall, John L., II, 583
Hall, Joseph G., 687
Hall, Karla D., 1183
Hall, Kelly, 3199
Hall, Kim, 2209
Hall, Lara A., 168
Hall, Lilisa, 2860
Hall, Lisa, 663
Hall, Mary, 1213
Hall, Matthew, 1285
Hall, Michael, 3568
Hall, Neil, 2997
Hall, O.B. Grayson, Jr., 3171
Hall, Patricia A. Hemingway, 2358
Hall, Pete, 3924
Hall, R. Randall, 373
Hall, Raymond L., Jr., 3924
Hall, Richard, 224
Hall, Robert J., 551, 2961
Hall, Shannon, 1587
Hall, Sophia, 2187
Hall, Steve R., 4034
Hall, Stuart A., 346
Hall, Ted W., 2916, 4079
Hall, Vern W., 3256
Hall, William A., 1695
Hall, William C., Jr., 1150
Hall, William K., 1626
Hall-Elerding, Bonnie R., 3256
Halla, Brian L., 818
Hallam, Rob, 871
Hallan, James P., 1078
Hallberg Family, L.P., 1704
Hallberg Marine, Inc., 1704
Hallberg, Dale R., 1077
Hallberg, Dana, 1704
Hallberg, Eugene C., 1704
Hallberg, Inc., 1704
Hallberg, Melissa, 1704
Hallberg, Michael, 1704
Hallelujah Acres, Inc., 1705
Hallene, James N., 2415
Haller Charitable Remander Trust, Marie, 2565
Haller, Karen, 3524

Haller, Karen S., 3524
Haller, Renee, 3397
Hallgrimson, Steven, 3767
Halliburton Co., 1173, 1706
Halliday, Stephen D., 180
Halligan, Mike, 3994
Hallingstad, Nicole D., 3380
Hallman, Gary D., 4047
Hallmark Cards, Inc., 1707, 2622
Hallock, Brooke, 676
Hallock, Raymond G., 882
Hallock, Robert, 577
Halloran, Jean M., 56
Halloran, Owen, 2162
Halloran, Robert J., Jr., 3086
Hallowin, Bob, 2173
Hallquist, Carol, 1707
Halls, Tim, 2557
Halpin, Kevin P., 1163
Halsey, Jeffrey L., 3230
Halstead Industries, Inc., 1708
Halstead, Catherine Frank, 1482
Halstead, Martha, 1708
Halstead, William, 1708
Haltaufderheid, Cora, 3061
Halter, Bill, 3366
Halton Co., 1709
Halton, E.H., Jr., 1709
Halton, Edward H., Jr., 1709
Halton, Susan, 1709
Halverson, Bradley M., 722
Halverson, Dierk, 1986
Halverson, Jack, 1464
Halverson, Steven T., 997, 3074
Halvey, John K., 2769
Halvorsen, Per-Kristian, 289
Halvorson, George C., 2086
Halyburton, Dan, 1260
Ham, Kerby S., 429
Ham, Rudman J., 1450, 2506
Hamachek, Tod R., 2747
Hamada, Richard, 304
Hamada, Richard P., 304
Hamano, Wayne Y., 342
Hambrick, James L., 2315
Hamburg, Marc D., 429
Hamby, Thomas L., 3066
Hamel, Matthew E., 592
Hamel, William, 242
Hamelin, Joseph L., 1159
Hamerlik, Michael, 4094
Hamersly, William L., 406
Hamill, John P., 2265
Hamill, Laura, 182
Hamilton, Alexander, 3217
Hamilton, Bud O., 1151
Hamilton, Fredrick M., 3873
Hamilton, Gail E., 249
Hamilton, Jeff, 1679, 2829
Hamilton, John M., 502
Hamilton, Judith H., 1155
Hamilton, Mark, 2707
Hamilton, Matthew, 260
Hamilton, Michael, 1283
Hamilton, Michael D., 565
Hamilton, Peter B., 2833, 3540
Hamilton, Robert-John, 21
Hamilton, Scott, 3977
Hamlin, John, 3150
Hamm, Donald, 267
Hamm, Jon H., 654
Hamm, Patricia, 1919
Hamm, Richard F., Jr., 1255
Hamm, Vinette, 3183
Hammack, Elizabeth M., 637
Hammelrath, Thomas P., 1029
Hammelrath, Tom, 1029
Hammen, Lea Ann, 2461
Hammer, Charles W., 3194
Hammer, Laurel, 2190
Hammer, Russ, 591
Hammer, Thomas J., 3704
Hammergren, John H., 1794, 2434
Hammersmith, Suann A., 1590
Hammersmith, Suann D., 1590
Hammerstein Music & Theater, Inc., 3250
Hammes, Jeffrey C., 2164
Hammes, Michael N., 2647
Hammet, Amir, 3300
Hammock, Kelli, 2600
Hammock, Kelli M., 2600
Hammond Machinery, Inc., 1711
Hammond, Christine, 3000
Hammond, Christine A., 1711
Hammond, Frank M., 344
Hammond, Jeremy, 1711
Hammond, John L., 3408
Hammond, Karen, 2659
Hammond, Paul, 2349
Hammond, Phyllis, 536
Hammond, Robert, 1711
Hammond, Robert E., 1711
Hammond-Whitney, Audrey, 931
Hammonds, Kim, 516
Hammons, Kevin J., 900
Hamnes, Vernon, 1535
Hamood, Samuel Allen, 3799
Hamory, Bruce, 501
Hamp, Sheila Ford, 1464
Hampden Bancorp, 1712
Hampden Savings Bank, 1713
Hampton, Clay, 2687
Hampton, James H., 1079
Hampton, Jim, 1079
Hampton, John, 386
Hampton, Sybil Jordan, 240
Hamrahi, Steve, 2684
Hamre, John J., 3311
Hamrick Mills Inc., 1715
Hamrick, A. W., 1715
Hamrick, C. F., II, 1715
Hamrick, Carlisle, 1715
Hamrick, Frank, 1432
Hamrick, J. L., 2525
Hamrick, Lyman W., 1715
Hamrick, S. Joan, 3140
Hamrick, W. C., 1715
Hamrick, Wylie L., 1715
Hamsa, William R., 2970
Han, Jong, 694
Hanafee, Susan, 1988
Hance, Elizabeth E., 2341
Hance, James H., Jr., 1189, 1464, 3556
Hancock County Savings Bank, FSB, 1716
Hancock, Dain M., 3731
Hancock, Ellen M., 48, 869
Hancock, Kristen, 3185
Hancock, Lain, 1169
Hancock, Lisa D., 1604
Hancock, William E., III, 1395
Hand, Carla Cerami, 3992
Hand, Robert E., 347
Handel, Nancy H., 579
Handleman, Gary, 4000
Handler, David A., 2923
Handler, Richard B., 2030
Handley, Thomas W., 1220, 1517
Handlon, Carolyn B., 2383
Handy & Harman, 1718
Handy, Alice W., 3433
Handy, F. Philip, 2842
Hanek, Mike, 924
Hanemann, Thomas S., 3815
Hanes Cos., Inc., 1719
Hanes, Daniel M., 678
Hanes, Joyce, 4095
Haney, David, 1578
Haney, Gary, 3474
Haney, Gary P., 3474
Haney, Michael P., 2502
Haney, Philip D., 2257
Haney, William, 3480
Hanford, Deirdre, 3673
Hanft, Adam, 3372
Hanft, Noah J., 2399
Hangemanole, Greg, 2482
Hank, Jeffrey, 1982
Hank, John L., Jr., 214
Hank, Sheri, 2067
Hanke, Peggy, 1414
Hankel, Brian K., 2504
Hankins, Kevin, 636
Hankins, Stephen M., 3350
Hankowsky, William P., 222
Hanks, W. Bruce, 751
Hanley, Chris, 161
Hanley, Steve, 2991
Hanlon, Charles R., 10
Hanlon, Pat, 2684
Hanlon, Paul, 491
Hanlon, Timothy G., 4028
Hann, Daniel P., 466
Hann, David C., 3938
Hanna Corporation, Howard, 1722
Hanna, Ashraf, 1549
Hanna, Debbie, 563
Hanna, Howard W., III, 1722
Hanna, Howard W., Jr., 1722
Hanna, Jack, 3387
Hanna, Nancy, 3274
Hanna, Steven R., 2125
Hannaford Bros. Co., 1723
Hannah, Ed, 2432
Hannah, Kenneth, 2459
Hannahs, R. Stephen, 2855
Hannaman, Tami, 2319
Hannan, James, 1568
Hannan, John P., 3529
Hannan, Kathy H., 2190
Hannan, Patrice S., 2795
Hannay, Lori B., 1564
Hanneman, LeRoy C., Jr., 3524
Hanner, Ken H., 697
Hannigan, Mike, 1583
Hanover Insurance Co., The, 1724
Hanrahan, Daniel J., 3172
Hanrahan, Paul T., 231, 1942
Hans, R. J., 3981
Hans, Rick, 3981
Hans, William, 2722
Hansard, Dale, Jr., 3726
Hanse, William, 283
Hanse, William C., 283
Hansen, Dan, 1173
Hansen, Eileen C., 4028
Hansen, J. Michael, 816
Hansen, Janet M., 2928
Hansen, Jean-Pierre, 1458
Hansen, Jill T., 4034
Hansen, Lyle, Jr., 286
Hansen, Marka, 1533
Hansen, Robert D., 1162
Hansen, Thomas J., 3719
Hansen, Vicki Bruce, 531
Hanser, Frederick O., 3568
Hanser, Timothy F., 3568
Hansford, V. Nathaniel, 3674
Hanson, Bill, 1674
Hanson, Dan, 831
Hanson, David J., 1645
Hanson, Gina, 367
Hanson, Greg, 1080
Hanson, John N., 249
Hanson, John Nils, 2070
Hanson, Larry, 2136
Hanson, Lyle, Jr., 286
Hanson, Margie, 880
Hanson, Paula C., 1053
Hanson, Peggy, 100
Hanson, Robert B., 1060
Hanson, Robert L., 140, 919
Hanson, Ron, 3279
Hanson, Sue, 2966
Hanson, Thomas L., 104, 4095
Hanson, Tom, 4095
Hanson, Victor H., 472
Hanstad, Marlin, 113
Hantke, William E., 2756
Hanway, H. Edward, 812, 2385
Hapij, Adam, 3400
Happe, Mike, 3775
Hara, Thomas I., 3909
Harad, George, 852
Haranas, Mark R., 1481
Harary, Joseph, 3345
Haraseth, Nancy, 3883
Haratunian, Melanie, 68
Harbage, Bob, 3530
Harbarger, Mark N., 2792
Harbarger, Terry E., 2792
Harbert, Raymond J., 1726
Harbert, Ted, 2649
Harbin, Cindy, 2139
Harbison, Earle H., Jr., 2605
Harbold, Michael R., 1053
Harbour Trust Investment Manangement Fiduciary, 1929
Harbour, Ronald, 3534
Harbrecht, Sandra W., 1035
Harcourt, Kathy S., 1764
Harczak, Harry J., Jr., 3876
Hard Rock Cafe International (USA) Inc., 1727
Hard, Brian, 3528
Hardage, Ginger C., 3522
Harden & Assocs., Inc., 1728
Harden, Gregory M., 3910
Harden, John, 1728
Harden, Lynn, 665
Harden, Marvin C., III, 1728
Harder, Ronald Richard, 261
Hardgrove, Ian F., 3
Hardin, Dan, 2235
Hardin, Heidi Walter, 2024
Hardin, Joseph S., Jr., 2948
Hardin, P. Russell, 2749
Hardin, Thomas, 3481
Harding, Dennis K., 3724
Harding, Jack, 40
Harding, Kyle, 3724
Harding, Samuel C., Jr., 385
Harding, Scott, 3837
Hardinge Inc., 1729
Hardis, Stephen R., 2258, 3057

Hardman Signs, 136
Hardman, Don, 1857
Hardman, Donald G., 1179
Hardwick, Catherine R., 1494
Hardwick, M. Susan, 3925
Hardwick, Mark K., 1410
Hardy, Alexander, 1549
Hardy, John D., Jr., 299
Hardy, Kathy, 2853
Hardy, Leslie M., 2466
Hardy, Marggie, 2913
Hardy, Richard B., 1103
Hare, Greg, 2251, 2319
Hare, Jeffrey R., 2563
Hare, Stephen E., 4030, 4031
Hareza, Dennis F., 3813
Hargate, Arthur, 3265
Hargrave, Jennifer D., 628
Hargrave, R.A., 3328
Hargrave, Richard A., 3328
Hargreaves, David D.R., 1747
Hargrove, Wes, 5
Harkavy, Tamara, 814
Harken, Inc, 1731
Harken, Olaf T., 1731
Harken, Peter, 1731
Harken, Peter O., 1731
Harken, Ruth F., 1731
Harker, Patrick T., 1895
Harker, Victoria D., 1032, 1532, 4139
Harker, William R., 3384
Harkey, Dee, 1470
Harkins, J. Daniel, 960
Harkins, Larry, 3525
Harkness, Matt, 1477
Harla, JoAnne, 1947
Harlan, Joseph E., 1447
Harlan, Robert E., 1651
Harless, Katherine J., 3775
Harley, Jill A., 853
Harley-Davidson, Inc., 1732
Harlin, Pam, 2455
Harlop, Janine, 2733
Harlow, Eric, 3940
Harlowe, Jeff, 3624
Harman, Fred, 728
Harman, Jeff, 2906
Harmeling, Mark M., 3887
Harmon Family Foundation, John, 2419
Harmon Foundation, 624
Harmon, Deborah L., 1467
Harmon, Debra A., 921
Harmon, Herbert N., 3298
Harmon, John Campbell, 1200
Harmon, Steve, 72
Harmon, W. Thomas, 1410
Harned, Christopher B., 3091
Harned, Elizabeth Quadracci, 3091
Harness, Hugh G., 1350
Harnett, Craig C., 2631
Harney, Gerard, 964
Harnischfeger Industries, Inc., 2070
Harnish Group, Inc., 1734
Harnish, Jennifer C., 1734
Harnish, John, 1734
Harnish, John J., 1734
Harnish, John W., 1734
Harnish, Katherine A., 1734
Harper Brush Works, 1735
Harper Collins Publishers, 3414
Harper Corp., 1735
Harper, Arthur H., 1532, 2559
Harper, Barry, 1735
Harper, Barry D., 1735
Harper, Conrad A., 2688
Harper, Craig, 1892
Harper, D. Scott, 107
Harper, Diane, 3659
Harper, Larry, 1748
Harper, Marian, 1871
Harper, Matt, 1313
Harper, Miles Douglas, III, 563
Harper-Taylor, Jeniffer, 3448
Harr, Ron, 507
Harrah's Operating Co., Inc., 650
Harrahs Entertainment, 1131
Harrel, Edward H., 3806
Harrel, Evan, 563
Harrell, Darlene, 1074
Harrell, Henry H., 3891
Harrell, Joanne, 3150
Harrell, John C., 470
Harrell, Terri, 1169
Harrigan, Arthur W., 1951
Harrigan, Robert B., 3466
Harrigian, Harold, 898
Harrington, Brad, 3418
Harrington, Brian C., 937
Harrington, Charles L., 2887
Harrington, Daniel P., 807
Harrington, James, 491, 3715
Harrington, Kurt, 1345
Harrington, Mark, 3921
Harrington, Matthew, 1224
Harrington, Michael J., 2274
Harrington, Patrick A., 1907
Harrington, Richard J., 48, 4136
Harrington, Robert J., 1481
Harrington, Russell D., Jr., 3944
Harrington, Susan W., 4070
Harrington, Teresa, 3616
Harrington, Tom, 1182
Harris Corp., 1736
Harris, Alan A., 2427
Harris, Alan F., 2216
Harris, Alan N., 3540
Harris, Ann, 2310
Harris, Brian, 977
Harris, Brian J., 376
Harris, C. Martin, 3733
Harris, Carla, 2570
Harris, Christy, 1970
Harris, Cory R., 4026
Harris, Danny P., 2794
Harris, David G., 1102
Harris, David M., 2601
Harris, Dennis J., 425
Harris, Douglas J., 1314
Harris, Elmer, 71
Harris, F.W., Inc., 138
Harris, Frank G., III, 2671
Harris, Frank W., 552
Harris, Glenda, 71
Harris, Isaiah, Jr., 812
Harris, Jack, 2274
Harris, James E., 861, 1501, 3432
Harris, Jay, 2229
Harris, Jeffrey A., 2176
Harris, Jeffrey P., 1693
Harris, John, 2711
Harris, John W., 1150, 2971, 3412
Harris, Joseph, 1078
Harris, Joseph C., 1078
Harris, Juanne Renee, 2689
Harris, Katherine, 1399
Harris, Katherine A., 1399
Harris, Keith, 962
Harris, Ken, 3418
Harris, Kevin, 3582
Harris, Kiffi, 2143
Harris, Kimberly J., 3081
Harris, King W., 221
Harris, Margery M., 211
Harris, Mel, 3504
Harris, Michael E, 1800
Harris, Neil, 924
Harris, Neil S., 924
Harris, Nelson G., 3693
Harris, Paul N., 2136
Harris, R. Jeffrey, 184
Harris, Rhonda, 2081
Harris, Richard H., 1486
Harris, Rob, 2968
Harris, Robert E., 934
Harris, Robert S., 826
Harris, Roladn J., 1118
Harris, Ronald J., 1118
Harris, Scott, 1227
Harris, Shane, 3072
Harris, Tandy, 213
Harris, Thomas, 310
Harris, Tom, 1
Harris, Tony, 3743
Harris, Walter L., 2296
Harris, William, 469
Harrison Ross, Phyllis, 185
Harrison, C. Lash, 1462
Harrison, Caroline Diamond, 2683
Harrison, Cheryl, 98
Harrison, Cole, 3641
Harrison, Gary, 72
Harrison, Hugh T., II, 1485
Harrison, J. Frank, III, 861
Harrison, J. Wade, 4097
Harrison, James M., Jr., 337
Harrison, Lisa, 1267
Harrison, Neil, 469, 1065
Harrison, Perry, 2470
Harrison, Robert S., 85, 1405
Harrison, Ronald, 3140
Harrison, Susan M., 3425
Harrison, William B., Jr., 2466
Harriss and Covington Hosiery Mills, Inc., 1740
Harry V. Quadracci 1998 Trust, 3091
Harsco Corp., 1741
Harshaw, Andy, 229
Harshman, Richard J., 91
Harson, Linn, 3230
Hart, Allyn, 3883
Hart, Bradley, 2823
Hart, Bridget-Ann, 2162
Hart, Cathy J., 4135
Hart, Cathy James, 4135
Hart, Craig J., 1971
Hart, Damon G., 4025
Hart, Deborah K., 898
Hart, Don, 1988
Hart, Gerard J., 656
Hart, Glenn, 2823
Hart, John, 3011
Hart, John K., 3931
Hart, Linda B., 1620
Hart, Marilyn, 2823
Hart, Mark, 3976
Hart, Matthew J., 3902
Hart, Maura, 4087
Hart, Michael A., 1532
Hart, Patti S., 1964
Hart, Rachel, 1517
Hart, W.F., 3404
Harte, Bruce, 1780
Harten, Ann, 1758
Hartenberger, Lisa, 2647
Hartenstein, Eddy W., 579
Hartig, Richard J., 2622
Hartigan, Paul V., 1820
Hartin, Chris, 1726
Hartings, Robert, 3199
Hartley, David E., 231
Hartley, Eric, 859
Hartley, J. R., 3812
Hartley, Mac, 3995
Hartley, Thomas D., 2559
Hartley-Leonard, Darryl, 2061
Hartline, Alan R., 3535
Hartman, Donna R., 74
Hartman, Graig W., 3474
Hartman, Jeffrey E., 2546
Hartman, Jerry J., 3910
Hartman, Kervin G., 2925
Hartman, Richard T., 3769
Hartman, Todd, 442
Hartman, Tracy L., 4105
Hartmann, George F., 1651
Hartmann, Michael W., 2519
Hartmann, Mike, 814
Hartog, Tunis Den, 3993
Harton, H. Lynn, 3866
Hartsock, Linda Dickerson, 2681
Hartsock, Robert, 892
Hartstein, Jaclyn, 2015
Hartung, David L., 402
Hartung, Raymond A., Jr., 3806
Hartwig, Chris J., 991
Hartwig, Evelyn, 991
Hartwig, Scott, 3874
Harty, Linda S., 2886
Harty, Sonia, 1767
Hartz, C. Scott, 1291
Hartzell Industries, Inc., 1745
Hartzell, David J., 1800
Hartzell, James Robert, 1745
Hartzfeld, Jim, 1953
Hartzog, Dan M., 971
Hartzog, Doug, 2257
Haruki, Warren H., 1405, 1672
Harvey Construction Co., 1746
Harvey Enterprises Inc., 3749
Harvey, Brien V., 1077
Harvey, Charlene, 4084
Harvey, Charles A., 2050
Harvey, F. Stephen, Jr., 380
Harvey, Frederick B., III, 1349
Harvey, J. Brett, 91
Harvey, Jerri Jeter, 1746
Harvey, Jim, 21
Harvey, Kent M., 2952
Harvey, Lucian A., 1746
Harvey, Margie, 2148
Harvey, Robin L., 1746
Harvey, Stuart C., Jr., 753
Harvey, Thomas H., 2415
Harvey, William, 3984
Harvey, William D., 854, 921
Harvey, William J., 2125
Harvey, William R., 2699
Harvey, William W., 2746
Harvey, William W., Jr., 2746
Harville, Kelly, 3325
Harwell, Aubrey B., Jr., 2971
Harwell, Janis, 1081
Harwood, Brain C., 2742
Harwood, Brent, 2445
Harwood, Randall R., 1640
Harwood, Rodene L., 4082

Harwood, Shawn, 4082
Harwood, Stanley A., 4082
Harwood, Vance, 4082
Harwood, Vance R., 4082
Hasbro, Inc., 1747
Hasek, William, 1542
Haseotes, Ari N., 1003
Haser, H. William, 3715
Hash, Bert J., Jr., 1008
Hashimoto, Tadaaki, 2713
Haskell, John E., 2814
Haskell, Katrina, 2475
Haskell, Robert G., 2855
Haskell, Wyatt R., 1748
Hasken, Sarah, 2426
Haskins-Conde, Judy, 3344
Haslam, Anne S., 3704
Hasler-Lewis, Clare M., 795
Hasnedl, Jerry, 802
Haspel, Susan, 2649
Hassan, Fred, 376, 3757
Hassan, Hass, 4066
Hassel, Jason P., 2993
Hassell, Gerald L., 344, 887
Hasseman, Dean M., 820
Hassenfeld, Alan, 3318
Hassenfeld, Alan G., 1747, 3318
Hassey, L. Patrick, 112, 3292
Hastert, J. Dennis, 853
Hastie, Fenanda, 2340
Hasting, Mark, 2199
Hastings Mutual Insurance Co., 1749
Hastings, Daniel E., 1171
Hastings, James, 2646
Hastings, Ken, 2850
Hatayama, Kuniki, 2144
Hatbouty, Thomas C., 2981
Hatch, Dave, 1548
Hatch, Don, Jr., 3820
Hatch, Mark, 3820
Hatch, Orrin, 1578
Hatchell, Dennis G., 2875
Hatcher, Samuel F., III, 3674
Hatfield, James R., 239
Hatfield, Joe M., 1373
Hatfield, Joseph M., 1373
Hatfield, Lance, 504
Hathaway, D. C., 1741
Hathihe Ramallah Magazine, 3124
Hattem, Gary S., 1099
Hattersley, Gavin, 2523, 2549
Hattman, David W., 226
Hatton, Vincent P., 945
Hattori, Kazushi, 2103
Hatzopoulos, Arthur, 1665
Hau, Robert, 3829
Haubenstricker, Thomas A., 4151
Haubiel, Charles W., 460
Hauck, Edward C., 3297
Hauck, William, 655
Hauenstein, Glen W., 1073
Hauenstein, Sandra J., 3062
Hauer, K. S., 722
Haugarth, Janel, 3920
Haugen, Janet B., 3859
Haugen, Rick, 1374
Haugen, Ronalee, 1491
Haugh, John, 46
Haugland, Kent, 615
Haun, Jay, 3376
Haupt, Mary, 4125
Hauptman, Andrew, 783
Hauselt, Denise A., 945
Hauser, Dan, 1095
Hauser, Marilyn, 2866
Haushill, Mark, 1165
Hausmann, Carl L., 612
Hausmann, Jim, 2672
Hauswald, Jeananne K., 919
Hautly Cheese Co., Inc., 1750
Hautly, Alan C., 1750
Hauwermeiren, Guido Van, 346
Havelock, Kevin, 3853
Havens, Samuel H., 491
Haver, Christopher, 1571
Haver, Maureen A., 2605
Haverkamp, Michael F., 2790
Haverty, Michael R., 2094
Haviland Plastic Products Co., 1752
Havlik, Clem, 2282
Havrilla, Bettina, 1801
Hawaii National Bank, 1753
Hawaii Nature Center, 1953
Hawaii Planing Mill, Ltd., 1754
Hawaiian Commercial and Sugar Co., 85
Hawaiian Electric Industries, Inc., 1755
Hawaiian Host, Inc., 1756
Hawaux, Andre, 3879
Hawes-Saunders, RoNita, 690
Hawfield, W.B., Jr., 2566
Hawk Industries, Inc., 662
Hawk, Anthony "Tony", 30
Hawk, Arlene F., 3658
Hawk, George W., Jr., 850
Hawk, Henry, 3658
Hawk, Jeffrey A., 3658
Hawk, Leo, 3658
Hawk, Leo J., 3658
Hawk, Lhotse, 30
Hawk, Patricia, 30
Hawk, Steve, 30
Hawke, Dave, 552
Hawke, John D., Jr., 2323
Hawkins Construction Co., 1757
Hawkins, Amy, 618
Hawkins, Benjamin, 3081
Hawkins, Chris, 1757
Hawkins, Fred, Jr., 1757
Hawkins, Fred, Sr., 1757
Hawkins, H. Clay, IV, 833
Hawkins, Jay L., 2500
Hawkins, Kim, 1757
Hawkins, Lawton, 862
Hawkins, Mark J., 289, 508
Hawkins, Wendy Ramage, 1950
Hawkins, William, 862
Hawley, David S., 3858
Hawley, Gary W., 3344
Hawley, Michael, 1214, 3902
Hawley, Nancy, 3200
Hawley, Raymond, 2615
Hawley, Richard L., 4039
Hawley, Rusty, 2684
Haworth, Howard H., 372
Haworth, Matthew R., 1758
Haworth, Richard G., 1758
Haxel, Geoffrey C., 817
Hay, Jess T., 3946
Hay, Laura, 2190
Hay, Lewis, III, 679, 1443, 1736
Hay, Thomas, 2543
Hayashi, Nancy, 1290
Hayashi, Wayne, 1290
Hayden, Bill, 2668
Hayden, James G., 1212
Hayden, John W., 2790, 3374
Hayden, Michael V., 2586
Haydon, John B., 3103
Hayes, Daniel K., 2241
Hayes, Edward J., Jr., 75
Hayes, Geralyn F., 612
Hayes, Gregory J., 3882
Hayes, James, 1170
Hayes, Jean, 1722
Hayes, Jimmy W., 959
Hayes, John, 4140
Hayes, John A., 328
Hayes, Michael J., 2699
Hayes, Mike, 1618
Hayes, Noreen J., 4040
Hayes, Peter C., 491
Hayes, Peter J., 460
Hayes, Robert F., 3771
Hayes, Simone, 2842
Hayes, Thomas M., 691
Hayes, Timothy M., 3554
Hayes, Tyan, 2184
Hayes-Giles, Joyce V., 1183
Hayford, Michael D., 1371
Hayhoe, Christopher S., 1356
Haynes and Boone, LLP, 1759
Haynes, Charles E., 2742
Haynes, Craig A., 3738
Haynes, Robert B., 1395
Haynes, Victoria F., 2760, 3025
Haynes, Wycliffe E., 1395
Haynie & Associates, Inc., 1760
Haynie, Dayna E., 1760
Haynie, Gilmore S., Jr., 2068
Haynie, Mary Daynese, 1760
Haynie, Randy K., 1760
Haynie, Ryan K., 1760
Hays Cos., 1761
Hays Group, The, 1761
Hays, James C., 1761
Hays, Kristin L., 2925
Hays, Pete, 1082
Hays, Sara L., 215
Hays, Suzy, 636
Hayson, Brian, 962
Haythornthwaite, Richard, 2399
Haythornthwaite, Richard N., 2399
Hayward, Richard R., Jr., 851
Haywood, George W., 1087
Hazel, Darryl B., 104, 4095
Hazel, Mark D., 1377
Hazen, Sam, 1762
HC Beck, Ltd., 396
HCA Inc., 1762
HCA—The Healthcare Co., 1762
HCB Jr. Lead Trust, 396
HCR Manor Care, Inc., 1763
Heacock, David K., 3728
Head, Holman, 2771
Head, Jim, 3533
Head, Lynn, 923
Head, R. Holman, 2771
Head, Robert L., 3866
Headington, Frank C., 2656
Headlines International Ltd., 838
Headrick, Roger L., 3118
Heagerty, Annie, 1702
Heagerty, Mary, 1702
Heagerty, Michael, 1702
Heagerty, Michael P., 1702
Heagerty, Riley, 1702
Healey, Melanie L., 3936
Healey, Sean M., 51
Health Care Management Consulting, Inc., 1764
Health Care Services Group, 1314
Health East Care Bethesda Hospital, 3944
Health Management Associates, Inc., 1765
Health Net, Inc., 1766
Health Options, Inc., 493
Healy, Bridget M., 1938
Healy, Daniel J., 2731
Healy, Daniel P., 1565
Healy, Doug, 814
Healy, Gary M., 493
Healy, Joseph, 3879
Healy, Karen L., 1071
Healy, Michael, 503, 3189
Healy, Michael J., 1915
Heaney, Eugene T., 3031
Heaney, James David, 4158
Heaney, James M., 3387
Heaney, John J., 2324
Heaps, John F., Jr., 1441
Heard, Gerry D., 3413
Heard, Marian L., 2265
Hearn, Bill, 1258
Hearn, Billy Ray, 1258
Hearn, Jeffrey A., 543
Hearn, Shawn E., 2494
Hearn-Whaley, Holly, 1258
Heath, Eric M., 1207
Heath, John, III, 3034
Heath, Leland, 3805
Heath, Robert F., 565
Heaton, Lissa, 1445
Heaton, Michael, 4002
Heaven, Diane, 1011
Heavin, Diane, 1011
Heavin, Gary, 1011
Heavin, Gary H., 1011
Heavin, H. Gary, 1011
Heavner, Daniel L., 1396
Hebb, Donald B., Jr., 3040
Hebel, Cheryl, 418
Hebenstreit, James B., 365, 890
Heberle, Donald J., 344
Hebert, Danny, 899
Hebrink, Rodney W., 59
Hecht, Beth, 3646
Hecht, Steven, 581
Hecht, Tom, 2527
Hecht, William F., 1089
Heck, Nancy, 2836
Heck, Patricia DelTorro, 915
Heck, Steve, 1569
Heckaman, Alton D., Jr., 3667
Heckart, Christine A., 2214
Heckel, Gary, 1191
Heckenlaible, Mick, 1080
Hecker, David, 2049
Hecker, Dennis, 30
Heckman, Alton D., Jr., 3667
Heckman, Art, 657
Heckman, Arthur S., 657
Heckman, Lois B., 1297
Hecktman, Melvin L., 3074
Hedberg, Joel, 1517
Hedden, Andrew S., 3358
Heddles, Will, 2401
Heddles, Willard P., 2401
Hedemark, N. Charles, 504, 1843
Hedemark, Norman Charles, 1843
Hederman, H. Doug, 250
Hederman, Hap, 250
Hedfors, Bo, 3709
Hedgebeth, Reginald D., 571
Hedgebeth, Reginald D., Jr., 3540

Henry, Robert H., 1102
Henry, Sean, 737, 2620
Henry, Stewart L., 2138
Henry, Susan A., 3406
Hensarling, John A., 2146
Henseler, Peter J., 1413
Hensgens, Valerie Moody, 2562
Henshaw, Leslie, 1062
Henshaw, Liz, 3606
Hensler, Tracy, 1071
Hensley, Jason M., 432
Hensley, Richard A., 2477
Hensley, Sue, 2638
Hensley, Thomas, 1373
Hensley, Thomas M., Jr., 1373
Hensley, Tim, 2800
Hensley, Tom, 3839
Henson, Christopher L., 385
Henson, Gregg L., 1102
Hensyn, Inc., 1782
Hentges, Mark, 1332
Henton, Douglas, 2027
Henton, June M., 1953
Henze, Daryl K., 4026
Henzler, Tom, 2424
Hepa, Raynita B., 3843
Hepburn, Michael, 2048
Hepfinger, David J., 4024
Hepfinger, David Jerome, 4024
Hepler, Cindy, 466
Hepler, Julie, 1151
Hepp, Jennifer, 1842
Heppelmann, James E., 2878
Heras, Gonzalo de Las, 3528
Herberger, Roy A., Jr., 216
Herbert, Bob, 147
Herbert, Dale M., 3171
Herbert, Gavin S., 99
Herbert, Kinneeveauk, Jr., 3751
Herbert, Michael, 1074
Herbert, Michael J., 1074
Herbert, Patrick J., 716
Herbert, Patrick J., III, 716
Herbig, Cheryl, 3225
Herbold, Robert J., 56
Herbstman, Sara, 4036
Herdegen, William P., 911
Herdman, Robert K., 1007
Herff Jones, Inc., 216
Herington, Charles M., 2549, 2709
Herink, Daniel D., 1944
Heritage Imports, Inc., 1784
Herlihy, Donagh, 305
Herlihy, Edward D., 3973
Herlihy, Edward M., 3973
Herlihy, Rebecca Pierce, 1839
Herling, Michael J., 571
Herma, John F., 2181
Herman Miller, Inc., 2517
Herman, Alexis M., 862, 1007, 1279, 2489
Herman, Bruce, 218
Herman, Cipora, 3326
Herman, Debi, 3824
Herman, Jason, 109
Herman, Joan E., 933
Herman, Michael R., 3134
Herman, Ronald D., 1264
Herman, Theodore L., 2605
Hermance, Frank S., 181
Hermance, Ronald E., 1880
Hermance, Ronald E., Jr., 1880
Hermann Cos., Inc., 1786
Hermann, Eliza, 567
Hermann, Jean E., 1786
Hermann, Mary Lee, 1786
Hermann, Phillip, 2483
Hermann, Robert R., 1786
Hermann, Robert R., Jr., 1786
Hermann, Robert R., Sr., 1786
Hermann, Robert Ringen, Jr., 1786
Hermanson, Pat, 1080
Hermens, Rosalee, 3815
Hermes, Robert A., 2600
Hermsen, Roger J., 2970
Hern, John J., Jr., 836
Hernandez, Alejandro J., 4028
Hernandez, Antonia, 655
Hernandez, Carlos, 229
Hernandez, Carlos M., 1448, 3069
Hernandez, Colleen, 3190
Hernandez, Elisa, 1442
Hernandez, Emmanuel T., 2459
Hernandez, Enrique, Jr., 780, 2427, 2724, 4028
Hernandez, Eric, 2305
Hernandez, Jesse, 1748
Hernandez, Robert, 24
Hernandez, Robert M., 1213
Hernandez, Roland A., 2489, 3835
Hernandez, Sandra, 655
Hernandez, Sheila, 3641
Hernandez, Teresa, 2870
Hernandez, William H., 78, 1214, 3905
Herndon, Alexa, 3998
Herndon, Dealey D., 406
Herndon, Ed, 805
Hernon, Robert, 46
Herold, Jo Ann, 228
Heron, Katrina, 2865
Herr, Edwin H., 1787
Herr, James M., 1787
Herr, Ken, 690
Herr, Randy, 3895
Herren, Pat, 1470
Herren, Vanessa, 3059
Herrera, George, 4132
Herres, Rebecca Gilbreth, 1302
Herrick, Dennis R., 177
Herrick, Joseph M., 1093
Herrick-Pacific Corporation, 1788
Herrig, Duane, 1987
Herrigel, Rodger K., 1984
Herrin, Jeff, 3527
Herrin, Tony E., 2729
Herring, Heather L., 1961
Herring, John W., 1053
Herring, Joseph L., 955
Herringer, Frank C., 182, 3310, 3363
Herringer, Maryellen C., 2952
Herrington, Marilyn A., 1419
Herrington, Philip, 1047
Herrington, Terri, 1968
Herrington, Terri L., 3711
Herrle, Joseph C., 1465
Herrman, Ernie L., 3765
Herrmann, Harold, Jr., 3177
Herron, John, 1279
Herron, John T., 1189
Hersch, Dennis S., 2277
Herschend, Chris, 1790
Herschend, Jim, 1790
Herschmann, Eric D., 3520
Hersey, Eleanor M., 2928
Hersh, Kenneth A., 2641
Hershey, Mark, 246, 3210
Hershey, Mark A., 1914
Hershiser, David, 2805
Hershman, Martha, 2561
Herson, Mendel, 3097
Hertel, Randall C., 2343
Herthaus, Donald H., 1880
Hertneky, Dianne C., 3636
Hertz, Paul, 1457
Hertz, Ronald, 1595
Hervey, Jay R., 372
Herz, Robert H., 1349, 2570
Herzan, Alexandra A., 1962
Herzog, Aaron, 3276
Herzog, David, 156, 3276
Herzog, David L., 156
Herzog, Eli, 3276
Herzog, Gary, 3276
Herzog, Herman, 3276
Herzog, Joseph, 3276
Herzog, Michael, 3276
Herzog, Michael B., 3276
Herzog, Mordechai, 3276
Herzog, Morris, 3276
Herzog, Nathan, 3276
Herzog, Phillip, 3276
Herzog, Robert, 3276
Hesalroad, Janice, 1645
Heseltine, Peter, 397
Hesgerberg, Greg, 1126
Heslop, James G., 901
Hess, Beverly B., 3142
Hess, Bill, 1986
Hess, David, 1890
Hess, David P., 3028
Hess, David Peter, Jr., 41
Hess, Donald, 3315
Hess, Glen E., 2164
Hess, Hal, 167
Hess, John B., 1160, 1793, 3879
Hess, Michael D., 314
Hess, Peter, 41
Hess, William C., 1986, 1987
Hessan, Diane, 2873
Hesse, Chad F., 1112
Hesse, Daniel R., 3556
Hessel, Katherine, 703
Hesselbein, Frances R., 2605
Hesselbrock, Steve, 3810
Hessels, Jan-Michiel, 2049, 2769
Hessler, David J., 2595
Hester, Donald, 2774
Hester, Roy, 511
Hesterberg, Earl J., 3572
Heston, June D., 624
Heston, W. Craig, 3910
Heth, Morrison, 1846
Heth, Tim, 1817
Hetzer, G. Scott, 1150
Heublein, Inc., 1107
Heuck, David, 2913
Heuer, Betsy, 436
Heuser, Henry V., Jr., 3966
Hewett, Charles E., 338
Hewett, Charles E., Ph.D., 338
Hewett, Wayne M., 1942
Hewitt, Bradford L., 3747
Hewitt, Conrad W., 346
Hewitt, Corey, 1509
Hewitt, Dennis E., 2808
Hewitt, Kirsten, 4056
Hewlett, Clothide, 3326
Hewlett, Clothilde, 3326
Hewlett-Packard Co., 1794
Hewson, Carolyn, 455
Hewson, Marillyn, 1184
Hewson, Marilyn A., 2292
Hexcel Corp., 1795
Heyano, John A., 797
Heydel, M. John, 952
Heydt, Stuart, 3026
Heyer, Steven J., 2807
Heyman, William H., 1382, 3802
Heyneman, Charles, 1409
Heyrman Construction Co., Inc., 1796
Heyrman, Christopher, 1796
Heyrman, Earl, 1796
Heyrman, Lawrence, 1796
Heyrman, Vernon, 1796
Heyse, Richard P, 3919
Heyward, Barney, 2829
Heywood, Thomas A., 544
Hiam, Robert P., 1405
Hiatt, Alison, 196
Hiatt, Mark A., 616
Hibbard, William, 4046
Hibberson, Sarah, 2203
Hibbing Taconite Co., 850
Hickey, Adam, 893
Hickey, Brian E., 2323
Hickey, Dennis, 869
Hickey, Kelly, 3140
Hickey, Mike, 3347
Hickey, Nancy W., 3597
Hickey, Phil, 2638
Hickey, Troy, 1734
Hickey, William M., Jr., 2223
Hickey, William V., 3077, 3381, 3408
Hickman, Mark, 3839
Hickman, Marty, 722
Hickman, Tommy L., 3200
Hickmann, William J., 3388
Hickory Tech Corp., 1797
Hicks, Alan, 959
Hicks, Arthur W., 3834
Hicks, Arthur W., Jr., 3834
Hicks, Christie, 3589
Hicks, David, 80
Hicks, Doug, 1018, 2331
Hicks, Gary, 3059
Hicks, H. Thomas, 3995
Hicks, Ken, 1459
Hicks, Ken C., 297, 1459
Hicks, Melissa, 1053
Hicks, Michael E., 2809
Hicks, Randall L., 1300
Hicks, Rob, 2991
Hicks, Thomas, 700
Hicks, Thomas O., 1023, 3729
Hicks, Thomas O., Jr., 3729
Hickson, Charles W., 1481
Hickton, Dawne S., 1318
Hiebert, Jeffrey, 2664
Hieda, Hisashi, 1515
Hieda, Hisoshi, 1515
Hiemstra, Doug, 2806
Hiestand, Jason, 1421
Higashi, Emiko, 2165
Higashi, Mildred, 1756
Higdem, Garry M., 758
Higgins, A. William, 2088
Higgins, Arthur J., 1220, 4157
Higgins, Denise, 2418
Higgins, John, 3686
Higgins, Kathy, 497, 698
Higgins, Melina, 2610
Higgins, Michael, 1246
Higgins, Molly, 3569
Higgins, Monsignor L., 2691
Higgins, Nigel, 3270
Higgins, Patricia L., 360, 3802

Higgins, Robert F., 3011
Higgins, Rod, 728
Higgs, Christopher, 2209
Higgs, John H., 2542
Highland Capital, 723
Highland, S. Craig, 2758
Highley, Randall, 3046
Highley, Randall M., 3046
Highmark Inc., 1799
Highmark West Virginia, Inc., 1799
Highsmith, Carlton L., 1419
Hightman, Carrie J., 2715
Highwoods Realty L.P., 1800
Higie, David G., 323
Higley, William, 1376
Hignam, Alec, 626
Higson, John P., 305
Hijkoop, Frans, 2481
Hilado, Tessa, 2935
Hilburn, Joe, 3978
Hilburn, Ray, 2235
Hild, Steven A., 3698
Hildenbrand, Wilt, 2336
Hildum, Keith P., 4048
Hile, Daniel, 2261
Hiler, Edward A., 856
Hilferty, Daniel J., 1926
Hilferty, Joan, 1926
Hilfiger U.S.A., Tommy, Inc., 1801
Hilgendorf, Ellen, 2439
Hilger, James K., 1044
Hill, Allen E., 3872
Hill, Andrew, 1669
Hill, Anne, 297
Hill, Barbara B., 1368, 3566
Hill, Betsy, 3519
Hill, Bonnie G., 67, 1842, 4150
Hill, Bruce, 3557
Hill, Bunny, 2588
Hill, C. Riley, 4135
Hill, Christie, 1190
Hill, Christie A., 1190
Hill, Chuck, 2950
Hill, Craig H., 1518
Hill, Dan J., 2763
Hill, David, 2756
Hill, David C., 1795
Hill, Deborah, 3071
Hill, Denise, 1458
Hill, Douglas A., 1235
Hill, Gregory P., 1793
Hill, J. Edward, 490
Hill, J. Tomilson, 477
Hill, James M., 413
Hill, Janet, 4030, 4031
Hill, Joan P., 3890
Hill, John, 2401, 2908
Hill, John A., 1102, 3085
Hill, John J.D., 2908
Hill, John T., II, 3078
Hill, Jonathan A., Sr., 2956
Hill, Julie A., 2303, 4027
Hill, Kathryn M., 2563
Hill, Kermit, 72
Hill, Kris L., 3306
Hill, Linda A., 542, 935, 3592
Hill, Michelle, 2298
Hill, Norman J., 966
Hill, Paul, 3839
Hill, Richard S., 249, 2314
Hill, Robert, 2359
Hill, Robert Dean, 1137
Hill, Robert K., 3890
Hill, Ruth, 3303
Hill, Susan M., 428
Hill, Thad, 661
Hill, V. Janet, 1054, 3556
Hill, W. Scott, 2089
Hill, Williard, 2416
Hillebrand, James A., 3610
Hillebrand, Jeffrey H., 3944
Hillegonds, Paul C., 1183
Hillenbrand, W. August, 1047, 1804
Hillenius, Steven J., 3403
Hiller, Russ, 3641
Hilliard Corp., The, 1805
Hilliard Farber & Co., Inc., 1806
Hilliard, Darren, 2775
Hilliard, Herb H., 1406
Hilliard, Herbert H., 507
Hillier, Peggy, 2945
Hillier, Scott, 2287
Hillman, Chip, 3199
Hillman, Jeanne, 4052
Hillman, Jeanne M., 4052
Hills Bank and Trust Co., 1808
Hills, Carla A., 1582
Hills, Mark, 3675
Hillside Capital, Inc., 1810
Hillside Hospital, 2270
Hilsabeck, Frank H., 269
Hilsheimer, Larry, 3372
Hilst, Homer, 1079
Hilt, Meredith, 3709
Hilton Chicago, 1634
Hilton, John Allen, Jr., 440
Hilton, John M., 3577
Hilton, Michael F., 2723, 3292
Hiltz, L. Thomas, 219
Hilzinger, Kurt J., 1886
Hilzinger, Matthew F., 1309, 3905
Himali, Joseph, 2482
Himebaugh, Ted, 2127
Himeno, Yoshinori, 2074
Hinchliffe, Lawrence, 3807
Hinchman, Martha R., 2740
Hinckle, Veronica, 694
Hinckley, Gregory K., 1955, 2462
Hinckley, Henry P., 3444
Hinckley, Robert C., 661
Hinderks, Mark D., 3608
Hinderliter, Mary, 267
Hindley, Graham, 3777
Hindman, James M., 99
Hine, Clarkson, 390
Hines, George N., 3946
Hines, Gerald D., 1813
Hines, Jeffrey C., 1813
Hines, Michael, 1191
Hines, Michael F., 3765
Hines, Rodney, 2501, 3585
Hinkel, Mark, 23
Hinkle, Amber, 131
Hinkle, Bill, 131
Hinkle, J. Steve, 61
Hinkle, Rosie, 131
Hinkley, Harold, 3637
Hinkley, Harold L., 3637
Hinrichs, Chuck A., 3167
Hinrichs, James F., 688
Hinshaw, John, 1794
Hinshaw, Juanita H., 4077
Hinson, Marianne, 601
Hinson, Ronnie, 2972
Hinson, W. Ron, 1567
Hinton, Greg, 3839
Hinton, Michael J., 1004
Hinton, Richard, 3526
Hintz, Donald C., 1279
Hintz, Gregory, 2468
Hintz, Gregory J., 2468
Hipp, Jonathan, 658
Hipp, Jonathan W., 658
Hippe, Alan, 1549
Hippeau, Eric, 3589
Hipple, Richard J., 1366
Hippler, Thomas, 3618
Hipwell, Todd, 1110
Hirabayashi, Shinichi, 2541
Hirata, Masayoshi, 4049
Hirji, Asiff S., 41
Hirota, Masao, 3639
Hirota, Sherry, 2865
Hirsberg, Josh, 546
Hirsch, Andrea S., 3879
Hirsch, Didier, 56
Hirsch, Elizabeth T., 3029
Hirsch, George, 2689
Hirsch, Morris W., 3854
Hirsch, Thomas J., 1427
Hirschfield, Ira, 3325
Hirschhorn, Daniel B., 168
Hirschmann, James W., 4041
Hirschy, Matthew G., 588
Hirshberg, Gary, 3617
Hirshberg, Mimi, 1313
Hirth, Dorian, 2658
Hirtler-Garvey, Karin, 46
Hiser, Rodena, 2442
Hiser, Vicki, 2914
Hitchcock, David W., 3672
Hitchcock-Gear, Salene, 21
Hitter, E. Paul, 2477
Hittner, Barry G., 183
Hitzemann, Mary, 1080
Hix, Thomas R., 1239
Hixon, James A., 2725
Hixon, Todd C., 3819
Hiyakumoto, Greg, 3782
Hiyakumoto, Greg H., 3782
Hjelm, Christopher T., 2195
Hjelseth, Nate, 692
Hjerpe, Edward, III, 1083
Hladky, Elizabeth, 3506
Hladky, Joe F., 3506
Hladky, John, 3506
Hladky, Joseph F., III, 3506
Hlavacek, James D., 2760
Hlay, Jean H., 2595
Hll, C.T., 3654
HMO Minnesota, 496
Hnat, James, 2041
Hnatin, Catherine B., 3766
HNI Corp., 1817
Ho, David H. Y., 63
Ho, David H.Y., 2926
Ho, Doreen Woo, 3835
Ho, Peter S., 342
Ho, Stuart, 1756
Hoag, Brent, 1130
Hoag, Greg, 3394
Hoag, Jay C., 1242
Hoag, John A., 1405
Hoaglin, Thomas E., 141
Hoak, Jonathan S., 1437
Hoard, Toni, 978
Hoare, Betty D., 3670
Hobbie, Lynn K., 2334
Hobbs, Cary D., 735
Hobbs, Franklin W., 2303, 2549
Hobbs, Helen H., 2950
Hobbs, Laura Lopez, 3524
Hobbs, Richard F., 3408
Hobby, Paul W., 2756, 3606
Hobson, Elana M., 2007
Hobson, Gilian A., 3957
Hobson, Jeff, 2223
Hobson, Mellody, 3585
Hobson, Mellody L., 1172, 2230
Hoch, Gordon B., 3157
Hochman, Marty, 660
Hochman, Russell, 2984
Hochschild, Roger C., 1125
Hock, A. Brooks, 4078
Hock, Doug, 1266
Hockaday, Irvine O., Jr., 1464, 2230
Hocken, Natalie L., 2860
Hockfield, Susan, 1552, 3095
Hockmeyer, Wayne T., 377
Hoctor, Susan F., 2126
Hodde, Debbie, 750
Hodge, Robert W., 1392
Hodges, Charles E., 4008
Hodges, Charles H., 875
Hodges, George W., 1518, 4103
Hodges, Larry A., 176
Hodges, Peter L., 2480
Hodgson, Patrick W.E., 2323
Hodgson, Thomas R., 3802
Hodnik, Alan R., 100
Hodnik, David F., 3437
Hodo, Edward Douglas, 3606
Hodson, John, 3794
Hodulik, Andrew G., 2341
Hoechner, Bruce D., 3253
Hoechst Corp., 730
Hoechst Marion Roussel, Inc., 3329
Hoecker, Thomas R., 3490
Hoefler, Karen E., 408
Hoeg, Krystyna T., 3643
Hoeg, Thomas E., 177
Hoehn-Saric, R. Christopher, 2231
Hoekenga, Craig T., 910
Hoeksema, Timothy E., 2371
Hoelmer, David R., 59
Hoepfner, Larry, 870
Hoernis, Jennifer, 3457
Hoeschen, Donald E., 2636
Hoeschler, Linda, 1645
Hoesly, Clarence, 835
Hofer, Andrew, 589
Hoff, Lawrence, 2450
Hoff, Susan S., 442
Hoffecker, Joe, 814
Hoffenberg, Stephen R., 937
Hoffenberg, Steven, 937
Hoffer Plastics Corp., 1821
Hoffer, Helen C., 1821
Hoffer, Robert A., 1821
Hoffer, Robert A., Jr., 1821
Hoffer, Taffy, 1629
Hoffer, W. Alex, 1821
Hoffer, William A., 1821
Hoffert, Kenneth, 3145
Hoffing, Ellen R., 2943
Hoffius, Dirk, 3923
Hoffman Adjustment Inc., 1822
Hoffman, Bill, 442
Hoffman, Brendan L., 521, 2973
Hoffman, Brock, 1822
Hoffman, Carol, 981
Hoffman, Gilbert, 2376
Hoffman, James, 2136
Hoffman, Janie, 2353
Hoffman, Joseph A., 1822
Hoffman, Joyce, 3047

Hoffman, Joyce N., 3047
Hoffman, Kathleen, 2200
Hoffman, Kent, 1822
Hoffman, Larry J., 1654
Hoffman, Lorey A., 70
Hoffman, Meyer, 2510
Hoffman, Michael, 511, 3626
Hoffman, Michael J., 1153, 3775
Hoffman, Paul J., 32
Hoffman, Philip, 2912
Hoffman, Rich, 2011
Hoffman, Richard W., 297
Hoffman, Robert, 657
Hoffman, Steven M., 1799
Hoffman, Susan, 986
Hoffmann, Andre, 1549
Hoffmann, Brian, 849
Hoffmann, Richard, 1264
Hoffmann, Richard W., 1264
Hoffmann-La Roche Inc., 1823
Hoffmeister, David F., 2268
Hoffner, Darin R., 3877
Hoffner, John F., 50
Hofmann 1987 Revocable Trust, The, 1824
Hofmann Co., The, 1824
Hofmann Foundation, 276
Hofmann, Kenneth H., 1824
Hofmann, Martha J., 1824
Hofmann, Martha Jean, 1824
Hofmann, Thomas W., 4038
Hofmann-Morgan, Lisa A., 1824
Hoga, Takashi, 1515
Hogan, Brad, 1079
Hogan, Brian J., 4044
Hogan, David O., 2795
Hogan, Jack, 3017
Hogan, John F., 851
Hogan, Michael, 7
Hogan, Michael P., 7
Hogan, Randall J., 2926
Hogan, Randall J., III, 956
Hogan, Thomas B., Jr., 3069
Hogan, William S., Jr., 1212
Hogben, Andrea, 2989
Hogberg, David E., 899
Hogel, Carol C., 917
Hogel, Catherine C., 917
Hogel, Elisabeth, 917
Hoglund, Robert N., 916
Hogue, Gordon, 1401
Hoguet, Karen M., 2333
Hohenstein, A. E., 2254
Hohenstein, A. Edward, 2254
Hohl, Doren E., 1338
Hojnacki, Christine, 521
Hojnacki, William, 3697
Hoke, John R., III, 2517
Hoke, Karen M., 3444
Hokin, Alexandra, 1957
Hokin, Amy, 1957
Hokin, Dana, 1957
Hokin, Justin, 1957
Hokin, Lauren, 1957
Hokin, Richard, 1956, 1957
Hokin, Tom, 1957
Hokin, William J., 1957
Holaday, A. Bart, 2441
Holaday, Alan, 4056
Holberg, Greg, 2762
Holbert, Ronald, 1399
Holbrook, James A. Stivender, Jr., 3602
Holbrook, James S., 3602
Holbrook, Richard E., 1209
Holce, Bonnie J., 1827
Holce, Evelyn L., 1827
Holce, Randall E., 1827
Holcim (US) Inc., 1828
Holcomb, H.T., 3116
Holcomb, Lavaughn, 72
Holcomb, Zelda J., 3910
Holcombe, Paul A., Jr., 1588
Holcombe, Tony, 3672
Holcombe, Tony G., 3672
Holden Trust, The, 340
Holden, Betsy D., 4045
Holden, Matt, 2312
Holden, Reg, 2945
Holden, S. Craig, 2777
Holden, William J., III, 1563
Holder Construction Co., 1829
Holder, David, 3675
Holder, Elizabeth D., 1829
Holder, JoAnn, 497
Holder, John R., 2847
Holder, Julie F., 1213
Holder, Thomas M., 1829
Holding, Frank B., 1395, 1396, 3515
Holding, Frank B., Jr., 1396, 2971
Holding, Frank B., Sr., 1396
Holdren, Larry E., 2929
Holdsworth, Mark K., 2887
Holdsworth, Raymond W., 4075
Holiday Auto & Truck Inc., 1830
Holiday Chrysler Dodge Jeep, Inc., 1831
Holiday Stationstores, Inc., 1832
Holiday, Bradley J., 660
Holiday, Edith E., 1793
Holiday, Tom, 131
Holien, Dennis D., 208
Holifield, Jerry, 1410
Holl, David B., 2392
Holland, Christopher S., 223, 358
Holland, Evans P., 2910
Holland, Evans P., Sr., 2910
Holland, G. Edison, 3516
Holland, G. Edison, Jr., 3516
Holland, Jan, 1262
Holland, John J., 626, 936
Holland, Judy, 4000
Holland, LJ, 1279
Holland, Mary Jane, 2910
Holland, Mary Jane P., 2910
Holland, Noel R., 882
Holland, Robert, Jr., 2258
Holland, Smith, 973
Holland, Stacy, 4028
Holland, Wendell F., 222
Hollander, Alan S., 505
Hollanders, Nicolas, 1458
Hollar, Mark R., 1336
Hollenbeck, Alan J., 3228
Hollenhorst, Tirza, 1912
Hollenkemp, Michael, 3453
Hollern, Michael P., 585, 1714
Hollex, Peter, 1195
Holley, Charles M., Jr., 3980
Holley, Rick R., 301, 2991
Hollfelder, Tom, 179
Hollick, Clive R., 1852
Holliday, Chad, 758
Holliday, Charles O., Jr., 340, 1061
Holliday, Steven John, 2630
Hollifield, Matthew V., 2312
Holling, Marcus, 3868
Holling, Marcus W., 3868
Hollingdale, Daniel L., 343
Hollinger, Mark, 1126
Hollinger, William R., 2105
Hollingsworth, Elizabeth, 234
Hollingsworth, J. Dianne, 337
Hollingsworth, J. Mark, 928
Hollingsworth, Thomas, 1196
Hollinshead, Barbara, 3193
Hollister, Caroline K., 391
Hollister, Thomas I., 583
Hollister, Thomas J., 1593
Hollman, Daniel, 1800
Holloman, J. Phillip, 816, 3246
Holloman, Scotty, 2442
Hollow, John Patton, 3818
Holloway, Janet M., 2559
Holloway, Jean, 358
Holloway, Shirley, 934
Holloway, Wes, 1607
Hollowell, F. Whit, Jr., 859
Hollowell, Harry H., 2639
Hollowell, William G., 749
Holm, George, 2938, 3255
Holm, George L., 2938
Holm, Krister, 901
Holman, David C., 144
Holman, Edwin J., 2205, 2875
Holman, Elise, 3998
Holman, Jennifer, 46
Holmberg, Douglas A., 2762
Holmberg, Gregory J., 2762
Holmberg, John, 1266
Holmes Automotive Group, 1838
Holmes, Bill, 1573
Holmes, Daisy, 344
Holmes, Gordon, 3781
Holmes, Grace B., 667
Holmes, Janelle L., 1838
Holmes, Julie, 1838
Holmes, Larry, 3450
Holmes, Max H., 1838
Holmes, Max Harvey, 1838
Holmes, Patsy, 72
Holmes, Stephen P., 4132
Holmes, W. Alexander, 2558
Holmes, William, 3159
Holmgren, Mark, 1167
Holmgren, Mike, 846
Holmstrom, Richard J., 2415
Holnam Inc., 1828
Holoch, Kristie, 943
Holst, Gregg, 2810
Holston, Michael J., 1794
Holsworth, Bill, 2387
Holt & Bugbee Co., 1839
Holt & Bugbee Hardwoods, Inc., 1839
Holt, Ben, 2762
Holt, Christopher, 3504
Holt, Connie, 2856
Holt, Jack, 2913
Holt, John, 2480
Holt, Matt, 1158
Holt, Peter M., 3321, 3557
Holt, Timothy A., 2488
Holt, Timothy J., 63
Holt, Winston, 2409
Holt, Winston, IV, 2409
Holtgrieve, Bill, 1963
Holthaus, Gerard E., 333
Holthaus, Stephanie, 3779
Holthus, C.G., 943
Holthus, Kelly, 943
Holthus, Kendell, 943
Holthus, Kristie, 943
Holthus, Marcy, 943
Holthus, Tom, 943
Holthus, Virginia, 943
Holton, Carlota Hermann, 1786
Holton, Donna D., 2635
Holtsberry, Robert, 1631
Holtz House of Vehicles Inc., 1840
Holtz, Alex, 364
Holtz, John D., 1840
Holtz, Kristine, 2378
Holtz, Seana, 1840
Holzmann, John A., 3499
Holzmann, Sarita, 3499
Holzshu, Chris, 2287
Homa, Michael, 2606
Homan, Andrew, 2409
Homasote Co., 1841
Hombach, Robert J., 377
Homcy, Charles J., M.D., 752
Home Federal Bancorp, Inc., 1843
Home Savings and Loan Co., 1845
Home State Bank, 1846
Homecall Hospice, 3884
Homecrest Industries, Inc., 1847
Homer, Michael W., 3633
HomeStar Bank, 1848
Homewood Corp., 1849
Hommert, Douglas D., 214
Homolka, James, 3140
Homonoff, Burt, 511
Homrighaus, Barry, 2032
HON INDUSTRIES Inc., 1817
Honan, Marc, 606
Honbarrier Co., R.L., 1850
Honbarrier, Archie L., 1850
Honda Cars of Bradenton, 1776
Honda Cars of Hickory, 1776
Honda of America Mfg., Inc., 1851
Honda Village, 3954
Honeycutt, Don, 3902
Honeycutt, J. Brian, 1576
Hong, Peter, 82
Honickman, Jeffrey A., 887, 2354
Honickman, Marjorie, 2354
Honig, David A., 4089
Honigfort, John, 1990
Honn, Bruce, 3222
Honnell, Hope H., 1396
Honnold, Scott, 1612
Honnold, Scott A., 1612
Honzal, Beth A., 1624
Hood, Amy, 2501
Hood, Cecil G., 373
Hood, Charles H., 3134
Hood, James W., 3171
Hood, Lynn, 1763
Hood, Vicki V., 2164
Hood, Warren A, Jr., 3516
Hoof, Tom, 3686
Hoogenboom, Paul G.P., 3278
Hoogendorn, Homer E., 422
Hoogendorn, Peggy, 422
Hook, Judith D., 1663
Hooker Furniture Corp., 1855
Hooker, A. Frank, Jr., 1855
Hooker, David J., 3740
Hooker, J. Clyde, 1855
Hooker, Mabel B., 1855
Hooley, Darlene, 3544
Hooley, John H., 3389
Hooley, Joseph L., 3592
Hoolihan, James J., 100
Hooper, Bobby, 72
Hooper, John A., 4052
Hooper, Michele J., 3025, 3884
Hoopes, Jeffrey C., 3668

Hoopes, Judith H., 4028
Hoopingarner, David W., 2913
Hoopingarner, Don, 2379
Hoops, Alan, 689
Hoops, Peter W., 910
Hooser, Nikki, 3553
Hooters of America, Inc., 1858
Hootkin, Pamela N., 3088
Hootwinc 100, 1858
Hoover, Monte L., 597
Hoover, R. David, 328, 1271, 2274, 3597
Hoover, Rose, 186
Hoover, W. Jeffrey, 3042
Hope Christian Community Foundation, 1857
Hope, Judith Richards, 1554, 3857
Hopkins Federal Savings Bank, 1859
Hopkins, Christopher C., 3370
Hopkins, David L., 861
Hopkins, Jan, 3978
Hopkins, Jane H., 862
Hopkins, John N., 2108
Hopkins, John P., 878
Hopkins, Marvin, 1893
Hopkins, Marvin B., 1893
Hopkins, Robert, 2310
Hopkins, Thomas E., 3437
Hopkins, Virginia, 1396
Hopkins, William F., 2784
Hopp, Jason, 3157
Hopper, David, 1065
Hopper, David W., 1399
Hopper, Dylan, 797
Hopper, John J., 1239
Hopper, Sidney, 3880
Hoppes, Jacquelyn, 3648
Hoppes, Michael D., 334
Hopping, Jamie E., 61
Hopson, Harry, 3525
Hopson, Kenneth, 362
Hopwood, Andy P., 547
Horan, Anthony J., 2071
Horan, Michael, 872
Horbach, Sandra, 1191
Horbaczewski, Henry Z., 3161
Horgan, William S., Jr., 1212
Horgen, Jay C., 51
Hori, Jim, 3455
Horikiri, Noriaki, 2144
Horiszny, Laurene H., 528
Horix Manufacturing Co., 1860
Horizon Beverage Co., Inc., 1862
Horizon Cash Management, LLC, 1864
Horizon Healthcare Services, Inc., 1863
Horizon-Five Star Enterprises, Inc., 1865
Hormaechea, Richard M., 3459
Hormel Foods Corp., 1866
Horn, Charles L., 101
Horn, D. Ralph, 3294
Horn, David C., 67
Horn, John, 238
Horn, Karen N., 2274, 2725, 3458
Horn, Randall C., 874
Horn, Rebecca, 2162
Horn, Rodney J., 3605
Horn, Sharon, 151
Horn, Terry, 3076
Hornaday, Ryan, 1259
Hornaday, Ryan A., 1259
Hornbaker, Renee J., 1213
Hornbarger, William Allen, 2557
Hornbrook, Sharon S., 1225
Hornbuckle, William J., 2489
Horne, Eleanor V., 4028
Horne, Rick, 1258
Horne, Vicki, 1258
Hornell, Art, 3726
Horner, C. Alan, 1403
Horner, Constance J., 2950, 3072
Horner, Donald G., 1405
Horner, Henry, 2615
Horner, Henry Igitaanuluk, Sr., 2615
Horner, Robert W., III, 2639
Horning, Sandra, 1549
Horrar, Robert A., 900
Horsley, Phillip, 2904
Horton Fund, Alan & Beverley, 3374
Horton, Amy D., 990
Horton, James A., 4028
Horton, John, 2234
Horton, Juana I., 491
Horton, Myra, 1987
Horton, Ozey K., 4124
Horton, Thomas W., 187, 3095
Horton, William L., Jr., 3936
Horwitz, Donald, 2427
Hosack, Carmen P., 2714
Hosack, Joseph V., Jr., 3036
Hoskins, Joe, 923
Hoskins, W.Wesley, 1347
Hoskyn, Thomas C., 3203
Hospira, Inc., 1867
Hospital Service Assn. of N.E. PA, 505
Hosseini-Kargar, Morteza, 1970
Hostetler, Hazel P., 319
Hostetter, Amos, 2625
Hotard, Lionel, 831
Hotarek, Brian, 456
Hotcaveg, Howard, 1901
Hotchkiss, James P., 1413
Hotopp, Thomas B., 2529
Houchens, Nell, 1543
Houchens, Ruel, 1543
Houchin, Jay, 3839
Houdlette, Kim, 7
Houghtaling, Ronald, 2920
Houghton, Amory, Jr., 945
Houghton, James R., 945
Houghton, Mary, 663
Houghton, Sean, 2465
Houk, Mike, 1080
Houle, Leo W., 801, 856
Houpt, Jeffrey L., M.D., 497
Houpt, Mary H., 1739
Hourigan, Tim, 1842
House, Paul D., 3753
Householder, Joseph A., 3405
Houseman, Dave, 611
Housen, Charles B., 1294
Housen, Majorie G., 1294
Housen, Morris, 1294
Houser, Daniel W., 1970
Houser, Douglas G., 2710
Houser, Jim, 1066
Houston McLane Co., Inc., 1871
Houston, Debbie, 1873
Houston, Harold, 1887
Houston, J. Wayne, 3972
Houston, Jonathan A., 1870
Houston, Julia A., 933
Houston, Margaret C., 1870
Houston, Robert A., 1870
Houston, Robert C., 1870
Houston-Philpot, Kimberly R., 1162
Houze, Gilbert L., 2951
Hovde, Eric D., 3655
Hovde, Robert, 3264
Hove, Rebecca, 563
Hover-Smoot, Scott, 4137
Hoverman, Ken, 487
Hovey, Chris A., 2995
Hovey, Gary, 3038
Hovey, James W., 65
Hovick, Kevin J., 1264
Hovis, James W., 2566
Howald, Matt, 3707
Howard Sloan Koller Group, Inc., 2183
Howard Trust, Jack R., 3374
Howard, Barbara C., 1165
Howard, Bob, 3356
Howard, Brent T., 4018
Howard, Bruce K., 2608
Howard, Carol, 2351
Howard, Chandler J., 2262
Howard, Charles S., 2508
Howard, Christian, 2206
Howard, D.L., 1788
Howard, Dave, 3601
Howard, David L., 2419
Howard, Jack L., 1718
Howard, Jim, 3457
Howard, John B., Jr., 102
Howard, John D., 46
Howard, John L., 1626
Howard, John W., 730
Howard, Kevin D., 765
Howard, Leslie Ann, 144
Howard, Mike, 3975
Howard, Richard P., 2813
Howard, Robert, 3634
Howard, Robert J., 745
Howard, Sue A., 1335
Howard, W. Kim, 1719
Howard, Waller K., 1719
Howard, William F., III, 432
Howard, William G., Jr., 4137
Howard-Potter, Jack, 3374
Howarth, Ron, 3655
Howatt, Thomas J., 4008
Howe, Dave, 2174
Howe, David H., 3302
Howe, G.M., 2174
Howe, H.R., 2174
Howe, H.T., 2174
Howe, John P., III, 385
Howe, Linda M., 85
Howe, Robert L., 1264
Howe, Robert M., 1130
Howell & Co., F.M., 1874
Howell, David, 2482
Howell, George L, 1874
Howell, George L., 1805, 1874
Howell, Henry W., Jr., 1962
Howell, James A., 2724
Howell, Keith J., 67
Howell, Kendra, 1050
Howell, Mary L., 1323
Howell, Melissa, 1555
Howell, Michael W.D., 4048
Howell, R. Leroy, 470
Howell, Rucker W., 2578
Howell, Samantha, 1719
Howell, Sarah B., 1874
Howell, Terry J., 1468
Howell, William, 415
Howen, Dennis, 991
Hower, Dale E., 2885
Hower, Matthew J., 188
Howey, Gregory B., 3253
Howl, Mike, 1079
Howland, Erin, 335
Howlett, C.A., 3902
Howmedica Osteonics Corp., 1875
Howson, Christopher S., 2698
Hoy, Charles, 3553
Hoy, Matt, 3827
Hoy, William L., 1410
Hoyem, David S., 3867
Hoyer, Thomas, 3563
Hoying, Joyce, 1804
Hoyt, Adam, 1018
Hoyt, Beverley, 1192
Hoyt, Donald A., 2506
Hoyt, James K., 1674
Hoyt, Jeffrey A., 2928
Hoyt, Kathleen C., 2394
Hoyt, Rebecca A., 211
Hoyt, Richard M., 2928
Hoyt, Robert F., 2996, 2997
Hrabowski, Freeman A., III, 332, 2423, 3040
Hrabowski, Jacqueline C., 3040
HRB Management, Inc., 1695
Hrevnack, Linda, 358
Hrizuk, Michael J., 256
Hruby-Mills, Elizabeth, 3206
HS Processing, LP, 1770
HSBC-North America, 3190
Hsia, Liang-Choo, 2969
Hsieh, An-Ping, 1879
Hsieh, Tony, 4153
Hsu, J. Carl, 3253
Hsu, Jonathan K., 3151
Hu, George, 3318
Huang, Claire A., 340
Huang, Jen-Hsun, 2767
Huang, Shauna, 82
Huang, Tao, 246
Hubach, Joseph F., 3728
Hubbard Broadcasting, Inc., 1877
Hubbard Farms, Inc., 1878
Hubbard, Allan B., 3458
Hubbard, David A., 1446
Hubbard, Karen H., 1877
Hubbard, Kenneth E., 492
Hubbard, Michael D., 98
Hubbard, R. Glenn, 2481
Hubbard, Robert Glenn, 291
Hubbard, Robert W., 1877
Hubbard, Samuel T., Jr., 3406
Hubbard, Stanley E., 1877
Hubbard, Stanley S., 1877
Hubbard, Walter W., 1132
Hubbell Inc., 1879
Hubberard, Bob, 644
Hubbert, Arabella, 2465
Hubbert, Charles, 771
Hubenette, Antoinette T., 1275
Huber, Creden W., 3637
Huber, David R., 1863
Huber, Edgar O., 2220
Huber, J. Kendall, 1724
Huber, Jeffrey T., 1242
Huber, Linda S., 2563
Huber, Michael, 2758
Huber, R. James, 2622
Huber, Rita, 2528
Huber, Stephen L., 470
Huber, Ted, 1062
Hubert, C.A. "Buck", 771
Hubex Corp., 3559
Huck, Paul E., 63
Huckabee, M.D., 2010
Huckfeldt, Paul A., 1855
Hudak, Don, 2845

Huddleston, Anita, 2886
Hudgins, Clay, 2171
Hudgins, Ron D., 2201
Hudson City Savings Bank, 1880
Hudson Liquid Asphalts, Inc., 1881
Hudson Neckwear Co., 1882
Hudson River Bank & Trust Co., 1419
Hudson Savings Bank, The, 298
Hudson, Bobby, 894
Hudson, David E., 2573
Hudson, Dawn, 99, 1974, 2209
Hudson, Dawn E., 2312
Hudson, Elizabeth J., 54
Hudson, Hank, 2738
Hudson, J. Clifford, 3498
Hudson, Joe P., 3087
Hudson, John J., 1881
Hudson, John O., III, 71
Hudson, Karen J., 1881
Hudson, Katherine M., 1962
Hudson, Lillian V., 1881
Hudson, Mary R., 10
Hudson, Michael, 491, 2669
Hudson, Michael T., 2669
Hudson, Nancy E., 1881
Hudson, R. Read, 3832
Hudson, Ryan M., 1881
Hudson, Sherrill W., 2250, 3079, 3701
Hudson, Thomas, 1881
Hudson, Thomas F., 1881
Hudson, Thomas J., 1881
Huebner, Fred, 2427
Huebner, Laurie, 1169
Huebner, Paul E., 21
Huebner, Thomas, 499
Huefner, Carl F., 3633
Hueneke, Terry A., 2358
Huey, Bruce E., 756
Huey, Morris Jack, II, 680
Huey, Ralph, 2229
Huey, Sandy, 672
Hufcor, 1883
Hufcor, Inc., 1883
Huff, A. Jackson, 977
Huff, Barry W., 2245
Huff, J.S., 2129
Huff, John R., 2106
Huff, Shawn, 2112
Huff, Thomas T., 774
Huff, William, 3850
Huffenus, Daniel S., 2101
Huffines, James R., 1273
Huffman, Ben, 2113
Huffman, Charmel, 3363
Huffman, David S., 3732, 3735
Huffman, Gary T., 2790
Huffman, Hap, 263
Huffman, Holly, 58
Huffman, John, 126
Huffman, Patrick, 3991
Hufstedler, Don, 166
Huge, Arthur W., 2461
Huggins, Pamela J., 2886
Hugh, Yoon J., 1141
Hughes Electronics Corp., 1124
Hughes, Alan, 497
Hughes, Angela M., 1484
Hughes, Bradley E., 936
Hughes, Brian, 1496, 1687
Hughes, Carla, 1763
Hughes, Carrie C., 3936
Hughes, Chuck, 3940
Hughes, David H., 1032
Hughes, Eileen, 787
Hughes, Frank, 942
Hughes, Frank H., 1640
Hughes, Greg, 279
Hughes, Hattie Hyman, 1496
Hughes, James, 1660
Hughes, John, 127
Hughes, Keith W., 1371
Hughes, Kenneth M., 1133
Hughes, Laura, 3418
Hughes, Michael H., 3306
Hughes, Michael J., 2635
Hughes, Nathaniel F., 942
Hughes, Patricia, 1823
Hughes, Raymond J., 3766
Hughes, Robert, 68
Hughes, Robert H., 2734
Hughes, Shirley, 496
Hughes, Thomas, 1589
Hughey, Kevin, 3205
Hugin, Robert J., 732
Hugley, David, 2632
Hugo-Martinez, Albert J., 2499
Huhndorf, Roy M., 934
Huhndorf, Thomas P., 934
Huisjen, Steve, 3969
Hulan, Henry, 2419
Hulihee, David C., 1405
Hull Storey Gibson Retail Group, 2573
Hull, Anthony E., 3145
Hull, Brett, 1023
Hull, Brian J., 3444
Hull, Gerald W., Jr., 2403
Hull, James, 763
Hull, Richard, 1031
Hull, Robert F., Jr., 2312
Hulman & Co., 1885
Hultquist, Douglas M., 3869
Humana Inc., 1886
Humane Society of the United States, The, 4066
Humann, L. Phillip, 863, 1288
Humble, Susan, 1409
Hume, Alexander J., 4158
Hume, D. William, 2924
Humenesky, Gregory S., 2973
Humer, Franz, 1107
Humer, Franz B., 821
Humes, Mike, 783
Humes, William D., 1941
Humeston, Joseph R., 2704
Humiston, Mary, 220
Huml, Paul J., 3732
Hummel, Albert F., 2776, 4007
Hummel, Dennis, 2376
Humphrey, Andrew, 1324
Humphrey, David, 487
Humphrey, G. Watts, 485
Humphrey, G. Watts, Jr., 485, 807, 4008
Humphrey, James D., 3865
Humphrey, James E., 194, 565
Humphrey, Kurt, 1932
Humphreys, David Craig, 3685
Humphreys, Ethelmae C., 3685
Humphries, Harold E., 166
Humphries, Paul, 1437
Humphries, Scott A., 1575
Huna Totem Corp., 1887
Hund, Thomas N., 618
Hund-Mejean, Martina, 2399, 3072
Hundley, Katherine Moody, 2562
Hundt, Reed E., 1950
Hundzinski, Ronald T., 528
Hunel, Jean-Claude, 236
Hung, John Song Yook, 4114
Hungate, Janelle, 1327
Hunger, C. J., 2758
Hunker, Fred D., 492
Hunkler, Bradley, 4040
Hunnicutt, Susan, 2573
Hunsaker, Jean, 1543
Hunstman, Jon M., Jr., 1895
Hunt Real Estate Corp., 1890
Hunt, B.G., 2759
Hunt, C. Stuart, 1890
Hunt, Charles, 1890
Hunt, Clark, 2091
Hunt, Clark K., 2091
Hunt, David K., 1371
Hunt, Donna Baldwin, 1423
Hunt, Douglas H., 231
Hunt, J. Bryan, Jr., 1892
Hunt, James W., Jr., 501
Hunt, Lamar, Jr., 2091
Hunt, M. Truman, 2759
Hunt, Marsha L., 1007
Hunt, Mary Jo, 1890
Hunt, Peter F., 1890
Hunt, Ray L., 1889, 2935
Hunt, Robert G., 1888
Hunt, Ronald F., 3478
Hunt, Timothy D., 999
Hunt, Timothy J., 3317
Hunt, W. M., 2711
Hunt, William R., 3545
Hunt, Zita, 117
Hunter Douglas, Inc., 1893
Hunter Roberts Construction, 136
Hunter, Beecher, 2267
Hunter, Conrad J., 2758
Hunter, G. William, 2624
Hunter, Heather, 3327
Hunter, J. Philip, 1729
Hunter, James, 2621
Hunter, Jennifer L., 120
Hunter, John C., III, 1271
Hunter, Kelli A., 174
Hunter, Kimberly A., 1942
Hunter, Larry D., 1124
Hunter, Laura B., 2776
Hunter, M. Scott, 1112
Hunter, Randy, 939
Hunter, Robert D., 118
Hunter, Scott D., 1845
Hunter, Steven L., 3572
Hunter, Tammy, 2190
Hunter, Tony, 788
Hunter, William C., 4026
Hunter, William Curt, 4136
Hunting, George L., Jr., 332
Hunting, Mary Anne, 3597
Huntington Bancshares Inc., 847, 1894
Huntington Bank, 1662
Huntington National Bank, 1662
Huntington National Bank, The, 1894
Huntington, Mike, 1956
Huntsman, Jon M., 1895
Huntsman, Jon M., Jr., 722, 1464
Huntsman, Peter R., 1895
Hupe, Roger L., 3275
Hupf, Cindy, 521
Hupprich, William R., 76
Hurand, Gary J., 827
Hurd, Jeffrey, 156
Hurd, Jeffrey J., 156
Hurd, Mark V., 2821
Huret, Robert A., 342
Hurley, Christa, 1203
Hurley, David, 1077
Hurley, Elizabeth M., 590
Hurley, Lori, 2279
Hurley, Maureen O., 3204
Hurley, Scott W., 3859
Hurley, Todd, 1421
Hurst, Robert J., 3913
Hurst, Rusty, 2673
Hurston, Karl A., 1624
Hurtley, Kathryn, 1887
Huseby, Michael, 765
Huseby, Michael P., 360
Huseby, Richard A., 806
Huss, Michael, 2606
Hussa, Benjamin M., 63
Hussey, Jeff, 3084
Hussey, Kent J., 170, 1519
Hussey, Richard W., Jr., 250
Hussey, Thomas H., 250
Hustad, Paul A., 424
Husted, Daniel, 2213
Huston, Eldon E., 4026
Huston, Mike, 1409
Hutchens, David G., 3819
Hutcheson, Jennifer, 3294
Hutchins, Bruce, 71
Hutchins, Glenn, 352
Hutchins, Glenn H., 2617
Hutchins, Priscilla, 71
Hutchinso, John L., 393
Hutchinson, David, 2467
Hutchinson, Howard G., 272
Hutchinson, John L., 393
Hutchinson, Rowland, 4054
Hutchinson, William R., 261
Hutchison Supply Co., 1898
Hutchison, Curtis R., 1898
Hutchison, Dian D., 1898
Hutchison, Mary, 2418
Hutchison, Michele, 434
Hutchison, Rick, 1834
Hutchison, William M., 1898
Hutson, Nancy J., 999, 1268
Hutson, Robert, 1023
Hutson, Tracey A., 4041
Hutt, Harry, 737
Hutta, Jane, 3480
Huttle, Frank, III, 114
Hutton Financial Advisors, 1899
Hutton, Gloria, 1899
Hutton, Thomas C., 773
Hutton, Tim, 1899
Hutton, Timothy, 1899
Hutton, William L., 3179
Huvane, Kevin S., 17
Huwaldt, Mary J., 246
Huzi, James, 1776
Hwang, Ben, 2268
Hwang, Jennie S., 1366
Hwee, Koh Boon, 56
Hy-Vee Food Stores, Inc., 1900
Hy-Vee, Inc., 1900
Hyatt Regency Chicago, 1634
Hyatt Regency McCormick Place, 1634
Hyatt, Lawrence E., 966
Hyatt, Max, 72
Hyatt, Michael, 1268
Hyatt, Wilbur A., 3316
Hyde Manufacturing Co., 1103
Hyde, Barbara, 1857
Hyde, J. R., III, 1857
Hyde, J.R., III, 294
Hyde, James A., 2758
Hyde, James S., 2758

Ishmael, Jeffrey, 3108
Ishrak, Omar, 2453
ISI International, 1858
Islamic Mission and Mosque, Inc., 303
Island Insurance Co., Ltd., 1996
Islands Fund, 624
Isler, Jonathan David, 1062
Isley, Brett, 179
Isom, Janis, 2122
Isom, Robert D., Jr., 3902
Issa Properties, 1997
Issa, Abdulaziz M., 1997
Issa, Anwar M., 1997
Issa, Mohammad, 1997
Issa, Mohammad M., 1997
Issa, Raed, 1997
Issa, Said, 1997
Issac, John, 2462
Istock, Verna G., 2393
Istock, Verne G., 2393, 3246
ITA Group Inc., 1998
Itani, Khalil, 3796
Itani, Samir, 2326
Itaya, Danessa, 2548
ITO EN, 4066
Ito, Joichi, 2690
Ito, Katsuhiro, 2539
Ito, Paul K., 85
Itokazu, John, 3854
ITT Industries, Inc., 1999
ITT Rayonier Inc., 3134
ITT Sheraton Corp., 3589
Ivanoff, Henry, 422
Ivanoff, Janis, 1586
Ivanoff, Stephen, 422
Ivascyn, Daniel W., 4017
Iverson, Ann, 2842
Iverson, Dave, 3940
Iveson, Karen B., 3184
Ivey, Craig S., 916
Ivey, G. Rouse, 3515
Ivey, Gilbert F., 2484
Ivey, James T., 2537
Ivins, Anthony R., 3104
Ivy, Gladys, 939
Iwamura, Tetsuo, 150
Iwashita, Fumio, 3631
Iwata, Hidenobu, 1851
Iwata, John C., 1960
Iwata, Jon C., 1960
Iwo Jima, Inc., 2003
Iyer, Balakrishnan S., 2268
Izatt, Troy, 3751
Izzo, Louis, 1890
Izzo, Ralph, 3077

J&M Holdings, Inc., 3056
J&S Construction Co., Inc, 135
J&S Precision Products Co., Inc., 2004
J-M Manufacturing Co., Inc., 2005
J.D. Posillico, Inc., 3014
J.F.W., Inc., 2043
Jack Carley, 872
Jack in the Box Inc., 2007
Jack, Ernest, 1887
Jackie, Joelle, 3585
Jackman, Dennis, 993
Jackman, Jonathan, 2663
Jackon, Gianna S., 812
Jacks, Tyler, 182, 3733
Jackson Iron & Metal Company, Inc., 2008
Jackson Paper Co., 2010
Jackson, Alexander, 3243
Jackson, Ann Rockler, 3243
Jackson, Barbara, 409
Jackson, C. Marshall, 306
Jackson, Carol M., 761
Jackson, Cathy, 1973
Jackson, Clarence, 3380
Jackson, Clarence, Sr., 3380
Jackson, Danny W., 4078
Jackson, Darren R., 39
Jackson, Deborah C., 1209
Jackson, Deborah J., 1207
Jackson, Denise L., 184
Jackson, Derek, 2491
Jackson, Dominick, 3848
Jackson, Douglas J., 3171
Jackson, Elizabeth, 335, 3243
Jackson, Gary, 957
Jackson, Gayle P.W., 128
Jackson, Guy C., 2269
Jackson, James C., 1532
Jackson, Jeanne P., 2427
Jackson, Jeffrey W., 3591
Jackson, Jimmy S., 2956
Jackson, John, 1527
Jackson, Judy S., 1210
Jackson, Kenneth G., 3426
Jackson, Laban P., Jr., 2071
Jackson, Laura, 1970
Jackson, Lawrence V., 266, 2887
Jackson, Lolita, 1567
Jackson, Louise, 1277
Jackson, Marianne, 655
Jackson, Mark, 1748
Jackson, Mark H., 1163
Jackson, Michael, 3893
Jackson, Michael J., 292
Jackson, Mozelle, 724
Jackson, Renee, 1140
Jackson, Robert M., 953
Jackson, Russell M., 3310
Jackson, Scott, 2250
Jackson, Sharon, 3544
Jackson, Shirley Ann, 1352, 1382, 1960, 2364, 2453, 3077
Jackson, Sonya Y., 3860
Jackson, Steve, 957
Jackson, Thomas W., 3251
Jackson, Tracy D., 3723
Jackson, Victoria Bridges, 2473
Jackson, Wes, 3880
Jackson, William C., 2050
Jackson, William W., 2506
Jackson, Yvonne R., 3535, 4087
Jackson-Shaw Company, 2013
Jacksonville Jaguars, Ltd., 2014
Jacksonville Savings Bank, N.A., 541
Jaclyn, Inc., 2015
Jacob, Bernard, 1689
Jacob, Beth M., 3691
Jacob, Kelly, 3053
Jacob, Kenneth, 652
Jacob, Linda, 2189
Jacob, P. Bernard, 1689
Jacob, Ravi, 1950
Jacob, Tom, 3190
Jacobi, Herbert H., 3520
Jacobi, Peter, 984, 3664
Jacobs Engineering Group Inc., 2016
Jacobs, Charlie, 537
Jacobs, Douglas C., 846
Jacobs, Electra, 1683
Jacobs, Howard, 2192
Jacobs, Janice, 788
Jacobs, Jeremy M., 1066
Jacobs, Jeremy M., Sr., 537
Jacobs, Julie, 209
Jacobs, Kim, 3181
Jacobs, Leonard, 910
Jacobs, M. Christine, 2434
Jacobs, Margaret, 3181
Jacobs, Mark M., 1563
Jacobs, Mary T., 1797
Jacobs, Paul E., 3095
Jacobs, Seth A., 655
Jacobs-Pratt, Vicki, 993
Jacobsen, Brian, 3781
Jacobsen, Dick, 84
Jacobsen, Jean, 2781
Jacobson, Anne, 1855
Jacobson, Craig A., 765, 1311
Jacobson, Jed J., 1078
Jacobson, Joyce, 272
Jacobson, Lyle G., 1797
Jacobson, Lynn, 615
Jacobson, Michael R., 1217
Jacobson, Mitchell, 2593
Jacobson, Nelson C., 2073
Jacobson, Paul, 1073
Jacobson, Rochelle M., 2472
Jacobson, Timothy, 2451
Jacquemin, John M., 2923
Jacquot, Mark, 2251, 2319
Jacuk, Katrina M., 934
Jadin, Ronald L., 1626
Jaedicke, Robert K., 637
Jaeger, Joseph, 2858
Jaeger, Kathleen, 2622
Jaehnert, Frank M., 552, 2723
Jaffe, David B., 1682
Jaffe, David R., 255
Jaffe, Elliot S., 255
Jaffe, Howard, 1582
Jaffe, Jon, 2250
Jaffe, Jonathan M., 2250
Jaffe, Pamela F., 2448
Jaffe, Roslyn E., 255
Jaffe, Roslyn S., 255
Jaffe, Seth, 4079
Jaffee, Elliot, 3835
Jaffee, Randy, 511
Jaffenagler, Alissa, 2753
Jaffy, Stanley A., 407
Jagger, Norman L., 1828
Jagiela, Mark E., 3718
Jahn, Greg, 1306
Jahne, John, 3344
Jahnel, Ferdinand, 3348
Jahner, Floyd, 1021
Jahnigen, Timothy, 2812
Jai Ma Creation Inc., 2017
Jain, Anshu, 1099
Jain, Dipak C., 1061, 2740
Jain, Elizabeth, 1469
Jain, Naveen K., 1951
Jaison, Susan, 2491
Jakins, E.A., 72
Jakobs, Nancy, 2822
Jakobsen, Peter Kasper, 2443
Jakobsson, Sten E., 4139
Jaksich, Daniel J., 429
Jaksich, Mark C., 3919
Jakubek, John, 1120
Jalapeno Corp., 2018
Jalosinski, Shawn, 888
JAM Securities Corp., 2019
Jamar, Thomas D., 3394
Jameel, Hasan, 2861
Jamerson, Hank, 2201
James, Alan W., 3081
James, Chuck, 3820
James, Don, 2712
James, Donald A., 1732
James, Donald M., 3516, 3972, 4028
James, Donna A., 2365, 3755
James, Donna Anita, 2277
James, Hamilton E., 477, 948
James, Harry, 2852
James, Jim, 1908
James, Juanita, 2984
James, Julie, 2979
James, Kay Coles, 171, 2996, 2997
James, Keryn, 1292
James, Laurens I., 823
James, Laurens I., Jr., 823
James, Lee Lee, 3674
James, Mark R., 1852
James, Marq, 1687
James, Phyllis, 1629
James, Renee J., 2417
James, Renne J., 2417
James, Ron, 3802
James, Ronald, 442
James, Stephan A., 508, 1371
James, Susan, 4140
James, Susan M., 220
James, Thomas A., 2021
James, Wilbert W., Jr., 3786
James, William E., 2907
James, William R., 3171
James-Brown, Christine, 2958
Jamieson, Adele, 2427
Jamieson, Jonathan M., 2742
Jamieson, Thomas J., 437
Jamil, Dhiaa M., 1189
Jamison, Greg, 3327
Jamison, Latrisha, 3171
Janatka, Lucille, 2645
Jancsy, Dennis, 2448
Jandahl, Keith E., 1749
Jandernoa, Michael J., 2943
Janet, Chiodi, 2234
Janeway, Dean, 2135
Janeway, William H., 3985
Janezic, Donald, 462
Jang, G. David, 540
Jankowski, Edward F., 3242
Jankowski, Tim, 3961
Jankowski, Timothy, 3961
Jankun, Richard P., 3936
Janney, Eric, 772
Janney, Stuart S., 485
Janning, James C., 2461
Jannotta, Edgar, 478
Jannotta, Edgar D., 210, 478
Janow, Merit E., 2618
JanPak, Inc., 2022
Jansen Foundation, Eleanor and Henry, 2320
Jansen, Han, 3193
Jansen, James H., 2320
Jansen, Jill, 2320
Jansen, Larry, 1668
Jansen, Mark D., 506
Janssen Pharmaceutica Inc., 2048
Janssen, Barbara, 2004
Janssen, David, 2004
Janssen, Steven, 2004
Jansson, Mats, 1458
Jantzen, Daniel P., 2394
Janus Capital Corp., 2024
Janus Capital Management LLC, 2024

Johnson, Felicia, 2716
Johnson, Frances H., 1768
Johnson, Gary M., 2330
Johnson, Gary R., 215
Johnson, Glenn S., 1861
Johnson, Gordon L., 2021
Johnson, Gordon W., Jr., 3625
Johnson, Gregory A. A., 2068
Johnson, Gregory E., 1487
Johnson, H. Fisk, 2049
Johnson, H. Fisk, III, 2049
Johnson, Hugh A., 2681
Johnson, Imogene Powers, 2049
Johnson, J., 1136
Johnson, J. Allen, 2344
Johnson, J. Thomas, 823
Johnson, Jacob, 3033
Johnson, James A., 1603, 1604, 3691
Johnson, James A., III, 700
Johnson, James C., 128, 777, 1720
Johnson, James J., 816
Johnson, Jana M., 2197
Johnson, Janissa, 2184
Johnson, Jeffrey, 2052
Johnson, Jeffrey B., 470
Johnson, Jeffrey M., 680
Johnson, Jennifer, 2053
Johnson, Jennifer M., 1487
Johnson, Jesse R., 671
Johnson, Jim, 1011, 1586
Johnson, Joanne, 1768
Johnson, Joe, 885
Johnson, Joel W., 1220, 2471, 3835
Johnson, Joia M., 1720
Johnson, Joseph B., 795
Johnson, Judith H., 1768
Johnson, Judy, 2505
Johnson, Julia L., 1424, 2748
Johnson, Justin, 131
Johnson, Kadant, 2083
Johnson, Kadant, Inc., 2083
Johnson, Kathleen C., 561
Johnson, Kathryn H., 1768
Johnson, Kathryn O., 2836
Johnson, Kathy, 552
Johnson, Keith, 1374
Johnson, Keith A., 1374
Johnson, Kenlon P., 504
Johnson, Kenneth S., 337
Johnson, Kevin, 2075, 3585
Johnson, Kirk, 3347
Johnson, Kirsten, 4033
Johnson, Kris, 2392
Johnson, Kristen A., 3245
Johnson, Kristina, 47
Johnson, Kristina M., 540, 818
Johnson, L. Robert, 4038
Johnson, LaVon, 776
Johnson, Lea, 3721
Johnson, Leon, 3721
Johnson, Lillian F., 2088
Johnson, Loretta, 671
Johnson, Loretta A., 671
Johnson, Margy K., 1415
Johnson, Marianne Boyd, 546
Johnson, Mark E., 561
Johnson, Mark J., 3672
Johnson, Mark L., 1472
Johnson, Marlene, 1887, 3380
Johnson, Matthew J., 671
Johnson, Matthew N., 1559
Johnson, Melinda, 2073
Johnson, Melinda E., 2073
Johnson, Mercedes, 2075, 2500
Johnson, Michael, 44, 2557
Johnson, Michael A., 777
Johnson, Michael O., 3331
Johnson, Michael P., 738
Johnson, Michael R., 962
Johnson, Miriam, 671
Johnson, Norman E., 832, 966
Johnson, Paula, 2965
Johnson, Paula A., 4038
Johnson, Philip H., 2323
Johnson, R. Milton, 1762
Johnson, Ralph, 823
Johnson, Ralph W., 823
Johnson, Ray A, 676
Johnson, Richard ("Rick"), 1817
Johnson, Richard A., 1459, 3840
Johnson, Richard E., 313
Johnson, Richard J., 2996, 2997
Johnson, Richard L., Jr., 2053
Johnson, Rick, 1832, 2941
Johnson, Rick L., 935, 2940
Johnson, Robbin S., 691
Johnson, Robert B., 54
Johnson, Robert L., 2105, 2312
Johnson, Robert Wood, IV, 2687
Johnson, Rolley, Dr., 3147
Johnson, Ronald, 2925
Johnson, Roz, 140
Johnson, Rupert H., Jr., 1487
Johnson, Ruth W., 2053
Johnson, Sally S., 254
Johnson, Scott W., 671
Johnson, Sean, 1549
Johnson, Sephen L., 1634
Johnson, Sharisse, 2330
Johnson, Sharisse L., 2330
Johnson, Sheila C., 2280
Johnson, Spencer, 502
Johnson, Spencer C., 502
Johnson, Stephen C., 2330
Johnson, Stephen L., 3372
Johnson, Steve, 1153
Johnson, Steven P., 3944
Johnson, Suzanne Nora, 1982, 2950
Johnson, Thomas H., 863, 1563
Johnson, Thomas P., 46
Johnson, Thomas S., 1155
Johnson, Timothy A., 460
Johnson, Timothy D., 756
Johnson, Timothy E., 2051
Johnson, Todd, 1227
Johnson, Tommy, 823
Johnson, Tracy, 92, 1382
Johnson, Tyler W., 935
Johnson, V. S., III, 73
Johnson, V.S., III, 73
Johnson, Van R., 1275
Johnson, Vicki Olson, 1409
Johnson, Victor S., III, 73
Johnson, Victoria R., 2330
Johnson, Vince, 72
Johnson, William D., 1189
Johnson, William P., 169
Johnson, William R., 1257, 2312, 3872
Johnson, William S., 3293
Johnson-Leipold, Helen, 2049
Johnson-Leipold, Helen P., 1130, 2049
Johnson-Leipold, Helen P., III, 1130
JohnsonDiversey, Inc., 2049
Johnsong, Christine, 3800
Johnsons, Kris, 2392
Johnsrud, David, 802
Johnston, David, 4009
Johnston, Gretchen, 2386
Johnston, Gretchen M., 2386
Johnston, Hugh F., 209, 2935, 3094
Johnston, Jack W., 2719
Johnston, James W., 3382, 3492
Johnston, Janet, 1745
Johnston, Julie A., 1180
Johnston, Lee, 1829
Johnston, Linda A., 428
Johnston, Michael F., 246, 1447, 4056
Johnston, Pat, 1766
Johnston, Philip W., 501
Johnston, Robert, 1044, 4092
Johnston, Stephen P., 3299
Johnston, Tom, 2171
Johnston, Vance C., 1519
Johnston, Verna Lee, 4028
Johnstone, Tom, 3473
Johri, Rajive, 904
Johst, David, 764
Joiner, Stephen N., 3263
Joines, Barbara, 1146
Jolibois, Marcus, 3240
Jolibois, Marcus P., 3240
Jolliffe, Lynn, 1941
Jollivette, Cyrus M. "Russ", 493
Jolloff Investments, Inc., 2379
Jolloff, Timothy C., 2379
Jollon, Katherine, 1604
Jolly, Jacqueline A., 3584
Jolly, Linda E., 945
Jolly, Molly Taylor, 200
Jolly, Paul, 2945
Joly, Hubert, 442, 3123
Jonas, Howard S., 1910
Jonas, Jeffery, 590
Jonas, Samuel, 1910
Jones & Co. Inc., R.A., 2056
Jones & Co., Edward D., L.P., 2055
Jones Apparel Group, Inc., 3123
Jones Fixture Co., J.R., 2060
Jones Soda, 30
Jones, Abigail L., 3104
Jones, Adam B., 2060
Jones, Adrian, 466
Jones, Adrian M., 1143
Jones, Alice P., 332
Jones, Allen W., 3861
Jones, Allen, Jr., 4074
Jones, Anita K., 3311
Jones, Ashley E., 2060
Jones, Barbara, 3788
Jones, Barry, 2201
Jones, Bill, 569, 2771
Jones, Bobby, 690
Jones, C. Todd, 886
Jones, Caren, 2344
Jones, Cedric, 3978
Jones, Charles E., 1424
Jones, Charles M., 1668
Jones, Charles W., 2771
Jones, Christopher, 398
Jones, Clayton M., 685, 1061, 3247
Jones, Craig B., 953
Jones, Curt D., 1122
Jones, Dale E., 2181, 2749
Jones, Damon T., 3998
Jones, Daniel, 1280
Jones, Daniel E., 2291
Jones, Daphne E., 1867
Jones, Daryl, 72
Jones, Dave, 2129
Jones, David, 743, 1601, 1873, 3999
Jones, David A., 1601, 1886, 2926
Jones, David A., Jr., 1886
Jones, David N., 1873
Jones, Deanna L., 2695
Jones, Donna D., 2291
Jones, Douglas J., 2060
Jones, Douglas M., 4106
Jones, Douglas R., 226
Jones, Earl, 645
Jones, Eli, 1944
Jones, Eric, 2060
Jones, Eric N., 2060
Jones, Ernie, 4028
Jones, Evon, 1376
Jones, Frank W., 3297
Jones, Frankie T., Sr., 2971
Jones, Fred, Jr., 1857
Jones, Gareth, 3822
Jones, Gladys, 2615
Jones, Glendell, Jr., Dr., 3514
Jones, Graham O., 3916
Jones, Greg C., 166
Jones, Hal S., Jr., 3999
Jones, Hannah, 2710
Jones, Harvey C., 2767
Jones, Helen, 409
Jones, Ingrid Saunders, 862
Jones, Isobel A., 2916
Jones, J. Thomas, 231
Jones, James, 2624
Jones, Jan, 650
Jones, Jana L., 3758
Jones, Jeanette, 1122, 3584
Jones, Jeffrey D., 3964
Jones, Jerral W., 1022
Jones, Jerral W., Jr., 1022
Jones, Jerry, 1022
Jones, John P., III, 291, 3650
Jones, John Stephen, 1022
Jones, John T., 4032
Jones, Judith, 48
Jones, Kathleen E., 2928
Jones, Kay, 1122
Jones, Kevin, 2344
Jones, Kevin J., 1927, 3242
Jones, Kim, 516
Jones, Kyle R., 898
Jones, Leslie A., 1089
Jones, Louis E., 2291
Jones, Lucius S., 1396
Jones, Mark, 378
Jones, Martha E., 1053
Jones, Mary K. W., 1061
Jones, Mary Sanders, 3857
Jones, Matt, 260
Jones, Matthew, 4064
Jones, Maurice D., 2355, 2356
Jones, Michael, 162
Jones, Michael J., 1946, 2232
Jones, Nancy E., 3317
Jones, Nicole S., 812
Jones, Patricia L., 380
Jones, Paul J., 1732
Jones, Paul W., 3484
Jones, Randall T., Sr., 3079
Jones, Raymond E., 3431
Jones, Rene F., 2323
Jones, Robert G., 231, 2798, 3925
Jones, Robert R., III, 3861
Jones, Ronald, 4064
Jones, Roy, 3978
Jones, Scott, 1080
Jones, Scott O., 1080
Jones, Sharon, 2108
Jones, Shelley, 4046
Jones, Shirley, 103

Jones, Sid, 1846
Jones, Stephen, 1022
Jones, Steve, 1304
Jones, Susan Short, 1762
Jones, Thomas N., 3893
Jones, Thomas W., 120
Jones, Tina, Sr., 646
Jones, Tom B., 1668
Jones, Tony (William H.), 1419
Jones, Tony, Jr., 2615
Jones, Tracey, 1122
Jones, Tracy, 1122
Jones, Trevor M., 99
Jones, Troy, 2078
Jones, Victoria, 852
Jones, W. Paul, 871, 3440
Jones, W. Wesley, 1568
Jones, W. Wilson, 3263
Jones, Walter A., 2656
Jones, Walter H., III, 3916
Jones, Wellington D., III, 2
Jones, William D., 3405
Jones, William H., 861
Jones, Wilson R., 2833
Jones, Zona, 3189
Jones-Walker, Delta F., 2344
Joo, Douglas, 2701
Joos, Ann, 591
Joos, David W., 42, 854, 921, 3597
Joos, Mark, 1687
Joppa, Sandra N., 1153
Jordache Enterprises, Inc., 2062
Jordache Ltd., 2062
Jordan Co., W.M., Inc., 2063
Jordan, D. Bryan, 1406
Jordan, Gregory B., 3163
Jordan, J. Craig, 3025
Jordan, J. Richard, 1957
Jordan, John, 891, 3817
Jordan, Joseph, 24
Jordan, Judy, 3065
Jordan, Michael, 512
Jordan, Patrick C., 2332
Jordan, Raymond C., 2048
Jordan, Robert E., 1909
Jordan, Tabitha, 58
Jordan, Vernon E., Jr., 143
Jordan-Kitt Music, Inc., 2064
Jording, Donald J., 1423
Jording, Michael, 1423
Jordon, Robert E., 1909
Jorge, Bob, 1602
Jorgensen Association, Roy, Inc., 2065
Jorgensen, Blake, 1242, 3624
Jorgensen, Cindy, 3523
Jorgensen, John J., 1657
Jorgensen, John S., 2065
Jorgensen, John S., Jr., 2065
Jorgensen, John S., Sr., 2065
Jorgensen, Tony E., 910
Jorgenson, G. Robert, 3297
Jornayvaz, Louisa, 1980
Jornayvaz, Louisa Craft, 1980
Jornayvaz, Robert, 1980
Jornayvaz, Robert P., III, 1980
Jorndt, L. Daniel, 3981
Josef, Ellyn, 3957
Josefowicz, Gregory, 3815
Josefowicz, Gregory P., 2948, 3272, 3876, 4087
Joseph, Cari, 1269
Joseph, Charles S., 493
Joseph, Edgar S., 2363
Joseph, Pamela A., 735, 2904
Josephs, Robin, 2991
Josephson, J., Inc., 2066
Joskow, Paul L., 1309
Joslyn Corp., 1027
Joss, Bob, 395
Joss, Robert L., 637, 821
Josse, Carmen, 1266
Jossi, Mike, 3708
Jostens, Inc., 2067
Joubert, Tracey, 2523
Joubran, David V., 33
Joubran, John, 3124
Joubran, Robert J., 3293
Joung, Chansoo, 211
Journal-Gazette Co., 2068
Jovi, Bon, 53
Jovon Broadcasting Corporation, 2069
Joy Global Inc., 2070
Joy, James, 613
Joy, Jean M., 4102
Joyal, Robert E., 2030
Joyce, Ann E., 46
Joyce, Bob, 2894
Joyce, Burton M., 2725
Joyce, Eugene, 3822
Joyce, Michael J., 91
Joyce, R. Todd, 4007
Joyce, Robert J., 4047
Joyce, Stephen P., 798, 1120
Joyce, Tom, 397
Joyner Becker, John, 2757
Joynor, Mike, 121
JP Morgan Chase, 624
JP Morgan Chase Foundation, 1538
JPMorgan Chase, 2684
JPMorgan Chase Bank, N.A., 421, 770, 1088, 1214, 1323, 2071, 2072, 2189, 3825, 3982
JSJ Corp., 2073
JTB Americas, Ltd., 2074
Juang, Charlie, 3762
Judas, Susanne, 1834
Juday, Dave, 1908
Juday, David W., 1908
Juday, Nancy, 1908
Juday, Patricia, 1908
Juday, Sally, 1908
Judd, Richard, 389
Judd, Troy, 3918
Judd, Virginia K., 1886
Judelson, Robert, 790
Judelson, Robert A., 785
Judge, Ann Powell, 578
Judge, James J., 2737
Judice, Kevin, 2765, 3076
Judkins, Peter, 1488
Judkins, Peter L., 1488
Juergens, Eric, 2104
Juergens, Ron, 1986
Juhlke, David P., 1866
Jukoski, Mary Ellen, 772
Julian, Janis, 4127
Julian, Paul C., 2434, 2622
Juliano, Robert, 412
Juliber, Lois D., 1184, 2556
Julien, Aaron D., 2702
Julien, Jeffrey P., 2021
Julien, Michael, 569
Julius, Adam, 3940
Julius, DeAnne, 2061
Jum'ah, Abdallah S., 1706
Jumper, John P., 3311
Junck, Mary E., 2241
Junek, John C., 174
Jung, Andrea, 217, 1552
Jung, Patrick J., 616
Jung, Simon, 3102
Jungels, Pierre H., 324
Junger, Ellen, 1707
Jungers, Mary Blanche, 891
Jungmann, Charles, 3183
Junkerman, Harry, 1122
Juno Healthcare Staffing, 2076
Junqueiro, Steve, 3342
Jurcic, James T., 1142
Jurcuvic, Goran, 1078
Jureller, John M., 1508
Jurgens, Richard N., 1900
Jurgensen, William G., 904
Jurgensmeyer, Charles, 2669
Juris, Leslie Nathanson, 176
Jurkovic, Goran, 1078
Jury, Victor R., Jr., 3641
Jussen, Robert C., 2681
Juster, Andrew A., 3458
Juster, Andy, 3458
Justice, William J., 3861
Justino, Jose Antonio, 2048
Juszkiewicz, Henry, 1578
Juszkiewicz, Henry E., 1578
Jutagir, Hattie K., `, 2381
Juusela, Jyrki, 2839
JWG Equipment Assocs., 1229

K N Energy, Inc., 2153
K-B Farms, Inc., 2081
K-Swiss Inc., 2082
Kabat, Donald J., 3348
Kabat, Kevin T., 1377, 3898
Kabbes, David G., 612
Kabel, Mary Ann, 4115
Kacer, Jim, 1723
Kachhia, Vipul, 1237
Kachmer, Michael J., 2356
Kachner, Michael J., 2356
Kackley, James R., 2517
Kaczka, Jeffrey, 2593
Kaczmarek, Kenneth, 3534
Kadambi, Vasu, 654
Kaden, Ellen Oran, 669
Kaden, Lewis B., 821
Kadenancy, Stephen M., 42
Kadia, Siddhartha, 2268
Kadic, Alan, 3081
Kadien, Thomas G., 3437
Kadoya, Tetsuo, 3776
Kaebnick, Julie H., 1745
Kaelin, William G., 2274
Kaerney, Daniel P., 2416
Kaesgen, Hartmut, 2595
Kaganoff, Moshe, 1910
Kagawa, Mirei, 3900
Kagay, Barry, 2486
Kahan, Bob, 30
Kahan, James S., 1508
Kahan, Marc, 1655
Kahl, Henry V., 331
Kahle, Gene, 3690
Kahle, John H., 2149
Kahler, Cynthia W., 3976
Kahler, Nancy, 2653
Kahn Construction Co., M.B., Inc., 2084
Kahn, Alan B., 2084
Kahn, Andrew, 2085
Kahn, Andrew L., 2085
Kahn, Gary, 1418
Kahn, Gary S., 1418
Kahn, Howard, 2085
Kahn, Jane B., 1418
Kahn, Peggy Anne, 2085
Kahn, Thomas Graham, 3070
Kahn, Todd, 858
Kahn-Lucas-Lancaster, Inc., 2085
Kahr, Julia, 1134
Kahrs, Kenneth L., 2649
Kahului Trucking and Storage, 85
Kailian, Vaughn M., 752
Kain, Robert L., 1162
Kain, Tucker, 2305
Kairey, Martin, 3313
Kaiser, Gerald J., 2335
Kaiser, James G., 2445, 3650
Kaiser, Kim J., 2086
Kaiser, Steve, 2133
Kaissar, Tal S., 156
Kaji, Gautam S., 642
Kajima International, Inc., 2087
Kakaty, Joe, 1234
Kalama, Corbett A.K., 1405
Kalantzis, Peter, 856
Kalathur, Rajesh, 1061
Kalawaski, Eva M., 3293
Kalawski, Eva M., 1095
Kaldas, Sally, 3343
Kaleak, George T., Sr., 234
Kalec, John J., 841
Kaleta, Paul J., 2765
Kalia, Kumud, 68
Kalil, Charles J., 1160, 1161
Kalinauskas, Brooke, 906
Kalinsky, Greg, 1621
Kalis, Todd, 3052
Kallander, Scott, 2581
Kallembach, Larry J., 2415
Kallery, Raichelle L., 3343
Kallet, Michael R., 2814
Kallgren, Pete, 3268
Kallick, Blackman, 1219
Kalman, Francis S., 2424
Kalmanson, Steven R., 3246
Kalnow, Andrew H., 2634
Kaloski, John F., 67
Kaltenbacher, Philip D., 3415
Kalvin, Greggory, 1120
Kalyani, Baba, 3473
Kam, Johnson, 2202
Kam, Kwock Yum, 2202
Kamali, Edmond, 1230
Kamali, Simone, 1230
Kamataris, Thomas, 2380
Kambeitz, Stephen J., 2881
Kamenetzky, David, 2384
Kamens, Matthew H., 2057
Kamensky, John, 1960
Kamer, Christopher, 3743
Kamer, Christopher R., 3743
Kamer, Joseph M., 2098, 3596
Kamerick, Anthony J., 3018
Kamerick, Eileen A., 261
Kameroff, Wassilie, 2200
Kamerschen, Robert, 3683
Kamerschen, Robert W., 1288
Kamil, Charles A., III, 4074
Kamin, John R., 2798
Kamins, Philip E., 2994
Kaminski, Jeff, 2105
Kaminski, Paul G., 1551
Kamlet, Mark S., 1799
Kammann, Gina, 2575
Kamon, Mark S., 1200
Kampfe, John, 3823

Kampling, Hermann, 3415
Kampling, Patricia L., 104, 565, 4095
Kampling, Patricia Leonard, 104
Kampouri-Monnas, Giovanna, 221
Kampouris, Emmanuel A., 1863
Kamsky, Virginia A., 1026
Kanai, Shingo, 1562
Kanaly Family Trust, 2089
Kanaly Trust Co. Inc., 2089
Kanaly, Andrew D., 2089
Kanaly, Drew, 2089
Kanaly, E. Deane, 2089
Kanaly, Jeffrey C., 2089
Kanaly, Steven P., 2089
Kanaly, Virginia L., 2089
Kanan, Michael, 3453
Kandarian, Steven A., 2481
Kane, Chad D., 4108
Kane, Cindy, 1736
Kane, David, 279
Kane, Deborah N., 4108
Kane, Dennis, 4134
Kane, Duncan, 3776
Kane, Edward J., 1894
Kane, Edward K., 1683
Kane, Jacqueline P., 852, 889
Kane, James F., 7
Kane, Kelly, 798
Kane, Linda, 1467
Kane, Linda M., 1467
Kane, Marion, 1083
Kane, Michael T., 1197
Kane, Patrick J., 1287
Kane, Robert, 1419
Kane, Steven E., 1197
Kane, Thomas B., 910
Kane, Tom, 246
Kane, William J., 3802
Kaneb, Gary R., 1854
Kaneb, John A., 1854
Kanemoto, Noele, 3189
Kaneti, Lubomir, 1522
Kang, Alvin D., 386
Kang, Donald B.S., 1811
Kang, Jan, 1009
Kangas, Edward A., 1982, 3713, 3882
Kangas, Paul, 3765
Kaniecki, Craig J., 3577
Kaniewski, James, 3736
Kaniewski, James S., 3736
Kann Sons Co., S., 2090
Kann, Gertrude, 2090
Kann, Sol, 2090
Kanofsky, Gordon R., 176
Kanovsky, Michael M., 1102
Kansas City Chiefs Football Club, Inc., 2091
Kanter, Allen, 2502
Kanter, Allen L., 2502
Kantor, Barbara, 3926
Kantor, Gregg S., 2747
Kantor, Jonathan D., 855
Kantor, Michael, 725
Kantrow, Byron, Jr., 977
Kany, A. William, Jr., 3302
Kanzelberger, Jeffrey, 3061
Kao, John, 689
Kao, Peter J., 4080
Kaouris, Demetrois G., 2512
Kaplan, Dan, 2958
Kaplan, Gilla, 732
Kaplan, Ira D., 1519
Kaplan, Jeff, 2677
Kaplan, Karen, 551, 1083, 1803
Kaplan, Kerri, 641
Kaplan, Lawrence H., 2303
Kaplan, Lawrence M., 2648
Kaplan, Lee, 1281
Kaplan, Mark E., 323, 1194, 2580
Kaplan, Mark N., 133
Kaplan, Mike, 260, 2620
Kaplan, Paula, 3097
Kaplan, Robert S., 3592
Kaplan, Stephen A., 3166
Kaplinsky, Andrew, 1664
Kapoor, Rohit, 638
Kapourelakos, Natalia, 3603
Kapp, M. Keith, 4078
Kapp, Steven H., 2409
Kappa, Kevin, 779
Kappauf, William J., Jr., 331
Kappelman, Peter, 2217
Kappler Safety Group, Inc., 2095
Kappler USA, Inc., 2095
Kappler, Gale N., 2095
Kappler, George, 2095
Kappler, George P., Jr., 2095
Kappler, Inc., 2095
Kappler-Roberts, Laura, 2095
Kappner, Johanna, 813
Kaprielian, Rachel, 501
Kapur, Jatindar, 1792
Kapusta, Susan M., 3877
Kara, Ron, 1699
Karakul, Kurt, 3732
Karalla, Cheryl, 1021
Karalson, Jerry, 814
Karam, Robert, 7
Karami, Zahra, 3673
Karande, Santosh S., 2778
Karande, Seema V., 2778
Karande, Shawn S., 2778
Karangelen, Nicholas, 3808
Karangelen, Nicholas E., 3808
Karaoglan, Alain, 1938
Karas, Devin M., 3173
Karas, Joe, 2581
Karavasilis, Alexander, 2482
Karayannopoulos, Constantine, 2550
Karb, Richard D., 1481
Karbowiak, Christine, 560
Karch, Nancy J., 1376, 1565, 2150, 2399
Karet, Laura S., 1571
Karhut, Guenter, 201
Karhut, Guenter D., 201
Kari, Ross J., 1348
Karickhoff, Brenda C., 3757
Karim, Jafar, 474
Karl, Herzog, 2696
Karlgaard, Richard P., 1951
Karlson, Lawrence C., 669
Karlson, Nancy L., 898
Karman, James A., 3278
Karmanos, Peter, Jr., 698, 4124
KarMART Automotive Group, 2096
Karmun, Gloria A., 3467
Karn, Robert B., III, 2907
Karna, Ajoy H., 3677
Karnal, Alex, 1062
Karnhaas, Robert J., Jr., 3344
Karol, Steven, 700
Karon, Robert, 3684
Karp, Allan, 2234
Karp, David W., 75
Karp, Roberta, 1376
Karpiak, Victor, 1404
Karpinski, Lois B., 996
Karr, David E., 2882
Karre, Paul J., 1968, 3711
Karriem, Sandra, 2869
Karsen, Perry A., 732
Karsh, Bruce, 728
Karsner, Alexander A., 220
Karst, Darren W., 3272
Karsunky, Robert, 83
Kartsotis, Tom, 624
Karvinen, Jouko, 3473
Kasai, Masahiro, 3632
Kasayulie, Willie, 657
Kasbar, Patrick, 1629
Kasbekar, Umesh M., 861
Kase, Karen, 243
Kaseff, Gary L., 1259
Kashevarof, Kimberly, 3397
Kashevaroff, Don, 3397
Kashevaroff, Don, Jr., 3397
Kasle Family, LLC, The, 2098
Kasle Steel Corp., 2098
Kasle, Julie, 2098
Kasle, Matthew, 2098
Kasle, Roger, 2098
Kasouf, David, 3675
Kasper, Dave, 1018
Kasper, F. Van, 637
Kasper, Thomas R., 3173
Kasriel, Bernard L.M., 2760
Kass, Dennis M., 2245
Kass, Steven A., 3271
Kassan, Glen K., 1718
Kassan, Glen M., 1718
Kassebaum, Denise, 878
Kassewitz, Darcie Glazer, 599
Kassis, Marc, 81
Kassling, William E., 2886, 4048
Kassoff, Eric S., 4074
Kast, Steve, 663
Kastelic, David A., 802
Kasten, Stanley H., 3998
Kaster, Eric, 1243
Kastin, David M., 3783
Kastner, Richard, 1517
Katayama, Russell, 3649
Katchman, Don E., 1366
Katehi, Linda P.B., 4072
Katen, Karen, 1736
Katen, Karen L., 1842
Kathy, Rainey, 2234
Katkov, David, 2995
Katleman, Steve, 3152
Katler, Gary M., 853
Katona, Michael, 640
Katopodis, Louis, 1375
Katovich, John, 2100
Katsirubus, Steve, 838
Katten Muchin Rosenman LLP, 2101
Katten Muchin Zavis, 2101
Katten Muchin Zavis Rosenman, 2101
Katula, Sharon E., 3298
Katz, Carolyn F., 167, 2709
Katz, Charles, Jr., 3150
Katz, Daniel, 1578
Katz, David, 3601
Katz, David S., 3887
Katz, Ezra, 2250
Katz, Karen W., 2657
Katz, Ken, 1429
Katz, Mark M., 235
Katz, Micheal, 3601
Katz, Richard, 3287
Katz, Robert J., 1603, 1604
Katz, Robert L., 1939, 3794
Katz, Ronald, 1147
Katz, Saul, 3601
Katzen, Larry, 2460
Katzenberg, Jeffrey, 1172
Katzoff, Jan, 3326
Kauai Coffee Co., 85
Kauai Commercial Co., Inc., 85
Kaudisch, Gerda, 935
Kauffman, Julia Irene, 2093
Kauffman, Richard L., 3624
Kauffman, Robert A., 1733
Kaufman Enterprises LLC, 2170
Kaufman, David L., 2584
Kaufman, Deborah, 3257
Kaufman, Harvey, 3103
Kaufman, Ilene, 511
Kaufman, Isaac, 2154
Kaufman, Jenneen, 3716
Kaufman, Jonah, 2170, 2427
Kaufman, Joshua, 1251
Kaufman, Jules, 950
Kaufman, Melinda, 2170
Kaufman, Monty, 1432
Kaufman, Robert, 511, 963
Kaufman, Stephen P., 1736, 2165
Kaufman, Victor A., 1311, 1903
Kaufmann, Barbara W., 3
Kaufmann, Joseph L., 3378
Kaufmann, Luiz, 2850
Kaufmann, Michael C., 2622
Kaul, Kaul, 2753
Kaull, Donald N., 2699
Kauten, Ralph, 1394
Kaval, Dave, 1206
Kavanagh, Malachy, 1961
Kavanagh, Mike, 3136
Kavanaugh, James J., 1960
Kawa, Masanori, 2713
Kawaguchi, Gary, 3900
Kawaguchi, Kenneth, 3900
Kawai, Mitsuhiko, 2541
Kawamata, Satoshi, 2144
Kawamura, Makoto, 306
Kawano, Nolan, 1996
Kawano, Nolan N., 1996
Kawasaki Heavy Industries (USA), Inc., 2103
Kawasaki Motors Corp., U.S.A., 2103
Kawasaki Motors Manufacturing Corp., U.S.A., 2103
Kawasaki Rail Car, Inc., 2103
Kawasaki Robotics (USA) Inc., 2103
Kawasaki Steel Investments, Inc., 67
Kawashima, Yoshiyuki, 2541
Kawula, Christopher, 4045
Kay, Colleen W., 1161
Kay, Kenneth J., 2225
Kay, Larry Alan, 1120
Kaye, Abbe, 2613
Kaye, Charles R., 3985
Kaye, Daniel G., 1365
Kaye, Judith S., Hon., 3470
Kaylie, Alicia, 3367
Kaylie, Gloria W., 3367
Kaylie, Harvey, 3367
Kaylie, Roberta, 3367
Kaylor, Craig W., 1712, 1713
Kayne, Alexander, 2807
Kayne, Alexander M., 2807
Kayser, David, 802
Kayser, Kraig H., 3406
Kaytee Products, Inc., 2104
Kazim, Essa, 2617
Kazmir, Munr, 3097

Kennedy, Cynthia M., 162
Kennedy, David L., 3202
Kennedy, Doris, 1822
Kennedy, Douglas L., 2909
Kennedy, Eileen T., 1030
Kennedy, Gary F., 187
Kennedy, Herlinda H., 3819
Kennedy, J. Donald, 2159
Kennedy, James A., 3040
Kennedy, James C., 958, 959
Kennedy, James C., Jr., 959
Kennedy, John, 804
Kennedy, Judith E., 1712
Kennedy, K. Daniel, 3203
Kennedy, Kevin A., 2646
Kennedy, Kevin J., 2165
Kennedy, Laura, 3142
Kennedy, Lesa France, 1970
Kennedy, Linda, 4037
Kennedy, Michael, 310, 3795
Kennedy, Michelle, 2620
Kennedy, Parker S., 1389, 1390
Kennedy, Pat, 2800
Kennedy, R. Michael, 3070
Kennedy, Rob, 2625
Kennedy, Robert, 2625
Kennedy, Robin, 2876
Kennedy, Sam, 538
Kennedy, Ted, 2548
Kennedy, Thomas A., 3135
Kennedy, Thomas C., 1812
Kennedy, Thomas L., 2635
Kennedy, Tim, 400
Kennedy, W. Keith, Jr., 903
Kennedy, William, 3037
Kennedy, William T., 1163
Kenney, Brandon, 1790
Kenney, Brian A., 1542, 3905
Kenney, Crane H., 784
Kenney, Donald, 1083
Kenney, Donald J., 1083
Kenney, Gerald, 2654
Kenney, James F., Hon., 1926
Kenney, James P., 4102
Kenney, Siobhan, 220
Kenney, Tom, 1699
Kennig, Michael, 1829
Kennis, Robert H., 2370
Kenny Electric Svcs., 2554
Kenny, David W., 4012
Kenny, Elizabeth, 4159
Kenny, Gregory B., 685, 1942
Kenny, John J., 2296
Kenny, Kenneth J., 3524
Kenny, Peter, 2039
Kensok, James M., 301
Kent, Cathy, 3698
Kent, Cathy A., 3698
Kent, Gage A., 2129
Kent, Greg, 2138
Kent, Jeffery, 704
Kent, Jerry, 2625
Kent, Kristy, 497
Kent, Michael J., 879
Kent, Muhtar, 3, 862, 2427
Kent, Philip I., 3823
Kent, Rodney D., 2814
Kent, Virginia H., 608
Kentuckiana Roofing Co., Inc., 2130
Kentz, Frederick C., III, 1549, 1823
Kenyon, Chuck, 807
Kenyon, Murray, 1620
Kenyon, Rebecca, 1077
Kenyon, V. Sheffield, 493
Keochstadt, Wolfgang, 439
Keogh, John, 24
Keogh, Tracy, 1794
Keough, Donald R., 93, 429, 1903
Keough, Mike, 242
Kepco, Inc., 2132
Kepler, Allen, 1359
Kepler, Dave E., 1161
Kepler, David E., 1161
Kepler, JoAnn, 1359
Keppers, Bonnie, 100
Keppner, Judy L., 3245
Keprta, Don, 3310
Keptner, Erik, 1572
Kercheral, Michael P., 1961
Kercheval, Michael P., 1961
Kerin, Andrew C., 249
Kerin, John J., 2370
Kerkhoff, Paul, 1818
Kerley, Robert P., 3984
Kerlin, William H., Jr., 1625
Kern, Kevin, 1400
Kern, Peter M., 1311
Kern-Knoblock, Deborah, 1688
Kernan, Richard T., 1173
Kerngan, Robert M., III, 3520
Kerns, Christopher, 1471
Kerr, David W., 3643
Kerr, Derek J., 3902
Kerr, Guy H., 406
Kerr, Janet E., 2205
Kerr, Mary, 521
Kerr, Steve, 2582
Kerr, William R., 1951
Kerr, William T., 227, 1974, 4056
Kerrey, J. Robert, 3713
Kerridge, Isaac C., 324
Kerrigan, Edward T., 2394
Kerrigan, Sylvia J., 2364
Kerschen, John R., 1749
Kerschen, Richard, 2233
Kerschen, Richard M., 1981
Kershaw, J.D., 870
Kershaw, Moichael, 3826
Kerska, Todd, 1679
Kersten, Kathy, 3117
Kertz, Marion, 2487
Kerwin, George F., 1651
Kerzner International Bahamas, 2133
Kerzner, Solomon, 2133
Kesler, Delores M., 3074
Kesner, Idalene, 2629
Kesner, Idalene F., 3643
Kess, Steve, 3348
Kesselman, Marc, 1506
Kesselman, Ronald C., 1922
Kessler, Bernd F., 2999
Kessler, Gary, 150
Kessler, John W., 17
Kessler, Murray S., 2304
Kessler, Stuart, 3955
Kestner, R. Steven, 319, 936, 3032, 3057
Ketcherside, James L., 1335
Ketchum Charitable Lead Annuity Trust, 2431
Ketchum, Brian C., 2431
Ketchum, Jason, 474
Ketchum, Kent H., 2431
Ketchum, Kevin B., 2431
Ketchum, Lewis Craig, 2431
Ketchum, Mark D., 2556
Ketchum, Richard G., 1382
Ketteler, Thomas R., 140
Kettering, Glen L., 2715
Kettleson, Rebecca L., 4108
Keudell, Kelly, 1546
Kever, Jim D., 3832
Keville, Michael T., 2814
Kew, Terry G., 3783
Kew-Prince, Ralph, 1471
Key Container Corp., 2134
Key Food Stores Cooperative, Inc., 2135
Key Trust Company of Indiana, N.A., 1195
Key, John W., 894
KeyBank Capital Markets, 136
KeyBank N.A., 560, 657, 867, 1216, 2136, 2279
KeyBank of Maine, 2136
KeyBank, N.A., 1112, 2136, 3830
KeyCorp, 2136
Keyes, J. Patrick, 4093
Keyes, James, 4010
Keyes, James E., 4010
Keyes, James H., 2647
Keyes, James W., 483
Keyes, John A., 4010
Keylon, Catherine A., 1838
Keys, Patricia M., 124
Keyser, Mark J., 2238
Keyser, Richard L., 3047
Keyser, William, 3932
KeySpan Corp., 2630
Keystone Foods Corp., 2137
Keystone Foods LLC, 2137
Keystone Nazareth Bank & Trust Co., 2635
Keyte, David H., 3166
Khalaf, Michel, 2481
Khaleel, Adeeb, 2665
Khaleel, Ghulam, 2665
Khaleel, Mohammed, 2665
Khalifa, Amin I., 2948
Khalil, Mark, 3502
Khan, Adil R., 4006
Khan, Ejaz A., 3972
Khan, Gordon, 1893
Khan, Mehmood, 2935
Khan, Murshid, 3606
Khan, Rob, 1418
Khan, Shahid, 2014
Khanna, Tarun, 47
Khing, Tony, 3327
Khosla, Sanjay, 442
Khosrowshahi, Dara, 1311
Khouri, Naif A., 1183
Khurana, Rakesh, 144
Kia, Neda, 728
Kiana, Chris, 1
Kiceluk, Michael S., 674
Kichiji, Katsuhiko, 2178
Kidd, Garland, 979
Kidder, C. Robert, 2466, 2570
Kidder, Rolland E., 2628
Kids Fund, The, 3955
Kids II Employees, 2141
Kids II Vendors, 2141
Kids II, Inc., 2141
Kieckhefer, John I., 4052
Kiedaisch, Maureen P., 2335
Kiefer, Donald F., 3371
Kiefer, Kathleen S., 3541, 4027
Kiefer, Lawrence J., 3371
Kiehl, Patricia, 2418
Kiehnle, Bob, 3053
Kielar, Walter, 1561
Kiely, Maryann S., 3858
Kiely, W. Leo, III, 120
Kiene, Lisa, 754
Kiernan, Donald E., 1765
Kiernan, Robert, 1345
Kiersey, Doug, 1168
Kiersey, Douglas A,, Jr., 1168
Kiersey, Douglas A., Jr., 1168
Kierstead, Ken, 3084
Kies, Peter S., 317
Kiesau, Thomas, 768
Kieschnick, Michael, 4116
Kiesling, William G., 996
Kiewit & Sons Co., Peter, 2142
Kiewit Construction Group Inc., 2142
Kiewit Diversified Group Inc., 2142
Kiewit Sons', Peter, Inc., 2142
Kiffe, Maryellen, 545
Kiffe, Sean, 545
Kiffin, Irvin A,, 2044
Kifton Development, Inc., 2143
Kiga, Frederick C., 1081
Kiggen, James D., 4138
Kight, Mike, 2136
Kight, Peter J., 1894
Kightlinger, Jeffrey, 2484
Kiguchi, Stafford J., 342
Kihlman, Dale, 3810
Kikkoman Foods, Inc., 2144
Kikugawa, Vincent E., 3538
Kilbane, Catherine, 3437
Kilbane, Catherine M., 149, 3437
Kilcoyne, Gerald, 1394
Kilcoyne, John F., 851
Kilcoyne, John J., 1967
Kiley, Joseph W. "Joe", III, 1404
Kiley, Michael, 3391
Kiley, Thomas R., 226
Kilgore, Bonnie, 3053
Kill, Stephen, 2532
Killen, John V., 3528
Killian, Ann E., 1366
Killian, Elizabeth A. Bell, 4108
Killian, John F., 1869
Killian, Kathy, 2964
Killian, Michael F., 3149
Killinger, Clayton E., 3915
Killingstad, H. Chris, 3714
Killingsworth, Cleve L., Jr., 3802
Killion, Theophlius, 4151
Killips, Rob, 1643
Killips, Robert E., 1643
Killoran, David J., 2073
Kilmartin Industries, 2145
Kilmartin, Betsey, 2145
Kilmartin, David F., 2145
Kilmartin, John D., III, 1967
Kilmartin, Paul F., 1967
Kilpatrick Life Insurance Co., 2146
Kilpatrick, Robert D., 3778
Kilts, James M., 1065, 2445, 2481, 2950
Kim, Charles G., 890
Kim, Christina, 2865
Kim, Helen L., 3909
Kim, Hyung D., 203
Kim, Hyung Don, 203
Kim, Jay, 3827
Kim, Jean, 1062
Kim, Jim Young, 1959
Kim, Keith, 3909
Kim, Keith K., 3909
Kim, Kenneth, 2449
Kim, Kenneth H,, 2449
Kim, Mi Hye, 203

Kim, Min, 386
Kim, N.K., 2140
Kim, Namjung, 3588
Kim, Neil Y., 579
Kim, Robert, 83
Kim, Shane S., 1530
Kim, Steven, 1191
Kim, Sun, 445
Kim, Sun Chong, 445
Kim, Thomas, 1694
Kim, Young Kil, 445
Kimball Co., Miles, 2148
Kimball International, Inc., 2149
Kimball, Jenny R., 1061
Kimball, Kevin M., 2383
Kimberly-Clark, 1186
Kimberly-Clark Corp., 2150
Kimble, Donald R., 1894
Kimbro, Becky, 3729
Kimbro, Kenneth J., 3832
Kimishima, Tatsumi, 2712
Kimley-Horn and Associates, Inc., 2151
Kimmel, Charlie, 2152
Kimmel, Joseph W., 2152
Kimmel, Roger H., 1268, 2952, 3270
Kimmel, Sidney, 2057
Kimmet, Pam, 863
Kimmet, Pamela O., 863
Kimsey, William L., 2887, 3273, 4042
Kimura, Kazumasa, 1088
Kinahan, Clare, 2106
Kincade, Joe, 1847
Kincaid, Bridget Baker, 1680
Kincaid, Marc, 2920
Kincaid, Marc E., 2920
Kincaid, Richard D., 3134
Kincer, R. Gregory, 2149
Kinch, Elizabeth, 1074
Kinder Morgan, Inc., 2153
Kinder, Richard D., 2153
Kindle, Carolyn, 1281
Kindle, Jo Ann Taylor, 1281
Kindler, Jeff, 2427
Kindred Healthcare Operating, Inc., 2154
Kindred Healthcare, Inc., 2154
Kindred Hospice Charities, Inc., 2154
King, Alan S., 4145
King, Allen B., 3891
King, Anne Kelly, 1926
King, Barbara E., 851
King, Bruce, 975, 3247
King, Bruce E., 975
King, Charles G., 85
King, Christine, 1907
King, Christopher, 245
King, Cris, 2836
King, David P., 685
King, Donald, 2863
King, Glenn R., 285
King, Gloria, 2308
King, Greg, 2678
King, Gwendolyn S., 2292, 2559
King, Heather A., 428
King, J. Luther, Jr., 3831
King, Jennifer, 4138
King, Jennifer Gill, 4138
King, Jesse, 3150
King, John W., 1541
King, Justin M., 3581
King, Kelly S., 385
King, Keri, 2489
King, Marie, 2323
King, Martin, 2962
King, Michael, 1085
King, Michael R., 1531
King, Patricia, 3618
King, Patricia M., 71
King, Richard A., 559
King, Richard G., 2323
King, Robert, 2935
King, Roderick K., 1083
King, Scott, 1332
King, Steven, 1251
King, Thomas B., 2630
King, Tiffany T., 333
King, Tom, 2524
King, Wendall, 1735
King-Lavinder, Joyce, 863
Kingik, George, 3751
Kingma, Todd W., 2943
Kingsbury Corp., 2160
Kingsbury, Arthur F., 1140
Kingsbury, Thomas, 617
Kingsley, Alfred D., 26
Kingsley, Juanita Allen, 1060
Kingsley, Lawrence D., 935, 3246
Kingsley, Tony, 465
Kingston, John, III, 51
Kington, Mark J., 1150
Kingzett, Robert, 2032
Kinnaird, Donna H., 3179
Kinnary, Michael T., 1749
Kinne, Kathleen, 1603
Kinnear, Peter D., 3614
Kinneen, Simon, 1586
Kinneeveauk, Herbert, Jr., 3751
Kinney Drugs, Inc., 2162
Kinney Trust, Mary, 2162
Kinney, Catherine R., 2481, 2769
Kinney, Daniel, 428
Kinnison, Donald L., 2973
Kinser, Thomas, 3898
Kinsey, Michelle, 2536
Kinsey, Paul, 3902
Kinsey, R. Steven, 1446
Kinsley, Thomas, 1924
Kinsolving, Dean, 2235
Kintzele, Jim, 489
Kinyon, Barry, 3721
Kinziger, Linda, 4019
Kip, Jeff, 1903
Kip, Jeffrey W., 2873
Kipfer, Kurt F., 1966
Kiplinger, Austin H., 2163
Kiplinger, Knight A., 2163
Kiralla, Gail, 2343
Kirban, Elise, 2650
Kirby, J. Scott, 3902
Kirby, Mark B., 2847
Kirby, Robert P., 2573
Kirby, Susan G., 3706
Kirby, SuzAnn, 3880
Kirchenbauer, Ronald W., 3247
Kircher, Christopher P., 904
Kircher, Kendall, 2486
Kirchman, Paula, 3061
Kireker, Charlie, 499
Kirk, Alan, 2823
Kirk, Chris, 725
Kirk, Cliff, 503
Kirk, J. Ellwood, 1419
Kirk, John, 1930
Kirk, Joseph A., 3297
Kirk, Kenneth C., 1287
Kirk, Paul G., Jr., 1742
Kirk, Rose M., 3936
Kirk, Rose Stuckey, 3936
Kirk, Stephen F., 3230
Kirkconnell, Kristin R., 144
Kirkendall, Bill, 1383
Kirker, James M., 1118
Kirkham, James F., 605
Kirkish, Mark S., 3221
Kirkland, George L., 780
Kirkpatrick, John F., 2164
Kirkpatrick, Margaret D., 2747
Kirkpatrick, Mark, 166
Kirkpatrick, Paul, 893
Kirkpatrick, Timothy L., 492
Kirkwood, Rhonda E., 32
Kirley, Francis P., 2705
Kirloskar, Virendra A., 2165
Kirsch, Eric M., 54
Kirsch, James F., 850, 1366
Kirschenbaum, Jennifer, 3325
Kirschner, Ann, 216
Kirsner, James D., 41
Kirstein, Greg, 870
Kirstein, Gregory, 870
Kirtley, Olivia F., 2876, 3835
Kiser, Ben, 2660
Kiser, Ellen A., 485
Kiser, Von Loy, 891
Kish Bank Asset Mgmt., 3577
Kish, Thomas C., 2873
Kisleiko, Irene M., 3093
Kispert, John H., 3532
Kiss Products, 1186
Kiss, Robert S., 544
Kissam, L., 78
Kissam, Luther C., IV, 78
Kissane, Janet M., 2769
Kissel, Frank A., 2909
Kissel, John D., 2909
Kissel, Richard O., II, 3458
Kissick, Robert M., 2553
Kissinger, Henry, 926
Kissinger, Karen G., 3819
Kissinger, Thomas F., 2371
Kissner, Matthew S., 4072
Kissner, Mike, 3053
Kist, Ewald, 2563
Kistenbroker, David H., 2101
Kistler, Gregory J., 745
Kita, John J., 3484
Kita, John M., 3484
Kitayama, Tomoo, 2768
Kitch, Thomas D., 1981
Kitchell, Hardison Downey, 136
Kitchen, William, III, 2930
Kitchens, George, 72
Kite, Charles W., 1146
Kitka, Julie E., 805
Kittelberger, Larry E., 227
Kitterman, James M., 3667
Kittoe, Larry T., 1057
Kittredge, Charles J., 969
Kittredge, John, 969
Kittredge, Robert P., 1322
Kittrell, Marty R., 2715
Kitz, Ed, 3272
Kitz, Edward G., 3272
Kitze, Chris, 1951
Kitzmiller, James K., 2402
Kivell, Thomas T., 3534
Kivisto, Nicole A., 2441
Kiwanis, 3015
KLA-Tencor Corporation, 2165
Klafter, Cary I., 1950
Klahr, Suzanne Mckechnie, 3470
Klammer, Mark, 1015
Klaphake, John, 77
Klappa, Gale E., 313, 2070, 4093
Klapstein, Julie D., 3576
Klarecki, Patrick, 1634
Klarner, David, 3074
Klarr, James P., 2205
KLAS-TV, 2218
Klasko, Stephen K., 3707
Klatt, James G., 62
Klauke, Joseph, 2556
Klawe, Maria M., 579, 2501
Klebanov, Lina, 2570
Klebe, Elizabeth L., 63
Kleberg, Richard M., III, 1512
Klee, Ted, 3560
Kleese, William R., 3915
Klein Diamonds Inc., Julius, 2167
Klein Tools, Inc., 2168
Klein's Super Markets, Inc., 2169
Klein, Abraham, 2167
Klein, Adam J., 1345
Klein, Andrew P., 2169
Klein, Barbara A., 1942
Klein, Bella, 2167
Klein, Bonnie M., 331
Klein, Bruce A., 832
Klein, Calvin, Inc., 2166
Klein, Charles D., 181
Klein, Christine, 657
Klein, Christopher, 1474
Klein, Christopher J., 1474
Klein, Dale E., 3516
Klein, Elmer, 331
Klein, Howard, 2169
Klein, Howard S., 2169
Klein, Irving, 2170
Klein, Jake, 3222
Klein, Joel, 2236
Klein, Joel I., 2700
Klein, John A., 215
Klein, John E., 1271
Klein, Jonathan, 1569
Klein, Kris, 980
Klein, Martin P., 1565
Klein, Mathias A., III, 2168
Klein, Michael, 839
Klein, Michael C., 331
Klein, Michael F., 3802
Klein, Michael J., 2169
Klein, Michael R., 3826
Klein, Moshe, 2167
Klein, Paul, 3204
Klein, Rachel, 2200
Klein, Ralph, 2169
Klein, Rebecca A., 301
Klein, Ron, 2333
Klein, Russell, 2347
Klein, Sara J., 2168
Klein, Shirley S., 2169
Klein, Starr T., 1132
Klein, Steven M., 2741
Klein, Thomas R., 2168
Klein, Ward M., 591, 1271
Klein-Kaufman Corp., 2170
Kleiner, Madeleine, 2744
Kleiner, Madleine, 2007
Kleinfeld, Klaus, 82, 2570
Kleinman, Mark H., 2981
Kleinschmidt, Amy, 1227
Kleinz, LouElla, 1262
Kleisner, Fred J., 2154
Kleisner, Ted J., 1424
Kleisterlee, Gerard J., 1068
Klema, Catherine M., 4007

Klesse, William R., 3915
Kletter, Jeff, 2155
Kleveland, Ronald, 4080
Kleven, Cynthia F., 3
Kliewer, Kendall G., 2748
Kligman, Richard, 3703
Klimczak, Sean, 477
Klimko, Justin G., 629
Kline, David, 2596
Kline, John C., 3858
Kline, John R., 857
Kline, Kenneth C., 1655
Kline, Lowry F., 1132
Kline, Roger, 745
Kline, Thomas, 1455
Kline, Wiliam, 412
Kling, Lewis M., 1213
Klinger, Leslie, 2225
Klinick, Theodore J., 1800
Klinkerman, David A., 2870
Klipper, Mitchell S., 360
Klitgaard, William E., 955
Klock, Brian L., 1434
Klocke, Tina, 608
Kloeppel, David C., 3294
Klopas, Frank, 783
Klopfenstein, John D., 1444
Klopfer, Jane, 1415
Kloppers, Marius, 455
Klose, Kevin, 3016
Klotsche, Allan, 552
Klotsche, Allan J., 552
Klotz, Caroline D., 1165, 1918
KLS Martin, L.P., 2171
Klug, Jonathan P., 273
Kluis, Gerry, 1787
KMTSJ, Inc., 2173
Knabusch, E. M., 2205
Knabush-Taylor, June E., 2205
Knakal, Robert, 2398
Knakal, Robert A., 2398
Knapp, Allison, 1648
Knapp, Ann H., 2309
Knapp, C. Clinton, 1488
Knapp, Charles B., 54
Knapp, Christian, 260
Knapp, D. R., 1366
Knapp, James, 3534
Knapp, Maynard, 1648
Knapp, Merle, 1586
Knapp, Scott, 2426
Knapstein, Annette S., 144
Knauss, Donald R., 852, 2120
Knecht, Randy, 802
Kneeley, Anita M., 2782
Kneidinger, Michael, 1727
Kneller, Patsy, 3274
Knepley, Katie, 3455
Knestrick, Walter, 3171
Knetter, Michael M., 144
Knickerbocker, Peggy, 2865
Knife River Corp., 2441
Knight Inc., 2153
Knight, Bobbie J., 71
Knight, Charles D., 3790
Knight, Dan, 786
Knight, David, 3598
Knight, Edward S., 2617
Knight, James B., 3531
Knight, Jeffrey A., 1682
Knight, Jessie J., Jr., 74
Knight, Jessie, Jr., 3405
Knight, Lester B., 210
Knight, Nancy Lopez, 3488
Knight, Philip H., 2710
Knight, Robert, 1359
Knight, Robert M., Jr., 3857
Knight, Roger A., 1248
Knight, Theresa, 3457
Knight, Timothy P., 786
Knight, W. Benton, 1859
Knight, W.H., Jr., 3591
Knisely, Philip W., 1130
Knitcraft Corp., 2175
Knitcraft, Inc., 2174
Knobel, Jeff A., 328
Knodel, Doreen, 3843
Knoell, Amanda B., 6
Knoeppel, Henry W., 3167
Knoll, Inc., 2176
Knoll, Jerome C., 3017
Knoll, Thomas G., 1668
Knopik, Stephen M., 389
Knorr, Eric T., 1981
Knorr, Johnny, 770
Knotts, Daniel L., 1155
Knowles, Marie L., 2434
Knowlton, Timothy S., 2120
Knowlton, Warren D., 174
Knox, Robert A., 1765
Knox, Wendell C., 1209
Knox, Wendell J., 1209, 1724
Knox, Wyck A., Jr., 57
Knudsen, Jeannette L., 3488
Knudson, Chris, 2743
Knudson, Jeanette L., 3488
Knudson, Laura, 2451
Knudson, Thomas C., 2441
Knudstorp, Jorge Vig, 2247
Knueppel, Henry W., 1741, 4093
Knueppel, Henry W., Jr., 3167
Knupp, C.O., 3981
Knutson, Dan, 2217
Knutson, Lisa A., 3374
Knutson, Paul, 2836
Knutson, Richard A., 2224
Knutson, Thomas K., 2457
KOA Speer Electronics, Inc., 2178
Kobak, Bernard S., 3732, 3735
Kobayashi, Bert T., Jr., 1405
Kobayashi, Kazuhiro, 2103
Kobayashi, Michael K., 3267
Kobayashi, Naomi H., 677
Kobayashi, Yotaro, 660
Kobe, Kenneth, 361
Kober, Steven, 3502
Kobin, Jenny, 3074
Kobori, Michael, 3624
Kobus, Thomas A., 1142
Kobus, Todd, 1857
Kobylenski, Sara L., 2394
Koc, Ali Y., 3125
Koch Enterprises, Inc., 2179
Koch Foundation, 1201
Koch Sons, George, Inc., 2179
Koch Sons, George, LLC, 2179
Koch, Ashley, 2310
Koch, C. James, 533
Koch, Charles G., 1981, 2180
Koch, Charles John, 266
Koch, Christopher H., 2673
Koch, Dave, 2401
Koch, David M., 2179
Koch, Kevin R., 2179
Koch, Kim, 938
Koch, Linda, 15
Koch, Robert J., 381
Koch, Robert L., II, 2179
Kocher, Brian W., 795
Kocher, Rick P., 795
Kochevar, Deborah, 764
Kochvar, Mark, 3297
Kocur, John A., 211
Kodosky, Jeffrey L., 2632
Koebelin, David J., 1012
Koeck, George A., 2836
Koehl, Hans K., 3545
Koehl, Jeffrey F., 3545
Koehler, Michael F., 1792
Koehler, William R., 2136
Koellner, Laurette T., 1809
Koeneke, Michael S., 965
Koenig Roloff, ReBecca, 3235
Koenig, Emery N., 2580
Koenig, John, 2540
Koenig, Linda, 286
Koenig, Peter, 1044
Koenig, Thomas J., 4115
Koenigs, Betty, 2503
Koeninger, David, 312
Koeper, Jay, 151
Koeppe, Alfred C., 1863
Koepsell, Pat, 11
Koerber, Hans-Joachim, 3677
Koerner, John E., III, 2245
Koerner, Philip D., 2629
Koerselman, James E., 1091
Koerselman, John, 3035
Koerselman, Robert, 1091
Kofisa Trading Co., S.A., 3125
Kofler, Kim, 954
Koga, Chester, 3782
Koga, Mike, 3773
Kogan, Richard J., 344, 869
Kogod, Dennis L., 1044
Kogovsek, John J., 4126
Kohl, Herb, 2528
Kohlberg, Andrew, 2968
Kohlberg, Elon, 1115
Kohlberg, James A., 2690
Kohler, David, 1651
Kohler, Herb, 2182
Kohler, Herbert V., Jr., 2182
Kohler, K. David, 1953, 2182
Kohler, Laura, 2182
Kohler, Mary S., 4086
Kohler, Terry J., 4086
Kohlhagen, Steven W., 181
Kohlhepp, Robert J., 816, 2886
Kohlwes, Gary F., 1404
Kohm, William J., 1053
Kohn, Arnold, 3044
Kohn, Barbara Shattuck, 2923
Kohn, Bradley, 2459
Kohn, Josef, 3044
Kohn, Leonard D., 1978
Kohn, Leonard D., Dr., 1978
Kohn, Mordechai, 2273
Kohn, Morty, 2273
Kohn, Sarah, 2273
Kohnstamm, Abby F., 3750
Kohorst, Elmer, 77
Koken, M. Diane, 2639
Kokot, Nadyne, 176
Kolanowski, Mark, 1749
Kolanowski, Mark A., 1749
Kolar, Derek J., 1
Kolb, Jerry W., 3984
Kolb, Jurgen, 3595
Kolde, Bert, 3793
Kollar, Ellen, 4125
Kollat, David T., 2277, 4106
Koller, Edward, 2183
Koller, Edward R., III, 2183
Koller, Edward R., Jr., 2183
Koller, Ross, 2183
Kolokotronis, Matina, 3303
Koltnow, Jenny, 1857
Koltz, Ron, 2321
Koltz, Ronald, 2321
Komakhuk, Kristel, 3694
Koman, James, 714
Komatsu, Koichi, 2539
Kombol, Danica, 2112
Kometer, Kevin, 853
Komnenovich, Dan P., 219
Komola, Christine T., 3581
Komoroski, Len, 724
Kompkoff, Gabriel, 805
Kompkoff, Gabriel D., 805
Kompkoff, Joyce L., 776
Kompkoff, Lloyd, 776
Komst, John C., 446
Koncz, Jeffrey, 2792
Konde, Ravi, 3678
Kondo, Hideo, 1756
Kondracke, Marguerite W., 566, 2270, 3315
Koneck, John M., 1491
Konen, Mark E., 2281
Koney, Robert, 415
Kong, Peter T., 1366
Koniag, Inc., 2184
Koniar, John, 3971
Konishi, Atsuo, 3480
Konkle, Barbara, 382
Kono, Hiroyo, 2496
Koo, George P., 2225
Koo, Grace J., 980
Kookesh, Albert M., 3380
Koonce, Neil W., 907, 1971
Koonce, Paul D., 1150
Koonin, Steven R., 1530
Koontz, Edward L., 393
Koontz, Fred, 947
Koontz, Gene, 1847
Koontz, Leah, 3522
Koontz, Richard L., Jr., 3434
Koop, Al, 189
Koop, Frans Hij, 2481
Kooy, Deanna V., 3868
Kopczick, E.M., 970
Kopczick, Elise M., 970
Kopec, Leon M., 4103
Kopelman, Kenneth P., 1376
Kopelson, Arnold, 727
Kopf, Richard S., 1497
Koplovitz, Kay, 638, 1376
Kopnisky, Jack L., 3070
Kopolovitz, Leonard, 1342
Kopp, Bob, 1269
Kopp, Bradford B., 2335
Kopp, Shirley, 1269
Koppel, Michael G., 2724
Koppelhus, Eva, 3893
Koppelman, Charles A., 2225
Koppelman, Rebecca, 335
Koppelsloen, Kurt, 615
Kopps-Wagner, Jennifer, 267
Koprowski, Doug, 3687
Kopsidas, Anastasios, 2017
Kopsidas, Satmata, 2017
Kopsidas, Shilpi, 2017
Koraleski, John J., 3857
Koranda, Kathleen, 3698
Korb, Brent L., 3100

Korbel, Edward, 2840
Korbey, John, 3316
Korde, Gerald, 3916
Kordeleski, Kirk, 446
Kordsmeier, John, 2749
Koreyva, Stanley J., 124
Korista, Stan, 3474
Korman, Harry A., 2610
Korman, James, 2958
Korn, Steven W., 591
Kornegay, Carl W., Jr., 3805
Kornegay, Carl, Jr., 3805
Kornegay, Tim, 367
Kornmann, Lynn, 1116
Kornstein, Don R., 330
Korologos, Ann McLaughlin, 187, 2120, 3972
Korpela, Richard A., 2320
Kors, Michael, 2186
Korstange, Jason E., 3695
Korth, Tricia, 991
Korum Automotive Group, Inc., 2187
Korum Family Limited Partnership, 2187
Korum Investments, Jerry, 2187
Korum, Germaine R., 2187
Korum, Jerome, 2187
Korum, Jerome M., 2187
Korum, Jerry, 2187
Korzilius, Paul, 53
Kos, Richard J., 1712
Kosecoff, Jacqueline B, 3600
Kosecoff, Jacqueline B., 688, 3381
Kosh, Mitchell, 3123
Kosh, Mitchell A., 3123
Koshel, Diana, 849
Koshijima, Keisuke, 2087
Koshima, Daisuke, 3422
Kosinski, Geyer, 3472
Kosinski, Gregory, 415
Koskinen, John, 47
Koss Corp., 2188
Koss, John C., 2188
Koss, John C., Jr., 2188
Koss, John C., Sr., 2188
Koss, Joseph, 1002
Koss, Michael J., 2188
Koss, Nancy L., 2188
Kossibel, John, 3758
Kossman, Charles R., 1139
Kossover, Victoria, 3070
Kost, T.G., 1673
Kostelich, Brad, 4103
Koster Insurance Agency, Inc., 1528
Koster, Barbara G., 3072
Koster, Gallagher, 1528
Koster, John F., 3944
Koster, Terasa, 1528
Koster, Teresa K., 1528
Kotek, James M., 2461
Kothari, Hansa, 3678
Kothari, Vimal, 3678
Kothiyal, Amit, 1995
Kotick, Bobby, 30
Kotick, Robert A., 30, 862
Kotke, Connie, 3775
Kouides, Peter A., 993
Kourtidis, Anastia, 3603
Kourtidis, Christos, 3603
Kourtidis, Efstathios, 3603
Koury, Frederick S., 2926
Kovac, James J., 2997
Kovacevich, Kathy, 2007
Kovacevich, Richard M., 691, 818
Kovach-Webb, Karen C., 211
Kovalsky, Don, 1816
Kowalchuk, E. J., 1448
Kowaleski, Tom, 509
Kowalik, Raymond J., 620
Kowalski Sausage Co., 2189
Kowalski, Agnes, 2189
Kowalski, Donald, 2189
Kowalski, Kenneth, 2189
Kowalski, Michael, 2189
Kowalski, Michael J., 344, 3750
Kowalski, Robert J., 1420
Kowalski, Ronald J., 2189
Kowalski, Stanley, Jr., 1712
Kowalski, Stephen, 2189
Kowalski, Stephen Z., 2189
Kowlzan, Mark W., 2861
Kozak, Charlie, 234
Kozak, John W., 2881
Kozak, Karl A., 2902
Kozel, David, 3088
Kozel, David F., 1801
Kozich, Gregory, 2996, 2997
Kozich, Ronald J., 3693
Koziel, Jeffrey, 1186
Kozik, P. Frank, 2924
Kozitza, William L., 684
Kozlak, Jodee, 3235
Kozlak, Jodeen A., 3691
Kozlowski, Wayne J., 1319
KPMG, 1858
KPMG LLP, 2190
Krabbenhoft, Kelby, 3944
Kracht, Hutch A., 1668
Kraegel, Frederick G., 3747
Kraemer, David A., 444
Kraemer, Harry M. Jansen, Jr., 3311
Kraemer, Richard A., 1345
Kraemer, Richard C., 3902
Kraetsch, Neil, 276
Krafcik, John, 1902
Kraft Foods Global, Inc., 2556
Kraft Total, 2687
Kraft, Daniel A., 2672
Kraft, David H., 2672
Kraft, Harold E., 3987
Kraft, James A., 2991
Kraft, Jonathan A., 2672
Kraft, Joshua M., 2672
Kraft, Robert K., 2672, 3945
Kraft, Roger, 3987
Kraft, Roger E., 3987
Kraft, Wanda, 3987
Krahling, David, 3035
Krajacic, Frederick M., 2323
Krajanowski, David, 3463
Krakauer, Mary Louise, 1253
Krakoff, Reed, 858
Krakora, Kevin J., 1112
Krakower, Ira J., 1795
Kramer, Amanda C., 3022
Kramer, Andrew M., 2058
Kramer, Anthony F., 1170
Kramer, Bob, 1407
Kramer, Bruce, 3977
Kramer, Curt A., 2647
Kramer, Dave, 1321
Kramer, Dennis, 15
Kramer, Denver, 2319
Kramer, Douglas, 1170
Kramer, Eddie M., 3022
Kramer, Edward M., 3022
Kramer, Ferdinand, 1170
Kramer, Jane, 382
Kramer, Jay S., 1360
Kramer, Jeffrey, 3022
Kramer, Jeffrey J., 3022
Kramer, Joyce A., 493
Kramer, Kelly A., 818
Kramer, Michael, 2642
Kramer, Michael W., 2121
Kramer, Mike, 2925
Kramer, Mitchell, 1079
Kramer, Nancy, 2277
Kramer, Patricia A., 3022
Kramer, Paul, 2103, 3118
Kramer, Regina, 238
Kramer, Richard J., 1612, 3437
Kramer, Richard N., 687
Kramer, Thomas, 388
Kramlich, Richard C., 3455
Krammer, Richard, 1019
Kranc, Lisa, 3572
Krane, Hilary, 2710
Krane, Hilary K., 3624
Krane, Howard G., 2164
Krangel, Stan, 2148
Krangel, Stanley E., 2148
Kranz, James C., 1880
Krapek, Karl J., 2744, 3072
Krapf, Robert J., 3207
Krapf, Scott Allen, 62
Krasas, Christopher P., 2733
Krasdale Foods, Inc., 2192
Krash, Abe, 248
Kraskouskas, Kristen, 476
Krasne, Charles, 2192
Krasne, Charles A., 2192
Krasne, Kenneth, 2192
Krasne, Thatcher, 2192
Krasner, Dan, 1095
Krasney, Martin, 2865
Krassin, Ron, 4159
Kratchman, Eden M., 24
Kratchmer, John E., 104
Kratochvil, Jim, 438
Krattebol, David, 780
Kraupp, Mike, 3476
Kraus, Carl E., 3134
Kraus, Carla, 896
Kraus, Eileen S., 2088, 3579
Kraus, Eric A., 956
Kraus, Jess F., 3505
Kraus, Margery, 2749
Kraus, Michael, 769
Kraus, Peter, 102
Kraus, Peter S., 102
Krause, Alan J., 2608
Krause, Arthur B., 4039
Krause, Charles H., 391
Krause, Claire, 2067
Krause, Dave, 2781
Krause, Jean, 739
Krause, Kyle J., 2199
Krause, Stefan, 1099
Krause, Stephen H., 391
Krause, W. A., 2199
Krauser, Frank W., 3052
Krausert, Gerry, 1821
Krauss, George H., 616, 1541
Kravis, Henry R., 1400
Krawitt, A.L., 970
Krawitt, Andrew L., 970
Krawitz, Harry, 675
Kreager, Kenton, 3839
Krebs, Robert D., 1555
Krebs, Thomas L., 1748
Krebs, Walter L., 773
Kreczko, Alan J., 1742
Kredi, Saul, 8
Kregor, Betty Baird, 894
Kreh, Richard K., 1210
Kreidler, Robert Chris, 3677
Kreienberg, William, 1840
Kreigel, Todd, 28
Kreiling, Scott, 665
Kreindler & Kreindler LLP, 2193
Kreindler, James, 2193
Kreindler, Ruth, 2193
Krejci, Frank R., 2171
Krema, Lawrence J., 3458
Kremchek, Tim, Dr., 814
Kremer, Lawrence J., 2179
Kremp, Charles F., III, 1419
Kremp, Laura, 1419
Krempa, Jerry, 407
Kremser, Steven, 529
Krenek, Wilfred M., 4020
Krenicki, John, Jr., 1552
Kresa, Kent, 1448
Kress, William F., 1651
Kretschmer, Charles, 1296
Kretschmer, R. David, 3541, 4027
Kretzschmar, David, 59
Krey, Julie, 2358
Krieg, Iris, 1187
Kriegel Holding Co., Inc., 28
Kriegel Holdings Inc., 28
Kriegel, David L., 28
Kriegel, Shirley C., 28
Krieger, David L., 3297
Krieger, James R., 178
Kriegshauser, Patrick A., 3984
Kriens, Scott, 2075
Krigstein, Alan, 1926
Krikorian, Lazarus, 175
Krishna, Suresh, 2999
Krishnan, Lata, 3455
Krisko, Diane, 2950
Krisowaty, Robert, 4047
Kristoff, Mark S., 2550
Kritz, Moses, 576
Krivacic, John, 3304
Krivulka, Joseph J., 2658
Krizan, Jim, 648
Kro, Lisa, 2517
Krodel, Thomas, 1985
Kroeger, Terry, 2606, 2806
Kroehler, Jon, 3478
Kroeker, Nathan, 3533
Kroenke, E. Stanley, 2194, 3569
Kroenke, Josh, 1090
Kroger Co., The, 2195
Kroger, Kevin, 1181
Krognes, Steve, 1549
Krohn, Marc, 103
Krohn, Scott D., 3
Krol, John A, 1071
Krol, John A., 1071
Krolick, Ronald S., 2335
Kroll, Edmund E., 735
Kroll, Teresa, 608
Kroloff, Mark, 1550
Krominga, Lynn, 299
Kronau, Kathleen M., 3433
Krone, Kevin M., 3522
Kroner, Ellen, 126
Krongard, Cheryl Gordon, 2245, 3902
Kronmiller, Kate B., 3874
Kroon, Gwenann, 1024
Kroon, M. Thomas, 1024
Kroonenberg, Sherri, 3363
Krop, Pamela S., 3566

LaHowchic, Nicholas J., 1313
Lahr, Carl, 2206
Lai, Koning, 3164
Lai, T.Y., 1048
Laidlaw Environmental Services, Inc., 3471
Laidley, David H., 1255
Laikin, Robert J., 567
Laimkuhler, Kathleen, 232
Laine, Erick, 1012
Laing, Sheila, 1900
Laipple, Don, 3212
Laird Norton Co. LLC, 2211
Laird, Benjamin W., 827
Laird, Brenda, 1078
Laird, John, 2853
Lake Region Electric Cooperative, 2213
Lake, Billy D., 3645
Lake, Charlene, 273
Lake, Christopher, 4043
Lake, Diane S., 4043
Lake, John W., 4043
Lake, Marianne, 2071
Lake, Robert, 4043
Lake, Stephen W., 2815
Lakefield, Bruce R., 3902
Lakeland Engineering Equipment Co., Inc., 3119
Lakeland Regional Medical, 4006
Laker, Robert L., 2951
Lakey, Ronald L., 3428
Lakritz, Isaac, 436
Lalas, Alexi, 2308
Lall, Sanjay, 1953
Lalla, Thomas R., Jr., 2942
Lally, Ann R., 3316
LaLonde, Curt, 1438
LaLonde, Timothy J., 704
Lalor, Angela S., 1027
Lam, Dales S., 3434
Lam, Shau-wai, 1048
Lam, Tracey, 1430
LaMacchia, John T., 2195
Lamach, Michael, 1939
Lamach, Michael W., 1939
LaManna, Frank A., 3740
Lamanna, Mathew C., 3893
Lamar, W. Bibb, Jr., 337
LaMarca, Gia, 2398
Lamattina, Chuck, 1819
Lamb Weston, 1858
Lamb, Brain, 2625
Lamb, Brian, 2625
Lamb, Chris, 1908
Lamb, Ed, 2206
Lamb, James R., 2909
Lamb, Jeff, 3522
Lamb, Patrick, 2206
Lamb, Philip A., 2606
Lamb, Raymond A., 2606
Lamb, Ron, 3199
Lambe, Christopher, 2580
Lambert, Blair W., 1693
Lambert, Clement T., 1481
Lambert, David W., 2991
Lambert, Ellen, 2466, 3077
Lambert, Janet, 2268
Lambert, Larry R., 361
Lambert, Michael D., 4042
Lambert, Peter, 2723
Lambert, Phelps L., 2798
Lambert, Sandra L., 2083
Lambert, Stephanie Shores, 3581
Lambert, Todd, 3567
Lambert, William M., 2529
Lamberth, Tom, 1136
Lamberti, Susan, 2741
Lambeth, Judy, 3200
Lambrow, Nicholas P., 2323
Lamel, Linda H., 3887
LaMendola, T.J., 870
LaMendola, Thomas J., 870
Lamere, David F., 344
Laming, Michael S., 1565
Lamkin, Janet W., 340
Lamm-Tennant, Joan M., 3399
Lamme, Kathryn A., 3576
Lammers, James D., 1033
Lamnin, Adam, 267
Lamon, James, 860
Lamont International, Inc., 2215
Lamont Ltd., 2215
Lamont, Gary F., 505
LaMontagne, Peter B., 2755
LaMoriello, Louis A., 2676
Lamoureux, Sheri, 1904
Lampe, William J., 1668
Lampereur, Andrew G., 3230
Lampert, Gregory S., 800
Lamphere, Gilbert H., 997
Lamping, Mark, 2014
Lampman, James S., 2212
Lampman, Sandra, 1394
Lamprey, Robert P., 1481
Lampton, Dorothy Lee, 1289
Lampton, Lee C., 1289
Lampton, Leslie B., 1289
Lampton, Leslie B., III, 1289
Lampton, Leslie B., Sr., 1289
Lampton, Mason H., 3674
Lampton, Robert H., 1289
Lampton, William W., 1289
Lamson, David, 298
Lamson, David F., 298
Lamutt, Marianne, 830
Lanaway, John, 856
Lanaway, John B., 801
Lancaster Industries, Inc., 670
Lancaster, George C., 1813
Lancaster, J.J., 555
Lancaster, Kathy, 2086
Lancaster, Natalie, 3606
Lance, Doug, 2279
Lance, Howard L., 1213, 1736, 3627
Lance, Inc., 3492
Lance, Jean, 540
Lance, Ryan M., 913
Lance, Thomas W., 533
Lancellot, Mike, 1012
Lancey, Paul, 2686
Land O'Lakes, Inc., 2217
Land, Jennifer M., 799
Land, Nick, 3965
Land, Peter, 209
Land, Stuart, 248
Landaker, Larry, 2914
Lande, James R., 3092
Landeche, Dean, 2356
Landegger, Renee, 769
Landenwich, Joseph L., 2154
Landes, Gary, 3848
Landgraf, Kurt M., 945, 2310
Landherr, James C., 1883
Landherr, Kenny, 3587
Landim, Rodolfo, 667
Landmann, Barbara, 81
Landmark Communications, Inc., 2218
Landmark Media Enterprises, 2218
Lando, Joey, 3712
Landol, Sam, 3380
Landon, Allan R., 342
Landon, Martin J., 2156
Landon, R. Kirk, 2250
Landry's Restaurants, Inc., 2219
Landry's Seafood Restaurants, Inc., 2219
Landry, Jim, 839
Landry, Kate, 199
Landry, Larry, 500
Landward, Stayner, 2028
Landy, Joseph P., 376, 3985
Landy, Richard, 1273
Lane, Amy B., 3765
Lane, Andrew R., 2431
Lane, Bob, 3459
Lane, Clark, Sr., 3751
Lane, David, 3720
Lane, Donald D., 2348
Lane, Elizabeth R., 1474
Lane, Jeffrey H., 2488
Lane, Lawrence J., 428
Lane, Margo, 283
Lane, Masuk M., 3751
Lane, Nancy Wolfe, 1129
Lane, Raymond J., 1794
Lane, Robert W., 1552, 2740, 3936
Lane, Scott, 394
Lane, Suzanne, 2771
Lane, Thomas H., 1162
Lane, Timothy, 2475
Laney, Sandra E., 773
Lang, Anne, 1633
Lang, Cheryl O., 3761
Lang, Ed, 2620
Lang, Helen, 6
Lang, Ian, 2385
Lang, John, 6
Lang, John D., 1286
Lang, John R., 6
Lang, Julie W., 6
Lang, Larry, 1969
Lang, Laura W., 3913
Lang, Linda A., 2007, 4011
Lang, Marshall, 57
Lang, Mike, 1852
Lang, Paul A., 231
Lang, Robert Todd, 4022
Lang, Roberta, 4066
Lang, Sandra P., 6
Lang, Susan, 1313
Langan, John P., 1815
Langan, Kathy, 1963
Lange, Brian, 443
Lange, Clement M., Jr., 443
Lange, Connie, 1269
Lange, David A., 3869
Lange, Elizabeth B., 491
Lange, Glenn A., 443
Lange, James, 1181
Lange, Joseph L., 443
Lange, Sylvia, 1317
Lange, Tom, 1269
Langel, Craig, 3679
Langelotti, James P., 3410
Langenbach, Jeff, 216
Langerman, Richard, 1627
Langevin, Eric T., 2083
Langham, Catherine A., 1383
Langhammer, Fred H., 1127
Langhorst, Rose, 1281
Langiotti, Patricia L., 2635
Langlais, Dennis, 2668
Langland, Marc, 2743
Langland, Marc R., 74
Langland, R. Marc, 3906
Langley, Donna, 3893
Langman, M. Steven, 3108
Langridge, Jack, 2674
Langrock, James M., 2560
Langton, Clara, 422
Langton, Edward, 2578
Langton, Edward J., 2578
Langton, Lynda, 2578
Langton, Lynda M., 2578
Langwell, Dennis J., 2265, 3306
Lanier, Douglas J., 3667
Lanier, J. Hicks, 2847
Lanier, J. Reese, Sr., 2847
Lanier, Robert, 3978
Lanigan, Bernard, Jr., 3281, 3727
Lanigan, Brian D., 2506
Lanigan, Susan, 1143
Lanigan, Susan S., 1143
Laninga, John, 1628
Laningham, Julie M., 3568
Lankey, Thomas, 2341
Lankton, Madelyn, 3802
Lannan, Robin, 947
Lannie, P. Anthony, 211
Lanning, C. Douglas, 1168
Lanning, James W., 1940
Lannon, David, 4066
Lanoga Corp., 2211
Lansing, Sherry, 1141, 3095
Lansky, Gregg I., 1406
Lant, Steven V., 757
Lanterman, A. Kirk, 3906
Lanuza, Celeste, 2449
Lanza, Michael H., 3399
Lanznar, Howard S., 2101
Lapati, Domenic, 2134
LaPerch, William, 1919
Lapham, John, 1569
Lapham-Hickey Steel Corp., 2223
Lapidus, Alvin M., 1859
Lapidus, Sidney, 2176, 2250
Lapierre, Susan, 666
Lapine, Mark, 1399
Lapine, Mark A., 1399
Lapinski, Vince, 1634
Laplante, Donald, 1441
Laporte, David, 3243
Lapp, Robert J., 3760
Lapso, Robert, 2913
LaPunzina, Carol J., 426
Lara Cantu, Gustavo, 167
Laramie GM Auto Center, 3291
Lare, Rebekah, 761
Large, Elizabeth, 2177
Largent, Edward, 4047
Largey, Marjorie L., 577
Lari, David A., 718
Larin, Anne T., 1555
Larizadeh, Daryoush, 2255
Lark, Freda, 2828
Larkey, Roslyn, 667
Larkin, Alfred S., Jr., 1594
Larkin, Hoffman, Daly & Lindgren, Ltd., 2224
Larkin, Marla, 502
Larkin, Terrence B., 2237
Larnard, Mary E., 1946
Larner, Carol L., 959
LaRocco, Michael, 1385
LaRose, Matthew, 3304
LaRossa, Ralph A., 3077

Larrimore, Randall W., 669, 2801
Larry, Harkins, 3525
Larsen, Andrew, 1920
Larsen, Brent, 1668
Larsen, Dallin A., 2555
Larsen, David W., 3764
Larsen, David Wayne, 3764
Larsen, Edward L., 3682
Larsen, Jack S., 484
Larsen, John, 104
Larsen, Kirk, 1371
Larsen, Marshall O., 398, 2312, 3882
Larsen, Melvin L., 502
Larsen, Ralph S., 1552
Larsen, Randy, 2555
Larsen, Victoria Coates, 3764
Larsen, Wayne E., 91
Larson, Brian A., 546
Larson, Bruce, 1748
Larson, Charles W., 256
Larson, Chris, 367
Larson, Christopher F., 3272
Larson, David, 3243
Larson, Donald, 1655
Larson, Dorothy M., 576
Larson, Eric J., 1335
Larson, Gloria C., 501, 3898
Larson, Jodi, 1149
Larson, Kent T., 4135
Larson, Kevin P., 3819
Larson, Kirk, 3254
Larson, Mary, 569
Larson, Mary Beth, 2378
Larson, Michael, 1220
Larson, Paul E., 4026
Larson, Peter N., 595
Larson, Richard C., 4005
Larson, Steve, 2853
Larson, Thomas J., 3775
Larson, Timothy M., 2067
Larson, Tom, 3827
Larson, Warren C., 1535
LaRue, David J., 1467
LaRusso, Michael L., 3916
LaSalandra, Len, 2369
LaSalle Steel Co., 3100
Lasater, D. Eugene, 1132
Lasater, Donald E., 1519
Laschinger, Mary A., 2120
Lasco Leasing, Inc., 2226
Laserson, Frances G., 2563, 2564
Lash, James A., 324
Lash, Joseph V., 2656
Lasher, Jeff, 984
Lashure, David A., 348
Laskawy, Philip A., 1349, 1555, 2296, 3348
Laskero, Dominic, 1191
Laskowitz, Steven, 2192
Lassalle, Paul J., 34
Lassus Brothers Oil Co., 2226
Lassus, Greg L., 2226
Lassus, Jon F., 2226
Lassus, Jon R., 2226
Lassus, Todd J., 2226
Lasswell, Christopher S., 3816
Latek, Rich, 2716
Latham Entertainment, Inc., 2229
Latham, Cindy, 3418
Latham, Mike, 3326
Latham, Walter, 2229
Lathrop, Arthur H., 2699
Latimer, Amy, 537
Latona, James, Sr., 1840
Latta, G. Michael, 3946
Lattan, Lisa H., 137
Lattanzio, Paul S., 1944
Lattimer, Jeffrey H., 1363
Lattu, Kimberly A., 691
Latushkin, Maria, 2916
Lau, Carl, 644
Lau, Constance H., 1755, 2404
lau, Daniel B.T., 1381
Lau, Jeffrey D., 1381
Lau, Lawrence J., 637
Lau, Michele, 2434
Lau, Russell J., 1381
Lauber, David E., 16
Lauber, Scott J., 4093
Lauck, Joseph, 2238
Laud, Katharine, 3069
Lauder, Aerin, 2230
Lauder, Jane, 2230
Lauder, Karyl H., 1446
Lauder, Leonard A., 2230
Lauder, William P., 2230
Lauderback, Brenda J., 460, 1087, 4106
Lauer, Allen J., 1955
Lauer, Jon Michael, 2488
Lauer, Len J., 4042
Laufer, Bob, 2689
Laufer, Harry, 262
Laughlin, John Mc, 3635
Laughlin, Paige, 131
Laughman, Larry R., 2190
Laughton, Kim, 3363
Laun, Max W., 82
Launer, Blanche, 2766
Launius, Leigh Ann, 959
Laurance, Dale R., 1941
Laureate Education, Inc., 2231
Laurel Hill Realty, 4060
Lauren, David, 3123
Lauren, Ralph, 3123
Laurent, Michael, 2401
Laurent, Michael J., 2401
Lauria, Del J., 4002
Laurino, Carl J., 2355, 2356
Lauro, Jeff, 871
Laursen, Soren Torp, 2247
Laursen, Thomas E., 4158
Lausch, R. Dale, 3223
Lausch, Shirley, 3223
Lauscha, Dennis, 2679
Lautenbach, Marc B., 2984
Lautenbach, Ned C., 1216
Lauth Property Group, Inc., 2232
Lauth, Edward J., III, 4024
Lauth, Robert L., 2232
Lauth, Robert L., Jr., 2232
Lauvergeon, Anne, 143
Laux, Gary T., 3649
Lauzon, Armand F., 3410
Lauzon, Armand F., Jr., 3410
LaVacca, John, 2911
Lavalette, Gordon, 2676
LaVallee, Dean, 506
Lavarone, Malio, 2691
LaVecchia, Jean M., 2737
Lavelle, Kate, 1191
Lavelle, Kate S., 3498
Lavelle, Larna, 2486
Laverentz, David, 2093
Laverne, Lance, 2688
Lavigne, Louis J., Jr., 99, 508
Lavigne, Mark S., 1271
Lavin, Angeline M., 4026
Lavin, Arthur, 2448
Lavin, Cathy, 3405
Lavin, Mark V., 4035
Lavin, Michael E., 3709
Lavin, Richard P., 1999, 3905
Lavitt, Mel S., 2006
Lavizzo-Mourey, Risa J., 1793
Lavoie, A. James, 2506
Lavoie, Anita B., 3416
Lavoie, Blair, 2608
Lavoie, Gerard R., 1060
Lavori, Nora, 2825
LaVoy, Kathy, 1077
Law Enforcement Legal Defense Fund, 1201
Law Offices of Peter F. Davis, 3425
Law, Amy, 3031
Law, Bruce W., 2339
Law, D. Brian, 2339
Law, Rhea F., 1479
Law, Robert "Buzz", 976
Lawer, Betsy, 1415
Lawhead, Jean, 878
Lawhon, W.M., 4014
Lawhon, William M. Mack, 4014
Lawhorn, Caron A., 2815
Lawing, John, 306
Lawler, Jim, 1573
Lawler, John J., 642
Lawler, Joseph D., 1388
Lawler, Julia M., 3047
Lawler, Katie, 1542
Lawler, Marnie, 2475
Lawler, Martin J., III, 3317
Lawler, Mary K., 1542
Lawler, Tammy, 1952
Lawler, Tommy, 4014
Lawler, Tommy D., 4014
Lawless, David A., 3078
Lawless, Deborah T., 1855
Lawless, Robert J., 333, 1309
Lawlor, Brian, 3374
Lawlor, Richard J., 1793
Lawrence, David M., 2434
Lawrence, David Mckinnon, 56
Lawrence, Denise Baraka, 1086
Lawrence, George D., 211
Lawrence, James A., 304
Lawrence, Pat, 3140
Lawrence, Richard A., 910
Lawrence, Sandra A.J., 4039
Lawrence, Steve, 838
Lawrence, William B., 1366
Lawrence-Apfelbaum, Marc, 3755
lawrence-Lightfoot, Sara, 566
Lawrie, J. Michael, 2075
Lawry, Seth W., 2558
Laws, D. P., 3913
Laws, Jason, 1809
Laws, Neal, Jr., 1326
Laws, Tom L., 2500
Lawson, Barbara, 761
Lawson, Beth, 1661
Lawson, James R., 1134
Lawson, John R., 2063
Lawson, Robert T., 2063
Lawson, Rodger A., 3884
Lawton, Alison, 999
Lawton, Bryan, 1139
Lawton, Edgar H., III, 3500
Lawton, Michael, 1151
Lawton, Patrick S., 4005
Lay, Brent, 3868
Lay, Jack B., 3179
Lay, Randall R., 2234
Laybourne, Geraldine B., 2925, 3669
Layden, Timothy M., 4042
Layman, Ira D., 3229
Layman, J. Allen, 3229
Laymon, Joe W., 780
Layton, Donald H., 1348
Layton, Kimberley, 3322
Lazar, Robert S., 2699
Lazar, Robert W., 2681
Lazaroff, Barbara, 3080
Lazaroff, Stephen J., 827
Lazaroff, Steve, 3744
Lazarus, Franz, 948
Lazarus, Michael P., 1359
Lazarus, Rochelle B., 1552, 2466
Lazarus, S., 2788
Lazarus, Shelly, 2788
Lazenby, Chip, 3544
Lazo, Ken W., 3037
Lazzaro, Victor, Jr., 878
LCR-M Corp., 917
Le Corre, Eric, 2495
Le, Chuck, 4
Le, Duy-Loan T., 2632
Le, Katherine Le, 3594
Lea County Electric Cooperative, Inc., 2235
Lea, Janice, 3344
Leach, Beth Ann, 1410
Leach, Dave, 1664
Leach, Susan E., 391
Leadbeater, Seth M., 890
Leader, K. C., 395
Leadform Est. LTD, 2231
League, John, 3016
Leahey, Jim, 276
Leahy, Christine A., 729
Leahy, Dennis F., 577
Leahy, Jim, 402
Leahy, Richard T., 4017
Leaman, Rick, 2834
Leamer, Marybeth N., 959
Leaming, Nancy L., 465
Lear Corp., 2237
Lear, Jim, 1332
Lear, William M., Jr., 2113
Learish, John, 3220
Learmond, Alexis A., 1034
Leary, John F., 1946
Leary, John F., III, 1946
Leary, Linda, 76
Leary, Robert G., 1938
Leatherberry, Tonie, 1070
Leatherby, Dennis, 3832
Leatherdale, Douglas W., 3884
Leatherman, Allen H., 588
Leatherman, Phyllis, 152
Leatherman, Robert, 152
Leatherman, Robert J., Jr., 152
Leatherman, Robert, Sr., 152
Leatherman, Sean, 152
Leathers, Betty Jane, 2858
Leathers, Jennifer, 2858
Leathers, Robert A., 2858
Leaverton, Clay, 166
Leavitt, Alan, 3257
Leavitt, Craig, 1376
Leavitt, David Maasak, Jr., 3843
Leavitt, Jeffrey S., 2058
Leavitt, Michael O., 2453
Lebanon Mutual Insurance Co., 2238
Lebda, Douglas R., 1214
Lebedoff, David, 3243

Leroy, Pierre E., 679
Lerum, Stephen, 1761
Lesar, David J., 1706
Lesco Services, Inc., 3445
Lesesne, Joe, 1576
Lesher, Donald W., Jr., 1518
LeSieur, Jim, 2250
Lesjak, Catherine A., 1794
Leslie, Ann Farrell, 910
Leslie, Bruce A., 2978
Leslie, Christopher J., 3081
Leslie, Kristina M., 2776
Leslie, Mark, 3669
Lesnau, J. Thomas, 1094
Lesnau, Thomas J., 1094
Lesnik, John W., 2124
Lesnik, Madeline S., 2124
Lesnik, Steven H., 2124
Less, Sirr, 4066
Lessard, Chantae, 2127
Lesser, Rich, 535
Lesser, Shawn, 4004
Lessin, Leeba, 689
Lester, Howard, 4079
Lester, Kevin, 2938
Lester, Tamara, 2310
Lester, William W., 178
Lester, William Wallace, 21
Letaconnoux, Francois, 2381
Letcher, John, 2939
Letcher, John R., 2939
Letendre, Daniel, 340
Letendre, Mark, 2345
Letham, Dennis J., 3715
LeTourneau, Inc., 667
Letson, Steve, 1021
Lettes, Louis, 915
Leucadia National Corporation, 1538
Leuliette, Timothy D., 3964
Leung, Mona, 103
Leung, Sandra, 578
Leuthold, Bruce, 1620
Levan, Alan B., 385
Levan, Jarett, 385
Levanduski, Joseph J., 3361
Levatich, Matthew S., 1257, 1732
Levato, Jeseph A., 4031
Levato, Joseph A., 4030
Level, Leon J., 3624
Leven, Michael A., 2225
Levenick, Stuart L., 1279, 1626
Levenson, Dana S., 3696
Levenson, Howard A., 1293
Levenson, Rodger, 4127
Leventhal, Richard A., 1259
Lever Bros. Co., 3853
Leverett, Allen L., 806, 4093
Leverett, Larry, 2869
Leveridge, Richard J., 1111
Levesque, Christine, 126
Levesque, David L., 1946
Levesque, Louise J., 3317
Levesque, Mia, 4144
Levesque, Tracy, 4144
Levett, Mark, 1007
Levi, Agnes E., 2254
Levi, Ray & Shoup, Inc., 2254
Levi, Richard H., 2254
Levi, Ryan M., 2254
Levia, Oz, 969
Levie, Mark R., 2826
LeVier, Jack K., 2850
Levin, Alan G., 1268
Levin, Jack S., 2164
Levin, Jacquelyn A., 1276
Levin, Jerry W., 1220, 3315, 3835
Levin, Marc S., 1026
Levin, Michael S., 3763
Levin, Richard C., 143
Levin, Robert, 3271
Levin, Steve, 768
Levine, Arnie, 2268
Levine, Ellen R., 3294
Levine, Howard R., 1330
Levine, Jay, 255, 3138
Levine, Jay N., 3138
Levine, Jeff M., 3858
Levine, Jeffrey M., 3858
Levine, Lawrence, 942
Levine, Lawrence D., 942
Levine, Michael J., 2682, 2683
Levine, Mike, 2676
Levine, Randy, 2691
Levine, Robert, 2523
Levinson Foundation, Anna, The, 3411
Levinson Foundation, Max, The, 3411
Levinson, Anne, 370
Levinson, Arthur D., 217, 1549
Levinson, Linda Fayne, 1792, 1941, 2016, 2650, 4045
Levinson, Richard G., 116
Levinson, Sara, 2333
Levinson, Sara L., 1732
Levinson, William, 417
Levinson, William A., 417
Levis, William, 3077
Levis, William E., 2844
Levison, A. Andrew, 1365
Leviton Manufacturing Co., Inc., 2255
Leviton, Shirley, 2255
Levoff, Jeffery, 1181
LeVrier, David, 1813
Levy, Erik, 2156
Levy, George, 2691
Levy, H. George, 2205
Levy, John F., 567
Levy, Jonathan A., 1894
Levy, Paul, 2953
Levy, Richard D., 4028
Levy, Richard M., 3664
Levy, Robert P., 2923
Levy, Stan I., 1633
Levy, William, 2502
Levy-Garboua, Vivien, 346
Lew, Diane, 133
Lewand, Tom, 1094
Lewandowski, Laurie, 3299
Lewent, Judy C., 2586, 3733
Lewick, Carol A., III, 3261
Lewin, Erin, 304
Lewiner, Colette, 423
Lewis, Alan E., 1627
Lewis, Andrew L., IV, 1926
Lewis, Aylwin B., 1127
Lewis, Barry, 3070
Lewis, Brian, 3401
Lewis, Dave, 962
Lewis, David B., 2195, 3600
Lewis, David Baker, 1695
Lewis, Delano E., 869, 1214
Lewis, Donald, 1818
Lewis, Elaine, 1097, 1915
Lewis, Erica, 3401
Lewis, Geoffrey M., 2819
Lewis, George R., 753
Lewis, Gordon, 336
Lewis, Gordon R., 336
Lewis, Gregory, 3401
Lewis, Guy, 4110
Lewis, Harriet R., 1627
Lewis, Harrison, 1699
Lewis, Herbert, Dr., 3501
Lewis, J. Lacey, 959
Lewis, J. Randolph, 4030, 4031
Lewis, Jennifer L., 2150
Lewis, Jeremiah T., 1946
Lewis, John H., Jr., 337
Lewis, John M., 3526
Lewis, Karen J., 669
Lewis, Kenneth A., 1487
Lewis, Kevin, 483
Lewis, Laura B., 2881
Lewis, Lemuel E., 1145, 2841
Lewis, Marc, 2753
Lewis, Margaret G., 3487
Lewis, Marlene, 3165
Lewis, Melody, 1726
Lewis, Michael P., 3964
Lewis, Nyree, 1636
Lewis, Peter B., 3057
Lewis, Raymond J., 3931
Lewis, Renee, 2414
Lewis, Robert J., 2514
Lewis, Roderick W., 2500
Lewis, Roger P., 4126
Lewis, S. Alex, 1087
Lewis, Scott, 1380
Lewis, Sherry L., 1129
Lewis, Stephen, 3736
Lewis, Stephen L., 3736
Lewis, Steve, 613
Lewis, Steven R., 1420
Lewis, Thomas J., 412
Lewis, Tom, 1347, 1450
Lewis, W. Walker, 174
Lewis, Warren, 2238
Lewis, Will, 1460
Lewis, William M., Jr., 1032
Lewis-Raymond, Jane R., 2971
Lewitt, Bert, 2572
Lewnes, Ann, 38
Lexington Furniture Industries, Inc., 2257
Ley, Marc, 1992
Ley, Peter D., 75
Leyden, Timothy M., 4042
Leyhe, Denise, 3137
Leyman Manufacturing Corp., 2259
Leyman, Ray B., 2259
Leyva, Anne, 4052
LG&E Energy Corp., 2260
LG&E Energy LLC, 2260
Li, Jennifer, 2962
Li, Sarah, 2944
Li, Victor, 3762
Li-Cor of Lincoln, 2261
Li-Cor of Lincoln LLC, 113
Li-Cor, Inc., 2261
Lian, Fred V., 2721
Liang, George, 1048
Liang, Samuel M., 2452
Liau, Jackie, 3585
Liaw, Jeffrey, 246, 1273
Libarle, Daniel G., 1306
Libby, Russell T., 3677
Libenson, Richard M., 948
Liberatore, Chris, 2894
Liberman, Alex, 2451
Liberman, Lee M., 1519
Liberty Bank, 2262
Liberty Carton Co., 1372
Liberty Diversified Industries, Inc., 1372
Liberty Media Corporation, 2264
Liberty Mutual, 216
Liberty Mutual Group, 1779
Liberty Mutual Insurance Co., 2265
Liberty Mutual Insurance Company, 2789
Liberty, Jason, 3273
Libman, Raquel, 1767
Liboff, Jerry, 576
Licata, Richard, 2649
Licciardo, Sandra, 2693
Lichenstein, John, 3959
Licht, Warren E., 491
Lichte, Rachel, 834
Lichte, Tim, 2486
Lichtenstein, Leslie, 1098
Lichtenstein, Warren G., 1548
Lichtiger, Ira, 4036
Lichty, Dana, 1676
Licklider, Rex A., 1059, 3550
Liddell, Carolyn, 1490
Liddell, Dick, 892
Liddell, Richard, 3912
Liddell, Richard D., 892
Liddle, David E., 2690
Liddle, Lynn M., 1151
Liddy, Edward, 13
Liddy, Edward M., 3, 516, 3838
Liding, Lawrence, Jr., 727
Lie, H., 1470
Lieb, Charles, 1651
Lieb, Charles R., 1651
Lieb, Peter, 210
Lieb, Randy, 3259
Liebenson, Paul, 229
Lieber, Dan, 3887
Lieber, Idii, 2893
Lieber, Joseph, 2893
Lieber, Leo, 1882
Lieberman Cos., Inc., 2266
Lieberman Music Co., 2266
Lieberman, Daniel, 2266
Lieberman, David, 2266
Lieberman, Ira, 663
Lieberman, Pamela Forbes, 716, 3575
Lieberman, Sara, 2266
Lieberman, Sheila, 2266
Lieberman, Stephen E., 2266
Lieberman, Susan, 2266
Lieberman, William K., 186
Liebersbach, John, 1894
Lieble, Randy F., 2636
Lieblein, Grace D., 1852
Liebman, Seymour, 672
Liedl, Heidi, 2173
Liedle, Heidi, 2173
Lieff, Ann Spector, 1519
Liem, Richard H., 2219, 3120
Liem, Rick, 3120
Lienert, James M., 2780
Lietz, Andrew, 3307
Lietz, Andrew E., 3307
Lievois, Jim, 2414
Life Care Centers of America Inc., 2267
Life Changing Lives, 30
Life Investors Insurance Co. of America, 45
Life Technologies Inc., 2268
Life Wise, 947
Lifepoint Corporate Services Group, 2270
LifePoint Hospitals, Inc., 2270
Lifshitz, Lisa, 1665
Liftman, Alexandra C., 340

Loftis, Harry E., 3203
Loftis, Thomas P., 3230
Lofton, Irene, 1587
Lofton, Kevin E., 1582
Lofton, Michael W., 2590
Loftus, Gerard A., 3115
Logan, Don, 3755
Logan, Harold R., Jr., 1635
Logan, Jim, 3534
Logan, Joe, 3673
Logan, Nancy, 1161
Logan, Winford L., 3590
Lograsso, John M., 3852
Lohbeck, David J., 773
Lohkamp, Joanna, 1081
Lohmann, Jens, 381
Lohmann, Steve, 3186
Lohr, David H., 3877
Lohr, Steve, 1545
Lohr, Walter G., Jr., 1027
Lohr, William James, 3409
Loiacono, Nicholas A., 2434
Loken, Darren, 1634
Loliger, Hans J., 988
Lomax, Rachel, 3179
Lomax, Thomas W., 1421
Lombard, Susan, 428
Lombardi, Dean, 2306
Lombardi, Don, 1359
Lombardi, John, 3955
Lombardi, Keith H., 2390
Lombardo, Patrick E., 1765
Lomeli-Azoubel, Raul, 3300
Lominac, Eve, 384
Lommen, Richard T., 261
Lommerin, Nils, 1065
Lonaker, Michelle, 1769
Londoff Chevrolet, Johnny, 2297
Londoff, John H., 2297
Londoff, John H., Jr., 2297
Londoff, John, Jr., 2297
London, J. Tate, 3380
London, Roberta, 2997
London, Terry E., 2973
Londono, Yolanda, 3821
Lonergan, Edward, 1130
Lonergan, Edward F., 795
Long Automotive Group, Phil, Inc., 2298
Long Ford Colorado Springs, Phil, 2298
Long Ford of Denver, Phil, LLC, 2298
Long Ford, Phil, LLC, 2298
Long Mitsubishi, Phil, LLC, 2298
Long Nissan, Phil, LLC, 2298
Long West, Phil, LLC, 2298
Long, Claranne R., 1009
Long, Dan, 2704, 3641
Long, David H., 2265, 3306
Long, David T., 476
Long, Deborah J., 3066
Long, Douglas J., 2171
Long, Elizabeth Valk, 403, 3488, 3597
Long, Erika, 2409
Long, Gary A., 2737, 3075
Long, George E., Jr., 3885
Long, George P., III, 2997
Long, Hal, 3426
Long, Henry P., 120
Long, John C., 1791
Long, John D., 1620
Long, Kim, 840
Long, Michael J., 175, 249
Long, Nicholas T., 4106
Long, Peter, 655
Long, R. Keith, 857
Long, Robert M., 2989
Long, Rose, 1986
Long, Sammie, 2120
Long, Theodore K., Jr., 1098
Long, Tom, 1438, 2523
Long, William C., 2323
Longaberger Co., The, 2299
Longaberger, Tamala, 2299
Longaberger, Tami, 2299
Longhi, Mario, 3877
Longoria, Janiece M., 738
Longval, Steve, 55
Longview Capital Corp., 2300
Longworth, Jo-Ann, 543
Lonn, Dana, 3775
Lonner, Matthew, 780, 3856
Lonon, Terrill A., 3319
Loo, Janice Luke, 1756
Look, Bryon, 2314
Loomis, Mickey, 2679
Loomis, Richard A., 3086
Loomis, William R., Jr., 2277, 2965
Loon, Wong, 1266
Looney, Carey Wilkenson, 1695
Loosbrock, Julie M., 1084
Loosbruck, Julie M., 1084
Lopardo, Nicholas A., 2939
Lopes, Lance, Sr., 1460
Lopez Morales, Ivan C., 268
Lopez, Evelyn, 1442
Lopez, Gerardo I., 125, 572
Lopez, Johnny O., 1095
Lopez, Lucia C., 2044
Lopez, Richard Y., 576
Lopez, Rosalio, 3034
Lopez, Tony, 783
Lopez, Yolanda, 3056
Lopez-May, Lucho, 1030
Lora, Melissa, 2105, 3679
Loranger, Daniel D., 3308
Loranger, Steven R., 1352, 4139
Lorber, David A., 1548
Lorberbaum, Jeffrey S., 2545
Lorch, George A., 2950
Lord and Taylor, LLC, 2302
Lord Trust Fund, Mary Louise and Marjori, 1763
Lord, Albert L., 2659, 3478
Lord, Gene D., 1446
Lord, Kevin, 1532
Lord, Richard C., 501
Loree, James M., 1741, 3579
Lorensen, Mike, 544
Lorenz, Arthur, 1893
Lorenzen, Shauna R., 1306
Loreto, Marty, 3524
Loretta, Mark, 2346
Loretto High School, 1042
Loria, Jeffrey H., 2491
Lorimer, Linda Koch, 2429
Lorimier, Bradley, 2268
Loring, James P., 183
Lorren, Stanly, 712
Lorson, John W., 231
Lorusso, Gerard C., 296
Lorusso, Joseph J., 296
Lorusso, Matthew J., 3054
Losch, William C., III, 1406
Losh, J. Michael, 210, 688, 1517, 2393, 3060
Lotano, Amy W., 2782
Lothrop, Dave, 1032
Lotman, Herbert, 2137
Lott, Raymond, 1152
Lotto, Bill, 771
Loudermilk, Joey M., 54
Loughlin, James, 732
Loughran, Dennis M., 3253
Loughrey, Joe, 3473
Loughridge, Mark, 1960
Louie, Mark, 2082
Louis, A. Andrew R., 928
Louis, Clifton D., 1130
Louis, John Jeffry, 1532
Louisiana-Pacific Corp., 2310
Lounsbury, Loren H., 1415
Louras, Peter N., Jr., 3461
Lourd, Bryan, 975, 1903
Louthan, Frank G., Jr., 3148
Louv, Bill, 1588
Lovallo, William P., 2190
Lovato, Ron, 2034
Love Family Charitable Lead Trust, 3049
Love, Dais, III, 2954
Love, Dan, 389
Love, Davis, 2954
Love, Dennis M., 57, 2847, 3049
Love, Frank, 2311
Love, Gay M., 3049
Love, Phillip E., 177
Love, Tom, 2311
Love, William G., 1214
Lovejoy, Joan D., 1276
Lovejoy, Mary F., 3731
Lovejoy, Wallace W., 2251
Lovelace, Glenn, 2920
Lovelace, James B., 677
Loveland, Catherine A., 910
Loveless, Keith, 74
Loveless, Tom, 2140
Lovell, Betsy, 1726
Lovell, Brad, 2113
Lovell, Stephanie, 501
Loveman, Gary W., 650, 858, 1352
Lovetro, Keith E., 1106
Lovett, James W., 955
Lovett, Richard, 975
Lovik, Kathryn, 3714
Low, Lisa, 3652
Low, Nathan A., 3652
Lowber, John, 1550
Lowden, John R., 1365
Lowder, James K., 71
Lowder, Kellie, 3523
Lowder, Maria, 1458
Lowe's, 1776
Lowe's Cos., Inc., 2312
Lowe, Alan L., 595
Lowe, Carol P., 3381
Lowe, David, 1624
Lowe, Gregg A., 1495
Lowe, John B., Jr., 4151
Lowe, John E., 2965
Lowe, Jonathan, 2306
Lowe, Ken, 3374
Lowe, Nancy S., 2150
Lowe, Robert J., 42
Lowell, Richard L., 2743
Lowenfeld, David, 4122
Lowenfels, Fred M., 3796
Lowenfield, Clay, 1464
Lowenstein, Elizabeth, 3181
Lowenthal, Edward, 136
Lower, Kathy, 1240
Lowery, Dolores J., 1424
Lowery, James W., Jr., 621
Lowery, Kay, 512
Lowery, William C., 3430
Lowery-Born, Beryl, 495
Lowndes III Trust, 3761
Lowndes, Henrietta M., 3761
Lowndes, Vincent, 3879
Lowndes, William, III, 3761
Lowndes, William, IV, 3761
Lowrance, Sid, 672
Lowrance, Tim, 3457
Lowrey, Charles F., 3072
Lowrey, Kathleen "Kate", 1296
Lowrey, Tom, 3369
Lowrey, William C., 3430
Lowrie, William G., 547
Lowrimore, Lawrence, 221
Lowry, J. E., 1309
Lowry, Scott T., 358
Lowsen, Dorrit, 58
Lowson, Steven R., 3410
Loy, James M., 2292
Loyalty Development Co., Ltd., 2198
Loyd, Kathy Brittain White, 2405
Loyello, P.J., 2491
Loyello, Peter J., 2491
Loynd, Michael R., 1519
Loynd, Richard B., 1519, 2070
Lozano, Cressida J., 3331
Lozano, Jose, 3470
Lozano, Jose Ignacio, 3150
Lozano, Monica C., 340, 1127
Lozier, Kaye R., 4034
LTC Properties, Inc., 1275
Lu, Ming, 2061
Lubar, David J., 2749
Lubin, Donald G., 2427
Lublin, Jason, 1267
Lubrizol Corp., The, 2315
Lubsen, Sigismundus W.W., 3707
Lucareli, Michael B., 2544
Lucarelli, Jay, 30
Lucas, G. Robert, 1300
Lucas, George W., Jr., 2316
Lucas, James M., 1448
Lucas, John T., 2292
Lucas, Mark E., 1919
Lucas, Ron D., 3572
Lucas, Rubye, 280
Lucas, Steve, 2914
Lucasfilm Foundation, 2316
Lucasfilm Ltd., 2316
Lucchese, Cynthia L., 567
Lucchese, John J., 2154, 2617
Lucchino, Frank J., 3877
Lucchino, Larry, 538
Lucchino, Lawrence, 538
Luce, Michael D., 1726
Lucent Technologies Inc., 81
Lucente, Rocco, II, 3214
Lucente, Sarah, 4097
Lucente, Tony, 2716
Luchetti, Linda, 2028
Luchetti, Linda Louise, 2028
Luciani, Vincent, 1903
Luciano, Juan R., 233
Luciano, Michael A., 1488
Lucien, Kent, 342
Lucien, Kent T., 342
Lucier, Gregory T., 688, 2268
Luck Stone Corp., 2317
Luck, Charles S., III, 2317
Luck, Charles S., IV, 2317
Luck, Mary Jane, 3624
Luck, Oliver, 43, 136
Luckacs, Joseph J., Jr., 2341
Lucke, James T., 2545

Macey, Christopher, 1112
Macey, Jonathan, 411
Macfariane, Gregory J., 1695
MacFarlane, Cathy, 1937
Macgarvie, D. Paul, 2137
MacGillivray, Robin Greenway, 3461
MacGowan, Bill, 2698
MacGowen, Florence, 1763
Machak, Kathy, 3818
Machias Savings Bank, 2332
Machicote, Joe, 3492
Machiels, Alec, 2550
Machost, Noel, 2010
Machtley, Ronald K., 183
Maciag, Sandra J., 3086
Maciag, Tom, 1696
MacInnes, Glenn, 4016
MacInnis, Frank, 1581, 1999
MacInnis, Frank T., 1255, 1999, 4077
MacInnis, Maureen J., 1089
MacIntyre, James, III, 2742
MacIntyre, Michael J., 1795
MacIntyre, Michael P., 1795
Mack, Ann Baker, 1680
Mack, Connie, 2605
Mack, Connie, III, 1032
Mack, Debra, 84
Mack, Edward J., II, 349
Mack, Michael P., 1534
Mack, Richard L., 2580
Mack, Richard L., Esq., 2580
Mack, Robert F., 4127
Mack, Stanley, 84
Mack, Thomas, 84
Mackay, A.D. David, 1474
Mackay, David, 390
Mackay, Graham, 2523, 2962
MacKay, Harold H., 2580
MacKay, John, 3343
MacKay, John J., Jr., 3343
Mackeand, Tanya, 1031
MacKeigan, John M., 502
Mackenna, Francisco Perez, 423
Mackenzie, Earle A., 3434
MacKenzie, George, 3307
Mackenzie, Mindy, 390
MacKenzie, Robert K., 183
MacKenzie, Tod, 1120
Mackesy, D. Scott, 376
Mackey, John, 4066
Mackey, John P., 4066
Mackey, Peter, 3940
Mackey, Steven R., 1774
Mackey, Warren A., 1485
Mackey, William P., 2335
Mackie, Bert H., 2815
Mackie, Jill, 3386
Mackin, Carol D., 492
Mackin, Craig L., 1954
Mackin, James E., 522
Mackin, Jay L., 1954
Mackin, Jay Lawrence, 1954
Mackin, Jeffrey L., 1954
Mackin, Kimberly Ann, 1954
Mackin, Michael J., 1954
MacKinnon, Elinor, 1298
Mackley, Pam, 2123
Macklin, Robert V., 2513
MacKrell, Patrick J., 2681
MacLachlan, Don, 3716
MacLean, Brian, 3802
MacLean, Brian W., 3802
Maclean, Elizabeth, 3741
Maclean, Mary Ann, 3560
MacLean, Pete, 1182
MacLeay, Thomas H., 2633
MacLellan, Robert F., 3040
MacLennan, David W., 691, 3235
Macleod, Ivor, 1823
Macleod, Lorna, 3812
MacLeod, Roderick C.G, 642
Maclin, Alan, 564
Maclin, Alan H., 564
Maclin, Joan, 3373
Macmanus, Michael, 1718
MacMilan, Marsha, 691
MacMillan, A.S., Jr., 3898
MacMillan, Stephen H., 668
Macnee, Walt M., 2399
Macnee, Walter M., 2399
Macneil, Bruce M., 2000
MacNeil, Malcolm F., 2000
Macomber, John D., 3992
Macor, Mark, 3394
MacQueen, R. M., 3198
Macricostas, Constantine S., 2969
Macricostas, George C., 2969
Madaj, Kim, 1088
Madar, Gregory S., 4016
Madaus, Martin D., 956
Maddalena, Susana Della, 2948
Maddaloni, Michael, 389
Madden, Beth A., 1966
Madden, Dougles M., 730
Madden, Teresa S., 4135
Madding, Bruce W., 637
Maddox, Elton, 3839
Maddox, Jeff, 1615
Maddrey, Greg, 768
Maddux, Richard H., 350
Madel, Christopher W., 3232
Madelain, Michel, 2564
Madelain, Michel F., 2563
Madere, Consuelo E., 2559
Madhaven, Ashok, 669
Madia, William J., 3904
Madigan, Daniel, 1353
Madigan, Daniel P., 1353
Madigan, John W., 1582
Madigan, Justin, 1353
Madigan, Laura, 1353
Madison Gas and Electric Co., 2334
Madison National Bank, 2335
Madison Tyler LLC, 853
Madison, Al, 602
Madison, Anne, 798
Madison, Michael H., 474
Madison, Scott, 713
Madland, Troy, 1466
Madonna, Jon C., 273, 1494, 3748
Madrazo, Jesus, 2559
Madri, Joseph A., 86
Madsen, Andrew H., 1032, 3682
Madsen, Dennis, 4037
Madsen, Gary C., 871
Madsen, Jacqueline, 2184
Madsen, Lorraine N., 1170
Madson, Brad, 2530
Madzula, John S., 2704
Maeda, Tatsumi, 306
Maedel, Michael, 3739
Mael, Joel, 2491
Mael, Joel A., 2491
Maestri, Luca, 3047
Maffei, Gregory, 765
Maffei, Gregory B., 360, 1242, 2264
Maffeo, Vincent A., 3311
Maffie, Michael O., 3524
Maffucci, David G., 2391
Magadauce, Donnie, 2966
Magao, Patricia A., 772
Magdalin, Dean, 783
Magdefrau, Stuart E., 3245
Magee, Karen, 3757
Magers, David A., 951
Maggert, Michael A., 1225
Maggin, Bruce, 3088
Maggioncalda, Jeff N., 3455
Maggiora & Ghilotti, Inc., 1570
Magid, Brent, 2241
Magill, Kent, 1809
Magill, Peter, 3474
Magill, William H., 3141
Maginn, Robert A., Jr., 2037
Magistretti, Elisabetta, 2319
Magleby, Shannon Savage, 3341
Magline, Inc., 2339
Magnacca, Joseph, 1186
Magner, Gwen, 3560
Magner, Marjorie, 1532
Magner, Patrick C., 1510
Magnetics, Inc., 3530
Magnolia Marine Transport Co., 1289
Magnolia Plantation Corp., 2340
Magnus, Diane S., 906
Magnus, Doug, 906
Magnus, James D., 906
Magnus, Matthew, 906
Magnus, Vanessa, 802
Magnuson, Michaelina, 1477
Magoon, Grace Previte, 1207
Magowan, Peter A., 722, 3324
Magri, Patrick, 2466
Magstadt, Brian, 3461
Maguire, Alan J., 44
Maguire, James J., Jr., 2960
Maguire, John M., 2873
Maguire, John P., 491
Magusin, Barbara, 3034
Magyar Bancorp, Inc., 2341
Mah, Sammy T., 588
Mahady, Joseph M., 78
Mahaffey, H. William, 1440
Mahan, Lucy, 1415
Mahany, Susan, 1698
Maher, Christopher D., 2782
Maher, John, 2531
Maher, Ken, 2148
Maheras, Thomas G., 1125
Mahill, Elizabeth, 2920
Mahlberg, Paul, 991
Mahler, Michael, 1402
Mahler, Michael W., 1402
Mahlke, Thomas K., 3235
Mahmoud, Adel A.F., 398
Mahnke, Dave, 14
Mahon, Bob, 263
Mahon, Casey D., 3869
Mahone, Cathy, 105
Mahoney, Anne, 2820
Mahoney, Carol L., 2704
Mahoney, Charles, 2820
Mahoney, Cornelius D., 428
Mahoney, Dan, 370
Mahoney, David C., 2064
Mahoney, David L., 3669
Mahoney, George R., Jr., 1330
Mahoney, James V., 1047
Mahoney, Janine, 1208
Mahoney, John J., 487
Mahoney, Joseph, 2820
Mahoney, Judy, 225
Mahoney, Kathleen M., 2619
Mahoney, Michael F., 540
Mahoney, Michael P., 2879
Mahoney, P. Michael, 2879
Mahoney, Peter, 2820
Mahoney, R. Scott, 1904
Mahoney, Sean O., 1071
Mahoney, Steve, 838
Mahoney, Terrence W., 3253
Mahoney, Thomas J., Jr., 1998
Mahoney, Thomas P., 2698
Mahony, Anne, 225
Mahony, Shelia A., 641
Mahony, Susan, 2274
Mahowald, Douglas A., 2441
Mahowald, Douglass A., 2441
Mahy, Helen, 2630
Mai, Johnny, 2005
Mai, Paul, 1430
Maibach, Benjamin C., III, 366
Maibach, Douglas, 366
Maibach, Ryan, 366
Maier, Donald R., 246
Maier, Howard S., 2335
Maier, Jean M., 2749
Mailer, Dee Jay A., 1405
Mailhot, Raymond E., 2126
Mailloux, J. Wayne, 1054
Mailman, Joshua, 16
Mailman, Susan M., 865
Main, Rebecca R., 341
Main, Timothy L., 2006
Maine Shellfish Co., Inc., 1989
Mainer, Matthew, 1296
Maiolino, Anna Maria, 1236
Mais, Stephen M., 1879
Maisch, Paul A., 3070
Maiz, Ricardo, 27
Majeske, Penelope K., 1078
Majestic Realty Co., 2343
Majestic Star Casinos & Hotel, 2344
Majewski, Alan M., 3577
Majka, Matt, 2531
Major, Barry, 2606
Major, John D., 2070
Major, John E., 579
Major, Paul, 148
Major, Rubysteen, 529
Major, Sean D., 2070
Majoras, Deborah Platt, 3055, 3915
Majoy, Constance A., 4113
Makal, Jeffrey T., 3408
Makepeace, A. D., 7
Makepeace, Christopher, 7
Maker's Mark, 2113
Makespeace Company, A.D., 7
Maki, Allison, 1094
Maki, Mark A., 1265
Maki, Tony, 2581
Maki, Val, 1259
Makin, Michael F., 1634
Makino, Inc., 2348
Makino, Jiro, 2348
Makinson, John, 2922
Makode, Gail, 2416
Makowski, Robert J., Jr., 2879
Makua, Elmer, 1
Malamud, Barry E., 1741
Malamud, Neil, 2350
Malamud, Neil N., 2350
Malamud, Sandra, 2350
Malanga, Victor, 1224
Malay, Ramal, 1777
Malburg, Angela, 3020

Malburg, Donald, 3020
Malco Industries, Inc., 2350
Malcolm, Jan K., 496
Malcolm, Robert M., 1791
Malcolm, Steve J., 2815
Malcolm, Waynewright, 2250
Maldavo, Callisto, 1959
Maldon, Alphonso, Jr., 3998
Malear, Cathy, 3852
Malebra, James J., 3592
Malek, Frederic V., 725
Malemute, Josephine, 1167
Malerba, James J., 3592
Malesich, Edward, 802
Malet, Philip L., 3599
Maletta, Matthew J, 99
Malfavon, Marco, 81
Malfettone, John P., 1186
Malheur Lumber Co., 2783
Malhorta, Sajid, 933
Malik Family, Fred, 1201
Malik, Andrew J., 2655
Malik, Rajiv, 2610
Malin, Donna, 2048
Malin-Peck, Nanci, 1591
Malinder, Elizabeth B., 962
Malinowski, Eugene P., 3693
Malis, Ira H., 2813
Malkin, Judd, 790
Malkmus, George, 1705
Malkmus, Paul, 1705
Malkmus, Paul H., 1705
Malkmus, Rhonda, 1705
Mallard Oil Company, 3749
Mallesch, Eileen A., 1300
Mallet, Conrad L., Jr., 2237
Malley, Claudia, 2689
Malliett, Julie, 569
Mallin, Lisa, 1266
Mallon, Laurel, 3118
Mallory, Bradley L., 323
Mallot, Bryon I., 74
Mallott, Anthony, 3380
Mallott, Byron I., 3380
Mallott, Philip E., 460
Malloy, John F., 1879, 3948
Malm, Steven E., 2707
Malmen, Jeffrey L., 1907
Malmgren, R. Scott, 144
Malo, Mike, 886
Malone, Chris, 912
Malone, Daniel, 4038
Malone, David J., 1318, 1799
Malone, David P., 898
Malone, Deborah L., 1118
Malone, Evan D., 2264
Malone, James R., 181, 3171
Malone, John, 765, 2263
Malone, John C., 1126, 1311, 2263, 2264
Malone, Keola, 3850
Malone, Mary Alice D., 669
Malone, Michael W., 2999
Malone, Rich, 2055
Malone, Robert, 368
Malone, Robert A., 1706, 2907
Malone, Ronald A., 1804
Maloney, Brown McClatchy, 2422
Maloney, Kimberley A., 4080
Maloney, Kimberly A., 4080
Maloney, Meghan, 3686
Maloney, Sean, 2455
Maloof, Thomas A., 1275
Malovany, Howard, 4125
Maltz, Allen P., 501
Mamiya, Richard T., 1405
Mamiye Brothers, Inc., 2352
Mamiye, Abraham, 2352
Mamiye, Charles D., 2352
Mamiye, Charles M., 2352
Mamiye, Hyman M., 2352
Mamiye, Hymie, 2352
Man, Debra C., 2484
Man-Dell Food Stores, Inc., 2135
Manager, Vada O., 258
Manago, Sharon, 1846
Manahan, Vincent D., III, 1984
Manby, Joel, 1790
Mancebo, Stephen, 2217
Manchester, Wayne F., 2126
Mancini, Lisa A., 997
Mancini,, Joseph H., Jr., 4136
Mancino, Douglas M., 1766
Mancino, Joseph L., 2335
Mancino, Lynn, 2882
Mancuso, Michael J., 3558
Mancuso, Peter, 3061
Mandanch, David D., 2324
Mandarich, David D., 2324
Mandekic, Anthony L., 2489
Mandel, Andrea J., 1179
Mandel, Irwin B., 785
Mandel, Lawrence, 2135
Mandel, Victor, 123
Mandelbaum, Barry R., 1863
Mandelbaum, Eric S., 1232
Mandell, Paula, 2323
Mandell, Robert A., 1648
Mandell, Zachary H., 1648
Manders, Matt, 812
Mandile, Patrick, 3232
Mandl, Alex J., 1068
Mandos, Robert R., Jr., 181
Mandragouras, Peter J., 1989
Mandsen, Dennis, 74
Maness, David J., 1993
Maness, Frank, 2752
Manfredi, Christine S., 41
Manfredi, Joseph A., 3855
Mangan, Michael D., 2423
Mangan, Richard K., 505
Manganello, Timothy M., 407, 528
Mangas, Thomas B., 246
Mangiagalli, Marco, 2319
Mangieri, Robin, 1256
Mangino, Jeff, 3187
Mangukiya, Piyush, 1231
Mangum, Gregory L., 1635
Mangum, Jim, 3978
Mangum, John K., 3822
Mangum, Myldred H., 871
Mangum, Mylle H., 362
Manhattan Beer Distributors, LLC, 2354
Maniaci, Debra, 2570
Manigault, Juan, 3697
Manigault, Pierre, 1302
Manion, James, 3840
Manion, Mark D., 2725
Manion, Melissa J., 3707
Manion, Melvin, 3421
Manitowoc Company, 2356
Manley, Rose Marie, 91
Manly, Marc E., 1189
Manly, Robert W., IV, 3487
Mann, Cathy, 1706
Mann, Jennifer, 3336
Mann, John, 3981
Mann, Lance, 1053
Mann, Neil, 92
Manning, Bill, 3549
Manning, Carol M., 2595
Manning, David F., 2279
Manning, Dennis J., 1683
Manning, Diane L., 2042
Manning, J. Terry, 215
Manning, Jack, 534
Manning, Jennifer, 1587
Manning, John P., 534, 2265
Manning, Katrina, 3860
Manning, Kenneth P., 3381, 3408
Manning, Lisa, 312
Manning, Mark, 337
Manning, Melissa Joy, 2458
Manning, Paul, 3408
Manning, Richard, 1652
Manning, Rick, 847
Mannion, Dennis, 2305
Mannion, Mel, 3421
Mannion, Melvin R., 3421
Mannis, Scott, 2121
Manns, Andrew, 2551
Mannucci, Pier, 382
Manocherian, Amir, 2357
Manocherian, Fraydun, 2685
Manocherian, Jed, 2357
Manocherian, John, 2685
Manocherian, Kimberly, 2685
Manocherian, Mireille, 2357
Manocherian, Robert, 2357
Manocherian, Rosita, 2357
Manogue, Caroline B., 1268
Manogue, Joseph, 2409
Manoogian, Richard A., 1464, 2393
Manor Care, Inc., 1763
Manos, John, 2302
Manpower Inc., 2358
Manring, Gene, 3637
Mansell, Kevin B., 2181
Mansfield, Christopher C., 2265, 3306
Mansfield, David E., 1410
Mansfield, William L., 407, 3920
Manson, Easton, 2944
Mansur, Bernadette, 2631
Manthy, Thomas A., 3388
Manti Operating Co., Inc., 2359
Mantlo, Bronwen, 2274
Manuel, Ethan, 2462
Manuel, Paul, 2377
Manufacturers and Traders Trust Co., 2323
Manus, Adam, 2689
Manwani, Harish, 4056
Manzi, Jim P., 926, 3733
Manzo, Robert J., 3964
Manzulli, Michael F., 2683
Manzur, Salman, 628
Mapes Industries Inc., 2360
Mapes, Christopher L., 2279
Mapes, Timothy W., 1073
Maples, Michael J., 2258, 3498
Mappin, Nancy Sue, 2239
Maquoketa State Bank, 2361
Mara, Francis X., 2684
Mara, John K., 2684
Mara, Martin J., 2671
Marac, John K., 2684
Maraffio, Melanie, 254
Marafino, Estelle R., 974
Maranga, Toby, 3185
Marathe, Paraag, 3326
Marathon Savings Bank, 2366
Marbach, Carl B., 3769
Marban, Lesly, 2451
Marberry, Michael L., 3453
Marblestone, Kenneth, 767
Marblestone, Philip K., 3431
Marburger, Robert, 116
Marbut, Bob, 3915
Marc-Aurele, Drew, 1946
Marc-aurele, R. Drew, 1946
MarcAurele, Joseph J., 4001
Marcell, Frederick A., Jr., 1419
March Buick, Tony, Inc., 2367
March, Anthony, 2367
March, Antony, 2367
March, Gail, 2367
March, Karen, 1947
March, Kevin P., 3728
March, Nancy, 2915
March, Vicki A., 3865
March-Aurele, R. Drew, 1946
Marchand, J.P., 2151
Marchetti, Roger, 688
Marchick, David M., 3410
Marchionne, Sergio, 801, 856, 2962
Marcho Farms, Inc., 2368
Marcho, Wayne, 2368
Marcho, Wayne A., 2368
Marchon Eyewear, Inc., 2369
Marciano, A. Carmen, 3317
Marciano, Maurice, 1685
Marciano, Paul, 1685
Marcil, James E., 4024
Marcin, Robert, 1026
Marcinelli, James A., 1854
Marco Family Limited Partnership, W. and M., 2368
Marco, Lori J., 1866
Marcous, Jeff, 1105
Marcuccilli, James C., 3595
Marcum, Brandi N., 1053
Marcum, R. Alan, 1102
Marcus & Millichap Co., The, 2370
Marcus Corp., The, 2371
Marcus, George M., 2370
Marcus, Gregory S., 2371
Marcus, Helen, 2711
Marcus, James S., 133
Marcus, Jeffrey A., 765
Marcus, Richard G., 133
Marcus, Robert D., 3755
Marcus, Roger S., 133
Marcus, Stephen H., 2371
Marcus, William M., 133
Marcy, Charles F., 1884
Marder, Adam K., 3863
Mardy, Michael J., 1653
Marena Group, Inc., 2372
Maresca, Bob, 530
Maresca, Robert, 530
Margaret, L.Brown, 75
Margetts, Robert, 1895
Margiotta, Charles, 3134
Margolies, Robert, 3250
Margolis, Jay, 533
Margolis, Judy O., 3548
Margolis, Robert J., 1044
Margolis, Sidney O., 3871
Margotta, Gisella L., 1208
Margulis, Heidi S., 1886
Marhenke, Michael C., 2379
Mariah Media Inc., 2373
Mariani Nut Co., Inc., 2374
Mariani, Dennis, 2374
Mariani, Frank, 2307
Mariani, Jack Dennis, 2374

Mariani, Jack N., 2374
Mariani, Linda L., 1118
Mariani, Martin, 2374
Mariani, Pedro Henrique, 328
Mariano, Robert A., 3272
Marican, Tan Sri Mohd Hassan, 913
Marin, Robert, 2869
Marinakos, Plato A., 1926
Marincel, Thomas W., 930
Marineau, Philip A., 2086, 2471
Marinello, Kathryn V., 1555
Mariner, Jonathan D., 1323, 2345
Marini, Guido Albi, 1236
Marino, George R., 2514
Marino, John, 3732
Marino, Michael, 809
Marino, Michael D., 1926
Marino, Patricia J., 1174
Marino, Robert A., 1863
Marino, Robert J., 3672
Marino, Thomas J., 866
Marino, V. James, 2786, 3088
Marino, William J., 1863, 3381
Marinos Charity, 1858
Marinovich, Robert F., 2815
Mario, Ernest, 540, 732
Marion General Hospital, 3944
Marion Merrell Dow Inc., 3329
Maris, Mahlon, 240
Maris, Mahlon O., 240
Maritan Memorial Hospital, 3944
Maritz, Johan, 2070
Maritz, W. Stephen, 2208, 2376
Mariucci, Anne L., 3524
Mark Gold L.P., 1605
Mark IV Industries, Inc., 2377
Mark, Alan Paul, 3721
Mark, Allen W., 1293
Mark, Richard J., 129
Mark, Tolliver J., 37
Markantonis, George, 2133
Markee, Richard L., 871
Markel, David, 3627
Markel, F. Lynn, 256
Markel, Robinson, 3916
Markel, Stacy, 3627
Markell, Peter K., 1209
Markell, Steve, 2783
Marker, Donald F., 1485
Markesan State Bank, 314
Markese, John D., 2617
Market Day Corpoaration, 2378
MarketSpan Corp., 2630
Markey, Edward, 1612
Markfield, Roger S., 140
Markgold, LP, 1605
Markham, Leah, 2542
Markham, Rudy H.P., 3872
Markham, Wade, 3640
Markham, Wesley D., 3285
Markins, Jane A., 3654
Markle, Beverly Jolloff, 2379
Markle, Timothy Jolloff, 2379
Markley, Christopher, 1197
Markley, John D., Jr., 765
Markoff, Richard M., 3458
Markos, Arthur C., 343
Markovich, Paul, 655
Markow, John C., 86
Markowitz, Alice, 3617
Markowitz, Eugene, 1605
Markowitz, Michael, 1864
Markowitz, Renee, 1605
Markowsky, James, 1272
Marks, Alan, 1217
Marks, Alan L., 1217
Marks, Irvin, 2011
Marks, Jonathan, 632
Marks, Judy, 3448
Marks, Michael, 1437
Marks, Murlin, 3673
Marks, Peter J., 529
Marks, Robert E., 1087
Marks, Steven A., 3456
Marks, Terrance M., 1858
Markus, Maura, 346
Markworth, Tom, 1235
Marlborough Country Club, 2380
Marlco Investment Corp., 414
Marlee, Carol A., 106
Marlen, James S., 2887
Marley, Brian T., 403
Marley, James E., 2473
Marlin Group, Inc., The, 3649
Marling, Kim, 4110
Marling, Robert, 4110
Marling, Robert E., Jr., 4110
Marlow, David J., 578
Marlow, Keith, 549
Marmalade, Inc., 2409
Marmer, Fran, 1961
Marmer, Lynn, 2195
Marmier, Jacques, 1133
Marmol, Guillermo G., 1459
Marmol, Robert, 4006
Maroon, Joseph C., 2610
Maroone, Michael E., 292
Maroone, Michael J., 292
Marquardt, David F., 2501
Marquardt, Kent S., 3034
Marquart, Leslie R., 2995
Marquart, Winifred J., 2049
Marquart, Winifred Johnson, 1130
Marquis, Charles K., 3750
Marr Equipment Corp., 2382
Marr Scaffolding Co., 2382
Marr, Daniel F., 2382
Marr, John S., Jr., 3831
Marr, Robert L., 2382
Marra, Nicole, 1684
Marram, Ellen R., 1464, 2274, 2690
Marren, Alexandria, 103
Marrie, Michael J., 3490
Marrie, Mike, 2407
Marriner, Kirsten, 2807
Marrion, Catherine A., 2688
Marriott International, 1252
Marriott, John W., III, 2383
Marriott, John W., Jr., 2383
Marrow Foundation, 1776
Marrs, Carl H., 2797
Marrs, Patrick M., 934
Marrs, Ron, 2745
Marry, Thomas F., 2544
Mars, Forrest E., Jr., 2384
Mars, Frank, 2384
Mars, Inc., 2384
Mars, Jacqueline B., 2384
Mars, John F., 2384
Mars, Tom, 3980
Marsalis, Wynton, 2596
Marsan, Bill, 1988
Marsan, William P., 1988
Marschall, McAlister C., II, 571
Marsh Assocs., 2386
Marsh Mortgage Co., 2386
Marsh Realty Co., 2386
Marsh, Andrew, 1278, 1279
Marsh, G. Alex, III, 2386
Marsh, Henry, 2555
Marsh, James, 2555
Marsh, Kevin B., 1395, 3346
Marsh, Laurie, 2613
Marsh, Martha H., 184
Marsh, Pat, 2419
Marsh, Steven D., 495
Marshal, Steven A., 1035
Marshall & Ilsley Trust Company, 1883
Marshall Motor Co., Inc., 2388
Marshall, Anna, 1600
Marshall, Barbara, 2388
Marshall, Barbara C., 2388
Marshall, Christine, 3840
Marshall, Jay, 2360
Marshall, Jim, 1286
Marshall, Joe, 3459
Marshall, Julie, 713
Marshall, Katherine, 1959
Marshall, Kenneth, 3683
Marshall, Larry L., 2388
Marshall, Lydia M., 2639, 3377
Marshall, M. C., 722
Marshall, McAlister C., II, 571
Marshall, Michael, 166
Marshall, Millie, 3784
Marshall, Paula, 145, 1774
Marshall, Richard N., 3520
Marshall, Robbie, 1173
Marshall, Ruth Ann, 904, 3171
Marshall, Siri S., 174, 1288
Marshall, Stephanie Pace, 3709
Marshall, Stephen W., 2388
Marshall, Steven A., 1035
Marshall, Terry, 3727
Marshall, Thurgood, Jr., 1559
Marshall, William P., 2734
Marshall, William W., 2255
Marshall-Blake, Lorina L., 1926
Marshalls of MA, Inc., 3765
Marsiglia, Gilbert D., 2482
Marsili, Daniel, 869
Marsing, Peter, 3335
Marsteller, William, 690
Martel, Alfredo V., 692
Martel, Lysane, 82
Martell, Debbie, 1188
Martell, S.A., 1673
Marten, Jon P., 2886
Marthey, Debra A., 3488
Marti, Kevin, 1590
Marti, Kevin A., 1590
Martin & Co., C.F., Inc., 2390
Martin Family Foundation, 4032
Martin Guitar Co., C.F., 2390
Martin Land Co., 1361
Martin Marietta Corp., 2292
Martin, Al, 1567
Martin, Alice A., 2707
Martin, Alison, 2722
Martin, Anthony, 3366
Martin, Arthur, 422
Martin, Barry, 3835
Martin, Bob L., 1533
Martin, Bradley P., 543
Martin, Brian K., 244
Martin, Brian M., 2165
Martin, Bruce E., 3725
Martin, Charles C., 811
Martin, Chris L., 2146
Martin, Christian F., IV, 2390, 2635
Martin, Christian Frederick, IV, 2390
Martin, Christopher, 3069
Martin, Christopher P., 3069
Martin, Clarence, 253
Martin, Craig L., 2016
Martin, Damon, 3518
Martin, Daniel P., 2607
Martin, Daryn A., 99
Martin, David W., 3414
Martin, Dennis J., 1817
Martin, Diane S., 2390
Martin, Doug, 3598
Martin, Douglas, 287
Martin, Douglas L., 2694
Martin, Edward N., 1651
Martin, Gordon G., 71
Martin, J. Landis, 1980
Martin, Jackie, 2666
Martin, James, 381
Martin, James G., 1330
Martin, Janice A., 3869
Martin, Jeff, 1572
Martin, Jim, 2154, 2194
Martin, JoAnn M., 178
Martin, John, 1212
Martin, John C., 1582
Martin, John C., Jr., 2666
Martin, John K., Jr., 3757
Martin, Joshua W., III, 3346
Martin, Judy, 1192
Martin, Karen C., 945
Martin, Kevin, 2053
Martin, Kristen H., 3910
Martin, Landis J., 1706
Martin, Lanny, 3279
Martin, Laura, Dr., 3902
Martin, Lauralee E., 2061
Martin, Lawanna S., 108
Martin, Lendell, 108
Martin, Linda, 434
Martin, Lois M., 753
Martin, Louise, 403
Martin, Melody, 191
Martin, Michael E., 3045
Martin, Micheal E., 2635
Martin, Murray D., 571, 2984
Martin, Patrick D., 1848
Martin, Paul, 3504, 3965
Martin, Paul E., 377
Martin, Pete, 3839
Martin, Quinn, 2531
Martin, R. Brad, 777, 1352, 1406
Martin, Ralph, 3806
Martin, Ralph C., II, 501
Martin, Ralph J., 3806
Martin, Rex, 2, 2707
Martin, Robert, 3380
Martin, Robert H., 3575
Martin, Robert J., 1863
Martin, Robert N., 2324
Martin, Rodney, 1938
Martin, Rodney O., Jr., 147
Martin, Roger D., 108
Martin, Roger L., 3741
Martin, Sam, 1457
Martin, Samuel M., III, 1642
Martin, Sandra J., 406
Martin, Sean B.W., 216
Martin, Shira D., 2696
Martin, Stanley, 3563
Martin, Susan H., 4093
Martin, Terence D., 1169
Martin, Tim, 2220
Martin, V. Larkin, 3134
Martin, Will, 1629
Martin, William G., 3531

Martin-Flickinger, Gerry, 38
Martindale, Ken, 3220
Martineau, James L., 2978
Martineau, Jean, 877
Martinek, Joel, 2408
Martinelli, Louis A., 3764
Martinetto, Joseph R., 3363
Martinez, Alfonso, 2709
Martinez, Angel R., 1059, 3821
Martinez, Arthur C., 156, 1376, 1903, 1962
Martinez, Danielle Tokai Moller, 3903
Martinez, Eduardo, 3872
Martinez, Edward P., 2660
Martinez, Gabriela, 3854
Martinez, Helen, 594
Martinez, Jorge, 446
Martinez, Kevin, 367
Martinez, Maria, 3726
Martinez, Mary, 657
Martinez, Melody, 1445
Martinez, Michael L., 986
Martinez, Roman, IV, 812
Martinez, Rudy, 705
Martinez, Toby, 705
Martinez-Helfman, Sarah, 2958
Martino, Lynn, 1821
Martino, Robert J., 3899
Martinovich, Robert F., 2815
Martins, Alex, 2824
Martinson, Nancy, 3357
Martiny, Mary Anne, 1732
Martire, Frank R., 1371
Martley, Susan E., 424
Martocci, Gino A., 2323
Martocci, John J., 2704
Martone, Craig, 2684
Martorana, Russel F., 577
Martore, Gracia C., 1323, 1532, 2445
Martrenchar, Yves, 346
Martuscelli, Eric, 713
Martz, Carrie, 2968
Martz, D. Stephen, 1318
Martz, Dayna, 2093
Martz, Gary R., 1663
Martz, Wesley A., 2083
Marugame, Hideya, 2087
Maruster, Robert, 2041
Marvin, Susan I., 1866
Marwitz, Steven, 1470
Marx, Franz, 1968
Marx, Franz J., 3711
Marx, James A., 814
Marx, Louis, Jr., 3950
Marx, Sean, 1583
Marxkors, David, 2418
Mary Kay Inc., 2392
Maryland-Delaware-D.C. Press Service, Inc., 3016
Marzano, Vincent, 4072
Marzec, Robert J., 215, 1008
Marziotti, John D., 2695
Masai, Toshiyuki, 2711
Masamitsu, Norie, 3773
Masamitsu, Stan, 3773
Masamitsu, Tony, 3773
Mascall, Graham, 3984
Mascaro, James, 1168
Mascaro, James V., 1168
Mascazzini, Matteo, 1684
Maschal, Jean, 688
Mascheroni, E., 2788
Mascheroni, Eleanor E., 1071
Masciangelo, Lindsey, 2959
Masco Corp., 2393
Mascolo, Lisa M., 22
Mascoma Savings Bank, 2394
Maser, Marc S., 146
Masferrer, Roberto, 937
Mashima, Karyn, 3348
Mashinsky, Alex, 3709
Masino, Melanie, 3598
Maslick, Joseph R., 1667
Maslick, Joseph R., Jr., 1667
Maslin, Kristy, 3181
Maslowe, Philip L., 2748
Mason State Bank, 2396
Mason, Dean J. Barry, 4046
Mason, J. Thomas, 2325
Mason, James E., 894
Mason, Janine, 1374
Mason, Jeanne K., 377
Mason, John C., 1937
Mason, Joyce J., 1910
Mason, Kathleen, 1559, 2785
Mason, Kelvin R., 1690
Mason, Linda A., 566
Mason, Marc, 2468
Mason, Mark, 3045
Mason, Rob, 3914
Mason, Robert A., 3914
Mason, Robert E., IV, 1396
Mason, Roger, 3279
Mason, Ron, 1870
Masrani, Bharat B., 3696
Mass, Gary, 1020
Massarelli, Richard J., 2506
Massaro, Anthony A., 893, 2996, 2997
Massaro, Anthony P., 674
Massaro, George A., 1209
Massaro, George E., 764, 1209
Massaro, Thomas, 2159
Massaroni, Ken, 3377
Masse, Gary A., 716
Masse, William D., 792
Massee, Ned W., 2445
Massela, Susan, 3458
Massengale, Martin A., 616
Massengill, Matthew E., 4042
Massengill, Scott, 1792
Massey Knakal Realty Services, 2398
Massey, Greg, 367
Massey, Joey, 2487
Massey, Michael J., 871
Massey, Paul, 2398
Massey, Paul J., Jr., 2398
Massey, Randy L., 885
Massey, Richard N., 1371
Massey, Robert A., 1712, 1713
Massey, Robert M., 1712
Massey, Walter E., 2427
Massiani, Luis, 3070
Massicotte, Jacques, 1140
Masson, Pamela Q., 1494
Mast, Kent, 1288
Mastaler, Richard M., 2447
Mastantuono, Gina, 1941
Masten, Bob, 2906
Masterson Co., Inc., The, 2400
Masterson, Althea, 4109
Masterson, Bill, Jr., 2344
Masterson, Joe A., 2400
Masterson, John H., 956
Masterson, Martin B., 2400
Masterson, Michael, 2400
Masterson, Nancy J., 2400
Mastorakis, Andrew, 1496
Mastrian, James, 3220
MAT Construction Service, 2403
Matalon, Eli, 731
Matalon, Michael, 731
Matalon, Morris D., 731
Matalon, Samuel, 731
Matejka, Robert, 3278
Material Sales Co., Inc., 1768
Material Service Corp., 2402
Mateschitz, Dietrich, 3152
Matesic, Jill, 783
Mathas, Theodore A., 2688
Matheny, Edward T., Jr., 1695
Mather, Ann, 1613
Mather, Kevin, 367
Matheson, Stephen H., 2088
Mathew, Sara, 1190
Mathew, Sara S., 669
Mathews, Barbara E., 1228
Mathews, Bob, 60
Mathews, Jessica Tuchman, 1720
Mathews, Mark, 3776
Mathews, Preston, 1326
Mathews, Suresh, 3859
Matheys, Steve, 3355
Mathias, Alice Hammerstein, 3250
Mathias, Alison, 1376
Mathiason, Dennis, 2213
Mathieson, David, 3714
Mathieu, Elizabeth L., Esq., 3879
Mathis Hill Robertson Agency, The, 2908
Mathis, Carol P., 3138
Mathis, Cecil, 172
Mathis, Charles, 3347
Mathis, Larry L., 86
Mathis, Mary, 2886
Mathis, Robert E., 2908
Mathison, Duncan, 2945
Mathur, Punam, 2489
Matis, Nina B., 2101
Matiuk, Greg, 3667
Matlock, Melissa, 2570
Matlock, Susan W., 3171
Matos, Maria, 4028
Matricaria, Ronald A., 2268
Matrix Realty, 2403
Matrix Special Events, 2403
Matsakis, Elias, 1834
Matschullat, Robert W., 852, 1127, 3960
Matson Navigation Co., Inc., 85
Matson, Russell, 3316
Matson, Susan, 2307
Matsubara, Fumiyoshi, 2348
Matsuda, Fujio, 1405
Matsukura, Hiroyuki, 2654
Matsumoto, Colbert M., 1996
Matsumoto, Iris Y., 1405
Matsumura, Norio, 2716
Matsuno, Nancy, 3782
Matsuno, Nancy K., 3782
Matsushita Electric Corp. of America, 2869
Matsushita Electronic Components Corp. of America, 2870
Matsushita, Masayuki, 2870
Matsuuara, Isao, 346
Matt, Jackie, 1838
Matt, Nicholas O., 3910
Mattel, 30
Mattel, Inc., 2405
Matter, David M., 1799
Mattera, Salvatore J., 4009
Mattern, Steve, 2505
Matteson, Tony L., 2215
Mattessich, Richard, 1190
Matthews International Corp., 2406
Matthews, Alvin, 1077
Matthews, Craig G., 1793, 2628
Matthews, Debra, 663
Matthews, John, 948
Matthews, Kalyn, 1189
Matthews, Kathleen, 2383
Matthews, L. White, 1919
Matthews, L. White, III, 753, 1919
Matthews, Lindsay M., 2254
Matthews, Norman S., 3348
Matthews, Reuben, 3978
Matthews, Robert, 3137
Matthews, Robert H., 3913
Matthews, Roger, 2873
Matthias, Rebecca C., 996
Mattina, Rob, 1096
Mattingly, Amber, 130
Mattoo, Sunil, 3029
Mattress Firm, Inc., 2407
Mattson, George N., 1073
Mattson, Lawrence S., 2188
Matulis, Mike, 2858
Matus, Kristi A., 48
Matus, Kristi Ann, 3873
Matweecha, Pamela, 2465
Mau, Leighton S.L., 1405
Maue, Richard A., 970
Mauer, Lisa A., 32
Mauff, Erich, 1099
Mauffray, David, 2536
Maughan, Deryck, 3741
Mauldin, Precilla, 3496
Mauldin, Prescilla, 3496
Maultsby, J. Thomas, 690
Maunz, Bettina, 83
Maupin, John E., Jr., 2270, 3171
Maupin, Stan A., 1921
Maurer, John A., 1459
Maurer, Mick, 3454
Maurere Mfg., 1091
Mauri, Frank, 3899
Maurices, 255
Mauriello, Anthony J., 1465
Mauro, Al, 1707
Mauro, Tony, 1684
Mautz Paint Co., Inc., 2408
Mautz, Allison J., 2408
Mautz, Bernhard F., IV, 2408
Mautz, Bernhard F., Jr., 2408
Mautz, Elsa M.S., 2408
Maverick Capital Charities, Ltd., 2409
Mavrakis, Carol Seidler, 1304
Maw, Deborah S., 1848
Mawae, Kevin, 2627
Maxa, John G., 987
Maxey, Cullen, 310
Maxey, Karen A., 1966
Maxfield, A. Melissa, 887
Maxfield, Kelly B., 3104
Maxfield, W. Dale, Sr., 811
Maxfield, William D., 811
Maximuck, Nancy A., 3143
MAXIMUS, Inc., 2410
Maxsted, Lindsay, 455
Maxwell, Carol B., 3972
Maxwell, Greg G., 2965
Maxwell, M. Craig, 2886
Maxwell, Marcelia, 711
Maxwell, Oscar N., 2829
Maxwell, Sara, 3347
Maxwell, William Keith, III, 3533
Maxwell-Hoffman, Ellen, 544

McComb, William L., 1376
McConahey, Stephen G., 1917
McConnell, Andrew, 624
McConnell, John P., 870, 4124
McConnell, Matthew, 1099
McConnell, Michael W., 3857
McConnell, Michelle, 1309
McConnell, R.J., 1410
McConnell, Sharon, 1167
McConnell, William T., 2881
McConville, Daniel, 2608
McCool, Robert J., 1593
McCord, Robert, 2757
McCord, Sharon DuPont, 2757
McCorey, William, 3889
McCorkendale, Christopher M., 1730
McCorkindale, Douglas H., 2292
McCormack, Dawn, 3888
McCormack, Jill B., 520
McCormack, Joe, 2307
McCormack, Judith B., 520
McCormack, Robert C., 1916
McCormick, Alan, 1079
McCormick, C. Alan, 1079
McCormick, Chris, 3587
McCormick, Christopher J., 392
McCormick, Courtney M., 3077
McCormick, Douglas W., 2002
McCormick, Fray, 3674
Mccormick, John, 477
McCormick, Thomas, 281
McCormick, William T., Jr., 3246
McCotter, Kevin, 2309
McCoubrey, Brian, 3343
McCoubrey, Brian D., 3343
McCourt, Frank H., Jr., 2305
McCourt, Jaime, 2305
McCourt, Marion, 272
McCown, J. Ross, 2653
McCoy, Alan H., 67
McCoy, Billy G., 546
McCoy, Charles Brent, 2309
McCoy, Deborah L., 1216
McCoy, Dolores G., 2034
McCoy, Dustan E., 595, 1494, 2310
McCoy, John B., 273, 2954
McCoy, Kirk, 1355
McCoy, Leslie, 3690
McCoy, Michael T., 680
McCoy, Ryan, 1442
McCoy, Sheri S., 305
McCoy, Stephen, 2162
McCoy, Steve, 2162
McCoy, Tim, 3726
McCracken, Merrick, 83
McCracken, Steven C., 660
McCrackin, Ben, 2359
McCrackin, Patrick D., 15
McCrae, Wendy, 476
McCranie, Daniel J., 2462
McCranie, John Daniel, 1495
McCrary, C. W., Jr., 29
McCrary, C.W., 29
McCrary, Charles D., 71, 3066, 3171
McCraven, Paul, 1419
McCray, Gregory J., 751
McCreary, James C., Jr., 1517
McCree, Douglas, 1407
McCree, Douglas I., 1407
McCroskey, Robert L., 931
McCuaig, Scott, 3567
McCubbin, Don A., 3431
McCullen, Randy, 3805
McCullers, Mark, 886
McCulley, Steven E., 1886
McCullough, F.H., III, 1272
McCullough, Frank H., III, 1272
McCullough, Greg, 1335
McCullough, John W., 1726
McCullough, Patrick, 1830
McCullough, Robert F., 3045
McCullough, Theodore J., 1689
McCullough-Berg, Nancy, 1831
McCully, Michael, 2048
McCune, Scott K., 1532
McCunniff, Donald A., 2391
McCurdy, Lindsey, 1726
McCurry, Chris, 1798
McCurry, Marty, 1798
McCuskey, Connie, 2983
McCutcheon, Hattie, 172
McCutcheon, Lawrence, 3569
McCutcheon, Mark W., 1601
McCutcheon, Stewart H., 1220
McCutcheon, Wayne C., 833
McCuthceon, Pam, 4127
McDade, Sandy D., 4052
McDaneld, David, 3584
McDaniel, Cleve, 471
McDaniel, Jim, 1317
McDaniel, Kristin, 3274
McDaniel, Layne R., 977
McDaniel, Liliana, 3674
McDaniel, Marvin E., Jr., 4135
McDaniel, Matthew P., 805
McDaniel, Pete, 148
McDaniel, Raymond W., Jr., 2563, 4072
McDaniel, Tom, 145
McDaniel, Tommie J., 145
McDaniels, Darryl, 2336
McDannold, Timothy J., 1112
McDavid, William, 1348
McDermott, Bill, 3334
McDermott, Doug, 286, 3116
McDermott, Douglas, 1846
McDermott, John, 3246
McDermott, John, III, 3070
McDermott, Laura, 2905
McDermott, Richard, 849
McDermott, Terrence, 2482
McDevitt, Daniel J., 3635
McDevitt, John, 2168, 3872
McDevitt, Thomas, 2701
McDevitt, Thomas F., 2579
McDonald Industries, A.Y., Inc., 2426
McDonald Investments, Inc., 847
McDonald, Alisa, 1189
McDonald, Bill, Jr., 3738
McDonald, Charles, 2419
McDonald, Charles P., 1592
McDonald, David S., 4089
McDonald, Debbie, 3459
McDonald, Debbie S., 3459
McDonald, Deborah, 4032
McDonald, Frank S., 942
McDonald, Greg, 2958
McDonald, Gregory C., 4032
McDonald, Hugh T., 1278
McDonald, J. M., III, 2426
McDonald, James A., 2042
McDonald, James F., 807
McDonald, James P., 344
McDonald, John, 3902
McDonald, John G., 2991, 3358
McDonald, Kenton, 2359
McDonald, Kim, 2474
McDonald, Michael, 1466
McDonald, Micheal J., 381
McDonald, Mike, 2426
McDonald, Paul, 1096
McDonald, Peter D., 3860
McDonald, R. Bruce, 2050
McDonald, R. D., II, 2426
McDonald, Rebecca A., 1632
McDonald, Rob, 2426
McDonald, Robert A., 4136
McDonald, Rod J., 483
McDonald, Sam E., Jr., 4032
McDonald, Sam, Jr., 4032
McDonald, Tom, 3324
McDonald, Wesley S., 2181
McDonald, William E., 2391
McDonald, William J., 1886
McDonnell, James P., 1955
McDonnell, Joseph W., 3575
McDonnell, Patrick J., 1413
McDonnell, Peter J., 99
McDonnell, Sherry, 1278
McDonnell, Thomas A., 2094
McDonough, C. Jean, 1436
McDonough, Charles, 1959
McDonough, David M., 3818
McDonough, James D., 786
McDonough, John F., 782
McDonough, Kerra, 2582
McDonough, Kevin C., 2462
McDonough, Kevin, Fr., 225
McDonough, Mark E., 2466
McDonough, Myles, 1436
McDonough, Neil, 1436
McDonough, Paul H., 2813
McDonough, Robert, 3157
McDougall, Duane C., 3574
McDougall, Elizabeth L., 2501
McDowell, J. Walter, 372
McDowell, Mary T., 289
McDowell, Suzanne, 2158
McEachern, Douglas J., 898, 4075
McElman, Ronald G., 2751
McElreath, Vicki W., 2971
McElroy, John, 2540
McElroy, Terry L., 2875
McElwee, Arthur H., Jr., 2798
McEnaney, Theresa, 315
McEnery, Terri, 315
McEnroe, Erika Varga, 3673
McEvoy, Bruce, 2938, 3255
McEvoy, Matthew, 551
McEwan, Bill, 1458
McEwen, Sally A., 2394
McFadden, Chris, 3824
McFadden, Chris A., 711, 3003
McFadden, Howard D., 2725
McFadden, Jeanmarie, 2570
McFadden, Jerry L., 2886
McFadden, Mary, 1686
McFadden, Michael, 344
McFadden, Timothy, 1686
McFadden, Wanda, 4084
McFadzen, Karen, 818
McFague, Warren M., 2734
McFarland, Duncan M., 1532, 2769
McFarland, William H., 1374
McFarlane, James G., 2607
McFarlane, Shawn, 1563
McFeetors, Raymond L., 1647
MCG Health, 2573
McGahan, Patrick, 2112
McGann, Edward T., 2766
McGarey, Jennifer C., 2744
McGarry, Chris, 1457
McGarry, William C., 3211
McGarvie, Blythe J., 3945
McGathey, Boyd H., 1365
McGavick, Michael S., 4134
McGeary, Roderick C., 818, 2850
McGee, B. Lee, 2231
McGee, Henry, 3757
McGee, Henry W., 175
McGee, Laura, 859
McGee, Liam E., 1742
McGee, Rick, 1547
McGee, Vicky, 3449
McGehee, Julie L., 3374
McGehee, Marie, 874
McGeough, Robert S., 1420
McGettrick, Mark F., 1150
McGhee, C. Andrew, 1142
McGhee, Michelle, 3978
McGill Toyota, Don, Inc., 1152
McGill, Dennis, 483
McGill, Donald R., 1152
McGill, James W., 1216
McGill, John O., 1152
McGill, Terrance L., 1265
McGill, Thomas J., 528
McGillicuddy, John K., 642
McGillicuddy, Rosemary, 3512
McGinley, J. Timothy, 3925
McGinley, Mark D., 3600
McGinn, Richard A., 143
McGinnes, Larry D., 2044
McGinnis, Karen K., 1016
McGinnis, Patricia G., 591
McGinnis, Terence A., 1209
McGinnis, W. Patrick, 591, 1271, 2662
McGinty, Kathleen A., 2756
McGiveren, Darrell, 1049
McGlade, John E., 63, 1612
McGlaun, Scott, 492
McGlennon, James M., 2265
McGlensey, Kevin, 930
McGlockton, Joan Rector, 3497
McGlothlin, Frances, 3864
McGlothlin, James W., 3864
McGlothlin-Gayle, Martha, 3864
McGlynn, Margaret G., 63
McGoldrick, John L., 4157
McGoldrick, Richard J., 338
McGonagle, Bill F., 3770
McGonigle, John W., 1351
McGovern, Gail J., 1183
McGovern, James F., 2887
McGovern, Jean, 2416
McGovern, John, 2108
McGovern, John F., 871, 2108
McGovern, John R., 3649
McGowan, Chris, 2306, 2308, 3793
McGowan, Gertude, 505
McGowan, Jeannine L., 2143
McGowan, Mark S., 493
McGowan, Peter F., 3512
McGowan, W. Brian, 1623
McGrail, Sean, 538
McGranaghan, M. R., 1299
McGrath, Brian T., 149
McGrath, Don J., 346, 1084
McGrath, Donald J., 1216
McGrath, Judy, 2596
McGrath, Mark G., 1542
McGrath, Marlene M., 3
McGrath, Nancy, 3775
McGrath, Sean, 1959
McGraw, Harold W., III, 2429, 2965, 3882
McGraw, James H., IV, 2429

McGraw, Robert P., 2429
McGraw, Ron, 722
McGraw-Hill Companies Inc., The, 2429
McGregor, Douglas J., 3972
McGregor, Justice Ruth, 3274
McGregor, Keli S., 879
McGregor, Scott, 579, 1941
McGregor, Scott A., 579
McGregor, Stephen D., 3520
McGroarty, Jeffrey B., 3307
McGroary, Colin, 2718
McGrory, Steve, 1292
McGuigan, Charles C., 2277
McGuigan, James, 2604
McGuiness, Patrick F., 3750
McGuinn, Martin G., 804
McGuire, C. Kent, 2869, 4028
McGuire, Charles L. "Lynn", 198
McGuire, Chelsea, 131
McGuire, Eileen, 2593
McGuire, Jim, 3363
McGuire, Mark, 784
McGuire, Mark M., 1216
McGuire, Patricia, 21
McGuire, Patricia A., 178
McGuire, Raymond J., 821
McGuire, Robert J., 2605
McGuirk, Terence F., 280
McGuirk, Terry, 280
McGuirt, Milford, 2190
McHale, Brandee, 821
McHale, David A., 1139
McHale, David R., 2737, 3075
McHale, John, Jr., 2345
McHale, Judith, 3123
McHale, Patrick J., 1624
McHaney, Martha Jean, 2573
McHenry, Donald F., 862
McHenry, John, 2259
McHenry, Margaret L., 2259
McHoul, Donald, 476
McHugh, David F., 996
McHugh, Jeanine, 2251
McHugh, Julie H., 1268
McHugh, Lawrence D., 2262
McHugh, Robert A., III, 345
Mchugh, Robert W., 1459
McInerney, Gary J., 502
McInerney, Ryan, 3960
McInerney, Thomas, 1938, 4140
Mcinerney, Thomas J., 1903
McInnis, Carol A., 2513
McInnis, Frank T., 4077
McInnis-Day, Brigette, 3334
McInteer, Marguerite R., 350
McIntire, Christopher, 4149
McIntire, Lee, 758
McIntire, Lee A., 758
McIntosh, Gary, 4014
McIntosh, John L., 2801
Mcintosh, Madeline, 2922
McIntosh, Ralph A., Jr., 3344
McIntosh, Robert B., 3239
McIntosh, William A., 2488
McIntyre, Diane, 1174
McIntyre, Edward J., 2836
McIntyre, James J., 806
McIntyre, John, 3016
McIntyre, Kevin, 1746
McIver, Frances, 3978
McJunkin Red Man Corp., 2431
McKallor, Alex, 2320
McKay, Judith E., 2980
McKay, Kay J., 500
McKay, Lamar, 547
McKay, Neil, 316
McKay, Olive B., 316
McKay, Rich, 2416
McKay, Richard, 277
McKay, Scott J., 1565
McKay, Shawn, 1668
McKean, Greg, 2119
McKee Foundation, James W. & Jayne A., 1942
McKee, Brandt F., 1026
McKee, E. Marie, 945, 1189
McKee, Leigh, 1053
McKee, Lynn B., 223
McKee, Lynnette, 2638
McKee, Michael, 1992
McKee, Michael D., 1389
McKee, Michael K., 2432
McKee, R. Ellsworth, 2432
McKeithan, Daniel F., Jr., 2371
McKellar, James W., 3738
McKelvey, Patricia, 2915
Mckelvey, Patti, 2915
McKelvy, Mike, 758
McKendrick, Ryan, 127
McKendrick, Ryan F., 127
McKenna, Andrew, 781
McKenna, Andrew J., 2427
McKenna, Dennis F., 3032
McKenna, Joann C., 2506
McKenna, John, 810
McKenna, Margaret, 3980
McKenna, Mary, 476
McKenna, Mary L., 476
McKenna, Matthew M., 1459
McKenna, Peter J., 18
McKenna, Ronald F., 970
McKenna, Thomas E., 907
McKenna, William A., Jr., 3211
McKenna, William P., 542
McKenney, Cecilia K., 1508
McKenney, Michael J., 2083
McKenney, Richard P., 3898
McKenzie, Diana, 182
McKenzie, Kimberly, 3892
McKenzie, Mary Alice, 2742
McKeown, Brad, 2320
McKeown, Daniel W., 3537
McKeown, Desmond, 3537
McKeown, Douglas, 4109
McKeown, Heidi Sandberg, 3537
McKeown, Millie, 84
McKernan, Heather, 2702
McKernan, John, 1869
McKernan, John R., Jr., 528
McKernan, Thomas V., 1389
McKesson Corp., 2434
McKesson HBOC, Inc., 2434
McKiffick, Smyth, 89
McKillip, Robert, 3138
McKim, Tony C., 1391
McKinley Revocable Trust, 3930
McKinley, Janet B., 3930
McKinley, John A., Jr., 1288
McKinley, Sara M., 3930
McKinley, Thomas G., 3930
McKinnell, Henry A., Jr 2563
McKinnell, Henry A., Jr., 2563
McKinney, Bill, 2242
McKinney, Carol, 957
McKinney, Tony M., 3627
McKinney, William C., 2242
McKinney-James, Rose, 2489
McKinnon, David G., 2548
McKinnon, Doug, 3223
McKinnon, John B., 2582
McKinnon, Mark A., 1060
McKinnon, Paul, 821
McKinstry Co., 2435
McKinstry, Harry, 26
McKinstry, Nancy, 13
McKissack, Eric T., 1629
McKissick, Ellison Smyth, III, 89
McKissick, James G., 59
McKleroy, John P., Jr., 1601
McKnight, H. James, 323
McKnight, Jeff, 1386
McKnight, Robert B., Jr., 3108
McKnight, Thomas F., 2667
McKown, David K., 1593
McKuin, Barry L., 3431
McLachlan, Neil A., 2445
McLain, Bobby, 3347
McLain, Susan, 3081
McLain, Timothy S., 2881
McLane Co., Inc., The, 2875
McLane Securities, 2684
McLane, Drayton, Jr., 1871
McLaren, C. Michael, 3275
McLarty, Thomas F., III, 3857
McLaughlin Body Company, 2436
McLaughlin, Chuck, 397
McLaughlin, Donald E., 2782
McLaughlin, Elmer G., 3865
McLaughlin, Gladys, 2919
McLaughlin, Hugh, 3635
McLaughlin, James A., 3999
McLaughlin, John Garvin, 3635
McLaughlin, Joseph J., 412
McLaughlin, Kathleen A., 3635
McLaughlin, Michael J., 3520
McLaughlin, Patrick, 1506
McLaughlin, Patrick J., 3887
McLaughlin, Peter J., 2436
Mclaughlin, Raymond L., 2436
McLaughlin, Richard D., 974
McLaughlin, Robert M., 65
McLaughlin, Seth, 2319
McLaughlin, Thomas, 3376
McLaughlin, W. Michael, 3865
McLaughlin, William P., 2237
McLaurin, Charles S., III, 1395
McLawhorn, Hunter Johnston, 2386
McLawhorn, James, 2386
McLawhorn, James H., 2386
McLean, Ben, 3279
McLean, Duane, 1097
McLean, Margaret B., 758
McLean, Mark, 2609
McLean, R. Bruce, 70
McLean, Rachel, 3279
McLeland, Allan H., 3500
McLellan, Richard, 2580
McLelland, Stan L., 2763
McLemore, David, 510
McLendon, Charles A., Jr., 1971
McLeod, Michael Preston, 1079
McLeod, Mike, 1079
McLeod, Robert B., 2991
McLeod, Scot M., 3107
McLeod, Tommy D., 239
McLester, Scott G., 4132
McLevish, Timothy R., 2125
McLin, Stephen T., 3363
McLoughlin, Hollis, 1348
McLoughlin, Keith R., 565
McLoughlin, Peter, 1460, 3793
McMackin, John J., Jr., 2844
McMahan, Lewis H., 3728
McMahon, Andrew, 307
McMahon, Bill, 2570
McMahon, Brian T., 2681
McMahon, Glenn Patrick, 3564
McMahon, John, 2440
McMahon, John D., 916
McMahon, John J., Jr., 3066
McMahon, Richard C., 399
McMahon, Vincent K., 4121
McMaken, Kurt B., 1216
McManaman, Lisa, 1455
McMannamy, Jerry, 117
McManus, James T., II, 1270
McManus, John M., 2489
McManus, Michael A., Jr., 3361
McManus, Patrick B., 2462
McManus, Patrick J., 3133
McManus, Roger, 678
McMaster, Carolyn, 3734
McMaster, Robert, 1017
McMaster, Robert R., 700
McMath, Charles, 3450
McMeel, Bridget J., 3895
McMeel, John P., 3895
McMeel, Maureen, 3895
McMeel, Susan S., 3895
McMillan, C. Steven, 2559
McMillan, Cary D., 140, 2427
McMillan, David J., 100
McMillan, John H., 2775
McMillan, L. Richards, II, 1494
McMillan, Nancy, 2775
McMillan, Robert R., 2335
McMillan, Stuart, 544
McMillan, Thomas E., Jr., 337
McMillen, Gayle C., 2553
McMillen, Jeff, 1707
McMillion, Raymos, 2536
McMonagle, James J., 2842
McMullen, Greer G., 3414
McMullen, Greerson G., 3414
McMullen, Karen, 3069
McMullen, Kevin, 2809
McMullen, Kevin M., 2809, 3600
McMullen, Mark J., 1651
McMullen, W. Rodney, 2195
McMullian, Amos R., 1446
McMurray, Charles J., 1153
McMurray, Michael, 2842
McMurray, Michael C., 2842
McNair, D. Cal, 1872
McNair, Daniel C., 1872
McNair, Janice S., 1872
McNair, Martin B., 2446
McNair, Robert C., 1872
McNair-Stoner, Francie, 754
McNairy, John O., 3749
McNairy, Leigh H., 3749
McNally, Alan G., 3981
McNally, Andrew, IV, 1879
McNally, Michael, 2247
McNally, Stephen A., 3685
McNamara Corley, Kathryn, 1125
McNamara, Brian, 2401
McNamara, Daniel J., 4134
McNamara, John J., 674
McNamara, John W., 1663
McNamara, Kevin, 3832
McNamara, Kevin J., 773
McNamara, Kyra, 131
McNamara, Michael, 1071
McNamara, Mike, 1437
McNamara, Stephen F., 246

McNamara, William J., 3858
McNamee, Brian M., 182
McNamee, Patrick, 1313
McNamme, Norman L., 3211
McNaney, Michael, 3157
McNaughton, Brian R., 2919
McNaughton, Stan W., 2919
McNaughton, Stanley William, 2919
McNeal, Beverly, 3012
McNeal, Glenda G., 3877
McNealus, Neal, 3940
McNeely, Lisa T., 827
McNeil, Barry F., 1759
McNeil, Beverly Blount, 3012
McNeil, Chris E., Jr., 3380
McNeil, John A., Jr., 3012
McNeil, Judson, 3775
McNeil, Mike, 1858
McNeill, Corbin A., Jr., 2844, 3010
McNelis, Donald T., 3070
McNerney, Peter H., 496
McNerney, W. James, Jr., 516, 1960, 3055
McNiff, Audrey, 1450
McNiff, Philip A., 2691
McNitt, Peter, 1739
McNorrington, Lorrie, 289
McNulty, Diane, 1594
McNulty, James F., 2887
McNulty, James J., 2769
McNulty, Jim, 2525
McNulty, Rich, 2162
McNulty, Richard, 2162
McNulty, Timothy, 3383
McNulty, Timothy F., 3383
McNutt, Gail, 3355
McNutt, Laura, 4014
McNutt, Robert M., 1663
McPadden, Kathleen, 2645
McPartland, Pete G., 3409
McPeak, Blaine E., 4062
McPeek, Daniel J., 80
Mcphee, Patricia, 442
McPherren, Ann, 2379
McPherson, Alan, 2976
McPherson, Caroline, 3354
Mcpherson, John, 3560
McPherson, John D., 997
McPherson, Michael, 1083
McQuade, Charles B., 3859
McQuade, Kathryn, 120
McQuade, Kathryn B., 3433
McQuade, Roberta, 1908
McQuaide, Jay, 501
McQueen, Todd, 3373
McQueston, James, 2633
McQuiston, Edwin T., 3873
McRae, Jim, 72
McRae, Lawrence D., 945
McRae, Nancy, 3222
McRae, Richard D., Jr., 3171
McRae, Willard, 2262
McShane Builders, Inc., 2439
McShane, Daniel P., 2439
McShane, James A., 2439
McShane, Mary G., 2439
McShane, Michael, 3540
McShea, Jeanine, 316
McSheffrey, Michael, 3175
McShepard, Randell, 3278
McSorley, M.J., 3515
McSwain, D. Jay, 2420
McSwain, Keith, 2419, 2420
McSwain, Ronald H., 2051
McTague, Dave, 867
McTier, Charles H., 57
McVay, Jim, 487
McVay, Larry D., 3029
McVeigh, David, 466
McVey, Bill, 3518
McVey, William R., 3518
McWain, Teresa L., 141
McWane, C. Phillip, 2440
McWane, Inc., 2440
McWaters, Michael, 72
McWhorter, David, 978
McWilliams, Larry, 2137
McWilliams, Larry S., 246
McWilliams, Mary O., 3081
MDCCP, 2211
MDU Construction Services Grp., 2441
MDU Resources Group, Inc., 2441
Me-Tex Oil & Gas, Inc., 2442
Meacher, Robert A., 2853
Mead, Christine B., 1565
Mead, Daniel S., 733
Mead, David L., 2929
Mead, Edward, 3758
Mead, James M., 1791
Mead, Michael, 3758
Mead, Peter, 2808
Mead, Robert M., 48
Mead, Tim, 200
Meade, Andrea, 3347
Meade, David C., 2468
Meade, Joseph F., III, 2468
Meade, Peggy M., 613
Meador, David E., 1183
Meadowlands Castle, The, 2449
Meadows, A. Stephen, 3239
Meadows, Amy M., 406
Meadows, David M., 331
Meadows, Doyle, 2419
Meadows, H., 2444
Meadows, H.G., 2444
Meadows, R., 2444
Meadows, Richard, 1835
Meadows, Robert, 463
Meadows, Stanley, 1857
Meadows, W.R., Inc., 2444
Meads, Lori F., 3383
Meagher, Andrew C.J., 380
Meagher, Laura C., 3913
Meakem, Glen T., 1799
Means, Brad, 2573
Means, Lawrence M., 3062
Means, Rick L., 3431
Means, Russell, 3331
Mears, Richard W., 2841
Meath, James V., 4078
Mebane, Reggie, 1578
Mechenbier, Jeff, 3076
Mechler, Harold P., 1922
Mecklenburg, Gary A., 398
Mecklenburg, William C., 3158
Mecklenburg, William C., Jr., 3158
Mecom, John W., Jr., 3413
Mecurio, Bob, 1490
Meddings, Chris, 2212
Medefinance, Inc., 2447
Medeiros, John E., 3383
Medema, Mike, 3128
Medford, Dale L., 3230
Medica, John K., 2632
Medical Mutual of Ohio, 847
Medieval Castle, Inc., 2449
Medieval Dinner & Tourmanent, Inc., 2449
Medieval Show, 2449
Medieval Times Management, Inc., 2449
Medieval Times Maryland, Inc., 2449
Medieval Times Myrtle Beach, Inc., 2449
Medina, Cesar, 3003
Medina, Cuauhtemoc, 1236
Medina, Jessica, 131
Medina, Manuel, 705
Medley, Francine, 54
Medley, Joellen, 13
Medlin, Billy Royce, 2235
Medlin, George L., 2605
Medlin, Lynn, 3259
Medlin, Meg, 3886
Medline Industries, Inc., 1275, 2451
Medtronic, 3329, 3501
Medtronic Neurological, 2171
Medtronic, Inc., 2453
Medusa Corp., 734
Medvecz, Patrick J., 4008
Medved, Gary, 3626
Medvin, Harvey N., 210
Medwick, Craig, 849
Medwid, Robert P., 226
Mee Corp. Capital Markets LLC, 2454
Mee Corp. Group, LLC, 2454
Mee, David G., 1892
Mee, Michael F., 2281
Meehan, Deborah, 496
Meehan, Jim, 251
Meehan, Michele, 3397
Meehan, Richard, 619
Meehan, William, 2075
Meek, Elizabeth, 3337
Meek, Terry O., 890
Meeker, David, 1566
MEEMIC Insurance Co., 2455
Meena, Hu, 636
Meena, V. Hugo, Jr., 636
Meenan, Patrick, 3902
Meenan, Robert, 501
Meenan, Robert F., 501
Meengs, Cindy, 611
Meeusen, Richard A., 313, 2461
Meezan, Erin, 1953
Megin, James L., 2565
Megrue, John F., Jr., 2156
Mehl, Cheryl, 844
Mehl, Timothy L., 854
Mehmel, Robert F., 1179
Mehmen, Dennis H., 1668
Mehrabian, Robert, 3025
Mehrberg, Randall E., 3077
Mehta, Shrikant, 3708
Mehta, Siddharth N., 3799
Meier, Deborah, 2869
Meier, John F., 219, 936
Meier, Richard A., 2841
Meier, Richard W., 326
Meier, Tara, 3279
Meier, William, 2982
Meiers, Margaret, 1348
Meijer, Doug, 2456
Meijer, Hendrick G., 2456
Meijer, Hendrik G., 2456
Meikle, Bruce E., 677
Meiklejohn, Mark, 349
Meiklejohn, Mark J., 349
Meil Revocable Trust, Leslie A., 2637
Meil, Barry R., 2637
Meil, Wendy E., 2637
Meiners, Diane, 45
Meinz, Thomas, 3061
Meisels, Isaac, 3041
Meisels, Joel, 3041
Meisenbach, John W., 948
Meisner, Christian, 3454
Meissner, Laurel, 210
Meissner, Thomas P., Jr., 3885
Meixelsperger, Mary, 3440
Mejaly, Joseph, 2473
Mekenna, Margaret, 3980
Mekhjian, Hagop, 1849
Mekrut, William A., 1323
Melaleuca, Inc., 2457
Melamed, A. Douglas, 1950
Melamed, Carol, 3016
Melamed, Leo, 853
Melampy, Linda, 484
Melancon, Paul, 2007
Melancon, Paul D., 2007
Meland, Mark G., 749
Melando, Edward J., 4072
Melani, Kenneth R., 1799
Melarkey, Michael J., 3524
Mele, Frank, 1370
Mele, Mario, 222, 1370
Mele, Mario V., 1370
Mele, Mike, 1370
Mele, Salvatore, 1370
Melen, Robert, 1893
Melendez, Ada, 1984
Melfi, Anthony, 587
Melidosian, Charlie, 316
Melidossian, Alan P., 349
Melillo, Samuel T., 2782
Meline, David W., 3
Meling, Eric M., 3649
Melisz, Rose, 1419
Mellies, Marla D., 3081
Mellin, Mark P., 3117
Mellon Bank, 344
Mellon Financial Corp., 344
Mellon Trust of New England, 2445
Mellor, James R., 3904
Mellowes, Charles A., 766
Mellowes, John A., 766
Mellowes, John W., 766
Mellowes, Linda T., 766
Melnick, Joseph J., 629
Meloa, Joe, 2816
Melody Music City, 2266
Melone, Martin, 3826
Meloy, Mark J., 1394
Melstrand, Dan, 2972
Melton, Steve, 3674
Melum, Mark, 261
Melville Corp., 1014
Melville Hope, H., III, 50
Melville, C.G., Jr., 751
Melville, James Clinton, 246
Melville, Melinda Savage, 3341
Melvin, Dubin, 3477
Melvin, Gary W., 1411
Melvin, Vincent P., 249
Melwani, Prakash, 2938, 3255
MEMC Electronic Materials, Inc., 2459
Men, Henry W., 590
Menaker, Frank H., Jr., 2391
Menapace, John J., 505
Menasce, Eduardo R., 1804, 2984, 4072
Menasha Corp., 2461
Mencoff, Samuel M., 2861
Mendel, John W., 150
Mendelow, Clive, 464
Mendelow, Clive G., 464

Mendelsohn, Karen R., 2393
Mendenhall, Samuel, 4089
Mendes, Aaron, 1178
Mendes, Estela M., 2335
Mendes, Stella M., 2335
Mendizabal, Andres, 1266
Mendlik, Paul M., 4035
Mendoza, Lou, 2279
Mendoza, Roberto G., 2358, 4045
Menedez, Manuel, Hon., 2691
Menefee, Dwight, 2920
Menezes, Ivan, 858
Menezes, Ivan M., 1107
Meng, John C., 1651
Mengacci, James A., 2646
Mengebier, David G., 854, 921
Menlove, Mary G., 1538
Mennem, Lynn, 1417
Menning, James R., 2591
Menon, Venu, 3728
Mense, Craig D., 855
Mense, D. Craig, 855
Menting, Steven, 1466
Mentor Graphics Corp., 2462
Menzel, Stephen, 839
Menzel, Susan L., 857
Menzer, John B., 2494
Mercer, Anne L., 3329
Mercer, Dianne, 2928
Merchan, Dario, 820
Merchant, David, 3736
Merchant, David V., 3736
Merchant, Fazal, 1124
Merchant, Kevin C., 2042
Merchant, Thomas C., 2245
Merchants Bancshares, Inc., 2465
Merchants Bank, 2465
Mercier, Camille, 3544
Merck, 3329
Merck & Co., Inc., 2466
Merck Sharp & Dohme Corp., 2466
Merculief, Boris, 84
Mercury Aircraft, Inc., 2468
Mercury Minnesota, Inc., 2468
Mercury Wire Products, Inc., 2470
Meredith Corp., 2471
Meredith, Kim, 2316
Meredith, Thomas C., 285
Merenbach, David, 1982
Merfeld, Susan, 2913
Merfish Pipe & Supply, 2472
Merfish, Abe, 2472
Merfish, Gerald, 2472
Merfish, Ida K., 2472
Mergenthaler, Frank, 1313, 1974
Merhab, Mark, 200
Merial, 3257
Merin, Mitchell M., 3643
Merino, Bruce, 3890
Merit Consulting LLC, 2597
Meritor Automotive, Inc., 2473
Merkatz, Ruth, 382
Merkle, Kevin, 3827
Merkrut, William A., 1323
Merksamer, Samuel, 2647
Merlo, Kristin, 1081
Merlo, Larry J., 1014, 2622
Merola, J. Robert, 1004
Merow, John E., 3634
Merriam, Dena, 3282
Merrick, Steve, 826
Merril, Don, 3840
Merrill Lynch, 136
Merrill Lynch & Co., Inc., 340
Merrill Lynch, Pierce, Fenner & Smith Inc., 2769
Merrill, Melinda, 2485
Merrimack County Savings Bank, 2474
Merrimack Valley Distributing Co., 2475
Merriman, Michael J., 2809, 3172
Merriman, Michael J., Jr., 149, 2723
Merriman, Ronald L., 2926
Merrin, Jeremy, 1751
Merritt, Carrie, 3455
Merritt, David C., 661, 765
Merritt, H. Kenneth, Jr., 2476
Merritt, Jennifer R., 1485
Merritt, Judy, 1748
Merritt, Judy M., 1270
Merritt, Randy, 3426
Merritt, Sharon J., 2476
Mershon, William, 1761
Merszei, Geoffery E., 1161
Merton, Edward A., 2909
Mertson, Eleanor, 2340
Merullo, Richard, 2475
Merz, Joe, 1849
Merzbacher, Celia I., 3403
Mesa Ford, L.P., 1464
Mesa, Alfredo, 2491
Meseck, Jane, 2501
Mesereau, Robert J., 2073
Meserve, Richard A., 2952
Mesina, Charmaine F., 220
Mesler, Jeffrey, 3156
Mesloh, James C., 1150
Mesquita, Jorge S., 2556
Messer Construction Co., 2477
Messer, David, 2190
Messer, John A., 2390
Messier, Andre J., Jr., 1210
Messina, Angelo, 2835
Messina, Elizabeth A., 500
Messina, Jim, 2376
Messman, Jack L., 3307
Messmer, Bernard, 2046
Messmer, Eric, 839
Mestre, Eduardo G., 299, 887
Mestres, Ricardo A., Jr., 3634
Metal Industries of California Foundation, Inc., 2478
Metal Industries, Inc., 2478
Metaltek International Inc., 4092
Metavante Technologies, Inc., 1371
Metcalf, James S., 3905
Metcalf, Roger G., 3647
Metevier, Jim, 2139
Methvin, S. P., 3430
MetPath Inc., 3103
Metrick, Mary Frances, 477
Metro Park, LLC, 3044
Metro, James de, 1056
Metrokin, Jason, 576
Metropolitan Bancorp, 2731
Metropolitan Bank Group, 2731
Metropolitan Edison Co., 1424
Metropolitan Life Insurance Co., 2481
Metropolitan Oklahoma City Motor Car Dealers and Association, 2480
Metropolitan Theatres Corp., 2483
MetroPower, Inc., 2972
Mettler, Robert L., 2057
Mettler, Robert Lewis, 3108
Metts, Steve, 3918
Metviner, Neil J., 1084
Metz, James H., 1008
Metzger, David M. K., 3140
Metzger, William L., 595
Metzinger, Bob, 1158
Meuleman, Ann E., 273
Meunier, Louis, 2333
Mey, J. Tracy, 3904
Meya, Wilhelm W., 772
Meybohm, Edward G., 3513
Meyer, Arthur G., 1047
Meyer, Barry M., 3989
Meyer, Brian K., 3394
Meyer, Carl E., 2681
Meyer, Christine, 1517
Meyer, David J., 301
Meyer, David M., 965
Meyer, Dennis, 2175
Meyer, Donald A., 15
Meyer, Douglas Robert, 3632
Meyer, Eric B., 2108
Meyer, Frederick R., 73
Meyer, Gregg, 2401
Meyer, Gregory S., 483
Meyer, James B., 774
Meyer, Jeff, 1355
Meyer, Jon P., 2718
Meyer, Jose Maria Garcia, 901
Meyer, Ken, 4066
Meyer, Kristine, 301
Meyer, Lawrence, 1469
Meyer, Lee D., 3361
Meyer, Marilyn Stiborek, 4137
Meyer, Melvin D., 2439
Meyer, Michael G., 2926
Meyer, Michael L., 1220
Meyer, Noa, 1604
Meyer, Pat, 2917
Meyer, Patrick J., 2917
Meyer, Paul, 552
Meyer, Paula R., 2607
Meyer, Ron, 2649, 3893
Meyer, Ronald, 3893
Meyer, Sarah, 2501
Meyer, Stephen P., 1900
Meyer, Steven J., 4112
Meyer, William F., 2671
Meyercord, F. Duffield, 2909
Meyercord, Wade F., 2499
Meyerhoeffer, Jason A., 1403
Meyerman, Harold J., 51
Meyers, Christopher, 2114
Meyers, David H., 3893
Meyers, Geoffrey G., 1762
Meyers, Jim, 1582
Meyers, Kenneth R., 3876
Meyers, Margaret J., 1651
Meyers, Robert, 2330
Meyersiek, Axel, 3781
Meyrowitz, Carol, 3765
Meyrowitz, Carol M., 3581, 3765
Mezger, Jeffrey T., 2105
Meziere, Daniel M., 285
Mezza, Livio, 502
MF Global, 853
MFA Inc., 2486
MFA Oil Co., 2486, 2487
MGM Mirage, 2489
MGough, Dennis R., 2801
MH Equipment Co., 2490
MH Logistics, 2490
Mhatre, Nitin J., 4016
MHC Investment Co., 2504
Mica, Barb, 3269
Micali, James M., 3500
Micali, James Michael, 3346
Micallef, Gary, 1902
Micelli, Frank, 3557
Michael, Alfred, 2530
Michael, Ellen A., 3066
Michael, Gary G., 1907, 3104
Michael, John, 96
Michael, Kirk B., 1988
Michael, Ralph S., III, 67, 1345
Michaelis, Kevin B., 63
Michaels, Jonathan, 3386
Michaels, Kenneth, 1696
Michaels, Paul S., 2384
Michaelson, John, 2655
Michalak, Michael H., 889
Michan, Jane, 1549
Michas, Alexis P., 528, 2939
Michaud, James, 850
Michaud, Thomas A., 2332
Michel, David S., 621
Michel, George, 536
Michel, Jean-Paul, 2834
Michel, Scott D., 681
Michel, Wayne A., 3142
Micheli, Carolyn, 3374
Michelotti, Carla, 619
Michels, Douglas A., 4038
Michels, Mike, 2972
Michelson, Jack, 4007
Michelson, Michael, 466
Michelson, Michael W., 1762
Michigan Cardiovascular Institute PC, 2497
Michigan Educational Employees Mutual Insurance Co., 2455
Michon, Edward J., 1989
Mickan, Carlos F., 2868
Mickinney, Pat, 1248
Mickle, Kathie, 3061
Miclot, John, 1089
Miclot, John L., 3193
Miclucci, Carolyn H., 272
Micro Analog, Inc., 2498
Microelectonics Advanced Research Corp., 3403
Micron Semiconductor Products, Inc., 2500
Micron Technology, Inc., 2500
Microsoft Corp., 2501
Mid Newark, LLP, 3712
Mid-Atlantic Packaging, Inc., 2502
Mid-States Aluminum, Inc., 2503
Midamerican Energy Holdings Co., 2504
Midcontinent Communications, 2505
Midcontinent Media, Inc., 2505
Middeke, Paul W., 3747
Middelhoff, Thomas, 2690
Middlesex Savings Bank, 2506
Middleton, Darrell E., 502
Middleton, Lori, 2229
Middleton, Michael L., 761
Middleton, Paul B., 3253
Midkiff, Mark W., 3854
Midkiff, Robin S., 1405
Midler, Laurence H., 725
Midmark, 3074
Midmark Corp., 2507
Midwestone Bank, 2508
Miehls, Jodi, 481
Miehls, Jodi L., 481
Mielbye, Susan J., 602
Mielke, Thomas J., 2150
Mieres, Jennifer H., 272
Miers, Mike, 2815
Mierswa, Charlie, 584
Mies, Admiral Richard W., 2607
Might, Thomas O., 2625

Migoya, Carlos A., 292
Mihaila, John Theodore, 3760
Mihalik, Trevor I., 3405
Mihm, Robert A., 2879
Mik, Anita D., 354
Mike's Train House, Inc., 2509
Mike, Campbell, 1621
Mike, Cheryl, 2188
Mike-Shannon Automotive, Inc., 1830
Mikells, Kathryn, 1742, 4136
Mikesell, Edwin A., 3518
Mikesell, Gordon, 3518
Mikesell, Gordon G., 3518
Mikesell, Gregory L., 3518
Mikesell, Kendall, 3518
Mikkilineni, Krishna, 1852
Miklas, Carl, 2530
Miklich, Jeffrey J., 3437
Mikosz, Michelle, 2548
Mikuen, Scott T., 1736
Milanese, Wendy A., 669
Milani, Joseph, 982
Milani, Joseph W., 982
Milano, Bernard J., 2190
Milano, Patricia, 820
Milazzo, Rick, 140
Milbar Corp., 3626
Milberg, Joachim, 1061
Milbourn, William L., 1225
Milburn, Carol S., 3619
Milch, Randal S., 3936
Miles, Amy E., 3166
Miles, Arthur, 2581
Miles, David P., 1695
Miles, George L., Jr., 156, 1287, 1732
Miles, John C., II, 1089
Miles, Mark, 438
Miles, Mark D., 1885, 2875
Miles, Michael A., 187
Miles, Micheal A., Jr., 4045
Miles, Mike, 3581
Miles, Peter, 509
Miletich, Joseph P., 182
Miley, Gwendolyn, 2048
Milford Bank, The, 2513
Milford National Bank and Trust Co., The, 2514
Milford, Scott, 3783
Milgram, Andrew, 49
Milgram, John S., 49
Milgram, Joseph B., Jr., 49
Milgram, Margaretta S.C., 49
Milgram, Thomas, 49
Milhollan, D. Jackson, 3996
Milholland, John, 1410
Miligan, Stephen D., 4042
Milinovich, John S., 3996
Militano, Joseph, 1179
Mill-Rose Company, 2515
Milledge, Eric, 2271
Millendorf, Howard, 1910
Miller Automobile Corp., 2518
Miller Brewing Co., 1858, 2523
Miller, Adam, 2649
Miller, Adam L., 887
Miller, Andrew C., Jr., 3467
Miller, Andrew M., 734
Miller, Bev Pratt, 1430
Miller, Bill, 556
Miller, Brad, 1256, 3866
Miller, Brian A., 47
Miller, Brian K., 3831
Miller, Brian, Hon., 3514
Miller, C. Alex, 2747
Miller, Carl, 1921
Miller, Carol, 2401
Miller, Carrol, 3918
Miller, Catherine B., 428
Miller, Chad, 1438
Miller, Charlene, 4149
Miller, Charles, 2799
Miller, Charles E., 433
Miller, Charles L., 351
Miller, Charlie, 1726
Miller, Craig, 3498
Miller, Dan, 1545
Miller, Dane A., 466
Miller, Dane A., Mrs., 466
Miller, Daniel P., 2144
Miller, David, 2199, 2477, 3924
Miller, David W., 1829
Miller, Dennis E., 684
Miller, Diane Duda, 1188
Miller, Don, 3365
Miller, Donald K., 3278
Miller, Doris, 1167
Miller, Duane K., 2279
Miller, E. Tyler, Jr., 873
Miller, Edward, 72
Miller, Edward D., 688
Miller, Edward J., 495
Miller, Elizabeth, 1561, 2518
Miller, Forrest E., 2952
Miller, Frank A., 2518
Miller, Franklin C., 1171
Miller, Fred, 2781
Miller, George Lloyd, 3453
Miller, Gerald, 3944
Miller, Gerald L., 424
Miller, Glenn, 1521
Miller, Grant, 3222
Miller, Greg S., 2028
Miller, Gregory N., 1804
Miller, Hans H., 3066
Miller, Harvey R., 4022
Miller, Heidi G., 1554, 3057
Miller, Henry M., Jr., 1914
Miller, Henry S., 156
Miller, Hinda, 1653
Miller, Howard, 267, 1136
Miller, Howard G., 2829
Miller, Irene R., 858
Miller, J. Randal, 536
Miller, James, 991
Miller, James B., Jr., 1953
Miller, James C., 3297
Miller, James H., 988, 3134
Miller, James M., 69
Miller, Jan A., 1209
Miller, Janson D., 1053
Miller, Jason D., 1053
Miller, Jeff, 1191, 1706
Miller, Jeffrey A., 2417
Miller, Jeffrey D., 1800
Miller, Jim, 1759
Miller, John, 2976
Miller, John C., 1087
Miller, John P., 3086, 4010
Miller, John R., 1635
Miller, John S., 2518
Miller, John W., 2702
Miller, Jonathan, 789
Miller, Judy, 1790
Miller, Kathy, 1256, 4101
Miller, Katrina Shum, 1652
Miller, Ken, 2296
Miller, Larry, 3587
Miller, Larry C., 626
Miller, Laurence G., 3707
Miller, Lawrence W., 2515
Miller, Lynne M., 3346
Miller, M. Victoria Wood, 1008
Miller, Marc D., 46
Miller, Marilynn, 1409
Miller, Mark, 28
Miller, Mark A., 2991
Miller, Marlin, 686
Miller, Mary Louise, 466
Miller, MaryAnn, 304
Miller, Mathew, 1757
Miller, Melanie E.R., 407
Miller, Merrill A., Jr., 777
Miller, Michael, 272, 551
Miller, Michael A., 569
Miller, Michael E., 894, 1425
Miller, Michael H., 302
Miller, Michael Jaye, 2153
Miller, Michael T., 564
Miller, Mike, 151, 263, 448, 2938, 2961, 3380
Miller, Natalie, 2409
Miller, Nigel, 863
Miller, Nina, 1578
Miller, Olivia A., 1274
Miller, P. Daniel, 2179
Miller, P. Michael, 551
Miller, Patricia, 551
Miller, Patricia R., 551
Miller, Paul, 3863
Miller, Paul David, 1153
Miller, Paul M., 2515
Miller, Phil, 221
Miller, Philip, 3519
Miller, Quincy, 3137
Miller, R. M., 3
Miller, R.N. "Bo", 1161
Miller, Rand K., 1015
Miller, Randall H., 1837
Miller, Randolph L., 3010
Miller, Richard A., 2837
Miller, Richard M., 2515
Miller, Richard S., 3916
Miller, Robert, 3659
Miller, Robert G., 79, 2724
Miller, Robert J., 1964
Miller, Robert L., 3826
Miller, Robert S., 156, 3669
Miller, Robert S., Jr., 156
Miller, Robyn C., 1015
Miller, Rodney G., 1274
Miller, Roger, 4138
Miller, Ron, 2588
Miller, Ronald C., 578
Miller, Ronald K., 1015
Miller, Rory L., 4077
Miller, Sandra, 1438
Miller, Sara, 4066
Miller, Sarah C., 4077
Miller, Scot A., 1647
Miller, Scott, 1314
Miller, Shari, 1421
Miller, Sharon, 2497
Miller, Sherman, 3839
Miller, Stephen F., 2028
Miller, Steve, 2028
Miller, Steven L., 1563
Miller, Stuart A., 2250
Miller, Sue, 1248
Miller, Susan, 4149
Miller, Susan C., 297
Miller, Suzan A., 1950
Miller, T. Michael, 2813
Miller, Ted B., Jr., 65
Miller, Ted C., 1146
Miller, Terri A., 1078
Miller, Thaddeus W., 661
Miller, Thomas R., 830
Miller, Tim, 1136
Miller, Todd E., 3325
Miller, Tom, 3448
Miller, Valerie, 3697
Miller, Victor F., 2515
Miller, W. Thaddeus, 661
Miller, William A., 1551
Miller, William C., Jr., 885
Miller, William D., 508
Miller, William I., 1007
Miller, William J., 2767, 4003
Miller, William P., II, 853
Miller-Davis Co., 2522
Miller-Out, Elisa, 3464
Miller-Out, Leon, 3464
Millet, Ernest M., Jr., 1188
Millett, Frank, 2138
Millett, Mark, 3595
Millett, Mark D., 3595
Millhiser Smith Agency, Inc., 2524
Milliard, Sheryl, 343
Millichap, William A., 2370
Milligan, Bill, 1636
Milligan, Brain, 2124
Milligan, Cynthia H., 2120, 4028
Milligan, David R., 4034
Milligan, George D., 3869
Milligan, Jim, 1312
Milligan, Joel, 1312
Milligan, John F., 1582
Milliken and Co., 2525
Milliken, Gerrish H., 2525
Milliken, James B., 3919
Millikin, Michael P., 1555
Millis, William B., 697
Millon, Jean-Pierre, 1014
Millos, Ronald A., 3700
Mills, Andrew, 2451
Mills, Andrew J., 2451
Mills, Charles N., 2451
Mills, Daniel, 1846
Mills, Don, 2486
Mills, J. William, III, 1926
Mills, James W., 1405
Mills, Jonathan B., 1004
Mills, Karen, 2853
Mills, Ken, 1458
Mills, Larry, 3557
Mills, Mandy, 516
Mills, Mary Lou, 3431
Mills, Rick J., 893, 1447
Mills, Scott M., 3945
Mills, Sharon, 1168
Mills, Steve, 3482
Mills, Steven A., 2385
Mills, Steven R., 474
Mills, William J., 821
Millsap, Colleen, 512
Millstein, Ira M., 4022
Milluzzo, Joni, 380
Millwood, Kevin, 3729
Milmoe, Michael W., 2814
Milne, George M., Jr., 764, 1171
Milne, James, 2689
Milner, Jeff, 3222
Milner, Michael, 1122
Milone, Francis M., 2571
Milroy, Douglas A., 1524, 2073
Milstein, Philip L., 2371

Milstein, Ronald S., 2304
Miltic, Kathleen C., 1217
Milton, John, 1444
Milwaukee Western Bank, 3388
Milyasevich, Joe, 1308
Milzcik, Gregory F., 362
Mims, John W., 572
Minaldi, Thad, 2309
Minardi, Eduardo, 560
Minardi, Giorgio, 1191
Minasi, Mike, 3310
Mincks, Jay E., 1944
Mine Safety Appliances Co., 2529
Minegar, Ron, 312
Minehan, Cathy Elizabeth, 3960
Minella, Lynn C., 63
Miner, John H.F., 2314
Minford, Louise, 123
Ming, Jenny J., 2086
Mingee, James C., 3547
Mings, Chris, 2104
Minich, Sophie, 934
Minichiello, Thomas P., 3709
Minicucci, Ben, 74
Minicucci, Robert A., 101
Mink, John, 1732
Mink, Victoria, 641
Minnesota Life Insurance Co., 3389
Minnesota Mining and Manufacturing Co., 3
Minnich, George E., Jr., 2088
Minnick, David, 3132
Minnick, Mary E., 3691
Minnick, Nicole G., 4076
Minniear, Randy, 3052
Minnis, Roland, 556
Minor, Oraetta, 150
Minot Chrysler Center Inc., 3291
Minow, Martha, 3470
Minson, Arthur T., Jr., 3755
Minster Machine Co., 2532
Minster, Barbara K., 3275
Minto Communities, Inc., 2533
Minto, Rebecca S., 337
Mintz, William A., 211
Minucci, Andrew, 1018
Minyard Food Stores, Inc., 1021
Miquelon, Eilleen, 1627
Miquelon, Wade D., 3981
Miracle Ear Inc., 2535
Miracle II, LLC, 3702
Miranda, Karen, 161
Mirenda, Anthony G., 2563
Mirgon, Thomas, 798
Mirkin, Nancy D., 1713
Miro, Jeffrey H., 2277
Miron, Robert, 2625
Miron, Robert J., 1126
Miron, Steve, 2625
Miron, Steven A., 1126
Mirosh, Walentin, 2600
Misad, Matthew J., 3890
Miscik, Jami, 1253
Misheff, Donald T., 1424
Miskell, Eileen C., 1927, 3242
Mislin, Kevin M., 1363
Misplon, James L., 3384
Mississippi Power Co., 2536
Missouri Valley Steel Co., 2840
Mistarz, Cecily, 1737
Mistretta, Nancy G., 3372
Mistry, Dinyar B., 2853, 2952
Mistysyn, Allen J., 3437
Mitarotonda, James A., 3361
Mitau, Lee R., 1517, 1624
Mitcham, Carla, 1563
Mitchell Industries, 2537
Mitchell, Bill, 2117
Mitchell, Craig S., 2573
Mitchell, David M., 2554
Mitchell, Donald D., 1946, 3344
Mitchell, Dorothy L., 2537
Mitchell, Edward, 1300
Mitchell, George, 1022
Mitchell, George K., 240
Mitchell, Guy, 3883
Mitchell, Guy K., III, 2537
Mitchell, Guy K., Jr., 2537
Mitchell, James R., 1933, 3056
Mitchell, Janet D., 2945
Mitchell, Joanne S., 3056
Mitchell, Jodi M., 3380
Mitchell, John C., 3031
Mitchell, Joseph W., 562
Mitchell, Kate D., 3455
Mitchell, Katherine J., 2537
Mitchell, Kelly, 3189
Mitchell, Ken, 3415
Mitchell, Krystin, 5
Mitchell, Lee, 3679
Mitchell, Lee Roy, 815
Mitchell, Leroy, 3052
Mitchell, Margaret N., 2394
Mitchell, Mark, 3370
Mitchell, Martha M., 966
Mitchell, Mary, 786
Mitchell, Max H., 970
Mitchell, Mike, 1174
Mitchell, Patricia E., 209
Mitchell, Ralph, 814
Mitchell, Rick, 3671
Mitchell, Rose Kleyweg, 1900
Mitchell, Sandra M., 3444
Mitchell, Sheila G., 120
Mitchell, Shirley, 2886
Mitchell, Stephen C., 215
Mitchell, Theodore R., 2422
Mitchell, William, 2117
Mitchell, William E., 592, 1886, 3253, 3532
Mitchelson, Mark A., 3317
Mitchelson, Peter L., 3466
Mitchelson, Timothy, 3512
Mitchelson, William H., 3317
Mitisek, Jeanne, 2047
Mitsubishi Corp., 2539
Mitsubishi Electric Corp., 2538
Mitsubishi International Corp., 2539
Mitsubishi Motors America, Inc., 2540
Mitsubishi Semiconductor America, Inc., 2538
Mitsui & Co. (U.S.A.), Inc., 2541
Mitsui, Mitsuhiro, 2510
Mittal Steel USA Inc., 229
Mittal, Aditya, 229
Mittal, Anuradha, 409
Mittal, Lakshmi N., 1603, 1604
Mittal, Lakshmi Niwas, 229
Mittan, Keith, 4043
Mitterholzer, Doug, 67
Mittman, Martin, 3649
Mitvalsky, Cheryle, 1679
Mix, Diane, 1864
Mixtacki, Steven, 1394
Miyaguchi, Toshiya, 3776
Miyata, Jon Y., 1754
Miyoshi, Rintaro, 3503
Miyun Park, 4066
Mizarrehi, Jack, 8
Mize, Jeffrey L., 2648
Mizel, Larry A., 2324
Mizell, Cynthia, 492
Mizell, Steven C., 2559
Mizeur, Mike, 498
Mizrachi, Murray, 1489
Mizrahi, Jack, 8
Mizuho Corporate Bank (USA), 2542
Mizuho Securities USA Inc., 2542
Mizuta, Nicky, 4141
Mjartan, Dominik, 3514
Mlotek, Mark E., 3348
Mo Villa Productions, Inc., 3123
Moberg, Paul, 1735
Mobley, Stacey J., 1968
MOC Holdco II, Inc., 887
Mock, Joseph M., 2019
Mock, Kathleen, 496
Moddelmog, Hala, 171, 228
Moddelmog, Hala G., 228
Modell, Mitchell B., 1781
Modell, William, 1781
Modern Leasing Corp., 4098
Modern Machinery, Inc., 3994
Modine Manufacturing Co., 2544
Modine, Matthew, 641, 2336
Modjeski, Pauline, 1864
Modrzynski, Chris, 2676
Moe, Palmer L., 3117
Moe, Paul, 2999
Moehler, Kim, 2785
Moellenhoff, Dave, 3318
Moeller, Frank H., 3747
Moeller, Jeanette, 3697
Moeller, Jon R., 2559, 3055
Moeller, Joseph W., 2180
Moeller, Matthew, 1196
Moellering, John H., 3873
Moen, Shirley A., 3226
Moen, Timothy P., 2740
Moench, Jennifer L., 2715
Moench, Mark C., 2860
Moerdyk, Carol B., 170
Moerland, Abe, Jr., 3928
Moerland, Abraham, Jr., 3928
Moesta, Bill, 3196
Moffett, David M., 819, 1217
Moffett, James R., 1494
Moffit, Timothy E., 1078
Moffitt, John, 2486
Moffitt, Larry, 2701
Moffitt, Scott, 2712
Mogg, Jim W., 2815
Moghadam, Hamid R., 3060
Mogi, Yuzaburo, 2144
Mogle, David B., 1318
Mograbi, Lio, 644
Mogul, Michael P., 1134
Mohapatra, Surya N., 4139
Mohasco Foundation, Inc., 946
Mohawk Industries, Inc., 2545
Mohl, William, 1279
Mohler, Hugh W., 332
Mohr, Ronnie, 2217
Moini, Ingrid A., 3817
Moir, Matthew, 3689
Moirao, Dave, 1174
Moison, Franck J., 869
Mojiea, Karen, 3347
Molander, Richard, 2848
Molavi, Niloufar, 3042
Moldenhauer, David, 849
Mole, Bernadette A., 2646
Molen, John Vander, 502
Molendorp, Dayton H., 169
Moler, Heather, 1296
Moles, Kenny, 2730
Moles, Robert, 1973
Moley, Kevin E., 752
Molina, V. Sue, 3274
Molinari, Guy V., 2682, 2683
Molinaro, Mary Ellen, 3993
Molinaro, Robert J., 3993
Molinaroli, Alex A., 2050
Molinini, Michael L., 65
Moll, Curtis E., 2595
Moll, Darrell, 2595
Moll, Robert T., 2595
Moll, Theodore S., 2595
Mollenkopf, Steven M., 3095
Moller, Austin, 3903
Moller, Elizabeth A., 1563
Moller, John J., 3903
Moller, Kristopher, 3903
Moller, Randy, 1442
Moller, Sandra, 2837
Mollner, Terrence J., 663
Mollner, Terry, 409
Molloy, Chip, 2948
Molloy, Joan C., 910
Molloy, Karen A., 2749
Moloney, Daniel M., 2585
Moloney, Herbert W., III, 2241
Moloney, Thomas E., 1565
Molson, Andrew T., 2549
Molson, Geoff, 2549
Molten, Donald C., Jr., 3452
Molyneux, Phil, 3503
Momeyer, Alan, 2296
Momtazee, James C., 1762
Mona, Dave, 2530
Monaco, John, 2112
Monadnock Paper Mills, Inc., 2551
Monaghan, Beth, 287
Monaghan, James D., 1546
Monaghan, Kevin, 1546
Monaghan, Lorna, 1546
Monahan, John J., 380
Monahan, John P., 690
Monahan, Michael, 2984
Monahan, Michael J., 1220
Monahan, Michael T., 854, 921
Monahan, Steve, 2455
Monahan, Steven D., 2455
Monahan, Thomas L., III, 933
Monahan, William T., 2580, 2926
Monarch Beverage Co., Inc., 2552
Monarch Cement Co., 2553
Monarch Corp., 2554
Monastesse, Lawrence J., 2902
Mondello, Mark T., 2006
Mondics, Benjamin J., 219
Mondor, Bernard G., 2903
Mondry, Connie, 3291
Mondry, Lawrence N., 2500
Monesmith, Heath B., 935
Money, David R., 1400
Moneymaker, Michael B., 2758
Monferino, Paolo, 856
Monfort, Charles K., 879
Monfort, Richard L., 879
Monge, Dimitri, 1326
Monge, Linda, 1326
Mongeau, Leo R., 2902
Mongillo, Antoinette, 870
Mongin, Don, 3087
Monico, Nickolas F., 3806

Monie, Alain, 122, 1941
Monitor Liability Managers, Inc., 426
Monkhouse, Bryan E., 2875
Monkton, Lang, 2385
Monreal, Marc, 1731
Monroe, Chris, 3522
Monroe, Pat, 3262
Monroe, Patrick C., 3262
Monroe, Paul, 1021
Monroe, Ray, 1762
Monroy, Ginger, 2658
Monsanto Co., 2559
Monser, Edward L., 1257
Monson, Jodie, 1517
Montag, Thomas K., 340
Montague, William P., 1268
Montaldo, Maurice J., 3298
Montana Dakota Utilities Co., 2441
Montana Rail Link, Inc., 3994
Montana Resources, L.L.P, 3994
Montanaro, Carl L., Jr., 3314
Montanaro, Craig, 2108
Montanaro, Craig L., 2108
Montanaro, Leopold W., 2108
Montaner, Pedro, 2449
Monte, Christopher J., 2270
Monte, Constance, 3973
Monteith, Timothy J., 2393
Monteleone, David G., 2675
Monteleone, William A., Jr., 2675
Montemayor, Jaime, 1506
Montemayor, Jose O., 855
Monterosso, Stefano, 1677
Montez, Ray, 1151
Montford, John T., 3522
Montgomery, Ann M., 563
Montgomery, C. Robert, 1053
Montgomery, Carolyn S., 2964
Montgomery, Cynthia A., 2694
Montgomery, David, 2964
Montgomery, Dirk A., 255
Montgomery, Graciela, 1059
Montgomery, John, 563, 3260
Montgomery, Marie, 1766
Montgomery, Michael J., 1172
Montgomery, Paul, 1213
Montgomery, Rebecca, 2536
Montgomery, Vincent, 1079
Montgomery, William C., 211
Montgomey-Rice, Robert S., 338
Montgoris, William, 2786, 3572
Montgoris, William J., 708
Montisano, Joseph, 2160
Montogomery, Debbie, 3194
Montoni, Richard A., 2410
Montoya, Benjamin F., 2016
Montoya, Jorge P., 1533, 2195
Montoya, Patrick, 2034
Montreuil, Benoit, 2401
Montross, Ted, 1558
Montupet, Jean-Paul L., 266, 2258
Montwani, Sanjay, 3330
Monumental Life Insurance Co., 2561
MONY Group, Inc., The, 307
Monz, David J., 3899
Monzo, James, 2176
Moody Co., The, 2562
Moody's Corp., 2416
Moody's Investors Service, Inc., 2563
Moody, Braxton I., III, 2562
Moody, James L., Jr., 2894
Moody, James, Jr., 2894
Moody, John S., 3017
Moody, Kevin, 2562
Moody, Paul, 2875
Moody, Raymond L., 373
Moody, Richard K., 2562
Moody, Sherwood C., 833
Moody, Stephen, 2562
Moody, Thelma H., 2562
Moon, Hyun-Jin, 2701
Mooney and Moses of Ohio, Inc., 1235
Mooney, Andrew P., 3108
Mooney, David, 103
Mooney, David W., 103
Mooney, Dee K., 2500
Mooney, Edward J., 1449, 2740
Mooney, J. Robert, 1921
Mooney, Joshua, 1290
Mooney, Kay D., 48
Mooney, Stephen R., 1550
Mooney, Thomas E., 451
Moonves, Leslie, 727, 2105
Moor, M. Eugene, 492
Moor, M. Eugene, Jr., 492
Moor, Mary Beth, 91
Moorad, Jeff, 3323
Moore & Co., Benjamin, 2565
Moore & Sons, B.C., Inc., 3572
Moore & Van Allen PLLC, 2566
Moore Co., The, 2567
Moore, Alexandra, 2567
Moore, Alice, Sr., 2615
Moore, Ann, 639
Moore, Ann S., 305, 3273
Moore, Bruce, Jr., 1762
Moore, C. Stephens, 3943
Moore, Charles R., 3668
Moore, Chip, 280
Moore, Christine C., 2648
Moore, Clyde R., 2195
Moore, David C., 3891
Moore, Dennis, 2906
Moore, Donald L., Jr., 2780
Moore, Dorothea B., 2567
Moore, Doug, 2435
Moore, Douglas G., 2019
Moore, Eddie N., Jr., 2841
Moore, Edward, 1873
Moore, Edward W., 3278
Moore, Elizabeth A., 2239
Moore, Eric L., 2042
Moore, Frank, 2308
Moore, Gary, 4126
Moore, Gary B., 818
Moore, Geoff, 1023
Moore, Geoffrey A., 68
Moore, George C., 3198
Moore, George C., Jr., 2567
Moore, Gwendolyn B., 199
Moore, H. Lynn, Jr., 3831
Moore, Isabelle, 896
Moore, J. A., 2600
Moore, J. David, 3431
Moore, Jack B., 667, 2106
Moore, James L., 3171
Moore, James R., 1895, 2019
Moore, James R., Jr., 2019
Moore, Jerry, 118
Moore, John, 2600
Moore, John G., 2246
Moore, John Graell, 2550
Moore, Kathleen O'Brien, 1712
Moore, Kristen, 672
Moore, Larry O., 2544
Moore, Lauren, 1217, 3585
Moore, Madison M., 3431
Moore, Malcolm F., 1545
Moore, Michael, 3281
Moore, Michael J., 219
Moore, Nathan, 2392
Moore, Nicholas G., 1582
Moore, Nick, 395
Moore, Patrick J., 233
Moore, Pattye L., 2815
Moore, Peggy Howard, 4095
Moore, Peter, 1242
Moore, Peter F., 2567
Moore, Robert A., 1051
Moore, Roger H., 4042
Moore, Roy S., III, 4146
Moore, Sheila, 783
Moore, Stacie, 2641
Moore, Susie, 166
Moore, Tammy R., 3413
Moore, Terence F., 774
Moore, Thom, 1337
Moore, W. Henson, 3904
Moore-Moore, Laurie, 3606
Moore-Morris, Rochardа, 756
Moorehead, Donald V., 2898
Moorhouse, Edward L., 2954
Moorman, Charles W., 780
Moorman, Charles W., IV, 2725
Moorman, Lew, 3117
Moorthy, Ganesh, 2499
Moose, Sandra O., 47, 3936
Mora, Alberto, 2384
Mora, Elizabeth, 1171
Mora, Lety, 1688
Mora, Melvin, 334
Mora, Robert A., 3404
Morales, Albert, 1960
Morales, Manuel, Jr., 3003
Morales, Maria C., 2665
Morali, Veronique, 863
Moramoto, Akio, 3121
Moran & Associates, Jim, Inc., 2044
Moran, Charles E., Jr., 1066
Moran, Courtney, 3726
Moran, David C., 987, 1922
Moran, David E., 1653
Moran, Jack, 365
Moran, James M., 2044, 2647
Moran, Janice M., 2044
Moran, Judith, 2799, 4002
Moran, Michael, 2482
Moran, Nicole, 679
Moran, Robert F., 871, 2948
Moran, Tami Grigsby, 652
Moran, Thomas E., 1216
Moran, Thomas J., 2605
Moran, Tom, 4037
Moran, Victor R., 3667
Moratti, Michelle, 768
Moravitz, Edward, 1571
Morcom, Jerry W., 3194
Moreau, Claude P., 3723
Morehouse, David, 2249
Morehouse, Frank, 1956
Morel, Donald E., Jr., 4038
Moreland, Kenneth V., 3040
Moreland, Patrick M., 806
Moreland, W. Benjamin, 661
Morelli, Fred J., Jr., 3297
Morelli, Richard J., 772
Morena, Christine A., 3315
Moreno, Albert F., 4135
Moreno, Arte, 200
Moreno, Carole, 200
Moreno, Glen, 2912
Moret, Pamela J., 588
Moreton, William W., 2873
Morey, Robert, 2143
Morey, Robert S., 2143
Morey, Sean, 2627
Morfitt, Martha A., 1624, 2269
Morfogen, Ann L., 3502
Morgado, Robert J., 30
Morgan Bradley LLC, 1095
Morgan Chase Foundation, J.P., 1279
Morgan Construction Co., 2568
Morgan Services, Inc., 2569
Morgan Stanley, 2570
Morgan Stanley & Co. Inc., 2570
Morgan Stanley Dean Witter & Co., 2570
Morgan Stanley Group Inc., 2570
Morgan Stanley, Dean Witter, Discover & Co., 2570
Morgan, Angela, 2200
Morgan, April, 3550
Morgan, Barrett, 2568
Morgan, Bennett J ., 2999
Morgan, Bennett J., 2999
Morgan, Bill, 2585
Morgan, Calvert A., Jr., 4127
Morgan, Catherine A., 3004
Morgan, Cathy, 1225
Morgan, Charles G., Jr., 1347
Morgan, Christina E., 458
Morgan, Christine R., 3004
Morgan, Clara, 2200
Morgan, Craig, 458
Morgan, Craig A., 458
Morgan, Daniel M., 2568
Morgan, David L., 2412
Morgan, Deborah L., 2341
Morgan, Donna M., 2065
Morgan, Dunia, 2200
Morgan, Eileen, 1066
Morgan, Gail M., 2568
Morgan, Harvey, 990, 1330
Morgan, Herman, 2200
Morgan, J. Grey, Jr., 3515
Morgan, James C., 220
Morgan, James H., 861
Morgan, Joe, 3576
Morgan, John F., Sr., 2991
Morgan, Joseph P., Jr., 3576
Morgan, Meredith, 1873
Morgan, Michael, 3249
Morgan, Michael C., 2153, 3004, 3366
Morgan, Paul S., 2568
Morgan, Peter, 1543
Morgan, Philip R., 2568
Morgan, Robert, 1225
Morgan, Sara S., 3004
Morgan, Stuart K., 749
Morgan, Suzy, 3978
Morgan, Terry E., 1458
Morgan, Thomas G., 1324
Morgan, Thomas I., 3134
Morgan, Vincent J., 458
Morgan, Vincent J., Jr., 458
Morgan, Wallace, 3839
Morgan, William J., 362
Morgan, William L., 3943
Morgan, William V., 3004
Morgan-Prager, Karole, 2422
Morganthall, Fred J., II, 1738
Morganthall, Frederick, II, 3535
Morgenweck, Donald, 2781
Morgenweck, Donald F., 2781
Morgridge, John P., 818
Mori, Ittetsu, 2538
Morial, Sybil H., 2309

Moriarty, John, 86
Moriarty, Kevin, 304
Moriarty, Rowland T., 3581
Moriarty, Thomas M., 1014
Moriguchi, Alison, 1672
Morikis, John G., 1474, 3437
Morikubo, Yukio, 1955
Morimoto, Akio, 3121
Morin, Eileen, 4123
Morin, Gary E., 3382
Morin, Wilma J., 1681
Morishita, Mayumi, 3900
Moritz, Jamie, 1963
Moritz, Robert E., 3042
Moritz., Robert E., 3042
Moriyama, Lisa, 3541, 4027
Mork, John F., 1272
Mork, Julie M., 1272
Mork, Kyl, 1272
Mork, Kyle M., 1272
Morlan, Robert C., 1264
Morley Group, Inc., 136, 2572
Morley, James E., Jr., 2629
Morley, James T., Jr., 2704
Mornarich, Carma, 957
Morneau, Michael J., 2088
Morns, Scott J., 2749
Moro-oka, Nobushi, 2538
Moroney, James M., 406
Morooka, Kenichi, 3480
Moroz, John, 1376
Morozoff, Coral, 2695
Morparia, Kalpana, 2962
Morrell, Jane McKay, 3011
Morrell, Michael W., 3936
Morrell, Phil, 3779
Morrelli, Jim, 2054
Morrill, Jerry T., 2588
Morris Communications Co., LLC, 2573
Morris Communications Corp., 2573
Morris USA Inc., Philip, 120
Morris, Clifton H., Jr., 1556, 3413
Morris, Diana, 2431
Morris, Donna, 38
Morris, Douglas, 727, 3380
Morris, George C., III, 231
Morris, Henry L., 3487
Morris, Herman, Jr., 2943
Morris, J. Tyler, 2573
Morris, James G., 680
Morris, James T., 169, 2798, 2855
Morris, Jeff, 1767
Morris, Jim, 1126, 2852
Morris, John G., 2711
Morris, John T., 2484
Morris, Katherine B., 403
Morris, Malcolm S., 3606
Morris, Maria, 2481
Morris, Matt, 3606
Morris, Matthew W., 3606
Morris, Michael G., 82, 141, 1742, 2277, 3540
Morris, Michael J., 412, 903, 1785
Morris, Pamela, 690
Morris, Pamela B., 690
Morris, Rick, 1144
Morris, Robert, 2507
Morris, Scott L., 301
Morris, Stephen A., 2126
Morris, Stephen B., 4025
Morris, Steven M., 3106
Morris, Stewart, Jr., 3606
Morris, Tim, 2762
Morris, Virginia H., 1877
Morris, W. Howard, 2842
Morris, Wes, 3839
Morris, William David, 160
Morris, William S., III, 2573
Morris, William S., IV, 2573
Morris, Williams S., IV, 2573
Morris-Tyndall, Lucille, 3668
Morrisette, N. Welch, 1395
Morrisey, Michael, 197
Morrison Knudsen Corp., 3995
Morrison, Albert, III, 1518
Morrison, Dale F., 1962
Morrison, Danny, 3209
Morrison, Denise, 669
Morrison, Denise M., 669
Morrison, Gregg S., 579
Morrison, Gregory B., 959
Morrison, J. Holmes, 385
Morrison, John L., 1866
Morrison, Kent, 986
Morrison, Lucian L., 1291
Morrison, Patricia, 685
Morrison, Robert S., 3, 210, 1916
Morrison, Scott C., 328
Morrison, Victoria A., 399
Morrison, William L., 2740
Morrisroe, Sylvia, 176
Morrissette, Harris V., 337
Morrissey, John J., 1927, 3242
Morrissey, Michael F., 1365, 4039
Morrissey, Michael J., 3399
Morrissey, Peter G., 637
Morrow, Dillard, 3615
Morrow, Mona, 2200
Morrow, Polly O'Brien, 2984
Morrow, Roy L., 2279
Morrow, Tim, 3553
Morrow, William E., 2735
Morrow, William T., 579
Morse, Andrew M., 3491
Morse, Carole E., 3010
Morse, Charles W., III, 2693
Morse, David L., 945
Morse, Herb, 3190
Morse, Janice C., 2693
Morse, Jay, Jr., 47
Morse, Phillip, 538
Morse, Phillip H., 538
Morte, Maria, 2514
Mortensen, Romy, 585
Mortenson Co., M.A., 2577
Mortenson, Alice D., 2577
Mortenson, Christopher D., 2577
Mortenson, David, 2577
Mortenson, David C., 2577
Mortenson, Mark, 2577
Mortenson, Mark A., 2577
Mortenson, Mathias H., 2577
Mortenson, Maurice A., Jr., 2577
Mortenson, Maurice, Jr., 2577
Mortenson, Mauritz A., Jr., 2577
Mortgage Funding Corp., 2578
Mortimer, Jennifer, 1388
Mortimer, Jim, 3165
Morton, Kelly, 2968
Morton, William B., Jr., 1601
Mosaic Company, The, 2580
Mosbacher, Robert A., Jr., 661, 1102
Moscardi, Nino, 2699
Mosch, James G., 1089
Mosco, John, 3670
Moscrop, Tony, 3137
Mose, Cheryl O., 493
Moseley, Joe L., 3431
Moseley, Terry, 72
Moselman, Stuart W., 1482
Moser, David, 2720
Moser, S. Thomas, 2688
Moses, Carl, 84
Moses, E. Linhart, 379
Moses, Jennifer F., 379
Moses, John P., 505
Moses, John S., 379
Moses, Marilyn, 1148
Moses, Marilyn N., 379
Moses, Thomas W., 1966
Moses, Victor, 3124
Mosier, Bill, 2979
Mosier, Susan, 28
Mosier, William, Jr., 2979
Mosiman, Louis E., 495
Moskal, Joseph T., 2048
Moskal, Stephen L., 3390
Moskalski, Noreen, 632
Moskow, Michael H., Ph.D., 1125
Moskowitz, Paul T., 3677
Mosley, Dave, 3377
Mosling, J. Peter, Jr., 2833
Moss, Debbie, 1848
Moss, Doug, 963
Moss, John O., 3148
Moss, Kenton K., 4026
Moss, Matt, 3289
Moss, Nancy, 1071
Moss, Patricia L., 2441
Moss, Richard D., Jr., 1720
Moss, Sara E., 2230
Moss, Slyvia F., 477
Moss, Susan E., 2154
Mosse, David, 1110
Mosse, David I., 1110
Most, Angela, 516
Moszkowski, Neal, 3781
Motamed, Thomas F., 855
Motch, Alan W., 2056
Motch, Arthur E., III, 2056
Motch, David W., 2056
Motch, Oliva DeBolt, 2056
Motiva, 3430
Motley, Sandra D., 81
Moto, Emerson, 2615
Moto, Ronald, Sr., 2615
Motor Castings Co., 2583
Motorists Mutual Insurance Co., 2584
Motorola Solutions Foundation, 2585
Motorola Solutions, Inc., 2586
Motorola, Inc., 2586
Mott, Frederick B., 2961
Mott, Randall D., 1555
Mottesheard, Andy, 2312
Motto, Bill, 3675
Motwani, Sanjay, 3330
Motyka, Michael P., 627
Moug, Kevin G., 2836
Moulder, Leon O., Jr., 999
Moules, Todd, 1419
Moulton, Eben S., 3885
Moulton, Paul G., 948
Moulton, R.W. Eli, III, 2476
Mound Printing, 838
Mounger, W. D., 1082
Mount Olive Pickle Co., Inc., 2594
Mount Sequoyah Conferance & Retreat Center, 1953
Mount Wheeler Power, Inc., 2588
Mountain Creek, 624
Mountain, Paul, 1167
Mountaineer Gas Co., 1272
Mountaire Corp., 2590
Mourges, Janet L., 70
Mouw, Randy, 1466
Mowatt, Margaret, 3559
Mowbray, Kevin D., 2241
Mowen, Mike, 129
Mower, Marshall, 3189
Mowry, Barbara, 1527
Mowry, John C., 3622
Mowry, Lee B., III, 3433
Moyer, Douglas C., 844
Moylan, Peter F., 2924
Moyles, Denise L., 542
Moynihan, Brian T., 340
Moynihan, Thomas F., 586
Mozingo, Glen R., 3655
MPB Corp., 2591
Mrkonic, George R., 572
Mrkonic, George R., Jr., 294
Mrotek, Richard P., 3248
Mrozek, Donald L., 1814
Mrozek, Ernest, 1524
Mrs. Fields' Original Cookies, Inc., 2592
MSS, Inc., 138
MTD Products, Inc., 2595
MTGLQ Investors, L.P., 1604
MTV Networks, 2596
Muarry Guard, Inc., 2601
Mubarak, Ahmad, 2326
Mucci, Louis M., 608
Mucci, Martin, 2904
Mucha, Zenia, 1127
Muchin, Allan, 790
Mucica, Glenn, 3155
Muckel, John, 1931
Muckel, Linda, 1931
Muckian, William M., 1542
Muckleshoot Indian Tribe, 1
Mudd, William E., 807
Muehl, Dale, 4091
Muehlbauer, Brad J., 2179
Muehlbauer, James H., 2179
Muehlbauer, James L., 3920
Muehlstein, Mary C., 3552
Mueller and Co., Inc., 2597
Mueller, Curt, 2553
Mueller, Edward A., 852, 2434
Mueller, Jack J., 213
Mueller, Josef M., 988
Mueller, Kim, 2890
Mueller, Klaus-Peter, 2886
Mueller, Margaret L., 2205
Mueller, Mark, 2597
Mueller, Moshe, 2597
Mueller, Randy, 28
Mueller, Ray, 2448
Muellner, George K., 2469
Muenster, G.E., 1296
Muenster, Gary E., 1296
Muessig, Cynthia M., 839
Muething, Paul V., 2109
Mufson, Kathleen Ryan, 2984
Mugford, Kristin W., 1450
Mughal, Nabil, 1046
Mugride, Jason, 993
Muhl, Edward J., 3898
Muhl, Shauna Sullivan, 959
Muhlberg, Judith A., 3591
Muhleisen, Angela L., 269
Muilenburg, Dennis A., 722
Muir, David F., 1628
Muir, Elizabeth M., 1628
Muir, Kathleen K., 1628
Muir, William D., Jr., 2006

Muir, William M., 1628
Muir, William W., 1628
Mujib, Farhan, 2106
Mujica-Larson, Evelyn, 576
Mukai, Toshio, 2541
Mukherjee, Anjan, 3708
Mukherjee, Debo, 3155
Mukumoto, Calvin, 939
Mulally, Alan, 1464
Mulbern, Timothy P., 3424
Mulcahey, Michael, 802
Mulcahy, Anne M., 2048, 3691, 3999
Mulcahy, J. Patrick, 1271, 1720
Mulcahy, John R., 2909
Mulcahy, Michael, 563
Mulder, Alfred J., 3604
Mulder, Jeffrey, 3156
Mulder, Jeri, 3156
Mulder, Karen, 3156
Mulder, Kimberly, 3156
Mulder, Michael, 3156
Muldoon, J. Patrick, 1884
Mulford, William J., 380
Mulhern, Laurence F., 7
Mulhern, Mark F., 1189, 1800
Mulhern, Timothy P., 3424
Mulholland, Shawn P., 597
Mulholland, Soapy, 2853
Mulkey, James C., 905
Mull, Daniel, 229
Mullaly, Alan R., 1464
Mullane, Peter E., 3954
Mullaney, James G., 3936
Mullany, Hank, 3414
Mullarkey, Maureen T., 2765
Mullen, Dennis M., 2681
Mullen, James C., 2939
Mullen, Mark William, 45
Mullen, Michael, 1772
Mullen, Michael G., 1555
Mullen, Patrick A., 100
Mullen, Paul, 3581
Mullen, Robert L., 495
Mullen, Stephanie, 466
Muller, Aaron P., 3142
Muller, Andy M., Jr., 3142
Muller, Christina J., 3142
Muller, Daniel E., 3760
Muller, Edward R., 1563, 2756
Muller, Michael, 1190
Muller-Levan, Christina, 3142
Mullett, C. Randal, 903
Mullice, Stephen, 859
Mulligan, Deanna M., 1683
Mulligan, Donal Leo, 1554, 3714
Mulligan, Donald T., 1085
Mulligan, John J., 3691
Mulligan, Richard C., 465
Mulligan, Stephen D., 4042
Mulligan, Terrence J., 4026
Mulligan, William Charles, 3732
Mullin, Bernard J., 279
Mullin, Bernie, 278
Mullin, Dave, 2237
Mullin, Jamey, 1031
Mullin, John H., III, 1793, 3500
Mullin, Leo F., 2048
Mullin, Mark William, 45
Mullin, Scott, 3696
Mullin, Siobhan, 3510
Mullin, Thomas J., 919, 3696
Mullinax, A.R., 1189
Mullings, Paul E., 1348
Mullins, Eric D., 190
Mullins, Jeffrey, 3138
Mullins, Kay, 3241
Mulloy, Martin J., 1464
Mulloy, Marty, 1464
Mulot, Regis, 3581
Mulpas, Joe, 1047
Mulroney, Brian, 477, 4132
Multicon Builders, Inc., 1235
Mulva, James J., 1552, 1555
Mulva, Patrick T., 1315
Mulvihill, John C., 2855
Muma, Leslie M., 2488
Mumford, Carol A., 491
Mumford, Constance, 3347
Mumm, Mark, 3644
Mumme, Ralph, 4090
Munder, Barbara A., 2948
Mundt, Kevin, 1065
Munger, Charles T., 429, 948
Munitz, Barry A., 3478
Muniz, Mary Theresa, 637
Munn, William J., 2660
Munoz, George, 120, 2383
Munoz, Judith T., 2945
Munoz, Oscar, 997
Munro, Kathryn L., 3034
Munsell, William A., 3884
Munshi, Imitiaz, 3678
Munson, Christine A., 742
Munson, Jon, 3586
Munson, Nina, 216
Munson, Wanda, 2236
Munstermann, Fried-Walter, 368
Munthe, Gert W., 3273
Munyan, Christopher J., 996
Munyon, Wendy, 1668
Munzenrider, Robert E., 3946
Murabito, John M., 812
Murakami, Karen, 3854
Murano, Elsa A., 1866
Murari, Radhika, 213
Murata, Masami, 3333
Murchie, Michael S., 2323
Murdoch, James R., 2700
Murdoch, Keith Rupert, 1480, 2700
Murdoch, Lachlan K., 2700
Murdoch, Rupert, 1163
Murdock, David H., 717, 718, 1141
Murdock, Justin, 1141
Murdy, Wayne, 455
Murdy, Wayne W., 4052
Murley, Robert S., 216, 3614
Murnane, Thomas M., 2875
Murnane, William P., 2234
Muro, Regina Biddings, 2344
Muroi, Masahiro, 2720
Murph, Alan, 1151
Murphy Brothers, Inc., 2599
Murphy Oil Corp., 2600
Murphy, Brian, 2697
Murphy, Brian J., 1844
Murphy, Bruce D., 2136
Murphy, C. Francis, 4074
Murphy, Christopher, 1696
Murphy, Christopher J., III, 2
Murphy, Daniel, 2950
Murphy, Daniel L., 2335
Murphy, David, 1031
Murphy, David D., 3154
Murphy, Dominic, 3981
Murphy, Donald, 3383
Murphy, Donald E., 3383
Murphy, Doris I., 3317
Murphy, Ed, 3630
Murphy, George M., 3308
Murphy, George P., 4008
Murphy, Glenn K., 1533
Murphy, Gregory E., 3399
Murphy, Henry L., Jr., 1209
Murphy, Jack, 3016
Murphy, Jennifer, 2245
Murphy, John F., 1124, 3439
Murphy, John M., 3858
Murphy, John M., Sr., 1844
Murphy, John R., 1134, 2808
Murphy, John V., 2245
Murphy, Joseph, 1881
Murphy, Judith, 3280
Murphy, Kenneth E., III, 2407
Murphy, Lawrence J., 2006
Murphy, Mark, 691, 2820
Murphy, Mark H., 1651
Murphy, Mark Hodge, 1651
Murphy, Mark W., 3566
Murphy, Mary G., 2262
Murphy, Michael, 858
Murphy, Michael W., 2007
Murphy, Michele, 3659
Murphy, Mike, 3824
Murphy, Patrick, 3563
Murphy, Robert M., 2769
Murphy, Robert Madison, 2600
Murphy, Sheri L., 32
Murphy, Shin, 4080
Murphy, Stephen, 1134
Murphy, Steven P., 3123
Murphy, Susan, 2262
Murphy, T. Chuck, 2599
Murphy, Thomas D., Jr., 910
Murphy, Thomas J., 2323
Murphy, Thomas P., Jr., 3563
Murphy, Thomas S., 429
Murphy, Thomas S., Jr., 1345
Murphy, W. Robert, 1879
Murphy, Walter J., Jr., 3298
Murphy, Wendell H., 3487
Murphy, Willam T., 2599
Murphy, William O., 2599
Murphy, William T., 2599
Murrane, William P., 2234
Murray, Bob, 2631
Murray, Cathy, 1687, 2267
Murray, David, 3840
Murray, Grant, 4160
Murray, Hilda S., 1132
Murray, James E., 1886
Murray, James J., 2054
Murray, Joanne, 3141
Murray, John F., 3261
Murray, John F., Jr., 3261
Murray, John H., 2512
Murray, John W., Jr., 2484
Murray, Judith, 2601
Murray, Katherine A., 1239
Murray, Malcolm T., Jr., 2594
Murray, Margaret, 1477
Murray, Mark A., 1183, 2456, 3890
Murray, Michael J., 903
Murray, Michael Q., 3382
Murray, Muffie B., 3948
Murray, Patrick J., Jr., 577
Murray, Robert C., 1563
Murray, Robert J., 1724, 3821
Murray, Roger, 2601
Murray, Timothy, 3888
Murray, Todd, 3664
Murren, James Joseph, 2489
Murrey, John W., III, 861, 1132
Murrin, Jeffrey, 2444
Murry, Paul Thomas, III, 2166
Murtagh, Sue, 831
Murtha, Patrick C., 2988
Murtlow, Ann D., 1988
Muscari, Joseph C., 1026
Muscatel, Dave, 2437
Muscatel, David, 2437
Muscheid, Kendis, 1077
Muschinsky, Alison W., 3149
Muschong, Lisa A., 1183
Muse, John R., 1054
Musial, Thomas G., 2355
Musictoday, LLC, 975
Mussatt, Lynn, 694
Mussell, Susan, 3587
Mussen, Ronald D., 2671
Mussman, Dave, 4035
Muth, Stefan, 4066
Muto, Allan A., 1297
Mutschler, Jay, 3581
Mutschler, Keith, 2705
Mutton, Nick, 1476
Mutual Distributing Co., 2523
Mutual Financial, Inc., 2603
Mutual Fire Foundation, 1370
Mutual Fire Marine and Inland Insurance Co., The, 2604
Mutual of America Life Insurance Co., 2605
Mutual of Omaha Insurance Co., 2607
Mutual Telephone Co., 3035
Muzzy, Luke, 2991
MWH Americas, Inc., 2608
MWH Global, Inc., 2608
MWI, 3257
Myara, Alicia, 1348
Myatt, Tom, 2361
Myer, Gayle, 1790
Myers and Sons, D., Inc., 2609
Myers, A. Maurice, 1755
Myers, Andrea, 2520
Myers, Christopher D., 824
Myers, Eric, 3243
Myers, Gillian, 1076
Myers, Greg, 2379
Myers, Jack A., 504
Myers, James M., 2007, 2945
Myers, James W., 4054
Myers, Jerry K., 3944
Myers, John, 3697
Myers, John H., 2245
Myers, Karlyn, 3031
Myers, Karlyn T., 3031
Myers, Kim, 1110
Myers, Larry, 2853
Myers, Lawrence O., 2719
Myers, Louise, 225
Myers, Marie, 3863
Myers, Max J., 2794
Myers, Melissa, 1267
Myers, P. Chad, 2009
Myers, Richard B., 210, 1061, 2744, 2814, 3882
Myers, Robert, 3888
Myers, Roger M., 1548
Myers, Ronald J., 3760
Myers, S. L., 3984
Myers, Stephanie, 529
Myers, Stewart C., 1279
Myers, Tim D., 82
Myers, William E., 704
Myers, Woodrow A., Jr., 1313
Myers-Miller, Diana J., 1878

Myhan, Ronald G., 1338
Myhers, Richard, 2636
Myhrvold, Nathan, 1172
Mylan Laboratories Inc., 2610
Mylan Pharmaceuticals, 2610
Myres, Albert, 1563
Myszka, Ken, 1284

N.E.W. Customer Service Cos., Inc., 2611
Na, Christian S., 4139
Naatz, Michael J., 2094
Nabholz, Dan, 240
Nabisco Brands, Inc., 3200
Naccarato, Vincent J., 1118
Naccarota, Vincent J., 1118
NACDS Charitable Foundation, 2622
Nachtsheim, Stephen P., 1084
Nachtwey, Peter H., 2245
Nack, Leonard, 1423
Nack, Leonard E., 1423
Nackard Bottling Co., 2612
Nackard Land Co., Fred, 2612
Nackard, P. Jewel, 2612
Nackard, Patrick M., 2612
Nackel, John G., 1275
Nadas, John, 796
Nadeau, Eric S., 1843
Nadeau, Melody, 3347
Nadeau, Richard J., 3562
Nadella, Venkat, 3678
Nader, Anthony, 2611
Nadler, David A., 2385
Nadler, Jeff, 678
Nadrchal, Don, 1987
Nadzick, Judith A., 3871
Nadzikewycz, Paul, 1422
Nafe, Rick, 3686
Nafranowicz, Steve, 2718
Nagaraja, Amita, 2429
Nagarkar, Devdutt, 3678
Nagarkatti, Jai P., 3453
Nagatani, Tsutomu, 2713
Nageak, Roy, 3843
Nagy, C. F., 936
Nagy, Louis, Jr., 934, 3397
Nahas, Caroline W., 1120
Nahas, John, 2606
Nahey, Brian L., 3933
Nahey, Nancy L., 3933
Naibert, James R., M.D., 947
Naidoff, Stephanie W., 4028
Naim, Moises, 47
Naimo-Fredette, Leesa, 2681
Nair, Balan, 765
Nair, Hari N., 3715
Naismith, Robert W., 2924
Naito, Tadashi, 3810
Najafi, Jahm, 2968
Najarian, Richard, 3133
Nakagaki, David, 723
Nakagawa, Ikouo, 2185
Nakagawa, Ikuo, 2185
Nakahara, Hideto, 2539
Nakamura, Alyson J., 85
Nakamura, Mayumi, 2857
Nakanishi, Hiroaki, 1816
Nakanishi, Ted, 241
Nakanishi, Toshinori, 241
Nakano, Hideo, 2870
Nakano, Tomoyuki, 2713
Nakash, Avi, 2062
Nakash, Joseph, 2062
Nakash, Ralph, 2062
Nakasone, Robert C., 1866, 3581
Nakayama, Dean A., 593
Nalco Chemical Co., 2613
Nalco Co., 2613
Nalebuff, Barry J., 2639
Nall, J. Wallace, Jr., 1601
Nalley, Rob, 3199
Nalley, Robert M., 1052
Nally, Sean, 1873
Namath, Donna, 377
Namen, Robert Van, 3904
NANC Partners, Ltd., 1697
Nance, Carlyle A., Jr., 3737
Nance, Frederick R., 846, 3278
Nance, Steven W., 4077
Nance, William, 3200
Nannes, Michael E., 1111
Nanney, Roger, 2953
Nansemond Insurance Svcs., 2616
Napier, A. Lanham, 3117
Napier, Iain, 2549
Napier, Katherine S., 1804
Napier, Lanham, 3117
Naples, Allen J., 2323, 2681
Napoli, Richard J., 2506
Napoliello, Gene F., 1075
Napolitan, Ray S., 135
Napolitano, Ken, 1619
Nappi, Mark, 3874
Nappi, Ralph, 1634
Nappi, Ralph J., 1634
Naqvi, Tehseen, 303
Nara Bank, 386
Narayen, Shantanu, 38, 1068
Narcisse, Sonja, 1772
Nardone, Henry J., 1551
Narey, Sally, 1385
Narum, Gene, 3883
Narum, Larry, 2997
Narvaez, Alejandro, 1081
Narveso, Robert J., 2622
Narveson, Bob, 2622
Narwold, Karen G., 78
Narzissenfeld, Bruce, 3701
Nasaw, David G., 3664
NASDAQ OMX PHLX, Inc., 2618
Nasdaq Stock Market, Inc., The, 2617
Nasella, Henry, 3088
Naselli, Diana, 976
Naselli, Joseph V., 976
Naseman, David, 986
Nash Finch Co., 2619
Nash, Avi M., 3453
Nash, Cathleen H., 827
Nash, David B., 1268, 1886
Nash, Joshua, 2784
Nash, Sarah E., 2176
Nash, Simon, 3146
Nason, Chuck, 1076
Nasser, Jacques, 455
Nasser, Jeff, 1966
Nasser, William E., 2208
Nassetta, Christopher J., 1812
Natale, Mike, 1426
Natarajan, Aravind, 213
Nathan, David, 2596
Nathan, Tharp, 3259
Nathanson, Greg A., 1259
Nathel, Gerald, 633
Nathel, Matheew, 633
Nation, Mike, 880
National Archery Association Foundation, Inc., The, 1215
National Association of Chain Drug Stores, Inc., 2622
National Association of Realtors, 1490
National Association of Securities Dealers, Inc., 1382
National Auto Care Corp., 1840
National Basketball Association, 1095
National Christian Foundation, 1577
National City, 1296
National Electronics Warranty Corp., 2611
National Football League, The, 2091, 2684
National Fuel Gas Company, 2628
National Grange Mutual Insurance Company, 2629
National Hockey League, 2631
National Instruments Corp., 2632
National Life Insurance Company, 2633
National Machinery Co., 2634
National Machinery LLC, 2634
National Maintenance Corp., 3825
National Park Service, 1887
National Park Svc., 3843
National Presto Industries, Inc., 2636
National Purchasing Corp., 1275
National Resources, Inc., 2637
National Vulcanized Fibre Co., 2766
Nationwide Corp., 2639
Nationwide Life Insurance Co. of America, 2639
Nationwide Mutual Insurance Co., 2639
Natoli, Frank A., Jr., 1112
Natori Co., The, 2640
Natori, Josie C., 2640
Natori, Ken, 2640
Natori, Kenneth, 2640
Natural Chemistry, Inc., 940
Natural Stone Bridge and Caves, Inc., 2643
Nature's Bounty Inc., 1186
Naugatuck Savings Bank, 2645
Naugatuck Valley Financial Corp., 2646
Naughton, Gail K., 358
Naughton, Marc G., 754
Naughton, Michael T., 3569
Naugle, Jeffrey A., 1421
Nautilus Insurance Company, 426
Navarro, Richard J, 79
Navarro, Richard J., 1843
Navikas, David, 3025
Navikas, David B., 3025
Navistar International Corp., 2647
Navistar International Transportation Corp., 2647
Navteq Corporation, 2648
Navteq North America, LLC, 2648
Naylor, Jeffrey G., 3765
Nayokpuk, Percy, 422
NBC Universal, Inc., 2649, 3893
NBT Bank, N.A., 3031
NC Machinery, 3475
NCFI Banhardt Foundation, 2730
NCR Corp., 2650
Neace Lukens Holding Co., 2651
Neace, John F., 2651
Neal, Daniel, 3889
Neal, Donna, 3726
Neal, Homer A., 1464
Neal, Howard, 2632
Neal, Jack E., 1081
Neal, Michael A., 1552
Neal, Patrick L., 120
Neal, Stephen C., 3624
Neal, Wendy, 3940
Neale, Gary L., 2544
Neale, JoAnne, 2347
Nealon, Kathleen A., 2699
Nealon, Thomas M., 3522
Nealson, Taylor Drayton, 2340
Nealy, Mike, 963
Neary, Daniel P., 2607, 3919
Neary, James C., 1371
Neave, Karen, 993
Neaves, William B., 754
Nebben, Dean A., 3848
NEBCO, Inc., 2653
Nebeker, Stephen B., 3131
Nebergall, Don, 1679
Neblett, Adonis, 1491
Neblett, Karen, 2141
NEC Corp., 2654
NEC USA, Inc., 2654
Nee, Anthony M., 3997
Neeb, Craig A., 1970
Neeb, Louis P., 1087
Neece, Dick R., 3649
Needham & Company, LLC, 2655
Needham, George A., 2655
Neel, Catherine, 2844
Neeley, Ruby, 72
Neely, Cam, 537
Neely, Jerry, 1272
Neely, Joseph F., 2842
Neely, William H., 2084
Neenah Foundry Co., 2656
Neeper, Andrea, 2234
Nees, Kenneth L., 3502
Neff, Daniel A., 3973
Neff, Robert, 2329
Neff, Robert H., 2329
Neff, Thomas J., 2303
Negrier, Claude, 382
Negron, Eduardo J., 3003
Negron, Patricia A., 2759
Nehra, John M., 1044
Nehring, Randy, 3291
Nehring, Randy J., 3291
Neidorff, Michael F., 591, 735
Neighborworks America, 3190
Neil, Dave, 4026
Neiner, A. Joseph, 3378
Neis, Douglas A., 2371
Neis, James, 3046
Neis, James M., 4089
Neitzel, Scott A., 2334
Nekritz, Edward S., 3060
Nell, Ross B., 1087
Nell, Steven E., 880
Nelles, Duane A., 3095
Nelms, David W., 1125
Nelnet, Inc., 2660
Nelsen, Brad, 310
Nelsen, Keith J., 442
Nelson Industries, Inc., 1006
Nelson, Allen, 3978
Nelson, Andrew, 1073
Nelson, Anita, 382
Nelson, Anna Spangler, 1450
Nelson, Betsy, 332
Nelson, Betty, 1924
Nelson, C. David, 693
Nelson, Carl A., Jr., 4124
Nelson, Carol K., 3034
Nelson, Celeste J., 1724
Nelson, Charley, 2067
Nelson, D.B., Jr., 2419
Nelson, David C., 3487

Nicholson, Bruce, 4109
Nicholson, Charles W., Jr., 897
Nicholson, Cynthia S., 3399
Nicholson, Gary, 2950
Nicholson, James B., 177, 1183
Nicholson, Jan, 328
Nicholson, John, 2658
Nicholson, Nick, 2113
Nicholson, Pamela M., 1271, 1281
Nicholson, Robin C., 2742
Nicholson, Sue, 1279
Niciforo, Joseph, 853
Nick, Nathan, 3378
Nickel, Daniel M., 2231
Nickel, Mark C., 3261
Nickels, Charlie, 3688
Nickels, Elizabeth A., 3535
Nickerson, Bruce G., 338
Nickerson, Gary, 972
Nickerson, Jennifer, 830
Nickerson, Matthew D., 3306
Nickl, Wolfgang, 4042
Nickl, Wolfgang U., 4042
Nickles, Donald L., 3915
Nicklin, Peter, 377
Nickloy, Lee R., 239
Nickolas, John, 2964
Nicodemo, John, 2942
Nicol, James, 1540
Nicola, S. F., 2406
Nicola, Steven F., 2406
Nicola, Terry F., 2070
Nicolaisen, Donald T., 2488, 2570, 3936
Nicoletti, Ralph, 812
Nicoletti, Ralph J., 899
Nicoli, David P., 272
Nicosia, Anthony S., 2680
Nictakis, William J., 1720
Niderno, Robert, 772
Nides, Thomas, 2570
Niederauer, Duncan L., 2769
Niefeld, Kenneth A., 3815
Niekamp, Cynthia, 936
Niekamp, Randall W., 987
Nieker, Mark, 2912
Nielsen, Chris, 4153
Nielsen, Claude B., 862
Nielsen, Gerald A., Jr., 1399
Nielsen, Jane, 858
Nielsen, Sarah N., 4088
Nielsen, Terry, 3116
Nielson, Denise, 828
Nielson, Jan, 2457
Nielson, Jane, 858
Nielson, Joani, 3692
Nielson, Steven M., 3886
Nieman, Chandra N., 214
Niemann Foods, Inc., 2708
Niemann, Bill, 2768
Niemann, Christopher, 2708
Niemann, Christopher J., 2708
Niemann, Craig, 3597
Niemann, Richard H., Jr., 2708
Niemann, Richard H., Sr., 2708
Niemann, Richard, Jr., 2708
Niemann, Richard, Sr., 2708
Niemen, Gary, 2842
Nieporent, Drew, 2336
Nieporent, Herb, Sr., 4159
Nierenberger, Janine L., 3534
Niesen, Linda, 1083
Niessen, Linda, 1089
Niessen, Linda C., 1083
Nieto, Luis P., 294
Nieto, Luis P., Jr., 3292
Nieves, Wilfredo, 2262
Niewenhous, August S., III, 3616
Nighbor, Beth J., 314
Nightingale, Paul C., 1854
Nigut, Elizabeth A., 1264
Niimi, Atsushi, 3784
Nike, 1383
NIKE, Inc., 2710
Nikias, Chrysostomos L., 3673
Nikon Inc., 2711
Nilan, Patrick F.X., 2683
Nill, Mike, 754
Nilsson, Patrick, 35
Nilsson, Sven-Christer, 3556
Nimocks, Suzanne P., 2842
NIPCO Student Loan Fund, 2714
Nippon Express U.S.A., Inc., 2713
Nise, George W., 412
Nishida, Hiroshi, 3784
Nishimoto, Russell, 3189
Nishio, Yukiyasu, 347
Nishiura, Lynne, 1996
Nishiwaki, Koji, 2542
Nishiyama, Shuji, 1020
Nishizawa, T., 3632
NiSource Corporate Services Co., 2715
Nissan Motor Corp. U.S.A., 2716
Nissan North America, Inc., 1538, 2716
Nissan Village, 3954
Niswonger, Scott M., 1406
Nita, Dan, 650
Nitido, Vincent, 3807
Nitta, Jeffrey W., 4052
Nitto, Paula, 2768
Nitzkowski, Greg, 2900
Niu Pia Land Company Ltd, 2717
Niven, James H., 4113
Nivica, Gjon N., Jr., 730
Nix, Craig L., 1395
Nix, Jerry W., 3674
Nix, Michael E., 2671
Nixon, P. Andrews, 1051
Nixon, Theodore H., 2188
NL Industries, Inc., 928
Nober, Roger, 618
Noble Chemical Inc., 662
Noble, Carlos, 1407
Nobles, Anne, 2274
Nobles, John E., 620
Noboa, Aric, 1126
Nobriga, Robert, 1753
Nocella, Andrew, 3902
Noddle, Jeffrey, 174, 852, 1153
Nodorft, Cynthia, 45
Noe, Gregory R., 1061
Noechel, Richard J., 1612
Noel, D. Jeffrey, 4056
Noel, Michael L., 301
Noel, W.J. "Dub", Jr., 977
Noffke, James, 261
Noffsinger, Jeff, 4115
Nofsinger, John, 2401
Nogaj, Florence, 3228
Nogaj, Richard J., 3228
Nogales, Luis G., 227, 1228, 2105
Nogueira, Gilda M., 1208
Nohra, Jude J., 1845
Noiri, Shrio, 2103
Nokes, James W., 3723
Nokes, Jim W., 78
Nolan, Curtis, 3637
Nolan, Danton, 228
Nolan, Ellen B., 27
Nolan, Jeffrey W., 2600
Nolan, Kevin, 2718
Nolan, Kim, 2145
Nolan, Mathew J., 1162
Nolan, Tracy, 893
Noland Co., 2719
Noland, Lloyd U., III, 2719
Noland, Richard A., 2044
Nolden, Dean J., 2355
Nolen, Darryl, 1464
Noll, Candice, 1308
Noll, Eric W., 2617, 2618
Noll, Richard A., 1720
Nolop, Bruce P., 2385
Nolte, A. M, 3430
Nomiyama, Shinji, 2074
Nomura Holding America Inc., 2720
Nomura Securities International, Inc., 2720
Nonaka, Hede, 3210
Nonomaque, Curt, 3944
Noonan, Frank R., 304
Noonan, Jim, 1332
Noonan, Mary, 878
Noonan, T.M., 970
Noordhoek, Jeff, 2660
Noordhoek, Jeffrey R., 2660
Noort, Hans E. Vanden, 3134
Nooyi, Indra K., 2935
Nora Johnson, Suzanne, 156, 3960
Norberg, Steve, 3274
Norby, R. Douglas, 86
Norcross, Gary, 1371
Norcross, Jeanne, 3535
Nord Capital Group, Inc., 2721
Nord, David G., 1879
Nordby, Eugene J., 4094
Norden, Jed L., 3414
Nordenberg, Mark A., 344
Nordhagen, Arlen D., 2721
Nordhagen, Wendy P., 2721
Nordic Group of Cos., Ltd., 2722
Nordling, Christopher, 2489
Nordquist, Lane, 1797
Nordson Corp., 2723
Nordstrom, Blake W., 2724
Nordstrom, Erik B., 2724
Nordstrom, Jamie, 4037
Nordstrom, Peter E., 2724
Nored, Anita, 343
Nored, Anita M., 343
Noren, Cynthia, 5
Norensberg, Ken, 1382
Norfolk Motor Co., 3291
Norfolk Southern Corp., 2725
Norgan, Kenneth, 2427
Norgren, Anneka, 2950
Norihama, Katsushi, 2087
Norland, Cynthia, 2441
Norland, Cynthia J., 2441
Norlander, Adam R., 32
Norling, James A., 1732
Norman, Christina, 2596
Norman, James, 113
Norman, Lewis, 432
Norman, Lewis G., 432
Norman, Michael, 3850
Norman, Paul, 2120
Normandin, Stephen, 3160
Norment, E. Sims, 1401
Norment, Philip Evan, 1095
Normile, Michael J., 1393
Normile, Robert, 2405
Norona, Michael A., 39
Norrell, Julia, 2573
Norrell, Julia J., 2573
Norrington, Lorrie, 1124
Norrington, Lorrie M., 2417
Norris Sucker Rods, 2981
Norris, Alisa C., 3575
Norris, Charles, 3550
Norris, Cindie, 1383
Norris, Derek J., 342
Norris, Marla Johnson, 240
Norris, Patricia C., 2445
Norris, Paul, 3382
Norris, Paul J., 1449
Norris, Robert B., 4097
Norris, Trevor J., 3816
Norsworthy, Alice, 3889
Norsworthy, Alice A., 3889
Nortex Corp., 2727
North & Schanz Consulting Group, Inc., 2732
North American Rescue Products, Inc., 2728
North Carolina Foam Industries, Inc., 2730
North Community Bank, 2731
North Group Consultants, Inc., 2732
North Jersey Media Group Inc., 2733
North Middlesex Savings Bank, 2734
North Star Ventures, 225, 2820
North, Jason Foster, 1461
North, John, 2287
North, Julia B., 900
North, Robert, 3228
North, Roger S., 2732
Northagen, Don, 3394
Northeast Nuclear Energy Co., 2737
Northeast Security Bank, 3394
Northeast Utilities, 2737
Northeastern Wyoming Bank Corp., 1423
Northern Arkansas Telephone Co., 2738
Northern Indiana Fuel and Light Co., Inc., 2739
Northern Life Insurance Co., 1938
Northern Plains Steel Co., 2840
Northern Trust, 1236
Northern Trust Co., The, 1257, 2740
Northfield Savings Bank, 2742
Northgate Gonzalez, LLC, 1608
Northrop Grumman Corp., 2744
Northrop, Mike, 1383
Northrup, Lori, 3626
Northshore Mining Co., 850
NorthSide Community Bank, 2745
Northwest Bancorp, MHC, 2746
Northwestern Mutual Life Insurance Co., The, 2749
Northwestern University, 3474
Norton Co., 3312
Norton Co., Matthew G., 2211
Norton, David, 2048, 2928
Norton, Helen A., 3661
Norton, Patrick J., 1663
Norton, Pierce H., II, 2815
Norton, Robert G., 491
Norton, Thomas, 2105
Norvik, Harald, 913
Norwalk Police Union Show Fund, 2631
Norwest Corp., 4028
Norwest Ltd., 4028
Norwood Cooperative Bank, 2751
Norwood, Ballard G., 3432
Norwood, Gregory W., 1419

O'Shaughnessy, Tim, 2290
O'Shea, Claire, 3624
O'Shea, Denny, 3607
O'Shea, Gerald, 3624
O'Shea, Kevin, 94, 1165
O'Shields, Lee, 3778
O'Such, Frederick M., 1788
O'Sullivan, James, 2414
O'Sullivan, James J., 2414, 2583
O'Sullivan, Michael B., 3267
O'Sullivan, Mort, 1689
O'Sullivan, Patrick, 240
O'Toole, Beverly L., 1603, 1604
O'Toole, Richard, 3070
O'Toole, Robert J., 565, 1323
O'Toole, Timothy T., 997
O-Z Gedney Co., LLC, 3558
Oak Hill Capital Management LLC, 1186
Oakley Industries, Inc., 2774
Oakley, David, 2774
Oakley, Gary A., 2774
Oakley, Gary Joann, 2774
Oakley, Harold B., 3110
Oakley, Michael, 2774
Oakley, Ralph M., 3110
Oakley, Thomas A., 3110
Oaks, Nancy, 1549
Oaksmith, Scott, 798
Oakwood Homes, Inc., 1782
Oates, Michael, 1371
Oates, R. Brad, 819
Oatey Supply Chain Services, Inc., 2775
Oatey, Gary, 2775
Oatey, Gary A., 3488
Oatey, Karen, 2775
Oatey, William, 2775
Oatway, Catherine L., 3317
Obendorf, Steven E., 188
Oberbeck, Christian L., 673
Oberdorfer, John L., 2898
Oberfeld, Steven J., 3437
Oberhelman, Douglas R., 722, 2274
Oberkrom, Scott, 137
Oberland, Gregory C., 2749
Oberlander, Michael, 591
Oberlander, Michael I., 591
Obermeyer, Paul R., 889
Oberndorf, William E., 661
Oberrender, Robert, 3884
Obert, Charles D., 1467
Obert, Steve, 191
Oberton, Willard, 1153
Oberweis, Julie, 2272
Oberyshyn, Jaroslaw, 3400
Objectwin Technology, Inc., 2778
Obourn, Candy M., 2886
Obrist, John H., 1287
Obssuth, Raymond K., 3271
Ocanas, Reymundo, 901
Ocean City Holding Company, 2781
Ocean City Home Bank, 2781
Ocean Federal Savings Bank, 2782
Ocean Financial Corp., 2782
OceanFirst Bank, 2782
OceanFirst Financial Corp., 2782
Ochoa-Brillembourg, Hilda, 1554, 2429
Ochoco Lumber Co., 2783
Ochs, Peter M., 1374
Ockenfels, Andrew, 829
Ockenfels, Andy, 829
Ockenfels, Christopher J., 829
Ockenfels, Deb, 829
Ockenfels, John L., 829
Ockenfels, Mark, 829
Ockenfels, Ralph, 3716
Ockenfels, Timothy A., 829
Octa Restoration Grant, 1992
OCWEN Loan Servicing, Inc., 3190
Oda, Masaru, 2539
Odake, Shin, 1343
Oddleifson, Christopher, 1927, 3242
Odeen, Philip A., 525, 933
Oder, Kenneth W., 3310
Odette, Debi, 3216
Odland, Steve, 1554
Odom, C.C., II, 853
Odom, Charles L., 1850
Odom, DeWayne, 150
Odom, Judy C., 2246
Odum, Marvin E., 3430
Odum, Steven P., 559
Odyssey Investment Partners, LLC, 2784
Oechsner, David, 4010
Oehrig, Susan, 123
Oei, Perry P., 723
Oeler, Robert P., 1142
Oesterle, Stephen N., 2453
Oestreich, Dean C., 104, 4095
Oestreich, Jonathan D., 589
Oetgen, Stephen, 2164
Oettinger, M. D., 3981
Ofer, Eyal M., 3273
Offen, Neil H., 2759
Offer, David Scott, 2585
Offit, Morris W., 156
Ogawa, Diane Harrison, 3076
Ogburn, Charles H., 692
Ogden, Roger, 3374
Ogden, Stan, 129
Ogg, Thomas C., 2584
Ogilvie, Dian, 3784
Ogilvie, Dian D., 3788
Ogilvy & Mather Worldwide, Inc., 2788
Ogles, Bill, Jr., 978
Oglesby, Ann M., 2965
Oglesby, Tony E., 2267
Oglesby, William S., 39
Ogletree, Powell G., Jr., 34
Ogun, Toyin, 4151
Ogunlesi, Adebayo O., 660, 1603, 1604
Oh Huber, Marie, 56
Oh, Christine, 386
Ohashi, Noriaki, 2087
Ohio Co., The, 1129
Ohio Edison Co., 1424
Ohio National Financial Svcs., 2790
Ohio National Life Insurance Co., The, 2790
Ohio Northwestern University, 3981
Ohio Power Co., 141
Ohio Savings Bank, 2791
Ohio Wholesale, Inc., 2792
Ohlig, Charles J., 3211
Ohringer, Mark, 2061
Ohtsubo, Fumio, 2870
Oi, Kazumori, 3785
Oilgear Co., The, 2793
Oiness, S. A., 3857
Ojakli, Ziad S., 1464
Ojeda, Jodi A., 3275
Oka, Ana, 3497
Oka, Hironori, 1020
Oka, Kensuke, 4042
Oka, Masashi, 3854
Okada, Takayuki, 2654
Okamoto, Kenneth T., 2198
Okamura, Kapsusha, 2726
Okamura, Kiyoshi, 4049
Okarma, Jerome D., 2050
Okazaki, Glen R., 1405
Oken, Marc D., 2385, 3500
Okenica, Kathleen, 2416
Okerstrom, Mark D., 1311
Okinow, Harold, 2266
Okinow, Sandra, 2266
Oklahoma Gas and Electric Co., 2794
Oklahoma Publishing Co., The, 2795
Okoroafor, Michael, 1772
Oktollik, Martin, 3751
Okuda, Petfuji, 3787
Okuda, Roy, 3673
Okuma America Corporation, 663
Okun, Andrew, 2939
Olabode, Lola, 1567
Olayan, Hutham S., 2570
Olczak, Jacek, 2962
Old Dominion Box Co., 2796
Old Harbor Native Corp., 2797
Old National Bank, 2798
Old National Trust Co., 3722
Old Westbury Golf & Country Club, 2799
Old, William A., Jr., 4078
Oldenburg, William R., 1174
Oldenburger, Waldemar, 2322
Oldham, William G., 1016
Oldroyd, Charlie, 1269
Oldroyd, Nancy, 1269
Olds, William, 4040
Ole South Properties, Inc., 2800
Olejniczak, Lonny, 45
Olejniczak, Thomas, 3061
Olejniczak, Thomas M., 1651
Oleksak, Michael, 428
Olemaun, Forrest D., 234, 3843
Olemaun, Ida, 234
Oleson, Sandra L., 4108
Oleynik, Leslie, 2482
Oliff, James E., 853
Olijnyk, Maria, 1422
Olin Corp., 2801
Olin, John A., 1732
Olin, Kathleen, 1628
Olin, William H., 1808
Olinde, Beau, 977
Olinger, Eric, 2025
Olinger, Thomas S., 3060
Olisa, Ken, 3741
Oliuares, Geraldo, 3560
Olivares, Jess, 3304
Olivares, Rosa, 3757
Olive, J. Terry, 811
Oliver, Augustus K., 3358
Oliver, Elizabeth J., 2136
Oliver, George, 3370
Oliver, Jerrold B., 1334
Oliver, Joe, 1110
Oliver, John, 392
Oliver, John J., Jr., 3016
Oliver, Jordan, 3363
Oliver, Leon J., 2737
Oliver, Sandy, 382
Oliver, Walter M., 144, 1551
Olivera, Armando J., 57, 1443, 1448
Oliveria, Dennis, 1445
Oliverio, John, 986
Oliverio, Lisa, 2051
Olivet, D. Scott, 871
Olivet, David Scott, 2774
Olivett, John, 341
Olivetti McMorrow, Jaffray K., 2802
Olivetti Office USA, 2802
Olivetti, Alfred C., 2802
Olivetti, Dino, 2802
Olivetti, Marc, 2802
Olivetti, Peter, 2802
Olivetti, Philip, 2802
Olivie, Marc, 2399
Olivier, Leon J., 2737, 3075
Olivieri, Jason, 511
Oliviero, Michael J., 2688
Olivo, Maria, 3802
Olli, Amy Fliegelman, 638
Ollila, Jorma, 3430
Olmsted, Frances C., III, 1239
Olmsted, Varner T., 2151
Olsen, Daryl, 286
Olsen, Dave, 3209
Olsen, Eric C., 2210
Olsen, Frederick, 1077
Olsen, James, 3241
Olsen, Jeffrey, 3218
Olsen, Kirk, 1168
Olsen, Lisa, 1828
Olsen, Michael J., 2836
Olsen, Michael S., 2070
Olsen, Mike L., 1797
Olsen, Robert, 4037
Olshansky, Joshua, 4151
Olson, Amy, 3241
Olson, Bruce J., 2371
Olson, Darlene, 797
Olson, David, 1766
Olson, Dean A., II, 3241
Olson, Doug, 1679
Olson, Edgar L., 1535
Olson, Frank A., 1793
Olson, Fred, 1077
Olson, Gary S., 1297
Olson, Gregg, 3793
Olson, Hjalmar E., 576
Olson, James P., 4087
Olson, Jayme D., 691
Olson, Jon, 4137
Olson, Keith D., 194
Olson, Kurt L., 32
Olson, Lyndon L., Jr., Amb., 1273
Olson, Mark, 2836
Olson, Mark K., 1785
Olson, Neil D., 3936
Olson, Patricia, 3241
Olson, Rich, 14
Olson, Richard, 14
Olson, Robert J., 4088
Olson, Ronald L., 429, 1228, 3999
Olson, Scott, 290
Olson, Steven C., 745
Olson, Tagar C., 1400
Olson, Teresa, 2067
Olson, Thomas F., 1551
Olson, Thomas L., 1651, 3500
Olson, Tiffany, 3458
Olson, Timothy P., 2748
Olsovsky, Jo-ann M., 618
Olszewski, Daniel, 1394
Olszewski, Veronica A., 1880
Olszewski, Zuzanna, 772
Oltjen, Larry, 55
Olympus America, Inc., 2804
Omachinski, David L., 193
Omaha Steaks International, Inc., 2805
Omaha World Herald Branching Out, 2806
Omaha World-Herald Co., 2806
Oman, Mark, 1389
Omega Financial Corp., 1318
Omenn, Gilbert S., 182

Omer, Russell J., 792
Omidyar, Pierre M., 1217
Omitsu, Takashi, 1923
Ommen, Kaye, 2966
Omnicare, Inc., 2807
Omron Electronics Components, LLC, 2810
Omron Electronics Inc., 2810
Omron Electronics LLC, 2810
Omron Healthcare, Inc., 2810
Omtvedt, Craig P., 1809, 2833
Once Upon A Time Foundation, 1021
Ondeo Nalco Co., 2613
One Valley Bank, N.A., 385
Oneglia, Gregory S., 3858
Oneglia, Raymond R., 3826
Oneida Financial Corp., 2814
ONEOK, Inc., 2815
Onesource Software, Inc., 1546
Oney, Nancy, 2650
Onken, Kristen M., 3377
Onken, Nancy, 1743
Online Testing Exchange, 1131
Onnembo, John, Jr., 3824
Onnink, Ludo, 1801
Ono, Kazuhiro, 2713
Ono, Leanne, 1916
Ono, Naoji, 150
Ono, Raymond S., 1405
Ono, Seiei, 2539
Onoe, Kiyoshi, 1515
Onorato, Don, 1799
Onorato, Joseph A., 2545
ONSPOT of North America, Inc., 2816
Onstead, R. Randall, Jr., 456
Oomittuk, Alzred, 3751
Open Society Institute, 2711
Opliger, Rod, 435
Oplin, William F. (Bill), 82
Oplinger, William F., 82
Oppenheimer, Deanna W., 2650
Oppenheimer, Martin, 2689
Oppenheimer, Peter, 217
Opperman, John R., 3696
Opperman, Vance K., 496, 3741
Opsahl, David, 3164
Optima Fund Management, Ltd., 2819
Optima Group Holdings, LLC, 2819
Optinuity Alliance Resources Corporation, 2416
Opus Corp., 225, 2820
Opus, LLC, 2820
Oral, Ray, 855
Orange Wood Children's Fdn., 1602
Orban, George P., 3267
Orchard, James C., 2377
Orcutt, Mike, 1151
Ord, John, 944
Orderest, Inc., 2882
Orders, David, 2882
Orders, Jimmy, 2882
Oren, Wes, 1517
OrePac Building Products, Inc., 2823
Oreson, Keith A., 2875
Oring, Nancy L., 1859
Orioles Reach, 334
Orlando Magic, Ltd., 2824
Orlando, John S., 727
Orleans Realty LLC, 2825
Orlen, Gregg F., 792
Orlinsky, Ethan, 2345
Ormlor, Richard J., 4149
Ormond, Melissa, 2336
Ormond, Paul A., 1763
Ornell, John, 4003
Orner, John, 496
Oros, John G., 2356
Orosz, Alan, 1913
Orr, Deano, 3711
Orr, Deano C., 1968
Orr, James F., 398, 2790
Orr, Kim, 832
Orr, L. Glenn, Jr., 1800
Orr, Robert M., 2869
Orr, San W., Jr., 4008
Orschein, William L., 2827
Orscheln Co., 2827
Orscheln, Barry L., 2827
Orscheln, D. W., 2827
Orscheln, Phillip A., 2827
Orscheln, R. J., 2827
Orscheln, W. C., 2827
Orscheln, W. L., 2827
Orsino, Jeannette M., 226
Ort, Charles G., 1486
Ortale, Gary J., 2508
Ortberg, Robert K. (Kelly), 3247
Ortec, Inc., 2828
Ortega, Bobby, 705
Ortega, Xavier, 1077
Ortenstone, Susan B., 1239
Ortho Biotech Inc., 2048, 3992
Ortho Biotech Products, L.P., 3992
Ortho Womens Health & Urology, 2048
Ortho-McNeil Pharmaceutical, Inc., 2048, 3329
Orthopaedic Center, The, 2829
Ortiz, Carlos, 1622
Ortiz, Jaun Carlos, 619
Ortiz, Maria Ester, 1608
Ortiz, Patrick T., 3076
Ortiz, Ron, 3626
Ortiz, Sylmarie, 1567
Orton, Laurence, 775
Ortsman, Illysa, 3863
Ortwine, Wanda S., 2317
Orullian, B. LaRae, 878
Orvis Co., Inc., The, 2830
Osako, John, 1679
Osani, Anthony, 1151
Osattin, Alison J., 540
Osbon Associates, 2573
Osborn, Debra, 648
Osborn, Karen, 2770
Osborn, Micheal R., 4126
Osborn, William A., 13, 722, 1551, 2740
Osborne, Alfred E., Jr., 1450
Osborne, Burl, 2925
Osborne, James C., 397
Osborne, Jaymie, 2028
Osburn, Maggie, 2945
OSCO Industries, Inc., 2832
Oscoda Plastics, 1196
Osheyack, Daniel J., 3757
Oshkosh Corp., 2833
Oshkosh Truck Corp., 2833
Oshman's Sporting Goods, Inc., 3548
Oshman, Marilyn, 3548
Oskey, LuEllen, 3355
Oskin, David W., 3134
Osmond, Justin, 3587
Ossing, Michael H., 2380
Ostby, Bryn Roe, 1982
Ostby, Helen Signe, 1982
Ostby, Signey, 1982
Ostdiek, Dave, 793
Ostenbridge, Paul Van, 283
Ostennk, Bruce, 1749
Oster, Ashley, 3902
Ostergard, Tonn M., 178
Osterink, Bruce J., 1749
Osterman, Tom, 3601
Ostermann, Douglas R., 233
Ostermiller, Marv, 937
Ostertag, Thomas, 2345
Ostfield, Alan, 1095, 2866
Ostling, Leif, 3473
Ostrander, Gregg A., 2493
Ostrander, Jane, 3715
Ostrander, Kevan A., 165
Ostrow, Gary J., 2265, 2789, 3306
Osusky, Frank P., 388
Oswald, Gerhard, 3334
Oswalt, Roy, 1871
Otaguro, Curt T., 1405
Otellini, Paul S., 1613, 1950
Otih, Otis O., 2384
Otis, Clarence, Jr., 1032, 3913, 3936
Otis, Thomas, 7
Oto, Hiroshi, 1515
Otsuka American Pharmaceutical, Inc., 578
Ott, Larry, 2473
Ott, Larry E., 2473
Ott, Nancy, 3091
Ottauquechee Health Foundation, 501
Otte, Patrick T., 2500
Ottensmeyer, Patrick J., 2094
Otto, Martin, 628
Otto, Norman A., 959
Otto, Tim, 2396
Ouchi, William G., 42, 3405
Ouimet, Matthew A., 871
Ounalashka Corp., 2837
Ouren, Eugene, 2883
Ousdahl, Kimberly, 1443
Outlaw, Jennings, 3805
Outlaw, Rhonda, 2229
OVB Charitable Trust, 385
Ovelmen, Karyn, 2322
Overgaard, Stan, 2213
Overhults, Joseph, 1053
Overlee, Steven, 615
Overlock, Willard J., Jr., 398
Overly, Alice, 1477
Overman, Norbert, 77
Overman, Worth, Jr., 3805
Overseas Adventure Travel, 1627
Overstreet, Dan, 979
Overstreet, James, 1192
Overstrom, Gunnar, 2409
Owen Industries, Inc., 2840
Owen, Angela, 3150
Owen, Charles, 2162
Owen, Kimberly J., 3109
Owen, Mary, 2626
Owen, Mary M., 606
Owen, Nicholas R., 1698
Owen, Richard, 802
Owen, Robert E., 2840
Owen, Tyler R., 2840
Owens Corning, 2842
Owens Group Ltd., 2843
Owens, B. Craig, 669
Owens, Ben, 240
Owens, Christine M., 3872
Owens, Herbert, 2843
Owens, James J., 1153
Owens, James W., 82, 1960
Owens, James W., Jr., 2570
Owens, Jim, 1517
Owens, Leonard, 1567
Owens, Mark C., 454
Owens, O'dell M., 3835
Owens, O. B., 72
Owens, Paul D., Jr., 337
Owens, Robert, 2843
Owens, Robert W., 3650
Owens, Walter, 1083
Owens, William A., 751, 1951
Owens, William Arthur, 751
Owens-Illinois, Inc., 2844
Owers, Helen, 3742
Owings Family Foundation, 3347
Owings, Steven H., 3347
Ownby, David H., 3166
Owner Revolution, Inc., 2845
Owoc, Jeff, 2452
Oxford Industries, Inc., 2847
Oxford Travel Inc., 2848
Oxford, Patrick, 549
Oxley, Scott, 338
Oyer, Timothy J., 4104
Oyler, Caroline, 2876
Oyler, Tennyson S., 2855
Ozan, Terrence R., 3732
Ozawa, Takashi, 2144
Ozer, Hope H., 310

P'Pool, William C., 2443
P.E.L., Inc., 2849
Paca, Dan, 2129
Paccapaniccia, Vincent A., 996
PACCAR Inc, 2850
Pacchini, Mark, 2531
Paccione, Philip, 3472
Pace Airlines, 1858
PACE Inc., 2851
Pace, Gary W., 3192
Pace, James C., Jr., 1943
Pace, Kaye, 4072
Pace, Nicholas J., 171
Pace, Thomas W., 478
Pace, Waymon, 72
Pace, Wayne H., 3755
Pacheco, Albert M., 1208
Pachella, Joseph, 46
Pachler, Christopher M., 2990
Pacific BMW, 723
Pacific Coast League, 3304
Pacific Gas & Electric Co., 3304
Pacific Gas and Electric Co., 2853
Pacific Gas and Electric Company, 2952
Pacific Giant, Inc., 2854
Pacific Life Insurance Co., 2855
Pacific Mutual Holding Co., 2855
Pacific Nissan Inc., 3773
Pacific Office Automation, Inc., 2856
Pacific World Corp., 2858
Pacificare Health Systems Foundation, 3884
Pacifico Airport Valet Svc., 2859
Pacifico Ford, 2859
Pacifico Hyundai, Inc., 2859
Pacifico, Joe D., 2859
Pacifico, Joseph R., 2859
Pacifico, Kerry, 2859
Pacifico, Kerry T., 2859
PacifiCorp, 2860
Pacious, Patrick, 798
Pack, Gary, 1762
Pack, Mike, 39
Packard, Ann, 2862
Packard, Crystal, 2862

Packard, Debra, 2862
Packard, Dennis, 2862
Packard, Flo, 2862
Packard, James L., 832, 2355
Packard, Jay, 2862
Packard, Lon D., 2862
Packard, Packard & Johnson, 2862
Packard, Ron, 2862
Packard, Ronald D., 2862
Packard, Seth, 2862
Packard, Von G., 2862
Packer, Gary D., 2695
Packham, Maura, 3091
Packwood, Jan B., 1907
Padden, James A., 3649
Padgett, John, III, 1551
Padgett, Tim, 1915
Padmanabhan, Ram, 210
Padrick, Kevin D., 1404
Paduano, Frances Ruth, 2955
Paese, Thomas G., 1926
Paetow, Gregory J., 1413
Paetow, William J., 1413
Pagano, Christopher J., 266
Pagano, Louis V., 1364
Pagano, Thomas A., 1364
Page, Alan, Justice, 2626
Page, G. Ruffner, Jr., 2440
Page, Gregory R., 691, 693, 1216
Page, Janice E., 140
Page, John, 888, 1602
Page, Larry, 1613
Page, Lawrence, 1613
Page, Lex F., 1505
Page, Raymond, 2506
Page, Raymond L., 2506
Page, Stephen F., 2265
Pagel, Benjamin G., 3394
Pagel, Gene, 2351
Paggi, Teresa, 2784
Paglia, Catherine James, 3919
Pagliuca, Stephen, 352
Pagliuca, Stephen G., 1762
Pagnillo, Jennifer M., 1046
Paige, Brad, 2126
Paige, Bradford C., 2126
Paige, Detra G., 276
Paik, Elaine, 869
Paik, Son-Jai, 85
Pain, George H., 2801
Painter, Craig, 2162
Painter, Craig C., 2162, 2622
Painter, Jonathan W., 2083
Paisley, Amanda, 1240
Paisner, Harold M., 1953
Pajak, Carol, 3942
Pajonas, Thomas L., 1447
Pajunen, Edward L., 3394
Palace of Auburn Hills, The, 1095
Palace Sports & Entertainment, Inc., 1095
Palacios, Mario, 176
Paladino, Steve, 3348
Paladino, Steven, 3348
Palafox, Mary, 3624
Palama Supermarket, 1694
Palandjian, Tracy P., 51
Palazzo, James, 3255
Palazzolo, Lori, 3060
Palen, Gregory P., 3920
Palensky, Frederick J., 127
Palermo, Christopher, 864
Palermo, James P., 344
Palestine, Lisa, 759
Palihapitiya, Chamath, 728
Paliotta, Mike, 980
Palisano, Donald J., 1139
Palkovic, Suzanne, 3191
Pallash, Robert C., 1449
Palleschi, Ralph F., 271
Pallotta, James, 352
Palm Bay Imports, Inc., 2867
Palm, Debra, 1269
Palm, Gregory K., 1603, 1604
Palm, Mike, 1269
Palmby, Paul L., 3406
Palmer First National Bank and Trust, 4028
Palmer, Adam J., 3410
Palmer, Alphonse, 1399
Palmer, Ann Page, 1083
Palmer, Anthony J., 1791, 2150
Palmer, Calandria, 989
Palmer, David, 3122
Palmer, Duncan J., 2833
Palmer, E. Perry, 1395
Palmer, James F., 2744
Palmer, John William, 756
Palmer, Kay Johnson, 1892
Palmer, Kaye A., 169
Palmer, Lesley, 2542
Palmer, Myrtle, 989
Palmer, Neil A., 749
Palmer, Ray, 989
Palmer, Richard, 801
Palmer, Richard K., 1155
Palmer, Rick, 3150
Palmer, Robert B., 40
Palmer, Roy, 4135
Palmer, Stephen R., 3607
Palmer, Thomas W., 1291
Palmer, Vicki R., 862, 1406
Palmer, Will, 2235
Palmer, William V., 2235
Palmetto Box Co., 2796
Palmisano, Donald J., 1139
Palmisano, Robert J., 376
Palmisano, Samuel J., 143, 1315, 1960
Palmore, Roderick A., 1554, 1612
Palms, John M., 1309
Paloian, John R., 1323
Palos Bank & Trust Co., 1413
Palotay, Marc, 3893
Palumbo, Nancy, 1261
Pambianchi, Christine M., 945
Pamela Equities Inc., 2685
Pamida, Inc., 3440
Pamon, Steve, 2689
Pan, Yi, 794
Panamaroff, Jon, 2184
Panasonic Corp. of North America, 2869
Panasonic Electronic Devices Corp. of America, 2870
Panda Management Co., Inc., 2871
Panda Restaurant Group, Inc., 2871
Panda, Soumitra, 2778
Paneak, Raymond, 234
Panega, Andrew B., 2315
Panera Bread Co., 2873
Pang, David J., 3960
Pang, Kathy, 3189
Pang, Sarah, 855
Pangea Leather Services Ltd, 838
Pangia, Robert, 2417
Pangia, Robert W., 465
Panico, Greg, 2048
Panigel, Michael, 3448
Pankau, David S., 498
Panke, Helmut, 2501
Pannabecker, Daryl G., 588
Panos, Jim, 743
Panosian Enterprises, Inc., 2874
Panosian, Daniel P., 2874
Panosian, David M., 2874
Panosian, Lucille A., 2874
Panosian, Manual N., 2874
Panosian, Ronald N., 2874
Panousopoulos, Constantine, 3002
Panousopoulos, Nelida, 3002
Pansini, Andrew, 3664
Pantages, Lisa, 3324
Pantalone, Brenda M., 2801
Panteleakos, David T., 2042
Pantry, Inc., The, 2875
Panzer, Marcy C., 412
Paoli, Peter P., 3841
Paolillo, Regina, 3708
Papa John's, 138
Papa, John A., 2048
Papa, Joseph, 4007
Papa, Joseph C., 2943
Papa, Mark G., 1282
Papa, Rosemarie Novello, 3245
Papadopoulos, Stelios, 465
Papageorge, Lisa, 1169
Papakyriacou, Peter, 316
Papandrew, Christopher, 3990
Papastephanou, Costa, 2828
Papenbrock, William A., 3278
Paper City Savings Association, 2877
Paper Conversions Inc., 2905
Paper Supply Co., 2022
Paper Supply Co. of Bristol, Inc., 2022
Papernick, Alan, 3297
Papp, Harry A., 500
Pappas, Chrissi, 1989
Pappas, Christopher D., 1424
Pappas, Daniel, 2455
Pappas, Tony, 4155
Pappert, Gerald J., 752
Pappous, Perry, 2538
Papuga, Henry C., 2514
Paquin, Natalye, 2635
Paradie, Terrance M., 850
Paradis, Bruce, 3190
Paradis, Bruce J., 3190
Paradis, Joseph A., 555
Paradis, Joseph A., III, 555
Paradis, Steven J., 555
Paradise, Will, 4066
Paramount Painting & Services, Inc., 1314
Paramount Pictures, 661, 3262
Parasida, Tony, 516
Parasiliti, Trina, 2319
Pardo, Jaime Chico, 273
Pardoe, Mike, 628
Pardun, Thomas E., 4042
Paredes, Domingo, 1266
Parekh, Harish, 2867
Parekh, Megha, 2014
Parent, Louise M., 143
Parente, Brian J., 414
Parente, Charles E., 414
Parente, Charles E., Jr., 414
Parente, John, 414
Parente, Mary M., 414
Parfet, Donald R., 3246
Parfet, William U., 2559, 3627
Parham, Joseph G., Jr., 1541
Parham, Michael, 3144
Parham, Monica G., 986
Pariseau, Edward P., 577
Parish, Glenn, 1602
Parish, Randy, 2595
Parisi, James E., 853
Parisot, Thomas G., 3736
Park Bank, 2879
Park Clipper Leasing Associates, 1431
Park Corp., 2880
Park National Bank, The, 2881
Park National Corp., 2881
Park Place Corporation, 2882
Park Region Mutual Telephone Co., 2883
Park, Charles B., III, 164
Park, Chong Sup, 3377
Park, Christine M., 2688
Park, Chul, 2854
Park, Dan K., 2880
Park, Daniel K., 2880
Park, Hyun, 2952
Park, Jaehoon, 2301
Park, Jerry, 241
Park, John, 2664
Park, John S., 377
Park, Jon, 4047
Park, Kelly C., 2880
Park, Laure E., 3103
Park, Miyun, 4066
Park, Patrick M., 2880
Park, Piper A., 2880
Park, Raymond P., 2880
Park, S. Leigh, 3331
Park, Wesley T., 1405
Parke, James A., 1565
Parker & Parsley Petroleum Co., 2981
Parker Development Co., 2884
Parker Investments, T&D, LLC, 1523
Parker, Barbara, 640
Parker, Bill, 2884
Parker, Brian, 298
Parker, Carol, 298
Parker, Carolyn Reynolds, 350
Parker, Dale, 1797
Parker, Dale, Jr., 1797
Parker, David, 46
Parker, David R., 3821
Parker, Deborah, 3820
Parker, Deborah S., 2715
Parker, Don, 880, 3336
Parker, Gary D., 2815
Parker, Gerhard H., 220
Parker, Harold, Jr., 763
Parker, James E., 2884
Parker, James M., 1396
Parker, John, 696
Parker, John O., Jr., 1313
Parker, John R., Jr., 863
Parker, Judy Ann, 3868
Parker, Kathy, 1902
Parker, Kim Marie, 1515
Parker, Lauren, 2884
Parker, Mark, 2710
Parker, Mark G., 2710
Parker, Mike, 1357
Parker, Nancy J., 1347
Parker, Nancy Karlson, 898
Parker, Richard H., 3868
Parker, Richard H., III, 3868
Parker, Richard H., Jr., 3868
Parker, Richard K., 937
Parker, Roland J., 2793
Parker, Runette, 859
Parker, Scott T., 819
Parker, Stuart B., 3873

Parker, Susan D., 2884
Parker, Theresa, 2622
Parker, Timothy, 2884
Parker, W. Douglas, 3902
Parker, Will, 644
Parker, William R., 2884
Parker-Hannifin Corp., 2886
Parkhill, Karen L., 889
Parkinson, Molly, 440
Parkinson, Robert L., Jr., 377
Parkinson, Scott, 969
Parkinson, Ward, 504
Parks, David A., 1053
Parks, Jack W., III, 1308
Parks, Jack W., Jr., 1308
Parks, Jim, 3778
Parks, Ronnie, 3805
Parks, Shannon, 82
Parks, Susan, 121
Parks, Tom, 3940
Parman, Angela M., 3890
Parman, James E., 3890
Parmer, Barbara J., 3191
Parmer, George A., 3191
Parnagian, Dennis, 1478
Parnagian, Ken, 1478
Parnagian, Philip, 1478
Parnagian, Randy, 1478
Parnell, Antony S., 78
Parra, Rosendo G., 572, 2709, 2952
Parravano, Carlo, 2466
Parrett, William G., 477, 1214, 3733
Parrini, Dante, 1517
Parriott, Ann B., 1517
Parrish Medical Center, 3944
Parrish, Charles S., 3723
Parrish, Mark W., 2610
Parrish, Sharon, 939
Parrott, John, 3779
Parrott, John C., Jr., 286
Parrott, Michael V., 1631
Parrs, Marianne Miller, 819, 3579
Parry, David C., 1916
Parsley, E. William, III, 2996, 2997
Parsons Trust, P.D. and Tracy, 2150
Parsons, Eric E., 3574
Parsons, Jerry, 3244
Parsons, Joanie, 2888
Parsons, John, 3648
Parsons, Joseph B., 2186
Parsons, Joseph D., 80
Parsons, Linda K., 900
Parsons, M. Brent, 2184
Parsons, Martin, 1317
Parsons, Richard D., 2230, 2336
Parsons, Robert R., 1595
Parsons, Stephen, 2184
Parsons, Stephen C., 1621
Parsons, Steve, 3220
Parsons, Susan E., 2179
Partain, Nathan I., 2836
Partenza, Louis, 1442
Parthenon Sportswear Ltd., Inc., 2889
Parton, Dolly, 1146
Partridge, John M., 812
Partridge, John W., Jr., 883
Partridge, Lamar J., 507
Partridge, Nancy M., 2734
Partridge, Ron, 2872
Parven, Alvin S., 86
Parvin, Margaret Ann P., 2594
Parvizian, Alan, 511
Pascal, Amy, 3504
Pascarelli, Charles, 3133
Pascoe, Edward R., 1601
Pascoe, J., 3430
Pascoe, Michele B., 2387
Pascoe, Ron J., 1409
Pasewaldt, Dieter C., 2128
Pash, Jeff, 2626
Pasha, Asim, 3546
Pashek, Shane, 1334
Paskevic, Shawn, 2653
Pasko, Anne W., 428
Pasquale, Douglas M., 85, 1120, 3931
Pasquale, Roger, 3157
Passarella, Michael J., 3898
Passen, Andrew J., 1467
Passero, Matthew, 3223
Passov, Richard, 2950
Pastime Amusement Co., 2891
Pastor, Pattie E., 57
Pastorello, Thomas J., 2262
Pata, Jacqueline Johnson, Sr., 3380
Patchen, Jeffrey H., 3458
Pate, Eric, 1386
Pate, F. Wayne, 1601
Pate, James, II, 1347
Pate, R. Hewitt, 780
Pate, Ronald D., 129
Pate-Cornell, M. Elisabeth, 1171
Patel, Jaymin, 1677
Patel, Kiran M., 2165
Patel, Pranay, 4006
Patel, Sandip, 48
Patel, Sheila, 1191
Patenaude, Mary E., 3086
Patenaude, Wayne, 666
Paternostro, Rick A., 3366
Paterson, Basil A., 2630
Paterson, Jill, 1385
Paterson, Lee, 957
Paterson, Lee T., 4089
Pathipati, Patrick, 3704
Patillo, Katy, 2896
Patillo, Robert A., 1099, 2896
Patkotak, Crawford, 234
Patoff, Kathy, 3854
Patram, Bruce, 29
Patricelli, Robert, 2697
Patrick, Charles F., 938
Patrick, Cory, 3347
Patrick, Dick, 2280
Patrick, Edward N., Jr., 3308
Patrick, Michael E., 667
Patrick, Richard, 2280
Patrick, Stephen C., 249
Patrick, Thomas, 2931
Patrick, Thomas H., 1061
Patrick, W.B., Jr., 952
Patriot Transportation Holding, Inc., 1444
Patsley, Pamela H., 1169, 2558, 3728
Pattarozzi, Richard A., 3614, 3748
Patterson Companies Inc., 3257
Patterson Mills Sales, 2893
Patterson, Anthony, 3935
Patterson, Aubrey B., 1519
Patterson, Aubrey B., Jr., 336
Patterson, Barry S., 2432
Patterson, Christopher W., 2544
Patterson, Dana L., 3577
Patterson, Deborah J., 2559
Patterson, Deidre, 3935
Patterson, J. Michael, 4137
Patterson, James Scott, 2673
Patterson, Jeffrey S., 1590
Patterson, Jill, 1385
Patterson, John J., 333
Patterson, Mark, 1589
Patterson, Mary Ann Morthland, 337
Patterson, Neal L., 754
Patterson, Patrick, III, 576
Patterson, Richard J., 910
Patterson, Sam, 3935
Patterson, Samuel J., 3935
Patterson, Suzanne D., 863
Patterson, Walt, 3514
Pattillo Properties, Robert A., Inc., 2896
Pattillo Properties, Robert, Inc., 2896
Pattillo, Robert A., 2896
Pattillo-Markaz Industrial Partners, 2896
Pattison, Jeff, 745
Pattison, Steve, 613
Patton's Inc., 2899
Patton, Beth A, 1149
Patton, Dennis, 3600
Patton, Douglas, 1088
Patton, Eric, 1122
Patton, Fran, 4084
Patton, James R., Jr., 2898
Patton, John C., 2899
Patton, Kenn, 2298
Patton, Lauren, 1609
Patton, Mary, 2898
Patton, Robert J., 2258
Patton, Rodman D., 211, 2763
Patton, Tom, 886
Patton, Willie D., 891
Patzer, Faye A., 1008
Patzer, Robert A., 502
Paukert, Maureen, 368
Paul, Bob, 902
Paul, Douglas L., 980
Paul, Elbert, 1949
Paul, Joseph R., 1035
Paul, Karen, 1259
Paul, Kathryn, 878, 937
Paul, Kathryn A., 878, 937
Paul, Laurence E., 186
Paul, Marie, 576
Paul, R. Chadwick, Jr., 2635
Paul, Robert A., 186
Paul, Robert C., 902
Paul, Robert G., 3253
Paul, Stephen E., 186
Paul, Steven, 3453
Paul, Vivek, 1242
Paul, Weiss, Rifkind, Wharton & Garrison LLP, 1186
Paules, Gretchen, 536
Pauley, Lisa A., 328
Paulhardt, Erick A., 2591
Paulhus, Robert, 851
Paulhus, Robert J., Jr., 851
Paulsen, Larry N., 2981
Paulsen, Wayne, 2714
Paulson, Brian, 4033
Paulson, Thomas, 3406
Paulson, Thomas J., 3714
Paulus, Henry P., 2670
Pauly, Marilyn, 1335
Paup, Bryce E., 1651
Pause, Samantha L., 2394
Pausic, Michael A., 2409
Pavelich, Gerald W., 1008
Pavelich, Nick, 2211
Paver, Robert L., 2006
Pavlock, Darlene, 1845
Pavlova, Irina, 584
Pawlicki, Ray, 465
Pawtucket Red Sox Baseball Club, Inc., 2903
Paxton & Vierling Steel Co., 2840
Paxton, John, 2401
Payless ShoeSource, Inc., 871
Payne, David, 278, 279
Payne, Donald M., 1126
Payne, Doyce, 942
Payne, Doyce G., 942
Payne, John, 650
Payne, Kevin, 2331
Payne, Kevin J., 1018
Payne, Lisa A., 2393
Payne, Michelle L., 3359
Payne, Richard, 3835
Payne, Shirley M., 2737, 3075
Payne, Stephen, 1355
Payne, Thomas, 2308
Payne, Ulice, Jr., 2358, 2749, 4093
Payne, William, 2768
Payne, William Porter, 2281
Paynter, Randy, 686
Paytas, Patricia, 2985
Paz, George, 1313, 1852
Pazour, Donald, 3863
PBA Construction, Inc., 982
PCCS, Inc., 2919
PE Corp., 2268
Peabody, Robert R., Jr., 3664
Peace, N. Brian, 2312
Peace, Nancy E., 1946
Peach, E. Russell, Jr., 3317
Peachtree Planning Corp., 2908
Peacock, Benjamin R., 4147
Peacock, Jonathan M., 182
Peak, John, 2072
Pearce, David, 1314
Pearce, Frank, 3978
Pearce, Harry J., 2383, 2441
Pearce, Randy, 3172
Pearce, Randy L., 255
Pearl, Erwin, 243
Pearle Vision, Inc., 2319
Pearlman, Brian, 1545
Pearlman, Emanuel R., 1261
Pearlstein, Seth L., 3604
Pearse, Diane M., 2529
Pearson, Daniel, 3902
Pearson, Daniel R., 1736
Pearson, Dave, 1460
Pearson, Denise, 1973
Pearson, Donald W., 127
Pearson, James F., 1424
Pearson, Jonathan, 1863
Pearson, Kevin J., 2323
Pearson, L. John, 333
Pearson, Luann, 2236
Pearson, Mark, 307
Pearson, Ronald D., 1900
Pease, Anne, 103
Pease, David, 199
Peaslee, Nicole, 1869
Peasley, Larry, 2883
Peat, Michael A., 3103
PEC Board of Directors, 2914
Pech, Jim, 1427
Pechman, Charles, 2613
Pechock, Christopher R., 1589
Pechota, Gary L., 474
Pechter, Richard S., 1382
Peck, Amy, 3199
Peck, Art, 1533
Peck, Charles H., 583
Peck, Patty, 2884

Peck, Rodney R., 346
Peck, Tom, 42, 3624
Pecora, Kristin L., 195
Pecora, Vincent, 331
Pecoux, Olivier, 3270
Peddie, Tom, 2710
Peden, Keith J., 3135
Pedernales Electric Cooperative, Inc., 2914
Pedersen, Brandon, 74
Pedersen, Brandon S., 74, 1861
Pedersen, Jamie, 2435
Pedersen, John, 111
Pederson, Jeff, 946
Pederson, Jeffery, 946
Pederson, Margaret E., 3946
Pedley, Martin, 3644
Pedreiro, Sergio, 950
Peel, Tesha, 839
Peercy, Paul S., 407
Peerless Publications, Inc., 2915
Peerman, Allyson W., 40
Peet, Shelly, 2723
Peet, Shelly M., 2723
Peeters, Steve, 2629
Peeters, Steven, 2629
Peets, Terry, 4087
Peetz, Karen, 344
Peetz, Karen B., 344
Pegado, Carlos, 1890
Pegau, Sharon M., 3017
Pegg, Jennifer, 3347
Pegram, John C., Jr., 3515
Pegram, John E., Jr., 3515
Pei, Edward, 2086
Peinhardt, William F., 1001
Peiper, Richard, 2972
Peirce, Mary, 3374
Peiros, Larry S., 3267
Peiros, Lawrence S., 3017
Peixotto, Robert, 392
Pekarek, Nancy J., 1588
Pekor, Allan J., 2250
Pela, L., 2319
Pelaccia, Joseph, 2513
Pelagio, Luanne, 576
Pelham, Judith C., 182
Pelino, Brigid V., 3753
Pell, Richard, Jr., 1561
Pella Corp., 2917
Pella, Steve, 474
Pellegrino, Michael, 3646
Pellegrom, Jeff, 2531
Peller, Philip, 2593
Peller, Philip R., 2128
Pelletier, Gary, 2950, 2976
Pelletier, John E., 2301
Pelletier, Ronald J., 3253
Pelletier, Thomas N., 2742
Pelletier, Tom, 2742
Pellitteri Waste Systems, Inc., 2918
Pellitteri's Container Haul Away, 2918
Pellitteri, Danielle, 2918
Pellitteri, Michele J., 2918
Pellitteri, Thomas J., 2918
Pelo, Jack, 862
Peloquin, Gary W., 2042
Pelta, Edward J., 1591
Peltier, Robert, 1227
Peltier, Ronald J., 3389
Pelton, M. Lee, 3010
Peltz, Nelson, 2245, 4030, 4031
Peltz, Richard H., 2370
Pelz, S., 97
Pelzer, Robert E., 2752
Pemberton, Brad, 918
PEMCO Corp., 2919
PEMCO Mutual Insurance Co., 2919
PEMCO Technology Services, Inc., 2919
Pena, Evelyn, 439
Pena, Federico F., 3498, 4028
Pena, Melinda dela, 44
Penasco Valley Telephone Cooperative Inc., 2920
Pence, Robin, 1532
Pence, Sean, 3108
Pendarvis, David, 3192
Pendell, Timothy A., 1094
Pendergast, Mary, 382
Pendergrass, David S., 1938
Pendleton Construction Corp., 2921
Pendleton, Edmund, 2921
Pendleton, H. Alexander, 3642
Pendleton, Michael, 1113
Pendleton, Tamara B., 3642
Pendleton, Trish, 811
Pendleton, William N., 2921
Pendley, Lehman, 2846
Pendrey, J.C., Jr., 1829
Peng, Teh Kok, 637
Penikas, Jim, 3199
Peninger, Michael J., 266
Penn National Gaming, Inc., 2923
Penn Security Bank & Trust Co., 2924
Penn, Loretta A., 3701
Penner, Gregory Boyd, 3980
Penney Co., J.C., Inc., 2925
Penney Corp., J.C., Inc., 2925
Penningroth, Ailey, 278, 279
Pennington, Kelvin J., 50
Pennington, Kevin, 1427
Pennington, Thomas, 236, 347
Pennsylvania Dutch Co., Inc., 3991
Pennsylvania Electric Co., 1424
Penrose, Sheila A., 2061, 2427
Penske, Roger S., 1552
Pensky, Wayne, 1795
Pensky, Wayne C., 1795
Pentair, Inc., 2926
People Reaching Out, 3304
People's United Bank, 2928
Peoples Bank, 2929
Peoples Bank, The, 2930, 2946, 3482
Peoples Mutual Telephone Co., 2932
Peoples Natural Gas Co., 1150
Peoples, D. Louis, 2748
Pepe, Marjorie, 1815
Peper, Cheri L., 211
Pepin, Tod, 1723
Peppard, Denise, 2744
Peppel, Alan, 1103
Pepper, Anthony M., 3029
Pepper, J. Stanley, 2439
Pepper, Jane G., 2996, 2997
Pepper, John J., 1793
Peppers, C. Alan, 1008
Peppes, Greg, 1074
Pepsi Bottling Group, Inc., The, 1131, 2935
Pepsico, 1858, 3585, 4066
Pepsico Inc., 624
PepsiCo, Inc., 1002, 2935, 3659
Perala, Michael A., 100
Percival, John, 2486
Percy, Steven W., 2809
Perda, Michael J., III, 4025
Perdue, David A., 104, 1635
Perdue, David A., Jr., 4095
Perdue, James A., 2936
Perea, Gary, 2588
Pereira, Bill, 1910
Pereira, John M., 2928
Pereira, Jorge G., 2323
Perella, Tom, 287
Perelman, Ronald O., 3202
Perenchio, John G., 1059
Perez, Anthony, 812
Perez, Antonio M., 1214
Perez, Arnaldo, 696
Perez, Beatriz, 862
Perez, Edith R., 903
Perez, Edward, 3876
Perez, Gilberto, 734
Perez, Hugo, 1585
Perez, Jorge, 1147
Perez, Juan Jose, 886
Perez, Ken, 2447
Perez, Laree E., 1563, 2391
Perez, Lissa, 1070
Perez, Luis, 1094
Perez, Norma Joan, 2553
Perez, Robert J., 999
Perez, William D., 2048, 4056
Perez-Ayala, Patricia, 305
Perforce Software, Inc., 2937
Peribere, Jerome A., 3381, 4139
Perich, Thomas J., 198
Perini Corp., 3826
Perini, Bart W., 3826
Perini, Charles B., 3826
Perini, Heather, 3826
Perini, Timothy, 3826
Perino, Barbara J., 4001
PerkinElmer, Inc., 2939
Perkins, B.D., 2048
Perkins, Brian D., 2048
Perkins, David D., 2830
Perkins, Erickson N., 801
Perkins, Georganne F., 1737
Perkins, Janice L., 2120
Perkins, Jerry F., Jr., 3972
Perkins, Joseph H., 4121
Perkins, Leigh H., Jr., 2830
Perkins, Leigh H., Sr., 2830
Perkins, Mary B., 2830
Perkins, Melissa M., 2830
Perkins, Perk, 2830
Perkins, Phil, 2486
Perkins, Robert, 272
Perkins, Robert W., 272
Perkins, Romi M., 2830
Perkins, Thomas J., 1549
Perks, A. C., 1219
Perks, Douglas C., 1219
Perks, Lachlan L., 1219
Perl, Aaron S., 1609
Perl, Richard, 16
Perles, Rick, 1937
Perlin, Gary L., 679
Perlman, Dana, 3088
Perlman, Dana A., 1801
Perlman, Ira, 2869
Perlman, Lawrence, 693
Perlman, Theodore, 2427
Perlmutter, Andy, 448
Permanente, Kaiser, 3673
Perna, Robert J., 716
Perna, Stephen, 53
Pernod Ricard USA, 1858
Pero, David, 1680
Perocchi, Nanci, 2913
Perocchi, William, 2913
Perot, Ross, Jr., 1068
Perrault, Paul, 349
Perrault, Paul A., 583, 3528
Perreault, Paul R., 993
Perreault, Roger, 3736
Perretta, Christopher (Chris), 3592
Perricone, Jaye, 2948
Perrigo Co., L., 2943
Perrin, Charles R., 669
Perrin, Michelle, 2409
Perrini, Sara Wolfe, 1129
Perrotti, John J., 1591, 1729
Perrotti, John T., 1591
Perry State Bank, 3116
Perry, A. Michael, 231
Perry, Amy, 2763
Perry, Andrew, 947
Perry, Barry W., 78, 249, 258
Perry, Brian M., 1591
Perry, Cecilia A., 3649
Perry, Charles A., 4005
Perry, Chris, 2914
Perry, Christopher J., 1555
Perry, Diane, 3122
Perry, Edward N., 407
Perry, Egbert L. J., 1349
Perry, Elliot, 1857
Perry, Emily S., 2924
Perry, Erinn, 2465
Perry, Harvey P., 751
Perry, J. Douglas, 1145
Perry, James H., 1548
Perry, John E., 3388
Perry, M. Marnette, 2195
Perry, Marilyn J., 4005
Perry, Mark, 2716
Perry, Mark L., 2767
Perry, Marnette, 2195
Perry, Michael W., 1756
Perry, Mike, 973
Perry, Richard, 3887
Perry, Sam, 891
Perry, Wayne, 367
Perry, William, 310
Persall, Cindy, 2771
Perschevitch, Elizabeth, 1042
Persis Corp., 2944
Persky, Marla, 515
Person, Bruce H., 428
Peru, Ramiro G., 3819, 4027
Perushek, Mary Lynne, 1153
Perzik, James L., 2307
Pesce, William J., 2667, 4072
Pescosolido, Vincent, 3296
Pescovitz, Ora H., 2268
Peskin, Mark, 3601
Pesko, Jon, 1466
Pessina, Stefano, 3981
Pestrikoff, Michael, 2184
Pestrikoff, Mike, 2184
Peszynski, Andrew F., 1042
Peszynski, I.G., 1042
Peterman, Donna C., 2997
Peters, Aulana L., 3, 1061, 2744
Peters, Carl, 2279
Peters, Charles A., 1257
Peters, Chuck, 3506
Peters, Elizabeth, 3639
Peters, Jason, 606
Peters, John N., 4030
Peters, Jon, 3116
Peters, Lauren B., 1459
Peters, Lisa B., 344
Peters, Mark A., 3200

Peters, Mary Lou, 2570
Peters, Michael P., 3388
Peters, Sara, 53
Peters, William E., 2006
Petersen, Cindy, 1567
Petersen, Ken, 1907
Petersen, Mary, 715
Petersen, Robert E., 873
Petersen, Roger, 2925
Petersen, Sue, 3324
Petersmeyer, Gary, 2369
Peterson Industries, Inc., 2946
Peterson, Angie, 3860
Peterson, Bart, 2274
Peterson, Brad, 2617
Peterson, Bruce, 3274
Peterson, Bruce D., 1183
Peterson, Christopher H., 3123
Peterson, Coleman, 608
Peterson, Coleman H., 966, 1892
Peterson, Conrad, 2184
Peterson, Cordell, 2282
Peterson, Cordell Q., 2282
Peterson, Curtis, 2946
Peterson, Dale G., 1843
Peterson, Daniel A., 6
Peterson, Dave, 208
Peterson, David A., 1678
Peterson, David O., 1678
Peterson, Donna, 6
Peterson, Doug, 1339
Peterson, Duana J., 2946
Peterson, DuWayne J., 898
Peterson, E. Joel, 1209
Peterson, Gail L., 3399
Peterson, Gregory, 1961
Peterson, Gregory J., 3524
Peterson, Gretchen A., 196
Peterson, James B., 2674
Peterson, James N., 328
Peterson, Jay, 885
Peterson, Jeffery, 2797
Peterson, Jennifer M., 458
Peterson, Jim, 3465
Peterson, Joel C., 2041
Peterson, Judy, 3673
Peterson, Karin, 2917
Peterson, Margaret C., 1678
Peterson, Marie-Pascale, 1496
Peterson, Marissa T., 1886
Peterson, Mark, 3679
Peterson, Mark A., 1678
Peterson, Mark L., 3302
Peterson, Mark W., 3198
Peterson, Mary L., 1678
Peterson, Michael, 2945
Peterson, Michele D., 955
Peterson, Per A., 2268
Peterson, Pete, 3092
Peterson, Renee J., 3775
Peterson, Richard C., 3003
Peterson, Robert, 896, 3726
Peterson, Robert J., 2880
Peterson, Robert R., Jr., 3433
Peterson, Robert T., 3833
Peterson, Roger, 2581, 2925
Peterson, Sandra E., 1190
Peterson, Scott, 3365
Peterson, Sharon, 1678
Peterson, Shirley D., 67, 1612, 4106
Peterson, Stephen M., 2503
Peterson, Terry D., 1084
Peterson, Timothy, 4026
Peterson, Vaughn D., 2946
Peterson, Vic A., 3608
Peterson-Nyren, Jayleen, 2200
Peterson-Nyren, Jaylene, 2200
Petillo, John, 4028
Petit, Anthony B., 2304
Petit, Geoffrey, 3778
Petit, Geoffroy, 3778
Petitt, Douglas, 3925
Petkau, Gerald, 497
Petne Parkman & Co., Inc., 2641
Petrakian, Raja, 4137
Petrarca, Mark A., 3484
Petratis, David D., 3100
Petrazzuoli, Anthony, 2928
Petrei, Guillermo, 783
Petrelia, Michael J., 2604
Petrella, Vincent K., 219, 2279
Petrelli, Charlene G., 1287
Petren, Carol Ann, 812
Petri, Mark G., 3221
Petrie, Thomas A., 1774
Petrillo, Thomas P., 3268
Petrillo, Tom, 295
Petroglyph Operating Co., 1957
Petroleum Products Corp., 2947
Petroskey, Dale, 3729
Petrovek, Brian S., 3011
Petrovich, Mary L., 2544
Petrovich, Stephen C., 61
Petrovich, Steve C., 61
Petrowski, Joseph, 1003
Petrucci, Laurie J., 1459
Petrucelli, Michael, 2185
Petsch, Gregory E., 1944
PetSmart, Inc., 2948
Petter, Mark, 703
Petterson, David S., 948
Petterson, John S., 3750
Pettigrew, Linda Y., 251
Pettingill, Richard R., 3713
Petty, L. Davis, Jr., 2084
Petway, Elizabeth P., 2014
Petz, Cordell, 229
Petzel, Jim, 2848
Petzold, Arthur, 2636
Pevehouse, Cynthia, 3581
Peverett, Jane L., 2747
Peverly, Francis W., 2822
Pew, Robert C., III, 3597
Pfaltzgraff Co., The, 3661
Pfau, Bruce N., 2190
Pfau, Kevin, 1246
Pfau, Michael, 2025
Pfau, Michael E., 1785
Pfeffer, David M., 24
Pfeffer, David Matthew, 2818
Pfeffer, James, 2840
Pfeffer, Michael, 2944
Pfeifer, Jim, 279
Pfeiffer, Beth, 3411
Pfeiffer, Darlene, 2139
Pfeiffer, Gary M., 3103, 3682
Pfeiffer, Greg, 1438
Pfeiffer, Nicholas D., 2508
Pfeiffer, Peter H., 221
Pfeiffer, Philip J., 3915
Pfirman, Drew J., 2323
Pfister & Vogel Tanning Co., Inc., 2949
Pfizer, 1201, 3329
Pfizer Equine Division, 3257
Pfizer Inc., 2950
Pflederer, Kent A., 2861
Pflughaupt, Randall J., 3789
Pforzheimer, Carl H., III, 186, 945
Pfotenhauer, James, 1908
Pfotenhauer, Jeanette, 3884
PFS Bancorp, Inc., 2951
PG&E Corp., 2853, 2952
PG&E Corporation, 2952
PG&E Gas Transmission, Texas Corp., 2952
PGA Tour Charities, Inc., 4087
Pharaoh, Andrew, 4125
Phares, Steve, 1466
Pharmaceutical Innovations, Inc., 2955
Pharmacy Network National Corp., 2956
Pharmacy Network National Corporation Trust, 2956
Pharo, Robert, 425
Phelan, David C., 3592
Phelan, Joseph, 1419
Phelan, William K., 2172, 3384
Phelps Dodge Corp., 1494
Phelps, Bob, 1674
Phelps, David E., 428
Phelps, Ken, 2972
Phelps, Mark, 3604
Phelps, Mark I., 3604
Phelps, Michael E. J., 2364
Phelps, Michael E.J., 3540
Phelps, Susan Bender, 1050
Phelps, Tom, 1211
Phieffer, James W., 1849
Philadelphia Eagles, 888
Philadelphia Gear Corp., 157
Philadelphia Insurance Company, 763
Philadelphia Phillies, 888
Philadelphia Stock Exchange, 2618
Philbin, Gary M., 1145
Philbrook, Dana S., 666
Philemonoff, Ron P., 3687
Philip, Edward M., 1747
Philip, Frances P., 551
Philip, George M., 1419, 3902
Philipp, Norbert, 2338
Philippi, Dan, 981
Philipps, Mike, 3374
Philippsen, John, 1463
Philips Electronics North America Corp., 2963
Philips, Lisa, 1236
Philips, Wally, 165
Phillips International, Inc., 1201
Phillips Petroleum Co., 913
Phillips Plastics Corp., 2966
Phillips Publishing International, Inc., 1201
Phillips Revocable Trust, Tom, 1201
Phillips, Arden T., 3997
Phillips, Betty, 712
Phillips, Charles E., Jr., 3945
Phillips, Craig, 1258
Phillips, David P., 3079
Phillips, Dean, 1258
Phillips, Don, 2588
Phillips, Donald, 4150
Phillips, Ellyn, 3036
Phillips, Graham H., 595
Phillips, Gregory D., 1154
Phillips, Jack, 3236
Phillips, James M., 507
Phillips, Jeanne, 1889
Phillips, Jeanne M., 1561
Phillips, John, 1429
Phillips, John R., 2790
Phillips, Jon, 2968
Phillips, Marilyn, 1122
Phillips, Michael W., 3869
Phillips, Mike, 1714
Phillips, Nick, 2745
Phillips, Sandra C., 2924
Phillips, Scott, 86
Phillips, Stephen R., 304
Phillips, Susan M., 2195, 3591
Phillips, Ted, 781
Phillips, Thomas L., 1201
Phillips, W., 2788
Phillips-Van Heusen Corp., 3088
Phinney, Jason T., 2570
Phipps, Chad F., 4157
Phipps, Gerald, 1081
Phipps, Gerald S., 1081
Phlegar, Janet, 2659
Phoenix Pharmaceuticals, Inc., 2967
Phoenix Racing, 1776
Phoenix Suns L.P., 2968
Photronics, Inc., 2969
Phyllis Lindsey, 1310
Physicians Mutual Insurance Co., 2970
Piancone, Louis G., 3255
Piancone, Louis M., 3255
Piancone, Stephen J., 3255
Piano, Steven, 2558
Piarowski, Pamela, 1739
Piasecki, Nicole W., 4052
Piatt, Rodney L., 2610
Piazzola, Sam, 446
Piburn, Patricia L., 1057
Picard, Robert A., 2819
Piccinini, Bob, 728
Piccinini, Robert M., 3342
Picciotto, John A., 687
Piccolomini, Jeffrey, 1778
Pichette, Patrick, 1613
Pichler, Joseph A., 2333
Pichler, Karl, 3117
Pick Quickfoods, Inc., 2135
Pickard, Mary, 225, 2820
Pickard, Vivian R., 1555
Pickering, Don, 166
Pickering, R.H., 166
Pickett, Cecil B., 4157
Pickett, Martin, 1669
Picknelly, Paul C., 792
Pidduck, Richard W., 3649
Pidgeon, Kathryn A., 2968
Pidgeon, Libby, 461
Pidgeon, Tina, 1550
Piechoski, Michael J., 2142
Piedmont Natural Gas Co., Inc., 2971
Piehler, Lisa, 380
Piell, Hilda Harris, 853
Pienitz, Eleenore, 4122
Pieper Electric, Inc., 2972
Pieper, Richard, Sr., 2972
Pieprz, Dennis, 3337
Pierazek, Suzanne, 739
Pierce, Beatrice, 993
Pierce, Edmund, 3207
Pierce, Everett F., 2436
Pierce, Gerard, 4021
Pierce, John, 3034
Pierce, Larry S., 2153
Pierce, Nancy L., 1621
Pierce, Pamela S., 323
Pierce, Phillip T., 1839
Pierce, Richard, 2660
Pierce, Roger C., Jr., 1839
Pierce, Vicki L., 2536
Pierce, Vickie, 2536
Piercey, Margery L., 4102
Piercey, Sherry, 2886

Piercy, Charlie, 3376
Piergallini, Alfred A., 889
Pierret, J. Kent, 3614
Pierson, Andrew, 2502
Pierson, R. Earl, 3098
Pierson, Steven T., 1938
Pierz, Ann K., 2814
Pietrafitta, Clifford E., 996
Pietroburgo, Linda, 2557
Pietrzak, John L., 853
Pietsch, Michael, 1696
Pifer, Jay S., 1272
Piggott, Julie A., 618
Pignataro, Ben, 675
Pignatelli, James S., 500
Pigott, Carol Berry, 490
Pigott, John M., 2850
Pigott, Mark C., 1487, 2850
Pihl, Marjorie J., 1832
Pike Realty LP, 1666
Pike, Robert W., 1139
Pikoganna, Vince, 3467
Piland, Robert, 2223
Pile, Maro Jo, 46
Pilkington, John, 3133
Pillai, Marie, 1554
Piller, Lynn J., 2770
Pilley, Wesley, 747
Pilnick, Gary H., 2120
Pilon, Lawrence J., 1626
Pilon, Mary Claudia Belk, 403
Pilotte, John, 13
Pimenta, Valerie, 2902
Pimentel, Albert A., 4137
Pinado, Jeanne, 1454
Pinard, Letty, 3449
Pinchev, Alex, 508
Pincus, Ronald, 2675
Pine Island Cranberry Co., Inc., 1701
Pine State Tobacco & Candy Co., Inc., 2976
Pine State Trading, 2976
Pineau, Jim, 3268
Pineci, Roy, 2780
Pineda, Patricia Salas, 3784
Pineda, Patricia Sales, 3624
Pinehurst Development, Inc., 553
Pineiro, Rosa Garcia, 82
Piness, Thomas, 529
Pinheiro, John, 1380
Pinion, Robert, 1705
Pinkard, Robert M., 715
Pinkard, Walter D., Jr., 333, 715
Pinkesz, Anthony, 3041
Pinkesz, Sara, 3041
Pinkett, Kathleen, 3389
Pinkston, Arnold A., 99
Pinnacle Communities, Ltd., 2977
Pinnacle Country Club, 2669
Pinnacle Entertainment, Inc., 2978
Pinnacle Realty, 2977
Pinnau, Thomas, 608
Pino, Dom, 2044
Pino, Eulogio Del, 820
Pinsker, Neal D., 3166
Pinsky, Jay, 790
Pinto, John J., 2682, 2683
Pinto, Michael P., 2323
Pinza, Gloria, 2974
Pioneer Federal Savings and Loan, 2979
Pioneer Hi-Bred International, Inc., 2980
Pioneer Natural Resources Co., 2981
Pioneer Natural Resources USA, Inc., 2981
Pioneer Trust Bank, N.A., 2982
Piotrowski, Stanley, 4006
Piper Jaffray Cos. Inc., 2983
Piper, Addison L., 2983
Piper, Gary, 2925
Pipkin, Phyllis, 776
Pippin, M. Lenny, 1524
Pippins, Dakota A., 1866
Pipski, John R., Jr., 91
Piqunik Management Corp., 234
Piraino, Thomas A., 2886
Pircio, Christopher, 1594
Piretti-Miller, Mary Jo, 428
Pirih, Michael P., 3996
Piro, James J., 3010
Piro, Jim, 3010
Pirron, Michael I., 1921
Pirtle, Terri A., 2815
Pirtle, William L., 3434
Pisano, Thomas R., 2759
Piscitelli, Francis M., 2834
Piscitello, Charlie, 2945
Pishka, Shawn J., 1118
Pistell, Timothy K., 1366
Pitassi, Doug, 2856
Pitcher, Michael L., 1276
Piterans, Marianne, 3732
Pitman, Charles J., 211
Pitman, James R., 2968
Pitman, Jim, 2968, 3902
Pitney Bowes Inc., 2984
Pitt, Gregory, 3201
Pittard, Patrick S., 2281
Pittman, Buddy, 1021
Pittman, Charles, 3507
Pittman, Jane D., 1681
Pittman, Jim A., 2156
Pittman, Robert W., 842
Pittman, Shelley, 495
Pittman, Sherri Q., 2349
Pittman, Tom, 1280
Pitts, Gregory C., 3045
Pitts, Laurette J., 1261
Pitts, Ralph A., 403
Pitts, Rodney D., 1981
Pittsburgh Forgings Foundation, 186
Pittston Co., The, 571
Pivirotto, Gregory A., 3819
Pizel, Kenneth L., 4033
Pizer, Howard, 790
Pizzi, Charles P., 1926, 3693
Pizzi, Charles R., 3693
Pizzi, Mark A., 2639
Pizzoli, Louis G., 1879
Place, Arthur, 341
Plake, Jim, 2985
Plakias, Dean P., 1060
Plank, Roger B., 211
Plant, John C., 2393
Plant, Mike, 280
Planters LifeSavers Co., 2556, 3200
Plaskey, Wade C., 1350
Plastatech Engineering, 1196
Platinum Performance, 3257
Platt - Manatt, Bob, 2206
Platt, Daniel J., 3650
Platt, Donna J., 805
Platt, Jeffrey M., 3748
Platt, Lorrie, 814
Platt, Melanie M., 57
Platt, Warren E., 3490
Platt-Rust, Patricia, 4055
Platts, Brad, 2117
Plautz, Jeannie, 746
Plautz, Leslie Jean, 746
Plavko, Ed, 4138
Plavko, Edward R., 4138
Plaxico, James S., 1417
Player, Thomas A., 177
Playtex Products, Inc., 3646
Plaza Bancorp, 2731
Plaza Cleaning Service Co. II LP, 1431
Plaza Nursing & Convalescent Center, Inc., 1250
Pleas, Charlie, III, 294
Pledge, Robert, 2711
Plepler, Andrew D., 340
Pleuhs, Gerhard, 2556
Plewacki, James, 420
Plewacki, James G., 420
Plews, Andy, 1739
Plimpton, Hollis W., Jr., 583
Pliska, Bernie, 2710
Ploetz, Joe, 231
Plotkin, Richard A., 183
Plotkin, Roger B., 397
Plott, Cody, 2913
Plouffe, Leo, 382
Plowman, Keith E., 521
Plukas, John M., 1209
Plum Creek Timber Co., Inc., 2991
Plum Creek Timber Co., L.P., 2991
Plummer, James D., 646, 1950
Plummer, Michelle M., 341
Plummer, Terry M., 2551
Plummer, William B., 4072
Plung, Louis, 1571
Plush, Gerald P., 4016
Plush, Mark J., 2115
Plutzik, Jonathan, 1349
Plybon, Bill, 863
Plybon, William T., III, 863
Plymouth Foam, Inc., 2993
Plymouth Rock Transportation Corp., 3812
PMC Global Inc., 2994
PMI Mortgage Insurance Co., 2995
PNC Bank, N.A., 1341, 1860, 1994, 2739, 2996, 2997, 3600
PNC Equity Partners, LP, 2997
PNC Financial Services Group, Inc., The, 2997
PNM Resources, Inc., 3076
Pober, Janice, 3502
Pocock, David, 3688
Podorowsky, Gary, 3502
Podzemny, Eugene, 3525
Poe, Ronald F., 1348
Poelker, John S., 1393
Poferl, Judy M., 4135
Poff, Howard, 978
Pogge, David L., 2590
Pohjola, Margaret P., 657
Pohlad, Bill, 3827
Pohlad, Bob, 3827
Pohlad, Jim, 3827
Pohlman, Tim, 1359
Pohlner, Roger E., 3203
Pohmer, Thomas, 3205
Poindexter, Cameron, 797
Poinsatte, Richard A., 3595
Poirier, Richard V., 806
Poirot, James W., 758
Poirot, Olivier, 3497
Pokriefka, Louis, 2785
Polacek, Steven, 2820
Poladian, Avedick B., 2780
Polan, Mary Lake, 3107
Polaris Industries Inc., 2999
Polen, Edward, 1254
Polen, Randall, 1254
Polen, Tamra, 1254
Polencheck, Audrey L., 1394
Polet, Robert B., 2962
Polhamus, Beatriz, 3003
Policano, Andrew J., 313, 3247
Policinski, Christopher J., 1866, 2217, 4135
Policy, Ed, 1651
Poliner, Gary A., 2749
Poling, Gregory E., 1623
Poling, J.M., III, 3525
Polish, Jack, 959
Polizzotto, Len, 1171
Polk, Barbara, 1252
Polk, Curtis J., 512
Polk, Michael B., 2694
Polk, Stephen R., 3000
Polke, Thomas P., 1364
Pollack, Kenneth, 1433
Pollack, Robert, 2419
Pollard, John O., 1940
Pollard, Robert D., 264
Pollard, Robert W., Jr., 3513
Polle, Gregg, 1261
Pollei, Scott J., 1140
Pollet, Richard, 3739
Pollichino, Robert, 2336
Pollichino, Robert M., 2336
Pollin, Abe, 4000
Pollini, Claire W., 4070
Pollitt, Byron H., 3960
Pollner, Michael, 2176
Pollner, Michael A., 2176
Pollnow, Keith C., 3388
Pollock, Alex J., 853, 1645
Pollock, Curtis A., 1665
Pollock, Robert B., 266
Pollom, Debbie, 3569
Polman, Paul, 1160, 1161
Polnaszek, Thomas J., 2833
Polo Ralph Lauren Corp., 3123, 3315
Polodna, Duane, 2806
Polsky, Lisa, 2983
Polyak, Philip G., 854
Pomer, Frank A., 515
Pomeroy, Scott A., 434
Pompa, Mark A., 1255
Pomranke, Darryl D., 756
Pomranke, Daryl D., 756
Pomykal, Ann, 3728
Pond, Dale C., 372, 1330
Pond, Peter B., 2410
Pond, Randy, 818
Pong, Mickey, 1902
Ponitz, Cathy, 690
Pontarelli, Kenneth, 1273
Pontarelli, Thomas, 855
Ponto, Michael A., 1324
Ponturo, Tony, 2209
Pony Sales, Inc., 3002
Pool, Joe D., 2899
Poole, Carl S., Jr., 1391
Poole, Clint, 574
Poole, Robert, 947
Pooler, John E., Jr., 2934
Pooler, M.J., 2361
Pooley, Deborah, 2789
Poon, Christine A., 3072
Poon, Linda, 2429
Popa, Nancy A., 921
Pope Foundation, John William, 1201

Pope, Alan J., 3910
Pope, C. Larry, 3487
Pope, Charles C., 2314
Pope, Emmett Judson, III, 2594
Pope, Jennifer, 2306
Pope, John C., 903, 1144, 1155, 2647
Pope, Lawrence J., 1706
Pope, Maria M., 3010, 3034
Pope, Nancy F., 2742
Pope, Terri, 3902
Poplar Foundation, The, 1857
Popoff, Frank P., 143
Popovich, Gregg, 3321
Popowich, James L., 2580
Popp, Tim, 2966
Poppe, Mike, 908
Poppell, James W., 1443
Poppell, Randall C., 3852
Poppen, Steve, 2530
Poppleton, Jay K., 2478
Porat, Ruth, 2570
Porcellato, Larry B., 1817, 2809
Poretz, Jeffery S., 2512
Porfido, Meg, 2086
Porges, David L., 1287
Pori, Jeffrey A., 3800
Porrino, Peter R., 4134
Portcullis Partners, L.P., 3004
Porte, Hubert, 423
Porteous, David L., 1894
Porter & Porter, 3005
Porter Corp., 3007
Porter, A. Alexander, Jr., 3478
Porter, Biggs C., 1448
Porter, Charles, 1571
Porter, Charles W., Jr., 1270
Porter, Grant, 3006
Porter, Inc., 3006
Porter, J. William, 3007
Porter, Jack, 2114
Porter, James, 693
Porter, James S., 215
Porter, James T., 496
Porter, Judith F., 3005
Porter, Kieren, 665
Porter, Marc, 2233
Porter, Michael C., 1183
Porter, Michael E., 2878, 3372
Porter, Neil A., 3005
Porter, Patricia Taylor, 3007
Porter, Paul B., 3007
Porter, Robert H., 833
Porter, Roger B., 2605, 2633, 2861, 3715, 4158
Porter, Ronald J., 3005
Porter, Scott, 3006, 3007
Porter, Susan J., 3374
Porter, Tom, 469
Porter, W. Arthur, 3606
Portera, Malcolm, 3066
Porterfield, Antonia, 2629
Porterfield, Toni, 2629
Porteus, Brent R., 2639
Portland General Electric Co., 3010
Portney, Paul R., 2049
Portnoy, James, 2556
Portnoy, Scott, 691
Portrait Brokers of America, Inc., 3012
Portugal, Susan, 340
Posada, Julian, 783
Posen Foundation, 2321
Poses, Frederic M., 777, 3135, 3794
Posey, David M., 1369
Posillico Civil, inc, 3014
Posillico Materials, LLC, 3014
Posillico, Joseph D., III, 3014
Posillico, Joseph K., 3014
Posillico, Mario, 3014
Posillico, Mario A., 3014
Posillico, Michael J., 3014
Posillico, Paul F., 3014
Posner, Brian S., 465
Post, Amber, 3459
Post, Glen F., III, 751
Post, Jeff, 1008
Post, Jeff H., 1008
Post, Richard A., 227
Post, Steven E., 258
Post, Tom, 3497
Post, William, 3902
Post, William J., 500
Post-Bulletin, Co., 3015
Post-Newsweek Media, Inc., 3016
Poste, George H., 2559
Postl, James J., 935, 3083
Postolos, George, 1871
Poston, Daniel T., 1377
Postorino, Michael, 1421
Posze, James L., Jr., 3134
Pot, Wiet H.M., 1920
Poteat, Amy Bodford, 1283
Poteshman, Michael, 3821
Pothoven, John P., 2508
Potlach Foundation II, 3017
Potlatch Corp., 3017
Potomic Edison, 1424
Potter, John, 1729
Potter, Lara, 3998
Potter, Mary, 960
Potter, Richard, 1683
Potter, Robert, 1180
Pottinger, Paula H., 2260
Pottorff, Gary W., 2715
Pottruck, David S., 1950
Potts, Grover, 4054
Potts, Randy, 4088
Potts, Randy J., 4088
Potts, W.A., 3515
Pottstown Mercury, 2915
Poturkovic, Christy, 896
Poucher, Nick, 3821
Poulos, Lise, 2560
Poulsen, Dennis C., 3262
Pound, Alan, 1286
Poundstone, Paula, 3463
Pounion, Steve, 2193
Poussot, Bernard, 691
Povich, Lisa, 4126
Povich, Lon F., 473
Powell Company, 511
Powell, Ben, 58
Powell, Charles D., 722
Powell, Cynthia A., 3590
Powell, Danni, 131
Powell, David D., 455
Powell, Dennis D., 220, 1982
Powell, Dick, 263
Powell, Dina H., 1603, 1604
Powell, Donald E., 340, 3614
Powell, Francis R., 2645
Powell, Gregg, 396
Powell, J. David, 2446
Powell, Justin, 626
Powell, Kendall J., 1554, 2453
Powell, Laura, 3199
Powell, Lord, 3731
Powell, Mary G., 499
Powell, Nigel, 2710
Powell, Paul, 1957
Powell, Paul R., 1956
Powell, Rodney O., 2737
Powell, Sarah, 39
Powell, Steve, 43
Powell, Susan, 1386
Powell, Thomas E., 3707
Powell, Todd, 2991
Powell, Weldon, 1070
Powell, William H., 1449, 1632
Power Equipment Distributors, Inc., 3020
Power Fuel & Transport, LLC, 3021
Power Service Products, Inc., 3022
Power Townsend Co., 3023
Power, Alan J., 1540
Power, Gerald J., 380
Power, James M., 1008
Powers Steel & Wire Products, Inc., 3024
Powers, Alice, 3024
Powers, Anne E., 491
Powers, George, 3560
Powers, John A., 3024
Powers, Kathleen T., 2544
Powers, Lynn, 1527
Powers, Marc, 1842
Powers, Mark, 2041
Powers, Mary Ellen, 2058
Powers, Maureen, 999
Powers, Michelle, 973
Powers, Peter J., 2605
Powers, Robert D., 71
Powers, Robert M., 141
Powers, Robert P., 141, 380
Powers, Thomas R., 1450
Powers, Tim, 1759
Powers, Timothy H., 1879, 2445
Powers, William, 1056
Powers, William T., III, 3254
Powlick, George, 2082
Powlus, Lee, 2928
Poyter, Rick, 3312
Pozen, Robert C., 2453
PPC Partners, Inc, 2972
PPG Industries, Inc., 3025
Prabhu, Vansant M., 3589
Prabhu, Vasant M., 2405, 3589
Prado, Danielle, 2306
Prado, Jose Luis, 2740
Prairie, Patti, 411
Pramaggiore, Anne R., 895, 2586
Prancia, Pete, 1857
Prange, Larry, 4056
Prappas Company, The, 3411
Prasch, Mike, 2851
Prather, Larry S., Sr., 3513
Prather, N. King, 497
Prather, Robert S., Jr., 3294
Pratt & Whitney Canada, 1953
Pratt, Gregory A., 700
Pratt, James G., 1808
Pratt, Pamela, 521
Pratt, Samuel W., 2717
Pratt, Timothy, 540
Pratt, Timothy A., 540
Praven, Scott, 103
Praxair, Inc., 3029
Pray, Joseph L., 3818
Prazeres, Joseph, 1191
Prebish, Ronald F., 3956
Precision Components, Inc., 1344
Prediger, Don, 1248
Predovich, Daniel, 3140
Preece, Craig S., 3875
Preete, Kerry J., 2559
Preferred Mutual Insurance Co., 3031
Preimesberger, David G., 1139
Premier Bank, N.A., 2072
Premier Dental Products Co., 3036
Premier Island Group, LLC, 152
Premier Medical Co., 3036
Premium Settlements of MD, LLC, 142
Premix, Inc., 3037
Prendegast, Sean, 2347
Prendergast, Franklyn G., 2274
Preneta, Megan C., 1879
Prenovost, Gary, 678
Prentice, E. Miles, 2633
Prentice, Sheldon, 2465
Prescot, Blane R., 593
Prescott, Bill, 2014
Prescott, Gordon, 428
Prescott, Michael K., 1677
Prescott, Stephen M., 145
Prescott, Thomas J., 3674
Preslar, Clyde, 2875
Presley Enterprises, Elvis, Inc., 3038
Presley, Lisa Marie, 3038
Pressel, Jerry R., 1617
Pressley, Kirk, 901
Pressley-Brown, Scarlet, 1073
Prest, George, 2401
Prest, George W., 2401
Prestage, John, 3839
Presti, Geralyn M., 1467
Presti, Richard M., 2506
Presti, Sheila, 3894
Presti, William, 1482
Preston, Anne F., 1539
Preston, David L., 3469
Preston, Ethel, 2267
Preston, Forrest L., 2267
Preston, John R., 3521
Preston, Margaret Mary V., 2423
Preston, Michael L., 4072
Preston, Stanley J., 3491
Pretasky, Michael J., Sr., 3388
Pretto, Christina, 156
Pretto, Christina L., 156
Preusker, Karen, 3818
Prevost, Keith, 2761
Prevost, Patrick, 642
Prevost, Patrick M., 642
Prevoznik, Michael E., 3103
Preymark, Jennifer, 2524
Prezbindowski, Gary, 62
Prezzano, Wilbur J., 3492
Pribyl, Marjorie, 3725
Pricara, 2048
Price Associates, T. Rowe, Inc., 3040
Price Group, T. Rowe, Inc., 3040
Price Watson, 1553
Price, Calvin K., 2262
Price, Charles H., 3604
Price, David B., Jr., 758, 3715
Price, Glenda D., 902
Price, Gretchen W., 390
Price, Helen Smith, 862
Price, Hugh B., 2481, 3936
Price, Kimberly F., 3
Price, Lisa K., 2447
Price, Matt L., 2444
Price, McKinley, 3805
Price, Mike, 3784
Price, Paula, 3618
Price, Phil, 3978
Price, Rebecca H., 3834

Rataj, Sue, 642
Ratcliff, Steve, 2234
Ratcliffe, David M., 997
Ratcliffe, G. Jackson, Jr., 1879
Ratcliffe, Peter G., 2443
Rath Trust, F.E., 3530
Rath, David F., 3530
Rath, Frank E., Jr., 3530
Rath, Kimberly, 2660
Rath, Tim, 352
Rathbone, John P., 2725
Rathburn, Lynn, 972
Rathert, Terry W., 2695
Rathje, Kendall, 3116
Rathke, Frances G., 1653
Ratio Architects, Inc., 3129
Ratnathicam, Chutta, 1487
Ratner Salzberg, Deborah, 1467
Ratner, Brian J., 1467
Ratner, Bruce, 584
Ratner, Bruce C., 1467
Ratner, Charles A., 149, 1467, 3278
Ratner, Dennis, 3130
Ratner, Dennis F., 3130
Ratner, Hank, 2336
Ratner, Hank J., 2336
Ratner, Ronald A., 1467
Ratner, Warren A., 3130
Rattie, Keith O., 3104
Rattner, Justin, 1950
Rau, Douglas W., 3453
Rau, John, 787
Rau, John E., 57, 787
Rau, Lisa, 1790
Raub, Philip J., 332
Rauch, Allan N., 399
Rauch, Scott H., 2596
Rauch, Thomas C., 2123
Rauenhorst, Gerald, 225
Rauenhorst, Gia, 225
Rauenhorst, Henriette, 225
Rauenhorst, Joe, 2820
Rauenhorst, Mark H, 2820
Rauenhorst, Mark H., 2820
Rauenhorst, Matthew G., 225
Rauenhorst, Michael, 1099
Rauenhorst, Sarah, 2820
Rauf, Zamir, 661
Rauh, B. Michael, Jr., 772
Rauh, Michael, 772
Rauh, Rob, 1126
Rausch, Daniel L., 2748
Rausch, David, 3632
Rausch, James, 3316
Rautio, Trudy, 693
Rautio, Trudy A., 1919, 3389
Ravech, Wendy Ziner, 68
Ravella, Venkata, 3673
Raver, William, 1785
Ravizza, Dianne, 1009
Ravizza, Eugene A., 1009
Ravn, Michael E., 806
Ravndal, Frank, 2137
Rawden, Louis, 218
Rawitch, Josh, 310, 2305
Rawl, Julian, 1776
Rawlings Sporting Goods Co., Inc., 3370
Rawlings, L.D., 2207
Rawlings, Lynn D., 2208
Rawlins, Randa C., 3431
Rawls, Kendra, 3000
Rawot, Billie K., 1216
Rawson, Richard G., 1944
Ray, Bobby, 1520
Ray, Bonnie, 1520
Ray, Bradford, 3596
Ray, Bradford T., 3596
Ray, Caroline B., 3902
Ray, Christopher, 2641
Ray, David C., 3507
Ray, Gilbert T., 39, 1120
Ray, Gloria S., 507
Ray, Matthew V. T., 1799
Ray, Michael, 654
Ray, Michael C., 551
Ray, Michael L., 2460
Ray, Paul H., 1527
Ray, Quinney & Nebeker Law Firm, P.C., 3131
Ray, Russell T., 99
Ray, Stuart, 3596
Ray, Tom, 2991
Ray-Carroll County Grain Growers, Inc., 3132
Rayball, Patrick, 1556
Rayborn, Karl, 72
Rayborn, Karl G., 72
Rayden, Michael W., 255
Rayfield, Mark, 3312
Raygorodetsky, Phillip, 3309
Raymond Corp., The, 3133
Raymond, Barbara, 2278
Raymond, Betsy, 2520
Raymond, George G., 3133
Raymond, Jean C., 3133
Raymond, Karen, 3133
Raymond, Lee R., 2071
Raymond, Louise R., 2429
Raymond, Pete, 3133
Raymond, Philip C., 71
Raymond, Scott H., 495
Raymond, Stephen S., 3133
Raymund, Steven A., 2006
Rayno, David, 659
Raynolds, Marlo, 1266
Rayonier Inc., 3134
Rayphole, Robert R., 211
Rayport, Jeffrey F., 2560
Razook, Bradley J., 1439
RBC Capital Markets, 136
RBC Capital Markets Corp., 3136
RBC Dain Rauscher Corp., 3136
RBS Citizens, N.A., 3137
Re, Mike, 3668
RE/MAX Equity Group, Inc., 3140
Read, Cheryl, 1762
Read, Frederick C., 12
Read, Ian C., 2150, 2950
Read, Paul, 1437, 1941
Read, Rory, 40
Reader's Digest Association, Inc., The, 3141
Reader, Kip, 3845
Reading Blue Mountain & Northern Railroad Co., 3142
Reading, Jimmie, 2486
Reagan, Jeff, 3979
Reagan, Mike, 3140
Reagent Chemical & Research, Inc., 3143
Reali, Heidi, 1607
RealNetworks, Inc., 3144
Ream, James B., 1542
Ream, Norman L., 1
Reandeau, Traci, 3793
Reardon, Edward J., II, 890
Reardon, Michael D., 2660
Reardon, Nancy J., 2394
Reardon, Robert P., 666
Reardon, Scott, 1099
Reardon, William E., 1089
Reasner, Amy, 1679
Reason, J. Paul, 182
Reasor, C. Clayton, 3572
Reaud, Wayne A., 1895
Reaugh, Kristin, 1023
Reaves, Donald J., 183
Reavis, Randall W., 3688
Rebagliati, Kathryn, 1709
Rebel, Jerry P., 2007
Rebelez, Darren, 5
Reber, Brett A., 1335
Reber, Tony, 77
Rebich, David, 4002
Rebman, Scott, 3228
Rebmann, David, 2538
Reboa, Marco, 2319
Rebolledo, Rogelio, 852
Rebolledo, Rogelio M., 2120
Rebula, Enzo, 1323
Recchia, Robert L., 3914
Rechin, Michael C., 1410
Recile, Shane, 652
Reckitt Benckiser Pharmaceuticals, Inc., 3147
RECO Constructors, Inc., 3148
RECO Industries, Inc., 3148
Record Journal Publishing Co., 3149
Record, Edward J., 3572
Record, Randy A., 2484
Recreational Equipment Inc., 1992, 3150
Rector, Ed, 2120
Red Bull North America, Inc., 3152
Red Devil, Inc., 3153
Red Man Charitable Trust, 2431
Red Rainbow Corp., 1236
Red Wing Shoe Co., Inc., 3154
Redd, Ellis, 3925
Redd, Kathleen E., 1548
Redd, L. Hugh, 1551
Reddig, Scott, 1687
Reddin, Michael S., 437
Reddin, Thomas J., 3914
Redding, Bill, 29
Redding, W. H., Jr., 29
Reddy, John Patrick, 3540
Reddy, Lata N., 3072
Reddy, Preetha, 2453
Redepenning, Charles W., Jr., 3625
Redgrave, Martyn R., 1084, 2277
Redies, Elizabeth J., 3113
Redies, Karen, 3113
Redies, R. Edward, 3113
Redies, Robert D., 3113
Redies, Thomas D., 3113
Redies, Tom, 3113
Redies, William D., 3113
Rediker, Dennis L., 2391
Rediker, J. Michael, 1748
Reding, John, 83
Redline Design, 1776
Redlum, Ltd., 3156
Redman, Clarence O., 127
Redman, Dodie, 1025
Redman, Monte N., 271
Redmon, Dwayne, 728
Redmond, Andrea, 107
Redmond, Billie, 698
Redmond, Jerry, 194
Redmond, Laura, 391
Redmond, Thomas, 1660
Redmond, Wynona, 3310
Redner's Markets, Inc., 3157
Redner, Earl W., 3157
Redner, Gary M., 3157
Redner, Richard E., 3157
Redner, Richard R., 3157
Redner, Ryan, 3157
Redstone, Shari E., 727, 3945
Redstone, Sumner M., 727, 3945
Redwoods Group, Inc., The, 3158
Reeber, Larke, 3673
Reebok International Ltd., 1383, 3159
Reece, Charlie, 2991
Reece, Matthew, 3995
Reed & Barton Corp., 3160
Reed Elsevier Inc., 3161
Reed Engineering Group, Inc., 3162
Reed, Beth, 2151
Reed, Bill J., 3203
Reed, Bruce, 2211
Reed, Christy Oliver, 2309
Reed, Colin V., 1406, 3294
Reed, Debra L., 1706, 3405
Reed, Duane, 3827
Reed, Frank E., 833
Reed, J. N., 1640
Reed, JoAnn A., 167, 4003
Reed, Kori E., 904
Reed, Marc C., 3936
Reed, Marsha, 1127
Reed, R. Brooks, 444
Reed, Rebecca C., 807
Reed, Reginald C., 2190
Reed, Robert A., 2970
Reed, Robert A., Jr., 2970
Reed, Robert A., Sr., 2970
Reed, Robert D., 3931
Reed, Ron, 3162
Reed, Ronald F., 3162
Reed, Samuel, 597
Reed, Sarah, 3162
Reed, Stephen N., 1369
Reed, Thomas L., 1277
Reed, Thomas M., 2991
Reed, Timothy R., 3910
Reed, W. Allen, 2245
Reeder, James A., Jr., 3957
Reeding, S. Steele, 29
Reedy, John D., 2493
Reedy, Tom, 694
Reef, Thomas W., 2022
Reel, Stephanie L., 333
Reen, Christopher P., 2795
Rees, Douglas R., 22
Rees, Mike, 624
Rees, Nigel A., 2434
Reese, Ann N., 4136
Reese, Beth, 57
Reese, C. Richard, 764
Reese, Cindy, 2821
Reese, Clay, 2896
Reese, Gary W., 2138
Reese, Mark E., 1264
Reese, Michael R., 1651
Reese, Richard L., 3441
Reese, Ron, 2225
Reese, Stuart H., 2397
Reese, William, 81
Reeve, Donald, 4021
Reeve, Kevin A., 1900
Reeve, Pamela, 1083
Reeve, Pamela D., 1508
Reeve, Pamela D.A., 167
Reeve, Thomas C., 3771

Reeves, Donald R., 3383
Reeves, Elizabeth, 4134
Reeves, Eric A., 1187
Reeves, G. Stuart, 3831
Reeves, Marta, 2868
Reeves, Norm, Inc., 3165
Reeves, Rip, 44
Reeves, Robert K., 190
Regal Entertainment Group, 3166
Regal, Kelly, 3823
Regal-Beloit Corp., 3167
Regan, Brian T., 1297
Regan, Chris, 768
Regan, John C., 3106
Regan, John F., 2108
Regan, Kevin, 461
Regan, Michael N., 3220
Reganato, Joseph, 2539
Regen, Albert J., 2741
Regenbaum, Howard, 1969
Regence Group, The, 665
Reger Family Owned Business, 3170
Reger Group, The, 3170
Reger, Rebekah, 3170
Reger, Tom, 3170
Reggio, Lorna K., 1404
Regier, Michael J., 3944
Regions Bank, 165, 3171
Regions Financial Corp., 3171
Regions Morgan Keegan Trust, 405, 3171
Regis Corp., 3172
Regis, Inc., 3172
Regnery, Alfred S., 1201
Regulinski, Mark, 3474
Reh, David, 2401
RehabCare Group, Inc., 2154
Reibstein, Saul, 2923
Reich, Joni, 3478
Reich, Victoria J., 1220, 1695
Reichert, Melissa M., 1872
Reichheld, Fred, 3117
Reichling, Darrell, 2361
Reid & Riege, P.C., 3173
Reid, Carter M., 1150
Reid, Christopher, 1925
Reid, Dale G., 91
Reid, Frank, 1655
Reid, Grant, 2384
Reid, Irvin D., 3361
Reid, J. S., Jr., 936
Reid, Janet, 1925
Reid, Karl, 913
Reid, Marjorie A., 1925
Reid, Morris L., 2596
Reid, Paul, 1719
Reid, Ralph, 3556
Reid, Robert T.F., 3010
Reid, Ryan, 136
Reid, Vernon A., Jr., 3040
Reier, Susan, 2561
Reif, Bob, 3569
Reifenheiser, Thomas V., 641
Reifert, Scott, 790
Reiff & Nestor Co., 3174
Reifsteck, John, 1674
Reigel, Ernest, 164
Reilley, Dennis H., 956, 1160, 1161, 2364
Reilley, Mary, 3190
Reilley, Shawn, 195
Reilly Electrical Contractors, Inc., 3175
Reilly, Don, 1902
Reilly, Donna, 2548
Reilly, Emmitt, 1028
Reilly, Jack, 3347
Reilly, James, 3175
Reilly, James J., 3175
Reilly, Joe, 4158
Reilly, John P., 3760
Reilly, Kevin, 1480
Reilly, Kevin G., 1028
Reilly, Michael, 123
Reilly, Patrick, 1028
Reilly, Patrick J., 1028
Reilly, Paul, 2021
Reilly, Paul C., 1363, 2021
Reilly, Paul J., 249, 266
Reilly, Thom, 650
Reilly, William K., 3273
Reilly, William R., 1273
Reilly-White, Patti, 1032
Reily Foods Co., 3177
Reily, Robert D., 3177
Reily, William B., III, 3177
Reim, John F., 687
Reimann, William O., IV, 2138
Reimer, Dennis J., 2605
Reimer, Gary, 3549
Reimer, Jeffrey A., 3388
Reimer, Nikki, 3549
Reimers, Arthur J., 1345
Rein, Andrew J., 1730
Rein, Catherine A., 344, 1424
Reinberger, Bill, 814
Reindel, Susan L., 2466
Reinders, G.F., 3956
Reinebach, Thomas J., 3790
Reinemund, Steven S., 143, 1315, 2383, 3980
Reiner, Gary M., 1794
Reiners, Derek S., 2815
Reinhard, J. Pedro, 869, 3453
Reinhard, Lisa A., 773
Reinhard, Michael, 2087
Reinhardsen, Jon Erik, 667
Reinhardt, Uwe E., 171, 540
Reinhart, Nancy A., 2681
Reinhart, Rick, 1828
Reiniche, Dominique, 862
Reinitz, Cheryl, 1517
Reinking, C. William, 1306
Reinsch, E. James, 1189
Reinsdorf, Jerry, 785
Reinsdorf, Jerry M., 785, 790
Reinsdorf, Michael, 785
Reinsurance Group of America, Inc., 3179
Reintjes, Robert J., Sr., 424
Reis, Gerard J., 3600
Reis, William, 912
Reischauer, Amy, 1180
Reiser, Blake, 1910
Reiser, James M., 1841
Reisinger, Sondra, 3822
Reisman, Lonny, 48
Reisner Corp., William H., 3180
Reisner, Harold H., 3180
Reisner, William M., 3180
Reissfelder, Bill, 352
Reissfelder, William J., 352
Reisz, Maurice E., 1925
Reitan, Bernt, 3273
Reitan, Scott, 2868
Reiten, Pat, 2860
Reiten, R. Patrick, 2860
Reiter, Bob, 1917
Reiter, Julie, 837
Reiter, Robert, 1917
Reitermann, Michael, 3448
Reithofer, Norbert, 509
Reitman Industries, 3181
Reitman, Alayne L., 3452
Reitz, Christopher M., 722
Reitz, Greg, 3195
Reitz, Mike, 2309
Reitz, Robert A., 1561
Reitzloff, Cheryl, 3942
Reliable Brokerage, Inc., 3182
Reliant Energy Ventures, Inc., 1563
Reliant Energy, Inc., 1563
ReliaStar Bankers Security Life Insurance Co., 1938
ReliaStar Financial Corp., 1938
ReliaStar Life Insurance Co., 1938
ReliaStar United Services Life Insurance Co., 1938
Relich, Geri, 809
Relich, Michael, 1685
Rell, M. Jodi, Hon., 2088
Rembolt, Jay, 4011
Remenapp, Donald, 2292
Remer, Jane, 675
Remick, David, 4109
Remke, Stephen, 3953
Remmele Engineering, Inc., 3183
Remondi, Jack, 3478
Remondi, John F., 2659, 3478
Rempell, Michael, 140
Remy, Antoine, 1030
Remy, James R., 2954
Renard, James S., 457
Renard, Jeanette, 2489
Rencheck, Michael W., 236
Rencher, Jared, 131
Renda, Larree, 3310
Renda, Susan, 2538
Render, Cecilia H., 2723
Rendino, Lee, 573
Rendulic, Mark, 1419
Rendulic, Mark, w, 1419
Renfro, John F., Jr., 1943
Renfro, Larry, 3884
Renfroe, Charles Hartley, 1203
Renfroe, Jed, 1203
Renfroe, Patricia, 1203
Renfroe, Robin, 1167
Renfrow, Paul, 2794
Renfrow, Paul L., 2794
Renjen, Punit, 1070
Renken, Keith W., 4075
Renna, Eugene A., 3292
Renneker, Nancy, 3726
Renner, Stacey A., 757
Renner, Troy A., 3235
Rennie, Missie, 3879
Rennoc Corp., 3184
Renovated Home, The, 3185
Renovitch, Sheila, 1376
Renschler, Scott A., 798
Renshaw, Alan, 3906
Rentz, Mark, 2853
Renwick, Glenn M., 1427, 3057, 3884
Renyi, Thomas A., 1742, 3077
Renzulli, Carmine, 3532
Renzulli, June, 3344
Renzulli, June A., 3344
Repass, Randolph K., 4037
Repella, Geoff, 631
Replogle, John B., 623, 3382, 3416
Reppa, Jerome J., 756
Represas, Carlos E., 2466
Republic of Tea, Inc., 3186
Republic of Tea, The, 3186
Resch, Edward J., 3592
Resch, Richard J., 2196
Reschke, Wayne A., 104
RESCO, Inc., 3189
Rescorla, Charles L., 1624
Resenblum, Robert, 2394
Resheske, Frances A., 916
Residential Funding Corp., 3190
Residential Warranty Corp., 3191
Residuary Trust, The, 2340
Reske, James R., 1845
Resler, Edward C., 3671
ResMed Inc., 3192
Resources for Human Development, 3559
Respironics, Inc., 3193
Responsys, 624
Ressler Chevrolet Inc., 3291
Ressler Motor Co., 3291
Restemayer, Brooke W., 3568
Restivo, Neal, 2775
Restrepo, Robert P., Jr., 3590
Restuccia, Robert, 501
Resweber, Christopher P., 3488
Retail Credit Co., 1288
Retemeyer, Deon, 2654
Rethore, Bernard G., 3984
Retsinas, Nicolas, 1348
Retsinas, Nicolas P., 1348
Rettig, Charles P., 678
Rettler, Thomas M., 2461
Retzlaff, Layne, 3015
Reum, Carter, 3927
Reum, Courtney, 3927
Reum, Robert W., 188
Reum, W. Robert, 188
Reuss, Lloyd, 1970
Reuss, Mark, 1555
Reusser, Bryan, 1079
Reuter, David, 2716
Reuther, Craig, 2356
Revai, Daniel L., 3409
Revelle, Charles L., Jr., 3515
Revere Copper and Brass, 31
Revere Graphics Worldwide, Inc., 31
Revuelta, Rodolfo J., 2868
Rewold, Frank, 3196
Rewold, Frank H., 3196
Rewold, Roy, 3196
Rexam Image Products Inc., 3197
Rexam Inc., 3197
Rexford Management, Inc., 3352
Rexford Offshore, LLC, 3352
Rexnord Corp., 3198
Reyes Lagunes, Jose Octavio, 2399
Reyes, Gregorio, 2314, 3377
Reyes, Luis, 705
Reyes, Toni, 2914
Reyes-Retana, Eugenio Clariond, 2050
Reyes-Retana, Eugenio Santiago Clariond, 3727
Reymann, Jeffrey S., 2769
Reynolds & Reynolds, 1776
Reynolds American, 3200
Reynolds and Reynolds Co., The, 3199
Reynolds Tobacco Co., R.J., 3200
Reynolds, Amanda, 2665
Reynolds, Arna, 3726
Reynolds, Barbara, 1722
Reynolds, Bob, 2952
Reynolds, Brett, 846
Reynolds, Catherine M., 854, 921

Reynolds, Chris, 3940
Reynolds, Craig B., 3193
Reynolds, Darline, 2518
Reynolds, Diane, 991
Reynolds, Donald E., 2332
Reynolds, Doug, 3172
Reynolds, Dudley C., 1270
Reynolds, Emily J., 507
Reynolds, Fredric G., 209, 2556
Reynolds, Gerald, 2260
Reynolds, Ginger, 3509
Reynolds, Harold, 350
Reynolds, James M., III, 350
Reynolds, Janet L., 237
Reynolds, Kenneth, 237
Reynolds, Kevin, 602
Reynolds, Mary B., 3765
Reynolds, Paul L., 1377
Reynolds, Paula Rosput, 190, 1073
Reynolds, Randy, 3785
Reynolds, Richard V., 215
Reynolds, Robert A., Jr., 1640
Reynolds, Robert L., 3085
Reynolds, Shelley L., 122
Reynolds, Stanley W., 5
Reynolds, Stephen P., 1955
Reynolds, Tim, 4056
Reynoso, Hector Gonzalez, 1608
Reynoso, Maria Teresa, 1608
Reynoso, Miguel Gonzalez, 1608
Rezich, Paul, 1080
Rezner, Ray G., 353
Rezza, Constance, 476
RG Industries, Inc., 3201
Rhatigan, Jessica, 2524
Rhea, John, 2681
Rheaume, Alain, 543
Rhee, Andrew Y., 466
Rhee, Suzane, 2570
Rhein, Kevin A., 4028
Rheney, Susan O., 738
Rhine, Diane F., 2782
Rhine, Rachel, 1165
Rhinelander Paper Mills Co., 4008
Rhines, Walden C., 2462
Rhoades, Ann, 2041
Rhoades, Scott, 3363
Rhoads, Rebecca R., 3135
Rhode, Brett J., 632
Rhode, Kim, 803
Rhode, Roy, 3544
Rhodes Development Group, Inc., 3062
Rhodes, Ann M., 1808
Rhodes, Bonnie F., 3062
Rhodes, J.W., 780
Rhodes, James T., 1189
Rhodes, Janice, 3356
Rhodes, John H., 3062
Rhodes, Joyce, 325
Rhodes, Marian, 310
Rhodes, Monica D., 3062
Rhodes, Rhonda, 3889
Rhodes, Thomas W., 3890
Rhodes, William C., III, 294, 1143
Riband, Herb F., 2453
Ribar, Geoffrey G., 646
Ribatt, Gregg, 3625
Ribatt, Gregg S., 3625
Ribeau, Sidney A., 4124
Ribeiro, Carl, 1927
Ribeiro, Carlos, 3242
Ricard, Corrine D., 2580
Ricca, Mark A., 711
Riccardelli, George, 3616
Riccardi, Mary Kay, 124
Ricciardello, Mary P., 1102
Ricciardi, Louis M., 577
Ricciardi, Marisa, 2769
Riccio, Louis M., Jr., 2205
Riccio, Louis, Jr., 2205
Riccio, Michael, 2869
Riccitiello, John, 1242
Rice, Brian J., 3273
Rice, Brian S., 2120
Rice, Christopher B., 3430
Rice, Chuck, 284
Rice, D. Douglas, 3393
Rice, Derica W., 2274, 3691
Rice, Donald B., 3972
Rice, Edwin C. "Cookie", 862
Rice, Jamison, 496
Rice, Jason, 2648
Rice, Jason S., 2648
Rice, Jeffrey, 1143
Rice, Jeffrey C., 2178
Rice, Jenny, 1567
Rice, John G., 1552
Rice, John L., 700
Rice, Karen, 1776
Rice, Laurie, 846
Rice, Lester, 2178
Rice, Linda Johnson, 2150, 2808
Rice, Nell M., 404
Rice, Richard, 3697
Rice, Rick, 3697
Rice, Robert C., 1776
Rice, Rod, 196
Rice, Ronald A., 3278
Rice, Scott, 2178
Rice, Steve, 1470
Rice, Steven, 2075
Rice, Terrie L., 1849
Rice, Thomas P., 773
Rice, Tim, 1047
Rice, Timothy D., 2178
Riceland Foods, Inc., 3203
Rich Products Corp., 3204
Rich, Andrea L., 2405
Rich, Bradford W., 2813
Rich, David, 3508
Rich, Harry, 2154
Rich, Jonathan, 438
Rich, MaryLisabeth, 3403
Rich, Melinda, 3204
Rich, Melinda R., 2323, 3204
Rich, Michael E., 1957
Rich, Robert E., Jr., 3204
Rich, Robert E., Sr., 3204
Rich, Ryan, 1244
Rich, Thomas N., 1618
Rich, Tracy L., 1683
Richard & Son, P.C., 3205
Richard, Aurelie, 3560
Richard, C., III, 2545
Richard, David W., 1053
Richard, Gary, 3205
Richard, Gregg, 3205
Richard, Gregg G., 3205
Richard, Henri Pascal, 1495
Richard, Jarod P., 1688
Richard, Jeffrey O., 3309
Richard, Robert J., 4026
Richards, Aileen, 2384
Richards, Brandt, Miller & Nelson, PC, 3206
Richards, Christine P., 1352
Richards, Clark, 80
Richards, Gerrie, 2472
Richards, H. Lee, 1901
Richards, James W., 502
Richards, Jerry, 4052
Richards, Joel, III, 112
Richards, John B., 2269
Richards, Mark, 2656
Richards, Mark W., 2928
Richards, Martin, 340
Richards, Merry K., 1901
Richards, Michael D., 3831
Richards, Pauline D.E., 4132
Richards, Roy, Jr., 3527
Richards, Thomas E., 729
Richardson, Andrew, 3443
Richardson, Andrew T., 3443
Richardson, Bradford, 3418
Richardson, Bradley C., 552, 1112
Richardson, Bruce, 3092
Richardson, Charles A., 1755
Richardson, Chet A., 1755
Richardson, Chris, 1039
Richardson, Collette, 2183
Richardson, Daniel E., 3443
Richardson, Drew, 678
Richardson, Frank E., 3498
Richardson, Gregory S., 3227
Richardson, Greta, 3189
Richardson, Howard V. "Rick", 4028
Richardson, J. William, 176
Richardson, Jeff, 2314
Richardson, John P., Jr., 2073
Richardson, Margaret Milner, 2245
Richardson, Pat, 3016
Richardson, Peter B., 3443
Richardson, R. Michael, 2724
Richardson, Sarah A., 3046
Richardson, Terry L., 3203
Richardson, Tony, 2627
Richardson, Traci, 3793
Richardson, William C., 344, 1309
Richardson, William M., 3148
Richardson, Williamson C., 1309
Richels, John, 1102
Richenhagen, Martin H., 3025
Richer, Clare S., 3085
Richer, John B., Jr., 2902
Richert, Melanie, 3247
Richeson, Brian, 3686
Richey, Erika, 1259
Richey, Vic, Jr., 1296
Richey, Victor L., Jr., 1296, 2723
Richieri, Kenneth A., 2690
Richland Trust Co., The, 2881
Richlovsky, Thomas A., 3866
Richman, Arnold I., 332
Richman, Keith, 3141
Richman, Lindy, 1259
Richman, Wayne, 2101
Richmond County Financial Corp., 2683
Richmond Hockey Fights Cancer, 2631
Richmond, Bradford C., 1032
Richmond, C. Bradford, 1032
Richmond, Jim, 636
Richmond, Kendall, 954
Richmond, Larry, 3635
Richmond, Michael H., 4110
Richmond, Vicki, 4110
Richter, Alice M., 1524, 3747, 4037
Richter, John C., 3025
Richter, Kirk A., 3453
Richter, Pat, 1651
Richter, Peter, 1743
Richter, Sid, 1419
Rickard, David B., 1143, 1736, 2061
Ricke, Beatrice, 663
Rickert, Dick, 2282
Ricketts, Laura, 784
Ricketts, Pete, 784
Ricketts, Todd, 784
Ricketts, Tom, 784
Rickey, Michael, 150
Rickmers, Erck R.C., 2721
Ricks, Charles V., 1776
Ricks, David A., 2274
Ricks, Thomas G., 2695
Ricord, Kathleen D., 1139
Ridder, Paul D., 3693
Riddick, Frank A., III, 4121
Riddle, Kevin R., 3649
Riddle, Pat, 555
Riddle, Ray, 1829
Riddle, Steve, 2730
Riddle, Timothy K., 3160
Riddle, W. Thomas, 3257
Ridenour, Julie, 3597
Ridenour, Mark E., 1770
Ridge, Garry O., 4011
Ridge, Thomas J., 567, 1309, 1791
Ridgeland Company, Inc., 905
Ridgewood Savings Bank, 3211
Ridler, Andy, 669
Ridley, Dawn, 1018
Ridley, Kristin R., 1624
Ridloff, Elena, 2409
Rieder, Randy, 196
Riederer, Richard K., 850
Riedman, M. Suzanne, 2154
Riege, John H., 3173
Riegel, Steve, 802
Rieke Corp., 3212
Rielly, John P., 1793
Rieman, Deborah D., 945
Riepe, James S., 332, 1565, 2617
Ries, Ann, 2609
Ries, Ann W., 2609
Ries, Catherine E., 3819
Ries, E. Carey, 2609
Ries, James M., 2609
Riesgo, Luis, 2058
Riewe, Paul R., 1429
Rife, John A., 3869
Rifiq, Babur, 3624
Rifle Church of Christ, 1520
Rigali, Dave, 3232
Rigby, Joseph M., 3018
Rigby, Kevin, 2753
Rigby, Nancy K., 959
Rigby, R. Michael, 1347
Rigby, Randy, 2028
Riggins, William G., 2092
Riggio, Leonard, 360
Riggio, Stephen, 360
Riggs Tractor Co., J.A., 3213
Riggs Trust, Lamar W., 3213
Riggs, Jack, III, 3213
Riggs, John A., III, 3213
Riggs, John A., IV, 3213
Riggs, Judson T., 3704
Riggs, Lamar W., 3213
Riggs, Sheila, 4026
Riggs, Susan G., 2695
Righteous Babe Records, Inc., 3214
Rigler, John B., 745
Rigney, John, 260
Rigsby, Ryann, 197
Rikleen, Lauren Stiller, 2506
Rilea, Ted, 786
Rilea, Theodore, 786

Roosevelt County Electric Cooperative, 3258
Roosevelt County Rural Telephone Cooperative, Inc., 3259
Roosevelt, Michael A., 3664
Root, Kevin D., 806
Rootes, Jamey, 1872
Roper, Jud, 3281
Roper, Martin F., 533
Roper, Pamela F., 953
Roper, William L., 1044, 1313
Ropietski, John J., Jr., 4024
Roque, Peter A., 476
Roque, Victor A., 1799
Roquemore, James W., 3346
Rorex, Rick, 3203
Rorick, Jeff, 2162
Ros, Francisco, 3095
Rosa, Carlos De La, 163
Rosales, Stephanie A., 3915
Rosanova, Donald S., 3272
Rosazza, Irving R., 1441
Rosborough, Mark N., 1391
Rosburg, Jerry, 335
Roscoe, Steve, 3337
Rose and Kiernan, Inc., 3261
Rose Hills Co., 3262
Rose Law Firm, P.A., The, 3263
Rose, B. Andrew, 4124
Rose, Debra J. Fields, 2592
Rose, Diana L., 2042
Rose, Ellen M., 1946
Rose, Ellen Mackey, 1946
Rose, Eric B., 1844
Rose, John, 77, 1998
Rose, John W., 1318
Rose, Kelly, 736, 892
Rose, Kenneth L., 1779
Rose, Kenton R., 390
Rose, Marya M., 1007
Rose, Matthew K., 187, 273, 618
Rose, Michael D., 1032, 1554, 3294
Rose, Mike, 4110
Rose, Mona Leigh, 1116
Rose, Patrick W., 1120
Rose, Peter, 477
Rose, Rick, 3170
Rose, Scott, 3726
Rose, Suzanne, 892
Rose, Traci, 3793
Roseborough, Terda Wynn, 1842
Rosebrough, Walter M., Jr., 3600
Rosen's Diversified, Inc., 3264
Rosen, Alan, 2668
Rosen, Barry F., 1616
Rosen, Charles L., 898
Rosen, Dan, 839
Rosen, Dennis, 1339
Rosen, Elaine D., 266
Rosen, Eric A., 3090
Rosen, Paul, 3539
Rosen, Paul R., 3539
Rosen, Richard H., 3264
Rosen, Roberta A., 3264
Rosen, Thomas J., 3264
Rosenbaum, Richard A., 1654
Rosenberg Associates, Gene, 511
Rosenberg, Barry, 1222
Rosenberg, Barry A., 1222
Rosenberg, Carla, 1023
Rosenberg, Cheryl, 1665
Rosenberg, David M., 3738
Rosenberg, Debbie, 946
Rosenberg, Donald J., 3095
Rosenberg, Eugene, 511
Rosenberg, Gene, 511
Rosenberg, Joseph W., 855
Rosenberg, Lon, 3054
Rosenberg, Marjorie, 1222
Rosenberg, Martin, 999
Rosenberg, Paul, 1368
Rosenberg, Robert M., 3498
Rosenberg, Ryan, 1380
Rosenberg, Samuel, 1431
Rosenberg, Sheli Z., 3931
Rosenberg, Stanley, 2679
Rosenberg, Stephen, 1665
Rosenblatt, David, 1903
Rosenblatt, Richard A., 2769
Rosenbloom, Chip, 3569
Rosenbloom, Dale, 3569
Rosenbloom, Jerry S., 1733
Rosenblum, Lisa, 2335
Rosenblum, Robert G., 2394
Rosencrans, Bob, 2625
Rosenfeld, Abram, 2514
Rosenfeld, Barry, 2753
Rosenfeld, Gerald, 819, 926
Rosenfeld, Irene B., 2556
Rosenfeld, Matt, 2306
Rosenfeld, Ronald A., 2682, 2683
Rosenfield, Richard L., 660
Rosenheim, John L., 3378
Rosenker, Mark V., 3410
Rosenquist, Iola, 615
Rosenstein, Howard, 1003
Rosenstock, Carl J., 3070
Rosensweig, Dan, 38
Rosentel, Stephen G., 3858
Rosenthal, David. S., 1315
Rosenthal, Donna, 3977
Rosenthal, James A., 2570
Rosenthal, Janie, 1115
Rosenthal, Jonathan, 2481
Rosenthal, Joyce A., 1077
Rosenthal, Morris, 2784
Rosenthal, Robert J., Ph.D., 3307
Rosenwinkel, Wayne, 103
Rosenzweig, Eric, 1534
Roshiem, Timothy M., 4105
Rosier, W. Grady, 2763
Roskens, Lisa Y., 616
Roskens, Lisa Yanney, 616
Roski, Edward P., Jr., 2343
Roski, Patricia Reon, 2343
Roslyn Bancorp, Inc., 2683
Ross Environmental Services, Inc., 3265
Ross Group Construction, The, 3266
Ross Stores, Inc., 276
Ross Willoughby Co., 1235
Ross, Brian A., 75
Ross, Cam, 2148
Ross, Carol, 1696
Ross, Cathy D., 3597
Ross, Christopher S., 1854
Ross, David A., III, 667
Ross, David E., 851
Ross, Donald L., 1281
Ross, Gary, 3090
Ross, George E., 1519
Ross, Jack, 2218
Ross, Jack J., 2218
Ross, Jay Kevin, 4050
Ross, Jesse H., 3266
Ross, Kara, 1147
Ross, Kimberly A., 305
Ross, Loretta T., 412
Ross, Pamela, 2877
Ross, Patricia A., 862
Ross, Randall R., 1524
Ross, Richard A., 850
Ross, Robert R., 756
Ross, Russell, 1571
Ross, Stan, 1467
Ross, Stephen M., 1147
Ross, Timothy M., 2742
Ross, Warren E., 3266
Ross, Wilbur L., Jr., 1971
Rossen, Bob, 3888
Rossetti, John, 3500
Rossetti-Delvaux, Tracy, 1722
Rossi, E. Jeffrey, 1420
Rossi, George J., 1140
Rossi, Kirk R., 1046
Rossi, Lynda M., 502
Rossi, Mark A., 342
Rossi, Nicola, 4132
Rossi, Sharon, 3853
Rossi, Walter, 1110
Rossin, Ada E., 1200
Rossin, Peter C., 1200
Rossiter, Peter L., 3350
Rossman, Gregory J., 3709
Rosson, Mark, 439
Rossotti, Charles O., 47, 340, 525
Rossum, Richard, 2883
Rost, Larry, 1326
Rost, Rynthia M., 1621
Rost, Shawn, 1409
Rostra Precision Controls, Inc., 3268
Rotelle, Michael W., III, 2619
Roth, C. Robert, 2635
Roth, Catherine A., 3889
Roth, Cathy, 3889
Roth, David E., 2815
Roth, Donald C., 2698
Roth, Doug, 1136
Roth, Eldon, 548
Roth, Eldon N., 548
Roth, Gary R., 1053
Roth, Harold R., 879
Roth, James J., 2605
Roth, Jane H., 1252
Roth, Margo, 2448
Roth, Mark, 786
Roth, Michael I., 1974, 2984, 3294
Roth, Regina, 548
Roth, Renee, 3674
Roth, Samuel A., 1420
Roth, Steve, 2689
Roth, Steven, 2925
Rothberg, Sheryl, 3902
Rothe, Christian E., 1624
Rothe, Thomas C., 500
Rothenberger, Tracey J., 1914, 3210
Rotherham, Gary M., 1651
Rotherham, Thomas G., 1633
Rothman, Marc, 2585
Rothman, Robert, 3054
Rothrock, Theresa, 2390
Rothschild Inc., 3270
Rothschild, Peter H., 4030, 4031
Rothschild, Sam, 1858
Rothstein, Daniel G., 3070
Rothstein, Joe, 2507
Rothstein, Kass & Company, 3271
Rothwell, Allan R., 2809
Rothwell, Sharon, 2393
Rothwell, Timothy, 3329
Roto-Rooter, Inc., 773
Rotondo, Joe, 427
Rottinger, Angie B., 3953
Rottinghaus, Cathy, 1397
Roubos, Gary L., 2808
Rouhier, Janet, 3332
Roulstone, Bonnie K., 1024
Roulstone, Douglas R., 1024
Roundy's Supermarkets, Inc., 3272
Roundy's, Inc., 3272
Roundy, Diane, 1651
Roundy, Diane L., 1651
Rounsaville, Guy, Jr., 1393
Rountree, George, III, 3520
Rountree, Michael W., 2930
Rouret, Hugues du, 988
Rouse, William R., 684
Roush, Wayne L., 1668
Rouson, Janine, 1552
Rousse, Sandra, 2742
Rousseau, David, 3319
Rousseau, Micheal S., 543
Routs, Robert J., 42
Rovelstad, Todd, 2612
Rovereto, Marjorie, 2681
Rovira, Alfredo L., 1517
Rowan, Irene Sparks, 2743
Rowan, Paul G., 79
Rowe, J. S., 3891
Rowe, Jeffrey D., 2980
Rowe, John W., 107, 1309, 2740
Rowe, Robert C., 2748
Rowell, Robert, 728
Rowinsky, Eric K., 465
Rowland, Douglas B., 3939
Rowland, G. Joyce, 3405
Rowland, Herman Goelitz, Sr., 2033
Rowland, Richard V., 3904
Rowland, Robert, 3731
Rowland, Thomas P., 829
Rowland, William S., 1411, 1412
Rowley, Jason, 2968
Rowley, Stuart, 1464
Roxane Laboratories, Inc., 515
Roy, C. R., 3198
Roy, Jenna, 2475
Roy, Rick R., 1008
Royal Caribbean International Celebrity cruises, 945
Royal Group Inc., 251
Royal Melbourne, 2124
Royal Savings Bank, 3275
Royal Wine Corp., 3276
Royal, Frank S., 3487
Royal, Pamela J., 1150
Royalnest Corp., 3277
Rozansky, Michael, 364
Roze, Frederic, 2203
Rozzell, Scott E., 738, 739
Ruan Transport Corporation, 3279
Ruan, John, 3279
Ruan, John, III, 3279
Rubba, Kathleen, 2781
Rubel, Matthew E., 3659
Rubel, Michael, 975
Rubenstein, Benjamin C., 1862
Rubenstein, James L., 1862
Rubenstein, Joshua S., 2101, 3250
Rubenstein, Samuel R., 1862
Rubin, Ann H., 695
Rubin, Brown, Gornstein & Co., LLP, 3280
Rubin, David B., 2513
Rubin, Harvey, 2146
Rubin, Kate, 3884
Rubin, L. M., 1315
Rubin, Lawrence, 3280

Rubin, Pamela, 3186
Rubin, Robert A., 222
Rubin, Ronald T., 3186
Rubin, Shelley, 2250
Rubin, Steven A., 937
Rubin, Steven M., 385
RubinBrown LLP, 3280
Rubinfeld, Arthur, 46
Rubino, Bill, 2046
Rubino, Nicholas, 1376
Rubino, Nick, 1376
Rubino, William, 2026, 2046
Rubins, Scott, 1560
Rubinstein, Jonathan, 122
Rubinstein, Jonathan J., 3095
Ruble, Jerred D., 3698
Rubright, James A., 57, 3239
Rubritz, Timothy G., 1318
Rubsam, Stacy, 2530
Rucci, William J., 1743
Ruch, Heinz, 2535
Ruchman, Marshall, 192
Ruckelshaus, Jill S., 948
Rucker, Bill, 2136
Rucker, Howell, 2578
Rudberg, Susan M., 3394
Ruddock, David P., 3297
Ruddy, Raymond B., 2410
Rude, Roberta, 3725
Rude, Tom, 1394
Ruder Finn, Inc., 3282
Rudicus, Catherine, 3635
Rudinsky, Charles A., 1593
Rudisill, Sonia G., 1536
Rudman, Anne Beane, 2689
Rudnick, Ellen A., 1413, 2265
Rudolf, Christoph, 400
Rudolph, Frank W., 1102
Rudolph, George, 103
Rudolph, Phil, 2007
Rudolph, Phillip H., 2007
Rudy's Food Products, Inc, 3284
Rudy, Paul L., III, 1625
Rudzik, John A., 740
Rue and Son, Chas E., Inc., 3285
Rue, Asley M., 3285
Rue, Charles L., Jr., 3285
Rue, Joan E., 3285
Rue, Lisa M., 3285
Rue, Richard A., 1998
Rue, William, 3285
Rue, William M., 3285, 3399
Rue, William M., Jr., 3285
Rue, William, Jr., 3285
Ruedy, Nichola, 2200
Ruelle, Mark A., 4039
Ruesch, Starla, 4013
Ruesch, Starla M., 4013
Ruettgers, Michael C., 3135
Ruff, Ellen T., 222
Ruffalo, Neal, 32
Ruffolo, Joseph A., 3595
Rufrano, Glenn J., 3931
Rug & Home, Inc., 3286
Rugen, Karen, 3220
Rugen, Peter C., 1399
Ruger, Richard, 2275
Ruger, Richard M., 2275
Ruggerio, Peter S., 973
Ruggieri, John T., 1581
Ruggiero, Denise E., 1338
Ruggiero, Peter, 3474
Ruhlman, Barbara P., 3032
Ruhlman, Randall M., 3032
Ruhlman, Robert G., 3032
Ruidl, Gregory A., 6
Ruisanchez, Carlos, 2978
Ruiz de Luzuriaga, Francesca, 2786
Ruiz, Donna, 3303
Ruiz, Fernando, 1161
Ruiz, Frederick R., 2422
Ruiz, Gisel, 3980
Ruiz, Joaquin, 3819
Rukin, Barnett, 3916
Rulli, John, 3458
Rulseh, James R., 4112
Rumble, Keith, 455
Rummelt, Andreas, 86
Rummler, Greg, 929
Rummler, Greg S., 929
Rump, Rick, 1763
Runde, James A., 2195
Rundorff, Jim, 2991
Runkel, John, 1772
Runkle, Donald L., 2237
Runstad, Judith M., 4028
Ruocco, Joseph B., 1612
Rupp, Joseph D., 2801, 3100
Rupp, Stefan, 1256
Ruppert, Ann, 2333
Ruppert, Roger G., 3564
Rupprecht, Daniel P., 3114
Rupprecht, Mark, 3114
Rupprecht, Phyllis M., 3114
Ruradan Corp., 3287
Rusch, Tim, 1006
Ruschau, Douglas M., 2735
Rusckowski, Stephen H., 3103
Rusckowski, Steve, 3193
Rusco Fixture Co., Inc., 3288
Rush, Leonard M., 317
Rush, Parker W., 3188
Rush, Parker William, 3188
Rush, Randy, 1948
Rush, Walter K., III, 937
Rushing, Coretha, 1288
Rushing, Roger, 2433
Rushmeyer, Lowell, 77
Ruskin, Elan, 3871
Ruskin, Uzi, 3871
Ruskin, Varda, 3871
Ruskoski, Eric S., 221
Rusnack, William C., 1447, 2907, 3405
Russ, Daryl, 829
Russ, Steve, 2966
Russ, Susan F., 3141
Russ, Susan Fraysse, 3141
Russak, Michael A., Jr., 3863
Russel, Christina Kay, 1011
Russell Harrington Cutlery, Inc., 1103
Russell, Cecil, 3342
Russell, Charles E., 1940
Russell, Dave E., 1541
Russell, David, 4150
Russell, Don, 3288
Russell, Don M., 3288
Russell, Franklin D., 2243
Russell, George A., Jr., 3592
Russell, George F., Jr., 3289
Russell, J. Shephard, 1501
Russell, Jackie, 2798
Russell, Jean, 2123
Russell, Jim, 1080
Russell, John G., 854, 921, 1879
Russell, Jonathan, 1665
Russell, Justine V.R., 2525
Russell, Keith P., 1755
Russell, Mark A., 4124
Russell, Mark C., 1631
Russell, Richard F., 177
Russell, Robert, 103
Russell, Sandra, 2396
Russell, Scott D., 1130
Russell, Timothy, 2243
Russell, Virginia W., 3288
Russell, Willard, 1418
Russman, Eliot D., 2088
Russo, Kimberly L., 132
Russo, Leslie, 544
Russo, Margaret, 1726
Russo, Patricia F., 82, 1555, 1794, 2466
Russo, Peter Dello, 562
Russo, Robert, 1179
Russo, Sam, 2678
Russo, Thomas A., 156
Russom, Kathleen M., 2681
Rust, Edward B., Jr., 722, 1774, 2429, 3591
Rust, James, 4055
Ruth, Angela M., 1834
Ruth, Gary R., 120, 2574
Ruth, John, 2486
Ruth, Steve, 1196
Rutherford, Eve, 1081
Rutherford, James R., 1137
Rutherford, James W., 1137
Rutherford, Jeffrey L., 1366
Rutherford, Jim, 698
Rutherford, Linda, 1173
Rutherford, Mark E., 1389
Rutherfurd, Winthrop, Jr., 475
Rutkowski, Lawrence R., 3988
Rutledge, Gary L., 202
Rutledge, Ronald E., 626
Rutledge, Stephen F., 1119
Rutledge, Stephen G., 87
Rutledge, Thomas M., 765
Rutledge, Tom, 2852
Rutledge, William P., 42, 3405
Rutrough, James E., 3591
Rutt, Sheila, 1112
Ruttenberg, Eric M., 1016
Ruttinger, George, 986
Ruzicka, Jerry, 3587
RW Asset Trust, 3044
Ryan Family Foundation, 3822
Ryan, Barbara, 3902
Ryan, Daniel J., 2903
Ryan, Diane M., 666
Ryan, E.R., 3328
Ryan, Edward A., 2383
Ryan, Edward R., 3328
Ryan, J. Stuart, 661
Ryan, James M., 1306
Ryan, James T., 1626
Ryan, Jamie, 886
Ryan, Janet, 642
Ryan, Jerry E., 1255
Ryan, John P., 1173
Ryan, John R., 641, 819
Ryan, John R., Jr., 3394
Ryan, John T., III, 2529
Ryan, Joseph, 590
Ryan, Joseph F., 590
Ryan, Michael E., 3873
Ryan, Michael S., 1720
Ryan, Nancy, 2853
Ryan, Nancy E., 2814
Ryan, Nolan, 3729
Ryan, Pat, 781
Ryan, Patrick T., 51
Ryan, Raymond, 2905
Ryan, Robert L., 821, 1554, 3579
Ryan, Robin, 2937
Ryan, Ruth, 3729
Ryan, Sharon R., 1968
Ryan, Stephen D., 256
Ryan, Steve, 312
Ryan, Thomas L., 777, 3413, 3727
Ryan, Thomas M., 4150
Ryan, Tim, 191, 2913
Ryan, Timothy, 2262
Ryan, Tom, 4138
Ryan, William J., 3898, 4027
Ryan-Cornelius, Stacey, 2788
Rycars Construction, LLC, 989
Rydell Chevrolet of Waterloo, 3291
Rydell Chevrolet Oldsmobile Cadillac, 3291
Rydell, David R., 421
Rydell, Earl, 2213
Rydell, Jim, 3291
Rydell, Wes, 3291
Ryder System, Inc., 3292
Ryder, E. Larry, 1855
Ryder, Robert, 919
Ryder, Thomas, 3091
Ryder, Thomas O., 122, 3589
Rydin, Craig, 3088
Ryerson Inc., 3293
Ryerson Tull, Inc., 3293
Ryker, Robert, 2581
Ryley, James S., 1009
Ryley, John S., 1009
Rynda, Scott W., 3802
Rysavy, Jirka, 1527
Rysdon, Jimmie, 3465
Rysdon, Phillip M., 3465
Rysdon, Scott, 3465

S & H Builders, Inc., 3295
S&S Kissimmee, LLC, 3963
S&S Worldwide, Inc., 3296
S&T Bancorp, Inc., 3297
S&T Bank, 3297
S.B.E. & S. Clients' Consolidated, 3298
S.D. Deacon of California, 1050
S.J. Electro Systems, Inc., 3299
S.L.S. & N., Inc., 598
Sa, Sophie, 2869
Saab City of Framingham, 3954
Saab, Joe, 1968
Saad, Joseph, 3309
Saathoff, Mardilyn, 2747
Saathoff, Tom, 2124
Saavedra, Alfred, 923
Saba, Marcel, 2711
Saba, Peter B., 3904
Sabanskas, Peggy, 3256
Sabathia, CC, 847
Sabatino, Thomas J., Jr., 3860, 3981
Sabbak, John J., 2130
Sabin, Michael, 1190
Sable, David M., 140
Sablosky Family Foundation, Inc., The, 1383
Sabochick, Carol, 463
Sabot, Jeffrey E., 2851
Sabourin, John E., 612
Sabourin, Steven, 7
Sac City State Bank, 1987
Sacca, Chris, 30
Saccaro, James K., 377
Saccary, Jim, 1572

Sacco, Matthew F., 1442
Saccomano, Jim, 2906
Saccucci-Radebach, Barbara, 2699
Sachdev, Rakesh, 3167, 3453
Sachs Electric Corp., 3301
Sachs Holdings, Inc., 3301
Sachs, David A., 3719
Sachs, Jonah, 1492
Sachs, Louis S., 3301
Sachs, Mary, 3301
Sachs, Mary L., 3301
Sachs, Samuel C., 3301
Sachs, Stephen C., 3301
Sachs, Susan E., 3301
Sachse, David, 3612
Sackett, Deanna, 934
Sacks, Ian, 3781
Sacks, Louis, 1493
Saco & Biddeford Savings Bank, 3302
Saco, Louis, 4006
Saco, Louis S., 4006
Sacramento River Cats Baseball Club, LLC, 3304
Sactson, James, 1989
Saddi, Karim, 3781
Saddlehorn, LLC, 3305
Saddler, Lyle, 1414
Sadigh, Mandana, 2405
Sadler, Dave, 2557
Sadler, Robert E., Jr., 2323
Sadlier, R. Daniel, 3925
Sadoski, Donald A., 3317
Sadove, Stephen I., 869, 3281, 3315
Sadowski, Ray, 304
Sadusky, Vincent L., 1964
Saenz, Stacy, 594
Safco Products Co., 1372
Safeco Corp., 3306
Safeco Insurance Co., 3306
Safeguard Scientifics, Inc., 3307
Safer, Albert, 2015
Safer, Donald, 878
Safer, Ronald S., 3350
Safety Insurance Company, Inc., 3308
Safety, Joe, 2206
Safety, Joseph, 2206
Safety-Kleen Corp., 3471
Safeway Co., 3310
Safeway Inc., 3310
Sagan, Paul, 68, 1253
Sagan, Rachel, 2990
Saganowich, Joe, 1908
Sagat, Mary, 3581
Sage, Daisy, 3751
Sage, David, 3697
Sage, Jim, 2950
Sage, John, 3084
Sage, Lowell, Jr., 2615
Sage, Mary, 2615
Sage-Gavin, Eva, 1533
Sagehorn, David M., 2833
Sager, Mike, 2161
Sager, Thomas L., 1184
Sagers, Elaine, 2917
Saggurti, Purna R., 340
Sagoonick, Fred, 422
Sahlberg, Jeffrey L., 455
Sahney, Nitin, 2807
Saia, Andrea, 810
Saia, Andrea L., 863
Saia, Dan, 1191
Sailer, Jim, 382
Saint, Laurie, 3886
Saint-Aignan, Patrick De, 3592
Saint-Gobain Corporation, 3312
Saint-Leger, Ursula, 221
Saito, Akinobu, 2540
Saito, Jiro, 1515
Saito, Michele K., 85
Sajak Foundation, Lesly & Pat, The, 1201
Sajdak, Guida R., 792
Saka, Charles, 3313
Saka, Jeffery, 3313
Saka, Jeffrey, 3313
Saka, Raymond, 3313
Saka, Sammy, 3313
Sakac, Ann, Sr., 3070
Sakaida, Hideya, 3776
Sakamoto, Hiroshi, 3904
Sakar International Inc., 3313
Sakas, Jeanne, 2703
Saker, Joseph J., Sr., 3314
Saker, Richard J., 3314
Sakkab, Nabil Y., 120
Saks Inc., 3315
Sakuta, Hisao, 2810
Saladen, Barbara, 793
Saladrigas, Carlos A., 39, 1189
Salamane, Denis J., 1880
Salamatof Native Association, 934
Salamone, Denis J., 1880
Salamy, George, 3124
Salandra, Michael, 92
Salatino, Cicely, 150
Salazar, Arsenio, 923
Salazar, David, 2034
Salazar, David R., 2034
Salazar, Deanna, 500
Salazer, John, 1347
Saldoff Charitable Trust, Ruth D., 192
Saldoff Family, Ruth D., 192
Saldoff, Ruth D., 192
Saldoff, Thomas S., 192
Saleeby, Jeff, 3678
Salem Co-operative Bank, 3316
Salem Five Cents Savings Bank, 3317
Salem, Enrique T., 291
Salem, Lee, 3895
Salerno, F. Robert, 299
Salerno, Frederic V., 68, 727, 2628, 3945
Sales, John, 1009
Sales, Wayne C., 3659
salesforce.com, inc., 3318
Saleski, Mary Ann, 888
Saleski, Mathew, 786
Saleski, Matthew A., 786
Salesky, Dawn, 3467
Salhus, Victoria D., 641
Saliba, Ken, 2064
Salice, Thomas P., 4003
Salierno, Tom, Jr., 3210
Saligram, Ravi K., 2786
Salizzoni, Frank L., 1695
Salka, Susan R., 184
Sallaffie, Moriah, 422
Sallas, Rhonda, 3281
Sallee, Jaclyn, 934
Sallee, Roxann, 2920
Sallerson, Samuel, 1655
Sally, Joe, 2525
Salmen, Richard C., 1356
Salmon, Peter M., 3408
Salo, Lynn D., 99
Salogiannis, Regina, 44
Salomonson, Carey, 1846
Salonek, Linda, 1976
Salonek, Thomas, 1976
Salonek, Tom, 1976
Salstrom, Heidi, 2501
Salter, Doug, 1279
Salters, Iris K., 502
Saltiel, Albert, 294
Saltiel, Karen Fine, 3045
Salts, Chris, 2837
Saltzman, Michael, 3844
Saltzman, Robert P., 2021
Salus, Eric, 965
Salva, Lawrence J., 887
Salvador Imaging, Inc., 1440
Salveson, Jon W., 990
Salvi, Julia, 2321
Salvi, Victor, 2321
Salzano, James, 838
Salzano, Jim, 838
Salzberg, Barry, 1070
Salzmann, Benjamin M., 32
Salzmann, Benjamin Michael, 32
Salzwedel, Jack C., 144
Sam Adams, 1858
Sam's Club Foundation, 1538
Samborsky, Ronald, 1548
Samford, John S. P., 1601
Samil, Dilek, 2765
Samil, Dimek, 2765
Sammon, Maureen E., 44, 2504
Sammons, Mary, 3220
Sammons, Mary F., 2622, 3220, 3574
Sammut, Dennis J., 254
Sammut, Helen, 254
Sample, Anne, 3747
Sample, Bill, 3653
Sample, Roger, 1846
Sample, Steven B., 1955
Samples, Lawrence R., 3351
Sampson, A. Patricia, 4135
Sampson, Gary, 2184
Sampson, Luke, 2615
Sampson, Patricia, 344
Sampson, Richard A., 285
Sampson, Robert, 2615
Sams, Charles Edgar, Jr., 1133
Sams, Charles, Jr., 1133
Sams, Lloyd, 2582
Sams, Susan, 129
Samsel-Deeming, Barbara, 111
Samson, David, 2491
Samson, David P., 2491
Samson, Lori, 24
Samuel, Anton, 1249
Samuel, George, 1
Samuel, Guy, 1762
Samuel, Isaac, 1249
Samuel, Joe, 1400
Samuel, Kitty, 2320
Samuel, Tamara, 1249
Samueli, Henry, 579
Samuelian, Harout, 2994
Samuels, Eric H., 1214
Samuels, Gary D., 3103
Samuels, Theodore R., 677
Samuelsen, H. Robin, Jr., 576
Samuelson-Nelson, Jenifer, 84
San Diego Union Shoe Fund, 938
San Francisco Chronicle, 3325
San Pedro, Claudia, 3498
Sanchez, Dolores, 580
Sanchez, George & Mary Ann, 3374
Sanchez, Manolo, 901
Sanchez, Manuel, 901
Sanchez, Max, 3525
Sanchez, Philip, 3757
Sanchez, Robert E., 3292, 3728
Sanchez, Tony, 2765
Sanchez, Tricia Grigsby, 652
Sancineto, Laura, 3707
Sandberg, Joe O., 1535
Sandberg, Sheryl, 1127
Sandblom, Marissa, 1672
Sandbo, Judith, 1235
Sander, Mark G., 1413
Sander, Norbert, 2689
Sander, Tony, 3995
Sandercock, Brett, 3192
Sanderg, Ellen, 1400
Sanderlin, Jacqueline, 3332
Sanderlin, Joanne, 3332
Sanderlin, W. M., 3332
Sanderlin, Waldron, 3332
Sanders, Barry W., 3372
Sanders, Carol, 1414
Sanders, Carol P., 104, 4095
Sanders, Carolyn, 3778
Sanders, Charles A., 752, 1588
Sanders, Corey, 1629
Sanders, Corey Ian, 2489
Sanders, Daniel S., 1220
Sanders, Dave, 3258
Sanders, David, 3259
Sanders, Doug, 745
Sanders, Jane, 1567
Sanders, Keith, 1894
Sanders, Kelly, 2127
Sanders, M. Jack, 3500
Sanders, Steven, 2738
Sanders, Steven G., Jr., 2738
Sanders, Susan N., 1302
Sanders, Thomas D., 3846
Sanders, Wayne R., 406, 1169, 3728
Sanders, William D., 4044
Sanderson, Bill, 1602
Sanderson, Edward J., Jr., 3311
Sanderson, Garry J., 2608
Sanderson, Veronica, 2067
Sandfort, Gregory A., 4011
Sandhurst Associates, 1431
Sandler, Ben, 3453
Sandler, David, 2593
Sandler, Faith, 3453
Sandler, Malvin G., 673
Sandler, Megan, 4097
Sandlin, Robert E., 1444
Sandman, Bill, 1117
Sandman, Gladys, 1117
Sandman, Randy, 1117
Sandman, Steve, 1117
Sandman, William P., 1117
Sandner, John F., 853
Sandness, Paul K., 2441
Sandor, Richard L., 141
Sandoval, Mathias F., 3484
Sandoz Corp., 2752
Sands, Anita M., 3842
Sands, Frank E., II, 2158
Sands, Jeffrey, 2799
Sands, Jeffrey J., 2799
Sands, Richard, 919
Sands, Robert, 919
Sands, Robert-John H., 21
Sands, Theodore D., 231
Sands, Vincent V., 344
Sandschafer, Scott A., 801
Sandstrom, Sven, 47
Sandt, Henry U., 425
Sandusky Foundry & Machine Co., 3328

Sandusky International Inc., 3328
Sandvik, Helvi, 2615
Sanfilippo, Anthony, 2978
Sanfilippo, Anthony M., 2978
Sanfillipo, Anthony M., 2978
Sanford, David, 2173
Sanford, G.W., Jr., 1871
Sanford, James H., 71
Sanford, Philip H., 692
Sanford, Wilma, 2588
Sangalis, Gregory T., 3413
Sanger, Stephen W., 2950, 4028
Sanghi, Steve, 2499
Sangiovanni-Vincentelli, Alberto, 646
Sangster, Claudia B., 1737
Sani, Suresh L., 3916
Sanna, Dina Kapur, 1046
Sannino, Louis J., 2424
Sano, Seiichiro, 3333
Sanofi-Aventis, 3329
Sanofi-Aventis US, LLC, 3329
Sansar Capital Management, LLC, 3330
Sansone, Daniel F., 3972
Sansone, Paul, 448
Sansone, Philip, 4066
Sansone, Robert, 3831
Sansone, Thomas A., 2006
Santa Fe Natural Tobacco Co., Inc., 3331
Santa Rosa Chamber of Commerce, 2952
Santander Consumer Inc., 1177
Santangelo, Rocco, 4126
Santarelli, Marino J., 3245
Santaren, Manuel De, 1236
Santee, Catherine M., 758
Santerini, Angela G., 1536
Santerini, William, 1536
Santerini, William A., III, 1536
Santi, E. Scott, 1916
Santi, Ernest Scott, 1916
Santi, Scott E., 1626, 1916
Santillan, Laura, 101
Santilli, Vincent E., 2928
Santivasci, Michael A., 996
Santivicca, Terry, 1620
Santo, Ronald D., 2415
Santoki, George, 3189
Santomero, Anthony M., 821
Santona, Gloria, 210, 2427
Santoro, Barbara A., 1939, 3794
Santoro, Brenda, 3455
Santos, Joe, 3028
Santos, Koreen A., 577
Santos, Scott, 3427
SanTrust, Ltd., 3332
Santry, Edward, 884
Santry, Molly, 2668
Santucci, Phillip J., 1077
Sanzari, Ben F., 114
Sanzari, David, 114
Sanzari, Joni, 114
Sanzari, Mary A., 114
Saoud, Joseph, 1006
SAP Global Marketing, Inc., 3327
Sapan, Josh, 126
Sapir, Amos, 3871
Sapona Manufacturing Co., Inc., 29
Sapp, Roger, 859
Sappah, Barbara, 1317
Sapsin, Shelley A., 2215
Saqi, Vinay, 2409
Saraswat, Krishna C., 2214
Sargen, Nicholas P., 4040
Sargent, Ronald L., 2195, 3581
Sari, Robert, 3220
Sari, Robert B., 2724
Sarigedik, Yonca, 3125
Sarin, Arun, 818, 3310, 3363, 3965
Sarkisian, Mark, 3474
Sarles, H. Jay, 174, 1083
Sarnoff, Richard, 30
Sarofim, Fayez, 2153
Sarosiek, James J., 2461
Sarrel, Lloyd, 3818
Sarrica, Lewis F., 385
Sarsam, Tony, 1174
Sartain, Elizabeth, 2916
Sartain, Elizabeth P., 2358
Sartarelli, Jose V., 2048
Sartori Food Corp., 3335
Sartori, James C., 3335
Sartori, Janet L., 3335
Sarvadi, Paul J., 1944
Sarver, Robert G., 3476
Sasaki Associates, Inc., 3337
Sasaki, Osamu, 2539
Sasek, Jeanne, 2190
Sasser, Bob, 1145
Sassi, Brian A., 3541, 4027
Sasso, William R., 3620
Sasson, Alan, 3345
Sasson, Ralph, 3313
Sastre, Maria A., 1032, 3079
Satcher, David, 2481
Sategna, Tom G., 3076
Satell, Edward J., 146
Satell, Edward M., 146
Satfin, Leslie A., 1089
Satkiewicz, Mark, 3479
Sato, Aaron, 1381
Sato, Kazuki, 2540
Sato, Mikio, 3189
Sato, Shun, 3210
Sato, Vicki L., 578, 2939
Satre, Philip G., 1964, 2724, 2765
Satter, Muneer A., 1603
Satterfield, Jay, 2771
Satterfield, L. Kent, 1133
Sattler, Brian, 3365
Saturday, Jeff, 2627
Saturn of Colorado Springs, LLC, 2298
Saturn of Denver, LLC, 2298
Saturn of St. Paul, Inc., 3291
Sauber, Theodore Pat, 2929
Saucedo, Pauline, 3738
Sauer Group Inc., 3824
Sauer, Brad T., 3832
Sauer, Dave, 3024
Sauer, Henry, 3117
Sauerbrei, Stephanie, 4019
Sauey, Floy A., 2722
Sauey, Todd L., 2722
Sauey, William R., 2722
Saul, Betsy, 1126
Saul, Jared, 1126
Saul, William J., 3183
Sauls, Henry, 2785
Saunders, Barry, 624
Saunders, Barry L., 3500
Saunders, Brent L., 376
Saunders, Donald E., 773
Saunders, Jill, 608
Saunders, John, 1970
Saunders, Michael M., 2121
Saunders, Michael M., III, 2121
Saunders, Thomas A., III, 1145
Saurage, H. N., IV, 899
Saurage, Matthew, 899
Saurage, Matthew C., 899
Sauter, George, 768
Sautter, William R., 1926
Savage Industries, Inc., 3341
Savage Services Corp., 3341
Savage, Anne, 135
Savage, Gregory James, 3341
Savage, Jeff, 3304, 4135
Savage, Joe, 3948
Savage, John K., 3341
Savage, Kevin P., 3302
Savage, Larae T., 3341
Savage, Matthew Trent, 3341
Savage, Nathan Neal, 3341
Savage, Patrick J., 3174
Savage, Rob, 3679
Savage, Rolland D., 1618
Savage, Susan, 3304, 3341
Savage, Terrence, 3341
Savage, Terry L., 853
Savage, Todd, 3341
Savage, Troy, 3341
Savage, Ty, 3341
Savage, W.R., III, 470
Savani, Patricia, 2482
Savannah Electric Foundation, Inc., 1567
Savarese, Dorothy A., 674
Savarise, Terry, 790
Saver, Jonathan A., 3721
Saver, Lisa, 3721
Savett, Cynthia, 920
Savings Bank of Danbury, 3344
Savings Bank of Maine, 343
Savings Bank, The, 3343
Savings Institutue Bank & Trust, 3444
Savini, Carl A., 752
Savitch, Jordan B., 2923
Savitch, Jordan B., Esq., 2923
Savo, Jack A., Jr., 797
Savoff, Mark T., 1279
Savoia, Sally A., 3029
Sawalich, Brandon, 3587
Sawchak, Rich, 2755
Sawdye, Carol, 2623
Sawhney, Ashwini, 1150
Sawyer, B., 2650
Sawyer, Bo, 2650
Sawyer, Caren, 1215
Sawyer, James S., 3029
Sawyer, Karen, 3343
Sawyer, Karen A., 3343
Sawyer, Patrick, 978
Sawyer, Thomas C., Sr., 2514
Sawyer-Jones, Grace, 2262
Sawyers, Clayton, 1238
Saxon, Andrew, 678
Saxon, Ken, 1333
Saxon, Stephen M., 1671
Sayed, Shaheda, 2912
Sayles, Helen E.R., 2265
Saylors, Charlotte, 216
Sayre, Charles E., 1987
Sayre, Scott E., 3946
SBC Communications Inc., 273
SBH Intimates, Inc., 3345
SC Johnson, 1131
Scagliotti, Nackey & Robert, 3374
Scaife Journalism Foundation, Richard J., 3806
Scaife, Richard Mellon, 3806
Scairato, Theodore, 888
Scala, Douglas E., 1881
Scalera, Tom, 1999
Scales, John, 1219
Scales, Tiffany, 415
Scalise, George M., 646
Scaminace, Joseph M., 816, 2886
SCANA Corp., 3346
Scangos, George A., 465
Scanlan, Dave, 3497
Scanlon, Bill, 813
Scanlon, Kathryn, 2914
Scanlon, Patricia M., 1367
Scanlon, Patrick, 2924
Scanlon, Patrick M., 2924
Scanlon, Raymond D., 2244
Scannavini, Michele, 950
ScanSource, Inc., 3347
Scarano, Glory, 1887
Scarborough, Dean A., 297, 2405
Scardina, Julie, 3387
Scarfone, Anthony C., 1084
Scarfone, Vincent A., 1186
Scarola, Susan, 1048
Scarpa, Michael, 3682
Scarpaci, Frank G., 3947
Scattaglia, Dorothea G., 3893
SCEcorp, 1228
Scelfo, John J., 1793
Schaab, Louis, 3816
Schaaf, Renee, 3047
Schaaf, Steve, 2980
Schacht, David, 3458
Schacht, Karen K., 1051
Schackert, Christa, 3270
Schaefer, Barbara W., 3857
Schaefer, Charles, 341
Schaefer, Charles H., 341
Schaefer, George A., 4027
Schaefer, George A., Jr., 258
Schaefer, Jack, 3751
Schaefer, Judy E., 1809
Schaefer, Lynn, 4127
Schaefer, R. Gregory, 231
Schaefer, Thomas, 2838
Schaefer, Tim, 420
Schaeffer, Leonard D., 182
Schaeffer, Stephanie L., 2904
Schafale, Mark A., 1271
Schafer, Lowell, 59
Schaffer, Archie, 3832
Schaffer, Cathie, 1419
Schaffer, Greg, 1371
Schaffner, Mary E., 4028
Schaller, George H., 825
Schaller, Harry P., 825
Schallert, Ralph, 2487
Schalliol, Charles E., 1410
Schalow, Laurie, 2139
Schamel, Dale, 1344
Schamel, Jannice, 1344
Schamel, V. Dale, 1344
Schanbel, Jerald, 3798
Schanwald, Steve, 785
Schanwald, Steven M., 785
Schaper, Carl James "Jim", 508
Schaper, Ryan, 3141
Schapiro, Ken, 2479
Schapiro, Morton O., 2385
Schappell, Joe, 2680
Schapperle, John, 1996
Schapperle, John F., 1996
Schar, Dwight, 3054
Scharf, Charles W., 3960
Scharf, David P., 377
Scharf, Michael M., 612

Scharff, Joseph T., 3631
Scharm, Anne D., 716
Scharmann, Jo-Anne, 4045
Scharmer, Neal R., 3869
Scharpf, George E., 124
Schatz, David, 1296
Schatzman, Charles, 1197
Schauer, Jay P., 97
Schauer, Laura, 100
Schauer, W. E., 3198
Schaufeld, Fred, 2611
Schaufeld, Frederick, 2611
Schaum, Richard O., 528
Schaumburg Castle, Inc., 2449
Schaumburg, Anne C., 2756
Schawe, Brian, 3584
Schea, Frederick E., 1421
Schechter, David, 2462
Schechter, Harold, 2015
Schechter, Robert P., 2878
Scheckiman, Dave, 2833
Schedler, Scott, 2582
Scheer, Brick, 1074
Scheer, Daniel J., 435
Scheerer, H. Richard, 838
Scheetz, Patrick C., 2524
Scheevel, David, 1466
Scheffel, William N., 735
Scheffey, Scott R., 2732
Scheffler, Diane, 3738
Scheibert, Celeste L., 2197
Scheible, David W., 1635
Scheidt, Kurt, 1769
Scheinthal, Steve, 3120
Scheinthal, Steve L., 2219
Scheinthal, Steven L., 3120
Scheirman, Scott T., 4045
Scheller, Paul, 3222
Scheller, Richard H., 1549
Scheller, Walter J., III, 3984
Schellinger, Ronald J., 1614
Schena, Joseph J., 4025
Schenk, Les, 1933
Schenk, Lynn, 465
Schenk, Lynn, Hon., 3405
Schenkel, Greg, 2852
Schenkenberg, Philip R., 564
Schenuit Investment, Inc., 3349
Schepman, Ellen Dierberg, 1393
Scher, Laura, 3318, 4116
Scherer, Allan D., 3520
Scherer, Chad C., 2608
Scherf, Willy, 381
Scherff, Scott A., 3760
Scherger, Joe, 1846
Scherger, Stephen R., 2445
Scherman, Carol, 3108
Schermbeck, Vickie, 318
Schermer, Gregory P., 2241
Scherrbaum, Joseph R., Jr., 3877
Scherting, Trudy, 2547
Schertle, Kurt A., 4024
Scheschuk, Peter, 2429
Schewel, Marc A., 3194
Schexnayder, Todd, 2309
Schiavo, Mary F., 4124
Schiavoni, Mark A., 239
Schichtel, Gerald F., 1805
Schick, Peter G., 2557
Schick, Peter Gregory, 2557
Schick, Thomas, 143
Schickler, Paul E., 2980
Schickler, Steven, 3385
Schickli, Dillon K., 1182
Schiek, Frederick, 1264
Schield, Clarice, 4013
Schield, Edward, 4013
Schield, Edward L., 4013
Schield, Edward Lee, 4013
Schield, Kevin, 4013
Schield, Kevin L., 4013
Schield, Mark A., 4013
Schierhorn, Joe, 2743
Schiesl, Andy, 3091
Schiesswohl, Patricia, 4047
Schievelbein, Thomas C., 571, 2688
Schiff Hardin LLP, 3350
Schiff, John J., Jr., 3576
Schiff, Margaret Scott, 687, 3999
Schiffenhaus Industries Inc., 3351
Schiffenhaus Packaging, Inc., 3351
Schiffenhaus, Laurence C., 3351
Schild, Penny, 474
Schildkraut, Lew, 3976
Schill, Michael H., 3470
Schiller, Derek, 280
Schiller, John C., 598
Schiller, Phillip W., 217
Schillinger, Sara, 2504, 2860
Schimmelmann, Wulf von, 3741
Schindhelm, Klaus, 3192
Schindler, Aaron, 2711
Schindler, Andrew J., 904, 1720
Schindler, Barbara J., 1600
Schindler, Kathleen, 3671
Schinella, Tom, 2966
Schipfer, Dan, 754
Schippers, D. Eric, 2923
Schiraldi, Richard J., 1845
Schirmer, Henry, 3853
Schiro, James J., 1603, 2935
Schlader, Ron, 981
Schlanger, Bill, 1237
Schlatter, Konrad, 1942
Schlatter, Martin, 4125
Schlattman, Daniel, 2396
Schlaybaugh, Rex E., Jr., 1199
Schleckser, Robert N., 1315
Schleich, Paul J., 684
Schlemmer, Brett G., 1756
Schlemmer, Jonathan J., 3167
Schlesinger, Lee R., 2646
Schlesinger, Rick, 2527
Schlessman, Lee E., 285
Schlichter, Susan, 1313
Schlichting, Nancy M., 3981
Schlicker, Carl, 1572, 3618
Schlieper, Bill, 1818
Schlifke, Bernard A., 1254
Schlifske, John E., 2181, 2749
Schloemer, James H., 2879
Schlonsky, Michael A., 460
Schlosberg, Richard T., III, 1217, 1228
Schloss & Co., Marcus, Inc., 3352
Schloss, Douglas, 3352
Schloss, Irwin, 3352
Schloss, John R., 3600
Schloss, Neil M., 1464
Schloss, Richard, 3352
Schlossberg, Wendy L., 1599
Schlotman, J. Michael, 2195, 2790
Schlotterbeck, David, 2075
Schlotterbeck, Steven T., 1287
Schlough, Bill, 3324
Schlueter, Richard J., 1257
Schluge, Daniel, 169
Schlundt, William, 3697
Schlussel, Edward, 212
Schmale, Neal E., 2600, 4011
Schmechel, Daniel J., 1220
Schmeeckie, William R., 269
Schmeeckle, William R., 269
Schmeling Construction Co., 3353
Schmeling, Judy A., 919
Schmeling, Roger E., 3353
Schmeling, Stephen E., 3353
Schmeltekopf, Mark, 3915
Schmeltz, Amy, 2950
Schmid, Jeffrey, 2606
Schmid, Jeffrey R., 2607
Schmid, John W., 472
Schmidleithner, Rudi, 1541
Schmidlin, John W., 1382
Schmidt, C.G., 1285
Schmidt, Carl G., 2241
Schmidt, Chris, 2581
Schmidt, Curtis R., 4008
Schmidt, Derek P., 1817
Schmidt, Eric E., 1613
Schmidt, Eric E., Ph.D., 1613
Schmidt, John A., 851
Schmidt, Joseph H., 1110
Schmidt, Kelly J., 2842
Schmidt, Lynn, 3222
Schmidt, Lynn D., 3025
Schmidt, Marj, 3896
Schmidt, Markus, 2401
Schmidt, Oscar, 2481
Schmidt, Ralph A., 4044
Schmidt, Richard, 350
Schmidt, Ron, 835
Schmidt, Rudi H., 1861
Schmiedel, Gary W., 2833
Schmitt, Caroline, 404
Schmitt, Christine, 2455
Schmitt, Harvey, 698
Schmitt, Mark, 591
Schmitt, Susan J., 3246
Schmitt, Thomas N., 2813
Schmitt, Wolfgang R., 2886
Schmitz, Jim, 3171
Schmitz, Ronaldo H., 642
Schmitzer, Loretta L., 687
Schmoke, Kurt, 3470
Schmoke, Kurt L., 2245, 2429
Schmon, Cynthia, 3721
Schmotter, James W., 3344
Schmuhl, William J., Jr., 2073
Schmults, Edward M., 551
Schnair, Gene, 3474
Schnall, Richard J., 1130
Schnapp, Carl W., 2506
Schnatter, John H., 2876
Schnaufer, Erich, 3293
Schneeberger, Carol A., 2929
Schneider Electric USA, Inc., 3560
Schneider Mills, Inc., 3354
Schneider National, Inc., 3355
Schneider Trading, Inc., 3354
Schneider, Agnes, 3354
Schneider, Albert, 3354
Schneider, Bernard, 191
Schneider, Edward P., 2447
Schneider, Frank, 2045
Schneider, Glenn, 1125
Schneider, James, 2282
Schneider, James M., 1550
Schneider, Jim, 2282
Schneider, Kathryn, 24
Schneider, Martin, 3913
Schneider, Mary Lee, Jr., 1455
Schneider, Neal, 857
Schneider, Neal C., 857
Schneider, Peter W., 3045
Schneider, Richard A., 1179
Schneider, Robert F., 2149
Schneider, Steven J., 1383
Schnell, Donald D., 828
Schnettler, Thomas P., 2983
Schnitzer, Alan D., 3802
Schnitzer, Bruce W., 2461, 3188
Schnoor, Lee, 2330
Schnoor, Stephen J., 1741
Schnuck, Craig D., Jr., 3835
Schnuck, Scott C., 3356
Schnuck, Todd R., 890, 3356
Schnurr, Thomas G., 1388
Schober, Gary M., 1820
Schober, Mark A., 100
Schoch, Alexander C., 2907
Schochet, Barry P., 2807
Schock, Todd, 3312
Schoeder, Jane, 1251
Schoellkopf, Wolfgang, 3478
Schoen, Anthony E., 4043
Schoen, William J., 1765
Schoenbaum, Alan, 3117
Schoenberger, Robert G., 3885
Schoenecker, Barbara, 3357
Schoenecker, Guy, 3357
Schoenecker, Larry, 3357
Schoeneckers, Inc., 3357
Schoenfeld, Marc, 3274
Schoenfelder, Brad, 2505
Schoenhals, Marvin N., 4127
Schoening, Robert, 2894
Schoettler, Gail, 878
Schoewe, Thomas, 3101
Schoewe, Thomas M., 1555, 2744
Schoff, Jonathan C., 1779
Schofield, Seth E., 2365, 3877
Scholer, Sue, 3632
Scholin, Margo, 1347
Scholl, Eric K., 3910
Schollaart, Ronald J., 3890
Scholten, Gary P., 3047
Scholtz, Stacy A., 2607
Scholund, Christian, 3093
Scholz, Mia M., 3981
Schommer, Bernard, 3883
Schonberg, Matthias, 927
Schoneman, Debbra L., 2983
Schoneman, Debra L., 2983
Schonherr, Mike, 2853
School Employees Credit Union of Washington, 2919
Schools, Bob, 1723
Schoonover Investments, L.P., 3359
Schoonover, Barbara Jean, 3359
Schoonover, Brett S., 3359
Schoonover, David L., 3359
Schoonover, John S., Jr., 1297
Schoonover, Steven L., 3359
Schorr, Judah, 1910
Schorr, Lawrence J., 1110
Schorr, Paul C., IV, 178
Schott Corp., 3360
Schott Foundation, Caroline and Sigmund, Inc., 3863
Schott, Elizabeth, 3506
Schott, James F., 4096
Schott, Owen W., 3360
Schott, Randy, 1365
Schott, Tom, 1009
Schott, Wendell, 3360
Schottenstein, Jay L., 140

Schottenstein, Robert H., 2325
Schowalter, Linda G., 3668
Schrader, William R., 1306
Schrage, Mitchell R., 2099
Schram, Lee J., 1084
Schramm, Lee J., 1084
Schreck, Mark R., 2999
Schreiber, Brian T., 156
Schreiber, Charles H., 589
Schreiber, Cheryl, 1716
Schreiber, Cheryl D., 1716
Schreiber, Mark F., 1855
Schreiner, Linda V., 2445
Schrimsher, Neil A., 219
Schriver, Michael, 1104
Schrock, Charles A., 4096
Schrock, Michael V., 2926
Schroder, Bruce E., 2020
Schroder, Soren W., 612
Schroeder, Bruce, 1763
Schroeder, Donald B., 3753
Schroeder, Fred, 3867
Schroeder, John C., 983
Schroeder, Kathy, 2785
Schroeder, Mark, 3852
Schroeder, Michelle R., 2149
Schroeder, Paul, 460
Schroeder, Richard A., 983
Schroeder, Stephen O., 936
Schroeder, William J., 903
Schroepfer, Mark, 4088
Schroeppel, Bobbi L., 2748
Schrott, Howard L., 1508
Schrum, R.P., 3500
Schubert, Gail, 422
Schubert, Gail R., 422
Schubert, John, 455
Schubert, Michael, 3282
Schuchart, Judy, 909
Schueler, Charles R., 641
Schueler, Dennis, 1655
Schueler, Judy, 3902
Schueneman, Daniel J., 940
Schueneman, John E., 940
Schueneman, Shane, 940
Schuerholz, John, 280
Schuerman, Janice, 2486
Schuessler, Tyler, 2148
Schuette, Joyce Nelson, 2836
Schuette, Rex S., 3866
Schuette, Stuart, 3838
Schuh, Dale Robert, 3409
Schuh, Kevin, 2461
Schuh, Michele, 1415
Schuitz, Rich, 2880
Schulaner, Felice, 858
Schuler, Barry, 3366
Schuler, Jack W., 2453, 3107
Schuler, Linda B., 1564
Schuler, Lynda, 4076
Schuler, Robert C., 1564
Schuler, Sharon, 838
Schuler, Wendy R., 32
Schuller Corp., 2047
Schuller, Brenda, 26
Schulman, Amy, 2950
Schulman, Daniel H., 3669
Schulman, Michael, 191
Schulman, Sammy, 1767
Schulte, Tamara, 3140
Schulte-Hillen, Gerd, 439
Schultz Family Foundation, 3585
Schultz, Alan F., 3914
Schultz, Daniel R., 144
Schultz, Howard, 370, 835, 3585
Schultz, Jerry, 3619
Schultz, John F., 1794
Schultz, Kenneth, 1918
Schultz, Kevin, 1276
Schultz, Kris, 1397
Schultz, Kurt L., 4089
Schultz, Richard G., 1647
Schultz, Roxanne, 1993
Schultz, Stuart L., 2300
Schultz, SueAnn, 1917
Schultz, Thomas J., 2117
Schulz, David, 45
Schulz, Mark A., 1026, 2850
Schulz, Philip J., 2801
Schulze, Richard L., 1629
Schum, Richard (Rick), 503
Schum, Rick, 503
Schumacher, Matthew A.P., 571
Schumacher, Michael, 1006
Schumann, William H., 127
Schumann, William H., III, 304
Schumeister, Steven A., 3232
Schunck, George J., 4146
Schupp, Joseph E., 3528
Schurr, Dan, 802
Schurr, Daniel, 802
Schurz Communications, Inc., 3507
Schurz, Todd, 1790
Schuster, Carl, 3080
Schuster, Marvin R., 54
Schutt, Aaron M., 1167
Schutte, Kathy J., 1966
Schutz, Don, 3553
Schutz, Jeffrey H., 3498
Schutz, John E., 643
Schutz, Ronald J., 3232
Schuyler, Shannon L., 3042
Schwab & Co., Charles, Inc., 3363
Schwab Corp., Charles, The, 3363
Schwab, Alan, 1911
Schwab, Carrie, 3363
Schwab, Charles R., 3363
Schwab, David E., II, 4030, 4031
Schwab, Frederick J., 546
Schwab, Nelson, III, 1790
Schwab, Susan C., 722, 1352
Schwab, Susan C., Amb., 516
Schwab-Pomerantz, Carrie, 3363
Schwager, Jeff, 3335
Schwalbach, John F., 32
Schwan Food Co., Inc., The, 3365
Schwan's Sales Enterprises, Inc., 3365
Schwan, Alfred, 3365
Schwan, Allan, 3365
Schwan, Paul M., 3365
Schwan, Severin, 1549
Schwan, Timothy T., 3747
Schwan-Okerlund, Lorrie, 3365
Schwaneke, Jeffrey A., 735
Schwarbach, Laura, 2849
Schwartz, A.J., 1957
Schwartz, Adam, 3296
Schwartz, Alan D., 641, 2336
Schwartz, Alan S., 1853
Schwartz, Barry K., 2166
Schwartz, Bart R., 266
Schwartz, Bernice Gailing, 2015
Schwartz, Carla R., 3296
Schwartz, Cathy L., 2855
Schwartz, Craig G., 120
Schwartz, Daniel S., 613
Schwartz, David, 3701
Schwartz, David A., 3853
Schwartz, David J., 3790
Schwartz, David Y., 3572, 3981
Schwartz, Deborah A., 3630
Schwartz, Dennis R., 1061
Schwartz, Doran N., 2441
Schwartz, Eugene M., 882
Schwartz, Gary W., 2149
Schwartz, Harvey M., 1603
Schwartz, Henry, 1782
Schwartz, Hy, 3296
Schwartz, Jeffrey H., 2225
Schwartz, Jodi D., 3973
Schwartz, Karl D., 91
Schwartz, Lisa, 1665
Schwartz, Mark, 2399
Schwartz, Mark S., 2296
Schwartz, Michael, 305
Schwartz, Mike, 1348
Schwartz, Raphe, 768
Schwartz, Richard W., 2719
Schwartz, Selma B., 436
Schwartz, Stephen L., 3296
Schwartz, Steven J., 3424
Schwartz, William, 3945
Schwartzkopf, Kurt, 3802
Schwartzman, James C., 1926
Schwarz, Diane K., 3731
Schwarz, Henryk, 1782
Schwarz, John G., 3673
Schwarz, Steven, 1782
Schwarzbach, Diane, 2849
Schwarzbach, Ellen, 2849
Schwarzbach, Howard, 2849
Schwarzbach, Peter, 2849
Schwarzman, Stephen A., 477
Schwarzwaelder, Steve, 1026
Schweertman, Shirley, 3993
Schwei, Russell P., 317
Schweier, Anthony E., 1301
Schweikert, Karrie E., 3936
Schweikhardt, R. Gary, 1081
Schweinhart, Martin G., 900
Schweinhart, Richard A., 3931
Schweizer, Paul H., 1805
Schwerdtman, Michael H., 1903
Schwieters, John T., 798, 1027, 3487
Schwimmer, Lance, 2945
Schwinger, Scott E., 1872
Scichili, Rob, 1023
Scientific Components Corp., 3367
Scientific-Atlanta Fdn. Inc., 818
Scilacci, William J., 1228
Scimone, George, 969
Sciortino, Anthony S., 1347
Scioscia, Anne, 200
Sclavos, Stratton, 3318
Scodari, Joseph, 955
Scodari, Joseph C., 1268
Scoggin, Andrew J., 79
Scoggins, Andy, 3281
Scolaro, Peter F., 1207
Score, Shawn, 442
Scott & Stringfellow, Inc., 3368
Scott Bridge Company, Inc., 3369
Scott Foundation, T.H. and Mayme P., 1279
Scott Technologies, Inc., 3370
Scott, Adam N., 1849
Scott, Bertram, 52
Scott, Bertram L., 398
Scott, Brain M., 184
Scott, Cheryl, 3150
Scott, Chris, 2910
Scott, David A., 887
Scott, David J., 182
Scott, Dennis W., 620
Scott, Diana, 1717
Scott, Diane, 4045
Scott, Edward J., 722
Scott, Elizabeth Davenport, 4078
Scott, Fred, 2126
Scott, George L., 1485
Scott, Gloria R., 2296
Scott, H. Al, 87
Scott, H. Lee, Jr., 3980
Scott, I.J., III, 3369
Scott, James, 1409
Scott, James H., 3747
Scott, James K., 1755
Scott, Jay, 191
Scott, Jerry, 1472
Scott, Kirby, 1080
Scott, Lorrie D., 3017
Scott, Lynette, 1409
Scott, Mary Ellen, 1712
Scott, Michael, 1095
Scott, Pamela Denise, 1579
Scott, Peggy B., 2309
Scott, Randy, 1409
Scott, Richard T., 1256
Scott, Richard W., 2296
Scott, Risa, 1409
Scott, Robert G., 2769
Scott, Robert J., 1417
Scott, Samuel C., III, 13, 344, 2586
Scott, Sidney Buford, 3368
Scott, Thomas, 1409
Scott, Thomas R., 3224
Scott, Todd, 3224
Scott, Tom, 1409, 2796
Scott, Valerie, 2260
Scott, Walter, Jr., 429, 3919
Scott, William H., Jr., 2716
Scott, William J., III, 1625
Scott, William M., 3369
Scott, Winston E., 1689
Scott, Yvette, 3457
Scottdale Bank & Trust Co., The, 3371
Scoular Co., The, 3373
Scoville, Roger D., 1209
Scowcroft, Brent, 3095
Scozzafava, Ralph, 3572
Scozzafava, Ralph P., 1519
Scranton, William W., III, 1733
Scribner, Thomas R., 3519
Scricco, Francis M., 3964
Scripps Co., E.W., The, 3374
Scripps Klenzing, Margaret, 3374
Scripps Vasquez, Virginia, 3374
Scripps, Cindy J., 3374
Scripps, Edward W. & Christy, 3374
Scripps, Henry R., 3374
Scripps, Paul K., 3374
Scripps, Robert P., 3374
Scripps, William H. & Kathryn, 3374
Scruggs, Patrick A., 966
Scrupps, Jay, 3222
Scudder, Michael L., 1413
Scullen, Stephen A., III, 1450
Scullion, Mary, Sr., 53
Scully, John H., 41
Scully, Kimberly, 2082
Scully, Robert W., 340
Scully, Terrance J., 3691
Scully, Thomas A., 3887
Scura, Patrick E., Jr., 2741
Seaboard, Inc., 3375
Seabourne, George, 3736

Seabourne, George P., 3736
Seafood Producers Cooperative, 3376
Seagate Technology LLC, 3327
Seagle, Miriam, 436
Seagle, Peter, 436
Seagle, Peter C., 436
SEAKR Engineering, Inc., 3379
Sealaska Corp., 3380
Sealaska Heritage Institute, 1887
Seale, Donald W., 2725
Sealright Co., Inc., 1884
Seaman, Tara L., 3667
Seaman, Wayne, 1846
Seamen's Bank, 3383
Searcy, Valerie D., 1567
Searl, Scott, 2806
Searls, Christine, 751
Sears Holdings Corp., 3384
Sears, Roebuck and Co., 3384
Seas, Bryan E., 57
Season of Sharing, 786
Seaton, David, 2953
Seaton, David T., 1448, 2580
Seaton, David Thomas, 1448
Seaton, Mark E., 1389
Seats Inc., 2722
Seats, Michael, 3190
Seats, Michael J., 3190
Seattle Coffee Co., 3385
Seattle Times Co., The, 3386
Seaver Holt, Carol, 2742
Seaver, Carol A., 2742
Seaver, G. Arthur, III, 517
Seaver, Michael L., 2928
Seavers, Janet, 3256
Seavers, Mark, 2242
Seawell, A. Brooke, 2767
SeaWorld Parks and Entertainment, 3387
Seay, J. Gary, 900
Sebair, Sam, 1067
Sebald, Christopher R., 3389
Sebasky, Gregory M., 2963
Sebastian Holdings, Inc., 2750
Sebastian, Teresa, 1032
Sebastiani, Dan, 1769
Sebring, Patti, 1918
Seccombe, Richard, 1116
Sechrest, Vita, 1824
Sechrest, William B., 2460
Seck, Gerald, 2224
Seckel, Doug, 1871
Seckington, Rita, 3980
Second Street Iron & Metal Co., Inc., 3425
Secondine, Josephine, 2268
Secor, Jamie, 2979
Secor, Teruko, 1515
Secrest, Tish, 340
Secrist, Steve R., 3081
Secru, Stephan, 270
Secunda, Thomas F., 486
Securant Bank & Trust, 3388
Securian Holding Co., 3389
Security Benefit Life Insurance Co., 3391
Security Finance Corp., 3392
Security Financial Life Insurance Co., 269
Security Mutual Life Insurance Co., 269
Security National Bank, 3393
Security State Bank, 3394
Security State Bank of Hibbing, 3394
Sedgewick, Robert, 38
Sedillo, Ronda, 3323
Sedlak, Pat, 2401
Sedwick, Dru A., 245
Sedwick, Jay L., 245
Sedwick, Linda, 245
Seeberger, James P., Jr., 333
Seeberger, Red, 2615
Seegal, Rhonda L., 4136
Seeger, Laureen E., 2434
Seeger, Vicky, 3147
Seegmiller, Dwight O., 1808
Seehorn, Terry, 672
Seelbach, William .R., 2809
Seeley, James R., 2124
Seelig, Jason, 281
Seelig, Jeffrey, 281
Seelig, Jonathan, 68
Seelig, Kay, 281
Seelig, Mac, 281
Seelig, Mac R., 281
Seeman, Charles, 1210
Seeman, Charles A., 1210
Seeno, Lisa H., 276
Seesz, Don, 3376
Sega, Ronald M., 4112
Segal, Hugh D., 3643
Segal, Richard M., 2945
Segal, Susan, 2281
Segarra, Ann, 1419
Segarra, Joseph W., 3204
Seggio, Kim, 2683
Segil, Larraine D., 1508
Segura, Gueri, 1092
Segura, Michael, 608
Segworth, Lorranine M., 3590
Sehgal, Dianne, 2906
Sehring, Richard P., 915
Seibel, Rob, 3483
Seiberlich, William C., 3312
Seibert, Gregg G., 641
Seibert, Mike, 3037
Seibert, Steven M., 2580
Seiden, Melvin R., 1450
Seidenberg, Ivan G., 3601
Seider, Bonnie, 2335
Seidler, Stan, 1304
Seidler, Stanley B., 1304
Seifel, Deneen, 3899
Seifert, James, 2025
Seifert, James A., 2025
Seifert, Kathi P., 2258, 2274
Seifert, Nancy, 1645
Seifert, Rachel A., 900
Seifert, Shelley J., 2997
Seifert, Thomas, 40
Seiff, Eric A., 2689
Seiffer, Jonathan A., 4066
Seigel, David, 2324
Seigfreid, Brad, 2786
Seigfreid, James T., 2091
Seiling, Amelia, 2556
Seip, Tom D., 1695
Seirer, Darren, 3398
Seistrup, Chris, 3274
Seith, Thomas W., 2051
Seitter, Dellmer B., III, 3049
Seitz, C. Richard, 1078
Seitz, David M., 4048
Seitz, Eugene B., 3865
Seitz, Eugene B., II, 3865
Seitz, George Michael, 3865
Seitz, Jay, 3450
Seitz, Kevin L., 502
Seitz, Michelle S., 478
Seiwald, Christopher, 2937
Seiwald, Trudi, 2937
Seksay, Edward H., 1927, 3242
Sekston, Angela, 13
Selanof, Patrick C., 776
Selanoff, Paul T., 776
Selati, Robin P., 729
Selby, Douglas, 2065
Selby, Thomas, 2429
Seldon, Angelo, 2625
Seldovia Native Association, Inc., 3397
Select Energy, Inc., 2737
Select Equity Group, Inc., 3398
Selective Insurance Group, Inc., 3399
Selemyer, Mark, 4105
Self Reliance NY FCU, 3400
Self, Anne Darden, 3106
Self, Leigh Anne, 131
Self, Sam, 3728
Selig Enterprises Inc., 3401
Selig Enterprises, Inc., 3401
Selig, Allan H., 2371
Selig, Robert C., Jr., 1297
Selig, Stephen, 3401
Selig, Stephen Scott, 3401
Selig, Steve, 3401
Selig-Prieb, Wendy, 2527
Seligman Distributing Co., Charles, Inc., 3402
Seligman, Chad, 3402
Seligman, Joel, 1214, 1382
Seligman, Naomi O., 68, 2821
Seligman, Nicole, 3502
Seligman-Doering, Ruth M., 3402
Sell-Shearer, June, 3544
Sellars, William E., 1395
Sellden, Todd, 1540
Selle, Donald S., 3571
Selle, Joan M., 3571
Selleck, Erin, 3854
Selleck, Pete, 2495
Sellers, M. Edward, 498
Sellers, Mary E., 342
Sellman, John, 3969
Sellner, Keith, 2883
Sells, Earlene A., 1884
Selner, Joe, 261
Selwood, Robert C., 2489
Selzer, Herbert, 2799
Selzer, Herbert M., 2799
Selzer, Lawrence A., 2991
Semedo, Tony B., 2453
Semel, Joel I., 2166
Semelsberger, Ken D., 1216
Semelsberger, Kenneth J., 1367
Sementelli, Anthony J., 1439
Semiconductor Industry Association, 3403
Semiconductor Research Corp., 3403
Semmelman, Joe, 1197
Sempra Energy, 3405
Semrau, Kelly M., 2049
Semtner, Katy, 370
Sen, Laura, 473
Sen, Laura J., 473
Sena, Kathryn E., 181
Senda, Kenryo, 2713
Seneca Foods Corp., 3406
Sener, Joseph W., 2245
Senerchia, Diane, 2741
Sengewald, Stefan, 509
Senglamb, Keith, 1355
Senglaub, Keith, 1355
Sengstack, Gregg C., 1484, 4112
Senior, Allen L., 2569
Senior, Diana M., 2569
Senior, Richard J.L., 2569
Senkler, Robert L., 3389
Sensient Technologies Corp., 3408
Senske, Kurt M., 3747
Sentry Insurance, 3409
Seong, Jacob, 2854
Sepanik, Heidi, 3964
Sepehri, Mouna, 423
Seppala, P.A., 1673
Sepulveda Realty & Development Co., Inc., 3550
Sequa Corp., 3410
Sera, Jean, 299
Serbin, Daniel S., 2886
Serck-Hanssen, Eilif, 2231
Serengeti Trading Company, The, 3411
Sergel, Richard P., 3592
Sergi, Vincent A.F., 2101
Serino, Joseph A., 1255
Serna, Isaac, 310
Seroka, Ken, 3949
Seroka, Todd, 1915
Serono, Inc., 1256
Serpico, Vincent, 2203
Serra, Jaime, 795
Serrano, Ruben, 1683
Serres, De, 3653
Sertich, Mark, 2930
Serure, Mal, 3604
Servco Pacific Inc., 3412
Servello, Aldo, 808
Service America Corp., 4084
Service Painting Corporation, 1314
ServiceMaster Co., The, 3414
Servodidio, Mark, 299
Servodidio, Mark J., 300, 604
Serwa, Walter, 2402
Serxner, Alan, 2955
Sescleifer, Daniel J., 1271
Seton Co., 3415
Settle, Bob, 981
Settles, James U., Jr., 502
Settles, Jimmy, 1464
Setzler, Brian C., 3809
Seufer, Howard, 544
Seuss, James, 867
Seventh Generation, 4066
Sever, Christopher J., 3902
Severino, Tom, 1259
Severson, Chris, 939
Seville-Jones, Sandra, 2598
Seward, Gerald, 3553
Sewell, D. Bruce, 217
Sewell, John L., 490
Sewers, Kat, 457
Sexton Can Co., Inc., 2001
Sexton, O. Griffith, 2570
Seybert, Daniel, 576
Seymann, Marilyn R., 2410
Seymour, David, 3902
Seymour, Kyle H., 4138
Seymour, Scott J., 1548
Sezer, Esat, 863
SFJTD Charitable Fund, 1520
Sfrisi, John, 888
Sgarlat, Marla Parente, 414
Sgarzi, Richard H., 1927, 3242
Sgirgnari, Michael, 956
Shabel, Fred, 888, 2957
Shabel, Fred A., 888, 2957
Shackouls, Bobby S., 2195
Shadaksharappa, Hamsa, 1988

Shadduck, David A., 3815
Shafer, Walt, 3839
Shaff, Karen E., 3047
Shaffer, David N., 2077
Shaffer, Jack, 421
Shaffer, Jim, 3777
Shaffer, Karen, 160
Shaffer, Michael A., 1801, 3088
Shaffer, Oren G., 1955, 3719
Shaffer, Penelope S., 493
Shaffer, Quentin, 3757
Shaffer, Steven, 286
Shaffer, Thomas H., 345
Shafir, Robert S., 980
Shah, Jen, 1053
Shah, Nirav, 1237
Shah, Rajat, 1066
Shaheen, Gabriel L., 3595
Shaheen, Gerald L., 1464
Shaich, Ronald M., 2873
Shaifer, Jerry, 350
Shain, Paul S., 144
Shakeel, Arif, 4042
Shaklee Corp., 3418
Shalam Imports Inc., 3420
Shalam, Abraham, 3420
Shalam, Janet, 3420
Shalam, Sasson, 3420
Shales, Jack, 2997
Shamah, Abraham, 1489
Shamah, Alan, 2889
Shamah, Ezra, 1489
Shamah, Harold, 2889
Shamah, Isaac, 2889
Shamah, Isadore, 2889
Shamah, Rachel, 1489
Shamaley Ford, L.P., 1464
Shames, Ervin R., 798
Shamey, Donald, 2706
Shammo, Francis J., 3936
Shamoon, Alan, 218
Shamrani Realty, 2889
Shamrock Industries, Inc., 1372
Shamrock Paving, 2599
Shams, Marc, 2328
Shams, Natham, 2328
Shan, Helen, 2984
Shanahan, Lauri, 1059
Shanahan, Mike, 3054
Shanahan, William, 3960
Shane, Julianna, 3687
Shane, Julie, 3687
Shang Hai Kotoni Shoe Co. Ltd, 838
Shank, Stephen G., 3714
Shanken Communications, M., Inc., 3421
Shanken, Marvin, 3421
Shanken, Marvin R., 3421
Shanks, David, 2912
Shanks, Earl C., 933
Shanks, Eugene B., Jr., 1348
Shanks, Gloria, 3888
Shanks, Robert L., 1464
Shanler, Amy, 3581
Shannon, Bill, 1044
Shannon, David M., 2767
Shannon, Joseph, 2114
Shannon, Kathleen, 156
Shannon, Kathleen E., 156
Shannon, Kenneth, 1981
Shannon, Lynn, 3673
Shannon, Michael, 1355
Shannon, Michael E., 1830
Shannon, Michael R., 1830
Shannon, Roger D., 2098, 3445, 3596
Shannon, Steve, 1902
Shapazian, Carole J., 377
Shaper, C. Park, 2153
Shapira, David S., 344, 1287, 1571
Shapiro Family, L.P., 1319
Shapiro, Arthur, 1319
Shapiro, David, 138
Shapiro, Isaac, 347
Shapiro, Joel A., 2255
Shapiro, Larry, 3179
Shapiro, Lois, 1319
Shapiro, Marc J., 2150
Shapiro, Mark, 1508
Shapiro, Mark L., 426
Shapiro, Mark S., 847, 2876
Shapiro, Michael, 3314
Shapiro, Neal, 1532
Shapiro, Paul E., 3769
Shapiro, Randy, 2703
Shapiro, Richard G., 734
Shapiro, Robert S., 2736
Shapiro, Steven J., 1239
Shapiro, Steven L., 3478
Shapiro, Steven M., 4129
Sharbono, Randy, 3365
Sharbutt, David E., 167
Share, Hugh, 3387
Sharer, Kevin W., 780, 2744
Sharlin, Norman, 1841
Sharnas, Michael K., 3964
Sharon Steel Corp., 673
Sharp, Arthur H., 3512
Sharp, Douglas S., 1944
Sharp, Isadore, 1476
Sharp, Jaime, 3347
Sharp, Jeffrey S., 2389
Sharp, Laura Ingle, 1940
Sharp, Michael J., 2030
Sharp, Philip R., 1189
Sharp, Richard, 1437
Sharp, Victoria, 3710
Sharpe, Charleen, 2679
Sharpe, Robert F., Jr., 174
Sharpe, William F., 637
Sharpstone, Lewis, 3463
Sharratt, Steve, 746
Sharrock, Todd, 870
Shasta, Theodore, 2416
Shattock, Matt, 390
Shattock, Matthew J., 390, 3913
Shattuck, Mayo A., II, 1309
Shattuck, Mayo A., III, 679, 1533
Shattuck, Mayo, III, 1309
Shatz, Schwartz & Fentin, P.C., 3424
Shatz, Stephen A., 3424
Shaughnessy & Ahearn Co., 3425
Shaughnessy Crane Service, Inc., 3425
Shaughnessy Trust, John J., 3425
Shaughnessy, Herbert A., Jr., 3425
Shaughnessy, Jack, Sr., 3425
Shaughnessy, John J., 3425
Shaughnessy, Mary E., 3425
Shaughnessy, Michael P., 3425
Shaughnessy, Stephen A., 3425
Shave, John E., III, 3307
Shavel, Lee, 2617
Shaver, Abigail, 3648
Shaver, Jimmy, 72
Shavers, Cheryl L., 3247
Shaw's Supermarkets, Inc., 3427
Shaw, Ann C., 753
Shaw, Brad, 1842
Shaw, Daren, 1275
Shaw, Dennis M., 2947
Shaw, Gail, 771
Shaw, Gary D., 3553
Shaw, Henry, 1564
Shaw, Hewitt B., 319
Shaw, James C., 3545
Shaw, James F., 1153
Shaw, Jane E., 2434
Shaw, Jeffrey A., 3048, 3396
Shaw, Jeffrey W., 3524
Shaw, John, 3569
Shaw, Keith S., 910
Shaw, Kenneth, 744
Shaw, Kevin, 3507
Shaw, L. Edward, Jr., 2529
Shaw, Lewis W., II, 2013
Shaw, Mark R., 3522
Shaw, Minor M., 498
Shaw, Minor Mickel, 2971
Shaw, Robert, 2213
Shaw, Robert E., 3426
Shaw, Ruth G., 1160, 1161, 1183
Shawlee, Jared, 1206
Shay, James C., 2092
Shay, James P., 1481
Shay, Joseph F., 1481
Shea Co., J.F., Inc., 3428
Shea, Charles, 2212
Shea, Edmund H., Jr., 3428
Shea, James L., 3929
Shea, John A., 3317
Shea, John F., 3428
Shea, K. Stuart, 3311
Shea, Natalie, 2409
Shea, Peter, 1210
Shea, Peter H., 1210
Shea, Peter O., 3428
Shea, Peter O., Jr., 3428
Shea, Thomas, 3900
Sheahan, Casey, 2892
Sheahan, Denis K., 1927, 3242
Sheakley, William "Ozzie", 1887
Sheakley, William O., 1887
Shean, Christopher W., 2264
Shearer, Grace O., 774
Shearer, Robert K., 3913
Sheares, Bradley T., 955, 1852, 3057, 3348
Shearing, John, 1079
Shearon, Howard, 1555
Shearrow, David, 3866
Sheboygan Beverage, Inc., 2240
Sheboygan Chevy, 3291
Shechtman, Ronald H., 3073
Shedd, Jack, 1821
Shedlarz, David L., 1791, 2984
Sheean, Jack, 1083
Sheehan, Daniel J., IV, 1565
Sheehan, James M., 3709
Sheehan, James N., 1866
Sheehan, Jay, 4109
Sheehan, Joe, 2557
Sheehan, John, 2894
Sheehan, John D., 2610
Sheehan, Joseph, 2557
Sheehan, Michael, 330
Sheehan, Michael J., 1803
Sheehan, Patrick, 3653
Sheehan, Paul, 298
Sheehan, Robert C., 3470
Sheehan, Thomas, 2875
Sheehy, Eugene J., 2323
Sheehy, Maureen A., 2147
Sheen, David J., 1874
Sheer, Brick, 1074
Sheerer, Brent, 1617
Sheets, Jeff, 913
Sheets, Joseph D., 1162
Sheets, Ruth A., 1207
Sheetz, Stanton R., 1318
Sheff, Barry, 4109
Sheffield, Bill, 76
Sheffield, Martin P., 1291
Sheffield, Scott, 2981
Sheffield, Scott D., 2981
Sheffield, Susan, 1556
Shefford S. Golband Charitable Gift Annuity, 3780
Shehee, Andrew M., 2146
Shehee, Andy, 2146
Shehee, Ann Shane, 2146
Shehee, Margaret, 2146
Shehee, Margaret S., 2146
Shehee, Nell, 2146
Shehee, Nell E., 2146
Shehee, Shane, 2146
Shehee, Virginia K., 2146
Sheils, James B., 3424
Shein, Jeffries, 3069
Shein, Oded, 3572
Shekhar, Charndra, 3678
Shelby County Trust Bank, 894
Shelby, Rhonda, 1430
Sheldon, Bryan King, 2275
Sheldon, Charles H., 3649
Sheldon, Donald, 2615
Sheldon, Donald G., 2615
Sheldon, Melvin R., Jr., 3820
Sheldon, Nellie, 2615
Shelk, Stuart J., Jr., 2783
Shell Exploration & Production, 3430
Shell Oil Co., 234, 3430
Shell, Frederick E., 1183
Shell, Owen G., Jr., 2270
Sheller, Patrick M., 1214
Shelley, Adrian D., 3667
Shelley, Edward, 3900
Shelnitz, Mark A., 1623
Shelnut, J. Timothy, 2573
Shelter Mutual Insurance Co., 3431
Shelto, Audrey, 501
Shelton Cos., The, 3432
Shelton, Charles M., 3432
Shelton, James, 2089
Shelton, James D., 2807, 3931
Shelton, Paul G., 1219
Shelton, R. Edwin, 3432
Shelton, Ralph K., 1396
Shelton, Steve, 3547
Shelton, Thomas M., 2063
Shenandoah Telecommunications Co., 3434
Shenker, Joseph, 3634
Shennan, James G., Jr., 3585
Shenton, Robert, 1548
Shepard, Charles E., 2461
Shepard, Donald C., 2461
Shepard, Donald C., III, 2461
Shepard, Donald J., 997, 2996, 2997, 3802
Shepard, Kathy, 1812
Shepard, Michael, 3386
Shepard, Michael B., 3386
Shepard, Randall T., 2798
Shepard, Timothy C., 2461
Shepard, William R., 853
Shephard, Edward, 2693
Shephard, Walter A., 1564

Shepherd, Constance D., 1669
Shepherd, Danny R., 3972
Shepherd, J. Michael, 346
Shepherd, Michael T., 1053
Shepherd, Mike, 1053
Sheppard, J. Joseph, 4135
Sheppard, James, 954
Sheppard, Valarie L., 3055
Sheptor, John C., 1922
Sheraton Chicago Hotel & Towers, 1634
Sheraton Corp., The, 3589
Sherbin, David M., 1071
Sherbrooke, Ross E., 1450
Sherburne, Jane, 344
Shere, Charles, 2865
Sherer, Marcia, 2200
Sherer, Marcie, 657
Sheridan, Brian, 3994
Sheridan, Joseph, 3979
Sherin, Keith, 2649
Sherin, Keith S., 1552
Sherman, Deanna S., 1051
Sherman, George, 39
Sherman, Harold L., 1655
Sherman, Jeff D., 1738
Sherman, Jeffrey B., 521
Sherman, Jeffrey S., 398
Sherman, Jeffrey W., 2270
Sherman, John Q., II, 3576
Sherman, John, Jr., 78
Sherman, L. J., 2426
Sherman, Mark, 2991
Sherman, Mark T., 3404
Sherman, Merrill, 491
Sherman, Merrill W., 349
Sherman, Michael, 1561
Sherman, Michael B., 1209
Sherman, Patrick A., 1410
Sherman, Peter C., 337
Sherman, Richard, 1172
Sherman, Roy, 2426
Sherman, Scott D., 99
Sherman, Spencer, 9
Sherman, Steve, 1655
Shern, Stephanie M., 1530, 3372
Sherrell, Lori, 98
Sherrill, Gregg M., 3715
Sherrill, Henry F., 1395
Sherwin, Stephen A., 465
Sherwin, Tim, 3052
Sherwin-Williams Co., The, 3437
Sherwood, Ann E., 2073
Sherwood, Lynne, 2073
Sherwood, Mark F., 2073
Sherwood, Michael S., 1603, 1604
Sheubrooks, Muriel W., 2971
Shewmake, Charles W., 618
Shewmaker, Adam, 1053
Shi, Christiana, 4037
Shi, David E., 2971
Shibata, Christa, 2649
Shibata, Christy Rupert, 3893
Shibuya, Toshifumi, 3639
Shick, Clinton, 506
Shick, Relda M., 1490
Shide, Charles F., 3878
Shields, Brian J., 2500
Shields, J.V., Jr., 1446
Shields, James D., 1171
Shields, Richard, 3108
Shields, Sterlin, 3525
Shields, Susan L., 2513
Shiely, John S., 565, 2833, 3091
Shiga, Shigenori, 4049
Shigemura, Dean Y., 342
Shih, Clara, 3585
Shih, Daniel T., 233
Shilo Inn, 723
Shimada, Minoru, 347
Shimizu, Hiroyuki, 2768
Shimizu, Kazuo, 2144
Shin, Hak Cheol, 3, 3077
Shin, Jeannie, 554
Shinagawa, Michihisa, 3639
Shinall, Heather, 4006
Shindler, Steven M., 2709
Shine, Kenneth I., 3884
Shinichiro, Sean F., 2087
Shinkle, Debra A., 1770
Shinn & Assocs., George, Inc., 2678
Shinn, Bryan A., 3840
Shinn, Chad, 2678
Shinn, Chris, 2678
Shinn, George, 2678
Shinn, Sheryl L., 1713
Shinn, Stephanie A., 377
Shinn, Tim, 2684
Shiota, Renee, 1549
Shiozaki, Richard, 1088
Shipley, Scott, 2552
Shipp, George, 3368
Shiraki, Seiji, 2539
Shirato, Hideki, 2542
Shircel, Diana L., 2993
Shire, Willow B., 3765
Shirk, Christopher C., 1162
Shirk, Richard D., 171
Shirley, Edward D., 3755
Shirley, James N., 930
Shirley, Marvin, 3116
Shirley, Michael J., 504
Shirley, Nelson D., 930
Shirley, Richard, 923
Shiroishi, Beth, 273
Shirrell, Angela R., 2608
Shive, Dunia A., 406
Shivell, Joseph, 7
Shiver, Allen L., 1446
Shivery, Charles W., 2737, 3075
Shlansky Free Loan Fund of BMG, 2597
Shlanta, Paul R., 57
Shneiderman, Jennifer, 1072
Shoaf, Debra, 1203
Shoaff, Thomas M., 4015
Shoemaker, Alvin V., 1895
Shoemaker, Anne M., Jr., 2847
Shoemaker, Edwin J., 2205
Shoemaker, Loren P., 1743
Shoen, Edward J., 3833
Shoji, Kazumasa, 3638
Shonka, Jeffrey, 1408
Shonka, Jeffrey A., 1408
Shontere, James G., 3428
Shoop, Randall A., 3075
Shoptaw, Robert L., 240
Shoquist, Debora, 2767
Shore, Maria, 2859
Shore, Melissa, 3581
Shore, Paul, 2366
Shore, William, 1588
Shorer, Teri L., 15
Shores, Thomas H., Jr., 840
Shorman, Gary, 495
Shorman, Gary D., 495
Shorr, E. Jack, 910
Short, Adam, 2309
Short, Andrea G., 2
Short, Barb, 3103
Short, Brian P., 3235
Short, Doris, 2816
Short, Ed, 72
Short, Gary F., 3394
Short, John, 2154
Short, Marianne, 367, 691
Short, Marianne D., 1157
Short, Michael J., 292
Short, Rick A., 1281
Short, Steve, 240
Shotley, Marsha, 496
Shott, John C., 2022
Shott, Michael R., 2022
Shott, Scott H., 2022
Shotts, Gerald, 748
Shou, Cecilia, 3051
Shou, Gen Chu ("Celia"), 3051
Shou, Philip M., 3051
Shoupe, Tom, 1851
Shouse, Clark L., 1417
Shouse, Clark L., Jr., 1417
Shouse, Clark, Jr., 1417
Shoval, Susan W., 1799
Shoven, John B., 646
Showers, Mark E., 3179
Shrack, Jordan, 3347
Shrader, Ralph W., 525
Shreiber, Nick, 669
Shrensky, Lewis F., 1471
Shreve, Robert, 939
Shribert, Mitch, 487
Shriram, K. Ram, 1613
Shriver, Michael F., 340
Shrontz, Frank, 367
Shropshire, Ronald T., 1644
Shtohryn, Dmytro, 1422
Shubilla, Stan, 3559
Shuey, John H., 936
Shuffler, Eric B., 1863
Shuford Development, Inc., 3441
Shuford Industries, Inc., 3441
Shuford, A. A., II, 3441
Shuford, C. H., 3441
Shuford, C. Hunt, Jr., 3441
Shuford, H. F., Jr., 3441
Shugak, Alex, Sr., 2797
Shugart Enterprises, LLC, 3442
Shugart Management Inc., 3442
Shugart, Grover F., Jr., 3442
Shugart, Kay W., 3442
Shugert, Wendy, 1320
Shula, Donald F., 1147
Shuler, Dennis W., 2120
Shulman, Irving J., 1019
Shulman, William, 3097
Shulruff, Stuart P., 2101
Shultz, Charles E., 2695
Shultz, George P., 1582
Shumaker, Gregory M., 2058
Shuman, Catherine E., 476
Shuman, Eric, 1869
Shuman, Jeffrey S., 1736
Shuman, Stanley S., 2700
Shumate, Alex, 2277, 3488
Shumway, Dave, 251
Shupp, Darby E., 216
Shupper, Judi E., 2291
Shur, Irwin M., 2356
Shure Manufacturing Corp., 3443
Shurick, Pricilla J., 2969
Shurte, Matthew R., 2216
Shuster, George W., 972
Shutzer, William A., 3750
SI Financial Group, Inc., 3444
Siadek, Leona Egeland, 1139
Sian, Sati, 1924
Sias, Thelma A., 4093
Sibert, Bob, 541
Sibert, Robert L., 541
Siboni, Roger S., 646
Sica, Frank V., 2041, 2181
Sicarddi, Tom, 3210
Sicchitano, Kenton J., 2481, 2939
Sichterman, Janet R., 2129
Siddle, Phil, 3567
Siddons, Ernest G., 186
Siddons, Mary Beth, 1818
Sidener Supply Co., 3445
Sidener, L.E., II, 3445
Sides, Delores C., 1971
Sidlik, Thomas W. SidlikThomas W., 1071
Sidon, Kenneth, 2448
Sidwell Materials, Inc., 3447
Sidwell, Adam, 3447
Sidwell, David H., 1349
Sidwell, Jeffrey, 3447
Sidwell, Jeffrey R., 3447
Sidwell, Jennie, 3447
Siebels, Keith, 2840
Siebels, Scott A., 411
Siebert, Lori A., 930
Siefert, James J., 1220
Siegel, Dana, 3181
Siegel, Deborah, 1685
Siegel, Henry, 3763
Siegel, Howard J., 853
Siegel, Irwin A., 2225
Siegel, Jason, 2676
Siegel, Jeff, 2523
Siegel, Jerome, 3763
Siegel, Jerome A., 3763
Siegel, Kenneth, 3589
Siegel, Kenneth S., 3589
Siegel, Laurie A., 751
Siegel, Morris J., 4066
Siegel, Nathan, 3016
Siegel, Ruth, 3763
Siegel, Sally R., 2851
Siegel, William J., 2851
Siegele, Stephen H., 1494
Siegert, P. Eric, 2070
Siegmund, Jan, 291
Sielak, George, 234
Sieloff, Paul, 3113
Siemens Corp., 3448
Siemon, George, 4066
Siener, Kimberly, 779
Sierks, Kevin J., 551
Sierra Alloys, 3449
Sierra Electric Cooperative, Inc., 3450
Sierra Pacific Industries, 3451
Sierra Pacific Resources, 2765
Sievers, Mary B., 2136
Sievers, Scott, 1846
Sievert, Frederick J., 857, 3179
Sieving, Charles E., 1443
Siewert, Patrick T., 2556
Siewert, Patrick Thomas, 297
SIFCO Industries, Inc., 3452
Sifferlen, Ned J., 1047
Sigafus, David, 1254
Sigal, Elliott, 578, 2443
Sigefried, Peter, 743
Sigel, John D., 936
Sigler, Mary Ann, 1095, 3293
Sigler, Rose, 1984
Sigloh, David, 615

Skinner, James A., 1916, 3981
Skinner, James E., 2657
Skinner, Paul W., 3475
Skinner, Randy, 1136
Skinner, Samuel, 1313
Skinner, Steven K., 2124
Skipper, Michael, 4127
Skjodt, Cindy Simon, 2852
Sklarsky, Frank S., 3025
Skogen, Mark, 1651
Skogen, Mark D., 1651
Skogland, Dennis, 2702
Skoglund, Peter, 980
Skogman, Kyle D., 3869
Skokan, Michael, 1900
Skolits, Adele M., 3434
Skonberg, Lorena, 2184
Skopil, Trace, 2581
Skornicka, Carol N., 3167
Skott, Allen, 159
Skowronski, Walter E., 3904
Skube, Dorothy, 103
Skube, Frank A., 2914
Skyler, Edward, 821
Slade, Colin, 3706
Slade, Jennifer K., 2179
Slade, Michael B., 3144
Slagle, Dennis, 3968
Slant/Fin Corp., 3477
Slark, Martin P., 2265, 2740
Slarsky, Stephen M., 2734
Slater, Richard J., 2106
Slater, Rodney E., 2094
Slater, Rodney Earl, 3936
Slater, Todd A., 2801
Slater, Tom, 2139
Slattery, Frank P., Jr., 2342
Slattery, James A., 1933
Slattery, John T., 1884
Slaughter, David, 3491
Slaughter, David W., 3491
Slaughter, Ken, 3506
Slaughter, Staci, 3324
Slaughter, William M., 1748
Slavik, James D., 1626
Slavinsky, Eric, 2260
Slawek, Eileen Heck, 23
Slawson, Stephen B., 1981
Slcap Head Start, 1538
Sledd, Robert C., 2841
Sledge, Charles M., 667
Sleeth, Mike, 350
Slepper, Eillen, 2474
Slevin, Colum, 2316
Slevin, Eileen T., 2688
Slezak, Edward, 46
Slezak, Edward M., 46
Slider, Robert, 1401
Slifer, Scott, 1995
Slifka, Alfred A., 1593
Slifka, Andrew, 1593
Slifka, Eric, 1593
Slifka, Richard, 1593
Slifstein, Barry M., 3278
Sliker, Chuck, 228
Slipsager, Henrik C., 565
Slivia, Raymond, 442
Slivka, Rich, 2906
Sliwkowski, Mary, 1549
Sloan, Hugh W., Jr., 3534
Sloan, Maceo K., 3346
Sloan, Melissa K., 1274
Sloan, O. Temple, Jr., 1800
Sloan, R.B., 2914
Sloan, Randy, 3522
Sloan, Robert, 1280
Sloan, Steve W., 495
Sloan, Sue, 3025
Sloan, Timothy J., 4028
Sloane, Deck S., 231
Sloane, Edward G., 2929
Slobodow, Brian, 3840
Slocum, David, 1158
Slominsky, Jack, 633
Slone, Deck S., 231
Slosberg, Mark, 1048
Slotnik, Joseph J., 583
Slutzky, Paul, 341
Sluzewski, Jim, 2333
Smach, Thomas, 984
Smagley, Norman, 2437
Small Business Service Bureau, Inc., 703
Small, Glenn R., 2323
Small, Larry K., 29
Small, Lawrence M., 804, 2383
Small, Michael J., 1413
Smalley, Gary, 1448
Smallpage, Benton, 1156
Smallpage, Charlotte Favrot, 1156
Smallpage, Jack L., 1156
Smallpage, John Benton, III, 1156
Smallpage, John Benton, Jr., 1156
Smallpage, Kathryn Carrere, 1156
Smallpage, Kathryn F., 1156
Smarr, Karen J., 542
Smart, David, 2917
Smart, George M., 328, 1424
Smart, Joyce, 456
SMBC Capital Markets, Inc., 3480
Smeby, Jason L., 1535
Smelter Service Corp., 3481
Smeltser, Jeremy, 3558
Smeltzer, David P., 222
Smickley, Robert J., 4092
Smidt, Carsten R., 3418
Smidt, Jonathan D., 1273
Smigelski, Alex, 1191
Smiley, Beverly L.P., 313
Smiley, Keith R., 3278
Smiley, Walter, 3514
Smirnov, Maxim, 82
Smit, Neil, 2625
Smith Construction, C.D., Inc., 3483
Smith Corp., A.O., 3484
Smith Corp., J M, 3485
Smith County State Bank & Trust Co., 3482
Smith, Abbie J., 1817, 3292
Smith, Adam, 1668
Smith, Alexander W., 2973
Smith, Alison, 389
Smith, Allen C., 1805
Smith, Angela, 2372
Smith, Anne Shen, 3405
Smith, Barbara, 859
Smith, Barbara R., 893
Smith, Benson F., 3707
Smith, Bonnie L., 3344
Smith, Brad D., 1982
Smith, Bradford L., 2501
Smith, Brain J., 3996
Smith, Brian, 2691
Smith, Brian J., 3996
Smith, Bruce, 1078
Smith, Bruce M., 3484
Smith, Bruce R., 1078
Smith, Cathy, 2125, 3980
Smith, Cece, 2973
Smith, Charles, 499
Smith, Christopher B., 2481
Smith, Claire H., 3649
Smith, Clarence H., 2847
Smith, Clint, 3679
Smith, Clyde W., Jr., 3667
Smith, Colleen Savage, 3341
Smith, Craig R., 2841
Smith, D. Scarborough, III, 3480
Smith, Dan F., 935
Smith, Daniel, 1359
Smith, Daniel C., Ph.D., 3458
Smith, Daniel T., 2842
Smith, Darnell, 493
Smith, David, 3552
Smith, David B., 1888, 1927, 3242
Smith, David B., Jr., 1916
Smith, David Donnan, 2188
Smith, David F., 2628
Smith, David H. B., Jr., 2740
Smith, David J.H., 2600
Smith, David L., 1200
Smith, David, II, 1266
Smith, Dean, 1520
Smith, DeForest W., 2513
Smith, DeMaunce, 2626
Smith, DeMaurice, 2627
Smith, Don, 2608
Smith, Donald, 3832
Smith, Donald E., 1555
Smith, Donna D., 71
Smith, Doug, 448, 3896
Smith, Douglas L., 3896
Smith, E. Follin, 1125, 3292
Smith, Elizabeth A., 487, 3581
Smith, Ellen M., 3797
Smith, Erron, 3980
Smith, Floyd, 3527
Smith, Frank, 1688
Smith, Frank A., 1688
Smith, Frank S., III, 525
Smith, Frederick W., 1352
Smith, Gary L., 907
Smith, Gary M., 3483
Smith, Gary W., 338
Smith, Geoffrey A., 3031
Smith, Gerald B., 935
Smith, Gibson, 2024
Smith, Gordon A., 798, 3879
Smith, Grady, 72
Smith, Graham V., 3318
Smith, Gregory, 516
Smith, Gregory C., 2237
Smith, Gregory H., 2551
Smith, Gregory L., 1612
Smith, Guy, 1107
Smith, H. B., 3891
Smith, Hap, 3759
Smith, Heflin, 72
Smith, Henry D., 3485
Smith, Hilary, 2002
Smith, Hudson D., 3452
Smith, Hugh C., 496
Smith, J. Albert, Jr., 3458
Smith, J. David, 893
Smith, James, 886, 1848
Smith, James B., Jr., 960
Smith, James C., 3741, 3985, 4016
Smith, James E., 720
Smith, Janice W., 3805
Smith, Jasmine, 497
Smith, Jay, 1981
Smith, Jeff, 2697
Smith, Jeffrey, 1105
Smith, Jeffrey C., 3172
Smith, Jerry, 3376
Smith, Jill D., 1268
Smith, Jim, 277
Smith, Joan H., 1907
Smith, Joanne, 221, 4160
Smith, Joanne C., 1804
Smith, Joe, 3637
Smith, John F., 1555
Smith, Joseph, 240
Smith, Joseph B., 1142
Smith, Joshua I., 107, 722, 1352
Smith, Judy, 3450
Smith, Julious P., Jr., 4078
Smith, Justin, 3483
Smith, Karen, 2412
Smith, Kaye B., 3745
Smith, Keith, 489, 597
Smith, Keith E., 546
Smith, Kelly, 2648
Smith, Kenneth W., 3873
Smith, Kevin, 1454, 2952, 3827
Smith, Kirsten D., 2991
Smith, Kyle, 3164
Smith, L. Stephen, 2995
Smith, Laura, 1081
Smith, Laura B., 2991
Smith, Laurence S., 1027
Smith, Lawrence S., 63
Smith, Lazane M., 1541
Smith, Louis A., 3890
Smith, Lowndes A., 2813
Smith, Lucy Lindsay, 3110
Smith, Lynn H., 833
Smith, M. Richard, 3904
Smith, Margaret, 3582
Smith, Mark, 66, 2287, 3331
Smith, Mark A., 66, 2550
Smith, Mark Alan, 2550
Smith, Mark D., 3484
Smith, Marquett, 733
Smith, Marshall I, 233
Smith, Martin C., 341
Smith, Mary, 3070
Smith, Mary Ann, 4033
Smith, Mary Lou, 3483
Smith, Mary Welles Mooers, 1805
Smith, Matthew, 400
Smith, Megan, 1613
Smith, Michael, 1368, 2224, 3150
Smith, Michael L., 567, 3925
Smith, Michael P., 2681
Smith, Michael T., 1941
Smith, Michelle, 360
Smith, Monica, 948
Smith, Murray D., 4077
Smith, Nate, 3756
Smith, Onnie Leach, 2461
Smith, Orin, 3585
Smith, Orin C., 1127, 2710
Smith, Otis, 2824
Smith, Pat, 1158
Smith, Patrick, 1732, 3686
Smith, Patrick S., 3483
Smith, Patty, 240
Smith, Paul E., 1837
Smith, Paul J., 3591
Smith, Paul L., 919
Smith, Peter, 176
Smith, Philip W., III, 2909
Smith, Phyllis M., 3668
Smith, Ralph, 4028
Smith, Ralph, Esq., 4028

Smith, Randolph R., 3513
Smith, Randy, 1470
Smith, Randy M., 1008
Smith, Raymond L., Jr., 3166
Smith, Richard, 1050, 2703
Smith, Richard A., 3145
Smith, Richard C., 3580
Smith, Richard F., 1288
Smith, Richard H., 1488
Smith, Richard M., 2703
Smith, Rick, 1872
Smith, Robert E., 2715, 3933
Smith, Robert H., 676
Smith, Robert Lee, 2274
Smith, Roger, 1908
Smith, Roger C., 153
Smith, Roger S., 3484
Smith, Roland, 1458
Smith, Roland C., 4030, 4031
Smith, Ronnie, 3171
Smith, Ruth M., 1872
Smith, Sarah, 131
Smith, Scott, 1699
Smith, Scott Alan, 153
Smith, Scott T., 779
Smith, Sean, 2969
Smith, Sean T., 2969
Smith, Shannon, 3189
Smith, Sharon P., 1382
Smith, Sherry M., 1061, 3659
Smith, Stacy J., 289, 1950
Smith, Stan, 288
Smith, Stepheanie, 1095
Smith, Stephen J., 149, 1668
Smith, Stephen M., 4072
Smith, Stephen P., 883, 2715
Smith, Stephen R., 188
Smith, Steve, 2738, 3177
Smith, Steve D., 1115
Smith, Steven J., 313
Smith, Stuart G., 1391
Smith, Stuart M., 3271
Smith, Susan M., 495
Smith, Suzan, 1716
Smith, Tao, 3940
Smith, Taylor, 131
Smith, Terry, 1347, 2392, 3759
Smith, Thad, 13
Smith, Tiina Bougas, 3879
Smith, Timothy A., 1054
Smith, Toby, 3703
Smith, Todd, 3664
Smith, Tom N., 3430
Smith, Turner, 942
Smith, Valerie, 3076
Smith, Vince J., 2801
Smith, Virginia L., 1441
Smith, W. Michael, 3831
Smith, Wayne T., 900, 3029
Smith, Wes, 2412
Smith, Whitney, 3162
Smith, William B., 859
Smith, William G., Jr., 676, 3516
Smith, William L., 585
Smith, William M., 1498
Smith, Wm. Randolph, 986
Smith, Yulonda, 2229
Smith, Zeke W., 71
Smith-Bogart, Karen A., 2545
Smith-Galloway, Bernice, 1317
Smith-Hams, Denise, 1549
Smith-Maclean, Joan, 3664
Smitham, Steven, 2036
Smithart-Oglesby, Debra, 1087
Smither, Nicholas J., 1464
Smithfield Foods, Inc., 3487
Smithhisler, Carolyn, 3694
SmithKline Beecham Corp., 1588
Smitley, Greg, 2379
Smitley, Gregory, 2379
Smits, Didier, 1458
Smits, Jim, 456
Smoke, Stefanie L., 996
Smokey Robinson Golf Classic, 2344
Smolan, Rick, 2711
Smolcic, Barry, 66
Smolenski, Don, 888, 2958
Smolenski, Donald, 2958
Smolenski, Eric M., 4124
Smoley, David E., 1437
Smoliga, Joseph, Jr., 3692
Smolik, Brent J., 1239
Smolski, Michael, 88
Smolyansky, Edward P., 2272
Smolyansky, Julie, 2272
Smolyansky, Ludmila, 2272
Smoncini, Mathew J., 2237
Smouse, H. Russell, 334
Smucker Co., J.M., The, 3488
Smucker, James, 468
Smucker, John E., II, 468
Smucker, John E., Jr., 468
Smucker, Mark T., 3488
Smucker, Richard K., 3437, 3488
Smucker, Timothy P., 3488
Smulders, Patrick, 3781
Smulekoff Furniture Co., 3489
Smulekoff Investment Co., 3489
Smulyan, Jeffrey H., 1259
Smylie, Sally, 2164
Smyre, Calvin, 3674
Smyth, D. Edward I., 2429
Smyth, Sylvia, 1070
Snabe, Jim Hagemann, 3334
Snapper, Suzanne D., 1275
Snead, Cheryl W., 183, 349
Snead, Rayner V., III, 3194
Snead, Rayner V., Jr., 3194
Sneden, Curtis, 871
Sneed, Norris P., 1213
Sneed, Paula A., 65, 3363
Sneed, R. Wayne, 3725
Sneed, Robert W., 3725
Sneed, Thomas K., 2364
Snell & Wilmer L.L.P., 3490
Snell, Dylan, 3940
Snell, Mark A., 3405
Snell, William E., Jr., 1336
Snelling, Gretchen E., 1885
Snetsinger, Robert J., 3653
Snider, Beth, 2620
Snider, Edward, 2957, 2959
Snider, Edward M., 888
Snider, John D., 231
Snider, Stephen A., 1270
Snively, David F., 2559
Snow, Christensen & Martineau, 3491
Snow, David B., Jr., 2984
Snow, Elizabeth, 7
Snow, John W., 171, 2365
Snow, Swanson, 2730
Snowsky, Mishka, 1319
Sny, Shawn, 1196
Snyder, Cheryl L., 2881
Snyder, Daniel M., 3054
Snyder, David, 2528
Snyder, Donald D., 2765, 3826
Snyder, Gail, 410
Snyder, James C., Jr., 1330
Snyder, James T., 2782
Snyder, K. Michael, 2704
Snyder, Maria, 173
Snyder, Paul L., 3389
Snyder, Randy, Jr., 1719
Snyder, Richard D., 1541
Snyder, Samuel, 3084
Snyder, Wallace S., 3914
Snyder, William W., 1281
Sobel, Andrea, 3313
Sobic, Dan, 2850
Soboleff, Vicki, 3380
Sobon, Leslie, 40
Sobon, Michael, 792
Soccodato, David, 2633
Socha, Scott, 1066
Society Capital Corp., 2136
Society Corp., 2136
Sockwell, Oliver R., 1155
Socorro Electric Cooperative, Inc., 3496
Soden, Jack R., 3038
Soderberg, Jess, 804
Soderlund, Clea Newman, 2697
Soderstrom, S. Carl, Jr., 4039
Sodexho Marriott Services, Inc., 3497
Sodexho, Inc., 3497
Soeters, Martin H., 999
Soffer, Robert M., 3253
Sofia, Zuheir, 2216
Sohi, Mohsen M., 3600
Sohn, Young K., 646, 1016
Soiland, Marlene K., 1306
Soileau, Linda, 34
Soin, Rajesh K., 1112
Soiron, Rolf, 230
Sokol, David L., 2504
Sokol, John S., 1149
Sokoloff, Jonathan D., 4066
Sokolov, Jacque J., 1867
Sokolov, Richard S., 3458
Sokolov, Stephen B., 2255
Sokolow, Stephen, 2255
Sokolow, Stephen B., 2255
Sokulski, Gary A., 3163
Solazzo, Mark J., 2736
Solberg, Jeff, 1674
Solberg, Jeffrey M., 1674
Solcher, Stephen B., 508
Solender, Michael S., 1293
Solheim, Jostein, 409
Soliday, Lance A., 1311
Solis, Jennifer, 1238
Solis, Pablo Albendea, 3227
Solitro, Mark, 538
Soljacich, Bob, 2229
Solley, L.W., 1296
Solmssen, Peter Y., 3448
Solomon, Darlene, 56
Solomon, Howard, 1468
Solomon, Sheila, 788
Solomon, Steven J., 1309
Solow, Mark G., 2782
Solso, Theodore M., 328, 1007, 1555
Solt, Russell, 460
Somerhalder, John W., II, 57
Somers, Daniel E., 804
Somers, David M., 3194
Somers, John A., 1683
Someya, Mitsuo, 2144
Somke, Doug, 1339
Somma, Tony, 4039
Sommer, Alfred, 398
Sommer, Alfred, Dr., 3040
Sommer, Anthony, 1248
Sommerhauser, Peter, 2583
Sommerhauser, Peter M., 2181, 2749
Sondergard, Dale J., 1335
Sondheim, William S., 1527
Sones, Bill, 1280
Sones, Randall D., Esq., 92
Sonic Automotive Inc., 1776
Sonkin, Mitchell, 2416
Sonlight Curriculum, Ltd., 3499
Sonnemaker, Scott A., 3677
Sonnenberg, Steven A., 3714
Sonnenfeld, Jeffrey, 2250
Sonoco Products Co., 3500
Sonsteby, Charles M., 2494
Sontrop, Mary, 993
Sony Corp. of America, 3502
Sony Electronics, Inc., 3502
SONY Playstation, 3327
Soonthornsima, Ob, 2309
Sopakco Inc., 3848
Soper, Willard, 343
Soper, Willard B., 343
Sopha, James R., 2009
Sophie Weber Trust, 3044
Sopp, Mark W., 3311
Sorckoff, Peter, 278
Sorden, Deborah, 2410
Sordoni, Andrew J., III, 222, 1741
Sorell, Thomas G., 1683
Sorensen, Jerry, 2991
Sorensen, Ken, 2329
Sorensen, Kenneth J., 2329
Sorensen, Lars Rebien, 3733
Sorensen, Vagn O., 3273
Sorenson, Arne M., 2383, 3980
Sorenson, John, 3671
Sorenson, Ralph Z., 4066
Sorge, Hans-Marti, 439
Sorgi, Cheryl L., 2879
Sorgi, Vincent, 3026
Sorley, Pippa, 1223
Soros Fellowship, Paul & Daisy, 3474
Sorrel, Lawrence B., 1259
Sorrell, Martin, 82
Sorrell, Robert W., 1926
Sorrenti, John, 2335
Sorrentino, Robert J., 439
Sosland, L. Joshua, 3846
Sosland, Morton, 926
Sosland, Morton I., 1695
Soubble, Stephen A., 2126
Soulder, Gerald, 1421
Soule, David B., Jr., 1391
Souleles, Thomas S., 2861
Soulliere, Anne-Marie, 1450
Sousa, Edward F., 562
Sousa, John P., II, 1239
Sousa, Steven M., 1481
Sousou, Ramez, 3781
South Bend Tribune Corp., 3507
South Carolina Electric & Gas Co., 3346
South Mississippi Home Health, Inc., 3509
South Shore Savings Bank, 3512
South Weymouth Savings Bank, 3512
South Weymouth Security Corp., 3512
Southcentral Foundation, 934
Southeastern Mutual Insurance Co., 3541
Southeastern Newspapers Corp., 2573
Southern Bancshares, Inc., 3515
Southern Bank & Trust Co., 3515
Southern Co., The, 3516

Southern Concrete Materials, Inc., 1768
Southern Furniture Co. of Conover, Inc., 3517
Southern Kansas Telephone Co., Inc., 3518
Southern Phenix Textiles, Inc., 2054
Southern States Brokerage, 4110
Southern Union Co., 3520
Southern Wine & Spirits of America, Inc., 3521
Southern, William B., 2310
Southstar, LP, 761
Southwest Business Corporation, 3523
Southwest Gas Corp., 3524
Southwestern Bell Corp., 273
Southworth, A. S., 3982
Soutter, Anne, 3045
Soutus, Sonya, 862
Souza, Paul M., 3383
Sovereign Bank, 3528
Sovey, Mara L., 1061
Sovine, Robert L., 2364
Sowalsky, Jerome, 1355
Sowar, Gerard D., 3576
Sowers, George, 4110
Soyster, Margaret Blair, 849
Space Mark Inc., 84
Spackler, Keith, 55
Spadafor, Christine J., 546
Spadafora, Charles A., 3297
Spadoni, Julia S., 447
Spadoni-Urquhart, Brenda L., 447
Spadorcia, Doreen, 3802
Spagnol, Tracy E., 381
Spagnoletti, Christopher, 2185
Spagnoletti, Joseph, 2185
Spagnoletti, Joseph C., 669
Spagnoletti, Maria, 2185
Spagnoletti, Mark, 2185
Spagnoletti, Paul, 2185
Spagnoletti, Richard, 2185
Spahn & Rose Lumber Co., Inc., 3529
Spain, Kent, 470
Spain, Tara N., 3802
Spain, Tim, 2483
Spain, Timothy G., 3869
Spain, W. J., Jr., 470
Spampinato, Gregory W., 341
Spandau, Michael, 1359
Spang and Co., 3530
Spangler Candy Co., 3531
Spangler, Dean L., 3531
Spann, Lucy, 1192
Spann, Stephen, 1192
Spanos, Alexander G., 3322
Spanos, Dean, 3322
Spanos, Dean A., 3322
Spar, Debora L., 1603, 1604
Sparaco, Jim, 3327
Sparkman, J.C., 2263
Sparkman, Janet, 3659
Sparks, Annette M., 395
Sparks, D. Shannon, 3414
Sparks, David, 2139
Sparks, Gary, 1735
Sparks, Ray Anthony, 1411
Sparks, William B., 3826
Spartan Motors, Inc., 3534
Spartan Stores, Inc., 3535
Spass, Robert A., 3887
Spatafora, Thomas, 3014
Spatz, D. Dean, 3453
Spaulding, Jean G., 685
Spaulding, Richard M., 3358
Speakes, Steve, 3873
Spear Pharmaceuticals, Inc., 3536
Spear, Jayne, 3536
Spear, K. L., 3536
Spear, K.L., 3536
Spears, Arthur C., 1208
Spears, Ronald E., 273
Spears, Stuart, 3716
Spears, Will D., 2312
Specht, Brian, 2247
Specht, Sandy, 954
Specht, William, 954
Specht, William F., 954
Specialty Manufacturing Co., The, 3537
Specker, Steven R., 3516
Specketer, Thomas B., 2504
Spector Gadon & Rosen, P.C., 3539
Spector, Alfred, 1613
SpectraCare, Inc., 3541
Speed, Jeffrey R., 4121
Speed, Leland R., 1082
Speed, Robert, 909
Speer, David B., 1916
Speer, John F., III, 1252
Speer, Phyllis, 2738
Speetzen, Mike, 4139
Speicher, Charles A., 2469
Speight, William, 179
Speirn, Sterling K., 2120
Speiser, Andy, 2957
Speiser, Anthony, 3730
Speiser, Anthony E., 3730
Speiser, Christine, 3730
Spell, Randy B., 2304
Spellings, J. M., 1315
Spellings, Margaret, 216
Spellman-Pollard, Latanya, 46
Spelts, Teresa, 3266
Spelts, Teresa A., 3266
Speltz, James M., 586
Spence Accounts, Inc., 3542
Spence, Benet, 3274
Spence, Benjamin, 3542
Spence, Kenneth F., III, 3802
Spence, Nash, 3542
Spence, Ralph, 3542
Spence, Ralph, III, 3542
Spence, Ralph, Jr., 3542
Spence, Tancy W., 3542
Spence, William H., 3026
Spencer, Amy, 1049
Spencer, Carlton, 2486
Spencer, Christina, 2802
Spencer, Craig, 53
Spencer, Irish, 2229
Spencer, James, 2162
Spencer, Janelle, 1049
Spencer, Jason, 1049
Spencer, Jim, 1767
Spencer, John, 1049
Spencer, John W., 1049
Spencer, Kathelen, 54
Spencer, Laura, 1049
Spencer, Michael, 3980
Spencer, Richard A., III, 333
Spencer, Robert (Bob) S., 320
Spencer, Steve R., 71
Spencer, Terry K., 2815
Spendlove, G. Scott, 3723
Spengeman, Craig C., 2909
Spengler, William F., 1268
Speranza, Paul S., Jr., 4021
Sperber, Cliff, 2689
Sperduti, Bruno, 1426
Sperling, Jac, 2531
Sperling, John G., 216
Sperling, Peter V., 216
Sperling, Scott M., 3733
Spero, Joan E., 821, 1960, 1968
Sperry, William R., 1879
Spherion, 1131
Spiegel, Eric A., 3448
Spiegel, John W., 3239
Spiegel, Noel J., 140
Spiegel, Steven M., 3172
Spiel, Eric J., 1781
Spierkel, Gregory M.E., 2850
Spies, Allan R., 3747
Spies, Gary J., 2836
Spieser, Matthew B., 3730
Spikes, Jesse J., 3066
Spilka, Susan, 4072
Spille, Kent W., 987
Spillman, Brenda L., 2628
Spilman, Robert H., Jr., 372, 1150
Spinazzo, Gary, 2619
Spinella, Mary, 1314
Spinello, John J., 2734
Spirit Mountain Gaming, Inc., 3544
Spiro, Richard G., 804
Spirol International Corp., 3545
Spiropoulos, Chris, 387
Spitz, C. A., 3981
Spitz, William T., 2397
Spitzberg, Marian, 406
Spivey, William R., 2214, 3135
Splaine, Thomas F., Jr., 1984
Splinter, Michael R., 220, 2617
Spolan, Harmon, 964
Sponem, Sandy, 2577
Spongberg, Roland C., 4100
Spongberg, Sandra, 4100
Sponholz, Joseph G., 1880
Spoon, Alan G., 1027, 1903
Spooner, Craig, 2257
Spoor, John, 253
Sports & Fitness Insurance Corp., 3547
Sports Club Co., Inc., The, 3550
Spotanski, Michael R., 2207, 2208
Spotanski, Micheal R., 2207
Spoto, Angelo, Jr., 4006
Spotts, Steve, 1987
Spradlin, James, 1674
Spradling, Mark R., 3957
Sprague, Charles W., 1427
Sprague, Derek, 2953
Sprague, Joseph, 74
Sprague, Michael, 2140
Sprague, Robert E., 1392
Sprague, Steven, 4155
Sprangers, Lynn, 2527
Spratlen, Susan A., 2981
Spratt, Randall N., 2434
Spray, Donna & Ed, 3374
Spray, Jane, 276
Spray, Steve, 2482
Sprecher, Ralph B., 3865
Sprieser, Judith A., 107
Spriggs, Otha T. "Ski"p, III, 540
Spriggs, Ray, 1668
Spring, Tony, 488
Springer Electric Cooperative, Inc., 3553
Springer, Barbara, 878, 1143
Springer, Barbara B., 878
Springer, Donald, 2104
Springer, Eileen, 2984
Springer, Stephen R., 285
Springer, Virginia B., 428
Springfield Lorton Dental Group, 138
Sprint Communications Co., LP, 3556
Sprint Corp., 3556
Sprint Nextel Corp., 3556
Spross, Jaci, 3673
Sproule, Michael E., 2688
Sproule, Simon, 2716
Sprouls, John, 3889
Sprouls, John R., 3889
Spruill, Rod, 29
Spudowski, Gloria, 3956
Spurck, Fredric C., 4018
Spurgeon, Allen, 3584
Spurr, John H., 3242
Spurr, John H., Jr., 1927
SPX Corp., 3558
Spychala, Darlene A., 2323
Spychala, Darlene R., 2323
Spychala, Michael R., 2323
Spyropoulos, Christos, 387
Spyropoulos, Stella, 387
SQA Pharmacy Services, LLC, 3559
Square D Co., 3560
Squeri, Stephen J., 143, 1683
Squibb & Sons, E.R., Inc., 578
Squibb & Sons, E.R., L.L.C., 578
Squier, David L., 3410
Squillante, Judith, 3332
Squires, James A., 2725
Sraberg, Bradley, 1328
Sraberg, Candace M., 1328
Sraberg, Gerald, 1328
Sraberg, Gerald A., 1328
Sraberg, Ilene, 1328
Srabian, Bryan, 3304
Srigley, Kevin, 1571
Srinivasan, Krishna, 1995
Srinivasan, Raj, 297
Srivastava, Alok, 382
Srivastava, Gautam, 2314
SRP Federal Credit Union, 2573
St. Angelo, Steve, 3784
St. Clair, Charles, 3673
St. Clair, Scott, 2692
St. Cyr, Kevin, 423
St. Francis Electric, 1570
St. George, Nicholas J., 2245
St. George, Peter, 510
St. James, Phillip, 3329
St. Jean, Phil S., 3804
St. John Knits, 3564
St. John Properties, Inc., 3565
St. John, Edward, 3565
St. John, Edward A., 3565
St. John, Emmett, 1604
St. John, Emmett C., 1603
St. John, Jonelle, 3434
St. John, Kellay, 3565
St. Jude Children's Research Hospital, 2270
St. Jude Medical, Inc., 3566
St. Juste, Robes, 613
St. Leger, Judy, 3387
St. Mary's Hispanic Ministry, 1675
St. Maurice, Louis M., 270
St. Onge, Timothy, 1248
St. Paul Companies, Inc., The, 3802
St. Paul Travelers Companies, Inc., The, 3802
St. Peter, David, 3827
St. Peter, David E., 3827
St. Wrba, John A., 928
Staab, John, 4043
Staab, Valari, 2649

Staat, Stacy, 3402
Staats, Paul, 2515
Stabler, Kristine M., 807
Stach, Joseph, 306
Stachler, Eric, 1894
Stachura, Paul, 1385
Stack, Edward W., 1110
Stack, Larry J., 726
Stackhouse, Brenda M., 3743
Stackhouse, Lucinda, 234
Stackhouse, Tom, 72
Stacy, Clyde, 3127
Stacy, Lee, 3165
Stadler, Mary K., 2094
Stadtmauer Bailkin LLP, 3570
Stadtmueller, Gerald, 2240
Staebler, Douglas A., 3997
Stafast Products, Inc., 3571
Stafeil, Jeff, III, 3964
Stafeil, Jeffrey M., 1195
Staff, Joel V., 2153
Staffieri, Victor A., 2260
Stafford, Dan, 2455
Stafslien, Joan B., 688
Staggs, Philip W., 612
Staglin, Garen K., 3455
Stagner, R. Stephen, 2407
Stagner, Steve, 2407
Stahl, Dale E., 127
Stahl, Jack J., 1169
Stahl, Jack L., 1458, 3315
Stahl, Lee J., 3185
Stahl, Wayne, 3573
Stainton, Mary, 3509
Stair., Richard C., 4157
Stake, James B., 2836, 3235
Stakel, John D., 3239
Staley, John C., 1867
Staley, Robert A., 1118
Staley, Warren R., 2850
Stalfort, John A., 2512
Stalippi, Jeanette, 1776
Staller, Alan, 664
Stallings, Faye L., 1239
Stallings, Norm, 2691
Stallings, Virginia A., 1030
Stallkamp, Thomas T., 377, 528
Staluppi, John, 1776
Stamas, George, 2280
Stamatopoulos, Stefanie, 287
Stamey, James R., 1843
Stamp, Charles R., Jr., 1061
Stamp, Darrell, 2714
Stamp, Scott, 2345
Stamper, Robert, 2257
Stamps, Jeffrey M., 2807
Stanage, Nick L., 1795
Stanbrook, Steven P., 795
Stancati, Joe, 1026
Stancorp Financial Group, Inc., 3574
Stanczak, Michael E., 2402
Standard Motor Products, Inc., 3575
Standard Products Co., The, 936
Standard Register Co., The, 3576
Standard Tube Co., 2138
Standiford, Jessica, 1769
Standland, David, 1118
Standley, Don, 1437
Standley, John, 2622
Standley, John T., 2894, 3220, 3659
Stanek Tool Corp., 3578
Stanek, Mary Ellen, 317, 2749, 4093
Stanford, Donald, 1677
Stanford, Mike, 3109
Stanford, Wayne T., 3207
Stang, Debbie, 2505
Stange, Lisa A., 1264
Stangeby, Alison, 2684
Staniar, Burton B., 2176
Stanisich, Tedd, 2979
Stanko, Ellen A., 3683
Stanland, David J., 1118
Stanley Consultants, Inc., 3580
Stanley, Heidi B., 301
Stanley, Joan, 1657
Stanley, John D., 63
Stanley, Kelly N., 2798
Stanley, Kenneth, 1657
Stanley, Nancy, 1657
Stanley, Robert A., 1118
Stanley, Susan D., 2928
Stansfield, Nigel, 1953
Stansik, Jim, 1151
Stanton, Domna, 4122
Stanton, Donna, 4122
Stanton, James, 4122
Stanton, Jim, 4122
Stanton, Julie A., 2197
Stanton, Kathryn A., 1455
Stanton, Michael, 4122
Stanton, Oliver K., 3796
Stanton, Paul E., 507
Stanton, Paul E., Jr., 507
Stanton, Ronald P., 3796
Stanzione, Dan C., 3103
Stapler, Howard, 3348
Staples, David M., 3535
Staples, Inc., 3581
Staples, Mitchell D., 3861
Stapleton, Craig R., 17
Stapleton, Steven, 2274
Stapley, Gregory K., 1275
Star Holdings, Inc., 3582
Star Industries, Inc., 3583
Star Ledger, 3205
Star Liquor Imports, Inc., 3583
Star Lumber & Supply Co., Inc., 3584
Star Technologies, Inc., 3582
Star Tribune Co., The, 2422
Star, Frank, 3860
Starbucks Coffee Co., 3585
Starbucks Corp., 3585
Stark, Arthur, 399
Stark, Brian Jay, 2371
Stark, C. Richard, Jr., 1388
Stark, Jeffrey S., 1248
Stark, Kenneth J., 2070
Stark, Michael, 940
Stark, Ron, 2756
Stark, Scott, 1902
Starkey Laboratories, Inc., 3587
Starkey, Matt, 886
Starks, Daniel J., 3566
Starling, David L., 2094
Starr Foundation, 156
Starr, Dan, 1136
Starr, Denise, 902
Starr, Frederick B., 3737
Starr, Gary, 2703
Starr, Robert D., 2088
Starrs, Michael E., 514
Staruck, James, 3837
Starwood Hotels & Resorts Worldwide, Inc., 3589
Stasse, David, 1495
Stasyszen, Richard E., 3572
State Automobile Mutual Insurance Co., 3590
State Bank of Kirkland, 2081
State Farm Mutual Automobile Insurance Co., 3591
State of Florida, 4006
State of Wisconsin Dept. of Adm., 4093
State Street Bank & Trust Co., 3592, 3731
Staton, Jimmy D., 2715, 2739
Staubach, Roger T., 187, 2061
Stauch, John L., 2926
Staudt, Denise, 4154
Stauffer Communications, Inc., 2573
Stauffer, Jared P., 574
Stauffer, Jerry, 325
Stauffer, Larry D., 774
Stautberg, Matt, 2333
Stautberg, Timothy E., 3374
Staver, Mary, 3274
Stawski, Willard S., 502
Stayer, Jacqueline F., 2050
Stayer, Ralph C., 595
Stayton, Sean, 2297
Stea, Gregory, 999
Stead, Jerre L., 567
Stead, Jerry L., 567
Steakley, John, 1762
Stearns Lending, Inc., 3594
Stearns, Dana, 1151
Stearns, Glenn B., 3594
Stearns, Howard, 1388
Stearns, Katherine, 663
Stebbins, Donald J., 1999, 3964
Stec, Vicki, 2746
Stecher, Paul W., 3239
Stecklein, Elizabeth E., 879
Stecko, Paul T., 2861, 3591, 3715
Stedman, Jaye G., 4070
Stedman, John, 2462
Stedman, Sandy, 2038
Steeg, Jim, 3322
Steel Dynamics, Inc., 3595
Steel Technologies, Inc., 3596
Steel, G. Donald, 1382
Steel, Wade, 3476
Steelcase Inc., 3597
Steele Guilfoile, Mary J., 1974, 3916
Steele, Edward R., 2377
Steele, Finley M., 1805
Steele, Glenn D., Jr., 4024
Steele, Gordon C., 2694
Steele, John M., 1762
Steele, Lee C., 2469
Steele, Pat, 1295
Steele, Robert A., 390
Steele, Thomas A., 7
Steele, Tom, 365
Steelman, Jeff, 3688
Steen, Ida Clement, 1512
Steen, John, 283
Steen, John L., 283
Steenland, Doug, 2938, 3255
Steenland, Douglas, 3255
Steenland, Douglas M., 156, 801
Steere, William C., Jr., 1765, 2950
Steers, William C., 229
Steeves, Frank L., 1257
Stefanik, Paul W., 3732
Stefanko, Robert A., 2809
Stefanov, Kenneth E., 847
Stefanski, Ben S., III, 3732
Stefanski, Floyd E., 3735
Stefanski, Marc A., 3732, 3735
Stefanski, Mark A., 3732
Steffan, William, 1088
Steffe, Ron, 1985
Steffen, Christopher J., 1623
Steffen, Mark, 941
Steffen, Phyllis, 1668
Steffens, Ray, 1674
Steffens, Roger S., 1567, 3516
Steffes, Lorene K., 2996, 2997
Stegeman, Klaus P., 3448
Stegemann, Klaus P., 3448
Steger, Charles W., 3433
Steger, Laurie, 4084
Stegman, Joe, 148
Stehy, R. Charles, 2635
Steigerwaldt, William, 2045
Stein, Avy H., 3272
Stein, Donald L., 4046
Stein, Jeffrey S., 123
Stein, John S., 1601
Stein, John S., III, 1601
Stein, Laura, 852, 1487
Stein, Martin A., 342
Stein, Robert W., 266
Stein, Roger, 2564
Stein, Ronald J., 3401
Stein, Sheldon I., 2460
Stein, Ted, 723
Stein, Ted, Mrs., 723
Steinbauer, Thomas M., 176
Steinberg, Ben, 3514
Steinberg, Burt B., 3070
Steinberg, Gregg M., 1969
Steinberg, Joan E., 2570
Steinberg, Joseph S., 2030
Steinberg, Leonard A., 75
Steinbock, Allen F., 4054
Steinbock, Anne, 4054
Steinbock, David J., 4054
Steinbock, R. Ted, 4054
Steinbock, Stuart, 4054
Steinbrenner, Harold, 2691
Steinbrenner, Harold Z., 2691
Steinbrenner, Henry, 2691
Steinbrenner, Henry G., 2691
Steinbrenner, Jessica, 2691
Steinbrenner, Joan, 2691
Steinbrink, William H., 3488
Steiner Corp., 115
Steiner Foods Inc., 1186
Steiner, David P., 1352
Steiner, Gerald A., 2559
Steiner, Judith, 1425
Steiner, Kevin K., 115
Steiner, Lisa, 592
Steiner, Richard R., 115
Steiner, Robert C., 115
Steinert, Frank, 2922
Steines, Ann Munson, 2333
Steinfeld, Allan, 2689
Steinhafel, Gregg W., 3691, 3775
Steinhart, Ronald G., 3727
Steinhaus, David M., 2453
Steinhauser, Susan, 945
Steinhorn, Jeffery L., 1793
Steinke, Bruce, 129
Steinke, Bruce A., 128
Steinl, Michael, 1269
Steinl, Mike, 1269
Steinman, Diane, 705
Steinmann, Jennifer, 1070
Steinmetz, Arthur P., 2818
Steinmetz, Chris, 3204
Steinmetz, William, 2518
Steinour, Stephen D., 1309, 1894
Steinwall, Susan D., 1491

Stone, Carolyn J., 4120
Stone, Cathy, 1999
Stone, Cosby, 3690
Stone, Donna, 4084
Stone, Fern, 1609
Stone, Hannah, 2292
Stone, Howard L., 1609
Stone, Jesse R., 4120
Stone, John, 2013
Stone, Kathryn W., 1289
Stone, Kent, 3835
Stone, Larry, 3520
Stone, Larry D., 1110, 2312
Stone, Mary E., 454
Stone, Rafael, 3240
Stone, Rafael A., 3240
Stone, Roger W., 2427
Stone, Steve K., 2573
Stoneburner, Richard K., 2695
Stonecutter Mills Corp., 3615
Stoneham Savings Bank, 3616
Stoner, John M., Jr., 909
Stoner, Jyme, 3918
Stonesifer, Patricia Q., 122
Stoney, Janice D., 4077
Stop & Shop Supermarket Co. LLC, The, 3618
Stop & Shop Supermarket Co., The, 3618
Storbeck, Cora, 1707
Storch, Gerald, 3790
Storch, Gerald L., 3790
Storch, Gerlad L., 578
Storey, Barry L., 3674
Storey, Bruce D., 1168
Storfer, Mark, 1811
Storino, Tammy, 3564
Storm, Brian, 2711
Storm, Kornelis J., 377
Storm, William R., 2436
Stormont-Vail Foundation, 3944
Stornant, Michael D., 4106
Storper, David H., 1971
Storts, William E., 1733
Story, Charles I., 565
Story, Luanne, 2601
Story, Susan N., 1689, 2021
Storz Ophthalmics, Inc., 3526
Stotlar, Douglas, 903
Stotlar, Douglas W., 903
Stott, John P., 233
Stott, Peter W., 903
Stottlemyer, Deb, 4149
Stough, John A., Jr., 894
Stoumpas, Nick, 1903
Stout Industries, Inc., 3619
Stout, Charlotte, 2325
Stout, Coy, 1582
Stout, David M., 65, 2006
Stout, Zach, 2890
Stover, Richard L., 1291
Stover, Sean, 1627
Stovesand, Kristen, 898
Stowe, Harold C., 3346
Stowers, James E., Jr., 137
Strabley, Rich, 3011
Stracener, Dan, 3791
Strachan, Michael G., 2314
Stracke, Christian, 2573
Straight, Samuel C., 3131
Strain, Frank, 1987
Strait, Melissa, 228
Straka, Angeline C., 727
Stram, Inc., 3622
Stranahan, Ann A., 1277
Stranahan, Stephen, 1277
Strandell, Peter, 2617
Strange, J. Terry, 2695, 3478
Strange, Karla, 3944
Strangfeld, John R., 3072
Strangfeld, John R., Jr., 3072
Stranghoener, Lawrence W., 2125, 2580
Strasner, Sherry, 547
Strasser, Joseph C., Sr., 3873
Strassler, Marc, 2894
Strassler, Marc A., 3220
Strategic Tax Advisors, Inc., 1969
Stratton, Frederick P., Jr., 565, 4051
Stratton, John G., 733
Strauch Family Foundation, The, 2655
Strauch, Charles S., 2655
Strauss & Co., Levi, 3624
Strauss, Audrey, 82
Strauss, Charles B., 1742
Strauss, David, 2134
Strauss, Iliana Kloesmeyer, 2958
Strauss, Kitty, 814
Strauss, Sylvia Sundel, 2134
Strauss-Levine, Debra, 2134
Strawn, Jeff, 3455
Strawn, Kathryn A., 2445
Strawsburg, Jon, 3199
Strawsburg, Stephen R., 3200
Strayer, Jacqueline F., 956
Strayhorn, Larry E., 2401
Strayton, George, 2681, 3070
Strayton, George L., 3070
Stred, Kristin H., 1081
Street, David, 3864
Street, Fay, 3864
Street, James E., 2153
Street, Joseph B., 1093
Street, Nicholas, 3864
Street, William M., 2876
Streeter, Bill, 2486
Streeter, Stephanie A., 1612, 2181
Streff, Ken, 1091
Streich, Brian, 754
Streker, Cathy, 3731
Strelitz, Renee D., 1368
Strem, Michael E., 1946
Streza, Richard E., 1608
Strickland, Frances, 350
Strickland, Frances R., 350
Strickland, Robert W., 3404
Strickland, Samuel R., 525
Strickland, Valerie, 3701
Strickland, William E., Jr., 344
Strickler, Sean, 72
Strickler, Thomas L., 1946
Strickler, William J., 1993
Stride Rite Charitable Foundation, Inc., The, 3625
Stride Rite Corp., The, 3625
Stride Tool Inc., 3626
Strigl, Dennis F., 1214, 2996, 2997, 3709
Strimbu, William J., 1318
Stringer, Carl, 3878
Stringer, Diane T., 2928
Stringer, Geoffrey L., 2149
Stringer, Mark, 3867
Stringer, Rochelle, 1884
Stringfield, Jo Anne, 504
Stringfield, Tracy D., 1274
Stritzke, Jerry, 858
Strizzi, Dave M., 3886
Strobel, David L., 700
Strobel, Pamela B., 1916, 3591
Strobel, Steven J., 2694
Strockis, John D., 3655
Stroh, Bryan, 2985
Strohm, David L., 1917
Strohm, David N., 1253
Strohman, Jessica, 3440
Strohman, Melissa, 1859
Strom, Arny, 3991
Strom, William, 918
Stromlund, Dana, 3714
Strong, Michael A., 861
Strong, Robert A., 338
Strong, Russ, 3995
Strong, Wendi E., 3873
Stronz, Terrence P., 1911
Stropki, John M., 3437
Stropki, John M., Jr., 2279
Strother, Jack W., Jr., 891
Strother, Jack W., Sr., 891
Strother, James M., 4028
Strother, Mark, 891
Stroucken, Albert P.L., 377, 2844
Stroud, Amber, 2069
Stroud, Dan, 2663
Stroud, Don, 2663
Stroud, Joseph, 2069
Stroud, Joseph A., 2069
Stroud, Vonesca, 2069
Stroud, Yvonne M., 2069
Strouse, George W., 772
Strouse, Rick, 2964
Strouse, Robert, 157, 1818
Strouse, Robert H., 157
Stroyd, Arthur H., Jr., 2401
Struble, Bryan, 1858
Struble, Scott, 2676
Struck, Laurie, 3122
Struckell, Elisabeth M., 1323
Strumwasser, Ira, 502
Strupp, Thomas J., 1484
Stryker Corporation, 3627
Stryker Orthopedics, 1875
Stryker, David, 368
Stryker, Ronda E., 3627
Strzynski, Richard C., 3865
Stuart, Bill, 1427
Stuart, Robert J., 1792
Stuart, Susan W., 3406
Stubblefield, Alfred G., 3944
Stubbs, Dace Brown, 592
Stubsten, Douglas, 1955
Stuchell, Harry, 2136
Stuck, David T., 1369
Stuck, James D., 1369
Stucker, Robert, 787
Stucker, Roy, 3059
Stuckey, John M., 694
Stuckey, Perry, 1213
Studenmund, Jaynie Miller, 2978
Studley, Donald T., 3858
Stueber, Frederick G., 2279
Stuermer, Sandra, 234
Stueven, Paul G., 1668
Stuhlsatz, Rebecca, 3584
Stuke, Bryan K., 2622
Stulb, Frank M., 1176
Stumiolo, Joseph S., 3629
Stumne, Deb, 1227
Stump, Denise S., 3372
Stumpf, John G., 780, 3691, 4028
Stuntz, Linda G., 3135
Stupak, Libby, 2636
Stupas, Tony, 2563
Stupp Bridge Co., 3628
Stupp Bros. Bridge & Iron Co., 3628
Stupp, John P., Jr., 2208, 3628
Stupp, Robert P., 3628
Sturdivant, Frederick D., 3575
Sturdivant, James M., 1525
Sturgeon, Nancy, 3200
Sturgeon, Stacy M., 2190
Sturgess, David E., 3899
Sturken, Craig C., 3535
Sturm, Denise, 3710
Sturm, Glen, 1985
Sturm, Glen M., 1985
Sturm, Greg, 1985, 2046
Sturm, Gregory, 1985
Sturm, Omer, 1985
Sturm, Scott, 2046
Sturniolo & Associates, Joseph S., Inc., 3629
Sturniolo, Joseph S., 3629
Stussi, Doug, 2311
Stute, Natalie, 2067
Stutts, Charles L., 1834
Stutz, Jeffrey, 2517
Stutz, Jeffrey M., 2517
Stutz, Richard J., 1524
Stuver, Douglas K., 2860
Stymiest, Barbara G., 3643
Styslinger, Lee J., III, 118, 3171
Styslinger, Lee J., Jr., 118
Su'a, Kelly M., 1174
Su, Jane J., 725
Su, Samuel Jing-Shyh, 4150
Suarez, Evelyn M., 4078
Sub-Zero Freezer Co., Inc., 3630
Subaru of America, Inc., 3631
Subaru of Indiana Automotive, Inc., 3632
Subaru-Isuzu Automotive Inc., 3632
Subotnick, Stuart, 696
Subourne, Mary Todd, 3153
Subramaniam, Shivan S., 1323
Suburban Communities, LLC, 1483
Suchecki, Tomek, 4125
Sucherman, Staurt, 3601
Sucic, Nicholas R., 1035
Sucre, Fernando R., 637
Sud, Inder, 1959
Sud, Jim, 4066
Sudbeck, Carol R., 2855
Sudders, Marylou, 1083
Sudderth, Gregory A., 502
Suddes, Adele, 3731
Suddes, Adele J., 3731
Sudduth, Kelly, 2669
Suellentrop, Steve, 1889
Suen, Samson, 4125
Sueoka, Jed, 1381
Suever, Catherine A., 2886
Suganuma, Hiroyuki, 150
Sugar, Ronald D., 182, 217, 780
Sugg, Laura A., 4077
Suggs, Stuart M., 2951
Sugi, Hikaru, 1088
Sugimori, Masato, 3639
Sugimoto, Mitsuo, 3681
Sugimura, Yuriko, 3773
Sugimura, Yuriko Jane, 3773
Sugiura, Yasuyuki, 2539
Suglia, Robert P., 183
Suh, Peters, 3965
Suits, Brenda L., 340
Suitter Axland & Hanson, P.C., 3633

Sujat, Frederick J., 3554
Sukeforth, James A., 3337
Sulentic, Bob, 725
Sulentic, Robert, 3581
Sulentic, Robert E., 725
Sulerzyski, Charles W., 2929
Suleski, James, 1075
Suleski, Steven R., 1008
Sullenberger, Mary Love, 3657
Sullivan & Cromwell LLP, 3634
Sullivan & McLaughlin Companies, Inc., 3635
Sullivan & McLaughlin Electrical Contractors, Inc., 3635
Sullivan, Aidan, 2711
Sullivan, Bill, 880
Sullivan, Chris T., 487
Sullivan, Dan, 503
Sullivan, Daniel J., Jr., 872
Sullivan, Daniel L., 3095
Sullivan, Darryl, 3450
Sullivan, David L., 3173
Sullivan, Deanna, 2738
Sullivan, Diane M., 591
Sullivan, Dolores, 2039
Sullivan, Elizabeth M., 601
Sullivan, Frank C., 3278, 3760
Sullivan, George F., 380
Sullivan, George F., Jr., 380
Sullivan, Glen, 375
Sullivan, John, 1423
Sullivan, John C., 1423
Sullivan, John J., 255
Sullivan, Joseph A., 2245
Sullivan, Joseph F., 498
Sullivan, Joseph P., 812
Sullivan, Katherine, 404
Sullivan, Kenneth M., 3487
Sullivan, Kerry H., 340
Sullivan, Louis W., 3348
Sullivan, Lynn, 3940
Sullivan, Lynne, 3940
Sullivan, M. Kevin, 3066
Sullivan, M. L., 722
Sullivan, Malcolm R., 3515
Sullivan, Margaret B., 298
Sullivan, Mark E., 530
Sullivan, Martha N., 297
Sullivan, Mary, 1158, 1450
Sullivan, Maura, 476
Sullivan, Meredith Key, 1423
Sullivan, Monica F., 756
Sullivan, Pat, 1136
Sullivan, Patrick, 3528
Sullivan, Patrick J., 428, 2939
Sullivan, Peggy, 860
Sullivan, Richard M., 428
Sullivan, Rob, 2183
Sullivan, Robert D., 1927, 3242
Sullivan, Sean S., 126
Sullivan, Shauna J., 959
Sullivan, Susan, 1981
Sullivan, Thomas, 3070
Sullivan, Thomas C., 3278
Sullivan, Timothy W., 2749
Sullivan, Trudy F., 3682
Sullivan, William P., 56, 304
Sullivan-Lent, Brenna, 1165
Sulphur Springs Valley Electric Cooperative, Inc., 3637
Sulpizio, Richard, 638, 3192
Sult, John R., 1239
Sultan, Ezra, 748
Sultan, Nader H., 1448
Sulva, Edward T., 2742
Sulzberger, Arthur O., Jr., 2690
Sumida, Richard, 3271
Sumida, Sheila M., 1405
Sumino, Takeo, 2720
Sumitomo Bank Capital Markets, Inc., 3480
Sumitomo Corporation of America "SCOA", 3639
Sumitomo Electric Wiring Systems, Inc., 3640
Summe, Gregory L., 291, 3592
Summer, Justin, 719
Summerlin, Jim, 2412
Summers, Jim, 1095
Summers, Kevin V., 2312
Summers, Patricia H., 2016
Summers, Stran, 497
Summers, Terry J., 37
Summers, William B., Jr., 3278
Summersett, Melodie Zamora, 2632
Summerwill, Suzanne, 2508
Summerwill, W. Richard, 2508
Summey, M. L., 3615
Summit Fund, LLC, The, 3864
Summit Tool Co., 3642
Sumner, Amanda, 1126
Sumner, George D., 1745
Sumner, Jill, 1921
Sumney, Larry W., 3403
Sumser, Chas, 2755
Sun Lumber Co., 3645
Sun, David, 2161
Sun, Frederick, 2615
Sun, Tony, 637
Sunbeam Development Corp., 3647
Sunbeam Properties, Inc., 3647
Sunbeam Television Corp., 3647
Sundaram, Eash, 2041
Sunday, Delena M., 2724
Sunday, Mark, 2821
Sundberg, Jim, 3729
Sundel, Claire, 2134
Sundel, Jacob, 2134
Sunderland, Charles T., 256
Sunderland, Kent W., 256
Sunderland, Kenton W., 256
Sunderman, John, 2840
Sundheim, Nancy S., 3859
Sunkin, Howard, 2305
Sunkist Growers, Inc., 3649
Sunoco, Inc., 3650
Sunrise Securities Inc., 3652
Sunrise Venture LLC, 2167
Sunset Ridge Church, 1520
Sunshine Makers, Inc., 3653
SunTrust Bank, 57, 591, 2573, 3127, 3654, 4129
Sununu, John E., 540, 3755
Sunwest Bank, 3655
Suomi, Marvin J., 2087
Supcoe, Donald C., 1272
Superba, Inc., 1801
Superior Metal Products, Inc., 3658
SUPERVALU INC., 3659
Supranowicz, Dianne M., 428
Suprenant, Mark N., 4009
Suquet, Jose S., 2868
Surber, Joe, 57
Surber, Sharen K., 4034
Sures, Jay, 3881
Surma, John P., 2365, 3877
Surma, John P., Jr., 3877
Surprenant, Mark C., 34
Survis Group, The, 3660
Sury, Ashok, 3963
Susan G. Komen Breast Cancer Foundation, Inc., The, 947
Susetka, William F., 2209
Susetka, William F. (Bill), 2209
Susik, W. Daniel, 3292
Suski, Richard D., 1712
Suskind, Dennis A., 853
Susman, Sally, 2950
Susquehanna Cable Co., 3661
Susquehanna Pfaltzgraff Co., 3661
Susquehanna Radio Corp., 3661
Sussman, Sam, 58
Sustana, Mark, 2250
Sutariya, Urvi, 150
Sutcliffe, James H., 3643
Sutcliffe, Lillian Bernhardt, 432
Sutherland, David S., 1542, 3877
Sutherland, L. Frederick, 223
Sutherland, Mary, 2320
Sutherland, Paul, 1527
Sutherland, Victoria D., 1098
Sutherlin, Michael, 2070
Sutherlin, Michael W., 2070
Sutter Medical Foundation North Bay, 2952
Sutter, Kathy, 1110
Sutton, Dave, 2853
Sutton, David E., 1590
Sutton, Deborah E., 1054
Sutton, Hal, 2954
Sutton, Howard G., 3068
Sutton, Howard G., II, 3068
Sutton, Mark, 1968
Sutton, Mark S., 3711
Sutton, Mary, 2247
Sutton, Nicholas J., 3748
Sutton, Thomas C., 1228
Suver, Susan M., 3877
Suwinski, Jan H., 3709
Suydam, Robin E., 2341
Suzuki, Toshifumi, 5
Svendsen, Kurt, 3775
Svensson, Ake, 2886
Svider, Raymond, 2785
Svitek, John, 3477
Svizeny, Susanne, 4028
Svoboda, Jeffrey A., 1718
Swain, Ruth, 3022
Swain, Ruth B., 3022
Swain, Susan, 2625
Swain, Susan M., 3682
Swain, Thomas, 878
Swain, Tom, 3775
Swainson, John A., 3960
Swalling, John C., 2743
Swan Manufacturing Co., 1235
Swan, Barb, 4095
Swan, Bob, 1217
Swan, James E., IV, 3346
Swan, Richard W., 1805
Swan, Robert H., 220
Swander, Dan C., 3492
Swango, Gary, 1674
Swanke, Patricia K., 1047
Swansen, Russell W., 3747
Swanson, Alice, 1168
Swanson, Allan, 3838
Swanson, Marc G., 3387
Swanson, Marlin, 3883
Swanson, Michael, 2093
Swanson, Ruth, 675
Swanson, Scott, 1505
Swanson, William H., 3135
Swanson, William R., 1481
Swarthout, Gerard, III, 3369
Swarthout, Jack, 3369
Swarts, James L., 890
Swartz, Brian, 216
Swartz, Harold, 1361
Swartz, Jeffrey B., 3754
Swartz, Neva, 1361
Swartz, Shawn, 3822
Swartz, Sidney W., 3754
Swearingen, Lee, 1716
Sweasy, William J., 3154
Sweatman, Rob, 2077
Sweatt, M. Brice, 1977
Swedish, Joseph R., 4027
Sweeney, Brian G., 641, 2336
Sweeney, Dawn, 2638
Sweeney, Donna J., 610
Sweeney, Eileen, 2585
Sweeney, J. B., 3
Sweeney, John J., 3312
Sweeney, John J., III, 3312
Sweeney, John K., 1922
Sweeney, Joseph J., 220
Sweeney, Mike, 4049
Sweeney, Patrick J., 2121
Sweeney, Sean, 3539
Sweeney, Stender E., 299
Sweeney, Timothy, 501
Sweet, Andrew W., 3108
Sweet, David C., 1845
Sweet, David G., 1855
Sweet, Ken, 1969
Sweet, Marc, 3367
Sweet, Robert, 1731
Sweetman, Mary E., 1519
Sweetnam, James E., 1216
Sweitzer, Donald R., 1677
Swenson, Nancy, 2474
Swenson, Peter, 1314
Swenson, Susan G., 4028
Swetich, Bob, 2588
Swick, Ron, 443
Swickard, Sherri D., 3066
Swidarski, Thomas W., 1112
Swider, Sandy, 3589
Swiech, Alan M., 775
Swienton, Gregory T., 1736, 3292
Swieringa, Robert J., 1552
Swierzewski, Jon, 2224
Swieskowski, David, 3710
Swift Co., John S., Inc., 3666
Swift Energy Company, 3667
Swift Limited Company, 1236
Swift, A. Earl, 3667
Swift, Bryan M., 3666
Swift, Christopher J., 1742
Swift, David, 3861
Swift, David W., 3861
Swift, Hampden M., 3666
Swift, John S., III, 3666
Swift, Richard J., 1014, 1879, 2088, 3077
Swift, Terry E., 3667
Swift, William, 3918
Swihart, Susannah M., 1051
Swilley, Reginald, 3673
Swinburn, Peter, 2523, 2549
Swindal, Jennifer Steinbrenner, 2691
Swindell, Murray J., 31
Swindells, Charles J., 3667
Swinerton Builders, 3668
Swinerton Inc., 3668

Swing, James & Arlene, 1776
Swiss Army Brands, Inc., 3950
Switz, Robert E., 579, 2500
Switz, Thomas R., 772
Switzer, Cathy R., 1925
Swope, Deborah, 1470
Swygert, H. Patrick, 1742, 3882
Swygert, Jeffrey Scott, 4006
SYB, Inc., 1601
Sydell, Gerald A., 1075
Syed, Ali, 303
Syed, Ali N., 303
Syed, Dure S., 303
Sykes, Charles O., 3515
Sykes, John, 2596
Sykes, William, 425
Sylla, Casey J., 1542
Syllaba, Chris, 2064
Sylvan Learning Systems, Inc., 2231
Sylvester, David C., 3597
Sylvester, Lois, 3892
Sylvester, Michael, 3892
Sylvester, Tom, 3892
Sylvester, Walter, 3892
Sylvestor, Thomas, 3892
Symantec Corp., 3669
Symens, Paul, 1339
Symmco Inc., 3670
Symons, Greg, 880
Syms, Marcy, 3220
Symson, Adam, 3374
Symson, Adam P., 3374
Syngenta Seeds, Inc., 3671
Synopsys Community Fund, 3673
Synopsys Foundation, 3673
Synopsys Technology Education
Opportunity Foundation, 3673
Synopsys, Inc., 3673
Synovus Financial Corp., 3674
Sypolt, Gary L., 1150
Syre Realty Corp., 3676
Syrvalin, Kristine C., 2809
Systel, Inc., 3678
Syta, Joseph, 3237
Szabatin, Stephen J., 1984
Szabo, Frank, 1511
Szabo, John, 2023
Szalkiewicz, Diane, 2123
Szalkowski, Charles, 321
Szczepanski, Gerald R., 1530
Szczepek, John, 251
Szczsponik, John, 3728
Szczupak, David T., 407
Szerlong, Timothy, 855
Szews, Charles L., 2833
Szkutak, Thomas J., 122
Szlosek, Theresa C., 792
Szmit, Helena, 1042
Sznewajs, John G., 2393
Szostak, M. Anne, 406, 1169, 3821
Szramowski, Linda M., 1860
Sztykiel, John E., 3534
Szudrowlcz, Stanley L., 2872
Szwajkowski, Leonard, 3275
Szwak, Tina, 2957
Szygenda, Ralph J., 902
Szymanczyk, Michael E., 1150
Szymanski, Betty B., 389
Szymanski, David M., 2786
Szynal, Michele M., 660

T-Mobile, 30
T. Abdul Wahid And Co., 838
T.P. Racing, LLP, 3822
Ta, Hung, 2498
Taber, Richard E., 1399
Taboni, Viola G., 1200
Tabori, Dan, 3189
Tabussi, Stephen J., 1408
Tabussi, Steve, 1408
Tacchetti, Gregory, 1385
Taccolini, David, 2548
Tachibana, Masaki, 3480
Tachiki, Karen, 2484
Tachimori, Takeshi, 3631
Tacka, David W., 1791
Tackaberry, Kevin, 2005
Taco Bell Corp., 3679
Tacoma News Inc., 3680
Tadler, Richard, 1450
Taff, Michael S., 1447
Taft, Christopher P., 3031
Taft, John, 3136
Taft, John Godfrey, 3136
TAG, 1541
Taggart, Harriett Tee, 78, 1724
Tagget, Patrick, 2497
Tagilabue, Paul, 2626
Tagliabue, Paul, 2626
Tagtow, Patrick K., 508
Tague, John P., 798
Tahiri, Khalid, 1920
Tai, Jackson P., 586, 2399
Tai, Jackson Peter, 2769
Tai, Pin, 723
Taibel, Basil, 1859
Taiclet, James D., Jr., 167
Taipei Hope Christian Association, 1290
Tait, John, 232
Takahashi, Hideyuki, 2720
Takahashi, Kenichi, 3480
Takahashi, Kozo, 3422
Takaki, Donald M., 342
Takamiya, Katsuya, 2538
Takase, Shigeru, 3776
Takeaki, Mori, 1020
Takeda Pharmaceuticals, 3329
Taketa, Kelvin H., 1755
Takeuchi, Mitsunobu, 3715
Takitani, Aiko, 1756
Takubo, Akihiro, 4049
Talamantes, Patrick J., 2422
Talbert, Eric, 1763
Talbert, J. Michael, 1239
Talbot, Randy, 1751
Talbot, Ron, 3076
Talbots, Inc., The, 3682
Talerman, Robert A., 674
Taliaferro, Lilton R., Jr., 1926
Taliaferro, Paul, 1335
Taliaferro, W. Paul, 1335
Talieri, Joe, 1620
Talieri, Joseph, 1620
Talla, D. Michael, 3550
Talla, David Michael, 3550
Tallarida, Louisa, 1769
Tallent, Jimmy C., 1567, 3866
Tallett, Elizabeth E., 2471, 3047
Talley, Emet C., 169
Tallichet, John D., 3538
Talwalkar, Abhi Y., 2314
Talwalkar, Abhjiti Y., 2214
TALX Corporation, 3683
Tam, Eric, 694
Tam, Gilbert, 2204
Tam, Raymond J., 2198
Tamakoshi, Ryosuke, 2570
Tamar Fink, Inc., 3684
Tamashasky, John, 2056
Tamayo, Carlos G., 1306
Tambakeras, Markos I., 4139
Tambornino, John L., 3119
Tamburro, Michael, 2903
Tamburro, Mike, 2903
Tamerlano, John, 1430
Tamke, George W., 1792
Tamler, Ronald, 3329
Tampa Products Co., 2696
Tamura, Mitsuyoshi, 2087
Tan's Holding Corp., 3860
Tan, Benjamin, 3796
Tan, Cho Yee, 998
Tan, Jerry, 998
Tan, Lip-Bu, 646
Tanabe, Barbara J., 342
Tanabe, Charles Y., 2264
Tanaka, Atsushi, 3776
Tanaka, Masa, 347
Tanaka, Masaaki, 2570
Tanawong, Virginia, 3893
Tandy, Bradley J., 466
Tandy, Daniel W., 2769
Tandy, Jack D., 2951
Tanenbaum, Marla L., 3998
Tanenbaum, Marla Lerner, 3998
Tang, Vance W., 170
Tang, Wilson, 723
Tang, Yvonne, 501
Tangney, Jay, 1828
Tangvik, Beverly, 226
Taniguchi, Barry K., 1755
Tankersley, Rayburn H., 3848
Tannenbaum, Michael, 2687
Tanner Cos., 3688
Tanner, Allen, 1674
Tanner, Allison Pell, 3688
Tanner, Bruce L., 2292
Tanner, Florence, 2884
Tanner, Gregg A., 533, 1054
Tanner, James T., 3688
Tanner, Michael S., 3688
Tanner, Neil Boyden, 3902
Tanner, O.C., 1538
Tano, Linda, 1766
Tanoue, Donna A., 342
Tanous, James J., 1291
Tanous, Will, 3990
Tanser, Toby, 2689
Tansey, Steve, 4145
Tansey, William A., III, 1984
Tansimore, Todd, 3806
Tanski, Ronald J., 2628
Tanzberger, Eric D., 3413
Tanzi, Lisa M., 727
Taormina, Jo Ann, 465
TAP Publishing, 3690
Tap South, Inc., 1247
Tapiero, Jacques, 2274
Tarapchak, Richard C., 2647
Tarapore, Kairus K., 753
Tarbutton, Charles K., 1567
Tardio, Juan Pablo, 1774
Target Corp., 3691
Target Corporation, 1538
Tarkoff, Rob, 41
Tarnok, Robert C., 2481
Tarola, Robert M., 3708
Taroni, John C., 307
Tarraf, Laila J., 2916
Tartikoff, William M., 663
Tarver, Lisa, 2812
Tasaki, Akira, 2538
Tash, Paul C., 3758
Tashjian, James, 298
Tashjian, Lee C., 1448
Tashma, Lauren, 1474
Tasker, Herbert B., 1389
Tassinari, Mark F., 725
Tassopoulos, Timothy, 791
Tasty Baking Co., 3693
Tata, Ratan N., 82
Tate, Billy, 1337
Tate, James H., 2070
Tate, Katherine, 2754
Tate, Sherman, 240
Tateishi, Fumio, 2810
Tatelman, Richard, 2475
Taten, Bruce M., 935
Tatitlek Corp., The, 3694
Tatko, Cindy, 1539
Tatlock, Anne M., 1487
Tattersfield, Michael, 692
Tattersfield, Michael J., 692
Tatum, Beverly Daniel, 1567
Tatum, Elinor, 185
Tatum, Nenetta Carter, 1472
Tatum, Susan, 185
Tatum, Wilbert, 185
Tau, Eng, 2967
Taub, David S., 2867
Taub, Henry, 291
Taub, Linda, 2867
Taub, Marc D., 2867
Taub, Richard, 2867
Taube, Ben, 4004
Taubman, Robert S., 889
Tauke, Thomas J., 3936
Taunton, Cyndee, 625
Taunton, Michael J., 2630
Taunton, Paul, 625
Taurel, Sidney, 1960, 2429
Tauscher, William Y., 3310
Taussig, Hal, 3897
Taussig, Harold E., 3897
Taussig, Norma L., 3897
Tauzin, W.J. Billy, 1279
Tavakoli, Nader, 123
Tavernise, Peter, 818
Tavernost, Nicolas de, 423
Tavers, David, 1338
Tawil, Ezra, 1489
Taxay, Marc, 2447
Taxter, Michael W., 2925
Taylor, Alexander B., 2403
Taylor, Alexander C., 959
Taylor, Amy, 3152
Taylor, Andrew C., 890, 1281
Taylor, Benjamin B., 1594
Taylor, Bob, 1136
Taylor, Cathy Mith, 495
Taylor, Chandler, 2557
Taylor, Christine, 3815
Taylor, Christopher J., 2681
Taylor, Cindy B., 3748
Taylor, D., 3198
Taylor, Daniel J., 2489
Taylor, David H., 2304
Taylor, Dean E., 3748
Taylor, Diana L., 821
Taylor, Dwight S., 3040
Taylor, Frank A., 564
Taylor, Gary J., 1279
Taylor, Gordon, 439
Taylor, Gregory, 2489
Taylor, Gregory D., 2315

Taylor, Gretchen S., 2394
Taylor, Howard, 2710
Taylor, Jack C., 1281
Taylor, Jack T., 3405
Taylor, James A., 10
Taylor, James H., Jr., 540
Taylor, Jean, 2983
Taylor, Jeff, 2912
Taylor, Jerry, 2486, 2487
Taylor, Joe, 2062
Taylor, John, 1968
Taylor, John C., 3833
Taylor, Joseph, 2869
Taylor, Joseph M., 2869
Taylor, Joseph S., 2403
Taylor, Karen D., 1563
Taylor, Kathleen, 1476
Taylor, Kathryn L., 3498
Taylor, Kim A., 3943
Taylor, Kris J., 1220
Taylor, Lennon, 2775
Taylor, Lyndon C., 1102
Taylor, Marilyn, 878
Taylor, Mark H., 620
Taylor, Mary Alice, 107
Taylor, Michael, 3893
Taylor, Michael L., 1411, 1412
Taylor, Norton, 2162
Taylor, Pat, 3888
Taylor, Peggy, 466
Taylor, Peter J., 1228
Taylor, Philip A., 1983
Taylor, Phyllis M., 3614
Taylor, R. John, 301
Taylor, Richard G. A., 1950
Taylor, Rick R., 2881
Taylor, Robert, 3880
Taylor, Ronald R., 3192, 4007
Taylor, Russel G., 176
Taylor, S. Martin, 502
Taylor, Sarah, 847, 2395
Taylor, Scott, 3669
Taylor, Sharon C., 3072
Taylor, Shelley M., 10
Taylor, Stuart A., II, 328
Taylor, Sue, 1955
Taylor, Susanne M., 2715
Taylor, Suzanne L., 3996
Taylor, Teresa A., 2715
Taylor, Thomas A., 183
Taylor, Tim, 1401
Taylor, Todd, 2852
Taylor, W. Kent, 2876
Taylor, Wayne D., 439
Taylor, Wesley M., 231, 1424
Taylor, William L., 1326
Taylor-Morley, Inc., 417
Tazon, Jose A., 1311
TCF Financial Corp., 3695
TCF National Bank, 3695
TCF National Bank Minnesota, 3695
TD Bank, N.A., 410
TD Banknorth Inc., 3696
Teachers Credit Union, 3697
Teachers Foundation, 2919
Tead, Barbara B., 570
Teal, Janice J., 258
Teal, Marc N., 534
Team Chevrolet, 3291
Team Chevrolet-Toyota Match, 3291
TEAM Industries, Inc., 663
Teammates for Kids, 334
Teammates for Kids Foundation, 276, 606, 2091
TeamQuest Corporation, 3698
Teany, Doug, 540
Tebaldi, Rosemary, 3327
Tech Deck, 30
Tech, Marilyn T., 3118
Techni-Core, Inc., 3699
TECO Energy, Inc., 3701
Tecson, Andrew P., 837
Tedco, Inc., 3702
Tedeschi, Brian S., 1927, 3242
Tedeton, Byron K., 3702
Tedeton, Byron Kirk, 3702
Tedeton, Byron Kirk, Jr., 3702
Tedeton, Pamela Sue, 3702
Tedo, Kunihiko, 672
Tedone, John J., 2088
Teel, James E., 3122
Teel, Joyce N. Raley, 3122
Teel, Michael J., 3122
Teel, Scott, 1689
Teeter, Geoff, 1549
Teets, Peter B., 1171
Teets, Richard P., 3595
Teffner, Carrie W., 3754
Tefft, Tom M., 2453
Tegeler, Gretchen H., 1264
Tehle, David M., 1143, 2007
Tehrani-Littrell, Penny, 2720
Teicher, Ben, 3130
Teichert & Son, A., Inc., 3704
Teichert, Frederick A., 3704
Teichert, Inc., 3704
Teichert, Melita M., 3704
Teitelbaum, Doug, 3141
Teitler & Teitler, 3705
Teitler, Michael F., 3705
Teixeira, Frank, 577
Teixido, Xavier, 2638
Tejada, Andrea M., 613
Tejada, Miguel, 334
Tektronix, Inc., 3706
Teleflex Inc., 3707
TeleTech Holdings, Inc., 3708
Telford, Nick, 2937
Tellabs, Inc., 3709
Telles, Cynthia A., 1555, 2086
Telles, Robert, 3594
Tellez, Luis, 3405
Tellman, Brenda A., 2837
Tellock, Glen E., 2355, 2356
Temares, Steven H., 399, 3601
Temmen, Robert P., 1532
Temperly, James E., 1061
Temple, Elaine, 3509
Temple-Inland Forest Products Corp., 3711
Temple-Inland Inc., 3711
Templeton, D. Jeffrey, 428
Templeton, Jeffrey D., 428
Templeton, Mark B., 1288
Templeton, Richard K., 3728
Templin, Donald C., 2362, 2365
Ten West Apparel, Inc., 3712
Tenaglia, Michael D., 851
Tencza, James J., 1053
Tener, James R., 460
Tenhaken, Mary Ten, 4086
Tenhulzen, Gaylen L., 1646
Tennant Co., 3714
Tennent, F.D., 1350
Tennessee Football, Inc., 3716
Tennessen, Rich, 1285
Tenney, Diane L., 1399
Tenney, Jolene D., 833
Tennihan, Jean M., 1060
Tennison, Lyndon L., 3857
Tension Envelope Corp., 3717
Tenzer, David, 3959
Tenzer, Judy, 143
Teodoro, Charmaine, 2076
Teodoro, Dante, 2076
Teodoro, Dante Raul, 2076
Teodoro, Nonette, 2076
Teodoro, Nonita, 2076
Teplicky, Bill, 2435
Teplicky, J. William, Jr., 2435
Teplin, Albert M., 3946
Teplitz, Edward D., 3737
Tepper, Marvin, 3601
Terada, Tetsuro, 2539
Teraherk, Jason, 1091
Teranishi, Dennis, 1756
Teranishi, Takeshi, 2102, 2103
Terashi, Shigeki, 3784, 3788
Terho, Randall P., 1591
Terlato Wine Group, Ltd., 3720
Terlato, Anthony, 3720
Terlato, Anthony J., 3720
Terlato, John, 3720
Terlato, John A., 3720
Terlato, Josephine P., 3720
Terlato, William A., 3720
Terlecky, Alice P., 2855
Terlizzi, Donald, 675
Terlizzi, Marc, 675
Terlizzi, Michael, 675
Terlizzi, Nicholas P., Jr., 675
Ternes, Donavon P., 3071
Ternoey Glassman, Jennifer, 3781
Terra Coastal Properties, Inc., 3721
Terra, Jean Lim, 182
Terracciano, Anthony P., 3478
Terre Haute Gas Corp., 3722
Terreberry, Roxanne, 2096
Terrell, Dorothy A., 1554, 2517
Terrell, Karenann K., 3980
Terrell, Michael, 3369
Terry, Benjamin C., 725
Terry, Bentina C., 1689
Terry, Hilliard C., III, 56
Terry, Phillip A., 2552
Terry, Thomas F., 2394
Terry, William A., 3066
Teruel, Javier, 2925
Teruel, Javier G., 3585
Teruya, Steven J., 1381
Terver, Bernard, 1828
Terver, Bernerd, 1828
Terwilliger, Tom, 2366
Terzariol, Giulio, 105
Tese, Vincent, 641
Tese, Vincent S., 2336
Tesija, Kathryn A., 3936
Tesjia, Kathee, 3691
Teske, Elizabeth, 1168
Teske, Todd, 313
Teske, Todd J., 565
Teskey, Kristen L., 340
Tesoriere, Steven, 2459
Tesoriero, Jean T., 2630
Tesoriero, Joseph S., 1141
Tesoro, Thomas S., 3575
Tessier, Janice M., 889
Tessier-Lavigne, Marc, 2950
Tessler, Allan R., 2277
Tessler, Lenard, 3659
Tessmer, Jim, 1858
Tessoni, Daniel D., 1971
Testa, Linda, 2501
Testwuide, Thomas R., Sr., 2993
Teter, Jeff, 4066
Tetler, George W., III, 3067
Tetrault, Denise Hallberg, 1704
Tetrault, Michael J., 4102
Tetreault, Phillip E., 2042
Tetreault, Phillips E., 2042
Teuber, William J., Jr., 1253, 3003
Tevrizian, Dickran, 3826
Tewnion, Lesley A., 1588
Tex, Belcher, 3259
Tex-Trude, Inc., 3724
Texaco Inc., 780
Texas Brine Co., LLC, 3725
Texas Feathers, Inc., 1735
Texas Industries, Inc., 3727
Texas Instruments Inc., 3728, 4042
Texas Stadium Corp, 1022
Texas Tech University, 3981
Texas Wings, 1858
Texor Petroleum Co., 3730
Texter, Michael W., 2925
Textor, Donald F., 1282
Textron Inc., 3731
TFS Financial Corp., 3732
Thacher, Carter, 4070
Thacher, Carter P., 4070
Thacher, John P., 4070
Thacker, Bradley D., 2716
Thacker, Charlotte, 2925
Thacker, William L., 1563
Thain, John A., 819
Thal, Gayla, 3857
Thalhimer, Robert L., 1921
Thaman, Michael H., 2842
Than, Ralph, 1026
Thandri, Ananthan, 2462
Tharin, Judson M., Jr., 3775
Tharpe, Rebecca, 859
Thatcher, Dale A., 3399
Thatcher, Jennifer, 802
Thatcher, K. Blake, 2810
Thatcher, Kathryn, 3637
Thatcher, Kathy, 3637
Thau, Andrew, 3881
Thawer, Amyn, 1217
Thawerbhoy, Nazim G., 2016
Thaxter, Shaun, 3147
Thaxton, Greg, 2723
Thaxton, Gregory A., 2723
Thayer, Jonathan W., 1309
The American Bottling Company, 1186
The Charles D. McCrary Family, 71
The IMA Financial Group Inc., 1917
The Michael Alan Group, 1186
The Walking Man Inc., 1186
Thebault, J. Brian, 3399
Theilmann, Michael T., 2925
Theisen, Henry J., 407
Thene, Tony R., 700
Theobald, Geri, 3113
Theobald, Thomas C., 2061
Theophilus, Nicole, 904
Therakos, Inc., 2048
Theriault, Timothy J., 3981
Thermo Realty, 3934
Theros, Louis, 629
Theurillat, Jacques, 856
Theus, Caroline G., 2600
Thibodeau, Laurie, 752
Thiel, Teresa, 3453
Thiele, Eric, 3025
Thielen, James E., 2282

Thielmann, Michael T., 2925
Thieman, Edward, 2675
Thier, Samuel O., 764
Thierer, Mark A., 1125
Thies, Mark T., 301
Thigpen, Carl S., 3066
Thigpen, Jonathan, 2151
Thigpen, Richard M., 3209
Thigpen, Richard T., 3077
Thigpen, Ronald L., 3513
Thill, Howard J., 2364
Third Federal Savings and Loan Association, MHC, 3732, 3735
Thiry, Kent, 1044
Thiry, Kent J., 1044
Thode, Mary Ann, 1139
Thom, Heidi K., 1220
Thoman, A. Randall, 3524
Thomann, Brad, 2038
Thomas, Bart, 3728
Thomas, Bill, 3380
Thomas, Brad, 1683, 1790
Thomas, Carl M., 894
Thomas, Carol Telgue Jean, 1541
Thomas, Cheryl, 3915
Thomas, Colleen, 104
Thomas, Dave, 3299
Thomas, David, 1474, 3266
Thomas, David L., 3710
Thomas, David M., 1974
Thomas, Deborah, 1747
Thomas, Deborah M., 1747
Thomas, Edward K., 3380
Thomas, Gary L., 1282
Thomas, Glen, 2883
Thomas, Glenn, 2883
Thomas, J. Darrell, 1732
Thomas, J. Grover, Jr., 3818
Thomas, Jack, 2991
Thomas, Jamie, 30
Thomas, Jeffery M., 3655
Thomas, Jennifer, 660
Thomas, Jerome, 3679
Thomas, Joe, 2338
Thomas, John, 3112, 3303
Thomas, John B., 13
Thomas, Jonathan Stuart, 137
Thomas, Joyce, 3324
Thomas, Kamne M., 3673
Thomas, Kevin, 2615
Thomas, L. Tarlton, III, 690
Thomas, Larry E., 1359
Thomas, Lee M., 65, 1184, 3134, 3166
Thomas, Lizanne, 2058
Thomas, Louis J., 91
Thomas, Lydia W., 642
Thomas, M. Ann, 4110
Thomas, Marjorie, 3503
Thomas, Marty, 3246
Thomas, Michael, 3289
Thomas, Michael E., 1957
Thomas, Mitzi, 588
Thomas, Peggy, 489
Thomas, Peter M., 546
Thomas, Peter T., 1366
Thomas, Robert, 89
Thomas, Robert H., 89
Thomas, Robert M., 3494
Thomas, Sally, 4013
Thomas, Silva, 2744
Thomas, Stephen, 1226
Thomas, Stephen J., 1527
Thomas, Suzanne, 1872
Thomas, Suzie, 1872
Thomas, Telford W., 3996
Thomas, Thomas A., 3524
Thomas, William R., 1282
Thomas-Graham, Pamela, 852
Thomason, Bill, 2113
Thomason, Ken, 3726
Thomason, Mike, 301
Thomason, Nancy, 2392
Thomason, William, 2113
Thomasson, Pat, 3743
Thomaston Savings Bank, 3736
Thomasville Furniture Industries, Inc., 3737
Thomco Enterprises, Inc., 989
Thome, Jim, 847
Thome, Layne, 1842
Thomison, Tom, 1826
Thomopulos, Gregs G., 3580
Thompsn, Ivan, 1169
Thompson Co., J. Walter, Inc., 3739
Thompson USA, J. Walter, Inc., 842
Thompson, Astrid I., 2919
Thompson, Billy, 2906
Thompson, Bruce R., 340
Thompson, Craig B., 2466
Thompson, D. Gary, 1567
Thompson, David, 415, 3918
Thompson, David Gary, 54
Thompson, David O., 551
Thompson, Dean, 1416
Thompson, Don, 2427
Thompson, Donald, 2427
Thompson, Donald N., 2394
Thompson, Doug, 1455
Thompson, Francis L., IV, 3431
Thompson, G. Kennedy, 2954
Thompson, Glenn, 2236
Thompson, Grant B., Jr., 3843
Thompson, Harry, 2486
Thompson, J. Kenneth, 2981
Thompson, Jack E., 2550, 3748
Thompson, James B., 2010
Thompson, James E., 795
Thompson, James R., 4089
Thompson, James R., Jr., 2410
Thompson, Jeffrey R., 680
Thompson, Jim, 2581
Thompson, John, 1973
Thompson, John David, 4045
Thompson, John M., 3741
Thompson, John R., 403, 2725
Thompson, John R., Jr., 2710
Thompson, John W., 2501, 3872
Thompson, Kathy C., 3610
Thompson, Keith, 2736
Thompson, Kennedy G., 1794
Thompson, Kenneth J., 74
Thompson, Kirk, 1892
Thompson, Larry D., 2935, 3516, 3999
Thompson, Laura, 2930
Thompson, Les, 3637
Thompson, Linda M. Silva, 1712
Thompson, Marcia A., 2176
Thompson, Mark, 337, 2690
Thompson, Mark E., 547
Thompson, Mark S., 833, 935
Thompson, Marsha, 3807
Thompson, Matthew A., 38
Thompson, Mella, 2363
Thompson, Michael L., 3840
Thompson, Norman, 977
Thompson, Peter J., 3741
Thompson, Richard L., 2715
Thompson, Robert T., 3011
Thompson, Ronald G., 1162
Thompson, Ronald L., 801
Thompson, Samme L., 167
Thompson, Scott L., 1144
Thompson, Shelley B., 342
Thompson, Simon R., 2698
Thompson, Thomas N., 385
Thompson, Tim, 2213
Thompson, Timothy, 74
Thompson, Timothy J., 1488
Thompson, Tommy, 72
Thompson, Tommy G., 358, 735
Thompson, Travis, 1135
Thompson, William S., Jr., 821
Thomsen, Jillian B., 2658
Thomsen, Laurie J., 3802
Thomson, Bob, 265
Thomson, David K. R., 3741
Thomson, David K.R., 3741
Thomson, Isobel, 1772
Thomson, James, 3312
Thomson, James A., 67
Thomson, Kris, 2067
Thomson, Martin, 1402
Thomson, Martin A., 1402
Thomson, Paul, 1924
Thomson, Richard, 3329
Thomson, Robert L., 2058
Thomson, Roger F., 572
Thomson, Traci L., 1259
Thoresson, Niklas, 3473
Thorington, Stephen A., 1287
Thormann, J.F., 197
Thorn, Matt, 3505
Thorn, Rod, 2957
Thorn, Stuart, 3527
Thornburgh, Richard E., 2429
Thorne, Michael G., 3574
Thornley, Anthony S., 660
Thornton Testamentary Trust, James E., 4128
Thornton, Bert, 3975
Thornton, David, 4128
Thornton, Diane, 4128
Thornton, Diane W., 4128
Thornton, Dixon, 2010
Thornton, Jerry Sue, 149, 219, 3278
Thornton, John L., 1464
Thornton, Leslie T., 3997
Thornton, Matthew A., 3743
Thornton, Robert M., 2751
Thornton, Roger, 3697
Thornton, Thomas E., Jr., 2332
Thornton, Timothy R., 564
Thorntons Inc., 3743
Thorp, Dean L., 4028
Thorpe, Bruce, 83
Thorpe, James, 972
Thorpe, Kathleen H., 1745
Thorpe, Patricia A., 2734
Thorrez Foundation, 3744
Thorrez Industries, C., Inc., 3744
Thorrez, Al, 3744
Thorrez, Albert F., 3744
Thorrez, Camiel, 3744
Thorrez, Camiel E., 3744
Thorrez, Michael, 3744
Thorrez, Morris C., 3744
Thorsen, Steven L., Jr., 2500
Thorson, Sondra J., 619
Thorson, Todd D., 3101
Thrall Car Manufacturing Co., 1187
Thrasher, Bennett, 415
Thrasher, Ken, 415
Thrasher, Kenneth, 2747
Thrasher, Kenneth L., 415
Thread Mill Athletic Assn., 860
Three Rivers Home Health Services, Inc., 3745
Three Z Printing Co., 3746
Thresher, Mark R., 2639
Thriffiley, Donald A., Jr., 1446
Thrivent Financial for Lutherans, 3747
Thronton, Dixon, 2010
Thrope, Susan A., 2688
Thulin, Inge G., 3
Thulin, Irene G., 3
Thunderbirds Charities, 1345
Thunell, Holly Ann, 2028
Thunstrom, Jason, 2269
Thurber, John, 4028
Thurber, Robert C., 3832
Thurman, Charles W., 377
Thurman, Robert, 3318
Thurston, Corydon L., 428
Thyen, James C., 1323, 2149
Thygeson, Marcus, 655
Tian, Edward Suning, 2399
Tibbetts, David A., 1946
Tibbetts, Linda, 3251
Tiberio, Paul, 1186
Tichenor, McHenry T., 406
Ticket, Allen, Sr., 2615
Ticketmaster Group, Inc., 1095, 3327
Ticketmaster LLC, 3303
Tickett, Michael, 2615
Ticknor, Carolyn M., 852
Tides Foundation, 872
Tidewater Transit Company, 3749
Tidwell, Cynthia, 3274
Tidwell, Isaiah, 2281, 3492
Tidwell, James M., 4020
Tidwell, Jim M., 4020
Tidwell, Steve A., 3413
Tiedemann, Julian A., 1977
Tieken, Robert W., 1635
Tienor, Lawrence J., 2636
Tierney, Brian X., 141
Tierney, David M., 1946
Tierney, James T., Jr., 3604
Tierney, Thomas J., 1217
Tierny, Brian P., 2961
Tiffany & Co., 3750
Tifft, Douglas C., 1729
Tigges, Dale C., 401
Tighe, John, 251
Tikigaq Corporation, 3751
Tilden Mining Co., 850
Tilden, Bradley D., 74, 1861
Tilden, Thomas, 797
Tilenius, Stephaine, 858
Tilger, Shawn, 888, 2959
Tilghman, Richard G., 3677
Tilghman, Shirley M., 1613
Tillerson, Rex W., 1315
Tillet, Andrew, 607
Tillet, Andrew B., 607
Tillett, Bryan E., 2946
Tilley, Donna, 811
Tilley, Paul S., 2382
Tillison-Dusenburg, Brenda, 489
Tillman Co., Inc., The, 3752
Tillman, Joseph E., 3752
Tillman, Thomas, Jr., 3752
Tillotson, Sandra N., 2759
Tilly, Jennifer, 1296
Tilman, Audrey, 54
Tilton, Glenn F., 13, 2965

Tilton, Gwen E., 1053
Tilton, Sumner B., Jr., 4060
Tim, Tatman, 4115
Timberman, Terri, 579
Timberman, Terri L., 579
Timbie, Mark T., 3693
Timblin, Danny, 507
Timboe, Ken J., 2721
Time Insurance Co., 266, 267
Time Warner Inc., 1801, 3757
Timemax International, Ltd., 3123
Times-Journal, Inc., 3759
Times-World Corp., 2218
Timken Co., The, 3760
Timken, John M., Jr., 3760
Timken, Ward J., 3760
Timken, Ward J., Jr., 3760
Timko, Thomas S., 1555
Timm, Dwane L., 1414
Timmerman, Douglas J., 193
Timmerman, James M., 2512
Timmerman, Mark D., 193
Timmins, Martin V., 4094
Timmons, Poe A., 1129
Timston Corp., 3287
Timyan, Philip J., 3275
Tinanoff, Norman A., 1083
Tindal, Bruce B., 1391
Tindal, Tracy E., 164
Tindall Corp., 3761
Tindell, William A., III, 4066
Tingey, Robert D., 2028
Tingo, Mike, 4013
Tinsley, Tom C., 508
Tinstman, Robert A., 1843, 1907
Tip Top Screw, 1196
Tippl, Thomas, 30
Tipsord, Michael L., 3591
Tireco, Inc., 3762
Tiru, Raghavan, 1995
Tirva, Robert L., 579
Tisch, Andrew H., 855, 2296
Tisch, James S., 855, 1552, 2296
Tisch, Jonathan, 2684
Tisch, Jonathan M., 2296
Tisch, Laurie, 2684
Tisch, Steve, 2684
Tischhauser, Thomas J., 2149
Tisdale, M. Paulette, 1873
Tisdale, Patrick, 2826
Tisher, Cynthia, 576
Tishkoff, Dennis B., 460
Tishman, Daniel R., 42
Tisone, Joseph J., 1271
Tissiere, Linda, 2317
Titan Industrial Corp., 3763
Titherington, Geoffrey, 2126
Title, Gail Migdal, 2101
Titley, Larry J., 3923
Titus, Lane, 615
Titzman, Donna Marie, 3915
TIV Operations Group, Inc., 3764
Tivnan, Mary, 3581
Tjaden, Kurt A., 1817
TJX Cos., Inc., The, 3765
Tkacz, Richard M., 3245
TMA Systems LLC, 1953
Toan, Barrett, 3453
Toan, Barrett A., 3453
Toba, Bert R., 3782
Toben, Doreen A., 1376, 2690
Tobias, Stephen C., 2991
Tobiason, Steve, 504
Tobin, John H., 2645
Tobin, Peter J., 819
Tobin, Richard, 856
Tobkin, Vincent H., 3709
Toburen, James, 1749
Toburen, James R., 1749
Tocco, Tony, 3497
Tocio, Mary Ann, 566
Tocklin, Adrian M., 3747
Todd Co., A.M., 3766
Todd, A.J., III, 3766
Todd, Allen, 1167
Todd, C. B., 2610
Todd, Carter R., 3294
Todd, Clarence B., 2610
Todd, Jessica L., 772
Todd, L. Tommy, 1587
Todd, Lee T., Jr., 1287
Todd, Rick, 1790
Todd, Robert L., Sr., 562
Todd, Scott, 2032
Todhunter, John A., 3653
Todman, Michael A., 2694, 4056
Todoroff, Christopher M., 1886
Toe, Sylvester, 1567
Toelle, Michael, 802
Toeniskoetter & Breeding, Inc., 3767
Toeniskoetter, Charles J., 3767
Toeniskoetter, Chuck, 3767
Toeniskoetter, Linda, 3767
Tofias PC, 3768
Toftgaard, Stig, 2247
Togashi, Kazuo, 3210
Togher, Renee, 2415
Tognoli, Thomas, 1973
Tognoli, Tom, 1973
Tokach, S. K., 3
Tokar, Edward T., 757
Tokarski, Steve, Fr., 1409
Tokarz, Michael T., 857, 3984
Tokich, Michael J., 3600
Tokin, Arthur C., 1753
Tokioka, Franklin M., 1996
Tokioka, Lionel Y., 1996
Tokioka, Tyler M., 1996
Tokunou, Masaaki, 2726
Toledano, John O. H., Jr., 29
Toledo Edison Co., The, 1424
Toler, Bill, 3481
Tolford, G.K., 4018
Tolger, Keith R., 1523
Tolk, David H., 3206
Toll, Bruce, 3769
Toll, Bruce E., 3769
Toll, Robert I., 3769
Tollefson, Denny, 2213
Tolliver, Fred, 4149
Tolliver, Harold J., 37
Tolliver, Mark, 37
Tolman, Gary C., 1298
Toloff, Tabetha, 422
Tom, Eric P., 1964
Tomasky, Susan, 141, 3077, 3723
Tomaszewski, Mike, 1438
Tombigbee Electric Cooperative, 72
Tomc, Richard W., 2262
Tome, Carol B., 1842, 3872
Tomkins Industries, Inc., 3771
Tomkins, Mark. E., 1623
Tomkins, Paul R., 3141
Tomlinson, Lawrence, 3318
Tomlinson, Phillip W., 3674
Tomlinson, Richard, 3474
Tomlinson, Van, 160
Tomoff, William, 4000
Tompkins, Alan W, 1891
Tompkins, Cathlyn L., 777
Tompkins, Jon D., 1016
Tompkins, Kristine, 475
Toms, David, 2954
Toms, David W., 2954
Toms, Paul B., Jr., 1855
Tomsicek, Michael, 999
Tomson, O. Jay, 1397
Tomson, Patricia A., 1397
Tonder, Daniel L., 100
Toner, Paul, 501
Toney, Robert L., 346
Tongue, Thomas H., 654
Tonkel, J. Rock, Jr., 1345
Tonokawa, Douglas M., 726
Tony Hawaii Automotive Group Ltd., 3773
Tony Hawaii Corp., 3773
Tony Hyundai, 3773
Tony Motors, Inc., 3773
Tookes, Hansel E., II, 945, 1736, 3292
Toomey, Denise M., 4102
Toomey, Mary, 3455
Toon, Albert L., Jr., 1651
Toop, R. Scott, 3753, 4030
Toothman, Walt, 3450
Toothman, Walter, 3450
Topalian, Krikor Gary, 264
Topel, Bob, 1466
Topham, H. Scott, 2405
Topinka, Joe, 3154
Toporek, Tony, 3822
Torell, Lena Treschow, 3473
Toretti, Christine J., 3297
Torgerson, James, 3870
Torgow, Gary H., 502
Tornaghi, Frank, 4137
Tornow, Larry, 771
Toro Co., The, 3775
Torre, Joe, 2345
Torres, Anselmo, 3637
Torres, George, 1147
Torres, Jose Maria, 1904
Torres, Martin Acosta, Sr., 3126
Torres, Robert, 4028
Torrison, Scott, 576
Torsone, Johnna G., 2984
Torti, Julio, 1292
Tortoli, Jacques, 2596
Tortora, John, 3327
Tortorelli, Joseph L., 2855
Toscano, Michael, 265
Tosches, Peter, 3414
Toshiba America, Inc., 3776
Toshiba Corporation, 3776
Tosi, Laurence A., 477
TOSOH Quartz, Inc., 3777
Total System Services, Inc., 3674
Totemoff, Charles W., 776
Totemoff, David J., Sr., 805
Totemoff, Roy, 3694
Toth, Linda, 246
Toth, Scott, 4062
Totino, Paul M., 2506
Totsy Manufacturing Co., Inc., 3780
Totusek, Jeffrey P., 3857
Touch Em All Foundation, 334
Touff, Michael, 2324
Tough, Doug, 2549
Tough, Douglas D., 1962
Tough, Douglas Davis, 1962
Tough, Steve, 1766
Toulouse, Sarah, 381
Toups, John M., 4075
Toups, Roland M., 3825
Touro University, 3981
Toussaint, Claudia S., 362
Tow, Leonard, 641
Towarak, Tim, 422
Towerbrook Capital Partners LP, 3781
Towers, Ed, 1020
Towers, James K., III, 1676
Towers, Jim, 1676
Towers, Robert, 2000
Towill Corporation, R.M., 3782
Towler, Fred, 1968
Towler, Fred A., 3711
Towler, Susan B., 493
Towles, Amor, 3398
Town Lake Partners, LLC, 2232
Town, Denice M., 2919
Towne, Ted, 3998
Townley, Dennis, 343
Townley, Steve, 3804
Townsend, Bill, 1050
Townsend, John L., III, 403, 1968
Townsend, Karen, 2402
Townsend, Kent G., 680
Townsend, Michele, 2855
Townsend, Michele A., 2855
Townsend, Patty, 1601
Townsend, Robert, 1088
Townsend, Ronald, 3134
Townsend, Thomas, 1402
Toyoda Machinety USA, 663
Toyoda, Kou, 1515
Toyota Motor Manufacturing North America, Inc., 3784
Toyota Motor Sales, U.S.A., Inc., 3784
Toyota of Wilmington, 1776
Toys "R" Us, Inc., 3790
Tozier, Scott A., Jr., 78
Tracey, Kevin, 2902
Tracey, Patricia A., 3877
Tracey, Vinnie, 3140
Trachimowicz, Richard J., 3245
Tractor & Equipment Co., Inc., 3791
Tracy, Colleen, 1434
Tracy, Don, 1158
Tracy, Jaclyn, 1158
Tracy, Jane, 1158
Tracy, Jim, 1158
Tracy, Joe, 1158
Tracy, John, 1158
Tracy, John J., 516
Tracy, Kristin, 3402
Tracy, Linda, 1158
Tracy, Patrick, 1158
Tracy, Patrick F., 1158
Tracy, Rob, 1158
Tracy, Thomas L., 1158
Tracy, Tom, 1158
Traczyk, Julie, 3173
Trader's Foundation Endowment Fund, 853
Tradition Development, LLC, 3792
Tradition Mortgage, LLC, 3792
Tradition Ventures, LLC, 3792
Traeger, Carrie, 3062
Traeger, Norman L., 2325
Traeger, Peter A., 2997
Trager, Mike, 2209
Trainer, Thomas, 2123
Traisman, Frances, 367
Trammell, Kenneth R., 3715
Tramontozzi, Mark, 1118
Tramontozzi, Mark E., 1118

Tran, Khanh T., 2855
Trane U.S. Inc., 3794
Tranen, Jeffrey D., 757
Trans-High Corp., 3795
Transammonia, Inc., 3796
Transco Inc., 3797
Transcontinental Realty Investors, Inc., 723
Transit Mix Concrete Co., 3798
Transmerica Financial Life Insurance Co., 45
Transwestern Investments Realty, 3800
Tranter, Gregory D., 1724
Trapani, Jennifer A., 3158
Trapani, Kevin A., 3158
Trapasso, Joseph "Jody", 801
Trask, Amy Jeanne, 2772
Trauschke, R. Sean, 2794
Trauscht, Donald C., 1296
Traut, Christopher D., 1455
Trautman, David L., 2881
Trautmann, Robert E., 2928
Traux, Tanya Wulff, 2704
Travasos, Scott, 655
Travelers Companies, Inc., The, 3802
Traveller, Michael D., 1403
Travers, Jeanne L., 1927
Travers, Mary Jean, 3349
Travers, Oliver, 3349
Travers, Oliver S., Jr., 3349
Travis, Mark, 2702
Travis, Nigel, 1191, 2304, 2785
Travis, Tracey T., 669, 2230
Travis, Tracy, 3123
Traynor, Sean M., 3887
Treacy, Dennis H., 3487
Treacy, Patrick, 3145
Treadway, Ingrid, 580
Treadwell, David L., 3964
Treasure Valley Business Group, Inc., 3803
Treasure Valley Sales & Marketing, Inc., 3803
Treat, Charles O., 1118
Trebilcock, James R., 1169
Trebing, Richard, 2462
Trechak, Perry, 3415
Tredway, Alfred, 3169
Tredway, Gary E., 145
Treff, Douglas J., 871
Treiber, Eric, 789
Treiber, Walter, 789
Treiber, Walter G., 789
Treiber, Walter G., Jr., 789
Treitler, William B., 3622
Treleaven, Carl W., 2117
Treleaven, Lina Z., 2117
Treliving, Brad, 963
Tremaine, Richard, 1586
Tremblay, Diane D., 1555
Tremble, Judith T., 792
Trempont, Dominique, 3144
Trenary, Lloyd R., 892
Trencher, Lewis J., 3739
Trends International, Inc., 3804
Trent, Keith B., 1189
Trent, Richard D., 3170
Trent, Tammy, 2246
Trentacosta, John F., 2704
Treschow, Michael, 3853
Trethewey, James A., 3595
Tretter, Kenneth, 2046
Tretter, Susan H., 1103
Treveloni, Dave, 3812
Trevenen, Denise D., 910
Treves, John S., 2171
Trezieres, Yves, 423
Triantafillopoulos, Nick, 2809
Trib Total Media, Inc., 3806
Tribbett, Charles A., III, 2740
Trible, Paul S., Jr., 3487
Tribolet, William A., 873
Tribune-Review Publishing Co., 3806
Tribune-Star Publishing Co., 3722
Trice, David A., 2695
Trick, David, 123
Trico Electric Cooperative, Inc., 3807
Tricon Global Restaurants, Inc., 4150
Trident Seafoods Corp., 3687
Trident Seapoods, 3687
Trident Systems, 3808
Trierweiler, Frank, 1466
Trifilio, Russ, 3477
Trifone, John, 499
Trigg, Lincoln, 3467
Trilling, Steve, 3669
Trim Masters Inc., 3810
Trimble, Ed, 3322
Trimmier, Leigh, 352
Trinity Health, 1131
Trinity Presbyterian Church, 1290
Tripeny, Tony, 1729
Tripi, Gregory, 3811
Tripi, Gregory G., 3811
Tripifoods, Inc., 3811
Tripp, Ann K., 1724
Tripp, Mark A., 1215
Trippe, Cathi, 2298
Triskel, S.A., 3125
Trittschuh, Diane, 3199
Triumph Leasing Corp., 3812
Trivers, Mollie C., 1262
Trivieri, Frank, 3967
Troen, Mark L., 1609
Troia, Sandra, 1973
Troiano, Becky, 3646
Troilo, Joseph C., 3314
Trojan, Gregory A., 1151
Troka, John, 3708
Trolli, Michele D., 2323
Trombley-Oakes, Martha, 2633
Trombly, Nicole, 1941
Tronchetti, Susan, 1846
Tropical Foods, 1186
Trosino, Vincent J., 3972
Trost, Lonn, 2691
Trost, Lonn A., 2691
Trostle, Michelle, 2280
Trotter, Lloyd G., 2935, 3731
Troubh, Raymond S., 4030, 4031
Trout, James H., 80
Trower, Alexandra C., 2230
Troxel, David B., 1139
Troxel, Tom, 1466
Troxil, William, 2185
Troy, George, 1059
Troy, Gregory T., 2088
Trpik, Joseph, Jr., 895
TRS Services, 661
Trubeck, William L., 753
Truchard, James J., 2632
Trudeau, Dawn, 370
Trudeau, Patricia J., 2163
Trudell, Cynthia M., 2935
True Oil LLC, 3814
True, Calvin E., 1051
True, H. A., III, 3814
True, H. A., Jr., 3814
True, H.A.'Hank', III, 3814
True, Jean D., 3814
Trueb, Martin, 1747
Trueb, Martin R., 1747
Trueblood, Rick, 1560
Truefit Solutions, 3816
Truesdell, Chris, 3109
Truess, James W., 171
Trujillo, Gary L., 500
Trujillo, Solomon D., 3691, 4045
Truland Systems Corp., 3817
Truland, Mary W., 3817
Truland, Robert W., 3817
Trulock, John W., Jr., 3513
Trumbull, R. Scott, 1484
Trummel, Rachel M., 353
Trumpy, Chris, 3081
Truncale, Joseph P., 1634
Trunk, Paul, 423
Trunzo, Robert, 1008
Truog, Mark, 1317
Truong, Jack, 1241
Trust A U/A of Ellison S. Mckissick, Jr., 89
Trustees of the Academy of Richmond County, 2573
Trustmark Insurance Co., 3818
Trusty, David, 2971
Truzinski, Dave, 2709
Trylko, Paul A., 3726
Tryniski, Mark E., 2681
Tryon, T. J., 2551
Trzepacz, Jennifer, 2290
Tsang, Katherine, 1533
Tscherter, Steve, 2282
Tschinkel, Victoria J., 2965
Tse, Alan K., 807
Tseng, Vivian S.Y., 4025
Tsimbinos, John M., 2683
Tsimbinos, John M., Jr., 2682, 2683
Tsimbinos, Steven J., 2782
Tsokris, Sue, 2935
Tsoumbanos, Anastasia, 3603
Tsugo, Yasushi, 2204
Tsugo, Yasutomi, 2204
Tsui, John K., 1405, 2198
Tsuji, Ryohei, Ph.D., 2144
Tsujihara, Kevin, 3989
Tsujiura, Steve, 3011
Tsurutani, Masatoshi, 2102
Tu, John, 2161
Tu, Lawrence P., 1068
Tubbs, Alan R., 2361
Tubbs, April, 1062
Tucci, Joseph M., 1253, 2904
Tuchman, Kenneth D., 3708
Tucker, Allen, 3121
Tucker, Arthur V., Jr., 773
Tucker, Bonnie, 832
Tucker, Christine A., 2855
Tucker, Faye, 3481
Tucker, Greg, 45
Tucker, Jeff, 3324
Tucker, Judy, 2699
Tucker, Kim, 3749
Tucker, Lance F., 2876
Tucker, Lee, 2054
Tucker, Mark, 3987
Tucker, Mark Edward, 1603, 1604
Tucker, Mary Ann, 1392
Tucker, Mel, 2948
Tucker, Michael, 299
Tucker, Michael K., 299, 300, 604
Tucker, R. Rand, 2205
Tucker, Rand, 2205
Tucker, Robert A., 411
Tucker, Ronnie, 2689
Tucker, Ruth, 3704
Tucker, Sara Martinez, 141, 4136
Tucker, Shannon, 1842
Tuckson, Reed V., 3884
Tuckson, Reed, Dr., 3884
Tudor, Fiona, 3192
Tueber, William J., Jr., 1253
Tufano, Paul A., 1926
Tufano, Paul J., 3718
Tufts, 501
Tuggle, Charles T., Jr., 1406
Tuggle, Clyde C., 862, 1567, 2847
Tuggle, James S., 3726
Tuin, Everett Vander, 3969
Tuite, Verne, 2168
Tulchin, Drew, 3493
Tulin, Stanley B., 3179
Tullis, James L.L., 970, 2303
Tully, Carol E., 4102
Tully, Herbert B., 4070
Tulsa Advertising Federation, Inc., 131
Tumlin, Clinton H., 3197
Tune, James F., 1081
Tunioli, Roberto, 2560
Tunkl, Clair, 30
Tunkl, David, 30
Tunney, Jason, 1196
Tunquist, Eric, 2007
Tuohy, Sean, 1857
Tuor, Nancy, 758
Tuor, Nancy R., 758
Tupperware Brands Corp., 3821
Tupperware U.S., Inc., 3821
Turan, Richard B., 446
Turano, Joseph J., 2655
Turba, Lawrence A., 2877
Turchin, Martin, 1548
Turco, Kelly, 1023
Turcotte, Brian, 2785
Turcotte, Deanna, 3542
Turf Paradise, Inc., 3822
Turilli, M. Louise, 3293
Turley, James, 1293
Turley, Robert, 2936
Turnbull, Craig, 1096
Turner & Turner, P.C., 2123
Turner Construction Co., 624, 3824
Turner Industries, Inc., 3825
Turner, Andrew L., 3550, 4007
Turner, B. Kevin, 2501, 2724
Turner, Burt S., 3825
Turner, C. Coolidge, 3805
Turner, Cal, 1143
Turner, Charles H., 2973
Turner, Cornelius, 1082
Turner, David G., 4127
Turner, David J., Jr., 3171
Turner, J. T., 744
Turner, J.T., 744
Turner, Jeffery H., 373
Turner, Jeffrey L., 1981, 3247
Turner, Jim L., 988, 1054
Turner, John D., 91, 2406
Turner, John F., 141, 258, 1968, 2907
Turner, John G., 857
Turner, Kathryn C., 700
Turner, Keena, 3326
Turner, Leslie M., 1791
Turner, M. Terry, 811
Turner, Mark A., 4127
Turner, Marshall, 2316

Turner, Marshall C., 2459
Turner, Marshall C., Jr., 4137
Turner, Mike, 35, 241
Turner, Phil, 4112
Turner, R. Gerald, 2925
Turner, Raymond, 2298
Turner, Reginald M., Jr., 889
Turner, Rhonda P., 823
Turner, Robert, 283
Turner, Robert F., 2032
Turner, Robert J., 283
Turner, Robert W., 3857
Turner, Ronald L., 571
Turner, Suzanne W., 3825
Turner, Terry, 3729
Turner, Thomas H., 3825
Turner, Thomas L., 3628
Turner, Tracy, 1829
Turner, W. Bruce, 2558
Turner, Wesley R., 1472
Turner, William, 3089
Turner, William D., 3089
Turner, William H., 174, 3575
Turney, Sharen Jester, 2325
Turnolo, Terrance, 632
Turpin, Cheryl Nido, 1459
Turpin, Kathleen J., 588
Turrini, Regis, 30
Turzenski, Michael P., 3272
Tuscai, T.J., 1443
Tusch, Carol, 1968, 3711
Tusiani, Michael J., 2691
Tutiakoff, Vincent M., Sr., 2837
Tutor, Ronald N., 3826
Tuttle, Donna, 1790
Tuttle, Ginny, 2556
Tuzroyluk, Sayers, 3751
Tuzroyluk, Sayers, Sr., 3751
Tuzun, Tayfun, 1377
Tweedy, Rusty, 39
Twellman, Beverly, 2487
Twigg-Smith, Benedict, 2944
Twigg-Smith, Christian, 2944
Twigg-Smith, David, 2944
Twigg-Smith, Lisa, 2944
Twigg-Smith, Louisa, 2944
Twigg-Smith, Magdalena, 2944
Twigg-Smith, Thurston, 2944
Twist, Gregory, 55
Twohig, Paul, 1191
Twohill, Lorraine, 4079
Twomey, Christopher A., 3775
Twomey, Robert J., 2403
TXI Operations LP, 3727
Tyabji, Hatim A., 442
Tykeson, Amy, 2625
Tyle, Craig Steven, 1487
Tyler Corp., 3831
Tyler Technologies, Inc., 3831
Tyler, Inc., W.S., 3830
Tyler, Michael R., 1541
Tyler, Robert D., 149
Tyler, Susan, 2448
Tylutki, Joseph P., 2427
Tymon, Deborah A., 2691
Tyonek Native Corp., 934
Tyransky, Jack T., 3858
Tyrrell, Jack, 3166
Tysoe, Ronald W., 816
Tyson, 1858
Tyson Foods, Inc., 3832
Tyson, Barbara A., 3832
Tyson, Bernard J., 2086
Tyson, George E., II, 4135
Tyson, Geroge E., II, 4135
Tyson, John, 3832
Tyson, John H., 3832
Tyson, Laura D'Andrea, 273, 725
Tyson, Laura D., 2570
Tyson, Mitchell G., 2969

U S WEST, Inc., 751
U'Prichard, David C., 2268
U-Ming, Dianne, 3888
U.M. Holding Ltd., 3834
U.S. Bancorp, 3835
U.S. Bank, N.A., 202, 1513, 2050, 2142, 2949, 3835, 3836
U.S. Borax Inc., 3218
U.S. Department of Energy, 3687
U.S. Dept. of Agriculture, 4095
U.S. Dist. Court Roanoke VA, 3127
U.S. Fiduciary Services, Inc., 3837
U.S. Paper Mills Corp., 3500
U.S. Postal Service, 3304
U.S. Poultry & Egg Association, 3839
U.S. Silica Company, 3840
Ubertino, Glenn, 2785
Ubinas, Luis, 1242
Uchikura, Ken, 2857
Udelhoven, Kevin, 1466
Udovic, Michael S., 2016
Udvar-Hazy, Steven F., 3476
Udvarhelyi, I. Steven, 1926
Ueberroth, Peter V., 862
Ueberroth, Virginia M., 1389
Uehlein, Curt, 216
Uffman, Kenneth E., 977
Uffman, Steve, 977
Uffman, Steven L., 977
Uhen, Greg, 1285
Uhing, Gregory S., 536
Uhler, Bill, 2787
Uhler, Paul R., 2529
Uhler, Robert B., 2608
Uhlich, Kevin, 2093
Uhlig, Janice K., 1555
Uhling, Terry T., 3459
Uhlmann, Paul, III, 3846
Uhrich, Marie A., 3747
UIC Construction LLC, 234, 3843
Uihlein Electric Co., Inc., 2554
Ujda, John, 448
Ujioka, Jim, 1317
Ujiri, Masai, 1090
Ujloka, Jim, 1317
Ukpeagvik Inupiat Corp., 3843
Ulatowski, Lois E., 3070
Ulewicz, Michael, 2098
Ulibarri, Milton, 3496
Ullem, Scott B., 407
Ullian, Elaine S., 3733
Ullman, Myron E., III, 2925, 3585
Ullmann, M.H., 2048
Ullmann, Michael H., 2048
Ulrich, Carl, 3902
Ulrich, David O., 2517
Ulrich, Lisa, 1122
Ulrich, Robert J., 3
Ulrich, S. M., 1309
Ulsh, Keith A., 2238
Ultimate Fighting Champion, 30
Ultramar Diamond Shamrock Corp., 3915
UM Power, 1424
UMB Bank, N.A., 516
Umosella, Jeff, 3894
Umosella, Jeffrey, 3894
Umosella, John, 3894
Umosella, Joseph F., III, 3894
Umosella, Joseph F., Jr., 3894
Umpqua Indian Development Corp., 957
Unaka Co., Inc., 3848
Unanue, Carlos A., 3003
Unanue, Robert I., 1622
Underhill, James F., 2431
Underwood, H. Ray, Jr., 3858
Underwood, Jeffrey, 482
Underwood, Jeffrey S., 482
Underwood, Peter C., 3167
Underwood, Roger C., 1383
Ungabrook, Richard, Sr., 3843
Ungarook, Richard, Sr., 3843
Unger, Kathleen, 2958
Unger, Laura S., 638, 819
Unger, Ron, 2184
Unger, Ronald, 2184
Uni, Kathy, 4127
UniGroup, Inc., 3852
Unilever Research, 3853
Unilever United States, Inc., 3853
Uninas, Luis A., 3914
Union Bank, 3854
Union Bank of California, N.A., 3854
Union County Savings Bank, 3855
Union Electric Co., 128
Union Insurance Company, 426
Union Oil Co. of California, 3856
Union Pacific Corp., 3857
Union Savings Bank, 3858
Union Water-Power Co., The, 1904
United Air Lines, Inc., 3860
United Bank, 3861
United Brass Works, Inc., 3862
United Business Media Ltd., 3863
United Business Media PLC, 3863
United Cities Gas Co., 285
United Coal Co., Inc., 3864
United Community Bancorp, 3865
United Community Bank, 3866
United Community Financial Corp., 1845
United Conveyor Corp., 3867
United Distillers & Vintners North America, Inc., 1107
United Finance Co., 3868
United Fire & Casualty Co., 3869
United Healthcare Services, Inc., 3884
United Illuminating Co., The, 3870
United Merchants and Manufacturers, Inc., 3871
United Parcel Service of America, Inc., 3872
United Pharmacy Cooperative Inc., 2956
United Press Syndicate, 3895
United Services Automobile Assn., 3873
United Shellfish Co., Inc., 1989
United Space Alliance, LLC, 3874
United States Steel Corp., 3877
United States Sugar Corp., 3878
United Talent Agency, Inc., 3881
United Telephone Co. of Pennsylvania, The, 3556
United Telephone Mutual Aid Corp., 3883
United Vision Foundation, 2701
United Way of Central Maryland, 2561
United Way of Central NM, 429
UnitedHealth Group Inc., 3884
Unitied States Achievement Academy, 3875
Univar Inc., 3886
Universal Care, Inc., 3888
Universal Computer Consulting, Inc., 1052
Universal Computer Network, Inc., 1052
Universal Computer Systems, Inc., 1052
Universal Foods Corp., 3408
Universal Forest Products, 3890
Universal Forest Products, Inc., 3890
Universal Leaf Tobacco Co., Inc., 3891
Universal Refractories, Inc., 3892
Universal Studios, Inc., 2649, 3893
Universal Supply Co., Inc., 3894
University Health Care System, 2573
University Hospital od Eastern Carolina, 3944
University Loft Co., 136
University Mechanical Contractors, Inc., 3896
Unkovic, John C., 2529
Unneland, Edmund, 2296
Uno, Karen, 1756
Unocal Corp., 3856
Unruh, Cathy, 3624
Unruh, Chad, 2327
Unruh, James A., 3072, 3713
Unruh, Jeannie, 2327
Unruh, Jeannie M., 2327
Unruh, Paul, 3669
Unruh, Travis, 2327
Unruh, Vickie, 468
Unruh, Victor, 2327
Unruh, Victor O., 2327
Unterthiner, Rudy, 3587
Upadhyay, Suketu, 398
Upbin, Hal J., 591
Upchurch, Julian E., 2956
Upchurch, Michael W., 2094
Updegraff, David, 2361
Updike, Kelly & Spellacy, P.C., 3899
Uphoff, Dan, 745
Upper Crust Enterprises, Inc., 3900
Upshaw, Eugene, 2627
Upton, Dennis, 587
Upton, Denny, 3213
Urbach, David, 632
Urban, Daniel, 3265
Urban, Luann, 957
Urban, Philip H., 1631
Urban, R.G., 12
Uribe, Alvaro, 2700
Uribe, Carlos Andres Cran, 2321
Urich, William F., 533
Urkiel, William S., 988
Urness, Kent D., 2813
Urselmann, Sabine, 1195
Urtasun, Frank, 3405
Urtin, Charles G., 3297
Ury, Burton, 790
US Agency for International Development, 2501
US Bank, 1314
US Foodservice, 1858
US Forest Service, 672
US Synthetic, 1538
USA Gasoline Corp., 3903
USA Interactive, 1903
USA Networks, Inc., 1903
USA Petroleum Corp., 3903
USAA Educational Foundation, The, 3873
Usdan, John, 255
Usdin, Stephen, 3177
USG Corp., 3905

Voigt, Steve, 2158
Voissem, Tim, 991
Voith, Garry H., 333
Voiture 327, 3015
Vold, Ron, 3222
Volgenau, Ernst, 3562
Volger, Ronald, 1738
Volk, Gerald N., 2814
Volk, James J., 1730
Volk, Stephen R., 926
Volkema, Michael A., 2517, 4106
Volkman, Jana L., 4014
Volkmann, W. Eric, 1225
Volkswagen of America, Inc., 3967
Voll, Sarah P., 3885
Vollick, Roberta B., 2386
Vollrath Co., LLC, The, 4086
Volmen, Len, 4002
Volpe, Jeff, 3952
Volpe, Vincent R., Jr., 1449
Volpi, Michele, 2983
Voltolina, Frank A., 2050
Voltz, Susan A., 2416
Volvo Village, 3954
Volz, Larry, 3028
Von Althann, Natica, 3026, 3696
von Autenried, Paul, 578
Von Derlinn, Denise, 2757
Von Furstenberg, Alexander, 1903
Von Furstenberg, Alexandre, 3604
von Gillern, Jeffry H., 3835
Von Hassel, Kristen A., 2733
Von Matthiessen, Malte, 4149
Von Metzsch, Ernst H., 1793
von Prondzynski, Heino, 1867
Von Schack, Wesley, 741
von Schack, Wesley W., 44, 344, 3237
Von Schimmelmann, Wulf, 4045
von Seldeneck, Judith M., 3693
Von Staats, Aaron C., 2878
VonCannon, Theresa, 2971
Vonder Haar, Judy, 202
Vonderhaar, Jerry, 2436
Vong, Phillip, 985
Vontalge, Alice, 981
Voorhees, Steven C., 3239
Vopak USA Inc., 3886
Vorsheck, Elizabeth Hirt, 1291
Vorst, Darren J., 3748
Vos Construction Co., Dan, 3969
Vos, Christine A., 3938
Vos, Ellen O'Connor, 2758
Vos, Gary, 3969
Vos, John L., 3938
Vos, Lauren, 3035
Vos, Mary, 3969
Vos, Peter, 625
Vos, Robin M., 3938
Vos, Tricia J., 3938
Vosbein, John, 1445
Voskuil, Steven E., 2150
Voss, Kim K., 136
Voss, Shiela, 3387
Voss, Steven, 2611
Voss, Thomas R., 128
Voss, William R., 2619
Vossler, Jennifer R., 2904
Votek, Glenn A., 1232
Vought, Robert D., 25
Voutsinas, Gerry, 2683
Voutsinas, Spiros J., 2682, 2683
Voves, Lucie H., 3858
Voyles, Bobby L., 350
Voyles, Carolyn Y., 4142
Voynich, S. Scott, 2749
Vrabeck, Kathy, 1530
Vrabel, Jean, 2281
Vrij, Robert, 81
Vrijsen, Peter, 691
Vroman, Gary J., 91
Vuckovich, Miki, 30
Vugrincic, Kellie, 728
Vujovich, Christine M., 2149
Vukich, Chris, 4087
Vulcan Lands Inc., 3972
Vulcan Materials Co., 3972
Vulcan, Inc., 3971

W.E.B. Construction Co., Inc., 553
Waack, Peter, 3675
Wabash Plastics, Inc., 983
Wach, Ken, 1982
Wachovia Bank, 2573
Wachovia Bank, N.A., 404, 2801, 2971, 3707, 3737, 3913, 4028
Wachovia Corp., 4028
Wachtell, Herbert M., 3973
Wachtell, Lipton, Rosen & Katz, 3973
Wachter, James, Dr., 839
Wachter, Ken, 3061
Wachter, Michael R., 2553
Wachter, Paul D., 3757
Wacker, David, 3115
Waddell, Don, 279
Waddell, Frederick H., 2740
Waddell, John C., 249
Waddle, Cy, 826
Wade, Bill, 2552
Wade, David, 3496
Wade, David P., 1921
Wade, Harry D., 3848
Wade, Jim, 39
Wade, Kathleen H., 533
Wade, Lori, 3534
Wade, Malcolm, Jr., 3878
Wade, Martin, 3141
Wade, Mike, 1053
Wade, Neal, 3563
Wade, Robert F., 3302
Wade, Valerie, 2536
Wade, William E., Jr., 913
Wade, William J., 3207
Wadhams, Timothy, 2393
Wadhams, Timothy J., 2393
Wadsworth Brothers Construction Company, Inc., 3974
Wadsworth, Guy L., 3974
Wadsworth, Helene Candi, 3974
Wadsworth, Jeffrey, 700
Wadsworth, Robert A., 3031
Waegelein, Robert A., 3887
Waffle House, Inc., 3975
Wageman, Patrick A., 3873
Wages, Leroy P., 4039
Wages, Robin A., 3832
Waghray, Ajay, 733
Wagler, Theresa E., 3595
Wagner Manufacturing Co., E.R., 3976
Wagner, A.J., 3984
Wagner, Barbara, 3815
Wagner, Barbara L., 3815
Wagner, Bruce, 2620, 4109
Wagner, Charles, 3496
Wagner, Charlie, 3496
Wagner, Chuck, 747
Wagner, Edward H., 177
Wagner, John A., 1891
Wagner, Jon, 1466
Wagner, Kenneth E., 569
Wagner, Kevin, 2471
Wagner, Laura, 96
Wagner, Mark, 2120
Wagner, Mike, 3251
Wagner, Richard M., 1089
Wagner, Ron, 1496
Wagner, Sylvia R., 266
Wagner, Vickie, 1477
Wagner, William J., 792, 2746
Wagner-Fleming, Susan, 2786
Wagoner, G. Richard, 3999
Wagstaff, Paul Smucker, 3488
Wagstaff, Susan S., 3488
Wahl Clipper Corp., 3977
Wahl, Earl K., Jr., 1318
Wahl, Edwin L., 214
Wahl, Greg, 3977
Wahl, Gregory S., 3977
Wahl, Jacqes H., 346
Wahl, Steven M., 443
Wahlstrom, Larry, 3427
Wahlstrom, Scott E., 4048
Waichler, Richard A., 1455
Waid, Richard, 317
Wainaina, Carol, 1126
Wainscott, James L., 67, 2886
Wainwright, Joan, 3829
Waite, Donald C., III, 1683
Waite, Michael K., 2461
Waitukaitis, Michael, 1602
Waitzman, James W., Jr., 3791
Wajsgras, David C., 3135
Wakefield, Chet, 1472
Wakefield, K. Terrence, 2879
Wakefield, Tom, 2217
Wako, Shinya, 2542
Wal-Mart Stores, Inc., 3980
Walchek Family, 1949
Walchek Integrity, LP, 1949
Walchek, Kelli, 1949
Walchek, Scott, 1949
Wald, Ashley, 1833
Wald, Danny, 2896
Waldhart, Wally, 32
Waldmann, Daniel, 3713
Waldock, David A., 2622
Waldrip, J.S., 2920
Waldron, Peter J., 2334
Wales, Bill, 1160
Wales, J.J., 1532
Walfield, Carolyn, 2475
Walgreen Co., 3981
Walgreen Co. and Subsidiaries, 3981
Walgreen, C.R., Jr., 3981
Walhstrom, Scott E., 4048
Walje, A. Richard, 2860
Walk Thru the Bible, 1312
Walk, Randy, 1215
Walke, Tracey, 625
Walkenshaw, Stephanie, 1833
Walker Machinery Co., Cecil I., 3982
Walker, Becky, 83
Walker, Brian C., 565, 2517
Walker, Brooks, Jr., 3363
Walker, Catherine, 3150
Walker, Clarice Dibble, 1348
Walker, Clayton, 2127
Walker, D. Stephen, 3982
Walker, David N., 2410
Walker, Don W., 3390
Walker, Donald L., 3760
Walker, Donna Lee, 3025
Walker, Genevieve, 1286
Walker, Harry M., 490
Walker, Joan H., 107
Walker, John E., 1073
Walker, John H., 2760, 3860
Walker, John L., 4078
Walker, John N., 3515
Walker, Justin, 415
Walker, Karen, 2164
Walker, Kevin E., 1904
Walker, Kimberly G., 890
Walker, Margie Sweet, 3012
Walker, Melinda P., 2717
Walker, Michael P., 2448
Walker, Neal, 3076
Walker, Paul, 1928, 3491
Walker, R. A., 738
Walker, R.A., 190
Walker, Richard, 1099, 3982
Walker, Richard B., 3982
Walker, Richard M., 1488
Walker, Robert, 4040
Walker, Samuel, 2523
Walker, Sidney H., 1576
Walker, Stacey, 1375
Walker, Steve, 3982
Walker, Steven G., 3066
Walker, T. Carl, 1884
Walker, Terry L., 1410
Walker, Wally, 370
Walker, Winston, 136
Wall, Arlene, 3023
Wall, Hugh E., III, 1617
Wall, Jenai Sullivan, 1405
Wall, John, 3023
Wall, John A., 3023
Wall, John W., 3068
Wall, Kevin, 3023
Wall, Mike, 3023
Wall, Mike A., 3023
Wallace Associates, Ltd., 3983
Wallace Preferred Stock Trust, 3141
Wallace, Ann, 3983
Wallace, Anna, 3983
Wallace, Bill, 3983
Wallace, Bruce, 3455
Wallace, Charles D., 2137
Wallace, Chuck, 3638
Wallace, Dennis A., 337
Wallace, Edward, 3502
Wallace, Henry D. G., 1112
Wallace, Henry D.G., 1112, 2237
Wallace, James D., 1687
Wallace, John C., 2374
Wallace, John F., 2618
Wallace, Judith, 3983
Wallace, Keith D., 1402
Wallace, Kelle, 1933
Wallace, Michael, 1496
Wallace, Michael J., 1496
Wallace, Peter C., 219, 3230, 3253
Wallace, Richard, 1528
Wallace, Richard P., 2165
Wallace, Rick, 2165
Wallace, Robert, 3034
Wallace, Sarah Reese, 2881
Wallace, Scott, 375, 507
Wallace, Scott E., 507
Wallace, Steve, 1734
Wallace, Thomas, 859
Wallace, Wilburn N., 3983
Wallace, William H., 1749
Wallace, William N., 3983
Wallace, William N., II, 3983

Weinreich, Steven, 2531
Weinrib, Jerome, 16
Weinrich, Tracy, 3011
Weinstein, Lynn A.M., 2902
Weinzimer, Andrea, 1696
Weir, Margaret Irvine, 2706
Weir, Roger, 393
Weir, Tom, 3902
Weirich, D., 1930
Weis, Jonathan H., 4024
Weis, Robert F., 4024
Weisberg, Arthur, 253
Weisberg, Joan, 253
Weisenbach, Paul, 3196
Weisenburger, Randall J., 696, 2808, 3915
Weisenfeld, Jason, 858
Weisenhoff, Scott M., 2963
Weisenthal, Bruce, 3350
Weisenthal, Bruce P., 3350
Weishaar, Henry, 1867
Weishan, James J., 3409
Weisman, James, 3784
Weiss Scientific Glass Blowing Co., 3777
Weiss, Allen, 216, 1110
Weiss, Andrea M., 966
Weiss, David E., 215
Weiss, Diane L., 882
Weiss, Ellen, 3374
Weiss, Fred G., 4007
Weiss, Gunther, 3777
Weiss, Jeffrey, 149
Weiss, Jerry, 1348
Weiss, Margie, Ph.D., 2461
Weiss, Michael A., 871
Weiss, Morry, 149
Weiss, Neil, 847
Weiss, Peter W., 3790
Weiss, Richard A., 1645
Weiss, Steven, 3424
Weiss, Zev, 149
Weisschuh, Jeannette, 1794
Weisser, Alberto, 2935
Weissman, Robert E., 2984, 3592
Weite, Marie, 1408
Weitz, Richard, 1267
Weitzel, Lyle, 1678
Weitzman, Elizabeth J., 3403
Weizenbaum, Norman, 1571
Welborn, Floyd, 3404
Welborn, Reich L., 2566
Welborn, Wesley Miller, 942
Welburn, Edward T., Jr., 1555
Welch, Bryan, 2787
Welch, Charles M., 3815
Welch, David H., 3614
Welch, Dennis, 141
Welch, Dennis E., 141
Welch, Doug, 1762
Welch, Edwin, 385
Welch, Edwin H., 385
Welch, Glenn S., 1712, 1713
Welch, Jack, 2127
Welch, James L., 3476
Welch, James S., Jr., 592
Welch, John, 4134
Welch, John K., 3904
Welch, John R., 708
Welch, Kevin, 1403
Welch, Mark, 1238
Welch, Mark F., 1946
Welch, Martha, 2329
Welch, P. Craig, Jr., 3597
Welch, Richard G., 4124
Welch, Robert F., Jr., 4112
Welch, Thomas G., 2979
Welch, Thomas H., 1631
Welch, Todd, 2552
Welch-Keller, Wendy, 898
Welding, Robert D., 936
Weldon, Raymond, 1810
Weldon, Raymond F., 1810
Weldon, William C., 804, 1014, 1315, 2071
Welgat, Michael, 3837
Well, Bob, 493
Wellborn, Christopher, 2545
Wellborn, Miller, 942
Wellborn, W. Christopher, 2545
Welle, E. Joseph, 1416
Welle, Paul N., 1416
Welle, Robert, 1416
Welle, Thomas E., 1416
Weller, Danielle, 2009
Weller, Mike L., 1651
Welling, Curtis R., 863
Wellington, Annetee, 1987
Wellington, Jeffrey A., 2323
Wellman, Peter, 3880
Wellmark, Inc., 4026
Wellness, Charlene A., 395
WellPoint, Inc., 4027
Wells Fargo, 918
Wells Fargo & Co., 4028
Wells Fargo Bank, 2573
Wells Fargo Bank Nebraska, N.A., 2806
Wells Fargo Bank, N.A., 524, 532, 973, 1189, 1409, 2501, 2680, 3666, 3798, 4028
Wells, Ann Cowley, 894
Wells, Darrell, 894
Wells, Darrell R., 807
Wells, Darren R., 1612
Wells, DeAngeloa, 3010
Wells, Garry, 1735
Wells, Gawen D., 3303
Wells, George M., 256
Wells, Greg, 3522
Wells, Irvin, 72
Wells, J. Kent, 2441
Wells, J. Lyle, Jr., 3846
Wells, James, 2441
Wells, James M., III, 3654
Wells, Jason P., 2853
Wells, Leeroy, Jr., 921
Wells, Lyndon, 1981
Wells, Margaret Ann, 894
Wells, Marsha, 3322
Wells, Michael A., 2009
Wells, Paula, 2716
Wells, Robert J., 3437
Wells, Trudy, 2800
Wells, Wayne, 894
Welsh, Beth, 2909
Welsh, Carden N., 3754
Welsh, Joe, 3204
Welsh, Kelly R., 2740
Welsh, W. Russell, 3001
Welsko, Donald, 2963
Welters, Anthony, 358, 3884, 4038
Welts, Rick, 728
Wenco, Inc. of North Carolina, 2032
Wenco, Inc. of Ohio, 2032
Wendell, Peter C., 2466
Wender, Ronald H., 1139
Wendholt, Sheila M., 443
Wendlandt, Gary E., 2688
Wendle, Lauren, 2711
Wendler, William F., II, 3040
Wendt, Barb, 3190
Wendt, Nancy J., 2032
Wendt, Roderick C., 2032
Wendy's International, Inc., 4031
Wendy's of Montana, Inc., 4032
Wenger Corp., 4033
Wenger, Brian, 564
Wenger, Brian D., 564
Wenger, Douglas E., 2809
Wenger, E. Philip, 1518
Wenger, Jerry A., 4033
Wenger, Kari, 4033
Wenger, Robin, 152
Wenger, Sonja H., 4033
Wennes, Timothy H., 3854
Wenthen, Jennifer, 1864
Wentworth, Jack R., 2149
Wentworth, Lynn A., 1635
Wentworth, Robert J., 1095
Wentzell, Stephen F., 865
Wentzell, Steve, 865
Wenz, Richard E., 246
Wenzel, Don, 3911
Wenzel, Donald, 3911
Wenzel, Donald P., 3911
Wenzel, Dustin, 3911
Wenzel, Jerome F., Jr., 3614
Wenzel, Mary Jo, 3378
Wenzel-Davlin, Angela, 3911
Wereszczak, Chrysta, 1422
Werle, Christopher J., 295
Werner, David P., 2879
Werner, Jay, 1365
Werner, Mark, 1588
Werner, Michael, 1936
Werner, Thomas, 538
Werner, Thomas C., 538
Werner, Thomas E., 1867
Werner, Tom, 538
Werneth, Tommie, 72
Werning, Joann, 657
Wertheimer, Barbara, 1088
Wertheimer, George, 2354
Wertheimer, Thomas C., 1427
Wertz, Russ, 3655
Wes Pak Sales, Inc., 3225
Wesaw, Mike, 2998
Wescott, David J., 853
Wesley, John W., 2150
Wesley, Norman H., 1474, 1653
Wesley, Rosalyn, 195
Wesley, Timothy R., 4048
Wesolowski, Lori-Ellen, 772
Wesolowski, Timothy M., 3374
Wessel, Jeff, 3777
Wessel, Michael R., 1612
Wessinger, Alesia, 373
Wessinger, Tommy, 1395
Wessman, Craig D., 806
West Bank, 4034
West Chester Savings Bank, 745
West Co., Inc., The, 4038
West Corporation, 4035
West Covina Auto Retail, Inc., 3165
West Essex Bancorp, Inc., 2108
West Manor Construction, 4036
West Penn Power, 1424
West Pharmaceutical Services, Inc., 4038
West United Way Pledge, 3507
West, Daniel, 2557
West, David J., 1065, 3693
West, Jeffrey P., 4093
West, Jerry, 728
West, Jim, 2151
West, John Kevin, 1287
West, Kanyon, 3569
West, Mary Beth, 2925
West, Michael B., 1337
West, Mindy K., 2600
West, Richard B., 2861
West, Rod K., 1279
West, Sandra, 1716
West, Steven M., 289, 818
West, Terri, 3728
West, Terry, 2938
West, Togo Dennis, Jr., 578
Westar Energy, Inc., 4039
Westbrook, Arlene, 3837
Westbrook, Dan, 1265
Westbrook, Kelvin R., 233
Westbrook, Sandra J., 3109
Westbrook, William C., 3031
Westenberger, Richard F., 708
Wester, Nelson G., 1323
Westerberg, Lars, 290
Westerdahl, John, 554
Westerfield, Randolph W., 1765
Westerhaus, William, 779
Westerhoff, Pete, 611
Westerhold, Norman J., III, 3248
Westerlind, Brian S., 4017
Westerlund, David A., 4135
Westerman, Rick, 2263
Western & Southern Life Insurance Co., The, 4040
Western Asset Mgmt. Co., 4041
Western Digital Corp., 4042
Western Digital Technologies, Inc., 4042
Western Massachusetts Electric Co., 2737
Western Oilfield Supply Co., 4043
Western Pacific Mutual Insurance Co., 3191
Western Resources, Inc., 4039
Western Union Co., 4045
Western Ventures, Inc., 2714
Westfall, Kevin P., 292
Westfall, Lance, 173
Westfall, Stephen, 1403
Westfall, Win, 4075
Westfield Group Foundation, 4047
Westfield Insurance Co., 4047
Westfield National Insurance Co., 4047
Westhoff, Theresa, 828
Westinghouse Air Brake Technologies Corp., 4048
Westinghouse Electric Corp., 727
Westinghouse Foundation, 727
Westlake Industries, Inc., 2117
Westlake, Lisa Simone, 2563
Westlake-Reich, Janice, 2615
Westman, Don B., 3714
Westman, Paul J., 1585
Westman, Stephen, 855
Westman, Timothy G., 1257
Weston, Charles, 487
Weston, Graham, 3117
Westphal, Bruce A., 378
Westphal, Graham, 378
Westphal, Matthew, 378
Westphal, Patricia A., 378
Westphal, Penny L., 378
Westphal, Robert S., 619
Westphal, Roger L., 378
Westport Corp., 4050

Wolszczak, Jay, 1727
Wolter, Gary J., 2334
Wolter, John F., 3899
Wolters, Kate Pew, 3597
Woltmann, Charles L., 3649
Wolverine World Wide, 4106
Wolz, John F., 937
Womack, Christopher C., 3516
Womack, Walter C., 620
Womble, Dustin R., 3831
Womble, Ralph, 1719
Wonder Transport, Inc., 4107
Wong, Andrea L., 2264
Wong, Cheryl, 3053
Wong, Gary, 717
Wong, Irwin, 723
Wong, Juanene L., 1121
Wong, Kurt, 3687
Wong, Mary, 2785
Wong, Paul, 276
Wong, Phillip W., 674
Wong, Sandra C.H., 3412
Wong-Chapman, Marguerite, 1239
Wonka, 30
Woo, Carolyn Y., 210, 2715
Woo, Tracy Timothy, 84
Wood County National Bank, 4108
Wood County Trust Co., 4108
Wood Prince, William Norman, 3046
Wood, Adam, 1427
Wood, Arthur M., Jr., 2740
Wood, Brad, 3568
Wood, Bradford S., 3568
Wood, Brett, 2401
Wood, Brian K., 3931
Wood, C. Martin, III, 1446
Wood, Christianna, 1695
Wood, David, 2600
Wood, David M., 2600
Wood, E. Jenner, III, 2847
Wood, Elizabeth, 3988
Wood, Ellen, 2101
Wood, Frank E., 773
Wood, Frank J., 112
Wood, Jenner, 3654
Wood, Jenner E., III, 3516
Wood, Keith, 113
Wood, Kristin K., 853
Wood, Michael B., 999, 3600
Wood, Mike J., 3135
Wood, Oscar Lee, 3450
Wood, Phoebe A., 863, 2246
Wood, Richard D., Jr., 4009
Wood, Ritch N., 2759
Wood, Rob, 1586
Wood, Robert L., 3029
Wood, Roger, 3777
Wood, Roger J., 595, 1026
Wood, Rogger, 3777
Wood, Susan Elizabeth, 2028
Wood, Ted G., 112
Wood, Thomas J., III, 3846
Wood, William, 2830
Wood, William E., 586
Wood, Yvonne M., 3840
Woodall, James, 1371
Woodall, Martin, 1021
Woodard, Elizabeth B., 3227
Woodard, Jack D., 128
Woodburn, Connie, 685
Woodbury, J. J., 1315
Woodbury, Timothy S., 3404
Woodcliff, Inc., 1782
Woodcock, James, 3567
Woodford, Michael C., 2804
Woodforest National Bank, 4110
Woodhouse, Hope, 2983
Woodhouse, Kathleen, 40
Woodhouse, Michael A., 966
Woodley, Loni Lyle, 180
Woodlief, John B., 1738
Woodman's, Inc., 2475
Woodman, Jonathan J., 1946
Woodring, A. Greig, 3179
Woodrow, Kenneth B., 1073
Woodruff, Bob, 2710
Woodruff, J. David, 1270
Woodrum, James D., 2861
Woods, Charles Dean, 1563
Woods, Daniel J., 154
Woods, Dorothy M., 882
Woods, Ed, 3591
Woods, Frank G., III, 797
Woods, Jacqueline F., 3760
Woods, James D., 1296
Woods, Jerry D., 1668
Woods, John, 544
Woods, John F., 3854
Woods, John R., Jr., 3619
Woods, John, III, 859
Woods, Judith, 3619
Woods, Kenton C., 3262
Woods, Laurel R., 154
Woods, Mary Jane, 154
Woods, Pat, 1337
Woods, Richard A., 679
Woods, Robert C., 1548
Woods, Teresa, 906
Woods, Tony, 2129
Woodside, Dennis, 2585
Woodson, Nathaniel D., 1419, 3870
Woodtrust Financial Corp., 4108
Woodward Governor Co., 4112
Woodward, Danielle, 3347
Woodward, Elizabeth Z., 1053
Woodward, Eric, 3476
Woodward, Inc., 4112
Woodward, Jim, 722
Woodward, Joan Kois, 3802
Woodward, Kelly, 2906
Woodward, Sara, 83
Woodward, Sharon, 3640
Woodward, Sharon V., 332
Woodward, Steve, 263
Woodward, W. Philip, 4113
Woodword, Joan K., 3802
Woodworth, Gregory D., 2633
Woodworth, J. K., 3
Woodworth, Richard, 3340
Woodworth, Richard J., 3340
Woody, Joe, 2156
Woody, Joe F., 2156
Woody, Kerry L., 91
Woolery, Roger L., 1547
Woolf, Arthur G., 2671
Woolf, Ryan, 290
Woollems, J. Michael, 40
Woolnough, Mark, 2771
Woolsey, Suzanne H., 1448
Woolson, Tyler, 1568
Woolway, Paul, 3363
Woori America Bank, 4114
Wooster Republican Printing Co., 1063
Wootton, Percy, 1485
Woram, Brian, 2105
Worek, Bob, 489
Workman, John L., 2807
Workman, Thomas E., 4047
Worl, Rod, 1317
Worl, Rosita F., 3380
Worl, Rosita, Dr., 3380
World of Chantilly, Inc., 4119
World Products, Inc., 4120
World Reach, 685
World-Wide Holdings Corp., 4122
WorldCom, Inc., 3327
Worley, Eric, 4084
Worman, Nancy H., 1425
Wormley, David N., 323
Worms, Vincent, 3930
Worrall, Bob, 2767
Worrell, Judy, 435
Worroll, David, 1138
Worsoe, Johannes, 347
Worsoe, Johannes H., 347
Wortel, Gary, 1472
Worth, David N., 2661
Worth, Jeffrey A., 3616
Worthen Industries, Inc., 4123
Worthen, David S., 4123
Worthen, Frederic P., 4123
Worthen, Frederic P., Jr., 4123
Worthen, Helen F., 4123
Worthen, Susan B., 4123
Worthing, Dave, Jr., 1438
Worthington, Beth A., 2929
Worthington, John M., 2181
Worthington, Michael, 927
Worthington, Scott, 3199
Wortley, Michael, 2981
Woudstra, F. Robert, 1338
Wowczuk, Yurd, 2001
Woys, James E., 1766
WPS Advisors, 3604
Wraase, Dennis R., 2737, 2933, 3018
Wrang, William E., 4016
Wrangler Apparel Corp., 3913
Wrassman, Owen, 814
Wray, William K., 491
Wren, John D., 2808
Wrench, M. Mervyn K., 285
Wrench, W. David, 2356
Wrenn, Frank, 1073
Wright Farms, Inc., 1414
Wright, Bradley J., 1345
Wright, Bruce, 23
Wright, Carolyn Savage, 3341
Wright, Charlie, 2194
Wright, Chuck, 2151
Wright, David, 934
Wright, Debbie, 3587
Wright, Deborah, 711
Wright, Deborah C., 711, 3757
Wright, Doreen, 984
Wright, Eddie, 1712, 1713
Wright, Elease E., 48
Wright, Emilee Savage, 3341
Wright, Georgianna, 2668
Wright, Harold B., 591
Wright, James, 88
Wright, James F., 1695
Wright, James W., 2879
Wright, Jeff, 1401
Wright, Jeffrey L., 1524
Wright, Joel, 3116
Wright, John, 3775
Wright, Julia V., 471
Wright, Karen Buchald, 237
Wright, Karen Buchwald, 237
Wright, Keith, 1953
Wright, Kimberly J., 757
Wright, Laura H., 854, 921
Wright, Mark, 160
Wright, Meg, 853
Wright, Michael W., 2049
Wright, Miranda, 1167
Wright, P.J., 606
Wright, Phillip D., 2971, 4077
Wright, Randy W., 1895
Wright, Robert C., 3123
Wright, Terrence L., 3524
Wright, Theodore, 908
Wright, Tracy, 1180
Wright, Wayne W., 2332
Wrighton, Mark S., 642, 945
Wrigley, 1186
Wrigley Jr. Co., Wm., 4125
Wrigley, William, Jr., 4125
Wroblewski, Jeff, 1517
Wronowski, Allen, 2954
Wronski, Maria, 579
Wronski, Marti, 2527
Wroten, Kimberly, 1620
Wry, Steve, 3940
WSBT, Inc., 3507
WSJV Television, Inc., 3110
WTVF-News Channel 5 Network, 2218
Wu, Grace T., 1202
Wu, Jack, 1470
Wu, Peter, 723
Wu, Simone, 798
Wu, Tom C., 1619
Wuebbels, Brian, 2459
Wuebbling, Don, 4040
Wuerch, Thomas, 3681
Wuest, James, 2162
Wuest, Timothy J., 314
Wuh, Hank C., 726
Wuite, Frans, 3992
Wujek, Lena, 423
Wulbrect, Edward, 3632
Wulf, Gene C., 3484
Wulf, Walter H., 2553
Wulf, Walter H., Jr., 2553
Wulff, John K., 775, 2563, 3650
Wulfsohn, Michael, 1582
Wulfsohn, William A., 700
Wunderlich, Ralf K., 221
Wunning, Steven H., 2125
Wunsch, Charles, 3556
Wuori, Stephen J., 1265
Wurmb, Robert O., 2486
Wurst, Bradley S., 89
Wurster Oil Co., Inc., 4128
Wurtzel, Patrick A., 459
Wurzburg, Inc., 4129
Wurzburg, Warren, Jr., 4129
WVVA Television, Inc., 3110
Wyatt, E. Lee, 1474
Wyatt, Joe B., 1941
Wyatt, John L., 1410
Wyatt, John T., 2007
Wyatt, Leslie, 240
Wyatt, Tom, 1533, 2177
Wyckoff, Richard L., 634
Wylie, Mike, 1898
Wyllie, Tony, 1872, 3054
Wyly, Evan A., 2409
Wyly, Evan Acton, 2409
Wyman, Richard E., 2474
Wyngarden, Allison Van, 3937
Wynkoop, Cynthia B., 594
Wynn's-Precision, Inc., 2886
Wynn, Donna, 1137
Wynne Building Corporation, 4133
Wynne, Brian, 862

Wynne, Christopher, 2707
Wynne, Deena L., 4133
Wynne, Dorothy, 4133
Wynne, Eric P., 4133
Wynne, James E., 629
Wynne, Joel F., 4133
Wynne, Matthew L., 4133
Wynne, Matthew Lyle, 4133
Wyoming Affiliate Of Susan G. Komen, 503
Wyrick, Cynthia G., 342
Wyrofsky, Randolph A., 1844
Wyrofsky, Randy A., 491
Wyrsch, Martha B., 3558
Wyrwicki, Doug, 1438
Wyse, Alden M., 2122
Wyse, Christopher, 1506
Wysham, Lark, 947
Wyshner, David, 299
Wyshner, David B., 299, 300, 604
Wyskiel, Christy, 2409
Wyss, Andre, 2753
Wyss, Jim, 1948
Wytana, Inc., 2142

Xcel Energy Inc., 4135
Xenos, Jim, 2311
Xerox Corp., 4136
XI Properties, 135
XL Global Services, Inc., 4134
XTEK, Inc., 4138
Xu, Xiao Ming, 794

Yabuki, Jeffrey W., 1427
Yackira, Michael W., 2765
Yacoby, Alicia Kaylie, 3367
Yaeger, Douglas H., 1393, 2207
Yager, Karrie, 3567
Yaglenski, John F., 157
Yagow, James, 1082
Yahia, Laurance H.S., 2265
Yakle, Steven B., 3667
Yale New Haven Health, 3944
Yale, David L., 2077
Yale, Phyllis R., 501, 2154
Yam, Osher, 3991
Yamada, Albert M., 1405
Yamada, Sayuri, 3076
Yamada, Tadataka, 56
Yamamoto, James, 3782
Yamamoto, Takuji, 2810
Yamamura, Masahiro, 4042
Yamanaka, Todd, 1996
Yamanishi, Kenichiro, 2538
Yamasato, Jon, 3189
Yanai, Tadashi, 1343
Yanarella, Mark C., 2645
Yancey, James D., 3674
Yancy, Luke, III, 1406
Yang, Geoffrey Y., 1487
Yang, Patrick Y., 3723
Yangkyu, Kim, 3320
Yaniga, Stephanie, 3070
Yankee Gas Services Company, 2737
Yanney, Gail Walling, 616
Yanney, Michael B., 616
Yannotti, Alexander, 1020
Yano, Michiko, 2190
Yano, Ron, 2295
Yantek, Dawn, 3995
Yantis, Tom, 3991
Yanussi, Linda, 1376
Yao, Lily K., 1405
Yao, Ming, 959
Yap, Keith, 1672
Yaqozinski, Steven, 3145
Yarbrough, Ethan, 109
Yarbrough, Hal, 2247
Yarbrough, Michael, 3569
Yard, Beverly, 2470
Yard, Chris, 2470
Yard, Christopher, 2470
Yard, Kenneth G., 2470
Yard, Robert, 2470
Yardley, James C., 1239, 3405
Yarmolinsky, Alex, 2370
Yarmouth Redemption Center, 867
Yarno, Wendy L., 3566
Yarrington, Patricia, 780
Yarrington, Patricia E., 780
Yasin, Ralph, 1445
Yasinsky, John B., 854, 921, 3361
Yaskowitz, Jerry, 1013
Yastine, Barbara A., 3045
Yates Petroleum Corp., 2018
Yates, Dick, 3731
Yates, Doug, 2316
Yates, Gary R., 3944
Yates, Harvey E., 2018
Yates, Harvey E., Jr., 2018
Yates, Lloyd M., 1189, 2385
Yates, Michael, 310
Yates, Michelle Crozier, 38
Yates, Richard L., 3731
Yates, Roy D., 412
Yates, Timothy T., 2560
Yates, William G., III, 4142
Yates, William G., Jr., 4142
Yates-Mack, Barrett E., 2018
Yavitz, Jessica, 783
Yawman, Gregory, 521
Yeadon, Cathy C., 962
Yeager, Frederick C., 1766
Yeager, J. Michael, 455
Yeaman, Eric K., 74, 85
Yeaman, John M., 3831
Yeamans, David G., 620
Yearley, Douglas C., Jr., 3769
Yeary, Frank D., 1950
Yeater, Max, 3053
Yeatman, Cynthia P., 2556
Yeatman, Harry, 626
Yeaton, Howard, 283
Yeaton, Howard R., 283
Yeaton, Violet F., 805
Yedid, Eli, 1013
Yedid, Jack, 1013
Yedid, Simon, 1013
Yee Tung Garment Co., Ltd., 3123
Yee, Donald, 506
Yee, James, 261
Yee, John F., 3324
Yee, Paul, 2916
Yeh, Charlotte S., 501
Yeldirim, Erdal, 3125
Yelencsics, Joseph A., 2341
Yelnosky, John, 1620
Yemenidjian, Alex, 1685, 3166
Yena, John A., 349
Yeomans, J. L., 3
Yeomans, Janet L., 3
Yeonopolus, Suzanne, 2038
Yerves, Ken, 2044
Yessick, Marsha, 942
Yeutter, Clayton K., 616
Yevich, Cynthia A., 505
Yevoli, Lewis, 2681
Yi, Sung, 3952
Yingling, Christopher, 1114
Yingling, Cindy Eni, 1114
Yingling, Cynthia Eni, 1114
Yingling, Robert S., 1589
Yingst, Tara, 2314
Yip, June, 1381
Yip, Leonard, 2871
Yockey, Ronald, 548
Yocum, Robert G., 1741
Yoder, Julie, 2368
Yoffie, David B., 1950
Yoh, Harold L., III, 3707
Yokoi, Masamichi, 1020
Yokoyama, Doug, 41
Yokozawa, Yoichi, 2540
Yomantas, Gary C., 2674
Yonker, Michael T., 1255, 4112
Yonng, Tamara S., 74
Yonz, Buddy, 3848
Yonz, L.A., 3848
Yoo, Tae, 818
Yoon, Gene Y.S., 1379
Yoon, John, 2140
Yoon, Kyung H., 3455
York Cable Television Co., 3661
York Container Co., 4145
York Graphic Services, Inc., 4143
York, Denise DeBartolo, 3326
York, Douglas W., 1303
York, Jed, 3326
York, Jill E., 2415
York, John C., II, 3326
York, Kelli, 1303
York, Susan, 1303
York, Susan E., 1303
York, Victoria, 1303
Yormark, Brett, 584
Yormark, Michael, 1442
Yory Produce, LLC, 3002
Yoshida, Blanche R., 1672
Yoshida, Makoto, 1923
Yoshida, Takuro, 54
Yoshihara, Grant M., 2747
Yoshimura, John, 2107
Yost, Jill, 1952
Yost, Larry D., 1955, 2125
Yost, R. David, 2385
Young Agency, Inc., The, 4146
Young Contracting/SE, Inc., 4147
Young Steel Products Co., 4148
Young, A. Thomas, 3311
Young, Abby, 624
Young, Abuhassanali, 2344
Young, Andrew C., 2746
Young, Austin P., III, 1944
Young, Babette S., 4148
Young, Beatriz Palomino, 3405
Young, Bill, 507
Young, Caroline McKissick, 89
Young, Daphne, 434
Young, Dave, 2401
Young, David, 1696
Young, Deborah, 3000
Young, Denise, 4125
Young, Dona D., 1459
Young, Donald, 3758
Young, Fran, 3690
Young, Frank M., III, 1748
Young, Gary W., 4147
Young, Gerald T., 542
Young, Glenn, 3387
Young, James R., 3857
Young, Jason, 849
Young, Jerry, 1554
Young, John F., 1273
Young, Joseph P., 3591
Young, Julie, 1073
Young, Kyle, 1416
Young, Larry D., 1169
Young, M. A., 4148
Young, Madeline, 3133
Young, Martin H., Jr., 437
Young, Maury, 4148
Young, Miles, 2788
Young, Mollie Hederman, 250
Young, P., 2788
Young, Paul, 3405, 3696
Young, Phil, 717
Young, Philip M., 717
Young, Ray G., 233
Young, Robert A., 4148
Young, Robert H., Jr., 65
Young, Ron, 2401
Young, Shirley, 3318
Young, Shirley A., 3708
Young, Steven K., 1189
Young, Suellen, 1121
Young, Thomas L., 1484, 2844
Young, Tricia, 663
Young, Walter R., Jr., 2756
Young, William B., 385
Young, William D., 465
Young, William J., 2287
Young, William M., 2229
Youngblood, Gary C., 1270
Youngblood, Kneeland, 1273
Youngblood, Rhonda, 1790
Younger, Gil, 763
Youngman, Judie, 11
Yourish, Brad, 3530
Youth Football Fund, 2091
Youth Football Fund, Inc., 1651
Yovovich, Paul G., 1542
Yowan, David L ., 143
Yox, Donna, 1037
YPW Asset Trust, 3044
YSI Inc., 4149
Yska, Dugald, 694
Yue, Drina, 4045
Yuen, Sharyl E. Lam, 1672
Yuen, Sharyl Lam, 1672
Yum Brands, Inc., 807
Yum! Brands, Inc., 4150
Yuth, Harold, 3397

Zabita, Frank, 3855
Zabriskie, John L., 2120
Zaccagnino, Joseph A., 956, 3944
Zaccaria, Adrian, 395
Zaccaro, Warren J., 3389
Zachary, Seth M., 2900
Zack, Stephen, 1018
Zadeh, Mansour T., 3487
Zafirovski, Mike S., 516, 1134
Zagel, Margaret M., 1633
Zahn, Kristie, 313
Zaidi, Ijlal Hussain, 303
Zalaznick, Lauren, 2002, 2649
Zale, Liz, 3458
Zalenski, Fred T., 1662
Zales, William E., Jr., 71
Zallie Supermarkets, Inc., 4152
Zallie, George, 4152
Zallie, George J., 4152
Zaloom, Richard P., 980
Zaltas, Arnold I., 2506

GEOGRAPHIC INDEX

This index lists corporations alphabetically by the states and cities in which their corporate giving programs, foundations, headquarters, subsidiaries, divisions, joint ventures, offices, and plants are located. Corporations are identified by abbreviated versions of their names and referenced by the sequence numbers assigned in the Descriptive Directory. Omitted from this index are the names of the individual corporate giving programs, foundations, subsidiaries, divisions, and joint ventures. This information can be found in the complete corporation entries of the Descriptive Directory.

ALABAMA

Albertville
Subsidiaries: Caterpillar 722, Regions 3171
Aliceville
Office: Westervelt 4046
Anniston
Office: Regions 3171
Plants: FMC 1449, SUPERVALU 3659
Athens
Office: Regions 3171
Plant: Steelcase 3597
Atmore
Corporate Giving Program: Poarch 2998
Foundation: United 3861
Corporate Headquarters: Poarch 2998, United 3861
Plant: Dixie 1132
Auburn
Plants: Briggs 565, Donaldson 1153
Bay Minette
Plant: Valmont 3919
Birmingham
Corporate Giving Programs: Alabama 71, Altec 118, Balch 327, Birmingham 472, Bradley 550, Burr 621, Energen 1270, Gulf 1689, Maynard 2413, O'Neal 2771, Protective 3066, Regions 3171, Vulcan 3972
Foundations: Alabama 71, Altec 118, Birmingham 471, Blue 492, Compass 901, Craft 967, Dunn 1192, Energen 1270, Golden 1601, Harbert 1726, Haskell 1748, Mayer 2412, McWane 2440, Mitchell 2537, Portrait 3012, Protective 3066, Regions 3171, Sterne 3602, Tractor 3791, Vulcan 3972
Corporate Headquarters: Alabama 71, Altec 118, Balch 327, Birmingham 471, Birmingham 472, Blue 492, Bradley 550, Burr 621, Compass 901, Craft 967, Dunn 1192, Energen 1270, Golden 1601, Harbert 1726, Haskell 1748, Mayer 2412, Maynard 2413, McWane 2440, Mitchell 2537, O'Neal 2771, Portrait 3012, Protective 3066, Regions 3171, Sterne 3602, Tractor 3791, Vulcan 3972, Walter 3984
Subsidiaries: Commercial 893, El Paso 1239, McWane 2440, Nucor 2760, Saks 3315, Schein 3348, Southern 3516, Synovus 3674, Walter 3984
Joint Venture: Alabama 71
Offices: Adams 34, AT&T 274, Baker 325, Balch 327, Bradley 550, Burr 621, Charter 765, Dixon 1133, Federal 1349, Ford 1462, Littler 2289, Regions 3171, State 3591, Wurzburg 4129
Plants: Butler 626, CA 638, McAfee 2417, Owens 2841
Blountsville
Subsidiary: Community 897
Brewton
Foundation: BancTrust 337
Calvert
Corporate Giving Program: First 1398
Chatom
Subsidiary: Interface 1953
Plant: Interface 1953
Citronelle
Plant: Worthington 4124
Columbiana
Office: Westervelt 4046
Columbus
Office: Regions 3171
Courtland
Plant: International 1968
Cuba
Plant: Westervelt 4046
Cullman
Foundation: Cullman 1001
Cororate Headquarters: Cullman 1001
Subsidiary: Superior 3658
Daphne
Corporate Giving Program: EAP 1204
Cororate Headquarters: EAP 1204
Decatur
Foundation: ITW 2001
Cororate Headquarters: ITW 2001
Office: Regions 3171
Demopolis
Plant: Westervelt 4046
Dothan
Subsidiary: Sony 3502
Office: Regions 3171
Enterprise
Subsidiary: Synovus 3674
Office: Regions 3171
Eufaula
Cororate Headquarters: American 135
Subsidiary: Teleflex 3707
Fayette
Corporate Giving Program: Ox 2846
Cororate Headquarters: Ox 2846
Florence
Plant: Hillshire 1809
Foley
Foundation: Vulcan 3971
Cororate Headquarters: Vulcan 3971
Division: DIRECTV 1124
Gadsden
Office: Regions 3171
Plant: Goodyear 1612
Gordo
Office: Westervelt 4046
Guntersville
Foundation: Kappler 2095
Cororate Headquarters: Kappler 2095
Hartselle
Plant: Sonoco 3500
Hueytown
Plants: Cliffs 850, Hunt 1892
Huntsville
Corporate Giving Program: Lanier 2222
Foundation: Orthopaedic 2829
Corporate Headquarters: Lanier 2222, Orthopaedic 2829
Subsidiaries: DRS 1179, Synovus 3674
Offices: Bradley 550, Draper 1171, Maynard 2413, Regions 3171
Plants: Kohler 2182, Mentor 2462, PPG 3025, Raytheon 3135, Rockwell 3247
Hurtsboro
Plant: U.S. 3840
Jasper
Subsidiary: Synovus 3674
Lincoln
Subsidiary: Honda 1851
Livingston
Subsidiary: Westervelt 4046
Luverne
Foundation: Airtek 66
Madison
Office: Wurzburg 4129
McIntosh
Plant: Olin 2801
Mobile
Foundations: Bay 379, Regions 3171
Corporate Headquarters: BancTrust 337, Bay 379
Subsidiary: Dixie 1132
Offices: Adams 34, Boh 517, Burr 621, GATX 1542, Littler 2289, Maynard 2413, Regions 3171, Univar 3886
Plant: Armstrong 246
Montevallo
Subsidiary: Leggett 2246
Montgomery
Corporate Giving Program: First 1398
Foundations: Alabama 72, Alfa 87, Caddell 645
Corporate Headquarters: Alabama 72, Alfa 87, Caddell 645
Subsidiaries: Alfa 87, Haskell 1748, Synovus 3674
Offices: Baker 325, Balch 327, Bradley 550, Burr 621, Maynard 2413, Regions 3171
Plants: STERIS 3600, Winn 4087
Moundville
Plant: Westervelt 4046

Opelika
Foundation: Scott 3369
Cororate Headquarters: Scott 3369
Pelham
Subsidiary: Danaher 1027
Plant: Owens 2841
Phenix City
Foundation: Johnston 2054
Cororate Headquarters: Johnston 2054
Subsidiary: Synovus 3674
Office: Regions 3171
Plant: Owens 2842
Prattville
Plant: International 1968
Rainsville
Foundation: Rainsville 3121
Cororate Headquarters: Rainsville 3121
Ralph
Plant: Westervelt 4046
Roanoke
Plant: Dixie 1132
Santa Rosa
Office: Regions 3171
Saraland
Plant: Dixie 1132
Selma
Subsidiary: Vulcan 3971
Offices: Regions 3171, Regis 3172
Plant: International 1968
Trinity
Subsidiary: Nucor 2760
Troy
Cororate Headquarters: Airtek 66
Office: Regions 3171
Tuscaloosa
Foundation: Westervelt 4046
Cororate Headquarters: Westervelt 4046
Subsidiaries: Hunt 1889, Nucor 2760, Rite 3220, Synovus 3674
Office: Regions 3171
Plant: Valmont 3919

ALASKA

Anchorage
Corporate Giving Programs: Alaska 75, Alaska 76, Alyeska 121, First 1415, General 1550, Northrim 2743
Foundations: Alaska 74, Aleut 84, Bristol 576, Calista 657, Chenega 776, Chugach 805, Cook 934, Eyak 1317, Glacier 1586, Koniag 2184, Kuskokwim 2200, Old 2797, Tanadgusix 3687, Ukpeagvik 3843
Corporate Headquarters: Alaska 75, Alaska 76, Aleut 84, Alyeska 121, Arctic 234, Bristol 576, Calista 657, Chenega 776, Chugach 805, Cook 934, First 1415, General 1550, Koniag 2184, Kuskokwim 2200, Northrim 2743, Old 2797, Seldovia 3397, Tanadgusix 3687, Tatitlek 3694, Tikigaq 3751, Ukpeagvik 3843
Subsidiaries: Arctic 234, AT&T 273, Bering 422, Choggiung 797, Chugach 805, ConocoPhillips 913, Lynden 2320, Premera 3034, Tesoro 3723
Offices: BP 547, Crowell 986, Davis 1041, Dorsey 1157, Eyak 1317, Humana 1886, K&L 2080, KeyBank 2136, Kiewit 2142, Lane 2221, Littler 2289, Patton 2898, Perkins 2940, Perkins 2941, Regis 3172, Stoel 3611, Ukpeagvik 3843
Aniak
Office: Kuskokwim 2200
Barrow
Foundation: Arctic 234
Subsidiary: Arctic 234
Cordova
Foundation: Tatitlek 3694
Cororate Headquarters: Eyak 1317
Dillingham
Foundation: Choggiung 797
Cororate Headquarters: Choggiung 797
Subsidiary: Choggiung 797
Fairbanks
Foundations: Doyon 1167, Usibelli 3906
Corporate Headquarters: Doyon 1167, Usibelli 3906
Subsidiary: Arctic 234
Healy
Corporate Giving Program: Usibelli 3906
Hoonah
Subsidiary: Huna 1887
Juneau
Foundations: Huna 1887, Sealaska 3380
Corporate Headquarters: Huna 1887, Sealaska 3380
Ketchikan
Subsidiary: Sealaska 3380
Kodiak
Office: Koniag 2184
Kotzebue
Foundation: NANA 2615
Cororate Headquarters: NANA 2615
Subsidiary: NANA 2615
Nome
Foundations: Bering 422, Sitnasuak 3467
Corporate Headquarters: Bering 422, Sitnasuak 3467
Subsidiaries: Bering 422, Caparo 673
Point Hope
Foundation: Tikigaq 3751
Seldovia
Foundation: Seldovia 3397
Unalaska
Foundation: Ounalashka 2837
Cororate Headquarters: Ounalashka 2837
Wasilla
Plant: Wal-Mart 3980

ARIZONA

Bullhead City
Foundation: Porter 3005
Cororate Headquarters: Porter 3005
Casa Grande
Office: Southwestern 3526
Plant: Hexcel 1795
Chandler
Corporate Giving Programs: Bashas' 369, Microchip 2499
Corporate Headquarters: Bashas' 369, Gould 1618, Microchip 2499
Subsidiary: Ergon 1289
Division: Rogers 3253
Offices: Applied 220, CDW 729, Fishel 1429
Plants: Hexcel 1795, Motorola 2586
Cottonwood
Office: Southwestern 3526
Dewey
Office: Fishel 1429
Flagstaff
Foundation: Nackard 2612
Cororate Headquarters: Nackard 2612
Glendale
Corporate Giving Program: Coyotes 963
Foundations: Coyotes 963, Delta 1077
Cororate Headquarters: Coyotes 963
Subsidiary: Corning 945
Kingman
Office: Southwestern 3526
Lake Havasu City
Office: Southwestern 3526
Lakeside
Office: Southwestern 3526
Marana
Foundation: Trico 3807
Cororate Headquarters: Trico 3807
Mesa
Foundations: Empire 1262, Sonoran 3501, Southwestern 3526
Corporate Headquarters: Empire 1262, Southwestern 3526
Division: Rogers 3253
Offices: Fishel 1429, Sonoran 3501
Plants: Arch 230, Motorola 2586, Univar 3886
Nogales
Foundation: Pony 3002
Cororate Headquarters: Pony 3002
Offices: Fennemore 1360, Southwestern 3526
Peoria
Office: Jennings 2036
Phoenix
Corporate Giving Programs: Arizona 239, Avnet 304, AZPB 310, Blue 500, Carter 706, Circle 817, Fennemore 1360, Gammage 1531, Gust 1691, Jennings 2036, Lewis 2256, Osborn 2831, Phoenix 2968, Snell 3490, SUMCO 3638, U-Haul 3833, US 3902
Foundations: Apollo 216, Arizona 239, AZPB 310, B & B 312, Brinkster 574, Ewing 1303, Fennemore 1360, Freeport 1494, Macayo 2330, PetSmart 2948, Phoenix 2968, Powers 3024, Snell 3490, Transit 3798, Turf 3822, US 3902, Viad 3946
Corporate Headquarters: Apollo 216, Arizona 239, Avnet 304, AZPB 310, Blue 500, Brinkster 574, Carter 706, Delta 1077, Ewing 1303, Fennemore 1360, Freeport 1494, Gammage 1531, Gust 1691, Jennings 2036, Lewis 2256, Macayo 2330, Osborn 2831, PetSmart 2948, Phoenix 2968, Powers 3024, Snell 3490, Sonoran 3501, SUMCO 3638, Turf 3822, U-Haul 3833, Viad 3946
Subsidiaries: Alcatel 81, Arizona 239, Associated 261, Belo 406, Clear 842, CORE 941, Farmers 1338, Gannett 1532, Lennar 2250, M.D.C. 2324, Meredith 2471, Opus 2820, Otter 2836, PerkinElmer 2939, Pulte 3083, Raymond 3133, Republic 3188, US 3902, Viad 3946, Washington 3999, Zions 4158
Divisions: Caesars 650, Cox 958
Offices: American 143, Applied 220, Ballard 329, Brownstein 593, Bryan 596, Federal 1349, Fennemore 1360, Fishel 1429, Ford 1462, Greenberg 1654, Gust 1691, Hays 1761, Holder 1829, Humana 1886, Husch 1896, Jennings 2036, Kiewit 2142, Kimley 2151, Lauth 2232, Lewis 2256, Liberty 2265, Littler 2289, Perkins 2940, Perkins 2941, Polsinelli 3001, Quarles 3101, SAS 3336, Sherman 3436, Snell 3490, Southwestern 3526, Squire 3561, Steptoe 3599, Stinson 3608, Thompson 3739, Tutor 3826, United 3873, US 3902, Vision 3961
Plants: Bassett 372, CA 638, Castle 716, Deluxe 1084, Golden 1602, Honeywell 1852, Lennar 2250, McAfee 2417, Novell 2754, Owens 2841, Pactiv 2863, Procter 3055, Southwest 3524, Sub-Zero 3630, UTC 3908, West 4038
Prescott
Office: Southwestern 3526
Rio Rico
Plant: Badger 313
Safford
Office: Southwestern 3526
Scottsdale
Corporate Giving Programs: Go 1595, Hunt 1888
Foundations: Mutual 2606, NRT 2757, Sprague 3551, Stardust 3586
Corporate Headquarters: Fender 1359, Go 1595, Hunt 1888, NRT 2757, Stardust 3586
Subsidiaries: Arctic 234, Nationwide 2639, New York 2688, Pacific 2855, West 4038
Office: Reinhart 3178
Plant: Motorola 2586
Sierra Vista
Office: Southwestern 3526
Sun City
Office: Southwestern 3526
Tempe
Corporate Giving Programs: B & B 312, Salt 3319
Corporate Headquarters: B & B 312, Circle 817, Salt 3319, US 3902
Subsidiaries: Health 1766, Lennar 2250, US 3902
Divisions: Bard 358, Rogers 3253, Safeway 3310
Offices: Mortenson 2577, Pulte 3083, State 3591
Plants: Coca 862, West 4038
Tolleson
Plant: Quaker 3094

Tucson
Corporate Giving Program: Tucson 3819
Foundations: Capri 682, Discovery 1126, Sundt 3648
Corporate Headquarters: Capri 682, Sundt 3648, Tucson 3819
Subsidiaries: Alcoa 82, Belo 406, Evening 1302, Kimberly 2150, M.D.C. 2324, Newmont 2698
Division: Lennar 2250
Offices: Fennemore 1360, Granite 1632, Gust 1691, Humana 1886, Intuit 1982, Kiewit 2142, Kimley 2151, Lewis 2256, Pulte 3083, Quarles 3101, Regis 3172, Snell 3490
Plants: Raytheon 3135, Sasol 3338, Southwest 3524, Texas 3728, Tomkins 3771
Willcox
Foundations: Sulphur 3637, Valley 3918
Corporate Headquarters: Sulphur 3637, Valley 3918
Yucca
Plant: Chrysler 801
Yuma
Office: Southwestern 3526

ARKANSAS
Arkadelphia
Cororate Headquarters: Southern 3514
Armorel
Subsidiary: Nucor 2760
Bauxite
Subsidiary: Manitowoc 2355
Plant: Alcoa 82
Bearden
Foundation: Anthony 206
Cororate Headquarters: Anthony 206
Bentonville
Corporate Giving Program: Wal-Mart 3980
Foundation: Wal-Mart 3980
Cororate Headquarters: Wal-Mart 3980
Office: Strauss 3624
Plant: Scotts 3372
Blytheville
Corporate Giving Program: Nucor-Yamato 2761
Cororate Headquarters: Nucor-Yamato 2761
Subsidiary: Nucor 2760
Plant: NIBCO 2707
Booneville
Subsidiary: Spang 3530
Camden
Plant: GenCorp 1548
Conway
Office: Univar 3886
Plant: FMC 1449
Crossett
Subsidiary: Georgia 1568
Plant: Bemis 407
De Queen
Subsidiary: Weyerhaeuser 4052
Dumas
Plant: Bassett 372
El Dorado
Corporate Giving Program: Murphy 2600
Foundation: Murphy 2600
Corporate Headquarters: Murphy 2600, Neurology 2665
Subsidiaries: Ergon 1289, Murphy 2600
Fayetteville
Offices: Littler 2289, RJN 3228
Plant: Campbell 669
Flippin
Foundation: Northern 2738
Cororate Headquarters: Northern 2738
Plant: Wal-Mart 3980
Fort Smith
Division: Quanex 3100
Plants: Owens 2842, Whirlpool 4056
Hardy
Subsidiary: CenturyLink 751
Hope
Plant: Scotts 3372
Jefferson
Office: Bionetics 467
Jonesboro
Plant: FMC 1449
Little Rock
Corporate Giving Program: Entergy 1278
Foundations: Arkansas 240, Friday 1501, Mountaire 2590, ProtechSoft 3065, Rose 3263, Southern 3514, Stephens 3598
Corporate Headquarters: Arkansas 240, Entergy 1278, First 1398, Friday 1501, ProtechSoft 3065, Riggs 3213, Rose 3263, Stephens 3598
Subsidiaries: Entergy 1279, First 1398, Leggett 2246, Regions 3171
Division: AEGON 45
Office: Kiewit 2142
Plants: Hunt 1892, Strauss 3624
Lowell
Corporate Giving Program: Hunt 1892
Cororate Headquarters: Hunt 1892
Subsidiary: Hunt 1892
Magnolia
Plant: Albemarle 78
Malvern
Plant: Pactiv 2863
Mountain Home
Subsidiaries: CenturyLink 751, Gannett 1532
Newport
Foundation: Arkansas 241
Cororate Headquarters: Arkansas 241
North Little Rock
Cororate Headquarters: Mountaire 2590
Plant: Timken 3760
Osceola
Subsidiary: Southwire 3527
Paragould
Plant: Tenneco 3715
Pine Bluff
Plants: Entergy 1279, International 1968
Prescott
Foundation: Firestone 1386
Subsidiary: Potlatch 3017
Rogers
Foundation: New 2669
Cororate Headquarters: New 2669
Plants: Clorox 852, Guardian 1682, Preformed 3032
Russellville
Plant: Procter 3055
Sheridan
Plant: Kohler 2182
Siloam Springs
Foundation: Allen 98
Cororate Headquarters: Allen 98
Subsidiary: Hallmark 1707
Plant: La-Z-Boy 2205
Springdale
Corporate Giving Program: Tyson 3832
Foundation: Tyson 3832
Cororate Headquarters: Tyson 3832
Stuttgart
Foundation: Riceland 3203
Cororate Headquarters: Riceland 3203
Texarkana
Plant: Cooper 936
Warren
Subsidiary: Potlatch 3017
Plant: Armstrong 246
White Hall
Foundation: Neurology 2665
Wynne
Division: Halstead 1708

CALIFORNIA
Agoura Hills
Foundation: Fender 1359
Cororate Headquarters: USA 3903
Subsidiaries: First 1400, Fiserv 1427
Alameda
Corporate Giving Program: Oakland 2772
Foundation: Perforce 2937
Corporate Headquarters: Oakland 2772, Perforce 2937
Subsidiary: Safeguard 3307
Office: State 3592
Alamo
Cororate Headquarters: Integrity 1949
Alhambra
Foundation: Alhambra 88
Cororate Headquarters: Alhambra 88
Subsidiary: Alcatel 81
Aliso Viejo
Foundation: Lennar 2250
Office: Safeco 3306
Alpine
Corporate Giving Program: Viejas 3951
Cororate Headquarters: Viejas 3951
Anaheim
Corporate Giving Programs: 7 4, Anaheim 191, Angels 200, Specialty 3538
Foundations: Angels 200, Bentley 416, Control 929, Gon 1608, Willdan 4075
Corporate Headquarters: 7 4, Anaheim 191, Angels 200, Control 929, Specialty 3538, Willdan 4075
Subsidiary: Tomkins 3771
Plants: Hexcel 1795, KB 2105, LyondellBasell 2322, Neville 2667, Procter 3055, Quad 3091
Anderson
Cororate Headquarters: Sierra 3451
Antelope Valley
Plant: Deluxe 1084
Antioch
Corporate Giving Program: EcoNexus 1221
Cororate Headquarters: EcoNexus 1221
Aptos
Subsidiary: Newman's 2697
Arcadia
Subsidiary: Safeway 3310
Office: Dilbeck 1116
Plant: Commercial 893
Arcata
Division: Sierra 3451
Arleta
Subsidiary: Kellwood 2121
Auburn
Plant: Carpenter 700
Azusa
Plant: Valspar 3920
Bakersfield
Foundation: Western 4043
Corporate Headquarters: Castle 718, Western 4043
Subsidiaries: Castle 717, Dole 1141, McGraw 2429, Occidental 2780
Division: Cox 958
Offices: Granite 1632, State 3591
Plants: Barnes 362, Chevron 780, General 1554, Groeniger 1670
Banning
Subsidiary: Deutsch 1098
Belvedere
Corporate Giving Program: Little 2288
Cororate Headquarters: Little 2288
Bennett Valley
Office: Exchange 1306
Berkeley
Corporate Giving Programs: Heller 1773, Mal 2349, Peet's 2916, Sun 3644
Foundation: Pagnol 2865
Corporate Headquarters: Mal 2349, Pagnol 2865, Sun 3644
Subsidiaries: Discovery 1126, Zions 4158
Beverly Hills
Foundations: Capital 678, Endeavor 1267, United 3881
Corporate Headquarters: Endeavor 1267, Puck 3080, United 3881
Subsidiaries: Fox 1480, Pacific 2855
Biola
Plant: Sealed 3381

Bonsall
Corporate Giving Program: Mamma 2353
Cororate Headquarters: Mamma 2353
Brea
Corporate Giving Program: Beckman 397
Foundation: Beckman 397
Cororate Headquarters: Beckman 397
Subsidiaries: Allegheny 91, Danaher 1027
Office: Richards 3208
Brisbane
Subsidiary: eBay 1217
Buena Park
Foundation: Medieval 2449
Cororate Headquarters: Medieval 2449
Burbank
Corporate Giving Programs: Disney 1127, Warner 3989
Foundations: Disney 1127, LJA 2291
Corporate Headquarters: Disney 1127, LJA 2291, Warner 3989
Subsidiary: ARAMARK 223
Offices: Dilbeck 1116, Turner 3823
Plant: Crane 970
Burlingame
Cororate Headquarters: Phoenix 2967
Subsidiary: AOL 209
Burney
Division: Sierra 3451
Calabasas
Plant: Emerson 1257
Calimesa
Division: Deutsch 1098
Campbell
Subsidiary: First 1389
Office: Mercury 2469
Carlsbad
Corporate Giving Programs: Callaway 660, Chuao 803, Drop 1178, Life 2268
Foundations: Callaway 660, Life 2268
Corporate Headquarters: Callaway 660, Chuao 803, Drop 1178, Life 2268, Stram 3622
Subsidiary: Nordson 2723
Plants: Indiana 1931, Rockwell 3247
Carpinteria
Subsidiary: Armstrong 246
Division: Zimmer 4157
Carson
Corporate Giving Program: Los Angeles 2308
Foundation: Los Angeles 2308
Corporate Headquarters: Indiana 1931, Los Angeles 2308
Subsidiaries: Emerson 1257, Leggett 2246
Plants: General 1554, Nalco 2613
Cerritos
Corporate Headquarters: Caremore 689, Reeves 3165
Subsidiary: First 1400
Chatsworth
Foundation: New Hampshire 2674
Subsidiaries: Kellwood 2121, New Hampshire 2674, Zions 4158
Plant: Deluxe 1084
Chico
Plant: Smucker 3488
Chula Vista
Plants: Panasonic 2869, Sealed 3381
City of Commerce
Subsidiary: Kellwood 2121
Plant: Dreyer's 1174
City of Industry
Foundations: Cacique 644, Majestic 2343
Cororate Headquarters: Majestic 2343
Subsidiary: Comerica 889
Plants: Campbell 669, Golden 1602, Goulds 1619, Steelcase 3597, Wal-Mart 3980
Cloverdale
Office: Exchange 1306
Coddingtown
Office: Exchange 1306
College
Office: Exchange 1306
Colton
Office: GATX 1542
Commerce
Joint Venture: McCormick 2423
Compton
Subsidiaries: Caterpillar 722, Kroger 2195
Plants: Owens 2842, Teleflex 3707
Concord
Foundation: Hofmann 1824
Corporate Headquarters: Hofmann 1824
Offices: Factory 1323, Kiewit 2142
Plant: Office 2785
Corning
Plant: Sierra 3451
Corona
Cororate Headquarters: Watson 4007
Subsidiaries: Spirol 3545, Watson 4007
Office: Dart 1033
Costa Mesa
Corporate Giving Program: Rutan 3290
Corporate Headquarters: Griswold 1669, Rutan 3290
Subsidiaries: Griswold 1669, NIKE 2710
Offices: Baker 319, Bingham 463, Blakely 480, BMC 508, California 655, Fitzpatrick 1434, Latham 2228, Paul 2900, Pillsbury 2975, Rutan 3290, Sheppard 3435
Cotati
Office: Exchange 1306
Covina
Foundations: Ameritec 179, Oxford 2848
Corporate Headquarters: Ameritec 179, Oxford 2848
Subsidiaries: Avery 297, PerkinElmer 2939
Culver City
Corporate Giving Programs: REthink 3195, Sony 3504
Corporate Headquarters: REthink 3195, Sony 3504
Subsidiary: Sony 3502
Office: Symantec 3669
Cupertino
Corporate Giving Program: Apple 217
Foundation: Intero 1973
Corporate Headquarters: Apple 217, Seagate 3377
Subsidiaries: Amazon.com 122, Cadence 646, Grace 1623, Mentor 2462
Plant: Hewlett 1794
Cypress
Corporate Giving Program: Yamaha 4141
Foundation: Mitsubishi 2540
Corporate Headquarters: Mitsubishi 2538, Mitsubishi 2540, Yamaha 4141
Subsidiaries: DRS 1179, Mitsubishi 2540
Plants: Mary 2392, Panasonic 2869, Rockwell 3247
Dana Point
Foundation: Guided 1686
Cororate Headquarters: Guided 1686
Danville
Foundation: Herrick 1788
Del Mar
Plant: Hexcel 1795
Delano
Plant: Thermo 3733
Diamond Bar
Subsidiary: Johnson 2048
Dinuba
Foundation: Rivermaid 3225
Dublin
Plant: KB 2105
Dutton
Office: Exchange 1306
Eagle Rock
Office: Dilbeck 1116
East Palo Alto
Offices: Bingham 463, Greenberg 1654
El Cajon
Cororate Headquarters: Whirl 4055
Subsidiaries: GKN 1585, PerkinElmer 2939
Plants: Carpenter 700, Toro 3775
El Dorado
Subsidiary: Murphy 2600
El Dorado Hills
Corporate Giving Program: Parker 2884
Foundation: Parker 2884
Cororate Headquarters: Parker 2884
Office: California 655
El Monte
Subsidiary: PerkinElmer 2939
El Segundo
Corporate Giving Programs: DIRECTV 1124, Los Angeles 2307, Mattel 2405
Foundations: Continental 922, DIRECTV 1124, Los Angeles 2306, Los Angeles 2307, Mattel 2405
Corporate Headquarters: Continental 922, DIRECTV 1124, Los Angeles 2307, Mattel 2405
Subsidiary: Chevron 780
Division: Los Angeles 2307
Office: California 655
Plants: Chevron 780, Raytheon 3135, Xerox 4136
Elk Grove
Plant: Sonoco 3500
Emeryville
Corporate Giving Program: Jamba 2020
Foundation: Clif 848
Corporate Headquarters: Clif 848, Jamba 2020, Medeanalytics 2447, Oaklandish 2773, Peet's 2916
Plant: Sherwin 3437
Encino
Cororate Headquarters: Securitas 3390
Escondido
Office: Mercury 2469
Eureka
Division: Cox 958
Fair Oaks
Office: Pan-American 2868
Fairfield
Corporate Giving Program: Jelly 2033
Cororate Headquarters: Jelly 2033
Subsidiary: Robbins 3230
Fallbrook
Corporate Giving Program: Focus 1451
Cororate Headquarters: Focus 1451
Fontana
Corporate Giving Program: Burrtec 622
Corporate Headquarters: Burrtec 622, Vista 3962
Foster City
Corporate Giving Program: Gilead 1582
Foundation: Gilead 1582
Cororate Headquarters: Gilead 1582
Offices: Hanson 1725, SAP 3334
Fountain Valley
Corporate Giving Programs: Kingston 2161, Noritz 2726
Corporate Headquarters: Fema 1358, Hyundai 1902, Kingston 2161, Noritz 2726
Fremont
Corporate Giving Programs: Fremont 1496, Greenlight 1658, Lam 2214
Foundations: Eagle 1202, Fremont 1496
Corporate Headquarters: Eagle 1202, Fremont 1496, Greenlight 1658, Lam 2214
Subsidiaries: Johnson 2048, Seagate 3377
Joint Venture: General 1555
Office: Men's 2460
Plant: KB 2105
French Camp
Office: Granite 1632
Fresno
Foundations: Bruno 594, Fowler 1478
Corporate Headquarters: Bruno 594, Fowler 1478
Subsidiary: Giant 1573
Offices: California 655, Granite 1632, Littler 2289
Plants: FMC 1449, Groeniger 1670, Illinois 1916, KB 2105, PPG 3025
Fullerton
Subsidiary: Emerson 1257
Plant: Guardian 1682
Garden Grove
Office: Costco 948

Gardena
Foundations: Ramona's 3126, Tireco 3762
Corporate Headquarters: Nissan 2716, Ramona's 3126, Tireco 3762
Subsidiaries: Canon 672, Deutsch 1098
Glendale
Corporate Giving Programs: DineEquity 1120, DreamWorks 1172, Nestle 2663
Foundations: CIBA 809, DreamWorks 1172, Nestle 2663
Corporate Headquarters: CIBA 809, DineEquity 1120, DreamWorks 1172, Nestle 2663
Subsidiaries: DineEquity 1120, Nestle 2663, Tension 3717
Offices: ACE 24, Dilbeck 1116
Gold River
Office: California 655
Goleta
Corporate Giving Program: Deckers 1059
Cororate Headquarters: Deckers 1059
Subsidiary: Robbins 3230
Divisions: Cox 958, DIRECTV 1124
Plant: Raytheon 3135
Hanford
Plant: Beneficial 411
Hawthorne
Division: Northrop 2744
Hayfork
Division: Sierra 3451
Hayward
Foundation: Groeniger 1670
Cororate Headquarters: Groeniger 1670
Plants: Cabot 643, Sealed 3381, Univar 3886
Healdsburg
Subsidiary: HCA 1762
Office: Exchange 1306
Hemet
Subsidiary: Deutsch 1098
Division: Deutsch 1098
Hercules
Corporate Giving Program: Mechanics 2446
Hermosa Beach
Office: Mercury 2469
Hollister
Subsidiary: Raymond 3133
Hollywood
Foundation: Red 3152
Subsidiaries: Eastman 1214, Mercedes 2463
Office: Boises 518
Huntington Beach
Corporate Giving Program: California 653
Foundations: Quiksilver 3108, Sunshine 3653
Corporate Headquarters: Quiksilver 3108, Sunshine 3653
Division: Sharp 3422
Plant: CA 638
Huntington Park
Subsidiary: Armstrong 246
Indian Wells
Offices: Best 441, Private 3050
Indio
Office: Granite 1632
Irvine
Corporate Giving Programs: Allergan 99, Broadcom 579, Detour 1092, Kia 2140, Mazda 2414, Taco 3679, Western 4042
Foundations: Allergan 99, Broadcom 579, Gateway 1541, Golden 1602, Griswold 1669, Integra 1947, Irvine 1992, St. John 3564, Sunwest 3655, Taco 3679, Western 4042
Corporate Headquarters: Allergan 99, Broadcom 579, Continental 925, Detour 1092, Fieldstone 1374, Gateway 1541, Golden 1602, Kawasaki 2102, Kia 2140, Mazda 2414, St. John 3564, Sunwest 3655, Taco 3679, Western 4042
Subsidiaries: Brink's 571, California 655, Edison 1228, M.D.C. 2324, Pacific 2855, Yum! 4150
Divisions: Parker 2886, ServiceMaster 3414
Offices: Allen 95, Best 441, Bryan 596, Canon 672, Cerner 754, Crowell 986, Dechert 1058, Dickstein 1111, Dorsey 1157, Gibson 1580, Grant 1633, Greenberg 1654, ITA 1998, Jones 2058, K&L 2080, Littler 2289, McDermott 2425, Morgan 2571, Opus 2820, Pepper 2934, SAP 3334, Sedgwick 3395, Shook 3439, Singerlewak 3463, Snell 3490, Whiting 4063
Plants: Katten 2101, Novell 2754, Panasonic 2869, Rockwell 3247
Irwindale
Foundation: Sierra 3449
Cororate Headquarters: Sierra 3449
Plant: Miller 2523
Jackson
Corporate Giving Program: Jackson 2011
Cororate Headquarters: Jackson 2011
Subsidiary: Georgia 1568
Kingsburg
Plant: Guardian 1682
La Canada
Foundation: Dilbeck 1116
Cororate Headquarters: Dilbeck 1116
La Canada Flintridge
Office: Dilbeck 1116
La Crescenta
Office: Dilbeck 1116
La Habra
Cororate Headquarters: Bentley 416
Plant: Chevron 780
La Jolla
Foundations: Copley 938, ResMed 3192
Cororate Headquarters: Copley 938
Office: Singerlewak 3463
La Mirada
Subsidiary: Miller 2517
La Palma
Office: BP 547
La Puente
Cororate Headquarters: Cacique 644
La Verne
Foundation: Micro 2498
Cororate Headquarters: Micro 2498
Lafayette
Foundation: Simpson 3461
Office: GATX 1542
Lake Forest
Cororate Headquarters: Pacific 2858
Office: Fishel 1429
Lakewood
Foundation: WKS 4100
Cororate Headquarters: WKS 4100
Larkfield
Office: Exchange 1306
Larkspur
Office: Hanson 1725
Lathrop
Subsidiary: Save 3342
Livermore
Subsidiary: Davey 1035
Office: Costco 948
Plants: Hexcel 1795, Intel 1950
Lodi
Cororate Headquarters: Rivermaid 3225
Subsidiary: GKN 1585
Offices: California 655, Dart 1033
Plant: General 1554
Long Beach
Corporate Giving Programs: Epson 1286, Obagi 2776
Corporate Headquarters: Epson 1286, Obagi 2776
Subsidiaries: Apex 214, Boeing 516, Occidental 2780, PerkinElmer 2939
Offices: Kimley 2151, Vision 3961
Plants: NYK 2768, Tenneco 3715, Valmont 3919
Los Altos
Foundations: Cupertino 1009, Packard 2862
Cororate Headquarters: Packard 2862
Los Angeles
Corporate Giving Programs: AECOM 42, Allen 95, California 656, Castle 718, City 830, Farmers 1338, Forever 1469, Gibson 1580, Hooper 1856, Irell 1991, Jeffer 2029, KB 2105, Leibowitz 2248, Loeb 2295, Los Angeles 2305, Los Angeles 2306, Metro 2479, Metropolitan 2484, Munger 2598, Occidental 2780, Paul 2900, Quinn 3111, Richards 3208, SABEResPODER 3300, Sheppard 3435, Sunkist 3649, Veev 3927
Foundations: Adir 36, Ann's 203, BBCN 386, Buchalter 600, California 656, Capital 677, Castle 717, Cathay 723, Chinese 794, Cohn 866, Creative 975, Delphos 1072, Fairmount 1328, Farmers 1338, Guess 1685, Hyundai 1902, J-M 2005, LAC 2206, Lim 2275, Los Angeles 2305, Metropolitan 2483, Network 2664, Puck 3080, Singerlewak 3463, Sports 3550, Upper 3900, Vista 3962, Wells 4028
Corporate Headquarters: Adir 36, AECOM 42, Allen 95, Ann's 203, BBCN 386, Buchalter 600, California 656, Capital 677, Castle 717, Cathay 723, CB 725, City 830, Creative 975, Fairmount 1328, Farmers 1338, Forever 1469, Gibson 1580, Guess 1685, Hooper 1856, Irell 1991, J-M 2005, Jeffer 2029, KB 2105, LAC 2206, Leibowitz 2248, Lim 2275, Loeb 2295, Los Angeles 2305, Los Angeles 2306, Metro 2479, Metropolitan 2483, Metropolitan 2484, Munger 2598, Occidental 2780, Paul 2900, Quinn 3111, Richards 3208, SABEResPODER 3300, Sheppard 3435, Singerlewak 3463, Sports 3550, Upper 3900, Veev 3927
Subsidiaries: Berkshire 429, Capital 677, CB 725, Chicago 787, Coca 863, Delta 1073, Dole 1141, Emmis 1259, Farmers 1338, Fox 1480, Grace 1623, Hunter 1893, Johnson 2048, KB 2105, Macy's 2333, Metropolitan 2481, Occidental 2780, Pacific 2855, Sempra 3405, Servco 3412, Viacom 3945
Offices: Abacus 9, Acumen 33, Akerman 69, Akin 70, Allen 95, Alston 116, Arent 235, Arnold 248, Baker 319, Ballard 329, Bessemer 440, Best 441, Bingham 463, Blakely 480, Brownstein 593, Bryan 596, C & C 633, Chadbourne 759, Clark 836, Cozen 964, Credit 980, Crowell 986, Davis 1041, Dechert 1058, Dickstein 1111, Drinker 1175, Duane 1185, Edelman 1224, Electronic 1242, Federal 1349, Fisher 1433, Foley 1453, Ford 1462, Fulbright 1516, Getty 1569, Gibson 1580, Gleacher 1589, Goodwin 1611, Grant 1633, Greenberg 1654, Hays 1761, Hogan 1825, Holland 1834, Holme 1837, Hooper 1856, Irell 1991, Jenner 2035, Jones 2058, K&L 2080, Katten 2101, Kelley 2118, Kirkland 2164, Kreindler 2193, Latham 2228, Littler 2289, Loeb 2295, Mayer 2411, McDermott 2425, McGuireWoods 2430, McKenna 2433, Milbank 2511, Mintz 2534, Morgan 2571, Morrison 2576, Munger 2598, NIBCO 2707, Opus 2820, Orrick 2826, Paul 2900, Perkins 2941, Pillsbury 2975, Polsinelli 3001, Presley 3038, Pryor 3073, Quinn 3111, Reed 3163, Richards 3208, Robins 3232, Robins 3233, Safety 3309, SAS 3336, Sedgwick 3395, Sheppard 3435, Sidley 3446, Simpson 3462, Skadden 3470, Skidmore 3474, Snell 3490, Squire 3561, State 3592, Steptoe 3599, Sullivan 3634, Thompson 3739, Venable 3929, White 4058, Winston 4089
Plants: adidas 35, Alcoa 82, Bassett 372, Chevron 780, Clorox 852, Coca 862, Donnelley 1155, Guardian 1682, Huhtamaki 1884, Indiana 1931, Interface 1953, International 1962, Katten 2101, Krueger 2196, Miller 2523, Mitsui 2541, Novell 2754, Owens 2841, Pactiv 2863, Rockwell 3247, Valassis 3914, Valmont 3919, Valspar 3920
Los Osos
Corporate Giving Program: Elemental Herbs 1244
Cororate Headquarters: Elemental Herbs 1244
Loyalton
Division: Sierra 3451
MacDoel
Foundation: Griswold 1669
Madera
Plant: FMC 1449
Malibu
Foundations: Morley 2572, Terra 3721
Cororate Headquarters: Terra 3721
Division: DIRECTV 1124
Manhattan Beach
Corporate Giving Program: Skechers 3472
Cororate Headquarters: Skechers 3472

Marina del Rey
Office: Quad 3091
McClellan
Subsidiary: Jacobs 2016
Mendota
Plant: Thermo 3733
Menlo Park
Cororate Headquarters: Harris 1737
Offices: Alston 116, Goodwin 1611, Jones 2058, Latham 2228, McDermott 2425, Needham 2655, Perkins 2940, Weil 4022
Milpitas
Corporate Giving Programs: LifeScan 2271, LSI 2314
Foundations: Flextronics 1437, KLA-Tencor 2165
Corporate Headquarters: KLA-Tencor 2165, LifeScan 2271
Subsidiaries: Johnson 2048, Scotts 3372, Seagate 3377
Plant: Lancaster 2216
Miraloma
Plant: Ingram 1941
Mission Viejo
Foundation: Ensign 1275
Cororate Headquarters: Ensign 1275
Subsidiary: Lennar 2250
Modesto
Corporate Giving Programs: Gallo 1529, Save 3342
Corporate Headquarters: Gallo 1529, Save 3342
Division: Gallo 1529
Office: Wendel 4029
Plants: American 135, Butler 626, Georgia 1568, Groeniger 1670, KB 2105, Procter 3055
Monrovia
Foundation: Bubalo 598
Cororate Headquarters: Bubalo 598
Subsidiary: Alcoa 82
Monterey
Corporate Giving Program: PRO*ACT 3053
Cororate Headquarters: PRO*ACT 3053
Plant: McGraw 2429
Monterey Park
Cororate Headquarters: Network 2664
Office: Singerlewak 3463
Montgomery Village
Office: Exchange 1306
Moorpark
Foundation: USA 3903
Subsidiary: Fiserv 1427
Morgan Hill
Cororate Headquarters: Intero 1973
Plant: Hospira 1867
Morro Bay
Plant: Chevron 780
Mountain View
Corporate Giving Programs: Fenwick 1362, Google 1613, Intuit 1982, Symantec 3669
Foundations: eBay 1217, Google 1613, Intuit 1982, Symantec 3669, Synopsys 3673
Corporate Headquarters: Fenwick 1362, Google 1613, Intuit 1982, Symantec 3669, Synopsys 3673
Subsidiaries: Activision 30, AOL 209, Bausch 376, eBay 1217, Intuit 1982, Johnson 2048
Offices: Dechert 1058, Fenwick 1362, Intuit 1982, Lewis 2256, Symantec 3669
Plants: Adobe 38, Hewlett 1794
Napa
Corporate Giving Program: One 2812
Foundation: Doctors 1139
Corporate Headquarters: Doctors 1139, One 2812
Subsidiary: First 1400
National City
Plant: PerkinElmer 2939
Nevada City
Plant: Menasha 2461
Newark
Plant: Morton 2579
Newbury Park
Plant: Hexcel 1795
Newport Beach
Corporate Giving Programs: Pacific 2855, Stradling 3621
Foundations: Fieldstone 1374, Pacific 2855, Reeves 3165
Corporate Headquarters: Irvine 1992, Pacific 2855, Stradling 3621
Subsidiaries: Danaher 1027, First 1389, Irvine 1992, Pacific 2855
Division: Griswold 1669
Offices: Buchalter 600, Google 1613, Irell 1991, Stradling 3621
Plant: KB 2105
Newport Coast
Foundation: Fema 1358
Nicasio
Cororate Headquarters: Lucasfilm 2316
Novato
Foundation: Fireman's 1385
Corporate Headquarters: Fireman's 1385, Republic 3186
Oakdale
Plant: Hershey 1791
Oakland
Corporate Giving Programs: CC 728, Clorox 852, Give 1583, Kaiser 2086, Katovich 2100, Melissa 2458, Oaklandish 2773, Wendel 4029
Foundations: Athletics 276, CC 728, Clorox 852, Dreyer's 1174
Corporate Headquarters: Athletics 276, CC 728, Clorox 852, Dreyer's 1174, Give 1583, Heller 1773, Kaiser 2086, Katovich 2100, Melissa 2458, Wendel 4029
Subsidiary: Clorox 852
Offices: Boises 518, Katten 2101, Kimley 2151, Reed 3163
Plant: Quaker 3094
Oceanside
Subsidiary: Emerson 1257
Office: Fishel 1429
Ontario
Corporate Giving Program: Citizens 824
Cororate Headquarters: Citizens 824
Subsidiaries: Biomet 466, Leggett 2246
Offices: Best 441, California 655, United 3872
Plants: Donaldson 1153, Sherwin 3437
Orange
Subsidiary: First 1389
Offices: Factory 1323, Kimley 2151, Pan-American 2868
Oxnard
Subsidiary: Duda 1188
Plants: Berry 437, Procter 3055, Smucker 3488
Pacheco
Corporate Giving Program: Bay 378
Foundation: Bay 378
Cororate Headquarters: Bay 378
Palm Coast
Cororate Headquarters: DeniseLawrence.Com 1086
Palm Desert
Subsidiary: Progressive 3057
Palm Springs
Subsidiary: Gannett 1532
Palmdale
Plant: KB 2105
Palo Alto
Corporate Giving Programs: Hewlett 1794, Wilson 4083, World 4118
Foundations: C.M. 637, Harris 1737, Hewlett 1794, Intuit 1982, Marchon 2369, Marcus 2370
Corporate Headquarters: C.M. 637, Hewlett 1794, Marcus 2370, Wilson 4083, World 4118
Subsidiaries: Amazon.com 122, Canon 672, Hoffmann 1823
Offices: Arnold 248, Baker 321, Credit 980, Dorsey 1157, Finnegan 1384, Foley 1453, Gibson 1580, Hogan 1825, Jones 2058, K&L 2080, Kirkland 2164, Mayer 2411, Mintz 2534, Morgan 2571, Morrison 2576, Paul 2900, Perkins 2941, Pillsbury 2975, Reed 3163, Rutan 3290, SAP 3334, Shearman 3429, Sheppard 3435, Sidley 3446, Simpson 3462, Squire 3561, Sullivan 3634, Vinson 3958, White 4058, Wilson 4083
Paramount
Plants: Castle 716, Coral 940
Pasadena
Corporate Giving Programs: Christie 800, Kaiser 2086, Parsons 2887
Foundations: Avery 297, Chapman 763, Community 898, Jacobs 2016, Western 4041
Corporate Headquarters: Avery 297, Chapman 763, Christie 800, Community 898, Jacobs 2016, Parsons 2887, Western 4041
Subsidiaries: Arctic 234, Avery 297, HCA 1762, Jacobs 2016, Legg 2245, Parsons 2887
Offices: Avon 305, Dilbeck 1116, Federal 1349, Private 3050
Plant: Schulman 3361
Paso Robles
Corporate Giving Program: Heritage 1785
Cororate Headquarters: Heritage 1785
Subsidiary: Heritage 1785
Plant: Lubrizol 2315
Pebble Beach
Foundation: Pebble 2913
Cororate Headquarters: Pebble 2913
Petaluma
Offices: Autodesk 289, Exchange 1306
Pico Rivera
Division: Northrop 2744
Pittsburg
Plant: Dow 1161
Placerville
Corporate Giving Program: Millennia 2516
Cororate Headquarters: Millennia 2516
Pleasanton
Corporate Giving Programs: Ross 3267, Safeway 3310
Foundations: Safeway 3310, Shaklee 3418
Corporate Headquarters: Ross 3267, Safeway 3310, Shaklee 3418, Simpson 3461
Subsidiaries: Automatic 291, Hoffmann 1823, PepsiCo 2935, VHA 3944
Division: Safeway 3310
Offices: AT&T 274, Kimley 2151, Liberty 2265, Opus 2820, Oracle 2821, Pan-American 2868, Whirlpool 4056
Plants: Clorox 852, Hexcel 1795
Poway
Subsidiary: Hunter 1893
Plant: Rockwell 3247
Quincy
Division: Sierra 3451
Rancho Cordova
Corporate Headquarters: GenCorp 1548, Vision 3961
Subsidiaries: Health 1766, M.D.C. 2324
Rancho Cucamonga
Plant: General 1551
Rancho Palos Verdes
Foundation: Indiana 1931
Rancho Santa Margarita
Foundations: Capital 678, Continental 925
Cororate Headquarters: Capital 678
Subsidiary: Capital 678
Red Bluff
Plant: Sierra 3451
Redding
Foundation: Sierra 3451
Subsidiary: Shea 3428
Division: Sierra 3451
Office: California 655
Plant: Groeniger 1670
Redlands
Subsidiary: Venturedyne 3933
Plant: La-Z-Boy 2205
Redwood City
Corporate Giving Programs: Care2.com 686, Electronic 1242, Oracle 2821, Rudolph 3283
Corporate Headquarters: Care2.com 686, Electronic 1242, Oracle 2821, Rudolph 3283, Vodafone 3965
Offices: Dickstein 1111, Fish 1428

Redwood Shores
Offices: Kasowitz 2099, King 2157, Quinn 3111, Weil 4023
Plant: Harris 1736
Richmond
Corporate Giving Program: Further 1521
Corporate Headquarters: Further 1521, Mechanics 2446
Office: International 1972
Plants: Chevron 780, Navistar 2647
Ripon
Foundation: Brocchini 580
Cororate Headquarters: Brocchini 580
Riverside
Corporate Giving Program: Best 441
Foundations: Bourns 542, Provident 3071
Corporate Headquarters: Best 441, Bourns 542, Provident 3071
Subsidiaries: Belo 406, HCA 1762
Division: Bourns 542
Office: Best 441
Plants: FMC 1449, Toro 3775
Rocklin
Subsidiary: First 1400
Rohnert Park
Offices: Exchange 1306, State 3591
Rolling Hills Estates
Division: Cox 958
Rosemead
Corporate Giving Programs: Edison 1228, Panda 2871
Foundations: Edison 1228, Panda 2871
Corporate Headquarters: Edison 1228, Panda 2871
Subsidiaries: Edison 1228, Panda 2871
Roseville
Office: Downey 1166
Plants: Fuller 1517, Groeniger 1670, Hewlett 1794, KB 2105, NEC 2654
Ross
Foundation: Pacific 2858
Rutherford
Subsidiary: Diageo 1107
Sacramento
Corporate Giving Programs: Blue 506, Downey 1166, Sacramento 3303, Sutter 3664
Foundations: American 134, Davison 1042, GenCorp 1548, McClatchy 2422, Raley's 3122, Sacramento 3303, Teichert 3704
Corporate Headquarters: American 134, Blue 506, Davison 1042, Downey 1166, McClatchy 2422, Sacramento 3303, Sutter 3664, Teichert 3704
Subsidiaries: Arctic 234, CLARCOR 832, GenCorp 1548, Jacobs 2016, McClatchy 2422
Offices: Best 441, Better 449, BMC 508, Brownstein 593, California 655, Downey 1166, Edelman 1224, Foley 1453, Granite 1632, Grant 1633, Greenberg 1654, Hanson 1725, Kimley 2151, Littler 2289, Morrison 2576, Opus 2820, Orrick 2826, Pan-American 2868, Pillsbury 2975, Stoel 3611, Stradling 3621, Sutherland 3663, Thompson 3739
Plants: Chevron 780, Edison 1228, Groeniger 1670, Novell 2754, Procter 3055
Saint Helena
Office: Farella 1331
Salinas
Subsidiaries: Dole 1141, Gannett 1532, Smucker 3488
Plant: Groeniger 1670
San Anselmo
Corporate Giving Program: Direct 1123
Cororate Headquarters: Direct 1123
San Bruno
Foundation: Artichoke 254
Cororate Headquarters: Artichoke 254
San Carlos
Foundation: Nektar 2658
Division: Genzyme 1566
San Clemente
Subsidiaries: Grace 1623, Zions 4158
Office: Brownstein 593
San Diego
Corporate Giving Programs: AMN Healthcare 184, Cymer 1016, Garden 1534, QUALCOMM 3095, Quidel 3107, San Diego 3322, San Diego 3323, SANYO 3333, Sempra 3405, Sony 3503, Underground 3850, Vianova 3947, WD-40 4011
Foundations: CareFusion 688, Collins 873, Jack 2007, PETCO 2945, Private 3050, San Diego 3322, Sempra 3405, Stram 3622
Corporate Headquarters: AMN Healthcare 184, California 653, CareFusion 688, Collins 873, Cymer 1016, Education 1232, Garden 1534, Jack 2007, PETCO 2945, Private 3050, QUALCOMM 3095, Quidel 3107, ResMed 3192, San Diego 3322, San Diego 3323, SANYO 3333, Schott 3360, Sempra 3405, Sony 3503, Underground 3850, Vianova 3947, WD-40 4011
Subsidiaries: Cardinal 685, Caterpillar 722, CIT 819, Copley 938, Eastman 1214, Education 1232, HCA 1762, McGraw 2429, PerkinElmer 2939, Sempra 3405, Service 3413, SKF 3473, Sony 3502
Divisions: Cox 958, QUALCOMM 3095
Offices: Allen 95, Ballard 329, Best 441, Better 449, Brownstein 593, California 655, Costco 948, Cozen 964, Duane 1185, Fieldstone 1374, Fish 1428, Foley 1453, Goodwin 1611, Hooper 1856, Intuit 1982, Jones 2058, K&L 2080, Kiewit 2142, Kimley 2151, Latham 2228, Littler 2289, McKenna 2433, Mintz 2534, Morrison 2576, Paul 2900, Perkins 2941, Pillsbury 2975, Print.Net 3048, Russell 3289, SAS 3336, SeaWorld 3387, Sheppard 3435, Stoel 3611, Stradling 3621, Thompson 3739, Wilson 4083
Plants: Castle 716, Coca 862, General 1551, Hewlett 1794, Hospira 1867, KB 2105, McAfee 2417, Novell 2754, Panasonic 2869, Sony 3502, Texas 3728
San Dimas
Plant: Bausch 376
San Francisco
Corporate Giving Programs: Advent 41, Bank 346, Brilliant 568, California 655, Del 1065, DFS 1104, Dharma 1105, Esurance 1298, Exgy 1316, Farella 1331, Farmland 1340, Gymboree 1693, Hanson 1725, Littler 2289, McKesson 2434, Morrison 2576, Orrick 2826, Pacific 2853, Partnership 2890, RCM 3139, Rimon 3217, San Francisco 3324, Sedgwick 3395, Shartsis 3423, Strauss 3624, Thinkshift 3734, Union 3854, Visa 3960, Wells 4028, Working 4116
Foundations: Bechtel 395, California 655, craigslist 968, Fremont 1497, Gap 1533, Genentech 1549, JAM 2019, Lucasfilm 2316, McKesson 2434, PG&E 2952, salesforce.com 3318, San Francisco 3324, San Francisco 3325, Schwab 3363, Strauss 3624, Swinerton 3668, Union 3854, Vendome 3930, Wilbur 4070, Williams-Sonoma 4079
Corporate Headquarters: Advent 41, Bank 346, Bechtel 395, Brilliant 568, California 655, craigslist 968, Del 1065, DFS 1104, Dharma 1105, Esurance 1298, Exgy 1316, Farella 1331, Farmland 1340, Fremont 1497, Gap 1533, Gymboree 1693, Hanson 1725, JAM 2019, Littler 2289, McKesson 2434, Morrison 2576, Nektar 2658, Orrick 2826, Pacific 2853, Partnership 2890, PG&E 2952, ProLogis 3060, RCM 3139, Rimon 3217, salesforce.com 3318, San Francisco 3324, San Francisco 3325, Schwab 3363, Sedgwick 3395, Shartsis 3423, Strauss 3624, Swinerton 3668, Thinkshift 3734, Union 3854, Visa 3960, Wells 4028, Wilbur 4070, Williams-Sonoma 4079, Working 4116
Subsidiaries: Alexander 85, Amazon.com 122, Bechtel 395, Berkshire 429, California 655, Chevron 780, Cornerstone 944, First 1400, Ford 1464, Fremont 1497, Gap 1533, Houghton 1869, Nestle 2663, Nippon 2713, PG&E 2952, Protective 3066, Schwab 3363, Tension 3717, Union 3857, United 3860
Division: GATX 1542
Offices: Abacus 9, ACE 24, Acumen 33, Akin 70, Allen 95, Arnold 248, Autodesk 289, Bessemer 440, Better 449, Bingham 463, Bryan 596, Buchalter 600, California 655, Campbell 668, Credit 980, Crowell 986, Davis 1041, Dechert 1058, Downey 1166, Drinker 1175, Duane 1185, Edelman 1224, Electronic 1242, Farella 1331, Fenwick 1362, Foley 1453, Ford 1462, Gibson 1580, Gleacher 1589, Good 1609, Goodwin 1611, Grant 1633, Greenberg 1654, Hanson 1725, Hays 1761, Hogan 1825, Holland 1834, Holme 1837, Hooper 1856, Jones 2058, K&L 2080, Kasowitz 2099, Kearney 2107, Keller 2116, King 2157, Kirkland 2164, Latham 2228, Littler 2289, McKenna 2433, Morgan 2571, Morrison 2576, Mound 2587, Munger 2598, Needham 2655, Paul 2900, Perkins 2940, Perkins 2941, Pillsbury 2975, Price 3040, Print.Net 3048, Quinn 3111, RBS 3138, Reed 3163, Richards 3208, Robins 3232, Ropes 3260, SAS 3336, Sasaki 3337, Schiff 3350, Sedgwick 3395, Shartsis 3423, Shearman 3429, Sheppard 3435, Shook 3439, Sidley 3446, Skadden 3470, Skidmore 3474, Squire 3561, State 3592, Stoel 3611, Stradling 3621, Thompson 3739, Vision 3961, West 4038, Whiting 4063, Wiley 4072, Wilson 4083, Winston 4089
Plants: Coca 862, Hexcel 1795, Interface 1953, Mitsui 2541, Novell 2754, Owens 2841, Quad 3091, Rockwell 3247
San Gabriel
Plant: Indiana 1931
San Jose
Corporate Giving Programs: Adobe 38, Cadence 646, Cisco 818, Xilinx 4137
Foundations: Cisco 818, San Jose 3327, Synopsys 3673, Toeniskoetter 3767
Corporate Headquarters: Adobe 38, Cadence 646, Cisco 818, Cupertino 1009, eBay 1217, Flextronics 1437, LSI 2314, San Jose 3327, Toeniskoetter 3767, Xilinx 4137
Subsidiaries: Boston 540, Danaher 1027, Rockwell 3247
Offices: BMC 508, California 655, Grant 1633, Kenyon 2131, Littler 2289, Opus 2820, SAS 3336, Singerlewak 3463, Sony 3502
Plants: Ecolab 1220, Groeniger 1670, Kellogg 2120, Mentor 2462, NEC 2654, Novell 2754, Texas 3728
San Juan Capistrano
Division: Cox 958
San Lorenzo
Plant: Hillshire 1809
San Luis Obispo
Subsidiary: Parker 2886
Plant: PerkinElmer 2939
San Marino
Office: Dilbeck 1116
San Mateo
Corporate Giving Programs: California 654, ForceBrain.com 1461, Franklin 1487
Foundation: Pacific 2853
Corporate Headquarters: California 654, ForceBrain.com 1461, Franklin 1487
Subsidiaries: Danaher 1027, Franklin 1487, Oracle 2821
San Rafael
Corporate Giving Programs: Autodesk 289, KINeSYS 2155
Foundations: Ghilotti 1570, Lucasfilm 2316
Corporate Headquarters: Autodesk 289, Ghilotti 1570, KINeSYS 2155
Subsidiary: Lucasfilm 2316
San Ramon
Corporate Giving Program: Chevron 780
Foundations: Bank 346, Chevron 780, Integrity 1949, Union 3856
Corporate Headquarters: Chevron 780, Herrick 1788, Union 3856
Subsidiary: Chevron 780
Plant: Navistar 2647

Santa Ana
Corporate Giving Programs: Ingram 1941, Kawasaki 2102
Foundations: Eberhard 1218, First 1389, First 1390
Corporate Headquarters: Eberhard 1218, First 1389, First 1390, Gon 1608, Ingram 1941, Stearns 3594
Subsidiaries: Dixie 1132, First 1389, Masco 2393, Textron 3731
Offices: Disney 1127, Ingram 1941
Plant: Indiana 1931
Santa Barbara
Foundation: Bragg 554
Cororate Headquarters: Bragg 554
Subsidiaries: Chubb 804, Ferro 1366
Offices: Brownstein 593, Granite 1632, Sheppard 3435, Stradling 3621
Santa Clara
Corporate Giving Programs: Agilent 56, Applied 220, Clarity 834, Earthquakes 1206, FileMaker 1380, Intel 1950, McAfee 2417, NVIDIA 2767, San Francisco 3326
Foundations: Agilent 56, Applied 220, San Francisco 3326, Silicon 3455
Corporate Headquarters: Agilent 56, Applied 220, Clarity 834, Earthquakes 1206, FileMaker 1380, Intel 1950, McAfee 2417, NVIDIA 2767, San Francisco 3326, Silicon 3455
Subsidiaries: Apple 217, Intel 1950, NEC 2654, Principal 3047
Offices: Applied 220, Canon 672, Granite 1632, Pulte 3083
Plants: Adobe 38, EMC 1253, FMC 1449, McAfee 2417, Owens 2842
Santa Clarita
Subsidiary: Grace 1623
Santa Fe Springs
Subsidiaries: Berkshire 429, Raymond 3133
Plants: Tension 3717, Univar 3886
Santa Maria
Subsidiary: Seagate 3377
Office: Littler 2289
Plant: Groeniger 1670
Santa Monica
Corporate Giving Program: Activision 30
Foundations: American 148, Morley 2572
Corporate Headquarters: Activision 30, American 148, Deutsch 1098, Morley 2572, Red 3152
Subsidiaries: Metro 2479, Morley 2572
Offices: Bingham 463, Boises 518, Google 1613, Perkins 2940
Santa Paula
Plant: Groeniger 1670
Santa Rosa
Foundations: Exchange 1306, PG&E 2952
Cororate Headquarters: Exchange 1306
Subsidiaries: Exchange 1306, Reagent 3143
Plant: Groeniger 1670
Santee
Foundation: Whirl 4055
Scotts Valley
Corporate Giving Program: Seagate 3377
Sebastopol
Office: Exchange 1306
Sherman Oaks
Cororate Headquarters: Sunkist 3649
Signal Hill
Foundation: Universal 3888
Cororate Headquarters: Universal 3888
Simi Valley
Foundation: Rasmussen 3128
Subsidiary: First 1400
Office: Farmers 1338
Solana Beach
Corporate Giving Program: Source 3505
Cororate Headquarters: Source 3505
Somis
Subsidiary: Shaklee 3418
Sonoma
Foundation: Woodward-Graff 4113
Corporate Headquarters: Woodward-Graff 4113, World 4120
Office: Exchange 1306
South Gate
Plants: Armstrong 246, Hunt 1892
South Pasadena
Office: Dilbeck 1116
South San Francisco
Corporate Giving Program: Genentech 1549
Foundations: Genentech 1549, Hoffmann 1823
Cororate Headquarters: Genentech 1549
Subsidiaries: Hoffmann 1823, Sumitomo 3639
St. Francis
Office: Exchange 1306
St. Helena
Subsidiary: Nestle 2663
Standard
Division: Sierra 3451
Stockton
Corporate Giving Program: Bank 345
Foundations: Bank 345, Florsheim 1445
Corporate Headquarters: Bank 345, Florsheim 1445
Offices: Downey 1166, Grant 1633, Harper 1735
Plants: Bassett 372, Castle 716
Stony Point
Office: Exchange 1306
Sun Valley
Foundation: PMC 2994
Cororate Headquarters: PMC 2994
Sunnyvale
Corporate Giving Programs: Blakely 480, Hewlett 1794, Juniper 2075, Spansion 3532, Yahoo! 4140
Corporate Headquarters: Advanced 40, Blakely 480, Juniper 2075, Spansion 3532, Yahoo! 4140
Subsidiaries: Boston 540, Philips 2963, Ripplewood 3219
Divisions: PerkinElmer 2939, Philips 2963
Office: Blakely 480
Plants: Harris 1736, Hewlett 1794
Susanville
Division: Sierra 3451
Sylmar
Corporate Headquarters: Tutor 3826
Subsidiary: St. Jude 3566
Division: DIRECTV 1124
Tarzana
Foundation: Associated 264
Subsidiary: Quest 3103
Office: Kimley 2151
Temecula
Plants: Merk 2467, Scotts 3372
Thousand Oaks
Corporate Giving Program: Amgen 182
Foundation: Amgen 182
Cororate Headquarters: Amgen 182
Subsidiary: HCA 1762
Thousand Palms
Subsidiary: SPX 3558
Torrance
Corporate Giving Programs: American 150, CTSI 998, Toyota 3789
Foundations: American 150, JTB 2074
Corporate Headquarters: American 150, CTSI 998, JTB 2074, Toyota 3789
Subsidiaries: American 150, Copley 938, Nissan 2716
Plants: Exxon 1315, Honeywell 1852
Truckee
Offices: Duane 1185, Stoel 3611
Tupman
Subsidiary: Occidental 2780
Turlock
Joint Venture: McCormick 2423
Office: Wal-Mart 3980
Plant: Sensient 3408
Tustin
Office: AT&T 274
Plants: Morton 2579, Rockwell 3247
Ukiah
Subsidiary: Gaiam 1527
Union City
Plants: Cabot 643, Dreyer's 1174
Universal City
Corporate Giving Program: Universal 3893
Foundation: Universal 3893
Cororate Headquarters: Universal 3893
Subsidiaries: CBS 727, General 1552, NBC 2649
Valencia
Foundation: Rasmussen 3128
Cororate Headquarters: Rasmussen 3128
Subsidiaries: Danaher 1027, Philips 2963, Textron 3731
Offices: Dilbeck 1116, GATX 1542
Plant: Boston 540
Valley Center
Plant: Scotts 3372
Van Nuys
Foundations: Easton 1215, Sunkist 3649
Corporate Headquarters: Associated 264, Easton 1215
Subsidiary: HNI 1817
Plant: Indiana 1931
Ventura
Cororate Headquarters: Patagonia 2892
Office: California 655
Plant: Indiana 1931
Vernon
Foundation: Pacific 2854
Cororate Headquarters: Pacific 2854
Subsidiary: Kellwood 2121
Victorville
Plants: Sherwin 3437, Southwest 3524
Visalia
Subsidiaries: Gannett 1532, Nash 2619
Plants: Butler 626, Jim's 2043, Jostens 2067
Vista
Corporate Giving Program: DJO 1134
Foundation: Activision 30
Corporate Headquarters: DJO 1134, UTI 3909
Subsidiary: Masco 2393
Division: Cox 958
Office: Pan-American 2868
Plant: DENSO 1088
Walnut
Corporate Giving Program: ViewSonic 3952
Foundation: Shea 3428
Corporate Headquarters: Shea 3428, ViewSonic 3952
Walnut Creek
Foundations: Heffernan 1769, PMI 2995
Corporate Headquarters: Heffernan 1769, PMI 2995
Subsidiary: Air 62
Division: Air 62
Offices: Allen 95, Best 441, California 655, Hanson 1725, Littler 2289
Plants: Chevron 780, Teradyne 3718
Watsonville
Corporate Giving Programs: Granite 1632, West 4037
Corporate Headquarters: Granite 1632, West 4037
Subsidiaries: NorthWestern 2748, Smucker 3488
Division: Granite 1632
West Hollywood
Subsidiary: IAC 1903
West Los Angeles
Cororate Headquarters: Chinese 794
West Sacramento
Corporate Giving Program: Raley's 3122
Foundation: Sacramento 3304
Corporate Headquarters: Raley's 3122, Sacramento 3304
Subsidiary: Raley's 3122
Westlake Village
Corporate Giving Program: Dole 1141
Foundations: K-Swiss 2082, Securitas 3390
Corporate Headquarters: Consolidated 917, Dole 1141, K-Swiss 2082
Subsidiaries: Avery 297, Dole 1141
Offices: Alston 116, Dilbeck 1116

Whittier
Corporate Giving Program: Marinello 2375
Foundation: Rose 3262
Corporate Headquarters: Marinello 2375, Rose 3262
Windsor
Office: Exchange 1306
Winters
Foundation: Mariani 2374
Cororate Headquarters: Mariani 2374
Woodland
Office: Regis 3172
Plant: Thermo 3733
Woodland Hills
Corporate Giving Program: Health 1766
Foundation: Health 1766
Cororate Headquarters: Health 1766
Subsidiaries: Health 1766, KB 2105
Offices: California 655, Dilbeck 1116, Federal 1348, Grant 1633, Singerlewak 3463

COLORADO

Aspen
Foundation: Aspen 260
Cororate Headquarters: Aspen 260
Offices: Holland 1833, Sherman 3436
Aurora
Foundation: Gold 1598
Cororate Headquarters: Gold 1598
Subsidiary: Lennar 2250
Office: Majestic 2343
Plants: CA 638, Subaru 3631, SUPERVALU 3659
Boulder
Corporate Giving Programs: Econscious 1223, GoLite 1606, Hutchinson 1897, Inspire 1945, Namaste 2614, Vedante 3926
Corporate Headquarters: Econscious 1223, Gaiam 1527, GoLite 1606, Hutchinson 1897, Inspire 1945, Namaste 2614, Vedante 3926
Subsidiaries: Hoffmann 1823, Masco 2393, Whole 4066
Offices: Holland 1833, Holme 1837
Plants: Amgen 182, Lexmark 2258
Brighton
Subsidiaries: Faribault 1332, O'Neal 2771
Broomfield
Corporate Giving Programs: Ball 328, Gaiam 1527, White 4062
Foundations: Cornerstone 944, MWH 2608
Corporate Headquarters: Ball 328, Cornerstone 944, MWH 2608, White 4062
Subsidiaries: Ball 328, Bausch 376, Cornerstone 944, Dean 1054
Division: Hunter 1893
Office: Fishel 1429
Centennial
Foundations: Fast 1344, SEAKR 3379
Cororate Headquarters: SEAKR 3379
Subsidiary: Regal 3166
Plant: McGraw 2429
Colorado Springs
Corporate Giving Program: Kaiser 2086
Foundations: Flir 1440, Integrity 1948, Long 2298
Corporate Headquarters: Flir 1440, Long 2298, Transit 3798
Subsidiaries: El Paso 1239, Long 2298, M.D.C. 2324, Philips 2963, Price 3040
Offices: El Paso 1239, Grant 1633, Hogan 1825, Holland 1833, Holme 1837, Rothgerber 3269, Sherman 3436, United 3873
Plants: Deluxe 1084, Harris 1736, Hewlett 1794, Illinois 1916, McGraw 2429
Commerce City
Corporate Giving Program: Kroenke 2194
Plant: Valmont 3919
Denver
Corporate Giving Programs: Berry 437, Brownstein 593, Colorado 877, Colorado 879, Davis 1039, Denver 1090, Gates 1540, Holme 1837, Kaiser 2086, Molson 2549, PDB 2906, Reilly 3176, Rothgerber 3269, Sherman 3436, Wheeler 4053
Foundations: Colorado 878, Colorado 879, COPIC 937, Encana 1266, Energy 1272, Hall 1703, Holland 1833, Intrepid 1980, Janus 2024, Johns 2047, M.D.C. 2324, ProLogis 3060, RE/MAX 3140, Sturniolo 3629, Tomkins 3771, Vodafone 3965
Corporate Headquarters: Berry 437, Brownstein 593, Colorado 877, Colorado 878, Colorado 879, Colorado 880, COPIC 937, Davis 1039, DaVita 1044, Denver 1090, Encana 1266, Energy 1272, Gates 1540, Hall 1703, Holland 1833, Holme 1837, Intrepid 1980, Janus 2024, Johns 2047, Kroenke 2194, M.D.C. 2324, Molson 2549, PENTAX 2927, RE/MAX 3140, Reilly 3176, Rothgerber 3269, Sherman 3436, Sturniolo 3629, Wheeler 4053
Subsidiaries: Anadarko 190, Berkshire 429, COPIC 937, Energy 1272, Fiserv 1427, Gates 1540, Grace 1623, IMA 1917, Johns 2047, Long 2298, M.D.C. 2324, Manitowoc 2356, McGraw 2429, Miller 2517, VHA 3944, Xcel 4135, Zions 4158
Divisions: Holcim 1828, MDU 2441
Offices: Akerman 69, Arnold 248, Baker 319, Ballard 329, Blakely 480, Brownstein 593, Cozen 964, Deere 1061, Dorsey 1157, Federal 1349, Fennemore 1360, Ford 1462, Fulbright 1516, Gibson 1580, Grant 1633, Greenberg 1654, Hays 1761, Hogan 1825, Holland 1833, Holme 1837, Humana 1886, Husch 1896, JPMorgan Chase 2071, KeyBank 2136, Kiewit 2142, Kimley 2151, Lauth 2232, Littler 2289, McKenna 2433, Merchant 2464, Morrison 2576, Mortenson 2577, Opus 2820, Patton 2898, Perkins 2940, Perkins 2941, Polsinelli 3001, Pulte 3083, Reilly 3176, Rothgerber 3269, SAP 3334, SAS 3336, Sherman 3436, Snell 3490, State 3592, Thompson 3739, Vision 3961, Wheeler 4053, Whirlpool 4056
Plants: Berry 435, BP 547, Coca 862, FMC 1449, Harris 1736, Nash 2619, Owens 2841, Owens 2842, Pactiv 2863, Univar 3886
Durango
Office: Regis 3172
Eagle
Subsidiary: Tyler 3831
Englewood
Corporate Giving Programs: CH2M 758, Sports 3548, Western 4045
Foundations: Chotin 799, Hackstock 1697, Jeppesen 2038, Liberty 2263, Liberty 2264, Oakley 2774, PDB 2906, Western 4045
Corporate Headquarters: CH2M 758, Fast 1344, Hackstock 1697, Jeppesen 2038, Liberty 2263, Liberty 2264, Oakley 2774, PDB 2906, Sports 3548, TeleTech 3708, Western 4045
Subsidiaries: Boeing 516, Chevron 780, Comcast 887, First 1400, Fiserv 1427, Freeport 1494, Nordstrom 2724, NorthWestern 2748, PerkinElmer 2939
Divisions: Safeway 3310, ServiceMaster 3414
Office: Google 1613
Plants: Binswanger 464, EMC 1253, McAfee 2417, Novell 2754
Fort Collins
Foundation: Universal 3890
Cororate Headquarters: Woodward 4112
Subsidiary: Danaher 1027
Division: Woodward 4112
Office: Wyatt 4130
Plant: Hewlett 1794
Glenwood Springs
Cororate Headquarters: Rocky 3249
Subsidiary: Kinder 2153
Golden
Corporate Giving Programs: Boston 536, PENTAX 2927
Cororate Headquarters: Boston 536
Subsidiaries: McDonald's 2427, PerkinElmer 2939, Synovus 3674
Office: Safeco 3306
Plant: International 1964
Greeley
Office: State 3591
Greenwood Village
Corporate Giving Programs: Great 1647, Molycorp 2550, Newmont 2698, Rio 3218
Foundation: First 1400
Corporate Headquarters: Chotin 799, Great 1647, Molycorp 2550, Newmont 2698, Rio 3218
Offices: Autodesk 289, Holland 1833, Reinhart 3178
Lakewood
Foundations: Kinder 2153, Rocky 3249
Subsidiary: Kinder 2153
Plant: Dreyer's 1174
Littleton
Foundation: Sonlight 3499
Cororate Headquarters: Sonlight 3499
Subsidiary: HCA 1762
Lone Tree
Foundation: Nord 2721
Lonetree
Cororate Headquarters: Nord 2721
Longmont
Subsidiary: Panasonic 2869
Division: White 4062
Plants: Amgen 182, Mentor 2462, Syngenta 3671
Louisville
Foundation: Rock 3238
Cororate Headquarters: Rock 3238
Office: Quad 3091
Plant: EMC 1253
Loveland
Cororate Headquarters: Home 1846
Subsidiary: Danaher 1027
Monument
Cororate Headquarters: Integrity 1948
Morrison
Foundation: Willow 4082
Cororate Headquarters: Willow 4082
Niwot
Corporate Giving Program: Crocs 984
Cororate Headquarters: Crocs 984
Parker
Foundation: EI 1237
Cororate Headquarters: EI 1237
Pueblo
Subsidiaries: Evening 1302, Health 1766
Plant: Jim's 2043
Steamboat Springs
Corporate Giving Program: SmartWool 3479
Cororate Headquarters: SmartWool 3479
Subsidiary: Timberland 3754
Office: Sherman 3436
Thornton
Subsidiary: Lennar 2250
Trinidad
Corporate Giving Program: Republic 3187
Vail
Office: Sherman 3436
Westminster
Corporate Giving Program: WSA 4126
Cororate Headquarters: WSA 4126
Wheat Ridge
Foundation: Caruso 709
Cororate Headquarters: Caruso 709
Subsidiary: Hershey 1791

CONNECTICUT

Berlin
Cororate Headquarters: Connecticut 911
Subsidiary: Northeast 2737
Bethel
Offices: Newtown 2704, Savings 3344
Bethlehem
Office: Thomaston 3736
Bloomfield
Corporate Giving Programs: CIGNA 812, Kaman 2088
Foundation: Kaman 2088
Cororate Headquarters: Kaman 2088
Subsidiaries: Danaher 1027, Kaman 2088
Plant: TJX 3765

Branford
Subsidiary: Nordson 2723
Bridgeport
Corporate Giving Program: People's 2928
Foundation: People's 2928
Corporate Headquarters: People's 2928, Pryor 3073
Subsidiaries: People's 2928, Sequa 3410
Plants: Public 3077, Warnaco 3988
Bristol
Foundation: Barnes 362
Cororate Headquarters: Barnes 362
Division: Barnes 362
Brookfield
Foundation: Photronics 2969
Cororate Headquarters: Photronics 2969
Offices: Newtown 2704, Savings 3344
Cheshire
Foundation: Alexion 86
Cororate Headquarters: Alexion 86
Office: Naugatuck 2645
Clinton
Plant: Campbell 669
Colchester
Foundation: S & S 3296
Cororate Headquarters: S & S 3296
Office: Eastern 1210
Danbury
Corporate Giving Program: IMS 1924
Foundations: Praxair 3029, Savings 3344, Union 3858
Corporate Headquarters: Praxair 3029, Savings 3344, Union 3858
Subsidiaries: Clorox 852, Dow 1161, Newmont 2698
Office: Newtown 2704
Plant: Sealed 3381
Danielson
Foundation: Spirol 3545
Cororate Headquarters: Spirol 3545
Darien
Corporate Giving Program: Zotos 4159
Foundation: Miller 2518
Corporate Headquarters: Miller 2518, Zotos 4159
Devon
Office: Milford 2513
East Hartford
Corporate Giving Program: Connecticut 912
Cororate Headquarters: Pratt 3028
Subsidiary: United 3882
East Windsor
Plant: CA 638
East Woodstock
Division: Rogers 3253
Enfield
Corporate Giving Program: Lego 2247
Foundation: Lego 2247
Cororate Headquarters: Lego 2247
Plant: Hallmark 1707
Fairfield
Corporate Giving Programs: Bigelow 462, General 1552
Foundation: General 1552
Corporate Headquarters: Bigelow 462, General 1552
Office: ACE 24
Farmington
Corporate Giving Program: Otis 2835
Foundation: Newman's 2697
Corporate Headquarters: Dowling 1165, Otis 2835
Subsidiaries: Diageo 1107, Otis 2835, United 3882
Division: United 3882
Office: GATX 1542
Glastonbury
Plant: Novell 2754
Greenwich
Foundations: Day 1046, Hillside 1810, Northwestern 2750
Corporate Headquarters: Berkley 426, U.S. 3841
Subsidiaries: Alcoa 82, Altria 120, Berkley 426, Berkshire 429, Marsh 2385, U.S. 3841, Unilever 3853
Offices: Cummings 1004, Day 1046, Gleacher 1589, Shipman 3438, State 3592, Wiggin 4068
Groton
Foundation: General 1551
Division: General 1551
Office: Chelsea 772
Guilford
Foundation: Seaboard 3375
Hartford
Corporate Giving Programs: Aetna 48, Connecticut 911, Day 1046, Hartford 1742, Hartford 1743, Murtha 2602, Shipman 3438, Travelers 3802, United 3882
Foundations: Aetna 48, Berkshire 428, Connecticut 912, Northeast 2737, Reid 3173, Updike 3899, X.L. 4134
Corporate Headquarters: Aetna 48, Connecticut 912, Day 1046, Hartford 1742, Hartford 1743, Imagineers 1918, March 2367, Murtha 2602, Reid 3173, Shipman 3438, United 3882, Updike 3899
Subsidiaries: American 156, Hartford 1742, Massachusetts 2397, Stanley 3579
Offices: Bingham 463, Bracewell 549, Brown 590, Day 1046, Dechert 1058, Federal 1349, Murtha 2602, SAS 3336, Shipman 3438, State 3592, Vision 3961, Wiggin 4068
Harwinton
Office: Thomaston 3736
Jewett City
Foundation: Jewett 2042
Cororate Headquarters: Jewett 2042
Office: Eastern 1210
Lakeville
Office: Shipman 3438
Lebanon
Plant: Scotts 3372
Madison
Office: Murtha 2602
Manchester
Corporate Giving Program: Bob's 511
Foundation: Bob's 511
Cororate Headquarters: Bob's 511
Divisions: Cox 958, Rogers 3253
Plant: Teleflex 3707
Meriden
Cororate Headquarters: Record 3149
Division: Cox 958
Office: Regis 3172
Plant: TJX 3765
Middlebury
Subsidiary: Chemtura 775
Office: Naugatuck 2645
Middletown
Foundation: Liberty 2262
Cororate Headquarters: Liberty 2262
Subsidiary: Liberty 2262
Milford
Corporate Giving Programs: Doctor's 1138, Milford 2513
Foundations: Milford 2513, Warnaco 3988
Corporate Headquarters: Doctor's 1138, Milford 2513
Subsidiaries: Energizer 1271, Windway 4086
Plant: Crystal 992
Monroe
Office: Newtown 2704
Mystic
Office: Chelsea 772
Naugatuck
Foundations: Naugatuck 2645, Naugatuck 2646
Corporate Headquarters: Naugatuck 2645, Naugatuck 2646
Subsidiary: Naugatuck 2646
Plant: Hershey 1791
New Britain
Corporate Giving Program: Stanley 3579
Foundation: Benedict-Miller 410
Corporate Headquarters: Stanley 3579, Westinghouse 4049
Office: Safeco 3306
Plant: Westinghouse 4049
New Fairfield
Offices: Mercury 2469, Savings 3344
New Haven
Corporate Giving Programs: United 3870, Wiggin 4068
Foundation: United 3870
Corporate Headquarters: United 3870, Wiggin 4068
Offices: Carmody 695, Day 1046, Littler 2289, Murtha 2602, Whiting 4063, Wiggin 4068
Plants: Beneficial 411, Kellogg 2120, Public 3077
New Milford
Office: Savings 3344
Newington
Subsidiary: Textron 3731
Newtown
Foundation: Newtown 2704
Cororate Headquarters: Newtown 2704
Subsidiary: Emerson 1257
Offices: Newtown 2704, Savings 3344
Niantic
Office: Chelsea 772
North Haven
Plant: Pactiv 2863
North Stonington
Office: Chelsea 772
Norwalk
Corporate Giving Programs: Arch 230, EMCOR 1255
Foundations: Diageo 1107, Xerox 4136
Corporate Headquarters: Arch 230, Diageo 1107, EMCOR 1255, IMS 1924, Xerox 4136
Subsidiaries: Franklin 1487, Georgia 1568, Life 2268, Pitney 2984
Office: Connecticut 910
Norwich
Foundations: Chelsea 772, Dime 1118, Eastern 1210
Corporate Headquarters: Chelsea 772, Dime 1118, Eastern 1210
Old Greenwich
Subsidiary: ConocoPhillips 913
Orange
Foundation: Hubbell 1879
Oxford
Office: Naugatuck 2645
Pawcatuck
Office: Chelsea 772
Plainfield
Office: Eastern 1210
Plainville
Subsidiary: Danaher 1027
Division: General 1552
Prospect
Office: Naugatuck 2645
Putnam
Foundation: Putnam 3086
Cororate Headquarters: Putnam 3086
Ridgefield
Foundation: Boehringer 515
Cororate Headquarters: Boehringer 515
Subsidiaries: Boehringer 515, Reader's 3141
Rockville
Foundation: Anocoil 204
Corporate Headquarters: Anocoil 204, Rockville 3245
Rocky Hill
Corporate Giving Program: Henkel 1778
Foundation: Connecticut 910
Corporate Headquarters: Connecticut 910, Henkel 1778
Subsidiaries: Fiserv 1427, Meredith 2471, Pratt 3028
Rogers
Corporate Giving Program: Rogers 3253
Cororate Headquarters: Rogers 3253
Salem
Office: Chelsea 772
Seymour
Cororate Headquarters: Seaboard 3375
Shelton
Corporate Headquarters: Hubbell 1879, Victorinox 3950
Subsidiaries: Health 1766, Philips 2963
Offices: CDW 729, Newtown 2704
Simsbury
Foundation: Ensign 1276
Cororate Headquarters: Ensign 1276
Subsidiary: Danaher 1027

Slimsbury
Subsidiary: Danaher 1027
South Windsor
Foundation: Rockville 3245
Subsidiary: O'Neal 2771
Division: United 3882
Southbury
Offices: Carmody 695, Naugatuck 2645, Newtown 2704
Sprague
Office: Chelsea 772
Stamford
Corporate Giving Programs: First 1398, Frontier 1508, General 1558, MeadWestvaco 2445, Pitney 2984, World 4121
Foundations: Consolidated 915, Cummings 1004, First 1399, Hexcel 1795, Pitney 2984, RBS 3138
Corporate Headquarters: Crane 970, Cummings 1004, First 1399, Frontier 1508, General 1558, Hexcel 1795, Pitney 2984, RBS 3138, World 4121, X.L. 4134
Subsidiaries: Altria 120, Berkshire 429, Fuji 1514, General 1552, Manpower 2358, Mead 2443, Philips 2963, SPX 3558
Divisions: Philips 2963, Pitney 2984
Offices: Cummings 1004, Day 1046, Dickstein 1111, Kelley 2118, Mintz 2534, Murtha 2602, Shipman 3438, Wiggin 4068
Stonington
Foundation: Wimpfheimer 4085
Cororate Headquarters: Wimpfheimer 4085
Stratford
Corporate Giving Program: Sikorsky 3454
Cororate Headquarters: Sikorsky 3454
Subsidiary: United 3882
Suffield
Subsidiaries: SUPERVALU 3659, Teleflex 3707
Plant: Hood 1854
Terryville
Subsidiary: Danaher 1027
Office: Thomaston 3736
Thomaston
Foundation: Thomaston 3736
Cororate Headquarters: Thomaston 3736
Trumbull
Division: Pitney 2984
Offices: Newtown 2704, Sun 3646
Uncasville
Corporate Giving Program: Mohegan 2546
Cororate Headquarters: Mohegan 2546
Unionville
Subsidiary: Danaher 1027
Wallingford
Corporate Giving Program: Edible 1226
Foundation: Edible 1226
Cororate Headquarters: Edible 1226
Plants: Allegheny 91, Bristol 578, Respironics 3193
Waterbury
Corporate Giving Programs: Carmody 695, Webster 4016
Foundations: Konica 2185, Webster 4016
Corporate Headquarters: Carmody 695, Webster 4016
Offices: Carmody 695, Savings 3344, Thomaston 3736
Plants: Illinois 1916, Olin 2801
Waterford
Foundation: Waterford 4002
Cororate Headquarters: Waterford 4002
Subsidiary: Waterford 4002
Office: Chelsea 772
Watertown
Offices: Naugatuck 2645, Thomaston 3736
Plant: Osram 2834
West Hartford
Offices: Cummings 1004, Day 1046
West Haven
Division: Bayer 382
Weston
Foundation: Dekker 1064
Westport
Corporate Giving Program: Terex 3719
Foundation: Sun 3646
Corporate Headquarters: Newman's 2697, Terex 3719
Office: State 3592
Willimantic
Foundation: SI 3444
Cororate Headquarters: SI 3444
Subsidiary: SI 3444
Division: Rogers 3253
Wilton
Foundation: Deloitte 1070
Cororate Headquarters: Sun 3646
Plants: Quad 3091, Valassis 3914
Windsor
Corporate Giving Programs: ING 1938, Redco 3155
Cororate Headquarters: ING 1938
Division: Barnes 362
Plants: Barnes 362, Westinghouse 4049
Windsor Locks
Subsidiaries: SUPERVALU 3659, United 3882
Woodbury
Offices: Naugatuck 2645, Newtown 2704
Woodmont
Office: Milford 2513

DELAWARE

Claymont
Corporate Giving Program: SocketLabs 3495
Cororate Headquarters: SocketLabs 3495
Delaware City
Plant: Formosa 1470
Dover
Office: Regis 3172
Plants: PPG 3025, Procter 3055
Georgetown
Offices: Archer 232, Wilson 4083
Greenville
Subsidiary: Sears 3384
Hockessin
Plant: Schulman 3361
Lewes
Subsidiary: Kiplinger 2163
Middletown
Office: Westfield 4047
Millsboro
Plant: Campbell 669
Newark
Cororate Headquarters: SLM 3478
Offices: Avon 305, Whiting 4063
Plant: FMC 1449
Rehoboth Beach
Subsidiary: Kiplinger 2163
Wilmington
Corporate Giving Programs: Ashby 257, Delmarva 1069, du Pont 1184, Morris 2575, Potter 3019, Richards 3207, WSFS 4127
Foundations: Adobe 38, AstraZeneca 272, Beneficial 411, Berkley 426, Burt's 623, Deutsch 1098, Dowling 1165, Encana 1266, Gelco 1546, Imagineers 1918, ING 1937, Laureate 2231, National 2636, Olivetti 2802, OrePac 2823, Stearns 3594, TeleTech 3708, Veridyne 3935, WSFS 4127
Corporate Headquarters: Ashby 257, AstraZeneca 272, Delmarva 1069, du Pont 1184, ING 1937, Morris 2575, Potter 3019, Richards 3207, WSFS 4127
Subsidiaries: Air 63, Apache 211, Armstrong 246, Beneficial 411, Campbell 669, Capital 679, Danaher 1027, Fulton 1518, HCA 1762, Jones 2057, Meritor 2473, Murphy 2600, National 2636, Pepco 2933, Philips 2963, U.S. 3835, Verizon 3936, WSFS 4127
Offices: Archer 232, Ballard 329, Benesch 413, Bessemer 440, Cole 868, Cozen 964, Dorsey 1157, Drinker 1175, Duane 1185, Fish 1428, Gibbons 1574, Greenberg 1654, Liberty 2265, Morgan 2571, Paul 2901, Pepper 2934, Polsinelli 3001, Potter 3019, Pulte 3083, Reed 3163, Richards 3207, Skadden 3470, Stradley 3620, Weil 4023, White 4059
Plant: Georgia 1568
Yorklyn
Cororate Headquarters: NVF 2766
Subsidiaries: Caparo 673, NVF 2766

DISTRICT OF COLUMBIA

Washington
Corporate Giving Programs: Agora 58, Akin 70, Arent 235, Arnold 248, Buckleysandler 603, Caplin 681, Crowell 986, D.C. 1018, Dickstein 1111, Dow 1164, Elevation 1245, Federal 1349, Finnegan 1384, Free 1492, Groom 1671, Hogan 1825, Hollingsworth 1836, International 1960, Keller 2116, Kiplinger 2163, LivingSocial 2290, Macfarlane-Chang 2331, McKenna 2433, National 2638, Patton 2898, Pepco 2933, Potomac 3018, Siemens 3448, Steptoe 3599, Washington 3997, Washington 3998, Washington 3999, Washington 4000, Wiley 4073, Williams 4076
Foundations: Arnold 248, Cassidy 715, Crowell 986, D.C. 1018, Eagle 1201, Financial 1382, Fort 1471, International 1959, Mazda 2414, National 2625, National 2627, News 2701, Patton 2898, sanofi-aventis 3329, SUPERVALU 3659, Washington 3998, Washington 3999, Whole 4066, Wilkes 4074
Corporate Headquarters: Agora 58, Akin 70, Arent 235, Arnold 248, Buckleysandler 603, Caplin 681, Cassidy 715, Crowell 986, D.C. 1018, Danaher 1027, Dickstein 1111, Dow 1164, Eagle 1201, Elevation 1245, Federal 1349, Financial 1382, Finnegan 1384, Fort 1471, Free 1492, Government 1621, Groom 1671, Hogan 1825, Hollingsworth 1836, International 1959, Keller 2116, Kiplinger 2163, Lincoln 2280, LivingSocial 2290, Macfarlane-Chang 2331, McKenna 2433, National 2625, National 2627, National 2638, News 2701, Patton 2898, Pepco 2933, Potomac 3018, Steptoe 3599, Washington 3997, Washington 3998, Washington 3999, Washington 4000, Wiley 4073, Wilkes 4074, Williams 4076
Subsidiaries: Berkshire 429, Danaher 1027, Grace 1623, Grant 1633, Kiplinger 2163, Marriott 2383, News 2701, Pepco 2933, Potomac 3018, Verizon 3936, Viacom 3945
Division: Washington 4000
Offices: Adams 34, Akerman 69, Akin 70, Alston 116, Andrews 198, Arent 235, Arnall 247, Arnold 248, Autodesk 289, Baker 319, Baker 321, Baker 325, Balch 327, Ballard 329, Bessemer 440, Best 441, Bingham 463, Boises 518, Bose 531, Bracewell 549, Bradley 550, Brinks 573, Brown 590, Brownstein 593, Bryan 596, Butzel 629, Cadwalader 649, Cahill 651, Caplin 681, Carter 707, Chadbourne 759, Clark 836, Cleary 843, Corning 945, Cozen 964, Crowell 986, Curtis 1010, Davis 1041, Day 1046, Debevoise 1055, Dechert 1058, Dickstein 1111, Dixon 1133, Dorsey 1157, Dow 1164, Drinker 1175, Duane 1185, Edelman 1224, Ellin 1251, Faegre 1324, Finnegan 1384, Fish 1428, Fitzpatrick 1434, Foley 1453, Foley 1454, Ford 1462, Fried 1502, Frommer 1507, Fulbright 1516, Garvey 1539, Gibson 1580, Godfrey 1596, Goodwin 1611, Grant 1633, Greenberg 1654, Haynes 1759, Hays 1761, Hogan 1825, Holland 1833, Holland 1834, Hooper 1856, Husch 1896, Ice 1905, Jenner 2035, Jennings 2036, Jones 2058, K&L 2080, Katten 2101, Kearney 2107, Keller 2116, Kelley 2118, Kenyon 2131, Kiewit 2142, King 2157, Kirkland 2164, Latham 2228, Leonard 2252, Littler 2289, Loeb 2295, Mal 2349, Mayer 2411, Mazda 2414, McDermott 2425, McGuireWoods 2430, McKenna 2433, Merchant 2464, Milbank 2511, Mintz 2534, Morgan 2571, Morrison 2576, Nelson 2661, Ober 2777, Orrick 2826, Parker 2885, Patton 2898, Paul 2900, Paul 2901, Pepper 2934, Perkins 2940, Perkins 2941, Pierce 2974, Pillsbury 2975, Polsinelli 3001, Porter 3009, Proskauer 3064, Quarles 3101, Quinn 3111, RBS 3138, Reed 3163,

Robins 3232, Ropes 3260, SAP 3334, Schiff 3350, Schulte 3362, Schwabe 3364, Sedgwick 3395, Seward 3417, Shearman 3429, Sheppard 3435, Shipman 3438, Shook 3439, Sidley 3446, Simpson 3462, Skadden 3470, Skidmore 3474, Squire 3561, Steptoe 3599, Stinson 3608, Stradley 3620, Sullivan 3634, Sullivan 3636, Sutherland 3663, Thompson 3740, Tonkon 3772, Toyota 3788, Turner 3823, Ungaretti 3851, Venable 3929, Vinson 3957, Vinson 3958, Weil 4022, Weil 4023, Weyerhaeuser 4052, White 4058, Whiting 4063, Wiley 4073, Williams 4076, Williams 4078, Willkie 4081, Wilson 4083, Winston 4089
Plants: Chevron 780, Edison 1228, Interface 1953, Katten 2101, Mitsui 2541, Northrop 2744, Raytheon 3135, Rockwell 3247, Vulcan 3972

FLORIDA

Altamonte Springs
Cororate Headquarters: Greater 1648
Subsidiary: Vilter 3956
Apopka
Division: Eclipse 1219
Plant: Scotts 3372
Atlantis
Subsidiary: HCA 1762
Aventura
Foundation: Celebrity 731
Bartow
Plants: Mosaic 2580, Valmont 3919
Belleair Bluffs
Office: ITA 1998
Boca Raton
Corporate Giving Program: Office 2785
Foundations: Acuity 31, Office 2785, Young 4148
Cororate Headquarters: Acuity 31, Office 2785, Palm 2867, Young 4148
Subsidiaries: Grace 1623, St. Joe 3563
Offices: Akerman 69, Duane 1185, Elevation 1245, Greenberg 1654, Proskauer 3064, Whirlpool 4056
Plants: Alro 113, GTECH 1677, Intel 1950
Bonita Springs
Office: Cummings 1004
Boynton Beach
Plants: Motorola 2586, Teleflex 3707
Bradenton
Corporate Giving Program: Tropicana 3813
Foundation: Beall's 389
Cororate Headquarters: Beall's 389, Tropicana 3813
Subsidiaries: Beall's 389, Oshkosh 2833, PepsiCo 2935
Bradley
Subsidiary: Mosaic 2580
Cape Canaveral
Office: Draper 1171
Clearwater
Foundation: Metal 2478
Cororate Headquarters: Metal 2478
Subsidiary: Lennar 2250
Offices: Humana 1886, Regis 3172, State 3592
Plants: Alro 113, Carpenter 700, Honeywell 1852, West 4038
Clewiston
Foundation: United 3878
Cororate Headquarters: United 3878
Subsidiary: United 3878
Cocoa
Plant: PerkinElmer 2939
Cocoa Beach
Subsidiary: Boeing 516
Coconut Creek
Foundation: Minto 2533
Cororate Headquarters: Minto 2533
Coral Gables
Foundation: BayView 384
Cororate Headquarters: BayView 384
Coral Springs
Subsidiary: First 1400
Plant: Univar 3886
Dania Beach
Corporate Giving Program: FirstService 1426
Cororate Headquarters: FirstService 1426
Davie
Cororate Headquarters: Dolphins 1147
Daytona
Office: Humana 1886
Daytona Beach
Corporate Giving Programs: International 1970, National 2621
Foundation: Ladies 2209
Corporate Headquarters: International 1970, Ladies 2209, National 2621
Plant: Coca 862
Deerfield Beach
Corporate Giving Program: JM 2044
Foundation: JM 2044
Cororate Headquarters: JM 2044
Office: RJN 3228
Deland
Office: Fishel 1429
Doral
Cororate Headquarters: International 1958
Edgewater
Subsidiary: Windway 4086
Estero
Plant: Florida 1444
Fernandina Beach
Subsidiary: Synovus 3674
Fort Lauderdale
Corporate Giving Programs: AutoNation 292, Dolphins 1147, Stiles 3607
Foundations: BB&T 385, Stiles 3607, Universal 3894
Cororate Headquarters: AutoNation 292, Pro 3052, Stiles 3607
Subsidiaries: Franklin 1487, Grace 1623
Division: Hunter 1893
Offices: Akerman 69, American 143, Boises 518, Fowler 1479, Grant 1633, Greenberg 1654, Hays 1761, Holland 1834, Humana 1886, Kimley 2151, Mound 2587, Pulte 3083, Rogers 3252, Whiting 4063
Plants: Guardian 1682, Novell 2754, Owens 2841
Fort Meade
Plant: Mosaic 2580
Fort Myers
Foundation: YGS 4143
Cororate Headquarters: Spear 3536
Offices: Fowler 1479, Hahn 1700, Humana 1886, KeyBank 2136, Kimley 2151, Pulte 3083, Rogers 3252, Sony 3502
Plant: Lennar 2250
Fort Walton Beach
Subsidiary: Cox 958
Joint Venture: Cox 958
Plant: Gulf 1689
Ft. Lauderdale
Office: Sedgwick 3395
Gainesville
Subsidiary: Cox 958
Division: Cox 958
Plants: Florida 1444, Fuller 1517
Goulds
Cororate Headquarters: Bernecker's 431
Heathrow
Office: Symantec 3669
Hialeah
Plant: International 1964
Holiday
Plant: Florida 1444
Homestead
Foundation: South 3508
Cororate Headquarters: South 3508
Jacksonville
Corporate Giving Programs: Blue 493, CSX 997, Jacksonville 2014, Winn 4087
Foundations: Allison-Erwin 106, Beaver 394, Blue 493, Fidelity 1371, Florida 1444, Harden 1728, Health 1764, Jacksonville 2014, PSS 3074, Rayonier 3134, Vestcor 3943, Winn 4087
Corporate Headquarters: Beaver 394, Blue 493, CSX 997, Fidelity 1371, Florida 1444, Harden 1728, Health 1764, Jacksonville 2014, KLS 2171, PSS 3074, Rayonier 3134, Vestcor 3943, Winn 4087
Subsidiaries: Berkley 426, Biomet 466, CSX 997, Leggett 2246, Miller 2517, Praxair 3029, Raymond 3133, St. Joe 3563, Vulcan 3972, Walter 3984
Offices: Akerman 69, Dixon 1133, Foley 1453, Ford 1462, Fowler 1479, Holland 1834, Humana 1886, Kimley 2151, Mazda 2414, McGuireWoods 2430, State 3591, State 3592
Plants: Commercial 893, Georgia 1568, Owens 2841, Owens 2842, Pactiv 2863
Juno Beach
Corporate Giving Program: Florida 1443
Foundation: Florida 1443
Cororate Headquarters: Florida 1443
Jupiter
Subsidiary: Philips 2963
Kennedy Space Center
Subsidiary: PerkinElmer 2939
Office: Bionetics 467
Kissimmee
Plant: Quaker 3094
Lake Buena Vista
Corporate Giving Program: Disney 1128
Cororate Headquarters: Disney 1128
Subsidiary: Disney 1127
Lake City
Office: GATX 1542
Lake Mary
Subsidiary: Fiserv 1427
Office: AT&T 274
Lake Wales
Plant: Bassett 372
Lakeland
Corporate Giving Program: Publix 3079
Foundation: Watson 4006
Cororate Headquarters: Publix 3079, Watson 4006
Office: Holland 1834
Plant: FMC 1449
Largo
Subsidiaries: DRS 1179, First 1389
Lithia
Foundation: Nursery 2762
Cororate Headquarters: Nursery 2762
LongBoat Key
Foundation: Frankel 1483
Longwood
Cororate Headquarters: American 154
Madeira Beach
Foundation: Keller-Crescent 2117
Maitland
Foundation: Wallace 3983
Cororate Headquarters: Wallace 3983
Offices: First 1400, Opus 2820, Safeco 3306
Plant: CA 638
Melbourne
Corporate Giving Program: Harris 1736
Foundation: Harris 1736
Cororate Headquarters: Harris 1736
Subsidiary: Duda 1188
Plant: Rockwell 3247
Miami
Corporate Giving Programs: Assurant 268, Burger 613, Carnival 696, Greenberg 1654, Heat 1767, Miami 2491, Royal 3273, Southern 3521
Foundations: Burger 613, EFC 1236, Kelly 2122, Lennar 2250, Miami 2491, Professional 3056, Ryder 3292, Southern 3521, Sunbeam 3647, Wynnne 4133
Corporate Headquarters: Assurant 268, Burger 613, Carnival 696, EFC 1236, Greenberg 1654, Heat 1767, Kelly 2122, Lennar 2250, Miami 2491, Professional 3056, Royal 3273, Ryder 3292, Southern 3521, Sunbeam 3647, Wynnne 4133
Subsidiaries: Assurant 266, Assurant 268, BayView 384, Beckman 397, Canon 672, Caterpillar 722,

Chemed 773, Goya 1622, Johnson 2048, Johnson 2049, Lennar 2250, Macy's 2333, Vilter 3956
Division: Sharp 3422
Offices: Akerman 69, American 143, Bessemer 440, Boises 518, Cozen 964, Credit 980, Duane 1185, Federal 1349, Foley 1453, Ford 1462, Grant 1633, Greenberg 1654, Hogan 1825, Holland 1834, Humana 1886, K&L 2080, Kasowitz 2099, Kiewit 2142, Kimley 2151, Littler 2289, McDermott 2425, Morgan 2571, SAS 3336, Shook 3439, Squire 3561, Thompson 3739, Turner 3823, Weil 4022, Weil 4023, White 4058
Plants: Bausch 376, Boston 540, Campbell 669, Katten 2101, McAfee 2417, Mitsui 2541, Navistar 2647, Rockwell 3247, Vulcan 3972

Miami Beach
Foundation: International 1958
Subsidiary: Hubbard 1877
Office: Kimley 2151

Miami Gardens
Foundation: Dolphins 1147

Miami Lakes
Subsidiary: Amazon.com 122
Office: Kimley 2151

Miramar
Subsidiaries: Caterpillar 722, SPX 3558
Office: Bressler 557

Miramar Beach
Foundation: Vermillion 3939

Moore Haven
Foundation: Glades 1587
Cororate Headquarters: Glades 1587

Naples
Foundations: DeVoe 1101, Health 1765, Henry 1780, Spear 3536
Cororate Headquarters: DeVoe 1101, Health 1765
Subsidiaries: CORE 941, Huntington 1894
Offices: Akerman 69, Bessemer 440, Bond 522, Cummings 1004, Hahn 1700, Porter 3009, Quarles 3101, Robins 3233, Rogers 3252, State 3592

New Port Richey
Cororate Headquarters: Manitowoc 2356

North Port
Office: Kimley 2151

Ocala
Foundation: C L D 635
Cororate Headquarters: C L D 635
Subsidiaries: Cox 958, SPX 3558
Joint Venture: McCormick 2423
Office: Kimley 2151

Orlando
Corporate Giving Programs: Akerman 69, Darden 1032, Lowndes 2313, Orlando 2824, Tupperware 3821, Universal 3889
Foundations: Darden 1032, Hard 1727, Maali 2326, Orlando 2824, Rapoca 3127, SanTrust 3332, SeaWorld 3387, SunTrust 3654, Tupperware 3821, Universal 3889, Wurzburg 4129
Corporate Headquarters: Akerman 69, Darden 1032, Hard 1727, Lowndes 2313, Maali 2326, Orlando 2824, SanTrust 3332, SeaWorld 3387, Tupperware 3821, Universal 3889
Subsidiaries: Anheuser 202, Comcast 887, Darden 1032, Dean 1054, First 1400, Manpower 2358
Offices: Akerman 69, Baker 319, Boises 518, Burr 621, Edelman 1224, Electronic 1242, Federal 1349, Foley 1453, Ford 1462, Greenberg 1654, Holland 1834, Humana 1886, Kimley 2151, Lauth 2232, Littler 2289, Lowndes 2313, Mercury 2469, SAS 3336, SeaWorld 3387, Whiting 4063
Plants: Alro 113, Florida 1444, FMC 1449, Lennar 2250, Owens 2841, Sherwin 3437, Univar 3886, Winn 4087

Ormond Beach
Subsidiaries: Flowserve 1447, JSJ 2073

Oviedo
Foundation: Duda 1188
Corporate Headquarters: Duda 1188, InfoSource 1936

Palm Bay
Subsidiary: DRS 1179
Plant: Harris 1736

Palm Beach
Offices: Akerman 69, Bessemer 440, Brown 589, Hodgson 1820

Palm Beach Gardens
Foundation: PGA 2953
Cororate Headquarters: PGA 2953
Subsidiary: Biomet 466
Office: Cummings 1004

Palm Coast
Corporate Giving Program: DeniseLawrence.Com 1086

Panama City
Plant: Gulf 1689

Pensacola
Foundations: Bear 393, Gulf 1689
Corporate Headquarters: Bear 393, Gulf 1689
Subsidiaries: Southern 3516, Synovus 3674
Division: Cox 958
Office: Opus 2820
Plants: Armstrong 246, International 1968

Pinellas Park
Office: Regal 3166

Plant City
Subsidiary: Smithfield 3487
Office: Dart 1033

Plantation
Corporate Giving Program: DHL 1106
Foundation: Kerzner 2133
Corporate Headquarters: DHL 1106, Kerzner 2133
Plant: Motorola 2586

Pompano Beach
Subsidiary: Hunter 1893
Plants: Illinois 1916, Winn 4087

Ponte Vedra Beach
Foundation: PGA 2954
Cororate Headquarters: PGA 2954

Port Manatee
Plant: Lafarge 2210

Punta Gorda
Foundation: A & E 6

Quincy
Subsidiary: Synovus 3674

Riverview
Plant: Mosaic 2580

Riviera Beach
Subsidiary: Philips 2963

Saint Petersburg
Cororate Headquarters: Konica 2185
Office: Adams 34

Sarasota
Corporate Giving Program: Green 1650
Foundations: Malco 2350, United 3871, Wells 4028
Corporate Headquarters: Green 1650, Malco 2350
Division: Bausch 376
Offices: Adams 34, Kimley 2151, Pulte 3083
Plants: Bausch 376, Berry 438

Scholz
Plant: Gulf 1689

Sebring
Subsidiaries: Huntington 1894, Koch 2180

Seffner
Foundation: Lazy 2234
Cororate Headquarters: Lazy 2234

Smith
Plant: Gulf 1689

South Bay
Foundation: Woerner 4101

St. Augustine
Subsidiary: St. Joe 3563
Division: Gates 1540

St. Petersburg
Corporate Giving Programs: Jabil 2006, James 2021, Tampa 3686
Foundation: Catalina 719
Corporate Headquarters: Catalina 719, Jabil 2006, James 2021, Tampa 3686, Times 3758
Subsidiaries: First 1389, Fiserv 1427, Hubbard 1877, IAC 1903, James 2021
Division: AEGON 45
Offices: Draper 1171, Grant 1633, Holder 1829, Humana 1886
Plants: Menasha 2461, Raytheon 3135, West 4038

Stuart
Subsidiary: Kiplinger 2163
Office: Kimley 2151

Summerland Key
Plant: Bausch 376

Sun City Center
Foundation: Convalescent 931
Cororate Headquarters: Convalescent 931

Sunrise
Corporate Giving Program: Florida 1442
Foundation: Florida 1442
Cororate Headquarters: Florida 1442
Subsidiary: NorthWestern 2748
Office: Opus 2820
Plant: Lennar 2250

Tallahassee
Foundation: Capital 676
Cororate Headquarters: Capital 676
Subsidiary: Synovus 3674
Offices: Akerman 69, Foley 1453, Fowler 1479, Greenberg 1654, Holland 1834, Kimley 2151, Nelson 2661, Wal-Mart 3980

Tampa
Corporate Giving Programs: Bloomin 487, Buccaneer 599, Center 737, Fowler 1479, Hill 1802, Seminole 3404, Sweetbay 3665, Syniverse 3672, TECO 3701, Walter 3984
Foundations: Baker 322, Bloomin 487, Buccaneer 599, Center 737, First 1407, Holland 1834, March 2367, New York 2691, Newman 2696, TECO 3701, Walter 3984
Corporate Headquarters: Baker 322, Bloomin 487, Buccaneer 599, Center 737, First 1407, Fowler 1479, Hill 1802, Holland 1834, Newman 2696, Seminole 3404, Sequa 3410, Sweetbay 3665, Syniverse 3672, TECO 3701
Subsidiaries: Bausch 376, Beneficial 411, Lennar 2250, Palace 2866, Progressive 3057, Walter 3984
Divisions: Bausch 376, Sweetbay 3665
Joint Venture: Watson 4007
Offices: Adams 34, Akerman 69, Draper 1171, Foley 1453, Ford 1462, Fowler 1479, GATX 1542, Grant 1633, Greenberg 1654, Humana 1886, Kiewit 2142, Kimley 2151, Liberty 2265, Opus 2820, Pan-American 2868, Price 3040, Quarles 3101, Russell 3289, SeaWorld 3387, Shook 3439, Squire 3561, United 3873, Vision 3961, Young 4147
Plants: Bausch 376, Clorox 852, Commercial 893, Dreyer's 1174, Lafarge 2210, Novell 2754, Valspar 3920, Winn 4087

Tampa Bay
Office: Pulte 3083

University Park
Foundation: Armbrust 243

Valparaiso
Subsidiary: Synovus 3674

Vero Beach
Foundation: Power 3021
Office: Kimley 2151

Watersound
Foundation: St. Joe 3563
Cororate Headquarters: St. Joe 3563

West Palm Beach
Foundation: Aberdeen 18
Corporate Headquarters: Aberdeen 18, Woerner 4101
Subsidiaries: DRS 1179, Pacific 2855
Offices: Grant 1633, Greenberg 1654, Holland 1834, Humana 1886, Kimley 2151, Squire 3561
Plant: Bassett 372

Weston
Foundation: NVF 2766
Office: Strauss 3624

Winter Garden
Office: Fishel 1429

Winter Haven
Office: State 3591
Plants: Packaging 2861, Sherwin 3437

Winter Park
Corporate Giving Program: InfoSource 1936
Foundation: Greater 1648
Office: Burr 621

Yulee
Subsidiary: Victaulic 3948

GEORGIA

Abbeville
Office: Three 3745

Albany
Subsidiary: Synovus 3674
Office: Fishel 1429
Plants: Cooper 936, Miller 2523, Procter 3055

Alpharetta
Corporate Giving Programs: Better 448, Colonial 876
Foundation: Mccar 2420
Corporate Headquarters: Better 448, Colonial 876, Kids 2141, Mccar 2419, Mccar 2420
Subsidiaries: Danaher 1027, Nucor 2760, Opus 2820, Synovus 3674, V.F. 3913
Offices: Deere 1061, GATX 1542, Pan-American 2868, State 3591
Plant: Clorox 852

Americus
Subsidiary: Synovus 3674

Athens
Foundations: Howmedica 1875, Tillman 3752
Cororate Headquarters: Tillman 3752
Subsidiaries: Johnson 2048, Synovus 3674

Atlanta
Corporate Giving Programs: AFC 50, AGL 57, Alston 116, Arnall 247, AT&T 274, Atlanta 278, Atlanta 280, Carter's 708, Carvel 710, Chick 791, Coca 862, Coca 863, Cox 959, Delta 1073, DS 1182, Ford 1462, Georgia 1568, Gray 1639, Home 1842, ifPeople 1912, Interface 1953, Invesco 1983, Kaiser 2086, Kilpatrick 2147, King 2157, Newell 2694, Rogers 3252, Southern 3516, SunTrust 3654, Superior 3657, Sutherland 3663, Turner 3823, United 3872, Weather 4012, Winter 4090
Foundations: AGL 57, Allen 96, Arby's 228, Atlanta 278, Atlanta 279, Atlanta 280, Bennett 415, Chick 791, Coca 862, Coca 863, Cousins 953, Cox 959, Equifax 1288, Georgia 1567, Georgia 1568, Greystone 1665, Holder 1829, Home 1842, Hooters 1858, ING 1938, Interface 1953, Invesco 1983, Kajima 2087, Keenan 2112, Kids 2141, Oxford 2847, Pattillo 2896, Peachtree 2908, Printpack 3049, SClenergy 3366, Selig 3401, Southern 3516, TALX 3683, United 3872, Young 4147
Corporate Headquarters: AFC 50, AGL 57, Allen 96, Alston 116, Arby's 228, Arnall 247, AT&T 274, Atlanta 278, Atlanta 279, Atlanta 280, Bennett 415, Cable 639, Carter's 708, Carvel 710, Chick 791, Coca 862, Coca 863, Consolidated 915, Cousins 953, Cox 958, Cox 959, Creative 976, Delta 1073, DS 1182, Equifax 1288, Exponential 1312, First 1400, Ford 1462, Georgia 1567, Georgia 1568, Gray 1639, Holder 1829, Home 1842, Hooters 1858, ifPeople 1912, Interface 1953, Kajima 2087, Keenan 2112, Kilpatrick 2147, King 2157, Newell 2694, Oxford 2847, Pattillo 2896, Peachtree 2908, Printpack 3049, Rogers 3252, Selig 3401, Southern 3516, SunTrust 3654, Superior 3657, Sutherland 3663, Turner 3823, United 3872, Weather 4012, Winter 4090, Young 4147
Subsidiaries: AGL 57, Alcoa 82, Assurant 266, AT&T 273, Berkshire 429, Caterpillar 722, Cox 958, Dean 1054, Delta 1073, Equifax 1288, Fortis 1473, HCA 1762, IMA 1917, Johns 2047, Koch 2180, Leggett 2246, Macy's 2333, Marriott 2383, Meredith 2471, Miller 2517, Philips 2963, SClenergy 3366, Southern 3516, Steelcase 3597, SUPERVALU 3659, Time 3757, Turner 3823, United 3872, Walter 3984
Divisions: AFC 50, American 132, General 1552, Leggett 2246
Offices: Alston 116, Arnall 247, Avon 305, Baker 325, Balch 327, Ballard 329, Bryan 596, Burr 621, Cerner 754, Cozen 964, Credit 980, CUNA 1008, Dixon 1133, Dow 1164, Duane 1185, Edelman 1224, Federal 1348, Federal 1349, Finnegan 1384, Fish 1428, Fisher 1433, Ford 1462, Gleacher 1589, Google 1613, Grant 1633, Greenberg 1654, Holland 1834, Humana 1886, ITA 1998, Jones 2058, Kasowitz 2099, Kearney 2107, Kiewit 2142, Kimley 2151, King 2157, Levi 2254, Liberty 2265, Littler 2289, Majestic 2343, McGuireWoods 2430, McKenna 2433, Merchant 2464, Nelson 2661, NIBCO 2707, Norfolk 2725, Paul 2900, Pulte 3083, Quad 3091, RBS 3138, Robins 3232, Robins 3233, SAP 3334, SAS 3336, Schiff 3350, State 3592, Stites 3609, Sutherland 3663, Thompson 3739, Thompson 3740, Turner 3823, Unum 3898, Vision 3961, Whiting 4063
Plants: BP 547, Cabot 642, Campbell 669, Chevron 780, Ecolab 1220, Guardian 1682, Hewlett 1794, Hunt 1892, Jim's 2043, Kellogg 2120, Lancaster 2216, McAfee 2417, Mitsui 2541, Navistar 2647, NEC 2654, Novell 2754, NYK 2768, Owens 2841, Owens 2842, Quaker 3094, Rayonier 3134, Rockwell 3247, Scotts 3372, Sherwin 3437, Valassis 3914, Vulcan 3972, Winn 4087

Augusta
Foundations: Morris 2573, Southeastern 3513
Corporate Headquarters: Morris 2573, Southeastern 3513
Subsidiaries: Cox 962, Textron 3731
Plants: BP 547, Deere 1061, International 1968, Martin 2391, Olin 2801, Owens 2841, Procter 3055

Austell
Plant: Subaru 3631

Baldwin
Foundation: Fieldale 1373
Cororate Headquarters: Fieldale 1373

Blairsville
Foundation: United 3866
Cororate Headquarters: United 3866

Bogart
Plant: Menasha 2461

Brunswick
Subsidiaries: Georgia 1568, Synovus 3674

Calhoun
Cororate Headquarters: Mohawk 2545
Subsidiary: Synovus 3674

Carnesville
Plant: Hunt 1892

Carrollton
Corporate Giving Program: Southwire 3527
Cororate Headquarters: Southwire 3527
Subsidiary: Synovus 3674

Cartersville
Plant: Clorox 852

Cedar Springs
Subsidiary: Georgia 1568

Chatsworth
Subsidiary: Synovus 3674

Claxton
Plant: Valmont 3919

Cochran
Subsidiary: Synovus 3674
Office: Three 3745

Columbus
Corporate Giving Program: Aflac 54
Foundations: Aflac 54, Gregory 1661, Synovus 3674
Corporate Headquarters: Aflac 54, Gregory 1661, Synovus 3674
Subsidiaries: Hallmark 1707, HCA 1762, Synovus 3674
Plant: Panasonic 2869

Conyers
Plant: Golden 1602

Covington
Division: Bard 358
Plants: Fuller 1517, General 1554, Valspar 3920

Dalton
Corporate Giving Program: Shaw 3426
Foundations: Mohawk 2545, Star 3582
Corporate Headquarters: Shaw 3426, Star 3582
Subsidiary: Berkshire 429

Decatur
Plant: TJX 3765

Doraville
Subsidiary: Victaulic 3948
Plant: Univar 3886

Douglasville
Subsidiary: Synovus 3674

Dublin
Corporate Giving Program: MAGE 2338
Cororate Headquarters: MAGE 2338
Office: Three 3745
Plants: Bassett 372, Rockwell 3246

Duluth
Corporate Giving Program: CIBA 810
Foundations: NCR 2650, Primerica 3045
Corporate Headquarters: CIBA 810, NCR 2650, Primerica 3045
Subsidiary: NCR 2650
Offices: ACE 24, Fishel 1429, Safeco 3306, State 3591
Plants: Nordson 2723, Rockwell 3246

East Point
Plant: PPG 3025

Eastman
Foundation: Three 3745
Corporate Headquarters: Three 3745

Eatonton
Foundations: Peoples 2930, Putnam 3087
Corporate Headquarters: Peoples 2930, Putnam 3087

Fairburn
Plant: Owens 2842

Flowery Branch
Corporate Giving Program: Atlanta 277
Cororate Headquarters: Atlanta 277
Plant: SKF 3473

Forest Park
Plant: Clorox 852

Fort Benning
Office: Bionetics 467

Fort Valley
Subsidiary: Synovus 3674

Gainesville
Foundation: Conditioned 906
Cororate Headquarters: Conditioned 906
Subsidiary: Lincoln 2279

Greensboro
Foundation: BankSouth 350
Cororate Headquarters: BankSouth 350
Plant: NIBCO 2707

Griffin
Subsidiary: Caterpillar 722

Hartwell
Plant: Tenneco 3715

Hazlehurst
Subsidiary: Synovus 3674

Helena
Office: Three 3745

Kennesaw
Corporate Giving Program: CryoLife 990
Corporate Headquarters: CarMax 694, CryoLife 990
Plant: Clorox 852

LaGrange
Subsidiaries: Keen 2111, Lancaster 2216, Synovus 3674
Division: DIRECTV 1124
Office: Regis 3172
Plant: Interface 1953
Lavonia
Plant: Sonoco 3500
Lawrenceville
Foundation: Marena 2372
Cororate Headquarters: Marena 2372
Subsidiaries: Cisco 818, Survis 3660
Office: Sharp 3422
Plant: Sherwin 3437
Leesburg
Plant: Martin 2391
Lithonia
Subsidiary: Raymond 3133
Division: Rogers 3253
Offices: Dart 1033, Fishel 1429
Plants: Coral 940, Sonoco 3500
Lyons
Plant: Oxford 2847
Macon
Cororate Headquarters: Eagle 1203
Subsidiary: Securian 3389
Division: Cox 958
Offices: Baker 325, GATX 1542, Wurzburg 4129
Plants: Armstrong 246, Bassett 372
Manchester
Plant: Sherwin 3437
Marietta
Foundations: Graphic 1635, Pro 3051, Times 3759
Corporate Headquarters: Graphic 1635, Pro 3051, Times 3759
Subsidiaries: Sonoco 3500, Synovus 3674
Plants: CA 638, Castle 716, Georgia 1568, Sealed 3381
Martinez
Subsidiary: Hunter 1893
McDonough
Foundation: Eagle 1203
Midland
Plant: Worthington 4124
Midway
Foundation: Coastal 859
Cororate Headquarters: Coastal 859
Monroe
Subsidiaries: Oxford 2847, Synovus 3674
Montezuma
Plant: Birds 469
Morrow
Plant: Sherwin 3437
Newnan
Subsidiary: Synovus 3674
Plant: Bassett 372
Norcross
Corporate Giving Programs: Herschend 1790, Rock 3239
Foundations: Survis 3660, Waffle 3975
Corporate Headquarters: Rock 3239, Waffle 3975
Subsidiaries: Hunter 1893, Ripplewood 3219, Schein 3348, Synovus 3674
Offices: Canon 672, Factory 1323, RJN 3228
Plants: Barnes 362, Donaldson 1153, Georgia 1568, Nordson 2723, Panasonic 2869, Sonoco 3500
Peachtree City
Corporate Giving Program: Global 1592
Cororate Headquarters: Global 1592
Subsidiaries: Global 1592, Synovus 3674
Plants: Newell 2694, Panasonic 2869
Rockmart
Plant: Interface 1953
Rome
Subsidiary: Synovus 3674
Savannah
Corporate Giving Program: Gulfstream 1690
Foundations: Brasseler 556, Byrd 631, Colonial 875
Corporate Headquarters: Brasseler 556, Byrd 631, Colonial 875, Gulfstream 1690
Subsidiaries: Colonial 875, General 1551, Harleysville 1733, Imperial 1922
Offices: BankSouth 350, Kiewit 2142
Plants: International 1968, Owens 2842
Smyrna
Subsidiary: Arch 230
Plant: Pactiv 2863
Social Circle
Plant: Goodyear 1612
Soperton
Office: Three 3745
Statesboro
Subsidiaries: Nash 2619, Synovus 3674
Plant: Briggs 565
Stone Mountain
Cororate Headquarters: Survis 3660
Suwanee
Plant: Mary 2392
The Rock
Plant: Quad 3091
Thomasville
Corporate Giving Program: Flowers 1446
Foundation: Tasty 3693
Cororate Headquarters: Flowers 1446
Subsidiaries: Smithfield 3487, Synovus 3674, Textron 3731
Tifton
Subsidiary: Synovus 3674
Tucker
Foundation: U.S. 3839
Cororate Headquarters: U.S. 3839
Subsidiaries: Ripplewood 3219, Synovus 3674
Division: ServiceMaster 3414
Plants: Bausch 376, Butler 626, Fuller 1517
Valdosta
Subsidiary: Synovus 3674
Warner Robins
Subsidiary: Synovus 3674
Plant: Rockwell 3247
Waycross
Subsidiary: Lancaster 2216
Office: GATX 1542
West Point
Foundation: Batson 373
Cororate Headquarters: Batson 373
Plant: Interface 1953

HAWAII

Aiea
Plant: Panasonic 2869
Anahola
Subsidiary: Cornerstone 944
Hilo
Foundation: Hawaii 1754
Office: Regis 3172
Plant: Hershey 1791
Honolulu
Corporate Giving Programs: Bank 342, Bays 383, Cades 647, CBI 726, First 1408, Hawaiian 1755, Hilo 1811, Kaiser 2086, Matson 2404
Foundations: Alexander 85, Bank 342, Finance 1381, First 1405, First 1408, H & K 1694, Hawaii 1753, Hawaiian 1755, Hawaiian 1756, Island 1996, Kukui 2198, L&L 2202, La Mariage 2204, Niu 2717, Persis 2944, RESCO 3189, Servco 3412, Towill 3782
Corporate Headquarters: Alexander 85, Bank 342, Bays 383, Cades 647, CBI 726, Finance 1381, First 1405, First 1408, H & K 1694, Hawaii 1753, Hawaiian 1755, Hawaiian 1756, Hilo 1811, Island 1996, Kukui 2198, L&L 2202, La Mariage 2204, Matson 2404, Niu 2717, Persis 2944, Servco 3412, Towill 3782
Subsidiaries: Alexander 85, Dole 1141, Fuji 1514, Hawaiian 1755, Servco 3412, Tesoro 3723
Offices: Canon 672, DFS 1104, Grant 1633, Kiewit 2142, Vision 3961
Plants: CA 638, Chevron 780, Owens 2841, Rockwell 3247
Kapolei
Corporate Giving Program: Campbell 668
Cororate Headquarters: Campbell 668
Keaau
Cororate Headquarters: Hawaii 1754
Keauhou
Corporate Giving Program: Natural 2642
Cororate Headquarters: Natural 2642
Kihei
Cororate Headquarters: Hotel 1868
Lanai City
Subsidiary: Castle 717
Lihue
Foundation: Grove 1672
Cororate Headquarters: Grove 1672
Subsidiary: Grove 1672
Mililani
Corporate Giving Program: Time 3756
Cororate Headquarters: Time 3756
Subsidiaries: Castle 717, Time 3757
Division: Time 3756
Plant: Wal-Mart 3980
Wailuku
Foundation: Hotel 1868
Waipahu
Foundation: Tony 3773
Cororate Headquarters: Tony 3773
Plant: Golden 1602

IDAHO

Boise
Corporate Giving Programs: Albertsons 79, Caprock 683, IDACORP 1907, Intermountain 1956, Micron 2500, Simplot 3459
Foundations: IDACORP 1907, Intermountain 1957, Micron 2500, Simplot 3459, SUPERVALU 3659, Washington 3995
Corporate Headquarters: Albertsons 79, Caprock 683, IDACORP 1907, Intermountain 1956, Intermountain 1957, Micron 2500, Simplot 3459, Syngenta 3671, Treasure 3803, Washington 3995
Subsidiaries: Alsco 115, Belo 406, Blue 504, IDACORP 1907, Intermountain 1957, Novartis 2752, SUPERVALU 3659
Offices: Applied 220, Fenwick 1362, Holland 1833, KeyBank 2136, Kiewit 2142, Perkins 2940, Perkins 2941, Stoel 3611, Wal-Mart 3980
Plants: Hewlett 1794, Syngenta 3671
Buhl
Office: First 1403
Plant: Seneca 3406
Burley
Foundation: First 1403
Office: First 1403
Coeur d'Alene
Plant: Avista 301
Eagle
Foundation: Treasure 3803
Idaho Falls
Foundations: Melaleuca 2457, Syngenta 3671
Cororate Headquarters: Melaleuca 2457
Subsidiary: PerkinElmer 2939
Jerome
Office: First 1403
Lewiston
Subsidiary: Potlatch 3017
Division: Potlatch 3017
Plant: Avista 301
Meridian
Foundation: Blue 504
Cororate Headquarters: Blue 504

Nampa
Foundation: Home 1843
Cororate Headquarters: Home 1843
Subsidiaries: Evening 1302, Home 1843
Payette
Subsidiary: Alsco 115
Pocatello
Subsidiary: Farmers 1338
Plant: FMC 1449
Ririe
Subsidiary: Otter 2836
Rupert
Office: First 1403
Salmon
Subsidiary: CenturyLink 751
Twin Falls
Cororate Headquarters: First 1403

ILLINOIS

Abbott Park
Corporate Giving Program: Abbott 13
Foundation: Abbott 13
Cororate Headquarters: Abbott 13
Addison
Subsidiary: Berkshire 429
Alsip
Foundation: Griffith 1667
Cororate Headquarters: Admiral 37, Griffith 1667
Subsidiaries: Griffith 1667, Venturedyne 3933
Plant: Smith 3484
Alton
Foundation: Simmons 3457
Office: Wal-Mart 3980
Arlington Heights
Cororate Headquarters: United 3860
Subsidiary: AMCOL 127
Plant: Motorola 2586
Aurora
Subsidiaries: Alsco 115, Farmers 1338, Ripplewood 3219
Plant: Caterpillar 722
Bannockburn
Cororate Headquarters: Terlato 3720
Barrington
Subsidiary: Bourns 542
Belleville
Foundation: Belleville 405
Cororate Headquarters: Belleville 405
Office: Greensfelder 1659
Bellwood
Subsidiary: Newell 2694
Belvidere
Foundation: K-B 2081
Plants: Chrysler 801, General 1554
Bensenville
Foundation: Chicago 789
Corporate Headquarters: Chicago 789, Victor 3949
Subsidiary: Transco 3797
Bloomington
Corporate Giving Programs: Country 951, State 3591
Foundations: Brady 553, Caterpillar 722, GROWMARK 1674, State 3591
Corporate Headquarters: Brady 553, Country 951, GROWMARK 1674, State 3591
Subsidiary: State 3591
Office: Levi 2254
Bourbonnais
Subsidiary: Nucor 2760
Office: HomeStar 1848
Bradley
Subsidiary: Bunge 612
Office: HomeStar 1848
Bridgeview
Corporate Giving Program: Chicago 783
Foundation: Chicago 783
Cororate Headquarters: Chicago 783
Plant: Quaker 3094
Buffalo Grove
Foundation: International Profit 1969
Corporate Headquarters: International Profit 1969, Swift 3666
Subsidiary: Miller 2517
Burr Ridge
Corporate Giving Program: CNH 856
Foundation: Vijuk 3953
Cororate Headquarters: CNH 856
Plant: Westinghouse 4049
Byron
Foundation: Quality 3098
Cororate Headquarters: Quality 3098
Cairo
Division: ServiceMaster 3414
Carlyle
Plant: Timken 3760
Carol Stream
Plants: Ingram 1941, Valspar 3920
Cary
Division: True 3815
Champaign
Joint Venture: Donaldson 1153
Chatsworth
Subsidiary: Quanex 3100
Chicago
Corporate Giving Programs: Arcelormittal 229, Baker 320, Bally 330, Banner 351, Barack 353, Blue 494, Boeing 516, Brinks 573, Butler 627, Chapman 762, Chicago 782, Chicago 784, Chicago 790, CNA 855, Commonwealth 895, Edelman 1224, Exelon 1309, First 1398, Four 1476, GATX 1542, Goldberg 1599, Harris 1739, Hillshire 1809, Hinshaw 1814, Jenner 2035, Jones 2061, Katten 2101, Kearney 2107, Kirkland 2164, Marshall 2389, Mayer 2411, McDermott 2425, McDonnell 2428, Miller 2523, Morton 2579, Neal 2652, North 2735, Northern 2740, Pattishall 2897, Peoples 2931, Pivotal 2987, Playboy 2990, Quaker 3094, Schiff 3350, Sidley 3446, TransUnion 3799, Ungaretti 3851, United 3860, United 3876, Urban 3901, Winston 4089, Wrigley 4125
Foundations: Accenture 22, Admiral 37, AGL 57, Alliant 103, Amsted 188, Aon 210, Arcelormittal 229, Azulay 311, Baird 316, Barack 353, Barbara 354, Bergstrom 421, Blair 478, Blommer 484, Burnett 619, CH2M 758, Chicago 785, Chicago 786, Chicago 787, Chicago 788, Chicago 790, Clarke 837, CME 853, CNA 855, Donnelley 1155, Draper 1170, DRW 1181, Duchossois 1187, Eastman 1214, Emerson 1257, Energizer 1271, Exelon 1309, Faber 1319, First 1422, GATX 1542, General 1553, Good 1609, Grand 1629, Grant 1633, Guth 1692, Horizon 1864, Horizon 1865, IMC 1920, Katten 2101, Kirkland 2164, Lapham 2223, Luster 2318, Lyon 2321, Material 2402, MB 2415, Morgan 2569, National 2638, NAVTEQ 2648, North 2731, Northern 2740, Prince 3046, Rockwood 3248, Royal 3275, Ryerson 3293, Schiff 3350, Skidmore 3474, Spraying 3552, Transco 3797, True 3815, United 3860, USG 3905, Victor 3949, Walker 3982, Winston 4089, Wrigley 4125
Corporate Headquarters: Alliant 103, Amsted 188, Aon 210, Arcelormittal 229, Azulay 311, Baird 316, Baker 320, Bally 330, Banner 351, Barack 353, Barbara 354, Blair 478, Blommer 484, Blue 494, Boeing 516, Brinks 573, Burnett 619, Butler 627, Chapman 762, Chicago 782, Chicago 784, Chicago 785, Chicago 786, Chicago 787, Chicago 788, Chicago 790, CME 853, CNA 855, Commonwealth 895, Donnelley 1155, Draper 1170, DRW 1181, Edelman 1224, Exelon 1309, Faber 1319, First 1422, Four 1476, GATX 1542, General 1553, Goldberg 1599, Grant 1633, Harris 1739, Hillshire 1809, Hinshaw 1814, Horizon 1864, IMC 1920, Jenner 2035, Jones 2061, Katten 2101, Kearney 2107, Kirkland 2164, Lapham 2223, Luster 2318, Lyon 2321, Marshall 2389, Material 2402, Mayer 2411, MB 2415, McDermott 2425, McDonnell 2428, Miller 2523, Morgan 2569, Morton 2579, NAVTEQ 2648, Neal 2652, North 2731, North 2735, Northern 2740, Pattishall 2897, Peoples 2931, Pivotal 2987, Playboy 2990, Prince 3046, Quaker 3094, Rockwood 3248, Royal 3275, Ryerson 3293, Schiff 3350, Sidley 3446, Skidmore 3474, Transco 3797, TransUnion 3799, True 3815, Ungaretti 3851, United 3876, Urban 3901, USG 3905, Ventas 3931, Winston 4089, Wrigley 4125
Subsidiaries: Alsco 115, American 149, Amsted 188, Archer 233, Associated 261, AT&T 273, Avnet 304, Baker 323, Bally 330, Berkshire 429, Berry 438, CB 725, Chicago 786, Chubb 804, CNA 855, CNO 857, Constellation 919, Donnelley 1155, DS 1182, Exelon 1309, Fiserv 1427, FMC 1449, Gannett 1532, GATX 1542, General 1551, Graybar 1640, Harley 1732, Harris 1739, HCA 1762, Lennar 2250, Loews 2296, Manpower 2358, Mars 2384, Massachusetts 2397, MAXIMUS 2410, Motorola 2586, New York 2688, Northern 2740, NYSE 2769, PepsiCo 2935, TJX 3765, Transco 3797, TransUnion 3799, U.S. 3838, USG 3905, Wrigley 4125
Divisions: Follett 1455, GATX 1542, Koch 2180
Offices: Autodesk 289, Baker 319, Bessemer 440, BP 547, Brinks 573, Brown 589, Bryan 596, CDW 729, CIBA 809, Cozen 964, Credit 980, DP 1168, Drinker 1175, Duane 1185, Elevation 1245, Faegre 1324, Federal 1348, Federal 1349, Foley 1453, Ford 1462, Getty 1569, Gleacher 1589, Good 1609, Google 1613, Greenberg 1654, Greensfelder 1659, Hays 1761, Heller 1773, Holland 1834, Humana 1886, Husch 1896, Ice 1905, Intertech 1976, Jenner 2035, Jones 2058, K&L 2080, Katten 2101, Kelley 2118, Kiewit 2142, Kimley 2151, Kirkland 2164, Latham 2228, Littler 2289, Loeb 2295, Mayer 2411, McDermott 2425, McDonnell 2428, McGuireWoods 2430, Michael 2492, Morgan 2571, NorthSide 2745, Paul 2900, Perkins 2940, Perkins 2941, Playboy 2990, Polsinelli 3001, Proskauer 3064, Quad 3091, Quarles 3101, Quinn 3111, RBS 3138, Reed 3163, Robins 3232, Rogers 3252, Ropes 3260, Russell 3289, SAS 3336, Sedgwick 3395, Sheppard 3435, Sidley 3446, Skadden 3470, State 3592, Steptoe 3599, Thompson 3739, Turner 3823, Ulmer 3845, Ungaretti 3851, Vision 3961, Winston 4089
Plants: Binswanger 464, Castle 716, Clorox 852, Crystal 992, FMC 1449, Interface 1953, International 1962, Mitsui 2541, Nalco 2613, Rockwell 3247, Sherwin 3437, Valassis 3914, Valmont 3919, Valspar 3920, Vulcan 3972
Chicago Heights
Subsidiaries: Chicago 786, Duchossois 1187
Chillicothe
Cororate Headquarters: MH 2490
Cicero
Corporate Giving Program: GreenChoice 1655
Cororate Headquarters: GreenChoice 1655
Collinsville
Office: RJN 3228
Countryside
Plant: Lubrizol 2315
Crystal Lake
Foundation: AptarGroup 221
Cororate Headquarters: AptarGroup 221
Division: Follett 1455
Danville
Plant: Quaker 3094
Davenport
Subsidiary: Quanex 3100
Decatur
Corporate Giving Program: Archer 233
Foundation: Ameren 129
Cororate Headquarters: Archer 233
Subsidiary: Archer 233
Offices: Baum 375, Keen 2111
Plant: Caterpillar 722

Deerfield
Corporate Giving Programs: Baxter 377, Beam 390, CF 755, Fortune 1474, Mondelez 2556, Walgreen 3981
Foundations: Baxter 377, Walgreen 3981
Corporate Headquarters: Baxter 377, Beam 390, CF 755, Fortune 1474, Mondelez 2556, Walgreen 3981
Subsidiaries: Georgia 1568, Grace 1623, Temple 3711
DeKalb
Office: Wiley 4072
Des Plaines
Subsidiaries: Danaher 1027, Novartis 2752, Otis 2835
Division: DIRECTV 1124
Plant: Deluxe 1084
Dixon
Plants: Donaldson 1153, Gates 1540
Downers Grove
Subsidiaries: Amsted 188, ServiceMaster 3414
Division: ServiceMaster 3414
Plants: Rexnord 3198, Syngenta 3671
Downs
Corporate Giving Program: Epiphany 1284
Cororate Headquarters: Epiphany 1284
Dwight
Plant: Donnelley 1155
East Alton
Cororate Headquarters: Simmons 3457
Plant: Olin 2801
East Dubuque
Foundation: Crescent 981
Cororate Headquarters: Crescent 981
East Moline
Plant: Deere 1061
East Saint Louis
Cororate Headquarters: Casino 714
East St. Louis
Foundation: Casino 714
Edwardsville
Offices: Bryan 596, Polsinelli 3001
Effingham
Plant: Sherwin 3437
El Paso
Plant: American 135
Elgin
Foundations: Elgin 1246, IHC 1913, PNC 2997
Corporate Headquarters: Elgin 1246, Grand 1629, IHC 1913
Subsidiaries: Copley 938, Safety 3309
Plants: Donnelley 1155, Panasonic 2869
Elk Grove Village
Subsidiaries: Philips 2963, Rogers 3253, United 3860
Offices: Mortenson 2577, Reynolds 3199
Plants: Ecolab 1220, Morton 2579
Elmhurst
Corporate Headquarters: Duchossois 1187, Vijuk 3953
Subsidiaries: Duchossois 1187, Follett 1455, Kellogg 2120, Raymond 3133
Evanston
Subsidiaries: Houghton 1869, Parsons 2887
Office: Pactiv 2863
Fairfield
Foundation: Fairfield 1326
Cororate Headquarters: Fairfield 1326
Flora
Plant: Sherwin 3437
Forest Park
Foundation: Ferrara 1364
Cororate Headquarters: Ferrara 1364
Frankfort
Plant: Illinois 1916
Franklin Park
Plants: Panasonic 2869, U.S. 3841
Freeport
Subsidiaries: Leggett 2246, Newell 2694
Galesburg
Subsidiary: Copley 938
Plant: Butler 626
Galva
Plant: Evans 1300
Geneseo
Foundation: Geneseo 1560
Cororate Headquarters: Geneseo 1560
Geneva
Subsidiary: Amsted 188
Office: Houghton 1869
Glencoe
Foundation: P.E.L. 2849
Glendale Heights
Cororate Headquarters: Spraying 3552
Subsidiary: Graybar 1640
Plant: Dreyer's 1174
Glenview
Corporate Giving Program: Mead 2443
Foundations: Abt 20, Illinois 1916
Corporate Headquarters: Abt 20, Illinois 1916, Mead 2443
Granite City
Subsidiary: Amsted 188
Gurnee
Foundation: NorthSide 2745
Corporate Headquarters: NorthSide 2745, Vermillion 3939
Subsidiary: Danaher 1027
Plant: Danaher 1027
Hampshire
Foundation: Meadows 2444
Cororate Headquarters: Meadows 2444
Hanover Park
Plant: Owens 2841
Harvard
Division: True 3815
Plant: Motorola 2586
Highland Park
Foundation: EMCO 1254
Cororate Headquarters: P.E.L. 2849
Hodgkins
Plant: Sealed 3381
Hoffman Estates
Corporate Giving Programs: Kmart 2172, Sears 3384
Foundations: AMCOL 127, Sears 3384
Corporate Headquarters: AMCOL 127, Kmart 2172, Sears 3384
Offices: AT&T 274, Factory 1323, ITA 1998, Pulte 3083, Safeco 3306, Strauss 3624
Plant: Mary 2392
Homewood
Plant: Sherwin 3437
Hoopeston
Plant: FMC 1449
Itasca
Corporate Giving Program: Fellowes 1357
Foundations: Boler 520, First 1413, Market 2378
Corporate Headquarters: Boler 520, Fellowes 1357, First 1413, Market 2378
Subsidiaries: First 1413, Houghton 1869, NEC 2654, Pacific 2855
Division: Fuji 1514
Offices: Ahern 60, Autodesk 289, Canon 672, Liberty 2265
Plant: Subaru 3631
Jacksonville
Foundation: Bound 541
Cororate Headquarters: Bound 541
Joliet
Subsidiary: Copley 938
Division: Caesars 650
Plants: BP 547, Caterpillar 722, Ecolab 1220, Exxon 1315
Joppa
Plant: Lafarge 2210
Kankakee
Plants: Armstrong 246, Merk 2467, Valspar 3920
La Grange
Foundation: Texor 3730
Division: Philips 2963
Lake Bluff
Foundation: Terlato 3720
Plant: Westinghouse 4049
Lake Forest
Corporate Giving Programs: Chicago 781, Grainger 1626, Packaging 2861, Pactiv 2863, Tenneco 3715
Foundations: Brunswick 595, Hospira 1867, Northern 2740, Trustmark 3818
Corporate Headquarters: Brunswick 595, Chicago 781, Grainger 1626, Hospira 1867, Packaging 2861, Pactiv 2863, Tenneco 3715, Trustmark 3818
Subsidiaries: Cargill 691, Mosaic 2580
Office: Schiff 3350
Lansing
Office: Royal 3275
Plant: Morton 2579
Libertyville
Foundation: Motorola 2585
Cororate Headquarters: Motorola 2585
Subsidiaries: Google 1613, Volkswagen 3967
Plant: Motorola 2586
Lincoln
Subsidiary: Copley 938
Lincolnshire
Foundation: Klein 2168
Cororate Headquarters: Klein 2168
Subsidiaries: Pactiv 2863, Quanex 3100, Staples 3581
Lisle
Foundation: GKN 1585
Corporate Headquarters: GKN 1585, Navistar 2647, U.S. 3837
Subsidiary: Unilever 3853
Plant: CA 638
Lombard
Subsidiaries: Kinder 2153, United 3869
Plants: NYK 2768, Sonoco 3500
Loves Park
Cororate Headquarters: Rockford 3241
Manteno
Foundation: HomeStar 1848
Cororate Headquarters: HomeStar 1848
Mapleton
Plant: Caterpillar 722
Marengo
Plant: Valspar 3920
Matteson
Foundation: Great 1644
Cororate Headquarters: Great 1644
Mattoon
Foundations: First 1411, First 1412
Corporate Headquarters: First 1411, First 1412
Subsidiary: First 1411
Plants: Donnelley 1155, Kellogg 2120
McGaw Park
Subsidiary: Cardinal 685
McHenry
Division: Follett 1455
Plant: Modine 2544
Melrose Park
Foundation: Avlon 303
Cororate Headquarters: Avlon 303
Plants: Alro 113, Navistar 2647
Mendota
Plant: Donnelley 1155
Metamora
Plant: Hallmark 1707
Mettawa
Office: CDW 729
Milan
Plant: Deere 1061
Mokena
Subsidiary: Manitowoc 2355
Office: HomeStar 1848
Moline
Corporate Giving Program: Deere 1061
Foundations: Deere 1061, McLaughlin 2436
Corporate Headquarters: Deere 1061, McLaughlin 2436
Subsidiary: Deere 1061
Division: Cox 958
Morris
Subsidiary: Leggett 2246
Plant: LyondellBasell 2322

Morton
Foundations: Baum 375, CORE 941
Corporate Headquarters: Baum 375, CORE 941
Subsidiaries: Caterpillar 722, CORE 941
Plant: Caterpillar 722
Morton Grove
Corporate Giving Program: Lifeway 2272
Foundation: ITT 1999
Cororate Headquarters: Lifeway 2272
Office: Avon 305
Mossville
Foundation: MH 2490
Subsidiary: Caterpillar 722
Plant: Caterpillar 722
Mount Prospect
Plant: Intel 1950
Mount Sterling
Corporate Giving Program: Dot 1158
Foundation: Dot 1158
Cororate Headquarters: Dot 1158
Mount Vernon
Plant: Continental 927
Mount Zion
Plant: PPG 3025
Mundelein
Foundation: Medline 2451
Cororate Headquarters: Medline 2451
Division: Medline 2451
Office: NorthSide 2745
Naperville
Corporate Giving Programs: OfficeMax 2786, Tellabs 3709
Foundations: Nalco 2613, OfficeMax 2786, Tellabs 3709
Corporate Headquarters: Horizon 1865, Nalco 2613, OfficeMax 2786, Tellabs 3709
Subsidiaries: Ecolab 1220, Quanex 3100, Wrigley 4125
Offices: Pan-American 2868, Whirlpool 4056
Plants: BP 547, Dannon 1030
Nashville
Foundation: Republic 3186
Newman
Foundation: Longview 2300
Cororate Headquarters: Longview 2300
Niles
Foundation: Block 482
Cororate Headquarters: Block 482
Division: Stride 3626
Office: NorthSide 2745
North Aurora
Cororate Headquarters: Air 64
Division: ServiceMaster 3414
Offices: Dart 1033, Farmers 1338
North Chicago
Cororate Headquarters: EMCO 1254
Subsidiary: Abbott 13
Northbrook
Corporate Giving Programs: Allstate 107, UL 3844
Foundations: Allstate 107, Consolidated 917, Frontier 1510, Kemper 2124
Corporate Headquarters: Allstate 107, Frontier 1510, Kemper 2124, UL 3844
Subsidiary: Consolidated 915
Office: Rockwood 3248
Plant: Motorola 2586
Northfield
Foundation: Mondelez 2556
Oak Brook
Corporate Giving Program: McDonald's 2427
Foundations: Castle 716, Jovon 2069, McDonald's 2427, Safeway 3310
Corporate Headquarters: Castle 716, Continental 924, McDonald's 2427
Office: Telligen 3710
Plant: Golden 1602
Oakbrook Terrace
Foundation: Graycor 1641
Cororate Headquarters: Graycor 1641
Plants: BP 547, McAfee 2417
Olympia Fields
Subsidiary: Securian 3389
Orland Park
Foundation: Air 64
Ottawa
Plants: Jim's 2043, U.S. 3840
Palatine
Foundation: Square 3560
Cororate Headquarters: Square 3560
Plants: Fuller 1517, Square 3560
Palos Heights
Foundation: First 1413
Paris
Foundations: Edgar 1225, First 1392
Corporate Headquarters: Edgar 1225, First 1392
Peoria
Corporate Giving Programs: Ameren 129, Caterpillar 722
Foundations: Caterpillar 722, Hagerty 1698
Corporate Headquarters: Ameren 129, Caterpillar 722, Hagerty 1698
Subsidiaries: Ameren 128, Caterpillar 722, Copley 938, Raymond 3133
Offices: CORE 941, Husch 1896, Levi 2254
Perkin
Office: Regis 3172
Plainfield
Office: HomeStar 1848
Pontiac
Plants: Caterpillar 722, Donnelley 1155, GKN 1585
Prairie View
Subsidiary: Philips 2963
Prospect Heights
Cororate Headquarters: Beneficial 411
Quincy
Foundations: Niemann 2708, Quincy 3110
Corporate Headquarters: Niemann 2708, Quincy 3110
Subsidiaries: Archer 233, Associated 261
Plant: Harris 1736
Ridgeway
Plant: Birds 469
Ringwood
Plant: Morton 2579
River Grove
Corporate Giving Program: Follett 1455
Foundation: Follett 1455
Cororate Headquarters: Follett 1455
Division: Follett 1455
Riverside
Cororate Headquarters: Texor 3730
Riverwoods
Corporate Giving Program: Discover 1125
Cororate Headquarters: Discover 1125
Office: NorthSide 2745
Robinson
Plant: Hershey 1791
Rock Island
Corporate Giving Program: Royal 3274
Foundation: Royal 3274
Cororate Headquarters: Royal 3274
Rockford
Corporate Giving Program: Rocknel 3244
Foundations: Anderson 195, Eclipse 1219, Kelley 2119, Rockford 3241, Schmeling 3353, Sjostrom 3469, Woodward 4112
Corporate Headquarters: Anderson 195, Bergstrom 421, Eclipse 1219, K-B 2081, Kelley 2119, Rocknel 3244, Schmeling 3353, Sjostrom 3469
Subsidiaries: Associated 261, CLARCOR 832, CNO 857, Eclipse 1219, Mylan 2610, Textron 3731
Division: Woodward 4112
Offices: Ahern 60, Reinhart 3178, United 3872
Plants: Barnes 362, Newell 2694, Sherwin 3437, Valspar 3920
Rolling Meadows
Subsidiaries: Berkley 426, Consolidated 915
Plants: Navistar 2647, Novell 2754
Romeoville
Foundation: Kehe 2114
Cororate Headquarters: Kehe 2114
Office: Sharp 3422
Roselle
Cororate Headquarters: Clarke 837
Division: Viad 3946
Rosemont
Corporate Giving Program: U.S. 3838
Foundations: McShane 2439, Popular 3003
Cororate Headquarters: McShane 2439
Subsidiaries: Opus 2820, Philips 2963
Salem
Plant: Sealed 3381
Schaumburg
Foundations: Motorola 2586, Omron 2810
Corporate Headquarters: Motorola 2586, Omron 2810
Subsidiaries: Canon 672, Lincoln 2281
Plant: Schulman 3361
Schiller Park
Plant: Square 3560
Silvis
Plant: Deere 1061
Skokie
Foundations: Continental 924, McNally 2437
Corporate Headquarters: McNally 2437, Techni 3699
Subsidiary: Allegheny 91
South Beloit
Subsidiary: Wisconsin 4095
South Elgin
Foundation: Hoffer 1821
Cororate Headquarters: Hoffer 1821
South Holland
Plant: Sherwin 3437
Springfield
Foundation: Levi 2254
Cororate Headquarters: Levi 2254
Subsidiaries: Ameren 128, Copley 938
Division: Cox 958
Offices: American 147, Ungaretti 3851
Sterling
Foundation: Wahl 3977
Cororate Headquarters: Wahl 3977
Subsidiary: Leggett 2246
Sycamore
Foundation: Ideal 1908
Cororate Headquarters: Ideal 1908
Teutopolis
Foundation: Three 3746
Cororate Headquarters: Three 3746
Thornton
Plant: Campbell 669
Tinley Park
Foundation: Panduit 2872
Corporate Headquarters: Jovon 2069, Panduit 2872
Plant: Fuller 1517
Trenton
Foundation: Jim's 2043
Cororate Headquarters: Jim's 2043
Tuscola
Plant: Cabot 642
Urbana
Subsidiary: SUPERVALU 3659
Vernon Hills
Corporate Giving Program: CDW 729
Cororate Headquarters: CDW 729
Subsidiaries: Manpower 2358, Masco 2393
Warrenville
Foundation: Navistar 2647
Subsidiary: Navistar 2647
Office: BP 547
Waukegan
Foundation: United 3867
Cororate Headquarters: United 3867
West Chicago
Subsidiary: Consolidated 915
Plants: General 1554, Navistar 2647
Westchester
Corporate Giving Program: Ingredion 1942
Foundation: Ingredion 1942
Cororate Headquarters: Ingredion 1942
Subsidiary: Exelon 1309
Office: SAP 3334
Plant: Navistar 2647

Westmont
Corporate Giving Program: Ty 3828
Cororate Headquarters: Ty 3828
Wheaton
Foundation: RJN 3228
Cororate Headquarters: RJN 3228
Wheeling
Plants: Clorox 852, Donnelley 1155, Valspar 3920
Wood Dale
Subsidiary: Nippon 2713
Plant: Illinois 1916
Woodridge
Subsidiary: Staples 3581
Woodstock
Foundation: Techni 3699
Subsidiary: Cardinal 685
Plant: Morton 2579
Zion
Foundation: Coral 940
Cororate Headquarters: Coral 940

INDIANA

Anderson
Foundation: Communications 896
Subsidiary: Churchill 807
Plant: Jim's 2043
Angola
Plant: Tenneco 3715
Auburn
Cororate Headquarters: Rieke 3212
Subsidiary: Nucor 2760
Aurora
Foundation: PFS 2951
Cororate Headquarters: PFS 2951
Subsidiary: PFS 2951
Batesville
Cororate Headquarters: Hill 1804
Bedford
Office: Regis 3172
Bloomington
Subsidiary: Hallmark 1707
Bluffton
Foundation: Franklin 1484
Cororate Headquarters: Franklin 1484
Bremen
Foundation: Graphix 1637
Cororate Headquarters: Graphix 1637
Brookville
Plant: Owens 2842
Brownsburg
Plant: TJX 3765
Butler
Subsidiary: Dura 1195
Carmel
Corporate Giving Program: CNO 857
Foundations: Indiana 1930, Lauth 2232
Corporate Headquarters: CNO 857, Lauth 2232
Subsidiary: CNO 857
Plant: Martin 2391
Charlestown
Subsidiary: Caterpillar 722
Plant: NIBCO 2707
Clinton
Plant: Lilly 2274
Columbus
Corporate Giving Program: Cummins 1007
Foundations: Cummins 1007, Johnson 2053
Corporate Headquarters: Cummins 1007, Johnson 2053
Plant: Meritor 2473
Connersville
Subsidiary: Gates 1540
Crawfordsville
Subsidiaries: Alcoa 82, Horizon 1865
Plants: Donnelley 1155, Wal-Mart 3980
Danville
Subsidiary: Bunge 612
Decatur
Foundation: Porter 3006
Cororate Headquarters: Porter 3006
East Chicago
Foundation: Ameristar 176
Subsidiaries: Caparo 673, Safety 3309
Eaton
Subsidiary: Lancaster 2216
Edinburgh
Plant: Sonoco 3500
Elkhart
Corporate Giving Programs: Conn 909, NIBCO 2707
Corporate Headquarters: Conn 909, NIBCO 2707
Subsidiary: Tomkins 3771
Office: Dura 1195
Plants: Fuller 1517, Tenneco 3715, Valmont 3919
Evansville
Corporate Giving Programs: Berry 438, Old 2798, Vectren 3925
Foundations: Crescent 983, Koch 2179, Old 2798, Springleaf 3554, Vectren 3925
Corporate Headquarters: Berry 438, Crescent 983, Keller-Crescent 2117, Koch 2179, Old 2798, Springleaf 3554, Vectren 3925
Subsidiaries: American 147, American 156, Goldman 1603, Handy 1718, Koch 2179, Old 2798, Vectren 3925
Plants: Bristol 578, Ferro 1366, PPG 3025, Schulman 3361, TJX 3765, Whirlpool 4056
Ferdinand
Foundation: Best 443
Cororate Headquarters: Best 443
Fishers
Foundation: SLM 3478
Floyds Knobs
Foundation: MAC 2327
Fort Wayne
Corporate Giving Programs: Do 1136, Lincoln 2281
Foundations: Bradley 551, Brotherhood 588, Journal 2068, Lassus 2226, Lincoln 2281, Steel 3595
Corporate Headquarters: Bradley 551, Brotherhood 588, Do 1136, Journal 2068, Lassus 2226, Steel 3595
Subsidiaries: American 141, Manitowoc 2356
Division: Superior 3657
Offices: Bose 531, Do 1136, Faegre 1324
Plants: Menasha 2461, Navistar 2647, Raytheon 3135, Schulman 3361, Univar 3886, Valspar 3920
Frankfort
Plants: Donaldson 1153, West 4038
Franklin
Subsidiary: Caterpillar 722
Fremont
Subsidiary: Leggett 2246
Ft. Wayne
Office: Humana 1886
Gary
Foundation: Majestic 2344
Gas City
Plant: Packaging 2861
Goshen
Plant: NIBCO 2707
Granger
Office: Univar 3886
Greencastle
Plant: Sherwin 3437
Greenfield
Cororate Headquarters: Indiana 1930
Plant: Lilly 2274
Greenwood
Foundation: Greenwood 1660
Cororate Headquarters: Greenwood 1660
Griffith
Division: Quanex 3100
Hammond
Subsidiary: Quanex 3100
Highland
Cororate Headquarters: Hoffman 1822
Subsidiary: Harsco 1741
Howe
Plant: Campbell 669
Huntington
Division: Quanex 3100
Plant: Square 3560
Indianapolis
Corporate Giving Programs: Barnes 361, Bose 531, Dow 1160, Ice 1905, Indianapolis 1932, IPALCO 1988, Lilly 2274, Marsh 2387, Pacers 2852, Roche 3236
Foundations: American 169, Andretti 197, BSA 597, Caremore 689, Emmis 1259, Emmis 1260, Finish 1383, General 1555, International 1966, IPALCO 1988, Jasper 2027, Lilly 2274, Marathon 2363, Monarch 2552, Pacers 2852, Ratio 3129, Simon 3458, SpectraCare 3541, Trends 3804, WellPoint 4027
Corporate Headquarters: American 169, Barnes 361, Bose 531, Brightpoint 567, BSA 597, Communications 896, Dow 1160, Emmis 1259, Emmis 1260, Finish 1383, Firestone 1386, Ice 1905, Indianapolis 1932, International 1966, IPALCO 1988, Lilly 2274, Marsh 2387, Monarch 2552, Pacers 2852, Ratio 3129, Roche 3236, Simon 3458, Trends 3804, WellPoint 4027
Subsidiaries: AES 47, Allete 100, Amsted 188, Aviva 302, Cardinal 685, Caterpillar 722, Chemtura 775, Covance 955, Dispatch 1129, Dow 1161, Emmis 1259, Gannett 1532, Handy 1718, Hoffmann 1823, Hunt 1888, Huntington 1894, IPALCO 1988, Marsh 2387, McGraw 2429, Meritor 2473, Praxair 3029, Securian 3389, STERIS 3600, Susquehanna 3661, Temple 3711, United 3882, Vectren 3925
Offices: AT&T 274, Benesch 413, Bose 531, Brinks 573, Faegre 1324, Frost 1511, Hahn 1700, Humana 1886, Ice 1905, ITA 1998, KeyBank 2136, Levi 2254, Littler 2289, Opus 2820, Pulte 3083, Safeco 3306, Thompson 3739, Vision 3961, Wiley 4072
Plants: CA 638, Chrysler 801, Marathon 2362, Olin 2801, Owens 2841, Quaker 3094, Rexnord 3198, Sensient 3408, Univar 3886
Jasper
Foundations: Inwood 1985, Jasper 2025, Jasper 2026, JOFCO 2046, Kimball 2149
Corporate Headquarters: Inwood 1985, Jasper 2025, Jasper 2026, JOFCO 2046, Kimball 2149
Subsidiary: Kimball 2149
Jeffersonville
Subsidiary: CLARCOR 832
Office: Stites 3609
Plant: Colgate 869
Kokomo
Division: Delphi 1071
Plants: Chrysler 801, Martin 2391
La Porte
Plant: Whirlpool 4056
Lafayette
Foundation: Subaru 3632
Cororate Headquarters: Subaru 3632
Division: Cox 958
Plants: Alcoa 82, Caterpillar 722, Lilly 2274, Mitsui 2541
LaGrange
Foundation: Hoffman 1822
Lawrenceburg
Foundation: United 3865
Cororate Headquarters: United 3865
Lebanon
Subsidiary: Reynolds 3199
Ligonier
Plant: Tenneco 3715
Logansport
Plant: Modine 2544
Marion
Foundation: Atlas 284
Cororate Headquarters: Atlas 284
Markle
Cororate Headquarters: MarkleBank 2379

Merrillville
Corporate Headquarters: NiSource 2715, Northern 2739
Subsidiary: NiSource 2715
Michigan City
Foundations: Blue 489, Indiana 1929
Cororate Headquarters: Blue 489
Plant: Illinois 1916
Mishawaka
Foundation: South Bend 3507
Monon
Plant: Vulcan 3972
Monticello
Plants: Donaldson 1153, Smith 3484
Muncie
Foundation: Mutual 2603
Corporate Headquarters: First 1410, Mutual 2603
Munster
Foundation: CFS 756
Cororate Headquarters: CFS 756
New Albany
Cororate Headquarters: MAC 2327
Office: Wyatt 4130
Plant: General 1554
New Castle
Plant: Allegheny 91
Newburgh
Subsidiary: Koch 2179
Plant: Alcoa 82
Noblesville
Foundation: Weaver 4015
Cororate Headquarters: Weaver 4015
North Vernon
Foundation: ONSPOT 2816
Cororate Headquarters: ONSPOT 2816
Ossian
Foundation: MarkleBank 2379
Paoli
Plant: Smith 3484
Peru
Plant: Square 3560
Plainfield
Corporate Giving Program: Brightpoint 567
Foundation: First 1410
Plymouth
Subsidiary: Jeld 2032
Plants: Ferro 1366, Valmont 3919
Porter
Plant: Worthington 4124
Portland
Corporate Giving Program: Graphic 1636
Cororate Headquarters: Graphic 1636
Princeton
Corporate Giving Program: Toyota 3785
Cororate Headquarters: Toyota 3785
Subsidiary: Emerson 1257
Rensselaer
Plant: Donaldson 1153
Richmond
Foundation: Vandor 3921
Cororate Headquarters: Vandor 3921
Subsidiary: Marsh 2387
Plant: Alcoa 82
Schererville
Subsidiary: Avery 297
Seymour
Plants: Cummins 1007, Donnelley 1155, Osram 2834
South Bend
Foundations: 1st 2, Teachers 3697
Corporate Headquarters: 1st 2, South Bend 3507, Teachers 3697
Subsidiary: 1st 2
Offices: Faegre 1324, Fiserv 1427, KeyBank 2136
Plants: Honeywell 1852, TJX 3765
Spencer
Plant: Boston 540
Terre Haute
Foundations: Hulman 1885, Terre 3722
Corporate Headquarters: Hulman 1885, Terre 3722
Office: GATX 1542
Plants: Bemis 407, International 1968, Sherwin 3437
Valparaiso
Plant: AMPCO 186
Vincennes
Office: Fishel 1429
Wabash
Foundation: Ford 1463
Cororate Headquarters: Ford 1463
Wakarusa
Subsidiary: Harley 1732
Wanatah
Plant: Pactiv 2863
Warsaw
Corporate Giving Programs: Biomet 466, Zimmer 4157
Corporate Headquarters: Biomet 466, Indiana 1929, Zimmer 4157
Subsidiary: Johnson 2048
Division: Zimmer 4157
Plant: Donnelley 1155
West Lafayette
Offices: Bose 531, State 3591
Whiting
Plant: BP 547
Winona Lake
Foundation: Biomet 466
Yorktown
Office: Fishel 1429

IOWA

Adair
Foundation: Owner 2845
Cororate Headquarters: Owner 2845
Allison
Office: Lincoln 2282
Alta Vista
Office: First 1397
Ames
Subsidiary: Tyler 3831
Office: Wiley 4072
Ankeny
Subsidiary: Hy-Vee 1900
Office: Wal-Mart 3980
Plant: Deere 1061
Aplington
Office: Lincoln 2282
Audubon
Foundation: Audubon 286
Cororate Headquarters: Audubon 286
Bellevue
Plant: Rockwell 3247
Bettendorf
Foundation: LeClaire 2239
Cororate Headquarters: LeClaire 2239
Plant: Alcoa 82
Boyden
Foundation: Dethmers 1091
Cororate Headquarters: Dethmers 1091
Burlington
Foundation: Lamont 2215
Cororate Headquarters: Lamont 2215
Subsidiary: Snyder's-Lance 3492
Carlisle
Plant: General 1554
Carroll
Foundation: Iowa 1986
Cororate Headquarters: Iowa 1986
Carter Lake
Cororate Headquarters: Owen 2840
Cedar Falls
Office: Lincoln 2282
Cedar Rapids
Corporate Giving Program: Rockwell 3247
Foundations: AEGON 45, Guaranty 1679, Millhiser-Smith 2524, Rockwell 3247, Smulekoff 3489, SourceMedia 3506, United 3869
Corporate Headquarters: AEGON 45, Guaranty 1679, Millhiser-Smith 2524, Rockwell 3247, Smulekoff 3489, SourceMedia 3506, United 3869
Subsidiaries: AEGON 45, Alliant 104, SourceMedia 3506, United 3869
Divisions: AEGON 45, Cox 958
Plants: General 1554, Nash 2619, Quaker 3094, Square 3560, Vulcan 3972
Centerville
Plant: Bemis 407
Chariton
Foundation: Johnson 2052
Cororate Headquarters: Johnson 2052
Subsidiary: Hy-Vee 1900
Clarinda
Foundation: Lisle 2286
Cororate Headquarters: Lisle 2286
Clarion
Office: First 1397
Clear Lake
Foundation: TeamQuest 3698
Cororate Headquarters: TeamQuest 3698
Clinton
Subsidiary: Bemis 407
Plant: LyondellBasell 2322
Clive
Foundation: Holmes 1838
Coralville
Subsidiary: SourceMedia 3506
Office: Midwestone 2508
Plant: Rockwell 3247
Cresco
Plant: Donaldson 1153
Cummings
Plant: Martin 2391
Davenport
Corporate Giving Program: Lee 2241
Foundations: Lee 2241, McCarthy 2421
Corporate Headquarters: Lee 2241, McCarthy 2421
Subsidiaries: McCarthy 2421, Quanex 3100
Offices: Ahern 60, Kiewit 2142
Plants: Deere 1061, Lafarge 2210
Decorah
Plant: Rockwell 3247
Des Moines
Corporate Giving Programs: Davis 1038, MidAmerican 2504, Principal 3047, Wellmark 4026
Foundations: Aviva 302, Betts 450, Employers 1264, Excell 1304, Meredith 2471, MidAmerican 2504, Principal 3047, RUAN 3279, Wellmark 4026, Wittern 4098
Corporate Headquarters: Betts 450, Davis 1038, Employers 1264, Excell 1304, Holmes 1838, Meredith 2471, MidAmerican 2504, Principal 3047, RUAN 3279, Wellmark 4026, Wittern 4098
Subsidiaries: Berkshire 429, Deere 1061, Employers 1264, Gannett 1532, Hy-Vee 1900, Lancaster 2216, Nationwide 2639, OneBeacon 2813, Philips 2963, Principal 3047
Offices: Ahern 60, Davis 1038, Dorsey 1157, Federal 1349, Kiewit 2142, State 3592
Plants: BP 547, Martin 2391, Owens 2841, SUPERVALU 3659, Tension 3717
Dubuque
Foundations: Lime 2276, McDonald 2426, Spahn 3529
Corporate Headquarters: Lime 2276, McDonald 2426, Spahn 3529
Subsidiary: RITE 3221
Plants: Deere 1061, Georgia 1568, McGraw 2429
Elkader
Subsidiary: Caterpillar 722
Fairfax
Foundation: Fairfax 1325
Cororate Headquarters: Fairfax 1325

Fairfield
Foundation: Harper 1735
Cororate Headquarters: Harper 1735
Forest City
Foundation: Winnebago 4088
Cororate Headquarters: Winnebago 4088
Fort Dodge
Foundation: First 1388
Cororate Headquarters: First 1388
Fort Madison
Plants: International 1968, Scotts 3372
Garwin
Office: Lincoln 2282
Greene
Office: Lincoln 2282
Grimes
Subsidiary: Faribault 1332
Grinnell
Foundation: Grinnell 1668
Cororate Headquarters: Grinnell 1668
Plant: Donaldson 1153
Guthrie Center
Plant: Illinois 1916
Harlan
Foundation: Nishnabotna 2714
Cororate Headquarters: Nishnabotna 2714
Hills
Foundation: Hills 1808
Cororate Headquarters: Hills 1808
Holstein
Cororate Headquarters: V-T 3912
Hudson
Office: Lincoln 2282
Independence
Foundation: Security 3394
Iowa City
Foundations: City 829, Midwestone 2508, River 3224
Corporate Headquarters: City 829, Midwestone 2508, River 3224
Plant: Procter 3055
Jefferson
Foundation: Home 1846
Johnston
Corporate Giving Program: Pioneer 2980
Foundation: Pioneer 2980
Cororate Headquarters: Pioneer 2980
Subsidiary: du Pont 1184
Kanawha
Office: First 1397
Keokuk
Office: Regis 3172
Lake Mills
Plant: Cummins 1006
Latimer
Office: First 1397
Lincoln
Office: Lincoln 2282
Manchester
Plants: Menasha 2461, Rockwell 3247
Maquoketa
Foundation: Maquoketa 2361
Cororate Headquarters: Maquoketa 2361
Marshalltown
Plants: Packaging 2861, Pactiv 2863
Mason City
Foundation: First 1397
Cororate Headquarters: First 1397
Subsidiary: Holcim 1828
Office: Principal 3047
Monticello
Plants: Georgia 1568, Menasha 2461
Mount Pleasant
Plant: Motorola 2586
Muscatine
Corporate Giving Program: Kent 2129
Foundations: Central 745, HNI 1817, Stanley 3580
Corporate Headquarters: Central 745, HNI 1817, Kent 2129, Stanley 3580
Subsidiary: HNI 1817
Nashua
Office: Lincoln 2282
New Hampton
Office: First 1397
Newton
Foundation: First 1418
Cororate Headquarters: First 1418
North Liberty
Office: Midwestone 2508
Oelwein
Plant: Donaldson 1153
Orange City
Foundation: DVK 1198
Cororate Headquarters: DVK 1198
Osage
Office: First 1397
Ottumwa
Plant: Deere 1061
Pella
Foundations: Djr 1135, Heritage 1784, Pella 2917, Vermeer 3937
Corporate Headquarters: Djr 1135, Pella 2917, Vermeer 3937
Plant: Wal-Mart 3980
Perry
Foundations: Progressive 3058, Raccoon 3116
Corporate Headquarters: Progressive 3058, Raccoon 3116
PERU
Subsidiary: Manpower 2358
Pocahontas
Foundation: Citizens 828
Reinbeck
Cororate Headquarters: Lincoln 2282
Robins
Plant: Vulcan 3972
Sac City
Foundation: Iowa 1987
Cororate Headquarters: Iowa 1987
Sioux Center
Foundation: Premier 3035
Cororate Headquarters: Premier 3035
Sioux City
Foundation: Security 3393
Corporate Headquarters: Bekins 401, Security 3393
Plant: Valmont 3919
Storm Lake
Foundation: Citizens 825
Cororate Headquarters: Citizens 825
Plant: Hillshire 1809
Tama
Office: Lincoln 2282
Washington
Plant: Modine 2544
Waterloo
Corporate Giving Program: Lincoln 2282
Foundations: Lincoln 2282, Warren 3993
Cororate Headquarters: Warren 3993
Offices: Lincoln 2282, Principal 3047
Plants: Deere 1061, DENSO 1088
Waverly
Subsidiaries: CUNA 1008, Terex 3719
West Des Moines
Corporate Giving Programs: Hy-Vee 1900, Kum 2199, Telligen 3710
Foundations: Fiserv 1427, Grubb 1675, GuideOne 1687, Hy-Vee 1900, ITA 1998, R & R 3114, West 4034
Corporate Headquarters: Aviva 302, Grubb 1675, GuideOne 1687, Hy-Vee 1900, ITA 1998, Kum 2199, R & R 3114, Telligen 3710, West 4034
Subsidiary: Hy-Vee 1900
Offices: Davis 1038, Fredrikson 1491
Winterset
Foundation: Farmers 1334
Cororate Headquarters: Farmers 1334
Wyoming
Cororate Headquarters: Citizens 828

KANSAS

Andover
Plant: Sherwin 3437
Atchison
Foundation: Exchange 1307
Cororate Headquarters: Exchange 1307
Blue Rapids
Plant: Georgia 1568
Bonner Springs
Cororate Headquarters: Berkel 424
Chanute
Plant: Wal-Mart 3980
Clearwater
Foundation: Southern 3518
Cororate Headquarters: Southern 3518
Coffeyville
Plants: Deere 1061, Sherwin 3437
De Soto
Foundation: Huhtamaki 1884
Cororate Headquarters: Huhtamaki 1884
Subsidiary: Huhtamaki 1884
Dodge City
Office: Regis 3172
El Dorado
Plant: Valmont 3919
Fort Scott
Foundation: Ward/Kraft 3987
Cororate Headquarters: Ward/Kraft 3987
Fredonia
Plant: Lafarge 2210
Goodland
Foundation: First 1414
Cororate Headquarters: First 1414
Humboldt
Foundation: Monarch 2553
Cororate Headquarters: Monarch 2553
Hutchinson
Subsidiary: Kroger 2195
Plant: Morton 2579
Junction City
Foundation: Central 742
Cororate Headquarters: Central 742
Kansas City
Foundation: Berkel 424
Subsidiaries: Kiewit 2142, Monarch 2553, Philips 2963, Tomkins 3771
Offices: Bryan 596, Levi 2254, Littler 2289, SAS 3336, Vision 3961
Plants: Colgate 869, Deluxe 1084, Hillshire 1809, Procter 3055
Lawrence
Plants: FMC 1449, Hallmark 1707, Wal-Mart 3980
Leavenworth
Plant: Hallmark 1707
Lenexa
Foundations: Control 930, O'Connor 2770
Corporate Headquarters: Control 930, O'Connor 2770
Subsidiary: CLARCOR 832
Offices: Deere 1061, Whirlpool 4056
Plants: Coca 862, Timken 3760
Liberal
Plant: Nash 2619
Manhattan
Subsidiary: STERIS 3600
Marysville
Plant: Tension 3717
McPherson
Foundation: Farmers 1335
Cororate Headquarters: Farmers 1335
Subsidiaries: CHS 802, Farmers 1335
Merriam
Subsidiary: V.F. 3913
Mission
Subsidiary: Farmers 1338
New Century
Subsidiary: Sprint 3556
Olathe
Subsidiary: Ash 256
Plant: Honeywell 1852

Ottawa
Subsidiary: Manpower 2358
Overland Park
Corporate Giving Programs: Ferrellgas 1365, Sprint 3556
Foundations: Ash 256, Delta 1074, Sprint 3556
Corporate Headquarters: Ash 256, Ferrellgas 1365, Sprint 3556
Subsidiaries: DineEquity 1120, ONEOK 2815, SPX 3558
Division: Sprint 3556
Offices: Bond 522, Bryan 596, Delta 1074, Farmers 1338, Littler 2289, Mortenson 2577, Opus 2820, Polsinelli 3001, Spencer 3543, Stinson 3608
Plants: Guardian 1682, McAfee 2417, Navistar 2647
Parsons
Plant: Smith 3484
Prairie Village
Foundation: Colt 881
Cororate Headquarters: Colt 881
Salina
Foundation: Marshall 2388
Cororate Headquarters: Marshall 2388
Plant: Jim's 2043
Shawnee Mission
Subsidiaries: Archer 233, Ash 256
Division: Bayer 382
Smith Center
Foundations: Peterson 2946, Smith 3482
Corporate Headquarters: Peterson 2946, Smith 3482
Spring Hill
Plant: Clorox 852
Tecumseh
Plant: Martin 2391
Topeka
Corporate Giving Programs: Capitol 680, Ogden 2787
Foundations: Blue 495, Capitol 680, Collective 871, Security 3391, Westar 4039
Corporate Headquarters: Blue 495, Capitol 680, Collective 871, Ogden 2787, Security 3391, Westar 4039
Subsidiaries: Capitol 680, Colgate 869, Emmis 1259, Farmers 1335, IMA 1917
Division: Caesars 650
Office: Polsinelli 3001
Plants: Goodyear 1612, Hallmark 1707, Jostens 2067, Martin 2391
Ulysses
Subsidiary: Occidental 2780
Wamego
Subsidiary: Caterpillar 722
Wichita
Corporate Giving Programs: Flint 1439, Koch 2180, Law 2233
Foundations: Berry 435, Builders 609, Dondlinger 1154, IMA 1917, INTRUST 1981, Star 3584
Corporate Headquarters: Berry 435, Builders 609, Delta 1074, Dondlinger 1154, Flint 1439, IMA 1917, INTRUST 1981, Koch 2180, Law 2233, Star 3584
Subsidiaries: Commerce 890, Emmis 1259, HCA 1762, IMA 1917, Koch 2180, Manpower 2358, Raytheon 3135, Textron 3731, Westar 4039
Offices: Delta 1074, Grant 1633, Stinson 3608
Plants: Castle 716, Guardian 1682, Kroger 2195, Rockwell 3247, Smith 3484, Valassis 3914, Vulcan 3972

KENTUCKY

Alexandria
Plant: Hillshire 1809
Anchorage
Office: Commonwealth 894
Ashland
Subsidiaries: American 141, Caterpillar 722
Division: Cox 958
Barbourville
Subsidiary: Manitowoc 2356
Berea
Plant: PPG 3025
Bowling Green
Foundation: Sumitomo 3640
Cororate Headquarters: Sumitomo 3640
Subsidiaries: American 165, Berkshire 429, HCA 1762
Office: Fishel 1429
Plants: Colgate 869, Sun 3646
Buckner
Plant: Boneal 523
Burlington
Plant: Scotts 3372
Burnside
Plant: Clorox 852
Calvert City
Plant: Lubrizol 2315
Covington
Corporate Giving Program: Ashland 258
Corporate Headquarters: Ashland 258, Jones 2056
Office: Huntington 1894
Danville
Plants: Donnelley 1155, Panasonic 2869
Edgewood
Plant: McAfee 2417
Elizabethtown
Plant: Barnes 362
Erlanger
Corporate Giving Program: Toyota 3784
Foundation: Toyota 3784
Corporate Headquarters: Toyota 3784
Office: Quad 3091
Plant: DENSO 1088
Florence
Subsidiary: Bemis 407
Office: Frost 1511
Plants: Smith 3484, Square 3560
Fort Knox
Plant: Vulcan 3972
Frankfort
Offices: Stites 3609, Stoll 3613, Wurzburg 4129
Georgetown
Corporate Giving Program: Toyota 3786
Cororate Headquarters: Toyota 3786
Glasgow
Foundation: Gaunce 1543
Cororate Headquarters: Gaunce 1543
Plant: Donnelley 1155
Grayson
Foundation: Commercial 891
Cororate Headquarters: Commercial 891
Harrodsburg
Cororate Headquarters: Trim 3810
Subsidiary: Johnson 2050
Plants: Corning 945, Modine 2544
Hebron
Plants: Owens 2841, Strauss 3624
Henderson
Subsidiaries: Koch 2179, Masco 2393
Office: Stoll 3613
Hopkinsville
Plant: U.S. 3841
Horse Cave
Office: Dart 1033
Lake City
Plant: Vulcan 3972
Lexington
Corporate Giving Program: Lexmark 2258
Foundations: Blood-Horse 485, Dean 1053, Keeneland 2113, Rood 3257, United 3875, Whitaker 4057
Corporate Headquarters: Blood-Horse 485, Dean 1053, Keeneland 2113, Lexmark 2258, Rood 3257, United 3875, Whitaker 4057
Subsidiaries: Boneal 523, NiSource 2715, Universal 3891, Yum! 4150
Offices: Fishel 1429, Frost 1511, Humana 1886, Littler 2289, Stites 3609, Stoll 3613, Wyatt 4130
Plants: Mitsui 2541, Square 3560
Louisville
Corporate Giving Programs: Brown 592, Churchill 807, LG&E Energy 2260, Papa 2876, Stites 3609, Stoll 3613, Thorntons 3743, Wyatt 4130, Yum! 4150
Foundations: Bramco 555, Churchill 807, Commonwealth 894, General 1552, Humana 1886, Interlock 1954, Kentuckiana 2130, KFC 2139, Kindred 2154, LG&E Energy 2260, Papa 2876, Steel 3596, Stock 3610, Thorntons 3743, Ventas 3931, Vogt 3966, Whip 4054, Yum! 4150
Corporate Headquarters: Bramco 555, Brown 592, Churchill 807, Commonwealth 894, Humana 1886, Interlock 1954, Kentuckiana 2130, KFC 2139, Kindred 2154, LG&E Energy 2260, Neace 2651, Papa 2876, SpectraCare 3541, Steel 3596, Stites 3609, Stock 3610, Stoll 3613, Thorntons 3743, Vogt 3966, Whip 4054, Wyatt 4130, Yum! 4150
Subsidiaries: AEGON 45, Belo 406, Brown 592, Churchill 807, Gannett 1532, HCA 1762, WellPoint 4027, Yum! 4150
Division: General 1552
Offices: Fishel 1429, Frost 1511, Huntington 1894, Stites 3609, Stoll 3613, Ventas 3931, Wyatt 4130
Plants: Lubrizol 2315, Marathon 2362, PPG 3025, Univar 3886, Valspar 3920, Winn 4087, Worthington 4124
Madisonville
Plant: Krueger 2196
Mayfield
Plant: Continental 927
Maysville
Plant: Emerson 1257
Means
Cororate Headquarters: Boneal 523
Morganfield
Office: Stoll 3613
Mount Sterling
Foundation: Boneal 523
Plant: Smith 3484
Murray
Plant: Briggs 565
Newport
Foundation: Goodman 1610
Cororate Headquarters: Goodman 1610
Nicholasville
Foundation: Trim 3810
Plants: Donaldson 1153, Westervelt 4046
Owensboro
Foundation: Independence 1925
Cororate Headquarters: Independence 1925
Subsidiary: Williams 4077
Paducah
Foundation: Dippin' 1122
Cororate Headquarters: Dippin' 1122
Plant: Fuller 1517
Pikeville
Plant: Kellogg 2120
Richmond
Plant: Sherwin 3437
Russellville
Plant: Illinois 1916
Shelbyville
Subsidiary: Landmark 2218
Office: Commonwealth 894
Plant: Pactiv 2863
Simpsonville
Office: Commonwealth 894
Somerset
Foundation: Citizens 826
Cororate Headquarters: Citizens 826
Subsidiary: LifePoint 2270
Plant: Armstrong 246
Summershade
Plant: Clorox 852
Versailles
Plant: Osram 2834
Walton
Foundation: Seligman 3402
Cororate Headquarters: Seligman 3402

Winchester
Plant: Osram 2834

LOUISIANA

Abita Springs
Corporate Giving Program: Abita 19
Cororate Headquarters: Abita 19
Alexandria
Offices: CenturyLink 751, Kilpatrick 2146
Plants: Procter 3055, Texas 3727
Amelia
Subsidiary: Tidewater 3748
Arcadia
Office: Kilpatrick 2146
Bastrop
Plant: International 1968
Baton Rouge
Corporate Giving Programs: Community 899, Louisiana 2309
Foundations: Albemarle 78, Cajun 652, Credit 977, Louisiana 2309
Corporate Headquarters: Albemarle 78, Cajun 652, Community 899, Credit 977, Louisiana 2309, Turner 3825
Subsidiary: Louisiana 2309
Offices: Adams 34, Baker 325, Boh 517
Plants: Albemarle 78, Exxon 1315, Formosa 1470, Honeywell 1852
Bossier City
Cororate Headquarters: Schoonover 3359
Plant: Texas 3727
Cameron
Subsidiary: Apache 211
Carville
Plant: Total 3778
Chalmette
Plant: Exxon 1315
Cotton Valley
Office: Hunt 1889
Coushatta
Office: Kilpatrick 2146
Dubberly
Plant: U.S. 3840
Franklin
Plant: Cabot 642
Garyville
Plants: Marathon 2362, Nalco 2613
Geismar
Office: GATX 1542
Plant: Vulcan 3972
Harahan
Foundation: Donovan 1156
Division: Cox 958
Office: Wurzburg 4129
Houma
Foundation: Gulf 1688
Jefferson
Plant: Univar 3886
Jena
Subsidiary: CenturyLink 751
Office: Kilpatrick 2146
Jonesville
Foundation: Wurster 4128
Cororate Headquarters: Wurster 4128
Kenner
Foundation: Crown 989
Cororate Headquarters: Crown 989
Lafayette
Corporate Giving Program: Stone 3614
Foundations: Haynie 1760, Moody 2562
Corporate Headquarters: Haynie 1760, Moody 2562, Stone 3614
Offices: Hunt 1889, Liskow 2285
Lake Charles
Office: Barrasso 363
Plants: LyondellBasell 2322, PPG 3025, Sasol 3338
Logansport
Office: Kilpatrick 2146
Mandeville
Office: Baker 325
Mansfield
Office: Kilpatrick 2146
Plant: International 1968
Marksville
Office: Kilpatrick 2146
Metairie
Corporate Giving Program: New 2679
Foundation: Gootee 1614
Corporate Headquarters: Gootee 1614, New 2679
Office: Pan-American 2868
Minden
Office: Kilpatrick 2146
Monroe
Foundations: CenturyLink 751, Entergy 1279
Cororate Headquarters: CenturyLink 751
Offices: Regis 3172, State 3591
Plant: Texas 3727
New Iberia
Plant: Morton 2579
New Orleans
Corporate Giving Programs: Adams 34, Barrasso 363, Entergy 1279, Feelgoodz 1354, Liskow 2285, Pan-American 2868, Whitney 4065
Foundations: Adams 34, Boh 517, Entergy 1279, International 1972, New 2675, New Orleans 2678, Reily 3177
Corporate Headquarters: Adams 34, Barrasso 363, Boh 517, Donovan 1156, Entergy 1279, Feelgoodz 1354, International 1972, Liskow 2285, New 2675, New Orleans 2678, Pan-American 2868, Reily 3177, Tidewater 3748, Whitney 4065
Subsidiaries: Belo 406, Entergy 1279, Freeport 1494, Procter 3055, Textron 3731, Tidewater 3748, United 3869
Division: Cox 958
Offices: ACE 24, Adams 34, Baker 325, Federal 1349, JPMorgan Chase 2071, Kiewit 2142, Liskow 2285, Proskauer 3064, SAS 3336, Thompson 3739
Plants: BP 547, Chevron 780, Coca 862, Lafarge 2210, Owens 2841
Norco
Office: GATX 1542
Oakdale
Office: Kilpatrick 2146
Perryville
Plant: Texas 3727
Pineville
Plant: International 1968
Plain Dealing
Subsidiary: CenturyLink 751
Plaquemine
Office: GATX 1542
Plant: Dow 1161
Shreveport
Foundations: Kilpatrick 2146, Schoonover 3359
Cororate Headquarters: Kilpatrick 2146
Subsidiary: Manitowoc 2356
Division: Caesars 650
Office: Wurzburg 4129
Springhill
Office: Kilpatrick 2146
Sterlington
Division: Koch 2180
Sulphur
Subsidiary: ConocoPhillips 913
Tallulah
Office: Bionetics 467
Thibodaux
Plant: Deere 1061
Ville Platte
Plant: Cabot 642
Welsh
Subsidiary: CenturyLink 751
West Monroe
Foundation: Tedco 3702
Cororate Headquarters: Tedco 3702
Plant: Georgia 1568
Westlake
Office: Boh 517
Zachary
Plant: Ferro 1366

MAINE

Auburn
Plant: Procter 3055
Augusta
Corporate Giving Program: Central 741
Corporate Headquarters: Central 741, Pine 2976
Subsidiaries: Central 741, Pine 2976
Offices: Bernstein 433, Pierce 2974
Baileyville
Office: Machias 2332
Bangor
Corporate Giving Program: Bangor 338
Foundations: Bangor 338, Dead 1051
Corporate Headquarters: Bangor 338, Dead 1051
Office: Regis 3172
Plant: Osram 2834
Bar Harbor
Office: Machias 2332
Berwick
Office: Kennebunk 2126
Biddeford
Plant: Teleflex 3707
Brunswick
Corporate Giving Program: Atayne 275
Cororate Headquarters: Atayne 275
Subsidiary: Susquehanna 3661
Bucksport
Plant: International 1968
Calais
Office: Machias 2332
Columbia Falls
Office: Machias 2332
Damariscotta
Corporate Giving Program: First 1391
Cororate Headquarters: First 1391
Subsidiary: First 1391
Danforth
Office: Machias 2332
Eliot
Office: Kennebunk 2126
Ellsworth
Office: Machias 2332
Falmouth
Subsidiaries: PVH 3088, Tyler 3831
Farmington
Foundation: Franklin 1488
Cororate Headquarters: Franklin 1488
Freeport
Corporate Giving Program: Bean 392
Cororate Headquarters: Bean 392
Gardiner
Foundations: Bank 343, Pine 2976
Cororate Headquarters: Bank 343
Greenville
Office: Iberdrola 1904
Houlton
Office: Machias 2332
Jay
Office: Franklin 1488
Plant: International 1968
Kennebunk
Corporate Giving Program: Tom's 3770
Foundation: Kennebunk 2126
Corporate Headquarters: Kennebunk 2126, Tom's 3770
Subsidiary: Colgate 869
Plant: Corning 945
Kittery
Office: Kennebunk 2126
Lewiston
Foundation: Androscoggin 199
Cororate Headquarters: Androscoggin 199
Plant: Philips 2963

Lincoln
Office: Machias 2332
Machias
Foundation: Machias 2332
Corporate Headquarters: Machias 2332
Medway
Plant: Scotts 3372
Mexico
Office: Franklin 1488
New Gloucester
Foundation: Iberdrola 1904
Corporate Headquarters: Iberdrola 1904
Norridgewock
Plant: New 2668
North Berwick
Office: Kennebunk 2126
Ogunquit
Office: Kennebunk 2126
Oxford
Subsidiary: Hannaford 1723
Pittsfield
Foundation: Cianbro 808
Corporate Headquarters: Cianbro 808
Portland
Corporate Giving Programs: Bernstein 433, Hannaford 1723, Pierce 2974, TD 3696
Foundations: Hannaford 1723, Portland 3011, TD 3696, Woodard 4109
Corporate Headquarters: Bernstein 433, Pierce 2974, Portland 3011, TD 3696, Woodard 4109
Subsidiaries: Georgia 1568, TD 3696
Offices: Bernstein 433, Bingham 463, KeyBank 2136, Pierce 2974, State 3592
Plant: Hood 1854
Princeton
Office: Machias 2332
Rangeley
Office: Franklin 1488
Rumford
Office: Franklin 1488
Saco
Foundation: Saco 3302
Corporate Headquarters: Saco 3302
Sanford
Office: Kennebunk 2126
Scarborough
Corporate Headquarters: Hannaford 1723
Skowhegan
Office: Franklin 1488
Plant: New 2668
South Portland
Plant: Pactiv 2863
Waldoboro
Plant: Osram 2834
Wells
Office: Kennebunk 2126
West Kennebunk
Subsidiary: Hallmark 1707
Westbrook
Plants: Bausch 376, Charles 764
Wilton
Office: Franklin 1488
Woodland
Subsidiary: Georgia 1568
Yarmouth
Corporate Headquarters: Cole 867
Subsidiary: NIKE 2710
York
Office: Kennebunk 2126

MARYLAND

Aberdeen
Plant: Clorox 852
Annapolis
Foundation: Post 3016
Office: Kimley 2151
Annapolis Junction
Foundation: Government 1620
Corporate Headquarters: Government 1620, PACE 2851
Baltimore
Corporate Giving Programs: American 168, Baltimore 334, Gordon 1616, Metropolitan 2482, Miles 2512, Ober 2777, Venable 3929, Whiting 4063
Foundations: Baltimore 331, Baltimore 332, Baltimore 334, Croft 985, Elite 1249, Ellin 1251, Exelon 1309, Hopkins 1859, Legg 2245, Miles 2512, Monumental 2561, Myers 2609, Price 3040, Questar 3105, St. 3565
Corporate Headquarters: American 168, Baltimore 331, Baltimore 332, Baltimore 334, Croft 985, Ellin 1251, Gordon 1616, Hopkins 1859, Laureate 2231, Legg 2245, Miles 2512, Monumental 2561, Myers 2609, Ober 2777, Price 3040, Questar 3105, Schenuit 3349, St. 3565, Venable 3929, Whiting 4063
Subsidiaries: AEGON 45, Citigroup 821, Price 3040, Stanley 3579, Verizon 3936
Division: AEGON 45
Offices: Ballard 329, Cole 868, Duane 1185, Federal 1349, Grant 1633, Hays 1761, Hogan 1825, McGuireWoods 2430, Miles 2512, Ober 2777, Pulte 3083, Thompson 3739, Venable 3929
Plants: Berry 438, FMC 1449, Nash 2619, Navistar 2647, Pactiv 2863, Sasol 3338, Sherwin 3437, Sun 3646, Worthington 4124
Belcamp
Office: Ellin 1251
Beltsville
Subsidiary: PerkinElmer 2939
Plant: Sherwin 3437
Bethesda
Corporate Giving Programs: AREVA 236, Lockheed 2292, Marriott 2383, USEC 3904
Foundations: Acacia 21, Calvert 663, Lockheed 2292
Corporate Headquarters: Acacia 21, AREVA 236, Calvert 663, International 1965, Lockheed 2292, Marriott 2383, USEC 3904
Subsidiary: Discovery 1126
Offices: Ballard 329, Holland 1834
Buckeystown
Foundation: Jorgensen 2065
Corporate Headquarters: Jorgensen 2065
Calverton
Plant: CA 638
Cambridge
Office: Miles 2512
Capitol Heights
Plant: Guardian 1682
Chevy Chase
Foundations: Government 1621, International 1965, Kann 2090
Corporate Headquarters: Kann 2090
Subsidiary: Berkshire 429
Clinton
Subsidiary: Caterpillar 722
College Park
Corporate Headquarters: Jordan 2064
Columbia
Corporate Giving Programs: Arbitron 227, Grace 1623
Foundations: Grace 1623, Mike's 2509
Corporate Headquarters: Arbitron 227, Grace 1623, Mike's 2509, U.S. 3838
Subsidiaries: Grace 1623, Republic 3188, Schein 3348
Offices: Miles 2512, Vision 3961
Plants: Coca 862, Honeywell 1852
Crisfield
Plant: Sherwin 3437
Crofton
Foundation: S.B.E. 3298
Corporate Headquarters: S.B.E. 3298
Darlington
Subsidiary: Exelon 1309
Easton
Corporate Giving Program: Lateral 2227
Corporate Headquarters: Lateral 2227
Office: Miles 2512
Eldersburg
Plant: Giant 1573
Elkridge
Office: Telligen 3710
Elkton
Subsidiary: Fulton 1518
Fallston
Office: Univar 3886
Forest Hill
Foundation: Klein's 2169
Corporate Headquarters: Klein's 2169
Frederick
Foundation: U.S. 3840
Offices: Ellin 1251, Miles 2512, State 3591
Plant: Bechtel 395
Gaithersburg
Corporate Giving Programs: MedImmune 2450, Sodexho 3497
Foundation: Sodexho 3497
Corporate Headquarters: MedImmune 2450, Post 3016, Sodexho 3497
Subsidiaries: Covance 955, Safeguard 3307, Washington 3999
Plant: Dreyer's 1174
Germantown
Plant: Texas 3728
Greenbelt
Office: AT&T 274
Hagerstown
Subsidiary: Fulton 1518
Plant: Valspar 3920
Hanover
Foundation: Allegis 92
Corporate Headquarters: Allegis 92
Plant: Owens 2841
Havre de Grace
Plant: Smucker 3488
Hunt Valley
Subsidiaries: Biomet 466, CSX 997, Procter 3055
Division: McCormick 2423
Hyattsville
Subsidiary: Kiplinger 2163
Jessup
Corporate Headquarters: Elite 1249
Subsidiary: Amsted 188
Plant: Owens 2842
Landover
Corporate Giving Program: Giant 1573
Foundation: Freedman 1493
Corporate Headquarters: Freedman 1493, Giant 1573
Subsidiary: Giant 1573
Lanham
Division: Safeway 3310
Largo
Foundation: Washington 4000
Laurel
Foundation: Vermeer 3938
Subsidiary: Grace 1623
Lutherville
Foundation: Legg 2245
Millersville
Corporate Giving Program: Travel 3801
Corporate Headquarters: Travel 3801
Division: Gould 1618
Owings Mills
Corporate Giving Programs: Baltimore 333, Baltimore 335, CareFirst 687
Foundation: Baltimore 335
Corporate Headquarters: Baltimore 333, Baltimore 335, CareFirst 687, Heritage 1784
Subsidiary: Baltimore 333
Office: Price 3040
Potomac
Foundations: Jordan 2064, National 2637
Corporate Headquarters: National 2637
Office: Pulte 3083
Riverwood
Subsidiary: Smithfield 3487

Rockville
Corporate Giving Program: Kaiser 2086
Foundations: Nasdaq 2617, PACE 2851
Cororate Headquarters: Metropolitan 2482
Subsidiaries: Financial 1382, First 1389, Fiserv 1427, General 1552, Opus 2820, PerkinElmer 2939, Raymond 3133
Offices: Cassidy 715, Dixon 1133, Miles 2512, SAS 3336, Venable 3929
Plants: Crystal 992, Scotts 3372, Westinghouse 4049
Salisbury
Corporate Giving Program: Perdue 2936
Cororate Headquarters: Perdue 2936
Subsidiaries: Perdue 2936, US 3902
Showell
Subsidiary: Perdue 2936
Silver Spring
Corporate Giving Program: Discovery 1126
Foundations: Choice 798, Discovery 1126
Cororate Headquarters: Choice 798, Discovery 1126
Sparks
Corporate Giving Programs: Fila 1379, McCormick 2423
Cororate Headquarters: Fila 1379, McCormick 2423
Subsidiaries: Danaher 1027, Florida 1444
Sparrows Point
Subsidiary: Worthington 4124
Plant: Illinois 1916
Sykesville
Foundation: Nexion 2705
Cororate Headquarters: Nexion 2705
Towson
Foundation: Schenuit 3349
Offices: Miles 2512, Ober 2777, Venable 3929
Waldorf
Foundations: Chaney 761, Phoenix 2967
Cororate Headquarters: Chaney 761
Subsidiary: Lennar 2250
Office: Regis 3172
Williamsport
Plant: Martin 2391

MASSACHUSETTS

Acton
Office: Cambridge 666
Plant: Corning 945
Agawam
Subsidiary: Handy 1718
Office: Hampden 1713
Plant: Hood 1854
Amherst
Division: Cox 958
Andover
Foundation: Philips 2963
Cororate Headquarters: Philips 2963
Office: Savings 3343
Plant: Raytheon 3135
Arlington
Office: Cambridge 666
Attleboro
Cororate Headquarters: Kilmartin 2145
Plant: Texas 3728
Attleboro Falls
Cororate Headquarters: Blackinton 476
Auburn
Foundations: Webster 4017, White 4060
Ausurn
Office: Bay 380
Avon
Cororate Headquarters: Horizon 1862
Ayer
Foundation: North 2734
Cororate Headquarters: North 2734
Bedford
Office: Cambridge 666
Plants: Merk 2467, Raytheon 3135
Belmont
Office: Cambridge 666
Berlin
Office: Clinton 851
Beverly
Subsidiary: Grace 1623
Billerica
Corporate Giving Program: Merk 2467
Cororate Headquarters: Merk 2467
Plant: Cabot 642
Bolton
Office: Clinton 851
Boston
Corporate Giving Programs: American 167, Autonomie 293, Bingham 463, Blue 501, Boston 533, Boston 535, Boston 537, Boston 538, Brown 590, Choate 796, Fish 1428, FMR 1450, Foley 1454, Goodwin 1611, Hachette 1696, Hancock 1717, Hill 1803, Houghton 1869, Liberty 2265, Loomis 2301, Mintz 2534, Nutter 2764, Ropes 3260, Sovereign 3528, State 3592, Stop 3618, Sullivan 3636, Wolf 4104
Foundations: Arbella 226, Banner 352, Blue 501, Boston 534, Boston 537, Boston 538, Boston 539, Boston 540, Brown 590, Cabot 642, Dedham 1060, Delta 1083, Devereaux 1100, Fallon 1329, Foley 1454, Globe 1594, Grand 1627, Jenzabar 2037, Liberty 2265, New 2668, Putnam 3085, Safety 3308, Starwood 3589, State 3592, Sullivan 3635, Tindall 3761, Tofias 3768, Village 3954, Wolf 4102
Cororate Headquarters: American 167, Autonomie 293, Banner 352, Bicon 458, Bingham 463, Blue 501, Boston 533, Boston 534, Boston 535, Boston 537, Boston 538, Boston 539, Brown 590, Cabot 642, Chartis 768, Choate 796, Delta 1083, Devereaux 1100, Eastern 1209, Fallon 1329, Fish 1428, FMR 1450, Foley 1454, Globe 1594, Goodwin 1611, Grand 1627, Hancock 1717, Hill 1803, Houghton 1869, Jenzabar 2037, Liberty 2265, Loomis 2301, Marr 2382, Mintz 2534, New 2668, Nutter 2764, Putnam 3085, Ropes 3260, Safety 3308, Shaughnessy 3425, Sovereign 3528, State 3592, Sullivan 3635, Sullivan 3636, Wolf 4102, Wolf 4104
Subsidiaries: Bank 340, Globe 1594, Hancock 1717, Hartford 1742, Kiewit 2142, Metropolitan 2481, Otis 2835, Parsons 2887, State 3592, Verizon 3936
Division: Shaughnessy 3425
Joint Venture: CB 725
Offices: Acumen 33, Bessemer 440, Bingham 463, Brown 589, Brown 590, Credit 980, Day 1046, Dechert 1058, Duane 1185, Elevation 1245, Federal 1349, Fish 1428, Foley 1453, Foley 1454, Gleacher 1589, Goodwin 1611, Google 1613, Grant 1633, Greenberg 1654, Hays 1761, Holland 1834, K&L 2080, Kreindler 2193, Latham 2228, Littler 2289, McDermott 2425, Mintz 2534, Morgan 2571, Murtha 2602, Needham 2655, Nelson 2661, Nutter 2764, Pepper 2934, Pierce 2974, Proskauer 3064, RBS 3138, RJN 3228, Robins 3232, Robins 3233, Ropes 3260, SAS 3336, Schiff 3350, Skadden 3470, Sullivan 3636, Vision 3961, Weil 4023, White 4059, Whiting 4063, Wolf 4104
Plants: Guardian 1682, Owens 2841, Rockwell 3247, Stride 3625, Valassis 3914
Braintree
Cororate Headquarters: Nellie 2659
Subsidiary: SLM 3478
Plants: Armstrong 246, Quad 3091
Brewster
Office: Cape 674
Brighton
Corporate Giving Program: New 2668
Subsidiary: Crystal 992
Brockton
Subsidiaries: Comcast 887, Kellwood 2121
Plant: Stride 3625
Brookline
Foundation: Brookline 583
Cororate Headquarters: Brookline 583
Subsidiary: Brookline 583
Burlington
Subsidiaries: PerkinElmer 2939, Teradyne 3718
Offices: Cambridge 666, Cerner 754
Plants: Merk 2467, Raytheon 3135
Cambridge
Corporate Giving Programs: Biogen 465, Digi 1115, Draper 1171
Foundations: Akamai 68, Cambridge 666, Genzyme 1566
Cororate Headquarters: Akamai 68, Cambridge 666, Digi 1115, Draper 1171, East 1208, Genzyme 1566, Tofias 3768
Subsidiaries: Activision 30, Fiserv 1427, Grace 1623, International 1960, Massachusetts 2397, Stride 3625
Office: Finnegan 1384
Canton
Corporate Giving Programs: Dunkin' 1191, Reebok 3159
Foundations: Dunkin' 1191, OneBeacon 2813, Reebok 3159
Cororate Headquarters: Dunkin' 1191, OneBeacon 2813, Reebok 3159
Subsidiaries: Colgate 869, Dunkin' 1191, Reebok 3159
Cataumet
Plant: PerkinElmer 2939
Centerville
Office: Cape 674
Chatham
Office: Cape 674
Chelmsford
Corporate Giving Program: Mercury 2469
Foundation: Demoulas 1085
Cororate Headquarters: Mercury 2469
Subsidiary: Leggett 2246
Chelsea
Cororate Headquarters: Hood 1854
Subsidiary: Cumberland 1003
Chicopee
Foundation: Chicopee 792
Cororate Headquarters: Chicopee 792
Clinton
Foundations: Clinton 851, Reisner 3180
Cororate Headquarters: Clinton 851, Reisner 3180
Cohasset
Foundation: Chartis 768
Concord
Corporate Giving Programs: Farm 1333, Hamilton 1710, Welch 4025
Cororate Headquarters: Farm 1333, Hamilton 1710, Welch 4025
Division: Welch 4025
Dalton
Foundation: Crane 969
Cororate Headquarters: Crane 969
Danvers
Corporate Giving Program: Osram 2834
Foundation: People's 2928
Cororate Headquarters: Merrimack 2475, Osram 2834
Plants: Illinois 1916, Merk 2467, Morton 2579
Dedham
Foundation: RBS 3137
Cororate Headquarters: Dedham 1060
Subsidiary: Kellwood 2121
East Cambridge
Foundation: East 1208
East Harwich
Office: Cape 674
Easthampton
Foundation: Easthampton 1212
Cororate Headquarters: Easthampton 1212
Subsidiary: Berry 438
Easton
Foundation: Reilly 3175
Erving
Foundation: Erving 1294
Cororate Headquarters: Erving 1294
Essex
Foundation: Merrimack 2475
Everett
Plant: Cabot 642

Fall River
Plants: PerkinElmer 2939, TJX 3765
Fitchburg
Subsidiary: Unitil 3885
Florence
Foundation: Florence 1441
Cororate Headquarters: Florence 1441
Foxboro
Foundations: New England 2672, Rodman 3251
Corporate Headquarters: Rodman 3251, Steve's 3603
Subsidiary: Grace 1623
Foxborough
Foundation: Steve's 3603
Cororate Headquarters: New England 2672
Framingham
Corporate Giving Programs: Cumberland 1003, Staples 3581, TJX 3765
Foundations: BOSE 530, Framingham 1481, Staples 3581, TJX 3765
Corporate Headquarters: BOSE 530, Cumberland 1003, Framingham 1481, Staples 3581, TJX 3765
Subsidiary: Avery 297
Division: Staples 3581
Gloucester
Office: Applied 220
Hanover
Foundations: Buckley 602, Rockland 3242
Cororate Headquarters: Buckley 602
Harwichport
Office: Cape 674
Hingham
Corporate Giving Program: Talbots 3682
Foundations: Building 610, Talbots 3682
Corporate Headquarters: Building 610, Talbots 3682
Holden
Office: Bay 380
Holyoke
Cororate Headquarters: Totsy 3780
Subsidiaries: Northeast 2737, NVF 2766
Office: Connecticut 910
Plant: Sonoco 3500
Hopkinton
Corporate Giving Program: EMC 1253
Cororate Headquarters: EMC 1253
Hudson
Foundation: Avidia 298
Cororate Headquarters: Avidia 298
Plant: Donnelley 1155
Hyannis
Offices: Cape 674, Nutter 2764, Regis 3172
Plant: Sealed 3381
Ipswich
Corporate Giving Program: New England 2670
Foundations: Institution 1946, Ipswich 1989, New England 2670
Corporate Headquarters: Ipswich 1989, New England 2670
Jamaica Plain
Foundation: Bicon 458
Lawrence
Subsidiary: Danaher 1027
Plants: New 2668, Stride 3625
Leominster
Office: Protector 3067
Lexington
Corporate Giving Program: Cubist 999
Foundations: Saucony 3340, Stride 3625
Corporate Headquarters: Cubist 999, Saucony 3340, Stride 3625
Subsidiary: Collective 871
Office: Cambridge 666
Plant: McGraw 2429
Lincoln
Foundation: ITW 2000
Littleton
Cororate Headquarters: Triumph 3812
Subsidiary: NEC 2654
Plant: Hewlett 1794
Longmeadow
Foundation: Totsy 3780
Office: Hampden 1713
Lowell
Subsidiaries: American 133, Textron 3731
Division: Bard 358
Lynn
Foundation: Eastern 1209
Lynnfield
Corporate Giving Program: Hood 1854
Offices: CUNA 1008, Savings 3343
Malden
Office: Wiley 4072
Mansfield
Corporate Giving Program: Covidien 956
Cororate Headquarters: Covidien 956
Marion
Foundation: Horizon 1862
Marlborough
Foundation: Marlborough 2380
Cororate Headquarters: Marlborough 2380
Plant: Raytheon 3135
Marshfield
Subsidiary: Hallmark 1707
Mashpee
Office: Cape 674
Metairie
Plant: CA 638
Methuen
Office: Savings 3343
Plant: General 1554
Milford
Corporate Giving Program: Waters 4003
Foundation: Milford 2514
Corporate Headquarters: Milford 2514, Waters 4003
Subsidiary: TJX 3765
Millbury
Office: Protector 3067
Millis
Subsidiary: U.M. 3834
Milton
Office: State 3592
Monson
Plant: Menasha 2461
Natick
Corporate Giving Program: Boston 540
Foundations: Boston 540, Middlesex 2506
Corporate Headquarters: Boston 540, Middlesex 2506
Plant: PerkinElmer 2939
Needham
Corporate Giving Program: Parametric 2878
Foundation: Universal 3893
Cororate Headquarters: Parametric 2878
Needham Heights
Plant: Coca 862
New Bedford
Foundation: Bufftree 607
Cororate Headquarters: Bufftree 607
Office: Tofias 3768
Newburyport
Corporate Giving Program: Cabot 643
Foundations: Institution 1946, Newburyport 2693
Corporate Headquarters: Cabot 643, Institution 1946, Newburyport 2693
Division: Gould 1618
Newton
Foundation: Reed 3161
Subsidiary: Washington 3997
Office: Cambridge 666
Newton Upper Falls
Foundation: Clarks 838
North Andover
Subsidiary: NIKE 2710
North Attleboro
Foundation: Blackinton 476
North Brookfield
Foundation: Quabaug 3090
Cororate Headquarters: Quabaug 3090
North Reading
Corporate Giving Program: Teradyne 3718
Cororate Headquarters: Teradyne 3718
Office: Savings 3343
North Truro
Foundation: Seamen's 3383
Northampton
Plant: Pactiv 2863
Norton
Subsidiary: Reed 3160
Norway
Plant: New 2668
Norwood
Foundation: Norwood 2751
Corporate Headquarters: Norwood 2751, Village 3954
Subsidiary: Praxair 3029
Orleans
Foundation: Cape 674
Cororate Headquarters: Cape 674
Osterville
Office: State 3592
Peabody
Foundation: East 1207
Cororate Headquarters: East 1207
Pittsfield
Corporate Giving Program: Berkshire 430
Foundation: Berkshire 428
Corporate Headquarters: Berkshire 428, Berkshire 430
Subsidiary: Guardian 1683
Divisions: General 1551, General 1552
Office: Draper 1171
Plainville
Foundation: Avelina 296
Cororate Headquarters: Avelina 296
Prides Crossing
Foundation: Affiliated 51
Cororate Headquarters: Affiliated 51
Provincetown
Cororate Headquarters: Seamen's 3383
Quincy
Foundations: Edvisors 1234, Gallagher 1528, Nellie 2659, Stop 3618
Corporate Headquarters: Arbella 226, Edvisors 1234, Gallagher 1528, Stop 3618
Subsidiary: General 1551
Joint Venture: State 3592
Raynham
Foundation: Bridgewater 562
Cororate Headquarters: Bridgewater 562
Subsidiary: Johnson 2048
Rentha
Office: FMC 1449
Rockland
Corporate Giving Program: Rockland 3242
Foundation: Independent 1927
Corporate Headquarters: EMD 1256, Independent 1927, Rockland 3242
Salem
Foundation: Salem 3317
Cororate Headquarters: Salem 3317
Subsidiaries: First 1400, PerkinElmer 2939
Division: PerkinElmer 2939
Saugus
Foundation: CB 725
Division: Henkel 1778
South Boston
Foundation: Marr 2382
South Easton
Cororate Headquarters: Reilly 3175
South Weymouth
Foundation: South 3512
Cororate Headquarters: South 3512
South Yarmouth
Office: Cape 674
Southbridge
Foundations: American 159, Dexter 1103
Corporate Headquarters: American 159, Dexter 1103
Subsidiary: Dexter 1103

Spencer
Foundation: Mercury 2470
Cororate Headquarters: Mercury 2470
Springfield
Corporate Giving Programs: Big 461, CSRwire 995, Massachusetts 2397, Social(k) 3494
Foundations: Big 461, Hampden 1712, Hampden 1713, Shatz 3424
Corporate Headquarters: Big 461, CSRwire 995, Hampden 1712, Hampden 1713, Massachusetts 2397, Northeast 2737, Shatz 3424, Social(k) 3494
Subsidiaries: Great 1642, Massachusetts 2397
Division: Shaughnessy 3425
Plant: Rexnord 3198
Sterling
Office: Clinton 851
Stoneham
Foundation: Stoneham 3616
Cororate Headquarters: Stoneham 3616
Stoughton
Cororate Headquarters: ITW 2000
Sudbury
Plant: Raytheon 3135
Taunton
Foundations: Bristol 577, Reed 3160
Corporate Headquarters: Bristol 577, Reed 3160
Division: Reed 3160
Tewksbury
Foundation: Holt 1839
Corporate Headquarters: Demoulas 1085, Holt 1839
Plant: Raytheon 3135
Wakefield
Foundation: Savings 3343
Cororate Headquarters: Savings 3343
Plants: McAfee 2417, PerkinElmer 2939
Waltham
Corporate Giving Programs: Holcim 1828, National 2630, Raytheon 3135, Thermo 3733
Foundations: Global 1593, Holcim 1828, PerkinElmer 2939
Corporate Headquarters: Global 1593, Holcim 1828, National 2630, PerkinElmer 2939, Raytheon 3135, Thermo 3733
Subsidiaries: Danaher 1027, Gates 1540, Globe 1594, Philips 2963
Offices: BMC 508, Foley 1454, SAP 3334
Plant: Raytheon 3135
Wareham
Foundation: A.D. 7
Cororate Headquarters: A.D. 7
Plant: Bergquist 420
Watertown
Foundation: Sasaki 3337
Corporate Headquarters: Bright 566, Sasaki 3337
Plants: PerkinElmer 2939, Sealed 3381
Webster
Cororate Headquarters: Webster 4017
Plants: Cranston 972, Guardian 1682
Wellesley
Offices: Connecticut 910, Protector 3067
Plant: Novell 2754
Wellesley Hills
Corporate Giving Program: Sun 3643
Foundation: American 133
Corporate Headquarters: American 133, Sun 3643
Wellfleet
Office: Cape 674
West Boylston
Office: Clinton 851
West Bridgewater
Corporate Giving Program: Shaw's 3427
Cororate Headquarters: Shaw's 3427
Subsidiary: Kellwood 2121
West Groton
Foundation: GenRad 1564
West Springfield
Subsidiary: Northeast 2737
Office: Hampden 1713
West Tisbury
Corporate Giving Program: South 3511
Foundation: South 3510
Corporate Headquarters: South 3510, South 3511
Westborough
Corporate Giving Program: BJ's 473
Cororate Headquarters: BJ's 473
Subsidiaries: National 2630, NiSource 2715
Offices: Porzio 3013, State 3592
Plant: EMC 1253
Westford
Cororate Headquarters: GenRad 1564
Subsidiary: Teradyne 3718
Weston
Foundations: Biogen 465, Triumph 3812
Cororate Headquarters: Biogen 465
Office: Liberty 2265
Westwood
Subsidiary: Johnson 2048
Offices: AT&T 274, State 3592
Plant: CA 638
Wilmington
Foundation: Charles 764
Cororate Headquarters: Charles 764
Subsidiaries: Bausch 376, Houghton 1869, Textron 3731
Plant: Lubrizol 2315
Woburn
Corporate Giving Program: Center 736
Cororate Headquarters: Center 736
Subsidiary: Raymond 3133
Office: Murtha 2602
Plants: Morton 2579, PerkinElmer 2939, TJX 3765
Worcester
Corporate Giving Program: Bay 380
Foundations: Bay 380, Carroll 703, Coghlin 864, Coghlin 865, Flexcon 1436, Hanover 1724, Morgan 2568, Protector 3067
Corporate Headquarters: Bay 380, Carroll 703, Coghlin 864, Coghlin 865, Hanover 1724, Morgan 2568, Protector 3067
Subsidiaries: Carroll 703, Coghlin 865, Danaher 1027, Hanover 1724, Harleysville 1733
Division: Shaughnessy 3425
Plants: Castle 716, TJX 3765

MICHIGAN

Ada
Corporate Giving Program: Amway 189
Foundation: Vos 3969
Corporate Headquarters: Amway 189, Vos 3969
Adrian
Corporate Giving Program: Gleaner 1590
Foundation: Gleaner 1590
Cororate Headquarters: Gleaner 1590
Subsidiary: Masco 2393
Albion
Subsidiary: Guardian 1682
Allegan
Foundation: Perrigo 2943
Cororate Headquarters: Perrigo 2943
Allen Park
Corporate Giving Program: Detroit 1094
Foundation: Detroit 1094
Cororate Headquarters: Detroit 1094
Subsidiary: SPX 3558
Alpena
Foundation: First 1402
Cororate Headquarters: First 1402
Subsidiary: First 1402
Plant: Lafarge 2210
Ann Arbor
Corporate Giving Programs: Con 903, Domino's 1151, IMRA 1923
Foundations: Domino's 1151, Issa 1997, Molly 2548, Stryker 3627
Corporate Headquarters: Con 903, Domino's 1151, Flint 1438, IMRA 1923, Issa 1997, Molly 2548
Subsidiaries: Comerica 889, Domino's 1151, Harley 1732, Nissan 2716, Philips 2963, Tyler 3831
Offices: Bodman 514, Brinks 573, Butzel 629, KeyBank 2136, Pan-American 2868
Plants: Boneal 523, Philips 2963, Rockwell 3247
Auburn
Plant: Dow 1162
Auburn Hills
Corporate Giving Programs: BorgWarner 528, Chrysler 801, Detroit 1095
Foundations: BorgWarner 528, Chrysler 801, Detroit 1095, Guardian 1682, MEEMIC 2455
Corporate Headquarters: BorgWarner 528, Chrysler 801, Detroit 1095, Guardian 1682, MEEMIC 2455, Palace 2866
Subsidiaries: Chrysler 801, ITT 1999, Palace 2866, Siemens 3448
Divisions: Delphi 1071, Palace 2866
Battle Creek
Corporate Giving Program: Kellogg 2120
Foundations: G & R 1523, Kellogg 2120
Cororate Headquarters: Kellogg 2120
Bay City
Foundation: Fabiano 1320
Belleville
Foundation: Visteon 3964
Subsidiary: Nucor 2760
Plant: Owens 2841
Benton Harbor
Foundation: Whirlpool 4056
Cororate Headquarters: Whirlpool 4056
Subsidiary: Chemical 774
Plant: Birds 469
Big Rapids
Division: Federal 1350
Bingham Farms
Subsidiary: Meritor 2473
Birmingham
Foundation: Kasle 2098
Subsidiary: Comerica 889
Plant: Schulman 3361
Bloomfield Hills
Corporate Giving Program: Pulte 3083
Cororate Headquarters: Pulte 3083
Subsidiaries: MAG 2337, Ryder 3292
Office: Butzel 629
Bridgeport
Plant: Campbell 669
Brighton
Division: Federal 1350
Office: Tim 3753
Buckley
Plant: Seneca 3406
Byron Center
Foundation: Buist 611
Cororate Headquarters: Buist 611
Cadillac
Subsidiary: Manitowoc 2356
Carleton
Plant: Guardian 1682
Charlotte
Foundation: Spartan 3534
Cororate Headquarters: Spartan 3534
Cheboygan
Office: Bodman 514
Chelsea
Division: Federal 1350
Plant: Chrysler 801
Coloma
Plant: Menasha 2461
Constantine
Foundation: Fibre 1369
Cororate Headquarters: Fibre 1369

Dearborn
Corporate Giving Program: Ford 1464
Foundation: Ford 1464
Corporate Headquarters: Ford 1464, Kasle 2098
Subsidiary: Ford 1464
Plants: CA 638, Caparo 673
Dearborn Heights
Foundation: Cablevision 640
Delton
Office: West 4038
Detroit
Corporate Giving Programs: Blue 502, Bodman 514, Butzel 629, Clark 836, Comerica 889, Compuware 902, Detroit 1096, Detroit 1097, DTE 1183, Dykema 1199, General 1555, Honigman 1853, Miller 2519
Foundations: Blue 502, Butzel 629, Comerica 889, Detroit 1093, DTE 1183, Ford 1464, General 1555, Hammond 1711, Ilitch 1915, Miller 2517
Corporate Headquarters: Blue 502, Bodman 514, Butzel 629, Clark 836, Compuware 902, Detroit 1093, Detroit 1096, Detroit 1097, DTE 1183, Dykema 1199, General 1555, Honigman 1853, Ilitch 1915, Kowalski 2189, Miller 2519
Subsidiaries: Comerica 889, DTE 1183, Gannett 1532, General 1555, Ilitch 1915, Kennametal 2125, Kimley 2151, Tomkins 3771, Washington 3999
Offices: Bodman 514, Butzel 629, Federal 1349, Foley 1453, Humana 1886, JPMorgan Chase 2071, Kearney 2107, Littler 2289, SAS 3336, Thompson 3739, Turner 3823, Urban 3901
Plants: Chrysler 801, Coca 862, Lafarge 2210, Marathon 2362, Office 2785, PPG 3025, Quaker 3093, Rockwell 3247
Dundee
Subsidiary: Holcim 1828
Plant: MAC 2329
Evart
Plant: PPG 3025
Farmington
Subsidiary: Raymond 3133
Farmington Hills
Corporate Giving Program: Amerisure 177
Foundations: Amerisure 177, Zatkoff 4154
Corporate Headquarters: Amerisure 177, Bosch 529, Zatkoff 4154
Plant: Guardian 1682
Fennville
Plant: Birds 469
Fenton
Plant: Newell 2694
Ferndale
Plant: Illinois 1916
Filer City
Plant: Pactiv 2863
Flat Rock
Plant: Mazda 2414
Flint
Foundation: Citizens 827
Cororate Headquarters: Citizens 827
Subsidiary: Meredith 2471
Division: Kasle 2098
Fremont
Subsidiary: Novartis 2752
Grand Haven
Foundation: JSJ 2073
Cororate Headquarters: JSJ 2073
Subsidiaries: Amazon.com 122, JSJ 2073
Office: Varnum 3923
Grand Rapids
Corporate Giving Programs: Gordon 1615, Meijer 2456, Miller 2520, Steelcase 3597, Varnum 3922, Varnum 3923
Foundations: Batts 374, Grand 1628, River 3223, Spartan 3535, Steelcase 3597, Todd 3766, Universal 3890, Velting 3928
Corporate Headquarters: Batts 374, Gordon 1615, Grand 1628, Meijer 2456, Miller 2520, River 3223, Spartan 3535, Steelcase 3597, Universal 3890, Varnum 3922, Varnum 3923, Velting 3928
Subsidiaries: Avery 297, Batts 374, Chemical 774, JSJ 2073, Steelcase 3597
Division: Steelcase 3597
Offices: Ahern 60, Humana 1886, Miller 2520, Varnum 3922
Plants: Fuller 1517, Schulman 3361, West 4038
Grass Lake
Plant: Tenneco 3715
Grosse Pointe Farms
Foundation: Buffalo 606
Hastings
Foundation: Hastings 1749
Corporate Headquarters: G & R 1523, Hastings 1749
Hemlock
Joint Venture: Dow 1162
Hillsdale
Subsidiary: Masco 2393
Plant: Evans 1300
Holland
Corporate Giving Program: Haworth 1758
Corporate Headquarters: Haworth 1758, Redlum 3156
Subsidiaries: Tennant 3714, Textron 3731, Venturedyne 3933
Plants: Great 1643, Sherwin 3437
Howell
Subsidiary: Hanover 1724
Hudson
Foundation: Rima 3216
Cororate Headquarters: Rima 3216
Ishpeming
Plant: Cliffs 850
Jackson
Corporate Giving Program: Consumers 921
Foundations: Alro 113, CMS 854, Consumers 921, Thorrez 3744
Corporate Headquarters: Alro 113, CMS 854, Consumers 921, Thorrez 3744
Subsidiaries: CMS 854, Consumers 921, Quanex 3100, Worthington 4124
Division: Quanex 3100
Plants: Tenneco 3715, Worthington 4124
Kalamazoo
Foundations: Fabri 1322, Miller 2522
Corporate Headquarters: Eliason 1248, Fabri 1322, Hammond 1711, Leet 2243, Miller 2522, Stryker 3627, Todd 3766
Subsidiaries: Flowserve 1447, Miller 2522
Offices: Miller 2520, Varnum 3922, Varnum 3923
Plant: Alro 113
Kalkaska
Subsidiary: Dart 1034
Lansing
Corporate Giving Program: Jackson 2009
Foundations: Delta 1078, Flint 1438
Corporate Headquarters: Henry 1780, Jackson 2009
Offices: Butzel 629, State 3592, Varnum 3922, Varnum 3923
Plants: Coca 862, Meijer 2456
Lawton
Plant: Welch 4025
Litchfield
Plant: Tenneco 3715
Livonia
Corporate Giving Program: Valassis 3914
Corporate Headquarters: ISGN 1995, Valassis 3914
Subsidiaries: Lennar 2250, Quanex 3100
Office: Factory 1323
Ludington
Foundation: Great 1643
Cororate Headquarters: Great 1643
Plant: Great 1643
Manistee
Plant: Morton 2579
Marshall
Subsidiary: BorgWarner 528
Office: State 3591
Plant: Tenneco 3715
Mason
Foundations: Dart 1033, Dart 1034, Mason 2396
Corporate Headquarters: Dart 1033, Dart 1034, Mason 2396
Office: Dart 1033
Menominee
Subsidiary: Caterpillar 722
Midland
Corporate Giving Programs: Chemical 774, Dow 1161, Dow 1162
Foundations: Bierlein 459, Dow 1161, Dow 1162
Corporate Headquarters: Bierlein 459, Chemical 774, Dow 1161, Dow 1162
Subsidiary: Chemical 774
Joint Ventures: Corning 945, Dow 1161
Office: GATX 1542
Plant: Lubrizol 2315
Monroe
Foundation: La-Z-Boy 2205
Cororate Headquarters: La-Z-Boy 2205
Plant: Tenneco 3715
Mount Pleasant
Foundation: Isabella 1993
Corporate Headquarters: Fabiano 1320, Isabella 1993
Muskegon
Subsidiary: Textron 3731
New Buffalo
Foundation: Four 1477
Cororate Headquarters: Four 1477
Northville
Foundation: ISGN 1995
Novi
Subsidiaries: Masco 2393, SPX 3558
Offices: Autodesk 289, Google 1613, Opus 2820, Varnum 3922
Oak Park
Subsidiary: Barton 366
Oakland
Cororate Headquarters: RESCO 3189
Okemos
Cororate Headquarters: Delta 1078
Otsego
Plant: Menasha 2461
Owosso
Plant: Georgia 1568
Parma
Corporate Giving Program: Michigan 2496
Cororate Headquarters: Michigan 2496
Paw Paw
Foundation: Eliason 1248
Pearl
Plant: Clorox 852
Pinconning
Subsidiary: CenturyLink 751
Plymouth
Subsidiary: Quadion 3092
Plant: SKF 3473
Pontiac
Subsidiary: Rite 3220
Port Huron
Subsidiaries: Caparo 673, Gannett 1532
Office: Regis 3172
Portage
Office: State 3591
Plants: Bausch 376, Charles 764
Quinnesec
Plant: International 1968
Redford
Plant: Alro 113
Reed City
Plant: General 1554
Richmond
Cororate Headquarters: Power 3020
Rochester
Foundation: Rewold 3196
Cororate Headquarters: Rewold 3196
Rochester Hills
Foundation: Dura 1195
Cororate Headquarters: Dura 1195
Subsidiaries: CLARCOR 832, Gates 1540, Mark 2377

Rockford
Foundation: Wolverine 4106
Cororate Headquarters: Wolverine 4106
Subsidiary: Wolverine 4106
Rockwood
Plant: U.S. 3840
Romulus
Division: Federal 1350
Plant: Univar 3886
Saginaw
Foundations: Duro-Last 1196, Michigan 2497
Corporate Headquarters: Duro-Last 1196, Michigan 2497
Subsidiary: Amsted 188
Division: Cox 958
Saint Clair Shores
Cororate Headquarters: Federal 1350
Saline
Foundation: R & B 3113
Cororate Headquarters: R & B 3113
Plant: Barnes 362
Sault Sainte Marie
Subsidiary: Wisconsin 4093
Shelby Township
Foundation: Power 3020
Sodus
Plant: Birds 469
South Lyon
Division: Quanex 3100
Southfield
Corporate Giving Programs: DENSO 1088, Polk 3000
Foundations: Barton 366, Berry 436, DENSO 1088, Lear 2237, Vesco 3942
Corporate Headquarters: Barton 366, Berry 436, DENSO 1088, Lear 2237, Olivetti 2802, Polk 3000, Vesco 3942
Subsidiaries: Barton 366, Comerica 889, CUNA 1008, Lafarge 2210
Division: Polk 3000
Offices: Cerner 754, CUNA 1008, Grant 1633, Pepper 2934, SAP 3334, Tutor 3826, Vision 3961
Plants: Mitsui 2541, Novell 2754
Spring Lake
Subsidiaries: JSJ 2073, Miller 2517
Springport
Subsidiary: Kadant 2083
St. Clair Shores
Foundation: Federal 1350
Standish
Foundation: Magline 2339
Cororate Headquarters: Magline 2339
Sterling Heights
Subsidiary: General 1551
Plants: Chrysler 801, Tenneco 3715
Taylor
Corporate Giving Program: Masco 2393
Foundation: Masco 2393
Cororate Headquarters: Masco 2393
Subsidiary: Worthington 4124
Three Rivers
Foundation: Kadant 2083
Cororate Headquarters: Kadant 2083
Subsidiary: Kadant 2083
Traverse City
Subsidiaries: Harleysville 1733, Textron 3731
Plant: Hillshire 1809
Trenton
Cororate Headquarters: Cablevision 640
Plant: Chrysler 801
Troy
Corporate Giving Program: Delphi 1071
Foundations: Cadillac 648, Delphi 1071, Kemp 2123, Meritor 2473
Corporate Headquarters: Cadillac 648, Delphi 1071, Kemp 2123, Meritor 2473
Subsidiaries: Caterpillar 722, Meritor 2473, PerkinElmer 2939, Textron 3731
Divisions: Delphi 1071, Kmart 2172
Offices: Bodman 514, ITA 1998, Quad 3091
Plants: Corning 945, Gleason 1591
Van Buren Township
Foundation: Dana 1026
Cororate Headquarters: Visteon 3964
Warren
Office: Huntington 1894
Plant: Chrysler 801
West Bloomfield
Cororate Headquarters: Frankel 1483
Wixom
Foundation: MAC 2329
Cororate Headquarters: MAC 2329
Woodhaven
Division: Kasle 2098
Wyandotte
Plant: BASF 368
Wyoming
Plant: Univar 3886
Ypsilanti
Plant: Barnes 362
Zeeland
Corporate Giving Program: Miller 2517
Foundation: Redlum 3156
Cororate Headquarters: Miller 2517
Subsidiary: Textron 3731
Plants: Bristol 578, Hillshire 1809

MINNESOTA

Albany
Foundation: Albany 77
Cororate Headquarters: Albany 77
Alexandria
Corporate Giving Program: Tastefully 3692
Cororate Headquarters: Tastefully 3692
Plant: Illinois 1916
Anoka
Plant: Graco 1624
Arden Hills
Cororate Headquarters: Land 2217
Austin
Corporate Giving Program: Hormel 1866
Foundation: Hormel 1866
Cororate Headquarters: Hormel 1866
Subsidiary: Hormel 1866
Bagley
Foundation: Calvert 663
Bayport
Corporate Giving Program: Andersen 194
Foundation: Andersen 194
Cororate Headquarters: Andersen 194
Subsidiary: Andersen 194
Becker
Plant: Plymouth 2993
Bemidji
Corporate Giving Program: First 1416
Foundation: First 1416
Cororate Headquarters: First 1416
Big Fork
Plant: Bergquist 420
Blaine
Corporate Giving Program: Aveda 295
Cororate Headquarters: Aveda 295
Bloomington
Corporate Giving Program: Toro 3775
Foundations: Riverway 3226, Toro 3775
Corporate Headquarters: Holiday 1832, Lieberman 2266, Riverway 3226, Toro 3775
Subsidiaries: Arbitron 227, Seagate 3377
Offices: Capstone 684, Kimley 2151, State 3592, Telligen 3710
Plants: CA 638, Novell 2754
Blue Earth
Plant: Seneca 3406
Bricelyn
Cororate Headquarters: Cannon 671
Burnsville
Office: Do 1136
Plant: UTC 3908
Cannon Falls
Plant: Bergquist 420
Chanhassen
Foundations: Bergquist 420, Business 625, Life 2269, Schott 3360
Corporate Headquarters: Bergquist 420, Business 625, Life 2269
Office: Mercury 2469
Chaska
Subsidiaries: Colgate 869, SUPERVALU 3659
Clearwater
Subsidiary: Otter 2836
Detroit Lakes
Foundation: S.J. 3299
Cororate Headquarters: S.J. 3299
Subsidiary: Otter 2836
Division: S.J. 3299
Dodge Center
Subsidiary: Oshkosh 2833
Duluth
Foundation: Allete 100
Cororate Headquarters: Allete 100
Subsidiaries: Allete 100, Black 475, Georgia 1568, Hubbard 1877
Plant: General 1554
Eagan
Corporate Giving Program: Thomson 3742
Foundations: Blue 496, Intertech 1976
Cororate Headquarters: Thomson 3742
Plants: Jostens 2067, Schulman 3361
Eden Prairie
Corporate Giving Programs: Minnesota 2530, Robinson 3235, SUPERVALU 3659
Foundations: Douglas 1159, Minnesota 2530, Starkey 3587
Corporate Headquarters: Douglas 1159, Minnesota 2530, Robinson 3235, Starkey 3587, SUPERVALU 3659
Subsidiaries: Robbins 3230, SUPERVALU 3659
Office: Regis 3172
Plant: Bausch 376
Edina
Corporate Giving Program: Capstone 684
Foundations: Edina 1227, Nash 2619
Subsidiaries: Edina 1227, Nash 2619
Offices: ProtechSoft 3065, Regis 3172
Elysian
Foundation: Cannon 671
Erskine
Foundation: Garden 1535
Cororate Headquarters: Garden 1535
Eveleth
Plant: Cliffs 850
Fairmont
Foundation: Rosen's 3264
Cororate Headquarters: Rosen's 3264
Faribault
Subsidiary: Faribault 1332
Farmington
Plant: Valmont 3919
Fergus Falls
Corporate Giving Program: Otter 2836
Cororate Headquarters: Otter 2836
Subsidiaries: Otter 2836, Park 2883
Division: Otter 2836
Forest Lake
Foundation: Hallberg 1704
Fridley
Plants: Cummins 1007, Fuller 1517
Golden Valley
Foundations: Jones 2060, Pentair 2926
Subsidiary: Novartis 2752
Division: Bausch 376
Hibbing
Foundation: Security 3394
Cororate Headquarters: Security 3394
Plant: Cliffs 850
Hopkins
Corporate Giving Program: Carlson 693
Plant: Menasha 2461

Windom
Plant: Toro 3775
Winona
Foundation: Knitcraft 2175
Cororate Headquarters: Knitcraft 2175
Woodbury
Office: State 3591
Worthington
Plant: Campbell 669
Wyoming
Cororate Headquarters: Hallberg 1704

MISSISSIPPI

Artesia
Subsidiary: Holcim 1828
Booneville
Plant: Bassett 372
Brandon
Foundation: Community 897
Cororate Headquarters: Community 897
Bruce
Subsidiary: Weyerhaeuser 4052
Canton
Plant: Strauss 3624
Clarksdale
Plant: Cooper 936
Coldwater
Subsidiary: Leggett 2246
Columbus
Subsidiary: Weyerhaeuser 4052
Plant: American 135
Fayette
Subsidiary: Thomasville 3737
Flowood
Foundation: Blue 490
Cororate Headquarters: Jackson 2010
Subsidiaries: Blue 490, Nucor 2760
Forest
Division: DIRECTV 1124
Fulton
Plant: Pactiv 2863
Grenada
Plant: Sealed 3381
Gulfport
Foundation: Mississippi 2536
Cororate Headquarters: Mississippi 2536
Subsidiary: Southern 3516
Office: Balch 327
Plant: International 1964
Hattiesburg
Foundations: Mortgage 2578, South 3509
Corporate Headquarters: Mortgage 2578, South 3509
Plant: Kohler 2182
Horn Lake
Subsidiary: Todd 3766
Houston
Subsidiary: Leggett 2246
Indianola
Subsidiary: SUPERVALU 3659
Iuka
Plant: Vulcan 3972
Jackson
Corporate Giving Programs: Entergy 1280, Irby 1990
Foundations: Delta 1082, Ergon 1289, Harvey 1746, Jackson 2008, Regions 3171
Corporate Headquarters: Blue 490, Delta 1082, Entergy 1280, Ergon 1289, Harvey 1746, Irby 1990, Jackson 2008
Subsidiaries: Blue 490, Consolidated 918, du Pont 1184, Entergy 1279, Ergon 1289, Saks 3315
Offices: Adams 34, Baker 325, Balch 327, Bradley 550, Burr 621, CUNA 1008, Federal 1349, JPMorgan Chase 2071, Wurzburg 4129, Wyatt 4130
Plants: Armstrong 246, Chevron 780, Modine 2544, Owens 2841
Laurel
Subsidiary: Delta 1082
Madison
Foundation: Sports 3547
Cororate Headquarters: Sports 3547
Meridian
Foundation: Jackson 2010
Natchez
Foundation: Leet 2243
Subsidiary: Ergon 1289
Newton
Plant: La-Z-Boy 2205
Okolona
Corporate Giving Program: First 1398
Olive Branch
Plant: Menasha 2461
Oxford
Plant: Whirlpool 4056
Pascagoula
Plant: Chevron 780
Philadelphia
Foundation: Yates 4142
Cororate Headquarters: Yates 4142
Picayune
Plant: Valspar 3920
Pontotoc
Plants: Illinois 1916, Krueger 2196
Poplarville
Subsidiary: Ergon 1289
Quitman
Office: Dart 1033
Ridgeland
Foundations: Arrowhead 250, C Spire 636
Corporate Headquarters: Arrowhead 250, C Spire 636
Subsidiary: Ergon 1289
Saltillo
Plants: Bassett 372, La-Z-Boy 2205
Senatobia
Plant: Donnelley 1155
Southaven
Subsidiary: First 1406
Starkville
Subsidiary: Ergon 1289
Summit
Subsidiary: Kellwood 2121
Taylorsville
Subsidiary: Ergon 1289
Plant: Georgia 1568
Tunica
Division: Caesars 650
Tupelo
Corporate Giving Program: First 1398
Foundation: BancorpSouth 336
Cororate Headquarters: BancorpSouth 336
Subsidiary: Furniture 1519
Plants: Cooper 936, FMC 1449, Krueger 2196
Verona
Office: Leggett 2246
Vicksburg
Division: Caesars 650
Plants: Armstrong 246, International 1968
Winona
Plant: Krueger 2196

MISSOURI

Ballwin
Cororate Headquarters: Fru 1513
Belle
Plant: Clorox 852
Belton
Subsidiary: QuikTrip 3109
Boonville
Subsidiary: UMB 3846
Branson
Foundation: Herschend 1790
Cororate Headquarters: Herschend 1790
Brookfield
Subsidiary: UMB 3846
California
Foundation: Burger's 614
Cororate Headquarters: Burger's 614
Camdenton
Plant: Modine 2544
Cape Girardeau
Plant: Procter 3055
Carthage
Foundation: Leggett 2246
Cororate Headquarters: Leggett 2246
Subsidiaries: Grace 1623, Leggett 2246, UMB 3846
Charleston
Plant: Gates 1540
Chesterfield
Corporate Giving Program: Reinsurance 3179
Foundations: McBride 2418, Reinsurance 3179, Sachs 3301
Corporate Headquarters: Kellwood 2121, McBride 2418, Reinsurance 3179, Sachs 3301
Subsidiary: Service 3413
Plant: McAfee 2417
Chillicothe
Plant: Donaldson 1153
Clayton
Foundations: Apex 214, Graybar 1640
Corporate Headquarters: First 1393, Moneta 2557, Olin 2801
Subsidiary: Commerce 890
Cleveland
Cororate Headquarters: Beyer 454
Columbia
Foundations: MFA 2486, MFA 2487, Shelter 3431
Corporate Headquarters: MFA 2486, MFA 2487, Shelter 3431
Office: State 3591
Plants: Quaker 3094, Square 3560
Creve Coeur
Cororate Headquarters: Benton 417
Cuba
Plants: Georgia 1568, Olin 2801
Des Peres
Cororate Headquarters: Jones 2059
Earth City
Corporate Giving Program: Forest 1468
Office: Factory 1323
Plant: Hillshire 1809
Ellisville
Foundation: Clarkson 839
Cororate Headquarters: Clarkson 839
Fenton
Corporate Giving Programs: Maritz 2376, UniGroup 3852
Foundations: Fabick 1321, Hautly 1750, International 1963, UniGroup 3852, Wolff 4105
Corporate Headquarters: Fabick 1321, International 1963, Maritz 2376, UniGroup 3852, Wolff 4105
Subsidiaries: Fabick 1321, Maritz 2376, UniGroup 3852
Plant: Tenneco 3715
Florissant
Foundation: Londoff 2297
Cororate Headquarters: Londoff 2297
Fulton
Plant: Stride 3625
Grandview
Foundation: Beyer 454
Division: Tomkins 3771
Hamilton
Plant: Stride 3625
Hannibal
Plant: General 1554
Hazelwood
Foundation: First 1393
Subsidiaries: Emerson 1257, SUPERVALU 3659
Office: State 3591
Independence
Cororate Headquarters: Knitcraft 2174
Plant: Olin 2801

Jefferson City
Offices: Bryan 596, Husch 1896, Polsinelli 3001, Spencer 3543, Stinson 3608
Plant: Modine 2544
Joplin
Corporate Giving Program: TAMKO 3685
Cororate Headquarters: TAMKO 3685
Plants: General 1554, Modine 2544, Westervelt 4046
Kansas City
Corporate Giving Programs: AMC 125, Fortis 1473, H & R 1695, Hallmark 1707, Husch 1896, Kansas 2091, Kansas 2092, Kansas 2093, Kansas 2094, Polsinelli 3001, Shook 3439, Spencer 3543, Sporting 3546, Stinson 3608, UMB 3846
Foundations: American 137, Bartlett 365, Boeing 516, Burns 620, Butler 626, Cerner 754, Commerce 890, DeBruce 1057, H & R 1695, Hallmark 1707, Highwoods 1800, Kansas 2091, Tension 3717, Universal 3895
Corporate Headquarters: AMC 125, American 137, Bartlett 365, Burns 620, Butler 626, Commerce 890, DeBruce 1057, Fortis 1473, H & R 1695, Hallmark 1707, Husch 1896, Kansas 2091, Kansas 2092, Kansas 2093, Kansas 2094, Polsinelli 3001, Shook 3439, Spencer 3543, Sporting 3546, Stinson 3608, Tension 3717, UMB 3846, Universal 3895
Subsidiaries: Assurant 266, Butler 626, Commerce 890, Jeld 2032, Kansas 2092, Kansas 2094, Meredith 2471, Otter 2836, UMB 3846
Offices: Federal 1349, Grant 1633, Hays 1761, Humana 1886, Husch 1896, Polsinelli 3001, Pulte 3083, Shook 3439, Spencer 3543, State 3592, Stinson 3608, Thompson 3739
Plants: Castle 716, General 1554, Honeywell 1852, Lafarge 2210, Novell 2754, Owens 2842, Procter 3055, Rockwell 3247, Tenneco 3715, Univar 3886
Kirksville
Subsidiary: Wolverine 4106
Lebanon
Foundation: Independent 1928
Cororate Headquarters: Independent 1928
Subsidiary: Leggett 2246
Liberty
Subsidiary: Ferrellgas 1365
Plant: Hallmark 1707
Maryland Heights
Division: Caesars 650
Plants: Scotts 3372, Univar 3886
Mercer
Plant: Martin 2391
Moberly
Foundation: Orscheln 2827
Cororate Headquarters: Orscheln 2827
Neosho
Plant: La-Z-Boy 2205
North Kansas City
Cororate Headquarters: Cerner 754
O'Fallon
Plant: Bausch 376
Pacific
Plant: U.S. 3840
Poplar Bluff
Plants: Briggs 565, Gates 1540
Richmond
Foundation: Ray 3132
Cororate Headquarters: Ray 3132
Richmond Heights
Foundation: Panera 2873
Saint Charles
Foundation: Our 2838
Saint Louis
Corporate Giving Programs: Bryan 596, Greensfelder 1659
Foundations: Build 608, Moneta 2557
Corporate Headquarters: Bryan 596, Greensfelder 1659
Subsidiary: Graybar 1640
Offices: Bryan 596, Fulbright 1516, Greensfelder 1659, Husch 1896
Savannah
Plant: Martin 2391
Springfield
Foundation: America's 130
Corporate Headquarters: America's 130
Offices: Husch 1896, Polsinelli 3001, Univar 3886
St. Charles
Foundation: ACF 26
Corporate Headquarters: ACF 26, Our 2838
Plant: Merk 2467
St. Joseph
Subsidiaries: AmerisourceBergen 175, Boehringer 515
Office: Polsinelli 3001
Plant: Hillshire 1809
St. Louis
Corporate Giving Programs: Ameren 128, Anheuser 202, Build 608, Charter 765, Emerson 1257, Intoximeters 1979, Jones 2059, Laclede 2208, Monsanto 2559, Nestle 2662, Panera 2873, Peabody 2907, Schnuck 3356, Senniger 3407, St. Louis 3567, St. Louis 3568, St. Louis 3569
Foundations: Ameren 128, American 142, Anheuser 202, Arch 231, Bakewell 326, Benton 417, Brown 591, Build 608, Bunge 612, Centene 735, CPI 965, Emerson 1257, Enterprise 1281, ESCO 1296, Express 1313, Fru 1513, Furniture 1519, Hermann 1786, Jones 2055, Kellwood 2121, Laclede 2207, Monsanto 2559, Nestle 2662, RubinBrown 3280, Sidener 3445, Sigma 3453, St. Louis 3567, St. Louis 3568, St. Louis 3569, Stout 3619, Stupp 3628
Corporate Headquarters: Ameren 128, American 142, Anheuser 202, Apex 214, Arch 231, Bakewell 326, Bodine 513, Brown 591, Build 608, Bunge 612, Centene 735, Charter 765, CPI 965, Emerson 1257, Energizer 1271, Enterprise 1281, ESCO 1296, Express 1313, Forest 1468, Furniture 1519, Graybar 1640, Guth 1692, Hautly 1750, Hermann 1786, Intoximeters 1979, Jones 2055, Laclede 2207, Laclede 2208, Monsanto 2559, Nestle 2662, Panera 2873, Peabody 2907, RubinBrown 3280, Schnuck 3356, Senniger 3407, Sidener 3445, Sigma 3453, St. Louis 3567, St. Louis 3568, St. Louis 3569, Stout 3619, Stupp 3628, TALX 3683
Subsidiaries: Ameren 128, Anheuser 202, Apex 214, AT&T 273, Belo 406, Berkshire 429, Boeing 516, Brown 591, Cardinal 685, Citigroup 821, CPI 965, DRS 1179, Equifax 1288, Jacobs 2016, Johnson 2049, Kellwood 2121, Lee 2241, Metropolitan 2481, Monsanto 2559, Nestle 2662, Nestle 2663, Sequa 3410, Sigma 3453, Toyota 3784, Valero 3915
Divisions: Koch 2180, PerkinElmer 2939
Offices: Ahern 60, AT&T 274, Federal 1349, Grant 1633, Hays 1761, Levi 2254, Littler 2289, Opus 2820, Polsinelli 3001, RJN 3228, SAP 3334, SAS 3336, Senniger 3407, Spencer 3543, State 3591, State 3592, Stinson 3608, Strauss 3624, Thompson 3739, Vision 3961
Plants: CA 638, International 1964, Lafarge 2210, Novell 2754, Owens 2841, Pactiv 2863, Procter 3055, Schulman 3361, Sensient 3408, Tension 3717
St. Peters
Foundation: MEMC 2459
Cororate Headquarters: MEMC 2459
St. Roberts
Plant: Wal-Mart 3980
Sugar Creek
Plant: Lafarge 2210
Sunset Hills
Office: Safeco 3306
Tipton
Plants: Bassett 372, Stride 3625
Trenton
Plant: Modine 2544
Troy
Corporate Giving Program: Bodine 513
Washington
Foundation: Shure 3443
Cororate Headquarters: Shure 3443
West Plains
Plant: Armstrong 246

MONTANA

Bigfork
Foundation: Saddlehorn 3305
Cororate Headquarters: Saddlehorn 3305
Billings
Corporate Giving Program: PPL 3027
Foundations: First 1409, Spence 3542, Wendy's 4032
Corporate Headquarters: PPL 3027, Spence 3542, Wendy's 4032
Subsidiaries: Evening 1302, PPL 3026, U.S. 3835
Office: Holland 1833
Plant: Exxon 1315
Bozeman
Subsidiary: Evening 1302
Butte
Subsidiary: Evening 1302
Deer Lodge
Office: Pioneer 2979
Dillon
Foundation: Pioneer 2979
Cororate Headquarters: Pioneer 2979
Emigrant
Corporate Giving Program: Mountain 2589
Cororate Headquarters: Mountain 2589
Eureka
Foundation: InterBel 1952
Cororate Headquarters: InterBel 1952
Great Falls
Subsidiary: Evening 1302
Plant: General 1554
Helena
Foundation: Power 3023
Cororate Headquarters: Power 3023
Subsidiary: Xcel 4135
Kalispell
Subsidiary: Fiserv 1427
Office: Applied 220
Livingston
Foundation: First 1423
Missoula
Foundation: Washington 3994
Cororate Headquarters: Washington 3994
Subsidiary: Evening 1302
Office: Dorsey 1157
Plant: International 1964

NEBRASKA

Auburn
Plant: Armstrong 246
Aurora
Subsidiary: Danaher 1027
Plant: Procter 3055
Beatrice
Subsidiary: Toro 3775
Office: Charter 765
Columbus
Cororate Headquarters: Flexcon 1436
Cozad
Plant: Tenneco 3715
Diller
Foundation: Diller 1117
Cororate Headquarters: Diller 1117
Doniphan
Subsidiary: Williams 4077
Fort Wayne
Foundation: Rieke 3212
Fremont
Plant: Oilgear 2793
Grand Island
Foundation: Chief 793
Cororate Headquarters: Chief 793
Office: Principal 3047
Plant: Nash 2619
Hastings
Foundation: Guarantee 1678
Cororate Headquarters: Guarantee 1678

Kearney
Subsidiary: CLARCOR 832
Plant: West 4038
Lincoln
Corporate Giving Program: Lincoln 2278
Foundations: Ameritas 178, Assurity 269, Kawasaki 2103, Li-Cor 2261, Mapes 2360, NEBCO 2653, Nelnet 2660
Corporate Headquarters: Ameritas 178, Assurity 269, Kawasaki 2103, Li-Cor 2261, Lincoln 2278, Mapes 2360, NEBCO 2653, Nelnet 2660
Subsidiaries: Fiserv 1427, Lee 2241, NEBCO 2653, Owen 2840
Offices: Federal 1349, Grant 1633, State 3591
Plant: Square 3560
McCook
Plant: Valmont 3919
Norfolk
Subsidiary: Nash 2619
Omaha
Corporate Giving Programs: Ag 55, Berkshire 429, Mutual 2607, Union 3857
Foundations: Burlington 616, ConAgra 904, Cox 959, Greater 1649, Hawkins 1757, Kiewit 2142, KLS 2171, Mutual 2607, Omaha 2805, Omaha 2806, Owen 2840, Physicians 2970, Scoular 3373, ShopKo 3440, Union 3857, Valmont 3919, West 4035
Corporate Headquarters: Ag 55, Berkshire 429, Burlington 616, ConAgra 904, Greater 1649, Hawkins 1757, Kiewit 2142, Mutual 2606, Mutual 2607, Omaha 2805, Omaha 2806, Physicians 2970, Scoular 3373, Union 3857, Valmont 3919, West 4035
Subsidiaries: Berkshire 429, Commerce 890, First 1400, Hy-Vee 1900, Metropolitan 2481, Mutual 2607, Owen 2840, Physicians 2970, Union 3857
Divisions: Cox 958, ServiceMaster 3414
Offices: Ahern 60, Bionetics 467, Grant 1633, Husch 1896, Spencer 3543, Stinson 3608
Plants: Bausch 376, Bemis 407, CA 638, Campbell 669, Kellogg 2120, Owens 2841, Pactiv 2863
Scottsbluff
Subsidiary: AMCOL 127
Office: Charter 765
Seward
Plant: Tenneco 3715
South Sioux City
Corporate Giving Program: Great 1646
Cororate Headquarters: Great 1646
Tecumseh
Plant: Campbell 669
Valley
Plant: Valmont 3919
Weeping Water
Plant: Martin 2391
West Point
Plant: Valmont 3919
York
Foundation: Cornerstone 943
Cororate Headquarters: Cornerstone 943

NEVADA

Carson City
Office: Holland 1833
Plants: American 135, Southwest 3524
Carson Valley
Plant: Starbucks 3585
Elko
Plant: International 1964
Ely
Foundation: Mount 2588
Cororate Headquarters: Mount 2588
Fallon
Plant: Kennametal 2125
Fernley
Plant: Sherwin 3437
Henderson
Corporate Giving Program: Zappos.com 4153
Cororate Headquarters: Zappos.com 4153
Subsidiaries: Amazon.com 122, HCA 1762, Meredith 2471, Station 3593
Plant: Strauss 3624
Lake Tahoe
Division: Caesars 650
Las Vegas
Corporate Giving Programs: Boyd 546, Caesars 650, Cotton 949, MGM 2489, NV 2765, Southwest 3524, Station 3593
Foundations: Caesars 650, Las Vegas 2225, MGM 2489, Pinnacle 2978, Southwest 3524, Transwestern 3800
Corporate Headquarters: Ameristar 176, Boyd 546, Caesars 650, Cotton 949, International 1964, Las Vegas 2225, Majestic 2344, MGM 2489, NV 2765, Pinnacle 2978, Southwest 3524, Station 3593, Transwestern 3800
Subsidiaries: Boyd 546, Caesars 650, Comerica 889, CORE 941, Landmark 2218, Lennar 2250, M.D.C. 2324, Mars 2384, MGM 2489, PerkinElmer 2939, Southwest 3524, Station 3593, Viad 3946, Zions 4158
Division: Caesars 650
Offices: Akerman 69, Ballard 329, Boises 518, Brownstein 593, CIBA 809, Cotton 949, Duane 1185, Federal 1349, Fennemore 1360, Greenberg 1654, Holland 1833, Kiewit 2142, Kimley 2151, Lewis 2256, Littler 2289, Majestic 2343, Pulte 3083, Sherman 3436, Snell 3490, Whiting 4063
Plants: International 1964, KB 2105, Southwest 3524, TJX 3765
Laughlin
Division: Caesars 650
Plant: International 1964
North Kansas City
Division: Caesars 650
North Las Vegas
Cororate Headquarters: Houston 1870
Subsidiary: Station 3593
Office: CDW 729
Reno
Corporate Giving Programs: International 1964, Patagonia 2892
Foundations: DP 1168, NV 2765
Cororate Headquarters: DP 1168
Subsidiaries: Armstrong 246, Deere 1061, FMC 1449, Gannett 1532, Lennar 2250, NV 2765, Oracle 2821
Division: Caesars 650
Offices: Brownstein 593, Cotton 949, Downey 1166, Grant 1633, Holland 1833, Kimley 2151, Lewis 2256, Littler 2289, Sherman 3436
Plants: Clorox 852, Donnelley 1155, FMC 1449, Hexcel 1795, Sherwin 3437
Sparks
Subsidiary: Diebold 1112
Office: Granite 1632
Plants: Antioch 207, Nestle 2662
Stateline
Plant: International 1964

NEW HAMPSHIRE

Amherst
Plants: Bassett 372, Sequa 3410
Bedford
Subsidiary: Teradyne 3718
Bennington
Foundation: Monadnock 2551
Cororate Headquarters: Monadnock 2551
Canaan
Office: Mascoma 2394
Claremont
Foundation: Claremont 833
Cororate Headquarters: Claremont 833
Concord
Foundations: Merrimack 2474, Newspapers 2702
Corporate Headquarters: Merrimack 2474, Newspapers 2702
Subsidiary: National 2630
Dover
Office: Liberty 2265
Enfield
Office: Mascoma 2394
Exeter
Plant: Osram 2834
Greenland
Subsidiary: NIKE 2710
Hampton
Corporate Giving Program: Unitil 3885
Cororate Headquarters: Unitil 3885
Subsidiaries: Thermo 3733, Unitil 3885
Hanover
Offices: Boises 518, Mascoma 2394
Hillsboro
Plant: Osram 2834
Hooksett
Subsidiary: CIGNA 812
Jaffrey
Foundation: Bean 391
Corporate Headquarters: Bean 391
Subsidiary: Bean 391
Plant: Merk 2467
Keene
Corporate Giving Program: C & S 634
Foundations: MPB 2591, National 2629
Corporate Headquarters: C & S 634, Kingsbury 2160, MPB 2591, National 2629
Subsidiaries: Corning 945, Liberty 2265, Timken 3760
Kensington
Subsidiary: Unitil 3885
Laconia
Plant: New Hampshire 2674
Lebanon
Foundation: Mascoma 2394
Cororate Headquarters: Mascoma 2394
Subsidiary: National 2630
Plant: Timken 3760
Londonderry
Corporate Giving Program: Stonyfield 3617
Corporate Headquarters: Stonyfield 3617
Subsidiary: Timberland 3754
Lyme
Office: Mascoma 2394
Manchester
Corporate Giving Program: Public 3075
Corporate Headquarters: Cityside 831, Public 3075
Subsidiaries: Northeast 2737, RBS 3137, TD 3696
Division: Shaughnessy 3425
Offices: Autodesk 289, Bernstein 433, Connecticut 910, State 3592
Plant: Osram 2834
Merrimack
Corporate Giving Programs: Brookstone 586, Cityside 831
Corporate Headquarters: Brookstone 586, White 4060
Subsidiary: Texas 3728
Nashua
Foundation: Worthen 4123
Cororate Headquarters: Worthen 4123
Plants: Raytheon 3135, Univar 3886
Newark
Office: Gibbons 1574
Newington
Plant: Westinghouse 4049
Peterborough
Cororate Headquarters: New Hampshire 2674
Office: West 4038
Pittsfield
Plants: Bausch 376, Charles 764
Portsmouth
Cororate Headquarters: Sprague 3551
Subsidiary: NiSource 2715
Offices: Liberty 2265, Pierce 2974

Salem
Foundations: FMR 1450, Salem 3316
Cororate Headquarters: Salem 3316
Stratham
Corporate Giving Program: Timberland 3754
Cororate Headquarters: Timberland 3754
Subsidiaries: Timberland 3754, V.F. 3913
Walpole
Foundation: Hubbard 1878
Cororate Headquarters: Hubbard 1878
West Lebanon
Office: Mascoma 2394

NEW JERSEY

Annandale
Foundation: Red 3153
Atlantic City
Foundation: Calvi 664
Cororate Headquarters: Calvi 664
Division: Caesars 650
Plant: International 1964
Avenel
Cororate Headquarters: Northfield 2741
Plant: Procter 3055
Basking Ridge
Corporate Giving Program: Verizon 3936
Foundations: Hilliard 1806, Verizon 3936
Cororate Headquarters: Cellco 733
Subsidiary: Verizon 3936
Division: Alcatel 81
Bayonne
Foundation: Royal 3276
Cororate Headquarters: Royal 3276
Office: International 1972
Plant: Public 3077
Bedminster
Corporate Giving Programs: Cellco 733, Peapack-Gladstone 2909
Cororate Headquarters: Celanese 730, Peapack-Gladstone 2909
Subsidiary: AT&T 273
Office: SAS 3336
Berkeley Heights
Division: Alcatel 81
Plant: Novell 2754
Blue Anchor
Plant: Kellogg 2120
Branchville
Foundations: Franklin 1486, Selective 3399
Cororate Headquarters: Franklin 1486, Selective 3399
Bridgeton
Plant: Owens 2841
Bridgewater
Corporate Giving Programs: Brother 587, sanofi-aventis 3329
Foundation: sanofi-aventis 3329
Cororate Headquarters: Brother 587, sanofi-aventis 3329
Subsidiary: Johnson 2048
Buena Vista Township
Plant: U.S. 3840
Burlington
Corporate Giving Program: Burlington 617
Cororate Headquarters: Burlington 617
Subsidiaries: Canon 672, DENTSPLY 1089
Plants: Panasonic 2869, Public 3077
Camden
Corporate Giving Program: Campbell 669
Foundation: Campbell 669
Cororate Headquarters: Campbell 669
Subsidiary: Campbell 669
Carlstadt
Subsidiary: Leggett 2246
Carteret
Cororate Headquarters: Pathmark 2894
Subsidiary: Great 1642
Plant: FMC 1449
Chatham
Subsidiary: Berkley 426
Chatsworth
Foundation: Haines 1701
Cororate Headquarters: Haines 1701
Cherry Hill
Foundation: Subaru 3631
Cororate Headquarters: Subaru 3631
Offices: Ballard 329, Cozen 964, Duane 1185, Hangley 1721, Stradley 3620, White 4059
Plants: Giant 1573, Subaru 3631
Clark
Foundation: D'Annunzio 1017
Cororate Headquarters: D'Annunzio 1017
Subsidiary: Harsco 1741
Clementon
Foundation: Zallie 4152
Cororate Headquarters: Zallie 4152
Clifton
Foundation: Goldmark 1605
Cororate Headquarters: Goldmark 1605
Subsidiaries: Dow 1161, O'Neal 2771
Cranbury
Foundation: Matrix 2403
Cororate Headquarters: Matrix 2403
Cranford
Foundation: Jersey 2039
Cororate Headquarters: Jersey 2039
Demarest
Foundation: Queen 3102
East Hanover
Foundation: Novartis 2753
Cororate Headquarters: Novartis 2753
Subsidiary: Novartis 2752
East Orange
Corporate Giving Program: Cox 958
East Rutherford
Corporate Giving Program: New York 2684
Foundations: AEGIS 44, New York 2684
Cororate Headquarters: AEGIS 44, New York 2684
Eatontown
Offices: CDW 729, Wilentz 4071
Edison
Foundations: Mamiye 2352, Sakar 3313
Cororate Headquarters: Parthenon 2889, Sakar 3313
Subsidiary: Leggett 2246
Office: Wiley 4072
Plants: Barnes 362, Public 3077
Egg Harbor Township
Foundation: Atlantic 281
Elizabeth
Foundation: Union 3855
Cororate Headquarters: Elizabeth 1250, Union 3855
Elmwood Park
Corporate Giving Program: Sealed 3381
Cororate Headquarters: Sealed 3381
Englewood
Foundation: C & C 633
Cororate Headquarters: C & C 633
Englewood Cliffs
Foundations: Bethel 445, Crane 970, Owens 2843, Unilever 3853
Cororate Headquarters: Owens 2843, Unilever 3853
Subsidiary: Unilever 3853
Division: Canon 672
Essex Fells
Foundation: Schiffenhaus 3351
Fair Lawn
Foundation: Columbia 882
Cororate Headquarters: Columbia 882
Subsidiaries: Biomet 466, Columbia 882
Plant: Sealed 3381
Fairfield
Foundations: Excellium 1305, Kearny 2108
Cororate Headquarters: Excellium 1305, Jesco 2040
Subsidiary: Mrs. Fields 2592
Farmingdale
Plant: Menasha 2461
Flemington
Office: Archer 232
Plant: Bemis 407
Florham Park
Corporate Giving Programs: BASF 368, Bressler 557, New York 2687
Foundation: New York 2687
Cororate Headquarters: BASF 368, Bressler 557
Offices: Bressler 557, Drinker 1175, Factory 1323, Greenberg 1654
Fort Lee
Foundation: Meecorp 2454
Cororate Headquarters: Meecorp 2454
Subsidiary: Franklin 1487
Franklin Lakes
Corporate Giving Program: Becton 398
Cororate Headquarters: Becton 398
Office: Kreindler 2193
Freehold
Corporate Giving Program: Saker 3314
Cororate Headquarters: Saker 3314
Subsidiary: Saker 3314
Gloucester City
Plant: Giant 1573
Hackensack
Corporate Giving Program: Cole 868
Foundations: Creamer 974, North 2733
Cororate Headquarters: Cole 868, Creamer 974
Offices: Archer 232, Cole 868
Plant: Tension 3717
Hackettstown
Subsidiary: Fulton 1518
Division: Mars 2384
Haddonfield
Corporate Giving Program: Archer 232
Foundation: U.M. 3834
Cororate Headquarters: Archer 232, U.M. 3834
Subsidiary: U.M. 3834
Office: Archer 232
Hamilton
Cororate Headquarters: Rue 3285
Plant: Public 3077
Hammonton
Cororate Headquarters: Universal 3894
Harrison
Corporate Giving Program: Anschutz 205
Plant: Public 3077
Hazlet
Subsidiary: International 1962
Plant: McAfee 2417
Hightstown
Plants: McGraw 2429, Sonoco 3500
Hillsborough
Office: Amboy 124
Hoboken
Corporate Giving Program: Wiley 4072
Foundation: Wiley 4072
Cororate Headquarters: Wiley 4072
Hope Creek
Plant: Public 3077
Hopewell
Office: Amboy 124
Plant: Bristol 578
Howell
Office: Amboy 124
Iselin
Foundation: Siemens 3448
Office: Satterlee 3339
Jamesburg
Office: Canon 672
Jersey City
Corporate Giving Program: Lord 2303
Cororate Headquarters: Bethel 445, Lord 2303, Provident 3069
Subsidiary: Provident 3069
Plant: Public 3077
Kearny
Cororate Headquarters: Kearny 2108
Plants: Owens 2842, Public 3077
Keasbey
Corporate Giving Program: Wakefern 3979
Cororate Headquarters: Wakefern 3979

Kenilworth
Cororate Headquarters: Benedict-Miller 410
Lakewood
Foundations: Mueller 2597, S & H 3295
Cororate Headquarters: Mueller 2597, S & H 3295
Laurence Harbor
Office: Amboy 124
Lawrenceville
Subsidiary: Brown 592
Leonia
Foundation: Quality 3097
Cororate Headquarters: Quality 3097
Livingston
Foundation: Education 1232
Cororate Headquarters: Formosa 1470
Subsidiary: CIT 819
Lumberton
Subsidiary: Robbins 3230
Lyndhurst
Corporate Giving Program: Citizen 822
Cororate Headquarters: Citizen 822
Subsidiary: Ralph 3123
Office: Ralph 3123
Madison
Corporate Giving Program: Quest 3103
Foundation: Quest 3103
Cororate Headquarters: Quest 3103
Mahwah
Corporate Giving Program: Sharp 3422
Corporate Headquarters: Howmedica 1875, Sharp 3422
Subsidiaries: AMETEK 181, Philips 2963
Manalapan
Office: Amboy 124
Marlton
Office: GATX 1542
Mauricetown
Plant: U.S. 3840
Maywood
Foundation: Jaclyn 2015
Cororate Headquarters: Jaclyn 2015
Medford
Foundation: J & S 2004
Cororate Headquarters: J & S 2004
Midland Park
Foundation: Atlantic 283
Cororate Headquarters: Atlantic 283
Subsidiary: ITT 1999
Millstone Township
Office: Amboy 124
Monroe
Office: Amboy 124
Monroe Township
Subsidiaries: Berry 438, O'Neal 2771
Montclair
Foundation: Pinnacle 2977
Cororate Headquarters: Pinnacle 2977
Montvale
Corporate Giving Programs: Food 1457, Great 1642, Mercedes 2463, Moore 2565, Pathmark 2894, Super 3656
Foundations: KPMG 2190, Moore 2565
Cororate Headquarters: Food 1457, Great 1642, Ingersoll 1939, Mercedes 2463, Moore 2565, Super 3656
Subsidiaries: Berkshire 429, Great 1642, Merck 2466
Moorestown
Subsidiaries: Harleysville 1733, Masco 2393
Division: American 133
Morristown
Corporate Giving Programs: Honeywell 1852, Porzio 3013, Riker 3215
Foundations: EMD 1256, Provident 3069, Seton 3415
Cororate Headquarters: Honeywell 1852, Porzio 3013, Riker 3215
Subsidiaries: Colgate 869, Jacobs 2016, SAIC 3311
Divisions: Alcatel 81, Bayer 382
Offices: Hays 1761, Porzio 3013, Riker 3215, SAP 3334
Plant: Colgate 869
Mount Arlington
Office: ITA 1998
Mount Laurel
Plants: Giant 1573, Navistar 2647
Mountain Lakes
Plant: Deluxe 1084
Mountainside
Foundation: Hensyn 1782
Cororate Headquarters: Hensyn 1782
Murray Hill
Corporate Giving Program: Alcatel 81
Foundations: Alcatel 81, Bard 358
Cororate Headquarters: Alcatel 81, Bard 358
Subsidiary: Bard 358
Division: Bard 358
Office: Hilliard 1806
Nassau Park
Office: Bristol 578
National Park
Plant: Public 3077
New Brunswick
Corporate Giving Program: Johnson 2048
Foundations: Johnson 2048, Magyar 2341
Cororate Headquarters: Johnson 2048, Magyar 2341
Subsidiary: Johnson 2048
Offices: Amboy 124, Bristol 578
New Providence
Corporate Giving Program: Bard 358
Newark
Corporate Giving Programs: Gibbons 1574, Horizon 1863, IDT 1911, New Jersey 2676, Prudential 3072, Public 3077, Sills 3456
Foundations: Edison 1229, Horizon 1863, IDT 1910, Pharmaceutical 2955, Pro 3052, Prudential 3072, Public 3077
Cororate Headquarters: Diversityinc 1131, Edison 1229, Gibbons 1574, Horizon 1863, IDT 1910, IDT 1911, New Jersey 2676, Pharmaceutical 2955, Prudential 3072, Public 3077, Schiffenhaus 3351, Sills 3456
Subsidiaries: Amazon.com 122, Delaware 1066, Schiffenhaus 3351, Verizon 3936
Offices: Duane 1185, Friedman 1504, Herrick 1789, K&L 2080, Kasowitz 2099, Latham 2228, Littler 2289, Mound 2587, Olshan 2803, Patton 2898, Proskauer 3064, Sedgwick 3395, Sills 3456, Skadden 3470, Thompson 3739, Winston 4089
Plant: LyondellBasell 2322
Newfield
Plants: Bausch 376, Charles 764
Newport
Plant: U.S. 3840
North Bergen
Plant: Fifth 1376
North Brunswick
Plant: Pactiv 2863
Nutley
Corporate Giving Program: Hoffmann 1823
Cororate Headquarters: Hoffmann 1823
Oakhurst
Office: Amboy 124
Oakland
Subsidiary: DRS 1179
Ocean City
Foundation: Ocean 2781
Cororate Headquarters: Ocean 2781
Old Bridge
Foundation: Amboy 124
Cororate Headquarters: Amboy 124
Office: Amboy 124
Ozone Park
Subsidiary: Key 2135
Paramus
Corporate Giving Program: Hudson 1880
Foundation: Hudson 1880
Cororate Headquarters: Hudson 1880
Subsidiaries: Fuji 1514, Harsco 1741, Macy's 2333
Office: White 4059
Park Ridge
Corporate Giving Program: Hertz 1792
Cororate Headquarters: Hertz 1792
Parsippany
Corporate Giving Programs: Avis 300, Budget 604, Reckitt 3146, Vision 3961, Watson 4007, Wyndham 4132
Foundations: Avis 299, Delta 1075, DRS 1179, Realogy 3145
Corporate Headquarters: Avis 299, Avis 300, Budget 604, Delta 1075, DRS 1179, Realogy 3145, Reckitt 3146, Wyndham 4132
Subsidiaries: Avis 299, Biomet 466, Chubb 804, New York 2688
Division: Alcatel 81
Offices: Day 1046, Grant 1633, Kelley 2118, State 3591, Vision 3961
Plant: Owens 2842
Paterson
Plant: Morton 2579
Paulsboro
Plants: Clorox 852, Nalco 2613
Peapack
Subsidiary: Pfizer 2950
Pedricktown
Foundation: Berkowitz 427
Cororate Headquarters: Berkowitz 427
Plant: Lubrizol 2315
Pilesgrove
Foundation: Nasdaq 2618
Pine Brook
Foundation: Westport 4050
Cororate Headquarters: Westport 4050
Piscataway
Foundations: Ingersoll 1939, Roma 3255, Trane 3794
Cororate Headquarters: Roma 3255, Trane 3794
Subsidiaries: Colgate 869, Ingersoll 1939, Johnson 2048, Performance 2938, Philips 2963
Plants: Illinois 1916, Schulman 3361
Plainsboro
Cororate Headquarters: Integra 1947
Office: Bristol 578
Pleasantville
Cororate Headquarters: Atlantic 281
Point Pleasant
Office: Mercury 2469
Port Elizabeth
Plant: U.S. 3840
Port Monmouth
Office: Amboy 124
Princeton
Corporate Giving Program: NRG 2756
Foundations: Covance 955, Diversityinc 1131, Scott 3370
Corporate Headquarters: Covance 955, NRG 2756
Subsidiaries: Bristol 578, Danaher 1027, NEC 2654, Pacific 2855
Offices: Archer 232, Dechert 1058, Drinker 1175, Duane 1185, Herrick 1789, Morgan 2571, Pepper 2934, Porzio 3013, Reed 3163, Sills 3456, State 3592
Plants: CA 638, FMC 1449
Rahway
Plant: Merck 2466
Raritan
Subsidiary: Johnson 2048
Red Bank
Office: Amboy 124
Ridgefield
Plant: Public 3077
Ridgefield Park
Corporate Giving Program: Samsung 3320
Cororate Headquarters: Samsung 3320
Ringoes
Foundation: Reagent 3143
Cororate Headquarters: Reagent 3143
Riverton
Subsidiary: GKN 1585
Rockaway
Plants: Dreyer's 1174, Hewlett 1794
Rockleigh
Subsidiary: Ford 1464

Rocky Hill
Office: Amboy 124
Roseland
Foundations: Automatic 291, Rothstein 3271
Corporate Headquarters: Automatic 291, Cohn 866, Rothstein 3271
Offices: AT&T 274, Gleacher 1589
Saddle Brook
Subsidiary: Masco 2393
Plant: Interface 1953
Saddle River
Subsidiary: Orange 2822
Sayreville
Office: Amboy 124
Secaucus
Corporate Giving Programs: Goya 1622, Hartz 1744, NYK 2768, Panasonic 2869
Foundations: Daffy's 1019, Kenneth 2128, Panasonic 2869
Corporate Headquarters: Anschutz 205, Daffy's 1019, Goya 1622, Hartz 1744, NYK 2768, Panasonic 2869
Office: Fisher 1433
Sewell
Foundation: Rennoc 3184
Short Hills
Foundation: Investors 1984
Corporate Headquarters: Dun 1190, Investors 1984
Subsidiaries: Chubb 804, Franklin 1487, Investors 1984
Sicklerville
Plant: Giant 1573
Skillman
Corporate Giving Program: ConvaTec 932
Cororate Headquarters: ConvaTec 932
Subsidiary: Johnson 2048
Somerset
Subsidiaries: Danaher 1027, Philips 2963
Offices: Mazda 2414, Whiting 4063, Wiley 4072
Plant: Mary 2392
Somerville
Subsidiary: Johnson 2048
South Amboy
Corporate Giving Program: DCH 1048
Cororate Headquarters: DCH 1048
Office: Amboy 124
South Brunswick
Plants: International 1962, Menasha 2461, Procter 3055
South Hackensack
Foundation: Alsan 114
Corporate Headquarters: Alsan 114, Josephson 2066
South Plainfield
Foundation: Jesco 2040
Subsidiary: Wrigley 4125
Division: Air 62
Plant: Campbell 669
Summit
Corporate Giving Program: Celgene 732
Cororate Headquarters: Celgene 732
Teaneck
Cororate Headquarters: United 3871
Tenafly
Subsidiary: Colgate 869
Thorofare
Subsidiary: CSS 996
Titusville
Corporate Giving Program: Janssen 2023
Cororate Headquarters: Janssen 2023
Subsidiary: Johnson 2048
Toms River
Foundation: OceanFirst 2782
Cororate Headquarters: OceanFirst 2782
Subsidiary: OceanFirst 2782
Totowa
Foundations: BC 387, Capezio 675
Corporate Headquarters: BC 387, Capezio 675
Plant: Sealed 3381
Township of Washington
Plant: Giant 1573
Trenton
Foundation: Rue 3285
Subsidiaries: American 133, PerkinElmer 2939
Offices: Gibbons 1574, Riker 3215
Union
Corporate Giving Program: Bed 399
Cororate Headquarters: Bed 399
Subsidiaries: Caparo 673, Comcast 887
Union Beach
Plant: International 1962
Upper Saddle River
Corporate Giving Program: Pearson 2911
Cororate Headquarters: Pearson 2911
Vineland
Cororate Headquarters: Rennoc 3184
Plants: Birds 469, General 1554
Voorhees
Office: CDW 729
Warren
Corporate Giving Program: Chubb 804
Cororate Headquarters: Chubb 804
Subsidiaries: Chubb 804, Johnson 2048
Washington
Corporate Giving Program: Herbalist 1783
Cororate Headquarters: Herbalist 1783
Wayne
Corporate Giving Program: Valley 3916
Foundations: Bayer 382, Toys 3790, Valley 3916
Corporate Headquarters: Bayer 382, Toys 3790, Valley 3916
Subsidiaries: Bayer 381, Valley 3916
Office: State 3591
West Caldwell
Corporate Giving Program: Ricoh 3210
Foundation: Reitman 3181
Corporate Headquarters: Reitman 3181, Ricoh 3210
West Trenton
Foundation: Homasote 1841
Cororate Headquarters: Homasote 1841
Westwood
Corporate Giving Program: BMW 509
Whitehouse Station
Corporate Giving Program: Merck 2466
Foundation: Merck 2466
Cororate Headquarters: Merck 2466
Windsor
Subsidiary: Fulton 1518
Wood Ridge
Plant: Carpenter 700
Woodbine
Subsidiary: U.S. 3840
Woodbridge
Corporate Giving Program: Wilentz 4071
Foundation: Bessemer 440
Cororate Headquarters: Wilentz 4071
Subsidiary: Hess 1793
Offices: Amboy 124, Bessemer 440, Wilentz 4071
Plant: Public 3077
Woodbury
Subsidiary: Fulton 1518
Woodcliff Lake
Cororate Headquarters: BMW 509
Woodland Park
Cororate Headquarters: North 2733
Woodstown
Subsidiary: Fulton 1518

NEW MEXICO

Albuerque
Plant: Owens 2841
Albuquerque
Corporate Giving Program: Summit 3641
Foundations: Berkshire 429, Jalapeno 2018, Public 3076
Corporate Headquarters: Abba 11, Jalapeno 2018, Public 3076, Summit 3641
Subsidiaries: Arctic 234, Hubbard 1877, Lockheed 2292, PerkinElmer 2939, Preformed 3032, Public 3076
Offices: Brownstein 593, Federal 1349, Kiewit 2142, Lewis 2256, Littler 2289
Plants: General 1554, SUMCO 3638, Thermo 3733
Artesia
Foundations: Central 747, Chase 770, Penasco 2920
Corporate Headquarters: Central 747, Chase 770, Penasco 2920
Subsidiary: Penasco 2920
Office: Fishel 1429
Clayton
Foundation: Southwestern 3525
Cororate Headquarters: Southwestern 3525
Clovis
Corporate Giving Program: Eastern 1211
Foundations: Eastern 1211, Farmers' 1337
Corporate Headquarters: Eastern 1211, Farmers' 1337
Subsidiary: Eastern 1211
Deming
Foundation: Columbus 885
Cororate Headquarters: Columbus 885
Elephant Butte
Foundation: Sierra 3450
Cororate Headquarters: Sierra 3450
Espanola
Foundation: Jemez 2034
Grants
Foundation: Continental 923
Cororate Headquarters: Continental 923
Hernandez
Cororate Headquarters: Jemez 2034
Hobbs
Foundations: Leaco 2236, Me-Tex 2442
Corporate Headquarters: Leaco 2236, Me-Tex 2442
Office: Leaco 2236
Las Cruces
Offices: Fishel 1429, GATX 1542
Los Alamos
Office: Abba 11
Lovington
Foundation: Lea 2235
Cororate Headquarters: Lea 2235
Moriarty
Cororate Headquarters: Central 744
Mountainair
Foundation: Central 744
Portales
Foundations: Roosevelt 3258, Roosevelt 3259
Corporate Headquarters: Roosevelt 3258, Roosevelt 3259
Subsidiary: Roosevelt 3259
Rio Rancho
Office: Applied 220
Plant: Intel 1950
Santa Fe
Corporate Giving Program: Social 3493
Foundations: Mariah 2373, Santa 3331
Corporate Headquarters: Mariah 2373, Santa 3331, Social 3493
Subsidiary: Pedernales 2914
Division: Genzyme 1566
Offices: Brownstein 593, Cozen 964, Holland 1833
Socorro
Foundation: Socorro 3496
Cororate Headquarters: Socorro 3496
Plant: GenCorp 1548
Springer
Foundation: Springer 3553
Cororate Headquarters: Springer 3553
Taos
Foundation: Carson 705
Cororate Headquarters: Carson 705

Tatum
Office: Leaco 2236
White Sands
Plant: Raytheon 3135

NEW YORK

Albany
Corporate Giving Programs: Callanan 659, McNamee 2438, Whiteman 4061
Foundation: New York 2681
Corporate Headquarters: Callanan 659, McNamee 2438, New York 2681, Whiteman 4061
Subsidiaries: Gleacher 1589, Securian 3389
Offices: Boises 518, Bond 522, Drinker 1175, GATX 1542, Gleacher 1589, Greenberg 1654, Hodgson 1820, KeyBank 2136, McKenna 2433, McNamee 2438, Whiteman 4061
Plant: Public 3077
Alton
Plant: Birds 469
Amherst
Corporate Giving Program: Taiyo 3681
Foundations: Davis 1037, Mark 2377
Corporate Headquarters: Davis 1037, Mark 2377, Taiyo 3681
Subsidiaries: Danaher 1027, Fiserv 1427
Office: Rose 3261
Amsterdam
Corporate Giving Program: Beech-Nut 400
Cororate Headquarters: Beech-Nut 400
Angola
Subsidiary: Goya 1622
Division: Flowserve 1447
Armonk
Corporate Giving Program: International 1960
Foundations: International 1960, MBIA 2416
Corporate Headquarters: International 1960, MBIA 2416
Subsidiary: VHA 3944
Office: Boises 518
Astoria
Cororate Headquarters: Astoria 270
Auburn
Subsidiary: Nucor 2760
Baldwin
Division: New York 2683
Baldwinsville
Office: Univar 3886
Plant: Goulds 1619
Ballston Spa
Office: State 3591
Barker
Plant: Birds 469
Beacon
Office: Rose 3261
Bellerose
Subsidiary: Key 2135
Bergen
Plant: Birds 469
Bethpage
Corporate Giving Programs: Bethpage 446, Cablevision 641, King 2159
Foundation: Cablevision 641
Corporate Headquarters: Bethpage 446, Cablevision 641, King 2159
Division: Northrop 2744
Big Flats
Plant: Corning 945
Binghamton
Foundation: Vista 3963
Cororate Headquarters: Vista 3963
Brewster
Subsidiary: Hubbell 1879
Briarcliff Manor
Subsidiary: Philips 2963
Brockport
Plant: Birds 469
Bronx
Corporate Giving Programs: Affinity 52, New York 2691
Foundation: New York 2691
Corporate Headquarters: Affinity 52, Manhattan 2354, New York 2691
Brooklyn
Corporate Giving Programs: Brooklyn 584, UncommonGoods 3849
Foundations: Brooklyn 584, Elizabeth 1250, Hudson 1882, Lighting 2273, Paterson 2893, Priceless 3041, Prime 3044, Ramallah 3124, Shalam 3420, Simpson 3460, Syre 3676, World 4119
Corporate Headquarters: Brooklyn 584, Hudson 1882, Lighting 2273, Paterson 2893, Priceless 3041, Prime 3044, Ramallah 3124, Scientific 3367, Simpson 3460, Syre 3676, UncommonGoods 3849, World 4119
Subsidiaries: National 2630, Occidental 2780
Buffalo
Corporate Giving Programs: Delaware 1066, Hockey 1819, Hodgson 1820, New 2673, Outokumpu 2839, Rich 3204, Tops 3774
Foundations: Ferguson 1363, First 1419, M&T 2323, Rich 3204, Righteous 3214, Tripifoods 3811
Corporate Headquarters: Delaware 1066, Ferguson 1363, First 1419, Hockey 1819, Hodgson 1820, M&T 2323, New 2673, Outokumpu 2839, Rich 3204, Righteous 3214, Tripifoods 3811
Subsidiaries: AMPCO 186, Berkshire 429, Bristol 578, Delaware 1066, Ferguson 1363, Gear 1544, National 2628
Division: Mead 2443
Offices: Bond 522, Federal 1349, Hodgson 1820, Ingram 1941, KeyBank 2136
Plants: DRS 1179, FMC 1449, General 1554, Georgia 1568, Hospira 1867, Pactiv 2863, Scott 3370
Canastota
Cororate Headquarters: Diemolding 1113
Canton
Plant: Corning 945
Catskill
Foundation: Bank 341
Cororate Headquarters: Bank 341
Centerport
Foundation: Hall 1702
Cororate Headquarters: Hall 1702
Chatham
Corporate Giving Program: davistudio 1043
Cororate Headquarters: davistudio 1043
Clifton Park
Office: McNamee 2438
Clinton
Cororate Headquarters: Indium 1933
Cohoes
Foundation: First 1419
Corning
Foundation: Corning 945
Cororate Headquarters: Corning 945
Subsidiary: Corning 945
Delhi
Foundation: Fulton 1518
Delmar
Plant: Owens 2842
Depew
Foundation: Hunt 1890
East Aurora
Foundation: Greene 1656
Cororate Headquarters: Greene 1656
Subsidiary: Mattel 2405
East Greenbush
Foundation: Rose 3261
Cororate Headquarters: Rose 3261
East Rochester
Office: Holtz 1840
East Syracuse
Subsidiary: Chubb 804
East Williamson
Plant: Seneca 3406
Ellicottville
Foundation: Stride 3626
Subsidiary: Stride 3626
Elma
Plant: Motorola 2586
Elmira
Foundations: Hardinge 1729, Hilliard 1805, Howell 1874, Panosian 2874
Corporate Headquarters: Hardinge 1729, Hilliard 1805, Howell 1874, Panosian 2874
Elmsford
Subsidiary: Baker 323
Division: Fuji 1514
Fairport
Subsidiary: Corning 945
Plant: CA 638
Farmingdale
Foundations: Posillico 3014, Richard 3205
Corporate Headquarters: Posillico 3014, Richard 3205
Fishkill
Foundation: Brinckerhoff 570
Cororate Headquarters: Brinckerhoff 570
Flushing
Foundations: Crystal 992, Kepco 2132, Sterling 3601
Corporate Headquarters: Crystal 992, Kepco 2132, Sterling 3601
Fort Edward
Subsidiary: United 3871
Fresh Meadows
Cororate Headquarters: West 4036
Fulton
Plants: Armstrong 246, Huhtamaki 1884
Fultonville
Subsidiary: Danaher 1027
Garden City
Subsidiary: Bertelsmann 439
Offices: Bond 522, Mound 2587
Geneva
Plant: Seneca 3406
Glencoe
Plant: Seneca 3406
Glendale
Foundation: Hemmerdinger 1775
Cororate Headquarters: Hemmerdinger 1775
Glens Falls
Office: Rose 3261
Plant: Bard 358
Gouverneur
Foundation: Kinney 2162
Cororate Headquarters: Kinney 2162
Grand Island
Subsidiary: Mark 2377
Granite Springs
Foundation: Klein 2166
Great Neck
Corporate Giving Program: North 2736
Foundation: Black 475
Corporate Headquarters: Black 475, North 2736
Greene
Foundation: Raymond 3133
Cororate Headquarters: Raymond 3133
Subsidiary: Raymond 3133
Greenvale
Foundation: Slant 3477
Cororate Headquarters: Slant 3477
Hamburg
Subsidiary: Raymond 3133
Hammondsport
Foundation: Mercury 2468
Cororate Headquarters: Mercury 2468
Hastings on Hudson
Foundation: West 4036
Hauppauge
Foundation: Madison 2335
Cororate Headquarters: Barron's 364
Subsidiary: Rock 3239
Plants: Bausch 376, Verby 3934
Hawthorne
Office: Tutor 3826
Hempstead
Foundation: Dan's 1025
Corporate Headquarters: Dan's 1025, New York 2687
Subsidiary: Key 2135

Hewlett
Foundation: Associated 262
Cororate Headquarters: Associated 262
Hewlett Harbor
Foundation: Verby 3934
Hicksville
Foundations: Econoco 1222, National 2630
Corporate Headquarters: Chesapeake 778, Econoco 1222
Holbrook
Plant: Verby 3934
Honeoye Falls
Plant: Emerson 1257
Hopewell Junction
Office: Applied 220
Horseheads
Plant: Corning 945
Hudson
Foundation: First 1419
Huntington Station
Foundation: Klein 2170
Cororate Headquarters: Klein 2170
Inwood
Foundation: Apex 212
Cororate Headquarters: Apex 212
Subsidiary: Avnet 304
Irvington
Corporate Giving Program: Fisher 1433
Cororate Headquarters: Fisher 1433
Office: Fisher 1433
Islandia
Corporate Giving Program: CA 638
Cororate Headquarters: CA 638
Ithaca
Corporate Giving Program: Singlebrook 3464
Cororate Headquarters: Singlebrook 3464
Offices: Autodesk 289, Bond 522
Plant: Emerson 1257
Jamaica
Corporate Giving Program: Pratt 3028
Cororate Headquarters: Verby 3934
Subsidiaries: Global 1592, Sumitomo 3639
Jamestown
Plant: Cummins 1007
Jericho
Corporate Giving Program: AMC 126
Foundation: Villency 3955
Cororate Headquarters: Villency 3955
Johnson City
Office: Rose 3261
Johnstown
Cororate Headquarters: FDI 1346
Office: Hodgson 1820
Kings Point
Foundation: Scientific 3367
Kingston
Office: Rose 3261
Lake Success
Corporate Giving Programs: Astoria 271, Canon 672
Corporate Headquarters: Astoria 271, Canon 672
Office: Hays 1761
Latham
Foundation: Goldman 1603
Le Roy
Plant: Seneca 3406
Leicester
Plant: Seneca 3406
Leroy
Foundation: Birds 469
Little Falls
Cororate Headquarters: Redco 3155
Lockport
Subsidiary: Harsco 1741
Plant: Allegheny 91
Long Island City
Corporate Giving Program: JetBlue 2041
Foundation: Citigroup 821
Corporate Headquarters: JetBlue 2041, Standard 3575
Subsidiary: Berkshire 429
Lynbrook
Subsidiary: Mutual 2607
Mamaroneck
Foundation: Titan 3763
Manhasset
Foundations: Royalnest 3277, United 3863
Corporate Headquarters: Royalnest 3277, United 3863
Manlius
Subsidiary: Philips 2963
Plant: Crystal 992
Marion
Foundation: Seneca 3406
Cororate Headquarters: Seneca 3406
Plant: Seneca 3406
Massena
Plant: Alcoa 82
Maybrook
Plant: Osram 2834
Medina
Plant: Newell 2694
Melville
Corporate Giving Programs: Arrow 249, MSC 2593, Schein 3348
Foundations: Leviton 2255, Schein 3348
Corporate Headquarters: Arrow 249, Leviton 2255, Madison 2335, Marchon 2369, MSC 2593, Nikon 2711, Schein 3348
Subsidiary: NEC 2654
Offices: Grant 1633, Littler 2289
Mexico
Foundation: Grandma 1630
Cororate Headquarters: Grandma 1630
Middleport
Plant: FMC 1449
Monroe
Cororate Headquarters: Reliable 3182
Monsey
Foundation: Klein 2167
Montebello
Foundation: Provident 3070
Cororate Headquarters: Provident 3070
Montgomery
Office: Do 1136
Monticello
Corporate Giving Program: Empire 1261
Cororate Headquarters: Empire 1261
Mount Kisco
Subsidiary: Brown 592
Mount Vernon
Subsidiary: Granite 1632
New Berlin
Foundation: GOLDEN 1600
Corporate Headquarters: GOLDEN 1600, Preferred 3031
New Hartford
Cororate Headquarters: Utica 3910
Subsidiary: Utica 3910
New Hyde Park
Subsidiary: Wendy's/Arby's 4030
New Paltz
Corporate Giving Program: CSRHUB 994
Cororate Headquarters: CSRHUB 994
New Rochelle
Corporate Giving Program: Frank 1482
Cororate Headquarters: Frank 1482
New York
Corporate Giving Programs: Accenture 22, Alcoa 82, Allen 93, Allen 94, AllianceBernstein 102, Ambac 123, American 143, American 156, AOL 209, Assurant 266, Axinn 308, Bank 344, Barclays 357, Barnes 360, Bloomberg 486, Bloomingdale's 488, Boises 518, Bristol 578, Cable 639, Cadwalader 649, Cahill 651, Carter 707, Carver 711, Catchafire 721, Chadbourne 759, CIT 819, Citigroup 821, Cleary 843, Coach 858, Colgate 869, Consolidated 916, Coty 950, Curtis 1010, Daiwa 1020, Davies 1036, Davis 1040, Debevoise 1055, Deloitte 1070, Deutsche 1099, Diamonds 1109, Dow 1163, Fast 1343, Fitzpatrick 1434, Foot 1459, Fox 1480, Freshfields 1500, Fried 1502, Friedman 1504, Frommer 1507, FXDD 1522, Godiva 1597, Goldman 1603, Guardian 1683, Havana 1751, Henry 1781, Herrick 1789, Hess 1793, HSBC 1876, Interpublic 1974, iVillage 2002, Jefferies 2030, Kasowitz 2099, Kelley 2118, Kenyon 2131, Kors 2186, Kramer 2191, L'Oreal 2203, Latham 2228, Lauder 2230, Let 2253, Linklaters 2283, Loews 2296, Madison 2336, Major 2345, Major 2347, Marsh 2385, McGraw 2429, Metropolitan 2481, Mikimoto 2510, Milbank 2511, Mitsubishi 2539, Monster 2560, Moody's 2564, Morgan 2570, Mound 2587, MTV 2596, National 2623, NBC 2649, New York 2688, News 2700, Newsweek 2703, NYSE 2769, Ogilvy 2788, Olshan 2803, Omnicom 2808, OppenheimerFunds 2818, Patterson 2895, Paul 2901, Penguin 2922, Pfizer 2950, Philip 2962, Pillsbury 2975, Plum 2992, PricewaterhouseCoopers 3042, Proskauer 3064, Pryor 3073, PVH 3088, RecycleBank 3151, RGI 3202, Satterlee 3339, Scholastic 3358, Schulte 3362, Seward 3417, Shearman 3429, Simpson 3462, Skadden 3470, Tiffany 3750, Time 3755, Time 3757, Toshiba 3776, Town 3783, Toyota 3788, Turner 3824, UBS 3842, Viacom 3945, Wachtell 3973, Weil 4023, White 4058, Willkie 4081
Foundations: A.J. 8, ABC 16, Aeropostale 46, Almar 110, American 143, American 156, American 163, Amnews 185, Assurant 266, Avon 305, AXA 307, Bank 347, Barber 356, Bertelsmann 439, Blackstone 477, Bristol 578, Brown 589, Candlesticks 670, Caparo 673, Carver 711, CBS 727, Century 748, Chadbourne 759, Chase 769, Clifford 849, Coach 858, Continental 926, Credit 980, Cutie 1013, Daiwa 1020, Deerfield 1062, Deutsche 1099, Duane 1186, Dun 1190, Edsim 1230, Ernst 1293, Fashion 1342, Fifth 1376, Fisher 1431, Foot 1459, Franshaw 1489, Fujisankei 1515, GJF 1584, Gleacher 1589, Goldman 1603, Goldman 1604, Guardian 1683, Gucci 1684, Hilfiger 1801, IAC 1903, Indus 1934, International 1961, International 1962, Iwo 2003, Jai 2017, Jordache 2062, Josephson 2066, JPMorgan Chase 2071, Juno 2076, Koller 2183, Kreindler 2193, Lodz 2294, Loews 2296, Mac 2328, Madison 2336, Major 2345, Major 2346, Manocherian 2357, Marnier-Lapostolle 2381, Massey 2398, McGraw 2429, Metropolitan 2481, Milliken 2525, Mitsubishi 2539, Mitsui 2541, Mizuho 2542, Moody's 2563, Morgan 2570, MTV 2596, Mutual 2605, National 2624, National 2626, National 2631, Natori 2640, NBC 2649, Needham 2655, New 2689, New York 2685, New York 2688, New York 2690, Nikon 2711, Nippon 2713, Nomura 2720, Novartis 2752, NYSE 2769, Odyssey 2784, Ogilvy 2788, Optima 2819, Orleans 2825, Pearson 2912, Pfizer 2950, PricewaterhouseCoopers 3042, Public 3078, PVH 3088, Ralph 3123, Ramerica 3125, Renovated 3185, Ripplewood 3219, Roberts 3231, Rodgers 3250, Rothschild 3270, Ruder 3282, Ruradan 3287, Saks 3315, Sansar 3330, SBH 3345, Schloss 3352, Select 3398, Self 3400, Shanken 3421, SMBC 3480, Sony 3502, Star 3583, Stewart 3604, Sullivan 3634, Sumitomo 3639, Sunrise 3652, Teitler 3705, Ten 3712, Thompson 3739, Thomson 3741, Tiffany 3750, Time 3757, Toshiba 3776, Towerbrook 3781, Toyota 3784, Trans 3795, Transammonia 3796, Turner 3824, Victorinox 3950, Wachtell 3973, Warburg 3985, Warner 3990, Weil 4022, Woori 4114, World 4122, Zilkha 4156, Zurich 4160
Corporate Headquarters: A.J. 8, ABC 16, Accenture 22, Aeropostale 46, Alcoa 82, Allen 93, Allen 94, AllianceBernstein 102, Almar 110, Ambac 123, AMC 126, American 143, American 156, American 163, Amnews 185, AOL 209, Apple 218, Assurant 266, Avon 305, AXA 307, Axinn 308, Bank 344, Bank 347, Barber 356, Barclays 357, Barnes 360, Bertelsmann 439, Bessemer 440, Blackstone 477, Bloomberg 486, Bloomingdale's 488, Boises 518, Bristol 578, Brown 589, Cadwalader 649, Cahill 651, Candlesticks 670, Carter 707, Carver 711, Catchafire 721, CBS 727, Celebrity 731, Century

748, Chadbourne 759, Chase 769, CIT 819, Citigroup 821, Cleary 843, Clifford 849, Coach 858, Colgate 869, Consolidated 916, Continental 926, Coty 950, Credit 980, Curtis 1010, Cutie 1013, Daiwa 1020, Davies 1036, Davis 1040, Debevoise 1055, Deerfield 1062, Dekker 1064, Deloitte 1070, Deutsche 1099, Diamonds 1109, Dow 1163, Duane 1186, Edsim 1230, Ernst 1293, Fashion 1342, Fast 1343, Fifth 1376, Fisher 1431, Fitzpatrick 1434, Foot 1459, Fox 1480, Franshaw 1489, Freshfields 1500, Fried 1502, Friedman 1504, Frommer 1507, Fujisankei 1515, FXDD 1522, GJF 1584, Gleacher 1589, Godiva 1597, Goldman 1603, Goldman 1604, Good 1609, Greystone 1665, Guardian 1683, Gucci 1684, Hachette 1696, Havana 1751, Henry 1781, Herrick 1789, Hess 1793, Hilfiger 1801, Hilliard 1806, Hillside 1810, HSBC 1876, IAC 1903, Indus 1934, International 1961, International 1962, Interpublic 1974, iVillage 2002, Jai 2017, Jefferies 2030, Jones 2057, Jordache 2062, JPMorgan 2072, JPMorgan Chase 2071, Juno 2076, Kahn 2085, Kasowitz 2099, Kelley 2118, Kenneth 2128, Kenyon 2131, Klein 2166, Klein 2167, Koller 2183, Kors 2186, KPMG 2190, Kramer 2191, Kreindler 2193, L'Oreal 2203, Latham 2228, Lauder 2230, Let 2253, Linklaters 2283, Lodz 2294, Loews 2296, Lord 2302, Mac 2328, Madison 2336, Major 2345, Major 2346, Major 2347, Mamiye 2352, Manocherian 2357, Marnier-Lapostolle 2381, Marsh 2385, Massey 2398, McGraw 2429, Metropolitan 2481, Mikimoto 2510, Milbank 2511, Mitsubishi 2539, Mitsui 2541, Mizuho 2542, Monster 2560, Moody's 2563, Moody's 2564, Morgan 2570, Mound 2587, MTV 2596, Mutual 2605, Nasdaq 2617, National 2623, National 2624, National 2626, National 2631, Natori 2640, NBC 2649, Needham 2655, New 2689, New York 2685, New York 2688, New York 2690, News 2700, Newsweek 2703, Nippon 2713, Nomura 2720, Novartis 2752, NYSE 2769, Odyssey 2784, Ogilvy 2788, Olshan 2803, Omnicom 2808, OppenheimerFunds 2818, Optima 2819, Orleans 2825, Patterson 2895, Paul 2901, Pearson 2912, Penguin 2922, Pfizer 2950, Philip 2962, Pillsbury 2975, Plum 2992, PricewaterhouseCoopers 3042, Proskauer 3064, Public 3078, PVH 3088, Queen 3102, Ralph 3123, Ramerica 3125, Reader's 3141, RecycleBank 3151, Reed 3161, Renovated 3185, RGI 3202, Ripplewood 3219, Roberts 3231, Rodgers 3250, Rothschild 3270, Ruder 3282, Ruradan 3287, Saks 3315, Sansar 3330, Satterlee 3339, SBH 3345, Schloss 3352, Schneider 3354, Scholastic 3358, Schulte 3362, Select 3398, Self 3400, Seward 3417, Shalam 3420, Shanken 3421, Shearman 3429, Siemens 3448, Simpson 3462, Skadden 3470, SMBC 3480, Sony 3502, Stadtmauer 3570, Stewart 3604, Sullivan 3634, Sumitomo 3639, Sunrise 3652, Teitler 3705, Ten 3712, Thompson 3739, Thomson 3741, Tiffany 3750, Time 3755, Time 3757, Titan 3763, Toshiba 3776, Towerbrook 3781, Town 3783, Toyota 3788, Trans 3795, Transammonia 3796, Travelers 3802, Turner 3824, UBS 3842, Verizon 3936, Viacom 3945, Wachtell 3973, Warburg 3985, Warnaco 3988, Warner 3990, Weil 4022, Weil 4023, White 4058, Willkie 4081, Woori 4114, World 4122, Zilkha 4156, Zurich 4160

Subsidiaries: Ambac 123, American 143, American 147, AOL 209, Arbitron 227, Avery 297, Avnet 304, Bank 340, Bank 344, Barnes 360, Bertelsmann 439, Brown 589, Cablevision 641, Canon 672, CBS 727, Chubb 804, CIT 819, Citigroup 821, CLARCOR 832, CNO 857, Colgate 869, Comcast 887, Deutsche 1099, Discovery 1126, Disney 1127, Eastman 1214, Evening 1302, Federated 1351, Financial 1382, First 1400, General 1552, Goldman 1603, Google 1613, Grace 1623, Grant 1633, Guardian 1683, IAC 1903, IDT 1910, Jacobs 2016, Jefferies 2030, Jones 2057, JPMorgan Chase 2071, Kellwood 2121, Kiplinger 2163, Klein 2166, Loews 2296, Macy's 2333, Manpower 2358, Marsh 2385, Massachusetts 2397, Mercedes 2463, Metropolitan 2481, Moody's 2563, Morgan 2570, NBC 2649, NEC 2654, New York 2688, New York 2690, Newmont 2698, Nippon 2713, NRG 2756, NYSE 2769, Omnicom 2808, Philips 2963, PVH 3088, Reader's 3141, Ripplewood 3219, Saks 3315, Scholastic 3358, Schwab 3363, Sony 3502, Time 3757, U.M. 3834, Unilever 3853, United 3871, V.F. 3913, Verizon 3936, Viacom 3945, Walgreen 3981, Washington 3999

Divisions: Hill 1803, L'Oreal 2203, Madison 2336, Mead 2443, MTV 2596, New York 2690

Offices: ACE 24, Acumen 33, Akerman 69, Akin 70, Allen 94, Alston 116, American 132, Andrews 198, Archer 232, Arent 235, Arnold 248, Avon 305, Baker 319, Baker 321, Bickel 457, Bingham 463, BMC 508, Boises 518, Bond 522, Bracewell 549, Bressler 557, Brown 590, Bryan 596, Butzel 629, C & C 633, Cadwalader 649, Cahill 651, Caplin 681, Carter 707, Clark 836, Cleary 843, Cole 868, Corning 945, Cozen 964, Crowell 986, Curtis 1010, Davies 1036, Davis 1041, Day 1046, Debevoise 1055, Dechert 1058, Dickstein 1111, Dorsey 1157, Drinker 1175, Duane 1185, Edelman 1224, Elevation 1245, Federal 1348, Federal 1349, Fish 1428, Fisher 1433, Fitzpatrick 1434, Foley 1453, Ford 1462, Fried 1502, Friedland 1503, Friedman 1504, Frommer 1507, Fulbright 1516, Garvey 1539, Getty 1569, Gibbons 1574, Good 1609, Goodwin 1611, Google 1613, Grant 1633, Haskell 1748, Haynes 1759, Heller 1773, Herrick 1789, Hill 1803, Hodgson 1820, Hogan 1825, Holland 1834, Houghton 1869, Intuit 1982, Jenner 2035, Jones 2058, K&L 2080, Kasowitz 2099, Katten 2101, Kearney 2107, Kelley 2118, Kenyon 2131, Kiewit 2142, King 2157, Kirkland 2164, Kramer 2191, Latham 2228, Liberty 2265, Linklaters 2283, Littler 2289, Loeb 2295, Mayer 2411, McDermott 2425, McGuireWoods 2430, McKenna 2433, Melissa 2458, Merchant 2464, Milbank 2511, Mintz 2534, Morgan 2571, Morrison 2576, Mound 2587, Olshan 2803, Orrick 2826, Patton 2898, Paul 2900, Paul 2901, Pepper 2934, Perkins 2941, Pillsbury 2975, Polsinelli 3001, Porzio 3013, Proskauer 3064, Pryor 3073, Quinn 3111, Reed 3163, Riker 3215, Robins 3233, Rogers 3252, Ropes 3260, Russell 3289, SAP 3334, SAS 3336, Satterlee 3339, Schiff 3350, Schulte 3362, Sedgwick 3395, Seward 3417, Shearman 3429, Sheppard 3435, Sidley 3446, Sills 3456, Simpson 3462, Skidmore 3474, State 3592, Steptoe 3599, Strauss 3624, Sullivan 3636, Sutherland 3663, Thompson 3740, Turner 3823, Union 3854, Unum 3898, Venable 3929, Vinson 3958, Wachtell 3973, Weil 4023, White 4058, White 4059, Wiggin 4068, Wilentz 4071, Wiley 4072, Willkie 4081, Wilson 4083, Winston 4089

Plants: adidas 35, Chevron 780, Crystal 992, Donnelley 1155, Fifth 1376, Interface 1953, Novell 2754, Oxford 2847, Quad 3091, TJX 3765, Warnaco 3988

Newark
Plant: Seneca 3406

Newburgh
Office: KeyBank 2136

Niagara Falls
Plants: Goodyear 1612, Olin 2801

North Tonawanda
Subsidiary: AMPCO 186

Norwich
Foundation: Preferred 3031

Nyack
Foundation: Parthenon 2889

Oakfield
Plant: Birds 469

Old Westbury
Foundation: Old 2799
Cororate Headquarters: Old 2799

Olean
Foundation: Cutco 1012
Cororate Headquarters: Cutco 1012

Oneida
Foundations: Diemolding 1113, Oneida 2814
Cororate Headquarters: Oneida 2814
Subsidiary: Oneida 2814
Plant: Hood 1854

Oneonta
Plant: Corning 945

Orangeburg
Foundation: Sequa 3410
Plant: Illinois 1916

Orchard Park
Corporate Giving Program: Buffalo 606
Cororate Headquarters: Buffalo 606

Ossining
Foundation: Warren 3992
Cororate Headquarters: Warren 3992

Oswego
Office: Bond 522

Oyster Bay
Foundation: Barron's 364

Painted Post
Plant: Corning 945

Pearl River
Corporate Giving Programs: Hunter 1893, Orange 2822
Foundation: Hunter 1893
Cororate Headquarters: Hunter 1893, Orange 2822

Pelham Manor
Foundation: Hilliard 1806

Penn Yan
Office: Seneca 3406
Plant: Ferro 1366

Phelps
Subsidiary: PerkinElmer 2939

Pittsford
Office: Rose 3261
Plant: Novell 2754

Plattsburgh
Offices: Rose 3261, Whiteman 4061

Pleasantville
Corporate Giving Program: Reader's 3141
Subsidiary: Reader's 3141
Office: White 4059

Port Henry
Office: Rose 3261

Port Washington
Foundation: Palm 2867
Plant: Charles 764

Potsdam
Office: Rose 3261

Pottersville
Foundation: Natural 2643
Cororate Headquarters: Natural 2643

Poughkeepsie
Corporate Giving Program: CH 757
Cororate Headquarters: CH 757
Subsidiary: CH 757

Purchase
Corporate Giving Programs: MasterCard 2399, PepsiCo 2935, Pernod 2942
Foundations: Central 743, PepsiCo 2935
Corporate Headquarters: Central 743, MasterCard 2399, PepsiCo 2935, Pernod 2942
Subsidiaries: AEGON 45, MasterCard 2399, PepsiCo 2935
Office: State 3592

Red Creek
Plant: Birds 469

Ridgewood
Foundation: Ridgewood 3211
Cororate Headquarters: Ridgewood 3211

Rochester
Corporate Giving Programs: Eastman 1214, Frontier 1509, Paychex 2904, Rochester 3237, Wegmans 4021
Foundations: Bausch 376, Gleason 1591, Holtz 1840
Corporate Headquarters: Bausch 376, Birds 469, Eastman 1214, Frontier 1509, General 1557,

Gleason 1591, Holtz 1840, Paychex 2904, Rochester 3237, Wegmans 4021
Subsidiaries: Bausch 376, Eastman 1214, Frontier 1508, Gleason 1591, Johnson 2048
Division: Bausch 376
Offices: Bond 522, KeyBank 2136, Littler 2289, Safeco 3306, Thompson 3739
Plants: Golden 1602, Harris 1736

Rockville Centre
Plant: McAfee 2417

Ronkonkoma
Subsidiary: Danaher 1027

Roslyn
Foundation: New York 2683

Rye
Cororate Headquarters: Iwo 2003
Office: Avon 305

Rye Brook
Corporate Giving Program: Universal 3887
Subsidiary: Mondelez 2556

Saratoga Springs
Plant: Quad 3091

Saugerties
Division: PerkinElmer 2939

Scarsdale
Corporate Giving Program: Apple 218

Schenectady
Corporate Giving Program: Price 3039
Foundation: Golub 1607
Corporate Headquarters: Golub 1607, Price 3039
Subsidiaries: Golub 1607, Lockheed 2292
Division: General 1552

Scotia
Plant: Sealed 3381

Scottsville
Foundation: Ward 3986
Cororate Headquarters: Ward 3986

Seneca Falls
Cororate Headquarters: Goulds 1619
Subsidiary: ITT 1999

Silver Springs
Plant: Morton 2579

Slingerlands
Foundation: FDI 1346

Somers
Foundation: PepsiCo 2935

Somerset
Subsidiary: PepsiCo 2935

South Glens Falls
Plant: NIBCO 2707

Spring Valley
Foundations: Reliable 3182, Stadtmauer 3570

Staten Island
Foundations: Key 2135, New York 2683, Northfield 2741
Cororate Headquarters: Key 2135
Division: New York 2683

Stone Ridge
Plants: Bausch 376, Charles 764

Suffern
Foundation: Ascena 255
Cororate Headquarters: Ascena 255
Subsidiary: Schiffenhaus 3351
Office: Avon 305

Syosset
Cororate Headquarters: Star 3583

Syracuse
Corporate Giving Programs: Bond 522, Carrols 704, Hiscock 1815
Foundations: Gear 1544, PCI 2905, Syracuse 3675, Young 4146
Corporate Headquarters: Bond 522, Carrols 704, Gear 1544, Hiscock 1815, PCI 2905, Syracuse 3675, Young 4146
Subsidiaries: Carrols 704, Highmark 1799, Lincoln 2281, Susquehanna 3661
Offices: Bond 522, KeyBank 2136, Telligen 3710
Plants: Barnes 362, Deluxe 1084

Tarrytown
Corporate Giving Program: Hitachi 1816
Corporate Headquarters: Hitachi 1816
Subsidiary: sanofi-aventis 3329
Division: Bayer 382

Ticonderoga
Plant: International 1968

Tonawanda
Foundation: Danforth 1028
Corporate Headquarters: Danforth 1028
Plants: Alro 113, Univar 3886

Uniondale
Corporate Giving Program: New York 2686
Corporate Headquarters: New York 2686

Utica
Foundations: Bank 348, Indium 1933, Utica 3910
Corporate Headquarters: Bank 348
Subsidiary: Utica 3910
Office: Bond 522

Valhalla
Corporate Giving Program: Fuji 1514
Corporate Headquarters: Fuji 1514

Vernon
Plant: Hood 1854

Vestal
Foundation: Dick's 1110

Victor
Corporate Giving Program: Constellation 919
Corporate Headquarters: Constellation 919

Voorheesville
Subsidiary: Raymond 3133

Warwick
Foundation: Provident 3070
Office: Mercury 2469

Waterloo
Subsidiary: Scotts 3372

Watertown
Subsidiary: Harleysville 1733
Office: Rose 3261

Watervliet
Subsidiary: Hunter 1893

Wayland
Subsidiary: HNI 1817

Webster
Plant: Xerox 4136

West Henrietta
Foundation: General 1557

West Seneca
Plant: Kellogg 2120

Westbury
Corporate Giving Program: New 2682
Corporate Headquarters: New 2682, New York 2683
Subsidiary: New 2682
Division: New York 2683

Westfield
Plant: Welch 4025

White Plains
Corporate Giving Programs: Dannon 1030, ITT 1999, Starwood 3589, United 3879, Xylem 4139
Foundations: Dannon 1030, Handy 1718, Krasdale 2192, Reader's 3141, Skadden 3470, United 3879
Corporate Headquarters: Dannon 1030, Handy 1718, ITT 1999, Krasdale 2192, Starwood 3589, United 3879, Universal 3887, Xylem 4139
Subsidiaries: Avery 297, International 1960, Jones 2057, Marsh 2385, Metropolitan 2481
Offices: Benesch 413, Greenberg 1654

Williamsville
Corporate Giving Program: National 2628
Foundation: National 2628
Corporate Headquarters: Hunt 1890, National 2628, Tops 3774
Subsidiary: GATX 1542

Wilson
Plant: Lancaster 2216

Woodbury
Plant: Philips 2963

Woodstock
Subsidiaries: AMETEK 181, PerkinElmer 2939

Yonkers
Foundation: Friedland 1503
Cororate Headquarters: Friedland 1503

NORTH CAROLINA

Aberdeen
Plant: FMC 1449

Albemarle
Plant: Preformed 3032

Arden
Plant: Barnes 362

Asheboro
Foundation: Acme 29
Corporate Headquarters: Acme 29, Bossong 532
Plants: Georgia 1568, Goodyear 1612, Timken 3760

Asheville
Corporate Giving Programs: Ingles 1940, Kimmel 2152
Cororate Headquarters: Kimmel 2152
Subsidiary: Hedrick 1768
Offices: Dixon 1133, Ford 1462
Plant: Square 3560

Badin
Subsidiary: Alcoa 82
Plant: Alcoa 82

Belmont
Foundation: Knitcraft 2174

Bessemer City
Plant: Martin 2391

Black Mountain
Cororate Headquarters: Ingles 1940

Boone
Plant: Vulcan 3972

Burlington
Foundation: Wishart 4097
Cororate Headquarters: Wishart 4097

Cary
Corporate Giving Programs: JustNeem 2079, SAS 3336
Foundations: Cary 712, Pantry 2875
Corporate Headquarters: Cary 712, JustNeem 2079, Kimley 2151, Pantry 2875, SAS 3336
Subsidiary: Safeguard 3307
Offices: Deere 1061, Kimley 2151

Chapel Hill
Office: Robinson 3234

Charlotte
Corporate Giving Programs: Bank 340, Belk 403, Bobcats 512, Coca 861, Electrolux 1241, Moore 2566, Nucor 2760, Parker 2885, Piedmont 2971, Richardson 3209, Robinson 3234
Foundations: American 162, American 164, Arrowpoint 251, Bank 340, Belk 403, Belk 404, Bobcats 512, Bonitz 524, Bossong 532, Coats 860, Conrail 914, Consolidated 918, Delta 1073, Duke 1189, Exponential 1312, Fonville 1456, Hendrick 1776, Material 2401, Moore 2566, New 2680, North 2730, Nucor 2760, Olin 2801, Patton's 2899, Piedmont 2971, Rexam 3197, SCANA 3346, Snyder's-Lance 3492, SPX 3558, Swift 3666, Teleflex 3707, Thomasville 3737, UTC 3908, V.F. 3913, Wells 4028
Corporate Headquarters: Allison-Erwin 106, American 162, American 164, Arrowpoint 251, Bank 339, Bank 340, Belk 403, Belk 404, Bobcats 512, Chiquita 795, Coats 860, Coca 861, Continental 927, Dixon 1133, Duke 1189, Electrolux 1241, Fonville 1456, Hendrick 1776, Marsh 2386, Material 2401, Moore 2566, Nucor 2760, Parker 2885, Patton's 2899, Piedmont 2971, Rexam 3197, Richardson 3209, Robinson 3234, Shelton 3432, Snyder's-Lance 3492, SPX 3558, UTC 3908, Vermeer 3938
Subsidiaries: Arrowpoint 251, Bank 340, Belk 403, Belo 406, Coats 860, Danaher 1027, Harris 1738, Hendrick 1776, Piedmont 2971, Raymond 3133, TransUnion 3799, VHA 3944
Division: Harris 1738
Offices: Alston 116, Bradley 550, Brown 589, Bryan 596, Cadwalader 649, Cozen 964, Cranfill 971, Dechert 1058, Deere 1061, Factory 1323, Federal 1349, Humana 1886, K&L 2080, Katten 2101,

Kimley 2151, King 2157, Lauth 2232, Littler 2289, Mayer 2411, McGuireWoods 2430, Moore 2566, Mortenson 2577, Parker 2885, Pulte 3083, Robinson 3234, Thompson 3739, Unum 3898, Vision 3961, Winston 4089

Plants: Alro 113, BASF 368, Binswanger 464, Castle 716, Frito 1506, Martin 2391, Novell 2754, Sonoco 3500, TJX 3765, UTC 3908, Winn 4087

Claremont

Plant: Westervelt 4046

Coleridge

Subsidiary: Cox 962

Columbus

Plant: Timken 3760

Concord

Plants: Corning 945, Martin 2391

Conover

Foundation: Southern 3517

Cororate Headquarters: Classic 840, Southern 3517

Joint Venture: Sealed 3381

Plant: Westervelt 4046

Cove City

Subsidiary: Cox 962

Covington

Plant: Seneca 3406

Cullowhee

Foundation: American 154

Davidson

Foundation: Miller 2523

Cororate Headquarters: JanPak 2022

Plant: McAfee 2417

Denver

Plant: Martin 2391

Dobson

Foundation: Shelton 3432

Dudley

Foundation: Tri 3805

Cororate Headquarters: Tri 3805

Durham

Corporate Giving Program: Blue 497

Foundation: Blue 497

Corporate Headquarters: Blue 497, Semiconductor 3403

Subsidiaries: Avnet 304, Eastman 1214

Joint Venture: Corning 945

Offices: Alston 116, Williams 4078

Plants: CA 638, Valassis 3914

Eden

Plant: Miller 2523

Fayetteville

Plant: Goodyear 1612

Fletcher

Foundation: Wilsonart 4084

Forest City

Subsidiary: American 149

Division: Leggett 2246

Gastonia

Subsidiaries: FMC 1449, Hunter 1893

Plants: FMC 1449, Lubrizol 2315

Goldsboro

Foundation: Borden 527

Cororate Headquarters: Borden 527

Greensboro

Corporate Giving Programs: Lorillard 2304, V.F. 3913, Volvo 3968

Foundations: Better 447, Cone 907, EPES 1283, Halstead 1708, International 1971, Latham 2229, Marsh 2386, V.F. 3913

Corporate Headquarters: Cone 907, EPES 1283, International 1971, Latham 2229, Lorillard 2304, V.F. 3913, Volvo 3968

Subsidiaries: Berkley 426, CLARCOR 832, Danaher 1027, Ecolab 1220, Gannett 1532, Keller-Crescent 2117, Landmark 2218, V.F. 3913

Offices: American 143, Kimley 2151, Pan-American 2868

Plants: Deluxe 1084, Dow 1162, Golden 1602, Martin 2391, PPG 3025, Procter 3055, Sherwin 3437

Greenville

Subsidiary: BB&T 385

Offices: Dixon 1133, Harper 1735

Henderson

Subsidiary: Universal 3891

Plants: Kennametal 2125, Procter 3055

Hendersonville

Office: Dixon 1133

Hickory

Foundations: Classic 840, Shuford 3441

Cororate Headquarters: Shuford 3441

Subsidiaries: Corning 945, Thomasville 3737

Plant: Bassett 372

High Point

Foundations: Carolina 697, Harriss 1740, Honbarrier 1850

Corporate Headquarters: Carolina 697, Harriss 1740, Honbarrier 1850

Subsidiaries: Leggett 2246, Steelcase 3597

Offices: Dixon 1133, La-Z-Boy 2205

Plants: Bassett 372, Kohler 2182, Krueger 2196, Leggett 2246, Newell 2694, Valspar 3920

Hildebran

Plant: Kohler 2182

Hudson

Subsidiary: La-Z-Boy 2205

Huntersville

Office: Univar 3886

Jamestown

Plant: Univar 3886

Kannapolis

Plant: Martin 2391

Kings Mountain

Plants: Martin 2391, Owens 2841

Kinston

Foundations: Carolina 699, Tidewater 3749

Corporate Headquarters: Carolina 699, Tidewater 3749

Plant: West 4038

Knightdale

Plant: Square 3560

Laurinburg

Cororate Headquarters: Rostra 3268

Plant: Butler 626

Lenoir

Foundation: Bernhardt 432

Cororate Headquarters: Bernhardt 432

Subsidiary: Furniture 1519

Plants: La-Z-Boy 2205, Sealed 3381

Lexington

Subsidiary: Chesapeake 778

Plant: PPG 3025

Lincolnton

Plant: Timken 3760

Louisburg

Plant: Scotts 3372

Lumberton

Plant: Nash 2619

Marion

Subsidiaries: Coats 860, Westervelt 4046

Matthews

Corporate Giving Programs: Family 1330, Harris 1738

Corporate Headquarters: Family 1330, Harris 1738

Subsidiary: Coats 860

Plant: Martin 2391

Maxton

Plant: Campbell 669

Mebane

Subsidiary: Snyder's-Lance 3492

Minot

Plant: Wal-Mart 3980

Monroe

Plants: Martin 2391, Square 3560

Mooresville

Corporate Giving Programs: Justacip 2078, Lowe's 2312

Foundations: Earnhardt 1205, Lowe's 2312

Corporate Headquarters: Earnhardt 1205, Justacip 2078, Lowe's 2312

Subsidiary: Masco 2393

Plant: Panasonic 2869

Morehead City

Plant: Owens 2842

Morganton

Plants: Pactiv 2863, Rexnord 3198

Morrisville

Corporate Giving Program: Redwoods 3158

Foundation: Redwoods 3158

Corporate Headquarters: Burt's 623, Redwoods 3158

Subsidiaries: Blue 498, Clorox 852

Office: K&L 2080

Mount Airy

Cororate Headquarters: North 2730

Plant: Bassett 372

Mount Olive

Corporate Giving Program: Mt. 2594

Foundations: Mt. 2594, Southern 3515

Corporate Headquarters: Mt. 2594, Southern 3515

Newton

Foundation: Lee 2242

Cororate Headquarters: Lee 2242

Plant: Bassett 372

Oakboro

Foundation: Rusco 3288

Cororate Headquarters: Rusco 3288

Patterson

Plant: Sealed 3381

Pine Hall

Plant: Halstead 1708

Pinehurst

Office: Dixon 1133

Raleigh

Corporate Giving Programs: Carolina 698, Cranfill 971, First 1396, Martin 2391, Nelson 2661, North 2729, Smith 3486

Foundations: BB&T 385, Carolina 698, Duke 1189, Howard 1873, Kimley 2151, Pharmacy 2956

Corporate Headquarters: Carolina 698, Cranfill 971, First 1396, Highwoods 1800, Howard 1873, Martin 2391, Nelson 2661, North 2729, Pharmacy 2956, Smith 3486

Subsidiaries: Bonitz 524, Danaher 1027, First 1396, Lennar 2250

Offices: Cranfill 971, Dixon 1133, Humana 1886, K&L 2080, Kiewit 2142, McGuireWoods 2430, Nelson 2661, Parker 2885, Pulte 3083, Smith 3486, Williams 4078

Plants: Bausch 376, Charles 764, Freescale 1495, Owens 2841, Rockwell 3247, Winn 4087

Randleman

Foundation: United 3862

Cororate Headquarters: United 3862

Office: Dart 1033

Reidsville

Plant: Miller 2523

Research Triangle Park

Corporate Giving Programs: Bayer 382, GlaxoSmithKline 1588

Foundations: GlaxoSmithKline 1588, Semiconductor 3403

Cororate Headquarters: GlaxoSmithKline 1588

Division: Bayer 382

Offices: Brinks 573, Moore 2566

Plant: Harris 1736

Riegelwood

Plant: International 1968

Roanoke Rapids

Plants: International 1968, Kennametal 2125

Rocky Mount

Foundations: Brewer 558, Fisher 1432, Guardian 1681

Corporate Headquarters: Brewer 558, Fisher 1432, Guardian 1681

Subsidiary: Universal 3891

Plants: American 135, Cummins 1007, Nash 2619

Rutherfordton

Foundation: Tanner 3688

Cororate Headquarters: Tanner 3688

Salem

Subsidiary: Leggett 2246

Salisbury
Corporate Giving Program: Food 1458
Foundations: Food 1458, Hedrick 1768
Corporate Headquarters: Food 1458, Hedrick 1768, Tyler 3830
Plant: Martin 2391
Shelby
Foundations: Hallelujah 1705, Porter 3007
Corporate Headquarters: Hallelujah 1705, Porter 3007
Plant: PPG 3025
Skyland
Office: Keen 2111
Smithfield
Foundation: First 1396
Subsidiaries: Avnet 304, Universal 3891
Spindale
Foundation: Stonecutter 3615
Cororate Headquarters: Stonecutter 3615
Spruce Pine
Corporate Giving Program: Highland 1798
Cororate Headquarters: Highland 1798
Statesville
Subsidiaries: Avery 297, Sonoco 3500
Plants: Armstrong 246, Bassett 372, Goodyear 1612, Valspar 3920
Swepsonville
Subsidiary: American 150
Tarboro
Plant: Hillshire 1809
Taylorsville
Foundation: Schneider 3354
Office: Schneider 3354
Plants: Bassett 372, La-Z-Boy 2205
Thomasville
Foundation: Lexington 2257
Corporate Headquarters: Lexington 2257, Thomasville 3737
Subsidiary: Furniture 1519
Trinity
Corporate Giving Program: Sealy 3382
Cororate Headquarters: Sealy 3382
Valdese
Plant: Hillshire 1809
Wake Forest
Foundations: Mitsubishi 2538, Wake 3978
Cororate Headquarters: Wake 3978
Warsaw
Subsidiary: Smithfield 3487
Wilmington
Foundation: Neuwirth 2666
Cororate Headquarters: Neuwirth 2666
Offices: Cranfill 971, McGuireWoods 2430, Williams 4078
Plant: Corning 945
Wilson
Foundation: Stage 3572
Subsidiary: Universal 3891
Plant: Merck 2466
Winston Salem
Subsidiary: Leggett 2246
Winston-Salem
Corporate Giving Programs: BB&T 385, Hanesbrands 1720
Foundations: BB&T 385, Hanes 1719, Reynolds 3200, Shugart 3442
Corporate Headquarters: BB&T 385, Hanes 1719, Hanesbrands 1720, Reynolds 3200, Shugart 3442
Subsidiaries: American 165, BB&T 385, Chesapeake 778, Leggett 2246, Masco 2393
Offices: Dixon 1133, Holder 1829, Nelson 2661
Plants: Jostens 2067, Sonoco 3500, Tension 3717, Vulcan 3972
Zebulon
Subsidiary: Caterpillar 722
Plants: GlaxoSmithKline 1588, Illinois 1916

NORTH DAKOTA

Bismarck
Foundation: MDU 2441
Cororate Headquarters: MDU 2441
Subsidiary: Allete 100
Division: MDU 2441
Offices: Fredrikson 1491, Leonard 2252
Plant: SUPERVALU 3659
Bismark
Division: MDU 2441
Columbus
Foundation: Burke 615
Cororate Headquarters: Burke 615
Fargo
Subsidiaries: Chrysler 801, Otter 2836, U.S. 3835
Offices: Dorsey 1157, Fredrikson 1491
Plants: Deere 1061, Nash 2619, SUPERVALU 3659
Grand Forks
Foundation: Rydell 3291
Cororate Headquarters: Rydell 3291
Office: Xcel 4135
Plant: Ecolab 1220
Kenmare
Plant: Burke 615
Langdon
Foundation: United 3883
Cororate Headquarters: United 3883
Mandan
Plant: BP 547
Minot
Plant: Nash 2619
Valley City
Plant: Deere 1061
West Fargo
Subsidiaries: Caterpillar 722, Otter 2836

OHIO

Akron
Corporate Giving Programs: Firestone 1387, FirstEnergy 1424, Goodyear 1612, Schulman 3361
Foundations: Albrecht 80, FirstEnergy 1424, Firstmerit 1425, Goodyear 1612, Summit 3642
Corporate Headquarters: Albrecht 80, Firestone 1387, FirstEnergy 1424, Firstmerit 1425, Goodyear 1612, Schulman 3361, Summit 3642
Subsidiaries: Albrecht 80, FirstEnergy 1424, Schulman 3361, Summit 3642
Offices: Ford 1462, Hahn 1700, KeyBank 2136, Rogers 3252
Plants: Coca 862, Koch 2180
Amherst
Plant: Nordson 2723
Anna
Plant: Honda 1851
Ashland
Plant: Timken 3760
Athens
Cororate Headquarters: Interthyr 1978
Avon Lake
Plant: Lubrizol 2315
Barberton
Plant: PPG 3025
Bay Village
Plant: Scotts 3372
Beachwood
Foundations: BASF 368, Ohio 2791
Cororate Headquarters: Scott 3370
Plant: Progressive 3057
Beavercreek
Plant: CA 638
Bedford Heights
Subsidiaries: Giant 1571, Lancaster 2216
Plants: Castle 716, Sherwin 3437
Bellefontaine
Subsidiary: Harsco 1741
Bellevue
Subsidiary: Schulman 3361
Berea
Corporate Giving Program: Cleveland 846
Foundation: Cleveland 846
Cororate Headquarters: Cleveland 846
Bidwell
Plant: Evans 1300
Blacklick
Plant: McGraw 2429
Bowling Green
Plant: Lubrizol 2315
Brecksville
Foundation: Industrial 1935
Cororate Headquarters: Industrial 1935
Plants: Lubrizol 2315, UTC 3908
Brooklyn
Foundations: Cole 867, Diebold 1112, KeyBank 2136, Tyler 3830
Bryan
Foundation: Spangler 3531
Cororate Headquarters: Spangler 3531
Plants: Continental 927, Olin 2801
Bucyrus
Subsidiaries: Park 2881, Transco 3797
Plant: Timken 3760
Cambridge
Plant: Colgate 869
Canfield
Foundation: WKBN 4099
Plant: Lafarge 2210
Canton
Corporate Giving Program: Diebold 1112
Foundations: Belden 402, Fresh 1499, Timken 3760
Corporate Headquarters: Belden 402, Gregory 1662, Timken 3760
Subsidiaries: American 141, Diebold 1112
Division: Fresh 1499
Joint Venture: Diebold 1112
Offices: KeyBank 2136, Vision 3961
Plant: Georgia 1568
Chagrin Falls
Division: Stride 3626
Cheshire
Plant: American 141
Cheviot
Cororate Headquarters: Cheviot 779
Chillicothe
Plant: PPG 3025
Cincinnati
Corporate Giving Programs: Cincinnati 813, Cincinnati 814, Cintas 816, Dinsmore 1121, Ethicon 1299, Fifth 1377, Frost 1511, Keating 2109, Kroger 2195, Macy's 2333, Procter 3055, Western 4040
Foundations: Bardes 359, Borcherding 526, Chemed 773, Cheviot 779, Chiquita 795, Cincinnati 814, Convergys 933, Evans 1301, Fifth 1377, FMR 1450, Gannett 1532, Hartzell 1745, Johnson 2051, Kroger 2195, Leyman 2259, Macy's 2333, Messer 2477, Neace 2651, Ohio 2790, Omnicare 2807, Scripps 3374, Western 4040, XTEK 4138
Corporate Headquarters: Bardes 359, Borcherding 526, Chemed 773, Cincinnati 813, Cincinnati 814, Cintas 816, Convergys 933, Dinsmore 1121, Ethicon 1299, Evans 1301, Fifth 1377, Frost 1511, Greyhound 1664, Johnson 2051, Keating 2109, Kroger 2195, Leyman 2259, Macy's 2333, Messer 2477, Ohio 2790, Omnicare 2807, Procter 3055, Scripps 3374, Western 4040, XTEK 4138
Subsidiaries: Berkshire 429, Chemed 773, CLARCOR 832, Duke 1189, Flowserve 1447, Johnson 2048, Lancaster 2216, Macy's 2333, Nucor 2760, Quest 3103, Raymond 3133, Smithfield 3487
Division: General 1552
Offices: Baker 319, Cheviot 779, Fishel 1429, Frost 1511, GATX 1542, Grant 1633, Humana 1886, Huntington 1894, KeyBank 2136, Porter 3009, Rogers 3252, Safeco 3306, SAP 3334, SAS 3336, Squire 3561, Thompson 3739, Thompson 3740, Ulmer 3845, West 4038
Plants: Castle 716, Emerson 1257, Fuller 1517, General 1554, Hewlett 1794, LyondellBasell 2322,

Morton 2579, Novell 2754, Owens 2841, PerkinElmer 2939, Sherwin 3437, SUMCO 3638
Circleville
Plant: PPG 3025
Clayton
Foundation: Anchor 192
Cororate Headquarters: Anchor 192
Cleveland
Corporate Giving Programs: American 149, Applied 219, Baker 319, Benesch 413, Cavaliers 724, Charter 767, Cleveland 847, Eaton 1216, Ferro 1366, Forest 1467, Hahn 1700, Jones 2058, Kaiser 2086, KeyBank 2136, Preformed 3032, Squire 3561, Thompson 3740, Ulmer 3845
Foundations: Baker 319, Beverage 452, Cleveland 847, Cliffs 850, Cooper 936, Eaton 1216, Horix 1860, Jones 2058, KeyBank 2136, Lincoln 2279, Medical 2448, MTD 2595, Northern 2739, Oatey 2775, Orvis 2830, Park 2880, Parker 2886, Plain 2989, Sherwin 3437, SIFCO 3452, Tap 3689, TFS 3732, Third 3735
Corporate Headquarters: American 149, Applied 219, Baker 319, Benesch 413, Beverage 452, Cavaliers 724, Charter 767, Cleveland 847, Cliffs 850, Eaton 1216, Forest 1467, Hahn 1700, Jones 2058, KeyBank 2136, Lincoln 2279, Medical 2448, Oatey 2775, Ohio 2791, Park 2880, Parker 2886, Plain 2989, Preformed 3032, Sherwin 3437, SIFCO 3452, Squire 3561, Tap 3689, TFS 3732, Third 3735, Thompson 3740, Ulmer 3845
Subsidiaries: Boehringer 515, CNO 857, Danaher 1027, Delaware 1066, Dominion 1150, FirstEnergy 1424, Gannett 1532, Grace 1623, Leggett 2246, Manitowoc 2356, Metropolitan 2481, Northrop 2744, Novartis 2752, Progressive 3057, TFS 3732, Tomkins 3771
Divisions: Cox 958, General 1552, Parker 2886, SIFCO 3452
Offices: Acumen 33, Baker 319, Benesch 413, Bricker 559, Federal 1349, Grant 1633, Hahn 1700, Ice 1905, Littler 2289, Pan-American 2868, Porter 3009, Pulte 3083, Rogers 3252, SAP 3334, SAS 3336, Squire 3561, Thompson 3739, Thompson 3740, Ulmer 3845, Urban 3901, West 4038, Whiting 4063, Wiley 4072
Plants: Alcoa 82, Clorox 852, Mitsui 2541, Novell 2754, PPG 3025
Clyde
Plant: Whirlpool 4056
Columbus
Corporate Giving Programs: American 141, Big 460, Bricker 559, Columbia 883, Columbus 886, Evans 1300, First 1398, Grange 1631, Huntington 1894, JPMorgan Chase 2071, Lancaster 2216, Limited 2277, Nationwide 2639, Porter 3009, Worthington 4124
Foundations: Altair 117, Altman 119, American 141, COLHOC 870, Columbus 886, Dispatch 1129, Dominion 1149, Edwards 1235, Fishel 1429, Gregory 1662, Homewood 1849, Huntington 1894, Limited 2277, M/I 2325, Motorists 2584, Nationwide 2639, NiSource 2715, State 3590
Corporate Headquarters: Altair 117, Altman 119, American 141, Big 460, Bricker 559, COLHOC 870, Columbia 883, Columbus 886, Dispatch 1129, Edwards 1235, Evans 1300, Fishel 1429, Grange 1631, Homewood 1849, Huntington 1894, Lancaster 2216, Limited 2277, M/I 2325, Motorists 2584, Nationwide 2639, Porter 3009, State 3590, Worthington 4124
Subsidiaries: American 141, Anheuser 202, AOL 209, Boehringer 515, Dispatch 1129, Emerson 1257, Farmers 1338, Grange 1631, Huntington 1894, Limited 2277, Masco 2393, Motorists 2584, NiSource 2715, Scotts 3372, State 3590, Utica 3910, Worthington 4124
Divisions: Abbott 13, Fishel 1429
Offices: Baker 319, Benesch 413, Bricker 559, Federal 1349, Frost 1511, Hahn 1700, Ice 1905, Jones 2058, KeyBank 2136, Littler 2289, NIBCO 2707, Plain 2989, Porter 3009, Rogers 3252, Squire 3561, State 3591, Thompson 3740, Ulmer 3845, Vision 3961
Plants: Bassett 372, Guardian 1682, Menasha 2461, Navistar 2647, Novell 2754, Pactiv 2863, Sherwin 3437, Timken 3760
Coshocton
Division: Cox 958
Crestline
Plant: PPG 3025
Dayton
Corporate Giving Programs: Berry 434, NCR 2650, Standard 3576
Foundations: CareSource 690, Dayton 1047, Dealer 1052, Gosiger 1617, Kuhns 2197, Reynolds 3199, Robbins 3230, Standard 3576, WorkflowOne 4115
Corporate Headquarters: Berry 434, CareSource 690, Dayton 1047, Gosiger 1617, Kuhns 2197, Standard 3576, Tomkins 3771, WorkflowOne 4115
Subsidiaries: MeadWestvaco 2445, Nash 2619, NCR 2650, Procter 3055, Reynolds 3199, Standard 3576, US 3902
Divisions: Flowserve 1447, Reynolds 3199
Offices: Fishel 1429, KeyBank 2136, Porter 3009, Thompson 3740, Whirlpool 4056
Plants: Kroger 2195, McAfee 2417
Defiance
Cororate Headquarters: Defiance 1063
Division: Cox 958
Delaware
Corporate Giving Program: Greif 1663
Foundation: Jeg's 2031
Corporate Headquarters: Greif 1663, Jeg's 2031
Plant: PPG 3025
Delphos
Cororate Headquarters: Delphos 1072
Dover
Subsidiary: Praxair 3029
Division: Zimmer 4157
Office: Huntington 1894
Dublin
Corporate Giving Programs: Cardinal 685, Tim 3753, Wendy's/Arby's 4030
Foundations: Cardinal 685, Wendy's 4031
Corporate Headquarters: Cardinal 685, Dominion 1149, Tim 3753, Wendy's 4031, Wendy's/Arby's 4030
Subsidiaries: AT&T 273, Harleysville 1733, Wendy's/Arby's 4030
Plant: DENSO 1088
Dundee
Plant: U.S. 3840
East Liberty
Plant: Honda 1851
Eastlake
Foundation: Gould 1618
Division: Gould 1618
Eaton
Plant: Timken 3760
Elyria
Corporate Giving Program: Ross 3265
Foundation: Ross 3265
Cororate Headquarters: Ross 3265
Plants: Carpenter 700, Crane 970
Euclid
Plant: PPG 3025
Fairborn
Plant: Northrop 2744
Fairfield
Foundation: Ohio 2789
Cororate Headquarters: Ohio 2789
Subsidiary: Ohio 2789
Fairlawn
Foundation: OMNOVA 2809
Cororate Headquarters: OMNOVA 2809
Division: OMNOVA 2809
Findlay
Corporate Giving Programs: Marathon 2362, Marathon 2365
Foundation: Cooper 936
Corporate Headquarters: Cooper 936, Marathon 2362, Marathon 2365
Subsidiaries: Cummins 1007, Marathon 2362, Marathon 2363, Marathon 2364
Plant: Whirlpool 4056
Fremont
Plant: Bemis 407
Gahanna
Subsidiary: Scotts 3372
Gallipolis
Subsidiary: Robbins 3230
Germantown
Foundation: Dupps 1193
Cororate Headquarters: Dupps 1193
Gettysburg
Subsidiary: Alcoa 82
Glenwillow
Cororate Headquarters: Stride 3626
Plant: Owens 2841
Granville
Plant: Owens 2842
Greenville
Subsidiaries: Martin 2391, Park 2881
Plant: Whirlpool 4056
Grove City
Plant: Sherwin 3437
Hamilton
Subsidiary: O'Neal 2771
Plants: Miller 2523, Univar 3886
Harrison
Office: Cheviot 779
Haviland
Foundation: Haviland 1752
Cororate Headquarters: Haviland 1752
Heath
Office: Bionetics 467
Hebron
Plant: Ecolab 1220
Hilliard
Foundation: Electric 1240
Cororate Headquarters: Electric 1240
Plant: Armstrong 246
Hudson
Office: Dixon 1133
Plants: Newell 2694, Terex 3719
Independence
Subsidiary: American 149
Plant: Novell 2754
Jackson
Plant: Campbell 669
Jamestown
Plant: American 135
Jefferson
Subsidiary: Worthington 4124
Kent
Foundation: Davey 1035
Cororate Headquarters: Davey 1035
Kettering
Foundation: Reynolds 3199
Cororate Headquarters: Reynolds 3199
Lancaster
Plants: Hexcel 1795, Newell 2694
Leipsir
Plant: Procter 3055
Lewisburg
Plant: Procter 3055
Lima
Foundation: Superior 3658
Cororate Headquarters: Superior 3658
Office: Huntington 1894
Plant: Procter 3055
London
Subsidiary: Worthington 4124
Lorain
Subsidiary: Grace 1623

Loveland
Subsidiary: O'Neal 2771
Division: International 1968
Office: West 4038
Macedonia
Plant: Parker 2886
Madison
Subsidiary: Hubbell 1879
Malta
Subsidiary: Tomkins 3771
Mansfield
Subsidiary: Park 2881
Plant: Emerson 1257
Marblehead
Plant: Lafarge 2210
Marietta
Foundation: Peoples 2929
Cororate Headquarters: Peoples 2929
Plants: BP 547, Chevron 780
Marion
Subsidiaries: Anheuser 202, Nucor 2760
Plant: Whirlpool 4056
Martel
Plant: General 1554
Marysville
Corporate Giving Programs: Honda 1851, Scotts 3372
Foundation: Honda 1851
Corporate Headquarters: Honda 1851, Scotts 3372
Subsidiary: Harsco 1741
Mason
Foundations: LensCrafters 2251, Makino 2348
Corporate Headquarters: LensCrafters 2251, Luxottica 2319, Makino 2348
Subsidiary: Cintas 816
Plants: Harris 1736, Worthington 4124
Massillon
Cororate Headquarters: Fresh 1499
Division: Fresh 1499
Masury
Office: GATX 1542
Maumee
Cororate Headquarters: Dana 1026
Subsidiaries: Eaton 1216, Turner 3824
Plant: Barnes 362
Mayfield Heights
Foundations: Danaher 1027, Ferro 1366
Cororate Headquarters: Ferro 1366
Subsidiaries: Danaher 1027, Progressive 3057
Plant: Rockwell 3246
Mayfield Village
Foundation: Progressive 3057
Cororate Headquarters: Progressive 3057
Medina
Corporate Giving Program: RPM 3278
Cororate Headquarters: RPM 3278
Subsidiary: STERIS 3600
Office: Plain 2989
Plants: Owens 2842, Valspar 3920
Mentor
Foundations: Aexcel 49, Mill 2515, STERIS 3600
Corporate Headquarters: Aexcel 49, Mill 2515, STERIS 3600
Subsidiary: STERIS 3600
Plant: Worthington 4124
Miamisburg
Corporate Giving Program: Reed 3161
Foundation: Danis 1029
Cororate Headquarters: Danis 1029
Subsidiaries: PerkinElmer 2939, Ripplewood 3219
Division: Reed 3161
Middlefield
Subsidiary: Masco 2393
Middletown
Plant: Quaker 3093
Milan
Plant: Tenneco 3715
Milbury
Subsidiary: Guardian 1682
Milford
Plant: PPG 3025
Minster
Foundation: Minster 2532
Cororate Headquarters: Minster 2532
Plant: Dannon 1030
Monroe
Plant: Worthington 4124
Mount Sterling
Plant: Tomkins 3771
Mount Vernon
Foundation: Ariel 237
Cororate Headquarters: Ariel 237
Subsidiary: Park 2881
Plant: Owens 2842
Napoleon
Plant: Tenneco 3715
New Albany
Corporate Giving Program: Abercrombie 17
Cororate Headquarters: Abercrombie 17
New Bremen
Corporate Giving Program: Crown 987
Cororate Headquarters: Crown 987
New Philadelphia
Plant: Timken 3760
New Richmond
Foundation: Jones 2056
Newark
Corporate Giving Program: Longaberger 2299
Foundations: Longaberger 2299, Park 2881
Corporate Headquarters: Longaberger 2299, Park 2881
Subsidiary: Park 2881
Division: Cox 958
Office: State 3591
Plants: Donnelley 1155, Owens 2842
Newcomerstown
Plant: Plymouth 2993
North Canton
Foundation: Diebold 1112
Cororate Headquarters: Diebold 1112
Plant: Graco 1624
North Kingsville
Foundation: Premix 3037
Cororate Headquarters: Premix 3037
North Olmstead
Office: Factory 1323
Northfield
Office: Plain 2989
Oregon
Plant: Marathon 2362
Orrville
Corporate Giving Program: Smucker 3488
Foundation: Smucker 3488
Cororate Headquarters: Smucker 3488
Plant: Smucker 3488
Orwell
Plant: Kennametal 2125
Ottoville
Cororate Headquarters: Acme 28
Oxford
Plant: Square 3560
Painesville
Foundation: Stafast 3571
Cororate Headquarters: Stafast 3571
Plants: Clorox 852, Lubrizol 2315, Morton 2579
Parma
Plant: Crystal 992
Paulding
Plant: Lafarge 2210
Pemberville
Plant: Modine 2544
Pepper Pike
Subsidiary: Danaher 1027
Perrysburg
Foundations: Entelco 1277, Owens 2844
Corporate Headquarters: Entelco 1277, Owens 2844
Division: Chrysler 801
Plant: Alro 113
Piqua
Cororate Headquarters: Hartzell 1745
Portsmouth
Foundation: OSCO 2832
Cororate Headquarters: OSCO 2832
Rittman
Plant: Morton 2579
Salem
Plant: Worthington 4124
Sandusky
Foundation: Sandusky 3328
Cororate Headquarters: Sandusky 3328
Seville
Foundation: Ohio 2792
Cororate Headquarters: Ohio 2792
Sharon Center
Plant: Schulman 3361
Sharonville
Plant: Sealed 3381
Sidney
Subsidiary: Alcoa 82
Plants: Alcoa 82, Emerson 1257
Solon
Foundation: Keithley 2115
Cororate Headquarters: Keithley 2115
Subsidiary: Nestle 2663
Plant: Kennametal 2125
South Charleston
Foundation: Buckeye 601
Cororate Headquarters: Buckeye 601
Springboro
Division: Flowserve 1447
Springdale
Office: Avon 305
Springfield
Subsidiaries: Marathon 2362, Robbins 3230
Plants: Evans 1300, Hunt 1892, Navistar 2647
St. Clair
Plant: Timken 3760
Stow
Subsidiary: Danaher 1027
Plant: Spirol 3545
Streetsboro
Plant: Deluxe 1084
Strongsville
Plants: Dow 1161, Univar 3886
Stryker
Plant: Ferro 1366
Tallmadge
Plant: Owens 2842
Tiffin
Foundations: National 2634, Webster 4018
Corporate Headquarters: National 2634, Webster 4018
Plant: Sonoco 3500
Tipp City
Plants: Illinois 1916, Smith 3484
Toledo
Foundations: Block 481, HCR 1763, Heidtman 1770, Owens 2842
Corporate Headquarters: Block 481, HCR 1763, Heidtman 1770, Owens 2842
Subsidiaries: Eclipse 1219, FirstEnergy 1424, Georgia 1568
Offices: GATX 1542, KeyBank 2136
Plants: Chrysler 801, Newell 2694, Univar 3886
Trenton
Plant: Miller 2523
Troy
Corporate Giving Program: Hobart 1818
Cororate Headquarters: Hobart 1818
Subsidiary: Illinois 1916
Plant: Panasonic 2869
Twinsburg
Subsidiary: CVS 1014
Plants: Carpenter 700, Chrysler 801, Rockwell 3246
Upper Sandusky
Plants: Guardian 1682, Smith 3484, Worthington 4124
Urbana
Plants: Menasha 2461, Nestle 2662
Valley City
Cororate Headquarters: MTD 2595

Van Wert
Foundation: Acme 28
Subsidiary: Teleflex 3707
Versailles
Foundation: Midmark 2507
Cororate Headquarters: Midmark 2507
Wadsworth
Foundation: American 152
Cororate Headquarters: American 152
Subsidiary: Hubbell 1879
Walton Hills
Plant: Ferro 1366
Wapakoneta
Subsidiary: Lancaster 2216
Warren
Foundation: First 1420
Cororate Headquarters: First 1420
Subsidiaries: First 1420, NVF 2766, Standard 3577
Division: Delphi 1071
Warrensville Heights
Corporate Giving Program: Heinens 1771
Cororate Headquarters: Heinens 1771
Wellston
Plant: General 1554
West Chester
Foundation: AK 67
Cororate Headquarters: AK 67
Offices: Bricker 559, Cheviot 779, Frost 1511
Westchester
Plant: Square 3560
Westerville
Subsidiaries: Dispatch 1129, Fiserv 1427, Harsco 1741
Offices: Opus 2820, Quandel 3099, Univar 3886
Plant: McGraw 2429
Westfield Center
Corporate Giving Program: Westfield 4047
Foundation: Westfield 4047
Cororate Headquarters: Westfield 4047
Westlake
Corporate Giving Program: Nordson 2723
Foundations: Fetzer 1367, Nordson 2723
Cororate Headquarters: Fetzer 1367, Nordson 2723
Subsidiary: Berkshire 429
Plant: Nestle 2662
Wickliffe
Foundation: Lubrizol 2315
Cororate Headquarters: Lubrizol 2315
Subsidiary: Berkshire 429
Willard
Plant: Donnelley 1155
Wooster
Foundation: Defiance 1063
Subsidiary: Newell 2694
Plant: Timken 3760
Worthington
Subsidiary: Kellogg 2120
Xenia
Subsidiary: Lafarge 2210
Plant: Evans 1300
Yellow Springs
Foundation: YSI 4149
Cororate Headquarters: YSI 4149
Subsidiary: Antioch 207
Division: Antioch 207
Youngstown
Foundation: Home 1845
Cororate Headquarters: Home 1845, WKBN 4099
Subsidiary: Lafarge 2210
Zanesville
Foundation: Sidwell 3447
Cororate Headquarters: Sidwell 3447
Subsidiaries: Cardinal 685, Nestle 2662, Park 2881

OKLAHOMA

Bartlesville
Foundation: ConocoPhillips 913
Broken Arrow
Subsidiary: PerkinElmer 2939
Catoosa
Office: GATX 1542
Claremore
Plants: Allegheny 91, Worthington 4124
El Reno
Foundation: Gemini 1547
Cororate Headquarters: Gemini 1547
Enid
Foundation: Cummins 1005
Cororate Headquarters: Cummins 1005
Jay
Plant: Wal-Mart 3980
Lawton
Plant: Goodyear 1612
Mill Creek
Plant: U.S. 3840
Moore
Plant: Wal-Mart 3980
Norman
Foundation: Commercial 892
Oklahoma City
Corporate Giving Programs: American 145, Chesapeake 777, Devon 1102, Love's 2311, Oklahoma 2794, Sonic 3498
Foundations: American 145, Century 750, Clements 845, Delta 1079, Dobson 1137, Metropolitan 2480, Oklahoma 2794, Oklahoma 2795
Corporate Headquarters: American 145, Century 750, Chesapeake 777, Clements 845, Delta 1079, Devon 1102, Dobson 1137, Love's 2311, Metropolitan 2480, Oklahoma 2794, Oklahoma 2795, Sonic 3498
Subsidiaries: Anadarko 190, Anheuser 202, Apache 211, Clements 845, Oklahoma 2795, Omnicare 2807, Republic 3188, Seagate 3377, Sonic 3498, Tyson 3832, VHA 3944
Divisions: Cox 958, Reynolds 3199
Offices: Bionetics 467, Federal 1349, Gable 1525, Gable 1526, Grant 1633, Humana 1886, Telligen 3710
Plants: Hunt 1892, Miller 2523, Owens 2841, Owens 2842, Quad 3091, Univar 3886
Pauls Valley
Plant: Bemis 407
Pawnee
Foundation: First 1417
Cororate Headquarters: First 1417
Pryor
Plants: Georgia 1568, Red 3153
Stillwater
Plant: Armstrong 246
Tulsa
Corporate Giving Programs: Dollar 1144, Gable 1526, Helmerich 1774, ONEOK 2815, Palace 2866, QuikTrip 3109
Foundations: American 131, Chandler 760, Colorado 880, Gable 1525, McJunkin 2431, ONEOK 2815, Ross 3266, Williams 4077
Corporate Headquarters: American 131, Chandler 760, Dollar 1144, Gable 1525, Gable 1526, Helmerich 1774, McJunkin 2431, ONEOK 2815, QuikTrip 3109, Red 3153, Ross 3266, Williams 4077
Subsidiaries: Badger 313, Dollar 1144, Franklin 1484, Goulds 1619, Handy 1718, Helmerich 1774, Mark 2377, Newfield 2695, Occidental 2780, ONEOK 2815, Robbins 3230
Joint Venture: Praxair 3029
Offices: Gable 1526, RJN 3228, State 3591, Thompson 3739
Plants: Badger 313, BP 547, Castle 716, Miller 2523, PerkinElmer 2939, Rockwell 3247, Terex 3719, Total 3778, Univar 3886, Valmont 3919
Vinita
Plant: General 1554
Wewoka
Cororate Headquarters: Commercial 892

OREGON

Albany
Subsidiary: Valmont 3919
Baker City
Office: Cascade 713
Beaverton
Corporate Giving Programs: NIKE 2710, Vernier 3941
Foundations: NIKE 2710, Pacific 2856, Tektronix 3706
Corporate Headquarters: NIKE 2710, Pacific 2856, Tektronix 3706, Vernier 3941
Subsidiary: Tektronix 3706
Offices: Blakely 480, Symantec 3669
Bend
Cororate Headquarters: Brooks 585
Subsidiaries: Brooks 585, Premera 3034
Offices: Cascade 713, Miller 2521, Schwabe 3364
Canby
Subsidiary: U.S. 3835
Clackamas
Division: Safeway 3310
Corvallis
Foundation: Corvallis 947
Cororate Headquarters: Corvallis 947
Plant: Hewlett 1794
Estacada
Foundation: Day 1045
Eugene
Foundations: Abby's 14, Guard 1680
Corporate Headquarters: Abby's 14, Guard 1680
Offices: Schwabe 3364, Strauss 3624
Gervais
Plant: Scotts 3372
Grand Ronde
Corporate Giving Program: Spirit 3544
Cororate Headquarters: Spirit 3544
Grants Pass
Subsidiary: Danaher 1027
Hermiston
Office: Cascade 713
Hillsboro
Foundation: Intel 1950
Offices: Applied 220, Farmers 1338
Plant: Intel 1950
Jasper
Cororate Headquarters: Jasper 2027
John Day
Subsidiary: Ochoco 2783
Klamath Falls
Cororate Headquarters: Jeld 2032
Lake Oswego
Foundation: DCI 1049
Offices: Autodesk 289, Safeco 3306
Lyons
Foundation: Freres 1498
Cororate Headquarters: Freres 1498
Medford
Corporate Giving Program: Lithia 2287
Cororate Headquarters: Lithia 2287
Subsidiary: Shaklee 3418
Plant: Avista 301
Milwaukie
Cororate Headquarters: Day 1045
Molalla
Plant: Scotts 3372
Newberg
Cororate Headquarters: DCI 1049
North Bend
Corporate Giving Program: Coquille 939
Cororate Headquarters: Coquille 939
Plant: Menasha 2461
Nyssa
Subsidiary: Alsco 115
Ontario
Office: Cascade 713
Pendleton
Office: Cascade 713
Portland
Corporate Giving Programs: adidas 35, Alima 90, Andersson 196, Eleek 1243, Green 1652, Hampton

1714, Idealist 1909, Kaiser 2086, Knowledge 2177, Meyer 2485, Miller 2521, Northwest 2747, PacifiCorp 2860, Portland 3010, PREM 3033, Regence 3168, Schwabe 3364, StanCorp 3574, Starbucks 3585, Stoel 3611, Sustainable 3662, Tonkon 3772, Trail 3793, TriLibrium 3809
Foundations: Alpenrose 111, American 155, Boyd 545, Cambia 665, Deacon 1050, Fisher 1430, Friesen 1505, Halton 1709, Jeld 2032, Kifton 2143, PacifiCorp 2860, Portland 3010, RE/MAX 3140, StanCorp 3574, TOSOH 3777, United 3868
Corporate Headquarters: Alima 90, Alpenrose 111, American 155, Andersson 196, Boyd 545, Cambia 665, Deacon 1050, Eleek 1243, Green 1652, Halton 1709, Hampton 1714, Idealist 1909, Kifton 2143, Knowledge 2177, Meyer 2485, Miller 2521, Northwest 2747, PacifiCorp 2860, Portland 3010, PREM 3033, Regence 3168, Schwabe 3364, StanCorp 3574, Stoel 3611, Sustainable 3662, Tonkon 3772, TOSOH 3777, Trail 3793, TriLibrium 3809, United 3868
Subsidiaries: Amsted 188, Belo 406, Berkshire 429, Danaher 1027, Donnelley 1155, Hampton 1714, Knowledge 2177, Kroger 2195, Lennar 2250, Northwest 2747, OneBeacon 2813, Raymond 3133, Regence 3168, StanCorp 3574, U.S. 3835, Zions 4158
Offices: Davis 1041, DP 1168, Edelman 1224, Federal 1349, Garvey 1539, Grant 1633, Hays 1761, Holland 1834, K&L 2080, KeyBank 2136, Lane 2221, Littler 2289, Miller 2521, Opus 2820, Perkins 2940, Perkins 2941, Schwabe 3364, Stoel 3611, Tonkon 3772, Vision 3961
Plants: CA 638, McAfee 2417, Mitsui 2541, Novell 2754, Owens 2841, Owens 2842, Rockwell 3247, Sherwin 3437, Square 3560, Subaru 3631, Univar 3886, Warnaco 3988

Prineville
Foundation: Ochoco 2783
Cororate Headquarters: Ochoco 2783
Office: Miller 2521

Roseburg
Corporate Giving Program: Cow 957
Corporate Headquarters: Cow 957, Umpqua 3847

Rosenberg
Corporate Giving Program: Umpqua 3847

Saint Helens
Cororate Headquarters: Friesen 1505

Salem
Foundations: Associated 263, Pioneer 2982
Corporate Headquarters: Associated 263, Gelco 1546, Pioneer 2982
Subsidiary: International 1962
Division: Fresh 1499
Offices: Halton 1709, Schwabe 3364, State 3591
Plants: SUMCO 3638, Valmont 3919

Springfield
Office: Symantec 3669
Plant: Clorox 852

St. Helens
Plant: Armstrong 246

The Dalles
Office: Halton 1709

Tigard
Subsidiary: Farmers 1338

Tualatin
Subsidiary: Arctic 234
Plant: Valmont 3919

Vancouver
Plant: Lafarge 2210

Vernonia
Foundation: Holce 1827
Cororate Headquarters: Holce 1827

Wilsonville
Foundation: Mentor 2462
Corporate Headquarters: Mentor 2462, OrePac 2823
Offices: Halton 1709, NIKE 2710
Plant: Coca 862

Woodburn
Office: Do 1136
Plants: International 1962, Smucker 3488

Yamhill
Plant: Bailey 315

PENNSYLVANIA

Aliquippa
Foundation: Universal 3892
Cororate Headquarters: Wonder 4107

Allentown
Corporate Giving Programs: Air 63, PPL 3026, Tees 3703
Foundation: Air 63
Corporate Headquarters: Air 63, PPL 3026, Tees 3703
Subsidiary: Air 63
Offices: Opus 2820, SKF 3473, Whiting 4063
Plants: Crystal 992, General 1554, Owens 2841

Ambler
Division: Henkel 1778

Ambridge
Subsidiary: O'Neal 2771

Annville
Plant: Butler 626

Ashland
Plant: Goulds 1619

Avoca
Subsidiary: Susquehanna 3661

Avondale
Plant: Scotts 3372

Bala Cynwyd
Corporate Giving Programs: Driscoll 1176, Philadelphia 2960
Corporate Headquarters: Conston 920, Driscoll 1176, Philadelphia 2960
Office: Factory 1323

Bangor
Cororate Headquarters: Berkheimer 425

Beaver
Subsidiary: Baker 323

Beaver Falls
Plant: Armstrong 246

Bedford
Plant: Kennametal 2125

Bedminster
Office: First 1421

Beech Creek
Plant: Armstrong 246

Ben Salem
Office: Whirlpool 4056

Bensalem
Subsidiary: CNO 857

Berwick
Subsidiary: CSS 996

Berwyn
Foundation: AMETEK 181
Cororate Headquarters: AMETEK 181
Subsidiary: Nationwide 2639
Offices: DaVita 1044, Liberty 2265, Pepper 2934, White 4059
Plant: Novell 2754

Bethlehem
Corporate Giving Program: Just 2077
Foundation: National 2635
Cororate Headquarters: Just 2077
Division: SKF 3473

Bird in Hand
Foundation: Bird 468
Cororate Headquarters: Bird 468

Blairsville
Plant: Westinghouse 4049

Blandon
Plant: Campbell 669

Bloomsburg
Foundation: Catawissa 720

Blue Bell
Corporate Giving Programs: Henkels 1779, Unisys 3859
Foundation: Henkels 1779
Corporate Headquarters: Henkels 1779, Unisys 3859
Subsidiary: Teleflex 3707

Boyertown
Cororate Headquarters: National 2635
Plant: Cabot 642

Brackenridge
Plant: Allegheny 91

Bradford
Foundation: KOA 2178
Cororate Headquarters: KOA 2178

Bridgeville
Plant: Carpenter 700

Bristol
Corporate Giving Program: Jones 2057
Subsidiary: Jones 2057

Brookville
Foundation: Symmco 3670

Broomall
Cororate Headquarters: Veridyne 3935

Bryn Mawr
Corporate Giving Program: Aqua 222
Corporate Headquarters: Aqua 222, Main 2342

Burnham
Cororate Headquarters: Standard 3577
Subsidiary: Standard 3577

Butler
Foundations: Armstrong 245, Nextier 2706
Corporate Headquarters: Armstrong 245, Nextier 2706
Subsidiaries: Harsco 1741, Spang 3530

Camp Hill
Foundation: Harsco 1741
Corporate Headquarters: Harsco 1741, Rite 3220, Warrell 3991
Subsidiaries: Harsco 1741, Highmark 1799

Canonsburg
Corporate Giving Program: Columbia 884
Foundations: CentiMark 740, Mylan 2610
Corporate Headquarters: CentiMark 740, Columbia 884, Mylan 2610
Subsidiary: NiSource 2715
Office: Fulbright 1516

Carbondale
Cororate Headquarters: Hendrick 1777

Carlisle
Corporate Giving Program: Giant 1572
Foundations: Keen 2111, Warrell 3991
Corporate Headquarters: Giant 1572, Keen 2111
Subsidiary: Sprint 3556
Plant: PPG 3025

Carnegie
Subsidiary: AMPCO 186

Center Valley
Foundation: Olympus 2804
Cororate Headquarters: Olympus 2804
Office: White 4059

Chadds Ford
Corporate Giving Program: Endo 1268

Chalfont
Foundation: Byers 630
Cororate Headquarters: Byers 630
Plant: FMC 1449

Chambersburg
Foundation: Farmers 1336
Cororate Headquarters: Farmers 1336
Subsidiary: AMETEK 181

Chesterbrook
Corporate Giving Program: AmerisourceBergen 175
Cororate Headquarters: AmerisourceBergen 175

Cheswick
Plant: Westinghouse 4049

Churchill
Plant: Westinghouse 4049

Cleona
Foundation: Lebanon 2238
Cororate Headquarters: Lebanon 2238

Collegeville
Corporate Giving Program: SunPower 3651
Cororate Headquarters: SunPower 3651

Concordville
Office: State 3591

Conemaush
Plant: Public 3077

Conshohocken
Corporate Giving Program: Quaker 3093
Foundation: Quaker 3093
Cororate Headquarters: Quaker 3093
Subsidiary: MedImmune 2450
Office: White 4059
Coraopolis
Foundation: Dick's 1110
Cororate Headquarters: Dick's 1110
Subsidiary: Baker 323
Plant: Univar 3886
Corry
Plant: Barnes 362
Cranberry Township
Corporate Giving Program: Westinghouse 4049
Foundations: Mine 2529, Truefit 3816
Corporate Headquarters: Mine 2529, Truefit 3816
Creighton
Plant: PPG 3025
Danville
Subsidiary: Fulton 1518
Delmont
Plant: Menasha 2461
Devon
Office: McKenna 2433
Dublin
Office: First 1421
Eagleville
Cororate Headquarters: Seton 3415
East Greenville
Foundation: Knoll 2176
Cororate Headquarters: Knoll 2176
East Stroudsburg
Subsidiary: Harsco 1741
Easton
Corporate Giving Program: Crayola 973
Foundation: Victaulic 3948
Corporate Headquarters: Crayola 973, Victaulic 3948
Subsidiaries: Fulton 1518, Hallmark 1707, Victaulic 3948
Ellwood City
Plant: Nalco 2613
Elverson
Plant: Newell 2694
Elysburg
Cororate Headquarters: Catawissa 720
Emmaus
Subsidiary: DRS 1179
Ephrata
Foundation: GSM 1676
Erie
Corporate Giving Program: Erie 1291
Foundation: Times 3758
Cororate Headquarters: Erie 1291
Subsidiaries: FirstEnergy 1424, National 2628
Division: General 1552
Office: FMC 1449
Evans City
Cororate Headquarters: Isaly's 1994
Exton
Foundations: ERM 1292, Mutual 2604, West 4038
Corporate Headquarters: ERM 1292, Mutual 2604, West 4038
Subsidiaries: Allegheny 91, Johnson 2048, O'Neal 2771
Fairless Hills
Plant: Castle 716
Farrell
Cororate Headquarters: Caparo 673
Plant: Caparo 673
Ford City
Subsidiary: S & T 3297
Fort Washington
Subsidiaries: Johnson 2048, sanofi-aventis 3329, Teleflex 3707
Joint Venture: Merck 2466
Franklin
Plant: Timken 3760
Frazer
Corporate Giving Program: Cephalon 752
Foundation: Cephalon 752
Cororate Headquarters: Cephalon 752
Fredericksburg
Plant: Sherwin 3437
Freeland
Subsidiary: Manitowoc 2356
Glenside
Foundation: FIDELIO 1370
Cororate Headquarters: FIDELIO 1370
Greensburg
Cororate Headquarters: Tribune 3806
Subsidiary: Tribune 3806
Plant: Owens 2841
Greenville
Subsidiary: NVF 2766
Hanover
Plants: Sealed 3381, SKF 3473
Harleysville
Corporate Giving Program: Harleysville 1733
Foundation: Marcho 2368
Corporate Headquarters: Harleysville 1733, Marcho 2368
Subsidiary: Harleysville 1733
Harmarville
Office: PPG 3025
Harrisburg
Foundations: Petroleum 2947, Quandel 3099, Residential 3191, Rite 3220, Tyco 3829
Corporate Headquarters: Quandel 3099, Residential 3191, Tyco 3829
Subsidiaries: Highmark 1799, NRG 2756
Offices: Cozen 964, CUNA 1008, Hangley 1721, K&L 2080, Morgan 2571, Pepper 2934, Stradley 3620
Havertown
Corporate Giving Program: Nolan 2718
Cororate Headquarters: Nolan 2718
Hazleton
Subsidiary: Westervelt 4046
Plants: Bemis 407, Hershey 1791, Owens 2842
Hermitage
Foundation: F.N.B. 1318
Cororate Headquarters: F.N.B. 1318
Hershey
Corporate Giving Program: Hershey 1791
Cororate Headquarters: Hershey 1791
Hilltown
Plant: Giant 1573
Homer City
Plant: FMC 1449
Horsham
Corporate Giving Program: Toll 3769
Foundations: Accupac 23, C & C 632
Corporate Headquarters: C & C 632, Toll 3769
Subsidiaries: Comcast 887, General 1555, Johnson 2048, STERIS 3600
Huntingdon
Plant: Owens 2842
Huntingdon Valley
Foundation: Griffith 1666
Cororate Headquarters: Griffith 1666
Indiana
Foundation: S & T 3297
Cororate Headquarters: S & T 3297
Ivyland
Subsidiary: Schein 3348
Jenkintown
Foundation: First 1419
Office: Grant 1633
Jersey Shore
Plant: West 4038
Johnstown
Joint Venture: DRS 1179
Jonestown
Plant: Ingram 1941
Kennett Square
Foundation: Genesis 1561
Corporate Headquarters: Clarks 838, Genesis 1561
Subsidiary: Exelon 1309
Plant: NVF 2766
Keystone
Plant: Public 3077
King of Prussia
Foundations: American 139, American 157, Arkema 242, CSL 993
Corporate Headquarters: American 139, American 157, Arkema 242, CSL 993
Subsidiaries: American 157, Fiserv 1427, Miller 2517
Offices: AT&T 274, ITA 1998
Plant: Crane 970
Kulpsville
Foundations: Clemens 844, Green 1657
Corporate Headquarters: Clemens 844, Green 1657
Lancaster
Corporate Giving Program: Fulton 1518
Foundations: Armstrong 246, Auntie 287, Calumet 662, Dutch 1197, Fulton 1518, Kahn 2085, North 2732
Corporate Headquarters: Armstrong 246, Auntie 287, Dutch 1197, Fulton 1518, GSM 1676, North 2732
Subsidiaries: Armstrong 246, Berry 438, CLARCOR 832, Danaher 1027, Fulton 1518, Goldman 1603, Highmark 1799, Universal 3891
Division: ServiceMaster 3414
Office: Westfield 4047
Plants: Armstrong 246, Donnelley 1155, Hershey 1791, Kellogg 2120, Packaging 2861, Pactiv 2863
Langhorne
Subsidiary: Brown 592
Office: SeaWorld 3387
Lansdale
Corporate Giving Program: SKF 3473
Cororate Headquarters: SKF 3473
Subsidiary: Armstrong 246
Latrobe
Corporate Giving Program: Kennametal 2125
Foundation: Kennametal 2125
Cororate Headquarters: Kennametal 2125
Subsidiary: Timken 3760
Plant: Kennametal 2125
Lebanon
Cororate Headquarters: New 2680
Subsidiaries: Fulton 1518, Gehl 1545
Plants: Alcoa 82, Bemis 407
Leechburg
Plant: Allegheny 91
Lemoyne
Foundation: Property 3062
Cororate Headquarters: Property 3062
Subsidiary: Property 3062
Plant: Crystal 992
Leola
Office: Dart 1033
Limerick
Foundation: Teleflex 3707
Cororate Headquarters: Teleflex 3707
Subsidiary: Teleflex 3707
Lititz
Cororate Headquarters: Esbenshade's 1295
Plant: West 4038
Lykens
Foundation: Reiff 3174
Cororate Headquarters: Reiff 3174
Madison
Plant: Westinghouse 4049
Mainland
Cororate Headquarters: Accupac 23
Malvern
Foundation: American 146
Corporate Headquarters: American 146, Endo 1268, IKON 1914
Office: Stradley 3620
Plant: Worthington 4124
Mapleton Depot
Plant: U.S. 3840

Marietta
Plant: Armstrong 246
McKees Rocks
Cororate Headquarters: Horix 1860
Plant: Horix 1860
McMurray
Foundation: Dynamet 1200
Meadville
Plant: PPG 3025
Media
Foundations: Main 2342, Untours 3897
Cororate Headquarters: Untours 3897
Mehoopany
Plant: Procter 3055
Middleburg
Subsidiary: Fulton 1518
Middletown
Cororate Headquarters: Petroleum 2947
Subsidiary: US 3902
Milford
Subsidiary: Orange 2822
Milford Square
Office: First 1421
Milton
Plant: GKN 1585
Minersville
Office: Quandel 3099
Mohnton
Foundation: Esbenshade's 1295
Monaca
Plant: Newell 2694
Monroeville
Office: PPG 3025
Montgomery
Subsidiaries: Springs 3555, Todd 3766
Montgomeryville
Foundation: Mid-Atlantic 2502
Cororate Headquarters: Mid-Atlantic 2502
Subsidiary: Todd 3766
Division: PerkinElmer 2939
Plant: Illinois 1916
Moon Township
Foundations: ANH 201, Baker 323, Wonder 4107
Corporate Headquarters: ANH 201, Baker 323
Moorestown
Plant: Subaru 3631
Morrisville
Plant: Univar 3886
Mount Pleasant
Plant: Sony 3502
Mountain Top
Plant: Quaker 3094
Muncy
Plant: Kellogg 2120
Murrysville
Foundation: Respironics 3193
Cororate Headquarters: Respironics 3193
Narberth
Foundation: Conston 920
Nazareth
Foundation: Martin 2390
Corporate Headquarters: Andretti 197, Martin 2390
New Bethlehem
Subsidiary: Smucker 3488
New Castle
Subsidiary: AMPCO 186
New Holland
Foundations: Berk 423, Quality 3096
Corporate Headquarters: Berk 423, Quality 3096
New Kensington
Plant: Alcoa 82
New Kingstown
Subsidiary: Keen 2111
New Stanton
Subsidiary: SUPERVALU 3659
Newtown
Office: ITA 1998
Newtown Square
Corporate Giving Program: SAP 3334
Foundations: Boiron 519, Creative 976
Corporate Headquarters: Boiron 519, SAP 3334
Plant: LyondellBasell 2322
Norristown
Subsidiary: Handy 1718
Office: Hangley 1721
North East
Plant: Welch 4025
Nottingham
Corporate Giving Program: Herr 1787
Cororate Headquarters: Herr 1787
Orwigsburg
Plant: Carpenter 700
Oxnard
Subsidiary: Teleflex 3707
Palmyra
Office: West 4038
Plant: Hershey 1791
Paoli
Corporate Giving Program: Naturescapes 2644
Cororate Headquarters: Naturescapes 2644
Peach Bottom
Plant: Public 3077
Pen Argyl
Foundation: Berkheimer 425
Pennsburg
Plant: Hershey 1791
Perkasie
Foundation: First 1421
Corporate Headquarters: First 1421
Philadelphia
Corporate Giving Programs: Abacus 9, ARAMARK 223, Azavea 309, Ballard 329, Chemtura 775, Comcast 887, Cozen 964, Crown 988, Dechert 1058, Drinker 1175, Duane 1185, First 1398, FMC 1449, Genji 1562, Hangley 1721, Morgan 2571, Pepper 2934, Philadelphia 2957, Philadelphia 2958, Philadelphia 2959, Philadelphia 2961, Praxis 3030, Stradley 3620, Sunoco 3650, White 4059, YIKES 4144
Foundations: ACE 24, AFL 53, BDP 388, Beneficial 412, Binswanger 464, CIGNA 812, Comcast 887, Comcast 888, Cozen 964, Crayola 973, Crescent 982, CSS 996, Dietz 1114, Erickson 1290, GlaxoSmithKline 1588, Independence 1926, Lefton 2244, Microsoft 2501, Pacifico 2859, Philadelphia 2958, Phillies 2964, Spector 3539, SQA 3559, Sunoco 3650, Wells 4028
Corporate Headquarters: Abacus 9, ACE 24, AFL 53, ARAMARK 223, Azavea 309, Ballard 329, BDP 388, Beneficial 412, Binswanger 464, Chemtura 775, CIGNA 812, Comcast 887, Comcast 888, Conrail 914, Cozen 964, Crescent 982, Crown 988, CSS 996, Dechert 1058, Dietz 1114, Drinker 1175, Duane 1185, Erickson 1290, FMC 1449, Genji 1562, Hangley 1721, Independence 1926, Lefton 2244, Morgan 2571, Nasdaq 2618, Pacifico 2859, Pepper 2934, Philadelphia 2957, Philadelphia 2958, Philadelphia 2959, Philadelphia 2961, Phillies 2964, Praxis 3030, Spector 3539, SQA 3559, Stradley 3620, Sunoco 3650, Tasty 3693, White 4059, YIKES 4144
Subsidiaries: Alsco 115, American 141, Cardinal 685, Comcast 887, Comcast 888, Conrail 914, Crown 988, Dow 1161, Exelon 1309, Fiserv 1427, Flowers 1446, Lincoln 2281, Manpower 2358, Nasdaq 2618, Norfolk 2725, Staples 3581, Sunoco 3650, Verizon 3936
Offices: Akin 70, Archer 232, Ballard 329, Benesch 413, Brown 589, Cozen 964, Credit 980, Dechert 1058, Drinker 1175, Duane 1185, Elevation 1245, Federal 1349, Gibbons 1574, GlaxoSmithKline 1588, Grant 1633, Greenberg 1654, Hangley 1721, Hogan 1825, Littler 2289, Morgan 2571, Pepper 2934, Reed 3163, SAS 3336, Stradley 3620, Thompson 3739, United 3872, Vision 3961, White 4059, Wiggin 4068, Wilentz 4071
Plants: Bemis 407, DP 1168, FMC 1449, Just 2077, Rexnord 3198, TJX 3765, Wal-Mart 3980
Pipersville
Office: First 1421
Pittsburgh
Corporate Giving Programs: American 140, Bayer 381, Dick's 1110, Duquesne 1194, Giant 1571, Heinz 1772, Highmark 1799, K&L 2080, Lemieux 2249, Morris 2574, Neville 2667, Pittsburgh 2985, Pittsburgh 2986, Print.Net 3048, Reed 3163, SEEDS 3396, StarKist 3588, U.S. 3841
Foundations: ABARTA 10, Alcoa 82, Allegheny 91, American 140, AMPCO 186, Bank 344, Bayer 381, Dollar 1142, Dominion 1150, Elias 1247, EQT 1287, Farrell 1341, Federated 1351, Giant 1571, Hanna 1722, Heinz 1772, Highmark 1799, Isaly's 1994, Matthews 2406, PNC 2996, PNC 2997, PPG 3025, Seneca 3406, Spang 3530, Tribune 3806, United 3874, United 3877
Corporate Headquarters: ABARTA 10, Allegheny 91, American 140, AMPCO 186, Bayer 381, Dollar 1142, Duquesne 1194, Elias 1247, EQT 1287, Farrell 1341, Federated 1351, Giant 1571, Hanna 1722, Heinz 1772, Highmark 1799, K&L 2080, Lemieux 2249, Matthews 2406, Neville 2667, Pittsburgh 2985, Pittsburgh 2986, PNC 2996, PNC 2997, PPG 3025, Print.Net 3048, Reed 3163, SEEDS 3396, Spang 3530, StarKist 3588, United 3877
Subsidiaries: Alcoa 82, Allegheny 91, AMPCO 186, Baker 323, Bard 358, Berkshire 429, Dominion 1150, Duquesne 1194, Eaton 1216, Emerson 1257, Fiserv 1427, Highmark 1799, Huntington 1894, Mine 2529, Occidental 2780, Omnicom 2808, PNC 2997, Sunoco 3650
Division: EQT 1287
Joint Venture: Corning 945
Offices: Duane 1185, Factory 1323, Jones 2058, K&L 2080, Liberty 2265, Littler 2289, McGuireWoods 2430, Pepper 2934, Reed 3163, SAP 3334, SAS 3336
Plants: Donnelley 1155, Georgia 1568, Novell 2754, Valspar 3920
Pittston Township
Plant: TJX 3765
Plymouth Meeting
Foundation: Premier 3036
Cororate Headquarters: Premier 3036
Subsidiaries: Comcast 887, eBay 1217, Teleflex 3707
Office: Opus 2820
Port Clinton
Foundation: Reading 3142
Cororate Headquarters: Reading 3142
Pottstown
Corporate Giving Program: Barber 355
Foundation: Peerless 2915
Corporate Headquarters: Barber 355, Peerless 2915
Plants: Bassett 372, Sonoco 3500
Pottsville
Plant: Hexcel 1795
Quakertown
Office: First 1421
Radnor
Corporate Giving Program: Airgas 65
Corporate Headquarters: Airgas 65, Lincoln 2281
Subsidiaries: Covance 955, Sunoco 3650
Reading
Foundation: Redner's 3157
Cororate Headquarters: Redner's 3157
Subsidiary: FirstEnergy 1424
Plants: Carpenter 700, Hershey 1791, Morton 2579
Reedsville
Foundation: Standard 3577
Richlandtown
Office: First 1421
Riegelsville
Office: First 1421
Rochester
Plant: Valspar 3920
Rydal
Foundation: Manhattan 2354
Sandy Lake
Division: Spang 3530

Scottdale
Foundation: Scottdale 3371
Cororate Headquarters: Scottdale 3371
Scranton
Foundation: Penn 2924
Cororate Headquarters: Penn 2924
Subsidiary: CSS 996
Plant: Menasha 2461
Shady Grove
Subsidiary: Manitowoc 2355
Sharon
Subsidiary: NVF 2766
Shenandoah
Plant: Beneficial 411
Shippensburg
Subsidiary: Keen 2111
Smoketown
Cororate Headquarters: Calumet 662
Souderton
Corporate Giving Program: One 2811
Cororate Headquarters: One 2811
Spring City
Corporate Giving Program: HolacracyOne 1826
Cororate Headquarters: HolacracyOne 1826
Springdale
Plant: PPG 3025
St. Marys
Plant: Osram 2834
State College
Plant: Jostens 2067
Stroudsburg
Foundation: Essa 1297
Cororate Headquarters: Essa 1297
Sunbury
Corporate Giving Program: Weis 4024
Cororate Headquarters: Weis 4024
Subsidiary: American 149
Sykesville
Cororate Headquarters: Symmco 3670
Templeton
Subsidiary: Caparo 673
Thompsontown
Plant: Armstrong 246
Tipton
Plant: PPG 3025
Titusville
Plant: Armstrong 246
Towanda
Plant: Osram 2834
Upper Darby
Plant: West 4038
Valley Forge
Foundations: IKON 1914, Saint 3312
Cororate Headquarters: Saint 3312
Subsidiary: Fiserv 1427
Vandergrift
Plant: Allegheny 91
Wampum
Cororate Headquarters: Universal 3892
Warren
Foundations: Betts 451, Northwest 2746
Corporate Headquarters: Betts 451, Northwest 2746
Subsidiary: Northwest 2746
Plants: Osram 2834, Rexnord 3198
Warrendale
Corporate Giving Program: Medrad 2452
Cororate Headquarters: Medrad 2452
Subsidiary: Joy 2070
Warrington
Plant: Crane 970
Washington
Foundation: Washington 3996
Corporate Headquarters: Dynamet 1200, Washington 3996
Subsidiary: Carpenter 700
Division: Cox 958
Plant: Carpenter 700
Wawa
Corporate Giving Program: Wawa 4009
Cororate Headquarters: Wawa 4009
Wayne
Foundation: Safeguard 3307
Cororate Headquarters: Safeguard 3307
Subsidiaries: Safeguard 3307, U.S. 3840
Division: ServiceMaster 3414
Wellsboro
Plant: Osram 2834
West Chester
Corporate Giving Programs: QVC 3112, Strategy 3623
Corporate Headquarters: QVC 3112, Strategy 3623
Subsidiary: Comcast 887
West Conshohocken
Foundation: Keystone 2137
Cororate Headquarters: Keystone 2137
Offices: BMC 508, Cozen 964
Plant: CA 638
West Elizabeth
Plant: Guardian 1682
West Grove
Foundation: Dansko 1031
Cororate Headquarters: Dansko 1031
West Mifflin
Plant: Lafarge 2210
West Point
Plant: Merck 2466
Whitehall
Subsidiary: Lafarge 2210
Plant: Lafarge 2210
Wilkes Barre
Foundation: Lord 2302
Corporate Headquarters: Benevento 414, Blue 505
Office: Cozen 964
Plants: Carpenter 700, Corning 945
Wilkes-Barre
Foundations: Benevento 414, Blue 505
Williamsport
Subsidiary: Textron 3731
Division: Cox 958
Plant: West 4038
Willow Grove
Subsidiary: Raymond 3133
Wilmerding
Foundation: Westinghouse 4048
Cororate Headquarters: Westinghouse 4048
Windsor
Subsidiary: Harsco 1741
Wyomissing
Corporate Giving Program: Carpenter 700
Foundations: Penn 2923, Sovereign 3528
Corporate Headquarters: Carpenter 700, Penn 2923
Yardley
Corporate Giving Program: Siw 3468
Cororate Headquarters: Siw 3468
York
Foundations: Bon 521, DENTSPLY 1089, Graham 1625, RG 3201, Susquehanna 3661, Wolf 4103, York 4145
Corporate Headquarters: Bon 521, DENTSPLY 1089, Graham 1625, RG 3201, Susquehanna 3661, Wolf 4103, YGS 4143, York 4145
Subsidiaries: Harsco 1741, Johnson 2050, Raymond 3133, Susquehanna 3661
Plants: Osram 2834, Starbucks 3585
Yukon
Plant: Menasha 2461
Zelienople
Foundation: Foreman 1465
Cororate Headquarters: Foreman 1465

PUERTO RICO

Aguadilla
Plant: Hewlett 1794
Barceloneta
Plant: Campbell 669
Caguas
Office: Avon 305
Plants: Clorox 852, Merck 2466, Panasonic 2869
Carolina
Subsidiary: Eastman 1214
Plant: Panasonic 2869
Cayey
Plants: Procter 3055, West 4038
Cidra
Plant: Merk 2467
Guaynabo
Subsidiaries: Biomet 466, Sealed 3381
Gurabo
Subsidiary: Praxair 3029
Hato Rey
Corporate Giving Program: Popular 3003
Subsidiary: Oracle 2821
Isabela
Subsidiary: Timberland 3754
Juncos
Subsidiary: Amgen 182
Las Piedras
Subsidiary: Sonoco 3500
Plant: Bard 358
Manati
Subsidiary: du Pont 1184
Mayaguez
Office: Humana 1886
Ponce
Office: Humana 1886
San Juan
Cororate Headquarters: Popular 3003
Subsidiaries: Bausch 376, Kimberly 2150, Nestle 2663
Offices: Humana 1886, Pan-American 2868
Plant: Bausch 376
Toa Baja
Subsidiary: Grace 1623

RHODE ISLAND

Central Falls
Plant: Osram 2834
Coventry
Subsidiary: GTECH 1677
Cranston
Foundation: Cranston 972
Cororate Headquarters: Cranston 972
Subsidiaries: Cranston 972, PerkinElmer 2939
Division: Cox 958
Plant: Bausch 376
East Providence
Subsidiary: Handy 1718
Glocester
Foundation: Kilmartin 2145
Johnston
Corporate Giving Program: Factory 1323
Foundation: Factory 1323
Cororate Headquarters: Factory 1323
Lincoln
Foundation: Amica 183
Cororate Headquarters: Amica 183
Subsidiary: Amica 183
Newport
Foundation: Newport 2699
Cororate Headquarters: Newport 2699
Office: Tofias 3768
North Kingstown
Subsidiary: Windway 4086
Pawtucket
Corporate Giving Programs: Hasbro 1747, Pawtucket 2902
Foundations: Collette 872, Hasbro 1747, International 1967, Key 2134, Pawtucket 2903
Corporate Headquarters: Collette 872, Hasbro 1747, International 1967, Key 2134, Pawtucket 2902, Pawtucket 2903
Portsmouth
Plant: Raytheon 3135

Providence
Corporate Giving Programs: Bank 349, Blue 491, Dimeo 1119, Gilbane 1581, GTECH 1677, RBS 3137, Textron 3731
Foundations: Bank 340, Dow 1163, Goulds 1619, Hudson 1881, Kingsbury 2160, Record 3149, Rostra 3268, Shaughnessy 3425, Shaw's 3427, Textron 3731, Tutor 3826
Corporate Headquarters: Armbrust 243, Bank 349, Blue 491, Dimeo 1119, Gilbane 1581, GTECH 1677, Hudson 1881, Providence 3068, RBS 3137, Textron 3731
Subsidiaries: American 133, Bank 340, Gilbane 1581, National 2630, Textron 3731
Division: Shaughnessy 3425
Offices: Brown 590, Littler 2289, Pierce 2974, State 3592, Tofias 3768, Weil 4023

Slatersville
Division: Philips 2963

Warren
Subsidiary: Avery 297

Warwick
Corporate Giving Program: Home 1844
Foundation: DeBlois 1056
Corporate Headquarters: DeBlois 1056, Home 1844
Subsidiaries: Jones 2057, Masco 2393, Metropolitan 2481, United 3871
Divisions: Bard 358, Dimeo 1119
Plants: Butler 626, PerkinElmer 2939

West Greenwich
Office: Tim 3753

West Kingston
Corporate Giving Program: American 161
Cororate Headquarters: American 161
Plant: Modine 2544

West Warwick
Division: Cox 958
Office: Connecticut 910

Westerly
Foundations: Moore 2567, Washington 4001
Corporate Headquarters: Moore 2567, Washington 4001

Woonsocket
Corporate Giving Program: CVS 1014
Foundation: CVS 1014
Cororate Headquarters: CVS 1014

SOUTH CAROLINA

Abbeville
Subsidiary: InterTech 1977

Aiken
Subsidiary: Evening 1302
Plants: Campbell 669, FMC 1449, Owens 2842

Anderson
Plant: Owens 2842

Beaufort
Subsidiary: Minster 2532

Bennettsville
Plant: Emerson 1257

Camden
Subsidiary: Blue 498

Cayce
Corporate Giving Program: SCANA 3346

Charleston
Foundations: Atlantic 282, Bosch 529, Evening 1302, Magnolia 2340, Pastime 2891
Corporate Headquarters: Evening 1302, Magnolia 2340, Pastime 2891
Subsidiaries: Amazon.com 122, MeadWestvaco 2445
Offices: Dixon 1133, Moore 2566, Nelson 2661, Parker 2885
Plant: Cummins 1007

Chester
Plants: PPG 3025, Scotts 3372, Sequa 3410

Clinton
Subsidiary: Avery 297

Columbia
Corporate Giving Program: Colonial 874
Foundations: Baker 318, Blue 498, Budweiser 605, First 1395, Kahn 2084
Corporate Headquarters: Baker 318, Blue 498, Bonitz 524, Budweiser 605, Colonial 874, Consolidated 918, First 1395, Kahn 2084, SCANA 3346
Subsidiaries: Blue 498, Bonitz 524, Commercial 893, Consolidated 918, First 1395, SCANA 3346, Snyder's-Lance 3492, Synovus 3674
Offices: Littler 2289, Nelson 2661, Parker 2885, United 3872, Unum 3898, Wyche 4131
Plants: Honeywell 1852, Square 3560, U.S. 3840, Westinghouse 4049

Cooper River
Plant: BP 547

Denmark
Plant: NIBCO 2707

Easley
Corporate Giving Program: Ortec 2828
Foundations: Alice 89, Ortec 2828
Corporate Headquarters: Alice 89, Ortec 2828

Eastover
Plant: International 1968

Florence
Foundation: Pearce 2910
Cororate Headquarters: Pearce 2910
Subsidiary: Hoffmann 1823

Fort Mill
Corporate Giving Program: Springs 3555
Foundation: Continental 927
Cororate Headquarters: Springs 3555

Fountain Inn
Foundation: AVX 306
Cororate Headquarters: AVX 306
Joint Venture: Corning 945
Plants: GKN 1585, Sherwin 3437, Sonoco 3500

Gaffney
Foundations: Hamrick 1715, Rug 3286
Corporate Headquarters: Hamrick 1715, Rug 3286
Plant: Timken 3760

Gaston
Plant: Starbucks 3585

Georgetown
Subsidiary: Evening 1302
Plant: International 1968

Greenville
Corporate Giving Programs: Bowater 543, Michelin 2495, Wyche 4131
Foundations: Gardner 1536, North 2728, Park 2882, ScanSource 3347
Corporate Headquarters: BI-LO 456, Bowater 543, Gardner 1536, Michelin 2495, Park 2882, ScanSource 3347, Wyche 4131
Subsidiaries: Bonitz 524, Meredith 2471
Divisions: Bausch 376, Bowater 543
Offices: Dixon 1133, Dow 1164, Hill 1803, Nelson 2661, Vision 3961, Wyche 4131
Plants: Bausch 376, Morton 2579

Greenwood
Foundation: County 952
Cororate Headquarters: County 952
Subsidiary: Fuji 1514

Greer
Foundation: Citizens 823
Corporate Headquarters: Citizens 823, North 2728
Office: Wurzburg 4129

Hanahan
Cororate Headquarters: Atlantic 282

Hartsville
Corporate Giving Program: Sonoco 3500
Foundation: Sonoco 3500
Cororate Headquarters: Sonoco 3500
Subsidiary: Sonoco 3500
Plants: Carpenter 700, Sonoco 3500

Hilton Head Island
Corporate Giving Program: Hargray 1730
Foundation: Mautz 2408
Cororate Headquarters: Hargray 1730

Inman
Foundation: Inman 1943
Cororate Headquarters: Inman 1943

Kingstree
Subsidiaries: Evening 1302, First 1395, Milliken 2525

Laurens
Plant: Jostens 2067

Lexington
Subsidiary: Caterpillar 722
Office: Do 1136
Plant: Golden 1602

Liberty
Plant: Vulcan 3972

Lyman
Plant: Vulcan 3972

Marietta
Division: Milliken 2525

Mauldin
Foundation: BI-LO 456

McBee
Plant: Smith 3484

Moncks Corner
Plant: Bard 358

Mullins
Subsidiary: Unaka 3848

Myrtle Beach
Cororate Headquarters: Better 447
Division: Cox 958
Offices: Nelson 2661, Parker 2885

Newberry
Subsidiary: Caterpillar 722

North Charleston
Foundation: InterTech 1977
Cororate Headquarters: InterTech 1977

Orangeburg
Foundation: Cox 962
Cororate Headquarters: Cox 962
Plants: Albemarle 78, Carpenter 700

Rock Hill
Office: Robinson 3234
Plants: BP 547, Worthington 4124

Seneca
Plant: Square 3560

Simpsonville
Subsidiary: Bardes 359
Office: Univar 3886

Spartanburg
Corporate Giving Programs: Dell Corning 1067, Denny's 1087
Foundations: Bridgewater 561, Gibbs 1576, Security 3392, Smith 3485
Corporate Headquarters: adidas 35, Bridgewater 561, Dell Corning 1067, Denny's 1087, Gibbs 1576, Milliken 2525, Security 3392, Smith 3485, Tindall 3761
Subsidiaries: Denny's 1087, Staples 3581
Division: Milliken 2525
Offices: Dixon 1133, Ford 1462, Parker 2885
Plants: adidas 35, Donnelley 1155, Georgia 1568, Kohler 2182, Lubrizol 2315, Westinghouse 4049

St. Matthews
Subsidiary: Worthington 4124

Stockton
Plant: Sonoco 3500

Summerville
Subsidiary: Caterpillar 722
Office: Dixon 1133

Sumter
Subsidiary: Cox 962
Plant: GKN 1585

Timmonsville
Subsidiary: American 150

Travelers Rest
Corporate Giving Program: Liquid 2284
Cororate Headquarters: Liquid 2284

West Columbia
Subsidiaries: Caterpillar 722, Harsco 1741

SOUTH DAKOTA

Dakota Dunes
Foundations: BPI 548, V-T 3912
Cororate Headquarters: BPI 548
Subsidiary: Tyson 3832
Office: Security 3393
Huron
Subsidiary: NorthWestern 2748
Madison
Plant: Gehl 1545
North Sioux
Plant: Procter 3055
Pierre
Foundation: Delta 1080
Cororate Headquarters: Delta 1080
Rapid City
Corporate Giving Program: Black 474
Foundation: Black 474
Cororate Headquarters: Black 474
Subsidiaries: Black 474, Nash 2619
Sioux Falls
Corporate Giving Program: NorthWestern 2748
Foundations: Robinson 3235, Sioux 3465
Corporate Headquarters: NorthWestern 2748, Sioux 3465
Subsidiaries: NorthWestern 2748, Target 3691
Offices: Wellmark 4026, Xcel 4135
Plants: Graco 1624, Nash 2619
Watertown
Foundation: ANZA 208
Cororate Headquarters: ANZA 208
Yankton
Subsidiary: Gehl 1545

TENNESSEE

Adamsville
Subsidiaries: CenturyLink 751, Masco 2393
Afton
Subsidiary: American 149
Alcoa
Plant: Alcoa 82
Athens
Subsidiary: HCA 1762
Plant: Vulcan 3972
Bartlett
Subsidiary: Brother 587
Brentwood
Foundations: Bright 566, EMI 1258, LifePoint 2270
Corporate Headquarters: EMI 1258, LifePoint 2270
Subsidiaries: Alcoa 82, Arbitron 227, Ceridian 753
Division: Meritor 2473
Bristol
Subsidiaries: Sprint 3556, Victaulic 3948
Charleston
Plant: Olin 2801
Chattanooga
Corporate Giving Program: Unum 3898
Foundations: BlueCross 507, Cornerstone 942, Dixie 1132, sanofi-aventis 3329
Corporate Headquarters: BlueCross 507, Cornerstone 942, Dixie 1132, Unum 3898
Subsidiaries: AGL 57, Danaher 1027, Unum 3898
Offices: Adams 34, Baker 325, CUNA 1008, Husch 1896
Plants: Commercial 893, Vulcan 3972, Westinghouse 4049
Clarksville
Foundation: Credit 978
Cororate Headquarters: Credit 978
Subsidiary: Anheuser 202
Plant: Jostens 2067
Cleveland
Foundation: Life 2267
Cororate Headquarters: Life 2267
Subsidiary: Alsco 115
Plant: Olin 2801
Clinton
Cororate Headquarters: Halstead 1708
Plant: Rexnord 3198
Collegedale
Corporate Giving Program: McKee 2432
Cororate Headquarters: McKee 2432
Collierville
Foundation: Hendrick 1777
Office: Univar 3886
Cookeville
Foundation: American 135
Division: Flowserve 1447
Plant: Cummins 1006
Copper Hill
Office: GATX 1542
Counce
Plant: Packaging 2861
Crossville
Foundation: TAP 3690
Cororate Headquarters: TAP 3690
Subsidiary: Evans 1300
Dayton
Plant: La-Z-Boy 2205
Ducktown
Subsidiary: Occidental 2780
Dyersburg
Plant: Sun 3646
Franklin
Corporate Giving Program: Nissan 2716
Foundations: Atmos 285, CLARCOR 832, Community 900, Nissan 2716
Corporate Headquarters: CLARCOR 832, Community 900
Subsidiary: Worthington 4124
Offices: Stites 3609, Univar 3886
Gallatin
Plants: Donnelley 1155, GKN 1585
Goodlettsville
Corporate Giving Program: Dollar 1143
Foundation: Dollar 1143
Cororate Headquarters: Dollar 1143
Subsidiary: Raymond 3133
Greeneville
Foundation: Unaka 3848
Cororate Headquarters: Unaka 3848
Subsidiary: Unaka 3848
Plants: Butler 626, Deere 1061, Donaldson 1153
Huntsville
Office: Baker 325
Jackson
Foundation: Murray 2601
Cororate Headquarters: Murray 2601
Plants: Armstrong 246, Owens 2842, Pactiv 2863, Procter 3055, U.S. 3840, Valspar 3920
Jamestown
Foundation: Progressive 3059
Cororate Headquarters: Progressive 3059
Jasper
Plant: Valmont 3919
Johnson City
Subsidiary: Thomasville 3737
Office: Baker 325
Plant: Kennametal 2125
Jonesborough
Plant: GenCorp 1548
Kingsport
Corporate Giving Program: Eastman 1213
Foundation: Eastman 1213
Cororate Headquarters: Eastman 1213
Subsidiary: American 141
Knoxville
Foundation: Regal 3166
Corporate Headquarters: Panasonic 2870, Regal 3166
Subsidiaries: Alcoa 82, Blue 498, Clayton 841, Philips 2963, Regal 3166, Sunoco 3650
Division: Alcoa 82
Offices: Baker 325, Bass 371, Kimley 2151, Merchant 2464, Strauss 3624, Univar 3886, Wurzburg 4129
Plants: Owens 2841, Panasonic 2869, Timken 3760, Vulcan 3972, Whirlpool 4056
La Vergne
Subsidiaries: Cardinal 685, Danaher 1027, Leggett 2246
Plant: Whirlpool 4056
Lawrenceburg
Plant: Modine 2544
Lebanon
Foundations: Cracker 966, Parker 2886
Cororate Headquarters: Cracker 966
Lenoir City
Subsidiary: Armstrong 246
Lewisburg
Plant: Newell 2694
Livingston
Subsidiary: LifePoint 2270
Lookout Mountain
Corporate Giving Program: Watershed 4004
Cororate Headquarters: Watershed 4004
Maryville
Corporate Giving Program: Clayton 841
Foundation: Ruby 3281
Corporate Headquarters: Clayton 841, Ruby 3281
Subsidiary: Berkshire 429
Plant: Donaldson 1153
Mc Kenzie
Subsidiary: Leggett 2246
Memphis
Corporate Giving Programs: ACI 27, AutoZone 294, Baker 325, FedEx 1352, First 1406, Hoops 1857, International 1968, ServiceMaster 3414
Foundations: American 165, First 1406, Hoops 1857, International 1968, Presley 3038, ServiceMaster 3414, Temple 3711
Corporate Headquarters: ACI 27, American 165, AutoZone 294, Baker 325, FedEx 1352, First 1406, Hoops 1857, International 1968, Presley 3038, ServiceMaster 3414, Wurzburg 4129
Subsidiaries: CSS 996, FedEx 1352, First 1406, L'Oreal 2203, Nucor 2760, Regions 3171, ServiceMaster 3414, Wurzburg 4129
Divisions: New York 2690, ServiceMaster 3414, Sharp 3422
Offices: Adams 34, Baker 325, Bass 371, Dixon 1133, Fishel 1429, Ford 1462, Humana 1886, Husch 1896, Kimley 2151, NIKE 2710, Pan-American 2868, Thompson 3739, Wyatt 4130
Plants: Cummins 1007, Hershey 1791, Kellogg 2120, Newell 2694, Novell 2754, Owens 2841, Owens 2842, Sherwin 3437, Smucker 3488, Tension 3717
Millington
Plant: Ingram 1941
Mount Pleasant
Foundation: Smelter 3481
Cororate Headquarters: Smelter 3481
Plants: Illinois 1916, Menasha 2461
Murfreesboro
Foundation: Ole 2800
Cororate Headquarters: Ole 2800
Office: State 3591
Plant: General 1554
Nashville
Corporate Giving Programs: Bass 371, Bridgestone 560, Genesco 1559, Louisiana 2310, Nashville 2620, Tennessee 3716
Foundations: AHS 61, Aladdin 73, American 160, Bridgestone 560, Cic 811, Gibson 1578, HCA 1762, Louisiana 2310, Nashville 2620, Ryman 3294
Corporate Headquarters: AHS 61, Aladdin 73, American 160, Bass 371, Bridgestone 560, Cic 811, Cummins 1006, Genesco 1559, Gibson 1578, HCA 1762, Louisiana 2310, Nashville 2620, Ryman 3294, Tennessee 3716
Subsidiaries: American 147, Cardinal 685, Caterpillar 722, Cummins 1007, Genesco 1559, Landmark 2218, Meredith 2471, Schulman 3361, Textron 3731, V.F. 3913
Offices: Adams 34, Baker 325, Bass 371, Bradley 550, Burr 621, Dixon 1133, Donnelley 1155, Fishel 1429, Frost 1511, Littler 2289, Loeb 2295,

Pan-American 2868, Safeco 3306, SAS 3336, Stites 3609, Unum 3898, Wurzburg 4129, Wyatt 4130
Plants: Mitsui 2541, Square 3560, U.S. 3841
New Tazewell
Subsidiaries: CenturyLink 751, La-Z-Boy 2205
Newbern
Plant: Hillshire 1809
Newport
Plant: Sonoco 3500
Oak Ridge
Subsidiary: PerkinElmer 2939
Office: Bionetics 467
Pigeon Forge
Foundation: Dollywood 1146
Cororate Headquarters: Dollywood 1146
Rossville
Plant: Kellogg 2120
Rutherford
Subsidiary: Kellwood 2121
Shelbyville
Foundation: Mccar 2419
Plants: Bemis 407, Jostens 2067
Smithville
Plant: Tenneco 3715
Smyrna
Subsidiary: Nissan 2716
Plant: Square 3560
Springfield
Subsidiary: Allegheny 91
Tullahoma
Subsidiary: Jacobs 2016
Union City
Plants: Goodyear 1612, Kohler 2182
Vonore
Plant: Panasonic 2869
White Bluff
Foundation: Interstate 1975
Cororate Headquarters: Interstate 1975
White House
Subsidiary: Leggett 2246
Winchester
Plant: Smith 3484

TEXAS

Abilene
Plant: Toro 3775
Addison
Corporate Giving Program: Mary 2392
Foundation: Mary 2392
Corporate Headquarters: Dresser 1173, Mary 2392
Subsidiary: Carlson 693
Offices: Mortenson 2577, Opus 2820
Plant: Quad 3091
Alamo
Plant: Birds 469
Alvin
Plants: BP 547, LyondellBasell 2322
Amarillo
Subsidiary: Xcel 4135
Plant: Owens 2842
Aransas Pass
Cororate Headquarters: Gulf 1688
Arlington
Foundation: Texas 3729
Cororate Headquarters: Texas 3729
Office: RJN 3228
Plants: Barnes 362, Dannon 1030, Sherwin 3437
Armstrong
Plant: Valero 3915
Athens
Subsidiary: Texas 3727
Austin
Corporate Giving Programs: Advanced 40, Freescale 1495, Whole 4066
Foundations: Abba 11, Advanced 40, American 136, Educational 1233, National 2632, Whitley 4064, Whole 4066
Corporate Headquarters: American 136, Educational 1233, Freescale 1495, National 2632, Temple 3711, Whitley 4064, Whole 4066
Subsidiaries: Belo 406, Commercial 893, Dell 1068, Farmers 1338, Fiserv 1427, GTECH 1677, International 1968, NCR 2650, Southern 3520
Divisions: Dresser 1173, Southern 3520
Offices: Akin 70, Andrews 198, Baker 321, Bracewell 549, Cox 961, Dechert 1058, Edelman 1224, Electronic 1242, Farmers 1338, Fish 1428, Fulbright 1516, Greenberg 1654, Haynes 1759, Humana 1886, Jackson 2012, K&L 2080, Kiewit 2142, Kimley 2151, King 2157, McGuireWoods 2430, Pulte 3083, RJN 3228, SAP 3334, SAS 3336, Sasol 3338, Sedgwick 3395, State 3591, Sutherland 3663, Vinson 3957, Vinson 3958, Weaver 4014, Wiley 4072, Wilson 4083
Plants: Applied 220, Bassett 372, CA 638, Chevron 780, Hospira 1867, Motorola 2586, Novell 2754
Autin
Subsidiary: Miller 2517
Bay City
Plant: LyondellBasell 2322
Bayport
Plant: Lubrizol 2315
Baytown
Subsidiary: Helmerich 1774
Plants: Chevron 780, Exxon 1315
Beaumont
Foundation: Conn 908
Subsidiary: Entergy 1279
Office: Packard 2862
Plants: Exxon 1315, Goodyear 1612, LyondellBasell 2322
Bellaire
Joint Venture: Praxair 3029
Boerne
Subsidiary: Fiserv 1427
Brenham
Plant: Valmont 3919
Brownsville
Plant: Panasonic 2869
Brownwood
Plant: Kohler 2182
Burnet
Cororate Headquarters: Gibraltar 1577
Caldwell
Foundation: Executive 1308
Carrollton
Subsidiaries: Miller 2517, SPX 3558
Plants: Ingram 1941, Mary 2392, McAfee 2417
Cedar Bayou
Plants: BP 547, Chevron 780
Center
Plants: Armstrong 246, Hallmark 1707
Channelview
Foundation: Tex 3724
Cororate Headquarters: Tex 3724
Plant: LyondellBasell 2322
Chocolate Bayou
Plant: BP 547
Clear Lake
Plant: Valero 3915
Cleburne
Subsidiary: Kimberly 2150
Clute
Plant: Commercial 893
Coppell
Foundation: Primary 3043
Cororate Headquarters: Primary 3043
Corpus Christi
Foundation: Manti 2359
Cororate Headquarters: Manti 2359
Offices: Humana 1886, Kiewit 2142
Plants: Commercial 893, LyondellBasell 2322, Valero 3915
Corsicana
Plant: Guardian 1682
Dallas
Corporate Giving Programs: 7-Eleven 5, Alliance 101, Austin 288, Brinker 572, Carrington Coleman 701, Dallas 1021, Dean 1054, Energy 1273, Federal 1347, Figari 1378, Frito 1506, Greyhound 1664, Hunt 1889, Jackson 2012, Neiman 2657, Pizza 2988, Republic 3188, Southwest 3522, Tenet 3713, Texas 3728, Thompson 3738
Foundations: AMR 187, AT&T 273, Bank 339, Bank 340, Beck 396, Belo 406, Bestway 444, Bickel 457, Boeing 516, Celanese 730, Contran 928, Dallas 1021, Dean 1054, Drive 1177, EnMark 1274, Haynes 1759, Houston 1870, Jackson-Shaw 2013, Lockheed 2292, Luxottica 2319, Mary 2392, Maverick 2409, Nestle 2663, Providence 3068, Reed 3162, Riggs 3213, Rudy's 3284, Texas 3727, Texas 3728, Thompson 3738, Tyler 3831
Corporate Headquarters: 7-Eleven 5, AT&T 273, Atmos 285, Austin 288, Beck 396, Belo 406, Bestway 444, Bickel 457, Blockbuster 483, Brinker 572, Carrington Coleman 701, Comerica 889, Contran 928, Dallas 1021, Dean 1054, Drive 1177, Energy 1273, EnMark 1274, Figari 1378, Haynes 1759, Hunt 1889, Hunt 1891, Jackson 2012, Jackson-Shaw 2013, Kimberly 2150, Maverick 2409, Neiman 2657, Pizza 2988, Reed 3162, Republic 3188, Rudy's 3284, SClenergy 3366, Southwest 3522, Tenet 3713, Texas 3727, Texas 3728, Thompson 3738, Tyler 3831
Subsidiaries: 7-Eleven 5, American 141, AT&T 273, Atmos 285, Austin 288, Baker 323, Bank 340, Belo 406, Boeing 516, Brown 589, CA 638, Citigroup 821, Commercial 893, Contran 928, Dean 1054, DRS 1179, Eastman 1214, Grace 1623, Intuit 1982, Kellwood 2121, Leggett 2246, Marathon 2363, NEC 2654, Occidental 2780, Omnicom 2808, Owens 2842, Philips 2963, Safeguard 3307, ServiceMaster 3414, Southern 3520, State 3591, Texas 3727, Turner 3824, Tyler 3831, Utica 3910, Yum! 4150
Divisions: Hunt 1889, Neiman 2657
Offices: Akerman 69, Akin 70, Alston 116, Andrews 198, AT&T 274, Baker 321, Bessemer 440, Bodman 514, Bracewell 549, Bryan 596, Cerner 754, CIBA 809, Cox 961, Cozen 964, Dixon 1133, Edelman 1224, Factory 1323, Federal 1348, Federal 1349, Fiserv 1427, Fish 1428, Ford 1462, Fulbright 1516, Gibson 1580, Grant 1633, Greenberg 1654, Hays 1761, Houghton 1869, Humana 1886, Jackson 2012, Jones 2058, JPMorgan Chase 2071, K&L 2080, Kearney 2107, Kiewit 2142, Kimley 2151, Lauth 2232, Littler 2289, Mercury 2469, Morgan 2571, Pactiv 2863, Pan-American 2868, Patton 2898, Perkins 2941, Polsinelli 3001, Pulte 3083, RJN 3228, SAP 3334, SAS 3336, Sedgwick 3395, Sharp 3422, Sidley 3446, Thompson 3739, Union 3854, United 3872, Vinson 3957, Vinson 3958, Vision 3961, Weaver 4014, Weil 4022, Weil 4023, Whiting 4063
Plants: Barnes 362, Coca 862, FMC 1449, Fuller 1517, Hunt 1892, Kroger 2195, Lafarge 2210, Lennar 2250, Motorola 2586, Navistar 2647, Novell 2754, Owens 2841, Oxford 2847, Quaker 3094, Raytheon 3135, Rockwell 3247, Sealed 3381, Univar 3886, Valassis 3914
Deer Park
Subsidiary: Safety 3309
Plants: Lubrizol 2315, Total 3778
Delmita
Plant: Valero 3915
Denton
Plant: Jostens 2067
DeSoto
Plant: McGraw 2429

Diboll
Subsidiary: Temple 3711
Dripping Springs
Foundations: Hutchison 1898, Serengeti 3411
Cororate Headquarters: Serengeti 3411
El Paso
Corporate Giving Program: Western 4044
Foundation: Ford 1464
Cororate Headquarters: Western 4044
Subsidiaries: Tomkins 3771, Western 4044
Offices: Cox 961, Univar 3886
Plants: Chevron 780, Cummins 1007, Raytheon 3135, Smith 3484, Toro 3775
Ennis
Plant: Sherwin 3437
Farmers Branch
Cororate Headquarters: Texas 3726
Fort Worth
Corporate Giving Programs: General 1556, Pier 2973, Quicksilver 3106
Foundations: ACE 25, Alcon 83, American 151, Burlington 618, Fort 1472, Keystone 2138, Morgan 2570, Weaver 4014
Corporate Headquarters: ACE 25, Alcon 83, American 151, AMR 187, Burlington 618, Fort 1472, General 1556, Hutton 1899, Keystone 2138, Pier 2973, Quicksilver 3106, Weaver 4014
Subsidiaries: AMR 187, Berkshire 429, Cummins 1007, Disney 1127, General 1555, Jacobs 2016
Offices: Cole 868, Haynes 1759, Jackson 2012, K&L 2080, Kiewit 2142, Kimley 2151, Pulte 3083, RJN 3228
Plants: Commercial 893, Dannon 1030, General 1551, Miller 2523, Motorola 2586, Panasonic 2869, Raytheon 3135, Rockwell 3247, Sealed 3381, Tension 3717, Winn 4087
Framers Branch
Foundation: Texas 3726
Freeport
Office: GATX 1542
Plants: Dow 1161, Nalco 2613
Frisco
Corporate Giving Programs: Dallas 1023, Hunt 1891
Foundation: Dallas 1023
Cororate Headquarters: Dallas 1023
Subsidiary: CORE 941
Offices: Kimley 2151, Strauss 3624
Galena Park
Office: GATX 1542
Galveston
Plant: Commercial 893
Garland
Office: First 1407
Plants: Coral 940, Ecolab 1220, Sherwin 3437, Valspar 3920
Gilmore
Plant: Valero 3915
Graham
Plant: Hexcel 1795
Grand Prairie
Foundation: El Dorado 1238
Plants: Castle 716, Valspar 3920
Grand Saline
Plant: Morton 2579
Grapeland
Plant: Nucor 2760
Grapevine
Corporate Giving Program: GameStop 1530
Cororate Headquarters: GameStop 1530
Plant: Total 3778
Greenville
Plants: Raytheon 3135, Snyder's-Lance 3492
Haltom City
Plant: Hillshire 1809
Harlingen
Foundation: Hygeia 1901
Plant: Owens 2841
Hearne
Office: GATX 1542
Hillsboro
Plant: Campbell 669
Houston
Corporate Giving Programs: AEG 43, American 147, Anadarko 190, Andrews 198, Apache 211, Aramco 224, Baker 321, BHP 455, BMC 508, BP 547, Bracewell 549, CenterPoint 738, CITGO 820, ConocoPhillips 913, Cooper 935, Enbridge 1265, EOG 1282, Fiesta 1375, Fulbright 1516, Gibbs 1575, Halliburton 1706, Hines 1813, Houston 1871, KBR 2106, LyondellBasell 2322, Marathon 2364, McDermott 2424, Men's 2460, New 2677, Phillips 2965, Porter 3008, Riviana 3227, Rocket 3240, Sasol 3338, Service 3413, Shell 3430, Spark 3533, Spectra 3540, Sysco 3677, Tidewater 3748, Vinson 3958
Foundations: Air 62, AllStyle 108, Apache 211, Arroyo 252, Astoria 270, Baker 324, BP 547, Bridgeway 563, Brochsteins 581, Calpine 661, CEMEX 734, CITGO 820, Cooper 935, El Paso 1239, GenOn 1563, Halliburton 1706, Houston 1871, Houston 1872, Kanaly 2089, Landry's 2219, Lockwood 2293, Mattress 2407, Merfish 2472, Newfield 2695, Nortex 2727, Portcullis 3004, Quanex 3100, Rainforest 3120, Rocket 3240, Shell 3430, Southern 3520, Sports 3548, Stewart 3606, Swift 3667, Systel 3678, Tennessee 3716, Texas 3725, Total 3778, United 3860, Vinson 3957, WEDGE 4020
Corporate Headquarters: AEG 43, Air 62, AllStyle 108, American 147, Andrews 198, Apache 211, Aramco 224, Arroyo 252, Baker 321, Baker 324, BHP 455, BMC 508, BP 547, Bracewell 549, Bridgeway 563, Brochsteins 581, Calpine 661, Cameron 667, CEMEX 734, CenterPoint 738, CITGO 820, ConocoPhillips 913, Cooper 935, Dealer 1052, El Paso 1239, Enbridge 1265, EOG 1282, Executive 1308, Fairmont 1327, Fiesta 1375, Fulbright 1516, GenOn 1563, Gibbs 1575, Halliburton 1706, Hines 1813, Houston 1871, Houston 1872, Invesco 1983, Kanaly 2089, KBR 2106, Kinder 2153, Landry's 2219, Lockwood 2293, LyondellBasell 2322, Marathon 2363, Marathon 2364, Mattress 2407, McDermott 2424, Men's 2460, Merfish 2472, New 2677, Nortex 2727, Objectwin 2778, Phillips 2965, Portcullis 3004, Porter 3008, Quanex 3100, Rainforest 3120, Republic 3187, Riviana 3227, Rocket 3240, Sasol 3338, Service 3413, Shell 3430, Southern 3520, Spark 3533, Spectra 3540, Stage 3572, Stewart 3605, Stewart 3606, Swift 3667, Sysco 3677, Texas 3725, Total 3778, United 3874, Vinson 3957, Vinson 3958, WEDGE 4020
Subsidiaries: AGL 57, Air 62, American 156, Apache 211, Arizona 239, Austin 288, Baker 323, Baker 324, Bechtel 395, Belo 406, Brunswick 595, Cardinal 685, CB 725, CenterPoint 738, CLARCOR 832, Contran 928, Duke 1189, El Paso 1239, First 1400, Fiserv 1427, FMC 1449, Grace 1623, Halliburton 1706, Hess 1793, Hewlett 1794, Jacobs 2016, Landry's 2219, Lennar 2250, Loews 2296, LyondellBasell 2322, Marathon 2364, Murphy 2600, National 2628, Newfield 2695, Newmont 2698, NRG 2756, Occidental 2780, Omron 2810, Parsons 2887, Praxair 3029, Riviana 3227, UBS 3842, Valero 3915, Williams 4077, Zions 4158
Divisions: American 147, EQT 1287, Hunt 1889
Joint Ventures: Boeing 516, Lockheed 2292, Praxair 3029
Offices: Adams 34, Akin 70, Andrews 198, Baker 319, Baker 321, Boh 517, Bracewell 549, Cadwalader 649, Cozen 964, Credit 980, Curtis 1010, Draper 1171, Duane 1185, Edelman 1224, Exxon 1315, Federal 1349, Fish 1428, Fishel 1429, FMC 1449, Fulbright 1516, GATX 1542, Grant 1633, Greenberg 1654, Haynes 1759, Hogan 1825, Humana 1886, Jackson 2012, Jones 2058, JPMorgan Chase 2071, Kasowitz 2099, Kearney 2107, Kiewit 2142, Kimley 2151, King 2157, Latham 2228, Liskow 2285, Littler 2289, Mayer 2411, McDermott 2425, McGuireWoods 2430, Morgan 2571, Opus 2820, Pillsbury 2975, Porter 3008, Pulte 3083, Reed 3162, SAP 3334, SAS 3336, Sedgwick 3395, Shook 3439, Simpson 3462, Skadden 3470, Squire 3561, Sutherland 3663, Thompson 3739, Vinson 3958, Vision 3961, Weaver 4014, Weil 4022, Weil 4023, Winston 4089
Plants: Bausch 376, BP 547, Castle 716, Chevron 780, Clorox 852, Commercial 893, Dow 1161, FMC 1449, Goodyear 1612, Hunt 1892, Interface 1953, Lafarge 2210, Lennar 2250, Lubrizol 2315, McAfee 2417, Mitsui 2541, Novell 2754, Owens 2841, Owens 2842, Rockwell 3247, Sun 3646, Texas 3728, Univar 3886
Huntsville
Plant: Scotts 3372
Hurst
Subsidiary: Textron 3731
Division: AEGON 45
Ingleside
Subsidiary: Occidental 2780
Irving
Corporate Giving Programs: Commercial 893, Dallas 1022, Exxon 1315, Flowserve 1447, Fluor 1448, Kimberly 2150, Michaels 2494, Pioneer 2981, Zale 4151
Foundations: Bekins 401, Dallas 1022, Exxon 1315, Fluor 1448, Kimberly 2150, Natural 2641, NEC 2654, Pioneer 2981, VHA 3944
Corporate Headquarters: Commercial 893, Dallas 1022, Exxon 1315, Federal 1347, Flowserve 1447, Fluor 1448, Michaels 2494, Natural 2641, NEC 2654, Pioneer 2981, VHA 3944, Zale 4151
Subsidiaries: Austin 288, CNO 857, VHA 3944, Zale 4151
Offices: Canon 672, Google 1613, ITA 1998, Katten 2101, Liberty 2265, SAP 3334
Plants: Mitsui 2541, NEC 2654, Owens 2842, Smith 3484
Jewett
Plant: Nucor 2760
Johnson City
Foundation: Pedernales 2914
Cororate Headquarters: Pedernales 2914
Junction
Subsidiary: International 1962
Katy
Foundation: Don 1152
Cororate Headquarters: Don 1152
Kerrville
Foundation: Butt 628
Kingwood
Corporate Giving Program: Insperity 1944
Cororate Headquarters: Insperity 1944
Kosse
Plant: U.S. 3840
La Porte
Plants: LyondellBasell 2322, PPG 3025
Lake Dallas
Subsidiary: CenturyLink 751
Laredo
Subsidiary: Coca 863
League City
Foundation: Canon 672
Lewisville
Foundation: Fairmont 1327
Subsidiary: Clements 845
Longview
Foundation: Cameron 667
Office: Kilpatrick 2146
Plant: Bemis 407
Lubbock
Corporate Giving Program: United 3880
Foundations: American 166, Gibson 1579
Corporate Headquarters: American 166, Gibson 1579, United 3880
Subsidiary: Tyler 3831
Division: Cox 958
Plant: Goulds 1619
Magnolia
Cororate Headquarters: Conn 908
Mansfield
Plant: Valmont 3919

Marble Falls
Foundation: Gibraltar 1577
McAllen
Foundation: Panasonic 2870
Cororate Headquarters: Hygeia 1901
Subsidiary: Duda 1188
Office: Cox 961
Plant: Donnelley 1155
McKinney
Corporate Giving Program: Blockbuster 483
Foundation: TIV 3764
Corporate Headquarters: El Dorado 1238, TIV 3764
Subsidiary: Tomkins 3771
Midland
Subsidiaries: Halliburton 1706, Occidental 2780
Division: Cox 958
Office: Hunt 1889
Midlothian
Subsidiary: Texas 3727
Mineral Wells
Subsidiary: CLARCOR 832
Mount Pleasant
Subsidiary: Lennar 2250
Nacogdoches
Plant: NIBCO 2707
Nederland
Office: GATX 1542
Needville
Foundation: Uticon 3911
Odessa
Plant: Univar 3886
Pampa
Plant: Cabot 642
Paradise
Foundation: Hutton 1899
Paris
Foundation: First 1401
Cororate Headquarters: First 1401
Pasadena
Plants: Albemarle 78, LyondellBasell 2322, Total 3778
Pearland
Foundation: Objectwin 2778
Plano
Corporate Giving Programs: Cinemark 815, Dr 1169, First 1398, Penney 2925, Safety 3309
Foundations: AmeriPlan 172, Dr 1169, Penney 2925
Corporate Headquarters: Alliance 101, AmeriPlan 172, Cinemark 815, Dr 1169, Frito 1506, Penney 2925, Safety 3309
Subsidiaries: Mark 2377, PepsiCo 2935, Tyler 3831
Offices: Autodesk 289, Safeco 3306
Plants: Georgia 1568, Navistar 2647, Texas 3728
Point Comfort
Plant: Formosa 1470
Port Arthur
Plants: Chevron 780, LyondellBasell 2322, Total 3778
Port Lavaca
Foundation: Formosa 1470
Poynor
Office: Hunt 1889
Richardson
Subsidiary: Evans 1300
Offices: Applied 220, Haynes 1759
Plants: Rockwell 3247, Tomkins 3771
Rockdale
Plant: Alcoa 82
Rosenberg
Cororate Headquarters: Uticon 3911
Division: Quanex 3100
Round Rock
Corporate Giving Program: Dell 1068
Cororate Headquarters: Dell 1068
Office: Opus 2820
San Angelo
Office: Jackson 2012
Plant: Goodyear 1612
San Antonio
Corporate Giving Programs: AT&T 273, Butt 628, Cox 961, Kinetic 2156, Rackspace 3117, San Antonio 3321, Spurs 3557, Tesoro 3723
Foundations: Clear 842, Cox 960, Frost 1512, Furr 1520, New 2679, NuStar 2763, Rackspace 3117, San Antonio 3321, Southwest 3523, United 3873, Valero 3915
Corporate Headquarters: Butt 628, Clear 842, Cox 960, Cox 961, Frost 1512, Furr 1520, Hutchison 1898, Kinetic 2156, NuStar 2763, Rackspace 3117, San Antonio 3321, Southwest 3523, Spurs 3557, Tesoro 3723, United 3873, Valero 3915
Subsidiaries: Anheuser 202, AT&T 273, Belo 406, Comcast 887, PerkinElmer 2939, Sequa 3410, Spurs 3557
Divisions: Bausch 376, Spurs 3557
Offices: Akin 70, AT&T 273, Bracewell 549, Cox 961, Federal 1349, Fieldstone 1374, Fulbright 1516, Haynes 1759, Humana 1886, Jackson 2012, Pulte 3083, RJN 3228, SeaWorld 3387, Weaver 4014
Plants: Bausch 376, Harris 1736, Univar 3886, Vulcan 3972
San Marcos
Plant: Butler 626
San Martin
Plant: Valero 3915
Seguin
Subsidiary: Commercial 893
Plants: Hexcel 1795, Illinois 1916, Jim's 2043, Motorola 2586
Sherman
Plants: Procter 3055, Raytheon 3135, Texas 3728
Shilling
Plant: Valero 3915
Shoup
Plant: Valero 3915
Sonora
Plant: Valero 3915
Southlake
Office: Fishel 1429
Stephenville
Plant: FMC 1449
Sugar Land
Corporate Giving Program: Imperial 1922
Corporate Headquarters: Imperial 1922, Systel 3678
Subsidiary: Amica 183
Office: Mazda 2414
Plants: Nalco 2613, Teleflex 3707
Taylor
Subsidiary: Newell 2694
Temple
Foundation: Wilsonart 4084
Cororate Headquarters: Wilsonart 4084
Terrell
Division: Butler 626
Texarkana
Plant: International 1968
Texas City
Subsidiary: Williams 4077
Plants: BP 547, Marathon 2362
The Woodlands
Corporate Giving Program: Huntsman 1895
Foundation: Woodforest 4110
Corporate Headquarters: Anadarko 190, Newfield 2695, Woodforest 4110
Subsidiary: Huntsman 1895
Offices: Andrews 198, Pan-American 2868
Thompsonville
Plant: Valero 3915
Tomball
Foundation: Stewart 3605
Tyler
Subsidiary: Manpower 2358
Victoria
Plants: Commercial 893, LyondellBasell 2322
Vinton
Plant: Commercial 893
Waco
Corporate Giving Program: American 153
Foundation: Curves 1011
Corporate Headquarters: American 153, Curves 1011
Plants: Raytheon 3135, Sherwin 3437, Westervelt 4046
Waxahachie
Foundation: Bernecker's 431
Office: Dart 1033
Plant: Owens 2842
Weatherford
Foundation: Power 3022
Cororate Headquarters: Power 3022
Westlake
Office: Strauss 3624
Wichita Falls
Subsidiary: Marathon 2363
Plant: PPG 3025
Willis
Cororate Headquarters: Robbins 3230
Subsidiary: Teleflex 3707

UTAH

American Fork
Subsidiary: Danaher 1027
Bingham Canyon
Cororate Headquarters: Kennecott 2127
Brigham City
Plants: Morton 2579, Nucor 2760
Castle Dale
Subsidiary: Savage 3341
Clearfield
Office: Leggett 2246
Draper
Foundation: Wadsworth 3974
Corporate Headquarters: Wadsworth 3974
Hill AFB
Office: Bionetics 467
Lindon
Plant: Valmont 3919
Logan
Corporate Giving Program: ICON 1906
Cororate Headquarters: ICON 1906
Subsidiary: ICON 1906
Plant: Bourns 542
Magna
Corporate Giving Program: Kennecott 2127
Midvale
Subsidiary: Blue 498
Plant: CA 638
Ogden
Corporate Giving Program: Autoliv 290
Cororate Headquarters: Autoliv 290
Office: Regence 3169
Plants: Parker 2886, Timken 3760, Westinghouse 4049
Orem
Subsidiary: Novell 2754
Office: Intuit 1982
Park City
Foundation: Mrs. Fields 2592
Plymouth
Plant: Nucor 2760
Provo
Corporate Giving Programs: Novell 2754, Nu 2759
Foundation: Nu 2759
Corporate Headquarters: Novell 2754, Nu 2759
Offices: Grant 1633, Kiewit 2142, Regence 3169
Salt Lake City
Corporate Giving Programs: Boart 510, Questar 3104, Regence 3169
Foundations: Alsco 115, Garff 1538, Jazz 2028, Questar 3104, Ray 3131, Richards 3206, Savage 3341, Snow 3491, Suitter 3633, Wells 4028, Zions 4158
Corporate Headquarters: Alsco 115, Garff 1538, Huntsman 1895, Jazz 2028, Mrs. Fields 2592, Questar 3104, Ray 3131, Regence 3169, Richards

3206, Savage 3341, Snow 3491, Suitter 3633, Zions 4158
Subsidiaries: Albertsons 79, Bard 358, Murphy 2600, Questar 3104, Raymond 3133, Ripplewood 3219, Target 3691, Zions 4158
Divisions: Alsco 115, Bosch 529
Offices: American 143, Ballard 329, Brinks 573, Cephalon 752, CUNA 1008, Dorsey 1157, Electronic 1242, Fieldstone 1374, Granite 1632, Grant 1633, Hays 1761, Holland 1833, Holme 1837, KeyBank 2136, Packard 2862, Snell 3490, Stoel 3611, Thompson 3739
Plants: BP 547, Chevron 780, Deluxe 1084, Lyon 2321, Morton 2579, Novell 2754, Owens 2841, Owens 2842, Pactiv 2863, Square 3560, Sun 3646
Sandy
Corporate Giving Program: Sports 3549
Cororate Headquarters: Sports 3549
Sigurd
Plant: Georgia 1568
South Jordan
Corporate Giving Program: Monavie LLC 2555
Foundations: Kennecott 2127, Rio 3218
Cororate Headquarters: Boart 510, Monavie LLC 2555
Springville
Corporate Giving Program: Neways 2692
Cororate Headquarters: Neways 2692
Subsidiary: Flowserve 1447
St. George
Corporate Giving Program: SkyWest 3476
Cororate Headquarters: SkyWest 3476
Tooele
Subsidiary: PerkinElmer 2939
West Jordan
Plant: Dannon 1030
Woods Cross
Plant: Univar 3886

VERMONT
Barre
Office: Northfield 2742
Plant: Hood 1854
Berlin
Cororate Headquarters: Blue 499
Bethel
Offices: Mascoma 2394, Northfield 2742
Burlington
Corporate Giving Programs: Gravel 1638, Lake 2212, Merritt 2476, Seventh 3416
Foundation: Burton 624
Corporate Headquarters: Burton 624, Gravel 1638, Lake 2212, Merritt 2476, Seventh 3416
Subsidiaries: Alcoa 82, Burton 624, Connecticut 910
Division: General 1551
Offices: KeyBank 2136, Northfield 2742
Cavendish
Foundation: Vermont 3940
Cororate Headquarters: Vermont 3940
Chelsea
Office: Mascoma 2394
Essex
Office: Northfield 2742
Essex Junction
Office: Northfield 2742
Hartland
Office: Mascoma 2394
Montpelier
Corporate Giving Program: Blue 499
Foundation: National 2633
Cororate Headquarters: National 2633
Subsidiary: National 2633
Office: Northfield 2742
Northfield
Corporate Giving Program: Northfield 2742
Foundation: Northfield 2742
Cororate Headquarters: Northfield 2742
Norwich
Corporate Giving Program: King 2158
Cororate Headquarters: King 2158
Office: Mascoma 2394
Proctor
Foundation: Carris 702
Cororate Headquarters: Carris 702
Putney
Corporate Giving Program: Venture 3932
Cororate Headquarters: Venture 3932
Randolph
Office: Northfield 2742
South Burlington
Corporate Giving Program: Ben 409
Foundations: Ben 409, Green 1653, Merchants 2465
Cororate Headquarters: Ben 409, Merchants 2465
Office: Northfield 2742
St. Albans
Subsidiary: Mylan 2610
Strafford
Office: Mascoma 2394
Sunderland
Cororate Headquarters: Orvis 2830
Waitsfield
Office: Northfield 2742
Waterbury
Corporate Giving Program: Green 1653
Cororate Headquarters: Green 1653
Office: Northfield 2742
White River Junction
Office: Mascoma 2394
Williston
Corporate Giving Program: New 2671
Cororate Headquarters: New 2671
Office: Northfield 2742
Windsor
Subsidiary: Spirol 3545

VIRGIN ISLANDS
St. Croix
Subsidiary: Hess 1793

VIRGINIA
Alexandria
Corporate Giving Programs: Motley 2582, Oblon 2779
Foundation: National 2622
Corporate Headquarters: Motley 2582, National 2622, Oblon 2779
Subsidiary: Intuit 1982
Offices: Bionetics 467, Oblon 2779, Stites 3609
Plants: Giant 1573, McAfee 2417, PerkinElmer 2939, Quad 3091
Altavista
Plant: Timken 3760
Amherst
Plant: Clorox 852
Arlington
Corporate Giving Programs: AES 47, Lincoln 2280
Foundations: Association 265, FBR 1345, Lincoln 2280, Mitsubishi 2538
Corporate Headquarters: AES 47, Association 265, FBR 1345
Subsidiaries: Gannett 1532, SRA 3562
Offices: Canon 672, Draper 1171, State 3592
Plants: Northrop 2744, UTC 3908
Ashburn
Corporate Giving Program: Pro 3054
Foundation: Pro 3054
Cororate Headquarters: Pro 3054
Ashland
Subsidiary: Danaher 1027
Bassett
Foundation: Bassett 372
Cororate Headquarters: Bassett 372
Bastian
Subsidiary: Schein 3348
Berryville
Subsidiary: Bertelsmann 439
Big Island
Plant: Georgia 1568
Blacksburg
Foundation: Burger 613
Bluefield
Cororate Headquarters: Concept 905
Plant: Nash 2619
Boykins
Subsidiary: Snyder's-Lance 3492
Bridgewater
Plant: TJX 3765
Bristol
Corporate Giving Program: Alpha 112
Foundation: United 3864
Corporate Headquarters: Alpha 112, Rapoca 3127, United 3864
Plant: Dana 1026
Buena Vista
Plant: Modine 2544
Burkeville
Plant: Bassett 372
Chantilly
Subsidiary: Quest 3103
Office: Whiting 4063
Charlottesville
Offices: McGuireWoods 2430, State 3591, Wiley 4072, Williams 4078, Woods 4111
Chesapeake
Corporate Giving Program: Dollar 1145
Cororate Headquarters: Dollar 1145
Subsidiary: Comcast 887
Office: Kimley 2151
Chester
Subsidiary: NiSource 2715
Office: Dixon 1133
Chesterfield
Plant: Honeywell 1852
Christiansburg
Subsidiary: Hubbell 1879
Plants: Bassett 372, Corning 945
Colonial Heights
Plant: Antioch 207
Culpeper
Plants: GenCorp 1548, Martin 2391
Dahlgren
Office: Bionetics 467
Daleville
Foundation: Roanoke 3229
Cororate Headquarters: Roanoke 3229
Danville
Subsidiary: Universal 3891
Offices: Dixon 1133, Woods 4111
Plants: Goodyear 1612, Loews 2296, Menasha 2461
Dillwyn
Foundation: Kyanite 2201
Cororate Headquarters: Kyanite 2201
Dulles
Subsidiary: AOL 209
Edinburg
Foundation: Shenandoah 3434
Cororate Headquarters: Shenandoah 3434
Elkton
Plant: Merck 2466
Fairfax
Corporate Giving Program: SRA 3562
Foundations: CORT 946, Ellucian 1252, Trident 3808, Zeta 4155
Corporate Headquarters: CORT 946, Ellucian 1252, SRA 3562, Trident 3808, Zeta 4155
Subsidiaries: Exxon 1315, M.D.C. 2324, Washington 3999
Offices: Electronic 1242, Exxon 1315, Holder 1829, Kimley 2151

Falls Church
Corporate Giving Programs: General 1551, Northrop 2744
Foundation: Northrop 2744
Corporate Headquarters: General 1551, Northrop 2744
Offices: Ober 2777, Reed 3163
Farmville
Subsidiary: Universal 3891
Franklin
Plant: International 1968
Fredericksburg
Corporate Giving Program: EduCare 1231
Foundations: BB&T 385, Fredericksburg 1490
Corporate Headquarters: EduCare 1231, Fredericksburg 1490
Plant: Bassett 372
Gainesville
Subsidiary: Sequa 3410
Galax
Foundation: Vaughan 3924
Cororate Headquarters: Vaughan 3924
Glen Allen
Foundation: Franklin 1485
Cororate Headquarters: Franklin 1485
Gretna
Foundation: Blair 479
Corporate Headquarters: Blair 479, Peoples 2932
Hampton
Subsidiary: Belo 406
Harrisonburg
Office: Wiley 4072
Plants: Donnelley 1155, Tenneco 3715
Herndon
Corporate Giving Program: First 1398
Foundations: Apex 213, Volkswagen 3967
Corporate Headquarters: Apex 213, Lafarge 2210, Volkswagen 3967
Subsidiaries: GTECH 1677, Hubbell 1879, Lennar 2250
Offices: CDW 729, Cerner 754
Plants: NEC 2654, Novell 2754
Hopewell
Plant: Honeywell 1852
Kenbridge
Subsidiary: Universal 3891
La Crosse
Plant: American 135
Lynchburg
Foundations: Old 2796, Retail 3194
Cororate Headquarters: Retail 3194
Subsidiaries: AMPCO 186, Genworth 1565
Plants: Donnelley 1155, Illinois 1916
Madison Heights
Cororate Headquarters: Old 2796
Manassas
Offices: Applied 220, Fishel 1429
Plant: Vulcan 3972
Martinsville
Foundation: Hooker 1855
Cororate Headquarters: Hooker 1855
Plant: Bassett 372
Mc Kenney
Subsidiary: Universal 3891
Mclean
Corporate Giving Programs: Acumen 33, Booz 525, Capital 679, Federal 1348, Hilton 1812, Mars 2384, Novetta 2755, SAIC 3311, Working 4117
Foundations: Capital 679, Federal 1348, Gannett 1532, Mars 2384
Corporate Headquarters: Acumen 33, Booz 525, Capital 679, Federal 1348, Gannett 1532, Hilton 1812, Mars 2384, Novetta 2755, SAIC 3311
Subsidiary: ITT 1999
Offices: Arnold 248, Autodesk 289, Better 449, BMC 508, Greenberg 1654, Hogan 1825, Holland 1834, Morrison 2576, Patton 2898, Pillsbury 2975, Wiley 4073
Mechanicsville
Cororate Headquarters: Owens 2841
Midlothian
Office: Safeco 3306
Milford
Plant: Georgia 1568
Montpelier
Plant: U.S. 3840
New Market
Subsidiary: Commercial 893
Plant: Kennametal 2125
Newport News
Foundations: Bionetics 467, Dixon 1133, Jordan 2063, Noland 2719
Corporate Headquarters: Bionetics 467, Jordan 2063, Noland 2719
Subsidiary: Canon 672
Offices: Dixon 1133, Williams 4078
Norfolk
Corporate Giving Programs: AmeriVision 180, Norfolk 2725
Foundations: FHC 1368, Landmark 2218, Norfolk 2725
Corporate Headquarters: AmeriVision 180, Landmark 2218, Norfolk 2725
Subsidiaries: AGL 57, Landmark 2218
Offices: McGuireWoods 2430, United 3873, Williams 4078
Plant: Nash 2619
North Chesterfield
Cororate Headquarters: Reckitt 3147
Oakton
Cororate Headquarters: Power 3021
Petersburg
Subsidiaries: Amsted 188, Boehringer 515
Plant: Honeywell 1852
Portsmouth
Office: Williams 4078
Plant: Sherwin 3437
Powhatan
Office: Univar 3886
Reston
Corporate Giving Programs: Better 449, Lafarge 2210, NII 2709, Rolls 3254
Foundations: Calkain 658, Graphic 1634, MAXIMUS 2410, Truland 3817
Corporate Headquarters: Better 449, Calkain 658, Graphic 1634, MAXIMUS 2410, NII 2709, Rolls 3254, Truland 3817, Working 4117
Subsidiaries: Miller 2523, Sprint 3556
Office: Finnegan 1384
Plant: CA 638
Richmond
Corporate Giving Programs: Altria 120, Chesapeake 778, Dominion 1150, Impact 1921, McGuireWoods 2430, Owens 2841, Performance 2938, Southern 3519, Williams 4078
Foundations: ACI 27, Altria 120, Brink's 571, CarMax 694, Century 749, Dominion 1148, Genworth 1565, Luck 2317, MeadWestvaco 2445, Peoples 2932, Reckitt 3147, RECO 3148, Scott 3368, Standard 3575, SunTrust 3654, Universal 3891, Williams 4078
Corporate Headquarters: Altria 120, Brink's 571, Century 749, Dominion 1148, Dominion 1150, Genworth 1565, Impact 1921, Luck 2317, McGuireWoods 2430, MeadWestvaco 2445, Morris 2574, Performance 2938, RECO 3148, Scott 3368, Southern 3519, Universal 3891, Williams 4078
Subsidiaries: Alcoa 82, Altria 120, BB&T 385, Chesapeake 778, Dominion 1150, Genworth 1565, Graybar 1640, Seagrave 3378, Verizon 3936
Offices: Dixon 1133, Intuit 1982, Jordan 2063, Kimley 2151, McGuireWoods 2430, Reed 3163, Thompson 3739, Whiting 4063, Williams 4078, Woods 4111
Plants: Campbell 669, Crystal 992, Timken 3760
Ridgeway
Joint Ventures: Bassett 372, Hooker 1855
Roanoke
Corporate Giving Programs: Advance 39, Shenandoah 3433, Woods 4111
Foundations: Berglund 419, Johnson 2048, Virginia 3959
Corporate Headquarters: Advance 39, Berglund 419, Credit 979, Shenandoah 3433, Virginia 3959, Woods 4111
Subsidiaries: American 141, HCA 1762, Johnson 2048, Landmark 2218, Orvis 2830, Shenandoah 3433
Division: Cox 958
Offices: Dixon 1133, Norfolk 2725, Woods 4111
Rockville
Plant: Martin 2391
Salem
Subsidiary: Caterpillar 722
Plant: Donnelley 1155
Smithfield
Corporate Giving Program: Smithfield 3487
Foundation: Smithfield 3487
Cororate Headquarters: Smithfield 3487
Subsidiary: Smithfield 3487
Springfield
Foundation: American 138
Cororate Headquarters: American 138
Subsidiaries: Florida 1444, Washington 3997
Stafford
Cororate Headquarters: Reger 3170
Sterling
Foundation: N.E.W. 2611
Cororate Headquarters: N.E.W. 2611
Office: Costco 948
Stuarts Draft
Subsidiary: Hershey 1791
Plant: NIBCO 2707
Suffolk
Foundations: Birdsong 470, Mondelez 2556, Nansemond 2616
Corporate Headquarters: Birdsong 470, Nansemond 2616
Plant: Golden 1602
Tysons
Office: Dixon 1133
Tysons Corner
Offices: Littler 2289, McGuireWoods 2430, Miles 2512, Squire 3561, Venable 3929, Williams 4078
Vienna
Corporate Giving Program: Feld 1355
Foundation: Ratner 3130
Cororate Headquarters: Feld 1355, Ratner 3130
Subsidiaries: AOL 209, Covance 955, Feld 1355
Offices: Akerman 69, Cassidy 715, Grant 1633, Mercury 2469, RJN 3228
Vinton
Foundation: Credit 979
Virginia Beach
Foundation: AMERIGROUP 171
Corporate Headquarters: AMERIGROUP 171, FHC 1368
Subsidiaries: Cox 958, Susquehanna 3661, WellPoint 4027
Offices: Dixon 1133, Williams 4078
Plant: Tenneco 3715
Wakefield
Plant: Scotts 3372
Waynesboro
Foundation: NTELOS 2758
Cororate Headquarters: NTELOS 2758
West Point
Subsidiary: Chesapeake 778
Williamsburg
Foundation: Williamsburg 4080
Cororate Headquarters: Williamsburg 4080
Subsidiary: Chesapeake 778
Office: SeaWorld 3387
Winchester
Foundation: American 170
Cororate Headquarters: American 170
Plants: Hood 1854, Newell 2694, Pactiv 2863
Wise
Subsidiary: HCA 1762

Wytheville
Foundation: Pendleton 2921
Cororate Headquarters: Pendleton 2921
Yorktown
Plant: BP 547

WASHINGTON

Aberdeen
Offices: Cascade 713, Wal-Mart 3980
Anacortes
Office: Cascade 713
Auburn
Subsidiary: Miller 2517
Plant: Barnes 362
Batavia
Plant: PPG 3025
Bellevue
Corporate Giving Programs: Expedia 1311, Intelius 1951, Pacific 2857, Puget 3081
Foundations: drugstore.com 1180, Exotic 1310, PACCAR 2850, Puget 3081
Corporate Headquarters: drugstore.com 1180, Expedia 1311, Intelius 1951, PACCAR 2850, Pacific 2857, Puget 3081
Subsidiaries: drugstore.com 1180, Puget 3081, VHA 3944, Walgreen 3981
Division: Safeway 3310
Offices: BMC 508, Cerner 754, Davis 1041, Factory 1323, KeyBank 2136, Mortenson 2577, Opus 2820, Perkins 2940, Perkins 2941, Quad 3091, SAP 3334
Plants: CA 638, Coca 862, McAfee 2417
Bellingham
Corporate Giving Programs: Haggen 1699, Moka 2547
Foundation: Seafood 3376
Corporate Headquarters: Haggen 1699, Moka 2547, Seafood 3376
Offices: Cascade 713, KeyBank 2136
Bothell
Subsidiary: Puget 3081
Plant: Panasonic 2869
Bremerton
Office: Cascade 713
Burlington
Foundation: KarMART 2096
Cororate Headquarters: KarMART 2096
Plant: Hexcel 1795
Camas
Subsidiary: Sharp 3422
Chehalis
Foundation: Chehalis 771
Cororate Headquarters: Chehalis 771
Plant: Bassett 372
Dayton
Plant: Seneca 3406
DuPont
Office: State 3591
Enumclaw
Plant: Birds 469
Everett
Foundations: Intermec 1955, KeyBank 2136
Cororate Headquarters: Intermec 1955
Subsidiaries: Danaher 1027, Granite 1632, Washington 3999
Federal Way
Corporate Giving Programs: Totem 3779, Weyerhaeuser 4052
Foundations: Damar 1024, Weyerhaeuser 4052
Corporate Headquarters: Totem 3779, Weyerhaeuser 4052
Grandview
Subsidiary: Smucker 3488
Plant: Welch 4025
Issaquah
Corporate Giving Program: Costco 948
Foundation: Costco 948
Corporate Headquarters: Costco 948, Rondys 3256
Kennewick
Office: Cascade 713
Plant: Welch 4025
Kent
Corporate Giving Program: Recreational 3150
Foundations: Diagnos-Techs 1108, Fleck 1435
Corporate Headquarters: Diagnos-Techs 1108, Exotic 1310, Recreational 3150
Subsidiaries: Best 442, Fiserv 1427, HNI 1817, Lynden 2320, Raymond 3133
Plants: Panasonic 2869, Square 3560, Starbucks 3585, Univar 3886
Kirkland
Corporate Giving Program: Allyis 109
Cororate Headquarters: Allyis 109
Subsidiary: Lennar 2250
Plants: Novell 2754, Rockwell 3247
Longview
Offices: Cascade 713, Halton 1709
Lynden
Subsidiary: Lynden 2320
Mead
Foundation: Cyan 1015
Cororate Headquarters: Cyan 1015
Mercer Island
Subsidiary: Farmers 1338
Monroe
Cororate Headquarters: Damar 1024
Moses Lake
Office: Cascade 713
Mount Vernon
Office: Cascade 713
Mountlake Terrace
Corporate Giving Program: Premera 3034
Cororate Headquarters: Premera 3034
Mukilteo
Foundation: University 3896
Cororate Headquarters: University 3896
Olympia
Offices: GATX 1542, Lane 2221, Perkins 2940
Plants: Georgia 1568, Menasha 2461
Othello
Plant: Seneca 3406
Pasco
Plant: Seneca 3406
Paterson
Plant: U.S. 3841
Port Townsend
Office: McDonnell 2428
Pullman
Plant: Avista 301
Puyallup
Foundation: Korum 2187
Cororate Headquarters: Korum 2187
Redmond
Corporate Giving Programs: Microsoft 2501, Nintendo 2712, Univar 3886
Foundation: Univar 3886
Corporate Headquarters: Microsoft 2501, Nintendo 2712, Univar 3886
Division: Nintendo 2712
Plants: Boston 540, GenCorp 1548
Renton
Corporate Giving Program: Football 1460
Foundation: First 1404
Corporate Headquarters: First 1404, Football 1460
Subsidiary: Hunter 1893
Division: Boeing 516
Plant: Rockwell 3247
Richland
Plant: Westinghouse 4049
Ritzville
Foundation: Ritzville 3222
Cororate Headquarters: Ritzville 3222
Seattle
Corporate Giving Programs: Alaska 74, Amazon.com 122, Baseball 367, Bristlecone 575, Cascade 713, Davis 1041, Foster 1475, Garvey 1539, Getty 1569, Hillis 1807, Holland 1835, Horizon 1861, Karr 2097, Lane 2221, Mills 2526, Nordstrom 2724, Parsons 2888, Perkins 2940, Perkins 2941, Russell 3289, Safeco 3306, Seattle 3386, Starbucks 3585, Vulcan 3970
Foundations: 13th 1, Baseball 367, Basketball 370, Delta 1081, Fisher 1430, Football 1460, Laird 2211, Lynden 2320, McKinstry 2435, Microsoft 2501, Moss 2581, PEMCO 2919, Plum 2991, Pura 3084, RealNetworks 3144, Safeco 3306, Seattle 3386, Skinner 3475, Starbucks 3585
Corporate Headquarters: 13th 1, Alaska 74, Amazon.com 122, Baseball 367, Basketball 370, Bristlecone 575, Cascade 713, Davis 1041, Delta 1081, Fisher 1430, Fleck 1435, Foster 1475, Garvey 1539, Getty 1569, Glacier 1586, Hillis 1807, Holland 1835, Horizon 1861, Karr 2097, Laird 2211, Lane 2221, Lynden 2320, McKinstry 2435, Mills 2526, Moss 2581, Nordstrom 2724, Parsons 2888, PEMCO 2919, Perkins 2940, Perkins 2941, Plum 2991, Pura 3084, RealNetworks 3144, Russell 3289, Safeco 3306, Seattle 3385, Seattle 3386, Skinner 3475, Starbucks 3585, Vulcan 3970
Subsidiaries: Amazon.com 122, Belo 406, Carnival 696, Cascade 713, Eclipse 1219, Hasbro 1747, Liberty 2265, Lynden 2320, Macy's 2333, Nucor 2760, Otis 2835, Recreational 3150, Vulcan 3970, Zions 4158
Division: Boeing 516
Offices: Better 449, Blakely 480, Bracewell 549, Cozen 964, Davis 1041, Deere 1061, Dorsey 1157, Edelman 1224, Federal 1349, Fenwick 1362, Foster 1475, Frommer 1507, Garvey 1539, GATX 1542, Google 1613, Grant 1633, K&L 2080, Lane 2221, Littler 2289, Merchant 2464, Miller 2521, Perkins 2941, SAS 3336, Schwabe 3364, Sedgwick 3395, Stoel 3611, Thompson 3739, Vision 3961, Wilson 4083
Plants: Adobe 38, Lafarge 2210, Mitsui 2541, Owens 2841, Rayonier 3134, Rockwell 3247, Smith 3484
Sedro Woolley
Subsidiary: General 1554
Sedro-Woolley
Plant: General 1554
Skagit Valley
Division: Caesars 650
Spokane
Corporate Giving Programs: Avista 301, Teck 3700
Foundations: Avista 301, Murphy 2599, Potlatch 3017
Corporate Headquarters: Avista 301, Murphy 2599, Potlatch 3017, Teck 3700
Subsidiaries: Avista 301, Belo 406, Fisher 1430, Plum 2991, Premera 3034
Divisions: Cox 958, Potlatch 3017
Offices: Foster 1475, K&L 2080, Principal 3047, Safeco 3306
Plant: Univar 3886
Sumner
Foundation: Recreational 3150
Plants: Golden 1602, Sonoco 3500
Sunnyside
Office: Cascade 713
Plant: Bailey 315
Tacoma
Foundations: DaVita 1044, Tacoma 3680
Cororate Headquarters: Tacoma 3680
Subsidiaries: Lennar 2250, Masco 2393, McClatchy 2422, Northwestern 2749, Weyerhaeuser 4052
Offices: KeyBank 2136, Kiewit 2142, Lane 2221
Plant: Birds 469
Tukwila
Foundation: Harnish 1734
Cororate Headquarters: Harnish 1734
Tulalip
Corporate Giving Program: Tulalip 3820
Cororate Headquarters: Tulalip 3820
Tumwater
Office: Dart 1033
Vancouver
Foundation: Rondys 3256
Subsidiaries: Farmers 1338, Panasonic 2869
Offices: CenturyLink 751, Kiewit 2142, Stoel 3611
Plants: Bemis 407, Fuller 1517, Hewlett 1794

Vashon Island
Foundation: Seattle 3385
Walla Walla
Subsidiary: Seattle 3386
Office: Cascade 713
Wenatchee
Subsidiary: Dole 1141
Office: Cascade 713
Woodinville
Foundation: Interthyr 1978
Subsidiary: U.S. 3841
Yakima
Subsidiary: Seattle 3386
Office: Cascade 713
Plants: Pactiv 2863, Seneca 3406
Yakima Valley
Plant: Welch 4025

WEST VIRGINIA

Belle
Cororate Headquarters: Walker 3982
Berkeley Springs
Cororate Headquarters: U.S. 3840
Beryl
Plant: Clorox 852
Bluefield
Foundations: Concept 905, JanPak 2022
Buckhannon
Foundation: Reger 3170
Buffalo
Corporate Giving Program: Toyota 3787
Cororate Headquarters: Toyota 3787
Subsidiary: Toyota 3784
Charleston
Foundation: Bowles 544
Cororate Headquarters: Bowles 544
Subsidiaries: Energy 1272, NiSource 2715, Verizon 3936
Offices: Dixon 1133, Frost 1511, Kimley 2151
Plant: Owens 2842
Chester
Foundation: Hancock 1716
Cororate Headquarters: Hancock 1716
Office: Hancock 1716
Clarksburg
Foundation: Beverage 453
Cororate Headquarters: Beverage 453
Grafton
Plant: Georgia 1568
Huntington
Foundation: Arthur's 253
Cororate Headquarters: Arthur's 253
Subsidiary: Arthur's 253
Office: Nelson 2661
Institute
Plant: FMC 1449
Logan
Foundation: Pyles 3089
Cororate Headquarters: Pyles 3089
Martinsburg
Plant: Quad 3091
Morgantown
Subsidiary: PerkinElmer 2939
Offices: Dixon 1133, Huntington 1894
Plant: Mylan 2610
Mount Hope
Plant: Georgia 1568
New Cumberland
Office: Hancock 1716
New Martinsville
Plant: PPG 3025
Newell
Subsidiary: Ergon 1289
Parkersburg
Plant: Guardian 1682
Parsons
Plant: Clorox 852
Pineville
Plant: Cliffs 850
South Charleston
Plants: FMC 1449, LyondellBasell 2322
Weirton
Office: Hancock 1716
Plant: Illinois 1916
Weston
Foundation: Sun 3645
Cororate Headquarters: Sun 3645
Wheeling
Foundation: Orrick 2826
Subsidiary: American 141
Williamstown
Foundation: Fenton 1361
Cororate Headquarters: Fenton 1361

WISCONSIN

Abbotsford
Foundation: AbbyBank 15
Cororate Headquarters: AbbyBank 15
Altoona
Cororate Headquarters: KMTSJ 2173
Appleton
Foundation: Thrivent 3747
Subsidiaries: Applied 219, V.F. 3913
Offices: Ahern 60, Godfrey 1596, Grant 1633, Wisconsin 4094
Plants: Bemis 407, Nash 2619
Arbor Vitae
Cororate Headquarters: Pukall 3082
Arcadia
Foundation: Ashley 259
Cororate Headquarters: Ashley 259
Baldwin
Plant: Donaldson 1153
Baraboo
Corporate Giving Program: Foremost 1466
Foundation: Nordic 2722
Corporate Headquarters: Foremost 1466, Nordic 2722
Subsidiary: Nordic 2722
Division: Foremost 1466
Plants: Olin 2801, Seneca 3406, Toro 3775
Beloit
Foundation: Regal 3167
Cororate Headquarters: Regal 3167
Plants: Ecolab 1220, Frito 1506
Berlin
Cororate Headquarters: Badger 314
Bonduel
Plants: Campbell 669, Krueger 2196
Brillion
Foundations: Ariens 238, Brillion 569
Corporate Headquarters: Ariens 238, Brillion 569
Brookfield
Foundation: Raabe 3115
Cororate Headquarters: Fiserv 1427
Subsidiary: Fiserv 1427
Offices: Grant 1633, Mortenson 2577
Plant: Brunswick 595
Butler
Foundation: Berghammer 418
Cororate Headquarters: Berghammer 418
Cedarburg
Subsidiary: Emerson 1257
Chilton
Foundation: Kaytee 2104
Cororate Headquarters: Kaytee 2104
Chippewa Falls
Subsidiary: Miller 2523
Plants: BP 547, Miller 2523
Clintonville
Foundation: Seagrave 3378
Cororate Headquarters: Seagrave 3378
Clyman
Plant: Seneca 3406
Cudahy
Foundations: Allegheny 91, Vilter 3956
Cororate Headquarters: Vilter 3956
Subsidiaries: Handy 1718, Smithfield 3487
Cumberland
Plant: Seneca 3406
Dane
Plant: Menasha 2461
De Pere
Foundation: Sonoco 3500
Subsidiary: Associated 261
Dodgeville
Corporate Giving Program: Lands' 2220
Cororate Headquarters: Lands' 2220
Subsidiary: Sears 3384
Eau Claire
Foundation: KMTSJ 2173
Cororate Headquarters: National 2636
Subsidiaries: Farmers 1335, National 2636
Offices: Ahern 60, Wisconsin 4094
Elm Grove
Foundation: WaterStone 4005
Fond du Lac
Foundations: Ahern 60, Holiday 1830, Holiday 1831, MAG 2337, Mid 2503, Smith 3483
Corporate Headquarters: Ahern 60, Holiday 1830, Holiday 1831, MAG 2337, Mid 2503, Smith 3483
Subsidiary: Danaher 1027
Division: Ahern 60
Offices: Ahern 60, Grant 1633
Fort Atkinson
Plant: Krueger 2196
Franklin
Office: Northwestern 2749
Germantown
Cororate Headquarters: WB 4010
Glendale
Corporate Giving Program: Johnson 2050
Grafton
Plant: Rexnord 3198
Green Bay
Corporate Giving Programs: Green 1651, Krueger 2196, ShopKo 3440
Foundations: Associated 261, FEECO 1353, Green 1651, Heyrman 1796, Promotional 3061, Schneider 3355, ShopKo 3440, Wisconsin 4096
Corporate Headquarters: Associated 261, FEECO 1353, Green 1651, Heyrman 1796, Krueger 2196, Promotional 3061, Schneider 3355, ShopKo 3440, Wisconsin 4096
Subsidiaries: Associated 261, Wisconsin 4096
Offices: Godfrey 1596, Humana 1886, Wisconsin 4094
Plants: FMC 1449, Procter 3055, SUPERVALU 3659
Green Lake
Plant: Menasha 2461
Greenwood
Foundation: Clark 835
Cororate Headquarters: Clark 835
Hartford
Plants: Menasha 2461, Quad 3091
Horicon
Plant: Deere 1061
Hudson
Corporate Giving Program: Armor 244
Corporate Headquarters: Armor 244, Phillips 2966
Jackson
Plant: Scotts 3372
Janesville
Foundations: Cullen 1000, Hufcor 1883
Corporate Headquarters: Cullen 1000, Hufcor 1883
Plant: Seneca 3406
Jefferson
Plant: Briggs 565
Kenosha
Foundation: Jockey 2045
Cororate Headquarters: Jockey 2045
Kewaunee
Subsidiary: Oshkosh 2833

Kiel
Foundation: Stoelting 3612
Cororate Headquarters: Stoelting 3612
Kohler
Corporate Giving Program: Kohler 2182
Cororate Headquarters: Kohler 2182
La Crosse
Subsidiaries: CenturyLink 751, JSJ 2073, Trane 3794
Lake Geneva
Foundation: Keefe 2110
Cororate Headquarters: Keefe 2110
Little Chute
Foundation: Crystal 991
Cororate Headquarters: Crystal 991
Lomira
Plant: Quad 3091
Madison
Corporate Giving Programs: Alliant 104, American 144
Foundations: Alliant 104, Central 746, CUNA 1008, Endres 1269, First 1394, Great 1645, Madison 2334, Pellitteri's 2918, Sub-Zero 3630
Corporate Headquarters: Alliant 104, American 144, Central 746, CUNA 1008, First 1394, Great 1645, Madison 2334, Mautz 2408, Pellitteri's 2918, Sub-Zero 3630, Wisconsin 4094, Wisconsin 4095
Subsidiaries: Alliant 104, Amazon.com 122, American 144, Associated 261, Brown 591, Covance 955, CUNA 1008, Deere 1061, Wisconsin 4094
Joint Venture: Lee 2241
Offices: Ahern 60, Akerman 69, CDW 729, Foley 1453, Godfrey 1596, Grant 1633, Humana 1886, Merchant 2464, Mercury 2469, Michael 2492, Perkins 2941, Quarles 3101, Reinhart 3178, Whyte 4067
Plants: Katten 2101, Newell 2694, Sonoco 3500
Manitowoc
Corporate Giving Program: Manitowoc 2355
Foundation: Manitowoc 2356
Cororate Headquarters: Manitowoc 2355
Subsidiaries: Associated 261, Manitowoc 2355
Office: Michael 2492
Plants: Krueger 2196, Newell 2694
Marinette
Subsidiary: Manitowoc 2355
Markesan
Foundation: Badger 314
Marshfield
Office: Associated 261
Mayville
Plant: Seneca 3406
Medford
Foundation: Weather 4013
Cororate Headquarters: Weather 4013
Menasha
Plant: Menasha 2461
Menomonee Falls
Corporate Giving Program: Kohl's 2181
Foundation: Cousins 954
Corporate Headquarters: Cousins 954, Kohl's 2181, Raabe 3115
Subsidiaries: Associated 261, Cousins 954
Office: Ahern 60
Plants: Alro 113, Briggs 565, International 1962
Mequon
Foundation: Allen 97
Cororate Headquarters: Charter 766
Plant: Rockwell 3246
Merrill
Corporate Giving Program: Church 806
Cororate Headquarters: Church 806
Middleton
Subsidiaries: Mattel 2405, Springs 3555
Milwaukee
Corporate Giving Programs: Foley 1453, Godfrey 1596, Harley 1732, MGIC 2488, Michael 2492, Milwaukee 2527, Milwaukee 2528, Quarles 3101, Reinhart 3178, Rockwell 3246, Roundy's 3272, Whyte 4067
Foundations: American 132, Assurant 267, Badger 313, Baird 317, Brady 552, Charter 766, Eppstein 1285, Extendicare 1314, Harley 1732, Johnson 2050, Joy 2070, JPMorgan 2072, Koss 2188, Kowalski 2189, Manpower 2358, Marcus 2371, Masterson 2400, Milwaukee 2527, Monarch 2554, Northwestern 2749, Oilgear 2793, Park 2879, Pfister 2949, Pieper 2972, Rexnord 3198, RITE 3221, Rockwell 3246, Roundy's 3272, Securant 3388, Sensient 3408, Smith 3484, Turner 3825, U.S. 3837, Usinger 3907, Wagner 3976, WB 4010, Weyco 4051, Wisconsin 4093
Corporate Headquarters: Abbot 12, American 132, Assurant 267, Badger 313, Baird 317, Brady 552, Eppstein 1285, Extendicare 1314, Foley 1453, Godfrey 1596, Harley 1732, Johnson 2050, Joy 2070, Koss 2188, Manpower 2358, Marcus 2371, Masterson 2400, MGIC 2488, Michael 2492, Milwaukee 2527, Milwaukee 2528, Monarch 2554, Motor 2583, Northwestern 2749, Oilgear 2793, Park 2879, Pfister 2949, Pieper 2972, Quarles 3101, Reinhart 3178, Rexnord 3198, RITE 3221, Rockwell 3246, Roundy's 3272, Securant 3388, Sensient 3408, Smith 3484, Usinger 3907, Wagner 3976, Weyco 4051, Whyte 4067, Wisconsin 4093
Subsidiaries: American 132, Associated 261, Assurant 266, CNO 857, Joy 2070, Koss 2188, Manpower 2358, Marcus 2371, MGIC 2488, Miller 2523, Northwestern 2749, Rockwell 3246, Roundy's 3272, Sigma 3453, Venturedyne 3933, Vilter 3956, Weyco 4051, Wisconsin 4093
Divisions: Badger 313, General 1552, RITE 3221, ServiceMaster 3414
Offices: American 147, Drinker 1175, Factory 1323, Foley 1453, Godfrey 1596, Hays 1761, Humana 1886, Littler 2289, Michael 2492, Opus 2820, Quarles 3101, Reinhart 3178, Russell 3289, Strauss 3624, Varnum 3923, Whyte 4067, Wisconsin 4094
Plants: Barnes 362, CA 638, Charter 766, General 1554, Lafarge 2210, Miller 2523, Newell 2694, Rockwell 3246
Monona
Foundation: Wisconsin 4094
Mosinee
Foundation: Wausau 4008
Cororate Headquarters: Wausau 4008
Neenah
Foundations: Bemis 407, Menasha 2461, Neenah 2656
Corporate Headquarters: Bemis 407, Menasha 2461, Neenah 2656
Subsidiaries: Associated 261, Kimberly 2150, Neenah 2656
New Berlin
Foundation: Stanek 3578
Corporate Headquarters: Northwestern 2750, Stanek 3578
Plants: Barnes 362, Univar 3886
New London
Plants: Bemis 407, Hillshire 1809
Oak Creek
Division: Henkel 1778
Plant: PPG 3025
Oregon
Plant: Bausch 376
Oshkosh
Foundations: Kimball 2148, Lee 2240, Oshkosh 2833
Corporate Headquarters: Kimball 2148, Lee 2240, Oshkosh 2833
Subsidiaries: Bemis 407, Oshkosh 2833, Tomkins 3771
Plant: Georgia 1568
Oskosh
Plant: Bemis 407
Pewaukee
Foundations: Harken 1731, Venturedyne 3933
Corporate Headquarters: Harken 1731, Venturedyne 3933
Plant: Quad 3091
Phillips
Corporate Giving Program: Phillips 2966
Plymouth
Foundations: Plymouth 2993, Sartori 3335
Corporate Headquarters: Plymouth 2993, Sartori 3335
Plants: Illinois 1916, Plymouth 2993, Toro 3775
Port Edwards
Plant: Vulcan 3972
Port Washington
Cororate Headquarters: Allen 97
Subsidiary: Allen 97
Prairie du Sac
Foundation: Culver 1002
Cororate Headquarters: Culver 1002
Prescott
Foundation: Phillips 2966
Plant: Bergquist 420
Racine
Corporate Giving Program: Johnson 2049
Foundations: Johnson 2049, Modine 2544
Corporate Headquarters: A & E 6, Johnson 2049, Modine 2544
Subsidiaries: Emerson 1257, GKN 1585, Textron 3731
Reedsburg
Subsidiary: Nordic 2722
Rice Lake
Subsidiary: Quanex 3100
Ripon
Foundation: Webster's 4019
Cororate Headquarters: Webster's 4019
Subsidiary: Smucker 3488
Sauk City
Foundation: Wisconsin 4095
Shawano
Subsidiary: Associated 261
Sheboygan
Foundations: Acuity 32, Wigwam 4069, Windway 4086
Corporate Headquarters: Acuity 32, Wigwam 4069, Windway 4086
Subsidiary: Windway 4086
Sheboygan Falls
Foundation: Bemis 408
Cororate Headquarters: Bemis 408
Stevens Point
Corporate Giving Program: Delta 1076
Foundation: Sentry 3409
Corporate Headquarters: Delta 1076, Sentry 3409
Subsidiaries: Associated 261, Leggett 2246, Sentry 3409
Plant: Donaldson 1153
Stoughton
Foundation: Cummins 1006
Sturtevant
Corporate Giving Program: Diversey 1130
Cororate Headquarters: Diversey 1130
Sun Prairie
Cororate Headquarters: AnchorBank 193
Superior
Subsidiary: Allete 100
Sussex
Corporate Giving Program: Quad 3091
Foundation: Quad 3091
Cororate Headquarters: Quad 3091
Tomah
Subsidiary: Acuity 32
Plant: Toro 3775
Tomahawk
Plant: Pactiv 2863
Verona
Foundation: AnchorBank 193
Walworth
Foundation: Kikkoman 2144
Cororate Headquarters: Kikkoman 2144
Plant: Bassett 372
Watertown
Plant: Menasha 2461

Waukesha
Foundations: Dresser 1173, Wisconsin 4092
Cororate Headquarters: Wisconsin 4092
Subsidiary: SPX 3558
Division: Dresser 1173
Offices: Godfrey 1596, Michael 2492, Reinhart 3178
Plant: Navistar 2647
Waunakee
Cororate Headquarters: Endres 1269
Wausau
Corporate Giving Program: Employers 1263
Foundations: Marathon 2366, Wipfli 4091
Corporate Headquarters: Employers 1263, Marathon 2366, Wipfli 4091
Subsidiaries: Associated 261, Liberty 2265
Office: Wisconsin 4094
Plant: Butler 626
Wauwatosa
Corporate Giving Programs: Briggs 565, WaterStone 4005
Foundations: Abbot 12, Briggs 565
Corporate Headquarters: Briggs 565, WaterStone 4005
Subsidiary: Great 1642
West Allis
Foundation: Motor 2583
Subsidiary: Schein 3348
Plant: Quad 3091
West Bend
Foundation: Gehl 1545
Cororate Headquarters: Gehl 1545
West Milwaukee
Plant: Rexnord 3198
Winneconne
Subsidiary: Wisconsin 4093
Wisconsin Rapids
Foundations: Paper 2877, Wood 4108
Corporate Headquarters: Paper 2877, Wood 4108
Woodruff
Foundation: Pukall 3082

WYOMING

Casper
Foundation: True 3814
Corporate Headquarters: First 1409, True 3814
Offices: Hunt 1889, Kiewit 2142, Rothgerber 3269, Sherman 3436
Cheyenne
Foundation: Blue 503
Cororate Headquarters: Blue 503
Subsidiary: Keen 2111
Office: Holland 1833
Clearmont
Subsidiary: Apache 211
Evanston
Cororate Headquarters: Vendome 3930
Gillette
Subsidiary: Black 474
Green River
Subsidiary: FMC 1449
Jackson
Foundation: Medeanalytics 2447
Office: Holland 1833
Lovell
Plant: Georgia 1568
Newcastle
Cororate Headquarters: First 1423
Subsidiary: Black 474
Riverton
Subsidiary: LifePoint 2270

INTERNATIONAL GIVING INDEX

List of terms: The names of countries, continents, or regions used in this index are drawn from the complete list below. Terms may appear on the list but not be present in the index.

Index: In the index itself, corporations are listed under the countries, continents, or regions in which they have demonstrated giving interests or made charitable contributions. Within these country or regional groupings, corporations are arranged alphabetically by abbreviated name and sequence number.

Afghanistan
Africa
Albania
Algeria
Andorra
Angola
Anguilla
Antarctica
Antigua & Barbuda
Arctic Region
Argentina
Armenia
Aruba
Asia
Australia
Austria
Azerbaijan
Bahamas
Bahrain
Balkans, The
Bangladesh
Barbados
Belarus
Belgium
Belize
Benin
Bermuda
Bhutan
Bolivia
Bonaire
Bosnia-Herzegovina
Botswana
Brazil
British Virgin Islands
Brunei
Bulgaria
Burkina Faso
Burma (Myanmar)
Burundi
Cambodia
Cameroon
Canada
Cape Verde
Caribbean
Cayman Islands
Central Africa
Central Africa Republic
Central America
Central Asia and the Caucasus
Chad
Chile
China
Colombia
Commonwealth of the Northern Mariana Islands
Comoros
Congo
Costa Rica
Croatia
Cuba
Curacao
Cyprus
Czech Republic
Democratic Republic of the Congo
Denmark
Developing countries
Djibouti
Dominica
Dominican Republic
East Africa/Horn of Africa
East Asia
East Jerusalem
East Timor
Eastern & Central Europe
Ecuador
Egypt
El Salvador
England
Equatorial Guinea
Eritrea
Estonia
Ethiopia
Europe
Federated States of Micronesia
Fiji
Finland
France
French Guiana
Gabon
Gambia
Georgia (Republic of)
Germany
Ghana
Gibraltar
Global programs
Greater Antilles
Greece
Greenland
Grenada
Guadeloupe
Guatemala
Guernsey
Guinea
Guinea-Bissau
Guyana
Haiti
Honduras
Hong Kong
Hungary
Iceland
India
Indonesia
Iran
Iraq
Ireland
Isle of Man
Israel
Italy
Ivory Coast
Jamaica
Japan
Jersey
Jordan
Kazakhstan
Kenya
Kiribati
Kosovo
Kuwait
Kyrgyzstan
Laos
Latin America
Latvia
Lebanon
Leeward Islands
Lesotho
Lesser Antilles
Liberia
Libya
Liechtenstein
Lithuania
Luxembourg
Macau
Macedonia
Madagascar
Malawi
Malaysia
Maldives
Mali
Malta
Marshall Islands
Martinique
Mauritania
Mauritius
Mexico
Middle East
Moldova
Monaco
Mongolia
Montenegro
Montserrat
Morocco and the Western Sahara
Mozambique
Namibia
Nauru
Nepal
Netherlands
Netherlands Antilles
New Caledonia
New Zealand
Nicaragua
Niger
Nigeria
North Korea
North Africa
Northern Ireland
Norway
Oceania
Oman
Pakistan
Palau
Panama
Papua New Guinea
Paraguay
Peru
Philippines
Poland
Portugal
Qatar
Romania
Russia
Rwanda
Saint Kitts-Nevis
Saint Lucia
Saint Vincent & the Grenadines
Samoa
Sao Tome and Principe
Saudi Arabia
Scandinavia
Scotland
Senegal

Serbia
Seychelles
Sierra Leone
Singapore
Slovakia
Slovenia
Solomon Islands
Somalia, Somaliland and Puntland
South Africa
South America
South Asia
South Korea
South Sudan
Southeast Asia
Southern Africa
Soviet Union (Former)
Spain
Sri Lanka
Sub-Saharan Africa
Sudan
Suriname
Swaziland
Sweden
Switzerland
Syria
Tahiti
Taiwan
Tajikistan
Tanzania, Zanzibar and Pemba
Thailand
Togo
Tonga
Trinidad & Tobago
Tunisia
Turkey
Turkmenistan
Turks & Caicos Islands
Tuvalu
Uganda
Ukraine
United Arab Emirates
United Kingdom
Uruguay
Uzbekistan
Vanuatu
Vatican City
Venezuela
Vietnam
Wales
West Bank/Gaza
Western Africa
Windward Islands
Yemen
Yugoslavia (Former)
Zambia
Zimbabwe

Afghanistan
Abbott 13, Callaway 660, Global 1592, Motorola 2585

Africa
Abbott 13, Alcoa 82, American 158, Amway 189, Bank 344, Becton 398, Brilliant 568, Bristol 578, Capstone 684, Coca 862, Cummins 1007, Deere 1061, EduCare 1231, Exxon 1315, General 1552, Georgia 1568, Gilead 1582, Goldman 1604, Grand 1627, Heinz 1772, Hess 1793, International 1960, International 1968, Johnson 2048, JPMorgan Chase 2071, Laird 2211, Linklaters 2283, Medtronic 2453, Merck 2466, Monsanto 2559, NIKE 2710, Parametric 2878, PepsiCo 2935, PPG 3025, Schein 3348, Standard 3575, Starbucks 3585, Strauss 3624, Whole 4066

Albania
Avon 305, Cisco 818, Procter 3055

Algeria
Cisco 818, Citigroup 821, Greif 1663, Hess 1793, Lexmark 2258, Mondelez 2556, Pfizer 2950, Procter 3055, Western 4045

Angola
Baker 324, Coca 862, Halliburton 1706, Ogilvy 2788, Pfizer 2950

Anguilla
Marriott 2383

Antigua & Barbuda
Diamonds 1109, Ecolab 1220, Marriott 2383

Argentina
3M 3, Abbott 13, AES 47, Air 63, Allergan 99, American 143, Amway 189, Apache 211, ARAMARK 223, Arrow 249, Assurant 266, Assurant 268, Avery 297, Avon 305, Baker 320, Baker 324, Bank 340, Becton 398, Biogen 465, Blockbuster 483, BMC 508, Boeing 516, Boston 540, CA 638, Cabot 642, Caterpillar 722, Chemtura 775, Chevron 780, Cisco 818, CITGO 820, Citigroup 821, Cleary 843, Clorox 852, Coca 862, Colgate 869, Covance 955, Cummins 1007, Dana 1026, Danaher 1027, Dart 1033, Deere 1061, Dell 1068, DENTSPLY 1089, Deutsche 1099, Diebold 1112, DIRECTV 1124, Disney 1127, Diversey 1130, Donnelley 1155, Dow 1161, du Pont 1184, Duke 1189, Dun 1190, Eastman 1213, Eastman 1214, Eaton 1216, Eclipse 1219, Ecolab 1220, Edelman 1224, El Paso 1239, Energizer 1271, Exxon 1315, Ferro 1366, First 1400, ForceBrain.com 1461, Franklin 1487, GenCorp 1548, General 1554, General 1555, Google 1613, Grace 1623, Graham 1625, Greif 1663, Harris 1736, Harsco 1741, Hartford 1742, Hewlett 1794, Hunt 1889, Huntsman 1895, IDT 1910, Illinois 1916, Imation 1919, Ingram 1941, Ingredion 1942, Intel 1950, International 1960, International 1962, International 1964, ITT 1999, James 2021, Johnson 2048, Johnson 2049, JPMorgan Chase 2071, Kellogg 2120, Manpower 2358, Marriott 2383, Masco 2393, MasterCard 2399, Mattel 2405, Medtronic 2453, Merck 2466, Mine 2529, Mondelez 2556, Monsanto 2559, Mosaic 2580, Motorola 2585, Motorola 2586, Nalco 2613, NCR 2650, New York 2688, Newell 2694, NII 2709, Novell 2754, Ogilvy 2788, Oracle 2821, Owens 2842, Parker 2886, Patagonia 2892, Pentair 2926, PepsiCo 2935, Pfizer 2950, Pinnacle 2978, Pioneer 2980, Pioneer 2981, Praxair 3029, Quaker 3093, Ralph 3123, Rio 3218, Robbins 3230, Rock 3239, Rockwell 3246, RPM 3278, Ryder 3292, Scholastic 3358, Sealy 3382, Sherwin 3437, St. Jude 3566, Stanley 3579, Tenneco 3715, Thompson 3739, Thomson 3742, Tyco 3829, Tyson 3832, UnitedHealth 3884, Universal 3893, Unum 3898, V.F. 3913, Viacom 3945, Waters 4003, West 4038, Western 4045, Whirlpool 4056, Whole 4066, Williams 4077, Yahoo! 4140

Armenia
Huntsman 1895, Marriott 2383, Mentor 2462

Aruba
CIT 819, Citigroup 821, Ecolab 1220, El Paso 1239, Marriott 2383, Wells 4028

Asia
Advanced 40, Alcoa 82, Amway 189, Autodesk 289, Bank 344, Becton 398, Capital 678, Cisco 818, Convergys 933, EduCare 1231, Exxon 1315, Flextronics 1437, Fuller 1517, Georgia 1568, Gibraltar 1577, Goldman 1604, Grand 1627, Ingram 1941, International 1960, JPMorgan Chase 2071, Kerzner 2133, Laird 2211, Lam 2214, Mead 2443, Monsanto 2559, Parametric 2878, PepsiCo 2935, PPG 3025, Praxair 3029, Quiksilver 3108, Ricoh 3210, salesforce.com 3318, SMBC 3480, Starbucks 3585, Strauss 3624, Timken 3760, Whole 4066

Australia
3M 3, Abbott 13, Activision 30, Adobe 38, AES 47, AK 67, Aladdin 73, Alcoa 82, Allegheny 91, Allen 94, Allergan 99, AMCOL 127, Amway 189, Apache 211, Armstrong 246, Ashland 258, Autodesk 289, Automatic 291, Avery 297, Avnet 304, Avon 305, Baker 320, Baker 324, Bank 340, Bausch 376, Becton 398, Berkshire 429, Biogen 465, Biomet 466, BMC 508, Boeing 516, BOSE 530, Boston 540, BP 547, Briggs 565, Brightpoint 567, CA 638, Cabot 642, Callaway 660, Campbell 669, Capital 678, Carlson 693, Caterpillar 722, CBS 727, Cephalon 752, Chemtura 775, Chevron 780, Cisco 818, CIT 819, Citigroup 821, CLARCOR 832, Clifford 849, Cliffs 850, Clorox 852, Coca 862, Colgate 869, Collective 871, Comcast 887, Commercial 893, ConocoPhillips 913, Cooper 935, Corning 945, Covance 955, Credit 980, Cummins 1007, Dana 1026, Danaher 1027, Dart 1033, Deere 1061, Delaware 1066, Dell 1068, Diebold 1112, Disney 1127, Diversey 1130, Donaldson 1153, Dorsey 1157, Dow 1161, Dow 1162, drugstore.com 1180, du Pont 1184, Duke 1189, Eastman 1213, Eaton 1216, eBay 1217, Ecolab 1220, Edelman 1224, Energizer 1271, Energy 1273, Exxon 1315, Ferro 1366, First 1389, First 1400, Fiserv 1427, Fluor 1448, FMC 1449, Ford 1462, Franklin 1487, Freshfields 1500, GameStop 1530, General 1551, General 1554, Genworth 1565, Gilead 1582, Google 1613, Grace 1623, Graco 1624, H & R 1695, Halliburton 1706, Hallmark 1707, Harris 1736, Harsco 1741, Haworth 1758, Heinz 1772, Hewlett 1794, Hillshire 1809, Honeywell 1852, Hormel 1866, Hospira 1867, Hubbell 1879, Huntsman 1895, IAC 1903, Ideal 1908, IDT 1910, Illinois 1916, Ingram 1941, Intel 1950, Interface 1953, International 1960, International 1962, International 1964, Interpublic 1974, Intuit 1982, ITT 1999, Johnson 2048, Johnson 2049, Jones 2058, Kearney 2107, Kellogg 2120, Kennametal 2125, Kids 2141, Kiewit 2142, Leggett 2246, Lexmark 2258, Life 2268, Lilly 2274, Manitowoc 2355, Manpower 2358, Mark 2377, Marriott 2383, MasterCard 2399, Mattel 2405, McCormick 2423, McDonald's 2427, McGraw 2429, Medtronic 2453, Mentor 2462, Merck 2466, Meritor 2473, Merk 2467, MGIC 2488, Microchip 2499, Miller 2517, Mine 2529, Modine 2544, Mondelez 2556, Monsanto 2559, Moody's 2563, Motorola 2586, Mylan 2610, Nalco 2613, Nasdaq 2617, NCR 2650, Newell 2694, Newmont 2698, Nordson 2723, Novell 2754, NRG 2756, Nu 2759, Ogilvy 2788, Oilgear 2793, Olin 2801, Omnicare 2807, Oracle 2821, Owens 2842, Oxford 2847, PACCAR 2850, Parker 2886, Peabody 2907, Pentair 2926, PepsiCo 2935, Pfizer 2950, Pioneer 2980, Pitney 2984, Polaris 2999, PPG 3025, Preformed 3032, Procter 3055, Quaker 3093, Quest 3103, Quiksilver 3108, Ralph 3123, Reader's 3141, ResMed 3192, Robbins 3230, Rockwell 3246, Rockwell 3247, Ruder 3282, Ryder 3292, SAIC 3311, SAS 3336, Schein 3348, Scholastic 3358, Sealed 3381, Sensient 3408, Sidley 3446, Simplot 3459, Sonoco 3500, SPX 3558, Squire 3561, St. Jude 3566, Stanley 3579, Staples 3581, Starbucks 3585, State 3592, Sullivan 3634, Susquehanna 3661, Teleflex 3707, Tenneco 3715, Terex 3719, Texas 3728, Thompson 3739, Thomson 3742, Tidewater 3748, Timken 3760, Toro 3775, Toys 3790, Tyco 3829, United 3882, UnitedHealth 3884, UTC 3908, Valmont 3919, Valspar 3920, Viacom 3945, Washington 3999, Waters 4003, WD-40 4011, West 4038, Western 4045, Whirlpool 4056, Wiley 4072, Wrigley 4125, Yahoo! 4140, Yum! 4150

Austria

3M 3, Abbott 13, AES 47, Air 63, Alcoa 82, Allergan 99, American 132, American 143, Amway 189, Armstrong 246, Autodesk 289, Avery 297, Avnet 304, Avon 305, Baker 320, Baker 324, Baxter 377, Bayer 382, Becton 398, Biogen 465, Biomet 466, BMC 508, Briggs 565, Brightpoint 567, Bristol 578, CA 638, Cisco 818, CIT 819, ConocoPhillips 913, Cummins 1007, Danaher 1027, Dell 1068, Diebold 1112, Diversey 1130, Donaldson 1153, Eaton 1216, eBay 1217, Ecolab 1220, Energizer 1271, Exxon 1315, Fifth 1376, First 1400, Foot 1459, Franklin 1487, Freshfields 1500, GameStop 1530, General 1551, General 1552, General 1554, General 1555, Genworth 1565, Gilead 1582, Google 1613, Harris 1736, Harsco 1741, Hexcel 1795, Huntsman 1895, Illinois 1916, Ingram 1941, International 1960, ITT 1999, Jabil 2006, Johnson 2048, Kearney 2107, Kellogg 2120, Leggett 2246, Lexmark 2258, Liberty 2263, Lilly 2274, Manpower 2358, Marriott 2383, Masco 2393, Matthews 2406, McDonald's 2427, Medtronic 2453, Merck 2466, Merk 2467, Microchip 2499, Modine 2544, Mondelez 2556, Motorola 2586, Mylan 2610, NCR 2650, Newell 2694, NIKE 2710, Nordson 2723, Novell 2754, Ogilvy 2788, Oracle 2821, Parametric 2878, Parker 2886, Patagonia 2892, Pfizer 2950, Pitney 2984, Polaris 2999, Praxair 3029, Procter 3055, Quiksilver 3108, Ralph 3123, Reader's 3141, Respironics 3193, Rockwell 3246, Rockwell 3247, RPM 3278, Schein 3348, St. Jude 3566, Stanley 3579, Staples 3581, State 3592, Teleflex 3707, Tennant 3714, Texas 3728, Thompson 3739, Toro 3775, Toys 3790, Tyco 3829, United 3877, Waters 4003, Western 4045, Whirlpool 4056, Williams 4077, Wrigley 4125, Xerox 4136

Azerbaijan

Baker 320, Hess 1793, McDermott 2424, Procter 3055

Bahamas

Abbott 13, AES 47, Anadarko 190, Bank 340, Chevron 780, Citigroup 821, ConocoPhillips 913, Credit 980, Diamonds 1109, eBay 1217, Ecolab 1220, Exxon 1315, H & R 1695, Hospira 1867, International 1960, Kenneth 2128, Marriott 2383, Martin 2391, Masco 2393, Mondelez 2556, PepsiCo 2935, Pfizer 2950, Pinnacle 2978, Pioneer 2981, Tidewater 3748, Viacom 3945, Vulcan 3972

Bahrain

Alcoa 82, Baker 320, CA 638, Cisco 818, Citigroup 821, Dell 1068, Freshfields 1500, Harsco 1741, Interpublic 1974, Kearney 2107, Kimberly 2150, Manpower 2358, Marriott 2383, Mondelez 2556, NCR 2650, Ogilvy 2788, Parsons 2887, Yum! 4150

Bangladesh

Abbott 13, Arch 230, Avery 297, Citigroup 821, First 1400, Harris 1736, Heinz 1772, Intel 1950, Mortenson 2577, NIKE 2710, PepsiCo 2935, Procter 3055, Thompson 3739, Whole 4066

Barbados

Abbott 13, Advanced 40, Applied 219, Becton 398, Boeing 516, Caterpillar 722, CIT 819, Clorox 852, Cooper 936, Crown 988, Cummins 1007, Danaher 1027, Dell 1068, Diamonds 1109, Diebold 1112, Diversey 1130, Donnelley 1155, Eastman 1214, Ecolab 1220, Energizer 1271, Fortune 1474, Hexcel 1795, Ingram 1941, International 1960, International 1962, Leggett 2246, Manitowoc 2355, MasterCard 2399, Merck 2466, Meritor 2473, Miller 2517, Modine 2544, Newell 2694, Nucor 2760, Ogilvy 2788, Oracle 2821, PepsiCo 2935, Pfizer 2950, Rockwell 3246, Rogers 3253, Sealed 3381, Smith 3484, Smucker 3488, Teleflex 3707, Texas 3728, Tidewater 3748, Wells 4028, Western 4045, Williams 4077, Xerox 4136

Belarus

Manpower 2358, Procter 3055

Belgium

3M 3, Abbott 13, Adobe 38, Advanced 40, Agilent 56, AK 67, Albemarle 78, Allegheny 91, Allen 94, Allergan 99, Alston 116, AMPCO 186, ARAMARK 223, Arch 230, Arnold 248, Arrow 249, Automatic 291, Avery 297, Avnet 304, Baker 320, Becton 398, Bemis 407, Berry 438, Biogen 465, Biomet 466, BMC 508, Boston 540, Brightpoint 567, Bristol 578, Broadcom 579, Brunswick 595, CA 638, Cabot 642, Cadwalader 649, Campbell 669, Cargill 691, Caterpillar 722, Chemtura 775, Cisco 818, CIT 819, Citigroup 821, Cleary 843, Clifford 849, Coca 862, Coca 863, Colgate 869, Comcast 887, Corning 945, Covance 955, Credit 980, Crowell 986, Crown 988, Cummins 1007, Danaher 1027, Dechert 1058, Dell 1068, Diebold 1112, Diversey 1130, Donaldson 1153, Donnelley 1155, Dow 1162, du Pont 1184, Dun 1190, Eastman 1213, Eastman 1214, Eaton 1216, eBay 1217, Ecolab 1220, Edelman 1224, Emerson 1257, Energizer 1271, Exxon 1315, Fifth 1376, Finnegan 1384, First 1400, FMC 1449, Foot 1459, Freshfields 1500, Gates 1540, General 1552, General 1554, General 1555, Genzyme 1566, Georgia 1568, Gibson 1580, Gilead 1582, Goodyear 1612, Google 1613, Grace 1623, Graco 1624, Graham 1625, Greif 1663, Griffith 1667, Hallmark 1707, Harris 1736, Harsco 1741, Haworth 1758, Heinz 1772, Hewlett 1794, Hexcel 1795, Hillshire 1809, Hilton 1812, Hogan 1825, Honeywell 1852, Hospira 1867, Huntsman 1895, IDT 1910, Illinois 1916, Ingram 1941, Intel 1950, International 1960, International 1964, Interpublic 1974, Jabil 2006, Johnson 2048, Johnson 2049, Jones 2058, K&L 2080, Keller 2116, Kelley 2118, Latham 2228, Leggett 2246, Lexmark 2258, Liberty 2263, Lilly 2274, Linklaters 2283, Lubrizol 2315, MAC 2329, Manpower 2358, Mark 2377, Marriott 2383, Mars 2384, Masco 2393, MasterCard 2399, Mayer 2411, McDermott 2425, McGuireWoods 2430, McKenna 2433, Medtronic 2453, Merck 2466, Meritor 2473, Merk 2467, Mine 2529, Mondelez 2556, Monsanto 2559, Morgan 2571, Morrison 2576, Motorola 2586, Mylan 2610, NCR 2650, Newell 2694, Novell 2754, Nu 2759, Ogilvy 2788, Omnicare 2807, Oracle 2821, Oshkosh 2833, Owens 2842, PACCAR 2850, Parker 2886, Patagonia 2892, Paul 2900, Pentair 2926, Pfizer 2950, Pitney 2984, PPG 3025, Praxair 3029, Procter 3055, QUALCOMM 3095, Quiksilver 3108, Ralph 3123, Reader's 3141, Rio 3218, Riviana 3227, Robbins 3230, Rockwell 3246, Rogers 3253, RPM 3278, SAS 3336, ScanSource 3347, Schein 3348, Schulman 3361, Sealed 3381, Sealy 3382, Shearman 3429, Sheppard 3435, Sidley 3446, Sonoco 3500, SPX 3558, Squire 3561, St. Jude 3566, Stanley 3579, Staples 3581, State 3592, Steptoe 3599, STERIS 3600, Teleflex 3707, Tennant 3714, Tenneco 3715, Texas 3728, Thompson 3739, Thomson 3742, Toro 3775, Toys 3790, United 3877, UnitedHealth 3884, V.F. 3913, Viacom 3945, Victaulic 3948, Western 4045, Westinghouse 4049, Whirlpool 4056, White 4058, Willkie 4081, Wilson 4083, Xerox 4136

Belize

New England 2670

Bermuda

Abbott 13, Activision 30, AES 47, Air 63, Allergan 99, American 156, AMETEK 181, Amgen 182, AMR 187, Anheuser 202, Assurant 266, Atmos 285, Avon 305, Bank 340, Bank 344, Barnes 360, BB&T 385, Becton 398, Biomet 466, Boeing 516, Boston 540, Brunswick 595, Burlington 618, Cadence 646, Caesars 650, Caterpillar 722, Cephalon 752, Chevron 780, Chubb 804, Cisco 818, CIT 819, Citigroup 821, Clorox 852, Collective 871, Comerica 889, ConocoPhillips 913, Cooper 935, Cooper 936, Costco 948, Dana 1026, Delta 1073, Dole 1141, Duke 1189, El Paso 1239, Ellucian 1252, Emerson 1257, Energizer 1271, First 1400, Ford 1464, Freeport 1494, Gap 1533, GenCorp 1548, General 1552, General 1554, General 1555, Genworth 1565, Gilead 1582, Google 1613, Great 1642, Greif 1663, Guess 1685, H & R 1695, Harris 1736, Harsco 1741, Hartford 1742, HCA 1762, Hillshire 1809, Honeywell 1852, IAC 1903, Illinois 1916, Ingram 1941, International 1960, International 1962, LSI 2314, Manitowoc 2355, Marriott 2383, Marsh 2385, Mattel 2405, Merck 2466, Morgan 2570, Mylan 2610, NCR 2650, Newmont 2698, Norfolk 2725, NRG 2756, Occidental 2780, Office 2785, Olin 2801, Oracle 2821, Parker 2886, PepsiCo 2935, Pfizer 2950, PPG 3025, Praxair 3029, Regions 3171, RPM 3278, Ryder 3292, Safeway 3310, Sedgwick 3395, Sigma 3453, Simon 3458, Smithfield 3487, Sprint 3556, St. Jude 3566, State 3591, SUPERVALU 3659, Texas 3728, Tidewater 3748, Toro 3775, Truland 3817, Tyson 3832, UnitedHealth 3884, Universal 3890, US 3902, Viacom 3945, Walter 3984, Wells 4028, Western 4045, Whirlpool 4056, Williams 4077, Xerox 4136

Bolivia

AES 47, Avon 305, Diebold 1112, Duke 1189, El Paso 1239, General 1554, International 1960, Kimberly 2150, Merck 2466, Mondelez 2556, New England 2670, Ogilvy 2788, Pfizer 2950, Praxair 3029, Rockwell 3246, Thompson 3739

Bosnia-Herzegovina

Avon 305, Cisco 818, Lexmark 2258, Merck 2466, Oracle 2821, PepsiCo 2935, Pfizer 2950, Procter 3055, Thompson 3739

Botswana

Cummins 1007, Heinz 1772, Ogilvy 2788, Sealed 3381

Brazil

3M 3, Abbott 13, Adobe 38, AES 47, Air 63, Alcoa 82, Allen 94, Allergan 99, Altria 120, American 158, American 167, Amway 189, Anheuser 202, Arkema 242, Arrow 249, Ashland 258, Assurant 266, Assurant 268, Autodesk 289, Automatic 291, Avery 297, Avnet 304, Avon 305, Baker 319, Baker 320, Baker 324, Bank 340, Bank 344, Bausch 376, Baxter 377, Becton 398, Bemis 407, Biogen 465, Biomet 466, BMC 508, Boeing 516, BorgWarner 528, BOSE 530, BP 547, Briggs 565, Bristol 578, Brown 591, Brunswick 595, Cabot 642, Capital 678, Caterpillar 722, CBS 727, Chemtura 775, Chevron 780, CHS 802, Cisco 818, CIT 819, Citigroup 821, Clark 836, Clifford 849, Cliffs 850, Clorox 852, CME 853, Coca 862, Colgate 869, Collette 872, Comcast 887, Comerica 889, Cooper 935, Credit 980, Crown 988, Cummins 1007, Dana 1026, Danaher 1027, Davis 1040, Deere 1061, Dell 1068, DENTSPLY 1089, Deutsche 1099, Devon 1102, Diebold 1112, DIRECTV 1124, Diversey 1130, Donaldson 1153, Donnelley 1155, Dow 1162, du Pont 1184, Dun 1190, Eastman 1213, Eaton 1216, Eclipse 1219, Ecolab 1220, Edelman 1224, EFC 1236, El Paso 1239, Energizer 1271, Equifax 1288, Ethicon 1299, Exxon 1315, Ferro 1366, Fifth 1376, First 1400, Flextronics 1437, FMC 1449, Franklin 1487, Freescale 1495, General 1551, General 1552, General 1554, General 1555, Gibson 1580, Goodyear 1612, Google 1613, Grace 1623, Graham 1625, Greif 1663, Harris 1736, Harsco 1741, Hartford 1742, Hershey 1791, Hewlett 1794, Hexcel 1795, Hillshire 1809, Hines 1813, Hospira 1867, Hubbell 1879, Huntsman 1895, Ideal 1908, IDT 1910, Illinois 1916, Ingram 1941, Ingredion 1942, Intel 1950, International 1960, International 1962, International 1964, International 1968, Interpublic 1974,

Jabil 2006, James 2021, Johnson 2048, Johnson 2049, Jones 2058, JPMorgan Chase 2071, Kearney 2107, Leggett 2246, Lexmark 2258, Linklaters 2283, Lubrizol 2315, Manitowoc 2355, Manpower 2358, Marriott 2383, MasterCard 2399, Mattel 2405, McDonald's 2427, MeadWestvaco 2445, Medtronic 2453, Merck 2466, Milbank 2511, Mine 2529, Modine 2544, Mondelez 2556, Monsanto 2559, Moody's 2563, Morgan 2568, Morgan 2570, Mosaic 2580, Motorola 2585, Motorola 2586, Nalco 2613, Navistar 2647, NCR 2650, New York 2690, Newell 2694, NII 2709, NIKE 2710, Nordson 2723, Novell 2754, Nu 2759, Occidental 2780, Ogilvy 2788, Olin 2801, Oracle 2821, Owens 2842, Owens 2844, PACCAR 2850, Parametric 2878, Parker 2886, Pentair 2926, Pfizer 2950, Pioneer 2980, Pitney 2984, PPG 3025, Praxair 3029, Preformed 3032, Procter 3055, Proskauer 3064, Prudential 3072, Quaker 3093, Quaker 3094, Quest 3103, Quiksilver 3108, Reader's 3141, Rio 3218, Robbins 3230, Rockwell 3246, Rockwell 3247, RPM 3278, Ryder 3292, Sealed 3381, Sealy 3382, Shearman 3429, Sherwin 3437, Simpson 3462, Sonoco 3500, Springs 3555, SPX 3558, Squire 3561, St. Jude 3566, Stanley 3579, Staples 3581, Starbucks 3585, Tennant 3714, Tenneco 3715, Texas 3728, Thompson 3739, Thomson 3742, Tidewater 3748, Timken 3760, Tyco 3829, United 3872, United 3877, UnitedHealth 3884, V.F. 3913, Valmont 3919, Valspar 3920, Viacom 3945, Waters 4003, Wells 4028, West 4038, Western 4045, Whirlpool 4056, White 4058, Xerox 4136, Yahoo! 4140, Yum! 4150

British Virgin Islands

AES 47, Anheuser 202, ARAMARK 223, Avery 297, Bank 340, Becton 398, Brightpoint 567, Brown 591, Cabot 642, Citigroup 821, Clorox 852, Colgate 869, Collective 871, Comerica 889, ConocoPhillips 913, Cooper 935, Crown 988, Dana 1026, Devon 1102, DIRECTV 1124, Disney 1127, Donnelley 1155, eBay 1217, First 1389, Franklin 1487, General 1554, Goldman 1603, Illinois 1916, Ingram 1941, James 2021, Lilly 2274, Manitowoc 2355, Manpower 2358, Masco 2393, Mondelez 2556, Oracle 2821, Owens 2841, Peabody 2907, Praxair 3029, QUALCOMM 3095, Regal 3167, Ryder 3292, Sonoco 3500, Tiffany 3750, Tyson 3832, Whirlpool 4056

Brunei

Avon 305, Citigroup 821, First 1400

Bulgaria

AES 47, Avery 297, Avon 305, Boston 540, Cisco 818, Citigroup 821, Danaher 1027, Dell 1068, Eaton 1216, Ecolab 1220, Hewlett 1794, Illinois 1916, International 1960, Lexmark 2258, Manpower 2358, Merck 2466, Mondelez 2556, Ogilvy 2788, PepsiCo 2935, Procter 3055, Tennant 3714, Thompson 3739, UnitedHealth 3884, Whirlpool 4056, Xerox 4136

Burkina Faso

Monsanto 2559

Cambodia

Abbott 13, Collette 872, Crown 988, Heinz 1772, Mortenson 2577

Cameroon

AES 47, Cisco 818, Citigroup 821, Exxon 1315, New England 2670, PPG 3025

Canada

3M 3, Abbott 13, Activision 30, Adobe 38, Advanced 40, Agilent 56, Air 63, Alcatel 81, Alcoa 82, Allergan 99, Altria 120, American 132, American 133, American 140, American 143, American 149, American 156, AmerisourceBergen 175, AMETEK 181, Amgen 182, Amsted 188, Amway 189, Andersen 194, AOL 209, Apache 211, Applied 219, Applied 220, ARAMARK 223, Archer 233, Arkema 242, Armstrong 246, Arrow 249, Ashland 258, Assurant 266, Assurant 268, Autodesk 289, Automatic 291, Avery 297, Avnet 304, Avon 305, Badger 313, Baker 320, Baker 324, Ball 328, Bank 340, Bank 344, Bard 358, Barnes 362, Baseball 367, Bausch 376, Bayer 382, Beam 390, Bechtel 395, Becton 398, Berkshire 429, Berry 438, Biomet 466, Blockbuster 483, BMC 508, Boeing 516, BorgWarner 528, BOSE 530, Boston 540, Bowater 543, Briggs 565, Bristol 578, Brown 591, Brunswick 595, Build 608, Burger 613, Burlington 618, CA 638, Cabot 642, Cadence 646, Callaway 660, Calpine 661, Campbell 669, Canon 672, Cargill 691, Carlson 693, Castle 716, Caterpillar 722, CBS 727, CDW 729, Ceridian 753, CF 755, Charles 764, Chemtura 775, Chevron 780, Chrysler 801, CHS 802, Cintas 816, Cisco 818, CIT 819, Citigroup 821, CLARCOR 832, Cliffs 850, Clorox 852, CNO 857, Coca 862, Coca 863, Colgate 869, Collective 871, Comcast 887, ConocoPhillips 913, Constellation 919, Convergys 933, Costco 948, Covance 955, Cox 959, Cozen 964, Crane 970, Credit 980, Crown 988, Cummins 1007, Dana 1026, Danaher 1027, Darden 1032, Dart 1033, Davey 1035, Davies 1036, Deere 1061, Delaware 1066, Dell 1068, Delta 1073, Deluxe 1084, Denny's 1087, DENSO 1088, DENTSPLY 1089, Deutsche 1099, Devon 1102, Diebold 1112, Disney 1127, Diversey 1130, Dole 1141, Donnelley 1155, Dorsey 1157, DRS 1179, drugstore.com 1180, du Pont 1184, Duke 1189, Dun 1190, Dura 1195, Eastman 1214, Eaton 1216, eBay 1217, Eclipse 1219, Ecolab 1220, Edelman 1224, Edison 1228, Electronic 1242, Ellucian 1252, Emerson 1257, Energizer 1271, Enterprise 1281, EOG 1282, Equifax 1288, Express 1313, Exxon 1315, Factory 1323, FedEx 1352, Ferro 1366, Fifth 1376, First 1389, First 1400, Fluor 1448, FMC 1449, FMR 1450, Foot 1459, ForceBrain.com 1461, Ford 1464, Fortune 1474, Franklin 1487, Freescale 1495, Fuller 1517, GameStop 1530, Gannett 1532, Gap 1533, General 1551, General 1552, General 1554, General 1555, General 1556, GenOn 1563, Genworth 1565, Georgia 1568, Gilead 1582, Goodyear 1612, Google 1613, Goulds 1619, Grace 1623, Graco 1624, Graham 1625, Grainger 1626, Green 1653, Greif 1663, Griffith 1667, Gucci 1684, Guess 1685, H & R 1695, Halliburton 1706, Hallmark 1707, Handy 1718, Hardinge 1729, Harris 1736, Harsco 1741, Hartford 1742, Haworth 1758, Heinz 1772, Hershey 1791, Hewlett 1794, Hillshire 1809, Hines 1813, HNI 1817, Hodgson 1820, Holcim 1828, Holland 1835, Home 1842, Honeywell 1852, Hormel 1866, Hospira 1867, HSBC 1876, Hubbell 1879, Hunt 1889, Huntington 1894, Huntsman 1895, IAC 1903, Ideal 1908, IKON 1914, Illinois 1916, Imation 1919, IMS 1924, Ingram 1941, Ingredion 1942, Intel 1950, Interface 1953, International 1960, International 1962, Interpublic 1974, Intuit 1982, ITT 1999, James 2021, JM 2044, Jockey 2045, Johns 2047, Johnson 2048, Johnson 2049, Johnson 2050, Jones 2057, JPMorgan Chase 2071, Kasle 2098, Kearney 2107, Kellogg 2120, Kellwood 2121, Kids 2141, Kiewit 2142, Kinder 2153, Koch 2180, L'Oreal 2203, La-Z-Boy 2205, Lafarge 2210, Lauder 2230, Leggett 2246, Leviton 2255, Lexmark 2258, Liberty 2265, Life 2268, LifeScan 2271, Limited 2277, Louisiana 2310, LSI 2314, Lubrizol 2315, M&T 2323, Manpower 2358, Marathon 2362, Maritz 2376, Mark 2377, Marriott 2383, Mars 2384, Marsh 2385, Masco 2393, Mattel 2405, McCormick 2423, McDermott 2424, McDonald's 2427, McGraw 2429, McWane 2440, Medtronic 2453, Men's 2460, Mentor 2462, Merck 2466, Meritor 2473, Michelin 2495, Microchip 2499, Miller 2517, Miller 2519, Miller 2521, Mine 2529, Mondelez 2556, MoneyGram 2558, Monsanto 2559, Moody's 2563, Moore 2565, Morgan 2570, Mosaic 2580, Motorola 2586, Murphy 2600, Mylan 2610, Nalco 2613, Nasdaq 2617, Navistar 2647, NCR 2650, New 2668, New 2673, Newell 2694, Newmont 2698, NIKE 2710, Nordson 2723, Novell 2754, Nu 2759, Nucor 2760, Occidental 2780, Office 2785, Ogilvy 2788, Olin 2801, Omnicare 2807, OMNOVA 2809, ONEOK 2815, Oracle 2821, Our 2838, Owens 2842, PACCAR 2850, Pactiv 2863, Panera 2873, Parametric 2878, Parker 2886, Parsons 2887, Patagonia 2892, Paul 2901, Pearson 2911, Penguin 2922, Pentair 2926, PepsiCo 2935, PerkinElmer 2939, PetSmart 2948, Pfizer 2950, Pier 2973, Pioneer 2980, Pitney 2984, Pizza 2988, Polaris 2999, PPG 3025, Praxair 3029, Preformed 3032, Procter 3055, Protective 3066, Pulte 3083, PVH 3088, QUALCOMM 3095, Quiksilver 3108, Rahr 3118, Ralph 3123, Raymond 3133, RBC 3136, Reader's 3141, Reebok 3159, Regis 3172, ResMed 3192, Respironics 3193, Reynolds 3199, Ricoh 3210, Robbins 3230, Rock 3239, Rockwell 3246, Rockwell 3247, RPM 3278, Ryder 3292, SAIC 3311, SAS 3336, ScanSource 3347, Schein 3348, Schneider 3355, Scholastic 3358, Schwabe 3364, Scotts 3372, Seagrave 3378, Sealed 3381, Sears 3384, Sensient 3408, ServiceMaster 3414, Shaklee 3418, Shearman 3429, Sherwin 3437, Slant 3477, Smith 3484, Smucker 3488, Sonoco 3500, Southwire 3527, Spectra 3540, Spirol 3545, SPX 3558, St. Jude 3566, Standard 3576, Stanley 3579, Staples 3581, Starbucks 3585, State 3591, State 3592, Steelcase 3597, STERIS 3600, Strauss 3624, Stride 3625, Sun 3643, Sun 3646, Syngenta 3671, Sysco 3677, Teleflex 3707, Terex 3719, Texas 3728, Textron 3731, Thompson 3739, Thomson 3742, Tidewater 3748, Timken 3760, TJX 3765, Toro 3775, Toshiba 3776, Toys 3790, Tyco 3829, Tyson 3832, U-Haul 3833, Unilever 3853, United 3872, United 3877, United 3882, UnitedHealth 3884, Universal 3890, Universal 3893, Unum 3898, V.F. 3913, Valassis 3914, Valero 3915, Valspar 3920, Viacom 3945, Viad 3946, Victaulic 3948, ViewSonic 3952, Vijuk 3953, Vulcan 3972, Washington 3999, WD-40 4011, Wells 4028, Wendy's 4031, Wendy's/Arby's 4030, Western 4042, Western 4045, Weyerhaeuser 4052, Whirlpool 4056, Whole 4066, Wiley 4072, Williams 4077, Wrigley 4125, Xerox 4136, Yahoo! 4140, Yum! 4150, Zale 4151

Caribbean

Alcoa 82, Carnival 696, Exxon 1315, Kerzner 2133, RBC 3136, Royal 3273

Cayman Islands

AES 47, Agilent 56, AK 67, Akamai 68, Allergan 99, Anheuser 202, Apache 211, Arrow 249, Assurant 266, AutoNation 292, Avon 305, Bank 340, Becton 398, Boeing 516, Brown 591, CA 638, Cadence 646, CIT 819, Citigroup 821, Clorox 852, Coca 862, Collective 871, Comerica 889, ConocoPhillips 913, Cooper 936, Corning 945, Danaher 1027, Dell 1068, Delta 1073, DENTSPLY 1089, Diamonds 1109, DIRECTV 1124, Diversey 1130, Donnelley 1155, Duke 1189, eBay 1217, Ecolab 1220, El Paso 1239, Energizer 1271, EOG 1282, Exxon 1315, First 1389, Franklin 1487, Genworth 1565, Goldman 1603, Halliburton 1706, Harris 1736, HCA 1762, Health 1766, Hess 1793, Hubbell 1879, Huntington 1894, Huntsman 1895, IAC 1903, Illinois 1916, Ingram 1941, Intel 1950, ITT 1999, Kansas 2094, Kennametal 2125, Kindred 2154, La-Z-Boy 2205, Las Vegas 2225, Limited 2277, LSI 2314, Lubrizol 2315, Manitowoc 2355, Marriott 2383, Marsh 2385, McCormick 2423, McGraw 2429, Medtronic 2453, Meritor 2473, Microchip 2499, Morgan 2570, Newell 2694, Occidental 2780, Oracle 2821, Owens 2842, PepsiCo 2935, Pfizer 2950, Pioneer 2981, Procter 3055, Pulte 3083, Sealed 3381, Sherwin 3437, Stanley 3579, Staples 3581, State 3592, SUPERVALU 3659, Tenet 3713, Tidewater 3748, Timken 3760, Tyson 3832, UnitedHealth 3884, Valero 3915, Viacom 3945, Wells 4028, Western 4042, Whirlpool 4056, Williams 4077, Yum! 4150

Central America

Agora 58, Alcoa 82, Autodesk 289, Canon 672, Hess 1793, Laird 2211, New England 2670, Seattle 3385

Chad

Exxon 1315

Chile

Abbott 13, AES 47, Allergan 99, American 167, Amway 189, Anheuser 202, ARAMARK 223, Assurant 266, Assurant 268, Avery 297, Avon 305, Baker 320, Bank 340, Bank 344, Biomet 466, CA 638, Caterpillar 722, Chemtura 775, Cisco 818, CIT 819, Citigroup 821, Clorox 852, Coca 862, Cummins 1007, Danaher 1027, Dell 1068, Deutsche 1099, Diebold 1112, DIRECTV 1124, Diversey 1130, Dole 1141, Donnelley 1155, Dow 1161, Eastman 1214, Eaton 1216, Eclipse 1219, Ecolab 1220, EFC 1236, El Paso 1239, Energizer 1271, Equifax 1288, Exxon 1315, First 1389, Fluor 1448, Freeport 1494, General 1554, General 1555, Goodyear 1612, Google 1613, Grace 1623, Grand 1627, Harris 1736, Harsco 1741, Hewlett 1794, Hospira 1867, Hunt 1889, IDT 1910, Illinois 1916, Ingram 1941, International 1960, International 1962, International 1964, ITT 1999, JPMorgan Chase 2071, Kimberly 2150, Lexmark 2258, Liberty 2263, Marriott 2383, MasterCard 2399, Mattel 2405, McGraw 2429, Merck 2466, Mine 2529, Mondelez 2556, Monsanto 2559, Mosaic 2580, NCR 2650, Newell 2694, NII 2709, Novell 2754, Occidental 2780, Ogilvy 2788, Oracle 2821, Parker 2886, Patagonia 2892, Pentair 2926, PepsiCo 2935, Pfizer 2950, Pioneer 2980, PPG 3025, Pulte 3083, Rock 3239, Rockwell 3246, RPM 3278, Sealed 3381, Sherwin 3437, Sonoco 3500, Stanley 3579, Teck 3700, Thompson 3739, Tidewater 3748, UnitedHealth 3884, V.F. 3913, Waters 4003, Western 4045, Whirlpool 4056, Xerox 4136, Yum! 4150

China

3M 3, Abbott 13, Activision 30, Adobe 38, Advanced 40, Advent 41, AES 47, Agilent 56, Air 63, Akamai 68, Akin 70, Alcoa 82, Allegheny 91, Allen 94, American 143, American 156, Amway 189, Andrews 198, Anheuser 202, Applied 220, ARAMARK 223, Ashland 258, Assurant 266, Assurant 268, Autodesk 289, Automatic 291, Avery 297, Avnet 304, Avon 305, Baker 320, Baker 321, Baker 324, Bank 340, Bausch 376, Baxter 377, Bayer 382, Becton 398, Bemis 407, Benesch 413, Biomet 466, BMC 508, Boeing 516, BorgWarner 528, Bourns 542, BP 547, Briggs 565, Bristol 578, Broadcom 579, Brown 589, Brunswick 595, Bryan 596, Butler 626, CA 638, Cabot 642, Cadence 646, Cadwalader 649, Campbell 669, Cardinal 685, Castle 716, Caterpillar 722, Chemtura 775, CHS 802, Cintas 816, Cisco 818, CIT 819, Citigroup 821, CLARCOR 832, Clark 836, Cleary 843, Clifford 849, Clorox 852, Coca 862, Colgate 869, Collective 871, Collette 872, Commercial 893, Convergys 933, Cooper 935, Cooper 936, Corning 945, Credit 980, Crown 988, Cummins 1007, Dana 1026, Danaher 1027, Davis 1040, Davis 1041, Debevoise 1055, Dechert 1058, Deckers 1059, Deere 1061, Dell 1068, DENTSPLY 1089, Diebold 1112, Disney 1127, Diversey 1130, Donaldson 1153, Donnelley 1155, Dorsey 1157, Dow 1160, Dow 1161, Dow 1162, Dow 1163, du Pont 1184, Dun 1190, Eastman 1213, Eastman 1214, Eaton 1216, eBay 1217, Eclipse 1219, Ecolab 1220, Edelman 1224, Energizer 1271, Erickson 1290, Ethicon 1299, Exxon 1315, Faegre 1324, Ferro 1366, Fifth 1376, Finnegan 1384, First 1389, First 1400, Fluor 1448, FMC 1449, Fortune 1474, Franklin 1487, Fredrikson 1491, Freshfields 1500, Fried 1502, Fulbright 1516, Fuller 1517, Furniture 1519, Garvey 1539, General 1552, General 1554, General 1555, Google 1613, Grace 1623, Graco 1624, Grand 1627, Greenberg 1654, Greif 1663, Griffith 1667, Harris 1736, Harsco 1741, Haworth 1758, Heinz 1772, Hershey 1791, Hewlett 1794, Hillshire 1809, Hines 1813, Hogan 1825, Holland 1834, Honeywell 1852, Hormel 1866, Hospira 1867, Huntsman 1895, IAC 1903, Ideal 1908, Illinois 1916, Ingram 1941, Intel 1950, International 1960, International 1962, Interpublic 1974, ITT 1999, Jabil 2006, Jefferies 2030, Johnson 2048, Johnson 2049, Jones 2058, Joy 2070, JSJ 2073, K&L 2080, Kearney 2107, Keller 2116, Kellwood 2121, Kennametal 2125, Kenneth 2128, Kids 2141, Kimball 2149, Kirkland 2164, Kohler 2182, Las Vegas 2225, Latham 2228, Leggett 2246, Lexmark 2258, Linklaters 2283, Loeb 2295, LSI 2314, Manitowoc 2355, Manpower 2358, Marriott 2383, Masco 2393, MasterCard 2399, Mattel 2405, Mayer 2411, McCormick 2423, McDermott 2424, McDermott 2425, McDonald's 2427, Medtronic 2453, Mentor 2462, Merck 2466, Meritor 2473, Merk 2467, Microchip 2499, Micron 2500, Milbank 2511, Miller 2517, Miller 2519, Mine 2529, Modine 2544, Mondelez 2556, Monsanto 2559, Moody's 2563, Morgan 2568, Morgan 2571, Morrison 2576, Mosaic 2580, Motorola 2585, Motorola 2586, Mylan 2610, Nalco 2613, Nasdaq 2617, NCR 2650, New York 2688, NIKE 2710, Nordson 2723, Novell 2754, Nu 2759, NVIDIA 2767, Ogilvy 2788, OMNOVA 2809, Oracle 2821, Owens 2842, PACCAR 2850, Parametric 2878, Parker 2886, Paul 2900, Paul 2901, Pentair 2926, PepsiCo 2935, Perkins 2940, Perkins 2941, Pfizer 2950, Photronics 2969, Pillsbury 2975, Pioneer 2980, Piper 2983, Pitney 2984, PPG 3025, Praxair 3029, Preformed 3032, Pro 3051, Procter 3055, Quaker 3093, QUALCOMM 3095, Quarles 3101, Quiksilver 3108, Reader's 3141, Reed 3163, Reell 3164, Regal 3167, Regions 3171, Ricoh 3210, Rio 3218, Robbins 3230, Rockwell 3246, Rockwell 3247, Rogers 3253, Ropes 3260, RPM 3278, Ruder 3282, Ryder 3292, Ryerson 3293, SAS 3336, Schein 3348, Schneider 3355, Scholastic 3358, Sealed 3381, Shearman 3429, Sheppard 3435, Sherwin 3437, Sidley 3446, Simpson 3462, Skidmore 3474, Smith 3484, Smucker 3488, Spansion 3532, SPX 3558, Squire 3561, St. Jude 3566, Stanley 3579, Staples 3581, Starbucks 3585, Steptoe 3599, Strauss 3624, Sullivan 3634, Sunkist 3649, Tellabs 3709, Tennant 3714, Tenneco 3715, Texas 3728, Thompson 3739, Timken 3760, Tyson 3832, United 3872, United 3882, Valmont 3919, Valspar 3920, ViewSonic 3952, Vinson 3958, Walgreen 3981, Washington 3999, Weil 4023, Wells 4028, West 4038, Western 4045, Weyerhaeuser 4052, Whirlpool 4056, White 4058, White 4059, Wilson 4083, Winston 4089, Wrigley 4125, Xerox 4136, Xilinx 4137, Xylem 4139, Yum! 4150

Colombia

Abbott 13, AES 47, Allergan 99, American 167, Amway 189, ARAMARK 223, Avery 297, Avon 305, Baker 320, Bank 340, Bayer 381, Becton 398, Boston 540, Brightpoint 567, Bristol 578, CA 638, Cabot 642, Cisco 818, CIT 819, Citigroup 821, Clorox 852, Coca 862, Collective 871, Cooper 935, Crown 988, Dana 1026, Dell 1068, Diebold 1112, DIRECTV 1124, Diversey 1130, Dow 1161, du Pont 1184, Eaton 1216, Eclipse 1219, Ecolab 1220, EFC 1236, Emerson 1257, Energizer 1271, Exxon 1315, Fifth 1376, First 1400, General 1554, General 1555, Goodyear 1612, Grace 1623, Griffith 1667, Hewlett 1794, Hospira 1867, Huntsman 1895, Illinois 1916, Imation 1919, Intel 1950, International 1960, International 1962, Johnson 2048, Johnson 2049, JPMorgan Chase 2071, Kellogg 2120, Kimberly 2150, Manpower 2358, McGraw 2429, Merck 2466, Mondelez 2556, Monsanto 2559, NCR 2650, Newell 2694, Nordson 2723, Novell 2754, Occidental 2780, Ogilvy 2788, Oracle 2821, Owens 2844, PepsiCo 2935, Pfizer 2950, Reader's 3141, Robbins 3230, RPM 3278, Sealed 3381, Sonoco 3500, St. Jude 3566, Stanley 3579, Thompson 3739, West 4038, Whirlpool 4056, Xerox 4136

Commonwealth of the Northern Mariana Islands

Citigroup 821

Congo

Citigroup 821, Mylan 2610

Costa Rica

Abbott 13, Allergan 99, Amway 189, Baxter 377, Caterpillar 722, Cisco 818, Citigroup 821, Coca 862, Collette 872, Cummins 1007, Dell 1068, Diebold 1112, Diversey 1130, Dole 1141, Donnelley 1155, Ecolab 1220, Equifax 1288, Fifth 1376, First 1400, Grand 1627, Greif 1663, Griffith 1667, Hewlett 1794, Illinois 1916, Intel 1950, International 1960, Johnson 2049, Kimberly 2150, Manpower 2358, Merck 2466, Mondelez 2556, Ogilvy 2788, Oracle 2821, Oxford 2847, Parsons 2888, Pfizer 2950, Procter 3055, Pura 3084, Riviana 3227, Seattle 3385, St. Jude 3566, Stanley 3579, Thompson 3739, UnitedHealth 3884, Western 4045, Whole 4066

Croatia

Abbott 13, Avon 305, Bubalo 598, Cisco 818, Commercial 893, Dell 1068, Ecolab 1220, First 1400, Hewlett 1794, Hogan 1825, Illinois 1916, International 1960, Leggett 2246, Lexmark 2258, Manpower 2358, Masco 2393, Merck 2466, Mondelez 2556, Ogilvy 2788, Oracle 2821, PepsiCo 2935, Pfizer 2950, Thompson 3739, UnitedHealth 3884, Whirlpool 4056

Cuba

Grace 1623, Procter 3055

Curacao

DIRECTV 1124, Sherwin 3437

Cyprus

AES 47, Boeing 516, CA 638, Cadence 646, Cisco 818, Danaher 1027, Donnelley 1155, Dun 1190, Ecolab 1220, General 1551, Heinz 1772, Johnson 2049, Masco 2393, McCormick 2423, Merck 2466, Moody's 2563, NCR 2650, Newmont 2698, Ogilvy 2788, Oracle 2821, Owens 2842, PepsiCo 2935, Quiksilver 3108, Tidewater 3748

Czech Republic

Abbott 13, Adobe 38, AES 47, Air 63, Allen 94, American 132, Amway 189, ARAMARK 223, Autodesk 289, Avery 297, Avnet 304, Avon 305, AVX 306, Badger 313, Baker 320, Becton 398, Bemis 407, Biogen 465, Biomet 466, Boeing 516, Boston 540, Briggs 565, CA 638, Cabot 642, Caterpillar 722, Cisco 818, Citigroup 821, Clifford 849, Colgate 869, ConocoPhillips 913, Cummins 1007, Danaher 1027, Dell 1068, Diebold 1112, Diversey 1130, Dole 1141, Donaldson 1153, Donnelley 1155, Eastman 1214, Eaton 1216, eBay 1217, Ecolab 1220, Energizer 1271, Exxon 1315, Fifth 1376, First 1400, Ford 1464, Freescale 1495, GenCorp 1548, General 1551, General 1554, Google 1613, Greif 1663, Harsco 1741, Hewlett 1794, Hillshire 1809, Hogan 1825, Honeywell 1852, Huntsman 1895, Illinois 1916, Intel 1950, International 1960, Johnson 2048, Kearney 2107, Lexmark 2258, Liberty 2263, Lilly 2274, Manitowoc 2355, Manpower 2358, Marriott 2383, Masco 2393, Medtronic 2453, Merck 2466, Meritor 2473, Mondelez 2556, Mylan 2610, NCR 2650, Nordson 2723, Novell 2754, Ogilvy 2788, Omnicare 2807, Oracle 2821, Parker 2886, Pentair 2926, Pfizer 2950, PPG 3025, Praxair 3029, Procter 3055, Quiksilver 3108, Reader's 3141, Rockwell 3246, RPM 3278, Schein 3348, Sealed 3381, SPX 3558, Squire 3561, Stanley 3579, Teleflex 3707, Tenneco 3715, Terex 3719, Texas 3728, Thompson 3739, Timken 3760, Tyco 3829, UnitedHealth 3884, Waters 4003, Weil 4023, White 4058, Wrigley 4125, Xerox 4136

Democratic Republic of the Congo

Citigroup 821

Denmark

3M 3, Abbott 13, Adobe 38, Advent 41, Allergan 99, AMETEK 181, Assurant 266, Automatic 291, Avery 297, Becton 398, Bemis 407, Biomet 466, BMC 508,

BOSE 530, Boston 540, Brightpoint 567, Broadcom 579, CA 638, Cephalon 752, Chemtura 775, Cisco 818, Citigroup 821, Colgate 869, Comcast 887, ConocoPhillips 913, Danaher 1027, Dell 1068, Donaldson 1153, Duke 1189, Eastman 1213, Eaton 1216, eBay 1217, Eclipse 1219, Ecolab 1220, Foot 1459, Freescale 1495, GameStop 1530, Gilead 1582, Google 1613, Handy 1718, Harris 1736, Harsco 1741, Hess 1793, Hewlett 1794, Hexcel 1795, Hillshire 1809, IDT 1910, Illinois 1916, Intel 1950, International 1960, International 1962, International 1964, Interpublic 1974, Johnson 2048, Kearney 2107, Leggett 2246, Lilly 2274, Manpower 2358, Mark 2377, Marriott 2383, Masco 2393, McDermott 2424, McDonald's 2427, Medtronic 2453, Mentor 2462, Merk 2467, MGIC 2488, Microchip 2499, Mondelez 2556, Motorola 2586, Mylan 2610, Nasdaq 2617, NCR 2650, Newell 2694, NIKE 2710, Novell 2754, Nu 2759, Ogilvy 2788, Omnicare 2807, Oracle 2821, Parker 2886, Patagonia 2892, PepsiCo 2935, Pfizer 2950, Pitney 2984, PPG 3025, Ralph 3123, Respironics 3193, Rockwell 3246, RPM 3278, SAS 3336, Sealed 3381, SPX 3558, Stanley 3579, Staples 3581, Teleflex 3707, Tennant 3714, Tenneco 3715, Texas 3728, Tyco 3829, Viacom 3945, ViewSonic 3952, Waters 4003, West 4038, Xerox 4136, Yahoo! 4140

Developing countries

Exxon 1315, LensCrafters 2251, New England 2670, NIKE 2710, Primary 3043, Whole 4066

Dominica

Ecolab 1220

Dominican Republic

AES 47, Assurant 266, Avery 297, Avon 305, Cardinal 685, Cisco 818, Citigroup 821, Clarkson 839, Clorox 852, Colgate 869, Collective 871, Danaher 1027, Diebold 1112, Diversey 1130, Eaton 1216, Energizer 1271, General 1554, Goya 1622, Ideal 1908, Lilly 2274, Manpower 2358, Marriott 2383, Mondelez 2556, NCR 2650, Ogilvy 2788, Pattillo 2896, PepsiCo 2935, Pfizer 2950, RPM 3278, Squire 3561, Thompson 3739, Timberland 3754

East Asia

Ann's 203, Exxon 1315, Johnson 2048

Eastern & Central Europe

Boeing 516, Timken 3760

Ecuador

Abbott 13, Avon 305, Chemtura 775, Cisco 818, Citigroup 821, Clorox 852, Colgate 869, Collective 871, Dell 1068, Diebold 1112, DIRECTV 1124, Dole 1141, Duke 1189, Ecolab 1220, Encana 1266, Energizer 1271, Exxon 1315, Ferro 1366, General 1554, Graham 1625, Harsco 1741, Hewlett 1794, Illinois 1916, International 1960, Johnson 2049, Kellogg 2120, Marriott 2383, Melaleuca 2457, Merck 2466, Mondelez 2556, New England 2670, Ogilvy 2788, PepsiCo 2935, Pfizer 2950, Procter 3055, Rockwell 3246, RPM 3278, Stanley 3579, Thompson 3739, Whirlpool 4056, Xerox 4136

Egypt

Abbott 13, Apache 211, Avon 305, Baker 320, Bechtel 395, Caterpillar 722, Cisco 818, Citigroup 821, Clorox 852, Coca 862, Crowell 986, Dell 1068, Diversey 1130, Eastman 1214, Energizer 1271, Exxon 1315, Google 1613, Grand 1627, Halliburton 1706, Harsco 1741, Heinz 1772, Hewlett 1794, Hilton 1812, Huntsman 1895, Intel 1950, International 1962, Johnson 2048, Johnson 2049, Lexmark 2258, Marriott 2383, Merck 2466, Mondelez 2556, Ogilvy 2788, One 2811, Oracle 2821, PepsiCo 2935, Pfizer 2950, Procter 3055, Thompson 3739, Western 4045, Xerox 4136

El Salvador

Abbott 13, AES 47, Avery 297, Avon 305, AVX 306, Cisco 818, Citigroup 821, Collective 871, Dell 1068, Diebold 1112, Donnelley 1155, Duke 1189, Ecolab 1220, Fifth 1376, Manpower 2358, Marriott 2383, McCormick 2423, Mondelez 2556, New England 2670, Ogilvy 2788, PepsiCo 2935, Pfizer 2950, Procter 3055, Seattle 3385, Stride 3626, Thompson 3739, Whirlpool 4056

England

Adobe 38, AMETEK 181, Apache 211, Assurant 266, Avnet 304, Avon 305, Bank 340, Bank 344, Bard 358, Boston 540, Brunswick 595, Cabot 642, Caterpillar 722, Chevron 780, Coca 863, Commercial 893, ConocoPhillips 913, Cooper 936, Disney 1127, Donnelley 1155, Duke 1189, Dun 1190, Eastman 1214, Equifax 1288, First 1389, ForceBrain.com 1461, Franklin 1487, Gap 1533, General 1551, Genzyme 1566, Graham 1625, Humana 1886, IAC 1903, Intel 1950, International 1962, Jabil 2006, Kellogg 2120, MasterCard 2399, McCormick 2423, Mentor 2462, Meritor 2473, Microchip 2499, Miller 2517, Moody's 2563, Morgan 2570, Motorola 2585, Motorola 2586, New 2668, Northern 2740, Parsons 2887, Peabody 2907, Pioneer 2981, Pitney 2984, PPG 3025, Rio 3218, Rockwell 3246, Rogers 3253, SAIC 3311, Scholastic 3358, Sheppard 3435, Sullivan 3634, Tidewater 3748, Timken 3760, United 3872, United 3882, Wal-Mart 3980, West 4038, Western 4042, Whirlpool 4056, Whole 4066, Williams 4077

Equatorial Guinea

Hess 1793

Estonia

Avnet 304, Avon 305, Cisco 818, Danaher 1027, Eastman 1213, eBay 1217, First 1400, Illinois 1916, International 1960, Lilly 2274, Manpower 2358, Merck 2466, Mondelez 2556, Nasdaq 2617, Ogilvy 2788, PepsiCo 2935, Procter 3055, Sonoco 3500, Thompson 3739, Valmont 3919, Waters 4003, Whirlpool 4056

Ethiopia

Cisco 818, Nu 2759, Ogilvy 2788, Pura 3084, Whole 4066

Europe

Alcoa 82, Amgen 182, Amway 189, Autodesk 289, Bank 344, Bayer 382, Becton 398, Bristol 578, Capital 678, Coca 862, Convergys 933, Exxon 1315, Flextronics 1437, Fuller 1517, General 1552, Genworth 1565, Georgia 1568, Goldman 1604, Grand 1627, Hess 1793, Ingram 1941, International 1960, JPMorgan Chase 2071, Lam 2214, Mead 2443, Monsanto 2559, New 2673, Parametric 2878, Patagonia 2892, PPG 3025, Quiksilver 3108, Ricoh 3210, salesforce.com 3318, Scotts 3372, Starbucks 3585, State 3592, Strauss 3624, TeleTech 3708

Finland

3M 3, Abbott 13, Ashland 258, Avery 297, Avon 305, Becton 398, Bemis 407, Biogen 465, Biomet 466, BMC 508, Boston 540, Brightpoint 567, Brunswick 595, CA 638, Cisco 818, Citigroup 821, Crown 988, Danaher 1027, Deere 1061, Dell 1068, Eastman 1214, Eaton 1216, Eclipse 1219, Ecolab 1220, Exxon 1315, Fifth 1376, Freescale 1495, GameStop 1530, General 1552, Gilead 1582, Google 1613, Graham 1625, Harsco 1741, Hewlett 1794, Hospira 1867, Illinois 1916, Intel 1950, International 1960, ITT 1999, Johnson 2048, Kearney 2107, Manpower 2358, Mars 2384, Medtronic 2453, Mentor 2462, Merck 2466, Merk 2467, Mondelez 2556, Mylan 2610, Nasdaq 2617, NCR 2650, Nordson 2723, Novell 2754, NVIDIA 2767, Ogilvy 2788, Omnicare 2807, Oracle 2821, Owens 2844, Parker 2886, Pfizer 2950, Pitney 2984, Procter 3055, QUALCOMM 3095, Reader's 3141, ResMed 3192, RPM 3278, SAS 3336, Sealed 3381, Sonoco 3500, Stanley 3579, Staples 3581, STERIS 3600, Tellabs 3709, Texas 3728, Thompson 3739, Towerbrook 3781, Tyco 3829, UnitedHealth 3884, Valmont 3919, Viacom 3945, ViewSonic 3952, Waters 4003, Whirlpool 4056, White 4058, Wrigley 4125, Xerox 4136

France

3M 3, Abbott 13, Activision 30, Adobe 38, Advanced 40, AES 47, Air 63, AK 67, Akamai 68, Alcoa 82, Allegheny 91, Allen 94, Allergan 99, American 143, American 156, American 161, Amway 189, Applied 220, Arch 230, Ashland 258, Autodesk 289, Automatic 291, Avery 297, Avnet 304, Avon 305, Badger 313, Baker 320, Bank 340, Bard 358, Barnes 362, Baxter 377, Bayer 381, Becton 398, Bemis 407, Biogen 465, Biomet 466, BMC 508, Boeing 516, BorgWarner 528, BOSE 530, Boston 540, Briggs 565, Brightpoint 567, Broadcom 579, Brunswick 595, Bryan 596, CA 638, Cabot 642, Cadence 646, Campbell 669, Caterpillar 722, CBS 727, Cephalon 752, Charles 764, Chemtura 775, Chevron 780, Cisco 818, CIT 819, Citigroup 821, CLARCOR 832, Cleary 843, Clifford 849, Coca 862, Coca 863, Colgate 869, Comcast 887, Cooper 935, Corning 945, Covance 955, Credit 980, Crown 988, Cummins 1007, Curtis 1010, Dana 1026, Danaher 1027, Davis 1040, Debevoise 1055, Dechert 1058, Deckers 1059, Deere 1061, Dell 1068, Delta 1073, Diebold 1112, Disney 1127, Diversey 1130, Dole 1141, Donaldson 1153, Donnelley 1155, Dow 1162, du Pont 1184, Dun 1190, Eastman 1213, Eastman 1214, Eaton 1216, eBay 1217, Eclipse 1219, Ecolab 1220, Edelman 1224, Emerson 1257, Energizer 1271, Exxon 1315, Fifth 1376, First 1400, Fiserv 1427, FMC 1449, Foley 1454, Foot 1459, Fortune 1474, Franklin 1487, Freescale 1495, Freshfields 1500, Fried 1502, GameStop 1530, GenCorp 1548, General 1551, General 1552, General 1554, Genworth 1565, Genzyme 1566, Georgia 1568, Gibson 1580, Gilead 1582, Goodyear 1612, Google 1613, Grace 1623, Graham 1625, Greif 1663, Guess 1685, Harris 1736, Harsco 1741, Haworth 1758, Heinz 1772, Hewlett 1794, Hexcel 1795, Hillshire 1809, Hines 1813, Hogan 1825, Honeywell 1852, Hospira 1867, Huntsman 1895, Ideal 1908, IDT 1910, IKON 1914, Illinois 1916, Ingram 1941, Intel 1950, International 1960, International 1962, International 1964, International 1968, Interpublic 1974, ITT 1999, Jabil 2006, Jefferies 2030, Johnson 2048, Jones 2058, K&L 2080, Kearney 2107, King 2157, Kohler 2182, Kramer 2191, Latham 2228, Leggett 2246, Lexmark 2258, Lilly 2274, Linklaters 2283, LSI 2314, Lubrizol 2315, Manitowoc 2355, Manpower 2358, Maritz 2376, Mark 2377, Marriott 2383, Mars 2384, Masco 2393, MasterCard 2399, Mattel 2405, Mayer 2411, McCormick 2423, McDermott 2425, McDonald's 2427, Medtronic 2453, Mentor 2462, Merck 2466, Mercury 2469, Meritor 2473, Merk 2467, Microchip 2499, Mine 2529, Mondelez 2556, Monsanto 2559, Moody's 2563, Morgan 2568, Morgan 2571, Motorola 2586, Mylan 2610, NCR 2650, Newell 2694, Newmont 2698, NIKE 2710, Nordson 2723, Novell 2754, Nu 2759, NVIDIA 2767, Office 2785, Ogilvy 2788, Oilgear 2793, Omnicare 2807, OMNOVA 2809, Oracle 2821, Owens 2842, Owens 2844, Parametric 2878, Parker 2886, Patagonia 2892, Paul 2900, Pentair 2926, PepsiCo 2935, Pfizer 2950, Pioneer 2980, Pitney 2984, Polaris 2999, PPG 3025, Praxair 3029, Procter 3055, Proskauer 3064, Quaker 3093, QUALCOMM 3095, Quiksilver 3108, Ralph 3123, Reader's 3141, RealNetworks 3144, Reed 3163, Regis 3172, ResMed 3192, Rio 3218, Robbins 3230, Rockwell 3246, Rockwell 3247, Rogers 3253, RPM 3278, Ruder 3282, SAIC 3311, SAS 3336, ScanSource 3347, Schein 3348, Seagate 3377, Sealed 3381, Sealy 3382, Sedgwick 3395, Shearman 3429, Smith 3484, Sonoco 3500, Spirol 3545, SPX 3558, Squire 3561, St. Jude 3566, Stanley 3579, Staples 3581, State 3592, Steelcase 3597, Sullivan 3634,

Teleflex 3707, Tenneco 3715, Terex 3719, Texas 3728, Thompson 3739, Thomson 3742, Timberland 3754, Timken 3760, Toro 3775, Toys 3790, Tyco 3829, Tyson 3832, United 3877, United 3882, UnitedHealth 3884, V.F. 3913, Valmont 3919, Valspar 3920, Viacom 3945, ViewSonic 3952, Waters 4003, Weil 4023, West 4038, Western 4042, Western 4045, Whirlpool 4056, White 4058, Willkie 4081, Winston 4089, Wrigley 4125, Xerox 4136, Yahoo! 4140, Yum! 4150

Gabon

Hess 1793, PPG 3025

Georgia (Republic of)

Danaher 1027

Germany

3M 3, Abbott 13, Activision 30, Adobe 38, Advanced 40, Agilent 56, Air 63, Akamai 68, Alcoa 82, Allegheny 91, Allen 94, Allergan 99, American 132, American 143, American 161, AMETEK 181, Amway 189, Applied 220, ARAMARK 223, Arch 230, Arkema 242, Armstrong 246, Ashland 258, Assurant 266, Assurant 268, Autodesk 289, Automatic 291, Avery 297, Avnet 304, Avon 305, Badger 313, Baker 320, Baker 324, Bank 340, Bemis 407, Bergquist 420, Bingham 463, Biogen 465, Biomet 466, BMC 508, Boeing 516, BorgWarner 528, BOSE 530, Boston 540, Bourns 542, BP 547, Briggs 565, Brightpoint 567, Bristol 578, Brunswick 595, Bryan 596, CA 638, Cabot 642, Cadence 646, Campbell 669, Caterpillar 722, Cephalon 752, Charles 764, Chemtura 775, Cisco 818, CIT 819, Citigroup 821, CLARCOR 832, Cleary 843, Clifford 849, Clorox 852, Coca 862, Colgate 869, Collective 871, Comcast 887, Commercial 893, ConocoPhillips 913, Cooper 935, Corning 945, Covance 955, Crane 970, Credit 980, Crown 988, Cummins 1007, Curtis 1010, Dana 1026, Danaher 1027, Debevoise 1055, Dechert 1058, Deere 1061, Dell 1068, Delta 1073, Disney 1127, Diversey 1130, Dole 1141, Donaldson 1153, Donnelley 1155, Dow 1161, Dow 1162, Dow 1163, du Pont 1184, Dun 1190, Eastman 1213, Eastman 1214, Eaton 1216, eBay 1217, Eclipse 1219, Ecolab 1220, Edelman 1224, Electronic 1242, Energizer 1271, Ethicon 1299, Exxon 1315, Ferro 1366, Fifth 1376, First 1400, Fish 1428, FMC 1449, Foot 1459, Franklin 1487, Freescale 1495, Freshfields 1500, Fried 1502, Fulbright 1516, GameStop 1530, Gehl 1545, General 1551, General 1552, General 1554, General 1555, Georgia 1568, Gibson 1580, Gilead 1582, Gleason 1591, Goldman 1603, Goodyear 1612, Google 1613, Grace 1623, Greif 1663, Guess 1685, Halliburton 1706, Hardinge 1729, Harris 1736, Harsco 1741, Haworth 1758, Heinz 1772, Hewlett 1794, Hexcel 1795, Hillshire 1809, Hines 1813, Hogan 1825, Honeywell 1852, Hospira 1867, Huntsman 1895, IAC 1903, Ideal 1908, IDT 1910, Illinois 1916, IMS 1924, Ingram 1941, Intel 1950, International 1960, International 1962, International 1964, Interpublic 1974, ITT 1999, Jabil 2006, Jefferies 2030, Jeppesen 2038, Johns 2047, Johnson 2048, Johnson 2049, Jones 2058, JPMorgan Chase 2071, K&L 2080, Kearney 2107, Kellogg 2120, Kennametal 2125, King 2157, Kirkland 2164, La-Z-Boy 2205, Lands' 2220, Latham 2228, Leggett 2246, Lexmark 2258, Liberty 2263, Life 2268, Lilly 2274, Lodz 2294, LSI 2314, Lubrizol 2315, Manitowoc 2355, Manpower 2358, Maritz 2376, Mark 2377, Marriott 2383, Mars 2384, Masco 2393, Mattel 2405, Matthews 2406, Mayer 2411, McDermott 2425, McDonald's 2427, Medtronic 2453, Mentor 2462, Merck 2466, Meritor 2473, Merk 2467, Microchip 2499, Micron 2500, Milbank 2511, Mine 2529, Modine 2544, Mondelez 2556, Moody's 2563, Morgan 2570, Morgan 2571, Motorola 2586, Mylan 2610, NCR 2650, Newell 2694, NIKE 2710, Nordson 2723, Novell 2754, NRG 2756, Nu 2759, NVIDIA 2767, Ogilvy 2788, Oilgear 2793, Oracle 2821, Owens 2842, Owens 2844, Pactiv 2863, Parametric 2878, Parker 2886, Patagonia 2892, Paul 2900, Paychex 2904, Pentair 2926, PepsiCo 2935, PerkinElmer 2939, Pfizer 2950, Philip 2962, Photronics 2969, Pitney 2984, Polaris 2999, PPG 3025, Praxair 3029, Procter 3055, QUALCOMM 3095, Quest 3103, Quiksilver 3108, Quinn 3111, Ralph 3123, Reader's 3141, RealNetworks 3144, Reed 3163, Regal 3167, Regis 3172, ResMed 3192, Respironics 3193, Rio 3218, Robbins 3230, Rockwell 3246, Rockwell 3247, Rogers 3253, RPM 3278, Ryder 3292, SAIC 3311, SAS 3336, ScanSource 3347, Schein 3348, Seagate 3377, Sealed 3381, Shearman 3429, Sidley 3446, Smith 3484, Smithfield 3487, Sonoco 3500, SPX 3558, Squire 3561, St. Jude 3566, Stanley 3579, Staples 3581, Starbucks 3585, State 3592, Steelcase 3597, Sullivan 3634, Teleflex 3707, Tennant 3714, Tenneco 3715, Terex 3719, Texas 3728, Thompson 3739, Timberland 3754, Timken 3760, TJX 3765, Toys 3790, Tyco 3829, United 3877, United 3882, UnitedHealth 3884, UTC 3908, V.F. 3913, Valmont 3919, Valspar 3920, Viacom 3945, Viad 3946, ViewSonic 3952, Waters 4003, Weil 4023, West 4038, Western 4042, Western 4045, Westinghouse 4049, Whirlpool 4056, White 4058, Wiley 4072, Willkie 4081, Wrigley 4125, Xerox 4136, Yahoo! 4140, Yum! 4150

Ghana

American 167, Becton 398, Citigroup 821, Crown 988, Cummins 1007, Dell 1068, Harris 1736, International 1960, Johnson 2049, Mortenson 2577, NCR 2650, New England 2670, Newmont 2698, Pattillo 2896, PepsiCo 2935, Pfizer 2950, Sunwest 3655, Thompson 3739, Western 4045

Gibraltar

Avery 297, Bank 340, Biomet 466, Boeing 516, Cooper 935, General 1551, General 1554, Harsco 1741, IDT 1910, IMS 1924, International 1962, International 1964, Lubrizol 2315, Mylan 2610, Parker 2886, Peabody 2907, Pfizer 2950, Toro 3775

Global programs

Chevron 780, Deere 1061, Western 4045

Greece

Abbott 13, AES 47, Allen 94, American 132, Amway 189, ARAMARK 223, Avnet 304, Avon 305, Becton 398, Biomet 466, Boeing 516, Boston 540, Bristol 578, Broadcom 579, CA 638, Cisco 818, Citigroup 821, Colgate 869, Comcast 887, Crown 988, Danaher 1027, Dell 1068, Diversey 1130, Duke 1189, Eclipse 1219, Ecolab 1220, Energizer 1271, Fifth 1376, First 1400, Foot 1459, General 1554, Gilead 1582, Grace 1623, Harsco 1741, Heinz 1772, Hewlett 1794, Hillshire 1809, International 1960, Interpublic 1974, ITT 1999, Johnson 2048, Johnson 2049, Leggett 2246, Manpower 2358, Marriott 2383, Medtronic 2453, Merck 2466, Mondelez 2556, Mylan 2610, NCR 2650, Ogilvy 2788, Oracle 2821, Parsons 2887, PepsiCo 2935, Pfizer 2950, Pinnacle 2978, Procter 3055, Reed 3163, Sealed 3381, Sonoco 3500, Stanley 3579, Staples 3581, Teleflex 3707, Thompson 3739, Waters 4003, Western 4045, Whirlpool 4056, Xerox 4136

Grenada

Abbott 13, American 154

Guatemala

Abbott 13, Amway 189, Arch 230, Avery 297, Avon 305, Becton 398, Brightpoint 567, Citigroup 821, Colgate 869, Collective 871, Dell 1068, Diebold 1112, Diversey 1130, Donnelley 1155, Duke 1189, Ecolab 1220, Exxon 1315, Harsco 1741, Hewlett 1794, Huntsman 1895, Illinois 1916, International 1960, Lilly 2274, Manpower 2358, Marriott 2383, Mondelez 2556, Monsanto 2559, Mortenson 2577, New England 2670, Nu 2759, Ogilvy 2788, Oxford 2847, PepsiCo 2935, Pfizer 2950, Philip 2962, Procter 3055, Pura 3084, PVH 3088, Riviana 3227, Rockwell 3246, Sealed 3381, Seattle 3385, TECO 3701, Thompson 3739, Western 4045, Whirlpool 4056, Whole 4066, Xerox 4136

Guernsey

AES 47, Bank 340, Caterpillar 722, Citigroup 821, Ecolab 1220, Genworth 1565, Harsco 1741, Pfizer 2950, Sealy 3382

Guinea

Ogilvy 2788

Guyana

Exxon 1315, Ogilvy 2788

Haiti

Abbott 13, Arch 230, Carnival 696, Citigroup 821, Heinz 1772, Savage 3341, Strauss 3624, Western 4045, Whole 4066, Xerox 4136

Honduras

AES 47, Arch 230, Avery 297, Avon 305, Booz 525, Cintas 816, Citigroup 821, Collective 871, Dell 1068, Diebold 1112, Dole 1141, Donnelley 1155, Ecolab 1220, Gap 1533, Harris 1736, Manpower 2358, Marriott 2383, Mondelez 2556, Monsanto 2559, Mortenson 2577, New England 2670, One 2811, Oxford 2847, Pentair 2926, PepsiCo 2935, Pfizer 2950, PVH 3088, Scott 3369, Thompson 3739, Whole 4066, Xerox 4136

Hong Kong

3M 3, Abbott 13, Activision 30, Adobe 38, Alcoa 82, Allen 94, Allergan 99, American 132, American 133, American 140, American 143, AMETEK 181, Anheuser 202, ARAMARK 223, Arch 230, Arrow 249, Avery 297, Avnet 304, Avon 305, Baker 321, Bank 340, Becton 398, Bergquist 420, Bingham 463, Biomet 466, BMC 508, Boeing 516, BorgWarner 528, Boston 540, Brown 589, Brown 591, Brunswick 595, Bryan 596, CA 638, Cadence 646, Cadwalader 649, Campbell 669, Caterpillar 722, Chemtura 775, CHS 802, Cintas 816, Cisco 818, CIT 819, Citigroup 821, Cleary 843, Clorox 852, Collective 871, Comcast 887, Comerica 889, Commercial 893, Covance 955, Crown 988, Cummins 1007, Dana 1026, Danaher 1027, Davis 1040, Debevoise 1055, Dechert 1058, Deckers 1059, Dell 1068, Diebold 1112, Disney 1127, Diversey 1130, Dollar 1143, Donnelley 1155, Dorsey 1157, Dow 1161, Dun 1190, Eastman 1213, Eaton 1216, eBay 1217, Ecolab 1220, Edelman 1224, Emerson 1257, Energizer 1271, Exxon 1315, Ferro 1366, Fifth 1376, First 1400, Fortune 1474, Franklin 1487, Freescale 1495, Fried 1502, Fulbright 1516, Furniture 1519, Gap 1533, General 1551, General 1554, Genworth 1565, Gibson 1580, Gilead 1582, Goldman 1603, Goodwin 1611, Google 1613, Grace 1623, Guess 1685, H & R 1695, Harris 1736, Hartford 1742, Hewlett 1794, Hexcel 1795, HNI 1817, Hogan 1825, Hospira 1867, Hubbell 1879, Huntington 1894, Huntsman 1895, IDT 1910, Illinois 1916, IMS 1924, Ingram 1941, Intel 1950, International 1960, International 1962, International 1964, Intuit 1982, ITT 1999, Jefferies 2030, Johnson 2048, Jones 2057, Jones 2058, K&L 2080, Kearney 2107, Kenneth 2128, Kids 2141, Kirkland 2164, KLA-Tencor 2165, Kroger 2195, Las Vegas 2225, Latham 2228, Leggett 2246, Life 2268, Lilly 2274, Limited 2277, Linklaters 2283, LSI 2314, Lubrizol 2315, Manpower 2358, Marriott 2383, MasterCard 2399, Mattel 2405, Mayer 2411, McDonald's 2427, McGraw 2429, Merck 2466, Microchip 2499, Milbank 2511, Modine 2544, Mondelez 2556, Morgan 2570, Morrison 2576, Motorola 2586, NCR 2650, New 2673, New York 2688, Newell 2694, Nu 2759, NVIDIA 2767,

Oracle 2821, Oxford 2847, Packaging 2861, Parametric 2878, Parker 2886, Paul 2900, Paul 2901, Pentair 2926, PepsiCo 2935, Pfizer 2950, Pitney 2984, PPG 3025, Proskauer 3064, PVH 3088, Quiksilver 3108, Rackspace 3117, Ralph 3123, ResMed 3192, Respironics 3193, Rockwell 3246, Rockwell 3247, Rogers 3253, Ropes 3260, RPM 3278, Ruder 3282, Ryder 3292, Schein 3348, Scholastic 3358, Seagate 3377, Sealed 3381, Sealy 3382, Shearman 3429, Sidley 3446, Simpson 3462, Skidmore 3474, Smucker 3488, SPX 3558, Squire 3561, St. Jude 3566, Stanley 3579, Staples 3581, Sullivan 3634, Sun 3643, Teleflex 3707, Tenneco 3715, Teradyne 3718, Texas 3728, Thomson 3742, Timberland 3754, Timken 3760, TJX 3765, Toys 3790, Tyco 3829, Tyson 3832, United 3882, UnitedHealth 3884, UTC 3908, V.F. 3913, Viacom 3945, Vinson 3958, Walgreen 3981, Wells 4028, Western 4042, Western 4045, Whirlpool 4056, White 4058, Wilson 4083, Winston 4089, Xerox 4136, Yahoo! 4140, YSI 4149, Yum! 4150

Hungary

Abbott 13, Advanced 40, AES 47, Alcoa 82, Allen 94, American 132, Amway 189, Autodesk 289, Avery 297, Avnet 304, Avon 305, Baker 320, Becton 398, Bemis 407, Biomet 466, BorgWarner 528, Boston 540, Bourns 542, Brunswick 595, Cadence 646, Caterpillar 722, Chemtura 775, Cisco 818, CIT 819, Citigroup 821, Clifford 849, Clorox 852, Comcast 887, Cooper 935, Corning 945, Covance 955, Crown 988, Dana 1026, Danaher 1027, Dell 1068, Diebold 1112, Diversey 1130, Donnelley 1155, Eastman 1213, Eastman 1214, Eaton 1216, Ecolab 1220, Energizer 1271, Exxon 1315, Fifth 1376, First 1389, First 1400, Foot 1459, Franklin 1487, General 1552, General 1554, Google 1613, Grace 1623, Greif 1663, Harris 1736, Harsco 1741, Haworth 1758, Hewlett 1794, Hillshire 1809, Hogan 1825, Huntsman 1895, Illinois 1916, Ingram 1941, International 1960, International 1962, ITT 1999, Jabil 2006, Johnson 2048, Leggett 2246, Lexmark 2258, Liberty 2263, Lilly 2274, LSI 2314, Manitowoc 2355, Manpower 2358, Masco 2393, Mattel 2405, Medtronic 2453, Mentor 2462, Merck 2466, Microchip 2499, Mine 2529, Modine 2544, Mondelez 2556, Mylan 2610, NCR 2650, Novell 2754, Ogilvy 2788, Oracle 2821, Parker 2886, Pentair 2926, PepsiCo 2935, Pfizer 2950, PPG 3025, Praxair 3029, Quaker 3093, Reader's 3141, RPM 3278, Ryder 3292, Sealed 3381, Smith 3484, Squire 3561, St. Jude 3566, Stanley 3579, Staples 3581, Teleflex 3707, Thompson 3739, Tyco 3829, UnitedHealth 3884, Viacom 3945, Waters 4003, Weil 4023, White 4058, Wrigley 4125

Iceland

Alcoa 82, Cisco 818, FMC 1449, Merck 2466, Nasdaq 2617, Schein 3348, Waters 4003

India

3M 3, Abbott 13, Activision 30, Adobe 38, Advanced 40, Advent 41, AES 47, Agilent 56, Akamai 68, Allegheny 91, Allen 94, Allergan 99, American 167, Ameriprise 174, Apex 213, Applied 220, AptarGroup 221, Arbitron 227, Autodesk 289, Avery 297, Avnet 304, Avon 305, Bank 340, Bausch 376, Bayer 382, Becton 398, Berry 438, Biogen 465, BMC 508, Boeing 516, BorgWarner 528, Boston 540, Brightpoint 567, Bristol 578, Broadcom 579, CA 638, Cabot 642, Cadence 646, Caterpillar 722, Cisco 818, Citigroup 821, Clifford 849, Coca 862, Colgate 869, Comcast 887, Convergys 933, Cooper 935, Cummins 1007, Dana 1026, Danaher 1027, Deere 1061, Dell 1068, Delta 1073, DENTSPLY 1089, Diebold 1112, DIRECTV 1124, Disney 1127, Diversey 1130, Donaldson 1153, Donnelley 1155, Dow 1160, Duke 1189, Dun 1190, Eastman 1213, Eastman 1214, Eaton 1216, eBay 1217, Eclipse 1219, Ecolab 1220, Edelman 1224, El Paso 1239, Electronic 1242, Emerson 1257, Energizer 1271, Ethicon 1299, Excellium 1305, Exxon 1315, First 1389, First 1400, Fiserv 1427, Fluor 1448, FMC 1449, ForceBrain.com 1461, Ford 1464, Franklin 1487, Freescale 1495, Gap 1533, General 1551, General 1552, General 1554, Genworth 1565, Gleason 1591, Goodyear 1612, Google 1613, Grace 1623, Graco 1624, H & R 1695, Halliburton 1706, Harris 1736, Harsco 1741, Haworth 1758, Heinz 1772, Hershey 1791, Hewlett 1794, Hillshire 1809, Hines 1813, Honeywell 1852, Hospira 1867, Huntsman 1895, Illinois 1916, Ingram 1941, Intel 1950, International 1960, International 1962, Interpublic 1974, Intuit 1982, ITT 1999, Jabil 2006, Jai 2017, Jefferies 2030, Johnson 2048, Jones 2058, Kearney 2107, Kellogg 2120, Kennametal 2125, Kohler 2182, Las Vegas 2225, Leggett 2246, Lexmark 2258, LSI 2314, Lubrizol 2315, Manitowoc 2355, Manpower 2358, Marriott 2383, Mattel 2405, McGraw 2429, Medtronic 2453, Mentor 2462, Merck 2466, Meritor 2473, Microchip 2499, Micron 2500, Modine 2544, Mondelez 2556, Monsanto 2559, Morgan 2568, Morgan 2570, Mosaic 2580, Motorola 2586, Mylan 2610, Nalco 2613, NCR 2650, Neurology 2665, New York 2688, Newell 2694, NIKE 2710, Nordson 2723, Novell 2754, Ogilvy 2788, Omnicare 2807, OMNOVA 2809, Oracle 2821, Owens 2842, PACCAR 2850, Parker 2886, Pattillo 2896, Pentair 2926, PepsiCo 2935, Pfizer 2950, Pioneer 2980, Pitney 2984, Praxair 3029, Procter 3055, ProtechSoft 3065, Prudential 3072, Quaker 3093, QUALCOMM 3095, Robbins 3230, Rockwell 3246, Rockwell 3247, RPM 3278, Ryerson 3293, SAIC 3311, Sansar 3330, Scholastic 3358, Sealed 3381, Sealy 3382, Sherwin 3437, Smith 3484, Sonoco 3500, SPX 3558, St. Jude 3566, Stanley 3579, Staples 3581, Starbucks 3585, State 3592, Systel 3678, Teleflex 3707, Tennant 3714, Tenneco 3715, Texas 3728, Thompson 3739, Thomson 3742, Tidewater 3748, Timken 3760, Tyson 3832, United 3882, UnitedHealth 3884, Vermillion 3939, Viacom 3945, Vista 3963, Walgreen 3981, Waters 4003, Wells 4028, West 4038, Western 4045, Whirlpool 4056, Whole 4066, Wrigley 4125, Xerox 4136, Xilinx 4137, Yahoo! 4140, Yum! 4150

Indonesia

Abbott 13, AES 47, Air 63, Allen 94, Amway 189, Avery 297, Avon 305, Baker 320, Bank 340, BP 547, Bryan 596, CA 638, Cabot 642, Campbell 669, Chevron 780, Cisco 818, Citigroup 821, ConocoPhillips 913, Dell 1068, Diebold 1112, Diversey 1130, Donaldson 1153, Dow 1161, Eastman 1213, Eaton 1216, Eclipse 1219, Ecolab 1220, Edelman 1224, Energizer 1271, Exxon 1315, Ferro 1366, FMC 1449, Freeport 1494, Furniture 1519, General 1554, General 1555, Goodyear 1612, Grace 1623, Halliburton 1706, Heinz 1772, Hess 1793, Hillshire 1809, Huntsman 1895, Illinois 1916, Intel 1950, International 1960, International 1962, ITT 1999, Johnson 2048, Johnson 2049, Kearney 2107, Kohler 2182, Marriott 2383, Mattel 2405, McDermott 2424, Merck 2466, Mondelez 2556, Monsanto 2559, NCR 2650, Ogilvy 2788, One 2811, Oracle 2821, Pfizer 2950, Philip 2962, Pioneer 2980, PPG 3025, Procter 3055, Quiksilver 3108, Rockwell 3246, Sun 3643, Thompson 3739, Waters 4003, Western 4045, Whole 4066

Iraq

Callaway 660, Disney 1127

Ireland

Abbott 13, Activision 30, Adobe 38, AES 47, Agilent 56, Air 63, Alcatel 81, Allergan 99, ARAMARK 223, Arch 230, Assurant 266, Assurant 268, Autodesk 289, Avery 297, Avnet 304, Avon 305, Bank 340, Bank 344, Bard 358, Baxter 377, Becton 398, Bergquist 420, Biogen 465, Blockbuster 483, BMC 508, Boeing 516, BorgWarner 528, Boston 540, Bourns 542, Brown 589, Brown 590, Brown 591, Cadence 646, Campbell 669, Caterpillar 722, Cephalon 752, Chemtura 775, Cisco 818, CIT 819, Citigroup 821, Coca 862, Colgate 869, Collective 871, ConocoPhillips 913, Cooper 935, Crown 988, Dana 1026, Danaher 1027, Dechert 1058, Dell 1068, Delta 1073, Diebold 1112, Diversey 1130, Donnelley 1155, Dow 1161, Duke 1189, Dun 1190, Eaton 1216, eBay 1217, Ecolab 1220, Edelman 1224, EMC 1253, Energizer 1271, Equifax 1288, Exxon 1315, Fifth 1376, First 1400, FMC 1449, Foot 1459, ForceBrain.com 1461, Franklin 1487, Gap 1533, General 1552, Genworth 1565, Genzyme 1566, Gilead 1582, Goldman 1603, Google 1613, Grace 1623, Greif 1663, Griffith 1667, Harsco 1741, Hartford 1742, Heinz 1772, Hewlett 1794, Hines 1813, Holme 1837, Hospira 1867, IAC 1903, IDT 1910, Illinois 1916, Imation 1919, Intel 1950, International 1960, International 1962, International 1964, ITT 1999, Johnson 2048, Lexmark 2258, Liberty 2263, Lilly 2274, LSI 2314, Manitowoc 2355, Manpower 2358, Marriott 2383, Mars 2384, MasterCard 2399, McKesson 2434, Medtronic 2453, Merck 2466, Meritor 2473, Merk 2467, Microchip 2499, Microsoft 2501, Mondelez 2556, Mylan 2610, Nasdaq 2617, NCR 2650, Newell 2694, Novell 2754, Ogilvy 2788, Oracle 2821, Parker 2886, Parsons 2887, Patagonia 2892, Pentair 2926, PepsiCo 2935, Pfizer 2950, Pitney 2984, PPG 3025, Praxair 3029, Procter 3055, QUALCOMM 3095, Quiksilver 3108, Ralph 3123, Rockwell 3246, RPM 3278, Schein 3348, Sealed 3381, Sherwin 3437, SIFCO 3452, Smith 3484, SPX 3558, Stanley 3579, Staples 3581, State 3592, Symantec 3669, Teradyne 3718, Texas 3728, Thompson 3739, Thomson 3742, Tyco 3829, U.S. 3835, United 3882, UnitedHealth 3884, Washington 3999, Waters 4003, Wells 4028, West 4038, Western 4042, Western 4045, Whirlpool 4056, Wrigley 4125, Xerox 4136, Xilinx 4137

Isle of Man

Bank 340, Manitowoc 2355, Whirlpool 4056

Israel

Adobe 38, Allegheny 91, American 156, Applied 220, Avnet 304, Avon 305, BMC 508, Boeing 516, Boston 540, Broadcom 579, CA 638, Cablevision 641, Cadence 646, Cisco 818, Citigroup 821, Convergys 933, Danaher 1027, Dell 1068, Diversey 1130, eBay 1217, Ecolab 1220, Edsim 1230, Fashion 1342, Fifth 1376, Freescale 1495, General 1553, General 1554, Google 1613, Greystone 1665, Hewlett 1794, IDT 1910, IMS 1924, Ingram 1941, Intel 1950, International 1960, International 1962, Interpublic 1974, Johnson 2048, Kimberly 2150, Life 2268, Manpower 2358, Marriott 2383, McGraw 2429, Medtronic 2453, Meecorp 2454, Mentor 2462, Merck 2466, Micron 2500, Mintz 2534, Motorola 2586, Novell 2754, Ogilvy 2788, Omnicare 2807, Oracle 2821, Pfizer 2950, Procter 3055, Ruder 3282, Schein 3348, Sealed 3381, Tamar 3684, Thompson 3739, Washington 3999, Waters 4003, West 4038, Xerox 4136

Italy

3M 3, Abbott 13, Activision 30, Adobe 38, Advanced 40, AES 47, Agilent 56, Air 63, AK 67, Akamai 68, Alcatel 81, Alcoa 82, Allegheny 91, Allen 94, Allergan 99, American 132, American 143, American 161, AMETEK 181, Amway 189, Arch 230, Ashland 258, Assurant 266, Assurant 268, Autodesk 289, Automatic 291, Avery 297, Avnet 304, Avon 305, Baker 320, Bayer 381, Biogen 465, Biomet 466, Blockbuster 483, BMC 508, Boeing 516, BorgWarner 528, BOSE 530, Boston 540, BP 547, Briggs 565, Brightpoint 567, Bristol 578, Brown 591, Brunswick 595, CA 638, Cabot 642, Cadence 646, Caterpillar 722, Cephalon 752, Charles 764, Chemtura 775, Cisco 818, CIT 819, CITGO 820, Citigroup 821, CLARCOR 832, Cleary 843, Clifford 849, Coca 862, Colgate 869, Comcast 887, Cooper 935, Credit 980, Crown 988, Cummins 1007, Curtis 1010, Dana 1026, Danaher 1027, Deere 1061, Dell 1068, Diebold 1112, Disney 1127, Diversey 1130, Dole 1141, Donaldson 1153, Donnelley

Ivory Coast

Jamaica

Japan

Jersey

Jordan

Kazakhstan

Kenya

Kuwait

Kyrgyzstan

Laos

Latin America

Latvia

Lebanon

Liberia

Liechtenstein

Lithuania

Luxembourg

Macau

Macedonia

Madagascar

Malawi

Malaysia

Mali

Malta

Martinique

Mauritania

Mauritius

Mexico

Middle East

Moldova

Monaco

Mongolia

Montenegro

Morocco and the Western Sahara

Mozambique

Namibia

Nepal

Netherlands

Netherlands Antilles

New Caledonia

New Zealand

Nicaragua

Niger

Nigeria

North Korea

Northern Ireland

Norway

Oceania

Oman

Pakistan

Palau

Panama

Papua New Guinea

Paraguay

Peru

Philippines

Poland

Portugal

Qatar

Romania

Russia

Saint Kitts-Nevis

Saint Lucia

Saudi Arabia

Scotland

Senegal

Serbia

Sierra Leone

Singapore

Pitney 2984, PPG 3025, Praxair 3029, Procter 3055, QUALCOMM 3095, Quiksilver 3108, Ralph 3123, Regal 3167, ResMed 3192, Rio 3218, Robbins 3230, Rockwell 3246, Rockwell 3247, RPM 3278, Ruder 3282, Ryder 3292, SAS 3336, Seagate 3377, Sealed 3381, Sealy 3382, Sensient 3408, Shearman 3429, Sherwin 3437, Sidley 3446, Smith 3484, Sonoco 3500, Spansion 3532, SPX 3558, St. Jude 3566, Stanley 3579, Starbucks 3585, State 3592, Symantec 3669, Teleflex 3707, Tennant 3714, Texas 3728, Textron 3731, Thompson 3739, Thomson 3742, Tidewater 3748, Timberland 3754, Timken 3760, Tyco 3829, United 3882, UnitedHealth 3884, Viacom 3945, ViewSonic 3952, Washington 3999, Wells 4028, West 4038, Western 4042, Western 4045, Whirlpool 4056, White 4058, Wiley 4072, Xerox 4136, Xilinx 4137, Yahoo! 4140, Yum! 4150

Slovakia

3M 3, Abbott 13, Air 63, Allen 94, Amway 189, Avnet 304, Badger 313, Bank 340, Becton 398, Biogen 465, Brightpoint 567, Cisco 818, Citigroup 821, Crown 988, Danaher 1027, Dell 1068, Diebold 1112, Diversey 1130, Donaldson 1153, Ecolab 1220, Energizer 1271, Exxon 1315, First 1400, General 1554, Harsco 1741, Hewlett 1794, Illinois 1916, International 1960, Johnson 2048, Liberty 2263, Manitowoc 2355, Manpower 2358, Mondelez 2556, Mylan 2610, Ogilvy 2788, Oracle 2821, PPG 3025, Praxair 3029, Quiksilver 3108, Schein 3348, Squire 3561, Stanley 3579, Teleflex 3707, Thompson 3739, Whirlpool 4056, White 4058

Slovenia

Amway 189, Avon 305, Biogen 465, Chemtura 775, Danaher 1027, Diversey 1130, Eclipse 1219, Ecolab 1220, Goodyear 1612, Hewlett 1794, Illinois 1916, International 1960, Johnson 2048, Manpower 2358, Merck 2466, Mylan 2610, Oracle 2821, PPG 3025, Procter 3055, Thompson 3739, Whirlpool 4056, Wrigley 4125, Xerox 4136

South Africa

3M 3, Abbott 13, Adobe 38, AES 47, Allergan 99, American 167, Amway 189, Arch 230, Arrow 249, Avery 297, Avnet 304, Avon 305, Bank 340, Becton 398, Berkshire 429, Biomet 466, Boeing 516, Boston 540, Briggs 565, Brightpoint 567, CA 638, Capital 678, Caterpillar 722, Chemtura 775, Cisco 818, Citigroup 821, CLARCOR 832, Clorox 852, Coca 862, Colgate 869, Collette 872, Crown 988, Cummins 1007, Dana 1026, Danaher 1027, Deere 1061, Dell 1068, Diebold 1112, Diversey 1130, Dole 1141, Donaldson 1153, Dow 1160, Dow 1161, Duke 1189, Eastman 1213, Eaton 1216, Eclipse 1219, Ecolab 1220, Exponential 1312, First 1400, Fluor 1448, Ford 1464, Franklin 1487, Gap 1533, General 1554, General 1555, Gilead 1582, Google 1613, Grace 1623, Greif 1663, Harris 1736, Harsco 1741, Hewlett 1794, Hillshire 1809, Huntsman 1895, IDT 1910, Illinois 1916, Ingram 1941, Intel 1950, International 1960, International 1962, International 1964, Interpublic 1974, Intuit 1982, Johnson 2048, Johnson 2049, Kearney 2107, Kennametal 2125, Leggett 2246, Manpower 2358, McCormick 2423, Medtronic 2453, Merck 2466, Meritor 2473, Mine 2529, Modine 2544, Mondelez 2556, MoneyGram 2558, Monsanto 2559, Mylan 2610, Nalco 2613, NCR 2650, Novell 2754, Ogilvy 2788, Omnicare 2807, Oracle 2821, Parker 2886, Pentair 2926, PepsiCo 2935, Pfizer 2950, Philip 2962, Pioneer 2981, Pitney 2984, PPG 3025, Preformed 3032, Procter 3055, Quaker 3093, Quiksilver 3108, Reader's 3141, Rockwell 3246, RPM 3278, Sealed 3381, SPX 3558, State 3592, Strauss 3624, Teleflex 3707, Tenneco 3715, Thompson 3739, Timken 3760, United 3872, Valmont 3919, Valspar 3920, Viacom 3945, Waters 4003, Western 4045, Whirlpool 4056, White 4058, Williams 4077, Yum! 4150

South America

Alcoa 82, Autodesk 289, Canon 672, Georgia 1568, Grand 1627, Hess 1793, Johnson 2048, New England 2670, Praxair 3029

South Asia

Exxon 1315, Johnson 2048

South Korea

3M 3, Abbott 13, Activision 30, Agilent 56, Air 63, Akamai 68, Allegheny 91, Allergan 99, Amway 189, Applied 220, ARAMARK 223, Autodesk 289, Avery 297, Avnet 304, Avon 305, Bank 340, Bausch 376, Becton 398, Bergquist 420, Biomet 466, BMC 508, Boeing 516, BorgWarner 528, Boston 540, Broadcom 579, CA 638, Cabot 642, Callaway 660, Chemtura 775, Cisco 818, CIT 819, Citigroup 821, Clorox 852, Corning 945, Cummins 1007, Dana 1026, Dell 1068, Disney 1127, Diversey 1130, Dole 1141, Donaldson 1153, Dow 1161, Dow 1162, Eastman 1213, Eastman 1214, eBay 1217, Eclipse 1219, Ecolab 1220, Edelman 1224, Electronic 1242, Ferro 1366, First 1389, First 1400, FMC 1449, Franklin 1487, Freescale 1495, General 1551, General 1555, Genworth 1565, Google 1613, Grace 1623, Guess 1685, Heinz 1772, Hewlett 1794, Huntsman 1895, Illinois 1916, Intel 1950, International 1960, International 1962, Interpublic 1974, ITT 1999, Johnson 2048, Johnson 2049, Kearney 2107, Kellogg 2120, Kennametal 2125, Kimberly 2150, Las Vegas 2225, Lear 2237, Leggett 2246, LSI 2314, Manitowoc 2355, Manpower 2358, Marriott 2383, Masco 2393, Medtronic 2453, Mentor 2462, Merk 2467, Metropolitan 2481, Micron 2500, Monsanto 2559, Morgan 2570, Nalco 2613, NCR 2650, New York 2688, Newell 2694, Nordson 2723, Novell 2754, Nu 2759, Ogilvy 2788, Oracle 2821, Owens 2842, Parker 2886, PepsiCo 2935, Pfizer 2950, Pitney 2984, PPG 3025, Praxair 3029, Procter 3055, Prudential 3072, QUALCOMM 3095, Rockwell 3246, Rogers 3253, RPM 3278, SAS 3336, Seagate 3377, Sealed 3381, Spansion 3532, SPX 3558, Stanley 3579, State 3592, Tenneco 3715, Texas 3728, Thompson 3739, Tyco 3829, United 3882, Viacom 3945, Wells 4028, Western 4042, Yahoo! 4140, Yum! 4150

Southeast Asia

Exxon 1315, General 1552, Hess 1793, Johnson 2048

Southern Africa

Arch 230

Soviet Union (Former)

Vinson 3958, White 4058, Winston 4089

Spain

3M 3, Abbott 13, Activision 30, Adobe 38, AES 47, Air 63, AK 67, Akamai 68, Alcoa 82, Allegheny 91, Allen 94, Allergan 99, American 132, American 143, American 161, Amway 189, Anheuser 202, ARAMARK 223, Armstrong 246, Ashland 258, Assurant 266, Assurant 268, Autodesk 289, Automatic 291, Avnet 304, Avon 305, Baker 320, Bank 340, Becton 398, Biogen 465, Biomet 466, Blockbuster 483, BMC 508, Boeing 516, BorgWarner 528, Boston 540, BP 547, Briggs 565, Brightpoint 567, Bristol 578, Broadcom 579, CA 638, Cabot 642, Castle 716, Caterpillar 722, Central 743, Cephalon 752, Chemtura 775, Cisco 818, CIT 819, Citigroup 821, CLARCOR 832, Clifford 849, Coca 862, Colgate 869, Collective 871, Cooper 935, Crown 988, Cummins 1007, Dana 1026, Danaher 1027, Davis 1040, Deere 1061, Dell 1068, DENTSPLY 1089, Diebold 1112, Diversey 1130, Dole 1141, Donaldson 1153, Donnelley 1155, du Pont 1184, Duke 1189, Eastman 1213, Eaton 1216, eBay 1217, Eclipse 1219, Ecolab 1220, Edelman 1224, EFC 1236, Emerson 1257, Energizer 1271, Exxon 1315, Ferro 1366, Fifth 1376, First 1400, Fluor 1448, FMC 1449, Foot 1459, Ford 1464, Franklin 1487, Freeport 1494, Freescale 1495, Freshfields 1500, GameStop 1530, General 1551, General 1554, General 1555, Genworth 1565, Gilead 1582, Google 1613, Goya 1622, Grace 1623, Greif 1663, Griffith 1667, Guess 1685, Harsco 1741, Haworth 1758, Heinz 1772, Hewlett 1794, Hexcel 1795, Hillshire 1809, Hines 1813, Hogan 1825, Hormel 1866, Hospira 1867, Huntsman 1895, IAC 1903, Illinois 1916, Ingram 1941, Intel 1950, International 1960, International 1962, Interpublic 1974, ITT 1999, Johnson 2048, Johnson 2049, Jones 2058, Kearney 2107, Kohler 2182, Latham 2228, Leggett 2246, Lexmark 2258, Lilly 2274, Linklaters 2283, Manitowoc 2355, Manpower 2358, Maritz 2376, Mark 2377, Marriott 2383, Masco 2393, Mattel 2405, McDonald's 2427, Medtronic 2453, Mentor 2462, Merck 2466, Meritor 2473, Merk 2467, Microchip 2499, Mine 2529, Mondelez 2556, Monsanto 2559, Moody's 2563, Mylan 2610, NCR 2650, NIKE 2710, Nordson 2723, Novell 2754, Ogilvy 2788, Oilgear 2793, Oracle 2821, Owens 2842, Parker 2886, Patagonia 2892, Pentair 2926, PepsiCo 2935, Pfizer 2950, Pitney 2984, Polaris 2999, PPG 3025, Praxair 3029, Preformed 3032, Procter 3055, Quaker 3093, QUALCOMM 3095, Quiksilver 3108, Ralph 3123, Reader's 3141, ResMed 3192, Rio 3218, Robbins 3230, Rockwell 3246, RPM 3278, SAS 3336, Schein 3348, Sealed 3381, Sealy 3382, Sonoco 3500, SPX 3558, Squire 3561, St. Jude 3566, Stanley 3579, Staples 3581, Steelcase 3597, Teleflex 3707, Tennant 3714, Tenneco 3715, Texas 3728, Thompson 3739, Thomson 3742, Timberland 3754, Timken 3760, Toys 3790, Tyco 3829, United 3882, UnitedHealth 3884, Valmont 3919, Viacom 3945, ViewSonic 3952, West 4038, Western 4045, Whirlpool 4056, Williams 4077, Wrigley 4125, Xerox 4136, Yahoo! 4140, Yum! 4150

Sri Lanka

3M 3, AES 47, Avery 297, Caterpillar 722, Citigroup 821, Donnelley 1155, Energizer 1271, First 1400, Hillshire 1809, Ingram 1941, Ogilvy 2788, Procter 3055, Thompson 3739

Sub-Saharan Africa

Bristol 578, General 1552

Suriname

Alcoa 82, Exxon 1315, PPG 3025

Swaziland

Winston 4089

Sweden

3M 3, Abbott 13, Activision 30, Adobe 38, Advanced 40, Advent 41, Akamai 68, Akin 70, Allergan 99, American 161, Armstrong 246, Autodesk 289, Avery 297, Avnet 304, Baker 320, Bank 340, Becton 398, Bemis 407, Biogen 465, Biomet 466, BMC 508, Boeing 516, Briggs 565, Brightpoint 567, Bristol 578, CA 638, Cadence 646, Campbell 669, Caterpillar 722, Cisco 818, CIT 819, Citigroup 821, Coca 862, Colgate 869, ConocoPhillips 913, Cooper 935, Covance 955, Danaher 1027, Deere 1061, Dell 1068, Diversey 1130, Dole 1141, du Pont 1184, Eaton 1216, eBay 1217, Eclipse 1219, Ecolab 1220, Edelman 1224, Electronic 1242, Energizer 1271, Exxon 1315, Fifth 1376, Franklin 1487, Freescale 1495, GameStop 1530, General 1552, General 1554, Gilead 1582, Google 1613, Grace 1623, Greif 1663, Harsco 1741, Hewlett 1794, Hillshire 1809, Hospira 1867, Huntsman 1895, IDT 1910, Illinois 1916, Ingram 1941, Intel 1950, International 1960, International 1962, International 1964, Interpublic 1974, ITT 1999, Johnson 2048, Johnson 2049, Kearney 2107, Kilpatrick 2147, Lear 2237, Lilly 2274, Linklaters 2283, LSI 2314, Manpower 2358, Mark 2377,

Switzerland

Syria

Taiwan

Tanzania, Zanzibar and Pemba

Thailand

Togo

Trinidad & Tobago

Tunisia

Turkey

Turkmenistan

Turks & Caicos Islands

Uganda

Ukraine

United Arab Emirates

Jones 2058, K&L 2080, Kearney 2107, King 2157, Latham 2228, Lexmark 2258, Linklaters 2283, LSI 2314, Manitowoc 2355, Manpower 2358, Marriott 2383, McDermott 2424, Mondelez 2556, Newell 2694, Novell 2754, Ogilvy 2788, Oracle 2821, Oshkosh 2833, Parker 2886, Parsons 2887, Patton 2898, PepsiCo 2935, Pfizer 2950, Pillsbury 2975, Procter 3055, Reed 3163, Rockwell 3246, RPM 3278, Schein 3348, Shearman 3429, Smith 3484, SPX 3558, Thompson 3739, Valmont 3919, Victaulic 3948, Vinson 3958, Western 4045, White 4058

United Kingdom

3M 3, Abbott 13, Activision 30, Acumen 33, Adobe 38, Advanced 40, Advent 41, AES 47, Agilent 56, Air 63, AK 67, Akamai 68, Akin 70, Aladdin 73, Alcatel 81, Alcoa 82, Allegheny 91, Allegis 92, Allen 94, Allergan 99, AMCOL 127, American 132, American 143, American 149, American 167, AMETEK 181, AMPCO 186, Amway 189, Andrews 198, Anheuser 202, Apache 211, ARAMARK 223, Arch 230, Armstrong 246, Arnold 248, Ashland 258, Assurant 266, Assurant 268, Autodesk 289, Automatic 291, Avery 297, Avnet 304, Baker 320, Baker 321, Baker 323, Baker 324, Baker 325, Bank 340, Bank 344, Barnes 362, Bausch 376, Bayer 381, Bechtel 395, Becton 398, Bemis 407, Ben 409, Bergquist 420, Berkshire 429, Best 442, Bingham 463, Biogen 465, Biomet 466, Blockbuster 483, BMC 508, Boeing 516, BorgWarner 528, BOSE 530, Bourns 542, BP 547, Bracewell 549, Bridgeway 563, Briggs 565, Bristol 578, Broadcom 579, Brown 589, Brown 590, Bryan 596, CA 638, Cabot 642, Cadence 646, Cadwalader 649, Cahill 651, Callaway 660, Campbell 669, Carlson 693, Castle 716, CB 725, Cephalon 752, Ceridian 753, Charles 764, Chemtura 775, Chesapeake 778, Cisco 818, CIT 819, Citigroup 821, CLARCOR 832, Clark 836, Cleary 843, Clifford 849, Clorox 852, CME 853, CNA 855, Coca 862, Coca 863, Colgate 869, Collective 871, Comcast 887, Commercial 893, ConocoPhillips 913, Cooper 935, Cooper 936, Corning 945, Covance 955, Cozen 964, Crane 970, Credit 980, Crowell 986, Crown 988, CryoLife 990, Cummins 1007, Curtis 1010, Dana 1026, Danaher 1027, Dart 1033, Davis 1040, Davison 1042, Dean 1054, Debevoise 1055, Dechert 1058, Deckers 1059, Deere 1061, Delaware 1066, Dell 1068, Delta 1073, Deluxe 1084, DENTSPLY 1089, Diebold 1112, DIRECTV 1124, Disney 1127, Diversey 1130, Dole 1141, Donaldson 1153, Donnelley 1155, Dorsey 1157, Dow 1161, Dow 1163, DRS 1179, drugstore.com 1180, du Pont 1184, Duane 1185, Duke 1189, Eastman 1213, Eastman 1214, Eaton 1216, eBay 1217, Eclipse 1219, Ecolab 1220, Edelman 1224, Edison 1228, El Paso 1239, Electronic 1242, Emerson 1257, Energizer 1271, Enterprise 1281, EOG 1282, Equifax 1288, Exxon 1315, Factory 1323, Ferro 1366, Fifth 1376, First 1389, First 1400, Fiserv 1427, Fluor 1448, FMC 1449, Foot 1459, Franklin 1487, Freescale 1495, Freshfields 1500, Fried 1502, Fulbright 1516, GameStop 1530, Gannett 1532, General 1551, General 1552, General 1554, General 1555, General 1558, Genworth 1565, Genzyme 1566, Georgia 1568, Gibson 1580, Gilead 1582, Gleason 1591, Goldman 1604, Goodwin 1611, Goodyear 1612, Google 1613, Grace 1623, Graham 1625, Greenberg 1654, Greif 1663, Griffith 1667, H & R 1695, Halliburton 1706, Hallmark 1707, Hardinge 1729, Harris 1736, Harsco 1741, Hartford 1742, Haworth 1758, HCA 1762, Heinz 1772, Hess 1793, Hewlett 1794, Hexcel 1795, Hillshire 1809, Hines 1813, Hogan 1825, Holme 1837, Honeywell 1852, Hospira 1867, Houghton 1869, Hubbell 1879, Hunt 1889, Huntsman 1895, Husch 1896, IAC 1903, Ideal 1908, IDT 1910, Illinois 1916, Imation 1919, IMS 1924, Ingram 1941, Intel 1950, Interface 1953, International 1960, International 1962, International 1964, Interpublic 1974, Intuit 1982, ITT 1999, James 2021, Jefferies 2030, Johnson 2048, Johnson 2049, Jones 2058, JPMorgan Chase 2071, K&L 2080, Katten 2101, KBR 2106, Kearney 2107, Kellogg 2120, Kennametal 2125, Kilpatrick 2147, Kimball 2149, King 2157, Kirkland 2164, Koch 2180, Kohler 2182, La-Z-Boy 2205, Landmark 2218, Lands' 2220, Lane 2221, Las Vegas 2225, Latham 2228, Lauder 2230, Leggett 2246, Lexmark 2258, Life 2268, Lilly 2274, Linklaters 2283, LSI 2314, Lubrizol 2315, Manitowoc 2355, Manpower 2358, Maritz 2376, Marriott 2383, Mars 2384, Masco 2393, MasterCard 2399, Mattel 2405, Matthews 2406, Mayer 2411, McDermott 2425, McDonald's 2427, McGraw 2429, McGuireWoods 2430, MedImmune 2450, Medtronic 2453, Mentor 2462, Merck 2466, Mercury 2469, Merk 2467, Micron 2500, Milbank 2511, Mine 2529, Mintz 2534, Modine 2544, Mondelez 2556, MoneyGram 2558, Monsanto 2559, Moody's 2563, Morgan 2568, Morgan 2570, Morgan 2571, Morrison 2576, Motorola 2586, Murphy 2600, Mylan 2610, Nasdaq 2617, NCR 2650, New York 2690, Newell 2694, Newmont 2698, NIKE 2710, Novell 2754, Nu 2759, NVIDIA 2767, Office 2785, Ogilvy 2788, Oilgear 2793, Olin 2801, Omnicare 2807, Omnicom 2808, OMNOVA 2809, Oracle 2821, Oshkosh 2833, Owens 2842, Owens 2844, Oxford 2847, PACCAR 2850, PACE 2851, Pactiv 2863, Papa 2876, Parametric 2878, Parker 2886, Parsons 2887, Patagonia 2892, Paul 2900, Paul 2901, Pentair 2926, PepsiCo 2935, Pfizer 2950, Photronics 2969, Pillsbury 2975, Piper 2983, Pitney 2984, Polaris 2999, PPG 3025, PPL 3026, Praxair 3029, Preformed 3032, Procter 3055, Proskauer 3064, PVH 3088, Quaker 3093, Quaker 3094, QUALCOMM 3095, Quest 3103, Quiksilver 3108, Quinn 3111, Rackspace 3117, Ralph 3123, RBC 3136, Reader's 3141, RealNetworks 3144, Reed 3163, Regal 3167, Regis 3172, ResMed 3192, Riker 3215, Riviana 3227, Rockwell 3246, Rockwell 3247, Ropes 3260, RPM 3278, Ruder 3282, Ryder 3292, Sandusky 3328, SAS 3336, ScanSource 3347, Schein 3348, Scholastic 3358, Schulman 3361, Schulte 3362, Seagate 3377, Sealed 3381, Sedgwick 3395, Sensient 3408, ServiceMaster 3414, Sherwin 3437, Shook 3439, Sigma 3453, Simon 3458, Simpson 3462, Skidmore 3474, Smith 3484, Smithfield 3487, Sonoco 3500, Spirol 3545, Springleaf 3554, SPX 3558, Squire 3561, St. Jude 3566, Stanley 3579, Staples 3581, Starbucks 3585, State 3592, STERIS 3600, Sutherland 3663, Sysco 3677, Teleflex 3707, Tenet 3713, Tennant 3714, Tenneco 3715, Terex 3719, Texas 3728, Thompson 3739, Thomson 3742, Tiffany 3750, Timberland 3754, TJX 3765, Toro 3775, Towerbrook 3781, Toys 3790, Tyco 3829, UBS 3842, Unisys 3859, United 3877, United 3882, UnitedHealth 3884, Unum 3898, V.F. 3913, Valero 3915, Valmont 3919, Valspar 3920, Viacom 3945, Viad 3946, ViewSonic 3952, Vinson 3958, Warburg 3985, Washington 3999, Waters 4003, WD-40 4011, Weil 4023, Wells 4028, Western 4042, Whirlpool 4056, White 4058, Whole 4066, Wiley 4072, Williams 4077, Williams 4078, Willkie 4081, Winston 4089, Wrigley 4125, Xerox 4136, Yahoo! 4140, Yum! 4150

Uruguay

3M 3, Abbott 13, AES 47, Amway 189, Avon 305, Bank 340, Becton 398, Blockbuster 483, Boston 540, Caterpillar 722, Citigroup 821, Clorox 852, Colgate 869, Collective 871, Credit 980, Dana 1026, Danaher 1027, Diebold 1112, DIRECTV 1124, Diversey 1130, Duke 1189, Dun 1190, Ecolab 1220, Energizer 1271, Equifax 1288, First 1400, General 1554, International 1960, James 2021, Leggett 2246, Lexmark 2258, Manpower 2358, MasterCard 2399, Merck 2466, Mondelez 2556, Monsanto 2559, Novell 2754, Ogilvy 2788, Owens 2842, PepsiCo 2935, Pfizer 2950, PPG 3025, Praxair 3029, Rockwell 3246, Sealed 3381, Sherwin 3437, Teleflex 3707, Tennant 3714, Thompson 3739, UnitedHealth 3884, Wells 4028, Weyerhaeuser 4052, Whirlpool 4056

Vanuatu

AK 67, Furniture 1519, Tidewater 3748

Venezuela

3M 3, Abbott 13, AES 47, Allergan 99, Arch 230, Autodesk 289, Avery 297, Avon 305, Baker 320, Baker 324, Bausch 376, Becton 398, Boston 540, Brightpoint 567, Bristol 578, CA 638, Cabot 642, Caterpillar 722, Cisco 818, CITGO 820, Citigroup 821, Clorox 852, Coca 862, ConocoPhillips 913, Dana 1026, Danaher 1027, Dell 1068, Diebold 1112, DIRECTV 1124, Diversey 1130, Donnelley 1155, Dow 1161, du Pont 1184, Dun 1190, Eastman 1214, Eaton 1216, Ecolab 1220, EFC 1236, Emerson 1257, Energizer 1271, Ferro 1366, Ford 1464, General 1551, General 1554, General 1555, Goodyear 1612, Grace 1623, Graham 1625, Greif 1663, Heinz 1772, Hewlett 1794, Hogan 1825, International 1960, International 1962, ITT 1999, Johnson 2048, Johnson 2049, Kellogg 2120, Kimberly 2150, Littler 2289, Manpower 2358, Marriott 2383, Mattel 2405, McGraw 2429, Merck 2466, Meritor 2473, Mondelez 2556, Newell 2694, Nordson 2723, Novell 2754, Ogilvy 2788, Oracle 2821, Owens 2844, Parker 2886, Peabody 2907, PepsiCo 2935, Pfizer 2950, Praxair 3029, Procter 3055, Quaker 3093, Robbins 3230, Rockwell 3246, RPM 3278, Sealed 3381, Sherwin 3437, Sonoco 3500, Stanley 3579, Thompson 3739, Tidewater 3748, Timken 3760, West 4038, Xerox 4136, Yum! 4150

Vietnam

3M 3, Avery 297, Avon 305, Baker 320, Cisco 818, Citigroup 821, Clarkson 839, Colgate 869, ConocoPhillips 913, Crown 988, Danaher 1027, Dell 1068, Duane 1185, Edelman 1224, Franklin 1487, Freshfields 1500, Grace 1623, Halliburton 1706, Hewlett 1794, Hogan 1825, Intel 1950, International 1960, Jabil 2006, Manpower 2358, Mayer 2411, Micro 2498, Ogilvy 2788, Oracle 2821, PepsiCo 2935, Procter 3055, Sherwin 3437, Thompson 3739, Waters 4003

Wales

Apache 211, Avnet 304, Avon 305, Brunswick 595, Cabot 642, Caterpillar 722, Chevron 780, Coca 863, Donnelley 1155, Dow 1162, Gap 1533, General 1551, Graham 1625, Humana 1886, IAC 1903, Intel 1950, KBR 2106, Meritor 2473, Peabody 2907, Whole 4066

Yemen

Clorox 852, Hunt 1889

Zambia

Citigroup 821, Cummins 1007, Mortenson 2577, NIKE 2710

Zimbabwe

Cummins 1007, Gilead 1582, Grand 1627, Heinz 1772, Hillshire 1809, International 1962, Mine 2529, NCR 2650, Ogilvy 2788, Pfizer 2950, Thompson 3739

TYPES OF SUPPORT INDEX

List of terms: Terms for the major types of support used in this index are listed below with definitions.

Index: In the index itself, corporations are identified by abbreviated versions of their names and referenced by the sequence numbers assigned in the Descriptive Directory.

Advocacy: cash grants for services related to advocacy, including advocating for better assistance in various program areas (for example school reform, full access to health care, legal reform, environmental clean-up work, etc.) and providing assistance in planning advocacy campaigns.

Annual campaigns: any organized effort by a nonprofit to secure gifts on an annual basis; also called annual appeals.

Building/renovation: money raised for construction, renovation, remodeling, or rehabilitation of buildings; may be part of an organization's capital campaign.

Camperships: funding to organizations to provide partial or full tuition subsidies to enable participants who would not otherwise be financially able to participate in fee-based camping programs.

Capital campaigns: a campaign, usually extending over a period of years, to raise substantial funds for enduring purposes, such as building or endowment funds.

Cause-related marketing: linking gifts to charity with marketing promotions. This may involve donating products which will then be auctioned or given away in a drawing with the proceeds benefiting a charity. The advertising campaign for the product will be combined with the promotion for the charity. In other cases it will be advertised that when a customer buys the product a certain amount of the proceeds will be donated to charity. Often gifts made to charities stemming from cause-related marketing are not called charitable donations and may be assigned as expenses to the department in charge of the program. Public affairs and marketing are the departments usually involved.

Computer technology: grants to acquire, upgrade or develop computer technology. Includes hardware, software, peripherals, systems, networking components and mobile devices.

Conferences/seminars: a grant to cover the expenses of holding a conference or seminar.

Consulting services: professional staff support provided by the foundation to a nonprofit to consult on a project of mutual interest or to evaluate services (not a cash grant).

Continuing support: a grant that is renewed on a regular basis.

Curriculum development: grants to schools, colleges, universities, and educational support organizations to develop general or discipline-specific curricula.

Debt reduction: also known as deficit financing. A grant to reduce the recipient organization's indebtedness; frequently refers to mortgage payments.

Donated equipment: surplus furniture, office machines, paper, appliances, laboratory apparatus, or other items that may be given to charities, schools, or hospitals.

Donated land: land or developed property. Institutions of higher education often receive gifts of real estate; land has also been given to community groups for housing development or for parks or recreational facilities.

Donated products: companies giving away what they make or produce. Product donations can include periodic clothing donations to a shelter for the homeless or regular donations of pharmaceuticals to a health clinic resulting in a reliable supply.

Emergency funds: a one-time grant to cover immediate short-term funding needs on an emergency basis.

Employee matching gifts: a contribution to a charitable organization by a corporate employee which is matched by a similar contribution from the employer. Many corporations support employee matching gift programs in higher education to stimulate their employees to give to the college or university of their choice. In addition, many foundations support matching gift programs for their officers and directors.

Employee volunteer services: an ongoing coordinated effort through which the company promotes involvement with nonprofits on the part of employees. The involvement may be during work time or after hours. (Employees may also volunteer on their own initiative; however, that is not described as corporate volunteerism). Many companies honor their employees with awards for outstanding volunteer efforts. In making cash donations, many favor the organizations with which their employees have worked as volunteers. Employee volunteerism runs the gamut from school tutoring programs to sales on work premises of employee-made crafts or baked goods to benefit nonprofits. Management of the programs can range from fully-staffed offices of corporate volunteerism to a part-time coordinating responsibility on the part of one employee.

Employee-related scholarships: a scholarship program funded by a company-sponsored foundation usually for children of employees; programs are frequently administered by the National Merit Scholarship Corporation which is responsible for selection of scholars.

Endowments: a bequest or gift intended to be kept permanently and invested to provide income for continued support of an organization.

Equipment: a grant to purchase equipment, furnishings, or other materials.

Exchange programs: usually refers to funds for educational exchange programs for foreign students.

Faculty/staff development: grants to institutions or organizations to train or further educate staff or faculty members

Fellowships: usually indicates funds awarded to educational institutions to support fellowship programs. A few foundations award fellowships directly to individuals.

Film/video/radio: grants to fund a specific film, video, or radio production.

General/operating support: a grant made to further the general purpose or work of an organization, rather than for a specific purpose or project; also called unrestricted grants.

Grants to individuals: awards made directly by the foundation to individuals rather than to nonprofit organizations; includes aid to the needy. (See also "Fellowships," "Scholarships—to individuals," and "Student loans—to individuals.")

In-kind gifts: a contribution of equipment, supplies, or other property as distinct from a monetary grant. Some organizations may also donate space or staff time as an in-kind contribution.

Income development: grants for fundraising, marketing, and to expand audience base.

Internship funds: usually indicates funds awarded to an institution or organization to support an internship program rather than a grant to an individual.

Land acquisition: a grant to purchase real estate property.

Lectureships: see "Curriculum development."

Loaned talent: an aspect of employee volunteerism. It differs from the usual definition of such in that it usually involves loaned professionals and executive staff who are helping a nonprofit in an area involving their particular skills. Loaned talents can assist a nonprofit in strategic planning, dispute resolution or negotiation services, office administration, real estate technical assistance, personnel policies, lobbying, consulting, fundraising, and legal and tax advice.

Loans: see "Program-related investments/loans" and "Student loans—to individuals."

Loans—to individuals: assistance distributed directly to individuals in the form of loans.

Management development/capacity building: grants for salaries, staff support, staff training, strategic and long-term planning, capacity building, budgeting and accounting.

Matching/challenge support: a grant which is made to match funds provided by another donor. (See also "Employee matching gifts.")

Mission-related investments/loans: Market-rate loans or other investments (as distinguished from grants) to organizations to finance projects related to the foundation's stated charitable purpose and interests. Organizations invested in may be for-profit entities.

Operating budgets: see "General/operating support."

Pro bono services: pro bono services rendered by a company, professional services firm, intermediary,association or individual professional leveraging the core competencies and expertise of the professional(s) engaged to meet the client's need.

Pro bono services-advocacy: pro bono consulting assistance related to advocacy, including advocating for better services in various program areas (for example school reform, full access to health care, legal reform, environmental clean-up work, etc.) and providing assistance in planning advocacy campaigns that will follow current legal guidelines preventing certain kinds of advocacy by nonprofits

Pro bono services-board: pro bono consulting assistance in board effectiveness assessment, board recruitment process design, board reporting, meeting facilitation, executive coaching, and performance review.

Pro bono services-communications/public relations: pro bono consulting assistance in external communications and public relations, including but not limited to assistance with the development of an annual report, brochure, newsletter design, and/or public service announcement.

Pro bono services-financial management: pro bono consulting assistance in financial management, including but not limited to program cost analysis, financial audit, financial controls assessment and design, budgeting process design, pricing strategy, and purchase and supply chain audit.

Pro bono services-fundraising: Pro bono consulting assistance in programs or projects directly relating to fundraising. These may include event planning and production, executive fundraising coaching, donor segmentation, in-kind opportunity assessment, capital campaign design and management, and the development of capital campaign materials.

Pro bono services-human resources: pro bono consulting assistance in the area of human resources, including a strategic assessment and recommendations for a human resources plan, organizational diversity plan, performance management system, back office systems implementation, staff compensation and incentive plan, staff training and development plan, and an internal communications plan.

Pro bono services-interactive/website technology: pro bono consulting assistance in website technology, including the design and development of a basic website, interactive website, intranet, and extranet.

Pro bono services-legal: pro bono consulting assistance in the area of legal support, including donation of legal services in court situations, review of various legal documents, including those related to incorporation and other law, justice, and counsel issues.

Pro bono services-marketing/branding: pro bono consulting assistance in marketing and branding. Programs or projects may cover issues such as a program marketing, organizational positioning and key messages, visual identity or re-naming.

Pro bono services-medical: pro bono consulting assistance in the medical area, including donation of medical services and equipment.

Pro bono services-strategic management: pro bono consulting assistance in the area of strategic management, including the development of a strategic plan, refined mission, environmental and sustainability policy and plan, internal capacity assessment, strengths, weaknesses, opportunities, and threats analysis, competitive analysis, earned income business plan, geographic expansion plan, and logic model design

Pro bono services-technology infrastructure: pro bono consulting assistance in technology infrastructure such as donor database implementation, the development of an organizational IT plan, installation of office networking, remote IT access set up, and program database implementation.

Professorships: a grant to an educational institution to endow a professorship or chair.

Program development: grants to support specific projects or programs as opposed to general purpose grants.

Program evaluation: grants to evaluate a specific project or program; includes awards both to agencies to pay for evaluation costs and to research institutes and other program evaluators.

Program-related investments/loans: a loan is any temporary award of funds that must be repaid. A program-related investment is a loan or other investment (as distinguished from a grant) made by a foundation to another organization for a project related to the foundation's stated charitable purpose and interests.

Public relations services: may include printing and duplicating, audio-visual and graphic arts services, helping to plan special events such as festivals, piggyback advertising (advertisements that mention a company while also promoting a nonprofit), and public service advertising.

Publication: a grant to fund reports or other publications issued by a nonprofit resulting from research or projects of interest to the foundation.

Renovation projects: see "Building/renovation."

Research: usually indicates funds awarded to institutions to cover costs of investigations and clinical trials. Research grants for individuals are usually referred to as fellowships.

Scholarship funds: a grant to an educational institution or organization to support a scholarship program, mainly for students at the undergraduate level. (See also "Employee-related scholarships.")

Scholarships—to individuals: assistance awarded directly to individuals in the form of educational grants or scholarships. (See also "Employee-related scholarships.")

Seed money: a grant or contribution used to start a new project or organization. Seed grants may cover salaries and other operating expenses of a new project. Also known as "start-up funds."

Special projects: see "Program development."

Sponsorships: endorsements of charities by corporations; or corporate contributions to all or part of a charitable event.

Student aid: see "Fellowships," "Scholarships—to individuals," and "Student loans—to individuals."

Student loans—to individuals: assistance awarded directly to individuals in the form of educational loans.

Technical assistance: operational or management assistance given to nonprofit organizations; may include fundraising assistance, budgeting and financial planning, program planning, legal advice, marketing, and other aids to management. Assistance may be offered directly by a foundation staff member or in the form of a grant to pay for the services of an outside consultant.

Travel awards: funding to organizations to provide awards to individuals to cover transportation and/or out-of-town living expenses while attending a conference or completing a period of studt or special project. Enrollment in a college or university is not a requirement.

Use of facilities: this may include rent free office space for temporary periods, dining and meeting facilities, telecommunications services, mailing services, transportation services, or computer services.

Annual campaigns

Acacia 21, Acuity 31, Adobe 38, Aflac 54, AGL 57, Ahern 60, Air 63, AK 67, Aladdin 73, Albemarle 78, Alcoa 82, Alexander 85, Allegheny 91, Allete 100, Alliant 104, Allianz 105, Alpha 112, AMC 126, Ameren 128, American 143, American 145, American 157, American 170, Ameritas 178, AMETEK 181, Amica 183, Andersen 194, Apache 211, Applied 220, ARAMARK 223, Arkema 242, Armstrong 246, Arrowpoint 251, Ash 256, Ashland 258, Associated 263, AstraZeneca 272, Autodesk 289, AutoZone 294, Avnet 304, Azulay 311, Baird 317, Baker 319, Bangor 338, Bank 341, Bank 342, Bank 346, Bardes 359, Barnes 362, Batson 373, Batts 374, Bay 378, BB&T 385, Beaver 394, Belden 402, Belk 403, Bemis 407, Beneficial 411, Beneficial 412, Berkheimer 425, Berkshire 428, Berry 435, Bickel 457, Bierlein 459, Bigelow 462, Biogen 465, Biomet 466, Blair 478, Blue 504, Boart 510, Boston 540, Bound 541, Bowater 543, Bridgestone 560, Bridgewater 562, Briggs 564, Briggs 565, Brooks 585, Brotherhood 588, Brown 591, Building 610, Burlington 618, Burns 620, Butler 626, Butzel 629, C Spire 636, Cambridge 666, Capitol 680, Carlson 693, Carpenter 700, Carter's 708, Cascade 713, Catalina 719, Caterpillar 722, Centene 735, CenterPoint 738, Central 745, Central 746, CH2M 758, Chaney 761, Charter 766, Charter 767, Chemed 773, Chesapeake 778, Chicago 787, Chicopee 792, Chrysler 801, CHS 802, CIGNA 812, Citizens 824, Citizens 828, CLARCOR 832, Clarkson 839, Clif 848, Cliffs 850, CME 853, CNH 856, Collective 871, Collette 872, Colonial 875, Commerce 890, Compass 901, Conditioned 906, Consolidated 917, Conston 920, Continental 924, Contran 928, Cooper 935, Crane 969, Crane 970, Creative 976, Cumberland 1003, Cummins 1007, Daiwa 1020, Dana 1026, Davis 1037, Dedham 1060, Deere 1061, Deluxe 1084, Demoulas 1085, Dethmers 1091, Detroit 1095, Dexter 1103, Diebold 1112, Dilbeck 1116, DineEquity 1120, Discover 1125, Discovery 1126, Disney 1127, Dispatch 1129, Dixie 1132, Dominion 1150, Donaldson 1153, Dot 1158, Dow 1163, Duchossois 1187, Duke 1189, Dun 1190, Eastern 1209, Easthampton 1212, Edison 1228, El Paso 1239, Electric 1240, Empire 1262, Entergy 1279, Ergon 1289, ERM 1292, Evening 1302, Faegre 1324, Faribault 1332, Farrell 1341, Federated 1351, Ferro 1366, Fifth 1376, Fifth 1377, First 1389, First 1393, First 1395, First 1397, First 1405, First 1406, First 1420, First 1421, FirstEnergy 1424, Firstmerit 1425, Fisher 1431, Fisher 1433, Florence 1441, Fluor 1448, Ford 1463, Ford 1464, Forest 1467, Franklin 1488, Freedman 1493, Freeport 1494, Fremont 1497, Fuller 1517, Fulton 1518, G & R 1523, GATX 1542, General 1555, General 1557, Genesis 1561, Georgia 1567, Georgia 1568, Global 1592, Golub 1607, Gould 1618, Graham 1625, Grand 1628, Grinnell 1668, Gulf 1689, H & R 1695, Halliburton 1706, Hampden 1713, Handy 1718, Hardinge 1729, Harken 1731, Harvey 1746, Hawkins 1757, HCA 1762, Heinz 1772, Henkel 1778, Hillshire 1809, Hillside 1810, Hofmann 1824, Holiday 1832, Home 1845, Honda 1851, Hormel 1866, Hubbell 1879, Huhtamaki 1884, Humana 1886, Hygeia 1901, Illinois 1916, Imation 1919, Independent 1927, Ingram 1941, Institution 1946, Interface 1953, International 1962, International 1963, International 1965, International 1971, Intoximeters 1979, Jaclyn 2015, Jacobs 2016, Jasper 2026, Jewett 2042, Johnson 2048, Johnson 2049, Johnson 2050, Jones 2056, Joy 2070, JSJ 2073, K-B 2081, Kahn 2084, Kaiser 2086, Kaman 2088, Kann 2090, Kansas 2094, Kennecott 2127, KeyBank 2136, Kiewit 2142, Kikkoman 2144, Kingsbury 2160, Kinney 2162, Klein's 2169, Kmart 2172, Koch 2179, Kohler 2182, Koss 2188, Laclede 2207, Landmark 2218, Larkin 2224, Laureate 2231, Lebanon 2238, Lefton 2244, LG&E Energy 2260, Lilly 2274, Lockheed 2292, Loews 2296, Longaberger 2299, Lubrizol 2315, Lucasfilm 2316, M&T 2323, M/I 2325, Macy's 2333, Main 2342, Major 2347, Mamiye 2352, Manti 2359, Marathon 2365, Maritz 2376, MarkleBank 2379, Mars 2384, Mary 2392, Masco 2393, Mascoma 2394, Massachusetts 2397, Material 2402, McClatchy 2422, McDermott 2424, McKinstry 2435, MDU 2441, Medtronic 2453, Men's 2460, Menasha 2461, Meredith 2471, MGIC 2488, Michael 2493, MidAmerican 2504, Miller 2523, Millhiser-Smith 2524, Mine 2529, Mississippi 2536, Mohawk 2545, Monadnock 2551, Moody's 2563, Morgan 2568, Motorists 2584, MSC 2593, MTD 2595, Myers 2609, National 2628, National 2634, National 2638, Nationwide 2639, Naugatuck 2645, Naugatuck 2646, NCR 2650, Nelnet 2660, Nestle 2662, Neville 2667, New York 2683, New York 2684, New York 2690, Newfield 2695, Newport 2699, Nextier 2706, NiSource 2715, Noland 2719, Nordic 2722, Nordson 2723, Nordstrom 2724, Norfolk 2725, Northern 2740, Northwestern 2749, NV 2765, NYSE 2769, OceanFirst 2782, Ohio 2789, Ohio 2790, Oklahoma 2794, Olin 2801, OMNOVA 2809, Opus 2820, Orscheln 2827, Oshkosh 2833, Otter 2836, Oxford 2847, PACCAR 2850, PacifiCorp 2860, Park 2879, Parker 2886, Peerless 2915, Penney 2925, People's 2928, Piedmont 2971, PPG 3025, Premier 3036, Premix 3037, Presley 3038, Principal 3047, Progressive 3057, Protective 3066, Pukall 3082, Putnam 3086, PVH 3088, Quad 3091, QUALCOMM 3095, Questar 3104, Quincy 3110, R & B 3113, Rahr 3118, Raymond 3133, Rayonier 3134, RBC 3136, RECO 3148, Red 3153, Redwoods 3158, Reed 3160, Regions 3171, Regis 3172, ResMed 3192, Retail 3194, Reynolds 3199, Reynolds 3200, Rich 3204, Riverway 3226, Rockville 3245, Roma 3255, Roundy's 3272, RPM 3278, Ryder 3292, Ryman 3294, S & T 3297, Sacramento 3304, Safeguard 3307, Saint 3312, Sandusky 3328, Sartori 3335, Scotts 3372, Scoular 3373, Sears 3384, Securian 3389, Security 3391, Sensient 3408, Servco 3412, Seventh 3416, Shaughnessy 3425, Sherwin 3437, SI 3444, Sigma 3453, Simplot 3459, Simpson 3461, Sioux 3465, Sit 3466, SLM 3478, SMBC 3480, Smith 3484, SourceMedia 3506, South Bend 3507, Southern 3515, Southern 3516, Southern 3517, Southern 3521, Southwest 3524, Sovereign 3528, Spahn 3529, Spartan 3535, Springleaf 3554, Sprint 3556, Square 3560, Standard 3575, Stanley 3580, Star 3584, State 3592, Stock 3610, Stupp 3628, SunTrust 3654, Superior 3658, SUPERVALU 3659, Symmco 3670, Synopsys 3673, Synovus 3674, TCF 3695, TD 3696, Tektronix 3706, Tenet 3713, Tennessee 3716, Terlato 3720, Texas 3728, Timberland 3754, Todd 3766, Tops 3774, Toro 3775, Totsy 3780, Towerbrook 3781, Toyota 3784, Triumph 3812, U.S. 3836, Union 3856, Union 3858, United 3860, United 3878, Unitil 3885, Univar 3886, Universal 3891, USG 3905, UTC 3908, Utica 3910, Valspar 3920, Vision 3961, Vulcan 3972, Wachtell 3973, Walgreen 3981, Walker 3982, Warburg 3985, Warrell 3991, Washington 3994, Washington 3999, Waterford 4002, Webster 4017, Wells 4028, Wenger 4033, West 4034, West 4038, Western 4040, Wiley 4072, Winn 4087, Winnebago 4088, Wisconsin 4096, Woodward 4112, XTEK 4138, YGS 4143, York 4145, Yum! 4150, Zappos.com 4153

Building/renovation

Abbott 13, AbbyBank 15, Activision 30, AEGON 45, Agilent 56, AGL 57, Albemarle 78, Alcoa 82, Alexander 85, Allen 98, Allete 100, Alliant 104, Alro 113, Altria 120, Ameren 128, American 141, American 143, American 155, American 165, American 170, AMERIGROUP 171, Ameristar 176, AMETEK 181, Amica 183, Amsted 188, AnchorBank 193, Andersen 194, Anheuser 202, Apex 214, Apple 218, Ariel 237, Ariens 238, Arkema 242, Armstrong 246, Ash 256, Associated 263, Autodesk 289, BancTrust 337, Bangor 338, Bank 340, Bank 341, Bank 342, Bank 346, Barnes 362, Batts 374, BB&T 385, Beck 396, Belk 403, Belo 406, Bemis 407, Bemis 408, Beneficial 412, Berkheimer 425, Berry 435, Betts 451, Bigelow 462, BJ's 473, Black 474, Blair 478, Blue 489, Blue 490, Boeing 516, Boh 517, Bridgestone 560, Bridgewater 562, Briggs 565, Bristol 577, Brooks 585, Brotherhood 588, Brown 590, Brunswick 595, Burlington 618, CA 638, Cabot 642, Caesars 650, Callanan 659, Calvert 663, Campbell 669, Cape 674, Capitol 680, Caterpillar 722, Centene 735, CFS 756, Chaney 761, Chase 770, Chelsea 772, Chemtura 775, Cheviot 779, Chicago 785, Chicago 787, Chicago 790, Chief 793, Chrysler 801, Cic 811, CITGO 820, Citizens 828, Clear 842, Clemens 844, Cliffs 850, CME 853, CMS 854, CNH 856, COLHOC 870, Collective 871, Collette 872, Colorado 880, Columbia 882, Commerce 890, Concept 905, Connecticut 912, Consumers 921, Contran 928, Control 929, Convergys 933, Cooper 935, Copley 938, Corning 945, Covidien 956, Cow 957, Credit 977, Croft 985, Cullen 1000, Cummins 1006, Cummins 1007, CUNA 1008, Cutco 1012, CVS 1014, Dana 1026, Danis 1029, Davison 1042, Dedham 1060, Deere 1061, Delta 1073, Delta 1074, Delta 1081, Delta 1083, Deluxe 1084, DENSO 1088, Dethmers 1091, Detroit 1095, Deutsche 1099, Dexter 1103, Dime 1118, Dispatch 1129, Diversey 1130, Dominion 1150, Donaldson 1153, Dow 1162, Duda 1188, Duke 1189, DVK 1198, Dynamet 1200, Eastern 1209, Eastern 1210, Easthampton 1212, Eaton 1216, Edina 1227, El Paso 1239, Empire 1262, Entergy 1279, Enterprise 1281, Equifax 1288, Evening 1302, Exchange 1306, Exelon 1309, Fabri 1322, Federated 1351, Ferro 1366,

Fifth 1377, Finish 1383, First 1393, First 1395, First 1397, First 1402, First 1403, First 1405, First 1406, First 1409, First 1419, First 1420, FirstEnergy 1424, Firstmerit 1425, Florence 1441, Florida 1443, Fluor 1448, FMR 1450, Ford 1463, Ford 1464, Forest 1467, Four 1477, Fremont 1496, Fuller 1517, Furr 1520, Georgia 1568, Golden 1602, Golub 1607, Grace 1623, Graco 1624, Graham 1625, Grand 1627, Grand 1628, Guard 1680, Guardian 1681, Gulf 1689, H & R 1695, Hallmark 1707, Hannaford 1723, Hanover 1724, Hardinge 1729, Hasbro 1747, Hastings 1749, Hawkins 1757, HCA 1762, Heat 1767, Heinz 1772, Hendrick 1776, Herschend 1790, Hess 1793, Hewlett 1794, Hilton 1812, HNI 1817, Hoffmann 1823, Honda 1851, Hoops 1857, Hormel 1866, Houston 1871, Hubbell 1879, Hudson 1880, Humana 1886, Illinois 1916, Indianapolis 1932, Institution 1946, Interlock 1954, International 1963, International 1971, INTRUST 1981, Inwood 1985, ITT 1999, Jazz 2028, Jeld 2032, JOFCO 2046, Johnson 2049, Johnson 2050, Jovon 2069, JPMorgan Chase 2071, JSJ 2073, K-B 2081, Kahn 2084, Kaman 2088, Kann 2090, Kappler 2095, Keeneland 2113, Kellogg 2120, Kennametal 2125, Kerzner 2133, KeyBank 2136, Kiewit 2142, Kinney 2162, Koch 2179, Kohler 2182, Korum 2187, Kukui 2198, La Mariage 2204, La-Z-Boy 2205, Laclede 2207, Land 2217, Landmark 2218, Lebanon 2238, Lee 2241, Levi 2254, LG&E Energy 2260, Liberty 2262, Limited 2277, Lincoln 2281, Lowe's 2312, Lubrizol 2315, Lucasfilm 2316, M&T 2323, M/I 2325, Main 2342, Mamiye 2352, Manitowoc 2356, Maquoketa 2361, Marnier-Lapostolle 2381, Mars 2384, Mary 2392, Masco 2393, Mascoma 2394, MasterCard 2399, Material 2402, MBIA 2416, McCormick 2423, McDonald's 2427, MDU 2441, Menasha 2461, Merchants 2465, Merck 2466, Mercury 2468, MFA 2487, Mid 2503, MidAmerican 2504, Midcontinent 2505, Midwestone 2508, Minnesota 2530, Mississippi 2536, Modine 2544, Mohawk 2545, Monadnock 2551, Morgan 2568, Morris 2573, Motorists 2584, MTD 2595, Mutual 2607, MWH 2608, Mylan 2610, National 2628, National 2635, Naugatuck 2646, NEBCO 2653, Neenah 2656, Nestle 2662, New England 2672, New York 2683, New York 2684, Newburyport 2693, Nextier 2706, NIBCO 2707, NiSource 2715, Nordson 2723, Norfolk 2725, Northern 2738, Northern 2740, Northfield 2741, NorthWestern 2748, Northwestern 2749, Nu 2759, OceanFirst 2782, Ohio 2789, Ohio 2790, Oklahoma 2794, Oklahoma 2795, Old 2798, Olin 2801, OMNOVA 2809, Omron 2810, ONEOK 2815, Opus 2820, Orscheln 2827, Otter 2836, PACCAR 2850, PacifiCorp 2860, Papa 2876, Parker 2886, Pella 2917, People's 2928, Perforce 2937, Perrigo 2943, PETCO 2945, Pfizer 2950, PFS 2951, PG&E 2952, Pharmacy 2956, Philip 2962, Plum 2991, PNC 2997, PPG 3025, Praxair 3029, Premix 3037, Principal 3047, Pro 3051, Provident 3069, Public 3076, Putnam 3086, Quality 3096, Questar 3104, Quincy 3110, R & B 3113, Raymond 3133, Raytheon 3135, Reed 3160, Regal 3167, Regis 3172, Reily 3177, Rexnord 3198, Riverway 3226, Robinson 3235, Rochester 3237, Rockford 3241, Rolls 3254, Rood 3257, RUAN 3279, Ryder 3292, S & T 3297, S.J. 3299, Saint 3312, Savings 3343, Scottdale 3371, Scoular 3373, Scripps 3374, Seattle 3385, Selective 3399, Seneca 3406, Shatz 3424, Shaw's 3427, Simplot 3459, Sioux 3465, Sjostrom 3469, Skinner 3475, Smith 3484, SourceMedia 3506, Southern 3515, Southern 3517, Southwest 3524, Sovereign 3528, Spahn 3529, Spartan 3535, Spirit 3544, Spirol 3545, Springleaf 3554, Square 3560, St. Joe 3563, St. Louis 3567, Stanley 3580, Star 3584, State 3592, Steel 3595, Steelcase 3597, Stonecutter 3615, Subaru 3632, SunTrust 3654, Sunwest 3655, Superior 3658, Synovus 3674, Talbots 3682, Techni 3699, Tellabs 3709, Tennessee 3716, Texas 3728, Textron 3731, Thomaston 3736, Timberland 3754, Time 3757, Timken 3760, Todd 3766, Totsy 3780, Trim 3810, Twins 3827, Tyson 3832, U.S. 3836, Union 3857, Union 3858, United 3863, United 3864, United 3868, United 3879, Univar 3886, US 3902, USG 3905, Utica 3910, Valero 3915, Valley 3917, Valspar 3920, Verizon 3936, Vermeer 3937, Victorinox 3950, Vogt 3966, Warrell 3991, Washington 3994, Washington 3996, Washington 4001, WEDGE 4020, West 4034, West 4038, Western 4040, Western 4045, Westfield 4047, Weyerhaeuser 4052, Williams 4077, Winn 4087, Winnebago 4088, Wisconsin 4096, Wolf 4103, Wood 4108, Wrigley 4125, York 4145, YSI 4149

Capital campaigns

3M 3, AbbyBank 15, Aberdeen 18, Acuity 31, AEGON 45, Aflac 54, AGL 57, Alabama 71, Aladdin 73, Alexander 85, Allegheny 91, Allete 100, Ameren 128, American 134, American 141, American 157, American 165, American 170, Ameristar 176, Ameritas 178, Amgen 182, Amica 183, Andersen 194, Apex 214, ARAMARK 223, Arbeit 225, Arch 231, Ariel 237, Arizona 239, Ash 256, Autodesk 289, Avidia 298, Avista 301, Baird 317, Bangor 338, Bank 342, Bank 346, Bardes 359, Batts 374, Bay 380, Bayer 381, BB&T 385, Belden 402, Belk 403, Belk 404, Belo 406, Bemis 407, Bemis 408, Beneficial 412, Berkheimer 425, Berkshire 428, Best 442, Betts 451, Bierlein 459, Birdsong 470, Black 474, Black 475, Blair 478, Blue 493, Blue 497, Boeing 516, Bowater 543, Bridgestone 560, Bridgewater 562, Bridgeway 563, Briggs 564, Briggs 565, Brillion 569, Brotherhood 588, Brown 591, Brunswick 595, BSA 597, Butler 626, Cabot 642, Caesars 650, Campbell 668, Cape 674, Capitol 680, Cargill 691, Carpenter 700, Caterpillar 722, CentiMark 740, CH2M 758, Chaney 761, Charter 766, Charter 767, Chemed 773, Chicago 786, Chief 793, Cianbro 808, CLARCOR 832, Claremont 833, Cliffs 850, CMS 854, CNH 856, Collective 871, Collette 872, Colorado 880, Columbia 882, Comerica 889, Commerce 890, Compuware 902, Conston 920, Consumers 921, Contran 928, Convergys 933, Cooper 935, Cooper 936, Copley 938, Corning 945, Covidien 956, Cow 957, Cox 959, Crane 969, Crayola 973, Credit 977, CUNA 1008, Cutco 1012, Dana 1026, Danis 1029, DeBlois 1056, Dedham 1060, Delta 1081, Deluxe 1084, DENSO 1088, Dexter 1103, Diebold 1112, Dime 1118, Disney 1127, Dixie 1132, Dominion 1150, Donaldson 1153, Dot 1158, Dow 1162, Dreyer's 1174, DTE 1183, Duchossois 1187, Dutch 1197, East 1207, Eastern 1209, Easthampton 1212, Eastman 1213, Eaton 1216, Econoco 1222, Edina 1227, Elias 1247, Empire 1262, Entelco 1277, Enterprise 1281, Equifax 1288, Essa 1297, Evening 1302, Exelon 1309, Express 1313, F.N.B. 1318, Fabiano 1320, Fabri 1322, Federal 1348, Federated 1351, Fenton 1361, Ferro 1366, Fifth 1377, Finish 1383, First 1391, First 1395, First 1397, First 1402, First 1403, First 1405, First 1406, First 1409, First 1416, First 1419, First 1420, First 1421, FirstEnergy 1424, Firstmerit 1425, Florida 1443, Fluor 1448, FMR 1450, Ford 1463, Ford 1464, Forest 1467, Framingham 1481, Fremont 1496, Fulton 1518, Gannett 1532, General 1554, General 1557, Georgia 1567, Georgia 1568, Gibbs 1576, GKN 1585, GlaxoSmithKline 1588, Golden 1602, Golub 1607, Grace 1623, Graco 1624, Graham 1625, Grand 1628, Grange 1631, Guard 1680, Gulf 1689, H & R 1695, Hallberg 1704, Hallmark 1707, Hampden 1713, Hannaford 1723, Hardinge 1729, Harris 1736, Hasbro 1747, Hawaiian 1755, Haynie 1760, HCA 1762, Heidtman 1770, Heinz 1772, Hexcel 1795, Hilliard 1805, HNI 1817, Hofmann 1824, Home 1845, Houston 1871, Hubbard 1877, Hubbell 1879, Hudson 1880, Huhtamaki 1884, Humana 1886, Huntington 1894, Hygeia 1901, IDACORP 1907, IHC 1913, Illinois 1916, IMA 1917, Independent 1927, Institution 1946, Integrity 1948, International 1958, International 1965, International 1971, INTRUST 1981, Investors 1984, Iowa 1986, Island 1996, Jacksonville 2014, Jasper 2025, Jazz 2028, Jeld 2032, Jewett 2042, Johnson 2049, Johnson 2050, Jones 2055, Journal 2068, JSJ 2073, K-B 2081, Kahn 2084, Kaiser 2086, Kaman 2088, Kann 2090, Kansas 2094, Keeneland 2113, KeyBank 2136, Kiewit 2142, Kimberly 2150, Kingsbury 2160, Kinney 2162, Klein's 2169, Koch 2179, Kohler 2182, Korum 2187, Koss 2188, Kroger 2195, Kukui 2198, Laclede 2207, Land 2217, Landmark 2218, Landry's 2219, Larkin 2224, Laureate 2231, Lebanon 2238, Lee 2241, Liberty 2262, Liberty 2265, LifePoint 2270, Lilly 2274, Limited 2277, Lubrizol 2315, M&T 2323, M/I 2325, Machias 2332, Macy's 2333, Main 2342, Majestic 2343, Manitowoc 2356, Mary 2392, Masco 2393, Massachusetts 2397, Material 2402, McClatchy 2422, McCormick 2423, McDermott 2424, McDonald 2426, McDonald's 2427, McLaughlin 2436, McWane 2440, MDU 2441, Menasha 2461, Merchants 2465, Meredith 2471, Metal 2478, MGIC 2488, MidAmerican 2504, Millhiser-Smith 2524, Mississippi 2536, Modine 2544, Monadnock 2551, Morgan 2568, Morris 2573, Mosaic 2580, Motorists 2584, Mt. 2594, MTD 2595, Mutual 2607, National 2628, National 2634, National 2635, National 2638, Nationwide 2639, Natural 2643, Naugatuck 2645, NEBCO 2653, Nestle 2662, New York 2683, Newburyport 2693, Newfield 2695, Nextier 2706, Noland 2719, Nordson 2723, Norfolk 2725, North 2730, Northern 2740, NorthWestern 2748, Northwestern 2749, Northwestern 2750, NV 2765, NYSE 2769, O'Neal 2771, OceanFirst 2782, Ohio 2789, Ohio 2790, Old 2798, Olin 2801, Omaha 2806, Omnicare 2807, OMNOVA 2809, ONEOK 2815, Opus 2820, Orleans 2825, Otter 2836, Oxford 2847, PACCAR 2850, Pacific 2853, Pacific 2855, Park 2879, Park 2880, Parker 2886, Pella 2917, Penn 2924, People's 2928, PETCO 2945, Physicians 2970, Piedmont 2971, Piper 2983, PNC 2997, PPG 3025, Premix 3037, Price 3040, Principal 3047, Protective 3066, Providence 3068, Provident 3069, Provident 3071, Prudential 3072, Puget 3081, Pulte 3083, Questar 3104, Quincy 3110, R & B 3113, Raymond 3133, Rayonier 3134, Raytheon 3135, RECO 3148, Red 3154, Reed 3160, Regal 3166, Regal 3167, Regions 3171, Regis 3172, Reily 3177, Reynolds 3200, RG 3201, Riverway 3226, Robbins 3230, Robinson 3235, Rockford 3241, Rockwell 3247, Roundy's 3272, RPM 3278, Ryder 3292, S & T 3297, Safeco 3306, Saint 3312, Savings 3343, Schloss 3352, Schneider 3355, Scoular 3373, Scripps 3374, Sears 3384, Seattle 3386, Securian 3389, Security 3391, Selective 3399, Sensient 3408, Sequa 3410, Servco 3412, Shatz 3424, Shaw's 3427, Sherwin 3437, SI 3444, Silicon 3455, Simplot 3459, Sioux 3465, Skinner 3475, Smith 3484, Sonoco 3500, SourceMedia 3506, South 3512, South Bend 3507, Southern 3515, Southern 3516, Southern 3517, Southwest 3523, Southwest 3524, Spahn 3529, SPX 3558, Square 3560, St. Joe 3563, Standard 3575, Standard 3577, Stanley 3580, State 3592, Steel 3595, Steelcase 3597, Stiles 3607, Stock 3610, Strauss 3624, Subaru 3632, SunTrust 3654, Superior 3658, SUPERVALU 3659, Susquehanna 3661, Sweetbay 3665, Synovus 3674, Tanner 3688, TCF 3695, TECO 3701, Teichert 3704, Tennant 3714, Tennessee 3716, Texas 3725, Texas 3728, Textron 3731, Tillman 3752, Todd 3766, Totem 3779, Totsy 3780, Travelers 3802, Trim 3810, Truland 3817, Tucson 3819, Tulalip 3820, Tupperware 3821, U.S. 3835, U.S. 3836, Unaka 3848, Union 3857, United 3864, United 3870, United 3877, United 3882, Unitil 3885, Univar 3886, Universal 3891, US 3902, USG 3905, V.F. 3913, Valero 3915, Vectren 3925, Vogt 3966, Vulcan 3972, Warrell 3991, Washington 3996, Washington 4001, Webster 4018, Wenger 4033, West 4034, West 4038, Western 4040, Westfield 4047, Weyerhaeuser 4052, Whole 4066, Wiley 4072, Williams 4077, Wisconsin 4093, Wisconsin 4096, Wolf 4103, Wood 4108, Woodward 4112, York 4145, YSI 4149

Cause-related marketing

7-Eleven 5, Abercrombie 17, Abita 19, Aflac 54, Allstate 107, Ameren 128, AmeriPride 173, AmeriVision 180, AOL 209, AutoNation 292, Bally 330, Bay 380, Belk 403, Big 460, Boston 536, Campbell 669, Chrysler 801, City 830, COLHOC 870, Columbia 884, Creative 975, Cumberland 1003, DeniseLawrence.Com 1086, Denver 1090, Dharma 1105, Diamonds 1109, DIRECTV 1124, Dollar 1143, Dr 1169, Econscious 1223, Fast 1343, Ferrellgas 1365, First 1408, Frontier 1508, Garden 1534, Getty 1569, Give 1583, Green 1650, Haggen 1699, Hancock 1717, Hannaford 1723, Harris 1738, Kohl's 2181, Macy's 2333, Marathon 2365, Maritz 2376, Mary 2392, MasterCard 2399, Motley 2582, New 2668, New York 2687, Newell 2694, One

2812, Playboy 2990, Plum 2992, Price 3039, Rochester 3237, Rockland 3242, RPM 3278, Sacramento 3303, Safeway 3310, Springs 3555, Sunkist 3649, Sysco 3677, Tesoro 3723, TJX 3765, Tops 3774, Tupperware 3821, Turner 3823, V.F. 3913, Winn 4087, Yahoo! 4140, Yum! 4150

Conferences/seminars

Abbott 13, Aetna 48, Agilent 56, Alcoa 82, Alliant 104, Allstate 107, AMC 126, Ameren 129, American 143, American 158, Archer 232, Bank 340, Baxter 377, Bayer 381, Bayer 382, Bering 422, Blue 497, Boeing 516, Booz 525, Boston 540, Bound 541, Bracewell 549, Bristol 578, Cablevision 640, California 655, Capezio 675, Capitol 680, Cardinal 685, CHS 802, CIGNA 812, City 830, Clear 842, Comcast 887, Commerce 890, Connecticut 910, Contran 928, Cook 934, COPIC 937, Crowell 986, CryoLife 990, Darden 1032, Deloitte 1070, Delta 1078, Delta 1080, Doctors 1139, Dominion 1150, DP 1168, Duke 1189, Eastman 1214, EMI 1258, Entergy 1278, Ethicon 1299, Exelon 1309, Farmers 1339, Farmers' 1337, Federal 1348, First 1406, First 1422, Fisher 1433, Florida 1443, FMR 1450, Four 1477, Gannett 1532, Genentech 1549, Georgia 1567, Georgia 1568, Gilead 1582, Graphic 1634, Halliburton 1706, Heller 1773, HSBC 1876, Integra 1947, Intel 1950, International 1961, Jazz 2028, JPMorgan Chase 2071, Kaiser 2086, KPMG 2190, L'Oreal 2203, Life 2268, Lilly 2274, Macy's 2333, Major 2345, McClatchy 2422, Medtronic 2453, Merck 2466, Mississippi 2536, Mitsubishi 2539, Mitsui 2541, Monsanto 2559, Naugatuck 2646, NEC 2654, Nellie 2659, New York 2683, News 2701, Norfolk 2725, Otter 2836, Pacific 2855, Panasonic 2869, Parametric 2878, Pattillo 2896, Pearson 2911, PETCO 2945, PetSmart 2948, Pioneer 2980, PricewaterhouseCoopers 3042, QUALCOMM 3095, Rayonier 3134, Rolls 3254, sanofi-aventis 3329, Sasaki 3337, Schwab 3363, Scripps 3374, Simplot 3459, Sonoran 3501, Southwestern 3526, St. Jude 3566, St. Louis 3569, Sulphur 3637, Synopsys 3673, Tellabs 3709, Thrivent 3747, Totsy 3780, Tribune 3806, Tulalip 3820, Union 3858, United 3882, Vulcan 3970, Weyerhaeuser 4052, Wiley 4072, Winn 4087

Consulting services

Alliant 104, Aspen 260, Blue 493, Blue 497, Boeing 516, Butt 628, Capital 679, City 830, Clif 848, Daiwa 1020, Entergy 1278, Federal 1348, FMR 1450, Focus 1451, Four 1477, IMS 1924, International 1960, Padilla 2864, Panasonic 2869, Riverway 3226, Sealed 3381, Superior 3658, Tulalip 3820

Continuing support

Abbott 13, Acuity 32, Adobe 38, Advanced 40, Aetna 48, Affinity 52, Agilent 56, Air 63, AK 67, Alabama 71, Alcatel 81, Alcoa 82, Alexander 85, Alima 90, Allen 94, Allen 97, Alliant 104, Ameren 128, American 141, American 143, American 150, American 170, AMERIGROUP 171, Ameritas 178, Amgen 182, Amica 183, Amsted 188, Anheuser 202, Applied 220, Aramco 224, Arbeit 225, Arch 231, Arkema 242, Aspen 260, Assurant 267, Assurant 268, AstraZeneca 272, Autodesk 289, AutoNation 292, Avery 297, Avidia 298, Avista 301, Aviva 302, Avon 305, Azulay 311, Badger 313, Baker 323, Bank 340, Bank 342, Batts 374, Bausch 376, Baxter 377, Bayer 381, BB&T 385, Beaver 394, Belk 403, Belo 406, Bemis 407, Beneficial 411, Berkshire 428, Best 442, Bigelow 462, Biogen 465, Blair 478, Blue 490, Blue 493, Blue 496, Blue 497, Blue 501, Blue 504, Boeing 516, Bowater 543, Brady 552, Bridgestone 560, Bridgewater 562, Briggs 564, Bristol 578, Broadcom 579, Brown 591, Brunswick 595, Buist 611, Butler 626, CA 638, Cabot 642, Caesars 650, Cajun 652, California 654, California 655, Calvert 663, Cape 674, Capezio 675, Capital 679, Capitol 680, Caplin 681, Cardinal 685, Cargill 691, Carrols 704, Catalina 719, Centene 735, Central 745, Century 748, CenturyLink 751, Chelsea 772, Chicago 790, Chick 791, Chicopee 792, Chrysler 801, Cisco 818, CIT 819, Citigroup 821, Claremont 833, CME 853, CNA 855, Coach 858, Coca 862, Collective 871, Collette 872, Comcast 887, Commerce 890, Compuware 902, Conditioned 906, Connecticut 910, Consolidated 917, Consumers 921, Contran 928, Cook 934, Cooper 935, Crane 970, Cumberland 1003, Cummins 1006, Cummins 1007, CUNA 1008, CVS 1014, Cymer 1016, Dana 1026, Dayton 1047, Dean 1054, Deere 1061, Delta 1073, Delta 1083, Deluxe 1084, Deutsche 1099, Diamonds 1109, Diebold 1112, Disney 1127, Dispatch 1129, Dixie 1132, Doctors 1139, Dollar 1142, Dominion 1150, Donaldson 1153, Dow 1162, Dow 1163, DP 1168, Dreyer's 1174, DRS 1179, DTE 1183, Duke 1189, Dun 1190, Easthampton 1212, Eastman 1213, Eastman 1214, Eaton 1216, El Paso 1239, Empire 1262, Energizer 1271, Evans 1300, Evening 1302, Exelon 1309, Express 1313, Faribault 1332, Federal 1348, FedEx 1352, Fifth 1377, First 1390, First 1398, First 1399, First 1405, First 1406, First 1420, Firstmerit 1425, Fisher 1433, Flextronics 1437, Foley 1454, Food 1458, Ford 1464, Four 1477, Fox 1480, Freeport 1494, Frontier 1510, Furniture 1519, Gardner 1536, Genentech 1549, General 1552, General 1555, Genesis 1561, GenRad 1564, Georgia 1567, Georgia 1568, Giant 1571, GKN 1585, Global 1592, Goldman 1604, Golub 1607, Grand 1627, Grand 1628, Grand 1629, Graybar 1640, Great 1644, Green 1651, Gulf 1689, H & R 1695, Halliburton 1706, Hallmark 1707, Hampden 1712, Handy 1718, Hardinge 1729, Harley 1732, Harsco 1741, Hasbro 1747, Hawaiian 1755, Herrick 1788, Hershey 1791, Hickory 1797, Highmark 1799, Hilton 1812, Horizon 1863, Hormel 1866, Humana 1886, Hygeia 1901, Ideal 1908, Illinois 1916, Indianapolis 1932, ING 1938, Institution 1946, Intel 1950, Interface 1953, International 1958, International 1960, Intoximeters 1979, INTRUST 1981, Investors 1984, IPALCO 1988, Island 1996, Jacksonville 2014, Janus 2024, Jazz 2028, Jewett 2042, JM 2044, Johnson 2048, Johnson 2050, Jordan 2063, Joy 2070, JPMorgan Chase 2071, JSJ 2073, Kaiser 2086, Kaman 2088, Kearny 2108, Kennametal 2125, Kennecott 2127, Kerzner 2133, KeyBank 2136, Kimberly 2150, Kinder 2153, Klein's 2169, Koss 2188, KPMG 2190, Laclede 2207, Landmark 2218, Leibowitz 2248, Liberty 2265, Life 2268, Lilly 2274, Lincoln 2278, Little 2288, Lockheed 2292, Lubrizol 2315, Lucasfilm 2316, M&T 2323, Macy's 2333, Main 2342, Majestic 2343, Major 2345, Manitowoc 2356, Mars 2384, Marsh 2387, Mascoma 2394, MasterCard 2399, Material 2402, MBIA 2416, McClatchy 2422, McKesson 2434, MDU 2441, Medrad 2452, Medtronic 2453, Menasha 2461, Merck 2466, Metropolitan 2481, Metropolitan 2484, MGIC 2488, Miami 2491, Micron 2500, Milford 2514, Millhiser-Smith 2524, Mine 2529, Mississippi 2536, Mitsubishi 2538, Mitsubishi 2539, Mizuho 2542, Modine 2544, Monadnock 2551, MoneyGram 2558, Monsanto 2559, Moody's 2563, Moody's 2564, Morgan 2568, Morgan 2570, Mosaic 2580, Mutual 2603, Nasdaq 2617, National 2632, Nationwide 2639, Naugatuck 2645, Nellie 2659, Nestle 2662, New 2668, New England 2672, New York 2681, New York 2683, New York 2688, New York 2690, Nextier 2706, NiSource 2715, Nord 2721, Nordson 2723, Norfolk 2725, Northeast 2737, Northern 2740, Northfield 2742, Northrim 2743, Northrop 2744, Northwest 2747, Northwestern 2749, Nu 2759, NV 2765, NVIDIA 2767, O'Neal 2771, OceanFirst 2782, Ogilvy 2788, Ohio 2789, Oklahoma 2794, Old 2796, Olin 2801, Omaha 2806, OMNOVA 2809, Omron 2810, Oracle 2821, Orscheln 2827, Oshkosh 2833, Otter 2836, Oxford 2847, PACCAR 2850, Pacific 2853, Pacific 2855, PacifiCorp 2860, Pan-American 2868, Park 2879, People's 2928, Peoples 2931, PepsiCo 2935, PETCO 2945, Pfizer 2950, PG&E 2952, Philip 2962, Physicians 2970, Piedmont 2971, Pitney 2984, PNC 2997, Popular 3003, Portland 3010, PPG 3025, Premix 3037, Price 3040, Principal 3047, Private 3050, Protective 3066, Provident 3069, Provident 3070, Public 3077, Puget 3081, Putnam 3086, PVH 3088, Quad 3091, QUALCOMM 3095, Questar 3104, Quiksilver 3108, QuikTrip 3109, Rahr 3118, Rayonier 3134, RBC 3136, RealNetworks 3144, Red 3153, Red 3154, Redwoods 3158, Regions 3171, Reily 3177, ResMed 3192, Reynolds 3199, Reynolds 3200, Rich 3204, Riverway 3226, Robbins 3230, Robinson 3235, Rockville 3245, Rockwell 3247, RPM 3278, Safeco 3306, Safeguard 3307, Saint 3312, San Francisco 3326, sanofi-aventis 3329, SAP 3334, Schneider 3355, Schwab 3363, SeaWorld 3387, Security 3391, Sentry 3409, Sequa 3410, Shaughnessy 3425, Sigma 3453, Smith 3484, Smith 3485, Sonoco 3500, Sony 3502, Southern 3516, Southwest 3524, Sovereign 3528, Spahn 3529, Springleaf 3554, Sprint 3556, Square 3560, St. Jude 3566, St. Louis 3567, St. Louis 3569, StanCorp 3574, Staples 3581, Star 3584, Starbucks 3585, State 3592, Stoneham 3616, Strauss 3624, Subaru 3631, Sunkist 3649, SunTrust 3654, Sunwest 3655, Superior 3658, Tanner 3688, TCF 3695, Teichert 3704, Tektronix 3706, Tennant 3714, Tesoro 3723, Texas 3728, Textron 3731, Tiffany 3750, TJX 3765, Todd 3766, Tom's 3770, Toro 3775, Toyota 3784, Toyota 3786, Toys 3790, U.S. 3836, UncommonGoods 3849, Union 3854, Union 3856, Union 3857, United 3872, United 3882, UnitedHealth 3884, Unitil 3885, Univar 3886, Urban 3901, USG 3905, Usibelli 3906, UTC 3908, Vodafone 3965, Vogt 3966, Vulcan 3972, Walker 3982, Washington 4001, Wausau 4008, Wellmark 4026, WellPoint 4027, Wells 4028, West 4038, Western 4040, Western 4045, Whirlpool 4056, Winn 4087, Wisconsin 4096, Woodward 4112, WorkflowOne 4115, Wrigley 4125, Xerox 4136, YSI 4149, Yum! 4150

Curriculum development

3M 3, Abbott 13, Agilent 56, Albemarle 78, Alcoa 82, Alcon 83, Allstate 107, Ameren 128, American 150, American 158, American 170, Applied 220, Aspen 260, Associated 263, AT&T 273, Autodesk 289, Avery 297, Avista 301, Baxter 377, Bayer 381, BB&T 385, Belo 406, Best 442, Birmingham 472, Blue 490, Blue 495, Blue 497, Blue 504, Boeing 516, Boston 540, Bristol 578, Brown 590, Cargill 691, Cascade 713, Caterpillar 722, Cavaliers 724, CH2M 758, Chevron 780, Chrysler 801, CHS 802, Cisco 818, City 830, Cleveland 846, CNA 855, Colorado 879, Commerce 890, Compass 901, Consumers 921, Contran 928, Corning 945, Cummins 1007, Dallas 1021, Dallas 1022, Deloitte 1070, Delta 1080, Deutsche 1099, Devon 1102, Digi 1115, DIRECTV 1124, Disney 1127, Dominion 1150, Dot 1158, Dow 1162, DTE 1183, Duke 1189, Eastern 1210, Ecolab 1220, Edina 1227, El Paso 1239, EMI 1258, Energy 1272, Ernst 1293, Extendicare 1314, Farmers 1338, First 1397, First 1398, First 1419, First 1420, Florida 1443, Fluor 1448, FMR 1450, Ford 1464, Four 1477, Freeport 1494, GenCorp 1548, Genentech 1549, General 1552, Gilead 1582, GlaxoSmithKline 1588, Grand 1627, Graphic 1634, Great 1647, Guard 1680, H & R 1695, Halliburton 1706, Harley 1732, Highmark 1799, Hoffmann 1823, Honeywell 1852, Horizon 1863, Houghton 1869, HSBC 1876, Humana 1886, Intel 1950, Interface 1953, International 1968, Janus 2024, Jazz 2028, Johnson 2048, JPMorgan Chase 2071, Kemp 2123, KeyBank 2136, Kimberly 2150, Kinder 2153, Klein's 2169, KPMG 2190, Landmark 2218, Liberty 2265, Life 2268, Lilly 2274, Long 2298, LyondellBasell 2322, M&T 2323, Major 2345, Mazda 2414, McDonald's 2427, Mead 2443, Medtronic 2453, Merchants 2465, Merck 2466, Miami 2491, Micron 2500, Mississippi 2536, Mitsubishi 2538, Monsanto 2559, Motorola 2585, Motorola 2586, Nasdaq 2617, NEC 2654, New England 2670, New York 2686, New York 2688, Northwestern 2749, Ohio 2789, Old 2798, Olin 2801, ONEOK 2815, PacifiCorp 2860, Parametric 2878, Pearson 2911, Peoples 2931, Pfizer 2950, Piedmont 2971, Pitney 2984, PNC 2997, Portland 3010, PPL 3026, Principal 3047, Provident 3069, Regions 3171, RPM 3278, Safeco 3306, San Antonio 3321, Savings 3343, Scripps 3374, Sony 3502, Sovereign 3528, Spirit 3544, St. Joe 3563, St. Louis 3569, Staples 3581, State 3591, Superior 3658, Teachers 3697, Teleflex 3707, Tellabs 3709, Texas 3728, Thrivent 3747, Time 3755, Toyota 3784, Tulalip 3820, U.S. 3836, UBS 3842, Union 3856, United 3863, United 3882, US 3902, Verizon 3936, Wellmark 4026, Wells 4028,

Weyerhaeuser 4052, Whole 4066, Wiley 4072, Xerox 4136, YSI 4149

Debt reduction

Delta 1080, First 1397, Kahn 2084, Riverway 3226, Southern 3515, York 4145

Donated equipment

Activision 30, Air 63, Ameren 128, Arbitron 227, AutoNation 292, AutoZone 294, Avista 301, Bally 330, Becton 398, Berkshire 428, Blue 493, Blue 504, Boart 510, Boeing 516, Butt 628, CA 638, Cadence 646, Canon 672, Cascade 713, Cellco 733, Central 741, Chesapeake 777, City 830, CNH 856, COLHOC 870, Columbia 884, Cooper 935, Cranfill 971, Crown 987, Delta 1073, Detroit 1097, Diebold 1112, Dow 1162, Eastman 1214, El Paso 1239, Energen 1270, Entergy 1279, Flint 1439, Flowserve 1447, Gap 1533, GATX 1542, GlaxoSmithKline 1588, Green 1653, Guard 1680, Hess 1793, Hilton 1812, HSBC 1876, Insperity 1944, International 1964, JPMorgan Chase 2071, Kennecott 2127, KLA-Tencor 2165, Kohler 2182, Lexmark 2258, Lincoln 2281, Loomis 2301, Lord 2303, MasterCard 2399, Miami 2491, Milford 2514, Miller 2523, MTV 2596, New York 2688, NIKE 2710, Nordson 2723, Norfolk 2725, Northfield 2742, Northwest 2747, Otter 2836, Pacific 2853, Pacific 2855, Packaging 2861, Parametric 2878, Playboy 2990, Prudential 3072, Questar 3104, QuikTrip 3109, Raley's 3122, Raytheon 3135, Rich 3204, Schneider 3355, Seagate 3377, Simplot 3459, Spansion 3532, Sprint 3556, Standard 3576, Starbucks 3585, Teachers 3697, Toro 3775, Toyota 3786, Turner 3823, U.S. 3836, UBS 3842, Unitil 3885, Volvo 3968, WD-40 4011, Wiley 4072

Donated land

Ameren 128, Bridgestone 560, Holcim 1828, Kennecott 2127, Norfolk 2725, Pacific 2853

Donated products

3M 3, 7-Eleven 5, Abbott 13, Abita 19, Activision 30, adidas 35, Adir 36, Adobe 38, AEG 43, Aeropostale 46, AFC 50, Alaska 76, Albertsons 79, Alcon 83, Alexion 86, Allergan 99, Alpha 112, Amazon.com 122, AMC 125, American 140, American 158, American 161, Amgen 182, Anaheim 191, Andersson 196, Anheuser 202, Apache 211, AT&T 273, Athletics 276, Atlanta 278, Autodesk 289, AutoNation 292, AutoZone 294, Avis 300, AZPB 310, Baltimore 335, Bard 358, Barnes 360, Baseball 367, BASF 368, Bashas' 369, Baxter 377, Bayer 382, Beam 390, Bean 392, Becton 398, Bed 399, Ben 409, Best 442, Better 448, Big 461, Biomet 466, Birmingham 472, Blue 497, Bobcats 512, Boehringer 515, Boston 533, Boston 536, Boston 540, Brady 552, Bridgestone 560, Bristol 578, Brooklyn 584, Brother 587, Buccaneer 599, Budget 604, Build 608, Burrtec 622, Butt 628, C & S 634, CA 638, Cablevision 641, Cabot 643, California 656, Callaway 660, Campbell 669, Canon 672, Capstone 684, Cardinal 685, Carnival 696, Carolina 698, Carter's 708, Cavaliers 724, CC 728, CDW 729, Celgene 732, Cellco 733, Center 737, Cephalon 752, Charter 765, Charter 767, Chicago 781, Chicago 782, Chicago 783, Chicago 784, Chicago 790, Chick 791, CIBA 810, Cincinnati 813, Cincinnati 814, Cinemark 815, Cintas 816, Cisco 818, City 830, Cleveland 846, Clif 848, Clorox 852, Coach 858, Coca 861, Coca 862, Colgate 869, Colorado 879, Community 899, ConAgra 904, Consumers 921, ConvaTec 932, Cooper 935, Covidien 956, Cox 958, Coyotes 963, Crayola 973, CryoLife 990, CVS 1014, D.C. 1018, Dallas 1021, Dallas 1022, Dallas 1023, Dannon 1030, Dean 1054, Deckers 1059, Del 1065, Delaware 1066, Dell 1068, Delmarva 1069, Delta 1073, Delta 1074, Delta 1077, Denny's 1087, Denver 1090, Dick's 1110, Digi 1115, DIRECTV 1124, Disney 1127, Disney 1128, DJO 1134, Doctor's 1138, Dole 1141, Domino's 1151, Dot 1158, Dow 1161, Dow 1162, Dr 1169, Dreyer's 1174, DS 1182, Dunkin' 1191, EAP 1204, Eastman 1214, Eaton 1216, Electronic 1242, EMC 1253, Endo 1268, Epson 1286, Ethicon 1299, Faribault 1332, Fast 1343, Feld 1355, Fiesta 1375, Fila 1379, FileMaker 1380, First 1398, Fisher 1433, Florida 1442, Flowers 1446, Follett 1455, Food 1457, Foremost 1466, Forest 1468, Four 1476, Fuji 1514, Gaiam 1527, Gap 1533, Garden 1534, GATX 1542, Genentech 1549, General 1552, General 1554, General 1555, Genesco 1559, Genzyme 1566, Georgia 1568, Getty 1569, Giant 1571, Giant 1572, Giant 1573, Give 1583, GlaxoSmithKline 1588, GoLite 1606, Golub 1607, Google 1613, Gordon 1615, Goya 1622, Green 1653, Greif 1663, Greyhound 1664, Guard 1680, Hachette 1696, Hallmark 1707, Hannaford 1723, Harris 1736, Hartz 1744, Hasbro 1747, Haworth 1758, Heat 1767, Heinens 1771, Heinz 1772, Henry 1781, Herr 1787, Hershey 1791, Hess 1793, Hewlett 1794, Hill 1804, Hillshire 1809, Hilton 1812, Holcim 1828, Hoops 1857, Hormel 1866, Hospira 1867, Houghton 1869, Houston 1871, Hunt 1888, Hy-Vee 1900, Imperial 1922, Indianapolis 1932, InfoSource 1936, Ingles 1940, Ingram 1941, Ingredion 1942, Insperity 1944, International 1960, International 1964, International 1968, Intuit 1982, Jelly 2033, JetBlue 2041, Johnson 2048, Johnson 2049, Just 2077, Kansas 2093, Kawasaki 2102, Kellogg 2120, Kimberly 2150, King 2158, Kmart 2172, Kohl's 2181, Kohler 2182, Kroger 2195, Lafarge 2210, Lake 2212, Lancaster 2216, Lands' 2220, Lauder 2230, Law 2233, Lego 2247, Let 2253, Lexmark 2258, Life 2268, LifeScan 2271, Lilly 2274, Limited 2277, Lithia 2287, Los Angeles 2308, Louisiana 2309, Louisiana 2310, Macfarlane-Chang 2331, Major 2347, Marriott 2383, Mars 2384, Marsh 2387, Mary 2392, Masco 2393, Matson 2404, Mattel 2405, McAfee 2417, Mead 2443, MeadWestvaco 2445, Medtronic 2453, Meijer 2456, Melissa 2458, Men's 2460, Merck 2466, Metro 2479, Meyer 2485, Michael 2493, Michigan 2497, Microsoft 2501, Millennia 2516, Miller 2523, Milwaukee 2527, Milwaukee 2528, Minnesota 2530, Miracle 2535, Mohegan 2546, Mondelez 2556, Monsanto 2559, Moore 2565, Mosaic 2580, Mt. 2594, Nash 2619, Nashville 2620, National 2638, Nestle 2662, Nestle 2663, New 2668, New 2679, New Jersey 2676, New York 2684, New York 2686, New York 2687, NIBCO 2707, NIKE 2710, Nintendo 2712, Norfolk 2725, Northwest 2747, Novartis 2753, Novell 2754, NV 2765, Oakland 2772, Oklahoma 2794, Orlando 2824, Pacific 2857, Packaging 2861, Palace 2866, Panasonic 2869, Panda 2871, Panera 2873, Parametric 2878, PDB 2906, Pearson 2911, Pearson 2912, Peet's 2916, Penguin 2922, PepsiCo 2935, Perdue 2936, Performance 2938, Pfizer 2950, Philadelphia 2957, Philadelphia 2958, Philadelphia 2959, Philip 2962, Phoenix 2968, Pier 2973, Pittsburgh 2985, Pittsburgh 2986, Playboy 2990, Portland 3010, Procter 3055, Quaker 3094, QUALCOMM 3095, Quiksilver 3108, QuikTrip 3109, Raley's 3122, Reckitt 3146, Recreational 3150, Reebok 3159, Rich 3204, Richardson 3209, Roundy's 3272, Royal 3273, RPM 3278, Sacramento 3303, Saker 3314, Samsung 3320, San Antonio 3321, San Diego 3322, San Diego 3323, San Francisco 3324, San Francisco 3326, sanofi-aventis 3329, Save 3342, Schein 3348, Schnuck 3356, Scholastic 3358, Schwan 3365, Scotts 3372, Seagate 3377, Sealed 3381, Sealy 3382, Sears 3384, Seattle 3386, Seminole 3404, Service 3413, ServiceMaster 3414, Sharp 3422, Shaw 3426, Shaw's 3427, Simplot 3459, SmartWool 3479, Smucker 3488, Sonic 3498, Sony 3503, Southwest 3522, Southwest 3524, Specialty 3538, Sporting 3546, Sports 3549, Sprint 3556, Spurs 3557, St. Louis 3567, St. Louis 3568, StanCorp 3574, Staples 3581, Starbucks 3585, Steelcase 3597, Stonyfield 3617, Stop 3618, Sunoco 3650, Super 3656, SUPERVALU 3659, Sweetbay 3665, Symantec 3669, Syniverse 3672, Sysco 3677, Talbots 3682, Tampa 3686, Target 3691, TeleTech 3708, Tennessee 3716, Texas 3729, Tiffany 3750, Tim 3753, Timberland 3754, Time 3755, Tom's 3770, Tops 3774, Toro 3775, Trail 3793, Travel 3801, True 3815, Tupperware 3821, Turner 3823, Tyson 3832, U-Haul 3833, U.S. 3836, U.S. 3838, United 3876, United 3880, United 3882, Unitil 3885, Universal 3889, Universal 3893, Wakefern 3979, Wal-Mart 3980, Walgreen 3981, Washington 3998, Washington 4000, Watson 4007, Wawa 4009, WD-40 4011, Wegmans 4021, Western 4042, White 4062, Whole 4066, Wiley 4072, Worthington 4124, Yahoo! 4140, Yamaha 4141, Yum! 4150, Zappos.com 4153, Zimmer 4157, Zotos 4159

Emergency funds

Aeropostale 46, Ag 55, AGL 57, Alcoa 82, Alliant 104, Allstate 107, Altria 120, Ameren 128, Ameren 129, American 143, American 156, Ameritec 179, Andersen 194, Apache 211, Arkema 242, Aspen 260, Autodesk 289, Avista 301, Bank 342, BB&T 385, Belk 403, Beneficial 412, Bloomberg 486, Boart 510, Boeing 516, BP 547, Bridgestone 560, Bridgeway 563, Capitol 680, Cascade 713, CenterPoint 738, Chrysler 801, City 830, CME 853, Coca 862, Commerce 890, ConocoPhillips 913, Contran 928, Cooper 935, Cox 959, Cummins 1007, Dana 1026, Deere 1061, Deluxe 1084, Dexter 1103, Diebold 1112, Dixie 1132, Dolan 1140, Dollar 1143, Domino's 1151, Dow 1161, eBay 1217, Ecolab 1220, Edina 1227, Entergy 1279, Enterprise 1281, ESCO 1296, Farmers 1338, Finish 1383, First 1397, Fisher 1433, Flextronics 1437, Florida 1443, Food 1458, Ford 1464, Four 1477, General 1555, Genesis 1561, GenRad 1564, Georgia 1567, Global 1592, Guard 1680, Guardian 1683, GuideOne 1687, Gulf 1689, H & R 1695, Harbert 1726, HCA 1762, Health 1765, Heinz 1772, Hess 1793, Hitachi 1816, Home 1842, Iberdrola 1904, Independence 1925, Ingersoll 1939, Intel 1950, International 1968, International 1971, Jack 2007, Johnson 2048, Johnson 2050, Kansas 2094, Kellogg 2120, KPMG 2190, Landmark 2218, Lincoln 2282, Lockheed 2292, M&T 2323, M.D.C. 2324, Macy's 2333, Marsh 2385, McDonald's 2427, Midcontinent 2505, Mohawk 2545, Morgan 2568, Mutual 2607, MWH 2608, National 2634, Nationwide 2639, New York 2690, Nord 2721, Nordson 2723, Northwestern 2749, OceanFirst 2782, Office 2785, OfficeMax 2786, Pacific 2853, PacifiCorp 2860, Penn 2923, Penney 2925, PETCO 2945, PetSmart 2948, Piedmont 2971, Pitney 2984, Polaris 2999, PPG 3025, Pro 3052, Prudential 3072, PVH 3088, Questar 3104, Rainforest 3120, Raytheon 3135, Riverway 3226, Rock 3238, Ruby 3281, Ryder 3292, Saint 3312, Schneider 3355, Scripps 3374, Sensient 3408, ServiceMaster 3414, Shaklee 3418, Sherwin 3437, Simplot 3459, Sodexho 3497, Southern 3514, Southern 3516, Southern 3520, Southern 3521, Southwest 3524, Sovereign 3528, Square 3560, Starbucks 3585, State 3592, Sullivan 3634, Superior 3658, Tiffany 3750, Totsy 3780, United 3863, United 3869, UnitedHealth 3884, Univar 3886, Volkswagen 3967, Wal-Mart 3980, Washington 3995, Weather 4013, Webster 4017, WellPoint 4027, West 4038, Weyerhaeuser 4052, Wiley 4072, Williams-Sonoma 4079, Woodward 4112, Xerox 4136, Yates 4142, YSI 4149

Employee matching gifts

3M 3, Abbott 13, ACE 24, ACF 26, Acumen 33, Advanced 40, AEGIS 44, AEGON 45, AES 47, Aetna 48, Agilent 56, Air 63, AK 67, Alaska 74, Albemarle 78, Alcoa 82, Alexander 85, Allegis 92, Alliant 104, Allstate 107, Allyis 109, Altria 120, Ameren 128, American 137, American 141, American 143, American 145, American 147, American 156, American 159, American 161, American 168, AMERIGROUP 171, Ameriprise 174, Amerisure 177, Amgen 182, Amica 183, Amsted 188, Anadarko 190, Andersson 196, Anheuser 202, Aon 210, Apache 211, Apple 217, AptarGroup 221, ARAMARK 223, Arch 230, Archer 233, Arizona 239, Arkema 242, Armstrong 246, Ascena 255, Ash 256, Ashland 258, Assurant 266, Assurant 267, Assurant 268, AT&T 273, Autodesk 289, Autoliv 290, Automatic 291, AutoNation 292, AutoZone 294, Avery 297, Avista 301, Aviva 302, Avon 305, AXA 307, Badger 313, Baird 317, Baker 323, Baker 324, Ball 328, Bank 340, Bank 344, Bard 358, Barnes 362, Baxter 377, Beam 390, Bechtel 395, Beckman 397, Becton 398, Bemis 407,

Ben 409, Berry 437, Biogen 465, Bloomberg 486, Boeing 516, Bon 521, BorgWarner 528, Bowater 543, BP 547, Bridgestone 560, Bristol 578, Bromelkamp 582, Brown 592, Brunswick 595, Bunge 612, Burlington 618, Burnett 619, Butler 626, C.M. 637, CA 638, Cadence 646, California 655, Callaway 660, Calpine 661, Campbell 669, Cannon 671, Capital 677, Capital 679, Capitol 680, Cardinal 685, CareFirst 687, Cargill 691, CarMax 694, Cascade 713, Castle 716, Caterpillar 722, CDW 729, Celanese 730, CFS 756, CH 757, Charter 767, Chevron 780, Chicago 788, Choice 798, Chrysler 801, Chubb 804, CIBA 809, CIGNA 812, Cisco 818, Clayton 841, Cliffs 850, Clorox 852, CME 853, CNA 855, Coach 858, Coca 862, Colgate 869, Colonial 874, Colonial 875, Community 900, ConAgra 904, ConocoPhillips 913, Consolidated 916, Consumers 921, Continental 926, Contran 928, Convergys 933, Cooper 935, Cooper 936, Copley 938, Corning 945, Covidien 956, Crane 970, Cranston 972, Crayola 973, Cummins 1007, CUNA 1008, Daiwa 1020, Dana 1026, Dannon 1030, Darden 1032, Davey 1035, Deacon 1050, Deckers 1059, Deere 1061, Dell 1068, Deloitte 1070, Delta 1073, Delta 1074, Deluxe 1084, Deutsche 1099, DFS 1104, Diageo 1107, DIRECTV 1124, Discover 1125, Discovery 1126, Disney 1127, Diversey 1130, Dominion 1150, Donaldson 1153, Dot 1158, Dow 1161, Dow 1162, DTE 1183, Duchossois 1187, Duke 1189, Dun 1190, Eastern 1209, Eaton 1216, Ecolab 1220, Edelman 1224, Edison 1228, El Paso 1239, Electronic 1242, Emerson 1257, Encana 1266, Endo 1268, Endres 1269, Energen 1270, Energizer 1271, Energy 1272, Energy 1273, Entergy 1279, Entergy 1280, EOG 1282, Equifax 1288, Ernst 1293, Exelon 1309, Expedia 1311, Express 1313, Exxon 1315, Factory 1323, Federal 1348, Federal 1349, Fieldstone 1374, Fifth 1376, Finance 1381, Fireman's 1385, First 1398, First 1400, First 1406, First 1409, First 1420, First 1421, FirstEnergy 1424, Fisher 1433, Florida 1443, Fluor 1448, FMC 1449, FMR 1450, Follett 1455, Ford 1464, Fortis 1473, Franklin 1485, Franklin 1487, Freeport 1494, Fremont 1497, Fuller 1517, Gallo 1529, Gannett 1532, Gap 1533, GATX 1542, GenCorp 1548, Genentech 1549, General 1552, General 1554, General 1555, General 1558, Genesco 1559, Genworth 1565, Georgia 1567, Getty 1569, Gilbane 1581, GKN 1585, GlaxoSmithKline 1588, Goldman 1603, Golub 1607, Google 1613, Government 1621, Grace 1623, Graco 1624, Grainger 1626, Grand 1627, Grand 1629, Grange 1631, Graybar 1640, Great 1647, Green 1653, Greif 1663, Grinnell 1668, GTECH 1677, Guardian 1683, Gulf 1689, H & R 1695, Hachette 1696, Hall 1703, Halliburton 1706, Hallmark 1707, Harley 1732, Harris 1736, Harsco 1741, Hartford 1743, Hasbro 1747, Hawaiian 1755, HCA 1762, HCR 1763, Heinz 1772, Heller 1773, Hewlett 1794, Hickory 1797, Highmark 1799, Hillshire 1809, Hobart 1818, Hofmann 1824, Hogan 1825, Holcim 1828, Holland 1835, Honda 1851, Honeywell 1852, Horizon 1861, Horizon 1863, Hormel 1866, Hospira 1867, HSBC 1876, Hubbell 1879, Huhtamaki 1884, Humana 1886, Huntington 1894, IAC 1903, IDACORP 1907, IDT 1910, IKON 1914, Illinois 1916, IMS 1924, ING 1938, Ingersoll 1939, Ingram 1941, Ingredion 1942, Intel 1950, Intelius 1951, Intermec 1955, Intermountain 1956, International 1960, International 1962, International 1968, International 1971, Intoximeters 1979, Intuit 1982, Island 1996, Jackson 2009, Janus 2024, Jefferies 2030, Johnson 2048, Johnson 2049, Johnson 2050, Jones 2061, Jostens 2067, JPMorgan Chase 2071, Juniper 2075, Kaiser 2086, Kansas 2094, Kawasaki 2102, KBR 2106, Kellogg 2120, Kennecott 2127, KeyBank 2136, Kimberly 2150, Kinder 2153, Kingsbury 2160, Kirkland 2164, KLA-Tencor 2165, Koch 2179, KPMG 2190, Laclede 2207, Lam 2214, Land 2217, Lands' 2220, Law 2233, Lego 2247, LG&E Energy 2260, Liberty 2265, Lilly 2274, Lincoln 2281, Lockheed 2292, Loews 2296, Loomis 2301, Louisiana 2309, Louisiana 2310, Lubrizol 2315, M&T 2323, Macy's 2333, MAG 2337, Majestic 2343, Mal 2349, Marathon 2365, Marsh 2385, Masco 2393, Massachusetts 2397, MasterCard 2399, Matson 2404, Mattel 2405, MBIA 2416, McAfee 2417, McClatchy 2422, McCormick 2423, McGraw 2429, McKee 2432, McKesson 2434, McNally 2437, MDU 2441, MeadWestvaco 2445, MedImmune 2450, Medrad 2452, Medtronic 2453, Menasha 2461, Mentor 2462, Mercedes 2463, Merck 2466, Meredith 2471, Meritor 2473, Merk 2467, Metropolitan 2481, MGIC 2488, Miami 2491, Michael 2493, Microchip 2499, Micron 2500, Microsoft 2501, MidAmerican 2504, Midcontinent 2505, Miller 2523, Mississippi 2536, Mitsubishi 2538, Mitsubishi 2539, Mitsui 2541, Mizuho 2542, Mohawk 2545, Mondelez 2556, MoneyGram 2558, Monsanto 2559, Monumental 2561, Moody's 2563, Moore 2565, Morgan 2568, Morgan 2570, Morris 2574, Motorola 2585, Mutual 2607, National 2629, National 2633, Nationwide 2639, NCR 2650, Nektar 2658, Nellie 2659, Nelnet 2660, New 2668, New York 2688, Newburyport 2693, Newsweek 2703, NIKE 2710, Nintendo 2712, Nordson 2723, Norfolk 2725, Northeast 2737, Northern 2740, Northfield 2742, Northrop 2744, NorthWestern 2748, Northwestern 2749, Novartis 2752, NRG 2756, NV 2765, NVIDIA 2767, NYK 2768, NYSE 2769, Occidental 2780, OceanFirst 2782, Ohio 2790, Oklahoma 2794, Olin 2801, OMNOVA 2809, Omron 2810, OneBeacon 2813, ONEOK 2815, OppenheimerFunds 2818, Oracle 2821, Orange 2822, Osram 2834, Otter 2836, Outokumpu 2839, Owens 2842, Owens 2844, Oxford 2847, PACCAR 2850, Pacific 2853, Pacific 2855, PacifiCorp 2860, Panera 2873, Parker 2886, Pattillo 2896, Peabody 2907, Peet's 2916, Pella 2917, Penguin 2922, Pentair 2926, Peoples 2931, PepsiCo 2935, PerkinElmer 2939, Pfizer 2950, PG&E 2952, Philadelphia 2960, Phillips 2965, Piedmont 2971, Pieper 2972, Pioneer 2980, Pioneer 2981, Piper 2983, Pitney 2984, Playboy 2990, Plum 2991, PMI 2995, PNC 2997, Porter 3006, Potomac 3018, PPG 3025, PPL 3026, Praxair 3029, Preformed 3032, Price 3040, PricewaterhouseCoopers 3042, Prince 3046, Principal 3047, Progressive 3057, ProLogis 3060, Protective 3066, Prudential 3072, Public 3076, Public 3077, Publix 3079, Puget 3081, Quad 3091, Quaker 3093, QUALCOMM 3095, Quanex 3100, Quest 3103, Questar 3104, Quidel 3107, QuikTrip 3109, Raley's 3122, Raytheon 3135, RBC 3136, RBS 3137, Reader's 3141, RealNetworks 3144, Reckitt 3146, Red 3154, Redwoods 3158, Reebok 3159, Reed 3160, Regions 3171, Reid 3173, Rexam 3197, Rexnord 3198, Reynolds 3200, Ricoh 3210, Riviana 3227, Robbins 3230, Robinson 3235, Rockwell 3246, Rockwell 3247, Royal 3273, RPM 3278, Rudolph 3283, Russell 3289, Ryder 3292, Safeco 3306, SAIC 3311, Saint 3312, salesforce.com 3318, sanofi-aventis 3329, SAP 3334, Schwab 3363, Schwan 3365, Scripps 3374, Seagate 3377, Securian 3389, Security 3391, Select 3398, Selective 3399, Sempra 3405, Sentry 3409, Servco 3412, Shell 3430, Shelter 3431, Sherwin 3437, Sikorsky 3454, SLM 3478, SMBC 3480, Smith 3484, Sonoco 3500, Sony 3504, Southern 3521, Southwest 3524, Sovereign 3528, Spectra 3540, Sprint 3556, SPX 3558, Square 3560, St. Jude 3566, StanCorp 3574, Stanley 3579, Starbucks 3585, State 3591, State 3592, Steelcase 3597, Strauss 3624, Subaru 3631, Subaru 3632, Sun 3643, Sunkist 3649, SunTrust 3654, Superior 3657, SUPERVALU 3659, Symantec 3669, Synopsys 3673, TCF 3695, TD 3696, Teachers 3697, Teichert 3704, Tektronix 3706, Teleflex 3707, Tellabs 3709, Tennant 3714, Teradyne 3718, Tesoro 3723, Texas 3728, Textron 3731, Thermo 3733, Thompson 3739, Thrivent 3747, Tiffany 3750, Time 3757, Toll 3769, Tomkins 3771, Toro 3775, Total 3778, Toyota 3786, Toys 3790, Trane 3794, Travelers 3802, Tupperware 3821, Turner 3823, U.S. 3835, U.S. 3841, UBS 3842, Unaka 3848, Unilever 3853, Union 3857, United 3863, United 3867, United 3872, United 3876, United 3877, United 3882, Universal 3895, Unum 3898, USG 3905, Usibelli 3906, UTC 3908, Utica 3910, V.F. 3913, Valspar 3920, Vectren 3925, Verizon 3936, Vernier 3941, Visa 3960, Vodafone 3965, Vulcan 3972, Wal-Mart 3980, Washington 3999, Waters 4003, Watson 4007, Wausau 4008, Wawa 4009, WD-40 4011, Weather 4013, Welch 4025, Wellmark 4026, WellPoint 4027, Wells 4028, West 4038, Westar 4039, Western 4040, Western 4042, Western 4045, Weyerhaeuser 4052, Whirlpool 4056, Wiley 4072, Winn 4087, Winston 4089, Wisconsin 4093, Wisconsin 4096, Wolverine 4106, Wrigley 4125, Wyndham 4132, Xcel 4135, Xerox 4136, Xylem 4139, YSI 4149, Yum! 4150, Zimmer 4157

Employee volunteer services

3M 3, 7-Eleven 5, Abbott 13, Abercrombie 17, Accenture 22, ACE 24, ACI 27, Acumen 33, Adams 34, adidas 35, Advance 39, Advanced 40, Advent 41, AECOM 42, AEGON 45, Aetna 48, Aflac 54, Ag 55, Agilent 56, AGL 57, Air 63, Airgas 65, Alabama 71, Alaska 74, Alaska 75, Albemarle 78, Albertsons 79, Alcatel 81, Alcoa 82, Alexander 85, Allen 94, Allen 95, Allergan 99, Alliant 104, Allianz 105, Allstate 107, Allyis 109, Alpha 112, Altria 120, Alyeska 121, Amazon.com 122, AMC 125, Ameren 128, Ameren 129, American 137, American 140, American 143, American 144, American 145, American 147, American 149, American 150, American 153, American 161, American 167, AmeriPride 173, Ameriprise 174, AmerisourceBergen 175, Amerisure 177, Amgen 182, Amica 183, AMN Healthcare 184, Amway 189, Anadarko 190, Andersson 196, Andrews 198, Angels 200, Anheuser 202, AOL 209, Aon 210, Apache 211, Apogee 215, Applied 219, Aramco 224, Arbella 226, Arbitron 227, Arcelormittal 229, Arch 230, Archer 232, Archer 233, Arent 235, Arizona 239, Armstrong 246, Arnall 247, Arrow 249, Assurant 266, Assurant 267, Assurant 268, AT&T 273, AT&T 274, Autodesk 289, AutoNation 292, AutoZone 294, Avery 297, Avista 301, Aviva 302, Avnet 304, AZPB 310, Baird 317, Baker 321, Baker 325, Balch 327, Baltimore 333, Baltimore 335, Bangor 338, Bank 340, Bank 342, Bank 344, Bank 345, Bank 346, Bank 349, Barnes 360, Barnes 362, Barrasso 363, BASF 368, Baxter 377, Bay 380, Bayer 381, Beam 390, Bechtel 395, Beckman 397, Becton 398, Belk 403, Berkshire 428, Berry 434, Berry 437, Berry 438, Better 449, BHP 455, Big 460, Big 461, Bigelow 462, Biogen 465, Black 474, Blockbuster 483, Bloomberg 486, Bloomingdale's 488, Blue 491, Blue 497, Blue 498, Blue 500, Blue 501, Blue 502, BMC 508, Boehringer 515, Boeing 516, Bon 521, Booz 525, BorgWarner 528, Boston 535, Boston 540, Bowater 543, Boyd 546, BP 547, Bracewell 549, Bressler 557, Bricker 559, Bridgestone 560, Briggs 565, Brightpoint 567, Brinker 572, Bristol 578, Broadcom 579, Bromelkamp 582, Brother 587, Brown 590, Brunswick 595, Burger 613, Burr 621, Burrtec 622, Butler 626, Butler 627, C & S 634, CA 638, Cablevision 641, Cadence 646, Caesars 650, California 655, Callaway 660, Calpine 661, Campbell 668, Campbell 669, Canon 672, Capital 677, Capital 679, Capitol 680, Caplin 681, Capstone 684, Cardinal 685, CareFirst 687, CareFusion 688, Cargill 691, Carlson 693, CarMax 694, Carmody 695, Carnival 696, Carpenter 700, Carrington Coleman 701, Carrols 704, Carter's 708, Cascade 713, Caterpillar 722, CDW 729, CenterPoint 738, CenterPoint 739, Central 741, CenturyLink 751, Cephalon 752, Ceridian 753, CH2M 758, Charter 765, Charter 767, Chemical 774, Chemtura 775, Chesapeake 777, Chevron 780, Chick 791, Choice 798, Chrysler 801, CHS 802, Chubb 804, Churchill 807, CIGNA 812, Cintas 816, Circle 817, Cisco 818, CIT 819, Citigroup 821, Citizens 824, City 830, Clark 836, Clayton 841, Clorox 852, CMS 854, CNA 855, CNO 857, Coach 858, Coca 861, Coca 862, Coca 863, Cole 868, Collette 872, Colonial 874, Colonial 876, Columbia 883, Columbia 884, Comcast 887, Comerica 889, Commerce 890, Commercial 893, Commonwealth 895, Compuware 902, Con 903, Connecticut 911, Connecticut 912, ConocoPhillips 913, Consolidated 916, Consumers 921, ConvaTec 932, Cooper 935, COPIC 937, Costco 948, Country 951, County 952, Covidien 956, Cranfill 971, Crayola 973, Creative 975, Credit 980, Crowell 986, CSX 997, Cubist 999, Cummins 1007, CUNA 1008, CVS 1014, Cymer 1016, D.C. 1018, Dannon 1030, Darden 1032, Davis 1041, Dayton 1047, Dean 1054, Deckers 1059, Deere 1061, Del 1065, Delaware 1066, Dell 1068, Delmarva 1069, Deloitte 1070, Delphi 1071, Delta 1073, Delta 1076, Deluxe 1084, Denny's 1087, DENSO 1088, Deutsche 1099, Devon 1102, DHL 1106, Diamonds 1109, Diebold 1112, DineEquity

1120, Discover 1125, Discovery 1126, Disney 1127, Disney 1128, Diversey 1130, DJO 1134, Dollar 1144, Dollar 1145, Dominion 1150, Donnelley 1155, Dow 1160, Dow 1163, Dr 1169, Dreyer's 1174, Driscoll 1176, DTE 1183, du Pont 1184, Duke 1189, Dunkin' 1191, Eastman 1213, Eaton 1216, eBay 1217, Edelman 1224, Edison 1228, El Paso 1239, Electronic 1242, EMC 1253, EMCOR 1255, Emerson 1257, Enbridge 1265, Endo 1268, Energen 1270, Entelco 1277, Entergy 1279, Entergy 1280, EOG 1282, EQT 1287, Esurance 1298, Ethicon 1299, Exelon 1309, Expedia 1311, Exxon 1315, Factory 1323, Faegre 1324, Farmers 1338, Fast 1343, Federal 1348, Federal 1349, FedEx 1352, Ferro 1366, Fifth 1377, First 1391, First 1396, First 1398, First 1400, First 1405, First 1406, First 1409, First 1415, First 1416, First 1419, FirstEnergy 1424, Fisher 1433, Flextronics 1437, Flint 1439, Florida 1442, Florida 1443, Flowserve 1447, Fluor 1448, FMC 1449, FMR 1450, Ford 1464, Fortis 1473, Fortune 1474, Fox 1480, Franklin 1487, Free 1492, Freeport 1494, Freescale 1495, Fremont 1497, Fuller 1517, Fulton 1518, Gallo 1529, GameStop 1530, Gap 1533, GATX 1542, GenCorp 1548, Genentech 1549, General 1551, General 1552, General 1554, General 1555, General 1556, Genesco 1559, Genworth 1565, Georgia 1568, Getty 1569, Giant 1571, Gibbons 1574, Gilbane 1581, Give 1583, GlaxoSmithKline 1588, Gleaner 1590, Global 1592, Golden 1602, GoLite 1606, Google 1613, Grace 1623, Graco 1624, Grand 1627, Grange 1631, Granite 1632, Great 1646, Great 1647, Green 1653, Greenberg 1654, Greyhound 1664, Grove 1672, GTECH 1677, Guardian 1683, Gulf 1689, Gulfstream 1690, H & R 1695, Haggen 1699, Halliburton 1706, Hallmark 1707, Hancock 1717, Hanesbrands 1720, Hanover 1724, Hanson 1725, Hargray 1730, Harley 1732, Harleysville 1733, Harris 1736, Harris 1739, Hartford 1742, Hartford 1743, Hasbro 1747, Haworth 1758, HCA 1762, HCR 1763, Heat 1767, Heinz 1772, Helmerich 1774, Heritage 1785, Herschend 1790, Hershey 1791, Hertz 1792, Hess 1793, Hewlett 1794, Hickory 1797, Highmark 1799, Hill 1803, Hillshire 1809, Hilton 1812, Hines 1813, Hitachi 1816, Hodgson 1820, Hogan 1825, Holcim 1828, Holland 1835, Holme 1837, Home 1842, Home 1844, Honda 1851, Honeywell 1852, Horizon 1861, Horizon 1863, Hormel 1866, HSBC 1876, Humana 1886, Hunt 1888, Hunt 1889, Huntington 1894, Huntsman 1895, Hy-Vee 1900, IDACORP 1907, Imation 1919, IMC 1920, Imperial 1922, IMS 1924, ING 1938, Ingles 1940, Ingram 1941, Ingredion 1942, Insperity 1944, Intel 1950, Intelius 1951, Intermec 1955, Intermountain 1956, International 1960, International 1962, International 1964, International 1968, International 1971, Interpublic 1974, Intuit 1982, Invesco 1983, IPALCO 1988, Irby 1990, ITT 1999, iVillage 2002, Jabil 2006, Jackson 2009, Jamba 2020, James 2021, Janssen 2023, JetBlue 2041, JM 2044, Johns 2047, Johnson 2049, Johnson 2050, Jones 2057, Jones 2059, Jones 2061, JPMorgan Chase 2071, Juniper 2075, Just 2077, Kaiser 2086, Kansas 2092, Kansas 2094, KB 2105, KBR 2106, Kellogg 2120, Kennametal 2125, Kent 2129, KeyBank 2136, Kimberly 2150, Kinetic 2156, King 2158, KLA-Tencor 2165, Kmart 2172, Knowledge 2177, Koch 2179, Koch 2180, Kohl's 2181, Kroger 2195, Krueger 2196, Lam 2214, Land 2217, Lands' 2220, Lauder 2230, Law 2233, Lee 2241, Lego 2247, Lexmark 2258, LG&E Energy 2260, Liberty 2265, Life 2268, LifeScan 2271, Lilly 2274, Limited 2277, Lincoln 2281, Lincoln 2282, Lithia 2287, Lockheed 2292, Loews 2296, Longaberger 2299, Loomis 2301, Louisiana 2309, Louisiana 2310, Lowe's 2312, LSI 2314, Lubrizol 2315, LyondellBasell 2322, M&T 2323, Macy's 2333, Majestic 2343, Major 2347, Marathon 2362, Marena 2372, Maritz 2376, Mars 2384, Marsh 2385, Marsh 2387, Martin 2391, Masco 2393, Massachusetts 2397, MasterCard 2399, Matson 2404, Mattel 2405, MBIA 2416, McAfee 2417, McClatchy 2422, McCormick 2423, McDermott 2424, McDonald's 2427, McGraw 2429, McKesson 2434, MDU 2441, Mead 2443, MeadWestvaco 2445, Mechanics 2446, MedImmune 2450, Medrad 2452, Medtronic 2453, Men's 2460, Menasha 2461, Merck 2466, Mercury 2469, Meredith 2471, Meritor 2473, Merk 2467, Metro 2479, Metropolitan 2481, Meyer 2485, MGM 2489, Miami 2491, Michael 2493, Michaels 2494, Michelin 2495, Micron 2500, Microsoft 2501, MidAmerican 2504, Miller 2517, Miller 2523, Minto 2533, Mitsubishi 2538, Mitsubishi 2539, Mitsui 2541, Mizuho 2542, Modine 2544, Mohegan 2546, Mondelez 2556, Monster 2560, Moody's 2563, Morgan 2570, Morris 2574, Morton 2579, Mosaic 2580, Motley 2582, Motorola 2585, Motorola 2586, MSC 2593, Mt. 2594, Murphy 2600, Mutual 2607, Nash 2619, National 2623, National 2630, National 2633, National 2638, Nationwide 2639, NBC 2649, NCR 2650, Nestle 2663, Neville 2667, New 2668, New England 2672, New York 2688, Newell 2694, Newmont 2698, Newsweek 2703, Nexion 2705, NIBCO 2707, NII 2709, NIKE 2710, Nintendo 2712, Nordson 2723, Nordstrom 2724, Northern 2740, Northfield 2742, Northrim 2743, Northrop 2744, Northwest 2747, NorthWestern 2748, Northwestern 2749, Novell 2754, Novetta 2755, NRG 2756, Nucor 2760, NV 2765, NVIDIA 2767, NYK 2768, NYSE 2769, Ogilvy 2788, Oklahoma 2794, Old 2798, Omnicom 2808, OMNOVA 2809, ONEOK 2815, OppenheimerFunds 2818, Oracle 2821, Orange 2822, Orlando 2824, Ortec 2828, Osram 2834, Otis 2835, Otter 2836, Outokumpu 2839, Owens 2841, Pacific 2853, PacifiCorp 2860, Packaging 2861, Padilla 2864, Pan-American 2868, Panasonic 2869, Panda 2871, Parametric 2878, Parsons 2887, Parsons 2888, Pathmark 2894, PDB 2906, Peabody 2907, Pearson 2911, Peet's 2916, Pella 2917, Penguin 2922, Penney 2925, People's 2928, Peoples 2931, PepsiCo 2935, Performance 2938, Perkins 2940, Pfizer 2950, Philadelphia 2960, Philip 2962, Phillips 2965, Piedmont 2971, Pier 2973, Pioneer 2980, Pioneer 2981, Piper 2983, Pitney 2984, Playboy 2990, Plum 2991, Portland 3010, Potomac 3018, PPG 3025, PPL 3026, Pratt 3028, Praxair 3029, Praxis 3030, Premera 3034, Price 3039, Price 3040, PricewaterhouseCoopers 3042, Procter 3055, Protective 3066, Prudential 3072, Public 3075, Public 3076, Public 3077, Puget 3081, Pulte 3083, QUALCOMM 3095, Quest 3103, Questar 3104, Quicksilver 3106, Quidel 3107, QuikTrip 3109, Rackspace 3117, Raley's 3122, Ralph 3123, Raytheon 3135, RBC 3136, RBS 3137, Reader's 3141, RealNetworks 3144, Reckitt 3146, Recreational 3150, Redwoods 3158, Reebok 3159, Reed 3161, Reell 3164, Regions 3171, Republic 3188, Rich 3204, Ricoh 3210, Robinson 3235, Roche 3236, Rock 3239, Rockland 3242, Rockville 3245, Rogers 3253, Rolls 3254, Ross 3265, Ross 3267, Royal 3273, RPM 3278, Rudolph 3283, Russell 3289, Ryder 3292, Saco 3302, Sacramento 3303, Safeco 3306, Safeway 3310, SAIC 3311, Salt 3319, Samsung 3320, Sandusky 3328, sanofi-aventis 3329, SANYO 3333, SAP 3334, SAS 3336, Sasol 3338, SCANA 3346, Schein 3348, Schneider 3355, Schwab 3363, Schwan 3365, Scotts 3372, Scripps 3374, Seagate 3377, Sealed 3381, Sealy 3382, Sears 3384, Seattle 3386, Securian 3389, Selective 3399, Seminole 3404, Sempra 3405, ServiceMaster 3414, Seventh 3416, Sharp 3422, Shaw's 3427, Shell 3430, Shenandoah 3433, ShopKo 3440, Siemens 3448, Sigma 3453, Sikorsky 3454, Silicon 3455, Singlebrook 3464, SkyWest 3476, SLM 3478, SmartWool 3479, Smith 3484, Smucker 3488, Sodexho 3497, Sonic 3498, Sonoco 3500, Sony 3503, Sony 3504, Southern 3514, Southern 3516, Southwest 3522, Southwest 3524, Southwire 3527, Sovereign 3528, Spansion 3532, Spectra 3540, Sprint 3556, SRA 3562, St. Louis 3569, Stahl 3573, StanCorp 3574, Standard 3576, Staples 3581, Starbucks 3585, Starwood 3589, State 3591, State 3592, Station 3593, Steelcase 3597, Stiles 3607, Stone 3614, Strauss 3624, SUMCO 3638, Sun 3643, Sun 3644, Superior 3657, SUPERVALU 3659, Sweetbay 3665, Swinerton 3668, Symantec 3669, Syniverse 3672, Sysco 3677, Tampa 3686, Target 3691, TCF 3695, TD 3696, TECO 3701, TeleTech 3708, Tenet 3713, Tennant 3714, Tenneco 3715, Tennessee 3716, Teradyne 3718, Terex 3719, Tesoro 3723, Textron 3731, Thermo 3733, Thomson 3742, Thrivent 3747, Tiffany 3750, Timberland 3754, Time 3755, Time 3756, Time 3757, TJX 3765, Toll 3769, Tom's 3770, Toro 3775, Toshiba 3776, Totem 3779, Toyota 3785, Toyota 3786, Toyota 3789, Trail 3793, Travel 3801, Travelers 3802, Tropicana 3813, Trustmark 3818, Tucson 3819, Tupperware 3821, Turner 3823, Tyco 3829, Tyson 3832, U.S. 3836, U.S. 3838, U.S. 3841, UBS 3842, UL 3844, UMB 3846, Union 3854, Unisys 3859, United 3860, United 3863, United 3870, United 3872, United 3876, United 3880, United 3881, United 3882, Unitil 3885, Universal 3889, Universal 3893, Unum 3898, US 3902, USEC 3904, UTC 3908, V.F. 3913, Valassis 3914, Valley 3916, Varnum 3923, Vectren 3925, Verizon 3936, Vernier 3941, Visa 3960, Vision 3961, Vulcan 3972, Wakefern 3979, Wal-Mart 3980, Walgreen 3981, Walter 3984, Washington 3997, Washington 3998, Waterford 4002, Watson 4007, Wawa 4009, WD-40 4011, Webster 4016, Wegmans 4021, Wellmark 4026, WellPoint 4027, Wells 4028, Wendel 4029, Wendy's/Arby's 4030, West 4037, Western 4040, Western 4042, Western 4044, Western 4045, Westfield 4047, Weyerhaeuser 4052, Whirlpool 4056, Whiting 4063, Whole 4066, Wiley 4072, Winter 4090, Wisconsin 4096, World 4121, Worthington 4124, Wrigley 4125, WSA 4126, WSFS 4127, Wyndham 4132, Xcel 4135, Xerox 4136, Xilinx 4137, Xylem 4139, Yahoo! 4140, Yum! 4150, Zale 4151, Zappos.com 4153

Employee-related scholarships

A & E 6, Air 62, AK 67, Aladdin 73, Albemarle 78, Alcoa 82, Alexander 85, Alhambra 88, Alliant 104, Alpha 112, AMCOL 127, American 141, American 143, American 146, American 156, American 159, Aon 210, ARAMARK 223, Arcelormittal 229, Arch 230, Arch 231, Arizona 239, Arkansas 241, Arkema 242, Armstrong 246, Arthur's 253, Ascena 255, Associated 261, AT&T 273, Atmos 285, Automatic 291, AutoZone 294, Avon 305, AXA 307, Badger 314, Bank 340, Barnes 362, Bashas' 369, Baxter 377, Bay 378, Beall's 389, Bechtel 395, Beckman 397, Bemis 407, Beneficial 411, Berk 423, Berkel 424, Berkowitz 427, Bertelsmann 439, Bestway 444, Big 461, Biomet 466, Black 474, Black 475, Block 481, Boart 510, Bonitz 524, Boston 540, Bridgestone 560, Briggs 565, Bristol 578, Brown 589, Brunswick 595, Burger 613, Burlington 618, Butler 626, Cacique 644, California 655, Callaway 660, Calvi 664, Campbell 669, Cardinal 685, Carroll 703, Central 743, Chase 770, Chevron 780, Chicago 789, Chick 791, Choice 798, Chrysler 801, Cianbro 808, Clorox 852, CNA 855, Coats 860, Coca 863, Cole 867, Compass 901, Con 903, ConAgra 904, Cone 907, Conn 908, ConocoPhillips 913, Conrail 914, Consolidated 915, Consolidated 918, Continental 926, Cooper 935, Cox 962, Cracker 966, Cranston 972, Creamer 974, Crown 988, CSS 996, Culver 1002, Cummins 1007, Curves 1011, CVS 1014, Daiwa 1020, Damar 1024, Dana 1026, Danis 1029, Dannon 1030, Dart 1034, Davey 1035, DaVita 1044, Day 1045, Detroit 1093, Diageo 1107, DIRECTV 1124, Disney 1127, Dixie 1132, Donaldson 1153, Donnelley 1155, Dot 1158, Dresser 1173, DRS 1179, Duke 1189, Dunkin' 1191, Dutch 1197, East 1208, Eastern 1211, Eastman 1213, El Paso 1239, Emerson 1257, Ensign 1276, Entergy 1279, Erving 1294, ESCO 1296, Evening 1302, Fabri 1322, Farmers 1336, Farmers 1339, Fifth 1377, Flint 1438, Flowers 1446, Fluor 1448, FMC 1449, Follett 1455, Ford 1464, Fort 1472, Franklin 1484, Freeport 1494, Fulton 1518, Gannett 1532, Gehl 1545, GenCorp 1548, General 1552, General 1554, Genesco 1559, GenOn 1563, Georgia 1568, GJF 1584, GKN 1585, Golden 1601, Golub 1607, Goulds 1619, Government 1621, Graco 1624, Graphic 1635, Grinnell 1668, Groeniger 1670, GSM 1676, Guardian 1682, H & R 1695, Halliburton 1706, Halton 1709, Hannaford 1723, Hanover 1724, Harris 1736, Harris 1738, Harsco 1741, Hawaiian 1755, Haworth 1758, Heffernan 1769, Helmerich 1774, Henry 1780, Hickory 1797, Holcim 1828, Homecrest 1847, HomeStar 1848, Honeywell 1852, Hooker 1855, Horix 1860, Hormel 1866, Houghton 1869, Humana 1886, Hunter 1893, Hy-Vee 1900, Hygeia 1901, IDACORP 1907, Illinois 1916, Ingles 1940, Ingredion 1942, Inman 1943, Interlock 1954, Intermec 1955, Intermountain 1956, International 1971, Intuit 1982, Inwood 1985,

Ipswich 1989, Jacobs 2016, Jefferies 2030, Johns 2047, Johnson 2049, Johnson 2050, Johnston 2054, Jostens 2067, JPMorgan Chase 2071, Kaman 2088, Keen 2111, Kelly 2122, Keystone 2137, Kimball 2149, Kimberly 2150, Kingsbury 2160, KMTSJ 2173, Knoll 2176, Koch 2179, Kohler 2182, Lake 2213, Lassus 2226, Lea 2235, Leet 2243, Leggett 2246, Lexington 2257, Lexmark 2258, LG&E Energy 2260, Liberty 2265, Lockheed 2292, Loews 2296, Londoff 2297, Lowe's 2312, Lynden 2320, Macy's 2333, MAG 2337, Main 2342, Manitowoc 2355, Manpower 2358, Market 2378, Marlborough 2380, MasterCard 2399, Mattel 2405, McDermott 2424, McKesson 2434, MDU 2441, Medline 2451, Menasha 2461, Merk 2467, Metropolitan 2481, MFA 2487, MGIC 2488, Michigan 2496, Midmark 2507, Mitsui 2541, MN 2543, Modine 2544, Mondelez 2556, Moody's 2563, Moore 2565, Morgan 2570, Murphy 2600, National 2628, National 2630, National 2634, National 2636, NCR 2650, Nelnet 2660, Nestle 2662, Nestle 2663, New 2669, New 2680, New York 2688, Nexion 2705, Nextier 2706, NIBCO 2707, Nordic 2722, Norfolk 2725, Northeast 2737, Northern 2739, Northwest 2746, Nucor 2760, Oilgear 2793, OMNOVA 2809, Omron 2810, OneBeacon 2813, Orscheln 2827, Oshkosh 2833, Osram 2834, Owens 2842, Papa 2876, Park 2882, Parker 2886, Pedernales 2914, Pella 2917, PepsiCo 2935, Peterson 2946, Pfister 2949, Pharmaceutical 2955, Philips 2963, Phillips 2966, Photronics 2969, Pine 2976, Pioneer 2981, Plum 2991, PMC 2994, PNC 2996, PPG 3025, PPL 3027, Price 3039, Protective 3066, Quad 3091, Quaker 3093, QUALCOMM 3095, Rahr 3118, Railway 3119, Rayonier 3134, Raytheon 3135, Reader's 3141, Reagent 3143, Record 3149, Red 3153, Reed 3161, Reed 3162, Remmele 3183, Republic 3186, Rexam 3197, Rexnord 3198, Reynolds 3199, Reynolds 3200, Rio 3218, Robinson 3235, Rocky 3249, Royal 3273, Ryder 3292, Ryerson 3293, S.J. 3299, Saks 3315, SAP 3334, ScanSource 3347, Schwan 3365, Scott 3368, Scripps 3374, Securian 3389, Sempra 3405, Servco 3412, Seton 3415, Shelter 3431, Sherwin 3437, ShopKo 3440, Siemens 3448, Sierra 3451, Sigma 3453, Simplot 3459, Smithfield 3487, Sonoco 3500, Sony 3502, Southern 3520, Southern 3521, Sovereign 3528, Spectra 3540, Square 3560, Stanley 3580, State 3591, Steelcase 3597, STERIS 3600, Stewart 3606, Strauss 3624, Stupp 3628, Subaru 3631, Sumitomo 3640, Sun 3645, Syngenta 3671, Tacoma 3680, TCF 3695, Tektronix 3706, Teleflex 3707, Temple 3711, Tension 3717, Teradyne 3718, Texas 3727, Texas 3729, Textron 3731, Thomasville 3737, Timken 3760, Toro 3775, Toshiba 3776, TOSOH 3777, Toyota 3784, Toyota 3786, Tractor 3791, Transit 3798, True 3814, True 3815, Trustmark 3818, Tutor 3826, U.S. 3840, UBS 3842, Unaka 3848, UniGroup 3852, Unilever 3853, United 3860, United 3867, United 3872, United 3877, Univar 3886, Universal 3890, Unum 3898, US 3902, Usibelli 3906, UTC 3908, Utica 3910, Valero 3915, Valspar 3920, Verizon 3936, Vermeer 3937, Vulcan 3972, Wahl 3977, Wal-Mart 3980, Washington 3994, Weather 4013, Wegmans 4021, West 4038, Weyerhaeuser 4052, Whirlpool 4056, Williams 4077, Williams-Sonoma 4079, Wilsonart 4084, Wisconsin 4094, Wisconsin 4096, X.L. 4134, Xerox 4136, YSI 4149

Endowments

Aflac 54, AGL 57, Alabama 71, American 134, American 141, AMETEK 181, Amgen 182, Amica 183, Arby's 228, Bank 342, Batson 373, Batts 374, BB&T 385, Belk 403, Belo 406, Berry 435, Blair 478, Bloomberg 486, BorgWarner 528, Bound 541, Bramco 555, Bridgestone 560, Burns 620, C Spire 636, Calvert 663, Connecticut 910, Consolidated 917, Convergys 933, Copley 938, County 952, Cummins 1007, Cutco 1012, DeBlois 1056, Demoulas 1085, Dexter 1103, Dixie 1132, Dutch 1197, Eastern 1209, Easthampton 1212, Eastman 1213, EMI 1258, First 1395, First 1405, First 1406, First 1410, Florence 1441, Florida 1443, Fluor 1448, Ford 1463, Fremont 1496, Gibbs 1576, GKN 1585, Heinz 1772, International 1958, Jeld 2032, Johnson 2049, JSJ 2073, Kahn 2084, Kann 2090, Keeneland 2113, Kellwood 2121, Kohler 2182, Lebanon 2238, Lee 2241, Lucasfilm 2316, M.D.C. 2324, M/I 2325, Main 2342, Mars 2384, Mautz 2408, McClatchy 2422, Merfish 2472, Mill 2515, Neenah 2656, New York 2683, Niemann 2708, Norfolk 2725, Northern 2740, O'Connor 2770, OMNOVA 2809, Omron 2810, Opus 2820, Otter 2836, Parker 2886, Pearce 2910, Pukall 3082, Quincy 3110, Raytheon 3135, Riverway 3226, Rockford 3241, Scripps 3374, Sensient 3408, Skinner 3475, South Bend 3507, St. Joe 3563, Stardust 3586, Stock 3610, Superior 3658, Teachers 3697, Totem 3779, Totsy 3780, United 3872, Usibelli 3906, Vulcan 3972, WEDGE 4020, Wiley 4072, Wisconsin 4092, Wisconsin 4093, Wood 4108, York 4145, YSI 4149

Equipment

AbbyBank 15, Activision 30, adidas 35, AEGON 45, AgStar 59, Alcoa 82, Alexander 85, Allergan 99, Allete 100, Alliant 104, Ameren 128, American 144, American 170, Ameritas 178, Ameritec 179, AMETEK 181, Amgen 182, Ariel 237, Arkema 242, Ash 256, Aspen 260, AT&T 273, Athletics 276, Atlanta 280, Autodesk 289, Avista 301, Avon 305, BancTrust 337, Bangor 338, Bank 341, Bank 342, Bayer 381, Bayer 382, BayView 384, Beneficial 412, Bergquist 420, Betts 451, BJ's 473, Blue 489, Blue 490, Blue 493, Blue 497, Blue 498, Boehringer 515, Boeing 516, Boston 540, Bristol 577, Brooks 585, Brown 590, Buccaneer 599, Buffalo 606, Cablevision 640, Cabot 642, Calvert 663, Campbell 668, Campbell 669, Cape 674, Capitol 680, Caterpillar 722, Cerner 754, CFS 756, Chaney 761, Chase 769, Chelsea 772, Cheviot 779, Chicago 785, Chicago 790, Churchill 807, Cisco 818, CITGO 820, Clark 835, Clarkson 839, Clemens 844, CME 853, CMS 854, COLHOC 870, Collette 872, Colonial 876, Colorado 880, Columbia 882, Comerica 889, Commerce 890, Commonwealth 894, Connecticut 912, Consumers 921, Contran 928, COPIC 937, Copley 938, Corning 945, Cow 957, Cracker 966, Credit 977, Cummins 1006, Cummins 1007, Dana 1026, Dealer 1052, Dedham 1060, Delta 1074, Delta 1079, Delta 1080, Delta 1081, Delta 1083, Deluxe 1084, DENSO 1088, Detroit 1097, Dexter 1103, Diebold 1112, Dime 1118, DIRECTV 1124, Dispatch 1129, Diversey 1130, Dominion 1150, Dow 1161, Dow 1162, DP 1168, Dreyer's 1174, Dutch 1197, East 1207, Eastern 1210, Eastern 1211, Eastman 1214, Eaton 1216, EMI 1258, Enterprise 1281, Essa 1297, Exchange 1306, Exponential 1312, Fabri 1322, Farmers 1338, Farmers 1339, Fifth 1377, Finish 1383, First 1395, First 1397, First 1399, First 1402, First 1403, First 1405, First 1406, First 1409, First 1419, First 1420, FirstEnergy 1424, Firstmerit 1425, Florence 1441, Fluor 1448, FMR 1450, Ford 1464, Formosa 1470, Four 1477, Freeport 1494, Fremont 1496, Fuller 1517, Gannett 1532, GenCorp 1548, Genentech 1549, General 1555, GenRad 1564, Georgia 1567, Georgia 1568, Give 1583, Golden 1602, Graco 1624, Grand 1627, Green 1651, Griswold 1669, Guard 1680, Gulf 1689, H & R 1695, Hallberg 1704, Halliburton 1706, Hallmark 1707, Hardinge 1729, Hastings 1749, HCA 1762, Heat 1767, Hewlett 1794, Highmark 1799, Home 1845, Horix 1860, IDACORP 1907, Independence 1925, Indianapolis 1932, Integra 1947, Intermec 1955, International 1968, Investors 1984, ITT 1999, Jazz 2028, Jeld 2032, Jewett 2042, Jim's 2043, JM 2044, Jockey 2045, JOFCO 2046, Johnson 2049, Johnson 2052, Jordan 2063, JPMorgan Chase 2071, Kaiser 2086, Kansas 2094, Keeneland 2113, Kennametal 2125, KeyBank 2136, Kingsbury 2160, Kinney 2162, Kmart 2172, Kohler 2182, Korum 2187, Laclede 2207, Land 2217, Landmark 2218, Levi 2254, Liberty 2262, LifePoint 2270, Lilly 2274, Lincoln 2279, Lincoln 2281, Long 2298, Longview 2300, Lubrizol 2315, M&T 2323, Main 2342, Major 2345, Manti 2359, Mars 2384, Mascoma 2394, Mason 2396, Mattel 2405, McBride 2418, McDonald's 2427, McKesson 2434, MDU 2441, Menasha 2461, Merchants 2465, MFA 2487, Miami 2491, Midcontinent 2505, Middlesex 2506, Milford 2514, Miller 2523, Millhiser-Smith 2524, Mississippi 2536, Monsanto 2559, Moody's 2563, Morgan 2568, Motorola 2585, Motorola 2586, MTD 2595, Mutual 2603, National 2631, National 2634, National 2635, Naugatuck 2645, Naugatuck 2646, Nestle 2662, New England 2672, New York 2683, New York 2684, Newburyport 2693, Niemann 2708, Nordson 2723, Norfolk 2725, Northern 2738, Northfield 2741, NorthWestern 2748, Nu 2759, OceanFirst 2782, Ohio 2789, Oklahoma 2794, Olin 2801, ONEOK 2815, OSCO 2832, Otter 2836, Pacific 2853, Pacific 2855, Pearce 2910, Penney 2925, PETCO 2945, PetSmart 2948, PFS 2951, Philadelphia 2958, Piedmont 2971, Pioneer 2980, Plum 2991, PPG 3025, Praxair 3029, Premix 3037, Provident 3069, Public 3076, Putnam 3086, Putnam 3087, Pyles 3089, QUALCOMM 3095, Questar 3104, R & B 3113, Rayonier 3134, RE/MAX 3140, Redwoods 3158, Reily 3177, Riverway 3226, Rockford 3241, Rockville 3245, Rudolph 3283, Salem 3316, salesforce.com 3318, San Francisco 3326, Saucony 3340, Savings 3343, Schneider 3355, Scottdale 3371, Scoular 3373, Scripps 3374, Security 3391, Selective 3399, Silicon 3455, Sioux 3465, Smith 3485, Southern 3514, Southern 3515, Spirit 3544, SQA 3559, St. Joe 3563, St. Louis 3569, Steel 3595, Steelcase 3597, Strauss 3624, Subaru 3632, Sulphur 3637, SunTrust 3654, Swinerton 3668, Synopsys 3673, Target 3691, Techni 3699, Tektronix 3706, Tennessee 3716, Texas 3725, Textron 3731, Thomaston 3736, Toshiba 3776, Towerbrook 3781, Toyota 3784, Tri 3805, Trim 3810, Twins 3827, U.S. 3836, Union 3857, Union 3858, United 3863, United 3879, US 3902, USG 3905, Utica 3910, Vectren 3925, Verizon 3936, Vogt 3966, Waffle 3975, Wake 3978, Washington 3995, Washington 3996, Webster 4018, Wells 4028, Western 4045, Westfield 4047, Weyerhaeuser 4052, Windway 4086, Winn 4087, Winnebago 4088, Wisconsin 4093, Wisconsin 4096, Wood 4108, Woodward 4112, Xylem 4139, YSI 4149

Exchange programs

AMETEK 181, JTB 2074, Mazda 2414, MedImmune 2450, Mitsui 2541, Panasonic 2870

Fellowships

Aflac 54, Allergan 99, American 158, Arnold 248, Bering 422, Blair 478, Bloomberg 486, Blue 501, Blue 502, Boeing 516, Boston 540, Bristol 578, Capitol 680, Chicago 790, Clif 848, Coca 862, Cook 934, Corning 945, Deloitte 1070, Delta 1078, du Pont 1184, Eagle 1201, ERM 1292, Ernst 1293, Exxon 1315, First 1398, Genentech 1549, GOLDEN 1600, Google 1613, Greenberg 1654, Hess 1793, Hoffmann 1823, IDACORP 1907, Intel 1950, International 1960, Johnson 2048, Johnson 2049, L'Oreal 2203, Lubrizol 2315, Marnier-Lapostolle 2381, Mazda 2414, MedImmune 2450, Medtronic 2453, Merck 2466, Merk 2467, Micron 2500, Mitsui 2541, Moody's 2563, Morgan 2570, Nasdaq 2617, Newman's 2697, Patton 2898, Pfizer 2950, PricewaterhouseCoopers 3042, Rahr 3118, Scripps 3374, Semiconductor 3403, Skadden 3470, Skidmore 3474, Skinner 3475, Sonoran 3501, St. Joe 3563, St. Jude 3566, Superior 3658, Symantec 3669, Synopsys 3673, Toro 3775, Ukpeagvik 3843, Universal 3893, Washington 3994, WEDGE 4020, Wiley 4072

General/operating support

1st 2, 3M 3, A & E 6, A.D. 7, A.J. 8, ABARTA 10, Abba 11, Abbot 12, Abbott 13, Abby's 14, Abercrombie 17, Aberdeen 18, Abt 20, Acacia 21, Accenture 22, Accupac 23, ACE 24, ACF 26, ACI 27, Acme 29, Acuity 31, Acuity 32, Adams 34, adidas 35, Adir 36, Admiral 37, Adobe 38, Advance 39, Advanced 40, Advent 41, AECOM 42, AEGON 45, Aeropostale 46, Aetna 48, Aexcel 49, Affinity 52, Aflac 54, Ag 55, Agilent 56, AGL 57, AgStar 59, AHS 61, Air 63, Air 64, Airgas 65, AK 67, Akamai 68, Alabama 71, Aladdin 73, Alaska 75, Albemarle 78, Albrecht 80, Alcatel 81, Alcoa 82, Alexander 85, Alfa 87, Alice 89, Allegheny 91, Allegis 92, Allen 93, Allen

94, Allen 95, Allen 96, Allen 97, Allete 100, Alliance 101, Alliant 104, Allianz 105, Allison-Erwin 106, Allstate 107, AllStyle 108, Allyis 109, Almar 110, Alpha 112, Alro 113, Alsan 114, Alsco 115, Altman 119, Altria 120, Alyeska 121, Amazon.com 122, Amboy 124, AMC 125, AMC 126, Ameren 128, Ameren 129, American 133, American 134, American 135, American 137, American 139, American 140, American 141, American 142, American 143, American 144, American 145, American 146, American 147, American 149, American 150, American 152, American 153, American 154, American 155, American 156, American 157, American 158, American 159, American 160, American 161, American 162, American 164, American 165, American 167, American 168, American 169, American 170, AMERIGROUP 171, AmeriPlan 172, AmeriPride 173, Ameriprise 174, AmerisourceBergen 175, Ameristar 176, Amerisure 177, Ameritas 178, AMETEK 181, Amgen 182, Amica 183, Amnews 185, AMR 187, Amsted 188, Amway 189, Anadarko 190, Anchor 192, Andersen 194, Anderson 195, Andersson 196, Andrews 198, ANH 201, Anheuser 202, Ann's 203, Anocoil 204, Antioch 207, ANZA 208, AOL 209, Aon 210, Apache 211, Apex 212, Apex 213, Apex 214, Apogee 215, Apollo 216, AptarGroup 221, Aqua 222, Arbeit 225, Arbella 226, Arbitron 227, Arcelormittal 229, Arch 231, Archer 233, Arent 235, AREVA 236, Ariel 237, Ariens 238, Arizona 239, Arkansas 240, Arkansas 241, Arkema 242, Armbrust 243, Armstrong 245, Armstrong 246, Arnall 247, Arnold 248, Arrow 249, Arrowhead 250, Arrowpoint 251, Arroyo 252, Artichoke 254, Ascena 255, Ash 256, Ashland 258, Ashley 259, Associated 262, Associated 264, Association 265, Assurant 266, Assurant 267, Assurant 268, Assurity 269, AstraZeneca 272, AT&T 273, Athletics 276, Atlantic 281, Atlantic 282, Atlantic 283, Atlas 284, Audubon 286, Austin 288, Autodesk 289, Autoliv 290, AutoNation 292, Autonomie 293, AutoZone 294, Aveda 295, Avelina 296, Avery 297, Avidia 298, Avis 299, Avis 300, Avista 301, Aviva 302, Avlon 303, Avnet 304, Avon 305, AVX 306, AXA 307, Azulay 311, B & B 312, Badger 313, Bailey 315, Baird 316, Baird 317, Baker 318, Baker 319, Baker 321, Baker 323, Baker 325, Bakewell 326, Ball 328, Baltimore 332, Baltimore 333, Baltimore 334, BancorpSouth 336, BancTrust 337, Bangor 338, Bank 340, Bank 341, Bank 342, Bank 343, Bank 344, Bank 345, Bank 346, Bank 347, Bank 348, Bank 349, BankSouth 350, Bard 358, Bardes 359, Barnes 362, Barrasso 363, Barron's 364, Bartlett 365, Barton 366, BASF 368, Bashas' 369, Bassett 372, Batson 373, Batts 374, Baum 375, Bausch 376, Baxter 377, Bay 378, Bay 379, Bay 380, Bayer 381, BayView 384, BB&T 385, BC 387, BDP 388, Beall's 389, Beam 390, Bean 391, Bean 392, Bear 393, Beaver 394, Bechtel 395, Beck 396, Beckman 397, Becton 398, Bekins 401, Belden 402, Belk 403, Belk 404, Belleville 405, Belo 406, Bemis 407, Bemis 408, Ben 409, Benedict-Miller 410, Beneficial 411, Benevento 414, Bennett 415, Bentley 416, Benton 417, Berghammer 418, Berglund 419, Bergquist 420, Berkley 426, Berkshire 428, Berkshire 429, Berkshire 430, Bernhardt 432, Berry 434, Berry 435, Berry 436, Berry 437, Bertelsmann 439, Best 442, Better 447, Better 448, Better 449, Betts 450, Betts 451, Beverage 452, Beyer 454, BHP 455, Bickel 457, Bierlein 459, Big 460, Biogen 465, Biomet 466, Bird 468, Birdsong 470, Birmingham 471, BJ's 473, Black 474, Black 475, Blair 478, Blakely 480, Block 481, Block 482, Blommer 484, Blood-Horse 485, Bloomberg 486, Bloomin 487, Bloomingdale's 488, Blue 490, Blue 491, Blue 492, Blue 493, Blue 494, Blue 495, Blue 497, Blue 498, Blue 499, Blue 500, Blue 501, Blue 502, BlueCross 507, BMC 508, BMW 509, Boart 510, Bob's 511, Bodine 513, Boehringer 515, Boeing 516, Boler 520, Bon 521, Booz 525, Borcherding 526, Borden 527, BorgWarner 528, BOSE 530, Bossong 532, Boston 533, Boston 534, Boston 535, Boston 540, Bound 541, Bourns 542, Bowater 543, Boyd 545, Boyd 546, BP 547, BPI 548, Bracewell 549, Brady 553, Bragg 554, Bramco 555, Brasseler 556, Bressler 557, Brewer 558, Bricker 559, Bridgestone 560, Bridgewater 561, Bridgewater 562, Bridgeway 563, Briggs 565, Bright 566, Brightpoint 567, Brilliant 568, Brillion 569, Brinckerhoff 570, Brink's 571, Brinker 572, Brinkster 574, Bristlecone 575, Bristol 578, Broadcom 579, Brocchini 580, Brochsteins 581, Bromelkamp 582, Brookline 583, Brooklyn 584, Brookstone 586, Brother 587, Brotherhood 588, Brown 590, Brown 591, Brown 592, Brunswick 595, BSA 597, Bubalo 598, Buchalter 600, Buckeye 601, Budget 604, Budweiser 605, Buffalo 606, Bufftree 607, Build 608, Building 610, Buist 611, Bunge 612, Burger 613, Burlington 616, Burnett 619, Burns 620, Burr 621, Burrtec 622, Butler 626, Butler 627, Butt 628, Butzel 629, Byers 630, Byrd 631, C & C 633, C & S 634, C Spire 636, C.M. 637, CA 638, Cablevision 640, Cabot 642, Cabot 643, Cacique 644, Caddell 645, Cadence 646, Cades 647, Cadillac 648, Caesars 650, Cajun 652, California 654, California 655, Callaway 660, Calpine 661, Calumet 662, Calvert 663, Cambridge 666, Cameron 667, Campbell 668, Campbell 669, Candlesticks 670, Cannon 671, Canon 672, Caparo 673, Capezio 675, Capital 676, Capital 677, Capital 679, Capitol 680, Caplin 681, Capstone 684, Cardinal 685, CareFirst 687, Cargill 691, Caribou 692, Carlson 693, Carmody 695, Carnival 696, Carolina 697, Carpenter 700, Carrington Coleman 701, Carris 702, Carroll 703, Carrols 704, Carson 705, Carter's 708, Cary 712, Cascade 713, Cassidy 715, Castle 716, Castle 717, Castle 718, Catalina 719, Caterpillar 722, Cathay 723, Cavaliers 724, CB 725, CBS 727, CC 728, CDW 729, Cellco 733, CEMEX 734, Centene 735, CenterPoint 738, CenterPoint 739, CentiMark 740, Central 741, Central 742, Central 743, Central 745, Central 746, Century 748, Century 750, CenturyLink 751, Cephalon 752, Ceridian 753, Cerner 754, CF 755, CFS 756, CH2M 758, Chadbourne 759, Chandler 760, Chaney 761, Chapman 763, Charles 764, Charter 765, Charter 766, Chartis 768, Chase 770, Chehalis 771, Chelsea 772, Chemed 773, Chemical 774, Chemtura 775, Chesapeake 777, Chesapeake 778, Cheviot 779, Chevron 780, Chicago 782, Chicago 786, Chicago 787, Chicago 788, Chicago 789, Chicago 790, Chick 791, Chicopee 792, Chinese 794, Choice 798, Chotin 799, Chrysler 801, CHS 802, Chubb 804, Churchill 807, CIBA 810, Cic 811, CIGNA 812, Cintas 816, Circle 817, Cisco 818, CIT 819, Citigroup 821, Citizens 824, Citizens 827, Citizens 828, City 829, City 830, CLARCOR 832, Claremont 833, Clarity 834, Clark 835, Clark 836, Classic 840, Clear 842, Cleary 843, Clemens 844, Clements 845, Cleveland 847, Clif 848, Cliffs 850, Clinton 851, Clorox 852, CME 853, CMS 854, CNA 855, CNO 857, Coach 858, Coca 861, Coca 862, Coca 863, Coghlin 864, Coghlin 865, Cohn 866, Colgate 869, Collette 872, Collins 873, Colonial 874, Colonial 875, Colonial 876, Colorado 880, Colt 881, Comcast 887, Comerica 889, Commerce 890, Commercial 891, Commercial 893, Commonwealth 894, Commonwealth 895, Communications 896, Community 897, Community 898, Community 900, Compass 901, Con 903, Concept 905, Conditioned 906, Cone 907, Conn 908, Connecticut 910, Connecticut 911, Connecticut 912, ConocoPhillips 913, Consolidated 915, Consolidated 917, Conston 920, Consumers 921, Continental 922, Continental 924, Continental 925, Continental 926, Continental 927, Contran 928, Control 929, ConvaTec 932, Cook 934, Cooper 935, Cooper 936, Coquille 939, Coral 940, CORE 941, Cornerstone 943, Corning 945, CORT 946, Corvallis 947, Costco 948, Country 951, County 952, Cousins 953, Cousins 954, Covance 955, Covidien 956, Cow 957, Cox 958, Cox 959, CPI 965, Cracker 966, Craft 967, Crane 969, Crane 970, Cranston 972, Crayola 973, Creative 975, Creative 976, Credit 979, Credit 980, Crescent 981, Crescent 982, Crescent 983, Croft 985, Crowell 986, Crown 987, Crown 988, Crystal 991, Crystal 992, CSRwire 995, CSS 996, CSX 997, Cubist 999, Cullen 1000, Cumberland 1003, Cummings 1004, Cummins 1005, Cummins 1007, CUNA 1008, Cupertino 1009, Curves 1011, Cutie 1013, CVS 1014, Cyan 1015, Cymer 1016, Daffy's 1019, Daiwa 1020, Dallas 1022, Damar 1024, Dan's 1025, Dana 1026, Danaher 1027, Danforth 1028, Danis 1029, Dannon 1030, Darden 1032, Dart 1033, Dart 1034, Davey 1035, Davis 1037, Davis 1041, Davison 1042, davistudio 1043, Dayton 1047, DCI 1049, Deacon 1050, Dead 1051, Dealer 1052, Dean 1053, Dean 1054, DeBruce 1057, Deckers 1059, Deere 1061, Deerfield 1062, Defiance 1063, Dekker 1064, Del 1065, Delaware 1066, Dell 1068, Dell Corning 1067, Delmarva 1069, Deloitte 1070, Delphi 1071, Delphos 1072, Delta 1073, Delta 1076, Delta 1079, Delta 1082, Deluxe 1084, Demoulas 1085, Denny's 1087, DENSO 1088, DENTSPLY 1089, Dethmers 1091, Detroit 1095, Detroit 1097, Deutsch 1098, Deutsche 1099, Devereaux 1100, Dexter 1103, Diageo 1107, Diagnos-Techs 1108, Diamonds 1109, Diebold 1112, Diemolding 1113, Dietz 1114, Dilbeck 1116, Dime 1118, Dimeo 1119, Dippin' 1122, DIRECTV 1124, Discover 1125, Disney 1127, Disney 1128, Dispatch 1129, Diversityinc 1131, Dixie 1132, Dixon 1133, DJO 1134, Djr 1135, Do 1136, Doctors 1139, Dole 1141, Dollar 1142, Dollar 1143, Dollar 1144, Dollar 1145, Dominion 1148, Dominion 1150, Dondlinger 1154, Donnelley 1155, Donovan 1156, Dot 1158, Douglas 1159, Dow 1160, Dow 1162, Dow 1163, Dowling 1165, Doyon 1167, DP 1168, Dr 1169, Draper 1170, Draper 1171, DreamWorks 1172, Dreyer's 1174, Drive 1177, DRW 1181, DTE 1183, du Pont 1184, Duane 1186, Duchossois 1187, Duda 1188, Duke 1189, Dun 1190, Dunkin' 1191, Dupps 1193, Dura 1195, Dutch 1197, DVK 1198, Dynamet 1200, Eagle 1202, Eagle 1203, East 1207, East 1208, Eastern 1209, Eastern 1211, Easthampton 1212, Eastman 1213, Eastman 1214, Easton 1215, Eaton 1216, eBay 1217, Eberhard 1218, Eclipse 1219, Ecolab 1220, Econoco 1222, Econscious 1223, Edelman 1224, Edgar 1225, Edible 1226, Edina 1227, Edison 1228, Edison 1229, EduCare 1231, Education 1232, Edwards 1235, EFC 1236, El 1237, El Dorado 1238, El Paso 1239, Electric 1240, Electronic 1242, Elemental Herbs 1244, Elias 1247, Eliason 1248, Elite 1249, EMC 1253, EMCOR 1255, Emerson 1257, EMI 1258, Emmis 1260, Empire 1262, Employers 1264, Enbridge 1265, Endeavor 1267, Endo 1268, Endres 1269, Energen 1270, Energizer 1271, Energy 1273, EnMark 1274, Ensign 1276, Entelco 1277, Entergy 1278, Entergy 1279, Entergy 1280, Enterprise 1281, Epson 1286, Equifax 1288, Ergon 1289, Erving 1294, Esbenshade's 1295, Essa 1297, Esurance 1298, Ethicon 1299, Evans 1300, Evening 1302, Excell 1304, Excellium 1305, Exchange 1306, Exchange 1307, Exelon 1309, Exotic 1310, Expedia 1311, Express 1313, Exxon 1315, F.N.B. 1318, Faber 1319, Fabiano 1320, Fabick 1321, Factory 1323, Faegre 1324, Fairfax 1325, Fairfield 1326, Family 1330, Farm 1333, Farmers 1334, Farmers 1335, Farmers 1338, Fashion 1342, Fast 1343, FDI 1346, Federal 1347, Federal 1348, Federal 1349, Federal 1350, Federated 1351, FedEx 1352, FEECO 1353, Feelgoodz 1354, Fellowes 1357, Fema 1358, Fenton 1361, Ferguson 1363, Ferrara 1364, Ferrellgas 1365, Ferro 1366, Fetzer 1367, FHC 1368, Fibre 1369, Fidelity 1371, Fidelity 1372, Fieldale 1373, Fieldstone 1374, Fiesta 1375, Fifth 1376, Fifth 1377, Fila 1379, Finance 1381, First 1388, First 1389, First 1390, First 1393, First 1394, First 1395, First 1396, First 1397, First 1398, First 1399, First 1400, First 1401, First 1404, First 1406, First 1407, First 1408, First 1409, First 1410, First 1411, First 1413, First 1414, First 1415, First 1416, First 1417, First 1418, First 1419, First 1420, First 1421, First 1422, FirstEnergy 1424, Firstmerit 1425, Fiserv 1427, Fishel 1429, Fisher 1431, Fisher 1433, Fleck 1435, Flextronics 1437, Flint 1439, Flir 1440, Florida 1444, Florsheim 1445, Flowserve 1447, Fluor 1448, FMC 1449, FMR 1450, Foley 1454, Fonville 1456, Food 1458, ForceBrain.com 1461, Ford 1463, Ford 1464, Foremost 1466, Forest 1467, Fort 1471, Fort 1472, Fortis 1473, Fortune 1474, Four 1477, Fowler 1478, Fox 1480, Frankel 1483, Franklin 1484, Franklin 1485, Franklin 1487, Franklin 1488, Franshaw 1489, Fredericksburg 1490, Freedman 1493, Freeport 1494, Freescale 1495, Fremont 1496, Fremont 1497, Freres 1498, Fresh 1499, Friday 1501, Friedland 1503, Friesen 1505, Frito 1506, Frontier 1509, Frontier 1510, Fru 1513, Fujisankei 1515, Fuller 1517, Fulton 1518, Furniture 1519, Furr 1520, G&K 1524, Gable 1525, Gallo 1529, GameStop 1530, Gannett 1532, Gap 1533, Garden 1535, Gardner 1536, Garff 1538, GATX 1542, Gaunce 1543, Gemini 1547, Genentech 1549, General 1550, General 1551, General 1552, General 1553, General 1554, General 1555, General 1556, General 1558, Genesco 1559, Geneseo 1560, GenOn

2935, Perdue 2936, Perforce 2937, Performance 2938, PerkinElmer 2939, Perkins 2940, Perrigo 2943, PETCO 2945, Petroleum 2947, Pfister 2949, Pfizer 2950, PFS 2951, PG&E 2952, Pharmaceutical 2955, Philadelphia 2957, Philadelphia 2960, Philip 2962, Phillips 2965, Phillips 2966, Phoenix 2968, Physicians 2970, Piedmont 2971, Pieper 2972, Pier 2973, Pinnacle 2977, Pioneer 2979, Pioneer 2980, Pioneer 2981, Piper 2983, Pitney 2984, Pizza 2988, Playboy 2990, Plum 2992, Plymouth 2993, PMI 2995, PNC 2997, Polaris 2999, Polk 3000, Popular 3003, Portcullis 3004, Porter 3006, Porter 3007, Portland 3010, Posillico 3014, Post 3015, Potomac 3018, Power 3020, Power 3022, Powers 3024, PPG 3025, PPL 3026, PPL 3027, Pratt 3028, Praxair 3029, Praxis 3030, Preferred 3031, Preformed 3032, Premera 3034, Premier 3035, Premier 3036, Premix 3037, Price 3040, Priceless 3041, PricewaterhouseCoopers 3042, Primary 3043, Prime 3044, Primerica 3045, Prince 3046, Principal 3047, Print.Net 3048, Printpack 3049, Private 3050, Pro 3051, PRO*ACT 3053, Procter 3055, Professional 3056, Progressive 3057, Progressive 3058, Progressive 3059, ProLogis 3060, Promotional 3061, Property 3062, Prophet 3063, ProtechSoft 3065, Protective 3066, Protector 3067, Providence 3068, Provident 3069, Provident 3070, Provident 3071, Prudential 3072, Public 3075, Public 3076, Public 3077, Public 3078, Publix 3079, Puget 3081, Pukall 3082, Putnam 3085, Putnam 3087, PVH 3088, Pyles 3089, Quabaug 3090, Quad 3091, Quadion 3092, Quaker 3093, Quaker 3094, QUALCOMM 3095, Quality 3096, Quality 3097, Quality 3098, Quandel 3099, Quanex 3100, Quest 3103, Questar 3105, Quicksilver 3106, Quidel 3107, Quiksilver 3108, QuikTrip 3109, Quincy 3110, R & R 3114, Rackspace 3117, Rahr 3118, Railway 3119, Raley's 3122, Ralph 3123, Ramallah 3124, Ramerica 3125, Rasmussen 3128, Ratio 3129, Ratner 3130, Ray 3131, Rayonier 3134, Raytheon 3135, RBC 3136, RBS 3137, RBS 3138, RCM 3139, RE/MAX 3140, Reader's 3141, Reckitt 3146, RECO 3148, Recreational 3150, Red 3153, Red 3154, Redco 3155, Redlum 3156, Redner's 3157, Redwoods 3158, Reebok 3159, Reed 3161, Reell 3164, Reeves 3165, Regal 3166, Regence 3168, Regence 3169, Regions 3171, Regis 3172, Reid 3173, Reiff 3174, Reilly 3175, Reily 3177, Reisner 3180, Reitman 3181, Rennoc 3184, Republic 3187, Republic 3188, RESCO 3189, Residential 3191, Respironics 3193, Retail 3194, Reynolds 3199, RG 3201, Riceland 3203, Rich 3204, Richard 3205, Richards 3206, Ricoh 3210, Ridgewood 3211, Rieke 3212, Riggs 3213, Rima 3216, Rio 3218, Ripplewood 3219, RITE 3221, River 3223, River 3224, Rivermaid 3225, Riverway 3226, RJN 3228, Roanoke 3229, Robbins 3230, Roberts 3231, Robins 3232, Robinson 3235, Roche 3236, Rock 3238, Rock 3239, Rockland 3242, Rockville 3245, Rockwell 3246, Rockwell 3247, Rodgers 3250, Rogers 3253, Rolls 3254, Rood 3257, Rose 3261, Rose 3263, Rosen's 3264, Ross 3265, Ross 3267, Rothschild 3270, Rothstein 3271, Roundy's 3272, Royal 3273, Royal 3274, Royal 3275, Royal 3276, Royalnest 3277, RPM 3278, RUAN 3279, RubinBrown 3280, Ruder 3282, Rudolph 3283, Rue 3285, Ruradan 3287, Rusco 3288, Russell 3289, Ryder 3292, Ryman 3294, S & H 3295, S & T 3297, S.B.E. 3298, S.J. 3299, Sachs 3301, Saco 3302, Sacramento 3303, Safeco 3306, Safeguard 3307, Safeway 3310, SAIC 3311, Saint 3312, Sakar 3313, Saks 3315, Salem 3317, Salt 3319, Samsung 3320, Sandusky 3328, sanofi-aventis 3329, Sansar 3330, Santa 3331, SanTrust 3332, SAP 3334, Sartori 3335, SAS 3336, Sasaki 3337, Sasol 3338, Saucony 3340, Savage 3341, Save 3342, SCANA 3346, Schein 3348, Schiff 3350, Schiffenhaus 3351, Schloss 3352, Schmeling 3353, Schneider 3354, Schneider 3355, Schoeneckers 3357, Schoonover 3359, Schott 3360, Schwab 3363, Schwan 3365, SCIenergy 3366, Scientific 3367, Scott 3368, Scott 3369, Scott 3370, Scottdale 3371, Scotts 3372, Scoular 3373, Scripps 3374, Seaboard 3375, Seagate 3377, Sealed 3381, Sealy 3382, Seamen's 3383, Sears 3384, Seattle 3385, Seattle 3386, SeaWorld 3387, Securant 3388, Securian 3389, Securitas 3390, Security 3392, Security 3393, Security 3394, Select 3398, Selective 3399, Selig 3401, Seligman 3402, Seminole 3404, Sempra 3405, Seneca 3406, Sensient 3408, Sentry 3409, Sequa 3410, Serengeti 3411, Servco 3412, ServiceMaster 3414, Seton 3415, Shakopee 3419, Shalam 3420, Shanken 3421, Shatz 3424, Shaughnessy 3425, Shaw 3426, Shaw's 3427, Shea 3428, Shell 3430, Shelter 3431, Shelton 3432, Shenandoah 3433, Shenandoah 3434, Sherwin 3437, ShopKo 3440, Shugart 3442, Shure 3443, SI 3444, Sidener 3445, Siemens 3448, Sierra 3449, Sierra 3451, SIFCO 3452, Sigma 3453, Sikorsky 3454, Silicon 3455, Simplot 3459, Simpson 3460, Simpson 3461, Singlebrook 3464, Sit 3466, Siw 3468, Sjostrom 3469, Skinner 3475, SkyWest 3476, Slant 3477, SmartWool 3479, SMBC 3480, Smith 3482, Smith 3483, Smith 3484, Smith 3485, Smithfield 3487, Smucker 3488, Smulekoff 3489, Snell 3490, Snow 3491, Snyder's-Lance 3492, Social(k) 3494, Sonic 3498, Sonoco 3500, Sony 3502, Sony 3504, South 3508, South 3509, South 3510, South 3511, South 3512, South Bend 3507, Southeastern 3513, Southern 3514, Southern 3515, Southern 3516, Southern 3517, Southern 3518, Southern 3519, Southern 3521, Southwest 3524, Southwestern 3526, Southwire 3527, Sovereign 3528, Spahn 3529, Spang 3530, Spangler 3531, Spansion 3532, Spark 3533, Spartan 3534, Spartan 3535, Spear 3536, Specialty 3537, Specialty 3538, Spector 3539, Spectra 3540, SpectraCare 3541, Spence 3542, Spirit 3544, Sports 3547, Sports 3548, Sprague 3551, Spraying 3552, Springleaf 3554, Springs 3555, Sprint 3556, SPX 3558, SQA 3559, Square 3560, St. 3565, St. John 3564, St. Jude 3566, St. Louis 3568, St. Louis 3569, Stadtmauer 3570, Stafast 3571, Stage 3572, Stahl 3573, StanCorp 3574, Standard 3575, Standard 3576, Standard 3577, Stanek 3578, Stanley 3579, Staples 3581, Star 3583, Starbucks 3585, Stardust 3586, Starwood 3589, State 3590, State 3591, State 3592, Station 3593, Steel 3595, Steelcase 3597, Stephens 3598, STERIS 3600, Sterne 3602, Steve's 3603, Stewart 3604, Stiles 3607, Stoelting 3612, Stone 3614, Stonecutter 3615, Stoneham 3616, Stonyfield 3617, Stop 3618, Stout 3619, Strauss 3624, Stride 3625, Stride 3626, Stupp 3628, Sturniolo 3629, Sub-Zero 3630, Subaru 3631, Suitter 3633, Sullivan 3634, Sullivan 3635, SUMCO 3638, Sumitomo 3639, Summit 3642, Sun 3644, Sunbeam 3647, Sunkist 3649, Sunoco 3650, Sunrise 3652, Sunshine 3653, SunTrust 3654, Sunwest 3655, Superior 3657, Superior 3658, SUPERVALU 3659, Sweetbay 3665, Swift 3666, Swift 3667, Symantec 3669, Symmco 3670, Synopsys 3673, Synovus 3674, Syracuse 3675, Sysco 3677, Systel 3678, Taco 3679, Taiyo 3681, Talbots 3682, TALX 3683, Tamar 3684, Tanner 3688, Tap 3689, TAP 3690, Target 3691, Tasty 3693, TCF 3695, TD 3696, Techni 3699, Teck 3700, TECO 3701, Tees 3703, Teichert 3704, Teitler 3705, Tektronix 3706, TeleTech 3708, Telligen 3710, Temple 3711, Tenet 3713, Tennant 3714, Tenneco 3715, Tennessee 3716, Tension 3717, Teradyne 3718, Terex 3719, Terlato 3720, Terre 3722, Tesoro 3723, Tex 3724, Texas 3725, Texas 3728, Textron 3731, TFS 3732, Thermo 3733, Thinkshift 3734, Third 3735, Thomaston 3736, Thomasville 3737, Thompson 3739, Thomson 3742, Thorntons 3743, Thorrez 3744, Three 3745, Three 3746, Thrivent 3747, Tidewater 3748, Tiffany 3750, Tillman 3752, Timberland 3754, Time 3755, Time 3757, Times 3759, Timken 3760, Tindall 3761, Titan 3763, TJX 3765, Toeniskoetter 3767, Toll 3769, Tom's 3770, Tomkins 3771, Tony 3773, Tops 3774, Toro 3775, Toshiba 3776, Total 3778, Totem 3779, Towerbrook 3781, Towill 3782, Toyota 3785, Toyota 3787, Toyota 3789, Tractor 3791, Tradition 3792, Trail 3793, Trane 3794, Trans 3795, Transammonia 3796, Transco 3797, TransUnion 3799, Travelers 3802, Tribune 3806, Trident 3808, TriLibrium 3809, Trim 3810, Tripifoods 3811, Triumph 3812, Tropicana 3813, True 3814, Truland 3817, Trustmark 3818, Tucson 3819, Tulalip 3820, Tupperware 3821, Turf 3822, Turner 3824, Tutor 3826, Twins 3827, Tyco 3829, Tyler 3831, Tyson 3832, U.M. 3834, U.S. 3835, U.S. 3836, U.S. 3839, UBS 3842, UL 3844, UMB 3846, Unaka 3848, UniGroup 3852, Unilever 3853, Union 3854, Union 3855, Union 3857, Union 3858, Unisys 3859, United 3860, United 3861, United 3862, United 3863, United 3864, United 3865, United 3867, United 3868, United 3869, United 3870, United 3871, United 3873, United 3874, United 3877, United 3878, United 3879, United 3880, United 3881, United 3882, Unitil 3885, Univar 3886, Universal 3887, Universal 3889, Universal 3890, Universal 3891, Universal 3893, Universal 3894, Universal 3895, Untours 3897, Unum 3898, Updike 3899, Upper 3900, Urban 3901, US 3902, USA 3903, USEC 3904, USG 3905, Usibelli 3906, Usinger 3907, UTC 3908, UTI 3909, Utica 3910, Uticon 3911, V-T 3912, V.F. 3913, Valassis 3914, Valero 3915, Valley 3916, Valley 3917, Valspar 3920, Vandor 3921, Varnum 3923, Vaughan 3924, Vectren 3925, Veev 3927, Velting 3928, Venturedyne 3933, Verby 3934, Veridyne 3935, Verizon 3936, Vernier 3941, Vesco 3942, VHA 3944, Victaulic 3948, Victor 3949, Victorinox 3950, ViewSonic 3952, Vijuk 3953, Vilter 3956, Virginia 3959, Visa 3960, Vision 3961, Vista 3962, Visteon 3964, Vodafone 3965, Volvo 3968, Vos 3969, Vulcan 3972, Wachtell 3973, Wadsworth 3974, Wagner 3976, Wake 3978, Wakefern 3979, Wal-Mart 3980, Walgreen 3981, Walker 3982, Wallace 3983, Walter 3984, Warburg 3985, Ward 3986, Warrell 3991, Warren 3993, Washington 3999, Washington 4001, Waterford 4002, Waters 4003, WaterStone 4005, Watson 4007, Wausau 4008, Wawa 4009, WB 4010, WD-40 4011, Weaver 4015, Webster 4016, Webster 4017, Webster's 4019, WEDGE 4020, Wegmans 4021, Weil 4022, Weis 4024, Welch 4025, Wellmark 4026, WellPoint 4027, Wells 4028, Wendel 4029, Wendy's 4031, Wendy's 4032, Wendy's/Arby's 4030, Wenger 4033, West 4034, West 4036, West 4038, Westar 4039, Western 4040, Western 4041, Western 4043, Western 4044, Westfield 4047, Westinghouse 4049, Westport 4050, Weyco 4051, Weyerhaeuser 4052, Whip 4054, Whirl 4055, Whirlpool 4056, White 4060, White 4062, Whiting 4063, Whitley 4064, Whitney 4065, Whole 4066, Wigwam 4069, Wiley 4072, Wilkes 4074, Willdan 4075, Williams 4077, Willow 4082, Wimpfheimer 4085, Winnebago 4088, Wisconsin 4092, Wisconsin 4093, Wisconsin 4094, Wisconsin 4095, Wisconsin 4096, Wishart 4097, Wittern 4098, WKBN 4099, Woerner 4101, Wolf 4102, Wolf 4103, Wolff 4105, Wolverine 4106, Wonder 4107, Wood 4108, Woodforest 4110, Woodward 4112, Working 4116, World 4118, World 4119, World 4122, Worthen 4123, Worthington 4124, Wrigley 4125, WSA 4126, WSFS 4127, Wurster 4128, Wurzburg 4129, Wyndham 4132, Wynnne 4133, Xcel 4135, Xerox 4136, Xilinx 4137, Xylem 4139, Yahoo! 4140, Yamaha 4141, YGS 4143, Young 4146, Yum! 4150, Zale 4151, Zallie 4152, Zappos.com 4153, Zilkha 4156, Zimmer 4157, Zions 4158, Zotos 4159

Grants to individuals

Abbott 13, Aeropostale 46, Airtek 66, Alcon 83, Aleut 84, Allstate 107, Altair 117, Ameren 129, American 151, AmeriPlan 172, Amgen 182, Ann's 203, Apache 211, Arch 231, Armstrong 246, Bank 339, Bank 340, Bay 380, Bayer 382, Bean 391, Belo 406, Bergquist 420, Blue 502, Blue 503, Boehringer 515, Boiron 519, Bon 521, Boston 540, Bristol 578, Buist 611, Burger 613, Butler 626, Butt 628, C Spire 636, Cable 639, Cannon 671, Capezio 675, Capital 678, Celgene 732, CenturyLink 751, CF 755, Charles 764, Chase 769, CNA 855, Coastal 859, Communications 896, Cook 934, Corvallis 947, Costco 948, Cox 959, Craft 967, Creative 976, Daiwa 1020, Delmarva 1069, Delta 1080, Diagnos-Techs 1108, Dippin' 1122, Discovery 1126, Dixie 1132, Doctors 1139, Dolan 1140, Dollar 1143, Domino's 1151, Dr 1169, Earnhardt 1205, Ecolab 1220, EFC 1236, EI 1237, EMI 1258, Equifax 1288, Erickson 1290, Fallon 1329, Fast 1344, Financial 1382, Fisher 1433, Food 1458, Ford 1464, Fort 1472, Fredericksburg 1490, G&K 1524, Genentech 1549, General 1551, Genesis 1561, Genzyme 1566, Georgia 1567, Getty 1569, GlaxoSmithKline 1588, GOLDEN 1600, Gon 1608, Government 1621, Greystone 1665, Grinnell 1668, Grubb 1675, Guardian 1683, Hall 1702, Harbert 1726, Hard 1727, Harper 1735, Haviland 1752, HCA 1762, Hill 1804, Holland 1834, Home 1842, Honeywell 1852, Houston 1871,

Howard 1873, Huna 1887, Huntsman 1895, Hutton 1899, Independence 1925, ING 1938, Ingersoll 1939, International 1968, International 1971, Intertech 1976, Interthyr 1978, IPALCO 1988, ITW 2001, Jack 2007, Johnson 2050, Juno 2076, Kaman 2088, Kellogg 2120, Keystone 2138, Koniag 2184, KPMG 2190, L'Oreal 2203, Latham 2229, Life 2268, Lilly 2274, Lincoln 2279, Lincoln 2282, Lockheed 2292, Lowe's 2312, Major 2345, Manti 2359, Marena 2372, MarkleBank 2379, McDonald's 2427, Me-Tex 2442, MEEMIC 2455, Merck 2466, Metropolitan 2480, Miller 2523, Miracle 2535, Murphy 2600, National 2634, National 2638, New England 2670, New York 2690, New York 2691, NIKE 2710, Nikon 2711, North 2729, NYSE 2769, Oaklandish 2773, Office 2785, Orthopaedic 2829, Our 2838, Packard 2862, Panasonic 2870, Papa 2876, Parametric 2878, Pebble 2913, Penn 2923, Penney 2925, Pitney 2984, Playboy 2990, Plum 2991, PricewaterhouseCoopers 3042, Pro 3052, Promotional 3061, Prudential 3072, PSS 3074, Quest 3103, Raytheon 3135, Recreational 3150, Rock 3238, Rostra 3268, Royal 3274, Ruby 3281, Rusco 3288, Ryder 3292, San Diego 3322, San Francisco 3325, sanofi-aventis 3329, Schwab 3363, Scott 3368, Scripps 3374, SEAKR 3379, Sealaska 3380, SeaWorld 3387, Sempra 3405, Seneca 3406, ServiceMaster 3414, Shaklee 3418, Shelter 3431, Sitnasuak 3467, Skadden 3470, South 3508, South 3509, Southern 3516, Southern 3520, Strauss 3624, Sullivan 3635, Sulphur 3637, Swift 3667, Target 3691, Tatitlek 3694, Times 3758, Toshiba 3776, Tri 3805, Turf 3822, Tyler 3830, U-Haul 3833, United 3869, United 3879, UnitedHealth 3884, Vermont 3940, Vernier 3941, VHA 3944, Villency 3955, Volkswagen 3967, Wal-Mart 3980, Walgreen 3981, Washington 3995, Washington 3999, Washington 4000, Weather 4013, Wiley 4072, Wonder 4107, Yates 4142

In-kind gifts

3M 3, 7-Eleven 5, Abercrombie 17, Abita 19, Adir 36, Advanced 40, AEG 43, Aeropostale 46, AFC 50, Ag 55, AGL 57, Air 63, Alaska 74, Alaska 75, Alaska 76, Alcon 83, Alexion 86, Alpha 112, Altria 120, Amazon.com 122, AMC 126, Ameren 128, American 150, American 153, American 158, Amgen 182, Amway 189, Anaheim 191, Andersen 194, Angels 200, Anschutz 205, Apache 211, Apple 218, ARAMARK 223, Arcelormittal 229, Arch 230, Arizona 239, AstraZeneca 272, Athletics 276, Atlanta 277, Atlanta 278, Atlanta 280, Austin 288, Autodesk 289, Autoliv 290, AutoNation 292, AutoZone 294, Avis 300, Avista 301, AZPB 310, B & B 312, Baltimore 334, Baltimore 335, Bank 342, Bank 349, Baseball 367, BASF 368, Bashas' 369, Basketball 370, Baxter 377, Bayer 381, BB&T 385, Becton 398, Bed 399, Ben 409, Berry 437, Berry 438, Big 460, Big 461, Biomet 466, Birmingham 472, Black 474, Blockbuster 483, Bloomberg 486, Blue 491, Blue 493, Blue 494, Blue 499, Bobcats 512, Boehringer 515, Boeing 516, Bosch 529, Boston 533, Boston 535, Boston 536, Boston 537, Boston 538, Boston 540, Boyd 546, Brady 552, Bristol 578, Brooklyn 584, Brown 590, Brown 592, Buccaneer 599, Budget 604, Buffalo 606, Burger 613, Burrtec 622, CA 638, Cadence 646, Caesars 650, Callaway 660, Campbell 669, Capstone 684, Cardinal 685, Carnival 696, Carolina 698, Carrols 704, Carter's 708, Cascade 713, Cavaliers 724, CC 728, CDW 729, Celgene 732, Center 737, CenterPoint 738, Cephalon 752, CH2M 758, Chemtura 775, Chesapeake 777, Chicago 781, Chicago 782, Chicago 783, Chicago 784, Chicago 790, Chick 791, Chicopee 792, Chiquita 795, Churchill 807, CIBA 810, Cincinnati 813, Cincinnati 814, Cinemark 815, Cintas 816, Circle 817, CITGO 820, City 830, Cleveland 846, Cleveland 847, CNA 855, CNH 856, Coca 861, Coca 862, Coca 863, Collective 871, Colonial 874, Colorado 877, Colorado 879, Columbia 884, Columbus 886, Commercial 893, Compuware 902, ConAgra 904, Conn 909, Connecticut 911, Consolidated 916, Consumers 921, Contran 928, Cooper 935, Costco 948, Covidien 956, Cox 958, Coyotes 963, Creative 975, Crown 987, CSX 997, CVS 1014, D.C. 1018, Dallas 1021, Dallas 1022, Dallas 1023, Darden 1032, Day 1046, Deere 1061, Delaware 1066, Dell 1068, Delmarva 1069, Deloitte 1070, Delta 1073, Delta 1075, Delta 1077, Delta 1080, Denver 1090, Detroit 1094, Detroit 1095, Detroit 1096, Detroit 1097, Devon 1102, DHL 1106, Diamonds 1109, DIRECTV 1124, Discovery 1126, Disney 1127, Disney 1128, Diversey 1130, Do 1136, Doctor's 1138, Dole 1141, Dollar 1143, Dolphins 1147, Dominion 1150, Dow 1161, Dr 1169, Draper 1171, DS 1182, DTE 1183, Duke 1189, Dunkin' 1191, Duquesne 1194, Earthquakes 1206, Eastern 1211, Eastman 1214, Eaton 1216, Edelman 1224, Edison 1228, Elevation 1245, EMC 1253, Entergy 1279, Epson 1286, EQT 1287, Esurance 1298, Exelon 1309, Faribault 1332, FedEx 1352, Fender 1359, Fennemore 1360, Ferrellgas 1365, Fila 1379, First 1398, Fisher 1433, Florida 1442, Florida 1443, Flowers 1446, Flowserve 1447, Follett 1455, Food 1458, Football 1460, ForceBrain.com 1461, Ford 1464, Foremost 1466, Forest 1468, Fox 1480, Gallo 1529, Gap 1533, Gates 1540, GATX 1542, General 1550, General 1554, General 1555, Genesco 1559, Georgia 1568, Giant 1571, Giant 1572, Giant 1573, Gibson 1578, Give 1583, GlaxoSmithKline 1588, Google 1613, Granite 1632, Great 1642, Green 1651, Green 1653, Greif 1663, Gulfstream 1690, Gymboree 1693, H & R 1695, Halliburton 1706, Hampton 1714, Hanesbrands 1720, Harris 1738, Hartz 1744, Hasbro 1747, Heat 1767, Heinz 1772, Helmerich 1774, Henry 1781, Herschend 1790, Hewlett 1794, Hill 1803, Hillshire 1809, Hilton 1812, Hockey 1819, Hoffmann 1823, HolacracyOne 1826, Holland 1835, Honda 1851, Hood 1854, Hoops 1857, Horizon 1861, Hormel 1866, Houston 1871, Houston 1872, HSBC 1876, Huna 1887, Hunt 1888, Hunt 1891, Huntington 1894, Hy-Vee 1900, IDACORP 1907, IMS 1924, Indianapolis 1932, ING 1938, Ingram 1941, Insperity 1944, Intel 1950, Interface 1953, Intermountain 1956, International 1960, International 1961, International 1964, International 1968, Intuit 1982, Jabil 2006, Jackson 2009, Jacksonville 2014, Jelly 2033, Johnson 2049, Jones 2059, JPMorgan Chase 2071, Juniper 2075, Kaiser 2086, Kansas 2091, Kansas 2093, Kansas 2094, KB 2105, KBR 2106, Kennecott 2127, Kent 2129, KeyBank 2136, Kimberly 2150, King 2159, KLA-Tencor 2165, Kmart 2172, Koch 2180, Kohler 2182, Kroenke 2194, Lake 2212, Lands' 2220, Lauder 2230, Lee 2241, Lemieux 2249, LensCrafters 2251, Lexmark 2258, Liberty 2265, Lilly 2274, Limited 2277, Lincoln 2280, Lincoln 2282, Lithia 2287, Loews 2296, Loomis 2301, Los Angeles 2305, Los Angeles 2306, Los Angeles 2308, Louisiana 2309, Louisiana 2310, LSI 2314, M&T 2323, Macfarlane-Chang 2331, Madison 2336, Main 2342, Major 2345, Major 2347, Marathon 2365, Maritz 2376, Mars 2384, Marsh 2385, Marsh 2387, Martin 2391, Mary 2392, Masco 2393, Massachusetts 2397, MasterCard 2399, Matson 2404, Mattel 2405, McCormick 2423, McDonald's 2427, McGraw 2429, McKee 2432, McKesson 2434, Mead 2443, Medtronic 2453, Meijer 2456, Men's 2460, Metropolitan 2481, Meyer 2485, Miami 2491, Michael 2493, Michelin 2495, Michigan 2496, Miller 2523, Milwaukee 2527, Milwaukee 2528, Minnesota 2530, Minnesota 2531, Mohegan 2546, Mondelez 2556, Monsanto 2559, Monster 2560, Moore 2565, Morris 2574, Morton 2579, Mosaic 2580, MSC 2593, Mutual 2607, Namaste 2614, Nashville 2620, National 2628, National 2638, Nationwide 2639, Nestle 2662, Nestle 2663, New 2668, New 2679, New England 2672, New Jersey 2676, New York 2684, New York 2686, New York 2690, New York 2691, Newell 2694, Newsweek 2703, NIBCO 2707, NIKE 2710, Nissan 2716, Nordson 2723, Northfield 2742, Northrim 2743, Northwest 2747, NorthWestern 2748, Novartis 2753, Novetta 2755, Nucor 2760, NV 2765, Oakland 2772, Office 2785, OMNOVA 2809, One 2812, OppenheimerFunds 2818, Oracle 2821, Orlando 2824, Otter 2836, Owens 2842, Pacers 2852, Pacific 2853, Pacific 2855, Palace 2866, Panda 2871, Panera 2873, Parametric 2878, Patagonia 2892, Pathmark 2894, Pawtucket 2902, PDB 2906, Pearson 2911, Pearson 2912, Peet's 2916, Penguin 2922, Penney 2925, People's 2928, PepsiCo 2935, Performance 2938, PETCO 2945, Pfizer 2950, PGA 2953, PGA 2954, Philadelphia 2957, Philadelphia 2958, Philadelphia 2959, Philadelphia 2961, Phoenix 2968, Pier 2973, Pittsburgh 2985, Pittsburgh 2986, Pizza 2988, Playboy 2990, Polaris 2999, Polk 3000, Portland 3010, Potomac 3018, Premera 3034, Pro 3054, Procter 3055, Prudential 3072, Publix 3079, QUALCOMM 3095, Questar 3104, Quiksilver 3108, QuikTrip 3109, Raley's 3122, Reckitt 3146, Reebok 3159, Reed 3161, Regal 3166, Rich 3204, Richardson 3209, Riviana 3227, Roche 3236, Rocket 3240, Rockwell 3246, Rolls 3254, Roundy's 3272, Royal 3273, RPM 3278, Ryder 3292, Sacramento 3303, Salt 3319, Samsung 3320, San Antonio 3321, San Diego 3322, San Diego 3323, San Francisco 3324, San Francisco 3326, SANYO 3333, SAS 3336, Save 3342, SCANA 3346, Schein 3348, Schneider 3355, Scholastic 3358, Schwab 3363, Scotts 3372, Seagate 3377, Sealy 3382, Sears 3384, Securian 3389, Seminole 3404, Shaklee 3418, Sharp 3422, Shaw's 3427, ShopKo 3440, Siemens 3448, Simplot 3459, SkyWest 3476, Smithfield 3487, Smucker 3488, Sodexho 3497, Sony 3503, Southern 3514, Southwest 3524, Spansion 3532, Spirit 3544, Sporting 3546, Sports 3548, Sports 3549, Sprint 3556, Spurs 3557, St. Louis 3567, St. Louis 3568, St. Louis 3569, StanCorp 3574, Staples 3581, Starbucks 3585, Starwood 3589, State 3591, State 3592, Steelcase 3597, Stiles 3607, Strauss 3624, Sunkist 3649, Sunoco 3650, Super 3656, Superior 3657, SUPERVALU 3659, Sweetbay 3665, Symantec 3669, Syniverse 3672, Sysco 3677, Talbots 3682, Tampa 3686, Target 3691, TD 3696, Teck 3700, Tennessee 3716, Tesoro 3723, Texas 3728, Tim 3753, Time 3755, Time 3756, TJX 3765, Toll 3769, Tom's 3770, Tops 3774, Toro 3775, Totem 3779, Toyota 3786, Toys 3790, Trail 3793, Trustmark 3818, Tucson 3819, Tupperware 3821, Turner 3823, Twins 3827, Tyson 3832, U.S. 3835, U.S. 3836, U.S. 3838, UBS 3842, UMB 3846, Union 3857, United 3860, United 3863, United 3870, United 3872, United 3880, United 3882, Unitil 3885, Universal 3889, Universal 3893, Urban 3901, US 3902, USEC 3904, UTC 3908, Valspar 3920, Volvo 3968, Wakefern 3979, Wal-Mart 3980, Walgreen 3981, Washington 3997, Washington 3998, Washington 3999, Washington 4000, Waterford 4002, Watson 4006, Watson 4007, Wawa 4009, Weather 4013, Wegmans 4021, Weis 4024, Welch 4025, West 4037, Western 4042, Westfield 4047, Weyerhaeuser 4052, Windway 4086, Winn 4087, Wisconsin 4093, World 4121, Worthington 4124, Wrigley 4125, Xilinx 4137, Yum! 4150, Zappos.com 4153, Zimmer 4157, Zotos 4159

Income development

Agora 58, Blue 502, Brooklyn 584, Capitol 680, Cavaliers 724, Center 737, D.C. 1018, Dallas 1021, Dallas 1023, Detroit 1095, Esurance 1298, Florida 1442, Hoops 1857, Houston 1871, Indianapolis 1932, Kansas 2093, Los Angeles 2308, M&T 2323, Macfarlane-Chang 2331, Marsh 2387, Middlesex 2506, Milwaukee 2527, Milwaukee 2528, Nashville 2620, New Jersey 2676, New York 2684, New York 2686, Oakland 2772, Palace 2866, Philadelphia 2957, Philadelphia 2958, Philadelphia 2959, Phoenix 2968, Pittsburgh 2986, San Antonio 3321, San Diego 3322, San Diego 3323, Sports 3549, Spurs 3557, St. Louis 3567, St. Louis 3569, Tennessee 3716, Timken 3760, UBS 3842, Washington 3998, Washington 4000, Wawa 4009, Wegmans 4021

Internship funds

Aleut 84, Avista 301, Bank 340, Blair 478, Boeing 516, Brinks 573, Brown 590, Capitol 680, Chenega 776, Convergys 933, Cook 934, Dow 1163, Doyon 1167, Florida 1443, Ford 1464, Freeport 1494, GlaxoSmithKline 1588, Hancock 1717, Heinz 1772, Johnson 2048, Koniag 2184, Long 2298, Merck 2466, Morgan 2570, Post 3016, Scripps 3374, Textron 3731

Land acquisition

Aspen 260, Avista 301, Equifax 1288, Four 1477, Grand 1629, Mitsubishi 2539, Morgan 2568

Loaned talent

Air 63, Alabama 71, Alliant 104, Allstate 107, Anschutz 205, AutoNation 292, Baltimore 335, Blue 493, Boeing 516, Brooklyn 584, Buffalo 606, Butt 628, Capital 679, Cavaliers 724, CC 728, Citizens 824, City 830, Colonial 874, Connecticut 911, Cooper 935, D.C. 1018, Deloitte 1070, Denver 1090, Detroit 1094, Detroit 1096, Detroit 1097, Diversey 1130, Edelman 1224, First 1398, Florida 1442, Fluor 1448, Focus 1451, GATX 1542, General 1554, Gulfstream 1690, Hanson 1725, Hartford 1743, Heat 1767, Holcim 1828, Hunt 1888, Huntington 1894, Idealist 1909, Imation 1919, Jacksonville 2014, Kansas 2093, Kroenke 2194, Law 2233, Los Angeles 2308, McDermott 2424, Milwaukee 2527, Milwaukee 2528, Minnesota 2530, Nashville 2620, New Jersey 2676, New York 2691, Newell 2694, Oakland 2772, Ogilvy 2788, Padilla 2864, Palace 2866, PDB 2906, People's 2928, Philadelphia 2959, Philip 2962, Pittsburgh 2986, Questar 3104, QuikTrip 3109, Rich 3204, Royal 3273, RPM 3278, Rudolph 3283, SAIC 3311, San Antonio 3321, San Diego 3322, SCANA 3346, Sears 3384, Securian 3389, Sports 3549, Spurs 3557, St. Louis 3567, StanCorp 3574, Tampa 3686, TCF 3695, TD 3696, Tennessee 3716, U.S. 3836, Unitil 3885, Vision 3961, Washington 3998, Washington 4000

Loans—to individuals

Bank 340, Chevron 780, Delta 1080, Guardian 1683, Haviland 1752, Morris 2573, Nord 2721, Rostra 3268, Sovereign 3528

Management development/capacity building

Abbott 13, Alcoa 82, Alcon 83, Allstate 107, American 143, Ameristar 176, Arby's 228, Aspen 260, Bank 340, Ben 409, Blue 493, Blue 496, Blue 497, Blue 501, Bristol 578, Brown 590, Burlington 618, California 655, Cambia 665, Capitol 680, Carlson 693, Chicago 790, Citigroup 821, Clif 848, Compass 901, ConAgra 904, Corning 945, Covidien 956, Credit 980, CVS 1014, Delta 1083, Deutsche 1099, Dot 1158, Duke 1189, Eastern 1210, Energy 1272, Equifax 1288, Federal 1348, Fieldstone 1374, FMR 1450, Four 1477, Freeport 1494, Gap 1533, General 1552, Genworth 1565, Gilead 1582, Graco 1624, Grand 1629, Guard 1680, Hastings 1749, Highmark 1799, HSBC 1876, Johnson 2048, JPMorgan Chase 2071, Kaiser 2086, Kerzner 2133, Laird 2211, Liberty 2262, Louisiana 2309, M&T 2323, McJunkin 2431, Medtronic 2453, Merck 2466, Middlesex 2506, Mizuho 2542, Moody's 2563, National 2626, New York 2683, Newman's 2697, NIKE 2710, Pacific 2853, Pacific 2855, Panasonic 2869, People's 2928, PepsiCo 2935, Pfizer 2950, Piedmont 2971, Primerica 3045, Provident 3069, Prudential 3072, Schwab 3363, St. Joe 3563, Steelcase 3597, Strauss 3624, Superior 3658, TD 3696, Tellabs 3709, Thrivent 3747, Tofias 3768, U.S. 3836, UBS 3842, Union 3854, Union 3857, United 3872, UTC 3908, Wal-Mart 3980, Wellmark 4026, Wells 4028

Matching/challenge support

Activision 30, Aetna 48, Air 63, Alabama 71, Alcoa 82, Allete 100, Alliant 104, Ameren 128, American 150, Ameritec 179, AMETEK 181, Amgen 182, Amica 183, Anheuser 202, Arizona 239, Arkema 242, Assurant 267, AT&T 273, Athletics 276, Autodesk 289, Bangor 338, Bank 342, Batts 374, BB&T 385, Belk 403, Biomet 466, Bloomberg 486, Blue 497, Blue 502, Blue 504, Boeing 516, Bridgestone 560, Bridgeway 563, Bristol 577, Build 608, Burlington 618, Callaway 660, Campbell 669, Capitol 680, Cardinal 685, Carlson 693, Cascade 713, Caterpillar 722, Centene 735, Chaney 761, Cleary 843, COLHOC 870, Collette 872, Compass 901, Contran 928, Cow 957, Cox 959, Cracker 966, Credit 980, Cummins 1007, Cutco 1012, Darden 1032, Delta 1077, Delta 1081, Deutsche 1099, Dime 1118, Dispatch 1129, Dominion 1150, Dow 1162, Duke 1189, Eastern 1211, Eaton 1216, Elevation 1245, Emerson 1257, Empire 1262, Endres 1269, Energy 1272, EQT 1287, Equifax 1288, ERM 1292, Exelon 1309, Fieldstone 1374, Fifth 1376, First 1403, First 1409, First 1419, First 1420, FMR 1450, Foley 1454, Four 1477, Framingham 1481, Freeport 1494, Fuller 1517, GATX 1542, General 1555, GlaxoSmithKline 1588, Globe 1594, H & R 1695, Hastings 1749, HCA 1762, HCR 1763, Herschend 1790, Highmark 1799, Humana 1886, Iberdrola 1904, Ingram 1941, Intel 1950, Investors 1984, Island 1996, Jack 2007, Jacksonville 2014, Jacobs 2016, Jeld 2032, Kellwood 2121, KeyBank 2136, Kingsbury 2160, Koch 2179, Korum 2187, Koss 2188, Kukui 2198, Land 2217, Landmark 2218, Larkin 2224, Lego 2247, LG&E Energy 2260, Liberty 2262, Lilly 2274, Lincoln 2281, Louisiana 2309, M&T 2323, Macy's 2333, Majestic 2343, Mars 2384, McClatchy 2422, Medeanalytics 2447, Merk 2467, Modine 2544, Mohawk 2545, Monsanto 2559, Mt. 2594, Mutual 2607, National 2632, National 2635, National 2638, Nationwide 2639, Nellie 2659, New 2668, New England 2670, New York 2683, Newman's 2697, Norfolk 2725, Northwestern 2749, NV 2765, OceanFirst 2782, ONEOK 2815, Osram 2834, Otter 2836, Owens 2844, Pacific 2853, PacifiCorp 2860, Pattillo 2896, Perforce 2937, Pioneer 2980, PNC 2997, Provident 3069, Quad 3091, Quaker 3093, QUALCOMM 3095, Raymond 3133, Rayonier 3134, Red 3154, Rich 3204, Riverway 3226, Rockville 3245, RPM 3278, Saint 3312, Schwab 3363, Scoular 3373, Scripps 3374, Sempra 3405, Sensient 3408, ShopKo 3440, Sioux 3465, Skinner 3475, Southern 3521, Spirit 3544, Square 3560, St. Louis 3569, Superior 3658, Tanner 3688, Teachers 3697, TECO 3701, Tennant 3714, Textron 3731, Thomasville 3737, Thrivent 3747, Toro 3775, Toys 3790, Trim 3810, Tulalip 3820, Tupperware 3821, Turner 3823, U.S. 3836, UBS 3842, UTC 3908, Utica 3910, Vulcan 3972, Wal-Mart 3980, Washington 3994, Washington 3996, Wells 4028, Wenger 4033, West 4038, Western 4045, Whirlpool 4056, Wiley 4072, Williams 4077, Winn 4087, Winnebago 4088, YSI 4149

Mission-related investments/loans

Boston 533, Deutsche 1099, Mitsubishi 2539, Pattillo 2896, Prudential 3072

Professorships

BB&T 385, Boeing 516, Capitol 680, Commerce 890, Deloitte 1070, First 1406, GlaxoSmithKline 1588, Humana 1886, Kahn 2084, KPMG 2190, Lee 2241, Micron 2500, Oklahoma 2794, PricewaterhouseCoopers 3042, Principal 3047, Respironics 3193, Scripps 3374, Square 3560, St. Joe 3563, U.S. 3836, Xerox 4136

Program development

3M 3, 7-Eleven 5, A.D. 7, Abbott 13, Abby's 14, AbbyBank 15, Abercrombie 17, Aberdeen 18, Accenture 22, ACE 24, Acme 29, Acuity 32, adidas 35, Adobe 38, Advanced 40, AEGON 45, Aeropostale 46, Aetna 48, Aflac 54, Agilent 56, AGL 57, AgStar 59, Air 63, Alabama 71, Alaska 74, Alaska 76, Albemarle 78, Albertsons 79, Alcatel 81, Alcoa 82, Alcon 83, Alexander 85, Allegheny 91, Allegis 92, Allen 94, Allergan 99, Allete 100, Alliant 104, Allstate 107, Alpenrose 111, Alro 113, Altria 120, Amboy 124, AMC 125, Ameren 128, Ameren 129, American 132, American 137, American 140, American 141, American 143, American 144, American 145, American 150, American 151, American 155, American 157, AMERIGROUP 171, Ameriprise 174, Amerisure 177, Ameritas 178, Ameritec 179, AMETEK 181, Amgen 182, AMPCO 186, AnchorBank 193, Andersen 194, Androscoggin 199, Anheuser 202, Aon 210, Apex 213, Apex 214, Apollo 216, Apple 218, Applied 220, Arbeit 225, Arbella 226, Arcelormittal 229, Archer 233, Arkansas 240, Arrow 249, Arrowpoint 251, Artichoke 254, Ashland 258, Aspen 260, Associated 261, Associated 264, Assurant 266, Assurant 267, Assurant 268, Astoria 270, AstraZeneca 272, AT&T 273, AT&T 274, Athletics 276, Autodesk 289, Avelina 296, Avery 297, Avidia 298, Avista 301, Avon 305, AZPB 310, Azulay 311, Badger 313, Baird 317, Baker 323, Baltimore 332, Bangor 338, Bank 340, Bank 341, Bank 342, Bank 344, Bank 346, Bank 347, Bank 348, Bard 358, Bardes 359, Barrasso 363, Barron's 364, Bassett 372, Batson 373, Batts 374, Bausch 376, Baxter 377, Bay 378, Bay 380, Bayer 381, BayView 384, BB&T 385, Bean 392, Bear 393, Bechtel 395, Beckman 397, Becton 398, Belk 403, Belk 404, Belo 406, Ben 409, Beneficial 411, Beneficial 412, Bergquist 420, Bergstrom 421, Berkley 426, Berkshire 428, Berry 434, Berry 436, Best 442, Better 448, Bickel 457, Biogen 465, Biomet 466, Birdsong 470, Birmingham 471, BJ's 473, Black 475, Blockbuster 483, Blue 489, Blue 490, Blue 492, Blue 493, Blue 495, Blue 496, Blue 497, Blue 498, Blue 501, Blue 502, Blue 504, Blue 505, Blue 506, BlueCross 507, BMC 508, BMW 509, Bobcats 512, Boehringer 515, Boeing 516, Boler 520, Bon 521, Boneal 523, Booz 525, Boston 540, Bound 541, Bourns 542, Boyd 545, BP 547, Brady 552, Bricker 559, Bridgestone 560, Bridgewater 562, Bridgeway 563, Briggs 564, Briggs 565, Brinks 573, Bristol 577, Bristol 578, Broadcom 579, Brooklyn 584, Brooks 585, Brotherhood 588, Brown 590, Brown 591, Brunswick 595, Buccaneer 599, Buffalo 606, Build 608, Bunge 612, Burger 613, Burlington 618, Burns 620, Butt 628, Byers 630, C Spire 636, Cabot 642, Caesars 650, Cajun 652, California 655, Callaway 660, Calvert 663, Cambia 665, Campbell 669, Canon 672, Caparo 673, Cape 674, Capezio 675, Capital 679, Capitol 680, Cardinal 685, CareFusion 688, Cargill 691, Carlson 693, CarMax 694, Carson 705, Carver 711, Cascade 713, Castle 716, Catalina 719, Caterpillar 722, Cavaliers 724, Centene 735, CentiMark 740, Central 745, CenturyLink 751, Cerner 754, CF 755, CFS 756, CH2M 758, Chandler 760, Chaney 761, Charles 764, Charter 767, Chase 769, Chase 770, Chelsea 772, Chevron 780, Chicago 785, Chicago 786, Chicago 787, Chicago 788, Chicago 790, Chick 791, Chicopee 792, Chiquita 795, Choice 798, Chotin 799, Chrysler 801, CHS 802, Chubb 804, Churchill 807, Cianbro 808, CIBA 809, Cic 811, CIGNA 812, Cisco 818, CIT 819, CITGO 820, Citigroup 821, Citizens 828, City 830, Claremont 833, Clarity 834, Clark 835, Clayton 841, Clemens 844, Clements 845, Cleveland 846, Clif 848, Clorox 852, CME 853, CMS 854, CNA 855, CNO 857, Coach 858, Coca 861, Coca 862, Coca 863, COLHOC 870, Collective 871, Collette 872, Colorado 879, Colorado 880, Columbia 882, Columbia 884, Comcast 887, Comerica 889, Commerce 890, Commercial 893, Community 898, Community 900, Compass 901, Compuware 902, ConAgra 904, Concept 905, Conditioned 906, Conn 909, Connecticut 911, Connecticut 912, Consolidated 917, Consumers 921, Continental 922, Contran 928, Control 929, Cook 934, Cooper 935, COPIC 937, Coquille 939, Coral 940, Corning 945, Corvallis 947, County 952, Cousins 953, Covidien 956, Cow 957, Cox 959, Cracker 966, Crayola 973, Creative 975, Credit 977, Credit 980, Crowell 986, CryoLife 990, Crystal 992, CSX 997, Cummins 1006, Cummins 1007, CUNA 1008, CVS 1014, Cymer 1016, Danis 1029, Dannon 1030, Darden 1032, Dayton 1047, Dean 1053, Dean 1054, DeBruce 1057, Dedham 1060, Deere 1061, Delphi 1071, Delphos 1072, Delta 1073, Delta 1074, Delta 1076, Delta 1077, Delta 1079, Delta 1080, Delta 1082, Delta 1083, Deluxe 1084, Demoulas 1085, DENSO 1088, Dethmers 1091, Detroit 1095, Deutsche 1099, Devon 1102, Diagnos-Techs 1108, Diebold 1112, Digi 1115, Dilbeck 1116, Dime 1118, Discovery 1126, Disney 1127, Doctors 1139, Dollar 1142, Dominion 1148, Dominion 1150, Dot 1158, Dow 1161, Dow 1162, DP 1168, Dreyer's 1174, DRS 1179, DRW 1181, DTE 1183, Duane 1186, Duke 1189, Dupps 1193, Duquesne 1194, Dutch 1197, Dynamet 1200, Eagle 1203, Earnhardt 1205, East 1207, East 1208, Eastern 1209, Eastern 1210, Easthampton 1212,

Eastman 1213, Eastman 1214, Eaton 1216, eBay 1217, Ecolab 1220, Edina 1227, Edison 1228, Edvisors 1234, EFC 1236, El Paso 1239, Elias 1247, Emerson 1257, EMI 1258, Emmis 1260, Empire 1262, Endeavor 1267, Energizer 1271, Energy 1272, Ensign 1276, Entelco 1277, Entergy 1278, Entergy 1279, Entergy 1280, Enterprise 1281, Epson 1286, EQT 1287, Ethicon 1299, Exchange 1306, Exelon 1309, Express 1313, Extendicare 1314, Exxon 1315, Farmers 1338, Farmers 1339, Farrell 1341, FBR 1345, Federal 1348, Federated 1351, FedEx 1352, Fender 1359, Ferro 1366, Fidelity 1371, Fieldstone 1374, Fifth 1376, Fifth 1377, Financial 1382, Finish 1383, Fireman's 1385, First 1389, First 1390, First 1391, First 1395, First 1397, First 1398, First 1399, First 1402, First 1405, First 1406, First 1409, First 1413, First 1416, First 1419, First 1420, First 1421, First 1422, FirstEnergy 1424, Firstmerit 1425, Fisher 1431, Fisher 1433, Flextronics 1437, Florence 1441, Florida 1443, Fluor 1448, FMR 1450, Foley 1454, Food 1458, Foot 1459, Ford 1464, Forest 1467, Formosa 1470, Fortis 1473, Four 1477, Framingham 1481, Franklin 1488, Freedman 1493, Freescale 1495, Fremont 1496, Fremont 1497, Friedland 1503, Friesen 1505, Frontier 1510, Fuller 1517, Fulton 1518, Furr 1520, G&K 1524, Gannett 1532, Gap 1533, Garden 1535, Gear 1544, Gemini 1547, GenCorp 1548, Genentech 1549, General 1552, General 1554, General 1555, GenOn 1563, GenRad 1564, Genworth 1565, Georgia 1567, Georgia 1568, Giant 1571, Gibbs 1576, Gibraltar 1577, Gilead 1582, GlaxoSmithKline 1588, Global 1593, Golden 1602, Goldman 1604, Golub 1607, Gon 1608, Google 1613, Grace 1623, Graco 1624, Graham 1625, Grand 1627, Grand 1628, Grand 1629, Graphic 1634, Great 1644, Green 1651, Gregory 1661, Grinnell 1668, Griswold 1669, Grubb 1675, GTECH 1677, Guard 1680, Guess 1685, GuideOne 1687, Gulf 1689, H & R 1695, Hallberg 1704, Halliburton 1706, Hallmark 1707, Hammond 1711, Hampden 1712, Hamrick 1715, Hancock 1717, Hannaford 1723, Hanover 1724, Hard 1727, Harley 1732, Hartford 1742, Hasbro 1747, Haskell 1748, Hastings 1749, Hawaiian 1755, HCA 1762, HCR 1763, Heffernan 1769, Heidtman 1770, Heinz 1772, Henkels 1779, Herschend 1790, Hershey 1791, Hess 1793, Hewlett 1794, Highmark 1799, Hilfiger 1801, Hitachi 1816, Hoffmann 1823, Holiday 1832, Home 1843, Home 1845, Honda 1851, Honeywell 1852, Hoops 1857, Horizon 1863, Hormel 1866, Hospira 1867, Houston 1871, HSBC 1876, Hubbard 1878, Hudson 1880, Humana 1886, Huna 1887, Hunt 1892, Iberdrola 1904, IDACORP 1907, IHC 1913, Illinois 1916, IMA 1917, Independence 1925, Independent 1927, ING 1937, ING 1938, Ingersoll 1939, Ingram 1941, Inman 1943, Institution 1946, Integra 1947, Integrity 1948, Intel 1950, Interface 1953, International 1958, International 1960, International 1962, International 1963, International 1968, International 1971, Intuit 1982, Investors 1984, Inwood 1985, Iowa 1986, Island 1996, Jabil 2006, Jack 2007, Jackson 2009, Jacksonville 2014, Janus 2024, Jasper 2025, Jasper 2026, Jazz 2028, Jeld 2032, Jenzabar 2037, Jewett 2042, JM 2044, Jockey 2045, JOFCO 2046, Johns 2047, Johnson 2048, Johnson 2049, Johnson 2050, Johnson 2052, Johnson 2053, Jostens 2067, Joy 2070, JPMorgan 2072, JPMorgan Chase 2071, JSJ 2073, JustNeem 2079, Kaiser 2086, Kajima 2087, Kaman 2088, Kann 2090, Kansas 2092, KBR 2106, Keeneland 2113, Kellogg 2120, Kellwood 2121, Kemp 2123, Kennecott 2127, Kerzner 2133, KeyBank 2136, Kilmartin 2145, Kimberly 2150, Kimley 2151, Kinder 2153, Kingsbury 2160, KLA-Tencor 2165, Koch 2179, Korum 2187, Kowalski 2189, KPMG 2190, Kroger 2195, Kukui 2198, Laclede 2207, Laird 2211, Landmark 2218, Lands' 2220, Laureate 2231, Lear 2237, Legg 2245, Lego 2247, LG&E Energy 2260, Liberty 2262, Liberty 2264, Liberty 2265, Life 2268, Life 2269, LifePoint 2270, LifeScan 2271, Lilly 2274, Limited 2277, Lincoln 2278, Lincoln 2279, Lincoln 2281, Lincoln 2282, Lockheed 2292, Loews 2296, Long 2298, Longaberger 2299, Loomis 2301, Louisiana 2309, Louisiana 2310, Lowe's 2312, LSI 2314, Lucasfilm 2316, Luck 2317, M&T 2323, M.D.C. 2324, M/I 2325, Machias 2332, Macy's 2333, Madison 2334, Main 2342, Majestic 2343, Major 2345, Mamiye 2352, Manhattan 2354, Manocherian 2357, Marcus 2370, Marcus 2371, Marnier-Lapostolle 2381, Marr 2382, Martin 2391, Mary 2392, Mascoma 2394, Massachusetts 2397, Material 2402, Mattel 2405, Mautz 2408, Maverick 2409, MAXIMUS 2410, Mazda 2414, MB 2415, MBIA 2416, McAfee 2417, McClatchy 2422, McDermott 2424, McDonald 2426, McDonald's 2427, McGraw 2429, McJunkin 2431, McKesson 2434, McKinstry 2435, MDU 2441, MeadWestvaco 2445, Mechanics 2446, MedImmune 2450, Medtronic 2453, Menasha 2461, Mentor 2462, Merchants 2465, Merck 2466, Meredith 2471, Merfish 2472, Meritor 2473, Merk 2467, Merrimack 2474, Metropolitan 2481, Metropolitan 2484, MFA 2487, Miami 2491, Michelin 2495, Micron 2500, Midcontinent 2505, Middlesex 2506, Midmark 2507, Midwestone 2508, Milford 2514, Mine 2529, Mississippi 2536, Mitsubishi 2538, Mitsubishi 2539, Mizuho 2542, Modine 2544, Monadnock 2551, Mondelez 2556, MoneyGram 2558, Monsanto 2559, Monster 2560, Moody's 2563, Moore 2565, Morgan 2568, Morgan 2570, Mortenson 2577, Mortgage 2578, Mosaic 2580, Motley 2582, Motorola 2585, Motorola 2586, MPB 2591, MTD 2595, MTV 2596, Murphy 2600, Mutual 2603, Mutual 2607, Nasdaq 2617, Nasdaq 2618, Nash 2619, National 2622, National 2626, National 2630, National 2631, National 2632, National 2633, National 2634, National 2635, Nationwide 2639, Naugatuck 2645, Naugatuck 2646, NBC 2649, NEBCO 2653, NEC 2654, Neenah 2656, Nektar 2658, Nellie 2659, Nestle 2662, Nestle 2663, New England 2670, New England 2672, New York 2683, New York 2684, New York 2687, New York 2688, Newburyport 2693, Newfield 2695, Newman's 2697, Niemann 2708, NIKE 2710, Nippon 2713, NiSource 2715, Nissan 2716, Nomura 2720, Nordson 2723, Norfolk 2725, North 2728, North 2730, Northeast 2737, Northern 2740, Northfield 2741, Northfield 2742, Northrop 2744, Northwestern 2749, NV 2765, NYSE 2769, Oaklandish 2773, OceanFirst 2782, Office 2785, Ogilvy 2788, Ohio 2789, Ohio 2791, Oklahoma 2794, Oklahoma 2795, Old 2796, Old 2798, Ole 2800, Olin 2801, Olivetti 2802, Olympus 2804, Omaha 2805, Omaha 2806, Omnicare 2807, OMNOVA 2809, Omron 2810, Opus 2820, Orlando 2824, Oshkosh 2833, Otter 2836, Owens 2842, Pacers 2852, Pacific 2853, Pacific 2855, Pacifico 2859, PacifiCorp 2860, Panda 2871, Park 2880, Pattillo 2896, Pawtucket 2902, Paychex 2904, PDB 2906, Pearce 2910, Pearson 2911, Pearson 2912, Pella 2917, PEMCO 2919, Penn 2923, Penney 2925, Pentair 2926, People's 2928, Peoples 2929, Peoples 2931, PepsiCo 2935, Perrigo 2943, PETCO 2945, PetSmart 2948, Pfizer 2950, PFS 2951, PG&E 2952, Philip 2962, Piedmont 2971, Pioneer 2979, Pioneer 2980, Piper 2983, Pitney 2984, Pizza 2988, Plum 2991, PMI 2995, PNC 2997, Polaris 2999, Popular 3003, Portcullis 3004, Porter 3007, Portland 3010, Post 3016, PPG 3025, PPL 3026, Praxair 3029, Premera 3034, Premier 3036, Premix 3037, Presley 3038, Price 3040, PricewaterhouseCoopers 3042, Primerica 3045, Principal 3047, Printpack 3049, Procter 3055, ProLogis 3060, ProtechSoft 3065, Protective 3066, Provident 3069, Provident 3070, Prudential 3072, Public 3075, Public 3076, Public 3077, Publix 3079, Puget 3081, Pukall 3082, Pulte 3083, Putnam 3085, Putnam 3086, PVH 3088, Pyles 3089, QUALCOMM 3095, Quest 3103, Questar 3104, Quiksilver 3108, Rahr 3118, Ralph 3123, Ramerica 3125, Ratner 3130, Raymond 3133, Rayonier 3134, Raytheon 3135, RBC 3136, RBS 3137, RBS 3138, RE/MAX 3140, RealNetworks 3144, RECO 3148, Recreational 3150, Red 3154, Redlum 3156, Reebok 3159, Regal 3166, Regions 3171, Reily 3177, Residential 3190, Retail 3194, Rexnord 3198, Reynolds 3199, Reynolds 3200, Rich 3204, Riverway 3226, Robins 3232, Robinson 3235, Rockville 3245, Rockwell 3246, Rockwell 3247, Rose 3261, Rosen's 3264, Ross 3265, Ross 3267, Roundy's 3272, RPM 3278, RubinBrown 3280, Rue 3285, Ryman 3294, S & T 3297, S.J. 3299, Sacramento 3304, Safeco 3306, Safety 3309, Saint 3312, Salem 3316, Salem 3317, salesforce.com 3318, San Antonio 3321, San Francisco 3324, San Francisco 3326, San Jose 3327, Santa 3331, SANYO 3333, Saucony 3340, Savings 3343, SCANA 3346, ScanSource 3347, Schneider 3354, Schneider 3355, Scoular 3373, Scripps 3374, Seamen's 3383, Sears 3384, Seattle 3386, SeaWorld 3387, Securian 3389, Security 3394, Select 3398, Selective 3399, Selig 3401, Sempra 3405, Seneca 3406, Sensient 3408, Shanken 3421, Shaughnessy 3425, Shaw's 3427, Shea 3428, Shell 3430, Sherwin 3437, ShopKo 3440, SI 3444, Sierra 3451, Silicon 3455, Skinner 3475, SLM 3478, SmartWool 3479, Smith 3484, Smith 3485, Smithfield 3487, Snell 3490, Sony 3502, South 3512, Southern 3514, Southern 3515, Southern 3516, Southwest 3524, Sovereign 3528, Spansion 3532, Spector 3539, Spirit 3544, Spraying 3552, Sprint 3556, St. 3565, St. Joe 3563, St. Louis 3567, St. Louis 3568, St. Louis 3569, StanCorp 3574, Standard 3575, Standard 3576, Staples 3581, Starbucks 3585, Starwood 3589, State 3592, Steelcase 3597, Sterne 3602, Strauss 3624, Stupp 3628, Sturniolo 3629, Sub-Zero 3630, Subaru 3631, Suitter 3633, Sunoco 3650, SunTrust 3654, Superior 3658, SUPERVALU 3659, Susquehanna 3661, Sweetbay 3665, Swift 3666, Swinerton 3668, Symantec 3669, Syniverse 3672, Synopsys 3673, Talbots 3682, Tastefully 3692, TCF 3695, TD 3696, Teachers 3697, TeamQuest 3698, Tektronix 3706, Teleflex 3707, TeleTech 3708, Tellabs 3709, Tennessee 3716, Terlato 3720, Texas 3725, Texas 3728, Textron 3731, TFS 3732, Thermo 3733, Thomaston 3736, Thomasville 3737, Thomson 3742, Thrivent 3747, Tiffany 3750, Tillman 3752, Time 3755, Time 3757, Titan 3763, TIV 3764, TJX 3765, Tofias 3768, Toro 3775, Toshiba 3776, Towerbrook 3781, Toyota 3784, Toyota 3786, Toyota 3788, Toyota 3789, Travelers 3802, Tri 3805, Trim 3810, Tripifoods 3811, True 3814, Trustmark 3818, Tulalip 3820, Tupperware 3821, Turner 3823, Turner 3824, Turner 3825, Twins 3827, Tyco 3829, Tyson 3832, U.S. 3835, U.S. 3836, U.S. 3837, U.S. 3839, UBS 3842, Unaka 3848, Unilever 3853, Union 3854, Union 3857, Union 3858, United 3860, United 3863, United 3864, United 3868, United 3869, United 3871, United 3872, United 3876, United 3878, United 3882, UnitedHealth 3884, Univar 3886, Universal 3891, Unum 3898, Urban 3901, US 3902, USA 3903, USG 3905, UTC 3908, Utica 3910, Valero 3915, Valley 3917, Valspar 3920, Vectren 3925, Veridyne 3935, Verizon 3936, VHA 3944, Victorinox 3950, Viejas 3951, Vilter 3956, Virginia 3959, Visteon 3964, Vodafone 3965, Vulcan 3972, Wachtell 3973, Waffle 3975, Wake 3978, Wal-Mart 3980, Warburg 3985, Warrell 3991, Washington 3994, Washington 3995, Washington 3998, Washington 4001, Waterford 4002, Wawa 4009, Webster 4017, Webster 4018, Wegmans 4021, Wellmark 4026, WellPoint 4027, Wells 4028, Wendy's 4032, West 4034, West 4037, Westar 4039, Western 4040, Western 4045, Westfield 4047, Weyco 4051, Weyerhaeuser 4052, Whirlpool 4056, Whitney 4065, Whole 4066, Windway 4086, Winn 4087, Wisconsin 4093, Wisconsin 4096, Wood 4108, Woodforest 4110, WorkflowOne 4115, Worthen 4123, Wrigley 4125, WSFS 4127, Wynnne 4133, Xcel 4135, Xerox 4136, Xilinx 4137, YSI 4149, Yum! 4150, Zions 4158

Program evaluation

Agilent 56, American 145, Amgen 182, Arkansas 240, Aspen 260, Blue 497, Blue 504, Boeing 516, Bristol 578, Brown 590, California 655, CHS 802, City 830, ConAgra 904, Corning 945, Delta 1074, Hallmark 1707, Johnson 2048, Louisiana 2309, Metropolitan 2481, Monsanto 2559, Nellie 2659, Orlando 2824, Pfizer 2950, Principal 3047, Riverway 3226, Savings 3343, Toyota 3784, Universal 3887, Wells 4028

Program-related investments/loans

Ashland 258, Blue 501, Calvert 663, Coats 860, Deutsche 1099, Eaton 1216, Four 1477, IDT 1910, JPMorgan Chase 2071, Laird 2211, Metropolitan 2481, Mitsubishi 2539, Pattillo 2896, Philip 2962, PNC 2997, Primary 3043, Prudential 3072, Questar 3104, Redwoods 3158, Regions 3171, Security 3391, Southern 3514, Untours 3897, Wells 4028

Public relations services

Alliant 104, Amazon.com 122, AutoNation 292, Bay 380, Bering 422, Blue 493, Boeing 516, C & S 634, Churchill 807, City 830, Edelman 1224, IDACORP 1907, iVillage 2002, Metropolitan 2484, National 2633, Padilla 2864, RBS 3137, Rich 3204, RPM 3278, Wegmans 4021, Yum! 4150

Publication

Amazon.com 122, Ameren 129, American 152, Bayer 382, BB&T 385, Berkshire 428, Boeing 516, Brown 590, Cabot 642, Chicago 790, Colorado 879, Comcast 887, Contran 928, Control 929, Cummins 1007, EFC 1236, Federal 1348, First 1422, FMR 1450, Ford 1464, General 1552, Graphic 1634, Guess 1685, IDACORP 1907, Independent 1927, International 1961, International 1962, International 1972, Life 2268, M&T 2323, Manitowoc 2356, Mascoma 2394, McDonald's 2427, Medtronic 2453, Merck 2466, Metropolitan 2481, NEC 2654, New York 2683, Packard 2862, Pinnacle 2977, PNC 2997, ResMed 3192, Retail 3194, St. Joe 3563, St. Louis 3569, Strauss 3624, UBS 3842, United 3872, United 3873, UnitedHealth 3884, Wellmark 4026, Wiley 4072, World 4121, YSI 4149

Research

Abbott 13, Aberdeen 18, Aetna 48, Aflac 54, Agilent 56, Alcoa 82, Alcon 83, Allegheny 91, Alliant 104, Allstate 107, American 145, American 158, AMERIGROUP 171, Ameritec 179, AMETEK 181, Amgen 182, Amica 183, Apollo 216, Arbeit 225, Arizona 239, Arkansas 240, Aspen 260, Associated 263, Avon 305, Bayer 382, Beneficial 411, Black 475, Bloomberg 486, Blue 498, Blue 502, Blue 504, Boehringer 515, Boeing 516, Boiron 519, BOSE 530, BP 547, Bradley 551, Bridgestone 560, Bristol 578, Broadcom 579, Buffalo 606, Build 608, Butt 628, Cablevision 641, Caesars 650, California 655, Cambia 665, Capital 678, Cardinal 685, Castle 717, Charles 764, Chase 769, Chevron 780, Chicago 790, Choice 798, Chotin 799, CHS 802, Citizens 828, CME 853, CNH 856, COLHOC 870, Compass 901, ConAgra 904, Connecticut 910, Connecticut 912, Contran 928, Convergys 933, Cook 934, Corning 945, Covance 955, CSL 993, Dannon 1030, Davey 1035, Deere 1061, Deloitte 1070, Delta 1073, Delta 1075, Delta 1078, Delta 1079, Diagnos-Techs 1108, Duchossois 1187, Duke 1189, Dynamet 1200, Eastern 1210, Eastern 1211, Eastman 1214, Edina 1227, Empire 1262, Endo 1268, Ensign 1276, Enterprise 1281, Ernst 1293, Ethicon 1299, Extendicare 1314, Farmers 1339, Federal 1348, Financial 1382, First 1398, First 1419, Fluor 1448, Foreman 1465, Formosa 1470, Four 1477, Freeport 1494, Fremont 1496, Genentech 1549, General 1552, General 1555, Graphic 1634, Hallberg 1704, Hard 1727, Hewlett 1794, Hoffmann 1823, Holiday 1832, Horizon 1863, Intel 1950, International 1961, International 1963, Interthyr 1978, Jeg's 2031, Johnson 2048, Kahn 2084, Keeneland 2113, Kellogg 2120, Kerzner 2133, Koch 2179, Kukui 2198, L'Oreal 2203, Laird 2211, Life 2268, Lockheed 2292, Louisiana 2309, Luxottica 2319, M&T 2323, Major 2345, Manitowoc 2356, Mars 2384, Mary 2392, Mazda 2414, McDermott 2424, McDonald's 2427, McKesson 2434, Medtronic 2453, Merck 2466, Metropolitan 2481, Micron 2500, Minnesota 2530, Mitsubishi 2539, Monsanto 2559, Moody's 2563, Moody's 2564, Nasdaq 2617, National 2622, National 2626, National 2630, NEC 2654, Nellie 2659, New 2668, New England 2670, New York 2683, Northwestern 2749, Nu 2759, NYSE 2769, O'Connor 2770, O'Neal 2771, Olin 2801, Olivetti 2802, Olympus 2804, Omnicare 2807, Orthopaedic 2829, Otter 2836, Pacific 2855, Packard 2862, Pattillo 2896, PETCO 2945, Pioneer 2980, Power 3022, Presley 3038, PricewaterhouseCoopers 3042, Private 3050, Protective 3066, Provident 3069, PVH 3088, QUALCOMM 3095, Quiksilver 3108, RECO 3148, Reinsurance 3179, ResMed 3192, Rich 3204, sanofi-aventis 3329, Sasaki 3337, Scripps 3374, SeaWorld 3387, Semiconductor 3403, Sensient 3408, Shanken 3421, Sigma 3453, Skidmore 3474, Sonoran 3501, Southwest 3524, St. Joe 3563, St. Jude 3566, Starkey 3587, Strauss 3624, Sumitomo 3639, Talbots 3682, Tanner 3688, Teachers 3697, Tellabs 3709, Temple 3711, Tex 3724, Texas 3728, Thrivent 3747, Tiffany 3750, Toro 3775, Toys 3790, Tyco 3829, U.S. 3837, U.S. 3839, UBS 3842, United 3860, United 3872, Universal 3893, USG 3905, Usibelli 3906, UTC 3908, Victorinox 3950, Watson 4006, WellPoint 4027, West 4038, Weyerhaeuser 4052, Whirlpool 4056, Whole 4066, Wiley 4072, Williams 4077, Windway 4086, Winn 4087, Wisconsin 4096, Xerox 4136, YSI 4149

Scholarship funds

3M 3, A.D. 7, Abbott 13, Aberdeen 18, Abt 20, Accenture 22, Acme 29, Acuity 31, Adobe 38, Aetna 48, Aflac 54, AGL 57, Ahern 60, Air 63, Alabama 71, Aladdin 73, Albrecht 80, Alcoa 82, Alice 89, Allegheny 91, Allegis 92, Allergan 99, Allete 100, Alliance 101, Alliant 104, Alpha 112, Alro 113, Alsco 115, AMC 126, Ameren 128, American 139, American 140, American 141, American 144, American 150, American 153, American 155, American 156, American 161, American 164, American 165, AmeriPlan 172, Ameristar 176, Ameritas 178, AMETEK 181, Amica 183, Anadarko 190, Anheuser 202, Apache 211, Apex 214, Apollo 216, Arbeit 225, Arbella 226, Arby's 228, Arcelormittal 229, Archer 232, Ariel 237, Ariens 238, Armstrong 246, Arrowhead 250, Artichoke 254, Ascena 255, Ashland 258, Assurant 268, Astoria 270, AT&T 273, Atlanta 280, Autodesk 289, AutoNation 292, Avelina 296, Avery 297, Avis 299, Avista 301, Aviva 302, AXA 307, AZPB 310, Badger 313, Baker 322, Baker 323, Baker 324, BancTrust 337, Bank 342, Bank 346, Bard 358, Barrasso 363, Barron's 364, Barton 366, BASF 368, Batts 374, Bay 380, Bayer 381, BB&T 385, Bechtel 395, Beck 396, Belk 403, Belk 404, Belo 406, Bemis 408, Beneficial 412, Benevento 414, Bergquist 420, Berkshire 428, Berry 435, Best 442, Betts 451, Biomet 466, Blair 478, Bloomberg 486, Blue 493, Bob's 511, Boeing 516, Bon 521, BorgWarner 528, Boston 538, Bound 541, BP 547, Bridgestone 560, Bridgeway 563, Brillion 569, Brink's 571, Bristol 577, Bristol 578, Brocchini 580, Brunswick 595, BSA 597, Bubalo 598, Buckley 602, Building 610, Buist 611, Burlington 618, Butzel 629, C Spire 636, Cabot 642, Cacique 644, Cades 647, Caesars 650, Cajun 652, California 655, Canon 672, Caparo 673, Capital 676, Capitol 680, Cardinal 685, Cargill 691, Carpenter 700, Cassidy 715, Catalina 719, Caterpillar 722, Centene 735, Central 745, CFS 756, CH2M 758, Chaney 761, Chase 770, Chelsea 772, Chemed 773, Chesapeake 777, Cheviot 779, Chevron 780, Chicago 790, Chick 791, Chicopee 792, Chief 793, Choice 798, Chrysler 801, CHS 802, Churchill 807, Cianbro 808, Cic 811, CIGNA 812, Citizens 826, Citizens 828, City 830, Clemens 844, Cleveland 847, Cliffs 850, Clinton 851, Clorox 852, CME 853, CNA 855, CNH 856, Coach 858, Coca 862, Coghlin 864, COLHOC 870, Collective 871, Collette 872, Collins 873, Colonial 875, Comcast 887, Comerica 889, Commerce 890, Commercial 891, Community 898, Community 900, Compass 901, Concept 905, Conditioned 906, Conn 908, Connecticut 910, Consolidated 915, Consolidated 917, Conston 920, Consumers 921, Continental 926, Contran 928, Cook 934, Cooper 935, COPIC 937, Copley 938, Coral 940, Corvallis 947, Costco 948, County 952, Cox 959, Cracker 966, Crane 970, Cranston 972, Creative 975, Creative 976, Credit 979, Crystal 992, Cullen 1000, Cumberland 1003, Cummins 1006, Cummins 1007, CUNA 1008, Cutco 1012, CVS 1014, Cymer 1016, Daffy's 1019, Damar 1024, Darden 1032, Dart 1034, Davis 1037, Dealer 1052, DeBruce 1057, Deere 1061, Delaware 1066, Deloitte 1070, Delta 1073, Delta 1074, Delta 1075, Delta 1078, Delta 1079, Delta 1081, Delta 1082, Demoulas 1085, Denny's 1087, DENTSPLY 1089, Dethmers 1091, Detroit 1095, Detroit 1097, Devereaux 1100, Diagnos-Techs 1108, Dietz 1114, Dime 1118, Dippin' 1122, Disney 1127, Dispatch 1129, Diversityinc 1131, Dixon 1133, Dollar 1142, Dollar 1145, Donaldson 1153, Dot 1158, Dow 1162, Dow 1163, Dowling 1165, DP 1168, DRS 1179, du Pont 1184, Duane 1186, Duke 1189, Dunkin' 1191, Duro-Last 1196, Dutch 1197, DVK 1198, Eagle 1203, Earnhardt 1205, East 1207, Eastern 1209, Eastern 1210, Eastman 1213, Eastman 1214, Easton 1215, Eaton 1216, Econoco 1222, Educational 1233, Edvisors 1234, El Paso 1239, Emerson 1257, EMI 1258, Emmis 1260, Endres 1269, Energen 1270, Energizer 1271, Energy 1272, Ensign 1276, Entergy 1279, Enterprise 1281, EQT 1287, Equifax 1288, Evening 1302, Excell 1304, Exelon 1309, Exotic 1310, Factory 1323, Fairfield 1326, Fairmount 1328, Farmers 1335, Farmers 1338, FBR 1345, FDI 1346, Federated 1351, Fieldale 1373, Fieldstone 1374, Fifth 1377, Finish 1383, First 1388, First 1389, First 1395, First 1396, First 1397, First 1398, First 1399, First 1402, First 1406, First 1409, First 1414, First 1416, First 1419, First 1420, Fisher 1431, Fleck 1435, Flextronics 1437, Florence 1441, Florida 1443, Florsheim 1445, Fluor 1448, Fonville 1456, Ford 1464, Four 1477, Franklin 1484, Freeport 1494, Fremont 1496, Fremont 1497, Fuller 1517, Fulton 1518, Furniture 1519, Furr 1520, Gallo 1529, Gannett 1532, Gap 1533, Gardner 1536, GATX 1542, GenCorp 1548, Genentech 1549, General 1552, General 1554, General 1555, General 1557, General 1558, Georgia 1567, Georgia 1568, Ghilotti 1570, Gibbs 1576, GlaxoSmithKline 1588, Golub 1607, Good 1609, Gosiger 1617, Grace 1623, Graco 1624, Graham 1625, Grainger 1626, Grand 1628, Graphic 1634, Graphix 1637, Greater 1649, Green 1653, GROWMARK 1674, GSM 1676, Guard 1680, Guardian 1681, Guess 1685, Gulf 1689, H & R 1695, Hackstock 1697, Hall 1703, Hallberg 1704, Halstead 1708, Hampden 1713, Hamrick 1715, Hanover 1724, Hardinge 1729, Harley 1732, Hawaiian 1756, Hawkins 1757, Hays 1761, HCA 1762, Heffernan 1769, Heidtman 1770, Heinz 1772, Hemmerdinger 1775, Hendrick 1776, Henkels 1779, Heritage 1785, Hess 1793, Hexcel 1795, Hickory 1797, Hilliard 1806, Hilton 1812, Holt 1839, Holtz 1840, Home 1844, Home 1845, Honda 1851, Honeywell 1852, Hood 1854, Horix 1860, Hormel 1866, Houston 1871, HSBC 1876, Hubbard 1878, Hudson 1880, Hudson 1881, Humana 1886, Hunt 1889, Huntsman 1895, Hygeia 1901, IDACORP 1907, IDT 1910, IHC 1913, Illinois 1916, IMA 1917, IMC 1920, Independence 1925, Industrial 1935, ING 1938, Ingersoll 1939, Institution 1946, Integra 1947, Intel 1950, Intermountain 1957, International 1963, International 1966, International 1971, Invesco 1983, Investors 1984, Iowa 1987, ITT 1999, Iwo 2003, Jacksonville 2014, Jacobs 2016, Janus 2024, Jasper 2025, Jasper 2026, Jazz 2028, Jeld 2032, Jesco 2040, Jewett 2042, Jim's 2043, JM 2044, JOFCO 2046, Johnson 2048, Johnson 2049, Johnson 2050, Johnson 2052, Jorgensen 2065, Journal 2068, Jovon 2069, JSJ 2073, Kahn 2084, Kajima 2087, Kanaly 2089, Keeneland 2113, Kellogg 2120, Kelly 2122, Kemper 2124, Kennametal 2125, Kennecott 2127, Key 2134, KeyBank 2136, Kiewit 2142, Kifton 2143, Kikkoman 2144, Kilmartin 2145, Klein's 2169, KOA 2178, Korum 2187, KPMG 2190, Kreindler 2193, Kukui 2198, Landmark 2218, Landry's 2219, Larkin 2224, LG&E Energy 2260, Liberty 2262, Liberty 2265, Life 2267, LifePoint 2270, Lilly 2274, Lincoln 2279, Lincoln 2281, Lockheed 2292, Loews 2296, Long 2298, Longaberger 2299, Lubrizol 2315, Lucasfilm 2316, M&T 2323, M.D.C. 2324, M/I 2325, Maali 2326, Macy's 2333, Majestic 2344, Major 2345, Mamiye 2352, Manhattan 2354, Manpower 2358, Manti 2359, Marathon 2366, Mariani 2374, Marnier-Lapostolle 2381, Marr 2382, Marsh 2385, Marsh 2386, Massachusetts 2397, MasterCard 2399, Mattel 2405, Maverick 2409, Mazda 2414, McBride 2418, McClatchy 2422, McCormick 2423, McDermott 2424, McDonald's 2427, McKesson 2434, McKinstry 2435, MDU 2441, Medtronic 2453, Melaleuca 2457, Menasha 2461, Mercedes 2463, Merchants 2465, Merck 2466, Merfish 2472, Metropolitan 2481, Metropolitan 2483, MFA 2486, Miami 2491, Michigan 2496, Michigan 2497, Micron 2500, MidAmerican 2504, Midmark 2507, Miller 2517, Miller 2518, Miller 2522, Milwaukee 2527, Mine 2529, Minster 2532, Mississippi 2536, Mitsubishi 2538,

Mitsui 2541, Modine 2544, Monsanto 2559, Moody's 2563, Morgan 2570, Morley 2572, Morris 2574, Mortgage 2578, Murphy 2600, Mutual 2603, Mutual 2604, MWH 2608, Nasdaq 2618, Nash 2619, National 2622, National 2628, National 2630, National 2631, National 2634, National 2635, Naugatuck 2646, Nelnet 2660, New 2668, New England 2672, New Hampshire 2674, New Orleans 2678, New York 2683, New York 2684, New York 2687, New York 2690, Newman 2696, Newport 2699, Newsweek 2703, Newtown 2704, Nextier 2706, Nordson 2723, Nordstrom 2724, Norfolk 2725, Northern 2740, Northfield 2741, Northrop 2744, NorthWestern 2748, Northwestern 2749, Northwestern 2750, Novell 2754, NV 2765, NYSE 2769, OceanFirst 2782, Ogilvy 2788, Ohio 2791, Oklahoma 2794, Old 2798, Olin 2801, Olivetti 2802, Omaha 2805, Omaha 2806, OMNOVA 2809, Omron 2810, Oneida 2814, Optima 2819, Opus 2820, Orlando 2824, Orscheln 2827, Osram 2834, Otter 2836, Owens 2842, Owens 2844, PACCAR 2850, Pacifico 2859, PacifiCorp 2860, Packard 2862, Panasonic 2869, Park 2880, Park 2881, Parker 2886, Parsons 2887, PCI 2905, Pearson 2911, Pella 2917, PEMCO 2919, Penguin 2922, Penn 2924, Penney 2925, Pentair 2926, People's 2928, PepsiCo 2935, Perrigo 2943, Pfizer 2950, PG&E 2952, Philip 2962, Phoenix 2967, Physicians 2970, Pioneer 2979, Pioneer 2980, PMI 2995, PNC 2997, Popular 3003, Porter 3006, Porter 3007, Portland 3010, PPG 3025, Praxair 3029, Premier 3035, Premier 3036, Presley 3038, Price 3040, Principal 3047, Printpack 3049, Progressive 3058, ProLogis 3060, ProtechSoft 3065, Protective 3066, Provident 3069, Provident 3071, Public 3075, Puget 3081, Putnam 3085, Putnam 3086, Putnam 3087, PVH 3088, Pyles 3089, Quabaug 3090, Quadion 3092, Quaker 3093, QUALCOMM 3095, Quality 3097, Quanex 3100, Questar 3104, Quiksilver 3108, Quincy 3110, R & B 3113, Ralph 3123, Raymond 3133, Rayonier 3134, RBS 3137, RE/MAX 3140, Reader's 3141, Reading 3142, RECO 3148, Red 3154, Redwoods 3158, Reed 3160, Regal 3166, Regions 3171, Regis 3172, Reiff 3174, Reisner 3180, Reitman 3181, RESCO 3189, Retail 3194, Reynolds 3199, Reynolds 3200, Riggs 3213, RJN 3228, Robbins 3230, Robins 3232, Rockland 3242, Rockwell 3246, Rockwell 3247, Rolls 3254, Rose 3261, Rose 3263, Ross 3265, Rothstein 3271, Royal 3273, Royalnest 3277, RPM 3278, Rudy's 3284, Rydell 3291, Ryder 3292, S & H 3295, S & T 3297, SAIC 3311, Sandusky 3328, Savage 3341, Schiffenhaus 3351, Schneider 3355, Schott 3360, Schwab 3363, Schwan 3365, Scoular 3373, Seagate 3377, Seamen's 3383, Seattle 3386, Securant 3388, Security 3394, Select 3398, Selective 3399, Seminole 3404, Seneca 3406, Sensient 3408, Sentry 3409, Seton 3415, Shakopee 3419, Shaughnessy 3425, Shell 3430, Shelter 3431, SI 3444, Siemens 3448, Sigma 3453, Simplot 3459, Simpson 3461, SLM 3478, SmartWool 3479, SMBC 3480, Smith 3484, Smith 3485, Smithfield 3487, Snyder's-Lance 3492, Sonoco 3500, Sonoran 3501, Sony 3502, Southern 3515, Southwestern 3526, Sovereign 3528, Spirol 3545, Sports 3547, Sprint 3556, Square 3560, St. 3565, St. Joe 3563, St. Louis 3568, St. Louis 3569, Stanek 3578, Star 3584, Starbucks 3585, Stardust 3586, Starwood 3589, State 3591, Steelcase 3597, Sterling 3601, Sterne 3602, Stonyfield 3617, Stop 3618, Strauss 3624, Stupp 3628, Sulphur 3637, Sunbeam 3647, SUPERVALU 3659, Symantec 3669, Synopsys 3673, Sysco 3677, TCF 3695, Teachers 3697, Teleflex 3707, Tennessee 3716, Texas 3725, Texas 3728, Textron 3731, Thomasville 3737, Thompson 3739, Thorntons 3743, Three 3745, Tillman 3752, Time 3757, Tomkins 3771, Tony 3773, Toro 3775, Towerbrook 3781, Trans 3795, Travelers 3802, Tri 3805, Trim 3810, Triumph 3812, True 3814, Tulalip 3820, Turner 3824, Tyson 3832, U.S. 3835, U.S. 3837, Unilever 3853, Union 3854, Union 3856, Union 3857, United 3860, United 3864, United 3868, United 3872, United 3874, United 3877, United 3878, United 3881, UnitedHealth 3884, Unitil 3885, Universal 3891, Universal 3895, Updike 3899, USEC 3904, USG 3905, Usibelli 3906, UTC 3908, Utica 3910, Uticon 3911, V.F. 3913, Venturedyne 3933, Veridyne 3935, Verizon 3936, Vermeer 3937, Victor 3949, Vijuk 3953, Vilter 3956, Vodafone 3965, Vulcan 3972, Wachtell 3973, Waffle 3975, Wake 3978, Wal-Mart 3980, Walker 3982, Wallace 3983, Washington 3994, Washington 3999, Wausau 4008, Weil 4022, WellPoint 4027, Wells 4028, Wendy's 4031, Wendy's/Arby's 4030, Wenger 4033, West 4034, Westar 4039, Western 4040, Western 4045, Weyco 4051, Whirlpool 4056, Wiley 4072, Wilkes 4074, Willdan 4075, Williams 4077, Windway 4086, Winn 4087, Winnebago 4088, Wisconsin 4092, Wisconsin 4093, Wisconsin 4094, Wisconsin 4095, Wisconsin 4096, Wolff 4105, Wolverine 4106, Wood 4108, Worthen 4123, Wrigley 4125, Xerox 4136, YSI 4149, Zallie 4152

Scholarships—to individuals

13th 1, Adir 36, AgStar 59, AK 67, Alabama 72, Albemarle 78, Aleut 84, Allen 94, Allen 98, Allete 100, Alliant 104, Altair 117, Ameren 129, American 131, American 138, American 166, Ameristar 176, AMN Healthcare 184, Ann's 203, Anocoil 204, Anthony 206, Aon 210, AptarGroup 221, Arctic 234, Ariel 237, Ariens 238, Arizona 239, Athletics 276, Atmos 285, AutoNation 292, Avery 297, Avlon 303, Avon 305, AVX 306, AXA 307, Badger 314, Baltimore 335, Bank 343, BankSouth 350, Basketball 370, BBCN 386, Beall's 389, Bean 391, Bemis 408, Bering 422, Berkshire 428, Berry 437, Bertelsmann 439, Best 443, Big 461, Blackinton 476, Blair 479, Boneal 523, Boston 538, Boston 540, Bound 541, Brewer 558, Briggs 565, Brillion 569, Bristol 576, Brooks 585, Buist 611, Burger 613, Burke 615, Burlington 618, Calista 657, Cambridge 666, Candlesticks 670, Canon 672, Cargill 691, Carroll 703, Carson 705, Carver 711, Catalina 719, Catawissa 720, Caterpillar 722, Cavaliers 724, Central 744, Central 747, Century 749, Ceridian 753, Chaney 761, Charles 764, Charter 765, Chase 770, Chenega 776, Chevron 780, Chicago 785, Chick 791, Choggiung 797, Choice 798, CHS 802, Chugach 805, Cic 811, Clarks 838, Cleveland 846, Coastal 859, Coca 862, COLHOC 870, Columbus 885, Comcast 887, Commercial 891, Communications 896, Conditioned 906, Continental 923, Cook 934, Corning 945, Corvallis 947, Cox 959, Crown 989, Cummins 1006, D'Annunzio 1017, Daiwa 1020, Dallas 1023, Delta 1078, Delta 1081, Detroit 1095, DeVoe 1101, Dick's 1110, Discovery 1126, Dixie 1132, Dobson 1137, Doctor's 1138, Dollywood 1146, Dominion 1148, Doyon 1167, Drive 1177, Eagle 1201, Earnhardt 1205, Eastern 1211, Edgar 1225, Edison 1228, Educational 1233, EFC 1236, El 1237, El Dorado 1238, Ellin 1251, Ellucian 1252, EMI 1258, EQT 1287, Excell 1304, Exotic 1310, Eyak 1317, Fairmont 1327, Fairmount 1328, Farmers' 1337, Farrell 1341, First 1392, First 1396, First 1398, First 1399, First 1412, First 1413, Fisher 1430, Fisher 1432, Flint 1438, Ford 1464, Foreman 1465, Formosa 1470, Four 1477, Franklin 1486, Franklin 1488, Fredrikson 1491, Freeport 1494, Gallagher 1528, Gehl 1545, Georgia 1568, Gilbane 1581, GJF 1584, Glades 1587, Gleaner 1590, Globe 1594, Golden 1601, Golub 1607, Gon 1608, Goulds 1619, Government 1620, Government 1621, Grandma 1630, Great 1643, Great 1646, Green 1651, Grove 1672, H & K 1694, H & R 1695, Halstead 1708, Hanover 1724, Harper 1735, Haviland 1752, Hawaiian 1756, Heat 1767, Holce 1827, Holland 1834, Holme 1837, Holt 1839, Home 1842, Homecrest 1847, HomeStar 1848, Homewood 1849, Honeywell 1852, Hotel 1868, Houghton 1869, Houston 1871, Hubbard 1878, Huna 1887, IDACORP 1907, Ilitch 1915, Independence 1925, Independent 1927, Institution 1946, InterBel 1952, International 1961, Iwo 2003, J & S 2004, Jabil 2006, Jemez 2034, Jesco 2040, Jorgensen 2065, Kadant 2083, Kajima 2087, Kansas 2091, Keen 2111, Kelly 2122, KeyBank 2136, KFC 2139, Kifton 2143, Kimmel 2152, KLA-Tencor 2165, KLS 2171, Kohl's 2181, Koniag 2184, KPMG 2190, Kuskokwim 2200, Kyanite 2201, LAC 2206, Ladies 2209, Lam 2214, Land 2217, Latham 2229, Leaco 2236, Lee 2242, Liberty 2262, Liberty 2265, Lilly 2274, Lim 2275, Lowe's 2312, Luxottica 2319, Main 2342, Manti 2359, Marathon 2362, Marathon 2365, Marchon 2369, Mariani 2374, Mary 2392, Material 2401, McDermott 2424, McDonald's 2427, Medline 2451, Merck 2466, Merrimack 2475, MFA 2486, Micron 2500, Middlesex 2506, Millennia 2516, Miller 2523, Mitsui 2541, Monarch 2553, Morgan 2570, Murphy 2600, NANA 2615, Nansemond 2616, Nashville 2620, National 2622, National 2634, National 2638, Needham 2655, Nelnet 2660, Network 2664, New 2671, New York 2690, Nishnabotna 2714, Nissan 2716, Nordic 2722, Northern 2738, Northfield 2742, Nucor 2760, NV 2765, Ochoco 2783, Old 2797, Orlando 2824, Orscheln 2827, Ounalashka 2837, Pacers 2852, Pacific 2854, Pacific 2856, Packard 2862, Papa 2876, Park 2882, Pawtucket 2902, PEMCO 2919, Penasco 2920, Peoples 2929, Peoples 2930, PepsiCo 2935, PFS 2951, PGA 2954, Pharmacy 2956, Phillips 2966, Phoenix 2967, Phoenix 2968, Pioneer 2980, PMC 2994, Portrait 3012, Post 3016, Potlatch 3017, Preferred 3031, Price 3039, Progressive 3059, Promotional 3061, Provident 3070, Pulte 3083, Quabaug 3090, Queen 3102, Questar 3104, Rainsville 3121, Ramona's 3126, Rapoca 3127, Ray 3132, Rayonier 3134, Record 3149, Regal 3166, Reiff 3174, Reynolds 3199, Ritzville 3222, Riviana 3227, Rockland 3242, Rockville 3245, Rockwell 3246, Rockwood 3248, Rocky 3249, Rondys 3256, Roosevelt 3258, Roosevelt 3259, Rosen's 3264, Royal 3274, San Antonio 3321, Scripps 3374, Seagrave 3378, Sealaska 3380, Seattle 3386, Security 3394, Seldovia 3397, Semiconductor 3403, Shanken 3421, Shelter 3431, ShopKo 3440, Siemens 3448, Sierra 3450, Simon 3458, Sitnasuak 3467, Socorro 3496, Sonlight 3499, Southwestern 3525, Spirol 3545, Sports 3547, Springer 3553, Standard 3577, Steve's 3603, Stoelting 3612, Stram 3622, Strauss 3624, Sulphur 3637, Sun 3645, Sunkist 3649, Superior 3657, Superior 3658, Synopsys 3673, Talbots 3682, Tanadgusix 3687, TAP 3690, Target 3691, Tatitlek 3694, Teachers 3697, Tedco 3702, Tension 3717, Texas 3728, Texas 3729, Thermo 3733, Tikigaq 3751, Trico 3807, Twins 3827, Ukpeagvik 3843, United 3864, United 3875, United 3879, United 3883, Universal 3892, Universal 3893, Unum 3898, Usibelli 3906, V-T 3912, Valley 3916, Valley 3918, Verizon 3936, Villency 3955, Vinson 3957, Vulcan 3971, Waffle 3975, Washington 3994, Washington 3996, Washington 3999, Watson 4006, Weaver 4015, Webster's 4019, Wells 4028, Wenger 4033, West 4035, West 4038, Western 4045, Williams-Sonoma 4079, Williamsburg 4080, Wisconsin 4096, Woodward-Graff 4113, Woori 4114, X.L. 4134, YGS 4143, YSI 4149, Zeta 4155

Seed money

Activision 30, Agilent 56, AGL 57, Alabama 71, Alexander 85, Alliant 104, Ameren 128, American 145, American 147, American 150, Androscoggin 199, Aspen 260, Avista 301, Azulay 311, Bayer 382, Blue 502, Bobcats 512, Boeing 516, Bristol 577, Bristol 578, Brooks 585, Butler 626, Capitol 680, Centene 735, Chase 769, CHS 802, Clayton 841, CME 853, Commerce 890, Convergys 933, Corning 945, Delta 1074, Delta 1077, Deutsche 1099, Dow 1161, Dow 1162, Empire 1262, EQT 1287, Extendicare 1314, Factory 1323, Farmers 1339, First 1402, First 1419, Fisher 1433, Foley 1454, Framingham 1481, GlaxoSmithKline 1588, Globe 1594, Guard 1680, Heinz 1772, Hoffmann 1823, International 1968, Investors 1984, Jewett 2042, Johnson 2049, Johnson 2050, Kahn 2084, Kaiser 2086, Kingsbury 2160, Kroger 2195, Land 2217, Landmark 2218, Machias 2332, Macy's 2333, McDonald's 2427, Medtronic 2453, Merck 2466, Midcontinent 2505, Mitsubishi 2538, Mizuho 2542, Monsanto 2559, Morgan 2568, National 2630, Nationwide 2639, Nellie 2659, New England 2670, Nord 2721, Nordson 2723, Pattillo 2896, Pawtucket 2902, PetSmart 2948, Principal 3047, Provident 3069, Prudential 3072, Robinson 3235, Rockford 3241, Saint 3312, Scripps 3374, South 3512, St. Joe 3563, St. Jude 3566, St. Louis 3569, Steelcase 3597, Superior 3658, Tellabs 3709, Thrivent 3747, Toys 3790, United 3863, Utica 3910, Vermeer

3937, Vulcan 3972, Wellmark 4026, Woodward 4112, Xerox 4136, YSI 4149

Sponsorships

7-Eleven 5, Abbott 13, Abby's 14, Activision 30, Acuity 32, Adams 34, Aetna 48, Agilent 56, AGL 57, AgStar 59, Air 63, Alabama 71, Alaska 74, Alaska 76, Alcoa 82, Allen 93, Allen 95, Allete 100, Alliant 104, Allstate 107, Altria 120, Amazon.com 122, Amboy 124, AMC 125, AMC 126, Ameren 128, American 140, American 141, American 142, American 143, American 144, American 145, American 149, American 150, American 161, American 162, American 165, AMERIGROUP 171, Ameriprise 174, Amerisure 177, Ameritas 178, AMN Healthcare 184, Andersen 194, Anheuser 202, Apache 211, Apollo 216, Apple 218, Applied 219, Applied 220, Aramco 224, Arch 230, Arch 231, AREVA 236, Arkansas 241, Arrowpoint 251, Assurant 266, Assurant 268, AT&T 273, Athletics 276, Autodesk 289, AutoNation 292, AutoZone 294, Avista 301, Avnet 304, AVX 306, Azulay 311, Baker 323, Balch 327, Bally 330, BancTrust 337, Bank 340, Bank 342, Bank 344, Bank 345, Bank 346, Bard 358, Barnes 360, Baxter 377, Bay 378, BayView 384, BB&T 385, Beam 390, Beaver 394, Beckman 397, Belk 403, Ben 409, Bergquist 420, Berkshire 428, Biogen 465, Biomet 466, Birdsong 470, Bloomberg 486, Bloomin 487, Bloomingdale's 488, Blue 490, Blue 491, Blue 493, Blue 494, Blue 499, Blue 500, Blue 501, Blue 504, Boart 510, Bob's 511, Boeing 516, Bon 521, Booz 525, Boston 536, Boston 540, Bound 541, Bowater 543, BP 547, Bressler 557, Bridgestone 560, Briggs 565, Brightpoint 567, Bristol 578, Broadcom 579, Brotherhood 588, Building 610, Bunge 612, Burger 613, Butzel 629, C & S 634, C Spire 636, Cadence 646, Caesars 650, Callanan 659, Calvert 663, Cape 674, Capital 679, CareFirst 687, Carlson 693, Carter's 708, Caterpillar 722, CBS 727, Cellco 733, Centene 735, CenterPoint 738, CenterPoint 739, Central 741, Central 745, Century 748, Century 750, CFS 756, CH2M 758, Charles 764, Charter 765, Charter 767, Chesapeake 777, Chick 791, Chicopee 792, Chrysler 801, CHS 802, Churchill 807, CIGNA 812, Circle 817, CITGO 820, City 830, Cleveland 846, Clorox 852, CME 853, CNH 856, CNO 857, Coca 861, Coca 862, Cole 868, COLHOC 870, Collective 871, Collette 872, Colonial 874, Colonial 875, Colonial 876, Columbia 884, Comcast 887, Comerica 889, Commonwealth 895, Community 899, Compass 901, Compuware 902, Consolidated 916, Convergys 933, Cooper 935, Cooper 936, Cornerstone 944, Corvallis 947, Country 951, Covidien 956, Cox 958, Cox 959, Cranfill 971, CryoLife 990, Cumberland 1003, Cummins 1007, Dannon 1030, Day 1046, DeBruce 1057, Dedham 1060, Deere 1061, Del 1065, Delaware 1066, Delmarva 1069, Deloitte 1070, Delta 1073, Delta 1077, Delta 1079, Delta 1081, Delta 1083, Denny's 1087, Detroit 1095, Deutsche 1099, Devon 1102, DHL 1106, Diamonds 1109, Dick's 1110, Diebold 1112, Discover 1125, DJO 1134, Do 1136, Doctor's 1138, Doctors 1139, Donnelley 1155, DP 1168, Dr 1169, Draper 1171, DS 1182, DTE 1183, Duane 1186, Duke 1189, Eastern 1209, Eastern 1211, Easthampton 1212, Eastman 1213, Edible 1226, Edison 1228, El Paso 1239, Elemental Herbs 1244, EMC 1253, Emerson 1257, EMI 1258, Employers 1263, Entergy 1278, Entergy 1280, Epson 1286, EQT 1287, Esurance 1298, Ethicon 1299, Evans 1300, Evening 1302, Exelon 1309, Exxon 1315, Family 1330, Faribault 1332, Farmers 1338, Farmers 1339, Federal 1348, Ferro 1366, Fifth 1377, Fila 1379, Fireman's 1385, First 1389, First 1391, First 1395, First 1396, First 1397, First 1398, First 1403, First 1405, First 1406, First 1419, Firstmerit 1425, Fisher 1433, Florence 1441, Florida 1443, Florsheim 1445, Flowserve 1447, FMR 1450, Follett 1455, Food 1458, Foot 1459, Ford 1464, Fox 1480, Franklin 1487, Franklin 1488, Freescale 1495, Fremont 1496, Frontier 1508, Fulton 1518, Gallo 1529, Gap 1533, Garden 1534, Genentech 1549, General 1550, General 1551, General 1555, Georgia 1567, Georgia 1568, Giant 1571, Giant 1572, Giant 1573, Gibraltar 1577, Golden 1602, Golub 1607, Gordon 1615, Government 1621, Grace 1623, Graham 1625, Great 1646, Great 1647, Gregory 1661, GTECH 1677, Guess 1685, GuideOne 1687, Haggen 1699, Hallmark 1707, Hampden 1713, Hannaford 1723, Hardinge 1729, Harley 1732, Harris 1736, Harris 1738, Harris 1739, Hartford 1742, Hartz 1744, Health 1765, Health 1766, Helmerich 1774, Henry 1781, Herr 1787, Hertz 1792, Hess 1793, Highmark 1799, Hilfiger 1801, Hill 1803, Hillshire 1809, Hilton 1812, Hoffmann 1823, Hofmann 1824, Home 1845, Homecrest 1847, Honeywell 1852, Horizon 1861, Horizon 1863, Hormel 1866, Houston 1871, HSBC 1876, Huna 1887, Hunt 1889, Huntington 1894, Iberdrola 1904, ICON 1906, IDACORP 1907, IDT 1910, Imation 1919, Independence 1925, Independent 1927, ING 1938, Insperity 1944, Institution 1946, Integra 1947, Intel 1950, Intermountain 1956, International 1962, International 1963, International 1964, International 1968, Invesco 1983, Inwood 1985, IPALCO 1988, Isabella 1993, ITT 1999, Jack 2007, Jackson 2009, Jacobs 2016, Jamba 2020, James 2021, Jelly 2033, JetBlue 2041, JM 2044, Jockey 2045, JOFCO 2046, Johnson 2048, Johnson 2049, Johnson 2050, Johnson 2053, Jones 2057, Jordan 2063, JPMorgan Chase 2071, Kaiser 2086, Kansas 2094, KB 2105, Kellogg 2120, Kellwood 2121, Kent 2129, KeyBank 2136, Kikkoman 2144, Kimberly 2150, Kingsbury 2160, Kinney 2162, Koch 2179, Koch 2180, Kohl's 2181, Korum 2187, KPMG 2190, L'Oreal 2203, Lake 2212, Lam 2214, Lauder 2230, Laureate 2231, Levi 2254, Lexmark 2258, LG&E Energy 2260, Liberty 2265, Life 2268, Lilly 2274, Lincoln 2281, Lincoln 2282, Lithia 2287, Lockheed 2292, Longaberger 2299, Loomis 2301, Lord 2303, Louisiana 2309, Louisiana 2310, Lowe's 2312, M&T 2323, Macy's 2333, Mamiye 2352, Manitowoc 2355, Manti 2359, Marcus 2370, Marnier-Lapostolle 2381, Marsh 2387, Martin 2391, Mary 2392, MasterCard 2399, Matson 2404, Mattel 2405, MBIA 2416, McKee 2432, McKesson 2434, Mechanics 2446, MedImmune 2450, Medtronic 2453, MEMC 2459, Menasha 2461, Mercedes 2463, Merck 2466, Mercury 2469, Merk 2467, Metro 2479, Metropolitan 2484, Meyer 2485, Michael 2493, Michelin 2495, Microchip 2499, Micron 2500, MidAmerican 2504, Midmark 2507, Milford 2513, Milford 2514, Millhiser-Smith 2524, Mitsubishi 2539, Mitsui 2541, Modine 2544, Mondelez 2556, Monsanto 2559, Morgan 2570, Morris 2574, Mosaic 2580, MPB 2591, MSC 2593, Mutual 2603, Namaste 2614, National 2628, National 2630, National 2631, National 2632, National 2634, National 2635, Nationwide 2639, Naugatuck 2645, NCR 2650, Nestle 2662, Nestle 2663, Neville 2667, New 2668, New 2671, New York 2683, New York 2688, Newport 2699, Newsweek 2703, Nexion 2705, Nextier 2706, Niemann 2708, NII 2709, NIKE 2710, Nordson 2723, Norfolk 2725, Northeast 2737, Northfield 2741, Northfield 2742, Northrim 2743, Northwest 2747, Northwestern 2749, Novetta 2755, Nu 2759, NV 2765, NYSE 2769, O'Connor 2770, Oakland 2772, OceanFirst 2782, Office 2785, Ohio 2790, Oklahoma 2794, Old 2798, Ole 2800, Omaha 2806, Omnicare 2807, Omnicom 2808, OneBeacon 2813, OppenheimerFunds 2818, Opus 2820, OrePac 2823, Orlando 2824, Orthopaedic 2829, Osram 2834, Otter 2836, Outokumpu 2839, Owens 2841, Pacific 2855, Packaging 2861, Padilla 2864, Pan-American 2868, Panasonic 2869, Papa 2876, Parametric 2878, Parker 2884, Parsons 2887, Patagonia 2892, Pathmark 2894, Pattillo 2896, Pawtucket 2902, Peabody 2907, Pearson 2911, Peet's 2916, Penney 2925, People's 2928, Peoples 2931, PepsiCo 2935, Perkins 2940, Pfizer 2950, Philadelphia 2960, Philadelphia 2961, Pinnacle 2977, Piper 2983, Pitney 2984, Plum 2992, PMI 2995, Polk 3000, Portland 3010, PPL 3026, Presley 3038, Price 3039, Principal 3047, Progressive 3059, Protective 3066, Provident 3071, Public 3075, Publix 3079, Puget 3081, Putnam 3086, Quaker 3094, Quality 3096, Questar 3104, Quicksilver 3106, Quincy 3110, Raymond 3133, Raytheon 3135, RBC 3136, RBS 3137, RE/MAX 3140, Recreational 3150, Red 3154, Reebok 3159, Regal 3166, RG 3201, RGI 3202, Rich 3204, Robins 3232, Robinson 3235, Rockville 3245, Rockwell 3246, Rockwell 3247, Rogers 3253, Rolls 3254, Royal 3273, RPM 3278, Ryder 3292, S & T 3297, Saco 3302, Safeco 3306, Safety 3309, SAIC 3311, Salem 3316, Salem 3317, Save 3342, Schwab 3363, Schwan 3365, Scoular 3373, Seattle 3386, Seminole 3404, Sempra 3405, Sentry 3409, Seventh 3416, Sharp 3422, Shaw's 3427, Shell 3430, ShopKo 3440, SI 3444, Sierra 3451, Simplot 3459, Smith 3484, Sonic 3498, Southern 3514, Southern 3521, Spansion 3532, Spirit 3544, Sports 3548, Springs 3555, Sprint 3556, Square 3560, St. Jude 3566, St. Louis 3569, Starbucks 3585, Starwood 3589, State 3591, State 3592, Station 3593, Steel 3595, Stock 3610, Stonyfield 3617, Strauss 3624, Sumitomo 3639, Sunkist 3649, Sunoco 3650, Sunshine 3653, Superior 3657, SUPERVALU 3659, Sweetbay 3665, Swinerton 3668, Symantec 3669, Synopsys 3673, Sysco 3677, Target 3691, TD 3696, TeleTech 3708, Tellabs 3709, Tenet 3713, Terlato 3720, Tesoro 3723, Texas 3728, Textron 3731, Thermo 3733, Thomson 3742, Thorntons 3743, Thorrez 3744, Tiffany 3750, Tim 3753, TJX 3765, Toll 3769, Tom's 3770, Toro 3775, Toshiba 3776, Totem 3779, Toyota 3784, Toyota 3785, Toyota 3786, Toyota 3787, Trail 3793, Travelers 3802, Tribune 3806, Trim 3810, Turner 3823, Turner 3824, Tyson 3832, U-Haul 3833, U.S. 3836, UBS 3842, Union 3854, Union 3857, United 3860, United 3864, United 3872, United 3876, United 3880, United 3882, Unitil 3885, Unum 3898, Urban 3901, UTC 3908, V.F. 3913, Valero 3915, Valley 3917, Valspar 3920, Vectren 3925, Verizon 3936, Vermeer 3937, Viejas 3951, ViewSonic 3952, Visa 3960, Vision 3961, Vulcan 3970, Wakefern 3979, Wal-Mart 3980, Walker 3982, Washington 3995, Waterford 4002, WaterStone 4005, Webster 4016, WEDGE 4020, Wegmans 4021, Wellmark 4026, WellPoint 4027, Wells 4028, Wendel 4029, Wendy's 4032, West 4034, West 4037, Western 4040, Western 4045, Whirl 4055, Whitney 4065, Whole 4066, Winn 4087, Winnebago 4088, Winter 4090, Wisconsin 4093, Wolf 4102, Wood 4108, World 4121, Wrigley 4125, WSFS 4127, Xerox 4136, Xylem 4139, Zotos 4159

Student loans—to individuals

Bank 345, Bering 422, First 1396, Fisher 1432, ITT 1999, Metal 2478, Stonecutter 3615, Strauss 3624

Technical assistance

Activision 30, adidas 35, AgStar 59, Airgas 65, Alliant 104, Allstate 107, Amazon.com 122, AMETEK 181, AOL 209, Aspen 260, AT&T 273, Avista 301, Bank 342, Bank 349, Beneficial 412, Blue 493, Blue 496, Blue 497, Blue 502, Boeing 516, Booz 525, Bristol 578, Bromelkamp 582, Cablevision 640, California 655, Cambia 665, Capitol 680, City 830, ConAgra 904, Corning 945, Cow 957, Cummins 1007, Delta 1083, Deutsche 1099, Dominion 1150, Eastern 1210, Elevation 1245, Entergy 1278, Equifax 1288, Federal 1348, Fifth 1376, FMR 1450, Focus 1451, Gateway 1541, Globe 1594, Google 1613, Graco 1624, Grand 1629, Hallmark 1707, Heinz 1772, Hoffmann 1823, Hoops 1857, Horizon 1863, Intel 1950, Jenzabar 2037, JPMorgan Chase 2071, Kaiser 2086, Kellogg 2120, Landmark 2218, Liberty 2262, Mattel 2405, Middlesex 2506, Mizuho 2542, NEC 2654, Nellie 2659, New York 2683, Nordson 2723, Panasonic 2869, Pfizer 2950, Premix 3037, Prudential 3072, Raytheon 3135, Robinson 3235, Roche 3236, salesforce.com 3318, Scripps 3374, Securian 3389, St. Louis 3569, Strauss 3624, Superior 3658, Textron 3731, Thorntons 3743, Totem 3779, United 3863, United 3872, United 3879, United 3882, UnitedHealth 3884, USG 3905, Verizon 3936, Wells 4028, Xerox 4136, YSI 4149

Use of facilities

Advanced 40, Air 63, AMC 125, Autodesk 289, AutoNation 292, Avista 301, Bank 349, Boeing 516, California 656, Cascade 713, Charter 767, CHS 802, City 830, Colonial 874, CryoLife 990, Entergy 1279, Fluor 1448, Getty 1569, Gulfstream 1690, HSBC 1876, International 1964, Lexmark 2258, Loews 2296,

SUBJECT INDEX

List of terms: Terms used in this index conform to the Foundation Center's Grants Classification System's comprehensive subject area coding scheme. The alphabetical list below represents the complete list of subject terms found in this edition.

Index: In the index itself, corporations are identified by abbreviated versions of their names and referenced by the sequence numbers assigned in the Descriptive Directory.

Abuse prevention
Accessibility/universal design
Adoption
Adult education—literacy, basic skills & GED
Adult/continuing education
Adults
Adults, men
Adults, women
African Americans/Blacks
Aging
Aging, centers/services
Agriculture
Agriculture, community food systems
Agriculture, farm bureaus/granges
Agriculture, farmlands
Agriculture, livestock issues
Agriculture, sustainable programs
Agriculture/food
Agriculture/food, alliance/advocacy
Agriculture/food, formal/general education
Agriculture/food, fund raising/fund distribution
Agriculture/food, management/technical assistance
Agriculture/food, public education
Agriculture/food, public policy
Agriculture/food, research
Agriculture/food, volunteer services
AIDS
AIDS research
AIDS, people with
Allergies research
ALS
Alzheimer's disease
Alzheimer's disease research
American Red Cross
Anatomy (animal)
Animal population control
Animal welfare
Animals/wildlife
Animals/wildlife, alliance/advocacy
Animals/wildlife, bird preserves
Animals/wildlife, endangered species
Animals/wildlife, fisheries
Animals/wildlife, management/technical assistance
Animals/wildlife, preservation/protection
Animals/wildlife, public education
Animals/wildlife, research
Animals/wildlife, sanctuaries
Animals/wildlife, special services
Animals/wildlife, training
Anti-slavery/human trafficking
Aquariums
Architecture
Art & music therapy
Arthritis
Arts
Arts councils
Arts education
Arts, alliance/advocacy
Arts, association
Arts, equal rights
Arts, public education
Arts, public policy
Arts, services
Arts, single organization support
Asians/Pacific Islanders
Assistive technology
Asthma
Asthma research
Athletics/sports, academies
Athletics/sports, amateur competition
Athletics/sports, amateur leagues
Athletics/sports, baseball
Athletics/sports, basketball
Athletics/sports, equestrianism
Athletics/sports, fishing/hunting
Athletics/sports, football
Athletics/sports, golf
Athletics/sports, Olympics
Athletics/sports, professional leagues
Athletics/sports, racquet sports
Athletics/sports, school programs
Athletics/sports, soccer
Athletics/sports, Special Olympics
Athletics/sports, training
Athletics/sports, water sports
Athletics/sports, winter sports
Autism
Autism research
Ballet
Big Brothers/Big Sisters
Biology/life sciences
Biomedicine
Biomedicine research
Bisexual
Blind/visually impaired
Botanical gardens
Botanical/horticulture/landscape services
Boy scouts
Boys
Boys & girls clubs
Boys clubs
Brain disorders
Brain research
Breast cancer
Breast cancer research
Buddhism
Business school/education
Business/industry
Camp Fire
Camps
Cancer
Cancer research
Catholic agencies & churches
Cemeteries/burial services, cemetery company
Cerebral palsy
Charter schools
Chemistry
Child abuse
Child development, education
Child development, services
Children
Children's rights
Children, services
Children/youth
Children/youth, services
Christian agencies & churches
Civic centers
Civil liberties, advocacy
Civil liberties, first amendment
Civil liberties, freedom of religion
Civil liberties, right to life
Civil/human rights
Civil/human rights, advocacy
Civil/human rights, alliance/advocacy
Civil/human rights, disabled
Civil/human rights, equal rights
Civil/human rights, immigrants
Civil/human rights, LGBTQ
Civil/human rights, minorities
Civil/human rights, women
Climate change/global warming
College
College (community/junior)
Community development, business promotion
Community development, men's clubs
Community development, neighborhood associations
Community development, neighborhood development
Community development, public/private ventures
Community development, real estate
Community development, service clubs
Community development, small businesses

Community development, women's clubs
Community/economic development
Community/economic development, equal rights
Community/economic development, fund raising/fund distribution
Community/economic development, management/technical assistance
Community/economic development, public education
Community/economic development, public policy
Community/economic development, volunteer services
Computer literacy/technology training
Computer science
Consumer protection
Continuing education
Correctional facilities
Courts/judicial administration
Crime/abuse victims
Crime/law enforcement
Crime/law enforcement, DWI
Crime/law enforcement, fund raising/fund distribution
Crime/law enforcement, police agencies
Crime/law enforcement, research
Crime/violence prevention
Crime/violence prevention, youth
Cultural/ethnic awareness
Cystic fibrosis
Cystic fibrosis research
Dance
Day care
Deaf/hearing impaired
Dental care
Dental school/education
Depression
Design
Developmentally disabled, centers & services
Diabetes
Diabetes research
Digestive diseases
Disabilities, people with
Disasters, 9/11/01
Disasters, domestic resettlement
Disasters, fire prevention/control
Disasters, floods
Disasters, Hurricane Katrina
Disasters, preparedness/services
Disasters, search/rescue
Dispute resolution
Domestic violence
Down syndrome
Drop-out prevention
Early childhood education
Economic development
Economically disadvantaged
Economics
Education
Education, alliance/advocacy
Education, association
Education, community/cooperative
Education, e-learning
Education, equal rights
Education, ESL programs
Education, formal/general education
Education, fund raising/fund distribution
Education, gifted students
Education, information services
Education, management/technical assistance
Education, PTA groups
Education, public education
Education, public policy
Education, reform
Education, research
Education, services
Education, single organization support
Education, special
Education, volunteer services
Electronic communications/Internet
Elementary school/education
Elementary/secondary education
Elementary/secondary school reform
Employment
Employment, equal rights
Employment, formal/general education
Employment, job counseling
Employment, management/technical assistance
Employment, public education
Employment, retraining
Employment, services
Employment, training
Employment, volunteer services
End of life care
Energy
Engineering
Engineering school/education
Engineering/technology
Environment
Environment, administration/regulation
Environment, air pollution
Environment, alliance/advocacy
Environment, association
Environment, beautification programs
Environment, ethics
Environment, forests
Environment, formal/general education
Environment, fund raising/fund distribution
Environment, government agencies
Environment, information services
Environment, land resources
Environment, legal rights
Environment, management/technical assistance
Environment, noise pollution
Environment, plant conservation
Environment, pollution control
Environment, public education
Environment, public policy
Environment, radiation control
Environment, reform
Environment, research
Environment, single organization support
Environment, toxics
Environment, volunteer services
Environment, water resources
Environmental education
Eye diseases
Eye research
Family planning
Family resources and services, disability
Family services
Family services, adolescent parents
Family services, home/homemaker aid
Family services, parent education
Film/video
Financial services
Folk arts
Food banks
Food distribution, groceries on wheels
Food distribution, meals on wheels
Food services
Food services, commodity distribution
Food services, congregate meals
Foreign policy
Foster care
Foundations (community)
Foundations (corporate)
Foundations (private grantmaking)
Foundations (public)
Fraternal societies (501(c)(8))
Freedom from violence/torture
Gay men
Genealogy
Genetic diseases and disorders
Geology
Geriatrics
Girl scouts
Girls
Girls clubs
Goodwill Industries
Government/public administration
Graduate/professional education
Gun control
Health care
Health care, alliance/advocacy
Health care, association
Health care, blood supply
Health care, clinics/centers
Health care, cost containment
Health care, emergency transport services
Health care, EMS
Health care, equal rights
Health care, financing
Health care, formal/general education
Health care, fund raising/fund distribution
Health care, home services
Health care, infants
Health care, information services
Health care, insurance
Health care, management/technical assistance
Health care, organ/tissue banks
Health care, patient services
Health care, public policy
Health care, reform
Health care, research
Health care, rural areas
Health care, support services
Health care, volunteer services
Health organizations
Health organizations, association
Health organizations, formal/general education
Health organizations, fund raising/fund distribution
Health organizations, public education
Health organizations, reform
Health organizations, research
Health organizations, single organization support
Health sciences school/education
Heart & circulatory diseases
Heart & circulatory research
Hematology research
Hemophilia
Hemophilia research
Higher education
Hinduism
Hispanics/Latinos
Historic preservation/historical societies
Historical activities
Historical activities, centennials
Historical activities, war memorials
History/archaeology
Holistic medicine
Home accessibility modifications
Homeless
Homeless, human services
Horticulture/garden clubs
Hospices
Hospitals (general)
Hospitals (specialty)
Housing/shelter
Housing/shelter, aging
Housing/shelter, development

Recreation
Recreation, adaptive sports
Recreation, association
Recreation, centers
Recreation, community
Recreation, fairs/festivals
Recreation, fund raising/fund distribution
Recreation, public education
Recycling
Religion
Religion, fund raising/fund distribution
Religion, interfaith issues
Religion, management/technical assistance
Reproductive health
Reproductive health, OBGYN/Birthing centers
Reproductive health, prenatal care
Reproductive rights
Residential/custodial care
Residential/custodial care, group home
Rural development
Rural studies
Safety, automotive safety
Safety, education
Safety, poisons
Safety/disasters
Safety/disasters, formal/general education
Safety/disasters, fund raising/fund distribution
Safety/disasters, information services
Safety/disasters, management/technical assistance
Safety/disasters, public education
Safety/disasters, volunteer services
Salvation Army
Schizophrenia
Scholarships/financial aid
Science
Science, formal/general education
Science, fund raising/fund distribution
Science, public education
Science, public policy
Science, research
Sculpture
Secondary school/education
Self-advocacy services, disability
Senior continuing care
Sexual abuse
Single parents
Skin disorders
Skin disorders research
Smoking
Social entrepreneurship
Social sciences
Social sciences, formal/general education
Social sciences, fund raising/fund distribution
Social sciences, interdisciplinary studies
Social work school/education
Space/aviation
Speech/hearing centers
Spine disorders
Spine disorders research
Spirituality
Stress
Student services/organizations
Students, sororities/fraternities
Substance abuse, prevention
Substance abuse, services
Substance abuse, treatment
Substance abusers
Suicide
Surgery
Surgery research
Teacher school/education
Television
Terminal illness, people with
Textile/fiber arts
Theater
Theater (playwriting)
Theological school/education
Transgender and gender nonconforming
Transportation
Tropical diseases
United Ways and Federated Giving Programs
University
Urban League
Urban studies
Urban/community development
Utilities
Venture philanthropy
Veterinary medicine
Veterinary medicine, hospital
Visitors/convention bureau/tourism promotion
Visual arts
Vocational education
Vocational education, post-secondary
Vocational rehabilitation
Voluntarism promotion
Volunteers of America
Voter education
Waste management
Water pollution
Web-based media
Women
Women, centers/services
YM/YWCAs & YM/YWHAs
Young adults
Young adults, female
Young adults, male
Youth
Youth development
Youth development, adult & child programs
Youth development, agriculture
Youth development, alliance/advocacy
Youth development, association
Youth development, business
Youth development, centers/clubs
Youth development, citizenship
Youth development, community service clubs
Youth development, equal rights
Youth development, formal/general education
Youth development, fund raising/fund distribution
Youth development, information services
Youth development, intergenerational programs
Youth development, public education
Youth development, services
Youth development, single organization support
Youth development, volunteer services
Youth, pregnancy prevention
Youth, services
Zoos/zoological societies

Abuse prevention

Acuity 32, Chicago 782, Fieldstone 1374, Fremont 1496, Mary 2392, Retail 3194, Seneca 3406

Accessibility/universal design

Bromelkamp 582, Nordson 2723

Adoption

Bristlecone 575, Carlson 693, Continental 925, Federal 1348, Gibraltar 1577, Hasbro 1747, International 1959, Jockey 2045, TJX 3765, ViewSonic 3952, Wendy's 4031, Wendy's 4032, Wendy's/Arby's 4030

Adult education—literacy, basic skills & GED

Berkshire 428, Bridgestone 560, Capital 679, Capstone 684, Dollar 1143, First 1419, FirstEnergy 1424, G&K 1524, H & R 1695, Kohler 2182, Lincoln 2281, Mutual 2607, Nellie 2659, Pitney 2984, RBC 3136, Reynolds 3199, San Francisco 3324, State 3592, TJX 3765, Union 3854, Verizon 3936, Visa 3960, Wal-Mart 3980, Xerox 4136

Adult/continuing education

Albemarle 78, Alcoa 82, Alyeska 121, Applied 220, Avidia 298, Capital 679, Cisco 818, Comerica 889, EQT 1287, Freeport 1494, IDACORP 1907, International 1960, Johnson 2050, JPMorgan Chase 2071, Kimball 2149, Kingsbury 2160, Kuskokwim 2200, Liberty 2262, Lincoln 2281, Middlesex 2506, Murphy 2600, Pitney 2984, Provident 3069, QUALCOMM 3095, SAP 3334, Sempra 3405, Shaughnessy 3425, Simplot 3459, UTC 3908, Wisconsin 4096

Adults

Abbott 13, Autodesk 289, Beneficial 412, Berkshire 428, Butt 628, Caterpillar 722, Chicago 788, Chrysler 801, CHS 802, Cow 957, Genesis 1561, GlaxoSmithKline 1588, Graco 1624, Great 1645, Guard 1680, Metropolitan 2481, Schwab 3363, Southern 3514, St. Joe 3563, Sundt 3648, U.S. 3835, WD-40 4011, Western 4045

Adults, men

Autodesk 289, Beneficial 412, Genesis 1561, Metropolitan 2481, Piedmont 2971

Adults, women

Autodesk 289, Avon 305, Beneficial 412, CA 638, Choice 798, Comerica 889, Fisher 1433, Genesis 1561, Metropolitan 2481, Piedmont 2971

African Americans/Blacks

Abbott 13, AK 67, Alliance 101, Allstate 107, Anheuser 202, Autodesk 289, Beneficial 412, Blue 496, Bristol 578, Chrysler 801, Crowell 986, Ford 1464, Genesis 1561, Hewlett 1794, Holland 1834, Intel 1950, Intoximeters 1979, KPMG 2190, Luster 2318, Merck 2466, Metropolitan 2481, Mondelez 2556, Piedmont 2971, PPG 3025, PricewaterhouseCoopers 3042, Semiconductor 3403, St. Joe 3563, Vinson 3957, Wachtell 3973, WD-40 4011, Xerox 4136

Aging

AGL 57, Allergan 99, Ameren 128, Ameren 129, AMERIGROUP 171, AmerisourceBergen 175, Andersen 194, Antioch 207, Apple 218, Athletics 276, Autodesk 289, Avista 301, Baxter 377, Beneficial 412, Blue 497, Blue 502, Blue 505, Bristol 578, Caesars 650, Calvert 663, Cardinal 685, CC 728, Chrysler 801, CME 853, CNO 857, Colorado 880, Columbia 884, Delta 1074, DP 1168, Duke 1189, Entergy 1279, EQT 1287,

Financial 1382, Florida 1443, Genesis 1561, Genworth 1565, Grand 1627, Granite 1632, HCR 1763, Highmark 1799, Horizon 1863, Humana 1886, Jackson 2009, JM 2044, Kansas 2093, Kennebunk 2126, Kennecott 2127, Kimball 2149, Lincoln 2281, Louisiana 2309, MDU 2441, Meredith 2471, Metropolitan 2481, Moneta 2557, National 2635, Newell 2694, Nexion 2705, Omnicare 2807, Penney 2925, Phoenix 2968, Principal 3047, Puck 3080, Questar 3104, Reynolds 3199, Savings 3343, Schwab 3363, Seneca 3406, ShopKo 3440, Skadden 3470, Square 3560, St. Joe 3563, Steelcase 3597, TECO 3701, Teichert 3704, United 3863, Universal 3887, Verizon 3936, Washington 3995, WD-40 4011

Aging, centers/services

Acuity 31, AK 67, Alabama 71, Allianz 105, Alpha 112, Altria 120, American 165, AMERIGROUP 171, AMR 187, Andersen 194, Avidia 298, Bank 342, Bank 347, Bristol 578, Brocchini 580, Burlington 616, Caesars 650, Calvert 663, Cape 674, Central 742, Chotin 799, CNO 857, Crayola 973, Curves 1011, Dedham 1060, Deluxe 1084, Deutsch 1098, Diageo 1107, Dime 1118, Dollar 1144, Dominion 1150, DTE 1183, DVK 1198, Dynamet 1200, East 1207, Eastern 1210, El Paso 1239, Fabri 1322, Family 1330, Fetzer 1367, First 1403, First 1415, Florida 1443, GenRad 1564, Genworth 1565, Gulf 1689, Halliburton 1706, Hampden 1712, Hanover 1724, HCR 1763, Horix 1860, Hubbard 1878, IDACORP 1907, IMA 1917, Institution 1946, Jackson 2009, Jackson 2011, JM 2044, Kaiser 2086, Kingsbury 2160, Kinney 2162, Levi 2254, Macy's 2333, Manhattan 2354, Merck 2466, Metropolitan 2481, Minto 2533, Newburyport 2693, Nexion 2705, NorthWestern 2748, OceanFirst 2782, Ohio 2790, Old 2796, Omron 2810, PacifiCorp 2860, Parker 2886, Penn 2923, Peoples 2931, Perkins 2940, Philadelphia 2961, Physicians 2970, Piedmont 2971, PMI 2995, Portland 3010, Public 3076, Pukall 3082, R & B 3113, Reynolds 3199, Rite 3220, Rosen's 3264, Rudolph 3283, Shenandoah 3433, ShopKo 3440, Sports 3548, Station 3593, Stoneham 3616, Tesoro 3723, Thomaston 3736, United 3876, Universal 3887, Universal 3891, Upper 3900, USEC 3904, Verby 3934, Viejas 3951, Vijuk 3953, Westinghouse 4049, Wisconsin 4096, Woodforest 4110, Wynnne 4133, Young 4146

Agriculture

Ag 55, AgStar 59, Albertsons 79, Altria 120, Bridgestone 560, Bunge 612, Chiquita 795, CHS 802, Continental 926, Country 951, Dean 1054, Dole 1141, Farmers 1339, First 1412, Flir 1440, Ford 1464, GROWMARK 1674, Hard 1727, Independence 1925, Kent 2129, Land 2217, MFA 2486, Mondelez 2556, Monsanto 2559, MTD 2595, Nu 2759, Perdue 2936, Pioneer 2980, Riceland 3203, Rockville 3245, Rosen's 3264, Sierra 3451, Starbucks 3585, Sunkist 3649, Toro 3775, Trim 3810, True 3814, U.S. 3839, UMB 3846, Union 3854, Welch 4025, Whole 4066, Wisconsin 4096

Agriculture, community food systems

Ben 409, Clif 848

Agriculture, farm bureaus/granges

Monsanto 2559

Agriculture, farmlands

AgStar 59, Ben 409, Clif 848, Dean 1054, Farmers 1339, Monsanto 2559, Mosaic 2580, Pioneer 2980, Wal-Mart 3980

Agriculture, livestock issues

Hubbard 1878, True 3814, Whole 4066

Agriculture, sustainable programs

AgStar 59, Archer 233, Ben 409, Blue 497, Blue 501, Cargill 691, Clif 848, Dean 1054, Deere 1061, Farmers 1339, Green 1653, Hannaford 1723, Hard 1727, Lake 2212, Land 2217, Mamma 2353, New England 2670, Philip 2962, Pioneer 2980, Stonyfield 3617, Sustainable 3662, Wal-Mart 3980, White 4062

Agriculture/food

A.D. 7, ACE 24, ACE 25, Aexcel 49, Aladdin 73, Ashley 259, Bartlett 365, BPI 548, Campbell 669, Capri 682, Clif 848, ConAgra 904, Connecticut 910, Cornerstone 942, Credit 979, Cupertino 1009, Deere 1061, Evans 1300, Executive 1308, Farmers 1339, First 1423, Foremost 1466, International 1958, Iowa 1986, Jewett 2042, JTB 2074, Land 2217, Mariani 2374, Marlborough 2380, Marriott 2383, Miller 2522, Mosaic 2580, Natural 2643, Nektar 2658, Pendleton 2921, PepsiCo 2935, Pioneer 2979, RBS 3137, Rivermaid 3225, Saco 3302, Safeway 3310, Shatz 3424, Simplot 3459, SUPERVALU 3659, Wallace 3983, Wegmans 4021, Wittern 4098

Agriculture/food, alliance/advocacy

GROWMARK 1674, Newman's 2697

Agriculture/food, formal/general education

AgStar 59, Archer 233, Cargill 691, Land 2217, Mosaic 2580, Shanken 3421, Southern 3519, Sustainable 3662, Woodward-Graff 4113

Agriculture/food, fund raising/fund distribution

National 2638

Agriculture/food, management/technical assistance

Eastern 1211, Farmers 1339

Agriculture/food, public education

CHS 802, ConAgra 904, Monsanto 2559, Pagnol 2865

Agriculture/food, public policy

ConAgra 904

Agriculture/food, research

Monsanto 2559, Mosaic 2580

Agriculture/food, volunteer services

Tesoro 3723

AIDS

Abbott 13, Bloomingdale's 488, Bristol 578, California 655, California 656, Carlson 693, Chevron 780, Coca 862, Discovery 1126, Duane 1186, Getty 1569, Gilead 1582, Gucci 1684, Guess 1685, Hewlett 1794, IAC 1903, International 1959, Jacksonville 2014, Johnson 2048, Kaiser 2086, Kenneth 2128, Klein 2166, Kohler 2182, Lauder 2230, Macy's 2333, Mattel 2405, Merck 2466, Pfizer 2950, Playboy 2990, Quest 3103, S & S 3296, Starbucks 3585, Strauss 3624, Watson 4007, Zappos.com 4153

AIDS research

Bristol 578, Gilead 1582, Guess 1685, Kenneth 2128, Kohler 2182, Macy's 2333, Security 3391, Strauss 3624, Wawa 4009

AIDS, people with

Abbott 13, Autodesk 289, Beneficial 412, Genesis 1561, S & S 3296, TJX 3765, WD-40 4011

Allergies research

Towerbrook 3781

ALS

Bay 378, Booz 525, CVS 1014, Duane 1186, Griswold 1669, Home 1844, Maritz 2376, Neenah 2656, Premier 3036, Rasmussen 3128, Transco 3797, Universal 3895

Alzheimer's disease

American 139, Caesars 650, California 655, Capital 676, CNO 857, Driscoll 1176, Extendicare 1314, First 1389, Genworth 1565, Gould 1618, Kindred 2154, Lincoln 2280, Metropolitan 2481, Orscheln 2827, Prophet 3063, Schmeling 3353, Shelter 3431, Smucker 3488, TJX 3765, Universal 3890

Alzheimer's disease research

Extendicare 1314, Metropolitan 2481

American Red Cross

Abbott 13, Acacia 21, ACE 24, Adir 36, Advance 39, AK 67, Alcoa 82, Alice 89, Allegis 92, Alro 113, American 143, American 156, American 169, AMETEK 181, AMPCO 186, Angels 200, Anheuser 202, Aon 210, Armstrong 246, Ascena 255, Avis 299, Baird 317, Baker 324, Barnes 362, Barton 366, Baum 375, Bayer 381, BB&T 385, Beckman 397, Berry 437, Birdsong 470, Bob's 511, BorgWarner 528, BOSE 530, BP 547, Bristol 578, Burlington 618, Caesars 650, Callaway 660, Calpine 661, Calumet 662, Capital 676, Carlson 693, Central 742, Central 745, CFS 756, Chaney 761, Chevron 780, Chrysler 801, CHS 802, CIGNA 812, CLARCOR 832, CNO 857, Coach 858, Collins 873, Columbia 883, Commerce 890, Community 900, Credit 980, Dana 1026, Darden 1032, Dayton 1047, Dean 1053, Dean 1054, Deere 1061, Delphi 1071, Delta 1073, DENTSPLY 1089, Dilbeck 1116, Discovery 1126, Doctor's 1138, Dollar 1143, Dollar 1144, DreamWorks 1172, DRS 1179, DTE 1183, Duke 1189, Dunkin' 1191, Eaton 1216, Emerson 1257, Employers 1264, Enbridge 1265, Farmers 1335, Farmers 1338, FedEx 1352, Fidelity 1371, Fifth 1377, First 1400, First 1404, First 1408, Franklin 1485, Fredericksburg 1490, Furniture 1519, GenCorp 1548, General 1555, GenOn 1563, GKN 1585, Greater 1649, GuideOne 1687, Haviland 1752, Hewlett 1794, Hilfiger 1801, Holcim 1828, Home 1842, Hooters 1858, Hormel 1866, Hulman 1885, Hy-Vee 1900, Illinois 1916, Ingersoll 1939, Institution 1946, International 1962, Island 1996, Jackson 2011, Jacobs 2016, Johns 2047, Johnson 2048, Jones 2055, Jones 2059, Kellogg 2120, Kimberly 2150, Kindred 2154, Kingsbury 2160, Kinney 2162, Kroger 2195, Kuhns 2197, Lauder 2230, Liberty 2265, Lilly 2274, Lincoln 2280, Lockheed 2292, Loews 2296, Lowe's 2312, Lucasfilm 2316, M&T 2323, Manitowoc 2356, McLaughlin 2436, Merck 2466, Midcontinent 2505, Mississippi 2536, Mondelez 2556, Morgan 2570, N.E.W. 2611, Nationwide 2639, NCR 2650, Nelnet 2660, Nestle 2663, Newport 2699, NIBCO 2707, Niemann 2708, NII 2709, North 2730, Northwestern 2749, Ohio 2790, Omron 2810, OneBeacon 2813, Oshkosh 2833, PEMCO 2919, Penguin 2922, Penney 2925, Perforce 2937, Perrigo 2943, PG&E 2952, Plain 2989, Plum 2991, PPG 3025, Pukall 3082, PVH 3088, Quad 3091, Quality 3096, Rayonier 3134, Realogy 3145, Recreational 3150, Red 3154, Regal 3166, Regions 3171, Robinson 3235, Ross 3267, Ryder 3292, S & T 3297, Scoular 3373, Sealy 3382, Sempra 3405, Sonic 3498, Sonoco 3500, Sprint 3556, Stanek 3578, STERIS 3600, Strauss 3624, SunTrust 3654, Synopsys 3673, Towerbrook

3781, Trane 3794, Turner 3824, Tyler 3831, United 3872, United 3873, United 3874, Universal 3891, USG 3905, Utica 3910, V.F. 3913, Valero 3915, Valspar 3920, Vectren 3925, VHA 3944, Wal-Mart 3980, Watson 4007, WEDGE 4020, Weil 4022, WellPoint 4027, Western 4040, Western 4041, Whirlpool 4056, Williams 4078, Wrigley 4125

Anatomy (animal)

Universal 3893

Animal population control

Magnolia 2340

Animal welfare

AGL 57, Albrecht 80, Allegheny 91, American 155, Ameritas 178, AMPCO 186, Arcelormittal 229, Aspen 260, Beaver 394, Betts 451, Black 475, Bloomingdale's 488, Bragg 554, Build 608, Charles 764, Cincinnati 814, CITGO 820, Creative 976, Darden 1032, davistudio 1043, Deacon 1050, Del 1065, Dharma 1105, Discover 1125, Discovery 1126, Econscious 1223, Edelman 1224, Elemental Herbs 1244, Energizer 1271, Ensign 1276, Exchange 1307, Exotic 1310, First 1397, Florida 1443, Fremont 1497, Friesen 1505, Go 1595, Green 1650, Green 1653, Groves 1673, Hackstock 1697, Haggen 1699, Hartz 1744, Hulman 1885, Indiana 1931, Insperity 1944, Kemp 2123, Kingsbury 2160, Magnolia 2340, Major 2346, Mars 2384, Merck 2466, Morton 2579, National 2634, Nestle 2662, North 2731, Perforce 2937, PETCO 2945, PetSmart 2948, Philadelphia 2958, Procter 3055, Questar 3104, Rahr 3118, Renovated 3185, Richard 3205, Rothstein 3271, Safeguard 3307, Schein 3348, SeaWorld 3387, Sierra 3449, Star 3584, Stiles 3607, Valassis 3914, Warren 3993, Weis 4024, Wendy's/Arby's 4030, Whole 4066, Wolf 4103

Animals/wildlife

A.D. 7, Alabama 71, Albrecht 80, Altec 118, American 143, American 155, Black 475, Boyd 545, BP 547, Budweiser 605, Build 608, Burlington 616, CME 853, Dansko 1031, DTE 1183, Fiserv 1427, Florida 1443, GenOn 1563, Google 1613, Graham 1625, Hermann 1786, Home 1843, Interface 1953, International 1958, Jackson-Shaw 2013, Kaytee 2104, Kerzner 2133, Kilmartin 2145, Lamont 2215, Morris 2573, Newman 2696, NV 2765, OSCO 2832, Philadelphia 2958, Pioneer 2982, PPL 3026, Redwoods 3158, Sasol 3338, SeaWorld 3387, Serengeti 3411, Sidener 3445, Sierra 3449, Sierra 3451, Stephens 3598, Swift 3666, Teleflex 3707, Textron 3731, Toeniskoetter 3767, Tulalip 3820, USA 3903, Vulcan 3972, Whole 4066, Wisconsin 4096, WKBN 4099, Working 4116, Worthen 4123, Young 4147

Animals/wildlife, alliance/advocacy

Xcel 4135

Animals/wildlife, bird preserves

Newport 2699

Animals/wildlife, endangered species

Edison 1228, Exxon 1315, Google 1613, Kerzner 2133, NEBCO 2653

Animals/wildlife, fisheries

GenOn 1563, Hannaford 1723, Lateral 2227, New England 2670, Pacific 2855, SeaWorld 3387

Animals/wildlife, management/technical assistance

Aspen 260

Animals/wildlife, preservation/protection

Bragg 554, Bridgestone 560, Build 608, Chase 769, Dharma 1105, Dow 1160, Earnhardt 1205, Edgar 1225, Edison 1228, Evening 1302, Hillside 1810, Hofmann 1824, IHC 1913, International 1958, Mars 2384, Miller 2518, Moore 2565, National 2636, Nestle 2662, New England 2670, North 2731, NorthWestern 2748, Orvis 2830, Rahr 3118, Reell 3164, SeaWorld 3387, Specialty 3538, Spirol 3545, Swift 3666, Terre 3722, Toyota 3787, Vulcan 3972, Wachtell 3973, Xcel 4135

Animals/wildlife, public education

Build 608, SeaWorld 3387, Xcel 4135

Animals/wildlife, research

Kerzner 2133, SeaWorld 3387

Animals/wildlife, sanctuaries

Herschend 1790, Kennebunk 2126, Longaberger 2299, SeaWorld 3387, Snyder's-Lance 3492, Star 3582, Swift 3666

Animals/wildlife, special services

Build 608, Copley 938, Green 1657, Kemp 2123, Nestle 2662

Animals/wildlife, training

American 155, Nestle 2662

Anti-slavery/human trafficking

Allen 94, Greenlight 1658, UncommonGoods 3849

Aquariums

American 150, Chicago 787, Herschend 1790, Illinois 1916, PerkinElmer 2939, PPG 3025, Union 3854, Union 3857, Williams 4078, WKBN 4099

Architecture

Andersen 194, Marcus 2371, Skidmore 3474

Art & music therapy

Crescent 982, CVS 1014

Arthritis

ABARTA 10, CNO 857, DJO 1134, Nasdaq 2618, Redner's 3157

Arts

1st 2, 3M 3, A.J. 8, ABARTA 10, Abbott 13, Acme 28, Acuity 32, Adobe 38, AEGON 45, Aetna 48, Aexcel 49, Aflac 54, AGL 57, Air 63, Airtek 66, Alabama 71, Aladdin 73, Alaska 74, Albemarle 78, Alexander 85, Allegheny 91, Allen 94, Allergan 99, Allete 100, Alliant 104, Alpha 112, Altec 118, Altria 120, Amazon.com 122, Amboy 124, AMC 126, Ameren 128, American 134, American 141, American 143, American 144, American 145, American 146, American 150, American 154, American 157, American 160, American 168, Ameriprise 174, Ameristar 176, Amerisure 177, Ameritas 178, AMETEK 181, Amgen 182, Amica 183, Amnews 185, Amsted 188, Amway 189, Andersen 194, Angels 200, Anocoil 204, Aon 210, Apache 211, Applied 220, AptarGroup 221, Arch 231, Archer 232, Arent 235, Ariel 237, Arizona 239, Arkema 242, Armbrust 243, Arrow 249, Associated 263, Associated 264, Assurant 267, Assurant 268, AT&T 273, AT&T 274, Austin 288, Autodesk 289, AutoNation 292, AutoZone 294, Avis 299, Avista 301, Aviva 302, Azavea 309, Badger 313, Bailey 315, Baird 316, Baird 317, Baker 321, Baker 324, Baker 325, Bangor 338, Bank 340, Bank 341, Bank 342, Bank 343, Bank 344, Bank 346, Bank 348, Bardes 359, Barnes 360, Barnes 362, Barrasso 363, BASF 368, Bassett 372, Baum 375, Bay 379, Bayer 381, BB&T 385, Bean 391, Bean 392, Bechtel 395, Bekins 401, Belden 402, Belk 403, Bemis 407, Bemis 408, Benedict-Miller 410, Beneficial 411, Berglund 419, Berkley 426, Berkshire 428, Berry 434, Berry 435, Beverage 452, BHP 455, Bickel 457, Bierlein 459, Binswanger 464, Biogen 465, Biomet 466, Birdsong 470, Black 474, Black 475, Blair 478, Block 481, Bloomberg 486, Bloomingdale's 488, Blue 493, Blue 494, Blue 500, BMW 509, Boart 510, Bobcats 512, Boeing 516, Boh 517, Bon 521, Booz 525, Boston 534, Bowater 543, BP 547, Bracewell 549, Bramco 555, Bricker 559, Bridgestone 560, Briggs 564, Briggs 565, Brightpoint 567, Brinckerhoff 570, Brinker 572, Brocchini 580, Brooklyn 584, Brooks 585, Brown 591, Brown 592, Brunswick 595, BSA 597, Buchalter 600, Budweiser 605, Bunge 612, Burger's 614, Burlington 616, Burlington 618, Burns 620, Butler 626, Butler 627, Butt 628, Cacique 644, Cades 647, Cajun 652, Calpine 661, Calumet 662, Cambridge 666, Cape 674, Capital 676, Capital 677, Capitol 680, Cargill 691, Carmody 695, Carnival 696, Carpenter 700, Carrington Coleman 701, Carroll 703, Carter's 708, Cascade 713, Caterpillar 722, Cathay 723, CBS 727, Centene 735, Central 745, Central 746, Century 750, Chaney 761, Chelsea 772, Chemed 773, Chevron 780, Chicago 786, Chicago 787, Chicago 788, Chicopee 792, Chief 793, Chinese 794, Chotin 799, Chrysler 801, Chubb 804, Churchill 807, Cianbro 808, CIGNA 812, Citizens 827, CLARCOR 832, Claremont 833, Clear 842, Clements 845, Cleveland 846, Clif 848, Cliffs 850, Clorox 852, CMS 854, Collective 871, Collette 872, Colonial 874, Colonial 875, Commerce 890, Commercial 893, Commonwealth 895, Compass 901, Compuware 902, ConocoPhillips 913, Consolidated 916, Consolidated 917, Consumers 921, Contran 928, Convergys 933, Cook 934, Cooper 935, Cooper 936, Copley 938, Coquille 939, Corning 945, Cousins 953, Cox 958, Coyotes 963, Cracker 966, Crane 969, Cranfill 971, Cranston 972, Crayola 973, Creative 975, Crown 987, Crystal 992, Cullen 1000, Cullman 1001, CUNA 1008, Cymer 1016, Dallas 1022, Dallas 1023, Dana 1026, Danaher 1027, Darden 1032, Davis 1041, davistudio 1043, Dayton 1047, Dean 1053, DeBruce 1057, Dedham 1060, Deere 1061, Delta 1073, Delta 1082, Demoulas 1085, DeniseLawrence.Com 1086, DENSO 1088, Deutsche 1099, Devon 1102, Dharma 1105, Diebold 1112, Dilbeck 1116, Dime 1118, Disney 1127, Dispatch 1129, Dollar 1142, Dollar 1145, Dominion 1150, Dondlinger 1154, DP 1168, Draper 1171, DTE 1183, du Pont 1184, Duke 1189, Dynamet 1200, East 1208, Eastman 1213, Eastman 1214, Eaton 1216, Ecolab 1220, Edelman 1224, Edison 1228, Edison 1229, Edsim 1230, Edvisors 1234, EFC 1236, El Paso 1239, Electronic 1242, EMC 1253, Emerson 1257, Employers 1264, Enbridge 1265, Endeavor 1267, Endres 1269, Energen 1270, EnMark 1274, Ensign 1276, Entelco 1277, Entergy 1279, Entergy 1280, Epson 1286, EQT 1287, Equifax 1288, Essa 1297, Evening 1302, Excell 1304, Exelon 1309, Express 1313, Faber 1319, Fabri 1322, FBR 1345, FDI 1346, Federated 1351, Fender 1359, Fenton 1361, Ferguson 1363, Ferro 1366, FIDELIO 1370, Fidelity 1371, Fieldstone 1374, Fifth 1377, First 1391, First 1395, First 1396, First 1397, First 1398, First 1403, First 1405, First 1406, First 1408, First 1409, First 1415, First 1416, First 1419, First 1420, First 1422, First 1423, FirstEnergy 1424, Fisher 1431, Florence 1441, Florida 1442, Florida 1443, Fluor 1448, FMC 1449, FMR 1450, Foley 1454, Ford 1463, Ford 1464, Forest 1467, Four 1477, Framingham 1481, Franklin 1485, Franklin 1488, Franshaw 1489, Freeport 1494, Fremont 1496, Friesen 1505, Fujisankei 1515, Fuller 1517, Fulton 1518, Furniture 1519, G & R 1523, Gable 1525,

Arts councils

Arts education

Arts, alliance/advocacy

Arts, association

Arts, equal rights

Arts, public education

Arts, public policy

Arts, services

Arts, single organization support
First 1419

Asians/Pacific Islanders
Abbott 13, Allstate 107, Autodesk 289, Beneficial 412, Calista 657, Chrysler 801, Crowell 986, Crystal 992, Fema 1358, Genesis 1561, Kajima 2087, Kawasaki 2103, Metropolitan 2481, Pacific 2857, Panda 2871, Vinson 3957, WD-40 4011

Assistive technology
CenturyLink 751, CVS 1014, Liberty 2265

Asthma
CVS 1014, Eastman 1214, General 1552, Merck 2466

Asthma research
Merck 2466

Athletics/sports, academies
New 2668, Vermont 3940

Athletics/sports, amateur competition
Football 1460, Holcim 1828

Athletics/sports, amateur leagues
7-Eleven 5, Abby's 14, Abt 20, Anaheim 191, Anderson 195, Ariens 238, Athletics 276, Atlanta 279, Baltimore 334, Bassett 372, Bay 378, Birdsong 470, Brightpoint 567, Brocchini 580, Brooklyn 584, Buccaneer 599, Burlington 616, C Spire 636, Cacique 644, California 656, Callaway 660, Carson 705, Catalina 719, CC 728, Centene 735, Center 737, Citizens 827, Clark 835, Collette 872, Cumberland 1003, Dallas 1022, Dart 1034, Denver 1090, Detroit 1095, Devereaux 1100, Dick's 1110, Dietz 1114, DS 1182, Farmers 1338, Finish 1383, First 1406, Food 1458, Foot 1459, Friday 1501, Fulton 1518, Genesco 1559, Gibbs 1576, Harris 1738, Henry 1781, Hoops 1857, Ilitch 1915, Independence 1925, Institution 1946, Integrity 1948, Kellogg 2120, Long 2298, M.D.C. 2324, Marena 2372, Mariani 2374, Mascoma 2394, Mattel 2405, McDonald's 2427, Mortgage 2578, National 2631, Neace 2651, New 2668, New Hampshire 2674, New York 2688, Newport 2699, Parker 2886, Price 3039, Progressive 3058, Quad 3091, R & R 3114, Redner's 3157, Reebok 3159, Reiff 3174, Rockville 3245, S & T 3297, San Francisco 3326, sanofi-aventis 3329, Schwan 3365, Sports 3548, Thomaston 3736, Tim 3753, Tops 3774, Trim 3810, United 3872, United 3880, Valero 3915, Wendy's 4032, Whitley 4064, Woerner 4101

Athletics/sports, baseball
Acme 29, Allegis 92, Angels 200, Athletics 276, Atlanta 280, AutoZone 294, Avidia 298, AZPB 310, Baltimore 334, Baseball 367, Carson 705, Cincinnati 814, Cleveland 847, Colorado 879, Dedham 1060, Delta 1073, Detroit 1097, DHL 1106, Doctor's 1138, Essa 1297, Florence 1441, Gould 1618, Hawkins 1757, Hofmann 1824, Houston 1871, Indus 1934, Kansas 2093, Law 2233, Legg 2245, Major 2345, Major 2346, Mariani 2374, Miami 2491, MidAmerican 2504, Milwaukee 2527, Mortgage 2578, New York 2688, New York 2691, Reiff 3174, S & T 3297, San Diego 3323, San Francisco 3324, Sterling 3601, Superior 3658, Tampa 3686, Texas 3729, Twins 3827, V.F. 3913, Washington 3998, Wendy's 4032

Athletics/sports, basketball
Basketball 370, Brooklyn 584, CC 728, Chicago 785, CNO 857, Dallas 1021, Denver 1090, Devereaux 1100, Heat 1767, Hoops 1857, Milwaukee 2528, Mohegan 2546, National 2623, Sacramento 3303, San Antonio 3321, Spurs 3557, Universal 3890, Washington 4000

Athletics/sports, equestrianism
Alfa 87, Churchill 807, Control 929, Golden 1601, Green 1657, Mary 2392, Provident 3070, Quanex 3100, Rood 3257, Turf 3822

Athletics/sports, fishing/hunting
Rich 3204

Athletics/sports, football
Buccaneer 599, Buffalo 606, Chicago 781, Chick 791, Dallas 1022, Employers 1263, First 1389, Indianapolis 1932, Minnesota 2530, National 2627, New York 2684, New York 2687, Nu 2759, Oakland 2772, PDB 2906, Philadelphia 2958, Pittsburgh 2986, Pro 3052, San Diego 3322, Tennessee 3716, Wilkes 4074

Athletics/sports, golf
AEGON 45, American 148, Bank 348, Callaway 660, CLARCOR 832, Devereaux 1100, Dietz 1114, DRW 1181, Easthampton 1212, Employers 1263, Exelon 1309, Fisher 1431, Jacobs 2016, Kahn 2084, Ladies 2209, Mariani 2374, PGA 2953, PGA 2954, Protector 3067, R & R 3114, Stonecutter 3615, Toro 3775, Tyler 3831, UBS 3842, Wendy's 4031, Winter 4090

Athletics/sports, Olympics
Hilton 1812

Athletics/sports, professional leagues
American 150, Dick's 1110, Long 2298, Pro 3052, Sports 3548

Athletics/sports, racquet sports
Astoria 270, Newport 2699, sanofi-aventis 3329, United 3879

Athletics/sports, school programs
Baltimore 335, BancTrust 337, Blue 497, Capital 676, Carmody 695, Carson 705, Coca 861, Concept 905, Coyotes 963, CVS 1014, Eastern 1211, Employers 1263, Farmers 1338, Food 1458, Franklin 1485, Inman 1943, Jamba 2020, Life 2269, Manitowoc 2355, Maquoketa 2361, Marena 2372, McCarthy 2421, McJunkin 2431, Mitchell 2537, Mylan 2610, New 2668, New Hampshire 2674, Newport 2699, NIKE 2710, Philips 2963, Progressive 3059, S & S 3296, sanofi-aventis 3329, Sierra 3451, Stiles 3607, TECO 3701, United 3864, Universal 3890, Winn 4087

Athletics/sports, soccer
Columbus 886, D.C. 1018, Danforth 1028, Earthquakes 1206, Florence 1441, Kohl's 2181, Los Angeles 2308, Major 2347, One 2812, Perforce 2937, Sports 3549, Toro 3775

Athletics/sports, Special Olympics
Alliance 101, Amerisure 177, Apogee 215, Arbella 226, Booz 525, Chicago 785, Delaware 1066, Denny's 1087, Dollar 1144, Dunkin' 1191, Esurance 1298, Fast 1343, Groves 1673, Hilton 1812, Hooters 1858, International 1967, International Profit 1969, Lime 2276, Mattel 2405, Michael 2493, Midmark 2507, Milwaukee 2528, Minnesota 2530, N.E.W. 2611, Nash 2619, New York 2684, NorthWestern 2748, Otis 2835, Patton's 2899, Philadelphia 2960, Robins 3232, ShopKo 3440, Sovereign 3528, Stride 3625, TD 3696, Tesoro 3723, United 3882, V.F. 3913, Washington 3994, Winter 4090, Zappos.com 4153

Athletics/sports, training
AZPB 310, Baltimore 335, New 2689, RBC 3136, Stop 3618, Trail 3793

Athletics/sports, water sports
Brunswick 595, Capital 678, Copley 938, Devereaux 1100, Harken 1731, Heat 1767, Highmark 1799, International 1958, Kellogg 2120, Madison 2334, ViewSonic 3952, Warnaco 3988, West 4037, Western 4041

Athletics/sports, winter sports
Atlanta 279, Center 737, Citizens 827, Dallas 1023, Danforth 1028, Franklin 1488, Hannaford 1723, Hubbard 1877, Lincoln 2280, Minnesota 2531, Nashville 2620, National 2631, New Jersey 2676, New York 2686, Philadelphia 2959, San Jose 3327, St. Louis 3567, U.M. 3834, Vermont 3940

Autism
AMC 125, Boler 520, Discovery 1126, Dunkin' 1191, Kepco 2132, Lincoln 2280, North 2728, Safeway 3310, Shanken 3421, Star 3583, YGS 4143, Zale 4151

Autism research
Detroit 1095, Quest 3103

Ballet
ABARTA 10, Baird 317, Darden 1032, Friesen 1505, Holder 1829, Huntington 1894, Illinois 1916, Intrepid 1980, Johnson 2052, Loomis 2301, Malco 2350, Marcus 2370, Mascoma 2394, MidAmerican 2504, Mine 2529, Mitchell 2537, Questar 3104, Regions 3171, Simplot 3459, Sports 3548, State 3590, Sterne 3602, Sunbeam 3647, United 3860

Big Brothers/Big Sisters
Alcatel 81, American 140, American 141, ANH 201, Arby's 228, Bob's 511, Brooklyn 584, Burger 613, Capitol 680, Carlson 693, Coca 862, Comcast 887, Copley 938, Credit 980, CUNA 1008, Dayton 1047, Discover 1125, Dollar 1144, Eastern 1210, Emerson 1257, Exchange 1307, Fidelity 1371, First 1401, First 1419, Giant 1571, Golden 1602, Hastings 1749, Heinz 1772, Intermec 1955, International 1959, Irby 1990, Jack 2007, JM 2044, Jones 2055, Liberty 2264, Manitowoc 2356, Nationwide 2639, Newfield 2695, Omaha 2805, Oshkosh 2833, Osram 2834, People's 2928, QuikTrip 3109, Rackspace 3117, RESCO 3189, Royal 3273, RUAN 3279, Shelter 3431, Sprint 3556, Sterne 3602, Teleflex 3707, TeleTech 3708, Tenneco 3715, Titan 3763, Tyler 3831, UBS 3842, Valero 3915, Visteon 3964, Whiting 4063

Biology/life sciences
Agilent 56, AMN Healthcare 184, Boston 540, Bristol 578, Cabot 642, L'Oreal 2203, Life 2268, Merck 2466, Merk 2467, New England 2670, Pfizer 2950, Universal 3893, Wiley 4072

Biomedicine
Life 2268, Merck 2466, Wiley 4072

Biomedicine research
Charles 764, McKinstry 2435

Bisexual
Allstate 107, Autodesk 289

Blind/visually impaired
Alcon 83, Allegheny 91, Autodesk 289, Bausch 376, Beneficial 412, Central 743, Chrysler 801, Clarkson 839, CVS 1014, Evening 1302, Genesis 1561, Kaman 2088, St. Joe 3563, StanCorp 3574, WD-40 4011, Xerox 4136

Botanical gardens
American 164, AMPCO 186, Baird 316, Bank 343, Bemis 408, Black 475, Bunge 612, Croft 985, Eliason 1248, Hermann 1786, Illinois 1916, Industrial 1935, International 1958, Kelly 2122, Magnolia 2340, Mine 2529, Mitsubishi 2539, P.E.L. 2849, Physicians 2970, Schloss 3352, Scotts 3372, Stardust 3586, Union 3854, Union 3857, Zions 4158

Botanical/horticulture/landscape services
Metropolitan 2484, Monsanto 2559, Tiffany 3750

Boy scouts
Acme 29, AK 67, Allegheny 91, Allegis 92, Alsco 115, American 135, Ameritas 178, AnchorBank 193, Armstrong 246, Ash 256, Baird 317, Bassett 372, Batson 373, Baum 375, Belk 403, Berry 437, Betts 451, Bridgestone 560, Bristol 577, Brown 591, Brunswick 595, Burlington 618, Center 737, Central 742, Cianbro 808, Clear 842, Convergys 933, Cooper 936, Crescent 983, Dayton 1047, Delmarva 1069, Dollar 1144, Dow 1162, Essa 1297, Fabick 1321, First 1401, Fremont 1497, Golden 1602, Graybar 1640, Gregory 1661, Hackstock 1697, Harriss 1740, Hartzell 1745, Hawkins 1757, Haynie 1760, Highwoods 1800, HNI 1817, IMA 1917, Independent 1927, Indiana 1929, International 1958, International 1959, International 1971, Island 1996, Jasper 2025, Kuhns 2197, Lauder 2230, Marsh 2387, McKinstry 2435, MidAmerican 2504, Midmark 2507, Milwaukee 2528, Mortgage 2578, National 2631, News 2701, North 2730, Ohio 2790, Omaha 2806, Oshkosh 2833, Parker 2886, Perrigo 2943, Physicians 2970, Printpack 3049, ProLogis 3060, Rasmussen 3128, RECO 3148, Regions 3171, RubinBrown 3280, Ryder 3292, S & T 3297, Scoular 3373, Sit 3466, Snyder's-Lance 3492, Southern 3517, Sprint 3556, Star 3584, Stupp 3628, Tennessee 3716, Trim 3810, United 3864, United 3868, Valero 3915, Weaver 4015, Western 4040, Wolf 4103, Xcel 4135, Young 4146

Boys
Abbott 13, Autodesk 289, Beneficial 412, Chrysler 801, Clorox 852, Hyundai 1902, Metropolitan 2481, Miami 2491, Piedmont 2971, Simpson 3461, WD-40 4011

Boys & girls clubs
Acacia 21, ACF 26, Advanced 40, Alaska 75, Alice 89, American 141, Amerisure 177, Amway 189, Angels 200, Applied 219, Armstrong 246, Avidia 298, AZPB 310, Baird 317, Baker 324, Bank 343, Barron's 364, BB&T 385, Belk 403, Bemis 408, Berkley 426, Berry 435, Best 442, Boston 540, Boyd 546, Briggs 565, Bristol 577, Brooklyn 584, Brooks 585, Burlington 618, Cadillac 648, Callaway 660, Capital 676, Capitol 680, Carpenter 700, Centene 735, Center 737, CFS 756, Chicago 786, Chicopee 792, Cleveland 847, Collette 872, Comcast 887, Consumers 921, Cooper 935, Cousins 953, craigslist 968, CUNA 1008, Dallas 1022, Dana 1026, Darden 1032, DeBruce 1057, Delaware 1066, Deluxe 1084, Demoulas 1085, Detroit 1095, Dilbeck 1116, DJO 1134, Dolphins 1147, Donnelley 1155, Eastern 1209, Easthampton 1212, Emerson 1257, Emmis 1260, Energizer 1271, Ensign 1276, Esurance 1298, First 1393, First 1399, First 1416, First 1419, Framingham 1481, Franklin 1484, Furniture 1519, Gap 1533, GenOn 1563, Gilbane 1581, Government 1621, Hawaiian 1756, Hawkins 1757, Heffernan 1769, Herrick 1788, Hoffer 1821, Hoops 1857, Houston 1871, Hufcor 1883, Huntington 1894, IDACORP 1907, IHC 1913, Illinois 1916, Independence 1925, Institution 1946, Intermountain 1957, International 1959, ISGN 1995, Jacobs 2016, Kansas 2093, Katten 2101, KeyBank 2136, Kimberly 2150, Lee 2240, Liberty 2264, Liberty 2265, Loomis 2301, Major 2345, Manitowoc 2356, Marcus 2371, Mascoma 2394, McDonald 2426, McKinstry 2435, Meritor 2473, Messer 2477, Mutual 2606, N.E.W. 2611, National 2636, Nationwide 2639, Nestle 2662, Nestle 2663, New England 2672, New Hampshire 2674, New York 2688, Nintendo 2712, North 2731, Northwestern 2749, Novetta 2755, Ole 2800, OMNOVA 2809, Opus 2820, Oshkosh 2833, Pacific 2853, Papa 2876, Parker 2884, PDB 2906, PEMCO 2919, Penney 2925, Perforce 2937, Pittsburgh 2986, PNC 2997, Progressive 3059, ProLogis 3060, Rahr 3118, Raytheon 3135, RBS 3138, Regal 3166, Regence 3168, Regence 3169, Regions 3171, Rockwell 3246, Ross 3267, S.J. 3299, San Diego 3323, San Jose 3327, Savings 3343, Schneider 3355, Schwab 3363, Sealy 3382, Sentry 3409, Shugart 3442, Simplot 3459, Skinner 3475, Smith 3485, Smucker 3488, Springleaf 3554, Sprint 3556, Spurs 3557, Staples 3581, Sunbeam 3647, Syniverse 3672, Taco 3679, Tampa 3686, Teichert 3704, Teleflex 3707, Temple 3711, Tennessee 3716, Tesoro 3723, TFS 3732, Tupperware 3821, Union 3855, Union 3857, United 3864, United 3872, Unum 3898, Valero 3915, Vandor 3921, Vijuk 3953, Vision 3961, Visteon 3964, Wake 3978, Wal-Mart 3980, Walter 3984, Washington 3998, Wausau 4008, WellPoint 4027, Wendy's 4032, Western 4043, Whirlpool 4056, Wisconsin 4093, Woodforest 4110

Boys clubs
California 655, Circle 817, Citizens 824, Dr 1169, Home 1844, Miller 2523, National 2623, Oracle 2821, Renovated 3185, Trail 3793, Zappos.com 4153

Brain disorders
Acuity 31, Bed 399, Wilkes 4074

Brain research
Palm 2867, Transco 3797

Breast cancer
Allergan 99, Alliant 104, American 142, AmeriPride 173, AMN Healthcare 184, Angels 200, Athletics 276, Avon 305, BDP 388, Belk 403, Beverage 452, Big 461, Blue 497, Boston 540, Bradley 551, Broadcom 579, Caterpillar 722, CIGNA 812, Coach 858, Cumberland 1003, Dallas 1022, Dell 1068, Delta 1073, Dietz 1114, DS 1182, Duane 1186, Edelman 1224, Edible 1226, Ethicon 1299, Faribault 1332, Foot 1459, Fort 1472, Giant 1571, Government 1621, Hackstock 1697, Hannaford 1723, Hubbell 1879, International 1962, Jones 2059, Kansas 2093, Kohl's 2181, Kroger 2195, Lauder 2230, LifePoint 2270, Maritz 2376, Massachusetts 2397, Mikimoto 2510, NII 2709, Ohio 2791, Omron 2810, Osram 2834, Palace 2866, Pathmark 2894, PDB 2906, Perforce 2937, Philadelphia 2958, Pittsburgh 2986, PVH 3088, Quest 3103, Ralph 3123, RGI 3202, Rothstein 3271, Safeguard 3307, San Diego 3322, ServiceMaster 3414, Shelter 3431, Snyder's-Lance 3492, Springs 3555, Spurs 3557, St. Louis 3569, Tampa 3686, TeleTech 3708, Tyler 3831, V.F. 3913, Warnaco 3988, Washington 3998, Washington 4000, Yahoo! 4140, Zale 4151

Breast cancer research
Amerisure 177, Aveda 295, Avon 305, Belk 403, Biomet 466, Bon 521, Bradley 551, Detroit 1095, Edible 1226, Ford 1464, Hard 1727, Holland 1835, Jones 2057, Kroger 2195, Longaberger 2299, Pier 2973, RGI 3202, Thorntons 3743, U.S. 3837, Valley 3916

Buddhism
Panda 2871, Upper 3900

Business school/education
3M 3, Alice 89, Amboy 124, American 131, Bangor 338, Bechtel 395, Burnett 619, Chaney 761, Chrysler 801, Cic 811, Comerica 889, Cone 907, Consumers 921, Cook 934, DeBruce 1057, Deloitte 1070, Deluxe 1084, DENSO 1088, Diageo 1107, Dominion 1150, DTE 1183, El Paso 1239, Employers 1263, Ernst 1293, Fifth 1377, First 1395, Fluor 1448, General 1552, Halstead 1708, Illinois 1916, Imation 1919, Intel 1950, International 1961, International 1964, Johnson 2053, KPMG 2190, Krasdale 2192, Kuskokwim 2200, Lincoln 2281, Marcus 2370, Marcus 2371, Material 2401, MDU 2441, Moody's 2563, Moss 2581, National 2638, Ogilvy 2788, Pattillo 2896, Peoples 2929, Pratt 3028, PricewaterhouseCoopers 3042, Principal 3047, Schneider 3355, Sealaska 3380, Shelter 3431, Sprint 3556, Steel 3595, SunTrust 3654, TECO 3701, Tektronix 3706, TFS 3732, Towerbrook 3781, Union 3854, Unisys 3859, United 3869, United 3872, United 3877, Univar 3886, Western 4040, Whirlpool 4056, Wisconsin 4096, Xcel 4135

Business/industry
AEGON 45, AGL 57, Allete 100, Alro 113, Amerisure 177, AMETEK 181, Andersen 194, Ascena 255, Astoria 270, Autonomie 293, Avery 297, Avis 299, Badger 314, Bangor 338, Bank 346, Berry 435, Boeing 516, BOSE 530, Boston 533, Bridgestone 560, Brilliant 568, Burlington 618, California 653, CEMEX 734, Central 743, Chrysler 801, Cianbro 808, Citigroup 821, Coach 858, Collective 871, Comerica 889, Compass 901, Cranston 972, Cummins 1007, Deutsche 1099, DHL 1106, Diebold 1112, Dispatch 1129, Dominion 1150, DTE 1183, Duke 1189, eBay 1217, Employers 1264, Entergy 1278, EQT 1287, Ernst 1293, Exxon 1315, Farmers 1335, First 1408, Fisher 1433, Flextronics 1437, Franklin 1485, Freeport 1494, Gear 1544, General 1555, Golub 1607, Graco 1624, Greater 1649, Green 1653, Guardian 1683, Guess 1685, Harsco 1741, Hewlett 1794, Highwoods 1800, Holder 1829, Huntsman 1895, Idealist 1909, International 1968, Intuit 1982, K-Swiss 2082, Kenneth 2128, Kimmel 2152, KPMG 2190, Kuskokwim 2200, L&L 2202, Laureate 2231, Lee 2241, Lincoln 2279, Lincoln 2281, Loews 2296, Meritor 2473, Modine 2544, MoneyGram 2558, Morgan 2570, Motorists 2584, MTD 2595, National 2638, Naugatuck 2645, Norfolk 2725, NYSE 2769, PEMCO 2919, Penney 2925, People's 2928, Physicians 2970, PNC 2997, Popular 3003, Potomac 3018, PVH 3088, Quanex 3100, Record 3149, RG 3201, Rich 3204, RubinBrown 3280, SAP 3334, Securian 3389, Selective 3399, Sempra 3405, Shanken 3421, Shugart 3442, SIFCO 3452, Simplot 3459, Southern 3521, Stanek 3578, State 3590, Strauss 3624, Stride 3625, Stupp 3628, Swinerton 3668, Tension 3717, Texas 3728, Toro 3775, Tyco 3829, U.S. 3836, United 3873, Untours 3897, Vulcan 3972, Washington 4001, Weil 4022, Western 4040, Western 4045, Weyco 4051, Weyerhaeuser 4052, Wiley 4072, Williams 4078, Wisconsin 4093, Wisconsin 4094, WSFS 4127, Xcel 4135

Camp Fire
Burlington 618, Fort 1472, PEMCO 2919, Sprint 3556

Camps
Alabama 71, Arch 230, Armstrong 245, Baum 375, Berry 437, Birmingham 471, Butt 628, Campbell 669, Control 929, CVS 1014, DCI 1049, Delaware 1066, East 1207, Endres 1269, Finish 1383, First 1398, Green 1653, Guess 1685, Harnish 1734, Hasbro 1747, Hillside 1810, Hunt 1888, Kellwood 2121, Levi 2254, Liberty 2265, LifeScan 2271, Long 2298, New York 2688, Palm 2867, Peerless 2915, Ratner 3130, RBS 3138, Sacramento 3303, Sealy 3382, Selig 3401, South Bend 3507, Tennessee 3716, Timberland 3754, V.F. 3913

Cancer
Abt 20, Acme 29, Acuity 31, Acuity 32, Aflac 54, AK 67, Alfa 87, Allegis 92, Alliant 104, American 152, American 155, AMETEK 181, AnchorBank 193, Angels 200, Apogee 215, Arbella 226, Ash 256, Associated 261, Associated 262, AstraZeneca 272, Athletics 276, Avis 299, Avon 305, BancTrust 337, Barnes 362, BASF 368, Bayer 381, Beaver 394, Berry 437, Birmingham 471, Blair 478, Block 482, Bloomingdale's 488, Blue 497, Blue 505, Bob's 511, Bon 521, Boston 533, Boston 540, Bragg 554, Bristol 578, Brown 591, Byers 630, Caddell 645, California 655, California 656, Celebrity 731, Center 737, CenterPoint 738, Chaney 761, Chicago 782, Chicago 790, Cianbro 808, CNO 857, COLHOC 870, Colonial 875, Corvallis 947, Cousins 953, Creative 976, Cummins 1006, Dallas 1023, Dana 1026, Danaher 1027, Danforth 1028, Davis 1037, Dean 1053, Dell 1068, Delta 1073, Delta 1078, Demoulas 1085, Diageo 1107, Dietz 1114, Discover 1125, Duchossois 1187, Dunkin' 1191, Eaton 1216, Edgar 1225, Eliason 1248, Ergon 1289, Ethicon 1299, Farmers 1338, Fellowes 1357, Fidelity 1371, First 1406, FirstEnergy 1424, Foot 1459, Foreman 1465, Fulton 1518, Gear 1544, Genentech 1549, Georgia 1567, Gibbs 1576, GKN 1585, Gould 1618, Government 1621, Green 1653, Gulf 1689, Hackstock 1697, Hartzell 1745, Heidtman 1770, Hendrick 1777, Highmark 1799, Homasote 1841, Hooters 1858, Horizon 1863, Houston 1871, Huntsman 1895, Hyundai 1902, IDT 1910, IMS 1924, Independence 1925, International 1959, International 1962, International 1967, International Profit 1969, Jacobs 2016, Jasper 2025, Jeg's 2031, Johnson 2052, Journal 2068, Kahn 2085, Katten 2101, Kellwood 2121, Kindred 2154, Kinney 2162, Klein 2166, Kohler 2182, Koller 2183, Kuhns 2197, L'Oreal 2203, Lefton 2244, Lennar 2250, Lilly 2274, Lincoln 2280, Lockheed 2292, M.D.C. 2324, Major 2347, Malco 2350, Manhattan 2354, Manitowoc 2356, Manocherian 2357, Marcus 2371, Mariani 2374, McKesson 2434, MedImmune 2450, Medtronic 2453, MEMC 2459, MidAmerican 2504, Midwestone 2508, Minto 2533, Mississippi 2536, Motorists 2584, N.E.W. 2611, National 2623, National 2629, National 2631, New 2675, New York 2686, North 2731, Northwestern 2749, Ogilvy 2788, Olivetti 2802, Panda 2871, Panduit 2872, Parametric 2878, Park 2880, Penney 2925, Perrigo 2943, Pfizer 2950, Philadelphia 2959, Pittsburgh 2986, Portcullis 3004, Presley 3038, Pukall 3082, PVH 3088, Quest 3103, Ralph 3123, RECO 3148, Redco 3155, Regal 3166, Regions 3171, RESCO 3189, Rich 3204, Richard 3205, Riggs 3213, Rudolph 3283, S.B.E. 3298, San Diego 3323, Save 3342, Schiff 3350, Security 3391, Select 3398, Shaw's 3427, Sierra 3449, Sit 3466, Spang 3530, Spartan 3535, Sports 3548, St. Louis 3567, St. Louis 3569, Star 3583, Stardust 3586, Stewart 3604, Stiles 3607, Stop 3618, SunTrust 3654, Thomasville 3737, TJX 3765, Tomkins 3771, Transco 3797, Trim 3810, Truland 3817, UBS 3842, Universal 3890, Universal 3891, Universal 3895, Vista 3962, Wadsworth 3974, Walgreen 3981, Washington 3998, Western 4040, Whiting 4063, Winn 4087, Wolverine 4106, Zappos.com 4153, Zions 4158

Cancer research
ACI 27, Aflac 54, AK 67, Angels 200, Apogee 215, Arbella 226, Avis 300, Avon 305, Blair 478, Blue 497, Bon 521, Bristol 578, Build 608, Cablevision 641, Chemical 774, Chicago 790, Compuware 902, Delta 1078, Duchossois 1187, Fellowes 1357, Ferrellgas 1365, Fidelity 1371, Foreman 1465, General 1555, Giant 1571, Giant 1572, Hard 1727, Haskell 1748, Hoffman 1822, Hooters 1858, IMS 1924, Ingersoll 1939, International 1962, Jefferies 2030, Jeg's 2031, Kohler 2182, Koller 2183, L'Oreal 2203, Limited 2277, Major 2345, Manitowoc 2355, Mary 2392, Milliken 2525, Mutual 2606, Olivetti 2802, OneBeacon 2813, Philadelphia 2960, Quest 3103, Rich 3204, Rood 3257, Safeway 3310, Smithfield 3487, Spang 3530, Stop 3618, Tap 3689, Turner 3824, Walgreen 3981, Wawa 4009

Catholic agencies & churches
Allegis 92, Allen 97, Arbeit 225, Associated 264, Beverage 452, Blair 478, Boh 517, CentiMark 740, Crayola 973, Creamer 974, Creative 976, Crescent 982, Davison 1042, Dondlinger 1154, Dot 1158, Exchange 1307, Fabiano 1320, Fabick 1321, Fidelity 1372, First 1393, First 1422, Gosiger 1617, Greater 1649, Haynie 1760, Henkels 1779, Hudson 1881, Jasper 2026, Koller 2183, Lapham 2223, Leet 2243, McCarthy 2421, McLaughlin 2436, Mercury 2468, Neace 2651, Orscheln 2827, Panduit 2872, Power 3020, R & R 3114, Royal 3275, S.B.E. 3298, Self 3400, Shaughnessy 3425, Shea 3428, Sierra 3449, Southwest 3523, Stanek 3578, Star 3584, Superior 3658, Texas 3725, Tripifoods 3811, Turner 3825, Warrell 3991, Warren 3993

Cemeteries/burial services, cemetery company
Tillman 3752

Cerebral palsy
Circle 817, COPIC 937, Dr 1169, Rose 3261

Charter schools
Albemarle 78, Arrowpoint 251, Crowell 986, CUNA 1008, DRW 1181, Ford 1464, Lincoln 2279, Lubrizol 2315, Maverick 2409, People's 2928, Public 3076, Reily 3177, TALX 3683, Urban 3901

Chemistry
Agilent 56, Arch 230, BASF 368, BDP 388, Bristol 578, Cabot 642, Dow 1161, L'Oreal 2203, Lubrizol 2315, Micron 2500, PPG 3025, Quaker 3093, Rayonier 3134, Siemens 3448, Univar 3886, Wiley 4072

Child abuse
Ameritas 178, Baxter 377, Bay 378, Burlington 618, C & S 634, Carlson 693, CC 728, Cow 957, DCI 1049, Emerson 1257, Fieldstone 1374, First 1413, Freeport 1494, Fremont 1496, Fremont 1497, Greater 1649, Haynes 1759, Ideal 1908, Journal 2068, Limited 2277, M.D.C. 2324, Major 2346, Maverick 2409, Miller 2523, National 2634, NRT 2757, Presley 3038, R & B 3113, Regal 3166, Retail 3194, Reynolds 3199, Seneca 3406, Shelter 3431, Stiles 3607, Thomasville 3737, Trim 3810, United 3867, V.F. 3913, Woerner 4101, Wrigley 4125

Child development, education
Abby's 14, Blue 496, Blue 505, Brady 552, Chick 791, Cole 868, Dannon 1030, Dollar 1145, Dolphins 1147, Earnhardt 1205, Entergy 1280, Fieldstone 1374, Hallmark 1707, Hewlett 1794, Kohler 2182, Lego 2247, New York 2688, Newell 2694, PNC 2997, Principal 3047, Reynolds 3200, SAP 3334, Scholastic 3358, Sovereign 3528

Child development, services
Blue 501, Bristlecone 575, Chick 791, Cole 868, Crane 970, Empire 1262, Kohler 2182, McDonald's 2427, Mead 2443, MGM 2489, Otis 2835, Procter 3055

Children
Abbott 13, adidas 35, Aetna 48, Allergan 99, Alliance 101, American 147, AMR 187, Amway 189, Antioch 207, Arbeit 225, Archer 233, Athletics 276, Atlanta 279, Autodesk 289, AutoNation 292, AZPB 310, B & B 312, BayView 384, Beneficial 412, Berkshire 428, Better 449, Blue 489, Blue 490, Blue 493, Blue 494, Blue 496, Blue 498, Blue 501, Blue 504, Blue 505, BlueCross 507, Bob's 511, Boler 520, BorgWarner 528, Boston 533, Boston 537, Boston 538, Bridgestone 560, Brilliant 568, Bristol 578, Build 608, Cable 639, California 654, California 656, Cardinal 685, Cargill 691, CDW 729, CenturyLink 751, Chick 791, Chrysler 801, Clorox 852, CME 853, CNA 855, Colgate 869, Collective 871, Collette 872, Columbia 884, ConAgra 904, Costco 948, Cow 957, CVS 1014, Dannon 1030, Dean 1054, Deerfield 1062, Delta 1074, Delta 1083, Disney 1128, Diversey 1130, DP 1168, Driscoll 1176, DRS 1179, Dunkin' 1191, EMCOR 1255, Empire 1262, Energy 1272, Entergy 1279, Express 1313, FedEx 1352, First 1419, Flowserve 1447, Food 1457, Giant 1571, Giant 1572, Gibraltar 1577, Gibson 1578, GlaxoSmithKline 1588, Goodyear 1612, Great 1642, Great 1644, Great 1645, Guard 1680, Hasbro 1747, Highmark 1799, Home 1845, Horizon 1863, Iberdrola 1904, International 1966, International 1968, Intero 1973, Jack 2007, Jackson 2009, Just 2077, Kaiser 2086, KB 2105, Kimball 2149, Kohl's 2181, Kroenke 2194, LAC 2206, Lazy 2234, Lego 2247, Let 2253, Life 2269, Lincoln 2281, Little 2288, Los Angeles 2306, Los Angeles 2308, Lucasfilm 2316, Macfarlane-Chang 2331, Madison 2336, Major 2347, Marriott 2383, Mattel 2405, MAXIMUS 2410, MBIA 2416, McDonald's 2427, McKesson 2434, Mead 2443, MedImmune 2450, Melissa 2458, Meredith 2471, Metropolitan 2481, Miami 2491, Mitsubishi 2538, Mondelez 2556, Monsanto 2559, Morgan 2570, National 2623, Nestle 2663, New 2668, New 2671, New York 2688, Newman's 2697, Nintendo 2712, Northern 2740, O'Neal 2771, Orlando 2824, Panda 2871, Pattillo 2896, Patton's 2899, Penney 2925, Piedmont 2971, Pitney 2984, Plum 2992, PNC 2997, PVH 3088, Quaker 3094, Quiksilver 3108, RBC 3136, Reckitt 3146, Regal 3166, Regence 3168, Royal 3273, Russell 3289, Saucony 3340, Simpson 3461, Singlebrook 3464, Spark 3533, St. Joe 3563, Stop 3618, Stride 3625, Sundt 3648, Sunshine 3653, Sunwest 3655, Super 3656, Teichert 3704, Thorntons 3743, Tim 3753, TJX 3765, Toys 3790, U.S. 3835, Universal 3889, Universal 3893, Verizon 3936, Walter 3984, Washington 3994, Wawa 4009, WD-40 4011, Wellmark 4026, Western 4045, Weyerhaeuser 4052, White 4062, Wrigley 4125, Wyndham 4132

Children's rights
AOL 209, Brilliant 568, Faegre 1324, Greenlight 1658, Hilton 1812, Spark 3533

Children, services
ABARTA 10, Adir 36, Advance 39, Aetna 48, Alfa 87, Alice 89, Allegis 92, Allen 94, Alliance 101, Almar 110, Alpha 112, AMC 125, American 142, American 169, AMERIGROUP 171, AmeriPride 173, Ameritas 178, Amway 189, Anaheim 191, Andersson 196, Angels 200, ANH 201, Antioch 207, AOL 209, Arbella 226, Atlanta 278, AutoZone 294, Avis 300, Avnet 304, B & B 312, Baker 323, Barron's 364, Barton 366, Bassett 372, BB&T 385, BDP 388, Beaver 394, Bergquist 420, Berry 435, Big 460, BJ's 473, Blockbuster 483, Booz 525, BorgWarner 528, Boston 536, Boston 537, Boston 540, Bridgestone 560, Brocchini 580, Brooks 585, Build 608, Burger 613, Burr 621, C & S 634, Calvert 663, Campbell 669, Capital 677, Carnival 696,

Catalina 719, Centene 735, Century 750, Charter 765, Chehalis 771, Chevron 780, Chick 791, Cisco 818, Citizens 824, Clear 842, Coach 858, Cole 868, Colorado 877, Con 903, Conditioned 906, Covidien 956, Cow 957, Crayola 973, Creative 976, CryoLife 990, Crystal 992, Dallas 1023, Davis 1037, Davis 1041, Dell 1068, Demoulas 1085, Denny's 1087, Deutsch 1098, Diagnos-Techs 1108, DineEquity 1120, DJO 1134, Dollar 1145, DreamWorks 1172, Dunkin' 1191, Eastern 1209, Elias 1247, Entergy 1279, Excell 1304, Express 1313, Fabiano 1320, Federated 1351, Fidelity 1371, First 1398, First 1413, First 1416, Flint 1439, Florence 1441, Florida 1442, Food 1457, Food 1458, Football 1460, Fort 1472, Franklin 1488, Giant 1571, Gibbons 1574, Golden 1602, Government 1621, Green 1650, Hannaford 1723, Hard 1727, Harnish 1734, Haskell 1748, Heinz 1772, Hendrick 1776, Henkels 1779, Highmark 1799, Holland 1834, Home 1844, Hood 1854, Hoops 1857, Horizon 1863, Houston 1871, Hubbell 1879, Humana 1886, Hy-Vee 1900, Indianapolis 1932, International 1962, Jackson 2009, Jackson 2011, James 2021, JM 2044, Johnson 2048, Jones 2059, Kaiser 2086, Kajima 2087, Kelly 2122, King 2159, Lamont 2215, Landry's 2219, Lauth 2232, Lee 2240, Liberty 2265, Limited 2277, Lincoln 2280, Lithia 2287, Loomis 2301, Lord 2303, Lucasfilm 2316, M.D.C. 2324, Magnolia 2340, Major 2346, Marathon 2365, Mattel 2405, Mayer 2412, McClatchy 2422, McCormick 2423, McWane 2440, Mead 2443, Mercedes 2463, Merck 2466, Metropolitan 2483, MidAmerican 2504, Midcontinent 2505, Mine 2529, Minnesota 2530, Minto 2533, MSC 2593, MTD 2595, Mutual 2607, Natural 2641, Neace 2651, Nestle 2663, NII 2709, Nu 2759, Office 2785, Ole 2800, Omaha 2806, Orlando 2824, Otter 2836, Our 2838, Owens 2841, Pacific 2855, PacifiCorp 2860, Panda 2871, Park 2880, Pathmark 2894, PEMCO 2919, Penney 2925, People's 2928, Peoples 2931, PepsiCo 2935, Pfizer 2950, PG&E 2952, Philadelphia 2960, Philadelphia 2961, Phoenix 2968, Pier 2973, Pinnacle 2977, Piper 2983, Presley 3038, Printpack 3049, QUALCOMM 3095, Quality 3096, QuikTrip 3109, Rackspace 3117, RBC 3136, RBS 3138, Regions 3171, RESCO 3189, Riggs 3213, Robins 3232, Rockville 3245, Rothstein 3271, Safeguard 3307, San Antonio 3321, Save 3342, ScanSource 3347, Scientific 3367, Sealy 3382, Security 3392, Select 3398, Sentry 3409, Sherwin 3437, ShopKo 3440, Shugart 3442, Sierra 3449, Snell 3490, Spark 3533, Spartan 3535, Stafast 3571, StanCorp 3574, Starbucks 3585, Stop 3618, SunTrust 3654, Swift 3666, Tap 3689, Target 3691, Terre 3722, Texas 3725, Texas 3729, Titan 3763, TJX 3765, Toys 3790, Trim 3810, True 3814, Tupperware 3821, Unaka 3848, Union 3857, United 3869, United 3880, Universal 3890, Unum 3898, Valassis 3914, ViewSonic 3952, Vision 3961, Vista 3963, Visteon 3964, Wachtell 3973, Wagner 3976, Wal-Mart 3980, Walter 3984, Watson 4007, Wells 4028, Wendy's 4031, Wendy's/Arby's 4030, Wisconsin 4093, Wood 4108, World 4121, Wrigley 4125, Wynnne 4133, Young 4146, Zappos.com 4153

Children/youth

3M 3, Abbott 13, Activision 30, Allstate 107, Andersen 194, Andretti 197, Assurant 268, Autodesk 289, Bank 342, Bay 378, Beneficial 412, Bloomingdale's 488, Bobcats 512, Burlington 618, Butt 628, California 654, Carlson 693, CarMax 694, Caterpillar 722, Chick 791, Chrysler 801, CHS 802, Cisco 818, Clorox 852, D.C. 1018, Dole 1141, Energy 1272, Equifax 1288, First 1419, GenCorp 1548, General 1554, GlaxoSmithKline 1588, Goodyear 1612, Graco 1624, Great 1645, Herr 1787, ICON 1906, IMC 1920, Imperial 1922, ING 1938, International 1959, Intoximeters 1979, Jazz 2028, Kellogg 2120, Korum 2187, Lexmark 2258, Louisiana 2309, Macfarlane-Chang 2331, Manitowoc 2355, McDonald's 2427, Miami 2491, MTV 2596, Nestle 2663, New York 2688, OceanFirst 2782, Ohio 2789, Panasonic 2869, Panda 2871, People's 2928, Piedmont 2971, Ross 3265, SAP 3334, Schwab 3363, Sherwin 3437, Siemens 3448, Southern 3514, St. Joe 3563, Starbucks 3585, Subaru 3631, True 3815, U.S. 3835, Union 3857, UnitedHealth 3884, Washington 3994, Washington 3998, WD-40 4011, Xerox 4136

Children/youth, services

ACI 27, Adobe 38, AEG 43, AEGON 45, Aflac 54, Ahern 60, AK 67, Albemarle 78, Alcoa 82, Alexander 85, Allegheny 91, Alro 113, Altec 118, Amboy 124, American 132, American 137, American 143, American 145, American 155, American 165, AMERIGROUP 171, Ameristar 176, Amerisure 177, Ameritec 179, Apex 213, Arbella 226, Arizona 239, Arkansas 240, Armstrong 246, Ascena 255, Assurant 266, Astoria 270, Avidia 298, AZPB 310, Baird 317, Baker 321, Baker 324, Bank 342, Bay 378, Bay 380, Bayer 381, BB&T 385, Belk 403, Belleville 405, Bemis 408, Ben 409, Berkley 426, Berry 434, Betts 451, Bickel 457, Bierlein 459, Biomet 466, Birmingham 471, Black 475, Blair 478, Blue 492, Blue 497, Blue 498, Bob's 511, Boh 517, Bon 521, Boston 540, Bridgeway 563, Bright 566, Bristol 578, Broadcom 579, Brooklyn 584, Buccaneer 599, Building 610, Burns 620, Butzel 629, Cacique 644, Cadence 646, California 655, Calpine 661, Campbell 669, Caparo 673, Cape 674, Capital 676, Carlson 693, Carter's 708, Cary 712, CentiMark 740, Central 742, Cerner 754, CH2M 758, Chaney 761, Chapman 763, Chelsea 772, Chicago 790, Chick 791, Chief 793, Chotin 799, Cic 811, CIGNA 812, CLARCOR 832, Cliffs 850, CME 853, CMS 854, Coca 861, Colgate 869, Collective 871, Collette 872, Colorado 879, Comcast 887, Community 900, Compass 901, Compuware 902, ConAgra 904, Contran 928, Convergys 933, Copley 938, Cox 959, Cracker 966, craigslist 968, Crane 970, CSS 996, CSX 997, Cummins 1006, CVS 1014, Dallas 1022, Dana 1026, Darden 1032, Dart 1034, Deacon 1050, Dean 1054, Deerfield 1062, Delta 1073, Delta 1077, Denver 1090, Detroit 1095, Deutsch 1098, Deutsche 1099, Devereaux 1100, Diageo 1107, Diamonds 1109, Diebold 1112, Dietz 1114, Dilbeck 1116, Dime 1118, Discover 1125, Disney 1127, Dispatch 1129, Donnelley 1155, Dot 1158, du Pont 1184, Duane 1186, Eastman 1214, Eaton 1216, Econscious 1223, Edison 1229, El Paso 1239, Eliason 1248, Employers 1264, Endeavor 1267, Endres 1269, Energizer 1271, Energy 1272, Ergon 1289, ESCO 1296, Essa 1297, Exelon 1309, Express 1313, Fabick 1321, Federal 1348, Fidelity 1372, Fieldstone 1374, First 1395, First 1397, First 1399, First 1400, First 1401, First 1403, First 1405, First 1408, First 1419, Fiserv 1427, Flexcon 1436, Florsheim 1445, Ford 1463, Forest 1467, Framingham 1481, Frankel 1483, Freeport 1494, Fremont 1496, Frito 1506, Fuller 1517, G&K 1524, GameStop 1530, GATX 1542, General 1555, Genesco 1559, GenOn 1563, GenRad 1564, Giant 1571, GKN 1585, GlaxoSmithKline 1588, Go 1595, Graybar 1640, Graycor 1641, Green 1657, Gregory 1662, Griffith 1667, Guess 1685, GuideOne 1687, Gulf 1689, Haggen 1699, Halliburton 1706, Hallmark 1707, Hampden 1712, Hannaford 1723, Harris 1736, Hasbro 1747, Haviland 1752, Hawkins 1757, Heffernan 1769, Heinz 1772, Hemmerdinger 1775, Hensyn 1782, Herrick 1788, Hershey 1791, Hewlett 1794, Highwoods 1800, Hofmann 1824, Holder 1829, Hooters 1858, Horizon 1864, Hubbard 1877, Hudson 1880, Huhtamaki 1884, Huntington 1894, Ideal 1908, IDT 1910, IMA 1917, Indus 1934, ING 1937, ING 1938, Institution 1946, Interlock 1954, International 1958, International 1964, Interstate 1975, INTRUST 1981, Intuit 1982, ISGN 1995, Island 1996, Jackson 2008, Janus 2024, Jasper 2026, JM 2044, Jones 2055, Jordan 2063, Journal 2068, JPMorgan Chase 2071, Kaman 2088, Kann 2090, Katten 2101, Kellogg 2120, Kellwood 2121, Kemp 2123, Kennecott 2127, Kepco 2132, Kids 2141, Kimball 2149, Kimberly 2150, Kindred 2154, Kingsbury 2160, Kinney 2162, Klein 2166, Klein's 2169, Kmart 2172, Kohl's 2181, Kohler 2182, Laclede 2207, Lapham 2223, Lauder 2230, Laureate 2231, Lennar 2250, Levi 2254, Liberty 2262, Liberty 2264, Limited 2277, Lockheed 2292, Loews 2296, Long 2298, Longaberger 2299, Los Angeles 2307, M&T 2323, M/I 2325, Mamiye 2352, Manitowoc 2356, Mapes 2360, Marcus 2370, Marcus 2371, Maritz 2376, MarkleBank 2379, Mars 2384, Marsh 2387, Mary 2392, Maverick 2409, McDonald 2426, McDonald's 2427, McKinstry 2435, Melaleuca 2457, MEMC 2459, Menasha 2461, Meredith 2471, Merfish 2472, Merrimack 2474, Metropolitan 2481, MH 2490, Milliken 2525, Milwaukee 2528, Miracle 2535, Mississippi 2536, Mitsubishi 2538, Monadnock 2551, Moneta 2557, Moore 2565, Mortenson 2577, Mrs. Fields 2592, Mutual 2605, Mutual 2606, Nasdaq 2618, Nash 2619, National 2631, National 2633, NBC 2649, Neenah 2656, New Jersey 2676, New York 2684, New York 2688, New York 2691, Newman's 2697, Nomura 2720, Nordic 2722, Nordson 2723, North 2728, North 2730, Northfield 2741, Northwest 2747, NRT 2757, Oakley 2774, OceanFirst 2782, Ohio 2790, Ohio 2791, Oklahoma 2795, Old 2798, Olin 2801, Omnicare 2807, Omnicom 2808, OMNOVA 2809, OneBeacon 2813, ONEOK 2815, Orscheln 2827, Owens 2844, Pacers 2852, Pacific 2853, PacifiCorp 2860, Padilla 2864, Papa 2876, Parker 2886, Pawtucket 2902, Paychex 2904, Pebble 2913, Peerless 2915, Penn 2923, Peoples 2929, Philadelphia 2958, Piedmont 2971, Pieper 2972, Plum 2991, Portcullis 3004, Portland 3010, Potomac 3018, Primerica 3045, Prince 3046, Procter 3055, ProLogis 3060, Prophet 3063, Protective 3066, Providence 3068, Provident 3070, Prudential 3072, Pura 3084, Putnam 3085, PVH 3088, Quad 3091, Questar 3104, Ralph 3123, Rayonier 3134, Reed 3161, Regions 3171, Reily 3177, Reitman 3181, Rexnord 3198, Riceland 3203, RJN 3228, Robinson 3235, Rodman 3251, Rose 3261, Rosen's 3264, Royal 3273, RUAN 3279, Ryman 3294, S & T 3297, Sacramento 3304, Safeway 3310, Sakar 3313, salesforce.com 3318, San Jose 3327, sanofi-aventis 3329, Schloss 3352, Schneider 3355, Scholastic 3358, Scott 3369, Scoular 3373, Sealy 3382, Security 3391, Selective 3399, Sempra 3405, Seneca 3406, Sensient 3408, Shaughnessy 3425, Shea 3428, Shelter 3431, Simplot 3459, Sit 3466, Smucker 3488, Southern 3521, Southwest 3524, Sovereign 3528, Sports 3548, Sports 3549, Sprague 3551, Springleaf 3554, Spurs 3557, St. Louis 3567, St. Louis 3568, StanCorp 3574, Standard 3576, Star 3584, Starbucks 3585, Stardust 3586, State 3590, Station 3593, Steel 3595, Sterne 3602, Stock 3610, Stupp 3628, Sumitomo 3639, Sun 3643, SUPERVALU 3659, Syniverse 3672, Synovus 3674, Tanner 3688, Teachers 3697, Tees 3703, Teichert 3704, Teleflex 3707, Temple 3711, Tennessee 3716, Tops 3774, Toro 3775, Trail 3793, Transco 3797, Trustmark 3818, Turner 3824, Tyler 3831, UBS 3842, UncommonGoods 3849, Unilever 3853, Union 3858, United 3864, United 3867, United 3870, United 3872, United 3874, United 3881, UnitedHealth 3884, Univar 3886, Universal 3891, Universal 3895, University 3896, USG 3905, Utica 3910, V.F. 3913, Valero 3915, Valmont 3919, Valspar 3920, Vectren 3925, Verizon 3936, Victaulic 3948, Virginia 3959, Vodafone 3965, Wadsworth 3974, Washington 3998, Washington 3999, Watson 4007, Weaver 4015, WEDGE 4020, Wegmans 4021, Weil 4022, Wenger 4033, Westar 4039, Western 4040, Western 4041, Westinghouse 4049, Weyco 4051, Woerner 4101, Wolverine 4106, Woodforest 4110, Woodward 4112, WorkflowOne 4115, World 4120, Wrigley 4125, Xerox 4136, Zurich 4160

Christian agencies & churches

Acme 28, Acuity 31, Alice 89, Allegheny 91, AllStyle 108, Alpenrose 111, Altec 118, American 135, American 152, American 165, AmeriVision 180, AnchorBank 193, Ann's 203, Archer 232, Armstrong 245, Atlantic 283, Baird 316, Batson 373, Bergquist 420, Bernecker's 431, Berry 435, Bierlein 459, Birmingham 471, Bragg 554, Brewer 558, Bridgewater 561, Bridgeway 563, Brillion 569, Brinkster 574, Brotherhood 588, Buist 611, Butt 628, Byers 630, C Spire 636, Calumet 662, Carlson 693, Cary 712, Central 742, Chapman 763, Chick 791, Cic 811, Classic 840, Colt 881, Commercial 892, Communications 896, Conditioned 906, Control 929, Craft 967, Croft 985, Curves 1011, Dallas 1022, DCI

1049, Dean 1053, Diageo 1107, DVK 1198, Eagle 1202, Eliason 1248, EMI 1258, Endres 1269, Ergon 1289, Erickson 1290, Exotic 1310, Fabick 1321, Federated 1351, Fenton 1361, Fieldstone 1374, Flir 1440, Friesen 1505, Furr 1520, Gaunce 1543, Gibbs 1576, Gibraltar 1577, Greenwood 1660, Griffith 1667, Grubb 1675, GuideOne 1687, Hallberg 1704, Harper 1735, Hartzell 1745, Haviland 1752, Heidtman 1770, Hendrick 1777, Henkels 1779, Herschend 1790, Hoffman 1822, Hofmann 1824, Hooters 1858, Houston 1871, Indiana 1931, Inman 1943, Integrity 1948, International 1959, ISGN 1995, J-M 2005, Johnson 2052, Juno 2076, Kahn 2084, Kehe 2114, Knitcraft 2174, L&L 2202, Lapham 2223, Legg 2245, Levi 2254, Li-Cor 2261, Marena 2372, MarkleBank 2379, MBIA 2416, McCarthy 2421, McShane 2439, Mercury 2468, MH 2490, Mid 2503, Miller 2517, Mitchell 2537, Monadnock 2551, Morris 2573, Mortgage 2578, MTD 2595, Murphy 2599, Neenah 2656, New Orleans 2678, Nord 2721, Nortex 2727, North 2728, Nursery 2762, Oakley 2774, Old 2796, Park 2880, Patton's 2899, Peoples 2932, Porter 3005, Power 3020, Premier 3035, Primary 3043, Printpack 3049, Prophet 3063, Pukall 3082, Quad 3091, Quality 3096, Regions 3171, Reiff 3174, Rennoc 3184, Residential 3191, Richard 3205, Riggs 3213, RITE 3221, Rosen's 3264, SanTrust 3332, Scott 3369, Shaughnessy 3425, Shelter 3431, Shugart 3442, Smith 3485, Smucker 3488, Sonlight 3499, South Bend 3507, Southern 3515, Southern 3517, Stafast 3571, Stahl 3573, Stewart 3605, Stiles 3607, Superior 3658, Thomaston 3736, Three 3746, Tillman 3752, Tomkins 3771, Tractor 3791, Truland 3817, Vandor 3921, Vermeer 3937, Vos 3969, Walker 3982, Walter 3984, Ward/Kraft 3987, WEDGE 4020, Whitley 4064, Willow 4082, Woerner 4101, Wolf 4103, Wonder 4107, Zatkoff 4154

Civic centers

ABARTA 10, AMPCO 186, Consumers 921, Dell Corning 1067, Employers 1264, First 1394, Fiserv 1427, Food 1458, General 1555, MidAmerican 2504, Tanner 3688, Westinghouse 4049, Weyco 4051

Civil liberties, advocacy

Federated 1351, PACE 2851, Playboy 2990, Tindall 3761

Civil liberties, first amendment

Chicago 788, Gannett 1532, McClatchy 2422, Playboy 2990, Post 3016, RealNetworks 3144, Scripps 3374, Working 4116, World 4122

Civil liberties, freedom of religion

Hackstock 1697

Civil liberties, right to life

Ariens 238, Federated 1351, Sartori 3335

Civil/human rights

Antioch 207, Baker 321, Ben 409, Bickel 457, Bressler 557, Bridgeway 563, Butler 627, C & C 632, Cable 639, Cacique 644, Citigroup 821, Continental 925, Contran 928, Cummins 1007, Deckers 1059, Denny's 1087, Eastern 1209, Foley 1454, General 1552, General 1555, Gold 1598, Google 1613, Green 1653, Hard 1727, JanPak 2022, Katten 2101, Keefe 2110, Lim 2275, Lord 2302, Major 2347, Mitsubishi 2539, Mitsubishi 2540, NAVTEQ 2648, Newman's 2697, Pearce 2910, Pendleton 2921, Playboy 2990, Questar 3105, RealNetworks 3144, Reid 3173, Rite 3220, Schiff 3350, Security 3394, Select 3398, Shanken 3421, Skadden 3470, Strauss 3624, Times 3759, TJX 3765, United 3872, UTI 3909, Visteon 3964, Weil 4022, Wells 4028, Windway 4086, Working 4116

Civil/human rights, advocacy

CIGNA 812, Skadden 3470, Strauss 3624

Civil/human rights, alliance/advocacy

Bridgestone 560

Civil/human rights, disabled

Marriott 2383, Sun 3643

Civil/human rights, equal rights

Aetna 48, Alabama 71, Alliant 104, Allstate 107, Alyeska 121, American 150, Arch 230, Arnold 248, AT&T 273, Baird 317, Bank 349, Blockbuster 483, Blue 493, Blue 494, Boeing 516, Burlington 618, Campbell 669, Chrysler 801, CIGNA 812, Citigroup 821, Coca 862, Coca 863, Comerica 889, Compuware 902, Cox 959, Crowell 986, Cummins 1007, Delta 1073, Dominion 1150, Donnelley 1155, DTE 1183, Exelon 1309, Federal 1348, Foley 1454, Ford 1464, Fortis 1473, Gannett 1532, Heinz 1772, Hilton 1812, Home 1844, ING 1938, Intel 1950, International 1960, IPALCO 1988, Kellogg 2120, KeyBank 2136, LG&E Energy 2260, Lincoln 2278, MasterCard 2399, Messer 2477, MGM 2489, Miller 2523, Moore 2565, Morgan 2570, New England 2672, Northrop 2744, NV 2765, NYSE 2769, Owens 2842, Peabody 2907, Penn 2923, PepsiCo 2935, Redwoods 3158, Seagate 3377, Seattle 3386, St. Louis 3567, St. Louis 3569, Starbucks 3585, Station 3593, Strauss 3624, Symantec 3669, Texas 3728, Toyota 3784, Toyota 3785, Toyota 3786, Toyota 3789, Unisys 3859, United 3872, Vulcan 3970, Wellmark 4026, Working 4116, Wrigley 4125

Civil/human rights, immigrants

Arbella 226, Ben 409, Berkshire 428, Crowell 986

Civil/human rights, LGBTQ

Avis 300, Esurance 1298, Miller 2523, Sempra 3405, Symantec 3669, Working 4116

Civil/human rights, minorities

Clear 842, Hilfiger 1801, J-M 2005, Marriott 2383, Penney 2925, Symantec 3669, Westinghouse 4049

Civil/human rights, women

Longaberger 2299

Climate change/global warming

3M 3, Alcoa 82, Aspen 260, Boeing 516, Booz 525, BP 547, CH2M 758, Chase 769, Clif 848, Cummins 1007, Deutsche 1099, Duke 1189, General 1552, Google 1613, National 2630, Public 3077, RealNetworks 3144, Stonyfield 3617, Unilever 3853, United 3872, Weyerhaeuser 4052

College

Alliance 101, Alpha 112, Berry 437, Bloomin 487, Boston 540, Cambridge 666, Capital 679, Coca 863, Deere 1061, Great 1645, Intel 1950, Liberty 2265, McCormick 2423, Mt. 2594, Natural 2641, NorthWestern 2748, Seminole 3404, Sonoco 3500, Stewart 3606, TECO 3701, Trico 3807, United 3868, Wal-Mart 3980, Webster's 4019, Wisconsin 4096

College (community/junior)

American 164, Bank 343, BASF 368, Duke 1189, GlaxoSmithKline 1588, Great 1645, Klein's 2169, Liberty 2262, LifePoint 2270, Lime 2276, Metropolitan 2481, Mutual 2603, Pedernales 2914, Piedmont 2971, Pioneer 2981, RUAN 3279

Community development, business promotion

Avis 300, Bank 346, Blackstone 477, Brother 587, Capital 679, Colonial 875, Cousins 953, Dayton 1047, Deere 1061, Diebold 1112, Ensign 1276, Entergy 1278, First 1406, Franklin 1487, Hawkins 1757, International 1971, Johnson 2053, Kindred 2154, Kingsbury 2160, KPMG 2190, MB 2415, Miller 2523, MoneyGram 2558, Ole 2800, Olin 2801, Penney 2925, People's 2928, PG&E 2952, Presley 3038, Progressive 3059, Smucker 3488, SunTrust 3654, Thomasville 3737, Wal-Mart 3980, Whole 4066

Community development, men's clubs

SunTrust 3654

Community development, neighborhood associations

Mutual 2607

Community development, neighborhood development

1st 2, Alabama 71, Allstate 107, Ameristar 176, AT&T 273, Bank 340, Butler 626, Capitol 680, CIGNA 812, Citigroup 821, Compass 901, Consumers 921, CSRwire 995, Deutsche 1099, Dollar 1142, Dominion 1150, DTE 1183, El Paso 1239, Entergy 1279, Fabri 1322, First 1390, First 1409, First 1419, Firstmerit 1425, Florida 1443, Gannett 1532, General 1552, Georgia 1567, Harley 1732, Harleysville 1733, Institution 1946, Jamba 2020, Joy 2070, JPMorgan Chase 2071, MB 2415, Miller 2517, Mizuho 2542, Mutual 2607, National 2635, Nestle 2663, New York 2683, Northwestern 2749, Opus 2820, People's 2928, Perkins 2940, PMI 2995, PNC 2997, Prudential 3072, State 3591, State 3592, Sunkist 3649, TFS 3732, Urban 3901, Wells 4028, Western 4040, Weyerhaeuser 4052

Community development, public/private ventures

Earnhardt 1205, Urban 3901

Community development, real estate

Urban 3901

Community development, service clubs

American 159, Artichoke 254, BASF 368, Firstmerit 1425, Green 1653, Gregory 1662, Hallberg 1704, Independence 1925, Indiana 1929, Kimball 2149, Newport 2699, Oklahoma 2795, Printpack 3049, Suitter 3633, Tyler 3831, U.M. 3834, U.S. 3837

Community development, small businesses

Accenture 22, Agora 58, AT&T 273, Bangor 338, Bank 340, Bank 346, Blackstone 477, Capital 679, Chevron 780, Cisco 818, Citigroup 821, Clif 848, Comerica 889, Deere 1061, Dell 1068, Deluxe 1084, Deutsche 1099, First 1419, Freeport 1494, Georgia 1568, Goldman 1604, Grand 1627, Hewlett 1794, Huntington 1894, Intuit 1982, JPMorgan Chase 2071, KeyBank 2136, MB 2415, Mizuho 2542, Northeast 2737, NYSE 2769, Pattillo 2896, People's 2928, Piper 2983, PNC 2997, Prudential 3072, RBS 3138, Regions 3171, Strauss 3624, Tastefully 3692, TD 3696, Travelers 3802, U.S. 3835, Union 3854, Urban 3901, Wal-Mart 3980, Western 4045, Whole 4066

Community development, women's clubs

Community/economic development

Community/economic development, equal rights

Community/economic development, fund raising/fund distribution

Community/economic development, management/technical assistance

Community/economic development, public education

Community/economic development, public policy

Nu 2759, Pacific 2853, Peoples 2931, PepsiCo 2935, Philadelphia 2961, Piedmont 2971, PNC 2997, PPG 3025, Premix 3037, Procter 3055, Prudential 3072, Public 3076, Public 3077, RBS 3137, Savings 3344, Securian 3389, Sempra 3405, Sovereign 3528, Steel 3595, Steelcase 3597, Sunoco 3650, Textron 3731, TFS 3732, Tindall 3761, Toyota 3787, Tucson 3819, U.S. 3835, UMB 3846, United 3873, Urban 3901, V.F. 3913, Vectren 3925, WD-40 4011, Wells 4028, Western 4045, Whole 4066, Williams 4077, Wisconsin 4093, Xcel 4135

Economically disadvantaged

3M 3, Abacus 9, Abbott 13, AbbyBank 15, ACE 24, Adir 36, Adobe 38, Aeropostale 46, Aetna 48, AFL 53, AGL 57, Agora 58, Air 63, Alabama 71, Alcatel 81, Alcon 83, Alexion 86, Allegis 92, Allen 94, Allstate 107, Alsco 115, Amboy 124, American 137, American 150, American 158, AMERIGROUP 171, Ameritec 179, Amgen 182, AMR 187, Andersen 194, Andersson 196, Anheuser 202, Antioch 207, Aon 210, Apex 213, Apollo 216, Applied 220, Arbeit 225, Arch 230, Arnall 247, AT&T 273, Athletics 276, Autodesk 289, AutoZone 294, Avery 297, Avista 301, Bank 339, Bank 341, Bank 342, Bank 346, Bank 347, Baxter 377, Bayer 382, Ben 409, Beneficial 412, Berkshire 428, Berry 438, Best 442, Bigelow 462, Blue 491, Blue 493, Blue 494, Blue 496, Blue 497, Blue 498, Blue 501, Blue 504, BlueCross 507, Boehringer 515, Boeing 516, Boston 540, BP 547, Bridgeway 563, Bristol 578, Brown 590, Buccaneer 599, Burlington 618, Butler 626, Butler 627, Butzel 629, California 655, Callaway 660, Capital 679, Cargill 691, CarMax 694, Caterpillar 722, CC 728, Cephalon 752, CH2M 758, Charter 767, Chemtura 775, Chicago 783, Chicopee 792, Chotin 799, Chrysler 801, Cincinnati 813, Circle 817, Cisco 818, CITGO 820, Citigroup 821, Clorox 852, CMS 854, CNA 855, Colgate 869, Collette 872, Columbia 882, Columbia 883, Comcast 887, Comerica 889, Communications 896, Compass 901, Continental 926, Corvallis 947, Covidien 956, Crane 970, Credit 980, Croft 985, Cummins 1007, CVS 1014, D.C. 1018, Deere 1061, Deerfield 1062, Delaware 1066, Dell 1068, Delta 1073, Delta 1074, Delta 1075, Delta 1076, Delta 1077, Delta 1078, Delta 1079, Delta 1083, Detroit 1095, Deutsche 1099, Diageo 1107, Dime 1118, Dollar 1143, Dollar 1145, Dominion 1150, Drive 1177, drugstore.com 1180, Duke 1189, Duquesne 1194, Eastman 1214, eBay 1217, Ecolab 1220, Edelman 1224, Edison 1228, EduCare 1231, El Paso 1239, Empire 1262, Energizer 1271, Entergy 1279, Enterprise 1281, EQT 1287, Equifax 1288, Exelon 1309, Family 1330, Federal 1348, Finish 1383, First 1390, First 1397, First 1399, First 1400, First 1409, First 1419, Fisher 1433, Flextronics 1437, Flint 1439, Flir 1440, Florida 1442, Florida 1443, FMR 1450, Forest 1468, Fox 1480, Framingham 1481, Freeport 1494, Frontier 1510, Fulton 1518, Gannett 1532, Gap 1533, GenCorp 1548, Genentech 1549, General 1552, General 1554, Genesis 1561, Genzyme 1566, Gibraltar 1577, Gilead 1582, Give 1583, GlaxoSmithKline 1588, Globe 1594, Google 1613, Great 1644, Great 1645, Green 1653, Greyhound 1664, Greystone 1665, Guardian 1683, Gulf 1689, H & R 1695, Haggen 1699, Hard 1727, Harris 1739, Hasbro 1747, Haviland 1752, Health 1764, Heinz 1772, Hewlett 1794, Highmark 1799, Hill 1804, Hillshire 1809, Hilton 1812, Home 1845, Houghton 1869, Hubbard 1878, Humana 1886, Huntsman 1895, Iberdrola 1904, Imation 1919, ING 1938, International 1958, Intoximeters 1979, Intuit 1982, Jack 2007, Jackson 2011, Jacksonville 2014, Janus 2024, Jazz 2028, JM 2044, Johnson 2048, JPMorgan Chase 2071, Juno 2076, Kaiser 2086, Kansas 2093, Kellogg 2120, KeyBank 2136, Kukui 2198, Landmark 2218, Las Vegas 2225, Lauder 2230, Lauth 2232, Lego 2247, Lemieux 2249, Lennar 2250, LG&E Energy 2260, Liberty 2262, Liberty 2264, Liberty 2265, Lilly 2274, Lincoln 2281, Lincoln 2282, Los Angeles 2308, Louisiana 2309, Major 2345, Marathon 2362, Marena 2372, Marsh 2385, Masco 2393, Maverick 2409, MAXIMUS 2410, MB 2415, McKesson 2434, McKinstry 2435, Medtronic 2453, Melissa 2458, Men's 2460, Merck 2466, Meredith 2471, Messer 2477, Metropolitan 2481, MGM 2489, Microsoft 2501, Middlesex 2506, Miles 2512, Miller 2517, Minnesota 2531, Mizuho 2542, Modine 2544, Moneta 2557, Monsanto 2559, Monster 2560, Morgan 2570, Mortenson 2577, Mount 2588, Nash 2619, Nationwide 2639, Natural 2641, Nestle 2662, New 2668, New York 2684, New York 2687, New York 2688, Newman's 2697, NIKE 2710, Nordson 2723, North 2735, Northern 2740, Northfield 2742, Northrim 2743, Northwest 2747, Northwestern 2749, Novartis 2753, NRG 2756, Nu 2759, NV 2765, NYSE 2769, O'Neal 2771, OceanFirst 2782, Ohio 2789, Old 2798, One 2812, ONEOK 2815, Pacific 2853, Pacific 2855, PacifiCorp 2860, Packard 2862, Park 2880, Pattillo 2896, Pawtucket 2902, Peerless 2915, Penn 2923, Penney 2925, Pentair 2926, People's 2928, Peoples 2929, Peoples 2931, PepsiCo 2935, Perdue 2936, Pfizer 2950, PG&E 2952, Philadelphia 2961, Philip 2962, Piedmont 2971, Pioneer 2981, Piper 2983, Pitney 2984, Pizza 2988, PMI 2995, PNC 2997, Portland 3010, Premera 3034, Primerica 3045, Pro 3052, Prophet 3063, Prudential 3072, PVH 3088, Pyles 3089, Quaker 3094, QUALCOMM 3095, Quality 3096, Quest 3103, Questar 3104, Ralph 3123, RBC 3136, RBS 3137, RealNetworks 3144, Reckitt 3146, Reebok 3159, Reed 3161, Regal 3166, Regions 3171, Reynolds 3199, Reynolds 3200, Ricoh 3210, RJN 3228, Rockwell 3246, Royal 3273, Ryman 3294, S & T 3297, Safeco 3306, salesforce.com 3318, San Francisco 3324, San Francisco 3325, San Jose 3327, sanofi-aventis 3329, SAP 3334, Savings 3343, Schein 3348, Schwab 3363, Scotts 3372, Seagate 3377, Seattle 3386, Securian 3389, Security 3391, Selective 3399, Sempra 3405, Seneca 3406, Sherwin 3437, ShopKo 3440, SI 3444, Silicon 3455, Skadden 3470, SKF 3473, Smithfield 3487, Sodexho 3497, Sony 3504, Southern 3514, Sovereign 3528, Sporting 3546, SQA 3559, Square 3560, St. 3565, St. Joe 3563, StanCorp 3574, Standard 3576, Staples 3581, State 3592, Steelcase 3597, Strauss 3624, Sun 3643, Sunwest 3655, Superior 3657, Synopsys 3673, Systel 3678, TALX 3683, TCF 3695, TD 3696, Terex 3719, Tesoro 3723, Textron 3731, TFS 3732, Thrivent 3747, TJX 3765, Tom's 3770, Trail 3793, Travelers 3802, U.S. 3835, Union 3854, United 3872, United 3876, UnitedHealth 3884, Universal 3889, USEC 3904, Valspar 3920, Varnum 3923, Verizon 3936, Visa 3960, Vision 3961, Wadsworth 3974, Waffle 3975, Wakefern 3979, Wal-Mart 3980, Walgreen 3981, Washington 3994, Washington 3995, Washington 4000, WD-40 4011, Webster 4016, Wells 4028, West 4034, Western 4042, Western 4045, Westinghouse 4049, Weyerhaeuser 4052, Whole 4066, Woodward 4112, Xcel 4135, Xerox 4136, Xylem 4139, Zappos.com 4153

Economics

3M 3, Amerisure 177, Aviva 302, Bangor 338, Comerica 889, Consumers 921, Dominion 1150, Equifax 1288, Ernst 1293, Financial 1382, Great 1647, Imation 1919, Moody's 2563, Nasdaq 2617, NYSE 2769, Piper 2983, Securian 3389, TFS 3732

Education

1st 2, 3M 3, 7-Eleven 5, A & E 6, A.D. 7, ABARTA 10, Abbot 12, Abbott 13, Abby's 14, AbbyBank 15, Aberdeen 18, Acacia 21, Accenture 22, Accupac 23, ACE 24, Acme 28, Acme 29, Acuity 31, Acuity 32, adidas 35, Adobe 38, Advance 39, Advanced 40, AEGON 45, Aetna 48, Affinity 52, Aflac 54, Ag 55, Agilent 56, AGL 57, AgStar 59, Ahern 60, Air 63, Airtek 66, Alabama 71, Aladdin 73, Alaska 74, Alaska 75, Alaska 76, Albemarle 78, Albertsons 79, Albrecht 80, Alcatel 81, Alcoa 82, Alcon 83, Alexander 85, Alice 89, Allegheny 91, Allegis 92, Allen 94, Allen 97, Allen 98, Allergan 99, Allete 100, Alliance 101, Alliant 104, Allison-Erwin 106, Almar 110, Alpha 112, Alro 113, Alsan 114, Alsco 115, Altec 118, Altman 119, Amboy 124, AMC 126, AMCOL 127, Ameren 128, America's 130, American 132, American 133, American 134, American 136, American 141, American 143, American 144, American 145, American 147, American 150, American 153, American 154, American 155, American 156, American 157, American 159, American 160, American 165, American 168, American 169, American 170, AMERIGROUP 171, AmeriPride 173, Ameristar 176, Amerisure 177, Ameritas 178, Ameritec 179, AMETEK 181, Amgen 182, Amica 183, Amnews 185, Amsted 188, Anadarko 190, Anaheim 191, Anchor 192, Andersen 194, Andretti 197, Andrews 198, Angels 200, Anheuser 202, Anocoil 204, ANZA 208, Aon 210, Apache 211, Apex 214, Apollo 216, Applied 220, AptarGroup 221, Arbella 226, Arby's 228, Arcelormittal 229, Arch 230, Archer 233, Arctic 234, Ariel 237, Arizona 239, Arkansas 241, Arkema 242, Armbrust 243, Armstrong 246, Arrow 249, Arrowhead 250, Artichoke 254, Ash 256, Ashland 258, Associated 262, Associated 264, Association 265, Assurant 266, Assurant 267, Assurant 268, Astoria 270, AstraZeneca 272, AT&T 273, AT&T 274, Athletics 276, Atlanta 278, Atlanta 279, Atlantic 281, Atlantic 282, Atlas 284, Atmos 285, Austin 288, Autodesk 289, Automatic 291, AutoNation 292, Avelina 296, Avidia 298, Avis 299, Avis 300, Avista 301, Aviva 302, Avlon 303, Avnet 304, AVX 306, AZPB 310, Azulay 311, Badger 313, Bailey 315, Baird 316, Baird 317, Baker 323, Baker 324, Baltimore 331, Baltimore 334, BancTrust 337, Bangor 338, Bank 340, Bank 342, Bank 343, Bank 344, Bank 346, Bank 348, Bank 349, BankSouth 350, Barbara 354, Bard 358, Barnes 360, Barnes 362, Barrasso 363, Barton 366, BASF 368, Basketball 370, Batson 373, Batts 374, Baxter 377, Bay 378, Bay 379, Bay 380, Bayer 381, BayView 384, BB&T 385, Beall's 389, Bean 392, Bear 393, Bechtel 395, Beck 396, Beckman 397, Bekins 401, Belden 402, Belk 403, Belk 404, Bemis 407, Bemis 408, Benedict-Miller 410, Beneficial 412, Benevento 414, Bentley 416, Bergstrom 421, Berkley 426, Berkshire 428, Bernhardt 432, Berry 434, Berry 435, Berry 436, Berry 437, Best 442, Better 449, Betts 450, Beverage 453, Beyer 454, BHP 455, Bickel 457, Bicon 458, Bierlein 459, Big 461, Bigelow 462, Biogen 465, Biomet 466, Bionetics 467, Birds 469, Birdsong 470, Birmingham 471, Birmingham 472, BJ's 473, Black 474, Black 475, Blair 479, Block 481, Blommer 484, Bloomberg 486, Blue 492, Blue 493, Blue 494, Blue 496, Blue 500, Blue 501, Blue 503, Blue 504, BMW 509, Bob's 511, Bobcats 512, Bodine 513, Boehringer 515, Boeing 516, Boh 517, Boler 520, Bon 521, Bonitz 524, Booz 525, BorgWarner 528, Bossong 532, Boston 534, Boston 538, Boston 539, Boston 540, Bound 541, Bourns 542, Bowater 543, BP 547, Brady 552, Bramco 555, Brasseler 556, Bressler 557, Brewer 558, Bricker 559, Bridgestone 560, Bridgewater 562, Bridgeway 563, Briggs 565, Bright 566, Brightpoint 567, Brillion 569, Brinckerhoff 570, Bristol 577, Bristol 578, Broadcom 579, Brocchini 580, Brochsteins 581, Brooklyn 584, Brooks 585, Brotherhood 588, Brown 590, Brown 591, Brown 592, Brunswick 595, Bubalo 598, Buccaneer 599, Buckeye 601, Buckley 602, Budweiser 605, Buffalo 606, Build 608, Building 610, Buist 611, Bunge 612, Burger 613, Burger's 614, Burlington 616, Burlington 618, Burnett 619, Burns 620, Butler 626, Butt 628, Butzel 629, Byrd 631, C L D 635, C Spire 636, C.M. 637, CA 638, Cabot 642, Cacique 644, Cades 647, Cajun 652, California 654, California 656, Calista 657, Callaway 660, Calpine 661, Calumet 662, Calvert 663, Cambridge 666, Cameron 667, Campbell 669, Caparo 673, Cape 674, Capital 676, Capital 677, Capital 678, Capital 679, Capitol 680, Capstone 684, Cardinal 685, Cargill 691, Carlson 693, CarMax 694, Carmody 695, Carolina 697, Carolina 699, Carrington Coleman 701, Carroll 703, Carson 705, Carver 711, Cary 712, Cassidy 715, Castle 716, Catalina 719, Catawissa 720, Caterpillar 722, Cathay 723, Cavaliers 724, CBS 727, CC 728, CDW 729, CEMEX 734, Centene 735, Center 737, CenterPoint 738, CentiMark 740, Central 741, Central 742, Central 745, Century 748, Century 749, CenturyLink 751, Ceridian 753, CFS 756, Chaney 761, Chapman 763, Charter 765, Chehalis 771, Chelsea 772, Chemed 773, Chemtura 775, Chesapeake 777, Chesapeake 778, Cheviot 779, Chevron 780, Chicago 781, Chicago 782, Chicago 783, Chicago 786, Chicago 789, Chicago 790, Chick 791, Chicopee 792, Chief 793, Choggiung 797, Choice 798, Chotin 799, Chrysler

801, CHS 802, Chubb 804, Churchill 807, Cianbro 808, CIBA 810, CIGNA 812, Cincinnati 814, Circle 817, Cisco 818, CITGO 820, Citizens 825, Citizens 827, Citizens 828, CLARCOR 832, Claremont 833, Clark 835, Classic 840, Clayton 841, Clear 842, Clemens 844, Clements 845, Cleveland 846, Cleveland 847, Clif 848, Clifford 849, Cliffs 850, Clinton 851, CME 853, CNA 855, CNO 857, Coach 858, Coastal 859, Coca 861, Coca 862, Coghlin 864, Cole 867, Colgate 869, COLHOC 870, Collective 871, Collette 872, Colonial 874, Colonial 875, Colonial 876, Colorado 879, Colt 881, Columbia 882, Columbia 883, Columbia 884, Columbus 885, Columbus 886, Comcast 887, Comcast 888, Comerica 889, Commerce 890, Commercial 891, Commercial 893, Communications 896, Compass 901, Compuware 902, Con 903, Concept 905, Connecticut 910, Connecticut 911, Connecticut 912, ConocoPhillips 913, Conrail 914, Consolidated 916, Conston 920, Consumers 921, Continental 922, Continental 923, Continental 924, Continental 925, Continental 926, Contran 928, Convalescent 931, ConvaTec 932, Convergys 933, Cook 934, Cooper 935, Cooper 936, Copley 938, Coquille 939, CORE 941, Cornerstone 942, Cornerstone 944, Corning 945, CORT 946, Corvallis 947, Costco 948, Cousins 953, Cousins 954, Cox 958, Cox 959, Coyotes 963, CPI 965, Cracker 966, craigslist 968, Crane 969, Creative 975, Creative 976, Credit 980, Crescent 981, Crescent 982, Crescent 983, Croft 985, Crowell 986, Crown 987, Crown 989, Crystal 992, CSS 996, Cullman 1001, Cummins 1007, CUNA 1008, Cupertino 1009, Curves 1011, Cutie 1013, Cymer 1016, Dallas 1021, Dallas 1022, Dallas 1023, Dana 1026, Danforth 1028, Danis 1029, Darden 1032, Dart 1034, Davis 1037, Dayton 1047, DCI 1049, Dead 1051, Dealer 1052, Dean 1053, Dean 1054, DeBlois 1056, DeBruce 1057, Dedham 1060, Deere 1061, Deerfield 1062, Dekker 1064, Delaware 1066, Dell Corning 1067, Delmarva 1069, Deloitte 1070, Delphi 1071, Delphos 1072, Delta 1082, Demoulas 1085, DeniseLawrence.Com 1086, Denny's 1087, Denver 1090, Dethmers 1091, Detroit 1093, Detroit 1094, Detroit 1095, Detroit 1097, Deutsche 1099, Devereaux 1100, Devon 1102, Dexter 1103, Dharma 1105, Diageo 1107, Diagnos-Techs 1108, Diebold 1112, Dietz 1114, Dilbeck 1116, Dime 1118, DineEquity 1120, Dippin' 1122, DIRECTV 1124, Discover 1125, Discovery 1126, Disney 1127, Dispatch 1129, Dixon 1133, Doctor's 1138, Dollar 1142, Dolphins 1147, Dominion 1148, Dominion 1149, Dominion 1150, Donaldson 1153, Donnelley 1155, Donovan 1156, Dot 1158, Douglas 1159, Doyon 1167, DP 1168, Draper 1171, Dresser 1173, Dreyer's 1174, Drive 1177, DRS 1179, DRW 1181, DTE 1183, du Pont 1184, Duda 1188, Duke 1189, Dunn 1192, Dupps 1193, Duro-Last 1196, Dutch 1197, Eagle 1202, Earnhardt 1205, Earthquakes 1206, East 1207, East 1208, Eastern 1209, Eastern 1210, Eastern 1211, Easthampton 1212, Eastman 1213, Eastman 1214, Eaton 1216, Eclipse 1219, Ecolab 1220, Edelman 1224, Edgar 1225, Edible 1226, Edison 1228, Edison 1229, Education 1232, Edvisors 1234, Edwards 1235, El 1237, El Paso 1239, Electric 1240, Electronic 1242, Elgin 1246, Ellucian 1252, EMC 1253, EMCO 1254, Emerson 1257, Emmis 1259, Empire 1262, Employers 1264, Enbridge 1265, Endeavor 1267, Endres 1269, Energizer 1271, Energy 1272, Ensign 1276, Entelco 1277, Entergy 1279, Epson 1286, EQT 1287, Equifax 1288, Ergon 1289, Ernst 1293, Erving 1294, Essa 1297, Evans 1300, Evans 1301, Evening 1302, Ewing 1303, Exchange 1306, Exchange 1307, Exelon 1309, Exotic 1310, Express 1313, Exxon 1315, Fabiano 1320, Fabick 1321, Fabri 1322, Factory 1323, Faegre 1324, Fairfax 1325, Fairfield 1326, Fairmont 1327, Farmers 1339, Farmers' 1337, Farrell 1341, Fashion 1342, FBR 1345, FDI 1346, Federal 1348, Federal 1350, Federated 1351, FEECO 1353, Feelgoodz 1354, Fender 1359, Ferguson 1363, Ferro 1366, Fetzer 1367, Fibre 1369, Fidelity 1371, Fidelity 1372, Fieldale 1373, Fieldstone 1374, Fiesta 1375, Fifth 1377, Finance 1381, Financial 1382, First 1389, First 1395, First 1396, First 1397, First 1398, First 1399, First 1400, First 1401, First 1402, First 1403, First 1405, First 1406, First 1408, First 1409, First 1412, First 1414, First 1415, First 1416, First 1417, First 1419, First 1420, First 1422, First 1423, FirstEnergy 1424, Firstmerit 1425, Fiserv 1427, Fishel 1429, Fisher 1432, Flextronics 1437, Flir 1440, Florence 1441, Florida 1442, Florida 1443, Florida 1444, Florsheim 1445, Flowserve 1447, Fluor 1448, FMC 1449, FMR 1450, Foley 1454, Fonville 1456, Foot 1459, Football 1460, Ford 1463, Ford 1464, Forest 1467, Fort 1471, Fort 1472, Fortis 1473, Four 1477, Framingham 1481, Frankel 1483, Franklin 1484, Franklin 1485, Franklin 1487, Franklin 1488, Franshaw 1489, Fredericksburg 1490, Freedman 1493, Freeport 1494, Fremont 1496, Fremont 1497, Freres 1498, Friedland 1503, Friesen 1505, Frontier 1510, Fuller 1517, Fulton 1518, Furniture 1519, G & R 1523, G&K 1524, Gable 1525, Gallo 1529, Gannett 1532, Gap 1533, Garelick 1537, GATX 1542, Gear 1544, GenCorp 1548, Genentech 1549, General 1551, General 1552, General 1553, General 1554, General 1555, Genesco 1559, Geneseo 1560, GenOn 1563, GenRad 1564, Genworth 1565, Georgia 1567, Georgia 1568, Getty 1569, Ghilotti 1570, Giant 1571, Giant 1572, Giant 1573, Gibbons 1574, Gibraltar 1577, Gibson 1578, Gilbane 1581, Give 1583, GJF 1584, GKN 1585, GlaxoSmithKline 1588, Globe 1594, Golden 1601, Golden 1602, Goldman 1604, Golub 1607, Gon 1608, Good 1609, Goodyear 1612, Google 1613, Gootee 1614, Gould 1618, Grace 1623, Graco 1624, Graham 1625, Grand 1627, Grand 1628, Grandma 1630, Grange 1631, Granite 1632, Graphic 1635, Graphix 1637, Graycor 1641, Great 1644, Great 1645, Great 1646, Greater 1649, Green 1651, Greene 1656, Gregory 1661, Greif 1663, Greystone 1665, Grove 1672, Groves 1673, GSM 1676, Guard 1680, Guess 1685, Gulf 1689, Gulfstream 1690, H & R 1695, Hackstock 1697, Hall 1702, Hall 1703, Hallberg 1704, Halliburton 1706, Hallmark 1707, Halstead 1708, Halton 1709, Hammond 1711, Hampden 1713, Hamrick 1715, Hancock 1716, Hancock 1717, Handy 1718, Hanes 1719, Hanna 1722, Hannaford 1723, Hanover 1724, Harden 1728, Hardinge 1729, Harley 1732, Harleysville 1733, Harper 1735, Harris 1736, Harsco 1741, Hartford 1742, Hartford 1743, Hartzell 1745, Harvey 1746, Havana 1751, Haviland 1752, Hawaii 1753, Hawaii 1754, Hawaiian 1755, Hawkins 1757, Haworth 1758, Hays 1761, HCA 1762, HCR 1763, Health 1765, Heat 1767, Hedrick 1768, Heffernan 1769, Heidtman 1770, Heinz 1772, Hemmerdinger 1775, Henkel 1778, Henkels 1779, Henry 1781, Heritage 1784, Heritage 1785, Hermann 1786, Herrick 1788, Hershey 1791, Hess 1793, Hewlett 1794, Hexcel 1795, Hickory 1797, Highmark 1799, Highwoods 1800, Hilfiger 1801, Hilliard 1806, Hills 1808, Hillside 1810, Hitachi 1816, HNI 1817, Hoffer 1821, Hoffmann 1823, Hofmann 1824, Holce 1827, Holder 1829, Holiday 1830, Holiday 1832, Holland 1834, Holmes 1838, Holt 1839, Holtz 1840, Home 1843, Home 1844, Home 1845, Home 1846, Homecrest 1847, Honda 1851, Honeywell 1852, Hood 1854, Hooker 1855, Hoops 1857, Hopkins 1859, Horix 1860, Horizon 1861, Horizon 1862, Horizon 1863, Horizon 1865, Hormel 1866, Houghton 1869, Houston 1871, HSBC 1876, Hubbard 1877, Hubbard 1878, Hubbell 1879, Hudson 1880, Hudson 1881, Hudson 1882, Huhtamaki 1884, Humana 1886, Huna 1887, Hunt 1889, Hunt 1890, Hunt 1892, Hunter 1893, Huntington 1894, Huntsman 1895, Hy-Vee 1900, Hygeia 1901, IAC 1903, Iberdrola 1904, ICON 1906, IDACORP 1907, Idealist 1909, IDT 1910, IHC 1913, Ilitch 1915, Illinois 1916, Imagineers 1918, Imation 1919, Independence 1925, Independent 1927, Independent 1928, Indianapolis 1932, Indium 1933, Indus 1934, Industrial 1935, ING 1938, Ingersoll 1939, Ingram 1941, Ingredion 1942, Insperity 1944, Institution 1946, Integrity 1948, Intel 1950, Intelius 1951, Interface 1953, Interlock 1954, Intermec 1955, Intermountain 1957, International 1958, International 1960, International 1962, International 1963, International 1965, International 1966, International 1967, International 1968, International 1971, International Profit 1969, Interstate 1975, InterTech 1977, Intrepid 1980, Intuit 1982, Invesco 1983, Investors 1984, Inwood 1985, Iowa 1986, Iowa 1987, IPALCO 1988, Ipswich 1989, Irby 1990, Isabella 1993, Isaly's 1994, ITA 1998, ITT 1999, ITW 2000, Iwo 2003, J & S 2004, Jabil 2006, Jack 2007, Jackson 2008, Jackson 2010, Jacksonville 2014, Jaclyn 2015, Jacobs 2016, Jai 2017, Jalapeno 2018, JAM 2019, Jamba 2020, James 2021, JanPak 2022, Janus 2024, Jasper 2026, Jasper 2027, Jazz 2028, Jefferies 2030, Jeld 2032, Jesco 2040, JetBlue 2041, Jim's 2043, JM 2044, Johns 2047, Johnson 2048, Johnson 2049, Johnson 2050, Jones 2055, Jones 2056, Jones 2057, Jones 2059, Jones 2060, Jordan 2063, Jordan 2064, Josephson 2066, Jostens 2067, Journal 2068, Joy 2070, JPMorgan Chase 2071, JTB 2074, Juno 2076, K-B 2081, Kahn 2084, Kaiser 2086, Kajima 2087, Kaman 2088, Kansas 2091, Kansas 2094, KarMART 2096, Katten 2101, KBR 2106, Kearny 2108, Keen 2111, Keeneland 2113, Kellogg 2120, Kellwood 2121, Kelly 2122, Kemp 2123, Kennebunk 2126, Kennecott 2127, Kepco 2132, Key 2134, Key 2135, KeyBank 2136, Kikkoman 2144, Kilmartin 2145, Kilpatrick 2146, Kimball 2149, Kimberly 2150, Kinder 2153, Kindred 2154, Kinetic 2156, Kingsbury 2160, Kingston 2161, KLA-Tencor 2165, Klein 2168, Klein's 2169, Kmart 2172, Knitcraft 2174, Knitcraft 2175, KOA 2178, Koch 2179, Koch 2180, Kohler 2182, Koniag 2184, Korum 2187, Koss 2188, Kowalski 2189, Kroger 2195, Kukui 2198, Kuskokwim 2200, L'Oreal 2203, La-Z-Boy 2205, Laclede 2207, Lake 2212, Lake 2213, Land 2217, Landmark 2218, Landry's 2219, Lands' 2220, Lapham 2223, Larkin 2224, Lauder 2230, Laureate 2231, Lebanon 2238, Lee 2241, Leet 2243, Legg 2245, Lemieux 2249, Lennar 2250, Levi 2254, Leviton 2255, Lexington 2257, Lexmark 2258, Leyman 2259, LG&E Energy 2260, Li-Cor 2261, Liberty 2262, Liberty 2264, Liberty 2265, Lieberman 2266, Life 2268, Life 2269, Lilly 2274, Lim 2275, Limited 2277, Lincoln 2279, Lincoln 2280, Lincoln 2281, Lincoln 2282, Lisle 2286, Lithia 2287, LJA 2291, Lockheed 2292, Lockwood 2293, Loews 2296, Long 2298, Longview 2300, Loomis 2301, Lord 2302, Lord 2303, Los Angeles 2305, Los Angeles 2306, Los Angeles 2308, Louisiana 2309, Louisiana 2310, Lowe's 2312, Lubrizol 2315, Lucasfilm 2316, Luck 2317, M&T 2323, M.D.C. 2324, M/I 2325, MAC 2327, MAC 2329, Machias 2332, Macy's 2333, Madison 2334, Magyar 2341, Majestic 2343, Majestic 2344, Major 2346, Major 2347, Makino 2348, Mamiye 2352, Manhattan 2354, Manitowoc 2356, Manocherian 2357, Manpower 2358, Manti 2359, Marathon 2362, Marathon 2363, Marathon 2365, Marcho 2368, Marcus 2371, Marena 2372, Mariani 2374, Maritz 2376, Marlborough 2380, Marnier-Lapostolle 2381, Mars 2384, Marsh 2385, Marsh 2387, Marshall 2388, Martin 2390, Martin 2391, Mary 2392, Mascoma 2394, Mason 2396, Massachusetts 2397, MasterCard 2399, Masterson 2400, Matrix 2403, Matson 2404, Mattel 2405, Mattress 2407, Maverick 2409, Mazda 2414, MBIA 2416, Mccar 2420, McCarthy 2421, McClatchy 2422, McCormick 2423, McDermott 2424, McDonald 2426, McDonald's 2427, McKee 2432, McKesson 2434, McKinstry 2435, McNally 2437, McShane 2439, McWane 2440, MDU 2441, Meadows 2444, MeadWestvaco 2445, Medieval 2449, MedImmune 2450, Medrad 2452, Medtronic 2453, MEEMIC 2455, Melaleuca 2457, Melissa 2458, Menasha 2461, Mentor 2462, Mercedes 2463, Merchants 2465, Merck 2466, Mercury 2468, Mercury 2470, Meredith 2471, Meritor 2473, Merk 2467, Merrimack 2474, Merrimack 2475, Messer 2477, Metropolitan 2480, Metropolitan 2481, Metropolitan 2483, MFA 2486, MFA 2487, MGIC 2488, MGM 2489, MH 2490, Miami 2491, Michael 2493, Michelin 2495, Michigan 2496, Michigan 2497, Micro 2498, Micron 2500, MidAmerican 2504, Midcontinent 2505, Middlesex 2506, Midmark 2507, Mill 2515, Millennia 2516, Miller 2517, Miller 2518, Miller 2522, Miller 2523, Millhiser-Smith 2524, Milliken 2525, Milwaukee 2527, Milwaukee 2528, Mine 2529, Minnesota 2530, Minster 2532, Minto 2533, Mississippi 2536, Mitsubishi 2538, Mitsui 2541, MN 2543, Modine 2544, Mohegan 2546, Monarch 2553, Moneta 2557, MoneyGram 2558, Monsanto 2559, Monster 2560, Moody 2562, Moody's 2563, Moore 2565, Moore 2566, Moore 2567, Morgan 2568, Morgan 2569, Morgan 2570, Morley 2572, Morris 2573, Morris 2574, Mortenson 2577, Mortgage 2578, Mosaic 2580, Motor 2583, Motorists 2584, Motorola 2585, Motorola 2586, Mt. 2594, Mueller 2597, Murphy

Education, alliance/advocacy

Education, association

Education, community/cooperative

Education, e-learning

Education, equal rights

Education, ESL programs

Education, formal/general education

Motorola 2586

Education, fund raising/fund distribution

Blue 497, CH2M 758, Chick 791, Darden 1032, Delta 1073, Haskell 1748, ITT 1999, Kohler 2182, Merck 2466, Penney 2925, Sensient 3408, West 4038

Education, gifted students

Siemens 3448, Urban 3901

Education, information services

SUPERVALU 3659

Education, management/technical assistance

Clear 842, TeleTech 3708, Texas 3728, Towerbrook 3781

Education, PTA groups

Dean 1053, Lowe's 2312

Education, public education

Altria 120, Aramco 224, Carpenter 700, Creative 975, CVS 1014, Exotic 1310, Great 1647, IMC 1920, MGM 2489, Panasonic 2869, Penguin 2922, Quaker 3094, State 3591, Strauss 3624, TECO 3701, Tesoro 3723, Time 3756, Union 3857, Western 4042

Education, public policy

Hillside 1810

Education, reform

Amerisure 177, General 1552, JPMorgan Chase 2071, Medtronic 2453, Nordson 2723, Panasonic 2869, Pattillo 2896, Piedmont 2971, Prudential 3072, Reily 3177, UTC 3908, Vulcan 3972

Education, research

Apollo 216, Golub 1607, Micron 2500, Sensient 3408

Education, services

3M 3, Alabama 71, Alcoa 82, Alsco 115, Andersen 194, Androscoggin 199, Apollo 216, Bangor 338, BayView 384, Belk 403, Boeing 516, Capital 679, Cargill 691, Carson 705, Chicago 786, Coca 862, Contran 928, Cummins 1007, Darden 1032, Deluxe 1084, Deutsche 1099, Dreyer's 1174, DTE 1183, Endeavor 1267, Energizer 1271, Excell 1304, Federal 1348, Fortis 1473, Genworth 1565, Herrick 1788, HNI 1817, JM 2044, JPMorgan Chase 2071, Kinder 2153, Liberty 2262, Liberty 2265, Lincoln 2281, Maverick 2409, Merck 2466, Metropolitan 2481, Nestle 2662, Old 2798, Pearson 2911, Pearson 2912, People's 2928, Pfizer 2950, Piedmont 2971, Pitney 2984, Provident 3069, Public 3076, Raytheon 3135, RBC 3136, Safeco 3306, Scientific 3367, Seneca 3406, StanCorp 3574, State 3592, Subaru 3631, TD 3696, Textron 3731, Thomaston 3736, Union 3854, Union 3857, United 3881, UTC 3908, Vectren 3925, Verizon 3936, Wal-Mart 3980, Washington 3994, Weyco 4051, Wynnne 4133

Education, single organization support

First 1419

Education, special

Alliance 101, Build 608, Columbia 882, Energizer 1271, Ergon 1289, Flextronics 1437, Groves 1673, Hewlett 1794, Makino 2348, Nasdaq 2618, Park 2880, People's 2928, Philadelphia 2960, SBH 3345, Tesoro 3723, Trane 3794, Xilinx 4137

Education, volunteer services

Booz 525, Scotts 3372, Tesoro 3723

Electronic communications/Internet

Focus 1451, Jenzabar 2037

Elementary school/education

1st 2, Alabama 71, American 145, AMETEK 181, Applied 219, Arkema 242, Baltimore 332, Bay 378, BB&T 385, Brady 552, Capstone 684, Carter's 708, Cavaliers 724, CC 728, Chick 791, CIGNA 812, Concept 905, Continental 925, Creative 975, Credit 980, Dallas 1021, Detroit 1095, Deutsch 1098, Digi 1115, Federal 1348, Federated 1351, Fenton 1361, Fidelity 1372, First 1403, Food 1458, Grand 1627, Great 1642, Heat 1767, Houston 1871, Humana 1886, IMC 1920, Independence 1925, Industrial 1935, Kepco 2132, Kingsbury 2160, Liberty 2265, Life 2269, Los Angeles 2308, Manhattan 2354, Maverick 2409, MBIA 2416, McGraw 2429, Medtronic 2453, Midcontinent 2505, Mississippi 2536, Moore 2566, Morris 2573, Nashville 2620, Neace 2651, Nestle 2663, New England 2670, New York 2686, Ohio 2791, Olin 2801, Omnicare 2807, Philadelphia 2957, Price 3040, ProLogis 3060, Protective 3066, Public 3077, Quaker 3093, RECO 3148, Reynolds 3200, Sacramento 3303, Safeco 3306, Sharp 3422, SIFCO 3452, Simpson 3461, Sprague 3551, Sprint 3556, Tampa 3686, Tap 3689, Teleflex 3707, Tennessee 3716, TFS 3732, United 3880, Universal 3889, Urban 3901, Wal-Mart 3980, Washington 3998, Weil 4022, Winn 4087, WorkflowOne 4115

Elementary/secondary education

3M 3, ABARTA 10, Abbott 13, Abby's 14, Abercrombie 17, ACI 27, Acuity 32, Adobe 38, Advent 41, Agilent 56, Akamai 68, Alabama 71, Alcatel 81, Alice 89, Allegheny 91, Allegis 92, Allen 97, Allete 100, Alsco 115, Altec 118, Altria 120, Alyeska 121, American 141, American 150, American 155, American 161, Ameristar 176, Andersen 194, Andersson 196, Applied 220, Arcelormittal 229, Arch 230, Arch 231, Arent 235, Astoria 270, Avery 297, Avista 301, Badger 313, Baker 321, Balch 327, Baltimore 335, BancTrust 337, Barnes 360, BASF 368, Batson 373, Baxter 377, Bay 380, Best 442, Bickel 457, Big 460, Birdsong 470, Birmingham 472, Blue 493, Bob's 511, Boeing 516, Boler 520, Boston 540, Bound 541, Brady 552, Brinks 573, Bristol 577, Broadcom 579, Brown 591, Burger 613, Burns 620, Butler 626, Butt 628, Cablevision 641, Cabot 642, Cabot 643, Cadence 646, California 654, California 656, Calvert 663, Campbell 668, Cannon 671, Cape 674, Capital 679, Cargill 691, CarMax 694, Carpenter 700, Carson 705, Castle 716, CenterPoint 738, CentiMark 740, CenturyLink 751, CF 755, CH2M 758, Chase 770, Chemed 773, Chicago 785, Cisco 818, Clarity 834, Clear 842, Cleary 843, Clorox 852, CNA 855, Colonial 875, Colonial 876, Colorado 879, Comerica 889, Community 899, Community 900, Compass 901, Conditioned 906, Contran 928, Cooper 936, Copley 938, Corning 945, Cow 957, Crane 970, Creative 975, Croft 985, Crowell 986, Cubist 999, Cumberland 1003, Cummins 1007, CVS 1014, Dallas 1021, Dallas 1022, Davison 1042, Dell 1068, Delphi 1071, Denver 1090, Deutsche 1099, Diebold 1112, Discover 1125, Discovery 1126, Dispatch 1129, Dole 1141, Dolphins 1147, Dominion 1150, Dot 1158, Dow 1160, Dow 1161, Dow 1162, Doyon 1167, DreamWorks 1172, Dreyer's 1174, DRS 1179, DTE 1183, du Pont 1184, Duke 1189, Eaton 1216, Ecolab 1220, Edgar 1225, Edison 1228, Edison 1229, EduCare 1231, El Paso 1239, Emerson 1257, Employers 1264, Endres 1269, Energizer 1271, Energy 1272, Ensign 1276, Epson 1286, EQT 1287, Ergon 1289, Exchange 1307, Express 1313, Exxon 1315, Factory 1323, Ferro 1366, First 1391, FirstEnergy 1424, Flint 1439, Florida 1443, Fluor 1448, FMR 1450, Food 1457, Football 1460, Ford 1464, Foremost 1466, Forest 1467, Franklin 1484, Freeport 1494, Freescale 1495, Fremont 1497, Fuller 1517, GenCorp 1548, General 1552, General 1554, Genworth 1565, Georgia 1568, Giant 1571, Giant 1573, Give 1583, GlaxoSmithKline 1588, Golden 1601, Great 1645, Great 1647, Green 1650, Groves 1673, GTECH 1677, Guardian 1681, Haggen 1699, Halliburton 1706, Hannaford 1723, Harris 1736, Harris 1738, Hartzell 1745, Hasbro 1747, Heidtman 1770, Helmerich 1774, Hendrick 1776, Hewlett 1794, Highmark 1799, Hilton 1812, Hines 1813, Hoffmann 1823, Holder 1829, Honda 1851, Hormel 1866, Houghton 1869, Hubbard 1877, Hudson 1881, Hunt 1892, IDT 1910, Illinois 1916, Imation 1919, Imperial 1922, InfoSource 1936, ING 1938, Ingersoll 1939, Ingles 1940, Institution 1946, Intel 1950, Intermec 1955, International 1960, International 1971, Interstate 1975, Invesco 1983, IPALCO 1988, Island 1996, Janus 2024, Johnson 2049, Johnson 2050, Jones 2056, Jostens 2067, JPMorgan Chase 2071, Just 2077, Kaiser 2086, Kajima 2087, Kellogg 2120, Kinder 2153, Knitcraft 2174, Kohl's 2181, Kroger 2195, Land 2217, Laureate 2231, Lauth 2232, Lazy 2234, Li-Cor 2261, Liberty 2265, Life 2268, LifePoint 2270, Lilly 2274, Lincoln 2281, Lincoln 2282, Lockheed 2292, Louisiana 2309, Louisiana 2310, Lowe's 2312, LSI 2314, Lucasfilm 2316, Luck 2317, LyondellBasell 2322, Malco 2350, Mamiye 2352, Manocherian 2357, Mapes 2360, Maritz 2376, Marnier-Lapostolle 2381, Mary 2392, Mason 2396, MasterCard 2399, Matson 2404, Mechanics 2446, MedImmune 2450, Medtronic 2453, Menasha 2461, Merck 2466, Micron 2500, Microsoft 2501, Mid 2503, Miller 2517, Milliken 2525, Minnesota 2531, Minto 2533, Modine 2544, Monsanto 2559, Moody's 2563, Morgan 2570, Motorola 2585, Motorola 2586, Mt. 2594, MTV 2596, Murphy 2600, Nasdaq 2617, Nash 2619, National 2630, National 2634, National 2635, Nestle 2663, New York 2688, New York 2691, Newell 2694, Nordson 2723, North 2729, Northrop 2744, Northwestern 2749, Nu 2759, Nucor 2760, Oakley 2774, Office 2785, Oklahoma 2794, OMNOVA 2809, ONEOK 2815, Oracle 2821, Otter 2836, Owens 2842, Pacific 2855, PacifiCorp 2860, Palm 2867, Panasonic 2869, Panda 2871, Park 2881, Peabody 2907, Penn 2923, Penney 2925, Pentair 2926, Peoples 2931, PerkinElmer 2939, Phillips 2965, Piedmont 2971, Pier 2973, Pioneer 2980, Pioneer 2981, Pizza 2988, Plum 2991, PMI 2995, PNC 2997, Portland 3010, PPG 3025, Premier 3035, Prime 3044, Prince 3046, Printpack 3049, Procter 3055, Provident 3069, Prudential 3072, Public 3076, Public 3077, Quad 3091, Quaker 3094, QUALCOMM 3095, Quanex 3100, Rayonier 3134, RBC 3136, Reed 3161, Regions 3171, Regis 3172, Residential 3191, Rexnord 3198, Riggs 3213, RJN 3228, Rockwell 3246, RPM 3278, RUAN 3279, Ryman 3294, S & T 3297, Safeco 3306, SAIC 3311, sanofi-aventis 3329, SAS 3336, Savings 3343, Schloss 3352, Seagate 3377, SeaWorld 3387, Seneca 3406, Siemens 3448, Sierra 3449, Smucker 3488, Sonic 3498, Sony 3503, Southern 3515, Southern 3517, Spansion 3532, Spirol 3545, Sprint 3556, St. Jude 3566, Stahl 3573, StanCorp 3574, State 3591, Station 3593, Stonecutter 3615, Stupp 3628, Subaru 3631, SunTrust 3654, Synopsys 3673, Target 3691, Tektronix 3706, TeleTech 3708, Temple 3711, Teradyne 3718, Texas 3728, Thomasville 3737, Thrivent 3747, Tillman 3752, Time 3755, Time 3756, Time 3757, Toshiba 3776, Towerbrook 3781, Toyota 3784, Toyota 3787, Trail 3793, Travelers 3802, Trim 3810, True 3815, Truland 3817, Tulalip 3820, Tyco 3829, U.S. 3835, U.S. 3841, United 3867, Unum 3898, Urban 3901, UTC 3908, V.F. 3913, Valero 3915, Valmont 3919, Vectren 3925, Verizon 3936, Vermeer 3937, Vernier 3941, Victaulic 3948, Vulcan 3972, Wachtell 3973, Walgreen 3981, Washington 3997, WD-40 4011, Wellmark 4026, Wells 4028, West 4034, Weyerhaeuser 4052, Whirlpool 4056, Wolff 4105,

World 4120, Wrigley 4125, Xcel 4135, Xilinx 4137, Zilkha 4156

Elementary/secondary school reform

Grand 1629, Intel 1950, Lucasfilm 2316

Employment

Accenture 22, AEGON 45, Alcoa 82, Allen 94, Alliant 104, Allstate 107, Alyeska 121, American 153, American 164, Ameriprise 174, Archer 233, AT&T 273, Autonomie 293, Bangor 338, Bank 340, Bank 344, Bank 346, Blockbuster 483, Blue 494, Blue 496, Boeing 516, Butler 626, California 656, Capital 679, CenterPoint 738, Chehalis 771, Chevron 780, Choice 798, Chrysler 801, Chubb 804, Clif 848, CNA 855, Columbia 882, Comerica 889, Cook 934, Deutsche 1099, Dime 1118, Disney 1127, Domino's 1151, DTE 1183, Duke 1189, eBay 1217, Ecolab 1220, Edison 1228, Emerson 1257, Evening 1302, FirstEnergy 1424, Ford 1464, Freeport 1494, G&K 1524, Gap 1533, Georgia 1568, Glacier 1586, Graco 1624, Grand 1627, Groves 1673, Harley 1732, Harris 1739, Imation 1919, International 1960, JPMorgan Chase 2071, Kaman 2088, KeyBank 2136, Liberty 2262, Lincoln 2281, Manpower 2358, Messer 2477, Microsoft 2501, Midmark 2507, Mizuho 2542, National 2636, NBC 2649, Newell 2694, NIKE 2710, Northeast 2737, Northfield 2742, Old 2798, Opus 2820, Pactiv 2863, Pentair 2926, Peoples 2931, PepsiCo 2935, Piedmont 2971, Pitney 2984, Primerica 3045, RBS 3137, RealNetworks 3144, Roberts 3231, Securian 3389, Seneca 3406, Silicon 3455, StanCorp 3574, Standard 3576, State 3592, Strauss 3624, Tennant 3714, Textron 3731, Thrivent 3747, Towerbrook 3781, Travelers 3802, U.S. 3835, V.F. 3913, Vectren 3925, Wal-Mart 3980, Westar 4039, Western 4045, Wisconsin 4093, Wisconsin 4096, Wood 4108, Xcel 4135, Xerox 4136

Employment, equal rights

Strauss 3624

Employment, formal/general education

Pratt 3028

Employment, job counseling

Edina 1227, Retail 3194, Seneca 3406, Wells 4028

Employment, management/technical assistance

Disney 1127

Employment, public education

Franklin 1487

Employment, retraining

Alliant 104, Cisco 818, Duke 1189, Piedmont 2971, Wal-Mart 3980, WD-40 4011, Xcel 4135

Employment, services

Agilent 56, Albemarle 78, Alcoa 82, Alliant 104, Allstate 107, Ameristar 176, Andersen 194, Ascena 255, Bangor 338, Bank 340, Bank 344, Baxter 377, Bayer 381, Berkshire 428, Capital 679, Cleveland 846, Convergys 933, Cook 934, CSS 996, Cummins 1007, Duke 1189, Eastern 1209, Edison 1228, Fidelity 1372, Fifth 1376, Framingham 1481, Gap 1533, Genentech 1549, Graco 1624, Johnson 2048, JPMorgan Chase 2071, KeyBank 2136, Men's 2460, Mitsubishi 2538, Moody's 2563, OMNOVA 2809, People's 2928, PG&E 2952, Pitney 2984, Provident 3069, Prudential 3072, Puget 3081, RealNetworks 3144, RUAN 3279, Securian 3389, Seneca 3406, State 3592, Strauss 3624, Tennant 3714, Thrivent 3747, TJX 3765, U.S. 3836, Union 3854, Untours 3897, Wal-Mart 3980, Wells 4028, Wisconsin 4093

Employment, training

Airgas 65, Alcatel 81, Alcoa 82, Alliant 104, Allstate 107, American 150, American 168, Ameristar 176, Arcelormittal 229, AT&T 273, Bank 340, Bank 344, Bank 346, Bank 349, Boeing 516, Brinks 573, Bromelkamp 582, Brother 587, Butler 626, Capital 679, Cathay 723, Chrysler 801, Chugach 805, Cisco 818, Clarity 834, CNA 855, Comcast 887, Comerica 889, Commercial 893, Cook 934, Dart 1034, Delta 1074, Deutsche 1099, Dime 1118, Diversey 1130, Duke 1189, Eastern 1209, Eastman 1214, Emerson 1257, Enterprise 1281, Exelon 1309, Federal 1348, Fifth 1376, Ford 1464, Framingham 1481, Freeport 1494, G&K 1524, Gap 1533, Genentech 1549, Georgia 1568, Green 1650, Groves 1673, Hancock 1717, Hilton 1812, JPMorgan Chase 2071, KeyBank 2136, Liberty 2262, Lincoln 2281, Manpower 2358, Marriott 2383, Matson 2404, Men's 2460, Messer 2477, Middlesex 2506, Midmark 2507, Mizuho 2542, Monster 2560, Nordson 2723, Northeast 2737, Northern 2740, NYSE 2769, OceanFirst 2782, Old 2798, Opus 2820, Pentair 2926, Peoples 2931, PepsiCo 2935, Philip 2962, Piedmont 2971, Pitney 2984, PMI 2995, PNC 2997, Portland 3010, Principal 3047, Prudential 3072, RBC 3136, RealNetworks 3144, Retail 3194, Salem 3317, Securian 3389, Sempra 3405, Shell 3430, SI 3444, Sovereign 3528, StanCorp 3574, Staples 3581, State 3592, Tastefully 3692, Tennant 3714, Textron 3731, Thomson 3742, Travelers 3802, U.S. 3835, U.S. 3836, Union 3854, Wal-Mart 3980, WD-40 4011, Wegmans 4021, Wells 4028, Western 4045, Xcel 4135

Employment, volunteer services

Alyeska 121

End of life care

Aetna 48, Cambia 665, HCR 1763, Iberdrola 1904, MedImmune 2450

Energy

AGL 57, Alcoa 82, Alliant 104, Alpha 112, Ameren 128, Ameren 129, Applied 220, Arcelormittal 229, Aspen 260, Avery 297, Avista 301, Bayer 381, Berry 437, BorgWarner 528, BP 547, Caesars 650, CH2M 758, CITGO 820, Clif 848, Columbia 883, Compass 901, Consumers 921, Cummins 1007, Deutsche 1099, Dominion 1150, DTE 1183, Duke 1189, Edison 1228, Entergy 1279, EQT 1287, Exelon 1309, Ferro 1366, Florida 1443, General 1555, Halliburton 1706, Johnson 2050, King 2158, Lafarge 2210, Matson 2404, National 2628, National 2630, NiSource 2715, Northeast 2737, Northwest 2747, NV 2765, Pacific 2853, PacifiCorp 2860, Pentair 2926, PG&E 2952, Phillips 2965, Piedmont 2971, Portland 3010, PPL 3026, Public 3076, Public 3077, Puget 3081, Redwoods 3158, Saint 3312, SANYO 3333, Seminole 3404, Sempra 3405, Sunoco 3650, TD 3696, Tucson 3819, Tyco 3829, Union 3854, United 3872, Vectren 3925, Verizon 3936, Weyerhaeuser 4052, Wisconsin 4096, Xcel 4135

Engineering

3M 3, Adobe 38, Ameren 129, Anadarko 190, Ariel 237, Bechtel 395, Boston 540, CH2M 758, Chaney 761, DENSO 1088, Dominion 1150, Earnhardt 1205, Freeport 1494, IDACORP 1907, Intel 1950, International 1960, Jacobs 2016, Jorgensen 2065, L'Oreal 2203, Lafarge 2210, Lincoln 2279, Lubrizol 2315, Mine 2529, National 2630, Novetta 2755, Pitney 2984, PPG 3025, Public 3075, Rayonier 3134, Rosen's 3264, Semiconductor 3403, Skidmore 3474, Sulphur 3637, Synopsys 3673, Tyco 3829, United 3877

Engineering school/education

3M 3, Alfa 87, Allegheny 91, American 132, Ariel 237, Badger 314, Bayer 381, Bechtel 395, BorgWarner 528, BOSE 530, Burns 620, CH2M 758, Charter 766, Chrysler 801, Colonial 875, Cook 934, Cummins 1007, DENSO 1088, Dominion 1150, DTE 1183, Duke 1189, Eaton 1216, Exxon 1315, Fluor 1448, Ford 1464, GenCorp 1548, General 1555, Guth 1692, Hewlett 1794, Hulman 1885, Intel 1950, Jorgensen 2065, Kadant 2083, Lam 2214, Micron 2500, Mitsubishi 2538, National 2632, Nucor 2760, Omron 2810, Oracle 2821, Pioneer 2981, Piper 2983, Questar 3104, Railway 3119, Rayonier 3134, Rockwell 3247, Sealaska 3380, Semiconductor 3403, Spirol 3545, Stanley 3579, Tektronix 3706, Tellabs 3709, Terre 3722, Towerbrook 3781, United 3874, United 3877, Vulcan 3971, Vulcan 3972, Wisconsin 4096

Engineering/technology

Abbott 13, Accenture 22, Adobe 38, Advanced 40, Agilent 56, Albemarle 78, Alcoa 82, Allete 100, American 150, Amgen 182, Andersen 194, Arch 230, Arrow 249, Association 265, AT&T 273, Autodesk 289, Avery 297, Avista 301, Avnet 304, AVX 306, Baker 323, Bayer 381, Beckman 397, Best 442, Booz 525, BorgWarner 528, BOSE 530, Boston 540, Bristol 578, Broadcom 579, Burns 620, CA 638, Cabot 642, Cadence 646, Calvert 663, Cargill 691, Carpenter 700, Caterpillar 722, Central 741, CenturyLink 751, CH2M 758, Chevron 780, Chrysler 801, Cisco 818, Compuware 902, Consumers 921, Cummins 1007, Deere 1061, Delphi 1071, DENSO 1088, Deutsche 1099, Dominion 1150, Dow 1162, Draper 1171, DTE 1183, du Pont 1184, Duke 1189, Eastern 1211, Edison 1228, El Paso 1239, EMC 1253, EQT 1287, Exelon 1309, FirstEnergy 1424, Flextronics 1437, Fluor 1448, Focus 1451, Freeport 1494, Freescale 1495, Fuller 1517, Gear 1544, GenCorp 1548, General 1552, General 1555, Google 1613, Halliburton 1706, Harris 1736, Hewlett 1794, Honeywell 1852, Ingram 1941, Intel 1950, Intermec 1955, International 1960, IPALCO 1988, ITT 1999, KBR 2106, Kennametal 2125, Kimmel 2152, Kingston 2161, KLA-Tencor 2165, Lam 2214, Lego 2247, Lexmark 2258, Liberty 2262, Life 2268, Lilly 2274, Lockheed 2292, MasterCard 2399, Material 2401, Matson 2404, Medtronic 2453, Mentor 2462, Merck 2466, Mercury 2469, Meritor 2473, Michelin 2495, Microchip 2499, Micron 2500, Microsoft 2501, Modine 2544, Motorola 2585, Motorola 2586, National 2632, NBC 2649, NEC 2654, Norfolk 2725, Northrop 2744, Nucor 2760, OMNOVA 2809, Oracle 2821, Parametric 2878, People's 2928, Piedmont 2971, Piper 2983, Portland 3010, PPG 3025, Pratt 3028, Procter 3055, Public 3077, QUALCOMM 3095, Rackspace 3117, Rayonier 3134, ResMed 3192, Rockwell 3246, Rockwell 3247, SAIC 3311, salesforce.com 3318, SAP 3334, SAS 3336, Seagate 3377, Sempra 3405, Siemens 3448, Sony 3504, Spirol 3545, St. Jude 3566, Stanley 3579, Symantec 3669, Syniverse 3672, Texas 3728, Textron 3731, Thermo 3733, Unisys 3859, United 3882, UTC 3908, Verizon 3936, Vernier 3941, Vodafone 3965, Washington 3995, West 4038, Western 4042, Western 4045, Wiley 4072, Williams 4078, Xerox 4136, Xilinx 4137, Yahoo! 4140

Environment

3M 3, A.D. 7, Abacus 9, Abbott 13, ACE 24, ACI 27, Adobe 38, Aflac 54, AgStar 59, Air 63, Alabama 71, Alaska 74, Alaska 75, Alcoa 82, Alexander 85, Alima 90, Allete 100, Alliant 104, Allyis 109, Alpha 112, Alyeska 121, Ameren 128, American 140, American 141, American 143, American 150, American 153, Ameriprise 174, AMETEK 181, Amica 183, Anheuser 202, Aon 210, Apache 211, Applied 220, Aqua 222, Aramco 224, Arcelormittal 229, Arch 230, Arch 231,

Archer 233, AREVA 236, Ariens 238, Arizona 239, Arrow 249, Ashland 258, Aspen 260, Associated 263, Atayne 275, Austin 288, Autodesk 289, AutoNation 292, Autonomie 293, Aveda 295, Avery 297, Azavea 309, Badger 314, Bailey 315, BancTrust 337, Bank 340, Bank 342, Bank 343, Bank 346, Barnes 362, BASF 368, Baxter 377, Bayer 381, BB&T 385, Bean 392, Ben 409, Berkshire 430, Better 449, BHP 455, Black 474, Black 475, Bloomberg 486, Blue 496, Blue 501, BMW 509, Bodine 513, Boeing 516, Booz 525, BorgWarner 528, BP 547, Bricker 559, Bridgestone 560, Briggs 565, Brilliant 568, Bristlecone 575, Brown 592, Bunge 612, Burlington 618, Burns 620, Cable 639, Caesars 650, Cajun 652, Candlesticks 670, Canon 672, Cape 674, Capital 677, Capital 678, Capstone 684, Caremore 689, Cargill 691, Carmody 695, Carnival 696, Cascade 713, Caterpillar 722, CenterPoint 738, CenterPoint 739, CF 755, CH2M 758, Chaney 761, Chase 769, Chesapeake 777, CIGNA 812, CITGO 820, Citigroup 821, Clif 848, CMS 854, Coach 858, Collective 871, Colonial 876, Commonwealth 895, Compass 901, Connecticut 911, Connecticut 912, ConocoPhillips 913, Consolidated 916, Consumers 921, Continental 922, Control 930, Cooper 935, Coquille 939, Cox 958, Cox 959, Cracker 966, Croft 985, CSX 997, Cummins 1007, Cymer 1016, Darden 1032, davistudio 1043, Deacon 1050, Dead 1051, Deckers 1059, Delaware 1066, Delmarva 1069, Delta 1073, DENSO 1088, Deutsche 1099, Devon 1102, Dharma 1105, Discovery 1126, Disney 1127, Dollar 1145, Dominion 1150, Dow 1161, Dow 1162, Dr 1169, DTE 1183, du Pont 1184, Duke 1189, Dupps 1193, Eastern 1209, Eastman 1214, Ecolab 1220, Econscious 1223, Edelman 1224, Edison 1228, Elemental Herbs 1244, Enbridge 1265, Encana 1266, Entergy 1279, Entergy 1280, ERM 1292, Esurance 1298, Exelon 1309, Expedia 1311, Exxon 1315, Fast 1343, FedEx 1352, Feelgoodz 1354, Ferro 1366, Finance 1381, First 1398, First 1419, FirstEnergy 1424, Flexcon 1436, Florida 1443, Fluor 1448, FMR 1450, Ford 1464, Fortis 1473, Fortune 1474, Four 1477, Fox 1480, Framingham 1481, Free 1492, Freeport 1494, Freescale 1495, Fremont 1496, Fremont 1497, GATX 1542, General 1552, General 1555, GenRad 1564, Georgia 1567, Georgia 1568, Gibson 1578, Give 1583, GoLite 1606, Google 1613, Grace 1623, Green 1650, Grove 1672, Guess 1685, Halliburton 1706, Halstead 1708, Harley 1732, Harleysville 1733, Hartford 1742, Hawaiian 1755, Haworth 1758, Heffernan 1769, Hershey 1791, Hess 1793, Hines 1813, Hitachi 1816, Hoffmann 1823, Holcim 1828, Holland 1835, Home 1844, Honda 1851, Honeywell 1852, Horizon 1861, HSBC 1876, Hy-Vee 1900, Iberdrola 1904, IDACORP 1907, Idealist 1909, Illinois 1916, Industrial 1935, ING 1938, Intel 1950, Interface 1953, International 1958, International 1965, InterTech 1977, Invesco 1983, IPALCO 1988, ITT 1999, Jabil 2006, JAM 2019, Jasper 2027, JetBlue 2041, JM 2044, Johnson 2048, Johnson 2049, Johnson 2050, Kansas 2092, Kaytee 2104, KBR 2106, Kennecott 2127, Kimberly 2150, King 2158, Kingsbury 2160, Kohler 2182, Krueger 2196, Lafarge 2210, Lake 2212, Landmark 2218, Lands' 2220, Lauder 2230, Legg 2245, Leibowitz 2248, LG&E Energy 2260, Life 2268, Lockheed 2292, Longaberger 2299, Louisiana 2310, Lowe's 2312, Lubrizol 2315, Luck 2317, LyondellBasell 2322, Macy's 2333, Major 2347, Marathon 2365, Maritz 2376, Mark 2377, Marriott 2383, Mars 2384, Marsh 2385, Mary 2392, Masco 2393, McDermott 2424, McGraw 2429, McKee 2432, MDU 2441, MeadWestvaco 2445, MedImmune 2450, Melissa 2458, Menasha 2461, Merck 2466, Merk 2467, Michelin 2495, Michigan 2496, MidAmerican 2504, Millennia 2516, Miller 2517, Miller 2523, Mississippi 2536, Mitsubishi 2539, Monsanto 2559, Moore 2565, Morgan 2570, Morley 2572, Morris 2574, Mortenson 2577, Motorola 2585, Murphy 2600, National 2628, National 2630, National 2633, National 2635, Natural 2642, NAVTEQ 2648, NBC 2649, NEBCO 2653, New 2668, Newfield 2695, Newmont 2698, NiSource 2715, Nissan 2716, Niu 2717, Nordson 2723, Nordstrom 2724, Norfolk 2725, North 2735, Northeast 2737, Northern 2740, Northfield 2742, Northrop 2744, Northwest 2747, NRG 2756, Nucor 2760, NV 2765, NYK 2768, Occidental 2780, OceanFirst 2782, Omnicom 2808, Orange 2822, Orvis 2830, Pacific 2853, Pacific 2855, PacifiCorp 2860, Palace 2866, Parsons 2887, Patagonia 2892, Peabody 2907, Pella 2917, Peoples 2931, PepsiCo 2935, Perdue 2936, Pfister 2949, PG&E 2952, Phillips 2965, Phoenix 2968, Piedmont 2971, Piper 2983, Plum 2991, PMI 2995, PNC 2997, Polaris 2999, Portland 3010, Potomac 3018, PPL 3026, PPL 3027, Pratt 3028, Praxair 3029, Principal 3047, Print.Net 3048, Public 3075, Public 3076, Public 3077, Publix 3079, Puget 3081, Pulte 3083, PVH 3088, Quad 3091, Quiksilver 3108, Raccoon 3116, Rainforest 3120, Raymond 3133, Rayonier 3134, RCM 3139, RealNetworks 3144, Recreational 3150, RecycleBank 3151, Redwoods 3158, Reell 3164, Regions 3171, Rennoc 3184, Riceland 3203, Ricoh 3210, Riverway 3226, Rochester 3237, Rockwell 3247, Rolls 3254, Rothstein 3271, Royal 3273, Safety 3309, Saint 3312, Salt 3319, Samsung 3320, sanofi-aventis 3329, SANYO 3333, SCANA 3346, Schloss 3352, Schott 3360, Scripps 3374, Seagate 3377, Sealed 3381, SeaWorld 3387, Security 3394, Select 3398, Sempra 3405, ServiceMaster 3414, Seventh 3416, Shaw's 3427, SI 3444, Siemens 3448, Sikorsky 3454, Singlebrook 3464, SmartWool 3479, Social(k) 3494, Sonoco 3500, Sony 3503, Sony 3504, South 3511, Southern 3516, Southwest 3524, Southwire 3527, Sovereign 3528, Specialty 3538, Spirit 3544, Sprint 3556, SRA 3562, St. Joe 3563, StanCorp 3574, Starbucks 3585, Steelcase 3597, Stonyfield 3617, Subaru 3631, SUMCO 3638, Sun 3644, Sunoco 3650, Sunshine 3653, Superior 3657, SUPERVALU 3659, Swift 3667, Swinerton 3668, Symantec 3669, Tastefully 3692, TD 3696, Teck 3700, Teichert 3704, Tellabs 3709, Tennant 3714, Tesoro 3723, Textron 3731, Thinkshift 3734, Tiffany 3750, Timberland 3754, Time 3755, Tom's 3770, Toro 3775, Toshiba 3776, Total 3778, Toyota 3784, Toyota 3785, Toyota 3786, Toyota 3787, Toyota 3788, Toyota 3789, Tulalip 3820, Tutor 3826, U.S. 3841, Unilever 3853, Union 3854, Union 3856, Union 3857, United 3863, United 3871, United 3872, United 3877, United 3882, USEC 3904, Usinger 3907, UTC 3908, Vectren 3925, Veev 3927, Verizon 3936, Vodafone 3965, Vogt 3966, Vulcan 3972, Washington 3995, Washington 4001, Wendel 4029, West 4036, Western 4042, Weyerhaeuser 4052, Whitney 4065, Wisconsin 4093, Wisconsin 4096, Wolverine 4106, Woodard 4109, Working 4116, World 4118, Wrigley 4125, Wyndham 4132, Xcel 4135, Xerox 4136, Yahoo! 4140, YSI 4149, Zions 4158, Zurich 4160

Environment, administration/regulation

Aspen 260

Environment, air pollution

AGL 57, Aspen 260, BP 547, Clif 848, DENSO 1088, Georgia 1567, Georgia 1568, Grand 1629, Indus 1934, International 1968, Toyota 3787, Washington 3997

Environment, alliance/advocacy

Aspen 260, Siw 3468, Xcel 4135

Environment, association

Aspen 260

Environment, beautification programs

AGL 57, Alabama 71, Altria 120, Aspen 260, BancTrust 337, Blue 501, Chaney 761, Cox 959, Discover 1125, DVK 1198, Esurance 1298, Exelon 1309, Fuller 1517, GoLite 1606, Houston 1872, Illinois 1916, Lowe's 2312, Mississippi 2536, National 2630, Owens 2844, Scotts 3372, Sony 3503, SRA 3562, Tiffany 3750, Toro 3775, United 3880, Xcel 4135

Environment, ethics

Aspen 260

Environment, forests

Alcoa 82, Aspen 260, Avery 297, Canon 672, Caterpillar 722, Chapman 763, Cianbro 808, Davey 1035, DTE 1183, Enterprise 1281, Freeport 1494, International 1968, Jasper 2025, Longaberger 2299, MeadWestvaco 2445, Mitsubishi 2539, OSCO 2832, Patagonia 2892, Rayonier 3134, Ricoh 3210, Sierra 3451, Simpson 3461, Sun 3645, UncommonGoods 3849, United 3872, Veev 3927, Weyerhaeuser 4052, Wisconsin 4096

Environment, formal/general education

Aspen 260, Interface 1953, PacifiCorp 2860, Phillips 2965, PPL 3026

Environment, fund raising/fund distribution

Aspen 260, Sunshine 3653

Environment, government agencies

Aspen 260

Environment, information services

Aspen 260

Environment, land resources

ACE 24, AGL 57, Alcoa 82, Alice 89, Altria 120, Anderson 195, Aspen 260, Assurity 269, Baird 316, Barnes 362, Black 475, Brooks 585, Caesars 650, Canon 672, Caterpillar 722, Clif 848, Consumers 921, Darden 1032, DENSO 1088, Disney 1127, Enterprise 1281, Exelon 1309, Fabri 1322, Four 1477, Freeport 1494, Georgia 1568, Graham 1625, Grand 1629, Industrial 1935, Jones 2055, Lamont 2215, Land 2217, Lucasfilm 2316, Marcus 2370, Mitsubishi 2539, Monadnock 2551, Morley 2572, Northeast 2737, Pacific 2853, Pacific 2855, PG&E 2952, Polaris 2999, Quad 3091, Recreational 3150, Rockwell 3247, Sempra 3405, Sierra 3449, Springs 3555, Tellabs 3709, Tiffany 3750, Toro 3775, Wolverine 4106, Wrigley 4125, Xcel 4135

Environment, legal rights

Aspen 260, Recreational 3150

Environment, management/technical assistance

Aspen 260, Sealaska 3380

Environment, noise pollution

Aspen 260

Environment, plant conservation

Aspen 260, Grand 1629, GROWMARK 1674, Herschend 1790, Land 2217, Newspapers 2702, PG&E 2952

Environment, pollution control

Alcoa 82, Alfa 87, Aspen 260, Blue 501, Boeing 516, Booz 525, BP 547, Clif 848, Exelon 1309, Green 1653, Monsanto 2559, Parsons 2887, Piedmont 2971, Working 4116

Environment, public education

Aspen 260, Fuller 1517, International 1958, Pacific 2853, PPL 3026, Sunshine 3653, TECO 3701, Xcel 4135

Environment, public policy

Alcoa 82, Aspen 260, Eagle 1201, HSBC 1876, Piedmont 2971, Weyerhaeuser 4052

Environment, radiation control

Aspen 260

Environment, reform

Aspen 260

Environment, research

Aspen 260, Bakewell 326, BP 547, Duke 1189, HSBC 1876, International 1958, Kerzner 2133, New England 2670, Otter 2836, Piedmont 2971, Tiffany 3750, Weyerhaeuser 4052

Environment, single organization support

Recreational 3150

Environment, toxics

Alima 90, Aspen 260, Blue 496, Plum 2992, Stonyfield 3617

Environment, volunteer services

Aspen 260, Expedia 1311, Sony 3503

Environment, water resources

Abbott 13, ACE 24, Aflac 54, Alcoa 82, Allegis 92, Altria 120, Anheuser 202, Arch 230, Aspen 260, Avery 297, Bakewell 326, Beck 396, Black 475, Bon 521, Bragg 554, Bristol 577, Canon 672, Capital 678, Cargill 691, Catalina 719, Caterpillar 722, CF 755, CH2M 758, Chaney 761, Coca 862, Coca 863, Consumers 921, Darden 1032, Dollar 1142, Edison 1228, Flir 1440, Freeport 1494, General 1552, GenOn 1563, Google 1613, Grand 1629, Indus 1934, Industrial 1935, ITT 1999, Johnson 2049, Johnson 2050, Kerzner 2133, Laird 2211, Land 2217, Legg 2245, Lennar 2250, Matson 2404, Metropolitan 2484, Miller 2517, Miller 2523, Mississippi 2536, Mitsubishi 2539, Moka 2547, Mosaic 2580, Nalco 2613, New England 2670, Newburyport 2693, NIBCO 2707, Northeast 2737, OceanFirst 2782, One 2811, Orvis 2830, Pacific 2855, Pentair 2926, PepsiCo 2935, Pyles 3089, Quiksilver 3108, RBC 3136, Rockwell 3247, SeaWorld 3387, Select 3398, Sempra 3405, Shell 3430, Starbucks 3585, Tellabs 3709, Tiffany 3750, Toro 3775, Unilever 3853, United 3881, Visteon 3964, West 4037, Xcel 4135, Xylem 4139, YSI 4149

Environmental education

3M 3, Alliant 104, Ameren 129, American 141, Anheuser 202, Applied 220, Ariens 238, Aspen 260, Bayer 381, Berkshire 428, Berkshire 430, Black 475, Bridgestone 560, Brother 587, Cajun 652, Capstone 684, CF 755, Chaney 761, Chesapeake 778, Colonial 876, Compass 901, Consumers 921, Croft 985, Darden 1032, Dollar 1145, Dominion 1150, Dr 1169, DTE 1183, Earnhardt 1205, Ecolab 1220, Econscious 1223, Edison 1228, El Paso 1239, EQT 1287, Exelon 1309, Florida 1443, Freeport 1494, Fuller 1517, General 1555, Georgia 1568, Grace 1623, Green 1653, Honeywell 1852, HSBC 1876, ING 1938, Interface 1953, International 1968, Just 2077, Kinder 2153, Kingsbury 2160, Landmark 2218, Lowe's 2312, Lubrizol 2315, Magnolia 2340, Metropolitan 2484, Michigan 2496, Mitsubishi 2539, Motorola 2585, National 2630, New England 2670, Otter 2836, Pacific 2853, Pacific 2855, Panasonic 2869, PG&E 2952, Piedmont 2971, Plum 2991, PPG 3025, PPL 3026, Public 3076, Public 3077, Quiksilver 3108, Rayonier 3134, Red 3154, Royal 3273, Scotts 3372, SeaWorld 3387, Sempra 3405, Sharp 3422, SmartWool 3479, Stonyfield 3617, Subaru 3631, Sunshine 3653, Tellabs 3709, Toro 3775, Tucson 3819, Union 3854, Vectren 3925, Verizon 3936, Weyerhaeuser 4052, Wisconsin 4093, Wrigley 4125, Xcel 4135

Eye diseases

Alcon 83, Allergan 99, CIBA 810, LensCrafters 2251, Luxottica 2319

Eye research

Alcon 83, CIBA 810, Kepco 2132, Luxottica 2319

Family planning

Alsco 115, Berkshire 429, Edgar 1225, Fabri 1322, Henkels 1779, Merfish 2472, Omaha 2805, PACE 2851, Playboy 2990, Quad 3091

Family resources and services, disability

Alabama 71, Berry 437, Chicago 782, Cumberland 1003, Dell 1068, Dunkin' 1191, Holland 1834, National 2623, Philip 2962, Timberland 3754, TJX 3765

Family services

Abbott 13, Adir 36, Advance 39, AEGON 45, Albemarle 78, Allen 97, Allyis 109, Alpha 112, Amboy 124, American 132, American 145, American 153, American 165, AMERIGROUP 171, Ameristar 176, Ameritas 178, AmeriVision 180, AMR 187, Anaheim 191, Androscoggin 199, AptarGroup 221, ARAMARK 223, Arbeit 225, Arbella 226, Arent 235, Arkansas 240, Armstrong 246, Arrowpoint 251, Assurant 266, AutoNation 292, Avidia 298, Baker 318, Baker 321, Baltimore 333, Baltimore 335, Bank 340, Bank 349, Belleville 405, Ben 409, Bergquist 420, Big 460, BJ's 473, Black 474, Blockbuster 483, Blue 493, Blue 496, Blue 505, Bob's 511, Boston 540, Bragg 554, Brooks 585, Build 608, Burlington 616, Cajun 652, Capital 677, CarMax 694, Carmody 695, Cathay 723, CC 728, CentiMark 740, Chicago 790, Chick 791, Chotin 799, Churchill 807, Cic 811, Clear 842, CMS 854, Coach 858, Coca 861, Cole 868, Collette 872, Consumers 921, Cow 957, Cox 959, Cracker 966, Crane 970, Credit 980, Cumberland 1003, CUNA 1008, Curves 1011, CVS 1014, Davis 1041, Deerfield 1062, Dime 1118, Disney 1127, Dollar 1143, Dot 1158, DP 1168, DreamWorks 1172, du Pont 1184, East 1207, Eastern 1209, Eastern 1210, Eastman 1214, Eaton 1216, Edina 1227, Elias 1247, Emerson 1257, Emmis 1260, Endeavor 1267, Entergy 1279, Entergy 1280, Ergon 1289, ESCO 1296, Essa 1297, Express 1313, Family 1330, Federal 1348, Fidelity 1372, Fieldstone 1374, First 1399, First 1413, First 1416, Florsheim 1445, Fluor 1448, Ford 1463, Fortune 1474, Frankel 1483, Freeport 1494, GATX 1542, General 1551, General 1554, Globe 1594, Golden 1602, Gon 1608, Gregory 1662, Greif 1663, Grubb 1675, Hard 1727, Hawaiian 1755, HCA 1762, Health 1766, Heffernan 1769, Heidtman 1770, Heinz 1772, Henkels 1779, Henry 1781, Hensyn 1782, Herrick 1788, Herschend 1790, Highmark 1799, Honeywell 1852, Hood 1854, Houston 1871, Humana 1886, IHC 1913, Independent 1927, ING 1938, Institution 1946, Intelius 1951, International 1964, Island 1996, Jacksonville 2014, JM 2044, Johnson 2053, JPMorgan Chase 2071, Just 2077, Kaiser 2086, Kann 2090, KB 2105, KeyBank 2136, Kimball 2149, Kimberly 2150, King 2159, Kingsbury 2160, Liberty 2262, Liberty 2264, Liberty 2265, Longaberger 2299, Loomis 2301, Majestic 2343, Maverick 2409, MAXIMUS 2410, MB 2415, MBIA 2416, McCarthy 2421, MeadWestvaco 2445, MedImmune 2450, Merchants 2465, Merck 2466, Meredith 2471, Merrimack 2474, Metropolitan 2480, Miller 2523, Mohegan 2546, Monadnock 2551, Moore 2566, Morley 2572, Mountain 2589, Mutual 2607, Mylan 2610, Nash 2619, National 2623, National 2633, Nationwide 2639, New 2668, New England 2672, New York 2683, New York 2684, New York 2686, NII 2709, Nintendo 2712, Nordic 2722, Nordson 2723, Northern 2740, Northfield 2742, Northrim 2743, Northwest 2747, Northwestern 2749, Novetta 2755, Ohio 2791, ONEOK 2815, Orlando 2824, Otter 2836, Our 2838, P.E.L. 2849, Packard 2862, Padilla 2864, Park 2879, Pathmark 2894, Paychex 2904, Pentair 2926, People's 2928, Peoples 2931, PepsiCo 2935, PG&E 2952, Popular 3003, Portland 3010, Premier 3035, Presley 3038, Primerica 3045, Principal 3047, Prophet 3063, Prudential 3072, Putnam 3085, PVH 3088, Questar 3104, RBC 3136, RECO 3148, RESCO 3189, Rich 3204, RJN 3228, Robinson 3235, Rose 3261, Roundy's 3272, Royal 3273, Royal 3275, RUAN 3279, Sacramento 3304, Safeco 3306, Salt 3319, San Jose 3327, Save 3342, Savings 3343, Schloss 3352, Scientific 3367, Scripps 3374, SEAKR 3379, Selective 3399, Selig 3401, Sempra 3405, Sensient 3408, Shaughnessy 3425, ShopKo 3440, Sigma 3453, Smucker 3488, Spark 3533, Spurs 3557, SRA 3562, Stafast 3571, StanCorp 3574, Stardust 3586, Station 3593, Steel 3595, Superior 3658, Tanner 3688, Target 3691, Tastefully 3692, Textron 3731, Thomson 3742, TJX 3765, Toyota 3787, UBS 3842, Union 3858, United 3873, United 3876, Utica 3910, Valero 3915, Valmont 3919, Valspar 3920, ViewSonic 3952, Vodafone 3965, Wachtell 3973, Walter 3984, Washington 4001, WD-40 4011, Weaver 4014, Webster 4016, Wells 4028, Western 4042, Western 4044, Westport 4050, Weyerhaeuser 4052, Whirlpool 4056, Williams 4077, Wolverine 4106, Xerox 4136, Zappos.com 4153

Family services, adolescent parents

Biomet 466

Family services, home/homemaker aid

Cary 712

Family services, parent education

Blue 497, Boeing 516, CVS 1014, Liberty 2262, MBIA 2416, Portland 3010, Thrivent 3747, Verizon 3936, Wellmark 4026

Film/video

Blockbuster 483, Brooks 585, Creative 975, Discovery 1126, Disney 1127, General 1553, Getty 1569, JPMorgan Chase 2071, Land 2217, Lucasfilm 2316, Marnier-Lapostolle 2381, Omaha 2805, Playboy 2990, Ramerica 3125, Reader's 3141, Red 3152, Regal 3166, Time 3757

Financial services

Alliant 104, Blue 501, Citigroup 821, Fifth 1377, Financial 1382, Harris 1739, JPMorgan Chase 2071, Mariani 2374, Motley 2582, NV 2765, Pattillo 2896, Schwab 3363, State 3591, Strauss 3624, TCF 3695, Webster 4016, Western 4045

Folk arts

Portcullis 3004

Food banks

ABARTA 10, Abbott 13, ACE 24, Adobe 38, Aetna 48, Albemarle 78, Allegheny 91, Altria 120, Ameren 128, American 141, American 142, American 143, American 153, American 165, Ameristar 176, Amgen 182, AMPCO 186, Angels 200, Applied 219, Applied 220,

Armstrong 246, Arrowpoint 251, AutoZone 294, Bank 340, Bank 342, Bank 344, Bayer 381, BB&T 385, Bemis 407, Bergquist 420, Berkley 426, Berry 437, Boston 540, Bromelkamp 582, Butt 628, C & S 634, Cape 674, CentiMark 740, Chicago 786, Churchill 807, Citizens 827, Clark 835, ConAgra 904, Consumers 921, Cooper 935, Credit 980, Danis 1029, Darden 1032, Dayton 1047, Dean 1054, Deere 1061, Diebold 1112, Dollar 1144, Dominion 1150, DP 1168, Dr 1169, DTE 1183, Dunkin' 1191, Eastern 1209, Easthampton 1212, Ecolab 1220, Esurance 1298, Evening 1302, Faribault 1332, First 1400, First 1402, First 1419, FirstEnergy 1424, Food 1458, Ford 1464, Framingham 1481, Franklin 1485, Fremont 1497, GATX 1542, Genentech 1549, General 1554, General 1555, Giant 1571, Give 1583, Gleacher 1589, Golden 1602, Gould 1618, Green 1653, Griswold 1669, GROWMARK 1674, GuideOne 1687, Haggen 1699, Hannaford 1723, Hanson 1725, Harris 1738, Hasbro 1747, Haviland 1752, Heffernan 1769, Heinz 1772, Hillshire 1809, Hilton 1812, Hoffman 1822, Hoffmann 1823, Hood 1854, Horix 1860, Hormel 1866, Huntington 1894, IDACORP 1907, Illinois 1916, Ingles 1940, Intermec 1955, International 1967, Jones 2055, Journal 2068, Kaiser 2086, Kellogg 2120, Kemp 2123, KeyBank 2136, King 2158, Kroger 2195, Lam 2214, Land 2217, Landmark 2218, Lapham 2223, Liberty 2262, Liberty 2265, Lincoln 2280, Lincoln 2281, Lockheed 2292, Loews 2296, Louisiana 2310, Macy's 2333, Mal 2349, Manitowoc 2355, Marcus 2370, Marsh 2387, Martin 2391, Mascoma 2394, Maverick 2409, Mazda 2414, MBIA 2416, McCormick 2423, Meijer 2456, Merck 2466, Metropolitan 2481, Meyer 2485, Miller 2523, Mondelez 2556, Morgan 2570, MTD 2595, Mutual 2603, Nash 2619, Nationwide 2639, Nestle 2663, New York 2684, Norfolk 2725, NRG 2756, NRT 2757, OceanFirst 2782, OMNOVA 2809, Omron 2810, OneBeacon 2813, Oracle 2821, Oshkosh 2833, Panera 2873, Pathmark 2894, People's 2928, PepsiCo 2935, Perforce 2937, Performance 2938, Plum 2991, Power 3020, Protective 3066, Provident 3069, Public 3076, Quad 3091, QuikTrip 3109, Rackspace 3117, Reader's 3141, RECO 3148, Regal 3166, Regence 3169, Robinson 3235, Roundy's 3272, Safeway 3310, ServiceMaster 3414, Seventh 3416, ShopKo 3440, Shugart 3442, Sit 3466, Smucker 3488, Sodexho 3497, Sovereign 3528, St. Louis 3569, Stardust 3586, Stop 3618, Sunwest 3655, Taco 3679, TD 3696, TeleTech 3708, Tennant 3714, Textron 3731, Tops 3774, Turner 3824, U.S. 3838, Unilever 3853, Union 3858, United 3864, United 3873, United 3880, United 3881, V.F. 3913, Valassis 3914, Valero 3915, Virginia 3959, Wachtell 3973, Wakefern 3979, Wal-Mart 3980, Warren 3993, Washington 3994, Washington 3998, Washington 4000, Wegmans 4021, Weis 4024, Weyerhaeuser 4052, White 4062, Whiting 4063, Whole 4066, Winn 4087, Woodforest 4110, Woodward 4112, WorkflowOne 4115, Yum! 4150

Food distribution, groceries on wheels

Wegmans 4021

Food distribution, meals on wheels

Acuity 32, American 143, Armstrong 246, Avis 300, BancTrust 337, Caesars 650, CentiMark 740, CNO 857, Dana 1026, DTE 1183, First 1419, Food 1458, Franklin 1485, Gleacher 1589, Inman 1943, Lockheed 2292, Merck 2466, Meyer 2485, Milliken 2525, Old 2796, Patton's 2899, Puck 3080, Shugart 3442, Smith 3485, Tesoro 3723, Union 3858, Valassis 3914, Wal-Mart 3980, Walter 3984, Whitley 4064

Food services

Abbott 13, ACE 24, Adobe 38, Aetna 48, Albertsons 79, Allegheny 91, Allete 100, Allianz 105, Almar 110, Alpha 112, Altria 120, American 141, American 143, American 144, American 145, American 146, Ameriprise 174, Ameristar 176, Andrews 198, Apex 213, Apogee 215, Applied 220, Arbella 226, Archer 233, Armstrong 246, Assurant 266, Assurant 268, Baker 324, Bank 340, Bank 342, Bank 347, Bemis 407, Bergquist 420, Beverage 452, Big 460, Big 461, Birdsong 470, BJ's 473, Bloomingdale's 488, Blue 497, Blue 501, Blue 504, Booz 525, BorgWarner 528, Boston 536, Brooks 585, Buccaneer 599, Butt 628, Butzel 629, C & S 634, Caesars 650, California 655, Calvert 663, Campbell 669, Cargill 691, Carmody 695, Cary 712, Catalina 719, Cathay 723, CenterPoint 738, CentiMark 740, Choice 798, Churchill 807, Circle 817, Cisco 818, CLARCOR 832, Clark 835, Clif 848, Coastal 859, Cole 868, Collette 872, Colonial 875, ConAgra 904, Consumers 921, Credit 980, Darden 1032, Dean 1054, Deere 1061, Del 1065, Delaware 1066, Dell 1068, Deluxe 1084, DeniseLawrence.Com 1086, Detroit 1095, Dime 1118, Dimeo 1119, Discovery 1126, Dominion 1150, Dow 1162, DP 1168, DRW 1181, Duane 1186, Dunkin' 1191, East 1207, Ecolab 1220, Econscious 1223, Edelman 1224, Elias 1247, Endres 1269, Evans 1300, Family 1330, Faribault 1332, Ferrellgas 1365, First 1398, First 1399, First 1409, Fluor 1448, Food 1458, Ford 1464, GATX 1542, Genentech 1549, General 1554, General 1555, Genworth 1565, Giant 1572, Giant 1573, Golden 1602, Grace 1623, Hanover 1724, Hard 1727, Harris 1736, Hasbro 1747, Hastings 1749, Havana 1751, HCA 1762, Heffernan 1769, Highwoods 1800, Hillshire 1809, Hilton 1812, Hooters 1858, Hormel 1866, Hudson 1880, Huntington 1894, Hy-Vee 1900, Imation 1919, Ingersoll 1939, Inman 1943, Institution 1946, Intermec 1955, International 1958, International 1968, Johnson 2048, Jones 2059, JPMorgan Chase 2071, Juno 2076, Kaiser 2086, Kellogg 2120, KeyBank 2136, King 2158, King 2159, Kroger 2195, Land 2217, Law 2233, Lear 2237, Lee 2240, Liberty 2262, Life 2269, Lincoln 2281, Loews 2296, Longaberger 2299, Macy's 2333, Manocherian 2357, Mars 2384, Marsh 2387, Masco 2393, Mascoma 2394, Maverick 2409, Merck 2466, Meyer 2485, Michael 2493, Miller 2517, Miller 2523, Mondelez 2556, Monsanto 2559, Moody's 2563, Morgan 2570, Mosaic 2580, MSC 2593, Mutual 2607, Nash 2619, National 2623, National 2638, Nationwide 2639, Nestle 2663, Neville 2667, New England 2670, New Jersey 2676, New York 2683, New York 2691, NII 2709, Nintendo 2712, Northern 2740, Northfield 2742, Novell 2754, NRG 2756, NYSE 2769, OMNOVA 2809, Orlando 2824, Ortec 2828, Oshkosh 2833, Otis 2835, Park 2879, Pawtucket 2902, Paychex 2904, PDB 2906, PepsiCo 2935, Perdue 2936, Performance 2938, Philip 2962, Pioneer 2980, Pizza 2988, Portland 3010, Power 3020, Prophet 3063, Provident 3069, Public 3076, Publix 3079, Pukall 3082, Quad 3091, Quaker 3094, Raley's 3122, RBC 3136, Reader's 3141, Reiff 3174, Rennoc 3184, Republic 3188, Retail 3194, Rexnord 3198, Reynolds 3199, Rich 3204, RJN 3228, Robinson 3235, Rock 3238, Rosen's 3264, Roundy's 3272, Safeco 3306, Salt 3319, San Diego 3322, Save 3342, Schwan 3365, Seagate 3377, Sealed 3381, Security 3391, Sensient 3408, Shaw's 3427, Sit 3466, Smith 3485, Smithfield 3487, Sodexho 3497, Sonoco 3500, Sony 3503, Spansion 3532, Spartan 3535, StanCorp 3574, Stop 3618, Sunwest 3655, SUPERVALU 3659, Sweetbay 3665, Sysco 3677, Taco 3679, Target 3691, Tastefully 3692, TeleTech 3708, Textron 3731, Timberland 3754, TJX 3765, Tops 3774, Tripifoods 3811, Tyson 3832, U-Haul 3833, U.S. 3838, UncommonGoods 3849, Unilever 3853, Union 3858, United 3860, United 3864, United 3872, United 3880, Universal 3891, Unum 3898, USEC 3904, Visa 3960, Wakefern 3979, Wal-Mart 3980, Washington 4000, Wawa 4009, Wegmans 4021, Weis 4024, Wellmark 4026, White 4062, Whole 4066, Winn 4087, Woodward 4112, Woodward-Graff 4113, Yum! 4150

Food services, commodity distribution

Anadarko 190, Cumberland 1003, FirstEnergy 1424

Food services, congregate meals

ConAgra 904

Foreign policy

First 1422, Lamont 2215, Mine 2529, Zilkha 4156

Foster care

Bank 342, BB&T 385, Bristlecone 575, Caparo 673, Chapman 763, Federal 1348, Fieldstone 1374, Florence 1441, Greater 1649, Guess 1685, Hewlett 1794, JM 2044, Pioneer 2981, Portland 3010, Station 3593, V.F. 3913, Wendy's/Arby's 4030, Western 4041

Foundations (community)

1st 2, Acuity 32, AK 67, Allete 100, American 137, American 143, Ash 256, Baker 318, Baltimore 334, BancTrust 337, Barton 366, BB&T 385, Better 447, Bowles 544, Bridgewater 561, Burns 620, Capital 677, Capitol 680, Central 745, Chandler 760, Chaney 761, Chotin 799, Concept 905, Consumers 921, Corning 945, Cousins 953, Cutco 1012, DeBruce 1057, Delta 1073, Dollar 1142, Dow 1162, eBay 1217, Farm 1333, First 1404, General 1555, GKN 1585, Graham 1625, Green 1651, Haynie 1760, Heidtman 1770, Hulman 1885, Interstate 1975, Jasper 2026, Johnson 2052, Keithley 2115, Kellogg 2120, Lee 2240, Legg 2245, LifePoint 2270, M/I 2325, Mayer 2412, McLaughlin 2436, MGM 2489, Midwestone 2508, Miller 2517, Minto 2533, Mortgage 2578, N.E.W. 2611, New England 2672, ONEOK 2815, Oshkosh 2833, Park 2880, Park 2881, Portcullis 3004, Property 3062, Reily 3177, RUAN 3279, sanofi-aventis 3329, SourceMedia 3506, Stardust 3586, State 3590, Stewart 3604, Tennessee 3716, Trane 3794, United 3874, Westport 4050, Wolf 4103, Wood 4108

Foundations (corporate)

SunTrust 3654

Foundations (private grantmaking)

Dart 1033, Vista 3962

Foundations (public)

CIGNA 812, Minto 2533, Ruder 3282, Spangler 3531

Fraternal societies (501(c)(8))

Gleaner 1590

Freedom from violence/torture

Working 4116

Gay men

Allstate 107, Autodesk 289

Genealogy

Packard 2862

Genetic diseases and disorders

AMERIGROUP 171, Amerisure 177, Arbella 226, Baker 318, Bon 521, CEMEX 734, Centene 735, CIGNA 812, First 1408, General 1556, Griswold 1669, Hannaford 1723, Hooters 1858, Hubbard 1878, International 1962, Jacobs 2016, LifePoint 2270, PerkinElmer 2939, TJX 3765, Washington 4000

Geology

Freeport 1494, Olin 2801, Pyles 3089, Rapoca 3127, Tiffany 3750

Geriatrics

Omnicare 2807, Principal 3047

Girl scouts

Alcatel 81, Alcoa 82, Berkheimer 425, Berry 437, Booz 525, Bridgestone 560, Center 737, Central 742, Chief 793, Coca 862, Dayton 1047, Delmarva 1069, Dollar 1144, Fabri 1322, Government 1621, Graybar 1640, International 1959, Kenneth 2128, Marsh 2387, Milwaukee 2528, Mutual 2605, Parker 2886, Perrigo 2943, Plum 2991, Sprint 3556, Swift 3666, Tennessee 3716, United 3872, Valero 3915, Walker 3982

Girls

Abbott 13, Alcoa 82, Autodesk 289, Beneficial 412, Chrysler 801, Cisco 818, Clorox 852, Exxon 1315, Fisher 1433, Freeport 1494, GenCorp 1548, General 1552, Guardian 1683, Hyundai 1902, Johnson 2048, Mary 2392, Mattel 2405, Melissa 2458, Metropolitan 2481, Miami 2491, Motorola 2586, NIKE 2710, PG&E 2952, Simpson 3461, St. Joe 3563, Symantec 3669, Tastefully 3692, Tupperware 3821, WD-40 4011

Girls clubs

Bay 378, Beall's 389, California 655, Circle 817, Citizens 824, Dr 1169, Greater 1649, Home 1844, ING 1938, Liberty 2264, Malco 2350, Miller 2523, National 2623, Oracle 2821, People's 2928, Simpson 3461, Trail 3793, Zappos.com 4153

Goodwill Industries

Dispatch 1129, Dondlinger 1154, Fabri 1322, First 1389, MTD 2595, United 3869, US 3902, Wagner 3976, Wal-Mart 3980, Wisconsin 4093

Government/public administration

Amsted 188, Berkshire 430, Blair 478, Boeing 516, Brillion 569, Chicago 789, Crane 969, Farmers' 1337, Florida 1443, Garelick 1537, Handy 1718, Jacobs 2016, Joy 2070, La-Z-Boy 2205, Pieper 2972, Red 3153, Tindall 3761

Graduate/professional education

Cook 934, Genentech 1549, Intel 1950, Interpublic 1974, National 2630, PMI 2995, Sempra 3405, Wiley 4072

Gun control

United 3881

Health care

3M 3, A.D. 7, ABARTA 10, Abbott 13, Abercrombie 17, Aberdeen 18, ACE 24, Acme 28, Admiral 37, Advance 39, AEGON 45, Aetna 48, Affinity 52, Aflac 54, Ahern 60, Air 63, AK 67, Alabama 71, Alaska 74, Albemarle 78, Albertsons 79, Alexander 85, Alexion 86, Alfa 87, Allegheny 91, Allen 95, Allen 98, Allergan 99, Allete 100, Alliant 104, Allianz 105, Alpha 112, Alro 113, Alsan 114, Amboy 124, Ameren 128, America's 130, American 137, American 141, American 143, American 144, American 145, American 151, American 153, American 155, American 156, American 165, AMERIGROUP 171, AmerisourceBergen 175, Ameristar 176, Amerisure 177, Ameritas 178, Amgen 182, Amica 183, AMN Healthcare 184, AMR 187, Amsted 188, Amway 189, Anadarko 190, Anaheim 191, Andersen 194, Andretti 197, Angels 200, ANH 201, Anocoil 204, Apache 211, Apex 212, Apex 214, AptarGroup 221, Aramco 224, Arbeit 225, Arcelormittal 229, Arizona 239, Arkansas 240, Armstrong 246, Arnold 248, Arrow 249, Arrowhead 250, Ascena 255, Assurant 266, Assurant 267, Assurant 268, Assurity 269, AstraZeneca 272, AT&T 273, Athletics 276, Atlanta 279, Atlantic 282, Atlantic 283, Audubon 286, Austin 288, Autodesk 289, Avelina 296, Avis 299, AVX 306, AZPB 310, Badger 313, Baird 317, Baker 324, Baker 325, Baltimore 332, Baltimore 334, Bangor 338, Bank 339, Bank 340, Bank 341, Bank 342, Bank 343, Bank 344, Bank 346, Bank 347, Banner 352, Bard 358, Barnes 362, Barrasso 363, Bartlett 365, Barton 366, BASF 368, Batson 373, Batts 374, Baxter 377, Bay 378, Bay 380, Bayer 382, BB&T 385, Beam 390, Bean 392, Bear 393, Beaver 394, Beckman 397, Becton 398, Belk 403, Belk 404, Bemis 407, Bentley 416, Bergquist 420, Bergstrom 421, Bernhardt 432, Berry 434, Berry 436, Beverage 453, BHP 455, Bickel 457, Bierlein 459, Bionetics 467, Birmingham 471, BJ's 473, Blair 478, Block 481, Block 482, Bloomberg 486, Blue 490, Blue 491, Blue 492, Blue 493, Blue 494, Blue 495, Blue 496, Blue 497, Blue 498, Blue 499, Blue 500, Blue 501, Blue 502, Blue 503, Blue 504, Blue 505, BlueCross 507, Bob's 511, Bobcats 512, Boehringer 515, Boeing 516, Boler 520, Bon 521, Borden 527, BorgWarner 528, BOSE 530, Boston 538, Boston 539, Boston 540, Bowater 543, Bracewell 549, Bricker 559, Bridgestone 560, Bridgewater 562, Bridgeway 563, Briggs 565, Brightpoint 567, Brillion 569, Brink's 571, Brinker 572, Bristol 577, Bristol 578, Broadcom 579, Brown 591, Bruno 594, Brunswick 595, BSA 597, Bubalo 598, Buccaneer 599, Buckeye 601, Build 608, Building 610, Buist 611, Burlington 618, Butler 626, Butt 628, Byers 630, C & C 632, C & S 634, C Spire 636, CA 638, Cable 639, Cabot 642, Caesars 650, Cajun 652, California 655, California 656, Callaway 660, Calumet 662, Calvert 663, Cambia 665, Cambridge 666, Cameron 667, Campbell 669, Cape 674, Capital 676, Capital 677, Capitol 680, Capri 682, Cardinal 685, CareFirst 687, CareFusion 688, Caremore 689, Cargill 691, Carter's 708, Caruso 709, Cary 712, Cascade 713, Catalina 719, Caterpillar 722, Centene 735, CenterPoint 738, CentiMark 740, Cephalon 752, Cerner 754, Chaney 761, Chapman 763, Charter 766, Chartis 768, Chelsea 772, Chemtura 775, Chesapeake 777, Cheviot 779, Chevron 780, Chief 793, Chotin 799, Chubb 804, CIBA 809, Cic 811, CIGNA 812, Cincinnati 814, Cisco 818, CITGO 820, Citizens 824, Citizens 828, Claremont 833, Clear 842, Clemens 844, Cleveland 846, Cliffs 850, Clinton 851, CME 853, CNA 855, Coach 858, Coastal 859, COLHOC 870, Collective 871, Collette 872, Colonial 874, Colonial 875, Columbia 882, Comerica 889, Commerce 890, Commercial 893, Communications 896, Community 900, Compass 901, Compuware 902, Con 903, Conditioned 906, ConocoPhillips 913, Continental 924, Contran 928, ConvaTec 932, Cooper 935, Cooper 936, COPIC 937, Copley 938, Coquille 939, Cornerstone 943, Cornerstone 944, Corvallis 947, Costco 948, Cousins 953, Covance 955, Covidien 956, Cox 959, Coyotes 963, Crane 969, Crane 970, Crayola 973, Creative 975, Credit 979, Crescent 981, Croft 985, CSS 996, Cullen 1000, Cumberland 1003, CUNA 1008, Curves 1011, CVS 1014, Cymer 1016, Daffy's 1019, Dallas 1021, Damar 1024, Danaher 1027, Danforth 1028, Dannon 1030, Davey 1035, Dayton 1047, Dealer 1052, DeBlois 1056, Dedham 1060, Deerfield 1062, Dell Corning 1067, Delmarva 1069, Delta 1073, Delta 1083, Demoulas 1085, DENTSPLY 1089, Denver 1090, Detroit 1094, Detroit 1095, Deutsch 1098, Devon 1102, Dharma 1105, Diageo 1107, Diagnos-Techs 1108, Diamonds 1109, Diemolding 1113, Dietz 1114, Dilbeck 1116, Dime 1118, Disney 1127, Dispatch 1129, Doctor's 1138, Doctors 1139, Dollar 1143, Dolphins 1147, Dominion 1150, Dot 1158, Dow 1162, Dowling 1165, Drive 1177, DRS 1179, drugstore.com 1180, DRW 1181, du Pont 1184, Duane 1186, Dunkin' 1191, Dunn 1192, Dutch 1197, DVK 1198, East 1207, Eastern 1209, Easthampton 1212, Eastman 1213, Eastman 1214, Eaton 1216, Ecolab 1220, Edelman 1224, Edgar 1225, Edina 1227, El Paso 1239, EMC 1253, Emerson 1257, Emmis 1260, Empire 1262, Employers 1264, Enbridge 1265, Endo 1268, Energen 1270, Energy 1272, Ergon 1289, Essa 1297, Esurance 1298, Ethicon 1299, Evans 1300, Evening 1302, Exchange 1306, Exelon 1309, Express 1313, Exxon 1315, F.N.B. 1318, Fairfax 1325, Fairfield 1326, Fallon 1329, Farmers 1335, Ferguson 1363, Ferro 1366, Fetzer 1367, Fibre 1369, Fidelity 1371, Fifth 1377, First 1391, First 1396, First 1397, First 1398, First 1399, First 1400, First 1403, First 1405, First 1406, First 1409, First 1415, First 1418, First 1419, First 1420, FirstEnergy 1424, Firstmerit 1425, Fiserv 1427, Fishel 1429, Fisher 1431, Fisher 1433, Flextronics 1437, Flir 1440, Florida 1442, Florida 1443, Florida 1444, FMR 1450, Food 1457, Food 1458, Football 1460, Ford 1463, Forest 1468, Fort 1472, Fortis 1473, Four 1477, Framingham 1481, Frankel 1483, Freedman 1493, Freeport 1494, Freescale 1495, Fremont 1496, Freres 1498, Fresh 1499, Fru 1513, Fuller 1517, Fulton 1518, Furniture 1519, G & R 1523, Gable 1525, Gallagher 1528, Gannett 1532, Garelick 1537, Gateway 1541, GATX 1542, Genentech 1549, General 1552, General 1555, Genesco 1559, Geneseo 1560, GenOn 1563, GenRad 1564, Genworth 1565, Genzyme 1566, Georgia 1567, Giant 1572, Gibbs 1576, Gibson 1578, Gilbane 1581, Gilead 1582, Give 1583, GKN 1585, GlaxoSmithKline 1588, Go 1595, Gold 1598, Golden 1602, Golub 1607, Goodyear 1612, Government 1621, Grace 1623, Grand 1627, Grand 1628, Grange 1631, Graphic 1634, Great 1642, Great 1644, Greater 1648, Green 1651, Gregory 1661, Greif 1663, Grinnell 1668, Griswold 1669, Grove 1672, GROWMARK 1674, Guaranty 1679, Guard 1680, Guess 1685, Gulf 1688, Gulf 1689, H & R 1695, Hackstock 1697, Halliburton 1706, Hancock 1717, Handy 1718, Hannaford 1723, Hanover 1724, Harden 1728, Hardinge 1729, Harley 1732, Harnish 1734, Harris 1736, Harsco 1741, Hartford 1743, Hartzell 1745, Hasbro 1747, Hastings 1749, Hawaii 1754, Hawkins 1757, Haynie 1760, HCA 1762, HCR 1763, Health 1766, Heidtman 1770, Heinz 1772, Helmerich 1774, Hendrick 1776, Herr 1787, Hershey 1791, Hess 1793, Hewlett 1794, Highmark 1799, Hilfiger 1801, Hilliard 1805, Hilliard 1806, Hillside 1810, HNI 1817, Hodgson 1820, Hoffer 1821, Hoffmann 1823, Hofmann 1824, Holder 1829, Holiday 1832, Homasote 1841, Home 1843, Home 1844, Home 1845, Hood 1854, Hooters 1858, Horizon 1861, Horizon 1862, Horizon 1863, Hospira 1867, Houston 1871, Hubbard 1877, Hubbard 1878, Hudson 1880, Huhtamaki 1884, Humana 1886, Huntington 1894, Hutchison 1898, Hutton 1899, Hy-Vee 1900, IAC 1903, Iberdrola 1904, ICON 1906, IDACORP 1907, IDT 1910, IHC 1913, Ilitch 1915, Illinois 1916, IMA 1917, Impact 1921, Imperial 1922, IMS 1924, Independent 1927, ING 1938, Inman 1943, Insperity 1944, Institution 1946, Integra 1947, Intelius 1951, Interlock 1954, Intermountain 1957, International 1958, International 1960, International 1962, International 1964, International 1966, International Profit 1969, Intertech 1976, Intuit 1982, Investors 1984, Inwood 1985, Island 1996, Issa 1997, Jack 2007, Jackson 2010, Jaclyn 2015, Jacobs 2016, Jasper 2025, Jasper 2026, Jeld 2032, Jesco 2040, JetBlue 2041, Jewett 2042, Johns 2047, Johnson 2048, Johnson 2049, Johnson 2050, Jones 2055, Jones 2056, Jordan 2063, Journal 2068, Joy 2070, Just 2077, Kahn 2084, Kahn 2085, Kaiser 2086, Kann 2090, Kansas 2094, Kasle 2098, Katten 2101, KBR 2106, Keeneland 2113, Kellogg 2120, Kellwood 2121, Kelly 2122, Kemp 2123, Kennecott 2127, Kepco 2132, Key 2135, KeyBank 2136, Kimball 2149, Kimberly 2150, Kindred 2154, Kinetic 2156, Kingsbury 2160, Kinney 2162, KLA-Tencor 2165, Klein 2166, Klein's 2169, Kmart 2172, KOA 2178, Koch 2179, Koch 2180, Kohl's 2181, Korum 2187, Krasdale 2192, Kroger 2195, Kukui 2198, Kuskokwim 2200, L'Oreal 2203, La-Z-Boy 2205, Laclede 2207, Lands' 2220, Lapham 2223, Las Vegas 2225, Lauder 2230, Laureate 2231, Lauth 2232, Legg 2245, LG&E Energy 2260, Liberty 2262, Liberty 2265, Life 2268, Life 2269, LifePoint 2270, Lilly 2274, Limited 2277, Lincoln 2282, Lithia 2287, Lockheed 2292, Lockwood 2293, Longaberger 2299, Loomis 2301, Lord 2302, Lord 2303, Louisiana 2309, M&T 2323, M.D.C. 2324, M/I 2325, Machias 2332, Macy's 2333, Madison 2334, Madison 2335, Magyar 2341, Majestic 2343, Majestic 2344, Major 2347, Mal 2349, Manhattan 2354, Manitowoc 2356, Marathon 2365, Mariani 2374, Maritz 2376, Mark 2377, MarkleBank 2379, Marr 2382, Mars 2384, Marsh 2385, Marsh 2386, Marsh 2387, Mary 2392, Mascoma 2394, Mattel 2405, Mautz 2408, Maverick

2409, MB 2415, MBIA 2416, McCormick 2423, McDonald 2426, McDonald's 2427, McGraw 2429, McKinstry 2435, McWane 2440, MDU 2441, Mechanics 2446, Medeanalytics 2447, Medical 2448, MedImmune 2450, Medrad 2452, Medtronic 2453, Menasha 2461, Mentor 2462, Mercedes 2463, Merck 2466, Mercury 2468, Mercury 2470, Meritor 2473, Merrimack 2474, Metropolitan 2480, Metropolitan 2481, MGIC 2488, MH 2490, Michael 2493, Michelin 2495, Michigan 2497, Mid-Atlantic 2502, Midcontinent 2505, Miller 2517, Miller 2518, Milliken 2525, Mine 2529, Minnesota 2531, Mississippi 2536, Modine 2544, Mohawk 2545, Monarch 2554, Mondelez 2556, Moody's 2563, Moore 2565, Moore 2566, Morgan 2570, Morley 2572, Motor 2583, Motorists 2584, Motorola 2585, Mrs. Fields 2592, MSC 2593, MTD 2595, Mutual 2605, Mutual 2606, Mylan 2610, N.E.W. 2611, Namaste 2614, National 2623, National 2626, National 2629, National 2631, National 2633, National 2634, National 2635, National 2636, National 2637, Nationwide 2639, Naugatuck 2645, NBC 2649, NCR 2650, Neace 2651, Nektar 2658, Nestle 2663, New 2668, New England 2672, New York 2683, New York 2684, New York 2686, New York 2687, Newfield 2695, Newmont 2698, Newport 2699, Newtown 2704, Nexion 2705, NIKE 2710, Nordstrom 2724, Norfolk 2725, Nortex 2727, North 2728, North 2730, North 2735, Northern 2740, Northfield 2741, Northfield 2742, Northrop 2744, Northwestern 2749, NTELOS 2758, Nu 2759, NV 2765, NYSE 2769, OceanFirst 2782, Odyssey 2784, Ohio 2789, Ohio 2791, Ohio 2792, Old 2798, Ole 2800, Olin 2801, Omaha 2806, Omnicare 2807, OMNOVA 2809, Omron 2810, ONEOK 2815, Optima 2819, Oracle 2821, OrePac 2823, Orscheln 2827, Oshkosh 2833, Otis 2835, Otter 2836, Owens 2841, Owens 2844, Oxford 2847, P.E.L. 2849, Pacers 2852, Pacific 2855, Pacifico 2859, PacifiCorp 2860, Palace 2866, Palm 2867, Pan-American 2868, Panda 2871, Park 2880, Park 2881, Parker 2886, Parsons 2887, Partnership 2890, PDB 2906, Peabody 2907, Penn 2923, Penney 2925, People's 2928, Peoples 2931, PepsiCo 2935, Perforce 2937, PerkinElmer 2939, Perrigo 2943, Pfizer 2950, PGA 2954, Pharmacy 2956, Philadelphia 2957, Philadelphia 2961, Philip 2962, Phoenix 2968, Piedmont 2971, Pieper 2972, Pioneer 2979, Pioneer 2980, Piper 2983, Pitney 2984, Plum 2991, PMI 2995, PNC 2997, Portland 3010, Potomac 3018, Powers 3024, PPL 3026, Praxair 3029, Preferred 3031, Premier 3035, Premix 3037, Price 3039, Primerica 3045, Principal 3047, Printpack 3049, ProtechSoft 3065, Protective 3066, Protector 3067, Provident 3069, Provident 3070, Publix 3079, Pukall 3082, Pulte 3083, Pura 3084, Putnam 3086, PVH 3088, Quad 3091, Quaker 3093, QUALCOMM 3095, Quality 3098, Quandel 3099, Quest 3103, Questar 3104, Quiksilver 3108, R & R 3114, Raley's 3122, Rasmussen 3128, Ratio 3129, Ray 3131, Rayonier 3134, RBC 3136, RBS 3138, RCM 3139, RE/MAX 3140, Reader's 3141, Reckitt 3146, Redwoods 3158, Reell 3164, Regal 3166, Regions 3171, Reid 3173, Reiff 3174, Reily 3177, Rennoc 3184, RESCO 3189, ResMed 3192, Retail 3194, Rewold 3196, Reynolds 3199, RG 3201, RGI 3202, Riceland 3203, Rich 3204, Richards 3206, Rieke 3212, Rite 3220, RITE 3221, Roberts 3231, Robins 3232, Robinson 3235, Rockland 3242, Rockville 3245, Rockwell 3246, Rodman 3251, Rolls 3254, Rood 3257, Rose 3261, Rose 3262, Royal 3275, Royalnest 3277, RPM 3278, RUAN 3279, Rudolph 3283, Rue 3285, Rug 3286, Ryder 3292, S & S 3296, S & T 3297, S.J. 3299, Sacramento 3303, Safeco 3306, Safeway 3310, Saint 3312, Saks 3315, Salem 3317, Salt 3319, Samsung 3320, San Francisco 3324, San Francisco 3326, San Jose 3327, sanofi-aventis 3329, Sartori 3335, Sasol 3338, Saucony 3340, Save 3342, Savings 3343, Savings 3344, Schein 3348, Schenuit 3349, Schiffenhaus 3351, Schloss 3352, Schneider 3355, Scientific 3367, Scott 3370, Scotts 3372, Seaboard 3375, Seagate 3377, Seamen's 3383, Securant 3388, Securian 3389, Security 3394, Select 3398, Selective 3399, Seligman 3402, Sempra 3405, Sensient 3408, Seton 3415, Seventh 3416, Shakopee 3419, Shaughnessy 3425, Shaw's 3427, Shenandoah 3433, Sherwin 3437, ShopKo 3440, Shugart 3442, SI 3444, Siemens 3448, Sierra 3451, Sigma 3453, Sikorsky 3454, Silicon 3455, Simplot 3459, Siw 3468, Sjostrom 3469, Skinner 3475, Slant 3477, Smith 3482, Smith 3484, Smucker 3488, Snow 3491, Sonoco 3500, South 3509, South 3512, Southeastern 3513, Southern 3514, Southern 3516, Southern 3517, Southern 3521, Southwest 3524, Sovereign 3528, Spahn 3529, Spang 3530, Spansion 3532, Spartan 3535, SpectraCare 3541, Spence 3542, Spirit 3544, Sports 3550, SPX 3558, SQA 3559, Square 3560, SRA 3562, St. Joe 3563, St. Jude 3566, St. Louis 3567, St. Louis 3569, StanCorp 3574, Standard 3575, Standard 3576, Stanley 3579, Starbucks 3585, State 3592, Steelcase 3597, Stephens 3598, STERIS 3600, Stewart 3604, Stock 3610, Stone 3614, Stop 3618, Strauss 3624, Stride 3625, Stupp 3628, Subaru 3632, Sullivan 3635, SunTrust 3654, Sunwest 3655, Super 3656, Superior 3658, SUPERVALU 3659, Sweetbay 3665, Swift 3667, Swinerton 3668, Synovus 3674, Systel 3678, Talbots 3682, Tanner 3688, Tap 3689, TD 3696, Teachers 3697, Teichert 3704, Teleflex 3707, Tellabs 3709, Telligen 3710, Temple 3711, Tenet 3713, Tenneco 3715, Tension 3717, Terex 3719, Terlato 3720, Texas 3725, Texas 3728, Textron 3731, Third 3735, Thomaston 3736, Thomasville 3737, Thrivent 3747, Tiffany 3750, Tillman 3752, Titan 3763, TJX 3765, Toeniskoetter 3767, Tops 3774, Toro 3775, Total 3778, Totem 3779, Towerbrook 3781, Toyota 3784, Toyota 3785, Toyota 3786, Toyota 3787, Toyota 3789, Toys 3790, Tractor 3791, Transammonia 3796, Trends 3804, Tri 3805, Trim 3810, Triumph 3812, True 3814, Truland 3817, Trustmark 3818, Tulalip 3820, Turner 3824, U.M. 3834, U.S. 3836, UncommonGoods 3849, Union 3854, Union 3856, Union 3857, Union 3858, Unisys 3859, United 3860, United 3863, United 3864, United 3866, United 3873, United 3877, United 3882, UnitedHealth 3884, Universal 3891, Universal 3895, Unum 3898, Updike 3899, Upper 3900, US 3902, USG 3905, UTC 3908, Utica 3910, V.F. 3913, Valassis 3914, Valero 3915, Valley 3917, Valmont 3919, Valspar 3920, Vaughan 3924, Vectren 3925, Verizon 3936, Vestcor 3943, VHA 3944, Victaulic 3948, Victorinox 3950, Vilter 3956, Virginia 3959, Visteon 3964, Vodafone 3965, Volvo 3968, Vulcan 3970, Waffle 3975, Wakefern 3979, Wal-Mart 3980, Walgreen 3981, Wallace 3983, Walter 3984, Warburg 3985, Washington 3994, Washington 3995, Washington 3996, Washington 3997, Washington 4000, Washington 4001, Waters 4003, WaterStone 4005, Watson 4006, Watson 4007, Wausau 4008, Wawa 4009, WD-40 4011, Weaver 4015, Webster 4018, WEDGE 4020, Weis 4024, Wellmark 4026, WellPoint 4027, Wells 4028, West 4038, Western 4040, Western 4041, Western 4042, Western 4043, Western 4044, Western 4045, Whitaker 4057, Whiting 4063, Whitney 4065, Wilbur 4070, Williams 4077, Winn 4087, Wisconsin 4092, Wisconsin 4096, Wishart 4097, Wolff 4105, Wood 4108, Woodforest 4110, Woodward 4112, Working 4116, World 4120, Worthington 4124, Wrigley 4125, Wurster 4128, Xilinx 4137, Xylem 4139, YGS 4143, Young 4147, Young 4148, Zatkoff 4154, Zimmer 4157, Zions 4158

Health care, alliance/advocacy

Blue 493

Health care, association

Allergan 99, Aviva 302, Boston 540, Diagnos-Techs 1108, GlaxoSmithKline 1588, LifeScan 2271, WEDGE 4020

Health care, blood supply

Advance 39, American 145, Angels 200, AutoZone 294, Badger 313, Blue 497, CenterPoint 738, COPIC 937, Deluxe 1084, Dollar 1144, Dunkin' 1191, Fort 1472, Giant 1571, Hunt 1888, Lam 2214, Law 2233, Mercury 2469, Neville 2667, New York 2691, NII 2709, Parsons 2887, PDB 2906, Ricoh 3210, RITE 3221, Sonic 3498, St. Louis 3569, Watson 4007

Health care, clinics/centers

Abbott 13, Aetna 48, AGL 57, AK 67, Alro 113, American 165, AMR 187, AnchorBank 193, Apex 214, Arkansas 240, Armstrong 245, Assurant 267, AVX 306, Bakewell 326, Bank 348, BB&T 385, Beaver 394, Belk 404, Bergquist 420, Beverage 452, Birdsong 470, Blue 493, Blue 495, Blue 496, Blue 497, Blue 498, Blue 501, Blue 505, BlueCross 507, Bob's 511, Boehringer 515, Boler 520, Bon 521, Boston 540, Bristol 578, Brooks 585, Brotherhood 588, Brown 591, Buccaneer 599, Caesars 650, California 655, Cambia 665, Cardinal 685, CareFusion 688, Catalina 719, CB 725, Chaney 761, Chapman 763, CITGO 820, Contran 928, Cooper 936, COPIC 937, Creative 976, Credit 980, CUNA 1008, CVS 1014, Danis 1029, Dead 1051, Dean 1054, Delta 1074, Delta 1077, Delta 1079, Delta 1083, Diagnos-Techs 1108, Disney 1127, Doctors 1139, Dominion 1150, Duane 1186, Eastern 1209, Eliason 1248, Essa 1297, Fabri 1322, Fidelity 1372, First 1397, First 1402, First 1406, Forest 1467, Franklin 1488, General 1552, Gilead 1582, GKN 1585, Government 1621, Hackstock 1697, Hannaford 1723, HCA 1762, Health 1766, Hewlett 1794, Highmark 1799, Hillside 1810, HNI 1817, Horizon 1863, Hormel 1866, Hubbard 1877, Hubbell 1879, Iberdrola 1904, Illinois 1916, Inman 1943, Integra 1947, Jacobs 2016, K-Swiss 2082, Kahn 2085, Kinney 2162, Koller 2183, Legg 2245, Levi 2254, Life 2269, LifePoint 2270, Loomis 2301, Louisiana 2309, Maquoketa 2361, Maverick 2409, McDonald 2426, McKesson 2434, McKinstry 2435, Medical 2448, Merck 2466, Morgan 2570, National 2631, National 2632, National 2636, New York 2683, Norfolk 2725, Northfield 2741, Ohio 2791, Ole 2800, Olympus 2804, Oshkosh 2833, Owens 2844, Park 2880, Parker 2886, PDB 2906, People's 2928, PerkinElmer 2939, Pfizer 2950, Pinnacle 2977, Powers 3024, Provident 3070, PVH 3088, QUALCOMM 3095, Rahr 3118, RECO 3148, Rich 3204, Robins 3232, Robinson 3235, Rose 3261, Royal 3275, S & T 3297, Safeco 3306, sanofi-aventis 3329, Scoular 3373, Shanken 3421, Shaw's 3427, Shea 3428, Sierra 3451, South Bend 3507, SQA 3559, Star 3584, Systel 3678, Tanner 3688, Tellabs 3709, Texas 3725, Tillman 3752, True 3814, Trustmark 3818, Union 3856, Union 3858, United 3864, UnitedHealth 3884, US 3902, Vectren 3925, VHA 3944, Virginia 3959, Wachtell 3973, Wal-Mart 3980, Warburg 3985, WEDGE 4020, Weis 4024, Western 4041, Western 4043, Winn 4087, Woodforest 4110, Woodward 4112

Health care, cost containment

Aetna 48, Assurant 267, Baxter 377, California 655, Johnson 2048, Pfizer 2950

Health care, emergency transport services

Griswold 1669, Medtronic 2453, Southwest 3522

Health care, EMS

Clark 835, Colonial 876, Eastern 1211, Emerson 1257, F.N.B. 1318, Kinney 2162, Medtronic 2453, Mercury 2468, Shakopee 3419, Thomaston 3736

Health care, equal rights

Aetna 48, Amgen 182, Baxter 377, Blue 493, Blue 496, Blue 501, Blue 505, Boehringer 515, Bristol 578, CIGNA 812, Compass 901, CVS 1014, Delta 1083, Highmark 1799, Kaiser 2086, McKesson 2434, Merck 2466, OceanFirst 2782, Peoples 2931, Principal 3047, Telligen 3710, Wal-Mart 3980

Health care, financing

Blue 493, California 655, Kaiser 2086, Retail 3194

Health care, formal/general education
AMN Healthcare 184, Genentech 1549, Gilead 1582, Kaiser 2086, LifeScan 2271, Pfizer 2950, Quidel 3107, Telligen 3710

Health care, fund raising/fund distribution
CVS 1014, Farmers 1338, LifeScan 2271, Maritz 2376, Stop 3618, Vision 3961

Health care, home services
Banner 352, Gear 1544, Huntington 1894, Kinney 2162, Union 3858

Health care, infants
Abbott 13, Aetna 48, Applied 219, Arkansas 240, BlueCross 507, CenterPoint 738, Chartis 768, Edina 1227, Farmers 1338, General 1552, Hewlett 1794, Jones 2059, Kmart 2172, Liberty 2262, MedImmune 2450, Quaker 3094, St. Louis 3569, TJX 3765, WellPoint 4027

Health care, information services
Amgen 182, Horizon 1863, Verizon 3936

Health care, insurance
AMERIGROUP 171, Assurity 269, Baxter 377, Blue 491, Blue 495, Blue 498, Blue 501, Blue 505, BlueCross 507, California 655, Callaway 660, Cambia 665, CareSource 690, Express 1313, Impact 1921, LifeScan 2271, Protector 3067, UnitedHealth 3884, WellPoint 4027

Health care, management/technical assistance
Delta 1083, Extendicare 1314

Health care, organ/tissue banks
CITGO 820

Health care, patient services
Aetna 48, Allergan 99, American 137, American 142, Amerisure 177, Amgen 182, AMR 187, ANH 201, Arkansas 240, Assurant 267, Avis 300, BDP 388, Birmingham 471, Blue 493, Blue 495, Blue 497, Blue 498, BlueCross 507, Bob's 511, BorgWarner 528, Boston 540, Bristol 578, Buccaneer 599, Caesars 650, Cambia 665, Cardinal 685, CareFusion 688, Cic 811, CIGNA 812, CITGO 820, CME 853, Colgate 869, COPIC 937, CVS 1014, Delta 1073, Diageo 1107, Doctors 1139, Duane 1186, Dynamet 1200, Eaton 1216, Ecolab 1220, Endo 1268, Express 1313, Extendicare 1314, Fidelity 1371, First 1398, First 1401, Fiserv 1427, Forest 1468, GameStop 1530, Genentech 1549, General 1552, Genzyme 1566, Gilead 1582, GKN 1585, Golden 1602, Green 1657, Haskell 1748, Haviland 1752, Highmark 1799, Highwoods 1800, Huntington 1894, ICON 1906, Interlock 1954, Jones 2055, Lapham 2223, Lilly 2274, Little 2288, Lockheed 2292, Manitowoc 2356, Marsh 2387, McDonald 2426, McKesson 2434, Medtronic 2453, Merfish 2472, Mitsubishi 2538, Mutual 2605, Mutual 2606, National 2631, Nestle 2663, New York 2684, New York 2691, Nintendo 2712, Nortex 2727, Oklahoma 2795, Olin 2801, OMNOVA 2809, Papa 2876, Pfizer 2950, Piedmont 2971, Pittsburgh 2986, ProLogis 3060, PVH 3088, Regal 3166, Regions 3171, Robinson 3235, Rood 3257, Save 3342, Schein 3348, Simplot 3459, Springleaf 3554, Sterne 3602, Stride 3625, Tap 3689, Terre 3722, Tyler 3831, UnitedHealth 3884, Valero 3915, VHA 3944, Weaver 4014, WEDGE 4020, Western 4040, Woodforest 4110, Young 4146

Health care, public policy
Aetna 48, Arkansas 240, Blue 493, Blue 501, Blue 502, Bristol 578, California 655, Delta 1083, Kaiser 2086, LifeScan 2271, Merck 2466, Pfizer 2950, Telligen 3710

Health care, reform
Amgen 182, Arkansas 240, California 655

Health care, research
ACI 27, Allergan 99, AMERIGROUP 171, Beckman 397, Blue 501, Blue 502, Booz 525, Endo 1268, Halliburton 1706, Harley 1732, Pathmark 2894, V.F. 3913, Wendy's/Arby's 4030

Health care, rural areas
Abbott 13, Colgate 869

Health care, support services
Avis 300, California 655, CITGO 820, Schein 3348

Health care, volunteer services
AK 67, Allegis 92, Ascena 255, Katten 2101, Perforce 2937, Turner 3824, Warburg 3985

Health organizations
Adams 34, Air 63, American 136, Apex 212, AstraZeneca 272, Baker 325, Baxter 377, Benton 417, Berry 436, Bloomingdale's 488, Blue 498, Blue 504, Bristol 578, Brochsteins 581, Bruno 594, Burr 621, Butler 627, C.M. 637, Cameron 667, Caribou 692, Caruso 709, Chesapeake 777, Coral 940, Covance 955, Covidien 956, Cranfill 971, Dansko 1031, Davis 1041, Dealer 1052, Douglas 1159, Dowling 1165, Emerson 1257, Ensign 1275, EPES 1283, Federal 1350, Ferrara 1364, First 1416, Football 1460, Fremont 1496, Fru 1513, Gardner 1536, General 1556, Gibbons 1574, Good 1609, Goodman 1610, Great 1643, Great 1647, Hawaii 1754, Health 1765, Highmark 1799, Hoffmann 1823, Home 1846, Houston 1870, InterTech 1977, Jasper 2027, Kanaly 2089, Keefe 2110, Key 2135, Kohler 2182, LeClaire 2239, Lilly 2274, Lisle 2286, MAC 2327, Marr 2382, Matthews 2406, McDonald's 2427, Merck 2466, Mercury 2470, Minto 2533, NYK 2768, Objectwin 2778, Omnicom 2808, Ortec 2828, Pro 3051, Public 3078, Rasmussen 3128, RE/MAX 3140, Republic 3188, ResMed 3192, River 3224, Rose 3263, Safety 3309, Schein 3348, Scott 3370, Selig 3401, Shenandoah 3434, Sidwell 3447, St. Jude 3566, Starwood 3589, Stout 3619, Sullivan 3635, Symmco 3670, Times 3759, Trans 3795, United 3861, Victor 3949, Walgreen 3981, Ward 3986, Williams 4078, WKBN 4099, York 4145

Health organizations, association
Altec 118, Amsted 188, M&T 2323, NuStar 2763, OneBeacon 2813, Safeway 3310, Seton 3415, Williams 4078

Health organizations, formal/general education
Allergan 99, ConvaTec 932

Health organizations, fund raising/fund distribution
Big 461, Blue 497

Health organizations, public education
Blue 505, ConAgra 904, Kaiser 2086, Principal 3047, St. Jude 3566

Health organizations, reform
California 655

Health organizations, research
ConAgra 904, Diamonds 1109

Health organizations, single organization support
California 655

Health sciences school/education
Allergan 99, AMERIGROUP 171, Boston 540, Cisco 818, Cook 934, Dow 1160, Eastern 1211, Ergon 1289, Kaiser 2086, Pacers 2852, Texas 3728, Whole 4066

Heart & circulatory diseases
Adir 36, AK 67, Allegis 92, Amerisure 177, Assurity 269, AstraZeneca 272, AVX 306, Barton 366, Blue 497, Blue 505, Boston 540, Capital 676, Chevron 780, Citizens 828, County 952, CryoLife 990, CVS 1014, Dallas 1022, Danis 1029, Dean 1053, Delmarva 1069, Demoulas 1085, Doctor's 1138, FMR 1450, Friesen 1505, General 1552, General 1555, Gilead 1582, Gould 1618, Groves 1673, Guess 1685, Health 1766, Highmark 1799, Horizon 1863, Houston 1871, IDACORP 1907, International 1959, Jones 2059, Kaiser 2086, Katten 2101, Kindred 2154, Kinetic 2156, Kinney 2162, Kohler 2182, Kuhns 2197, Landry's 2219, Lilly 2274, Madison 2334, Marcus 2370, Marcus 2371, Maritz 2376, Medtronic 2453, Mississippi 2536, National 2629, Nu 2759, Ole 2800, Omron 2810, PDB 2906, Printpack 3049, Regence 3168, S.J. 3299, Spurs 3557, St. Jude 3566, STERIS 3600, SUPERVALU 3659, TeleTech 3708, Truland 3817, Turner 3824, USG 3905, Walgreen 3981, Wawa 4009, WellPoint 4027, West 4036, Wilkes 4074

Heart & circulatory research
California 655, General 1555, Kohler 2182, Merck 2466, SUPERVALU 3659, Walgreen 3981

Hematology research
CSL 993

Hemophilia
Baxter 377, Bayer 382

Hemophilia research
Bayer 382, CSL 993

Higher education
1st 2, 3M 3, ABARTA 10, Abbott 13, Accupac 23, ACE 24, ACF 26, Acme 28, Adir 36, Advanced 40, AEGON 45, Agilent 56, AGL 57, AgStar 59, Air 62, Air 63, Alabama 72, Albemarle 78, Albrecht 80, Alcatel 81, Alcoa 82, Alfa 87, Alice 89, Allegheny 91, Allen 97, Allete 100, Alliant 104, Alro 113, Alsco 115, Altec 118, Altria 120, Amboy 124, Ameren 128, Ameren 129, American 132, American 135, American 138, American 140, American 141, American 143, American 145, American 146, American 150, American 155, American 156, American 157, American 161, American 164, American 165, American 169, AMERIGROUP 171, Amerisure 177, Ameritas 178, Ameritec 179, AMETEK 181, Amgen 182, AMPCO 186, AnchorBank 193,

Specialty 3537, SpectraCare 3541, Spirol 3545, Sports 3547, Sports 3548, Sprague 3551, Springer 3553, Springleaf 3554, St. 3565, Standard 3577, Stanek 3578, Star 3584, Stardust 3586, State 3590, State 3591, Station 3593, STERIS 3600, Stewart 3604, Stiles 3607, Stock 3610, Stoelting 3612, Stonecutter 3615, Stram 3622, Strauss 3624, Stupp 3628, Sumitomo 3639, Sunbeam 3647, Sunkist 3649, SunTrust 3654, Superior 3658, Swift 3666, Syngenta 3671, Synopsys 3673, Synovus 3674, Sysco 3677, TALX 3683, TAP 3690, Target 3691, Tatitlek 3694, TECO 3701, Tedco 3702, Tektronix 3706, Teleflex 3707, Telligen 3710, Temple 3711, Tennant 3714, Tennessee 3716, Tension 3717, Terre 3722, Texas 3725, Texas 3727, Texas 3729, Textron 3731, TFS 3732, Thomasville 3737, Tikigaq 3751, Time 3757, Timken 3760, Tindall 3761, Tireco 3762, Titan 3763, Tomkins 3771, Toro 3775, TOSOH 3777, Towerbrook 3781, Toyota 3784, Tractor 3791, Trane 3794, TransUnion 3799, Trico 3807, Trim 3810, True 3814, True 3815, Truland 3817, Turner 3824, Tyler 3831, U.S. 3835, U.S. 3837, U.S. 3839, U.S. 3840, UBS 3842, Ukpeagvik 3843, UniGroup 3852, Unisys 3859, United 3864, United 3867, United 3868, United 3869, United 3870, United 3872, United 3873, United 3874, United 3877, United 3880, Univar 3886, Universal 3890, Universal 3891, Universal 3892, Universal 3895, US 3902, USG 3905, Usibelli 3906, UTC 3908, Utica 3910, V-T 3912, V.F. 3913, Valero 3915, Valley 3916, Valmont 3919, Valspar 3920, Vectren 3925, Verby 3934, Verizon 3936, Vermeer 3937, Victaulic 3948, Vijuk 3953, Vodafone 3965, Vulcan 3972, Wachtell 3973, Waffle 3975, Wahl 3977, Wake 3978, Wal-Mart 3980, Walker 3982, Walter 3984, Warburg 3985, Warrell 3991, Warren 3993, Washington 3994, Washington 3999, Washington 4001, Wausau 4008, WD-40 4011, Weather 4013, Weaver 4015, WEDGE 4020, Wegmans 4021, Weil 4022, Wells 4028, Wendy's 4032, Wenger 4033, West 4034, West 4035, West 4038, Western 4040, Western 4041, Western 4043, Westfield 4047, Westport 4050, Weyco 4051, Weyerhaeuser 4052, Whirlpool 4056, Whitley 4064, Williams 4078, Williamsburg 4080, Wilsonart 4084, Windway 4086, Winn 4087, Wisconsin 4093, Wisconsin 4094, Wisconsin 4096, WKBN 4099, Wolf 4103, Wolff 4105, Wolverine 4106, Wood 4108, Woodward 4112, Woori 4114, Wrigley 4125, Wynnne 4133, Xerox 4136, YGS 4143, YSI 4149, Yum! 4150, Zatkoff 4154, Zilkha 4156

Hinduism

Systel 3678

Hispanics/Latinos

Abbott 13, Allstate 107, Anheuser 202, Autodesk 289, Beneficial 412, Burlington 618, Chrysler 801, Ford 1464, Genesis 1561, Gon 1608, Hewlett 1794, Intel 1950, KPMG 2190, Merck 2466, Metropolitan 2481, Mondelez 2556, Pan-American 2868, Piedmont 2971, Ramona's 3126, Rudy's 3284, Semiconductor 3403, Simpson 3461, St. Joe 3563, Vinson 3957, WD-40 4011, Xerox 4136

Historic preservation/historical societies

A.D. 7, American 143, American 152, American 157, Arent 235, Ashley 259, Baird 316, Bank 343, Bemis 408, Birdsong 470, Black 475, Bound 541, Bristol 577, Brooklyn 584, Burns 620, Byers 630, Calpine 661, Cape 674, Chaney 761, Cianbro 808, Colonial 875, Columbia 884, Cook 934, Coquille 939, Cranston 972, Creative 976, Cummins 1006, davistudio 1043, Dedham 1060, Delaware 1066, Delta 1073, Discovery 1126, Eagle 1202, Evening 1302, Expedia 1311, Federated 1351, First 1393, First 1416, First 1419, Flexcon 1436, Franklin 1488, Fulton 1518, Gable 1525, Georgia 1568, Hilton 1812, HNI 1817, Hopkins 1859, Johnson 2053, Kimball 2149, Kingsbury 2160, Kohler 2182, Lefton 2244, Levi 2254, Magnolia 2340, Mars 2384, Mazda 2414, MB 2415, Midmark 2507, Miller 2518, Modine 2544, Moore 2565, NCR 2650, Nordson 2723, Omaha 2805, ONEOK 2815, Orvis 2830, Osram 2834, PacifiCorp 2860, Penn 2923, Peoples 2931, Price 3039, Provident 3070, RECO 3148, Regions 3171, Ryman 3294, Santa 3331, Sit 3466, Southern 3515, Specialty 3537, Spirit 3544, Suitter 3633, SunTrust 3654, Teichert 3704, Terre 3722, Truland 3817, Turner 3825, U.S. 3835, U.S. 3836, Union 3857, Universal 3891, Wenger 4033, WKBN 4099

Historical activities

American 159, Central 745, Dedham 1060, Delta 1073, Edvisors 1234, Fabiano 1320, Ford 1464, HCA 1762, Indiana 1931, Journal 2068, Magnolia 2340, Republic 3187, Rolls 3254, Southern 3517, Spirit 3544, Walter 3984

Historical activities, centennials

Delta 1073, Hilfiger 1801

Historical activities, war memorials

Guardian 1681, IPALCO 1988

History/archaeology

Cook 934, Eagle 1201, Kohler 2182

Holistic medicine

Kinetic 2156

Home accessibility modifications

Sears 3384, Shaw's 3427

Homeless

Autodesk 289, Beneficial 412, Boston 540, Chrysler 801, Cisco 818, Coach 858, Croft 985, Edina 1227, ESCO 1296, Federal 1348, Genesis 1561, Haggen 1699, Hilton 1812, Huntsman 1895, Iberdrola 1904, Kennecott 2127, Kohler 2182, Lennar 2250, Los Angeles 2307, Metropolitan 2481, Nordson 2723, Novell 2754, NYSE 2769, Pacific 2855, Piedmont 2971, Presley 3038, Primerica 3045, Procter 3055, Questar 3104, Reynolds 3199, Rock 3238, Safeco 3306, Security 3391, Sensient 3408, Spark 3533, St. Joe 3563, Union 3854, Washington 3994, WD-40 4011, Woodward 4112, Xerox 4136

Homeless, human services

Abbott 13, Allen 94, Allergan 99, Almar 110, Alpenrose 111, Alsco 115, American 156, Andersson 196, Androscoggin 199, Apex 213, Applied 220, Arbella 226, Arnall 247, Ash 256, Baker 321, Bank 340, Bank 346, BB&T 385, Birdsong 470, BJ's 473, Bloomingdale's 488, Booz 525, Bracewell 549, Bristlecone 575, Bristol 578, Brotherhood 588, Butler 627, Cadence 646, Calpine 661, Calumet 662, Caplin 681, Carter's 708, CentiMark 740, Chicago 782, Chief 793, Churchill 807, Clear 842, Coach 858, Collette 872, Consumers 921, Contran 928, Crowell 986, Deutsche 1099, Dime 1118, DJO 1134, Dominion 1150, DTE 1183, East 1207, Eastern 1209, Edina 1227, Ergon 1289, Fabick 1321, Federal 1349, First 1394, First 1399, First 1400, Florida 1443, Fort 1472, Fremont 1496, Furniture 1519, Global 1593, Green 1657, Hanover 1724, Hastings 1749, Heat 1767, Holland 1834, Hudson 1880, Ideal 1908, Indiana 1931, International 1958, ISGN 1995, JM 2044, Johnson 2049, Kaiser 2086, Lam 2214, Landmark 2218, Lennar 2250, Li-Cor 2261, Liberty 2262, Liberty 2265, LifePoint 2270, Lincoln 2281, Lockheed 2292, M.D.C. 2324, Masco 2393, Men's 2460, MH 2490, MidAmerican 2504, Miller 2523, Milliken 2525, Mizuho 2542, Mutual 2603, Mutual 2605, Mutual 2607, Namaste 2614, Nash 2619, Nationwide 2639, New 2668, NII 2709, Nordic 2722, Norfolk 2725, NRG 2756, NRT 2757, O'Connor 2770, OceanFirst 2782, OMNOVA 2809, Orscheln 2827, Osram 2834, Owens 2844, Pacific 2858, Patton's 2899, Pawtucket 2902, Paychex 2904, PDB 2906, Peoples 2931, Perforce 2937, PerkinElmer 2939, Perrigo 2943, Philadelphia 2961, Piedmont 2971, Pioneer 2981, Portland 3010, Power 3020, Prophet 3063, Provident 3069, QUALCOMM 3095, Reader's 3141, Renovated 3185, Retail 3194, RJN 3228, Robinson 3235, Rood 3257, Rudolph 3283, Safeco 3306, Savings 3343, Sensient 3408, Shaughnessy 3425, Shelter 3431, Silicon 3455, Sit 3466, Smucker 3488, Snyder's-Lance 3492, Southwest 3523, Spark 3533, Stanek 3578, Stardust 3586, Station 3593, Steelcase 3597, Sunwest 3655, TALX 3683, Textron 3731, Thrivent 3747, United 3864, United 3873, United 3881, Univar 3886, Valero 3915, Virginia 3959, Wachtell 3973, Warrell 3991, Warren 3993, Washington 4000, Western 4042, Weyerhaeuser 4052, Woodforest 4110, Woodward 4112

Horticulture/garden clubs

Bailey 315, Magnolia 2340, Scotts 3372

Hospices

Acme 29, Acuity 32, Aetna 48, American 152, American 165, Amerisure 177, ANH 201, Apex 214, Bank 341, Bemis 408, Beneficial 411, Bergquist 420, Bristol 578, Cabot 642, Calvert 663, Cape 674, Capital 676, Cephalon 752, CFS 756, Cic 811, Citizens 828, Cone 907, Corning 945, East 1207, Emerson 1257, Essa 1297, Fiserv 1427, Four 1477, Gaunce 1543, GKN 1585, Griswold 1669, Haynie 1760, HCR 1763, Heffernan 1769, Hoffer 1821, Hoffman 1822, Illinois 1916, Institution 1946, International 1959, Kaiser 2086, Kemp 2123, Lapham 2223, Leyman 2259, Magnolia 2340, Miller 2518, MTD 2595, Mutual 2606, Newburyport 2693, North 2730, Northwest 2746, OMNOVA 2809, Parker 2886, Powers 3024, Protector 3067, Provident 3069, Provident 3070, Pukall 3082, Quad 3091, Questar 3105, R & B 3113, Rennoc 3184, Sartori 3335, Sensient 3408, Sjostrom 3469, Snyder's-Lance 3492, Southern 3515, Southern 3517, Tanner 3688, Thomasville 3737, TJX 3765, True 3814, Trustmark 3818, Union 3855, United 3869, V.F. 3913, Wilkes 4074

Hospitals (general)

1st 2, ABARTA 10, Abbott 13, Abercrombie 17, ACI 27, Acme 29, Adir 36, Aetna 48, AK 67, Albemarle 78, Allegheny 91, Allergan 99, Allstate 107, Almar 110, Alro 113, Amboy 124, Ameren 128, American 132, American 137, American 141, American 143, American 155, American 157, American 164, Ameritas 178, AMETEK 181, Andersen 194, ANH 201, Apex 214, Arbella 226, Arizona 239, Arkansas 240, Armstrong 246, Arrowpoint 251, Ascena 255, Associated 261, Astoria 270, Athletics 276, Avidia 298, Avis 299, AVX 306, Baird 317, Baker 323, Bakewell 326, Bank 340, Bank 341, Bank 343, Barton 366, Bay 378, BB&T 385, BDP 388, Beaver 394, Belk 403, Belk 404, Beneficial 411, Berry 434, Berry 437, Birmingham 471, Blair 478, Block 482, Blue 492, Blue 501, Blue 504, BlueCross 507, Booz 525, Boston 540, Bristol 577, Bristol 578, Brown 591, BSA 597, Buccaneer 599, Building 610, Burlington 618, Butler 626, Cacique 644, Caesars 650, Calvert 663, Cambia 665, Cape 674, Capital 676, Capital 677, Cardinal 685, CareFusion 688, Cary 712, Catalina 719, Caterpillar 722, Centene 735, CentiMark 740, Central 743, Chapman 763, Charter 766, Chelsea 772, Chicago 787, Chotin 799, Cic 811, CITGO 820, Citizens 824, Cliffs 850, CME 853, Coach 858, Coca 862, Collette 872, Comcast 888, Community 900, Contran 928, Copley 938, Corning 945, Covidien 956, Crane 970, Cranston 972, Creamer 974, Cumberland 1003, Curves 1011, Cutco 1012, CVS 1014, Davey 1035, Delta 1073, Demoulas 1085, DENTSPLY 1089, Deutsche 1099, Dexter 1103, Dietz 1114, Dime 1118,

Dispatch 1129, Dow 1162, Dunkin' 1191, Dynamet 1200, Easthampton 1212, Eastman 1214, Eaton 1216, Econoco 1222, Edgar 1225, Eliason 1248, Emerson 1257, Ergon 1289, F.N.B. 1318, Fabick 1321, Fidelity 1371, Fidelity 1372, First 1393, First 1405, First 1406, First 1408, First 1419, First 1421, Firstmerit 1425, Fiserv 1427, Fisher 1431, Foremost 1466, Frankel 1483, Franklin 1485, Freeport 1494, Fulton 1518, GenRad 1564, Giant 1571, Gilead 1582, Global 1593, Golden 1601, Golub 1607, Government 1621, Grace 1623, Graycor 1641, Green 1651, Hannaford 1723, Hartzell 1745, Hasbro 1747, Hastings 1749, Hautly 1750, HCR 1763, Hensyn 1782, Highmark 1799, Highwoods 1800, HNI 1817, Hoffer 1821, Hofmann 1824, Hoops 1857, Hubbard 1877, IDACORP 1907, IDT 1910, IHC 1913, Illinois 1916, IMA 1917, Industrial 1935, Integra 1947, Interlock 1954, International 1958, International 1962, International 1966, ISGN 1995, J-M 2005, Jack 2007, Jacobs 2016, Jasper 2025, Jasper 2026, Jeld 2032, Johnson 2048, Johnson 2050, Johnson 2052, Jones 2055, Jones 2056, Jordan 2063, Josephson 2066, Kahn 2085, Kann 2090, Katten 2101, Kelly 2122, Kepco 2132, Kimball 2149, Kimberly 2150, Kingsbury 2160, Kinney 2162, KOA 2178, Kukui 2198, Land 2217, Leet 2243, Leyman 2259, LifePoint 2270, Lilly 2274, Lincoln 2279, Lockheed 2292, Louisiana 2309, M&T 2323, Madison 2334, Main 2342, Mamiye 2352, Manhattan 2354, Mapes 2360, Mariani 2374, Mascoma 2394, Mattel 2405, Mayer 2412, Mazda 2414, McClatchy 2422, McCormick 2423, McKinstry 2435, MDU 2441, Medtronic 2453, Merchants 2465, Mercury 2468, Miller 2518, Milwaukee 2528, Mine 2529, Monadnock 2551, Moody's 2563, Morgan 2570, MTD 2595, N.E.W. 2611, National 2631, National 2634, National 2635, National 2636, Nationwide 2639, Naugatuck 2645, Nestle 2663, New 2668, New York 2683, Newtown 2704, North 2728, North 2730, Northfield 2741, Northwest 2746, NTELOS 2758, Odyssey 2784, Ohio 2790, Olympus 2804, Omaha 2806, OMNOVA 2809, ONEOK 2815, PACCAR 2850, Panda 2871, Park 2879, Park 2881, Parker 2886, Pathmark 2894, Perforce 2937, Perrigo 2943, Pfizer 2950, Pittsburgh 2986, Plum 2991, Portcullis 3004, Praxair 3029, Premier 3035, Price 3039, Professional 3056, Progressive 3058, ProLogis 3060, Prophet 3063, Protective 3066, Providence 3068, Provident 3069, Provident 3070, Putnam 3085, Putnam 3086, Quad 3091, Quaker 3093, Quest 3103, R & B 3113, Ralph 3123, Rayonier 3134, Regal 3166, Regions 3171, ResMed 3192, Respironics 3193, RG 3201, Riggs 3213, Robins 3232, Robinson 3235, Rose 3261, Royal 3275, Ryder 3292, S & T 3297, Sachs 3301, San Diego 3322, San Diego 3323, sanofi-aventis 3329, Sartori 3335, Schiff 3350, Schoonover 3359, Security 3392, Selective 3399, Sensient 3408, Shaughnessy 3425, Shelter 3431, Smith 3484, Smucker 3488, South 3512, Southern 3515, Spahn 3529, Spang 3530, Spartan 3535, Sports 3548, Square 3560, St. Louis 3567, Stanley 3579, STERIS 3600, Sterne 3602, Stewart 3604, Stock 3610, Stupp 3628, Sunbeam 3647, SunTrust 3654, SUPERVALU 3659, Swift 3666, Synovus 3674, TECO 3701, Tellabs 3709, Tennant 3714, Tennessee 3716, Terre 3722, Textron 3731, Titan 3763, Tripifoods 3811, True 3814, Truland 3817, Turner 3824, U.S. 3836, Union 3857, United 3870, United 3873, Universal 3891, Universal 3895, Unum 3898, USG 3905, V.F. 3913, Valero 3915, VHA 3944, Victaulic 3948, Vulcan 3972, Wagner 3976, Wal-Mart 3980, Walter 3984, Warburg 3985, Washington 4000, Washington 4001, Wausau 4008, Wendy's 4031, Wenger 4033, West 4038, Western 4041, Western 4043, Winn 4087, Wisconsin 4096, WKBN 4099, Wolff 4105, World 4120, Young 4146, Zilkha 4156

Hospitals (specialty)

Abercrombie 17, Alcon 83, AutoZone 294, AZPB 310, Build 608, Chicago 782, Citizens 824, Discover 1125, DJO 1134, Dr 1169, Friesen 1505, Giant 1571, Hawkins 1757, Home 1844, Intrepid 1980, Kmart 2172, Major 2347, National 2623, Palm 2867, Panda 2871, Safeway 3310, Security 3392, Trail 3793

Housing/shelter

A.D. 7, Adobe 38, AEGON 45, Affinity 52, AFL 53, Alliant 104, Allison-Erwin 106, Altman 119, Amboy 124, American 141, American 144, American 164, American 170, Ameriprise 174, Andersen 194, Anheuser 202, Apple 218, Applied 220, Arcelormittal 229, Assurant 266, Assurant 268, Baltimore 332, Bank 340, Bank 341, Bank 342, Bank 344, Bank 346, Bank 348, Banner 352, Batson 373, Bay 380, Bayer 381, BB&T 385, Bean 391, Beck 396, Berghammer 418, Berglund 419, Berkshire 428, Berry 438, Blue 496, Brown 592, Buist 611, Butler 626, California 653, Calpine 661, Cambridge 666, Candlesticks 670, Capital 676, Capital 679, Capitol 680, Caplin 681, Carpenter 700, Cathay 723, CenterPoint 739, CentiMark 740, CFS 756, Charter 767, Chemed 773, Chemical 774, Chicopee 792, Choice 798, Cisco 818, Citizens 827, Claremont 833, Clayton 841, Cleary 843, Clif 848, Coastal 859, Columbia 882, Comerica 889, Communications 896, Compass 901, Cornerstone 943, CORT 946, Country 951, Delmarva 1069, Delphos 1072, DeniseLawrence.Com 1086, Deutsche 1099, Dime 1118, Diversey 1130, Dollar 1142, Dollar 1144, DVK 1198, East 1207, Eastern 1209, Eaton 1216, Eberhard 1218, Ecolab 1220, Emerson 1257, Ensign 1276, Entergy 1279, ESCO 1296, Essa 1297, Federal 1347, Federal 1348, Federal 1349, Fieldstone 1374, Fifth 1377, First 1390, First 1399, First 1400, First 1406, First 1407, First 1409, First 1410, FirstEnergy 1424, Florida 1443, Fluor 1448, Framingham 1481, Fredericksburg 1490, Freeport 1494, Genentech 1549, Genworth 1565, Georgia 1568, Gilbane 1581, Golden 1602, Guarantee 1678, Guess 1685, H & R 1695, Hanover 1724, Harris 1739, Hasbro 1747, HCA 1762, Heffernan 1769, Hilton 1812, Holiday 1830, Holland 1834, Homasote 1841, Home 1844, Honeywell 1852, Hudson 1880, Huntington 1894, IDACORP 1907, Indium 1933, Institution 1946, International 1959, Intertech 1976, Investors 1984, Issa 1997, JPMorgan Chase 2071, KB 2105, KeyBank 2136, Kilmartin 2145, Kinetic 2156, Kohler 2182, Konica 2185, Lafarge 2210, Lebanon 2238, Lennar 2250, Liberty 2262, Lincoln 2281, Louisiana 2310, Lowe's 2312, M/I 2325, MAC 2329, Madison 2335, Magyar 2341, Marlborough 2380, Marriott 2383, Masco 2393, Material 2402, Matrix 2403, MAXIMUS 2410, MB 2415, McBride 2418, Merk 2467, Merrimack 2474, Metropolitan 2481, MGIC 2488, Milford 2513, Mill 2515, Mississippi 2536, Mizuho 2542, Moneta 2557, Moody's 2563, Moore 2565, National 2633, National 2635, Nationwide 2639, Naugatuck 2645, New Hampshire 2674, New York 2683, NIBCO 2707, Nordson 2723, Northern 2740, Northfield 2742, OceanFirst 2782, Owens 2842, Penn 2923, Pentair 2926, People's 2928, Peoples 2931, Philadelphia 2961, Piedmont 2971, Plymouth 2993, PMI 2995, PNC 2997, Pony 3002, Popular 3003, Presley 3038, Primerica 3045, Principal 3047, Provident 3069, Provident 3071, Pulte 3083, Putnam 3086, Quandel 3099, RBS 3137, Realogy 3145, Redwoods 3158, Regence 3169, Regions 3171, Retail 3194, RJN 3228, Robinson 3235, Rose 3262, Royal 3275, Saint 3312, San Francisco 3325, Seagate 3377, Sears 3384, Selective 3399, SI 3444, Sidener 3445, Silicon 3455, South 3510, South 3511, Southern 3514, Sovereign 3528, Spansion 3532, Sports 3550, SRA 3562, Stanley 3579, State 3591, Steve's 3603, Stiles 3607, Sun 3644, Sunwest 3655, Target 3691, Tastefully 3692, TCF 3695, TD 3696, Texor 3730, Textron 3731, Third 3735, Thrivent 3747, Trail 3793, Transammonia 3796, Travelers 3802, Tri 3805, U-Haul 3833, U.S. 3835, U.S. 3836, Union 3854, United 3863, Universal 3895, Untours 3897, USEC 3904, Valley 3916, Valspar 3920, Vectren 3925, Vermeer 3938, Vodafone 3965, Vulcan 3970, Wal-Mart 3980, Washington 4001, Waterford 4002, Wells 4028, Westfield 4047, Weyerhaeuser 4052, Whiting 4063, Whitney 4065, Winn 4087, Woodward 4112, Zappos.com 4153, Zions 4158

Housing/shelter, aging

Bridgestone 560, Genworth 1565, Union 3854

Housing/shelter, development

Adobe 38, Aetna 48, Albemarle 78, Amboy 124, American 141, American 165, Amerisure 177, Anheuser 202, Armstrong 246, Ash 256, AT&T 273, Bank 347, Barton 366, BOSE 530, Bridgestone 560, Calpine 661, Calvert 663, Catalina 719, CFS 756, Charter 766, Chicopee 792, Cisco 818, CNO 857, Columbia 882, Credit 980, D.C. 1018, Dart 1034, Delta 1073, Deutsche 1099, Eastern 1210, Easthampton 1212, Eaton 1216, Emerson 1257, Energizer 1271, Entergy 1279, EQT 1287, Exelon 1309, Fidelity 1372, First 1394, First 1406, First 1419, First 1421, Fort 1472, General 1555, GenOn 1563, Genworth 1565, Georgia 1568, Guardian 1683, GuideOne 1687, Harleysville 1733, Harris 1736, Harsco 1741, Hartzell 1745, Haynes 1759, HCA 1762, Heffernan 1769, Hess 1793, Hoffman 1822, Honeywell 1852, Hudson 1880, Independence 1925, JPMorgan Chase 2071, Kelly 2122, KOA 2178, Lapham 2223, Lee 2240, Liberty 2262, Louisiana 2310, Masco 2393, MB 2415, Midcontinent 2505, Mutual 2603, Mutual 2606, National 2634, Naugatuck 2645, Newtown 2704, NRT 2757, Ohio 2790, Omron 2810, Oshkosh 2833, Otis 2835, Owens 2842, Pawtucket 2902, PMI 2995, Popular 3003, Prophet 3063, Provident 3070, Ralph 3123, RBS 3137, Red 3154, RESCO 3189, Retail 3194, Rood 3257, Rothstein 3271, Schneider 3355, Springleaf 3554, Square 3560, Stiles 3607, Sunwest 3655, Tanner 3688, Tap 3689, TD 3696, Teleflex 3707, Tennant 3714, Terre 3722, Tesoro 3723, Textron 3731, Timken 3760, Tyler 3831, U.S. 3835, U.S. 3836, United 3882, V.F. 3913, Valspar 3920, Vectren 3925, Wadsworth 3974, Wells 4028, Westfield 4047, Wolf 4103, Wolverine 4106

Housing/shelter, expense aid

Ameren 129, Assurant 266, Capital 679, Edina 1227, Primerica 3045, RBS 3137, SI 3444, TD 3696, Weyerhaeuser 4052

Housing/shelter, formal/general education

First 1390, First 1419, Home 1842

Housing/shelter, home owners

Bank 340, Bank 346, Berkshire 428, Bridgestone 560, Columbia 882, Federal 1348, First 1390, First 1419, JPMorgan Chase 2071, Liberty 2262, Mizuho 2542, New York 2683, Old 2798, Pawtucket 2902, People's 2928, PNC 2997, Sovereign 3528, State 3591, Thrivent 3747, U.S. 3835, Wells 4028

Housing/shelter, homeless

Adobe 38, AEGON 45, Altria 120, Ariens 238, Assurant 266, AZPB 310, Berkshire 428, Bromelkamp 582, California 655, Capital 679, Chicago 782, Cleary 843, Coach 858, East 1207, Edina 1227, Federal 1348, Green 1653, Guardian 1683, Hancock 1717, Hasbro 1747, International 1959, Kaiser 2086, Lennar 2250, Nash 2619, OceanFirst 2782, Orlando 2824, Pawtucket 2902, PDB 2906, Textron 3731, Thrivent 3747, Union 3854, Universal 3893

Housing/shelter, information services

First 1419

Housing/shelter, management/technical assistance

First 1419

Housing/shelter, owner/renter issues

Andersen 194

Housing/shelter, public education

First 1390, First 1419

Housing/shelter, public policy

Guardian 1683

Housing/shelter, rehabilitation

Booz 525, Capital 679, First 1419, Guardian 1683, MB 2415, Old 2798, PacifiCorp 2860, Retail 3194, Stanley 3579, TCF 3695, TD 3696, Trail 3793, U.S. 3835, Valspar 3920

Housing/shelter, repairs

Bigelow 462, Bridgestone 560, Dominion 1150, Mississippi 2536, Sears 3384, Trail 3793

Housing/shelter, services

Alpha 112, Columbia 882, Dominion 1150, Loews 2296, People's 2928, Sovereign 3528, Wells 4028

Housing/shelter, single organization support

First 1419

Housing/shelter, temporary shelter

Andersen 194, Berkshire 428, Federal 1348, Genworth 1565, Green 1653, Lennar 2250, Liberty 2262, Lincoln 2281, Nationwide 2639, Piedmont 2971, PNC 2997, RECO 3148, TJX 3765, Union 3854, Weyerhaeuser 4052, Zappos.com 4153

Housing/shelter, volunteer services

ACI 27, Alabama 71, Alliant 104, Anadarko 190, Applied 219, Aramco 224, Bigelow 462, Bridgestone 560, Broadcom 579, Churchill 807, Circle 817, Dow 1160, Farmers 1338, Federal 1348, FirstEnergy 1424, Halliburton 1706, Kaiser 2086, NII 2709, PacifiCorp 2860, Parsons 2887, Peet's 2916, Pioneer 2981, Publix 3079, Rudolph 3283, Sealy 3382, ServiceMaster 3414, Sovereign 3528, TECO 3701, Tesoro 3723, Timberland 3754, Turner 3824, United 3880, Vision 3961

Human services

1st 2, 3M 3, A & E 6, ABARTA 10, Abbot 12, Abbott 13, AbbyBank 15, Abercrombie 17, Abt 20, ACE 25, ACI 27, Acme 29, Adams 34, Adir 36, Advanced 40, AEGON 45, Aexcel 49, Affiliated 51, AFL 53, Aflac 54, AgStar 59, Ahern 60, Air 63, Air 64, AK 67, Alabama 71, Aladdin 73, Alaska 74, Albemarle 78, Albrecht 80, Alcon 83, Alexander 85, Allegheny 91, Allegis 92, Allen 95, Allen 96, Allergan 99, Allete 100, Alliant 104, Allison-Erwin 106, Almar 110, Alpha 112, Alsco 115, Altair 117, Altec 118, Amboy 124, Ameren 128, America's 130, American 132, American 133, American 134, American 137, American 141, American 143, American 144, American 145, American 150, American 155, American 156, American 165, American 169, Ameristar 176, Amerisure 177, Ameritas 178, Ameritec 179, AMETEK 181, Amgen 182, Amica 183, AMN Healthcare 184, Amnews 185, AMPCO 186, Amsted 188, Anadarko 190, Anchor 192, Andersen 194, Andrews 198, Androscoggin 199, ANH 201, Anheuser 202, Antioch 207, Aon 210, Apache 211, Apex 213, Apex 214, Applied 220, AptarGroup 221, Arbeit 225, Arbella 226, Archer 232, AREVA 236, Ariel 237, Ariens 238, Arizona 239, Armstrong 245, Armstrong 246, Arrow 249, Artichoke 254, Ascena 255, Ash 256, Ashley 259, Assurant 266, Assurity 269, Astoria 270, AT&T 273, AT&T 274, Atlantic 281, Atlas 284, Audubon 286, Auntie 287, Autodesk 289, Avelina 296, Avidia 298, Avis 299, Avis 300, Avlon 303, Azavea 309, Badger 313, Baird 316, Baird 317, Baker 321, Baker 324, Baker 325, Baltimore 331, Baltimore 332, Baltimore 334, BancorpSouth 336, BancTrust 337, Bangor 338, Bank 340, Bank 341, Bank 342, Bank 343, Bank 344, Bank 346, Bank 349, BankSouth 350, Bard 358, Bardes 359, Bartlett 365, BASF 368, Batts 374, Baum 375, Bay 379, Bay 380, Bayer 381, BB&T 385, Beam 390, Bean 391, Bean 392, Bear 393, Beaver 394, Bechtel 395, Becton 398, Belden 402, Belk 403, Belk 404, Bemis 407, Benedict-Miller 410, Beneficial 412, Benevento 414, Bentley 416, Berghammer 418, Berglund 419, Bergquist 420, Bergstrom 421, Berkley 426, Berkshire 428, Berry 435, Best 442, Bethel 445, Betts 450, Betts 451, Beverage 452, Beverage 453, Beyer 454, BI-LO 456, Bickel 457, Bierlein 459, Big 460, Biogen 465, Biomet 466, Bionetics 467, Birdsong 470, Birmingham 471, Black 474, Black 475, Blair 478, Block 482, Bloomberg 486, Blue 493, Blue 494, Blue 496, Blue 500, Blue 501, Blue 505, BlueCross 507, BMC 508, Bob's 511, Boehringer 515, Boeing 516, Bon 521, Booz 525, Borden 527, BorgWarner 528, Bosch 529, Bossong 532, Boston 539, Boston 540, Bound 541, Bowater 543, Boyd 545, BP 547, Brady 553, Bragg 554, Bramco 555, Brewer 558, Bricker 559, Bridgestone 560, Bridgewater 562, Bridgeway 563, Briggs 565, Brinker 572, Bristol 577, Bristol 578, Broadcom 579, Brocchini 580, Brooklyn 584, Brooks 585, Brotherhood 588, Brown 591, Brunswick 595, Bubalo 598, Buccaneer 599, Buckeye 601, Bufftree 607, Builders 609, Building 610, Buist 611, Burger 613, Burger's 614, Burlington 618, Burns 620, Burr 621, Butzel 629, C & C 632, C L D 635, C Spire 636, C.M. 637, CA 638, Cabot 642, Cacique 644, Cades 647, Caesars 650, Cajun 652, California 655, California 656, Calkain 658, Calpine 661, Calumet 662, Calvert 663, Cambridge 666, Campbell 669, Candlesticks 670, Caparo 673, Cape 674, Capital 676, Capital 677, Capitol 680, Caplin 681, Capri 682, Caremore 689, Cargill 691, Caribou 692, Carlson 693, CarMax 694, Carmody 695, Carolina 697, Carolina 698, Carolina 699, Carpenter 700, Carrington Coleman 701, Carter's 708, Cary 712, Cascade 713, Castle 716, Caterpillar 722, Cathay 723, Cavaliers 724, CEMEX 734, Centene 735, CenterPoint 738, CentiMark 740, Central 745, Century 748, CF 755, CFS 756, Chaney 761, Chapman 763, Charter 765, Charter 767, Chase 770, Chehalis 771, Chelsea 772, Chemed 773, Chemtura 775, Chesapeake 777, Cheviot 779, Chicago 786, Chicago 789, Chicago 790, Chicopee 792, Chief 793, Choice 798, Chotin 799, Chrysler 801, Churchill 807, CIBA 809, Cic 811, CIGNA 812, Cincinnati 814, Cintas 816, Cisco 818, CITGO 820, Citizens 823, Citizens 827, CLARCOR 832, Claremont 833, Clark 835, Clarke 837, Clear 842, Clif 848, Cliffs 850, Clinton 851, CME 853, CMS 854, CNA 855, CNO 857, Coastal 859, Coghlin 865, Collective 871, Collette 872, Colonial 875, Colorado 880, Colt 881, Columbia 882, Columbia 883, Columbia 884, Commerce 890, Commercial 893, Commonwealth 894, Community 900, Compass 901, Connecticut 911, Conston 920, Consumers 921, Continental 924, Continental 926, Contran 928, Convergys 933, Cooper 935, COPIC 937, Copley 938, Coral 940, CORE 941, Cornerstone 942, Corning 945, Costco 948, Country 951, Cousins 954, Cox 959, Cox 960, CPI 965, Cracker 966, craigslist 968, Crane 969, Crane 970, Cranfill 971, Crayola 973, Creamer 974, Creative 975, Creative 976, Credit 979, Credit 980, Crescent 981, Crescent 982, Crowell 986, CSS 996, Cullen 1000, Cullman 1001, Cumberland 1003, Cummings 1004, Cummins 1006, Cummins 1007, CUNA 1008, Cupertino 1009, Curves 1011, D.C. 1018, Daffy's 1019, Dallas 1022, Damar 1024, Dana 1026, Danforth 1028, Danis 1029, Dansko 1031, Darden 1032, Dart 1034, Davis 1041, Davison 1042, Dayton 1047, DCI 1049, Deacon 1050, Dean 1053, DeBlois 1056, Dedham 1060, Deere 1061, Deerfield 1062, Dekker 1064, Delta 1073, Delta 1077, Deluxe 1084, Demoulas 1085, DENSO 1088, DENTSPLY 1089, Dethmers 1091, Detroit 1094, Deutsch 1098, Deutsche 1099, Devereaux 1100, Devon 1102, Dexter 1103, Dharma 1105, Diageo 1107, Diamonds 1109, Dick's 1110, Diebold 1112, Diemolding 1113, Dietz 1114, Dilbeck 1116, Dime 1118, Discovery 1126, Dispatch 1129, Dixie 1132, Dolan 1140, Dollar 1142, Dollar 1144, Dominion 1148, Dominion 1149, Dominion 1150, Donnelley 1155, Donovan 1156, Dot 1158, Douglas 1159, Dowling 1165, Draper 1171, DRS 1179, drugstore.com 1180, DRW 1181, DTE 1183, du Pont 1184, Duane 1186, Duchossois 1187, Duda 1188, Duke 1189, Dunkin' 1191, Dunn 1192, Dutch 1197, DVK 1198, East 1207, East 1208, Eastern 1209, Eastern 1210, Eastman 1213, Eastman 1214, Eaton 1216, Eberhard 1218, Eclipse 1219, Edelman 1224, Edina 1227, Edison 1229, Edsim 1230, El 1237, El Paso 1239, Electric 1240, Elias 1247, Eliason 1248, EMC 1253, EMCO 1254, Emerson 1257, Employers 1264, Endo 1268, Endres 1269, Energen 1270, Energizer 1271, EnMark 1274, Entelco 1277, Entergy 1279, EPES 1283, Eppstein 1285, Epson 1286, Equifax 1288, Ergon 1289, Esbenshade's 1295, Essa 1297, Evening 1302, Exchange 1307, Executive 1308, Exelon 1309, Exxon 1315, Faber 1319, Fabick 1321, Fabri 1322, Factory 1323, Fairfax 1325, Fairfield 1326, Family 1330, Farrell 1341, FBR 1345, Federal 1350, Federated 1351, FEECO 1353, Fenton 1361, Ferro 1366, Fetzer 1367, FHC 1368, Fidelity 1372, Fieldstone 1374, Fifth 1376, Fifth 1377, Finance 1381, First 1391, First 1393, First 1394, First 1395, First 1396, First 1397, First 1398, First 1399, First 1400, First 1401, First 1402, First 1403, First 1404, First 1405, First 1406, First 1407, First 1408, First 1409, First 1410, First 1411, First 1413, First 1415, First 1416, First 1419, First 1420, First 1421, FirstEnergy 1424, Fiserv 1427, Fleck 1435, Flexcon 1436, Flint 1439, Flir 1440, Florida 1443, Florida 1444, Florsheim 1445, Fluor 1448, FMR 1450, Fonville 1456, Food 1458, Forest 1467, Formosa 1470, Fort 1472, Fortis 1473, Four 1477, Framingham 1481, Franklin 1485, Fredericksburg 1490, Freeport 1494, Freescale 1495, Fremont 1496, Fremont 1497, Freres 1498, Frito 1506, Fuller 1517, Fulton 1518, Furniture 1519, G&K 1524, Gable 1525, Gannett 1532, Gap 1533, Gardner 1536, Gateway 1541, Gelco 1546, Gemini 1547, General 1551, General 1552, General 1553, General 1554, General 1555, General 1557, General 1558, Genesco 1559, Geneseo 1560, GenOn 1563, GenRad 1564, Genworth 1565, Georgia 1567, Giant 1571, Gibbons 1574, Gibbs 1576, Gibraltar 1577, Gibson 1579, Give 1583, GKN 1585, Gleaner 1590, Gleason 1591, Global 1592, Go 1595, Golub 1607, Gon 1608, Goodman 1610, Goodyear 1612, Gosiger 1617, Gould 1618, Grace 1623, Graco 1624, Graham 1625, Grand 1627, Grandma 1630, Grange 1631, Granite 1632, Graphix 1637, Graybar 1640, Graycor 1641, Great 1643, Green 1650, Green 1651, Green 1653, Greene 1656, Gregory 1661, Gregory 1662, Greif 1663, Griffith 1666, Grinnell 1668, Griswold 1669, Grove 1672, GSM 1676, Guarantee 1678, Guaranty 1679, Guard 1680, Guess 1685, GuideOne 1687, Gulf 1688, Gulf 1689, Gulfstream 1690, H & R 1695, Hagerty 1698, Hall 1703, Halliburton 1706, Hallmark 1707, Hampden 1712, Hamrick 1715, Hancock 1716, Hancock 1717, Hannaford 1723, Hanover 1724, Hanson 1725, Harbert 1726, Hard 1727, Harden 1728, Hardinge 1729, Harley 1732, Harleysville 1733, Harris 1736, Harriss 1740, Harsco 1741, Hartford 1742, Hartford 1743, Hartzell 1745, Harvey 1746, Haskell 1748, Hastings 1749, Haviland 1752, Hawaii 1753, Hawkins 1757, Haynes 1759, Heffernan 1769, Heidtman 1770, Heinz 1772, Helmerich 1774, Henkels 1779, Herr 1787, Herrick 1788, Herschend 1790, Hershey 1791, Hewlett 1794, Heyman 1796, Hickory 1797, Highwoods 1800, Hilliard 1806, HNI 1817, Hodgson 1820, Hoffer 1821, Hoffmann 1823, Hofmann 1824, Holder 1829, Holiday 1830, Holiday 1831, Holmes 1838, Holtz 1840, Homasote 1841, Home 1843, Home 1845, Honda 1851, Hoops 1857, Hooters 1858, Horizon 1861, Hormel 1866, Houston 1870, Hubbard 1877, Hubbard 1878, Hudson 1880, Hufcor 1883, Huhtamaki 1884, Humana 1886, Hunt 1890, Huntington 1894, Hutchison 1898, Hutton 1899, IAC 1903, IDACORP 1907, Idealist 1909, IDT 1910, IHC 1913, Illinois 1916, IMA 1917, Imation 1919, Independent 1927, Independent 1928, Indiana 1931, Indium 1933, Indus 1934, ING 1938, Ingersoll 1939, Ingredion 1942, Insperity 1944, Institution 1946, Integrity 1949, Interlock 1954, Intermountain 1957, International 1958, International 1960, International 1962, International 1963, International 1964, International

Human services, alliance/advocacy

Human services, emergency aid

Human services, financial counseling

Capital 679, Charter 767, Cisco 818, Citigroup 821, Columbia 882, Comerica 889, Compass 901, Country 951, Credit 977, Deutsche 1099, Discover 1125, Eastern 1209, Emmis 1260, Entergy 1279, Federal 1348, Fifth 1377, First 1390, First 1396, First 1400, First 1406, Fluor 1448, FMR 1450, Fortis 1473, Franklin 1485, Franklin 1487, Fremont 1496, Genworth 1565, Huntington 1894, ING 1938, Intuit 1982, Johnson 2050, JPMorgan Chase 2071, KeyBank 2136, KPMG 2190, Liberty 2262, Lincoln 2278, Lincoln 2281, MasterCard 2399, MB 2415, McGraw 2429, Merrimack 2474, Metropolitan 2481, Middlesex 2506, Mizuho 2542, Morgan 2570, Motley 2582, Mutual 2607, Nasdaq 2617, New 2671, New York 2688, NIKE 2710, NYSE 2769, Old 2798, PACCAR 2850, Pacific 2855, People's 2928, PNC 2997, PPG 3025, Primerica 3045, Principal 3047, Provident 3069, RBC 3136, RBS 3137, Regions 3171, Russell 3289, Salem 3317, Savings 3343, Schwab 3363, Sovereign 3528, StanCorp 3574, Strauss 3624, SunTrust 3654, TCF 3695, TD 3696, Thrivent 3747, TransUnion 3799, U.S. 3835, U.S. 3836, Union 3854, Union 3858, United 3872, Visa 3960, Wal-Mart 3980, Webster 4016, Wells 4028, Western 4042, Western 4045

Human services, fund raising/fund distribution

Advance 39, Alliant 104, Aramco 224, Bigelow 462, Boston 540, Broadcom 579, Chicago 782, Cumberland 1003, Delaware 1066, DineEquity 1120, FirstEnergy 1424, Give 1583, Halliburton 1706, Harris 1736, Hartford 1743, Louisiana 2309, Macy's 2333, Mt. 2594, Northwest 2747, People's 2928, RBC 3136, Reed 3161, Ricoh 3210, Sealy 3382, Shenandoah 3433, SUPERVALU 3659, TJX 3765, Tops 3774, U.S. 3838, Zappos.com 4153

Human services, gift distribution

Alabama 71, Allianz 105, Almar 110, AmeriPride 173, Ameritec 179, Ascena 255, AZPB 310, Barnes 360, Berry 437, Boston 540, Brooklyn 584, Carter's 708, Cavaliers 724, Chicago 782, CryoLife 990, Denny's 1087, Discovery 1126, Dollar 1145, Dunkin' 1191, FMR 1450, GATX 1542, Gulf 1689, Heat 1767, Hilton 1812, Hunt 1888, Jones 2059, Kahn 2085, Kmart 2172, Lam 2214, Levi 2254, Life 2268, Lockheed 2292, Martin 2391, Miller 2523, Milwaukee 2528, Neville 2667, New Jersey 2676, New York 2684, New York 2686, Nortex 2727, Orlando 2824, Otis 2835, Philadelphia 2958, Pioneer 2981, Pittsburgh 2986, Reader's 3141, Regal 3166, Rood 3257, San Diego 3322, St. Louis 3567, Trail 3793, Tyler 3831, Univar 3886, ViewSonic 3952, Wadsworth 3974, Wal-Mart 3980, Washington 4000, Watson 4007, Wendy's 4031, Zappos.com 4153

Human services, mind/body enrichment

Caesars 650, Fisher 1433, Nortex 2727, Orlando 2824, South 3510, Wal-Mart 3980

Human services, personal services

G&K 1524, Nordson 2723

Human services, public education

Bigelow 462

Human services, reform

Nordson 2723

Human services, volunteer services

Cary 712, Texas 3729

Humanities

Alliant 104, Amica 183, Bank 344, Bloomberg 486, Brightpoint 567, Cajun 652, Corvallis 947, First 1420, Jeld 2032, Kohler 2182, NEBCO 2653, New 2668, Oxford 2847, Peoples 2929, Schott 3360, Vulcan 3970, Williams 4077

Immigrants/refugees

Autodesk 289, Beneficial 412, Blue 496, Deutsche 1099, State 3592, Western 4045

Immunology

Baxter 377, MedImmune 2450, Walgreen 3981

Independent housing for people with disabilities

Alliance 101, Bridgestone 560, Lincoln 2281, Union 3854

Independent living, disability

Allergan 99, AMERIGROUP 171, Andersen 194, Apache 211, Blue 497, CH2M 758, CVS 1014, Esurance 1298, Fuller 1517, Law 2233, Lincoln 2281, Madison 2334, Mitsubishi 2538, PacifiCorp 2860, StanCorp 3574, TJX 3765, Unum 3898, Waffle 3975

Indigenous peoples

Autodesk 289, Bank 342, Calista 657, Chrysler 801, NANA 2615, Sitnasuak 3467, WD-40 4011, Xerox 4136

Infants/toddlers

Autodesk 289, Blue 501, Chrysler 801, Cow 957, Metropolitan 2481, Piedmont 2971, Principal 3047, St. Joe 3563, Washington 3994, WD-40 4011

Infants/toddlers, female

Autodesk 289, Beneficial 412, Chrysler 801, Metropolitan 2481, WD-40 4011

Infants/toddlers, male

Autodesk 289, Beneficial 412, Chrysler 801, Metropolitan 2481, WD-40 4011

Insurance, providers

Lincoln 2281, UnitedHealth 3884

International affairs

A.J. 8, American 146, AMETEK 181, Fremont 1497, Gap 1533, General 1552, Johnson 2048, Kasle 2098, Miller 2517, Mitsui 2541, Tireco 3762, Tulalip 3820, Union 3856, Warburg 3985

International affairs, equal rights

Symantec 3669

International affairs, goodwill promotion

First 1408, Sealaska 3380, Sit 3466

International affairs, management/technical assistance

Cisco 818

International affairs, U.N.

General 1552, Johnson 2048, PricewaterhouseCoopers 3042, Western 4045

International agricultural development

Renovated 3185

International conflict resolution

Ascena 255, Bridgeway 563

International development

Abbott 13, Accenture 22, Archer 233, Azavea 309, Cargill 691, Clarity 834, Community 900, Dharma 1105, Hilfiger 1801, Huntsman 1895, Jenzabar 2037, Johnson 2048, Laureate 2231, Leibowitz 2248, McKinstry 2435, Panda 2871, Pfizer 2950, Pura 3084, Quality 3096, Ramerica 3125, Towerbrook 3781, Warburg 3985, Whole 4066

International economic development

Econscious 1223, One 2811, Pattillo 2896, Primary 3043, Select 3398, Starbucks 3585, Visa 3960, Whole 4066

International economics/trade policy

American 153, Better 449, General 1552, Kikkoman 2144

International exchange

JTB 2074, Panasonic 2870

International exchange, students

Kikkoman 2144, Merck 2466, Mitsui 2541, Sony 3502

International human rights

Alima 90, Allen 94, Brilliant 568, Cleary 843, Econscious 1223, Hilton 1812, Kann 2090, Leibowitz 2248, Omnicom 2808, Skadden 3470, Working 4116

International migration/refugee issues

ACE 24, Fast 1343, Visa 3960

International peace/security

Bridgeway 563, Friedland 1503, Working 4116

International relief

Abbott 13, ACE 24, AK 67, Allegis 92, Allen 94, Applied 220, Ascena 255, Associated 264, AVX 306, BP 547, Bridgeway 563, Brookstone 586, Brotherhood 588, Capital 677, Cary 712, Cintas 816, Collette 872, Community 900, Danaher 1027, Deutsch 1098, DreamWorks 1172, Eastman 1214, FedEx 1352, Hendrick 1777, Hoffmann 1823, Holland 1834, Huntsman 1895, IDT 1910, Interpublic 1974, Johnson 2048, Katten 2101, Kimberly 2150, McShane 2439, Miller 2517, Nissan 2716, Nomura 2720, Ohio 2791, Omnicom 2808, Power 3020, ProLogis 3060, Pukall 3082, Quality 3096, Southern 3517, Spark 3533, Turner 3824, United 3872, Warburg 3985, Weil 4022, Yum! 4150

International relief, 2004 tsunami

DreamWorks 1172

International studies

JTB 2074, Panasonic 2870

Islam

Continental 925, Edible 1226, Issa 1997

LGBTQ

Abbott 13, Allstate 107, Arnold 248, Autodesk 289, Chrysler 801, Globe 1594, KeyBank 2136, Metropolitan 2481, PG&E 2952

Libraries (public)

Abbott 13, AbbyBank 15, Acuity 31, AgStar 59, Allegheny 91, Alliant 104, Ariel 237, Artichoke 254, Ash 256, BancTrust 337, Bank 343, Bank 348, Barron's 364, BB&T 385, Berkshire 428, Best 442, Blue 496, BP 547, Buccaneer 599, Capital 677, Central 745, Chicago 785, Chicago 787, Clark 835, Concept 905, Consumers 921, CUNA 1008, Dean 1053, Dedham 1060, Dime 1118, Dominion 1150, Donnelley 1155, Eastern 1210, Easthampton 1212, Edison 1229, Emerson 1257, Energizer 1271, EQT 1287, Essa 1297, Evening 1302, F.N.B. 1318, Four 1477, Genentech 1549, Graycor 1641, Harken 1731, HNI 1817, Hubbell 1879, IDT 1910, Industrial 1935, Janus 2024, Johnson 2050, Kimball 2149, Kinder 2153, KOA 2178, Land 2217, Lefton 2244, Manitowoc 2356, McDonald 2426, MDU 2441, Mercury 2468, Mid 2503, Midmark 2507, Midwestone 2508, Miller 2518, Mine 2529, Monsanto 2559, National 2635, National 2636, Nestle 2663, New York 2683, Newspapers 2702, Niemann 2708, Northern 2740, Ohio 2790, Pacific 2858, Parker 2886, People's 2928, Phillips 2966, Plum 2991, PPG 3025, Praxair 3029, Price 3040, Providence 3068, Provident 3069, Quad 3091, Regis 3172, Reiff 3174, Rockville 3245, Rodgers 3250, Safeco 3306, San Diego 3322, Simpson 3461, Southern 3515, Sovereign 3528, Synovus 3674, Target 3691, Tension 3717, Thomaston 3736, Timken 3760, Trim 3810, Union 3857, United 3869, Valero 3915, Verizon 3936, Washington 3998, Washington 4001, Williams 4077, Wisconsin 4093, Wolf 4103, World 4122

Libraries (school)

Cablevision 641, F.N.B. 1318, OceanFirst 2782, Oklahoma 2794

Libraries (special)

Copley 938, Dallas 1022

Libraries/library science

Arbitron 227, Bound 541, Bridgestone 560, Corning 945, Harper 1735, Joy 2070, NorthWestern 2748, Peoples 2931, Piedmont 2971, Target 3691, Wiley 4072

Literature

Amazon.com 122, Bertelsmann 439, Cook 934, Hachette 1696, Johnson 2050, Kukui 2198, Land 2217, Monsanto 2559, Peoples 2929, Skidmore 3474, Starbucks 3585

Lung diseases

Calpine 661, Chevron 780, Kindred 2154, Lincoln 2279, Medtronic 2453, Pfizer 2950, Wagner 3976

Lung research

AMC 125, Respironics 3193

Lupus

New York 2687

Marine science

Capital 678, Hannaford 1723, Herschend 1790, Holland 1835

Mathematics

3M 3, Abbott 13, Advanced 40, AGL 57, Akamai 68, Alcoa 82, American 150, Amgen 182, Andersen 194, Applied 220, AT&T 273, Avery 297, Baxter 377, Bayer 381, Bechtel 395, Beckman 397, Boehringer 515, Boeing 516, Boston 540, Bristol 578, Broadcom 579, Burns 620, Cabot 642, Calvert 663, Carpenter 700, Caterpillar 722, Cavaliers 724, Central 741, CH2M 758, Chevron 780, Cisco 818, Commonwealth 895, Consumers 921, Cook 934, Cubist 999, Cummins 1007, Deere 1061, Deutsche 1099, Digi 1115, Dominion 1150, Dow 1162, Draper 1171, DTE 1183, du Pont 1184, Duke 1189, Edison 1228, El Paso 1239, Electronic 1242, EMC 1253, EQT 1287, Ernst 1293, Exelon 1309, Express 1313, Exxon 1315, FirstEnergy 1424, Flextronics 1437, Flint 1439, Fluor 1448, Freeport 1494, Freescale 1495, Fuller 1517, GenCorp 1548, General 1552, General 1555, GlaxoSmithKline 1588, Google 1613, Harris 1736, Hewlett 1794, Honeywell 1852, Intel 1950, International 1960, IPALCO 1988, KBR 2106, KLA-Tencor 2165, L'Oreal 2203, Lam 2214, Lexmark 2258, LG&E Energy 2260, Lilly 2274, Lincoln 2281, Lockheed 2292, LSI 2314, LyondellBasell 2322, Medtronic 2453, Mentor 2462, Merck 2466, Mercury 2469, Michelin 2495, Microchip 2499, Micron 2500, Microsoft 2501, Modine 2544, Monsanto 2559, Moody's 2563, Motorola 2586, New 2671, Nordson 2723, Norfolk 2725, Northrop 2744, NorthWestern 2748, Nucor 2760, Oklahoma 2794, Old 2798, OMNOVA 2809, Oracle 2821, Pacific 2855, Parametric 2878, Pearson 2911, Pentair 2926, People's 2928, Pfizer 2950, Piedmont 2971, Piper 2983, PNC 2997, Portland 3010, PPG 3025, Procter 3055, Public 3077, QUALCOMM 3095, Rackspace 3117, Raytheon 3135, ResMed 3192, Rockwell 3246, Rockwell 3247, Rosen's 3264, SAIC 3311, SAP 3334, Seagate 3377, Securian 3389, Sempra 3405, Siemens 3448, Spansion 3532, St. Jude 3566, Stanley 3579, Subaru 3631, Symantec 3669, Synopsys 3673, TD 3696, Tellabs 3709, Texas 3728, Thermo 3733, Time 3755, Toshiba 3776, Toyota 3784, Tyco 3829, United 3882, USEC 3904, UTC 3908, Verizon 3936, Vulcan 3972, Washington 3995, Western 4042, Westinghouse 4049, Xcel 4135, Xilinx 4137

Media/communications

Acuity 32, AMC 126, American 139, Andersen 194, Arkema 242, Athletics 276, Cablevision 640, Caterpillar 722, Clear 842, Corning 945, Disney 1127, Emerson 1257, Federated 1351, Fiserv 1427, Fisher 1430, Gannett 1532, Harsco 1741, Homasote 1841, IAC 1903, Jacksonville 2014, Milliken 2525, National 2625, PACE 2851, Pacific 2858, Playboy 2990, Record 3149, Robins 3232, Scripps 3374, Sovereign 3528, Time 3757, Toro 3775, United 3881, Williams 4077, Wolf 4103, World 4122

Medical care, community health systems

Abbott 13, Assurant 267, Blue 497, Boston 540, Bristol 578, Cambia 665, Cardinal 685, CareSource 690, CVS 1014, Hewlett 1794, Kaiser 2086, Lilly 2274, Medical 2448, Medtronic 2453, Merck 2466, Pfizer 2950, sanofi-aventis 3329, Springs 3555, SunTrust 3654, UnitedHealth 3884

Medical care, in-patient care

Boart 510, C & S 634, Cambia 665, Foremost 1466, Hasbro 1747, Klein's 2169, Merfish 2472, Piedmont 2971

Medical care, outpatient care

LifePoint 2270

Medical care, rehabilitation

Aetna 48, Alice 89, Bridgestone 560, Callaway 660, CVS 1014, Government 1621, Mapes 2360, StanCorp 3574, Teichert 3704, Temple 3711, True 3814

Medical research

Abt 20, American 150, American 158, Arbella 226, Beckman 397, Beneficial 411, Bloomberg 486, Blue 502, Boston 540, Build 608, Center 737, Coach 858, COPIC 937, Cox 959, CSL 993, Danforth 1028, Davis 1037, Doctors 1139, DRW 1181, EMD 1256, Emerson 1257, Exxon 1315, Fellowes 1357, FHC 1368, First 1418, Florida 1442, Fortune 1474, General 1555, Greene 1656, Gucci 1684, Hanover 1724, Hargray 1730, Hopkins 1859, Howmedica 1875, Hunt 1892, Integra 1947, International 1958, International Profit 1969, Interthyr 1978, Joy 2070, JPMorgan 2072, Kohler 2182, L'Oreal 2203, Lamont 2215, Leviton 2255, Manocherian 2357, Mary 2392, Maverick 2409, Mazda 2414, MBIA 2416, McDonald 2426, McKinstry 2435, Medtronic 2453, Merck 2466, Nasdaq 2618, National 2626, Nu 2759, NYSE 2769, Olympus 2804, Palm 2867, Quad 3091, Quest 3103, ResMed 3192, Rexnord 3198, Smith 3484, Southern 3521, Sub-Zero 3630, TJX 3765, United 3871, USEC 3904, Walgreen 3981, Whiting 4063, Zimmer 4157

Medical research, fund raising/fund distribution

AMN Healthcare 184, Disney 1127, Hyundai 1902, IMS 1924, Jefferies 2030, Quest 3103, ServiceMaster 3414

Medical research, institute

Allergan 99, Ameritec 179, Blue 502, Boiron 519, ICON 1906, Manocherian 2357, McDonald's 2427, Merck 2466, Reinsurance 3179, sanofi-aventis 3329, Sensient 3408, Seton 3415, Watson 4006

Medical research, public education

American 158, Arch 230

Medical research, single organization support

Jones 2059

Medical school/education

Aetna 48, Alcon 83, Allergan 99, Amgen 182, Arnold 248, Badger 313, Bausch 376, Block 482, Blue 502, Blue 505, BlueCross 507, Bon 521, Boston 540, Bristol 578, BSA 597, Charter 766, Community 900, COPIC 937, Corvallis 947, CVS 1014, Dietz 1114, Eastern 1211, Evening 1302, Express 1313, Genentech 1549, Gilead 1582, Indiana 1929, Integra 1947, Jacobs 2016, K-Swiss 2082, Kadant 2083, Krasdale 2192, Kuskokwim 2200, Lilly 2274, Luxottica 2319, Marcus 2371, Mary 2392, McKesson 2434, North 2730, Olympus 2804, Orthopaedic 2829, Pacers 2852, Respironics 3193, sanofi-aventis 3329, Scientific 3367, Titan 3763, United 3867, UnitedHealth 3884, Wagner 3976, Wolverine 4106, Zimmer 4157

Medical specialties

Bard 358

Medical specialties research

American 158, sanofi-aventis 3329

Medicine/medical care, public education

ACI 27, Blue 505, CVS 1014, Delta 1083, Express 1313, Kaiser 2086, Lilly 2274, Louisiana 2309, Pfizer 2950, Principal 3047

Men
Abbott 13, Autodesk 289, Beneficial 412, Chrysler 801, Genesis 1561, Metropolitan 2481, Piedmont 2971

Mental health, addictions
Commercial 892

Mental health, association
International 1959

Mental health, counseling/support groups
Blue 493, Kimball 2149, OceanFirst 2782, Scientific 3367, TJX 3765

Mental health, disorders
Lilly 2274, RBC 3136

Mental health, gambling addiction
Churchill 807, Coquille 939, Spirit 3544

Mental health, grief/bereavement counseling
Baird 317, Belleville 405, Highmark 1799, Neace 2651, New York 2688, Regence 3168, Rosen's 3264

Mental health, treatment
Andersson 196, Blue 505, Bristol 578, RBC 3136

Mental health/crisis services
ABARTA 10, ACF 26, Aetna 48, Amerisure 177, Andersen 194, Androscoggin 199, Bangor 338, Baxter 377, Blue 493, Blue 496, Blue 498, Bristol 578, Butt 628, Caesars 650, Chaney 761, CUNA 1008, Deluxe 1084, Duchossois 1187, First 1421, Forest 1467, Freeport 1494, Fremont 1496, H & R 1695, Hasbro 1747, Health 1766, Highmark 1799, Horizon 1863, Kaiser 2086, Lilly 2274, Mascoma 2394, MB 2415, McClatchy 2422, Miller 2518, Mutual 2607, OceanFirst 2782, Patton's 2899, Piedmont 2971, Portland 3010, Power 3022, Provident 3069, RBC 3136, Redwoods 3158, Rose 3263, RUAN 3279, Sensient 3408, Shakopee 3419, Todd 3766, Toyota 3784, Trans 3795, Wadsworth 3974, Wagner 3976, Walter 3984, Warren 3993, Western 4040, Wisconsin 4096, Woodward 4112

Mental health/crisis services, formal/general education
American 158

Mental health/crisis services, public education
Blue 505, RBC 3136

Mentally disabled
Autodesk 289, Bank 347, Beneficial 412, Commercial 893, CVS 1014, Genesis 1561, Gilbane 1581, Knitcraft 2174, Spark 3533, St. Joe 3563, WD-40 4011, Xerox 4136

Microfinance/microlending
Abacus 9, ACE 24, Bank 346, Beck 396, Caterpillar 722, Cisco 818, Citigroup 821, Credit 980, eBay 1217, Flir 1440, JPMorgan Chase 2071, McGraw 2429, McKinstry 2435, Moody's 2563, NIKE 2710, Pattillo 2896, Philip 2962, Starbucks 3585, Union 3854, United 3872, Urban 3901, Visa 3960, Whole 4066

Middle schools/education
AbbyBank 15, Biogen 465, Capital 677, Crowell 986, General 1552, International 1967, Jack 2007, Lennar 2250, P.E.L. 2849, Public 3076, Urban 3901, Wal-Mart 3980

Migrant workers
Autodesk 289, WD-40 4011, Western 4045

Military/veterans
Activision 30, Airgas 65, Anheuser 202, AT&T 273, Autodesk 289, Baxter 377, Beam 390, Beneficial 412, Berkshire 428, Bloomin 487, Bristol 578, Cadence 646, Callaway 660, Carlson 693, Chrysler 801, Cintas 816, Community 899, Delmarva 1069, Deluxe 1084, Detroit 1095, Dollar 1143, DRS 1179, EMCOR 1255, Express 1313, Ferrellgas 1365, Ford 1464, General 1551, Genesis 1561, Giant 1572, Grainger 1626, Health 1766, Longaberger 2299, Masco 2393, Metropolitan 2481, National 2628, Newman's 2697, North 2728, Packaging 2861, Penney 2925, Questar 3104, Safety 3309, SAIC 3311, Schwab 3363, SEAKR 3379, Sears 3384, Spark 3533, Union 3857, Valassis 3914, Verizon 3936, Viejas 3951, Wal-Mart 3980, WD-40 4011, Western 4042, Xerox 4136

Military/veterans' organizations
Anheuser 202, AT&T 273, Avis 300, Boston 536, Boston 540, California 655, CenterPoint 738, Cisco 818, Comcast 887, CVS 1014, Discover 1125, Discovery 1126, Dollar 1145, Dr 1169, DRS 1179, Dunkin' 1191, Ensign 1276, Express 1313, First 1389, Fisher 1431, Food 1458, Garff 1538, General 1553, General 1555, Global 1592, Government 1621, Harris 1736, Hasbro 1747, Hooters 1858, Hy-Vee 1900, Insperity 1944, Kmart 2172, Lockheed 2292, Maritz 2376, Masco 2393, McGraw 2429, Men's 2460, Miller 2523, MSC 2593, National 2638, Newman's 2697, North 2728, Northrop 2744, Orlando 2824, Raytheon 3135, SAP 3334, Sempra 3405, Shaw's 3427, Sit 3466, SRA 3562, Star 3583, Stoneham 3616, Towerbrook 3781, United 3873, Valero 3915, Wal-Mart 3980, Washington 3998, Wendy's/Arby's 4030, Western 4042, World 4121

Minorities
3M 3, Abbott 13, Aetna 48, Aflac 54, Agilent 56, AGL 57, Alabama 71, Alcoa 82, Alliance 101, Alliant 104, Allstate 107, Ameren 129, American 150, Anheuser 202, Aon 210, Apex 213, Arnold 248, AT&T 273, Austin 288, Autodesk 289, Avis 299, Avis 300, Avista 301, AXA 307, B & B 312, Bank 349, Bayer 381, Beneficial 412, Blue 493, Blue 496, Bracewell 549, Bressler 557, Broadcom 579, Burlington 618, Butler 626, Caterpillar 722, Centene 735, Chicago 788, Chrysler 801, Cisco 818, Citigroup 821, Colgate 869, Columbia 884, Comerica 889, Compass 901, Compuware 902, Cox 958, Crane 970, Deere 1061, Deutsche 1099, DTE 1183, Eastman 1214, Enterprise 1281, Exxon 1315, Family 1330, First 1398, Fisher 1430, Ford 1464, Gannett 1532, GenCorp 1548, General 1554, Genesis 1561, Georgia 1568, GlaxoSmithKline 1588, Globe 1594, Golub 1607, Graco 1624, Great 1645, Greyhound 1664, Heinz 1772, Hewlett 1794, Highmark 1799, Hubbard 1878, ING 1938, Intel 1950, International 1960, Intoximeters 1979, JPMorgan Chase 2071, KeyBank 2136, KPMG 2190, Kroger 2195, Ladies 2209, Las Vegas 2225, LG&E Energy 2260, Macy's 2333, Mazda 2414, Medtronic 2453, Metropolitan 2481, Moody's 2563, Moore 2565, Morgan 2570, Motorola 2586, National 2638, North 2735, NYSE 2769, Pactiv 2863, Pawtucket 2902, Penney 2925, People's 2928, PepsiCo 2935, PG&E 2952, Piedmont 2971, Pitney 2984, PPG 3025, Seagate 3377, Semiconductor 3403, Sensient 3408, SI 3444, Siemens 3448, Simpson 3461, Southern 3514, St. Joe 3563, St. Louis 3567, Steelcase 3597, Sysco 3677, Textron 3731, Total 3778, Toyota 3784, Toyota 3786, Travelers 3802, United 3872, United 3882, Wal-Mart 3980, WD-40 4011, Western 4045, Wisconsin 4094, Wisconsin 4096, Xerox 4136

Minorities/immigrants, centers/services
Andersen 194, B & B 312, Butler 627, Cleary 843, Crowell 986, Eastern 1209, Popular 3003, Sempra 3405, Tesoro 3723, Western 4045

Multiple sclerosis
Allegheny 91, AmeriPride 173, Cummins 1006, Giant 1572, Global 1593, IAC 1903, International 1971, K-Swiss 2082, Kuhns 2197, Manocherian 2357, MEMC 2459, Minto 2533, Patton's 2899, Regal 3166, Rexnord 3198, Rothstein 3271, S.B.E. 3298, Swift 3666, TeleTech 3708, V.F. 3913, Valero 3915, Western 4040

Multiple sclerosis research
Haggen 1699, Novetta 2755, Schoonover 3359

Multipurpose centers/programs
U.S. 3835, Urban 3901

Muscular dystrophy
CITGO 820, Denny's 1087, Dr 1169, Harley 1732, Hooters 1858, International Profit 1969, Kuhns 2197, Safeway 3310, Save 3342, Valero 3915, Wolverine 4106, Zappos.com 4153

Museums
Abbott 13, ACI 27, Acuity 31, AEGON 45, Aflac 54, AK 67, Alice 89, Allegheny 91, Allstate 107, Altria 120, American 143, American 145, American 159, American 164, American 169, AMETEK 181, Andersen 194, Arkema 242, Associated 264, AutoZone 294, Avis 299, Avista 301, Aviva 302, AVX 306, Badger 313, Bailey 315, Baker 318, Bakewell 326, Baum 375, Bausch 376, Bayer 381, Belk 404, Beneficial 411, Berkshire 428, Berry 437, Boh 517, BP 547, Bridgestone 560, Brooks 585, Buccaneer 599, Burlington 618, C Spire 636, Calpine 661, Capital 677, Caterpillar 722, Centene 735, Churchill 807, Cianbro 808, CLARCOR 832, Cliffs 850, Colonial 875, Compass 901, Concept 905, Consolidated 917, Cooper 936, Copley 938, Corning 945, Crane 969, Crescent 983, Dallas 1022, Dean 1053, Delaware 1066, Delta 1073, Deluxe 1084, Deutsche 1099, Dollar 1142, Dominion 1150, Donnelley 1155, Dow 1162, Econoco 1222, Edison 1229, Emerson 1257, Empire 1262, Endeavor 1267, Energizer 1271, Entergy 1279, EQT 1287, Evening 1302, Factory 1323, Federated 1351, Fidelity 1371, First 1393, First 1395, First 1402, First 1406, First 1421, First 1422, Fisher 1431, Fluor 1448, Food 1458, Ford 1464, Fort 1472, Friesen 1505, GenCorp 1548, General 1555, Giant 1571, GlaxoSmithKline 1588, Golub 1607, Gould 1618, Grace 1623, Hoffmann 1823, Hubbard 1877, IDACORP 1907, Industrial 1935, Intermec 1955, International 1958, Jacobs 2016, Johnson 2049, Johnson 2050, Jones 2056, Joy 2070, JPMorgan Chase 2071, Katten 2101, Landmark 2218, Laureate 2231, Lee 2240, Liberty 2265, Lubrizol 2315, Lucasfilm 2316, Marnier-Lapostolle 2381, Marsh 2387, Mascoma 2394, MBIA 2416, McCarthy 2421, McCormick 2423, MDU 2441, MeadWestvaco 2445, Mentor 2462, Mercury 2468, Mine 2529, Mississippi 2536, Monadnock 2551, Morgan 2568, Morgan 2570, National 2629, National 2631, National 2635, Natural 2641, Naugatuck 2645, Nestle 2663, New York 2683, Newfield 2695, Newsweek 2703, Nissan 2716, Norfolk 2725, NorthWestern 2748, Northwestern 2749, NTELOS 2758, OceanFirst 2782, Ohio 2790, Oklahoma 2794, Old 2796, Omaha 2805, OMNOVA 2809, PACE 2851, PacifiCorp 2860, Peoples 2931, PerkinElmer 2939, Physicians 2970, Piedmont 2971, Pinnacle

2977, Plain 2989, Plum 2991, Presley 3038, Prince 3046, ProLogis 3060, Provident 3069, PVH 3088, Quaker 3093, Questar 3104, Rasmussen 3128, Ratner 3130, Rayonier 3134, Riggs 3213, SCANA 3346, Schloss 3352, Servco 3412, Smucker 3488, Snell 3490, South Bend 3507, Southern 3515, Sovereign 3528, Specialty 3537, Specialty 3538, Springleaf 3554, Sprint 3556, Stardust 3586, State 3590, Stiles 3607, SunTrust 3654, Synovus 3674, Tanner 3688, Target 3691, TECO 3701, Temple 3711, Texas 3725, Tiffany 3750, Time 3757, Titan 3763, True 3814, U.S. 3835, UBS 3842, Union 3854, Union 3857, United 3860, United 3864, United 3868, United 3869, United 3870, United 3882, US 3902, USEC 3904, Usibelli 3906, V.F. 3913, Valero 3915, Wachtell 3973, Washington 4001, Weil 4022, Western 4040, Western 4043, Wiley 4072, Williams 4077, Williams 4078, Wisconsin 4093, Wisconsin 4096, Wolverine 4106, Woodward 4112

Museums (art)

American 132, American 141, American 157, Anderson 195, Arch 231, Assurant 266, AVX 306, Baird 317, Barron's 364, BB&T 385, Booz 525, BP 547, Brown 591, Bunge 612, Capital 677, Contran 928, Cooper 936, Crystal 992, CSS 996, CUNA 1008, Dallas 1022, Dana 1026, DeBruce 1057, Deutsche 1099, Dynamet 1200, Eaton 1216, EFC 1236, Eliason 1248, Energizer 1271, First 1421, Flexcon 1436, Forest 1467, Franklin 1485, Fujisankei 1515, Furniture 1519, Gable 1525, GenRad 1564, GlaxoSmithKline 1588, Global 1593, Haynie 1760, Highwoods 1800, Holder 1829, Huntington 1894, IMA 1917, International 1962, JPMorgan Chase 2071, Kawasaki 2103, Kenneth 2128, Lee 2241, Lefton 2244, Legg 2245, Loews 2296, M&T 2323, Makino 2348, Manhattan 2354, McClatchy 2422, McKinstry 2435, Metropolitan 2481, Mississippi 2536, Mitchell 2537, Monadnock 2551, Morris 2573, Motorists 2584, National 2629, O'Connor 2770, Oakley 2774, Ohio 2790, Ohio 2791, Orleans 2825, Owens 2844, Pacific 2858, Pan-American 2868, Price 3040, Protective 3066, Quad 3091, Regal 3166, Rexnord 3198, S & S 3296, SClenergy 3366, Scoular 3373, Simplot 3459, Simpson 3461, Skinner 3475, State 3590, Stewart 3604, SunTrust 3654, Tap 3689, Teachers 3697, TECO 3701, Terre 3722, United 3864, Universal 3895, Valero 3915, Virginia 3959, Wausau 4008, Wendy's 4032, Weyco 4051

Museums (children's)

Ameritas 178, Imperial 1922, MidAmerican 2504, Terre 3722, United 3868

Museums (ethnic/folk arts)

Giant 1571

Museums (history)

1st 2, American 146, Century 750, Flexcon 1436, Ford 1463, Ideal 1908, Illinois 1916, Loews 2296, TECO 3701, Wolf 4103

Museums (marine/maritime)

Alexander 85, AnchorBank 193, Truland 3817

Museums (natural history)

Bassett 372, F.N.B. 1318, Orleans 2825, Orvis 2830

Museums (science/technology)

3M 3, Abbott 13, American 155, Bailey 315, Bayer 381, Biogen 465, Burns 620, Cadence 646, Cargill 691, Dondlinger 1154, Ferro 1366, Flexcon 1436, Illinois 1916, Jones 2055, Kepco 2132, Life 2268, McWane 2440, Medtronic 2453, MEMC 2459, Northeast 2737, Oklahoma 2794, PPG 3025, Red 3154, Regions 3171, Stardust 3586, Texas 3728, Union 3857, Unisys 3859, United 3874, UTC 3908, Valspar 3920

Museums (specialized)

Alaska 74, Corning 945, Exotic 1310, Jeppesen 2038, Kawasaki 2103, Orvis 2830, Sierra 3449, Verizon 3936

Museums (sports/hobby)

Baltimore 334, General 1555, Mccar 2419

Music

AbbyBank 15, AEGON 45, American 141, Andersen 194, Arkansas 241, Assurant 267, Bertelsmann 439, Black 475, BOSE 530, Caddell 645, Chevron 780, Chicago 786, Citizens 827, Consolidated 917, Deutsche 1099, Dollywood 1146, EMI 1258, Ensign 1276, Excell 1304, Fender 1359, FMR 1450, Ford 1464, General 1558, Gibson 1578, Hampden 1712, Hard 1727, Homecrest 1847, IAC 1903, Issa 1997, JPMorgan Chase 2071, Kawasaki 2103, Kingsbury 2160, Kukui 2198, Lee 2241, Lincoln 2281, Lyon 2321, M&T 2323, Marnier-Lapostolle 2381, Martin 2391, McCarthy 2421, MTV 2596, Nomura 2720, Nortex 2727, Nu 2759, OceanFirst 2782, Pacific 2855, Pentair 2926, Presley 3038, RBC 3136, Red 3154, Regions 3171, Rodgers 3250, SANYO 3333, Shure 3443, SIFCO 3452, SunTrust 3654, Transco 3797, Tulalip 3820, United 3860, United 3867, Washington 3994, Wenger 4033, Wiley 4072

Music (choral)

Prince 3046

Music ensembles/groups

Imperial 1922

Native Americans/American Indians

13th 1, Aleut 84, Allstate 107, Arctic 234, Autodesk 289, Bering 422, Blue 496, Bristol 576, Burlington 618, Calista 657, Chenega 776, Chrysler 801, Chugach 805, Cook 934, Coquille 939, Cow 957, Doyon 1167, Four 1477, Freeport 1494, Genesis 1561, Hewlett 1794, Holland 1834, Huna 1887, Intel 1950, Intoximeters 1979, Koniag 2184, KPMG 2190, Kuskokwim 2200, Land 2217, Metropolitan 2481, Santa 3331, Sealaska 3380, Seldovia 3397, Semiconductor 3403, Shakopee 3419, Spirit 3544, St. Joe 3563, Tatitlek 3694, Tulalip 3820, Viejas 3951, Vinson 3957, Washington 3994, WD-40 4011, Xerox 4136

Natural resources

3M 3, A.D. 7, AGL 57, Alabama 71, Alcoa 82, Alexander 85, Allete 100, Alliant 104, Altria 120, American 140, American 141, AMETEK 181, Andersen 194, Anheuser 202, Apache 211, Aramco 224, Arch 231, Ash 256, Aspen 260, Avery 297, Badger 314, Bakewell 326, Barnes 362, Beneficial 411, Black 475, Boeing 516, Bound 541, BP 547, Bridgestone 560, Cajun 652, Canon 672, Cape 674, Capital 678, Cargill 691, Cascade 713, Caterpillar 722, CH2M 758, Charter 766, Chiquita 795, Clif 848, Columbia 884, Compass 901, Consumers 921, Continental 926, Contran 928, Cox 959, Crane 969, Cummins 1007, CVS 1014, Darden 1032, Delta 1073, Disney 1127, Dollywood 1146, Dominion 1150, Dow 1160, Dow 1162, Dr 1169, DTE 1183, Duke 1189, Ecolab 1220, Edison 1228, El Paso 1239, Emerson 1257, EQT 1287, Evening 1302, Exelon 1309, Exxon 1315, First 1419, Flint 1439, Freeport 1494, Fremont 1497, Gannett 1532, General 1555, GenOn 1563, Georgia 1567, Georgia 1568, GoLite 1606, Gosiger 1617, Grace 1623, Grand 1629, Heffernan 1769, Hilton 1812, IDACORP 1907, ING 1938, Intel 1950, Interface 1953, International 1958, IPALCO 1988, Johnson 2049, Johnson 2050, Kennebunk 2126, Kerzner 2133, Kimball 2149, Kimberly 2150, King 2158, Kingsbury 2160, Koch 2180, Kohler 2182, Lamont 2215, Longaberger 2299, Luck 2317, Magnolia 2340, Maquoketa 2361, Mars 2384, Martin 2391, Matson 2404, Mazda 2414, MDU 2441, Menasha 2461, Miller 2517, Mississippi 2536, Mitsubishi 2539, Monadnock 2551, Morley 2572, Murphy 2600, National 2630, National 2635, National 2636, NEBCO 2653, New England 2670, Newspapers 2702, Norfolk 2725, Northfield 2742, Northwest 2747, NV 2765, Orvis 2830, OSCO 2832, Otter 2836, Owens 2844, Pacific 2855, Patagonia 2892, PG&E 2952, Philip 2962, Piedmont 2971, Public 3076, Public 3077, Puget 3081, Quad 3091, Rahr 3118, Rayonier 3134, Recreational 3150, Redwoods 3158, Reell 3164, Rockwell 3247, Schott 3360, Sealaska 3380, Sempra 3405, SI 3444, Sierra 3449, Spirit 3544, Spirol 3545, Springs 3555, Stardust 3586, Subaru 3631, Sunshine 3653, SUPERVALU 3659, TD 3696, Tektronix 3706, Tellabs 3709, Tiffany 3750, Timberland 3754, Toro 3775, Toyota 3784, Toyota 3787, U.S. 3841, Unilever 3853, Union 3854, Union 3856, United 3872, United 3881, United 3882, Universal 3891, V.F. 3913, Vectren 3925, Vulcan 3972, Washington 4001, Western 4042, Westinghouse 4049, Weyerhaeuser 4052, Wisconsin 4093, Wisconsin 4096, Wolf 4103, Wolverine 4106, Wrigley 4125, YSI 4149

Neighborhood centers

Arent 235

Nerve, muscle & bone diseases

Allergan 99, Brocchini 580, Dietz 1114, Highmark 1799, Lilly 2274, Redner's 3157, sanofi-aventis 3329, Towerbrook 3781

Neuroscience

Amerisure 177, Bristol 578, KLS 2171, Lilly 2274, Mayer 2412, St. Jude 3566

Neuroscience research

Aramco 224, Integra 1947, KLS 2171

Nonprofit management

Abba 11, American 143, Elevation 1245, JPMorgan Chase 2071, Mississippi 2536, United 3872

Nursing care

Beneficial 411, Blue 498, Bristol 578, Corvallis 947, HCR 1763, Kindred 2154, Protector 3067, STERIS 3600

Nursing home/convalescent facility

Midcontinent 2505

Nursing school/education

Aetna 48, AMN Healthcare 184, Blue 493, Blue 504, Community 900, Corvallis 947, Fairmount 1328, Gregory 1662, Guardian 1682, HCR 1763, Johnson 2048, Kadant 2083, LifePoint 2270, McKesson 2434, New 2671

Nutrition

Abbott 13, Adobe 38, AEGON 45, Aetna 48, Amway 189, Arbeit 225, Assurant 266, Bank 340, Birdsong 470, Blue 490, Blue 493, Blue 494, Blue 496, Blue 497, Blue 501, Blue 502, Blue 504, Blue 505, Brooklyn 584, Butt 628, Caesars 650, Calvert 663, Campbell 669, Cargill 691, Cavaliers 724, CC 728, Chiquita 795, Coca 862, Coca 863, ConAgra 904, Dannon 1030, Dean 1054, Denver 1090, Dole 1141, DTE 1183,

Eastern 1209, Evans 1300, Food 1458, Freeport 1494, Fremont 1496, General 1554, Hannaford 1723, Heinz 1772, Highmark 1799, Hillshire 1809, Hood 1854, Horizon 1863, Humana 1886, Indianapolis 1932, Jacksonville 2014, Jamba 2020, Kaiser 2086, Kellogg 2120, King 2158, Land 2217, Life 2269, Louisiana 2309, Mead 2443, Merck 2466, Meyer 2485, Mondelez 2556, Monsanto 2559, Morgan 2570, Nash 2619, Nestle 2663, New 2668, Newman's 2697, Pagnol 2865, Palace 2866, PepsiCo 2935, Philadelphia 2957, Philadelphia 2959, Pioneer 2980, Plum 2992, Principal 3047, Quaker 3094, Questar 3105, RBS 3137, Redwoods 3158, Roundy's 3272, San Antonio 3321, Scotts 3372, Sensient 3408, Shaw's 3427, Smithfield 3487, Spurs 3557, Starbucks 3585, Stonyfield 3617, Stop 3618, SUPERVALU 3659, Sweetbay 3665, TJX 3765, Trustmark 3818, Unilever 3853, Upper 3900, Wal-Mart 3980, Wegmans 4021, Wellmark 4026, White 4062, Whole 4066, Wrigley 4125

Obstetrics/gynecology research
EMD 1256

Offenders/ex-offenders
Cleary 843, Lear 2237

Offenders/ex-offenders, rehabilitation
Colt 881

Offenders/ex-offenders, services
Men's 2460

Opera
Abba 11, Baird 317, Bridgestone 560, Capital 677, Centene 735, Chicago 787, Chicago 789, Consolidated 917, Demoulas 1085, Dondlinger 1154, Federated 1351, Fort 1472, Frankel 1483, Gosiger 1617, HCA 1762, Johnson 2049, Lee 2240, Lime 2276, Meritor 2473, Ohio 2790, Prince 3046, Questar 3104, Rahr 3118, Rodgers 3250, Southwest 3523, Spang 3530, Specialty 3537, Synovus 3674, U.M. 3834, World 4122, Zilkha 4156

Optometry/vision screening
Alcon 83, Bausch 376, Blue 493, Buccaneer 599, CIBA 810, Deutsche 1099, LensCrafters 2251, Luxottica 2319, Sacramento 3303, ShopKo 3440

Orchestras
3M 3, Acme 29, Allegheny 91, American 169, AMPCO 186, ANH 201, Apex 214, Arbella 226, Assurity 269, AVX 306, Baker 319, Baltimore 334, Bardes 359, Batson 373, BB&T 385, Berkley 426, Bridgestone 560, Brown 591, Caddell 645, Calumet 662, Cargill 691, CLARCOR 832, Cliffs 850, Consolidated 917, Cooper 936, Copley 938, Crescent 983, Dallas 1022, Dana 1026, Delta 1073, Dollar 1142, Eaton 1216, Ecolab 1220, Employers 1264, First 1406, First 1408, First 1416, Firstmerit 1425, Fluor 1448, Ford 1464, Forest 1467, Frankel 1483, Franklin 1484, Franklin 1485, Gable 1525, Giant 1571, Gosiger 1617, Graybar 1640, Graycor 1641, Hampden 1712, Harken 1731, Hubbard 1877, Huntington 1894, Illinois 1916, Institution 1946, Intermountain 1957, Interstate 1975, James 2021, Jones 2056, Laureate 2231, Lee 2240, Legg 2245, Liberty 2265, Lieberman 2266, Madison 2334, Marcus 2371, Marsh 2387, McDonald 2426, Meritor 2473, Mine 2529, Nasdaq 2618, National 2629, O'Connor 2770, Ohio 2790, Owens 2844, Pan-American 2868, Parker 2886, Prince 3046, Protective 3066, Red 3154, Regions 3171, Reily 3177, Rockwell 3246, RUAN 3279, SIFCO 3452, Simplot 3459, Simpson 3461, Sit 3466, Spang 3530, Springleaf 3554, Sprint 3556, Stardust 3586, SunTrust 3654, Superior 3658, Tap 3689, TeleTech 3708, Tennant 3714, Texas 3728, Tillman 3752, UBS 3842, Unaka 3848, United 3867, United 3870, V.F. 3913, Valspar 3920, Walter 3984, Wendy's 4032, Wenger 4033, Western 4041, Western 4043, Wolverine 4106, Zions 4158

Organ diseases
Kohler 2182

Orthodox agencies & churches
Demoulas 1085

Orthopedics
Hackstock 1697

Orthopedics research
Orthopaedic 2829

Painting
GOLDEN 1600, Skinner 3475

Palliative care
Aetna 48, ANH 201, Bristol 578, Cambia 665, HCR 1763, Hofmann 1824, MedImmune 2450, North 2730, Wachtell 3973

Parasitic diseases
Exxon 1315

Parkinson's disease
Avis 300, Sachs 3301, World 4122

Parkinson's disease research
Quanex 3100

Parks/playgrounds
Activision 30, Alabama 71, Alcoa 82, Allegis 92, Ariel 237, Belo 406, Black 475, Bloomberg 486, Blue 494, Brooklyn 584, Burlington 618, CH2M 758, Chicago 785, CIGNA 812, Clear 842, Concept 905, Consumers 921, Cooper 935, Cox 959, Credit 980, Cummins 1006, CVS 1014, Darden 1032, Delaware 1066, Dominion 1150, Dow 1162, Dunkin' 1191, Emerson 1257, Essa 1297, Exelon 1309, Four 1477, GATX 1542, Hasbro 1747, Jackson 2011, Journal 2068, Land 2217, Loews 2296, Lowe's 2312, Mutual 2607, MWH 2608, National 2623, NIBCO 2707, NV 2765, Orlando 2824, Pacific 2853, PG&E 2952, Piedmont 2971, Quad 3091, R & B 3113, Ralph 3123, RG 3201, RubinBrown 3280, Scotts 3372, Shelter 3431, Tiffany 3750, Trim 3810, Turner 3825, United 3879, Warburg 3985, Weyerhaeuser 4052, Williams 4078

Pathology
Gilead 1582

Patients' rights
American 158, Baxter 377, Blue 501, Endo 1268, Genentech 1549

Pediatrics
Aflac 54, AMR 187, COLHOC 870, CryoLife 990, Cumberland 1003, CVS 1014, Ethicon 1299, Genentech 1549, Giant 1572, Haggen 1699, Mattel 2405, MedImmune 2450, Merck 2466, Moore 2565, Morgan 2570, Trustmark 3818

Pediatrics research
Build 608, MedImmune 2450, Minnesota 2530, Quest 3103, Swift 3666

Performing arts
AEGON 45, AGL 57, Alabama 71, Allegheny 91, Altec 118, Altria 120, American 143, Andersen 194, Anderson 195, AptarGroup 221, Assurity 269, Aviva 302, Badger 313, Baird 317, Bank 343, Bank 348, Batson 373, BB&T 385, Bemis 407, Bemis 408, Berkley 426, Berry 434, Bickel 457, Boeing 516, Bon 521, Booz 525, Briggs 564, Briggs 565, Burlington 618, Burns 620, Caddell 645, Cajun 652, Campbell 669, Capital 677, Centene 735, Charter 766, Chicago 787, Clorox 852, Consumers 921, Cook 934, Crane 970, Crescent 983, Dayton 1047, Delta 1073, Deluxe 1084, Dime 1118, DTE 1183, Emerson 1257, Ensign 1276, Entergy 1279, EQT 1287, F.N.B. 1318, Fidelity 1371, Firstmerit 1425, Fluor 1448, Ford 1464, Fort 1472, Four 1477, Frankel 1483, Fremont 1496, General 1554, Giant 1571, Gould 1618, Hallberg 1704, Hanover 1724, Haskell 1748, Horizon 1863, Hubbell 1879, Hudson 1880, Huntington 1894, IDACORP 1907, Illinois 1916, Independent 1927, Institution 1946, Johnson 2049, Johnson 2050, Jones 2056, Joy 2070, JPMorgan Chase 2071, Katten 2101, Kikkoman 2144, Kimball 2149, Kohler 2182, Lake 2212, Land 2217, Lee 2241, Lime 2276, M&T 2323, M.D.C. 2324, Manhattan 2354, Masco 2393, Mascoma 2394, McCarthy 2421, Mentor 2462, Meredith 2471, Metropolitan 2483, MidAmerican 2504, Miller 2523, Mitchell 2537, Modine 2544, Monsanto 2559, Morris 2573, Myers 2609, N.E.W. 2611, National 2629, National 2635, NEBCO 2653, Nissan 2716, Nordson 2723, Norfolk 2725, Nortex 2727, Northfield 2741, Northfield 2742, NorthWestern 2748, Northwestern 2749, OMNOVA 2809, Orscheln 2827, PacifiCorp 2860, Park 2881, Peoples 2929, Peoples 2931, Piedmont 2971, Plain 2989, Plum 2991, PNC 2997, PPG 3025, Printpack 3049, Professional 3056, Pukall 3082, Putnam 3086, Questar 3104, Rahr 3118, Rayonier 3134, Rich 3204, Robins 3232, Rockwell 3246, Rodgers 3250, RUAN 3279, Ryder 3292, Ryman 3294, Safeco 3306, Security 3391, Sensient 3408, Sentry 3409, SIFCO 3452, Simpson 3461, Sit 3466, Sovereign 3528, Spang 3530, Specialty 3537, Sprint 3556, Sumitomo 3639, TECO 3701, Teleflex 3707, Temple 3711, Tennant 3714, Texas 3728, Timken 3760, Titan 3763, U.S. 3835, UBS 3842, United 3877, Universal 3891, Universal 3895, Urban 3901, USG 3905, Vodafone 3965, Walker 3982, Washington 3995, Washington 3999, Weaver 4014, Webster 4016, Wiley 4072, Wisconsin 4093, Wisconsin 4096, Zions 4158

Performing arts centers
Capitol 680, Centene 735, Dallas 1022, Davis 1037, DeBruce 1057, Edison 1229, Fisher 1431, Graham 1625, Hubbell 1879, International 1962, Kenneth 2128, KOA 2178, Marcus 2371, Microsoft 2501, National 2629, Northfield 2741, Oshkosh 2833, Peet's 2916, RG 3201, SunTrust 3654, TECO 3701, Universal 3895, USEC 3904

Performing arts, education
Black 475, Conn 909, Consolidated 917, EMI 1258, Miller 2523, Trail 3793

Pharmacy/prescriptions
Alexion 86, AstraZeneca 272, Bayer 382, Blue 505, Bristol 578, Cardinal 685, CareSource 690, Celgene 732, CVS 1014, Express 1313, Forest 1468, Genentech 1549, Hewlett 1794, Merck 2466, National

2622, Pfizer 2950, Pharmacy 2956, Piedmont 2971, sanofi-aventis 3329, Walgreen 3981, Watson 4007

Philanthropy/voluntarism

Abba 11, Acuity 31, American 140, Beverage 452, Birdsong 470, Chase 770, Crane 970, Danaher 1027, FMR 1450, Harris 1737, Hasbro 1747, Idealist 1909, International 1959, Johnson 2048, Johnson 2051, JSJ 2073, KPMG 2190, M.D.C. 2324, Major 2345, Meecorp 2454, Newman's 2697, Pfizer 2950, Recreational 3150, SAP 3334, Schwab 3363, Towerbrook 3781, University 3896

Philanthropy/voluntarism, information services

AOL 209, Rackspace 3117

Philanthropy/voluntarism, management/ technical assistance

Elevation 1245

Philanthropy/voluntarism, single organization support

New York 2690

Philanthropy/voluntarism, volunteer services

Avnet 304, Zale 4151

Philosophy/ethics

Cook 934

Photography

Getty 1569, Nikon 2711

Physical therapy

CVS 1014, Pacers 2852

Physical/earth sciences

American 150, Avista 301, Freeport 1494, Halliburton 1706, L'Oreal 2203, Quaker 3093, Texas 3728

Physically disabled

Autodesk 289, Bank 347, Beneficial 412, Chrysler 801, CVS 1014, Ford 1464, Genesis 1561, Hendrick 1776, Iberdrola 1904, KeyBank 2136, Metropolitan 2481, Mitsubishi 2538, Security 3391, St. Joe 3563, Washington 3994, WD-40 4011, Xerox 4136

Physics

International 1960, ITT 1999, Siemens 3448, Wiley 4072

Planetarium

Illinois 1916

Political science

Consumers 921

Pregnancy centers

Applied 219, Biomet 466, Buist 611, CentiMark 740

Print publishing

Allstate 107, Amazon.com 122, Belo 406, Burnett 619, Chicago 788, Danaher 1027, Dow 1163, Eagle 1201, Fulton 1518, Gannett 1532, Guard 1680, Homasote 1841, Hubbard 1877, Kenneth 2128, Lee 2241, McClatchy 2422, Meredith 2471, News 2701, Newsweek 2703, Nikon 2711, Philadelphia 2961, Playboy 2990, Post 3016, Primary 3043, Reader's 3141, Record 3149, Ruder 3282, Scripps 3374, Washington 3999

Protestant agencies & churches

Bay 379, Belk 404, Don 1152, Hagerty 1698, Homewood 1849, Raabe 3115, Scott 3369, SUPERVALU 3659, Thrivent 3747

Psychology/behavioral science

S.J. 3299

Public affairs

1st 2, AEGON 45, Aetna 48, Aflac 54, Allergan 99, Alliant 104, Amboy 124, Ameren 128, American 143, American 145, American 150, American 156, Ameriprise 174, Apache 211, Arkema 242, Astoria 270, AT&T 273, AutoNation 292, Aviva 302, Baird 316, Bangor 338, Bank 341, Bank 346, Barnes 362, BASF 368, Bechtel 395, Bemis 407, Bickel 457, Black 474, Blair 478, Boart 510, Boeing 516, Bossong 532, Bowater 543, Bricker 559, Briggs 565, Bristol 578, Brown 591, Brown 592, Buchalter 600, Butler 627, C Spire 636, Caesars 650, Cargill 691, Cascade 713, Castle 717, Caterpillar 722, CenterPoint 738, Chicago 786, Chicago 788, Citigroup 821, Citizens 824, Claremont 833, Cliffs 850, CNA 855, Coca 862, Commerce 890, Compuware 902, ConocoPhillips 913, Contran 928, Crayola 973, Credit 978, Cummings 1004, Cymer 1016, Davis 1041, Dayton 1047, Dell Corning 1067, Devon 1102, Dharma 1105, Dilbeck 1116, Dominion 1150, Donovan 1156, DRS 1179, du Pont 1184, Eastman 1213, Eaton 1216, Ecolab 1220, Edison 1228, El Paso 1239, Emerson 1257, Energen 1270, Entergy 1279, Epson 1286, Exelon 1309, Exxon 1315, FEECO 1353, Ferro 1366, Fieldale 1373, Fieldstone 1374, First 1391, First 1403, First 1406, First 1415, FirstEnergy 1424, Fluor 1448, Free 1492, Freeport 1494, Genentech 1549, General 1551, Genesco 1559, Grace 1623, Grandma 1630, Grange 1631, Green 1651, GSM 1676, Gulf 1689, Halliburton 1706, Hancock 1717, Hanna 1722, Hannaford 1723, Harris 1736, Hartford 1743, Hemmerdinger 1775, Henkel 1778, Heritage 1784, Hershey 1791, Hillshire 1809, Hilton 1812, Hodgson 1820, Honbarrier 1850, Honda 1851, Humana 1886, Hy-Vee 1900, IDACORP 1907, Ingredion 1942, Interlock 1954, Intermountain 1957, International 1964, International Profit 1969, Jacobs 2016, Jeld 2032, Jones 2055, JPMorgan Chase 2071, Kaiser 2086, Kennebunk 2126, KeyBank 2136, Kimball 2149, Koch 2179, Koch 2180, Laclede 2207, Land 2217, Liberty 2265, Lockheed 2292, Lord 2303, M&T 2323, Madison 2334, Major 2347, Manitowoc 2355, Marathon 2365, Masco 2393, Matson 2404, MB 2415, McCormick 2423, McDermott 2424, MeadWestvaco 2445, Mechanics 2446, Medtronic 2453, Meritor 2473, Metropolitan 2481, MFA 2487, MGIC 2488, Microsoft 2501, Miller 2518, Modine 2544, Monsanto 2559, Moody's 2563, Nationwide 2639, NBC 2649, NCR 2650, New York 2684, News 2701, Nordson 2723, Northfield 2741, Novartis 2752, Ohio 2789, OMNOVA 2809, Orleans 2825, Owens 2842, Oxford 2847, Pacific 2855, PacifiCorp 2860, Parker 2886, Pattillo 2896, Peabody 2907, Pella 2917, Penn 2923, Penney 2925, PFS 2951, Philadelphia 2961, Piedmont 2971, Pitney 2984, Plum 2991, Potomac 3018, PPG 3025, PPL 3026, Premix 3037, Principal 3047, Printpack 3049, Protective 3066, Provident 3069, Rayonier 3134, RBC 3136, RealNetworks 3144, Reily 3177, Rieke 3212, Rockwell 3246, Ross 3265, RPM 3278, Ryder 3292, Salt 3319, sanofi-aventis 3329, Sasol 3338, Scripps 3374, Seagate 3377, Selective 3399, Sempra 3405, Sikorsky 3454, Smith 3484, Springleaf 3554, Sprint 3556, SPX 3558, Square 3560, St. Jude 3566, Stone 3614, Strauss 3624, SunTrust 3654, TeamQuest 3698, Teichert 3704, Toro 3775, Total 3778, Toyota 3784, Toyota 3785, Toyota 3787, Toyota 3789, Tulalip 3820, Union 3857, United 3865, United 3877, United 3880, USG 3905, Usibelli 3906, Vectren 3925, Verizon 3936, Vodafone 3965, Volvo 3968, Waffle 3975, Walgreen 3981, Ward 3986, Warrell 3991, Washington 3995, Washington 3999, WD-40 4011, Wellmark 4026, Western 4042, Western 4044, Western 4045, Weyerhaeuser 4052, Whitney 4065, Willdan 4075, Williams 4077, Windway 4086, Working 4116, Worthington 4124, Wrigley 4125, Xerox 4136, Zotos 4159

Public affairs, alliance/advocacy

Federated 1351, First 1422

Public affairs, association

Jacobs 2016

Public affairs, citizen participation

Ben 409, Brotherhood 588, Nordson 2723, Philadelphia 2961, Piper 2983, RBC 3136, Vodafone 3965, World 4121

Public affairs, equal rights

Newman's 2697

Public affairs, finance

Comerica 889, Financial 1382, Hemmerdinger 1775, Jones 2055

Public affairs, formal/general education

Patton 2898

Public affairs, fund raising/fund distribution

National 2622

Public affairs, political organizations

American 153, Sempra 3405, Unisys 3859

Public affairs, public education

OMNOVA 2809

Public affairs, reform

Grand 1629, International 1960

Public health

7-Eleven 5, Aetna 48, American 150, AMERIGROUP 171, AmerisourceBergen 175, Ameristar 176, AMN Healthcare 184, Andersen 194, Assurant 267, Beam 390, Becton 398, Blue 490, Blue 493, Blue 494, Blue 495, Blue 496, Blue 497, Blue 498, Blue 501, Blue 502, Blue 504, Blue 505, BlueCross 507, BMC 508, Booz 525, Bristol 578, Cambia 665, Cardinal 685, CareFirst 687, CareSource 690, Carmody 695, Chaney 761, Chotin 799, Churchill 807, CIGNA 812, CITGO 820, Colgate 869, COLHOC 870, Compass 901, COPIC 937, Covidien 956, Del 1065, DIRECTV 1124, Dominion 1149, Dot 1158, DTE 1183, Enbridge 1265, Entergy 1280, Evans 1300, Express 1313, Flint 1439, Fremont 1496, Giant 1573, GlaxoSmithKline 1588, Google 1613, Halliburton 1706, Hancock 1717, Health 1766, Highmark 1799, Horizon 1863, Hospira 1867, Ingredion 1942, Interthyr 1978, Johnson 2048, Johnson 2049, Kaiser 2086, Kellogg 2120, Lemieux 2249, Liberty 2262, LifeScan 2271, Lilly 2274, Lithia 2287, Louisiana 2309, McKesson 2434, Medical

2448, Medtronic 2453, Merck 2466, Metropolitan 2481, Morton 2579, Mutual 2607, Orlando 2824, Peoples 2931, PepsiCo 2935, Pfizer 2950, Plain 2989, Premera 3034, Price 3039, Principal 3047, Procter 3055, Reinsurance 3179, ResMed 3192, San Francisco 3324, Schwan 3365, Scoular 3373, Strauss 3624, SUPERVALU 3659, Sweetbay 3665, Target 3691, Tellabs 3709, Texas 3728, Textron 3731, Towerbrook 3781, UMB 3846, United 3877, Verizon 3936, VHA 3944, Wal-Mart 3980, Webster 4016, Wellmark 4026, WellPoint 4027, Westinghouse 4049

Public health school/education

Kaiser 2086, Kinney 2162, Springs 3555, Xylem 4139

Public health, clean water supply

CH2M 758, Cisco 818, Coca 862, General 1552, Google 1613, Laird 2211, Monsanto 2559, Mosaic 2580, Pentair 2926, PepsiCo 2935, Philip 2962, RBC 3136, Starbucks 3585, Xylem 4139

Public health, communicable diseases

Arch 230, Bristol 578, Gilead 1582, Lilly 2274, Major 2347, MedImmune 2450, WellPoint 4027

Public health, environmental health

Blue 496, Blue 501

Public health, hygiene

Beck 396, Diversey 1130, Strauss 3624

Public health, obesity

Aetna 48, Allergan 99, Blue 490, Blue 493, Blue 495, Blue 497, Blue 498, Blue 504, Blue 505, BlueCross 507, Campbell 669, Cisco 818, Coca 862, Covidien 956, Dallas 1022, Ethicon 1299, Heinz 1772, Highmark 1799, Hillshire 1809, Horizon 1863, Humana 1886, Jacksonville 2014, Kaiser 2086, Kellogg 2120, Louisiana 2309, Maverick 2409, Mondelez 2556, Nestle 2663, New 2668, New York 2687, Pacers 2852, sanofi-aventis 3329, Saucony 3340, St. Louis 3569, Stop 3618, Stride 3625, Wellmark 4026, WellPoint 4027

Public health, occupational health

CVS 1014

Public health, physical fitness

Abbott 13, Aetna 48, Athletics 276, Atlanta 278, Bangor 338, Bemis 407, Blue 490, Blue 493, Blue 494, Blue 495, Blue 497, Blue 502, Blue 504, Blue 505, Brooklyn 584, Brunswick 595, Buffalo 606, Cardinal 685, Cavaliers 724, CC 728, Chicago 781, Coca 862, Coca 863, Collective 871, ConAgra 904, Cox 959, CVS 1014, Dallas 1022, Denver 1090, Dr 1169, Freeport 1494, General 1554, Henry 1781, Highmark 1799, Hillshire 1809, Horizon 1863, Humana 1886, Indianapolis 1932, Jacksonville 2014, Jamba 2020, Kaiser 2086, Kellogg 2120, Louisiana 2309, Major 2347, Mattel 2405, Mondelez 2556, National 2623, New 2668, New 2689, New York 2684, New York 2687, Pacers 2852, Palace 2866, PDB 2906, PepsiCo 2935, Philadelphia 2957, Philadelphia 2958, Philadelphia 2959, Philadelphia 2960, Pittsburgh 2986, Premera 3034, San Antonio 3321, San Diego 3322, San Diego 3323, Saucony 3340, Sports 3548, Spurs 3557, Stride 3625, Tennessee 3716, TJX 3765, Trail 3793, Unilever 3853, Washington 4000, Wegmans 4021, Wellmark 4026, WellPoint 4027, Wrigley 4125

Public health, sanitation

Coca 862, General 1552, Laird 2211, Monsanto 2559, Starbucks 3585

Public health, STDs

Bristol 578, Jacksonville 2014

Public policy, research

American 153, Armstrong 245, Assurant 267, Berkley 426, Bickel 457, Caterpillar 722, Chrysler 801, CIGNA 812, Community 897, Exxon 1315, Factory 1323, Fluor 1448, General 1552, Hilton 1812, International 1960, Jeld 2032, JPMorgan Chase 2071, Laureate 2231, Lilly 2274, M&T 2323, MeadWestvaco 2445, Otis 2835, Piedmont 2971, PMI 2995, Redwoods 3158, Reily 3177, Strauss 3624, Tindall 3761, United 3877, Vodafone 3965, Wausau 4008, WEDGE 4020, WellPoint 4027, Xerox 4136, Zilkha 4156

Public utilities, sewage

Xylem 4139

Public utilities, water

Arch 230, Metropolitan 2484, Xylem 4139

Race/intergroup relations

Allstate 107, Ben 409, Compass 901, du Pont 1184, Foley 1454, Fortis 1473, Hilton 1812, JPMorgan Chase 2071, Kann 2090, LG&E Energy 2260, Lincoln 2278, Mazda 2414, Praxair 3029, Redwoods 3158, Sealaska 3380

Radio

Athletics 276, Bridgestone 560, Capital 677, Curves 1011, Fisher 1430, Fluor 1448, Gibbs 1576, Illinois 1916, Johnson 2050, Jones 2055, Medtronic 2453, Piedmont 2971, PMI 2995, Providence 3068, Stafast 3571, Union 3857, Valspar 3920, Western 4041

Rape victim services

Stoneham 3616, UncommonGoods 3849, United 3881

Reading

AbbyBank 15, Abercrombie 17, Acacia 21, AEGON 45, AGL 57, Alexander 85, Alliance 101, American 145, American 150, Ameristar 176, Andersson 196, Androscoggin 199, Angels 200, Applied 220, Arbitron 227, Avnet 304, AZPB 310, Bank 346, Bank 347, Barnes 360, Bayer 381, Beall's 389, Better 448, Bigelow 462, Bloomberg 486, Blue 493, Blue 505, Bobcats 512, Boeing 516, Boston 540, Bound 541, Bromelkamp 582, Brooklyn 584, Buccaneer 599, Build 608, C & S 634, Cabot 642, Calvert 663, Capital 677, Capital 679, Capstone 684, Cavaliers 724, CC 728, Chelsea 772, Chicago 782, Chicago 786, Cisco 818, CITGO 820, Citigroup 821, Clarity 834, Colorado 879, Comcast 887, Continental 926, Convergys 933, Dallas 1021, Deluxe 1084, Denver 1090, Detroit 1095, Dime 1118, Discovery 1126, Dolphins 1147, Donnelley 1155, DRW 1181, El Paso 1239, EMC 1253, Entergy 1279, Entergy 1280, EQT 1287, Express 1313, Fieldstone 1374, FMR 1450, Follett 1455, Food 1458, Four 1477, Freeport 1494, G&K 1524, Georgia 1568, GlaxoSmithKline 1588, Grand 1627, Guard 1680, Hachette 1696, Heat 1767, Herrick 1788, Herschend 1790, Hilton 1812, Hitachi 1816, Hoops 1857, Houston 1871, IAC 1903, Indianapolis 1932, International 1960, International 1968, JM 2044, Jostens 2067, JPMorgan Chase 2071, Kaman 2088, Kemp 2123, Kimball 2149, Kohler 2182, KPMG 2190, Lauder 2230, Lincoln 2281, Loews 2296, MasterCard 2399, Mattel 2405, Mazda 2414, MEEMIC 2455, Milwaukee 2528, Mitsubishi 2538, Nash 2619, Nashville 2620, Nestle 2663, New Jersey 2676, New York 2684, New York 2686, New York 2688, Newburyport 2693, Nordic 2722, Nordson 2723, Northrop 2744, Northwestern 2749, Nu 2759, Old 2798, Orlando 2824, Otis 2835, Owens 2844, Pacific 2855, PacifiCorp 2860, Packaging 2861, PDB 2906, Pearson 2911, Pearson 2912, Penguin 2922, People's 2928, Peoples 2931, Philadelphia 2957, Philadelphia 2958, Philadelphia 2961, Phoenix 2968, Piedmont 2971, Pitney 2984, Pizza 2988, PMI 2995, Portland 3010, Public 3076, Quad 3091, Quanex 3100, Rayonier 3134, RBC 3136, RECO 3148, RESCO 3189, Rockville 3245, Roundy's 3272, Safeco 3306, San Antonio 3321, San Jose 3327, Schmeling 3353, Scholastic 3358, Scripps 3374, Sentry 3409, Shaughnessy 3425, SI 3444, Siw 3468, SLM 3478, Sonic 3498, Spartan 3535, Spurs 3557, St. Louis 3567, St. Louis 3569, StanCorp 3574, Staples 3581, Starbucks 3585, Subaru 3631, SunTrust 3654, Symantec 3669, Target 3691, TD 3696, Teachers 3697, Teleflex 3707, TeleTech 3708, Textron 3731, Thomaston 3736, Trail 3793, Union 3854, Union 3858, United 3872, United 3881, Vectren 3925, Verizon 3936, Wal-Mart 3980, Warburg 3985, Washington 3998, Washington 4000, Wegmans 4021, Weyco 4051, WorkflowOne 4115, World 4121

Recreation

ABARTA 10, ACI 27, Activision 30, Allegis 92, AmeriPride 173, Andersen 194, Angels 200, Atlanta 277, Atlanta 278, Bean 392, Biomet 466, Blue 490, Bobcats 512, Boston 538, Brunswick 595, Buccaneer 599, Builders 609, Burlington 616, Burlington 618, Butt 628, California 656, Cambridge 666, Campbell 669, Cavaliers 724, Chicago 789, Chicago 790, Chick 791, Churchill 807, Clark 835, Cleveland 847, Coca 861, Coghlin 864, Colonial 876, Concept 905, Copley 938, Coral 940, Cornerstone 944, Cox 960, Crane 970, Credit 978, Cummins 1005, CVS 1014, Dallas 1023, Danforth 1028, Dedham 1060, Detroit 1095, Detroit 1097, Dick's 1110, DRW 1181, DS 1182, Easton 1215, Eclipse 1219, EMCO 1254, Essa 1297, Fiesta 1375, First 1398, First 1403, First 1409, First 1418, Foley 1454, Foot 1459, Formosa 1470, Fortis 1473, Four 1477, Franklin 1488, Freeport 1494, Fuller 1517, General 1554, Ghilotti 1570, Granite 1632, Gregory 1661, Guard 1680, Hagerty 1698, Hasbro 1747, Hawaii 1753, Hermann 1786, Hofmann 1824, Hubbard 1878, Hy-Vee 1900, Hygeia 1901, Ilitch 1915, Independence 1925, International 1958, Invesco 1983, Iowa 1986, Jackson-Shaw 2013, Jacksonville 2014, Jersey 2039, KarMART 2096, Korum 2187, Latham 2229, Lincoln 2282, Lockwood 2293, Long 2298, Los Angeles 2305, Los Angeles 2306, Los Angeles 2307, Marena 2372, Mary 2392, Masterson 2400, Material 2402, Me-Tex 2442, Medeanalytics 2447, Midcontinent 2505, Millhiser-Smith 2524, Milwaukee 2527, Mohegan 2546, Monarch 2552, Morley 2572, Mt. 2594, Mutual 2607, National 2624, National 2626, National 2636, NIBCO 2707, NIKE 2710, Noland 2719, NorthSide 2745, Oklahoma 2794, Oneida 2814, Optima 2819, Owen 2840, Pacers 2852, Pacific 2853, Pebble 2913, Phillips 2966, Phoenix 2968, Pinnacle 2978, Polaris 2999, Preferred 3031, Principal 3047, Progressive 3059, Provident 3069, Quincy 3110, Ratio 3129, Record 3149, Recreational 3150, Red 3153, Regal 3167, Reid 3173, Ripplewood 3219, Rockler 3243, San Diego 3322, San Francisco 3324, Save 3342, Schenuit 3349, Scottdale 3371, Seagate 3377, Selig 3401, Serengeti 3411, Sierra 3451, SmartWool 3479, Sports 3548, Spurs 3557, St. Louis 3567, St. Louis 3569, Steel 3596, Sterling 3601, Syracuse 3675, TD 3696, TeamQuest 3698, Three 3745, Tractor 3791, Trends 3804, Tribune 3806, Triumph 3812, Tulalip 3820, Turner 3825, Twins 3827, United 3879, V.F. 3913, Valero 3915, Ventas 3931, Virginia 3959, Wake 3978, Washington 3998, Waters 4003, Wausau 4008, Whirl 4055, Winnebago 4088, Worthen 4123

Recreation, adaptive sports
PG&E 2952, Philadelphia 2960

Recreation, association
Dick's 1110

Recreation, centers
McDonald 2426, Midcontinent 2505, Wood 4108

Recreation, community
Ashley 259, Baseball 367, Black 474, Chicago 783, Dr 1169, Duquesne 1194, First 1419, Holcim 1828, New 2668, New 2689, San Francisco 3324, United 3879

Recreation, fairs/festivals
AgStar 59, American 143, Bank 343, Biomet 466, Burrtec 622, Caddell 645, Capezio 675, Centene 735, CH2M 758, Chicago 787, Cooper 935, Dayton 1047, Dr 1169, DS 1182, First 1395, Food 1458, Foremost 1466, Four 1477, Graybar 1640, Life 2268, Maritz 2376, MidAmerican 2504, Miller 2523, Newport 2699, Nu 2759, Oakland 2772, Oklahoma 2794, P.E.L. 2849, sanofi-aventis 3329, Sierra 3451, Tim 3753, Timberland 3754, Trim 3810, UBS 3842, United 3867, ViewSonic 3952

Recreation, fund raising/fund distribution
Law 2233, Major 2347

Recreation, public education
St. Louis 3569

Recycling
Albertsons 79, Alcoa 82, Anheuser 202, Aspen 260, Avery 297, Berry 438, Boeing 516, Burrtec 622, Coca 862, Coca 863, EQT 1287, Four 1477, Georgia 1568, Interface 1953, International 1968, NV 2765, Sempra 3405, Sunshine 3653, Union 3854

Religion
A.J. 8, Abbot 12, Aberdeen 18, Allen 98, American 133, American 160, American 165, Anchor 192, ANZA 208, Apex 212, Armbrust 243, Arrowhead 250, Associated 262, Atlantic 281, Atlantic 282, Atlantic 283, Atlas 284, Audubon 286, Avlon 303, Azulay 311, BankSouth 350, Barbara 354, BB&T 385, BC 387, Bekins 401, Belk 404, Benevento 414, Bennett 415, Benton 417, Bethel 445, Betts 450, Beyer 454, Bird 468, Borden 527, Bourns 542, Brochsteins 581, C L D 635, Carroll 703, Chapman 763, Chick 791, Citizens 823, Citizens 825, Clemens 844, Coghlin 865, Comcast 888, Conston 920, Cummins 1005, Cyan 1015, Delphos 1072, Demoulas 1085, Devereaux 1100, Dharma 1105, Diageo 1107, Dispatch 1129, Dominion 1148, Duda 1188, Eagle 1202, Eberhard 1218, Edsim 1230, El 1237, Electric 1240, Elizabeth 1250, Ensign 1275, EPES 1283, Esbenshade's 1295, Excellium 1305, Exchange 1307, Executive 1308, Exponential 1312, Faber 1319, Fast 1344, FDI 1346, Ferrara 1364, Fibre 1369, FIDELIO 1370, Fidelity 1372, First 1405, First 1410, First 1412, Fishel 1429, Fleck 1435, Foldcraft 1452, Formosa 1470, Fowler 1478, Freedman 1493, Fru 1513, Furniture 1519, Gelco 1546, Gemini 1547, General 1557, Ghilotti 1570, Gibson 1579, Gleason 1591, Gold 1598, Goldmark 1605, Goodman 1610, Griffith 1666, Griswold 1669, Guarantee 1678, Hackstock 1697, Hall 1702, Hamrick 1715, Hancock 1716, Heritage 1784, Hilliard 1806, Holiday 1831, Holiday 1832, Holmes 1838, Home 1846, Horizon 1865, Houston 1871, Howell 1874, Huhtamaki 1884, Hunt 1890, Hutton 1899, Independent 1928, Indiana 1930, Industrial 1935, Integrity 1948, Integrity 1949, Interlock 1954, International 1963, Inwood 1985, Iowa 1987, Isabella 1993, Jaclyn 2015, Jai 2017, Jasper 2025, KarMART 2096, Kemper 2124, Kentuckiana 2130, Key 2134, Kilpatrick 2146, Kimball 2149, Koch 2179, Koss 2188, Lapham 2223, Larkin 2224, Manti 2359, Mark 2377, Marsh 2386, Marshall 2388, Massey 2398, Material 2402, Matrix 2403, MBIA 2416, McBride 2418, McCarthy 2421, Meadows 2444, Mercury 2468, Mike's 2509, Milford 2514, Moody 2562, Morris 2573, Nackard 2612, Nash 2619, National 2636, Natori 2640, Natural 2643, Neace 2651, Neuwirth 2666, New York 2685, North 2732, NVF 2766, Pacific 2858, Panosian 2874, Parker 2886, Parthenon 2889, Paterson 2893, Peachtree 2908, Pellitteri's 2918, Pharmaceutical 2955, Pioneer 2982, Plymouth 2993, Porter 3006, Porter 3007, Posillico 3014, Power 3020, Primary 3043, Printpack 3049, Pro 3051, Professional 3056, Reell 3164, Reisner 3180, Rewold 3196, Ridgewood 3211, Roanoke 3229, Rockford 3241, Rockler 3243, Ross 3266, Royalnest 3277, Rug 3286, Rusco 3288, S & H 3295, Savage 3341, Schneider 3354, Schoonover 3359, SCIenergy 3366, Scott 3369, Scottdale 3371, Seaboard 3375, Selig 3401, Shelton 3432, Slant 3477, South 3508, Stage 3572, Stoelting 3612, Stonecutter 3615, Stout 3619, Stupp 3628, SUPERVALU 3659, Teitler 3705, Ten 3712, Thomaston 3736, Three 3745, TIV 3764, Tofias 3768, Totsy 3780, Trans 3795, Treasure 3803, Truefit 3816, Tulalip 3820, United 3871, United 3880, UTI 3909, Uticon 3911, Veridyne 3935, Vesco 3942, Vista 3962, WB 4010, Whirl 4055, White 4060, Wigwam 4069, Wishart 4097, Wurster 4128, Wurzburg 4129, Young 4148

Religion, fund raising/fund distribution
Thrivent 3747

Religion, interfaith issues
Primary 3043

Religion, management/technical assistance
Thrivent 3747

Reproductive health
AMERIGROUP 171, Brotherhood 588, General 1552, Lapham 2223, Primary 3043, Strauss 3624, Valero 3915, Wellmark 4026, Working 4116

Reproductive health, OBGYN/Birthing centers
Abbott 13

Reproductive health, prenatal care
AMERIGROUP 171, Highmark 1799, Mead 2443, Pathmark 2894, Syniverse 3672, TJX 3765, Wellmark 4026, WellPoint 4027

Reproductive rights
Working 4116

Residential/custodial care
American 155, Baum 375, Birmingham 471, Burlington 618, Commercial 892, Conditioned 906, Creative 976, Diagnos-Techs 1108, First 1419, Ford 1463, Graybar 1640, Harnish 1734, Lennar 2250, Melaleuca 2457, MEMC 2459, Molly 2548, Ohio 2790, RUAN 3279, Stafast 3571, State 3590, Terre 3722, TJX 3765, United 3864, United 3869, Universal 3891, Valero 3915, Victaulic 3948, Walter 3984

Residential/custodial care, group home
Birmingham 471, Ergon 1289, Hudson 1880, JM 2044, Ratner 3130

Rural development
AgStar 59, Bangor 338, Blue 497, Calvert 663, Cargill 691, CHS 802, Clarity 834, Grand 1627, Green 1653, Land 2217, Philip 2962

Rural studies
AgStar 59

Safety, automotive safety
Allstate 107, Arbella 226, Avis 300, BMW 509, Bridgestone 560, Chrysler 801, Con 903, FedEx 1352, Ford 1464, General 1555, Government 1621, GuideOne 1687, Honda 1851, Michelin 2495, Progressive 3057, Safeco 3306, Schiff 3350, Selective 3399, State 3591, Toyota 3788, United 3872, United 3873, Volvo 3968, Westfield 4047

Safety, education
BJ's 473, Blue 492, Build 608, ConocoPhillips 913, Georgia 1568, Goodyear 1612, Lincoln 2278, Lowe's 2312, Monsanto 2559, Pioneer 2980, PMI 2995, Safeco 3306, State 3591, Tucson 3819, United 3877

Safety, poisons
Valspar 3920

Safety/disasters
3M 3, 7-Eleven 5, Accenture 22, adidas 35, Adobe 38, Advance 39, Air 63, Alcoa 82, Alliant 104, Allstate 107, Alyeska 121, American 141, American 145, American 156, Ameristar 176, Anadarko 190, Andersen 194, Apache 211, Aramco 224, AutoNation 292, Baltimore 333, Blue 496, BP 547, Broadcom 579, Buccaneer 599, C Spire 636, Cardinal 685, Carter's 708, CNA 855, Colonial 876, Columbia 884, Coquille 939, Cox 959, CSX 997, Dell 1068, Delmarva 1069, Diemolding 1113, Discover 1125, Dolan 1140, Dr 1169, Duke 1189, Dunkin' 1191, Duquesne 1194, Eastern 1211, Enbridge 1265, Federal 1348, FedEx 1352, Firestone 1386, FirstEnergy 1424, Flint 1439, Florida 1443, Food 1458, Freeport 1494, General 1552, General 1554, Georgia 1568, Grange 1631, Harleysville 1733, Haynes 1759, HCA 1762, Health 1765, Hilton 1812, Home 1842, Honda 1851, Honeywell 1852, Horizon 1863, Hubbell 1879, IDACORP 1907, IMS 1924, Ingredion 1942, Jack 2007, Jackson 2011, JanPak 2022, Jefferies 2030, KPMG 2190, Liberty 2265, Lincoln 2282, Lisle 2286, Lowe's 2312, Major 2347, McDonald's 2427, McGraw 2429, McWane 2440, Menasha 2461, Merk 2467, MGM 2489, Monsanto 2559, Mosaic 2580, Motorola 2586, MSC 2593, National 2626, National 2630, National 2638, Natural 2643, NBC 2649, New York 2685, Newell 2694, Nexion 2705, NIKE 2710, NiSource 2715, North 2733, North 2734, NorthWestern 2748, NYSE 2769, Office 2785, Oklahoma 2794, OMNOVA 2809, Opus 2820, Oracle 2821, Orange 2822, Parsons 2887, Penn 2923, PepsiCo 2935, Perdue 2936, Philip 2962, Pioneer 2981, Pitney 2984, Portland 3010, PricewaterhouseCoopers 3042, PSS 3074, Puget 3081, Quabaug 3090, Raytheon 3135, RE/MAX 3140, Reeves 3165, Royal 3273, Royal 3274, Ruby 3281, Ryder 3292, Safeco 3306, San Jose 3327, Scott 3370, Selective 3399, Sempra 3405, Shaklee 3418, Sidwell 3447, SLM 3478, Sony 3504, Southern 3516, Sprint 3556, SRA 3562, Steel 3596, Swift 3667, Symantec 3669, Target 3691, Texas 3726, Thomaston 3736, Timberland 3754, Toyota 3786, Toyota 3789, Trustmark 3818, U-Haul 3833, UL 3844, United 3872, United 3873, Volkswagen 3967, Wal-Mart 3980, Walgreen 3981, Watson 4007, Westfield 4047,

Westinghouse 4049, Weyerhaeuser 4052, Yahoo! 4140

Safety/disasters, formal/general education

CSX 997

Safety/disasters, fund raising/fund distribution

Alabama 71, Amazon.com 122, Mrs. Fields 2592, Yahoo! 4140

Safety/disasters, information services

Google 1613, New 2679, Sonic 3498

Safety/disasters, management/technical assistance

Cisco 818, Intel 1950, Target 3691

Safety/disasters, public education

Diversey 1130, DTE 1183, Farmers 1338, FedEx 1352, Symantec 3669, West 4037

Safety/disasters, volunteer services

Arch 230, Bridgestone 560, Carnival 696, Deere 1061, New York 2688

Salvation Army

Acuity 32, Ameren 128, Amerisure 177, AMPCO 186, ANH 201, Applied 219, AutoZone 294, Bank 342, BB&T 385, BDP 388, Bemis 407, Bemis 408, Berry 438, Birdsong 470, Building 610, Byers 630, Caplin 681, Cary 712, CentiMark 740, Central 742, Churchill 807, Consumers 921, Curves 1011, Dallas 1022, Danis 1029, Davison 1042, Dayton 1047, Delta 1073, Eaton 1216, Edison 1229, Emerson 1257, Ergon 1289, Evening 1302, Fabick 1321, FedEx 1352, Fetzer 1367, First 1394, First 1397, First 1399, First 1403, First 1406, Fiserv 1427, Florida 1443, Franklin 1485, Franklin 1488, General 1556, Georgia 1567, Giant 1571, Gould 1618, Graybar 1640, Gregory 1662, Gulf 1689, Hallberg 1704, Highwoods 1800, Hoffman 1822, Hooters 1858, Hufcor 1883, IDACORP 1907, International 1959, ISGN 1995, JM 2044, Jones 2055, KeyBank 2136, Kimberly 2150, Kroger 2195, Kuhns 2197, Lauder 2230, Lee 2240, Levi 2254, Li-Cor 2261, Liberty 2265, Milwaukee 2528, Mondelez 2556, MTD 2595, National 2629, National 2634, NCR 2650, Neenah 2656, NiSource 2715, North 2730, Northeast 2737, Oklahoma 2794, Olin 2801, Park 2881, Parker 2886, Patton's 2899, Penney 2925, Pittsburgh 2986, Price 3040, Puget 3081, Pukall 3082, Raley's 3122, Regions 3171, Retail 3194, Rite 3220, Ryder 3292, Save 3342, SCANA 3346, Schneider 3355, Scoular 3373, Sealy 3382, ShopKo 3440, Shugart 3442, Sit 3466, Sjostrom 3469, Smucker 3488, South Bend 3507, Southern 3515, Spang 3530, Spartan 3535, Stafast 3571, State 3590, SunTrust 3654, Target 3691, TECO 3701, Thorntons 3743, Timken 3760, Tops 3774, Trail 3793, Turner 3824, U.S. 3836, Union 3858, United 3864, United 3867, United 3872, Utica 3910, Valero 3915, Virginia 3959, Waffle 3975, Wal-Mart 3980, Walter 3984, Warren 3993, Washington 3995, Western 4040, Wynnne 4133, Zale 4151

Schizophrenia

Lilly 2274

Scholarships/financial aid

AK 67, Alcoa 82, Altria 120, Ameren 129, American 138, AMETEK 181, Anheuser 202, Apex 214, Arby's 228, Arthur's 253, Associated 261, AT&T 273, Baker 322, Bank 348, BASF 368, Beall's 389, Berkowitz 427, BP 547, Bridgestone 560, Brunswick 595, Catalina 719, Coca 862, Continental 923, Cook 934, Crowell 986, CVS 1014, Denny's 1087, Detroit 1095, DeVoe 1101, Discovery 1126, Disney 1127, Eastern 1211, Educational 1233, Energizer 1271, EQT 1287, Exelon 1309, Factory 1323, Farmers' 1337, Fidelity 1371, Florence 1441, Fluor 1448, Ford 1464, Franklin 1484, Freeport 1494, Gannett 1532, General 1552, Georgia 1568, Government 1621, Hallberg 1704, Harsco 1741, Henkels 1779, Holcim 1828, Horix 1860, HSBC 1876, Hubbell 1879, Independent 1927, Ingersoll 1939, Johnson 2050, Jostens 2067, Kelly 2122, KFC 2139, Kimmel 2152, Leet 2243, Manpower 2358, Marathon 2365, MasterCard 2399, MFA 2486, Mine 2529, Morgan 2570, Murphy 2600, National 2622, National 2630, Navistar 2647, Nelnet 2660, Network 2664, New York 2690, Newtown 2704, NYSE 2769, Owens 2844, Packard 2862, Pearson 2911, Pearson 2912, Penney 2925, Philips 2963, Phillips 2966, Phoenix 2967, PPG 3025, ProLogis 3060, Quality 3097, R & B 3113, Rosen's 3264, Royal 3274, SAP 3334, Servco 3412, Simplot 3459, Smithfield 3487, Sony 3502, Teleflex 3707, Texas 3729, Thomasville 3737, Tomkins 3771, Trico 3807, Union 3854, United 3874, United 3883, Wal-Mart 3980, Washington 3994, Western 4045, Whirlpool 4056, Xcel 4135, YSI 4149

Science

3M 3, Abbott 13, Advanced 40, Agilent 56, AgStar 59, Alcoa 82, American 150, Amgen 182, Anadarko 190, Andersen 194, Angels 200, Applied 220, Ariel 237, Arkema 242, AT&T 273, Autodesk 289, Avery 297, Avista 301, BASF 368, Baxter 377, Bayer 381, Bechtel 395, Beckman 397, Berkshire 428, Biogen 465, Bloomberg 486, Boehringer 515, BorgWarner 528, Boston 540, Bourns 542, Bristol 578, Broadcom 579, Burns 620, Cabot 642, Canon 672, Carpenter 700, Central 741, Chevron 780, Chrysler 801, Cisco 818, Consumers 921, ConvaTec 932, Cubist 999, Cummins 1007, Deere 1061, Delphi 1071, DENSO 1088, Deutsche 1099, Discovery 1126, Disney 1127, Dow 1162, Draper 1171, DTE 1183, du Pont 1184, Duke 1189, EQT 1287, Exelon 1309, Express 1313, Ferro 1366, FirstEnergy 1424, Flextronics 1437, Freeport 1494, Freescale 1495, Fuller 1517, Furniture 1519, GenCorp 1548, Genentech 1549, General 1552, General 1555, Gilead 1582, GlaxoSmithKline 1588, Google 1613, Guth 1692, Harris 1736, Haworth 1758, Hewlett 1794, Hoffmann 1823, Holland 1834, Honeywell 1852, Hubbard 1878, Illinois 1916, Intel 1950, Intermec 1955, International 1960, International 1968, IPALCO 1988, ITT 1999, Kadant 2083, KBR 2106, Kennametal 2125, Kingston 2161, KLA-Tencor 2165, Kukui 2198, L'Oreal 2203, Lam 2214, Lexmark 2258, Life 2268, Lilly 2274, Lockheed 2292, Lowe's 2312, LSI 2314, LyondellBasell 2322, Matson 2404, MedImmune 2450, Medtronic 2453, MEEMIC 2455, Merck 2466, Mercury 2469, Meritor 2473, Merk 2467, Michelin 2495, Microchip 2499, Micron 2500, Microsoft 2501, Modine 2544, Monsanto 2559, Motorola 2585, Motorola 2586, National 2632, New 2668, New 2671, Newmont 2698, NiSource 2715, Nomura 2720, Norfolk 2725, Northrop 2744, Nucor 2760, Oatey 2775, Oklahoma 2794, OMNOVA 2809, Oracle 2821, Parametric 2878, Pearson 2911, Pentair 2926, People's 2928, Peoples 2929, Perforce 2937, Pfizer 2950, Piedmont 2971, Pioneer 2980, Pioneer 2981, Piper 2983, PNC 2997, Portland 3010, PPG 3025, Public 3077, Quaker 3093, QUALCOMM 3095, Quiksilver 3108, Rackspace 3117, Ratner 3130, Rayonier 3134, Raytheon 3135, ResMed 3192, Rockwell 3246, Rockwell 3247, SAIC 3311, SAP 3334, SAS 3336, Seagate 3377, Semiconductor 3403, Seminole 3404, Sempra 3405, Siemens 3448, Sigma 3453, Southern 3521, Spirol 3545, St. Jude 3566, Stanley 3579, Subaru 3631, Sulphur 3637, Symantec 3669, Synopsys 3673, Tellabs 3709, Texas 3728, Thermo 3733, Time 3755, Toshiba 3776, Toyota 3784, Tyco 3829, Unisys 3859, United 3877, United 3882, Univar 3886, Universal 3893, USEC 3904, UTC 3908, Verizon 3936, Vernier 3941, Washington 3995, Waters 4003, West 4038, Western 4042, Westinghouse 4049, Wiley 4072, Xerox 4136, YSI 4149

Science, formal/general education

3M 3, Agilent 56, AGL 57, American 150, Amgen 182, Bayer 381, Beckman 397, Boehringer 515, Boeing 516, Bristol 578, Cargill 691, CH2M 758, Chevron 780, Deere 1061, Delphi 1071, Devon 1102, Discovery 1126, Dominion 1150, Dow 1162, Edison 1228, El Paso 1239, EMC 1253, Exelon 1309, Exxon 1315, Fluor 1448, Freeport 1494, Genentech 1549, GlaxoSmithKline 1588, Hoffmann 1823, Honeywell 1852, Intel 1950, International 1960, International Profit 1969, Kennametal 2125, LG&E Energy 2260, Life 2268, Lockheed 2292, Medtronic 2453, Mentor 2462, Merck 2466, Merk 2467, Micron 2500, Monsanto 2559, Motorola 2585, NEC 2654, NiSource 2715, Nordson 2723, OMNOVA 2809, Parametric 2878, Pfizer 2950, Pioneer 2980, Piper 2983, PPG 3025, Procter 3055, Public 3077, Rockwell 3246, Rockwell 3247, Seagate 3377, Siemens 3448, Spansion 3532, Subaru 3631, Synopsys 3673, Texas 3728, Thermo 3733, Toshiba 3776, Toyota 3784, Vernier 3941, Vulcan 3972, Xcel 4135, Xilinx 4137

Science, fund raising/fund distribution

CH2M 758

Science, public education

Arch 230, Boston 540, Commonwealth 895, Flint 1439, Fuller 1517, NorthWestern 2748, Sony 3503, Teradyne 3718, Western 4042

Science, public policy

Life 2268

Science, research

Association 265, L'Oreal 2203, Mazda 2414, Merck 2466

Sculpture

Gannett 1532

Secondary school/education

Acacia 21, Accupac 23, Acuity 31, AEGON 45, AGL 57, Alfa 87, Allegheny 91, Amazon.com 122, American 140, American 155, American 157, Ameritas 178, Apex 214, Ariens 238, AT&T 273, Athletics 276, AutoZone 294, AVX 306, Baird 317, Bank 340, Barron's 364, Belk 403, Belk 404, Beneficial 411, Berry 435, Biogen 465, Biomet 466, Boh 517, Boston 540, Bowles 544, Brocchini 580, Building 610, Buist 611, C Spire 636, Cacique 644, Canon 672, Caparo 673, Capital 677, Capital 679, Carlson 693, Cavaliers 724, Centene 735, Central 745, CFS 756, Chick 791, Cianbro 808, Clear 842, CME 853, CMS 854, Coach 858, Collette 872, Collins 873, Concept 905, Continental 926, Creative 976, Credit 980, Crescent 982, Croft 985, CUNA 1008, Darden 1032, Davis 1037, Dayton 1047, DCI 1049, Dedham 1060, Demoulas 1085, Detroit 1095, Devereaux 1100, Diageo 1107, Diagnos-Techs 1108, Doctor's 1138, Dondlinger 1154, Donnelley 1155, Dot 1158, East 1207, Eaton 1216, Edvisors 1234, Exotic 1310, Fabiano 1320, Farmers 1338, Federal 1348, Federated 1351, Fetzer 1367, First 1395, First 1402, First 1409, Florence 1441, Fort 1472, Framingham 1481, Franklin 1488, Friesen 1505, Gap 1533, General 1553, General 1555, Giant 1571, GJF 1584, Gosiger 1617, Graham 1625, Green 1651, Guided 1686, H & R 1695, Hallberg 1704, Harnish 1734, Hautly 1750, Haviland 1752, Haynie 1760, HCR 1763, Heat 1767, Henkels 1779, Herrick 1788, Highwoods 1800, Hofmann 1824, Hoops 1857, Houston 1871, IDACORP 1907, IKON 1914, Independence 1925, Independent

1927, Industrial 1935, Inman 1943, Institution 1946, International 1967, Jack 2007, JM 2044, Jordan 2063, Josephson 2066, Kennametal 2125, Kikkoman 2144, Kindred 2154, Konica 2185, KPMG 2190, Laclede 2207, Lam 2214, Landry's 2219, Leet 2243, Levi 2254, Loomis 2301, M&T 2323, Magnolia 2340, Manhattan 2354, Mariani 2374, Martin 2391, Mascoma 2394, Maverick 2409, McCarthy 2421, McLaughlin 2436, MDU 2441, Mercury 2469, Meritor 2473, Micron 2500, Monadnock 2551, Moody's 2563, Morgan 2570, Morley 2572, Morris 2573, Motley 2582, MTD 2595, Murphy 2600, Mutual 2605, Mutual 2607, MWH 2608, Nasdaq 2618, National 2625, National 2629, NBC 2649, Neace 2651, NEC 2654, Neenah 2656, Nelnet 2660, New York 2687, Niemann 2708, NIKE 2710, North 2728, North 2731, Northern 2740, NorthWestern 2748, Novetta 2755, Odyssey 2784, Omron 2810, Orscheln 2827, Owens 2844, P.E.L. 2849, Pacific 2858, Parametric 2878, Parker 2886, PEMCO 2919, People's 2928, Perforce 2937, PG&E 2952, Portcullis 3004, Post 3016, Premier 3036, Price 3040, PricewaterhouseCoopers 3042, Primerica 3045, Providence 3068, Provident 3070, R & R 3114, Raabe 3115, Ralph 3123, Redner's 3157, Regal 3166, Reiff 3174, Rennoc 3184, ResMed 3192, Rich 3204, Rockville 3245, Ross 3266, Royal 3275, S.B.E. 3298, Sakar 3313, San Antonio 3321, Sartori 3335, SBH 3345, Scientific 3367, Scoular 3373, Select 3398, Selig 3401, Shaughnessy 3425, Shea 3428, Shelter 3431, Shure 3443, Siemens 3448, Sierra 3451, Simon 3458, Simplot 3459, Smith 3485, St. 3565, StanCorp 3574, Stanek 3578, State 3592, Stewart 3604, Stoneham 3616, Sun 3643, Sunbeam 3647, Superior 3658, Swift 3666, Synovus 3674, Taco 3679, TAP 3690, TECO 3701, Tennessee 3716, Texas 3725, Texas 3728, TFS 3732, Tripifoods 3811, Turner 3823, U.S. 3836, Union 3855, United 3881, United 3882, Universal 3895, Urban 3901, Waffle 3975, Wake 3978, Wal-Mart 3980, Walter 3984, Warrell 3991, Washington 3999, Weaver 4015, Western 4045, Weyco 4051, Wood 4108, WorkflowOne 4115

Self-advocacy services, disability

American 156, Maritz 2376, StanCorp 3574, Westinghouse 4049

Senior continuing care

CFS 756, Mine 2529, Stoneham 3616, Upper 3900

Sexual abuse

Baxter 377, Carlson 693, Parker 2884, Providence 3068, V.F. 3913, Wawa 4009, Zappos.com 4153

Single parents

Autodesk 289, Beneficial 412, Chrysler 801, Diagnos-Techs 1108, Genesis 1561, Marena 2372, WD-40 4011

Skin disorders

Allergan 99, Hubbard 1877

Skin disorders research

Nu 2759

Smoking

Blue 504, Lorillard 2304, QuikTrip 3109, WellPoint 4027

Social entrepreneurship

American 156, Bangor 338, Cisco 818, CSRwire 995, Dominion 1149, eBay 1217, Farm 1333, Feelgoodz 1354, Georgia 1568, Grand 1627, Haynes 1759, Hewlett 1794, Melissa 2458, NIKE 2710, Primary 3043, Starbucks 3585, United 3872, Urban 3901, Western 4045, Whole 4066

Social sciences

Peoples 2929

Social sciences, formal/general education

Sempra 3405

Social sciences, fund raising/fund distribution

Aramco 224

Social sciences, interdisciplinary studies

Hackstock 1697

Social work school/education

Rocket 3240

Space/aviation

Alaska 74, Honeywell 1852, Jeppesen 2038, United 3874, UTC 3908

Speech/hearing centers

Boler 520, CITGO 820, CVS 1014, Jones 2056, People's 2928, Skinner 3475, Western 4043

Spine disorders

DJO 1134, DRW 1181, ProLogis 3060, Sonoran 3501

Spine disorders research

Ameritec 179, Sonoran 3501

Spirituality

HolacracyOne 1826, Jai 2017

Stress

Premera 3034

Student services/organizations

Jenzabar 2037, Sacramento 3303

Students, sororities/fraternities

Beall's 389, Dallas 1022

Substance abuse, prevention

Alpha 112, Altria 120, American 140, Andersen 194, Athletics 276, Blue 505, Colorado 879, Freeport 1494, IDACORP 1907, Integrity 1948, Pacers 2852, Perrigo 2943, Principal 3047, QuikTrip 3109, Rich 3204, Vodafone 3965

Substance abuse, services

Alsco 115, Apple 218, Armstrong 246, Baxter 377, Blue 505, Bridgestone 560, Burlington 618, Cardinal 685, Chase 770, Cic 811, Control 929, Cooper 936, Dime 1118, Fieldstone 1374, Fortune 1474, Guess 1685, Hard 1727, Herrick 1788, Kelley 2119, Mascoma 2394, Men's 2460, Mutual 2607, Nationwide 2639, PacifiCorp 2860, Paychex 2904, Piedmont 2971, Portland 3010, Principal 3047, Retail 3194, Snell 3490, Star 3583, Stewart 3604, TJX 3765, True 3814, Viejas 3951, Western 4043, Woodward 4112

Substance abuse, treatment

American 152, Armstrong 246, Blue 505, Carmody 695, Harnish 1734, Neenah 2656, Principal 3047, Regions 3171, Rennoc 3184, Union 3854, Univar 3886, Utica 3910

Substance abusers

Autodesk 289, Beneficial 412, Gilbane 1581, St. Joe 3563, WD-40 4011

Suicide

Esurance 1298, Questar 3105

Surgery

CryoLife 990, Ethicon 1299, General 1552, St. Jude 3566

Surgery research

Howmedica 1875, Integra 1947

Teacher school/education

3M 3, Alabama 71, Alcoa 82, Amgen 182, Baxter 377, Compass 901, Creative 976, Credit 980, Duke 1189, Freeport 1494, Hoffmann 1823, Honeywell 1852, ING 1938, Intel 1950, JPMorgan Chase 2071, Kadant 2083, Laureate 2231, Lexmark 2258, Life 2268, Medtronic 2453, Merck 2466, Micron 2500, Northern 2740, Pattillo 2896, Pearson 2911, People's 2928, PNC 2997, Siemens 3448, Subaru 3631, Target 3691, Texas 3728, Thermo 3733, Toshiba 3776, Vernier 3941, Vodafone 3965, Wal-Mart 3980, Whole 4066

Television

1st 2, Aramco 224, Associated 261, Aviva 302, Biomet 466, Bridgestone 560, Brown 591, Capital 677, Caterpillar 722, Curves 1011, Disney 1127, Fisher 1430, Fluor 1448, Franklin 1484, Harken 1731, IDACORP 1907, Ingersoll 1939, Johnson 2050, Kuhns 2197, Land 2217, Lincoln 2279, Neenah 2656, Niemann 2708, PEMCO 2919, Piedmont 2971, Playboy 2990, PMI 2995, Texas 3725, Time 3757, Union 3857, United 3867

Terminal illness, people with

Autodesk 289, Chrysler 801, Genesis 1561, WD-40 4011

Textile/fiber arts

Cranston 972

Theater

ABARTA 10, Acuity 32, Allegheny 91, Alsco 115, Amazon.com 122, American 146, Applied 220, Arch 231, Assurant 267, Assurity 269, AutoZone 294, Beneficial 411, Betts 451, Brooks 585, Brown 591, Burns 620, Caddell 645, Capezio 675, Capital 676, Capital 677, Century 750, Chicago 787, Chief 793, Cliffs 850, Collette 872, Community 897, Contran 928, Cooper 936, Copley 938, Creative 975, Dana 1026, DeBruce 1057, Dedham 1060, Dominion 1150, Eaton 1216, Endres 1269, Ensign 1276, F.N.B. 1318, Fabri 1322, Fenton 1361, First 1416, Forest 1467, Frankel 1483, Giant 1571, Graycor 1641, Hallberg 1704, Home 1844, Hubbard 1877, Hubbell 1879, Industrial 1935, Intermec 1955, Interstate 1975, James 2021, JPMorgan Chase 2071, Katten 2101, Laureate 2231, Lieberman 2266, Loews 2296, MDU 2441, Monadnock 2551, Mutual 2603, National 2629, National 2634, Naugatuck 2645, OceanFirst 2782, ONEOK 2815, Orscheln 2827, Pacific 2855, Pacific 2858, Parker 2886, Prince 3046, Questar 3104, RBC 3136, Regal

3166, Rodgers 3250, RUAN 3279, Schneider 3355, Schwan 3365, Scoular 3373, Sierra 3451, Specialty 3537, Sprint 3556, Star 3584, STERIS 3600, Stoneham 3616, Sunbeam 3647, Target 3691, Tennant 3714, Time 3757, United 3860, United 3864, United 3869, Upper 3900, US 3902, Victaulic 3948, Warburg 3985, Washington 3994, Wendy's 4032, Wenger 4033, Western 4043, Wiley 4072, Williams 4078, Yum! 4150

Theater (playwriting)

Amazon.com 122

Theological school/education

Butt 628, Century 748, Community 897, Dead 1051, Elite 1249, Ergon 1289, Fabick 1321, Fisher 1432, Gaunce 1543, General 1553, Giant 1571, Gosiger 1617, Homewood 1849, IDT 1910, Jasper 2025, Jasper 2026, Jordache 2062, Miller 2517, Morris 2573, MTD 2595, Omnicare 2807, Opus 2820, Pinnacle 2977, Premier 3036, Printpack 3049, Rothschild 3270, Southern 3517, SunTrust 3654, Tripifoods 3811, Willow 4082, Wolff 4105, YGS 4143

Transgender and gender nonconforming

Autodesk 289

Transportation

Alcoa 82, Arcelormittal 229, Avis 300, Freeport 1494, GoLite 1606, Grand 1629, Matson 2404, Teichert 3704, Volvo 3968

Tropical diseases

Abbott 13, Carlson 693, Chevron 780, Coca 862, Detroit 1095, General 1552

United Ways and Federated Giving Programs

1st 2, 3M 3, Abbott 13, ACE 24, Acme 28, Acme 29, Acuity 32, Advance 39, AEGON 45, Aflac 54, AGL 57, Air 63, AK 67, Alabama 71, Alaska 75, Alexander 85, Alfa 87, Alice 89, Allegheny 91, Allergan 99, Allete 100, Alliant 104, Alro 113, Altec 118, Ameren 128, American 132, American 137, American 143, American 145, American 146, American 149, American 159, AMERIGROUP 171, AmerisourceBergen 175, Amerisure 177, AmeriVision 180, AMETEK 181, Amgen 182, Amica 183, AMPCO 186, Amsted 188, Anadarko 190, Anheuser 202, ANZA 208, Apogee 215, Applied 219, AptarGroup 221, Arbeit 225, Arbella 226, Arcelormittal 229, Archer 233, Ariel 237, Arkema 242, Arrowpoint 251, Assurant 267, Assurant 268, Assurity 269, AutoZone 294, Avery 297, Avis 299, Aviva 302, Baird 316, Baird 317, Baker 318, Baker 323, Baker 324, Baltimore 332, Baltimore 335, Bangor 338, Bank 340, Bank 343, Bank 348, Bard 358, Bardes 359, Barnes 362, Barton 366, BASF 368, Baum 375, BB&T 385, Beaver 394, Bechtel 395, Belk 403, Belk 404, Belleville 405, Bemis 407, Berry 435, Berry 437, Best 442, Beverage 452, Bierlein 459, Biomet 466, Black 474, Bloomingdale's 488, Blue 492, Blue 497, Blue 505, Boehringer 515, BOSE 530, Boston 540, Bound 541, Boyd 546, Bridgestone 560, Briggs 564, Briggs 565, Bristol 577, Brookline 583, Brown 591, Bunge 612, Burlington 618, Burns 620, Butler 626, Butler 627, C & S 634, Cabot 642, Caddell 645, Cades 647, Campbell 669, Caparo 673, Capital 676, Capitol 680, Cargill 691, Carpenter 700, Carris 702, Castle 716, Catalina 719, Caterpillar 722, Centene 735, Central 742, Central 743, Central 745, CenturyLink 751, Ceridian 753, Chaney 761, Charter 766, Chelsea 772, Chemed 773, Chemical 774, CHS 802, CITGO 820, Citizens 824, Citizens 827, CLARCOR 832, Clayton 841, Cliffs 850, CMS 854, CNO 857, Coghlin 865, Collective 871, Colonial 875, Colt 881, Columbia 883, Comcast 887, Commerce 890, Commonwealth 895, Community 900, Compass 901, Cone 907, Consumers 921, Contran 928, Convergys 933, Cooper 935, Cooper 936, Corning 945, County 952, Cousins 953, Crane 969, Crane 970, Cranston 972, Credit 980, Crescent 983, CSS 996, Cummins 1007, CUNA 1008, Dana 1026, Danforth 1028, Darden 1032, Dayton 1047, Dead 1051, Dean 1053, Deere 1061, Delaware 1066, Delphi 1071, Deluxe 1084, DENTSPLY 1089, Diageo 1107, Diebold 1112, Dime 1118, Dispatch 1129, Dollar 1142, Dolphins 1147, Dominion 1150, Donaldson 1153, Donnelley 1155, Dow 1161, Dow 1162, Dow 1163, Duke 1189, DVK 1198, Eastern 1209, Easthampton 1212, Eaton 1216, Ecolab 1220, Edison 1229, El Paso 1239, Eliason 1248, Emerson 1257, Employers 1264, Energen 1270, Energizer 1271, Ensign 1276, Entergy 1279, Enterprise 1281, Evening 1302, Excell 1304, Exelon 1309, Fabri 1322, Factory 1323, Faegre 1324, Federated 1351, Fenton 1361, Ferro 1366, Fetzer 1367, Fifth 1377, First 1389, First 1393, First 1395, First 1396, First 1398, First 1399, First 1400, First 1402, First 1405, First 1406, First 1408, FirstEnergy 1424, Firstmerit 1425, Florida 1443, Fluor 1448, FMC 1449, Food 1458, Ford 1464, Forest 1467, Frankel 1483, Franklin 1484, Franklin 1488, Freeport 1494, Furniture 1519, Gear 1544, General 1552, General 1554, General 1555, General 1556, GenOn 1563, Georgia 1568, Gibbs 1576, GKN 1585, Golub 1607, Goodyear 1612, Gosiger 1617, Gould 1618, Government 1621, Grace 1623, Graco 1624, Graham 1625, Graybar 1640, GROWMARK 1674, GuideOne 1687, Gulf 1689, Hackstock 1697, Handy 1718, Hannaford 1723, Harley 1732, Harris 1736, Harris 1738, Harsco 1741, Hartford 1743, Hartzell 1745, Hawkins 1757, Haynes 1759, Haynie 1760, HCA 1762, Hermann 1786, Hewlett 1794, Highmark 1799, HNI 1817, Hoffer 1821, Holder 1829, Holme 1837, Homasote 1841, Home 1845, Honda 1851, Hood 1854, Hoops 1857, Hormel 1866, Houston 1871, Hubbard 1878, Hubbell 1879, Hunt 1888, Huntington 1894, IDACORP 1907, Ideal 1908, Illinois 1916, IMA 1917, Imation 1919, Independent 1927, Indianapolis 1932, Ingersoll 1939, Inman 1943, Intel 1950, Intermec 1955, Intermountain 1957, International 1958, International 1962, International 1967, International 1971, INTRUST 1981, Irby 1990, Island 1996, Jack 2007, James 2021, Jeld 2032, Johnson 2048, Johnson 2049, Johnson 2050, Jones 2055, Jones 2059, Jordan 2063, Journal 2068, Kann 2090, Katten 2101, Kawasaki 2103, Keithley 2115, Kellogg 2120, Kellwood 2121, Kennametal 2125, KeyBank 2136, Kimberly 2150, Kindred 2154, Kingsbury 2160, Klein's 2169, KOA 2178, Kroger 2195, La-Z-Boy 2205, Laclede 2207, Lake 2212, Land 2217, Landmark 2218, Laureate 2231, Lear 2237, Lee 2240, Lee 2241, Legg 2245, Lennar 2250, Levi 2254, Lexmark 2258, LG&E Energy 2260, Liberty 2262, Lieberman 2266, Lilly 2274, Limited 2277, Lincoln 2279, Lincoln 2281, Lincoln 2282, Lockheed 2292, Loews 2296, Longaberger 2299, Louisiana 2309, M&T 2323, Macy's 2333, Madison 2334, MAG 2337, Manitowoc 2355, Manitowoc 2356, Manpower 2358, Marathon 2362, Marathon 2365, Marcus 2371, Maritz 2376, MarkleBank 2379, Marsh 2387, Massachusetts 2397, Matson 2404, McCarthy 2421, McClatchy 2422, McDonald 2426, McJunkin 2431, McKesson 2434, Medtronic 2453, Menasha 2461, Mercury 2468, Mercury 2469, Meredith 2471, Merfish 2472, Meritor 2473, Michael 2493, Michigan 2496, Microchip 2499, MidAmerican 2504, Midcontinent 2505, Miller 2523, Milliken 2525, Mine 2529, Mississippi 2536, Modine 2544, Morgan 2568, Motorists 2584, Motorola 2585, MSC 2593, Mt. 2594, MTD 2595, Murphy 2600, Mutual 2603, Mutual 2605, Myers 2609, Mylan 2610, N.E.W. 2611, National 2629, National 2630, National 2634, National 2636, Naugatuck 2645, Navistar 2647, NCR 2650, NEBCO 2653, Neenah 2656, Nelnet 2660, Nestle 2662, Nestle 2663, Neville 2667, New 2668, New 2675, New England 2672, New Orleans 2678, New York 2684, New York 2687, NIBCO 2707, NiSource 2715, Nordson 2723, Norfolk 2725, North 2730, Northfield 2742, NorthWestern 2748, Northwestern 2749, NTELOS 2758, NV 2765, O'Connor 2770, Ohio 2789, Ohio 2790, Oklahoma 2795, Ole 2800, Olin 2801, Omaha 2805, Omaha 2806, Omron 2810, OneBeacon 2813, ONEOK 2815, Orscheln 2827, OSCO 2832, Oshkosh 2833, Osram 2834, Otis 2835, Owens 2842, Owens 2844, Oxford 2847, PACCAR 2850, PacifiCorp 2860, Pan-American 2868, Park 2879, Park 2881, Parker 2886, PDB 2906, Peabody 2907, PEMCO 2919, Penney 2925, Pentair 2926, People's 2928, Peoples 2929, PepsiCo 2935, Perkins 2940, Perrigo 2943, Pfizer 2950, Physicians 2970, Piedmont 2971, Pieper 2972, Pier 2973, Piper 2983, Portland 3010, Potomac 3018, PPG 3025, PPL 3026, Praxair 3029, Premier 3036, Premix 3037, Presley 3038, Price 3039, Price 3040, PricewaterhouseCoopers 3042, Printpack 3049, Progressive 3059, Protective 3066, Providence 3068, Public 3075, Publix 3079, Puget 3081, Quad 3091, Quaker 3093, Quanex 3100, QuikTrip 3109, R & R 3114, Rayonier 3134, RBS 3138, RECO 3148, Red 3154, Regal 3166, Regions 3171, Regis 3172, Reily 3177, Republic 3188, RESCO 3189, Retail 3194, Rexnord 3198, Reynolds 3200, Ricoh 3210, Riggs 3213, Rio 3218, Rite 3220, RITE 3221, Robins 3232, Robinson 3235, Rockwell 3246, Rose 3261, Ryder 3292, S & T 3297, S.J. 3299, Sachs 3301, Safeco 3306, Safety 3308, sanofi-aventis 3329, Sasol 3338, Schiff 3350, Schmeling 3353, Schneider 3355, Schwan 3365, Scotts 3372, Sealy 3382, Securian 3389, Selective 3399, Sempra 3405, Seneca 3406, Sensient 3408, Sentry 3409, Seton 3415, Shaw's 3427, Shea 3428, Shell 3430, Shelter 3431, ShopKo 3440, Shugart 3442, Sigma 3453, Silicon 3455, Simplot 3459, Sit 3466, Sjostrom 3469, Smith 3484, Smith 3485, Smucker 3488, Smulekoff 3489, Snell 3490, Snyder's-Lance 3492, SourceMedia 3506, South Bend 3507, Sovereign 3528, Spahn 3529, Spartan 3535, Springleaf 3554, St. Louis 3567, Stanley 3580, Star 3584, Stardust 3586, State 3590, STERIS 3600, Stewart 3604, Stupp 3628, Sunbeam 3647, Sunoco 3650, SunTrust 3654, SUPERVALU 3659, Syniverse 3672, Synovus 3674, Talbots 3682, Tanner 3688, Tap 3689, Target 3691, TD 3696, TECO 3701, Tektronix 3706, Tennant 3714, Tenneco 3715, Tennessee 3716, Tension 3717, Tesoro 3723, Texas 3728, Textron 3731, Thomasville 3737, Thompson 3738, Timken 3760, Tops 3774, Toro 3775, Total 3778, Tractor 3791, Trane 3794, Transco 3797, Trim 3810, True 3814, Trustmark 3818, Tyco 3829, U.S. 3835, U.S. 3836, Unisys 3859, United 3860, United 3867, United 3868, United 3869, United 3870, United 3872, United 3873, United 3874, United 3880, United 3882, Universal 3891, Unum 3898, US 3902, USG 3905, UTC 3908, Utica 3910, V.F. 3913, Valero 3915, Valspar 3920, Vectren 3925, Victaulic 3948, Virginia 3959, Volvo 3968, Wagner 3976, Wal-Mart 3980, Walgreen 3981, Washington 4001, Wausau 4008, Webster 4016, Wegmans 4021, Weil 4022, Weis 4024, Wellmark 4026, Wenger 4033, West 4038, Western 4040, Western 4042, Westfield 4047, Weyco 4051, Weyerhaeuser 4052, Whirlpool 4056, Whiting 4063, Williams 4077, Wisconsin 4093, WKBN 4099, Wolf 4103, Wolverine 4106, Woodward 4112, Wrigley 4125, Wynnne 4133, Xcel 4135, Xerox 4136, XTEK 4138, Young 4146, YSI 4149, Yum! 4150, Zatkoff 4154, Zions 4158

University

Alpha 112, Berry 437, Bloomin 487, CH2M 758, Chartis 768, Coca 863, Great 1645, Iberdrola 1904, Lam 2214, Liberty 2265, Matson 2404, MedImmune 2450, NorthWestern 2748, Ross 3266, SAP 3334, Sonoco 3500, United 3880

Urban League

Dolphins 1147

Urban studies

Skidmore 3474

Urban/community development

Alabama 71, Alcoa 82, Bank 347, Berkshire 428, Blackstone 477, Calvert 663, Collette 872, Coyotes 963, Dominion 1149, DTE 1183, Eaton 1216, Federal 1349, First 1420, Forest 1467, H & R 1695, Hallmark 1707, Johnson 2050, JPMorgan Chase 2071, MeadWestvaco 2445, Metropolitan 2481, PacifiCorp 2860, Public 3077, Sensient 3408, SunTrust 3654, Tiffany 3750, Union 3854, Urban 3901, Valspar 3920, WD-40 4011, Wells 4028, Wolverine 4106

Utilities

Ameren 129, Black 474, Columbia 883, Consumers 921, Delmarva 1069, Duquesne 1194, Gulf 1689, Liberty 2262, Mount 2588, Oklahoma 2794, ONEOK 2815, PG&E 2952, SCANA 3346, Sears 3384

Venture philanthropy

Bristlecone 575, Farm 1333, Towerbrook 3781

Veterinary medicine

Keeneland 2113

Veterinary medicine, hospital

American 155

Visitors/convention bureau/tourism promotion

Choice 798, Factory 1323, Freeport 1494, Hilton 1812, Lincoln 2282, Northwestern 2749, Principal 3047

Visual arts

Adobe 38, Alabama 71, Altria 120, American 143, Andersen 194, Avery 297, Aviva 302, Berry 434, Boeing 516, Burlington 618, Cajun 652, Clorox 852, Cook 934, Corning 945, Crayola 973, CVS 1014, Danaher 1027, Deutsche 1099, EFC 1236, First 1406, Fluor 1448, Getty 1569, Hanover 1724, Haskell 1748, HCA 1762, IDACORP 1907, James 2021, Johnson 2050, Joy 2070, JPMorgan Chase 2071, Kimball 2149, Kohler 2182, Land 2217, Lefton 2244, Luck 2317, McClatchy 2422, Mentor 2462, Meredith 2471, Metropolitan 2481, Monsanto 2559, National 2635, Nordson 2723, Oaklandish 2773, Old 2796, Omaha 2805, Owens 2844, PacifiCorp 2860, Peoples 2929, Peoples 2931, Piedmont 2971, RBC 3136, Sentry 3409, Skinner 3475, Sovereign 3528, Sports 3548, Sprint 3556, Tiffany 3750, UBS 3842, Universal 3895, Urban 3901, Washington 3995, Washington 3999

Vocational education

Accenture 22, Allete 100, Altria 120, American 150, Ameristar 176, Arctic 234, Avery 297, Bob's 511, Bristol 576, Brunswick 595, Burlington 618, Cadence 646, CarMax 694, Chenega 776, Chevron 780, Chrysler 801, Chugach 805, Cisco 818, CNA 855, Coca 863, Connecticut 911, Cook 934, Cooper 935, Doyon 1167, Dreyer's 1174, Duke 1189, Eaton 1216, El Paso 1239, Entergy 1279, Farmers' 1337, First 1398, Freeport 1494, G&K 1524, General 1555, Grainger 1626, Guardian 1682, Hitachi 1816, Home 1842, Huna 1887, IDACORP 1907, KeyBank 2136, Kingsbury 2160, Kuskokwim 2200, Lowe's 2312, Material 2401, Middlesex 2506, Newell 2694, Nucor 2760, Panda 2871, Peabody 2907, Penney 2925, Pentair 2926, Piedmont 2971, QUALCOMM 3095, Remmele 3183, Rockville 3245, Safeco 3306, Safety 3309, Sempra 3405, Shanken 3421, ShopKo 3440, Simplot 3459, Stanley 3579, Staples 3581, State 3592, STERIS 3600, TJX 3765, Universal 3890, Western 4045, Wisconsin 4096, Woodward-Graff 4113, Zale 4151

Vocational education, post-secondary

Aon 210, Bering 422, Berkel 424, Berkshire 428, Chugach 805, Cracker 966, ESCO 1296, First 1413, Four 1477, Government 1620, Grainger 1626, Green 1651, Koniag 2184, Middlesex 2506, National 2638, Nexion 2705, Ounalashka 2837, Pedernales 2914, Peterson 2946, Portland 3010, Reed 3162, Royal 3274, State 3592, Strauss 3624, True 3815, Ukpeagvik 3843, Wisconsin 4096

Vocational rehabilitation

Baum 375, G&K 1524, Lord 2303

Voluntarism promotion

American 143, AOL 209, BJ's 473, Boston 533, Clorox 852, Comcast 887, Creative 975, Credit 980, Fluor 1448, Kemp 2123, Loews 2296, Metropolitan 2481, Mutual 2606, Newman's 2697, News 2701, Nordson 2723, Parametric 2878, Security 3391, Sensient 3408, State 3591, SunTrust 3654, Teachers 3697, Texas 3725, Towerbrook 3781, United 3872

Volunteers of America

Major 2346

Voter education

Philadelphia 2961, Working 4116

Waste management

Alcoa 82, Aspen 260, Avery 297, Burrtec 622, Clif 848, Tellabs 3709, Unilever 3853, Union 3854, Wrigley 4125

Water pollution

Aspen 260, Bed 399, Booz 525, BP 547, Bridgestone 560, Capital 678, Coca 862, DENSO 1088, Dunkin' 1191, Georgia 1567, Green 1653, Indus 1934, International 1968, Monsanto 2559, Nalco 2613, Neville 2667, PepsiCo 2935, RBC 3136, Royal 3273, V.F. 3913, YSI 4149

Web-based media

Allstate 107, Fisher 1430

Women

Abbott 13, Aetna 48, Agilent 56, AGL 57, Alcoa 82, Alima 90, Allergan 99, American 142, Arnold 248, Ascena 255, Autodesk 289, B & B 312, Bayer 381, Bayer 382, Bed 399, Beneficial 412, Bloomingdale's 488, Blue 505, Bressler 557, Bristol 578, Broadcom 579, Burlington 618, Butler 626, Chevron 780, Chrysler 801, Cisco 818, Citigroup 821, Coach 858, Collective 871, Columbia 884, Compuware 902, Cox 958, Danaher 1027, Diversey 1130, DTE 1183, Exxon 1315, Fifth 1376, Fisher 1433, Freeport 1494, Gannett 1532, Gap 1533, Genesis 1561, Georgia 1568, Globe 1594, Greyhound 1664, Haynes 1759, Heinz 1772, Homasote 1841, Intel 1950, International 1962, iVillage 2002, Johnson 2048, Katten 2101, Kimball 2149, Kohler 2182, Kroger 2195, L'Oreal 2203, Ladies 2209, Limited 2277, Longaberger 2299, Macy's 2333, Mary 2392, MasterCard 2399, Medtronic 2453, Melissa 2458, Mercedes 2463, Metropolitan 2481, Moody's 2563, Newell 2694, North 2735, Northern 2740, Pactiv 2863, Palace 2866, People's 2928, PepsiCo 2935, Pfizer 2950, PG&E 2952, Piedmont 2971, Pitney 2984, PPG 3025, PVH 3088, RESCO 3189, RGI 3202, Rite 3220, Rockwell 3246, Royal 3274, Seattle 3386, Security 3391, Semiconductor 3403, SpectraCare 3541, Sterne 3602, Strauss 3624, Symantec 3669, Talbots 3682, Tanner 3688, Tastefully 3692, Textron 3731, TJX 3765, Tupperware 3821, United 3882, Verizon 3936, Wal-Mart 3980, WD-40 4011, Winn 4087, Wisconsin 4096, Wyndham 4132, Xerox 4136

Women, centers/services

American 142, AMPCO 186, Apex 213, AutoZone 294, Avis 300, B & B 312, Cadence 646, Caplin 681, CEMEX 734, CITGO 820, Coach 858, Contran 928, craigslist 968, Davison 1042, DCI 1049, Eastern 1210, Food 1458, Friedland 1503, General 1554, Herrick 1788, Johnson 2049, Limited 2277, MidAmerican 2504, Quad 3091, Quaker 3094, Safeway 3310, Seventh 3416, Shaughnessy 3425, Skinner 3475, Talbots 3682, TECO 3701, Whitley 4064, Woodforest 4110, Working 4116, Xylem 4139, Zappos.com 4153

YM/YWCAs & YM/YWHAs

1st 2, Acme 29, AK 67, Albrecht 80, Alfa 87, Allegheny 91, Allen 97, American 143, AMERIGROUP 171, Ameritas 178, Ameritec 179, Ariel 237, Armstrong 245, Assurity 269, Avidia 298, Badger 313, Baird 317, Baker 324, Bank 341, Bank 342, Bank 343, BB&T 385, Belk 403, Belleville 405, Bemis 408, Betts 451, Bon 521, Boston 540, Bound 541, Bridgestone 560, Briggs 565, Bristol 577, Brown 591, Burlington 618, Butzel 629, Cargill 691, Cary 712, Center 737, Central 742, Central 745, CFS 756, Chief 793, Cianbro 808, CIGNA 812, Citizens 824, CLARCOR 832, Classic 840, Coca 861, Colonial 875, Comcast 887, Commerce 890, Concept 905, Conditioned 906, Contran 928, Cooper 936, Corning 945, Cranston 972, CUNA 1008, Dead 1051, Dean 1053, Defiance 1063, Deluxe 1084, Demoulas 1085, Denver 1090, Deutsche 1099, Dilbeck 1116, Dime 1118, Dollar 1144, Donnelley 1155, Dot 1158, DVK 1198, Dynamet 1200, East 1207, Easthampton 1212, Eaton 1216, Edgar 1225, Essa 1297, Exotic 1310, Fabiano 1320, Fabri 1322, Farmers 1335, Fidelity 1372, First 1395, First 1397, First 1421, Firstmerit 1425, Fort 1472, General 1554, Giant 1571, Golub 1607, Graham 1625, Graybar 1640, Greater 1649, Green 1651, Griswold 1669, Hampden 1712, Hannaford 1723, HCA 1762, Hendrick 1777, HNI 1817, Hoffer 1821, Home 1845, Horizon 1863, Hubbard 1878, Hudson 1880, Hudson 1881, Hufcor 1883, Huntington 1894, Ideal 1908, Illinois 1916, Inman 1943, Institution 1946, Intermountain 1957, International 1958, Jacksonville 2014, Johnson 2049, Jones 2055, Journal 2068, JPMorgan Chase 2071, Kellogg 2120, KeyBank 2136, KOA 2178, Kuhns 2197, Kukui 2198, L&L 2202, Lee 2240, Lee 2241, LifePoint 2270, Lilly 2274, Luck 2317, Madison 2334, Majestic 2343, Manitowoc 2356, Mapes 2360, Marcus 2370, Mary 2392, McCarthy 2421, McKinstry 2435, McWane 2440, Midcontinent 2505, Midmark 2507, Milliken 2525, Milwaukee 2528, Mondelez 2556, Morris 2573, MTD 2595, Mutual 2603, National 2629, National 2634, National 2636, Naugatuck 2645, NEBCO 2653, Newburyport 2693, Newport 2699, Newspapers 2702, Niemann 2708, Northwest 2746, NTELOS 2758, Oklahoma 2795, Old 2796, Orscheln 2827, Oshkosh 2833, Pan-American 2868, Park 2879, Park 2881, Parker 2884, Parker 2886, People's 2928, Peoples 2929, PepsiCo 2935, Physicians 2970, PPG 3025, Protective 3066, Protector 3067, Recreational 3150, Red 3154, Redwoods 3158, Regal 3166, Regions 3171, Reiff 3174, Retail 3194, Rite 3220, RITE 3221, Robins 3232, Robinson 3235, Rockville 3245, Rose 3261, Rudolph 3283, S & T 3297, Safeco 3306, Safeway 3310, Schiff 3350, Schloss 3352, Sealy 3382, Selective 3399, Sentry 3409, Shaw's 3427, Simplot 3459, Smith 3483, Smith 3485, Smucker 3488, Southern 3517, Spartan 3535, Springleaf 3554, Sterne 3602, Stop 3618, Stupp 3628, SunTrust 3654, Superior 3658, Synovus 3674, Tampa 3686, Tanner 3688, Teleflex 3707, TeleTech 3708, Thompson 3738, Tillman 3752, Titan 3763, Trim 3810, UBS 3842, Union 3858, United 3864, United 3867, United 3869, Universal 3891, Utica 3910, Valero 3915, Valspar 3920, Vectren 3925, Vijuk 3953, Waffle 3975, Walker 3982, Washington 4001, Wausau 4008, Weaver 4015, WellPoint 4027, Wendy's 4032, Weyco 4051, Whirlpool

4056, Wisconsin 4093, Wolf 4103, Wolverine 4106, Wood 4108, Woodward 4112, Young 4146

Young adults

Abbott 13, Archer 233, Autodesk 289, Beneficial 412, Caterpillar 722, Chrysler 801, CHS 802, First 1419, Genesis 1561, Guard 1680, Iberdrola 1904, Metropolitan 2481, Piedmont 2971, Schwab 3363, Security 3391, Southern 3514, St. Joe 3563, U.S. 3835, WD-40 4011

Young adults, female

Alcatel 81, Autodesk 289, Avon 305, Beneficial 412, Chrysler 801, Colgate 869, Fisher 1433, Genesis 1561, Guardian 1683, Metropolitan 2481, Simpson 3461, WD-40 4011

Young adults, male

Autodesk 289, Beneficial 412, Chrysler 801, Genesis 1561, Metropolitan 2481, WD-40 4011

Youth

Abbott 13, Abby's 14, adidas 35, Aeropostale 46, Alcatel 81, American 150, Androscoggin 199, Aon 210, Atlanta 277, Austin 288, Autodesk 289, AutoNation 292, Avis 299, AXA 307, Bayer 381, Beneficial 412, Best 442, Biogen 465, Blue 498, Blue 500, Blue 501, Blue 502, Broadcom 579, Brooklyn 584, Buccaneer 599, Buffalo 606, Butt 628, Callaway 660, Calvert 663, Cambridge 666, Cardinal 685, Cargill 691, CC 728, Center 737, Chicago 786, Chicago 788, Chrysler 801, CHS 802, Citigroup 821, Cleveland 847, Clorox 852, Coca 862, Colgate 869, Colorado 880, Cox 958, CUNA 1008, Dallas 1021, Dayton 1047, Dean 1054, Delphi 1071, Deluxe 1084, Detroit 1095, Deutsche 1099, Dick's 1110, Donnelley 1155, Dreyer's 1174, Emerson 1257, Energy 1272, Equifax 1288, Exelon 1309, Finish 1383, First 1419, Frontier 1510, Fuller 1517, GameStop 1530, Gap 1533, General 1554, Georgia 1568, Green 1651, Hanover 1724, Herschend 1790, Highmark 1799, Hilfiger 1801, Illinois 1916, IMA 1917, Intel 1950, Intelius 1951, International 1968, Jacksonville 2014, JM 2044, Kansas 2093, Kinder 2153, Kohl's 2181, Land 2217, Lauth 2232, Liberty 2264, Liberty 2265, Los Angeles 2308, Lubrizol 2315, MAXIMUS 2410, Mazda 2414, McKesson 2434, Medtronic 2453, Metropolitan 2481, MFA 2487, Miami 2491, Mitsubishi 2538, Monsanto 2559, Motorola 2585, Motorola 2586, Mountain 2589, Nashville 2620, National 2635, NEC 2654, Nelnet 2660, Nestle 2662, Nestle 2663, New England 2672, New York 2684, New York 2687, Nordson 2723, Northrop 2744, O'Neal 2771, Pacific 2853, People's 2928, Philadelphia 2957, Philadelphia 2958, Philadelphia 2959, Pitney 2984, Pittsburgh 2986, Polaris 2999, Protective 3066, Prudential 3072, Quiksilver 3108, RBC 3136, Reebok 3159, Reell 3164, Reynolds 3199, Robinson 3235, Rockwell 3247, RubinBrown 3280, Ryman 3294, Safeco 3306, San Diego 3323, San Jose 3327, Security 3391, Seneca 3406, ShopKo 3440, Sierra 3451, Simpson 3461, Spirit 3544, Sporting 3546, Sprint 3556, Staples 3581, State 3592, Station 3593, Steelcase 3597, Sulphur 3637, Taco 3679, TALX 3683, Tampa 3686, Teichert 3704, TeleTech 3708, Tennessee 3716, Thorntons 3743, Toyota 3784, Toyota 3786, Tulalip 3820, U.S. 3835, Union 3857, United 3860, United 3863, Waffle 3975, Washington 3994, Washington 3995, Washington 3998, Washington 4000, WD-40 4011, Westar 4039, Xerox 4136

Youth development

3M 3, 7-Eleven 5, A & E 6, Acacia 21, ACF 26, Adams 34, AEG 43, Aeropostale 46, Affinity 52, Aflac 54, Alaska 75, Alaska 76, Albertsons 79, Alcatel 81, Alcoa 82, Allen 94, Allen 95, Allete 100, Alpha 112, Altria 120, Ameren 128, American 134, American 136, American 140, American 144, American 150, American 154, American 155, AmeriPride 173, Ameristar 176, Amica 183, Androscoggin 199, Angels 200, Aon 210, Arby's 228, Associated 263, Atlanta 278, Atlanta 280, Auntie 287, AZPB 310, Baker 325, Balch 327, Baltimore 334, BancorpSouth 336, Bank 340, Bank 349, Barrasso 363, BASF 368, Bay 380, Beall's 389, Bemis 407, Bennett 415, Benton 417, Best 442, Beverage 452, BHP 455, Binswanger 464, Black 474, Blue 501, Blue 506, Bobcats 512, Bodine 513, Boh 517, Boneal 523, Boston 540, Boyd 545, Bracewell 549, Brinks 573, Build 608, Builders 609, Burger 613, Burr 621, Butler 626, Butler 627, California 654, Callaway 660, Campbell 668, Campbell 669, Canon 672, Capital 677, Capital 679, Caribou 692, CarMax 694, Carolina 699, Carpenter 700, CC 728, CF 755, CFS 756, Chase 770, Chemical 774, Chicago 789, Chicago 790, Chick 791, Chrysler 801, CHS 802, Chubb 804, Churchill 807, Cincinnati 814, Circle 817, Clorox 852, Coca 862, Coca 863, Coghlin 864, Colorado 879, Colt 881, Columbus 886, Comcast 887, Comcast 888, Compuware 902, ConocoPhillips 913, Continental 922, Cooper 936, CORE 941, Cow 957, Cox 958, Credit 978, Crescent 983, Crowell 986, CSRwire 995, Cummins 1005, CVS 1014, D.C. 1018, Dallas 1021, Dallas 1022, Dead 1051, Dell 1068, Delmarva 1069, Delta 1082, Denver 1090, Dethmers 1091, Detroit 1095, Detroit 1097, Devon 1102, Diamonds 1109, Dick's 1110, Discovery 1126, Dispatch 1129, Do 1136, Dominion 1149, Dot 1158, DTE 1183, Dun 1190, Earthquakes 1206, Eastern 1209, Edelman 1224, Emerson 1257, Emmis 1260, Energizer 1271, EnMark 1274, Epson 1286, Esbenshade's 1295, ESCO 1296, Esurance 1298, Exchange 1306, Family 1330, Federal 1348, Ferrara 1364, Fieldstone 1374, Fifth 1377, Finish 1383, First 1391, First 1398, First 1401, First 1415, First 1416, First 1419, First 1421, Fleck 1435, Florida 1442, Foley 1454, Fonville 1456, Foot 1459, Football 1460, Ford 1463, Ford 1464, Fortune 1474, Frontier 1510, Fuller 1517, Furniture 1519, G&K 1524, Gallo 1529, Gannett 1532, Gap 1533, Gemini 1547, General 1550, Genesco 1559, Georgia 1568, Give 1583, Gleaner 1590, Golub 1607, Google 1613, Grace 1623, Graco 1624, Grand 1627, Granite 1632, Graphic 1634, Graybar 1640, Greater 1649, Greif 1663, Guardian 1683, H & R 1695, Hall 1702, Hancock 1717, Hanover 1724, Hargray 1730, Harris 1738, HCA 1762, Hedrick 1768, Henry 1781, Heritage 1785, Hewlett 1794, Heyrman 1796, Highmark 1799, Hilliard 1805, Hilton 1812, Hines 1813, Holtz 1840, Home 1844, Hoops 1857, Horizon 1862, Houston 1872, Hubbard 1878, Hunt 1891, Hunt 1892, IHC 1913, Institution 1946, Intermountain 1956, International 1964, International 1971, Investors 1984, Isaly's 1994, Jack 2007, Jackson-Shaw 2013, Jamba 2020, Johnson 2050, Jostens 2067, JPMorgan Chase 2071, JSJ 2073, K-B 2081, Kansas 2092, Kemper 2124, Kennecott 2127, Kent 2129, Key 2134, Kiewit 2142, Kimball 2148, Kimley 2151, Klein 2168, Knowledge 2177, Koss 2188, Land 2217, Las Vegas 2225, Latham 2229, Laureate 2231, Lee 2242, Lemieux 2249, Liberty 2265, Lilly 2274, Lincoln 2280, Lincoln 2281, Long 2298, Los Angeles 2306, Los Angeles 2307, Los Angeles 2308, Lowe's 2312, Lubrizol 2315, Luck 2317, Major 2345, Major 2347, Manpower 2358, Marathon 2363, Marathon 2366, Mattel 2405, Maverick 2409, McShane 2439, Mechanics 2446, Mercedes 2463, Metropolitan 2481, Metropolitan 2483, Meyer 2485, MFA 2486, Miami 2491, Micro 2498, Middlesex 2506, Mike's 2509, Milford 2514, Milwaukee 2527, Minnesota 2531, Minster 2532, Mohawk 2545, Monarch 2552, Monsanto 2559, Morgan 2569, Morley 2572, Morris 2574, Mortenson 2577, Motorists 2584, Mountain 2589, MTV 2596, Murray 2601, N.E.W. 2611, Nashville 2620, National 2623, National 2626, Naugatuck 2646, Nestle 2662, Nestle 2663, New 2668, New England 2672, New York 2686, New York 2688, New York 2691, NIKE 2710, North 2732, North 2735, Northern 2738, Northfield 2742, NorthWestern 2748, NRG 2756, NuStar 2763, NV 2765, NYSE 2769, Oakland 2772, OceanFirst 2782, Oklahoma 2794, One 2812, Opus 2820, Orlando 2824, Oshkosh 2833, Owen 2840, Owner 2845, Pacific 2853, Padilla 2864, Pawtucket 2902, Pawtucket 2903, PDB 2906, Pearce 2910, PEMCO 2919, Penney 2925, People's 2928, Peoples 2929, PepsiCo 2935, PGA 2954, Philadelphia 2957, Philadelphia 2959, Philadelphia 2961, Phillips 2966, Piedmont 2971, Piper 2983, Pizza 2988, Plain 2989, Plum 2991, PNC 2997, Polaris 2999, Pony 3002, Porter 3006, Potomac 3018, Price 3040, Principal 3047, Printpack 3049, Provident 3070, Quadion 3092, RBC 3136, Regions 3171, Riceland 3203, Ricoh 3210, Riggs 3213, Rima 3216, Rockford 3241, Rockland 3242, Rockwell 3247, Rolls 3254, Rudolph 3283, Rue 3285, Salem 3317, San Antonio 3321, San Diego 3322, San Francisco 3326, San Jose 3327, SANYO 3333, SAS 3336, Savage 3341, Schwan 3365, Seattle 3386, Securian 3389, Security 3393, Select 3398, Seneca 3406, Servco 3412, Shakopee 3419, Shelton 3432, ShopKo 3440, Sidwell 3447, Sigma 3453, Simplot 3459, Sioux 3465, Slant 3477, SmartWool 3479, Sony 3502, Southern 3516, Southern 3518, Southern 3519, Southwest 3524, Southwire 3527, Spahn 3529, Spartan 3535, Sports 3549, Sprint 3556, St. Louis 3567, St. Louis 3568, St. Louis 3569, Standard 3576, Staples 3581, Starbucks 3585, State 3592, Stiles 3607, Stone 3614, Stride 3625, Sulphur 3637, Superior 3657, Target 3691, TCF 3695, TD 3696, Tees 3703, Teichert 3704, Tennessee 3716, Terlato 3720, Texas 3729, Texor 3730, Textron 3731, TFS 3732, Thomson 3742, Thorntons 3743, Thrivent 3747, Time 3757, TJX 3765, Totem 3779, Towerbrook 3781, Tractor 3791, Trail 3793, Triumph 3812, Turner 3824, Twins 3827, Tyson 3832, U.S. 3835, U.S. 3836, U.S. 3841, Union 3858, United 3860, United 3879, Universal 3889, Usibelli 3906, Vodafone 3965, Vulcan 3970, Washington 3994, Washington 3998, Washington 4000, WaterStone 4005, WD-40 4011, Weaver 4014, Wegmans 4021, West 4037, Weyerhaeuser 4052, Wimpfheimer 4085, Wolf 4102, Worthen 4123, Wrigley 4125, Young 4147

Youth development, adult & child programs

Alcatel 81, American 140, Androscoggin 199, Applied 220, Berkshire 428, Blue 501, Carlson 693, Coyotes 963, Deluxe 1084, Emerson 1257, EQT 1287, Exelon 1309, First 1419, Fluor 1448, Fortis 1473, Freeport 1494, Gap 1533, Hoops 1857, Hubbell 1879, Jack 2007, Lear 2237, Liberty 2262, Liberty 2265, MasterCard 2399, Metropolitan 2481, Motorists 2584, New York 2688, NIKE 2710, Northwestern 2749, OceanFirst 2782, Ohio 2789, Pacific 2855, People's 2928, Piedmont 2971, Pitney 2984, PPG 3025, Principal 3047, ProLogis 3060, Provident 3069, Raytheon 3135, RBC 3136, Seneca 3406, Sprint 3556, TD 3696, Textron 3731, U.S. 3835, United 3872, Vectren 3925, Vodafone 3965, Wisconsin 4096

Youth development, agriculture

AgStar 59, CHS 802, ConAgra 904, GROWMARK 1674, Land 2217, MFA 2486, Monsanto 2559, Riggs 3213

Youth development, alliance/advocacy

First 1419

Youth development, association

Brady 552

Youth development, business

AbbyBank 15, Acuity 32, Alcatel 81, Alcoa 82, Ameren 128, American 146, Amerisure 177, AnchorBank 193, Ariens 238, Armstrong 246, Associated 261, AT&T 273, Beaver 394, Brown 591, Burlington 618, Catalina 719, Caterpillar 722, Charter 766, Chemical 774, Chicago 787, Citigroup 821, Colonial 875, Control 929, Credit 980, Crescent 983, Dana 1026, Deere 1061, Diebold 1112, Dollar 1144, Dow 1162, Eaton 1216, El Paso 1239, Energizer 1271, EQT 1287, Exelon 1309, Fidelity 1371, First 1406, Ford 1463, Fresh 1499, General 1552, Georgia 1568, GKN 1585, Great 1647, H & R

1695, HCA 1762, Hewlett 1794, Highwoods 1800, Illinois 1916, ING 1938, Intel 1950, Jack 2007, James 2021, Jones 2055, Lexmark 2258, Mapes 2360, Marcus 2371, MasterCard 2399, McDonald 2426, Meritor 2473, Metropolitan 2481, Midcontinent 2505, Mine 2529, Motley 2582, Mutual 2606, Neenah 2656, Nelnet 2660, Olin 2801, OppenheimerFunds 2818, Otis 2835, Papa 2876, Parker 2886, Patton's 2899, PEMCO 2919, Penney 2925, Physicians 2970, Popular 3003, PricewaterhouseCoopers 3042, ProLogis 3060, Quad 3091, RITE 3221, RubinBrown 3280, SCANA 3346, Smucker 3488, State 3590, TALX 3683, Tap 3689, Thomasville 3737, Thorrez 3744, Thrivent 3747, Timken 3760, TransUnion 3799, Tupperware 3821, United 3860, US 3902, Visteon 3964, Wal-Mart 3980, Wausau 4008, Wegmans 4021, Whirlpool 4056, Wolverine 4106

Youth development, centers/clubs

Altec 118, American 155, Build 608, Chicago 790, Colt 881, Credit 980, Evening 1302, Herrick 1788, Mississippi 2536, Nashville 2620, New Hampshire 2674, Provident 3069, Superior 3657, Temple 3711, Urban 3901, V.F. 3913, Warnaco 3988, World 4120

Youth development, citizenship

Kohler 2182, Laureate 2231, Lauth 2232, Luck 2317, New York 2688

Youth development, community service clubs

Basketball 370, Build 608, Chicago 785, HCA 1762, Kohl's 2181, Rocket 3240

Youth development, equal rights

Avis 300

Youth development, formal/general education

Chicago 790, Nellie 2659, Toyota 3785

Youth development, fund raising/fund distribution

PacifiCorp 2860, Trail 3793

Youth development, information services

Lorillard 2304

Youth development, intergenerational programs

Macy's 2333

Youth development, public education

Booz 525, Capital 679, Nellie 2659, Plum 2992

Youth development, services

Arby's 228, Capital 679, Comcast 887, Community 900, Cumberland 1003, Fisher 1433, Foot 1459, Kellogg 2120, Lauth 2232, Metropolitan 2484, Orlando 2824, PDB 2906, Sprint 3556, Tesoro 3723

Youth development, single organization support

First 1419

Youth development, volunteer services

American 140, Bigelow 462, Kohl's 2181, Reebok 3159, Scotts 3372

Youth, pregnancy prevention

Jacksonville 2014, Vodafone 3965

Youth, services

Advanced 40, Allen 97, Allstate 107, Alpenrose 111, Altria 120, Ameren 128, American 164, AMETEK 181, Androscoggin 199, Apollo 216, Applied 220, Avery 297, Avista 301, Baltimore 335, Bangor 338, Barnes 362, Baseball 367, Baxter 377, Bayer 381, Birdsong 470, Boehringer 515, Bosch 529, Brillion 569, Brooklyn 584, Brotherhood 588, Caesars 650, California 656, Cannon 671, Capitol 680, Cavaliers 724, CC 728, Chicago 786, Churchill 807, Clif 848, Columbia 884, Contran 928, Control 929, Cooper 935, Corning 945, Cummins 1007, Dallas 1023, Dedham 1060, Delaware 1066, Dolphins 1147, Dr 1169, East 1207, Ecolab 1220, Emmis 1260, Family 1330, First 1406, First 1419, FirstEnergy 1424, Florida 1442, Fluor 1448, Football 1460, Fortis 1473, Fox 1480, Friesen 1505, Furniture 1519, Gable 1525, Genworth 1565, Globe 1594, Hallberg 1704, Hastings 1749, Hawaiian 1756, Heat 1767, Hulman 1885, IDACORP 1907, Imation 1919, Independence 1925, Independent 1927, Indiana 1929, International 1964, Johns 2047, Johnson 2049, Johnson 2050, KeyBank 2136, Kikkoman 2144, Koch 2180, Lincoln 2282, Los Angeles 2307, M&T 2323, Majestic 2343, Major 2347, Mariani 2374, Mascoma 2394, MasterCard 2399, McDonald's 2427, MDU 2441, MeadWestvaco 2445, Men's 2460, Milwaukee 2527, Minnesota 2530, Mohegan 2546, Morley 2572, Mortgage 2578, Myers 2609, National 2634, National 2636, Nationwide 2639, New 2679, New Orleans 2678, New York 2684, Newburyport 2693, Newmont 2698, NorthWestern 2748, NV 2765, Omaha 2805, P.E.L. 2849, Palace 2866, PDB 2906, Peabody 2907, Pearson 2911, Pentair 2926, People's 2928, Phillips 2966, PMI 2995, PricewaterhouseCoopers 3042, Primary 3043, Provident 3069, Provident 3070, Prudential 3072, Publix 3079, R & B 3113, Rackspace 3117, RECO 3148, Recreational 3150, Reebok 3159, Reynolds 3199, San Francisco 3324, Sony 3504, Specialty 3537, Square 3560, Staples 3581, Swinerton 3668, Terex 3719, Texas 3729, Thomaston 3736, Thomson 3742, Toyota 3784, Travelers 3802, U.M. 3834, Union 3854, United 3868, United 3876, Viejas 3951, Warburg 3985, Washington 4000, Washington 4001, WaterStone 4005, Western 4043, Windway 4086, Wisconsin 4094, Yum! 4150

Zoos/zoological societies

Acme 29, Albrecht 80, Altec 118, American 169, AMPCO 186, Berry 435, Blue 489, Bristol 577, Caterpillar 722, CME 853, Consumers 921, Contran 928, DS 1182, Emerson 1257, Ensign 1276, First 1395, Garff 1538, Giant 1571, Graybar 1640, Hasbro 1747, Heidtman 1770, Holder 1829, Hubbard 1877, International 1958, Jones 2055, Journal 2068, Kellogg 2120, Midcontinent 2505, Pan-American 2868, Piedmont 2971, PPG 3025, Providence 3068, sanofi-aventis 3329, Spang 3530, Specialty 3537, Union 3857, Valero 3915, Western 4043

TYPES OF BUSINESS INDEX

This index is an alphabetical listing of the products and services provided or the types of businesses conducted by the corporations in this edition of the *Directory*. Corporations are identified by abbreviated versions of their names and referenced by the sequence numbers assigned in the Descriptive Directory.

Abrasive, asbestos, and nonmetallic mineral products, 3M 3, American 159, Armstrong 246, Johns 2047, Martin 2391, Owens 2842, Transco 3797, USG 3905, Walter 3984

Accounting, auditing, and bookkeeping services, AgStar 59, Bennett 415, Cohn 866, Dean 1053, Deloitte 1070, Dixon 1133, Ellin 1251, Ernst 1293, Grant 1633, KPMG 2190, Moss 2581, Paychex 2904, Porter 3005, PricewaterhouseCoopers 3042, Rothstein 3271, RubinBrown 3280, Singerlewak 3463, Tofias 3768, Weaver 4014, Wipfli 4091, Wolf 4102

Administration/environmental quality program, Burns 620

Advertising, AMC 126, American 131, Berry 434, Burnett 619, Catalina 719, CBS 727, Clear 842, Hill 1803, Interpublic 1974, Landmark 2218, Lefton 2244, LivingSocial 2290, Midcontinent 2505, Monster 2560, Moody's 2563, Morris 2573, Ogilvy 2788, Omnicom 2808, Ruder 3282, Thompson 3739, Valassis 3914

Agricultural production crops, Chiquita 795, Pony 3002

Agricultural services—crop, Archer 233

Aircraft and parts, Allegheny 91, Ball 328, Barnes 362, Boeing 516, Boston 539, Brunswick 595, Exotic 1310, Gulfstream 1690, Honeywell 1852, Industrial 1935, Kaman 2088, Parker 2886, Raytheon 3135, Remmele 3183, Rockwell 3246, Sequa 3410, SIFCO 3452, Sikorsky 3454, Teleflex 3707, Textron 3731, United 3882, UTC 3908, Whirl 4055, Woodward 4112

Ammunition, ordinance, and accessories, Duchossois 1187, FMC 1449, Olin 2801

Amusement and recreation services/miscellaneous, American 148, Andretti 197, Anheuser 202, Artichoke 254, Bally 330, Baltimore 334, Boyd 546, Caesars 650, Capital 678, CBS 727, Colorado 879, Comcast 888, Coquille 939, Cow 957, Curves 1011, Disney 1127, Dollywood 1146, Empire 1261, Feld 1355, Four 1477, Grand 1629, GTECH 1677, Herschend 1790, IAC 1903, Jackson 2011, Jacksonville 2014, Ladies 2209, Life 2269, Magnolia 2340, Majestic 2344, Marlborough 2380, MGM 2489, Natural 2643, NBC 2649, NEBCO 2653, New 2669, New York 2684, New York 2685, New York 2687, Old 2799, Owner 2845, Penn 2923, PGA 2953, Pinnacle 2978, Presley 3038, Roberts 3231, Sacramento 3304, SeaWorld 3387, Shakopee 3419, Spirit 3544, Sports 3550, Station 3593, Town 3783, Tulalip 3820, Turf 3822, United 3879, Universal 3889, Universal 3893, Viejas 3951

Animal services, except veterinary, Charles 764, PetSmart 2948

Apparel and accessories/miscellaneous, Greenlight 1658

Apparel and accessory stores, Aeropostale 46, American 163, Andersson 196, Bean 392, Men's 2460

Apparel and accessory stores/miscellaneous, Gap 1533

Apparel and other finished products made from fabrics and similar materials, Atayne 275, Autonomie 293, Gymboree 1693, Jordache 2062, NIKE 2710, Patagonia 2892, Reebok 3159, SmartWool 3479, Timberland 3754

Apparel, piece goods, and notions—wholesale, adidas 35, Ann's 203, Brown 591, Business 625, Celebrity 731, Clarks 838, Cutie 1013, Dansko 1031, Deckers 1059, Dollar 1143, Fifth 1376, Fila 1379, Franshaw 1489, Genesco 1559, Heritage 1784, Jaclyn 2015, Jai 2017, Jim's 2043, Jockey 2045, Myers 2609, Oaklandish 2773, Parthenon 2889, PVH 3088, Queen 3102, Saucony 3340, SBH 3345, St. John 3564, Strauss 3624, Stride 3625, Ten 3712, Weyco 4051, Wolff 4105

Apparel—girls' and children's outerwear, A.J. 8, Candlesticks 670, Carter's 708, Kahn 2085, Mamiye 2352, Oxford 2847

Apparel—hats, caps, and millinery, New 2673

Apparel—men's and boys' coats and suits, Belleville 405, Genesco 1559

Apparel—men's and boys' outerwear, adidas 35, Bethel 445, Cintas 816, Guess 1685, Hilfiger 1801, Hudson 1882, Indiana 1930, Jockey 2045, Jones 2057, Kahn 2085, Klein 2166, New 2668, Oxford 2847, PVH 3088, Quiksilver 3108, Ralph 3123, Rennoc 3184, V.F. 3913, Warnaco 3988

Apparel—women's outerwear, Capezio 675, Fashion 1342, Fifth 1376, Fisher 1433, Genesco 1559, Guess 1685, Hilfiger 1801, Jones 2057, Kahn 2085, Kellwood 2121, Klein 2166, Kors 2186, Oxford 2847, Tanner 3688, V.F. 3913, Warnaco 3988

Apparel—women's, girls', and children's undergarments, Candlesticks 670, Guess 1685, Hanesbrands 1720, Jockey 2045, Natori 2640, Warnaco 3988

Appliance stores/household, Abt 20, Best 442, Conn 908, Lowe's 2312, Richard 3205

Appliances/household, Allegheny 91, Bemis 408, Bosch 529, Dollar 1143, Electrolux 1241, Eliason 1248, Fetzer 1367, National 2636, Philips 2963, Sub-Zero 3630, Tomkins 3771, Whirlpool 4056

Asphalt and roofing materials, Ashland 258, Callanan 659, Ergon 1289, Firestone 1386, Harsco 1741, Johns 2047, Koch 2180, Monarch 2553

Audio and video equipment/household, BOSE 530, EMI 1258, Koss 2188, Millennia 2516, Philips 2963, Reader's 3141, Righteous 3214, Sharp 3422, Sony 3502, Sony 3503, Time 3757, Warner 3990

Auto and home supplies—retail, Advance 39, AutoZone 294, Bridgestone 560, Dollar 1143, Fairmount 1328, Jeg's 2031, MFA 2487, Servco 3412

Automotive dealers and gasoline service stations, Lithia 2287, Pantry 2875

Bakeries, Bird 468, Publix 3079

Bakery products, Byrd 631, Clif 848, Frito 1506, Kellogg 2120, McKee 2432, Rich 3204, Snyder's-Lance 3492, Tasty 3693, Upper 3900, World 4119

Bands, orchestras, and entertainers, Creative 975, Endeavor 1267, Latham 2229, Madison 2336, United 3881, World 4121

Banks/commercial, 1st 2, AbbyBank 15, Amboy 124, American 166, Apple 218, Associated 261, Atlantic 283, Audubon 286, BancorpSouth 336, BancTrust 337, Bangor 338, Bank 340, Bank 342, Bank 343, Bank 344, Bank 345, Bank 346, Bank 347, Bank 348, Bank 349, BankSouth 350, Barclays 357, BB&T 385, BBCN 386, Beneficial 411, Berkshire 428, Brown 589, California 653, Cape 674, Capital 676, Capital 679, Cathay 723, Central 742, Central 745, Charter 767, Chemical 774, Citigroup 821, Citizens 824, Citizens 825, Citizens 826, Citizens 827, Citizens 828, City 830, Colorado 880, Colt 881, Columbia 882, Comerica 889, Commerce 890, Commercial 891, Commonwealth 894, Community 897, Community 898, Compass 901, Cornerstone 942, Cornerstone 943, County 952, Edgar 1225, Exchange 1307, F.N.B. 1318, Fairfax 1325, Fairfield 1326, Farmers 1336, Fifth 1377, First 1388, First 1391, First 1393, First 1394, First 1395, First 1396, First 1397, First 1398, First 1402, First 1405, First 1406, First 1409, First 1410, First 1411, First 1412, First 1413, First 1414, First 1415, First 1416, First 1417, First 1418, First 1423, Firstmerit 1425, Framingham 1481, Fremont 1496, Frost 1512, Fulton 1518, Great 1644, Guaranty 1679, Hampden 1712, Harris 1739, Hawaii 1753, Heritage 1785, Hills 1808, Home 1846, HomeStar 1848, Hopkins 1859, HSBC 1876, Huntington 1894, Independence 1925, Independent 1927, Integrity 1948, INTRUST 1981, Iowa 1986, Iowa 1987, Isabella 1993, JPMorgan 2072, JPMorgan Chase 2071, KeyBank 2136, Longview 2300, M&T 2323, Madison 2335, Maquoketa 2361, MarkleBank 2379, Mascoma 2394, Mason 2396, MB 2415, Mechanics 2446, Midwestone 2508, Milford 2513, Milford 2514, Mutual 2606, National 2635, Nextier 2706, North 2731, Northern 2740, Northrim 2743, NorthSide 2745, Old 2798, Park 2879, Park 2881, Peapack-Gladstone 2909, Penn 2924, Peoples 2929, Peoples 2930, Pioneer 2982, PNC 2996,

Angeles 2307, Los Angeles 2308, Macfarlane-Chang 2331, Madison 2336, Major 2345, Major 2346, Major 2347, Miami 2491, Milwaukee 2527, Milwaukee 2528, Minnesota 2530, Minnesota 2531, Mohegan 2546, Nashville 2620, National 2621, National 2623, National 2624, National 2626, National 2627, National 2631, NEBCO 2653, New 2679, New England 2672, New Jersey 2676, New Orleans 2678, New York 2686, New York 2687, New York 2691, Oakland 2772, Orlando 2824, Pacers 2852, Palace 2866, Pawtucket 2903, PDB 2906, PGA 2953, PGA 2954, Philadelphia 2957, Philadelphia 2958, Philadelphia 2959, Phillies 2964, Phoenix 2968, Pittsburgh 2985, Pittsburgh 2986, Portland 3011, Pro 3052, Pro 3054, Richardson 3209, Rocket 3240, Sacramento 3303, San Antonio 3321, San Diego 3322, San Diego 3323, San Francisco 3324, San Francisco 3326, San Jose 3327, Sporting 3546, Sports 3549, Spurs 3557, St. Louis 3567, St. Louis 3568, St. Louis 3569, Sterling 3601, Tampa 3686, Tennessee 3716, Texas 3729, Trail 3793, Turf 3822, Turner 3823, Twins 3827, United 3879, Washington 3998, Washington 4000

Communications, Energy 1273, Hargray 1730

Communications equipment, Alcatel 81, Ameritec 179, ANZA 208, Avnet 304, Canon 672, Corning 945, Danaher 1027, Emerson 1257, ESCO 1296, General 1557, Harris 1736, Intermec 1955, Motorola 2585, Motorola 2586, NEC 2654, Philips 2963, Preformed 3032, Pro 3051, QUALCOMM 3095, Rockwell 3246, Rockwell 3247, Sony 3502, Syniverse 3672, Tellabs 3709

Communications services/miscellaneous, American 167, Cox 958, craigslist 968, Working 4116, Zeta 4155

Computer and office equipment, Apple 217, Cadence 646, Canon 672, Cisco 818, Contran 928, Dell 1068, Diebold 1112, EMC 1253, Epson 1286, Fellowes 1357, Gateway 1541, Gould 1618, Hewlett 1794, Hitachi 1816, International 1960, Juniper 2075, Kingston 2161, Lexmark 2258, Matthews 2406, Mercury 2469, NCR 2650, NEC 2654, Nordic 2722, Olivetti 2802, Philips 2963, Pitney 2984, Reell 3164, Remmele 3183, Reynolds 3199, Sakar 3313, Seagate 3377, Sharp 3422, Sony 3502, Systel 3678, Texas 3728, ViewSonic 3952, Western 4042, Xerox 4136

Computer services, Abba 11, Abt 20, Activision 30, Acumen 33, Adobe 38, Advent 41, Akamai 68, Alcatel 81, Allyis 109, American 140, AOL 209, Apex 213, Arbitron 227, Autodesk 289, Automatic 291, Barnes 360, Bean 392, Belo 406, Best 442, Bloomberg 486, BMC 508, Bromelkamp 582, CA 638, Cadence 646, Cardinal 685, Cerner 754, Cianbro 808, Compuware 902, Control 930, Convergys 933, Cyan 1015, Dealer 1052, Diebold 1112, Disney 1127, Drop 1178, drugstore.com 1180, eBay 1217, EI 1237, Electronic 1242, Elevation 1245, Ellucian 1252, Equifax 1288, Fidelity 1371, FileMaker 1380, First 1400, Fiserv 1427, Focus 1451, Follett 1455, Gaiam 1527, GameStop 1530, Gannett 1532, GenRad 1564, Give 1583, Go 1595, Google 1613, GTECH 1677, H & R 1695, Heller 1773, Houghton 1869, IAC 1903, Idealist 1909, Imation 1919, Impact 1921, IMS 1924, InfoSource 1936, Intel 1950, International 1965, Intuit 1982, ISGN 1995, iVillage 2002, Jenzabar 2037, Jeppesen 2038, Landmark 2218, Laureate 2231, Lee 2241, Levi 2254, Lucasfilm 2316, McAfee 2417, McGraw 2429, McNally 2437, Mentor 2462, Meredith 2471, Microsoft 2501, Midcontinent 2505, Monster 2560, Moody's 2563, Motley 2582, MTV 2596, National 2632, NAVTEQ 2648, NBC 2649, New York 2690, North 2733, Novell 2754, Novetta 2755, Objectwin 2778, Oracle 2821, Our 2838, Parametric 2878, Penney 2925, Perforce 2937, PETCO 2945, PetSmart 2948, Playboy 2990, Post 3016, Presley 3038, ProtechSoft 3065, Rackspace 3117, RealNetworks 3144, Recreational 3150, Reed 3161, Reynolds 3199, Safeguard 3307, SAIC 3311, salesforce.com 3318, SAP 3334, SAS 3336, ScanSource 3347, Schein 3348, SCIenergy 3366, Singlebrook 3464, Smith 3485, SocketLabs 3495, Sony 3502, South Bend 3507, SRA 3562, Star 3582, Symantec 3669, Synopsys 3673, Talbots 3682, TALX 3683, TeamQuest 3698, Telligen 3710, Teradyne 3718, Thomson 3741, Thomson 3742, Time 3757, Tribune 3806, Trident 3808, Truefit 3816, Tyler 3831, Unisys 3859, United 3863, Veridyne 3935, Vernier 3941, Viacom 3945, West 4037, Yahoo! 4140

Concrete, gypsum, and plaster products, Ash 256, Ashland 258, Callanan 659, CEMEX 734, Delta 1082, Lafarge 2210, NEBCO 2653, Simpson 3461, Teichert 3704, Texas 3727, Tindall 3761, Transit 3798, USG 3905, Vulcan 3972

Construction/highway and street (except elevated), Ashland 258, Boh 517, Cummins 1005, D'Annunzio 1017, Fort 1471, Ghilotti 1570, Groves 1673, Jorgensen 2065, KBR 2106, McCarthy 2421, Murphy 2599, NEBCO 2653, Pendleton 2921, Posillico 3014, Rasmussen 3128, Sjostrom 3469, Transit 3798, Velting 3928, Wadsworth 3974, Ward 3986

Construction/miscellaneous heavy, American 139, Boh 517, Bubalo 598, Cajun 652, Dondlinger 1154, Fort 1471, Groves 1673, Hawkins 1757, Irby 1990, KBR 2106, Rasmussen 3128, Scott 3369, Shea 3428, Sundt 3648, Thermo 3733, Tutor 3826, University 3896, Velting 3928, Ward 3986, White 4060

Consumer electronics and music stores, Abt 20, Activision 30, Adir 36, Barnes 360, Best 442, CDW 729, GameStop 1530, Jordan 2064, Lowe's 2312, Pacific 2856, Richard 3205

Contractors/concrete work, Berkel 424, Gelco 1546, Morley 2572, Stewart 3605

Contractors/electrical work, Ahern 60, Block 482, Buist 611, Calvi 664, Coghlin 865, Continental 924, Cupertino 1009, Electric 1240, EMCOR 1255, Ferguson 1363, Guarantee 1678, Leet 2243, Pieper 2972, Reilly 3175, Sullivan 3635, Truland 3817

Contractors/general nonresidential building, ACI 27, Austin 288, Barton 366, Bechtel 395, Beck 396, Berghammer 418, Blair 479, Bufftree 607, Century 749, Cianbro 808, Cullen 1000, Danis 1029, Deacon 1050, Dondlinger 1154, Dunn 1192, Eagle 1203, Erickson 1290, Fishel 1429, Gilbane 1581, Gootee 1614, Graycor 1641, Harvey 1746, Heyrman 1796, Holder 1829, Jackson-Shaw 2013, Jordan 2063, Kahn 2084, Kajima 2087, KBR 2106, Lauth 2232, Law 2233, McBride 2418, McShane 2439, Morley 2572, Mortenson 2577, Opus 2820, Quandel 3099, Questar 3105, Rewold 3196, Ross 3266, Schmeling 3353, Sjostrom 3469, Swinerton 3668, Taiyo 3681, Turner 3824, Turner 3825, Waterford 4002, Winter 4090, Yates 4142

Contractors/general residential building, ACI 27, Benton 417, Berghammer 418, Brady 553, Devereaux 1100, Dominion 1149, Fisher 1432, Grubb 1675, Hawkins 1757, Hensyn 1782, Homewood 1849, KB 2105, Law 2233, M.D.C. 2324, McBride 2418, Mccar 2419, Mccar 2420, Morley 2572, Questar 3105, S & H 3295, Tutor 3826, Vos 3969, Walter 3984, Washington 3997, Waterford 4002, West 4036, Willow 4082, Winter 4090, Young 4147

Contractors/miscellaneous special trade, American 139, Berkel 424, Bierlein 459, Creamer 974, Danforth 1028, Groves 1673, KBR 2106, RECO 3148, Renovated 3185, Shaughnessy 3425, Velting 3928

Contractors/plumbing, heating, and air-conditioning, Ahern 60, Air 64, Conditioned 906, Control 929, Danforth 1028, Gibson 1579, Kajima 2087, McKinstry 2435, Pieper 2972

Contractors/roofing, siding, and sheet metal work, CentiMark 740, Crown 989, Duro-Last 1196, GSM 1676, Kentuckiana 2130

Credit institutions/business, American 143, BayView 384, CarMax 694, CIT 819, Deere 1061, General 1555, Meecorp 2454, New York 2681, Springleaf 3554

Credit institutions/federal and federally-sponsored, Education 1232, Federal 1347, Federal 1349, Norwood 2751

Credit institutions/personal, American 143, American 147, Beneficial 411, Capital 679, CIT 819, Deere 1061, Discover 1125, Drive 1177, Education 1232, Ford 1464, General 1555, General 1556, JM 2044, Mitsubishi 2540, Morgan 2570, Nellie 2659, Nelnet 2660, Paper 2877, Republic 3188, Sears 3384, Security 3392, SLM 3478, United 3868

Credit reporting and collection agencies, Cic 811, Credit 977, Credit 978, Credit 979, Dun 1190, Equifax 1288, Great 1645, Moody's 2563, Moody's 2564, TransUnion 3799

Credit unions, Alliant 103, Bethpage 446, New 2671, Pawtucket 2902, Self 3400, Teachers 3697

Cutlery, hand and edge tools, and hardware, A & E 6, Contran 928, Cooper 935, Cutco 1012, Dexter 1103, Energizer 1271, Fetzer 1367, Handy 1718, Ideal 1908, Ingersoll 1939, Klein 2168, Lisle 2286, Newell 2694, PACE 2851, Red 3153, Stanley 3579, Stride 3626, Summit 3642, United 3862, Wagner 3976, Windway 4086

Dairy products, Alpenrose 111, Ben 409, Cacique 644, Dannon 1030, Dean 1054, Dreyer's 1174, Hood 1854, Hygeia 1901, Isaly's 1994, Sartori 3335, Schwan 3365, Shaklee 3418, Starbucks 3585, Stonyfield 3617, White 4062

Day care services/child, Bright 566, Knowledge 2177, National 2637

Department stores, Beall's 389, Belk 403, Belk 404, Bloomingdale's 488, Bon 521, Century 748, Kohl's 2181, Lord 2302, Macy's 2333, Meijer 2456, Neiman 2657, Odyssey 2784, Penney 2925, Saks 3315, Sears 3384, ShopKo 3440, Stage 3572, Toys 3790

Depository banking/functions related to, First 1400, Inspire 1945, Merchants 2465, U.S. 3837, Viad 3946, Western 4045

Drug stores and proprietary stores, Albertsons 79, Albrecht 80, Corvallis 947, CVS 1014, drugstore.com 1180, Duane 1186, Hannaford 1723, Hy-Vee 1900, Kinney 2162, Limited 2277, Omnicare 2807, Raley's 3122, Rite 3220, ShopKo 3440, SQA 3559, Walgreen 3981

Drugs, Abbott 13, Accupac 23, Alcon 83, Alexion 86, Allergan 99, Amgen 182, Amway 189, AstraZeneca 272, BASF 368, Bayer 381, Bayer 382, Becton 398, Biogen 465, Boehringer 515, Boiron 519, Bristol 578, Celgene 732, Cephalon 752, CIBA 810, Covidien 956, CSL 993, Cubist 999, du Pont 1184, EMD 1256, Endo 1268, Excellium 1305, Forest 1468, Genentech 1549, Genzyme 1566, Gilead 1582, GlaxoSmithKline 1588, Griffith 1667, Hoffmann 1823, Hospira 1867, Janssen 2023, Justacip 2078, Life 2268, LifeScan 2271, Lilly

2274, Mead 2443, MedImmune 2450, Merck 2466, Mylan 2610, Nektar 2658, New England 2670, Novartis 2752, Novartis 2753, Obagi 2776, Perrigo 2943, Pfizer 2950, Pioneer 2980, Quidel 3107, sanofi-aventis 3329, Sensient 3408, Shaklee 3418, Spear 3536, Warren 3992

Drugs, proprietaries, and sundries—wholesale, Albrecht 80, Alima 90, Almar 110, AmerisourceBergen 175, Avon 305, Cardinal 685, Hy-Vee 1900, McKesson 2434, Phoenix 2967, Reckitt 3147, Smith 3485, Tripifoods 3811

Durable goods—wholesale, Almar 110, Callaway 660, Central 743, City 829, Do 1136, Faber 1319, General 1553, International 1964, Jackson 2008, Kaman 2088, Klein 2167, Lieberman 2266, Nintendo 2712, Polaris 2999, Prophet 3063, Reed 3160, Shalam 3420, Victorinox 3950, Virginia 3959, Yamaha 4141

Education services, International 1965, Landmark 2218, Laureate 2231

Educational services/miscellaneous, Altair 117, Andretti 197, Reynolds 3199, Sonlight 3499

Electric services, AES 47, Alabama 71, Alexander 85, American 141, Arizona 239, Astoria 270, Black 474, Burke 615, Calpine 661, Carson 705, CenterPoint 738, Central 741, Central 744, Central 747, Clark 835, Coastal 859, Columbus 885, Commonwealth 895, Connecticut 911, Continental 923, Cow 957, Dominion 1150, DTE 1183, Duke 1189, Duquesne 1194, Edison 1228, El Paso 1239, Energy 1273, Entergy 1278, Entergy 1279, Entergy 1280, Exxon 1315, Farmers' 1337, FirstEnergy 1424, Florida 1443, GenOn 1563, Georgia 1567, Glades 1587, Gulf 1689, Hawaiian 1755, IDACORP 1907, Jemez 2034, Kansas 2092, Kinder 2153, Lake 2213, Lea 2235, MidAmerican 2504, Mississippi 2536, Mount 2588, National 2630, Nishnabotna 2714, North 2729, Northeast 2737, NRG 2756, Oklahoma 2794, ONEOK 2815, Otter 2836, Pacific 2853, PacifiCorp 2860, Pedernales 2914, Portland 3010, Potomac 3018, PPL 3026, PPL 3027, Public 3075, Puget 3081, Rochester 3237, Roosevelt 3258, Salt 3319, SCANA 3346, Seminole 3404, Sierra 3450, Socorro 3496, Southern 3516, Southwestern 3525, Spark 3533, Springer 3553, Sulphur 3637, Sun 3644, TECO 3701, Thermo 3733, Tri 3805, Trico 3807, Tucson 3819, Union 3856, United 3870, Wake 3978, Westar 4039, Wisconsin 4093, Wisconsin 4096

Electric transmission and distribution equipment, Hitachi 1816, Hubbell 1879, Kepco 2132, Leviton 2255, Schott 3360, Spang 3530, Square 3560

Electrical equipment and supplies, Energizer 1271, Fema 1358, Hubbell 1879, Imation 1919, International 1964, Motorola 2586, Nestle 2662, Railway 3119, Standard 3575, Textron 3731

Electrical goods—wholesale, Allison-Erwin 106, Arrow 249, Arthur's 253, Avnet 304, Brightpoint 567, Consolidated 917, Crescent 981, Do 1136, Fuji 1514, Grainger 1626, Graybar 1640, Lighting 2273, Mayer 2412, Microsoft 2501, Nintendo 2712, Priceless 3041, Servco 3412, Summit 3641, World 4120

Electrical industrial apparatus, American 161, AMETEK 181, Danaher 1027, Electric 1240, Emerson 1257, Franklin 1484, Hitachi 1816, Honeywell 1852, Kennametal 2125, Lincoln 2279, Railway 3119, Regal 3167, S.J. 3299, Smith 3484, Square 3560

Electronic and other electrical equipment and components, AMETEK 181, Bergquist 420, Bourns 542, Coghlin 864, Delphi 1071, Eaton 1216, Flextronics 1437, General 1552, Mitsubishi 2538, Panasonic 2869, Siemens 3448, SPX 3558, Toshiba 3776, Tyco 3829

Electronic components and accessories, Advanced 40, Agilent 56, Allegheny 91, Applied 220, Avnet 304, AVX 306, Bergquist 420, Broadcom 579, Chief 793, Douglas 1159, Ergon 1289, Flextronics 1437, Freescale 1495, Gould 1618, Handy 1718, Harris 1736, Hitachi 1816, Hubbell 1879, Intel 1950, ITT 1999, Jabil 2006, Kimball 2149, KOA 2178, Koss 2188, Leviton 2255, LSI 2314, MAGE 2338, Matthews 2406, MEMC 2459, Mercury 2469, Micro 2498, Microchip 2499, Micron 2500, Motorola 2586, NEC 2654, NVIDIA 2767, Panasonic 2870, Panduit 2872, Photronics 2969, Rexnord 3198, Samsung 3320, Schott 3360, Scientific 3367, SEAKR 3379, Spang 3530, Spansion 3532, SUMCO 3638, Texas 3728, Xilinx 4137, XTEK 4138

Engineering, accounting, research, management, and related services, Paychex 2904

Engineering, architectural, and surveying services, AECOM 42, Allen 96, Apex 213, Baker 323, Barton 366, Bechtel 395, BSA 597, Burns 620, CH2M 758, Eppstein 1285, ERM 1292, Factory 1323, Fluor 1448, Foreman 1465, Gardner 1536, Hartford 1743, Henkels 1779, Jacobs 2016, Kajima 2087, KBR 2106, McShane 2439, MWH 2608, Opus 2820, Parsons 2887, Ratio 3129, Reed 3162, RJN 3228, SAIC 3311, Sasaki 3337, Skidmore 3474, South 3510, Stanley 3580, Towill 3782, Washington 3995, Willdan 4075, Woodard 4109

Engines and turbines, Amsted 188, Briggs 565, Brunswick 595, Cameron 667, Caterpillar 722, Cummins 1007, Detroit 1093, Hilliard 1805, Honda 1851, Kohler 2182, McDermott 2424, Navistar 2647, Oilgear 2793, Otter 2836, Pratt 3028, Rolls 3254, Textron 3731, Woodward 4112

Equipment rental and leasing/miscellaneous, AgStar 59, Atlantic 282, Bestway 444, Calumet 662, CORT 946, DVK 1198, Empire 1262, GATX 1542, Halton 1709, Hertz 1792, International 1958, Kelly 2122, Marr 2382, Nordic 2722, North 2728, Turner 3825, Ward 3986

Executive and legislative offices combined, Poarch 2998

Extraction/natural gas liquids, BP 547, ConocoPhillips 913, Koch 2180, Occidental 2780, ONEOK 2815, Phillips 2965, Quicksilver 3106

Extraction/oil and gas, ABARTA 10, Anadarko 190, Apache 211, Aramco 224, Berry 437, BHP 455, BP 547, Calpine 661, Chesapeake 777, Chevron 780, ConocoPhillips 913, Dart 1034, Devon 1102, El Paso 1239, Encana 1266, Energy 1272, EOG 1282, Ergon 1289, Exxon 1315, Hess 1793, Hunt 1889, Intermountain 1957, Loews 2296, Manti 2359, Marathon 2363, Marathon 2364, Me-Tex 2442, Murphy 2600, Nalco 2613, National 2628, Newfield 2695, Nortex 2727, Occidental 2780, ONEOK 2815, Phillips 2965, Pioneer 2981, Questar 3104, Quicksilver 3106, Shell 3430, Stone 3614, Swift 3667, True 3814, Union 3856, Walter 3984, Williams 4077

Fabric finishing, Cone 907, Cranston 972, Hanes 1719, Springs 3555

Fabricated metal products (except machinery and transportation equipment), Anchor 192, Boneal 523, Consolidated 918, Handy 1718, Herrick 1788, Johnson 2052, Superior 3658

Fabricated textile products/miscellaneous, Autoliv 290, Blackinton 476, Klein 2168, Longaberger 2299, Springs 3555, Trim 3810, Windway 4086

Fabrics/broadwoven natural cotton, Alice 89, Cone 907, Hamrick 1715, Inman 1943, Milliken 2525, Springs 3555, United 3871

Fabrics/broadwoven natural wool, Odyssey 2784

Fabrics/broadwoven synthetic and silk, Inman 1943, Johnston 2054, Milliken 2525, Schneider 3354, Springs 3555, United 3871, Wimpfheimer 4085

Family apparel and accessory stores, Abercrombie 17, American 140, Burlington 617, Daffy's 1019, Fast 1343, Gap 1533, Hilo 1811, Nordstrom 2724, Ross 3267

Farm-product raw materials—wholesale, Ag 55, Archer 233, Bartlett 365, Birdsong 470, Birmingham 471, Blue 506, Bunge 612, CHS 802, Coats 860, DeBruce 1057, GROWMARK 1674, International 1963, Mariani 2374, Ray 3132, Riceland 3203, Ritzville 3222, Scoular 3373, Universal 3891, Wilbur 4070

Farms, except cash grains/field crop, Alexander 85, Duda 1188, NEBCO 2653, Pioneer 2980, Scotts 3372, United 3878

Farms/animal and livestock specialty, Charles 764

Farms/fruit and nut, A.D. 7, Alexander 85, Baker 322, Brocchini 580, Chiquita 795, Coquille 939, Dole 1141, Duda 1188, Fowler 1478, Gallo 1529, Haines 1701, Mariani 2374, Rivermaid 3225

Farms/general crop, K-B 2081

Farms/livestock, Bartlett 365, Continental 926, Duda 1188, Koch 2180, Simplot 3459, Smithfield 3487

Farms/miscellaneous cash grain, NEBCO 2653, Pioneer 2980

Farms/poultry and egg, Continental 926, Fieldale 1373, Hubbard 1878, Mountaire 2590, Perdue 2936

Farms/vegetable and melon, Baker 322, Chiquita 795, Dole 1141, Duda 1188

Fats and oils, Archer 233, Bragg 554, Bunge 612, Farmers 1339, International 1963, Reily 3177, Todd 3766, Unilever 3853

Fertilizers and agricultural chemicals, Atlantic 282, BASF 368, Bayer 381, Cargill 691, CF 755, Dow 1160, Dow 1161, Ecolab 1220, FMC 1449, GROWMARK 1674, Johnson 2049, Koch 2180, Monsanto 2559, Mosaic 2580, Occidental 2780, Pioneer 2980, Scotts 3372, Simplot 3459, Teck 3700, Transammonia 3796

Fish hatcheries and preserves, Continental 926

Fishing/commercial, Glacier 1586, Ipswich 1989, Pacific 2854, Rondys 3256

Fixtures/office and store, Fidelity 1372, Foldcraft 1452, Hooker 1855, Hufcor 1883, Industrial 1935, Jones 2060, Leggett 2246, Midmark 2507, Rusco 3288, Shure 3443

Food and kindred products, Altria 120, Campbell 669, Cargill 691, ConAgra 904, Evans 1300, Faribault 1332, Flowers 1446, Hallelujah 1705, Hillshire 1809, Hormel 1866, Isaly's 1994, Kroger 2195, Longaberger 2299, Mars 2384, Michael 2493, Mondelez 2556, Nestle 2663, PepsiCo 2935, Riviana 3227, Todd 3766, Tyson 3832, Unaka 3848

Footwear/rubber and plastic, Belleville 405, Crocs 984, NIKE 2710, Reebok 3159

Forest products, Louisiana 2310

Forestry—timber tracts, National 2628, Pactiv 2863, Plum 2991, Potlatch 3017, Rayonier 3134, St. Joe 3563, Sun 3645, Temple 3711

Fuel dealers—retail, Andretti 197, Ferrellgas 1365, Seaboard 3375, Vesco 3942

Funeral services, Service 3413

Furniture and fixtures, Cox 962, Kohler 2182

Furniture and fixtures/miscellaneous, Fidelity 1372, Hill 1804, Homecrest 1847, Knoll 2176, Miller 2517, Newell 2694, Shure 3443

Furniture and home furnishing stores, ABC 16, Bob's 511, Dollar 1143, Mattress 2407, QVC 3112, Rug 3286, Saks 3315, Smulekoff 3489, Star 3584, Villency 3955, Williamsburg 4080

Furniture and home furnishings—wholesale, Allen 96, Allison-Erwin 106, Ann's 203, Armstrong 246, Bed 399, Fidelity 1372, Mautz 2408, Ohio 2792, Ramallah 3124

Furniture/household, Armstrong 246, Ashley 259, Bassett 372, Bernhardt 432, Best 443, Carris 702, Classic 840, Furniture 1519, Homecrest 1847, Hooker 1855, Inwood 1985, Kimball 2149, Kohler 2182, La-Z-Boy 2205, Lamont 2215, Lee 2242, Leggett 2246, Lexington 2257, Longaberger 2299, Park 2882, Sealy 3382, Southern 3517, Thomasville 3737, Vaughan 3924

Furniture/office, Brochsteins 581, Classic 840, Fidelity 1372, Haworth 1758, HNI 1817, Hooker 1855, Jasper 2025, Jasper 2026, JOFCO 2046, JSJ 2073, Kimball 2149, Krueger 2196, Miller 2517, Shure 3443, Steelcase 3597

Furniture/public building, Jasper 2026, Johnson 2050, Krueger 2196, Lear 2237

Games, toys, and sporting and athletic goods, Brunswick 595, Burton 624, Callaway 660, Digi 1115, Easton 1215, Hasbro 1747, ICON 1906, Kids 2141, Lateral 2227, Lego 2247, Mac 2328, Mattel 2405, Mike's 2509, NIKE 2710, Nintendo 2712, Orvis 2830, Reagent 3143, Reebok 3159, S & S 3296, Sakar 3313, Spang 3530, Totsy 3780, Ty 3828

Garden supplies—retail, Esbenshade's 1295, Nursery 2762, Saker 3314

Gas production and distribution, AGL 57, Atmos 285, BP 547, Cascade 713, CenterPoint 739, Chevron 780, Columbia 883, Columbia 884, Connecticut 912, DeBlois 1056, DTE 1183, El Paso 1239, Energen 1270, Energy 1273, EQT 1287, Exxon 1315, Global 1593, IDACORP 1907, Intermountain 1956, Intermountain 1957, Kinder 2153, Laclede 2207, Laclede 2208, Marathon 2363, MFA 2487, National 2628, North 2735, Northern 2739, Northwest 2747, ONEOK 2815, Pacific 2853, Peoples 2931, Piedmont 2971, Questar 3104, Quicksilver 3106, Rochester 3237, Rocky 3249, SCANA 3346, Shell 3430, Southern 3520, Southwest 3524, Spectra 3540, Terre 3722, Union 3856, Washington 3997, Williams 4077, Wisconsin 4093, Wisconsin 4096

Gaskets, packing and sealing devices, and rubber hose and belting, Bentley 416, Cooper 936, Dana 1026, Gates 1540, Green 1657, Rieke 3212, SKF 3473, Zatkoff 4154

Gasoline service stations, Cary 712, Cow 957, Cumberland 1003, Golub 1607, Kelley 2119, Lassus 2226, Love's 2311, Marathon 2364, MFA 2487, QuikTrip 3109, Shell 3430, Stram 3622, Tesoro 3723, Thorntons 3743, USA 3903, Wurster 4128

General merchandise stores, Albertsons 79, Delaware 1066, Family 1330, Target 3691

Glass products/miscellaneous, ACI 27, Apogee 215, Byers 630, Guardian 1682, Pella 2917

Glass/flat, ACI 27, Berkowitz 427, Fenton 1361, Guardian 1682, PPG 3025

Glass/pressed or blown, ACI 27, Aladdin 73, Corning 945, Guardian 1682, Lancaster 2216, Newell 2694, Owens 2844, PPG 3025, TOSOH 3777

Government establishments/miscellaneous, Seldovia 3397

Grain mill products, including pet food, Archer 233, Bartlett 365, General 1554, GROWMARK 1674, Hartz 1744, Ilitch 1915, Ingredion 1942, Kaytee 2104, Kellogg 2120, Kent 2129, King 2158, Malt 2351, Mars 2384, Nestle 2662, Quaker 3094, Riviana 3227, Simplot 3459

Greeting cards, American 149, CSS 996, Hallmark 1707, Kimball 2148

Groceries—retail, 7-Eleven 5, Albertsons 79, Albrecht 80, Bashas' 369, BI-LO 456, Big 461, Butt 628, Circle 817, Clemens 844, Cumberland 1003, Dan's 1025, Demoulas 1085, Fiesta 1375, Food 1457, Food 1458, G & R 1523, Giant 1571, Giant 1572, Giant 1573, Golub 1607, Gon 1608, Great 1642, H & K 1694, Haggen 1699, Hannaford 1723, Harris 1738, Heinens 1771, Holiday 1832, Hy-Vee 1900, Ingles 1940, Kelley 2119, Key 2135, King 2159, Klein's 2169, Kroger 2195, Lassus 2226, Marsh 2387, MFA 2487, Nash 2619, Niemann 2708, Odyssey 2784, Pantry 2875, Pathmark 2894, Price 3039, Publix 3079, QuikTrip 3109, Raley's 3122, Redner's 3157, Safeway 3310, Saker 3314, Save 3342, Schnuck 3356, Shaw's 3427, Spartan 3535, Stop 3618, Super 3656, SUPERVALU 3659, Sweetbay 3665, Tesoro 3723, Thorntons 3743, Tops 3774, United 3880, Wawa 4009, Webster's 4019, Wegmans 4021, Weis 4024, Whole 4066, Winn 4087, Zallie 4152

Groceries—wholesale, Albrecht 80, Associated 262, Beaver 394, Boyd 545, C & S 634, Dole 1141, Dot 1158, Dreyer's 1174, FDI 1346, Foremost 1466, Giant 1571, Golden 1601, Golden 1602, Gordon 1615, Goya 1622, Hannaford 1723, Hartz 1744, Hautly 1750, Hy-Vee 1900, Ilitch 1915, Kehe 2114, Keystone 2137, Kowalski 2189, Krasdale 2192, Land 2217, Lifeway 2272, Lime 2276, Marsh 2387, Nash 2619, Omaha 2805, Performance 2938, PRO*ACT 3053, Reily 3177, Roma 3255, Roundy's 3272, Scoular 3373, Seafood 3376, Serengeti 3411, Southern 3521, Sunkist 3649, SUPERVALU 3659, Sysco 3677, Treasure 3803, Tripifoods 3811, U.S. 3838, Waffle 3975, Wakefern 3979, Winn 4087

Guided missiles and space vehicles, Boeing 516, Brunswick 595, GenCorp 1548, Lockheed 2292, Raytheon 3135, Sequa 3410, Textron 3731, UTC 3908

Hardware stores, Power 3023, Rockler 3243

Hardware, plumbing, and heating equipment—wholesale, Buckley 602, Do 1136, Elias 1247, Golub 1607, Grainger 1626, Groeniger 1670, Hagerty 1698, Indiana 1931, Lowe's 2312, Merfish 2472, Noland 2719, Noritz 2726, O'Connor 2770, Sidener 3445, True 3815, Victorinox 3950

Health services, Caremore 689

Heavy construction other than building construction contractors, Fluor 1448, Granite 1632, Halliburton 1706, Jacobs 2016, Kiewit 2142, MAC 2327, Parsons 2887, SanTrust 3332, Teichert 3704, Washington 3995

Holding company, ABARTA 10, Acuity 31, AGL 57, Ameren 128, American 141, American 144, American 155, American 156, Anheuser 202, Aon 210, Arbeit 225, Arrowpoint 251, Associated 261, Assurant 268, AT&T 273, Audubon 286, Aviva 302, AXA 307, Bank 340, Bank 344, Bardes 359, Batts 374, Beneficial 411, Berkley 426, Berkshire 429, BMW 509, Boston 534, Bristol 576, Brookline 583, Brown 592, Burger 613, Burlington 618, C.M. 637, Cablevision 641, Capital 679, Capitol 680, CenterPoint 738, Central 742, CFS 756, CH 757, Chemical 774, Chubb 804, Citigroup 821, Citizens 827, CMS 854, Columbia 882, Comerica 889, Commerce 890, Community 897, Contran 928, CUNA 1008, Deutsche 1099, DTE 1183, Edison 1228, Edwards 1235, Energy 1273, Entergy 1279, Exelon 1309, F.N.B. 1318, Ferrellgas 1365, First 1391, First 1393, First 1396, First 1402, First 1406, First 1411, First 1413, First 1414, First 1419, First 1420, FirstEnergy 1424, Fluor 1448, Fulton 1518, Furr 1520, General 1550, Goldman 1603, Goldman 1604, Granite 1632, H & R 1695, Harleysville 1733, Hartzell 1745, Hawaiian 1755, Heritage 1785, Hickory 1797, Hill 1804, Home 1843, Horizon 1865, Hunt 1888, Hunt 1892, Huntington 1894, IDACORP 1907, Intermountain 1957, InterTech 1977, Investors 1984, IPALCO 1988, James 2021, JPMorgan Chase 2071, Kann 2090, Kansas 2094, KB 2105, Lafarge 2210, Legg 2245, LG&E Energy 2260, Loews 2296, Longview 2300, McBride 2418, MGIC 2488, Mitsubishi 2539, Moody 2562, Moore 2567, Morgan 2570, National 2628, Naugatuck 2646, New 2682, NII 2709, Northfield 2741, Northwest 2746, OceanFirst 2782, Odyssey 2784, Old 2798, Omnicom 2808, Oneida 2814, Peoples 2931, PFS 2951, PNC 2997, Porter 3007, Prince 3046, Progressive 3057, Provident 3069, Putnam 3087, Regions 3171, Reinsurance 3179, Republic 3187, Republic 3188, Ripplewood 3219, Rockville 3245, S & T 3297, Safeguard 3307, Saint 3312, SCANA 3346, Schoonover 3359, Schwan 3365, Sempra 3405, Shenandoah 3434, SI 3444, Skinner 3475, SLM 3478, Southeastern 3513, Southern 3514, Sprint 3556, StanCorp 3574, Standard 3577, State 3592, Synovus 3674, TD 3696, TFS 3732, Travelers 3802, U.S. 3835, UMB 3846, Unitil 3885, Unum 3898, US 3902, USG 3905, Valley 3916, Vectren 3925, Vendome 3930, Vulcan 3970, Waters 4003, WB 4010, Wells 4028, Wendy's/Arby's 4030, Windway 4086, Wisconsin 4093, Woodforest 4110, World 4122, WSFS 4127, Zions 4158

Home furniture, furnishings, and equipment stores, Pier 2973, Williams-Sonoma 4079

Home healthcare services, American 151, American 152, Guided 1686, Health 1764, Quality 3097, South 3509, SpectraCare 3541, Three 3745

Horticultural specialties, Bernecker's 431, Duda 1188, Syngenta 3671

Hosiery and knitted fabrics, Acme 29, Bossong 532, Harriss 1740, Jockey 2045, Knitcraft 2174, Knitcraft 2175, V.F. 3913, Warnaco 3988, Wigwam 4069

Hospitals, Community 900, FHC 1368, HCA 1762, Health 1765, Kaiser 2086, Kindred 2154, LifePoint 2270, Main 2342, North 2736, Sutter 3664, Tenet 3713

Hotels and lodging places/membership organization, Wyndham 4132

Hotels and motels, American 152, Ameristar 176, Aspen 260, Bird 468, Blue 489, Caesars 650, Carlson 693, Casino 714, Castle 717, Choice 798, Coquille 939, Cow 957, CSX 997, Disney 1127, Disney 1128, Four 1476, Four 1477, Hilton 1812, Hotel 1868, Hubbard 1877, Jackson 2011, Kerzner 2133, Kohler 2182, Las Vegas 2225, Loews 2296, Marcus 2371, Marriott 2383, MGM 2489, Nestle 2662, New 2675, Nordic 2722, Pebble 2913, Presley 3038, Ryman 3294, Sodexho 3497, Starwood 3589, Station 3593, Vista 3963, Waterford 4002

Industrial and commercial machinery and computer equipment, Chemtura 775, Damar 1024, Mark 2377, Oakley 2774, Omron 2810, Otter 2836, SPX 3558, Teleflex 3707, Westinghouse 4049

Industrial machinery and equipment—wholesale, ACF 26, Air 62, American 164, Applied 219, Barnes 362, Berry 435, BMW 509, Boler 520, Bramco 555, Donovan 1156, Eberhard 1218, Fabick 1321, Fidelity 1372, Freedman 1493, Gibbs 1576, Gosiger 1617, Grainger 1626, Halton 1709, Harnish 1734, Jesco 2040, Kaman 2088, Kelly 2122, Lockwood 2293, Meadows 2444, MH 2490, MSC 2593, National 2636, Patton's 2899, Power 3020, RG 3201, Riggs 3213, Sidener 3445,

Stafast 3571, Tractor 3791, Valmont 3919, Vermeer 3938, West 4037, Yamaha 4141

Insurance agents, brokers, and services, AEGIS 44, Aon 210, Baltimore 332, Chapman 763, CIBA 809, Colt 881, Edina 1227, FIDELIO 1370, Government 1620, Greene 1656, Hall 1702, Hannaford 1723, Harden 1728, Hays 1761, Heffernan 1769, Hoffman 1822, IMA 1917, International 1966, LJA 2291, Marsh 2385, Millhiser-Smith 2524, Nansemond 2616, Neace 2651, Owens 2843, Protector 3067, Reliable 3182, Rockwood 3248, Rue 3285, Southwest 3523, Sports 3547, WellPoint 4027, X.L. 4134, Young 4146

Insurance carriers, Alfa 87, American 169, Amica 183, BB&T 385, Berkshire 429, Brinckerhoff 570, Caterpillar 722, Chandler 760, Employers 1263, Fireman's 1385, First 1408, First 1411, Grinnell 1668, GuideOne 1687, Hancock 1717, Johnson 2049, Mutual 2607, Nationwide 2639, Sears 3384, Servco 3412, StanCorp 3574, Temple 3711, Thrivent 3747

Insurance/accident and health, Acuity 32, AEGON 45, Aetna 48, Affinity 52, Aflac 54, AgStar 59, American 144, American 145, American 153, AMERIGROUP 171, AmeriPlan 172, Ameritas 178, Aon 210, Arkansas 240, Assurant 266, Assurant 267, Berkshire 430, Blue 490, Blue 491, Blue 492, Blue 493, Blue 494, Blue 495, Blue 496, Blue 497, Blue 498, Blue 499, Blue 500, Blue 501, Blue 502, Blue 503, Blue 504, Blue 505, BlueCross 507, California 655, Cambia 665, CareFirst 687, CareSource 690, Centene 735, Century 750, CIGNA 812, CNA 855, CNO 857, Colonial 874, Colorado 878, Country 951, Cow 957, CUNA 1008, Delta 1074, Delta 1075, Delta 1076, Delta 1077, Delta 1078, Delta 1079, Delta 1080, Delta 1081, Delta 1083, Farmers 1338, Fortis 1473, Gallagher 1528, General 1558, Genworth 1565, Great 1647, Guardian 1683, Health 1766, Highmark 1799, Horizon 1863, Humana 1886, Independence 1926, ING 1938, Kaiser 2086, Kilpatrick 2146, KMTSJ 2173, Louisiana 2309, Massachusetts 2397, McWane 2440, Medical 2448, Mutual 2605, National 2633, Northwestern 2749, Northwestern 2750, Pacific 2855, Pan-American 2868, Pharmacy 2956, Physicians 2970, Premera 3034, Principal 3047, Progressive 3057, Prudential 3072, Regence 3168, Regence 3169, Reinsurance 3179, Republic 3188, Rose 3261, Shenandoah 3433, StanCorp 3574, State 3591, Textron 3731, Trustmark 3818, UnitedHealth 3884, Universal 3887, Universal 3888, Unum 3898, Vision 3961, Wellmark 4026, WellPoint 4027, Wisconsin 4094

Insurance/fire, marine, and casualty, ACE 24, AgStar 59, Allstate 107, American 144, American 156, Amerisure 177, Arbella 226, Arrowpoint 251, Assurant 266, Berkley 426, Brotherhood 588, California 654, Chubb 804, Church 806, Clayton 841, CNA 855, COPIC 937, Doctors 1139, Edina 1227, Employers 1264, Erie 1291, Esurance 1298, Fairmont 1327, Farmers 1335, Farmers 1338, Franklin 1486, General 1555, Government 1621, Grange 1631, Great 1646, Hanover 1724, Harleysville 1733, Hartford 1742, Hartford 1743, Hastings 1749, Island 1996, JM 2044, Kennebunk 2126, Kilpatrick 2146, Lebanon 2238, Liberty 2265, Loews 2296, McWane 2440, MEEMIC 2455, Motorists 2584, Mutual 2604, National 2629, National 2633, Northwestern 2750, Ohio 2789, OneBeacon 2813, PEMCO 2919, Philadelphia 2960, Preferred 3031, Progressive 3057, Public 3078, Redwoods 3158, Rose 3261, Safeco 3306, Safety 3308, Selective 3399, Sentry 3409, Shelter 3431, Springleaf 3554, State 3590, State 3591, Travelers 3802, United 3869, United 3873, Utica 3910, Westfield 4047

Insurance/life, Acacia 21, AEGON 45, AgStar 59, Allianz 105, American 144, American 145, American 147, American 153, American 156, Ameritas 178, Aon 210, Assurant 266, Assurant 268, Assurity 269, Aviva 302, AXA 307, Baltimore 333, Blue 497, Century 750, CIGNA 812, CNA 855, CNO 857, Colonial 874, Country 951, CUNA 1008, Farmers 1338, FMR 1450, Fortis 1473, Genworth 1565, Gleaner 1590, Grange 1631, Great 1647, Guardian 1683, Hancock 1717, Hartford 1742, Hill 1804, ING 1938, Jackson 2009, Kilpatrick 2146, Lincoln 2278, Lincoln 2281, Loews 2296, Massachusetts 2397, McWane 2440, Metropolitan 2481, Monumental 2561, Mutual 2605, National 2633, New York 2688, Northwestern 2749, Northwestern 2750, Ohio 2790, Pacific 2855, Pan-American 2868, Physicians 2970, Primerica 3045, Principal 3047, Progressive 3057, Protective 3066, Prudential 3072, Reinsurance 3179, Republic 3188, Rose 3261, Royal 3274, Securian 3389, Security 3391, Sentry 3409, Shelter 3431, Shenandoah 3433, Springleaf 3554, State 3591, Sun 3643, Tamar 3684, Trustmark 3818, United 3873, Unum 3898, WellPoint 4027, Western 4040, WSA 4126

Insurance/surety, Ambac 123, Assurant 266, Beneficial 411, Century 750, Genworth 1565, MBIA 2416, MGIC 2488, National 2629, NEBCO 2653, PMI 2995, Residential 3191, Rose 3261, Travelers 3802, United 3868

Insurance/title, Aetna 48, Chicago 787, Connecticut 910, First 1389, First 1390, Lennar 2250, Stewart 3606, Westfield 4047

Investment offices, AllianceBernstein 102, Arbeit 225, Graham 1625, Greystone 1665, Hillside 1810, IMC 1920, Integrity 1949, Johnson 2049, Lord 2303, Optima 2819, Putnam 3085, Sansar 3330, Schenuit 3349, Young 4148

Investors/miscellaneous, Aberdeen 18, Allen 93, American 136, Arrowhead 250, BayView 384, Ben 409, Berry 436, Blackstone 477, C L D 635, Caterpillar 722, Choice 798, Cornerstone 944, Curves 1011, DineEquity 1120, Disney 1127, Doctor's 1138, Earnhardt 1205, Entelco 1277, FBR 1345, Florida 1444, Graham 1625, Hooters 1858, IMC 1920, Integrity 1949, Jack 2007, JAM 2019, Keystone 2138, Laird 2211, Lucasfilm 2316, Luxottica 2319, Marsh 2386, Maverick 2409, McDonald's 2427, Mitsubishi 2539, Mitsui 2541, Natural 2641, Odyssey 2784, Papa 2876, Partnership 2890, Persis 2944, Plum 2991, Portcullis 3004, Potlatch 3017, Presley 3038, Prince 3046, ProLogis 3060, Puck 3080, Ramerica 3125, Rodgers 3250, Scripps 3374, Sealy 3382, Shelton 3432, Simon 3458, Social(k) 3494, Sumitomo 3639, Transwestern 3800, Ventas 3931, Viacom 3945, Waffle 3975, Warburg 3985, WEDGE 4020, Wendy's 4031, Wendy's/Arby's 4030, World 4121

Iron and steel foundries, Alhambra 88, Amsted 188, Atlas 284, Betts 451, Brillion 569, Great 1643, McWane 2440, Monarch 2554, Motor 2583, Neenah 2656, OSCO 2832, Progressive 3058, Titan 3763, Webster 4018, Worthington 4124

Irrigation systems services, Ewing 1303

Jewelry and notions/costume, C & C 633, Jones 2057, United 3871

Jewelry/precious metal, Diamonds 1109, Goodman 1610, Jostens 2067, Kilmartin 2145, Klein 2167, Melissa 2458, Mikimoto 2510, Reed 3160

Labor organization, Major 2346, National 2624, National 2627

Laboratories/medical and dental, Corvallis 947, Diagnos-Techs 1108, Genzyme 1566, Hoffmann 1823, Quest 3103, West 4038

Laboratory apparatus, Agilent 56, Air 63, Badger 313, Beckman 397, Danaher 1027, Dresser 1173, Ford 1463, GenRad 1564, Goulds 1619, Hitachi 1816, Honeywell 1852, Kadant 2083, Keithley 2115, KLA-Tencor 2165, Li-Cor 2261, Merk 2467, Mine 2529, National 2632, Nikon 2711, PerkinElmer 2939, Rockwell 3246, S.J. 3299, Sakar 3313, Starkey 3587, Tektronix 3706, Teradyne 3718, Thermo 3733, Venturedyne 3933, Waters 4003, YSI 4149

Landscape and horticultural services, Davey 1035, Evans 1301, Kemper 2124, Sasaki 3337

Laundry, cleaning, and garment services, Alsco 115, AmeriPride 173, Cintas 816, G&K 1524, Morgan 2569

Leather footwear, Allen 97, Brown 591, Capezio 675, Clarks 838, Cole 867, Fila 1379, Genesco 1559, Gold 1598, Jones 2057, K-Swiss 2082, Kenneth 2128, New 2668, PVH 3088, Red 3154, Skechers 3472, Stride 3625, Timberland 3754, Wolverine 4106

Leather goods/miscellaneous, Klein 2168

Leather goods/personal, Bradley 551, Coach 858, Westport 4050

Leather luggage, Bradley 551

Leather tanning and finishing, Edsim 1230, Pfister 2949, Seton 3415

Legal services, Adams 34, Akerman 69, Akin 70, Allen 94, Allen 95, Alston 116, Andrews 198, Archer 232, Arent 235, Arnall 247, Arnold 248, Ashby 257, Axinn 308, Azulay 311, Baker 319, Baker 320, Baker 321, Baker 325, Balch 327, Ballard 329, Banner 351, Barack 353, Barnes 361, Barrasso 363, Bass 371, Bays 383, Benesch 413, Bernstein 433, Best 441, Bickel 457, Bingham 463, Blakely 480, Bodman 514, Boises 518, Bond 522, Bose 531, Bowles 544, Bracewell 549, Bradley 550, Bressler 557, Bricker 559, Briggs 564, Brinks 573, Brown 590, Brownstein 593, Bryan 596, Buchalter 600, Buckleysandler 603, Burr 621, Butler 627, Butzel 629, Cades 647, Cadwalader 649, Cahill 651, Caplin 681, Carmody 695, Carrington Coleman 701, Carter 707, Chadbourne 759, Chapman 762, Choate 796, Christie 800, Clark 836, Cleary 843, Clifford 849, Cole 868, Cotton 949, Cox 960, Cox 961, Cozen 964, Cranfill 971, Crowell 986, Cummings 1004, Curtis 1010, Davies 1036, Davis 1038, Davis 1039, Davis 1040, Davis 1041, Day 1046, Debevoise 1055, Dechert 1058, Dickstein 1111, Dinsmore 1121, Dorsey 1157, Dow 1164, Downey 1166, Drinker 1175, Duane 1185, Dykema 1199, Faegre 1324, Farella 1331, Felhaber 1356, Fennemore 1360, Fenwick 1362, Figari 1378, Finnegan 1384, Fish 1428, Fitzpatrick 1434, Foley 1453, Foley 1454, Ford 1462, Foster 1475, Fowler 1479, Fredrikson 1491, Freshfields 1500, Friday 1501, Fried 1502, Friedman 1504, Frommer 1507, Frost 1511, Fulbright 1516, Gable 1525, Gable 1526, Gammage 1531, Garvey 1539, Gibbons 1574, Gibbs 1575, Gibson 1580, Godfrey 1596, Goldberg 1599, Goodwin 1611, Gordon 1616, Gravel 1638, Greenberg 1654, Greensfelder 1659, Groom 1671, Gust 1691, Hahn 1700, Hall 1703, Hamilton 1710, Hangley 1721, Hanson 1725, Haskell 1748, Haynes 1759, Herrick 1789, Hill 1802, Hillis 1807, Hinshaw 1814, Hiscock 1815, Hodgson 1820, Hogan 1825, Holland 1833, Holland 1834, Hollingsworth 1836, Holme 1837, Honigman 1853, Hooper 1856, Husch 1896, Hutchinson 1897, Ice 1905, Irell 1991, Jackson 2012, Jeffer 2029, Jenner 2035, Jennings 2036,

Jones 2058, K&L 2080, Karr 2097, Kasowitz 2099, Katten 2101, Keating 2109, Keenan 2112, Keller 2116, Kelley 2118, Kemp 2123, Kenyon 2131, Kilpatrick 2147, King 2157, Kirkland 2164, Kramer 2191, Kreindler 2193, Lane 2221, Lanier 2222, Larkin 2224, Latham 2228, Leonard 2252, Lewis 2256, Lim 2275, Linklaters 2283, Liskow 2285, Littler 2289, Loeb 2295, Lowndes 2313, Marshall 2389, Maslon 2395, Mayer 2411, Maynard 2413, McDermott 2425, McDonnell 2428, McGuireWoods 2430, McKenna 2433, McNamee 2438, Merchant 2464, Michael 2492, Milbank 2511, Miles 2512, Miller 2519, Miller 2520, Miller 2521, Mills 2526, Mintz 2534, Moore 2566, Morgan 2571, Morris 2575, Morrison 2576, Mound 2587, Munger 2598, Murtha 2602, Neal 2652, Nelson 2661, Nutter 2764, Ober 2777, Oblon 2779, Olshan 2803, Oppenheimer 2817, Orrick 2826, Osborn 2831, Packard 2862, Parker 2885, Patterson 2895, Pattishall 2897, Patton 2898, Paul 2900, Paul 2901, Pepper 2934, Perkins 2940, Perkins 2941, Pierce 2974, Pillsbury 2975, Polsinelli 3001, Porter 3009, Porzio 3013, Potter 3019, PricewaterhouseCoopers 3042, Proskauer 3064, Pryor 3073, Pyles 3089, Quarles 3101, Quinn 3111, Ray 3131, Reed 3163, Reid 3173, Reilly 3176, Reinhart 3178, Richards 3206, Richards 3208, Riker 3215, Rimon 3217, Robins 3232, Robins 3233, Robinson 3234, Rogers 3252, Ropes 3260, Rose 3263, Rothgerber 3269, Rutan 3290, S.B.E. 3298, Satterlee 3339, Schiff 3350, Schulte 3362, Schwabe 3364, Sedgwick 3395, Senniger 3407, Seward 3417, Shartsis 3423, Shatz 3424, Shearman 3429, Sheppard 3435, Sherman 3436, Shipman 3438, Shook 3439, Sidley 3446, Sills 3456, Simmons 3457, Simpson 3462, Skadden 3470, Smith 3486, Snell 3490, Snow 3491, Spector 3539, Spencer 3543, Squire 3561, Stadtmauer 3570, Steptoe 3599, Stinson 3608, Stites 3609, Stoel 3611, Stoll 3613, Stradley 3620, Stradling 3621, Suitter 3633, Sullivan 3634, Sullivan 3636, Sutherland 3663, Teitler 3705, Thompson 3738, Thompson 3740, Tonkon 3772, Ulmer 3845, Ungaretti 3851, Updike 3899, Varnum 3922, Varnum 3923, Venable 3929, Vinson 3957, Vinson 3958, Wachtell 3973, Weil 4022, Weil 4023, Wendel 4029, Wheeler 4053, White 4058, White 4059, Whiteman 4061, Whyte 4067, Wiggin 4068, Wilentz 4071, Wiley 4073, Wilkes 4074, Williams 4076, Williams 4078, Willkie 4081, Wilson 4083, Winston 4089, Wishart 4097, Wolf 4104, Woods 4111, Wyatt 4130, Wyche 4131

Lighting and wiring equipment/electric, Alcoa 82, Armstrong 246, Bardes 359, Betts 451, Cooper 935, Energizer 1271, Guth 1692, ITW 2000, Leviton 2255, Micron 2500, Osram 2834, Preformed 3032, Sumitomo 3640

Liquor stores, Hy-Vee 1900, P.E.L. 2849, Raley's 3122, Saker 3314

Logging, Associated 263, Bowater 543, Georgia 1568, Hampton 1714, Holce 1827, International 1968, National 2628, Sealaska 3380, Westervelt 4046, Weyerhaeuser 4052

Lumber and construction materials—wholesale, American 134, Avelina 296, Chaney 761, Do 1136, Guardian 1682, Hartzell 1745, Hawaii 1754, Hudson 1881, Hutchison 1898, Lafarge 2210, Lowe's 2312, OrePac 2823, Sidwell 3447, Simpson 3461, TAMKO 3685, Universal 3890, Universal 3894, Verby 3934, Ward 3986

Lumber and other building materials—retail, Caruso 709, Hawaii 1754, Home 1842, Houston 1870, Lowe's 2312, Spahn 3529, Star 3584, Wolf 4103

Lumber and wood products, Anthony 206, Bowater 543, Catawissa 720, Freres 1498, Friesen 1505, Holt 1839, Louisiana 2310, Ochoco 2783, Pukall 3082, Rayonier 3134, Sonoco 3500

Lumber and wood products (except furniture), Cox 962, Georgia 1568, Hampton 1714, Homasote 1841, Jasper 2027, Louisiana 2310, Potlatch 3017, Temple 3711, Westervelt 4046, Weyerhaeuser 4052

Machinery/construction, mining, and materials handling, ACE 25, Air 62, Altec 118, Baker 324, Boart 510, Cameron 667, Caterpillar 722, Crown 987, FEECO 1353, Gehl 1545, Ingersoll 1939, Joy 2070, Kennametal 2125, Leyman 2259, Magline 2339, Manitowoc 2355, Oshkosh 2833, Otis 2835, PACCAR 2850, Pactiv 2863, Raymond 3133, RITE 3221, Sioux 3465, Terex 3719, Tomkins 3771, United 3867, United 3882, Venturedyne 3933, Vermeer 3937, Walker 3982, Webster 4018

Machinery/farm and garden, Ariens 238, Brillion 569, CNH 856, Deere 1061, Dethmers 1091, Gehl 1545, Kawasaki 2102, MTD 2595, Specialty 3537, Toro 3775, Valmont 3919, Vermeer 3937, Vulcan 3971, Western 4043

Machinery/general industry, Abbot 12, American 157, AMPCO 186, Amsted 188, AptarGroup 221, Ariel 237, Avery 297, Baker 324, Cameron 667, CLARCOR 832, Contran 928, Dana 1026, Dethmers 1091, Eagle 1202, Emerson 1257, Fetzer 1367, Flowserve 1447, FMC 1449, Ford 1463, Gear 1544, Goulds 1619, Graco 1624, Great 1643, Hammond 1711, Hilliard 1805, Hitachi 1816, Horix 1860, Illinois 1916, Industrial 1935, Ingersoll 1939, ITT 1999, Jones 2056, Kadant 2083, Matthews 2406, Minster 2532, Monarch 2554, MPB 2591, New Hampshire 2674, Nordson 2723, Oakley 2774, Pentair 2926, Regal 3167, Remmele 3183, Rexnord 3198, Rieke 3212, Robbins 3230, SKF 3473, Sonoco 3500, Symmco 3670, Timken 3760, Tomkins 3771, Webster 4018, Woodward 4112, XTEK 4138, Xylem 4139

Machinery/industrial and commercial, Amsted 188, Applied 219, Bardes 359, Dana 1026, Deutsch 1098, Donaldson 1153, Dynamet 1200, Eaton 1216, Flowserve 1447, Hilliard 1805, ITT 1999, Kadant 2083, McDonald 2426, Midmark 2507, Parker 2886, Remmele 3183, Rima 3216, Techni 3699, Walter 3984, XTEK 4138

Machinery/metalworking, Air 62, Allegheny 91, AMPCO 186, ANZA 208, Bosch 529, Gleason 1591, Hammond 1711, Hardinge 1729, InterTech 1977, Kennametal 2125, Kingsbury 2160, Klein 2168, Lincoln 2279, MAG 2337, Makino 2348, Minster 2532, Monarch 2554, Morgan 2568, MTD 2595, National 2634, Park 2880, R & B 3113, Reiff 3174, SPX 3558, Stanek 3578, Stanley 3579, XTEK 4138

Machinery/refrigeration and service industry, AllStyle 108, AMPCO 186, Amsted 188, Baker 324, Chief 793, Emerson 1257, Hubbell 1879, Ingersoll 1939, Manitowoc 2355, Manitowoc 2356, Mars 2384, Mercury 2468, Metal 2478, Parker 2886, Philips 2963, RG 3201, Shaklee 3418, Slant 3477, Stout 3619, Tennant 3714, Thermo 3733, Trane 3794, United 3882, Venturedyne 3933, Vilter 3956, Vogt 3966, Wittern 4098

Machinery/special industry, AMPCO 186, Applied 220, Cardinal 685, Chief 793, Cranston 972, Cymer 1016, Dupps 1193, Flowserve 1447, Hobart 1818, Lam 2214, Monarch 2554, Nordson 2723, Old 2796, Pentair 2926, R & B 3113, Sandusky 3328, Spirol 3545, Stoelting 3612, Thermo 3733, Tyler 3830, Venturedyne 3933, Vijuk 3953

Mailing, reproduction, commercial art, photography, and stenographic service, American 138, Goldmark 1605, Moody's 2563, Print.Net 3048, Staples 3581, United 3873

Management and public relations services, Aberdeen 18, Accenture 22, AgStar 59, AHS 61, Allegis 92, American 132, Atlantic 282, Baker 323, Barber 356, Barton 366, BayView 384, Bionetics 467, Black 475, Booz 525, Boston 535, Bright 566, Butler 626, Capri 682, Cardinal 685, Cargill 691, Carlson 693, Carroll 703, Ceridian 753, Chartis 768, Chehalis 771, Chotin 799, Delaware 1066, Deloitte 1070, Dimeo 1119, Dixon 1133, Donnelley 1155, DP 1168, Driscoll 1176, Edelman 1224, Edison 1229, Ellin 1251, EMC 1253, ERM 1292, Ernst 1293, FedEx 1352, Foreman 1465, Frontier 1510, Further 1521, Haynie 1760, Hays 1761, Health 1764, International 1960, International Profit 1969, ITA 1998, Kearney 2107, Kemper 2124, Kimley 2151, KPMG 2190, Maritz 2376, Marsh 2385, MAXIMUS 2410, McDermott 2424, Medeanalytics 2447, Microsoft 2501, Monster 2560, Nasdaq 2618, Network 2664, Nord 2721, North 2732, Padilla 2864, Panosian 2874, Parsons 2888, PricewaterhouseCoopers 3042, Pro 3052, Promotional 3061, Reed 3162, Reger 3170, Retail 3194, RJN 3228, RubinBrown 3280, Ruder 3282, SANYO 3333, Schoeneckers 3357, Stanley 3580, Station 3593, Steelcase 3597, Survis 3660, Synopsys 3673, Tikigaq 3751, TIV 3764, Tofias 3768, Toyota 3788, U.M. 3834, Underground 3850, Unisys 3859, Vermillion 3939, VHA 3944, Wallace 3983, Washington 3994, Washington 3995, Waterford 4002, Woerner 4101

Manufacturing/miscellaneous, American 149, ANZA 208, Atlantic 281, Bean 391, Brady 552, Bridgewater 561, Douglas 1159, Fabri 1322, Hallmark 1707, Harper 1735, Hartz 1744, Herrick 1788, Hill 1804, Interlock 1954, International 1964, Lancaster 2216, Matthews 2406, Mill 2515, PerkinElmer 2939, Sherwin 3437, Shure 3443, Stout 3619, True 3815, Vandor 3921, Vulcan 3971, Wahl 3977

Measuring, analyzing, and controlling instruments, Intoximeters 1979

Meat and seafood markets, Publix 3079

Meat packing plants and prepared meats and poultry, BPI 548, Burger's 614, ConAgra 904, Cow 957, Dietz 1114, Fresh 1499, Greater 1649, Hillshire 1809, Hormel 1866, Keystone 2137, Kowalski 2189, Marcho 2368, Smithfield 3487, Tyson 3832, Usinger 3907

Medical instruments and supplies, Alcon 83, American 158, Bard 358, Baxter 377, Bayer 381, Becton 398, Bicon 458, Biomet 466, Boston 540, CareFusion 688, ConvaTec 932, Covidien 956, CryoLife 990, Danaher 1027, DCI 1049, DENTSPLY 1089, DJO 1134, Ethicon 1299, Garelick 1537, Hill 1804, Howmedica 1875, Integra 1947, Johnson 2048, Kappler 2095, Kinetic 2156, KLS 2171, Marena 2372, Medline 2451, Medrad 2452, Medtronic 2453, Midmark 2507, Mine 2529, Miracle 2535, Pharmaceutical 2955, Philips 2963, PSS 3074, ResMed 3192, Respironics 3193, Roche 3236, Scott 3370, St. Jude 3566, STERIS 3600, Stryker 3627, Teleflex 3707, West 4038, Whip 4054, Zimmer 4157

Medical offices and clinics/miscellaneous, Chinese 794, Clarkson 839, U.M. 3834

Membership organization/miscellaneous, New 2689, Semiconductor 3403, Texas 3726

Men's and boys' apparel and accessory stores, Foot 1459, Lands' 2220, Limited 2277, Men's 2460

Merchandise stores/general, Building 610, Kmart 2172, Kum 2199, Meyer 2485, Raley's 3122

Tobacco products—cigarettes, Altria 120, Loews 2296, Lorillard 2304, Morris 2574, Philip 2962, Reynolds 3200, Santa 3331
Tobacco products—cigars, Newman 2696
Transportation by air, Lynden 2320
Transportation equipment/miscellaneous, Chief 793, Dethmers 1091, General 1551, Harsco 1741, Kawasaki 2102, Nordic 2722, Polaris 2999
Transportation services, Expedia 1311, GATX 1542
Transportation services/freight, Alexander 85, AMCOL 127, BDP 388, Con 903, JTB 2074, Nippon 2713, Robinson 3235
Transportation services/miscellaneous, EPES 1283, Power 3021, Ryder 3292, United 3874
Transportation services/water, Alexander 85, Atlantic 282, Hallberg 1704, Riverway 3226, TECO 3701, Tidewater 3748
Transportation/deep sea domestic freight, Alexander 85, Nippon 2713, TECO 3701, Totem 3779
Transportation/deep sea foreign freight, Alexander 85, NYK 2768
Transportation/intercity and rural bus, Greyhound 1664
Transportation/nonscheduled air, Global 1592
Transportation/railroad, Alaska 76, Burlington 618, Conrail 914, CSX 997, Hunt 1892, Kansas 2094, NEBCO 2653, Norfolk 2725, Reading 3142, Union 3857
Transportation/scheduled air, Alaska 74, AMR 187, Brink's 571, Delta 1073, DHL 1106, FedEx 1352, Horizon 1861, JetBlue 2041, MN 2543, Nippon 2713, SkyWest 3476, Southwest 3522, United 3860, United 3872, US 3902
Transportation/water freight, CTSI 998, Riverway 3226
Transportation/water passenger, Carlson 693, Carnival 696, Disney 1128, Holland 1835, Royal 3273
Travel and tour arrangers, Carlson 693, Collette 872, Grand 1627, JTB 2074, Maritz 2376, Oxford 2848, Travel 3801, United 3873, Untours 3897
Trucking and courier services, except by air, Alexander 85, AMCOL 127, Castle 717, Central 746, Con 903, CSX 997, FedEx 1352, Florida 1444, Hunt 1892, Keen 2111, Lynden 2320, New 2680, RUAN 3279, Ryder 3292, Savage 3341, Schneider 3355, TECO 3701, Tidewater 3749, UniGroup 3852, United 3872, Warren 3993, Wonder 4107
Trusts, Exchange 1307, Kanaly 2089
Variety stores, Albrecht 80, Beall's 389, Big 460, BJ's 473, Costco 948, DFS 1104, Dollar 1145, Kmart 2172, Target 3691, Wal-Mart 3980
Veterinary services, PetSmart 2948, Rood 3257
Video tape rental, Blockbuster 483
Vocational schools, Intertech 1976, Marinello 2375, Washington 3999
Warehousing and storage, Alexander 85, Atlantic 282, Birdsong 470, Bunge 612, Cow 957, Edison 1229, International 1972, NEBCO 2653, Prince 3046, Savage 3341, Scoular 3373, TECO 3701, U-Haul 3833, Unaka 3848
Watches, clocks, and parts, Citizen 822, Nintendo 2712
Water suppliers, Allete 100, Alliant 104, Aqua 222, Metropolitan 2484
Water transportation, Alexander 85, Lynden 2320, Matson 2404, Tidewater 3748
Wholesale trade—durable goods, Gaiam 1527
Women's apparel stores, Ascena 255, Conston 920, Foot 1459, Forever 1469, Gucci 1684, La Mariage 2204, Lands' 2220, Limited 2277, Talbots 3682, Tanner 3688, United 3871
Women's specialty and accessory stores, BC 387, Gucci 1684, Lands' 2220, Limited 2277, Talbots 3682, United 3871
Wood buildings and mobile homes, Clayton 841, KB 2105
Wood containers, Buckeye 601, Carris 702, Independent 1928, Key 2134
Wood millwork, American 170, Andersen 194, Carris 702, Freres 1498, Hartzell 1745, Jeld 2032, Jones 2060, Louisiana 2310, Masco 2393, OMNOVA 2809, Pella 2917, Quality 3096, Sierra 3451, Weather 4013
Wood products/miscellaneous, American 149, Bemis 408, Carris 702, Homasote 1841, Independent 1928, Longaberger 2299, Louisiana 2310, Moore 2567, Sierra 3451, Sonoco 3500
Yarn and thread mills, Borden 527, Coats 860, Dixie 1132, Milliken 2525, United 3871

CORPORATION AND CORPORATE GRANTMAKER INDEX

This index is a list of corporations, subsidiaries, and corporate grantmakers found in this edition. They are cross-referenced to the sequence number assigned to the corporation in the Descriptive Directory. Those corporations which have entries in the Descriptive Directory and are also subsidiary organizations are referenced to their individually-assigned sequence numbers and further cross-referenced to the sequence numbers of their parent companies.

Graybar Financial Services, Inc., see 1640
Graybar Foundation, 1640
Graybar International, Inc., see 1640
Graybar Services, Inc., see 1640
Graycor Inc., 1641
Great American Reserve Insurance Co., see 857
Great Atlantic & Pacific Tea Company, Inc., The, 1642
Great Atlantic & Pacific Tea Company, The, see 1457
Great Lakes Bank, see 1644
Great Lakes Bank Foundation, 1644
Great Lakes Castings Corporation, see 1643
Great Lakes Castings Corporation Foundation, 1643
Great Lakes Castings LLC, 1643
Great Lakes Cement Region, see 2210
Great Lakes Chemical Corporation, see 775
Great Lakes Financial Resources Charitable Foundation, Inc., see 1644
Great Lakes Financial Resources Inc., 1644
Great Lakes Higher Education Corporation, 1645
Great Northern Nekoosa Corp., see 1568
Great Oaks Insurance Co., see 1733
Great Plains Meter, Inc., see 1027
Great Source Education Group, see 1869
Great Southern Paper, see 1568
Great West Casualty Company, 1646
Great West Casualty Company Contributions Program, 1646
Great Western Financial Corp., see 4158
Great-West Life & Annuity Insurance Company, 1647
Great-West Life & Annuity Insurance Company Contributions Program, 1647
Greater Berkshire Charitable Foundation, see 428
Greater Community Bancorp Charitable Foundation, Inc., see 3916
Greater Community Educational Foundation, Inc., 3916
Greater Construction Corp. Charitable Foundation, Inc., The, see 1648
Greater Construction Corp., The, 1648
Greater Homes, see 1648
Greater Omaha Packing Co. Foundation, 1649
Greater Omaha Packing Co., Inc., 1649
Greater Washington Publishing, Inc., see 3999
Green Awakening Coffee, 1650
Green Awakening Coffee Corporate Giving Program, 1650
Green Bay Packers Foundation, 1651
Green Bay Packers, Inc., 1651
Green Bay Packers, Inc. Corporate Giving Program, 1651
Green Building Services, Inc., 1652
Green Building Services, Inc. Contributions Program, 1652
Green Mountain Coffee Roasters Foundation, see 1653
Green Mountain Coffee Roasters, Inc., 1653
Green Mountain Coffee Roasters, Inc. Corporate Giving Program, 1653
Green Mountain Coffee, Inc., see 1653
Green Mountain Coffee, Inc. Corporate Giving Program, see 1653
Greenberg Financial Insurance Services, Inc., see 3057
Greenberg Traurig Fellowship Foundation, 1654
Greenberg Traurig, P.A., 1654
GreenChoice Bank, 1655
GreenChoice Bank Corporate Giving Program, 1655
Greene & Associates, W. H., Inc., 1656
Greene Foundation, W. H., Inc., 1656
Greene, Tweed & Co., Inc., 1657
Greenlee Textron, see 3731
Greenlight Apparel, 1658
Greenlight Apparel Corporate Giving Program, 1658
Greensboro News Co., see 2218
Greensfelder, Hemker & Gale, P.C., 1659
Greensfelder, Hemker & Gale, P.C. Pro Bono Program, 1659
Greenview Hospital, Inc., see 1762
Greenwich Capital Foundation, see 3138
Greenwich Capital Markets, Inc., see 3138
Greenwood Dermatology, Inc., 1660
Greenwood Dermatology, P.C., see 1660
Gregory Enterprises Inc., Carl, 1661
Gregory Family Foundation, T. Raymond, 1662
Gregory Foundation, Carl, Inc., The, 1661
Gregory Galvanizing & Metal Processing Inc., see 1662
Gregory Industries, Inc., 1662
Greif, Inc., 1663
Greif, Inc. Corporate Giving Program, 1663
Greyhound Lines, Inc., 1664
Greyhound Lines, Inc. Corporate Giving Program, 1664
Greyhound Racehorses, see 1066
Greystone Construction, Inc., see 2250
Greystone Funding Corporation, 1665
Greystone Homes of Nevada, Inc., see 2250
Greystone Homes, Inc., see 2250
Greystone Nevada, L.L.C., see 2250
Griffin Pipe Products Co., see 188
Griffin Wheel Co., see 188
Griffin Williamson Foundation, 2119
Griffith Laboratories Foundation, Inc., 1667
Griffith Laboratories, Inc., 1667
Griffith, Inc., 1666
Grigsby Foundation, Merice "Boo" Johnson, The, 652
Grinnell Mutual Group Foundation, 1668
Grinnell Mutual Reinsurance Company, 1668
Griswold Industries, Inc., 1669
Groeniger & Co., 1670
Groeniger College Scholarship Fund, Mike & Bev, 1670
Groom Law Group, 1671
Groom Law Group, Chartered Pro Bono Program, 1671
Gross Foundation, Donald & Linda, Inc., 1025
Grove Farm Company, Inc., 1672
Grove Farm Foundation, 1672
Grove U.S. LLC, see 2355
Groves and Sons Company, S. J., 1673
Groves Foundation, 1673
Growing Family Foundation, Inc., 2838
Growing Family, Inc., see 2838
GROWMARK Foundation, The, 1674
GROWMARK, Inc., 1674
Grubb Charitable Foundation Inc., Stephen R., 1675
Grubb Construction, Stephen R., Inc., 1675
GSB, see 1583
GSD Packaging, LLC, see 4046
GSF Foundation, 1602
GSM Industrial, Inc., 1676
GT Foundation, 1657
GTECH Holdings Corporation, 1677
GTECH Holdings Corporation Contributions Program, 1677
GTL Truck Lines, Inc., see 2619
Guarantee Electric Company Inc., 1678
Guaranty Bank and Trust Company, 1679
Guaranty Bank and Trust Company Charitable Trust, 1679
Guard Publishing Company, 1680
Guardian Corp., 1681
Guardian Industries Corp., see 1682
Guardian Industries Corporation, 1682
Guardian Industries Educational Foundation, 1682
Guardian Insurance & Annuity Co., Inc., The, see 1683
Guardian Investor Services LLC, see 1683
Guardian Life Insurance Company of America Corporate Giving Program, The, 1683
Guardian Life Insurance Company of America, The, 1683
Guardian Life Welfare Trust, The, see 1683
Guardian Transportation Corp., see 1682
Gucci America, Inc., 1684
Gucci Foundation, The, 1684
Guess? Foundation, 1685
Guess?, Inc., 1685
Guided Alliance Healthcare Service Inc., 1686
Guided Alliance Pharmacy, see 1686
GuideOne Insurance Foundation, Inc., The, 1687
GuideOne Life Insurance Co., 1687
Guinness UDV North America, Inc., see 1107
Guitar Center Music Foundation, The, see 1359
Gulf Marine Fabricators Employee Foundation, 1688
Gulf Marine Fabricators, LP, 1688
Gulf Oil L.P., see 1003
Gulf Power Company, 1689
Gulf Power Company, see 3516
Gulf Power Company Contributions Program, 1689
Gulf Power Foundation, Inc., 1689
Gulf States Paper Corporation, see 4046
Gulf States Tube Div., see 3100
Gulfstream Aerospace Corporation, 1690
Gulfstream Aerospace Corporation, see 1551
Gulfstream Aerospace Corporation Contributions Program, 1690
Gulfstream Aerospace, Corp., see 1690
Gunlocke Co., The, see 1817
Gust Rosenfeld PLC, 1691
Gust Rosenfeld PLC Pro Bono Program, 1691
Guth Charitable Trust, Edwin F., 1692
Guth Company Charitable Trust, Edwin F., see 1692
Guth Lighting Co., see 1692
Guth Lighting Systems, Inc., 1692
Guy Carpenter & Co., Inc., see 2385
Gwaltney of Smithfield, Ltd., see 3487
GWCC, see 1646
Gygi and von Wyss Foundation, 1828
Gygi Foundation, Hans, see 1828
Gymboree Corporation Contributions Program, The, 1693
Gymboree Corporation, The, 1693

H & K Inc., 1694
H & R Block Foundation, The, 1695
H & R Block, Inc., 1695
H & R Block, Inc. Corporate Giving Program, 1695
H-C Industries, Inc., see 82
H-D Michigan, Inc., see 1732
H.E.I. Charitable Foundation, see 1755
H.U.G.S., Inc., 34
Habig Foundation, The, see 2149
Hach Company, see 1027
Hach Ultra Analytics Inc., see 1027
Hachette Book Group USA, Inc., 1696
Hachette Book Group USA, Inc. Corporate Giving Program, 1696
Hackstock Family Foundation, 1697
Hackstock Properties Inc., 1697
Hagerstown Trust Co., see 1518
Hagerty Brothers Company, 1698
Hagerty Brothers Company Foundation, 1698
Haggen, Inc., 1699
Haggen, Inc. Corporate Giving Program, 1699
Hahn Loeser & Parks LLP, 1700
Hahn Loeser & Parks LLP Pro Bono Program, 1700
Haines & Haines, Inc., 1701
Haines Family Foundation, Inc., The, 1701
Haldewang Family Charitable Foundation, 1929
Half.com, Inc., see 1217
Hall & Company, Edward E., 1702
Hall & Evans L.L.C. Foundation, 1703
Hall & Evans, LLC, 1703
Hall Memorial Music Scholarship, Joyce, 3256
Hall Surgical Div., see 4157
Hallberg Family Foundation, 1704
Hallberg, Inc., 1704
Hallelujah Acres, Inc., 1705

NetDeposit, L.L.C., *see* 4158
Netherlands Insurance Company, The, *see* 2265
Nets Foundation, Inc., The, 584
Netscape Communications Corp., *see* 209
Network Air Medical Systems, Inc., *see* 857
Network Management Group, Inc., 2664
Network Systems Div., *see* 81
Networks Associates, Inc., *see* 2417
Networks Associates, Inc. Corporate Giving Program, *see* 2417
Neurol, *see* 2665
Neurology Clinic of South Arkansas, 2665
Neusport Football Club, 3800
Neutrogena Corporation, *see* 2048
Neuwirth Motors, Inc., 2666
Nevada State Bank, *see* 4158
Neville Chemical Company, 2667
Neville Chemical Company Contributions Program, 2667
New Balance Athletic Shoe, Inc., 2668
New Balance Athletic Shoe, Inc. Corporate Giving Program, 2668
New Balance Foundation, 2668
New Champions Golf & Country Club Inc., 2669
New Course Charity Foundation Inc., 2454
New England Biolabs Foundation, 2670
New England Biolabs, Inc., 2670
New England Electric Resources, Inc., *see* 2630
New England Electric System, *see* 2630
New England Electric Transmission Corp., *see* 2630
New England Energy Inc., *see* 2630
New England Federal Credit Union, 2671
New England Federal Credit Union Contributions Program, 2671
New England Hydro-Transmission Corp., *see* 2630
New England Hydro-Transmission Electric Co., Inc., *see* 2630
New England Life Insurance Company, *see* 2481
New England Patriots Charitable Foundation, Inc., The, 2672
New England Patriots LP, 2672
New England Power Co., *see* 2630
New England Power Service Co., *see* 2630
New Era Cap Co., Inc., 2673
New Era Cap Company Contributions Program, 2673
New Frontiers Foundation, 1510
New Hampshire Ball Bearings Foundation, 2674
New Hampshire Ball Bearings, Inc., 2674
New Hotel Monteleone, LLC, 2675
New Jersey Basketball LLC, *see* 584
New Jersey Devils LLC Corporate Giving Program, 2676
New Jersey Devils, LLC, 2676
New Jersey Nets Corporate Giving Program, *see* 584
New Linden Price Rite, Inc., *see* 3314
New Living, 2677
New Living Corporate Giving Program, 2677
New Marriott MI, Inc., *see* 2383
New Mavericks Foundation, The, *see* 1021
New Orleans Hornets NBA L.P., 2678
New Orleans Louisiana Saints, L.P., 2679
New Orleans Saints, *see* 2679
New Orleans Saints Corporate Giving Program, 2679
New Orleans Saints Hurricane Katrina Relief Fund, The, 2679
New Penn Motor Express Scholarship Foundation, 2680
New Penn Motor Express, Inc., 2680
New United Motor Manufacturing, Inc., *see* 1555
New Vision Santa Rosa Foundation, 2952
New York Amsterdam News, *see* 185
New York and Mississippi Valley Printing Telegraph Company, *see* 4045
New York Business Development Corporation, 2681
New York Casualty Insurance Co., *see* 1733
New York Community Bancorp, Inc., 2682
New York Community Bancorp, Inc. Contributions Program, 2682
New York Community Bank, 2683
New York Community Bank, *see* 2682
New York Community Bank Foundation, The, 2683
New York Football Giants, Inc., 2684
New York Frozen Foods, Inc., *see* 2216
New York Giants, *see* 2684
New York Giants Corporate Giving Program, 2684
New York Health and Racquet Club, 2685
New York Health and Racquet Club Foundation, 2685
New York Islanders Hockey Club, L.P., 2686
New York Islanders Hockey Club, LP Corporate Giving Program, 2686
New York Jets Corporate Giving Program, 2687
New York Jets Football Club, Inc., 2687
New York Jets Foundation, Inc., 2687
New York Knicks, *see* 2336
New York Life Foundation, 2688
New York Life Insurance and Annuity Corporation, *see* 2688
New York Life Insurance Company, 2688
New York Life Insurance Company, *see also* 2688
New York Life Insurance Company Contributions Program, 2688
New York Life International, Inc., *see* 2688
New York Life Investment, *see* 2688
New York Mercantile Exchange Charitable Foundation, *see* 853
New York Mets, *see* 3601
New York Mets Foundation, Inc., 3601
New York Rangers, *see* 2336
New York Red Bulls Corporate Giving Program, 205
New York Road Runners, Inc., 2689
New York Self Reliance Foundation Ltd., 3400
New York Stock Exchange Fallen Heroes Fund, 2769
New York Stock Exchange Foundation, Inc., *see* 2769
New York Stock Exchange, L.L.C., *see* 2769
New York Stock Exchange, L.L.C. Corporate Giving Program, *see* 2769
New York Times Company Foundation Inc., The, 2690
New York Times Company, The, 2690
New York Times Media Group, The, *see* 2690
New York Times Neediest Cases Fund, Inc., The, 2690
New York Vegetable Research Association Inc., 469
New York Yankees Corporate Giving Program, The, 2691
New York Yankees Foundation, Inc., 2691
New York Yankees Partnership, 2691
New York Yankees Tampa Foundation, Inc., 2691
New York/New Jersey MetroStars Corporate Giving Program, *see* 205
Neways, Inc., 2692
Neways, Inc. Contributions Program, 2692
Newburyport Five Cents Savings Bank, The, 2693
Newburyport Five Cents Savings Charitable Foundation Inc., 2693
NewCastle Industries, Inc., *see* 186
Newell Co., *see* 2694
Newell Co. Contributions Program, *see* 2694
Newell Operating Co., *see* 2694
Newell Rubbermaid Inc., 2694
Newell Rubbermaid Inc., *see also* 2694
Newell Rubbermaid Inc. Corporate Giving Program, 2694
Newfield Exploration Company, 2695
Newfield Exploration Mid-Continent Inc., *see* 2695
Newfield Foundation, 2695
Newfield Gulf Coast Inc., *see* 2695
Newlin, Sr. Memorial Trust, Robert "Aqqaluk", 2615
Newman Cigar Company, J. C., 2696
Newman Foundation, Inc., 2696
Newman's Own Foundation, 2697
Newman's Own Organics, Inc., *see* 2697
Newman's Own, Inc., 2697
Newmont Exploration, Ltd., *see* 2698
Newmont Mining Corporation, 2698
Newmont Mining Corporation, *see also* 2698
Newmont Mining Corporation Contributions Program, 2698
Newmont Oil Co., *see* 2698
Newport Bancorp, Inc., 2699
Newportfed Charitable Foundation, 2699
News Corporation, 2700
News Corporation Contributions Program, 2700
News Tribune, *see* 3680
News Tribune Scholarship Foundation, 3680
News World Communications, Inc., 2701
Newspaper Foundation, The, 2702
Newspapers of New England, Inc., 2702
Newsweek, Inc., *see* 2703
Newsweek, Inc. Corporate Giving Program, *see* 2703
Newsweek/Daily Beast Company LLC Contributions Program, The, 2703
Newsweek/Daily Beast Company LLC, The, 2703
Newtown Savings Bank, 2704
Newtown Savings Bank Foundation Inc., 2704
Nexans USA Inc., *see* 423
Nexion Health Foundation, 2705
Nexion Health, Inc., 2705
Nextel Communications, Inc., *see* 3556
Nextel Community Connect Program, 3556
NextEra Energy Foundation, Inc., 1443
NexTier Bank, 2706
Nextier Bank Foundation, 2706
NFC Foundation, 2619
NFL Charities, 2626
NHL, *see* 2631
Niagara Bancorp, Inc., *see* 1419
NIBCO Inc. Corporate Giving Program, 2707
NIBCO, Inc., 2707
Nichols Aluminum, *see* 3100
Nichols Company Charitable Trust, 1800
Nichols-Homeshield, *see* 3100
Nichols-Homeshield Casting, *see* 3100
Nick and Terry's Foundation, 2792
Nickelodeon, *see* 2596
Nickelodeon Corporate Giving Program, 2596
Nicolai Memorial Scholarship Fund, David K., *see* 657
Niemann Foods Foundation, 2708
Niemann Foods, Inc., 2708
Night Vision Equipment Co., Inc., *see* 1179
NII Holdings, Inc., 2709
NII Holdings, Inc. Corporate Giving Program, 2709
Niject Services Co., *see* 3029
NIKE Employee Disaster Relief Foundation, 2710
NIKE Foundation, 2710
NIKE P.L.A.Y. Foundation, *see* 2710
NIKE, Inc., 2710
NIKE, Inc., *see also* 2710
NIKE, Inc. Corporate Giving Program, 2710
Nikon Inc., 2711
Nine West Group Inc., *see* 2057
Ninety Commerce Road, Inc., *see* 2443
Nintendo of America Inc. Corporate Giving Program, 2712
Nintendo of America, Inc., 2712
Nippon Express Foundation, Inc., 2713
Nippon Express Travel USA Inc., *see* 2713
Nippon Express U.S.A., Inc., 2713
Nippon Express USA (Illinois), Inc., *see* 2713
NIPSCO, *see* 2739
NIPSCO Industries, Inc., *see* 2715
Nishnabotna Valley Foundation, 2714
Nishnabotna Valley Rural Electric Cooperative, 2714
NiSource Charitable Foundation, 2715
NiSource Inc., 2715
NiSource Inc., *see also* 2715
Nissan Foundation, The, 2716

TALX Corporation, 3683
TALX Corporation, *see* 1288
Tamar Fink, Inc., 3684
TAMKO Building Products, Inc., 3685
TAMKO Building Products, Inc. Contributions Program, 3685
Tampa Bay Bowl Association, Inc., 487
Tampa Bay Buccaneers, *see* 599
Tampa Bay Buccaneers Corporate Giving Program, 599
Tampa Bay Devil Rays, Ltd., *see* 3686
Tampa Bay Devil Rays, Ltd. Corporate Giving Program, *see* 3686
Tampa Bay Lightning, *see* 737
Tampa Bay Lightning Corporate Giving Program, 737
Tampa Bay Rays Baseball Corporate Giving Program, 3686
Tampa Bay Rays Baseball, Ltd., 3686
TAN, *see* 3801
TAN Corporate Giving Program, 3801
Tanadgusix Corporation, 3687
Tangram Enterprise Solutions, Inc., *see* 3307
Tanner Companies, 3688
Tanner Foundation, Inc., 3688
Tap Packaging Solutions, 3689
TAP Publishing, 3690
Tape Products Div., *see* 133
Tapoco, Inc., *see* 82
Target Bank, *see* 3691
Target Corporation, 3691
Target Corporation, *see also* 3691
Target Corporation Contributions Program, 3691
Target Foundation, 3691
Target Foundation, *see* 3691
Target National Bank, *see* 3691
Target Stores, Inc., *see* 3691
TASQ Corp., *see* 1400
Tastefully Simple Corporate Giving Program, 3692
Tastefully Simple, Inc., 3692
Tasty Baking Company, 3693
Tasty Baking Company, *see* 1446
Tasty Baking Foundation, 3693
Tatitlek Corporation, The, 3694
Taub Family Foundation, Inc., 2867
Taurus World Stunt Awards (USA) Foundation, 3152
Taxware, LP, *see* 1400
Taylor Bros., *see* 165
Taylor Charitable Trust, Sally Smith, 540
Taylor Co. Inc., J.P., *see* 3891
Taylor-Wharton Gas Equipment, *see* 1741
Tazo Corporate Giving Program, 3585
TBS, *see* 3823
TBS Corporate Giving Program, 3823
TCF Foundation, 3695
TCF National Bank, 3695
TCU, *see* 3697
TCU Foundation, Inc., 3697
TD Bank, N.A., 3696
TD Bank, N.A. Corporate Giving Program, 3696
TD Banknorth, *see* 3696
TD Banknorth Charitable Foundation, *see* 3696
TD Banknorth Inc. Corporate Giving Program, *see* 3696
TD Charitable Foundation, 3696
TDX, *see* 3687
TDX Foundation, 3687
Teachers Credit Union, 3697
Team Aerotek Foundation, Inc., *see* 92
TEAM Foundation, 663
TeamQuest Corporation, 3698
TeamQuest Foundation, 3698
Tearoom in Utica Square, Inc., The, *see* 1774
Tech Group, Inc., *see* 4038
TechAdvantage Program, The, *see* 1451
Techni-Core, Inc., 3699
Technology Center, *see* 869
Technology Leaders Management, Inc., *see* 3307
Techsonic Industries, Inc., *see* 3707
Teck Cominco American Incorporated, *see* 3700
Teck Cominco American Incorporated Corporate Giving Program, *see* 3700
Teck Resources Limited, 3700
Teck Resources Limited Corporate Giving Program, 3700
TECO Energy Foundation, Inc., 3701
TECO Energy, Inc., 3701
TECO Energy, Inc. Corporate Giving Program, 3701
Tedco, Inc., 3702
Tedeton Memorial Scholarship Foundation, Easy, 3702
Tees At Risk LLC Contributions Program, 3703
Tees At Risk, LLC, 3703
Teichert Foundation, 3704
Teichert, Inc., 3704
Teitler & Teitler, L.L.P., 3705
Teitler Foundation, Inc., 3705
Tektronix Development Co., *see* 3706
Tektronix Foundation, 3706
Tektronix, Inc., 3706
Telcordia Technologies, Inc., *see* 3311
TeleCheck Services, Inc., *see* 1400
Teleflex Automotive Manufacturing Corp., *see* 3707
Teleflex Control Systems, Inc., *see* 3707
Teleflex Fluid Systems, Inc., *see* 3707
Teleflex Foundation, 3707
Teleflex Incorporated, 3707
TeleTech Community Foundation, 3708
TeleTech Foundation, *see* 3708
TeleTech Holdings, Inc., 3708
Tellabs Foundation, 3709
Tellabs, Inc., 3709
Tellabs, Inc. Corporate Giving Program, 3709
Telligen, 3710
Telligen Community Initiatives Program, 3710
Tempil Div., *see* 62
Temple Memorial Foundation, William F., 2378
Temple-Inland Forest Products Corp., *see* 3711
Temple-Inland Foundation, 3711
Temple-Inland Inc., 3711
Temple-Inland Inc., *see also* 3711
Temple-Inland Inc., *see* 1968
Templeton Investment Counsel, Inc., *see* 1487
Ten Talents International Ministries, Inc., 1660
Ten West Apparel Inc., 3712
Tenet Healthcare Corporation, 3713
Tenet Healthcare Corporation Contributions Program, 3713
Tennant Company, 3714
Tennant Company Foundation, *see* 3714
Tennant Foundation, 3714
Tenneco Automotive Inc., *see* 3715
Tenneco Automotive Inc. Corporate Giving Program, *see* 3715
Tenneco Inc., 3715
Tenneco Inc., *see also* 3715
Tenneco Inc. Corporate Giving Program, 3715
Tenneco Packaging Inc., *see* 2863
Tenneco Packaging Inc. Corporate Giving Program, *see* 2863
Tennessee Football, Inc., 3716
Tennessee Health Foundation, Inc., 507
Tennessee Titans, *see* 3716
Tennessee Titans Corporate Giving Program, 3716
Tennessee Titans Foundation, 3716
Tennessee Walking Horse Foundation, Inc., *see* 2419
Tennessee Walking Horse National Foundation, Inc., 2419
Tension Envelope Corporation, 3717
Tension Envelope Foundation, 3717
TEP, *see* 3819
TEP Corporate Giving Program, 3819
Teradyne, Inc., 3718
Teradyne, Inc. Corporate Giving Program, 3718
Terex Corporation, 3719
Terex Corporation Contributions Program, 3719
Terlato Family Foundation, 3720
Terlato Wine Group, The, 3720
Terminix Corp., The, *see* 3414
Terra Coastal Properties, Inc., 3721
Terre Haute Gas Corporation, 3722
Terry Scholarship Foundation, C. D., 424
Tesoro Alaska Co., *see* 3723
Tesoro Corporation, 3723
Tesoro Corporation, *see also* 3723
Tesoro Corporation Contributions Program, 3723
Tesoro Hawaii Corporation, *see* 3723
Tesoro Petroleum Corporation, *see* 3723
Tesoro Petroleum Corporation Contributions Program, *see* 3723
Tex-Trude Charities, Inc., 3724
Tex-Trude, Inc., 3724
Texas Brine Company, LLC, 3725
Texas Credit Union Foundation, 3726
Texas Credit Union League, 3726
Texas Farmers Insurance Co., *see* 1338
Texas Gas Transmission Corporation, *see* 4077
Texas Industries Foundation, 3727
Texas Industries, Inc., 3727
Texas Instruments Foundation, 3728
Texas Instruments Incorporated, 3728
Texas Instruments Incorporated, *see also* 3728
Texas Instruments Incorporated Corporate Giving Program, 3728
Texas Rangers Baseball Foundation, 3729
Texas Rangers, Ltd., The, 3729
Texas Station, LLC, *see* 3593
Texor Petroleum Company, 3730
Textron Aerostructures, *see* 3731
Textron Charitable Trust, The, 3731
Textron Defense Systems, *see* 3731
Textron Financial Corp., *see* 3731
Textron Inc., 3731
Textron Inc., *see also* 3731
Textron Inc. Corporate Giving Program, 3731
Textron Lycoming Reciprocating Engines, *see* 3731
Textron Marine & Land Systems, *see* 3731
Textron Specialty Materials, *see* 3731
TFS Financial Corporation, 3732
TFX Equities Inc., *see* 3707
TFX Medical Inc., *see* 3707
TGC, Inc., *see* 887
TGI Friday's, Inc., *see* 693
Thaw & Edgeworks, Inc., *see* 3150
THDF II, Inc., 1842
The Berry, Co., *see* 434
The Davey Tree Surgery Co., *see* 1035
The Duriron Co., Inc. Foundry Div., *see* 1447
The Duriron Co., Inc. Rotating Equipment Grp., *see* 1447
The Duriron Co., Inc. Valve Div., *see* 1447
The Evening Record, *see* 2733
The Kimley-Horn Group, Inc., *see* 2151
The Rams Football Company, Inc., *see* 3569
Therakos, Inc., *see* 2048
Therapeutics and Genetics Div., *see* 1566
Thermal Systems, *see* 1071
Thermo Electron Corporation, *see* 3733
Thermo Fisher Foundation for Science, *see* 3733
Thermo Fisher Scientific Inc., 3733
Thermo Fisher Scientific Inc., *see also* 3733
Thermo Fisher Scientific Inc. Contributions Program, 3733
Thermotron Industries, Inc., *see* 3933
Thin Film Technology Div., *see* 376
Thinkshift Communications, 3734